THE ELEMENTARY SCHOOL LIBRARY COLLECTION

A GUIDE TO BOOKS AND OTHER MEDIA
TWENTY-FIRST EDITION   PHASES 1-2-3

Linda L. Homa - Editor
Ann L. Schreck - Editorial Assistant
Maureen Hoebener - Bibliographer

Assisted by

Eileen Palmer Burke

Margaret Bush

Ruth I. Gordon

Virginia G. Kalb

Sue Kimmel

Ethel Kutteroff

Mary D. Lankford

Barbara Perrotti

Joanne Troutner

BRODART CO.
WILLIAMSPORT, PENNSYLVANIA
1998

Library of Congress Cataloging-in-Publication Data

The elementary school library collection : a guide to books and
    other media, phases 1-2-3 / Linda L. Homa, editor ; Ann L.
    Schreck, editorial assistant ; Maureen Hoebener, bibliographer ;
    assisted by Eileen Palmer Burke ...(et al.). — 21st ed.
        p.   cm.
    Includes bibliographical references and indexes.
    ISBN 0-87272-114-0 : $139.95
        1.   Children's literature—Bibliography.   2. Elementary
school libraries—United States — Book Lists.   3. Audio-
visual materials—United States — Catalogs.
    I. Homa, Linda L., 1951-   . II. Schreck, Ann L., 1954-   .
III. Hoebener, Maureen,   1948-   .
Z1037.E4   1998
(PN1009.A1)
011.62--dc21
                                                                          97-35627
                                                                          CIP

CONTENTS

Acknowledgements V

Introduction VI

Selection Policies VII

How To Use This Selection Tool XVIII

Selectors' Choice XXIV

Sample Entry XXVII

SECTION I — Classified Catalog

    Professional Collection 1

    Reference 33

    Periodicals 45

    Nonfiction 51

    Easy 395

    Fiction 519

SECTION II — Indexes

    Author Index 615

    Title Index 723

    Subject Index 815

SECTION III — Appendixes

    Materials for Preschool Children 1049

    Books for Independent Reading 1060

        Level 1-1 1060

        Level 1-2 1060

        Level 2-1 1062

        Level 2-2 1066

    Author's Series 1071

    Publisher's Series 1079

Directory of Publishers and Producers 1105

This edition of *THE ELEMENTARY SCHOOL LIBRARY COLLECTION* is dedicated to Mary Virginia Gaver (1906-1991), the founding editor who served from 1965 to 1973. As librarian, educator, author, researcher, and editor, she has made a distinguished contribution to the world of books. Her enthusiasm for children's literature and long dedication to library services for children and youth have provided inspiration for countless librarians and media specialists. It is with deep appreciation and fond memories that we humbly continue the legacy she founded.

And to Christina Glass Woll (1934-1996), who served as an advisor from 1972-1974 and as the selector for social studies and social sciences materials from 1988-1996. A knowledgeable and dedicated librarian, she will be remembered for her graciousness and generosity. Her caring nature has touched many lives. One of her last selections, SACRED RIVER by Ted Lewin, has been designated as a Selectors' Choice title in her memory.

COUNT OF TITLES IN THE TWENTY-FIRST EDITION

BOOKS
Professional 292
Reference 137
Nonfiction..4,017
Easy..2,041
Fiction 1,320

    TOTAL BOOKS **7,807**

PERIODICALS 127

TOTAL PRINT MATERIALS **7,934***

AUDIOVISUAL MATERIALS
Art/Study print sets ....36 **
CD-ROM products 104
Kits (read-along book and audio) 225
Microcomputer programs 55
Multimedia kits 5
Sound recordings (cassette or compact disc) 228
Talking Books (recorded books on cassette or compact disc) 138
Videocassettes 747
Videodiscs 13

    TOTAL AUDIOVISUAL............................**1,551**
    TOTAL TITLES......................................**9,485**

* This count includes titles available in multiple formats including board books, big books, large type books, bilingual books, and books in foreign languages.

** In certain formats, the count represents the number of recommended sets. The number of separate titles within sets varies.

ACKNOWLEDGEMENTS

Through their participation in **Advisory Committee** meetings and through correspondence, the following members of the education and library professions contributed to the production of this list. Their guidance and advice in 1) the revision of the selection policy, 2) curriculum trends, 3) the development and continuous revision of the list, 4) the reevaluation of specific sections of the list, and their constructive suggestions for the overall improvement of *The Elementary School Library Collection* are greatly appreciated.

Dale W. Brown
  Supervisor of Libraries
  Arlington Public Schools
  Arlington, VA

Hugh Durbin
  Swedenborg Memorial
    Library
  Urbana University
  Urbana, OH

Dorothy Fix
  Retired School Librarian
  Former Selector, ESLC
  Naples, FL

Sharon Harvey
  Children/Young Adult
    Services Consultant
  Alabama Public Library
    Service
  Montgomery, AL

Karen James
  Manager of Children's
    Services
  Louisville Free Public Library
  Louisville, KY

Carol-Ann Page
  Consultant
  Vancouver, British Columbia
  Canada

Dr. Lotsee Patterson
  Associate Professor
  School of Library and
    Information Services
  University of Oklahoma
  Norman, OK

Marilyn Goodrich Peterson
  Consultant
  Olathe, KS

The members of the **Selection Committee** are responsible for specific activities to develop and assess the collection. They identify and review new materials, and each annually reevaluates a specific area of the collection. Their ability to evaluate materials and their knowledge of children provide the basis for the recommendations found in this list.

Eileen Palmer Burke
  Consultant
  Denver, CO

Margaret Bush
  Associate Professor
  Graduate School of
    Library and Information
    Science
  Simmons College
  Boston, MA

Ruth I. Gordon
  Critical Reviewing, Unltd.
  Sonoma County, CA

Linda L. Homa
  Editor, ESLC
  Brodart Company
  Williamsport, PA

Virginia G. Kalb
  Consultant
  Fountain Valley, CA

Sue Kimmel
  Former Bibliographer, ESLC
  Librarian
  Brunson Elementary School
  Winston Salem, NC

Ethel Kutteroff
  Consultant
  Richmond, VA

Mary D. Lankford
  Consultant
  Irving, TX

Barbara Perrotti
  School Librarian
  Buckingham County
    Public Schools
  Buckingham, VA

Joanne Troutner
  Director of Technology
    and Media
  Tippecanoe School
    Corporation
  Lafayette, IN

INTRODUCTION

PURPOSE

The Elementary School Library Collection is a primary resource for the continuous development, evaluation, and maintenance of existing collections as well as for the establishment of new library media centers. High quality materials have been selected to meet the curricula related needs and personal interests of preschool through sixth grade children. The Professional Collection section, which focuses on child development and curriculum areas, helps adults in their professional and personal contacts with young people.

Public and academic librarians also find *The Elementary School Library Collection* useful. Public libraries, after all, serve the same clientele – children, teachers, caregivers, and parents – and often for the same purposes. Academic libraries which support programs in library science and/or teacher education use *ESLC* to identify titles for their collections of children's materials and as a reference tool for students and faculty.

Providing both interest and reading level estimates, *ESLC* functions effectively as a reading, listening, and viewing guidance tool. It is also a cataloging and bibliographic aid.

Collection development is an ongoing process. It involves three stages of evaluation:

> accuracy, currency, and appeal of the individual title;
> comparison of the title with others on the same subject or theme for the same audience;
> determination of the need for the title in the collection.

While very few, if any, library media centers have the financial resources to reevaluate the total collection annually, a regularly scheduled program to target specific sections or segments is wise practice. Analysis for currency and condition of materials as well as for breadth and depth of coverage helps pinpoint materials which need to be discarded/replaced/augmented. *The Elementary School Library Collection* provides information for a systematic program of collection development and maintenance.

SCOPE

The materials included are in a variety of formats: books (including board books, big books, and large type), periodicals, art and study prints (pictures), sound recording cassettes, talking books, compact discs, kits (read-along book and audio), multimedia kits, videocassettes, microcomputer software, videodiscs, and CD-ROM products.

The collection is limited to those items which have a range of applied use and are generally housed in the building level library media center. Therefore textbooks, workbooks, most novelty books, 16mm films, maps, and realia are excluded. Toy and movable books which are sturdily constructed and have educational content are considered for inclusion.

The Elementary School Library Collection offers recommendations for elementary schools in a wide variety of settings and at different levels of collection development. *The building level library media specialist must adapt this, or any other basic list, to local needs.*

CONTINUOUS REVISION

The twenty-first edition of *ESLC* contains: 1) new titles published or produced between July 1995 and June 1997; 2) titles which were formerly included and judged, upon review, to be of current value; 3) older titles published prior to 1995, not listed previously, and found to be useful. Other titles, previously recommended, have been dropped from this edition because 1) they are out of print; 2) their contents have become outdated; or 3) newer, better titles have been published.

For this edition, the members of the selection committee and the editor have evaluated 9,900 new items. Twenty-six percent (2,594 titles) were added.

AVAILABILITY OF TITLES

As the twenty-first edition goes to press, all titles in the collection are, to the best of our knowledge, readily available for purchase. However, publishers' and producers' inventories are in constant flux. Publishers' trade and library bindings are available for different lengths of time. Gaps develop in reprinting schedules. Hardcover binds may or may not be available when the paperback edition is in print. The paperback book may have the same publisher but another imprint or may be available from a different publisher. As publishers and producers continue to merge, finding a specific title in a specific bind or configuration on any given day is very often a matter of persistence. Contact the publisher or your vendor for current information.

ESLC was first published 33 years ago. Over this period, it has remained a satisfying professional challenge to develop and maintain a full media collection to meet children's needs.

SELECTION POLICIES

This section describes the considerations affecting selectors' decisions. It is arranged in three broad categories: General Policies; Policies for Specific Collection Areas; Policies for Specific Formats.

General Policies

EVALUATIVE CRITERIA

Materials are selected on the basis of generally accepted criteria: quality, appeal to children, excellence in format type, authenticity of content, and suitability for the range of reading, listening, and viewing abilities usually represented in a Pre-K - 6 elementary school.

In some cases, items which are timely in appeal may not meet the criteria, but are included for their current value.

The titles reflect respect for, and understanding of, the multiethnic, pluralistic nature of the population in the United States and Canada. Recognition of cultural diversity involves far more than the mere avoidance of stereotypes; it also involves inclusion of items by authors/illustrators/producers of varying backgrounds, items with characters from diverse backgrounds, and items representing many viewpoints. Terminology for various ethnic groups, however, may reflect the common language of the period of the item. Bibliographies and other resources in the Professional Collection section present various viewpoints of multiculturalism.

TRENDS IN ELEMENTARY EDUCATION

School curricula and teaching methods are dynamic, not stagnant, and this calls for a similarly dynamic school media center collection. *ESLC* selectors study these trends and evaluate materials in light of changing needs and accept materials to support current practices.

The whole language movement continues to be a driving force in elementary education. As teaching strategies shift away from practices which emphasize isolated language skills (basal readers, phonics worksheets, spellers, and workbooks) and incorporate language arts instruction which integrates the teaching of reading, writing, listening, and speaking skills,[1] library materials have become central to the curriculum and are no longer being used merely to supplement texts. The natural outgrowth of this integrated instruction has been the development of thematic units which introduce concepts across the content areas. This webbing across the curriculum allows children to discover natural connections and interrelationships among the disciplines. In this language rich environment, the role of the school media specialist has evolved into that of literature consultant and curriculum consultant. "There appear[s] to be a renewed focus on traditional roles such as providing resources, providing reading guidance, and teaching children how to find information."[2]

Literature-based curricula encourage active inquiry, and as a result, children, even very young children, visit school media centers more frequently for both research and recreational use. In response to increased classroom use and personal use, collections need to cover a broader range of topics while providing depth in topics, genres, and authors who are studied in the school curriculum.[3]

The relationship between free reading and reading ability has been widely demonstrated. To achieve this positive outcome from reading and books, access is essential. More reading occurs in schools when there is a school library with a print-rich environment, an enthusiastic library media specialist, free volunteer reading time, a resource-based curriculum, and flexible access to the school library.

Flexible scheduling has been a natural outgrowth of the literature-based curriculum. "Most significant changes in library media programs occur when the library media specialist moves to flexible scheduling and curriculum integrated instruction."[4]

"Flexible access gives full visibility to the creative capabilities of librarians. The role of the librarian as teacher, organizer, leader, resource specialist, reading consultant, and curriculum wizard becomes obvious through planning sessions with teachers and other new responsibilities."[5] At the same time, flexible scheduling has a positive impact on literacy development, reading comprehension, and vocabulary.

Flexible access is also a vital part of collaboration. Open schedules enable classroom teachers and library media specialists to schedule time for collaborative planning. Combining their unique perspectives, they can create instructional units which incorporate a variety of resources, which meet the goals and objectives of both the curriculum and library instruction, and which positively effect student comprehension and performance. The collaborative process, though time consuming, is beneficial to students, teachers, and school library media specialist as teaching and learning become more integrated.

As schools more frequently adopt pre-kindergarten programs as well as daycare programs, the need for quality materials for preschoolers increases. In addition, the whole language program stresses reading aloud which encourages parents to borrow materials from the school library media center.

There is also a renewed national emphasis on family literacy as research increasingly indicates that the educational success of children begins with parental expectations and parental involvement in children's education. Yet, significant numbers of children have few, if any, print resources at home. As a result, in many communities the school library media center is serving as the library for the entire family unit.

Homeschooling continues to be a popular option for parents who, for a variety of reasons, choose to teach their children themselves. These homeschooling families frequently use school library media centers as a resource for both teaching and recreational materials.

These factors make it critical that materials are available not only with a wide range of reading levels but also in a variety of formats. Students have become increasingly visually oriented. As sophisticated audiovisual materials have become more affordable, more schools have incorporated them into their programs. Recently some states have adopted multimedia textbooks as official state texts.

Materials which reflect our culturally and ethnically diverse nation and world remain important. Teaching a multicultural world view gives students an understanding of the uniqueness of cultures while exploring their similarities and differences. At the same time, it enhances feelings of self-confidence and self-worth.

Despite the clear need for not only more materials but also a wider range of materials and formats, budgets have remained stagnant. During the 1995-1996 school year, the average book expenditure remained the same as in the 1993-1994 school year -- a mere $4,000.[6] Considering that the average price for a book is $15.65 and has been steadily increasing, it is not difficult to determine that book collections are deteriorating.[7] Funds for other formats -- AV, periodicals, microforms and CD-ROM products -- have dropped slightly. Only spending for microcomputer software has increased. The mean expenditure for a total materials budget was $15,707 while the median was $11,144 approximately $600 less than in 1993-1994. These figures represent expenditures for not only print and AV materials but also AV equipment and computer hardware.[8] *ESLC* selectors understand the difficult decisions that must be made in regard to allocation of resources and have tried to present a broad spectrum of affordable, high quality materials in a variety of formats with priority for acquisition indicated.

While a higher percentage of funding continues to be allocated for books, a steady increase in the use of computers and the expansion of telecommunications are apparent in school library media centers. Sixty-six percent now have a Local Area Network while only 38.8% did in 1993-1994. Access to the Internet has jumped from 21.3% of school media centers in 1993-1994 to 34% in 1995-1996.[9]

Though computers have been acquired relatively recently, school library media centers have become the technological centers for many schools. With the advent of the World Wide Web in 1991, the Internet introduced an open-ended system which required teachers and students to learn a completely new method of locating and using materials. It quickly has become the reference tool of choice. Print sources are frequently consulted only after computer resources have been exhausted. In fact, it is becoming more common for print materials to list Web sites in their bibliographies both as sources and as resources for additional information.

School library media specialists have learned to use the Web as a professional resource for access to professional publications, listservs, and even links to library catalogs. In some states, a statewide union catalog is now available on the Web.

The challenge for school library media specialists is to efficiently integrate the Web into the existing curriculum, to learn new search strategies, and to critically evaluate Web sites for accuracy, currency, and lack of bias. Even more importantly, the school library media specialist must teach these new found skills to teachers and students, enabling them to become informed users of the Net.

Library media specialists make a singular contribution to the improvement of teaching and learning, especially in a school with site-based management. Their role in cooperative planning and teaching can reduce fragmentation and repetition of effort. Increasingly library media specialists are helping to establish curriculum, not just supporting it. Their work with teachers, administrators, and the community promotes cohesive instruction and learning. Of equal importance, individual students become excited about reading and learning because of personal relationships with the librarian who shares her/his knowledge of the varied materials available through the library media center.

Considering this, it is not at all surprising that a recent study by the Colorado Department of Education, THE IMPACT OF SCHOOL LIBRARY MEDIA CENTERS ON ACADEMIC ACHIEVEMENT, revealed that the strength of the school library media center is a clear predictor of academic achievement. The study found that not only was the size of the school library media center's staff and collection the best school predictor of academic achievement but also that among school and community predictors it was second after the absence of at-risk conditions. Furthermore, students with high standardized tests scores tend to come from schools with more library staff and materials.[10]

Clearly, the school library media center and the school library media specialist are essential components of an effective educational system.

**MATERIALS FOR THE
READING PROGRAM
IN THE SCHOOL**

The benefits derived from reading entire works reinforce the need for the elementary school library media center to provide as broad a selection of excellent materials as current publishing and production make possible. Fictional and informational materials on all subjects of interest to children and at many levels of difficulty and maturity are, therefore, included.

ESLC avoids abridgments and simplified versions except in instances where the edition meets the criteria of other independent work. Talking books which have abridged texts are generally excluded unless the text has been approved by the author. Classic titles, translated or retold for children, are evaluated as original contributions and are included when standards of literary merit are met.

BOOKS FOR PRIMARY GRADES AND PRESCHOOL CHILDREN

Books designated for the young child are placed in the Nonfiction section as well as the Easy section of the list. Consideration is given to literary and artistic merit, plot and character development, clarity of exposition, and general excellence of design. Wordless Picture Books, which help to develop imagination and language skills, are included in materials for this age group. Such titles can be identified by looking in the subject index under the heading "Stories without words."

PICTURE BOOKS

The majority of picture books (fiction titles in which the illustrations are equal to or greater than the amount of text) are entered in the Easy section. However, many books with complicated plots and sophisticated illustrations are published in picture book format. Since these picture books appeal to older readers, they are listed in the Fiction section. Informational books in picture book format are placed in the Nonfiction section according to the appropriate Dewey Decimal classification.

BIG BOOKS

Increasingly, picture books are being published as oversize volumes for classroom use with groups. Picture book entries indicate when titles are also available in big book format. Big books published as original titles are not included.

BOARD BOOKS

Board books with simple text that is suitable for beginning readers are included. Board books designed for babies and toddlers are considered to be out of scope and are excluded. When a board book is published as an original title, it is assigned a main entry. When a board book is a facsimile of a previously listed picture book, it is entered as a note in the main entry for the title as an alternative format.

MATERIALS FOR BLIND & PHYSICALLY HANDICAPPED CHILDREN

To meet the needs of visually impaired children, a note before the annotation shows the availability of recorded and/or braille editions from the National Library Service for the Blind and Physically Handicapped. These items are available on loan to eligible individuals through participating institutions. Large print editions of recommended titles are also shown in a similar note.

Books which have also been produced in an audio format such as talking books, kits, and videocassettes are identified as combined entries (CE) in the Classified Catalog. Titles indicated as combined entries (CE) are sold as separate items and are frequently available from different publishers/producers. Videos that are closed captioned for the hearing impaired are indicated as such.

CANADIAN MATERIALS

Canadian imprints, as available, are shown for recommended titles. In addition, a number of Canadian publications (books and periodicals) and productions (video-cassettes) which have special value for Canadian libraries and/or have value or appeal to readers in Canada and the United States are included. If, in the selector's opinion, the title is limited in appeal to the Canadian reader, the title is designated Phase 3 (special regional value). If the appeal of the item is broader, the phase is assigned on the same basis as any other material. Library media specialists interested in identifying the best in this field should consult the Professional Collection section for selection tools directly related to Canadian materials.

OMNIBUS ENTRIES

Author's series (e.g. Beverly Cleary's "Beezus and Ramona" books), in which familiar characters are carried through many different experiences, serve a real purpose in maintaining children's interests and developing reading fluency. To conserve space, many sequels are noted in the annotation, rather than being given a separate citation. These "omnibus" entries are used when the subject headings, the reading level, and interest level of each of the titles remain the same. The "Author's Series" appendix identifies series with three or more volumes.

PUBLISHER'S SERIES — Individual titles are evaluated without regard to the series as a whole and are included where they meet standards of literary quality, appeal and interest, pertinence to the elementary school collection, authenticity, and need. The "Publisher's Series" appendix lists recommended titles within a given series. For some series, particularly geography series which have numerous titles, only representative examples are included.

ART — In selecting art materials, a major aim is to choose items which emphasize the creative approach in drawing and other art activities.

A concurrent emphasis is to identify materials that extend children's appreciation of art. Books and art prints are identified for this purpose. Sculpture reproductions are another means for children to experience art. Local art museums and galleries or the catalogs of companies which handle reproductions should be checked by library media specialists.

BIOGRAPHY — Emphasis is placed on those individuals whose lifeworks made a long-standing impact and, secondarily, on those contemporary figures who may inspire students. Particular efforts are made to include works on individuals who are likely to be covered in the school curriculum. While coverage of subjects has improved, significant gaps remain.

FOREIGN LANGUAGE — Print and audiovisual materials with text or narrative in a foreign language serve different audiences. There is a great need for materials for students whose primary language is not English and for the increasing number of students in Foreign Language in the Elementary School programs.

Library media specialists in schools with either a program for children for whom English is a second language or a FLES program must work closely with involved faculty to identify the special criteria for the evaluation and utilization of materials for their particular program.

In *ESLC*, foreign language materials are classified in the appropriate Dewey section for the subject of the work (e.g., 567.9 for a book on dinosaurs), rather than the language in which they are written. Translations of fiction titles are listed as a note in the entry for the original work. Access is provided through the subject index, e.g., Spanish language materials; Bilingual materials -- French; etc.

The titles represent outstanding materials to form a foundation for either of these programs. The selection tools and bibliographies listed in the Professional Collection section identify additional resources.

POETRY — A broad selection of poetry—both in anthologies and in single volumes—is provided so that the range of poetry and the works of individual poets can be explored. Such materials are included for independent reading by children and for introduction by adults. A selection of versions or translations, both new and old, of works of world literature is also recommended.

FOLKLORE — Folklore is selected primarily with the child user in mind. It is read as a form of literature and used in country and multicultural studies. To increase access to appropriate titles, subject headings that show the source of the tale(s) are given and are also reversed (e.g., Folklore--France/France--Folklore). The annotations indicate titles which are also resources for the adult storyteller and which have particular curriculum applications.

**HISTORY AND
DESCRIPTION OF
GEOGRAPHICAL
AREAS**

ESLC selectors recognize that materials on cities, states, regions, countries, and continents can become quickly dated in this era of rapid political changes. While efforts are made to include only the most current and accurate materials at the time of publication, it is still important for library media specialists to review an item's validity at the time of purchase or use. These items are listed as Phase 3 titles (special regional interest).

LOCAL HISTORY

Materials on state and local history are essential in the elementary school library media center. Although it has not proved possible to locate works about every state of sufficiently broad interest to include in a national list, many local or regional titles of general value and interest are included. These are listed as titles of special regional interest (Phase 3). Additional sources for specific locales need to be purchased.

MUSIC

Access to a range of traditional and contemporary musical literature should be available to children. In addition to anthologies of musical scores and picture books of individual songs, *ESLC* includes selected sound recordings of classical, folk, and contemporary music which represent quality for their form of music. Additional selections should be made by library media specialists to meet particular needs.

PERIODICALS

Periodicals and appropriate indexes recommended for children are included. The periodicals for adults, including those that review materials and/or keep teachers and library media specialists abreast of timely educational issues, are listed in the Professional Collection section. Prices of periodicals are subject to change. Subscription addresses and URLs (Uniform Resource Locators) for Internet access to subscription information are given in the Directory of Publishers and Producers, but most of the recommended periodicals are also available through subscription agents.

Increasingly periodicals are becoming available on the Internet. The URLs (Uniform Resource Locators) for Web sites which list the full text of a periodical, include additional issues, post supplemental articles or other significant information, or index backlist issues are supplied as a note in the main entry.

PROFESSIONAL

In addition to children, the elementary school library media center must serve two groups of adults: those who work with children—teachers, administrators, library media specialists, and other staff members; and the adults who live with them—their parents or caregivers. Toward this end, audiovisual materials, books, periodicals, indexes, and bibliographies that aid adults in their work have been recommended. These titles emphasize the practical, the innovative, and discussions of recent trends and problems. The aim is to include titles in all areas of concern to elementary school educators. When available, paperback editions of professional titles have been listed to reduce costs.

Increasingly school libraries are being used by families in the community. Therefore materials have also been selected to reflect the spectrum of parental concerns. These titles are identified by the parenthetical phrase (Parents' Shelf) following the annotation.

REFERENCE COLLECTION

Reference materials, those items particularly designed to locate specific facts as opposed to being read in their entirety, appear in a separate section. Encyclopedias, dictionaries, bibliographies, biographical dictionaries, etc. are recommended for children and adults.

RELIGION

Information on customs and traditions of all major religious faiths, stories from religious literature, mythology, legends, and information on religious holidays are selected when they meet standards of quality and appropriateness for elementary school use. Materials which proselytize religious belief rather than provide information on religious belief and practice are excluded.

FAMILY LIFE, SEX EDUCATION, CHILD SAFETY, SUBSTANCE ABUSE & AIDS AWARENESS

Major attention is now being paid to education in these areas. Community and family values are of particular concern. The importance of the individual child's self-esteem is recognized. The materials included on these subjects meet the criteria of scientific and medical authority and appeal at the elementary level.

AUDIOVISUAL MATERIALS

The primary emphasis of *ESLC* is on printed materials. However, the selectors recognize the increasingly important role that audiovisual materials play in the collection. Therefore a basic list of outstanding and classic audiovisual materials is included. These listings represent materials designed for use by teachers or students in support of the school curriculum. Materials produced solely for student entertainment are not listed. Many audiovisual presentations based on, or adapted from, a book serve a motivational purpose. As a rule a sound recording, videocassette, videodisc, microcomputer software, or CD-ROM product based on a book is not recommended unless the book itself can be recommended.

Exceptions occur when:

1. the book is out of print;

2. the nonprint item is judged to be clearly superior to the book or to have values independent of the printed format;

3. a recording of a fine book, written at a high reading level, is suitable for a child's listening level;

4. a picture book of limited appeal has been interpreted in a visually interesting format.

All of the policies stated previously apply to audiovisual materials as well as to printed materials.

16MM FILMS

For most elementary schools, access to 16mm films remains more economical through district or regional collections or from rental sources. As material is increasingly available on videocassettes, many school library media specialists are discontinuing the use of 16mm films. Therefore materials in this format are not included.

FILMSTRIPS

Likewise many filmstrip productions have been transferred to videocassettes. Availability of filmstrips has decreased dramatically. Fewer producers are now marketing this format. The remaining producers are seldom creating new titles. Many sound filmstrips, though available, had been dropped from the collection because their contents were judged to be outdated. Although many schools continue to use this format, it has become increasingly difficult to identify quality productions that are still available. Therefore materials in this format are no longer listed.

VIDEOCASSETTES

Prices for videocassettes vary widely. Some producers transfer film or filmstrips to videocassettes at a reasonable price. Others establish agreements for duplication licensing. Videocassettes designed for the consumer market are not included except when copyright and use provisions allow. Public performance rights are noted when available. It is, of course, the responsibility of each school library media specialist or teacher to follow fair use practices. Titles in the Professional Collection section address copyright and use regulations.

Production considerations sometimes mandate high costs. However, many videocassettes are still priced extravagantly, transferred from poor films, or transferred from filmstrips or slide shows with little action provided, thus denigrating a main advantage of the format. These productions are not included. Iconographic productions are generally excluded.

The Advisory Committee and Selection Committee members have been sensitive to costs and have been conservative in adding expensive materials. *ESLC* remains a building level tool and prices for individual items must be set realistically for building level budgets. Therefore costly productions which, nevertheless, meet a curriculum need are listed as Phase 3 (special interest) acquisitions.

MICROCOMPUTER SOFTWARE & CD-ROM PRODUCTS

Microcomputer use is commonplace. Programs are available for the constantly changing spectrum of hardware. The trend toward networking continues. Software publishers are addressing this trend as well as the need for excellent simulations, problem-solving software, and tool programs.

Classic microcomputer software for children as well as the best of the new programs are included in this edition. Utility software products and other programs useful for classroom management are listed in the Professional Collection section.

CD-ROM products have become more widespread and, while most address an older audience, many are suitable for elementary age children. The best of these products is included in this edition. The combination of information through text, audio, and video makes these items particularly versatile and appealing. A recent innovation allows an Internet site connection to be embedded into a CD-ROM product. Products with this feature include a statement in the annotation that identifies the Web site(s).

Increasingly, microcomputer software and CD-ROM products are being simultaneously released in multiple versions which run on a variety of hardware. The system requirements for the version which was reviewed are given. Availability of additional versions is listed as a note.

Many microcomputer software programs and CD-ROM products are now being released with multiple platforms on the same product. The system requirements for each platform are given. Availibility of additional versions is listed as a note.

Microcomputer software and CD-ROM programs can be identified through the subject index under the heading Software--(Subject area) and (Subject area)--Software.

Monographic and periodical literature related to the capabilities, use, and evaluation of microcomputers, microcomputer software, and CD-ROM products are included in the Professional Collection section.

VIDEODISCS

The videodiscs which best address the needs of the elementary school curriculum are included in this edition. Those videodiscs which are able to be used both by teachers for lessons and by students for reports are given priority. Videodiscs appear to be a fading format. The cost of a separate projection device and the increased availability of less expensive CD-ROM products have made the videodisc less attractive.

KITS

A kit is defined as a read-along book and audio product that is packaged together as a unit. Kits primarily consist of a book with sound recording cassette(s). However, kits may also include a book with compact disc(s). Whenever possible, kits are listed with a paperback edition of the book. However, in some instances, a kit is only available with a hardback edition of the book and is listed accordingly. The collation statement indicates the bind of the book. Kits are listed as a note in the main entry for the title. These titles are identified as combined entries (CE) in the Classified Catalog.

MULTIMEDIA KITS

The ever increasing number of kits takes many forms. ANGLO-AMERICAN CATALOGUING RULES, 2nd edition (AACR2) has defined a kit as "an item containing two or more categories of material, no one of which is identifiable as the predominate constituent of the item; also designated 'multimedia item.'" (p. 619) When determination of a predominate component can be made, the item is listed by that format, e.g. a CD-ROM product with a teacher's guide and student workbooks is listed as a CD-ROM. When none of the items of a set is predominate and the items can be used separately, the set has been assigned the general material designation (GMD) "Multimedia kit" and the material type code MMK.

BOOK WITH AUDIO
BOOK WITH COMPUTER FILE

Books with accompanying materials, which are not defined as read-along or multimedia kits, are classed as books when the book is the predominate component. These include books with an accompanying audio component [sound recording cassette(s), or compact disc(s)], or books with an accompanying computer file (microcomputer software or CD-ROM product). "Book with audio" carries the material type code BA; "Book with computer file" carries the material type code BC. No general material designation (GMD) is assigned in either case. The ancillary item will appear in the collation. System requirements will be listed for books which are accompanied by a computer file.

SOUND RECORDINGS

When a recording is a single item, the cassette (SRC) format will be indicated first with a note indicating availability of a compact disc (CD) format. Single recording items available only on compact discs are designated (CD). The widespread availability of cassettes and compact discs has virtually eliminated the 12 inch disc. Therefore the format sound recording disc (SRD) is no longer listed. Entries for classic disc recordings of children's music have been updated to list either the cassette (SRC) or the compact disc (CD) versions.

TALKING BOOKS

A book which has been recorded on either sound recording cassette(s) or on compact disc(s) is listed as a note in the main entry for the title. These may be either works of fiction or nonfiction. Talking books (TB) which have abridged texts are generally excluded unless the texts have been approved by the authors. Read-along books which have been recorded and are packaged as a book and cassette(s) or compact disc(s) set are listed as kits.

REALIA AND GAMES

The need for, and interest in, realia and educational games as part of the library media center varies widely. These formats are excluded from *ESLC,* and little evaluation of them has been done. Accordingly, a file of dealers' catalogs should be developed for selection, and items must be previewed.

GOVERNMENT DOCUMENTS

A number of these publications are included in *ESLC.* This resource can be maintained by requesting the free bimonthly publication NEW BOOKS from the Superintendent of Documents, USGPO, Washington, D.C. U.S. GOVERNMENT BOOKS, also available at no cost from the same source, is a quarterly catalog of popular documents.

PAPERBACK BOOKS, PAMPHLETS AND VERTICAL FILE MATERIALS

Availability of fiction and easy juvenile titles in paperback editions is now common. The increased demand by the general public for quality children's materials is leading to increased publication of nonfiction paperback editions.

Paperback use continues to be strongly recommended to teachers and library media specialists for personal libraries and to provide duplicates for the library media center, for classroom use, and for discussion groups. Paperback editions for library use have been suggested when the title is an original publication, is obtainable in no other form, and/or when the hardcover edition is out of print and its contents are needed. Occasionally a title is published in a quality trade paperback judged capable of withstanding circulation demands without prebinding. Where the price difference is significant, these trade paperback binds have been recommended. Many trade paperback editions have been listed in the Professional Collection section.

Tools such as *CHILDREN'S BOOKS IN PRINT* and publisher's catalogs identify titles recommended in *ESLC* in library or trade bindings that are also available as mass market paperbacks.

With few exceptions no effort is made to list pamphlets (less than fifty pages in length) which should be a part of the vertical file collection of a library. The establishment of such a resource is another responsibility of the library media specialist in each school. The Professional Collection section lists sources for these materials.

HOW TO USE THIS SELECTION TOOL

CLASSIFIED CATALOG

This list has been prepared in book catalog format, organized as follows:

SECTION I

The Classified Catalog contains bibliographic information for each title in the collection. Titles in this section are divided into six headings: Professional Collection, Reference, Periodicals, Nonfiction, Easy, and Fiction. Titles are arranged according to the Dewey Decimal Classification system with B (individual biography) following the 920s. Audiovisual materials are integrated with books on the same subject. When the recommended audiovisual material is based on or adapted from a single book, its availability is shown by a note, with complete ordering information, in the primary entry. The letters CE in the call number aid in the easy identification of these Combined Entries.

Each main entry contains the following information when applicable: 1) type of material code; 2) Dewey classification; 3) recommended phase of acquisition; 4) interest level; 5) reading level; 6) price; 7) bind and purchasing information; 8) citation number; 9) author, compiler, or editor; 10) title; 11) adapter or translator; 12) illustrator; 13) publisher or producer; 14) ISBN, product number, or ISSN; 15) distribution in Canada; 16) date of publication; 17) collation; 18) series name; 19) special features such as a chronology, directory, bibliography, index, or glossary; 20) system requirements for audiovisual materials; 21) availability in other formats; 22) critical annotation; 23) sequels or related titles; 24) subject headings.

A composite sample entry is printed at the beginning of the Classified Catalog.

SECTION II

INDEXES

Separate Author, Title, and Subject Indexes are provided. Author index includes illustrators. Joint authors and illustrators are listed separately.

In addition to the basic index access points, publication date, interest and reading level estimates, and citation number are included for each index entry.

Titles beginning with numeric characters are entered as they are presented on the title page. Thus they may be filed either as spelled or numerically at the end of the title index.

The subject index is filed as indicated:

>Animals -- Wit and humor.
>
>Animals, Mythical.
>
>Animals, Mythical -- Poetry.
>
>Animals, Mythical, in Art.
>
>Animals and civilization.

Letters are filed before numbers thus:

>United States -- History.
>
>United States -- History -- Civil War, 1861-1865.
>
>United States -- History -- Colonial period, ca. 1600-1775.
>
>United States -- History -- French and Indian War, 1755-1763.
>
>United States -- History -- 1783-1815.

SECTION III

APPENDIXES

MATERIALS FOR PRESCHOOL CHILDREN is an alphabetical listing of books and audiovisual materials for use with and of particular appeal to children three and four years of age.

BOOKS FOR INDEPENDENT READING is an alphabetical listing of titles judged by application of the Spache Reading Formula to be at:

>Independent Reading Level 1 - 1
>
>Independent Reading Level 1 - 2
>
>Independent Reading Level 2 - 1
>
>Independent Reading Level 2 - 2

AUTHOR'S SERIES provides an alphabetical listing by author and series name. The series name is created, if necessary, using the name(s) of the primary character(s). For the purpose of this appendix, a series is defined as three or more books written by an author about a particular character or characters.

PUBLISHER'S SERIES is an alphabetical listing by series name showing the publisher and recommended titles. For some series, particularly geography series with numerous titles, only representative titles are listed.

CATALOGING PRINCIPLES

Titles in *THE ELEMENTARY SCHOOL LIBRARY COLLECTION* are classified according to the *ABRIDGED DEWEY DECIMAL CLASSIFICATION AND RELATIVE INDEX, EDITION 13*. Many titles, particularly those with interdisciplinary topics, can be classified correctly in more than one area. When materials are cataloged, efforts are made to assign classifications which best reflect the content of the work and which group similar titles together according to previous *ESLC* practices. Simplifications required to meet the needs of elementary school libraries have been made in keeping with the principles.

The following classifying options have been exercised:

— North American native groups are classified in 970.1-970.5. This includes contemporary Native American groups.

— Forms of music are listed in 789.

— Jokes and riddles, except for those few showing folklore sources, are classed in 793.735.

— Individual biographies are placed in B.

— Collective biographies are cataloged according to the primary subject of the work, e.g., a collective biography about composers would be located in 780. When a collective biography encompasses a variety of topics, it is classed in 920.

— Natural history books are placed in geographic classification when a specific geographic location is identified, e.g., a work depicting the Sonoran Desert is listed in 979.1. General works on natural environments are classed in 508 for general natural history and description or 577 for specific ecosystems, e.g., rain forests.

— Religious literature from all cultures is placed in the 200s, e.g., Jataka stories, Buddhist moral tales, are cataloged in 294.3.

— Mythology from all cultures is classified in the 290s.

— Books depicting the social life and customs of contemporary ethnic groups in the United States (with the exception of the aforementioned Native American groups) are placed in 305.8.

— Geographical references are sometimes not included.

The ABRIDGED EDITION 13 includes major revisions in public administration (350-354) and the life sciences (560-599), significant changes in education (370-379) and religion (230-270, 279), and expansions for numerous popular topics and for several countries. Titles newly accepted for the 21st edition have been classified according to these revised tables. As many classification changes as possible have been made to previously accepted titles to reflect these revisions as *ESLC* went to press. Classification of materials will continue to be reevaluated and updated according to the reductions and relocations recommended in the ABRIDGED EDITION 13.

The subject authority is the LIBRARY OF CONGRESS ANNOTATED CARD SUBJECT HEADINGS FOR CHILDREN'S LITERATURE. To increase accessibility, additional headings are sometimes added to the headings provided by CIP.

ANNOTATIONS

The annotations for titles in this list have been written by members of the Selection Committee, except where quotations have been indicated and a source acknowledged. The critically descriptive annotations indicate particular audiences and/or uses of the recommended title.

ACQUISITION AIDS

Several acquisition aids (phase of acquisition recommendation, estimate of interest or appeal level, and estimate of reading level) have been added to the entries in the Classified Catalog and are explained in greater detail below.

PHASE NOTATION

Phase indications (Ph-1, Ph-2, or Ph-3) are suggested priorities for acquisitions and are noted on the right above the body of the entry. These recommendations are based on the quality and appeal of the title in relation to other titles on the same theme or subject.

Phase 1 represents those items which, in the opinion of the selectors, should be on the shelves of all library media centers. Some areas are not as well represented in the Phase 1 listing as would be desirable because materials are not currently available.

Phase 2 recommends items for continuing development of the collection to provide for a broad range of needs and interests.

Phase 3 identifies items whose cost, limited usage, regional interest, or appeal to special audiences makes them less important for all schools, although their value and significance for some schools may be equally as great as titles in Phase 1 or 2.

INTEREST LEVEL

Specific grade levels indicate estimated range of interest or appeal.

P	Preschoolers (3 and 4 year olds)
K	Kindergartners (5 year olds)
1	First graders (6 year olds)
2	Second graders (7 year olds)
3	Third graders (8 year olds)
4	Fourth graders (9 year olds)
5	Fifth graders (10 year olds)
6	Sixth graders (11 year olds)
A	Advanced readers—not necessarily restricted to advanced 6th graders.

Various combinations are used including, occasionally, the comprehensive symbol P-A meaning elements of appeal and usability at all levels for which this bibliography is prepared.

READABILITY LEVEL ESTIMATE

A number indicating the readability level estimate has been added to the alpha/numeric symbol(s) which indicates estimate of reader appeal (e.g., P-K/3, K-2/4, 3-5/4, 5-6/7). A slash separates the interest level and the readability level estimates. Interest level and readability level estimates are indicated by grade levels.

Readability level estimates have been obtained through the use of one of two reading formulas. For materials where the readability level estimate is third grade or higher, the Fry Formula for Estimating Readability [11] has been used. This method has been validated for use in elementary grade levels.

Readability level estimates for grades one and two are based on the Spache formula,[12] which provides finer distinctions than Fry and enables identification of four independent reading levels within grades one and two.

As a rule, readability level estimates are not given for the following: audiovisual materials, periodicals, professional materials, reference materials, songbooks, poetry, anthologies, foreign language titles, and books which are primarily directions, such as cookbooks and craft books.

Sometimes appeal and reading level estimates are seemingly disparate, which can reflect an author's style, the use of specialized vocabulary, and/or material requiring greater comprehension. These indicators are always second to knowledge of the needs, abilities, and interests of the individual child. As Fry points out, "High motivation overcomes high readability level"[13] and "A child's interest level tends to follow chronological age level and is not related to reading level."[14]

PRICES

The list prices for titles are shown to the right above the annotation and reflect the binding that is recommended. While the prices shown are accurate as copy goes to press, changes occur frequently.

ORDER DIRECT

"OD" indicates a title which must be ordered directly from the publisher or producer. The directory for these publishers, as well as producers of audiovisual materials, can be found following the appendixes. In addition to addresses and phone numbers, FAX numbers, e-mail addresses and URLs (Uniform Resource Locators) are listed as available.

ISBN/ISSN PRODUCER'S CODE NUMBER

This ordering aid information is found in the bibliographic record directly following the publisher's and/or producer's name.

These ISBN codes refer to country of publication - publisher - specific title in a specific bind. The rapid growth in the number of book titles published in the United States means that some publishers have more than one ISBN prefix. Sometimes the number for titles published in the United States begins with a one rather than a zero. Ordering a title by ISBN only may result in the purchaser being told a work is out of print when it is available in another binding or has recently been reprinted and assigned a new ISBN. It is good practice to contact the publisher or a vendor for the most current information.

This edition of *The Elementary School Library Collection* continues the practice of responding to the suggestions and needs of users. As always, comments are welcomed.

Linda L. Homa, Editor
THE ELEMENTARY SCHOOL LIBRARY COLLECTION
500 Arch Street, Williamsport, PA 17705
(800) 233-8467, Ext. 572

FOOTNOTES

1. Silva, Cecilia and Delgado-Larocco, Esther L. "Facilitating Learning Through Interconnections: A Concept Approach to Core Literature Units." *LANGUAGE ARTS*, Vol. 70, October 1993, pp. 469-474.

2. Hughes, Sandra M. "The Impact of Whole Language on Four Elementary School Libraries." *LANGUAGE ARTS*, Vol. 70, September, 1993, pp. 393-399.

3. Ibid.

4. Haycock, Ken. "Research in Teacher-Librarianship and the Institutionalization of Change." *SCHOOL LIBRARY MEDIA QUARTERLY*, Summer 1995, pp. 227-233.

5. Lankford, Mary D. "Flexible Access: Foundation for Achievement." *SCHOOL LIBRARY JOURNAL*, August 1994, pp. 21-23.

6. Miller, Marilyn L. and Shontz, Marilyn. "Small Change: Expenditures for Resources in School Library Media Centers, FY 1995-96." *SCHOOL LIBRARY JOURNAL*, October 1997, pp. 28-37.

7. Gerhardt, Lillian N. "Average Book Prices '97." *SCHOOL LIBRARY JOURNAL*, March 1997, p. 77.

8. Miller, Marilyn L. and Shontz, Marilyn. "Small Change: Expenditures for Resources in School Library Media Centers, FY 1995-96." *SCHOOL LIBRARY JOURNAL*, October 1997, pp. 28-37.

9. Ibid.

10. Loertscher, David V. "Objective: Achievement. Solution: School Libraries." *SCHOOL LIBRARY JOURNAL*, May 1993, pp. 30-33.

11. Fry, Edward B. *FRY READABILITY SCALE*. Jamestown Publishers, 1978.

12. Spache, George D. *GOOD READING FOR POOR READERS*. 10th ed. Garrard, 1978, pp. 185-197.

13. Fry, Edward B. "The Readability Principle." *LANGUAGE ARTS*. September 1975, p. 847.

14. Ibid., p. 849

SELECTORS' CHOICE

The books and audiovisual materials on this list make a valuable contribution to meeting the special needs of children. They represent unusual, if not unique, approaches to subject areas. The list is arranged alphabetically by main entry within appeal level. Full information for each title may be found in the Classified Catalog Section. To the authors, illustrators, publishers and producers, we extend our deepest appreciation for their outstanding contributions to materials for children.

PRESCHOOL - PRIMARY GRADES

398.24	Aardema, Verna. *HOW THE OSTRICH GOT ITS LONG NECK: A TALE FROM THE AKAMBA OF KENYA.* Scholastic.
421	Bender, Robert. *A TO Z BEASTLY JAMBOREE.* Dutton/Lodestar.
EASY	Byars, Betsy Cromer. *MY BROTHER, ANT.* Viking.
EASY	Edwards, Pamela Duncan. *SOME SMUG SLUG.* HarperCollins.
EASY	Ehlert, Lois. *SNOWBALLS.* Harcourt Brace.
EASY	Fanelli, Sara. *MY MAP BOOK.* HarperCollins.
EASY	Henkes, Kevin. *LILLY'S PURPLE PLASTIC PURSE.* Greenwillow.
EASY	Kirk, Daniel. *TRASH TRUCKS.* Putnam.
591	MacDonald, Suse. *PECK SLITHER AND SLIDE.* Gulliver/Harcourt Brace.
EASY	Pilkey, Dav. *PAPERBOY.* Orchard.
EASY	Pinkney, J. Brian. *ADVENTURES OF SPARROWBOY.* Simon & Schuster.
811	Prelutsky, Jack. *MONDAY'S TROLL: POEMS.* Greenwillow.
621.8	Rotner, Shelley. *WHEELS AROUND.* Houghton Mifflin.
EASY	Stewart, Sarah. *GARDENER.* Farrar Straus Giroux.
CDR 529	*TRUDY'S TIME AND PLACE HOUSE.* School version (CD-ROM). Edmark.
EASY	Wells, Rosemary. *BUNNY CAKES.* Dial.

MIDDLE GRADES

966.7	Angelou, Maya. *KOFI AND HIS MAGIC.* Clarkson Potter.
513.4	Anno, Mitsumasa. *ANNO'S MAGIC SEEDS.* Philomel.
598.9	Arnosky, Jim. *ALL ABOUT OWLS.* Scholastic.
959.404	Cha, Dia. *DIA'S STORY CLOTH.* Lee & Low/Denver Museum of Natural History.
B MANDELA, N.	Cooper, Floyd. *MANDELA: FROM THE LIFE OF THE SOUTH AFRICAN STATESMAN.* Philomel.
398.27	Duncan, Lois. *MAGIC OF SPIDER WOMAN.* Scholastic.
398.2	Hamilton, Virginia. *HER STORIES: AFRICAN-AMERICAN FOLKTALES, FAIRY TALES, AND TRUE TALES.* Blue Sky Press/Scholastic.

398.24	Lewis, Paul Owen. *STORM BOY.* Beyond Words Publishing.
EASY	Martin, Jacqueline Briggs. *GRANDMOTHER BRYANT'S POCKET.* Houghton Mifflin.
970.1	McLain, Gary. *INDIAN WAY: LEARNING TO COMMUNICATE WITH MOTHER EARTH.* John Muir.
940.53	Mochizuki, Ken. *PASSAGE TO FREEDOM: THE SUGIHARA STORY.* Lee & Low.
VCR B POLACCO, P.	Polacco, Patricia. *DREAM KEEPER* (Videocassette). Philomel.
FIC	Say, Allen. *ALLISON.* Houghton Mifflin.
EASY	Scieszka, Jon. *MATH CURSE.* Viking.

UPPER GRADES - ADVANCED

FIC	Alcock, Vivien. *RED-EARED GHOSTS.* Houghton Mifflin.
FIC	Alexander, Lloyd. *IRON RING.* Dutton.
579.6	Arnold, Katya. *KATYA'S BOOK OF MUSHROOMS.* Henry Holt.
FIC	Avi. *BEYOND THE WESTERN SEA.* Books one and two. Orchard.
331.3	Bartoletti, Susan Campbell. *GROWING UP IN COAL COUNTRY.* Houghton Mifflin.
FIC	Coman, Carolyn. *WHAT JAMIE SAW.* Front Street.
FIC	Cooper, Susan. *BOGGART AND THE MONSTER.* McElderry.
FIC	Cushman, Karen. *BALLAD OF LUCY WHIPPLE.* Clarion.
398.27	Demi. *ONE GRAIN OF RICE: A MATHEMATICAL FOLKTALE.* Scholastic.
FIC	Freeman, Suzanne. *CUCKOO'S CHILD.* Greenwillow.
REF 423	*HARCOURT BRACE STUDENT DICTIONARY.* 2nd ed. Harcourt Brace.
639.9	Johnson, Sylvia A. *RAPTOR RESCUE!: AN EAGLE FLIES FREE.* Dutton.
FIC	Konigsburg, E. L. *VIEW FROM SATURDAY.* Atheneum.
551.55	Lauber, Patricia. *HURRICANES: EARTH'S MIGHTIEST STORMS.* Scholastic.
294.5	Lewin, Ted. *SACRED RIVER.* Clarion.
624	Mann, Elizabeth. *BROOKLYN BRIDGE.* Mikaya Press.
641.3	Micucci, Charles. *LIFE AND TIMES OF THE PEANUT.* Houghton Mifflin.
986.6	Myers, Lynne Born. *GALAPAGOS: ISLANDS OF CHANGE.* Hyperion.
FIC	Skurzynski, Gloria. *VIRTUAL WAR.* Simon & Schuster.
860.9	*TREE IS OLDER THAN YOU ARE: A BILINGUAL GATHERING OF POEMS AND STORIES FROM MEXICO WITH PAINTINGS BY MEXICAN ARTISTS.* Selected by Naomi Shihab Nye. Simon & Schuster.
940.53	Tunnell, Michael O. *CHILDREN OF TOPAZ: THE STORY OF A JAPANESE-AMERICAN INTERNMENT CAMP: BASED ON A CLASSROOM DIARY.* Holiday House.

970.1	Viola, Herman J. *NORTH AMERICAN INDIANS.* Crown.
B WATSON, L.	Watson, Lyall. *WARRIORS, WARTHOGS, AND WISDOM: GROWING UP IN AFRICA.* Kingfisher.
FIC	Young, Ronder Thomas. *MOVING MAMA TO TOWN.* Orchard.

FOR ALL AGES

811.008	*FOR LAUGHING OUT LOUDER: MORE POEMS TO TICKLE YOUR FUNNYBONE.* Selected by Jack Prelutsky. Knopf.
523.3	Gibbons, Gail. *MOON BOOK.* Holiday House.
VCR 635	*LOOK WHAT I GREW: WINDOWSILL GARDENS* (Videocassette). Intervideo.
811	Prelutsky, Jack. *PIZZA THE SIZE OF THE SUN: POEMS.* Greenwillow.
811	Silverstein, Shel. *FALLING UP: POEMS AND DRAWINGS.* HarperCollins.
789.2	*SONGS FOR SURVIVAL: SONGS AND CHANTS FROM TRIBAL PEOPLES AROUND THE WORLD.* Compiled by Nikki Siegen-Smith. Dutton.
895.6	*SPRING: A HAIKU STORY.* Selected by George Shannon. Greenwillow.
546	Wick, Walter. *DROP OF WATER: A BOOK OF SCIENCE AND WONDER.* Scholastic.

PROFESSIONAL

PROF 011.62	Ammon, Bette DeBruyne. *WORTH A THOUSAND WORDS: AN ANNOTATED GUIDE TO PICTURE BOOKS FOR OLDER READERS.* Libraries Unlimited.
PROF 028.1	Horning, Kathleen T. *FROM COVER TO COVER: EVALUATING AND REVIEWING CHILDREN'S BOOKS.* HarperCollins.
PROF 372.3	Jurenka, Nancy E. Allen. *BEYOND THE BEAN SEED: GARDENING ACTIVITIES FOR GRADES K-6.* Teacher Ideas Press.
PROF 372.3	*RESOURCES FOR TEACHING ELEMENTARY SCHOOL SCIENCE.* National Academy Press.
PROF 809	Sutherland, Zena. *CHILDREN AND BOOKS.* 9th ed. Longman.

SAMPLE ENTRY

The composite sample entry below is keyed for elements which occur in entries for both books and audiovisual materials.

Type of Material
- BA Book with audio
- BB Board book
- BC Book with computer file
- CD Compact disc (audio)
- CDR CD-ROM (computer product)
- CE Combined entry (book and audiovisual material)
- KIT Kit (read-along book and audio)
- MCP Microcomputer program
- MMK Multimedia kit
- PIC Picture (art or study print)
- SRC Sound recording cassette
- TB Talking book
- VCR Videocassette
- VD Video disc

Interest Level
- P Preschoolers
- K Kindergarteners
- 1 First graders
- 2 Second graders
- 3 Third graders
- 4 Fourth graders
- 5 Fifth graders
- 6 Sixth graders
- A Advanced readers (not necessarily restricted to advanced sixth graders.)

Phase of Acquisition
- Ph-I For all libraries
- Ph-2 Continuing development
- Ph-3 Specialized significance

Dewey Classification

Readability Estimate (books)

Price

Purchasing Information
- (L) Library or Reinforced edition
- (T) Trade edition
- (P) Paperback
- (OD) Must be ordered direct

CE   398.25   Ph-1   4-A/3 $14.89   L   KB694 - Citation Number

Main entry — SCHWARTZ, ALVIN. | Scary stories to tell in the dark. — Title

Expanded author/illustrator statement — Illus. by Stephen Gammell. | HarperCollins ISBN 0-397-31927-4,

1981. | 111p. ill. — Collation (Publisher's Series, if any)

Publisher(s)/Producer
- ISBN book
- Product No. audiovisual
- ISSN periodical
- Date

Includes bibliography.
Talking book available from HarperAudio/ Caedmon (ISBN 0-89845-758-0, 1986). 1 sound cassette, (42 min), $11.95. Available from National Library Service for the Blind and Physically Handicapped in Braille BR06199 and on sound recording cassette RC22330.

— Notes

Annotation

"Telling scary stories is something people have done for thousands of years, for most of us like being scared in that way" (Intro.) and contained in this collection are some of the best scary tales for telling and reading. The documentation provided for the tales could lead to an interesting social studies or language arts experience for gifted students.

Followed by MORE SCARY STORIES TO TELL IN THE DARK (ISBN 0-397-32082-5, c1986); and SCARY STORIES 3: MORE TALES TO CHILL YOUR BONES (ISBN 0-06-021795-2, 1991).

— Notes

Subject Headings — SUBJ: Ghosts - Folklore./ Folklore - United States./ United States - Folklore.

PROFESSIONAL
COLLECTION

MMK PROF 004.67   Ph-3 $249.00   OD KA001
EDUCATORS' ESSENTIAL INTERNET TRAINING SYSTEM (Multimedia kit). Classroom Connect LETS02, 1996. 4 3.5" disks, 2 1/2" VHS videocassettes color (42min).
> Includes trainer's guide, workbooks and certificates.
> This set of training materials makes a good addition to a district office collection. The videotapes explore the vast educational wealth of the Internet. The ready-made workshop materials make it simple for a trainer to introduce the Internet and the various e-mail and listserv functions, explore the World Wide Web, and briefly discuss integration of this tool into the curriculum. Good overview for teachers or parents.
> SUBJ: Internet (Computer network)--Handbooks, manuals, etc./ World Wide Web (Information retrieval system)--Handbooks, manuals, etc.

MCP PROF 006.6   Ph-1 $79.95   OD KA002
PRINT SHOP DELUXE I (Microcomputer program). Broderbund, 1992. 5 3.5" program disks, 1 3.5" teacher's guide disk, 1 3.5" bonus disk.
> Includes user's guide, graphic reference guide, and teacher's guide.
> Also available for Macintosh.
> System requirements: DOS/Windows 386 or faster: DOS 3.0 or higher; 2MB RAM; hard drive; high density floppy disk drive; VGA monitor; Mouse recommended.
> This upgraded version of a classic program includes options for greeting cards, signs, banners, letterheads, and calendars. Options for more fonts, rotating graphics and text, as well as shaping text blocks add variety to creations. Still an easy-to-use software creation package. Superb teaching tool suggestions will be helpful to classroom teachers.
> SUBJ: Graphics--Software./ Software--Graphics.

PROF 011   Ph-3   FREE   P OD KA003
AIT CATALOG OF EDUCATIONAL MATERIALS. Agency for Instructional Technology, 1962-. Annual (Sept).
> A well-designed catalog of instructional television programs. All are available in broadcast videotape or videocassettes, some as 16mm film. Most can be rented, a few available for purchase only. This catalog, free to libraries on request, will be useful wherever videotape is used.
> SUBJ: Videocassettes--Catalogs./ Television programs--Catalogs./ Motion pictures--Catalogs.

PROF 011   Ph-2 $59.95   T KA004
NEWBERY AND CALDECOTT MEDALISTS AND HONOR BOOK WINNERS: BIBLIOGRAPHIES AND RESOURCE MATERIAL THROUGH 1991. 2nd ed. By Muriel W. Brown and Rita Schoch Foudray. Edited by Jim Roginski. Neal-Schuman ISBN 1-55570-118-3, 1992. 511p.
> Includes bibliographies and index.
> Lists alphabetically authors and illustrators who have won Newbery or Caldecott awards or honors. Each entry includes the titles which received the awards as well as a bibliography of the complete works of the author or illustrator. Bibliographies of background reading about the recipients and locations of collections which house their original artwork and manuscripts complete the package. Useful for author studies in whole language programs.
> SUBJ: Children's literature, American--Awards./ Children's literature, American--Illustrators--Awards./ Illustrated books, Children's--Bibliography./ Bibliography--Best books--Children's literature./ Caldecott Medal books./ Newbery Medal books./ Literary prizes.

PROF 011   Ph-1 $45.00   T KA005
RECOMMENDED REFERENCE BOOKS FOR SMALL AND MEDIUM-SIZED LIBRARIES AND MEDIA CENTERS. Edited by Bohdan S. Wynar and Anna Grae Patterson. Libraries Unlimited ISSN 0277-5948, 1981-. annual.
> Includes index.
> Designed to aid small libraries in selecting suitable reference tools for their collections. Titles have been selected from AMERICAN REFERENCE BOOKS ANNUAL. All types of reference books are included. Code letters "C", "P", and "S" indicate recommended purchase for college (C), public (P) or school media center (S). Complete bibliographic information plus in-depth annotation make this an excellent guide.
> SUBJ: Reference books--Bibliography./ Reference services (Libraries).

PROF 011   Ph-2 $26.00   P KA006
REFERENCE BOOKS BULLETIN, 1994-1995: A COMPILATION OF EVALUATIONS APPEARING IN "REFERENCE BOOKS BULLETIN," SEPTEMBER 1, 1992 - AUGUST, 1993. Edited by Sandy Whiteley. American Library Association ISBN 0-8389-7816-9, 1995. 178p.
> Includes index.
> The 22nd annual cumulation of evaluations which have appeared in "Reference Books Bulletin" (RBB), published jointly with "Booklist." The purpose of RBB is "to provide critical reviews that librarians can use in making selection decisions and in providing guidance to users contemplating personal purchases for their home libraries." Includes indexes by subject, type of material and title.
> SUBJ: Reference books--Reviews.

PROF 011   Ph-2 $40.00   T KA007
WYNAR, CHRISTINE GEHRT. Guide to reference books for school media centers. 4th ed. Libraries Unlimited ISBN 0-87287-833-3, 1992. 463p.
> Includes index.
> "Designed to be a comprehensive guide to current reference materials that are suitable for several categories of users: (1) students in elementary, middle, and high schools; (2) teachers K-12; (3) school library media specialists; and (4) educators in the areas of teachers' preservice and inservice, information resources, and children's and young adult literature." The main entry for each work offers standard bibliographic information (does not include ISBN). The annotations are broad enough to provide needed information about the usefulness and scope of the work cited. The format is pleasing to read. The index is extensive and provides access through multiple entries. A particular strength is the number of media sources cited.
> SUBJ: Children's reference books--Bibliography./ Bibliography--Best books--Children's literature./ School libraries--Book lists./ Instructional materials centers.

PROF 011.008   Ph-2 $28.00   P KA008
CORETTA SCOTT KING AWARDS BOOK: FROM VISION TO REALITY. Edited by Henrietta M. Smith. American Library Association ISBN 0-8389-3441-2, 1994. 115p. ill. (some col.).
> Includes index.
> A celebration of the twenty-fifth anniversary of the Coretta Scott King Awards showcases the rich diversity of African-American literature for children and the artists and authors who create it. Award-winning and honor titles are discussed in detail along with profiles of the award

recipients. For multicultural studies.
SUBJ: Coretta Scott King Award--Bibliography./ Afro-American authors--Bio-bibliography./ Afro-American artists--Bio-bibliography./ American literature--Afro-American authors--Bibliography.

PROF 011.62   Ph-1 $22.95   P   KA009
ADVENTURING WITH BOOKS: A BOOKLIST FOR PRE-K-GRADE 6. 1997 ed. Edited by Wendy K. Sutton and the Committee to revise the Elementary School Booklist. With a forward by Patricia MacLachlan. National Council of Teachers of English ISBN 0-8141-0080-5, 1997. 401p. ill. (NCTE bibliography series).
Includes directory and indexes.
Annotated bibliography, arranged by genre, lists high quality literature for children. Includes complete bibliographic information along with interest level stated as ages. Art medium used in illustrations is indexed in subject index. Excellent resource for collection development and curriculum enhancements.
SUBJ: Children's literature--Bibliography./ Bibliography--Best books--Children's literature./ Elementary school libraries--Book lists.

PROF 011.62   Ph-1 $26.50   P   KA010
AMMON, BETTE DEBRUYNE. Worth a thousand words: an annotated guide to picture books for older readers. By Bette D. Ammon and Gale W. Sherman. Libraries Unlimited ISBN 1-56308-390-6, 1996. 210p.
Includes bibliography and indexes.
Selectors' Choice, 21st ed.
Begins with the "top ten reasons why teachers, librarians, and parents should provide picture books for older readers." Symbols are used with each annotated entry to point out books that are "extraordinary" or "include a combination of sophisticated themes, language, and illustrations." Other icons identify books for writing, math, science, history, research, and reading aloud. Entries are arranged alphabetically by author and provide bibliographic information (no ISBN). Excellent for interdisciplinary studies and for parents. (Parents' Shelf).
SUBJ: Illustrated books, Children's--Bibliography./ Picture books for children--Bibliography./ Children--Books and reading.

PROF 011.62   Ph-3 $47.00   T   KA011
BARSTOW, BARBARA. Beyond picture books: a guide to first readers. 2nd ed. By Barbara Barstow and Judith Riggle. Bowker ISBN 0-8352-3519-X, 1995. 501p.
Includes indexes.
Somewhat unusual (and a little confusing) in organization and format, this identifies 2500 easy-to-read books for young independent readers. Each title is numbered and entered alphabetically under the author's name. Reading level is provided as is a descriptive annotation. Out of print titles are included, but not noted.
SUBJ: Children's literature--Bibliography./ Libraries, Children's--Book lists./ Children--Books and reading.

PROF 011.62   Ph-1 $105.00   L OD KA012
CHILDREN'S CATALOG. 17th ed. Ed. by Anne Price and Juliette Yaakov. Wilson ISBN 0-8242-0893-5, 1996. 1373p. (Standard catalog series).
Includes indexes and directory.
Includes annual supplements.
A fully classified bibliography of materials for children ages preschool through grade six. Useful collection development tool to identify fiction and nonfiction books, magazines, and CD-ROM reference works for children as well as professional materials for librarians and school media specialists.
Contents: Pt 1: Classified catalog; Pt 2: Author, title, subject, and analytical index; Pt 3: Select list of recommended CD-ROM reference works; Pt 4: Directory of publishers and distributors.
SUBJ: Children's literature--Bibliography./ Cataloging of children's literature--Specimens./ Children's literature--Book lists./ School libraries--Book lists.

PROF 011.62   Ph-1 $139.95   T   KA013
ELEMENTARY SCHOOL LIBRARY COLLECTION: A GUIDE TO BOOKS AND OTHER MEDIA, PHASES 1-2-3. 21st ed. Brodart Co. ISBN 0-87272-114-0, 1998.
Includes indexes and directory.
Editor: 1965-73, Mary V. Gaver; 1974-77, Phyllis Van Orden; 1978-90, Lois Winkel; 1991-1994, Lauren K. Lee; 1995- , Linda L. Homa.
A classified catalog of recommended print and audiovisual materials for library media centers serving preschool through sixth-grade children. Main arrangement covers materials in the professional collection, reference materials, periodicals, and the general circulating collection, followed by author, title, and subject indexes. Each citation includes: bibliographic data, price and recommended binding, recommended phase of acquisition, interest and reading levels, and a critically descriptive annotation frequently with suggestions for use.

Special features include: Selection Policies, How To Use This Selection Tool, Selectors' Choice, and Appendices identifying materials for use with preschool children, books for beginning independent readers (1-1 - 2-2), Author's Series, and Publisher's Series.
SUBJ: Children's literature--Bibliography./ Audio-visual materials--Catalogs./ Elementary school libraries--Book lists.

CDR PROF 011.62   Ph-1 $199.00   OD KA014
ELEMENTARY SCHOOL LIBRARY COLLECTION: A GUIDE TO BOOKS AND OTHER MEDIA, PHASES 1-2-3. 21st ed. (CD-ROM). Brodart Co., Automation Division ISBN 0-87272-115-9, 1998. 1 CD-ROM color.
Version 2.1.
Includes user's manual.
Annual supplement available at additional price.
Network version also available (ISBN 0-87272-116-7), $299.00.
Editor: 1994, Lauren K. Lee; 1995- , Linda L. Homa.
System requirements: IBM PC, AT, or 100% compatible (386 or higher); VGA color monitor; 640K RAM; MS-DOS 3.3 or higher; any double-speed CD-ROM drive with MS-DOS extensions.
Contains the same comprehensive information as the printed 21st edition. Recommends print and audiovisual materials for library media centers serving preschool through sixth-grade children, including reference and professional materials. Items can be searched through numerous access points -- author/illustrator, title, subject, Dewey range, publication date, publisher, series, format, phase of acquisition, section, appeal level, reading level, and independent reading level. Combined searching and keyword searching capability is provided. Bibliography function permits saving to a list or a file, sorting, and printing. Especially useful to identify materials for specific levels including high/low and materials for interdisciplinary subjects such as environmental studies and multicultural studies. Use to create individualized readers' advisory lists.
SUBJ: Children's literature--Bibliography--Software./ Audio-visual materials--Catalogs--Software./ Elementary school libraries--Book lists--Software./ Software--Children's literature--Bibliography./ Software--Audio-visual materials--Catalogs./ Software--Elementary school libraries--Book lists.

PROF 011.62   Ph-1 $39.00   T   KA015
FREEMAN, JUDY. Books kids will sit still for: the complete read-aloud guide. 2nd ed. Bowker ISBN 0-8352-3010-4, 1990. 660p.
Includes bibliography and indices.
This is a book that should be highlighted (books you have in your collection); improved (by writing to the author - at her invitation in the preface); shared with teachers and students; and discussed at staff meetings. The excellent section on techniques of reading aloud includes "pitfalls" and "using props and other gimmicks." Examples of other sections are Storytelling, Booktalking, and 101 Ways to Celebrate Books. The annotated read-aloud lists are arranged by grade and provide brief information on ideas and other books that will "connect."
SUBJ: Children's literature--Bibliography./ Bibliography-Best books--Children's literature./ School libraries--Book lists./ School libraries--Activity programs./ Oral reading.

PROF 011.62   Ph-1 $38.00   T   KA016
HARMS, JEANNE MCLAIN. Picture books to enhance the curriculum. By Jeanne McLain Harms and Lucille J. Lettow. Wilson ISBN 0-8242-0867-6, 1996. 523p.
Includes index and bibliography.
An index of picture books, organized by theme. Criteria for inclusion includes "literary and artistic quality, curriculum application, appeal to youth, and availability." (p.x) Review sources include: CHILDREN'S CATALOG, 16th ed., CHILDREN'S LITERATURE IN THE ELEMENTARY SCHOOL, SCHOOL LIBRARY JOURNAL, BOOKLIST, HORN BOOK MAGAZINE, and BULLETIN OF THE CENTER FOR CHILDREN'S BOOKS. Titles are included under a "Themes Index" and under a "Picture Book Index." A "Title Index" is also included. Weakness, lack of an author index. Useful resource for creating thematic units for storytimes or classrooms.
SUBJ: Children's literature--Bibliography./ Picture books for children--Educational aspects--Indexes./ Picture books for children--Educational aspects--Bibliography.

PROF 011.62   Ph-2 $65.00   T   KA017
LIMA, CAROLYN W. A to zoo: subject access to children's picture books. 5th ed. By Carolyn W. and John A. Lima. Bowker ISBN 0-8352-3916-0, 1998. 1250p.
Includes indexes.
Designed to assist teachers to better utilize the wealth of material in informational and fictional picture books, this listing of over 15,000 titles is divided into five sections: Subject Headings; Subject Guide; Bibliographic Guide; Title Index; and Illustrator Index. Inclusive listing that contains a broad collection of titles, including out-of-print books.

Recommended for use in major collections.
SUBJ: Picture books for children--Bibliography./ Children's literature--Bibliography.

PROF 011.62   Ph-2 $15.95   P   KA018
MAGAZINES FOR KIDS AND TEENS: Rev. ed. Edited by Donald R. Stoll. Educational Press Association of America/International Reading Association ISBN 0-87207-243-6, 1997. 118p.
Formerly MAGAZINES FOR CHILDREN, 1990.
Includes indexes.
Opens with an article justifying magazines by Bernice E. Cullinan, former president of IRA. Alphabetically arranged, annotated notes for 249 magazines include target audience, subject, distribution, and editorial and ordering addresses. Includes subject and age/grade indexes as well as index of magazines that publish readers' work.
SUBJ: Children's periodicals--Bibliography./ Youths' periodicals--Bibliography./ Periodicals--Bibliography.

PROF 011.62   Ph-1 $175.00   T OD KA019
MIDDLE AND JUNIOR HIGH SCHOOL LIBRARY CATALOG. 7th ed. Edited by Anne Price and Juliette Yaakov. Wilson ISBN 0-8242-0880-3, 1995. 988p. (Standard catalog series).
Rev. ed. of: JUNIOR HIGH SCHOOL LIBRARY CATALOG. 6th ed.
Includes indexes and directory.
Includes annual supplements.
A basic bibliography of materials provides broad coverage including classic, contemporary, and genre fiction and nonfiction which reflects the developmental interests of middle and junior high school students. Special emphasis was placed on "cultural diversity, technology, personal values, and contemporary social and political issues." (p. v) Useful tool for collection development, curriculum support, and reader's advisory in the upper elementary grades.
SUBJ: Young adult literature--Bibliography./ Junior high school libraries--Book lists.

PROF 011.62   Ph-2 $39.95   T   KA020
MILLER-LACHMANN, LYN. Our family, our friends, our world: an annotated guide to significant multicultural books for children and teenagers. Bowker ISBN 0-8352-3025-2, 1992. 710p. ill.
Includes bibliographies, directory and indexes.
Bibliography of multicultural materials lists over 1,000 fiction and nonfiction titles published between 1970-1990 for children in preschool through twelfth grade which accurately reflect 18 major geographical regions or ethnic groups. Critical annotations written by selectors who have expertise on the culture being represented include suggestions for use and descriptions of illustrations and point out errors or flaws in the work. Use as a readers' advisory guide and collection development tool. For multicultural studies.
SUBJ: Children's literature--Bibliography./ Young adult literature--Bibliography./ Pluralism (Social sciences) in literature--Bibliography./ Ethnic groups in literature--Bibliography./ Minorities in literature--Bibliography.

PROF 011.62   Ph-2 $39.50   T   KA021
PETERSON, CAROLYN SUE. Reference books for children, 4th ed. By Carolyn Sue Peterson and Ann D. Fenton. Scarecrow ISBN 0-8108-2543-0, 1992. 399p.
Includes indexes.
An excellent source for collection development, this selection tool "...includes more than 1,000 annotated entries for reference books and selection tools appropriate for school and public libraries." (Preface) The book also provides information on evaluating reference books and conducting the reference interview.
SUBJ: Children's reference books--Bibliography./ Libraries, Children's--Book lists./ School libraries--Book lists.

PROF 011.62   Ph-2 $12.50   KA022
RICHARDSON, SELMA K. Magazines for children, a guide for parents, teachers, and librarians. American Library Association ISBN 0-8389-0392-4, 1983. 147p.
Includes appendices and index.
Planned to alert adults, parents and professionals to the variety of magazines available for children, this edition features lengthier and more detailed annotations. Curiously, no magazines about computers are listed.
SUBJ: Periodicals.

PROF 011.62   Ph-3 $37.50   T   KA023
SUTHERLAND, ZENA. Best in children's books: the University of Chicago guide to children's literature, 1985-1990. Written and edited by Zena Sutherland, Betsy Hearne and Roger Sutton. University of Chicago ISBN 0-226-78064-3, 1991. 492p.
Includes indexes.
Includes the most important reviews from the University of Chicago's

BULLETIN OF THE CENTER FOR CHILDREN'S BOOKS from 1985-1990. Organization is alphabetical by author. The six indexes provide access by title, developmental values, curricular use, reading level, subject, and type of literature. Useful tool for collection development as well as readers' advisory.
SUBJ: Bibliography--Best books--Children's literature./ Children's literature--Bibliography./ Children's literature--Book reviews.

PROF 011.62   Ph-1 $25.00   P   KA024
VENTURE INTO CULTURES: A RESOURCE BOOK OF MULTICULTURAL MATERIALS AND PROGRAMS. Edited by Carla D. Hayden. American Library Association ISBN 0-8389-0579-X, 1992. 165p. ill.
Includes bibliographies and index.
Presents a wealth of resources for programs and suggested activities to introduce cultural diversity into the curriculum. Cultures represented include African, American, Arabic, Asian, Hispanic, Jewish, Native American, and Persian. Cultural orientation and background present distinguishing aspects of each culture. Bibliographies with each chapter include fiction, picture books, folklore, nonfiction, and audiovisual resources. Useful for multicultural studies as well as interdisciplinary units.
SUBJ: Children's literature--Bibliography./ United States--Ethnic relations--Bibliography./ Minorities--United States--Bibliography./ Pluralism (Social sciences) in literature--Bibliography./ Ethnic groups in literature--Bibliography./ Minorities in literature--Bibliography.

PROF 016.1559   Ph-2 $49.00   T   KA025
RUDMAN, MASHA K. Books to help children cope with separation and loss: an annotated bibliography. 4th ed. By Masha K. Rudman, Kathleen Dunne Gagne, and Joanne E. Bernstein. Bowker ISBN 0-8352-3412-6, 1993. 514p. (Serving special needs).
Includes bibliography, directory and indexes.
Valuable resource for librarians, teachers, guidance counselors, and parents seeking to identify books on topics ranging from acceptance of a new sibling to death. Over 750 entries, more than half of which are new to this edition, include complete bibliographic information, an extensive descriptive annotation with critical remarks, interest and reading levels, and suggestions for use. (Parents' Shelf).
SUBJ: Separation (Psychology)--Bibliography./ Bereavement--Psychological aspects--Bibliography.

PROF 016.372   Ph-2 $15.00   P   KA026
ROUTMAN, REGIE. Blue pages: resources for teachers from Invitations. Updated, expanded, and rev. By Regie Routman with Susan Hepler...[et al.]. Heinemann ISBN 0-435-08835-1, 1994. 256p. ill.
Includes index.
Annotated resource list of professional books, journal articles, journals, newsletters, and literacy extension resources which will provide professional growth for educators. "Recommended Literature by Grade Level, K-12" should be especially helpful in planning units. These "blue pages" are also included in the author's book INVITATIONS: CHANGING AS TEACHERS AND LEARNERS K-12.
SUBJ: Language experience approach in education--Bibliography./ Language arts--Bibliography./ Teaching--Bibliography./ Teachers--Bibliography.

PROF 016.3982   Ph-3 4-6 $99.00   T   KA027
MACDONALD, MARGARET READ. Storyteller's sourcebook: a subject, title, and motif index to folklore collections for children. Gale ISBN 0-8103-0471-6, 1982. 818p.
Includes bibliography.
Brings together "variants of each folktale, and supplies descriptions of them. It aims to fill a long-felt need in the school, public, and university library, and is specifically designed for quick and easy access by the teacher or librarian who wants to locate (1) tales about a given subject, (2) the location of a specific tale title in collections, (3) tales from an ethnic or geographical area, (4) variants of a specific tale." Indexes 556 folktale collections and 389 picture books.
SUBJ: Folklore--Classification./ Folklore--Indexes.

PROF 016.5   Ph-2 $24.00   P   KA028
SCIENCE BOOKS AND FILMS' BEST BOOKS FOR CHILDREN, 1992-1995. Edited by Tracy Gath and Maria Sosa. American Association for the Advancement of Science ISBN 0-87168-586-8, 1996. 286p.
Includes indexes.
Includes top ranked reviews published in SCIENCE BOOKS & FILMS, a review journal published by the American Association for the Advancement of Science. Useful selection tool for librarians and teachers who are seeking books with accurate scientific content. Lengthy annotations provide standard bibliographic information, age level, and name of the reviewer. Divided in broad topics with separate reviewer, author, and title indexes. Lack of a subject index is the only weakness.
SUBJ: Science--Bibliography./ Science--Study and teaching--Audio-

PROFESSIONAL COLLECTION

visual aids--Bibliography./ Best books--Children's literature--Bibliography./ School libraries--Book lists.

PROF 016.7893   Ph-2 $25.00   P   KA029

REID, ROB. Children's jukebox: a subject guide to musical recordings and programming ideas for songsters ages one to twelve. American Library Association ISBN 0-8389-0650-8, 1995. 225p.

Includes filmography, directories, bibliography and index.
Indexes 2,400 contemporary recorded songs according to 35 popular themes for children's programs. Includes selections for audience participation such as cumulative songs, call and response songs, and rounds. Annotation gives a summary of the song's lyrics, interest level, and suggestions for use with children. A welcome resource for teachers, librarians, performers, and parents. Especially useful in libraries with large collections of sound recordings. (Parents' Shelf).
SUBJ: Children's songs--Discography--Indexes./ Children's songs--Reviews./ Children's libraries--Activity programs.

PROF 016.791   Ph-3 $305.00   T OD   KA030

VIDEO SOURCE BOOK. National Video Clearinghouse/dist. by Gale ISSN 0748-0881, 1979-. 2v. annual.

Includes index and directory of distributors.
Having as its objective bibliographic control of videotape and videodisc titles, this tool includes over 30,000 entries--listed alphabetically and indexed under 400 subject headings; for each indicates date of production, running time, color, caption or sign for deaf, format, use availability (ex. home, school), appropriate audience age, brief content description, language, producer, and distributor. Price not given. A unique reference, very useful where video equiment is used.
SUBJ: Videotapes--Catalogs./ Video discs--Catalogs./ Audio-visual materials--Catalogs.

PROF 016.80883   Ph-1 $60.00   T   KA031

COLBORN, CANDY. What do children read next?: a reader's guide to fiction for children. Gale Research ISBN 0-8103-6448-4, 1997. 1135p.

Includes indexes.
A "readers advisory tool designed to match readers from Grades 1 through 8 with books that reflect their interests and concerns." (Preface p.VII) Includes approximately 2000 entries--over half were published within the past five years, others have withstood the "test of time." Arranged alphabetically by author, entries include complete bibliographic information, review citations, other books by the author, and additional titles on a similar theme. The ten indexes cover: Awards, Time Period, Geographic, Subject, Character Name, Character Description, Age level, Illustrator, Author, and Title. Excellent tool for teachers, librarians, and students.
SUBJ: Children--Books and reading--Bibliography./ Children's stories--Bibliography.

PROF 016.80883   Ph-3 $52.00   T   KA032

LYNN, RUTH NADELMAN. Fantasy literature for children and young adults: an annotated bibliography. 4th ed. Bowker ISBN 0-8352-3456-8, 1994. 1092p.

Includes indexes.
Excellent overview of fantasy will provide teachers and librarians with new ideas about the importance of this essential genre. Bibliography is extensive, selective, and annotated. Indexed by author and illustrator, title, and subject. Includes bibliographic references for author studies, educational resources on fantasy literature, critical and historical studies, and biographical and reference sources.
SUBJ: Children--Books and reading./ Children's literature--Bibliography./ Young adult literature--Bibliography./ Fantastic literature--Bibliography.

PROF 016.809   Ph-3 $156.00   T   KA033

CHILDREN'S AUTHORS AND ILLUSTRATORS: AN INDEX TO BIOGRAPHICAL DICTIONARIES. Gale ISSN 1082-7390, 1976-. v. irregular. (Gale biographical index series).

Indexes biographies of 25,000 authors and illustrators in over 450 reference works. Each entry gives the author's name--with cross references to pseudonyms and variant spellings--birth and death dates, and a list of reference sources. A key to index with abbreviations is conveniently printed on the end papers. Usefulness of this index will depend on local availability of the biographical references cited.
SUBJ: Authors--Biography--Indexes./ Illustrators--Biography--Indexes./ Children's literature--Indexes.

PROF 016.809   Ph-2 $11.95   P   KA034

LITERARY LAURELS: KIDS' EDITION: A READER'S GUIDE TO AWARD-WINNING CHILDREN'S BOOKS. Edited by Laura Carlson, Sean Creighton, Sheila Cunningham. Hillyard ISBN 0-9647361-1-X, 1996. 138p.

Includes directory and indexes.

Lists over 1200 children's books which have won major book awards. Includes awards that are well known in the United States such as Caldecott, Newbery, and Coretta Scott King awards as well as less familiar genre awards such as the Scott O'Dell Award for historical fiction; Edgar Allan Poe Award for suspense, detective, and spy stories; and the Western Heritage Award for books about the American West. A representative group of Children's Choice awards is provided--William Allen White Children's Book Award (Kansas), Mark Twain Award (Missouri), and Dorothy Canfield Fisher Children's Book Award (Vermont). Major awards from Great Britian and Canada such as the Carnegie Medal, the Kate Greenaway Medal, and the Governor General's Literary Award are also given. While not a complete list of award-winning children's books (many state awards are omitted and in most cases, honor books are not mentioned), this will serve as a handy tool for both collection development and reader's advisory.
SUBJ: Literary prizes--Bibliography./ Children's literature--Bibliography.

PROF 016.813   Ph-1 $48.00   T   KA035

GILLESPIE, JOHN THOMAS. Newbery companion: booktalk and related materials for Newbery Medal and Honor Books. By John T. Gillespie and Corinne J. Naden. Libraries Unlimited ISBN 1-56308-356-6, 1996. 406p.

Includes bibliographies and indexes.
Excellent sourcebook for Newbery Award books. A chronological listing for all award and honor books follows background information on John Newbery and the establishment of the award. Plot summary, theme, subject, incidents for booktalking, and related titles are provided for each book.
SUBJ: Newbery Medal--Bibliography./ Best books--Children's literature--Bibliography./ Children's literature, American--Bibliography.

PROF 016.974   Ph-1 $24.95   P   KA036

EXPLORING THE NORTHEAST STATES THROUGH LITERATURE. Edited by P. Diane Frey; state editors, Judith W. Whitcomb...[et al.]. Oryx ISBN 0-89774-779-8; In Canada: Oryx, 1994. 260p. (Exploring the United States through literature).

Includes directory and indexes.
This useful, annotated regional guide identifies print and nonprint resources for grades K-8, which cover both the history and contemporary culture of Connecticut, Delaware, the District of Columbia, Maine, Maryland, Massachusetts, New Hampshire, New Jersey, New York, Pennsylvania, Rhode Island, and Vermont. Arranged by state in Dewey sequence, entries list materials related to history, culture, geography, resources, industries, literature, legends, and famous personalities. Annotations provide a brief description, comment on usefulness in the curriculum, and suggest at least one learning activity. Supports interdisciplinary studies and the discovery approach to social studies.
SUBJ: Northeastern States--Bibliography./ Children's literature--Bibliography.

PROF 016.975   Ph-1 $24.95   P   KA037

EXPLORING THE SOUTHEAST STATES THROUGH LITERATURE. Edited by Linda Veltze; state editors, Judith V. Lechner...[et al.]. Oryx ISBN 0-89774-770-4; In Canada: Oryx, 1994. 205p. (Exploring the United States through literature).

Includes directory and indexes.
This useful, annotated regional guide identifies print and nonprint resources for grades K-8, which cover both the history and contemporary culture of Alabama, Arkansas, Florida, Georgia, Kentucky, Louisiana, Mississippi, North Carolina, South Carolina, Tennessee, Virginia, and West Virginia. Arranged by state in Dewey sequence, entries list materials related to history, culture, geography, resources, industries, literature, legends, and famous personalities. Annotations provide a brief description, comment on usefulness in the curriculum, and suggest at least one learning activity. Supports interdisciplinary studies and the discovery approach to social studies.
SUBJ: Southern States--Bibliography./ Children's literature--Bibliography.

PROF 016.976   Ph-1 $24.95   P   KA038

EXPLORING THE SOUTHWEST STATES THROUGH LITERATURE. Edited by Pat Tipton Sharp; state editors, Cathy C. Bonnell...[et al.]. Oryx ISBN 0-89774-765-8; In Canada: Oryx, 1994. 107p. (Exploring the United States through literature).

Includes directory and indexes.
This useful, annotated regional guide identifies print and nonprint resources for grades K-8, which cover both the history and contemporary culture of Arizona, New Mexico, Oklahoma, and Texas. Arranged by state in Dewey sequence, entries list materials related to history, culture, geography, resources, industries, literature, legends, and famous personalities. Annotations provide a brief description, comment on usefulness in the curriculum, and suggest at

least one learning activity. Supports interdisciplinary studies and the discovery approach to social studies.
SUBJ: Southwestern States--Bibliography./ Children's literature--Bibliography.

PROF 016.977   Ph-1 $24.95   P   KA039
EXPLORING THE GREAT LAKES STATES THROUGH LITERATURE. Edited by Kathy Howard Latrobe; state editors, LaVonne Hayes Sanborn...[et al.]. Oryx ISBN 0-89774-731-3; In Canada: Oryx, 1994. 149p. (Exploring the United States through literature).
Includes directory and indexes.
This useful, annotated regional guide identifies print and nonprint resources for grades K-8, which cover both the history and contemporary culture of Illinois, Indiana, Michigan, Minnesota, Ohio, and Wisconsin. Arranged by state in Dewey sequence, entries list materials related to history, culture, geography, resources, industries, literature, legends, and famous personalities. Annotations provide a brief description, comment on usefulness in the curriculum, and suggest at least one learning activity. Supports interdisciplinary studies and the discovery approach to social studies.
SUBJ: Lake States--Bibliography./ Children's literature--Bibliography.

PROF 016.978   Ph-1 $24.95   P   KA040
EXPLORING THE MOUNTAIN STATES THROUGH LITERATURE. Edited by Sharyl G. Smith; state editors, Deborah K. Reum...[et al.]. Oryx ISBN 0-89774-783-6; In Canada: Oryx, 1994. 157p. (Exploring the United States through literature).
Includes directory and indexes.
This useful, annotated regional guide identifies print and nonprint resources for grades K-8, which cover both the history and contemporary culture of Colorado, Idaho, Montana, Nevada, Utah, and Wyoming. Arranged by state in Dewey sequence, entries list materials related to history, culture, geography, resources, industries, literature, legends, and famous personalities. Annotations provide a brief description, comment on usefulness in the curriculum, and suggest at least one learning activity. Supports interdisciplinary studies and the discovery approach to social studies.
SUBJ: Rocky Mountains Region--Bibliography./ Children's literature--Bibliography.

PROF 016.978   Ph-1 $24.95   P   KA041
EXPLORING THE PLAINS STATES THROUGH LITERATURE. Edited by Carolyn S. Brodie; state editors, Bonnie Raasch...[et al.]. Oryx ISBN 0-89774-762-3; In Canada: Oryx, 1994. 124p. (Exploring the United States through literature).
Includes directory and indexes.
This useful, annotated regional guide identifies print and nonprint resources for grades K-8, which cover both the history and contemporary culture of Iowa, Kansas, Missouri, Nebraska, North Dakota, and South Dakota. Arranged by state in Dewey sequence, entries list materials related to history, culture, geography, resources, industries, literature, legends, and famous personalities. Annotations provide a brief description, comment on usefulness in the curriculum, and suggest at least one learning activity. Supports interdisciplinary studies and the discovery approach to social studies.
SUBJ: Great Plains--Bibliography./ Children's literature--Bibliography.

PROF 016.9795   Ph-1 $24.95   P   KA042
EXPLORING THE PACIFIC STATES THROUGH LITERATURE. Edited by Carol A. Doll; state editors, Katherine L. Spangler...[et al.]. Oryx ISBN 0-89774-771-2; In Canada: Oryx, 1994. 151p. (Exploring the United States through literature).
Includes directory and indexes.
This useful, annotated regional guide identifies print and nonprint resources for grades K-8, which cover both the history and contemporary culture of Alaska, California, Hawaii, Oregon, and Washington. Arranged by state in Dewey sequence, entries list materials related to history, culture, geography, resources, industries, literature, legends, and famous personalities. Annotations provide a brief description, comment on usefulness in the curriculum, and suggest at least one learning activity. Supports interdisciplinary studies and the discovery approach to social studies.
SUBJ: Pacific States--Bibliography./ Hawaii--Bibliography./ Alaska--Bibliography./ Children's literature--Bibliography.

PROF 016.98   Ph-1 $20.00   T   KA043
SCHON, ISABEL. Hispanic heritage, series II. Scarecrow ISBN 0-8108-1727-6, 1985. 164p.
Includes indexes.
A carefully selected guide to books on the history, culture, and economy of Latin American countries, for students from kindergarten through high school. Critical annotations include suggested grade level. Entries are arranged by country; outstanding books are designated. Author, title, and subject indices. Useful to teachers and librarians.
Other titles in this series are HISPANIC HERITAGE I (1980, OPC), HISPANIC HERITAGE, SERIES III (ISBN 0-8108-2133-8, 1988), HISPANIC HERITAGE, SERIES IV (ISBN 0-8108-2462-0, 1991, OPC), LATINO HERITAGE, SERIES V (ISBN 0-8108-3057-4, 1995).
SUBJ: Latin America--Bibliography./ Spain--Bibliography.

PROF 020   Ph-3 $22.50   T   KA044
LANDS OF PLEASURE: ESSAYS ON LILLIAN H. SMITH AND THE DEVELOPMENT OF CHILDREN'S LIBRARIES. Edited by Adele M. Fasick, Margaret Johnston and Ruth Osler. Scarecrow ISBN 0-8108-2266-0, 1990. 176p.
Includes index.
This collection represents a quiet pause in the midst of our exploding technology. The essays on Ms. Smith and her work as a prominent children's librarian in the first half of the 20th century are thought provoking and present a balanced collection of ideas and concerns on topics from popular fiction and storytelling to intellectual freedom and creating literature.
SUBJ: Smith, Lillian H./ Librarians--Biography./ Children--Books and reading./ Libraries, Children's./ Children's literature--Authorship.

CDR PROF 025   Ph-3 $40.00   OD   KA045
AASL ELECTRONIC LIBRARY. 1997 ed. (CD-ROM). Edited by Daniel Callison and Robert Grover. American Library Association 78649 ISBN 0-8389-7864-9, 1997. 1 CD-ROM.
Includes user's guide.
System requirements: IBM compatible 80386 PC with 4MB RAM and CD-ROM drive; an 80486/25SX PC or above, with 8MB, is recommended; 10MB free hard disk space; Windows 3.1x or Windows 95.
Historical information about the American Association of School Librarians; sections on children's literature, trends and issues, grant and research reports; a portion of the organization's publications; and several ERIC documents are included on this CD-ROM. Information can be accessed via a series of query and search templates or the table of contents. Useful for the sections on information literacy and other current topics.
SUBJ: American Association of School Librarians./ Library science literature./ Information science literature./ Children's literature.

PROF 025.04   Ph-1 $24.95   P OD   KA046
HARRIS, JUDI. Way of the ferret: finding and using educational resources on the Internet. 2nd. ed. International Society for Technology in Education ISBN 1-56484-085-9, 1995. 290p. ill. (Spiral bound).
Includes index and directories.
To effectively use this book, you must have access to an Internet account; use telnet and FTP commands, Gopher tools, and World Wide Web browsers; have modem and telephone line access; and be comfortable with operation of full-featured word processor. Chapter 10, "Teleresearch Activities," will be extremely useful for teachers and librarians. The author cites the problem of information versus knowledge. The research process based on the Maine Educational Media Association model is outlined. Excellent source book.
SUBJ: Education--Computer network resources--Directories./ Internet (Computer network)--Directories./ World Wide Web (Information retrieval system)--Directories./ Online information services--Directories.

PROF 025.06   Ph-1 $26.50   P   KA047
BARRON, ANN E. Internet and instruction: activities and ideas. By Ann E. Barron and Karen S. Ivers. Libraries Unlimited ISBN 1-56308-331-0, 1996. 159p. ill.
Includes glossary and indexes.
Both readable and practical, this book is designed to be used as a resource, a guide for staff development, or a textbook. Graphics clearly define both hardware and software. Reproducible masters are included. An excellent source for the novice, teacher, librarian, or student who wants to explore this aspect of technology.
SUBJ: Teaching--Computer network resources./ Education--Computer network resources./ Internet (Computer network)./ Computer managed instruction.

PROF 025.06   Ph-1 $35.00   P   KA048
BENSON, ALLEN C. Connecting kids and the Internet: a handbook for librarians, teachers, and parents. By Allen C. Benson and Linda Fodemski. Neal-Schuman ISBN 1-55570-244-9, 1996. 382p. ill. (Neal-Schuman NetGuide series).
Includes bibliographies and index.
Everything you ever wanted to know about all the technology available to parents, teachers, librarians and students. Information is extended through black and white illustrations of screens and World Wide Web home pages. The size is foreboding, but used in small doses, it is most understandable. (Parents' Shelf)
SUBJ: Internet (Computer network) in education--Handbooks, manuals,

etc./ Internet (Computer network)--Study and teaching--Handbooks, manuals, etc./ Education--Computer network resources.

BC PROF 025.06 Ph-1 $29.95 P KA049
GIAGNOCAVO, GREGORY. Educator's Internet companion: CLASSROOM CONNECT's complete guide to educational resources on the Internet. 4th ed. By the staff of CLASSROOM CONNECT. Ed. by Gregory Giagnocavo...[et al.]. Classroom Connect ISBN 0-932577-47-4, 1996. 271p. ill., 1 3.5" disk, 1 1/2" VHS videocassette color (10min).
Includes glossary and index.
Software available in either Windows or Macintosh format.
System requirements: Macintosh System 6.0.7 or higher; 1.44MB 3.5" disk drive; 4MB RAM; text editor.
System requirements: IBM compatible PC; MS-DOS 5.0 or higher; 1.44MB 3.5" disk drive; 4MB RAM; text editor.
This volume contains a wealth of information for would-be Internet educators. Over 30 lesson plans, a number of virtual tours, a myriad of educational resources, as well as information on securing funding for using Internet with students are included. A good compendium of stable Internet sites.
SUBJ: Education--Computer network resources--Directories./ Internet (Computer network)--Directories./ World Wide Web (Information retrieval system)--Directories./ Online information services--Directories.

PROF 025.1 Ph-1 $27.50 P KA050
KARPISEK, MARIAN E. Policymaking for school library media programs. American Library Association ISBN 0-8389-0520-X, 1989. 164p.
Includes bibliography and index.
An excellent guide for librarians and school administrators who need to review, develop, or re-evaluate library policies. The book "is intended to help practicing library media specialists develop the foundations of philosophy and policy upon which to build exciting, relevant, and resourceful programs for the school community." (Preface p.ix)
SUBJ: School libraries--Administration--Decision making./ Media programs (Education)--Management--Decision making.

PROF 025.2 Ph-3 $42.50 T KA051
BURRESS, LEE. Battle of the books: literary censorship in the public schools, 1950-1985. Scarecrow ISBN 0-8108-2151-6, 1989. 385p.
Includes bibliography and index.
The continuing education of school librarians should include information on the topic of censorship. This title provides a comprehensive survey of the increasing censorship problems facing schools.
SUBJ: Censorship./ Children's literature--Censorship./ School libraries--Censorship.

PROF 025.2 Ph-1 $35.00 P KA052
INTELLECTUAL FREEDOM MANUAL. 5th. ed. Comp. by the Office for Intellectual Freedom of the American Library Association . American Library Association ISBN 0-8389-0677-X, 1996. 393p.
The basic resource for Intellectual Freedom and Freedom to Read issues is arranged in seven sections. This is essential in every library.
SUBJ: Libraries--Censorship--Handbooks, manuals, etc./ Censorship--Handbooks, manuals, etc./ Freedom of Information--Handbooks, manuals, etc.

PROF 025.2 Ph-1 $18.00 P KA053
REICHMAN, HENRY. Censorship and selection: issues and answers for schools. Rev. ed. American Library Association ISBN 0-8389-0620-6, 1993. 140p.
This should be considered first purchase for the professional collection and then form the basis for a series of staff development workshops for administrators, teachers and students. Information is included on topics ranging from "What Is Censorship?" to "What Do We Do If...?" A wide range of appendices include sample selection policies, sample letters to complainants. A splendid effort from ALA and AASL.
SUBJ: Censorship./ Children's literature--Censorship./ School libraries--Censorship./ Teaching, Freedom of./ Education--Curricula--Censorship./ School libraries--Book selection.

PROF 025.2 Ph-2 $32.50 P KA054
VAN ORDEN, PHYLLIS. Collection program in schools: concepts, practices, and information sources. 2nd ed. Libraries Unlimited ISBN 1-56308-334-5, 1995. 376p. ill.
Includes appendix and index.
"The purpose is to provide an overview of the processes and procedures associated with developing, maintaining, and evaluating a collection at the building level. To achieve this goal, the processes and procedures practiced in school library media centers are discussed in relation to educational theory and principles of collection development." Part I, The Setting; Part II, Selection of Materials: Part

III, Administrative Concerns. Extensive bibliographic citations should also prove useful.
SUBJ: School libraries--Collection development.

PROF 025.3 Ph-1 $12.00 P KA055
AMERICAN LIBRARY ASSOCIATION. FILING COMMITTEE. ALA filing rules. American Library Association ISBN 0-8389-3255-X, 1980. 50p.
Includes appendices, glossary and index.
The final authority for filing catalog cards or for arranging the display of a library's contents in another format such as the book catalog.
SUBJ: Alphabetizing.

PROF 025.3 Ph-1 $72.00 T OD KA056
ANGLO-AMERICAN CATALOGUING RULES. 2ND ED., 1988 REVISION. Edited by Michael Gorman and Paul W. Winkler. Canadian Library Association/Library Association/American Library Association ISBN 0-8389-3361-0, 1988. 677p. (loose-leaf).
Includes glossary and index.
Integrates the complete text of the 1978 edition and all the changes authorized since 1978 by the Joint Steering Committee for Revision of AACR. Includes additional rules and examples for new nonprint formats, wider coverage of materials for the visually handicapped, additional examples of many existing rules, and revised appendixes and glossary. The loose-leaf format is recommended for ease of updating.
ANGLO-AMERICAN CATALOGUING RULES, 2ND ED., 1988 REVISION. AMENDMENTS 1993 (ISBN 0-8389-3431-5, 1993).
SUBJ: Cataloging.

PROF 025.3 Ph-2 $39.95 P KA057
FECKO, MARY BETH. Cataloging nonbook resources: a how-to-do-it manual for librarians. Neal-Schuman ISBN 1-55570-124-8, 1993. 204p. (How-to-do-it manuals for libraries).
Includes bibliography and index.
A handy guide for librarians to use in conjunction with AACR2R when cataloging nonbook materials. Covers the major formats: visual materials, sound recordings, maps, computer software, kits, and electronic resources. Examples of bibliographic records, MARC tagging, AACR2R rules, and Library of Congress rule interpretations are provided.
SUBJ: Cataloging of nonbook materials--Handbooks, manuals, etc./ Cataloging of audio-visual materials--Handbooks, manuals, etc./ Audio-visual library service--Handbooks, manuals, etc.

PROF 025.4 Ph-1 $90.00 T KA058
DEWEY, MELVIL. Abridged Dewey decimal classification and relative index. Ed. 13. Devised by Melvil Dewey. Edited by Joan S. Mitchell...(et al.). Forest Press/OCLC ISBN 0-910608-59-8, 1997. 1023p.
Includes bibliography, glossary and indexes.
The latest revised edition of Dewey's famous and ubiquitous system for arranging library collections, in an abridged form for use in small libraries. Contains updated classification tables and terminology as well as new topics and additional index terms. Numbering is compatible with corresponding unabridged, full edition.
SUBJ: Classification, Dewey Decimal.

PROF 025.4 Ph-1 $48.00 T KA059
FOUNTAIN, JOANNA F. Subject headings for school and public libraries: an LCSH/Sears companion. 2nd ed. Libraries Unlimited ISBN 1-56308-360-4, 1996. 177p.
Rev. ed. of: HEADINGS FOR CHILDREN'S MATERIALS, 1993.
A valuable cataloging tool as libraries merge or move from SEARS LIST OF SUBJECT HEADINGS to LIBRARY OF CONGRESS SUBJECT HEADINGS. Based on more than 20,000 bibliographic records (print and nonprint) from a public school district, it also serves as a "first check" source for daily subject cataloging.
SUBJ: Subject headings--Children's literature./ Children's literature--Abstracting and indexing.

PROF 025.4 Ph-1 $75.00 P KA060
OLSON, NANCY B. Cataloging of audiovisual materials and other special materials: a manual based on AACR2. New 4th ed. Edited by Sheila S. Intner and Edward Swanson. Media Marketing Group & Minnesota Scholarly Press Inc. ISBN 0-933474-53-9, 1998. 310p. ill.
Includes index.
Complete guide to cataloging all types of special materials includes MARC coding and tagging information as well as card format. Examples range from the common maps and audiocassettes to the newer formats of interactive media and monographic and serial Internet resources. Bibliographic authority is based on AACR2, and the descriptive cataloging examples include rule citations. Plentiful illustrations provide valuable insight on the relationships between location of cataloging information and product packaging and presentation.

SUBJ: Cataloging of audio-visual materials--Handbooks, manuals, etc./ Audio-visual library service--Handbooks, manuals, etc./ Cataloging of nonbook materials--Handbooks, manuals, etc.

PROF 025.4   Ph-1 $54.00   T   KA061
SEARS LIST OF SUBJECT HEADINGS. 16th ed. Edited by Joseph Miller. Wilson ISBN 0-8242-0920-6, 1997. 786p.
   Practical tool to serve small and medium-sized libraries suggests subject headings suitable to provide access to the collection. Conforms to the National Information Standards Organization (NISO) standards for thesauri approved in 1993, and labels the references BT, NT, RT, SA, and UF for broader, narrower, related terms, see also, and used for. Also included is a list of canceled and replacement headings useful for updating catalogs.
The SEARS LIST OF SUBJECT HEADINGS: CANADIAN COMPANION. 5th ed. (ISBN 0-8242-0879-X, 1995) lists additional subject headings pertaining to Canadian topics.
   SUBJ: Subject headings--Children's literature.

PROF 025.4   Ph-1 $80.00   P   KA062
SUBJECT HEADINGS FOR CHILDREN: A LIST OF SUBJECT HEADINGS USED BY THE LIBRARY OF CONGRESS WITH DEWEY NUMBERS ADDED. 2nd ed. Edited by Lois Winkel. Forest Press/OCLC ISBN 0-910608-58-X, 1998. 2 v.
   Provides a simple and authoritative source of Library of Congress juvenile subject headings, suggested Dewey numbers, and an index that provides access to words within subject headings. Volume 1 is an alphabetical list of the headings with recommended classification numbers (based on the ABRIDGED DEWEY DECIMAL CLASSIFICATION AND RELATIVE INDEX, Edition 13). Volume 2, an alphabetical keyword index, assists in determining the correct form of the subject headings. A must purchase cataloging aid.
   Contents: v.1. List of headings -- v.2. Keyword index.
   SUBJ: Subject headings--Children's literature./ Subject headings, Library of Congress./ Classification--Books--Children's literature./ Classification, Dewey Decimal.

PROF 025.5   Ph-1 $22.95   P   KA063
EISENBERG, MICHAEL B. Information problem-solving: the Big Six Skills approach to library and information skills instruction. By Michael B. Eisenberg and Robert E. Berkowitz. Ablex ISBN 0-89391-757-5, 1990. 156p. (Information management, policy, services).
   Includes bibliography and index.
   Presents a systematic approach to teaching information seeking behavior. Information problem-solving is taught through integration with subject area curriculum. Filled with ideas and approaches. A must for every school library.
   SUBJ: Library orientation./ School children--Library orientation./ Information retrieval--Study and teaching./ Information services--User education./ Problem solving--Study and teaching.

PROF 025.5   Ph-1 $22.50   T   KA064
URBANIK, MARY KAY. Curriculum planning and teaching using the library media center. Scarecrow ISBN 0-8108-2148-6, 1989. 164p.
   Includes bibliography and index.
   If librarians and administrators had read and heeded the advice of this small volume, perhaps reduction in force and budget cuts for libraries would not take place. The author's purpose includes helping the classroom teacher "become a more active and effective user of school library media center services, resources and materials in curriculum planning and teaching." (Intro.) The book effectively describes integration of the library and classroom activities.
   SUBJ: Teachers--Library orientation./ Media programs (Education)./ Teaching--Aids and devices./ Libraries and education./ Curriculum planning./ School libraries.

PROF 026.371   Ph-1 $15.00   P   KA065
BROSTROM, DAVID C. Guide to homeschooling for librarians. Highsmith ISBN 0-917846-46-X, 1995. 85p.
   Includes directories, bibliographies and index.
   Presents an overview of the homeschool movement and an outline of the role libraries and librarians can play in assisting parents. Extensive appendixes include lists of homeschool organizations, resources, supply sources, and online connections. (Parents' Shelf)
   SUBJ: Libraries and education./ Home schooling.

PROF 027.62   Ph-1 $29.00   T   KA066
BAUER, CAROLINE FELLER. Leading kids to books through magic. Illus. by Richard Laurent. American Library Association ISBN 0-8389-0684-2, 1996. 128p. ill. (Mighty easy motivators).
   Includes directories, filmography and bibliographies.
   Describes simple tricks or effects which accompany stories and poems. Clear black and white illustrations extend written explanations. Hints for most situations are given. Activities to enliven storytimes.
SUBJ: Libraries, Children's--Activity programs./ Book talks./ Conjuring./ Children's literature--Bibliography.

PROF 027.62   Ph-1 $45.00   T   KA067
BAUER, CAROLINE FELLER. Read for the fun of it: active programming with books for children. Illus. by Lynn Gates Bredeson. Wilson ISBN 0-8242-0824-2, 1992. 372p. ill.
   Includes index.
   Inventive programming ideas and activities designed to promote the joys of reading. Provides bibliographies of "surefire" books to read, suggestions for involving the community, storytelling techniques, methods for promoting poetry, as well as splendid ideas for featuring books and stimulating interest. Useful compendium for the experienced or the novice programmer.
   SUBJ: Libraries, Children's--Activity programs./ Children's literature--Appreciation--Problems, exercises, etc./ Children--Books and reading.

PROF 027.62   Ph-2 $7.50   P   KA068
GAGNON, ANN. Guidelines for children's services. Canadian Library Association ISBN 0-88802-221-2; In Canada: Canadian Library Association, 1989. 20p. ill. (Library service to children).
   Includes bibliography.
   The suggestions provided in this pamphlet outline the steps which can be taken to both evaluate and improve library service to children. Patterns for setting goals, identifying objectives and establishing costs are outlined.
   SUBJ: Libraries, Children's./ Library science.

PROF 027.62   Ph-1 $24.50   P   KA069
MCELMEEL, SHARRON L. Author a month (for pennies). Illus. by Deborah L. McElmeel. Libraries Unlimited ISBN 0-87287-661-6, 1988. 224p. ill.
   Includes index.
   The author states: "Using literature in the classroom or library is not as easy as gathering activity suggestions into your teaching files. Some type of instructional structure is necessary in order to reach your prescribed objectives.... Focusing on an author to provide a structure for the sharing of literature does several things for the teacher/librarian and the students in the classroom or library." These "several things" are clearly outlined in the practical suggestions which introduce authors such as Marcia Brown, Eric Carle, Carol Carrick, Tomie DePaola, and others.
AUTHOR A MONTH (FOR NICKELS) (ISBN 0-87287-827-9, 1990) provides biographical information on popular children's authors such as Pat Hutchins, John Steptoe, and Hilary Knight and suggests helpful hints for introducing and sharing their books. AUTHOR A MONTH (FOR DIMES) (ISBN 0-87287-952-6, 1993) introduces 12 popular children's authors including Anthony Browne, Joanna Cole, and Jan Brett and suggests activities to accompany their work.
   SUBJ: School libraries--Activity programs./ Children--Books and reading./ Children's literature--Study and teaching.

PROF 027.62   Ph-3 $15.95   T   KA070
PELLOWSKI, ANNE. Family storytelling handbook. Illus. by Lynn Sweat. Macmillan ISBN 0-02-770610-9; In Canada: Collier Macmillan, 1987. 150p. ill.
   The introduction of why, how, and when to tell stories should encourage parents, teachers and librarians to learn the storytelling basics. All of the activities included are easy to do, and can be presented with a minimum of preparation and materials. If you are searching for a simple introduction for bilingual students the "Finger Story" of "Don't Touch the Baby" is given (some phonetically) in nine languages. (Parents' Shelf).
   SUBJ: Storytelling./ Family recreation.

PROF 027.62   Ph-1 $8.00   P   KA071
WATKINS, JAN. Programming author visits. Association for Library Service to Children/American Library Association ISBN 0-8389-5766-8, 1996. 19p. (ALSC program support publications).
   Includes bibliography and filmography.
   A very brief paperback succinctly outlines the necessary steps to ensure a successful author visit to a public library, school, or other location.
   SUBJ: Children-s libraries--Activity programs./ Literature--Study and teaching./ Children--Books and reading./ Lectures and lecturing--Planning.

PROF 027.8   Ph-2 $19.50   T   KA072
DOLL, CAROL A. Nonfiction books for children: activities for thinking, learning and doing. Teacher Ideas Press/Libraries Unlimited ISBN 0-87287-710-8, 1990. 117p.
   Includes indexes.
   A reminder that nonfiction titles can be used to tie activities to reading. The author presents units based on fifty-seven titles. The

appendices include Selected Sources; Selected 1989 Titles from Science and Social Studies Lists; Grade Level Index (for activities outlined in the book); and Subject/Activity Index.
SUBJ: School libraries--Activity programs./ Children's literature--Bibliography./ Children--Books and reading.

PROF 027.8   Ph-3 $24.50   P   KA073
FARMER, LESLEY S. J. Cooperative learning activities in the library media center. Libraries Unlimited ISBN 0-87287-799-X, 1991. 183p.
Includes glossary and index.
Although the focus of this book is middle and high school, it has excellent information that can easily be adapted for use in the elementary school. Beginning with theory and practice of cooperative learning, the author then provides read-to-use activities in a variety of curriculum areas. Appendixes include: subjects table, information skills table, and benchmark projects media table.
SUBJ: School libraries--Activity programs./ Media programs (Education)./ Libraries and education.

PROF 027.8   Ph-2 $16.95   P   KA074
FARMER, LESLEY S. J. Creative partnerships: librarians and teachers working together. Linworth Publishing ISBN 0-938865-13-7, 1993. 1 v. (various pagings). (Professional growth series).
"A publication of THE BOOK REPORT & LIBRARY TALK."
An idea-filled, three-hole-punched paperback compilation provides practical solutions for increasing teacher/librarian communication. The readings "35 good reasons to send a student to the library" and "68 ways to catch a teacher" are valuable, however, the reading on censorship battles will be invaluable.
SUBJ: School libraries./ Media programs (Education).

PROF 027.8   Ph-2 $18.50   P   KA075
HART, THOMAS L. Creative ideas for library media center facilities. Libraries Unlimited ISBN 0-87287-736-1, 1990. 75p. col. ill.
Includes bibliography.
Color photographs illustrate ideas for transforming library media centers into unique, exciting places to visit and learn. You do not need a complete remodeling job to incorporate some of these "face lifts" for the facility in your school. Information is also included on the effect of environment (color, light, ergonomics) on learning.
SUBJ: School libraries--Activity programs./ Media programs (Education).

PROF 027.8   Ph-1 $26.50   P   KA076
LOERTSCHER, DAVID V. Taxonomies of the school library media program. Illus. by Mark Loertscher. Libraries Unlimited ISBN 0-87287-662-4, 1988. 336p. ill.
Includes appendix and index.
The author equates the development of an exemplary library media program to erecting a magnificent structure. "Each component part of the structure must be in its proper place if the building is to be functional and permanent." Serves as an excellent starting point for this dedication of effort with readable and practical ideas ranging from attitude of the Library Media Specialist to how to spend the budget.
SUBJ: School libraries./ Media programs (Education).

PROF 027.8   Ph-2 $41.00   T   KA077
MORRIS, BETTY J. Administering the school library media center. 3rd ed. By Betty J. Morris with John T. Gillespie and Diana L. Spirt. Bowker ISBN 0-8352-3092-9, 1992. 567p.
Includes bibliographies, appendices and index.
Everything you ever wanted to know about the development, implementation, and problem resolution of a school library media program. Handy one source reference for "key documents" such as Library Bill of Rights.
SUBJ: School libraries--Administration./ Media programs (Education).

PROF 027.8   Ph-3 $32.50   P   KA078
POWER UP YOUR LIBRARY: CREATING THE NEW ELEMENTARY SCHOOL LIBRARY PROGRAM. By Sheila Salmon...[et al.]. Libraries Unlimited ISBN 1-56308-357-4, 1996. 292p. ill.
Includes bibliographies and index.
Written as an aid for implementation of the New York City Library Power Program, this handbook addresses the topics of administration, collection development, technology, budgeting, teaching, and flexible scheduling. Although the text is based on the vision of the "new" school library, none of the photographs reflect a library ready for the next century. Photographs are dark and add little to text. There are useful ideas included, but it is not a step-by-step outline for building the library of the future.
SUBJ: Elementary school libraries.

PROF 027.8   Ph-1 $38.00   T   KA079
WILSON, PATRICIA POTTER. Professional collection for elementary educators. Wilson ISBN 0-8242-0873-0, 1996. 295p.
Includes bibliography and indexes.
Designed as an elementary school professional library selection tool. Includes both professional books and journals. Also includes citations for professional readings in various content areas; administrative materials; and suggestions, based on research, which may be used for promotion of the district professional collection.
SUBJ: Education libraries./ Media programs (Education).

PROF 027.8   Ph-1 $22.00   P   KA080
WRIGHT, KIETH. Challenge of technology: action strategies for the school library media specialist. American Library Association ISBN 0-8389-0604-4, 1993. 122p. (School library media programs. Focus on trends and issues).
Includes bibliographies, directory and index.
An important book for library media specialists and everyone working in the field of education. Research based, but practical. Explores questions educators should ask about technology and its role in improving education.
SUBJ: School libraries--Data processing./ Libraries--Special collections--Databases./ Libraries--Special collections--Software./ School libraries--Collection development./ Computer-assisted instruction./ Computer managed instruction.

PROF 027.8   Ph-1 $17.00   P   KA081
ZINGHER, GARY. At the Pirate Academy: adventures with language in the library media center. American Library Association ISBN 0-8389-3384-X, 1990. 132p. (School library media programs. Focus on trends and issues).
Includes bibliographical references.
Help for media specialists who are trying to establish consulting partnerships with the teachers in their schools. Excellent ideas about choosing the theme, planning, beginning, taking, and celebration of the journey. Any library/school moving into interdisciplinary or resource based teaching will welcome this book.
SUBJ: School libraries--Activity programs./ Media programs (Education).

PROF 028   Ph-1 $15.00   P   KA082
KRASHEN, STEPHEN. Power of reading: insights from the research. Libraries Unlimited ISBN 1-56308-006-0, 1993. 119p.
Includes bibliography and indexes.
Powerful words and research to support the need for more books, more free reading time, and libraries--the essential link that makes readers.
SUBJ: Books and reading.

PROF 028.1   Ph-2 $49.95   P   KA083
BEST OF BOOKFINDER: A GUIDE TO CHILDREN'S LITERATURE ABOUT INTERESTS AND CONCERNS OF YOUTH AGED 2-18. By Sharon Spredemann Dreyer. American Guidance Service CV7592 ISBN 0-88671-439-7, 1992. 451p.
Includes indexes and directory.
"Describes and categorizes 676 children's books according to more than 450 psychological, behavioral, and developmental topics of concern to children and adolescents, ages 2 and up... Written primarily for parents, teachers, librarians, counselors, psychologists, psychiatrists, and other adults who want to identify books that may help children to cope with the challenges of life." (Intro.) Detailed annotated entries describe quality materials on sensitive topics such as peer relationships, divorce, loneliness, moving, and death. Useful as a readers' guide as well as a bibliotherapy tool for guidance counselors.
SUBJ: Children's literature--Book reviews./ Children--Books and reading.

PROF 028.1   Ph-1 $48.00   T   KA084
GILLESPIE, JOHN THOMAS. Best books for children: preschool through grade 6. 5th ed. By John T. Gillespie and Corinne J. Naden. Bowker ISBN 0-8352-3455-X, 1994. 1411p.
Includes indexes.
Presents 17,140 titles for preschool through sixth grade arranged in broad subject categories. Selection for inclusion is based on major reviewing periodicals and standard selection tools (THE ELEMENTARY SCHOOL LIBRARY COLLECTION, CHILDREN'S CATALOG). Book is designed to be used "(1) as a tool to evaluate the adequacy of existing collections; (2) as a book-selection instrument for beginning and expanding collections; (3) as an aid for giving reading guidance to children; and (4) as a base for the preparation of bibliographies and reading lists." (Preface) Brief annotations give bibliographic information, appeal levels, and recommendation sources.
SUBJ: Bibliography--Best books--Children's literature./ Children's

literature--Bibliography./ Libraries, Children's--Book lists./ School libraries--Book lists.

PROF 028.1   Ph-1 $12.95   P   KA085

HORNING, KATHLEEN T. From cover to cover: evaluating and reviewing children's books. HarperCollins ISBN 0-06-446167-X; In Canada: HarperCollins, 1997. 230p.

Includes bibliographies and index.

Selectors' Choice, 21st ed.

An outstanding tool to assist librarians, teachers, and parents in the difficult task of evaluating books. Information on book production will be helpful to those interested in writing and useful in explaining the process to students. Chapters include evaluation techniques for: Books of Information; Traditional Literature; Poetry, Verse, Rhymes, and Songs; Picture Books, Easy Readers and Transitional Books; and Fiction. Distinguishes between reviewing and literary criticism. First purchase. (Parents' Shelf).

SUBJ: Book reviewing./ Children's literature--History and criticism.

PROF 028.1   Ph-1 $21.00   P   KA086

MCELMEEL, SHARRON L. Great new nonfiction reads. Libraries Unlimited ISBN 1-56308-228-4, 1995. 225p. ill.

Includes bibliographies and indexes.

Most of the 120 titles listed are suitable for reading aloud. Each entry provides complete bibliographic data and target audience while some titles have suggestions for further reading. Good advice on sharing information books, selection, and encouraging research. Includes a list of 25 response activities for information books.

SUBJ: Children--Books and reading./ Oral reading.

PROF 028.1   Ph-3 $29.95   T   KA087

SHARKEY, PAULETTE BOCHNIG. Newbery and Caldecott Medal and Honor books in other media. Neal-Schuman ISBN 1-55570-119-1, 1992. 142p.

Includes bibliographies, directory and index.

A comprehensive list of materials based on Newbery and Caldecott Award winners contains audiovisuals such as sound filmstrips, films, sound recordings, talking books, videos, and software; print materials such as large print and braille; and realia such as dolls, posters, bookmarks, and calendars. Entries include bibliographic information, review citations, recommendations in standard bibliographies, and additional awards. For libraries that maintain large media collections or schools where Caldecott and Newbery titles are incorporated into the curriculum.

SUBJ: Newbery Medal books--Audio-visual aids./ Caldecott Medal books--Audio-visual aids./ Children's books, Illustrated--Audio-visual aids./ Children's literature./ Nonbook materials.

PROF 028.1   Ph-1 $34.95   T   KA088

THOMAS, JAMES L. Play, learn, and grow: an annotated guide to the best books and materials for very young children. Bowker ISBN 0-8352-3019-8, 1992. 439p.

Includes bibliographies, directories and indexes.

Evaluates over 1,000 print and nonprint items suitable for young children--infants, toddlers, preschoolers, and kindergartners. Introductory sections describe the role of adults in developing emerging literacy and how to choose materials. Includes a useful chart of child development which lists characteristics of the various stages and appropriate types of materials for each characteristic. Entries contain bibliographic information, age of appeal, category (concept, folklore, story, wordless, etc.), priority of purchase, citations to reviews and awards, and a critically descriptive annotation. A list of professional materials completes this highly selective collection development tool which will be of particular interest to libraries which have pre-K programs. (Parents' Shelf).

SUBJ: Bibliography--Best books--Children's literature./ Preschool children--Books and reading./ Children's literature--Bibliography./ Audio-visual materials--Catalogs.

PROF 028.5   Ph-1 $45.00   T   KA089

BAUER, CAROLINE FELLER. This way to books. Illus. by Lynn Gates. Wilson ISBN 0-8242-0678-9, 1983. 363p. ill.

Includes appendix and index.

Delineates a host of adaptable ideas, suggestions and techniques "to get children and books together." Offers ideas for all grade levels, for all teachers and librarians. Books cited are current and should be readily available.

SUBJ: Books and reading.

PROF 028.5   Ph-1 $32.00   P   KA090

BOOKTALK! 5: MORE SELECTIONS FROM THE BOOKTALKER FOR ALL AGES AND AUDIENCES. Edited by Joni Richards Bodart. Wilson ISBN 0-8242-0836-6, 1993. 282p. (Booktalk!).

Includes bibliography, directory and index.

These collections were taken, in part, from articles from the "Booktalker" published in WILSON LIBRARY BULLETIN. Each entry, one or two paragraphs in length, gives title, author, and grade level. Useful for both booktalking and collection development. Complete bibliographic information includes a "P & Q" (popularity and quality level) listing by age level, and a selective bibliography by theme and genre.

BOOKTALK! 2: BOOKTALKING FOR ALL AGES AND AUDIENCES. 2ND ED. (ISBN 0-8242-0716-5, 1985).

BOOKTALK! 3: MORE BOOKTALKS FOR ALL AGES AND AUDIENCES (ISBN 0-8242-0764-5, 1988).

BOOKTALK! 4: SELECTIONS FROM THE BOOKTALKER FOR ALL AGES AND AUDIENCES (ISBN 0-8242-0835-8, 1992).

SUBJ: Book talks./ Public relations--Libraries./ Libraries and readers./ Books and reading.

PROF 028.5   Ph-1 $42.00   T   KA091

GILLESPIE, JOHN THOMAS. Juniorplots 4: a book talk guide for use with readers ages 12-16. By John T. Gillespie and Corinne J. Naden. Bowker ISBN 0-8352-3167-4, 1993. 450p. (Plots series).

Includes indexes.

Provides librarians and teachers guidance for book talks and serves as a collection development tool. Entries give summary plots for 81 titles, brief descriptions of recommended related titles, thematic materials, book talk suggestions, review citations, and sources for biographical information about the author. Volume includes separate author, title, and subject indexes. Separate cumulative author, title, and subject indexes include all citations from JUNIORPLOTS, MORE JUNIORPLOTS, JUNIORPLOTS 3, and JUNIORPLOTS 4. Libraries with larger, established collections will be interested in earlier volumes.

JUNIORPLOTS: A BOOK TALK MANUAL FOR TEACHERS AND LIBRARIANS (ISBN 0-8352-0063-9, 1967).

MORE JUNIORPLOTS: A GUIDE FOR TEACHERS AND LIBRARIANS (ISBN 0-8352-1002-2, 1977).

JUNIORPLOTS 3: A BOOK TALK GUIDE FOR USE WITH READERS AGES 12-16 (ISBN 0-8352-2367-1, 1987).

SUBJ: Teenagers--Books and reading./ Young adult literature--Stories, plots, etc./ Young adult literature--Bibliography./ Book talks.

PROF 028.5   Ph-1 $42.00   T   KA092

GILLESPIE, JOHN THOMAS. Middleplots 4: a book talk guide for use with readers ages 8-12. By John T. Gillespie and Corinne J. Naden. Bowker ISBN 0-8352-3446-0, 1994. 434p. (Plots series).

Includes indexes.

Divided by subjects or genre popular with middle grade readers, the 80 entries provide excellent plot summaries, a one sentence summary of related books, thematic material, book talk suggestions, review citations, and sources for biographical information about the author. Useful for book talks and as a collection development tool. Includes cumulative author, title, and subject indexes for previously published books in this series. Libraries with larger, established collections will be interested in earlier volumes.

INTRODUCING BOOKS: A GUIDE FOR THE MIDDLE GRADES (ISBN 0-8352-0215-1, 1970, OPC).

INTRODUCING MORE BOOKS: A GUIDE FOR THE MIDDLE GRADES (ISBN 0-8352-0988-1, 1978).

INTRODUCING BOOKPLOTS 3: A BOOK TALK GUIDE FOR USE WITH READERS AGES 8-12 (ISBN 0-8352-2345-0, 1988).

SUBJ: Children's literature--Stories, plots, etc./ Children's literature--Bibliography./ Children--Books and reading./ Book talks.

PROF 028.5   Ph-1 $42.00   T   KA093

THOMAS, REBECCA L. Primaryplots 2: a book talk guide for use with readers ages 4-8. Bowker ISBN 0-8352-3411-8, 1993. 431p. (Plots series).

Includes indexes.

Focusing on recent picture books (featured titles have been published between 1988 and 1992) selected from "best books" and "notable" lists, and standard evaluation tools, these 150 titles can be used at "different levels from preschool to the middle grades." Organized into eight chapters: Enjoying Family and Friends; Developing a Positive Self-Image; Celebrating Everyday Experiences; Finding the Humor in Picture Books; Exploring the Past; Learning about the World Around You; Analyzing Illustrations; and Focusing on Folktales. Each title cited includes: Bibliographic Information; Plot Summary; Thematic Material; Book Talk Material and Activities; Audiovisual Adaption; Related Titles; and Author/Illustrator Information.

PRIMARYPLOTS: A BOOK TALK GUIDE FOR USE WITH READERS AGE 4-8 (ISBN 0-8352-2514-3, 1989).

SUBJ: Children's literature--Stories, plots, etc./ Libraries, Children's--Activity programs./ Children--Books and reading./ Book talks./ Children's literature--Book reviews.

VCR PROF 028.5   Ph-3 $49.95   OD KA094
WHAT'S A GOOD BOOK? (Videocassette). Weston Woods MN435V, 1993. 1/2" VHS videocassette color (27min).
    Children's librarians, professors of children's literature, authors, and children themselves give their opinions on what makes a good children's book. This series of interviews offers a range of evaluative criteria as well as the view that a good book is in the eye of the beholder. A bit dry, but useful for teachers and librarians.
    SUBJ: Children's literature./ Book selection.

PER PROF 050   Ph-1 $48.50 yr   OD KA095
APPRAISAL: SCIENCE BOOKS FOR YOUNG PEOPLE. Northeastern University, Children's Science Book Review Comm.; Dept. of Science and Mathematics Education ISSN 0003-7052, 1967-. v. quarterly.
    Editorial policy states: "The Children's Science Book Review Committee believes that science books deserve the same careful attention as literary works for children and that they should be entirely worthy of a child's attention." Reviews current books in the field of the sciences and technology for elementary grades and junior high. Each entry is reviewed by both a librarian and a science specialist. Recommendations are made for age levels and ratings, from excellent to unsatisfactory are included.
    SUBJ: Science--Bibliography--Periodicals.

PER PROF 050   Ph-1 $24.95 yr   OD KA096
ARTS AND ACTIVITIES: CREATIVE ACTIVITIES FOR THE CLASSROOM. Arts and Activities ISSN 0004-3931, 1932-. v. ill. 10 nos. per yr.
    Formerly: ARTS AND ACTIVITIES: THE TEACHER'S ARTS AND CRAFTS GUIDE.
    Creative activities for the classroom. Indexed in EDUCATION INDEX.
    SUBJ: Art--Study and teaching--Periodicals./ Arts and crafts--Periodicals./ Project method in teaching.

PER PROF 050   Ph-1 $20.00 yr   OD KA097
BOOK LINKS: CONNECTING BOOKS, LIBRARIES AND CLASSROOMS. American Library Association ISSN 1055-4742, 1991-. v. bimonthly.
    Excellent bimonthly magazine which provides a multitude of ideas for creating curriculum connections, promoting new uses for standard titles, and showcasing new titles. A good balance between fiction and nonfiction. Particularly useful in areas with whole language programs. Bibliographies will be an asset for colleciton development. An essential professional periodical for all libraries.
    SUBJ: Children's literature--Bibliography--Periodicals./ School libraries--Periodicals./ Books and reading--Best books./ Books--Reviews.

PER PROF 050   Ph-1 $60.00 yr   OD KA098
BOOKLIST. American Library Association ISSN 0006-7385, 1905-. v. semi-monthly.
    Title varies.
    This ALA publication provides a current buying list of recent books and non-print media with brief annotations designed to assist librarians in selection. Only recommended books are included. The separate section for children's books includes grade levels. Once a month the children's book section includes reviews of easy reading books. Reviews in Reference Books Bulletin are of reference books and include both those recommended for purchase and those which are not, with long critical commentary. Reviews of AV materials, including frequent subject lists of media, are very useful to all grades.
    SUBJ: Books and reading--Best books./ Books--Reviews./ Reference books.

PER PROF 050   Ph-1 $40.00 yr   OD KA099
BULLETIN OF THE CENTER FOR CHILDREN'S BOOKS. University of Illinois ISSN 0008-9036, 1947-. v. monthly.
    A review journal of books for children ages four to fourteen. Covers about 75 titles per month, evaluated by both educators and librarians on the University faculty. Recommendations are both favorable and negative.
    URL: http://www.uiuc.edu/providers/uipress -- on-line publication available
    SUBJ: Children's literature--Bibliography--Periodicals.

PER PROF 050   Ph-3 $39.00 yr   OD KA100
CANADIAN CHILDREN'S LITERATURE. Canadian Children's Press/ Canadian Children's Literature Assoc. ISSN 0319-0080, 1975-. v. quarterly.
    Thoughtfully written articles on Canadian children's literature, interviews with Canadian writers and illustrators, specialized bibliographies and in-depth reviews of current works make this an informative journal for both Canadian and American readers. Issues are usually focused on a theme, such as an author or a subject.
    URL: http://www.uoguelph.ca/englit/ccl/ -- on-line issue updates including table of contents, sample reviews, and on-line index
    SUBJ: Children's literature--Periodicals./ Children's literature--Bibliography--Periodicals./ Canadian literature--Periodicals./ Books--Reviews.

PER PROF 050   Ph-1 $60.00 yr   OD KA101
CBC FEATURES. Children's Book Council ISSN 0008-0721, 1945-. v. ill. approx. every 6 months.
    Supersedes CALENDAR.
    One time charge for placement on mailing list.
    An invaluable leaflet for teachers and librarians giving information about new books, ways to relate television and books, awards and prizes, free and inexpensive materials about books, etc. Produced by the organization which furnishes material for celebration of Children's Book Week.
    SUBJ: Children's literature--Periodicals./ Literary prizes./ Authors.

PER PROF 050   Ph-2 $39.00 yr   OD KA102
CLASSROOM CONNECT. Classroom Connect ISSN 1078-6430, 1994-. v. ill. 9 nos. per yr.
    Practical tips printed on good, three-hole punched paper provide "netiquette," e-mail addresses, new-user basics, network news, and lesson plans. It is not necessary to be a technical computer whiz to understand the information.
    SUBJ: Internet (Computer network)--Periodicals./ Online information services--Periodicals./ World Wide Web (Information retrieval system)--Periodicals.

PER PROF 050   Ph-2 $20.00 yr   OD KA103
CONNECT: HANDS-ON SCIENCE AND MATH GUIDE FOR K-8 EDUCATORS. Teacher's Laboratory ISSN 1041-682X, 1988-. v. ill. 5 nos. per year.
    A three-hole punched newsletter designed "to support hands-on science and math curriculum." The focus of each issue might be fruits, geology, water, time, or animals. The interdisciplinary approach is supported with ideas, activities, book reviews and investigative suggestions.
    SUBJ: Science--Study and teaching./ Science--Periodicals./ Mathematics--Study and teaching./ Mathematics--Periodicals.

PER PROF 050   Ph-1 $45.00 yr   OD KA104
EDUCATION DIGEST. Prakken ISSN 0013-127X, 1935-. v. monthly (Sept-May).
    In the familiar digest form, presents summaries and abridgements of articles from the education press. Many related to elementary school though administrative point of view also predominant. Regular columns: With Education in Washington; Education Briefs; New Educational Materials.
    SUBJ: Education--Periodicals.

PER PROF 050   Ph-1   Varies   OD KA105
EDUCATION INDEX. Wilson ISSN 0013-1385, 1929-. v. monthly (Sept-June).
    With annual and biennial cumulations.
    If the elementary school library is to serve the faculty adequately, an index to the professional journals is essential as a starting point for any investigation for educational projects or faculty research. This is the primary key, listing and indexing not only journal literature but also many other types of serials, workbooks, curriculum guides, and the like, important to educators.
    SUBJ: Education--Bibliography./ Education--Periodicals--Indexes.

PER PROF 050   Ph-1 $69.94 yr   OD KA106
EDUCATION WEEK. Editorial Projects in Education ISSN 0277-4232, 1981-. v. 41 nos. per yr.
    Reports on issues in education occurring in the United States. Exceedingly useful for its synthesis and natural perspective. Highly recommended as regular reading by all faculty and interested parents.
    URL: http://www.edweek.org -- includes current issue, archives, and daily updates on education issues and on-line forums
    SUBJ: Education--Periodicals.

PER PROF 050   Ph-1 $14.95 yr   OD KA107
EDUCATIONAL SOFTWARE PREVIEW GUIDE. Developed by the Educational Software Preview Guide Consortium at the Annual Software Evaluation Forum. International Society for Technology in Education ISSN 0898-2694, 1982-. v. annual.
    Includes directories.
    Compiled from results of software evaluations done by a number of state and regional agencies, this guide is a good starting place for those wanting to find curriculum related software. Brief annotations are included as well as a publisher's address listing.
    SUBJ: Computer-assisted instruction--Catalogs./ Computer software--Catalogs.

PER PROF 050   Ph-1 $49.00 yr   OD KA108
EMERGENCY LIBRARIAN. Rockland Press/Ken Haycock & Associates
ISSN 0315-8888, 1973-. v. ill. 5 nos. per yr.
> A lively magazine with news and reviews of interest to librarians
> serving children and young adults. Useful to school as well as public
> librarians.
> SUBJ: Libraries, Children's--Periodicals./ School libraries--Periodicals.

PER PROF 050   Ph-1 5-A $12.95 yr   OD KA109
FAMILY PC. Disney Computer Magazine/Ziff Communications ISSN
1076-7754, 1994-. v. col. ill. 10 nos. per yr.
> Provides information for beginning computer users as well as reviews
> of hardware and materials for children. (Parents' Shelf).
> SUBJ: Computers--Periodicals./ Microcomputers--Periodicals.

PER PROF 050   Ph-1 $35.00 yr   OD KA110
FIVE OWLS. Five Owls ISSN 0892-6735, 1986-. v. ill. bimonthly.
> This publication states on the masthead that it is "A publication for
> readers personally and professionally involved in children's literature."
> Each issue offers an in-depth article on a variety of topics.
> Bibliographies are included which relate to the article. The remainder
> of the 44-page newsletter/magazine is devoted to "New Books of
> Merit." These reviews are signed and offer full bibliographic
> information together with an in-depth evaluation.
> SUBJ: Children's literature--Periodicals.

PER PROF 050   Ph-3 $20.00 yr   OD KA111
FREE MATERIALS FOR SCHOOLS AND LIBRARIES. Dyad Services
ISSN 0836-0073, 1979-. v. 5 nos. per yr.
> Includes sources of free materials in the U.S. and Canada. Since free
> materials are often of transient availability and interest, this current
> source of information will be of some value. Although materials are
> selected and fully described, librarians must be on guard against bias
> in those from commercial sources.
> SUBJ: Free material.

PER PROF 050   Ph-1 $42.00 yr   OD KA112
FUTURIST. World Future Society ISSN 0016-3317, 1967-. v. ill.
bimonthly.
> "A journal of forecasts, trends and ideas about the future,"
> published by the World Future Society, an Association for the Study
> of Alternative Futures. "The Society acts as an impartial
> clearinghouse for a variety of different views and does not take
> positions on what will happen or should happen in the future."
> Covers concerns of today and tomorrow. Will be helpful to teachers
> involved in "future studies."
> URL: http://www.wfs.org/wfs -- special features and articles from
> each issue
> SUBJ: Future--Periodicals.

PER PROF 050   Ph-1 $29.95 yr   OD KA113
GIFTED CHILD TODAY. G-C-T Publishing ISSN 0892-9580, 1978-. v.
bimonthly.
> Formerly: G-C-T/GIFTED, CREATIVE, TALENTED CHILDREN.
> "The world's most popular magazine for parents and teachers of
> gifted, creative, and talented children." Offers teachers, parents and
> librarians ideas on programs, curriculum, seminars, and an overview
> of the "state of the art" of gifted and talented programs.
> URL: http://www.prufrock.com -- complete issues
> SUBJ: Gifted children--Education.

PER PROF 050   Ph-2 $42.00 yr   OD KA114
HORN BOOK GUIDE TO CHILDREN'S AND YOUNG ADULT BOOKS.
Horn Book ISSN 1044-405X, 1990-. v. semi-annual.
> "Short critical annotations of all hard-cover trade children's and
> young adult books published in the United States in one season (a six
> month period)... in order of quality." (Editorial vol. 1, no. 1). Fiction
> is arranged by grade level or genre and nonfiction is by Dewey
> classification. Rating system is from 1 (outstanding) to 6 (not
> recommended). This is another selection tool that should prove most
> useful.
> SUBJ: Children's literature--Bibliography--Periodicals.

PER PROF 050   Ph-1 $36.00 yr   OD KA115
HORN BOOK MAGAZINE: ABOUT BOOKS FOR CHILDREN AND
YOUNG ADULTS. Horn Book ISSN 0018-5078, 1924-. v. col. ill.
bimonthly.
> Indexed in CHILDREN'S MAGAZINE GUIDE.
> Indispensable to teachers for articles on authors and illustrators and
> for discriminating reviews.
> SUBJ: Children's literature--Bibliography--Periodicals.

PER PROF 050   Ph-1 $14.95 yr   OD KA116
INSTRUCTOR: PRIMARY. Instructor Publications ISSN 0020-4285,
1891-. v. ill. 8 nos. per yr.
> Title varies.
> Indexed in CHILDREN'S MAGAZINE GUIDE.
> Practical articles for the classroom teacher with much illustrative
> material, booklists, guides for activities. Special issues on elementary
> school libraries and the like have made this an outstanding periodical
> and one with high appeal to teachers.
> SUBJ: Education--Periodicals.

PER PROF 050   Ph-2 $95.00 yr   OD KA117
INTERVENTION. Pro-Ed Publishing ISSN 1053-4512, n.d. v. ill. 5 nos.
per yr.
> Individual subscription price, $35.00 per yr.
> A useful journal for teachers of children with learning disabilities such
> as dyslexia. While most articles are directed to specialists in the field,
> some are intended to help the regular classroom teacher with
> mainstreamed LD students.
> SUBJ: Handicapped--Education--Periodicals.

PER PROF 050   Ph-1 $40.00 yr   OD KA118
JOURNAL OF YOUTH SERVICES IN LIBRARIES. American Library
Association ISSN 0739-5086, 1946-. v. quarterly.
> Formerly: TOP OF THE NEWS.
> Covers news and timely articles for teachers and media specialists
> interested in evaluating materials or planning programs for children.
> SUBJ: Children's literature--Periodicals./ Libraries, Children's--
> Periodicals.

PER PROF 050   Ph- $40.00 yr   OD KA119
KNOWLEDGE QUEST. American Association of School Librarians ISSN
1094-9046, 1997-. v. 5 nos. per yr.
> Available free to AASL members.
> This journal brings together certain elements of both SCHOOL
> LIBRARY MEDIA QUARTERLY and HOTLINE/CONNECTIONS. An
> excellent source for keeping up with the latest in research and
> practices for your library media program.
> SUBJ: School libraries--Periodicals./ Media programs (Education)--
> Periodicals.

PER PROF 050   Ph-1 $50.00 yr   OD KA120
LANGUAGE ARTS. National Council of Teachers of English ISSN 0360-
9170, 1924-. v. ill. 8 nos. per yr.
> Formerly: ELEMENTARY ENGLISH.
> Membership includes subscription.
> Individual subscription price, $35.00 yr.
> Official journal of the Elementary Section of the National Council of
> Teachers of English.
> Contains many articles of interest to teachers and media specialists.
> Regular features are the review columns: Books in the Classroom,
> Instructional Materials, and Nonprint Media. Indexed in EDUCATION
> INDEX. Subscription included in membership fee.
> SUBJ: English language--Study and teaching--Periodicals./ English
> literature--Study and teaching--Periodicals.

PER PROF 050   Ph-1 $61.00 yr   OD KA121
LEARNING AND LEADING WITH TECHNOLOGY. International Council
for Technology in Education ISSN 1082-5754, 1979-. v. 8 nos. per yr.
> "A journal for persons interested in the instructional use of
> computers." Every issue contains material of interest to classroom
> teachers. A first priority purchase in schools where microcomputers
> are available for use with students.
> SUBJ: Computers--Periodicals./ Microcomputers--Periodicals.

PER PROF 050   Ph-2 $20.00 yr   OD KA122
LEARNING: SUCCESSFUL TEACHING TODAY. Education Center, Inc.
ISSN 0090-3167, 1972-. v. ill. 6 nos. per yr.
> Formerly: LEARNING: THE MAGAZINE FOR CREATIVE TEACHING.
> Indexed in CHILDREN'S MAGAZINE GUIDE.
> Articles with ideas and resources of interest to elementary and middle
> school teachers. A special feature is a monthly poster with
> accompanying teaching suggestions. Includes reviews of professional
> books.
> URL: http://www.theeducationcenter.com -- on-line issues include
> samplings from features and departments, reviews
> SUBJ: Teaching--Periodicals./ Education--Periodicals.

PER PROF 050   Ph-2 $44.00 yr   OD KA123
LIBRARY TALK: THE MAGAZINE FOR ELEMENTARY SCHOOL
LIBRARIANS. Linworth Publishing ISSN 1043-237X, 1988-. v. ill. 5 nos.
per yr.
> Published five times each school year, each issue highlights a
> particular concern of the elementary school library. Themes have

included: Booktalks; Bulletin Boards and Working with Classroom Teachers. Regular columns include: Picture books early readers, Fiction for Grades 3-6, Nonfiction, Reference Books & Series, Audiovisuals, Paperbacks for Young Readers, Good Ideas & Helpful Hints, Professional Reading.
URL: http://www.linworth.com -- on-line issue includes special features and index
SUBJ: School libraries--Periodicals.

PER PROF 050 Ph-3 $255.00 yr OD KA124
MEDIA REVIEW DIGEST. Pierian ISSN 0363-7778, 1970-. v. annual with 1 supplement.
Includes indices.
An index of reviews from over 160 sources of nonbook media, including non-classical records and tapes, slides, transparencies, filmstrips and films. Gives bibliographic and purchasing/renting information for each title, as well as a short descriptive annotation, Dewey classification number, and LC subject headings. Each review cited is assigned a symbol to show recommendation or to signify that the review was descriptive only. A new feature is a section of books that deal with nonprint media. Indices give access by title, subject and Dewey number. On the whole a comprehensive and professional tool; essential for district collections.
SUBJ: Audio-visual materials--Reviews--Indexes.

PER PROF 050 Ph-1 $59.00 yr OD KA125
MULTICULTURAL REVIEW: DEDICATED TO A BETTER UNDERSTANDING OF ETHNIC, RACIAL, AND RELIGIOUS DIVERSITY. Greenwood ISSN 1058-9236, 1992-. v. ill. quarterly.
Includes directory and indexes.
Individual subscription rate $29.95.
Formerly JOURNAL OF MULTICULTURAL LIBRARIANSHIP.
Provides critical reviews on multicultural books and audiovisual materials for children and adults. Covers the diverse cultures comprising the United States and other countries today. Featured articles are aimed at instructing educators how to accurately portray people of different cultural backgrounds with a stress on similarities rather than differences. For multicultural studies.
SUBJ: Multicultural education--Periodicals./ Pluralism (Social sciences)--Periodicals./ Ethnicity--Periodicals.

PER PROF 050 Ph-3 $80.00 yr OD KA126
MUSIC EDUCATORS JOURNAL. Music Educators National Conference ISSN 0027-4321, 1934-. v. ill. 6 nos. per year.
Includes TEACHING MUSIC magazine, 6 issues per year, alternating months.
This publication is representative of all phases of music education in schools, colleges, universities, and teacher-education institutions. Although the format and illustrations seem dated the information provides sound information and ideas.
URL: http://www.menc.org -- on-line issue includes index and featured articles
SUBJ: Music--Periodicals./ Music--Study and teaching.

PER PROF 050 Ph-2 $45.00 yr OD KA127
NEW ADVOCATE. Christopher-Gordon ISSN 0895-1381, 1988-. v. quarterly.
A professional journal which would appeal equally to the librarian and classroom teachers. A good balance of information about children's literature, techniques in teaching reading, extending the basal through literature, and book reviews in readable format.
SUBJ: Children's literature--Periodicals.

PER PROF 050 Ph-2 $16.00 yr KA128
NEWBERY AND CALDECOTT AWARDS: A GUIDE TO THE MEDAL AND HONOR BOOKS. Association for Library Service to Children, A.L.A. ISSN 1070-4493, n.d. v. ill. annual.
Includes indexes.
A complete annotated listing of Newbery and Caldecott Award and Honor books. Provides information on the media used to illustrate the Caldecott books.
SUBJ: Bibliography--Best books--Children's literature--Periodicals./ Children's literature--Bibliography--Periodicals./ Illustrated books, Children's--Bibliography--Periodicals./ Caldecott Medal books--Periodicals./ Newbery Medal books--Periodicals./ Literary prizes--Periodicals.

PER PROF 050 Ph-1 $66.50 yr OD KA129
ONLINE--OFFLINE: THEMES AND RESOURCES K-8. Rock Hill Press ISSN 1090-1930, 1996-. v. ill. 9 nos. per yr.
An annotated list of materials identifies resources for interdisciplinary studies. Expands curriculum connections to include thought-provoking themes and to incorporate many formats--books, periodicals, videos, microcomputer software, CD-ROMs, and Web sites. Subject index provides access to specific topics. A useful tool for whole language programs and collection development.
URL: http://www.rockhillpress.com -- entire issue plus additional indexing capabilites
SUBJ: Teaching--Periodicals./ Education--Periodicals./ Interdisciplinary approach in education--Periodicals.

PER PROF 050 Ph-1 FREE OD KA130
PARENTS' CHOICE: A REVIEW OF CHILDREN'S MEDIA. Parent's Choice Foundation ISSN 0161-8146, 1978-. v.
Once published in newspaper format, this highly respected reviewing magazine is now only available on the Internet via the Children's Television Workshop's Web site. Offers reviews of children's books and other media including toys, videos, sound recordings, computer programs, Web sites, etc. and several articles/essays. Helpful resource for teachers, librarians, and parents. (Parents' Shelf).
URL: http://www.ctw.org./parents -- full text issues; continuously updated
SUBJ: Children's literature--Reviews./ Audio-visual materials--Reviews.

PER PROF 050 Ph-1 $39.00 yr OD KA131
PHI DELTA KAPPAN. Phi Delta Kappa Educational Foundation ISSN 0031-7217, 1915-. v. ill. 10 nos. per yr.
The magazine read by leaders in education at all levels, to keep up with policy, news, and trends. Articles, emphasizing public schools and research are interesting, well-written, and of high professional quality. Highly recommended.
URL: http://www.pdkintl.org/kappan.htm -- on-line selected articles
SUBJ: Education--Periodicals.

PER PROF 050 Ph-1 $55.00 yr OD KA132
PRIMARY VOICES K-6. National Council of Teachers of English ISSN 1068-073X, 1993-. v. quarterly.
Individual memberships $40.00.
This professional journal is devoted to exploring alternative methods of teaching language arts. Each issue focuses on a theme or concept such as inquiry-based instruction and writing across the curriculum. Articles are written by teams of experienced teachers who share personal practices in support of the featured theories. The practical, teacher-centered publication achieves a good balance of theory and practice.
SUBJ: Language arts (Elementary)--Periodicals./ English language--Study and teaching--Periodicals./ Teaching--Periodicals.

PER PROF 050 Ph-1 $50.00 yr OD KA133
READING TEACHER. International Reading Association ISSN 0034-0561, 1957-. v. ill. 8 nos. per yr. (Sept.-May).
Individual subscription price, $45.00 yr.
Price includes membership.
Official journal of International Reading Association; this has rapidly become an essential tool for teachers of reading at any level. Indexed in EDUCATION INDEX.
SUBJ: Reading (Elementary)--Periodicals.

PER PROF 050 Ph-1 $49.00 yr OD KA134
RESOURCE LINKS: CONNECTING CLASSROOMS, LIBRARIES AND CANADIAN LEARNING RESOURCES. Council for Canadian Learning Resources ISSN 1201-7647, 1995-. v. ill. bimonthly.
Focus is on review and promotion of Canadian resources that will be useful for teachers and librarians. Six issues per year review resources based on the acronym EGAP (Excellent, Good, Average, Problematic). Reviews cover print resources from grades P-12. Audiovisual materials include: videos and recordings, computer software and CD-ROMs, internet resources, and French language resources. Canadian author profile is also included.
SUBJ: Children's literature--Bibliography--Periodicals./ Children's literature--Periodicals./ Canadian literature--Periodicals./ Children's literature--Reviews--Periodicals.

PROF 050 Ph-1 $22.00 yr OD KA135
REVIEWS. Parent Council, Ltd. ISSN 1073-5895, 1993-. v. ill. semiannual.
Includes indexes.
Useful guide to new children's books, audio and video cassettes, CD-ROMs, software, and parenting books is published twice yearly by an independent review organization of librarians, teachers, child development specialists, and other professionals who are also experienced parents. Each of the over 300 entries gives bibliographic information, subjects, annotation, and interest level. (Parents' Shelf).
SUBJ: Children--Books and reading--Periodicals./ Children's literature--Reviews--Periodicals./ Audio-visual materials--Reviews--Periodicals.

PER PROF 050   Ph-3 $24.50 yr OD KA136
SCHOOL ARTS MAGAZINE. Davis ISSN 0036-6463, 1901-. v. ill. 10 nos. per yr.
Aims to present in each issue "balanced...in-depth here's how activities within a framework of sound, creative art philosophy". Appears to provide also a balance between the theoretical and practical, aimed at being of assistance to the classroom teacher rather than the specialist. Contains occasional interviews with artists, such as the children's book illustrator Antonio Frasconi, and the like.
SUBJ: Art--Study and teaching--Periodicals.

PER PROF 050   Ph-3 $44.99 yr OD KA137
SCHOOL LIBRARIAN'S WORKSHOP. Library Learning Resources ISSN 0271-3667, 1980-. v. 10 nos. per yr.
Practical suggestions on management, public relations, scheduling, reference, plus bibliographies. Punched for three ring binder this publication offers many ideas for improving library service.
SUBJ: School libraries--Periodicals.

PER PROF 050   Ph-3 $35.00 yr OD KA138
SCHOOL LIBRARIES IN CANADA. Canadian School Library Association ISSN 0227-3780, 1974-. v. quarterly.
Formerly: MOCASSIN TELEGRAPH.
The official journal of the Canadian School Library Association. A source of policy statements, association news, articles on programs and services in Canadian school libraries and reviews of professional materials.
SUBJ: School libraries--Periodicals.

PER PROF 050   Ph-1 $87.50 yr OD KA139
SCHOOL LIBRARY JOURNAL: FOR CHILDREN'S, YOUNG ADULT, AND SCHOOL LIBRARIES. Bowker ISSN 0362-8930, 1954-. v. ill. 12 nos. per yr.
Indexed in CHILDREN'S MAGAZINE GUIDE.
The journal most widely used by school librarians for its numerous book reviews and its articles and news about librarianship.
SUBJ: School libraries--Periodicals./ Children's literature--Bibliography--Periodicals.

PER PROF 050   Ph-1 $49.00 yr OD KA140
SCHOOL LIBRARY MEDIA ACTIVITIES MONTHLY. LMS Associates ISSN 0889-9371, 1984-. v. ill. 10 nos. per yr.
Splendid activities from how to use an author's books to a day by day outline for a month of library promotion. This is a professional journal which the librarian should share with teachers. Production techniques include: goal, objectives, and process. The "Computer Cache" column is "designed to provide useful information on microcomputers in library media centers, particularly in connection with teaching library media skills."
SUBJ: School libraries--Periodicals./ Media programs (Education)--Periodicals.

PER PROF 050   Ph-1 $45.00 yr KA141
SCHOOL LIBRARY MEDIA ANNUAL. Libraries Unlimited ISSN 0739-7712, 1983-. v. annual.
Includes index.
Divided into sections which cover concerns and issues facing the school library media specialist, this compilation of papers provides insight into current research, implementation of national standards, and reports from national and state agencies. It is an information packed volume covering topics which should be of interest to all practitioners.
SUBJ: School libraries--Periodicals./ Instructional materials centers--Periodicals./ Media programs (Education)--Periodicals./ Audio-visual library service--Periodicals.

PER PROF 050   Ph-3   free OD KA142
SCHOOL LIBRARY MEDIA QUARTERLY. American Association of School Librarians, 1972-. v. ill. 4 nos. per yr.
Formerly: SCHOOL LIBRARIES and SCHOOL MEDIA QUARTERLY.
Official journal of the American Association of School Librarians, containing news of the Association, reviews of professional publications, and articles on programs and services in school media centers.
URL: http://www.ala.org/aasl/SLMQ -- on-line issue contains full text; continuously updated
SUBJ: School libraries--Periodicals.

PER PROF 050   Ph-3 $43.00 yr OD KA143
SCHOOL SCIENCE AND MATHEMATICS. School Science and Mathematics Association ISSN 0036-6803, 1901-. v. ill. monthly (Oct-May).
Available to individuals for $30.00 a year.
This is the official journal of the publishing society, and is devoted to the improvement of teaching of the sciences and mathematics at all grade levels. Its emphasis is more for the upper grades than elementary school level, but would be of stimulating interest to teachers. The scholarly articles are contributed by members of the profession and cover methods of teaching and research in the field. Books and Teaching Aids Received are listed under subject headings, followed by evaluative reviews of a relatively small proportion of those items received.
SUBJ: Science--Study and teaching--Periodicals./ Mathematics--Study and teaching--Periodicals.

PER PROF 050   Ph-2 $56.00 yr OD KA144
SCIENCE AND CHILDREN. National Science Teachers Association ISSN 0036-8148, 1963-. v. ill. 8 nos. per yr.
Subscription included with membership.
Individual subscription price, $52.00 yr.
A journal of science directed specifically to the elementary school teacher. Contributors are primarily working science educators at a variety of levels. Articles include practical suggestions for classroom methods and projects, information on events and trends of interest to the teacher, professionally, and reviews of science resource materials for student use and at professional level.
SUBJ: Science--Study and teaching--Periodicals.

PER PROF 050   Ph-3 $40.00 yr OD KA145
SCIENCE BOOKS AND FILMS. American Association for the Advancement of Science ISSN 0098-342X, 1975-. v. 9 nos. per yr.
Formerly: SCIENCE BOOKS: A QUARTERLY REVIEW.
Reviews trade, text, reference books, 16mm films, videocassettes, and filmstrips related indirectly or directly to the pure sciences. Books are arranged by Dewey Classification within appeal ranges. Films, videos, filmstrips are in separate sections.
SUBJ: Books--Reviews./ Audio-visual materials--Reviews./ Science--Bibliography--Periodicals.

PER PROF 050   Ph-1 $59.00 yr OD KA146
SOCIAL EDUCATION. National Council for the Social Studies ISSN 0037-7724, 1937-. v. 7 nos. per yr.
The official journal of the National Council for the Social Studies and therefore essential for any teacher who wished to be informed on professional matters in this field, whether at the elementary or secondary level. Currently has many issues devoted to specific topics, which cut across grade levels, but with a special section on the elementary school. Departments: Notes and news, Sight and sound, Books.
SUBJ: Social sciences--Periodicals.

PER PROF 050   Ph-1 $37.00 yr OD KA147
SOCIAL STUDIES AND THE YOUNG LEARNER: A QUARTERLY FOR CREATIVE TEACHING IN GRADES K-6. National Council for the Social Studies ISSN 1056-0300, 1988-. v. ill. quarterly.
Department editors combine efforts in an excellent publication for teachers and librarians. A pull-out feature provides specific lessons for integrating the topic (example in this issue was economics) across the curriculum. Procedure, discussion, and extension activities are clearly written. The Children's Literature feature combines science, technology and society. Teacher's Bookshelf recommends resources of all types.
SUBJ: Social sciences--Study and teaching./ Social sciences--Periodicals.

PER PROF 050   Ph-3 $57.00 yr OD KA148
TEACHING CHILDREN MATHEMATICS. National Council of Teachers of Mathematics ISSN 0004-136X, 1954-. v. monthly (Sept.-May).
Formerly ARITHMETIC TEACHER.
Official journal for arithmetic teachers and an essential in this specialty. Indexed in EDUCATION INDEX.
SUBJ: Arithmetic--Study and teaching--Periodicals.

PER PROF 050   Ph-1 $50.00 yr OD KA149
TEACHING ELEMENTARY PHYSICAL EDUCATION. Human Kinetics ISSN 1045-4853, 1990-. v. ill. 6 nos. per yr.
Available for individuals, $18.00.
Informative, readable newsletter geared exclusively for elementary physical education teachers, specialists, and administrators. Each issue of TEPE will include: Profile (interviews with successful elementary physical educators); News (brief items of interest on a local and national level); Instruction (practical ideas for teaching activities and games); Curriculum (articles on program content); Professional issues (topics such as public relations, certification, continuing education); Resources & Events (reviews of video and books); listings of important events; and Viewpoint (opinions on various topics).
SUBJ: Physical education and training--Study and teaching./ Physical education and training--Periodicals.

PER PROF 050   Ph-1 $58.00 yr   OD KA150
TEACHING EXCEPTIONAL CHILDREN. Council for Exceptional Children
ISSN 0040-0599, 1968-. v. ill. quarterly.
An incomparably useful periodical for the teacher involved in
mainstreaming. Well-illustrated articles provide appropriate teaching
ideas and techniques for the regular classroom teacher whose class
includes handicapped children.
SUBJ: Mainstreaming in education./ Handicapped--Education.

PER PROF 050   Ph-1 $19.77 yr   OD KA151
TEACHING K-8. Early Years ISSN 0891-4508, 1971-. v. ill. 8 nos. per
yr.
Formerly: EARLY YEARS.
Indexed in CHILDREN'S MAGAZINE GUIDE.
Geared to primary and pre-school education, this is intended to assist
the classroom teacher with practical ideas, articles, explanations of
new theories, etc. Sponsored by a list of well-known educators as the
Editorial Advisory Board. Departments include features, classroom
management, exceptional children, curriculum materials, along with
special reports on such subjects as educational advertisers.
SUBJ: Education, Elementary--Periodicals./ Nursery schools--
Periodicals.

PER PROF 050   Ph-1 $24.00 yr   OD KA152
TECHNOLOGY AND LEARNING. Miller Freeman ISSN 0746-4223,
1980-. v. ill. 9 nos. per yr.
Formerly CLASSROOM COMPUTER LEARNING.
Indexed in CHILDREN'S MAGAZINE GUIDE.
A slender journal for teachers and other educators directed toward
the use of microcomputers in the classroom.
SUBJ: Microcomputers--Periodicals.

PER PROF 050   Ph-2 $40.00 yr   OD KA153
TECHTRENDS: FOR LEADERS IN EDUCATION AND TRAINING.
Association for Educational Communication and Technology ISSN 8756-
3894, 1956-. v. bimonthly.
Formerly: AUDIOVISUAL INSTRUCTOR and INSTRUCTIONAL
INNOVATOR.
Official journal of the Association for Educational Communication and
Technology.
Includes news of the association, reviews of the professional literature,
and timely articles for teachers and media specialists. Regular columns
cover such topics as news of ERIC activities and publications,
copyright, and techniques.
SUBJ: Audio-visual education--Periodicals.

PER PROF 050   Ph-1 $12.00 yr   OD KA154
WONDERSCIENCE: FUN PHYSICAL SCIENCE ACTIVITIES FOR
CHILDREN AND ADULTS TO DO TOGETHER. American Chemical
Society/American Institute of Physics, 1987-. v. col. ill. 8 nos. per yr.
Includes teacher's guide.
Colorful, simple experiments in a readable format provide the teacher
and student with scientific challenges. Materials needed for the
experiments are highlighted in a box. A very inexpensive way to
reinforce scientific principles. Adult supervision is recommended.
SUBJ: Science--Periodicals./ Science--Study and teaching.

PER PROF 050   Ph-1 $95.00 yr   OD KA155
WORLD NEWSMAP OF THE WEEK: HEADLINE FOCUS. Weekly
Reader Corp ISSN 0043-874X, 1938-. v. col. ill. 30 nos. per yr.
Formerly: WORLD NEWSMAP OF THE WEEK.
Provides information on contemporary world events and profiles of
nations accompanied by cartographic illustrations. An excellent
teaching aid for social studies or current events.
SUBJ: Social sciences--Periodicals./ Current events--Periodicals./
Spanish language materials.

PROF 153.4   Ph-1 $14.95   P OD KA156
POLETTE, NANCY. ABC's of books and thinking skills. Book Lures ISBN
0-913839-61-2, 1987. 142p. ill.
Includes index.
Nancy Polette continues to offer creative ways to incorporate good
literature in activities based on the various types of thinking skills. This
is not a "fill in the blank" book. Most libraries will have the book
titles mentioned in the activities.
SUBJ: Children's literature./ Books and reading./ Thought and
thinking.

PROF 155.4   Ph-2 $29.95   P KA157
CHAPMAN, CAROLYN. If the shoe fits...how to develop multiple
intelligences in the classroom. IRI/Skylight ISBN 0-932935-64-8, 1993.
242p. ill.
Includes bibliography and index.
Provides background on how to expand methods from incorporating
two intelligences, verbal/linguistic and logical/mathematical, to
including the seven intelligences identified in Howard Gardner's book
FRAMES OF MIND. Each chapter demonstrates a variety of ways to
understand and implement Gardner's theory.
SUBJ: Intellect./ Cognitive learning./ Cognition in children.

PROF 170   Ph-1 $20.50   T KA158
LETTERS FOR OUR CHILDREN: FIFTY AMERICANS SHARE LESSONS
IN LIVING. Edited by Erica Goode, with Jeannye Thornton. Forword by
James Fallows. Photos by Jim Lo Scalzo. Random House ISBN 0-679-
45011-4; In Canada: Random House, 1996. 256p. ill.
"U.S. News & World Report book."
Loving, heartfelt messages to children cover many pitfalls of growing
up: resisting authority, depression, teen pregnancy, and repercussions
of divorce. Adults from different walks of life and racial backgrounds
confirm their love of and pride in children. Inspirational but not
preachy, it conveys valuable advice. For reading aloud in segments
for values education.
SUBJ: Conduct of life--Case studies./ Children--Conduct of life./ Role
models--Correspondence./ Role models--Biography./ Success.

PROF 177   Ph-3 $12.95   P KA159
KINCHER, JONNI. First honest book about lies. Free Spirit ISBN
0-915793-43-1, 1992. 170p. ill.
Includes bibliography and index.
Lessons, anecdotes, and exercises demonstrate how people often
massage the truth. Shows how to separate fact from fiction and
encourages students to make decisions based on the best available
information. Most valuable when used in directed discussions which
explore situational ethics and personal responsibility. Also useful for
exploring cultural differences.
SUBJ: Honesty.

PROF 200   Ph-1 $25.00   P KA160
HUBBARD, BENJAMIN JEROME. America's religions: an educator's
guide to beliefs and practices. By Benjamin J. Hubbard, John T. Hatfield,
and James A. Santucci. Teacher Ideas Press ISBN 1-56308-469-4, 1997.
162p.
Includes bibliographies, filmography, directory and index.
Admirable guide written in language which should be understandable
for both students and teachers. Chapters highlight specific religions
and include information on origins, basic beliefs, sacred books,
subgroups, common misunderstandings and stereotypes, classroom
concerns, and population data. Annotated bibliographies include
books, periodicals, videotapes, CD-ROMs and Web sites. Appendixes
include sample school district policy covering recognition of religious
beliefs and customs, calendar of religious holidays for 1997-1998;
and subject index.
SUBJ: United States--Religion./ Religions--Study and teaching./
Religion in the public schools.

PROF 303.6   Ph-2 $35.95   P OD KA161
BODINE, RICHARD J. Creating the peaceable school: a comprehensive
program for teaching conflict resolution: program guide. By Richard J.
Bodine, Donna K. Crawford and Fred Schrumpf. Research Press ISBN
0-87822-346-0, 1994. 362p.
Includes bibliography and index.
Two volumes present a plan for guiding students to identify
cooperative solutions to conflict. Exercises focus on mediation,
negotiation, and group problem solving. Useful resource for classroom
teachers and guidance counselors.
CREATING THE PEACEABLE SCHOOL: A COMPREHENSIVE
PROGRAM FOR TEACHING CONFLICT RESOLUTION: STUDENT
MANUAL (ISBN 0-87822-350-9, 1994), $14.95.
SUBJ: Conflict management./ Classroom environment./ Conduct of
life./ Interpersonal relations.

PROF 303.6   Ph-1 $7.00   P KA162
SLABY, RONALD G. Early violence prevention: tools for teachers of
young children. By Ronald G. Slaby...[et. al.]. National Association for
the Education of Young Children ISBN 0-935989-65-X, 1995. 198p. ill.
Includes bibliographies and directory.
One response to the concern of all educators coping with the impact
of violence on young people. Strategies are presented to aide
teachers, parents, and administrators to empower students to
"develop the patterns of thought, feeling, and action that can
effectively prevent violence." (viii) Focusing on children ages two to
six, this research based book provides many topics and specific
examples to stimulate discussion between teachers, parents, and
young people. A comprehensive resource for teaching nonviolent
conflict resolution and social competence. No index. (Parents' Shelf).
SUBJ: Conflict management./ Conduct of life./ Interpersonal relations.

VCR PROF 303.6   Ph-3 $99.95   OD KA163
STUDENT WORKSHOP: MEDIATION SKILLS (Videocassette). Sunburst 2550-03 ISBN 0-7805-4209-6, 1996. 1/2" VHS videocassette color (30min).
>   Includes teacher's guide.
>   An engaging, clearly modeled video with a realistic scenario gives students an opportunity to observe and practice a five-step mediation process: introduction and ground rules, getting the story, brainstorming for solutions, choosing solutions, and closing the mediation. Teacher guide contains an extensive bibliography, supplementary information, and additional opportunities for review and practice. For schools where nonviolent conflict resolution is encouraged, this will be a practical tool in programs designed to train student mediators.
>   SUBJ: Conflict management./ Interpersonal relations./ Conduct of life.

VCR PROF 303.6   Ph-1 2-6 $99.95   OD KA164
STUDENT WORKSHOP: SOLVING CONFLICTS (Videocassette). Sunburst 2448 ISBN 0-7805-4150-2, 1994. 1/2" VHS videocassette color (25min).
>   Includes teacher's guide and 20 reproducible student worksheets.
>   Super sleuth Les Struggle offers primary grade students techniques which help in solving conflicts satisfactorily. Support materials include script, worksheets, and suggestions for use. Preview and planning required for lasting positive outcomes.
>   STUDENT WORKSHOP: CONFLICT RESOLUTION SKILLS (ISBN 0-7805-4110-3, 1994) provides a complete package to be used in teaching basic skills of conflict resolution to intermediate and junior high student.
>   SUBJ: Conflict management./ Interpersonal relations./ Conduct of life.

VCR PROF 303.6   Ph-2 K-2 $79.95   OD KA165
WE CAN WORK IT OUT!: CONFLICT RESOLUTION (Videocassette). Sunburst Communicatons 2455 ISBN 0-7805-4149-9, 1994. 1/2" VHS videocassette color (14min), 1 sound cassette (2min).
>   Includes teacher's guide, nine reproducible student worksheets, games, songs and poster.
>   Introduces concepts of resolving peer conflict. Script, worksheets, music tape, and score are included. Useful in aiding student growth and as classroom management support.
>   SUBJ: Conflict management./ Interpersonal relations./ Conduct of life.

PROF 305.4   Ph-1 $24.00   P   KA166
HAVEN, KENDALL. Amazing American women: 40 fascinating 5-minute reads. Forward by Molly Murphy MacGregor. Libraries Unlimited ISBN 1-56308-291-8, 1995. 305p.
>   Includes bibliographies, chronology and index.
>   A splendid collection of 40 brief stories of American women from the seventeenth century to the twentieth century who made a significant difference in American history, who were trendsetters, and who worked to expand opportunities for other women. Each story is followed by questions to explore and a bibliography for young people and adults. Stories are grouped in broad categories of civil rights, politics, sports, science and exploration, education, medicine, military service, business, and visual, written, and performing arts. Appendixes give a timeline of stories and major events in American history and additional significant women in our history. For women's studies.
>   SUBJ: Women--Biography./ United States--History--Biography.

PROF 306   Ph-2 $12.95   P   KA167
MILORD, SUSAN. Hands around the world: 365 creative ways to build cultural awareness and global respect. Williamson ISBN 0-913589-65-9; In Canada: Williamson/dist. by Fitzhenry & Whiteside, 1992. 158p. ill.
>   "Williamson Kids Can! book."
>   Includes directory, bibliography and index.
>   Promotes cultural awareness by offering daily suggestions, grouped by theme, of activities, games, and ideas which will aid in breaking down stereotypes and in increasing appreciation of each other. Back matter includes addresses, suppliers and bibliography. Though directed to students, this is a bonafide teacher-pleaser for multicultural studies. (Parents' Shelf)
>   SUBJ: Culture./ Games.

PROF 346.73   Ph-1 $5.95   P OD KA168
OFFICIAL FAIR-USE GUIDELINES: COMPLETE TEXT OF FOUR OFFICIAL DOCUMENTS ARRANGED FOR USE BY EDUCATORS. Assn. for Educational Communications & Technology ISBN 0-914143-04-2, 1987. 32p.
>   The author states "In consulting with school districts, I frequently discover my clients are distributing incomplete or inaccurate texts of the federal fair-use guidelines teachers are expected to observe. Unfortunately, the inaccurate or truncated versions of the documents frequently distort the purpose and scope of the original documents.

Those documents have been gathered in this booklet in the hope the booklet will facilitate an accurate application of the guidelines." Includes fair use guidelines for books and periodicals, music, off-air videotaping, ICCE policy statement on network and multiple machine software, sample suggested district policy on software copyright, bibliography.
>   SUBJ: Copyright.

PROF 346.73   Ph-1 $14.95   P   KA169
TALAB, R. S. Commonsense copyright: a guide to the new technologies. McFarland ISBN 0-89950-224-5, 1986. 162p.
>   Includes index.
>   A concise, understandable, explanation of the confusing law which guides use of copyright resources. The charts on pages 114-116 offer simplified guidelines for educational institutions. Simplified chart explanation for single and multiple copy library duplication guidelines include books, periodicals, audiovisual news programs and computer software documentation. Motion picture and television off-air taping compares live transmission to classroom and taping for limited retention periods.
>   SUBJ: Copyright./ Fair use (Copyright).

VCR PROF 362.7   Ph-1 K-3 $59.95   OD KA170
MY BODY BELONGS TO ME (Videocassette). Sunburst Communications 2379 ISBN 0-7805-4092-1, 1992. 1/2" VHS videocassette color (25min).
>   Includes teacher's guide.
>   Includes Paul Glickman's book, "My body belongs to me," (illus. by Mina Yamashita) a story on the same topic but about different characters.
>   Counselor and puppets discuss ways for children to respond to inappropriate types of touches. The format works well in delivering information; accompanying guide includes suggestions for use, script, and follow-up questions. Preview a must.
>   SUBJ: Child sexual abuse--Prevention./ Self-protection.

PROF 370   Ph-1   Free   P OD KA171
NATIONAL EDUCATION GOALS REPORT: BUILDING A NATION OF LEARNERS. National Education Goals Panel ISSN 1062-1962 ISBN 0-16-045194-9, 1991-. v. annual.
>   Includes bibliography.
>   "Focuses on 16 policy-actionable core indicators to convey to parents, educators, and policymakers how far we are from where we should be and what we must do in order to reach our destination." (Forward) Provides invaluable information about the educational progress of individual states and the nation as schools strive to meet Goals 2000.
>   NATIONAL EDUCATION GOALS REPORT: DATA VOLUMES (ISBN 0-16-045203-1, 1994-) supply pertinent statistics, graphs, and charts. Volume one lists national information in detail; volume two lists information by individual states.
>   SUBJ: Education--Aims and objectives--Statistics--Periodicals./ Education--Statistics--Periodicals./ Educational evaluation--States--Statistics--Periodicals.

PROF 370.11   Ph-1 $3.00 ea. P   KA172
PHI DELTA KAPPA EDUCATIONAL FOUNDATION. Fastback series. Phi Delta Kappa, 1972. v. ill.
>   A series of over 140 compact and readable paperbacks designed to bring to readers authoritative and timely summaries on significant subjects relating to schools today. Sponsored by an honorary educational fraternity.
>   SUBJ: Education.

PROF 370.117   Ph-3 $19.00   P   KA173
VANDERHEYDEN-TRESCONY, CATHERINE. Faxing friends; a resource guide for forming international friendships among students, age 5-9. Illus. by Barbara Knutson. Teacher Ideas Press/Libraries Unlimited ISBN 1-56308-061-3, 1992. 101p. ill.
>   Includes directory, bibliography and index.
>   Introduce students to one of the latest methods of communication. The author's goal is "to help students ages five through nine learn about a different country and culture through regular communication with another class via facsimilie (fax) machine." (Intro.) Appendixes include: Lesson Expansion Ideas; Year End Suggestions; Chart of World Languages and Academic Year Dates; Telephone and Facsimilie Dialing Information; Cost Estimates for Faxing Items Internationally; Troubleshooting; and Evaluation Forms. Ideas for correspondence can be easily adapted for traditional pen pals as well. For teachers interested in initiating international exchanges and for multicultural studies.
>   SUBJ: Intercultural education./ Education, Primary./ Facsimile transmission./ Teaching--Aids and devices./ Pen pals.

PROF 370.15   Ph-2 $15.95   P   KA174
LAZEAR, DAVID G. Seven pathways of learning: teaching students and parents about multiple intelligences. By David Lazear. Foreword by Arthur L. Costa. Zephyr Press ISBN 0-913705-92-6, 1994. 225p. ill.
    Includes bibliography and index.
    This is the author's third book on the seven intelligences. This title is "devoted to teaching about multiple intelligences and thus presents the metacognitive dimension of this work." (p.xiii) Lesson procedures to expand intelligent behavior are given for both elementary and secondary levels. (Parents' Shelf).
    SUBJ: Learning./ Intellect./ Cognitive styles./ Teaching./ Activity programs in education.

PROF 371.04   Ph-1 $10.00   P   KA175
KENYON, MARY POTTER. Home schooling from scratch. Gazelle ISBN 0-930192-35-4, 1996. 127p. ill.
    Includes bibliographies, directory and index.
    A brief, practical guide for those wanting to home school. Topics range from how important the public library is as a resource to how to "beg, barter, and borrow." Extensive resource list is included, along with information on finding and using support groups. (Parents' Shelf).
    SUBJ: Home schooling./ Education--Parent participation.

PROF 371.3   Ph-1 $32.50   P   KA176
BARRON, ANN E. New technologies for education: a beginner's guide. 3rd ed. By Ann E. Barron and Gary W. Orwig. Libraries Unlimited ISBN 1-56308-477-5, 1997. 276p. ill.
    Includes glossaries, directories, bibliographies and index.
    Designed with multiple uses: resource book, guide for staff development, or textbook. Readable with excellent illustrations and bibliographies, this book is an outstanding primary source for school librarians who must continue to assume a leadership role in the technology race. Must purchase handbook for all school library media specialists.
    SUBJ: Educational technology./ Teaching--Aids and devices.

PROF 371.3   Ph-1 $ P   KA177
BOSMA, BETTE. Fairy tales, fables, legends and myths: using folk literature in your classroom. 2nd ed. Teachers College Press, 1992.
    Includes bibliography and index.
    "The teaching strategies in this book address the questions: How do we teach reading as a thinking process? How do we foster interaction between the reader, the reading materials and writing?" (Preface) The lively and readable presentation of over 50 imaginative teaching ideas has value for librarians and teachers.
    SUBJ: Folk literature--Study and teaching (Elementary)./ Reading (Elementary)./ English language--Composition and exercises.

PROF 371.3   Ph-3 $25.50   P   KA178
LANKFORD, MARY D. Successful field trips. ABC-CLIO ISBN 0-87436-638-0, 1992. 129p.
    Includes bibliography and index.
    Serves as a source of sample field trip policies, ideas for locations, and commonsense suggestions for planning effective field trips. Creative teachers will find ideas for pretrip and posttrip activities particularly useful.
    SUBJ: School excursions./ Language experience approach in education./ English language--Composition and exercises--Study and teaching./ Thought and thinking--Study and teaching./ Education, Elementary.

PROF 371.3   Ph-1 $25.00   P   KA179
MILLER, ELIZABETH B. Internet resource directory for K-12 teachers and librarians. Libraries Unlimited ISSN 1084-5798, 1994-. v. annual.
    Includes indexes.
    Annual directory of K-12 Internet resources. Criteria for inclusion states a resource: supports and enriches K-12 curriculum of science, math, social studies, language arts, and foreign language studies; supplements school library media core collections; is free; is current and updated regularly and is specifically designed to assist educators develop professionally, collaborate with peers, and share information and ideas.
    URL: http://www.lu.com -- contains updated addresses.
    SUBJ: Internet (Computer network)--Directories./ Databases--Directories./ Education, Elementary--Information services--Directories./ Education, Secondary--Information services--Directories.

PROF 371.3   Ph-1 $12.00   P   KA180
PAPERT, SEYMOUR. Children's machine: rethinking school in the age of the computer. BasicBooks ISBN 0-465-01063-6; In Canada: HarperCollins, 1993. 242p. ill.
    Includes directory, bibliography and index.
    Poses the question: "How does the relationship between children and computers affect learning? Understanding this relationship will be crucial to our ability to shape the future." (Preface) Explores where the love affair with the computer is going, if the older generation can guide its direction whether constructive or destructive, and if the evolution is already out of control. (Parents' Shelf).
    SUBJ: Computer-assisted instruction./ Education--Data processing.

PROF 371.3   Ph-1 $14.95   P   KA181
RADENCICH, MARGUERITE C. How to help your child with homework: every caring parent's guide to encouraging good study habits and ending the Homework Wars: for parents of children ages 6-13. Rev. and updated ed. By Marguerite C. Radencich and Jeanne Shay Schumm. Edited by Pamela Espeland. Free Spirit ISBN 1-57542-006-6, 1997. 199p. ill.
    Includes bibliographies, directory and index.
    A welcome resource for parents who will find the tips for scheduling and planning homework completion to be most useful. Suggestions for parental assistance in all core curriculum areas (reading, writing, spelling, math, science, and social studies) are included. The section on resources and tools for parents contains helpful reproducible forms and checklists. (Parents' Shelf).
    SUBJ: Homework./ Education--Parent participation./ Study skills.

PROF 371.3028   Ph-1 $12.00   P   KA182
KROPP, PAUL. Raising a reader: make your child a reader for life. Main Street Books/Doubleday ISBN 0-385-47913-1; In Canada: Bantam Doubleday Dell, c1993, 1996. 206p.
    Includes index.
    Author explains why there are no "pat" answers to the problems of poor reading skills and lack of reading motivation. Includes suggestions to reinforce methods for avoiding the pitfalls of a student becoming a "nonreader." Provides information that will be useful to promote support for libraries. (Parents' Shelf).
    SUBJ: Reading--Parent participation./ Children--Books and reading./ Teenagers--Books and reading.

PROF 371.826   Ph-1 $7.95   P   KA183
TOWER, CYNTHIA CROSSON. Homeless students. By Cynthia Crosson Tower and Donna J. White. National Education Association ISBN 0-8106-0245-8, 1989. 47p. (NEA Professional library).
    Includes glossary, appendices and bibliography.
    This book begins with the unbelievable statement: "Today homeless families are the fastest-growing population in the United States." (p.6). Factors which lead to this situation for young people, and ways those in education can respond are presented. Appendixes include: An American Tragedy: Homeless Children; Advocacy Organizations for the Homeless; Sample forms; Bibliography.
    SUBJ: Homeless students./ Homeless students--Education.

PROF 371.9   Ph-2 $9.95   P   KA184
DUNN, KATHRYN BOESEL. Trouble with school: a family story about learning disabilities. By Kathryn Boesel Dunn and Allison Boesel Dunn. Illus. by Rick Stromoski. Woodbine House ISBN 0-933149-57-3, 1993. unp. col. ill.
    Includes directory.
    Empathetically portrays what it is like to be diagnosed as learning disabled. Dual narrative of a parent and child provides a variation in point of view. Particularly useful when read with parents. (Parents' Shelf).
    SUBJ: Learning disabilities--Case studies./ Education, Primary--Case studies.

VCR PROF 371.92   Ph-1 $69.95   KA185
EDUCATING PETER (Videocassette). Ph-1. HBO/dist. by Ambrose Video ISBN 1-55980-608-7, 1993. 1/2" videocassette color (30min).
    Peter's year in third grade serves as a testimonial for mainstreaming as being beneficial for both special students and their classmates. Vignettes illustrate the difficulties as well as the rewards of this educational process. Useful for teachers, parents, and fellow students of developmentally challenged children. (Parents' Shelf).
    SUBJ: Mainstreaming in education./ Down's syndrome.

PROF 371.92   Ph-1 $13.95   P   KA186
STEVENS, SUZANNE H. Classroom success for the LD and ADHD child. John F. Blair ISBN 0-89587-159-9, 1997. 342p.
    Rev. ed. of: CLASSROOM SUCCESS FOR THE LEARNING DISABLED, 1984.
    Includes directory, bibliographies and index.
    Excellent guide that presents many solutions to assist teachers and parents in coping with children with learning disabilities and attention deficit disorders. (Parents' Shelf).
    SUBJ: Learning disabled children--Education--United States--Case studies./ Attention-deficit-disordered children--Education--United States./ Slow learning children--United States--Case studies./ Educational change--United States.

VCR PROF 371.95   Ph-3 $1195.00   OD KA187
EDUCATING ABLE LEARNERS (Videocassette). Agency for Instructional Technology 343-VVV, 1991. 12 1/2" VHS videocassettes color (29min ea.). (Educating able learners).
Includes study guide.
Individual titles available separately, $150.00 ea.
A thorough look at teaching gifted students both in and outside the regular classroom. Includes information on the five types of giftedness (intellectual, academic, creative, artistic, leadership). Expensive but useful for teachers at all levels and for teacher education programs.
SUBJ: Gifted children--Education./ Talented students.

PROF 371.95   Ph-3 $19.95   P   KA188
PATTERNS OF INFLUENCE ON GIFTED LEARNERS: THE HOME, SELF, AND THE SCHOOL. Edited by Joyce L. VanTassel-Baska and Paula Olszewski-Kubilius. Teachers College Press ISBN 0-8077-2937-X, 1989. 250p. (Education and psychology of the gifted).
Includes index.
Descriptions of how parents, the individual and school influence the development of talent in children and young adults. Provides current research on the development, both from a psychological and sociological perspective of the influences on an individual's growth toward intellectual fulfillment. Useful not only for parents but also for school administrators and guidance counselors.
SUBJ: Gifted children--Education./ Gifted children--Family relationships./ Gifted children--Psychology.

PROF 371.95   Ph-2 $12.95   P   KA189
SAUNDERS, JACQULYN. Bringing out the best: a resource guide for parents of young gifted children. Rev. and updated. By Jacqulyn Saunders with Pamela Espeland. Free Spirit ISBN 0-915793-30-X, 1991. 234p. ill.
Includes directories, bibliographies and index.
Although the bibliographies for children are dated, the book provides practical suggestions for identifying resources and for working with a gifted child. (Parents' Shelf).
SUBJ: Gifted children--Education (Preschool)./ Parent and child.

PROF 372   Ph-2 $7.95   P   KA190
DIMIDJIAN, VICTORIA JEAN. Early childhood at risk: actions and advocacy for young children. National Education Association ISBN 0-8106-1481-2, 1989. 63p. (NEA Professional library).
Includes bibliography.
The problems of a "lost" generation of young people in our society are examined in this monograph which presents a portrait of children "whose bodies have been inadequately nurtured, whose personalities have been inadequately socialized, and whose minds have been incompletely or inappropriately stimulated." (Introduction). The conclusion explores directions for changing the future for the young people.
SUBJ: Readiness for school./ Early childhood education./ Early childhood education--Case studies./ Performance in children./ Academic achievement.

PROF 372.1   Ph-3 $37.16   P   KA191
CROFT, DOREEN J. Activities handbook for teachers of young children. 5th ed. By Doreen J. Croft and Robert D. Hess. Houghton Mifflin ISBN 0-395-43207-3, 1990. 447p. ill.
Includes bibliographies.
Covers activities for pre-primary school children in the following curriculum areas: language abilities, pre-science, the arts, pre-math, and cooking. Includes annotated bibliographies of materials for both children and the teachers. Materials needed for the various activities are those readily available.
SUBJ: Creative activities and seatwork./ Nursery schools./ Teaching--Handbooks, manuals, etc.

PROF 372.11   Ph-1 $19.95   T   KA192
KIDDER, TRACY. Among schoolchildren. Houghton Mifflin ISBN 0-395-47591-0, 1989. 340p.
Includes bibliography.
Available from National Library Service for the Blind and Physically Handicapped on sound recording cassette, RC 30238.
Teacher Chris Zajac's fifth grade class in Holyoke, Mass. is followed through a school year. Mrs. Zajac's aspirations, frustrations and disciplinary and teaching techniques reflect those of many other teachers. Whether the reader comes to admire her or not, the portrayal of Mrs. Zajac's small world effectively transmits the best and worst aspects of American education. For both teachers and parents.
SUBJ: Elementary school teaching--United States--Case studies./ Fifth grade (Education)--United States--Case studies.

PROF 372.13   Ph-1 $22.95   T   KA193
CHILD'S SEASONAL TREASURY. Complied and written by Betty Jones. Tricycle Press ISBN 1-883672-30-9; In Canada: Publishers Group West, 1996. 136p. ill. (some col.).
Includes bibliographies and indexes.
Poetry, fingerplays, games, riddles, and activities involving movement, cooking, music and art are presented based on a seasonal theme. These ideas will be especially useful for preschool teachers and parents. Resource list includes books and catalogs. Useful for planning preschool storytimes. (Parents' Shelf).
SUBJ: Creative activities and seatwork./ Early childhood education--Activity programs./ Children's poetry./ Children's songs./ Waldorf method of education.

PROF 372.13   Ph-2 $10.95   P   KA194
RICE, MELANIE. Complete book of children's activities. Illus. by Chris Barker. Kingfisher/dist. by Raintree Steck-Vaughn ISBN 1-85697-907-5, 1993. 120p. col. ill.
This useful compendium of simple activities for young children includes number and word games, cooking projects, handicrafts, and nature study suggestions. Projects require little preparation, use readily available materials, and are presented in easy-to-follow directions. Use to develop manual dexterity and listening and observation skills in preschoolers and kindergarteners. (Parents' Shelf).
SUBJ: Creative activities and seatwork./ Amusements./ Educational games./ Handicraft.

PROF 372.19   Ph-2 $29.95   P OD KA195
MEINBACH, ANITA MEYER. Complete guide to thematic units: creating the integrated curriculum. By Anita Meyer Meinbach, Liz Rothlein, Anthony D. Fredericks. Christopher-Gordon ISBN 0-926842-42-0, 1995. 227p.
Includes bibliographies and index.
An excellent sourcebook for teachers and librarians who need a framework to support thematic teaching. Includes information on how to select and organize the theme, gather materials, design activities and projects, and implement the unit. Use for interdisciplinary studies.
SUBJ: Interdisciplinary approach in education./ Education--Curricula./ Elementary school teaching--United States./ Group work in education.

PROF 372.21   Ph-2 $39.95   T   KA196
BROSTERMAN, NORMAN. Inventing kindergarten. Photos by Kiyoshi Togashi. Abrams ISBN 0-8109-3526-0, 1997. 160p. ill. (some col.).
Includes bibliography and index.
A fascinating and comprehensive book about the original kindergarten developed by the German educator Friedrich Froebel in the 1830s. His program of blocks, tiles, origami, clay, sewing, and design projects may have influenced important artists such as Mondrian, Klee, and Frank Lloyd Wright. An informative book on a part of education that helps shape education.
SUBJ: Kindergarten--History--19th century./ Kindergarten--History--20th century./ Kindergarten--Methods and manuals./ Frobel, Friedrich./ Art, Abstract--History--20th century./ Architecture, Modern--20th century.

PROF 372.21   Ph-2 $29.95   P   KA197
GIANT ENCYCLOPEDIA OF CIRCLE TIME AND GROUP ACTIVITIES FOR CHILDREN 3 TO 6: OVER 600 FAVORITE CIRCLE TIME ACTIVITES CREATED BY TEACHERS FOR TEACHERS. Edited by Kathy Charner. Gryphon House ISBN 0-87659-181-0, 1996. 510p. ill.
Includes indexes.
Created from suggestions by teachers from all over the world, these 600 circle time, or group activities, are for children ages three to six. Each entry includes a list of materials required, step-by-step directions, and related books, songs, and poems. Table of contents and index provide easy access to broad themes such as holidays, shapes, self-concept, and senses. Edge of each page displays a header that identifies the subject area. Includes an index both of books cited and materials.
SUBJ: Early childhood education--Activity programs./ Creative activities and seatwork./ Group work in education.

PROF 372.3   Ph-2 $9.95   P   KA198
BOURNE, BARBARA. Exploring space: using Seymour Simon's astronomy books in the classroom. By Barbara Bourne and Wendy Saul. Morrow ISBN 0-688-12723-1, 1994. 96p. col. ill.
Includes bibliographies, directories and index.
Successfully integrates children's literature and science through lessons that build on Seymour Simon's marvelous astronomy books. Chapters include "Exploring our solar system," "Exploring the stars," and "Exploring the universe." Each lesson states: materials needed, procedure, extension activities, journal recording, and additional reading. An excellent resource for teachers assigning science projects, group investigations, and independent study. Using this innovative

book will be a springboard to exciting, active teaching and learning.
SUBJ: Astronomy--Study and teaching--Activity programs./ Outer space--Study and teaching.

PROF 372.3   Ph-3 $12.95   P   KA199
BOWDEN, MARCIA. Nature for the very young: a handbook of indoor and outdoor activities. Illus. by Marilyn Rishel. Wiley ISBN 0-471-62084-X; In Canada: Wiley, 1989. 232p. ill.
Includes bibliography and index.
Dividing activities into the four seasons, the author presents ideas for linking home and school as children learn methods of discovery with nature as the focus. Helpful for teachers, parents, camp counselors and librarians working with preschool to second grade children.
SUBJ: Nature study./ Education, Preschool.

PROF 372.3   Ph-1 $24.95   P   KA200
HEFNER, CHRISTINE ROOTS. Literature-based science: children's books and activities to enrich the K-5 curriculum. By Christine Roots Hefner and Kathryn Roots Lewis. Oryx ISBN 0-89774-741-0; In Canada: Oryx, 1995. 186p.
Includes bibliographies and index.
Organized by grades: K-1, 2-3, 4-5, the handy resource provides activities and books to intertwine literature and science. Further division is by Life Science--Animals, Life Science--Plants, Human Body, Earth Science, Space, Energy and Motion, Ecology, and Nonprint Sources including videocassettes, CD-ROMs, and microcomputer software.
SUBJ: Science--Study and teaching./ Science--Bibliography./ Children--Books and reading./ Children's literature--Study and teaching./ Education, Elementary--Activity programs.

PROF 372.3   Ph-1 $24.00   P   KA201
IRVING, JAN. Mudluscious: stories and activities featuring food for preschool children. By Jan Irving and Robin Currie. Illus. by Robert B. Phillips. Libraries Unlimited ISBN 0-87287-517-2, 1986. 259p. ill.
Includes bibliography and index.
The authors have combined language and reading and food into a sourcebook that should be of value not only to preschool students but to primary grades as well. Two special sections will be useful: breakdown of activities by skills area, and an alphabetical index of activities showing associated skills. The skills cited include: role and dialogue invention; word recognition; following directions; sequencing; group cooperation; gross motor; counting; size and shape recognition; classification, etc.
SUBJ: Food--Study and teaching (Elementary)./ Nutrition--Study and teaching (Elementary).

PROF 372.3   Ph-1 $26.00   P   KA202
JURENKA, NANCY E. ALLEN. Beyond the bean seed: gardening activities for grades K-6. By Nancy Allen Jurenka and Rosanne J. Blass. Teacher Ideas Press ISBN 1-56308-346-9, 1996. 195p. ill.
Includes bibliography and indexes.
Selectors' Choice, 21st ed.
Authors provide creative lessons which combine language arts, science, and gardening. Each lesson begins with book sharing. Chapters are divided into broad topics: Botany, Flowers, Vegetables, Fruits, Plant variety, Getting ready to garden, Gardening gadgets, Garden inhabitants: friend or foe, Garden habitats, and City gardening. Excellent annotated bibliography gives approximate reading levels. Also has an activities index and an author, title, subject index. Good resource for interdisciplinary curriculum.
SUBJ: Children's gardens./ Gardening--Experiments./ Botany--Experiments./ Botany--Study and teaching--Activity programs./ Teaching--Aids and devices.

PROF 372.3   Ph-1 $17.95   P   KA203
RESOURCES FOR TEACHING ELEMENTARY SCHOOL SCIENCE. National Science Resources Center, National Academy of Sciences, Smithsonian Institution. National Academy Press ISBN 0-309-05293-9, 1996. 289p. ill.
Rev. ed. of: SCIENCE FOR CHILDREN, 1988.
Includes bibliographies, directories and indexes.
Selectors' Choice, 21st ed.
Based on the NATIONAL EDUCATION STANDARDS, this guide is "packed with carefully gathered and reviewed information about hands-on, inquiry-based curriculum materials and resources for teaching science in kindergarten through sixth grade." (p.IX) An excellent resource guide to assist in selecting instructional materials. Chapters include Life Science; Earth Science; Physical Science; and Multidisciplinary and Applied Science. Within each chapter, categories include core materials, supplementary materials, and science activity books. Appendixes provide access to publishers and suppliers; evaluation criteria used for curriculum materials; review forms. Indexes include: title, names (authors, series, curriculum projects); curriculum

topics; grade levels of curriculum materials by scientific area covered; scientific areas of curriculum materials by grade level; subject index; index of ancillary resources (places to visit/organizations).
SUBJ: Science--Study and teaching (Elementary)--Bibliography.

PROF 372.3   Ph-1 $19.95   P   KA204
TAYLOR, BEVERLEY A. P. Teaching physics with toys: activities for grades K-9. By Beverley A. P. Taylor, James Poth, Dwight J. Portman. Learning Triangle Press ISBN 0-07-064721-6, 1995. 296p. ill.
Includes bibliographies and indexes.
A collection of the physics activities used in the Teaching Science with Toys project based at Miami University, Ohio. Divided into three grade-level groupings: K-2, 4-6, and 7-9, the activities have complete instructions. Photographs of toys extend the text. Suggestions are provided for webbing and charting. Typical topic includes grade level, key science concepts, student background knowledge, key process skills, time required, list of materials, introduction, procedure, explanation, multidisciplinary integration, references, and contributor. Fun filled resource that will give students and teachers a new perspective on play. For interdisciplinary studies.
SUBJ: Physics--Study and teaching (Elementary)--Activity programs./ Toys--Study and teaching.

PROF 372.4   Ph-1 $5.60   P   KA205
ANDERSON, RICHARD C. Becoming a nation of readers: the report of the Commission on Reading. Prepared by Richard C. Anderson, et al. National Institute of Education/dist. by International Reading Association, 1985. 147p.
Includes bibliography.
"Summarizing the knowledge acquired from research and drawing implications for reading instruction this report" (p. 3) also provides strong support for the school library program. This is critically important reading for professionals and parents alike.
SUBJ: Reading.

PROF 372.4   Ph-1 $19.95   P   KA206
COUNT ON READING HANDBOOK: TIPS FOR PLANNING READING MOTIVATION PROGRAMS. Compiled and edited by Susan D. Ballard. American Association of School Librarians ISBN 0-8389-7892-4, 1997. 84p.
The American Association of School Librarians national initiative is described in stirring words from former Presidents of AASL. Includes descriptions of state reading projects.
SUBJ: Reading./ Motivation in education.

PROF 372.4   Ph-2 $3.98   P   KA207
COUNTERPOINT AND BEYOND: A RESPONSE TO BECOMING A NATION OF READERS. Edited by Jane L. Davidson. National Council of Teachers of English ISBN 0-8141-0876-8, 1988. 112p.
Includes bibliography.
Nine essays critique "Becoming a Nation of Readers." "Issues in BNR that are considered to be controversial, incomplete, or inconsistent are addressed; reactions and alternative recommendations for the improvement of literacy are set forth." (Intro.)
SUBJ: Reading (Elementary)./ Literacy.

PROF 372.4   Ph-1 $9.95   P   KA208
HARSTE, JEROME C. New policy guidelines for reading: connecting research and practice. National Council of Teachers of English ISBN 0-8141-3342-8, 1989. 80p.
Twenty factors are described which improve reading instruction and learning. This slender, clearly written volume should be used to evaluate and determine the course of every reading program.
SUBJ: Reading--Research.

PROF 372.4   Ph-1 $35.00   T   KA209
ITZKOFF, SEYMOUR W. Children learning to read: a guide for parents and teachers. Praeger ISBN 0-275-95436-6, 1996. 198p. ill.
Includes bibliographies and index.
Written in understandable terms, the practicle text outlines the many steps (and pitfalls) leading to reading readiness and reading systems and relates advice to avoid reading problems. Discusses the roles of parents, television, and the school. (Parents' Shelf).
SUBJ: Reading./ Reading readiness.

PROF 372.4   Ph-1 $29.95   P   KA210
LAUGHLIN, MILDRED KNIGHT. Literature-based reading: children's books and activities to enrich the K-5 curriculum. By Mildred Knight Laughlin and Claudia Lisman Swisher. Oryx Press ISBN 0-89774-562-0, 1990. 149p.
Includes glossary, bibliography and index.
A very practical approach for integrating literature throughout the curriculum. For each reading concept (e.g. predicting, sequencing, vocabulary) objectives are indicated and followed by recommended

children's works and suggested activities.
SUBJ: Reading--Language experience approach./ Children--Books and reading./ Activity programs in education.

PROF 372.4   Ph-1 $7.95   P   KA211
NAGY, WILLIAM E. Teaching vocabulary to improve reading comprehension. NCTE/IRA/ERIC ISBN 0-8141-5238-4, 1988. 42p.
Includes bibliography.
This is a succinct "practitioner-oriented text developed by ERIC/RCS in cooperation with NCTE and IRA." The author states as his purpose: "how one can use vocabulary instruction most effectively to improve reading comprehension... Although the focus is on improving reading comprehension, some connections will be made to other aspects of instruction, linking vocabulary instruction and reading comprehension with broader goals of the language arts program."
SUBJ: Vocabulary--Study and teaching.

PROF 372.4   Ph-1 $25.00   P   KA212
OLSEN, MARY LOU. More creative connections: literature and the reading program, grades 4-6. Teacher Ideas Press/Libraries Unlimited ISBN 1-56308-027-3, 1993. 319p.
Includes bibliography and indexes.
Based on books that will be found in most school library media centers, activities are well defined and are as basic as a "writing prompt." Inventive methods for tying math to folk literature, making a computer connection, and critical thinking questions are just a few of the thousands of ideas included. In addition to suggested activities, each entry offers information about the author and illustrator, additional titles by the author, and related titles. A well-presented package.
SUBJ: Reading./ Children--Books and reading.

MCP PROF 372.4   Ph-2 $29.97   OD KA213
READABILITY ANALYSIS (Microcomputer program). Gamco Educational Materials 1051, 1994. 1 3.5" disk.
Includes user's guide.
Version 6.1.6.
Also available on 5.25" disk.
Also available for Apple II 105A on 3.5" and 5.25" disk, $29.97.
System requirements: IBM PC/XT/AT or true compatible; 256K RAM; color/graphics card; DOS 2.0 or higher.
Using keyed passages of 100 words, this program analyzes the reading level of any written material based on three commonly used readability tests--Spache, Dale-Chall, and Fry. Tests may be run individually or concurrently, with an option to print the results. Although the DOS based program is not technologically up-to-date, this is one of the few available computer-based programs which provides reliable readability tests, as opposed to time-consuming manual calculations.
SUBJ: Readability (Literary style)--Software./ Software--Readability (Literary style)./ Books and reading--Software./ Software--Books and reading.

PROF 372.4   Ph-2 $28.50   P   KA214
ROUTMAN, REGIE. Invitations: changing as teachers and learners K-12. Updated, expanded, and rev. resources and Blue pages. Heinemann ISBN 0-435-08836-X, c1991, 1994. 502, 256p. ill.
Includes bibliographies and index.
This lengthy book was written in response to teachers who have made the transition to whole language and need more assistance in going further with literature. Touching on all aspects of a literature-based reading and writing program, the author uses anecdotal material, research results, and examples of student writing to support the activities outlined. The "Blue pages," included at the end of the book, give annotated listings for various subject areas. Appendices include practical materials for classroom use. Professional books, journals, newsletters, and articles cited are annotated.
SUBJ: Reading--Language experience approach./ Children--Books and reading.

PROF 372.4   Ph-1 $15.00   P   KA215
SLAUGHTER, JUDITH POLLARD. Beyond storybooks: young children and the shared book experience. International Reading Association ISBN 0-87207-377-7, 1993. 167p. ill.
Includes bibliographies and indexes.
Intended for all those who work with primary age children. Topics include how children acquire literacy, the shared book experience, predictable literature, writing activities, and how the shared book experience can be integrated into the curriculum. Appendix describes 120 widely available, predictable books.
SUBJ: Reading (Primary)--Language experience approach./ English language--Composition and exercises--Study and teaching (Primary)./ Children--Books and reading.

PROF 372.5   Ph-1 $23.00   P   KA216
MARKS, DIANA F. Glues, brews, and goos: recipes and formulas for almost any classroom project. Illus. by Donna L. Farrell. Teacher Ideas Press ISBN 1-56308-362-0, 1996. 179p. ill.
Includes bibliography.
From basic concoctions for art activities to experiments for science classes to baking recipes for multicultural celebrations, this book has it all. The practical, easy-to-follow recipes and formulas are classroom tested, and they will be popular with students, teachers, group leaders for 4-H and scouts, and parents. A good resource for interdisciplinary studies. (Parents' Shelf).
SUBJ: Activity programs in education--Handbooks, manuals, etc.

PROF 372.5   Ph-1 $33.50   T   KA217
TOPAL, CATHY WEISMAN. Children and painting. Davis Publications ISBN 0-87192-241-X, 1992. 168p. col. ill.
Includes glossary, bibliography and index.
A very readable, practical guide for teachers and parents who want to provide open-ended painting activities. The basic concepts such as line, texture, shape, color, and value are incorporated into the various techniques. (Parents' Shelf).
SUBJ: Painting--Study and teaching./ Children as artists.

PROF 372.6   Ph-1 $23.00   P   KA218
BARCHERS, SUZANNE I. Creating and managing the literate classroom. Illus. by Leann Mullineaux. Teacher Ideas Press/Libraries Unlimited ISBN 0-87287-705-1, 1990. 187p.
Includes bibliographies, appendices and index.
The author, a teacher, starts at the right place to support the title of her book--the library and the librarian. Practical suggestions explore location of inexpensive and effective materials; managing the program (reading, researching, writing); sample handouts and bibliographies. This is an excellent sourcebook, and well worth the purchase price, if only for the example of how to critique a worksheet. This book can empower both librarians and teachers.
SUBJ: Language arts (Elementary)./ Teaching./ Activity programs in education./ Reading (Elementary)./ Classroom management.

PROF 372.6   Ph-2 $25.00   T   KA219
CHALL, JEANNE STERNLICHT. Reading crisis: why poor children fall behind. By Jeanne S. Chall, Vicki A. Jacobs, and Luke E. Baldwin. Harvard University Press ISBN 0-674-74884-0, 1990. 191p.
Includes appendices, references and index.
If librarians want to assist students in reading achievement, they must know the research, the problems, and the solutions for the complex problem of literacy in the schools. Jeanne Chall, renowned reading specialist, points out the crucial time in grade four, "when students confront text containing unfamiliar words and ideas that are beyond the range of their own experience." (text). Chapters cover language development and the influence of the home environment on it.
SUBJ: Language arts (Elementary)./ Reading./ Underachievers./ Literacy.

VCR PROF 372.6   Ph-2 $30.00   OD KA220
CREATIVE DRAMA IN THE EARLY CHILDHOOD CLASSROOM (Videocassette). InterAct Story Theatre, 1991. 1/2" VHS videocassette color (54min).
Lenore Blank Kelner explains and shows techniques for using dramatic games to help students learn and retain information. She uses puppets, miniature toys, "Coffee Can Theatre", and a simple version of role-playing to teach colors, shapes, math, directional words, etc. Provides good ideas for P-1 teachers who want to instill more fun into learning.
Similar ideas for slightly older children are given in CREATIVE DRAMA IN THE ELEMENTARY CLASSROOM (Videocassette, 1990).
SUBJ: Activity programs in education./ Drama in education.

PROF 372.6   Ph-1 $11.95   P   KA221
FOCUS ON COLLABORATIVE LEARNING: CLASSROOM PRACTICES IN TEACHING ENGLISH. By Jeff Golub, Chair, and the Committee on Classroom Practices. National Council of Teachers of English ISBN 0-8141-1753-8, 1988. 170p.
"None of Us is as Smart as All of Us" is the first chapter in this important book. The techniques of collaborative learning are outlined as not just "mere teaching techniques for a slow day" but as "the group process is the life process." This learning process does not "just happen." The first section of the book includes articles that provide ideas for guiding students in group skills. The second section "provides descriptions of cooperative learning activities dealing with the study of literature."
SUBJ: Learning.

PROF 372.6 Ph-1 $7.95 P KA222

GEIGER, EVE. TNT: two hundred and ninety-two activites for literature and language arts! Fearon ISBN 0-8224-6746-1, 1989. 96p. ill.

Includes bibliography.

Use the suggested activities contained in this small paperback book and apply them to books currently in your collection. The skills relate to "comprehension, sequencing, plot development, vocabulary growth, character analysis, and creative writing." (Intro.) Divided into General Activities, Poetry Activities, Thematic Activities, Questions to Stimulate Book Discussions, and Suggestions for Successful Group Work, this is a small gem of literature and language arts ideas.

SUBJ: Literature--Study and teaching./ Language arts (Elementary).

PROF 372.6 Ph-2 $22.50 P KA223

IRVING, JAN. Full speed ahead: stories and activities for children on transportation. By Jan Irving and Robin Currie. Illus. by Karen Wolf. Teacher Ideas Press/Libraries Unlimited ISBN 0-87287-653-5, 1988. 244p. ill.

Includes bibliography and index.

Highlighting books and activities appropriate for students in preschool through third grade the authors use transportation as the basis for the encouragement of reading and enjoyment of literature. Moving from the most basic form of transportation, Feet, to Magic Carpets and Merry Go Rounds the reader is provided with ideas, patterns for flannel board figures, comprehensive, annotated bibliographies, and games. Splendid for both the teacher and librarian.

SUBJ: Storytelling./ Children--Books and reading./ Transportation in literature./ Transportation--Study and teaching (Elementary)./ Children's literature--Study and teaching.

PROF 372.6 Ph-2 $22.50 P KA224

LAUGHLIN, MILDRED KNIGHT. Social studies readers theatre for children: scripts and script development. By Mildred Knight Laughlin, Peggy Tubbs Black, and Margery Kirby Loberg. Teacher Ideas Press/Libraries Unlimited ISBN 0-87287-865-1, 1991. 189p.

Includes bibliography and index.

Readers theatre presentations provide an opportunity for students reading from historical fiction and biographies to understand social relationships of people of the past. Part I sketches an overview of readers theatre techniques; Part II outlines uses of tall tales with bibliography; Part III bases programs on books by Laura Ingalls Wilder; Part IV includes sixty readers theatre starters.

SUBJ: Readers' Theater--Study and teaching (Elementary)./ Drama in education./ Social sciences--Study and teaching (Elementary)./ Children's plays.

PROF 372.6 Ph-1 $21.00 P KA225

MCELMEEL, SHARRON L. McElmeel booknotes: literature across the curriculum. Illus. by Deborah L. McElmeel. Teacher Ideas Press/Libraries Unlimited ISBN 0-87287-951-8, 1993. 217p. ill.

Includes bibliographies and index.

Ideas will help make the connection between a variety of subject areas and literature. The author provides interesting activities that incorporate fiction and nonfiction titles which can be found in most libraries. Reproducible pages offer writing ideas.

SUBJ: Language arts./ Literature--Study and teaching./ Interdisciplinary approach in education./ Activity programs in education.

PROF 372.6 Ph-1 $14.95 P KA226

MELTON, DAVID. Written & illustrated by... a revolutionary two-brain approach for teaching students how to write and illustrate amazing books. Landmark ISBN 0-933849-00-1, 1985. 95p. ill.

Provides a step-by-step outline for a successful student author program. Creativity, language skills, and interpersonal skills are intertwined. Definitely promotes good writing.

SUBJ: Creative writing./ English language--Composition and exercises./ Children as authors.

PROF 372.6 Ph-2 $17.95 P KA227

POLETTE, NANCY. Brain power through picture books: help children develop with books that stimulate specific parts of their minds. McFarland ISBN 0-89950-708-5, 1992. 138p. ill.

Includes bibliographies and index.

Explores how reading aloud stimulates mental activity in the listener which develops thinking processes. Includes chapters such as "Developing early childhood thinking skills," "The power of fairy tales and fantasy," and "Expanding the horizons of young thinkers." Suggestions are practical, adaptable, and based on many books found in library collections. (Parents' Shelf).

SUBJ: Reading (Elementary)./ Thought and thinking--Study and teaching./ Cognition in children./ Learning./ Children--Books and reading.

PROF 372.6 Ph-2 $8.95 P KA228

SHELNUTT, EVE. Magic pencil: teaching children creative writing: exercises and activities for children, their parents, and their teachers. Illus. by Paulette L. Lambert. Peachtree ISBN 1-56145-045-6, 1994. 125p. ill.

Includes bibliography.

Provides exercises and activities which support the writing process. Skills and concepts being taught are clearly outlined. An asset in working with the reluctant writer. (Parents' Shelf).

SUBJ: Creative writing (Elementary education)./ English language--Composition and exercises--Study and teaching.

PROF 372.6 Ph-1 $29.95 P KA229

SPILLMAN, CAROLYN V. Integrating language arts through literature in elementary classrooms. Oryx ISBN 0-89774-897-2; In Canada: Oryx, 1996. 201p.

Includes bibliographies and index.

The author states "I wrote this book for teachers who believe that language arts should be united for communication purposes, not separated into its various components....Teachers also know, however, they cannot possibly read every children's book that is published." (p.viii) Majority of selections included are summaries of books published within last four years. Presented by genre including folk literature, fantasy, contemporary realistic fiction, historical realistic fiction, poetry, and nonfiction. Includes nine themes related to interpersonal interactions. First purchase for teachers and librarians.

SUBJ: Language arts (Elementary)./ Children's literature--Study and teaching (Elementary)./ Interdisciplinary approach in education.

PROF 372.6 Ph-1 $39.00 T KA230

STANEK, LOU WILLETT. Whole language: literature, learning, and literacy: a workshop in print. Wilson ISBN 0-8242-0837-4, 1993. 244p.

Includes bibliographies and index.

The words "whole language" often create concern and argument and seem to defy definition. In four sections, the author covers whole language theory, practice, implementation, and success stories. The whole language activities will assist librarians and teachers with ideas for using a variety of books.

SUBJ: Language experience approach in education.

VCR PROF 372.6 Ph-3 $29.95 OD KA231

STORY STARTERS. Vol. 1 (Videocassette). Barbara Lawrence Productions LE200T ISBN 0-9641538-1-5, 1995. 1/2" VHS videocassette color (37min). (Let's explore series).

Includes teacher's guide.

Video also available with parent's guide (LE200P, ISBN 0-9641538-3-1, $24.95).

Presents three possible formats for writing stories and follows with 17 story ideas. Difficulty of material requires thorough preview and careful planning to achieve success.

SUBJ: English language--Composition and exercises--Study and teaching./ Creative writing--Study and teaching./ Education, Primary--Activity programs./ Teaching--Aids and devices.

PROF 372.6 Ph-1 $16.95 P KA232

WATSON, DOROTHY J. Ideas and insights: language arts in the elementary school. National Council of Teachers of English ISBN 0-8141-2259-0, 1987. 243p. ill.

Includes bibliography.

Hooray for our side! "It won't take long for readers of this book to discover that there are no skill, drill, and fill-in-the-blank exercises to be found on these pages, for this is not the way children learn to write, read, listen, and speak. What you will find however, are activities that encourage language in its fullness, activities that are based on the whole language approach to learning." Each section or activity gives the "Why", "Who", and "How" for teacher and student. The bibliography is divided in sections which include broad headings such as: Read-Aloud Books, Wordless Books, Predictable Language, and Extending Literature: Reading Leading to Writing.

SUBJ: Language arts (Elementary)./ Reading (Elementary).

PROF 372.6 Ph-1 $16.95 P KA233

WHOLE LANGUAGE: BELIEFS AND PRACTICES, K-8. Edited by Gary and Maryann Manning. National Education Association ISBN 0-8106-1482-0, 1989. 240p. (Aspects of learning).

"This anthology includes the ideas of many of the leading authorities on whole language. It contains chapters in several areas: the meaning of whole language, the skills movement and its lack of sound theory on how students construct knowledge about reading and writing, reading and writing development, and teacher autonomy. Each chapter begins with a brief overview. Although not every facet of whole language is discussed references are provided for readers who would like additional information." (Intro.) An essential tool for librarians who need to understand this movement.

SUBJ: Language experience approach in education./ Language arts (Elementary)./ Reading (Elementary)--Language experience approach.

PROF 372.64   Ph-1 $45.00   T   KA234
BAUER, CAROLINE FELLER. Poetry break: an annotated anthology with ideas for introducing children to poetry. Illus. by Edith Bingham. Wilson ISBN 0-8242-0852-8, 1995. 347p. ill.
Includes bibliography and indexes.
The author has been promoting her idea for poetry breaks throughout the world in her workshops for librarians and teachers. This "how to" book provides all the necessary information to create interest in poetry in a variety of situations. Poems are divided into categories: for acting out; with art activities; to recite with props; for contemplating; for writing; in pairs; with themes; as Mother Goose rhymes; for short breaks; and for final musings.
SUBJ: Children's poetry--Study and teaching./ Oral interpretation of poetry.

PROF 372.64   Ph-1 $21.00   P   KA235
BOOK TALK AND BEYOND: CHILDREN AND TEACHERS RESPOND TO LITERATURE. Edited by Nancy L. Roser and Miriam G. Martinez. International Reading Association ISBN 0-87207-129-4, 1995. 246p. ill.
Includes bibliographies and indexes.
This fine publication adds to our knowledge of responding to literature. Divided into four sections: Getting ready for story talk; Tools of story talk; Guiding book talk; and Other responses to literature, the book offers practical suggestions for engaging students in literature. Index by author; subject index includes titles of books cited.
SUBJ: Literature--Study and teaching (Elementary)./ Children--Books and reading./ Reader-response criticism.

PROF 372.64   Ph-1 $29.95   P   KA236
BORDERS, SARAH G. Children talking about books. By Sarah G. Borders and Alice Phoebe Naylor. Oryx ISBN 0-89774-737-2; In Canada: Oryx, 1993. 241p.
Includes bibliographies and indexes.
Includes 34 book dialogues and commentary on the discussion process. Encouraged by only three discussion prompts, students respond with something more than "It was interesting." Creates many opportunities for higher level thinking skills. Books cited are standard titles; arrangement is alphabetical by author; bibliographic information, audience level, themes, and values to target are provided. Includes an excellent chapter on the role of the adult leader.
SUBJ: Literature--Study and teaching (Elementary)./ Children--Books and reading.

PROF 372.64   Ph-1 $28.50   P   KA237
CHATTON, BARBARA. Using poetry across the curriculum: a whole language approach. Oryx ISBN 0-89774-715-1; In Canada: Oryx, 1993. 214p.
Includes bibliographies, directory and index.
Provides opportunities for interdisciplinary approach in planning thematic units. Includes a chapter on poems authored by poets from various ethnic and cultural groups which will be useful for multicultural studies. Bibliographies of poetry in standard disciplines such as science, mathematics, social studies, etc. are further subdivided into sections that support or enhance the study of individual concepts, e.g. the senses, counting, transportation, etc.
SUBJ: Poetry--Study and teaching./ Language experience approach in education./ Interdisciplinary approach in education.

PROF 372.64   Ph-2 $27.95   T   KA238
CHILDREN'S LITERATURE IN THE CLASSROOM: WEAVING CHARLOTTE'S WEB. Edited by Janet Hickman and Bernice E. Cullinan. Christopher-Gordon ISBN 0-926842-00-5, 1989. 274p.
Includes references.
A rare insight into the contributions made to the teaching/library profession by Charlotte S. Huck is followed by a "discussion of her philosophy, perspectives on literary quality, early literacy, reading aloud, literature as a foundation and source for children's writing, and literature across the curriculum. Part II deals with four selected genres---Part III includes discussions of how literature becomes a part of the school curriculum." (Preface) Bibliographic information on books cited does not include ISBN.
SUBJ: Children's literature--Study and teaching./ Education, Elementary--Curricula.

PROF 372.64   Ph-1 $18.50   P   KA239
MCELMEEL, SHARRON L. Latest and greatest read-alouds. Illus. by Deborah L. McElmeel. Libraries Unlimited ISBN 1-56308-140-7, 1994. 210p. ill.
Includes indexes.
Excellent resource for teachers, parents, and librarians. Focus is on books published since 1988. The 109 entries are arranged within six suggested listening level categories. Each entry includes standard

bibliographic information, ISBN, Listening Level, Read-Alone Level, lengthy annotation, and other suggested titles with ideas for showing their relationships to the entry. Concludes with twenty-one steps for building a family/classroom of readers. Author, illustrator, title index. Separate subject index. (Parents' Shelf).
SUBJ: Oral reading./ Children--Books and reading.

PROF 372.64   Ph-2 $14.95   P   KA240
RAINES, SHIRLEY C. Story stretchers for the primary grades: activities to expand children's favorite books. By Shirley C. Raines and Robert J. Canady. Gryphon House ISBN 0-87659-157-8, 1992. 256p. ill. (Story stretchers).
Includes index.
Contains activities appropriate for literature-based curriculum for popular children's books, both classics and new favorites. Brief synopsis of each book is accompanied with: suggestions for reading aloud, and art, cooking, science, nature, talent, hobby show, and writing center activities. Index is followed by subject arrangement of centers or activities.
MORE STORY STRECHERS: MORE ACTIVITIES TO EXPAND CHILDREN'S FAVORITE BOOKS (ISBN 0-87659-153-5, 1991).
450 MORE STORY STRETCHERS FOR THE PRIMARY GRADES: ACTIVITIES TO EXPAND CHILDREN'S FAVORITE BOOKS (ISBN 0-87659-167-5, 1994).
SUBJ: Children's literature--Study and teaching./ Education, Primary--Activity programs--Handbooks, manuals, etc./ Children--Books and reading--Handbooks, manuals, etc./ Teaching--Aids and devices--Handbooks, manuals, etc.

PROF 372.64   Ph-2 $18.95   P   KA241
STORIES AND READERS: NEW PERSPECTIVES ON LITERATURE IN THE ELEMENTARY CLASSROOM. Edited by Charles Temple and Patrick Collins. Christopher-Gordon ISBN 0-926842-10-2, 1992. 282p. ill.
Includes index.
An excellent compilation of essays on readers and reading. The text is thought provoking and readable. Use any part of this book for staff development.
SUBJ: Literature--Study and teaching (Elementary)./ Education, Elementary--Curricula.

PROF 372.64   Ph-1 $12.95   P   KA242
TRELEASE, JIM. Read-aloud handbook. 4th ed. Illus. by Virginia Norey. Penguin ISBN 0-14-046971-0; In Canada: Penguin, 1995. 387p. ill.
Rev. ed. of: NEW READ-ALOUD HANDBOOK, Penguin, 1989.
Includes bibliography and indexes.
Identifies titles "with a proven track record" that have been read and enjoyed by the author and lists "the kind of book that will inspire children to want to read another one just like it, or even the same book over again." The revised edition of the earlier best seller will continue to encourage parents and teachers to make time for reading aloud. Unfortunately the author's bias against nonfiction as exciting reading continues unabated. (Parents' Shelf)
SUBJ: Children--Books and reading./ Oral reading.

PROF 372.64   Ph-1 $9.95   P   KA243
USING LITERATURE IN THE ELEMENTARY CLASSROOM. Rev. ed. Edited by John Warren Stewig and Sam Leaton Sebesta. National Council of Teachers of English ISBN 0-8141-5618-5, 1989. 132p.
Includes bibliography.
The authors provide ideas that should entice any teacher or librarian. Playing with words, pictures to assist in developing a child's reading vocabulary, reading critically, developing visual literacy, and responding in writing are all detailed in very readable style. Bibliographies and related readings conclude each chapter.
SUBJ: Children's literature--Study and teaching./ Education, Elementary--Curricula.

PROF 372.67   Ph-1 $39.00   T   KA244
BAKER, GREENEA. Storytelling, art and technique. 3rd ed. Bowker ISBN 0-8352-3458-4, 1995. 182p.
Concentrating on pure storytelling, this practical and straightforward manual is primarily designed for the novice storyteller. Tracing the history of storytelling in libraries in this country the authors, both well-known storytellers, address themselves to selection, preparation, presentation, planning, in both usual and differing settings. The Appendices: In-Service Education, Sources for the Storyteller, and Glossary are useful. Indexed.
SUBJ: Storytelling.

VCR PROF 372.67   Ph-2 $55.00   KA245
FOLKTELLERS. Storytelling: tales and techniques (Videocassette). Folktellers/Mama-T Artists, 1994. 1/2" VHS videocassette color (60min).
Two well-known storytellers demonstrate their techniques before a

group of librarians. Includes how to select a story, use props dramatically, tandem telling, and using stories to introduce books to young readers.
SUBJ: Storytelling.

VCR PROF 372.67 Ph-3 $24.95 OD KA246
JENKINS, SANDY. Storytelling: learning and sharing (Videocassette). Coyote Creek, 1995. 1/2" VHS videocassette color (45min).
Selecting, learning, and presenting a story are demonstrated by a talented storyteller who also explains how to gear material to groups which differ in age and interest. Several stories are told, and Jenkins, an elementary school teacher, tells why her experiences have proven to her that storytelling is a vital skill for all teachers to master. Useful for novice storytellers or for in-service training.
SUBJ: Storytelling.

PROF 372.67 Ph-3 $17.50 P KA247
LIVO, NORMA J. Storytelling activities. By Norma J. Livo and Sandra A. Rietz. Libraries Unlimited ISBN 0-87287-566-0, 1987. 140p.
A practical, readable manual outlines how to find, and design the story presentation. If you are looking for support material to justify this storytelling activity Appendix "C" provides a matrix which matches the activities with the kind of educational skill they utilize. This splendid tool should be available for teachers in all grade levels plus the librarian.
SUBJ: Storytelling.

PROF 372.67 Ph-1 $9.95 P KA248
PELLOWSKI, ANNE. Story vine: a source book of unusual and easy-to-tell stories from around the world. Illus. by Lynn Sweat. Simon & Schuster ISBN 0-02-044690-X; In Canada: Distican, 1984. 116p. ill.
Includes bibliography.
"This unusual collection of stories requires the storyteller to use string, nesting dolls, sandpainting, drawings, or musical instruments." Each of the six parts offers several stories from various parts of the world. Also includes "Suggestions for Storytellers" and "Sources of Stories."
SUBJ: Storytelling./ Folklore.

PROF 372.67 Ph-1 $16.00 L KA249
PELLOWSKI, ANNE. Storytelling handbook: a young people's collection of unusual tales and helpful hints on how to tell them. Illus. by Martha Stoberock. Simon & Schuster ISBN 0-689-80311-7; In Canada: Distican, 1995. 122p. ill.
Includes bibliography and index.
Although the language of the book is aimed at young people, this will be an asset for teachers, librarians, and parents who are trying to initiate a storytelling festival or improve skills. Many of the stories have a surprise ending. Stories are grouped by type: cumulative, objects used in telling, holidays, etc.
SUBJ: Storytelling./ Storytelling--Collections./ Folklore.

PROF 372.7 Ph-2 $7.50 P KA250
ARTZT, ALICE F. How to use cooperative learning in the mathematics class. By Alice F. Artzt and Claire M. Newman. National Council of Teachers of Mathematics ISBN 0-87353-293-7, 1990. 73p. ill.
Includes bibliography.
What is cooperative learning and how can it be used in math classes? The authors explain it clearly and give sample exercises.
SUBJ: Mathematics--Study and teaching.

PROF 372.7 Ph-1 $24.50 P KA251
BURGUNDER, ANNE. Zoolutions: a mathematical expedition with topics for grades 4 through 8. By Anne Stanko Burgunder and Vaunda Nelson. Scarecrow ISBN 0-8108-3075-2, c1993, 1996. 127p. ill. (School library media series).
Includes bibliographies.
"Zoolutions is a team-taught interdisciplinary program which takes place in the school library and uses the study of animals as a basis for problem solving." (p.1) Goals of the program plus curricular benefits reflect the five major shifts in the environment of mathematics classrooms that are recommended in standards from NCTM. Questions for each topic are based on student interests and should provide models for independent research. Appendixes list supplies, cooperative behaviors' checklist, student writing samples, and examples of Zoolutions currency.
SUBJ: Mathematics--Study and teaching (Elementary).

PROF 372.7 Ph-1 $25.00 T OD KA252
CURRICULUM AND EVALUATION STANDARDS FOR SCHOOL MATHEMATICS. National Council of Teachers of Mathematics ISBN 0-87353-273-2, 1989. 255p. ill.
Includes bibliography.
Responding to the need "to help improve the quality of school

mathematics" (Preface) these standards for curriculum and evaluation for grades K-4, 5-8, and 9-12 are grouped under the headings Problem solving, Communication, Reasoning and Mathematical Connections. Each standard summarizes objectives, establishes the focus and features a discussion that includes sample activities. Essential reading for each teacher in the elementary school.
SUBJ: Mathematics--Study and teaching.

PROF 372.7 Ph-1 $19.95 P KA253
KOHL, MARY ANN F. MathArts: exploring math through art for 3 to 6 year olds. By Mary Ann F. Kohl and Cindy Gainer. Illus. by Cindy Gainer. Gryphon House ISBN 0-87659-177-2, 1996. 255p. ill.
"Mary Ann Kohl book."
Includes indexes.
Organized to simplify selecting appropriate activities, the book uses a series of icons to indicate age, planning or preparation, assistance, and caution and a table of contents to outline concepts, skill, art medium, age, preparation, help, and caution. Explorations include math concepts such as patterns, shapes, order, sequence, number value, symmetry, time, money, and measuring. A list of collage materials and sources is provided. The horizontal format allows the book to lie flat for easy reference. Each activity is presented on one page. Indexes include art medium, math skills, and materials. An excellent choice for combining a child's interest in creating and math. (Parents' Shelf).
SUBJ: Art in mathematics education./ Mathematics--Study and teaching (Early childhood).

PROF 372.7 Ph-1 $12.95 P KA254
MATH FOR THE VERY YOUNG: A HANDBOOK OF ACTIVITIES FOR PARENTS AND TEACHERS. By Lydia Polonsky...[et al.]. Illus. by Marcia Miller. Wiley ISBN 0-471-01647-0; In Canada: Wiley, 1995. 210p. ill.
Includes bibliography and index.
Replete with activities organized around the young child's world. Take advantage of daily happenings and seize the teaching moment by using housekeeping (sorting laundry), growing up (charting inches), calendar events, trips, and animals to demonstrate math concepts. Invaluable early childhood resource. (Parents' Shelf).
SUBJ: Mathematics--Study and teaching (Primary).

PROF 372.7 Ph-2 $22.00 T KA255
NEW DIRECTIONS FOR ELEMENTARY SCHOOL MATHEMATICS, 1989 YEARBOOK. Edited by Paul R. Trafton and Albert P. Shulte. National Council of Teachers of Mathematics ISBN 0-87353-272-4, 1989. 245p. ill.
Includes references.
This 1989 Yearbook coincides with the publication of the NCTM's CURRICULUM AND EVALUATION STANDARDS FOR SCHOOL MATHEMATICS which "present a coherent vision of what it means to know and do mathematics, of the content of the curriculum in the age of information, and of the roles of teachers and students in the teaching and learning of mathematics. The yearbook shares the vision of the "Standards" and offers additional insights into the meaning of the standard for K-6 mathematics programs. The yearbook consists of five secitons, with samples of children's work appearing between sections. These examples reinforce the active, dynamic approaches to learning mathematics that are portrayed in the articles." (Preface)
SUBJ: Mathematics--Study and teaching (Elementary).

PROF 372.7 Ph-1 $20.00 P KA256
PERRY, PHYLLIS JEAN. Guide to math materials: resources to support the NCTM standards. By Phyllis J. Perry. Teacher Ideas Press ISBN 1-56308-491-0, 1997. 127p.
Includes bibliographies, directory and index.
A priority purchase to support math curriculum reform. Includes the six basic assumptions made by the NCTM groups who governed selection of the standards and the 13 standards published by the National Council of Teachers of Mathematics, March 1989. Bibliography includes books, manipulatives, games, sets, reproducibles, videos, and computer programs to support each standard. An invaluable resource for collection development for librarians to serve as a guide for teachers and for parents. (Parents' Shelf).
SUBJ: Mathematics--Study and teaching--Audio-visual aids--Catalogs./ Mathematics--Study and teaching (Elementary)./ NCTM Standards.

PROF 372.7 Ph-1 $25.00 P KA257
PROFESSIONAL STANDARDS FOR TEACHING MATHEMATICS. National Council of Teachers of Mathematics ISBN 0-87353-307-0, 1991. 195p. ill.
Includes list of references.
This book "is designed, along with the "Curriculum and Evaluation Standards for School Mathematics", to establish a broad framework to guide reform in school mathematics in the next decade." (Preface)
SUBJ: Mathematics--Study and teaching--Standards.

PROF 372.7   Ph-1 $21.50   P   KA258
WHITIN, DAVID J. It's the story that counts: more children's books for
mathematical learning, K-6. By David J. Whitin and Sandra Wilde.
Heinemann ISBN 0-435-08369-4, 1995. 224p. ill.
>Includes bibliographies.
>Believing that children's literature has a powerful role to play in
restoring stories to the teaching and learning of mathematics, the
author focuses on books that can be used in teaching a wide range
of math topics. A bibliography of over 300 math books expands titles
cited in an earlier book READ ANY GOOD MATH LATELY? Excellent
source for collection development and interdisciplinary studies.
>SUBJ: Mathematics--Study and teaching (Elementary)./ Children's
literature in mathematics education.

PROF 372.7   Ph-1 $23.50   P   KA259
ZASLAVSKY, CLAUDIA. Multicultural math classroom: bringing in the
world. Heinemann ISBN 0-435-08373-2, 1996. 239p. ill.
>Includes bibliographies, directory and index.
>This book is deceptive, from its title to its size. It is an excellent book
for raising consciousness levels and for integrating math into all areas
of the curriculum. Using the focus of NCTM CURRICULUM AND
EVALUATION STANDARDS FOR SCHOOL MATHEMATICS,
emphasis is on the problem-solving process, connections to
development of math skills with reasoning/communication, and use of
manipulatives and technology. Arranged by various mathematical
functions, lists of resources include titles found in most library
collections. It is amazing to find this much information in such a small
package. A rich resource for math activities, multicultural studies, and
interdisciplinary curriculum.
>SUBJ: Mathematics--Study and teaching (Elementary)./ Multicultural
education.

PROF 372.83   Ph-2 $24.00   P   KA260
FREDERICKS, ANTHONY D. Social studies through children's literature:
an integrated approach. Illus. by Rebecca N. Fredericks. Teacher Ideas
Press/Libraries Unlimited ISBN 0-87287-970-4, 1991. 191p.
>Includes bibliographies and index.
>For teachers who use a process approach to learning, this is an
excellent resource for integrating whole language into social studies,
building on critical thinking skills, and using thematic units. Useful for
grades K-6, ability ranges from high to low. Included are Caldecott
winners and honors, Reading Rainbow selections, and titles suggested
by teachers and children's librarians. Organized around seven major
areas of elementary social studies curriculum - self/child, family,
community/neighborhood, city/country, states/regions, nation/
country, and world. Includes critical thinking questions and activities
which can easily be adapted to use with many titles.
>SUBJ: Social studies--Study and teaching (Elementary)./ Language
experience approach in education./ Children's literature.

PROF 372.83   Ph-1 $27.50   P   KA261
LAUGHLIN, MILDRED KNIGHT. Literature-based social studies: children's
books and activities to enrich the K-5 curriculum. By Mildred Knight
Laughlin and Patricia Payne Kardaleff. Oryx Press ISBN 0-89774-605-8,
1991. 148p.
>Includes appendix and index.
>Everyone now seems to acknowledge what librarians have understood
for years, that the textbook is just another resource book. The author
provides units that are suggested ideas for "extending the social
studies curriculum beyond the adopted text." (Introduction).
>SUBJ: Social sciences--Study and teaching (Elementary)./ Social
sciences--Study and teaching (Elementary)--Bibliography./ Activity
programs in education./ Teaching--Aids and devices.

PROF 372.89   Ph-2 $23.50   P   KA262
HELTSHE, MARY ANN. Multicultural explorations: joyous journeys with
books. By Mary Ann Heltshe and Audrey Burie Kirchner. Teacher Ideas
Press/Libraries Unlimited ISBN 0-87287-848-1, 1991. 276p. ill.
>Includes bibliographies.
>An excellent resource for the study of other countries and their
geography, identification of innovative strategies for teaching social
studies, developing an appreciation of other cultures. This book
provides everything from lesson plans to recipes, vocabulary and
bibliographies for: Hawaii, Australia, Japan, Italy, Kenya, and Brazil.
The outline offered by the authors is an excellent model for
developing units on other countries.
>SUBJ: Social sciences--Study and teaching (Elementary)./
Geography--Study and teaching (Elementary)./ Reading
(Elementary)--Language experience approach./ Intercultural education.

PROF 372.89   Ph-1 $24.95   P   KA263
PEREZ-STABLE, MARIA A. Understanding American history through
children's literature: instructional units and activities for grades K-8. By
Maria A. Perez-Stable and Mary Hurlbut Cordier. Oryx ISBN 0-89774-

795-X; In Canada: Oryx, 1994. 312p.
>Includes bibliography and index.
>Provides usable activities for grades K-8; cites objectives, activities,
and resources. Good annotated list of suggested materials.
Annotations and bibliography combine to make this a good selection
tool. Excellent source for integrated curriculum study.
>SUBJ: United States--History--Study and teaching (Elementary)./
Children's literature--Study and teaching (Elementary)./ United
States--History--Juvenile literature--Bibliography.

PROF 394.2   Ph-1 $29.95   T   KA264
CHASE, WILLIAM D. Chase's calendar of annual events: special days,
weeks and months. Compiled by William D. and Helen M. Chase.
Contemporary Books, 1958-. v. ill. annual.
>Includes appendices and index.
>More than 3,000 special days, weeks or months are noted in this
famous list which is revised each year. A handy reference tool for
teachers.
>SUBJ: Calendars./ Almanacs./ Holidays./ Festivals.

PROF 398.2   Ph-1 $17.50   P   KA265
BALTUCK, NAOMI. Apples from heaven: multicultural folk tales about
stories and storytellers. Linnet ISBN 0-208-02434-4, 1995. 143p.
>Includes index.
>A wide variety of tales from all parts of the world explores
"stories." Some tell of tellers, some relate the impact a story makes
on a listener or listeners, and others stir memories of wisdom learned
from a well told story. The diversity and brevity of the material make
this a tool for teachers and librarians--both novice and veteran
storytellers. For multicultural studies.
>SUBJ: Folklore./ Storytelling.

PROF 398.2   Ph-3 $14.95   P   KA266
EDMONDS, MARGOT. Voices of the winds: Native American legends.
By Margot Edmonds and Ella E. Clark. Illus. by Molly Braun. Facts On
File ISBN 0-8160-2749-8; In Canada: Facts On File, 1989. 368p. ill.,
map.
>Includes glossary, bibliography and index.
>"The Indian myths and legends collected in this volume represent
most of the tribes of longtime North American Indian cultures in the
six major regions of the United States of America... Representative
legends from various sources preserved in government documents, old
histories, periodicals and reports from anthropoligists in the field
[were chosen]." (Intro.) Complete collection for storytellers and for
units on Native Americans.
>SUBJ: Indians of North America--Folklore.

PROF 398.2   Ph-2 $17.00   P   KA267
FAVORITE FOLKTALES FROM AROUND THE WORLD. Edited by Jane
Yolen. Pantheon ISBN 0-394-75188-4; In Canada: Random House, 1986.
498p. (Pantheon fairy tale & folklore library).
>Available from National Library Service for the Blind and Physically
Handicapped on sound recording cassette RC25529.
>"This collection comes more directly from the folk archives where
tales are basic, with a metaphoric content that must be read into the
story by sophisticated listeners, where the language has been honed
by centuries of tongue-polishing, where the stories are not personal
history artfully disguised...." (p. 7) Divided into the following
categories: Telling Tales; The Very Young and the Very Old; True
Loves and False; Tricksters, Rogues and Cheats; The Fool: Numbskulls
and Noodleheads; Heroes: Likely and Unlikely; Wonder Tales, Tall
Tales and Brag; Shape Shifters; Not Quite Human; Fooling the Devil;
The Getting of Wisdom; Ghosts and Revenants; Death and the
World's End, and each tale is identified by country. Lack of a title
index is not detrimental to the utilization of this outstanding collection.
A fine resource for the storyteller.
>SUBJ: Folklore.

PROF 398.2   Ph-2 $27.00   T   KA268
KIRCHNER, AUDREY BURIE. In days gone by: folklore and traditions of
the Pennsylvania Dutch. By Audrey Burie Kirchner and Margaret R.
Tassia. Illus. by Erin Kirk. Libraries Unlimited ISBN 1-56308-381-7, 1996.
123p. ill. (some col.). (World folklore series).
>Includes bibliography.
>Presents folklife and folklore of the Pennsylvania Germans. Part I
gives a history of this group and information such as "dialect, family
and home life, folk art, holidays, beliefs, superstitions, and
contributions." Part II includes folklore from rhymes to tales. Recipes
and information on customs round out the presentation. No index. For
multicultural studies.
>SUBJ: Pennsylvania Dutch--Folklore./ Pennsylvania Dutch./ Folklore--
Pennsylvania./ Pennsylvania--Folklore.

PROFESSIONAL COLLECTION

PROF 398.2 Ph-1 $23.50 P KA269
KNOCK AT THE DOOR. Compiled by George Shannon. Illus. by Joanne Caroselli. Oryx ISBN 0-89774-733-X; In Canada: Oryx, 1992. 174p. ill. (Oryx multicultural folktale series).
Includes bibliographies and index.
Presents 35 tales from 34 cultures including one Spanish language version from Mexico which explore the universal theme of a stranger knocking at the door. Representing cultures from Europe, Asia, Africa, the Middle East, and the Americas, the tales range from comic to terrifying. Extensive source notes identify more than 40 additional variants. Suggestions for integrating folktales into the curriculum are included. Welcome resource for storytelling, social studies curriculum, and multicultural studies.
SUBJ: Fairy tales./ Folklore.

PROF 398.2 Ph-1 $40.00 T KA270
MACDONALD, MARGARET READ. Celebrate the world: twenty tellable folktales for multicultural festivals. Illus. by Roxane Murphy Smith. Wilson ISBN 0-8242-0862-5, 1994. 225p. ill.
Includes bibliography and index.
Includes 20 easy-to-learn, easy-to-tell ethnopoetic tales with performance notes. Arranged chronologically by date of festival, this collection should provide resources for programs throughout the year. A brief description of holiday traditions and suggested activities are also provided. Welcome addition for social studies and multicultural studies.
SUBJ: Folklore./ Storytelling./ Festivals.

PROF 398.2 Ph-3 $15.95 P KA271
MACDONALD, MARGARET READ. Peace tales: world folktales to talk about. Linnet ISBN 0-208-02329-1, 1992. 116p.
Includes bibliographies and index.
The many stories collected here will aid teachers and librarians who are discussing peace, war, cooperation, and problem solving. Bibliography of additional materials and source notes complete the book. Entries from a wide variety of cultures make it also useful for multicultural studies.
SUBJ: Folklore./ War--Folklore./ Peace--Folklore.

PROF 398.2 Ph-1 $19.95 P KA272
READY-TO-TELL TALES: SURE-FIRE STORIES FROM AMERICA'S FAVORITE STORYTELLERS. Ed. by David Holt and Bill Mooney. August House ISBN 0-87483-381-7, 1994. 224p. ill. (American storytelling).
A wide variety of stories which well-known storytellers have successfully used with audiences in schools, libraries, etc. have been compiled with source notes, musical scores, and invaluable hints on how to enrich the telling of the tales. Useful volume for reading aloud as well as a source book for beginning and seasoned storytellers.
SUBJ: Folklore./ Storytelling--Collections.

PROF 398.2 Ph-2 $12.99 T KA273
SCANDINAVIAN FOLK & FAIRY TALES. Edited by Claire Booss. Avenal Books/dist. by Crown ISBN 0-517-43620-5, 1984. 666p. ill.
Citing that Scandinavian tales have the "power to terrify, haunt and delight," Claire Booss has gathered here a definitive collection of titles from Norway, Sweden, Denmark, Finland, and Iceland. This book will supply storytellers with tales of all types and lengths.
SUBJ: Folklore--Scandinavia./ Storytelling./ Scandinavia--Folklore.

PROF 398.2 Ph-3 $29.95 T KA274
THOMPSON, STITH. One hundred favorite folktales. Chosen by Stith Thompson. Illus. by Franz Altschuler. Indiana University Press ISBN 0-253-15940-7, c1968. 439p. ill.
Includes bibliography.
An extensive collection of tales for the story teller who wants collected into one volume many of the tales for story telling. The editor has selected the tales which have become universal favorites. He has chosen a version which "belongs in the geographical area where the tale is best known" and is well told. For the beginning storyteller this collection will have great use for here are the best, in a good version, and ready for the telling.
SUBJ: Folklore./ Fairy tales.

SRC PROF 398.8 Ph-2 $11.95 OD KA275
GLASS, HENRY. Children's all-time Mother Goose favorites (Sound recording cassette). By Henry "Buzz" Glass and Rosemary Hallum. Educational Activities AC 639, 1989. 1 sound recording cassette (29min).
A booklet of activities to accompany the singing of fourteen Mother Goose rhymes provides teachers with ideas for using the rhymes to develop skills in language arts, music, and movement. Frees the teachers to participate with the pre-school and beginning primary grade children.
SUBJ: Nursery rhymes./ Singing games.

PROF 398.8 Ph-3 $19.95 T KA276
I SAW ESAU: THE SCHOOLCHILD'S POCKET BOOK. Edited by Iona and Peter Opie. Illus. by Maurice Sendak. Candlewick ISBN 1-56402-046-0; In Canada: Candlewick/dist. by Douglas & McIntyre, 1992. 160p. col. ill.
Originally published as I SAW ESAU: TRADITIONAL RHYMES OF YOUTH, 1947.
The wit and wisdom of generations of school children are preserved in this classic text which now includes detailed notes and Sendak's devilishly delightful illustrations. His caricatures of mischievous children and boisterous adults extend the text and add to its irreverent tone. Over 170 folk rhymes ranging from the ridiculous to the vulgar include puns, insults, tongue twisters, riddles, and jump-rope rhymes. Inspiration for playground taunts as well as creative writing exercises.
SUBJ: Nursery rhymes./ English poetry--Collections./ Children's writings.

PROF 398.8 Ph-1 $16.95 T KA277
JANE YOLEN'S MOTHER GOOSE SONGBOOK. Selected, edited and introduced by Jane Yolen. Musical arrangements by Adam Stemple. Illus. by Rosekrans Hoffman. Caroline House/Boyds Mills ISBN 1-878093-52-5, 1992. 95p. col. ill.
Includes index.
All the familiar nursery rhymes are set to music in a charmingly illustrated format. Brief histories of rhymes preface the music. An invaluable treasury of songs for teachers and parents. (Parents' Shelf).
SUBJ: Nursery rhymes.

PROF 398.8 Ph-2 $7.95 P KA278
KNAPP, MARY. One potato, two potato: the folklore of American children. By Mary and Herbert Knapp. Norton ISBN 0-393-09039-6, 1978. 274p.
Includes bibliographical references and index.
The culture of the child as seen through their jokes, riddles, clapping games, jump rope rhymes, and parodies. This collection and analysis of the folklore of children in the United States provides a fresh look at the world of today's child.
SUBJ: Nursery rhymes./ Folklore--United States./ United States--Folklore.

PROF 419 Ph-1 $29.95 P KA279
HAFER, JAN CHRISTIAN. Come sign with us: sign language activities for children. 2nd. ed. By Jan C. Hafer and Robert M. Wilson. Illus. by Paul Setzer. Clerc Books/Gallaudet University Press ISBN 1-56368-051-3, 1996. 156p. ill.
Includes bibliographies, directory and glossary.
Provides 20 lessons to teach beginning sign language as well as information on the history of sign language. Lesson plans focus on topics that make signing more relevant to students. Facts about deafness are included with each lesson. Illustrations with step-by-step directions for arm and hand movements are clear. The inclusion of Spanish speaking words will make the book appealing to Spanish children and reinforces the concept that many languages are commonly used in the United States.
SUBJ: Sign language--Study and teaching (Elementary)--Activity programs./ Deaf--Means of communication./ Bilingual materials--Spanish./ Spanish language materials.

PROF 428 Ph-1 $9.95 P KA280
JONES, BEAU FLY. Teaching thinking skills: English/language arts. By Beau Fly Jones, Margaret Tinzmann, Lawrence B. Friedman, Beverly B. Walker. National Education Association ISBN 0-8106-0204-0, 1987. 104p. (Building students' thinking skills).
Includes glossary and index.
"Increasingly teachers are teaching thinking and integrating language arts skills in order to improve student understanding of specific works of literature...reading comprehension and writing across the curriculum (is being taught) as a means to understanding the information in content courses." The two parts of the book present a framework for teaching language arts as thinking. Part 1 defines the essential concept--strategic teaching. Part 2 presents "five examples for teaching specific content and skills objectives."
SUBJ: Thought and thinking--Study and teaching./ English language--Study and teaching./ Language arts.

PROF 428 Ph-2 $12.95 P KA281
WHEN THEY DON'T ALL SPEAK ENGLISH: INTEGRATING THE ESL STUDENT INTO THE REGULAR CLASSROOM. Edited by Pat Rigg and Virginia G. Allen. National Council of Teachers of English ISBN 0-8141-5693-2, 1989. 156p. ill.
"This book is written for the teacher who...at some time during his or her career will have at least one student who speaks English as another language." (Intro.). Answers about integration of these

students into the classroom, and other important principles about language learners and language learning are presented in ten articles. Unfortunately an index is not included.
SUBJ: English language--Study and teaching--Foreign speakers.

PROF 500.5   Ph-2 $29.95   P   KA282
SUMNERS, CAROLYN. Toys in space: exploring science with the astronauts. Foreword by John Casper. McGraw-Hill/Learning Triangle Press ISBN 0-07-069489-3; In Canada: McGraw-Hill Ryerson, 1997. 1 v. (various pagings). ill.
Includes directory, glossary and index.
What happens if you fly a paper plane or throw a ball in zero gravity? Learn how the motions of physical reaction/action, magnetism inertia, gyroscopic action, etc. of 40 toys were tested in space and on earth, and then have your students try it! Dr. Sumners is both the author and Project Director for the Toys in Space Program. After three introductory chapters, she divides toys into categories: swimming, flying, rolling, and more. Space contests and games are also part of the action. Contains information on astronauts and three shuttle missions, 300 activity sheets, 15 reproducible flip books, directions for making some toys, background science information along with lists of: NASA resources, quiz answers, and science concepts. For innovative teachers wanting new approaches.
SUBJ: Weightlessness--Experiments./ Toys--Study and teaching (Elementary)./ Space shuttles--Experiments.

PROF 507   Ph-1 $8.95   P   KA283
MUNSON, HOWARD R. Science experiences with everyday things. Fearon Teacher Aids/David S. Lake ISBN 0-8224-6846-8, 1988. 91p. ill.
The author states that "science is something people do." By actively involving students in observing, recording, predicting, comparing, inferring and concluding they are given experience in problem solving and drawing conclusions. The activities require very simple and easy to obtain materials.
SUBJ: Science--Experiments./ Experiments.

PROF 507   Ph-1 $19.95   P   KA284
NATIONAL SCIENCE EDUCATION STANDARDS: OBSERVE, INTERACT, CHANGE, LEARN. National Academy Press ISBN 0-309-05326-9, 1996. 262p. ill.
Includes bibliographies and index.
This essential tool for all libraries provides more than just the National Science Educaton Standards. Also included are broad principals and definitions of terms which precede chapters covering: standards for science teaching; standards for professional development for teachers of science; standards for assessment in science education; standards for science content; standards for science education programs; and standards for science education systems.
SUBJ: Science--Study and teaching--Standards--United States.

PROF 507.8   Ph-1 $29.95   P   KA285
BOSAK, SUSAN V. Science is...2nd ed. By Susan V. Bosak with Douglas A. Bosak and Brian A. Puppa. Scholastic ISBN 0-590-74070-9; In Canada: Scholastic Canada/Communication Project, 1991. 515p. ill.
Includes bibliographies and index.
This "has been designed...to jump off the shelf and scream. 'Use me!'" (p.5) Activity after activity attests to the fun of adventure and discovery. Offers 480 pages of step-by-step procedures to explore matter, environment, plants, animals, weather, and more. Handy chart interrelates activities for all elementary science topics. Thumb index directs user to sections--Quickies, Make Time, and One Thing Leads to Another. Both index and resource guides are extensive. Each teacher will want her own copy.
SUBJ: Science--Experiments./ Scientific recreations./ Experiments.

PROF 507.8   Ph-1 $8.95   P   KA286
FREDERICKS, ANTHONY D. Complete science fair handbook. By Anthony D. Fredericks and Isaac Asimov. Illus. by Phyllis Disher Fredericks. Good Year Books/Scott, Foresman ISBN 0-673-38800-X, 1990. 82p. ill.
Includes bibliography.
Addressed to both teacher and parent, this book is a "systematic guide to the design and development of a successful science fair. It is intended to stimulate higher levels of participation, well-designed and functional projects,...and...an abundance of originality." (IX)
Coverage ranges from selection of a topic to presenting the project. Perforated pages and reproduction clearance will enable teachers to share information with students and parents. Resources include books and periodicals for students and teachers, government agencies, and science supply companies.
SUBJ: Science fairs.

PROF 507.8   Ph-1 $12.95   P   KA287
VECCHIONE, GLEN. 100 amazing make-it-yourself science fair projects. Sterling ISBN 0-8069-0367-8; In Canada: Sterling c/o Canadian Manda, 1995. 224p. ill.
Includes index.
Although some of these experiments may be beyond elementary school students' capability, the author provides a wide range of activities--from electricity to chemistry and from ecology to eye and mind tricks. Each experiment clearly outlines materials needed and defines scientific terms. Some activities, like spider-web collecting, are excellent nature study ideas.
SUBJ: Science projects./ Science--Experiments./ Experiments.

PROF 508   Ph-2 $15.95   P   KA288
DUENSING, EDWARD. Talking to fireflies, shrinking the moon: nature activities for all ages. Fulcrum ISBN 1-55591-310-5, 1997. 136p.
Originally published by Plume, 1990.
Written by a naturalist who shares his expertise and love of nature by explaining how to interact with wild critters and plants to reveal our amazing world. Over 35 imaginative activities such as hypnotizing frogs, calling worms from their tunnels, and using found clay to make thumbprint plaques will have children demanding to know more. Nurtures a love of the outdoors and a respect for all creatures. Use with scouting programs, outdoor classrooms, or just for fun. Everyone learns, even the teacher! (Parents' Shelf).
SUBJ: Natural history--Outdoor books./ Nature study--Activity programs.

PROF 508   Ph-1 $19.50   P   KA289
HILLMAN, LAWRENCE E. Nature puzzlers. Teacher Ideas Press/Libraries Unlimited ISBN 0-87287-778-7, 1989. 151p. ill.
Includes bibliography and index.
Development of higher level thinking skills and problem solving abilities are utilized and stressed heavily in this book that focuses on situations or occurrences in nature. Puzzles range from relatively easy to difficult.
SUBJ: Natural history--Study and teaching./ Educational games./ Puzzles.

PROF 510   Ph-1 $18.00   P   KA290
ERICKSON, TIM. Get it together: math problems for groups, grades 4-12. Curriculum developers, Bill Finzer...[et al.]. Illus. by Rose Craig. EQUALS/Lawrence Hall of Science ISBN 0-912511-53-2, 1989. 180p. ill.
Includes bibliography and index.
Based on the EQUALS teacher education program from Berkeley, California, this collection of math problems for groups, called "cooperative logic" problems, is an easy way for teachers to begin to use group instruction. The "clue" cards provide each member of the group with a different piece of information. Everyone must cooperate to solve the problem. Problems are presented in "families." The concept area, materials required, description, and possible debriefing questions are included. Permission to reproduce is granted for home, workshop, or classroom use only. Despite the problems of a spiral binding, the book should be welcome by teachers and parents. (Parents' Shelf).
SUBJ: Mathematics--Study and teaching./ Group work in education.

VCR PROF 530   Ph-3 5-A $79.00   OD   KA291
WATER ROCKETS I (Videocassette). Insights Visual Productions 701, 1994. 1/2" VHS videocassette color (53min).
Includes teacher's guide.
Includes public performance rights.
Combine two scientists with two liter plastic bottles and the teaching possibilities are endless. Opens with a safety segment, giving clear concise directions, then follows the students outside as they begin to experiment with water rockets. Builds on beginner knowledge to demonstrate other concepts by varying design, changing water volume and pressure, finding altitude using astrolabes, launching payloads with different loads, and more. Appendix shows how to build the basic launch pad. A super resource for teachers. "The excitement over water rockets is contagious for apathetic terminal science students, hormone driven middle level students, and...for advanced physics students." (p.1 handbook)
Also available: WATER ROCKETS II (67min), $79.00.
SUBJ: Physics--Experiments./ Water--Experiments./ Scientific recreations.

VCR PROF 530.4   Ph-3 3-A $69.00   OD   KA292
BUBBLEOLOGY I AND II (Videocassette). Insights Visual Productions 403, 1988. 1/2" VHS videocassette color (60min).
Includes teacher's guide.
Includes public performance rights.
Everyone plays with bubbles, but structured inquiry can revel the

dynamics and physics behind simple soap and water. Here are children learning to form questions and investigate answers. Begin with blowing, sealing, and recycling a bubble; advance to the giant bubble machine, bubbles filled with natural gas, and a giant bubble parachute. Wonderful, inexpensive fun that assures learning. Perfect match for Zubrowski's BUBBLES: A CHILDREN'S MUSEUM ACTIVITY BOOK.
SUBJ: Bubbles./ Experiments./ Physics--Experiments.

PROF 551.5   Ph-2 $14.95   P   KA293
LOCKHART, GARY. Weather companion. Wiley ISBN 0-471-62079-3; In Canada: Wiley, 1988. 230p. ill. (Wiley science editions).
Includes bibliography and index.
This fascinating book will provide teachers with many ideas involving folklore, superstition, and legends that can supplement any lesson on weather.
SUBJ: Meteorology--Miscellanea./ Weather--Miscellanea.

PROF 551.6   Ph-1 $22.00   P   KA294
PERRY, PHYLLIS J. World's regions and weather: linking fiction to nonfiction. Teacher Ideas Press ISBN 1-56308-338-8, 1996. 157p. (Literature bridges to science series).
Includes bibliographies and index.
Designed to provide discussion ideas, interdisciplinary activities, and skills in research. Divided by types of weather: snow, hail, and ice; drought, dust, and dunes; clouds, rain, and floods; winds: hurricanes, tornadoes, and typhoons. Each section includes both fiction and nonfiction titles. Most titles will appeal to a wide range of interests. Books cited are for upper elementary and junior high school students. Useful for interdisciplinary studies.
SUBJ: Weather--Study and teaching./ Meteorology--Study and teaching./ Weather--Bibliography./ Meteorology--Bibliography./ Interdisciplinary approach in education.

MMK PROF 570   Ph-1 K-A $19.95   KA295
HORTON, BOBBY. Lyrical life science (Multimedia kit). Text and lyrics by Doug Eldon. Illus. by Eric Altendorf. Lyrical Learning ISBN 0-9646367-0-0, 1995. 1 paperback book, 1 workbook, 1 sound cassette (30min).
Includes lyrics and music.
ALA notable recording, 1996.
Clever lyrics put to familiar traditional, patriotic, and camp tunes offer a crafty way to teach and learn. Content rich songs have plenty of technical terms (commensal, symbiosis, vascular) and cover a vast array of scientific concepts. Volume 1 includes tunes on the scientific method, various plants, genetics, and more. Volume 2 covers mammals, ecology, and biomes. The two books contain all the lyrics and music along with fairly comprehensive, related text. There are two workbooks with objective and essay questions, fill in the blanks, and matching sheets, all using song lyrics. For environmental studies. LYRICAL LIFE SCIENCE. VOL. 2: MAMMALS, ECOLOGY, AND BIOMES (ISBN 0-9646367-2-7, 1996), $19.95.
SUBJ: Life sciences--Songs and music./ Songs.

PROF 591   Ph-2 $23.50   P   KA296
LIVO, LAUREN J. Of bugs and beasts: fact, folklore, and activities. By Lauren J. Livo, Glen McGlathery and Norma J. Livo. Illus. by David Stallings. Photos by Lauren J. Livo and Steve Wilcox. Teacher Ideas Press/Libraries Unlimited ISBN 1-56308-179-2, 1995. 217p. ill. (Learning through folklore).
Includes bibliographies, glossary and index.
A wonderful combination of folklore and scientific facts profiles 15 animals grouped within their normal habitat. Activities, which provide connections to other areas of study such as drama, language arts, mathematics, social studies, geography, etc., may be completed by individuals, classes, or small groups. Annotated resource lists include books, magazines, journal articles, tapes, and compact discs. Interesting and informative resource for interdisciplinary studies.
SUBJ: Animals./ Animals--Folklore./ Animals--Study and teaching--Activity programs.

PROF 607   Ph-2 $21.50   P   KA297
FLACK, JERRY D. Inventing, inventions, and inventors: a teaching resource book. Illustrated by Adam Burton. Teacher Ideas Press/Libraries Unlimited ISBN 0-87287-747-7, 1989. 148p. ill. (Gifted treasury).
Includes appendix and index.
This is the first book of a series being prepared for use with gifted and talented students that will provide teaching strategies and activities centered around a single theme. Numerous illustrations and figures enhance this well suited topic. Excellent ideas, creative teaching activities, and cross-curriculum areas combine to provide a comprehensive treatment of the topic of inventors and inventions.
SUBJ: Technology--Study and teaching./ Gifted children--Education./ Inventions--Study and teaching./ Talented students--Education.

VCR PROF 613.81   Ph-2 $70.00   OD KA298
BROKEN PROMISES (Videocassette). Clearvue/EAV CL741, 1991. 1/2" VHS videocassette color (34min).
Includes teacher's guide.
Children of alcoholic parents appear in three group sessions which focus on feelings and coping skills. As the children respond to the two counselors, the film intercuts to realistic scenes of their family lives. The cultural mix of children and the simple honesty of their remarks will reassure students that they are indeed not alone. Counselors and teachers may find the film, the discussion pointers in the guide, and the substantial bibliography very useful in helping children cope with this widespread problem.
SUBJ: Alcoholism./ Family life./ Family problems.

PROF 641.59   Ph-3 $25.95   P   KA299
ALBYN, CAROLE LISA. Multicultural cookbook for students. By Carole Lisa Albyn and Lois Sinaiko Webb. Oryx ISBN 0-89774-735-6; In Canada: Oryx, 1993. 287p., maps.
Includes glossary and index.
More than 300 recipes offer a quick glimpse of foods eaten in 122 countries. Large sections by region--Africa, Middle East, Asia, and the South Pacific, etc.--list each country with a small map, an introductory paragraph, and one or two recipes. Intended for children, this plain, dense volume will best serve as an added source on countries not covered in other materials on national foods and cultures. For multicultural studies.
SUBJ: Cookery, International./ Food habits./ Food crops.

VCR PROF 649   Ph-3 $19.95   KA300
CHANGE FOR THE BETTER: TEACHING CORRECT BEHAVIOR (Videocassette). Boys Town ISBN 0-938510-14-2, 1989. 1/2" VHS videocassette color (11min). (Videos for parents).
Includes parents' guide.
Based on the principles developed at Boys Town homes and schools, this video shows parents how to react to misbehavior, coaching their children into proper behavior. Dramatized scenes provide examples of various situations and how to handle them. (Parents' Shelf)
SUBJ: Parenting./ Behavior.

PROF 649   Ph-2 $3.95   P   KA301
CULLINAN, BERNICE E. Read to me: raising kids who love to read. Scholastic ISBN 0-590-45206-1; In Canada: Scholastic, 1992. 152p.
Includes bibliographies.
In a nonthreatening manner, this excellent resource for librarians, teachers, and parents presents ideas for building a sound reading foundation in preschoolers through twelve-year-olds. The techniques are simple, yet filled with potential. Includes recommended children's magazines and "Surefire Hits" by grade level. (Parents' Shelf).
SUBJ: Children--Books and reading./ Reading--Parent participation.

VCR PROF 649   Ph-3 $19.95   KA302
IT'S GREAT TO BE ME! INCREASING YOUR CHILD'S SELF-ESTEEM (Videocassette). Boys Town ISBN 0-938510-12-6, 1989. 1/2" VHS videocassette color (12min). (Videos for parents).
Includes parents' guide.
The pre-adolescent years can be hard on a child's self-esteem. Based on the principles developed at Boys Town homes and schools, this video can help parents have a positive impact on their child's self-esteem. (Parents' Shelf)
SUBJ: Parenting./ Behavior./ Self-acceptance.

PROF 649   Ph-2 $12.95   P   KA303
KENNEDY, PATRICIA. Hyperactive child book. By Patricia Kennedy, Leif Terdal, and Lydia Fusetti. St. Martin's ISBN 0-312-11286-6; In Canada: St. Martin's, 1994. 276p.
Includes bibliography, directories and index.
Thorough coverage of the issues faced by children diagnosed with Attention Deficit-Hyperactivity Disorder (ADHD). Provides practical information and advice particularly dealing with schools and developing an individual educational program (IEP). (Parents' Shelf).
SUBJ: Attention deficit disorders./ Hyperactive child syndrome.

PROF 649   Ph-1 $17.95   P   KA304
MENDLER, ALLEN N. Smiling at yourself: educating young children about stress and self-esteem. Illus. by Marcia Quackenbush. Network Publications ISBN 0-941816-90-7, 1990. 145p. ill.
Includes appendices.
A sensitive and well-developed approach to reducing stress through a number of activities that center on self-image, relaxation, problem-solving, healthy anger release, and special problems that can cause stress (divorce, illness, death or disabilties). Additional resources provide depth beyond these simple activities that can be used by teachers or counselors.
SUBJ: Stress (Psychology)./ Self-acceptance./ Problem solving--Study and teaching.

PROF 649 Ph-2 $14.95 P KA305
ORLICK, TERRY. Free to feel great: teaching children to excel at living. Creative Bound/dist. by BookWorld Services ISBN 0-921165-26-9; In Canada: Creative Bound, 1993. 174p.
Includes bibliography, discographies and filmography.
Simple techniques for use with students to build self confidence, ease stress, shift focus, and have a positive outlook are described. Examples are interesting, practical, and show how even the youngest child can gain a positive perspective. (Parents' Shelf).
SUBJ: Children--Conduct of life./ Success./ Stress in children./ Child rearing.

VCR PROF 649.8 Ph-3 $69.95 OD KA306
MEETING THE CHALLENGE: PARENTING CHILDREN WITH DISABILITIES (Videocassette). Karol Media, 1992. 1/2" VHS videocassette color.
Includes teacher's guide.
Includes public performance rights.
Several sets of parents discuss the stresses of parenting special needs children and offer practical advice in this supportive presentation. Occasional scenes of the children are included as the conversations cut back and forth among people talking about the grief process, making decisions about institutional care, approaches to parenting, and finding professional services. Libraries serving parents and social services specialists may find this useful for group discussions or viewing by individual families, particularly those in the early years of dealing with profound disabilities. (Parents' Shelf).
Contents: Part I: Lost dreams (23min); Part II: Rebuilding dreams (17min); Part III: The challenge of parenting (26min); Part IV: The professional puzzle (28min).
SUBJ: Parenting./ Handicapped children--Care.

PROF 703 Ph-1 FREE P OD KA307
DETROIT INSTITUTE OF ARTS. Catalogue of color reproductions. Detroit Institute of Arts, n.d. 112p.
Mail or fax your request on letterhead.
List of over 3000 2"x2" color slides from the Detroit Institute of Arts with instructions for ordering. Arranged under headings such as paintings, sculpture, graphic arts, ceramics, etc. with national subdivisions. High quality of slide reproduction.
SUBJ: Slides (Photography)--Catalogs./ Art--Catalogs.

PROF 703 Ph-3 FREE P OD KA308
NATIONAL GALLERY OF ART (U.S.). Catalogue of color reproductions: books and catalogues, educational materials. National Gallery of Art, n.d. 58p.
Gives for each item listed the number, the artist, the title, price, etc. Includes such materials of interest to schools as a 60-fr set of 35mm slidestrips on American Painting in History at the National Gallery, along with a disc recording and a paperbound text of the recording plus suggestions to teachers. Sculpture, reproductions of jewelry and many other kinds of material valuable for an appreciation of art are listed.
SUBJ: Art--Catalogs.

PROF 736 Ph-2 $11.50 P KA309
KALLEVIG, CHRISTINE PETRELL. Holiday folding stories: storytelling and origami together for holiday fun. Photos by Terey Page. Storytime Ink International ISBN 0-9628769-1-7, 1992. 93p. ill.
Includes directory, bibliographies, glossary and index.
Using the term "storigami," the author combines origami and storytelling through nine brief multicultural stories. These stories can be interactive, and will provide opportunities to improve listening, visualization, and motor skills. Useful not only for librarians and teachers, but also for parents who may be seeking club activities. (Parents' Shelf).
SUBJ: Origami./ Storytelling./ Holidays./ Handicraft.

PROF 741.6 Ph-3 $25.00 P KA310
BRODIE, CAROLYN S. Bookmark book. By Carolyn S. Brodie, Debra Goodrich, and Paula K. Montgomery. Libraries Unlimited ISBN 1-56308-300-0, 1996. 100p. ill. (Cut 'n clip series).
Includes bibliography.
Includes 280 reproducible bookmarks which are not just decorative, but are designed as puzzles, alphabets, phrases in many languages, statistics, state facts, biographical information, questions on various topics, and useful information about various reference tools. A simple way to provide customized bookmarks to supplement the curriculum.
SUBJ: Bookmarks./ Teaching--Aids and devices.

PROF 741.6 Ph-2 $35.95 T KA311
ILLUSTRATORS OF CHILDREN'S BOOKS, 1967-1976. Compiled by Lee Kingman, Grace Allen Hogarth and Harriet Quimby. Horn Book ISBN 0-87675-018-8, 1978. 290p. ill.
Includes appendix.
A fourth in the series all entitled "Illustrators of children's books" including in this case four essays on the current state of the arts in Europe and Japan as well as the United States, followed by the list of annotated biographies (p90-173), and two bibliographies of illustrators active 1967-1976 and authors.
SUBJ: Children's literature--History and criticism./ Illustration of books./ Illustrators.

PROF 741.6 Ph-2 $49.00 T KA312
STEWIG, JOHN WARREN. Looking at picture books. Highsmith Press ISBN 0-917846-29-X, 1995. 269p. ill. (some col.).
Includes bibliographies and indexes.
Designed for teachers and librarians without a background in visual art, this overview introduces methods to evaluate and understand the art in picture books. Examines visual components, compositional principles, and numerous media. Includes activities to engage children beyond the verbal experience to become more skilled observers. For classroom teachers and librarians interested in visual literacy as well as for art teachers.
SUBJ: Picture books for children--Authorship./ Illustration of books./ Children's stories--History and criticism.

PROF 745.5 Ph-2 $10.95 P KA313
STANGL, JEAN. Recycling activities for the primary grades. Fearon Teacher Aids/Simon & Schuster ISBN 0-86653-938-7, 1993. 95p. ill.
Arts and crafts projects enhance the interdisciplinary curriculum with science, math, art, and drama activities using newspapers, paper bags, and boxes and cartons. Fosters the integration of recycling into every curricular area.
SUBJ: Handicraft./ Recycling (Waste)--Study and teaching./ Creative activities and seatwork./ Teaching--Aids and devices.

VCR PROF 780 Ph-1 $19.95 KA314
LANGSTAFF, JOHN. Let's sing!: John Langstaff sings with children, ages 3-7 (Videocassette). Produced and directed by Elizabeth Lloyd Mayer. Langstaff Video Project ISBN 1-886380-15-5, 1997. 1/2" VHS videocassette color (45min). (Making music with John Langstaff).
Public performance rights available at additional charge.
Teacher's guide with lyrics and music available (ISBN 1-886380-22-8, 1997), $4.95.
An enthusiastic, sing along video certain to engage young children in musical activities encourages audience participation with clapping songs, call and response songs, and singing games. Songs include familiar tunes such as "Muffin Man" and "Over in the meadow" as well as less familiar ones like "Ally Bally" and "Santy Maloney." Can be used alone or after personally viewing the companion video MAKING MUSIC WITH CHILDREN, AGES 3-7. Invaluable for music teachers, it is also suitable for use in homes, libraries, elementary schools, and preschools. (Parents' Shelf).
SUBJ: Music--Study and teaching./ Songs.

VCR PROF 780 Ph-1 $29.95 KA315
LANGSTAFF, JOHN. Making music with children, ages 3-7 (Videocassette). Elizabeth Lloyd Mayer, Director. Langstaff Video Project ISBN 1-886380-10-4, 1995. 1/2" VHS videocassette color (60min). (Making music with John Langstaff).
Includes teacher's guide with lyrics and music.
Public performance rights available at additional charge.
Using modeling and positive reinforcement, Langstaff demonstrates how to teach every child to sing. Simple step-by-step instructions effectively convey such musical concepts as singing on pitch and rhythm. Incorporating traditional songs and chants such as "Jim along, Josie" and "Sally go round the moon," he introduces percussion and movement and audience participation activities including singing games and dance drama. His enthusiasm is contagious, and his practical ideas will inspire music educators as well as classroom teachers, librarians, and parents. (Parents' Shelf).
SUBJ: Music--Study and teaching./ Songs.

BA PROF 789.2 Ph-2 $29.95 OD KA316
BURTON, BRYAN. Moving within the circle: contemporary Native American music and dance. World Music Press ISBN 0-937203-65-3, 1993. 1 paperback book, 1 compact disc (64min).
Includes discography, bibliography, filmography, directories and index.
Also available in book/CD/slide set (ISBN 0-937203-66-1) and book/sound cassette/slide set (ISBN 0-937203-50-5), $63.00.
Also available with sound recording cassette (ISBN 0-937203-43-2, 1993). 1 paperback book, 1 sound cassette (64min), $29.95.
Collection of 24 social songs and dances provides listening experiences as well as information on Native American cultures. Movement directions plus a CD are included to expand text. Useful for social studies and multicultural studies.
SUBJ: Indians of North America--Music./ Indians of North America--Dances./ Folk music--United States./ Folk dancing--United States.

PROFESSIONAL COLLECTION

BA PROF 789.2 Ph-2 $20.95 KA317
NGUYEN, PHONG THUYET. From rice paddies and temple yards: traditional music of Vietnam. By Phong Thuyet Nguyen and Patricia Shehan Campbell. Photos by Phong Thuyet Nguyen...[et al.]. World Music Press ISBN 0-937203-34-3, c1990, 1992. 1 paperback book, 1 sound cassette (33min).
> Includes bibliography, discography, filmography and index.
> Also available with compact disc (ISBN 0-937203-73-4, 1992). 1 paperback book, 1 compact disc (33min), $20.95.
> An extensive introduction to the music and culture of Vietnam presents 12 traditional and contemporary folk songs, game songs and dance music. Text provides history and cultural background as well as descriptions of musical instruments and musical forms. Each song includes background, translation, transliteration, suggested activities, and recommended age levels. Unique contribution to multicultural studies and music education.
> SUBJ: Folk music--Vietnam./ Folk songs./ Singing games.

BA PROF 789.2 Ph-2 $24.95 KA318
SAM, SAM-ANG. Silent temples, songful hearts: traditional music of Cambodia. By San-Ang Sam and Patricia Shehan Campbell. Illus. by Yang Sam and Tho "Tony" Sangphet. Photos by Bonnie Periale...[et al.]. World Music Press ISBN 0-937203-36-X, 1991. 1 paperback book, 1 sound cassette (45min).
> Includes glossary, bibliography, discography, filmography and index.
> Also available with compact disc (ISBN 0-937203-74-2, 1991). 1 paperback book, 1 compact disc (45min), $24.95.
> Seventeen game songs, story songs, instrumental music arrangements, and dance accompaniments provide a thorough overview of Khmer music and musical instruments. Introductory chapters detail the history, geography, and culture of Cambodia. Fourteen musical selections accompany text which includes transcriptions, transliterations, extensive background information, and suggested activities. Welcome resource for multicultural studies and music education.
> SUBJ: Folk music--Cambodia./ Folk songs--Cambodia./ Singing games.

BA PROF 789.2 Ph-2 $17.95 OD KA319
SERWADDA, W. MOSES. Songs and stories from Uganda. Transcribed and edited by Hewitt Pantaleoni. Illus. by Leo and Diane Dillon. World Music Press ISBN 0-937203-17-3; In Canada: Fitzhenry & Whiteside, c1974, 1987. 1 paperback book, 1 sound cassette (60min).
> Also available with compact disc (ISBN 0-937203-85-8, 1987). 1 paperback book, 1 compact disc (60min), $17.95.
> Thirteen authentic story songs of the Baganda people provide a representative sampling of audience participation songs frequently used by African storytellers. Background notes, transcriptions, phonetic spellings, and translations are included. Valuable resource for storytelling, multicultural studies, and music education.
> SUBJ: Folk songs--Uganda./ Folk music--Uganda./ Folklore--Uganda./ Uganda--Folklore.

BA PROF 789.3 Ph-1 $29.95 OD KA320
CAMPBELL, PATRICIA SHEHAN. Roots and branches: a legacy of multicultural music for children. By Patricia Shehan Campbell, Ellen McCullough-Brabson and Judith Cook Tucker. World Music Press ISBN 0-937203-55-6, 1994. 1 paperback book, 1 compact disc (42min).
> Includes bibliography and index.
> Also available as a book and sound recording cassette set (ISBN 0-937203-52-1).
> A very broad sampling of songs and singing games from many continents. The companion CD provides an excellent accompaniment to lyrics and lines of music. Background about each country provides valuable social studies material. Pages describing the songs also give information about musical instruments and directions for playing, singing, and pronunciation. Includes bibliography, facts and figures for each country, and index. Book does not included track number for songs on CD, but it is provided on CD cover. For multicultural studies.
> SUBJ: Children's songs./ Singing games./ Folk songs.

CE PROF 789.3 Ph-1 $12.95 P KA321
NELSON, ESTHER L. Everybody sing and dance. Scholastic Professional ISBN 0-590-49041-9, 1989. 192p. ill.
> Includes index.
> Sound recording cassette available from Dimension 5 D511 (ISBN 0-945110-09-X, 1988). (50min), $10.95.
> Nelson provides teaching strategies for incorporating music and movement into early childhood education. The activities are designed to develop coordination, rhythm, and creativity. Songs include such favorites as "Noble Duke of York", "A Hunting We Will Go", and "The Clothes in the Washer."
> SUBJ: Songs./ Dance music./ Finger play.

PROF 789.3 Ph-3 $19.95 P OD KA322
WORLD OF CHILDREN'S SONGS. Edited by Mary Lu Walker. Illus. by Gloria Ortiz. Friendship Press ISBN 0-377-00260-7, 1993. 191p. ill. (Children's world series).
> Includes bibliography and indexes.
> Piano renditions of children's songs from around the world. Contains material from the seven major geographical-cultural regions, including folksongs from Asia, Africa, Middle East, Americas, South Pacific, and Europe. Gives cultural information on each area. For multicultural studies.
> SUBJ: Children's songs./ Folk songs.

PROF 790.1 Ph-1 $14.95 P KA323
ORLANDO, LOUISE. Multicultural game book: more than 70 traditional games from 30 countries. Scholastic Professional Books ISBN 0-590-49409-0; In Canada: Scholastic, 1993. 110p. ill., maps. (Instructor Books).
> "Grades 1-6."
> Includes bibliography.
> Seventy games requiring few supplies are included. Some games may be played alone or in pairs while others are group activities. Games are from: Africa, Asia, Australia, Europe, North America, and South America. Useful for multicultural studies.
> SUBJ: Educational games./ Multicultural education.

PROF 790.1 Ph-1 $12.95 P KA324
PERRY, SUSAN K. Playing smart: a parent's guide to enriching offbeat learning activities for ages 4-14. Edited by Pamela Espeland. Illus. by L.T. Anderson. Free Spirit ISBN 0-915793-22-9, 1990. 211p. ill.
> Includes bibliography and index.
> An excellent collection of enrichment activities to develop critical thinking, creative thought processes, and problem solving. Organization allows easy access and use of contents. A delightful compendium from diaries to tongue-twisters to what-if's to cultural diversity that will provide hours of interesting activities. (Parents' shelf).
> SUBJ: Family recreation./ Creative thinking (Education).

PROF 790.1 Ph-2 $19.95 P KA325
SILBERG, JACKIE. 500 five minute games: quick and easy activities for 3-6 year olds. Illus. by Rebecca Jones. Gryphon House ISBN 0-87659-172-1, 1995. 270p. ill.
> Includes indexes.
> A plethora of fun games for youngsters three to six years of age. Physically active and quiet activities foster concentration, coordination, counting, memory, and observation skills. Skills index identifies games to develop specific proficiencies. An excellent resource for parents and teachers. (Parents' Shelf).
> SUBJ: Educational games./ Early childhood education--Activity programs./ Motor ability.

PROF 791.5 Ph-3 $13.95 P KA326
BUCHWALD, CLAIRE. Puppet book: how to make and operate puppets and stage a puppet play. Illus. by Audrey Jakubiszyn. Plays, Inc. ISBN 0-8238-0293-0, 1990. 125p. ill.
> Poor organization hampers the utilization of 5 original plays and their use in school settings. The complexity of sets, props, puppets, stages and scenes would limit this book's use to only a very involved program of enrichment and supplemental activities. The plays, however, are unique and can provide new ideas in a school that has utilized puppetry in the past and is seeking new material.
> SUBJ: Puppets./ Puppet plays./ Plays.

PROF 791.5 Ph-1 $20.95 P OD KA327
HUNT, TAMARA. Puppetry in early childhood education. By Tamara Hunt and Nancy Renfro. Nancy Renfro Studios ISBN 0-931044-04-9, 1982. 258p. ill. (Puppetry in education).
> Includes bibliographies.
> Basic--down to earth ideas for utilizing, making, playacting, "puppeteaching," storing, and building a collection of puppets. Not only offers bibliography of other books on the subject, but an excellent list of library books which can be introduced with puppets. The teaching ideas abound: self concept, measuring, nature appreciation, seasons, counting, etc. The line drawings and many photographs beautifully compliment the text.
> SUBJ: Puppets./ Puppet plays.

PROF 791.5 Ph-3 $17.95 T OD KA328
RENFRO, NANCY. Puppetry, language, and the special child: discovering alternate languages. Nancy Renfro Studios ISBN 0-931044-12-X, 1984. 152p. ill. (Puppetry in education).
> The author, herself hearing impaired, presents creative methods for utilizing puppetry "as a tool to discover alternate languages with the special child. Six major disability areas are covered in the multimedia

approach that includes a wide range of practical ideas for puppetmaking, music, rhythm, story presentation and creative dramatics."
SUBJ: Puppets./ Handicapped./ Physically handicapped./ Mentally handicapped.

PROF 792 Ph-1 $45.00 T KA329
BAUER, CAROLINE FELLER. Presenting reader's theater: plays and poems to read aloud. Illus. by Lynn Gates Bredeson. Wilson ISBN 0-8242-0748-3, 1987. 238p. ill.
This rich panoply of scripts and poetry will promote the fun of reading in general and reading aloud in particular. Drawn from folk literature and the works of contemporary authors, these activities require little if anything in the way of props and should encourage students of varying abilities to participate. Reader's theater is a fine way to develop and reenforce language arts and speaking objectives.
SUBJ: Drama in education./ Readers' Theater--Study and teaching (Elementary)./ Language arts.

PROF 792 Ph-1 $7.95 P KA330
MORIN, ALICE. Newspaper theatre: creative play production for low budgets and no budgets. Fearon Teacher Aids/David S. Lake ISBN 0-8224-6349-0, 1989. unp. col. ill.
An excellent sourcebook of ideas for converting newspapers into costumes, backdrops, masks, decorations for plays and dramatic activities. The newspaper itself is not forgotten. Ideas for creating stories about photographs and cartoons is also included.
SUBJ: Scenery./ Costume.

PROF 796 Ph-1 $24.50 P KA331
SIERRA, JUDY. Children's traditional games: games from 137 countries and cultures. By Judy Sierra and Robert Kaminski. Oryx ISBN 0-89774-967-7; In Canada: Oryx, 1995. 232p. ill.
Includes bibliographies and indexes.
This treasury of 204 games from 137 various countries gives a brief history of games and describes their similarities and development. Types of traditional games are arranged alphabetically, followed by descriptions of games by country. Black line drawings illustrate patterns when needed. Each entry cites procedures, playing area required, number of players, and materials. Plans for 12 classroom projects (for third through sixth grade) using games in the library and a multicultural games festival are included. Useful resource for multicultural studies, math activities, and physical education classes. Group leaders for after school activities such as scouts will want to borrow this. (Parents' Shelf).
SUBJ: Games--Cross-cultural studies./ Games--Study and teaching./ Children and folklore.

PROF 796.1 Ph-1 $8.95 P KA332
ROWEN, LAWRENCE. Beyond winning: sports and games all kids want to play. Fearon ISBN 0-8224-3380-X, 1990. 94p. ill.
Includes appendix and index.
Integration of good teaching techniques with physical activities that all children can enjoy result in a very useful title for any physical education program or for recess activities. Clear and simple format and directions enhance usefulness.
SUBJ: Games./ Recreation.

PROF 808 Ph-2 $25.00 P KA333
ROBERTSON, DEBORAH. Super kids publishing company. By Deborah Robertson and Patricia Barry. Teacher Ideas Press/Libraries Unlimited ISBN 0-87287-704-3, 1990. 354p.
Includes appendices, bibliography and index.
Today's emphasis on the writing process is translated into structural activities, and learning centers that make heavy use of children's literature. Practical and yet innovative, this is a useful guide for teachers at all grade levels.
SUBJ: English language--Composition and exercises--Study and teaching.

PROF 808 Ph-1 $9.95 P KA334
ZARNOWSKI, MYRA. Learning about biographies: a reading-and-writing approach for children. National Council of Teachers of English/National Council for the Social Studies ISBN 0-8141-2778-9, 1990. 94p.
Includes bibliography and appendices.
This book "shows teachers in elementary and middle schools how to use biography as a vehicle for developing children's natural curiosity about people and the world around them to the point where they themselves investigate a particular life and, through the artful use of language, tell that human story to others." (Foreword). The activities outlined are simple, and can easily be incorporated into teaching at any grade level. This book may assist teachers in preventing students from developing the belief that biographical research equates to copying the first paragraph from the encyclopedia.
SUBJ: Biography (as a literary form)--Study and teaching (Elementary)./ Heroes--Biography--Methodology.

PROF 808.06 Ph-2 $23.50 T KA335
ROGINSKI, JIM. Behind the covers: interviews with authors and illustrators of books for children and young adults, Vol. I. Libraries Unlimited ISBN 0-87287-506-7, 1985. 249p.
Includes appendices and bibliography.
Following a format which begins with a biographical note, a perspective on the individual's work by the author, an interview and a bibliography of works and listing of awards and honors follow. Twenty-two authors and illustrators are included and librarians, teachers and older students should find this a useful resource in author studies.
Interviews with another 19 authors and illustrators follow in BEHIND THE COVERS, Vol. II (ISBN 0-87287-627-6, 1989).
SUBJ: Children--Books and reading./ Children's literature--Authorship./ Authors, American--20th century--Interviews./ Illustrators, American--20th century--Interviews.

PROF 808.3 Ph-2 $29.95 T KA336
BEST CHILDREN'S BOOKS IN THE WORLD: A TREASURY OF ILLUSTRATED STORIES. Edited by Byron Preiss. Project editor, Kathy Huck. Introduction by Jeffrey Garrett. Abrams ISBN 0-8109-1246-5, 1996. 319p. col. ill.
"Byron Preiss book."
This collection provides an opportunity for everyone to see some of the popular, beautifully illustrated stories from around the world. Most continents are represented with either an original story or a folktale. Hopefully this book will not be relegated to a "special" shelf, but will be on display for students and teachers to enjoy. Many of the books are award winners in country of origin. For multicultural studies.
SUBJ: Children's stories.

PROF 808.5 Ph-1 $35.00 T KA337
DAILEY, SHEILA. Putting the world in a nutshell: the art of the formula tale. Wilson ISBN 0-8242-0860-9, 1994. 118p.
Includes bibliographies.
A book about storytelling techniques which will be useful in helping teachers define and identify formula tales such as chain, cumulative, circle, endless, catch, compound triad, question, air castles, and good/bad. The ROVER (read, organize, visualize, energize, rehearse) technique for learning stories is excellent. Includes examples of formula tales.
SUBJ: Storytelling./ Tales--Classification./ Oral-formulaic analysis.

PROF 808.5 Ph-1 $11.00 P KA338
HEY! LISTEN TO THIS: STORIES TO READ ALOUD. Edited by Jim Trelease. Penguin ISBN 0-14-014653-9; In Canada: Penguin, 1992. 414p. ill.
Includes bibliographies and directory.
A collection of 48 read-aloud chapters which will be useful for teachers, librarians, and parents reading aloud to children, ages five through nine. Includes favorite folktales and fairy tales as well as chapters from classic children's books such as WHERE THE RED FERN GROWS and MR. POPPER'S PENGUINS. (Parents' Shelf).
SUBJ: Children's literature.

PROF 808.5 Ph-3 $17.50 P KA339
LAUGHLIN, MILDRED KNIGHT. Readers theatre for children: scripts and script development. By Mildred Knight Laughlin and Kathy Howard Latrobe. Teacher Ideas Press/Libraries Unlimited ISBN 0-87287-753-1, 1990. 138p.
Includes bibliography and index.
Share sixty-seven favorite books with readings taken or adapted from them that involve students. Techniques for scripting works are included. For use where this type of activity is not already ongoing.
SUBJ: Readers' Theater./ Plays--Presentation./ Stage adaptations.

PROF 808.5 Ph-2 $34.00 P KA340
LIVO, NORMA J. Storytelling folklore sourcebook. By Norma J. Livo and Sandra A. Rietz. Libraries Unlimited ISBN 0-87287-601-2, 1991. 384p.
Includes bibliography and index.
This book "aims to bring understanding to how folklore of ancient times still influences us in our speech and actions today. It is by no means comprehensive but it contains information and folklore material that can make us all more multiculturally literate." (Introduction). Contents include information of the technique of storytelling, customs, heroes, cultural artifacts, and patterns.
SUBJ: Storytelling./ Tales./ Folklore.

PROF 808.5   Ph-1 $15.00   P   KA341
MALLAN, KERRY. Children as storytellers. Photos by Mick Mallan.
Primary English Teaching Association/Heinemann ISBN 0-435-08779-7,
1992. 87p. ill.
    Originally published: Primary English Teaching Association, Newtown,
    NSW, Australia, 1991.
    Includes bibliographies.
    Explores ways for teachers to give children opportunities to create
    and retell oral stories. Includes exercises and presentation techniques.
    Story mapping as a memory aid is discussed.
    SUBJ: Storytelling--Study and teaching./ Language arts.

PROF 808.8   Ph-1 $45.00   T   KA342
BAUER, CAROLINE FELLER. Celebrations: read-aloud holiday and theme
book programs. Illus. by Lynn Gates Bredeson. Wilson ISBN 0-8242-
0708-4, 1985. 301p. ill.
    Includes bibliographies and index.
    Holiday programming ideas that are "pre-packaged and ready-to-go;
    no defrosting or cooking needed!...Each chapter, or program, follows
    the same general order: prose selections, poems, activities (crafts,
    treats, creative writing, etc.) and a booklist." The programs which
    can be used in the library or classroom present fresh ideas and utilize
    materials that are readily available. The bibliographies can be used as
    a selection aid.
    SUBJ: Children--Books and reading./ Libraries, Children's--Activity
    programs./ Activity programs in education./ Holidays.

PROF 808.8   Ph-3 $17.00   T   KA343
BOOK OF VIRTUES FOR YOUNG PEOPLE: A TREASURY OF GREAT
MORAL STORIES. Edited with commentary by William J. Bennett. Illus.
by Andrea Wisnewski. Simon & Schuster ISBN 0-689-81613-8; In
Canada: Distican, 1997. 374p. ill.
    Originally published: Silver Burdett, 1996.
    Includes index.
    A compilation of newly illustrated stories, folktales, and poems that
    exhibit positive character traits. Each section is devoted to a single
    virtue which is defined in a brief note. The treasury depicts such
    morals as courage, perseverance, loyalty, honesty, compassion, and
    self-discipline. Useful tool in schools where values education is part of
    the curriculum. For reading aloud. (Parents' Shelf).
    SUBJ: Conduct of life--Literary collections.

VCR PROF 808.8   Ph-3 $175.00   OD   KA344
LITERATURE TO ENJOY AND WRITE ABOUT, SERIES 1
(Videocassette). Pied Piper/AIMS Multimedia QLWA01/VGE3, 1989. 5
1/2" VHS videocassettes color.
    Includes teacher's guides and bibliographies.
    Over ten different books in genres such as adventure, mystery,
    biography, realistic fiction and humorous stories spark whole language
    activities. There are opportunities for the use of higher level thinking
    skills and for cooperative learning experiences as students are
    involved in the study of these books. An enrichment activity that
    would have benefited from being in another format.
    Contents: Diary - journal; realistic fiction (19min); New endings:
    adventure (19min); Problem solving: humorous stories (/18min);
    Mapping: mysteries (20min); Interviewing: biographies (22min).
    SUBJ: Literature--Study and teaching (Elementary).

VCR PROF 808.8   Ph-3 $175.00   OD   KA345
LITERATURE TO ENJOY AND WRITE ABOUT, SERIES 2
(Videocassette). Pied Piper/AIMS Multimedia QL-2V, 1990. 5 1/2"
VHS videocassettes color.
    Includes teacher's guides and bibliographies.
    Recommended for use with middle graders, this second series of
    LITERATURE TO ENJOY AND WRITE ABOUT introduces five
    additional writing activities that enrich the reading process. Each video
    presents excerpts from two books in the genres of realistic fiction,
    non-fiction, fantasy, animal stories and historical fiction; the first
    presentation followed by examples of the writing mode clearly
    presented by three students and an adult; the second excerpt is meant
    for student participation. Requiring teacher support, this series
    encourages cooperative learning, enhanced reading comprehension,
    and provides a refreshing approach to creative writing projects.
    Contents: Friendly letter: realistic fiction (23min); Persuasive writing:
    non-fiction (18min); Book review: fantasy (24min); Sequel: animal
    stories (22min); Readers theatre: historical fiction (26min).
    SUBJ: Literature--Study and teaching (Elementary).

PROF 808.81   Ph-1 $6.00   P   KA346
KOCH, KENNETH. Wishes, lies, and dreams: teaching children to write
poetry. By Kenneth Koch and the students of P.S. 61 in New York City.
HarperCollins ISBN 0-06-080530-7, c1970, 1980. 309p. (Perennial
library).
    Results of an experiment conducted by the poet Kenneth Koch at P.

S. 61, on the Lower East Side of New York. Pages 1-55 recount how
it was done. The rest of the book consists of an astonishingly
spontaneous and imaginative collection of the poems the children
wrote, grouped by the "ideas" he used as assignments--metaphors,
dreams, noises, wishes, class collaborations, etc. Both practical and
inspiring.
    SUBJ: Poetry--Study and teaching./ Children's writings.

PROF 809   Ph-1 $19.95   P   KA347
AMMON, BETTE DEBRUYNE. Handbook for the Newbery Medal and
Honor Books, 1980-1989. By Bette D. Ammon and Gale W. Sherman.
Alleyside Press ISBN 0-913853-15-1, 1991. 274p.
    Includes bibliography, directory and indexes.
    Provides background information on award winning and honor books,
    on the selection process, and on John Newbery. Each title is shown
    with: genre, theme, readability, interest level, reviews, author
    information, citation for the text of the acceptance speech, plot
    summary, reading aloud tips, booktalk outlines, and curriculum
    implications for various subjects. Each chapter concludes with a list of
    comparable books and of other works by the author. Titles can be
    accessed through an author/illustrator/title index and subject index
    which includes curriculum areas.
    SUBJ: Newbery Medal books./ Children's literature--Bibliography./
    Children's literature--Reviews./ Books and reading--Best books.

PROF 809   Ph-1 $31.00   T   KA348
CULLINAN, BERNICE E. Literature and the child. 3rd ed. Harcourt Brace
Jovanovich ISBN 0-15-500985-0, 1993. 755p. ill.
    Includes bibliographies and indices.
    This should prove an invaluable tool for teachers and librarians who
    seek to bring child and literature together. "The text is divided into
    three segments. Part I, 'The Child,' describes the developmental
    foundations, according to Piagetian theory, of the study of children's
    literature. Part II, 'The Books,' is organized according to genre and
    builds around themes that complement and expand the school
    curriculum. Part III, 'The World of Children's Books,' contains chapters
    on the literature of many cultures and on the history of children's
    literature." The content of this book is very important, however, the
    "Teaching Ideas" are invaluable tools for generating interest in the
    best of literature. The "Landmark" boxes include discussions of
    books that exemplify a standard in the genre. Extensive bibliographies
    and appendices (Children's Book Awards, Book Selection Aids, Books
    about Authors and Illustrators, Children's Periodicals, Publishers of
    Children's Books, Holiday books, birthdays of Selected Authors and
    Illustrators).
    SUBJ: Books and reading./ Children's literature.

PROF 809   Ph-2 $21.95   P   KA349
EGOFF, SHEILA. New republic of childhood: a critical guide to Canadian
children's literature in English. Rev. ed. Oxford ISBN 0-19-540576-5,
1990. 392p.
    An outstanding student of Canadian children's literature--that is, that
    by Canadian authors and about Canadian subjects--analyzes the
    Canadian contribution to this field of literature. Focuses particularly on
    Indian legends and folklore, history and biography, and fiction--
    historical, realistic, and animal tales. Selective bibliographies. Essential
    reading for the teacher and librarian who would be really
    knowledgeable about children's literature in English.
    SUBJ: Canadian literature--History and criticism./ Children's literature-
    -Bibliography.

PROF 809   Ph-2 $32.50   P   KA350
GREESON, JANET. Name that book! Questions and answers on
outstanding children's books. By Janet Greeson and Karen Taha.
Scarecrow ISBN 0-8108-3151-1, 1996. 247p.
    Includes index.
    Based on the renewed popularity of "Battle of the Books," the
    authors provide questions, suggestions and rules for conducting the
    game. Additional curriculum-related activities are also included.
    SUBJ: Children's literature--Miscellanea./ Educational games./ Literary
    recreations.

PROF 809   Ph-1 $11.95   P   KA351
HAZARD, PAUL. Books, children and men. 5th ed. Translated by
Marguerite Mitchell. Horn Book ISBN 0-87675-059-5, 1983. 176p.
    Includes index and bibliography.
    Short but compact critique of children's literature and reading; a
    "delightful and discerning study" essential for knowledgeability in
    this field!
    SUBJ: Books and reading./ Children's literature--History and criticism.

PROF 809   Ph-3 $22.95   T   KA352
HORN BOOK MAGAZINE. Newbery and Caldecott medal books,
1966-1975: with acceptance papers & related material chiefly from the

Horn Book Magazine. Edited by Lee Kingman. Horn Book ISBN 0-87675-003-X, 1975. 321p. ill.

Supplements earlier volumes including Newbery and Caldecott Medal books: 1956-1965 and follows same pattern of information about prize-winning authors and illustrators. Additional contents: A decade of Newbery books in perspective, John Rowe Townsend; Picture books, art and illustration, Barbara Bader; The Honor Books: 1966-1975; Honoring the Honor Books, Elizabeth Johnson. NEWBERY AND CALDECOTT MEDAL BOOKS, 1976-1985 (ISBN 0-87675-004-8, 1986).
SUBJ: Newbery Medal books./ Caldecott Medal books.

PROF 809   Ph-3 $22.95   T   KA353
HORN BOOK MAGAZINE. Newbery Medal books: 1922-1955: with their authors' acceptance papers, biographies, and related materials chiefly from the Horn Book Magazine. Edited by Bertha Mahony Miller and Elinor Whitney Field. Horn Book ISBN 0-87675-000-5, c1957. 458p. ill. (Horn Book papers).

An anthology of information on the books selected annually to receive the Newbery Medal for "the most distinguished contribution to American literature for children." For 34 winners there is given a book note, an excerpt from the book, a biographical note, and (where available) the acceptance paper.
SUBJ: Newbery Medal books./ Children's literature--History and criticism./ Literary prizes.

PROF 809   Ph-3 $94.00   T   KA354
JONES, DOLORES BLYTHE. Children's literature awards and winners: a directory of prizes, authors, and illustrators. 3rd ed. Neal-Schuman in association with Gale Research ISBN 0-8103-6900-1, 1994. 671p.

Includes bibliography and index.

Provides "quick access to the complete award history of an individual author or illustrator. It also documents the award history of a particular title...Contains descriptions for 211 awards. More than 5,000 titles and nearly 7,000 authors and illustrators are listed." Part one, Directory of Awards; Part two, Authors and Illustrators; Part three, Selected Bibliography, Award Index, Subject Index of Awards, Author/Illustrator Index, Title Index.
SUBJ: Children's literature./ Literary prizes.

PROF 809   Ph-1 $6.95   P   KA355
KOBRIN, BEVERLY. Eyeopeners II: children's books to answer children's questions about the world around them. Scholastic ISBN 0-590-48402-8; In Canada: Scholastic, 1995. 305p.

Includes bibliographies and indexes.

An update of EYEOPENERS, this nonfiction selection tool provides ideas on how to use nonfiction and the role of librarian as teacher. The Quick-Link Index combines subject headings and titles. The heart of the book is the annotated citations for 800 books which are arranged by subjects. A solid resource for interdisciplinary studies.
SUBJ: Children's literature--History and criticism.

PROF 809   Ph-2 $18.95   T   KA356
SENDAK, MAURICE. Caldecott and Co.: notes on books & pictures. Farrar, Straus & Giroux ISBN 0-374-22598-2; In Canada: HarperCollins, 1988. 216p. ill.

Writing about a variety of topics based on the theme of picture books, illustration, and authors and illustrators, the noted author/illustrator shares his views about children's literature. Also included are autobiographical essays, interviews, and speeches.
SUBJ: Authorship./ Children's literature.

PROF 809   Ph-1 $25.95   T   KA357
SMITH, LILLIAN. Unreluctant years: a critical approach to children's literature. With a new introduction by Kay E. Vandergrift. American Library Association ISBN 0-8389-0557-9, c1953, 1991. 183p.

Includes index.

A new introduction reaffirms the continuing importance of Smith's guide to book selection for children. First published in 1953, this small book reinforces the importance of critical selection for both the young person and the library program.
SUBJ: Childrens' literature--History and criticism./ Libraries, Children's--Book selection.

PROF 809   Ph-1 $38.05   T   KA358
SUTHERLAND, ZENA. Children and books. 9th ed. Longman ISBN 0-673-99733-2, 1997. 720p. col. ill.

Includes bibliographies, directory and indexes.

Selectors' Choice, 21st ed.

"The ninth edition is meant for all adults who are interested in bringing children and books together, but it is designed particularly for children's literature classes in education and English departments in library schools, colleges, and universities." (Preface, p.xi) Anyone working in the field of children's literature--librarians, public or school,

and teachers in any educational setting--should purchase this book. Edition has been revised and updated. Bibliographies have been enlarged to include new genres and new selection aids. In part four, the "Areas and Issues" section, topics addressed include "Effects of Computers on Reading and Literature;" "Censorship: Issues and Solutions;" "Make Way for Books;" "Children's Book Awards;" "Windows and Mirrors: International Children's Books and the American Child." An important book for all school collections.
SUBJ: Children's literature--History and criticism./ Children--Books and reading.

PROF 809   Ph-3 $25.00   T   KA359
TOUCHSTONES: REFLECTIONS ON THE BEST IN CHILDREN'S LITERATURE, VOL. 1. Edited by Perry Nodelman. Childrens Literature Association ISBN 0-937263-01-X, 1985. 309p.

Twenty-nine essays discuss fiction titles placed on the Children's Literature Association "Touchstones" list because of unanimous agreement as to their merit and significance. The list includes (in part): LITTLE WOMEN, THE SECRET GARDEN, THE MOFFATS, THE WIND IN THE WILLOWS, and the Narnia books. The essays about the selection and work itself will serve as the basis for booktalks to teachers and students.
Vol. 2: FAIRY TALES, FABLES, MYTHS, LEGENDS, AND POETRY (ISBN 0-937263-02-8, 1987), "Seeking to show why and how some myths, legends, folktales and poetry are better, why and how some works of literature are deemed touchstones" (v) these 20 essays provide valuable continuing education for librarians and language arts teachers.
Vol. 3: PICTURE BOOKS (ISBN 0-937263-03-6, 1989) examines the contributions the art has made to particular picture books, e.g. WHERE THE WILD THINGS ARE, THE FIVE HUNDRED HATS OF BARTHOLOMEW CUBBINS, and MILLIONS OF CATS through nineteen essays.
SUBJ: Children's literature--Criticism./ Children's literature--Study and teaching.

PROF 809   Ph-2 $24.00   P   KA360
TUTEN-PUCKETT, KATHARYN E. My name in books: a guide to character names in children's literature. Libraries Unlimited ISBN 0-87287-979-8, 1993. 242p.

Includes indexes.

An alphabetical listing by character's first name. Each citation includes author, title, illustrator, publisher, publication date, number of pages, type of book, LC catalog number, ISBN, and brief annotation. Awards and honors the book has won are cited. Unique feature is listing of Reader's Choice Awards. Useful to identify titles when only the characters' names are known as well as to locate books for children which contain characters with their names or those of their friends.
SUBJ: Children's literature--History and criticism--Dictionaries./ Characters and characteristics in literature--Dictionaries./ Names, Personal, in literature--Dictionaries.

PROF 812   Ph-2 $25.00   P   KA361
ANDERSON, DEE. Amazingly easy puppet plays: 42 new scripts for one-person puppetry. American Library Association ISBN 0-8389-0697-4, 1997. 235p. ill.

Includes bibliographies, directory and index.

Step-by-step instructions for developing puppet skits which require 27 different puppets. Tips are included on bringing puppets to life, body language for puppets, and how to stage the skits. Skits are divided into Miggs and Jiggs; From the Library's Shelves; and About Books, Reading, and Libraries. Appendixes: Alphabetical list of puppets and skits; how to make almost no-sew, inexpensive puppets; picture books to present with puppets; patterns and scripts; puppet supplies; and an index of play titles.
SUBJ: Puppet plays./ Puppet theater.

PROF 812   Ph-2 $19.50   P   KA362
FREDERICKS, ANTHONY D. Frantic frogs and other frankly fractured folktales for readers theatre. Illus. by Anthony Allan Stoner and Joan Garner. Teacher Ideas Press/Libraries Unlimited ISBN 1-56308-174-1, 1993. 123p.

Includes bibliographies and directory.

Splendid ideas that combine readers theater and folktale parodies. Brief section outlines the value of readers' theatre and presentation techniques. Combine with contemporary "folktales" such as THE STINKY CHEESE MAN and THE TRUE STORY OF THE THREE LITTLE PIGS.
SUBJ: Readers' Theater./ Fairy tales--Parodies, imitations, etc.

PROF 812   Ph-2 $40.00   T   KA363
STORIES ON STAGE: SCRIPTS FOR READER'S THEATER. Edited by Aaron Shepard. Wilson ISBN 0-8242-0851-X, 1993. 162p.

Includes bibliography and directory.
Based on quality children's literature, these selections range from primary grades to junior high school. Each selection is identified by genre, culture, theme, grade level, number of roles, and time. Useful for literature-based curriculum.
SUBJ: Plays./ Readers' Theater.

PROF 812   Ph-2 $25.00   P   KA364
VIGIL, ANGEL. Teatro!: Hispanic plays for young people. Teacher Ideas Press ISBN 1-56308-371-X, 1996. 169p. ill.
Includes glossary and bibliography.
Presents 14 plays for grades 1-8 which reflect the Hispanic culture of the American Southwest. Subject areas include: folktales, animal fables, holiday plays, and an historical play. Rights for production and limited reproduction of scripts for nonprofessionals are granted. For multicultural studies.
SUBJ: Hispanic Americans--Drama./ Plays.

PROF 812   Ph-2 $19.50   P   KA365
WRIGHT, DENISE ANTON. One-person puppet plays. Illus. by John Wright. Teacher Ideas Press/Libraries Unlimited ISBN 0-87287-742-6, 1990. 236p. ill.
Includes appendices.
As the title implies, simple scripts, puppets, stages and presentation ideas constitute this useful addition to a collection of professional titles. Teachers and librarians will find an easy entry into the use of puppetry as an enhancement for a variety of teaching and enrichment applications. Adaptations from folklore, fables, seasonal themes and reading and library emphasis can be found for children ages 2-9.
SUBJ: Puppet plays./ Puppet making.

PROF 820.8   Ph-1 $15.95   T   KA366
JUBA THIS AND JUBA THAT. Selected by Virginia Tashjian. Illus. by Nadine Bernard Westcott. Little, Brown ISBN 0-316-83234-0; In Canada: Little, Brown, 1995. 106p. ill.
Includes index.
Available from National Library Service for the Blind and Physically Handicapped as talking book TB02998.
A classic collection of chants, poetry, rhymes, fingerplays, riddles, songs (with melody), and tongue twisters. Selected by an experienced storyteller for use in the "stretch period." Directions are provided along with text of a few special stories such as "The Hobyahs," "The Snooks Family, and the like.
SUBJ: Storytelling--Collections./ Literature--Collections./ Finger play./ Songs.

PROF B COURLAND   Ph-1 $16.95   T   KA367
JAFFE, NINA. Voice for the people: the life and work of Harold Courlander. Henry Holt ISBN 0-8050-3444-7; In Canada: Fitzhenry & Whiteside, 1997. 177p. ill.
Includes chronology, bibliographies, discography, directory and index.
Harold Courlander first journeyed to the Caribbean to write, but he found the folklore of the people so interesting that he began gathering the material which later developed into his well-known anthologies. He moved on to delve into the stories of Native Americans and African Americans living in the South. His contributions to storytelling and literature were great. This biography presents him as a warm, creative author as well as a scholar. For multicultural studies.
SUBJ: Courlander, Harold./ Folklorists--Biography./ Afro-Americans--Folklore./ Folklore--Caribbean Area./ Caribbean Area--Folklore./ Folklore--Africa./ Africa--Folklore./ Indians of North America--Southwest, New--Folklore.

PROF B GAVER, M   Ph-3 $25.00   T   KA368
GAVER, MARY VIRGINIA. Braided cord: memoirs of a school librarian. Scarecrow ISBN 0-8108-2032-3, 1988. 233p. ill.
Includes appendix, bibliography and index.
Spanning a fifty year period this respected librarian and first editor of ESLC tells of the development of elementary school libraries and her major contributions to this happening.
SUBJ: Gaver, Mary Virginia./ Librarians--Biography./ School libraries--History--20th century.

PROF B POTTER,B   Ph-2 3-5/4 $15.95   L   KA369
WALLNER, ALEXANDRA. Beatrix Potter. Holiday House ISBN 0-8234-1181-8, 1995. unp. col. ill.
Beatrix Potter's early love of animals, her artistic skills, and her attempts to become independent from her parents are all covered in this pictorial study of her life. Useful tool for introducing Potter's books to the middle grades.
SUBJ: Potter, Beatrix./ Authors, English./ Artists./ Women authors, English./ Women artists.

PROF 973   Ph-2 $39.00   T   KA370
BLACK HISTORY MONTH RESOURCE BOOK. Edited by Mary Ellen Snodgrass. Foreward by Bertha Calloway. Gale Research ISBN 0-8103-9151-1, 1993. 430p.
Includes bibliography, directory and indexes.
An extensive collection of activities arranged by broad subject areas such as art and architecture, cooking, math, religion, sewing and fashion, speech and drama, and storytelling. Each entry cites grade level or audience followed by procedures, resources, budget, and alternative applications. An appendix includes: books, articles, publishers, films, videos, video distributors, music distributors, dance ensembles, theater companies, software packagers, computer networks, supplies, and resource centers. Indexes include: entry, age/grade level, and budget. Excellent resource book for multicultural studies.
SUBJ: Afro-Americans--Study and teaching--Activity programs.

PROF 973   Ph-2 $14.95   P   KA371
MANY VOICES: TRUE TALES FROM AMERICA'S PAST. By the National Storytelling Association. National Storytelling Press ISBN 1-879991-17-9, 1995. 206p. ill.
Includes directory and indexes.
Teacher's guide available separately (ISBN 1-879991-20-9, 1995), $7.95.
Individual voices of many storytellers and tales from the oral tradition are arranged chronologically from 1640 to the present and cover political, economic, and social events and personalities in America's history. Teacher's guide in separate volume contains additional background information, introductory activities, provocative discussion questions, and engaging follow-up activities. Stories will serve well as independent reading selections, storytelling sources, or for reading aloud; and both stories and guide will be excellent resources for interdisciplinary curriculum for social studies units on American history.
SUBJ: United States--History--Anecdotes./ Storytelling--Collections.

REFERENCE

REF 006.7   Ph-1 A $24.95 T KA372
MULTIMEDIA, THE COMPLETE GUIDE. DK Publishing ISBN 0-7894-0422-2, 1996. 192p. col. ill.
    Includes bibliographies, glossary and index.
    A comprehensive overview of multimedia technology includes five chapters covering software, workings of computers and multimedia machines, creation of multimedia, and future predictions. Terms are defined and backed up with intricate diagrams. Familiar titles (Encarta, Myst, Cinemania, etc.) on business, education, reference, and entertainment are used to explain and illustrate how multimedia is created and functions. Glossary makes the specialized vocabulary user friendly.
    SUBJ: Interactive multimedia./ Computers./ High technology.

REF 011.62   Ph-2 5-A $21.95 P KA373
YOUR READING: AN ANNOTATED BOOKLIST FOR MIDDLE SCHOOL AND JUNIOR HIGH. 1995-96 ed. Edited by Barbara G. Samuels and G. Kylene Beers. Foreword by Joan Lowery Nixon. National Council of Teachers of English ISBN 0-8141-5943-5, 1996. 381p. (NCTE bibliography series).
    Includes directory and indexes.
    Bibliography of recommended books selected from recent publishing seasons includes a broad range of topics including coming-of-age fiction, fantasy and horror, historical fiction, science fiction, drama, poetry, short stories, history, science, sports, and trivia. Descriptive annotations are directed toward young people. Students will be able to easily use this format to identify books for reports or leisure reading.
    SUBJ: Young adult literature--Bibliography./ Junior high school libraries--Book lists./ Middle school libraries--Book lists.

REF 016.811   Ph-3 5-6 $58.00 T KA374
INDEX TO POETRY FOR CHILDREN AND YOUNG PEOPLE: 1988-1992. Compiled by G. Meredith Blackburn III. Wilson ISBN 0-8242-0861-7, 1994. 400p.
    An index by author, title, subject, and first line to poems in collections for children. Approximate grade levels are noted for each anthology included.
    INDEX TO CHILDREN'S POETRY (ISBN 0-8242-0021-7, 1942).
    INDEX TO CHILDREN'S POETRY, FIRST SUPPLEMENT (ISBN 0-8242-0022-5, 1954).
    INDEX TO CHILDREN'S POETRY, SECOND SUPPLEMENT (ISBN 0-8242-0023-3, 1965).
    INDEX TO POETRY FOR CHILDREN AND YOUNG PEOPLE: 1964-1969 (ISBN 0-8242-0435-2, 1972).
    INDEX TO POETRY FOR CHILDREN AND YOUNG PEOPLE: 1970-1975 (ISBN 0-8242-0621-5, 1978).
    INDEX TO POETRY FOR CHILDREN AND YOUNG PEOPLE: 1976-1981 (ISBN 08242-0681-9, 1984).
    INDEX TO POETRY FOR CHILDREN AND YOUNG PEOPLE: 1982-1987 (ISBN 0-8242-0773-4, 1988).
    SUBJ: Poetry--Indexes./ Children's poetry--Indexes.

REF 016.811   Ph-3 A $25.00 P KA375
SNOW, KATHLEEN. Subject index for children & young people to Canadian poetry in English. 2nd ed. Compiled by Kathleen Snow, Esther Gorosh, and Margaret Harper. Canadian Library Association ISBN 0-88802-202-6, 1986. 182p.

Includes collections of Canadian poetry in English listed in print. Chosen to fit curricula of Canadian school systems and interests of ages six to fourteen.
    SUBJ: Canadian poetry (English)--Indexes./ Children's poetry, Canadian (English)--Indexes.

CDR REF 028.7   Ph-1 3-A $54.95 OD KA376
MICROSOFT BOOKSHELF: MULTIMEDIA REFERENCE LIBRARY, 1998 ed. School ed. (CD-ROM). Microsoft ISBN 1-57231-619-5; In Canada: Microsoft Canada, 1997. 1 CD-ROM color.
    Includes user's guide and teacher's activity guide.
    Also available for Macintosh, $54.95.
    System requirements: Multimedia PC with a 486SX/33 MHz or higher processor; Microsoft Windows 95 operating system or Microsoft Windows NT Workstation operating system version 4.0; 8MB of memory, 12MB for Windows NT Workstation 4.0; at least 10MB of available hard-disk space; double-speed CD-ROM drive; audio board and headphones or speakers; SVGA 256-color monitor; Microsoft Mouse or compatible pointing device recommended; modem required for Internet and monthly updates.
    A superb reference tool which includes a zip code directory and eight other standard references such as the WORLD ALMANAC, ROGET'S THESAURUS, THE AMERICAN HERITAGE DICTIONARY, a dictionary of quotations, a world atlas, a chronology, and a desk encyclopedia. In conjunction with the Internet interface, this edition also includes an Internet directory and a computer and Internet dictionary. The interface is straightforward and easily accessible by students and adults.
    SUBJ: Reference books--Software./ Software--Reference books./ Encyclopedias and dictionaries--Software./ Software--Encyclopedias and dictionaries./ Atlases--Software./ Software--Atlases./ Internet (Computer network)--Directories--Software./ Software--Internet (Computer network)--Directories.

REF 030   Ph-1 4-A $11.95 P OD KA377
ANTHONY, SUSAN C. Facts plus: an almanac of essential information. New 3rd ed. Instructional Resources Company ISBN 1-879478-10-2, 1995. 250p. ill., maps.
    Includes activity book.
    Includes bibliography and index.
    What better way to introduce students to research than this readable, fact-filled, illustrated compilation. Information is divided into ten chapters: Time and Space; Science and Health; The Earth and its People; The United States; Maps; Libraries and Books; The English Language; Writing, Music and Art; Math and Numbers; and Handbook (study skills). Recommended purchase for reference collections and individual classroom use.
    SUBJ: Almanacs./ Miscellanea.

REF 031   Ph-1 P-2 $218.00 L OD KA378
CHILDCRAFT: THE HOW AND WHY LIBRARY. World Book, Inc., 1964-. 15v. col. ill., maps, annual.
    Includes bibliographies.
    A browsing and informational set especially designed for preschool and primary grade use in choice of content, vocabulary, illustration, and typographical format. Can be read to and with children of these ages and alone by better readers; it does not talk down to the child. Recent editions enlarged and improved. Includes CHILDCRAFT

DICTIONARY available only with the encyclopedia set. Highly recommended as a useful source for creative teaching.

Contents: v1 Once upon a time; v2 Time to read; v3 Stories and poems; v4 World and space; v5 About animals; v6 The Green kingdom; v7 Story of the sea; v8 About us; v9 Holidays and birthdays; v10 Places to know; v11 Make and do; v12 How things work; v13 Mathemagic; v14 About me; v15 Guide and index. Supplements available are DINOSAURS (ISBN 0-7166-0687-9, 1987); PEOPLE TO KNOW (ISBN 0-7166-0689-5, 1989); I WAS WONDERING (ISBN 0-7166-0691-7, 1991); PETS AND OTHER ANIMALS (ISBN 0-7166-0692-5, 1992); A LOOK INTO SPACE (ISBN 0-7166-0694-1, 1994); OUR AMAZING BODIES (ISBN 0-7166-0695-X, 1995); EXPLORING THE OCEAN (ISBN 0-7166-0696-8, 1996); SCIENCE, SCIENCE EVERYWHERE (ISBN 0-7166-0697-6, 1997).

SUBJ: Children's literature--Collections./ Encyclopedias and dictionaries.

REF 031　　　　　　Ph-3 3-5　　$199.00　L OD KA379

CHILDREN'S BRITANNICA. 4th ed., (1995 revision). Encyclopedia Britannica ISBN 0-85229-242-2, 1995. 20v. col. ill.

Includes index.

Over 30,000 topics focus on important people, places, events and things. Unsigned articles, detailed illustrations, and a full-color atlas in volume 19 provide basic information in a readable style and good sized type face. Certainly not as extensive in scope as other encyclopedias, it does have a very useful and extensive index volume and will serve the majority of middle grade student's research needs.

SUBJ: Encyclopedias and dictionaries.

REF 031　　　　　　Ph-3 5-6　　$395.00　L OD KA380

COMPTON'S ENCYCLOPEDIA AND FACT-INDEX. Compton c/o Contemporary Books, 1968-. 26v. col. ill., maps, annual.

Original title: COMPTON'S PICTURED ENCYCLOPEDIA.

Illustrated fact-index in every volume.

Includes bibliographies.

Yearbook available for $17.00 OD.

Authoritative general encyclopedia which utilizes a regular program of revision and up-dating. Particularly useful for the subject outlines and quick fact outlines for the states.

SUBJ: Encyclopedias and dictionaries.

CDR REF 031　　　　　Ph-1 3-6　　$108.00　　OD KA381

COMPTON'S MULTIMEDIA ENCYCLOPEDIA (CD-ROM). Compton c/o Contemporary Books ISBN 1-55730-125-5, 1994. 1 CD-ROM.

Also available for Macintosh and Windows.

Pricing varies.

System requirements: 80286 IBM or IBM compatible with 20 megabyte hard drive, 640K VGA card, color monitor, CD-ROM drive with controller card, speech adapter and card, mouse.

Switch from text to pictures to maps to sound with ease in this 5,000 plus article interactive encyclopedia. Special features include: Picture Explorer, World Atlas, Idea search, Topic tree, U.S. History Timeline and the text of the Merriam-Webster dictionary. An encyclopedia on the cutting edge.

SUBJ: Encyclopedias and dictionaries--Software./ Software-- Encyclopedias and dictionaries.

REF 031　　　　　　Ph-1 4-6　　$95.00　T　KA382

KANE, JOSEPH NATHAN. Famous first facts. 5th ed. By Joseph Nathan Kane, Steven Anzovin, and Janet Podell. Wilson ISBN 0-8242-0930-3, 1997. 1350p.

Includes index.

"A record of first happenings, discoveries, and inventions in American history" are arranged chronologically within clearly delineated subject headings. Additional indexes include year, month, and day of occurence; personal names; and geographical location. A basic reference source.

SUBJ: Encyclopedias and dictionaries.

REF 031　　　　　　Ph-2　　$29.95　T　KA383

KINGFISHER CHILDREN'S ENCYCLOPEDIA. REV. ED. Edited by John Paton. Kingfisher ISBN 1-85697-800-1, 1992. 902p. col. ill., maps.

Includes indexes.

Students should be introduced to quick reference books and this is an outstanding one. If you only need a small bit of information and a picture or a map, this book will do. Coverage is comprehensive, though brief. Although the information is arranged alphabetically, the indexes clearly illustrate to students the need for consulting an index even in an encyclopedia.

SUBJ: Encyclopedias and dictionaries.

CDR REF 031　　　　　Ph-1 4-A　　$69.95　　OD KA384

MICROSOFT ENCARTA 97 ENCYCLOPEDIA. Deluxe school ed. (CD-ROM). Microsoft ISBN 1-57231-481-8; In Canada: Microsoft Canada, 1996. 2 CD-ROMs color.

Includes user's guide and teacher's guide.

Also available for Macintosh (ISBN 1-57231-482-6, 1996), $69.95.

System requirements: Multimedia PC with a 486DX/33 MHz or higher microprocessor; Microsoft Windows 95 operating system, Windows 3.1 or later operating system, or Windows NT version 3.51 or later operating system; 8MB of memory (RAM) for Windows 95 or Window 3.1, 12MB for Windows NT; 14MB of available hard-disk space for Windows 95 or Windows NT, 21MB for Windows 3.1; double-speed or faster CD-ROM drive; SVGA, 256-color monitor supporting 640x480 or higher resolution; local bus video with 1MB or more of VRAM; Microsoft Mouse or compatible pointing device; audio board and speakers or headphones. To use Encarta Yearbook, Web Links, and monthly on-line updates: Modem (9600 bps or faster); Access to the Internet; 4MB of additional hard-disk space, plus 1MB for each monthly installment.

This two CD multimedia encyclopedia is a much improved reference tool. Over 30,000 articles and a vast array of new media features are included. The switching of CDs is logical and not cumbersome for students. The integrated on-line functions are easy to configure and use.

URL: http://www.encarta.com -- Encarta Yearbook and monthly on-line updates.

SUBJ: Encyclopedias and dictionaries--Software./ Software-- Encyclopedias and dictionaries./ Interactive media.

REF 031　　　　　　Ph-2 4-6　　$479.00　T OD KA385

NEW BOOK OF KNOWLEDGE. Grolier ISBN 0-7172-8028-2, 1997. 21v. col. ill.

Yearbook available for $21.95 OD.

A completely new and up-to-date encyclopedia intended to serve the curricular and interest needs of intermediate grades. Information arranged alphabetically in unit letter volumes retaining the how-to-do-it and story-features beloved from the former set. Outstanding for its format, with a wealth of appealing and authentic illustrations in full color, with very legible type. Articles somewhat longer and under fewer headings than in other comparable sets, but copious cross-references and a fact-index in each volume on colored paper guide to other headings in entire set. Teachers should note preface; pronunciation guide and note on use of index is only in A-volume. Separate index (reprinted from each volume) available only to school and libraries.

SUBJ: Encyclopedias and dictionaries.

REF 031　　　　　　Ph-1 5-A　　$644.00　L OD KA386

WORLD BOOK ENCYCLOPEDIA. World Book, Inc., 1931-. 22v. ill. annual.

Yearbook available for $21.95 OD.

Extensively updated and set in a new san serif typeface, this fourth major revision of this standard reference work is even more attractive and comprehensive. The latter factor, however, tends to place the usability of this tool at a higher level than earlier editions. The smaller typeface and writing style support the needs of upper elementary school and above students.

SUBJ: Encyclopedias and dictionaries.

REF 031　　　　　　Ph-1　　$160.00　T OD KA387

WORLD BOOK ENCYCLOPEDIA OF PEOPLE AND PLACES. World Book, Inc. ISBN 0-7166-3796-0, 1997. 6v. col. ill., maps.

Includes index.

This six volume series presents "individual nations and other political or geographic units through an article or series of articles. All articles are covered within a two-page spread." Running heads, colorful and appealing illustrations, fact boxes, and timelines, and a comprehensive index make this a very accessible reference tool.

SUBJ: Encyclopedias and dictionaries.

CDR REF 031　　　　　Ph-1 3-A　　$65.00　　OD KA388

WORLD BOOK 1997 MULTIMEDIA ENCYCLOPEDIA. Deluxe ed. (CD-ROM). World Book/IBM ISBN 0-7166-8421-7; In Canada: World Book Educational Products of Canada, 1997. 3 CD-ROMs color.

Includes user's guide.

Also available for Macintosh (ISBN 0-7166-8522-1), $65.00 and Windows network (ISBN 0-7166-8420-9), $1300.00.

Third disc, RESEARCH HELPER AND INTERNET BONUS KIT, available separately for Macintosh (ISBN 0-7166-8523-X), $39.95.

Third disc, RESEARCH HELPER AND INTERNET BONUS KIT, available separately for Windows (ISBN 0-7166-8422-5), $39.95.

System requirements: Microsoft Windows 95 or Windows 3.1 or higher; 486SX/25MHz (or higher) IBM or 100% compatible PC; 8MB RAM (minimum), 16MB RAM recommended; 10MB free hard

disk space; SVGA, 256 colors or higher (800x600 recommended); 16-bit sound card; double-speed or faster CD-ROM drive; mouse. For on-line access: 8MB additional free hard-disk space; modem; Internet connection.
WORLD BOOK has matured into a fully functioning multimedia encyclopedia complete with exclusive Internet connections and web addresses. Search features include options for selecting just videos or animations. Navigation features also include subject area screens, world maps, and a time frame screen. Users do have to switch CD's to access some of the multimedia features.
SUBJ: Encyclopedias and dictionaries--Software./ Software--Encyclopedias and dictionaries.

REF 031 Ph-3 A $345.00 T OD KA389
WORLDMARK ENCYCLOPEDIA OF THE NATIONS. 9th ed. Gale ISBN 0-7876-0074-1, 1997. 5v. col. ill., maps.
Includes index.
Provides thorough, current information on the geography, history, politics, social life, economic conditions through text, illustrations, and maps. Parallel construction of entries allows drawing of comparisons. Recommended for use by advanced students and teachers.
SUBJ: Encyclopedias and dictionaries./ Geography./ History./ Political science.

REF 031.02 Ph-1 6-A $29.95 T KA390
CORBEIL, JEAN-CLAUDE. Facts on File visual dictionary. Facts on File ISBN 0-8160-1544-9, 1986. 797p. ill.
Includes bibliography and index.
A great source for identifying the object and relating terminology. There are twenty-eight major subjects (themes) which are then divided into many categories. The black line drawings are labeled, but offer no interpretation other than the precise term. Access is provided through general, thematic, and specialized indexes.
SUBJ: Picture dictionaries./ Vocabulary./ English language--Terms and phrases.

REF 031.02 Ph-2 4-A $29.95 L OD KA391
TESAR, JENNY. New view almanac: the first all-visual resource of vital facts and statistics! Premiere edition. Computer graphics by David C. Bell. Text by Jenny Tesar. Edited by Bruce S. Glassman. Blackbirch ISBN 1-56711-123-8, 1996. 608p. ill. (some col.), maps.
Includes index.
Knowledge in the blink of an eye! Charts, graphs, and maps allow the reader to quickly absorb statistical information about government, sports, crime, health, and more. Students will pore over facts and figures that interest them. A unique reference tool to lend authenticity to reports, debates, and essay writing.
SUBJ: Almanacs./ United States--Statistics.

REF 291.1 Ph-3 5-A $10.00 P KA392
BIERHORST, JOHN. Mythology of North America. Morrow ISBN 0-688-06666-6, 1985. 198p. (Mythology of the Americas).
Includes index.
Describing the important characters found in the various myths of the major Indian tribes and the familiar stories connected with the raven, coyote and others, John Bierhorst develops for the reader a background to the mythology of the North American Indian tribes. This reference book will be useful to storytellers who are seeking background for the stories they are telling.
The second book in this three-part series, THE MYTHOLOGY OF SOUTH AMERICA (ISBN 0-688-06722-0, 1988) provides extensive background information, divided into seven mythological regions, on the native beliefs of that continent.
THE MYTHOLOGY OF MEXICO AND CENTRAL AMERICA (ISBN 0-688-06721-2, 1990) "is different from its companions in that it surveys the myths of just one, more or less unified area...", "...incorporating an anthology of basic myths..." (Preface)
SUBJ: Indians of North America--Religion and mythology./ Religion and mythology./ Mythology.

REF 291.1 Ph-2 4-6 $31.35 T KA393
GODDESSES, HEROES, AND SHAMANS: THE YOUNG PEOPLE'S GUIDE TO WORLD MYTHOLOY. Kingfisher/dist. by Raintree Steck-Vaughn ISBN 1-85697-999-7, 1994. 160p. col. ill., maps.
Includes chronologies, glossary and index.
Gathers in one easily accessible volume the mythical characters from many cultures. Brief biographical sketches are preceded by a map and a timeline for each region. Lack of cross references may limit use. For multicultural studies.
SUBJ: Mythology./ Folklore.

REF 291.1 Ph-2 5-A $19.95 T KA394
PHILIP, NEIL. Illustrated book of myths: tales and legends of the world. Retold by Neil Philip. Illus. by Nilesh Mistry. Dorling Kindersley ISBN

0-7894-0202-5, 1995. 192p. col. ill., maps.
Includes glossary and index.
The major myths of the world are divided into types such as Creation, Gods and People, Gods and Animals, Visions of the End, etc. The myth is briefly told and border inserts augment the tale. The arrangement of the material allows similar stories from various cultures to be compared, making this a good volume for multicultural studies.
SUBJ: Mythology.

REF 292 Ph-1 6-A $16.95 L KA395
SWITZER, ELLEN. Greek myths: gods, heroes and monsters, their sources, their stories and their meanings. By Ellen Switzer and Costas. Photos by Costas. Atheneum ISBN 0-689-31253-9; In Canada: Collier Macmillan, 1988. 208p. ill.
Includes bibliography and index.
Selectors' Choice, 17th ed.
Covering the Greek gods and goddesses, the heroes, the Trojan War and many legends, this scholarly text will answer all questions on the subjects. For teachers and students.
SUBJ: Mythology, Greek.

REF 296 Ph-3 5-6 $27.95 T KA396
JUNIOR JEWISH ENCYCLOPEDIA. 11th rev. ed. Edited by Naomi Ben-Asher and Hayim Leaf. Shengold ISBN 0-88400-154-7, 1991. 350p. ill., maps, music.
Includes bibliography.
A lucid explanation, lavishly illustrated with pictures, drawings, and maps, answering questions relating to the Jewish heritage and its contribution to our culture, literature, legal structure, as well as the religious backgrounds.
SUBJ: Jews--Dictionaries.

REF 305.4 Ph-1 5-A $85.00 T KA397
WOMEN'S ALMANAC. Edited by Linda Schmittroth and Mary Reilly McCall. UXL ISBN 0-7876-0656-1, 1997. 3 v. ill.
Includes glossary, bibliography, index and chronologies.
Three volumes focus on historical and contemporary information about the life and culture of women in the United States and around the world. Information is arranged within broad topics such as women in developing countries, civil rights, education, science, and exploration. Biographical boxes provide information on women relating to the subject being discussed. A welcome reference for women's studies.
Contents: v.1. History--v.2. Society--v.3. Culture.
SUBJ: Women--Miscellanea./ Women--History--Miscellanea./ Almanacs.

REF 305.8 Ph-2 5-A $112.00 T KA398
AFRICAN AMERICAN BIOGRAPHY. UXL ISBN 0-8103-9234-8, 1994. 4 v. ill. (African American reference library).
Includes index.
Although aimed at the middle school audience, this should be useful for upper elementary grades. Includes profiles of three hundred African Americans, living and deceased, who are prominent in their fields in careers ranging from politics to storytelling. Each entry includes a black and white photograph and a quotation by or about the person.
SUBJ: Afro-Americans--Biography.

REF 305.8 Ph-2 5-A $60.00 T KA399
ASIAN AMERICAN BIOGRAPHY. Edited by Helen Zia and Susan B. Gall. UXL ISBN 0-8103-9687-4, 1995. 2 v. ill.
Includes bibliographies and index.
Includes profiles of more than 130 Americans, both living and deceased, who can trace their ancestry to Asia or the Pacific Islands. Article usually begins with a statement of philosophy, occupation, birth, and death dates. Profilees are notable for their achievements in a broad range of fields including politics, civil rights, sports, entertainment, science, academia, and the military. A cumulative Field of Endeavor Index is included in each volume. For multicultural studies.
SUBJ: Asian Americans--Biography./ Pacific Islander Americans--Biography.

REF 305.8 Ph-1 5-A $55.00 T KA400
HISPANIC AMERICAN BIOGRAPHY. Edited by Rob Nagel and Sharon Rose. UXL ISBN 0-8103-9828-1, 1995. 2 v. ill.
Includes bibliographies and index.
Profiles more than 90 Hispanic Americans, living and deceased. People prominent in fields from construction to athletics, politics to literature, and entertainment to science are included. A black and white portrait accompanies each article, and most articles include citations for additional information. Field of endeavor index is included. For multicultural studies.
SUBJ: Hispanic Americans--Biography./ Biography--Dictionaries.

REF 305.8 Ph-2 $26.95 T KA401
KRANZ, RACHEL. Biographical dictionary of Black Americans. By Rachel C. Kranz. Facts On File ISBN 0-8160-2324-7; In Canada: Facts On File, 1992. 190p. ill.
Includes index and bibliography.
Snapshot biographies of almost 200 African Americans from politicians and religious leaders to sports and military heroes. Alphabetical entries depict contemporary as well as historical figures with good coverage of African-American women. Some black and white photographs and line drawings are included.
SUBJ: Afro-Americans--Biography.

REF 306 Ph-2 4-A $30.00 P KA402
MANY PEOPLE, MANY WAYS: UNDERSTANDING CULTURES AROUND THE WORLD. Compiled by Chris Brewer and Linda Grinde. Zephyr Press ISBN 1-56976-017-9, 1995. 238p. ill., maps.
Includes bibliographies, filmographies, discographies and directories.
Beginning with an introduction to the term "culture," the book includes many activities to assist students to experience aspects of diverse cultures. Each chapter provides general information and possibilities for integrating information across the curriculum. Many activities are open-ended and require additional research--art, writing, and role playing. Very good for social studies, multicultural units, and interdisciplinary studies. Lack of index limits access.
SUBJ: Ethnology./ Culture./ Multiculturalism.

REF 310 Ph-1 4-6 $23.95 T KA403
GUINNESS BOOK OF WORLD RECORDS. Facts on File ISSN 0300-1679, 1955-. v. ill. annual.
Formerly: THE GUINNESS BOOK OF RECORDS/GUINNESS BOOK OF WORLD RECORDS.
Includes index.
Available from National Library Service for the Blind and Physically Handicapped on sound recording cassette RC19296, and in Braille BRA13072.
Collection of quantitative facts covering the natural world; the animal kingdom; outer space, science, mechanics; business, sports and other fields wherever there is a highest, lowest, coldest, hottest, lightest or heaviest of anything.
SUBJ: Encyclopedias and dictionaries./ Statistics./ Curiosities and wonders.

REF 310 Ph-1 4-6 $16.00 P OD KA404
UNITED STATES. BUREAU OF PUBLIC AFFAIRS, DEPT. OF STATE. Background notes of the countries of the world. U.S. Government Printing Office, n.d. Looseleaf.
Short, factual "Notes" for 160 countries, written by staff members of the Department of State, provide information on each country's land, people, history, government, politics, economy. Also included: map, travel notes, list of government officials, and a reading list. An indispensable resource for the school library.
SUBJ: Statistics./ World politics.

REF 317.3 Ph-1 4-6 $6.95 P KA405
INFORMATION PLEASE ALMANAC, ATLAS & YEARBOOK. Houghton Mifflin, 1947-. v illus maps annual.
Includes index.
A yearbook summarizing events of the past year, worldwide, and a source book of well-indexed statistics and facts. Its larger print and more readable format make it more useful for young students than the venerable WORLD ALMANAC, but there is enough difference in their coverage to make both almanacs useful purchases for a school library.
SUBJ: Almanacs./ Atlases./ Statistics--Yearbooks.

REF 317.3 Ph-2 4-6 $27.95 T KA406
WORLD ALMANAC AND BOOK OF FACTS. World Almanac, 1868-. v. ill., maps, annual.
An annual, general compendium of information, primarily useful for identification of sports events and persons, population and economic data on the U. S. as well as other nations, data on important institutions and organizations, and even many scientific facts. Indexed in the front.
SUBJ: Almanacs./ United States--Statistics./ Statistics--Yearbooks.

REF 350 Ph-1 4-6 $36.00 T KA407
BIOGRAPHY TODAY WORLD LEADERS SERIES: PROFILES OF PEOPLE OF INTEREST TO YOUNG READERS. Edited by Laurie Lanzen Harris and Cherie D. Abbey. Omnigraphics ISSN 1094-2823, 1997-. v. ill. annual.
Includes bibliographies and indexes.
Profiles 16 twentieth century African leaders, both living and deceased. Each entry includes a photographic portrait, personal history, career highlights and background on the country of each ruler. Alphabetic arrangement is supported by complete indexing which includes dates and places of birth. Suitable for units on contemporary political activity and multicultural studies.
Contents: v.1 Environmental leaders--v.2 Modern African leaders.
SUBJ: Heads of state./ Kings, queens, rulers, etc./ Political leadership./ Presidents.

REF 350 Ph-1 5-A $57.00 T KA408
WORLD LEADERS: PEOPLE WHO SHAPED THE WORLD. Ed. by Rob Nagel and Anne Commire. UXL ISBN 0-8103-9768-4, 1994. 3 v. ill., maps.
Includes chronology and index.
Three to five page biographies of 120 world leaders. Set is sequentially paginated; each volume includes a cumulative index, index by country, and time line. Good cross section of both cultural and historical backgrounds. Good coverage of non-European history makes it useful for multicultural studies.
v1: Africa and Asia; v2: Europe; v3: North and South America.
SUBJ: Kings, queens, rulers, etc./ Heads of state./ Revolutionaries./ Statesmen./ Biography--Dictionaries.

REF 353 Ph-3 A $21.00 P KA409
UNITED STATES GOVERNMENT MANUAL. Government Printing Office, 1935-. v. annual charts.
Title varies: 1935-48, "U. S. Government Manual"; 1949-1972/3, "U. S. Government Organization Manual"; 1973/4-, "U. S. Government Manual".
Authoritative account of executive, legislative and judicial branches of the federal government, with supplementary histories of agencies whose functions have been abolished or transferred since March 4, 1933, and brief descriptions of quasi-official agencies and selected international organizations. Includes also a useful list of several hundred representative publications available from government agencies.
SUBJ: United States--Executive departments./ United States--Politics and government./ United States. Office of the Federal Register.

REF 363.7 Ph-1 6-A $14.95 L KA410
FLEISHER, PAUL. Ecology A to Z. Dillon ISBN 0-87518-561-4; In Canada: Maxwell Macmillan, 1994. 224p. ill.
Includes directory, bibliographies and index.
Using the dictionary ready reference format, 350 entries cite problems threatening our planet. Entries are complete enough to explain places, people, laws, concepts, and terms related to ecology. Alphabetical order is given increased access through many cross references and an index. Listing of national environmental organizations includes addresses and telephone numbers. Includes bibliographies for young people and adults. Welcome addition for environmental studies.
SUBJ: Environmental sciences--Encyclopedias.

REF 371.2 Ph-2 5-A $25.00 P KA411
GUIDE TO SUMMER CAMPS AND SUMMER SCHOOLS. 26th ed. Porter Sargent ISBN 0-87558-134-X, 1995. 500p.
Includes index.
Lists 1100 plus academic, tutorial, travel, specialized study, adventure, and other programs for K-12 children. A useful resource for parents and/or guidance counselors. (Parents' Shelf).
SUBJ: Camps--Handbooks./ Schools--Handbooks.

REF 394.2 Ph-2 4-6 $87.00 T KA412
AMERICAN BOOK OF DAYS. 3rd ed. Compiled and edited by Jane M. Hatch. Wilson ISBN 0-8242-0593-6, 1978. 1214p.
Includes index.
A standard reference, revised and updated with careful research. Chronological organization. For each day gives current celebrations--including regional events, background on traditional holidays, important events in U. S. history, biographies of famous Americans who were born or died on that date. A detailed index is key to this rich source of information.
SUBJ: Holidays--United States./ Fasts and feasts--United States./ Festivals--United States.

REF 394.26 Ph-3 5-A/7 $16.95 T KA413
BARKIN, CAROL. Holiday handbook. by Carol Barkin and Elizabeth James. Illus. by Melanie Marder Parks. Clarion ISBN 0-395-65011-9, 1994. 240p. ill.
Includes directory, bibliography and index.
Describes the origin of more than 30 holidays and suggests activities suitable for celebration of the day. Includes mention of the holidays of major religions and offers an excellent bibliography. Solid information for adopt-a-holiday projects.
SUBJ: Holidays.

REF 394.26 Ph-1 4-6 $80.00 T KA414
FOLKLORE OF WORLD HOLIDAYS. Edited by Margaret Read
McDonald. Gale Research ISBN 0-8103-7577-X, 1992. 739p.
Includes bibliographies and index.
Selectors' Choice, 19th ed.
The cost of this reference tool is money well invested. Not only is
information provided for many cultures, there are quotations about
the celebrations and splendid bibliographies of additional sources.
Chronological arrangement and excellent index provide access.
Exceptional resource for multicultural studies whether to introduce
international celebrations to students or to compare holiday traditions
among cultures.
SUBJ: Holidays./ Festivals./ Folklore.

REF 398.23 Ph-3 5-6 $27.95 T KA415
ITALIAN FOLKTALES. Compiled by Italo Calvino. Translated by George
Martin. Harcourt Brace Jovanovich ISBN 0-15-145770-0, 1980. 763p.
Includes bibliography.
Available from National Library Service for the Blind and Physically
Handicapped in Braille BRA17304.
Two hundred tales from all parts of Italy, from all times and from the
rich memories of people, young and old, are retold here. The source
of each tale is given in an appendix. The book is primarily of value to
the storyteller.
SUBJ: Folklore--Italy./ Italy--Folklore.

REF 398.8 Ph-3 5-6 $35.00 T KA416
OXFORD DICTIONARY OF NURSERY RHYMES. Edited by Iona and
Peter Opie. Oxford ISBN 0-19-860088-7, 1997. 467p. ill.
Includes bibliographic material.
Definitive work about the Mother Goose canon, which will enable
teachers to have greater understanding of the more than 500 rhymes
and songs studied by the Opies, their variants and parallels, and
origin.
SUBJ: Nursery rhymes.

REF 423 Ph-1 3-6 $17.00 T KA417
AMERICAN HERITAGE CHILDREN'S DICTIONARY. Houghton Mifflin
ISBN 0-395-85762-7, 1997. 842p. col. ill.
The introduction to the use of the dictionary is an excellent overview.
Topics covered include: preview of the dictionary, introduction,
alphabetical order, guidewords, homographs, spelling, parts of
speech, meanings (definitions), idioms, syllabication, pronunciation,
homophones, word endings, word parts, synonyms and antonyms,
word histories, language detective notes (interesting facts about
words), and pronunciation key. Edge of page coloration divides the
contents into three sections. Though it does not include geographic
names, this is an excellent dictionary for intermediate grades, including
37,000 entries with 800 color photographs and drawings.
SUBJ: English language--Dictionaries.

REF 423 Ph-1 1-3 $15.00 T KA418
AMERICAN HERITAGE FIRST DICTIONARY. By the editors of the
American Heritage dictionaries. Houghton Mifflin ISBN 0-395-85761-9,
1997. 362p. col. ill.
Clear typeface and bright colors will appeal to beginning readers for
whom this first dictionary is intended. Simple definitions are supplied
along with forms of each word such as plurals and tenses. Each word
is used in a sentence, and frequent illustrations and photographs
reinforce word recognition.
SUBJ: English language--Dictionaries.

REF 423 Ph-2 6-A $17.95 T KA419
AMERICAN HERITAGE STUDENT DICTIONARY. Houghton Mifflin ISBN
0-395-55857-3, 1994. 1094p. ill.
Compiled for students in grades six through nine, entries are derived
from materials commonly used in schools--books, magazines, and
encyclopedias. Over 5,000 new entries have been included as well as
thousands of new definitions for existing entries such as mouse.
Features like synonyms, word entymology, usage notes, and regional
notes provide more than adequate information for each entry.
"Elements of the dictionary" pages would make very effective
transparencies for teaching dicitonary skills. Lack of color illustrations
is a drawback.
SUBJ: English language--Dictionaries.

REF 423 Ph-2 5-A $27.95 T KA420
FACTS ON FILE STUDENT'S THESAURUS. Edited by Paul Hellweg.
Facts on File ISBN 0-8160-1634-8, 1991. 287p.
Includes listings for more than 5,000 words. Utilizing a dictionary
arrangement, each entry gives part of speech, synonyms, antonyms
and a sample sentence. Although words are "appropriate for junior
and senior high school students" the format, type size, and
vocabulary make it accessible to elementary students.
SUBJ: English language--Synonyms and antonyms.

REF 423 Ph-1 4-6 $17.95 T KA421
HARCOURT BRACE STUDENT DICTIONARY. 2nd ed. Harcourt Brace
ISBN 0-15-200187-5; In Canada: Harcourt Brace c/o Canadian Manda,
1994. 902p. col. ill.
Previous edition as: THE LINCOLN WRITING DICTIONARY FOR
CHILDREN, 1988.
Companion volume: THE HARCOURT BRACE STUDENT THESAURUS,
1994.
Selectors' Choice, 21st ed.
Unique dictionary uses quotations from the works of 500 different
writers to expand word definitions. Word selection is based on
computerized survey of over ten million words from library books,
textbooks, magazines, and newspapers. The 35,000 entry words
include the latest accepted terms from various subject fields. Includes
many full-color illustrations and colored letter tabs.
SUBJ: English language--Dictionaries.

REF 423 Ph-1 4-6 $16.00 T KA422
HARCOURT BRACE STUDENT THESAURUS. 2nd ed. Edited by
Christopher Morris. Harcourt Brace ISBN 0-15-200186-7, 1994. 312p.
col. ill.
Includes index.
A single A-Z list of 800 main entries is supplemented by an index of
synonyms. Basic terms used by students provide easy access to a
more exact or expanded use of the words. Examples of word use for
synonyms are listed in order of relationship to the word. Illustrations
depict entry word and a synonym. Ease of use and good type size
make this an excellent addition to the writing corner. For creative
writing activities or report writing.
SUBJ: English language--Synonyms and antonyms.

REF 423 Ph-1 P-1 $11.95 T KA423
HILLERICH, ROBERT L. American Heritage picture dictionary. Illus. by
Maggie Swanson. Houghton Mifflin, 1994. 138p. col. ill.
The first in a new series of dictionaries, this dictionary was compiled
from "an analysis of ten different word counts." Proper names for
children and animals illustrated are continued through the book.
Words are listed in alphabetical order. The entry word, when used in
a sentence, is printed in the same color as shown in the main entry.
Some words (astronauts, body, classroom, dinosaur, farm, games and
fun, supermarket, word, and zoo) are given in the main text,
highlighted with green. This word is then illustrated. "The almost 650
illustrations are in bright, clear colors. There are several family
groupings of different races whose members and pets appear
frequently in the illustrations and example sentences. The illustrations
are nonsexist." (Booklist 2/15/87)
SUBJ: Picture dictionaries.

REF 423 Ph-1 1-2 $21.36 L OD KA424
KINGFISHER FIRST DICTIONARY. Ed. by John Grisewood and Angela
Crawley. Kingfisher/dist. by Raintree Steck-Vaughn ISBN 1-85697-645-9,
1995. 180p. col. ill.
Easily accessible by students just learning to read: type size is good,
and the combination of drawings and color photographs adds visual
meaning. Definitions are clear and examples of word usage are
simple, but not condescending. Many full pages show an extended
definition for words such as aircraft, boats, clothes. A string of
alphabet letters on the outer margin of each page indicates placement
of the initial letter within the alphabet. Special features: a list of
naming, counting, and measuring words plus a simple section on
grammar.
SUBJ: English language--Dictionaries./ Vocabulary.

REF 423 Ph-2 2-4 $16.95 T KA425
MACMILLAN DICTIONARY FOR CHILDREN. 3rd. rev. ed. Edited by
Robert B. Costello. Simon & Schuster ISBN 0-689-81384-8; In Canada:
Distican, 1997. 864p. col. ill., maps.
An attractive dictionary with over 30,000 entries, many accompanied
by color illustrations. Large print, simplified format, and a carefully
controlled reading level provide ease-of-use for young readers.
SUBJ: English language--Dictionaries.

CDR REF 423 Ph-1 K-3 $23.95 OD KA426
MY FIRST AMAZING WORDS AND PICTURES (CD-ROM). DK
Multimedia ISBN 1-56458-902-1, 1994. 1 CD-ROM color.
Also available for Macintosh (ISBN 0-7894-0094-4).
ALA notable computer software, 1995.
Selectors' Choice, 20th ed.
System requirements: IBM or compatible PC, with 386SX or higher
microprocessor, 4MB of RAM, CD-ROM drive, sound card, mouse,
SVGA 256-color display, and loudspeakers or headphones. Microsoft
Windows version 3.1 or later.
This dictionary is a superb example of quality multimedia. Limited
vocabulary is fully defined, illustrated, and read to the user. Cross

references are abundant as are other word games. Draws youngsters into learning about language!
SUBJ: English language--Dictionaries--Software./ Software--English language--Dictionaries./ Interactive media.

REF 423   Ph-3 6-A $69.50   T   KA427
PALMATIER, ROBERT A. Speaking of animals: a dictionary of animal metaphors. Greenwood Press ISBN 0-313-29490-9, 1995. 472p.
Playing with language is part of the joy of reading. This dictionary is filled with information about language and clearly explains the origin of animal metaphors. Organized alphabetically by metaphor, rather than by animal.
SUBJ: Animals--Folklore--Dictionaries./ English language--Etymology./ English language--Terms and phrases./ Metaphor--Dictionaries.

REF 423   Ph-1 6-A $23.95   T   KA428
RANDOM HOUSE WEBSTER'S COLLEGE DICTIONARY. 2nd ed. Random House ISBN 0-679-45570-1; In Canada: Random House, 1997. 1568p. ill.
Includes index.
The "first book to benefit from the Random House Living Dictionary Project, the most sophisticated merging of traditional lexicography and high technology in American publishing." (Preface) Described as both a dictionary and "micro-encyclopedia", the large volume has over 180,000 entries including 7,000 geographical entries, and 4,000 biographical entries. Guide words clearly indicate both the beginning and ending word for that page. Special section at the end includes: "Guide for Writers," " Avoiding Sexist Language" and "From Sounds to Spellings."
SUBJ: English language--Dictionaries.

REF 423   Ph-1 4-6 $11.95   T   KA429
SCHILLER, ANDREW. In other words: a beginning thesaurus. By Andrew Schiller and William A. Jenkins. Scott Foresman ISBN 0-673-12486-X, 1987. 240. col. ill.
Several synonyms are given for the 102 most often used words by elementary students. Sentences illustrate meaning and antonyms are also listed. The first part of the book explains how to use a thesaurus; second part lists words in alphabetical order; and the third part presents sets of related words which are not interchangeable.
SUBJ: English language--Synonyms and antonyms.

REF 423   Ph-1 4-6 $16.95   T   KA430
SCHOLASTIC CHILDREN'S DICTIONARY. Rev. ed. By the editors of Scholastic Inc. Scholastic Reference ISBN 0-590-25271-2; In Canada: Scholastic, 1996. 648p. col. ill., maps.
Includes index.
Many unique features create a most usable tool for upper grade readers. Edge of page colored "tabs" indicate initial letter placement. Guide words, complete with arrows, indicate first and last entry words on a page. Hanging indention gives main entry added emphasis. Phonetic symbols are replaced with letter combinations to indicate pronunciation. First line of entry usually has part of speech label. Cross references, sample sentences, related words, and clear definitions complete entries in this accessible dictionary.
SUBJ: English language--Dictionaries.

REF 423   Ph-2 4-6 $15.95   L   KA431
TERBAN, MARVIN. Scholastic dictionary of idioms. Scholastic Reference ISBN 0-590-27549-6; In Canada: Scholastic, 1996. 245p. ill.
Includes indexes.
An easy-to-use dictionary presents over 600 idioms with meanings, origins, and examples of use. Provides a fascinating look at the idiosyncrasies of the English language which will intrigue browsers. A handy resource for both language arts classes and creative writing activities.
SUBJ: English language--Idioms--Dictionaries./ Figures of speech--Dictionaries.

REF 423   Ph-1 5-6 $87.00   T OD KA432
WORLD BOOK DICTIONARY. Edited by Clarence L. and Robert K. Barnhart. World Book, Inc. ISBN 0-7166-0296-2; In Canada: World Book Educational of Canada, 1996. 2v. ill. (Thorndike-Barnhart dictionary).
Original title: THE WORLD BOOK ENCYCLOPEDIA DICTIONARY. Designed to be used with the other World Book reference tools, the dictionary gives meanings, usage notes, word history, and illustrative words and sentences for 225,000 entries. Words are treated in accordance with the age at which a person first encounters them. Continuously revised with new words and new meanings.
SUBJ: English language--Dictionaries.

REF 503   Ph-3 5-6 $239.00   T OD KA433
NEW BOOK OF POPULAR SCIENCE. Rev. ed. Grolier ISBN 0-7172-1221-1, 1998. 6v. col. ill.
Includes bibliography and index.
Contents: 1 Astronomy & space science; 2 Earth sciences, energy, environmental sciences; 3 Physical sciences biology; 4 Plant life, animal life; 5 Mammals, human sciences; 6 Technology, index.
A revised and updated edition of this authoritative reference set containing articles written by eminent scientists.
SUBJ: Science./ Technology./ Natural history.

REF 503   Ph-2 3-5 $541.43   L   KA434
RAINTREE STECK-VAUGHN ILLUSTRATED SCIENCE ENCYCLOPEDIA. Newly revised. Raintree Steck-Vaughn ISBN 0-8172-3943-X; In Canada: Nelson, 1997. 24v. col. ill.
Revised edition of RAINTREE ILLUSTRATED SCIENCE ENCYCLOPEDIA, 1991.
Includes bibliographies and indexes.
In this appealing science resource, articles ranging from a paragraph to several pages cover a broad spectrum of science disciplines including math and psychology. Numerous color photographs, drawings, and diagrams are used throughout the articles to highlight the text. Volume 24 contains 75 science experiments which relate to one or more articles as well as an index to activities described within the articles. Contains thorough coverage, yet the appearance and format will attract reluctant readers.
SUBJ: Science--Encyclopedias./ Encyclopedias and dictionaries.

REF 505   Ph-3 A $29.40   T OD KA435
SCIENCE YEAR: THE WORLD ANNUAL SCIENCE SUPPLEMENT. World Book, 1965-. v. col. ill. annual.
A survey of each year's highlights in scientific fields, stressing such subjects as increasing danger from pollution of the environment, featuring transparent overlays for selected subjects, and a science file of articles, arranged alphabetically by subject, and reporting on the year's work in science and technology. The superb photography will appeal to the browser; teachers and mature students will find it a useful reference source.
SUBJ: Science--Yearbooks./ Technology--Yearbooks.

REF 508   Ph-1 5-A $30.00   T   KA436
KEENE, ANN T. Earthkeepers: observers and protectors of nature. Oxford ISBN 0-19-507867-5, 1994. 222p. ill. (some col.), maps.
Includes directory, glossary, bibliography and index.
Introduces over 100 naturalists and environmentalists, 44 of whom are presented in articles longer than an encyclopedia entry. Fast-facts sidebars supply basic information while well-chosen photographs personify the noted individuals. Divided into four historical periods from the 1700s to the present, coverage includes familiar figures such as James Audubon, Charles Darwin, and John Muir as well as lesser-known figures like Anna Botsford Comstock, Gifford Pinchot, and Katharine Ordway. Welcome edition for environmental studies.
SUBJ: Naturalists--Biography./ Conservationists--Biography./ Nature conservation.

REF 508   Ph-2 5-A $30.00   T   KA437
LIVING WORLD. Oxford ISBN 0-19-910142-6; In Canada: Oxford, 1993. 160p. col. ill., map.
Includes index.
Attractively designed for browsing and research. Illustrations, diagrams, and photographs are detailed and clearly labeled. The human senses are compared with the same sensory organs of an animal. Broad subject categories include: mammals, birds, reptiles, amphibians and fish, animals without backbones, animals bodies at work, plants, and evolution.
SUBJ: Natural history./ Animals./ Plants./ Body, Human.

REF 509   Ph-1 4-6 $36.00   T   KA438
BIOGRAPHY TODAY SCIENTISTS AND INVENTORS SERIES: PROFILES OF PEOPLE OF INTEREST TO YOUNG PEOPLE. Edited by Laurie Lanzen Harris and Cherie D. Abbey. Omnigraphics ISSN 1091-3939, 1996-. v. ill. annual.
Includes bibliographies and indexes.
Scientists from archaeologists to zoologists are presented in biographical sketches which depict both personal lives and professional achievements. Each entry includes a photographic portrait as well as a bibliography of further readings. The alphabetical listings are fully indexed, including dates and places of birth.
SUBJ: Scientists./ Women scientists./ Inventors.

REF 509   Ph-2 A/11 $22.50   P   KA439
CELEBRATING WOMEN IN MATHEMATICS AND SCIENCE. Edited by Miriam P. Cooney. Illus. by Kevin C. Chadwick. National Council of Teachers of Mathematics ISBN 0-87353-425-5, 1996. 223p.

Includes bibliographies.
Short biographies of 22 gifted women detail their hard work, contributions, and struggles to overcome discrimination. Some people are well known, Jane Goodall and Florence Nightingale; others are fairly obscure, Evelyn Boyd Granville and Sophie Germain. All inspire. Includes bibliographies for each person. For women's studies.
SUBJ: Women mathematicians./ Women scientists.

REF 509 Ph-1 5-A $27.07 P KA440
LAROUSSE DICTIONARY OF SCIENTISTS. Edited by Hazel Muir. Larousse/dist. by Raintree Steck-Vaughn ISBN 0-7523-0036-9, 1996. 595p.
Includes index.
A welcome addition to reference collections includes scientists who "have made their mark in the traditional natural sciences (physics, chemistry, biology, astronomy, Earth sciences) and their applications, and includes an extensive selection of mathematicians." Over 2,200 entries give a biographical profile and achievements. Provides an index of scientific concepts plus listing of Nobel Prize winners; arranged by topic.
SUBJ: Scientists--Dictionaries.

REF 509 Ph-2 5-A $34.50 T KA441
MOUNT, ELLIS. Milestones in science and technology: the ready reference guide to discoveries, inventions, and facts. 2nd ed. By Ellis Mount and Barbara A. List. Oryx Press ISBN 0-89774-671-6, 1994. 216p. ill.
Includes indexes.
From abacus to zoology this is an excellent reference tool for a wide range of scientific discoveries. Each entry is placed under the appropriate broad area of science, facilitating further research. The citation also includes information for additional reading. These citations are expanded in the bibliography following the alphabetical entries. A "Personal Name Index" lists names of scientists and inventors with page reference to main entry. The Chronological Index begins in 25,000 BC, citing the "Abrasive" entry on page 1 and concludes with "Supernova" entry on page 81. The Geographical Index includes both names of countries and continents. The last index is a "Field of Study Index." This slim volume will seem more accessible than FAMOUS FIRST FACTS.
SUBJ: Science--Dictionaries./ Inventions--Dictionaries.

REF 509 Ph-1 5-A $99.95 T KA442
SCIENTISTS: THE LIVES AND WORKS OF 150 SCIENTISTS. Edited by Peggy Saari and Stephen Allison. UXL ISBN 0-7876-0959-5, 1996. 3 v. ill.
Includes chronology, glossary, bibliographies and index.
Information beyond the 150 detailed biographies of scientists is provided in this three volume set. Scientists whose "theories, discoveries, and inventions revolutionized science and society" are included. An "Impact" box identifies the most important effects of each scientist's work. Each volume includes a timeline of scientific breakthroughs, a Field of Specialization index, and Words to Know (scientific definitions). Each entry concludes with a brief bibliography.
SUBJ: Scientists.

REF 551 Ph-2 A/7 $19.95 T KA443
VAN ROSE, SUSANNA. Earth atlas. Illus. by Richard Bonson. DK Publishing ISBN 1-56458-626-X, 1994. 64p. col. ill.
Includes index.
Examines geologic processes as it provides a journey through the mountains, valleys, coastlines, and deserts of the earth. Cross-sections provide intriguing detail. Rich source for advanced students.
SUBJ: Geology--Maps./ Atlases.

REF 567.9 Ph-1 3-6 $24.95 L KA444
SATTLER, HELEN RONEY. New illustrated dinosaur dictionary. Rev. ed. Illustrated by Joyce Powzyk. Lothrop, Lee & Shepard ISBN 0-688-08462-1, c1983, 1990. 363p. col. ill.
Includes For Further Reading, and Reference by Location.
Consistent format, simple illustrations, readable entries and good cross-references all combine to provide an excellent dictionary for elementary library users. Even the youngest readers will be able to use this resource to locate information about their favorite dinosaurs or subtopics, such as speed, tracks and fossils.
SUBJ: Dinosaurs--Dictionaries./ Extinct animals--Dictionaries.

REF 570 Ph-1 3-A $19.95 T KA445
BURNIE, DAVID. Dictionary of nature. DK Publishing ISBN 1-56458-473-9, 1994. 192p. col. ill.
Includes index.
Here is a dictionary packed with information for both the neophyte and the sophisticate and replete with illustrations and explanatory artwork that will keep the curious turning pages. A thematic

arrangement of over 2,000 words is grouped under several headings, the largest two being "Plants" and "Animals." Elementary users may just want to review the scientific method or the classification system. Older students might use the human anatomy diagrams to better understand bodily functions. The beauty of the arrangement is its intellectual lure. A search for vitamins will send the reader off to chemical reaction, inorganic/organic compounds, and metabolism. Science teachers will be especially responsive to this volume.
SUBJ: Biology--Encyclopedias./ Biology--Dictionaries.

REF 578.68 Ph-1 5-A $399.95 L OD KA446
ENDANGERED WILDLIFE OF THE WORLD. Marshall Cavendish ISBN 1-85435-489-2; In Canada: Marshall Cavendish, 1993. 11 v. col. ill., maps.
Includes glossaries, indexes, directories and bibliographies.
This set has been described as "a printed zoo." Information provided includes common name, class, order, family, subfamily, tribe, and description. Readable type size is complemented with color photographs, drawings, and range maps. Glossary is listed in each volume. The last volume is devoted to indexes, address lists, and bibliographies. Fast facts provide easy access to vital statistics for report writers. Welcome resource for environmental studies.
SUBJ: Rare animals./ Rare birds./ Wildlife conservation.

REF 595.7 Ph-3 A/12 $21.95 T KA447
BORROR, DONALD J. Field guide to the insects of America north of Mexico. By Donald J. Borror and Richard E. White. Houghton Mifflin ISBN 0-395-07436-3, 1970. 404p. ill. (Peterson field guide series).
Includes glossary, bibliography and index.
Physical characteristics of numerous species in major insect families are described in brief, technical paragraphs, accompanied by line drawings and full-color illustrations. The catalog of insects is preceded by brief chapters on collecting and preserving insects, working with living insects, and structure, growth and development, and classification of insects. Difficult to read, but exceptionally informative and authoritative.
SUBJ: Insects.

REF 598 Ph-2 5-6/8 $29.95 T KA448
FORSHAW, JOSEPH. Birding. By Joseph Forshaw, Steve Howell, Terence Lindsey, Rich Stallcup. Nature Company/Time Life ISBN 0-7835-4752-8, c1994, 1995. 288p. col. ill., maps. (Nature Company guide).
"Weldon Owen Production."
Includes bibliography, directory, glossary and index.
This substantial guide to understanding birds and observing them is a fine handbook with a survey of many common species by major types of habitats. Informative sections cover history, the naming of birds, anatomy, attracting birds to the backyard, equipping oneself for birdwatching, and beautifully photographed guide entries to numerous species. Too heavy for a field guide, this is a fine compendium for library and home reference use, and it makes absorbing reading for serious birdwatchers.
SUBJ: Birds./ Birds--Attracting./ Bird watching.

REF 598 Ph-1 4-6/9 $19.95 T KA449
TAYLOR, BARBARA. Bird atlas. Illus. by Richard Orr. DK Publishing ISBN 1-56458-327-9, 1993. 64p. col. ill., maps.
Includes index.
Numerous birds, common and unusual, appear in this worldwide survey arranged by regions of each continent. Introductory sections discuss the use of the atlas, the physical characteristics and flight of birds, and various types of bird habitats. Two-page entries introduce the geography and physical history of the large region and include numerous photographs and information bits. This oversize volume is an informative compendium of both geography and bird life, offering quick use for specific information and inviting more thorough reading by anyone seriously interested in birds.
SUBJ: Birds.

CDR REF 599 Ph-1 2-A $69.95 OD KA450
MAMMALS: A MULTIMEDIA ENCYCLOPEDIA (CD-ROM). National Geographic 80922, 1990. 1 CD-ROM.
Also available for Macintosh.
Selectors' Choice, 19th ed.
System requirements: 640K IBM PS/2 or compatible with DOS V3.3 or higher; IBM PS/2 mouse or compatible; IBM PS/2 color monitor or compatible; IBM PS/2 CD-ROM drive or compatible with audio capability using Microsoft Extensions Version 2.1 or higher; amplified speaker.
Students learn about mammals from aardvarks to zorillas with this icon driven program. Text, visuals, sound, and graphics are intertwined to provide an excellent source of information which is extremely easy to use. A classification game reinforces student

learning and a pop-up glossary makes learning simple.
SUBJ: Mammals--Software./ Software--Mammals./ Animals--
Software./ Software--Animals.

REF 608   Ph-1 4-7 $99.95   T   KA451
EUREKA! Edited by Linda Schmittroth, Mary Reilly McCall and Bridget
Travers. UXL ISBN 0-8103-9802-8, 1995. 6 v. ill.
Includes index.
Includes 600 entries "on scientific inventions and discoveries that have
made a great impact on the world." (vii) Person responsible for the
discovery is identified. Entry gives background and resulting change.
Arranged alphabetically, each volume cites inventions and discoveries
by subject and includes a master index. Illustrations are black and
white, and volumes include many diagrams and sidebar information.
SUBJ: Inventions./ Inventors./ Discoveries in science.

REF 670   Ph-2 5-A $44.95   T   KA452
CDs, SUPER GLUE, AND SALSA: HOW EVERYDAY PRODUCTS ARE
MADE. Edited by Sharon Rose and Neil Schlager. UXL ISBN 0-8103-
9791-9, 1995. 2 v. ill.
Includes bibliographies and index.
Despite black and white photographs (some of which are not sharply
focused), the information is interesting and concisely written. Topics
provide a wide variety of manufactured products from bar code
scanners to salsa. For reference collections which need additional
information on products, inventions, and inventors.
CDs, SUPER GLUE, AND SALSA: HOW EVERYDAY PRODUCTS
ARE MADE. SERIES 2 (ISBN 0-7876-0870-X, 1996) continues with
more information about inventions such as air bags, fireworks,
ketchup and umbrellas. Edited by Kathleen L. Whitman, Kyung Lim
Kalasky, and Neil Schlager.
SUBJ: Manufactures.

REF 709.2   Ph-1 4-6 $36.00   T   KA453
BIOGRAPHY TODAY ARTISTS SERIES: PROFILES OF INTEREST TO
YOUNG READERS. Edited by Laurie Lanzen Harris and Cherie D.
Abbey. Omnigraphics ISSN 1091-3947, 1996-. v. ill. annual.
Includes bibliographies and index.
Features 18 artists whose work represents a variety of techniques e.g.
photographer Margaret Bourke-White, architect I.M Pei, muralists
Diego Riera, and pop artist Andy Warhol. Each entry gives personal
and professional background with a photographic portrait and
provides a bibliography for further reading. Indexing includes date
and place of birth.
SUBJ: Artists./ Women artists.

REF 792.5   Ph-1 4-A $10.95   P   KA454
SIMON, HENRY W. 100 great operas and their stories. Rev. ed.
Anchor/Doubleday ISBN 0-385-05448-3, c1957, 1989. 554p.
Revised and abridged edition of FESTIVAL OF OPERA. (1957).
Cites setting, characters and voice type, composer and librettist, first
performance as well as a solid synthesis for each opera. The text is
readable, and accessible for upper elementary students. Arranged
alphabetically by opera title with a chronology by composer which
serves as an index.
SUBJ: Operas--Stories, plots, etc.

REF 793.734   Ph-3 4-6 $42.95   T   KA455
EISS, HARRY EDWIN. Dictionary of language games, puzzles, and
amusements. Greenwood Press ISBN 0-313-24467-7, 1986. 278p.
Includes index.
Selectors' Choice, 17th ed.
For students and teachers who are searching for another "Stinky
Pinky" game this book will provide the answer. The term used for the
study of language games is "logology." Most entries give the
explanation of the game, historical significance, examples, similar
puzzles, and a bibliography. The information is like peanuts--you can't
read just one.
SUBJ: Word games--Dictionaries./ Puzzles--Dictionaries./ Literary
recreations--Dictionaries.

REF 796   Ph-1 4-6 $36.00   T   KA456
BIOGRAPHY TODAY SPORTS SERIES: PROFILES OF PEOPLE OF
INTEREST TO YOUNG READERS. Edited by Laurie Lanzen Harris and
Cherie D. Abbey. Omnigraphics, 1996-. v. ill. annual.
Includes bibliographies and indexes.
Alphabetically arranged sketches of 16 well-known athletes include
personal histories, career highlights, and, at least, one photograph.
Individuals, both historical and contemporary, from Hank Aaron to
Tiger Woods are covered. Fully indexed with special indexes for date
and place of birth. Each entry includes an extensive bibliography.
SUBJ: Athletes./ Women athletes./ Sports--Biography.

REF 796   Ph-1 5-A $49.95   T   KA457
PARE, MICHAEL A. Sports stars. UXL ISBN 0-8103-9859-1, 1994. 2 v.
ill.
Includes directories, bibliographies and index.
These volumes may entice students to spend time in the reference
section. Criteria for inclusion includes: currently active or recently
retired from amateur or professional sports; top performers in their
fields; role models who have overcome physical obstacles or societal
constraints. Arranged alphabetically, each entry includes information
from childhood through star status. Sidebars include honors and
awards. Addresses to write the athletes at the end of each article will
be a popular resource for letter writing activities.
SPORTS STARS. SERIES 2. UXL (ISBN 0-7876-0867-X), 1996. 2 v.,
$49.95.
SUBJ: Athletes./ Sports--Biography./ Biography--Dictionaries./
Women athletes.

REF 803   Ph-1 A $40.00   T   KA458
BARTLETT, JOHN. Bartlett's familiar quotations: a collection of passages,
phrases and proverbs traced to sources in ancient and modern literature.
16th ed. Little, Brown ISBN 0-316-08277-5, 1992. 1540p.
An index to identification of many thousands of memorable
quotations. An established tool, first published in 1855, this complete
revision includes memorable quotes from President Kennedy, Dr.
Martin Luther King and many other great spokesmen in many walks
of life.
SUBJ: Quotations.

REF 803   Ph-1 5-6 $45.00   T   KA459
BREWER'S DICTIONARY OF PHRASE AND FABLE. 15th ed. Edited by
Ivor H. Evans. HarperCollins ISBN 0-06-270133-9, 1995. 1264p.
The standard reference tool for information on literature, customs,
sayings provides "the derivation, source, or origin of common
phrases, allusions, and words that have a tale to tell." The three
hundred new entries in this revised entry add to its usefulness, though
with creative introduction this title because of its eminently readable
style could become a favorite browsing title.
SUBJ: Literature--Dictionaries./ Folklore--Dictionaries./ English
language--Etymology.

REF 809   Ph-1 5-A $59.50   T   KA460
AUTHORS OF BOOKS FOR YOUNG PEOPLE. 3RD ED. Martha E.
Ward...[et al.]. Scarecrow ISBN 0-8108-2293-8, 1990. 780p.
Alphabetical listing of short biographies of over 3500 authors and
illustrators of books for children and young people. Strives to include
classic writers and artists as well as contemporary ones, particularly
those about whom biographical information is difficult to locate. Lists
representative titles not complete works. Includes cross-references for
pseudonyms.
SUBJ: Authors--Dictionaries./ Illustrators--Dictionaries./ Children's
literature--Bio-bibliography.

REF 809   Ph-1 4-6 $34.00   T   KA461
BIOGRAPHY TODAY AUTHOR SERIES: PROFILES OF PEOPLE OF
INTEREST TO YOUNG READERS. Edited by Laurie Lanzen Harris.
Omnigraphics ISSN 1082-9989, 1996-. v. ill. annual.
Includes indexes.
First volume of a series which will cover authors, artists, scientists and
inventors, sports figures, and world leaders. The format is similar to
information found in BIOGRAPHY TODAY. However, there will be no
duplication. Each entry includes a black and white photograph.
Information is divided by broad subject headings including birth, early
memories, education, career information, and marriage and family.
Each citation concludes with a selected bibliography, honors and
awards, additional biographical citations, periodicals and address.
Indexes include names of individuals profiled in BIOGRAPHY TODAY,
general index, places of birth index, birthday index, list of people to
appear in future issues. Use in literature and creative writing classes
to encourage students to write to a favorite author.
SUBJ: Authors./ Women authors./ Children's literature--Bio-
bibliography.

REF 809   Ph-2 A $205.00   T   KA462
JUNIOR AUTHOR SERIES. Wilson, 1951-. 7v.
Available from National Library Service for the Blind and Physically
Handicapped in Braille BRA06871.
Combining biographical and autobiographical sketches, each of these
volumes contains information about approximately 250 noted authors
and illustrators of children's books.
Contents: Stanley J. Kunitz and Howard Haycraft eds. JUNIOR
BOOK OF AUTHORS (2nd rev. ed. ISBN 0-8242-0028-4 1971);
Muriel Fuller ed. MORE JUNIOR AUTHORS (ISBN 0-8242-0036-5
1969); Doris de Montreville and Donna Hill eds. THIRD BOOK OF
JUNIOR AUTHORS (ISBN 0-8242-0408-5 1972); Doris de

Montreville and Elizabeth D. Crawford eds. FOURTH BOOK OF JUNIOR AUTHORS AND ILLUSTRATORS (ISBN 0-8242-0568-5 1978); Sally Holmes Holtz ed. FIFTH BOOK OF JUNIOR AUTHORS AND ILLUSTRATORS (ISBN 0-8242-0694-0, 1983); Sally Holmes Holtze ed. SIXTH BOOK OF JUNIOR AUTHORS AND ILLUSTRATORS (ISBN 0-8242-0777-7, 1989); Sally Holmes Holtze ed. SEVENTH BOOK OF JUNIOR AUTHORS AND ILLUSTRATORS (ISBN 0-8242-0874-9, 1996).
SUBJ: Authors--Dictionaries./ Illustrators--Dictionaries.

CDR REF 809   Ph-3 5-A $325.00   OD KA463
JUNIOR DISCOVERING AUTHORS: BIOGRAPHIES AND PLOTLINES ON 300 MOST-STUDIED AND POPULAR AUTHORS FOR YOUNG READERS (CD-ROM). UXL ISBN 0-8103-5896-4, 1994. 1 CD-ROM color.
DOS version 1.0.
Includes user's guide and help card.
Also available for Macintosh (ISBN 0-8103-5850-0), $325.00.
System requirements: IBM XT, AT, PS/2, or compatible (80386 or faster processor recommended); MS-DOS or PC-DOS 3.1 or higher; MS-DOS CD-ROM Extension (MSCDEX) version 2.0 or higher (or MSCDEX version 2.1 or higher with MS-DOS 4.0 or higher); 640K bytes of RAM with 480K available; hard disk with 1 MB of free space (for optimal usage) or floppy disk drive (5 1/4" - 1.2MB or 3 1/2" - 720K), requires additional hard disk or floppy disk space for temporary storage information downloaded or saved; monochrome, CGA, EGA, VGA, or better monitor (color recommended), 16-color EGA monitor (640 x 480 pixels) or better required to view photos; ISO 9660-compatible CD-ROM drive with cables and interface card; parallel or serial printer port for printing (optional).
Biographical information on over 300 well-known authors for intermediate and middle grade students is included. Brief plotlines on most of the authors' works are also provided along with additional reading suggestions. The text-based, DOS interface allows for searching by author, title, subject, character, personal data on authors, or any word in the full text. The lack of a graphical interface dates the program.
SUBJ: Authors--Software./ Software--Authors./ Children's literature--Software./ Software--Children's literature./ Plots (Drama, novel, etc.)--Software./ Software--Plots (Drama, novel, etc.).

REF 809   Ph-2 $265.00   T   KA464
MAJOR AUTHORS AND ILLUSTRATORS FOR CHILDREN AND YOUNG ADULTS: A SELECTION OF SKETCHES FROM SOMETHING ABOUT THE AUTHOR. Edited by Laurie Collier and Joyce Nakamura. Gale Research ISBN 0-8103-7702-0, 1993. 6 vols.
Designed to meet the needs of small public and school libraries this six volume reference source contains "updated and revised sketches on nearly 800 of the most widely read authors and illustrators appearing in Gale's SOMETHING ABOUT THE AUTHOR series." (Intro.) Covers classic and contemporary American, Canadian, and British authors as well as international authors whose works are available in English translations. In addition to biographical information, entries contain complete bibliographies of published works and works in progress.
SUBJ: Children's literature--Bio-bibliography./ Authors./ Illustrators.

REF 809   Ph-3 5-6 $76.00 ea T   KA465
SOMETHING ABOUT THE AUTHOR. Current editor, Anne Commire. Gale Research, 1971-. vol. ill.
Includes cumulative index in each volume.
Each volume includes introductions to more than 200 authors with illustrations from their books and often with a photograph of the author. Entries give biographical information, a list of their writings, and in many cases a brief autobiographical sketch. Beginning with v16, SATA includes authors who died before 1961, which was the original cut-off date.
SUBJ: Children's literature--Bio-bibliography./ Children's literature--Illustrators./ Authors.

REF 809   Ph-3 4-6 $85.00   T   KA466
SOMETHING ABOUT THE AUTHOR AUTOBIOGRAPHY SERIES. Current editor, Joyce Nakamura. Gale Research, 1986-. vol. ill.
Includes cumulative index in each volume.
Designed "to complement 'Something About the Author' SAAS presents a 'close up' view of some of these fascinating people." The autobiographies are readable, and include a number of black and white photographs. Each volume will include twenty essays by current authors of books for young people. "A bibliography appears at the end of each essay, listing the writer's book-length works in chronological order of publication."
SUBJ: Authors.

REF 811.008   Ph-3 5-6 $19.95   T   KA467
FERRIS, HELEN. Favorite poems, old and new, selected for boys and girls. Illus. by Leonard Weisgard. Doubleday ISBN 0-385-07696-7, c1957. 598p. ill.
Sparingly illustrated, this volume is a bulky collection of over 700 traditional poems, most of which are familiar standards strong in rhyme, rhythm, mood, and drama. The thematic organization and indexes to title, first line, and poet make it useful for reference at all grade levels.
SUBJ: Poetry--Collections.

REF 822.3   Ph-3 A $99.00   L   KA468
SHAKESPEARE, WILLIAM. Riverside Shakespeare. Textual editor, G. Blackmore Evans. With an essay on stage history by Charles H. Shattuck. Houghton Mifflin ISBN 0-395-17226-8, 1974. 2v. ill. (some col.).
Includes chronology, appendices, bibliography, index and genealogical tables.
A handsome edition of the complete works of Shakespeare with footnotes to explain those words and phrases that will not be understood by 20th century readers. Scholarly introductions to the collection and to each play enhance the reader's appreciation. A handsome edition and recommended for teachers and able students.
SUBJ: Plays.

REF 909   Ph-3 5-6 $259.00   T OD KA469
LANDS AND PEOPLES. Rev. ed. Grolier ISBN 0-7172-8020-9, 1997. 6v col. ill., maps.
Arranged geographically, information is given about the sociology, history, geography, anthropology, economics, political science, culture, religion and the arts. Useful for both comparative and individual studies of the countries. Good for browsing or independent study.
SUBJ: Geography--Pictorial works.

REF 910   Ph-1 5-A $76.00   T   KA470
EXPLORERS AND DISCOVERERS: FROM ALEXANDER THE GREAT TO SALLY RIDE. Ed. by Peggy Saari and Daniel B. Baker. UXL ISBN 0-8103-9787-8, 1995. 4 v. ill., maps.
Includes chronology and index.
Biographies of 171 men, women, and machines "who have expanded the horizons of our world and universe." Alphabetical arrangement, black and white photographs or drawings, and sidebars provide background information on the "why" of the quest or interest of the biographee. Goes beyond the familiar figures to profile subjects who are not normally found in books.
SUBJ: Explorers./ Discoveries in geography./ Biography--Dictionaries.

REF 910.3   Ph-1 5-6 $29.95   T   KA471
WEBSTER'S GEOGRAPHICAL DICTIONARY. 3rd. ed. Merriam-Webster ISBN 0-87779-546-0, 1997. 1568p. maps.
Original title: WEBSTER'S GEOGRAPHICAL DICTIONARY.
"New edition of Webster's Geographical Dictionary which has been entirely reexamined and revised throughout to update the compact, easy-to-use gazetteer." (Preface) This edition contains over 47,000 entries and 217 maps (all black and white). Statistical data from the early '70's is given.
SUBJ: Geography--Dictionaries.

CDR REF 912   Ph-1 3-A $44.95   OD KA472
MICROSOFT ENCARTA 97 WORLD ATLAS (CD-ROM). Microsoft ISBN 1-57231-478-8; In Canada: Microsoft Canada, 1996. 1 CD-ROM color.
Version 4.0.
Includes user's guide.
System requirements: Multimedia PC with a 486DX/33 MHz or higher processor; Microsoft Windows 95 operating system or Windows NT Workstation version 4.0 or later; 8MB of memory (RAM) on Windows 95, 12MB on Windows NT; 10MB of available hard-disk space; double-speed or faster CD-ROM drive; SVGA, 256-color monitor supporting 640x480 or higher resolution; Microsoft Mouse or compatible pointing device; Sound card with speakers or headphones. To use Microsoft Encarta 97 WebLinks: 9600 bps or faster modem; Internet service provider and access to the Internet.
A superb reference tool, this multimedia atlas includes a number of 360 degree panoramic views, street maps for fifty cities, and a wealth of other map formats. Internet links, various media features, family portraits from various countries, and world music options are easily accessible. Culture articles include information on the people, life styles, arts, government, economy, education, and other almanac type information. Navigation is simple through a series of menus.
URL: http://www.encarta.msn.com/evg98 -- updated maps and information.
SUBJ: Atlases--Software./ Software--Atlases./ Geography--Software./ Software--Geography./ Maps--Software./ Software--Maps./ Interactive media.

REF 912   Ph-1 4-6 $90.00   T OD KA473
NATIONAL GEOGRAPHIC ATLAS OF THE WORLD. 6th ed., Rev. ed.
National Geographic C02038 ISBN 0-87044-835-8, 1995. 404p. maps.
>   Includes index.
>   "First published in 1963, this atlas presents general-reference political
>   maps that have become world famous for accuracy and usefulness."
>   Features include updated information on urbanization, world resource
>   maps showing locations of energy sources and food growing regions.
>   Beginning with a section on astronomy and earth sciences the atlas
>   concludes with a pocket for the annual supplement sheet indicating an
>   update on political changes since the last edition.
>   SUBJ: Atlases.

REF 912   Ph-1 5-A $9.25   P OD KA474
NYSTROM DESK ATLAS. Ed. by Charles Novosad and Joan Pederson.
Nystrom ISBN 0-7825-0349-7, 1994. 176p. col. ill., maps.
>   Includes glossary and index.
>   Also available in a set of 30 for $239.00.
>   This soft cover desk atlas can be purchased as a set or single item.
>   Reference information begins on the inside cover with world facts.
>   Table of contents is clearly marked, leading the reader to areas,
>   continents, or the final entry, geographic facts and index. Thematic
>   maps and graphs give a quick overview of topics such as:
>   environmental concerns, culture and history, ethnicity and indigenous
>   peoples, quality of life, and relative location and travel. A cross
>   section of the country not only gives an idea of land forms, but also
>   indicates relationships to surrounding countries. The index cites name,
>   and in parentheses: name of state or country, latitude and longitude,
>   and some pronunciations. An excellent teaching tool for teachers and
>   librarians which is also accessible to students. Keep copies in the
>   circulating collection for country reports.
>   SUBJ: Atlases./ Geography.

REF 912.73   Ph-1 4-A $35.50   L OD KA475
NATIONAL GEOGRAPHIC PICTURE ATLAS OF OUR FIFTY STATES.
Prepared by National Geographic Book Division. National Geographic
ISBN 0-87044-859-5, 1994. 264p. col. ill., maps.
>   Includes index.
>   Provides general reference and physical maps for each state as well
>   as United States territories. Photographs, fact boxes, and flag-flower-
>   bird information also are included. A useful, standard resource.
>   SUBJ: Atlases./ United States--Maps.

REF 920   Ph-1 3-5 $40.00   T KA476
BIOGRAPHY FOR BEGINNERS: SKETCHES FOR EARLY READERS.
Edited by Laurie Lanzen Harris. Omnigraphics ISSN 1081-4973, 1995-.
v. ill. semiannual.
>   "Favorable impressions."
>   Includes indexes.
>   Each volume, published in April and September, includes about 15
>   illustrated biographical profiles of people easily recognized by
>   children. Approximately half of the articles feature children's authors.
>   Contains cumulative name, subject, and birthday indexes. Address of
>   subject is listed in each article, making it a useful resource for letter
>   writing units.
>   SUBJ: Biography--Dictionaries.

REF 920   Ph-1 5-6 $45.00   T KA477
CURRENT BIOGRAPHY YEARBOOK. Edited by Charles Moritz, et al.
Wilson, 1967-. vol. ill. annual.
>   Index, 1940-1985, $15.00.
>   Autobiographical sketches, with photographs of persons who are
>   newsworthy in many walks of life. Includes list of additional references
>   on each person and indexes subjects by profession. Index of each
>   volume is cumulated for the decade.
>   SUBJ: Biography--Dictionaries.

REF 970.004   Ph-1 5-A $35.00   T KA478
PATTERSON, LOTSEE. Indian terms of the Americas. By Lotsee
Patterson and Mary Ellen Snodgrass. Illus. by Dan Timmons. Libraries
Unlimited ISBN 1-56308-133-4, 1994. 275p. ill., maps.
>   Includes bibliography and indexes.
>   An encyclopedic dictionary of names for objects, methods of doing
>   things, and significant people, places and events is enhanced by
>   guides, drawings, and maps. Endpaper maps indicate location of
>   tribes by name. Additional details about tribes and their locations,
>   and languages are included in text. Designed to represent a realistic
>   picture of Native American lore, this is a welcome addition to
>   multicultural studies.
>   SUBJ: Indians--Terminology./ Indians--Dictionaries./ Reference books--
>   Indians--Dictionaries.

REF 970.004   Ph-1 6-A $39.95   T KA479
PEOPLES OF THE WORLD: NORTH AMERICANS. Edited by Joyce
Moss and George Wilson. Illus. by Lynn Van Dam. Gale ISBN 0-8103-
7768-3, 1991. 441p. ill.
>   Includes glossary, bibliography and index.
>   Although the level may be a little above elementary, most school
>   libraries will find this title useful for its even-handed and consistent
>   reporting of the key elements of life styles, history, geographical
>   setting and culture of the many ethnic groups in North America. This
>   well-organized and clearly formatted book will provide a useful
>   source about the diverse cultural make up of North America's settlers.
>   SUBJ: Ethnology--North America./ North America--Social life and
>   customs.

REF 970.1   Ph-1 5-A $25.00   L KA480
GRIFFIN-PIERCE, TRUDY. Encyclopedia of Native America. Viking ISBN
0-670-85104-3; In Canada: Penguin, 1995. 192p. ill. (some col.), maps.
>   Includes bibliographies and index.
>   Divided into seven cultural and geographical areas, this thorough
>   resource provides information on languages of the tribes, art,
>   costumes, traditions, literature, ceremonies, history, and contemporary
>   events. Both color and black and white photographs are used to
>   effectively enhance an in-depth survey of the first Americans. For
>   multicultural studies.
>   SUBJ: Indians of North America--History./ Indians of North America--
>   Social life and customs.

REF 970.1   Ph-3 6-A $60.00   T KA481
NATIVE NORTH AMERICAN BIOGRAPHY. Edited by Sharon
Malinowski and Simon Glickman. UXL ISBN 0-8103-9821-4, 1996. 2 v.
ill.
>   Includes bibliographies and index.
>   Canadians and North Americans, both living and deceased, "who are
>   notable in their achievements in fields ranging from civil rights to
>   sports, politics and tribal leadership to literature, entertainment to
>   religion, science to military" (p.xiii) are included. Begins with a listing
>   of Tribal Groups/Nations, however, biographies are arranged
>   alphabetically by person. Each profile includes a black and white
>   photograph or drawing with brief bibliography. For multicultural
>   studies.
>   SUBJ: Indians of North America--Biography./ Biography--Dictionaries.

REF 970.1   Ph-1 5-A $34.00   T KA482
NATIVE NORTH AMERICAN VOICES. Edited by Deborah Gillan
Straub. UXL ISBN 0-8103-9819-2, 1997. 235p. ill.
>   Includes chronology, bibliographies and index.
>   Profiles 112 Native North Americans from the United States and
>   Canada, living and deceased. The "voice" may be that of a sports
>   figure, politician, entertainer, or military figure. Black and white
>   portraits, list of sources, and index of individuals by field of endeavor
>   complement biographical material. Excellent for primary source
>   material, background information, and accurate information about the
>   first Americans. For multicultural studies.
>   SUBJ: Speeches, addresses, etc.--Indian authors./ Indians of North
>   America--Biography./ Indians of North America--History.

REF 970.4   Ph-3 4-A $40.00   T KA483
WALDMAN, CARL. Encyclopedia of Native American tribes. Illus. by
Molly Braun. Facts on File ISBN 0-8160-1421-3, 1988. 293p. col. ill.
>   Includes glossary, bibliography and index.
>   Discusses over 150 Indian tribes of North America. Culture areas,
>   language families, and tribes are cited before the alphabetical list of
>   tribes and peoples. Earth tone illustrations depict many of the tools,
>   clothes, and artifacts.
>   SUBJ: Indians of North America--Dictionaries.

REF 971   Ph-3 5-6 $117.20   T KA484
CORPUS ALMANAC AND CANADIAN SOURCEBOOK. Corpus; In
Canada: Corpus, 1964-. 2v annual.
>   Details current events, business and governmental affairs in Canada.
>   Comprehensive table of contents and index assist in locating specific
>   information being sought.
>   SUBJ: Almanacs./ Canada--Directories.

REF 971   Ph-3 A/12 $22.95   P KA485
JENNESS, DIAMOND. Indians of Canada. 7th ed. University of Toronto
Press ISBN 0-8020-6326-8, 1977. 432p. ill.
>   Includes index.
>   A classic work by an eminent anthropologist, with new irreplaceable
>   photographs. A wealth of information on Canada's Indians and
>   Eskimos--their economy, customs, food, dwellings, art, religion, politics.
>   Tribes are described by location from eastern woodland to Pacific
>   Coast. Written in interesting style, set in very readable type.
>   SUBJ: Indians of North America--Canada.

REF 973   Ph-1 5-A $165.00 T KA486
AFRICAN AMERICAN ALMANAC. 7th ed. Compiled and edited by
Harry A. Ploski and James Williams. Gale ISBN 0-8103-7867-1, 1997.
1270p. ill.
    Previously published as NEGRO ALMANAC.
    Includes chronologies, bibliography and index.
    Information about the status and contributions of African Americans
as well as sections on African nations and Blacks in the Western
Hemisphere are updated through spring 1997. Extensive tables and
charts are very helpful. Curiously, some biographical information has
not been revised but the scope of this standard resource makes it
essential for all libraries. For multicultural studies.
    SUBJ: Afro-Americans./ Civil rights./ Afro-Americans--History./ Afro-
Americans--Biography./ Almanacs.

REF 973   Ph-1 5-A $60.00 T KA487
AFRICAN AMERICAN VOICES. Edited by Deborah Gillan Straub. UXL
ISBN 0-8103-9497-9, 1996. 2 v. ill.
    Includes chronology, bibliographies and index.
    Two volumes of well-known speeches by orators of the African-
American culture are accompanied by biographical and historical
information. Arrangement is alphabetical by speaker. The brief
biography indicates the historical perspective of the era in which the
speaker lived. Bibliographies are included, but are a bit dated.
Primary source material for multicultural studies.
    SUBJ: Afro-Americans--History--Sources./ Speeches, addresses, etc.--
Afro-American authors./ Afro-Americans--Biography.

REF 973   Ph-2 4-6 $39.00 T OD KA488
ALABAMA TO WYOMING: STATE FACT CARDS. Toucan Valley
Publications ISBN 1-884925-51-0, 1997. 1 v. (loose-leaf) ill., maps.
    Includes bibliography.
    Brief facts, statistics, and Internet addresses for further information
about each of the 50 states is presented on heavy card stock in a
loose-leaf binder. While most of the information is available in
encyclopedias and almanacs and includes little depth of detail, the
format may be useful as a starting place for students doing reports.
Includes single copy permission for students.
    SUBJ: United States.

REF 973   Ph-3 5-6 $310.00 L OD KA489
ALBUM OF AMERICAN HISTORY. Rev. ed. Edited by James Truslow
Adams. Library Reference Services, Simon & Schuster ISBN 0-684-
16848-0, 1981. 3v. ill.
    An indispensable collection of photographs, portraits, facsimiles of
contemporary prints illustrative of important events and personages in
American history.
    SUBJ: United States--History--Pictorial works./ United States--Social
life and customs.

REF 973   Ph-3 $65.00 T KA490
HORNSBY, JR., ALTON. Chronology of African-American history:
significant events and people from 1619 to the present. 2nd ed. Gale
Research ISBN 0-8103-8573-2, 1997. 526p. ill.
    Includes bibliography and index.
    An overview of the events and people that shaped African-American
history is subdivided into the 11 most significant eras which effected
African-Americans in the United States. Information can be accessed
both by date or through the index. Appendixes offer information on
Virginia Slave Laws, Supreme Court decisions, and statistics on
African-American issues. Includes some black and white illustrations.
Selected bibliography is arranged chronologically.
    SUBJ: Afro-Americans--History--Chronology.

CDR REF 973   Ph-1 2-A $99.00 OD KA491
PRESIDENTS: IT ALL STARTED WITH GEORGE (CD-ROM). National
Geographic 80930, 1991. 1 CD-ROM.
    Includes user's guide.
    Selectors' Choice, 19th ed.
    System requirements: IBM PS/1, PS/2, or 100% compatible
computer with 640K and VGA; color monitor (IBM PS/2 or
compatible); mouse (IBM PS/2 or other Microsoft compatible); CD-
ROM Drive (IBM PS/2 or compatible); audio adapter (and
associated speakers); printer (optional). DOS 3.3 or higher, Microsoft
CD-ROM Extensions version 2.10 or higher.
    This CD-ROM encyclopedia provides a wealth of information on all
the U.S. Presidents. Famous moments on video, audio clips from
speeches, election maps, captioned photographs, photo essays, and a
historical perspective are provided for each president. A timeline
feature helps students understand the context of each president's
term. In addition, the program provides an excellent introduction to
hypermedia for youngsters.
    SUBJ: Presidents--Software./ Encyclopedias and dictionaries--
Software./ Software--Presidents./ Software--Encyclopedias and
dictionaries.

REF 973   Ph-1 4-A $17.95 T KA492
RUBEL, DAVID. Scholastic encyclopedia of the presidents and their times.
Updated ed. Scholastic Reference ISBN 0-590-49366-3; In Canada:
Scholastic, 1997. 232p. ill., maps.
    "Agincourt Press book."
    Includes index.
    The many features of this book warrant a copy in the circulating
collection and a copy in reference. The "How to Look Up..." guide
provides an excellent teaching tool, not only for this reference work,
but others. Words in red lead readers to other access points where
topics are discussed in detail. Listing for each president has basic
facts, followed by information on the United States at the time of his
presidency, myths about the person, and other people who were
important at that time in history. Presidential Election Results chart
cites president, vice president, term, election date, candidates, popular
vote, electoral vote, and president's birthplace.
    SUBJ: Presidents--History./ Presidents--Encyclopedias./ United States--
History--Encyclopedias.

REF 973   Ph-2 4-A $49.95 T KA493
SHEARER, BENJAMIN F. State names, seals, flags, and symbols: a
historical guide. Rev. and expanded ed. By Benjamin F. Shearer and
Barbara S. Shearer. Illus. by Jerrie Yehling Smith. Greenwood Press
ISBN 0-313-28862-3, 1994. 438p. col. ill.
    Includes bibliography and index.
    Well researched and documented information about the history of all
fifty United States names, birds, animals, mottoes, flowers, trees, state
songs and other official state designations. Color plates are found in
the middle of the book and include seals, flags, flowers, trees, and
birds. The index is useful but does not refer to color plates.
    SUBJ: Names, Geographical--States./ Emblems, State./ Flags--United
States--States--History./ State birds./ State songs.

REF 973   Ph-3 A $135.00 T KA494
WORLDMARK ENCYCLOPEDIA OF THE STATES. 3rd ed. Gale ISBN
0-8103-9877-X, 1995. 758p. ill., maps.
    Includes bibliography and glossary.
    Detailed information, arranged under 50 distinct headings, is
presented for each of the United States and the District of Columbia,
Puerto Rico, and the U. S. Caribbean and Pacific Dependencies.
Useful for students searching for extensive and/or comparative
information on the states.
    SUBJ: United States--Dictionaries and encyclopedias.

REF 973.03   Ph-1 5-6 $39.95 T KA495
ENCYCLOPEDIA OF AMERICAN HISTORY. 7th ed. Edited by Richard B.
Morris. HarperCollins ISBN 0-06-016481-6, 1992. 1328p maps index.
    Arranged in three major sections: Basic Chronology (the political
history), Topical Chronology (the arts, the sciences, etc.), and Five
Hundred Notable Americans (brief biographical sketches) this
"provide(s) in a single handy volume the essential historical facts
about American life and institutions".
    SUBJ: Chronology, Historical./ United States--History--Dictionaries.

PERIODICALS

PER 050   Ph-2 3-6 $112.00yr   OD KA496
ABRIDGED READERS' GUIDE TO PERIODICAL LITERATURE, AUTHOR
AND SUBJECT INDEX TO A SELECTED LIST OF PERIODICALS. Wilson
ISSN 0001-334X, 1935-. v. monthly (Sept-May).
> Plus annual and quarterly cumulations.
> Designed especially for school and small public libraries. Children in
> middle grades can easily learn how to use this index for information
> on current events scientific subjects, authors, illustrators, and the like.
> SUBJ: Periodicals--Indexes.

PER 050   Ph-2 A $24.00 yr   OD KA497
ALASKA: THE MAGAZINE OF LIFE ON THE LAST FRONTIER. Alaska
Publishing Properties ISSN 0002-4562, 1935-. v. col. ill. monthly.
> Formerly ALASKAN SPORTSMAN.
> A beautifully illustrated magazine both in color and black and white
> and covering all aspects of life today and past history of this frontier
> state. Has much the same kind of appeal as NATIONAL
> GEOGRAPHIC, although articles are more extensive.
> SUBJ: Alaska--Periodicals.

PER 050   Ph-1 3-5 $19.95 yr   OD KA498
AMERICAN GIRL. Pleasant Company Publications ISSN 1062-7812,
1993-. v. col. ill. bimonthly.
> Designed for preadolescent girls, this magazine depicts active and
> self-confident young women. Attractive layout is filled with rich,
> colorful photographs and illustrations, many of which are contributed
> by well-known children's book illustrators. Includes excerpts from
> award-winning children's books. Regularly features letters from
> readers including comments received on-line, readers' opinions page,
> activities page, crafts, word games, and advice column. The enclosed
> pop-out paper dolls that may prove problematic for library collections
> can be easily removed. Despite its affliation with the Pleasant
> Company, the periodical includes no advertisement.
> SUBJ: Children's periodicals./ Girls--Periodicals.

PER 050   Ph-3 5-6 $20.00 yr   OD KA499
AMERICAN INDIAN ART MAGAZINE. American Indian Art ISSN
0192-9968, 1975-. v. col. ill. quarterly.
> Superb illustrations are an integral part of this magazine which
> focuses on the various forms and techniques American Indian art has
> taken historically and currently.
> SUBJ: Indians of North America--Art--Periodicals.

PER 050   Ph-2 P-A $17.00 yr   OD KA500
ARIZONA HIGHWAYS. Arizona Highways ISSN 0004-1521, 1925-. v.
col. ill., ports., maps. monthly.
> Fascinating for browsing by all ages because of its superb color
> photography. Useful also in units on desert life and western history,
> geography, or animal life.
> URL: http://www.arizhws.com -- issue updates including table of
> content, hike of the month, and various departments
> SUBJ: Arizona--Description and travel--Periodicals.

PER 050   Ph-3 5-6 $20.00 yr   OD KA501
AUDUBON MAGAZINE: THE MAGAZINE OF THE NATIONAL
AUDUBON SOCIETY. National Audubon Society ISSN 0004-7694,
1899-. v. ill. bimonthly.
> Addressed to young people and adults and illustrated profusely, this

magazine is "devoted to the conservation of our wildlife, wilderness,
scenic areas, plants, soil and water."
SUBJ: Birds--Periodicals./ Birds--Protection.

PER 050   Ph-1 4-6 $22.00 yr   OD KA502
BASEBALL DIGEST. Century ISSN 0005-609X, 1941-. v ill. monthly.
> An almost pocket-sized monthly of 100 packed pages devoted
> entirely to baseball with feature articles about individual players or
> teams and historical baseball milestones. Regular departments include
> Tips for Budding Baseball Players by Lou Boudreau (where he
> answers letters from young readers), a baseball quiz and puzzle, and
> four or five interesting statistical charts. This is must reading for the
> baseball fan.
> SUBJ: Baseball--Periodicals.

PER 050   Ph-2 A $27.50 yr   OD KA503
BEAVER: EXPLORING CANADA'S HISTORY. Hudson's Bay ISSN 0005-
7517; In Canada: Hudson's Bay, 1920-. v. ill. 6 nos. per yr.
> Indexed in CHILDREN'S MAGAZINE GUIDE.
> A magazine replete with many interesting articles and stories about
> Canadian geography and history, illustrated in black and white. Useful
> with units on Canada, especially because of scarcity of authentic book
> materials.
> SUBJ: Canada--Description and travel--Periodicals.

PER 050   Ph-1 2-A $18.00 yr   OD KA504
BOYS' LIFE. Boy Scouts of America ISSN 0006-8608, 1911-. v. ill.
monthly.
> Indexed in CHILDREN'S MAGAZINE GUIDE.
> Available from the National Library Service for the Blind and
> Physically Handicapped in braille.
> A magazine designed to appeal to boys between eight and fourteen,
> whether or not they are Boy Scouts. There are articles on science,
> sports, nature and outdoor activities such as camping and hiking.
> There are regular features on Scoutcraft, short stories, projects,
> puzzles, games and hints on hobbies. Because of the wide range of
> subjects touched upon, BOYS' LIFE is both useful and popular.
> SUBJ: Boy Scouts--Periodicals.

PER 050   Ph-1 4-6 $26.95 yr   OD KA505
CALLIOPE: WORLD HISTORY FOR YOUNG PEOPLE. Cobblestone
Publishing ISSN 1050-7086, 1990-. v. ill., maps. 9 nos. per yr.
> Indexed in CHILDREN'S MAGAZINE GUIDE.
> Thematic in scope, each issue offers students readable articles. Text is
> supplemented with illustrations and photographs. Back issues on topics
> such as Epic Heroes, Great Explorers, Hinduism, and Lost Cities are
> also available. Excellent resource for older readers.
> SUBJ: History--Periodicals./ Children's periodicals.

PER 050   Ph-3 P-3 $14.95 yr   OD KA506
CHICKADEE: THE CANADIAN MAGAZINE FOR YOUNG CHILDREN.
Young Naturalist Foundation ISSN 0707-4611; In Canada: Young
Naturalist Foundation, 1979-. v. col. ill. 10 nos. per yr.
> Indexed in CHILDREN'S MAGAZINE GUIDE.
> Designed for children ages four through eight, this younger version of
> "Owl" contains a mixture of fiction, stories about wildlife, games
> and puzzles, stories about Canada and in each issue a special
> "surprise"--something to make and/or keep. Accpets children's

original artwork.
SUBJ: Nature study--Periodicals./ Wildlife--Periodicals./ Outdoor life-
-Periodicals.

PER 050   Ph-2 2-4 $17.95 yr   OD KA507
CHILD LIFE. Children's Better Health Institute ISSN 0009-3971, 1921-. v.
8 nos. per yr.
Indexed in CHILDREN'S MAGAZINE GUIDE.
A diversified magazine of health topics with stories, poems,
informational articles, naturelore, recipes, activities and contributions
from readers.
SUBJ: Children's periodicals.

PER 050   Ph-1 3-A $59.95 yr   OD KA508
CHILDREN'S MAGAZINE GUIDE: SUBJECT INDEX TO CHILDREN'S
MAGAZINES. Bowker ISSN 0743-9873, 1948-. v. monthly.
Formerly: SUBJECT INDEX TO CHILDREN'S MAGAZINES.
Cumulated semi-annually in February and August.
Follows the same form of entry as ABRIDGED READERS' GUIDE;
indexes wide range of magazines--local history, science, classroom--
not covered by ARG. These two indexes should form basis for
selection of current periodical subscriptions.
SUBJ: Children's periodicals--Indexes.

PER 050   Ph-2 1-3 $17.95 yr   OD KA509
CHILDREN'S PLAYMATE. Children's Better Health Institute ISSN 0009-
4161, 1929-. v. 8 nos. per yr.
Indexed in CHILDREN'S MAGAZINE GUIDE.
Stories, poems, recipes, science information, jokes, and riddles,
contributions by other readers, and "Things to do" are geared to
appeal to and entertain the young reader.
SUBJ: Children's periodicals.

PER 050   Ph-1 5-6 $29.95 yr   OD KA510
COBBLESTONE: THE HISTORY MAGAZINE FOR YOUNG PEOPLE.
Cobblestone Publishing ISSN 0199-5197, 1978-. v. ill. 9 nos. per yr.
Supplement available: COBBLESTONE COMPANION: A TEACHER'S
MANUAL.
Indexed in CHILDREN'S MAGAZINE GUIDE.
An outstanding periodical for both young people and teachers. The
articles are well written and readable. Many pictures and drawings
are included. Puzzle relates to articles in the issue. Students are
offered an opportunity to "Dig Deeper" through other books and
past issues of COBBLESTONE.
SUBJ: United States--History--Periodicals.

PER 050   Ph-2 4-A $19.95 yr   OD KA511
CREATIVE KIDS. G/C/T Publishing ISSN 0744-3420, n.d. v. 8 nos. per
yr.
Formerly: CHART YOUR COURSE.
Provides students an opportunity to be published. Submission
guidelines include: "We are looking for the very best material
(cartoons, reviews, songs, articles, puzzles, comic strips,
interviews, stories, art work, poems, activities, games, editorials, plays,
etc.) we can find by gifted, creative, and talented children for gifted,
creative, and talented children.
URL: http://www.prufrock.com/ -- complete issue
SUBJ: Children's periodicals./ Children as authors--Periodicals.

PER 050   Ph-1 3-6 $32.97 yr   OD KA512
CRICKET: THE MAGAZINE FOR CHILDREN. Carus Publishing Company
ISSN 0090-6034, 1973-. v. col. ill. monthly.
Indexed in CHILDREN'S MAGAZINE GUIDE.
Selectors' Choice, 8th ed.
Under the prestigious editorial board and staff headed by Clifton
Fadiman, this literary magazine for children provides from well-known
authors short stories, poems, articles, puzzles, and jokes. The
magazine encourages reader participation through its "Letter-box"
and "Cricket League" (Where Children's work appears). Teachers
and librarians will want to encourage children to appreciate the
artistic and literary qualities of this magazine.
SUBJ: Children's literature--Periodicals.

PER 050   Ph-2 5-6 $7.45 yr   OD KA513
CURRENT SCIENCE. Field Publications ISSN 0011-3905, 1927-. v. col.
ill. 18 nos. per yr.
Indexed in CHILDREN'S MAGAZINE GUIDE.
Articles on recent developments in the various science disciplines as
well as experiments, puzzles, and games are included in this illustrated
periodical.
SUBJ: Science--Periodicals.

PER 050   Ph-1 5-A $26.95 yr   OD KA514
FACES: THE MAGAZINE ABOUT PEOPLE. Cobblestone ISSN 0749-
1387, 1984-. v. col. ill. 9 nos. per yr.
Indexed in CHILDREN'S MAGAZINE GUIDE.
Selectors' Choice, 15th ed.
Published in cooperation with the American Museum of Natural
History this offers the student information on various aspects of
anthropology. Using a single theme for each issue (i.e. Pueblo
Indians) the reader is given information on mythology, food, dolls,
recipes, art, and housing. A welcome addition from the publishers of
COBBLESTONE. Accepts contributions from readers.
SUBJ: Anthropology--Periodicals.

PER 050   Ph-2 5-6 $23.94 yr   OD KA515
FOOTBALL DIGEST. Century Publishing ISSN 0015-6760, 1971-. v. ill.
10 nos. per yr.
Written by newspaper reporters this fast-paced periodical features
articles on teams and individual players, letters and queries from
readers, and statistical tables so beloved by sports fans.
SUBJ: Football--Periodicals.

PER 050   Ph-1 4-6 $14.95 yr   OD KA516
GIRLS' LIFE: THE NEW MAGAZINE FOR GIRLS. Monarch Avalon ISSN
1078-3326, 1994-. v. col. ill. bimonthly.
A contemporary look enhances the content of this magazine which
resembles popular women's magazines. Articles are timely and
frequently include an address for additional information. Regular
features range from movie and book reviews, recipes, profiles of
entertainment personalities, fashions, career information, and an
advice column to a pen pal page.
URL: http://www.girlslife.com -- video and music reviews, contests,
and departments: "Hanging with," "Bytes & bits," and "Cyber
pals"
SUBJ: Children's periodicals./ Girls--Periodicals.

PER 050   Ph-1 P-A $29.64 yr   OD KA517
HIGHLIGHTS FOR CHILDREN. Highlights for Children ISSN 0018-165X,
1946-. v. ill. 11 nos. per yr.
Indexed in CHILDREN'S MAGAZINE GUIDE.
Excellent for arts and crafts and activities; of interest to all grade
levels. Much of the material may be used in work with retarded or
handicapped children. Accepts children's original art work and
writings.
SUBJ: Arts and crafts--Periodicals./ Games--Periodicals./ Children's
periodicals.

PER 050   Ph-1 2-6 $15.00 yr   OD KA518
HOPSCOTCH: THE MAGAZINE FOR GIRLS. Hopscotch ISSN 1044-
0488, 1990-. v. ill. bimonthly.
Good paper and large type are features of this magazine created
and published by a school librarian for girls, ages 6 to 12. Includes
both articles and stories on a variety of subjects.
SUBJ: Children's periodicals.

PER 050   Ph-1 P-1 $17.95 yr   OD KA519
HUMPTY DUMPTY'S MAGAZINE. Children's Better Health Institute ISSN
0273-7590, 1952-. v. col. ill. 8 nos. per yr.
Formerly: HUMPTY DUMPTY'S MAGAZINE FOR LITTLE CHILDREN.
Indexed in CHILDREN'S MAGAZINE GUIDE.
Designed for the young reader, this periodical includes stories based
on health topics at varying levels of difficulty, puzzles and easy
science activities.
SUBJ: Children's periodicals.

PER 050   Ph-1 4-6 $16.00 yr   OD KA520
INTERNATIONAL WILDLIFE. National Wildlife Federation ISSN 0020-
9112, 1971-. v col. ill. bimonthly.
Indexed in CHILDREN'S MAGAZINE GUIDE.
Established by the National Wildlife Federation in recognition "that
thoughtful concern for the future of Man's environment does not stop
at any national border". The threat of the fashion industry to the
great cats, how great cities poison their atmosphere and change the
weather, interviews with leaders such as Lord Snow, and a story of
life in the Netherlands written and illustrated by Peter Spier, are
among the articles in this excellent magazine.
SUBJ: Wildlife conservation--Periodicals.

PER 050   Ph-1 1-5 $17.95 yr   OD KA521
JACK AND JILL: THE MAGAZINE FOR BOYS AND GIRLS. Children's
Better Health Institute ISSN 0021-3829, 1938-. v. col. ill., music. 8 nos.
per yr.
Indexed in CHILDREN'S MAGAZINE GUIDE.
Also available from the National Library Service for the Blind and
Physically Handicapped in braille and on sound recording cassette.

Stories, articles, verses and things to do for children in grades 1 to 5. Accepts children's original art work and writings.
SUBJ: Children's periodicals.

PER 050   Ph-1 A $24.00 yr   OD KA522
JUNIOR SCHOLASTIC. Scholastic ISSN 0022-6688, 1937-. v. ill., music. 18 nos. per yr. (Sept.-May).
Indexed in CHILDREN'S MAGAZINE GUIDE.
Includes: JUNIOR REVIEW.
Excellent classroom magazine on wide range of topics of current interest to boys and girls.
SUBJ: Current events--Periodicals.

PER 050   Ph-2 2-4 $19.90 yr   OD KA523
KID CITY. Children's Television Workshop ISSN 0899-4293, 1988-. v. col. ill. 10 nos. per yr.
Formerly: ELECTRIC COMPANY MAGAZINE.
Indexed in CHILDREN'S MAGAZINE GUIDE.
Contents will have wide appeal despite the title of the magazine. Some good color photographs, an overview of a country followed by a folktale from its culture, a science experiment, a few riddles, simple games, book reviews, and new products for kids are typical of each issue.
SUBJ: Children's periodicals.

PER 050   Ph-1 P-2 $32.97 yr   OD KA524
LADYBUG: THE MAGAZINE FOR YOUNG CHILDREN. Carus Publishing Company, 1990-. v. col. ill. monthly.
Includes Parents' Guide with each issue.
Format, type size, and general appearance reinforce the subtitle - this is an outstanding magazine for young children. The quality of illustrations, choice of poetry, and concepts provide an almost book-like quality.
SUBJ: Children's literature--Periodicals./ Children's periodicals.

PER 050   Ph-3 4-A $39.95 yr   OD KA525
MODEL AIRPLANE NEWS. Air Age ISSN 0026-7295, 1929-. v. ill. monthly.
Articles, diagrams, illustrations, much highly technical information about the hobby of model airplanes, along with profuse advertisements. By no means a hobby just for children, this magazine is reported as being very popular and subscribed to by many elementary schools.
SUBJ: Airplanes--Models--Periodicals.

PER 050   Ph-3 4-A $34.95 yr   OD KA526
MODEL RAILROADER. Kalmbach ISSN 0026-7341, 1934-. v. ill. monthly.
For the boy (or man) engrossed in the hobby of model railroading, this magazine is undoubtedly a goldmine. Articles on specific model railroad systems, on production of realistic sound, on the building of specific equipment for model railroads, tools for model railroading, etc. etc. are among the topics treated in the issues examined. Copious advertisements, of course, abound.
Accepts children's original writings.
URL: http://www.modelrailroader.com/~ -- preview of annuals, preview of next issue, current issue details, and links to other related subjects
SUBJ: Railroads--Models--Periodicals.

PER 050   Ph-1 4-6 $24.00 yr   OD KA527
MUSE. Carus Publishing ISSN 1090-0381, 1997-. v. col. ill. bimonthly.
Nonfiction articles intended to inspire readers to seek further information cover an array of topics including art, history, and science. Illustrated with high quality photographs and drawings, the eclectic subjects are drawn from the numerous collections of the Smithsonian. Also features readers' letters, book reviews, and brief biographical sketches.
URL: http://www.musemag.com -- selected monthly articles.
SUBJ: Children's periodicals./ History--Periodicals./ Science--Periodicals./ Art--Periodicals.

PER 050   Ph-1 4-A $29.95   OD KA528
NATIONAL GEOGRAPHIC INDEX, 1888-1988. National Geographic 00764, 1989. 1216p. col. ill.
A one stop source for referencing articles in National Geographic.
SUBJ: Geography--Periodicals--Indexes.

PER 050   Ph-1 4-A $27.00 yr   OD KA529
NATIONAL GEOGRAPHIC MAGAZINE. National Geographic ISSN 0027-9358, 1888-. v. col. ill., maps. monthly.
Six month indexes available free on request.
Indexed in ABRIDGED READER'S GUIDE and CHILDREN'S MAGAZINE GUIDE.

Available from the National Library Service for the Blind and Physically Handicapped on sound recording cassette.
Includes quarterly "Geoguide" editorial page enhancing the study of the issue's main topic. Single copy detailed lesson plans for the main topic of the quarterly issue are available upon request.
Standard reference on scientific expeditions, animal life, people of other lands, people of other times.
URL: http://www.nationalgeographic.com -- complete index from 1888-present
SUBJ: Geography--Periodicals.

PER 050   Ph-1 2-4 $17.95 yr   OD KA530
NATIONAL GEOGRAPHIC WORLD. National Geographic ISSN 0361-5499, 1975-. v. col. ill. monthly.
Formerly known as WORLD, MONTHLY MAGAZINE FOR CHILDREN.
Indexed in CHILDREN'S MAGAZINE GUIDE.
Selectors' Choice, 11th ed.
Available from the National Library Service for the Blind and Physically Handicapped on sound recording cassette.
Colorfully illustrated with many photographs, this magazine appeals to children with its articles about wildlife, people, and travels around the world. Frequently articles give practical tips on sports, such as backpacking. Other popular features are the science puzzles, games, tricks, and monthly poster.
URL: http://www.nationalgeographic.com -- current issue plus individual archival articles
SUBJ: Children's periodicals.

PER 050   Ph-3 5-A $25.00 yr   OD KA531
NATIONAL PARKS. National Parks and Conservation Association ISSN 0276-8186, 1919-. v. ill. bimonthly.
Formerly: NATIONAL PARKS AND CONSERVATION MAGAZINE.
Available to institutions for $22.00 yr. and students for $18.00 yr.
Journal of the National Parks and Conservation Association, a private, public service organization whose "responsibilities relate primarily to protecting the national parks and monuments of America." Effectively illustrated with black and white photographs, this journal presents timely and thoughtful articles on topics of ecology, endangered species, and environmental concerns. Indexed in READER'S GUIDE TO PERIODICAL LITERATURE.
URL: http://www.npca.org -- on-line issues are a month behind
SUBJ: National parks and reserves--Periodicals./ Environmental protection--Periodicals.

PER 050   Ph-1 A $16.00 yr   OD KA532
NATIONAL WILDLIFE. National Wildlife Federation ISSN 0028-0402, 1962-. v. col. ill. bimonthly.
Subscription included in membership.
Indexed in CHILDREN'S MAGAZINE GUIDE.
Covers every aspect of the enjoyment and conservation of the nation's outdoors resources, in articles written by experts in every field and illustrated lavishly with colored and black-and-white photographs.
SUBJ: Wildlife conservation--Periodicals./ Natural resources--Periodicals.

PER 050   Ph-2 A $28.00 yr   OD KA533
NATURAL HISTORY. American Museum of Natural History ISSN 0028-0712, 1900-. v. col. ill., maps. 10 nos. per yr.
Title varies.
Indexed in ABRIDGED READERS' GUIDE.
Available from the National Library Service for the Blind and Physically Handicapped on sound recording cassette.
Useful for a wide range of topics in natural history, ancient cultures, conservation, etc. For advanced students and teachers this has high interest and usefulness.
SUBJ: Natural history--Periodicals.

PER 050   Ph-1 3-5 $26.95 yr   OD KA534
ODYSSEY. Cobblestone ISSN 0163-0946, 1992-. v. col. ill. 9 nos. per yr.
Focus theme for each issue is on various aspects of space exploration and astronomy such as science fiction, exploring the edge of the solar system, cyberspace, or women in astronomy. Timely information presented in a readable style is augmented by numerous full-color photographs and drawings. Each issue includes a monthly star chart, astronomy projects, biographical sketches, and feature articles. Useful for backyard astronomers as well as for science classes.
SUBJ: Astronomy--Periodicals./ Outer space--Periodicals.

PER 050   Ph-2 2-4 $14.95 yr   OD KA535
OWL: THE DISCOVERY MAGAZINE FOR CHILDREN. Young Naturalist Foundation ISSN 0382-6627, 1976-. v. col. ill. 10 nos. per year.

Formerly: THE YOUNG NATURALIST.
Indexed in CHILDREN'S MAGAZINE GUIDE.
Colorful drawings and photographs, charts, diagrams, puzzles, stories and informational articles to capture the interest and attention of young naturalists. "All Your Own" provides a column for sharing of illustrations and letters from the readers. An attractive magazine that is not limited in appeal to Canadian readers.
SUBJ: Nature study--Periodicals./ Wildlife--Periodicals./ Outdoor life--Periodicals.

PER 050   Ph-3 5-A $29.00 yr   OD KA536
PLAYS: THE DRAMA MAGAZINE FOR YOUNG PEOPLE. Plays ISSN 0032-1540, 1941-. v. 7 nos. per yr.
Indexed in CHILDREN'S MAGAZINE GUIDE and READER'S GUIDE TO PERIODICAL LITERATURE.
The text of non-royalty plays useful in work with children and young people.
SUBJ: Drama--Periodicals.

PER 050   Ph-1 5-A $17.94 yr   OD KA537
POPULAR SCIENCE: THE WHAT'S NEW MAGAZINE. Times Mirror Magazines ISSN 0161-7370, 1872-. v. ill. monthly.
Indexed in ABRIDGED READER'S GUIDE.
This informational magazine has articles on cars and driving, science and inventions, space and aviation, electronics, photography, the home and shop, sports, boats and boating. Regular features include answers to readers' questions on the above subjects and reports of new science developments and inventions. Both articles and how-to features are illustrated with numerous photographs and drawings.
SUBJ: Science--Periodicals.

PER 050   Ph-1 K-3 $17.00 yr   OD KA538
RANGER RICK. National Wildlife Federation ISSN 0033-9229, 1967. v. ill. 12 nos. per yr.
Formerly: RANGER RICK'S NATURE MAGAZINE.
Indexed in CHILDREN'S MAGAZINE GUIDE.
Issued "to give boys and girls a year-round program of activities, adventure and knowledge which will help them enjoy nature."
Attractive format, illustrated in color, with stories, articles, nature legends, puzzles, how-to-do-it projects, and a book review column. Available only through membership; a very useful teaching aid. Accepts children's original art work and writings.
SUBJ: Nature study--Periodicals.

PER 050   Ph-1 4-6 $49.50 yr   OD KA539
SCIENCE NEWS. Science Service ISSN 0036-8423, 1921-. v. ill. weekly.
Indexed in ABRIDGED READER'S GUIDE.
Also available 39 issues (school year) for $37.50.
Each issue combines summaries of current events and articles explaining recent developments in the various scientific disciplines.
URL: http://www.sciencenews.org -- highlights from current and past issues
SUBJ: Science--Periodicals./ Current events--Periodicals.

PER 050   Ph-3 P $19.90 yr   OD KA540
SESAME STREET MAGAZINE. Children's Television Workshop ISSN 0049-0253, 1971-. v. col. ill. 10 nos. per yr.
Indexed in CHILDREN'S MAGAZINE GUIDE.
A 34-page magazine in colored cartoon style on newspaper stock almost entirely made up of pictures (cartoons) with very few words. A very good tool for Headstart, day-care centers and other agencies which have Puerto Rican and Mexican-American children in their groups. Instructions to children given in both English and Spanish. Accepts children's original art work.
SUBJ: Children's periodicals./ Education, Preschool--Periodicals./ Bilingual materials--Spanish.

PER 050   Ph-3 A $22.00 yr   OD KA541
SMITHSONIAN. Smithsonian Association ISSN 0037-7333, 1970-. v. col. ill. monthly.
Indexed in READER'S GUIDE TO PERIODICAL LITERATURE.
An extremely handsome periodical whose articles cover anything that falls under the broad headings of science, history or art. Additional features include what's going on at the Smithsonian, book reviews, and capsule summaries on unusual research.
URL: http://www.smithsonianmag.si.edu -- columns and article summaries
SUBJ: History--Periodicals.

PER 050   Ph-1 1-3 $32.97 yr   OD KA542
SPIDER: THE MAGAZINE FOR CHILDREN. Carus Publishing ISSN 1070-2911, 1993-. v. col. ill. monthly.
Using quality paper, illustrations, and text, this magazine for first

through third grade readers includes fiction by well-known authors and articles on subjects ranging from art to science.
SUBJ: Children's literature--Periodicals./ Children's periodicals.

PER 050   Ph-3 4-6 $19.94 yr   OD KA543
SPORT. Sport Magazine Associates ISSN 0038-7797, 1946-. v. ill. monthly.
Institutions available at $9.97 per year.
Covering the sports by season of activity this periodical also includes background information on major personalities. Sports quizzes are a regular feature of this fast paced magazine.
SUBJ: Sports--Periodicals.

PER 050   Ph-3 5-A $80.46 yr   OD KA544
SPORTS ILLUSTRATED. Time Inc. ISSN 0038-822X, 1954-. v. col. ill. weekly.
Outstanding news magazine covering events and personalities in a wide range of activities--auto racing, golf, school athletics, boat racing--fully illustrated in color and black and white.
URL: http://cnnsi.com/ -- some issue features, some original content; continually updated
SUBJ: Sports--Periodicals.

PER 050   Ph-1 2-4 $27.95 yr   OD KA545
SPORTS ILLUSTRATED FOR KIDS. Time Inc. ISSN 1042-394X, 1989-. v. ill. 12 nos. per yr.
Filled with photographs and brief articles about young people who are involved with sports. Departments include "Letters, Training room, What's the call." Each issue includes a poster and detachable sports cards. Decidedly light weight in comparison to its parent.
URL: http://www.pathfinder.com/SIFK/ -- some issue features, some original content; continually updated
SUBJ: Sports--Periodicals.

PER 050   Ph-1 2-A $32.00 yr   OD KA546
STONE SOUP: A MAGAZINE BY CHILDREN. Children's Art Foundation ISSN 0094-579X, 1973-. v. ill. 6 nos. per yr.
Stories, poems, illustrations and book reviews by children ages 6-12. The "Editors Notebook" ($1.25) is a companion volume to help teachers use "Stone Soup" in writing and art programs. Occasional stories in Spanish or Chinese with translations.
URL: http://www.stonesoup.com -- individual monthly articles
SUBJ: Children's periodicals./ Children as authors--Periodicals.

PER 050   Ph-1 3-6 $24.95 yr   OD KA547
TIME FOR KIDS. Time Inc. ISSN 1084-0168, 1995-. v. col. ill. 26 nos. per yr.
Specify Primary Edition (grades 3-4) or Intermediate Edition (grades 5-6).
Includes teacher's guide (with class subscription only).
Although both subscription rate and guides are designed for classroom use, this should be a valuable library resource for current events, science news, and background information on government issues. Provides timely information in an appealing format.
SUBJ: Current events--Periodicals./ Children's periodicals.

PER 050   Ph-1 4-A $59.94 yr   OD KA548
TIME: THE WEEKLY NEWSMAGAZINE. Time Inc. ISSN 0040-781X, 1923-. v. col. ill. weekly.
Indexed in ABRIDGED READER'S GUIDE.
Summaries of current events throughout the world in a variety of areas are reported in a popular style.
URL: http://cgi.pathfinder.com/time/daily/ -- some issue features, some original content; continually updated
SUBJ: History--Periodicals.

PER 050   Ph-2 2-4 $21.95 yr   OD KA549
U*S* KIDS: A WEEKLY READER MAGAZINE. Children's Better Health Institute ISSN 0895-9471, 1987-. v. ill. 11 nos. per yr.
Colorful illustrations and photographs surround games, puzzles, articles, and stories for the intermediate grades.
SUBJ: Children's periodicals.

PER 050   Ph-2 K-6   Varies   OD KA550
WEEKLY READER. Weekly Reader Corp., 1947-. v. col. ill. 27 nos. per yr.
This series of newspaper-like periodicals designed for Kindergarten-sixth graders frequently subscribed to in the classroom also has a place in the library media center. Articles about current events in a range of subject areas, games, and other activities are included in these heavily illustrated newsletters.
Contents: WEEKLY READER-EDITION K ($2.95); WEEKLY READER-EDITION 1 ($2.95); WEEKLY READER-EDITION 2 ($2.95); WEEKLY READER-EDITION 3 ($3.15); WEEKLY READER-EDITION 4 ($3.20);

WEEKLY READER-EDITION 5 ($3.40); WEEKLY READER-SENIOR
EDITION ($3.50).
SUBJ: Current events--Periodicals.

PER 050   Ph-1 K-A $17.95 yr   OD KA551
WILDLIFE CONSERVATION. NYZS/Wildlife Conservation Society ISSN
0003-3537, 1897-. v. col. ill. bimonthly.
Formerly: ANIMAL KINGDOM.
Brilliant photographs are the highlight of this periodical which seeks to
develop and further an appreciation of wildlife. Frequently featuring
articles on endangered species this periodical will be helpful in nature
study and ecology curriculum projects.
URL: http://www.wcs.org/news/magazine -- updates with special
articles and index
SUBJ: Animals--Habits and behavior--Periodicals./ Nature study--
Periodicals./ Wildlife conservation--Periodicals.

050   Ph-1 4-6 $12.50 yr   OD KA552
YES MAG: CANADA'S SCIENCE MAGAZINE FOR KIDS. Peter Piper
Publishing ISSN 1203-8016, 1996-. v. col. ill. quarterly.
Published in partnership with YES (Youth Engineering and Science)
Camps of Canada which are a nationwide network of science
promotion programs seeking to stimulate enthusiasm for science,
technology, engineering, and mathematics. The issue examined
included colorful, well-written articles ranging on topics from an ants'
eye view of the world to rocks and minerals. Includes reviews of
science software and books, puzzles, and contests.
URL: http://www.islandnet.com/~yesmag -- issue updates including
articles, experiments, and projects
SUBJ: Science--Periodicals./ Technology--Periodicals./ Mathematics--
Periodicals.

PER 050   Ph-2 3-5 $16.00 yr   OD KA553
ZILLIONS. Consumers Union of the United States, 1980-. v. col. ill. 6
nos. per yr.
Formerly: PENNY POWER.
Activity guide for teachers comes with each edition.
Indexed in CHILDREN'S MAGAZINE GUIDE.
The publishers of CONSUMER REPORTS produce this child's guide to
spending and saving. Articles, in attractive format, advise on small
purchases (food), large purchases (bicycles), and ways to save by
making things at home (Halloween costumes). Could be used in
teaching math, social studies, and nutrition.
SUBJ: Consumer education--Periodicals./ Consumer protection--
Periodicals./ Economics--Periodicals.

PER 050   Ph-1 4-6 $15.00 yr   OD KA554
ZOONOOZ. Zoological Society of San Diego ISSN 0044-5282, 1926-.
v. col. ill. monthly.
Available in Canada, $18.00 per year.
A beautiful magazine describing the activities and exhibits of the
world-famous San Diego Zoo. The Zoo's staff and Research Council
are responsible for articles in their special fields of interest, and each
topic is enhanced by many illustrations. The regular column, Around
the Zoo, describes current news and events. An invaluable and
fascinating resource for the study of natural history.
SUBJ: Zoos--Periodicals./ Animals--Periodicals.

PER 050   Ph-1 3-5 $19.90 yr   OD KA555
3-2-1 CONTACT. Children's Television Workshop ISSN 0195-4105,
1979-. v. ill. 10 nos. per yr.
Indexed in CHILDREN'S MAGAZINE GUIDE.
Appealing, both in quality of photographs and choice of topics, issues
include articles and activities on a wide range of subjects. Methods of
animation, short features on topics which ranged from the appendix
to why February has only 28 or 29 days were included in the issue
examined. Accepts contributions from readers.
SUBJ: Children's periodicals.

NONFICTION

001.9 Ph-3 5-A/9 $8.95 P KA556
GOLDBERG, M. HIRSH. Blunder book: colossal errors, minor mistakes, and surprising slipups that have changed the course of history. Illustrated by Ray Driver. Morrow ISBN 0-688-07757-9, 1984. 271p.
  Includes index.
  Available from National Library Service for the Blind and Physically Handicapped in Braille BR06038.
  Find out why the Pilgrims landed in the wrong place; how an arrogant official caused the U.S. to abandon neutrality; and where the most dangerous place is. Author recounts historic, medical, business, sports, library goofs and more. Good for adding fun and humor to social studies and science, browsing and selective reading aloud.
  SUBJ: Errors, Popular.

001.9 Ph-3 A/8 $22.80 L KA557
GRAHAM, IAN. Fakes and forgeries. Raintree Steck-Vaughn ISBN 0-8114-3843-0, 1995. 46p. col. ill. (Science spotlight).
  Includes glossary, bibliography and index.
  No one likes to be fooled, especially the experts! Yet it happens all the time: copies of fashion items are sold at a discount, a publisher claims to have the authentic diaries of Hitler, and witnesses swear they have seen Bigfoot. Exposes fakery including mimicking of metals, forgeries with paints and inks, and paper tricks. Scientists scurry to keep one step ahead with radiocarbon dating, thermoluminescence, and dendrochronology. Enticing text with wonderful illustrations makes this enjoyable for reading aloud.
  SUBJ: Fraud in science./ Impostors and imposture.

001.9 Ph-3 4-6/8 $16.00 L KA558
KETTELKAMP, LARRY. ETs and UFOs: are they real? Morrow ISBN 0-688-12868-8; In Canada: Hearst Book Group, 1996. 86p. ill., maps.
  Includes directory, bibliography and index.
  Are we alone?...a query that tantalizes the imagination. Kettlecamp discusses unexplained sightings and possible abductions, detailing physical evidence and first-person encounters (including possible human/alien interbreeding). Details what our government has investigated, refuted, and compiled. First chapter explores controversial claims that: space flights have been monitored by extraterrestrials, UFOs have been observed and photographed from space, and a human face appears in Martian photographs. Overall tone gives credence to UFO sightings. Pages inform and delight all inquiring minds, then raise more questions.
  SUBJ: Unidentified flying objects./ Human-alien encounters./ Extraterrestrial beings.

001.9 Ph-2 4-A/8 $13.95 T KA559
PERL, LILA. Don't sing before breakfast, don't sleep in the moonlight: everyday superstitions and how they began. Illus. by Erika Weihs. Clarion ISBN 0-89919-504-0, 1988. 90p. ill.
  Includes bibliography and index.
  Available from National Library Service for the Blind and Physically Handicapped on sound recording cassette RC30799.
  Superstitious adages involving numbers, animals, weather, habits and more are traced from forgotten origins to their current applications and interpretations. Children and adults will have much to discuss about belief/unbelief, phraseology, and predictions.
  SUBJ: Superstition.

001.94 Ph-3 4-6/4 $12.95 L KA560
ABELS, HARRIETTE. Bermuda triangle. Crestwood House ISBN 0-89686-340-9, 1987. 47p. col. ill. (Mystery of...).
  Includes glossary and index.
  A chronological listing of unknown phenomena in the Atlantic Ocean triangle off the coasts of Bermuda and Miami. All readers will wonder about missing ships, planes and the lost city of Atlantis. Even psychics have some ideas. Ideal for reluctant readers.
  SUBJ: Bermuda Triangle.

001.94 Ph-3 4-6/7 $16.00 L KA561
SIMON, SEYMOUR. Strange mysteries from around the world. Rev. ed. Morrow ISBN 0-688-14636-8; In Canada: Hearst Book Group, 1997. 58p. ill.
  "Describes nine strange natural phenomena and possible explanations for them, including the day it rained frogs, an atomic explosion that occurred forty years before the atom bomb, and an eerie crystal skull." (CIP)
  SUBJ: Curiosities and wonders.

001.944 Ph-3 3-6/7 $15.95 L KA562
BACH, JULIE S. Bigfoot. Lucent ISBN 1-56006-160-X, 1995. 48p. col. ill., map. (Exploring the unknown).
  Includes glossary, bibliography and index.
  Recants Bigfoot's elusiveness, tracing sightings from the earliest accounts in 1811 to 1988. Lists some obvious hoaxes; discusses cryptozoology (study of unseen animals); concludes that a worldwide searching of evidence still yields too many unknowns for scientific conclusions. Rational adults will say, "There's no such thing!" but students are forever fascinated by this beast and will heartily enjoy this book.
  SUBJ: Sasquatch.

001.944 Ph-3 3-6/9 $15.95 L KA563
STEFFENS, BRADLEY. Loch Ness Monster. Lucent ISBN 1-56006-159-6, 1995. 48p. col. ill., map. (Exploring the unknown).
  Includes glossary, bibliography and index.
  Reports sightings of the legendary "monster" in Lock Ness and hypothesizes what type of creature "Nessie" could be. Straightforward account clearly distinguishes fact from conjecture.
  SUBJ: Loch Ness monster./ Monsters.

001.944 Ph-3 4-6/6 $15.95 T KA564
WALKER, PAUL ROBERT. Bigfoot and other legendary creatures. Illus. by William Noonan. Harcourt Brace Jovanovich ISBN 0-15-207147-4; In Canada: Harcourt Brace Jovanovich, 1992. 56p. col. ill.
  Includes bibliography.
  Seven monsters on different continents entice readers to speculate. Each story is invented and based upon people's firsthand accounts and impressions. Following each are scientific conjectures as to the monster's probability and possible evolutionary history. Straightforward with little skepticism, the text is convincing. Good addition to this topic and sure to be read.
  SUBJ: Monsters.

002 Ph-1 4-A/9 $16.99 L KA565
BROOKFIELD, KAREN. Book. Photos by Laurence Pordes. Knopf ISBN 0-679-94012-X, 1993. 64p. col. ill. (Eyewitness books).

NONFICTION

"Borzoi book."
Includes index.
The story of language and print unfolds in glorious illustrations that take the mystery out of--cuneiform, manuscript, Asian and Islamic books, the evolution of printing, and bookbinding. Concludes with pages on the book market and libraries. No mention is made of word processors or the current technology that produces daily newspapers. A book to refer to again and again as historic topics are introduced in social studies. Worthy inclusion of non-Western coverage offers multicultural studies information. Students will need assistance to find the buried nuggets.
SUBJ: Books--History.

004 Ph-2 4-A/9 $14.95 P KA566
BORMAN, JAMI LYNNE. Computer dictionary for kids...and their parents. Illus. by Yvette Santiago Banek. Barron's ISBN 0-8120-9079-9; In Canada: Barron's, 1995. 253p. col. ill.
Softcover dictionary defines 700 key computer terms coupled with examples and (sometimes) directions (how to rearrange an AUTOEXEC.BAT file!). No pronunciations are given. Useful in the jargon-filled computer world, giving all readers some expertise.
SUBJ: Computers--Dictionaries.

004 Ph-3 5-6/9 $13.90 L KA567
KAPLAN, ANDREW. Careers for computer buffs. Interviews by Andrew Kaplan. Photos by Edward Keating and Carrie Boretz. Millbrook ISBN 1-56294-021-X, 1991. 64p. ill. (Choices).
Includes directory, bibliography, and glossary/index.
Profiles 14 computer-related careers including a video game designer and a repairman. Each person tells what they do; how they got started; how they feel about their work; and what the reader should know about training, education, and salary. Good addition to the computer shelf.
SUBJ: Computers--Vocational guidance./ Vocational guidance--Computers./ Data processing--Vocational guidance./ Vocational guidance--Data processing.

MCP 004 Ph-1 K-A $24.95 OD KA568
KIDDESK (Microcomputer program). Edmark 1303, 1993. 1 3.5" disk.
Includes teacher's guide.
Also available for IBM.
System requirements: Macintosh Plus or later; hard disk; System 6.0.7 or later. For System 6.0.x: 1MB for monochrome and 2MB for color. For System 7.0 or later: 2MB for monochrome and 4MB for color. TouchWindow, printer, microphone (optional).
This menu program limits student access to hard drives while providing a number of desk accessories including a calculator, talking clock, calendar, and message machine. Ease of use and the ability to develop group activities to provide simple access to software make the program valuable for teachers and students.
SUBJ: Utilities (Computer programs)--Software./ Software--Utilities (Computer programs)./ Computer programs--Software./ Software--Computer programs.

CDR 004 Ph-1 P-A $24.95 OD KA569
KIDDESK. School version (CD-ROM). Edmark 1086, 1995. 1 CD-ROM color.
Includes teacher's guide.
Version 1.3.
System requirements: Color Macintosh (256 colors); 4MB RAM; CD-ROM drive for installation; System 7.0.1 or higher; hard drive; 13" monitor or larger; microphone (optional), printer (optional), Edmark TouchWindow (optional).
System requirements: Windows 3.1, Windows 95 or later; 386 or better; hard drive; 4MB RAM (8MB recommended); floppy drive for installation (CD-ROM version requires CD-ROM drive for installation); 256-color SVGA; mouse; Windows-compatible sound-output device; microphone required for sound input; TouchWindow (optional); printer (optional).
Product (1086) runs on either Macintosh or Windows compatible hardware.
This menu program limits student access to hard drives while providing a number of desk accessories including a calculator, talking clock, calendar, address card file, and note pad, as well as text and voice message machines. Ease of use and the ability to develop groups and to provide simple access to software make the program valuable for teachers and students.
SUBJ: Utilities (Computer programs)--Software./ Software--Utilities (Computer programs)./ Computer programs--Software./ Software--Computer programs./ Interactive media.

004.67 Ph-2 4-6/8 $21.00 L KA570
COCHRANE, KERRY. Internet. Watts ISBN 0-531-20200-3, 1995. 64p. col. ill. (First book).

Includes glossary and index.
Explains how the Internet works, its major functions, and how to locate the best sites. File transfer protocol (FTP), newsgroups, and mailing lists are discussed. Half the text is devoted to Archie, Gopher, Veronica, World Wide Web, and fun places on the Internet. The many computer screen illustrations will help readers be productive on-line. Offers a wealth of background information.
SUBJ: Internet (Computer network)./ Computers.

004.67 Ph-2 2-4/7 $20.00 L KA571
KAZUNAS, CHARNAN. Internet for kids. By Charnan and Tom Kazunas. Childrens Press ISBN 0-516-20334-7; In Canada: Children's Press, 1997. 48p. col. ill. (True book).
Includes bibliography, glossary and index.
Basic introduction to the Internet: how it started, how it is used, and how providers allow users to connect to sites. Explains addresses, protocol, safety rules, news groups, chat rooms, and e-mail. Evenly balanced, giving beginners some idea of the information and enjoyment waiting for net users.
SUBJ: Internet (Computer network)./ Computers.

004.67 Ph-1 3-6/6 $5.99 P KA572
SALZMAN, MARIAN. Kids on-line: 150 ways for kids to surf the net for fun and information. By Marian Salzman and Robert Pondiscio. Avon ISBN 0-380-78231-6; In Canada: Avon, 1995. 245p.
Includes glossary, directory and index.
Aside from the Web addresses and tips on participating in on-line discussions and using e-mail, this stresses the importance of privacy and on-line safety, explains 'netiquette, and covers all you really need to know while navigating cyberspace. Useful to students who have access to the net. Necessarily, some information will become quickly dated, but this is a worthwhile purchase.
SUBJ: Internet (Computer network)./ World Wide Web (Information retrieval system).

005.265 Ph-1 3-A $24.00 P KA573
FARMER, LESLEY S. J. I speak HyperCard. By Lesley S.J. Farmer and Jean Hewlett. Libraries Unlimited ISBN 0-87287-977-1, 1992. 11 individually numbered sections.
Includes appendices, bibliography and glossary.
Teachers and students wanting to learn about HyperCard will find this self-paced tutorial useful. Concise directions guide the user through developing a stack with text, graphics and some scripting. One of the best instructional books available for beginners.
SUBJ: Macintosh (Computer)--Programming./ HyperCard (Computer program)./ Programming (Computers).

MCP 006.7 Ph-2 2-A $199.95 OD KA574
HYPERSTUDIO (Microcomputer program). Roger Wagner Publishing ISBN 0-927796-32-5, 1990. 7 3.5" disks, manuals, microphone, sound digitizing hardware card.
Version 3.1.
Also available on Macintosh 3.0 and Windows 3.1.
System requirements: Apple IIGS with 1MB RAM.
This hypermedia construction software allows students and teachers to produce their own learning and reporting materials. Paint tools, text editor, sound editor, sound digitizing hardware card, and a microphone are included. The program offers an alternative to paper and pencil communication and works well with an entire class, small groups, or individuals.
SUBJ: Software--Multimedia./ Multimedia--Software./ Software--Hypermedia./ Hypermedia--Software.

BC 025.04 Ph-1 3-A/8 $19.95 P KA575
AHMAD, NYLA. Cybersurfer: the Owl Internet guide for kids. Directory researched and written by Keltie Thomas. Illus. by Martha Newbigging. Owl Books/dist. by Firefly ISBN 1-895688-50-7; In Canada: Greey de Pencier Books/Owl/dist. by Firefly, 1996. 1 paperback book, 1 3.5" disk.
Includes chronology, glossary, index and directory.
System requirements for Windows: 386SX processor or higher; 3.5" floppy drive; 1MB hard disk space; at least 4MB RAM; Windows 3.1 or Windows for Workgroups 3.11 or Windows 95 or Windows NT; full color monitor recommended.
Systems requirements for Macintosh: 68020 processor or higher; 3.5" floppy drive; 2MB hard disk space; at least 4MB RAM; Macintosh System 7.x or MAC OS; full color monitor recommended. Disk runs on either Windows or Macintosh compatible hardware.
A brief overview of the Internet, tips for accessing, and ideas for searching for information are provided. The safety section is worthy reading for children and parents. The disk provides a good starting point for surfing the 'Net as it is filled with worthwhile web page addresses. (Parents' Shelf).
SUBJ: Internet (Computer network)./ World Wide Web (Information retrieval system).

025.04   Ph-1   A/10 $19.00   P OD KA576
BOE, TOM. World desk: a student handbook to the Internet.
By Tom Boe, Cheryl B. Graubart, Marge Cappo. Learning In Motion
ISBN 1-889775-00-2, 1996. 144p. ill.
    Includes bibliographical references and glossary.
    "Written specifically for the student who wants to utilize the Internet
to improve his or her schoolwork and to become a participating
member of the information age..." (Preface) Explains how to do
effective searches, to be safe and considerate, to evaluate data, and
to write Internet citations for formal papers. Gives address, contents,
and ideas for using over 40 Internet sources involving science,
language, math, and social studies, stating this is "just the tip of the
iceberg." (p. 96) Appendix of Internet terms lends precision to
technical jargon. Useful for teaching research skills and for students
doing independent study.
    SUBJ: Online information services./ Internet (Computer network).

025.04   Ph-2 2-6/6 $20.00   L   KA577
BRIMNER, LARRY DANE. World Wide Web. Childrens Press ISBN
0-516-20345-2; In Canada: Children's Press, 1997. 48p. col. ill. (True
book).
    Includes bibliographies, glossary and index.
    A beginners' introduction to the components and procedures that
make the World Wide Web work. Gives information on Web
addresses, hypertext, home pages, and bookmarks. Encourages safe
surfing and lists a Web site rating system. Helpful to students and
teachers with Web access. Not sterling, but certainly useful.
    SUBJ: World Wide Web (Information retrieval system).

025.04   Ph-1 3-A/4 $29.95   T   KA578
GRALLA, PRESTON. Online kids: a young surfer's guide to cyberspace.
Wiley ISBN 0-471-13546-1; In Canada: Wiley, 1996. 282p. ill.
    Includes glossary and index.
    Surf's up in cyberspace, and here is all you need to know about
connecting online. Discusses the basics (netiquette, choosing a service,
e-mail, etc.) and reviews the best educational and entertainment sites.
Site listings rate programs by usefulness and coolness, give directions
to locate programs, describe programs' contents, and offer tips and
insights. Diverseness reigns. Users can find a key pal (keyboard pen
pal), print a historical map for a report, travel to the National
Museum of the American Indian, get handicraft directions, or preview
MTV's upcoming CDs. Purchase multiple copies of this Rosetta Stone!
(Parents' Shelf).
    SUBJ: Online information services./ Internet (Computer network).

025.04   Ph-1 3-A/7 $14.95   P   KA579
KIDS RULE THE NET: THE ONLY GUIDE TO THE INTERNET
BY KIDS. Wolff New Media/dist. by National Book Network ISBN
1-889670-08-1; In Canada: Wolff New Media, 1996. 179p. ill.
(NetBooks).
    Includes index.
    Nine chapters demonstrate how to surf the net for animals, heroes,
science facts, games, sports, and more. Includes tips for on-line pen
pals, instructions for constructing a Web site, and frequently asked
adult questions. Most topics yield more than one Web address. Site
reviewers are young people who cite their ages (early teens) and
names. Useful for school assignments and a gold mine for students
with unlimited Web access. Teachers will find many curriculum related
activities.
    SUBJ: Internet (Computer network)./ World Wide Web (Information
retrieval system).

BC 025.04   Ph-2 4-A $19.99   P   KA580
TECH GIRL'S INTERNET ADVENTURE. By Girl Tech. IDG Books
Worldwide ISBN 0-7645-3046-1, 1997. 178p. col. ill., 1 CD-ROM.
    Includes glossary and index.
    System requirements: 486-66 MHz DX; 8MB of RAM, 16MB
recommended; 1 gigabyte hard drive; color VGA monitor; mouse;
Microsoft Windows 3.1 or, preferably, Windows 95; 28.8Bps internal
or external modem (slower modem will take longer to download
graphics).
    System requirements: 68040 processor or Power Macintosh; 8MB of
RAM, 16MB recommended; 1 gigabyte hard drive; color VGA
monitor; mouse; System 7.x operating system; internal or external
modem.
    Supplemental CD-ROM runs on either Windows or Macintosh
compatible hardware.
    Presents a number of fascinating Internet sites which will be especially
of interest to girls. The well done explanations of various segments of
the Internet are useful for all students. Included CD has Internet
Explorer web browser on it.
    SUBJ: Internet (Computer network)--Directories./ Women's computer
network resources.

VCR 025.5   Ph-3 3-6 $79.00   OD KA581
ANIMATED ALMANAC (Videocassette). Society for Visual Education
95382-HAVT, 1990. 1/2" VHS videocassette color (15min), 12 skill
sheets. (SVE basic skill booster).
    Includes Teacher's Manual.
    Various claymation almanacs explain their strengths, organization and
use. Highlights topics that interest students and illustrates that you
don't need a research assignment to have fun with this special
reference book. Study questions refer to the 1990 WORLD
ALMANAC BOOK OF FACTS and are mostly for advanced readers.
    SUBJ: Almanacs.

VCR 025.5   Ph-3 4-6 $79.00   OD KA582
ANIMATED ATLAS (Videocassette). Society for Visual Education
95383-HAVT, 1990. 1/2" VHS videocassette color (20min), 12 skill
sheets. (SVE basic skill booster).
    Includes Teacher's Manual.
    Begins with the history of mapmaking, then advances to today's
technology which creates the most accurate maps imaginable.
Cartographers, drafters and artists continually update and add to
general historical, nature and other atlases. Viewers are shown how
to use the table of contents, index and map coordinates while study
page questions refer to the RAND MCNALLY CLASSROOM ATLAS.
Video outlines salient points and encourages browsing but does not
eliminate the need for each student to examine a general atlas.
    SUBJ: Atlases.

VCR 025.5   Ph-2 3-6 $79.00   OD KA583
ANIMATED ENCYCLOPEDIA (Videocassette). Society for Visual
Education 95381-HAVT, 1990. 1/2" VHS videocassette color (17min),
12 skill sheets. (SVE basic skill booster).
    Includes Teacher's Manual.
    Lively claymation encyclopedia volumes work as a team to deliver
accurate information. Discusses the alphabetical organization, guide
words and index. Helpful for both introductory lessons on using the
encyclopedia and at the beginning of research assignments as a
refresher that emphasizes encyclopedias as the first source for general
information and topic overview.
    SUBJ: Encyclopedias and dictionaries.

VCR 027   Ph-2 2-6 $50.00   OD KA584
FIND IT ALL AT THE LIBRARY: AN INTRODUCTION TO THE LIBRARY
FOR CHILDREN (Videocassette). ALA Video/Library Video Network
10312F ISBN 1-56641-031-2, 1996. 1/2" VHS videocassette color
(10min).
    Closed captioned.
    Introduces the electronic catalog and demonstrates how to locate
materials by title, subject, and author. After giving a brief overview of
the Dewey arrangement, the young narrator explains how trained
librarians answer questions and order books and materials and how
support staff shelve the collection, so that all users can find the
information they are seeking. The introduction to public library
services and materials can be easily adapted for school media centers.
    SUBJ: Libraries./ Online bibliographic searching.

CE 027   Ph-1 1-3/3 $12.95   L   KA585
GIBBONS, GAIL. Check it out!: the book about libraries. Harcourt Brace
Jovanovich ISBN 0-15-216400-6, 1985. unp. col. ill.
    Opens the library world to the young user by explaining about
different libraries, catalogs, and materials. Gibbons' bold colored
illustrations complement her clearly written text.
    SUBJ: Libraries.

VCR 027.4   Ph-2 1-4 $79.00   OD KA586
LIBRARY (Videocassette). National Geographic 51473, 1991. 1/2" VHS
videocassette color (14min). (Your town).
    Includes teacher's guide.
    A father takes his two children to the Montgomery County Library.
While one child gets homework assistance, the other attends
storytime. Briefly introduces the types of materials and services
available and shows the process of obtaining a library card and
checking out materials. Can be used in community units or as a
preface to assignments that require use of the public library.
    SUBJ: Libraries, Public.

027.5   Ph-2 3-6/11 $19.00   L   KA587
FOWLER, ALLAN. Library of Congress. Children's Press ISBN 0-516-
20137-9; In Canada: Children's Press, 1996. 48p. col. ill. (True book).
    Includes bibliographies, directory, glossary and index.
    Gives the history of our national library: how it blazed the way for
public library service; the invention of Putnam's Library of Congress
classification system; some idea of its priceless holdings; and its
service to Congress. Useful as an introduction to a national treasure.
Readers may want to access the listed web sites for up-to-date

NONFICTION

information.
SUBJ: Library of Congress./ Libraries.

VCR 028.7   Ph-3 3-5 $79.00   OD KA588
ANIMATED DICTIONARY (Videocassette). Society for Visual Education
95652-HAVT, 1992. 1/2" VHS videocassette color.
Includes teacher's guide and 12 skill sheets.
Reviews dictionary facts such as guide words, alphabetical order,
pronunciation guides, definitions, and synonyms. Discusses specialized
dictionaries and gives pointers to assist dictionary users. Breezy
animated format and talking books hold student's attention. Use for
review and to hone skills.
SUBJ: Reference books./ Encyclopedias and dictionaries./ Libraries.

031   Ph-2 4-A $8.50   P KA589
NEW AMERICAN DESK ENCYCLOPEDIA. 3RD REV. New American
Library ISBN 0-451-17566-2, 1993. 1374p. ill. (some col.), maps.
"Signet book."
Designed for quick ready reference, this mini encyclopedia includes a
sixteen page color atlas of the earth and universe. Allows for
browsing and enjoyment outside the assigned encyclopedia topics. A
duplicate copy is recommended for the reference collection.
SUBJ: Encyclopedias and dictionaries./ Atlases.

031.02   Ph-3 2-4/6 $9.59   L KA590
MATTHEWS, RUPERT. Record breakers of the sea. Troll ISBN 0-8167-
1925-X, 1990. 31p. col. ill. (Record breakers).
The calmest seas, the biggest jellyfish, the deepest ocean are among
the biggest, smallest, most unusual facts presented in this collection.
Brief explanations and an illustration accompany the 3 to 5 facts
found on each page. Fun for those not quite ready for THE
GUINNESS BOOK OF WORLD RECORDS.
The companion titles RECORD BREAKERS OF THE LAND (ISBN
0-8167-1923-3, 1990) and RECORD BREAKERS OF THE AIR (ISBN
0-8167-1921-7, 1990) follow the same pattern.
SUBJ: Curiosities and wonders./ World records.

031.02   Ph-2 4-A/6 $15.95   P KA591
PETERSON, PATRICIA R. Know it all: resource book for kids. Zephyr
Press ISBN 0-913757-45-4, 1989. 144p b&w illus.
From common abbreviations to a world map, this alphabetical list of
curricula topics offers brief definitions and informative drawings.
Good for browsing and refreshing memories, especially in math,
language arts, and science. Great desk reference for students and
teachers alike.
SUBJ: Miscellanea./ Encyclopedias and dictionaries./ Questions and
answers.

069   Ph-3 3-6/6 $8.95   P KA592
GRIER, KATHERINE. Discover: investigate the mysteries of history with
40 practical projects probing our past. Illustrated by Pat Cupples.
Addison-Wesley ISBN 0-201-52322-1; In Canada: Addison-Wesley,
1990. 96p. ill. (Royal Ontario Museum book).
Includes glossary and index.
Activities, loosely arranged around museum exhibits, invite children to
investigate and learn. Includes puzzles and crafts such as weaving
and mask making. A "back door" approach to scientific inquiry that
makes learning fun in and out of the classroom or for youth groups
such as scouts.
SUBJ: Scientific recreations./ Archaeology--Experiments./ Fossils--
Experiments./ Experiments.

070.4   Ph-3 6-A/7 $13.90   L KA593
KAPLAN, ANDREW. Careers for wordsmiths. Interviews by Andrew
Kaplan. Photos by Edward Keating and Carrie Boretz. Millbrook ISBN
1-56294-024-4, 1991. 64p. ill. (Choices).
Includes directory, bibliography and glossary/index.
Interviews 14 people from songwriter to lexicographer. First person
accounts give unique slant and meaning to language-related careers.
Subjects come from a wide range of backgrounds. Solid addition to
career units.
SUBJ: Journalism--Vocational guidance./ Vocational guidance--
Journalism./ Reporters and reporting--Vocational guidance./
Vocational guidance--Reporters and reporting.

CDR 070.4   Ph-2 4-A $149.95   OD KA594
OWENS, PETER. Classroom newspaper workshop (CD-ROM). By Dr.
Peter Owens. Tom Snyder Productions CNW-J, 1995. 1 CD-ROM color.
Version 1.0.
Includes teacher's guide, student reporter's notebooks and sponsorship
kit.
Also available on Macintosh 3.5" disks or Appleshare network
version 3.5" disks.
System requirements: Color Macintosh with at least 4MB of RAM;

hard drive with 9MB of space; minimum 12" color monitor set to
256 colors or gray scales; System 7.0 or higher; CD-ROM drive.
Designed to be used by individual students or small groups, the
program provides skills modules and practice lessons on generating
ideas, doing interviews, writing stories, developing headlines,
generating layouts, and editing. An electronic mail allows for ease of
sending messages, and a built-in Internet connection is included.
Excellent tool for teaching students the parts of newspaper
production.
SUBJ: Newspapers--Software./ Software--Newspapers./ Journalism--
Software./ Software--Journalism./ Interactive media.

VCR 070.4   Ph-3 5-6 $195.00   KA595
SO YOU WANT TO BE?: NEWSPAPER ARTIST (Videocassette).
Pyramid Media 02493, 1994. 1/2" VHS videocassette color (15min).
(So you want to be?).
Explores the responsibilities of a newspaper artist and discusses the
skills necessary in the job. Lively graphics, question-and-answer
format, and a cheerful host keep matters moving. Fits with career
studies activities.
SUBJ: Journalism--Vocational guidance./ Vocational guidance--
Journalism./ Graphic arts--Vocational guidance./ Vocational
guidance--Graphic arts./ Occupations.

071   Ph-1 3-6/5 $14.99   L KA596
GRANFIELD, LINDA. Extra! extra!: the who, what, where, when and why
of newspapers. Illus. by Bill Slavin. Orchard ISBN 0-531-08683-6; In
Canada: Kids Can Press, 1994. 72p. ill.
Includes index.
Here's everything you ever wanted to know about setting up a
neighborhood or school newspaper: gathering, discovering, publishing,
and recycling the news. Coverage includes an interview with cartoonist
Lynn "For better or for worse" Johnson, the specialized, abbreviated
advertising lingo, page paste up, and craft activities to recycle
wastepaper. Perfect for neophyte publishers.
SUBJ: Newspapers./ Handicraft.

080   Ph-3 4-A/7 $15.95   T KA597
BURLEIGH, ROBERT. Who said that?: famous Americans speak. Illus. by
David Catrow. Henry Holt ISBN 0-8050-4394-2; In Canada: Fitzhenry &
Whiteside, 1997. 45p. ill.
Presents 21 quotations tied to American history along with their
significance and thumbnail sketches of the people who uttered them
such as United States presidents, other historical figures, artists,
actors, and musicians. Cartoon illustrations capture the spirit of the
text and offer an extended invitation to stay and browse. Use as a
back door entry to the past.
SUBJ: Quotations./ Celebrities.

133.1   Ph-3 5-6/5 $13.99   T KA598
COHEN, DANIEL. Ghost in the house. Illus. by John Paul Caponigro.
Cobblehill/Dutton ISBN 0-525-65131-4, 1993. 60p. ill.
Discusses nine hauntings worldwide and the fuel that spiritualism fed
to nightmare happenings. Reporting is straightforward without
conjecture or reasonable explanations. Readers are left to wonder
about some rather strange occurrences. Perfect for Halloween and
sleepovers.
SUBJ: Haunted houses./ Ghosts.

133.1   Ph-3 4-6/7 $14.99   T KA599
COHEN, DANIEL. Ghostly warnings. Illus. by David Linn. Cobblehill/
Dutton ISBN 0-525-65227-2; In Canada: McClelland & Stewart, 1996.
64p. ill.
The cover guarantees a horde of readers waiting to be frightened,
and they will be--beginning with tales of deadly doubles that
prophesy doom and ending with a Middle Eastern legend of the lady
in black. Cohen's writing is sparce and to the point. Let teachers
know they can insert some ghosts when discussing Napoleon or Guy
de Maupassant. Try on reluctant readers!
SUBJ: Ghosts./ Parapsychology.

133.1   Ph-3 4-6/7 $14.95   T KA600
COHEN, DANIEL. Ghosts of the deep. Putnam ISBN 0-399-22435-1; In
Canada: Putnam, 1993. 103p.
Meet nautical ghosts, who haunt lighthouses, inns, and ships in 16
tales that will add salt to any oceangoing unit. Murder and mayhem
are kept to a minimum, and there are no accompanying creepy
drawings that might entice reluctant readers. Fun to read aloud;
landlubbers will pick up a seaworthy vocabulary.
SUBJ: Ghosts./ Supernatural./ Sea stories./ Shipwrecks.

133.1   Ph-2 4-A/6 $14.95   T KA601
COHEN, DANIEL. Ghosts of War. Putnam ISBN 0-399-22200-6; In
Canada: Putnam, 1990. 82p.

Ghosts speak from Civil War locations and dead soldiers appear at home before their loved ones are even notified of their demise. Eighteen chapters of captivating stories pique the reader's curiosity. Social studies teachers who share the tales related to teaching units can't miss.
SUBJ: Ghosts.

133.1   Ph-3 4-6/4 $13.00   T   KA602
COHEN, DANIEL. Great ghosts. Illustrated by David Linn. Cobblehill/ Dutton ISBN 0-525-65039-3, 1990. 48p. ill.
Matter-of-fact renditions of nine famous ghosts including the Flying Dutchman. No explanations are given. Enticing for the reluctant reader.
SUBJ: Ghosts.

133.1   Ph-3 4-A/9 $13.99   T   KA603
COHEN, DANIEL. Young ghosts. Rev ed. Cobblehill/Dutton ISBN 0-525-65154-3, c1978, 1994. 106p. ill.
Includes bibliography and index.
Accounts of children and young people who have either seen ghosts or become ghosts. Black and white photographs and prints enhance text.
SUBJ: Ghosts.

133.1   Ph-3 4-A/7 $13.95   T   KA604
DEEM, JAMES M. How to find a ghost. Illus. by True Kelley. Houghton Mifflin ISBN 0-395-46846-9, 1988. 138p. ill.
Includes bibliography and index.
Documented sightings, categories of ghosts, and instructions for doing research as well as hunting for ghosts are included in this lively and interesting approach. The author's belief in ghosts is apparent throughout. Likely to appeal to the curious without being overly scary.
SUBJ: Ghosts./ Supernatural./ Psychical research.

133.1   Ph-1 A/9 $9.95   P   KA605
JONES, LOUIS C. Things that go bump in the night. Illustrated by Erwin Austin. Syracuse University Press ISBN 0-8156-0184-0, c1959, 1983. 208p. ill. (York state book).
Includes notes and index.
Telling over 200 stories of unbelievable happenings, this book is a gold mine for storytellers, American folklore buffs, and spook fans. Especially worthwhile is a chapter on haunted history, certain to spark social studies.
SUBJ: Ghosts./ Folklore--United States./ United States--Folklore.

133.4   Ph-2 3-5/4 $3.50   P   KA606
KRENSKY, STEPHEN. Witch hunt: it happened in Salem Village. Illus. by James Watling. Random House ISBN 0-394-81923-3; In Canada: Random House, 1989. 48p. col. ill. (Step into reading).
Recounts the events of the late seventeenth century Salem Village witch hunts, sparked by a group of ten girls, which eventually caused nineteen persons to be hanged for practicing witchcraft. Describing events of the witch hunt as "a time when fear and hate ruled over common sense," the author provides a high interest/easy reading text useful in curriculum units.
SUBJ: Witchcraft--Massachusetts--Salem./ Salem (Mass.)--History-- Colonial period, ca. 1600-1775.

133.4   Ph-1 A/7 $19.95   L   KA607
WILSON, LORI LEE. Salem witch trials. Lerner ISBN 0-8225-4889-5, 1997. 112p. ill. (some col.), map. (How history is invented).
Includes bibliography and index.
Three-hundred-year-old events in Salem, Massachusetts continue to haunt and pique curiosity. The author returns to historical court documents, diaries, and letters to recreate the texture of the time and chronicle events. Describes revisionist views, Robert Calef's Rationalist arguments, Freud's studies of hysteria, Arthur Miller's CRUCIBLE and the House Committee on Un-American Activities, and current feminist beliefs. Final chapters reveal how the town has capitalized on its lurid reputation and the Halloween migration of Wicca believers. Outstanding historical research written on a subject with much appeal. For mature readers.
SUBJ: Witchcraft--Massachusetts--Salem./ Trials (Witchcraft)-- Massachusetts--Salem.

133.5   Ph-1 K-6/4 $15.95   T   KA608
YOUNG, ED. Cat and Rat: the legend of the Chinese zodiac. Henry Holt ISBN 0-8050-2977-X; In Canada: Fitzhenry & Whiteside, 1995. unp. col. ill.
Animals race for the Jade Emperor to gain one of the twelve immortal places in the Chinese zodiac. Full-page charcoal and chalk drawings depict the strength and fierceness of the contest. Includes a chart of the Chinese calendar. The pourquoi tale will be useful when discussing the Chinese New Year.
SUBJ: Astrology, Chinese./ Zodiac./ China--Folklore./ Folklore--China.

133.8   Ph-3 4-6/3 $14.95   L   KA609
GREEN, CARL R. Mysterious mind powers. By Carl R. Green and William R. Sanford. Illus. by Keith Robinson. Enslow ISBN 0-89490-455-8, 1993. 48p. ill. (Exploring the unknown).
Includes glossary, bibliography and index.
Describes telepathy and psychokinesis as well as tests used by scientists who study the phenomena. Includes tests for readers to use to discover their own psychic abilities.
SUBJ: Telepathy./ Psychokinesis.

133.8   Ph-3 4-6/5 $14.95   L   KA610
GREEN, CARL R. Seeing the unseen. By Carl R. Green and William R. Sanford. Illus. by Keith Robinson. Enslow ISBN 0-89490-454-X, 1993. 48p. ill. (Exploring the unknown).
Includes glossary, bibliography and index.
Examines the mysterious phenomena of precognition and clairvoyance using documented experiences. Evenhanded presentation of a highly appealing topic.
SUBJ: Clairvoyance./ Precognition./ Extrasensory perception.

133.9   Ph-3 4-6/3 $14.95   L   KA611
GREEN, CARL R. Recalling past lives. By Carl R. Green and William R. Sanford. Illus. by Keith Robinson. Enslow ISBN 0-89490-458-2, 1993. 48p. ill. (Exploring the unknown).
Includes glossary, bibliography and index.
Traces the puzzles of reincarnation, hypnotic regression, and deja vu, citing case studies and possible explanations. Evenly presented with the caution that there is much about the human brain that is still to be discovered. Topic is appealing, well researched, and documented.
SUBJ: Reincarnation.

152.14   Ph-2 4-A/5 $10.95   P   KA612
DOHERTY, PAUL. Cheshire cat and other eye-popping experiments on how we see the world. By Paul Doherty, Don Rathjen and the Exploratorium Teacher Institute. Wiley ISBN 0-471-11516-9; In Canada: Wiley, 1995. 114p. ill. (Exploratorium science snackbook series).
Includes index.
Explore visual perception and discover that what you "see" is not always what you "get." Experiments originally designed as hands-on activities for science museum exhibits are presented for classroom and home use. Each includes a list of materials and the time needed to conduct. Sessions requiring adult help are indicated.
SUBJ: Visual perception--Experiments./ Experiments.

152.14   Ph-1 P-A $12.88   L   KA613
HOBAN, TANA. Dots, spots, speckles, and stripes. Greenwillow ISBN 0-688-06863-4, 1987. unp. col. ill.
Exquisite photography explores the commonplace, focussing on pattern, color and size relationships in animals, vegetables and minerals. Pages to be explored and enjoyed by all ages.
SUBJ: Shape./ Form perception.

152.14   Ph-2 P $16.00   T   KA614
HOBAN, TANA. Is it red? Is it yellow? Is it blue? An adventure in color. Greenwillow ISBN 0-688-80171-4, 1978. unp. col. ill.
Color circles at the bottom of the page identify the major colors shown in the brilliantly executed photographs of city life. Very useful for visual perception as well as color identification.
SUBJ: Color./ Size./ Space perception./ Shape.

152.14   Ph-2 P-2 $15.93   L   KA615
HOBAN, TANA. Just look. Greenwillow ISBN 0-688-14041-6, 1996. unp. col. ill.
Just look through die-cut circles that focus on one small portion of a photograph and try to guess what is pictured. Shiny black frames the wordless pages and quality photographs that comprise this surprising guessing game. Objects pictured are less common than those in Hoban's earlier work.
SUBJ: Visual perception./ Toy and movable books.

152.14   Ph-1 P-3 $12.88   L   KA616
HOBAN, TANA. Look! look! look! Greenwillow ISBN 0-688-07240-2, 1988. unp. col. ill.
Handsome, full page color photographs are viewed first through a small, square, cutout hole then when the page is turned the entire picture is seen.
SUBJ: Visual perception.

152.14   Ph-1 P-1 $13.95   L   KA617
HOBAN, TANA. Shapes and things. Macmillan ISBN 0-02-744060-5, c1970. unp. ill.
Common household objects take on new meanings in this wordless collection of silhouettes on black background. Great for encouraging observation in tots, this can double as a creative spur to any child

aspiring to create artistic work, but not knowing where to begin.
SUBJ: Silhouettes./ Size./ Shape.

152.14 Ph-2 P-A $15.93 L KA618
HOBAN, TANA. Take another look. Greenwillow ISBN 0-688-84298-4,
1981. unp. ill.
As in "Look Again" Hoban's photography allows the viewer an
unfamiliar view of the familiar. Nine black & white subjects are first
presented completely covered except for a small circular opening.
Turning the page shows the entire subject by itself; turning once again
shows the subject as part of its total environment.
SUBJ: Visual perception.

152.14 Ph-3 P-K/2 $14.95 T KA619
JENKINS, SANDRA. Flip-flap. Photos by Andy Crawford...[et al.]. Illus.
by John Hutchinson. DK Publishing ISBN 0-7894-0121-5, 1995. 23p. col.
ill.
Match shapes, colors, and numbers in this oversized presentation with
lots of color and pizzazz. Beginners will have fun manipulating a
number wheel and numerous flaps to discover the wealth of pictured
toys, foods, and familiar objects.
SUBJ: Concepts./ Visual perception./ Toy and movable books.

152.14 Ph-1 3-A $12.95 T KA620
MAGIC EYE: A NEW WAY OF LOOKING AT THE WORLD. 3D
illusions by N.E. Thing Enterprises. Andrews and McMeel ISBN 0-8362-
7006-1; In Canada: Gage, 1993. 32p. col. ill. (Magic eye).
With a little practice staring at these pages, amazing three-
dimensional objects leap off the paper. Effects are made possible by
the computer-generated "Salitsky Dot" patterns. This new and
popular craze refutes the old saw: "There's nothing new under the
sun." Art and computer teachers will enjoy challenging classes to
come up with their own versions based upon a modern, mechanized
Seurat. Include in discussions of optical illusions, color, and graphics.
Also recommended: MAGIC EYE II: NOW YOU SEE IT... (ISBN
0-8362-7009-6, 1994).
SUBJ: Visual perception./ Optical illusions.

152.14 Ph-2 1-6/7 $13.95 T KA621
WESTRAY, KATHLEEN. Picture puzzler. Ticknor & Fields ISBN 0-395-
70130-9, 1994. unp. col. ill.
Optical illusions fool the eye and fascinate all ages. Here are puzzles
based on American folk art. This is a unique and innovative approach
to a perennially favorite topic. Use to explore the deception of
perception.
SUBJ: Optical illusions./ Visual perception.

VCR 152.4 Ph-3 4-6 $245.00 KA622
ANGRY JOHN (Videocassette). Pyramid Media 01265 ISBN 1-55981-
385-7, 1994. 1/2" VHS videocassette color (23min).
A violent cartoon character, Angry John, comes out of the TV and
goads a young (African-American male) viewer. The boy gets
involved with spray paint vandalism and is sent to the school
counselor who teaches him better methods for dealing with anger.
Highly entertaining and powerful in depicting the affects of media
violence. Youngsters are going to root for the superhero mischief
maker unless the teacher has done a lot of preparation before
viewing.
SUBJ: Anger./ Emotions./ Behavior.

152.4 Ph-1 P-2/6 $15.95 T KA623
BROWN, TRICIA. Someone special, just like you. Photos by Fran Ortiz.
Henry Holt ISBN 0-8050-0481-5; In Canada: Fitzhenry & Whiteside,
1984. 64p. ill.
Includes bibliography.
Captures through brief text and multiple large b/w photographs the
joyous moods as physically and mentally handicapped young students
participate in all parts of life. A good read aloud for understanding
how handicapped enjoy the same things that others do.
SUBJ: Physically handicapped./ Mentally handicapped./
Handicapped.

152.4 Ph-3 4-6/8 $12.95 L KA624
FLEMING, ALICE. What, me worry?: how to hang in when your
problems stress you out. Scribner's ISBN 0-684-19277-2; In Canada:
Maxwell Macmillan, 1992. 88p.
Includes index.
Sound advice on how to fend off depression and anxiety. Inserts
anecdotes of historical and celebrity worriers who faced stress with
humor, courage, and grace. Gives advice on harnessing problems,
developing moral courage, and getting along with parents, teachers,
and friends. Useful book for the introspective.
SUBJ: Worry./ Conduct of life.

PIC 152.4 Ph-3 1-3 $107.00 OD KA625
HOW DO I FEEL? (Picture). Shorewood Reproductions 0128, 1974. 12
art prints in case, color 27x22in.
Also available mounted $143.00.
Includes teacher's guide.
Prints of works of well-known artists are used as a stimulus for
discussions between teachers and children concerning personal
emotions and feelings. Includes paintings by such artists as Munch,
Nast, Picasso, Wyeth.
SUBJ: Emotions--Pictorial works./ Paintings.

VCR 152.4 Ph-2 K-3 $59.95 OD KA626
I GET SO MAD! (Videocassette). Sunburst Communicatons 2417 ISBN
0-7805-4100-6, 1993. 1/2" VHS videocassette color (13min), 1 sound
cassette (5min).
Includes teacher's guide and reproducible worksheets.
Also available in Spanish 241796-PJ.
Recognizes that children experience intense anger and that the
seemingly hopelessness of situations often increases aggression. Shows
three methods of self help: talk, thought, and action. Suggestions
include compromise, screaming into a pillow, and physical activity.
Will help very young children learn to deal confidently with their
anger without resorting to violence.
SUBJ: Anger./ Behavior.

VCR 152.4 Ph-3 1-3 $59.95 OD KA627
I'M SO FRUSTRATED! (Videocassette). Sunburst Communicatons 2489
ISBN 0-7805-4166-9, 1994. 1/2" VHS videocassette color (20min).
Includes teacher's guide, sound recording cassette and reproducible
worksheets.
Learning new things often causes frustration. Although youngsters may
not know the name for this condition, they certainly have experienced
it. Video offers this advice: count to ten, take a break, try to do one
step at a time, get someone to help. Depicts children building with
plastic blocks, tackling a two step math problem, and making a bird
house. Even the clown narrator learns to ask for juggling advice.
Shows that initial failure is part of learning and offers attainable self-
help.
SUBJ: Frustration./ Emotions./ Behavior.

VCR 152.4 Ph-3 4-6 $99.00 OD KA628
IT'S NOT MY FAULT: A PROGRAM ABOUT CONFLICT RESOLUTION
(Videocassette). Disney Educational 68927, 1981. 1/2" VHS
videocassette color (18min).
Includes teacher's guide.
A young boy and his brother begin the day arguing and teasing.
Their fighting escalates into trouble at school, hurt feelings, and an
almost ruined friendship. Students will see themselves in the painful
situations in which everybody is so busy being angry that the other
person's side is never considered. Finally the boy's mother gently
coaxes him into expressing his feelings verbally and hearing both
sides of an argument. Characters are likable and real though their
problems are solved too simply. Some of the incidences are painted in
such broad strokes that students may view it as a comedy. Teacher
preview is necessary to prepare the class.
SUBJ: Anger./ Self-control./ Behavior.

SRC 152.4 Ph-3 K-1 $10.95 OD KA629
MURPHY, JANE. Songs for you and me: kids learn about feelings and
emotions (Sound recording cassette). Kimbo KIM 8085C, n.d. 1 sound
cassette.
Includes teacher's guide.
Songs about tolerance, friendship, honesty, school spirit and handling
fear are here with easy to learn lyrics which should encourage
emotional growth. There is some unevenness; teachers may not want
the suggestion "put thumbtacks on his chair" for getting even with a
bully or the idea that everyone's family has a mother, father, sister,
brother, etc. The majority of songs are helpful.
SUBJ: Emotions./ Behavior./ Fear.

152.4 Ph-1 P-2/2 $12.95 T KA630
SIMON, NORMA. I was so mad. Illus. by Dora Leder. Whitman ISBN
0-8075-3520-6, 1974. 40p. col. ill.
A comfortable portrayal of many familiar, everyday situations that are
experienced by children and cause them to feel anger and hostilities.
By showing children experiencing parental domination, sibling rivalry,
school pressures, peer relationships, humiliation, anxiety, etc., young
readers are helped to understand why they get angry and frustrated
and what to do about it.
SUBJ: Emotions.

VCR 152.4 Ph-3 5-6 $135.00 OD KA631
WHEN I GET MAD (Videocassette). Film Ideas WCM 68, 1994. 1/2"
VHS videocassette color (14min). (Life lessons).

Includes teacher's guide.
Closed captioned.
Conveys that all emotions are acceptable and illustrates positive ways to deal with anger. Demonstrates that children can depend upon themselves to find solutions to troubling situations and learn to control their anger. Good for group discussion.
SUBJ: Anger./ Emotions./ Behavior.

VCR 152.4 Ph-3 4-6 $99.95 OD KA632
WHEN YOU'RE MAD, MAD, MAD!: DEALING WITH ANGER (Videocassette). Sunburst Communications 2365, 1993. 1/2″ VHS videocassette color (33min).
Includes teacher's guide.
Three stories show how disappointed and angry people become when expectations aren't met, when friends let them down, and when parents won't listen. Discussion questions allow students to explore problem solving away from the heat of anger, a sensible approach to nonviolent resolutions.
SUBJ: Anger./ Behavior.

153 Ph-2 A/8 $9.95 P KA633
BARRETT, SUSAN L. It's all in your head: a guide to understanding your brain and boosting your brain power. Rev. ed. Illus. by Jackie Urbanovic. Free Spirit ISBN 0-915-793-45-8, 1992. 151p. ill.
Includes bibliography and index.
Teacher's guide available (ISBN 0-915793-46-6), $6.95.
Uses current scientific discoveries to explain the human brain. Includes exercises to increase memory and hone thinking skills along with useful ideas for hooking up to biofeedback. Teachers working with creative writing, problem solving, and national contests such as Invent America will want this book.
SUBJ: Brain./ Intellect.

153.14 Ph-2 P-1/2 $14.89 L KA634
MURPHY, STUART J. Pair of socks. Illus. by Lois Ehlert. HarperCollins ISBN 0-06-025880-2; In Canada: HarperCollins, 1996. 33p. col. ill. (MathStart).
Includes bibliography.
Brightly colored socks with geometric patterns allow the reader to seek and find a match. Rhyming text involves familiar encounters with a washing machine and a pet pooch.
SUBJ: Pattern perception.

MCP 153.4 Ph-1 2-4 $59.95 OD KA635
FACTORY: EXPLORATIONS IN PROBLEM SOLVING (Microcomputer program). Sunburst 6475, 1983. 3.5″disk, backup disk.
Includes teacher's guide.
Network versions available.
Also available for IBM PC & PCjr; IBM PS/2 Model 25; Tandy 1000; MS Windows 3.1 or higher, and Apple family.
Available in Spanish LA FABRICA for Macintosh 4038 and Apple 6398 only.
System requirements: Macintosh family (1MB), hard drive or 2 800K disk drives required.
Spanish version LA FABRICA 6908 available.
Designed to develop problem solving skills, the three programs focus on experimentation and sequencing by involving the student first in finding out the capabilities of three machines; second in creating an assembly line of up to eight machines and noting the resulting product; and third, upon being given a product, being challenged to replicate the unknown assembly line. Creative graphics hallmark these programs, which may be used by individuals or a small group.
Contents: 1: Test a machine; 2: Build a factory; 3: Make a product.
SUBJ: Problem solving--Software./ Logic--Software./ Software--Problem solving./ Software--Logic.

MCP 153.4 Ph-1 P-1 $59.00 OD KA636
SNAPDRAGON (Microcomputer program). MECC MS325, 1992. 2 3.5″ disks.
Version 1.0.
Includes teacher's guide and ready reference card.
Also available for MacIntosh Plus or later, 1MB, MS225.
System requirements: MS-DOS 386 or higher, DOS 5.0 or higher, 256-color VGA or SVGA, 460K, 1MB RAM and DOS 5.0 or higher for Novell.
The discovery learning program provides practice in classifying objects as well as allowing for active play. Youngsters play with objects on a farm, in the bathtub, in space, and a variety of other scenes. A radio plays a number of songs and a coloring book option allows for creation and printing of those creations. Ease of use and a wealth of options make this usable in a learning center environment or at home with a parent. (Parents' Shelf)
SUBJ: Reasoning--Software./ Software--Reasoning./ Problem solving--Software./ Software--Problem solving./ Educational games--Software./ Software--Educational games.

MCP 153.7 Ph-2 4-A $65.00 OD KA637
BUILDING PERSPECTIVE: STRATEGIES IN PROBLEM SOLVING (Microcomputer program). Wings for Learning/Sunburst 6529, 1986. 3.5″ disk, 1 backup disk.
Includes teacher's guide.
Network versions available.
IBM and Tandy 1000 (256K) available.
Apple II family (64K) available.
System requirements: Macintosh family (4MB); color monitor required; Ethernet or other network with comparable transmission rates recommended for Network Version.
Also available for IBM and Tandy 1000 (256K), color graphics adapter and color monitor required; Windows 3.1 or higher (4MB), SVGA color monitor recommended; Apple II family (64K).
Problem solving skills such as scanning for clues, looking for a pattern, and gathering information are practiced with this software. The object is to develop a bird's-eye view of a grid of skyscrapers. Arrays of 3, 4, or 5 squares can be used. Visual perception/thinking skills are improved when using this program. Excellent choice for use with girls. Works well with pairs at the computer.
SUBJ: Visual perception--Software./ Problem solving--Software./ Software--Visual perception./ Software--Problem solving.

SRC 155.2 Ph-3 P-1 $9.95 KA638
EPSTEIN-KRAVIS, ANNA. Happy to be me (Sound recording cassette). Self esteem songs by Rita Gold and Anna Epstein Kravis. Anna Epstein-Kravis GG 101, 1993. 1 sound cassette (31min).
Includes lyrics.
Snappy little tunes with a variety of background accompaniment allow youngsters to sing about manners, safety, self-worth, and more. Easily learned lyrics will reinforce much of the early childhood curriculum.
SUBJ: Self-perception./ Individuality./ Songs.

VCR 155.2 Ph-3 3-6 $59.95 OD KA639
EVERYBODY'S DIFFERENT (Videocassette). Sunburst Communications 2481 ISBN 0-7805-4164-2, 1994. 1/2″ VHS videocassette color (14min).
Includes teacher's guide, sound recording cassette and reproducible worksheets.
A young boy brings a sandwich to school made with Russian black bread. A girl has to wear a patch over one eye and doesn't like her appearance. Both children have a difference that sets them apart. Helpful teachers give advice: all people are different, that's what makes us interesting. Could lead to discussions about disabilities and ethnic differences. The message is you are what you are and that's acceptable. Use in units on persons with disabilities.
SUBJ: Individuality./ Self-acceptance.

VCR 155.2 Ph-3 3-6 $59.95 OD KA640
NO ONE QUITE LIKE ME...OR YOU (Videocassette). Sunburst Communicatons 2395, 1992. 1/2″ VHS videocassette color (17min).
Includes teacher's guide and 8 reproducible activity sheets.
Four vignettes illustrate that people have different interests and come in various colors, sizes, and shapes. One shows a class learning about their ethnic heritages. Another encourages children to explore their own interests. The last episode depicts a physical handicap singling out someone different. The message is to accept and enjoy yourself and not try to change what you cannot. The idea is presented that individual differences are real and should not be reasons for hurt feelings or embarrassment. Video will encourage personal examples. Perfect for classrooms where getting along is sometimes a chore.
SUBJ: Individuality./ Self-acceptance.

SRC 155.2 Ph-1 P-1 $11.95 OD KA641
PALMER, HAP. Getting to know myself (Sound recording cassette). Educational Activities AC 543, 1972. 1 sound cassette (30min).
Includes teacher's guide.
Compact disc available from Educational Activities CD 543, 1972 (30min), $14.95.
Hap Palmer's snappy lyrics involve young children in learning about emotions (anger, sadness, fear) and directions (forward, back, left, right). Musical arrangements insure lots of fun and audience participation. Many opportunities for free ranging expression and creative movement.
SUBJ: Individuality./ Songs./ Singing games.

VCR 155.4 Ph-3 3-6 $59.95 OD KA642
IT'S NOT FAIR! (Videocassette). Sunburst Communications 2437 ISBN 0-7805-4108-1, 1994. 1/2″ VHS videocassette color (14min).
Includes teacher's guide and reproducible student worksheets.
Kids make their own rules to decide what's fair on the playground, in the classroom, and at home. Encourages talking about and understanding both sides of a conflict. Shows that young people are old enough to set their own rules and consequences. Although some

of the actors seem wise beyond their years, students will relate to common childhood conflicts. "You-solve-it" plots encourage classroom discussion.
SUBJ: Fairness./ Conduct of life.

155.4   Ph-2 K-2/2 $13.99   L   KA643
SENISI, ELLEN B. Secrets. With an afterword by Carolyn Edwards, Ed.D. Dutton ISBN 0-525-45393-8, 1995. unp. col. ill.
As young children grow in independence, they discover the exclusiveness, pleasure and the sometimes burden of secrets. Large color photographs show how secets enter our thoughts and alert our conscience, as in the case of a stolen candy bar. Teachers will find this a useful discussion starter for reading aloud.
SUBJ: Secrets.

155.4   Ph-2 P-4/2 $13.95   L   KA644
SIMON, NORMA. I am not a crybaby. Illus. by Helen Cogancherry. Whitman ISBN 0-8075-3447-1; In Canada: General, 1989. unp. col. ill.
Insensitive adults, cruel words, unfortunate circumstances and childhood fears lead to crying--a natural escape mechanism. Here the young child learns that all people cry and it's okay; hurting is part of being human. A nice book for classroom sharing to foster self understanding.
SUBJ: Crying.

155.42   Ph-1 6-A/7 $13.95   L   KA645
YEPSEN, ROGER. Smarten up! how to increase your brain power. Little, Brown ISBN 0-316-96864-1; In Canada: Little, Brown, 1990. 117p. ill.
Includes index.
Smarten up by eating right, exercising, meditating, and applying the myriad of suggestions presented here. Some of the activities such as brainstorming and translating unfamiliar languages would be super used as teacher directed class activities to promote both the book and self-actualization.
SUBJ: Intellect./ Brain.

155.5   Ph-1 A/6 $17.95   T   KA646
JOHNSTON, ANDREA. Girls speak out: finding your true self. With an introduction by Gloria Steinem. Scholastic ISBN 0-590-89795-0; In Canada: Scholastic, 1997. 210p. ill.
Includes bibliography.
Written by a feminist to help girls navigate the maze of cultural expectations, media hype, and peer pressures. Ms. Johnson has outlined lessons from her Green Stone classroom (named after Alice Walker's story "Finding the green stone"). The stone represents the true inner person where no one else can go. Girls are taught to think for themselves regardless of neglect, sexual and/or verbal abuse, racial bias, etc. Includes women's and girls' written responses as they learn to become their stronger selves. All issues are dealt with honestly. Emphasis is on self worth. Most useful when both a caring adult and girl can read and discuss together.
SUBJ: Self-esteem./ Self-perception./ Adolescence.

155.9   Ph-1 5-6/5 $13.95   L   KA647
BRATMAN, FRED. Everything you need to know when a parent dies. Rosen ISBN 0-8239-1324-4; In Canada: Rosen, 1992. 64p. ill. (some col.). (Need to know library).
Includes glossary, directory, bibliography and index.
Explains how to deal with conflicting emotions of anger and grief. Discusses caring for the terminally ill, visiting the hospital, and attending the funeral. Demonstrates how, with love and friendship, the process of healing will evolve. For children and their teachers who are either experiencing tragedy firsthand or helping someone else cope.
SUBJ: Death./ Parent and child.

155.9   Ph-1 K-4/5 $14.95   L   KA648
BROWN, LAURENE KRASNY. When dinosaurs die: a guide to understanding death. By Laurie Krasny Brown and Marc Brown. Little, Brown ISBN 0-316-10917-7; In Canada: Little, Brown, 1996. 32p. col. ill.
Includes glossary.
Written in comic book format and illustrated with humanoid dinosaurs, this book presents facts and sorrows of death on a level very young children can understand. Matter-of-fact openness is useful in defusing confusion and grief. Will help classmates to empathize with friends and families who have experienced irrevocable loss. Diverse religions and secular beliefs are respected. (Parents' Shelf).
SUBJ: Death./ Grief.

155.9   Ph-3 K-3/4 $13.95   T   KA649
GREENLEE, SHARON. When someone dies. Illus. by Bill Drath. Peachtree ISBN 1-56145-044-8, 1992. unp. col. ill.
Gently reminds children that when someone dies everyone feels sad, that sometimes it helps to cry or write all your thoughts in a letter,

and that people can hold onto dear memories to help them deal with their hurt. May help a student through painful and confused mourning. Simply written and delicately illustrated.
SUBJ: Death./ Grief.

155.9   Ph-1 4-6/6 $15.95   L   KA650
KID'S BOOK ABOUT DEATH AND DYING. By and for kids, by Eric E. Rofes and the Unit of FayerweatherStreet School. Little, Brown ISBN 0-316-75390-4; In Canada: Little, Brown, 1985. 119p.
Includes bibliography.
Available from National Library Service for the Blind and Physically Handicapped on sound recording cassette RC24641.
Written to help children understand death is part of life, that it often comes without warning and no age is immune, the authors relate personal conversations with fourteen young people and stress the need for open, honest communication. Along with ageing and illness, the book covers accidents, homicide and suicide. It does not mention hospice nor does it deal directly with keeping patients alive on machines. Approach is personalized and centered on the thoughts and misgivings of those left behind. Should be very helpful.
SUBJ: Death./ Children's writings.

155.9   Ph-1 5-6/7 $13.95   L   KA651
LESHAN, EDA. Learning to say goodbye: when a parent dies. Illus. by Paul Giovanopoulos. Macmillan ISBN 0-02-756360-X, c1976. 85p. ill.
Includes bibliography.
Selectors' Choice, 11th ed.
Available from National Library Service for the Blind and Physically Handicapped on sound recording cassette RC15363.
A direct, simple, and honest discussion of the questions, reactions, fears and fantasies children and young people face when a parent or other person close to them dies. Gives suggestions for coping with grief and other related problems and provides many actual examples illustrating the points discussed.
SUBJ: Death./ Parent and child.

VCR 155.9   Ph-3 2-4 $59.95   OD KA652
SAYING GOOD-BYE (Videocassette). Sunburst Communcations 2394, 1993. 1/2" VHS videocassette color. (12min).
Includes teacher's guide and 2 reproducible activity sheets.
A teacher deals with questions and grief following the death of her class' pet rabbit. Concerns are handled with tact and respect as different children relate their experiences with death and mourning. Although theological concerns are omitted entirely, they are the most difficult to respond to and the video misses out by not addressing them. However, this is a worthwhile purchase because many teachers are not comfortable with discussions on death--especially with primary children.
SUBJ: Death./ Grief.

VCR 155.9   Ph-3 3-6 $59.95   OD KA653
STRESSBUSTERS (Videocassette). Sunburst Communications 2419 ISBN 0-7805-4104-9, 1994. 1/2" VHS videocassette color (15min).
Includes teacher's guide and reproducible student worksheets.
Offers advice on handling three stressful situations: peer rejection, parental squabbles, and overcommitting your time. Advice is down-to-earth with adults supplying understanding and support. Direct, no-frills presentation will hit home for students and offer nonthreatening help to many who may not even realize they need it.
SUBJ: Stress (Psychology).

VCR 158   Ph-3 3-5 $169.00   KA654
CHOOSE TO REFUSE: SAYING NO AND KEEPING YOUR FRIENDS (Videocassette). Human Relations Media 112 ISBN 1-55548-524-3, 1993. 1/2" VHS videocassette color (19min).
Includes teacher's guide.
Commonsense guidance for youngsters fighting daily battles of peer pressure. Allows children the power to take control by teaching five strategies: suggest a better idea, leave, give an excuse, ignore and walk away, or challenge the challenger. Also has tips for how to say "no" and mean it. Practice skills in the classroom until students are comfortable asserting themselves. Down-to-earth presentation with realistic advice.
SUBJ: Interpersonal relations./ Assertiveness (Psychology)./ Decision making.

VCR 158   Ph-3 4-6 $59.95   OD KA655
COOPERATION (Videocassette). Featuring Michael Pritchard. Live Wire Video, 1990. 1/2" VHS videocassette color (28min). (You can choose).
Includes teacher's guide.
Sold as a set of 10, $549.50.
Entertaining playlets about life skills are performed for a student audience which then discusses the topics. Differing views are explored through honest, spontaneous conversations led by Michael Pritchard.

Excellent for values education.
Additional videocassettes in this series include: BEING RESPONSIBLE (28min); DEALING WITH FEELINGS (28min); SAYING NO (28min); DOING THE RIGHT THING (28min); DEALING WITH DISAPPOINTMENT (28min); APPRECIATING YOURSELF (28min); ASKING FOR HELP (28min); BEING FRIENDS (28min); RESOLVING CONFLICTS.
SUBJ: Interpersonal relations./ Values./ Cooperation.

158   Ph-3 5-A/4 $10.95   P KA656
ERLBACH, ARLENE. Best friends book: true stories about real best friends... Photos by Stephen J. Carrera. Ed. by Pamela Espeland. Free Spirit ISBN 0-915793-77-6, 1995. 89p. ill.
Includes index.
First person accounts of young teenagers' experiences are coupled with advice on the care and feeding of friendships. Presents information on how to solve best friend problems, make new friends, and keep established friendships strong and growing. Lots of material for classroom discussions and much guidance to steer young people through emotional mazes.
SUBJ: Friendship.

VCR 158   Ph-3 4-6 $99.95   OD KA657
GO, GO, GOALS!: HOW TO GET THERE (Videocassette). Sunburst Communications 2430 ISBN 0-7805-4103-0, 1993. 1/2" VHS videocassette color (25min).
Includes teacher's guide.
With their teacher's help, a class learns how to set goals, brainstorm, take the first steps, reevaluate and succeed. Personal goals range from making new friends to remodeling a storage room into a bedroom. Demonstrates that self motivation is the key to achieving. Affirms the value of individual and group efforts as students help keep each other on track and often offers new approaches and insights. Will work well shown in segments, allowing class time for discussion, journal writing, and personal goal setting.
SUBJ: Motivation (Psychology)./ Success.

158   Ph-3 P-1/2 $14.95 T KA658
KALMAN, BOBBIE. Fun with my friends. Crabtree ISBN 0-86505-063-5, 1985. 32p col illus. (In my world).
Play with friends indoors or outside, play any one of a number of types of games--just be fair, follow the rules and you'll have fun. The format of a large illustration, brief text and thought questions results in 14 self-contained units that, though pedantic, have been used successfully with very young children.
SUBJ: Friendship.

158   Ph-2 6-A/6 $8.95 P KA659
KAUFMAN, GERSHEN. Stick up for yourself!: every kid's guide to personal power and positive self-esteem. By Gershen Kaufman and Lev Raphael. Edited by Pamela Espeland. Free Spirit ISBN 0-915793-17-2, 1990. 81p. ill.
Includes index.
Teacher's guide available separately (ISBN 0-915793-31-8, 1991), $14.95.
Assertiveness manual for elementary students discusses responsiblity, making choices, self-awareness, and self-esteem. Offers down-to-earth advice for handling bullies, friendship, and the demands of school and family. An evenhanded presentation that allows insight. Dynamite if used for class discussions and/or counseling.
SUBJ: Assertiveness (Psychology)./ Self-respect.

158   Ph-2 K-3/3 $15.95 L KA660
LEEDY, LOREEN. How humans make friends. Holiday House ISBN 0-8234-1223-7, 1996. unp. col. ill.
Cartoons of aliens and kids on large doublespreads demonstrate how to make friends, how to relate to friends, and how to be a friend. Also discusses conflicts and angry feelings in a manner young children can understand. Useful in discussions on conflict resolution.
SUBJ: Friendship.

VCR 158   Ph-2 3-4 $59.95   OD KA661
NO MORE TEASING! (Videocassette). Sunburst Communications 2490 ISBN 0-7805-4168-5, 1995. 1/2" VHS videocassette color (14min).
Includes teacher's guide and reproducible worksheets.
Join the No More Teasing Team and learn effective methods to deal with insensitive peers: walk away, ignore the teaser, and tell people how you feel and what you want. Teacher's guide has some alternate suggestions such as "Be a Pal Day" and role playing. Every child can use the tactics and good advice to gain confidence when facing teasing bullies.
SUBJ: Assertiveness (Psychology)./ Interpersonal relations./ Conflict management./ Bullies.

MCP 158   Ph-1 1-6 $99.95   OD KA662
ON THE PLAYGROUND (Microcomputer program). Tom Snyder Productions ISBN 0-926891-05-7, 1988. 1 3.5" disk, backup disk. (Choices, choices).
Includes teacher's guide.
Version 5.0 now available for Macintosh or Windows computers. Macintosh and Windows network versions: AppleShare or Novell based.
System requirements: Macintosh LC II or better; System 7.1 or higher; 4megs of available RAM; 256-color 13" monitor or larger.
An excellent simulation about accepting a new student who is very different. Playground scenarios are used for the simulation. Superb teaching tools and lesson plans are included. For use with the entire class at one time.
SUBJ: Interpersonal relations--Software./ Individuality--Software./ Software--Interpersonal relations./ Software--Individuality.

VCR 158   Ph-2 3-5 $59.95   OD KA663
SAY NO AND MEAN IT (Videocassette). Sunburst Communications 2359, 1991. 1/2" VHS videocassette color (17min).
Includes teacher's guide and 6 reproducible activity sheets.
Four contemporary plots feature techniques to deal politely but firmly with uncomfortable situations such as refusing to be conned into doing an unwanted job, or allowing friends to get you into trouble with threats of loss of friendship and taunts of "chicken". Stresses the need to know your own mind and hold firm against pressure. Teachers will need to state that children do not have the no option with parents and teachers. Be prepared for lively discussions and many true-life anecdotes.
SUBJ: Assertiveness (Psychology)./ Decision making.

158   Ph-3 5-A/6 $4.95 P KA664
SIMMONS, CASSANDRA WALKER. Becoming myself: true stories about learning from life. Free Spirit ISBN 0-915793-69-5, 1994. 137p.
A chatty, first-person account of a young girl facing the trials and tribulations of adolescence. Chapters on peer, family, and school pressures are evenhanded with the message: always stay true to yourself. Preteens enduring teasing, gossip, and worry will find solace.
SUBJ: Self-esteem./ Self-perception./ Adolescence.

MCP 158   Ph-1 1-6 $99.95   OD KA665
TAKING RESPONSIBILITY (Microcomputer program). Tom Snyder Productions ISBN 0-926891-07-3, 1988. 1 3.5" disk, backup disk. (Choices, choices).
Includes teacher's guide.
Also available for Windows 3.1 or higher.
Macintosh and Windows network versions: AppleShare or Novell based.
System requirements: Macintosh LC II or better; System 7.1 or higher; 4 megs of available RAM; 256-color 13" monitor or larger.
A vase broken while a trick on the teacher is being set up presents a predicament. A decision about telling the complete story and/or protecting a close friend must be made. The simulation itself, discussion ideas and lesson plans are extremely useful in this extraordinary tool for use with the entire classroom.
SUBJ: Responsibility--Software./ Decision making--Software./ Values--Software./ Software--Responsibility./ Software--Decision making./ Software--Values.

VCR 158   Ph-3 5-6 $135.00 OD KA666
THAT'S WHAT FRIENDS ARE FOR (Videocassette). Film Ideas WAFF 59, 1994. 1/2" VHS videocassette color (15min). (Life lessons).
Includes teacher's guide.
Closed captioned.
Young actors demonstrate that friends talk, share and do things together...that people who think alike gravitate towards one another. Offers a few condolences to those who encounter unfriendliness. Viewing live-action sequences will open the climate to helpful discussions, conflict resolution, and tolerance.
More "Life lessons" in HURTFUL WORDS HFW 146, 1993 (12min), $135.00.
SUBJ: Friendship./ Interpersonal relations.

MCP 172   Ph-1 5-A $149.95 OD KA667
COLONIZATION (Microcomputer program). Tom Snyder Productions COL ISBN 0-926891-50-2, 1986. 1 3.5" disk, backup disk. (Decisions, decisions).
Includes teacher's guide and student reference books.
Macintosh and Windows network versions: AppleShare or Novell based.
System requirements: Macintosh LC II or better; System 7.1 or higher; 4 megs of available RAM; 256-color 13" monitor or larger.
System requirements: Windows 3.1 or higher; 8 megs of RAM; 256-color VGA monitor.

NONFICTION

Assume the role of President of the U.S. and make a decision about allowing a private company to start a colony in outer space. While completing the simulation, students learn a great deal about the development of the American colonies in the 17th and 18th centuries and the reality of ethical decisions. The computer manages the simulation which also incorporates concerns about energy resources and is excellent for use with an entire class.
SUBJ: Colonization--Software./ Ethics--Software./ Energy--Software./ Problem solving--Software./ Software--Colonization./ Software--Ethics./ Software--Energy./ Software--Problem solving.

MCP 172   Ph-1 5-A $149.95   OD KA668
REVOLUTIONARY WARS: CHOOSING SIDES (Microcomputer program). Tom Snyder Productions ISBN 0-926891-56-1, 1986. 1 5.25" disk, backup disk. (Decisions, decisions).
Includes teacher's guide and student reference books.
Macintosh and Windows network versions: AppleShare or Novell based.
System requirements: Macintosh LC II or better; System 7.1 or higher; 4 megs of available RAM; 256-color 13" monitor or larger.
System requirements: Windows 3.1 or higher; 8 megs of RAM; 256-color VGA monitor.
Decide whether the country of Catalan will have a revolution to become an independent nation. Keeping with the tradition seen in this series of computer managed simulations this is excellent for teaching group problem-solving, history, and cooperative learning. Works well with an entire class and one computer.
SUBJ: Problem solving--Software./ Ethics--Software./ Revolutions--Software./ Software--Problem solving./ Software--Ethics./ Software--Revolutions.

VCR 177   Ph-3 5-6 $150.00   OD KA669
CHEATING, LYING AND STEALING (Videocassette). Film Ideas CLS 12, 1993. 1/2" VHS videocassette color (22min). (Life lessons).
Includes teacher's guide.
Closed captioned.
Three episodes explore dishonest actions and their consequences--a tennis player cheats in a match, a student claims credit for an outstanding computer project that his lab partner conducted alone, and a teenager shoplifts a bracelet. Realistic situations will encourage group discussion.
SUBJ: Honesty.

177   Ph-2 3-6/2 $16.95 L KA670
CRARY, ELIZABETH. Finders, keepers? Illustrated by Rebekah Strecker. Parenting Press ISBN 0-943990-39-4, 1987. 59p. ill. (Decision is yours book).
Two boys find a wallet lying along a path in the park. Their decision about how to deal with the wallet and its contents is presented in an enticing, very easy to read choose-your-own-solution format that should prove useful in the values curriculum when honesty is being discussed.
SUBJ: Honesty.

177   Ph-1 6-A/9 $13.95 T KA671
WEISS, ANN E. Lies, deception and truth. Houghton Mifflin ISBN 0-395-40486-X, 1988. 143p.
Includes index.
Selectors' Choice, 17th ed.
Discusses the ethics of lying and the rationale for white lies of deception, propaganda, censorship and apocryphal fables. Talks about judging the weight of a lie by its consequences and examines moral conundrums of politics, education, religion, media, medicine and more. Includes timely references to Presidents Reagan and Nixon; AIDS and abortion. A thought provoking book extremely useful for values education and social studies.
SUBJ: Honesty.

179   Ph-1 5-A/8 $14.95 L KA672
BLOYD, SUNNI. Animal rights. Lucent ISBN 1-56006-114-6, 1990. 128p. ill. (Overview).
Includes glossary, directory, bibliographies and index.
Covers current concerns over animal welfare in laboratory testing, experimental surgery, agribusiness, and schools. Outlines a ten step proposal (authored by the Animal Legal Defense Fund) that students can follow if they object to participating in animal experimentation. As public attitudes change, consciousness is raised, and people lobby for reforms. Graphic pictures are held to a minimum. Educated view of a timely controversy.
SUBJ: Animal rights./ Animals--Treatment.

179   Ph-1 3-6/7 $6.99 P KA673
NEWKIRK, INGRID. Kids can save the animals!: 101 easy things to do. Warner ISBN 0-446-39271-5, 1991. 234p. ill.

Includes directory.
This handbook empowers by suggesting constructive actions students can take to halt cruelty to animals: science fair guidelines, informed shopping, lobbying law makers, cleaning up the environment, and becoming a vegetarian. Also includes ideas for fund-raising and publicity. Will be useful to ecology clubs and other groups interested in protecting animals.
SUBJ: Animals--Treatment./ Animal rights.

179   Ph-3 6-A/9 $17.50 L KA674
OWEN, MARNA. Animal rights: yes or no? Lerner ISBN 0-8225-2603-4, 1993. 112p. ill. (some col.) (Pro/Con).
Includes directory, glossary, bibliography and index.
Explains how human attitudes towards animals are influenced by culture, beliefs, and occupations. Discusses how laws governing research and medicine are evolving. Not for the squeamish, but useful in tandem with current events and ethical debates.
SUBJ: Animal rights./ Animals--Treatment.

179   Ph-2 A/7 $17.95 L KA675
YOUNG, ED. Voices of the heart. Scholastic ISBN 0-590-50199-2; In Canada: Scholastic, 1997. unp. col. ill.
Invites readers to explore feelings such as joy and respect by analyzing 26 Chinese characters, each containing the heart symbol. Full-page, cut-paper collages reinterpret the Chinese characters, giving them a decidedly modern texture. Perfect blend of creativity and cultural awareness. Will serve as a resource for values education as well as inspiration for art classes. For multicultural studies.
SUBJ: Conduct of life./ Emotions./ Chinese language--Vocabulary.

220   Ph-3 4-6/5 $19.95 T KA676
HASTINGS, SELINA. Children's illustrated Bible. Stories retold by Selina Hastings. Illus. by Eric Thomas and Amy Burch. DK Publishing ISBN 1-56458-472-0, 1994. 320p. col. ill., maps.
Includes indexes.
The major stories of the Bible are retold in a simple, direct manner with dramatic illustrations to further the young reader's understanding of the text. Text is augmented by historical information and maps.
SUBJ: Bible stories--N.T./ Bible stories--O.T.

221.9   Ph-2 3-4/3 $15.95 L KA677
FISHER, LEONARD EVERETT. Moses. Retold from the Bible and illus. by Leonard Everett Fisher. Holiday House ISBN 0-8234-1149-4, 1995. unp. col. ill., map.
Includes bibliography.
A faithful retelling of the life of Moses is accompanied by dramatic paintings which show the plight of the Isralites as they flee Egypt to find the Promised Land. Excellent map prefaces the text.
SUBJ: Moses (Biblical leader)./ Bible stories--O.T.

221.9   Ph-3 4-6/6 $15.00 L KA678
GELLMAN, MARC. God's mailbox: more stories about stories in the Bible. Illus. by Debbie Tilley. Morrow ISBN 0-688-13169-7, 1996. 111p. ill.
Sequel to: DOES GOD HAVE A BIG TOE?, HarperCollins, 1989.
Rabbi Gellman conveys the wisdom of the Bible through several midrashim, stories about biblical stories. The reteller humorously presents anachronistic language and old stories with modern faces. The writing throughout is pedestrian, although the variety of tales and their morals will be useful, especially in religious schools where the Old Testament is studied. Tilley's black and white illustrations add dimension. Biblical chapter, verse, and lines are given. For reading aloud.
SUBJ: Bible. O.T.--Wit and humor./ Humorous stories.

221.9   Ph-2 P-2/6 $14.95 L KA679
HUTTON, WARWICK. Moses in the bulrushes. Retold and illustrated by Warwick Hutton. Atheneum ISBN 0-689-50393-8; In Canada: Collier Macmillan, 1986. unp. col. ill.
A simple retelling of the story of the infant Moses. Full-paged watercolor paintings and striking double-paged spreads add beauty to the beloved story.
SUBJ: Moses (Biblical leader)./ Bible stories--O.T.

221.9   Ph-2 3-4/7 $14.93 L KA680
MCDONOUGH, YONA ZELDIS. Eve and her sisters: women of the Old Testament. Illus. by Malcah Zeldis. Greenwillow ISBN 0-688-12513-1, 1994. 32p. col. ill.
The events of the lives of 14 women from the Bible are told from their point of view. Leaves the reader reassured that in Biblical times women were major figures. The folk art which accompanies the text is childlike and will encourage young artists. For women's studies.
SUBJ: Women in the Bible./ Bible stories--O.T.

221.9   Ph-1 P-2 $16.95   T   KA681
NOAH'S ARK. Translated from the Dutch and illustrated by Peter Spier. Doubleday ISBN 0-385-09473-6, c1977. 46p. col. ill.
Caldecott Medal Award.
Superb, action filled and minutely detailed watercolors with original touches of humor illustrate the age old Biblical story of Noah who builds an ark, fills it with animals and rides out the Great Flood. Almost textless except for the one-page translation of Jacobus Revius' seventeenth-century poem, "The Flood".
SUBJ: Noah's ark./ Bible stories--O.T./ Stories without words.

VCR 221.9   Ph-1 P-2 $9.95   KA682
NOAH'S ARK (Videocassette). Narrated by James Earl Jones. Music by Stewart Copeland. Lightyear Entertainment 54001-3 ISBN 1-879496-45-3, c1989, 1996. 1/2" VHS videocassette color (27min). (Stories to remember).
Closed captioned.
A fully animated version of Peter Spier's Caldecott Award winning picture book depicts Noah's heroic task of rescuing the animals. The talents of well-known actor James Earl Jones and Grammy winner Stewart Copeland combine to create an entertaining adaptation of the familiar Bible story.
SUBJ: Noah's ark./ Bible stories--O.T.

222   Ph-1 1-4/6 $16.99   L   KA683
DE REGNIERS, BEATRICE SCHENK. David and Goliath. Illus. by Scott Cameron. Orchard ISBN 0-531-08796-4, 1996. unp. col. ill.
The text for this book originally appeared in 1965 and now appears with fine oil paintings as it illustrations. It is the traditional biblical tale of David slaying the giant Goliath. The author has added several psalms which are fitting to the text. A handsome retelling of a favorite Bible tale.
SUBJ: David, King of Israel./ Goliath (Biblical giant)./ Bible stories--O.T.

222   Ph-2 K-2/4 $14.95   T   KA684
GAUCH, PATRICIA LEE. Noah. Illus. by Jonathan Green. Philomel ISBN 0-399-22548-X; In Canada: Putnam, 1994. unp. col. ill.
Told in verse and illustrated with pictures which reflect the Gullah people of South Carolina, the familiar story of Noah's ark building and survival becomes vividly alive.
SUBJ: Noah (Biblical figure)./ Bible stories--O.T.

VCR 222   Ph-2 5-6 $12.98   KA685
GLEESON, BRIAN. Joseph and his brothers (Videocassette). Told by Ruben Blades. Music by Strunz & Farah. Illus. by Garnet Henderson. Rabbit Ears ISBN 1-56668-848-5, 1993. 1/2" VHS videocassette color (30min). (Greatest stories ever told).
"Family classics from the stars."
Faithful retelling of Joseph's betrayal by his brothers, his servitude in Egypt and his final reunion with his family. Appropriate music fills in the background.
SUBJ: Joseph (Son of Jacob)./ Bible stories--O.T.

VCR 222   Ph-3 2-4 $12.98   KA686
METAXAS, ERIC. David and Goliath (Videocassette). Told by Mel Gibson. Illus. by Douglas Fraser. Music by Branford Marsalis. Rabbit Ears/dist. by Microleague Multimedia, Inc. (MMI) ISBN 1-56668-196-0, 1992. 1/2" VHS videocassette color (30min). (Greatest stories ever told).
Read-along kit available from Rabbit Ears/dist. by Simon & Schuster (ISBN 0-689-80604-3, 1996) 1 paperback book, 1 sound cassette (23min), $10.95.
Talking book available from Rabbit Ears/dist. by Microleague Multimedia, Inc. (MMI) (ISBN 157099999-6, 1996). 1 sound cassette (24min), $10.95.
David, a young shepherd, goes to the army to see how his brothers are fairing, and he discovers that no one will fight the giant, Goliath. His valiant battle with the giant is retold with pictures of traditional scenes.
SUBJ: David, King of Israel./ Goliath (Biblical giant)./ Bible stories--O.T.

222   Ph-2 1-2/2 $3.50   P   KA687
ORGEL, DORIS. Flower of Sheba. By Doris Orgel and Ellen Schecter. Illus. by Laura Kelly. Bantam ISBN 0-553-37235-1; In Canada: Bantam Doubleday Dell, 1994. 32p. col. ill. (Bank Street ready-to-read).
"Byron Preiss book."
The Queen of Sheba tests King Solomon's wisdom by filling a room with paper, silk, and glass flowers and one real one. The king proves his knowledge with the aid of a bee. Beginning readers will enjoy solving the many riddles woven into the familiar legend.
SUBJ: Solomon, King of Israel./ Jews--Folklore./ Bible--Folklore.

222   Ph-2 2-3/4 $16.00   L   KA688
STORY OF THE CREATION: WORDS FROM GENESIS. Illus. by Jane Ray. Dutton ISBN 0-525-44946-9, 1993. unp. col. ill.
Also available in Spanish HISTORIA DE LA CREATION: SEGUN EL GENESIS (ISBN 0-525-45055-6, 1993, OD).
The story of creation as told in the King James Version of the Bible is presented with exquisitely detailed illustrations. Vibrantly colored artwork depicts the harmonious relationships of all living things.
SUBJ: Creation./ Bible stories--O.T.--Genesis.

222   Ph-2 2-4/5 $13.95   T   KA689
WILLIAMS, MARCIA. Joseph and his magnificent coat of many colors. Candlewick ISBN 1-56402-019-3; In Canada: Candlewick/dist. by Douglas & McIntyre, 1992. unp. col. ill.
Sprightly colored cartoon drawings retell the story of Joseph's rejection by his brothers and final rise to power in Egypt. An attractive introduction to a biblical story.
SUBJ: Joseph (Son of Jacob)./ Bible stories--O.T.

222   Ph-1 4-A/4 $14.93   L   KA690
WOLKSTEIN, DIANE. Esther's story. Illus. by Juan Wijngaard. Morrow ISBN 0-688-12128-4, 1996. unp. col. ill.
Relates Esther's trials as she becomes the wife and queen of King Ahasuerus in Persia. How she saves her uncle and her people is a drama which is fleshed out by the author, a storyteller. Each of the full-page illustrations are portraits on their own. Two extraordinary talents have created a jewel. Use as background information for the feast of Purim.
SUBJ: Esther, Queen of Persia./ Bible stories--O.T.

223   Ph-2 P-A/3 $16.00   T   KA691
PSALM TWENTY-THREE. Illus. by Tim Ladwig. Eerdmans ISBN 0-8028-5160-6, 1997. unp. col. ill.
An urban interpretation of a familiar psalm shows its relevance to today's world. For multicultural studies.
SUBJ: Bible. O.T. Psalms XXIII.

224   Ph-2 P-2/4 $14.00   T   KA692
PATTERSON, GEOFFREY. Jonah and the whale. Lothrop, Lee & Shepard ISBN 0-688-11238-2, 1992. unp. col. ill.
Retelling of the trials of Jonah who attempted to avoid God's wishes, landed in a whale's stomach, and upon release followed God's desires. Strong vigorous paintings depict the scenes of this remarkable biblical story.
SUBJ: Jonah (Biblical prophet)./ Bible stories--O.T.

229   Ph-3 1-3/2 $15.99   T   KA693
MARK, JAN. Tale of Tobias. Retold by Jan Mark. Illus. by Rachel Merriman. Candlewick ISBN 1-56402-692-2; In Canada: Candlewick/dist. by Douglas & McIntyre, 1996. unp. col. ill.
The story of Tobias' travels with Azarias to a far away city to regain his blind father's money is told from the perspective of his dog. Their journey is eventful, and Azarias reveals his powers to demolish demons and cure blindness. The Biblical story of faith and devotion from the Apocrypha is portrayed with cartoon-like drawings.
SUBJ: Tobias (Biblical figure)./ Bible stories--O.T.

231   Ph-3 K-2/2 $15.00   T   KA694
KROLL, VIRGINIA L. I wanted to know all about God. Illus. by Debra Reid Jenkins. Eerdmans ISBN 0-8028-5078-2, 1994. unp. col. ill.
A simple presentation of a child's experience of God in his/her world. The paintings show children of all cultures.
SUBJ: God.

232.9   Ph-3 5-6/7 $15.95   L   KA695
DE PAOLA, TOMIE. Miracles of Jesus. Holiday House ISBN 0-8234-0635-0, 1987. unp. col. ill.
Twelve of the miracles performed by Jesus Christ are retold in this handsomely illustrated work. The companion book THE PARABLES OF JESUS (Holiday House ISBN 0-8234-0636-9, 1987) features seventeen of the stories used by Christ in his teachings. Unfortunately the look of the books is considerably younger than the appropriate audience.
SUBJ: Jesus Christ--Miracles./ Jesus Christ--Parables./ Bible stories--N.T.

232.9   Ph-1 4-A/5 $16.00   L   KA696
JESUS OF NAZARETH: A LIFE OF CHRIST THROUGH PICTURES. Illus. with paintings from the National Gallery of Art, Washington, D.C. Simon & Schuster ISBN 0-671-88651-7; In Canada: Simon & Schuster, 1994. 37p. col. ill.
Includes index.
The life of Christ is told through "excerpts from the King James version of the Bible, and the illustrations of paintings by European

artists who lived between the fourteenth and seventeenth centuries."
(Intro.) A handsome volume.
SUBJ: Jesus Christ--Biography./ Jesus Christ--Art.

232.9   Ph-3 4-A/6 $19.95   L   KA697
L'ENGLE, MADELEINE. Glorious impossible. Illustrated with frescoes
from the Scrovegni Chapel by Giotto. Simon & Schuster ISBN 0-671-
68690-9, 1990. unp. col. ill.
The magnificent frescoes of the Scrovegni Chapel are reproduced
here to dramatize 25 of the major happenings in the life of Jesus.
L'Engle's text offers an explanation of the elements in Christian life
which are impossible and are accepted by faith. This beautifully
illustrated book will aid the Christian reader in understanding his/her
religion and give others insight into the tenets which direct this
religion. It can also be used for art history studies.
SUBJ: Jesus Christ--Biography./ Jesus Christ--Art.

232.91   Ph-1 1-4/6 $15.95   L   KA698
DE PAOLA, TOMIE. Lady of Guadalupe. Holiday House ISBN 0-8234-
0373-4, 1980. unp. col. ill.
Includes author's note.
Also available in Spanish NUESTRA SENOR DE GUADALUPE (ISBN
0-8234-0374-2, 1980).
A humble Indian living in Mexico was chosen many years ago to
carry a message to the Bishop that the Mother of God wished a
church built on the hillside of Tepeyac. His trials before the message
was acknowledged, are pictured in this book in handsome full color
illustrations. The story can be used in picture book hours and story
hours.
SUBJ: Guadalupe, Nuestra Senora de./ Diego, Juana./ Spanish
language materials.

232.91   Ph-2 3-6/5 $16.95   L   KA699
DE PAOLA, TOMIE. Mary: the mother of Jesus. Holiday House ISBN
0-8234-1018-8, 1995. unp. col. ill.
Skillfully combines legends and the few references to Mary found in
the Bible with simple, dignified paintings to explain the life of the
woman who became a central and beloved figure in the Christian
faith.
SUBJ: Mary, Blessed Virgin, Saint./ Saints./ Bible stories--N.T.

232.92   Ph-2 P-K $14.89   L   KA700
BROWN, MARGARET WISE. Christmas in the barn. Illus. by Barbara
Cooney. Crowell/HarperCollins ISBN 0-690-19272-X, c1952. unp. col. ill.
Available from the National Library Service for the Blind and
Physically Handicapped on sound recording cassette RC27144.
A gently beautiful telling of the Nativity story done with great
simplicity and effectiveness.
SUBJ: Jesus Christ--Nativity./ Christmas.

232.92   Ph-2 2-3/4 $15.95   L   KA701
CHRISTMAS STORY. Adapted and illus. by Kay Chorao. Holiday House
ISBN 0-8234-1251-2, 1996. unp. col. ill.
Traditional interpretation of the story of the birth and early childhood
of Christ. The text is adapted from the New Testament: the Books of
Luke and Matthew. The artist cites the Renaissance painters who
inspired her work.
SUBJ: Jesus Christ--Nativity./ Bible stories--N.T.

232.92   Ph-3 P-4/7 $15.95   T   KA702
DE PAOLA, TOMIE. First Christmas. Putnam ISBN 0-399-21070-9; In
Canada: General, 1984. unp. col. ill.
Starting with the visitation of Mary by the angel, Gabriel, this pop-up
book relates the story of the birth of Jesus in six scenes. The book
will have use in the Christmas season as a display item but will be
limited in use because of its construction.
SUBJ: Christmas./ Toy and movable books.

232.92   Ph-3 2-3/2 $16.00   L   KA703
DUNBAR, JOYCE. This is the star. Illus. by Gary Blythe. Harcourt Brace
ISBN 0-15-200851-9; In Canada: Harcourt Brace c/o Canadian Manda,
1996. unp. col. ill.
First published in Great Britain, Transworld Publishers Ltd., 1996.
Stunning oil paintings which show the journey of Mary and Joseph to
a manger where the baby Jesus is born are accompanied by rhyming
verses. The cumulative story and rhyming text make this a good
selection for reading aloud.
SUBJ: Jesus Christ--Nativity./ Christmas./ Stories in rhyme.

232.92   Ph-3 6-A/5 $16.00   T   KA704
FIRST CHRISTMAS. Illus. with paintings from The National Gallery,
London. Simon & Schuster ISBN 0-671-79364-0; In Canada: Simon &
Schuster, 1992. 29p. col. ill.
Words from several books of the King James Version of the Bible are

accompanied by paintings from the National Gallery of London to
retell the birth of Jesus. A handsome book for art classes as well as
use in holiday displays.
SUBJ: Jesus Christ--Nativity./ Bible. N.T. Luke.

KIT 232.92   Ph-2 3-5 $19.95   KA705
GLEESON, BRIAN. Savior is born (Kit). Told by Morgan Freeman.
Music by Christ Church Cathedral Choir, Oxford. Illus. by Robert Van
Nutt. Rabbit Ears/dist. by Simon & Schuster ISBN 0-88708-284-X; In
Canada: Vanwell, 1992. 1 hardcover book, 1 sound cassette (54min).
(Greatest stories ever told).
ALA notable recording, 1994.
Read-along kit, book and compact disc is available (ISBN 0-689-
81098-9, 1992). 1 hardcover book, 1 compact disc (54min), $19.95.
Morgan Freeman's reading of this telling of the conception, birth, and
early life of Jesus is augmented by the book's illustrations which are
reminiscent of European stained glass windows. The tape and book
combination will enrich this material which is frequently overlooked in
holiday celebrations.
SUBJ: Jesus Christ--Nativity./ Bible stories--N.T.

232.92   Ph-1 P-2/3 $13.99   L   KA706
HENNESSY, B. G. First night. Illus. by Steve Johnson with Lou Fancher.
Viking ISBN 0-670-83026-7; In Canada: Penguin, 1993. unp. col. ill.
A simple, dignified text retells the biblical Christmas story. The
illustrations, carved and painted on wood, provide a timeless quality
and beauty.
SUBJ: Jesus Christ--Nativity.

232.92   Ph-1 K-2/5 $16.00   T   KA707
HOGROGIAN, NONNY. First Christmas. Greenwillow ISBN 0-688-
13579-X, 1995. unp. col. ill.
Using passages from the Gospels of St. Matthew and St. Luke in the
King James version of the Bible, Nonny Hogrogian quietly and
reverently tells the story of the birth of Jesus in simple and moving oil
paintings.
SUBJ: Jesus Christ--Nativity./ Bible stories--N.T.

CE 232.92   Ph-3 4-6/7 $7.95   P   KA708
KURELEK, WILLIAM. Northern Nativity: Christmas dreams of a prairie
boy. Tundra ISBN 0-88776-099-6; In Canada: Tundra, c1976. 40p. col.
ill.
The Christmas message of love and humanity is expressed through a
series of dreams experienced by the author when he was 12 years
old. Truly brilliant illustrations.
SUBJ: Jesus Christ--Nativity.

232.92   Ph-2 3-5/5 $5.99   P   KA709
NATIVITY. Illus. by Juan Wijngaard. Candlewick ISBN 1-56402-981-6; In
Canada: Candlewick/dist. by Douglas & McIntyre, 1996. 29p. col. ill.
Originally published by Lothrop, Lee & Shepard, 1990.
Tasteful, somber drawings augment the story of the birth of Jesus
from the time the angel spoke to Mary until the flight into Egypt. A
good choice for children seeking the traditional telling from the King
James Bible.
SUBJ: Jesus Christ--Nativity./ Bible stories--N.T.

232.96   Ph-3 5-6/5 $11.95   T   KA710
HEYER, CAROL. Easter story. Retold and illus. by Carol Heyer. Ideals
ISBN 0-8249-8439-0; In Canada: Ideals, 1990. unp. col. ill.
Retells the events that preceded and followed the crucifixion of Jesus
Christ to explain some of the basic beliefs of Christianity.
SUBJ: Jesus Christ--Passion./ Bible stories--N.T./ Easter.

232.96   Ph-1 5-6/7 $15.95   L   KA711
WINTHROP, ELIZABETH. He is risen: the Easter story. Illus. by Charles
Mikolaycak. Holiday House ISBN 0-8234-0547-8, 1985. unp. col. ill.
Adapted from the Books of Matthew and Luke in the King James
version of the Bible, this retelling of the Last Supper, trial, crucifixion,
and resurrection of Christ has the flavor of the Biblical text and is
richly illustrated in large full-toned watercolor and colored pencil
drawings.
SUBJ: Jesus Christ--Crucifixion./ Jesus Christ--Resurrection./ Bible
stories--N.T./ Easter.

242   Ph-2 3-6 $12.95   T   KA712
BAYNES, PAULINE. Thanks be to God: prayers from around the world.
Selected and illustrated by Pauline Baynes. Macmillan ISBN 0-02-
708541-4; In Canada: Collier Macmillan, 1990. unp. col. ill.
Charming drawings augment a collection of prayers drawn from many
cultures and religions.
SUBJ: Prayers.

242 Ph-2 K-3/4 $11.95 L KA713
FIELD, RACHEL. Prayer for a child. Illustrated by Elizabeth Orton Jones. Macmillan ISBN 0-02-735190-4, 1973. unp. col. ill.
Caldecott Medal Award.
A very simple prayer that the author wrote for her own child and now shares with all children.
SUBJ: Prayers.

263 Ph-2 2-3/2 $14.95 T KA714
FISHER, AILEEN LUCIA. Story of Easter. By Aileen Fisher. Illus. by Stefano Vitale. HarperCollins ISBN 0-06-027296-1; In Canada: HarperCollins, 1997. unp. col. ill.
Following an explanation of the Christian belief in the Resurrection of Christ are descriptions of customs associated with the Easter celebration and directions for decorating Easter eggs and making hot cross buns. Colorful, mural-like paintings face each page of text.
SUBJ: Easter./ Jesus Christ--Resurrection.

265 Ph-2 5-6/7 $14.40 L KA715
LANKFORD, MARY D. Quinceanera: a Latina's journey to womanhood. Photos by Jesse Herrera. Millbrook ISBN 1-56294-363-4, 1994. 47p. col. ill.
Includes bibliography and index.
Traces the traditional celebration marking the fifteenth birthday of a young Hispanic girl. Planning, church ceremony, and the following fiesta are captured in black-and-white and color photographs. Interesting as a browser and useful in discussion of coming-of-age customs for multicultural studies.
SUBJ: Quinceanera (social custom)./ Hispanic Americans--Rites and ceremonies.

270 Ph-3 5-A/10 $17.00 T KA716
ARMSTRONG, CAROLE. Lives and legends of the saints: with paintings from the great museums of the world. Simon & Schuster ISBN 0-689-80277-3, 1995. 45p. col. ill.
Includes index.
Twenty of the saints venerated by the Catholic Church are presented in brief biographies and reproductions of world renowned paintings found in the Louvre, the national Gallery in Washington, D.C., and other museums. The clear reproductions of well-known paintings make this a text useful in art classes and religious studies. A calendar of the principal feast days of the saints is included on the endpapers.
SUBJ: Saints./ Art appreciation.

289 Ph-1 4-6/8 $15.95 L KA717
BIAL, RAYMOND. Shaker home. Houghton Mifflin ISBN 0-395-64047-4, 1994. 39p. col. ill.
Includes bibliography.
A pictorial study, true to Shaker philosophy, simply and cleanly explains the birth of the Shaker movement, its guiding figures, and the numerous inventions which sprung from their communal activities. Color photographs eloquently capture their residences, inside and out, and their handicrafts.
SUBJ: Shakers.

289 Ph-2 5-6/8 $13.85 L KA718
BOLICK, NANCY O'KEEFE. Shaker villages. By Nancy O'Keefe Bolick and Sallie G. Randolph. Illus. by Laura LoTurco. Walker ISBN 0-8027-8210-8; In Canada: Thomas Allen, 1993. 79p. ill., map.
Includes chronology and index.
Details the origin and growth of the Shaker movement with further information on the practices of the Shakers and the few practicing members of the faith.
SUBJ: Shakers.

289.7 Ph-2 5-A/8 $14.95 L KA719
BIAL, RAYMOND. Amish home. Houghton Mifflin ISBN 0-395-59504-5, 1993. 40p. col. ill.
Includes bibliography.
Captures Amish life through use of photographs of memorable quality. Text is carefully integrated with illustrative material and details Amish attitudes, dress, and lifestyle. Valuable to expand knowledge and in "how-people-live" units. Priority purchase for communities with Amish populations.
SUBJ: Amish.

289.7 Ph-1 4-6/7 $17.95 T KA720
KENNA, KATHLEEN. People apart. Photos by Andrew Stawicki. Houghton Mifflin ISBN 0-395-67344-5, 1995. 64p. ill.
Includes bibliography.
The author and photographer visited Mennonite communities for several years and engaged in the activities found there. This book is the result of the trust they developed with the people. The photographs show all aspects of the Old Order Mennonite life: work,

religious practices, education, dress, and recreation. A serious study of a group of people who maintain their way of life in spite of outside pressures.
SUBJ: Old Order Mennonites./ Mennonites.

289.7 Ph-2 5-A/9 $20.00 L KA721
WILLIAMS, JEAN KINNEY. Amish. Watts ISBN 0-531-11275-6; In Canada: Grolier Ltd., 1996. 111p. ill. (American religious experience).
Includes bibliography, directory and index.
Explains the origin of Amish beliefs, the flight of followers of these beliefs to America, and where the Amish settled. Photographs show the way the people dress, worship, and pursue their livelihoods. Text shows respect for this group of people who are capable of leading productive lives without cars, telephones, or electricity. Includes many little known facts which make this title fascinating reading.
SUBJ: Amish.

VCR 291 Ph-2 5-A $89.95 KA722
FAITH AND BELIEF: FIVE MAJOR WORLD RELIGIONS (Videocassette). Knowledge Unlimited ISBN 1-55933-101-1, 1992. 1/2" VHS videocassette color (21min).
Includes teacher's guide.
A brief introduction to the major religions of the world, stressing their similarities. It may be used in its entirety or as an overview of a specific religion.
SUBJ: Religions./ Judaism./ Christianity./ Islam./ Hinduism./ Buddhism.

291 Ph-2 3-5/9 $18.95 T KA723
GANERI, ANITA. Religions explained: a beginner's guide to world faiths. Henry Holt ISBN 0-8050-4874-X; In Canada: Fitzhenry & Whiteside, 1997. 69p. col. ill. (Your world explained).
"Henry Holt reference book."
Includes glossary and index.
The major religions of the world are explored in text and color photographs and drawings of the places of worship, artifacts, and rites. The easy to access, attractive volume focuses on the history, worship, and festivals of each faith.
SUBJ: Religions.

291 Ph-2 5-A/4 $15.00 L KA724
GELLMAN, MARC. How do you spell God?: answers to the big questions from around the world. By Rabbi Marc Gellman and Monsignor Thomas Hartman. With a foreword by His Holiness the Dalai Lama. Illus. by Jos. A. Smith. Morrow ISBN 0-688-13041-0, 1995. 206p. ill.
In this introduction to religions, the commonalities of the world's religions are discussed as well as the practices and beliefs which make each distinctive. Filled with puns and humor as well as serious discussions of why religions exist.
SUBJ: Religions.

291 Ph-1 3-4/9 $15.00 L KA725
MAESTRO, BETSY. Story of religion. Illus. by Giulio Maestro. Clarion ISBN 0-395-62364-2, 1996. 48p. col. ill., map.
Includes glossaries and index.
Explains the origin of the major religious ideas and beliefs. Also explores how different eras have produced distinct leaders and practices in lands all over the world. The author's premise is that to understand one another, people must study various faiths and the evolution of these faiths. Drawings capture major religious symbols. A brief summary lists festivals, holidays, and sacred texts. For multicultural studies.
SUBJ: Religions.

291 Ph-1 4-A/7 $26.99 L KA726
OSBORNE, MARY POPE. One world, many religions: the ways we worship. Knopf ISBN 0-679-93930-X; In Canada: Random House, 1996. 86p. col. ill., map.
"Borzoi book."
Includes glossary, chronology, bibliography and index.
The seven major religions of the world are discussed, and their beliefs, practices, and locations are detailed. The major theme of the book, however, is what the religions have in common. Outstanding color photographs complement the basic title for world religions classes.
SUBJ: Religions.

VCR 291 Ph-2 3-6 $79.00 OD KA727
RELIGION (Videocassette). National Geographic C51565, 1992. 1/2" VHS videocassette color (19min). (Celebrating our differences).
Includes teacher's guide.
As the variety of religions practiced in the United States are explored, viewers discover that "whatever a person believes" is protected by

the United States Constitution. Depicts some of the more colorful rites of many religions.
SUBJ: Religions.

291   Ph-2 4-A/10 $19.95   L   KA728
SITA, LISA. Worlds of belief: religion and spirituality. Published in cooperation with the Denver Museum of Natural History. Blackbirch ISBN 1-56711-125-4, 1995. 80p. col. ill., maps. (Our human family).
Includes glossary, bibliography and index.
The why and how of religious beliefs are clearly explained, so readers will better understand the diversity of faiths found in the world. Color photographs, index, glossary, and a bibliography add to the value of this text. For units on world religions and multicultural studies.
SUBJ: Religions./ Manners and customs.

291.1   Ph-3 3-6/5 $18.00   L   KA729
GANERI, ANITA. Out of the ark: stories from the world's religions. Illus. by Jackie Morris. Harcourt Brace ISBN 0-15-200943-4; In Canada: Harcourt Brace c/o Canadian Manda, 1996. 96p. col. ill.
Includes glossary.
Numerous stories from many of the world's religions are retold to explain events, the lives and practices of leaders, and the beliefs (morals) that are part of the religious practices. The stories are brief and suitable for reading aloud in conjunction with units on world religions and multicultural studies.
SUBJ: Religions./ Mythology.

291.2   Ph-1 4-5/4 $18.95   T   KA730
ANDERSON, DAVID A. Origin of life on Earth: an African creation myth. Retold by David A. Anderson/Sankofa. Illus. by Kathleen Atkins Wilson. Designed by Pete Traynor. Sights ISBN 0-9629978-5-4, 1991. unp. col. ill.
Includes glossary.
Coretta Scott King Award.
"In Yoruba religion, Olorun is God-Almighty. Olorun lives in the sky with many assistants or agents." (Intro.) This is the story of the agent Obatala who was sent to make Earth and the first people. Each drawing is handsomely conceived and could stand on its own.
SUBJ: Yoruba (African people)--Folklore./ Creation--Folklore./ Folklore--Africa./ Africa--Folklore.

291.2   Ph-2 5-6/4 $22.95   T   KA731
HAMILTON, VIRGINIA. In the beginning: creation stories from around the world. Illus. by Barry Moser. Harcourt Brace Jovanovich ISBN 0-15-238740-4, 1988. 161p. col. ill.
Includes bibliography.
Newbery Honor Book.
Striking illustrations supplement myths in this collection. Sources are given and the compiler stresses that these tales are more than "pourquoi" stories; they are truths to the people who believed in them and lived by them. An effective complement to the social studies curriculum that will need to be introduced to young people.
SUBJ: Creation./ Mythology./ Folklore.

291.2   Ph-1 4-6/8 $17.95   T   KA732
WALDHERR, KRIS. Book of goddesses. Introduction by Linda Schierse Leonard. Beyond Words Publishing ISBN 1-885223-30-7, 1995. unp. col. ill.
Includes glossary and bibliography.
For each letter of the alphabet, the author-illustrator has chosen a goddess from various cultures. The women personify character traits, and their roles in the myths of their cultures is pivotal. The legend is presented on the left-hand side of the two-page spread, and a striking watercolor portrait of the goddess is on the right-hand side. The stories can be used for reading aloud individually or as a group for mythology studies, multicultural studies, or women's studies.
SUBJ: Goddesses./ Mythology./ Folklore./ Alphabet.

292   Ph-3 4-5/5 $16.00   T   KA733
ALIKI. Gods and goddesses of Olympus. HarperCollins ISBN 0-06-023530-6; In Canada: HarperCollins, 1994. 48p. col. ill., map.
While explaining how the gods gained their thrones on Olympus, the author-illustrator describes how the gods came into being and some of their trials and adventures.
SUBJ: Mythology, Greek.

292   Ph-3 A/9 $14.95   L   KA734
BULFINCH, THOMAS. Book of myths: selections from Bulfinch's Age of fable. Illus. by Helen Sewell. Macmillan ISBN 0-02-782280-X, c1942. 126p. col. ill.
Available from National Library Service for the Blind and Physically Handicapped in Braille BRA08007.
Thirty Greek myths with illustrations that are like Greek sculpture.
SUBJ: Mythology, Greek.

292   Ph-1 3-6/4 $15.95   T   KA735
CLIMO, SHIRLEY. Atalanta's race: a Greek myth. Retold by Shirley Climo. Illus. by Alexander Koshkin. Clarion ISBN 0-395-67322-4, 1995. 32p. col. ill.
Selectors' Choice, 20th ed.
Atalanta's superior skill in running makes it difficult for any young man to match her speed. In a familiar mythological romance, Melanion is given three golden apples by the goddess Aphrodite to help him win a race with Atalanta and her hand in marriage. Well told with accompanying watercolor, tempera and gouache illustrations which capture the ancient Greek world.
SUBJ: Atalanta (Greek mythology)./ Mythology, Greek.

292   Ph-3 5-6/6 $15.95   T   KA736
COLUM, PADRAIC. Golden fleece and the heroes who lived before Achilles. Illus. by Willy Pogany. Macmillan ISBN 0-02-723620-X, c1949. 316p. ill.
Newbery Honor Book.
Available from National Library Service for the Blind and Physically Handicapped on sound recording cassette RC14881.
Many of the best known myths and legends of Greece are brought into this dramatic account of Jason's search for the Golden Fleece.
SUBJ: Jason (Greek mythology)./ Mythology, Greek.

292   Ph-2 4-5/6 $15.93   L   KA737
CRAFT, M. CHARLOTTE. Cupid and Psyche. Illus. by K. Y. Craft. Morrow ISBN 0-688-13164-6, 1996. unp. col. ill.
The lovely Psyche was hated by Venus for her beauty. Venus sent her mischievous son Cupid to wound Psyche and cause her to fall in love with the "most frightening creature in the world." Accidentally pricking himself, Cupid falls in love with the maiden, and she is taken to his castle where she reigns, never seeing her lover. How envy and curiosity bring her further grief completes this tale of love and devotion. Exquisite watercolors painted over with oils create the dreamlike world in which the lovers dwell.
SUBJ: Cupid (Roman deity)./ Psyche (Greek deity)./ Mythology, Greek.

CE 292   Ph-1 2-6/7 $20.00   T   KA738
D'AULAIRE, INGRI. Ingri and Edgar Parin d'Aulaire's Book of Greek myths. By Ingri and Edgar Parin D'Aularie. Doubleday ISBN 0-385-01583-6, c1962. 192p. col. ill.
Available from National Library Service for the Blind and Physically Handicapped on sound recording cassette RC10718.
Many beautiful pictures in full color highlight the brief stories. A good selection for first readers of mythology.
SUBJ: Mythology, Greek.

292   Ph-2 1-6/4 $14.95   L   KA739
FISHER, LEONARD EVERETT. Cyclops. Holiday House ISBN 0-8234-0891-4, 1991. unp. col. ill.
As Odysseus traveled home from the Trojan War, he was shipwrecked on the Isle of Sicily. There he fell into the hands of the Cyclops but through cleaver maneuvers fooled the monster and escaped. Text and dramatic drawings capture all the horrors of this adventure for readers discovering it for the first time.
SUBJ: Polyphemus (Greek mythology)./ Cyclops (Greek mythology)./ Odysseus (Greek mythology)./ Mythology, Greek.

292   Ph-1 5-6/7 $14.95   L   KA740
FISHER, LEONARD EVERETT. Olympians: great gods and goddesses of Ancient Greece. Holiday House ISBN 0-8234-0522-2, 1984. unp. col. ill.
Includes bibliography.
Accompanying handsome, dramatic portraits of each of the Greek gods is a brief paragraph which describes the origin of the god, his distinctive dress and the characteristics for which he is best known. The book will be a source for language arts, art and social studies classes.
SUBJ: Mythology, Greek.

292   Ph-2 5-6/6 $14.95   L   KA741
FISHER, LEONARD EVERETT. Theseus and the Minotaur. Holiday House ISBN 0-8234-0703-9, 1988. unp. col. ill.
Includes bibliography.
After proving he is King Aegus' son, Theseus offers to slay the fearsome half man/half bull monster known as the Minotaur. Long one of the most popular of the Greek myths, this edition features a dramatic and comprehensive text set against strikingly vibrant double paged spread full color acrylic paintings.
SUBJ: Theseus (Greek mythology)./ Minotaur (Greek mythology)./ Mythology, Greek./ Jason (Greek mythology).

292   Ph-2 3-6/5 $15.95   T   KA742
GERINGER, LAURA. Pomegranate seeds: a classic Greek myth. Retold by Laura Geringer. Illus. by Leonid Gore. Houghton Mifflin ISBN 0-395-68192-8, 1995. 48p. col. ill.
Left at home while her mother, Demeter, flew around the world scattering seeds, Persephone falls into the hands of her uncle, Hades, king of the underworld. She refuses to eat because once food touches her lips, she is under his control. Zeus finally agrees to reunite her with her mother, but since Persephone had eaten three seeds from a pomegranate, she must return each year for three months to her uncle. Moody full-color illustrations capture the darkness of the underworld and the warmth of sunshine. The ancient tale of the origin of winter is useful for units on the seasons.
SUBJ: Persephone (Greek deity)./ Mythology, Greek.

SRC 292   Ph-1 5-6 $9.98   KA743
GREEK MYTHS (Sound recording cassette). As told by Jim Weiss. Greathall Productions 1124-02 ISBN 1-882513-02-9, 1989. 1 sound cassette (60min).
Compact disc available 1124-002 (ISBN 1-882513-27-4, 1989). 1 compact disc (60min), $14.95.
Four well-known myths are retold by a gifted storyteller who brings new interpretations and insight to the tales. For readers of myths who are seeking variety in presentations.
SUBJ: Mythology, Greek.

292   Ph-2 5-6/5 $14.95   L   KA744
HUTTON, WARWICK. Persephone. Retold and illus. by Warwick Hutton. McElderry ISBN 0-689-50600-7; In Canada: Maxwell Macmillan, 1994. unp. col. ill.
Hades, god of the underworld, kidnaps Persephone to keep as his own wife. When her mother demands her return, Zeus intercedes. His decree that each year Persephone spend six months with Hades and six months on earth is why to this day we have summer and winter.
SUBJ: Persephone (Greek deity)./ Mythology, Greek.

292   Ph-2 5-6/4 $15.95   L   KA745
HUTTON, WARWICK. Perseus. Retold and illus. by Warwick Hutton. McElderry ISBN 0-689-50565-5; In Canada: Maxwell Macmillan, 1993. unp. col. ill.
Retells the Greek myth of Perseus who was cast off to sea by his grandfather as an infant and who slays the monsterous Medusa. Lyrically interpreted in text and illustrations.
SUBJ: Perseus (Greek mythology)./ Medusa (Greek mythology)./ Mythology, Greek.

292   Ph-2 5-6/6 $14.95   L   KA746
HUTTON, WARWICK. Theseus and the Minotaur. McElderry ISBN 0-689-50473-X; In Canada: Collier Macmillan, 1989. unp. col. ill.
Returning home to his father's court at Athens, Theseus discovers that 14 young people are being sent to Crete to be fed to the half man, half bull, the Minotaur. Replacing one of the young men, he kills the monster and frees his people from this dreadful punishment. Lyrical drawings of the court at Crete and the isle of Naxos make this retelling a pictorial delight.
SUBJ: Theseus (Greek mythology)./ Minotaur (Greek mythology)./ Mythology, Greek.

292   Ph-1 5-6/4 $15.89   L   KA747
LASKY, KATHRYN. Hercules: the man, the myth, the hero. Illus. by Mark Hess. Hyperion ISBN 0-7868-2274-0; In Canada: Little, Brown, 1997. unp. col. ill.
Hercules tells his own tale in this picture book version of the well-known myth. At times, his brutality and madness is overwhelming, but the sweep of the tale carries the reader. The author has succeeded in stressing the strengths of this hero, and the dynamic drawings done in acrylics make the book unforgettable.
SUBJ: Heracles (Greek mythology)./ Mythology, Greek.

292   Ph-1 4-6/6 $18.95   L   KA748
MCCAUGHREAN, GERALDINE. Greek myths. Retold by Geraldine McCaughrean. Illus. by Emma Chichester Clark. McElderry ISBN 0-689-50583-3; In Canada: Maxwell Macmillan, 1993. 96p. col. ill.
Sixteen major Greek myths are sprightly retold with colorful illustrations filled with humor, fantasy, and realism. This anthology will replace older less attractive works.
SUBJ: Mythology, Greek.

VCR 292   Ph-2 3-6 $9.95   KA749
PEGASUS (Videocassette). Narrated by Mia Farrow. Music by Ernest Troost. Lightyear Entertainment 5105-3-LR ISBN 1-879496-62-3, 1990. 1/2" VHS videocassette color (25min). (Stories to remember).
Closed captioned.
Pegasus, the winged horse, was created to carry a warrior to do battle with the serpent-headed Medusa. How this heroic victory took place and how the magnificent horse was later misused makes an exciting story tenderly related by Mia Farrow. A good introduction to mythology.
SUBJ: Pegasus (Greek mythology)./ Mythology, Greek.

292   Ph-2 2-5/6 $15.93   L   KA750
ROCKWELL, ANNE F. One-eyed giant and other monsters from the Greek myths. By Anne Rockwell. Greenwillow ISBN 0-688-13810-1, 1996. 32p. col. ill.
Ten of the monsters from the Greek myths are pictured and their adventures or misadventures are related. The concise stories are a good introduction to the myths. Suitable for reading aloud.
SUBJ: Mythology, Greek.

292   Ph-1 3-6/6 $17.93   L   KA751
ROCKWELL, ANNE F. Robber baby: stories from the Greek myths. By Anne Rockwell . Greenwillow ISBN 0-688-09741-3, 1994. unp. col. ill.
A wide selection of Greek myths are retold with appealing, childlike illustrations. Pronunciation guide provides Classical Greek pronunciations.
SUBJ: Mythology, Greek.

SRC 292   Ph-2 5-6 $9.98   KA752
SHE AND HE: ADVENTURES IN MYTHOLOGY (Sound recording cassette). As told by Jim Weiss. Greathall Productions 1124-09 ISBN 1-882513-09-6, 1991. 1 sound cassette (60min).
Following an introduction about the relevance of Greek myths in today's world, Jim Weiss calmly and surely retells six of the better known myths. For collections where there is a large interest in mythology.
SUBJ: Mythology, Greek.

292   Ph-2 4-6/6 $14.89   L   KA753
WALDHERR, KRIS. Persephone and the pomegranate: a myth from Greece. Dial ISBN 0-8037-1192-1, 1993. unp. col. ill.
The haunting myth of a mother's search for her daughter who is abducted by Pluto and forced to spend the remainder of her life in the underworld is retold with illustrations that capture the devotion of the mother and daughter. For reading aloud as spring approaches.
SUBJ: Persephone (Greek deity)./ Mythology, Greek.

292   Ph-1 5-6/4 $6.00   P   KA754
YOLEN, JANE. Wings. Illus. by Dennis Nolan. Harcourt Brace Jovanovich ISBN 0-15-201567-1, c1991, 1997. unp. col. ill.
Selectors' Choice, 19th ed.
Daedalus, famed for his inventions, kills his young nephew and is exiled to the island of Crete. There he builds a great maze to hold the Minotaur but reveals the maze's secret to a Greek prince. His subsequent imprisonment in a tower causes him to create wings for himself and his son. This familiar tale of "pride preceding a fall" is heroically retold and pictured here.
SUBJ: Daedalus (Greek mythology)./ Mythology, Greek.

293   Ph-1 4-5/5 $15.95   L   KA755
CLIMO, SHIRLEY. Stolen thunder: a Norse myth. Retold by Shirley Climo. Illus. by Alexander Koshkin. Clarion ISBN 0-395-64368-6, 1994. 32p. col. ill.
Selectors' Choice, 20th ed.
Thor's magic hammer is stolen by Thrym, king of the frost giants. Loki proves his worth by conceiving an ingenious plan to regain the hammer. Heroic illustrations match the drama and humor of the legend.
SUBJ: Thor (Norse deity)./ Mythology, Norse.

293   Ph-1 4-6/6 $17.95   L   KA756
OSBORNE, MARY POPE. Favorite Norse myths. Retold by Mary Pope Osborne. Illus. by Troy Howell. Scholastic ISBN 0-590-48046-4; In Canada: Scholastic, 1996. 88p. col. ill.
Includes glossaries, bibliography and index.
Fourteen of the best known Norse legends are retold with oil and acrylic illustrations which introduce images from early Viking art. The full-page illustrations use the early drawings as a starting point and elaborate on them. The author and illustrator have made these rarely retold legends come vividly alive. The book is well researched and is basic to any collection.
SUBJ: Mythology, Norse.

293   Ph-1 3-A/6 $19.95   T   KA757
PHILIP, NEIL. Odin's family: myths of the Vikings. Retold by Neil Philip. Illus. by Maryclare Foa. Orchard ISBN 0-531-09531-2, 1996. 124p. col. ill.
Includes glossary and bibliographies.
Culling the best of the legends from the Icelandic PROSE EDDA,

Philip retells the stories in a simple, direct prose which brings them into contemporary times. The masterful oil paintings are reminiscent of the work of the Expressionists and are perfectly suited to the text.
SUBJ: Mythology, Norse.

294.3   Ph-1 2-6/6 $18.95   T   KA758
DEMI. Buddha. Henry Holt ISBN 0-8050-4203-2; In Canada: Fitzhenry & Whiteside, 1996. unp. col. ill.
    The full story of Siddhartha's life is retold in this handsome book. The numerous figures in the watercolor illustrations were found in paintings and sculptures of Asian countries. The author-illustrator is a Buddhist and paid great care to the smallest details in the paintings.
    SUBJ: Buddha./ Buddhism--Biography.

294.3   Ph-2 3-4/6 $15.95   L   KA759
HODGES, MARGARET. Hidden in sand. Retold by Margaret Hodges. Illus. by Paul Birling. Scribner's ISBN 0-684-19559-3; In Canada: Maxwell Macmillan, 1994. unp. col. ill.
    Rejected by the guide of a caravan crossing the desert, a young boy proves his worth when he finds water for the desperate and dying group. A faithful retelling of a Jataka tale.
    SUBJ: Jataka stories.

294.3   Ph-1 3-4/4 $14.95   L   KA760
MARTIN, RAFE. Foolish rabbit's big mistake. Illus. by Ed Young. Putnam ISBN 0-399-21178-0; In Canada: General, 1985. unp. col. ill.
    Hearing a crash behind him, a silly rabbit ran to all his friends telling them that "the earth's breaking up." The lion was the one who realized that the animals were running in fright and brought them to their senses. This Indian tale which is similar to "Chicken Little" stories will find a place in units on India, folklore and art appreciation.
    SUBJ: Jataka stories.

294.3   Ph-2 5-A/10 $23.95   L   KA761
STEWART, WHITNEY. 14th Dalai Lama: spiritual leader of Tibet. Lerner ISBN 0-8225-4926-3, 1996. 128p. ill. (some col.), map. (Newsmakers).
    Includes bibliography and index.
    In addition to providing an explanation of how a Dalai Lama is found, trained, and elevated to be the leader of his people, the author describes Tibet and the political upheaval since the country was claimed by the Chinese. Many black and white photographs chronicle the youth of the Dalai Lama and his activities in the various regions of the world.
    SUBJ: Tenzin Gyatso, Dalai Lama XIV./ Dalai lamas./ Buddhism--Biography./ Tibet (China)--History.

294.5   Ph-2 5-A/9 $18.95   T   KA762
GANERI, ANITA. What do we know about Hinduism? Peter Bedrick ISBN 0-87226-385-1, 1995. 45p. col. ill., maps. (What do we know about).
    Includes chronology, glossary and index.
    All aspects of the Hindu religion are explained in this pictorial study. The book will be useful in related areas such as language arts, music, and art as these aspects of the religion are covered. Wonderful, colorful illustrations make this good for browsing.
    SUBJ: Hinduism.

294.5   Ph-2 4-6/7 $21.40   L   KA763
KADODWALA, DILIP. Holi. Raintree Steck-Vaughn ISBN 0-8172-4610-X, 1997. 31p. col. ill. (World of holidays).
    Includes glossary, bibliography and index.
    Filled with color photographs, this slim volume explains Hinduism and the importance of the holiday, Holi. Much of the material shows Hindus in India, but there is a discussion of how Holi is celebrated outside India.
    SUBJ: Holi (Hindu festival)./ Hinduism./ Fasts and feasts--Hinduism.

294.5   Ph-2 3-4/4 $19.95   T   KA764
KRISHNASWAMI, UMA. Broken tusk: stories of the Hindu god Ganesha. Retold by Uma Krishnaswami. Illus. by Maniam Selven. Linnett ISBN 0-208-02442-5, 1996. 101p. ill.
    Includes glossary and bibliography.
    The elephant-headed Hindu god Ganesha is an appealing hero with a gigantic appetite. The compiler relates many of his adventures based on her childhood memories and careful research. Brief stories can be read individually. For multicultural studies.
    SUBJ: Ganesha (Hindu deity)./ Mythology, Hindu.

294.5   Ph-2 4-6/6 $14.95   L   KA765
LEWIN, TED. Sacred river. Clarion ISBN 0-395-69846-4, 1995. unp. col. ill.
    Selectors' Choice, 21st ed.
    Brilliant watercolor illustrations capture the reverence and rapture of a

Hindu pilgrimage to Benares, a city on the most sacred river--the Ganges. Rand's skillful use of light sets the mood while his palette depicts the colorful pageantry of the pilgrims. Useful for world religions classes and multicultural studies.
    SUBJ: Hinduism--Customs and practices./ Ganges River (India and Bangladesh)--Description and travel.

294.5   Ph-2 3-4/4 $15.95   L   KA766
SHEPARD, AARON. Savitri: a tale of ancient India. Illus. by Vera Rosenberry. Whitman ISBN 0-8075-7251-9; In Canada: General, 1992. unp. col. ill.
    Savitri weds a handsome prince who is doomed to die within a year. How she outwits fate and gains great joy for herself, her husband, and his family is a fine introduction to the stories found in the Indian epic, THE MAHABHARATA.
    SUBJ: Savitri (Hindu mythology)./ Mythology, Hindu./ Mahabharata.

294.5   Ph-3 2-5/5 $14.95   T   KA767
VISHAKA. Our most dear friend: Bhagavad-gita for children. Torchlight Publishing ISBN 1-887089-04-7; In Canada: Torchlight Publishing, 1996. unp. col. ill.
    Includes directory.
    A very brief summary of the Bhagavad-gita with contemporary photographs to illuminate the text. This introduction to a major sacred work of Hinduism will be useful in units on India as well as on world religions.
    SUBJ: Bhagavadgita./ Hinduism.

296.1   Ph-2 6-A/8 $15.00   L   KA768
COOPER, ILENE. Dead Sea Scrolls. Illus. by John Thompson. Morrow ISBN 0-688-14300-8; In Canada: Hearst Book Group, 1997. 58p. ill., map.
    Includes chronologies, glossary, bibliographies and index.
    The author explains where and how the scrolls were found, the difficulties in obtaining them for study and preservation, and the impact they have had on Biblical studies. She raises many questions, answers some, and piques interest in a subject which to date has not been fully explored. For mature readers.
    SUBJ: Dead Sea scrolls./ Manuscripts--History./ Bible--History.

296.1   Ph-3 5-6/7 $14.93   L   KA769
PODWAL, MARK. Book of tens. Greenwillow ISBN 0-688-12995-1, 1994. unp. col. ill.
    Explains the importance of the number 10 in Jewish history as found in the Bible. Supplements units on Jewish holidays and traditions.
    SUBJ: Bible--Folklore./ Ten (The number)./ Midrash--Legends./ Jews--Folklore.

296.4   Ph-1 5-6/8 $6.95   P   KA770
CHAIKIN, MIRIAM. Light another candle: the story and meaning of Hanukkah. Illus. by Demi. Clarion/Ticknor & Fields ISBN 0-89919-057-X, c1981, 1987. 80p. col. ill.
    Includes glossary and pronunciation guide, chronology of the Temple, bibliography and index.
    Available from National Library Service for the Blind and Physically Handicapped on sound recording cassette RC23325.
    An extensive history of the Maccabees and the building of the temple precedes the explanation of how the holiday Hanukkah was and is celebrated. Numerous black and white drawings highlighted with red surround the text.
    SHAKE A PALM BRANCH (ISBN 0-89919-254-8, 1984, OPC) relates the origin of Sukkot, how it is celebrated today and how it was celebrated in the past.
    ASK ANOTHER QUESTION (ISBN 0-89919-281-5, 1985 OSI) tells of the Passover celebration and its customs and SOUND THE SHOFAR (ISBN 0-89919-427-3, 1986) tells the story and meaning of Rosh Hashannah and Yom Kippur.
    SUBJ: Hanukkah./ Judaism--Feasts and holidays./ Sukkot./ Passover./ Rosh Hashanah./ Yom Kippur.

SRC 296.4   Ph-3 K-6 $10.95   OD KA771
CHANUKAH AT HOME (Sound recording cassette). Rounder Records 8017C, 1988. 1 sound cassette (30min).
    Fourteen traditional favorites and popular modern classics celebrate the Jewish holiday of Chanukah. The songs are alternately playful and amusing or nostalgic and moving. Includes "The Dreydle Song" and "Chanukah Oh Chanukah."
    SUBJ: Hanukkah--Songs and music.

296.4   Ph-1 2-6/6 $22.95   T   KA772
DRUCKER, MALKA. Family treasury of Jewish holidays. Illus. by Nancy Patz. Little, Brown ISBN 0-316-19343-7; In Canada: Little, Brown, 1994. 180p. col. ill.
    Includes music, glossary, bibliography and index.

Selectors' Choice, 20th ed.
All inclusive collection of stories, songs, recipes, and games to be used as an explanation of the various Jewish holidays. In addition to the more familiar holidays of Hanukkah and Passover, it includes Tu B'Sh'vat, Pesah, Yom HaShoah and Yom Ha'atzmaut. (Parents' Shelf).
SUBJ: Fasts and feasts--Judaism./ Judaism--Customs and practices.

296.4   Ph-2 5-A/10 $14.99   T   KA773
GOLDIN, BARBARA DIAMOND. Bat mitzvah: a Jewish girl's coming of age. Illus. by Erika Weihs. Viking ISBN 0-670-86034-4; In Canada: Penguin, 1995. 139p. ill.
Includes glossary and index.
The origin of the bat mitzvah for girls, practices connected to the ceremony, heroines of the bible, and the place of women in Jewish culture are all covered. The attractive, well-written book serves a dual purpose. Girls approaching their own bat mitzvahs will find much information to enrich the experience, and others seeking information about the Jewish faith will find it useful. Also useful for discussion of coming-of-age practices in women's studies.
SUBJ: Bat mitzvah./ Women in Judaism./ Judaism--Customs and practices./ Jews--Rites and ceremonies.

VCR 296.4   Ph-2 2-5 $69.95   KA774
HANUKKAH (Videocassette). Coleman Communications/dist. by United Learning 10242V ISBN 1-56007-248-2, 1994. 1/2" VHS videocassette color (10min).
Includes teacher's guide.
Current practices of a typical Jewish family celebrating Hanukkah are augmented by a brief history of the origin of the holiday. All terms connected with the traditions are explained by the narrator. Excellent introduction to the Jewish faith and a strong plea for religious freedom.
SUBJ: Hanukkah./ Judaism--Feasts and holidays.

296.4   Ph-2 3-4/7 $16.95   T   KA775
HOYT-GOLDSMITH, DIANE. Celebrating Hanukkah. Photos by Lawrence Migdale. Holiday House ISBN 0-8234-1252-0, 1996. 32p. col. ill.
Includes glossary and index.
Presents the history and traditions of Hanukkah. Photographs follow one family's preparations for and enjoyment of the holiday. Glossary and sidebars give additional facts.
SUBJ: Hanukkah./ Judaism--Feasts and holidays.

296.4   Ph-1 5-A/7 $15.00   L   KA776
KIMMEL, ERIC A. Bar mitzvah: a Jewish boy's coming of age. Illus. by Erika Weihs. Viking ISBN 0-670-85540-5; In Canada: Penguin, 1995. 143p. ill.
Includes glossary and index.
Combining a history of Jewish faith and rituals with warm and amusing anecdotes, the author presents a book for boys preparing for their bar mitzvah and for children who are curious about the Jewish faith. The title may appear to limit the use of the book, but it is a comprehensive study which will serve as a basic book in any collection on religious faiths and coming-of-age ceremonies.
SUBJ: Bar mitzvah./ Judaism--Customs and practices./ Jews--Rites and ceremonies.

296.4   Ph-3 4-6/5 $13.95   L   KA777
KIMMEL, ERIC A. Days of awe: stories for Rosh Hashanah and Yom Kippur. Adapted from traditional sources by Eric A. Kimmel. Illus. by Erika Weihs. Viking ISBN 0-670-82772-X; In Canada: Penguin, 1991. 48p. col. ill.
Three stories concerning the Jewish High Holidays, Rosh Hashanah and Yom Kippur, are illustrated with stylized oil paintings. Kimmel provides the backgrounds of the stories and indicates where he changed them. Good for reading aloud and for units dealing with religion.
SUBJ: Rosh Hashanah./ Yom Kippur./ Jews--Folklore.

296.4   Ph-2 3-4/4 $5.95   P   KA778
KUSKIN, KARLA. Great miracle happened there: a Chanukah story. Illus. by Robert Andrew Parker. HarperCollins ISBN 0-06-443426-5; In Canada: HarperCollins, c1993, 1995. unp. col. ill.
"Willa Perlman books."
When Henry visits his friend across the street, he is included in the ceremony of lighting the menorah on the first night of Chanukah. He hears the story of the Maccabees and their fight to reopen the great Temple on Mount Moriah in Jerusalem. Pleasant introduction to an important chapter of Jewish history.
SUBJ: Hanukkah.

296.4   Ph-2 K-2/2 $5.95   P   KA779
SCHOTTER, RONI. Hanukkah! Illus. by Marylin Hafner. Joy Street/Little, Brown ISBN 0-316-77469-3; In Canada: Little, Brown, 1993. unp. col. ill.
One evening in the life of a warm loving family is pictured here as they light the menorah, make gifts and latkes and share a meal and gift giving. A good introduction to the holiday for beginning readers.
SUBJ: Hanukkah.

296.4   Ph-2 3-6/7 $16.99   T   KA780
SCHWARTZ, HOWARD. Next year in Jerusalem: 3000 years of Jewish stories. Retold by Howard Schwartz. Illus. by Neil Waldman. Viking ISBN 0-670-86110-3; In Canada: Penguin, 1996. 58p. col. ill.
Includes glossary.
Available from the National Library Service for the Blind and Physically Handicapped on sound recording cassette RC 42925.
Presents legends and stories concerning the city of Jerusalem or the longing to go there. Sources for the material are given and reflect the variety of areas from which the tales were collected. The author carefully augments the stories with explanations which give greater depth to the stories. Dreamlike watercolors are fitting to the material. Background reading for understanding the Jewish search for a homeland.
SUBJ: Jews--Folklore./ Jerusalem--Folklore./ Folklore--Jerusalem./ Folklore.

296.4   Ph-2 2-4/3 $14.95   T   KA781
SIMON, NORMA. Story of Passover. Illus. by Erika Weihs. HarperCollins ISBN 0-06-027062-4; In Canada: HarperCollins, 1997. unp. col. ill.
The story of Moses and the flight of the Hebrews from Egypt is retold, and then an explanation of the significance of the event to the Jewish people is given in this small book. Current customs and recipes for traditional Seder dishes complete the text.
SUBJ: Passover./ Seder.

296.6   Ph-2 5-6/7 $12.95   T   KA782
COWAN, PAUL. Torah is written. Photos by Rachel Cowan. Jewish Publication Society ISBN 0-8276-0270-7, 1986. 32p. ill.
Longing since childhood to be a sofer (scribe), Rabbi Chapman's unique ability and how he developed it are described here. Each step in making a Torah is described and numerous photographs graphically show the process. An aid in explaining the Jewish faith and distinctive careers.
SUBJ: Torah scrolls./ Scribes, Jewish--Handbooks, manuals, etc.

296.6   Ph-2 3-6/7 $12.95   T   KA783
ROSENBLUM, RICHARD. Old synagogue. Jewish Publication Society ISBN 0-8276-0322-3, 1989. unp. ill.
Available from National Library Service for the Blind and Physically Handicapped on sound recording cassette RC31666.
Established by a group of Jewish immigrants, a synagogue is eventually deserted by its congregation and becomes a factory. Rebirth comes as young people rediscover the area and restore the synagogue. All aspects of the life of this building are pictured in line drawings which capture the busy and cyclical life common to many cities.
SUBJ: Synagogues./ Cities and towns--History.

297   Ph-2 5-A/6 $16.95   L   KA784
CHILD, JOHN. Rise of Islam. Peter Bedrick ISBN 0-87226-116-6, 1995. 64p. col. ill., maps. (Biographical history).
Includes index.
The Prophet Muhammad's life and teachings are fully explained, followed by a description of the spread of Islam and its impact on science, politics, and art. Numerous biographies of important figures in Islamic history and color photographs of shrines and art works round out the presentation. Where Muslims are found in today's world and their interactions with Christians are also examined.
SUBJ: Islam--History./ Civilization, Islamic./ Islamic Empire--History./ Islamic Empire--Biography.

297   Ph-2 3-5/7 $15.95   L   KA785
GHAZI, SUHAIB HAMID. Ramadan. Illus. by Omar Rayyan. Holiday House ISBN 0-8234-1254-7, 1996. unp. col. ill.
Includes glossary.
Ramadan is a month of prayer and atonement in the Muslim year during which those who practice this faith fast during the day. Various rituals of the season and the meals which are eaten before dawn and after twilight are described. The watercolor illustrations show one boy's trials and joys during this special month.
SUBJ: Ramadan./ Fasts and feasts--Islam./ Islam--Customs and practices.

297   Ph-2 4-6/9 $18.95   L   KA786
HUSAIN, SHAHRUKH. What do we know about Islam? Peter Bedrick
ISBN 0-87226-388-6, 1996. 45p. col. ill., maps. (What do we know
about).
Includes chronology, glossary and index.
Answers questions about the origins, beliefs, practices, and leaders of
the Islamic religion and where the majority of Muslims live. Clear,
informative photographs add to the worth of the book.
SUBJ: Islam.

297   Ph-2 3-5/7 $21.40   L   KA787
KERVEN, ROSALIND. Id-ul-Fitr. Raintree Steck-Vaughn ISBN 0-8172-
4609-6, 1997. 31p. col. ill. (World of holidays).
Includes glossary, bibliography and index.
An explanation of the fasting practiced by Muslims during Ramadan
and the adornments and dress, feasting and worship services on Id-
ul-Fitr, the day after Ramadan ends. Color photographs show Muslims
at home, at worship, and with friends.
SUBJ: Fasts and feasts--Islam./ Islam--Customs and practices./
Ramadan.

297   Ph-2 5-6/3 $16.00   L   KA788
OPPENHEIM, SHULAMITH LEVEY. And the Earth trembled: the creation
of Adam and Eve. Illus. by Neil Waldman. Harcourt Brace ISBN 0-15-
200025-9; In Canada: Harcourt Brace c/o Canadian Manda, 1996. unp.
col. ill.
The creation of Adam and Eve as found in Islamic writings is told in
text and pictures. God makes man in spite of the protest of the
angels who foresaw man creating havoc in the world. The illustrations
done in acrylic paints on cold-pressed watercolor paper are
impressionistic in style and fitting to the material.
SUBJ: Koran stories./ Adam (Biblical figure)./ Eve (Biblical figure).

297   Ph-2 4-5/4 $15.95   L   KA789
OPPENHEIM, SHULAMITH LEVEY. Iblis. Retold by Shulamith Levey
Oppenheim. Illus. by Ed Young. Harcourt Brace ISBN 0-15-238016-7; In
Canada: Harcourt Brace c/o Canadian Manda, 1994. unp. col. ill.
Presents the Islamic version of the banishment of Adam and Eve from
the garden. The pastel and watercolor artwork is impressionistic and
allows the reader's own interpretation of the action. Creation story
for multicultural studies.
SUBJ: Islamic stories./ Adam (Biblical figure)./ Eve (Biblical figure).

299   Ph-2 4-6/7 $11.90   L   KA790
LIPTAK, KAREN. North American Indian ceremonies. Watts ISBN 0-531-
20100-7; In Canada: Watts, 1992. 63p. col. ill. (First book).
Includes glossary, bibliography and index.
The numerous ceremonies which are part of the lives of Native
Americans are explained. Tribal differences are clarified, but
similarities are emphasized.
SUBJ: Indians of North America--Rites and ceremonies./ Indians of
North America--Social life and customs.

VCR 299   Ph-3 1-3 $100.00   OD KA791
ROUGHSEY, DICK. Giant devil dingo (Videocassette). Weston Woods
MVP192, n.d. 1/2" VHS videocassette color (10min).
Based on the book of the same title (o.p.).
According to aborigine legend, Gaiya, the giant devil-dingo, was
savage, bigger than a horse, killed men for food, and was controlled
by Eelgin, the grasshopper woman. One day the two butcher-bird
brothers outran Gaiya and managed to kill the fierce beast. The
whole tribe celebrated and feasted. From the skin, bones, kidney and
head Woodbral, the medicine man, created two small dingoes who
for all time were to be friends and helpers of man.
SUBJ: Australian aborigines--Folklore.

299   Ph-3 6-A/7 $16.95   T   KA792
SEYMOUR, TRYNTJE VAN NESS. Gift of Changing Woman. Henry Holt
ISBN 0-8050-2577-4; In Canada: Fitzhenry & Whiteside, 1993. 38p. col.
ill.
Includes bibliography and glossary.
When an Apache girl matures into a young woman, she participates
in a ritual dance which retells the stories of creation and the powers
of Changing Woman. Illustrations of the coming-of-age dance and
costumes were drawn by Apache artists. For use in units on Native
Americans, puberty, and multicultural studies.
SUBJ: Apache Indians--Rites and ceremonies./ Apache Indians--
Folklore./ Indians of North America--Rites and ceremonies.

299   Ph-1 3-6/5 $14.89   L   KA793
STROUD, VIRGINIA A. Path of the Quiet Elk: a Native American
alphabet book. Dial ISBN 0-8037-1718-0, 1996. unp. col. ill.
A quiet, contemplative introduction to Native American teachings.
Looks Within, a young child, accompanies an older woman, Wisdom

Keeper, on a walk through a forest. For each letter of the alphabet,
the guide names an object and explains its use in the Native
American culture or a hidden truth which can be found through study
and thought. The author-illustrator is a Native American, and her art
is her means of making her culture survive. Book is not a simple
alphabet, but rather a dignified explanation of Native American
beliefs for mature readers to study and ponder. For multicultural
studies.
SUBJ: Indians of North America--Religion and mythology./ Indian
philosophy--North America./ Alphabet.

302.2   Ph-1 K-6/4 $13.93   L   KA794
ALIKI. Communication. Greenwillow ISBN 0-688-11248-X, 1993. unp.
col. ill.
Uses cartoon panels and a warm, deft touch to offer the basics of
communication between people. Though appearing to be for the
youngest, it also works well with older students. For individual use or
as the basis for role-playing activities. Endpapers contain charts of
upper case, lower case, braille, and sign language alphabets.
SUBJ: Communication.

302.2   Ph-2 5-6/9 $19.95   L   KA795
GAN, GERALDINE. Communication. Chelsea House ISBN 0-7910-2845-
3, 1997. 102p. ill. (some col.). (Life in America 100 years ago).
Includes bibliography and index.
An account of modes of communication in the United States at the
turn of the century and their impact on American society and culture.
Included are the postal service, books, newspapers, magazines,
telegraph, and telephone. Illustrated with period photographs; posters;
and drawings, a few of which are in color. Use to add detail to units
on late nineteenth century and early twentieth century United States
history. Use to compare and contrast with contemporary methods of
communication.
SUBJ: Communication./ United States--History--19th century.

302.2   Ph-2 1-4/4 $14.93   L   KA796
GIBBONS, GAIL. Puff...flash...bang!: a book about signals. Morrow
ISBN 0-688-07378-6, 1993. unp. col. ill.
"Describes ways people say things to each other without using
spoken or written words..." (CIP) Fresh illustrations lead the reader
through more than 50 examples of the nonverbal signaling of today
and yesterday. Use in communication activities which identify signals.
SUBJ: Signs and symbols.

302.2   Ph-3 P-1 $14.93   L   KA797
HOBAN, TANA. I read symbols. Greenwillow ISBN 0-688-02332-0,
1983. unp. col. ill.
Presents through clear color photographs twenty-eight signs which
through symbols rather than words give information. An exceptional
presentation for the very young and perhaps a refresher for older
students.
SUBJ: Traffic signs and signals./ Signs and signboards./ Signs and
symbols.

302.2   Ph-2 2-4/4 $13.93   L   KA798
HOFSINDE, ROBERT. Indian sign language. Written and illustrated by
Robert Hofsinde (Gray-Wolf). Morrow ISBN 0-688-31610-7, c1956.
96p. ill.
"Indian names and totems:" p87-89.
How to form gestures representing more than 500 words in sign
language, the universal language of American Indian tribes. Words
are arranged alphabetically in index.
SUBJ: Indians of North America--Sign language.

VCR 302.23   Ph-2 2-4 $79.00   OD KA799
COMMUNICATIONS (Videocassette). National Geographic 51494,
1992. 1/2" VHS videocassette color (15min). (Your town).
Includes teacher's guide.
Emphasizes television, newspapers, computers and the telephone as
communication tools. Production quality is good and educational
design is solid. Can be used above recommended grade levels.
SUBJ: Mass media./ Newspapers./ Television./ Computers.

302.23   Ph-2 P-1 $13.93   L   KA800
HOBAN, TANA. I read signs. Greenwillow ISBN 0-688-02318-5, 1983.
unp. col. ill.
Directing people and activities, this collection of full page colorful
photographs of signs is well suited for safety and awareness lessons.
SUBJ: Traffic signs and signals./ Street signs./ Signs and
signboards./ Signs and symbols.

VCR 302.23   Ph-2 5-6 $89.95   OD KA801
READING THE NEWSPAPER INTELLIGENTLY (Videocassette).
Knowledge Unlimited 5496VD ISBN 1-55933-190-9, 1995. 1/2" VHS

videocassette color (25min).
Includes teacher's guide.
Includes public performance rights.
Closed captioned.
A clearly narrated, informative overview of the history and importance of the newspaper, comparisons with television news, specific examples of differences between fact and opinion, and practical tips for getting the most out of reading the newspaper. Good production values alternate live action with archival images. A basic introduction for current events units and to supplement local Newspapers in Education programs.
SUBJ: Newspapers./ Mass media./ Current events.

MCP 302.23   Ph-2 5-A $149.95   OD KA802
VIOLENCE IN THE MEDIA (Microcomputer program). Tom Snyder MED-J, 1994. 1 3.5" disk. (Decisions, decisions).
Includes teacher's guide, activity guide, and 24 student reference books.
Macintosh and MS-DOS network versions: AppleShare or Novell based.
System requirements: Macintosh - Black and white version runs on all Macintosh computers with at least 1MB of internal memory and a hard disk; color version runs on all color Macintosh computers with at least 2MB of internal memory and a hard disk, monitor must be set to 16 or 256 colors.
Students take on the role of advertising executives as they develop an advertising campaign for a new product. Controversy erupts concerning the television show where the campaign will be launched. Cooperative learning and critical thinking skills are used. Works best with small groups or an entire class.
SUBJ: Violence in mass media--Software./ Software--Violence in mass media./ Mass media--Influence--Software./ Software--Mass media--Influence./ Mass media--Moral and ethical aspects--Software./ Software--Mass media--Moral and ethical aspects.

VCR 303.3   Ph-3 5-6 $89.00   OD KA803
AND YOU CAN'T COME: PREJUDICE HURTS (Videocassette). Rainbow Educational RB8317, 1996. 1/2" VHS videocassette color (17min). (Prejudice series).
Includes teacher's guide.
Includes public performance rights.
When Mia's friends exclude her from a sleepover because she is "different," her soccer coach leads her through an exploration of prejudice that includes a group discussion by students with first-hand experience. Good production values, and opportunities to interrupt viewing for classroom discussion of issues raised. Brief teacher guide will need to be supplemented with other materials, and extensive planning and class preparation will be needed before using this video.
SUBJ: Prejudices./ Discrimination.

VD 303.48   Ph-3 5-A $249.95   OD KA804
MINDS-ON SCIENCE: FOR THE SAKE OF THE NATION (Videodisc). Smithsonian Institution/Tom Snyder Productions SAK-J, 1995. 1 12" CAV single-sided videodisc color. (Minds-on science).
Includes teacher's guide and student portfolios.
Level I interactive with barcodes.
Optional 3.5" Macintosh or Windows software (Level III interactive) available, $49.95.
System requirements (Level I): CAV videodisc player with monitor (large video monitor for whole-class viewing recommended).
System requirements for optional Macintosh software (Level III): Macintosh computer (LC series or better); System 7.0 or later; QuickTime system extension; 4MB RAM; hard disk with at least 4MB free space; 256 (8-bit) color monitor.
This cooperative learning activity allows youngsters to take on the role of science advisor for the President of the United States. Various scenarios allow for government involvement in biotechnology, space exploration, or environmentally friendly cars. Assessment strategies and various extended activities are included. Excellent for large groups. For environmental studies.
SUBJ: Technology and civilization./ Technology--Government policy./ Science--Moral and ethical aspects./ Man--Influence on nature./ Interactive media.

303.48   Ph-1 6-A/11 $17.98   L   KA805
PASCOE, ELAINE. Mexico and the United States: cooperation and conflict. Twenty-First Century ISBN 0-8050-4180-X; In Canada: Fitzhenry & Whiteside, 1996. 126p. col. ill., map.
Includes chronology, bibliography and index.
A balanced account of political, social, and economic relations between the United States and Mexico covers early territorial disputes and contemporary issues relating to drugs, immigration, and international economics and trade. Use with advanced readers for social studies units, multicultural studies, and contemporary economic and political issues.
SUBJ: United States--Relations--Mexico./ Mexico--Relations--United States.

303.6   Ph-3 5-A/7 $18.90   L   KA806
BLUE, ROSE. People of peace. By Rose Blue and Corinne J. Naden. Millbrook ISBN 1-56294-409-6, 1994. 80p. ill. (some col.).
Includes glossary, bibliography and index.
Eleven courageous individuals who have dedicated their lives and energies to finding peaceful solutions to world problems are briefly described in a well designed volume. For units on conflict resolution and current events.
SUBJ: Pacifists./ Peace.

VCR 303.6   Ph-3 K-3 $79.00   OD KA807
BULLY UP: FIGHTING FEELINGS (Videocassette). Britannica ISBN 0-8347-5512-2, c1990, 1991. 1/2" VHS videocassette color (15min).
Includes teacher's guide.
Examines techniques for dealing with name-calling and bullies. Presented by appealing stuffed animal characters, possible solutions to problems are reasonable. A good addition to large collections with strong budgets.
SUBJ: Conflict management./ Bullies./ Quarrels.

VCR 303.6   Ph-1 3-5 $59.00   OD KA808
CASEY'S REVENGE: A STORY ABOUT FIGHTING AND DISAGREEMENTS (Videocassette). Kids' Media Group/dist. by Guidance Associates 60172, 1991. 1/2" VHS videocassette color (25min). (Human Race Club).
Includes activity guide.
Based on the books by Joy Berry.
Human Race Club member Casey O'Reilly finds a method of retaliation for the indignities heaped upon him by his older sister in this story of sibling arguments. Appealing format and teacher's guide are pluses. Use this presentation as the cornerstone for students learning about alternatives to fighting and ways to handle or avoid fights.
SUBJ: Conflict management./ Conduct of life./ Interpersonal relations.

VCR 303.6   Ph-3 5-A $179.95   OD KA809
GETTING TO THE HEART OF IT (Videocassette). Tom Snyder GTH-Y, 1993. 1/2" VHS videocassette color (60min).
Includes teacher's guide, student workbooks, role-play cards.
1/2" VHS videocassette color Take-Home version and guide (30min).
A comprehensive conflict resolution curriculum based on identifying Demands, "Really Wants," and Creative Solutions with opportunities for role playing and discussion. Although conflict situations have some elements which may stretch credibility, teacher materials are complete and self explanatory. Video defines vocabulary and concepts, models strategies, and will actively engage middle grade students. Kit includes a take home video and guide in English and Spanish for family use, student workbooks, role-play cards, and extensive opportunities for extended activities. (Parents' Shelf).
SUBJ: Conflict management./ Interpersonal relations./ Conduct of life.

VCR 303.6   Ph-2 1-3 $69.95   OD KA810
GROARK LEARNS ABOUT BULLYING (Videocassette). Featuring Randel McGee. Elkind & Sweet Communications/dist. by Live Wire Media, 1996. 1/2" VHS videocassette color (30min). (Prevent violence with Groark).
Includes teacher's guide.
Groark (a green dragon puppet), his puppet friends, a live studio audience, song, and story combine to discuss various aspects of interpersonal relations, how to peacefully handle conflict resolution, and get along with others. Good production values with appealing puppet characters and insightful student audience. Use in the classroom as a discussion starter about similar situations and issues. (Parents' Shelf).
SUBJ: Conflict management./ Bullies./ Conduct of life.

VCR 303.6   Ph-2 1-3 $69.95   OD KA811
GROARK LEARNS TO WORK OUT CONFLICTS (Videocassette). Featuring Randel McGee. Elkind & Sweet Communications/dist. by Live Wire Media, 1996. 1/2" VHS videocassette color (30min). (Prevent violence with Groark).
Includes teacher's guide.
Groark (a green dragon puppet), his puppet friends, a live studio audience, song, and story combine to discuss various aspects of interpersonal relations, how to peacefully handle conflict resolution, and get along with others. Good production values with appealing puppet characters and insightful student audience. Use in the classroom as a discussion starter about similar situations and issues. (Parents' Shelf).
SUBJ: Conflict management./ Interpersonal relations./ Conduct of life.

303.6   Ph-2 P-2/5 $13.95   L   KA812
SCHOLES, KATHERINE. Peace begins with you. Illus. by Robert Ingpen. Sierra Club/Little, Brown ISBN 0-316-77436-7; In Canada: Little, Brown, 1990. unp. col. ill.
> Examines concepts of peace and conflict. Approach to concepts and the text are offered in simple terms; final page gives suggestions on how to be a peacemaker. Effective as a one-to-one or small group item with young students.
> SUBJ: Peace.

VCR 303.6   Ph-3 5-6 $99.95   OD KA813
WORKING IT OUT: CONFLICT RESOLUTION (Videocassette). Sunburst Communications 2396, 1993. 1/2" VHS videocassette color (28min).
> Includes teacher's guide.
> Dr. Advice, a popular disk jockey, is on the air to help resolve conflicts between parents, students, and friends. The rules are: no blaming, choose a good time to talk, and get the facts straight. Role-playing, brainstorming, and resolution groups are all depicted accentuating the positive. Many school counselors use these techniques while some schools have students trained in resolution processes, but it helps to expose all children to positive handling of potentially explosive situations. An excellent start towards self-discipline and self-reliance.
> SUBJ: Conflict management./ Self-control./ Self-reliance./ Behavior.

304.2   Ph-2 2-6/7 $19.99   T   KA814
HOFFMAN, MARY. Earth, fire, water, air. Illus. by Jane Ray. Dutton ISBN 0-525-45420-9, 1995. 76p. col. ill.
> Originally published in Great Britain, Orion Children's Books.
> The title elements are featured in stories, myths, legends, and brief poems that demonstrate how ancient cultures endowed them with power and magic. Each section ends with a comment on how modern cultures have misused these basic elements and efforts to restore them. Luminous, full-color paintings provide striking detail and add interest. Use for a different perspective on mythology and for an interdisciplinary approach to environmental studies.
> SUBJ: Four elements (Philosophy)./ Earth./ Fire./ Water./ Air./ Folklore.

304.6   Ph-3 A/7 $25.27   L   KA815
BLASHFIELD, JEAN F. Too many people? By Jean F. Blashfield and Wallace B. Black. Childrens Press ISBN 0-516-05513-5; In Canada: Childrens Press, 1992. 127p. col. ill. (Saving planet Earth).
> Includes directory, glossary and index.
> "Presents opposing views on the effects of the earth's rising population." (CIP) Difficult appearance will slow circulation of this resource. However, the advanced student who uses it will find it evenhanded. For environmental studies.
> SUBJ: Population./ Natural resources.

304.6   Ph-2 5-6/9 $21.50   L   KA816
WINCKLER, SUZANNE. Our endangered planet: population growth. By Suzanne Winckler and Mary M. Rodgers. Lerner ISBN 0-8225-2502-X, 1990. 64p. col. ill. (Our endangered planet).
> Includes directory, glossary and index.
> Examines the causes of overpopulation and the problems that result from an ever increasing population using ever decreasing resources. Valuable for projects with advanced students.
> SUBJ: Population./ Environmental policy.

VCR 305   Ph-2 1-3 $45.00   OD KA817
BEHIND THE MASK. Rev. ed. (Videocassette). By Daniel Salazar. Anti-Defamation League of B'nai B'rith, 1987. 1/2" VHS videocassette color (9min).
> Includes study guide.
> Rhythmic language and colorful child-made masks show each person is different in a positive way. Quite effective as a discussion starter about the problems connected with forming judgements based on superficial characteristics. Study guide suggests a variety of correlated worthwhile activities.
> SUBJ: Prejudices./ Individuality.

305   Ph-1 3-6/5 $16.95   L   KA818
COHN, JANICE. Christmas menorahs: how a town fought hate. Illus. by Bill Fransworth. Whitman ISBN 0-8075-1152-8; In Canada: General, 1995. 40p. col. ill.
> When rocks are thrown through the windows of Jewish families who display menorahs, the community of Billings, Montana, joins together to fight hate and prejudice, and hundreds of families, Jews and non-Jews, put menorahs in their windows. Full-page, color illustrations help bring the story to life. This will be an unforgettable addition to units on prejudice, community involvement, and holidays.
> SUBJ: Prejudices./ Antisemitism./ Hate crimes./ Hanukkah./ Jews--Billings (Mont.).

VCR 305   Ph-2 1-3 $69.95   OD KA819
GROARK LEARNS ABOUT PREJUDICE (Videocassette). Featuring Randel McGee. Elkind & Sweet Communications/dist. by Live Wire Media, 1996. 1/2" VHS videocassette color (30min). (Prevent violence with Groark).
> Includes teacher's guide.
> Groark (a green dragon puppet), his puppet friends, a live studio audience, song, and story combine to discuss responding to people who appear to be different, the causes and effects of prejudice, and demonstrate ways to overcome it. Good production values with appealing puppet characters and insightful student audience. Use in the classroom as a discussion starter about similar situations and issues. (Parents' Shelf)
> SUBJ: Prejudices./ Individuality.

MCP 305   Ph-2 5-A $149.95   OD KA820
PREJUDICE (Microcomputer program). Tom Snyder Productions PJD-J, 1992. 2 3.5" disks. (Decisions, decisions).
> Includes teacher's guide and student reference books.
> Macintosh and Windows network versions: AppleShare or Novell based.
> System requirements: Macintosh LC II or better; System 7.1 or higher; 4 megs of available RAM; 256-color 13" monitor or larger.
> System requirements: Windows 3.1 or higher; 8 megs of RAM; 256-color VGA monitor.
> Students assume the role of the mayor of Spring Falls during an election year and must deal with a racism issue. The simulation is superb and quite open-ended. Requires teacher preparation and debriefing of students. Works with an entire class or small groups.
> SUBJ: Prejudices--Software./ Software--Prejudices./ Racism--Software./ Software--Racism./ Emotions and social attitudes--Software./ Software--Emotions and social attitudes.

VCR 305   Ph-1 3-5 $59.00   OD KA821
UNFORGETTABLE PEN PAL: A STORY ABOUT PREJUDICE AND DISCRIMINATION (Videocassette). Kids' Media Group/dist. by Guidance Associates 60174, 1991. 1/2" VHS videocassette color (28min). (Human Race Club).
> Includes activity guide.
> Based on the books by Joy Berry.
> Tells of a friendship formed between a Human Race Club member and a pen pal and the difficulty which develops between the two as the result of a head-on encounter with prejudice. Cartoon format, creative design, and a solid teacher's guide make this an appealing resource which can serve easily as the foundation for a discussion of prejudice and discrimination.
> SUBJ: Prejudices./ Discrimination./ Interpersonal relations.

305.23   Ph-1 2-5/7 $18.95   L   KA822
AJMERA, MAYA. Children from Australia to Zimbabwe: a photographic journey around the world. By Maya Ajmera and Anna Rhesa Versola. With a foreword by Marian Wright Edelman. Charlesbridge ISBN 0-88106-999-X, 1997. unp. col. ill., maps.
> Originally published: Durham, N.C.: SHAKTI for Children, 1996.
> Includes directory.
> Overviews of countries of the world in an alphabetical format include interesting information about each; give consistent facts such as capital, languages, number of children in the general population, sports, and something about the environment; and list other countries in the world beginning with the same letter of the alphabet. Attractive photographs, maps, and flags complete each doublepage spread. Use for multicultural studies, as a supplement to geography units, and as a model for additional classroom writing and research activities.
> SUBJ: Human geography./ Alphabet.

305.23   Ph-2 4-A/7 $35.00   L   KA823
BRILL, MARLENE TARG. Extraordinary young people. Children's Press ISBN 0-516-00587-1; In Canada: Children's Press, 1996. 212p. ill. (Extraordinary people).
> Includes glossary, bibliography, directory and index.
> Brief profiles depict a multicultural mix of historical (Phillis Wheatley, Louis Braille, Thomas Alva Edison) and contemporary (Midori, Zlata Filipovic, Tiger Woods) figures who accomplished extraordinary feats at a young age. Includes artists, athletes, scientists, entertainers, and social activists. An inspirational book for browsing.
> SUBJ: Gifted children.

305.23   Ph-1 4-6/8 $15.45   L   KA824
FREEDMAN, RUSSELL. Children of the wild west. Clarion ISBN 0-89919-143-6, 1983. 104p. ill.
> Selectors' Choice, 15th ed.
> Available from National Library Service for the Blind and Physically Handicapped on sound recording cassette RC22740.
> Experience all aspects of daily life faced by children of pioneer

families as they traveled in a wagon train and during the early days of settlement in the West. The readable text with quotes from primary sources is enhanced by many well reproduced old photographs. A first-hand look at culture as it was in the settlement of the West which will be an excellent source for browsing or research reports.
SUBJ: West (U.S.)--Social life and customs./ West (U.S.)--History.

305.23   Ph-1 2-6/8 $16.95   T   KA825
KINDERSLEY, BARNABAS. Children just like me. By Barnabas and Anabel Kindersley. Compiled and written by Sue Copsey. UNICEF/DK Publishing ISBN 0-7894-0201-7, 1995. 80p. col. ill., maps.
Includes index.
Interviews and photographs of children from all over the world are organized by continent and feature information about families, friends, school, food, likes, dislikes, and other interesting personal information. Format encourages comparisons among the cultures of our human family and provides opportunities for readers to identify and appreciate diversity and commonalities. Commemorates the fiftieth anniversary of UNICEF. For multicultural studies.
SUBJ: Children--Pictorial works./ Children--Foreign countries./ Geography.

305.232   Ph-2 P-K/2 $13.95   T   KA826
ANHOLT, CATHERINE. Here come the babies. By Catherine and Laurence Anholt. Candlewick ISBN 1-56402-209-9; In Canada: Candlewick/dist. by Douglas & McIntyre. unp. col. ill.
Offers a lighthearted report on the characteristics of babies as seen through the eyes of a toddler. Lively illustrations reminiscent of early Sendak and a rhyming text make this a happy choice for reading aloud to a small group or one-to-one.
SUBJ: Babies./ Brothers and sisters.

305.232   Ph-2 P-K/3 $14.95   T   KA827
STEIN, SARA. Oh, baby! Photos by Holly Anne Shelowitz. Walker ISBN 0-8027-8261-2; In Canada: Thomas Allen & Son, 1993. unp. col. ill.
Details characteristics of newborns and follows their development. Text is simple; photographs are appealing. Useful for reading aloud with preschoolers and of interest to older browsers.
SUBJ: Babies./ Child development.

305.3   Ph-2 3-A/9 $19.95   T   KA828
HAZELL, REBECCA. Heroes: great men through the ages. Abbeville Press ISBN 0-7892-0289-1, 1997. 80p. col. ill., maps.
First published in Great Britain, Barefoot Books Ltd., 1996.
Includes bibliography.
This book has "many kinds of heroes, from all around the world and from different periods of history." (Introduction) Following a brief presentation of the hero's life is a summary of the world in which he lived, an important event in his life, and a map of the area in which he was active. This title will be useful in many social studies units, and each of the sections can be used individually during a birthday celebration. For multicultural studies.
SUBJ: Heroes.

305.4   Ph-2 4-A/10 $19.95   T   KA829
HAZELL, REBECCA. Heroines: great women through the ages. Abbeville Press ISBN 0-7892-0210-7, 1996. 79p. col. ill., maps.
First published in Great Britain, Barefoot Books Ltd., 1996.
Includes bibliography.
Twelve diverse women who have had important roles in history and the world in which they lived are described. All of the women are role models and their activities span numerous areas: medicine, politics, science, art, etc. Full-page portrait of the heroine plus a map of the geographical area in which she functioned are included. Biographies are full and can be read individually. For women's studies and multicultural studies.
SUBJ: Heroines.

305.42   Ph-2 3-5/6 $14.95   L   KA830
BLUMBERG, RHODA. Bloomers!. Illus. by Mary Morgan. Bradbury ISBN 0-02-711684-0; In Canada: Maxwell Macmillan, 1993. unp. col. ill.
Recounts the development of a more comfortable style of dress as women of the 1800s began a shift which included simpler clothing as well as efforts to increase women's rights. Simple text is joined by good-humored illustrations. Strong starting point for a costume project in American history and for women's studies.
SUBJ: Women's rights--History./ Costume--History.

VCR 305.42   Ph-2 5-A $95.00   OD   KA831
WOMEN OF RURAL AMERICA (Videocassette). United Learning 10350V ISBN 1-56007-482-5, 1995. 1/2" VHS videocassette color (23min).
Includes teacher's guide.
Includes public performance rights.

Daily routines and life of American farm women in the first half of the twentieth century are shown through archival film and photographs, some reenactments, movie film clips, interviews, and stories of family memories. Use for women's studies as well as social studies units covering this time period.
SUBJ: Rural families./ Women in agriculture./ Women--History./ United States--History--20th century.

305.48   Ph-2 3-5/7 $16.95   T   KA832
PRESILLA, MARICEL E. Mola: Cuna life stories and art. Henry Holt ISBN 0-8050-3801-9; In Canada: Fitzhenry & Whiteside, 1996. unp. col. ill.
In the matriarchal Cuna Indian society of the San Blas Islands off the coast of Panama, women pass their property to their children and tell the stories of their cultural heritage through colorful designs created for their molas, or blouses. Illustrated with intricate mola designs, this can be paired with DIA'S STORY CLOTH and the author's LIFE AROUND THE LAKE for cross cultural comparisons of needle art. For multicultural studies.
SUBJ: Cuna Indians--Social life and customs./ Indians of Central America--Panama--Social life and customs./ Cuna women--Industries./ Embroidery--Panama./ San Blas Islands (Panama)--Social life and customs.

305.5   Ph-2 A/6 $16.95   T   KA833
ATKIN, S. BETH. Voices from the fields: children of migrant farmworkers tell their stories. Interviews and photos by S. Beth Atkin. Joy Street/ Little, Brown ISBN 0-316-05633-2; In Canada: Little, Brown, 1993. 96p. ill.
Includes bibliography.
Reveals hardships and hopes of nine Hispanic young people living in the Salinas Valley of California. Photographs, poems in Spanish and English, and first-person narratives are used in depicting the difficult lives of these children of migrant workers. Valuable used alone or in conjunction with other materials.
SUBJ: Migrant labor./ Agricultural laborers./ Mexican Americans./ Children's writings.

305.5   Ph-2 4-6/6 $17.50   L   KA834
BRIMNER, LARRY DANE. Migrant family. Text and photos by Larry Dane Brimner. Lerner ISBN 0-8225-2554-2, 1992. 40p. ill.
Includes bibliography.
Portrays the life of twelve-year-old Juan Medina in a migrant camp near San Diego. Black and white photographs provide a sense of the hardships and uncertainties faced by the boy and his family. Useful as a discussion-starter and in combination with other titles in examining patterns of American life.
SUBJ: Migrant labor./ Agricultural laborers./ Mexican Americans./ Medina, Juan.

305.5   Ph-2 5-A/7 $15.99   L   KA835
STANLEY, JERRY. Children of the Dust Bowl: the true story of the school at Weedpatch Camp. Crown ISBN 0-517-58782-3, 1992. 85p. ill., maps.
Includes index.
Traces the plight of children of migrant workers during the Depression as their families moved from the Dust Bowl and traveled to California. Emphasis of the second half of the work is on education and development of Weedpatch School. A strong background-builder reinforced by good graphic design and outstanding photographs.
SUBJ: Migrant labor./ Agricultural laborers./ Depressions--1929./ Schools--History.

305.8   Ph-2 5-6/8 $16.99   T   KA836
ASHABRANNER, BRENT. To seek a better world: the Haitian minority in America. Photos by Paul Conklin. Cobblehill/Dutton ISBN 0-525-65219-1; In Canada: McClelland & Stewart, 1997. 88p.
Includes bibliography and index.
Through historical background and interviews with Haitian Americans who have made a difference in their communities, the author explores the efforts of immigrants and refugees from Haiti to build a better life for themselves and their families in the United States. Photographs of the Miami community and of Haitians from many walks of life illustrate the text. For multicultural studies, for units examining the immigrant experience, and for regional studies.
SUBJ: Haitian Americans./ United States--Emigration and immigration.

PIC 305.8   Ph-2 4-6 $39.95   OD   KA837
BLACK INNOVATORS (Picture). Knowledge Unlimited 7058P ISBN 1-55933-174-7, 1994. 10 study prints color (17"x22").
Includes teacher's guide.
Also available as individual posters, $7.95 each.
Introduces ten African-American men and women notable for their achievements. Teacher's guide expands the text provided on each poster and suggests student activities. Useful display and teaching material. For multicultural studies.

Contents: Matthew Henson -- Charlie Parker -- Katherine Dunham -- Elijah McCoy -- Mary McLeod Bethune -- Granville T. Woods -- Dr. Charles Drew -- George Washington Carver -- Benjamin Banneker -- Madame C. J. Walker.
SUBJ: Afro-Americans--Biography.

VCR 305.8   Ph-3 4-6 $89.00   OD KA838
BLACK IS MY COLOR: THE AFRICAN AMERICAN EXPERIENCE (Videocassette). Rainbow Educational RB8180, 1992. 1/2" VHS videocassette color (15min).
Includes teacher's guide.
Offers a brief, simple overview of early African-American history. Question and answer segments with elementary students reinforce points developed. For large collections.
SUBJ: Afro-Americans--History./ Slavery--History./ Segregation./ Afro-Americans--Civil rights.

305.8   Ph-2 3-5/4 $15.95   T   KA839
BROWN, TRICIA. Konnichiwa!: I am a Japanese-American girl. Photos by Kazuyoshi Arai. Henry Holt ISBN 0-8050-2353-4; In Canada: Fitzhenry & Whiteside, 1995. unp. col. ill.
Includes glossary and bibliography.
Offers a view of the life of a Japanese-American girl living in San Francisco. Handsome photographs capture preparations for the Cherry Blossom Festival; text is written in first person and at times is disconcerting. Use with author's CHINESE NEW YEAR, HELLO, AMIGOS!, and LEE ANN to display diverse bicultural settings or draw from the excellent bibliography to identify several books featuring Japanese Americans. For multicultural studies.
SUBJ: Kamiya, Lauren Seiko./ Japanese Americans--California--San Francisco--Social life and customs./ Japanese Americans--Social life and customs./ San Francisco (Calif.)--Social life and customs./ Asian Americans--Social life and customs.

305.8   Ph-3 5-6/7 $14.90   L   KA840
CAVAN, SEAMUS. Irish-American experience. Millbrook ISBN 1-56294-218-2, 1993. 64p. ill. (some col.), map. (Coming to America).
Includes bibliography and index.
Describes the wave of Irish immigrants during the Potato Famine, the conditions they endured to emigrate to America, and the hardships they overcame in the United States. Includes information about famous Irish Americans such as John Kennedy, Eugene O'Neill, and F. Scott Fitzgerald.
SUBJ: Irish Americans--History.

305.8   Ph-2 3-4/4 $14.95   L   KA841
COOPER, MARTHA. Anthony Reynoso: born to rope. Photos by Martha Cooper. Text by Ginger Gordon. Clarion ISBN 0-395-71690-X, 1996. 32p. col. ill.
Appealing photographic study of a boy whose talent is roping. He performs with his father on weekends, but during the week he is just an average school boy. For multicultural studies.
SUBJ: Mexican Americans--Social life and customs./ Rodeos./ Reynoso, Anthony./ Hispanic Americans--Social life and customs./ Trick roping.

305.8   Ph-2 5-6/7 $14.95   L   KA842
DAWSON, MILDRED LEINWEBER. Over here it's different: Carolina's story. Photos by George Ancona. Macmillan ISBN 0-02-726328-2; In Canada: Maxwell Macmillan, 1993. unp. ill.
Compares the New York life of eleven-year-old Carolina with her earlier experiences growing up in the Dominican Republic. Descriptions of the extended family are difficult to follow at times, but black-and-white photographs by George Ancona help keep matters straight. Use in "how we live" units and in discussion of immigration. For multicultural studies.
SUBJ: Dominican Americans--Social life and customs./ Dominican Americans--New York (N.Y.)./ United States--Emigration and immigration.

305.8   Ph-1 P-1/1 $16.00   L   KA843
FOX, MEM. Whoever you are. Illus. by Leslie Staub. Harcourt Brace ISBN 0-15-200787-3; In Canada: Harcourt Brace c/o Canadian Manda, 1997. unp. col. ill.
Emphasizes the similarities of people all over the world who unite in love, joy, and pain despite differences in language, culture, and skin color. Bold, colorful oil paintings edged with jeweled frames complement the simple text. For multicultural studies and for introducing young students to concepts of the human family.
SUBJ: Ethnicity./ Multiculturalism./ Individuality.

305.8   Ph-3 3-6/4 $14.95   T   KA844
GORDON, GINGER. My two worlds. Photos by Martha Cooper. Clarion ISBN 0-395-58704-2, 1993. unp. col. ill.

Follows Kirsy Rodriguez from her home in New York to the Dominican Republic where she celebrates Christmas and her eighth birthday with her grandparents and friends. Color photographs support the text and aid in contrasting the two very different settings and lifestyles. Useful for multicultural studies or as the basis for discussion of intergenerational cross-cultural visits.
SUBJ: Dominican Republic--Social life and customs./ United States--Emigration and immigration./ Dominican Americans./ Family life./ Family.

305.8   Ph-1 4-6/7 $16.95   L   KA845
GRAFF, NANCY PRICE. Where the river runs: a portrait of a refugee family. Photos by Richard Howard. Little, Brown ISBN 0-316-32287-3; In Canada: Little, Brown, 1993. 71p. ill.
Describes the experiences of a family of Cambodian refugees as they adjust to life in the United States. Sensitive, well-written text combines effectively with black and white photographs. Sampling of questions from citizenship examinations provides a thought-provoking finish. Has read-aloud potential.
SUBJ: Cambodian Americans./ Refugees.

PIC 305.8   Ph-2 4-6 $39.95   OD KA846
GREAT BLACK AMERICANS. Set I (Picture). Knowledge Unlimited 7003PN ISBN 0-915291-97-5, 1996. 10 study prints color (17"x22").
Includes teacher's guide.
Also available as individual posters, $7.95 each.
Presents brief biographical profiles of African-Americans from post-Revolutionary War times to the present in the fields of science, politics, government, the arts, and sports. Teacher's guide contains additional information on people pictured and suggested classroom activities. For multicultural studies.
GREAT BLACK AMERICANS. Set II (Picture). Knowledge Unlimited 7015PN ISBN 1-55933-056-2, 1991), $39.95.
Contents: Set I: Harriet Tubman -- Booker T. Washington -- George Washington Carver -- Louis Armstrong -- Langston Hughes -- Jesse Owens -- Jackie Robinson -- Ralph Bunche -- Thurgood Marshall -- Dr. Martin Luther King, Jr. Set II: Benjamin Banneker -- Sojourner Truth -- Frederick Douglass -- W.E.B. Du Bois -- Ralph Ellison -- Ella Fitzgerald -- Leroy "Satchel" Paige -- Charles Drew -- Rosa Parks -- Shirley Chisholm.
SUBJ: Afro-Americans--Biography.

305.8   Ph-3 5-A/7 $13.95   L   KA847
HASKINS, JAMES. One more river to cross: the stories of twelve Black Americans. Scholastic ISBN 0-590-42896-9, 1992. 215p. ill.
Includes bibliography and index.
Available from the National Library Service for the Blind and Physically Handicapped on sound recording cassette RC 38023.
A diverse group of individuals who fought prejudice and poverty and stood up for freedom and individual rights is studied in this collective biography of leading African-American men and women. Includes historical (Crispus Attucks) as well as contemporary figures (Shirley Chisolm). For mature readers.
SUBJ: Afro-Americans--Biography.

PIC 305.8   Ph-3 4-6 $44.95   OD KA848
HISPANIC HERITAGE (Picture). Knowledge Unlimited 7007PN ISBN 1-55933-217-4, 1997. 12 study prints color (17"x22").
Includes teacher's guide.
Also available as individual posters, $7.95 each.
Brief biographical portraits of 12 Hispanics who have had an impact on American and global society in the fields of government, politics, labor, the arts, and early exploration. Teacher's guide contains additional information on people pictured and suggested classroom activities. For multicultural studies.
Contents: Henry Cisneros -- Cesar Chavez -- Gloria Estefan -- Rita Moreno -- Juan Ponce De Leon -- Pablo Picasso -- Pablo Casals -- Roberto Clemente -- Simon Bolivar -- Gabriel Garcia Marquez -- Nancy Lopez -- Antonia Novello.
SUBJ: Hispanic Americans--Biography./ United States--Civilization--Spanish influences.

305.8   Ph-2 3-6/6 $14.95   L   KA849
HOYT-GOLDSMITH, DIANE. Hoang Anh: a Vietnamese-American boy. Photos by Lawrence Migdale. Holiday House ISBN 0-8234-0948-1, 1992. 32p. col. ill. map.
Includes glossary and index.
Description of the daily activities of young Hoang Anh Chau's life in San Jose. The text interweaves information about Vietnamese customs and the recent history of the family of Hoang Anh; a glossary assists with pronunciation. Works well with the author's TOTEM POLE and PUEBLO STORYTELLER in units examining American culture today. For multicultural studies.
SUBJ: Hoang, Anh Chau./ Vietnamese Americans.

305.8 Ph-1 1-3/5 $13.95 L KA850
KUKLIN, SUSAN. How my family lives in America. Bradbury ISBN 0-02-751239-8; In Canada: Maxwell Macmillan, 1992. unp. col. ill.
 Selectors' Choice, 19th ed.
 Introduces three young Americans who describe life in their family groups which are African American, Hispanic American, and Chinese American. Color photographs and first-person narratives emphasize the uniqueness of the individuals while effectively depicting similarities of the family groupings. Stretch this one upward and use it as a starting point for cultural study projects with upper elementary students.
 SUBJ: Afro-Americans--Social life and customs./ Asian Americans--Social life and customs./ Hispanic Americans--Social life and customs.

VCR 305.8 Ph-3 4-6 $450.00 OD KA851
MANY VOICES (Videocassette). TVOntario/Journal Films/Altschul Group; In Canada: TVOntario, 1991. 9 1/2" VHS videocassettes color. (Many voices).
 Teacher's guide available for $3.45.
 Includes public performance rights.
 Individual videocassettes available $49.00.
 Series of nine videos depicts children from various ethnic heritages learning to accept their cultures. Open-ended storylines serve as a foundation for group discussion or examination of attitudes. Separate purchase of teacher's guide is recommended. Ideal for multicultural studies.
 Series contents: What's in a name 388201 (14min); To Jew is not a verb 388202 (14min); Quick to judge 388203 (14min); Food for thought 388204 (14min); Hair scare 388205 (14min); Sari tale 388206 (14min); Mother tongue 388207 (14min); World at my door 388208 (14min); Positively native 388209 (14min).
 SUBJ: Ethnic groups./ Ethnic attitudes./ Prejudices.

305.8 Ph-2 K-2/5 $14.95 L KA852
MEDEARIS, ANGELA SHELF. Our people. Illus. by Michael Bryant. Atheneum ISBN 0-689-31826-X; In Canada: Maxwell Macmillan, 1994. unp. col. ill.
 "Parent and child discuss their African-American heritage and the contributions made to civilization by their people." (CIP) Effective chalk drawings illustrate a repetitive text which introduces an achievement and follows with the phrase "I wish I could have been there." For reading aloud and multicultural studies.
 SUBJ: Afro-Americans--History.

VCR 305.8 Ph-2 5-A $199.00 OD KA853
OUR HISPANIC HERITAGE (Videocassette). Society for Visual Education C95915-HAVT, 1991. 5 1/2" VHS videocassettes color.
 Includes teacher's manual.
 Individual videocassettes available separately, $49.00 ea.
 Provides a thorough discussion of the diverse cultural background and history of Hispanic people. Learning objectives, blackline masters, scripts, and bibliographies are included in total teaching package. Use alone or in conjunction with other social studies resources.
 Contents: Spain comes to America (12min); Mexico's heritage (13min); Mexican and Mexican American heroes (11min); Caribbean contributors (11min); Central and South American achievers (11min).
 SUBJ: Hispanic Americans.

VCR 305.8 Ph-1 4-6 $599.00 OD KA854
PLAYING FAIR (Videocassette). National Film Board of Canada, 1991. 4 1/2" VHS videocassettes color. (Playing fair).
 Includes teacher's guide.
 Individual videocassettes are available, $200.00.
 Four offerings depict white racial prejudice against blacks, Chinese and students from India. While enduring taunts and abuse, the young targets sometimes make peace with their classmates and sometimes only with themselves. Each video forcefully shows how cruel and relentless prejudice is.
 Contents: Carol's mirror (15min); Mela's lunch (15min); Hey, Kelly (15min); and Walker (15min).
 SUBJ: Racism./ Minorities./ Prejudices.

VCR 305.8 Ph-3 A $79.00 KA855
RACE (Videocassette). National Geographic C51564, 1993. 1/2" VHS videocassette color (17min). (Celebrating our differences).
 Includes teacher's guide.
 Discusses differences in skin color and gently attempts to counter misconceptions about race. Presentation returns throughout to a skilled youth orchestra which provides an effective, though unmentioned, example of individual abilities and unified effort across racial groups. Useful as an awareness-increaser.
 SUBJ: Race awareness./ Color of man./ Prejudices.

305.8 Ph-3 6-A/7 $18.95 L KA856
RAGAZA, ANGELO. Lives of notable Asian Americans: business, politics, science. Chelsea House ISBN 0-7910-2189-0, 1995. 142p. ill. (Asian American experience).
 Includes bibliography and index.
 Twelve Asian Americans who have made their way in business, the media, politics, and medicine are covered in this collected biography. The biographies are detailed, and black and white photographs capture the individuals at work and at leisure activities. For advanced readers. For multicultural studies.
 SUBJ: Asian Americans.

SRC 305.8 Ph-2 1-6 $10.00 KA857
SACRE, ANTONIO. Looking for Papito: family stories from Latin America (Sound recording cassette). Woodside Avenue Music Productions WA 007-4 ISBN 1-886283-09-5, 1996. 1 sound cassette (42min). (American story series).
 A masterful storyteller presents a combination of family reminiscences, sometimes humorously exaggerated, about his experiences growing up Hispanic in America, and retellings of traditional Latin American tales. English and Spanish are effortlessly integrated, and the stories will delight both listeners who have had similar experiences and those who have not. Use for multicultural studies.
 SUBJ: Cuban Americans./ Hispanic Americans./ Bilingual materials--Spanish./ Spanish language materials.

305.8 Ph-1 3-6/5 $15.95 L KA858
SEWALL, MARCIA. People of the breaking day. Atheneum ISBN 0-689-31407-8; In Canada: Collier Macmillan, 1990. 48p. col. ill.
 Includes glossary.
 Available from the National Library Service for the Blind and Physically Handicapped on sound recording cassette RC35485.
 Poetic text and light-filled illustrations recreate the lifeways of the Wampanoags in the time before the "Mayflower." Presented as a companion book to the prizewinning THE PILGRIMS OF PLIMOTH, this title works particularly well as a read-aloud.
 SUBJ: Wampanoag Indians./ Indians of North America.

305.8 Ph-2 5-A/8 $31.93 L KA859
SINNOTT, SUSAN. Extraordinary Asian Pacific Americans. Childrens Press ISBN 0-516-03052-X; In Canada: Childrens Press, 1993. 270p. ill. (Extraordinary people).
 Includes bibliography and index.
 This widely diverse collection about Asian Americans includes brief historical information and biographies. Text explains who these individuals are, their contributions, and how they or their ancestors came to the United States. For reports and browsing.
 SUBJ: Asian Americans./ Pacific Islander Americans.

305.8 Ph-3 5-A/7 $30.60 L KA860
SINNOTT, SUSAN. Extraordinary Hispanic Americans. Childrens Press ISBN 0-516-00582-0; In Canada: Childrens Press, 1991. 277p. ill. (Extraordinary people).
 Includes notes, bibliography and index.
 Available from the National Library Service for the Blind and Physically Handicapped on sound recording cassette RC 37974.
 Beginning with Columbus' crew, this book reviews over seventy-five Hispanic Americans and their impact on American life. Brief, yet inclusive, the biographies will be useful for assignments and to lead readers to more extensive studies. Each biography includes a portrait plus other related sketches and photographs. Consider for reference as well as circulation.
 SUBJ: Hispanic Americans--Biography./ United States--Civilization--Spanish influences.

305.8 Ph-2 4-6/7 $10.50 L KA861
STANEK, MURIEL. We came from Vietnam. Photos by William Franklin McMahon. Whitman ISBN 0-8075-8699-4; In Canada: General, 1985. 46p. ill.
 Describes the life of a Vietnamese refugee family in Chicago as they move toward being a part of a culture new to them. Vietnamese language, food, games, and clothing receive brief mention in the text which is illustrated with black and white photographs. The appended pronunciation guide is a valuable feature.
 SUBJ: Vietnamese--United States./ United States--Emigration and immigration.

VCR 305.8 Ph-2 3-6 $99.95 OD KA862
WHITEWASH (Videocassette) Michael Sporn Animation, Inc./dist. by SVE/Churchill Media 81192-HAVT, 1994. 1/2" VHS videocassette color (20min).
 Includes teacher's guide.
 Includes public performance rights.
 Andrew Carnegie Medal, 1995.

Based on a true incident, the story portrays a young African-American girl who is waylaid with her brother on her way home from school and spray painted with white shoe polish. Animated format, contemporary music, and voices of Ruby Dee and Linda Lavin hold attention. Use for multicultural studies, discussions of interpersonal and community relationships, conflict resolution, and connections to the civil rights movement of the 1960s.
SUBJ: Racism./ Prejudices./ Afro-Americans--Social conditions.

PIC 305.8　　Ph-2 4-6　$39.95　OD KA863
WOMEN OF HOPE: AFRICAN AMERICANS WHO MADE A DIFFERENCE (Picture). Developed by Network of Educators on the Americas (NECA). Edited by Diane Yarbro-Swift and Lynda Tredway. Bread and Roses Cultural Project/dist. by Knowledge Unlimited 7048PN, 1994. 12 study prints color (17"x22").
Includes teacher's guide.
Each poster features a photograph or artistic rendering of an African-American woman who has challenged injustice and contributed to both the African-American community and society at large. Extensive and helpful study guide includes added information about each, suggestions for classroom activities, additional resources, and bibliographies. Excellent visuals for multicultural studies and women's studies.
Contents: Maya Angelou -- Ella J. Baker -- Alexa Canady -- Septima Poinsette Clark -- Ruby Dee -- Sarah and Annie Elizabeth Delany -- Marian Wright Edelman -- Fannie Lou Hamer -- Mae C. Jemison -- Toni Morrison -- Alice Walker -- Ida B. Wells-Barnett.
SUBJ: Afro-American women--Biography./ Afro-Americans--Biography.

305.8　　Ph-3 5-6/8　$14.90　L　KA864
WU, DANA YING-HUI. Chinese-American experience. By Dana Ying-Hui Wu and Jeffrey Dao-Sheng Tung. Millbrook ISBN 1-56294-271-9, 1993. 64p. ill. (some col.), map. (Coming to America).
Includes bibliography and index.
"Traces the history of Chinese immigration to the United States, discussing why they emigrated, their problems in a new land, and their contributions to American culture." (CIP) Text is difficult, but well-organized and pleasingly written. Useful in support of immigration units, multicultural studies, and in general social studies classes.
SUBJ: Chinese Americans--History.

306.4　　Ph-2 5-A/7　$19.95　L　KA865
MILLER, THOMAS ROSS. Taking time out: recreation and play. Published in cooperation with the Denver Museum of Natural History. Blackbirch ISBN 1-56711-128-9, 1996. 80p. col. ill. (Our human family).
Includes glossary, bibliography and index.
Compares kinds of play, social play, playing to learn, and fun and leisure among societies in the Americas, Africa, Europe and the Middle East, Asia, and Australia and the South Pacific. Illustrated with active, engaging color photographs from each region. Will add a new and interesting dimension to reports on geographic areas and multicultural studies. For advanced readers.
SUBJ: Games--Social aspects./ Play--Social aspects./ Leisure--Social aspects.

306.85　　Ph-2 2-5/6　$13.95　L　KA866
GARZA, CARMEN LOMAS. Family pictures: Cuadros de familia. Paintings and stories by Carmen Lomas Garza, as told to Harriet Rohmer. Spanish version by Rosalma Zubizarreta. Children's Book Press ISBN 0-89239-050-6, 1990. 30p. col. ill.
Reflects the life of a Mexican-American family in South Texas in the era of the author's childhood. Brightly colored, primitive illustrations echoing the detail and technique of Mexican folk art support a bilingual text. Potential for art and regional social studies units.
SUBJ: Mexican Americans./ Bilingual materials--Spanish./ Spanish language materials.

306.85　　Ph-1 3-6　$29.95　T　KA867
IN PRAISE OF OUR FATHERS AND OUR MOTHERS: A BLACK FAMILY TREASURY BY OUTSTANDING AUTHORS AND ARTISTS. Compiled by Wade Hudson and Cheryl Willis Hudson. Just Us Books ISBN 0-940975-59-9; In Canada: Publishers Group West, 1997. 131p. col. ill.
More than 40 African-American writers and illustrators share their family remembrances and celebrate their cultural heritage in stories, prose, poetry, interviews, and pictures, which reflect feelings of pride and familial bonding and, in some cases, anger and frustration. Illustrations include linocuts, photographs, paintings, collages, and graphics. Readers will find many of their favorite authors and illustrators represented in this well-crafted anthology that will be a welcome addition to multicultural studies and literature units.
SUBJ: Afro-American families./ Afro-American authors./ Afro-American artists./ Afro-Americans--Literary collections.

306.85　　Ph-3 4-6/5　$13.95　T　KA868
JENNESS, AYLETTE. Families: a celebration of diversity, commitment, and love. Houghton Mifflin ISBN 0-395-47038-2, 1990. 47p. ill.
Includes bibliography.
Depicts the lives of seventeen American families joined in a variety of non-traditional configurations - step relationships, gay parents, foster homes, communes, and others. Handsome black-and-white photography is a significant feature of this work based on a traveling exhibition from the Children's Museum of Boston. For collections wishing emphasis in this area.
SUBJ: Family life.

306.85　　Ph-2 K-2/2　$15.95　L　KA869
LEEDY, LOREEN. Who's who in my family. Holiday House ISBN 0-8234-1151-6, 1995. unp. col. ill.
Includes glossary.
Visits a primary classroom in which young students describe their family trees and relationships among family members. Noteworthy features are lighthearted illustrations of a furry cast of characters and clear definitions of "second cousins" and "first cousins once removed." Addresses relationships within nuclear families as well as blended families.
SUBJ: Family./ Genealogy.

306.85　　Ph-2 2-5/6　$15.95　L　KA870
LOMAS GARZA, CARMEN. In my family./En mi familia. Paintings and stories by Carmen Lomas Garza; as told to Harriet Rohmer; edited by David Schecter; translated by Francisco X. Alarcon. Children's Book Press ISBN 0-89239-138-3, 1996. unp. col. ill.
The second book of bilingual stories based on the author's recollections and experiences growing up in a Mexican-American family in Texas. Illustrated with brightly colored, detailed paintings that evoke the feelings of the stories. For multicultural units and regional studies.
SUBJ: Hispanic Americans--Social life and customs./ Spanish language materials./ Bilingual materials--Spanish.

VCR 306.85　　Ph-2 K-2　$59.95　OD KA871
MY FAMILY, YOUR FAMILY (Videocassette). Sunburst 2425-03 ISBN 0-7805-4111-1, 1994. 1/2" VHS videocassette color (16min).
Includes teacher's guide and eight reproducible student worksheets. Presents three short vignettes which depict different family structures. Can be used in toto or as individual segments; support materials are above average. Useful for classroom discussion.
SUBJ: Family./ Family life./ Domestic relations.

306.85　　Ph-2 4-6/6　$14.95　L　KA872
ROSENBERG, MAXINE B. Living with a single parent. Bradbury ISBN 0-02-777915-7; In Canada: Maxwell Macmillan, 1992. 113p. ill.
Includes bibliographies, directory and index.
Contains interviews with 17 children who live in single parent homes. Family configurations vary widely but emphasis is on successful coping patterns in one-parent settings rather than on type of parent. Guidelines, addresses, and bibliography are included. Particularly appealing to individual readers.
SUBJ: Single-parent family.

306.85　　Ph-2 1-3/5　$13.95　L　KA873
SIMON, NORMA. All kinds of families. Illus. by Joe Lasker. Whitman ISBN 0-8075-0282-0, c1976. 40p. col. ill.
Explores the various structures and lifestyles of the family unit in gentle, flowing text accompanied by alternating soft color and black-and-white expressive illustrations. Emphasizes the supportive nature of the family, with many ethnic groups included.
SUBJ: Family./ Domestic relations.

VCR 306.85　　Ph-3 3-5　$99.95　OD KA874
WE'RE A FAMILY (Videocassette). Sunburst 2409-03 ISBN 0-7805-4088-3, 1992. 1/2" VHS videocassette color (15min).
Includes teacher's guide and reproducible student worksheets. Depicts different family structures and shows children successfully adjusting to new family situations. Guide provides suggestions for video use, activities, and script. Useful supplementary material.
SUBJ: Family./ Family life./ Domestic relations.

306.87　　Ph-2 P-1/2　$14.95　T　KA875
KNIGHT, MARGY BURNS. Welcoming babies. Illus. by Anne Sibley O'Brien. Tilbury House ISBN 0-88448-123-9, 1994. unp. col. ill.
Explores ways in which diverse cultures welcome and celebrate the birth of a baby. Closing notes provide supportive material and expand the text. Can be used with older students in multicultural studies.
SUBJ: Birth customs./ Babies.

306.874 Ph-2 P-1/2 $12.95 T KA876
ALPERT, LOU. You and your dad. Whispering Coyote Press ISBN
1-879085-36-4, 1992. unp. col. ill.
 Offers a warm picture of a variety of father and child activities.
 Rhymed text and colorful illustrations make this a natural for small
 group or one-to-one sharing. Use as the basis for a class-illustrated
 book about fathers.
 SUBJ: Father and child./ Stories in rhyme.

306.874 Ph-2 4-6/4 $19.95 L KA877
GREENBERG, KEITH ELLIOT. Zack's story: growing up with same-sex
parents. Photos by Carol Halebian. Lerner ISBN 0-8225-2581-X, 1996.
32p. col. ill.
 Includes glossary, bibliography and directory.
 As eleven-year-old Zack matter-of-factly describes life in a
 nontraditional family headed by his mother and her lesbian
 companion, he points out some specific attitudes he finds offensive
 and relates how he copes with hurtful remarks. Photographs depict
 both very ordinary events and unique experiences directly connected
 to being part of a family that participates actively in the gay and
 lesbian community. Use as a discussion starter for building
 understanding of families who do not fit the traditional mold and for
 fostering understanding of gay and lesbian people. (Parents' Shelf).
 SUBJ: Mothers and sons./ Gay parents./ Lesbians./ Family./
 Homosexuality.

306.874 Ph-3 1-3/4 $15.95 L KA878
GREENSPUN, ADELE ARON. Daddies. Philomel ISBN 0-399-22259-6; In
Canada: Putnam, 1991. unp. ill.
 Offers a collection of black and white photographs depicting warm
 moments between fathers and young children. A poignant, personal
 note provides an introduction. Use in developing writing and
 photography projects about fathers.
 SUBJ: Fathers./ Father and child.

306.874 Ph-2 4-6/9 $13.95 T KA879
LESHAN, EDA. Grandparents: a special kind of love. Illustrated by Tricia
Taggart. Macmillan ISBN 0-02-756380-4; In Canada: Collier Macmillan,
1984. 119p. ill.
 Identifies the special relationship between grandparents and
 grandchildren and discusses ways of loving and handling conflicts
 when they occur. Conversational style communicates ideas on a
 personal basis. Will be useful in understanding the special place of
 grandparents in our family structure.
 SUBJ: Grandparents./ Conflict of generations.

306.874 Ph-2 1-3/2 $13.88 L KA880
MORRIS, ANN. Loving. Photos by Ken Heyman. Lothrop, Lee &
Shepard ISBN 0-688-06341-1, 1990. 32p. col. ill.
 Includes index to photographs.
 Emphasizes the universality of love as warm relationships between
 children and parents, friends, and pets are depicted. An afterword
 provides additional information about each photograph and its
 subject. Good discussion starter.
 SUBJ: Love./ Parent and child./ Friendship./ Family.

306.874 Ph-1 P-1/2 $12.89 L KA881
ROTNER, SHELLEY. Lots of dads. By Shelley Rotner and Sheila M. Kelly.
Photos by Shelley Rotner. Dial ISBN 0-8037-2089-0; In Canada:
McClelland & Stewart, 1997. unp. col. ill.
 Lots of multicultural dads are pictured in full-color photographs in a
 variety of daily activities, showing how they teach, take care of, play
 with, and love their kids. Readers will be reassured by the loving
 relationships depicted and will enjoy identifying things they do with
 their own fathers. Pair with LOTS OF MOMS for family units and as
 an appealing addition to Father's Day units.
 SUBJ: Fathers./ Father and child.

306.874 Ph-1 P-1/1 $12.89 L KA882
ROTNER, SHELLEY. Lots of moms. By Shelley Rotner and Sheila M.
Kelly. Photos by Shelley Rotner. Dial ISBN 0-8037-1892-6, 1996. unp.
col. ill.
 An array of multicultural moms are pictured in full-color photographs
 in a variety of daily activities which show how they teach, take care
 of, play with, and love their children. Readers will be reassured by
 the loving relationships depicted and will enjoy identifying things they
 do with their own mothers. Use for family studies and as an
 appealing addition to Mother's Day units.
 SUBJ: Mothers./ Mother and child.

VCR 306.874 Ph-3 A $99.95 OD KA883
WHEN THERE'S TROUBLE AT HOME (Videocassette). Sunburst
Communicatons 2374, 1991. 1/2" VHS videocassette color (34min).
 Includes teacher's guide.

Formerly WHEN HOME MEANS TROUBLE (Videocassette).
 Offers three vignettes designed to help the viewer develop coping
 skills in difficult home situations including unemployment, divorce, and
 stepfamilies. Settings are middle class; participants are seventh and
 eighth graders. Most useful with mature students.
 SUBJ: Family problems./ Parent and child./ Emotions.

VCR 306.875 Ph-2 P-3 $34.90 OD KA884
HEY, WHAT ABOUT ME? (Videocassette). TMA/Kidvidz, 1987. 1/2"
VHS videocassette color (25min).
 Includes reader's guide, and activity sheets.
 Includes public performance rights.
 While playing with the new baby in their family, children describe
 their feelings about the infant. The well-paced, well-planned and well
 developed video, marred only by its length, is useful for stimulating
 discussion of family and helping a child with a new sibling.
 SUBJ: Babies./ Brothers and sisters.

306.875 Ph-1 5-A/6 $13.90 L KA885
LANDAU, ELAINE. Sibling rivalry: brothers and sisters at odds. Illus. by
Anne Canevari Green. Millbrook ISBN 1-56294-328-6, 1994. 48p. col.
ill.
 Includes bibliography and index.
 Investigates sibling rivalry and its causes, and suggests ways to lessen
 its damage. Interviews and vignettes set the stage for the discussion
 sections which follow; cheerful cartoons lighten the text. A useful
 bibliography lists both fiction and nonfiction and offers the basis for a
 special unit on families.
 SUBJ: Sibling rivalry./ Brothers and sisters.

VCR 306.875 Ph-2 P-1 $9.95 KA886
NEW BABY IN MY HOUSE (Videocassette). Children's Television
Workshop/dist. by Sony Wonder, 1993. 1/2" VHS videocassette color
(30min).
 Offers Muppets and Sesame Street quality as a story within a story
 demonstrates how older brothers and sisters feel when a new baby
 arrives on the scene. No teacher's guide is supplied, but the warmth
 of the message speaks for itself. Use with preschoolers and primary
 students or as a trigger for a language arts activity with upper
 elementary students. (Parents' Shelf).
 SUBJ: Babies./ Brothers and sisters.

306.875 Ph-1 1-4/4 $14.95 L KA887
ROSENBERG, MAXINE B. Brothers and sisters. Photos by George
Ancona. Clarion ISBN 0-395-51121-6, 1991. 32p. col. ill.
 "Follows the ever-changing and growing relationships of brothers and
 sisters in three different families." (CIP) Color photographs
 accompany the text which is presented from the points of view of
 oldest, middle, and youngest children. Valuable discussion-starter.
 SUBJ: Brothers and sisters.

CE 306.89 Ph-1 K-3/6 $14.95 L KA888
BROWN, LAURENE KRASNY. Dinosaurs divorce: a guide for changing
families. By Laurene Krasny Brown and Marc Tolon Brown. Joy Street/
Little, Brown ISBN 0-316-11248-8, 1986. 31p. col. ill. (Children's
literature series).
 Includes glossary.
 Selectors' Choice, 16th ed.
 Covers, with surprising completeness and good-humored matter-of-
 factness, children's feelings as they react to divorce in their families.
 Marked by a reassuring warmth, the text and illustrations bring
 information about stepparents, special occasions, telling friends,
 having two homes, and other areas of concern to the large number of
 children affected by divorce. Of value to students and parents.
 SUBJ: Divorce.

VCR 306.89 Ph-2 P-1 $99.95 OD KA889
DADDY DOESN'T LIVE WITH US (Videocassette). Sunburst 2463-03
ISBN 0-7805-4143-X, 1994. 1/2" VHS videocassette color (13min).
 Includes teacher's guide and reproducible student worksheets.
 Designed to give young children an understanding of their feelings
 about divorce. Preview before use. (Parents' Shelf).
 SUBJ: Divorce./ Emotions./ Parent and child.

VCR 306.89 Ph-2 4-6 $79.95 OD KA890
WHEN MOM AND DAD DIVORCE (Videocassette). Rainbow
Educational RB8235, 1994. 1/2" VHS videocassette color (12min).
 Includes teacher's guide.
 Discusses the guilt, loneliness, depression, and anger young people
 frequently feel when their parents divorce. Offers commonsense
 suggestions for coping with uncomfortable feelings. Can be used one-
 on-one or in a group setting.
 SUBJ: Divorce./ Emotions.

306.9   Ph-2   A/7 $14.95   T   KA891
HYDE, MARGARET O. Meeting death. By Margaret O. and Lawrence E. Hyde. Walker ISBN 0-8027-6873-3; In Canada: Thomas Allen, 1989. 129p. ill.
Includes bibliography and index.
Offers a straightforward, unemotional discussion of death. Included are suggestions for ways to deal with grief or to interact with a suicidal person. Most useful with mature students.
SUBJ: Death./ Grief.

CDR 307   Ph-1   1-4 $29.95   OD KA892
MICROSOFT EXPLORAPEDIA: THE WORLD OF PEOPLE. Academic ed. (CD-ROM). Microsoft ISBN 1-57231-092-8; In Canada: Microsoft Canada, 1994. 1 CD-ROM color. (Microsoft Explorapedia series).
Version 1.00.
Includes user's guide and teacher's guide.
System requirements: Multimedia PC with a 486SX or higher processor; 4MB of memory (8MB recommended); at least 8MB of available hard-disk space; double-speed CD-ROM drive; audio board; 256-color Super VGA monitor; MS-DOS operating system version 3.1 or later; Microsoft Windows operating system version 3.1 or later; Microsoft Mouse or compatible pointing device; headphones or speakers.
This superb CD-ROM provides a wealth of information and encourages the user to actively seek knowledge. Over 3,600 text entries with 35 videos, 29 animations, and over 17 hours of sound are available as youngsters explore scenes related to backstage, a city, a classroom, a neighborhood, a transportation museum, and many other environments. Excellent reference tool or learning center activity. Use to augment community helper units or for career studies.
SUBJ: Culture--Software./ Software--Culture./ Occupations--Software./ Software--Occupations./ Interactive media.

307.3   Ph-2   P-1 $12.88   L   KA893
FLORIAN, DOUGLAS. City street. Greenwillow ISBN 0-688-09544-5, 1990. 32p. col. ill.
Depicts familiar elements of urban neighborhood life; streets, games, police, stores, bus, and pigeons. Black outlines and water colors are used in the illustrations. Useful as a naming book or as the basis for a project in which young students design their own books illustrating their surroundings.
SUBJ: City and town life--Pictorial works./ Streets--Pictorial works.

VCR 307.76   Ph-3   4-6 $195.00   OD KA894
BERGIN, DANIEL PIERCE. Zero Street (Videocassette). Written and directed by Daniel Pierce Bergin. Produced by Marie Domingo and Emily Stevens. Dist. by Direct Cinema ISBN 1-55974-572-X, 1995. 1/2" VHS videocassette color (30min).
Includes public performance rights.
Depicts survival in an African-American inner city community combining fantasy and reality and focuses on violence, racism, and the need to make a difference. Provokes in-depth discussion of issues and understanding of day-to-day realities of urban neighborhoods. Use for multicultural studies and for promoting self-esteem.
SUBJ: Inner cities./ Self-esteem./ Afro-Americans--Social conditions.

307.76   Ph-3   A/11 $14.95   T   KA895
HERNANDEZ, XAVIER. Barmi: a Mediterranean city through the ages. By Xavier Hernandez and Pilar Comes. Translated by Kathleen Leverich. Illus. by Jordi Ballonga. Houghton Mifflin ISBN 0-395-54227-8, 1990. unp. ill.
Includes index.
Traces the development of a fictional southern European city from the fourth century B.C. through the late 20th century. Fourteen black-and-white overviews detail the growth of the city; each two-paged spread is followed by text, diagrams, and cutaway expansion. An intriguing, large format knowledge-expander for advanced students.
SUBJ: Cities and towns--History.

307.76   Ph-3   A/10 $16.95   T   KA896
HERNANDEZ, XAVIER. Lebek: a city of Northern Europe through the ages. By Xavier Hernandez and Jordi Ballonga. Translated by Kathleen Leverich. Illus. by Francesco Corni. Houghton Mifflin ISBN 0-395-57442-0, 1991. unp. ill.
Includes index.
Traces the development of a fictional, coastal city in northern Europe from the tenth century B.C. to the late twentieth century. Fourteen two-page spreads depict various stages of the city's growth and provide fascinating details. Has strong appeal as a browser and potential as the basis for compare-and-contrast projects both self-contained and with its companion volume BARMI: A MEDITERRANEAN CITY THROUGH THE AGES.
SUBJ: Cities and towns--Europe, Northern--History.

307.76   Ph-3   A/8 $16.95   T   KA897
HERNANDEZ, XAVIER. San Rafael: a Central American city through the ages. Translated by Kathleen Leverich. Illus. by Jordi Ballonga and Josep Escofet. Houghton Mifflin ISBN 0-395-60645-4, 1992. 61p. ill.
Includes index.
Follows the evolution of fictitious San Rafael from 1000 B.C. through today. Finely detailed black-and-white drawings record changes in the tropical site as climate and cultures take their toll. Intriguing book for browsing for advanced learners.
SUBJ: Cities and towns--Central America--History.

307.76   Ph-3   K-2/3 $14.93   L   KA898
SOENTPIET, CHRIS K. Around town. Lothrop, Lee & Shepard ISBN 0-688-04573-1, 1994. unp. col. ill.
Offers an idyllic depiction of big city life as a young girl and her mother spend time together on the streets of the boroughs of New York, ride in a hansom cab, and visit Central Park. Illustrative quality is a highpoint in this nostalgic presentation. Useful in city/country units and as a one-to-one read-aloud.
SUBJ: City and town life./ Cities and towns.

320   Ph-1   6-A/12 $17.98   L   KA899
LINDOP, LAURIE. Political leaders. Twenty-First Century ISBN 0-8050-4164-8; In Canada: Fitzhenry & Whiteside, 1996. 128p. col. ill. (Dynamic modern women).
Includes bibliography and index.
Well documented, in-depth profiles of ten American women who have achieved prominence in contemporary politics and who have made significant contributions to government as legislators, governors, jurists, and other positions of note. Each profile is illustrated with one full-page color photograph. Advanced readers will find this a useful resource for American politics, women's studies, and multicultural studies.
SUBJ: Women in politics./ Politicians.

323   Ph-2   6-A/7 $22.95   L   KA900
JACOBS, WILLIAM JAY. Great lives: human rights. Scribner's ISBN 0-684-19036-2; In Canada: Collier Macmillan, 1990. 278p. ill. (Great lives).
Includes bibliography and index.
Who has stood up for the rights of the individual since the founding of our country? This question is answered fully in this collection of twenty-nine concise biographies. Many of the well selected b&w photographs and a few drawings show the individuals in action. Present in a book talk.
SUBJ: Reformers./ Human rights.

323   Ph-1   5-6/6 $16.95   T   KA901
PARKS, ROSA. Dear Mrs. Parks: a dialogue with today's youth. By Rosa Parks, with Gregory J. Reed. Lee & Low ISBN 1-880000-45-8, 1996. 112p. ill.
Includes chronology and directory.
Rosa Parks responds to letters written to her by young people across the country and addresses issues of courage, freedom, religion, the power of education, and standing up for what you believe. A few black and white photographs accompany her personal answers to a wide range of questions. Use for study of the civil rights movement, women's studies, multicultural studies, and for units on contemporary issues.
SUBJ: Parks, Rosa--Correspondence./ Conduct of life./ Letters.

323.1   Ph-2   2-5/4 $13.95   L   KA902
COLES, ROBERT. Story of Ruby Bridges. Illus. by George Ford. Scholastic ISBN 0-590-57281-4; In Canada: Scholastic, 1995. unp. col. ill.
Available from the National Library Service for the Blind and Physically Handicapped on sound recording cassette RC 41709.
Details the experiences of six-year-old Ruby Bridges as she becomes one of the first African-American children to attend an all-white school in New Orleans in 1960. Watercolor and acrylic illustrations accompany a text which emphasizes Ruby's deep religious beliefs and her courage. For multicultural studies.
SUBJ: School integration--Louisiana--New Orleans./ Bridges, Ruby./ Afro-Americans--Biography./ New Orleans (La.)--Race relations.

323.1   Ph-2   3-6/8 $16.95   L   KA903
DUNCAN, ALICE FAYE. National Civil Rights Museum celebrates everyday people. Photos by J. Gerard Smith. BridgeWater ISBN 0-8167-3502-6; In Canada: BridgeWater/dist. by Vanwell, 1995. 64p. ill. (some col.).
Includes chronology, bibliographies and index.
A tour of the exhibits from the National Civil Rights Museum at the Lorraine Motel, site of Martin Luther King, Jr.'s assassination, covers such events as the Montgomery Bus Boycott, Freedom Riders, March

on Washington, and sit-ins. Illustrated with photographs of exhibits, snapshots of young people visiting them, and some archival photographs. Although the narrative has no chapter headings or other delineated organizing structure, this will be a useful addition to units on civil rights, multicultural studies, African-American history, and Martin Luther King, Jr.
SUBJ: National Civil Rights Museum./ Afro-Americans--Civil rights./ Civil rights movements--History./ United States--Race relations.

323.1   Ph-2 5-6/10 $17.98   L   KA904
GOLD, SUSAN DUDLEY. Indian treaties. Twenty-First Century ISBN 0-8050-4813-8; In Canada: Fitzhenry & Whiteside, 1997. 128p. ill. (some col.), maps. (Pacts & treaties).
Includes bibliography and index.
An overview of land and peace treaties between Native Americans and settlers from the early 1600s to the late 1800s that describes the efforts of settlers to acquire Indian land by any means, the effects of expansion on tribal life and culture, and relationships between Native Americans and whites. Illustrated with engravings, maps, and paintings, and includes source notes. Use for American history units from early settlement to modern times, for study of current issues, and for multicultural studies.
SUBJ: Indians of North America--Treaties./ Indians of North America--Government relations.

323.1   Ph-2 5-6/7 $15.99   T   KA905
ROCHELLE, BELINDA. Witnesses to freedom: young people who fought for civil rights. Lodestar/Dutton ISBN 0-525-67377-6; In Canada; McClelland & Stewart, 1993. 97p. ill.
Includes bibliography and index.
Profiles eight young people who were involved in the civil rights movement of the 1950s and 1960s. Pluses include well-written text and current comments from many of the eight subjects. Useful in reports and in study of the twentieth century. For multicultural studies.
SUBJ: Civil rights movements--History./ Afro-Americans--Civil rights./ Race relations.

323.1   Ph-2 A/7 $15.95   P   KA906
WEBB, SHEYANN. Selma, Lord, Selma: girlhood memories of the civil-rights days. By Sheyann Webb and Rachel West Nelson, as told to Frank Sikora. University of Alabama Press ISBN 0-8173-0898-9, c1980, 1997. 158p. ill.
The way two young girls, one eight and one nine, are caught up in Martin Luther King's nonviolent protest in Selma, Alabama, is vividly retold here from the recollections of the girls, Sheyann Webb and Rachel Webb. The book is illustrated by photographs taken during that historic week.
SUBJ: Webb, Sheyann./ Nelson, Rachel West./ Afro-Americans--Civil rights./ Selma (Ala.)--Race relations.

VCR 323.4   Ph-2 4-A $14.95   KA907
MARTIN LUTHER KING: I HAVE A DREAM (Videocassette). MPI Home Video/Premiere Video MPI 1350, 1986. 1/2" VHS videocassette color (25min).
The massive Civil Rights March in Washington, D.C. in 1963 was rallied by Dr. Martin Luther King, Jr.'s inspirational speech. Footage from black & white and colored newsreels of the time places the speech in the context of the civil rights movement, the Birmingham, Alabama church bombing and King's later assassination and Robert Kennedy's eulogy. While the film quality is poor, this is important primary source material for civil rights studies and for understanding the reason behind the national holiday in honor of Dr. King.
SUBJ: Civil rights workers./ King, Martin Luther, Jr.

323.44   Ph-2 4-6/12 $19.90   L   KA908
SHERROW, VICTORIA. Freedom of worship. Millbrook ISBN 0-7613-0065-1, 1997. 48p. col. ill. (Land of the free).
Includes glossary, bibliography and index.
Discusses the First Amendment's guarantee of freedom of religion in terms of historical context, Supreme Court decisions, and specific political examples of separation of Church and State. Includes color photographs. Use for units on American government, the Constitution, and contemporary issues.
SUBJ: Freedom of religion.

CE 323.6   Ph-2 2-5/4 $14.95   L   KA909
SWANSON, JUNE. I pledge allegiance. Illus. by Rick Hanson. Carolrhoda ISBN 0-87614-393-1, 1990. 40p. col. ill. (Carolrhoda on my own book).
Read-along kit available from Live Oak (ISBN 0-87499-202-8, 1991).
1 hardbound book, 1 sound cassette (15min), $19.95.
Traces the Pledge of Allegiance from its origin in 1892 when Francis Bellamy drafted it for use in a celebration honoring the 400th anniversary of Columbus' voyage to the New World. Period

illustrations support the text. Valuable in units celebrating patriotic symbols and documents.
SUBJ: Pledge of Allegiance./ United States--History.

324.6   Ph-2 4-6/12 $14.90   L   KA910
PASCOE, ELAINE. Right to vote. Millbrook ISBN 0-7613-0066-X, 1997. 48p. ill. (some col.). (Land of the free).
Includes glossary, bibliography and index.
Discusses the evolution of the right to vote from the time of the writing of the Constitution to the present day, including extending suffrage to women and African Americans, the Voting Rights Act of 1965, and lowering the voting age to 18. Illustrated with photographs and engravings. Use for units on American government, the Constitution, and contemporary issues.
SUBJ: Suffrage./ Voting.

324.6   Ph-2 5-6/9 $16.98   L   KA911
SMITH, BETSY COVINGTON. Women win the vote. Silver Burdett ISBN 0-382-09837-4, 1989. 64p. col. ill. (Turning points in American history).
Includes bibliography and index.
Traces the history of the women's suffrage movement. Photographs, political cartoons, and reproductions of pamphlets and reports add information and interest; an afterword discusses the women's movement of today. Valuable background builder and research source for strong readers.
SUBJ: Women--Suffrage./ Women's rights.

324.6   Ph-2 5-6/7 $13.90   L   KA912
STEINS, RICHARD. Our elections. Millbrook ISBN 1-56294-446-0, 1994. 48p. col. ill. (I know America).
Includes chronology, bibliography, and index.
Describes campaigns and elections in the two-party system of the United States. Closing chapter discusses four national elections of particular significance. Useful in support of social studies.
SUBJ: Elections--United States./ Politics, Practical./ United States--Politics and government.

VCR 324.973   Ph-2 6-A $99.00   OD KA913
ELECTING A PRESIDENT: THE PROCESS (Videocassette). Rainbow Educational RB870 ISBN 1-56701-011-3, 1993. 1/2" VHS videocassette color (22min).
Includes teacher's guide.
Describes the processes by which American presidents are chosen. Network clips, archival prints, and a solid script add up to an effective presentation. Most useful with advanced students.
SUBJ: Presidents--Election./ Elections--United States.

VCR 324.973   Ph-2 6-A $89.95   OD KA914
ELECTING A PRESIDENT (Videocassette). Knowledge Unlimited ISBN 1-55933-182-8, 1995. 1/2" VHS videocassette color (25min).
Includes teacher's guide.
Presents an overview of the election process using film clips and stills to describe the complicated procedure of electing a president. Covers campaigns, primaries and caucuses, political parties and political conventions, voting in general elections, and the Electoral College. Highlights of recent campaigns, including the 1996 Presidential primary, are combined with information about campaign finances, media coverage, third party candidates, and voting rights to make a good discussion starter.
SUBJ: Presidents--Election./ Elections--United States.

324.973   Ph-1 4-6/8 $15.93   L   KA915
MAESTRO, BETSY. Voice of the people: American democracy in action. Illus. by Giulio Maestro. Lothrop, Lee & Shepard ISBN 0-688-10679-X, 1996. 48p. col. ill., maps.
Discusses the concepts of democracy, organization of our government, and the responsibility of citizens to participate in the voting process in clear, understandable language. Full-color illustrations depict places and events in our nation's history from the days of early settlement to the present. A welcome addition to social studies units on government and civic responsibility.
SUBJ: Voting./ Elections./ Presidents--Election.

325   Ph-2 4-6/7 $14.99   L   KA916
I WAS DREAMING TO COME TO AMERICA: MEMORIES FROM THE ELLIS ISLAND ORAL HISTORY PROJECT. Selected and illus. by Veronica Lawlor. Foreword by Rudolph W. Giuliani, Mayor, New York City. Viking ISBN 0-670-86164-2; In Canada: Penguin, 1995. 40p. col. ill.
Offers the recollections and feelings of new Americans as they arrived through Ellis Island. Based on Ellis Island Oral History Project interviews, the excerpts used are from immigrants who came to the United States in the early decades of the twentieth century. Useful supplement to other Ellis Island materials. May inspire oral history

projects.
SUBJ: Ellis Island Immigration Station (New York, N.Y.)--History./ United States--Emigration and immigration--History.

MCP 325 Ph-1 5-A $149.95 OD KA917
IMMIGRATION (Microcomputer program). Tom Snyder Productions IMM-C, 1996. 4 3.5" program disks. (Decisions, decisions). Version 5.0.
Includes teacher's guide and student reference books.
Also available in Windows disks and Macintosh/Windows CD-ROM.
System requirements: Macintosh LC II or better, or Macintosh PowerPC; System 7.1 or higher; 5MB RAM, 8MB for PowerPC; 256-color, 640x480 monitor resolution or higher; hard disk; large-screen projection device (optional).
While tens of thousands of boat people are approaching the country, students take on the role of the President of the United States. What decisions will they make regarding immigration? This simulation allows the computer to manage the student-made decisions and for the teacher to view the components of such a simulation. Works very well with the entire class or with small groups.
SUBJ: Emigration and immigration--Software./ Software--Emigration and immigration./ Problem solving--Software./ Software--Problem solving.

PIC 325 Ph-2 5-6 $41.50 OD KA918
IMMIGRATION (Picture). Documentary Photo Aids 89G, n.d. 40 study prints (11"x14").
Authentic captioned photographs of immigrants on shipboard, arriving at Ellis Island, being processed, standing in line, waiting to be examined, eating. Shows how they dressed, their luggage and possessions, and how they lived immediately after arrival.
SUBJ: United States--Emigration and immigration.

325 Ph-1 3-6/6 $13.95 L KA919
JACOBS, WILLIAM JAY. Ellis Island: new hope in a new land. Scribner's ISBN 0-684-19171-7; In Canada: Collier Macmillan, 1990. 34p. ill.
Includes index.
Available from the National Library Service for the Blind and Physically Handicapped on sound recording cassette RC35719.
"Traces the history of Ellis Island and immigration to America..." (CIP) in an accessible text which features short, vigorous sentences. Period black-and-white photographs make an important contribution to the work's effectiveness. Strong curriculum support for immigration study and a happy companion to Fisher's more difficult ELLIS ISLAND and Siegel's SAM ELLIS'S ISLAND.
SUBJ: Ellis Island Immigration Station (New York, N.Y.)--History./ United States--Emigration and immigration--History.

325 Ph-2 2-4/10 $15.95 L KA920
KROLL, STEVEN. Ellis Island: doorway to freedom. Illus. by Karen Ritz. Holiday House ISBN 0-8234-1192-3, 1995. 32p. ill. (some col.), maps.
Includes glossary and index.
Discusses the history of Ellis Island and its place at the center of American immigration between 1892 and 1954, and details the experiences of immigrants who entered through its doors. Illustrations are modeled on early engravings and re-creations of photographs from the museum at Ellis Island. Will be a useful introduction to concepts of immigration, and may engender discussion of family experiences.
SUBJ: United States--Emigration and immigration./ Ellis Island Immigration Station (New York, N.Y.)--History.

325 Ph-1 1-3/8 $15.95 L KA921
MAESTRO, BETSY. Coming to America: the story of immigration. Illus. by Susannah Ryan. Scholastic ISBN 0-590-44151-5; In Canada: Scholastic, 1996. unp. col. ill.
Includes chronology.
Traces the history of immigration in America from the earliest prehistoric crossing of the Asian land bridge through early European settlement, African slave trade, late nineteenth century influx through Ellis Island, and present day arrival. Active, multiethnic illustrations complement the text. An excellent introduction to concepts of immigration for the early grades. Good discussion starter for multicultural studies.
SUBJ: Immigrants--United States--History./ United States--Emigration and immigration--History./ Ellis Island Immigration Station (New York, N.Y.)--History.

325 Ph-2 5-A/7 $21.95 T KA922
SANDLER, MARTIN W. Immigrants. Introduction by James H. Billington, Librarian of Congress. HarperCollins ISBN 0-06-024507-7; In Canada: HarperCollins, 1995. 92p. ill. (some col.).
"Library of Congress book."
Includes index.

Employs vintage photographs and quotations from immigrants entering the United States through Ellis Island to provide an overview of the immigration of more than 35 million people in the 100 years between 1820 and 1920. Appealing browser and background-builder.
SUBJ: Immigrants--United States--History./ United States--Emigration and immigration--History./ Immigrants--United States--Pictorial works./ United States--Emigration and immigration--Pictorial works.

PIC 325.73 Ph-2 4-6 $36.95 OD KA923
AMERICA: A NATION OF IMMIGRANTS (Picture). Knowledge Unlimited 7082PN ISBN 1-55933-219-0, 1996. 8 study prints color (19"x25").
Brief overview of major concepts of immigration history from East Asia, Southeast Asia, South Asia and the Middle East, Eastern Europe, Western Europe, West Africa, Mexico and Central America, and the Caribbean Islands is accompanied by world locator map, timelines, pictures of cultural significance, and photographs of famous members of the culture. Text is clear and legible, and photographs, drawings, and timelines are of good quality. These will provide bright multicultural room environment, and both text and illustrations will provide a starting place for discussion, research, and exploration. For multicultural studies.
SUBJ: United States--Emigration and immigration--History./ Immigrants--United States--History.

325.73 Ph-1 5-6/12 $16.99 T KA924
ASHABRANNER, BRENT. Our beckoning borders: illegal immigration to America. Photos by Paul Conklin. Cobblehill/Dutton ISBN 0-525-65223-X; In Canada: Penguin, 1996. 99p. ill.
Includes bibliography and index.
A comprehensive examination of the legal, economic, and social issues surrounding illegal immigration uses many personal stories to emphasize the need for enforcement, understanding, and compassion. Photo captions are detailed and add interest to the discussion of illegal border crossers, visa abusers, asylum seekers, and other undocumented aliens. Bibliography cites many up-to-date newspaper and periodical sources in this readable, useful resource for exploration of a current social issue much in today's headlines. For multicultural studies.
SUBJ: Illegal aliens./ United States--Emigration and immigration.

325.73 Ph-3 2-4/2 $12.00 L KA925
BERGER, MELVIN. Where did your family come from?: a book about immigrants. By Melvin and Gilda Berger. Illus. by Robert Quackenbush. Ideals ISBN 0-8249-8647-4; In Canada: Ideals, 1993. 48p. col. ill. (Discovery readers).
Includes index.
Introduces basic facts about immigration to the United States and provides a simple report of the immigration of four individual children. Easy-to-read format and Quackenbush illustrations will help students for whom the subject is formidable. Useful in conjunction with other resources.
SUBJ: Immigrants./ United States--Emigration and immigration.

VCR 326 Ph-3 6-A $39.95 OD KA926
AMISTAD REVOLT: "ALL WE WANT IS MAKE US FREE" (Videocassette). Produced and directed by Karyl K. Evans. Amistad Committee/dist. by Linnet/Shoe String Press, 1996. 1/2" VHS videocassette color (33min).
Includes teacher's guide, FREE MEN: THE AMISTAD REVOLT AND THE AMERICAN ANTI-SLAVERY MOVEMENT by Priscilla Searles.
Story of the capture of 53 African slaves who revolted and took over the ship "Amistad" in 1839, efforts of abolitionists to aid them, their struggle for freedom in Connecticut courts and the United States Supreme Court, and their eventual return to Africa. Presented with a storyteller narrating events to an audience of young people on the recreated ship. An excellent resource to extend studies of slavery and abolition and for multicultural units.
SUBJ: Amistad (Schooner)./ Slavery./ Antislavery movements.

326 Ph-1 4-6/7 $16.99 L KA927
HAMILTON, VIRGINIA. Many thousand gone: African Americans from slavery to freedom. Illus. by Leo and Diane Dillon. Knopf ISBN 0-394-92873-3; In Canada: Random House, 1993. 151p. ill.
Includes bibliography and index.
Selectors' Choice, 19th ed.
Traces the history of slavery in America from earliest slave trading through the Emancipation Proclamation. Moving, individual profiles and vignettes detailed in graceful, spare text build to powerful cumulative effect. Valuable read-aloud, awareness-builder, and discussion-starter.
SUBJ: Underground railroad./ Fugitive slaves.

326   Ph-1 A/7 $14.95 T KA928
LESTER, JULIUS. To be a slave. Illus. by Tom Feelings. Dial ISBN
0-8037-8955-6, c1968. 160p. ill.
Includes bibliography.
Newbery Honor Book.
Available from National Library Service for the Blind and Physically
Handicapped in Braille BR7247.
This vivid account of how it felt to be a slave is based on material
gathered from men and women who themselves had been slaves. The
quotations which are arranged in chronological order begin in the
time of the African slave trade and conclude with the Reconstruction
Period. The editor's commentary a historical background for these
moving statements by black Americans.
SUBJ: Slavery--Collections.

326   Ph-1 4-6/7 $14.95 L KA929
MCKISSACK, PAT. Rebels against slavery: American slave revolts. By
Patricia C. McKissack and Fredrick L. McKissack. Scholastic ISBN 0-590-
45735-7; In Canada: Scholastic, 1996. 182p. ill.
Includes chronology, bibliography and index.
Coretta Scott King Author Honor book, 1997.
Stories of slave revolts, those who led them, their planning, and
outcomes are presented in a smooth, readable narrative that is both
interesting and informative. Documented with an extensive
bibliography of sources, and illustrated with black and white
photographs, paintings, and graphics. This provides a perspective on
African-American history not often emphasized and will be a valuable
addition to units on periods of United States history up to the Civil
War and for multicultural studies.
SUBJ: Slavery--Insurrections, etc./ United States--History.

326   Ph-2 6-A/10 $19.95 T KA930
ZEINERT, KAREN. Amistad slave revolt and American abolition. Linnet
Books ISBN 0-208-02438-7, 1997. 101p. ill., map.
Includes chronology, bibliographies and index.
An engrossing account of the circumstances and events surrounding a
group of African slaves who revolted and took over the ship
"Amistad" in 1839, the efforts of abolitionist committees to aid
them, their struggle for freedom in Connecticut courts and the United
States Supreme Court, and their eventual return to Africa.
Documented with chapter notes, a timeline, and bibliography. Use in
conjunction with the video AMISTAD REVOLT to extend studies of
slavery and abolition and for multicultural units.
SUBJ: Amistad (Schooner)./ Antislavery movements.

PIC 328.3   Ph-2 5-6 $14.95 OD KA931
HOW A BILL BECOMES A LAW (Picture). Knowledge Unlimited 7009P
ISBN 1-55933-218-2, 1989. 1 study print color (34"x22").
Visual flowchart depicts the legislative process from bill to law
through both houses of Congress and the President. Useful for
display, introduction, and review of concepts in American government.
SUBJ: Legislation./ Law.

328.73   Ph-1 5-A/10 $18.95 L KA932
KRONENWETTER, MICHAEL. Congress of the United States. Enslow
ISBN 0-89490-745-X, 1996. 104p. ill. (American government in action).
Includes glossary, bibliography and index.
Discusses the history and development of the United States Congress,
and features in-depth analysis of health care legislation, one of the
major issues of the 1990s. A few photographs of political figures are
included. Use in studies of contemporary government and for units on
Constitutional history.
SUBJ: United States. Congress./ United States--Politics and
government.

VCR 328.73   Ph-2 5-A $99.00 OD KA933
OUR FEDERAL GOVERNMENT: THE LEGISLATIVE BRANCH
(Videocassette). Rainbow Educational RB869, 1993. 1/2" VHS
videocassette color (28min).
Includes teacher's guide.
Offers an overview of the history, structure, and function of Congress.
Express powers, responsibilities, and member qualifications are
discussed. Also explains how a bill becomes a law. Solid support for
advanced students.
SUBJ: United States. Congress./ Legislative bodies.

331.3   Ph-1 4-6/8 $16.95 T KA934
BARTOLETTI, SUSAN CAMPBELL. Growing up in coal country.
Houghton Mifflin ISBN 0-395-77847-6, 1996. 127p. ill.
Includes bibliography.
Selectors' Choice, 21st ed.
Depicts the realities of life for the men and boys in the coal mines of
Pennsylvania; filled with interesting details and personal remembrances
of breaker boys, nippers, spraggers, mule divers, miners, and butties

as they meet the dangers and challenges of life in the mines and daily
life in surrounding towns. Black and white contemporary and archival
photographs and an entensive source bibliography accompany the
informative text. For units on the industrial revolution, child labor, and
personal history.
SUBJ: Coal miners./ Coal mines and mining./ Children--Employment--
History./ Pennsylvania--History.

331.3   Ph-3 4-6/7 $15.40 L KA935
COLMAN, PENNY. Mother Jones and the march of the mill children.
Millbrook ISBN 1-56294-402-9, 1994. 47p. ill. (some col.).
Includes chronology, bibliography, directory and index.
Text and photographs retell how Mary Harris Jones organized and
led a 20 day protest march to make the president and America
aware of how very young children were abused as laborers in the
mills. For women's studies.
SUBJ: Children--Employment--History./ Jones, Mother./ Reformers./
Women social reformers.

331.3   Ph-2 5-6/8 $19.95 L KA936
CURRIE, STEPHEN. We have marched together: the working children's
crusade. Lerner ISBN 0-8225-1733-7, 1997. 88p. ill., map. (People's
history).
Includes bibliography and index.
In the summer of 1903, legendary labor activist Mother Jones led a
small army of children employed in the Philadelphia textile mills on a
protest march across New Jersey to New York in an attempt to have
laws passed and enforced to stem the use of child labor in factories.
Illustrated with archival photographs. Use for units on economics, and
to extend units on labor, industry, and turn-of-the-century issues.
SUBJ: Children--Employment--History./ Jones, Mother.

331.3   Ph-1 5-A/8 $16.95 T KA937
FREEDMAN, RUSSELL. Kids at work: Lewis Hine and the crusade against
child labor. With photos by Lewis Hine. Clarion ISBN 0-395-58703-4,
1994. 104p. ill.
Includes bibliography and index.
While he was teaching school, Hine discovered photography and
introduced it to his students. He then went on to photograph children
laboring in all types of industries in America. His heartbreaking
photographs stirred action to enact child labor laws and free children
to attend school. An unsung hero whose work speaks for his fight for
children's rights.
SUBJ: Children--Employment--History./ Hine, Lewis Wickes./ Social
reformers./ Photographers.

331.4   Ph-2 5-A/7 $16.99 L KA938
COLMAN, PENNY. Rosie the Riveter: women working on the home front
in World War II. Crown ISBN 0-517-59791-8, 1995. 120p. ill.
Includes chronology, bibliography and index.
Provides a lively look at women's participation in the work force
during World War II. Highlights include a Norman Rockwell cover,
interesting tidbits in photo captions, and solid notes and bibliography.
Use in period studies and women's studies or as background for oral
history projects.
SUBJ: Women--Employment--History./ World War, 1939-1945--United
States.

331.4   Ph-2 6-A/8 $15.95 L KA939
DASH, JOAN. We shall not be moved: the women's factory strike of
1909. Scholastic ISBN 0-590-48409-5; In Canada: Scholastic, 1996.
165p. ill.
Includes bibliography and index.
Examines the background, causes, social and economic conditions,
personalities, and leadership of the strike of New York garment
workers in the shirtwaist industry in 1909. Illustrated with black and
white photographs of people and events, this is a highly readable
account of a landmark episode in the development of labor unionism.
Discusses related suffragist efforts, and explores the struggle for the
rights of women within the labor movement.
SUBJ: Women--Employment--History./ Labor unions--Clothing
workers--History./ Strikes and lockouts.

331.7   Ph-2 2-6/6 $10.95 T KA940
CIVARDI, ANNE. Things people do. Illustrated by Stephen Cartwright.
EDC Publishing ISBN 0-86020-864-8, 1986. 38p. col. ill.
Utilizes humorous, cartoonlike drawings to depict the imaginary island
community of Banilla and more than 100 of its citizens at work. The
librarian wears glasses and has her hair in a bun, but job roles shown
generally avoid gender stereotypes. Elementary students will enjoy
browsing in this work and the cast of characters presented can form
the base for an ongoing career investigation activity.
SUBJ: Occupations.

331.7   Ph-2 P-K/3 $15.00   L   KA941
KALMAN, MAIRA. Chicken soup, boots. Viking ISBN 0-670-85201-5,
1993. unp. col. ill.
   Offers a free-form examination of the world of work in a presentation
which is most effective as a one-on-one read-aloud with the youngest.
Has potential as a trigger for creative career exploration activities
with older students.
   SUBJ: Occupations./ Vocational guidance.

331.7   Ph-2 P-1/4 $12.95   T   KA942
MAYNARD, CHRISTOPHER. Jobs people do. DK Publishing ISBN
0-7894-1492-9, 1997. 32p. col. ill.
   Includes index.
   Brief descriptions of over 30 career choices including standards like
police officer, firefighter, and mail carrier (British uniforms and post
boxes) to less familiar ones like stockbroker, veterinary surgeon, and
electrician. Bright, colorful photographs of children dressed for work
are interspersed with other photographic images relating to the
professions being discussed. Use for community helper units.
   SUBJ: Vocational guidance./ Occupations.

331.7   Ph-1 P-K $12.88   L   KA943
MILLER, MARGARET. Who uses this? Greenwillow ISBN 0-688-08279-3,
1990. unp. col. ill.
   Selectors' Choice, 18th ed.
   Colorful photographs of the tools of nine trades offer impetus for a
satisfying question and answer learning session between parent/child,
teacher/child, or child/child. Useful in expanding vocabulary and
career awareness or as the pattern for a class project in which other
tools and occupations are explored.
   SUBJ: Tools./ Occupations./ Questions and answers.

331.88   Ph-3 4-6/6 $19.92   L   KA944
DE RUIZ, DANA CATHARINE. Causa: the migrant farmworkers' story.
By Dana Catharine de Ruiz and Richard Larios. Illus. by Rudy Gutierrez.
Raintree Steck-Vaughan ISBN 0-8114-7231-0, 1993. 92p. ill. (Stories of
America).
   "Describes the efforts in the 1960s of Cesar Chavez and Dolores
Huerta to organize migrant workers in California into a union..."
(CIP) Readable narrative text is supported by black and white
drawings; no index is provided. Useful material on an often neglected
subject.
   SUBJ: Chavez, Cesar./ Huerta, Dolores./ United Farm Workers--
History./ Labor leaders./ Migrant labor./ Mexican Americans--
Biography.

VCR 332.024   Ph-1 4-6 $14.95   KA945
PIGGY BANKS TO MONEY MARKETS: A KID'S VIDEO GUIDE TO
DOLLARS AND SENSE (Videocassette). KidVidz ISBN 1-878231-06-5,
1993. 1/2" VHS videocassette color (30min).
   Includes activity guide.
   Introduces topics related to money--barter, coins, business, savings,
planning, and making choices. Acting is strong and production values
are good. Particularly useful as a closing activity for a unit on money.
   SUBJ: Finance, Personal./ Money.

332.024   Ph-1 2-5/5 $15.93   L   KA946
SCHWARTZ, DAVID M. If you made a million. Illus. by Steven Kellogg.
Lothrop, Lee & Shepard ISBN 0-688-07018-3, 1989. unp. col. ill.
   Includes "A Note from the Author."
   Explores the world of money as four youngsters and assorted animals
team up with Marvelosissimo the Mathematical Magician in an
explanation of the value of pennies, nickels, dimes, quarters and bills.
Imaginative, humorous illustrations attract young readers and a closing
note from the author provides additional information for strong
readers and adults. A solid aid in understanding money concepts.
   SUBJ: Finance, Personal./ Money.

332.4   Ph-2 3-6/3 $13.95   L   KA947
ADAMS, BARBARA JOHNSTON. Go-around dollar. Illus. by Joyce
Audy Zarins. Four Winds ISBN 0-02-700031-1; In Canada: Maxwell
Macmillan, 1992. unp. col. ill.
   Uses a slight fictional narrative as a vehicle to provide facts about the
United States one-dollar bill. Endpapers are noteworthy as they
provide a guided tour of the many elements of the dollar. A good
brush up for teachers and fine report material for students.
   SUBJ: Dollar, American./ Money.

332.4   Ph-2 2-4/2 $12.00   L   KA948
BERGER, MELVIN. Round and round the money goes: what money is
and how we use it. By Melvin and Gilda Berger. Illus. by Jane
McCreary. Ideals ISBN 0-8249-8640-7; In Canada: Ideals, 1993. 48p.
col. ill. (Discovery readers).
   Includes index.

Offers a simple explanation of the origins of money and its uses
today. Easy reading level is the distinguishing feature in an otherwise
routine presentation. Useful as a supplement to other resources.
   SUBJ: Money.

332.4   Ph-1 4-6/8 $15.99   L   KA949
CRIBB, JOE. Money. Knopf ISBN 0-679-90438-7, 1990. 63p. col. ill.
(Eyewitness books).
   Includes index.
   Goose weight, stone weight, flower silver, bank notes, pieces of
eight, and today's plastic cards are all units of money. Coverage
includes history of money and offers two-page spreads depicting
development of coins and bills of various countries; the final pages
give examples of money currently issued by more than 60 countries
worldwide. Appeals as a browser and in early economics activities.
   SUBJ: Money.

332.4   Ph-2 3-6/5 $15.95   L   KA950
MAESTRO, BETSY. Story of money. Illus. by Giulio Maestro. Clarion
ISBN 0-395-56242-2, 1993. 48p. col. ill.
   Reports the history of money and its development from the bartering
of earliest times to the use of credit cards and ATM services today.
Coins and bills depicted are actual size in most instances; closing
pages contain trivial facts related to money. Great resource for early
units on economics and general social studies curriculum.
   SUBJ: Money--History.

332.4   Ph-1 K-3/2 $15.95   L   KA951
MCMILLAN, BRUCE. Jelly beans for sale. Text and photos by Bruce
McMillan. Scholastic ISBN 0-590-86584-6; In Canada: Scholastic, 1996.
unp. col. ill.
   Pennies, nickels, dimes, quarters, and jelly beans are used to show
numerical combinations from one to 25. Endnotes include a history of
jelly beans, how they are made, and other brief facts. Illustrated with
full-color photographs of mathematical patterns and a multicultural
cast of children obviously enjoying their purchases. Use for
interdisciplinary studies, units on counting money, and as a model for
class activities.
   SUBJ: Money./ Addition./ Coins./ Jelly beans.

333.7   Ph-2 4-A/8 $4.95   P   KA952
KAPLAN, ANDREW. Careers for outdoor types. Interviews by Andrew
Kaplan. Photos by Edward Keating and Carrie Boretz. Millbrook ISBN
1-56294-770-2, 1991. 64p. ill. (some col.). (Choices).
   Includes directory, bibliography, and glossary/index.
   Interviews with 14 people who like to work in the great outdoors
include a marine archaeologist, windsurfing teacher, and landscape
architect. Excellent for interesting young people in a wide variety of
career choices. Unfortunately, double-columned text may be difficult
for some readers.
   SUBJ: Vocational guidance./ Outdoor recreation--Vocational
guidance./ Vocational guidance--Outdoor recreation./ Agriculture--
Vocational guidance./ Vocational guidance--Agriculture.

333.7   Ph-2 4-6/7 $15.95   P   KA953
SIRCH, WILLOW ANN. Eco-women: protectors of the earth. Fulcrum
Kids ISBN 1-55591-252-4, 1996. 89p. ill.
   Includes index.
   Profiles of nine women who have had a profound effect on how we
view and care for our environment include information about their
early lives as well as brief summaries of their lives and work.
Illustrations include black and white photographs, some from family
albums, and environmental graphics. Each chapter ends with
suggestions for "What You Can Do" activities that range from
further reading to local activities and supporting national foundations.
A well-documented source for women's studies and environmental
issues.
   SUBJ: Environmentalists./ Women environmentalists.

333.73   Ph-2 4-6/7 $23.20   L   KA954
WILLIS, TERRI. Healing the land. Technical consultant, Terry Gips.
Childrens Press ISBN 0-516-05541-0; In Canada: Childrens Press, 1994.
96p. col. ill. (Restoring nature: success stories).
   Includes directory, glossary and index.
   Describes efforts worldwide to restore damaged land. Backmatter
includes addresses of Canadian and United States organizations which
can provide additional information. Useful resource for environmental
studies.
   SUBJ: Environmental degradation./ Environmental policy./ Man--
Influence on nature.

333.74   Ph-2 4-6/7 $23.20   L   KA955
GOLDSTEIN, NATALIE. Rebuilding prairies and forests. Technical
consultants, Jerry J. Crockett and Jill Mahon. Childrens Press ISBN

0-516-05542-9; In Canada: Childrens Press, 1994. 96p. col. ill., maps. (Restoring nature: success stories).
Includes directory, glossary and index.
Delivers an ecological message while describing successful growth rebuilding projects worldwide. Boxed insets provide anecdotes and special information. Useful in environmental studies and current events activities.
SUBJ: Prairie conservation./ Forest conservation./ Prairie ecology./ Ecology./ Man--Influence on nature.

VCR 333.79   Ph-2 4-6 $89.00   OD KA956
POWER UP?: ENERGY IN OUR ENVIRONMENT (Videocassette).
Rainbow Educational Video RB862, 1992. 1/2" VHS videocassette color (22min).
Includes Teacher's Guide.
Offers a framework for understanding fossil fuel issues such as global warming, air pollution, and acid rain. Teacher's guide includes script, activities, and energy-saving suggestions. Use in support of science and current events programming.
SUBJ: Power resources./ Energy conservation./ Pollution.

VCR 333.791   Ph-2 4-6 $89.00   OD KA957
SIMPLE THINGS YOU CAN DO TO SAVE ENERGY IN YOUR SCHOOL (Videocassette). Produced by Joy Cohen and Stu McGowan. Noodlehead Network/dist. by Video Project SIS-060-A, 1995. 1/2" VHS videocassette color (15min).
Includes public performance rights.
Sara escorts viewers through her school as she and other student actors demonstrate bright ideas for saving energy in the areas of heating and cooling, lighting, recycling, and conservation. Will raise consciousness on the part of both students and adults and suggests potential activities. For environmental studies.
SUBJ: Energy conservation./ Energy resources./ Power resources.

333.91   Ph-2 4-6/7 $14.95   L   KA958
ANCONA, GEORGE. Riverkeeper. Macmillan ISBN 0-02-700911-4; In Canada: Collier Macmillan, 1990. unp. col. ill.
Delivers a strong environmental message as it examines the duties and challenges of work as riverkeeper of the Hudson River. Black-and-white photographs by the talented author/photographer capture the daily routines of John Cronin as he challenges polluters and talks with lawmakers and citizen groups. Particularly useful in activities which focus on the growing involvement of society with environmental issues.
SUBJ: Riverkeepers--Hudson River (N.Y. and N.J.)./ Hudson River (N.Y. and N.J.)./ Water--Pollution--Hudson River (N.Y. and N.J.)./ Conservation of natural resources.

333.91   Ph-2 5-6/8 $21.50   L   KA959
HOFF, MARY KING. Our endangered planet: groundwater. By Mary King Hoff and Mary M. Rodgers. Lerner ISBN 0-8225-2500-3, 1991. 64p. col. ill. (Our endangered planet).
Includes directory, glossary and index.
Discusses how groundwater works and why it is endangered. Fact boxes provide information and trivia beyond the text; a list of groundwater protection suggestions is a valuable feature. Fine support for conservation and ecological awareness activities.
OUR ENDANGERED PLANET: OCEANS (ISBN 0-8225-2505-4, 1992).
SUBJ: Water, Underground.

333.91   Ph-2 4-6/8 $6.95   P   KA960
LIPTAK, KAREN. Saving our wetlands and their wildlife. Watts ISBN 0-531-115648-6; In Canada: Watts, 1991. 63p. col. ill. (First book).
Includes appendix, glossary, bibliography and index.
Describes North American wetlands and examines their ecological importance. Color photographs accompany the text which closes with a list of suggestions for those visiting a swamp; an appendix provides addresses of organizations of interest. Useful in support of regional and/or environmental studies.
SUBJ: Wetlands./ Wetland ecology./ Ecology./ Conservation of natural resources.

333.95   Ph-2 4-6/7 $23.20   L   KA961
BLASHFIELD, JEAN F. Rescuing endangered species. Technical consultant, Dr. Onnie Byers. Childrens Press ISBN 0-516-05544-5; In Canada: Childrens Press, 1994. 96p. col. ill. (Restoring nature: success stories).
Includes directory, glossary and index.
Offers reports of successful return of endangered species to their native habitats. Boxed insets provide special material, and an address list suggests sources for additional information. Solid curriculum support for environmental studies.
SUBJ: Wildlife conservation./ Wildlife reintroduction./ Endangered species./ Man--Influence on nature.

333.95   Ph-2 5-6/8 $21.50   L   KA962
HOFF, MARY KING. Our endangered planet: life on land. By Mary Hoff and Mary M. Rodgers. Lerner ISBN 0-8225-2507-0, 1992. 72p. col. ill. (Our endangered planet).
Includes directory, glossary and index.
Delivers a convincing environmental message as ecological balance is described and examined. Strong graphic design and informational sidebars combine effectively. Valuable for project ideas and in environmental units.
SUBJ: Extinction (Biology)./ Rare animals./ Rare plants./ Man--Influence on nature./ Ecology./ Wildlife conservation.

333.95   Ph-2 2-A/4 $14.88   L   KA963
JONAS, ANN. Aardvarks, disembark! Greenwillow ISBN 0-688-07207-0, 1990. unp. col. ill.
Includes list of extinct and endangered animals.
After calling forth many of the animals from the ark, Noah discovers that a great number remain. This book is a striking pictorial presentation of rare and extinct animals. Teachers will need to explain the names of these animals to children. Best used in ecology and conservation units.
SUBJ: Noah's ark./ Bible stories--O.T./ Rare animals./ Wildlife conservation./ Alphabet.

333.95   Ph-2 5-6/9 $17.95   T   KA964
PATENT, DOROTHY HINSHAW. Biodiversity. Photos by William Munoz. Clarion ISBN 0-395-68704-7, 1996. 109p. col. ill.
Includes glossary and index.
Explores the concept of biodiversity and its importance to the health of the world, preservation and survival of species, the relationships and connections of ecological systems, the dangers of man-made extinction, and our responsibilities for preserving the well-being of our planet. Use for environmental studies and interdisciplinary science and social science units.
SUBJ: Biological diversity./ Biological diversity conservation.

333.95   Ph-2 5-6/8 $14.95   L   KA965
PATENT, DOROTHY HINSHAW. Buffalo: the American Bison today. Photos by William Munoz. Clarion ISBN 0-89919-345-5, 1986. 73p. ill.
Includes index.
Describes the preservation and history of the American bison of today. Black and white photographs accompany the text which uses a seasonal approach in discussing the fewer than 100,000 "buffalo" which live in parks and private preserves. Browsers, animal lovers, and creative report writers will use this title.
SUBJ: Bison./ Wildlife management.

333.95   Ph-2 4-6/7 $15.95   L   KA966
PATENT, DOROTHY HINSHAW. Places of refuge: our national wildlife refuge system. Photos by William Munoz. Clarion ISBN 0-89919-846-5, 1992. 80p col photos.
Includes directory and index.
Available from the National Library Service for the Blind and Physically Handicapped on sound recording cassette RC 41865. Tells of the mission and efforts of the National Wildlife Refuge System started in 1903 by President Theodore Roosevelt. The text focuses on refuges in Texas, North Dakota, and California. Handsome color photographs by William Munoz bring interest and emphasis to the work. Use in study of governmental services and environmental studies.
SUBJ: Wildlife refuges./ National parks and reserves./ Wildlife conservation.

PIC 338.5   Ph-2 A $51.50   OD KA967
GREAT DEPRESSION (Picture). Documentary Photo Aids 88G, n.d. 32 study prints (11"x14").
Includes Teacher's Guide.
Thirty-two black and white editorial cartoons or photographs work together to portray the difficulties of the Great Depression. Captions on each print expand the impact of the materials. Valuable, versatile teaching resource.
SUBJ: Depressions--1929--Pictorial works.

VCR 341.23   Ph-2 5-A $59.95   OD KA968
COMMON GOAL: AN INTRODUCTION TO THE UN (Videocassette). Films for the Humanities & Sciences FFH 6395, 1996. 1/2" VHS videocassette color (14min).
Includes public performance rights.
Uses the metaphor of a soccer game played fairly and by the rules to explain the basic concepts and operations of the United Nations as they relate to peacekeeping, health care, the environment, and human rights. Excellent visuals use examples from a wide variety of cultures and countries. Use for social studies and for international units.
SUBJ: United Nations.

341.23   Ph-2 4-6/7 $16.40   L   KA969
STEIN, R. CONRAD. United Nations. Rev. ed. Childrens Press ISBN 0-516-06677-3; In Canada: Childrens Press, 1994. 32p. ill. (some col.). (Cornerstones of freedom).
> Includes index.
> Traces the history of the United Nations in brief, matter-of-fact fashion. Illustrations include photographs and drawings.
> SUBJ: United Nations.

341.23   Ph-2 5-A/8 $15.95   P   KA970
WORLD IN OUR HANDS: IN HONOR OF THE FIFTIETH ANNIVERSARY OF THE UNITED NATIONS. Written, illus., and edited by young people of the world. Produced by Peace Child International in association with Paintbrush Diplomacy. Tricycle Press ISBN 1-883672-31-7, 1995. 96p. col. ill., maps.
> Includes chronology and index.
> A celebration of the fiftieth anniversary of the United Nations in the narratives, poetry, and pictures of young people from 115 countries around the world, with focus on the history of the organization and visions of the future. Numerous original paintings, drawings, and graphics complement the text, sidebars, and poetry. Use for international relations and multicultural studies.
> SUBJ: United Nations.

CE 342.73   Ph-1 3-6/6 $14.95   T   KA971
FRITZ, JEAN. Shh! We're writing the Constitution. Illus. by Tomie De Paola. Putnam ISBN 0-399-21403-8; In Canada: General, 1987. 64p. ill.
> Includes notes and appendix.
> Bickering among themselves, the fifty-five delegates to the Constitutional Congress managed to produce a document that established the unique form of government still in operation today. Impeccable research is transformed into lively narrative that vividly recreates the time, effort, and concerns of the delegates. The entire text of the Constitution proper is appended.
> SUBJ: United States. Constitutional Convention (1787)./ United States--Constitution.

342.73   Ph-1 4-6/7 $14.90   L   KA972
KING, DAVID C. Freedom of assembly. Millbrook ISBN 0-7613-0064-3, 1997. 48p. col. ill. (Land of the free).
> Includes glossary, bibliography and index.
> Discussion of the right of assembly and petition uses many specific examples that show democracy in action and make concepts clear and understandable. Includes court decisions, applications in women's suffrage, abolition, civil rights movement, protections for private property, and public safety. Illustrated with photographs and engravings. Use for social studies units on American government, the Constitution, and contemporary issues.
> SUBJ: Assembly, Right of./ Freedom of speech.

342.73   Ph-1 4-6/7 $14.90   L   KA973
KING, DAVID C. Right to speak out. Millbrook ISBN 0-7613-0063-5, 1997. 48p. col. ill. (Land of the free).
> Includes glossary, bibliography and index.
> Discusses the First Amendment right of freedom of expression in terms of historical perspective, Supreme Court decisions, and contemporary issues, including those related to rap music, tabloid newspapers, cigarette advertising, and Internet access. Illustrated with photographs, not all of which match placement of text. Use for units on American government, the Constitution, and contemporary issues.
> SUBJ: Freedom of speech./ Freedom of the press.

342.73   Ph-1 4-6/8 $15.93   L   KA974
MAESTRO, BETSY. More perfect union: the story of our constitution. By Betsy and Giulio Maestro. Lothrop, Lee & Shepard ISBN 0-688-06840-5, 1987. 49p. col. ill.
> Describes events of the Constitutional Convention and efforts to ratify the document. Colorful illustrations are skillfully integrated with the text and additional information provided in the back matter includes summaries of the Constitution and its amendments, a list of signers, a chronology, and notes on the Connecticut Compromise. A useful, readable source.
> SUBJ: United States--Constitutional Convention (1787)./ United States--Constitutional history.

VCR 342.73   Ph-2 5-A $89.00   OD KA975
OUR CONSTITUTION: THE DOCUMENT THAT GAVE BIRTH TO A NATION (Videocassette). Rainbow Educational Video RB815, 1988. 1/2" VHS videocassette color (26min).
> Includes Teacher's Guide.
> From its drafting in 1787 to its bicentennial in 1987, the U.S. Constitution and its amendments have guided the country, its lawmakers and citizens. Excerpts of speeches by Warren Burger and James Earl Jones are intermingled with narration to cover the history

and meaning of the document. Fairly complex, but a possible supplement to U.S. history and government studies.
> SUBJ: United States--Constitutional Convention (1787)./ United States--Constitution.

VCR 342.73   Ph-2 5-A $49.00   OD KA976
U.S. CONSTITUTION: A DOCUMENT FOR DEMOCRACY (Videocassette). Society for Visual Education 95034-HAVT, 1986. 1/2" VHS videocassette color (25min).
> Includes teacher's guide.
> Recreates the events during the three month long Constitutional Convention in Philadelphia which resulted in the written United States Constitution. Solidly and engagingly narrated this overview provides appropriate background for further study.
> SUBJ: United States--Constitutional Convention (1787)./ United States--Constitution.

VCR 347   Ph-3 5-6 $195.00   KA977
SO YOU WANT TO BE?: JUDGE (Videocassette). Pyramid Media 02491, 1994. 1/2" VHS videocassette color (15min). (So you want to be?).
> Offers an overview in the life of a judge and delivers a strong read-and-stay-in-school message. Lively graphics and upbeat sound track are featured. Useful in career studies units.
> SUBJ: Judges./ Occupations./ Vocational guidance--Law./ Law--Vocational guidance.

347.73   Ph-1 5-A/10 $18.95   L   KA978
KRONENWETTER, MICHAEL. Supreme Court of the United States. Enslow ISBN 0-89490-536-8, 1996. 112p. ill. (American government in action).
> Includes glossary, bibliography and index.
> An account of the history, powers, duties, and personalities of the nation's highest court includes specific issues and landmark decisions. Use for units on Constitutional history and American government.
> SUBJ: United States. Supreme Court.

VCR 347.73   Ph-3 A $99.00   OD KA979
OUR FEDERAL GOVERNMENT: THE SUPREME COURT (Videocassette). Rainbow Educational RB868 ISBN 1-56701-025-3, 1993. 1/2" VHS videocassette color (22min).
> Includes teacher's guide.
> Describes the origin of the Supreme Court and examines some of the most famous cases the Supreme Court has decided. Production quality is good; script and narration are straightforward. For advanced students.
> SUBJ: United States. Supreme Court./ United States--Constitutional law.

VCR 352.23   Ph-2 5-A $89.00   OD KA980
OUR FEDERAL GOVERNMENT: THE PRESIDENCY (Videocassette). Rainbow Educational RB867, 1993. 1/2" VHS videocassette color (22min).
> Includes teacher's guide.
> Focuses on the powers and responsibilities of the presidency while also providing examples of balance between governmental branches. Strong educational design is supported by archival prints, films, and network clips. Valuable social studies material which can do double duty in adult citizenship classes.
> SUBJ: Presidents./ Executive power--United States.

355   Ph-1 5-6/5 $18.60   L   KA981
APPLEGATE, KATHERINE. Story of two American generals: Benjamin O. Davis, Jr.; Colin L. Powell. Gareth Stevens ISBN 0-8368-1380-4; In Canada: Saunders, 1995. 108p. ill. (Famous lives).
> Originally published by Parachute Press, Inc., 1992.
> Includes chronologies, bibliography, filmography and index.
> Biographical accounts of two African-American generals who made significant contributions to their country through distinguished military service and personal integrity. Text is accompanied by black and white photographs. Useful for multicultural studies and as a resource for students with a general interest in the military.
> SUBJ: United States--Armed Forces--Afro-Americans./ United States--History, Military./ Davis, Benjamin O. (Benjamin Oliver)./ Powell, Colin L./ Afro-Americans--Biography.

355   Ph-2 5-6/6 $14.98   L   KA982
REEF, CATHERINE. Black fighting men: a proud history. Twenty-First Century ISBN 0-8050-3106-5; In Canada: Fitzhenry & Whiteside, 1994. 80p. ill. (African-American soldiers).
> Includes chronology, index and bibliography.
> Traces contributions of African-American patriots through a series of vignettes of African-American soldiers from the Revolutionary War through the Persian Gulf War. A 1770-1990 chronology follows the

text. For multicultural studies.
SUBJ: United States--Armed Forces--Afro-Americans./ United States--History, Military./ Soldiers./ Afro-Americans--Biography.

355.02   Ph-2 4-6/8 $16.89   L   KA983
MELTZER, MILTON. Weapons and warfare: from the stone age to the space age. Illus. by Sergio Martinez. HarperCollins ISBN 0-06-024876-9; In Canada: HarperCollins, 1996. 85p. ill.
Includes bibliography and index.
An informative, interesting history of the evolution and development of weapons and warfare from prehistory to the present, with emphasis on how and why they developed, how they are used, and their impact on society and culture. Black and white drawings show details. A browser that will have high appeal and stimulate discussion about issues of war and peace. Use in units on conflict resolution as well as in history classes.
SUBJ: Weapons./ Military art and science./ Military weapons.

355.1   Ph-3 4-8/12 $15.95   L   KA984
LLOYD, MARK. Military badges and insignia. Grange Books ISBN 1-85627-792-5, 1995. 46p. col. ill. (Concise collection).
For readers fascinated with military symbols, this offers information on 40 units worldwide. Although only eight are from the United States, readers will often be interested in insignia from other countries through current events. Each page has an illustration of the badge or insignia, a brief history, and usually a picture of the troops who wear it.
SUBJ: Military decorations./ Decorations of honor./ Armed Forces--History.

355.1   Ph-2 4-A/8 $15.99   L   KA985
VISUAL DICTIONARY OF MILITARY UNIFORMS. DK Publishing ISBN 1-56458-011-3, 1992. 64p. col. ill. (Eyewitness visual dictionaries).
Includes index.
Presents military clothing and accoutrements from the Imperial Gallic helmet of the Roman legionary to the flying boots of jet aircrews. Precise index provides access to special items displayed in the thematic arrangement common to the Eyewitness series. The depiction of modern military uniforms is marred by the lack of female models. Valuable browser.
SUBJ: Military uniforms.

355.8   Ph-2 A/10 $15.99   L   KA986
BYAM, MICHELE. Arms and armor. Knopf ISBN 0-394-99622-4, 1988. 64p. col. ill. (Eyewitness books).
Includes index.
Spanish version ARMAS Y ARMADURAS available from Santillana (ISBN 84-372-3723-8, n.d.).
Examines armor and handheld weapons from the Stone Age through the close of the nineteenth century. Crisp graphic design using color photographs, historic illustrations, and trivia-filled descriptive captions showcases the arms of many cultures and many centuries. A high appeal import which is useful as a browser, background builder, or report source.
SUBJ: Arms and armor./ Spanish language materials.

356   Ph-2 4-A/8 $15.99   L   KA987
VISUAL DICTIONARY OF SPECIAL MILITARY FORCES. DK Publishing ISBN 1-56458-189-6, 1993. 64p. col. ill. (Eyewitness visual dictionaries).
Includes index.
Displays the paraphernalia of spies, spooks, and special services. Detailed index provides access; photographs provide the museum-like presentation common to Eyewitness books. A high-appeal browser and information tool.
SUBJ: Special forces (Military science).

359.1   Ph-2 4-6/7 $16.95   T   KA988
BIESTY, STEPHEN. Man-of-war. Text by Richard Platt. DK Publishing ISBN 1-56458-321-X, 1993. 32p. col. ill. (Stephen Biesty's cross-sections).
Includes glossary and index.
Spanish version BARCO DE GUERRA DEL SIGLO XVIII available from Santillana (ISBN 84-372-4536-2, 1995).
"...depict(s) life aboard a British warship of the Napoleonic era, covering such topics as work, leisure, discipline, navigating, and fighting." (CIP) Large format and detailed drawings create a high-appeal browser for naval and war buffs.
SUBJ: Great Britain, Royal Navy--Sea life./ Sea life./ Spanish language materials.

VCR 359.9   Ph-2 4-6 $14.95   KA989
BIG AIRCRAFT CARRIER (Videocassette). VanDerKloot Film & Television/Little Mammoth Media, 1995. 1/2" VHS videocassette color (45min).

Includes public performance rights.
Two children narrate an informative tour of the USS Nimitz, explaining the training and work of many of the nearly 6,000 people who staff the gigantic ship. The firsthand view includes the many types of aircraft served on the carrier, the training of pilots and crew members, the building of carriers, and much more about life and work aboard the Nimitz. The thoughtfully constructed tour is an intriguing look at this special kind of work and the ship and air operations. For career studies.
SUBJ: Aircraft carriers./ Jet planes, Military./ Nimitz (Aircraft carrier).

359.9   Ph-3 5-6/7 $22.95   L   KA990
WARNER, J. F. U.S. Marine Corps. Lerner ISBN 0-8225-1432-X, 1991. 88p. ill. (some col.). (Lerner's armed services).
Includes index.
Available from the National Library Service for the Blind and Physically Handicapped on sound recording cassette RC 38277. Reads like a visit to the recruiter's office as it sets forth information on today's Marine Corps. Early chapters provide a history of this military branch which was established in 1775. Useful in career activities and as the basis for a military history display.
SUBJ: United States. Marine Corps.

361.2   Ph-1 3-6/6 $14.95   P   KA991
LEWIS, BARBARA A. Kid's guide to social action: how to solve the social problems you choose--and turn creative thinking into positive action. Illus. by Steve Michaels. Free Spirit ISBN 0-915793-29-6, 1991. 185p. ill.
Includes bibliography and index.
Offers techniques and suggestions designed to aid students in working toward solutions to local and national social problems. Format is lively; recommendations are knowledgeable; and some of the pages (e.g. petition form) are reproducible. Solid resource for those interested in social change projects.
SUBJ: Social action./ Political participation./ Politics, Practical.

361.7   Ph-2 4-6/8 $21.50   L   KA992
BURGER, LESLIE. Red Cross/Red Crescent: when help can't wait. By Leslie Burger and Debra L. Rahm. Lerner ISBN 0-8225-2698-0, 1996. 80p. ill. (some col.), maps. (International cooperation).
Includes directory and index.
Presents the history of the Red Cross and Red Crescent Societies as they are organized nationally and internationally. For social studies units and units on current events.
SUBJ: Red Cross--History.

362.1   Ph-2 2-6/2 $13.95   L   KA993
BE A FRIEND: CHILDREN WHO LIVE WITH HIV SPEAK. Art and writing compiled by Lori S. Wiener, Ph.D; Aprille Best; Philip A. Pizzo, M.D. Whitman ISBN 0-8075-0590-0; In Canada: General, 1994. 40p. col. ill.
Features thought-provoking drawings and writings by children who have HIV infection and AIDS. Foreword and introduction provide valuable insights to material which follows. Valuable as an awareness-builder and as the base for discussion of a difficult topic.
SUBJ: AIDS (Disease)--Patients./ Children's writings./ Children's art.

CE 362.1   Ph-1 3-6/4 $17.95   L   KA994
COERR, ELEANOR. Sadako. Illus. by Ed Young. Putnam ISBN 0-399-21771-1; In Canada: Putnam, 1993. unp. col. ill.
Teacher's guide available separately.
SADAKO AND THE THOUSAND PAPER CRANES, 1/2" VHS videocassette color (30min) available from Informed Democracy (ISBN 1-879368-00-5, 1990), $195.00. Effective video features Liv Ullmann and the solo guitar of George Winston.
"Hospitalized with the dreaded atom bomb disease, leukemia, a child in Hiroshima races against time to fold one thousand paper cranes to verify the legend that by doing so a sick person will become healthy." (CIP) Moving text and illustrations combine to good effect. Valuable as a discussion starter. A companion video, HOW TO FOLD A PAPER CRANE, demonstrates origami techniques used to make a crane, an international symbol of peace. For multicultural studies and conflict resolution units.
SUBJ: Leukemia./ Sasaki, Sadako./ Atomic bomb--Physiological effect./ Hiroshima-shi (Japan)--History--Bombardment, 1945./ Death.

VCR 362.1   Ph-2 1-4 $79.00   OD KA995
HOSPITAL (Videocassette). National Geographic 51436, 1990. 1/2" VHS videocassette color (13min). (Your town).
Includes teacher's guide.
Watch a medical crew handle an emergency, observe lab procedures, and visit the children's ward. A calm look at the efforts hospitals make to help sick and injured people. For community helpers units or for children about to go to the hospital.
SUBJ: Hospitals.

362.1 Ph-1 3-6/6 $12.95 L KA996
MOORE, ADAM. Broken Arrow boy. Landmark ISBN 0-933849-24-9, 1990. 29p. ill. (Landmark editions).
Selectors' Choice, 19th ed.
Autobiographical account of eight-year-old Adam's life-threatening accident that sends him and his family headlong into the world of doctors, hospitals and therapy. A riveting story of real courage and family love that all elementary students will relate to.
SUBJ: Moore, Adam./ Brain--Wounds and injuries--Patients./ Children's writings.

VCR 362.29 Ph-2 K-4 $145.00 OD KA997
KID'S GUIDE TO DRUG, ALCOHOL AND SMOKING AWARENESS (Videocassette). Learning Tree/dist. by Clearvue/eav LT 351-CV, 1985. 4 programs on 1 1/2" VHS videocassette color.
Includes teacher's guide.
Explains good (medicine) and bad drug use in unanimated cartoon-like drawings--including drugs used for physical and mental illness, smoking, caffeine, cocaine, heroin, marijuana, recreational illegal drugs, alcohol and alcoholism addiction. Emphasizing the importance of taking drugs only from parents and each person's responsibility for his/her own health, this well paced video is effective in the drug abuse curriculum.
Contents: Good drugs-bad drugs (12min); Drugs (11min); Alcohol (11min); Smoking (10min); Your health-your responsibility (10min).
SUBJ: Drugs./ Alcohol./ Smoking.

362.29 Ph-1 4-6/9 $16.00 L KA998
PRINGLE, LAURENCE P. Smoking: a risky business. By Laurence Pringle. Morrow ISBN 0-688-13039-9; In Canada: Hearst Books, 1996. 124p. ill.
Includes directory, glossary, bibliography and index.
Detailed exploration of the history, use, and effects of tobacco with emphasis on scientific studies, industry responses, and changing attitudes of society. Illustrated with black and white photographs and full-page graphics and sidebars. Use for study of contemporary issues and health units.
SUBJ: Tobacco habit./ Smoking.

362.29 Ph-3 5-6/5 $13.85 L KA999
WAX, WENDY. Say no and know why: kids learn about drugs. Photos by Toby McAfee. Walker ISBN 0-8027-8141-1; In Canada: Thomas Allen, 1992. 71p. ill.
Includes glossary.
Follows a group of sixth graders through an anti-drug program in which they visit a hospital maternity ward, meet with law enforcement personnel, and witness drug-related trials in criminal court. Text format uses a conversational approach. Useful as a browser and in drug prevention programs.
SUBJ: Drug abuse./ Narcotics, Control of.

362.292 Ph-1 4-6/7 $15.00 T KB000
SEIXAS, JUDITH S. Living with a parent who drinks too much. Greenwillow ISBN 0-688-80196-X, 1979. 116p.
Explains what it is like to live with a parent who drinks too much by describing alcoholism, behavior of alcoholics and problems which the family faces. Suggests ways to cope with medical emergencies for the alcoholic and counseling help for the child.
SUBJ: Alcoholism./ Alcoholics.

VCR 362.292 Ph-2 3-5 $99.95 OD KB001
SOMETHING WRONG AT HOME: THE ALCOHOLIC FAMILY (Videocassette). Sunburst 2432, 1994. 1/2" VHS videocassette color (14min).
Includes teacher's guide and 4 student worksheets.
Promotes a general understanding of the experiences of children from alcoholic families. Guide includes script, questions, discussion topics, and a caution against probing for personal information. Valuable with adequate preparation.
SUBJ: Alcoholism./ Alcoholics./ Family life./ Family problems.

362.3 Ph-2 1-4/6 $12.95 T KB002
CAIRO, SHELLEY. Our brother has Down's syndrome: an introduction for children. By Shelley, Jasmine and Tara Cairo. Photos by Irene McNeil. Annick/dist. by Firefly ISBN 0-920303-30-7; In Canada: Annick/dist. by Firefly, 1985. unp. col. ill.
Describes in a simple photographic album the everyday experiences of a family whose toddler son has Down's syndrome. Narrated by one of the older sisters, this includes a simple explanation of the chromosome difference in Down's children and emphasizes the child's capabilities and the need for love and extra support. A very positive treatment of a handicapping condition which minimizes frustrations and problems, this is an attractive introduction to this condition.
SUBJ: Down's syndrome./ Mentally handicapped.

362.4 Ph-2 2-4/3 $14.95 L KB003
ALEXANDER, SALLY HOBART. Mom's best friend. Photos by George Ancona. Macmillan ISBN 0-02-700393-0; In Canada: Maxwell Macmillan, 1992. unp. ill.
Tells of the author's adjustment to a new guide dog. Narrated in the voice of the author's daughter, this sequel to MOM CAN'T SEE ME offers an understanding of the interaction among owner, guide dog, and family. Works well in animal helper and other special units.
SUBJ: Guide dogs.

362.4 Ph-2 1-3/3 $15.95 T KB004
MCMAHON, PATRICIA. Listen for the bus: David's story. Photos by John Godt. Boyds Mills ISBN 1-56397-368-5; In Canada: McClelland & Stewart, 1995. unp. col. ill.
Portrays the typical school day of a young kindergartner who is blind. Warm text, color photographs, and an appealing subject combine to good effect. Use as a browser, as a one-on-one read aloud, or as supplemental material for units on persons with disabilities.
SUBJ: Blind./ Kindergarten./ Physically handicapped.

362.4 Ph-1 2-5/7 $16.95 T KB005
MCMAHON, PATRICIA. Summer tunes: a Martha's Vineyard vacation. Photos by Peter Simon. Boyds Mills ISBN 1-56397-572-6; In Canada: McClelland & Stewart, 1996. 48p. col. ill.
Photo-essay documents the summer vacation with his family on Martha's Vineyard of Conor Healy, who loves music and has cerebral palsy. Conor's physical challenges, his zest for life, and full participation in a warm family environment are clearly shown. Use for social studies units on families and relationships within them, and as an example of how persons with disabilities adapt to daily living.
SUBJ: Physically handicapped./ Cerebral palsy./ Martha's Vineyard (Mass.)--Biography.

362.4 Ph-1 1-3/3 $3.99 P KB006
MOORE, EVA. Buddy: the first seeing eye dog. Illus. by Don Bolognese. Scholastic ISBN 0-590-26585-7; In Canada: Scholastic, 1996. 48p. col. ill. (Hello reader!).
"Cartwheel books."
A high interest account of the training of Buddy, the first seeing eye dog to be a companion to a blind American, and Morris Frank, his owner. Colorful drawings depict the high points of the story. An appealing story for beginning readers who are interested in learning more about guide dogs. Use in units on persons with disabilities.
SUBJ: Buddy (dog)./ Guide dogs--Training./ Dogs./ Blind./ Physically handicapped.

362.4 Ph-1 2-4/4 $13.89 L KB007
PETERSON, JEANNE WHITEHOUSE. I have a sister--my sister is deaf. Illus. by Deborah Kogan Ray. HarperCollins ISBN 0-06-024702-9, c1977. 32p. ill.
Soft charcoal drawings create a warm positive approach as a young girl describes how her deaf sister experiences everyday things. Provides information on the ways that the deaf compensate: lip reading, vibrations (cat purring.)
SUBJ: Deaf./ Brothers and sisters.

362.4 Ph-2 4-6/8 $12.95 T KB008
ROSENBERG, MAXINE B. Finding a way: living with exceptional brothers and sisters. Photos by George Ancona. Lothrop, Lee & Shepard ISBN 0-688-06873-1, 1988. 48p. ill.
Explores the feelings of three young people who have brothers or sisters who are handicapped. Emphasis is on sibling relationships and both positive and negative attitudes are discussed. Valuable for individual or group use.
SUBJ: Brothers and sisters./ Physically handicapped.

362.5 Ph-2 3-6/4 $17.00 T KB009
HUBBARD, JIM. Lives turned upside down: homeless children in their own words and photographs. Simon & Schuster ISBN 0-689-80649-3; In Canada: Distican, 1996. 40p. ill.
Includes directory.
Four children present different perspectives and ways of coping emotionally with homelessness through their own narratives that discuss their hopes, dreams, families, and the circumstances of being homeless. Uncaptioned photographs, taken by the narrators, will provoke discussion of issues and conditions surrounding homelessness. Use for units on contemporary issues.
SUBJ: Homeless persons./ Shelters for the homeless.

362.5 Ph-2 4-6/4 $16.99 L KB010
WOLF, BERNARD. Homeless. Text and photos by Bernard Wolf. Orchard ISBN 0-531-08736-0, 1995. unp. col. ill.
Follows eight-year-old Mikey as he and his family members face the challenge of being homeless in New York City. Quality of

photography is high as the photo-essay records the family's placement in a transitional housing project and the beginning of stability in their lives. Useful background builder.
SUBJ: Homeless persons./ Poor--New York (N.Y.)./ Family life--New York (N.Y.).

362.73   Ph-1 2-4/3 $13.89   L   KB011
BANISH, ROSLYN. Forever family. Story and pictures by Roslyn Banish with Jennifer Jordan-Wong. HarperCollins ISBN 0-06-021674-3; In Canada: HarperCollins, 1992. 44p. ill.
Includes glossary.
Describes with words and photographs an eight-year-old girl's adoption and her adjustment to her new, extended family. Engaging narrative is told in first person; former foster parents and social workers are included as she describes the experience and her feelings.
SUBJ: Adoption./ Foster home care./ Family life./ Jordan-Wong, Jennifer./ Children's writings.

362.73   Ph-1 1-3/2 $14.93   L   KB012
COLE, JOANNA. How I was adopted: Samantha's story. Illus. by Maxie Chambliss. Morrow ISBN 0-688-11930-1, 1995. unp. col. ill.
Sam explains what it means to be adopted, including having a separate birth mother, the anticipation felt by her adoptive parents, and the loving family they have formed. Forthright in text and illustrations, the book includes a lengthy note to parents and details about pregnancy and birth. A book for families to share and discuss. (Parents' Shelf).
SUBJ: Adoption.

362.73   Ph-2 5-6/7 $13.95   T   KB013
ROSENBERG, MAXINE B. Growing up adopted. Bradbury ISBN 0-02-777912-2; In Canada: Collier Macmillan, 1989. 107p.
Includes bibliography, sources of help and index.
Offers first person narrative from 14 adoptees, children and adults, as they describe their feelings about being adopted. The sensitively edited text reflects society's changes in the matter of revealing adoption to children and, perhaps unintentionally, provides a striking example of individual differences. Useful as an item of interest to individual readers and as a group discussion tool.
SUBJ: Adoption.

362.73   Ph-2 3-6/6 $19.95   L   KB014
SCHWARTZ, PERRY. Carolyn's story: a book about an adopted girl. Text and photos by Perry Schwartz. Lerner ISBN 0-8225-2580-1, 1996. 40p. col. ill.
Includes glossary, bibliography and directories.
Nine-year-old Carolyn, born in Honduras and adopted as an infant by an American family, shares her insights into adoption, multiracial families, and cultural experiences. Illustrated with family photographs, the book also includes general information about adoption. Useful for students and families where this issue is important and for building general understanding.
SUBJ: Adoption./ Intercountry adoption./ Honduran Americans.

362.73   Ph-2 4-6/8 $15.95   T   KB015
WARREN, ANDREA. Orphan train rider: one boy's true story. Houghton Mifflin ISBN 0-395-69822-7, 1996. 80p. ill.
Includes bibliography and index.
Lee Nailling has been given an award by the Orphan Train Heritage Society for helping people learn about the orphan trains and the poverty which prompted their development. This is his story. It explains how a lonely, frightened boy found a loving, supportive family. This bit of American history has been covered before in fiction, but in this book the heartbreak of orphanages and displaced children is factually discussed.
SUBJ: Orphan trains./ Nailling, Lee./ Orphans./ Abandoned children.

VCR 362.76   Ph-1 P-2 $150.00   KB016
CRITTER JITTERS (Videocassette). Columbia-Green Rape Crisis Center/ dist. by Media Bus, 1986. 1/2" VHS videocassette color (20min).
Includes teacher's guide.
Available in two versions: Version A contains specific mention of genitalia; Version B does not.
Guided by the physical education teacher, preschool and primary grade children talk about proper and improper touching and ways to respond to improper touching. Reinforced with mime, music, movement and catchy lyrics, the simple and complete explanations incorporate children's feelings. The full range of correlated activities are presented in the teacher's guide.
SUBJ: Child abuse./ Child sexual abuse.

362.76   Ph-3 A/10 $19.95   T   KB017
MUFSON, SUSAN. Straight talk about child abuse. By Susan Mufson and Rachel Kranz. Facts On File ISBN 0-8160-2376-X; In Canada: Facts

On File, 1991. 104p.
Includes index.
Defines and discusses physical, emotional, and sexual abuse. Particular strengths are the evenhandedness of the forthright text and a listing of organizations and referral programs dealing with prevention and treatment of child abuse.
SUBJ: Child abuse.

VCR 362.76   Ph-1 5-6 $99.95   OD   KB018
WHEN SHOULD YOU TELL?: DEALING WITH ABUSE (Videocassette). Sunburst 2530-03 ISBN 0-7805-4182-0, 1995. 1/2" VHS videocassette color (15min).
Includes teacher's guide.
Karen relates her experience with abuse by an older male cousin; describes her feelings of discomfort, sadness, and preoccupation; and her details ultimate decision to share her secret with an understanding adult. Provides specific information while giving insight into a difficult, delicate subject. Will reassure students who may be victims of abuse and encourage them to seek help. Excellent, low-key approach is suitable for middle grade students. Teacher's guide provides assistance in meaningful follow-up discussion and activities. (Parents' Shelf).
SUBJ: Child sexual abuse./ Sexually abused children.

362.87   Ph-1 4-A/5 $14.90   L   KB019
WILKES, SYBELLA. One day we had to run!: refugee children tell their stories in words and paintings. Millbrook ISBN 1-56294-557-2, 1994. 63p. col. ill., maps.
Originally published in Great Britain, Evans Brothers Limited.
Includes bibliography, directory and index.
Children from Sudan, Somalia, and Ethiopia portray their experiences as refugees in vivid, heart-stopping stories, paintings, and personal experiences. Enhanced with maps, photographs, historical background, and descriptions of everyday life in refugee camps, this striking volume will find a place in multicultural studies and units on African history and contemporary issues.
SUBJ: Refugees--Kenya./ Refugees--Africa, East./ Children's writings./ Children's art.

363.1   Ph-1 P-3/3 $7.95   P   KB020
BROWN, MARC TOLON. Dinosaurs, beware: a safety guide. By Marc Tolon Brown and Stephen Krensky. Joy Street/Little, Brown ISBN 0-316-11219-4; In Canada: Little, Brown, 1982. 32p. col. ill.
Selectors' Choice, 14th ed.
Colorful illustrations are packed with delightful detail as dinosaurs warn of the consequences of not following safety rules. Approximately 60 tips are grouped by situation--at home, in case of fire, in the cold, etc. Useful for both individuals or group discussions and will surely delight and educate.
SUBJ: Safety.

363.1   Ph-1 1-3/6 $11.95   L   KB021
GIRARD, LINDA WALVOORD. Who is a stranger and what should I do? Illus. by Helen Cogancherry. Whitman ISBN 0-8075-9014-2; In Canada: General, 1985. 32p. col. ill. (Concept book).
Includes "Note to Parents".
Stresses the importance of safety in dealing with strangers, providing rules to follow in many situations. Easy-going tone will not frighten but provide positive suggestions. Suitable for reading aloud in a group situation or one-to-one basis.
SUBJ: Strangers./ Safety.

363.1   Ph-2 5-6/7 $15.98   L   KB022
GUTMAN, BILL. Hazards at home. Twenty-First Century ISBN 0-8050-4141-9; In Canada: Fitzhenry & Whiteside, 1996. 80p. col. ill. (Focus on safety).
Includes bibliography, directory and index.
Sensible discussion of many common types of dangers and accidents includes advice on safety procedures for parents and children caring for themselves and younger siblings. Falls, fires and burns, poisons, firearms, swimming pools and other drowning dangers, tools and machinery, and further tips on accidents and first aid are all covered methodically and illustrated with occasional photographs. This practical presentation on accident prevention and response will be useful for classroom studies on safety and public library programs on babysitting. (Parents' Shelf).
SUBJ: Safety./ Accidents--Prevention.

VCR 363.1   Ph-2 P-1 $29.95   OD   KB023
K.C.'s first bus ride (Videocassette). KidSafety of America SE 1665 ISBN 1-884413-06-4, 1994. 1/2" VHS videocassette color (10min).
Provides suggestions and safety rules for riding the school bus. Appealing script and cheerful puppets deliver a solid message designed to allay anxiety as well as to deliver safety instruction. Most

NONFICTION

useful with very young students.
SUBJ: Buses--Safety measures./ Safety education./ Accidents--Prevention.

VCR 363.1 Ph-2 P-1 $34.95 OD KB024
SAFETY ON WHEELS (Videocassette). Films for the Humanities & Sciences FFH 4691, 1994. 1/2" VHS videocassette color (15min). (Calling all safety scouts).
Includes public performance rights.
Combines good information about bike safety, explaining general rules of the road, street signs, and hand signals with information about safety near trains, in buses, and in cars. Lively puppet presentation will appeal to young student audiences. Good vehicle for beginning discussion of safety rules, or for review.
SUBJ: Safety./ Accidents--Prevention./ Bicycles and bicycling--Safety measures./ Automobiles--Safety measures.

363.12 Ph-1 4-6/8 $6.95 P KB025
BALLARD, ROBERT D. Exploring the Titanic. Illustrated by Ken Marschall. Scholastic/Madison Press ISBN 0-590-41952-8; In Canada: Madison Press, 1988. 64p. col. ill.
Includes glossary, timeline and bibliography.
Meshes photographs, realistic paintings and cutaway drawings in fine fashion as the leader of the 1985 French-American expedition which found the "Titanic" describes the events of the 1912 disaster and the discovery and exploration of the legendary ship some decades later. Though occasionally leaning toward the melodramatic, the overall impact of the book is strong. Can be used effectively as a stimulus for research or as the basis for creative writing activities.
SUBJ: Titanic (Steamship)./ Shipwrecks./ Underwater exploration.

363.12 Ph-2 4-6/7 $16.40 L KB026
KENT, DEBORAH. Titanic. Childrens Press ISBN 0-516-06672-2; In Canada: Childrens Press, 1993. 32p. ill. (some col.). (Cornerstones of freedom).
Includes index.
Offers a straightforward report of the 1912 sinking of the world's largest ocean liner after it struck an iceberg during its maiden voyage. Closing pages mention Ballard's research after locating the long-lost remains of the ship in 1985. Supplements EXPLORING THE TITANIC and meets a need for high-interest, nonsensational materials on the subject.
SUBJ: Titanic (Steamship)./ Shipwrecks.

363.12 Ph-2 4-A/6 $16.95 T KB027
TANAKA, SHELLEY. On board the Titanic. Illus. by Ken Marschall. Hyperion ISBN 0-7868-0283-9; In Canada: Madison Press, 1996. 48p. col. ill., map. (I was there).
"Hyperion/Madison Press book."
Includes glossary and bibliography.
Details the grandeur and the sinking of the "unsinkable" Titanic through the experiences of seventeen-year-old passenger Jack Thayer of Philadelphia. The account is accompanied by full-color illustrations, detailed diagrams, and photographs.
SUBJ: Titanic (Steamship)./ Shipwrecks./ Thayer, Jack./ Bride, Harold.

363.2 Ph-2 4-6/7 $18.95 L KB028
BALLINGER, ERICH. Detective dictionary: a handbook for aspiring sleuths. Lerner ISBN 0-8225-0721-8, 1994. 144p. ill.
Includes index.
Supplies an alphabetic handbook which lists terms of interest to young sleuths. Approach is tongue-in-cheek and somewhat idiosyncratic. High-appeal browser with language arts potential.
SUBJ: Criminal investigation--Dictionaries./ Crime--Dictionaries./ Detectives--Dictionaries.

363.2 Ph-3 5-6/7 $22.83 L KB029
GRAHAM, IAN. Crime-fighting. Raintree Steck-Vaughn ISBN 0-8114-3840-6, 1995. 46p. col. ill. (Science spotlight).
Includes glossary, bibliography and index.
Discusses the work of forensic scientists and briefly describes some of the tests and techniques in use today. Photographs and drawings illustrate the rather difficult text of this imported title. Of particular interest to crime buffs. Use to introduce a less commonly studied occupation for career studies.
SUBJ: Criminal investigation.

VCR 363.2 Ph-2 5-6 $95.00 OD KB030
WOMEN IN POLICING (Videocassette). Produced by Jocelyn Riley. Her Own Words 17001 ISBN 1-877933-52-X, 1994. 1/2" VHS videocassette color (15min). (Women's history and literature media).
Includes public performance rights.
Effectively uses still photographs to portray the multifaceted duties of

police officers while emphasizing the role of women in the police force. Presents an overview of the different services provided by uniformed patrol officers, neighborhood police officers, detectives, special operations police officers, mounted patrol officers, and uniformed special investigators. Depicts police work as a challenging but rewarding career. For career studies and women's studies.
SUBJ: Policewomen./ Police./ Occupations.

VCR 363.3 Ph-3 2-4 $79.00 OD KB031
FIRE STATION (Videocassette). National Geographic 51437, 1990. 1/2" VHS videocassette color (13min). (Your town).
Includes teacher's guide.
Shows examples of the duties of fire fighters--providing emergency medical assistance, rescuing pets, inspecting buildings, teaching fire safety, and fighting fires. Also shows life at the fire station in calm as well as in exciting times. Includes minimal information on personal safety in case of fire.
SUBJ: Fire departments./ Fire fighters.

363.3 Ph-2 P-1/6 $15.95 L KB032
GIBBONS, GAIL. Emergency! Holiday House ISBN 0-8234-1128-1, 1994. unp. col. ill.
Introduces boats, trucks, and other vehicles used in responding to emergencies. Simple, brightly colored illustrations carry the day in an otherwise routine presentation. Useful in community helper units.
SUBJ: Emergency vehicles./ Vehicles.

VCR 363.3 Ph-2 6-A $150.00 OD KB033
HANDGUNS: MADE FOR KILLING, NOT FOR KIDS (Videocassette). Produced by Allen Mondell and Cynthia Salzman Mondell. Media Projects ISBN 1-880898-15-2, 1996. 1/2" VHS videocassette color (19min).
Closed captioned.
Graphically depicts in docudrama style three true episodes involving handguns--an angry confrontation, an accidental shooting, and a drive-by shooting. Realistically portrays the juveniles involved and the aftermath of their actions. Though an even-handed presentation of the dangers of firearms, the sensitive subject matter makes previewing essential.
SUBJ: Gun control./ Firearms--Safety measures.

363.3 Ph-1 4-6/9 $15.95 L KB034
VOGEL, CAROLE GARBUNY. Great Midwest flood. Little, Brown ISBN 0-316-90248-9; In Canada: Little, Brown, 1995. 32p. col. ill., maps.
In 1993, flooding from the Mississippi and its tributaries devastated communities in at least ten states, and this well-organized account covers causes, events, and effects on people and the environment. Color photographs provide visual focus, and maps, including endpapers with flood areas clearly identified, satellite photographs, and cutaways enhance the text. A relevant addition to collections for studies of natural disasters, weather, and environmental issues.
SUBJ: Floods--Middle West./ Natural disasters.

363.34 Ph-1 4-6/4 $18.95 T KB035
LAUBER, PATRICIA. Flood: wrestling with the Mississippi. National Geographic/dist. by Publishers Group West ISBN 0-7922-4141-X, 1996. 63p. col. ill., maps.
Includes index.
Describes the history of the Mississippi River, the floods of 1993 and 1927, their effects on nearby communities, and efforts to control both flooding and the course of the river. Full-color and black and white photographs, satellite images, and diagrams illustrate the text. Pair this with Carole Vogel's GREAT MIDWEST FLOOD for environmental studies and interdisciplinary science and social science units.
SUBJ: Floods--Mississippi River./ Mississippi River.

363.34 Ph-2 4-6/7 $15.98 L KB036
OTFINOSKI, STEVEN. Blizzards. Twenty-First Century ISBN 0-8050-3093-X; In Canada: Fitzhenry & Whiteside, 1994. 64p. col. ill. (When disaster strikes).
Includes glossary, bibliographies and index.
Reviews major North American blizzards of the nineteenth and twentieth centuries and discusses causes of the severe storms. Sidebars provide specialized information and safety suggestions. Background builder for current events and high appeal report material.
SUBJ: Blizzards./ Natural disasters.

363.34 Ph-2 4-6/7 $15.98 L KB037
ROZENS, ALEKSANDRS. Floods. Twenty-First Century ISBN 0-8050-3097-2; In Canada: Fitzhenry & Whiteside, 1994. 64p. col. ill., map. (When disaster strikes).
Includes glossary, bibliographies and index.
Tells of American floods from one which imperiled the DeSoto

expedition in 1539 through the Midwest floods of 1993. Advances in flood forecasting and a listing of flood preparation considerations are included. Use for specialized study units.
SUBJ: Floods./ Natural disasters.

363.34   Ph-2 4-6/7 $15.98   L   KB038
SPIES, KAREN BORNEMAN. Earthquakes. By Karen Spies. Twenty-First Century ISBN 0-8050-3096-4; In Canada: Fitzhenry & Whiteside, 1994. 64p. col. ill. (When disaster strikes).
Includes glossary, bibliographies and index.
Discusses earthquakes and their causes. Emphasis is on North American temblors. Useful browser and background builder.
SUBJ: Earthquakes./ Natural disasters.

363.34   Ph-2 3-6/10 $15.95   L   KB039
VOGEL, CAROLE GARBUNY. Shock waves through Los Angeles: the Northridge earthquake. Little, Brown ISBN 0-316-90240-3; In Canada: Little, Brown, 1996. 32p. col. ill., maps.
Examines the aftereffects of the Northridge, California, earthquake in 1994 on people, communities, resource services, and structures. Full-color photographs document the devastation. Use for units on natural disasters and for general interest reading.
SUBJ: Earthquakes--California--Northridge (Los Angeles)./ Natural disasters.

363.37   Ph-2 4-A/6 $19.95   L   KB040
CONE, PATRICK. Wildfire. Carolrhoda ISBN 0-87614-936-0, 1997. 48p. col. ill. (Nature in action).
Includes glossary and index.
Presents convection and conduction; details latest thinking on wildfire and forest management; and describes the ecological stages of change and regrowth. Good photographs along with safety tips and fire facts sustain reader interest. Useful for weather units, environmental studies, and all forest fire discussions.
SUBJ: Wildfires./ Forest fires./ Fires./ Fire ecology.

363.37   Ph-2 3-6/7 $14.93   L   KB041
SIMON, SEYMOUR. Wildfires. Morrow ISBN 0-688-13936-1, 1996. unp. col. ill.
Since the 1988 Yellowstone firestorm, scientists have come to a new understanding about fire's crucial role in maintaining the balance of nature. This well-organized presentation explains the force and necessity of forest fires and describes what happens when well-meaning people prevent large scale fires from burning themselves out. Use for units on fire, forests, trees, and environmental studies.
SUBJ: Forest fires./ Fire ecology./ Fires./ Ecology.

363.37   Ph-2 4-6/7 $15.98   L   KB042
WOOD, LEIGH. Fires. Twenty-First Century ISBN 0-8050-3094-8; In Canada: Fitzhenry & Whiteside, 1994. 64p. col. ill. (When disaster strikes).
Includes glossary, bibliographies and index.
Discusses major North American fires of the nineteenth and twentieth centuries. A chapter on fire fighting and fire prevention is included. Use as a resource for student reports.
SUBJ: Fires./ Natural disasters.

363.4   Ph-2 5-6/12 $19.95   L   KB043
HINTZ, MARTIN. Farewell, John Barleycorn: prohibition in the United States. Lerner ISBN 0-8225-1734-5, 1996. 88p. ill. (People's history).
Includes bibliography and index.
A history of alcohol use in the United States covers colonial times, the nineteenth century Temperance Movement, and an in-depth look at the Prohibition Era. Illustrated with photographs, engravings, graphics, and cartoons. Will add depth to United States history units on the time periods covered, and will be useful background for discussion of current social issues.
SUBJ: Prohibition./ United States--History./ Alcoholic beverages--Law and legislation.

363.7   Ph-2 A/9 $17.95   T   KB044
ANDERSON, JOAN. Earth keepers. Photos by George Ancona. Harcourt Brace ISBN 0-15-242199-8; In Canada: Harcourt Brace c/o Canadian Manda, 1993. unp. ill.
"Gulliver Green book."
Includes directory.
Chronicles the efforts of three environmentalists who respectively work with water, urban land, and animals. Rather complex text meshes closely with strong black and white photographs. Good for environmental studies.
SUBJ: Environmental protection.

CE 363.7   Ph-2 1-4/4 $14.95   L   KB045
BROWN, LAURENE KRASNY. Dinosaurs to the rescue!: a guide to protecting our planet. By Laurene Krasny Brown and Marc Tolon Brown. Joy Street/Little, Brown ISBN 0-316-11087-6; In Canada: Little, Brown, 1992. unp. col. ill.
Available from the National Library Service for the Blind and Physically Handicapped on sound recording cassette RC 38103.
Delivers a simple, basic environmental message through use of Brown's familiar cast of dinosaur characters. Use as the foundation for a primary grade discussion activity in which students develop their own suggestions for protecting the environment.
SUBJ: Environmental protection.

CDR 363.7   Ph-1 1-5 $99.95   OD KB046
HALPERN, NAOMI ANGORN. Kids and the environment: taking responsibility for our surroundings (Microcomputer program). Tom Snyder Productions KID-Y, 1994. 2 3.5" disks. (Choices, choices).
Includes teacher's guide.
5.0 version in Macintosh and Windows computers.
System requirements: Macintosh black and white version--any Macintosh computer with at least 1MB of internal memory and a hard disk; color version--any color Macintosh computer with at least 2MB of internal memory and a hard disk.
Version 1.0.
An excellent simulation in which youngsters deal with keeping a playground clean. Superb teaching tools and lesson plans are included. Intended for use with the entire class at one time. For environmental studies.
SUBJ: Environmental protection--Software./ Software--Environmental protection./ Refuse and refuse disposal--Software./ Software--Refuse and refuse disposal./ Recycling (Waste)--Software./ Software--Recycling (Waste)./ Decision making--Software./ Software--Decision making.

VCR 363.7   Ph-1 3-6 $49.95   OD KB047
KIDS BY THE BAY (Videocassette). Produced by Judy Irving and Chris Beaver. IDG Films/dist. by Video Project KID-147-P, 1997. 1/2" VHS videocassette color (20min).
Includes public performance rights.
Video field trips by diverse groups of students to islands, marshes, and other wildlife habitats in the San Francisco Bay area demonstrate that kids can make a personal difference in restoring land and water damaged by pollution. Close-ups of endangered wildlife, effects of pollution, environmental activities in progress, and lively music add to student appeal. Although regional in setting, this can be used effectively for environmental studies in any area of the country.
SUBJ: Environmental protection./ Conservation of natural resources--San Francisco Bay Area (Calif.).

363.7   Ph-1 4-6/7 $16.95   L   KB048
MCVEY, VICKI. Sierra Club kid's guide to planet care and repair. Illus. by Martha Weston. Sierra Club ISBN 0-87156-567-6; In Canada: Sierra Club, 1993. 84p. ill.
Includes glossary and index.
Outstrips most of its environmental competitors in providing a readable text filled with activities, vignettes, and thought-provoking discussion. Unassuming sketches illustrate each of twelve chapters. Useful for ecobuffs, project planners, and general readers.
SUBJ: Environmental protection./ Man--Influence on nature.

VCR 363.7   Ph-2 3-6 $59.95   OD KB049
MISH, MICHAEL. Kid's eye view of ecology (Videocassette). KCET-TV and Lubin/Mish Productions/dist. by Video Project, 1991. 1/2" VHS videocassette color (28min).
Includes teacher's guide and lyrics.
Includes public performance rights.
Introduces major environmental issues such as pollution, waste, recycling, energy use, water conservation, ozone depletion, and deforestation while encouraging children to take an active role in solutions. Practical suggestions and lively songs will engage listeners. Good discussion starter for environmental studies.
SUBJ: Environmental protection./ Ecology.

SRC 363.7   Ph-1 P-2 $9.95   OD KB050
MISH, MICHAEL. Kid's eye view of the environment (Sound recording cassette) Mish Mash Music MMM 2003, 1989. 1 sound cassette (40min).
At head of title: Michael Mish presents.
Includes lyrics.
Spirited rhythms and meaningful lyrics teach about recycling, rain forest depletion, and pollution of the rivers. The winsome voices of young children ask questions about the environment and sing songs based on the answers creating humorous, enjoyable lyrics. Includes a bilingual song in French and English. Excellent vehicle for provoking

discussion.
SUBJ: Environmental protection--Songs and music./ Songs.

VCR 363.7   Ph-2 4-6 $89.00   OD KB051
REDUCING, REUSING AND RECYCLING: ENVIRONMENTAL
CONCERNS (Videocassette). Rainbow Educational Video RB853, 1992.
1/2" VHS videocassette color (20min).
Includes Teacher's Guide.
Discusses the problems of solid waste and examines patterns which
can reduce the consequences of careless use of resources. Teacher's
guide includes script, review questions, student activities, glossary, and
a list of addresses. Use to provide an overview of the subject.
SUBJ: Refuse and refuse disposal./ Conservation of natural resources.

KIT 363.72   Ph-3 1-3 $41.00   OD KB052
CAPTAIN CONSERVATION: ALL ABOUT RECYCLING (Kit). National
Geographic C30856, 1992. 30 ill. booklets, 1 sound cassette (12min).
(Wonders of learning).
Includes teacher's guide with 6 activity sheets, and a Spanish
supplement.
Simplified overview of recycling of paper, glass, aluminum, plastic,
and organic materials. Uses read-along booklets with spoken cassette;
teacher's guide suggests additional activities. For individual use as
well as a group setting.
SUBJ: Recycling (Waste)./ Refuse and refuse disposal.

363.72   Ph-2 3-6/10 $16.98   L   KB053
CHANDLER, GARY. Recycling. By Gary Chandler and Kevin Graham.
Twenty-First Century ISBN 0-8050-4622-4; In Canada: Fitzhenry &
Whiteside, 1996. 64p. col. ill. (Making a better world).
Includes directories, glossary, bibliography and index.
Brief essays on recycling efforts of specific individuals, agencies, and
companies feature a variety of materials from ordinary paper and
plastic bottles to more unusual salmon skin and used computer parts.
Illustrated with photographs of both people and products, it includes
addresses for further information at the end of each essay. Use to
spark ideas for student developed projects in environmental studies in
which young scientists can participate.
SUBJ: Recycling (Waste)./ Recycled products.

VCR 363.72   Ph-2 5-A $89.95   OD KB054
GARBAGE STORY (Videocassette). United Learning 10209V ISBN
1-56007-599-6, 1996. 1/2" VHS videocassette color (21min).
Includes teacher's guide and reproducible worksheets.
Includes public performance rights.
Closed captioned.
Discusses modern systems for managing landfills, incineration methods
that produce energy, and recovery of materials that can be recycled
and reused. Identifies issues and questions surrounding efforts to
reduce dangers of pollution from all forms of garbage disposal. For
environmental studies.
SUBJ: Refuse and refuse disposal./ Recycling (Waste).

VCR 363.72   Ph-2 2-4 $79.00   OD KB055
PUBLIC WORKS (Videocassette). National Geographic 51491, 1992.
1/2" VHS videocassette (15min). (Your town).
Includes teacher's guide.
Examines community public works services such as trash collection and
landfills, water treatment systems, wastewater facilities, and street
maintenance and lighting. Serves as a valuable overview to city
services often ignored. Can be used above recommended grade
levels.
SUBJ: Refuse and refuse disposal./ Water treatment plants./ Public
works./ Community service.

VCR 363.72   Ph-2 5-6 $79.00   OD KB056
RECYCLING: IT'S EVERYBODY'S JOB (Videocassette). National
Geographic 51513, 1992. 1/2" VHS videocassette color (20min).
Includes teacher's guide.
Burning, landfills, and recycling are the common means of getting rid
of garbage. A competent narration by a child follows class exercises
which examine family garbage and paper recycling. Includes
informative segments on each method of garbage treatment.
Interesting examples of products manufactured from recycled material
and advice on how to reduce, reuse, and recycle materials round out
the well constructed presentation.
SUBJ: Refuse and refuse disposal./ Recycling (Waste)./ Environmental
protection.

363.73   Ph-3 1-4/4 $14.89   L   KB057
BERGER, MELVIN. Oil spill! Illus. by Paul Mirocha. HarperCollins ISBN
0-06-022912-8; In Canada: HarperCollins, 1994. 32p. col. ill., map.
(Let's-read-and-find-out science book).
Presents basic information on causes of oil spills and methods of

cleanup. Final pages offer suggestions for conserving oil and supply a
sample lobbying letter urging stronger laws related to oil spills. For
environmental studies.
SUBJ: Oil spills./ Pollution.

VCR 363.73   Ph-1 5-A $29.95   KB058
BLUE PLANET (Videocassette). By the Smithsonian Institute and Lockheed
Corp. in association with IMAX. IMAX/dist. by Finley Holiday V165; In
Canada: IMAX, 1993. 1/2" VHS videocassette color (42min).
Selectors' Choice, 20th ed.
Spectacular photography filmed during five space shuttle missions
delivers a powerful message about forces effecting Earth's ecology.
Developed by the Smithsonian's National Air and Space Museum and
Lockheed Corporation for use in IMAX theaters, production quality is
high; length requires special planning. A bargain buy which offers
strong support for environmental studies.
SUBJ: Pollution./ Earth.

MCP 363.73   Ph-1 5-A $149.95   OD KB059
ENVIRONMENT (Microcomputer program). Tom Snyder Productions
ISBN 1-55998-151-2, 1990. 1 3.5" disk, backup disk. (Decisions,
decisions).
Includes teacher's guide, 24 student reference books, and
reproducible worksheets.
Macintosh and Windows network versions: AppleShare or Novell
based.
Available on Windows/Macintosh CD-ROM, $149.95.
Spanish version available for Macintosh and MS-DOS systems.
System requirements: Macintosh LC II or better; System 7.1 or higher;
4 megs of available RAM; 256-color 13" monitor or larger.
System requirements: Windows 3.1 or higher; 8 megs of RAM; 256-
color VGA monitor.
This simulation guides students through solving pollution and
environmental issues in a town. Cooperative learning, research skills,
and critical thinking are all practiced. Works best in small groups or
with an entire class.
SUBJ: Pollution--Software./ Software--Pollution./ Refuse and refuse
disposal--Software./ Software--Refuse and refuse disposal./
Environmental protection--Software./ Software--Environmental
protection.

VCR 363.73   Ph-2 6-A $99.00   OD KB060
FRESH WATER: RESOURCE AT RISK (Videocassette). National
Geographic Society C51579, 1993. 1/2" VHS videocassette color
(28min).
Includes teacher's guide.
Young people in different regions of the country study the use and
pollution of water in rivers, aquifers, and dams. This informative
survey alternates scenes featuring students and Future Farmers of
America with explanations of the sources of fresh water, the
problems, and some solutions. The excellent photography and
substantial explanations offer good instructional materials, and the film
effectively encourages participation and further study by students.
SUBJ: Water--Pollution./ Water quality management./ Water supply./
Pollution.

363.73   Ph-1 4-6/8 $21.50   L   KB061
HOFF, MARY KING. Our endangered planet: atmosphere. By Mary Hoff
and Mary M. Rodgers. Lerner ISBN 0-8225-2509-7, 1995. 72p. col. ill.
(Our endangered planet).
Includes directory, glossary and index.
Discusses the greenhouse effect and global warming, explores their
impact on our planet, and includes possible solutions, both global and
personal. Illustrated with full-color photographs and clear diagrams.
Full-page boxed features provide additional information of interest.
Useful resource for reports and discussions in environmental studies.
SUBJ: Atmosphere./ Ozone layer./ Global warming./ Greenhouse
effect, Atmospheric./ Man--Influence on nature.

363.73   Ph-2 5-6/8 $21.50   L   KB062
HOFF, MARY KING. Our endangered planet: rivers and lakes. By Mary
King Hoff and Mary M. Rodgers. Lerner ISBN 0-8225-2501-1, 1991.
64p col photos and illus. (Our endangered planet).
Includes directory, glossary and index.
Discusses the current dangers of surface water pollution and examines
ways to keep waters fresh. A list of concerned organizations is
appended as are glossary and index.
SUBJ: Water--Pollution./ Pollution./ Water.

VCR 363.73   Ph-2 5-A $99.00   OD KB063
INVESTIGATING GLOBAL WARMING (Videocassette). National
Geographic 52671, 1997. 1/2" VHS videocassette color (24min).
Includes teacher's guide.
Closed captioned.

Scientific accounts of climate history based on glacier and deep sea core samples, computer generated models of the climate system, and global climate simulations are used to speculate on causes of global warming, make predictions of future effects of current trends, and explore ways to reduce greenhouse gases. Use for environmental studies and interdisciplinary units in science and social science.
SUBJ: Global warming./ Greenhouse effect, Atmospheric.

VCR 363.73   Ph-2 3-5 $125.00   OD KB064
OUR WATERY WORLD (Videocassette). Agency for Instructional Technology/Slim Goodbody Corp., 1991. 1/2" VHS videocassette color (15min). (Outside story with Slim Goodbody).
Includes teacher's guide.
Delivers an effective environmental message as Slim Goodbody guides viewers through a discussion of water and its role in our world. Lively production design, songs, and a dinosaur rap add to the package.
A similar format is used in IT ALL ADDS UP, 1991, an examination of recycling issues.
SUBJ: Water--Pollution./ Pollution./ Water.

363.73   Ph-2 5-6/9 $14.93   L   KB065
PRINGLE, LAURENCE P. Oil spills: damage, recovery, and prevention. By Laurence Pringle. Morrow ISBN 0-688-09861-4, 1993. 56p. ill. (Save-the-Earth book).
"Save-the-earth book."
Includes glossary, bibliography and index.
Provides an evenhanded examination in which both problems and solutions of man-made and natural oil spills are discussed. Valuable as background for current events and science curriculum.
SUBJ: Oil spills./ Petroleum./ Environmental protection.

363.73   Ph-2 5-6/7 $16.95   L   KB066
RYBOLT, THOMAS R. Environmental experiments about water. By Thomas R. Rybolt and Robert C. Mebane. Enslow ISBN 0-89490-410-8, 1993. 96p. ill. (Science experiments for young people).
Includes index.
Water acidity and density, the water cycle, acid rain, types of pollution, and aspects of purification are included in this handy compendium. Each of the 16 experiments includes a materials list, explanation of procedures including safety warnings, suggested observations, a discussion of results, and suggestions for added things to try. Practical addition for experiments collections and for use in environmental studies.
SUBJ: Water--Experiments./ Water--Pollution--Experiments./ Water--Purification--Experiments./ Acid rain--Experiments./ Experiments.

363.73   Ph-2 3-6/9 $15.89   L   KB067
SIMON, SEYMOUR. Earth words: a dictionary of the environment. Illus. by Mark Kaplan. HarperCollins ISBN 0-06-020234-3; In Canada: HarperCollins, 1995. 48p. col. ill., maps.
Provides careful, clear definitions of 66 environmental terms. Colorful drawings aid in understanding. Useful in environmental studies.
SUBJ: Ecology--Dictionaries./ Pollution--Dictionaries.

VCR 363.73   Ph-1 4-6 $89.00   OD KB068
SOURCE OF LIFE?: WATER IN OUR ENVIRONMENT (Videocassette). Rainbow Educational Video RB861, 1992. 1/2" VHS videocassette color (22min).
Includes Teacher's Guide.
Discusses pollution of Earth's water and the careless or wasteful use of the fresh water supply. Strong teacher's guide and good production values add to the impact of the effort. Useful in science, social studies, or current events units.
SUBJ: Water--Pollution./ Water supply.

363.73   Ph-1 4-6/8 $21.50   L   KB069
YOUNT, LISA. Our endangered planet: air. By Lisa Yount and Mary M. Rodgers. Lerner ISBN 0-8225-2510-0, 1995. 64p. col. ill. (Our endangered planet).
Includes directory, glossary and index.
Presents the essential nature of air, its structure, and processes before exploring effects of pollution and acid rain and discussing possible solutions, both global and personal. Captions for many of the full-color photographs add interest and detail while full-page boxed features complement the general narrative. A useful resource for reports and discussions in environmental studies.
SUBJ: Air--Pollution./ Pollution./ Man--Influence on nature.

VCR 364.1   Ph-3 A $85.95   OD KB070
GANGS: DECISIONS AND OPTIONS (Videocassette). Rainbow Educational RB8132, 1993. 1/2" VHS videocassette color (17min).
Includes teacher's guide.
Presents three vignettes which highlight reasons students choose

involvement with gangs. Teacher's guide suggests strategies for use with each segment. Valuable as a discussion starter.
SUBJ: Gangs.

364.1   Ph-3 4-6/6 $17.50   L   KB071
GREENBERG, KEITH ELLIOT. Out of the gang. Illus. by Carol Halebian. Lerner ISBN 0-8225-2553-4, 1992. 40p. ill.
Includes bibliography.
Offers insight into gang life through the experiences of a twenty-eight-year-old former gang member and a sixth grader who is resisting membership. Not as strong as other Lerner books on social conditions, but will be useful nonetheless.
SUBJ: Gangs./ Young, Butch.

364.36   Ph-2 A/8 $13.99   T   KB072
HYDE, MARGARET O. Kids in and out of trouble. Cobblehill/Dutton ISBN 0-525-65149-7, 1995. 104p.
Includes directory, glossary, bibliography and index.
Provides a sobering discussion of the ways young people get into trouble and what happens when they are arrested. A directory supplies sources for additional information and a listing of toll-free (800) hotline numbers. Solid, useful resource for students, parents, and teachers. (Parents' Shelf).
SUBJ: Juvenile delinquents./ Justice, Administration of.

369.43   Ph-1 4-6/6 $7.95   P   KB073
BIRKBY, ROBERT C. Boy Scout handbook. 10th ed. By William Hillcourt in association with Boy Scouts of America. Boy Scouts of America ISBN 0-839-53229-6, 1990. 672p. col. ill.
Includes bibliography and index.
Available from National Library Service for the Blind and Physically Handicapped on sound recording cassette RC18897.
Contains information and instruction in the four major skill areas in scouting: camping and hiking activities, nature, communication, and citizenship. Explains activities of scouting program and is abundantly illustrated with full-color drawings.
SUBJ: Boy Scouts--Handbooks, manuals, etc./ Scouts and scouting.

369.43   Ph-1 4-5/5 $7.50   P   KB074
BOY SCOUTS OF AMERICA. Big Bear Cub Scout book. Rev. ed. Boy Scouts of America ISBN 0-8395-3228-8, 1984. 256p. col. ill.
Available from the National Library Service for the Blind and Physically Handicapped on sound recording cassette RC 41936.
Handbook of requirements for the nine-year-old boy in Cub Scouting. Includes basic cub scouting information, achievements to earn the rank of Bear and electives for earning gold and silver arrow points. Parents' supplement accompanies handbook.
SUBJ: Boy Scouts--Handbooks, manuals, etc./ Scouts and scouting.

369.43   Ph-1 4-6/3 $7.95   P   KB075
BOY SCOUTS OF AMERICA. Webelos Scout book. Rev. ed. Boy Scouts of America ISBN 0-8395-3235-0, 1987. 416p. col. ill.
Handbook of requirements for the 10-year-old boy in scouting. Webelos bridges the gap between Cub Scouts and Boy Scouts. Includes general information and requirements for activity badges.
SUBJ: Boy Scouts--Handbooks, manuals, etc./ Scouts and scouting.

369.43   Ph-1 3-4/4 $3.50   P   KB076
BOY SCOUTS OF AMERICA. Wolf Cub Scout book. Rev. ed. Boy Scouts of America ISBN 0-8395-3234-2, 1986. 224p. col. ill.
Available from the National Library Service for the Blind and Physically Handicapped on sound recording cassette RC 41935.
Handbook of requirements for the eight-year-old boy who is beginning in scouting. Includes basic cub scouting information, achievements to earn the rank of Wolf and electives for earning gold and silver arrow points. Parents' supplement accompanies handbook.
SUBJ: Scouts and scouting./ Boy Scouts--Handbooks, manuals, etc.

369.43   Ph-2 2-4/6 $8.10   P   KB077
KENOWER, FELICIE T. Cub Scout fun book. By Felicie T. and Felicie C. Kenower with Bill and Bernard Martin. Boy Scouts of America ISBN 0-8395-3213-X, c1956, 1986. 88p. ill.
Easy to follow directions for projects which Cub Scouts can complete for arrow point credits.
SUBJ: Cub Scouts./ Boy Scouts./ Handicraft.

369.463   Ph-1 1-3 $9.25   P OD KB078
GIRL SCOUTS OF THE UNITED STATES OF AMERICA. Brownie Scout handbook. Girl Scouts of the United States of America 20-910 ISBN 0-88441-279-2, 1993. 288p. col. ill.
The basic resource for young girls involved in this organization. Illustrated in full color with activities keyed as starter or advanced.
SUBJ: Brownie Scouts./ Girl Scouts./ Scouts and scouting.

369.463   Ph-1 4-6 $9.25   P OD KB079
GIRL SCOUTS OF THE UNITED STATES OF AMERICA. Junior Girl
Scout handbook. Girl Scouts of the United States of America 20-912
ISBN 0-88441-281-4, 1994. 208p. col. ill.
> Available from National Library Service for the Blind and Physically
> Handicapped in Braille BR06893 and on sound recording cassette
> RC25369.
> The basic resource for girls involved in this organization. Heavily
> illustrated with lots of how-tos.
> SUBJ: Girl Scouts./ Scouts and scouting.

MCP 370.15   Ph-1 K-3 $59.95   OD KB080
THINKIN' THINGS COLLECTION 1 (Microcomputer program). Edmark
702-1465, 1993. 3 3.5" disks. (Thinkin' things series).
> Includes teacher's guide, user's guide and reproducible activity sheets.
> Also available in Windows/DOS disk (702-1447, $59.95), and
> Macintosh/Windows CD-ROM (702-1176, $59.95).
> ALA notable computer software, 1994.
> Selectors' Choice, 20th ed.
> System requirements: Macintosh 256-color; 4MB RAM (5MB for
> System 7.5); hard-disk drive with 6MB free; System 6.0.7 or higher;
> high density floppy drive; microphone (optional); TouchWindow
> (optional).
> Youngsters gain practice in the thinking skills of memory, critical
> thinking, problem solving, and creativity while using the six activities in
> the software. Superb graphics, animation, and sound make the
> program enjoyable and allow youngsters to use it without adult help.
> SUBJ: Thought and thinking--Software./ Software--Thought and
> thinking./ Problem solving--Software./ Software--Problem solving./
> Interactive media.

CDR 370.15   Ph-1 1-6 $59.95   OD KB081
THINKIN' THINGS COLLECTION 2. School version (CD-ROM). Edmark
702-1177, 1995. 1 CD-ROM color. (Thinkin' things series).
> Version 1.43.
> Includes teacher's guide.
> Also available in Macintosh disk (702-1440, $59.95), and Windows/
> DOS disk (702-1441, $59.95).
> System requirements: Color Macintosh (256 colors); System 6.0.7 or
> higher; 4MB RAM (5MB required for System 7.5), 1900K minimum
> free; CD-ROM drive; microphone (optional); TouchWindow (optional).
> System requirements: MS-DOS 3.1 or later or Windows 3.1; SVGA
> monitor with 1MB RAM (VESA drivers are included); 560K free
> conventional memory (2MB extended memory [XMS] strongly
> recommended); Microsoft-compatible mouse and driver; CD-ROM
> drive; third-party sound-output device or card (with external speaker);
> hard disk with 1MB free; 25 MHz 386 or better; microphone
> (optional); TouchWindow (optional).
> Product (702-1177) runs on either Windows or Macintosh compatible
> hardware.
> The five extraordinary activities in this program allow students to
> exercise their musical and artistic creativity, memory, visual and spatial
> awareness as well as listening and problem-solving skills. A create
> mode and a question and answer option are available. The difficulty
> level can be set on each activity. Works well with individual students,
> small groups, or for an entire class with a projection device.
> SUBJ: Problem solving--Software./ Software--Problem solving./
> Thought and thinking--Software./ Software--Thought and thinking./
> Creative ability--Software./ Software--Creative ability./ Interactive
> media.

CDR 370.15   Ph-1 3-A $59.95   OD KB082
THINKIN' THINGS COLLECTION 3. School version (CD-ROM). Edmark
702-1084, 1995. 1 CD-ROM color. (Thinkin' things series).
> Version 1.0.2.
> Includes teacher's guide.
> System requirements: Color Macintosh (256 colors required); 4MB
> RAM, 5MB required for System 7.5 (8MB recommended); CD-ROM
> drive (double-speed or faster recommended); System 7.0.1 or higher;
> 13" monitor or larger; microphone (optional); TouchWindow
> (optional).
> System requirements: Windows 3.1 (enhanced mode), Windows 95 or
> later; 8MB RAM; CD-ROM drive (double-speed or faster
> recommended); 486 processor (33 MHz or better recommended);
> Super VGA, 640x480 (256 colors, or more); hard disk with 2MB
> free; mouse; Windows-compatible sound-output device; microphone
> (optional); TouchWindow (optional).
> Product (702-1084) runs on either Windows or Macintosh compatible
> hardware.
> The five extraordinary activities in this program allow students to
> exercise logical reasoning, practice analyzing and synthesizing
> information, and continue to develop problem solving skills. A create
> mode and a question and answer option are available. The difficulty
> level can be set on each activity. Works well with individual students,
> small groups, or for an entire class with a projection device.
> SUBJ: Problem solving--Software./ Software--Problem solving./
> Thought and thinking--Software./ Software--Thought and thinking./
> Interactive media.

371.1   Ph-2 3-6/7 $14.95   L OD KB083
FISHER, LEONARD EVERETT. Schoolmasters. Benchmark Books ISBN
0-7614-0480-5, 1997. 47p. ill. (Colonial craftsmen).
> Originally published in New York, F. Watts, 1967.
> Includes index.
> Traces development of education in Colonial America. Distinguished
> reverse scratch illustrations add to the interest of the text which can
> be used for reading aloud to support units on the Colonial era. Useful
> as the basis for an activity recreating an eighteenth century classroom
> or for student research.
> SUBJ: Teachers--History./ Schools--History./ Education--History./
> United States--History--Colonial period, ca. 1600-1775--Education.

371.19   Ph-2 3-6/7 $14.95   L KB084
HAUSHERR, ROSMARIE. One-room school at Squabble Hollow. Four
Winds/Macmillan ISBN 0-02-743250-5, 1988. 73p b&w photos.
> Portrays day-to-day activities in a one-room elementary school in
> Vermont. Black and white photographs coupled with a skillfully written
> text lift the work above the average as they capture the spirit of a
> disappearing approach to education. Useful as a discussion starter or
> as the basis for a comparison and contrast exercise.
> SUBJ: Squabble Hollow School (Caledonia County, Vt.)./ Schools.

CDR 371.3   Ph-1 P-2 $59.95   OD KB085
PLAYROOM (CD-ROM). Broderbund, 1990. 1 CD-ROM color.
> Includes program guide, and teacher's guide.
> System requirements: Macintosh and Power Macintosh; System 7.0.1
> or higher; 25MHz 68030 processor or faster, Power Macintosh; 8MB
> RAM; 5MB free; requires 2MB hard disk space; 2X CD-ROM drive or
> faster required; monitor: 13-inch or larger color, 256 colors; printer
> support: works with most popular Macintosh compatible printers
> (monochrome and color).
> System requirements: Windows 3.1 or Windows 95; 25MHz 386 or
> faster required; 4MB RAM for Windows 3.1, 8MB RAM for
> Windows 95; requires 2MB hard disk space; 2X CD-ROM drive or
> faster required; SVGA monitor/display card 640 x 480, 256 colors;
> Windows compatible sound device; printer support: works with most
> popular printers (monochrome and color) supported Windows.
> Product runs on either Macintosh or Windows compatible hardware.
> Youngsters will not only learn how to use a computer but will also
> gain skills in language, art, music, and problem solving as they
> explore the many activities found in this electronic playroom. The
> activity format is enticing for youngsters and works well with
> independent users or as a family activity. Playroom also works well in
> a learning center environment and with small cooperative groups.
> SUBJ: Educational games--Software./ Software--Educational games./
> Problem solving--Software./ Software--Problem solving./ Music--
> Software./ Software--Music.

CDR 371.3   Ph-1 K-4 $59.95   OD KB086
TREEHOUSE (CD-ROM). Broderbund, 1991. 1 CD-ROM color.
> Includes teacher's guide, program guide, kid's guide, and songbook.
> System requirements: Macintosh and Power Macintosh; System 7.0.1
> or higher; 25MHz 68030 processor or faster, Power Macintosh; 8MB
> RAM, 5MB free; requires 2MB hard disk space; 2X CD-ROM drive or
> faster required; monitor: 13-inch or larger color, 256 colors; printer
> support: works with most popular Macintosh compatible printers
> (monochrome and color).
> System requirements: Windows 3.1 or Windows 95; 33MHz 486 or
> faster required; 8MB RAM; requires 2MB hard disk space; 2X CD-
> ROM drive or faster required; SVGA monitor/display card 640 x
> 480, 256 colors; Windows compatible sound device; printer support:
> works with most popular printers (monochrome and color) supported
> by Windows.
> Product runs on either Macintosh or Windows compatible hardware.
> Designed as a sequel to PLAYROOM, this software provides activities
> in language, math, science, art, music, and problem solving. The
> exploration of each area of the treehouse and the backyard provides
> well designed, exciting activities for the user. Works well with
> individual users or small groups.
> SUBJ: Educational games--Software./ Software--Educational games./
> Problem solving--Software./ Software--Problem solving./ Music--
> Software./ Software--Music.

VCR 371.302   Ph-3 5-6 $33.10   OD KB087
HOW TO STUDY (Videocassette). World Book, 1988. 1/2" VHS
videocassette color (45min).
> Includes teacher's guide.
> Delivers a solid presentation of study and listening skills. Appendix

includes four practice activities for listening and note-taking. Particularly useful in small group or individual viewing settings.
SUBJ: Study skills.

371.302   Ph-2 4-6/7 $11.93   L   KB088
JAMES, ELIZABETH. How to write a great school report. By Elizabeth James and Carol Barkin. Lothrop, Lee & Shepard ISBN 0-688-02283-9, 1983. 79p.
    Includes index.
    Identifies the steps in writing a report and explains each part--choosing a topic, collecting information, taking notes, organizing information, writing and revising the final draft. Includes sample pages of reference books and suggested charts for organizing information. Will be a good basis for independent use in developing writing skills.
    SUBJ: Report writing./ Research./ English language--Composition and exercises./ Homework.

371.302   Ph-3 5-A/6 $14.95   L   KB089
MCINERNEY, CLAIRE. Tracking the facts: how to develop research skills. Illus. by Harry Pulver. Lerner ISBN 0-8225-2426-0, 1990. 64p. col. ill. (Study skills).
    Includes bibliography and index.
    Discusses the development of research skills from finding a topic to writing the final paper. Includes brainstorming, note taking, outlining and computer searches.
    SUBJ: Report writing./ Research./ Study skills.

MCP 371.302   Ph-3 5-A $99.95   OD   KB090
OWENS, PETER. Research paper writer (Microcomputer program). By Dr. Peter Owens. Tom Snyder Productions ISBN 1-55998-195-4, c1990. 4 3.5" program disks.
    Version 2.0, color.
    Includes teacher's guide with lesson plans and reproducible worksheets.
    Also available for Windows on 3.5" disks, or CD-ROM for Macintosh or Windows.
    System requirements: Macintosh (1MB), 2 drives, hard drive, printer.
    This simulation guides students through the process of writing a research paper. Taking notes, doing library research, developing a bibliography, doing interviews, reading tutorials on research, and saving notecards in text files all relate to solving the mystery of the hijacking of Flight 102. Works well with individuals and small groups.
    SUBJ: Report writing--Software./ Software--Report writing./ Research--Software./ Software--Research.

CDR 371.302   Ph-1 4-A $99.00   OD   KB091
STUDENT WRITING AND RESEARCH CENTER WITH COMPTON'S CONCISE ENCYCLOPEDIA (CD-ROM). Learning Company WRC3344AE, 1995. 1 CD-ROM color. (Interactive writing tools).
    Version 1.0.
    Includes user's guides and graphics reference card.
    System requirements: Windows IBM and compatibles; 486/33 MHz or better; 8MB RAM; hard disk (20MB free); 256-color SVGA; double-speed CD-ROM drive; DOS 3.1 or higher; Windows 3.1 or higher (including Windows '95); Windows-compatible sound card; mouse; keyboard. Supports all Windows-compatible printers.
    This superb tool combines COMPTON'S CONCISE ENCYCLOPEDIA with the word processor, STUDENT WRITING CENTER. The encyclopedia containing more than 8,000 pictures, 75 multimedia presentations, and over 15 hours of sound is easily accessed while the student is developing a report. Five document types, a bibliography maker, grammar and writing tips, a title page maker, and a journal feature with password protection as well as other features are included in the word processor.
    SUBJ: Report writing--Software./ Software--Report writing./ Research--Software./ Software--Research./ Desktop publishing--Software./ Software--Desktop publishing./ Encyclopedias and dictionaries--Software./ Software--Encyclopedias and dictionaries./ Interactive media.

VCR 371.302   Ph-2 5-A $99.95   OD   KB092
STUDY SKILLS PLUS ATTITUDE: THE WINNING COMBINATION (Videocassette). Sunburst Communicatons 2213, 1989. 2 programs on 1 1/2" VHS videocassette color.
    Find out how to recognize and work with your individual learning style. Strategies to improve study skills and test taking are presented also through real life situations. Can be used effectively by individuals or as a whole class activity. Price is a limiter.
    Contents: What's your study style? (15min); Getting good grades (15min).
    SUBJ: Study skills.

371.92   Ph-2 4-6/4 $10.95   P   KB093
CUMMINGS, RHODA WOODS. School survival guide for kids with LD (Learning differences). By Rhoda Woods Cummings and Gary L. Fisher. Ed. by Pamela Espeland. Free Spirit ISBN 0-915793-32-6, 1991. 164p. ill. (Self-help for kids).
    Includes directory, bibliographies and index.
    Provides commonsense suggestions of ways to improve school life and learning for children with learning differences. Bibliographies include references and listings of recommended learning and teaching materials. Useful for students, teachers, and parents. (Parents' Shelf)
    SUBJ: Learning disabilities.

371.92   Ph-1 4-6/4 $9.95   P   KB094
FISHER, GARY L. Survival guide for kids with LD (Learning differences). By Gary L. Fisher and Rhoda Woods Cummings. Edited by Nancy J. Nielsen. Illus. by Jackie Urbanovic. Free Spirit ISBN 0-915793-18-0, 1990. 97p. ill.
    Includes discography, bibliographies, directories and index.
    Discusses the issues of learning disabilities and offers realistic suggestions for getting along in school and at home. Tone is casual and easygoing; final chapter is directed to parents and teachers. Valuable resource in collections of all sizes. (Parents' Shelf).
    SUBJ: Learning disabilities.

371.92   Ph-3 K-3/2 $14.95   T   KB095
GEHRET, JEANNE. Don't-give-up Kid and learning differences. 2nd ed. Illus. by Sandra Ann DePauw. Verbal Images Press ISBN 1-88428-115-X, 1996. unp. ill.
    Includes glossary, directory and bibliography.
    A first-person account of a young boy with attention deficit disorder. Gives a clear understanding of the difficulties faced by children with ADD. Can be used as bibliotheraphy. Provides a parents' resource section. (Parents' Shelf).
    SUBJ: Learning disabilities.

371.92   Ph-2 4-6/6 $13.95   L   KB096
ROBY, CYNTHIA. When learning is tough: kids talk about their learning disabilities. Photos by Elena Dorfman. Whitman ISBN 0-8075-8892-X; In Canada: General, 1994. 56p. ill.
    Includes directory.
    Provides first-person interviews with eight young people who have learning disabilities. Black-and-white photographs illustrate the text which provides child-to-child tips for coping with LD.
    SUBJ: Learning disabilities.

372.21   Ph-2 P-K/2 $14.93   L   KB097
HOWE, JAMES. When you go to kindergarten. Rev. and updated ed. Photos by Betsy Imershein. Morrow ISBN 0-688-12913-7, 1994. unp. col. ill.
    Answers questions preschoolers may have about kindergarten life. Photographs support a text which is designed to improve a child's confidence as he enters the world of "big school." Works well as a parent-child one-on-one. (Parents' Shelf).
    SUBJ: Kindergarten./ Schools.

372.21   Ph-2 P-3/2 $12.95   L   KB098
KUKLIN, SUSAN. Going to my nursery school. Bradbury ISBN 0-02-751237-1; In Canada: Collier Macmillan, 1990. unp col photos.
    Includes "What to Look For in a Nursery School."
    Offers a you-are-there photographic tour of nursery school as experienced by a four-year-old boy. An afterword for parents discusses considerations in selecting a nursery school. Helpful with parents and a happy choice for a young reader to take home to share with a younger brother or sister. (Parents' Shelf).
    SUBJ: Nursery schools./ Schools.

VCR 372.4   Ph-1 P-2 $24.95   OD   KB099
ABC'S AND SUCH (Videocassette). Waterford Institute ISBN 0-9634283-4-9, 1993. 1/2" VHS videocassette color (35min). (Rusty and Rosy).
    Features multisensory approach, concept strength, and classical music. A high-appeal item in any collection serving the young. "...with a design, delivery, and price that both teachers and parents can love..." (BL 2/1/94) (Parents' Shelf).
    SUBJ: Reading (Preschool)--Phonetic method./ Alphabet.

CDR 372.4   Ph-1 P-2 $59.95   OD   KB100
BAILEY'S BOOK HOUSE (CD-ROM). Edmark, 1995. 1 CD-ROM color. (Early learning house).
    Includes user's guide.
    Version 2.0.
    System requirements: Windows 3.1 (enhanced mode), Windows 95 or later; 4MB required (8MB highly recommended); CD-ROM drive (double-speed or faster recommended); 386DX/33 MHz required

(486/33 MHz or better recommended); super VGA, 640x480 (256 colors, or more, required); hard disk with 2MB free; mouse; Windows-compatible sound-output device; Windows compatible printer (optional); TouchWindow (optional).
System requirements: Macintosh: color Macintosh (256 colors required); 4MB (8MB recommended); CD-ROM drive (double-speed or faster recommended); System 7.0.1 or higher; 13" or larger monitor; printer (optional); TouchWindow (optional).
Product runs on either Windows or Macintosh compatible hardware. The animation, graphics, and clear sound make this program a superb method for introducing preschoolers to the computer and literacy. Seven activities help the user learn about letters, words, and writing. The excellent speech makes adult help unnecessary.
SUBJ: Reading (Preschool)--Software./ Software--Reading (Preschool)./ Writing--Software./ Software--Writing./ Interactive media.

MCP 372.4   Ph-1 P-2 $49.95   OD KB101
BAILEY'S BOOK HOUSE (Microcomputer program). Edmark 406-1302, 1993. 3 3.5" high density disks. (Early learning house).
Includes teacher's guide and reproducible activity sheets.
Also available for Windows/DOS.
Selectors' Choice, 20th ed.
System requirements: Macintosh Plus or later; hard disk drive with 8MB available during installation; System 6.0.7 or later, 1MB RAM--black and white, 2MB RAM--color; System 7 or later, 2MB RAM--black and white, 4MB RAM--color. Printer, TouchWindow (optional).
The animation, graphics, and clear sound make this program a superb method for introducing preschoolers to the computer and literacy. Five activities help the user learn about letters, words, and writing. The excellent speech makes adult help unnecessary.
SUBJ: Reading (Preschool)--Software./ Software--Reading (Preschool)./ Writing--Software./ Software--Writing.

SRC 372.4   Ph-2 K-2 $18.95   OD KB102
GALLINA, MICHAEL. Alphabet in action: consonants and vowels taught through song and motor activities (Sound recording cassette). Words and music by Jill Gallina. Kimbo KIM 1210XC, 1978. 1 sounce cassette (30 duplicating masters.
Includes guide.
Encourages the listener to identify the beginning consonant and vowel sounds of words and participate in a motor activity when the correct sound is identified. An enjoyable learning activity with clever songs and pleasant narration. Will be useful in early childhood programs in reading readiness preparation.
SUBJ: Reading games.

372.4   Ph-2 P-1/2 $16.99   L   KB103
MILES, BETTY. Hey! I'm reading!: a how-to-read book for beginners. Illus. by Sylvie Wickstrom. Knopf ISBN 0-679-95644-1; In Canada: Random House, 1995. 59p. col. ill.
"Borzoi book."
Offers reassuring answers about reading and helpful suggestions to the anxious. Closing portions provide casual opportunity for practice and success. Will be a popular resource for parents of preschoolers and those just beginning to read. (Parents' Shelf).
SUBJ: Reading./ Readers.

VCR 372.4   Ph-1 P-2 $24.95   OD KB104
NURSERY SONGS AND RHYMES (Videocassette). Waterford Institute ISBN 0-9634283-5-7, 1993. 1/2" VHS videocassette color (37min).
Twenty-six nursery rhymes teach basic reading concepts in a lively computer animated presentation. Stresses word and letter recognition using lyrics from popular songs. Useful in whole language classrooms or home environments. (Parents' Shelf).
SUBJ: Reading (Preschool)./ Nursery rhymes./ Songs.

CDR 372.4   Ph-1 K-2 $99.95   OD KB105
READ, WRITE AND TYPE! (CD-ROM). Learning Company 25094, 1996. 1 CD-ROM color. (Interactive writing tools).
Includes user's guides.
System requirements: IBM PC and compatibles; 486SX/33MHz minimum processor; 256-color display; 4MB RAM (8MB recommended if running Windows 95); MS-DOS 5.0 or later; Windows 3.1 or later (including Windows 95); PC sound card; hard disk; mouse; double-speed CD-ROM drive.
System requirements: Macintosh 68030 minimum processor; 256-color display; 4MB RAM; 4MB for System 7.0.1, 5MB for System 7.5; hard disk; mouse; double-speed CD-ROM drive.
Product (25094) runs on either Windows or Macintosh compatible hardware.
Over 200 game activities not only help youngsters learn to type but also sharpen phonics and reading skills. Each key has a speech sound, a story, and another memory booster to help the user memorize the

keyboard. As the keyboard is learned, keys are also rescued from Vexor the Virus and returned to the Storytellers. Youngsters are entranced with this program. (Parents' Shelf).
SUBJ: Reading (Primary)--Software./ Software--Reading (Primary)./ Writing--Software./ Software--Writing./ Typewriting--Software./ Software--Typewriting./ Interactive media.

MCP 372.4   Ph-1 1-3 $79.95   OD KB106
READER RABBIT 3 (Microcomputer program). Learning Company 24096, 1993. 2 3.5" disks.
Includes user's guide.
Also available on Macintosh.
System requirements: IBM, AT and compatibles with 640K; 80286 or better; Hard disk with 3MB free; 3.5" drive; DOS 3.3 or greater; 256-color VGA; 10 MHz minimum clock speed; Mouse, Sound Blaster and compatible sound cards, Laser, inkjet, or dot matrix printer (Laser printer must have at least 1MB of memory, (Optional).
The third member of the series follows a newspaper motif while students search for the who, what, when, and where of the stories in four activities. When the youngster has completed one story from each activity, the paper is ready to print. Works well with individual students as a learning center. (Parents' Shelf).
SUBJ: Reading (Primary)--Software./ Software--Reading (Primary)./ Writing--Software./ Software--Writing./ Newspapers--Software./ Software--Newspapers.

MCP 372.4   Ph-1 P-1 $35.00   OD KB107
READER RABBIT'S READY FOR LETTERS (Microcomputer program). Learning Company, 1994. 1 3.5" disk and 1 5.25" disk.
Includes user's guide.
Version 1.1.
Also available for Macintosh.
System requirements: IBM or compatibles with 640K; 3.5" or 5.25" high-density drive; 8 MHz; hard disk with 1MB free (optional); color monitor; (256-color VGA or MCGA, 16-color EGA or TGA); DOS 2.0 or higher; mouse (optional); Windows 3.1 (optional); Sound Blaster or compatible sound cards (optional).
Youngsters will be delighted with the activities which help build visual discrimination, letter recognition, and simple word understanding. The easy-to-understand speech makes this program truly one for a nonreader. Superb graphics and animation make the program appealing to preschoolers. (Parents' Shelf).
SUBJ: Reading (Preschool)--Software./ Software--Reading (Preschool)./ Reading games--Software./ Software--Reading games.

MCP 372.6   Ph-1 5-A $139.00   OD KB108
BRIDGE TO TERABITHIA: A MULTI-MEDIA STUDY (Microcomputer program). Humanities Software/dist. by Sunburst IM307-M, 1993. 1 3.5" disk. (Write on!).
Includes teacher's guide.
Also available in MS-DOS (IM307-D) and Windows (IM307-W) disks, and Macintosh/Windows CD-ROM (IM316), $139.00.
System requirements: Macintosh Classic or later; 4MB RAM; Operating System 6.0.7 or above; hard drive, 3.5" high density floppy disk drive; 200k to 1MB of hard disk space; Macintosh compatible printer.
Program contains a series of 11 writing activities tied to the book and video versions of this literary classic. Young writers work on describing the setting, writing dialogue, comparing the book and the video, as well as other activities. Loads easily on a network or stand-alone computer. Software is sold separately from the book and video.
SUBJ: Writing--Software./ Software--Writing./ English language--Composition and exercises--Software./ Software--English language--Composition and exercises.

MCP 372.6   Ph-3 2-6 $139.00   OD KB109
BROWN, MARC TOLON. Arthur's teacher trouble (Microcomputer program). Humanities Software/dist. by Sunburst PM225, 1994. 1 3.5" data disk, 1 CD-ROM, 1 paperback book. (Write on!).
Includes teacher's guide and supplemental manual.
Also available in Apple II, MS-DOS and Windows versions.
CD-ROM available separately from Broderbund.
System requirements: any Macintosh system with a word processing package.
Well-developed writing activities extend Broderbund's ARTHUR'S TEACHER TROUBLE for those using whole language approaches. Files can be used by all major word processors and ASCII files are also included. Excellent for use with peer editing groups.
SUBJ: Writing--Software./ Software--Writing./ Spanish language materials--Software./ Software--Spanish language materials./ Bilingual materials--Spanish--Software./ Software--Bilingual materials--Spanish.

MCP 372.6　　　　　　　Ph-1 3-6　　$139.00　　OD KB110
CHARLOTTE'S WEB: A WRITE ON! MULTI-MEDIA STUDY
(Microcomputer program). Humanities Software/dist. by Sunburst
EM227, 1992. 1 3.5″ disk. (Write on!).
　　Includes teacher's manual, supplemental manual, instruction card,
　　student disk labels and reproducibles.
　　Includes 1/2″ VHS videocassette color (94min) and 1 paperback
　　book.
　　Also available on 5.25″ disk.
　　System requirements: Apple MacIntosh computer, printer
　　recommended, video tape player, LCD or Large screen monitor or
　　overhead transparency viewer.
　　The Paramount Picture version of CHARLOTTE'S WEB is combined
　　with 13 superb writing exercises. The word processing files will work
　　with most standard software programs. Good activities to support
　　whole language learning and provide peer editing practice.
　　SUBJ: Writing--Software./ Software--Writing./ English language--
　　Composition and exercises--Software./ Software--English language--
　　Composition and exercises.

CDR 372.6　　　　　　　Ph-1 1-A　　$39.95　　OD KB111
DESTINATION: OCEAN. School version (CD-ROM). Edmark 602-1085,
1995. 1 CD-ROM color. (Imagination express).
　　Includes teacher's guide.
　　Version 2.0.
　　System requirements: Color Macintosh (256 colors required); 8MB
　　RAM required; CD-ROM drive (doublespeed or faster recommended);
　　System 7 or higher; 13″ or larger monitor; hard disk with 4MB free;
　　printer and microphone recommended.
　　System requirements: Windows 3.1 (enhanced mode) or later; 8MB
　　RAM required; CD-ROM drive (doublespeed or faster recommended);
　　25 MHz 386 or better; Super VGA, 640x480 (256 colors or more,
　　required); hard disk with 4MB free; mouse; Windows-compatible
　　sound-output device; Windows-compatible printer and microphone
　　(recommended).
　　Product (602-1085) runs on either Windows or Macintosh compatible
　　hardware.
　　This program enables writers to create electronic stories for sharing
　　with classmates via large monitors or learning centers. Excellent
　　graphics are used for backgrounds; tools help youngsters learn
　　perspective as well as visual presentation skills. Good introduction for
　　oral presentations with visual aids.
　　DESTINATION: CASTLE. SCHOOL VERSION (CD-ROM) Edmark
　　602-1607, 1994. 1 CD-ROM color, $39.95.
　　DESTINATION: NEIGHBORHOOD. SCHOOL VERSION (CD-ROM)
　　Edmark 602-1605, 1994. 1 CD-ROM color, $39.95.
　　DESTINATION: RAIN FOREST. SCHOOL VERSION (CD-ROM)
　　Edmark 602-1608, 1994. 1 CD-ROM color, $39.95.
　　DESTINATION: PYRAMIDS. SCHOOL VERSION (CD-ROM)
　　Edmark/Harcourt Brace 602-1606, 1996. 1 CD-ROM color, $39.95.
　　DESTINATION: TIME TRIP, USA. SCHOOL VERSION (CD-ROM)
　　Edmark/Harcourt Brace 602-1634, 1996. 1 CD-ROM color, $39.95.
　　SUBJ: Writing--Software./ Software--Writing./ English language--
　　Composition and exercises--Software./ Software--English language--
　　Composition and exercises./ Interactive media.

MCP 372.6　　　　　　　Ph-1 2-5　　$139.00　　OD KB112
ECOLOGY WITH SEUSS (Microcomputer program). Humanities
Software/dist. by Sunburst E218, 1990. 1 3.5″ data disk. (Write on!).
　　With 1 copy of LORAX, $86.95.
　　Includes 1 reproducible data disk, 1 instruction card, 32 student disk
　　labels, teacher's manual and supplement.
　　Also available on Apple II family and MS-DOS.
　　System requirements: Macintosh; 1 disk drive (2 preferred); monitor;
　　word processing program (MaxWrite I and II, Microsoft Word,
　　Microsoft Works, WordPerfect, Word Weaver, Write Now, or any
　　text-base word processor); data disks.
　　Valuable for use with a whole language approach, the thirteen
　　activities included with this software engage youngsters in writing
　　through literature. Experiences in making predictions, writing poems,
　　developing advertisements, and solving moral dilemmas are included.
　　Materials work well with individual students or cooperative group
　　writing.
　　SUBJ: Writing--Software./ Software--Writing./ Ecology--Software./
　　Software--Ecology.

MCP 372.6　　　　　　　Ph-1 4-6　　$139.00　　OD KB113
INDIAN IN THE CUPBOARD (Microcomputer program). Humanities
Software/dist. by Sunburst I308, 1991. 1 3.5″ data disk. (Write on!).
　　Includes class set of disk labels, user's manual, teacher's manual, and
　　teacher's manual supplement.
　　Also available on Apple II family and MS-DOS.
　　System requirements: Macintosh, disk drive, monitor, printer preferred,
　　compatible word processing program, blank disks.

Valuable for use with a whole language approach, the eighteen
activities included with this software engage youngsters in writing
through literature. Experiences in making predictions, writing poems,
comparing and contrasting, dealing with irony, and solving moral
dilemmas are included. Materials work well with individual students or
cooperative group writing.
　　SUBJ: Writing--Software./ Software--Writing.

CDR 372.6　　　　　　　Ph-1 2-A　　$29.95　　OD KB114
MICROSOFT CREATIVE WRITER 2. School ed. (CD-ROM). Microsoft
ISBN 1-57231-472-9; In Canada: Microsoft Canada, 1996. 1 CD-ROM
color.
　　Version 2.0.
　　Includes user's guide and teacher's guide.
　　ALA notable computer software, 1997.
　　System requirements: Multimedia PC with a 486/33 MHz or higher
　　processor; Microsoft Windows 95 operating system or Windows NT
　　4.0 operating system; 8MB of memory (RAM), 16MB optimal; 16MB
　　of available hard-disk space, 22MB optimal; double-speed CD-ROM
　　drive; Super VGA, 256-color monitor; Audio board with speakers or
　　headphones; Microsoft Windows-compatible modem and on-line
　　service required for e-mail and Web pages.
　　This is an easy-to-use word processor that includes backgrounds,
　　stamps, special printing effects, and sounds. The web publishing
　　features allow for easy creation and publishing of intranet and
　　Internet web sites. The on-line tools are simple to configure and use.
　　Newsletters, cards, banners, and stories can be created, illustrated,
　　and printed. An idea workshop contains more than 8,000 story
　　starters for creative writing activities.
　　SUBJ: Desktop publishing--Software./ Software--Desktop publishing./
　　Writing--Software./ Software--Writing./ English language--
　　Composition and exercises--Software./ Software--English language--
　　Composition and exercises./ Interactive media.

CDR 372.6　　　　　　　Ph-1 3-A　　$99.95　　OD KB115
MULTIMEDIA WORKSHOP. Teacher ed. (CD-ROM). Davidson 3172
ISBN 0-7849-0516-9, 1996. 1 CD-ROM color. (Cool tools).
　　Includes teacher's guide.
　　Also available in Windows CD-ROM (1803), $99.95.
　　System requirements: LC II, Performa, Centris and Quadra Series and
　　PowerBooks with color or grayscale capabilities supports 256-color
　　graphics and 4MB of RAM (with 2MB free); supports thousands of
　　colors with 8MB of RAM; System 7.0 or higher; CD-ROM drive; hard
　　drive; microphone and printer highly recommended.
　　This tool allows students to create a variety of print and multimedia
　　projects. Authors can easily add still pictures, QuickTime movies, and
　　sound to any project. Logical operation requires little instruction for
　　average computer users.
　　Also available in Spanish/English MULTIMEDIA WORKSHOP
　　BILINGUAL (2288), $149.95.
　　SUBJ: Desktop publishing--Software./ Software--Desktop publishing./
　　Writing--Software./ Software--Writing./ Design--Software./
　　Software--Design./ Spanish language materials--Software./ Software-
　　-Spanish language materials./ Bilingual materials--Spanish--Software./
　　Software--Bilingual materials--Spanish./ Interactive media.

MCP 372.6　　　　　　　Ph-2 1-3　　$139.00　　OD KB116
MY FIRST SENTENCES (Microcomputer program). Humanities
Software/dist. by Sunburst P275, 1987. 1 3.5″ data disk. (Write on!).
　　Includes teacher's guide and supplemental manual.
　　Also available in Apple II, MS-DOS and Windows versions.
　　System requirements: any Macintosh system with a word processing
　　package.
　　Writing activities are designed to allow experimenting with nouns,
　　verbs, adverbs, pronouns, and adjectives. Separate student and
　　teacher files make management easy. Files are included for all major
　　word processors as well as an ASCII version. Excellent for use with
　　peer editing groups.
　　SUBJ: Writing--Software./ Software--Writing./ English language--
　　Grammar--Software./ Software--English language--Grammar.

CDR 372.6　　　　　　　Ph-1 P-2　　$59.95　　OD KB117
STANLEY'S STICKER STORIES. School version (CD-ROM). Edmark/
Harcourt Brace 702-1078, 1996. 1 CD-ROM color. (Early learning
house).
　　Version 1.03.
　　Includes teacher's guide.
　　System requirements: System 7 or higher; 68040, 68030, or
　　PowerPC; hard disk with 4MB free; 8MB RAM, 4100K free; 13″
　　monitor or larger (256 colors); double-speed or faster CD-ROM
　　drive; microphone (optional); printer (optional); TouchWindow
　　(optional).
　　System requirements: Windows 3.1 (enhanced mode), Windows 95 or
　　later; 486, Pentium, or better; hard disk with 4MB free; 8MB RAM;

Super VGA, 640x480 (256 colors); double-speed or faster CD-ROM drive; Windows-compatible sound card; microphone (optional); Windows-compatible printer (optional); TouchWindow (optional). Product (702-1078) runs on either Windows or Macintosh compatible hardware.
Part of the superb Early Learning Series, Stanley introduces budding authors to the world of writing and illustrating. Animated stories with music and narration can be easily created with the various backgrounds and over 325 stickers. The excellent audio help feature makes the program easy to use for beginning readers.
SUBJ: Writing--Software./ Software--Writing./ Creative writing--Software./ Software--Creative writing./ Desktop publishing--Software./ Software--Desktop publishing./ Interactive media.

CDR 372.6 Ph-2 1-5 $79.00 OD KB118
STORYBOOK WEAVER DELUXE (CD-ROM). MECC CD-642 ISBN 0-7929-0866-X, 1995. 1 CD-ROM color.
Version 1.1.
Includes teacher's guide.
System requirements: color-capable Macintosh; 5MB RAM; System 7.1 or later; hard disk; 13-inch or larger color display; CD-ROM drive; mouse; printer (optional).
Product (CD742) runs on either Macintosh or Windows compatible hardware.
This is the combination of MECC's MY OWN STORIES and STORYBOOK WEAVER. The easy-to-use desktop publishing features and the ability to add up to 99 sound effects, to incorporate original artwork, and to have stories read aloud with a computerized voice make the writing process come alive for the user. Stories can be read in English or Spanish. Enhanced features allow Version 1.1 to use add-on graphics, sounds, music, and borders via STORY PACKS, which will not work with Version 1.0.
Microcomputer supplemental programs are: STORY PACK FOR STORYBOOK WEAVER DELUXE FEATURING HOLLYWOOD HOUNDS and STORY PACK FOR STORYBOOK WEAVER DELUXE FEATURING DINKYTOWN DAY CARE KIDS. 3.5" disk, $14.95 ea.
SUBJ: English language--Composition and exercises--Software./ Software--English language--Composition and exercises./ Writing--Software./ Software--Writing./ Spanish language materials--Software./ Software--Spanish language materials./ Bilingual materials--Spanish--Software./ Software--Bilingual materials--Spanish./ Interactive media.

MCP 372.6 Ph-1 4-6 $139.00 OD KB119
TUCK EVERLASTING (Microcomputer program). Humanities Software/ dist. by Sunburst I302, 1989. 1 3.5" data disk. (Write on!).
Includes class set of disk labels, handout (1 sheet), user's guide, and teacher's manual and teacher's manual supplement.
Also available on Apple II family, Windows, and MS-DOS.
System requirements: Macintosh, disk drive, monitor, printer preferred, blank disks preferred.
Valuable for use with a whole language approach, the fifteen activities included with this software engage youngsters in writing through literature. Experiences in descriptive writing, character sketches, plot development, point of view, and dealing with moral dilemmas are included. Materials work well with individual students or cooperative group writing.
SUBJ: Writing--Software./ Software--Writing.

CDR 372.6 Ph-1 K-5 $69.95 OD KB120
ULTIMATE WRITING AND CREATIVITY CENTER. School ed. (CD-ROM). Learning Company 65118, 1996. 1 CD-ROM color. (Interactive writing tools).
Version 1.2.
Includes user's guide, teacher's guide and activity sheets.
System requirements: Macintosh 68040/33 MHz or better, including the following models: any Power Macintosh, Centris, Quadra, Performa 460 or greater, LC 550 or greater, and IIfx or greater; 12MB memory (RAM), 16MB for Power Macintosh; hard disk with 15MB free disk space; double-speed or higher CD-ROM drive; 256-color monitor (13" or larger); System 7.0.1 or higher; mouse; any Macintosh-compatible printer (optional).
System requirements: IBM PC and compatibles (486DX/33 MHz or better); 8MB memory (RAM); hard disk with 30MB free disk space; double-speed or higher CD-ROM drive; 256-color VGA monitor (640x480); DOS 5.0 or higher; Windows 3.1 or higher (including Windows 95); Windows-compatible sound card; mouse; any Windows-compatible printer, except plotters (optional).
Product (65118) runs on either Macintosh or Windows compatible hardware.
This word processing program includes a wide range of drawing tools, a variety of clip art, and a presentation mode in which the document is read by the computer. Options for a spelling checker, a story starter feature, and ideas for writing projects involving research

are included. Compare with the AMAZING WRITING MACHINE. A useful tool for creative writing activities.
SUBJ: Writing--Software./ Software--Writing./ Desktop publishing--Software./ Software--Desktop publishing./ Interactive media.

MCP 372.6 Ph-3 4-A $69.00 OD KB121
WRITING ALONG THE OREGON TRAIL (Microcomputer program). MECC MC236 ISBN 0-7929-0782-5, 1994. 4 3.5" disks.
Version 1.0.
Companion software to THE OREGON TRAIL.
Includes user's manual.
Also available for Windows (MW436).
System requirements: Macintosh Plus or later; System 6.0.8 or later, 2 MB of free RAM for color or 1 MB free RAM for black and white; 4 MB of free RAM is desirable if working with two or more of the integrated ClarisWorks or Microsoft Works applications at the same time; ClarisWorks 2.0, or Microsoft Works 3.0, or Word Weaver 2.0. Hard disk; printer, high-density disk drive.
These writing activities are based on thematic curriculum designed to enrich the simulation program OREGON TRAIL. 45 projects as well as publishing templates and databases are included. Excellent materials to use with individual students and small groups.
SUBJ: English language--Composition and exercises--Software./ Software--English language--Composition and exercises./ Creative writing--Software./ Software--Creative writing./ Oregon Trail--Software./ Software--Oregon Trail./ Overland journeys to the Pacific--Software./ Software--Overland journeys to the Pacific.

VCR 372.67 Ph-3 1-3 $145.00 OD KB122
STOTTER, RUTH. Origami stories (Videocassette). Chip Taylor Communications, 1993. 1/2" VHS videocassette color (12min). (Master storyteller series).
Noted storyteller, Ruth Stotter, adds another dimension to her tales by incorporating origami. Using simple paperfolding techniques, she enlivens such stories as "Rain hat" and "Hot lips."
SUBJ: Storytelling./ Origami.

372.973 Ph-2 4-6/8 $13.95 L KB123
LOEPER, JOHN J. Going to school in 1776. Atheneum ISBN 0-689-30089-1; In Canada: Collier Macmillan, 1973. 79p illus.
Includes bibliography.
Explores the education and everyday life of children in the early days of our country. Begins by giving an overview vignettes of the everyday life and education of children from many parts of the colonies.
SUBJ: Education--United States--History--Colonial period, ca. 1600-1775./ Schools--History./ Frontier and pioneer life--United States./ United States--Social life and customs--To 1775.

372.973 Ph-2 3-6/7 $13.95 L KB124
LOEPER, JOHN J. Going to school in 1876. Atheneum ISBN 0-689-31015-3; In Canada: Collier Macmillan, 1984. 83p b&w illus.
Includes bibliography.
Describes the education and everyday life of school children in 1876. Personal accounts based on primary sources with supportive period drawings lend authenticity. As a sequel to GOING TO SCHOOL IN 1776, this will provide a more complete picture for social studies curriculum.
SUBJ: Schools--History./ United States--Social life and customs--1865-1918.

VCR 373.2 Ph-2 5-6 $99.95 OD KB125
HOW TO SUCCEED IN MIDDLE SCHOOL (Videocassette). Sunburst Communications 2446 ISBN 0-7805-4144-8, 1994. 1/2" VHS videocassette color (22min).
Includes teacher's guide.
Offers strategies and suggestions designed to help students make a successful transition to middle school. Ideas presented are practical and workable; annotated bibliography leads to additional resources. Useful with student and parent groups. (Parents' Shelf).
SUBJ: Middle schools./ Schools.

381 Ph-1 1-3/2 $18.00 L KB126
FLANAGAN, ALICE. Busy day at Mr. Kang's grocery store. By Alice K. Flanagan. Photos by Christine Osinski. Reading consultant, Linda Cornwell. Children's Press ISBN 0-516-20047-X; In Canada: Children's Press, 1996. 32p. col. ill. (Our neighborhood).
Depicts everyday events in the life of Mr. Kang, recently emigrated from Korea, as he and his family operate a neighborhood store. Full-color photographs with lots of close-ups add appeal. For multicultural studies and community helper units.
SUBJ: Grocery trade./ Occupations.

381   Ph-2 1-4/6 $15.99   L   KB127
HAUTZIG, DAVID. At the supermarket. Orchard ISBN 0-531-08682-8, 1994. unp. col. ill.
Takes the reader behind the scenes of a large supermarket as deliveries are received and store employees carry out the specialized tasks which make a complicated system work. Use for career studies and in discussions of community economics.
SUBJ: Supermarkets.

381   Ph-1 1-3/6 $15.93   L   KB128
LEWIN, TED. Market! Lothrop, Lee & Shepard ISBN 0-688-12162-4, 1996. unp. col. ill.
An intriguing visit to markets of the world from Equador, Nepal, and Ireland to Uganda, New York, and Morocco. Detailed, vibrant illustrations capture the excitement and activity of buyer and seller and convey a flavor of the uniqueness of each market. Use in multicultural studies and to compare and contrast details of a universal cultural experience.
SUBJ: Markets./ Culture.

383   Ph-1 2-5/8 $16.00   T   KB129
HARNESS, CHERYL. They're off!: the story of the Pony Express. Simon & Schuster ISBN 0-689-80523-3; In Canada: Distican, 1996. unp. col. ill., maps.
Includes bibliography.
Presents the exciting saga of the Pony Express from its inception in 1860 to its replacement by the telegraph in 1861, with details of its founding and individual rider's adventures. Illustrated with lively watercolors and informative maps. An appealing choice to supplement units on communications, the United States Postal Service, and the American West.
SUBJ: Pony express./ West (U.S.)--History./ Postal service--United States--History.

383   Ph-1 4-6/6 $16.95   L   KB130
KROLL, STEVEN. Pony Express! Illus. by Dan Andreasen. Scholastic ISBN 0-590-20239-1; In Canada: Scholastic, 1996. 40p. col. ill., maps.
Includes bibliography and index.
"Discusses the eighteen month history, officially beginning April 3, 1860, of the mail delivery between Saint Joseph, Missouri, and Sacramento, California, known as the Pony Express." (CIP) Full-page illustrations capture the flavor of the text; also includes a map of route stations and a few archival photographs. This will have high appeal for students interested in the Old West, and it can be used to provide background and comparisons for units on the Post Office.
SUBJ: Pony express./ West (U.S.)--History./ Postal service--United States--History.

VCR 383   Ph-2 1-4 $79.00   OD KB131
POST OFFICE (Videocassette). National Geographic 51472, 1991. 1/2" VHS videocassette color (15min). (Your town).
Includes Teacher's Guide.
Follows a birthday card on its journey to its recipient, displaying modern postal technology en route. Technical quality is good in this video which extends its life by avoidance of specific postage rates. Valuable as a knowledge expander.
SUBJ: Postal service.

VCR 383   Ph-2 K-4 $34.95   OD KB132
POSTAL STATION (Videocassette). TVOntario/dist. by Films for the Humanities, 1991. 1/2" VHS videocassette color (10min). (Here's how!).
Includes teacher's guide.
Offers a brief history of letter writing and then tours an automated postal station in Canada. Script is solid and production values are good.
SUBJ: Postal service--Canada./ Letter writing.

383   Ph-3 1-4/4 $13.95   L   KB133
SKURZYNSKI, GLORIA. Here comes the mail. Bradbury/Macmillan ISBN 0-02-782916-2; In Canada: Maxwell Macmillan, 1992. unp. col. ill.
Follows Stephanie's letter to her cousin from idea to delivery. Final pages show preferred form for addressing envelopes and provide state abbreviations. Useful in support of language arts.
SUBJ: Postal service.

384.3   Ph-2 2-4/3 $19.00   L   KB134
BRIMNER, LARRY DANE. E-mail. Children's Press ISBN 0-516-20332-0; In Canada: Grolier Ltd., 1997. 48p. col. ill.
Includes bibliographies.
An introduction to e-mail with information about how it works, parts of an address, abbreviations and symbols, mailing lists, and netiquette. Illustrated with photographs and graphics, some of which show addresses of various organizations of interest. Beginning e-mailers will find this clear and informative.

SUBJ: Electronic mail systems./ Internet (Computer network)./ Information superhighway.

VCR 384.6   Ph-1 2-5 $80.00   KB135
EMERGENCY 911 (Videocassette). National Geographic 51602, 1994. 1/2" VHS videocassette color (22min).
Includes teacher's guide.
Describes the 911 network, and explains how children and adults can use it to save lives and property. Activities suggested in the brief guide are for primary students. Valuable in safety units.
SUBJ: Telephone./ Emergency medical services./ Rescue work.

VCR 384.6   Ph-2 2-6 $19.95   OD KB136
USING 911: PROTECT YOURSELF (Videocassette). Lucent Technologies/AT&T, 1995. 1/2" VHS videocassette color (18min).
Includes teacher's guide.
Includes public performance rights.
A basic introduction to 911 emergency service uses enactments and role-playing to demonstrate how emergencies are handled by police, fire, and other agencies, gives procedures for making emergency calls, and shows appropriate behavior and responses while on the line. A straightforward, information-filled production that will be useful to introduce students to correct and confident use of 911 emergency service.
SUBJ: Telephone./ Emergency medical services./ Rescue work.

385   Ph-1 4-6/10 $18.95   T   KB137
BLUMBERG, RHODA. Full steam ahead: the race to build a transcontinental railroad. National Geographic ISBN 0-7922-2715-8, 1996. 159p. ill., maps.
Includes bibliographies and index.
A detailed, readable account of the intricacies, political maneuverings, use of Chinese labor, challenges of construction, and rivalries between competing companies in the planning and building of the transcontinental railroad. Illustrated with period photographs, cartoons, graphics, and maps. A valuable resource in units on westward expansion and United States history units covering the period from 1859-1869.
SUBJ: Union Pacific Railroad Company--History./ Central Pacific Railroad Company--History./ Railroads--History.

PIC 385   Ph-2 5-6 $43.00   OD KB138
BUILDING THE FIRST TRANSCONTINENTAL RAILROAD (Picture). Documentary Photo Aids 21E, n.d. 25 study prints (11"x14").
Authentic period photographs showing the construction of the first transcontinental railroad. With captions.
SUBJ: Railroads--History.

385   Ph-1 5-6/7 $6.95   P   KB139
FRASER, MARY ANN. Ten mile day and the building of the transcontinental railroad. Henry Holt ISBN 0-8050-4703-4; In Canada: Fitzhenry & Whiteside, c1993, 1996. unp. col. ill., map.
Includes bibliography and glossary.
Details events of a record ten mile day as the Central Pacific Railroad crews pushed to join the Union Pacific in the 1869 completion of the first transcontinental rail route. Endpapers include a map, glossary, elevations, and depiction of railroad tools. Strong support for Westward Movement studies and of high interest to railroad buffs.
SUBJ: Railroads--History.

385   Ph-3 6-A/8 $16.95   T   KB140
MURPHY, JIM. Across America on an emigrant train. Clarion ISBN 0-395-63390-7, 1993. 150p. ill., map.
Includes bibliography and index.
Because his funds were so limited, Robert Louis Stevenson traveled across America on an emigrant train and suffered the discomforts that the immigrants endured. His memoir is supplemented with historical details about the laying of the railroad lines, the laborers, and the displacement of Native Americans. For true train buffs and units on westward expansion.
SUBJ: Railroads--History./ United States--Description and travel./ Stevenson, Robert Louis.

386   Ph-2 2-4/6 $19.00   L   KB141
ARMBRUSTER, ANN. St. Lawrence Seaway. Children's Press ISBN 0-516-20016-X; In Canada: Children's Press, 1996. 48p. col. ill., maps. (True book).
Includes bibliography, directories, glossary and index.
An account of the construction of the seaway connecting the Great Lakes with the Atlantic Ocean and its effects on commerce in both the United States and Canada. Color photographs, maps, and engravings illustrate the text; and the bibliography includes web sites. For social studies units and regional studies.
SUBJ: Saint Lawrence Seaway.

386 Ph-1 2-5/6 $15.00 T KB142
GIBBONS, GAIL. Great St. Lawrence Seaway. Morrow ISBN 0-688-06984-3, 1992. unp. col. ill.
Selectors' Choice, 19th ed.
Available from the National Library Service for the Blind and Physically Handicapped on sound recording cassette RC 38409.
Tells of the early exploration and history of the St. Lawrence River and then traces today's systems of locks and canals on the waterway. Effective watercolor, ink, and pencil artwork add pleasure as well as support to the text. Combines nicely with Maestro's FERRYBOAT and BIG CITY PORT in thematic units on harbors, boats, and waterways.
SUBJ: Saint Lawrence Seaway.

386 Ph-2 3-6/8 $16.00 L KB143
HARNESS, CHERYL. Amazing impossible Erie Canal. Macmillan ISBN 0-02-742641-6; In Canada: Distican, 1995. unp. col. ill., maps.
Includes bibliography.
Describes the development of the 363-mile-long Erie Canal and the festive ten-day celebratory trip which marked its completion in 1825. Colorful illustrations add to the excitement and support a text which at times is disjointed. Useful supplement to other works on the subject.
SUBJ: Erie Canal (N.Y.)--History.

386 Ph-1 P-3/2 $14.89 L KB144
MAESTRO, BETSY. Ferryboat. By Betsy and Giulio Maestro. Crowell/HarperCollins ISBN 0-690-04520-4, 1986. unp. col. ill.
Traces activity as a family crosses the Connecticut River on the Chester-Hadlyme Ferry. Handsome watercolor drawings illustrate the text which takes a close look at a ride on a ferryboat. Useful in support of transportation units.
SUBJ: Ferries.

386 Ph-2 5-6/11 $16.95 L KB145
MCNEESE, TIM. Panama Canal. Lucent ISBN 1-56006-425-0, 1997. 96p. ill., maps. (Building history series).
Includes chronology, bibliographies and index.
A detailed, straightforward account of the history of the building of the Panama Canal, including early attempts, political aspects, challenges, eventual completion, and current status. Illustrated with black and white photographs and drawings of varying quality. A useful resource for report writers.
SUBJ: Panama Canal (Panama)--History.

PIC 386 Ph-2 5-6 $26.00 OD KB146
PANAMA CANAL (Picture). Documentary Photo Aids 119G, n.d. 12 study prints (11"x14").
Authentic period photos, with captions, picturing the background and the construction of the Panama Canal.
SUBJ: Panama Canal (Panama)--History.

386 Ph-2 3-5/7 $16.00 L KB147
PARKER, NANCY WINSLOW. Locks, crocs, and skeeters: the story of the Panama Canal. Greenwillow ISBN 0-688-12241-8, 1996. 32p. col. ill., maps.
Includes index.
Following a poem by James Stanley Gilbert, the author presents a series of one or two page essays on the history, personalities, and challenges involved in building the Panama Canal. Drawings and detailed maps illustrate the text. An excellent addition to social studies units covering the building of the canal, medical discoveries, and late nineteenth century political relationships with South and Central America.
SUBJ: Panama Canal (Panama)--History./ Panama--History.

387.1 Ph-2 4-6/6 $13.95 L KB148
FLEMING, CANDACE. Women of the lights. Illus. by James Watling. Whitman ISBN 0-8075-9165-3; In Canada: General, 1996. 80p. ill.
Includes bibliographies and index.
"Chronicles the lives of women lighthouse keepers, who braved seas and storms, rescued people from icy waters, and lovingly cared for their lights." (CIP) Contains some photographs and occasional drawings. A well-documented source for women's studies. Use as a companion to LIGHTHOUSES by Brenda Guiberson.
SUBJ: Lighthouse keepers./ Lighthouses./ Women lighthouse keepers.

387.1 Ph-2 3-6/6 $16.00 T KB149
GIBBONS, GAIL. Beacons of light: lighthouses. Morrow ISBN 0-688-07379-4, 1990. unp. col. ill.
Available from the National Library Service for the Blind and Physically Handicapped on sound recording cassette RC35397.
High appeal topic and fresh design join in a brief, colorful presentation which depicts lighthouses past and present. Power sources and foghorn use are discussed and a final page offers random bits of lighthouse lore. A pleasant entry in a subject area with few books.
SUBJ: Lighthouses.

387.1 Ph-3 5-6/8 $15.95 T KB150
GUIBERSON, BRENDA Z. Lighthouses: watchers at sea. Henry Holt ISBN 0-8050-3170-7; In Canada: Fitzhenry & Whiteside, 1995. 70p. ill. (Redfeather book).
Includes bibliography and index.
Recounts the history, operation, and challenges facing keepers of lighthouses from the earliest stone structure at Pharos in ancient Egypt to their importance in American history from the Revolution to World War II. Illustrated with black and white photos, sketches, and graphic representations that clarify and extend the text. Contains science connections in discussion of light projection and includes high interest accounts of shipwrecks and piracy.
SUBJ: Lighthouses.

387.2 Ph-2 P-1/2 $14.89 L KB151
BARTON, BYRON. Boats. Crowell/HarperCollins ISBN 0-690-04536-0, 1986. unp. col. ill.
Depicts rowboats, sailboats, ferryboats, tugboats and more in a book for the very young. Primary colors, bold lines and simple text with sentences presented in phrases contribute to a cleancut style. Can be used in naming colors and objects with a child.
SUBJ: Boats and boating./ Ships.

387.2 Ph-2 P-2/3 $14.95 L KB152
GIBBONS, GAIL. Boat book. Holiday House ISBN 0-8234-0478-1, 1983. unp. col. ill.
Identifies primarily through bold, colorful illustrations many kinds of boats and how they are powered. Minimum text describes type of boat as a pleasure craft or a work vessel. To be shared with a group.
SUBJ: Boats and boating./ Ships.

VCR 387.2 Ph-2 2-4 $135.00 OD KB153
TUGBOATS: MASTERS OF OUR HARBORS (Videocassette). Film Ideas TUG-60 ISBN 1-57557-022-X, 1996. 1/2" VHS videocassette color (13min). (Transportation series).
Includes public performance rights.
Shows tugboats as they assist barges, oil tankers, passenger ships, and cargo ships in navigating harbors and other waterways. Good production values allow students to observe different operations in progress. Use for transportation units.
SUBJ: Tugboats./ Boats and boating.

387.2 Ph-2 4-A/6 $18.95 T KB154
VISUAL DICTIONARY OF SHIPS AND SAILING. DK Publishing ISBN 1-879431-20-3, 1991. 64p. col. ill. (Eyewitness visual dictionaries).
Includes index.
Offers vivid photographs of the objects of sailing. Though the work is a thematic collection rather than a dictionary, the items displayed are readily accessible through the thorough index. A pleasure for browsers and knowledge-seekers.
SUBJ: Ships./ Sailing ships.

387.7 Ph-2 P-1/2 $14.89 L KB155
BARTON, BYRON. Airplanes. Crowell/HarperCollins ISBN 0-690-04532-8, 1986. unp. col. ill.
Introduces the young child to a cropduster, a helicopter, and a seaplane as a jet flies overhead; final illustrations depict the jet landing and ultimately reloading for takeoff. Bright, simple illustrations make this appealing.
SUBJ: Airplanes.

387.7 Ph-2 5-6/8 $16.99 T KB156
SULLIVAN, GEORGE. How an airport really works. Lodestar/Dutton ISBN 0-525-67378-4; In Canada: McClelland & Stewart, 1993. 122p. ill.
Includes glossary and index.
Provides a behind-the-scenes look at facets of airport operation. Air traffic control, safety, weather, baggage handling, turnaround times, and more are covered in a rather casually written but thorough text. Valuable in transportation and career units.
SUBJ: Airports.

VCR 388 Ph-2 1-4 $14.95 OD KB157
HERE WE GO AGAIN! (Videocassette). Narrated by Lynn Redgrave. JSK Enterprises CHE 3015, 1986. 1/2" VHS videocassette color (60min).
Includes public performance rights.
Uses real life situations and strong production qualities to introduce tow trucks, airplanes, cable cars, river barge life, and farm tractors. Settings are in Great Britain and the United States; design allows easy use of desired portions rather than total tape. Useful in

transportation units and as a trigger for language arts writing
activities.
SUBJ: Transportation.

VCR 388　　　　　Ph-2 1-4　　$19.95　　　　KB158
HERE WE GO. VOL. 1 (Videocassette). Narrated by Lynn Redgrave.
JSK Enterprises CHE 3011, 1986. 1/2" VHS videocassette color
(33min).
Includes public performance rights.
From the giggles in the introduction through completion, this video
offers exciting moments depicting transportation experiences ranging
from helicopters to road graders. Useful as a stand-alone or in
conjunction with other resources.
In HERE WE GO, volume 2 (JSK Enterprises, CHE 3012, 1/2" VHS
videocassette color (33min), also narrated by Lynn Redgrave) viewers
ride on seven vehicles including an ocean liner and a milk truck.
SUBJ: Transportation.

VCR 388　　　　　Ph-2 2-4　　$79.00　　OD KB159
TRANSPORTATION (Videocassette). National Geographic 51492, 1992.
1/2" VHS videocassette color (15min). (Your town).
Includes teacher's guide.
Illustrates ways in which transportation impacts upon our lives. Mass
transit and movement of goods by land, air, and sea receive attention
in this solid introduction which features excellent photography, a
carefully crafted script, and strong production values. Valuable
curriculum support.
SUBJ: Transportation.

388.1　　　　　Ph-2 4-A/10 $19.95　L　KB160
WHITMAN, SYLVIA. Get up and go!: the history of American road
travel. Lerner ISBN 0-8225-1735-3, 1996. 88p. ill. (People's history).
Includes bibliography and index.
A highly readable account of the history of American roads,
highways, and turnpikes from Colonial times to the present is filled
with interesting anecdotes and insights into the influence of roads for
foot traffic, horses, wagons, stagecoaches, bicycles, automobiles,
trucks, and other vehicles on the development of American social and
economic life. Illustrated with black and white archival drawings and
photographs. Use to extend study of all periods of American history
and for general interest reading.
SUBJ: Roads--History./ Travel--History./ Transportation--History.

388.3　　　　　Ph-2 P-1/2　$14.89　L　KB161
BARTON, BYRON. Trucks. Crowell/HarperCollins ISBN 0-690-04530-1,
1986. unp. col. ill.
Brightly colored illustrations depict trucks, usually in urban settings,
carrying out tasks that undergird everyday life. Good as a teaching
tool or discussion device with the very young.
SUBJ: Trucks.

388.4　　　　　Ph-3 5-6/7　$14.95　L　KB162
YEPSEN, ROGER. City trains: moving through America's cities by rail.
Macmillan ISBN 0-02-793675-9; In Canada: Maxwell Macmillan, 1993.
96p. ill.
Includes bibliography and index.
Supplies a thorough discussion of the history of urban trains--
yesterday's horsecars through today's maglev trains. Emphasis is on
North America. Useful for general readers and in transportation
studies.
SUBJ: Street-railroads./ Subways./ Transportation./ City and town
life.

391　　　　　Ph-3 4-6/4　$14.95　T　KB163
CHRISTIAN, MARY BLOUNT. Hats are for watering horses: why the
cowboy dressed that way. Illus. by Lyle Miller. Hendrick-Long ISBN
0-937460-89-3, 1993. 64p. ill.
Describes cowboy gear from hat to boots and throws in spurs,
slickers, and bedrolls for good measure. Text set in a format normally
reserved for verse is a distraction, but much solid information is
provided. Use in a unit on styles of American dress.
SUBJ: Cowboys--Costume./ Costume--West(U.S.)--History.

391　　　　　Ph-2 4-6/6　$15.95　L　KB164
KALMAN, BOBBIE. 18th century clothing. Crabtree ISBN 0-86505-492-4;
In Canada: Crabtree, 1993. 32p. col. ill. (Historic communities).
Includes glossary and index.
Discusses clothing styles, accessories, and hygienic patterns of the
people of eighteenth century North America. Color photographs from
historic villages and line drawings illustrate the text. A useful resource
in curriculum units about wearing apparel or American studies.
Companion volume 19TH CENTURY CLOTHING (ISBN 0-86505-493-
2, 1993) gives the same coverage to clothing of the nineteenth
century.
SUBJ: Costume--History.

391　　　　　Ph-1 4-6/8　$19.00　T　KB165
ROWLAND-WARNE, L. Costume. Knopf ISBN 0-679-81680-1, 1992.
64p. col. ill. (Eyewitness books).
"Dorling Kindersley book."
Includes index.
Displays clothing from many eras in a visually rich presentation
featuring the familiar graphic design effects of the "Eyewitness
Books." Intriguing, but not exhaustive, detail offers a strong,
chronologically arranged overview of European and American clothing
through the ages.
SUBJ: Costume--History./ Fashion--History.

391.4　　　　　Ph-1 P-K　$13.93　L　KB166
MILLER, MARGARET. Whose hat? Greenwillow ISBN 0-688-06907-X,
1988. unp. col. ill.
Excellent color photographs of people working at various occupations
provide the answers to the frequently asked question "Whose hat?"
A similarly effective approach is used in the author's WHOSE SHOE?
(ISBN 0-688-10009-0, 1991).
SUBJ: Hats.

391.4　　　　　Ph-1 1-4/1　$13.93　L　KB167
MORRIS, ANN. Hats, hats, hats. Photos by Ken Heyman. Lothrop, Lee &
Shepard ISBN 0-688-06339-X, 1989. 29p. col. ill.
Includes index.
Selectors' Choice, 17th ed.
Uses handsome color photographs to depict 29 types of hats worn in
the United States or other countries. A picture-keyed index provides
additional and valuable information. Has potential as the keystone of
a classroom hat day celebration.
SUBJ: Hats.

391.4　　　　　Ph-2 4-6/6　$14.95　T　KB168
YUE, CHARLOTTE. Shoes: their history in words and pictures. By
Charlotte and David Yue. Houghton Mifflin ISBN 0-395-72667-0, 1997.
92p. ill.
Includes bibliography and index.
A lively history of shoes from the Stone Age to the present relates
how they are made, the cultural customs they reflect, and the
influences of social and political changes. Detailed black and white
sketches of styles show evolutionary changes. Use for multicultural
studies, as a supplement to units on historical time periods, and for
general interest.
SUBJ: Shoes.

391.5　　　　　Ph-3 4-6/6　$17.20　L　KB169
BADT, KARIN LUISA. Hair there and everywhere. Childrens Press ISBN
0-516-08187-X; In Canada: Childrens Press, 1994. 32p. col. ill. (World
of difference).
Includes glossary and index.
Explores a variety of hairstyles in cultures around the world.
Photographs and captions provide most of the appeal and supply
most of the information; text is pedestrian. Useful in exposition of
similarities and differences for multicultural studies.
SUBJ: Hair./ Hairstyles.

392.1　　　　　Ph-2 1-2/7　$15.00　L　KB170
BERNHARD, EMERY. Ride on mother's back: a day of baby carrying
around the world. Illus. by Durga Bernhard. Gulliver/Harcourt Brace
ISBN 0-15-200870-5; In Canada: Harcourt Brace c/o Canadian Manda,
1996. unp. col. ill.
"Explores the ways in which people from a variety of cultures carry
their young ones, and describes what children see and learn as they
are carried." (CIP) Full-color illustrations picture aspects of life in
each culture, end notes provide additional information, and endpapers
show a world map with each culture located. For multicultural studies
and discussions about family relationships.
SUBJ: Infant carriers./ Cross-cultural studies./ Manners and customs./
Babies.

392.3　　　　　Ph-2 6-A/7　$14.95　T　KB171
MONROE, JEAN GUARD. First houses: Native American homes and
sacred structures. By Jean Guard Monroe and Ray A. Williamson. Illus.
by Susan Johnston Carlson. Houghton Mifflin ISBN 0-395-51081-3,
1993. 150p. ill.
Includes glossary, bibliographies and index.
In their creation myths, Native Americans told how the first houses
were conceived and then proceeded to use these patterns for their
own dwellings. Line drawings of the houses open each chapter and
are followed by the myths which reveal why and how the house came
to be. For inclusion in units on Native Americans, multicultural studies,
creation stories, and architecture.
SUBJ: Indians of North America--Dwellings./ Indians of North
America--Rites and ceremonies./ Indians of North America--Folklore./
Creation--Folklore./ Sacred space--North America.

392.3   Ph-3 4-6/7 $13.95   T   KB172
SHEMIE, BONNIE. Mounds of earth and shell: the Southeast. Tundra ISBN 0-88776-318-9; In Canada: Tundra, 1993. 24p. col. ill. (Native dwellings).
Includes bibliography.
Discusses North American mound structures found from Florida to Ontario and from the Atlantic coast to the Mississippi. Crayon drawings illustrate a text which provides an introduction to early mound cultures. For large collections.
SUBJ: Indians of North America--Dwellings./ Indians of North America--Southern states.

393   Ph-1 4-6/6 $14.89   L   KB173
ALIKI. Mummies made in Egypt. Crowell/HarperCollins ISBN 0-690-03859-3, 1979. unp. col. ill.
Selectors' Choice, 13th ed.
Describes step-by-step the ancient art of mummy making. Details the removal of the inner organs, wrapping of the body, coffin and funeral procession and placement in the tomb. Many of the color illustrations were adapted from paintings and sculptures found in ancient tombs.
SUBJ: Mummies--Egypt./ Egypt--Antiquities./ Funeral rites and ceremonies.

393   Ph-2 3-5/8 $21.00   L   KB174
BENDICK, JEANNE. Tombs of the ancient Americas. Watts ISBN 0-531-20148-1; In Canada: Grolier Ltd., 1993. 64p. col. ill., maps. (First book).
Includes glossary, bibliography and index.
Describes ancient burial customs, tombs, and archeological sites in South, Central, and North America. Illustrated with photographs and graphic renderings. Will add dimension to social studies units on Aztecs, Maya, and Native Americans. For multicultural studies.
SUBJ: Indians--Funeral customs and rites./ Tombs--America./ Archaeology.

393   Ph-2 4-6/8 $14.95   L   KB175
DEEM, JAMES M. How to make a mummy talk. Illus. by True Kelley. Houghton Mifflin ISBN 0-395-62427-4, 1995. 184p. ill., maps.
Includes bibliography and index.
A lively discussion of mummies, both human and animal, found throughout the world, the scientific process of their investigation, and the need for respectful treatment are presented with a humorous, light touch. Sketches of scientific finds and cartoons depicting concepts enliven the text. Includes references to museums where mummies are exhibited. Will appeal to students who are intrigued by mummies and will broaden their perspective on the subject.
SUBJ: Mummies.

393   Ph-2 4-6/8 $16.99   L   KB176
PUTNAM, JAMES. Mummy. Photos by Peter Hayman. Knopf ISBN 0-679-93881-8, 1993. 64p. col. ill. (Eyewitness books).
"Dorling Kindersley book."
Includes index.
Offers an examination of mummies, natural and man-made, from many cultures. Major emphasis in this handsome import is on ancient Egyptian preservation techniques. Complements MUMMIES AND THEIR MYSTERIES and holds the same high appeal to readers.
SUBJ: Mummies.

393   Ph-2 5-6/6 $22.95   L   KB177
WILCOX, CHARLOTTE. Mummies and their mysteries. Carolrhoda ISBN 0-87614-767-8, 1993. 64p. col. ill., map.
Includes glossary and index.
"...takes readers on a hunt for mummies and their mysteries around the world." (Jacket) Author successfully avoids sensationalism and provides a carefully written text which discusses mummies from many cultures and climes. Book with high appeal for browsers or information seekers.
SUBJ: Mummies./ Antiquities.

394   Ph-1 5-6/9 $19.95   L   KB178
BRAINE, SUSAN. Drumbeat...heartbeat: a celebration of the powwow. Text and photos by Susan Braine. Lerner ISBN 0-8225-2656-5, 1995. 48p. col. ill. (We are still here: Native Americans today).
Includes glossary and bibliography.
Detailed description of the history and tradition of the powwow with emphasis on historical roots of elements of modern celebrations, including dancing, costumes, drum groups, songs, and giveaways. Text illustrated with descriptive contemporary photographs. For multicultural studies.
SUBJ: Powwows./ Indians of North America--Rites and ceremonies./ Indians of North America--Social life and customs.

394   Ph-2 4-6/7 $14.95   P   KB179
BURSTEIN, CHAYA M. Jewish kids catalog. Jewish Publication Society ISBN 0-8276-0215-4, 1983. 224p. ill.
Includes index.
Contains a potpourri of Jewish culture and history including customs, language, holidays, crafts, recipes, beliefs, literature, music, folklore and landmarks. A mini-encyclopedia and index locate items in the text, which is illustrated with many black/white drawings and photographs. Not intended to be comprehensive, this miscellany encompasses a wide range of Jewish-related information in a single volume.
SUBJ: Jews--Miscellanea./ Judaism--Miscellanea.

394   Ph-2 1-3/6 $15.93   L   KB180
LEWIN, TED. Fair! Lothrop, Lee & Shepard ISBN 0-688-12851-3; In Canada: Hearst Book Group, 1997. unp. col. ill.
Describes the excitement of a county fair with the arrival and set-up of carnival rides and games; the gathering of farm animals, jams, vegetables, quilts, and other items for judging; opening day celebrations; and the activities that follow. Full-color illustrations capture the thrills and enjoyment of each aspect. For units on the farm and American life.
SUBJ: Fairs./ Agriculture--Exhibitions.

394   Ph-1 1-3/3 $21.50   L   KB181
RENDON, MARCIE R. Powwow summer: a family celebrates the circle of life. Photos by Cheryl Walsh Bellville. Carolrhoda ISBN 0-87614-986-7, 1996. 48p. col. ill.
Photo-essay follows the Downwind family through a summer of ceremonial powwows and gives insights into Anishinabe traditions, old and new. Comparisons with celebrations of other cultures and description of daily life will be useful in helping students make comparisons with their own families and lives. For multicultural studies.
SUBJ: Powwows./ Ojibwa Indians--Social life and customs./ Indians of North America--Social life and customs.

KIT 394   Ph-2   P $9.95   KB182
TURNER, MARGRET. Come on everybody! Let's go to the fair (Kit). By Margret Turner and Alyson Scott. LifeWorks ISBN 0-9630453-0-X, 1991. 1 paperback book, 1 sound cassette (9min).
Animal noises abound in an aural adventure as a young girl visits the fair. Primary value will be as a source of rooster crows, cow moos, pig oinks, and horse whinnies. Use as a one-to-one developmental activity.
SUBJ: Fairs./ Animal sounds.

CE 394.1   Ph-1 2-5/5 $14.89   L   KB183
ALIKI. Medieval feast. Crowell/HarperCollins ISBN 0-690-04246-9, 1983. unp. col. ill.
Describes the preparation and celebration of a medieval feast held at an English manor house toward the end of the Middle Ages, about 1400. The story unfolds through lavish illustrations in rich colors and fine detail which are reminiscent of tapestries. For all ages: younger children will enjoy the ample menu and lovely drawings; older readers will gather the facts about the medieval world.
SUBJ: Visits of state./ Courts and courtiers./ Civilization, Medieval.

394.1   Ph-3 3-5/7 $17.20   L   KB184
BADT, KARIN LUISA. Good morning, let's eat! Childrens Press ISBN 0-516-08190-X; In Canada: Childrens Press, 1994. 32p. col. ill. (World of difference).
Includes glossary and index.
Describes breakfast customs and foods in various countries of the world. Pictures are not closely related to the text; caption information is indexed. Useful as a browser and in food or "how we live" units. For multicultural studies.
SUBJ: Food habits./ Breakfast.

394.1   Ph-2 5-6/8 $12.89   L   KB185
GIBLIN, JAMES CROSS. From hand to mouth, or how we invented knives, forks, spoons, and chopsticks & the table manners to go with them. Crowell/HarperCollins ISBN 0-690-04662-6, 1987. 86p. ill.
Includes bibliography and index.
Traces the history and use of eating utensils from early times to the present as it points out that, regardless of location or era, the purpose of eating tools and table manners has been to get food from hand to mouth "swiftly, gracefully and as neatly as possible." An examination of the index suggests many topics for reports and/or discussion.
SUBJ: Flatware--History./ Tableware--History./ Eating customs--History./ Table etiquette--History./ Dinners and dining--History.

394.1 Ph-1 3-6/4 $14.95 L KB186
PENNER, LUCILLE RECHT. Eating the plates: a Pilgrim book of food and manners. Macmillan ISBN 0-02-770901-9; In Canada: Maxwell Macmillan, 1991. 117p b&w illus.
Includes glossary, bibliography and index.
Presents a vivid picture of Pilgrim life, eating habits, and customs. Chapter titles "Bugs for Dinner" and "Don't Throw your Bones on the Floor" give a hint of the lively appeal of the contents. Accessible text, recipes, and read-aloud potential make this a valuable addition to all collections serving young readers.
SUBJ: Pilgrims (New Plymouth Colony)--Social life and customs./ Cookery, American./ Food habits--United States.

394.1 Ph-1 4-6/6 $14.95 L KB187
PENNER, LUCILLE RECHT. Native American feast. With illus. selected by the author. Macmillan ISBN 0-02-770902-7; In Canada: Maxwell Macmillan, 1994. 99p. ill.
Includes bibliography and index.
Provides a pleasing combination of Native American recipes, cooking techniques, customs, and lore from many regions of the country. Printing quality is high, and black and white illustrations are well chosen. Particularly useful in multicultural studies and holiday units.
SUBJ: Indians of North America--Food./ Cookery, Indian./ Indians of North America--Social life and customs.

394.2 Ph-1 P-2/4 $15.95 L KB188
CREWS, DONALD. Parade. Greenwillow ISBN 0-688-01996-X, 1983. unp. col. ill.
Selectors' Choice, 15th ed.
Depicts an all-American event--a parade--from the "No Parking--Parade Today" sign to cleaning up afterwards in bright, colorful, and mood-catching art. An exciting title for the younger child.
SUBJ: Parades--Pictorial works.

394.2 Ph-1 2-5/9 $16.95 L KB189
HOYT-GOLDSMITH, DIANE. Potlatch: a Tsimshian celebration. Photos by Lawrence Migdale. Holiday House ISBN 0-8234-1290-3, 1997. 32p. col. ill., map.
Includes glossary and index.
Thirteen-year-old David, a member of the Tsimshians of Metlakatla, Alaska, relates the history, culture, and heritage of his people, and gives details of concepts about and preparation for the recently revived tradition of potlatch. Excellent color photographs illustrate and amplify the text. Use for Native American studies and multicultural studies.
SUBJ: Potlatch./ Tsimshian Indians--Social life and customs./ Indians of North America--Northwest, Pacific--Social life and customs.

394.2 Ph-1 K-3/6 $15.88 L KB190
PENNINGTON, DANIEL. Itse Selu: Cherokee harvest festival. Illus. by Don Stewart. Charlesbridge ISBN 0-88106-852-7, 1994. unp. col. ill.
Uses the celebration of the Green Corn Festival as a central focus to portray many aspects of the Cherokee culture, village life, and vocabulary. Large, bold illustrations depict scenes from the narrative and close-ups of artifacts. Use with materials on Thanksgiving and New Year celebrations to make cultural comparisions. For multicultural units and Native American studies.
SUBJ: Harvest festivals./ Cherokee Indians./ Indians of North America.

394.2 Ph-1 2-5/11 $15.93 L KB191
VIESTI, JOSEPH F. Celebrate! in South Asia. By Joe Viesti and Diane Hall. Photos by Joe Viesti. Lothrop, Lee & Shepard ISBN 0-688-13775-X, 1996. unp. col. ill., map.
These brief, one-page descriptions of holidays celebrated in India, Sri Lanka, Bangladesh, Pakistan, Myanmar, and Nepal are accompanied by vibrant, detailed photographs and an outline map of the areas covered. A useful source of information about cultural celebrations not usually featured in holiday books. For multicultural studies.
SUBJ: Festivals--South Asia./ Holidays--South Asia./ South Asia--Social life and customs.

394.2 Ph-1 2-5/11 $15.93 L KB192
VIESTI, JOSEPH F. Celebrate! in Southeast Asia. By Joe Viesti and Diane Hall. Photos by Joe Viesti. Lothrop, Lee & Shepard ISBN 0-688-13489-0, 1996. unp. col. ill., map.
These brief, one-page descriptions of holidays celebrated in Thailand, Malaysia, Singapore, Indonesia, Philippines, Vietnam, Laos, and Cambodia are accompanied by vibrant, detailed photographs and an outline map of the areas covered. A useful source of information about cultural celebrations not usually featured in holiday books. For multicultural studies.
SUBJ: Festivals--Asia, Southeastern./ Holidays--Asia, Southeastern./ Asia, Southeastern--Social life and customs.

394.26 Ph-1 3-6/5 $14.93 L KB193
ANCONA, GEORGE. Pablo remembers: the Fiesta of the Day of the Dead. Lothrop, Lee & Shepard ISBN 0-688-11250-1, 1993. 48p. col. ill.
Includes bibliography and glossary.
Spanish edition available PABLO RECUERDA (ISBN 0-688-12894-7, 1993).
Follows Pablo and his family as they prepare for El Dia de los Muertos, the three-day celebration honoring loved ones who have died. Photographed in Oaxaca in southern Mexico, the book provides a solid exposition of an important cultural observance. Both illustrations and text avoid sensationalism. Strong resource for holiday units and multicultural studies.
SUBJ: All Souls' Day--Mexico./ Mexico--Social life and customs./ Spanish language materials.

394.26 Ph-2 3-6/6 $16.95 L KB194
ANCONA, GEORGE. Powwow. Photos and text by Geroge Ancona. Harcourt Brace Jovanovich ISBN 0-15-263268-9; In Canada: Harcourt Brace c/o Canadian Manda, 1993. unp. col. ill.
Captures the cultural strength of a colorful Native American celebration as dancers gather at the summer Crow Fair in Montana. Distinguished color photographs highlight a text which describes Traditional, Fancy, Grass, and Jingle-dress dancing. Use with other titles in a thematic unit or in a display of resources reflecting American customs and celebrations.
SUBJ: Powwows./ Indians of North America--Rites and ceremonies.

VCR 394.26 Ph-2 3-A $59.00 OD KB195
BLACK HERITAGE HOLIDAYS (Videocassette). Society for Visual Education 95552-HAVT, 1992. 1/2" VHS videocassette color (20min).
Includes teacher's guide.
Divided into two segments, one introduces the nonreligious, cultural holiday Kwanzaa, and the other offers the history of African-American freedom celebrations in North America. The Kwanzaa presentation targets a primary-intermediate audience; freedom celebrations, intermediate and older. Valuable addition to all collections.
SUBJ: Afro-Americans--Social life and customs./ Kwanzaa./ Juneteenth (Holiday).

394.26 Ph-3 5-6 $30.00 T KB196
CARNEGIE LIBRARY SCHOOL ASSOCIATION. Our holidays in poetry. Comp. by M.P. Harrington, J.H. Thomas & the Carnegie Library School Association. Wilson ISBN 0-8242-0039-X, 1965. 479p.
Anthology of religious and secular poems for observance of Lincoln's Birthday, Washington's Birthday, Easter, Arbor Day, Mother's Day, Memorial Day, Thanksgiving and Christmas.
SUBJ: Holidays--Poetry./ Poetry--Collections.

394.26 Ph-1 5-A/5 $16.95 L KB197
CRUM, ROBERT. Eagle drum: on the powwow trail with a young grass dancer. Four Winds ISBN 0-02-725515-8; In Canada: Maxwell Macmillan, 1994. 48p. col. ill.
Follows young grass dancer Louis Pierre as he participates in a weekend powwow in Montana. Color photographs accompany a detailed text that examines the role of dancing in today's Native American culture. Expand by using with Ancona's POWWOW and Smithsonian/Folkways DANCES OF NORTH AMERICAN INDIANS. For multicultural studies.
SUBJ: Powwows./ Kalispel Indians./ Pierre, Louis./ Indians of North America--Dances.

394.26 Ph-2 4-6/7 $15.95 L KB198
HOYT-GOLDSMITH, DIANE. Day of the Dead: a Mexican-American celebration. Photos by Lawrence Migdale. Holiday House ISBN 0-8234-1094-3, 1994. 32p. col. ill.
Includes glossary and index.
Describes the Dia de los Muertos celebration of Latinos living in the Sacramento area of California. Special features include the creation story of how the Aztecs came to be and a history of this important holiday. Use with Ancona's PABLO REMEMBERS for a comparison and contrast activity for multicultural studies.
SUBJ: All Souls' Day./ Mexican Americans--Social life and customs./ Fasts and feasts--Mexico./ Spanish language materials.

CD 394.26 Ph-1 P-3 $14.00 OD KB199
JENKINS, ELLA. Holiday times (Compact disc). Smithsonian/Folkways CD SF 45041, 1996. 1 compact disc (33min).
Includes lyrics.
Sound recording cassette available CS SF 45041, 1996. 1 sound cassette (33min), $8.50.
A variety of winter holidays including Christmas, Hanukkah, Kwanzaa, Chinese New Year, and St. Patrick's Day are represented in this appealing collection of songs, poems, chants, and instrumentals from

Ella Jenkins and friends. Guide includes words to all selections and brief explanations for some.
SUBJ: Holidays--Songs.

394.26   Ph-2 5-6/6 $15.89   L   KB200
LASKY, KATHRYN. Days of the Dead. Photos by Christopher G. Knight. Hyperion ISBN 0-7868-2018-7, 1994. 48p. col. ill.
Includes glossary.
Depicts the traditional Days of the Dead observance of a family in the mountains of central Mexico. Text is more difficult than that of Ancona's PABLO REMEMBERS and Hoyt-Goldsmith's DAY OF THE DEAD, but treatment is solid and provides insight into lifeways of a rural family in Mexico. Useful in multicultural or regional studies and in holiday units.
SUBJ: All Souls' Day--Mexico./ All Saints' Day--Mexico./ Mexico--Social life and customs.

394.26   Ph-2 4-6/7 $15.95   L   KB201
PENNER, LUCILLE RECHT. Celebration: the story of American holidays. Illus. by Ib Ohlsson. Macmillan ISBN 0-02-770903-5; In Canada: Maxwell Macmillan, 1993. 79p. col. ill.
Provides information about 13 holidays, nine of which are unique to the United States. Searchers will be particularly pleased to find chapters about Labor Day, Veterans Day, and Martin Luther King Day.
SUBJ: Holidays.

394.26   Ph-2 4-6/6 $13.95   L   KB202
PERL, LILA. Pinatas and paper flowers, holidays of the Americas in English and Spanish/ Pinatas y flores de papel, fiestas de las Americas en ingles y espanol. Illustrated by Victoria de Larrea. Clarion ISBN 0-89919-112-6, 1983. 91p. ill.
Includes index.
Identifies and describes eight Hispanic holidays that are celebrated in the Americas. Bilingual text alternates between full page of English and Spanish.
SUBJ: Holidays./ Hispanic Americans./ Bilingual materials--Spanish.

394.26   Ph-3 4-6/7 $13.90   L   KB203
SILVERTHORNE, ELIZABETH. Fiesta!: Mexico's greatest celebrations. Illus. by Jan Davey Ellis. Millbrook ISBN 1-56294-055-4, 1992. 64p. col. ill.
Includes glossary, bibliography and index.
Presents information on patriotic and religious fiestas of Mexico. Instructions for crafts and simple recipes are included as are brief sections dealing with the history and culture of the country. Useful as a supplementary source.
SUBJ: Festivals--Mexico./ Mexico--Social life and customs.

394.26   Ph-2 P-A/4 $18.00   T   KB204
TUDOR, TASHA. Time to keep: the Tasha Tudor book of holidays. Simon & Schuster ISBN 0-689-81162-4; In Canada: Distican, 1996. unp. col. ill.
Month by month description of holidays in New England as remembered by Tasha Tudor from her childhood. Soft watercolors depict the events and form delicate seasonal (pussywillow, apples, pumpkins, etc.) borders for each page.
SUBJ: Holidays./ New England--Social life and customs.

394.261   Ph-2 1-3/7 $14.99   T   KB205
BERNHARD, EMERY. Happy New Year! Illus. by Durga Bernhard. Lodestar/Dutton ISBN 0-525-67532-9; In Canada: McClelland & Stewart, 1996. unp. col. ill.
Includes glossary.
Brief sketches of New Year celebrations in various cultures around the world show origins, traditions, and time of year observances occur. Colorful, cheerful illustrations of festivities and artifacts related to them will appeal to young readers. Use for holiday units and multicultural studies.
SUBJ: New Year./ Festivals.

394.261   Ph-2 2-4/2 $10.95   T   KB206
CHOCOLATE, DEBORAH M. NEWTON. My first Kwanzaa book. Illus. by Cal Massey. Scholastic ISBN 0-590-45762-4; In Canada: Scholastic, 1992. unp. col. ill.
"Cartwheel books."
Includes glossary.
Describes family activities during an African-American Kwanzaa celebration. Useful features include a day-by-day description of the seven principles of Kwanzaa, a pronunciation guide, and information about symbols and words of Kwanzaa. Use in support of units about holidays celebrated in the United States. For multicultural studies.
SUBJ: Kwanzaa./ Afro-Americans--Social life and customs.

CE 394.261   Ph-2 1-6/5 $14.95   L   KB207
GIBBONS, GAIL. Valentine's Day. Holiday House ISBN 0-8234-0572-9, 1986. unp. col. ill.
Also available as read-along kit from Live Oak Media (ISBN 0-87499-006-8, 1986). 1 hardback book, 1 sound cassette (5min), $22.95.
Captures the feeling of Valentine's day as it traces with cheerful forthrightness both current customs and the history of the day. An added plus is the illustrated set of instructions on how to make valentines or a valentine box.
SUBJ: Valentine's Day./ Valentines.

394.261   Ph-2 2-6/6 $19.95   T   KB208
GOSS, LINDA. It's Kwanzaa time! By Linda and Clay Goss. Illus. by Ashley Bryan...[et al.]. Putnam ISBN 0-399-22505-6; In Canada: BeJo Sales, 1995. 72p. col. ill.
Includes music and bibliography.
Available from the National Library Service for the Blind and Physically Handicapped on sound recording cassette RC 42923.
A story for each of the seven days of Kwanzaa, suitable for reading aloud, mirrors that day's theme and features fables, traditional retellings, contemporary stories, and nonfiction. Each story contains a single-page illustration by a well-known African-American illustrator. Also includes a history of the holiday, games, activities, recipes and music. Use for multicultural and holiday studies. (Parents' Shelf).
SUBJ: Kwanzaa./ Afro-Americans--Social life and customs.

394.261   Ph-3 5-6/8 $13.95   L   KB209
GRAHAM-BARBER, LYNDA. Mushy! the complete book of Valentine words. Illus. by Betsy Lewin. Bradbury ISBN 0-02-736941-2; In Canada: Collier Macmillan, 1991. 122p. ill.
Includes timeline, bibliography and index.
Dishes out information about the words, history, customs, and sayings of Valentine's Day. Good-humored drawings add to the pleasure of this book which is of considerable appeal to teachers as well as to students.
SUBJ: Valentine's Day./ English language--Etymology.

394.261   Ph-2 4-6/7 $15.95   L   KB210
HOYT-GOLDSMITH, DIANE. Celebrating Kwanzaa. Photos by Lawrence Migdale. Holiday House ISBN 0-8234-1048-X, 1993. 32p. col. ill., map.
Includes glossary and index.
Tells of the Kwanzaa celebration of a Chicago family. Text describes the observance of the seven Kwanzaa principles and supplies a quotation appropriate for each; glossary is notable for its quality. For holiday units and multicultural studies.
SUBJ: Kwanzaa./ Afro-Americans--Social life and customs.

394.261   Ph-2 3-5/6 $15.40   L   KB211
JACKSON, ELLEN. Winter solstice. Illus. by Jan Davey Ellis. Millbrook ISBN 1-56294-400-2, 1994. unp. col. ill.
Traces customs of winter solstice observations in many cultures and provides background for discussion of today's Christmas and Hanukkah celebrations. A Cherokee creation tale complements and expands factual material presented. Useful in study of seasons and holidays.
SUBJ: Winter solstice./ Seasons.

VCR 394.261   Ph-2 3-6 $69.95   KB212
KWANZAA (Videocassette). United Learning 10243V, 1994. 1/2" VHS videocassette color (10min).
Includes teacher's guide.
Offers an overview of Kwanzaa and describes the seven principles basic to the observance of the seven-day, modern holiday. Teacher's guide includes script. Useful in holiday units and for multicultural studies.
SUBJ: Kwanzaa./ Afro-Americans--Social life and customs.

VCR 394.261   Ph-2 1-4 $29.95   OD KB213
NEW YEAR'S DAY (Videocassette). GPN 568.001, 1994. 1/2" VHS videocassette color (14min). (America's special days).
Includes series teacher's guide.
Discusses the relationship of day and night, seasons, and moon and sun to solar and lunar calendars. Demonstrations of concepts and explanations of New Year's resolutions are clear and understandable. Lively scenes of a New Year's celebration in Times Square and a Chinese Dragon Parade will hold interest and add to the usefulness of this well-presented discussion.
SUBJ: New Year.

394.261   Ph-1 2-6/7 $14.89   L   KB214
PINKNEY, ANDREA DAVIS. Seven candles for Kwanzaa. Illus. by Brian Pinkney. Dial ISBN 0-8037-1293-6, 1993. unp. col. ill.
Includes bibliography.

"Describes the origins and practices of Kwanzaa, the seven-day festival during which people of African descent rejoice in their ancestral values." (CIP) Handsome scratchboard illustrations depict each of the seven Kwanzaa principles; pronunciation help and a brief bibliography are welcome features. Best of the several Kwanzaa titles now available.
SUBJ: Kwanzaa./ Afro-Americans--Social life and customs.

VCR 394.261　　Ph-2 2-5　$29.95　OD KB215
PRESIDENTS' DAY (Videocassette). GPN 568.003, 1994. 1/2" VHS videocassette color (14min). (America's special days).
Includes series teacher's guide.
Features visits of schoolchildren to the Washington Monument, Lincoln Memorial, Mount Vernon, and homes of Lincoln in New Salem and Springfield. Although the section on Washington offers very little new or freshly presented information, the Lincoln section is informative and interesting. The field trip by proxy will appeal to students and hold interest.
SUBJ: Presidents' Day.

394.261　　Ph-2 1-4/2　$14.95　L KB216
SAINT JAMES, SYNTHIA. Gifts of Kwanzaa. Whitman ISBN 0-8075-2907-9; In Canada: General, 1994. unp. col. ill.
Includes glossary.
Uses bright, colorful artwork to present the seven principles of Kwanzaa. Text is simple and offers possibilities for student discussion and presentations. Joins SEVEN CANDLES FOR KWANZAA at the top of the group of recently produced titles about this holiday which was created in 1966. For multicultural studies.
SUBJ: Kwanzaa./ Afro-Americans--Social life and customs.

394.261　　Ph-2 1-4/2　$13.95　L KB217
WATERS, KATE. Lion dancer: Ernie Wan's Chinese New Year. By Kate Waters and Madeline Slovenz-Low. Photos by Martha Cooper. Scholastic ISBN 0-590-43046-7; In Canada: Scholastic, 1990. unp. col. ill.
Includes Chinese horoscope.
Young Ernie Wan describes his first time out as a lion dancer in a Chinese New Year parade in New York. Brightly colored photographs support an easy-to-read text. Closing pages display a Chinese lunar calendar and a Chinese horoscope.
SUBJ: Chinese New Year.

394.262　　Ph-2 5-6/7　$15.95　L KB218
BARTH, EDNA. Shamrocks, harps, and shillelaghs: the story of the St. Patrick's Day symbols. Illus. by Ursula Arndt. Clarion ISBN 0-395-28845-2, c1977. 96p. ill.
Explores the meaning of the symbols and legends relating to St. Patrick's Day. Explains the origins of these symbols which have religious, political or folklore background. Bibliography of Irish stories is appended.
SUBJ: St. Patrick's Day.

394.262　　Ph-1 2-5/2　$15.95　L KB219
GIBBONS, GAIL. St. Patrick's Day. Holiday House ISBN 0-8234-1119-2, 1994. unp. col. ill.
Joins other popular holiday books by the author as it traces the origins and customs of St. Patrick's Day. Fresh, clean lined illustrations bordered in green add appeal. Useful as a seasonal item and in "favorite holiday" projects.
SUBJ: St. Patrick's Day.

394.263　　Ph-1 5-A/A　$3.99　P KB220
GRAHAM-BARBER, LYNDA. Doodle Dandy!: the complete book of Independence Day words. Illus. by Betsy Lewin. Avon ISBN 0-380-72100-7; In Canada: Distican, 1992. 122p. ill.
Includes chronology, bibliographies and index.
Available from the National Library Service for the Blind and Physically Handicapped on sound recording cassette RC 38933.
Examines the etymology of words related to the Fourth of July ranging from independence to watermelon. Vigorous black and white drawings enliven the proceedings. Works as a browser for teachers or students researching patriotic symbols or for "favorite holiday" projects.
SUBJ: Fourth of July./ English language--Etymology.

394.264　　Ph-2 3-6/6　$13.88　L KB221
BARKIN, CAROL. Happy Thanksgiving! By Carol Barkin and Elizabeth James. Illustrated by Giora Carmi. Lothrop, Lee & Shepard ISBN 0-688-06801-4, 1987. 80p. ill.
Includes index.
Suggests simple crafts, recipes, and community service projects for the Thanksgiving season. A brace of riddles of appeal to elementary school students closes each chapter. Strong ideas for tradition-building activities.
SUBJ: Thanksgiving Day./ Thanksgiving cookery.

394.264　　Ph-1 3-6/4　$13.95　L KB222
DALGLIESH, ALICE. Thanksgiving story. Illus. by Helen Sewell. Scribner's ISBN 0-684-18999-2, c1954. unp. col. ill.
Newbery Honor Award.
Available from National Library Service for the Blind and Physically Handicapped in Braille BR02187.
Presents in simple, graceful language a fictionalized story of the Pilgrims and settlers who sailed on the Mayflower, their first year in the New World, and their celebration of a special day of thanks. Teachers have long used this 1955 Newbery Honor book as a holiday read-aloud, but an easy reading level broadens its accessibility to a wide range of student readers.
SUBJ: Thanksgiving Day./ Pilgrims (New Plymouth Colony).

394.264　　Ph-1 4-6/6　$15.95　L KB223
GEORGE, JEAN CRAIGHEAD. First Thanksgiving. Illus. by Thomas Locker. Philomel ISBN 0-399-21991-9; In Canada: Putnam, 1993. unp. col. ill.
Combines a strong narrative with light-swept illustrations to tell the story of Squanto and the Pilgrims as they joined in a celebraton which they respectively called the Green Corn Dance and the Harvest Feast. Valuable for reading aloud.
SUBJ: Thanksgiving Day./ Pilgrims (New Plymouth Colony)./ Massachusetts--History--New Plymouth, 1620-1691.

CE 394.264　　Ph-1 P-2/7　$14.95　L KB224
GIBBONS, GAIL. Halloween. Holiday House ISBN 0-8234-0524-9, 1984. unp. col. ill.
Read-along kit available from Live Oak Media (ISBN 0-941078-87-6, 1984). 1 hardback book, 1 sound cassette (5min), $22.95.
Videocassette available from Live Oak Media (ISBN 0-87499-281-8, 1993). 1/2" VHS videocassette color (6min), $36.95.
Captures the many historical and traditional activities of the Halloween holiday in text and bold bright illustrations. A useful holiday title for reading aloud or independently.
SUBJ: Halloween.

CE 394.264　　Ph-1 P-2/4　$14.95　L KB225
GIBBONS, GAIL. Thanksgiving Day. Holiday House ISBN 0-8234-0489-7, 1983. unp col. ill.
Read-along kit available from Live Oak (ISBN 0-941078-63-9, 1984). 1 hardcover book, 1 sound cassette (6min), $22.95.
Videocassette available from Live Oak (ISBN 0-87499-312-1, 1993). 1/2" VHS videocassette color (6min), $36.95.
Presents the background for celebrating Thanksgiving and discusses activities and foods which are part of the holiday today. Illustrations, large and bold with seasonal color, are vintage work by a well-known author/illustrator.
SUBJ: Thanksgiving Day.

CD 394.264　　Ph-2 K-2　$15.98　OD KB226
GOLD, ANDREW. Andrew Gold's Halloween howls (Compact disc). Music for Little People R272532 ISBN 1-56628-095-8, 1996. 1 compact disc (42min).
ALA notable recording, 1997.
Sound recording cassette available R472532 (ISBN 1-56628-096-6, 1996). 1 sound cassette (42min), $9.98.
Good music, great sound effects, funny accents--all combine to create a delightful holiday addition.
SUBJ: Halloween--Songs and music.

CE 394.264　　Ph-3 1-4/2　$7.99　L KB227
HAYWARD, LINDA. First Thanksgiving. Illus. by James Watling. Random House ISBN 0-679-90218-X; In Canada: Random House, 1990. 48p. col. ill. (Step into reading).
Offers a straightforward telling of the traditional Indian-Pilgrim first Thanksgiving story. The easy reading text is accompanied by undistinguished, muddy illustrations. Useful in collections needing additional Thanksgiving materials.
SUBJ: Thanksgiving Day./ Pilgrims (New Plymouth Colony)./ Massachusetts--History--New Plymouth, 1620-1691.

394.264　　Ph-2 2-3/2　$14.95　L KB228
SCOTT, GEOFFREY. Labor Day. Illustrated by Cherie R. Wyman. Carolrhoda ISBN 0-87614-178-5, 1982. 48p. col. ill. (Holiday on my own book).
The working conditions of the 19th century and the origin of Labor Day in New York in 1882 are described as well as how its celebration spread to other cities and became a national holiday.
SUBJ: Labor Day./ Holidays.

NONFICTION

VCR 394.264   Ph-2 3-6 $29.95   OD KB229
THANKSGIVING DAY (Videocassette). GPN 568.010, 1994. 1/2"
VHS videocassette color (14min). (America's special days).
 Includes series teacher's guide.
 The emphasis of this student-narrated video is on the observance of
Thanksgiving in America today. Striking visuals, including parades,
overflowing produce bins, and illustrations from THE FIRST
THANKSGIVING by Thomas Locker, provide a starting place for
discussions of why and how we celebrate Thanksgiving and for
comparing the abundance of some with the needs of others. The last
part of the video features an unnarrated segment showing families
from several cultures as they celebrate Thanksgiving, offering students
and teachers opportunities for interactive discussion while viewing. For
multicultural studies.
 SUBJ: Thanksgiving Day.

394.266   Ph-2 P-2 $9.95   T   KB230
ANGLUND, JOAN WALSH. Christmas is a time of giving. Harcourt
Brace Jovanovich ISBN 0-15-217863-5, c1961. unp. col. ill.
 Presents Christmas as a time of sharing, with its songs, prayers, joys,
family reunions, memories and peace.
 SUBJ: Christmas.

394.266   Ph-3 5-6/7 $15.95   L   KB231
BARTH, EDNA. Holly, reindeer and colored lights: the story of Christmas
symbols. Illus. by Ursula Arndt. Clarion ISBN 0-395-28842-8, c1971.
96p. col. ill.
 Includes bibliography.
 Available from National Library Service for the Blind and Physically
Handicapped on sound recording cassette RC12187.
 Explains the meaning of the holiday symbols which are seen at
Christmas time, many of which have been used since the first
Christmas or even long before. Included are the Christmas tree and its
ornaments, Christmas greens and flowers, the Yule log, Santa Claus
and his ancestors, the custom of giving gifts, the Christmas manger,
the three kings, traditional food, Christmas bells, cards and colors.
Appended is a bibliography of Christmas stories and poems.
 SUBJ: Christmas./ Signs and symbols.

394.266   Ph-3 4-6/10 $18.50   T   KB232
CHRISTMAS IN CANADA. World Book ISBN 0-7166-0894-4; In
Canada: World Book of Canada, 1994. 80p. col. ill. (Christmas around
the world).
 Canadian Christmas customs and traditions are arranged by culture,
including French Canadian, British, German, Ukrainian, and Native
American. Includes recipes, crafts, and carols. Illustrated with
contemporary photographs and graphics and a few archival materials.
Although the lack of an index limits comparisons among cultures, this
will be an interesting addition to holiday collections.
 SUBJ: Christmas--Canada./ Canada--Social life and customs.

394.266   Ph-2 4-6/8 $15.95   T   KB233
CHRISTMAS IN COLONIAL AND EARLY AMERICA. World Book ISBN
0-7166-0875-8; In Canada: World Book, c1996. 80p. col. ill. (Christmas
around the world).
 Includes music and index.
 Compares and contrasts early holiday customs in Massachusetts and
Virginia and shows the influences of Dutch and German immigrants.
Includes development of customs and traditions through the nineteenth
century, the evolution of Santa Claus, craft projects, recipes, and
carols. Illustrated with photographs from Williamsburg and archival
photographs, paintings, drawings and lithographs. Use for seasonal
connections to American history units and for general holiday interest.
 SUBJ: Christmas--United States./ United States--Social life and
customs--To 1775./ United States--History--Colonial period, ca. 1600-
1775.

394.266   Ph-2 2-4/6 $14.95   L   KB234
DE PAOLA, TOMIE. Family Christmas tree book. Holiday House ISBN
0-8234-0416-1, c1980, 1984. unp. col. ill.
 Provides historical background on the development of the decoration
of a tree at Christmas. Also describes where the tree was obtained,
order of adding decorations and meaning of the star on the top.
 SUBJ: Christmas trees./ Christmas.

394.266   Ph-1 2-6/8 $14.95   L   KB235
GRAHAM-BARBER, LYNDA. Ho Ho Ho!: the complete book of Christmas
words. Illus. by Betsy Lewin. Bradbury ISBN 0-02-736933-1; In Canada:
Maxwell Macmillan, 1993. 119p. ill.
 Includes chronology, bibliographies and index.
 Supplies background information for 48 Christmas words and
customs. Good-natured, black-and-white drawings add Christmas
cheer. Introduces customs from various countries, making it useful for
multicultural studies. A worthy addition to other holiday word books

by the same team.
 SUBJ: Christmas./ English language--Etymology.

394.266   Ph-2 4-6/7 $12.00   L   KB236
KENNEDY, PAMELA. Christmas celebration: traditions and customs from
around the world. Art research by F. Lynne Bachleda. Ideals ISBN
0-8249-8587-7; In Canada: Ideals/dist. by Vanwell, 1992. 32p. col. ill.
 Includes index.
 Combines handsome illustrations and gently-paced text to review
Christmas traditions and customs from all parts of the world. An index
helps provide access for fact-seekers; art credits identify illustrative
material.
 SUBJ: Christmas.

394.266   Ph-2 3-6/7 $15.93   L   KB237
LANKFORD, MARY D. Christmas around the world. Illus. by Karen
Dugan. Morrow ISBN 0-688-12167-5, 1995. 47p. col. ill., map.
 Includes chronology, bibliography and index.
 Tells of Christmas customs in 12 countries. Special features include a
chronology, a ten-page crafts section, and a multilingual pronunciation
guide. Useful for both library and home collections. For multicultural
studies.
 SUBJ: Christmas./ Christmas decorations./ Handicraft.

394.266   Ph-2 5-A/7 $6.95   P   KB238
PRESILLA, MARICEL E. Feliz nochebuena, feliz navidad: Christmas feasts
of the Hispanic Caribbean. Illus. by Ismael Espinosa Ferrer. Henry Holt
ISBN 0-8050-4905-3; In Canada: Fitzhenry & Whiteside, c1994, 1996.
unp. col. ill., map.
 Includes glossary and bibliography.
 Describes the foods and customs of Christmas in the Hispanic
Caribbean of Cuba, Puerto Rico, and the Dominican Republic.
Detailed watercolor and ink illustrations add color and excitement. For
multicultural studies.
 SUBJ: Christmas--Caribbean Area./ Christmas cookery--Caribbean
Area.

395   Ph-1 1-6/2 $13.88   L   KB239
ALIKI. Manners. Greenwillow ISBN 0-688-09199-7, 1990. unp. col. ill.
 Packs a multi-layered, velvet-gloved wallop as it describes good
manners in a variety of situations. Cheerful drawings will attract
browsers who will stay around to consider the message. Works well
as a source for role-playing activities.
 SUBJ: Etiquette.

395   Ph-3 P-3/6 $15.00   T   KB240
LEAF, MUNRO. Four-and-twenty watchbirds. Linnet/Shoe String ISBN
0-208-02208-2, c1939, 1990. unp. col. ill.
 Resurrects twenty-four unpleasant creatures from Munro Leaf's works
of the 1940s. Ever present, the good watchbirds observe such
despicable beings as the sneak, the show-off, the plotter, the floor-
piler and other reprehensible types and share with the reader
paragraphs describing the unfortunates' characteristics. Nostalgic for
adults but useful with young listeners.
 SUBJ: Etiquette./ Conduct of life.

VCR 395   Ph-3 3-5 $79.95   OD KB241
MINDING YOUR MANNERS AT SCHOOL (Videocassette). Rainbow
Educational RB849, 1996. 1/2" VHS videocassette color (12min).
(Minding your manners series).
 Includes teacher's guide and reproducibles.
 Includes public performance rights.
 A multicultural cast of student reporters narrate and demonstrate the
basics of good manners relating to caring about others, courtesy, and
being careful. In addition to the informational content, this can serve
as a model for a class project.
 SUBJ: Etiquette./ Behavior./ Conduct of life.

SRC 395   Ph-2 1-3 $11.95   OD KB242
SLONECKI, CATHERINE. Dog ate my homework: social skills for today
(Sound recording cassette). Educational Activities AC 684, 1995. 1
sound cassette (30min).
 Includes lyrics.
 Compact disc available CD 684, 1995. 1 compact disc (30min),
$14.95.
 A rockin', rappin' approach to basics of good manners and self-
esteem with catchy lyrics and sprightly music. This will be useful for
review and reinforcement of concepts and for stimulating discussion.
 SUBJ: Etiquette./ Conduct of life./ Behavior.

395.3   Ph-1 4-6/6 $14.95   T   KB243
JAMES, ELIZABETH. Social smarts: manners for today's kids. By
Elizabeth James and Carol Barkin. Illus. by Martha Weston. Clarion ISBN
0-395-66585-X, 1996. 103p. ill.

Advice columnist K. T. (Knows The) Answers gives students practical advice and explains the reasons for good social manners in situations ranging from meeting and introducing people to table manners, behavior at parties, relationships with peers and adults, and telephone etiquette. Breezy style and illustrative cartoons make points about a wide variety of social interactions without being preachy or heavy-handed.
SUBJ: Etiquette./ Conduct of life.

395.4 Ph-2 P-1/2 $14.93 L KB244
ALIKI. Hello! Good-bye! Greenwillow ISBN 0-688-14334-2, 1996. unp. col. ill.
Describes many of the ways people throughout the world say hello and good-bye, both verbally and through body language. Colorful illustrations tell more of the stories than the text. Use with beginning readers for vocabulary activities, for cultural comparisons, and for fun.
SUBJ: Salutations./ Manners and customs./ Interpersonal communication.

395.4 Ph-3 3-5/6 $17.20 L KB245
BADT, KARIN LUISA. Greetings! Childrens Press ISBN 0-516-08188-8; In Canada: Childrens Press, 1994. 32p. col. ill. (World of difference).
Includes glossary and index.
Discusses greetings and goodbyes in various cultures. Accompanying photographs are not closely correlated with the text, and this may limit its value in some settings. Useful as a browser or in a charting activity. For multicultural studies.
SUBJ: Salutations./ Vocabulary./ Manners and customs.

395.4 Ph-2 2-5/2 $14.95 L KB246
LEEDY, LOREEN. Messages in the mailbox: how to write a letter. Holiday House ISBN 0-8234-0889-2, 1991. unp. col. ill.
Explains the basics of letter writing in a cheerful, cartoon format as Mrs. Gator and her students (a curious mix of animals and multiethnic children) prepare letters of various types. Provides a painless primer in an area in which materials are limited. Includes a list of state and territory abbreviations.
SUBJ: Letter writing.

395.5 Ph-1 2-6/5 $10.00 P KB247
BRAINARD, BETH. Soup should be seen, not heard!: the kids' etiquette book. By Beth Brainard and Sheila Behr. Dell ISBN 0-440-50333-7; In Canada: Bantam, c1988, 1990. 152p. col. ill.
Cartooned illustrations and spiral binding are part of the lively treatment in this title which covers introductions, telephone manners, table behavior, proper dress, and more. Useful as a manners lesson aid for teachers and as a painless and simple confidence builder for interested students.
SUBJ: Etiquette.

395.5 Ph-2 2-6/2 $14.89 L KB248
BUEHNER, CARALYN. It's a spoon, not a shovel. Illus. by Mark Buehner. Dial ISBN 0-8037-1495-5, 1995. unp. col. ill.
Offers the reader a quick, multiple-choice test to determine whether his manners are "monstrous or marvelous." Reinforcement of correct (and obvious) answers is hidden in colorful illustrations which accompany the questions. Corny but useful presentation of a sometimes resisted subject.
SUBJ: Etiquette--Wit and humor./ Questions and answers.

395.5 Ph-2 1-3/4 $4.95 P KB249
LEAF, MUNRO. Manners can be fun. Rev. ed. HarperCollins ISBN 0-06-443053-7, 1985. 47p. ill. (Can be fun books).
Funny pictures illustrate simple advice on how to act when introduced to people, how to behave at home and at school and when playing with other boys and girls.
SUBJ: Etiquette./ Behavior.

395.5 Ph-2 1-3 $4.95 P KB250
PARISH, PEGGY. Mind your manners! Illus. by Marylin Hafner. Mulberry ISBN 0-688-13109-3, 1994. 55p. ill. (Mulberry read-alones).
Originally published by Greenwillow Books, 1978.
Presents proper manners with grown-ups, on the telephone, at the table, at parties, and in other situations involving a proper response. Illustrations liven the routine rules.
SUBJ: Etiquette.

VCR 395.5 Ph-2 3-6 $99.95 OD KB251
PHONE MANNERS (Videocassette). South Central Bell/Sunburst 2442, 1991. 1/2" VHS videocassette color (26min).
Includes teacher's guide.
Uses an MTV format to present the basics of phone manners.
Teacher's guide includes objectives, synopsis, script, activities, and a

quiz. Lively support for discussion of phone use.
SUBJ: Telephone etiquette./ Etiquette.

CDR 398 Ph-1 K-3 $34.95 OD KB252
P.J.'S READING ADVENTURES (CD-ROM). Microsoft/Rabbit Ears ISBN 1-57231-391-9; In Canada: Microsoft Canada, 1996. 3 CD-ROMs color. Version 1.0.
Includes user's guide.
System requirements: Multimedia PC with a 486SX/33 MHz or higher microprocessor; either MS-DOS operating system version 5.0 or later with Microsoft Windows operating system version 3.1 or later, or Windows 95; 4MB of memory (RAM); 6MB of available hard-disk space for each CD; double-speed CD-ROM drive; Windows-compatible sound card; headphones or speakers; Super VGA, 256-color monitor; Microsoft Mouse or compatible pointing device.
This package includes three interactive stories--"Paul Bunyan" told by Jonathan Winters, "Koi and the kola nuts" told by Whoopi Goldberg, and "How the leopard got his spots" told by Danny Glover. All three include a variety of games and animations on various pages of the stories. Works well as a learning center or with individual students.
Contents: Koi and the kola nuts -- Paul Bunyan -- How the leopard got his spots.
SUBJ: Folklore--Africa--Software./ Software--Folklore--Africa./ Africa--Folklore--Software./ Software--Africa--Folklore./ Folklore--United States--Software./ Software--Folklore--United States./ United States--Folklore--Software./ Software--United States--Folklore./ Bunyan, Paul (Legendary character)--Software./ Software--Bunyan, Paul (Legendary character)./ Leopard--Fiction--Software./ Software--Leopard--Fiction./ Interactive media.

398.2 Ph-3 5-A/7 $20.00 L KB253
ALDERSON, BRIAN. Arabian nights, or, Tales told by Sheherezade during a thousand nights and one night. Retold by Brian Alderson. Illus. by Michael Foreman. Books of Wonder/Morrow ISBN 0-688-14219-2, 1995. 192p. col. ill.
Elaborate edition of the tales which Sheherezade told to the king to entertain him, so he would not behead her. All of the favorite tales are retold with drawings outlined and detailed in gold, giving the book the appearance of a Persian manuscript. For mature readers.
SUBJ: Fairy tales./ Folklore--Arab countries./ Arab countries--Folklore.

SRC 398.2 Ph-2 4-5 $9.95 KB254
ARABIAN NIGHTS (Sound recording cassette). As told by Jim Weiss. Greathall Productions 1124-03 ISBN 1-882513-03-7, 1991. 1 sound cassette (60min).
Explaining how Scheherazade entranced the king with her tales of adventure and romance, Jim Weiss tells several of the best-known stories from the Arabian Nights. Listeners soon know why the king pardoned her from death. Excellent introduction to this treasure house of Arabian tales.
SUBJ: Fairy tales./ Folklore--Arab countries./ Arab countries--Folklore.

398.2 Ph-1 5-A/9 $25.00 L KB255
ARABIAN NIGHTS: THEIR BEST-KNOWN TALES. Edited by Kate Douglas Wiggin and Nora A. Smith. Illus. by Maxfield Parrish. Scribner's ISBN 0-684-19589-5; In Canada: Maxwell Macmillan, c1909, 1994. 344p. col. ill.
Tales originally told in the Persian marketplace are presented so that every reader may know the adventures of Aladdin, Sinbad, and Ali Baba. Published in 1909, this edition has the distinguished illustrations by Maxfield Parrish. A classic!
SUBJ: Fairy tales./ Folklore--Arab countries./ Arab countries--Folklore.

398.2 Ph-2 2-3/3 $16.95 T KB256
ARAUJO, FRANK P. Nekane, the lamina and the bear: a tale of the Basque Pyrenees. Illustrated by Xiao Jun Li. Rayve Productions ISBN 1-877810-01-0, 1993. unp. col. ill. (Toucan tales).
Includes glossary.
A Basque version of "Red Riding Hood" in which a young girl is sent to deliver fish and olive oil to her uncle. A supernatural being tries to fool her, but she depends upon her own ingenuity rather than the help of others to outwit it. Gentle watercolors by an internationally known Chinese illustrator make this book a meeting of two cultures.
SUBJ: Basques--Folklore./ Spain--Folklore./ Folklore--Spain./ France--Folklore./ Folklore--France.

398.2 Ph-3 3-4/7 $13.95 T KB257
BAHOUS, SALLY. Sitti and the cats: a tale of friendship. Illus. by Nancy Malick. Roberts Rinehart ISBN 1-879373-61-0; In Canada: Key Porter, 1993. 24p. col. ill.
"Odyssey book."
Includes glossary.

A kitten in a lavender dress and yellow scarf, a kindhearted elderly woman, and a greedy neighbor make a story which proves that goodness will be rewarded and greed punished. Some Palestinian words and customs are explained. For multicultural studies.
SUBJ: Fairy tales./ Folklore--Palestine./ Palestine--Folklore.

SRC 398.2   Ph-1 2-4 $12.95   KB258
BARCHAS, SARAH. Giant and the rabbit: six bilingual folktales from Hispanic culture (Sound recording cassette). Selected and adapted by Sarah Barchas. High Haven Music HHM-106C ISBN 0-9632621-6-5, 1996. 1 sound cassette (70min).
Includes teacher's guide.
ALA notable recording, 1997.
Intermingling Spanish words in the text, Sarah Barchas makes these Hispanic folktales come alive for English-speaking listeners as well as Spanish-speaking children who are learning English. Sources for the materials are given. A useful tool for instruction and individual enjoyment. For multicultural studies.
SUBJ: Folklore./ Spanish language materials./ Bilingual materials--Spanish.

VCR 398.2   Ph-2 K-3 $9.95   KB259
BEAUTY AND THE BEAST (Videocassette). Narrated by Mia Farrow. Music by Ernest Troost. Lightyear Entertainment 54000-3 ISBN 1-879496-44-5, c1989, 1996. 1/2" VHS videocassette color (27min). (Stories to remember).
Closed captioned.
Beauty sojourns with the Beast to fulfill her father's promise when he took a rose from the Beast's garden. A separation makes her realize that she has learned to love the creature because of his kindness to her. Her belated return releases him from the spell which held him, and the two find happiness. The dream-like drawings of Mordicai Gerstein illustrate the story which is poignantly read by Mia Farrow.
SUBJ: Fairy tales./ Folklore--France./ France--Folklore.

SRC 398.2   Ph-3 2-A $10.00   OD KB260
BEN IZZY, JOEL. Beggar King and other tales from around the world (Sound recording cassette). Old City Press JBI-2 ISBN 0-9631129-1-0, 1993. 1 sound cassette (55min).
Retellings of tales from Ireland, Poland, China, Israel, and England in which Joel Ben Izzy amuses and gently teaches his audiences. The teller uses variety in his voice and includes a number of musical pieces as background and introduction to the stories. For group listening sessions and multicultural studies.
SUBJ: Folklore.

SRC 398.2   Ph-3 3-A $10.00   OD KB261
BEN IZZY, JOEL. Buried treasures: a storyteller's journey (Sound recording cassette). Old City Press JBI-3CS ISBN 0-9631129-2-9, 1995. 1 sound cassette (55min).
Compact disc available JBI-3CD, 1995. 1 compact disc (55min), $15.00.
The stories retold here are a mixed bag with material from Israel, Haiti, and the Ukraine. The smooth and enjoyable retellings are about tricksters, the best known being Herschel. The tape was originally recorded before a live audience in San Francisco. Useful for group listening sessions for multicultural studies.
SUBJ: Folklore.

SRC 398.2   Ph-3 3-A $10.00   OD KB262
BEN IZZY, JOEL. Stories from far away (Sound recording cassette). Old City Press JBI-1 ISBN 0-9631129-0-2, 1991. 1 sound cassette (56min).
ALA notable recording, 1992.
Joel Ben Izzy has traveled widely. The stories he tells come from Israel, Japan, and Europe. Wisdom that is ageless is mixed with humor. For storytelling sessions and multicultural studies.
SUBJ: Folklore.

398.2   Ph-2 2-4/4 $15.95   T KB263
BERENZY, ALIX. Rapunzel. Retold and illus. by Alix Berenzy. Henry Holt ISBN 0-8050-1283-4; In Canada: Fitzhenry & Whiteside, 1995. unp. col. ill.
Based on a German version which predates the Grimm version, this retelling has stunning illustrations created with colored pencil and gouache on black paper. The final reunion of Rapunzel and her prince is a gleeful, happy ending.
SUBJ: Fairy tales./ Folklore--Germany./ Germany--Folklore.

SRC 398.2   Ph-1 2-6 $10.00   OD KB264
BIRCH, CAROL. Careful what you wish for (Sound recording cassette). Frostfire 104, 1993. 1 sound cassette (62min).
Five amusing tales demonstrate the results of poor wishing. Includes a beautiful rendition of Ruth Sawyer's story "Wee Meg Barnileg and the fairies."
SUBJ: Folklore./ Short stories.

SRC 398.2   Ph-3 2-6 $10.00   OD KB265
BIRCH, CAROL. Happily-ever-after love stories...more or less (Sound recording cassette). Frostfire, 1987. 1 sound cassette (47min).
ALA notable recording.
Four stories show the varied forms of love. The teller's clear enunciation and use of dramatic pauses capture the listener's attention and make the material memorable.
SUBJ: Folklore./ Short stories.

SRC 398.2   Ph-1 3-6 $10.00   OD KB266
BIRCH, CAROL. Nightmares rising (Sound recording cassette). Frostfire 100, 1984. 1 sound cassette (48min).
Four scary stories are skillfully told by Carol Birch. All material is suitable for use at Halloween or to develop listening skills. "Mary Culhane and the Dead Man" is long and must be heard in one sitting to maintain the suspense.
SUBJ: Folklore./ Short stories.

398.2   Ph-1 K-2/3 $14.95   L KB267
BIRDSEYE, TOM. Soap! soap! don't forget the soap!: an Appalachian folktale. Retold by Tom Birdseye. Illus. by Andrew Glass. Holiday House ISBN 0-8234-1005-6, 1993. unp. col. ill.
Poor Plug Honeycut! He can't remember his name, let alone the directions his mother gives him when he is sent to the store. Rollicking humor with illustrations to match.
SUBJ: Folklore--Appalachian Region./ Appalachian Region--Folklore.

398.2   Ph-2 4-5/6 $15.95   L KB268
BRETT, JAN. Beauty and the Beast. Retold and illustrated by Jan Brett. Clarion ISBN 0-89919-497-4, 1989. nnp. col. ill.
Based on the version by Sir Arthur Quiller-Couch.
Stealing a rose from the beast's garden, a merchant must return one of his daughters to the strange palace where she develops a fondness for the beast. Ornate drawings portray a fairy tale land which can only exist in one's imagination.
SUBJ: Fairy tales./ Folklore--France./ France--Folklore.

398.2   Ph-1 P-3/6 $16.95   T KB269
BROOKE, L. LESLIE. Golden goose book: a fairy tale picture book. Clarion ISBN 0-395-61303-5, 1992. 96p. ill. (some col.).
Four favorite nursery tales are told here with time-honored drawings by L. Leslie Brooke. First published in the United States in 1905, this classic of children's literature has been reissued with an afterword of its history by Neil Philip.
SUBJ: Fairy tales./ Folklore.

398.2   Ph-3 5-A/5 $16.00   L KB270
BRUCHAC, JOSEPH. Between earth and sky: legends of Native American sacred places. Illus. by Thomas Locker. Harcourt Brace ISBN 0-15-200042-9; In Canada: Harcourt Brace c/o Canadian Manda, 1996. unp. col. ill.
Includes bibliography.
A Native American boy and his uncle, Old Bear, discuss what makes a sacred place. They soon decide that there are special places in all parts of the Native American world remembered by the people for varied reasons. Luminous paintings create a haunting setting for legends succinctly told in prose facing the illustrations. For the special audience who recognizes the beauty of nature and how it became basic to Native American beliefs. For multicultural studies.
SUBJ: Indians of North America--Legends./ Folklore--North America./ North America--Folklore./ Indians of North America--Religion and mythology.

398.2   Ph-2 2-6/3 $18.95   L KB271
BRUCHAC, JOSEPH. Four ancestors: stories, songs, and poems from Native North America. Illus. by S. S. Burrus...[et al.]. BridgeWater ISBN 0-8167-3843-2, 1996. 96p. col. ill.
Bruchac notes in his introduction that Native Americans believe that fire, earth, water, and air are all a part of a human being and are thus his/her ancestors just as each person has four grandparents. The stories about these elements come from many sources, but all read smoothly and are suitable for reading aloud. Handsome illustrations and borders make this an attractive book. Invaluable for science as well as Native American units and multicultural studies.
SUBJ: Indians of North America--Folklore./ Folklore--North America./ North America--Folklore.

398.2   Ph-2 3-5/6 $14.99   T KB272
BRUCHAC, JOSEPH. Gluskabe and the four wishes. Retold by Joseph Bruchac. Illus. by Christine Nyburg Shrader. Cobblehill/Dutton ISBN 0-525-65164-0, 1995. unp. col. ill.
Gluskabe lives on a far island, but four Abenaki men seek him to ask for great gifts. Three of the men are unable to restrain themselves from looking in the pouches they received, but the fourth waits to

open his pouch and gains the ability to hunt and provide for his people. Strong teaching tale which is entertaining as well as instructional. Subtle watercolors are appropriate to the atmosphere and locale of the tale. For multicultural studies.
SUBJ: Abenaki Indians--Folklore./ Indians of North America--Folklore.

SRC 398.2 Ph-3 4-5 $9.95 OD KB273
BRUCHAC, JOSEPH. Gluskabe stories (Sound recording cassette). Yellow Moon Press 006 ISBN 0-938756-26-5, 1990. 1 sound cassette (80min).
Six stories from the Abenaki, the native inhabitants of northern New England, are told by a renowned storyteller who presents this material orally and in written form. Tape can be used in conjunction with Bruchac's book THE FOUR WISHES. For multicultural studies.
SUBJ: Indians of North America--Folklore./ Abenaki Indians--Folklore.

VCR 398.2 Ph-3 P-3 $149.95 OD KB274
CALDECOTT VIDEO LIBRARY. VOL. IV (Videocassette). Weston Woods HMPV495V ISBN 0-89719-322-9, 1992. 1/2" VHS videocassette color (46min).
Includes public performance rights.
Four African folktales which have won the Caldecott Award are presented. Useful for collections where limited space or budgets prohibit purchase of individual videocassettes.
Contents: STORY-A STORY, Gail E. Haley; VILLAGE OF ROUND AND SQUARE HOUSES, Ann Grifalconi; WHY MOSQUITOES BUZZ IN PEOPLE'S EARS, retold by Verna Aardema; MUFARO'S BEAUTIFUL DAUGHTERS, John Steptoe.
SUBJ: Caldecott Medal books./ Folklore--Africa./ Africa--Folklore.

398.2 Ph-2 2-4/3 $14.89 L KB275
CLIMO, SHIRLEY. Irish Cinderlad. Illus. by Loretta Krupinski. HarperCollins ISBN 0-06-024397-X; In Canada: HarperCollins, 1996. unp. col. ill.
With the help of a giant's sword, a kindly lad rescues a princess from a dragon. In his haste to leave, he loses his boot. The princess engages a royal messenger to comb the countryside in search of the owner of the boot. Readers will enjoy this masculine version of the universal Cinderella story.
SUBJ: Fairy tales./ Folklore--Ireland./ Ireland--Folklore.

398.2 Ph-1 3-4/4 $13.95 L KB276
COOPER, SUSAN. Tam Lin. Retold by Susan Cooper. Illus. by Warwick Hutton. McElderry ISBN 0-689-50505-1; In Canada: Collier Macmillan, 1991. unp. col. ill.
The ballad of Margaret and Tam Lin is retold by Cooper and Hutton as part three of their Celtic trilogy. Good for storytelling and an introduction to ballads.
SUBJ: Fairy tales./ Scotland--Folklore./ Folklore--Scotland.

398.2 Ph-3 3-6/6 $7.95 P KB277
COURLANDER, HAROLD. Fire on the mountain and other stories from Ethiopia and Eritrea. By Harold Courlander and Wolf Leslau. Illus. by Robert Kane. Henry Holt ISBN 0-8050-3652-0; In Canada: Fitzhenry & Whiteside, c1950, 1995. 133p. ill.
Includes glossary.
The people, animals, and countryside of the ancient land of Ethiopia are brought to life in this collection of tales, gathered at firsthand from the lips of wayside storytellers. A historically important book for large folktale collections. For multicultural studies.
SUBJ: Ethiopia--Folklore./ Folklore--Ethiopia./ Eritrea--Folklore./ Folklore--Eritrea./ Africa--Folklore./ Folklore--Africa.

398.2 Ph-2 1-A/5 $9.95 P KB278
COURLANDER, HAROLD. People of the short blue corn: tales and legends of the Hopi Indians. Illus. by Enrico Arno. Henry Holt ISBN 0-8050-3511-7; In Canada: Fitzhenry & Whiteside c1970, 1996. 184p. ill.
"Owlet book."
Originally published by Harcourt Brace Jovanovich, 1970.
Includes glossary.
The short ear of blue corn symbolized to the Hopi Indians that their life would be long and full of struggles. The 17 legends explain this belief and the ways of the animals and people who are part of Hopi Indian life in the American Southwest. Extensive notes tell the origin of tales, and a pronunciation guide and glossary aid the reader. For multicultural studies.
SUBJ: Hopi Indians--Folklore./ Indians of North America--Arizona--Folklore./ Folklore--Arizona./ Arizona--Folklore.

398.2 Ph-2 3-5/7 $10.95 P KB279
COURLANDER, HAROLD. Tiger's whisker and other tales from Asia and the Pacific. Illus. by Enrico Arno. Henry Holt ISBN 0-8050-3512-5; In Canada: Fitzhenry & Whiteside, c1959, 1995. 170p. ill.

First published by Harcourt, Brace & World, 1959.
"Owlet book."
Thirty-one brief tales from Asia and the Pacific are simply retold. They capture the places from which the stories originated, and full notes give more insight into the material. A basic collection which will be useful in units on the Far Eastern countries and multicultural studies.
SUBJ: Folklore--Asia, Southeastern./ Asia, Southeastern--Folklore./ Folklore--Middle East./ Middle East--Folklore./ Folklore--Oceania./ Oceania--Folklore.

398.2 Ph-2 4-6/6 $8.00 P KB280
D'AULAIRE, INGRI. D'Aulaires' trolls. By Ingri and Edgar Parin d'Aulaire. Dell ISBN 0-440-40779-6; In Canada: Bantam Doubleday Dell, c1972, 1993. 62p. col. ill.
"Yearling book."
In the old days, the Norwegian mountains belonged to the trolls. The habits of these trolls, their appearance, and some of their best known adventures are related here. The text is illustrated by full-page lithographs which picture the trolls as truly frightening creatures.
SUBJ: Trolls--Fiction./ Folklore--Norway./ Norway--Folklore.

CE 398.2 Ph-3 5-A $12.95 P KB281
DAVENPORT, TOM. From the Brothers Grimm: a contemporary retelling of American folktales and classic stories. By Tom Davenport and Gary Carden. Highsmith ISBN 0-917846-20-6, 1992. 105p. ill.
Teacher's guide available, $4.00.
Videocassettes available as a set 95537, $600.00.
Appalachian and other American regional settings give fresh perspective to ten familiar tales in which characters prove themselves by overcoming adversity. Companion volume to Davenport's award-winning films is adapted from his screenplays and illustrated with photographs of his live-action scenes.
Individual titles also available on videocassette with public performance rights: ASHPET 95527 (45min), $89.00; BEARSKIN 95528 (20min), $60.00; BRISTLELIP 95529 (19min), $60.00; FROG KING 95530 (27min), $60.00; GOOSE GIRL 95531 (18min), $60.00; HANSEL AND GRETEL 95532 (16min), $60.00; JACK AND THE DENTIST'S DAUGHTER 95533 (38min), $60.00; MUTZMAG 95534 (53min), $89.00; RAPUNZEL, RAPUNZEL 95535 (15min), $60.00; SOLDIER JACK 95536 (40min), $89.00.
SUBJ: Fairy tales./ Folklore--Germany./ Germany--Folklore.

398.2 Ph-2 4-5/6 $14.95 L KB282
DE BEAUMONT, MARIE LEPRINCE. Beauty and the Beast. Translated by Richard Howard. Illus. by Hilary Knight. Simon & Schuster ISBN 0-671-70720-5, 1990. 36p. col. ill.
A request that her father bring a rose back to her from his business venture, plunges Beauty and her father into the power of the Beast. Proving that she prefers virtue over beauty and wit, Beauty wins her handsome Prince while her selfish sisters are doomed because of their wicked and envious hearts. This oversized book is done in the romantic style typical of the art nouveau period and is totally in keeping with the tale.
SUBJ: Fairy tales./ Folklore--France./ France--Folklore.

398.2 Ph-3 4-5/6 $18.95 L KB283
DELACRE, LULU. Golden tales: myths, legends, and folktales from Latin America. Scholastic ISBN 0-590-48186-X; In Canada: Scholastic, 1996. 74p. col. ill., map.
Spanish edition available DE ORO Y ESMERALDAS: MITOS, LEYENDAS Y CUENTOS POPULARES DE LATINOAMERICA (ISBN 0-590-67683-0, 1996).
This compilation is useful in social studies units on South American history (particularly the early civilizations). The stories are grouped by culture--Taino, Zapotec, Muisca, and Inca. Illustrations show native life, folk motifs, and artifacts. Good map, notes, and pronunciation guide provide background information. For multicultural studies.
SUBJ: Latin America--Folklore./ Folklore--Latin America./ Indians--Folklore./ Spanish language materials.

398.2 Ph-2 3-5/2 $17.95 T KB284
DEMI. Magic gold fish: a Russian folktale. By Aleksandr Pushkin. Adapted and illus. by Demi. Translated by Louis Zelikoff. Henry Holt ISBN 0-8050-3243-6; In Canada: Fitzhenry & Whiteside, 1995. unp. col. ill.
A Russian version of the tale of the fisherman who caught a fish which could fulfill any desire. The fisherman's wife soon discovers this gift and gets whatever she wants until her wishes become unreasonable. A wide band of gold encircles the drawings done in traditional Chinese inks (with powdered jade for good luck).
SUBJ: Fairy tales./ Folklore.

NONFICTION

398.2   Ph-3 2-3/6 $14.95   L   KB285
DE PAOLA, TOMIE. Legend of the Persian carpet. Retold by Tomie De Paola. Illus. by Claire Ewart. Putnam ISBN 0-399-22415-7; In Canada: Putnam, 1993. unp. col. ill.
"Whitebird book."
The story of how the first Persian carpet came into existence is told with illustrations of the old palaces and workplaces of Persia (Iran).
SUBJ: Folklore--Iran./ Iran--Folklore./ Carpets--Folklore.

398.2   Ph-2 3-5/7 $7.95   P   KB286
DESPAIN, PLEASANT. Eleven nature tales: a multicultural journey. Illus. by Joe Shlichta. August House ISBN 0-87493-458-9, 1996. 91p. ill.
Simple tales from diverse cultures show respect for the natural world. The format will encourage browsers to sample these stories. Good choice for reading aloud when celebrating Earth Day. For multicultural studies and environmental studies.
SUBJ: Folklore./ Storytelling--Collections./ Ecology--Folklore.

398.2   Ph-2 2-5/3 $15.95   L   KB287
DESPAIN, PLEASANT. Strongheart Jack and the beanstalk. Illus. by Joe Shlichta. August House LittleFolk ISBN 0-87483-414-7; In Canada: Monarch Books, 1995. unp. col. ill.
A full retelling of JACK AND THE BEANSTALK in which his father's death is explained and a cat and a lively maid play important roles in Jack's slaying of the giant. This version, based on the earliest known British stories, will interest any reader who seeks variations of familiar tales since it contains several elements which are unique.
SUBJ: Fairy tales./ Folklore--England./ England--Folklore./ Giants--Folklore.

SRC 398.2   Ph-3 K-2 $12.00   KB288
DESPAIN, PLEASANT. Tales to tell from around the world. Vol. 1 (Sound recording cassette). August House ISBN 0-87483-417-1, 1995. 1 sound cassette (57min).
Twenty short tales which reflect the diversity of material around the world are retold. The tales are brief, witty, and ideal for primary grades. The storyteller stresses that these tales are easy to learn and tell. For multicultural studies.
TALES TO TELL FROM AROUND THE WORLD, VOL. 2 (ISBN 0-87483-418-X, 1995). 1 sound cassette (43min), $12.00.
SUBJ: Folklore./ Storytelling.

398.2   Ph-3 4-5/7 $14.95   T   KB289
DUGIN, ANDREJ. Dragon feathers. By Andrej Dugin and Olga Dugina. Lickle Publishing/dist. by PRI ISBN 1-56566-047-1, 1993. unp. col. ill.
To win his ladylove, Henry must pluck three golden feathers from a dragon and find solutions to problems troubling those he meets on his travels. Detailed, fanciful illustrations make this a book for the perceptive reader who will pore over the pictures to find the mythical creatures.
SUBJ: Fairy tales./ Folklore--Austria./ Austria--Folklore.

398.2   Ph-1 2-5/5 $17.95   T   KB290
EARLY, MARGARET. Sleeping Beauty. Retold and illus. by Margaret Early. Abrams ISBN 0-8109-3835-9, 1993. unp. col. ill.
Annoyed at being overlooked and uninvited to the royal christening, an old fairy casts a spell over the princess and predicts that one day she will prick her finger and die. In order to protect the princess from harm, another fairy alters the spell so that she will not die, but sleep for 100 years until wakened by a prince. Vivid, jewel-like drawings, which show the area of France where the story originated, accompany this faithful retelling.
SUBJ: Fairy tales./ Folklore--France./ France--Folklore.

CD 398.2   Ph-1 3-5 $14.95   OD KB291
ELLIOTT, DOUG. Crawdads, doodlebugs and creasy greens: songs, stories and lore celebrating the natural world (Compact disc). Native Ground Music NG-CD-600 ISBN 1-883206-15-4, 1996. 1 compact disc (59min).
ALA notable recording, 1996.
Sound recording cassette available NG600 (ISBN 1-883206-10-3, 1995). 1 sound cassette (59min), $9.95.
Tales of mosquitos, lobsters, woodpeckers, etc. are accompanied by songs sung by the storyteller. Many of the tales are Native American legends, but others are from the mountains and across the ocean. A wonderful collection of nature lore to incorporate into interdisciplinary science units or multicultural studies.
SUBJ: Folklore./ Songs./ Nature--Songs and music.

398.2   Ph-2 3-4/6 $19.95   T   KB292
EVETTS-SECKER, JOSEPHINE. Mother and daughter tales. Retold by Josephine Evetts-Secker. Illus. by Helen Cann. Abbeville Kids ISBN 0-7892-0281-6, 1996. 80p. col. ill. (Abbeville anthology).
Originally published in Great Britain, Barefoot Book, Ltd.
"These (ten) stories explore themes universal to the mother/daughter experience. They reflect what it is to be a natural and spiritual woman; to be in the home and alone in the wild; to distinguish the false from the true; to honor the process of birth and death." (Notes p.80) Carefully selected stories bring to life the relationships of daughters to mothers. The multicultural collection includes familiar and lesser known tales. For women's studies and for reading aloud.
SUBJ: Mothers and daughters--Folklore./ Folklore.

TB 398.2   Ph-2 2-4 $8.95   OD KB293
FAIRY TALES FROM THE PICTURE BOOK PARADE (Talking book). Weston Woods WW735C, 1986. 1 sound cassette (48min).
Four tales--two from folklore and two modern fairy tales--are skillfully told for middle grade listeners.
Contents: Side 1: Beauty and the beast, retold by Warwick Hutton, narrated by Pauline Brailsford (12min); The selfish giant, by Oscar Wilde, narrated by Charles Cioffi (13min); Side 2: Red riding hood; adapted by Beatrice Schenk De Regnier, narrated by Carol Birch, (7min); The ugly duckling, by Hans Christian Andersen, adapted by Sven Otto S., narrated by Pauline Brailsford, (17min).
SUBJ: Folklore./ Fairy tales.

SRC 398.2   Ph-2 K-3 $9.95   KB294
FAIRYTALE FAVORITES IN STORY AND SONG (Sound recording cassette). As told by Jim Weiss. Greathall Productions 1124-12 ISBN 1-882513-12-6, 1993. 1 sound cassette (60min).
Four of the best loved fairy tales are retold here with modern touches which will please the listener. Weiss tells his stories without a script and with the addition of original songs.
Contents: Stone soup -- Puss in boots -- The shoemaker and the elves -- Rapunzel.
SUBJ: Fairy tales./ Folklore.

398.2   Ph-2 4-6/5 $16.00   T   KB295
FANG, LINDA. Ch'i-lin purse: a collection of ancient Chinese stories. Retold by Linda Fang. Illus. by Jeanne M. Lee. Farrar Straus Giroux ISBN 0-374-31241-9; In Canada: HarperCollins, 1995. 127p. ill.
Includes glossary.
Nine stories from the author's childhood were either told to her or came from novels or popular operas. The material is well suited to telling and will please those seeking new tales which are not easily found in popular collections. For a discriminating audience. For multicultural studies.
SUBJ: Folklore--China./ China--Folklore.

398.2   Ph-3 2-5/5 $15.95   T   KB296
FLOOD, NANCY BOHAC. From the mouth of the monster eel: stories from Micronesia. By Bo Flood. Illus. by Margo Vitarelli. Fulcrum Kids ISBN 1-55591-245-1, 1996. 56p. ill. (World stories).
Includes glossary.
Tales from the Micronesian Islands explain the origins of the breadfruit and coconut trees and the outrigger canoe. Other stories depict monsters and sea creatures. Decorative woodcuts complement the material. For units on oceans and the Pacific Islands and multicultural studies.
SUBJ: Folklore--Micronesia./ Micronesia--Folklore.

SRC 398.2   Ph-2 5-A $10.00   OD KB297
FOLKTELLERS. Stories for the road (Sound recording cassette). Mama-T Artists MTA-5C, 1992. 1 sound cassette (40min).
Six selections, some funny, told in two voices. Many are traditional, but the best are from Richard Kennedy: THE DANCING MAN and COME AGAIN IN THE SPRING. Almost everyone will enjoy the hilarious non-literary "Peanut butter."
SUBJ: Folklore--United States./ United States--Folklore.

SRC 398.2   Ph-2 K-3 $10.00   OD KB298
FOLKTELLERS. Tales to grow on (Sound recording cassette). By Connie Regan-Blake and Barbara Freeman. Mama-T Artists, c1981. 1 sound cassette (48min).
Presents traditional Appalachian Mountain tales, many of which have been collected by Richard Chase, along with humorous contemporary stories. The Folktellers' unique tandem storytelling brings the tales to life with vivid images, audience participation chants, and street rhymes. Good resource for beginning storytellers.
SUBJ: United States--Folklore./ Folklore--United States./ Appalachian Region--Folklore./ Folklore--Appalachian Region.

398.2   Ph-1 K-3/4 $14.95   T   KB299
FORD, BERNETTE. Hunter who was king and other African tales. Adapted by Bernette Ford. Illus. by George Ford. Hyperion ISBN 1-56282-585-2; In Canada: Little, Brown, 1994. unp. col. ill.
A pop-up book which consists of three tales: the traditional story of how a turtle fools an elephant and a hippopotamus into believing that

he is equal to them, a romance in which a prince loses his princess because of curiosity, and the moralistic tale of the youngest son who discovers that his father's small gift is the greatest of all. Well constructed with pop-up figures that amaze and delight. For reading aloud with small groups in storytimes and multicultural studies.
SUBJ: Folklore--Africa./ Africa--Folklore./ Toy and movable books.

398.2   Ph-3 3-5/6 $16.95   P   KB300
FOREST, HEATHER. Wonder tales from around the world. Illus. by David Boston. August House ISBN 0-87483-422-8, 1995. 155p. ill.
Heather Forest as a storyteller uses a "minstrel performance style [which] interweaves original poetry, guitar, and the sung and spoken word." She incorporates these practices into the 27 tales retold in this anthology. Though multicultural in scope, the tales share common themes of human hopes, fears, and dreams. Good choices for reading aloud for multicultural studies.
SUBJ: Folklore.

398.2   Ph-2 K-2/2 $15.95   T   KB301
FRENCH, VIVIAN. Lazy Jack. Retold by Vivian French. Illus. by Russell Ayto. Candlewick ISBN 1-56402-130-0; In Canada: Candlewick/dist. by Douglas & McIntyre, 1995. unp. col. ill.
Lazy Jack can do a day's work, but he is never able to get his pay (a coin, milk, cheese, puppy, fish, or donkey) home safely. His misadventures cause the village to laugh as will readers. Cartoon-like illustrations capture the humor. For reading aloud.
SUBJ: Fairy tales./ Folklore--England./ England--Folklore.

398.2   Ph-2 2-3/6 $15.89   L   KB302
GERINGER, LAURA. Seven ravens. By the Brothers Grimm. Adapted by Laura Geringer. Illus. by Edward S. Gazsi. HarperCollins ISBN 0-06-023553-5; In Canada: HarperCollins, 1994. 32p. col. ill.
Freely adapted retelling of a young girl's search for her seven brothers who were turned into ravens by her father's thoughtless curse. Drawings depict a make-believe world of caves, glass castles, and underground treasure troves.
SUBJ: Fairy tales./ Folklore--Germany./ Germany--Folklore.

398.2   Ph-2 K-2/3 $17.95   L   KB303
GONZALEZ, LUCIA M. Senor Cat's romance and other favorite stories from Latin America. Retold by Lucia M. Gonzalez. Illus. by Lulu Delacre. Scholastic ISBN 0-590-48537-7; In Canada: Scholastic, 1997. 48p. col. ill.
Includes glossaries.
Six of the best known stories from Latin America are retold. The illustrator depicts scenes from her childhood home, Puerto Rico, to dramatize the tales. Notes affixed to each story further explain the origins and motifs of the material. For reading aloud.
SUBJ: Latin America--Folklore./ Folklore--Latin America./ United States--Folklore./ Folklore--United States.

398.2   Ph-2 2-4/5 $15.95   L   KB304
GREENE, ELLIN. Billy Beg and his bull: an Irish tale. Retold by Ellin Greene. Illus. by Kimberly Bulcken Root. Holiday House ISBN 0-8234-1100-1, 1994. unp. col. ill.
After his mother's death, Billy's closest companion is his bull. Driven from his home by his stepmother, Billy is cared for by his companion even after the bull dies in a mighty battle. Familiar Irish folktale with new illustrations.
SUBJ: Fairy tales./ Folklore--Ireland./ Ireland--Folklore.

398.2   Ph-2 2-4/5 $13.95   L   KB305
GREENE, JACQUELINE DEMBAR. What his father did. Illus. by John O'Brien. Houghton Mifflin ISBN 0-395-55042-4, 1992. 32p. col. ill.
A weary traveler appears at an inn and asks for food and a place to sleep. When the innkeeper refuses to give him something to eat, the traveler's reply that he would do what his father did brings surprising results. A story to keep readers guessing to the end which can easily be adapted for reader's theater.
SUBJ: Jews--Folklore./ Humorous stories.

398.2   Ph-3 5-A/7 $9.95   P   KB306
GRIMM, JACOB. Juniper tree and other tales from Grimm. Selected by Lore Segal and Maurice Sendak. With four tales translated by Randall Jarrell. Illus. by Maurice Sendak. Farrar, Straus and Giroux ISBN 0-374-51358-9; In Canada: HarperCollins, c1973, 1992. 332p. ill.
From the 210 tales in the complete collection of Grimm, Lore Segal and Maurice Sendak have chosen 27 tales, some very familiar and some not too well known. Each of the stories is illustrated with a handsome full page pen-and-ink sketch by Maurice Sendak. The drawings are filled with German hausfraus, cunning animals and willing but not-too-clever peasants. The book is distinguished in all respects--design, translation, and illustration.
SUBJ: Fairy tales./ Folklore--Germany./ Germany--Folklore.

398.2   Ph-2 2-4/4 $14.95   L   KB307
GRIMM, JACOB. Rapunzel. Retold from the Brothers Grimm by Barbara Rogasky. Illus. by Trina Schart Hyman. Holiday House ISBN 0-8234-0454-4, 1982. unp. col. ill.
Longing for rampion (lettuce), a woman sends her husband into a witch's garden to gather some for her. When caught, the man promises to give to the witch his unborn child. The witch hides the girl in a tower but a prince finds her there. Following a series of misfortunes, the two escape to the prince's kingdom and happiness.
SUBJ: Fairy tales./ Folklore--Germany./ Germany--Folklore.

398.2   Ph-2 K-2/2 $15.95   T   KB308
GRIMM, JACOB. Rumpelstiltskin. By the Brothers Grimm. Retold and illus. by Marie-Louise Gay. Groundwood/dist. by Publishers Group West ISBN 0-88899-279-3; In Canada: Groundwood/Douglas & McIntyre, 1997. unp. col. ill.
Marie-Louise Gay's lighthearted, whimsical drawings are well suited to this familiar tale of a poor girl who must discover the name of the little man who helps her spin gold out of straw. The pictures which spill over borders are done in graphite and colored pencils.
SUBJ: Fairy tales./ Folklore--Germany./ Germany--Folklore.

398.2   Ph-2 3-5/7 $15.88   L   KB309
GRIMM, JACOB. Seven ravens: a fairy tale. By the Brothers Grimm. Illustrated by Henriette Sauvant. Translated by Anthea Bell. North-South Books ISBN 1-55858-459-5; In Canada: North-South Books, 1995. unp. col. ill.
Their father's unkind words spoken at the time of their sister's baptism cause seven boys to be turned into ravens. The sister's search for them and their reunion is captured in text and oil paintings which are a mixture of humor and fantasy. For reading aloud.
SUBJ: Fairy tales./ Folklore--Germany./ Germany--Folklore.

398.2   Ph-2 3-4/6 $5.95   P   KB310
GRIMM, JACOB. Snow-White and the seven dwarfs. Translated from the Brothers Grimm by Randall Jarrell. Illus. by Nancy Ekholm Burkert. Farrar, Straus & Giroux ISBN 0-374-46868-0, 1972. unp. col. ill.
Caldecott Honor Book.
Her stepmother's evil jealousy forces Snow White to find shelter with seven dwarfs deep in the woods. Luminously hued and deeply detailed drawings expand upon the rich text of the beloved folktale. Skilled middle grade readers enjoy this edition.
SUBJ: Folklore--Germany./ Germany--Folklore./ Fairy tales./ Jealousy--Folklore.

398.2   Ph-2 3-4/6 $16.88   L   KB311
GRIMM, JACOB. Twelve dancing princesses: a fairy tale. By Jacob and Wilhelm Grimm. Translated from the German by Anthea Bell. Illus. by Dorothee Duntze. North-South Books ISBN 1-55858-217-7; In Canada: North-South Books/dist. by Vanwell, 1995. unp. col. ill.
Lured by the promise that he would gain a princess as a bride and eventually rule a kingdom, a poor soldier with magical gifts sets out to find why the princesses have holes in their shoes each night. This fanciful, romantic tale has stylized drawings which show the princesses in gowns which will delight the reader.
SUBJ: Fairy tales./ Folklore--Germany./ Germany--Folklore.

398.2   Ph-1 4-6/3 $19.95   L   KB312
HAMILTON, VIRGINIA. Her stories: African-American folktales, fairy tales, and true tales. Illus. by Leo and Diane Dillon. Blue Sky Press/Scholastic ISBN 0-590-47370-0; In Canada: Scholastic, 1995. 112p. col. ill.
Includes bibliography.
Coretta Scott King Author Award, 1996.
Coretta Scott King Illustrator Honor book, 1996.
Selectors' Choice, 21st ed.
A compilation of stories from the "vast treasure store of traditional black folklore." (p.xi) The tales are a mixture of animal stories, fairy tales, supernatural tales, legends, and true narratives. All are brief and express another facet of the African-American woman's experiences. A fine selection for reading aloud. For multicultural studies and women's studies.
SUBJ: Afro-Americans--Folklore./ Women--Folklore.

398.2   Ph-2 K-3/5 $14.89   L   KB313
HAN, OKI S. Kongi and Potgi: a Cinderella story from Korea. Adapted by Oki S. Han and Stephanie Haboush Plunkett. Illus. by Oki S. Han. Dial ISBN 0-8037-1572-2, 1996. unp. col. ill.
A second marriage brings a harsh stepmother and a wicked stepsister into the life of Kongi, a Korean maiden. Animals ease her hard work, and spirits provide finery and transportation to a party being given for a prince. A lost slipper brings the prince and maid together. Watercolor illustrations depict Korean rural life, and a preface gives a fuller explanation of what life was like in Korea pre-1900. For

reading aloud.
SUBJ: Fairy tales./ Folklore--Korea./ Korea--Folklore.

398.2   Ph-3 1-2/2 $3.99   P   KB314
HAUTZIG, DEBORAH. Aladdin and the magic lamp. Retold by Deborah Hautzig. Illus. by Kathy Mitchell. Random House ISBN 0-679-83241-6; In Canada: Random House, 1993. 48p. col. ill. (Step into reading).
    Aladdin is led to believe that a magician is his long-lost uncle. When he helps the sorcerer find a magic lamp, he gains the services of a powerful genie. This familiar tale is simply retold for beginning readers.
SUBJ: Fairy tales./ Folklore--Arab countries./ Arab countries--Folklore.

398.2   Ph-2 2-5/4 $10.95   P   KB315
HAYES, JOE. Watch out for clever women!/Cuidado con las mujeres astutas!: Hispanic folktales. Illus. by Vicki Trego Hill. Cinco Puntos Press ISBN 0-938317-20-2, 1994. 77p. ill.
    Five stories from the Southwest are retold by storyteller Joe Hayes in a simple and direct fashion that makes the material easy to read and to tell. In each story, a woman saves a man or herself from being denied a rightful reward or property. For multicultural units.
SUBJ: New Mexico--Folklore./ Folklore--New Mexico./ Southwest, New--Folklore./ Folklore--Southwest, New./ Women--Folklore./ Spanish language materials./ Bilingual materials--Spanish.

398.2   Ph-2 3-5/5 $14.95   T   KB316
HEDLUND, IRENE. Mighty Mountain and the three strong women. English version by Judith Elkin. Volcano Press ISBN 0-912078-86-3, 1990. unp. col. ill.
    Can you imagine having wife, mother-in-law and grandmother-in-law stronger than you? This Japanese folktale relates how a mighty wrestler learns from his women folk and gains honors and a fortune. Good for reading aloud. Pictures show Japanese countryside and a far from average family.
SUBJ: Fairy tales./ Folklore--Japan./ Japan--Folklore.

398.2   Ph-2 2-3/4 $14.95   L   KB317
HONG, LILY TOY. Two of everything. Retold and illus. by Lily Toy Hong. Whitman ISBN 0-8075-8157-7; In Canada: General, 1993. unp. col. ill.
    A magic pot provides two of everything for a poverty-stricken couple until they tumble into the pot. How they solve this dilemma makes delightful reading. For reading aloud.
SUBJ: Fairy tales./ Folklore--China./ China--Folklore.

398.2   Ph-2 2-3/4 $15.95   L   KB318
HOOKS, WILLIAM H. Snowbear Whittington: an Appalachian Beauty and the Beast. Illus. by Victoria Lisi. Macmillan ISBN 0-02-744355-8; In Canada: Maxwell Macmillan, 1994. unp. col. ill.
    Seeking to please his youngest daughter, Nell, a father plucks a Christmas rose for her when he journeys to town. A bear, the owner of the rosebush, demands the daughter in payment. Thus begins a haunting romance set in the Appalachian mountains.
SUBJ: Fairy tales./ Folklore--United States./ United States--Folklore./ Folklore--Appalachian Region./ Appalachian Region--Folklore.

398.2   retro   Ph-1 2-3/3 $15.93   L   KB319
HUCK, CHARLOTTE S. Toads and diamonds. By Charlotte Huck. Illus. by Anita Lobel. Greenwillow ISBN 0-688-13681-8, 1996. unp. col. ill.
    The rewards for kindness and cruelty are shown in this traditional tale of two sisters and their treatment of a stranger. Full-color watercolor and gouache paintings dance with the vibrant countryside and costumes in this variant of Perrault's "The fairies."
SUBJ: Fairy tales./ Folklore--France./ France--Folklore.

398.2   Ph-2 3-4/6 $14.99   L   KB320
JAFFE, NINA. Older brother, younger brother: a Korean folktale. Retold by Nina Jaffe. Illus. by Wenhai Ma. Viking ISBN 0-670-85645-2; In Canada: Penguin, 1995. unp. col. ill.
    One of the best-known Korean folktales demonstrates kindness and family loyalty. The younger brother personifies gentleness and faithfulness, while the older brother reveals negative characteristics. Delicate watercolor illustrations are well suited to the tale.
SUBJ: Folklore--Korea./ Korea--Folklore.

398.2   Ph-3 5-6/6 $14.95   T   KB321
JAFFE, NINA. Patakin: world tales of drums and drummers. Illus. by Ellen Eagle. Henry Holt ISBN 0-8050-3005-0; In Canada: Fitzhenry & Whiteside, 1994. 144p. ill.
    Includes glossary, bibliographies, discography and directory.
    While including information about the various drums used around the world, the author presents folktales which show the importance of the drums to the diverse cultures and the major role they play in many stories. Incorporate into multicultural studies and units on traditional

music.
SUBJ: Drum--Folklore./ Folklore.

398.2   Ph-3 2-4/7 $1.00   P   KB322
JAPANESE FAIRY TALES. Edited by Philip Smith. Illus. by Kakuzo Fujiyama. Dover ISBN 0-486-27300-8; In Canada: General, 1992. 90p. ill. (Dover children's thrift classics).
    Five of the best-known Japanese folktales are reproduced with traditional ink-brush illustrations. Selected from a 1903 edition of Japanese fairy tales, the stories each present a moral lesson stressing such values as obedience, respect, courage, and integrity.
SUBJ: Fairy tales./ Folklore--Japan./ Japan--Folklore.

398.2   Retro   Ph-2 3-4/5 $13.95   T   KB323
JOSEPH, LYNN. Mermaid's twin sister: more stories from Trinidad. Illus. by Donna Perrone. Clarion ISBN 0-395-64365-1, 1994. 63p. ill.
    The author retells traditional tales she learned from her aunt (Tantie) while growing up in the West Indies. Tantie's stories capture the flavor of life in Trinidad long ago when magical beings and spirits were part of everyday occurrences. Welcome addition to Caribbean folklore for multiculturals studies.
SUBJ: Folklore--Trinidad and Tobago./ Trinidad and Tobago--Folklore.

398.2   Ph-3 3-4/4 $15.95   L   KB324
KEENS-DOUGLAS, RICHARDO. Diablesse and the baby: a Caribbean folktale. Illus. by Marie Lafrance. Annick Press ISBN 1-55037-993-3; In Canada: Annick Press/dist. by Firefly, 1994. unp. col. ill.
    Relates the origin of the devil-like folk figure, the Diablesse, and what happened when she visited the storyteller's family. A frightening, cautionary tale from the Caribbean for multicultural studies.
SUBJ: Caribbean Area--Folklore./ Folklore--Caribbean Area.

398.2   Ph-2 2-3/4 $14.88   L   KB325
KELLOGG, STEVEN. Jack and the beanstalk. Retold and illus. by Steven Kellogg. Morrow ISBN 0-688-10251-4, 1991. unp. col. ill.
    Tricked by a comically appearing fellow, Jack is berated by his mother for the five beans he received in exchange for his cow. He soon finds wealth when he climbs the vine which grows from the beans. An ogre to end all ogres graces the illustrations which enhance this favorite tale.
SUBJ: Fairy tales./ Folklore--England./ England--Folklore./ Giants--Folklore.

CD 398.2   Ph-1 3-5 $15.00   OD   KB326
KENNEDY, SHARON. Irish folk tales for children (Compact disc). Rounder Records CD 8040 ISBN 1-886767-14-9, 1996. 1 compact disc (59min).
    Sound recording cassette available C 8040 (ISBN 1-886767-15-7, 1996). 1 sound cassette (59min), $9.98.
    Four tales from Ireland are told by Sharon Kennedy who incorporates bits of Irish lore into her tellings. Clear enunciation, appropriate music, and outstanding material make this a delight. To be used with any unit featuring Ireland.
SUBJ: Ireland--Folklore./ Folklore--Ireland.

398.2   retro   Ph-2 2-4/4 $15.95   L   KB327
KIMMEL, ERIC A. Bearhead: a Russian folktale. Adapted by Eric A. Kimmel. Illus. by Charles Mikolaycak. Holiday House ISBN 0-8234-0902-3, 1991. unp. col. ill.
    Part bear, part human, the hero of this tale outfoxes a witch because he carries out her instructions literally. The artist's bold illustrations of an ugly goblin, conniving witch, and a warmhearted Bearhead make this title a good choice for picture book hours.
SUBJ: Fairy tales./ Folklore--Soviet Union./ Soviet Union--Folklore.

398.2   Ph-2 3-5/5 $15.95   L   KB328
KIMMEL, ERIC A. Goose girl: a story from the Brothers Grimm. Retold by Eric A. Kimmel. Illus. by Robert Sauber. Holiday House ISBN 0-8234-1074-9, 1995. unp. col. ill.
    A princess is forced by her maid to swap roles as the pair journeys to the princess's wedding. The maid becomes a princess, and the lovely princess is set to tending the geese. Their fates are overturned when the goose boy reports the head of a horse that talks and the beauty of the goose girl's tresses. A compassionate father-in-law is portrayed in this familiar fairy tale. Large portraits of the main characters dominate the illustrations.
SUBJ: Fairy tales./ Folklore--Germany./ Germany--Folklore.

398.2   Ph-3 3-4/6 $16.95   L   KB329
KIMMEL, ERIC A. I-know-not-what, I-know-not-where: a Russian tale. Adapted by Eric A. Kimmel. Illus. by Robert Sauber. Holiday House ISBN 0-8234-1020-X, 1994. 63p. col. ill.
    After an archer wounds a dove, he becomes enchanted with the bird

while tending it. Thus begins the fantastic adventure which takes the archer to strange lands with extraordinary companions. For mature fairy tale readers who enjoy involved plots.
SUBJ: Fairy tales./ Folklore--Russia./ Russia--Folklore.

398.2   *retro*   Ph-3 4-5/4 $15.95   L   KB330
KIMMEL, ERIC A. Iron John. Adapted from the Brothers Grimm. Illus. by Trina Schart Hyman. Holiday House ISBN 0-8234-1073-0, 1994. unp. col. ill.
A wild man befriends a young prince and teaches him the ways of the forest. When the youth sets out to prove his worth, he still needs the assistance of the wild man. The golden prince frees his friend from an enchantment, but almost loses his life.
SUBJ: Fairy tales./ Folklore--Germany./ Germany--Folklore.

398.2   Ph-2 3-4/4 $15.95   L   KB331
KIMMEL, ERIC A. Rimonah of the Flashing Sword: a North African tale. Adapted by Eric A. Kimmel. Illus. by Omar Rayyan. Holiday House ISBN 0-8234-1093-5, 1995. unp. col. ill.
An African version of Snow White in which the heroine finds a haven with a band of thieves who become her protectors. A prince awakens her after she succumbs to her stepmother's spells, and together-- princess, prince, robbers, and a restored king--they regain the kingdom from the sorceress. The illustrator combined influences from Egypt, Persia, and other middle eastern countries to create a background fitting to the story.
SUBJ: Fairy tales./ Folklore--Egypt./ Egypt--Folklore.

398.2   Ph-2 3-4/6 $15.95   L   KB332
KIMMEL, ERIC A. Tale of Ali Baba and the forty thieves: a story from the Arabian Nights. Illus. by Will Hillenbrand. Holiday House ISBN 0-8234-1258-X, 1996. unp. col. ill.
Ali Baba's discovery of a treasure belonging to 40 thieves intrigues his brother who falls into the thieves' hands and is killed. When the thieves attempt to gain back their wealth from Ali Baba, he seeks revenge which results in their deaths. Illustrations done in watercolor, plaka, and oil pastel on vellum are humorous and add the right touch to this tale of murder and robbery.
SUBJ: Fairy tales./ Arabs--Folklore./ Folklore--Arab countries./ Arab countries--Folklore.

KIT 398.2   Ph-3 3-5 $19.95   KB333
KUNSTLER, JAMES HOWARD. Aladdin and the magic lamp (Kit). Adapted by James Howard Kunstler. Read by John Hurt. Music by Mickey Hart. Illus. by Greg Couch. Rabbit Ears/Simon & Schuster ISBN 0-689-80063-0, 1995. 1 hardback book, 1 sound cassette (25min). (We all have tales).
ALA notable recording, 1996.
Retelling of the familiar saga of the poor boy who is fooled into assisting a magician and ends up keeping the lamp which the magician desires. Aladdin's marriage to a princess and his loss of the lamp is also related. John Hurt's reading of the tale is well-paced, and the tape can be used independently.
SUBJ: Fairy tales./ Folklore--Arab countries./ Arab countries--Folklore.

398.2   *retro*   Ph-2 3-5/6 $16.89   L   KB334
LATTIMORE, DEBORAH NOURSE. Arabian nights: three tales. Retold and illus. by Deborah Nourse Lattimore. HarperCollins ISBN 0-06-024734-7; In Canada: HarperCollins, 1995. 64p. col. ill.
"Joanna Cotler books."
Three of the compiler-illustrator's favorite tales from the ARABIAN NIGHTS are stunningly illustrated in this volume. "Aladdin" leads the reader to discover "The Queen of the Serpents" and "The Lost City of Ubar." An author's note sets the framework for the book.
SUBJ: Fairy tales./ Folklore--Arab countries./ Arab countries--Folklore.

398.2   *retro*   Ph-2 5-6/6 $5.95   P   KB335
LESTER, JULIUS. How many spots does a leopard have? and other tales. Illus. by David Shannon. Scholastic ISBN 0-590-41972-2, c1989, 1994. 72p. col. ill.
Includes author's note pp 69-71 and bibliography.
Twelve stories--some about animals--others about human frailties are retold in fluid, yet dramatic prose. The detailed author's note explains the sources for the stories and the changes made by the reteller. Large, powerful paintings add to the appeal of the collection.
SUBJ: Folklore--Africa./ Africa--Folklore./ Jews--Folklore.

398.2   *retro*   Ph-2 4-6/6 $21.50   T   KB336
LEWIS, I. MURPHY. Why ostriches don't fly and other tales from the African bush. Forward by Izak Barnard. Libraries Unlimited ISBN 1-56308-402-3, 1997. 105p. ill. (some col.), map. (World folklore series).
Includes glossary, bibliography, filmography and discography.
A group of brief stories told among the Bushmen is preceded by explanations of the Bushman's way of life, why he has been driven into a restricted area in Africa, and how near his talents and customs are to extinction. The simplicity of the tales make them appropriate for reading aloud. A multifaceted view of a unique people for interdisciplinary units and multicultural studies.
SUBJ: San (African people)--Folklore./ San (African people)--Social life and customs./ Africa--Folklore./ Folklore--Africa./ Kalahari Desert--Social life and customs.

398.2   Ph-2 3-6/7 $19.95   T   KB337
LION'S WHISKERS: AND OTHER ETHIOPIAN TALES. Rev. ed. Edited by Brent Ashabranner and Russell Davis. Illus. by Helen Siegl. Linnet ISBN 0-208-02429-8, 1997. 96p. ill.
Rev. ed. of THE LION'S WHISKERS: TALES OF HIGH AFRICA, 1959.
Includes glossary.
While working in Ethiopia in the 1950s, Brent Ashabranner and Russell Davis collected the material found in this anthology. The 16 stories are prefaced by editor's notes about where the stories were found and the tellers. Many of the tales are favorites of storytellers and have appeared elsewhere. To make the material come alive, the reader must travel with the author to this unique land in the pages of this book. A treasure!
SUBJ: Folklore--Ethiopia./ Ethiopia--Folklore.

398.2   Ph-2 P-1/2 $15.95   L   KB338
LOTTRIDGE, CELIA BARKER. Ten small tales. Retold by Celia Barker Lottridge. Illus. by Joanne Fitzgerald. McElderry ISBN 0-689-50568-X; In Canada: Maxwell Macmillan, 1994. 64p. col. ill.
A founding member of the Storytellers School of Toronto, the author retells gentle tales which will please young listeners. Preschool and kindergarten teachers will find the material great for reading aloud.
SUBJ: Folklore.

398.2   *retro*   Ph-2 4-5/7 $15.95   T   KB339
MADRIGAL, ANTONIO HERNANDEZ. Eagle and the rainbow: timeless tales from Mexico. Illus. by Tomie De Paola. Fulcrum Kids ISBN 1-55591-317-2, 1997. 57p. col. ill. (World stories).
Includes glossary.
The author retells stories of bravery from five different cultures of Mexico. The central figure might be a child or a ruler, but each influenced how his people lived. Brief information about the location of the tribe and their way of life follows each story. For multicultural studies.
SUBJ: Indians of Mexico--Folklore./ Folklore--Mexico./ Mexico-- Folklore.

398.2   Ph-3 2-4/4 $12.95   T   KB340
MARSHALL, JAMES. Hansel and Gretel. Retold by James Marshall. Dial ISBN 0-8037-0827-0, 1990. unp. col. ill.
Concerned for her own well-being, a wife convinces her husband to take his children into the forest and forsake them. The children fall into the hands of a hideous witch but outsmart her and gain their freedom. Another version of the well-known tale with unconventional drawings.
SUBJ: Fairy tales./ Folklore--Germany./ Germany--Folklore.

TB 398.2   Ph-2 K-4 $9.95   KB341
MARTIN, RAFE. Rafe Martin tells his children's books (Talking book). Yellow Moon Press ISBN 0-938756-49-4, 1994. 1 sound cassette.
Martin reads his books with great expression making them come alive to the listener. The tape can be used to introduce his works and for the child with limited vision.
Contents: The rough-face girl (14min); Foolish rabbit's big mistake (15min); The boy who lived with the seals (11min); The boy who loved mammoths (16min).
SUBJ: Folklore./ Indians of North America--Folklore./ Short stories.

398.2   Ph-2 3-5/5 $15.93   L   KB342
MAYER, MARIANNA. Turandot. Illus. by Winslow Pels. Morrow ISBN 0-688-09074-5, 1995. unp. col. ill.
Turandot is an icy princess who executes her suitors if they cannot answer her three riddles until Calaf, a stranger in the city, is successful. The formal design and chilly illustrations match the haunting mood of the story. Based on a Persian folktale, Turandot has been a theatrical and an operatic production.
SUBJ: Fairy tales./ Princesses--Folklore./ Problem solving--Folklore./ Folklore--Arab countries./ Arab countries--Folklore.

398.2   *retro*   Ph-3 4-5/6 $19.99   T   KB343
MAYO, MARGARET. Magical tales from many lands. Retold by Margaret Mayo. Illus. by Jane Ray. Dutton ISBN 0-525-45017-3, 1993. 128p. col. ill.
A wide selection of tales from all over the world (sources given) is

augmented with illustrations by the talented artist Jane Ray. Representing a wide variety of traditions, the collection will be useful for multicultural studies and for readers seeking unusual tales.
SUBJ: Fairy tales./ Folklore.

398.2   Ph-2 2-5/7 $19.95   T   KB344
MCCAUGHREAN, GERALDINE. Golden hoard: myths and legends of the world. Illus. by Bee Willey. McElderry ISBN 0-689-80741-4, 1996. 130p. col. ill.
First published in Great Britain by Orion Children's Books, 1995.
A true mixture of well-known and little known tales from all parts of the world. Notes give the sources of the stories, and the illustrations incorporate objects and motifs which are part of the cultures from which the tales are drawn. For multicultural studies.
SUBJ: Mythology./ Legends./ Folklore.

398.2   Ph-1 K-6/6 $19.95   T   KB345
MCCAUGHREAN, GERALDINE. Silver treasure: myths and legends of the world. Illus. by Bee Willey. McElderry ISBN 0-689-81322-8; In Canada: Distican, 1996. 130p. col. ill.
First published in London, Orion Children's Books.
A magnificent collection of tales from all over the world. The title of the collection comes from the first story about the silver mines of Peru and how their treasures were secreted away from the Spaniards. Notes are provided for each of the stories which are brief and excellent for reading aloud.
SUBJ: Folklore./ Mythology./ Legends.

TB 398.2   Ph-3 5-6 $11.00   KB346
MCNEIL, HEATHER. Hyena and the moon: stories to listen to from Kenya (Talking book). Libraries Unlimited ISBN 1-56308-397-3, 1995. 1 sound cassette (60min). (World folklore series).
ALA notable recording, 1996.
Retelling selected, traditional tales she collected in Kenya, the author includes percussion instruments and native language to enhance the storytelling. Teachers will use in conjunction with multicultural studies while students will enjoy numerous entertaining tales.
SUBJ: Kenya--Folklore./ Folklore--Kenya./ Africa--Folklore./ Folklore--Africa.

398.2   Ph-3 5-6/7 $23.00   T   KB347
MCNEIL, HEATHER. Hyena and the moon: stories to tell from Kenya. Libraries Unlimited ISBN 1-56308-169-5, 1994. 171p. ill. (some col.), map. (World folklore series).
Includes glossary, bibliography and index.
Retelling traditional tales she collected in Kenya, the author includes background information about the various cultures, original translations of the stories, source notes, and tips for storytelling. Teachers will find a wealth of information for multicultural studies while students will enjoy numerous entertaining tales. Good resource for beginning storytellers, child or adult.
SUBJ: Kenya--Folklore./ Folklore--Kenya./ Africa--Folklore./ Folklore--Africa.

398.2   Ph-3 4-5/7 $16.95   L   KB348
MEDICINE STORY. Children of the Morning Light: Wampanoag tales. As told by Manitonquat (Medicine Story). Illus. by Mary F. Arquette. Macmillan ISBN 0-02-765905-4; In Canada: Maxwell Macmillan, 1994. 72p. col. ill.
An elder from the Wampanoag tribe from southeastern Massachusetts recorded tales he learned from his grandfather and has retold numerous times. The legends cover creation tales, traditional practices, and animal stories. Illustrations were drawn by a Native American artist. For multicultural studies.
SUBJ: Wampanoag Indians--Folklore./ Wampanoag Indians--Religion and mythology./ Indians of North America--Massachusetts--Folklore./ Indians of North America--Massachusetts--Religion and mythology./ Creation--Folklore.

VCR 398.2   Ph-2 K-2 $9.95   KB349
METAXAS, ERIC. Jack and the beanstalk (Videocassette). Retold by Eric Metaxas. Read by Michael Palin. Music by David A. Stewart. Illus. by Edward Sorel. Rabbit Ears ISBN 1-56204-003-0, 1991. 1/2" VHS videocassette color (30min).
JACK AND THE BEANSTALK (ISBN 0-88708-188-6, 1991).
Read-along kit JACK AND THE BEANSTALK available from Simon & Schuster (ISBN 0-689-81583-2, 1997). 1 paperback book, 1 sound cassette (27min), $10.95.
A well done rendition of a favorite tale. The telling is clear and the still pictures come alive by varied camera movements. The section of Jack climbing up the beanstalk is particularly well done.
SUBJ: Fairy tales./ Folklore--England./ England--Folklore./ Giants--Folklore.

398.2   Ph-2 3-4/6 $15.95   L   KB350
MILLS, LAUREN A. Tatterhood and the hobgoblins: a Norwegian folktale. Retold and illus. by Lauren Mills. Little, Brown ISBN 0-316-57406-6; In Canada: Little, Brown, 1993. unp. col. ill.
Two sisters, one beautiful and quiet, the other untidy and willful, encounter hobgoblins on their twelfth birthday. The misfortune that befalls them results in a tale of adventure and romance. Subdued, ethereal illustrations decorate the Norwegian story. For the fairy tale reader looking for a well-plotted, unfamiliar story.
SUBJ: Fairy tales./ Folklore--Norway./ Norway--Folklore.

398.2   Ph-2 2-3/5 $15.95   L   KB351
MOSER, BARRY. Tucker Pfeffercorn: an old story retold. Little, Brown ISBN 0-316-58542-4; In Canada: Little, Brown, 1994. unp. col. ill.
A retelling of the "Rumpelstiltskin" story. It is set in the South, and the heroine is a young widow with a small child. The illustrations show the despair of the young widow, the brutality of her captor, and the nastiness of her benefactor, Tucker Pfeffercorn. This traditional story in new dress portrays a strong female protagonist with gumption and appeal. For reading aloud.
SUBJ: Fairy tales./ Folklore--Germany./ Germany--Folklore.

398.2   Ph-1 4-6/7 $19.95   T   KB352
MURPHY, CLAIRE RUDOLF. Prince and the Salmon People. Retold by Claire Rudolf Murphy. Illus. by Duane Pasco. Rizzoli ISBN 0-8478-1662-1, 1993. 48p. ill. (some col.), map.
Reproductions of artifacts used by the Tsimshian are central to the value of this retelling of a Tsimshian Indian tale of why salmon stop coming to the waters near a village. A smooth flowing narrative suits the material as do the black and white drawings. For multicultural studies.
SUBJ: Tsimshian Indians--Folklore./ Indians of North America--Folklore.

398.2   Ph-2 4-6/5 $17.00   L   KB353
NESS, CAROLINE. Ocean of story: fairy tales from India. Retold by Caroline Ness. Chosen with an introduction and notes by Neil Philip. Illus. by Jacqueline Mair. Lothrop, Lee & Shepard ISBN 0-688-13584-6, 1996. 123p. col. ill.
Includes bibliography.
An anthology of popular folklore from India. Many of the tales resemble stories like "Cinderella," "Princess and the pea," and "Aladdin." "India's ocean of story has encircled the world." (Introduction) Readers curious about how similar tales appear in various cultures will find this collection fascinating. Good discussion starter to compare and contrast variants. For multicultural studies.
SUBJ: Fairy tales./ India--Folklore./ Folklore--India.

398.2   Ph-1 P-2/7 $19.95   L   KB354
NURSERY TALES AROUND THE WORLD. Selected and retold by Judy Sierra. Illus. by Stefano Vitale. Clarion ISBN 0-395-67894-3, 1996. 114p. col. ill.
Includes bibliography.
The collector of these stories stresses that "the age-old nursery tales from the oral tradition are...attuned to the needs of young listeners" (two to four year olds). She has gathered tales in six thematic sections of related stories to prove her point. The folk motifs used to illustrate each tale are representative of the country from which the story came. A very attractive volume and invaluable collection for multicultural studies, it can be used with older students to compare and contrast related tales. For reading aloud.
SUBJ: Folklore.

398.2   Ph-1 3-4/6 $18.95   T   KB355
PERRAULT, CHARLES. Complete fairy tales of Charles Perrault. Newly translated by Neil Philip and Nicoletta Simborowski. Illus. by Sally Holmes. Clarion ISBN 0-395-57002-6, 1993. 156p. col. ill.
Includes bibliography.
Fine introduction explains how Perrault rewrote these "simple stories of the people" to entertain the court of Louis XIV. Decorative pastel drawings capture the rural countryside and courtly scenes which are the settings for these familiar tales. For all collections.
SUBJ: Fairy tales./ Folklore--France./ France--Folklore.

SRC 398.2   Ph-1 4-6 $11.00   OD KB356
PERRAULT, CHARLES. Story of Sleeping Beauty (Sound recording cassette). Read by Claire Bloom. Adapted by Ward Botsford. Music by Peter Ilyich Tchaikovsky. HarperAudio/Caedmon CPN1546; In Canada: Heath, 1980. 1 sound cassette (51min).
With the background filled with Tchaikovsky's ballet music, Claire Bloom fluently and lovingly tells the famed story. The record is a perfect blend of music and text. It can be used in music and literature classes.
SUBJ: Folklore--France./ France--Folklore.

398.2   Ph-2 2-4/3 $14.89   L   KB357
PETERSON, JULIENNE. Caterina, the clever farm girl: a tale from Italy. Retold by Julienne Peterson. Illus. by Enzo Giannini. Dial ISBN 0-8037-1182-4, 1996. unp. col. ill.
When her father finds a golden mortar, he plans to give it to the king. The daughter warns him that the king will also want a golden pestle. Learning that the clever daughter has forseen his request, the king sets several tasks for the girl. She outwits him every time and finally becomes his loving wife. Her cleverness helps him to become a just king. Caterina is a welcome addition to strong heroines in folk literature. The illustrations reflect Tuscany.
SUBJ: Fairy tales./ Folklore--Italy./ Italy--Folklore.

398.2   Ph-2 5-6/6 $19.95   T   KB358
PHILIP, NEIL. Arabian nights. Retold by Neil Philip. Illus. by Sheila Moxley. Orchard ISBN 0-531-06868-4, 1994. 157p. col. ill.
Telling stories for a thousand and one nights, the young Sheherazade eventually persuades her husband, the king, to break his vow to wed and behead a wife daily. The stories, classic ones of adventure, also accurately reflect the human condition. A handsome edition recommended for reading aloud and multicultural studies.
SUBJ: Fairy tales./ Folklore--Arab countries./ Arab countries--Folklore.

398.2   Ph-2 2-4/4 $14.95   L   KB359
PLUME, ILSE. Shoemaker and the elves. Retold and illus. by Ilse Plume from a tale by the Brothers Grimm. Harcourt Brace Jovanovich ISBN 0-15-274050-3, 1991. unp col illus.
Befriended by clever, hard working elves, Antonio, an empoverished shoemaker gains a new start in his business and rewards his small helpers with gifts at Christmas. A new version set in Italy!
SUBJ: Fairy tales./ Folklore--Germany./ Germany--Folklore.

398.2   Ph-1 2-6/8 $20.00   L   KB360
RAINBOW FAIRY BOOK. Edited by Andrew Lang. Selected and illus. by Michael Hague. Morrow ISBN 0-688-10878-4, 1993. 288p. ill. (some col.).
"Books of wonder."
Includes bibliography.
The purpose of this collection is... "to introduce a new generation to the breadth and depth of the fairy tales in Lang's books--in short, the very best of Lang." (Intro). Handsomely illustrated with full-color plates and 47 pencil drawings, the collection includes favorites such as "Cinderella" and "Rumpelstiltzkin" as well as lesser known works like "Father Grumbler" and "Master Cat."
SUBJ: Fairy tales./ Folklore.

398.2   Ph-1 4-6/4 $11.95   L   KB361
RAW HEAD, BLOODY BONES: AFRICAN-AMERICAN TALES OF THE SUPERNATURAL. Selected by Mary E. Lyons. Scribner's ISBN 0-684-19333-7; In Canada: Maxwell Macmillan, 1991. 88p.
Includes bibliographies.
Tales of goblins, ghosts, monsters and superhumans will delight the reader of this collection. Many come from Africa or are African-American adaptations. All have hidden meanings fully explained in notes at the end of each tale. A storyteller's treasure.
SUBJ: Afro-Americans--Folklore./ Supernatural--Folklore./ Blacks--Folklore.

398.2   Ph-2 P-2/2 $15.93   L   KB362
ROCKWELL, ANNE F. Acorn tree and other folktales. Retold and illus. by Anne Rockwell. Greenwillow ISBN 0-688-13723-7, 1995. 40p. col. ill.
The collector-illustrator has gathered ten tales from around the world to introduce the young listener and beginning reader to the joys of folklore. Several selections are variations of familiar stories which will alert the reader that stories come in many guises. Sources given. For multicultural studies.
SUBJ: Folklore.

398.2   Ph-2 P-K/2 $15.88   L   KB363
ROWE, JOHN A. Gingerbread Man: an old English folktale. North-South Books ISBN 1-55858-543-5; In Canada: North-South Books/dist. by Vanwell, 1996. unp. col. ill.
"Michael Neugebauer book."
A stylized version of the familiar tale in which a cookie is able to elude all pursuers until he comes upon a wily fox.
SUBJ: Fairy tales./ England--Folklore./ Folklore--England.

398.2   Ph-1 2-4/6 $14.95   T   KB364
SAN JOSE, CHRISTINE. Cinderella. Retold by Christine San Jose. Illus. by Debrah Santini. Boyds Mills ISBN 1-56397-152-6; In Canada: McClelland & Stewart, 1994. unp. col. ill.
Retold and revitalized, the traditional fairy tale is placed in New York City at the turn of the century with the costuming and home interiors from that time and place. All of the elements of the original story are here, including the stepsisters, fairy godmother, horse drawn carriage created from a pumpkin, the royal ball, and the glass slipper. The sepia-toned illustrations framed in marbled endpapers place the story of enchantment in a real time and place that is at least as romantic as any in make believe. Compare and contrast with the many other artistic interpretations of the story as well as variants found in other cultures.
SUBJ: Fairy tales./ France--Folklore./ Folklore--France.

398.2   Ph-2 3-4/6 $15.99   T   KB365
SAN SOUCI, ROBERT D. Samurai's daughter: a Japanese legend. Illus. by Stephen T. Johnson. Dial ISBN 0-8037-1135-2, 1992. unp. col. ill.
When her father is exiled to a distant island, Tokoyo is determined to join him. Her travels which bring her upon bandits, ghost ships, and serpents are carefully detailed in this picture book tale of a courageous woman. For units on Japanese culture and folklore.
SUBJ: Folklore--Japan./ Japan--Folklore.

398.2   Ph-3 3-5/7 $14.95   T   KB366
SCHROEDER, ALAN. Lily and the wooden bowl. Illus. by Yoriko Ito. Doubleday ISBN 0-385-30792-6; In Canada: Bantam Doubleday Dell, 1994. unp. col. ill.
Warned by her grandmother to hide her beauty, Lily wears a wooden bowl over her face. When she works for a wealthy farmer and his jealous wife, the eldest son falls in love with her. In spite of his mother's devious scheming, the two are wed, and the secret underneath the wooden bowl is revealed. Japanese costumes and countryside are captured in the elegant illustrations. For multicultural studies.
SUBJ: Fairy tales./ Folklore--Japan./ Japan--Folklore.

398.2   Ph-3 2-3/4 $14.89   L   KB367
SCHROEDER, ALAN. Smoky Mountain Rose: an Appalachian Cinderella. Illus. by Brad Sneed. Dial ISBN 0-8037-1734-2; In Canada: McClelland & Stewart, 1997. unp. col. ill.
Freely adapted from Perrault's "Cinderella," this version is set in the Appalachian Mountains. The fairy godmother is a pig. The ball is a square dance, and the prince is a rich feller who settles down with his Rose in the Smoky Mountains. Illustrations are watercolors with all the figures elongated.
SUBJ: Fairy tales./ Folklore--France./ France--Folklore./ Appalachian Region--Folklore./ Folklore--Appalachian Region.

398.2   Ph-1 3-4/6 $17.00   T   KB368
SCHWARTZ, HOWARD. Diamond tree: Jewish tales from around the world. Selected and retold by Howard Schwartz and Barbara Rush. Illus. by Uri Shulevitz. HarperCollins ISBN 0-06-025239-1; In Canada: HarperCollins, 1991. 120p. col. ill.
Includes source notes.
Available from the National Library Service for the Blind and Physically Handicapped on sound recording cassette RC 36065.
All the tales retold in this collection come from authenic Jewish sources and are about basic character traits - honesty, faith, charity, and cooperation. The full-color plates add to the humor and wisdom of the stories. A storyteller's delight!
SUBJ: Jews--Folklore.

398.2   Ph-2 2-4/5 $16.89   L   KB369
SCHWARTZ, HOWARD. Wonder child and other Jewish fairy tales. Selected and retold by Howard Schwartz and Barbara Rush. Illus. by Stephen Fieser. HarperCollins ISBN 0-06-023518-7; In Canada: HarperCollins, 1996. 66p. col. ill.
Includes glossary.
Eight stories make up this collection and "each of these stories draws on well-known fairy tale figures, such as kings and queens, princes and princesses, and every kind of supernatural being, but colors them according to the Jewish time and place from which they emerged." (Introduction) Similar in theme to the Grimm tales, the stories can be compared and contrasted with the more familiar variants. Extensive sources and a glossary make this a useful collection.
SUBJ: Fairy tales./ Jews--Folklore./ Folklore.

SRC 398.2   Ph-2 3-4 $10.00   OD   KB370
SOME DOG AND OTHER KENTUCKY WONDERS (Sound recording cassette). Retold by Mary Hamilton. Hidden Spring, 1992. 1 sound cassette (60min).
Mary Hamilton's carefully chosen stories from Kentucky and Appalachia are told with vigor and humor. "Some Dog" becomes so alive that after hearing his adventures, listeners will be on the look out to return him to his home in Kentucky.
SUBJ: Folklore--Kentucky./ Kentucky--Folklore./ Folklore--Appalachian Region./ Appalachian Region--Folklore.

398.2   Ph-2 2-5/6 $16.95 T KB371

SPIDER SPINS A STORY: FOURTEEN LEGENDS FROM NATIVE AMERICA. Edited by Jill Max. Illus. by Robert Annesley...[et al.]. Rising Moon ISBN 0-87358-611-5, 1997. 63p. col. ill.

> Fourteen legends in which Spider plays a central role are retold with full-page paintings by illustrators with Native American backgrounds. Preceding each story is a description of the tribe from which the material originated. Good material for storytelling or reading aloud. For multicultural studies.
> SUBJ: Indians of North America--Legends./ Folklore--North America./ North America--Folklore./ Spiders--Folklore.

398.2   Ph-3 3-4/5 $16.95 T KB372

STEWIG, JOHN WARREN. Princess Florecita and the iron shoes: a Spanish fairy tale. Illus. by K. Wendy Popp. Apple Soup/Knopf ISBN 0-679-84775-8; In Canada: Random House, 1995. unp. col. ill.

> A long search which takes Princess Florecita to the homes of the Winds enables her to find her sleeping prince and restore him to life. The romantic fairy tale, similar to "Sleeping Beauty," features a strong female protagonist.
> SUBJ: Fairy tales./ Spain--Folklore./ Folklore--Spain./ Princesses--Folklore.

TB 398.2   Ph-2 3-4 $8.95 OD KB373

STORIES FROM MANY LANDS FROM THE PICTURE BOOK PARADE (Talking book). Weston Woods WW736C, 1986. 1 sound cassette (42min).

> Stressing kindness, humility, courage and trust, these six tales come from varied cultures. The musical backgrounds are distinctive and add to the appeal the stories will have for individual listeners.
> Contents: The silver cow (Welsh); The stonecutter (Japanese); The treasure (Yiddish); Tikki Tikki Tembo (Chinese); The hole in the dike (Dutch); One fine day (Armenian).
> SUBJ: Folklore.

SRC 398.2   Ph-2 2-4 $10.00 OD KB374

STORYTELLING TIME IS HERE (Sound recording cassette). Told by Toni Simmons. Toni Simmons, 1992. 1 sound cassette (35min).

> Four familiar stories are told here in a clear direct manner.
> Contents: If I had a story; Anansi and Turtle; Gunniwolf; Terrible creature.
> SUBJ: Folklore./ Storytelling.

SRC 398.2   Ph-3 3-4 $9.98 KB375

TALES FROM CULTURES FAR AND NEAR (Sound recording cassette). As told by Jim Weiss. Greathall Productions 1124-08 ISBN 1-882513-08-8, 1990. 1 sound cassette (60min).

> In a deliberate, well-paced voice, Jim Weiss retells six tales from around the world. The relatively unknown stories combine humor and wisdom. For multicultural studies.
> SUBJ: Folklore.

398.2   Ph-2 P-3/2 $2.95 P KB376

TARCOV, EDITH H. Frog prince. Retold by Edith H. Tarcov. Illus. by James Marshall. Scholastic ISBN 0-590-46571-6; In Canada: Scholastic, c1974, 1993. unp. col. ill. (Hello reader!).

> "Cartwheel books."
> A greedy princess loses her golden ball in a well. An obliging frog returns the ball, but the princess refuses to live up to her promise to take him into her home. How she is finally forced to accept the frog, who turns into a handsome prince, is captured in warm, silly illustrations.
> SUBJ: Fairy tales./ Germany--Folklore./ Folklore--Germany./ Frogs--Folklore./ Princes--Folklore./ Princesses--Folklore.

398.2   Ph-2 4-5/4 $20.60 L KB377

TAYLOR, C. J. How we saw the world: nine Native stories of the way things began. Tundra ISBN 0-88776-302-2; In Canada: Tundra, 1993. 32p. col. ill.

> Selecting the legends because they were ideal for illustrating, the compiler retells how natural wonders were created as well as the origins of the small creatures which flourish in the world. Sweeping scenes make this a book for visual enjoyment. Native American creation stories for reading aloud and multicultural studies.
> SUBJ: Indians of North America--Folklore./ Creation--Folklore.

398.2   Ph-2 P-3/6 $5.99 P KB378

TOM TIT TOT: AN ENGLISH FOLK TALE. Illus. by Evaline Ness. Aladdin ISBN 0-689-81398-8; In Canada: Distican, c1965, 1997. unp. col. ill.

> Caldecott Honor Book, 1966.
> A foolish old woman promises a greedy king that her daughter can spin five skeins of flax a day. He weds the girl and asks that she produce the skeins every day for one month. Help arrives in the form

of an ugly little thing with a long tail who loses to her in a name guessing contest. A classic Rumpelstilskin variant.
> SUBJ: Fairy tales./ Folklore--Great Britain./ Great Britain--Folklore.

398.2   Ph-2 2-4/4 $15.95 L KB379

UCHIDA, YOSHIKO. Magic purse. Retold by Yoshiko Uchida. Illus. by Keiko Narahashi. McElderry ISBN 0-689-50559-0; In Canada: Maxwell Macmillan, 1993. unp. col. ill.

> A dreamlike story of a peasant who meets a beautiful maid who asks him to deliver a letter for her in a frightening swamp. His courage and faithfulness are rewarded, and the reader leaves the story with a reassurance that good will be repaid.
> SUBJ: Fairy tales./ Folklore--Japan./ Japan--Folklore.

CE 398.2   Ph-3 5-6/4 $28.00 T KB380

VIGIL, ANGEL. Corn woman: stories and legends of the Hispanic Southwest/La mujer del maiz: cuentos y leyendas del sudoeste Hispano. Retold by Angel Vigil. Translated by Jennifer Audrey Lowell and Juan Francisco Marin. Libraries Unlimited ISBN 1-56308-194-6, 1994. 234p. col. ill., map. (World folklore series).

> Includes glossary and bibliography.
> Talking book available from Libraries Unlimited (ISBN 1-56308-396-5, 1995). 2 sound cassettes (90min), $19.50.
> The compiler of this collection traveled in New Mexico and Colorado to gather native folktales. His interest was spurred by his memories of stories told by his Hispanic grandparents. The collection contains a wide variety of tales in English and Spanish. For Spanish teachers, teachers of bilingual classes, and multicultural studies.
> SUBJ: Hispanic Americans--Folklore./ Indians of North America--Southwest, New--Folklore./ Southwest, New--Folklore./ Spanish language materials./ Bilingual materials--Spanish.

398.2   Ph-2 4-6/7 $17.00 T KB381

WALKER, PAUL ROBERT. Giants!: stories from around the world. Illus. by James Bernardin. Harcourt Brace ISBN 0-15-200883-7; In Canada: Harcourt Brace c/o Canadian Manda, 1995. 73p. col. ill.

> Includes bibliography.
> Long ago tall beings inhabited the earth! In this collection, the reteller presents some of the great legends about these gigantic humans. The stories come from many cultures and eras. Full-page gouache and colored pencil illustrations match the tales and bring the giants to life.
> SUBJ: Giants--Folklore./ Folklore.

VCR 398.2   Ph-2 K-2 $11.99 OD KB382

WHITE CAT (Videocassette). Narrated by Emma Thompson. Music by Joe Jackson. Written by Eric Metaxas. Illus. by Barbara McClintock. Rabbit Ears/Microleague Multimedia Inc. (MMI)/dist. by Ingram Library Services ISBN 157099982-1, 1997. 1/2" VHS videocassette color (30min).

> Includes public performance rights.
> Talking book available from Rabbit Ears/Microleague Multimedia Inc. (MMI)/dist. by Ingram Library Services (ISBN 157099997-X, 1997). 1 sound cassette (30min), $7.99.
> Seeking gifts for his father, the youngest son stumbles upon a castle owned by a handsome white cat. Each time he returns to his father with his gifts, he regrets leaving the cat until at last he stays and fights the ogre who has bewitched her. Based on the tale by Comtesse d'Aulnoy. Poignantly told by Emma Thompson.
> SUBJ: Fairy tales./ France--Folklore./ Folklore--France./ Cats--Folklore.

398.2   Ph-2 2-3/6 $14.95 L KB383

WILSON, BARBARA KER. Wishbones: a folk tale from China. Retold by Barbara Ker Wilson. Illus. by Meilo So. Bradbury ISBN 0-02-793125-0; In Canada: Maxwell Macmillan, 1993. unp. col. ill.

> A Chinese Cinderella is befriended by a small fish in this tale of hardship, cunning, and greed. Primitive drawings show Chinese life in caves and palaces. A refreshing retelling of a familiar tale.
> SUBJ: Fairy tales./ Folklore--China./ China--Folklore.

398.2   Ph-1 3-4/4 $14.95 L KB384

YOLEN, JANE. Tam Lin. Illus. by Charles Mikolaycak. Harcourt Brace Jovanovich ISBN 0-15-284261-6, 1990. unp. col. ill.

> Includes "About Tam Lin."
> Selectors' Choice, 18th ed.
> A haunting ballad is retold here with stunning illustrations which capture the heroine's defense of her beloved as she rescues him from the fairies' magic. By introducing this legend to young listeners they can be led to appreciate the early ballads from other lands.
> SUBJ: Fairy tales./ Scotland--Folklore./ Folklore--Scotland.

CE 398.2   Ph-2 1-4/7 $14.00 L KB385

ZELINSKY, PAUL O. Rumpelstiltskin. Retold and illustrated by Paul O. Zelinsky from the Brothers Grimm. Dutton ISBN 0-525-44265-0; In

Canada: Fitzhenry & Whiteside, 1986. unp. col. ill.
Caldecott Honor Book.
Available in Spanish EL ENANO SALTARIN (ISBN 0-525-44903-5, 1992).
Videocassette available from SRA/McGraw-Hill 87-005000; 1/2" VHS videocassette color (12min), $43.00.
Available from National Library Service for the Blind and Physically Handicapped in Braille BR07108 and on sound recording cassette RC25470.
Videocassette available from SRA/McGraw-Hill 87-509257, 1989.1/2" iconographic VHS videocassette color (12min), $39.00. (Caldecott video collection).
Fruitlessly attempting to spin straw into gold, a miller's daughter strikes a bargain with a strange little man who succeeds but demands her first child in payment. How the girl outwits the man and saves her baby is an old favorite which in this version has stunning illustrations filled with haunting details.
SUBJ: Fairy tales./ Folklore--Germany./ Germany--Folklore./ German language materials./ Spanish language materials.

398.2   Ph-2 2-3/4 $16.00   T   KB386
ZEMACH, MARGOT. Three wishes: an old story. Farrar, Straus and Giroux ISBN 0-374-37529-1, 1986. unp. col. ill.
Spanish version TRES DESEOS: UN VIEJO CUENTO (ISBN 0-374-34662-3, 1993, Mirasol/Farrar, Straus & Giroux).
The familiar story could be entitled "Three wasted wishes" as it humorously illustrates that it is best to think before you speak. Great for telling or reading aloud.
SUBJ: Fairy tales./ Folklore--France./ France--Folklore./ Spanish language materials.

398.21   Ph-2 2-3/3 $14.88   L   KB387
ARNOLD, KATYA. Baba Yaga: a Russian folktale. Retold and illus. by Katya Arnold. North-South Books ISBN 1-55858-209-6; In Canada: North-South Books, 1993. unp. col. ill.
Tishka, a clever lad born from a piece of wood, outwits Baba Yaga. Decorated with drawings done in a folk art style popular in Russia in the seventeenth century.
Another clever young person outsmarts the fearsome witch Baba Yaga in BABA YAGA AND THE LITTLE GIRL: A RUSSIAN FOLKTALE (ISBN 1-55858-288-6, 1994, OPC).
SUBJ: Baba Yaga (Legendary character)./ Fairy tales./ Folklore--Russia./ Russia--Folklore.

398.21   Ph-2 2-3/2 $13.95   L   KB388
BADEN, ROBERT. And Sunday makes seven. Illustrated by Michelle Edwards. Whitman ISBN 0-8075-0356-8; In Canada: General, 1990. unp. col. ill.
Includes glossary.
Also available in Spanish Y DOMINGO, SIETE (ISBN 0-8075-9355-9, 1990).
A kindly peasant stumbles upon a group of witches who repay his contribution of a rhyme by removing his wart and giving him a treasure. His greedy brother fares less well. The use of Spanish words in a simple verse makes this an entertaining introduction to the language.
SUBJ: Folklore--Costa Rica./ Costa Rica--Folklore./ Witches--Folklore./ Spanish language materials.

398.21   Ph-2 1-3/2 $14.00   T   KB389
BANG, MOLLY. Wiley and the Hairy Man: adapted from an American folk tale. By Molly Garrett Bang. Simon & Schuster ISBN 0-689-81141-1; In Canada: Distican, c1976, 1987. 64p. ill. (Ready-to-read).
Available from the National Library Service for the Blind and Physically Handicapped in Braille BR03383.
Wiley and his mother lived near a swamp where the hairy man, who captured children, hid. Each time Wiley ventured into the swamp, he took his hound dog who frightened off the hairy man. However, wanting to rid the swamp forever of the monster, Wiley and his mother plotted to fool him three times and drive him away. For multicultural studies.
SUBJ: Folklore--United States./ United States--Folklore./ Monsters./ Mothers and sons--Folklore./ Problem solving--Folklore.

398.21   Ph-2 2-4/6 $14.95   L   KB390
CECH, JOHN. First snow, magic snow. Illus. by Sharon McGinley-Nally. Four Winds ISBN 0-02-717971-0; In Canada: Maxwell Macmillan, 1992. unp. col. ill.
Snowflake, a child molded out of snow, stays with her new parents until the coming of spring. Longing for their lost child, the couple travels to the coldest regions to claim her again. Love, loneliness, and the changing of the seasons are featured in this traditional Russian tale.
SUBJ: Folklore--Soviet Union./ Soviet Union--Folklore./ Snow--Folklore.

VCR 398.21   Ph-2 K-2 $49.95   OD KB391
CRYING RED GIANT: A JAPANESE FOLKTALE (Videocassette). Pied Piper/AIMS Multimedia Q8001, n.d. 1/2" VHS videocassette color (18min).
Blue Giant aids Red Giant in proving to the villagers that he is kindly. In their endeavor, however, Red Giant loses Blue Giant, the best friend he had. For classes investigating human relationships.
SUBJ: Japan--Folklore./ Folklore--Japan./ Friendship--Folklore./ Giants--Folklore.

398.21   Ph-1 1-3/4 $14.95   L   KB392
DE PAOLA, TOMIE. Fin M'Coul: the giant of Knockmany Hill. Retold and illustrated by Tomie De Paola. Holiday House ISBN 0-8234-0384-X, 1981. unp. col. ill.
Selectors' Choice, 13th ed.
Fin M'Coul was terrified of the giant Cucullin but his wife devised a scheme which proved that Fin might not be stronger than the giant but he and his wife were certainly smarter. The full page brightly inked drawings make this a delight for picture book hours.
SUBJ: Finn MacCool./ Folklore--Ireland./ Giants--Folklore./ Ireland--Folklore.

398.21   Ph-1 P-3/4 $14.95   L   KB393
DE PAOLA, TOMIE. Jamie O'Rourke and the big potato: an Irish folktale. Retold and illus. by Tomie De Paola. Putnam ISBN 0-399-22257-X; In Canada: Putnam, 1992. unp. col. ill.
"Whitebird Book."
Available from the National Library Service for the Blind and Physically Handicapped on sound recording cassette RC 37999.
Jamie, a large fellow, is forced to find food when his wife becomes ill. His chance encounter with a leprechaun results in a magnificent potato and a constant food supply. A warm Irish tale to read for St. Patrick's day or in concert with STONE SOUP.
SUBJ: Folklore--Ireland./ Ireland--Folklore.

CE 398.21   Ph-1 1-4/6 $13.95   L   KB394
DE PAOLA, TOMIE. Strega Nona: an old tale. Retold and illustrated by Tomie de Paola. Prentice-Hall ISBN 0-671-66283-X, 1975. 32p. col. ill.
Caldecott Honor Book.
Videocassette available from Weston Woods HMPV198V. 1/2" VHS videocassette color (9min), $49.95.
Big book available from Scholastic (ISBN 0-590-65967-7, 1992).
Read-along kit available from Weston Woods PBC198, 1993. 1 paperback book, 1 sound cassette (26min), $16.95. Side one with page turn signal, side two without signal.
A magic pasta pot fascinates Big Anthony, a young boy in the employ of Strega Nona, "Grandma Witch". One day, while the witch is away, Big Anthony decides to treat the town to pasta, but as he doesn't know the complete spell to start and stop the pot, his treat almost brings disaster to the town. The witch's timely return and her just punishment of Anthony brings the tale to a satisfying end.
SUBJ: Folklore--Italy./ Witches--Folklore./ Italy--Folklore.

398.21   Ph-1 2-4/3 $15.95   L   KB395
FISHER, LEONARD EVERETT. Kinderdike. Macmillan ISBN 0-02-735365-6; In Canada: Maxwell Macmillan, 1994. unp. col. ill.
Poetic explanation of why a town in southern Holland bears the name "Kinderdike." Strong, dynamic illustrations show dikes, windmills, and the life of the people who depend on these structures to exist.
SUBJ: Folklore--Netherlands./ Netherlands--Folklore./ Stories in rhyme.

398.21   Ph-3 3-4/5 $14.95   L   KB396
FOREST, HEATHER. Woman who flummoxed the fairies: an old tale from Scotland. Illustrated by Susan Gaber. Harcourt Brace Jovanovich ISBN 0-15-299150-6, 1990. unp. col. ill.
Known for the delicious cakes that she alone can bake, a woman is stolen by the fairies. How she fools them but still wins fairy gold makes a tale which will please readers and tellers alike. The watercolor, acrylic, and colored pencil on board illustrations are dark--limiting the book's appeal.
SUBJ: Folklore--Scotland./ Scotland--Folklore./ Cake--Folklore.

398.21   Ph-2 2-3/6 $15.99   L   KB397
GERSHATOR, PHILLIS. Iroko-man: a Yoruba folktale. Retold by Phillis Gershator. Illus. by Holly C. Kim. Orchard ISBN 0-531-08660-7, 1994. unp. col. ill.
"Richard Jackson book."
The Iroko-man grants fertility to the women of the village in exchange for suitable gifts. One woman has no gift but the child she will have. How her husband outwits the spirit makes an entertaining tale which shows that thought can find answers to problems. For multicultural studies.
SUBJ: Yoruba (African people)--Folklore./ Nigeria--Folklore./ Folklore--Nigeria.

398.21   Ph-2 K-2/5 $15.99 L KB398

GERSHATOR, PHILLIS. Tukama Tootles the flute: a tale from the Antilles. Retold by Phillis Gershator. Illus. by Synthia Saint James. Orchard ISBN 0-531-08661-5, 1994. unp. col. ill.

"Richard Jackson book."

A naughty boy evades his grandmother, stays out too late, falls into the hands of a two-headed giant, escapes, and determines never to leave his grandmother's loving care again. The rapidly paced tale with large impressionistic paintings is good for reading aloud. For multicultural studies.

SUBJ: Folklore--Virgin Islands of the United States./ Virgin Islands of the United States--Folklore./ Giants--Folklore.

398.21   Ph-2 2-4/3 $15.95 L KB399

GERSON, MARY-JOAN. People of corn: a Mayan story. Retold by Mary-Joan Gerson. Illus. by Carla Golembe. Little, Brown ISBN 0-316-30854-4; In Canada: Little, Brown, 1995. unp. col. ill.

The Mayan civilization flourished because the people had abundant corn crops. This dependence prompted a creation story in which the gods attempted to make men from different materials who would honor them, but finally fashioned a creature from corn to fulfill their desires. Vibrant colors recreate the Mayan land and practices. For multicultural studies.

SUBJ: Mayas--Folklore./ Indians of Central America--Folklore./ Folklore--Guatemala./ Guatemala--Folklore./ Creation--Folklore./ Corn--Folklore.

398.21   Ph-2 2-4/2 $14.95 L KB400

KIMMEL, ERIC A. Boots and his brothers: a Norwegian tale. Retold by Eric A. Kimmel. Illus. by Kimberly Bulcken Root. Holiday House ISBN 0-8234-0886-8, 1992. unp col illus.

Available from the National Library Service for the Blind and Physically Handicapped on sound recording cassette RC 38578.

When two brothers set out to seek their fortunes, the youngest wins in the end because he persists in finding answers to his questions. Minor changes from Thorne-Thomsen make the tale more acceptable for those seeking less violence in folktales.

SUBJ: Folklore--Norway./ Norway--Folklore.

398.21   Ph-2 2-4/7 $15.95 L KB401

KIMMEL, ERIC A. One Eye, Two Eyes, Three Eyes: a Hutzul tale. Retold by Eric A. Kimmel. Illus. by Dirk Zimmer. Holiday House ISBN 0-8234-1183-4, 1996. unp. col. ill.

Promising to give his most precious possession to an old woman who showed him the way out of a forest, a woodsman realizes that he is relinquishing his beloved daughter. The daughter takes her goat with her, and the goat's sacrifice of its life gains her freedom and a handsome prince. For reading aloud.

SUBJ: Hutsuls--Folklore./ Folklore--Ukraine./ Ukraine--Folklore.

398.21   Ph-3 3-5/2 $15.95 L KB402

KIMMEL, ERIC A. Witch's face: a Mexican tale. Adapted by Eric A. Kimmel. Illus. by Fabricio Vanden Broeck. Holiday House ISBN 0-8234-1038-2, 1993. unp. col. ill.

A young girl is destined to be a witch but is saved when a young man promises to marry her. He had also promised to destroy the witch's face which protected her identity when she was with the witches. The mask was so beautiful, however, that he failed to do so and brought grief to both of them. For multicultural studies.

SUBJ: Folklore--Mexico./ Mexico--Folklore./ Witches--Folklore.

398.21   Ph-2 3-5/5 $13.95 L KB403

MARTINEZ, ALEJANDRO CRUZ. Woman who outshone the sun: the legend of Lucia Zenteno./La mujer que brillaba aun mas que el sol: la leyenda de Lucia Zenteno. From a poem by Alejandro Cruz Martinez. Story by Harriet Rohmer and David Schecter. Translated into Spanish by Rosalma Zubizarreta. Illus. by Fernando Olivera. Children's Book Press ISBN 0-89239-101-4, 1991. 31p. col. ill.

A haunting retelling of a tale well known to the Zapotec Indians of Mexico. A beautiful woman visits a small village, and when the villagers drive her away, she carries the river (their source of water) in her hair. Mural-like paintings by an internationally recognized Mexican painter illustrate the text.

SUBJ: Zenteno, Lucia (Legendary character)./ Zapotec Indians--Folklore./ Indians of Mexico--Folklore./ Spanish language materials./ Bilingual materials--Spanish.

398.21   Ph-3 3-4/4 $13.00 T KB404

MCCARTHY, RALPH F. Moon princess. Retold by Ralph F. McCarthy. Illus. by Kancho Oda. Kodansha ISBN 4-7700-1756-1, 1993. 47p. col. ill. (Kodansha children's classics).

Told in verse, this tale relates the finding of a baby girl in a bamboo shoot by an aged Japanese couple. She becomes the delight of their old age. Her beauty is renowned throughout the land though she rejects all suitors. Eventually she must return to her true home on the moon. Full-page illustrations show the interiors of Japanese homes and elaborate dress.

SUBJ: Stories in rhyme./ Folklore--Japan./ Japan--Folklore.

398.21   Ph-2 3-5/5 $16.95 L KB405

MERMAID TALES FROM AROUND THE WORLD. Retold by Mary Pope Osborne. Illus. by Troy Howell. Scholastic ISBN 0-590-44377-1; In Canada: Scholastic, 1993. 84p. col. ill.

Includes bibliography.

Twelve little-known tales from different cultures and eras are authentically retold. Text is well researched, and the striking illustrations reflect the lands in which the stories are set. For multicultural studies.

SUBJ: Mermaids./ Folklore.

398.21   Ph-3 4-5/4 $15.95 T KB406

MOLLEL, TOLOLWA M. Orphan boy: a Maasai story. Illus. by Paul Morin. Clarion ISBN 0-89919-985-2, 1990. unp. ill. (some col.).

Selectors' Choice, 18th ed.

Available from the National Library Service for the Blind and Physically Handicapped on sound recording cassette RC 36511.

A haunting tale from the Maasai people of the origins of their name for the planet Venus. A story of devotion and a broken trust which is as memorable as the drawings of the stark countryside where the story is set.

SUBJ: Africa--Folklore./ Folklore--Africa./ Masai (African people)--Folklore.

398.21   Ph-3 3-5/5 $13.95 L KB407

MORONEY, LYNN. Elinda who danced in the sky: an Estonian folktale. Adapted by Lynn Moroney. Illus. by Veg Reisberg. Children's Book Press ISBN 0-89239-066-2, 1990. 31p. col. ill.

Elinda rejected all her suitors until Prince Borealis, Lord of the Northern Lights wooed and won her. She began to weave her wedding veil and when the Prince failed to return for her, she carried it with her to the sky, where it can be seen as the Milky Way. This handsomely illustrated book is valuable for astronomy classes in addition to units on Russia.

SUBJ: Sky--Folklore./ Estonia--Folklore./ Folklore--Estonia.

398.21   Ph-2 4-6/7 $14.93 L KB408

PODWAL, MARK. Golem: a giant made of mud. Greenwillow ISBN 0-688-13812-8, 1995. unp. col. ill.

A rabbi is fascinated by a spoon given to him by an emperor. The spoon, as the legend went, could create a golem, a huge figure of mud which comes to life. When the Jewish townspeople are persecuted, the rabbi uses the spoon to make a golem to protect them. The mystery of where and if the golem exists today makes this a timeless tale. Sources are listed.

SUBJ: Golem./ Jews--Folklore./ Folklore.

398.21   Ph-3 2-3/4 $14.89 L KB409

RAPPAPORT, DOREEN. Long-haired girl: a Chinese legend. Retold by Doreen Rappaport. Illus. by Yang Ming-Yi. Dial ISBN 0-8037-1412-2, 1995. unp. col. ill.

Available from the National Library Service for the Blind and Physically Handicapped on sound recording cassette RC 42883.

The people of Ah-mei's village suffered because there was no water. When she reveals a hidden waterfall, a god punishes her by having her hair turn pure white. How her beauty is restored makes a haunting folktale for reading aloud. For multicultural studies.

SUBJ: Folklore--China./ China--Folklore.

398.21   Ph-2 2-3/6 $14.89 L KB410

ROSS, GAYLE. Legend of the Windigo: a tale from native North America. Retold by Gayle Ross. Illus. by Murv Jacob. Dial ISBN 0-8037-1898-5, 1996. unp. col. ill.

Combining a number of Native American tales, the author relates how a scheme to destroy an evil creature made of stone was successful, but resulted in the coming of a pesky creature called "mosquito." A pourquoi tale which will fit into many units: nature, multicultural studies, and the seasons; this monster tale is good for reading aloud and can be paired with Aardema's WHY MOSQUITOES BUZZ IN PEOPLE'S EARS.

SUBJ: Windigos./ Algonquin Indians--Folklore./ Indians of North America--Folklore.

398.21   Ph-2 4-6/5 $16.00 L KB411

SAN SOUCI, ROBERT D. Faithful friend. Illus. by Brian Pinkney. Simon & Schuster ISBN 0-02-786131-7; In Canada: Distican, 1995. unp. col. ill.

Includes glossary.

Caldecott Honor book, 1996.

Coretta Scott King Illustrator Honor book, 1996.

Two young men, companions from birth, travel to a young woman's home seeking her hand in marriage. The future bride's uncle is a wizard who sets before the young men many trials which they succeed in overcoming. The scratchboard and oil artwork captures life on the Caribbean island of Martinique. Elements of romance, wizards, and zombies will appeal to older folklore fans. Great for reading aloud.
SUBJ: Folklore--Martinique./ Martinique--Folklore./ Folklore--Caribbean Area./ Caribbean Area--Folklore.

398.21   Ph-1 3-4/3 $15.89   L   KB412
SAN SOUCI, ROBERT D. Hired hand: an African-American folktale. Retold by Robert D. San Souci. Illus. by Jerry Pinkney. Dial ISBN 0-8037-1297-9; In Canada: McClelland & Stewart, 1997. unp. col. ill.
Lazy and greedy, Young Sam tries to work the magic New Hand, the hired hand, performed upon an old man to make him spry and youthful again. The experiment almost turns into disaster when the old woman ends up dead instead of regaining her youth. New Hand believes that Young Sam is truly repentant for his deed and the tale ends well. Based on an African-American folktale which has roots in Greece and Rome. Drawings done in pencil and watercolor capture the era of the late 1700s. For multicultural studies.
SUBJ: Afro-Americans--Folklore./ Folklore--United States./ United States--Folklore.

398.21   Ph-1 2-5/6 $14.89   L   KB413
SAN SOUCI, ROBERT D. Nicholas Pipe. Illus. by David Shannon. Dial ISBN 0-8037-1765-2; In Canada: McClelland & Stewart, 1997. unp. col. ill.
Nicholas Pipe, a merman, lives with the land-folk whom he protects in a small fishing village. His only concern is that he must touch the sea everyday, or he will die. He is loved by Margaret, a lovely maid whose father almost brings about his death. The father has him captured as a curiosity for the king and carried away from the sea. Margaret's rescue of her lover is breathtaking. The old legend, first recorded in the twelfth century, features a determined, resourceful heroine for women's studies.
SUBJ: Mermen--Folklore./ Folklore.

398.21   Ph-3 3-9/5 $14.99   T   KB414
SAN SOUCI, ROBERT D. Snow wife. Illus. by Stephen T. Johnson. Dial ISBN 0-8037-1409-2, 1993. unp. col. ill.
In this Japanese tale, the value of keeping a promise haunts a young woodcutter as he loses his young wife to the land of snow. Watercolor and pastel illustrations set a sombre mood, showing ogres, monsters, and a barren landscape. For the exceptional reader.
SUBJ: Folklore--Japan./ Japan--Folklore.

CE 398.21   Ph-1 3-5/5 $15.89   L   KB415
SAN SOUCI, ROBERT D. Talking eggs. Illus. by Jerry Pinkney. Dial ISBN 0-8037-0620-0; In Canada: Fitzhenry & Whiteside, 1989. unp. col. ill.
Caldecott Honor Book, 1990.
Videocassette available from SRA/McGraw-Hill 87-909932 (ISBN 0-07-909932-7, 1991). 1/2" iconographic VHS videocassette color (21min), guide, $42.00.
Spanish version available HUEVOS HABLANTES (ISBN 0-8037-1991-4, 1996).
Adapted from a Creole folktale, this lavishly illustrated story tells of two sisters, one kind and careful to follow directions, the other, selfish and prone to disregard instructions. Their adventures when they come upon multicolored chicks, a cow with two heads, and an old crone who removes her head to arrange her hair will please readers and storytellers alike. For multicultural studies.
SUBJ: Sisters--Folklore./ Folklore--United States./ United States--Folklore./ Spanish language materials.

398.21   Ph-1 1-3/4 $14.99   L   KB416
SAWYER, RUTH. Remarkable Christmas of the cobbler's sons. Told by Ruth Sawyer. Illus. by Barbara Cooney. Viking ISBN 0-670-84922-7; In Canada: Penguin, 1994. unp. col. ill.
A cobbler is forced to leave his three sons alone on Christmas eve when he goes to an army encampment to mend shoes. While he is away, the boys are visited by King Laurin, a goblin, who heaps gifts upon them after first frightening them. Newly illustrated version of a story from Sawyer's 1941 book THE LONG CHRISTMAS.
SUBJ: Folklore--Austria./ Austria--Folklore./ Christmas--Folklore.

398.21   Ph-1 K-3/4 $15.99   T   KB417
SIERRA, JUDY. Wiley and the Hairy Man. Retold by Judy Sierra. Illus. by Brian Pinkney. Lodestar ISBN 0-525-67477-2; In Canada: McClelland & Stewart, 1996. unp. col. ill.
Wiley and his mother lived near a swamp where the Hairy Man hid and carried off people. Each time Wiley ventured into the swamp, he took his hound dog that frightened off the Hairy Man. However,

wanting to rid the swamp forever of the monster, Wiley and his mother plotted to fool him three times and drive him away. For reading aloud. For multicultural studies.
SUBJ: Afro-Americans--Folklore./ Folklore--United States./ United States--Folklore./ Mothers and sons--Folklore./ Problem solving--Folklore.

398.21   Ph-2 4-6/3 $14.93   L   KB418
SINGER, MARILYN. Maiden on the moor. Illus. by Troy Howell. Morrow ISBN 0-688-08675-6, 1995. unp. col. ill.
Two shepherds find a maiden nearly frozen to death on the moor. The younger one tends her lovingly, and when she fails to respond, he becomes despondent. After the maiden begs his dog to kill her, she is transformed into a snow goose, and the dog becomes a young female companion for the shepherd. Reminiscent of a medieval manuscript, the colored pencil illustrations capture the mood of the story.
SUBJ: Ballads, English./ Folklore--England./ England--Folklore.

398.21   Ph-1 K-3/5 $14.99   L   KB419
SLOAT, TERI. Hungry giant of the tundra. Retold by Teri Sloat. Illus. by Robert and Teri Sloat. Dutton ISBN 0-525-45126-9, 1993. unp. col. ill.
When a group of children stay too long in the tundra, they are captured by a hungry giant. Their escape is aided by a chickadee and a clever crane. This cautionary tale from Alaska will delight listeners and readers. For multicultural studies.
SUBJ: Eskimos--Folklore./ Giants--Folklore./ Indians of North America--Folklore.

VCR 398.21   Ph-1 2-5 $44.95   OD KB420
TALKING EGGS (Videocassette). An animated story by Michael Sporn, narrated by Danny Glover. SVE/Churchill Media C81149-HAVT ISBN 0-7932-3030-6, 1993. 1/2" VHS videocassette color (25min).
Includes teacher's guide.
After befriending an old woman, Selina brings home three talking eggs. Wade, her brother, tries to gain equal treasures for himself but gets into a mess of trouble instead. Loosely based on a Creole folktale, this animated fable uses an inner-city setting.
SUBJ: Brothers and sisters--Folklore./ Friendship--Folklore./ Self-realization--Folklore./ Folklore--United States./ United States--Folklore.

398.21   Ph-2 4-5/4 $14.95   L   KB421
WAHL, JAN. Tailypo! Illus. by Wil Clay. Henry Holt ISBN 0-8050-0687-7; In Canada: Fitzhenry & Whiteside, 1991. unp. col. ill.
In a one room cabin, an old man chops off the tail of a monster who invades his home one night. The monster's return in search of his tail makes a horror story which will hold audiences spellbound when told or read aloud.
SUBJ: Folklore--United States./ United States--Folklore.

398.21   Ph-2 4-6/6 $13.88   L   KB422
WISNIEWSKI, DAVID. Elfwyn's saga. Lothrop, Lee & Shepard ISBN 0-688-09590-9, 1990. unp. col. ill.
Viking folk sail safely into a harbor but are pursued by a warrior who pronounces a curse upon them and gives them a crystal in which they see themselves in more fortunate situations. The story revolves around a blind child who frees the people from the curse and the enchantment of the stone. The cut-paper technique gives a 3-D effect to the illustrations in this Icelandic legend in stunning dress.
SUBJ: Vikings--Folklore./ Iceland--Folklore./ Folklore--Iceland./ Fairy tales.

398.21   Ph-1 2-6/5 $15.95   L   KB423
WISNIEWSKI, DAVID. Golem. Clarion ISBN 0-395-72618-2, 1996. unp. col. ill.
Caldecott Medal Award, 1997.
Formed from clay by a rabbi of Prague in the Middle Ages, the Golem is an enormous man who protects the Jews housed in a ghetto. When the emperor promises the safety of the Jews, the rabbi returns the figure to clay, but many believe that he can exist again. The horror of persecution and pain is depicted in the three-dimensional cut-paper illustrations. Notes supply information on the legend and history of the persecution of the Jews through the ages.
SUBJ: Golem./ Jews--Czech Republic--Folklore./ Folklore--Czech Republic./ Czech Republic--Folklore.

398.21   Ph-3 4-5/5 $14.95   T   KB424
WOLFSON, MARGARET. Marriage of the rain goddess: a South African myth. By Margaret Olivia Wolfson. Illus. by Clifford Alexander Parms. Marlowe & Company ISBN 1-56924-774-9, 1996. unp. col. ill.
First published in Great Britain, Barefoot Books Ltd.
Using a fragment of a Zulu myth, storyteller Wolfson has created a tale in which the rain goddess chooses a mortal man to be her husband. When she tests his knowledge of her powers, he proves his

love and understanding, and she makes him immortal. Beadwork which is often used to express love and deep feelings is central to the story.
SUBJ: Zulu (African people)--Folklore./ South Africa--Folklore./ Folklore--South Africa.

398.21 Ph-2 2-4/3 $15.95 L KB425
YEP, LAURENCE. Junior thunder lord. Illus. by Robert Van Nutt. BridgeWater ISBN 0-8167-3454-2; In Canada: BridgeWater/dist. by Vanwell, 1994. unp. col. ill.
As a youngster, Yue was helped in his studies and learned that "Those at the top should help those at the bottom." Yue lived this creed. When he came upon an ugly giant, he fed him and treated him with kindness. The giant soon became attached to Yue. Thus began a series of adventures in which the drought of an entire countryside is relieved because of the act of kindness. Larger than life cartoon-like illustrations bring drama and humor to the retelling.
SUBJ: Folklore--China./ China--Folklore.

CE 398.21 Ph-1 2-4/7 $17.00 T KB426
ZEMACH, HARVE. Duffy and the devil, a Cornish tale. Retold by Harve Zemach. Illus. by Margot Zemach. Farrar Straus & Giroux ISBN 0-374-31887-5, c1973. unp. col. ill.
Caldecott Medal Award.
Selectors' Choice, 9th ed.
Available from National Library Service for the Blind and Physically Handicapped in Braille BR06265.
A delightful variation of the Rumpelstiltskin story which was presented in play form in Cornwall in the 19th century. Squire Lovel of Trove seeks a maid to aid his housekeeper. When set to do the spinning, she turns to the devil for help. When she discovers the devil's name, all his knitting turns to ashes, but by this time the maid is wed to the squire and all are happy.
SUBJ: Folklore--Cornwall (England)./ Devil--Folklore./ Cornwall (England)--Folklore.

398.22 Ph-2 1-2/2 $14.00 T KB427

BERNIER-GRAND, CARMEN T. Juan Bobo: four folktales from Puerto Rico. Illus. by Ernesto Ramos Nieves. HarperCollins ISBN 0-06-023389-3; In Canada: HarperCollins, 1994. 64p. col. ill. (I can read book).
Four funny stories about Juan Bobo are retold for beginning readers with colorful drawings of a typical Puerto Rican house and farm. Spanish translations of the traditional tales in which the young hero outwits his mother are provided in an appendix.
SUBJ: Juan Bobo (Legendary character)./ Folklore--Puerto Rico./ Puerto Rico--Folklore./ Bilingual materials--Spanish./ Spanish language materials.

398.22 Ph-3 5-6/6 $12.95 T KB428
BROWN, MARCIA. Backbone of the king: the story of Paka'a and his son Ku. University of Hawaii Press ISBN 0-8248-0963-7, 1984. 180p. ill. (Kolowalu book).
Available from National Library Service for the Blind and Physically Handicapped in Braille BRA02172 and as talking book TB02143.
Based on an old myth, this epic tells of a father and son, powers behind the throne in Hawaii, and how each in his turn became "the backbone of the king". Excellent for storytelling. Detailed, basic history of Hawaii with the quality of folklore.
SUBJ: Folklore--Hawaii./ Hawaii--Folklore.

398.22 Ph-2 2-4/3 $14.95 T KB429
BRUSCA, MARIA CRISTINA. Pedro fools the gringo and other tales of a Latin American trickster. By Maria Cristina Brusca and Tona Wilson. Illus. by Maria Cristina Brusca. Henry Holt ISBN 0-8050-3827-2; In Canada: Fitzhenry & Whiteside, 1995. 54p. ill. (Redfeather book).
Includes bibliography.
Pedro, a South American trickster, has numerous adventures in this collection of brief humorous tales. Pedro reminds the reader of Robin Hood as he outwits the rich and influential. The cartoon-like illustrations are a perfect match for the stories. Sources supplied. For multicultural studies.
SUBJ: Folklore--Latin America./ Latin America--Folklore./ Tricksters--Folklore./ Short stories.

398.22 Ph-3 3-5/4 $13.95 L KB430
CHIN, CHARLIE. China's bravest girl: the legend of Hua Mu Lan = [Chin kuo ying hsiung Hua Mu-lan]. Illus. by Tomie Arai. Chinese translation by Wang Xing Chu. Children's Book Press ISBN 0-89239-120-0, 1993. 31p. col. ill.
When the Emperor called for a soldier from every household, Hua Mu Lan went in place of her elderly father. Her illustrious career in the army, while she was disguised as a man, is retold in verse. Told in English with the Chinese translation on each page, the tale is useful for students studying English as a second language. Incorporate into

women's studies units and multicultural studies.
SUBJ: Hua, Mu-lan (Legendary character)./ China--Folklore./ Folklore--China./ Bilingual materials--Chinese./ Chinese language materials./ Stories in rhyme.

398.22 Ph-2 2-3/5 $14.95 L KB431
CHOCOLATE, DEBORAH M. NEWTON. Imani in the belly. Illus. by Alex Boies. BridgeWater ISBN 0-8167-3466-6; In Canada: BridgeWater/dist. by Vanwell, 1994. unp. col. ill.
Imani (Faith) must leave her children each day while she journeys to the market. One day the children are eaten by the King of Beasts, Simba. It is Imani's courage and ingenuity which finally frees the children and other villagers from the beast's stomach. Bold gouache illustrations capture the action of the story. For multicultural studies.
SUBJ: Folklore--Africa./ Africa--Folklore./ Animals--Folklore.

398.22 Ph-3 3-5/6 $16.89 L KB432
CLIMO, SHIRLEY. Treasury of princesses: princess tales from around the world. Collected and retold by Shirley Climo. Illus. by Ruth Sanderson. HarperCollins ISBN 0-06-024533-6; In Canada: HarperCollins, 1996. 76p. col. ill.
In this treasury, seven stories from all corners of the world tell how princesses find true happiness. Sources are given for the tales. Full-page paintings show the princesses in the culture in which the story is found. For reading aloud. For multicultural studies.
SUBJ: Fairy tales./ Folklore./ Princesses--Folklore.

398.22 Ph-2 2-4/4 $15.95 L KB433
COHEN, BARBARA. Robin Hood and Little John. Retold by Barbara Cohen. Illus. by David Ray. Philomel ISBN 0-399-22732-6; In Canada: Putnam, 1995. unp. col. ill.
A simplified version of the comical meeting of Robin Hood with the gigantic fellow who later was christened Little John. The ripening of their friendship is captured in large sculptured drawings done in woodland colors.
SUBJ: Robin Hood (Legendary character)./ Folklore--England./ England--Folklore.

398.22 Ph-1 6/6 $24.95 L KB434
CRESWICK, PAUL. Robin Hood. Illus. by N. C. Wyeth. Scribner's ISBN 0-684-18162-2; In Canada: Collier Macmillan, 1984. 362p. col. ill.
Available from National Library Service for the Blind and Physically Handicapped in Braille BRA08283, on sound recording cassette RC26766, and as talking book TB03586.
As a youth, Robin Hood gazes into a globe and sees his future life in Sherwood Forest with Maid Marian and his company of men. This retelling of the beloved tale is filled with adventure and wisdom. The illustrations are world-known and handsomely reproduced.
SUBJ: Robin Hood (Legendary character)./ Folklore--Great Britain./ Great Britain--Folklore.

398.22 Ph-2 2-5/3 $14.95 L KB435
CURRY, JANE LOUISE. Christmas Knight. Illus. by DyAnne DiSalvo-Ryan. McElderry ISBN 0-689-50572-8; In Canada: Maxwell Macmillan, 1993. unp. col. ill.
When he had wealth to spare, people flocked around Sir Cleges to share in his bounty. This tale relates how a rare gift restores wealth to the good man and causes him to become "The Christmas Knight." Filled with humor and good feeling, this warmly illustrated picture book is a good choice for reading aloud at the holiday season.
SUBJ: Folklore--England./ Knights and knighthood--Folklore./ Christmas--Folklore./ England--Folklore.

398.22 Ph-3 3-5/3 $13.95 L KB436
CURRY, JANE LOUISE. Robin Hood and his Merry Men. Retold by Jane Louise Curry. Illus. by John Lytle. McElderry ISBN 0-689-50609-0; In Canada: Distican, 1994. 42p. ill.
Includes glossary.
Forced to live in Sherwood Forest, Robin joins a group of bandits and becomes their leader. His practices and tenets soon become theirs, and the group is known for standing for justice and as benefactors of the poor. This concise retelling of selected episodes may lead readers to fuller editions of the Robin Hood saga.
SUBJ: Robin Hood (Legendary character)./ Folklore--England./ England--Folklore.

398.22 Ph-3 3-5/3 $15.00 L KB437
CURRY, JANE LOUISE. Robin Hood in the greenwood. Retold by Jane Louise Curry. Illus. by Julie Downing. McElderry ISBN 0-689-80147-5; In Canada: Distican, 1995. 53p. ill.
Includes glossary.
In a companion volume to ROBIN HOOD AND HIS MERRY MEN, the author retells seven of the well-known legends about the notorious outlaw. Robin Hood's merry band enlarges to include the legendary

Friar Tuck and Maid Marion who is hiding from the Sheriff of Nottingham. Daring deeds of danger and fast paced adventures will lure reluctant readers, who may be overwhelmed by more complete editions, to this episodic volume.
SUBJ: Robin Hood (Legendary character)./ Folklore--England./ England--Folklore.

398.22   Ph-1 2-3/4 $15.95   L   KB438
DE PAOLA, TOMIE. Christopher: the holy giant. Holiday House ISBN 0-8234-0862-0, 1994. unp. col. ill.
A gentle giant wishes to serve the greatest king of all. This familiar legend of how he finds the king and earns the name Christopher (the Bearer-of-Christ) is told in a memorable fashion. De Paola's succinct retelling doesn't use an excess word, and the large drawings, typical of his work, are well-suited to the subject.
SUBJ: Christopher, Saint./ Saints.

398.22   Ph-1 2-4/5 $14.95   L   KB439
DIANE GOODE BOOK OF AMERICAN FOLK TALES AND SONGS. Collected by Anne Durell. Dutton ISBN 0-525-44458-0; In Canada: Fitzhenry & Whiteside, 1989. 63p. col. ill.
Stories people love to tell and songs that people love to sing from all parts and all cultures of the United States are gathered here and illustrated by gay, brightly colored, animated drawings.
SUBJ: Folklore--United States./ United States--Folklore./ Folk songs.

398.22   Ph-1 4-6/6 $17.95   T   KB440
EARLY, MARGARET. William Tell. Retold and illus. by Margaret Early. Abrams ISBN 0-8109-3854-5, 1991. unp. col. ill.
Available from the National Library Service for the Blind and Physically Handicapped on sound recording cassette RC 36317.
With illustrations which are very like those found in early manuscripts, the story of one man's valiant stand against a cruel dictator is retold. A visual treasure!
SUBJ: Tell, William--Legends./ Folklore--Switzerland./ Switzerland--Folklore.

TB 398.22   Ph-2 3-5 $11.00   KB441
EVANS, RON. Inktomi and the ducks and other Assiniboin trickster stories (Talking book). Parabola ISBN 0-930407-33-4; In Canada: Atrium Publishing Group, 1994. 1 sound cassette (60min). (Parabola storytime series).
Iktomi is a favorite character in the legends of the Native Americans. He tricks, blunders, and gets into impossible situations (e.g., losing his eyes) but always teaches a lesson of respect for the land and its people. A welcome adjunct to Paul Goble's books. For multicultural studies.
SUBJ: Indians of North America--Folklore./ Assiniboine Indians--Folklore./ Dakota Indians--Folklore.

398.22   Ph-1 3-5/4 $16.00   T   KB442
FISHER, LEONARD EVERETT. William Tell. Farrar, Straus and Giroux ISBN 0-374-38436-3; In Canada: HarperCollins, 1996. unp. col. ill.
A senseless decree by the royal governor, Herr Gessler, is disobeyed by a marksman, William Tell. His punishment is to shoot an apple from his son's head. His success gains his son's freedom, but he is imprisoned. Tell escapes his captors and kills the cruel dictator to conclude the story. Oversized figures against rugged countryside capture the drama of this traditional legend.
SUBJ: Tell, William--Legends./ Folklore--Switzerland./ Switzerland--Folklore.

398.22   Ph-2 3-5/4 $15.95   L   KB443
GIBLIN, JAMES CROSS. Dwarf, the giant, and the unicorn: a tale of King Arthur. Retold by James Cross Giblin. Illus. by Claire Ewart. Clarion ISBN 0-395-60520-2, 1996. 48p. col. ill.
Based on a little known Arthurian romance "Le Chevalier du Papegau ("The Knight of the Parrot"). Arthur and his knights find themselves shipwrecked on an island inhabited by a dwarf, a giant, and a unicorn. The strange trio have led a peaceful existence dependent on one another, and Arthur presents a threat to them. How they meet, work together, and finally returned to Camelot is an amazing tale sure to delight fans of King Arthur.
SUBJ: Arthur, King./ Dwarfs--Folklore./ Giants--Folklore./ Unicorns--Folklore./ Knights and knighthood--Folklore./ Folklore--England./ England--Folklore.

398.22   Ph-1 2-4/6 $14.95   L   KB444
GINSBURG, MIRRA. King who tried to fry an egg on his head: based on a Russian tale. Illus. by Will Hillenbrand. Macmillan ISBN 0-02-736242-6; In Canada: Maxwell Macmillan, 1994. unp. col. ill.
A king, desperate to provide food for his family, promises his three daughters to Sun, Moon, and Raven. The three sons-in-law are wise, but the foolish king misuses their talents. A rollicking tale, great for

reading aloud.
SUBJ: Folklore--Soviet Union./ Soviet Union--Folklore.

VCR 398.22   Ph-1 3-5 $9.95   KB445
GLEESON, BRIAN. Finn McCoul (Videocassette). Told by Catherine O'Hara. Music by Boys of the Lough. Illus. by Peter De Seve. Rabbit Ears ISBN 1-56204-013-8, 1991. 1/2" VHS videocassette color (30min). (We all have tales).
"Children's classics from around the world."
Read-along kit available from Rabbit Ears/Simon & Schuster (ISBN 0-689-80201-3, 1995). 1 hardback book, 1 sound cassette (25min), $19.95.
Finn, a fearsome giant in his own right, trembles at the thought of the "super" giant, Cucullin. This beautifully told legend shows how a clever woman can outwit the greatest of giants and protect her beloved mate. An outstanding production in which music and narration take the viewer back to Ireland in the time of giants.
SUBJ: Finn MacCool./ Folklore--Ireland./ Ireland--Folklore./ Giants--Folklore.

KIT 398.22   Ph-2 2-5 $19.95   KB446
GLEESON, BRIAN. Koi and the kola nuts (Kit). Told by Whoopi Goldberg. Music by Herbie Hancock. Illus. by Reynold Ruffins. Rabbit Ears/dist. by Simon & Schuster ISBN 0-88708-282-3; In Canada: Vanwell, 1992. 1 hardcover book, 1 sound cassette (50min). (We all have tales).
A young prince is denied his just share of the kingdom when his father, the chief, dies, but his kindness and courage gain him respect and rewards in a neighboring village. The accompanying reading will please the listener and the musical effects are suited to the text.
SUBJ: Folklore--Africa./ Africa--Folklore.

VCR 398.22   Ph-2 3-5 $14.95   KB447
GLEESON, BRIAN. Paul Bunyan (Videocassette). Adapted by Brian Gleeson. Read by Jonathan Winters. Music by Leo Kottke with Duck Baker. Illus. by Rick Meyerowitz. Rabbit Ears, 1990. 1/2" VHS videocassette color (30min).
Combines many of the familiar legends of Paul Bunyan but concludes with an ecological note as Paul returns to the forests to plant trees to replace those he had cut down. Excellent animation and good musical background.
SUBJ: Bunyan, Paul (Legendary character)./ Folklore--United States./ United States--Folklore.

398.22   Ph-2 3-5/7 $16.99   L   KB448
GOBLE, PAUL. Remaking the earth: a creation story from the Great Plains of North America. Orchard ISBN 0-531-08874-X, 1996. unp. col. ill.
"Richard Jackson book."
Combining legends from many tribes, Goble tells how the Earth Maker made the earth and the animals, people, landscape, and birds who live there. Because in Native American mythology the world is recreated many times, the tale ends with decline, but with the possibility that it will all reoccur. A calm, beautiful explanation of how the world was created for people to use and appreciate. For multicultural studies.
SUBJ: Algonquin Indians--Folklore./ Indians of North America--Great Plains--Folklore./ Folklore--Great Plains./ Creation--Folklore.

398.22   Ph-2 4-6/6 $15.99   L   KB449
HALEY, GAIL E. Mountain Jack tales. Told by and illus. by Gail E. Haley. Dutton ISBN 0-525-44974-4, 1992. 131p. ill.
Includes glossary and bibliography.
A superior collection of tales from the North Carolina Mountains features Jack, the clever mountain lad, and has its origins in familiar European stories. The dialect, local settings, and humor add to the appeal of the material which begs to be told.
SUBJ: Folklore--United States./ United States--Folklore.

398.22   Ph-1 6/6 $16.00   T   KB450
HASTINGS, SELINA. Sir Gawain and the green knight. Illus. by Juan Wijngaard. Lothrop, Lee & Shepard ISBN 0-688-00592-6, 1981. unp. col. ill.
This slim volume relates how Sir Gawain took up the challenge of the Green Knight to strike off his head with the condition that one year later the Green Knight could do the same to him. Illustrated with spectacular drawings of the court and countryside, this retelling of a familiar Arthurian legend is a gem.
SUBJ: Arthur, King--Fiction./ Knights and knighthood--Folklore./ Gawain (Legendary character).

398.22   Ph-2 3-5/6 $15.95   L   KB451
HODGES, MARGARET. Hero of Bremen. Retold by Margaret Hodges. Illus. by Charles Mikolaycak. Holiday House ISBN 0-8234-0934-1, 1993.

unp. col. ill., map.

Tale of a disabled shoemaker who wins for his townspeople land on which to expand their city. The inclusion of material on the medieval hero Roland makes this a tale of many uses. Smoothly presented with heroic watercolor illustrations. Useful for units on persons with disabilities.

SUBJ: Folklore--Germany--Bremen./ Germany--Bremen--Folklore.

398.22   Ph-2 4-5/6 $14.95   L   KB452
HODGES, MARGARET. Of swords and sorcerers: the adventures of King Arthur and his knights. By Margaret Hodges and Margery Evernden. Woodcuts by David Frampton. Scribner's ISBN 0-684-19437-6; In Canada: Maxwell Macmillan, 1993. 96p. ill.

Arthur's birth, childhood, coronation, formation of the Round Table, and marriage as well as his knights' search for the Holy Grail are simply retold. A smooth retelling for reading aloud.

SUBJ: Arthur, King./ Folklore--England./ Knights and knighthood--Folklore./ England--Folklore.

CE 398.22   Ph-1 5/7 $15.95   L   KB453
HODGES, MARGARET. Saint George and the dragon: a golden legend. Adapted by Margaret Hodges from Edmund Spenser's Faerie Queene. Illus. by Trina Schart Hyman. Little, Brown ISBN 0-316-36789-3; In Canada: Little, Brown, 1984. 32p. col. ill.

Caldecott Medal Award.

Available from National Library Service for the Blind and Physically Handicapped on sound recording cassette RC22236.

Sent by the Queen of the Fairies to fight a fierce dragon, the Red Cross Knight knew that by destroying this monster, he would save a terrified country and bring honor to the maid Una. Well crafted drawings bring life to this bit of English legend which can be incorporated in language arts units and art classes.

SUBJ: George, Saint./ Folklore--England./ Knights and knighthood--Folklore./ Dragons--Folklore./ England--Folklore.

398.22   Ph-2 3-4/5 $16.95   T   KB454
HODGES, MARGARET. Saint Patrick and the peddler. Illus. by Paul Brett Johnson. Orchard ISBN 0-531-05489-6, 1993. unp. col. ill.

"Richard Jackson book."

Following the dictates of St. Patrick, who appears to him in a dream, a peddler gains great wealth. Irish countryside and folk are handsomely evoked in the illustrations. Includes information on St. Patrick and the origin of the tale. Welcome story for St. Patrick's day.

SUBJ: Patrick, Saint./ Folklore--Ireland./ Ireland--Folklore.

398.22   Ph-1 5-6/6 $15.95   L   KB455
HOWE, JOHN. Knight with the lion: the story of Yvain. Retold and illus. by John Howe. Little, Brown ISBN 0-316-37583-7; In Canada: Little, Brown, 1996. unp. col. ill.

An adventuresome knight sets forth to free a spring guarded by a Black Knight. When he kills the Black Knight, he wins the hand of the knight's wife, but loses her love by spending too much time away from her side. The remainder of the tale tells of his efforts to regain her affection and of his adventures with a worthy companion, a lion. Full-page paintings of castles, battles, and knights capture the heroic adventures which fill this Arthurian story originally recorded by Chretien de Troyes.

SUBJ: Yvain (Legendary character)./ Arthur, King./ Folklore--England./ England--Folklore./ Knights and knighthood--Folklore.

398.22   Ph-1 3-4/5 $14.93   L   KB456
KELLOGG, STEVEN. Mike Fink. Retold and illus. by Steven Kellogg. Morrow ISBN 0-688-07004-3, 1992. unp col illus.

As an infant, Mike Fink was determined to be a keelboatman. The story of how he gains his goal by learning to be a marksman and wrestler makes him one of the greatest folk heroes ever. Dynamite illustrations bustling with the life of the river and settling of the West.

SUBJ: Tall tales./ Folklore--United States./ United States--Folklore./ Fink, Mike--Legends.

398.22   Ph-1 4-6/7 $15.93   L   KB457
KELLOGG, STEVEN. Paul Bunyan, a tall tale. Retold and illustrated by Steven Kellogg. Morrow ISBN 0-688-03850-6, 1984. unp. col. ill.

Selectors' Choice, 15th ed.

Spanish edition PAUL BUNYAN: UN CUENTO FANTASTICO (ISBN 0-688-13614-1, 1994).

Big book available from Mulberry (ISBN 0-688-12610-3, 1993), $18.95.

Being oversized from birth, Paul Bunyan was both a joy and a problem for his family. The Bunyan family business, lumbering, was soon taken over by Paul, and his enormous lumbering crew soon cleared the midwest of wood. The exaggerations of the tales are matched by the drawings which are filled with monsters and ingenious

woodsmen. This tallest of tales is a delight for the viewer as much as the reader.

Another tall tale PECOS BILL (ISBN 0-688-05872-8, 1986) (Spanish version PECOS BILL: UN CUENTO FANTASTICO ISBN 0-688-14036-X, 1995 available from Mulberry; and also available from National Library Service for the Blind and Physically Handicapped on sound recording cassette RC25297) is told in the same extravagant fashion with humorous, action-filled illustrations.

SUBJ: Bunyan, Paul (Legendary character)./ Folklore--United States./ Tall tales./ United States--Folklore./ Spanish language materials.

398.22   Ph-1 2-5/5 $14.93   L   KB458
KELLOGG, STEVEN. Sally Ann Thunder Ann Whirlwind Crockett: a tall tale. Retold and illus. by Steven Kellogg. Morrow ISBN 0-688-14043-2, 1995. unp. col. ill.

A rollicking tall tale of Davy Crockett's wife who was born talking, grinning, and running. She outwits bears, rescues Davy, and protects their home from an invasion by alligators. Kellogg's drawings abound with action and humor. A welcome heroine for units on tall tales.

SUBJ: Crockett, Sally Ann Thunder Ann Whirlwind--Legends./ Crockett, Davy--Legends./ Fink, Mike--Legends./ United States--Folklore./ Folklore--United States./ Tall tales.

398.22   Ph-2 2-4/7 $15.95   T   KB459
KIMMEL, ERIC A. Adventures of Hershel of Ostropol. Retold by Eric A. Kimmel. Illus. by Trina Schart Hyman. Holiday House ISBN 0-8234-1210-5, 1995. 64p. ill.

Available from the National Library Service for the Blind and Physically Handicapped on sound recording cassette RC 42583. Kimmel has collected ten stories about Hershel, a poor man who could make fun of the common events of life. His wit, cunning, and acceptance of God have endeared him to the Jewish people. This anthology makes the exploits of the Jewish folk hero available to all. For reading aloud.

SUBJ: Ostropoler, Hershele, 18th cent.--Legends./ Jews--Folklore./ Folklore.

398.22   Ph-3 4-5/5 $16.00   L   KB460
KIMMEL, ERIC A. Billy Lazroe and the King of the Sea: a tale of the Northwest. Illus. by Michael Steirnagle. Browndeer/Harcourt Brace ISBN 0-15-200108-5; In Canada: Harcourt Brace c/o Canadian Manda, 1996. unp. col. ill.

Billy, born to be a sailor, lived to play his concertina and sing. Davy Jones enjoyed his singing too and asked him to come to his world under the sea. Reluctantly, Billy visits this eerie world and is given a bride in payment for his music. This haunting legend from Oregon is based on an old Russion Tale, SADKO, THE MERCHANT OF NOVGOROD. Pastel drawings depict the world frequented by this legendary seaman. For inclusion in units on the sea and American folklore.

SUBJ: Folklore--Oregon./ Oregon--Folklore.

398.22   Ph-2 2-3/4 $15.95   L   KB461
KIMMEL, ERIC A. Three princes: a tale from the Middle East. Retold by Eric A. Kimmel. Illus. by Leonard Everett Fisher. Holiday House ISBN 0-8234-1115-X, 1994. unp. col. ill.

Unable to decide which prince to wed, a princess sends them into the world to find a "great wonder." Each one finds a rare treasure, but the actions of one of the princes proves that he would give all he owns to his beloved and thus becomes her choice. A haunting story with bold stark paintings which show the bare desert and its inhabitants. For multicultural studies.

SUBJ: Fairy tales./ Folklore--Arab countries./ Arab countries--Folklore.

SRC 398.22   Ph-2 5-6 $9.95   KB462
KING ARTHUR AND HIS KNIGHTS (Sound recording cassette). As told by Jim Weiss. Greathall Productions 1124-06 ISBN 1-882513-06-1, 1991. 1 sound cassette (60min).

ALA notable recording.

Compact disc available 1124-006 (ISBN 1-882513-31-2, 1991). 1 compact disc (60min), $14.95.

Sir Bedivere, the last of the knights of the Round Table, relates his memories which capture many of the highlights of King Arthur's reign. The storyteller uses several voices to make the material become vividly alive. For mature listeners. Incorporate into units on the Middle Ages or legends.

SUBJ: Arthur, King./ Knights and knighthood--Folklore./ Great Britain--Folklore./ Folklore--Great Britain.

398.22   Ph-2 3-5/6 $13.95   L   KB463
LATIMER, JIM. Irish piper. Illus. by John O'Brien. Scribner's ISBN 0-684-19130-X; In Canada: Collier Macmillan, 1991. unp. col. ill.

Full explanation of how an Irish piper from County Clare traveled to Saxony where he delivered the town from the mice who had invaded

it and also stole away the children taking them back to Ireland. A humorous supplement to the traditional Pied Piper story.
SUBJ: Pied Piper of Hamelin (Legendary character)./ Folklore--Germany--Hamelin./ Germany--Hamelin--Folklore.

398.22 Ph-1 2-5/4 $16.89 L KB464
LESTER, JULIUS. John Henry. Illus. by Jerry Pinkney. Dial ISBN 0-8037-1607-9, 1994. unp. col. ill.
Caldecott Honor book, 1995.
Selectors' Choice, 20th ed.
John Henry's mighty battle against a steam drill is captured in words and pictures which show the strength, physical and emotional, of this tall tale hero. Striking book for multicultural studies will find a place in all collections.
SUBJ: John Henry (Legendary character)./ Folklore--United States./ United States--Folklore./ Afro-Americans--Folklore.

398.22 Ph-2 4/7 $13.95 P KB465
LISTER, ROBIN. Story of King Arthur. Retold by Robin Lister. Illus. by Alan Baker. Kingfisher/dist. by Raintree Steck-Vaughn ISBN 0-7534-5101-8, 1997. 96p. col. ill.
The birth of Arthur, his creation of the Round Table, and the search for the Holy Grail are described through the eyes of Merlin. Each page is decorated with a color drawing which shows Arthur's court, the countryside, and the principal characters in the narrative.
SUBJ: Arthur, King./ Knights and knighthood--Folklore./ Folklore--England./ England--Folklore.

398.22 Ph-1 3-5/5 $15.99 L KB466
MAYER, MARIANNA. Baba Yaga and Vasilisa the Brave. Illustrated by K. Y. Craft. Morrow ISBN 0-688-08501-6, 1994. unp. col. ill.
A few months before she died, Vasilisa's mother gave her a small doll which helped her through the trials of her new life with her stepmother. Her adventure as she seeks light from the witch Baba Yaga is filled with terror and romance. Decorated in the style of an old Russian manuscript, the book is visually a delight.
SUBJ: Baba Yaga (Legendary character)./ Fairy tales./ Folklore--Russia./ Russia--Folklore.

398.22 Ph-1 4-6/6 $11.95 T KB467
MCCORMICK, DELL J. Paul Bunyan swings his axe. Caxton Printers ISBN 0-87004-093-6, c1936, 1962. 111p. ill.
Available from National Library Service for the Blind and Physically Handicapped in Braille BRA13812.
Tall tale of America's Paul Bunyan from his boyhood days in Maine through some of his western adventures.
SUBJ: Bunyan, Paul (Legendary character)./ Folklore--United States./ Lumber and lumbering--Folklore./ United States--Folklore.

398.22 Ph-1 4-6/6 $7.95 T KB468
MCCORMICK, DELL J. Tall timber tales: more Paul Bunyan stories. Illustrated by Lorna Livesley. Caxton Printers ISBN 0-87004-094-4, c1939. 155p. ill.
More stories of Paul Bunyan, Babe, his blue ox and some of his good friends such as Johnnie Inkslinger and Sourdough Sam.
SUBJ: Bunyan, Paul (Legendary character)./ Folklore--United States./ Lumber and lumbering--Folklore./ United States--Folklore.

VCR 398.22 Ph-2 2-5 $9.95 KB469
METAXAS, ERIC. Peachboy (Videocassette). Told by Sigourney Weaver. Music by Ryuichi Sakamoto. Illus. by Jeffrey Smith. Rabbit Ears REV 10244 ISBN 1-56204-002-2, 1991. 1/2" VHS videocassette color (30min). (We all have tales).
Read-along kit available from Rabbit Ears/Simon & Schuster (ISBN 0-689-80192-0, 1995). 1 hardback book, 1 sound cassette (28min), $19.95.
From a large peach comes a baby boy who delights an elderly Japanese couple. As he matures, he becomes a national hero as he vanquishes ogres who have long terrorized the country. One of the best known legends of Japan is dramatically retold with music well suited to the setting of the story.
SUBJ: Folklore--Japan./ Japan--Folklore.

KIT 398.22 Ph-2 2-5 $19.95 KB470
METAXAS, ERIC. Stormalong (Kit). Read by John Candy. Music by NRBQ. Illus. by Don Vanderbeek. Rabbit Ears/dist. by Simon & Schuster ISBN 0-689-80194-7, 1995. 1 hardcover book, 1 sound cassette (23min). (American heroes and legends).
Videocassette available from Rabbit Ears MMI 20055 (ISBN 1-56204-018-9, 1992). 1/2" VHS videocassette color (30min), $9.99.
The baby, Stormalong, came on a wave that crested in the front parlor. His amazing size and feats as a child and an adult are captured in this robust retelling of his life. The cartoonish illustrations

show him on, under, and away from the sea he loved and mastered. A whopper to augment collections on the sea and tall tales.
SUBJ: Stormalong, Alfred Bulltop (Legendary character)./ Tall tales./ Folklore--United States./ United States--Folklore.

398.22 Ph-2 5-A/7 $22.00 T KB471
PERHAM, MOLLY. King Arthur: the legends of Camelot. Illus. by Julek Heller. Viking ISBN 0-670-84990-1; In Canada: Penguin, 1993. 176p. col. ill.
Stunning pictures augment this faithful retelling of the legends surrounding King Arthur.
SUBJ: Arthur, King./ Knights and knighthood--Folklore./ England--Folklore./ Folklore--England.

398.22 Ph-2 A/9 $18.95 T KB472
PYLE, HOWARD. Story of King Arthur and his knights. Scribner's ISBN 0-684-14814-5, c1933, 1984. 312p. ill.
Available from National Library Service for the Blind and Physically Handicapped in Braille BRA12338, and as talking book TB01435.
When Arthur draws the sword from an anvil before the Cathedral he gains his birth right as the son of Uther-Pendragon and becomes High King of Britain.
Further adventures of the Knights of the Round Table and King Arthur are found in THE STORY OF THE CHAMPIONS OF THE ROUND TABLE (ISBN 0-684-18171-1); THE STORY OF SIR LAUNCELOT AND HIS CHAMPIONS (Doubleday ISBN 0-486-26701-6, 1991); and THE STORY OF THE GRAIL AND THE PASSING OF ARTHUR (ISBN 0-684-18483-4).
SUBJ: Arthur, King./ Knights and knighthood--Folklore./ Great Britain--Folklore./ Folklore--Great Britain.

398.22 E Ph-1 4-A/3 $14.99 T KB473
RAPPAPORT, DOREEN. New king. Illustrated by E. B. Lewis. Dial ISBN 0-8037-1460-2, 1995. unp. col. ill.
Selectors' Choice, 20th ed.
Available from the National Library Service for the Blind and Physically Handicapped on sound recording cassette RC 42058.
When his father dies, a young African prince seeks help from a doctor, wizard, counselor, and finally a wise woman. The wise woman counsels him with a Malagasy tale which helps him to understand the king's death. This book is useful in explaining death and is based upon the stages of grief as described by Dr. Kubler-Ross. For multicultural studies.
SUBJ: Folklore--Madagascar./ Madagascar--Folklore./ Folklore--Africa./ Africa--Folklore./ Death--Folklore.

398.22 Ph-2 K-2/6 $15.95 L KB474
RATTIGAN, JAMA KIM. Woman in the moon: a story from Hawaii. Retold by Jama Kim Rattigan. Illus. by Carla Golembe. Little, Brown ISBN 0-316-73446-2; In Canada: Little, Brown, 1996. unp. col. ill.
Includes glossary and bibliography.
Hina, the best tapa maker in Hawaii, was married to a lazy husband who spent his days hunting and fighting. She longed for a new home where she need not work all the time. This retelling of a well-known Hawaiian legend traces her search until she finds a place in the moon. Brilliant pictures painted in gouache on Victoria cover, a 100-percent rag black paper, capture the plants, birds, and fruits of the islands. For reading aloud.
SUBJ: Polynesians--Folklore./ Folklore--Hawaii./ Hawaii--Folklore./ Moon--Folklore.

398.22 Ph-2 2-3/4 $14.89 L KB475
RENBERG, DALIA HARDOF. King Solomon and the bee. Adapted by Dalia Hardof Renberg. Illus. by Ruth Heller. HarperCollins ISBN 0-06-022902-0; In Canada: HarperCollins, 1994. unp. col. ill.
A bee stings a king's nose and begs forgiveness. How the bee repays the king is a charming legend which could have come from the Talmud.
SUBJ: Solomon, King of Israel./ Jews--Folklore.

398.22 E Ph-2 2-4/4 $14.98 L KB476
ROTH, SUSAN L. Brave Martha and the dragon. Dial ISBN 0-8037-1853-5, 1996. unp. col. ill.
Clever collages illustrate this French tale of Saint Martha who aids a village in which animals are being eaten by a fierce dragon. This legend from Provencal has many facets from different centuries. The illustrator has chosen not to set the story in any particular period, but rather to capture the gay prints of the area.
SUBJ: Martha, Saint--Legends./ Dragons--Folklore./ France--Folklore./ Folklore--France.

398.22 Ph-1 4-6/7 $14.95 T KB477
ROUNDS, GLEN. Ol' Paul, the mighty logger: being a true account of the seemingly incredible exploits and inventions of the great Paul Bunyon.

Profusely illustrated with drawings made at the scene by the author.
Holiday House ISBN 0-8234-0269-X, 1976. 93p. ill.

Out of the North woods came a gigantic lumberman by the name of Paul Bunyan. He fashioned the land to meet his needs, and developed animals and people to carry out his work. The tall tales of his adventures have delighted people for many years and this collection is one of the best.
SUBJ: Bunyan, Paul (Legendary character)./ Folklore--United States./ Lumber and lumbering--Folklore./ United States--Folklore.

398.22   Ph-2 3-5/3 $14.95   L   KB478
RUBALCABA, JILL. Uncegila's seventh spot: a Lakota legend. Retold by Jill Rubalcaba. Illus. by Irving Toddy. Clarion ISBN 0-395-68970-8, 1995. 31p. col. ill.

In this Native American legend about twins, one brother is blind, but together they seek a way to destroy a wicked serpent. They kill the monster and gain its heart which demands such constant attention that the tribal activities are forgotten. The legend stresses "wealth is sweet through effort, and slavery is too high a price to pay for security." (Author's note) Features realistic paintings of the quest of the twins. For multicultural studies.
SUBJ: Dakota Indians--Folklore./ Indians of North America--Folklore.

398.22   Ph-2 3-5/5 $16.00   L   KB479
SABUDA, ROBERT. Arthur and the sword. Retold and illus. by Robert Sabuda. Atheneum ISBN 0-689-31987-8; In Canada: Distican, 1995. unp. col. ill.

Retells the tale of Arthur's ascendancy to the throne when he removes the sword from the rock which encased it. Boldly colored illustrations done in the form of stained glass windows are fitting for the medieval period. Vivid colors sparkle from the pages, and the reader develops a respect for this art form as well as receives an introduction to one of the best-loved stories. Notes on the origin of the King Arthur legend complete this book.
SUBJ: Arthur, King./ Folklore--England./ England--Folklore./ Knights and knighthood--Folklore.

398.22   Ph-2 3-6/5 $8.95   P   KB480
SANFIELD, STEVE. Adventures of High John the Conqueror. Illus. by Wendell E. Hall. August House ISBN 0-87483-433-3, 1989. 113p. ill.
Includes bibliography.
The High John of these stories personifies all the character traits which slaves admired during those long years when their bodies were owned by others. John was clever and could outwit his master at every turn. Highly amusing, these stories read and tell well, making them good choices for reading aloud or storytelling. Brief sections interspersed between the tales give bits of folklore which provide background for the stories. For multicultural studies.
SUBJ: Afro-Americans--Folklore./ Folklore--United States./ United States--Folklore.

398.22   Ph-3 5-6/6 $16.95   T   KB481
SAN SOUCI, ROBERT D. Cut from the same cloth: American women of myth, legend, and tall tale. Collected and told by Robert D. San Souci. Illus. by Brian Pinkney. Philomel ISBN 0-399-21987-0; In Canada: Putnam, 1993. 140p. ill.
Includes bibliography.
The collector/reteller, Robert San Souci, feels that tales of vital heroines have too long languished on book shelves. He has compiled stories from Anglo-American, African-American, Spanish-American, and Native American traditions to prove his point. Full-page black and white drawings picture these almost forgotten women.
SUBJ: Folklore--United States./ Tall tales./ Women--Folklore./ United States--Folklore.

398.22   Ph-2 3-4/6 $16.95   T   KB482
SAN SOUCI, ROBERT D. Young Guinevere. Illus. by Jamichael Henterly. Doubleday ISBN 0-385-41623-7; In Canada: Bantam Doubleday Dell, 1993. unp. col. ill.

Guinevere's childhood is portrayed in this large picture book. Her willfulness and courage foretell the problems which will develop in her marriage to Arthur. Encourages readers to further explore Arthurian material.
SUBJ: Guinevere, Queen (Legendary character)./ Arthur, King./ Folklore--England./ England--Folklore.

398.22   Ph-2 4-5/6 $15.95   T   KB483
SAN SOUCI, ROBERT D. Young Lancelot. Illus. by Jamichael Henterly. Doubleday ISBN 0-385-32171-6; In Canada: Bantam Doubleday Dell, 1996. unp. col. ill.

The son of good King Ban and Queen Helen, Lancelot is raised by the Lady of the Lake when his parents die while he is just a babe. He acquires all the knightly skills and a heart that is diamond-hard. The role the Lady of the Lake plays in helping him gain a generous heart

as well is related in a large picture book illustrated with stirring paintings.
SUBJ: Lancelot (Legendary character)./ Knights and knighthood--Folklore./ Folklore--England./ England--Folklore.

398.22   Ph-2 4-5/6 $5.99   P   KB484
SAN SOUCI, ROBERT D. Young Merlin. Illus. by Daniel Horne. Dell ISBN 0-440-41159-9; In Canada: Bantam, Doubleday, Dell, c1990, 1996. unp. col. ill.

Raised by nuns because his mother was deserted before his birth, Merlin became known as the devil's own child. Sought out by kings, he proved his magical powers and became the mentor of the early English kings. Stirring paintings dramatize this remarkable legend and will bring Merlin into center stage for students reading the Arthurian legends.
SUBJ: Merlin (Legendary character)./ Folklore--England./ England--Folklore.

398.22   Ph-2 1-2/2 $3.99   P   KB485
SCHECTER, ELLEN. Warrior maiden: a Hopi legend. Illus. by Laura Kelly. Bantam Doubleday Dell ISBN 0-553-37022-7; In Canada: Bantam Doubleday Dell, 1992. 48p. col. ill. (Bank Street ready-to-read).
"Byron Preiss book."
"Bantam little rooster book."
Told by her father to be alert for an Apache raid to steal corn, Huh-ay-ay is the first to hear and see the attacking party. She also formulates a plan to fool the attackers and runs to bring help. A simple tale of a courageous Hopi girl for multicultural studies.
SUBJ: Hopi Indians--Folklore./ Indians of North America--Folklore.

398.22   Ph-2 5-6/7 $13.00   L   KB486
SEREDY, KATE. White stag. Viking ISBN 0-670-76375-6, c1937. 94p. col. ill.
Newbery Medal Award.
Available from National Library Service for the Blind and Physically Handicapped in Braille BRA01680, on sound recording cassette RC23270, and as talking book TB00821.
The story of the flight to their "promised land" of the Hungarian people under the leadership of the twins Hunor and Magyar and their descendants, guided sometimes by a white stag, sometimes by a red eagle.
SUBJ: Folklore--Hungary./ Hungary--Folklore.

398.22   Ph-1 K-2/4 $15.00   L   KB487
SHEPARD, AARON. Baker's dozen: a Saint Nicholas tale. Retold by Aaron Shepard. Illus. by Wendy Edelson. Atheneum ISBN 0-689-80298-6; In Canada: Distican, 1995. unp. col. ill.

A good, but miserly, baker gives only twelve cookies to a dozen until an old woman (St. Nicholas in disguise) teaches him that a full measure is thirteen. A bit of Americana and an explanation of a tradition make a good story for reading aloud during the holiday season.
SUBJ: Folklore--United States./ United States--Folklore./ Nicholas, Saint, Bp. of Myra--Legends./ Bakers and bakeries--Folklore.

398.22   Ph-2 2-3/2 $16.00   L   KB488
SHEPARD, AARON. Gifts of Wali Dad: a tale of India and Pakistan. Retold by Aaron Shepard. Illus. by Daniel San Souci. Atheneum ISBN 0-684-19445-7; In Canada: Distican, 1995. unp. col. ill.

A gold bracelet given to the noblest of queens and her reciprocation with a far larger gift begins a chain of events which places the grass-cutter, Wali Dad, in the midst of a great romance and prompts him to resolve never to give another gift. Presents a unique hero with whom the reader soon sympathizes. Drawings capture the humor of the tale. For multicultural studies.
SUBJ: Fairy tales./ Folklore--India./ India--Folklore./ Folklore--Pakistan./ Pakistan--Folklore.

398.22   Ph-2 3-5/3 $14.95   L   KB489
SHEPARD, AARON. Legend of Slappy Hooper: an American tall tale. Retold by Aaron Shepard. Illus. by Toni Goffe. Scribner's ISBN 0-684-19535-6; In Canada: Maxwell Macmillan, 1993. unp. col. ill.

Slappy Hooper painted such extraordinary billboards and signs that they came alive. His final responsibility was painting sunrises and sunsets which are enjoyed by all today. A whopper with an upbeat ending.
SUBJ: Folklore--United States./ United States--Folklore./ Tall tales.

398.22   Ph-2 4-5/6 $15.93   L   KB490
TALBOTT, HUDSON. King Arthur and the Round Table. Books of Wonder/Morrow ISBN 0-688-11341-9, 1995. unp. col. ill. (Tales of King Arthur).

After he sees Guinevere tending the wounded at a battle, Arthur longs for her in spite of Merlin's vigorous wishes that he forget her.

Later aiding another king, Arthur is given Guinevere's hand and a magnificent round table which becomes the rallying place for Arthur's knights. Filled with battle scenes and seiges of castles, this picture book version of the Arthur story will attract browsers as much as readers.
SUBJ: Arthur, King./ Folklore--England./ England--Folklore./ Knights and knighthood--Folklore.

398.22   Ph-3 4-5/4 $8.50   P   KB491
THOMPSON, VIVIAN L. Hawaiian tales of heroes and champions. Illustrated by Herbert Kawainui Kane. University of Hawaii Press ISBN 0-8248-1076-7, c1971, 1986. 128p. ill. (Kolowalu book).
Includes glossary and bibliography.
Battling and playing tricks on each other, Kapuas (supernatural beings) helped Hawaiian peoples understand the unexplainable. The twelve stories are dramatic and are appropriate for use in the social studies curriculum.
Additional tales of how men and boys find answers to unsolvable riddles and fool tricksters can be found in HAWAIIAN LEGENDS OF TRICKSTERS AND RIDDLERS, illustrated by Patricia A. Wozniak (ISBN 0-8248-1302-2, c1969, 1991).
SUBJ: Folklore--Hawaii./ Hawaii--Folklore.

398.22   Ph-1 2-4/5 $14.95   L   KB492
UCHIDA, YOSHIKO. Wise old woman. Retold by Yoshiko Uchida. Illus. by Martin Springett. McElderry ISBN 0-689-50582-5; In Canada: Maxwell Macmillan, 1994. unp. col. ill.
Selectors' Choice, 20th ed.
Because of his devotion to his aged mother, a son refuses to abandon her. When she solves the three impossible tasks set by a powerful warring overlord, she proves the value of respecting age and experience. A haunting tale illustrated with dramatic prints. For units on aging, family, and multicultural studies.
SUBJ: Folklore--Japan./ Japan--Folklore./ Old age--Folklore.

398.22   Ph-3 4-A/7 $16.95   T   KB493
WALKER, PAUL ROBERT. Big men, big country: a collection of American tall tales. Illus. by James Bernardin. Harcourt Brace Jovanovich ISBN 0-15-207136-9; In Canada: Harcourt Brace c/o Canadian Manda, 1993. 79p. col. ill.
Includes bibliography.
With explanations of the sources used and background about the real people around whom tall tales grew, the author tells nine amazing adventures which will tickle funny bones. Illustrations and descriptive language are outstanding.
SUBJ: Tall tales./ Folklore--United States./ United States--Folklore.

398.22   Ph-1 2-4/6 $17.00   T   KB494
WALKER, PAUL ROBERT. Little folk: stories from around the world. Illus. by James Bernardin. Harcourt Brace ISBN 0-15-200327-4; In Canada: Harcourt Brace c/o Canadian Manda, 1997. 72p. col. ill.
Includes bibliography.
Little folk, who lived in the past and cruised the fields of the countryside of Ireland, Hawaii, and Japan make fascinating reading to the "little folk" of today. This collection of eight stories from many cultures has full source notes and distinctive paintings done in acrylic and colored pencil. Good choice for reading aloud. For multicultural studies.
SUBJ: Fairies--Folklore./ Leprechauns--Folklore./ Dwarfs--Folklore./ Folklore.

398.22   Ph-1 3-5/4 $15.95   L   KB495
WISNIEWSKI, DAVID. Sundiata: Lion King of Mali. Photos of cut-paper illus. by Lee Salsbery. Clarion ISBN 0-395-61302-7, 1992. unp. col. ill.
Selectors' Choice, 19th ed.
How a youth, unable to walk or talk in his early years, rises to become the ruler of the Mali empire in Africa almost 800 years ago is vividly related through text and detailed paper designs. A visual drama which incorporates folklore with history to make a little known period come alive.
SUBJ: Mandingo (African people)--Folklore./ Kings, queens, rulers, etc.--Folklore./ Mali--Folklore./ Folklore--Mali./ Keita, Soundiata.

398.22   Ph-2 3-5/5 $13.89   L   KB496
YEP, LAURENCE. Shell woman and the king: a Chinese folktale. Retold by Laurence Yep. Paintings by Yang Ming-Yi. Dial ISBN 0-8037-1395-9, 1993. unp. col. ill.
A ruthless, selfish king kidnaps Shell, the magical woman from the sea, and tries to keep her for himself. When he demands three matchless gifts, she outwits him in this retelling of an old Chinese tale. Illustrator, who comes from China, beautifully shows palaces, old customs, and handicrafts in fluid watercolor paintings.
SUBJ: Fairy tales./ Folklore--China./ China--Folklore.

398.22   Ph-1 K-2/4 $15.95   L   KB497
YOUNG, ED. Little Plum. Philomel ISBN 0-399-22683-4; In Canada: Putnam, 1994. unp. col. ill.
Small as a plum seed, the Chinese boy in this story helps his father in the fields, outwits the lord of the city who plunders and beats the people of Little Plum's village, and brings peace to the countryside. Chinese version of TOM THUMB. Good choice for reading aloud. For multicultural studies.
SUBJ: Folklore--China./ China--Folklore.

398.23   Ph-1 2-4/6 $14.95   L   KB498
BROWN, MARCIA. Dick Whittington and his cat. Told and cut in linoleum by Marcia Brown. Scribner's ISBN 0-684-18998-4, c1950, 1988. unp. col. ill.
Caldecott Honor Book.
Available from National Library Service for the Blind and Physically Handicapped in Braille BR04673.
Dick Whittington owns nothing but a cat which he sells for a great fortune.
SUBJ: Folklore--Great Britain./ Cats--Folklore./ Great Britain--Folklore.

398.23   Ph-1 5-6/6 $7.95   P   KB499
DEARMOND, DALE. Seal oil lamp. Adapted from an Eskimo folktale and illus. with wood engravings by Dale DeArmond . Sierra Club Books ISBN 0-87156-858-6, 1988. 32p. ill.
"Yolla Bolly Press book."
Includes glossary.
When Alluga is deserted by his parents because his blindness will limit his usefulness to them, he is befriended by Mouse Woman. Her help and advice aid him in killing a mighty whale and proving his value. A moving story illustrated by beautifully designed woodcuts.
SUBJ: Eskimos--Folklore./ Indians of North America--Folklore./ Blind--Folklore.

398.23   Ph-3 K-3/5 $14.95   L   KB500
DE PAOLA, TOMIE. Tony's bread. Whitebird/Putnam ISBN 0-399-21693-6; In Canada: Putnam, 1989. unp. col. ill.
Available from the National Library Service for the Blind and Physically Handicapped on sound recording cassette RC33732.
Outside the city of Milan lived a baker who longed to become famous. How he achieved his goal, created a delicious Christmas treat and found a husband for his cherished daughter is related in this retelling of an Italian folktale. A tale for all seasons, but especially for the Christmas season.
SUBJ: Folklore--Italy./ Italy--Folklore./ Bread--Folklore.

398.23   Ph-2 2-3/2 $13.93   L   KB501
DE REGNIERS, BEATRICE SCHENK. Little Sister and the Month Brothers. Retold by Beatrice Schenk de Regniers. Illus. by Margot Tomes. Lothrop, Lee & Shepard ISBN 0-688-05293-2, c1976, 1994. unp. col. ill.
Mistreated by her stepmother and stepsister, Little Sister is forced to search for violets and strawberries in winter. She is befriended by the Month Brothers whose magic helps her to accomplish the impossible task. When her greedy tormentors set out to find the Month Brothers and their gifts, they never return. Large drawings as well as numerous small sketches depict the action.
SUBJ: Fairy tales./ Folklore--Slavic Countries./ Slavic Countries--Folklore.

SRC 398.23   Ph-2 4-5 $8.95   OD KB502
HAYES, JOE. Tales from the Southwest (Sound recording cassette). Weston Woods WW726C, 1984. 1 sound cassette.
Drawing from Hispanic and American Indian cultures, these six tales sparkle with humor. The storyteller's expressive voice and excellent sense of pacing add to the inherent appeal of the stories. Applicable to the social studies curriculum and multicultural studies.
Contents: Side I: La Mariposa (The Butterfly) (10min); La Hormiguita (8min); Donde Hay Ganas, Hay Manas (6min); Side 2: Soft Child (6min); Rain (6min); Homes for the People (6min).
SUBJ: Folklore--United States./ Indians of North America--Folklore./ Folklore--Spain./ United States--Folklore./ Spain--Folklore.

398.23   Ph-2 2-4/5 $16.00   T   KB503
JAFFE, NINA. Golden flower: a Taino myth from Puerto Rico. Retold by Nina Jaffe. Illus. by Enrique O. Sanchez. Simon & Schuster ISBN 0-689-80469-5; In Canada: Distican, 1996. unp. col. ill.
A Puerto Rican legend explains how a barren mountain becomes a fertile land when a child planted seeds and two men fought over a pumpkin, releasing water. The illustrations are mosaics filled with vivid colors of the earth and sky. Creation story for multicultural studies.
SUBJ: Taino Indians--Folklore./ Indians of the West Indies--Puerto Rico--Folklore./ Creation--Folklore./ Folklore--Puerto Rico./ Puerto Rico--Folklore.

398.23   Ph-1 3-5/5 $15.95   L   KB504
KIMMEL, ERIC A. Count Silvernose: a story from Italy. Retold by Eric A. Kimmel. Illus. by Omar Rayyan. Holiday House ISBN 0-8234-1216-4, 1996. unp. col. ill.
> When her two younger sisters foolishly ride off to work for Count Silvernose, they are reported dead. It is up to the older sister Assunta to outwit the count, rescue her sisters (if they are alive), and bring the story to a happy ending. Bursting with life and vigor, the paintings appear to be part of an old sketchbook which explained the disappearance of washerwomen in the fourteenth century. The little known tale, which has a Blue Beard theme, features a strong female protagonist.
> SUBJ: Folklore--Italy./ Italy--Folklore./ Problem solving--Folklore.

398.23   Ph-2 3-4/5 $15.95   L   KB505
KURTZ, JANE. Miro in the Kingdom of the Sun. Illus. by David Frampton. Houghton Mifflin ISBN 0-395-69181-8, 1996. unp. col. ill.
> A courageous maiden, talented in understanding the language of the birds, finds her way to a mythical lake to get water to cure the Prince. Bold woodcuts, colored in earthy hues, depict many of the symbols connected with the Inca civilization. An engaging tale with a strong female protagonist for multicultural studies.
> SUBJ: Incas--Folklore./ Folklore--Peru./ Peru--Folklore./ Indians of South America--Folklore.

398.23   Ph-3 4-5/6 $16.00   L   KB506
OODGEROO. Dreamtime: aboriginal stories. Illus. by Bronwyn Bancroft. Lothrop, Lee & Shepard ISBN 0-688-13296-0, 1994. 95p. col. ill.
> Two sections relate events from the author's childhood and some of the legends familiar to the aboriginal people. Striking full-page illustrations were drawn by an artist recognized in Australia as a faithful interpretor of aboriginal art.
> SUBJ: Australian aborigines--Folklore./ Australia--Folklore./ Folklore--Australia./ Authors, Australian.

398.23   Ph-2 1-3/2 $3.99   P   KB507
OPPENHEIM, JOANNE. Christmas Witch: an Italian legend. Retold by Joanne Oppenheim. Illus. by Annie Mitra. Bantam ISBN 0-553-37187-8; In Canada: Bantam Doubleday Dell, 1993. 48p. col. ill. (Bank Street ready-to-read).
> "Byron Preiss book."
> Befana lived a long time ago in Italy. She had no family or friends, so her neighbors called her a witch. One night she saw a bright star in the sky, and three kings who were seeking the Baby Jesus traveled by her door. She failed to join their group, but to this day, many believe that she too searches for the Baby and travels through Italy distributing gifts. The familiar legend is written for beginning readers with cartoon-like illustrations.
> SUBJ: Befana (Legendary character)./ Folklore--Italy./ Italy--Folklore./ Christmas--Folklore.

398.23   Ph-2 K-3/3 $19.95   T   KB508
RIORDAN, JAMES. Stories from the sea. Compiled by James Riordan. Illus. by Amanda Hall. Abbeville Kids ISBN 0-7892-0282-4, 1996. 80p. col. ill. (Abbeville anthology).
> First published in Great Britain, Barefoot Books Ltd., 1996.
> Nine stories about the oceans of the world create a delightful collection which is illustrated with full-color, doublespread paintings that dance across the text. Sources for the tales are given. Good choice for reading aloud. For multicultural studies.
> SUBJ: Ocean--Folklore.

398.23   Ph-1 2-4/6 $143.95   L   KB509
ROBBINS, RUTH. Baboushka and the three kings. Adapted from a Russian folktale. Illus. by Nicolas Sidjakov. Parnassus Press ISBN 0-395-27673-X, c1960. unp. col. ill.
> Caldecott Medal Award.
> Available from National Library Service for the Blind and Physically Handicapped on sound recording cassette RC23548 and in Braille BRA06638.
> "The Russian legend of the old woman who refused to follow the three kings in search of the Holy Child" is retold here and illustrated in a striking, unusual manner.
> SUBJ: Babouska (Legendary character)./ Christmas--Folklore./ Folklore--Soviet Union./ Soviet Union--Folklore.

398.23   Ph-1 6-A/7 $15.95   T   KB510
SANFIELD, STEVE. Feather merchants and other tales of the fools of Chelm. Illus. by Mikhail Magaril. Orchard ISBN 0-531-05958-8, 1991. 102p. ill.
> "Richard Jackson book."
> Includes glossary and bibliography.
> How the town of Chelm came into existence is humorously explained. Contains wonderful tales from Jewish folklore of the "wise" and the

"foolish" who populated the town. Stories beg to be told.
> SUBJ: Jews--Folklore./ Chelm (Chelm, Poland)--Folklore./ Folklore-- Chelm (Chelm, Poland)./ Folklore--Europe, Eastern./ Europe, Eastern- -Folklore.

398.23   Ph-3 4-6/6 $4.95   P   KB511
SCHWARTZ, HOWARD. Sabbath lion: a Jewish folktale from Algeria. Retold by Howard Schwartz and Barbara Rush. Illus. by Stephen Fieser. HarperCollins ISBN 0-06-443382-X; In Canada: HarperCollins, 1992. unp. col. ill.
> A youth accompanying a caravan to a far city to collect his family's inheritance is forsaken in the desert when he stops to worship on the Sabbath. His amazing rescue by a lion and its effects on those who see it are depicted in bright full-color illustrations. The story, which is well-known and told in the Middle East, is a good introduction to the customs of the Jewish faith. For multicultural studies.
> SUBJ: Jews--Folklore./ Folklore--Algeria./ Algeria--Folklore./ Sabbath--Folklore.

398.23   Ph-3 4-5/7 $22.50   T   KB512
TREASURY OF TURKISH FOLKTALES FOR CHILDREN. Retold by Barbara K. Walker. Linnet/Shoe String ISBN 0-208-02206-6, 1988. 155p.
> Includes glossary.
> Selecting from the 3000 Turkish tales that she and her husband have collected, Barbara Walker presents here a wide variety of material which will delight storytellers and teachers introducing the culture.
> SUBJ: Folklore--Turkey./ Turkey--Folklore.

398.23   Ph-2 1-3/4 $15.88   L   KB513
VOJTECH, ANNA. Marushka and the Month Brothers: a folktale. Retold by Anna Vojtech and Philemon Sturges. Illus. by Anna Vojtech. North-South Books ISBN 1-55858-629-6; In Canada: North-South Books/dist. by Vanwell, 1996. unp. col. ill.
> Sent into a storm to find violets for her selfish stepmother and stepsister, Marushka stumbles upon the 12 Month Brothers. Further quests bring strawberries and apples. Her selfish stepsister, desiring more apples, sets out to find the brothers, but her search only results in her death and her mother's. A smooth retelling with haunting illustrations for reading aloud.
> SUBJ: Folklore--Slavic Countries./ Slavic Countries--Folklore./ Fairy tales.

398.24   Ph-1 P-2/4 $15.99   L   KB514
AARDEMA, VERNA. Borreguita and the coyote: a tale from Ayutla, Mexico. Retold by Verna Aardema. Illus. by Petra Mathers. Knopf ISBN 0-679-90921-4; In Canada: Random House, 1991. unp. col. ill.
> Includes glossary.
> Humorous tale of a clever "little lamb" who bests a coyote who is left to howl at the moon. Mexican folktale with a taste of Aesop.
> SUBJ: Folklore--Mexico./ Mexico--Folklore./ Animals--Folklore.

CE 398.24   Ph-1 P-2/6 $14.95   L   KB515
AARDEMA, VERNA. How the ostrich got its long neck: a tale from the Akamba of Kenya. Retold by Verna Aardema. Illus. by Marcia Brown. Scholastic ISBN 0-590-48367-6; In Canada: Scholastic, 1995. unp. col. ill.
> Selectors' Choice, 21st ed.
> Talking book available from Recorded Books 95090 (ISBN 0-7887-1086-9, 1997). 1 sound cassette (15min), $10.00.
> Once Ostrich had a short neck and had difficulty eating and drinking, but then she helped Crocodile with his bad toothache. Crocodile returned her kindness by trying to eat her when she placed her head in his mouth. Ostrich's strength overcame Crocodile, but a mark of her adventure is still evident today: a wonderful, useful long neck. Large watercolors highlighted with pen and ink augment the lively pourquoi story.
> SUBJ: Akamba (African people)--Folklore./ Folklore--Kenya./ Kenya-- Folklore.

398.24   Ph-2 K-2/3 $18.99   L   KB516
AARDEMA, VERNA. Lonely lioness and the ostrich chicks: a Masai tale. Illus. by Yumi Heo. Knopf ISBN 0-679-96934-9; In Canada: Random House, 1996. unp. col. ill.
> "Borzoi book."
> A lioness attempts to adopt a family of new born ostrich chicks and almost succeeds until she is outwitted by a crafty mongoose. Stylized primitive paintings glow with the light and colors of the African savannah. A simple tale of a mother desperately trying to win back her young. For reading aloud.
> SUBJ: Masai (African people)--Folklore./ Folklore--Africa./ Africa-- Folklore.

398.24   Ph-2 K-2/2 $14.89   L   KB517
AARDEMA, VERNA. This for that: a Tonga tale. Retold by Verna Aardema. Illus. by Victoria Chess. Dial ISBN 0-8037-1554-4; In Canada: McClelland & Stewart, 1997. unp. col. ill.
     During a drought in Africa, wily Rabbit tricks other animals and people into giving her gifts in exchange for the goods she currently has. This maneuver works well until her last possession escapes, and her fellow animals recognize her as a liar and trickster. The Tonga trickster tale is based on a folktale from Northern Rhodesia. Artwork is done in watercolors and with Pelikan sepia. For multicultural studies.
     SUBJ: Tonga (Zambesi people)--Folklore./ Folklore--Africa./ Africa--Folklore./ Animals--Folklore.

VCR 398.24   Ph-1 K-3 $60.00   OD KB518
AARDEMA, VERNA. Who's in Rabbit's house? (Videocassette). Weston Woods VC279V, 1995. 1/2" VHS videocassette color (13min).
     Includes teacher's guide.
     Includes public performance rights.
     Rabbit, coming home, discovers that his home is occupied by the Long One, who refuses to vacate. All the animals suggest ways to drive the Long One out, but it is Frog's scheme to scare him which finally drives Caterpillar out and up a tree. The story is told in the form of a play presented before a group of Masai villages. Use as a model for a readers' theater production or as inspiration for mask making activities.
     SUBJ: Masai (African people)--Folklore./ Africa--Folklore./ Folklore--Africa./ Animals--Folklore.

CE 398.24   Ph-1 1-3/5 $15.99   T   KB519
AARDEMA, VERNA. Why mosquitoes buzz in people's ears: a West African tale. Retold by Verna Aardema. Illustrated by Leo and Diane Dillon. Dial ISBN 0-8037-6089-2, 1975. 30p. col. ill.
     Caldecott Medal Award.
     Selectors' Choice, 10th ed.
     Available from Weston Woods as 1/2" VHS videocassette color HMPV199V (10min), $49.95.
     Available from National Library Service for the Blind and Physically Handicapped in Braille BR05916 and on sound recording cassette RC22905.
     Big book available from Penguin (ISBN 0-14-054589-1, 1993).
     This is a West African cumulative tale which is set in action by a buzzing mosquito. The animals are all involved and concerned because Mother Owl refuses to wake the sun. The illustrations are bold and employ several unique techniques.
     SUBJ: Folklore--Africa, West./ Animals--Folklore./ Africa, West--Folklore.

TB 398.24   Ph-3 2-4 $11.00   OD KB520
AARDEMA, VERNA. Why mosquitoes buzz in people's ears (Talking book). HarperAudio/Caedmon ISBN 0-694-51187-0, 1978. 1 sound cassette.
     Ruby Dee and Ossie Davis read five African tales adapted from the author's books WHY MOSQUITOES BUZZ IN PEOPLE'S EARS and TALES FOR THE THIRD EAR from Equatorial Africa.
     Contents: Why mosquitoes buzz in people's ears; Ol-Ambu and He-of-the-Long Sleeping Place; Ananse and the King's Cow; Kindai and the apes; Ikpoom.
     SUBJ: Folklore--Africa, West./ Animals--Folklore./ Africa, West--Folklore.

398.24   Ph-2 K-2/2 $15.95   T   KB521
ADA, ALMA FLOR. Mediopollito/Half-Chicken. Illus. by Kim Howard. Translated by Rosalma Zubizarreta. Doubleday ISBN 0-385-32044-2; In Canada: Bantam Doubleday Dell, 1995. unp. col. ill.
     A mother hen has 12 perfect chicks, but the last born is only half of a chick. Scorned in the farmyard, Half-Chicken sets off for Mexico City to see the court of the Viceroy. On his way, he befriends water, fire, and wind who save his life and find a safe place for him on a tower of the palace. Thus Half-Chicken became the first weather vane. The pourquoi tale in Spanish and English is illustrated with brightly colored folk art. For multicultural studies.
     SUBJ: Folklore--Mexico./ Mexico--Folklore./ Weather vanes--Folklore./ Spanish language materials./ Bilingual materials--Spanish.

CDR 398.24   Ph-1 P-A $39.95   OD KB522
AESOP'S FABLE: THE TORTOISE AND THE HARE (CD-ROM). Random House/Broderbund, 1993. 1 CD-ROM, 1 paperback book. (Living books).
     Includes teacher's guide and coloring book.
     Also available for Windows.
     System requirements: Macintosh and Power Macintosh; System 6.0.7 or higher; 16MHz 68020 processor faster; Power Macintosh; 4MB RAM, 2.5MB free; CD-ROM drive required; Monitor: 12 inch or larger color, 256 colors.

System requirements: Windows 3.1 or Windows 95; 16MHz 386 or faster required; 4MB RAM for Windows 3.1; 8MB RAM for Windows 95; CD-ROM drive or faster required; SVGA monitor/display card 640x480, 256 colors; Windows compatible sound device.
     Product runs on either Macintosh or Windows compatible hardware. Based on Aesop's fable, this multimedia version contains the complete story and is greatly enhanced with animation and voice. Easy to navigate, the program requires a minimum of adult intervention. Youngsters may explore at their own pace with the play option or choose to have the story read to them page by page. English and Spanish versions are included.
     SUBJ: Fables--Software./ Software--Fables./ Interactive media./ Bilingual materials--Spanish--Software./ Software--Bilingual materials--Spanish./ Spanish language materials--Software./ Software--Spanish language materials.

SRC 398.24   Ph-2 P-2 $9.95   KB523
ANIMAL TALES (Sound recording cassette). As told by Jim Weiss. Greathall Productions 1124-07 ISBN 1-882513-07-X, 1990. 1 sound cassette (60min).
     Goats, cats, roosters, and many other animals and birds abound in these tellings of familiar and not so familiar stories. For entertainment and development of listening skills.
     SUBJ: Animals--Folklore.

398.24   Ph-2 2-3/5 $6.95   P   KB524
ARKHURST, JOYCE COOPER. Adventures of Spider: West African folktales. Retold by Joyce Cooper Arkhurst. Illus. by Jerry Pinkney. Little, Brown ISBN 0-316-05107-1; In Canada: Little, Brown, c1964, 1992. 58p. ill. (some col.).
     Six of Spider's best-known adventures are retold with rib-tickling illustrations. Children will relate to the scrapes that Spider encounters in this classic anthology of Anansi tales. Ideal for reading aloud.
     SUBJ: Anansi (Legendary character)./ Folklore--Africa, West./ Africa, West--Folklore./ Spiders--Folklore.

398.24   Ph-2 P-K/2 $16.00   T   KB525
ARUEGO, JOSE. Rockabye crocodile. By Jose Aruego and Ariane Dewey. Greenwillow ISBN 0-688-06738-7, 1988. unp. col. ill.
     Two boars--one kind and one spiteful--are neighbors. Annabel kindly offers to tend crocodile's cranky baby in return for fish while Netti scolds the baby and receives a basket of loathsome insects, rat and bats. She repents her behavior and the two agree to share from then on. The bright and bouncy illustrations add humor and make this ideal to share in picture book hours.
     SUBJ: Pigs--Folklore./ Behavior--Folklore./ Folklore--Philippines./ Philippines--Folklore.

398.24   Ph-2 2-4/6 $17.95   T   KB526
BARBOSA, ROGERIO ANDRADE. African animal tales. English language adaptation by Feliz Guthrie. Illus. by Cica Fittipaldi. Volcano Press ISBN 0-912078-96-0, 1993. 62p. col. ill.
     Ten unique African fables collected by a United Nations volunteer are accompanied by bold illustrations based on Yoruba art. Distinctive easy-to-tell stories for multicultural studies.
     SUBJ: Folklore--Africa./ Africa--Folklore./ Animals--Folklore.

398.24   Ph-1 P-K/1 $12.89   L   KB527
BARTON, BYRON. Three bears. HarperCollins ISBN 0-06-020424-9; In Canada: HarperCollins, 1991. unp. col. ill.
     This simple retelling of the adventures of Goldilocks and the three bears will find a place in preschool collections and in picture book hours where youngsters are encouraged to tell the story by viewing the pictures.
     SUBJ: Bears--Folklore./ Folklore.

398.24   Ph-2 K-1/1 $17.28   L   KB528
BENITEZ, MIRNA. How spider tricked snake. Illustrated by Dorothea Sierra. Raintree ISBN 0-8172-3524-8, 1989. 30p. col. ill. (Real readers).
     Using every trick he knows, spider is unable to capture snake until snake willingly stretches himself out to be measured and falls into spider's hands. Retold for beginning readers this doesn't use Anansi's name even though it, clearly, is one of his stories.
     SUBJ: Folklore--Jamaica./ Jamaica--Folklore.

398.24   Ph-2 1-2/4 $15.95   L   KB529
BERNHARD, EMERY. How Snowshoe Hare rescued the Sun: a tale from the Arctic. Retold by Emery Bernhard. Illus. by Durga Bernhard. Holiday House ISBN 0-8234-1043-9, 1993. unp. col. ill.
     When Bear and Wolf fail to capture the Sun, the animals of the Arctic turn to Snowshoe Hare. His determination and ingenuity are proven as he succeeds. Simple illustrations capture the Arctic landscapes in this tale which will be appreciated by young listeners.
     SUBJ: Eskimos--Russia--Folklore.

398.24   Ph-3   3/3 $15.95   L   KB530
BIERHORST, JOHN. Doctor Coyote: a Native American Aesop's fables. Retold by John Bierhorst. Illus. by Wendy Watson. Macmillan ISBN 0-02-709780-3; In Canada: Collier Macmillan, 1987. unp. col. ill.
> Available from National Library Service for the Blind and Physically Handicapped on Braille BR7679.
> Recast by the Aztecs in the 16th century, the traditional fables focus on Coyote who was clever, compassionate and sometimes foolish. Active panel drawings and well presented text make this an unusual adjunct in units on fables. The sophistication of the title will require initial introduction.
> SUBJ: Coyote (Legendary character)./ Fables./ Aztecs--Folklore./ Indians of Mexico--Folklore.

398.24   Ph-3   3-4/4 $13.00   L   KB531
BIERHORST, JOHN. Monkey's haircut and other stories told by the Maya. Edited by John Bierhorst. Illus. by Robert Andrew Parker. Morrow ISBN 0-688-04269-4, 1986. 151p. ill.
> Includes bibliography.
> Following an extensive introduction which develops background for many of the stories, the famed collector retells twenty-two tales of the Maya people. The stories reveal much of the way of life of the people, their customs and beliefs, including interpretations of Christian doctrine. A little known treasure house of material is found in this well designed book.
> SUBJ: Mayas--Folklore./ Indians of Central America--Folklore.

398.24   Ph-2   K-2/5 $14.93   L   KB532
BODNAR, JUDIT Z. Wagonload of fish. Translated and adapted by Judit Z. Bodnar. Illus. by Alexi Natchev. Lothrop, Lee & Shepard ISBN 0-688-12173-X, 1996. unp. col. ill.
> An old woman had all she could ever want, but she wanted "fish." How a fox foiled her husband's efforts to satisfy her is a humorous tale for reading aloud to primary groups. Humorous, oversized drawings of the old man and woman, the ox, and the fox will please the youngest readers.
> SUBJ: Folklore--Hungary./ Hungary--Folklore./ Foxes--Folklore.

TB 398.24   Ph-2   3-A $10.95   OD KB533
BRER RABBIT AND BOSS LION (Talking book). Told by Danny Glover. Music by Dr. John. Rabbit Ears ISBN 1-56668-837-X, 1992. 1 sound cassette (51min). (American heroes and legends).
> ALA notable recording, 1994.
> Danny Glover's lively retelling of how wily (and cowardly) Brer Rabbit outwits mean Boss Lion is full of humor. Narration with music by Dr. John on one side; full musical score with no narration on the other side. For multicultural studies.
> SUBJ: Afro-Americans--Folklore./ Animals--Folklore./ United States--Folklore./ Folklore--United States.

398.24   Ph-1   K-2/3 $15.95   L   KB534
BRETT, JAN. Mitten. Putnam ISBN 0-399-21920-X, 1989. unp. col. ill.
> A lost mitten becomes home for many of the forest animals until a bear's sneeze sends it into the air and into the hands of its owner. Rich, action packed drawings of animals and winter scenes.
> SUBJ: Folklore--Ukraine./ Ukraine--Folklore./ Mittens--Folklore./ Animals--Folklore.

398.24   Ph-1   K-3/3 $15.95   L   KB535
BRETT, JAN. Town Mouse, Country Mouse. Putnam ISBN 0-399-22622-2; In Canada: Putnam, 1994. unp. col. ill.
> Town mice longing to see the countryside again swap houses with two country mice. However, they soon discover the discomforts and terrors in the country while the country mice find unexpected dangers in the city. Detailed scenes of the countryside and the interior of an elegant Victorian house provide additional enjoyment for the reader. Lavish artwork is as entertaining as the familiar fable.
> SUBJ: Fables./ Mice--Folklore.

CE 398.24   Ph-1   1-3/6 $13.95   L   KB536
BROWN, MARCIA. Once a mouse. Scribner's ISBN 0-684-12662-1, c1961. unp. col. ill.
> Caldecott Medal Award.
> Available from National Library Service for the Blind and Physically Handicapped in Braille BR05912, on sound recording cassette RC22903, and as talking book TB01117.
> Fable of the arrogant tiger who turned into a mouse. Magnificently vigorous woodcuts.
> SUBJ: Animals--Folklore./ Folklore--India./ India--Folklore.

CE 398.24   Ph-1   2-4/4 $15.89   L   KB537
BRUCHAC, JOSEPH. Boy who lived with the bears: and other Iroquois stories. Illus. by Murv Jacob. HarperCollins ISBN 0-06-021288-8; In Canada: HarperCollins, 1995. 63p. col. ill.

Talking book available from HarperAudio CPN 1897 (ISBN 1-55994-541-9, c1990, 1991). 1 sound cassette (63min), $11.95.
> Bruchac creates the mood of sitting around a fire and listening to a respected Native American storyteller tell legends of birds and animals, which subtly teach lessons about caring, sharing, and using one's wits to stay alive. The pourquoi stories are intended for young listeners and are great for reading aloud. For multicultural studies.
> SUBJ: Iroquois Indians--Folklore./ Indians of North America--Folklore./ Animals--Folklore./ Folklore--North America./ North America--Folklore.

398.24   Ph-1   1-3/4 $13.89   L   KB538
BRUCHAC, JOSEPH. First strawberries: a Cherokee story. Retold by Joseph Bruchac. Illus. by Anna Vojtech. Dial ISBN 0-8037-1332-0, 1993. unp. col. ill.
> A Cherokee couple live in peace and harmony until the man's thoughtless words cause the woman to flee their home. Sun's creation of strawberries brings the pair together again. This simple story will delight readers whenever strawberries appear in the spring.
> SUBJ: Cherokee Indians--Folklore./ Indians of North America--Folklore./ Strawberries--Folklore.

398.24   Ph-2   2-4/2 $14.99   T   KB539
BRUCHAC, JOSEPH. Great ball game: a Muskogee story. Retold by Joseph Bruchac. Illus. by Susan L. Roth. Dial ISBN 0-8037-1539-0, 1994. unp. col. ill.
> Unfortunately, the Birds lose the ball game with the Animals in this familiar Native American pourquoi tale that explains how Bat came to be accepted as an Animal. Illustrated with creative collages, which will inspire young artists, the tale can be incorporated into lessons on the seasons or science units on migration. For multicultural studies.
> SUBJ: Creek Indians--Folklore./ Indians of North America--Folklore./ Animals--Folklore./ Birds--Folklore.

398.24   Ph-3   4-6/5 $12.95   P   KB540
BRUCHAC, JOSEPH. Native American animal stories. From KEEPERS OF THE ANIMALS by Michael J. Caduto and Joseph Bruchac. Illus. by John Kahionhes Fadden and David Kanietakeron Fadden. Fulcrum ISBN 1-55591-127-7, 1992. 135p. ill., maps.
> Includes glossary and bibliography.
> Twenty-four brief legends are presented under the headings: Creation; Celebration; Vision; Feathers and Fur, Scales and Skin; and Survival. A small map affixed to each story explains the origin of the tale. Contains background information on Tribal Nations represented in the stories as well as source notes. Though primarily for use by teachers and librarians, the book will attract students because of its appealing design and illustrations. An ideal resource for storytellers and units on Native Americans.
> SUBJ: Indians of North America--Folklore./ Animals--Folklore.

398.24   Ph-2   2-3/5 $16.95   T   KB541
BRUSCA, MARIA CRISTINA. When jaguars ate the moon: and other stories about animals and plants of the Americas. By Maria Cristina Brusca and Tona Wilson. Henry Holt ISBN 0-8050-2797-1; In Canada: Fitzhenry & Whiteside, 1995. unp. col. ill., map.
> Includes bibliography.
> The author/illustrator shows the many animals and plants of the Americas in small drawings which head each page, followed by a brief story from one of the continents. Notes on the tales give the source and brief information about the animal or plant in the story. For reading aloud, multicultural studies, and units on the people and animals of South America, the United States, and Canada.
> SUBJ: Indians--Folklore./ America--Folklore./ Folklore--America./ Plants--Folklore./ Animals--Folklore./ Alphabet.

398.24   Ph-2   4-6/4 $15.95   T   KB542
BRYAN, ASHLEY. Beat the story-drum, pum-pum. Retold and illustrated by Ashley Bryan. Atheneum ISBN 0-689-31356-X; In Canada: Collier Macmillan, 1980. 68p. ill.
> Coretta Scott King Award.
> The five tales from Nigeria found in this collection are about animals who show human traits and weaknesses. Stylistically told and illustrated, these stories should prove popular for telling.
> SUBJ: Folklore--Nigeria./ Nigeria--Folklore./ Animals--Folklore.

398.24   Ph-1   K-3/2 $11.95   L   KB543
BRYAN, ASHLEY. Cat's purr. Atheneum ISBN 0-689-31086-2; In Canada: Collier Macmillan, 1985. 42p. ill.
> Rat and Cat are best friends until Rat tricks Cat, plays Cat's family drum and is almost eaten by Cat, who instead swallows the small drum. Since that day, if Cat is stroked gently the purring-purrum, purrum, purrum of Cat's drum is heard. Based on an old West Indian folktale.
> SUBJ: Cats--Folklore.

398.24   Ph-3 4-6/3 $14.95 T KB544
BRYAN, ASHLEY. Lion and the ostrich chicks and other African folk tales. Retold and illustrated by Ashley Bryan. Atheneum ISBN 0-689-31311-X, 1986. 87p. ill.
Four stories from the Hausa, Angolan, Masai and Bushmen people of Africa are found in this collection. Stylistically told and illustrated, these stories should prove popular for telling.
SUBJ: Folklore--Africa./ Africa--Folklore./ Animals--Folklore.

398.24   Ph-1 K-3/6 $14.95 L KB545
BRYAN, ASHLEY. Turtle knows your name. Atheneum ISBN 0-689-31578-3; In Canada: Collier Macmillan, 1989. unp. col. ill.
Retold from "Turtle Tells Her Name" in FOLKLORE OF THE ANTILLES by Elsie Clews Parsons.
Having mastered his own long name, a young boy must now learn his granny's name or go without dessert. Colorful, exuberant, full page watercolor paintings match the chant filled rhythmic text. Be prepared - as with TIKKI TIKKI TEMBO - to have duplicates of the names on hand after the story is told.
SUBJ: Folklore--West Indies./ West Indies--Folklore./ Names, Personal--Folklore./ Grandmothers--Folklore.

398.24   Ph-2 3-4/6 $6.95 P KB546
CAMERON, ANNE. Raven and Snipe. Illus. by Gaye Hammond. Harbour ISBN 1-55017-037-6; In Canada: Harbour, 1991. 29p. ill.
Knowing that Raven is a glutton, Snipe promises her endless food if she learns a bit of magic. The magic causes Raven great pain, and to this day she leaves the snipe alone. Based on an Indian legend from the Pacific Northwest, this is great for telling.
SUBJ: Indians of North America--Canada--Folklore./ British Columbia (Canada)--Pacific Coast--Folklore./ Folklore--British Columbia (Canada)--Pacific Coast./ Ravens--Folklore.

398.24   Ph-3 3-4/6 $6.95 P KB547
CAMERON, ANNE. Raven goes berrypicking. Illus. by Gaye Hammond. Harbour ISBN 1-55017-036-8; In Canada: Harbour, 1991. 31p. ill.
Sly old Raven is up to her old tricks in this story of how she steals all the fruits of her friends' efforts but is found out in the end. Stark black and white drawings augment this well-known trickster tale. Excellent material for telling.
SUBJ: Indians of North America--Canada--Folklore./ British Columbia (Canada)--Pacific Coast--Folklore./ Folklore--British Columbia (Canada)--Pacific Coast./ Ravens--Folklore.

398.24   Ph-2 1-3/2 $16.00 L KB548
CECIL, LAURA. Frog princess. Retold by Laura Cecil. Illus. by Emma Chichester Clark. Greenwillow ISBN 0-688-13506-4, 1995. unp. col. ill.
Three sons are sent out into the world to find the perfect bride. All of the girls are talented, but it is the bride of the youngest son, a frog, who surpasses the others. The sprightly drawings are exaggerated, human, and delightful.
SUBJ: Fairy tales./ Folklore--Russia./ Russia--Folklore.

398.24   Ph-2 2-3/5 $14.95 L KB549
CHANG, MARGARET. Cricket warrior: a Chinese tale. Retold by Margaret and Raymond Chang. Illus. by Warwick Hutton. McElderry ISBN 0-689-50605-8; In Canada: Maxwell Macmillan, 1994. unp. col. ill.
The only means a Chinese family has to save their land is to provide the emperor with a fighting cricket. When their son accidently releases the family's cricket, the son magically becomes one and restores the family fortune. Gentle tale with subdued watercolors which match its message of family love and dedication. For reading aloud in the primary grades. For multicultural studies.
SUBJ: Folklore--China./ China--Folklore.

398.24   Ph-2 K-3/3 $15.95 L KB550
COMPTON, JOANNE. Sody sallyratus. Illus. by Kenn Compton. Holiday House ISBN 0-8234-1165-6; 1995. unp. col. ill.
Ma discovers that her sody sallyratus is gone when she starts to bake biscuits. She sends Will and Tom to fetch some sody sallyratus, but it is Jack who fools the bear and rescues his entire family. A popular "Jack" tale for reading aloud.
SUBJ: Folklore--United States./ United States--Folklore.

CE 398.24   Ph-1 3-4/6 $14.95 L KB551
COOPER, SUSAN. Selkie girl. Retold by Susan Cooper. Illus. by Warwick Hutton. McElderry ISBN 0-689-50390-3, 1986. unp. col. ill.
Available from National Library Service for the Blind and Physically Handicapped on sound recording cassette RC26263.
Iconographic videocassette available from Weston Woods HMPV319V, 1991. 1/2" VHS videocassette color (14min), $49.95.
Capturing a selkie girl (seal maiden) from the sea, Donallan marries her and they have a family of three boys and two girls. When the mother's sealskin is found in its hiding place by the youngest boy, she

returns to the sea but continues to protect her clan. A notable team has produced this hauntingly beautiful book which captures the Scottish landscape. Useful for storytelling.
SUBJ: Folklore--Great Britain./ Seals (Animals)--Folklore./ Great Britain--Folklore.

398.24   Ph-3 P-2/2 $13.95 L KB552
COWLEY, JOY. Mouse bride. Illus. by David Christiana. Scholastic ISBN 0-590-47503-7; In Canada: Scholastic, 1995. unp. col. ill.
An appealing tiny mouse, lamenting her smallness, sets out to find "the strongest husband in the world." Her search is captured in watercolors which faithfully portray her stature in contrast to the wind, sun, clouds, and man-made structures. Based on African, Asian, and Central American versions.
SUBJ: Mice--Folklore./ Marriage--Folklore./ Japan--Folklore./ Folklore--Japan.

398.24   Ph-2 K-3/7 $14.89 L KB553
CZERNECKI, STEFAN. Cricket's cage: a Chinese folktale. Retold by Stefan Czernecki. Hyperion ISBN 0-7868-2234-1, 1997. unp. col. ill.
The emperor who built the Forbidden City in Beijing, China, wished to complete the great wall around the city with four towers. Designs for these structures displeased him until a lowly cricket provided plans for his own cage. These plans ultimately became the model for the stupendous watchtowers protecting the Forbidden City. Author provides full notes on the story told by generations of Beijing storytellers. The artwork was prepared using Chinese mineral and vegetable pigments, and the border details, representing the emperor's robe, create the impression of exquisite brocade cloth. For multicultural studies.
SUBJ: Crickets--Folklore./ Folklore--China./ China--Folklore.

398.24   Ph-1 K-2/4 $14.95 L KB554
DABCOVICH, LYDIA. Polar bear son: an Inuit tale. Retold and illus. by Lydia Dabcovich. Clarion ISBN 0-395-72766-9, 1997. 37p. col. ill.
Unable to hunt for her own food, an old Inuit woman is dependent upon the people of the village, until she adopts a little white bear cub. As the cub grows, so does his ability to hunt and provide food for the two of them. Villagers, jealous of the bear, threaten to kill him. The children and the old woman force the bear to flee, but he continues over the years to pay visits to the old woman and care for her. Based on several stories. The author-illustrator has used Inuit sculpture as models for her drawings. For multicultural studies.
SUBJ: Inuit--Folklore./ Eskimos--Folklore./ Folklore--Arctic regions./ Arctic regions--Folklore./ Polar bear--Folklore.

398.24   Ph-3 2-4/5 $15.95 L KB555
DAVIS, DONALD. Jack and the animals: an Appalachian folktale. Illus. by Kitty Harvill. August House LittleFolk ISBN 0-87483-413-9; In Canada: Monarch Books, 1995. unp. col. ill.
Teacher's guide available upon request.
This Jack tale is a retelling of the familiar BREMEN-TOWN MUSICIANS. Large illustrations convey the action and humor of the story.
SUBJ: Folklore--Appalachian Region./ Appalachian Region--Folklore.

398.24   Ph-2 2-3/2 $16.00 T KB556
DAY, NOREHA YUSSOF. Kancil and the crocodiles: a tale from Malaysia. Illus. by Britta Teckentrup. Simon & Schuster ISBN 0-689-80954-9; In Canada: Distican, 1996. unp. col. ill.
Originally published in Great Britain, ABC, All Books for Children. Longing to get to some juicy fruit on a far shore, Kancil, the mouse deer, and Kura-Kura, the tortoise, fool the crocodiles into forming a bridge which they can use to cross to the other side. When the crocodiles realize that they have been tricked, they leave the pair with the problem of how to get back again. The cut-paper collages which dramatize the tale dance with vivid colors. For multicultural studies.
SUBJ: Folklore--Malaysia./ Malaysia--Folklore./ Animals--Folklore.

398.24   Ph-3 3-5/6 $18.95 T KB557
DE LA MARE, WALTER. Turnip. Illus. by Kevin Hawkes. Godine ISBN 0-87923-934-4, 1992. unp. col. ill.
A unique turnip grows in a poor farmer's field, and he gives it to his king. His jealous brother attempts to rival him by giving the king a gigantic ruby but soon discovers that his gift isn't appreciated. A familiar Grimm tale retold by a famed poet. A classic!
SUBJ: Fairy tales./ Folklore--Germany./ Germany--Folklore.

CE 398.24   Ph-1 2-4/4 $14.95 L KB558
DE PAOLA, TOMIE. Legend of the Bluebonnet: an old tale of Texas. Retold and illustrated by Tomie De Paola. Putnam ISBN 0-399-20937-9; In Canada: General, 1983. unp. col. ill.
Selectors' Choice, 14th ed.
Spanish version available LA LEYENDA DE LA FLOR EL CONEJO:

UNA ANTIGUA LEYENDA DE TEXAS (ISBN 0-698-11361-6, 1993). One spring, the Comanche Indians suffered from a great drought. The shaman prayed to the Great Spirits for rain and were told the spirits wanted the people to give up their most valuable possession. A small orphan sacrificed her beloved warrior doll which was all she had to remember her parents. The spirits replied by covering the hills with beautiful bluebonnet (lupine) flowers. A haunting tale with typical De Paola illustrations. A good choice for picture book hours.
Similar in theme is THE LEGEND OF THE INDIAN PAINTBRUSH (ISBN 0-399-21534-4, 1988); Spanish version LA LEYENDA DEL PINCEL INDIO (ISBN 0-698-11362-4, 1988). This flower dots the landscape of Western states.
SUBJ: Comanche Indians--Folklore./ Indians of North America--Texas--Folklore.

398.24   Ph-3 2-3/4 $12.95   T   KB559
DESPAIN, PLEASANT. Eleven turtle tales: adventure tales from around the world. Illus. by Joe Shlichta. August House ISBN 0-87843-388-4, 1994. 106p. ill.
Simple tales from many cultures prove the turtle to be steadfast, intelligent, and kind. Chosen because they are very tellable, the stories are also good for reading aloud. For multicultural studies.
SUBJ: Turtles--Folklore./ Folklore.

398.24   Ph-1 2-3/5 $15.95   L   KB560
DIAKITE, BABA WAGUE. Hunterman and the crocodile: a West African folktale. Retold and illus. by Baba Wague Diakite. Scholastic ISBN 0-590-89828-0; In Canada: Scholastic, 1997. unp. col. ill.
When four crocodiles stray from their river, they beg a hunter to carry them home. His efforts are rewarded by the crocodiles' threat to eat him. Many animals agree that he should be eaten because man has never been kind to them, but the rabbit saves the man and later his wife. Lesson learned by all: man must live amongst all living things and not be above them. The artist created his unique drawings on ceramic tiles.
SUBJ: Folklore--Africa, West./ Africa, West--Folklore./ Crocodiles--Folklore.

398.24   Ph-1 P-2/3 $16.00   L   KB561
EHLERT, LOIS. Cuckoo: a Mexican folktale./Cucu: un cuento folklorico mexicano. Translated by Gloria de Aragon Andujar. Harcourt Brace ISBN 0-15-200274-X; In Canada: Harcourt Brace c/o Canadian Manda, 1997. unp. col. ill.
Proud Cuckoo proves her courage when a fire sweeps across the field and she alone saves the seeds for the next year's planting. Cuckoo looses her plummage and voice, but proves again that "You can't tell much about a bird by looking at its feathers." Bold illustrations were inspired by Mexican crafts and folk art. For multicultural studies.
SUBJ: Mayas--Folklore./ Indians of Mexico--Folklore./ Folklore--Mexico./ Mexico--Folklore./ Spanish language materials./ Bilingual materials--Spanish.

398.24   Ph-1 K-2/3 $14.95   L   KB562
EHLERT, LOIS. Mole's hill: a woodland tale. Harcourt Brace ISBN 0-15-255116-6; In Canada: Harcourt Brace c/o Canadian Manda, 1994. unp. col. ill.
When the animals ask Mole to move her tunnel and its hill, she finds a colorful way to prove to them that her hill is a treasure. Gigantic cut-paper collages, based on Native American beadwork and ribbon applique, create stunning illustrations. For multicultural studies.
SUBJ: Woodland Indians--Folklore./ Indians of North America--Folklore./ Moles (Animals)--Folklore.

398.24   Ph-3 1-3/2 $14.95   L   KB563
EHLERT, LOIS. Moon rope: a Peruvian folktale/Un lazo a la luna: una leyenda Peruana. Translated into Spanish by Amy Prince. Harcourt Brace Jovanovich ISBN 0-15-255343-6; In Canada: Harcourt Brace Jovanovich, 1992. unp. col. ill.
Large papercuts of a fox, a mole, the moon, and birds tell this Peruvian pourquoi tale for beginning readers. Told in Spanish and English, the story moves swiftly, and the illustrations incorporate elements of Peruvian folkart.
SUBJ: Folklore--Peru./ Moon--Folklore./ Peru--Folklore./ Bilingual materials--Spanish./ Spanish language materials.

398.24   Ph-3 3-4/6 $14.95   L   KB564
ESBENSEN, BARBARA JUSTER. Great buffalo race: how the buffalo got its hump: a Seneca tale. Retold by Barbara Juster Esbensen. Illus. by Helen Davie. Little, Brown ISBN 0-316-24982-3; In Canada: Little, Brown, 1994. unp. col. ill.
When drought causes unrest among the members of a buffalo herd, Old Buffalo counsels patience, for rain will come and the grass will be green again. Young Buffalo challenges his advice, and a contest results in which Young Buffalo overcomes Old Buffalo, and most of

the herd thunders off seeking the rain. How and why all buffalo bear the punishment of the Great Spirit is poetically told and accompanied by illustrations of the plains and the plant and animal life found there. For multicultural studies.
SUBJ: Seneca Indians--Folklore./ Indians of North America--Folklore./ Bison--Folklore.

398.24   Ph-2 K-2/4 $14.95   L   KB565
FARRIS, PAMELA J. Young Mouse and Elephant: an East African folktale. Adapted by Pamela J. Farris. Illus. by Valeri Gorbachev. Houghton Mifflin ISBN 0-395-73977-2, 1996. unp. col. ill.
Mouse thinks himself to be so strong! Fortuitous events help him to impress other animals with his powers until he meets up with Elephant. Then, true to form, Young Mouse convinces himself that he scared Elephant away. A humorous tale with drawings perfectly suited to the material. For reading aloud.
SUBJ: Folklore--Africa./ Africa--Folklore./ Mice--Folklore./ Elephants--Folklore.

TB 398.24   Ph-2 2-4 $8.95   OD KB566
FOLKTALES FROM THE PICTURE BOOK PARADE (Talking book). Weston Woods WW717C, 1981. 1 sound cassette.
Based on books of the same titles, five of the world's best folktales are retold here. The first, "Story, a story," comes from Africa and sets the scene for stories from Mongolia, France, America, and Europe. A variety of voices read the stories.
Contents; Story, a story, by Gail Haley (11min); Suho and the white horse, by Yuzo Otsuka (10min); Stone soup, by Marcia Brown (10min); Arrow to the sun, by Gerald McDermott (7min); Great big enormous turnip, by Alexei Tolstoy (4min).
SUBJ: Folklore.

398.24   Ph-2 1-3/3 $15.95   L   KB567
FOSTER, JOANNA. Magpies' nest. Retold by Joanna Foster. Illus. by Julie Downing. Clarion ISBN 0-395-62155-0, 1995. unp. col. ill.
The magpies attempt to show the other birds how to build a proper nest, but the impatient birds fly off, thinking they have heard enough. The result of the half-heard instructions is the variety of nests found today. Drawings done in watercolor and color pencil show numerous birds, their nests, and eggs. Based on a Joseph Jacobs' story, this pourquoi tale can be incorporated into interdisciplinary science units.
SUBJ: Birds--Nests--Folklore./ Nest building--Folklore./ Animals--Habitations--Folklore./ England--Folklore./ Folklore--England.

398.24   Ph-1 K-3/4 $15.95   T   KB568
FRENCH, FIONA. Lord of the animals: a Miwok Indian creation myth. Millbrook ISBN 0-7613-0112-7; In Canada: Millbrook/dist. by Vanwell, 1997. unp. col. ill.
First published in Great Britain, Frances Lincoln Limited.
Fiona French retells a creation myth in which the animals incorporate all of their best traits into one who will rule over them--a human. The boldly colored illustrations include many geometric designs like those found on Native American pottery. A good choice for reading aloud. For multicultural studies.
SUBJ: Miwok Indians--Folklore./ Indians of North America--California--Folklore./ Coyote (Legendary character)./ Creation--Folklore.

398.24   Ph-2 K-2/7 $14.89   L   KB569
FROESE, DEBORAH L. Wise washerman: a folktale from Burma. By Deborah Froese. Illus. by Wang Kui. Hyperion ISBN 0-7868-2232-5, 1996. unp. col. ill.
In a humorous tale of jealousy, a potter is envious of his neighbor, a washerman. He convinces the ruler that the washerman is capable of scrubbing his dingy, gray elephant white. How the washerman outwits him and turns the scheme back upon the potter is great fun for reading aloud. For multicultural studies.
SUBJ: Folklore--Burma./ Burma--Folklore./ Elephants--Folklore.

398.24   Ph-2 1-3/4 $15.00   T   KB570
GATES, FRIEDA. Owl eyes. Illus. by Yoshi Miyake. Lothrop, Lee & Shepard ISBN 0-688-12472-0, 1994. unp. col. ill.
Pesty Owl gets his comeuppance in this legend which tells why the Master of All Spirits made Owl the way he did. A humorous telling which illustrates that it is often best to keep our advice to ourselves. The creatures featured in the illustrations are appealing, and the story begs to be read aloud. For multicultural studies.
SUBJ: Mohawk Indians--Folklore./ Iroquois Indians--Folklore./ Indians of North America--Folklore./ Owls--Folklore.

398.24   Ph-3 5-A/7 $6.95   P   KB571
GIBLIN, JAMES CROSS. Truth about unicorns. Illus. by Michael McDermott. HarperCollins ISBN 0-06-446147-5; In Canada: HarperCollins, c1991, 1996. 113p. ill. (some col.).

Includes bibliography and index.
Available from the National Library Service for the Blind and
Physically Handicapped on sound recording cassette RC35381.
Traces the entire history of the "snow beast with the single horn"
which has fascinated people since the writings of the early Greeks.
The author explores myths found in Chinese, Indian and Biblical
literature which depict the magical animal. A dramatic account of the
unicorn hunt portrayed in the Unicorn Tapestries from the Cloisters
Collection of the New York Metropolitan Museum of Art is included.
For curious, mature readers. Extensive bibliography.
SUBJ: Unicorns--Folklore.

KIT 398.24   Ph-2 3-5 $19.95   KB572
GLEESON, BRIAN. Anansi (Kit). Told by Denzel Washington. Music by
UB40. Illus. by Steven Guarnaccia. Rabbit Ears/dist. by Simon &
Schuster ISBN 0-88708-231-9; In Canada: Vanwell, 1992. 1 hardcover
book, 1 sound cassette (52min). (We all have tales).
Videocassette available from Rabbit Ears/dist. by Uni 10261, 1991.
1/2" VHS videocassette color (30min), $9.95.
Two of the best known Anansi stories are told with brightly decorated
pictures of the spider and the animals who share his adventures. The
reading is well paced and the music is fitting. Readers will be able to
read along with the tape.
SUBJ: Anansi (Legendary character)./ Folklore--Jamaica./ Jamaica--
Folklore.

398.24   Ph-1 3-4/4 $14.99   L   KB573
GOBLE, PAUL. Crow Chief: a Plains Indian story. Orchard ISBN 0-531-
08547-3, 1992. unp. col. ill.
Available from the National Library Service for the Blind and
Physically Handicapped on sound recording cassette RC 38567.
Crows were once white. Then Crow Chief, who warned the buffaloes
of approaching hunters, was captured and forced to sit in the smoke
until he knew hunger as desperate as that of the Native Americans
when they were without buffalo meat. A pourquoi tale which
incorporates beliefs and practices of the Plains Indians.
SUBJ: Dakota Indians--Folklore./ Indians of North America--Great
Plains--Folklore.

398.24   Ph-1 3-5/4 $5.99   P   KB574
GOBLE, PAUL. Great race of the birds and animals. Aladdin ISBN
0-689-71452-1, 1991. unp. col. ill.
Available from National Library Service for the Blind and Physically
Handicapped on sound recording cassette RC24365.
Seeing the distress of the people as the buffalo ate them, the Creator
set up a race. The result of the race was that whoever won would
eat the other. How the people won out over the buffalo is told in
sparse text and beautiful pictures. The book will please storytellers
and find a place in units on the Plains Indians.
SUBJ: Cheyenne Indians--Folklore./ Dakota Indians--Folklore./ Indians
of North America--Folklore.

398.24   Ph-2 3-5/3 $15.95   T   KB575
GOBLE, PAUL. Return of the buffaloes: a Plains Indian story about
famine and renewal of the Earth. National Geographic ISBN 0-7922-
2714-X, 1996. unp. col. ill.
Famine comes to a group of Native Americans because the buffalo
herd has not returned. Two young men go to a great cave where a
woman shows them the walls which are filled with paintings of
buffalo. She promises to send these herds to the tribe and does. This
tale is associated with the Wind Cave in the Black Hills of South
Dakota and has great significance in the mythology of the Lakota
tribe. It could be a statement of belief in the constant renewal of the
earth. Haunting story with many interpretations for enviromental
studies and multicultural studies.
SUBJ: Teton Indians--Folklore./ Indians of North America--Great
Plains--Folklore./ Folklore--Great Plains./ Buffaloes--Folklore.

398.24   Ph-2 2-4/2 $15.00   L   KB576
GOLDIN, BARBARA DIAMOND. Coyote and the fire stick: a Pacific
Northwest Indian tale. Illus. by Will Hillenbrand. Gulliver/Harcourt Brace
ISBN 0-15-200438-6; In Canada: Harcourt Brace c/o Canadian Manda,
1996. unp. col. ill.
Set in the time before people had fire, this Coyote tale finds him
devising a scheme (with advice from his sisters) to take a burning
torch from the three evil spirits who guard fire. Coyote is joined in his
quest by the Mountain Lion, Deer, Squirrel, and Frog. The illustrations
in oil and oil pastels are filled with action, and the spirits are fittingly
gruesome. For reading aloud and multicultural studies.
SUBJ: Indians of North America--Northwest, Pacific--Folklore./ Coyote
(Legendary character).

398.24   Ph-2 K-2/4 $14.95   L   KB577
GONZALEZ, LUCIA M. Bossy gallito/el gallo de bodas: a traditional
Cuban folktale. Retold by Lucia M. Gonzalez. Illus. by Lulu Delacre.
Scholastic ISBN 0-590-46843-X; In Canada: Scholastic, 1994. unp. col.
ill.
Includes glossary.
A traditional cumulative story which is known to most children in Cuba
is told in English and Spanish. Illustrated with scenes from Little
Havana, the heart of Miami's Cuban community.
SUBJ: Folklore--Cuba./ Cuba--Folklore./ Spanish language materials./
Bilingual materials--Spanish.

VCR 398.24   Ph-1 K-3 $29.95   OD   KB578
GREEDY CAT (Videocassette). Signed in American sign language by Billy
Seago. Narrated by T.R. Hinkey. Sign-A-Vision/dist. by Modern Signs
Press, 1987. 1/2" VHS videocassette color (15min). (Stories from the
attic).
Includes teacher/student resource packet.
Also available in signed English, 101SE.
The story of a greedy cat who ate 499 cookies, a lady washing
clothes, a company of soldiers, a family of elephants and a mouse
sewing is told through American sign language and voice-over
narration. The explanation of the meaning of the actions and
expressions is included on the tape. Useful for deaf and hearing
students.
SUBJ: Storytelling./ Sign language./ Cats--Folklore.

398.24   Ph-2 1-2/4 $15.88   L   KB579
GRIMM, JACOB. Wolf and the seven little kids: a fairy tale. By Jacob
and Wilhelm Grimm. Translated from the German by Anthea Bell. Illus.
by Bernadette Watts. North-South Books ISBN 1-55858-446-3; In
Canada: North-South Books, 1995. unp. col. ill.
Old Mother Goat warns her seven little kids not to let the wolf in the
house, but he finally fools the kids and gobbles them up. It is the
mother who rescues them and brings this favorite tale to a happy
ending. The drawings are filled with tiny details to pore over and
enjoy.
SUBJ: Fairy tales./ Folklore--Germany./ Germany--Folklore.

CE 398.24   Ph-1 3-5/5 $15.95   L   KB580
HALEY, GAIL E. Story, a story: an African tale. Retold and illustrated by
Gail E. Haley. Atheneum ISBN 0-689-20511-2, c1970. unp. col. ill.
Caldecott Medal Award.
Also available as 1/2" VHS videocassette color from Weston Woods
HMPV123V, $49.95.
Available from National Library Service for the Blind and Physically
Handicapped in Braille BR06103, as a talking book TB03784, and
sound recording cassette RC 41943.
Talking book available from Weston Woods RAC123, 1993. 1 sound
cassette (22min), $8.95.
Ananse, the spider man, longs for the stories owned by the Sky God.
The Sky God sets as his price, Asebo the leopard, Mmboro the
hornet and Mmoatia the fairy. By trickery, Ananse, so small, captures
the three and gains the stories which were scattered to the corners of
the world. Strong woodcuts illustrate this familiar tale. Ananse is
portrayed as a man rather than as a spider and it seems a logical
transferral for him to be pictured as a thin, spidery figure. The Sky
God is richly robed and dominates the pages on which he appears.
SUBJ: Folklore--Africa./ Leopards--Folklore./ Africa--Folklore.

398.24   Ph-1 2-4/4 $15.95   T   KB581
HAMANAKA, SHEILA. Screen of frogs: an old tale. Retold and illus. by
Sheila Hamanaka. Orchard ISBN 0-531-05464-0, 1993. unp. col. ill.
"Richard Jackson book."
A wealthy man wastes his fortune until a huge frog awakens him to
his responsibilities. The unexpected reward given to him by the frogs
makes this a good tale for telling. Art students will appreciate the art
of the frogs and want to create screens of their own.
SUBJ: Folklore--Japan./ Japan--Folklore./ Frogs--Folklore.

398.24   Ph-1 2-5/2 $17.95   T   KB582
HAMILTON, VIRGINIA. When birds could talk and bats could sing: the
adventures of Bruh Sparrow, Sis Wren, and their friends. Told by
Virginia Hamilton. Illus. by Barry Moser. Blue Sky Press/Scholastic ISBN
0-590-47372-7; In Canada: Scholastic, 1996. 65p. col. ill.
These stories were first written by Martha Young, a journalist, as she
heard them on her father's plantation. In the first story, the birds fuss
over a vine which produces a pumpkin too large for them "to tote."
Many of the tales are pourquoi stories explaining such things as why
bats hide, why cardinals are red, and why swallows are allowed to
nest near warm chimneys. Hamilton has recast the stories so that they
will be easy-to-read and produce smiles. An excellent collection for
reading aloud. For multicultural studies.
SUBJ: Afro-Americans--Folklore./ Folklore--Southern States./ Southern
States--Folklore./ Birds--Folklore.

JKO 495.7

398.24   Ph-2 P-2/3 $15.95   T   KB583
HAN, SUZANNE CROWDER. Rabbit's escape/Kusa ilsaenghan tookki.
Illus. by Yumi Heo. Henry Holt ISBN 0-8050-2675-4; In Canada:
Fitzhenry & Whiteside, 1995. unp. col. ill.
> When the Dragon King of the East Sea felt ill, the court physician
> told him to eat the fresh raw liver of a rabbit. Rabbit is enticed into
> the underwater kingdom by Turtle, but manages to escape by a
> clever lie. The Korean people gain a remarkable cure when a god
> takes pity on Turtle. Story is told in English and Korean. Childlike
> illustrations filled with small creatures complete the tale. For reading
> aloud.
> SUBJ: Folklore--Korea./ Korea--Folklore./ Korean language
> materials./ Bilingual materials--Korean.

398.24   Ph-2 P-2/3 $13.95   T   KB584
HANSARD, PETER. Jig, Fig, and Mrs. Pig. Illus. by Francesca Martin.
Candlewick ISBN 1-56402-540-3; In Canada: Douglas & McIntyre, 1995.
unp. col. ill.
> Mrs. Pig and her son, Fig, are unpleasant, rude, and especially mean
> to their servant, Jig. Jig's warmhearted generosity is rewarded by a
> wizard's spell that causes gold and diamonds to fall from his mouth.
> Hoping for similar results, Mrs. Pig sends her son out to fetch pails of
> milk from town, but his cruelty and selfishness are rewarded with
> snakes and toads falling from his mouth. The traditional folktale is
> recreated with pigs for characters and illustrated with small watercolor
> paintings.
> SUBJ: Fairy tales./ Folklore--France./ France--Folklore.

398.24   Ph-1 3-4/6 $7.00   P   KB585
HARRIS, JOEL CHANDLER. Jump! The adventures of Brer Rabbit.
Adapted by Van Dyke Parks and Malcolm Jones. Illus. by Barry Moser.
Harcourt Brace ISBN 0-15-201493-4, 1997. 40p. col. ill.
> Available from National Library Service for the Blind and Physically
> Handicapped on sound recording cassette RC25570.
> Working together, a composer, a journalist, and a distinguished
> illustrator present five of the favorite Brer Rabbit tales. The wily
> trickster "jumps" from the pages and once again readers and
> listeners will discover the folk literature brought to this country by
> people free in their minds if not in their bodies. The modified dialect
> is easily comprehensible. Five further adventures of Brer Rabbit are in
> JUMP AGAIN (ISBN 0-15-241352-9, 1987, OPC).
> JUMP ON OVER! THE ADVENTURES OF BRER RABBIT AND HIS
> FAMILY (ISBN 0-15-241354-5, 1989, OPC) shows how Brer Rabbit
> tricked the other animals and protected his family during an extended
> drought.
> SUBJ: Animals--Folklore./ Afro-Americans--Folklore.

398.24   Ph-2 2-3/6 $16.95   T   KB586
HASTINGS, SELINA. Reynard the Fox. Retold by Selina Hastings. Illus.
by Graham Percy. Tambourine/Morrow ISBN 0-688-09949-1, 1991.
76p. col. ill.
> How Reynard tricked the King, a lion, and escaped all punishment for
> his many misdeeds is unfolded in a humorous tale with life like
> pictures of his foes. A chapter book which sweeps along from
> adventure to adventure.
> SUBJ: Reynard the Fox (Legendary character)./ Fables./ Foxes--
> Folklore.

398.24   Ph-3 3-4/5 $14.95   T   KB587
HAUSMAN, GERALD. Eagle boy: a traditional Navajo legend. Retold
by Gerald Hausman. Illus. by Cara and Barry Moser. HarperCollins ISBN
0-06-021100-8; In Canada: HarperCollins, 1996. unp. col. ill.
> This is a legend which explains the Navajo Eagle Way, a healing
> ceremony to show respect for the power and majesty of the eagle. It
> is a simple tale of a boy who is carried into the sky to the Eagle
> Chief. There he is fooled by Coyote. For a brief time, he is turned
> into a coyote but is restored and returns to earth. For mythology units
> and multicultural studies.
> SUBJ: Navajo Indians--Folklore./ Indians of North America--Folklore./
> Coyote (Legendary character).

398.24   Ph-2 K-3/3 $14.89   L   KB588
HAUSMAN, GERALD. How Chipmunk got tiny feet: Native American
animal origin stories. Collected and retold by Gerald Hausman. Illus. by
Ashley Wolff. HarperCollins ISBN 0-06-022907-1; In Canada:
HarperCollins, 1995. 41p. col. ill.
> Seven pourquoi stories tell how various animals and birds acquired
> distinctive traits which they still have today. The simplicity of the
> material makes it suitable for reading aloud. The stories come from
> the Koasati Creek, Navajo, and Tsimshian traditions. Decorative
> borders representing the individual native groups surround the text.
> For multicultural studies.
> SUBJ: Indians of North America--Folklore./ Animals--Folklore.

398.24   Ph-1 P-2/2 $14.95   L   KB589
HEO, YUMI. Green frogs: a Korean folktale. Retold by Yumi Heo.
Houghton Mifflin ISBN 0-395-68378-5, 1996. unp. col. ill.
> No matter what their mother told them to do, two green frogs did
> the reverse. In despair, the mother turned to telling them to do just
> the opposite of what she wanted them to do. At her death, their final
> desire to follow her wishes resulted in near disaster. The frogs are
> captured in stylized oils and pencil. For reading aloud.
> SUBJ: Folklore--Korea./ Korea--Folklore./ Frogs--Folklore.

398.24   Ph-2 1-3/3 $14.95   T   KB590
HICKOX, REBECCA. Zorro and Quwi: tales of a trickster guinea pig.
Illus. by Kim Howard. Doubleday ISBN 0-385-32122-8; In Canada:
Bantam Doubleday Dell, 1997. unp. col. ill.
> Quwi is a clever guinea pig who must constantly find ways to outwit
> Zorro, a hungry fox. As in many stories, the smallest wins in the end,
> but in so doing encounters many adventures. Striking colors portray
> the corn fields, farms and countyside of Peru where guinea pigs have
> been domesticated for centuries.
> SUBJ: Folklore--Peru./ Peru--Folklore./ Guinea pigs--Folklore.

SRC 398.24   Ph-2 1-3 $11.50   KB591
HOLT, DAVID. Why the dog chases the cat: great animal stories (Sound
recording cassette). By David Holt and Bill Mooney. High Windy Audio
HW 1209 ISBN 0-942303-07-5, 1994. 1 sound cassette (40min). (Time
for a tale storytelling series).
> ALA notable recording, 1995.
> Six rib-tickling pourquoi stories of animals in farfetched situations are
> told by master storytellers. The youngest listeners will relate to the
> tales and delight in the musical accompaniments. Sources for the
> stories are found on the insert.
> SUBJ: Animals--Folklore./ Storytelling.

398.24   Ph-1 2-4/5 $14.95   T   KB592
HOOKS, WILLIAM H. Three little pigs and the fox. Illus. by S. D.
Schindler. Macmillan ISBN 0-02-744431-7; In Canada: Collier Macmillan,
1989. unp. col. ill.
> Rooter and Oinky are too involved with food and fail to take their
> mother's advice; "Watch out for the mean, tricky old drooly-mouth
> fox; build a safe, strong house; come home every Sunday." Their
> sister, Hamlet, fares better in this variant of THE THREE LITTLE PIGS
> set in Appalachia. Colorful, humorous illustrations add to the fun.
> SUBJ: Pigs--Folklore./ Foxes--Folklore./ Appalachian Region--
> Folklore./ Folklore--Appalachian Region./ Folklore--United States./
> United States--Folklore.

398.24   Ph-2 3-4/7 $15.89   L   KB593
HUNTER, MOLLIE. Gilly Martin the Fox. Illus. by Mollie Hunter. Illus.
by Dennis McDermott. Hyperion ISBN 1-56282-518-6, 1994. 36p. col.
ill.
> Gilly uses his ability as a shape-shifter to befriend a prince who is
> under the spell of a wicked witch. Their quest for the Blue Falcon
> leads them through a series of perilous tasks until finally the prince is
> freed from his enchantment. Celtic fairy tale of adventure, treasure
> seeking, and wily goodness overcoming great odds.
> SUBJ: Fairy tales./ Folklore--Scotland./ Scotland--Folklore.

398.24   Ph-2 2-3/2 $16.00   T   KB594
JACKSON, ELLEN. Precious gift: a Navaho creation myth. Illus. by
Woodleigh Marx Hubbard. Simon & Schuster ISBN 0-689-80480-6; In
Canada: Distican, 1996. unp. col. ill.
> When the first people came to the earth, they lacked water. The
> creatures that struggled to bring back water and failed are described
> as is the small snail that succeeded. A pourquoi tale which points out
> the importance of the smallest animal. The warm colors in gouache
> are an excellent example of how hues set the tone of the action.
> Author's note gives a full explanation of the sources of the tale. For
> multicultural studies.
> SUBJ: Creation--Folklore./ Snails--Folklore./ Navajo Indians--Folklore./
> Indians of North America--Folklore./ Southwest, New--Folklore./
> Folklore--Southwest, New.

CE 398.24   Ph-1 1-3/2 $13.95   L   KB595
JACOBS, JOSEPH. King of the cats. Retold and illustrated by Paul
Galdone. Houghton Mifflin ISBN 0-395-29030-9, 1980. unp. col. ill.
> An old grave digger reports when he arrives home that he has
> witnessed the burial of the King of the Cats. His cat, Tom, listens to
> his recital and then bolts from the house to reign as the new king to
> the amazement of his master and mistress. An excellent tale for telling
> at Halloween.
> SUBJ: Folklore--Great Britain./ Cats--Folklore./ Great Britain--Folklore.

(Iref)

398.24 Ph-2 2-3/2 $14.95 L KB596
JOHNSTON, TONY. Tale of Rabbit and Coyote. Illus. by Tomie De Paola. Putnam ISBN 0-399-22258-8; In Canada: Putnam, 1994. unp. col. ill.
Includes glossary.
When Rabbit steals chiles and is caught, he fakes Coyote into exchanging places with him and then uses his wits to escape the furious pursuer. His final retreat is the moon and that is why Coyote howls at the moon. A fast-moving tale which will satisfy young readers who puzzle over the familiar stance of the coyote. Mexican setting and Spanish phrases make this a good selection for multicultural studies.
SUBJ: Coyote (Legendary character)./ Indians of Mexico--Folklore./ Animals--Folklore./ Bilingual materials--Spanish./ Spanish language materials.

398.24 Ph-2 P-1/4 $13.95 L KB597
JONES, CAROL. Hare and the Tortoise. Houghton Mifflin ISBN 0-395-81368-9, 1996. unp. col. ill.
Originally published in Australia, HarperCollins.
"Walter Lorraine books."
Hare, a fervent jogger, feels that the slow Tortoise should be easily defeated in a race staged by their animal friends. However, overconfidence loses in the end. Die-cuts provide a glimpse of the action on the next page, and the illustrations, full of animals involved in the race, will give the reader as much pleasure as the tale.
SUBJ: Fables./ Toy and movable books.

398.24 Ph-3 3/3 $11.95 T KB598
KANI, SARU. Monkey and the crab. Retold by Seishi Horio. Illustrated by Tsutomu Murakami. Heian ISBN 0-89346-246-2, 1985. unp. col. ill.
Tricking Mrs. Crab out of her rice ball, Mr. Monkey leaves her with a single persimmon seed. When the seed becomes a fruitful tree, he once again steals from the crab and kills her. Colorful, action-filled illustrations show how revenge comes to this villain and right prevails. This folktale from Japan is a delight to read and tell. The afterword traces similarities in this story to materials found in other cultures.
SUBJ: Folklore--Japan./ Monkeys--Folklore./ Crabs--Folklore./ Japan--Folklore.

KIT 398.24 Ph-2 3-A $10.95 KB599
KESSLER, BRAD. Brer Rabbit and Boss Lion (Kit). Told by Danny Glover. Collected by Joel Chandler Harris. Illustrated by Bill Mayer. Music by Dr. John. Rabbit Ears/Simon & Schuster ISBN 0-689-80606-X, 1996. 1 paperback book, 1 sound cassette (26min). (American heroes and legends).
Danny Glover's lively retelling of how wily (and cowardly) Brer Rabbit outwits mean Boss Lion is full of humor. Narration with music by Dr. John. For multicultural studies.
SUBJ: Afro-Americans--Folklore./ Animals--Folklore./ United States--Folklore./ Folklore--United States.

CE 398.24 Ph-2 1-2/4 $14.95 L KB600
KIMMEL, ERIC A. Anansi and the moss-covered rock. Illus. by Janet Stevens. Holiday House ISBN 0-8234-0689-X, 1988. unp. col. ill.
Read-along kit available from Live Oak (ISBN 0-87499-171-4, 1991). 1 hardbound book, 1 sound cassette (11min), $19.95.
Coming upon a moss covered rock Anansi discovers that the rock can cause anyone to fall down unconscious. How he uses his knowledge to fool others and is finally tricked himself makes an amusing story. Bold, bright amusing drawings make the book a welcome addition to picture book collections.
SUBJ: Anansi (Legendary character)./ Africa, West--Folklore./ Folklore--Africa, West./ Spiders--Folklore.

CE 398.24 Ph-2 2-3/2 $15.95 L KB601
KIMMEL, ERIC A. Anansi and the talking melon. Retold by Eric A. Kimmel. Illus. by Janet Stevens. Holiday House ISBN 0-8234-1104-4, 1994. unp. col. ill.
Videocassette available from Live Oak Media (ISBN 0-87499-338-5, 1994). 1/2" VHS videocassette color (11min), $37.95.
Read-along kit available from Live Oak Media (ISBN 0-87499-339-3, 1995). 1 paperback book, 1 sound cassette (10min), $15.95.
When Anansi the Spider gets too fat dining on a melon, he solves his problem by convincing Elephant, Hippo, Warthog, and finally the king that the melon can talk. Illustrations capture the humor of this story for devotees of Anansi tales.
SUBJ: Anansi (Legendary character)./ Folklore--Africa./ Africa--Folklore.

CE 398.24 Ph-1 K-2/2 $14.95 L KB602
KIMMEL, ERIC A. Anansi goes fishing. Retold by Eric A. Kimmel. Illus. by Janet Stevens. Holiday House ISBN 0-8234-0918-X, 1991, c1992. unp. col. ill.
Videocassette available from Live Oak (ISBN 0-87499-248-6, 1992). 1/2" VHS videocassette color (12min), $31.95.
Read-along kit available from Live Oak (ISBN 0-87499-250-8, 1993) 1 hardcover book, 1 sound cassette (12min), $19.95.
Available from the National Library Service for the Blind and Physically Handicapped on sound recording cassette RC 38207.
Anansi longs to learn how to fish, but all he learns is that turtle can easily outwit him and gain a scrumptous fish dinner. Large, colorful drawings make the tale come alive and a good choice for picture book hours.
SUBJ: Anansi (Legendary character)./ Folklore--Africa./ Africa--Folklore./ Spiders--Folklore.

398.24 Ph-2 K-2/2 $14.95 L KB603
KIMMEL, ERIC A. Old woman and her pig. Adapted by Eric A. Kimmel. Illus. by Giora Carmi. Holiday House ISBN 0-8234-0970-8, 1992. unp col illus.
The trials of an old woman as she tries to get her pig over a stile are humorously pictured in this retelling of an old English folktale.
SUBJ: Folklore--England./ England--Folklore.

398.24 Ph-1 3-4/6 $6.95 P KB604
KIRSTEIN, LINCOLN. Puss in boots. Retold by Lincoln Kirstein. Illus. by Alain Vaes. Little, Brown ISBN 0-316-89501-6; In Canada: Little, Brown, c1992, 1994. unp. col. ill.
A regal cat earns a bride and estates for his young master in this handsomely illustrated retelling of Perrault's popular tale. The detailed drawings introduce readers to spectacular castles and the glory of seventeenth century court life.
SUBJ: Fairy tales./ Folklore--France./ France--Folklore./ Cats--Folklore.

398.24 Ph-2 K-2/4 $14.95 L KB605
KWON, HOLLY H. Moles and the Mireuk: a Korean folktale. Retold by Holly H. Kwon. Illus. by Woodleigh Hubbard. Houghton Mifflin ISBN 0-395-64347-3, 1993. unp. col. ill.
In search of the perfect husband for their daughter, two moles consider the sky, sun, cloud, wind, and a Mireuk, a massive stone statue, as a mate. It is the statue, however, who directs them to the suitable spouse. A Korean retelling of a familiar theme with childlike, boldly colored illustrations.
SUBJ: Folklore--Korea./ Korea--Folklore./ Moles (Animals)--Folklore.

398.24 Ph-3 2-4/5 $14.95 T KB606
LACAPA, MICHAEL. Antelope Woman: an Apache folktale. Retold and illus. by Michael Lacapa. Northland ISBN 0-87358-543-7, 1992. 42p. col. ill.
When her tribe rejects her newborn twins, Antelope Woman leaves them and joins her husband's people--the antelopes. A poetic explanation of why the Apache people respect all forms of life. For reading aloud.
SUBJ: Apache Indians--Folklore./ Indians of North America--Folklore./ Antelopes--Folklore.

398.24 Ph-3 4-5/3 $14.95 T KB607
LESTER, JULIUS. Man who knew too much: a moral tale from the Baila of Zambia. Retold by Julius Lester. Illus. by Leonard Jenkins. Clarion ISBN 0-395-60521-0, 1994. 32p. col. ill.
A father, suspicious about what an eagle was doing near his child, shoots an arrow at the bird. The arrow misses the bird and hits the child. Thus murder comes into the world. Lester uses the child as a symbol of wonder and marvel, and in the endnotes, he urges all to consider how often these traits are destroyed.
SUBJ: Folklore, Ila./ Folklore--Zambia./ Zambia--Folklore.

398.24 Ph-2 4-5/5 $18.99 T KB608
LESTER, JULIUS. Tales of Uncle Remus: the adventures of Brer Rabbit. Illus. by Jerry Pinkney. Dial ISBN 0-8037-0271-X, 1987. 151p. ill.
Coretta Scott King Award.
Available from National Library Service for the Blind and Physically Handicapped on sound recording cassette RC26183.
Searching for the best of the Uncle Remus stories to retell and the dialect (voice) in which to tell them became for Julius Lester a labor of love, which is reflected here. Some may be bothered by the "updating" of some of the tales, but they are extremely tellable and should be attempted by children as well as adults. For reading aloud. Additional adventures of Brer Rabbit and his friends, enemies and others are found in MORE TALES OF UNCLE REMUS (ISBN 0-8037-0419-4, 1987); FURTHER TALES OF UNCLE REMUS: THE MISADVENTURES OF BRER RABBIT, BRER FOX, BRER WOLF, THE DOODANG, AND OTHER CREATURES (ISBN 0-8037-0610-3, 1990); LAST TALES OF UNCLE REMUS (ISBN 0-8037-1304-5, 1994).
SUBJ: Animals--Folklore./ Afro-Americans--Folklore.

398.24 Ph-1 2-4/4 $15.89 L KB609
LEVINE, ARTHUR A. Boy who drew cats: a Japanese folktale. Illus. by Frederic Clement. Dial ISBN 0-8037-1173-5, 1993. unp. col. ill.
Failure follows Kenji, a frail Japanese boy, whose only talent is drawing cats until he stumbles upon a haunted temple. There he filled empty screens with drawings of cats. An ensuing battle between the cats of the panels and the evil rats frees the temple from its curse. In triumph, he receives a position in the temple where he becomes a great artist. Exquisite art work distinguishes this famous Japanese tale without which no collection is complete.
SUBJ: Folklore--Japan./ Cats--Folklore./ Japan--Folklore.

398.24 Ph-1 2-4/3 $14.95 T KB610
LEWIS, PAUL OWEN. Storm boy. Beyond Words Publishing ISBN 1-885223-12-9, 1995. unp. col. ill.
Selectors' Choice, 21st ed.
During a storm, a chief's son finds himself cast into the sea and washes ashore in a strange land. There he meets huge men who befriend him and teach him their dances. Sensing his loneliness, the giants send him back to his family. Powerful drawings show the masks and robes of the Native Americans of the Northwest Coast. Stunning illustrations and a suspenseful story make this a good choice for reading aloud. For multicultural studies.
SUBJ: Haida Indians--Folklore./ Indians of North America--Folklore./ Folklore--Northwest, Pacific./ Northwest, Pacific--Folklore./ Killer whales--Folklore./ Whales--Folklore.

398.24 Ph-3 3-4/4 $13.95 T KB611
LONDON, JONATHAN. Fire race: a Karuk Coyote tale about how fire came to the people. Retold by Jonathan London and Lanny Pinola. Illus. by Sylvia Long. Chronicle ISBN 0-8118-0241-8; In Canada: Raincoast, 1993. unp. col. ill.
Cooperation is the message of this Native American legend which explains how the animals stole fire from the bees and finally released it from the tree where frog had reposited it. Handsome, action-filled pictures accompany the text.
SUBJ: Karuk Indians--Folklore./ Indians of North America--California--Folklore./ Fire--Folklore./ Coyote (Legendary character).

398.24 Ph-2 2-3/2 $15.99 T KB612
LONG, JAN FREEMAN. Bee and the dream: a Japanese tale. Adapted by Jan Freeman Long. Illus. by Kaoru Ono. Dutton ISBN 0-525-45287-7; In Canada: Penguin, 1996. unp. col. ill.
A hardworking peasant buys a fellow worker's dream. He follows the dictates of the dream only to end up with an empty jar, from which a swarm of bees have flown. Feeling that he has been disgraced, he returns home to find that the bees have brought him great wealth. The illustrations of the Japanese village and countryside were done in a Japanese style of painting known as iwa-enogu. For multicultural studies.
SUBJ: Folklore--Japan./ Japan--Folklore./ Treasure hunts--Folklore.

CE 398.24 Ph-3 K-2/2 $4.99 P KB613
MARSHALL, JAMES. Three little pigs. Puffin ISBN 0-14-055742-3; In Canada: Penguin Books Canada, 1989. unp. col. ill.
Videocassette available from Weston Woods VC343V, 1992. 1/2" VHS videocassette color (12min), $60.00.
Setting out in the world to build their own homes, three pigs suffer misadventures with a wily wolf. The third and smartest pig matches wits with the wolf and wins out in the end. For independent readers in the beginning grades.
SUBJ: Folklore./ Pigs--Folklore.

398.24 Ph-3 2-4/6 $14.95 L KB614
MARTIN, RAFE. Boy who lived with the seals. Illus. by David Shannon. Putnam ISBN 0-399-22413-0; In Canada: Putnam, 1993. unp. col. ill.
A young boy strays from his parents and finds a life with the sea animals. His struggle to readjust to life with humans is beautifully portrayed in this legend from the Chinook Indians of the Northwest. For mature readers and listeners.
SUBJ: Chinook Indians--Folklore./ Indians of North America--Folklore.

398.24 Ph-1 P-2/3 $17.00 L KB615
MAYO, MARGARET. Tortoise's flying lesson. Illus. by Emily Bolam. Harcourt Brace ISBN 0-15-200332-0; In Canada: Harcourt Brace c/o Canadian Manda, 1995. 76p. col. ill.
Selectors' Choice, 20th ed.
Eight animal tales from all parts of the world are simply retold for preschool and kindergarten students to enjoy. Stories read smoothly and the exuberant illustrations dance on the pages. The simple drawings will inspire children to create artwork of their own. For multicultural studies.
SUBJ: Folklore./ Animals--Folklore.

398.24 Ph-1 1-3/2 $15.95 L KB616
MCDERMOTT, GERALD. Anansi the spider: a tale from the Ashanti. Adapted and illustrated by Gerald McDermott. Henry Holt ISBN 0-8050-0310-X, c1972. unp. col. ill.
Caldecott Honor Book.
Available from National Library Service for the Blind and Physically Handicapped in Braille BR05391 and on sound recording cassette RC19896.
An adaptation from the 1970 Blue Ribbon film. The book tells two adventures of Anansi, the first concerning his adventures while lost and the second his problems in deciding which of his six sons should have the moon as reward for saving him. The stunning designs come from the graphics of the Ashanti people and are reproduced in bold, sharp colors.
SUBJ: Spiders--Folklore./ Folklore--Africa, West./ Africa, West--Folklore./ Anansi (Legendary character).

398.24 Ph-2 P-2/2 $14.95 L KB617
MCDERMOTT, GERALD. Coyote: a trickster tale from the American Southwest. Told and illus. by Gerald McDermott. Harcourt Brace ISBN 0-15-220724-4; In Canada: Harcourt Brace c/o Canadian Manda, 1994. unp. col. ill.
Coyote, always in trouble, comes upon a flock of crows and asks to dance and fly with them. The crows, not liking his boasting and rudeness, play a trick on him. They supply him with their feathers and then take them back while he is in flight. The large drawings, done in gouache, colored pencil, and pastel, capture the motifs of the Southwest. For multicultural studies.
SUBJ: Coyote (Legendary character)./ Indians of North America--Southwest, New--Folklore.

398.24 Ph-1 1-3/3 $14.95 L KB618
MCDERMOTT, GERALD. Raven: a trickster tale from the Pacific Northwest. Told and illus. by Gerald McDermott. Harcourt Brace Jovanovich ISBN 0-15-265661-8; In Canada: Harcourt Brace Jovanovich c/o Canadian Manda, 1993. unp. col. ill.
Caldecott Honor book, 1994.
Dramatic pictures and simple language depict Raven's plan to steal the sun to give people the gift of light. The transformation of Raven into a boy child is a delightful variation on the familiar legend sure to entrance beginning readers or listeners.
SUBJ: Indians of North America--Northwest, Pacific--Folklore./ Ravens--Folklore.

398.24 Ph-1 K-2/1 $14.95 T KB619
MCDERMOTT, GERALD. Zomo the rabbit: a trickster tale from West Africa. Harcourt Brace Jovanovich ISBN 0-15-299967-1; In Canada: Harcourt Brace Jovanovich, 1992. unp. col. ill.
Big book available from Harcourt Brace (ISBN 0-15-201011-4, 1996), $22.00.
Three tasks are set by the Sky God for Zomo the rabbit. If he carries them out successfully, this clever fellow will gain wisdom. Striking colors fill the pages of this African folktale which proves that the "smallest" can be the brightest. For multicultural studies.
SUBJ: Folklore--Africa, West./ Africa, West--Folklore.

KIT 398.24 Ph-3 1-4 $19.95 KB620
METAXAS, ERIC. Puss in Boots (Kit). Told by Tracey Ullman. Music by Jean Luc Ponty. Illus. by Pierre Le-Tan. Rabbit Ears/dist. by Simon & Schuster ISBN 0-88708-286-6; In Canada: Vanwell, 1992. 1 hardcover, 1 sound cassette (48min). (We all have tales).
An amusing version of the story of how an inventive cat saves his own skin and provides wealth for his master. Tracey Ullman's reading is lighthearted and convinces the listener that anything is possible in the world of make-believe.
SUBJ: Folklore--France./ France--Folklore./ Cats--Folklore.

398.24 Ph-2 3-4/3 $15.99 T KB621
MOHR, NICHOLASA. Song of el coqui and other tales of Puerto Rico. By Nicholasa Mohr and Antonio Martorell. Viking ISBN 0-670-85837-4; In Canada: Penguin, 1995. unp. col. ill.
Includes glossary.
Spanish edition available CANCION DEL COQUI Y OTROS CUENTOS DE PUERTO RICO (ISBN 0-670-86296-7, 1995).
Three tales represent the three groups of people who make up Puerto Rico--the indigenous inhabitants, the Africans, and the Spaniards. The first is a creation tale, and the second tells of a guinea hen which is imported to the island. At first it is hated, but later it inspires native art. The last story is about a mistreated mule which helps a slave escape to freedom. Vivid oranges, greens, and blues are used in the flowing, dramatic paintings created by a Puerto Rican artist to interpret the tales.
SUBJ: Folklore--Puerto Rico./ Puerto Rico--Folklore./ Animals--Folklore./ Spanish language materials.

398.24   Ph-2 K-2/3 $14.95   L   KB622

MOLLEL, TOLOLWA M. Ananse's feast: an Ashanti tale. Retold by Tololwa M. Mollel. Illus. by Andrew Glass. Clarion ISBN 0-395-67402-6, 1997. 32p. col. ill.

> In a time of drought, Ananse, the crafty spider, has an abundance of food which he refuses to share with Akye, the turtle, claiming that the turtle's feet are too dusty to touch the food. The turtle gets his just desserts when he feasts on crabmeat in his watery home which Ananse can't reach. The drawings done in oils and colored pencil are a riot of colors and are well suited to this tale of cunning and one upmanship. For multicultural studies.
> SUBJ: Anansi (Legendary character)./ Ashanti (African People)--Folklore./ Ghana--Folklore./ Folklore--Ghana.

398.24   Ph-2 2-3/3 $14.95   T   KB623

MOLLEL, TOLOLWA M. Flying tortoise: an Igbo tale. Retold by Tololwa M. Mollel. Illus. by Barbara Spurll. Clarion ISBN 0-395-68845-0; In Canada: Oxford University Press, 1994. unp. col. ill.

> An angry group of birds rewards a wily tortoise for his deceit and theft with a punishment that tortoises carry to this day. Sprightly text and colorful illustrations of a personable tortoise make this pourquoi tale a good choice for reading aloud.
> SUBJ: Igbo (African people)--Folklore./ Folklore--Nigeria./ Nigeria--Folklore./ Turtles--Folklore.

398.24   Ph-3 2-3/4 $14.95   L   KB624

MOLLEL, TOLOLWA M. King and the tortoise. Illus. by Kathy Blankley. Clarion ISBN 0-395-64480-1, 1993. unp. col. ill.

> The king sets an impossible task--to make a robe of smoke. He thinks that he has outsmarted all the animals and people of his kingdom, but the ingenious tortoise goes him one better by asking for thread of fire to fashion the robe. Humorous tale for telling or reading aloud.
> SUBJ: Animals--Folklore./ Folklore--Cameroon./ Cameroon--Folklore.

398.24   Ph-2 P-3/4 $14.95   T   KB625

MOLLEL, TOLOLWA M. Rhinos for lunch and elephants for supper!: a Masai tale. Illus. by Barbara Spurll. Clarion ISBN 0-395-60734-5, 1991. unp. col. ill.

> An intruder in hare's cave holds all the animals at bay with his boasts until a frog out shouts the "monster" who is a weary caterpillar looking for a place to snooze. Large, merry pictures of jungle animals make this a wise choice for picture book hours.
> SUBJ: Masai (African people)--Folklore./ Animals--Folklore.

VCR 398.24   Ph-2 3-4 $49.95   OD   KB626

OTSUKA, YUZO. Suho and the white horse: a legend of Mongolia (Videocassette). Retold by Yuzo Otsuka. Illus. by Suekichi Akaba. Weston Woods HMPV188V, 1981. 1/2" VHS videocassette color (10min).

> Based on the book of the same title, now o.p.
> This is the story of a poor shepherd boy, Suho, who rescues a newborn foal and nurses it to health. He enters his horse in a race to win the governor's daughter, but instead of winning the girl, his horse is taken from him and he is beaten. Later the horse escapes and returns to Suho but he dies from his wounds and Suho makes a musical instrument from the horse's bones and soon many horse-headed fiddles are found in Mongolia.
> SUBJ: Folklore--Mongolia./ Horses--Folklore./ Mongolia--Folklore.

398.24   Ph-3 2-4/3 $14.95   L   KB627

OUGHTON, JERRIE. Magic weaver of rugs: a tale of the Navajo. Illus. by Lisa Desimini. Houghton Mifflin ISBN 0-395-66140-4, 1994. 32p. col. ill.

> Spider Woman aides two Navajo women to discover how to weave blankets for their people. The skill not only provides warmth for the people, but in time brings survival. A quiet story for multicultural studies which can also be used for crafts units.
> SUBJ: Navajo Indians--Folklore./ Indians of North America--Folklore./ Weaving--Folklore.

398.24   Ph-1 2-4/4 $14.89   L   KB628

OYONO, ERIC. Gollo and the lion. Illus. by Laurent Corvaisier. Hyperion ISBN 0-7868-2034-9; In Canada: Little, Brown, 1995. unp. col. ill.

> Originally published in France, GOLLO ET LE LION, 1994.
> A crafty lion manages to get into the hut belonging to Gollo and his sister. When the lion eats his sister, Gollo cuts off the lion's tail in an attempt to rescue her. To find the injured lion, the boy holds all the water in a gourd, causing a drought. A happy ending to this tale of cunning will please readers. For reading aloud and multicultural studies.
> SUBJ: Folklore--Cameroon./ Cameroon--Folklore./ Brothers and sisters--Folklore.

SRC 398.24   Ph-2 K-3 $8.95   OD   KB629

PARENT, MICHAEL. Tails and childhood (Sound recording cassette). Weston Woods WW731C, 1985. 1 sound cassette.

> Combining tales from folkloric and original sources, Parent recreates "the gentle, magic passing from one world...to another" of his boyhood.
> Contents: Why bear sleeps all winter (5min); Angela the mud girl (17min); Why rabbit has a short tail (4min); The kite story (15min).
> SUBJ: Storytelling.

398.24   Ph-3 2-3/5 $8.95   P   KB630

PARKE, MARILYN. Quetzalcoatl tale of corn. Retold by Marilyn Parke and Sharon Panik. Illus. by Lynn Castle. Fearon Teacher Aids/Simon & Schuster ISBN 0-86653-965-4, 1992. 48p. col. ill. (Legends from Mexico and Central America).

> Book also available with teacher's guide.
> Spanish version QUENTZALCOATL ACERCA DEL MAIZ (ISBN 0-86653-964-6, 1992).
> How an understanding god brought corn to his people is explained in a simple book which is published in both English and Spanish editions. For instructional use in English/Spanish language classes and as introduction to the culture of Mexico.
> SUBJ: Folklore--Mexico./ Folklore--Central America./ Mexico--Folklore./ Central America--Folklore./ Corn--Folklore.

398.24   Ph-1 2-3/6 $15.00   T   KB631

PATERSON, KATHERINE. Tale of the mandarin ducks. Illustrated by Diane and Leo Dillon. Lodestar/Dutton ISBN 0-525-67283-4, 1990. unp. col. ill.

> Selectors' Choice, 18th ed.
> Entranced by the beauty of the plumage of a mandarin duck, an emperor carries him away to beautify his court. When the duck droops as he longs to be with his mate, a kitchen maid frees him and brings misfortune upon herself and her lover. The illustrations are done in the ukiyo-e style, or "pictures of the floating (or passing) world." To be used in art classes, social studies units and to delight younger listeners.
> SUBJ: Fairy tales./ Japan--Folklore./ Ducks--Folklore./ Folklore--Japan.

398.24   Ph-2 3-4 $13.93   L   KB632

PAXTON, TOM. Aesop's fables. Retold in verse by Tom Paxton. Illus. by Robert Rayevsky. Morrow ISBN 0-688-07361-1, 1988. unp. col. ill.

> Available from National Library Service for the Blind and Physically Handicapped on sound recording cassette RC31158.
> Lyrical verses retell 10 of the best known Aesop fables. Full-color illustrations show the animals as sly, enraged, wise and all knowing. For enjoyment and incorporation into language arts programs.
> BELLING THE CAT AND OTHER AESOP'S FABLES (ISBN 0-688-08158-4, 1990, also available from the NLSBPH on sound recording cassette RC35351) presents another ten fables in the same witty style; continuing with ANDROCLES AND THE LION AND OTHER AESOP'S FABLES (ISBN 0-688-09683-2, 1991, OPC).
> SUBJ: Fables./ Stories in rhyme.

398.24   Ph-1 3-4/4 $16.00   L   KB633

PERRAULT, CHARLES. Puss in boots. Translated by Malcolm Arthur. Illus. by Fred Marcellino. Farrar, Straus & Giroux ISBN 0-374-36160-6, 1990. unp. col. ill.

> Caldecott Honor Book.
> Also available in Spanish, EL GATO CON BOTAS (ISBN 0-374-36158-4, 1990).
> Determined to prove his worth to his master, Puss invents situations which show off his master, the Marquis of Carabas, before the king and his daughter. Elaborate castles and attractive countrysides fill this handsomely illustrated version.
> SUBJ: Folklore--France./ France--Folklore./ Cats--Folklore./ Spanish language materials.

398.24   Ph-1 K-3/5 $15.88   L   KB634

PERRAULT, CHARLES. Puss in boots: a fairy tale. Retold and supplemented with necessary explanations and illus. by Hans Fischer. Translated by Anthea Bell. Afterword by Hans ten Doornkaat. North-South ISBN 1-55858-643-1; In Canada: North-South/dist. by Vanwell, 1996. unp. ill. (some col.).

> Hans Fischer reworked Perrault's tale to make Puss more appealing and certain elements of the story less scary. His final version with his trademark cats cavorting across the pages is a classic. For all collections.
> SUBJ: Fairy tales./ Folklore--France./ France--Folklore./ Cats--Folklore.

398.24   Ph-2 4-6/7 $15.90   L   KB635
PIPE, JIM. In the footsteps of the werewolf. Illus. by Susanna
Addario...[et al.]. Copper Beech ISBN 0-7613-0450-9, 1996. 40p. col.
ill.
> Includes glossary and index.
> This book is made up of two sections. One is a story of a man who
> was a werewolf, which is recounted on the left-hand pages. As the
> story unfolds, explanations are given on the right-hand pages of how
> beliefs in werewolves have arisen, their habits, and werewolf myths
> found in literature and motion pictures. For mature readers interested
> in the supernatural.
> SUBJ: Werewolves./ Supernatural--Folklore.

398.24   Ph-2 1-3/4 $5.99   P   KB636
PLUME, ILSE. Bremen-Town musicians. Retold and illustrated from the
Brothers Grimm by Ilse Plume. Delacorte ISBN 0-440-41456-3, 1998.
unp. col. ill.
> Caldecott Honor Book.
> Realizing that their masters intend to do away with them because
> they're old a donkey, dog, cat, and rooster band together intending
> to become musicians. The full page primitively styled pictures are just
> right for sharing with a group.
> SUBJ: Folklore--Germany./ Germany--Folklore./ Animals--Folklore.

CE 398.24   Ph-3 K-2/6 $12.50   L   KB637
REASONER, CHARLES. Night owl and the rooster: a Haitian legend.
Retold and illus. by Charles Reasoner. Troll ISBN 0-8167-3749-5, 1995.
32p. col. ill. (Legends of the world).
> Talking book available, 1996. 1 sound cassette (8min), $9.95.
> Coucou, the owl, thinks he is ugly. He is enamored with a swallow
> who likes his stories. When he takes her dancing, he hides behind an
> enormous hat. Eventually, he reveals his face and discovers that she
> likes him for himself. A Haitian legend in which self-doubt is
> overcome. For multicultural studies.
> SUBJ: Folklore--Haiti./ Haiti--Folklore.

KIT 398.24   Ph-3 P-1 $9.98   KB638
ROBBINS, SANDRA. Growing rock: a Southwest Native American tale
(Kit). Adapted by Sandra Robbins. Inspired by a tale from the Miwok
tribe. Illus. by Iku Oseki. See-More's Workshop ISBN 1-882601-15-7,
1993. 1 paperback book, 1 sound cassette (32min).
> "See-More book."
> Lively verse tells the story of how three baby birds are stranded on
> top of a rock when Crow convinces Growing Spirit to make the rock
> grow. The animals try to rescue the birds, but it is Medicine Man who
> succeeds. The read-along, move-along tape includes a narrated
> version and a creation musical which encourages children to act out
> the story. For multicultural studies and creative dramatics.
> SUBJ: Indians of North America--Southwest, New--Folklore./ Readers'
> Theater.

398.24   Ph-3 3-4/5 $14.95   L   KB639
RODANAS, KRISTINA. Dance of the sacred circle: a Native American
tale. Adapted and illus. by Kristina Rodanas. Little, Brown ISBN 0-316-
75358-0; In Canada: Little, Brown, 1994. unp. col. ill.
> Based on a Blackfeet myth, this picture book tells how and why the
> horse was created to aid a Native American tribe in the search for
> the buffalo. A quiet tale which reinforces the belief that all must work
> together to produce good. In this instance, it is the animals giving to
> the horse the best trait that each possesses. For multicultural studies.
> SUBJ: Sihasapa Indians--Folklore./ Indians of North America--
> Folklore./ Horses--Folklore.

398.24   Ph-2 2-4/4 $14.95   L   KB640
ROSEN, MICHAEL. How the animals got their colors: animal myths from
around the world. Illus. by John Clementson. Harcourt Brace Jovanovich
ISBN 0-15-236783-7, 1992. unp col illus.
> The origins of nine distinctive animals and their colors are explained in
> the stories in this collection. Bold collages illustrate the stories and a
> final section provides the sources. Good for storytellers or for units
> on myths and legends from various cultures.
> SUBJ: Folklore./ Animals--Folklore.

CE 398.24   Ph-1 2-4/6 $16.89   L   KB641
ROSS, GAYLE. How Rabbit tricked Otter and other Cherokee trickster
stories. Told by Gayle Ross. With a foreward by Chief Wilma Mankiller.
Illus. by Murv Jacob. HarperCollins ISBN 0-06-021286-1; In Canada:
HarperCollins, 1994. 79p. col. ill.
> Talking book available from HarperChildren's Audio (ISBN 1-55994-
> 542-7, c1991, 1996). 1 sound cassette (60min), $11.95.
> Gayle Ross, descendant of John Ross (principal chief of the Cherokee
> nation during the infamous "Trail of Tears"), retells pourquoi tales
> from Cherokee folklore. For introducing units on animals and Native
> Americans or multicultural studies.

SUBJ: Rabbit (Legendary character)./ Cherokee Indians--Folklore./
Indians of North America--Folklore.

398.24   Ph-2 4-5/5 $15.99   T   KB642
ROSS, GAYLE. How Turtle's back was cracked: a traditional Cherokee
tale. Retold by Gayle Ross. Illus. by Murv Jacob. Dial ISBN 0-8037-
1728-8, 1995. unp. col. ill.
> Available from the National Library Service for the Blind and
> Physically Handicapped on sound recording cassette RC 41522.
> When Possum kills Wolf, Turtle claims the honor and carries Wolf's
> ears as trophies. The wolves band together to punish Turtle. Although
> he outwits them, he gains a cracked back for his efforts. A pourquoi
> tale useful for multicultural studies.
> SUBJ: Cherokee Indians--Folklore./ Indians of North America--
> Folklore./ Turtles--Folklore.

398.24   Ph-2 2-3/2 $15.00   L   KB643
ROTH, SUSAN L. Biggest frog in Australia. Simon & Schuster ISBN
0-689-80490-3; In Canada: Distican, 1996. unp. col. ill.
> Includes glossary.
> Illustrated in bold, bright cut-paper collages, Roth's retelling of an
> Australian folktale will be good to use in storytimes. In the
> Dreamtime, the biggest frog in Australia woke up thirsty and
> swallowed every drop of water. It is up to the other animals to make
> the frog spit out the water--and finally the eels succeed. The story
> tells smoothly, and the art is textured and appealing.
> SUBJ: Frogs--Folklore./ Australia--Folklore./ Folklore--Australia./ Tall
> tales.

398.24   Ph-2 P-1/2 $14.95   KB644
ROUNDS, GLEN. Three billy goats Gruff. Retold and illus. by Glen
Rounds. Holiday House ISBN 0-8234-1015-3, 1993. unp. col. ill.
> The heroic battle between the third Billy Goat Gruff and the troll is
> captured in larger-than-life illustrations by a respected artist in this
> retelling of a familiar story. For reading aloud to preschoolers and
> kindergarten students.
> SUBJ: Fairy tales./ Folklore--Norway./ Norway--Folklore.

398.24   Ph-2 K-3/4 $14.95   L   KB645
ROUNDS, GLEN. Three little pigs and the big bad wolf. Holiday House
ISBN 0-8234-0923-6, 1992. unp. col. ill.
> A mangy wolf and three pigs share misadventures in this large picture
> book whose simplicity makes the wolf more frightening and his end
> more deserving. Not for the fainthearted!
> SUBJ: Folklore./ Pigs--Folklore./ Wolves--Folklore.

398.24   Ph-2 3-4/6 $15.95   L   KB646
SANDERSON, RUTH. Papa Gatto: an Italian fairy tale. Retold and illus.
by Ruth Sanderson. Little, Brown ISBN 0-316-77073-6; In Canada: Little,
Brown, 1995. unp. col. ill.
> Two sisters, one selfish, the other warm and diligent, are tested by
> caring for eight kittens. The beauty of the selfish girl almost wins her
> a prince, but the father of the playful kittens upsets her plans. Richly
> detailed oil paintings portray the playfulness of the kittens. A tale
> mixing humans and wily cats will please fairy tale readers as well as
> cat enthusiasts.
> SUBJ: Fairy tales./ Folklore--Italy./ Italy--Folklore./ Cats--Folklore.

398.24   Ph-3 3-4/6 $5.99   P   KB647
SAN SOUCI, ROBERT D. Hobyahs. Illus. by Alexi Natchev. Doubleday
ISBN 0-440-41212-9; In Canada: Bantam Doubleday Dell, 1996. unp.
col. ill.
> The Hobyahs lived deep in a forest; nearby was a tiny house. In the
> house lived an old man, old woman, and an orphan. Five dogs
> protected the house, but each night when the Hobyahs came, the
> dogs disturbed the sleep of the old folk. One by one the dogs were
> driven into the forest by the old man. This tale, which has roots in
> many cultures, describes how the faithful dogs prevent the Hobyahs
> from capturing the young girl.
> SUBJ: Fairy tales./ Folklore--England./ England--Folklore.

398.24   Ph-2 3-5/5 $14.95   T   KB648
SAN SOUCI, ROBERT D. Little seven-colored horse: a Spanish American
folktale. Illus. by Jan Thompson Dicks. Chronicle ISBN 0-8118-0412-7; In
Canada: Raincoast, 1995. unp. col. ill.
> Includes glossary.
> The youngest son, Juanito, discovers a colt with a multicolored coat
> eating corn growing in his father's fields. Because of his kindness, the
> horse promises that help will be given to him whenever it is needed.
> His brother's mistreatment of him results in a series of impossible tasks
> which he is only able to accomplish with the horse's help. A retelling
> of a Mexican tale with watercolors which capture the beauty of the
> desert and life in the pueblo. For multicultural studies.
> SUBJ: Folklore--Southwest, New./ Southwest, New--Folklore./
> Folklore--Latin America./ Latin America--Folklore.

398.24   Ph-2 3-4/2 $15.93   L   KB649
SAN SOUCI, ROBERT D. Pedro and the monkey. Retold from Filipino
folklore by Robert D. San Souci. Illus. by Michael Hays. Morrow ISBN
0-688-13744-X, 1996. unp. col. ill.
PUSS IN BOOTS, but in a different locale (Philippines). In this
variant, a wily monkey, instead of the well-known cat, gains riches
and a bride for his master. Acrylics painted on linen give the
impression that the book was printed on cloth.
SUBJ: Folklore--Philippines./ Philippines--Folklore./ Monkeys--Folklore.

398.24   Ph-1 K-3/2 $16.00   T   KB650
SHULEVITZ, URI. Golden goose. By the Brothers Grimm; retold and with
pictures by Uri Shulevitz. Farrar Straus Giroux ISBN 0-374-32695-9; In
Canada: HarperCollins, 1995. unp. col. ill.
An old man befriends a simpleton by giving him a golden goose.
When three girls try to get one of the golden feathers, they become
stuck to the goose as do a parson, a sexton, and a peasant and his
wife. What a sight they make! This scene so tickles the princess, who
never laughed, that her chuckles ring out, and the simpleton wins her
for his wife. Forlorn and silly in appearance, the characters pictured in
this tale will produce loads of smiles and laughter.
SUBJ: Fairy tales./ Folklore--Germany./ Germany--Folklore.

398.24   Ph-2 K-2/2 $15.93   L   KB651
SHUTE, LINDA. Rabbit wishes. Lothrop, Lee & Shepard ISBN 0-688-
13180-6, 1995. unp. col. ill.
Includes glossary.
Rabbit wants to be bigger, and Father God promises to change his
size if he can gain three objects from an eagle, a snake, and a lion.
His success gains for him a change which has stayed with him to this
day--long, long ears. Humorous Afro-Cuban pourquoi tale with a
smattering of Spanish words incorporated into the text. For
multicultural studies.
SUBJ: Rabbit (Legendary character)./ Rabbits--Folklore./ Folklore--
Cuba./ Cuba--Folklore./ Blacks--Folklore.

398.24   Ph-1 P-2/4 $14.00   T   KB652
SIERRA, JUDY. Elephant's wrestling match. Illus. by J. Brian Pinkney.
Lodestar/Dutton ISBN 0-525-67366-0, 1992. unp. col. ill.
A pesty bat proves that he can beat the "mighty" elephant in this
African folktale which is dramatized by large scratchboard drawings
of the animals.
SUBJ: Animals--Folklore./ Pride and vanity--Folklore./ Africa--
Folklore./ Folklore--Africa.

398.24   Ph-1 1-3/5 $15.99   T   KB653
SLOAT, TERI. Sody sallyratus. Retold and illus. by Teri Sloat. Dutton
ISBN 0-525-45609-0; In Canada: McClelland & Stewart, 1997. unp. col.
ill.
Out of baking soda or sody sallyratus needed for biscuits, a boy, a
girl, an old man, and an old woman each go to the store to buy
some, but end up being eaten by a big black bear. Their pet squirrel
leads the bear on a chase through the trees that lands the bear on
the ground with such a thud that everyone pops out. In this variation
of the traditional story, the bear makes a safe getaway, and a recipe
for biscuits follows. Woodsy illustrations and frames set the story in
the Appalachian Mountains.
SUBJ: Folklore--United States./ United States--Folklore./ Folklore--
Appalachian Region./ Appalachian Region--Folklore./ Squirrels--
Folklore./ Bears--Folklore.

398.24   Ph-1 P-1/2 $14.95   L   KB654
SOUHAMI, JESSICA. Leopard's drum: an Asante tale from West Africa.
Little, Brown ISBN 0-316-80466-5; In Canada: Little, Brown, 1995. unp.
col. ill.
First published in Great Britain by Frances Lincoln Limited, 1995.
A shy little turtle tricks a boastful leopard into climbing into the
magnificent drum that the leopard has constructed. The drum is then
carried to Nyame, the Sky-God, and the turtle gains the shell which
he carries to this day. Fun pourquoi story for reading aloud and
enacting in primary grades.
SUBJ: Africa, West--Folklore./ Folklore--Africa, West./ Animals--
Folklore./ Drum--Folklore.

398.24   Ph-2 3-4/4 $13.95   L   KB655
SPAGNOLI, CATHY. Judge Rabbit and the tree spirit: a folktale from
Cambodia. Told by Lina Mao Wall; adapted by Cathy Spagnoli. Illus. by
Nancy Hom. Children's Book Press ISBN 0-89239-071-9, 1991. 31p. col.
ill.
A tree spirit masquerades as a young soldier who has gone to war.
When the soldier returns home, it is the Judge Rabbit who saves the
day by proving which one is the true husband and soldier. Bilingual -
English and Khmer.
SUBJ: Cambodia--Folklore./ Folklore--Cambodia./ Bilingual materials--
Khmer./ Khmer language materials.

CE 398.24   Ph-1 4-5/5 $14.93   L   KB656
STEPTOE, JOHN. Story of Jumping Mouse: a Native American legend.
Retold and illustrated by John Steptoe. Lothrop, Lee & Shepard ISBN
0-688-01903-X, 1984. 40p. ill.
Caldecott Honor Book.
Selectors' Choice, 15th ed.
Available from National Library Service for the Blind and Physically
Handicapped on sound recording cassette RC23246.
Longing to know what the far-off land was like, a young mouse
began his voyage to see it. Along the way, aided by magic frog, he
met many animals and helped them, giving up his ability to see and
smell, but was rewarded by being turned into an eagle. This haunting
Indian legend teaches confidence, unselfishness, and love. The large
black and white drawings make it a good selection for picture-book
hours.
SUBJ: Indians of North America--Great Plains--Folklore./ Mice--
Folklore.

398.24   Ph-1 2-4/2 $15.95   L   KB657
STEVENS, JANET. Coyote steals the blanket: a Ute tale. Retold and
illus. by Janet Stevens. Holiday House ISBN 0-8234-0996-1, 1993. unp.
col. ill.
Available from the National Library Service for the Blind and
Physically Handicapped on sound recording cassette RC 38478.
Poor Coyote! His theft of a blanket results in the spirit of the desert
(in the form of a rock) chasing after him. Friends try to save him, but
it is the pesky little Hummingbird that rescues him in the end. Large
pictures and a humorous escapade make this a good selection for
reading aloud.
SUBJ: Coyote (Legendary character)./ Ute Indians--Folklore./ Indians
of North America--Folklore.

398.24   Ph-2 2-3/4 $14.95   L   KB658
STEVENS, JANET. How the Manx cat lost its tail. Retold and illustrated
by Janet Stevens. Harcourt Brace Jovanovich ISBN 0-15-236765-9,
1990. unp. col. ill.
As the time came to close the door to the ark Noah discovers that
the Manx cat is missing. It is at the very last moment that the cat
attempts to enter and suffers an accident which can still be seen
today--a missing tail. Warm, humorous watercolor wash illustrations
keynote this original view of life on Noah's ark.
SUBJ: Folklore./ Cats--Folklore./ Noah's ark--Folklore.

398.24   Ph-1 1-3/2 $15.95   L   KB659
STEVENS, JANET. Old bag of bones: a coyote tale. Retold and illus. by
Janet Stevens. Holiday House ISBN 0-8234-1215-6, 1996. unp. col. ill.
Coyote is old, just a bag of bones; and he envies Young Buffalo's
youth and vitality. Young Buffalo changes Coyote into a Buffote (a
powerless animal). Instead of being satisfied with his new youth,
Buffote tries to reinvigorate other old animals, looses his temporary
youth, and learns little. Humorous tale which points out the
advantages of old age. For multicultural studies.
SUBJ: Shoshoni Indians--Folklore./ Indians of North America--
Folklore./ Coyote (Legendary character).

398.24   Ph-1 K-2/2 $15.00   L   KB660
STEVENS, JANET. Tops and bottoms. Adapted and illus. by Janet
Stevens. Harcourt Brace ISBN 0-15-292851-0; In Canada: Harcourt
Brace c/o Canadian Manda, 1995. unp. col. ill.
Caldecott Honor book, 1996.
When hardship forces Father Hare to go into a gardening partnership
with lazy Bear, he cleverly gets Bear to agree to an even split of their
crops--tops and bottoms. The first season Hare keeps the bottoms of
the root crops they plant, giving Bear the tops. The next year he
takes the tops of the broccoli, celery, and lettuce. Although in the
third year Bear takes the tops and bottoms, he still loses to his crafty
partner. A rollicking African-American folktale by a renowned
illustrator in a unique format as the pictures flow down the pages
from top to bottom, making the book easy to share with a large
group. For reading aloud.
SUBJ: Afro-Americans--Folklore./ Hares--Folklore./ Bears--Folklore.

398.24   Ph-1 K-2/2 $14.99   T   KB661
SUMMERS, KATE. Milly and Tilly: the story of a town mouse and a
country mouse. Illus. by Maggie Kneen. Dutton ISBN 0-525-45801-8,
1997. unp. col. ill.
Originally published in Great Britain, Orion Children's Books, 1996.
Presents the familiar story of two mouse cousins who visit each other
in their different environments. Small watercolor illustrations feature
details like acorn caps for bowls and tiny dollhouse furniture. A
charming page layout focuses attention on the mice and their
environs.
SUBJ: Fables./ Mice--Folklore.

398.24   Ph-2 2-3/5 $15.00   L   KB662
TAYLOR, HARRIET PECK. Coyote and the laughing butterflies. Retold and illus. by Harriet Peck Taylor. Macmillan ISBN 0-02-788846-0; In Canada: Distican, 1995. unp. col. ill.
> Once butterflies played a trick on Coyote and carried him back home each time he arrived at the lake to gather salt for his wife, and they are still laughing over their prank. A simple pourquoi story from Native American legend which explains why butterflies flitter to and fro. Batik illustrations give the feeling of New Mexico, the origin of the tale. For multicultural studies.
> SUBJ: Coyote (Legendary character)./ Indians of North America--Folklore./ Folklore--North America./ North America--Folklore./ Tewa Indians--Folklore.

398.24   Ph-2 2-3/2 $15.99   L   KB663
TEMPLE, FRANCES. Tiger soup: an Anansi story from Jamaica. Retold and illus. by Frances Temple. Orchard ISBN 0-531-08709-3, 1994. unp. col. ill.
> "Richard Jackson book."
> Available from the National Library Service for the Blind and Physically Handicapped on sound recording cassette RC 39838. Anansi not only fools the tiger and steals his soup, but he also convinces him that it was the little monkeys who were the thieves. Note: a play script of the story is on the underside of the jacket.
> SUBJ: Folklore--Jamaica./ Jamaica--Folklore./ Anansi (Legendary character).

SRC 398.24   Ph-1 2-5 $9.95   KB664
THOMASON, DOVIE. Lessons from the animal people (Sound recording cassette). Music by Ulali. Yellow Moon Press ISBN 0-938756-50-8, 1996. 1 sound cassette (83min).
> ALA notable recording, 1997.
> Compact disc available (ISBN 0-938756-51-6, 1996). 1 compact disc (83min), $15.00.
> Nine Native American stories about animals explain their origins, their character traits, and how foolish and how wise they can be. The teller has a wide range and cleverly uses her voice to speak for an individual animal. Sources for the stories are provided on the insert. For multicultural studies.
> SUBJ: Animals--Folklore./ Indians of North America--Folklore.

VCR 398.24   Ph-1 P-K $9.98   KB665
THREE BILLY GOATS GRUFF; AND, THE THREE LITTLE PIGS (Videocassette). Read by Tom Roberts. Adapted by Tom Roberts. Music by Art Lande. Illus. by David Jorgensen. Rabbit Ears H0703, 1989. 1/2" VHS videocassette color (30min). (Storybook classics).
> Modernized versions of "Three Billy Goats Gruff" and "The Three Little Pigs" will appeal to the youngest viewers. Contemporary language brings the stories into today's world. Holly Hunter's reading is well paced and calming.
> SUBJ: Animals--Folklore./ Pigs--Folklore./ Goats--Folklore.

SRC 398.24   Ph-3 4-5 $9.00   OD KB666
TORRENCE, JACKIE. Brer Rabbit stories (Sound recording cassette). Weston Woods WW725C, 1984. 1 sound cassette.
> Fooling his friends is Brer Rabbit's greatest delight and in the five stories told on this record, the listener finds him outwitting the fox, the bear, and the wolf. The last story, "The Wonderful Tar Baby," is an American favorite and is told by Jackie Torrence with humor and understanding.
> Contents: Brer Rabbit builds a home (7min); Brer Rabbit goes hunting (6min); Brer Wolf catches Brer Rabbit (4min); Brer Rabbit pays his respects (6min); The Wonderful tar baby (10min).
> SUBJ: Folklore--United States./ United States--Folklore./ Rabbits--Folklore.

SRC 398.24   Ph-1 P-1 $10.95   OD KB667
TORRENCE, JACKIE. Classic children's tales (Sound recording cassette). Told by Jackie Torrence. Rounder Records 8015C; In Canada: Oak Street Music, 1989. 1 sound cassette.
> Also available on compact disc 123CD, $10.95.
> Six of childhood's best loved stories are retold on this record by a recognized storyteller whose comforting manner will assure the listeners that there is much to be learned from these simple tales. For the youngest listeners.
> Contents: Introductory poem (1min); Little red hen (5min); Three Billy Goats Gruff (5min); Gingerbread man (7min); Introductory poem (1min); Goldilocks & the three bears (6min); Introductory poem (1min); Little Red Riding Hood (8min); Introductory poem (1min); The three little pigs (12min).
> SUBJ: Folklore.

SRC 398.24   Ph-1 2-3 $9.98   OD KB668
TORRENCE, JACKIE. Traditions: a potpourri of tales (Sound recording cassette). Rounder Records RO 8030, 1994. 1 sound cassette.
> ALA notable recording, 1995.
> Six tales from Africa and America are told in Jackie's easy style. Encourages audiences to develop listening skills while enjoying spellbinding stories.
> Contents: Side A: Sody Salleradus (18min), The fresher the better (8min), The Ku bird (6min); Side B: Why spiders hang in corners (10min), The big hairy toe (9min), Brer Rabbit builds a house (13min).
> SUBJ: Folklore--United States./ United States--Folklore./ Afro-Americans--Folklore.

398.24   Ph-2 4-5/6 $14.95   T   KB669
UDE, WAYNE. Maybe I will do something. Illus. by Abigail Rorer. Houghton Mifflin ISBN 0-395-65233-2, 1993. 75p. ill.
> The many sides of Coyote are explored in these seven legends which the author claims are based on stories told to him by Native Americans. Coyote is creative, resentful, and, at times, compassionate, but always Coyote. This attractive entertaining volume reads smoothly and will create a desire to know more about this wily fellow. For multicultural studies.
> SUBJ: Coyote (Legendary character)./ Indians of North America--Folklore.

398.24   Ph-1 4-5 $15.93   L   KB670
WAITE, MICHAEL P. Jojofu. Illus. by Yoriko Ito. Lothrop, Lee & Shepard ISBN 0-688-13661-3, 1996. unp. col. ill.
> A young hunter owns many hunting dogs, but his favorite was Jojofu. This exciting tale relates how she saves his life a number of times, but it is his promise that he will never lose faith in her which finally proves her devotion to him. Based on a medieval Japanese folktale, this saga with masterful illustrations will please all dog lovers. Excellent material for reading aloud. For multicultural studies.
> SUBJ: Folklore--Japan./ Japan--Folklore./ Dogs--Folklore.

398.24   Ph-3 2-4/3 $15.95   T   KB671
WALLIS, DIZ. Something nasty in the cabbages. A tale from Roman de Renard. Written in the 12th century by Pierre de Saint-Cloud. Retold and illus. by Diz Wallis. Caroline House/Boyds Mills ISBN 1-878093-10-X, 1991. unp. col. ill.
> The adventures of Reynard the Fox unfold in this gay, witty retelling of his search for a good dinner and how his "big mouth" caused him to lose the tender dish. The figures spring out from the bold drawings, and Reynard becomes a memorable character in this sprightly version.
> SUBJ: Reynard the Fox (Legendary character)./ Foxes--Folklore./ Fables.

398.24   Ph-2 2-3/3 $14.89   L   KB672
WARDLAW, LEE. Punia and the King of Sharks: a Hawaiian folktale. Adapted by Lee Wardlaw. Illus. by Felipe Davalos. Dial ISBN 0-8037-1683-4; In Canada: McClelland & Stewart, 1997. unp. col. ill.
> Includes glossary.
> Longing for lobster meat to augment his diet of poi and yams, Punia devises a series of schemes to fool the sharks that guard the lobster cave. How he outwits the monsters and escapes being eaten alive makes a scary and fast moving tale. The island vocabulary precedes the story, and the watercolor and ink illustrations catch the flavor of the islands.
> SUBJ: Folklore--Hawaii./ Hawaii--Folklore./ Sharks--Folklore.

398.24   Ph-1 3-5/4 $15.00   L   KB673
WILLIAMS, CAROL ANN. Tsubu the little snail. Illus. by Tatsuro Kiuchi. Simon & Schuster ISBN 0-671-87167-6; In Canada: Distican, 1995. unp. col. ill.
> A Japanese couple long for a child. Their wish is fulfilled when they are given a snail. The snail carries out tasks for his father and, in time, is married to a beautiful maiden. At a festival, she fears that she has lost him in a rice paddy only to discover that her love has turned him into a real person. For multicultural studies.
> SUBJ: Folklore--Japan./ Japan--Folklore.

398.24   Ph-1 P-1/5 $14.90   L   KB674
WOOD, A. J. Lion and the mouse: an Aesop's fable. Retold by A. J. Wood. Illus. by Ian Andrew. Millbrook ISBN 1-56294-658-7, 1995. unp. ill.
> "Templar book."
> The kindness a lion shows to a small mouse is repaid many times over as the mouse frees the lion when he is held captive in a net. Black and white line drawings skillfully placed on large white pages capture the drama and simplicity of the tale.
> SUBJ: Fables./ Animals--Folklore.

398.24   Ph-1 3-5/4 $16.00   L   KB675
WOOD, AUDREY. Rainbow bridge: inspired by a Chumash tale. Retold by Audrey Wood. Illus. by Robert Florczak. Harcourt Brace ISBN 0-15-265475-5; In Canada: Harcourt Brace c/o Canadian Manda, 1995. unp. col. ill.
> A legend handed down by the Chumash Indians to explain their exodus from Santa Cruz Island to Santa Barbara, California. Overpopulation prompted the earth goddess to make a rainbow bridge to carry them from the island. Unfortunately, a few fell from the bridge and were transformed into dolphins which explains the closeness of the Chumash Indians to the sea creatures. The illustrations, done in layers of transparent oil glazes, show the beauty of the people, landscape, and the sea. For multicultural studies and California history units.
> SUBJ: Chumash Indians--Folklore./ Indians of North America--Folklore./ Dolphins--Folklore.

SRC 398.24   Ph-3 3-5 $9.95   KB676
WOPILA--A GIVEAWAY: LAKOTA STORIES (Sound recording cassette). Retold by Dovie Thomason. Yellow Moon Press 036 ISBN 0-938756-44-3, 1993. 1 sound cassette (60min).
> A wide variety of Lakota stories (including Iktomi tales) are told by Dovie Thomason, who has presented this Native American folklore to groups throughout the Northeast. For multicultural studies.
> SUBJ: Dakota Indians--Folklore./ Indians of North America--Great Plains--Folklore./ Animals--Folklore.

398.24   Ph-2 P-3/4 $13.95   L   KB677
XIONG, BLIA. Nine-in-one, grr! grr! a folktale from the Hmong people of Laos. Told by Blia Xiong. Adapted by Cathy Spagnoli. Illus. by Nancy Hom. Children's Book Press ISBN 0-89239-048-4, 1989. 30p. col. ill.
> The world would be overrun with tigers had not the earliest tiger become confused in reciting the message given to her by the great Shao. This is a humorous story from Laos illustrated by vivid drawings which mimic story cloth (multi-imaged embroidery).
> SUBJ: Folklore--Laos./ Laos--Folklore./ Tigers--Folklore.

398.24   Ph-2 1-2/5 $16.00   L   KB678
YOUNG, ED. Donkey trouble. Atheneum ISBN 0-689-31854-5; In Canada: Distican, 1995. unp. col. ill.
> As an old man and his grandson attempt to take their donkey to the market place, they discover that listening to the advice of others can cause problems! Set in the barren desert which is captured in pastel and paper collages, this familiar La Fontaine fable is given a new look.
> SUBJ: Fables./ Donkeys--Folklore./ Animals--Folklore.

398.24   Ph-1 3-4/4 $14.95   L   KB679
YOUNG, ED. Lon Po Po: A Red-Riding Hood story from China. Translated and illustrated by Ed Young. Philomel ISBN 0-399-21619-7; In Canada: Philomel, 1989. unp. col. ill.
> Caldecott Medal Award.
> Left alone in their home in the countryside three sisters manage to trick the wolf who wants to eat them. This variant of the well known story is handsomely illustrated and is enjoyed as an artistic as well as literary experience. Best used in story hours.
> SUBJ: Folklore--China./ China--Folklore./ Wolves--Folklore.

398.24   Ph-1 2-3/4 $15.95   L   KB680
YOUNG, ED. Night visitors. Philomel ISBN 0-399-22731-8; In Canada: Putnam, 1995. unp. col. ill.
> His father's threat to destroy the ants that are stealing grain from his storehouse drives Ho Kuan to find a way to seal the walls and floor. His dream in which he enters the world of the ants, falls in love, and marshals troops to fight off invaders may at times appear unreal. When he finds a treasure to provide a means to safeguard his father's grain, the reader knows what is true and what is fantasy. The drawings are done in shades of brown with highlights which capture the shadow world of the ant kingdom.
> SUBJ: Folklore--China./ China--Folklore./ Dreams--Folklore.

398.24   Ph-1 K-3/2 $16.95   L   KB681
YOUNG, ED. Seven blind mice. Philomel ISBN 0-399-22261-8; In Canada: Putnam, 1992. unp. col. ill.
> Caldecott Honor Book, 1993.
> In this version of THE BLIND MEN AND THE ELEPHANT, seven mice explore different parts of an elephant and prove "Knowing in part may make a fine tale, but wisdom comes from seeing the whole." Extraordinary collage illustrations will inspire art students.
> SUBJ: Fables./ Elephants--Folklore./ Folklore--India./ India--Folklore./ Stories in rhyme.

398.24   Ph-3 P-2/4 $14.00   T   KB682
ZEMACH, MARGOT. Three little pigs. Farrar, Straus and Giroux ISBN 0-374-37527-5; In Canada: HarperCollins, 1988. unp. col. ill.
> Only one of the three pigs followed his mother's advice and "built a strong house and watched out for the wolf." How he tricked the wolf is told in this matter of fact retelling of this traditional story. Large, simple drawings make this a wise choice for preschool story hours.
> SUBJ: Pigs--Folklore.

398.24   Ph-2 K-1/1 $3.50   P   KB683
ZIEFERT, HARRIET. Turnip. Retold by Harriet Ziefert. Illus. by Laura Rader. Penguin ISBN 0-14-038082-5; In Canada: Penguin, 1996. unp. col. ill. (Viking easy-to-read).
> "Viking easy-to-read classic."
> A stubborn turnip resists the efforts of an old man, a woman, a little girl, a dog, and a cat to pull it out of the ground. It is a tiny mouse that gives the man power to finally free the turnip. The easy-to-read, predictable book is a rollicking tale of teamwork for beginning readers.
> SUBJ: Folklore--Russia./ Russia--Folklore.

CE 398.25   Ph-3 3-6/6 $5.99   P   KB684
DEFELICE, CYNTHIA C. Dancing skeleton. Illus. by Robert Andrew Parker. Aladdin ISBN 0-689-80453-9, 1996. unp. col. ill.
> Adapted from "Daid Aaron II" in THE DOCTOR TO THE DEAD by John Bennett.
> Videocassette available from SRA/McGraw-Hill 87-002682, 1991. 1/2" VHS videocassette color (9min), $43.00. (Children's literature series).
> Ornery Aaron Kelly's widow can't get him to stay in his grave until a fiddler tries to court her. Vibrant watercolor wash illustrations and the robust retelling make this a delight particularly at Halloween.
> SUBJ: Skeleton--Folkore./ Folklore--United States./ United States--Folklore.

398.25   J 808.81   Ph-1 2-5/5 $15.99   T   KB685
DIANE GOODE'S BOOK OF SCARY STORIES AND SONGS. Illus. by Diane Goode. Selections collected by Lucia Monfried. Dutton ISBN 0-525-45175-7, 1994. 64p. col. ill.
> Varied collection of stories, poems, and songs which can be told and sung at Halloween. As scary stories, this attractive compilation will be read year 'round.
> SUBJ: Ghosts--Literary collections./ Folklore./ Songs.

SRC 398.25   Ph-1 2-4 $10.00   KB686
HAMILTON, MARY. Haunting tales: live from the Culberson Mansion State Historic Site (Sound recording cassette). Retold by Mary Hamilton. Hidden Springs ISBN 1-885556-04-7, 1996. 1 sound cassette (54min).
> Six tales, some familiar and some new, all make good listening at Halloween. Sources are given. Superstition about the counting compulsion of ghosts is attributed to the teller's grandmother.
> SUBJ: Ghosts--Fiction./ United States--Folklore./ Folklore--United States.

398.25   Ph-2 4-5/4 $13.89   L   KB687
HASKINS, JAMES. Headless haunt and other African-American ghost stories. Collected and retold by James Haskins. Illus. by Ben Otero. HarperCollins ISBN 0-06-022997-7; In Canada: HarperCollins, 1994. 116p. ill.
> Includes bibliography.
> Many of the tales in the anthology are 50 years old or older and are a mixture of African and European folklore. Brief section which includes recollections of private individuals adds variety to the material. For multicultural studies.
> SUBJ: Afro-Americans--Folklore./ Folklore--United States./ United States--Folklore./ Ghosts--Folklore.

398.25   Ph-1 K-3/3 $16.00   T   KB688
HODGES, MARGARET. Molly Limbo. Illus. by Elizabeth Miles. Atheneum ISBN 0-689-80581-0; In Canada: Distican, 1996. unp. col. ill.
> Mr. Means moves into an old haunted house and hires his next door neighbor, Mrs. Handy, to clean and cook for him. The work is too much for Mrs. Handy, and surprisingly she finds help from an extra pair of hands in the form of Molly Limbo, the ghost-in-residence. Mr. Means tries to get along with just a ghost to care for him, but soon finds he needs two women to keep him content. Perfect watercolors capture the charm of the old house and occupants.
> SUBJ: Folklore--England./ England--Folklore./ Ghosts--Folklore.

SRC 398.25   Ph-1 3-6 $9.95   OD   KB689
MARTIN, RAFE. Ghostly tales of Japan (Sound recording cassette). Yellow Moon Press 025 ISBN 0-938756-23-0, 1989. 1 sound cassette (80min).
> Four traditional Japanese stories are retold on Side one by Rafe

Martin, who is both an author and storyteller. Side two is an original tale by Martin. Eerie and poetic, the material will find a place in units on Japan and during the Halloween season. For multicultural studies.
SUBJ: Ghosts--Folklore./ Japan--Folklore./ Folklore--Japan./ Ghosts--Fiction.

398.25   Ph-1 3-5/3 $18.95   L   KB690
MARTIN, RAFE. Mysterious tales of Japan. Illus. by Tatsuro Kiuchi. Putnam ISBN 0-399-22677-X; In Canada: Putnam, 1996. 74p. col. ill.
Includes bibliography.
Ten eerie tales from Japan are well told in this collection. The author gives complete notes and acknowledges his debt to Lafcadio Hearn, earlier compiler of Japanese material. The book will be popular with lovers of "ghost stories."
SUBJ: Fairy tales./ Folklore--Japan./ Japan--Folklore./ Ghosts--Folklore.

398.25   Ph-2 2-4/2 $12.95   L   KB691
SCARY BOOK. Compiled by Joanna Cole and Stephanie Calmenson. Illus. by Chris Demarest, et al. Morrow ISBN 0-688-10654-4, 1991. 127p. ill.
Includes indexes.
Divided into four sections--stories, poems, tricks and games, and jokes and riddles, this book will delight beginning readers all year long not just at Halloween. For all collections.
SUBJ: Folklore./ Ghosts--Folklore./ Supernatural--Folklore./ Supernatural--Literary collections.

CE 398.25   Ph-2 1-2/2 $15.89   L   KB692
SCHWARTZ, ALVIN. Ghosts!: ghostly tales from folklore. Retold by Alvin Schwartz. Illus. by Victoria Chess. HarperCollins ISBN 0-06-021797-9; In Canada: HarperCollins, 1991. 63p. col. ill. (I can read book).
Read-along kit available from HarperChildren's Audio (ISBN 0-69470-026-6, 1995). 1 paperback book, 1 sound cassette (15min), $7.95.
Presents seven brief ghostly stories for the beginning reader to read and tell. Sources of the original stories are given.
SUBJ: Ghosts--Folklore./ Folklore.

398.25   Ph-1 K-3/1 $13.89   L   KB693
SCHWARTZ, ALVIN. In a dark, dark room and other scary stories. Retold by Alvin Schwartz. Illus. by Dirk Zimmer. HarperCollins ISBN 0-06-025274-X; In Canada: HarperCollins, 1984. 63p. col. ill. (I can read book).
Evoke ghosts, pirates, skeletons, and eerie happenings through these six spooky stories and one poem which the reteller says are best told "at night--in front of a fire or in the dark." (p.9) The darkish colored pictures complement the stories which are just scary enough and also humorous. Fun for young primaries but also very useful for older, reluctant readers with limited skills.
SUBJ: Folklore./ Horror--Folklore./ Ghosts--Folklore.

CE 398.25   Ph-1 4-A/3 $14.89   L   KB694
SCHWARTZ, ALVIN. Scary stories to tell in the dark. Illus. by Stephen Gammell. HarperCollins ISBN 0-397-31927-4, 1981. 111p. ill.
Includes bibliography.
Talking book available from HarperAudio/Caedmon (ISBN 0-89845-758-0, 1986). 1 sound cassette (42min), $11.95.
Available from National Library Service for the Blind and Physically Handicapped in Braille BR06199, and on sound recording cassette RC22330.
"Telling scary stories is something people have done for thousands of years, for most of us like being scared in that way" (Intro.) and contained in this collection are some of the best scary tales for telling and reading. The documentation provided for the tales could lead to an interesting social studies or language arts experience for gifted students.
Followed by MORE SCARY STORIES TO TELL IN THE DARK (ISBN 0-397-32082-5, c1986); and SCARY STORIES 3: MORE TALES TO CHILL YOUR BONES (ISBN 0-06-021795-2, 1991).
SUBJ: Ghosts--Folklore./ Folklore--United States./ United States--Folklore.

398.25   Ph-2 2-4/4 $19.89   L   KB695
SPOOKY STORIES FOR A DARK AND STORMY NIGHT. Compiled by Alice Low. Illus. by Gahan Wilson. Hyperion ISBN 0-7868-2008-X, 1994. 128p. col. ill.
"Byron Preiss book."
Gathers a wide variety of tales, some new and many which have caused chills over the years. Decorated with colorful drawings which amuse as much as they scare. Subject and format will attract readers.
SUBJ: Folklore./ Horror stories./ Ghosts--Fiction.

398.25   Ph-3 2-5/4 $17.27   L   KB696
TAYLOR, C. J. Ghost and Lone Warrior: an Arapaho legend. Childrens Press ISBN 0-516-08167-5; In Canada: Tundra, 1991. unp col illus.
Includes notes on the Arapaho.
Available in French: GUERRIER-SOLITAIRE ET LE FANTOME (ISBN 0-88776-264-6, 1991).
Starvation, pain, freezing weather and a ghost are the trials which face Lone Warrior and prove him to be worthy of leading his tribe. A gripping story illustrating the values of the Arapaho Indians and life before the advent of horses.
SUBJ: Indians of North America--Folklore./ Arapaho Indians--Folklore./ Ghosts--Folklore./ French language materials.

398.25   Ph-2 1-3/4 $15.95   T   KB697
YEP, LAURENCE. Man who tricked a ghost. Illus. by Isadore Seltzer. BridgeWater ISBN 0-8167-3030-X; In Canada: BridgeWater/dist. by Vanwell, 1993. unp. col. ill.
Sung is afraid of no one, not even a ghost! This retelling of a Chinese story from the third century AD is dramatically illustrated and is a perfect selection for use in units on China and at Halloween.
SUBJ: Folklore--China./ China--Folklore./ Ghosts--Folklore.

SRC 398.25   Ph-3 4-6 $12.00   KB698
YOUNG, RICHARD. Head on the high road: ghost stories from the Southwest (Sound recording cassette). By Richard and Judy Dockrey Young. August House Audio ISBN 0-87483-334-5, 1993. 1 sound cassette (55min).
A variety of ghost stories from the Southwest, including traditional tales and many urban legends, are told by a husband and wife team of storytellers. Presents primary resource materials from fieldwork collections.
SUBJ: Ghosts--Folklore./ Horror stories./ Folklore--United States./ United States--Folklore./ Southwest, New--Folklore./ Folklore--Southwest, New.

398.26   Ph-3 3-4/5 $15.95   L   KB699
BERNHARD, EMERY. Tree that rains: the flood myth of the Huichol Indians of Mexico. Retold by Emery Bernhard. Illus. by Durga Bernhard. Holiday House ISBN 0-8234-1108-7, 1994. unp. col. ill., map.
A farmer toils in his fields trying to chop down trees which strangely reappear whole the next day. Spying on the spirit who is bringing back life to the plants he uproots, the farmer learns of the approaching flood and is saved to start human life again on the planet. Gouache paintings with childlike qualities decorate this flood myth for multicultural studies.
SUBJ: Huichol Indians--Folklore./ Indians of Mexico--Folklore./ Deluge--Folklore.

398.26   Ph-3 3-4/3 $15.88   L   KB700
BISHOP, GAVIN. Maui and the Sun: a Maori tale. Retold and illus. by Gavin Bishop. North-South Books ISBN 1-55858-578-8; In Canada: North-South Books/dist. by Vanwell, 1996. unp. col. ill.
Dissatisfied at the speed with which the sun travels across the sky, Maui, a trickster, determines to catch it in a net woven from flax. While captured, the sun reveals his secret name and falls under the power of Maui. Trying to curb the sun, Maui ties him to the moon and regulates time. The author-illustrator has a Maori background and uses traditional design in his pen and ink watercolors.
SUBJ: Maori (New Zealand people)--Folklore./ Folklore--New Zealand./ New Zealand--Folklore./ Sun--Folklore.

398.26   Ph-1 2-3/3 $14.89   L   KB701
BRUCHAC, JOSEPH. Story of the Milky Way: a Cherokee tale. By Joseph Bruchac and Gayle Ross. Illus. by Virginia A. Stroud. Dial ISBN 0-8037-1738-5, 1995. unp. col. ill.
This pourquoi tale explains the formation of the Milky Way as passed down through the years by the Cherokee. Corn was vital to the people, and an old couple kept their stock of cornmeal in bins behind their house. When some of the meal is stolen, it is their grandson who discovers the thief. With the help of the Beloved Women, he drives the scoundrel into the sky. Stresses community spirit and family caring. For multicultural studies.
SUBJ: Cherokee Indians--Folklore./ Milky Way--Folklore./ Indians of North America--Folklore.

398.26   Ph-1 K-2/2 $14.95   L   KB702
BRYAN, ASHLEY. Story of lightning and thunder. Atheneum ISBN 0-689-31836-7; In Canada: Maxwell Macmillan, 1993. unp. col. ill.
"Jean Karl book."
When Ma Sheep Thunder and her son Ram Lightning lived on Earth, the youngster caused the villagers so much trouble they were banished to the sky. Bryan's warm drawings and rhythmic text cause this African folktale to come alive. Perfect choice for reading aloud on a rainy day. Pourquoi story for multicultural studies.

SUBJ: Folklore--Africa, West./ Africa, West--Folklore./ Lightning--Folklore./ Thunderstorms--Folklore.

398.26 Ph-2 2-4/7 $14.89 L KB703
CZERNECKI, STEFAN. Pancho's pinata. By Stefan Czernecki and Timothy Rhodes. Illus. by Stefan Czernecki. Hyperion ISBN 1-56282-278-0, 1992. 40p. col. ill.
When he was a boy, a kindly peasant freed a star which was caught on a cactus, and the star rewarded him with happiness. Wanting to share his good fortune, he converts a clay jar filled with gifts into a replica of the star to give to the children of his village on Christmas Eve. Flat, stylized drawings capture the essence of Mexican folk art. Combine with NINE DAYS TO CHRISTMAS for holiday celebrations using pinatas or for units on Mexico.
SUBJ: Stars--Folklore./ Christmas--Folklore./ Folklore--Mexico./ Mexico--Folklore.

CE 398.26 Ph-1 K-3/6 $4.95 P KB704
DAYRELL, ELPHINSTONE. Why the sun and the moon live in the sky: an African folktale. Illus. by Blair Lent. Houghton Mifflin ISBN 0-395-53963-3, c1968. unp. col. ill.
Caldecott Honor Book.
Videocassette available from Pied Piper/AIMS Multimedia Q4099, n.d. 1/2" VHS videocassette color (11min), study guide, $49.95.
"Many years ago the sun and water were great friends, and both lived on the earth together." This telling of how the sun and his wife, the moon, left the earth and water and came to live in the sky is as it might have been told by African tribesmen wearing ceremonial masks to represent the elements and sea creatures.
SUBJ: Sun--Folklore./ Moon--Folklore./ Folklore--Nigeria./ Nigeria--Folklore.

398.26 Ph-2 2-4/5 $15.95 L KB705
GERSON, MARY-JOAN. Why the sky is far away: a Nigerian folktale. Retold by Mary-Joan Gerson. Illus. by Carla Golembe. Joy Street/Little, Brown ISBN 0-316-30852-8; In Canada: Little, Brown, 1992. unp col illus.
Indiscriminate nibbling of the sky causes it to desert the people that it had sheltered and fed in this early ecology tale from Nigeria. Incorporates Nigerian folk art in the illustrations.
SUBJ: Folklore--Nigeria./ Nigeria--Folklore./ Sky--Folklore.

398.26 Ph-1 2-5/4 $15.95 L KB706
GOBLE, PAUL. Adopted by the eagles: a Plains Indian story of friendship and treachery. Told and illus. by Paul Goble. Bradbury ISBN 0-02-736575-1; In Canada: Maxwell Macmillan, 1994. unp. col. ill.
Two friends, who love the same maiden, go to find a herd of horses. White Hawk leaves Tall Bear on a cliff where only a nest of young eagles is perched and returns home to claim his bride. How the eagles aid Tall Bear in outwitting the traitorous White Hawk make a tale of devotion and courage. Typical Goble illustrations compliment the Lakota legend for multicultural studies.
SUBJ: Dakota Indians--Folklore./ Indians of North America--Folklore.

398.26 Ph-1 3-5/5 $14.95 L KB707
GOBLE, PAUL. Lost children: the boys who were neglected. Bradbury ISBN 0-02-736555-7; In Canada: Maxwell Macmillan, 1993. unp. col. ill.
Explanation of the origin of the constellation Pleiades which can be seen clearly in the open sky. It is also a reminder that children are to be loved and nurtured. Typical Goble drawings capture Native American life and the beauty of the western states.
SUBJ: Siksika Indians--Folklore./ Indians of North America--Folklore./ Stars--Folklore.

398.26 Ph-2 3-4/5 $16.00 L KB708
HULPACH, VLADIMIR. Ahaiyute and Cloud Eater. Illus. by Marek Zawadzki. Translated by Pauline Hejl. Harcourt Brace ISBN 0-15-201237-0; In Canada: Harcourt Brace c/o Canadian Manda, 1996. unp. col. ill.
A young Native American boy longs to prove himself as a warrior. His grandmother tells him about a monster who eats the clouds which bring rain. With her aid and that of his small friend, Mole, he kills the monster and frees the clouds. A handsome book with source notes that capture the Southwest. A Zuni legend for multicultural studies.
SUBJ: Zuni Indians--Folklore./ Indians of North America--New Mexico--Folklore./ New Mexico--Folklore./ Folklore--New Mexico.

398.26 Ph-3 2-3/4 $16.00 T KB709
LARRY, CHARLES. Peboan and Seegwun. Retold and illus. by Charles Larry. Farrar, Straus and Giroux ISBN 0-374-35773-0; In Canada: HarperCollins, 1993. unp. col. ill.
An Ojibwa Indian explanation of how Spring comes into the tent of Old Man Winter and each discusses his impact on the earth. For multicultural studies.

SUBJ: Ojibwa Indians--Folklore./ Indians of North America--Folklore./ Seasons--Folklore.

398.26 Ph-2 5-6/8 $6.95 P KB710
LURIE, ALISON. Heavenly zoo: legends and tales of the stars. Retold by Alison Lurie. Illus. by Monika Beisner. Farrar, Straus and Giroux ISBN 0-374-42927-8; In Canada: HarperCollins, c1979, 1996. 63p. col. ill.
"Sunburst book."
"Our ancestors saw all sorts of things in the stars.... But what they saw most often were beasts, birds, and fish. And for most of these creatures there was a legend of how they came to be there." (Preface) Many of the legends are gathered here with clear diagrams of the stars. Pourquoi stories to enhance astronomy units.
SUBJ: Stars--Folklore./ Constellations.

CE 398.26 Ph-1 2-4/3 $16.99 L KB711
MCDERMOTT, GERALD. Arrow to the sun. Viking ISBN 0-670-13369-8; In Canada: Penguin, 1974. 42p. col. ill.
Caldecott Medal Award.
Available in Spanish, FLECHA AL SOL (ISBN 0-670-83748-2, 1991) $15.95.
According to the Pueblo Indians, the Lord of the Sun sent the spark of life to the earth in the form of a boy. Taunted by the other boys about not having a father, Boy journeys to the heavens to find his father. There he is subjected to the four chambers of ceremony to prove his relationship. When the trials are over, Boy returns to Earth and the Indians celebrate his return with the Dance of Life.
SUBJ: Pueblo Indians--Folklore./ Indians of North America--Folklore./ Spanish language materials.

398.26 Ph-2 K-2/5 $14.89 L KB712
OLIVIERO, JAMIE. Day Sun was stolen. Illus. by Sharon Hitchcock. Hyperion ISBN 0-7868-2026-8, 1995. unp. col. ill.
A pourquoi tale explains hibernation and the different thicknesses of various animals' coats. Bold drawings by a Haida artist are elementary and will appeal to young children. For multicultural studies.
SUBJ: Haida Indians--Folklore./ Indians of North America--Folklore./ Animals--Folklore.

398.26 Ph-2 K-2/4 $15.99 L KB713
SANFIELD, STEVE. Just rewards, or, Who is that man in the moon and what's he doing up there anyway? Illus. by Emily Lisker. Orchard ISBN 0-531-08885-5, 1996. unp. col. ill.
When a farmer cares for an injured bird, his kindness is rewarded with a magical seed which produces a vine on which jewel-filled watermelons grow. A jealous neighbor injures a bird, so he might care for it. His only reward is a vine which he climbs to the sky--where he still remains. Primitive drawings are rendered in oils on canvas. For multicultural studies.
SUBJ: China--Folklore./ Folklore--China./ Moon--Folklore.

398.26 Ph-3 5-6/6 $13.93 L KB714
SHANNON, GEORGE. Stories to solve. Illus. by Peter Sis. Greenwillow ISBN 0-688-04304-6, 1985. 55p ill.
Available from National Library Service for the Blind and Physically Handicapped on sound recording cassette RC25059.
Solving puzzles is always fun and particularly when the characters in the stories come from different countries and cultures. The stories could be introduced in mathematics units to explain logic. Stories are excellent short ones to add variety to story hours. For multicultural studies.
More puzzles are found in MORE STORIES TO SOLVE: FIFTEEN FOLKTALES FROM AROUND THE WORLD (ISBN 0-688-09161-X, 1991); and STILL MORE STORIES TO SOLVE: FOURTEEN FOLKTALES FROM AROUND THE WORLD (ISBN 0-688-04619-3, 1994).
SUBJ: Folklore./ Literary recreations./ Riddles./ Logic--Folklore.

398.26 Ph-2 2-4/2 $14.89 L KB715
SIMMS, LAURA. Moon and Otter and Frog. Illus. by Clifford Brycelea. Hyperion ISBN 0-7868-2022-5; In Canada: Little, Brown, 1995. unp. col. ill.
Haunting tale of a lonesome moon who seeks a wife amongst the earthly creatures and finds the perfect mate in Little Green Ugly Frog. The pourquoi tale of the Modoc Indians explains why the moon wanes and then becomes full again. A delight for reading aloud. Useful for units on astronomy and multicultural studies.
SUBJ: Modoc Indians--Folklore./ Indians of North America--Folklore./ Moon--Folklore.

398.26 Ph-2 3-4/2 $13.95 T KB716
TAYLOR, C. J. How Two-Feather was saved from loneliness: an Abenaki legend. Tundra ISBN 0-88776-254-9; In Canada: Tundra, 1990. unp. col. ill.

Also available in French DEUX-PLUMES ET LA SOLITUDE DISPARUE (ISBN 0-88776-344-8, 1990).
Three tales of origins are interwoven into one in this poetic telling of a young man's struggle to overcome loneliness. The Abenaki Indian legends for the origin of fire, corn, and communal living are dramatically presented. Creation stories for multicultural studies.
SUBJ: Indians of North America--Canada--Folklore./ Abenaki Indians--Folklore./ French language materials.

398.26   Ph-3 3-5/7 $13.89   L   KB717
VUONG, LYNETTE DYER. Sky legends of Vietnam. Illus. by Vo Dinh Mai. HarperCollins ISBN 0-06-023001-0; In Canada: HarperCollins, 1993. 103p. ill.
Includes glossary.
Stories from Vietnam about the moon, sun, and stars illustrate that many themes in folklore can be found in all cultures. Contemporary environmental messages are included in these traditional tales which read smoothly. For multicultural studies.
SUBJ: Fairy tales./ Folklore--Vietnam./ Vietnam--Folklore.

398.26   Ph-2 3-5/2 $16.95   L   KB718
WOLF-SAMPATH, GITA. Mala: a women's folktale. Adapted by Gita Wolf. Illus. by Annouchka Galouchko. Annick/dist. by Firefly ISBN 1-55037-491-5; In Canada: Annick/dist. by Firefly, 1996. unp. col. ill.
Originally published in Madras, TARA Publishing, 1994.
An Indian folktale told by gypsies in which a young girl longs to be a boy, so she might defeat a demon. Having her wish fulfilled, she discovers that it is her own wisdom and kindness which outwits the demon and brings rain back to her village. Adapted from the film "Girya," this tale of a resourceful young woman will be useful in units on India, multicultural studies, and women's studies.
SUBJ: India--Folklore./ Folklore--India.

398.27   Ph-2 2-4/6 $13.95   L   KB719
ASBJORNSEN, P. C. Man who kept house. By P.C. Asbjornsen and J.E. Moe. Illus. by Svend Otto S. McElderry ISBN 0-689-50560-4; In Canada: Maxwell Macmillan, 1992. unp. col. ill.
Dissatisfied with his hard work in the fields, a farmer swaps jobs with his wife. Humorous pictures show the disasterous results of the exchange. Large pictures make this an excellent choice for picture book hours.
SUBJ: Folklore--Norway./ Norway--Folklore.

398.27   Ph-3 3-5/3 $15.95   L   KB720
BERNHARD, EMERY. Girl who wanted to hunt: a Siberian tale. Retold by Emery Bernhard. Illus. by Durga Bernhard. Holiday House ISBN 0-823-1125-7, 1994. unp. col. ill.
A stepmother asks her husband to make toys which will teach his daughter household tasks, but the daughter begs for toys which are miniatures of ones he uses to hunt. The story depicts a strong heroine and demonstrates that women are able to succeed at tasks which are frequently considered to be for men only.
SUBJ: Folklore--Russia (Federation)--Siberia./ Russia (Federation)--Siberia--Folklore.

CE 398.27   Ph-1 K-3/2 $13.95   L   KB721
BROWN, MARCIA. Stone soup: an old tale. Retold and illustrated by Marcia Brown. Scribner's ISBN 0-684-92296-7, c1947. unp. col. ill.
Caldecott Honor Book.
Available in Spanish SOPA DE PIEDRAS (Lectorum ISBN 0-9625162-1-X, 1991).
Available from National Library Service for the Blind and Physically Handicapped in Braille BRA06859.
Read-along kit available in Spanish: SOPA DE PIEDRAS from Live Oak Media (ISBN 0-87499-279-6, 1992). 1 hardcover book, 1 sound cassette (16min), $22.95.
Three hungry soldiers sup with villagers on tasty soup made with stones.
SUBJ: Folklore--France./ Spanish language materials./ France--Folklore.

TB 398.27   Ph-3 4-6 $11.00   OD KB722
BUDBERG, MOURA. Russian fairy tales (Talking book). Retold in English by Moura Budberg and Amabel Williams-Ellis. Read by Morris Carnovksy. HarperAudio/Caedmon ISBN 1-55994-399-8; In Canada; dist. by HarperCollins, n.d. 1 sound cassette. (Caedmon children's classic).
Based on a book of the same title, six tales from Russia tell of the common man who because of wits, goodness, and perseverance wins over poverty, greed and unkindness. The tales are found in collections of folktales of many lands, but on this recording, they take place in Russian villages and happen to Russian peasants. The tales are clearly and expressively read by the actor Morris Carnovsky.
Contents: The King who liked fairy tales; The chatterbox; The doctor who knew everything; The town of fools; Two brothers; The stolen turnips.
SUBJ: Folklore--Soviet Union./ Soviet Union--Folklore.

398.27   Ph-1 K-A/4 $16.95   T   KB723
CHASE, RICHARD. Grandfather tales: American-English folk tales. Selected and edited by Richard Chase. Illustrated by Berkeley Williams, Jr. Houghton Mifflin ISBN 0-395-06692-1, c1948. 239p. ill.
Available from National Library Service for the Blind and Physically Handicapped as talking book TB01433.
"How Bobtail beat the devil" and other stories told in North Carolina and Virginia. A good source for the storyteller.
SUBJ: Folklore--United States./ United States--Folklore.

398.27   Ph-1 K-A/3 $13.95   T   KB724
CHASE, RICHARD. Jack tales. Set down from these sources and edited by Richard Chase. Illustrated by Berkeley Williams, Jr. Houghton Mifflin ISBN 0-395-06694-8, c1943. 201p. ill.
Includes glossary and appendix.
Available from National Library Service for the Blind and Physically Handicapped in Braille BRJ00406.
Jack has several adventures with giants before and after he climbs the bean tree. A good source for the storyteller.
SUBJ: Folklore--United States./ United States--Folklore.

SRC 398.27   Ph-1 K-A $9.98   OD KB725
CHASE, RICHARD. Richard Chase tells three "Jack" tales from the Southern Appalachians (Sound recording cassette). Folk-Legacy Records FTA-6, n.d. 1 sound cassette.
Selectors' Choice, 11th ed.
Richard Chase gathered tales from the people living in the Appalachian Mountains in the 1940s and gathered them into two volumes which children have loved for a long time. Now, we have three of the best of the tales retold by Richard Chase himself with an appreciative audience of mountain children.
Contents: Jack and the robbers; Jack and the King's girl; Jack and the three sillies.
SUBJ: Folklore--United States./ United States--Folklore.

398.27   Ph-1 2-4/5 $14.89   L   KB726
CLIMO, SHIRLEY. Korean Cinderella. Illus. by Ruth Heller. HarperCollins ISBN 0-06-020433-8; In Canada: HarperCollins, 1993. unp. col. ill.
A jealous stepmother is unkind to her lovely stepdaughter in this handsomely illustrated Korean version of the familiar Cinderella story. The illustrations overflow with traditional motifs and are visually delightful.
SUBJ: Fairy tales./ Folklore--Korea./ Korea--Folklore.

398.27   Ph-2 2-3/4 $15.95   L   KB727
COMPTON, JOANNE. Ashpet: an Appalachian tale. Retold by Joanne Compton. Illus. by Kenn Compton. Holiday House ISBN 0-8234-1106-0, 1994. unp. col. ill.
Set in Appalachia, this retelling of Cinderella depicts Asphet's fairy godmother as an old granny who lives over the ridge and the prince as the doctor's son. The cartoonlike illustrations are well suited to this updating of a traditional tale.
SUBJ: Fairy tales./ Folklore--United States./ United States--Folklore./ Folklore--Appalachian Region./ Appalachian Region--Folklore.

398.27   Ph-3 4-6/7 $14.95   T   KB728
COURLANDER, HAROLD. Cow-tail switch and other West African stories. By Harold Courlander and George Herzog. Illustrated by Madye Lee Chastain. Henry Holt ISBN 0-8050-0288-X, c1947, 1987. 143p. ill.
Newbery Honor book.
Named after an African symbol of authority, these stories are full of laughter and food for thought.
SUBJ: Folklore--Africa, West./ Africa, West--Folklore.

TB 398.27   Ph-3 K-A $9.98   OD KB729
COURLANDER, HAROLD. Uncle Bouqui of Haiti (Talking book). Read by Augusta Baker. Smithsonian Folkways FC7107, 1959. 1 sound cassette.
Notes in case.
The renowned story-teller and former children's librarian of New York Public Library presents a group of humorous tales centering about the perennial clown of Haitian folk literature. From the book: UNCLE BOUQUI OF HAITI.
Contents: Uncle Bouqui gets Whee-ai; Uncle Bouqui rents a horse; Uncle Bouqui and Godfather Malice.
SUBJ: Folklore--Haiti./ Haiti--Folklore.

398.27   Ph-3 2/2 $2.50   P   KB730
CRAIG, M. JEAN. Three wishes. Retold by M. Jean Craig. Illustrated by Yuri Salzman. Scholastic ISBN 0-590-41744-4; In Canada: Scholastic, c1968, 1986. 32p. col. ill.

Granted three wishes, a woodcutter wasted two wishes by asking for a sausage and then wanting it on his wife's nose. The final wish brought peace but not the treasure that the two had hoped for. A delightful tale for beginning readers.
SUBJ: Folklore.

398.27   Ph-1 3-6/6 $19.95   L   KB731
DEMI. One grain of rice: a mathematical folktale. Scholastic ISBN 0-590-93998-X; In Canada: Scholastic, 1997. unp. col. ill.
Selectors' Choice, 21st ed.
In a time of extreme starvation, a clever village girl begs the raja to give her one grain of the rice she had saved when his servants spilled his supply. But he must also double the grain each day. The next day she would get two, the following day four, etc. The raja's agreement causes him to deplete his storage houses. For in 30 days, Rani had received one billion grains of rice. A mathematical fable in which the theory of geometric progression is vividly pictured. The illustrations dramatically depict the increasing numbers until the huge supply of grain can only be shown on foldout pages. A concluding chart outlines the number theory. An ideal choice for interdisciplinary math units and multicultural studies.
SUBJ: Folklore--India./ India--Folklore./ Mathematics--Folklore.

CE 398.27   Ph-1 P-2 $4.95   P   KB732
DE REGNIERS, BEATRICE SCHENK. Red Riding Hood. Retold in verse by Beatrice Schenk de Regniers. Illus. by Edward Gorey. Aladdin/Macmillan ISBN 0-689-71373-8; In Canada: Collier Macmillan, c1972, 1990. 42p. col. ill.
While taking a cake to her Grandma, Red Riding Hood meets a wolf. He persuades her to pick some flowers, while he gallops ahead and gobbles Grandma up. Red Riding Hood meets the same fate, but is rescued by a passing hunter. This retelling is told in simple verse and Gorey's illustrations add to the fun.
SUBJ: Folklore--Germany./ Germany--Folklore.

398.27   Ph-1 4-5/6 $14.95   L   KB733
DUNCAN, LOIS. Magic of Spider Woman. Illus. by Shonto Begay. Scholastic ISBN 0-590-46155-9; In Canada: Scholastic, 1996. unp. col. ill.
Selectors' Choice, 21st ed.
A young, willful maiden misses the instructions of the Spirit Being about how to survive on earth because she is tending her sheep in the hills. When winter comes, she returns to her people. Her suffering from the elements prompts Spider Woman to teach her how to weave blankets from the wool of her sheep, but she is warned not to become obsessive about her craft. She disobeys and this is the foundation for the practice of making a spirit trail in the blankets woven by Navajo women. The perceptive reader will note that no border is unbroken in the illustrations. A haunting tale which teaches in addition to explaining. For multicultural studies.
SUBJ: Navajo Indians--Folklore./ Indians of North America--Folklore./ Folklore--Southwest, New./ Southwest, New--Folklore.

398.27   Ph-2 K-3/2 $15.95   L   KB734
FARLEY, CAROL J. Mr. Pak buys a story. By Carol Farley. Illus. by Benrei Huang. Whitman ISBN 0-8075-5178-3; In Canada: General, 1997. unp. col. ill.
Long, boring nights prompt an old couple to send their servant, Mr. Pak, to buy a story. A thief creates a tale as he watches a stork and sells it to Mr. Pak. How the story comes back to haunt the thief and protect the old couple is a satisfying tale from Korea.
SUBJ: Folklore--Korea./ Korea--Folklore.

SRC 398.27   Ph-2 2-4 $8.95   OD KB735
FOREST, HEATHER. Songspinner: folktales and fables sung and told (Sound recording cassette). Weston Woods WW721C, 1982. 1 sound cassette. (Storytelling circle).
Accompanying herself on the guitar, wooden drum, recorder, zither, and/or bell tree, Heather Forest singingly retells eleven "folktales and fables which contain a kernel of homespun wisdom passed down through oral tradition." Sources for the tales and fables come from all over the world.
TALES OF WOMENFOLK (1985) contains five tales which offer a positive view of women taken from Ethel Johnston Phelps's TATTERHOOD AND OTHER TALES.
SUBJ: Folklore./ Fables./ Women--Folklore.

CE 398.27   Ph-1 P-2/4 $14.95   L   KB736
GALDONE, PAUL. Gingerbread boy. Clarion ISBN 0-395-28799-5, 1975. unp. col. ill.
Sound filmstrip from Listening Library GSF700, 1984, (OPC). 52fr color, 1 sound cassette (10min) $32.98.
Large, vigorous and humorous pictures illustrate the familiar and popular old tale of the gingerbread boy who springs to life and runs

away from the little old woman, the little old man, a cow, a horse, threshers and mowers, but is finally outwitted by a clever fox.
SUBJ: Folklore./ Animals--Folklore.

398.27   Ph-2 1-3/3 $14.95   L   KB737
GILMAN, PHOEBE. Something from nothing: adapted from a Jewish folktale. Scholastic ISBN 0-590-47280-1; In Canada: Scholastic, 1993. unp. col. ill.
Joseph could always count on his grandfather to create a new coat, vest, tie, or button from the smallest bit of cloth. Finally, he realizes it is up to him to create the lasting treasure: a story. Illustrations show the myriad activities of Joseph's home and village. A delightful Jewish tale retold with humor and insight. Repetitive phrases make it a good choice for reading aloud.
SUBJ: Jews--Folklore.

CE 398.27   Ph-1 3-5/6 $14.95   L   KB738
GOBLE, PAUL. Love flute. Bradbury/Macmillan ISBN 0-02-736261-2; In Canada: Maxwell Macmillan, 1992. unp. col. ill.
Videocassette available from Reading Adventures RA 1006 (ISBN 1-882869-55-9, 1993) 1/2" VHS color (9min), $42.50.
Read-along kit available from Reading Adventures RA 1393, 1992. 1 hardback book, 1 sound cassette (9min), $25.95.
Shyness drives a Native American youth to wander away from his people and the girl he worships. Coming to his aid, two Elk men give him a magical flute which helps him gain his heart's desire. Poignant, romantic tale will be a good choice for Valentine's Day.
SUBJ: Indians of North America--Great Plains--Folklore.

CE 398.27   Ph-1 3-4/6 $16.95   L   KB739
GRIFALCONI, ANN. Village of round and square houses. Little, Brown ISBN 0-316-32862-6; In Canada: Little, Brown, 1986. unp. col. ill.
Caldecott Honor book.
Selectors' Choice, 16th ed.
Unanimated 1/2" VHS videocassette from Weston Woods HMPV326V (12min), 1989, $49.95.
Pourquoi stories are usually fanciful but this one explains why the men and women of Tos, a small isolated village in Cameroon near a volcano, live in separate differently shaped houses. The pastel and watercolor wash illustrations are rich in detail, tone and texture as they interpret the text which is excellent to share with a group.
SUBJ: Folklore--Cameroon./ Folklore--Africa./ Cameroon--Folklore./ Africa--Folklore.

CE 398.27   Ph-1 5/6 $14.95   T   KB740
GRIMM, JACOB. Hansel and Gretel: a tale from the Brothers Grimm. Retold by Rika Lesser. Illus. by Paul O. Zelinsky. Putnam ISBN 0-399-21733-9; In Canada: Putnam, 1984. unp. col. ill.
Caldecott Honor.
Available from National Library Service for the Blind and Physically Handicapped on sound recording cassette RC22393.
Made desperate by the fear of starving, a man and his wife take their two children into the forest and leave them. Stumbling upon a house made of cake, the children begin to devour it, only to discover that the house belongs to a witch who plans to devour them. Their escape with jewels is courageously executed and they return to their father. Full-page detailed oil paintings show the world of the starving peasants and the make-believe world of gingerbread cottages.
SUBJ: Folklore--Germany./ Witches--Folklore./ Germany--Folklore.

CE 398.27   Ph-1 1-4/6 $14.95   L   KB741
GRIMM, JACOB. Little Red Riding Hood. By the Brothers Grimm. Retold and illustrated by Trina Schart Hyman. Holiday House ISBN 0-8234-0470-6, 1983. unp. col. ill.
Caldecott Honor Book.
Selectors' Choice, 15th ed.
Available from National Library Service for the Blind and Physically Handicapped in Braille BR03030.
Sent by her mother to take some bread, butter, and wine to her ill grandmother, young Elizabeth meets a wolf in this faithful retelling of the familiar folktale. Highlighted by an extravagance of detailed full-color illustrations, this is recommended for sharing with a group.
SUBJ: Folklore--Germany./ Germany--Folklore.

398.27   Ph-1 2-5/5 $14.99   T   KB742
HALEY, GAIL E. Two bad boys: a very old Cherokee tale. Retold and illus. by Gail E. Haley. Dutton ISBN 0-525-45311-3; In Canada: McClelland & Stewart, 1996. unp. col. ill.
Boy lives peacefully with his parents Kanati (First Hunter) and Selu (Corn Mother) until he brings to life his reflection from the river. Wild Boy proves willful and destructive, driving away the father and mother. The pair were forced to hunt and plant for themselves; and still do to this day. Gouache paintings capture this tale of good and evil. For multicultural studies.

SUBJ: Cherokee Indians--Folklore./ Indians of North America--Folklore./ Folklore--United States./ United States--Folklore.

398.27   Ph-3 5-6/5 $6.95   P   KB743
HIGHWATER, JAMAKE. Anpao: an American Indian odyssey. Illus. by Fritz Scholder. HarperCollins ISBN 0-06-440437-4, c1977, 1992. 256p. ill.

Includes bibliography.
Newbery Honor book.
Selectors' Choice, 12th ed.
Anpao and his twin brother Oapana spent long years in search of their origin and their destiny. Knowing he loved Ko-ko-mik-e-is above all others Anpao journeyed to the Sun to gain his beloved's freedom from a pledge to marry the Sun. In telling the story of Anpao's search, Jamake Highwater has selected tales which reflect American Indian religious beliefs and their explanation of historical events. The book is illustrated with stark and mystifying lithographs.
SUBJ: Indians of North America--Folklore./ Indians of North America--Religion and mythology.

398.27   Ph-1 3-5/5 $12.93   L   KB744
HOGROGIAN, NONNY. Contest. Greenwillow ISBN 0-688-84042-6, c1976. unp. col. ill.

Caldecott Honor Book.
Selectors' Choice, 11th ed.
Two thieves are engaged to the same, winsome maid, Ehleezah. One shares her company during the day, the other at night. When they decide to move to a new province to try their thieving skills, they discover their mutual love. To prove who is the better thief, they carry out two highly successful pieces of trickery, but only find that they could get along without the maid and she without them.
SUBJ: Folklore--Armenia./ Robbers and outlaws--Folklore./ Armenia--Folklore.

CE 398.27   Ph-2 3-4/6 $13.93   L   KB745
HUCK, CHARLOTTE S. Princess Furball. Retold by Charlotte Huck. Illus. by Anita Lobel. Greenwillow ISBN 0-688-07838-9, 1989. unp. col. ill.
Videocassette available from Weston Woods HMPV347V. 1/2" VHS iconographic videocassette color (17min), $49.95.
Read-along kit available from Weston Woods HPRA347. 1 paperback book, 1 sound cassette (17min), $12.00.
Talking book available from Weston Woods RAC347, 1993. 1 sound cassette (17min), $8.95.
Unwilling to wed the ogre her father has chosen for her, a princess flees in a coat made from the skins of a thousand different animals with three walnut shells holding treasures. She works in the kitchen of a king and dazzles him when she appears at balls in spectacular gowns. Another "Cinderella" tale, perhaps disturbing because of the wholesale animal slaughter, lovingly retold with striking watercolor and gouache portrait-like paintings.
SUBJ: Folklore--England./ England--Folklore.

TB 398.27   Ph-1 4-6 $19.95   OD KB746
KAULA, EDNA MASON. African village folktales, vols 1-3 (Talking book). Read by Brock Peters and Diana Sands. HarperAudio/Caedmon ISBN 1-55994-946-5; In Canada: dist. by HarperCollins, n.d. 3 sound cassettes.

Based on a book of the same title, each cassette contains seven stories from as many different parts of Africa. Many of the tales are pourquoi tales, while others are traditional or tales used to teach customs. Two skilled storytellers, one male and one female, present factual introductions to the tales and then tell the stories. They will be useful in units on Africa, for storytelling and for sheer pleasure listening.
Contents: v1 From the Ashanti, Mashona, Nyakyusa, Gogo, Chagga, Sukuma, Baganda people; v2 From the Baluba, Bemba, Zulu, Swazi, Bavenda, Bushman, Pygmy people; v3 From the Masai, Swahili, Gaila, Amhara and Egyptian tribes.
SUBJ: Folklore--Africa./ Africa--Social life and customs./ Africa--Folklore.

398.27   Ph-1 2-4/6 $15.00   L   KB747
KURTZ, JANE. Fire on the mountain. Illustrated by E. B. Lewis. Simon & Schuster ISBN 0-671-88268-6; In Canada: Simon & Schuster, 1994. unp. col. ill.

An ill-tempered rich man refuses to reward a young shepard boy for accomplishing the difficult task he was assigned. A serving maid proves the man's reasoning to be wrong and gains for her young brother his rightful reward. A touching tale of the warm relationship of a brother and sister as well as a positive picture of a girl who outwits a crafty, powerful man.
SUBJ: Folklore--Ethiopia./ Ethiopia--Folklore./ Brothers and sisters--Folklore.

398.27   Ph-2 K-2/3 $15.00   L   KB748
KURTZ, JANE. Trouble. Illus. by Durga Bernhard. Gulliver/Harcourt Brace ISBN 0-15-200219-7; In Canada: Harcourt Brace c/o Canadian Manda, 1997. unp. col. ill.
Includes glossary.
A humorous, circular story in which a boy is given a game board to keep him out of trouble while he tends his father's goats. He loses the gebeta board before he gets to the hills where the goats are to graze, but his misadventures turn out well in the end. The reader can follow his wanderings on the endpapers. Source notes provide background information about the story and the country of Eritrea. Instructional as well as entertaining, the story will be useful for interdisciplinary units and multicultural studies.
SUBJ: Folklore--Eritrea./ Eritrea--Folklore./ Folklore--Africa./ Africa--Folklore.

398.27   Ph-2 K-3/6 $15.93   L   KB749
LANG, ANDREW. Flying ship. Retold by Andrew Lang. Illus. by Dennis McDermott. Morrow ISBN 0-688-11405-9, 1995. unp. col. ill.
In this version of the Russian folktale retold from Andrew Lang, a "fool" wins a princess because of his willingness to share and the magical talents of his crew. The drawings are comforting and filled with men who are comical and endearing. For reading aloud and sharing with small groups.
SUBJ: Folklore--Soviet Union./ Soviet Union--Folklore./ Ships--Folklore.

398.27   Ph-2 3-5/6 $14.95   L   KB750
LOUIE, AI-LING. Yeh-Shen, a Cinderella story from China. Retold by Ai-Ling Louie. Illus. by Ed Young. Philomel ISBN 0-399-20900-X, c1982, 1990. unp. col. ill.
This Chinese Cinderella predates the versions known and beloved by American children. However, the tale contains the same elements: the lonely, lovely child, mistreated by a cruel stepmother finds a way to have beautiful clothes in which to appear at a local festival. The haunting artwork by Ed Young is a fine compliment to this tale. Certainly a prime example to be used in a story hour which presents Cinderella tales from many countries.
SUBJ: Folklore--China./ China--Folklore.

398.27   Ph-2 3-4/4 $13.93   L   KB751
MANTINBAND, GERDA. Blabbermouths: adapted from a German folktale. Illus. by Paul Borovsky. Greenwillow ISBN 0-688-10604-8, 1992. unp. col. ill.
A talkative farmer is saved from a jail sentence by his clever wife who proves that his stories can't be true--especially the one about the chest of gold given to him by a kindly old woman. A great story to prove that idle talk may bring about misfortune.
SUBJ: Folklore./ Gossip--Folklore.

398.27   Ph-1 3-5/4 $14.95   L   KB752
MARTIN, RAFE. Rough-face girl. Illus. by David Shannon. Putnam ISBN 0-399-21859-9; In Canada: Putnam, 1992. unp col illus.
In this version of Cinderella from the Algonquin Indians, inner strength and beauty find their own rewards. For storytellers and units on Native Americans.
SUBJ: Algonquin Indians--Folklore./ Indians of North America--Folklore.

398.27   Ph-3 2-3/3 $13.00   T   KB753
MCCARTHY, RALPH F. Grandfather Cherry-Blossom. Retold by Ralph F. McCarthy. Illus. by Eiho Hirezaki. Kodansha ISBN 4-7700-1759-6, 1993. 47p. col. ill. (Kodansha children's classics).
An elderly couple befriends a lost dog. After he is killed by a mean neighbor, they continue to benefit from the gifts he sends to them. The jealous neighbor gains only misfortune through his greed. Illustrations are richly colored reproductions of classic Japanese book illustrations.
SUBJ: Stories in rhyme./ Fairy tales./ Folklore--Japan./ Japan--Folklore.

398.27   Ph-3 3-4/4 $13.00   T   KB754
MCCARTHY, RALPH F. Inch-high samurai. Retold by Ralph F. McCarthy. Illus. by Shiro Kasamatsu. Kodansha ISBN 4-7700-1758-8, 1993. 47p. col. ill. (Kodansha children's classics).
Adapted from ISSUN-BOSHI.
Stunned at his birth by Inchy Bo's small size, his parents love and care for him and fear for his life when he sets off to visit the capital. There he protects the princess and fights a demon and proves that size is not important. For reading aloud.
SUBJ: Stories in rhyme./ Fairy tales./ Folklore--Japan./ Japan--Folklore.

398.27 Ph-1 2/2 $12.95 L KB755
MCDERMOTT, GERALD. Daniel O'Rourke: an Irish tale. Viking Penguin ISBN 0-670-80924-1; In Canada: Penguin, 1986. unp. col. ill.
Falling asleep after eating too much at a grand party, Daniel O'Rourke meets the birds that he has mistreated and befriended as they harass and care for him. A rollicking adventure which will please children and storytellers seeking a good Irish tale.
Another tale of a poor Irish man, Tim O'Toole, who must learn to keep his mouth closed is TIM O'TOOLE AND THE WEEFOLK (ISBN 0-14-050675-6, 1992).
SUBJ: Folklore--Ireland./ Ireland--Fiction.

VCR 398.27 Ph-1 2-4 $49.95 OD KB756
MCDERMOTT, GERALD. Stonecutter (Videocassette). Weston Woods HMPV178V, 1976. 1/2" VHS videocassette color (6min).
Based on book of the same title (now o.p.).
A humble stonecutter is happy at his work, until a prince passed by one day. He asked from the spirit within the mountain to become a prince, then the sun, a cloud and finally a mountain. In his final form he realized that he was not all powerful for a stonecutter could cut into his very being.
SUBJ: Folklore--Japan./ Japan--Folklore.

398.27 Ph-2 4-5/6 $15.95 L KB757
MEDEARIS, ANGELA SHELF. Singing man: adapted from a West African folktale. Illus. by Terea Shaffer. Holiday House ISBN 0-8234-1103-6, 1994. unp. col. ill.
Coretta Scott King Illustrator Honor book, 1995.
After his manhood ceremony, Banzar decides to follow his love of music and nature, and the elders expel him from the village. This well-developed tale relates how his talent led him to fame while he retained his humility. A folktale which interprets traditions and history. For multicultural studies.
SUBJ: Folklore--Africa, West./ Africa, West--Folklore./ Music--Folklore.

398.27 Ph-2 2-4/4 $15.00 T KB758
MOODIE, FIONA. Nabulela: a South Africa folk tale. Retold and illus. by Fiona Moodie. Farrar, Straus and Giroux ISBN 0-374-35486-3, 1997. unp. col. ill.
First published in Great Britain, Andersen Press Ltd., 1996.
Angered when the king favors his daughter, a group of girls plot against his daughter and push her into a deep pit. She is rescued by her dog, but the king demands that the girls pay for their cruelty. They must bring to the king the skin of Nabulela, a man-eating monster who lives in a deep lake. The girls lull the monster from the lake and capture him. They have learned their lesson, and the king has, too--all the girls must be treated equally.
SUBJ: Nguni (African people)--Folklore./ Folklore--South Africa./ South Africa--Folklore.

398.27 Ph-1 P-2/5 $14.95 L KB759
MOSEL, ARLENE. Tikki Tikki Tembo. Illus. by Blair Lent. Henry Holt ISBN 0-8050-0662-1, 1967. 32p. col. ill.
Available from National Library Service for the Blind and Physically Handicapped as talking book TB02753.
Big book available (ISBN 0-8050-2345-3, 1992).
A little Chinese boy with a great long name falls into a well and the length of his name delays his rescue. Perfect for reading aloud with the children chorusing "Tikki Tikki Tembo No-Sa Rembo Chari Bari Ruchi Pip Peri Pembo."
SUBJ: Names, Personal--Folklore./ Folklore--China./ China--Folklore.

398.27 Ph-3 K-2/7 $14.95 L KB760
NIC LEODHAS, SORCHE. Always room for one more. Illus. by Nonny Hogrogian. Henry Holt ISBN 0-8050-0331-2, 1965. unp. col. ill.
Includes glossary.
Caldecott Medal Award.
Available from National Library Service for the Blind and Physically Handicapped in Braille BR00216.
A Scottish tale told in rhyme of a big-hearted man who invites so many travelers into his house on a stormy night that it crashes down, is illustrated in lively crosshatch pen and ink drawings.
SUBJ: Folk songs--Scotland./ Folklore--Scotland./ Scotland--Folklore.

398.27 Ph-2 3-4/6 $14.95 L KB761
O'BRIEN, ANNE SIBLEY. Princess and the beggar: a Korean folktale. Adapted and illus. by Anne Sibley O'Brien. Scholastic ISBN 0-590-46092-7; In Canada: Scholastic, 1993. unp. col. ill.
A tenderhearted princess is banished by her father to dwell with an illiterate peasant when she refuses to marry her father's choice. The retelling demonstrates how a punishment can resolve into a victory. Illustrations show the Korean countryside and the dress and customs of the Yi Dynasty.
SUBJ: Folklore--Korea./ Korea--Folklore.

398.27 Ph-1 1-3/7 $13.95 L KB762
PERRAULT, CHARLES. Cinderella, or the little glass slipper. Illus. by Marcia Brown. Scribner's ISBN 0-684-12676-1, 1954. unp. col. ill.
Caldecott Medal Award.
Available from National Library Service for the Blind and Physically Handicapped in Braille BRA04738.
The King's son is desperate to know the beautiful princess with whom he has danced three nights. Whose foot will fit the little glass slipper?
SUBJ: Folklore--France./ Fairy tales./ France--Folklore.

398.27 Ph-2 2-4/2 $13.99 L KB763
PITRE, FELIX. Juan Bobo and the pig: a Puerto Rican folktale. Retold by Felix Pitre. Illus. by Christy Hale. Lodestar/Dutton ISBN 0-525-67429-2; In Canada: McClelland & Stewart, 1993. unp. col. ill.
Juan Bobo (a fool) proves his mother to be more of a fool than he when she leaves him to care for their pig. Many Spanish phrases are incorporated into the humorous text about the Puerto Rican folk hero. Bright, stylized illustrations capture the Puerto Rican countryside. An attractive folk hero for multicultural studies in the spirit of Goose Hans and Epaminondas.
SUBJ: Juan Bobo (Legendary character)./ Folklore--Puerto Rico./ Puerto Rico--Folklore.

398.27 Ph-2 2-4/6 $16.95 T KB764
POLLOCK, PENNY. Turkey girl: a Zuni Cinderella story. Retold by Penny Pollock. Illus. by Ed Young. Little, Brown ISBN 0-316-71314-7; In Canada: Little, Brown, 1996. unp. col. ill.
A poor maiden who cares for the turkeys feels that she will be unable to go to the Dance of the Sacred Bird because of her miserable clothing. This unique Native American legend holds true to the European Cinderella story until the girl procrastinates on her pledge to the turkeys and loses all. Compare and contrast with the many other versions of this universal tale. For multicultural studies.
SUBJ: Zuni Indians--Folklore./ Indians of North America--New Mexico--Folklore.

398.27 Ph-1 2-5/5 $16.00 T KB765
RANSOME, ARTHUR. Fool of the world and the flying ship: a Russian tale. Retold by Arthur Ransome. Illus. by Uri Shulevitz. Farrar, Straus & Giroux ISBN 0-374-32442-5, c1968. unp. col. ill.
Caldecott Medal Award.
Available in Spanish TONTIMUNDO Y EL BARCO VOLADOR (ISBN 0-374-32443-3, 1991).
Available from National Library Service for the Blind and Physically Handicapped in Braille BR00949, and as sound recording cassette RC16474.
The Fool of the World is the youngest of three sons. His parents expect little of him but least of all do they expect him to win the hand of the Czar's daughter. The Fool, however, does find a flying ship because of his generosity and with eight peasants with great powers to help him, he outwits the Czar. The princess loves him to distraction and all ends well.
SUBJ: Folklore--Soviet Union./ Ships--Folklore./ Soviet Union--Folklore./ Spanish language materials.

398.27 Ph-3 5-6/6 $3.50 P KB766
RANSOME, ARTHUR. Old Peter's Russian tales. Illus. by Faith Jaques. Puffin/Penguin ISBN 0-14-030696-X, 1975. 243p. ill.
Available from National Library Service for the Blind and Physically Handicapped on sound recording cassette RC30848.
Retold "in his own way, writing mostly from memory," these favorite Russian folktales from the great folklorist Afanasev entertain not only Vanya and Maroosia the two children being told the stories but children everywhere. Basic for any story-telling collection.
SUBJ: Folklore--Soviet Union./ Soviet Union--Folklore.

398.27 Ph-2 2-3/4 $14.95 L KB767
RODANAS, KRISTINA. Dragonfly's tale. Retold and illustrated by Kristina Rodanas. Clarion ISBN 0-395-57003-4, 1992. unp col illus.
Two children create a cornstalk toy in a time of famine. Transformed into a dragonfly, the toy restores bountiful harvest to their people. An adaptation of a Zuni story with full-page paintings of the Native Americans and their habitat.
SUBJ: Zuni Indians--Folklore./ Indians of North America--New Mexico--Folklore.

398.27 Ph-2 3-4/5 $15.95 L KB768
RODANAS, KRISTINA. Eagle's song: a tale from the Pacific Northwest. Adapted and illus. by Kristina Rodanas. Little, Brown ISBN 0-316-75375-0; In Canada: Little, Brown, 1995. unp. col. ill.
Ermine lives with his brothers among a people who keep to themselves. When his brothers disappear, the boy is befriended by eagles who teach him to dance and open himself to others. He brings his new found talents to his people and prompts them to dance and

NONFICTION

love each other. A legend which tells of the importance of sharing and loving, this haunting story is suitably illustrated with drawings of the Indians of the Northwest: their dress, houses, and motifs. The animals and birds are equally well drawn. For multicultural studies.
SUBJ: Indians of North America--Northwest, Pacific--Folklore./ Folklore--North America./ North America--Folklore.

398.27   Ph-3 4-5/5 $13.95   L   KB769
ROHMER, HARRIET. Atariba and Niguayona: a story from the Taino people of Puerto Rico. Adapted by Harriet Rohmer and Jesus Guerrero Rea. Revised Spanish version by Rosalma Zubizarreta. Illustrated by Consuelo Mendez. Children's Book Press ISBN 0-89239-026-3, c1976, 1988. 23p. col. ill. (Tales of the Americas).
Includes pronunciation guide and author's note.
Available from National Library Service for the Blind and Physically Handicapped in Braille BR04477 and on sound recording cassette RC17752.
The search for a fruit that will cure his friend takes Niguayona through many dangers and adventures. Boldly colored and designed illustrations add vigor to the straightforward text. Particularly helpful in foreign language, ESL, and social studies classes.
SUBJ: Taino Indians--Folklore./ Indians of the West Indies--Puerto Rico--Folklore./ Bilingual materials--Spanish./ Spanish language materials.

398.27   Ph-2 2-4/2 $13.95   L   KB770
ROHMER, HARRIET. Uncle Nacho's hat: a folktale from Nicaragua/El sombrero de Tio Nacho: un cuento de Nicaragua. Adapted by Harriet Rohmer. Illustrated by Veg Reisberg. Children's Book Press ISBN 0-89239-043-3, 1989. 31p. col. ill.
A humorous tale of an elderly gentleman who has difficulty adjusting to a new hat given to him by his niece. Bright drawings fill the pages which retell this Nicaraguan folktale in both English and Spanish.
SUBJ: Folklore--Nicaragua./ Nicaragua--Folklore./ Hats--Folklore./ Bilingual materials--Spanish./ Spanish language materials.

398.27   Ph-2 2-4/3 $14.89   L   KB771
ROTHENBERG, JOAN. Yettele's feathers. Hyperion ISBN 0-7868-2081-0; In Canada: Little, Brown, 1995. 32p. col. ill.
A widow is taught a lesson about unkind words which she discovers are as difficult to recall as pillow feathers flying about on a windy day. A humorous folktale with an important message.
SUBJ: Jews--Folklore./ Folklore--Europe, Eastern./ Europe, Eastern--Folklore.

398.27   Ph-2 K-2/2 $15.95   L   KB772
SANFIELD, STEVE. Bit by bit. Illus. by Susan Gaber. Philomel ISBN 0-399-22736-9; In Canada: Putnam, 1995. unp. col. ill.
When his favorite coat wears out, Zundel the tailor fashions it into a jacket, then a cap, a pocket, and a button until finally there is nothing left but this story. Based on a Yiddish folksong, the predictable book features a catchy refrain for listeners to repeat. Bright illustrations convey an additional story about Zundel's marriage and growing family.
SUBJ: Clothing and dress--Folklore./ Jews--Folklore.

398.27   Ph-2 2-3/4 $14.99   L   KB773
SANFIELD, STEVE. Strudel, strudel, strudel. Illus. by Emily Lisker. Orchard ISBN 0-531-08729-8, 1995. unp. col. ill.
"Richard Jackson book."
A teacher and his wife in Chelm long for apple strudel which they only eat at special feasts. They decide to save money in a large trunk, so that in the spring they will have all the strudel they want. Discovering that neither one has put coins in the trunk, they argue, become entangled in the trunk, and roll wildly through the town. Lots of fun.
SUBJ: Jews--Folklore./ Chelm (Chelm, Poland)--Folklore./ Folklore--Chelm (Chelm, Poland)./ Folklore--Europe, Eastern./ Europe, Eastern--Folklore.

398.27   Ph-2 1-3/6 $16.95   L   KB774
SAN SOUCI, ROBERT D. Sootface: an Ojibwa Cinderella story. Retold by Robert D. San Souci. Illus. by Daniel San Souci. Doubleday ISBN 0-385-31202-4; In Canada: Bantam Doubleday Dell, 1994. unp. col. ill.
Mistreated by her two sisters, Sootface is an unlikely prospect to wed the mighty warrior who lives across the lake. However, when they visit his wigwam, her sisters fail to see him (he is invisible to most), and Sootface in her forest costume made of birch bark earns his love. A Native American version of Cinderella for multicultural studies.
SUBJ: Ojibwa Indians--Folklore./ Indians of North America--Folklore.

398.27   Ph-1 3-4/6 $14.95   L   KB775
SAN SOUCI, ROBERT D. Sukey and the mermaid. Illus. by Brian Pinkney. Four Winds/Macmillan ISBN 0-02-778141-0; In Canada:

Maxwell Macmillan, 1992. unp. col. ill.
Coretta Scott King honor book.
Available from the National Library Service for the Blind and Physically Handicapped on sound recording cassette RC 43029.
Disheartened by the mistreatment given to her by her stepfather, Sukey slips away to the seashore where she is befriended by a mermaid. This haunting story from the lore of the sea isles off South Carolina will prove that Cinderella tales can take many guises.
SUBJ: Mermaids./ Afro-Americans--Folklore.

398.27   Ph-1 P-3/5 $4.99   P   KB776
SAWYER, RUTH. Journey cake, ho. Illus. by Robert McCloskey. Puffin/Penguin ISBN 0-14-050275-0, c1953, 1989. 45p. col. ill.
Caldecott Honor Book.
A humorous telling of Johnny's pursuit of the journey cake which leads him and several barnyard animals back home to the farm and better times.
SUBJ: Folklore--United States./ United States--Folklore.

398.27   Ph-2 P-1/5 $13.95   T   KB777
SAY, ALLEN. Under the cherry blossom tree: an old Japanese tale. Retold and illus. by Allen Say. Houghton Mifflin ISBN 0-395-84546-7, 1997. 32p. ill.
"Walter Lorraine books."
Originally published as ONCE UNDER THE CHERRY BLOSSOM TREE; AN OLD JAPANESE TALE, Harper & Row, 1974.
When a miserly old man swallows a cherry pit, it settles in the top of his head and grows into a tree. In anger, he pulls the tree from his head, but now a great hole remains. The hole fills with water where boys attempt to fish. While chasing the boys, the miser stumbles and falls. The children soon discover that all that remains of him is a lovely pond in the valley. Intricately detailed woodcuts complement the classic Japanese tale.
SUBJ: Folklore--Japan./ Japan--Folklore.

398.27   Ph-1 2-4/4 $15.95   T   KB778
SHULEVITZ, URI. Treasure. Farrar, Straus & Giroux ISBN 0-374-37740-5; In Canada: McGraw-Hill Ryerson, 1978. unp. col. ill.
Caldecott Honor Book.
Available in Spanish EL TESORO (ISBN 0-374-37422-8, 1992).
Isaac, a poor old man, is told in a dream to go to the capital city and look for a treasure under the bridge by the Royal Palace. After great hardships, he arrives at the city and finds only a jovial captain of the guards, who tells Isaac of his dream of a treasure hidden under the stove in Isaac's house. Finding the treasure where the dream had revealed it would be, Isaac realized "Sometimes one must travel far to discover what is near".
SUBJ: Jews--Folklore./ Dreams--Folklore./ Spanish language materials.

398.27   Ph-3 4-6/6 $11.95   T   KB779
SINGER, ISAAC BASHEVIS. Mazel and Shlimazel; or, The milk of a lioness. Translated from the Yiddish by Isaac Bashevis Singer and Elizabeth Shub. Illus. by Margot Zemach. Farrar, Straus & Giroux ISBN 0-374-34884-7, 1967. 42p. col. ill.
Mazel, good luck, and Shlimazel, bad luck, make a bet one day. Whatever good Mazel can do in a year, Shlimazel will undo in a second, and win a barrel of the wine of forgetfulness. Mazel helps Tam, an impoverished boy, gain the confidence of the king and the love of the princess. But when Tam gets some lioness' milk to cure the ailing king, Shlimazel takes control of Tam's tongue when he presents the milk, and it seems that Shlimazel has won. However, Shlimazel, drunk with the wine, forgets Tam, and Mazel again offers help.
SUBJ: Jews--Folklore./ Good and evil--Folklore.

398.27   Ph-2 2-4/6 $14.99   T   KB780
STANLEY, DIANE. Petrosinella: a Neapolitan Rapunzel. Retold and illus. by Diane Stanley. Dial ISBN 0-8037-1712-1, 1995. unp. col. ill.
An ogress claims a young maiden as her payment for the parsley stolen by her mother and hides her away in a tall tower. A prince rescues her, but it is the ogress' own enchanted acorns which gain freedom for the lovers. In this Italian version of the familiar tale, published 200 years before the German story of "Rapunzel," the heroine plays a more active role in her escape. Good choice for compare and contrast activities.
SUBJ: Fairy tales./ Folklore--Italy./ Italy--Folklore.

SRC 398.27   Ph-3 4-6 $8.95   OD   KB781
TORRENCE, JACKIE. Story lady (Sound recording cassette). Weston Woods WW720C, 1982. 1 sound cassette. (Storytelling circle).
Four stories: "Jack and the Varmints," "Tilly," "Brer Possum's Dilemma," and "Kate the Bell Witch of Tenna" are told with vigor and humor here. Two of the tales are traditional ones (found in numerous collections) while the other two come from Jackie's own explorations.
SUBJ: Folklore--United States./ United States--Folklore.

VCR 398.27 Ph-2 K-3 $29.95 OD KB782
VILLAGE STEW (Videocassette). Signed in American sign language by Billy Seago. Narrated by T.R. Hinkey. Sign-A-Vision/dist. by Modern Signs Press, 1987. 1/2" VHS videocassette color (15min). (Stories from the attic).
Includes teacher/student resource packet.
Also available in signed English, 104SE.
This Scottish version of the folktale, "Stone Soup" is told through American sign language and voice-over narration. The explanation of the meaning of the actions and expressions is included on the tape. Useful for deaf and hearing students.
SUBJ: Folklore--Scotland./ Scotland--Folklore./ Storytelling./ Sign language.

398.27 Ph-2 2-3/2 $14.00 T KB783
WAHL, JAN. Little Eight John. Illus. by Wil Clay. Lodestar/Dutton ISBN 0-525-67367-9; In Canada: McClelland & Stewart, 1992. unp col illus.
Coretta Scott King honor book.
Each time Little Eight John's mother warned him not to do something, he did exactly what she warned against and brought disaster down upon the house. Large drawings of a very human farm family bring life to this tale of a perverse boy.
SUBJ: Folklore--North Carolina./ North Carolina--Folklore./ Afro-Americans--Folklore./ Mothers and sons--Folklore.

398.27 Ph-3 2-3/6 $14.95 T KB784
WANG, ROSALIND C. Magical starfruit tree: a Chinese folktale. Adapted by Rosalind C. Wang. Illus. by Shao Wei Liu. Beyond Words ISBN 0-941831-89-2, 1993. unp. col. ill.
To quench his thirst, an elderly gentleman asks a fruit seller for his smallest starfruit. The miserly peddler refuses, but a young acrobat shares his few coins to buy the fruit and is magically rewarded by the old man. Reteller bases the tale on stories told to her as a child to reinforce Chinese culture and moral values. For multicultural studies.
SUBJ: Folklore--China./ China--Folklore.

398.27 Ph-1 2-4/3 $16.00 T KB785
WELLS, RUTH. Farmer and the Poor God: a folktale from Japan. Retold by Ruth Wells. Illus. by Yoshi. Simon & Schuster ISBN 0-689-80214-5; In Canada: Distican, 1996. unp. col. ill.
A family plans to leave their home and Poor God who lives in their attic. He overhears their plans and begins to make sandals for the trip. His craftsmanship soon provides the family with an income and they prosper. When Rich God threatens to replace Poor God, the family discovers its true happiness and clings to its benefactor. Exquisite paintings done in color dyes on silk create textured illustrations with the appearance of cloth.
SUBJ: Folklore--Japan./ Japan--Folklore.

398.27 Ph-2 1-3/2 $16.00 L KB786
WOLKSTEIN, DIANE. White Wave: a Chinese tale. Rev. ed. Retold by Diane Wolkstein. Illus. by Ed Young. Gulliver/Harcourt Brace ISBN 0-15-200293-6, 1996. unp. ill.
A Chinese farmer finds a lovely snail and takes it home. From that time on, the creature inside the snail cares for him. One day he spies on the snail and sees a moon goddess escape from the shell. His spying prompts the goddess to flee, but she promises to help him when he is in need. He builds a shrine in her memory, but it too has disappeared. All that remains is this story. For multicultural studies.
SUBJ: Folklore--China./ China--Folklore.

398.27 Ph-1 2-4/6 $16.95 L KB787
YEP, LAURENCE. Khan's daughter: a Mongolian folktale. Illus. by Jean and Mou-Sien Tseng. Scholastic ISBN 0-590-48389-7; In Canada: Scholastic, 1997. unp. col. ill.
When Mongke, a poor man's son, is told that one day he will marry a Khan's daughter, he sets out to find her. Fortunately, the daughter is attracted to the country bumpkin and helps him fulfill the tasks assigned him by her parents. The hero of the tale in his simplicity wins the maid who proves that she is clever, but loves him for his respect for her. The watercolor paintings portray the Mongolian countryside and costumes.
SUBJ: Folklore--Mongolia./ Mongolia--Folklore./ Princesses--Folklore.

398.27 Ph-1 5-A/4 $4.50 P KB788
YEP, LAURENCE. Rainbow people. Illus. by David Wiesner. HarperCollins ISBN 0-06-440441-2; In Canada: HarperCollins, c1989, 1991. 194p. ill.
Selectors' Choice, 17th ed.
Some of these twenty folktales gathered from Chinese immigrants carry familiar folkloric themes but others reflect the difficult times they faced in coming to the "Golden Mountain." Expressively retold, they add understanding to cultural heritage and social studies units.
SUBJ: Folklore--China./ China--Folklore.

398.27 Ph-2 1-3/6 $15.95 L KB789
YEP, LAURENCE. Tiger Woman. Illus. by Robert Roth. BridgeWater ISBN 0-8167-3464-X; In Canada: BridgeWater/dist. by Vanwell, 1995. unp. col. ill.
A selfish old woman refuses to share her bean curd with a beggar saying, "I'm a tiger, when I'm famished," and a tiger she becomes. Her stupid remarks whenever she sees food prompt several other transformations. This rollicking account of a greedy old lady will become a favorite for reading aloud.
SUBJ: Folklore--China./ China--Folklore./ Greed--Folklore.

398.27 Ph-2 4-6/3 $13.95 L KB790
YEP, LAURENCE. Tree of dreams: ten tales from the garden of night. Illus. by Isadore Seltzer. BridgeWater ISBN 0-8167-3498-4; In Canada: BridgeWater/dist. by Vanwell, 1995. 93p. col. ill.
A dream is the central focus of each of the ten stories which Yep has retold from the writings of India, Japan, China, Greece, and Senegal. Sources for the tales and comments on some of the scholars who have studied dreams complete the book. A single full-page painting precedes each story. For multicultural studies.
SUBJ: Dreams--Folklore./ Folklore.

398.27 Ph-2 2-3/6 $15.95 T KB791
YOLEN, JANE. Emperor and the kite. Illus. by Ed Young. Philomel ISBN 0-399-21499-2, 1988. unp. col. ill.
Available from National Library Service for the Blind and Physically Handicapped in Braille BR00728.
Forced to play by herself because of her small size, a Chinese princess shows great resourcefulness by rescuing her imprisoned father. This haunting tale proves that smallness is not a handicap. Multiple uses for this Chinese tale on kites and courage.
SUBJ: Folklore--China./ China--Folklore./ Fathers and daughters--Folklore./ Kites--Folklore.

CE 398.27 Ph-3 2-4/4 $17.00 T KB792
ZEMACH, MARGOT. It could always be worse: a Yiddish folk tale. Retold and illustrated by Margot Zemach. Farrar, Straus & Giroux ISBN 0-374-33650-4; In Canada: McGraw-Hill Ryerson, 1976. 32p. col. ill.
Caldecott Honor Book.
Available in Spanish SIEMPRE PUEDE SER PEOR: UN CUENTO FOLKLORICO YIDDISH (ISBN 0-374-36907-0, 1992).
A poor unfortunate man lived with his mother, his wife and his six children in a little one-room hut. Hoping to relieve the crowding, he turned to the Rabbi for advice. "Take into the house your chickens, the goose, the rooster, the cow and the goat" said the Rabbi. Having endured the discomfort produced by these extra animals and birds in the house the man realized when he released them how roomy and peaceful his home really was.
SUBJ: Jews--Folklore./ Spanish language materials.

398.8 Ph-1 P-1/1 $13.95 L KB793
BIG FAT HEN. Illus. by Keith Baker. Harcourt Brace ISBN 0-15-292869-3; In Canada: Harcourt Brace c/o Canadian Manda, 1994. unp. col. ill.
The familiar nursery rhyme "One, two, buckle my shoe" is illustrated with a big fat hen, several of her friends, and all of their chicks. Each doublespread illustration offers items to count; the final illustration includes all of the chicks and their egg shells for ambitious counters. Ideal introduction to counting for young primaries.
SUBJ: Nursery rhymes./ Counting.

398.8 Ph-2 P-3 $6.95 P KB794
CHINESE MOTHER GOOSE RHYMES. Edited by Robert Wyndham. Illus. by Ed Young. Philomel ISBN 0-399-21718-5, c1968, 1989. unp. col. ill.
Includes "List of first lines".
Riddles and rhymes reflect the universality of nursery rhymes in this welcomed reissue. Stunning illustrations are paired with the bilingual text.
SUBJ: Nursery rhymes./ Bilingual materials--Chinese./ Chinese language materials.

398.8 Ph-2 3-5 $14.93 L KB795
COLE, JOANNA. Six sick sheep: 101 tongue twisters. Compiled by Joanna Cole and Stephanie Calmenson. Illus. by Alan Tiegreen. Morrow ISBN 0-688-11140-8; 1993. 64p. ill.
Includes bibliography and index.
An abundance of hilarious tongue twisters guaranteed to evoke gales of laughter.
SUBJ: Tongue twisters.

398.8 Ph-2 P-1 $18.95 T KB796
DE PAOLA, TOMIE. Tomie De Paola's Mother Goose. Putnam ISBN 0-399-21258-2; In Canada: General, 1985. 127p. col. ill.
Includes index of first lines.

Available from National Library Service for the Blind and Physically Handicapped in Braille BR06635.

Well placed drawings filled with children and animals decorate the pages of this abundant collection of Mother Goose rhymes. The book will please nursery and kindergarten children.

Companion volume is FAVORITE NURSERY TALES (ISBN 0-399-21319-8, 1986) (available from National Library Service for the Blind and Physically Handicapped on sound recording cassette RC26369), a well-rounded selection of stories and poems for the nursery and kindergarten child.

SUBJ: Nursery rhymes.

398.8   Ph-1 P-1/1 $15.88   L   KB797
FIVE LITTLE DUCKS: AN OLD RHYME. Illus. by Pamela Paparone. North-South Books ISBN 1-55858-474-9; In Canada: North-South Books, 1995. unp. col. ill.
    Presents the traditional countdown song about five little ducks who disappear one by one until all are gone. Mama Duck calls one last time, and happily, all the ducks come back. Acrylic illustrations expand the story to show Mother Duck busy with various tasks including baking a pie for her reunited family. The predictable book is a pleasant source for sharing the song with children.
    SUBJ: Nursery rhymes./ Ducks--Poetry./ Counting.

398.8   Ph-2 P-1/5 $13.95   L   KB798
GALDONE, PAUL. Three little kittens. Clarion ISBN 0-89919-426-5, 1986. unp. col. ill.
    Available from National Library Service for the Blind and Physically Handicapped in Braille BR07119.
    Describes the misadventures of three active kittens who lose and soil their mittens. Large, action-filled pictures will please young listeners.
    SUBJ: Cats--Folklore./ Nursery rhymes.

398.8   Ph-2 P-2 $14.95   T   KB799
GRANDMOTHER'S NURSERY RHYMES: LULLABIES, TONGUE TWISTERS, AND RIDDLES FROM SOUTH AMERICA/NANAS DE ABUELITA: CANCIONES DE CUNA, TRABALENGUAS Y ADIVINANZAS DE SURAMERICA. Compiled by Nelly Palacio Jaramillo. Illus. by Elivia. Henry Holt ISBN 0-8050-2555-3; In Canada: Fitzhenry & Whiteside, 1994. unp. col. ill.
    A bilingual collection of rhymes, riddles, and lullabies. The South American traditional verses provide an introduction to the Spanish language, making multicultural studies lively.
    SUBJ: Nursery rhymes, Spanish American./ Riddles, Spanish American./ Spanish language materials./ Bilingual materials--Spanish.

398.8   Ph-1 P-1 $23.99   L   KB800
LOBEL, ARNOLD. Arnold Lobel book of Mother Goose. Random House ISBN 0-679-98736-3; In Canada: Random House, 1997. 176p. col. ill.
    Originally published as THE RANDOM HOUSE BOOK OF MOTHER GOOSE, Random House, 1986.
    "Borzoi book."
    Includes index.
    Available from the National Library Service for the Blind and Physically Handicapped, RANDOM HOUSE BOOK OF MOTHER GOOSE, on sound sound recording cassette RC 26342.
    Gathering familiar and unfamiliar Mother Goose rhymes, Arnold Lobel has illustrated a delightful anthology with unique pictures of plump ladies, crying babes, and humorous animals. A standard collection for preschool and kindergarten students.
    SUBJ: Nursery rhymes.

398.8   Ph-3 P-1/2 $14.88   L   KB801
MANSON, CHRISTOPHER. Tree in the wood: an old nursery song. Adapted and illus. by Christopher Manson. North-South Books ISBN 1-55858-193-6; In Canada: North-South Books, 1993. unp. col. ill.
    A simple cumulative rhyme tells how a tree comes from an acorn, a twig on the tree shelters a nest for a bird, the bird produces a feather for a pillow on which a mother and child rest, and the child grows to plant an acorn in the ground--then the cycle begins again. An ecological message for reading aloud. For environmental studies.
    SUBJ: Folk songs./ Nursery rhymes.

398.8   Ph-2 P-2 $13.95   L   KB802
MARTIN, SARAH CATHERINE. Comic adventures of Old Mother Hubbard and her dog. Illus. by Tomie De Paola. Harcourt Brace Jovanovich ISBN 0-15-219541-6, 1981. unp. col. ill.
    This familiar folk rhyme is presented here as if being acted out on a stage with numerous back drops. The old woman constantly attempts to please her poodle with gifts and he constantly turns to a variety of occupations around the house which amuse and surprise the poor woman. Large pictures make this book perfect for picture book hours.
    SUBJ: Nursery rhymes.

398.8   Ph-2 P-K $15.95   L   KB803
MOTHER GOOSE. Glorious Mother Goose. Selected by Cooper Edens. Atheneum ISBN 0-689-31434-5; In Canada: Collier Macmillan, 1988. 88p. col. ill.
    Many of the talented artists of the past who have illustrated Mother Goose rhymes are represented in this book. Single verses are accompanied by two pictures by different artists. Valuable addition to historical collections.
    SUBJ: Nursery rhymes.

398.8   Ph-1 P-1 $19.95   T   KB804
MOTHER GOOSE. Michael Foreman's Mother Goose. Foreword by Iona Opie. Harcourt Brace Jovanovich ISBN 0-15-255820-9, 1991. 157p. col. ill.
    Includes index.
    The perfect book to introduce nursery rhymes! The selection is extensive and the illustrations are whimsical. Includes favorites such as Little Jack Horner and Little Miss Muffet as well as less familiar characters such as Sulky Sue and Billy Button.
    SUBJ: Nursery rhymes.

KIT 398.8   Ph-2 P-K $12.95   KB805
MOTHER GOOSE. Olde Mother Goose (Kit). Performed by the Hubbards. Illus. by Anita Carroll-Welden. August House Audio ISBN 0-87483-213-6, 1993. 1 paperback book, 1 sound cassette (40min).
    Includes lyrics.
    Twenty-one classic nursery rhymes are set to Old English arrangements and accompanied by traditional instruments. Lyrics booklet includes information about the various acoustical instruments heard on the tape such as the bowed psaltery, the melodeon, and the recorder. A fresh rendition of Mother Goose suitable for homes and classrooms. (Parents' Shelf).
    SUBJ: Nursery rhymes./ Songs.

398.8   Ph-2 P-2 $8.95   T   KB806
MOTHER GOOSE. Real Mother Goose. Illus. by Blanche Fisher Wright. Scholastic ISBN 0-590-22517-0; In Canada: Scholastic, c1944, 1994. 128p. col. ill.
    Available from National Library Service for the Blind and Physically Handicapped in Braille BRA08300 and as talking book TB01122.
    Still popular after fifty years, although old-fashioned in appearance, this collection of seventy-some rhymes is just right for both preschool and primary grades.
    SUBJ: Nursery rhymes.

398.8   Ph-1 P-K $16.95   T   KB807
MOTHER GOOSE. Ring o'roses: a nursery rhyme picture book. Illus. by L. Leslie Brooke. Clarion ISBN 0-395-61304-3, 1992. 96p. ill. (some col.).
    Includes index.
    Delightful animals cavort over the quiet, beautiful English countryside in Brooke's illustrations of these favorite Mother Goose rhymes. Originally published in 1922, this is one of the classics of children's literature with an afterword of its history by Neil Philip.
    SUBJ: Nursery rhymes.

398.8   Ph-1 P-K/2 $19.99   T   KB808
MY VERY FIRST MOTHER GOOSE. Edited by Iona Opie. Illus. by Rosemary Wells. Candlewick ISBN 1-56402-620-5; In Canada: Candlewick/dist. by Douglas & McIntyre, 1996. 107p. col. ill.
    An inclusive collection of rhymes gathered by Iona Opie, the expert in the field of children's rhymes and games. Rabbits, pigs, cats, and other critters abound in sprightly watercolor illustrations. A treasure that is sure to become a classic. (Parents' Shelf).
    SUBJ: Nursery rhymes.

398.8   Ph-2 P-K $13.95   T   KB809
OLD MOTHER HUBBARD AND HER WONDERFUL DOG. Illus. by James Marshall. Farrar, Straus & Giroux ISBN 0-374-35621-1; In Canada: HarperCollins, 1991. unp. col. ill.
    A versatile bulldog and a fashionable mistress cavort through all kinds of adventures in this comical version of a familiar rhyme. Children will delight in the array of hats worn by the dog.
    SUBJ: Nursery rhymes.

398.8   Ph-1 K-2 $13.95   L   KB810
PETERSHAM, MAUD. Rooster crows: a book of American rhymes and jingles. Compiled and illustrated by Maud and Miska Petersham. Macmillan ISBN 0-02-773100-6, c1945. unp. col. ill.
    Caldecott Medal Award.
    Available from National Library Service for the Blind and Physically Handicapped in Braille BRA04368 and on sound recording cassette RC21585.
    A wide and varied collection of favorite American rhymes is

delightedly illustrated in this book. Nursery rhymes are supplemented by finger games, rope skipping rhymes and games. Truly this book is "An American Mother Goose."
SUBJ: Nursery rhymes./ Folklore--United States./ Finger play./ United States--Folklore.

398.8 Ph-2 P-2 $11.99 T KB811
REAL MOTHER GOOSE BOOK OF AMERICAN RHYMES. Selected by Debby Slier. Illus. by Patty McCloskey-Padgett, Bernice Loewenstein, Nan Pollard. Scholastic ISBN 0-590-50955-1; In Canada: Scholastic, 1993. 124p. col. ill.
"Cartwheel books."
Includes indexes.
A very complete collection of nursery rhymes and poems from the American oral tradition. The rhymes can be accessed by the indexes to first lines, titles, and poets.
SUBJ: Nursery rhymes./ Poetry--Collections.

398.8 Ph-1 2-6 $14.95 T KB812
REES, ENNIS. Fast Freddie Frog and other tongue-twister rhymes. Illus. by John O'Brien. Caroline House/Boyds Mills ISBN 1-56397-038-4, 1993. unp. col. ill.
An enchanting combination of maddening tongue twisters, tongue-twister rhymes, and hilarious illustrations. Great fun for reading aloud.
SUBJ: Tongue twisters.

398.8 Ph-2 P-K/2 $19.95 T KB813
RING-A-RING O' ROSES AND A DING, DONG, BELL: A BOOK OF NURSERY RHYMES. Selected and illus. by Alan Marks. North-South ISBN 1-55858-363-7; In Canada: North-South/dist. by Vanwell, 1991. 97p. col. ill.
"Michael Neugebauer book."
Includes index.
Extensive collection of classic nursery rhymes with watercolor illustratons to amuse the reader or listener presents familiar rhymes, and some not so familiar ones, in an attractive package. (Parents' Shelf).
SUBJ: Nursery rhymes.

398.8 Ph-1 P-2/2 $15.95 L KB814
ROSEN, MICHAEL. We're going on a bear hunt. Illus. by Helen Oxenbury. McElderry ISBN 0-689-50476-4, 1989. unp. col. ill.
Selectors' Choice, 18th ed.
Available from the National Library Service for the Blind and Physically Handicapped on sound recording cassette RC34744.
Available in Spanish, VAMOS A CAZAR UN OSO (Ekare ISBN 980-257-106-7, n.d.).
Setting out to find a bear, a father, his four children and the family dog go through a field, river, forest, and a cave before they come upon their prey. Wonderfully active, oversized illustrations and scrumptious onamatapoeic words make this edition of the traditional story in rhyme a delight to share with a group. Beginning readers can have fun with it also.
SUBJ: Nursery rhymes./ Spanish language materials./ Stories in rhyme.

398.8 Ph-2 P-K $5.95 P KB815
SENDAK, MAURICE. Hector Protector and As I went over the water: two nursery rhymes with pictures. HarperCollins ISBN 0-06-443237-8, c1965, 1990. unp. col. ill.
Two short nursery rhymes are so expansively and creatively illustrated that they assume new dimensions. To share with a group.
SUBJ: Nursery rhymes.

398.8 Ph-1 1-3 $14.95 L KB816
TORTILLITAS PARA MAMA AND OTHER SPANISH NURSERY RHYMES. Selected and translated by Margot C. Griego, et al. Illus. by Barbara Cooney. Henry Holt ISBN 0-8050-0285-5; In Canada: Fitzhenry & Whiteside, 1981. unp. col. ill.
All the rhymes and lullabies collected here have come from the Spanish communities in America. The book has a two-fold purpose--to preserve the material and to introduce others to its charm and beauty. Handsomely illustrated with full page drawings filled with bright golds, browns and blues.
(The title of the second rhyme sould be "Rima de la hermana vistiendose".).
SUBJ: Nursery rhymes, Spanish American./ Bilingual materials--Spanish./ Spanish language materials.

398.8 Ph-2 P-K/2 $7.95 T KB817
VAN RYNBACH, IRIS. Five little pumpkins. Boyds Mills/dist. by St. Martins ISBN 1-56397-452-5; In Canada: McClelland & Stewart, 1995. unp. col. ill.
Sprightly drawings in autumn colors show the five little pumpkins

described in the familiar finger rhyme. The predictable book will be a welcome addition to holiday collections.
SUBJ: Nursery rhymes./ Finger play./ Halloween--Poetry.

398.8 Ph-2 P-1 $13.95 L KB818
WESTCOTT, NADINE BERNARD. Lady with the alligator purse. Joy Street/Little, Brown ISBN 0-316-93135-7; In Canada: Little, Brown, 1988. unp. col. ill.
When all else fails, call the lady with the alligator purse! Zany drawings show the lady coming to the rescue and will delight youngsters as much as the verse.
SUBJ: Nonsense verses./ Jump rope rhymes.

411 Ph-1 2-4 $13.95 L KB819
BROWN, RUTH. Alphabet times four: an international ABC: English, Spanish, French, German. Dutton ISBN 0-525-44831-4, 1991. unp. col. ill.
A lavishly illustrated alphabet book for older readers provides an introduction to languages. Each letter of the alphabet is represented by a framed detailed painting below which the name of an object is written in English, Spanish, French, and German. Readers can easily compare words in the four languages and see common roots as well as words that are identical in each language such as the Maori term, kiwi. A simple pronunciation guide on each page assists with saying the words aloud. For multicultural studies and language arts.
SUBJ: Alphabet./ Spanish language materials./ French language materials./ German language materials./ Polyglot materials.

419 Ph-1 K-A $14.95 T KB820
ANCONA, GEORGE. Handtalk zoo. By George Ancona and Mary Beth Miller. Four Winds ISBN 0-02-700801-0; In Canada: Maxwell Macmillan, 1989. unp. col. ill.
Kids at the zoo learn both American Sign Language and finger spelling for the names of the animals. This continues the lessons from Charlip's HANDTALK in an entertaining fashion.
SUBJ: Zoo animals./ Deaf./ Sign language.

419 Ph-3 K-3 $14.95 T KB821
BAKER, PAMELA J. My first book of sign. Illus. by Patricia Bellan Gillen. Kendall Green/Gallaudet University Press ISBN 0-930323-20-3, c1986, 1995. 76p. col. ill.
Includes glossary and index.
Bright illustrations depict 150 common words with their corresponding symbols in American Sign Language. The fingerspelling symbol for each letter of the alphabet is shown along with upper and lower case letters. Includes a discussion of fingerspelling and general rules for signing. (Parents' Shelf).
SUBJ: Sign language--Dictionaries./ Picture dictionaries.

VCR 419 Ph-1 3-A $599.40 OD KB822
BEGINNING AMERICAN SIGN LANGUAGE VIDEOCOURSE (Videocassette). Sign Enhancers, Inc., 1991. 15 1/2" VHS videocassettes color.
Learn American Sign Language with the fictional Bravo family as they watch television, shop, and go to school, the doctor, and the bank. Each episode opens with new vocabulary and closes with grammatical information and practice sessions with sentences and stories. The lessons are well presented and enhanced with humor and with cultural notes on the hearing impaired community. Can be used with both hearing impaired and hearing students.
Meet the Bravo family: morning routine signs (40min); Breakfast with the Bravos: breakfast & dining signs (40min); Where's the TV remote?: household signs (30min); Let's go food shopping!: food signs (40min); Review and practice session: lessons 1-4 (60min); Any good fingers lately?: colors & fingerspelling (35min); School daze: school related signs (40min); School daze, the sequel: school related signs (45min); Dollar signs: money & banking signs (50min); Review & practice session: lessons 6-9 (60min); Playing in the park: nature & sports signs (45min); Doctor is in?: medical signs (45min); Business as Unusual: work related signs (45min); Lets go clothes shopping!: clothing signs (40min); Review & practice session: lessons 11-14 (65min).
SUBJ: Sign language--Study and teaching./ Deaf--Means of communication./ Video recordings for the hearing impaired.

419 Ph-1 K-A $15.95 T KB823
CHARLIP, REMY. Handtalk: an ABC of finger spelling and sign language. By Remy Charlip and Mary Beth Miller. Illustrated by George Ancona. Four Winds/Macmillan ISBN 0-02-718130-8; In Canada: Collier Macmillan, c1974, 1984. unp col illus.
Explains two methods that deaf people use to talk: finger spelling - where each word is spelled out letter by letter with the fingers, and signing - where an entire word or idea is covered by making a picture or sign with one or both hands. Begins with the alphabet in finger

signs followed by a double-page spread for each letter which includes finger signs and words beginning with the letter spelled out in sign for translating. The exaggerated expressions of the models for the excellent color photographs further communicate the meanings of finger spelling and signing. A 20" x 14" color poster featuring the alphabet and finger spelling chart is included in each library edition.
SUBJ: Sign language./ Alphabet.

419   Ph-1 K-3 $15.95   L   KB824
CHARLIP, REMY. Handtalk birthday: a number and story book in sign language. By Remy Charlip, Mary Beth Miller, and George Ancona. Four Winds/Macmillan ISBN 0-02-718080-8; In Canada: Collier Macmillan, 1987. unp. col. ill.
Mary Beth is surprised by friends on her birthday, tries to guess what her gifts are, and makes a birthday wish all with sign language and finger spelling. Color photographs show an expressive Mary Beth and her friends communicating the surprise and fun of a birthday using the language of the deaf.
SUBJ: Sign language./ Deaf./ Birthdays.

419   Ph-2 5-A/9 $10.90   L   KB825
GREENE, LAURA. Sign language talk. By Laura Greene and Eva Barash Dicker. Watts ISBN 0-531-10597-0; In Canada: Watts, 1989. 95p b&w illus. (First book).
Includes index.
Describes American Sign Language, and how the parts of sign formation signal distinctions between words and how the structure of the language differs from English. Helpful diagrams and well displayed text detail the language.
SUBJ: Sign language./ Deaf./ Physically handicapped.

419   Ph-2 4-A/5 $17.71   L   KB826
LIPTAK, KAREN. North American Indian sign language. Illustrated by Don Berry. Watts ISBN 0-531-10869-4, 1990. 64p. col. ill. (First book).
Includes bibliography and index.
American Indians used sign language to communicate silently while hunting or with other tribes who spoke different languages. This easy-to-use guide provides background information, plus the signs for more than 100 words and simple sentences. Useful for units on language and American Indians.
SUBJ: Indians of North America--Sign language./ Indians of North America--Social life and customs.

419   Ph-1 K-A $14.95   L   KB827
MILLER, MARY BETH. Handtalk school. By Mary Beth Miller and George Ancona. Photos by George Ancona. Four Winds ISBN 0-02-700912-2; In Canada: Maxwell Macmillan, 1991. unp. col. ill.
Includes directory.
Appealing full-color photographs show the daily activities of a group of students at a residential school for the deaf as they prepare for a Thanksgiving Day play. Text is presented in both print and American Sign Language (ASL). A positive presentation of children who are hearing impaired as well as an introduction to ASL. Directory of schools for the deaf is appended.
SUBJ: Sign language./ Deaf.

VCR 419   Ph-2 3-5 $14.95   OD KB828
PARKER, DAVID. Sign for friends (Videocassette). Yellin Tabor Visual Productions, 1991. 1/2" VHS videocassette color (33min).
David Parker employs humor, music and repetition to teach a young class how to sign. An entertaining overview rather than a practical lesson in signing.
SUBJ: Sign language.

419   Ph-1 K-3 $14.00   T   KB829
RANKIN, LAURA. Handmade alphabet. Dial ISBN 0-8037-0974-9, 1991. unp. col. ill.
Selectors' Choice, 19th ed.
Distinctive colored pencil drawings eloquently portray the manual alphabet used in American Sign Language. Hands of various people of many ages and races form the shape of each letter, and an object whose name begins with the letter is imaginatively incorporated into each illustration. Visually appealing, artistic introduction to a fascinating form of communication.
SUBJ: Alphabet./ Sign language./ Deaf.

421   Ph-1 K-2 $15.99   T   KB830
BENDER, ROBERT. A to Z beastly jamboree. Dutton/Lodestar ISBN 0-525-67520-5; In Canada: McClelland & Stewart, 1996. unp. col. ill.
Selectors' Choice, 21st ed.
Two-word sentences describe the action as the letters of the alphabet are engaged in a series of animal antics. Turtles tickle, iguanas illuminate, and yaks yank. Energetic illustrations capture the details including a nose-to-tail menagerie that forms a border around each

scene. Bright, luminous colors combine with more subdued tones of gray and brown for a dazzling effect. Beginning readers who have mastered letter recognition will pore over this lively romp.
SUBJ: Alphabet./ Animals./ English language--Verb.

421   Ph-1 2-6 $14.95   L   KB831
HEPWORTH, CATHERINE. ANTics!: an alphabetical anthology. Putnam ISBN 0-399-21862-9; In Canada: Putnam, 1992. unp. col. ill.
An imaginative combination of wordplay and art presents 26 alphabetical portraits of ants, each representing a word which contains "ant" in its letters. Off-beat illustrations depict the personalities of such ants as ObservANT, EnchANTer, and ANTique. Colored pencil drawings are filled with whimsical details. This alphabet for older readers offers fANTastic fun for creative writing and vocabulary enrichment.
SUBJ: Alphabet./ Word games.

421   Ph-2 2-4/2 $17.95   T   KB832
PELLETIER, DAVID. Graphic alphabet. Orchard ISBN 0-531-36001-6, 1996. unp. col. ill.
Caldecott Honor book, 1997.
Bold colors and spare lines portray the letters of the alphabet. Single word clues give the context for the portrait, the design of which, in many instances, is at a dramatic angle. A sophisticated presentation for children who have already mastered letter recognition, this has potential for art activities.
SUBJ: Alphabet./ Graphic arts.

423   Ph-2 1-2 $14.00   T   KB833
CAT IN THE HAT BEGINNER BOOK DICTIONARY. By the Cat himself and P.D. Eastman. Beginner Books/Random House ISBN 0-394-81009-0, c1964, 1984. 133p. col. ill. (Beginner books).
An illustrated storybook which explains word meaning through pictures and sentences.
SUBJ: English language--Dictionaries.

423   Ph-1 K-2 $12.95   L   KB834
MACMILLAN FIRST DICTIONARY. Edited by Judith S. Levey. Macmillan ISBN 0-02-761731-9, 1990. 402p. col. ill.
"How words came to be" p. vi-ix.
"How writing came to be" p. x-xiii.
"How to use your dictionary": p. xiv.
A revised and expanded edition of MACMILLAN VERY FIRST DICTIONARY.
Alphabetical list of over 2100 common words defined through a series of sentences in more direct and specific entries than usually found in dictionaries for this age level. Attractive photographs, drawings and collages are used in tandem with some of the sample sentences.
SUBJ: English language--Dictionaries.

423   Ph-2 P-2 $16.95   T   KB835
ROOT, BETTY. My first dictionary. Illus. by Jonathan Langley. DK Publishing ISBN 1-56458-277-9, 1993. 96p. col. ill.
Includes index.
The everyday language of children is presented with concise definitions and bright photographs and detailed drawings which provide attractive visual clues. The majority of the entries are familiar concrete objects, while others successfully describe abstract concepts such as equal, new, and same or actions such as mix, pull, and play. Suggested dictionary games encourage vocabulary development and dictionary skills. Useful for point-and-say activities with preschoolers, beginning readers, and ESL students. (Parents' Shelf)
SUBJ: English language--Dictionaries./ Vocabulary.

423   Ph-1 2-4 $17.95   T   KB836
SCOTT FORESMAN BEGINNING DICTIONARY. By E.L. Thorndike and Clarence A. Barnhart. Scott Foresman ISBN 0-673-12387-1, c1983, 1994. 770p. ill. (some col.).
Includes section "How to use this dictionary" pp7-62.
First published in 1945 under title: THORNDIKE CENTURY BEGINNING DICTIONARY; 1952-1974 ed. published under title: THORNDIKE-BARNHART BEGINNING DICTIONARY.
Includes pronunciation, syllabication, definition, examples of the word used in sentences, and parts of speech for each of over 21,000 entries. Introduction presents 24 lessons on reading a citation, alphabetizing, finding plurals as well as using guide words and the pronunciation key. Answers are included in the back of the dictionary.
SUBJ: English language--Dictionaries.

423   Ph-1 4-6 $15.95   T   KB837
WEBSTER'S INTERMEDIATE DICTIONARY: A NEW SCHOOL DICTIONARY. Merriam ISBN 0-87779-479-0, c1977, 1994. 960p. ill.
Provides definition, pronunciation, etymology and part of speech for

more than 65,000 entries. A "using the dictionary" section precedes the main body.
SUBJ: English language--Dictionaries.

423   Ph-1 3-5 $16.95   T   KB838
WEBSTER'S NEW WORLD CHILDREN'S DICTIONARY. New ed. Victoria Neufeldt, editor in chief; Fernando de Mello Vianna, project editor. Runner's World ISBN 0-02-861888-2; In Canada: Webster's New World/dist. by H. B. Fenn, 1997. 896p. col. ill., maps.
Entries for 33,000 words commonly used by elementary students are indexed. Vocabulary was selected from words used in textbooks as well as those used by students in compositions. Lists all the countries of the world, United States state capitals, and major world cities. Compound words, abbreviations, prefixes, suffixes, and contractions are all given main-entry status. Appendix provides a wealth of information for reports including maps, United States' presidents, and state flowers and birds. Colorful illustrations and photographs augment the text of this appealing, accessible dictionary.
SUBJ: English language--Dictionaries.

423   Ph-2 P-2 $12.95   T   KB839
WILKES, ANGELA. My first word book. DK Publishing ISBN 1-879431-21-1, 1991. 64p. col. ill.
Available in Spanish MI PRIMER LIBRO DE PALABRAS EN ESPANOL (ISBN 1-56458-262-0, 1993). Limited by lack of pronunciation guides and English translations.
Available in French MON PREMIER LIVRE DE MOTS EN FRANCAIS (ISBN 1-56458-261-2, 1993). Limited by lack of pronunciation guides and English translations.
Crisp photographs and drawings create a bountiful catalog of a child's world. Items are grouped by type and include familiar objects such as food, toys, clothing, and animals as well as concepts such as colors, size, shape, and opposites. Access to individual pictures is also available through an index. Though primarily for use by individuals, the large clearly labeled photographs are suitable to use with groups. Good point-and-say dictionary for developing vocabulary with preschoolers, new readers, and ESL students. (Parents' Shelf).
SUBJ: Vocabulary.

423   Ph-1 3-5 $31.00   P OD KB840
WORLD BOOK STUDENT DICTIONARY. REV. ED. World Book ISBN 0-7166-1595-9, 1995. 900p. col. ill.
Includes 16 pages of student exercises.
Highly readable type and frequent color illustrations provide easy access to 30,000 entries. Brief definitions, phonetic pronunciation, speech part, plural form and example of use are included. The reference section provides listings of geographic, political, and measurement data.
SUBJ: English language--Dictionaries.

423.1   Ph-2 3-5 $16.00   T   KB841
HBJ STUDENT THESAURUS. Harcourt Brace Jovanovich ISBN 0-15-200186-7; In Canada: Harcourt Brace c/o of Canadian Manda, 1994. 312p. col. ill.
Includes index.
A basic thesaurus for young writers. Alphabetical entries give definitions, name parts of speech, and list synonyms from familiar words to more specific terms. Synonyms are defined in the context of example sentences. Antonyms are listed but not defined. Simple entries to complement other more formal representations in reference books.
SUBJ: English language--Synonyms and antonyms.

423.1   Ph-3 5-A $14.95   T   KB842
YOUNG, SUE. Scholastic rhyming dictionary. Scholastic ISBN 0-590-49460-0; In Canada: Scholastic, 1994. 213p. ill.
"Scholastic Reference."
Includes index.
Introduces the concepts of perfect rhyme, imperfect rhyme, and slant rhyme then presents an extensive alphabetical list of rhyming sounds. Index provides easy access to over 15,000 words and their rhyming patterns. Fun resource for creative writing classes. Unfortunately, the textbook-like appearance may limit appeal.
SUBJ: English language--Rhyme--Dictionaries.

428   Ph-2 1-3 $11.95   T   KB843
KAHN, MICHELE. Mi libro de palabras Inglesas de todos los dias. Translated by Michael Mahler. Illustrated by Benvenuti. Barrons ISBN 0-8120-5431-8, 1982. 41p. col. ill.
Includes index.
An attractive colorfully illustrated introduction to English vocabulary for Spanish-speaking children, featuring 28 groups of things, activities and experiences common to children. The index doubles as a brief dictionary.
SUBJ: Bilingual materials--Spanish./ English language--Vocabulary.

428   Ph-2 P-1 $12.95   T   KB844
MCMILLAN, BRUCE. Dry or wet? Lothrop, Lee & Shepard ISBN 0-688-07100-7, 1988. 29p. col. ill.
Photographs of a variety of children in a range of settings show different ways of being wet and dry. A start for creative activities as well as an excellent guide to an important concept.
SUBJ: English language--Synonyms and antonyms--Pictorial works.

428.1   Ph-1 K-2/3 $15.95   L   KB845
GREENWAY, SHIRLEY. Two's company. Photos by Oxford Scientific Films. Charlesbridge ISBN 0-8810-6963-9, 1997. unp. col. ill.
Sharply focused, full-color photographs of groups of animals depict collective nouns. Familiar animals introduce such unfamiliar terms as shoal, skulk, and pod and appear in photographs large enough for storytimes. Concluding paragraphs include interesting facts about each animal and give their scientific names.
SUBJ: English language--Collective nouns./ English language--Terms and phrases./ Animals.

428.1   Ph-2 P-3 $13.95   T   KB846
HELLER, RUTH. Cache of jewels and other collective nouns. Grosset & Dunlap ISBN 0-448-19211-X, c1987, 1989. unp. col. ill.
Brightly colored illustrations and brief phrases convey the names for twenty-eight groups of things. The concluding author's note explains that "one collective noun can describe many groups...and...one group can be described by more than one collective noun." Can be used in picture book hours.
SUBJ: English language--Collective nouns.

428.1   Ph-1 P-1 $12.88   L   KB847
HOBAN, TANA. Exactly the opposite. Greenwillow ISBN 0-688-08862-7, 1990. unp. col. ill.
Tana Hoban's camera captures fourteen pairs of opposites, all wide open for interpretation and discussion, in this wordless pictorial of familiar scenes.
SUBJ: English language--Synonyms and antonyms.

428.1   Ph-2 P-3/3 $14.95   L   KB848
MAESTRO, BETSY. All aboard overnight: a book of compound words. Illus. by Giulio Maestro. Clarion ISBN 0-395-51120-8, 1992. 32p. col. ill.
Introduces the concept of compound words in the context of a train trip. Examples of compound words appear in boldface type in the text while others are found only in the illustrations. Useful for language arts as well as for transportation units.
SUBJ: English language--Compound words.

428.1   Ph-1 P $13.95   L   KB849
ROCKWELL, ANNE F. What we like. By Anne Rockwell. Macmillan ISBN 0-02-777274-8; In Canada: Maxwell Macmillan, 1992. 24p. col. ill.
Rockwell uses familiar settings to convey concepts such as the five senses, things to wear, and things to make. Clear, attractive layout of colorful illustrations makes this accessible to the youngest readers. Use with groups or with individuals.
SUBJ: Vocabulary.

428.1   Ph-2 3-6/6 $13.95   T   KB850
TERBAN, MARVIN. Superdupers! really funny real words. Illus. by Giulio Maestro. Clarion ISBN 0-89919-804-X, 1989. 63p. col. ill.
Includes bibliography and index.
Kowtow, wingding, fuddy-duddy and harum-scarum are among the 100 specially made up words that are fun to hear. The origins of the words are combined with comedic illustrations which make the work fun for a book talk as well as an effective means to enliven vocabulary lessons.
SUBJ: Vocabulary./ Play on words./ English language--Etymology.

428.2   Ph-2 1-3 $13.95   L   KB851
HELLER, RUTH. Many luscious lollipops: a book about adjectives. Grosset & Dunlap ISBN 0-448-03151-5; In Canada: Putnam, 1989. unp. col. ill.
Rhymed couplets describe different uses and types of adjectives. The large bright illustrations allow the book to be read aloud and shared with a group as a part of language arts studies.
SUBJ: English language--Adjectives.

428.2   Ph-2 1-3 $13.95   T   KB852
HELLER, RUTH. Up, up and away: a book about adverbs. Grosset & Dunlap ISBN 0-448-40249-1, 1991. unp. col. ill.
Vibrant watercolor illustrations and catchy rhyming text introduce the concept of adverbs. The meaning of such words as superlatives and irregular adverbs are clear from the context as well as the large captivating drawings. An English lesson on parts of speech in a fun-to-read format.
SUBJ: English language--Adverb.

428.2 Ph-2 P-1 $13.88 L KB853
HOBAN, TANA. All about where. Greenwillow ISBN 0-688-09698-0, 1991. unp. col. ill.
Bright photos serve as a springboard for choosing and understanding prepositions. Word lists (above, behind, under, etc.) are visible from all the pages.
SUBJ: English language--Prepositions.

428.2 Ph-2 K-2/2 $16.00 T KB854
ROTNER, SHELLEY. Action alphabet. Atheneum ISBN 0-689-80086-X; In Canada: Distican, 1996. unp. col. ill.
Crisp, full-color photographs capture children in motion while oversized white block letters name the physical activity. Introduces action words to students who have already mastered letter recognition. Use for creative writing activities and in language arts units on verbs. Compare and contrast with another alphabet book of verbs--ADD IT, DIP IT, FIX IT.
SUBJ: English language--Verb./ Alphabet.

428.2 Ph-2 K-2/2 $13.95 L KB855
SCHNEIDER, R. M. Add it, dip it, fix it: a book of verbs. Houghton Mifflin ISBN 0-395-72771-5, 1995. unp. col. ill.
A playful jaunt through the alphabet introduces action verbs. Colorful cut-paper collages dramatically depict such terms as kick, sew, and unlock. For students who have mastered letter recognition and who understand abstract concepts, this has potential for creative writing and art activities. Compare and contrast with another alphabet book of verbs--ACTION ALPHABET.
SUBJ: English language--Verb./ Alphabet.

428.2 Ph-2 5-A $10.95 T KB856
TERBAN, MARVIN. Checking your grammar. Scholastic ISBN 0-590-49454-6; In Canada: Scholastic, 1993. 144p. ill. (Scholastic guides).
"Scholastic Reference."
Includes index.
Concise grammar guide covers sentence structure, parts of speech, and style and usage including rules for spelling, punctuation, and capitalization. Also defines use of troublesome words such as affect and effect, further and farther, immigrate and emigrate. Clear examples are provided, and highlighted boxes display important information, exceptions to rules, notes on usage, and helpful tips. Textbook-like appearance may limit the appeal of this thorough and useful guide.
SUBJ: English language--Grammar./ English language--Usage.

463 Ph-3 K-2/2 $15.95 L KB857
EMBERLEY, REBECCA. Let's go: a book in two languages./Vamos: un libro en dos lenguas. Little, Brown ISBN 0-316-23454-0; In Canada: Little, Brown, 1993. unp. col. ill.
Doublespreads of brightly colored, cut-paper collages labeled in English and Spanish present a series of fun places to go--the beach, the circus, the aquarium, the art museum, etc. Simple, repetitive bilingual text describes each scene. Appealing format for beginning readers of either language and a springboard for creative writing or art activities about "how I spent my summer vacation."
Unfortunately, no pronunciation guide is provided.
SUBJ: Vocabulary./ Spanish language materials./ Bilingual materials--Spanish./ Vacations.

463 Ph-3 K-2 $15.95 T KB858
EMBERLEY, REBECCA. My house: a book in two languages/Mi Casa: un libro en dos lenguas. Little, Brown ISBN 0-316-23637-3; In Canada: Little, Brown, 1990. unp col illus.
Collage illustrations, labels, and simple sentences describe the parts and rooms of a house in both English and Spanish. The companion title TAKING A WALK/CAMINANDO (ISBN 0-316-23471-0, 1994) follows the same format and describes a variety of items, buildings and structures seen in a city. Unfortunately there is no pronunciation guide.
SUBJ: Dwellings./ Vocabulary./ Bilingual materials--Spanish./ Spanish language materials.

463 Ph-1 3-A $5.95 P KB859
LIPTON, GLADYS C. Beginning Spanish bilingual dictionary: a beginner's guide in words and pictures. 2nd rev. ed. By Gladys C. Lipton and Olivia Munoz. Barron's ISBN 0-8120-4274-3, 1989. 405p b&w illus.
For each of the 1300+ words in Spanish and/or English, gives phonemic transcription, part of speech, definition, use of word in a sentence and translation of sentence. Verbs are conjugated in the present tense, vocabulary is beginning level for FLES programs, and illustrations are included. A fine dictionary for FLES and bilingual programs.
SUBJ: Spanish language--Dictionaries--English./ English language--Dictionaries--Spanish.

463 Ph-3 4-6 $7.95 P KB860
PARNWELL, E. C. Oxford picture dictionary of American English. English/Spanish ed. Illustrated by Bernard Case, Corinne Clarke, and Ray Burrows. Oxford ISBN 0-19-502333-1, c1978, 1988. 77p. col. ill.
Includes index.
Each page features detailed pictures of common objects, persons, places and/or activities. The items in the pictures are numbered and a key at the bottom of each page provides both the Spanish and the English term for each item. Indexes for both Spanish and English allow the reader to go from the term to the picture if desired. Useful for students of either language.
SUBJ: English language--Vocabulary./ Bilingual materials--Spanish./ Spanish language--Vocabulary.

468 Ph-2 1-3 $10.95 T KB861
KAHN, MICHELE. My everyday Spanish word book. Translated by Michael Mahler and Gwen Marsh. Illus. by Benvenuti. Barron's ISBN 0-8120-5429-6, 1982. 41p. col. ill.
Includes index.
An attractive colorfully illustrated introduction to Spanish vocabulary for 28 groups of things, activities and experiences common to children. The index doubles as a brief dictionary showing noun gender and meanings.
SUBJ: Spanish language--Vocabulary./ Bilingual materials--Spanish.

468.1 Ph-2 K-2/3 $14.95 T KB862
ELYA, SUSAN MIDDLETON. Say hola to Spanish. Illus. by Loretta Lopez. Lee & Low ISBN 1-880000-29-6, 1996. unp. col. ill.
Includes glossary.
Over 70 basic Spanish words are introduced in rhyming text. A Southwestern theme is carried throughout the boldly colored gouache and colored pencil illustrations which provide visual clues. Singsong sentences and zany cartoon drawings create a lively language lesson. Fun for both Spanish speaking and English speaking students.
SUBJ: Spanish language--Vocabulary./ Bilingual materials--Spanish./ Stories in rhyme.

491.7 Ph-3 4-6 $11.95 T KB863
AMERY, HEATHER. First thousand words in Russian. By Heather Amery and Katrina Kirilenko. Illustrated by Stephen Cartwright. Usborne/EDC ISBN 0-86020-769-2, 1983. 63p. col. ill. (First picture word book).
Includes pronunciation guide.
Containing explanations, phonetic pronunciations, and illustrations, this introduction to Russian will captivate children interested in the language. The pages are very cluttered and the "index," although it gives the English equivalent of the Russian words (which are not found in the text), lacks page references.
SUBJ: Russian language--Vocabulary./ Bilingual materials--Russian.

492.4 Ph-3 1-3 $15.00 T KB864
EDWARDS, MICHELLE. Alef-bet: a Hebrew alphabet book. Lothrop, Lee & Shepard ISBN 0-688-09724-3, 1992. unp. col. ill.
Introduces the modern Hebrew alphabet as it depicts the everyday activities of a loving family. Each page features a word and letter of the Hebrew alphabet and shows the Hebrew characters with their pronunciations and their transliteration into Roman letters. Boldly colored, humorous illustrations convey the interactions of the three siblings including a toddler, preschooler, and a nine-year-old boy who was born with spina bifida and uses a wheelchair. For language units as well as multicultural studies.
SUBJ: Hebrew language--Alphabet./ Alphabet.

493 Ph-3 5-A/7 $15.89 L KB865
GIBLIN, JAMES CROSS. Riddle of the Rosetta Stone: key to ancient Egypt. Crowell/HarperCollins ISBN 0-690-04799-1; In Canada: HarperCollins, 1990. 85p. ill.
Includes bibliography and index.
Available from the National Library Service for the Blind and Physically Handicapped on sound recording cassette RC35382.
Egyptian history was a mystery until the Rosetta Stone was found and deciphered. This is the story of the painstaking process of deciphering the hieroglyphics. For advanced students who are intrigued by ancient history or codes and ciphers.
SUBJ: Rosetta stone./ Egyptian language--Writing, Hieroglyphic.

493 Ph-3 5-6/9 $13.95 T KB866
KATAN, NORMA JEAN. Hieroglyphs, the writing of ancient Egypt. By Norma Jean Katan with Barbara Mintz. Atheneum ISBN 0-689-50176-5; In Canada: Collier Macmillan, 1981. 96p. ill.
Includes index.
Text and numerous photographs and drawings show where and how hieroglyphs were used as well as their origins and meanings.
SUBJ: Egyptian language--Writing, Hieroglyphic./ Hieroglyphics.

VCR 500 Ph-3 1-6 $68.95 OD KB867
HENDERSON AVENUE BUG PATROL (Videocassette). Media Projects
ISBN 1-880898-03-9, 1984. 1/2" VHS videocassette color (15min).
A group of young friends are enticed away from video games and
into exploring backyards and alley ways. With the help of a
knowledgeable adult, the children discover the just-out-of-sight worlds
of bees, birds, ants and slugs. A few scenes are highlighted by
animation, such as laying of wood lice eggs. This is not an in-depth
nature study, but an informal backyard field trip that will nurture
curiosity.
SUBJ: Insects./ Birds./ Urban ecology (Biology).

500 Ph-3 3-6/7 $7.95 P KB868
MYERS, JACK. What makes popcorn pop?: and other questions about
the world around us. Boyds Mills ISBN 1-56397-402-9, c1991, 1994.
64p. col. ill.
Includes index.
Questions from HIGHLIGHTS FOR CHILDREN refer to daily
phenomena such as: Why does the sun follow me when I'm riding in
a car? Why is my hair darker wet than it is dry? Text is clearly
written; illustrations are large and colorful. Not organized for
research, but good for leisure reading and excellent for reading aloud
five minutes before the bell. Encourages curiosity and could lead to
further investigations.
SUBJ: Science--Miscellanea./ Questions and answers.

VD 500 Ph-1 K-3 $249.95 OD KB869
PIP AND ZENA'S SCIENCE VOYAGE (Videodisc). Tom Snyder/MCET
PIP-A, 1996. 12" double-sided CAV videodisc.
Includes teacher's guide, student workbooks and pogs.
Level I interactive with barcodes.
Spanish version available PIY-A, $299.95.
System requirements: CAV videodisc player with monitor (large video
monitor for whole-class viewing recommended).
The story of spending the weekend with Grandpa and his fishing boat
serves as a wonderful vehicle for the cartoon characters who guide
the viewer through a wealth of science and interdisciplinary activities
related to the ocean. Superb off-computer activities are provided.
Works well with an entire class or cooperative learning groups.
Multipurpose resource for integrated curriculum that demonstrates
science is everywhere.
SUBJ: Science./ Ocean.

CDR 500 Ph-1 K-3 $59.95 OD KB870
SAMMY'S SCIENCE HOUSE (CD-ROM). Edmark 505-1178, 1994. 1
CD-ROM color. (Early learning house).
Includes teacher's guide.
Also available for Macintosh or Windows/DOS in 3.5" disks,
$59.95.
Selectors' Choice, 20th ed.
System requirements: Windows 3.1 or Windows 95 or later; 4MB
RAM (8MB recommended); CD-ROM drive (doublespeed or faster);
386DX/33MHz (486 recommended); super VGA (640x48, 256-color
or more required); hard disk with 2MB free space; mouse; Windows
compatible sound output device; printer (optional); TouchWindow
(optional); microphone (optional).
Product (505-1178) runs on either Macintosh or Windows compatible
hardware.
The animation, graphics, and clear sound make this program a superb
method for introducing youngsters to science. Five activities help the
user learn about sequencing, problem solving, observing, classifying,
constructing, comparing and contrasting, and vocabulary related to
plants, animals, seasons, and weather. Excellent speech and easy-to-
use interface make adult help unnecessary.
SUBJ: Science--Software./ Software--Science./ Problem solving--
Software./ Software--Problem solving.

CDR 500 Ph-2 K-3 $79.95 OD KB871
SCIENCE BLASTER JR. Teacher ed. (CD-ROM). Davidson 3287, 1997. 1
CD-ROM color.
Includes teacher's guide and user's guide.
System requirements: Windows 95 or 3.1; 66 MHz 486 or faster
processor; 8MB RAM; 256-color Super VGA graphics; double-speed
or higher CD-ROM drive; Mouse; hard drive; Windows-compatible
sound card.
System requirements: Pentium processor with MMX technology; 16MB
RAM; Windows 95; 4X or higher CD-ROM drive; DirectDraw-
compatible HiColor (32K) or above video card; DirectSound-
compatible sound card and driver.
System requirements: Performa 575, Quadra, Power Mac or higher
(minimum 68040 processor); System 7 or higher; 13" monitor (256-
color system and 640x480 resolution); 12MB RAM (8MB free RAM);
double-speed or higher CD-ROM drive.
Product (3287) runs on either Windows, Windows MMX, or

Macintosh compatible hardware.
Exploration, sequencing, categorizing, and classifying are all concepts
learned as youngsters play the various games included in this
program. There is ample educational content, and game format will
hold young user's attention. Works well as a learning center or with
small groups.
SUBJ: Science--Software./ Software--Science./ Problem solving--
Software./ Software--Problem solving./ Interactive media.

500 Ph-2 4-6/7 $9.95 P KB872
SOUCIE, GARY. What's the difference between lenses and prisms and
other scientific things? Illus. by Jeff Domm. Wiley ISBN 0-471-08626-6;
In Canada: Wiley, 1995. 88p. ill. (What's the difference).
Includes glossary and index.
Answers the trickier questions of science with brief, careful definitions
of terms such as tons/tonnes, fission/fusion, mathematics/arithmetic,
and other sticklers. Perfect for the literal and trivia minded.
Encourages precise thinking and speaking.
SUBJ: Science--Miscellanea./ Technology--Miscellanea./ Questions
and answers.

500 Ph-2 2-A/5 $9.95 P KB873
STEIN, SARA. Science book. Workman ISBN 0-89480-120-1, 1979.
285p. ill.
Includes glossary and index.
This book "begins at home and stays there" (p12). Investigate
persons, pets and pests in your own environment, conducting all
experiments and observations with items readily at hand. A book to
refer to over and over which will provide hours of learning and family
fun.
SUBJ: Biology./ Science./ Experiments.

500 Ph-2 4-8/6 $11.95 P KB874
WOLLARD, KATHY. How come? Illus. by Debra Solomon. Workman
ISBN 1-56305-324-1; In Canada: Thomas Allen, 1993. 308p. ill.
Includes index.
Science questions and answers that investigate light and color, force
and particles, astronomy, weather, animals, and humans. An index
quickly directs the reader to topics such as mirages, fruit, and
dreaming. Explanations are straightforward, lengthy when necessary,
and reflect state of the art research. For example, high cholesterol
can cause tinnitus (ear ringing) (p.261). A book to pick up and
browse through anytime, anywhere.
SUBJ: Science--Miscellanea./ Questions and answers.

VD 502 Ph-3 5-A $249.95 OD KB875
MINDS-ON SCIENCE: THE IMPACT OF DISCOVERY (Videodisc).
Smithsonian Institution/Tom Snyder IMP, 1995. 1 12" CAV single-sided
videodisc color. (Minds-on science).
Includes teacher's guide and student portfolios.
Level I interactive with barcodes.
Optional 3.5" Macintosh or Windows software (Level III interactive)
available, $49.95.
System requirements (Level I): CAV videodisc player with monitor
(large video monitor for whole-class viewing recommended).
System requirements for optional Macintosh software (Level III):
Macintosh computer (LC series or better); System 7.0 or later;
QuickTime system extension; 4MB RAM; hard disk with at least 4MB
free space; 256 (8-bit) color monitor.
This cooperative learning activity allows youngsters to take on the
role of a research scientist who has discovered a memory enhancer.
Various scenarios allow for publishing the results, calling a press
conference, or starting a company. Assessment strategies and various
extended activities are included. Excellent for large groups.
SUBJ: Science--Models./ Research--Scientific applications./ Science--
Moral and ethical aspects./ Interactive media.

VCR 502.8 Ph-3 6-A $75.00 OD KB876
HOW TO USE THE COMPOUND MICROSCOPE (Videocassette).
Clearvue/EAV CL318, 1991. 1/2" VHS videocassette (20min).
(Introduction to the microscope).
Includes teacher's guide.
After a brief historical introduction, viewers learn the parts and care
of a microscope. Stressing proper use and care, directions are given
for adjusting magnification and illumination. Video will need to be
shown in segments over several class periods. After students become
familiar with parts and procedures, video will be valuable for review.
SUBJ: Microscopes.

503 Ph-2 4-6/7 $18.95 L KB877
RUBEL, DAVID. Science. Scholastic Reference ISBN 0-590-49367-1; In
Canada: Scholastic, 1995. 192p. col. ill., maps. (Scholastic kid's
encyclopedia).
"Agincourt Press book."

Includes glossary and index.
Oversized, alphabetical presentation of subjects from the fields of astronomy, biology, earth science, anatomy, physics, and chemistry. Each topic has its own table of contents. Topics begin with a brief definition; then salient points are discussed and illustrated. Additional cross references appear on every page. Attractive format ensures hours of browsing and learning.
SUBJ: Science--Encyclopedias.

503   Ph-3 4-6/9 $9.79 L KB878
STONE, JEANNE. Julian Messner illustrated dictionary of science. Messner ISBN 0-671-54548-5, 1986. 196p. col. ill.
Brief definitions of 2,000-plus science words and terms. Appendices show information about the planets, history of life on earth, forty famous scientists and inventors, the chemical periodic table, standard measurements, and the Beaufort scale for measuring wind. Useful as a starting point.
SUBJ: Science--Dictionaries.

507   Ph-2 2-6/6 $11.95 T KB879
BJORK, CHRISTINA. Linnea's almanac. Illus. by Lena Anderson. R&S/dist. by Farrar Straus & Giroux ISBN 91-29-59176-7, c1982, 1989. 61p. col. ill.
City girl, Linnea, follows the seasons observing plants and animals around her. Numerous small projects such as making a bird feeder, a dish garden, flower garlands, collector's notebooks and Christmas presents are included. Linnea's happiness and curiosity are contagious and will inspire young readers.
SUBJ: Nature study.

507   Ph-1 5-6/6 $15.00 T KB880
COBB, VICKI. Bet you can't: science impossibilities to fool you. By Vicki Cobb and Kathy Darling. Illus. by Martha Weston. Lothrop, Lee & Shepard ISBN 0-688-410905-4, 1980. 128p. ill.
Includes index.
New York Academy of Sciences Children's Science Book Award.
Available from National Library Service for the Blind and Physically Handicapped on sound recording cassette RC19715.
Fascinating tricks offer an entertaining introduction to the basic scientific principles of gravity, mechanics, fluids, logic, energy, and perception.
SUBJ: Science--Experiments./ Scientific recreations./ Experiments.

507   Ph-1 A/6 $11.98 L KB881
GARDNER, ROBERT. Science in your backyard. By Robert Gardner and David Webster. Messner ISBN 0-671-55565-0, 1987. 114p b&w photos.
Includes appendix and index.
Learn how much science goes on all around. Projects: trapping small insects, accumulating inanimate collections, building weather and astronomy instruments are ingenious simple ways to foster curiosity and wonder. A worthy resource for the individual student and the teacher.
SUBJ: Science--Experiments./ Scientific recreations.

MCP 507   Ph-1 3-6 $49.95 OD KB882
GIZMOS AND GADGETS! (Microcomputer program). Learning Company, 1993. 1 3.5" program disk, 1 3.5" data disk. (Super solvers).
Includes user's guide.
ALA notable computer software, 1994.
System requirements: IBM PC, AT, PS/1, PS/2, and compatibles with 640K; 80286 or better; hard disk with 2 MB free; mouse; 3.5" high-density floppy disk drive; DOS 3.3 or higher; color monitor; 256-color VGA; 10 MHz minimum clock speed; Sound Blaster or compatible sound card (optional).
As with other Super Solvers programs, the goal is to outwit Morty, the Master of Mischief. This activity provides 15 different vehicles which must be constructed by reading blueprints and gathering the correct pieces and which are then raced against Morty's vehicle. Works well with small groups and in a learning center environment.
SUBJ: Science--Study and teaching--Software./ Software--Science--Study and teaching./ Problem solving--Software./ Software--Problem solving./ Educational games--Software./ Software--Educational games.

507   Ph-1 4-6/6 $14.89 L KB883
KRAMER, STEPHEN P. How to think like a scientist: answering questions by the scientific method. Illus. by Felicia Bond. Crowell/HarperCollins ISBN 0-690-04565-4, 1987. 48p. ill.
Brings home scientific thinking by linking it to real life dramas such as skipping homework in favor of the movies, and farming out chickens during summer vacation. Five steps are discussed: 1, pose a question; 2, gather information; 3, form a hypothesis; 4, test; 5, distribute findings. A compact guide to a basic survival skill.

SUBJ: Science--Methodology./ Science--Experiments./ Thought and thinking./ Experiments.

507   Ph-1 5-A/9 $9.35 P KB884
SCIENCE ACTIVITIES FOR YOUNG PEOPLE. Edited by Elizabeth Lai and Monica Schwalbe. Hummingbird Children's Books ISBN 0-919952-19-4; In Canada; Hummingbird Children's Books, 1983. 74p. ill.
Includes bibliography and index.
Carefully presented and illustrated science experiments explore many current environmental issues such as pollution, solar energy, and soil erosion along with fourteen other topics. Each activity is methodically organized and procedure and record keeping are stressed. An excellent resource for independent or class projects.
SUBJ: Science--Experiments./ Experiments.

CDR 507   Ph-1 4-A $79.00 OD KB885
SCIENCE SLEUTHS. VOL. 1: THE MYSTERIES OF THE BLOB AND THE EXPLODING LAWNMOWERS (CD-ROM). Videodiscovery SCIMAX12CD ISBN 1-56307-387-0, 1995. 1 CD-ROM color, 1 3.5" disk.
Includes teacher's guide.
Also available for Macintosh.
System requirements: Multimedia PC with 486 DX; 25-MHz processor or higher; 8MB RAM; doublespeed CD-ROM; 256-color display or higher; 16-bit sound card; Microsoft Windows 3.1 or later; MS-DOS 3.1 or later; mouse; headphones or speakers; printer (optional).
Students become scientific investigators as they solve the two mysteries found on each CD-ROM, which are much like the videodisc versions by the same names. Six levels of difficulty are included in each mystery. Makes good use of multimedia features. Works well with an entire class, small groups, or as a learning center activity.
SCIENCE SLEUTHS. VOL. 2: THE MYSTERIES OF THE BIOGENE PICNIC AND THE TRAFFIC ACCIDENT (CD-ROM) SCIMAX08CD (ISBN 1-56307-388-9, 1995), $79.00.
SUBJ: Science--Study and teaching--Software./ Software--Science--Study and teaching./ Problem solving--Software./ Software--Problem solving.

VCR 507   Ph-2 5-6 $79.00 OD KB886
SCIENTIFIC METHOD (Videocassette). National Geographic 51569, 1993. 1/2" VHS videocassette color (20min).
Includes teacher's guide.
Looks at three research projects: first, a ten-year-old study involving elephant urine, next how zooplankton hear underwater, and finally collecting data on volcanic eruptions. Each exciting tale illustrates how the scientific method of observing, hypothesizing, experimenting, and forming conclusions applies to real life situations outside the lab. The first and third studies are not finished, so the ideals of continuous inquiry and dedication are reinforced. Students can read about the scientific method, memorize the steps, do a science project, and this video will still convey meaningful learning. Use to reinforce the concepts of the scientific method and for career studies.
SUBJ: Science--Experiments./ Science projects./ Experiments.

507   Ph-2 K-4/2 $11.38 L KB887
WYLER, ROSE. Science fun with mud and dirt. Messner ISBN 0-671-55569-3, 1986. 48p. col. ill.
It is a small step from making mud pies to experimenting with dirt--and just as much fun. Book includes recipes for making adobe bricks and sticker mud pies. What could be a less expensive and a more prolific medium than mud? Children learn from doing. Can also be used in upper grades for environmental studies.
SUBJ: Science--Experiments./ Experiments./ Earth.

507   Ph-2 4-A/7 $12.88 L KB888
ZUBROWSKI, BERNIE. Balloons: building and experimenting with inflatable toys. Illustrated by Roy Doty. Morrow ISBN 0-688-08325-0, 1990. 79p. ill. (Boston Children's Museum activity book).
Transform ordinary balloons into rockets or submarines with easy-to-follow instructions using handy, inexpensive materials. With little adult help, children will delight in learning about propulsion and air pressure. For inquisitive minds who like to tinker.
SUBJ: Balloons--Experiments./ Science--Experiments./ Experiments.

507.8   Ph-1 A/8 $27.95 T KB889
BEN FRANKLIN BOOK OF EASY AND INCREDIBLE EXPERIMENTS. Ed. by Lisa Jo Rudy. Illus. by Cheryl Kirk Noll. Wiley ISBN 0-471-07639-2; In Canada: Wiley, 1995. 131p. ill.
"Franklin Institute Science Museum book."
Includes chronology, bibliographies, glossary and index.
Tying science and social studies together is an effective way to learn about a great American. In chapter five, Paper and Printing, readers learn how to make homemade paper, mold and deckle, and create a gelatin sizing. Chapters on weather, electricity, music, and light make

this a perfect fit with interdisciplinary curriculum and a must for the "hands on" science class.
SUBJ: Science--Experiments./ Engineering--Experiments./ Experiments./ Franklin, Benjamin.

507.8   Ph-2 A/7 $13.89   L   KB890
COBB, VICKI. More science experiments you can eat. Illus. by Giulio Maestro. Lippincott/HarperCollins ISBN 0-397-31878-2, 1979. 126p. ill.
Describes food experiments which investigate spoilage, dehydration, ripening, acidity, flavorings and extracts. In discussing additives, the author relies on FDA's questionable GRAS (Generally Regarded As Safe) list.
SUBJ: Science--Experiments./ Cookery./ Nutrition./ Experiments.

507.8   Ph-2 3-5/7 $14.89   L   KB891
COBB, VICKI. Science experiments you can eat. Rev. and updated. Illus. by David Cain. HarperCollins ISBN 0-06-023551-9; In Canada: HarperCollins, 1994. 214p. ill.
Includes glossaries and index.
The experiments/recipes are designed to get you started as a scientist in your own kitchen. Basic concepts such as solutes, suspensions, and precipitates are introduced through food preparations. Sometimes you can even eat your completed experiments. Materials and equipment for each experiment are listed, procedures are clearly stated, and results are analyzed.
SUBJ: Science--Experiments./ Experiments./ Cookery.

507.8   Ph-3 P-4/7 $12.95   P   KB892
HIRSCHFELD, ROBERT. Kids' science book: creative experiences for hands-on fun. By Robert Hirschfeld and Nancy White. Illus. by Loretta Trezzo Braren. Williamson ISBN 0-913589-88-8; In Canada: Williamson/dist. by Fitzhenry & Whiteside, 1995. 158p. ill.
"Williamson Kids Can! book."
Includes index.
Over 100 experiments to delight young readers include simple directions, lists of supplies, and plenty of black and white illustrations. Have fun making a shoe box diorama with movable cardboard figures attached to small magnets or making marbleized paper with liquids that layer. Activities help children to question, observe, and predict.
SUBJ: Science--Experiments./ Experiments.

507.8   Ph-3 3-8/7 $9.95   P   KB893
LEVINE, SHAR. Silly science: strange and startling projects to amaze your family and friends. By Shar Levine and Leslie Johnstone. Wiley ISBN 0-471-11013-2; In Canada: Wiley, 1995. 95p. ill.
Includes glossary and index.
Grow fruit in a bottle (as they did in LIKE JAKE AND ME) or create some contraptions that sell in novelty stores, such as a sand puzzle and a gooey looking egg timer. Read the clear directions and use an assortment of household objects to get the job done. Students will love the experiments, and science teachers will find plenty of activities to pique students' interest and learning.
EVERYDAY SCIENCE: FUN AND EASY PROJECTS FOR MAKING PRACTICAL THINGS (ISBN 0-471-11014-0, 1995).
SUBJ: Science--Experiments./ Experiments./ Scientific recreations./ Science projects.

507.8   Ph-3 3-6/8 $14.89   L   KB894
MARKLE, SANDRA. Creepy spooky science. Illus. by Cecile Schoberle. Hyperion ISBN 0-7868-2178-7; In Canada: Little, Brown, 1996. 72p. ill.
Whip up some fake blood (the kind actors use) with corn syrup or write a secret message with lemon juice. Combines creepy experiments with weird facts such as people buried alive and the discovery of a glacier mummy. Use at Halloween.
SUBJ: Science--Miscellanea./ Science--Experiments./ Experiments.

507.8   Ph-2 4-8/6 $14.89   L   KB895
MARKLE, SANDRA. Icky squishy science. Illus. by Cecile Schoberle. Hyperion ISBN 0-7868-2177-9; In Canada: Little, Brown, 1996. 70p. ill.
Presents 22 experiments beginning with Foam at the mouth. Some, such as make your own marshmallows, will need an adult's help, but most can be done independently. By highlighting the disgusting, Markle is able to capture and retain attention. (Who wouldn't want to delve into a page that warns "This is disgusting!"). A nifty way to involve students who "hate" science.
SUBJ: Science--Experiments./ Experiments./ Scientific recreations.

507.8   Ph-3 6-A/8 $15.95   L   KB896
MARKLE, SANDRA. Science to the rescue. Atheneum ISBN 0-689-31783-2; In Canada: Maxwell Macmillan, 1994. 48p. col. ill.
Includes index.
Examines scientific frontiers from constructing artificial offshore islands to genetically altering foods. Each topic is fully explained, research problems are examined, and the reader is challenged to conduct

complementary projects. "See for yourself" activities demonstrate concepts, e.g. creating earthquake waves in a cake pan or making a bundle of optical fibers out of fishing line. An exciting and challenging book to stretch young minds. Several activities are useful for environmental studies.
SUBJ: Science./ Science projects.

507.8   Ph-3 6-A/7 $19.14   L   KB897
RAINIS, KENNETH G. Exploring with a magnifying glass. Watts ISBN 0-531-12508-4; In Canada: Watts, 1991. 144p. ill. (Venture book).
Includes directory and index.
Using a hand lens, readers are invited to investigate the structure and function of fibers, mold, pond water, computer barcodes, and other familiar objects. Black and white layout is not eye-catching and text is sometimes daunting. However, with a little guidance, a young learner can pick and choose exactly what interests from the animal, vegetable, or mineral worlds.
SUBJ: Magnifying glasses--Experiments./ Science--Experiments./ Experiments.

VCR 507.8   Ph-2 5-A $89.00   OD KB898
SCIENCE FAIR PROJECTS (Videocassette). Cambridge Educational CCP0226V-Y, 1995. 1/2" VHS videocassette color (30min).
Includes public performance rights.
A youthful narrator guides students though a detailed presentation of what makes a successful science fair project, how to compete, and the rewards of independent learning. Involved procedures are carefully explained so that novices will want to take on the challenge. Emphasizes that winners are not overnight sensations with killer ideas and that failed projects can be valuable. Covers topic selection, scientific method, organization, display tips, oral presentations, and more. A variety of young people testify to the rewards of time and effort well spent. Teachers can use this to motivate students, keep them on track, and review the involved processes of worthwhile research. The complexity and mastery demonstated by junior and senior high school students should not deter beginners. This inspires.
SUBJ: Science projects./ Science--Experiments./ Experiments./ Science fairs.

507.8   Ph-2 3-6 $14.95   P   KB899
VANCLEAVE, JANICE PRATT. Janice VanCleave's guide to the best science fair projects. By Janice VanCleave. Wiley ISBN 0-471-14802-4; In Canada: Wiley, 1997. 156p. ill.
Includes bibliographies, directories, glossary and index.
Fifty science fair projects for the beginner require easily available materials and explore concepts in astronomy, biology, earth and physical sciences, engineering, and math. Each project is given two pages of procedures, an explanation of what is occurring, and questions to further explore. Both familiar topics (homemade volcano) and unique (erasing cassette tapes with a magnet) are examined. Discusses the scientific method, research, and displays and includes a detailed example of a completed project. Well-written directions insure success although adult input is needed.
SUBJ: Science fairs./ Science projects.

508   Ph-3 P-A $25.95   T   KB900
ABC'S OF NATURE: A FAMILY ANSWER BOOK. Reader's Digest/dist. by Random House ISBN 0-89577-169-1, 1984. 336p. col. ill.
Displaying the wonders of wildlife in four sections devoted to: the physical world, plants, animals and interactions of flora and fauna in various environments, this volume is packed with scientific information. Beautifully illustrated, the book is oriented toward sharing and/or for browsing. Excellent index assures easy access to text.
SUBJ: Natural history--Miscellanea./ Questions and answers.

508   Ph-1 P-A/5 $16.00   L   KB901
BUSCH, PHYLLIS S. Backyard safaris: 52 year-round science adventures. Illus. by Wayne J. Trimm. Simon & Schuster ISBN 0-689-80302-8; In Canada: Distican, 1995. 142p. ill.
Includes bibliography and index.
In spring, summer, winter, and fall there are exciting adventures waiting for the person who knows how to observe nature. Some ideas such as reading snow tracks and catching fireflies are well-known, but others such as mapping a beetle's trail under the bark of a fallen log, finding a pixie in a violet, or making sumacade are new adventures that will nuture budding naturalists. There is something here for the whole family...just lie on your backs watching clouds or listen to squirrels and frogs, and your lives are enriched! A treasure trove to use for scout camping trips, guided nature walks, and family fun. (Parents' Shelf.)
SUBJ: Nature study./ Seasons./ Scientific recreations.

NONFICTION

VCR 508   Ph-2 3-6 $49.95   OD KB902
EARTH'S SEASONS/CLIMATES (Videocassette). Disney Educational Productions 68A27VL00, 1995. 1/2" VHS videocassette color (52min). (Bill Nye the science guy: classroom edition).
Includes teacher's guide.
Includes public performance rights.
50 volume series also available for purchase as a set, 6P27VL00, $949.00.
Closed captioned.
Lively presentation examines the reasons for seasons and why different climates occur. Science experiments demonstrate basic concepts such as the changing angle of the sun's rays and condensation. Additional experiments are suggested in the teacher's guide. Flashy graphics, music, and live-action photography are sure to capture the interest of even reluctant scientists.
SUBJ: Nature study./ Seasons./ Climate./ Experiments.

508   Ph-3 5-A/7 $22.95   L   KB903
FABER, DORIS. Great lives: nature and the environment. By Doris and Harold Faber. Scribner's ISBN 0-684-19047-8; In Canada: Distican, 1991. 296p. ill. (Great lives).
Includes bibliography and index.
An international roster of leaders in the field of conservation and environmental concerns. Includes twenty-six biographies of individuals who have struggled to make the world aware of the problems facing our natural world. For perceptive readers.
SUBJ: Naturalists./ Conservationists./ Environmentalists.

508   Ph-2 K-3 $15.93   L   KB904
GARDNER, BEAU. Guess what? Lothrop, Lee & Shepard ISBN 0-688-04983-4, 1985. unp. col. ill.
Bold graphics in a wordless format provide a pleasant guessing game as children are invited to identify the animal suggested by spare brightly colored shapes. The answer is provided on the back of each page as a gray silhouette and the name of the animal. Unlike similar games in a photographed format, this provides abstraction and seems likely to encourage children to also draw animals in this attractive graphic form.
SUBJ: Animals--Pictorial works./ Picture puzzles.

508   Ph-2 4-8/10 $27.07   T   KB905
GATES, PHIL. Nature got there first. Kingfisher/dist. by Raintree Steck-Vaughn ISBN 1-85697-587-8, 1995. 80p. col. ill.
Includes glossary and index.
Eight well illustrated chapters explain the connections between the living world and man-made products such as: Velcro, conveyer belts, filters, and jet propulsion. Through careful observation, scientists/inventors have built upon nature's designs. Sidebars, color illustrations, and capsulated text sustain interest and increase knowledge. Perfect for those who think science is boring and others who are nascent inventors. Easy to booktalk.
SUBJ: Nature--Miscellanea./ Technology--Miscellanea./ Inventions--Miscellanea.

508   Ph-1 K-4/4 $15.95   L   KB906
GRAHAM-BARBER, LYNDA. Toad or frog, swamp or bog?: a big book of nature's confusables. Illus. by Alec Gillman. Four Winds ISBN 0-02-736931-5; In Canada: Maxwell Macmillan, 1994. 48p. col. ill.
Includes index.
Places tricky look-alikes (frogs and toads) side by side to examine their finer distinguishing features. Younger readers will target their favorite animals while older children will devour the entire book, and everyone, including teachers, will learn something. Piques curiosity and educates with wonderful illustrations and perfect explanatory text.
SUBJ: Natural history./ Animals.

508   Ph-1 3-A/9 $15.95   T   KB907
HILLER, ILO. Young naturalist, from Texas Parks and Wildlife Magazine. Texas A & M University Press ISBN 0-89096-163-8, 1983. 160p. ill.
Includes index.
Selectors' Choice, 15th ed.
Acting on the premise "you are never too young or too old to explore the world of nature" (Preface) this book encourages all to observe, learn and enjoy. Includes puzzles, projects and animal lore galore. Very useful for elementary nature studies. Regional focus does not detract from universal appeal.
SUBJ: Natural history.

508   Ph-1 1-5/6 $16.95   L   KB908
LESLIE, CLARE WALKER. Nature all year long. Greenwillow ISBN 0-688-09183-0, 1991. 56p. col. ill.
Includes bibliography and index.
Four pages narrate and display each month's uniqueness. Filled with orderly labeled nature drawings, craft projects, and lists of facts, this offers a windfall of learning both in and out of the classroom. Of special value to young learners who want to explore on their own.
SUBJ: Nature study./ Months.

CDR 508   Ph-1 1-4 $29.95   OD KB909
MICROSOFT EXPLORAPEDIA: THE WORLD OF NATURE. Academic ed. (CD-ROM). Microsoft ISBN 1-57231-085-5; In Canada: Microsoft Canada, 1995. 1 CD-ROM color. (Microsoft Explorapedia series).
Version 1.00.
Includes user's guide and teacher's guide.
System requirements: Windows 3.1 or later, MS-DOS version 3.1 or later, multimedia PC or compatible with a 386SX or higher processor, 4MB of RAM (8MB recommended), 2.5 - 5MB available hard disk space (actual requirements will vary based on features you choose to install), CD-ROM, VGA or higher resolution graphics card (256 color), Microsoft Mouse or compatible pointing device (optional), audio card/speakers for sound (optional).
Based on THE RANDOM HOUSE ENCYCLOPEDIA FOR CHILDREN, this multimedia reference tool is narrated by children and contains approximately 4,000 entries. Wise Cracker games and 26 structured activities are also included. Works well as a learning station and as a large classroom activity.
SUBJ: Nature study--Software./ Software--Nature study./ Animals--Software./ Software--Animals./ Plants--Software./ Software--Plants./ Interactive media.

508   Ph-2 4/6 $12.95   P   KB910
MILORD, SUSAN. Kids' nature book: 365 indoor/outdoor activities and experiences. Rev. ed. Williamson ISBN 1-885593-07-4; In Canada: Williamson/dist. by Fitzhenry & Whiteside, 1996. 157p. ill.
"Williamson Kids Can! book."
Includes bibliographies and index.
A science book of days that will ensure learning throughout the year with simple (play in some mud) and not-so-simple (set up an aquarium) activities. Best used along with a supportive adult. Lots of activities for teachers, scout leaders, and parents, so be sure to introduce this title at a PTA meeting. (Parents' Shelf).
SUBJ: Nature study./ Natural history--Outdoor books.

508   Ph-1 4-A/7 $15.95   T   KB911
QUINLAN, SUSAN E. Case of the mummified pigs and other mysteries in nature. Illus. by Jennifer Owings Dewey. Boyds Mills ISBN 1-878093-82-7; In Canada: McClelland & Stewart, 1995. 128p. ill.
Includes bibliography and index.
Selectors' Choice, 20th ed.
Presents 17 ecological investigations that prove nature's webs are secret and intricate. Alert scientists observe oddities then dig, experiment, and arrive at startling conclusions concerning plant chemicals and pigments, symbiotic relationships, and animal populations. The title story proves that there is a lot more going on with mummy preservation than just hot, dry weather. Each fantastic account reads like a well-written detective story and testifies that hard work and research are exciting. Captivating scientific mysteries for environmental studies. For reading aloud.
SUBJ: Nature./ Science--Miscellanea.

508   Ph-1 P-1/4 $14.95   L   KB912
ROTNER, SHELLEY. Nature spy. By Shelley Rotner and Ken Kreisler. Macmillan ISBN 0-02-777885-1; In Canada: Maxwell Macmillan, 1992. unp. col. ill.
Handsome photographs attract children to close-up views of animals and plants in order to appreciate the beauty surrounding all of us. Follow up reading by supplying everyone with a hand lens and marching outside. Especially useful in seasonal studies.
SUBJ: Nature.

VCR 508   Ph-2 K-3 $99.00   OD KB913
SEEING THINGS (Videocassette). Film Images/dist. by Beacon Films/Altschul Group 8217, 1987. 1/2" VHS videocassette color (14min). (Science walk with David Suzuki).
Includes teacher's guide.
Includes public performance rights.
Commonplace animals and plant life are explored and discussed by three children and scientist David Suzuki. Colorful and well paced, this is a most attractive guide to backyard nature study.
SUBJ: Animals./ Plants./ Nature study.

508   Ph-1 3-A/7 $14.89   L   KB914
THOMSON, PEGGY. Auks, rocks and the odd dinosaur: inside stories from the Smithsonian's Museum of Natural History. Crowell/HarperCollins ISBN 0-690-04492-5; In Canada: HarperCollins, 1985. 120p. ill.
Includes index.
Selectors' Choice, 16th ed.

Available from National Library Service for the Blind and Physically Handicapped on sound recording cassette RC24434.
Treasures including a collection of 5-foot worms, a freeze dried Komodo dragon, Allende meteorites, a bull mummy, and the Hope diamond are among the items housed and studied at the Museum of Natural History. The individual chapters are lively reading and well documented by photographs. Testifying to the spirit of scientific sleuthing, this should be part of every museum field trip.
SUBJ: National Museum of Natural History./ Museums.

508   Ph-3 3-A/7 $19.95   P   KB915
WEBER, LARRY. Backyard almanac. Illus. by Judy Gibbs. Pfeifer-Hamilton ISBN 1-57025-071-5, 1996. unp. ill. (Appointment with nature).
Includes index.
Experience a wildlife adventure right where you live! One page is devoted to each day of the year and highlights a familiar plant or animal with three paragraphs of text and a black and white drawing. Fosters an awareness of nature that is often taken for granted. When children become more knowledgeable of their surroundings, they will take pride in and care of the environment. Use year round for reading aloud or to celebrate a special day. Though set in Minnesota, most of the entries are applicable to other states. For environmental studies.
SUBJ: Natural history--Miscellanea./ Animals./ Plants./ Almanacs.

SRC 508   Ph-2 P-1 $11.95   OD KB916
ZEITLIN, PATTY. Spin, spider, spin: songs for a greater appreciation of nature (Sound recording cassette). Written and sung by Patty Zeitlin and Marcia Berman. Sung and accompanied by David Zeitlin. Educational Activities AC 551, 1974. 1 sound cassette.
Nature songs (beautifully accompanied by guitar, mandolin, flute, and harmonica) encourage children to bypass the negative conditioning which causes distaste in many adults for such harmless creatures as spiders, lizards, turtles, snails, earthworms, bees, snakes, and salamanders. Also included are songs to relieve fears of death (in this case, a bird) and night sounds. The teacher's guide has lyrics and 8-1/2x11" study prints of the animals discussed in the songs.
SUBJ: Nature--Songs and music.

508.2   Ph-3 P-2/2 $12.60   L   KB917
FOWLER, ALLAN. How do you know it's fall? Childrens Press ISBN 0-516-04922-4; In Canada: Childrens Press, 1992. 32p. col. ill. (Rookie read-about science).
Includes index.
Also available in Spanish COMO SABES QUE ES OTONO? (ISBN 0-516-34922-8, 1992).
Big book available (0-516-49623-9, 1992), and in Spanish COMO SABES QUE ES OTONO? (ISBN 0-516-59623-3, 1992).
Lots of pictures and simple text portray familiar seasonal happenings. Primary students will enjoy the colorful presentation that they can read independently.
See also HOW DO YOU KNOW IT'S WINTER? (ISBN 0-516-04915-1, 1991), HOW DO YOU KNOW IT'S SUMMER? (ISBN 0-516-04923-2, 1992, also available in Spanish COMO SABES QUE ES VERANO? ISBN 0-516-34923-6, 1992, available in Spanish Big book ISBN 0-516-59624-1, 1992), and HOW DO YOU KNOW IT'S SPRING? (ISBN 0-516-04914-3, 1991, also available in Spanish COMO SABES QUE ES PRIMAVERA? ISBN 0-516-34914-7, 1994). Big books available for HOW DO YOU KNOW IT'S SPRING? (ISBN 0-516-49474-0, 1991), HOW DO YOU KNOW IT'S SUMMER? (ISBN 0-516-49624-7, 1992) and HOW DO YOU KNOW IT'S WINTER? (ISBN 0-516-49475-9, 1991).
SUBJ: Autumn.

508.2   Ph-3 4-6/7 $14.89   L   KB918
SIMON, SEYMOUR. Autumn across America. Hyperion ISBN 1-56282-468-6; In Canada: Little, Brown, 1993. unp. col. ill. (Seasons across America).
Leaves change colors; animals migrate, burrow, or die; and plants spew their seeds to the wind. From New England to Yellowstone National Park to Alaska, amazing changes unfold as nature gets ready for winter. Beautiful photographs accompany a detailed text suitable for reading aloud. Book looks deceptively simple, but the information on leaf color, endangered species, and migrating monarch butterflies will promote a variety of independent research assignments.
SUBJ: Autumn./ North America--Climate./ Seasons./ United States--Description and travel.

508.2   Ph-3 5-8/7 $15.89   L   KB919
SIMON, SEYMOUR. Spring across America. Hyperion ISBN 0-7868-2056-X; In Canada: Little, Brown, 1996. unp. col. ill. (Seasons across America).
Traces the progress of the season as spring unfolds from the southern

borders to the northern edges of the continental United States. Highlights familiar flora like pussywillows and skunk cabbage and other harbingers of spring such as nesting birds and insect hatchings. Poetic text and stunning photographs will instill appreciation for the season of new beginnings.
SUBJ: Spring./ North America--Climate./ Seasons./ United States--Description and travel.

508.2   Ph-3 4-6/6 $14.89   L   KB920
SIMON, SEYMOUR. Winter across America. Hyperion ISBN 0-7868-2015-2; In Canada: Little, Brown, 1994. unp. col. ill. (Seasons across America).
Describes how animals throughout the United States adapt to the frequently frigid conditions of winter. Sharply focused photographs capture the crystalline appearance of ice and snow.
SUBJ: Winter./ North America--Climate./ Seasons./ United States--Description and travel.

508.2   Ph-3 6-A/8 $12.45   P   KB921
STOKES, DONALD W. Guide to nature in winter, northeast and north central North America. Illustrated by Deborah Prince and Donald W. Stokes. Little, Brown ISBN 0-316-81723-6; In Canada: Little, Brown, c1976, 1979. 374p. ill.
Includes bibliography and index.
Wrap up, walk into winter with this guide to introduce weeds, trees, birds, tracks, snow crystals--a landscape full of surprises opens to the educated viewer. Very thorough, serves as an excellent adjunct for biology, nature studies, scouts and 4-H.
SUBJ: Natural history./ Winter./ Nature study.

508.3   Ph-3 P-1 $12.88   L   KB922
FLORIAN, DOUGLAS. Nature walk. Greenwillow ISBN 0-688-08269-6, 1989. 32p. col. ill.
Three children take a walk in a woods with one word printed on each two-page spread. Use before and after nature walks. Topic vocabulary is presented in a creative context ideally suited for beginners.
SUBJ: Nature.

509   Ph-3 6-A/6 $13.95   L   KB923
HAYDEN, ROBERT C. 7 African-American scientists. Rev. and expanded ed. Illus. by Richard Loehle. Twenty-First Century/Henry Holt ISBN 0-8050-2134-5, 1992. 171p. ill. (Achievers: African Americans in science & tech.).
Includes index.
Discussing seven African-American scientists' lives and scientific research, the author demonstrates their important contribution to American life. For studies in African-American history.
SUBJ: Scientists./ Afro-Americans--Biography.

509   Ph-3 4-6/7 $17.90   L   KB924
MCKISSACK, PAT. African-American scientists. By Patricia and Fredrick McKissack. Millbrook ISBN 1-56294-372-3, 1994. 96p. ill. (Proud heritage).
Includes bibliography and index.
Inspiring stories of frequently overlooked scientists in the fields of astronomy, medicine, biology, and chemistry. Documents how young African-American men and women overcame prejudice, prevailed to become educated, and contributed selflessly to their areas of expertise. Authoritative enough for research; interesting enough for pleasure reading. For multicultural studies.
SUBJ: Scientists./ Afro-Americans--Biography.

509   Ph-3 6-A/9 $20.00   T   KB925
STEFOFF, REBECCA. Scientific explorers: travels in search of knowledge. Oxford ISBN 0-19-507689-3, 1992. 151p. ill. (some col.), maps. (Extraordinary explorers).
Includes chronology, bibliography and index.
Explores the persistence and inquisitiveness of the human spirit from Galileo to the astronauts which has unlocked the secrets of our world. Book is divided into several parts: the first scientific expeditions such as La Condamine's trek into South America in 1735; great naturalists such as Alexander von Humboldt (1798) and Charles Darwin (1830's); undersea explorers such as Matthew Maury (1850's), Jacques Cousteau (mid 1900's) and Sylvia Earl (today), and finally space exploration. Wonderful personal and detailed information bring textbook heroes alive and will inspire all readers to investigate surroundings as inconsequential as an ant colony or as momentous as the solar system. A special book for the gifted or advanced student.
SUBJ: Scientific expeditions--History./ Explorers.

CDR 510   Ph-1 K-2 $59.95   OD KB926
CARNIVAL COUNTDOWN. School version (CD-ROM). Edmark/Harcourt Brace 702-1077, 1996. 1 CD-ROM color. (Mighty math).

Version 1.11.
Includes teacher's guide.
System requirements: Windows 3.1, Windows 95 or later; 486, Pentium or better (33 MHz or faster recommended); hard disk with up to 5MB free; 8MB memory (RAM); Super VGA graphics, 640x480, 256 colors or more; double-speed or faster CD-ROM drive; Windows-compatible sound card; Windows-compatible printer (optional); TouchWindow (optional).
System requirements: Macintosh System 7.0.1 or higher; 68040, 68030 (25 MHz or faster recommended), or PowerPC; 4MB memory (RAM), 1900K unused, 5MB for System 7.5 or later, 8MB highly recommended; 13" or larger monitor, 256 or more colors; double-speed or faster CD-ROM drive; printer (optional); TouchWindow (optional).
Product (702-1077) runs on either Windows or Macintosh compatible hardware.
Youngsters encounter five delightful activities which help them practice problem solving, addition, subtraction, beginning multiplication and division skills, as well as understand place value, sorting, and classification. An exploration mode and a question-and-answer mode are included; difficulty levels can be changed. Works well with individual students and small groups.
SUBJ: Mathematics--Software./ Software--Mathematics./ Arithmetic--Software./ Software--Arithmetic./ Geometry--Software./ Software--Geometry./ Problem solving--Software./ Software--Problem solving./ Interactive media.

510   Ph-1 1-6/5 $18.60   L   KB927
CLEMENT, ROD. Counting on Frank. Gareth Stevens ISBN 0-8368-0358-2; In Canada: Saunders, 1991. unp col illus.
An off-the-wall look at measurement and comparison. Frank, a dog, cavorts with his young master as they explore how long it would take the bathroom to fill with water, how many whales would fit inside a house, and how long a line an ink pen can draw before running dry. Use for brainstorming ideas for scientific investigations or just to see students' reactions to the droll humor.
SUBJ: Mathematics./ Size.

510   Ph-1 3-6/7 $14.95   L   KB928
MARKLE, SANDRA. Math mini-mysteries. Atheneum ISBN 0-689-31700-X; In Canada: Maxwell Macmillan, 1993. 58p. ill.
Includes index.
Explore mathematics with grids, patterns, surveys, and paper cutouts. Students won't want to wait to try things out for themselves. Encourages the curious and motivates learning. All activities were created under the National Council of Teachers of Mathematics curriculum standards. For students to use independently and for teachers to fire up their lessons.
SUBJ: Mathematics./ Mathematical recreations./ Problem solving.

CDR 510   Ph-1 3-6 $59.95   OD KB929
NUMBER HEROES. School version (CD-ROM). Edmark/Harcourt Brace 702-1076, 1996. 1 CD-ROM color. (Mighty math).
Version 1.11.
Includes teacher's guide.
System requirements: Windows 3.1, Windows 95 or later; 486, Pentium or better (33 MHz or faster recommended); hard disk with up to 5MB free; 8MB memory (RAM); Super VGA graphics, 640x480, 256 or more colors; double-speed or faster CD-ROM drive; Windows-compatible sound card; Windows-compatible printer (optional); TouchWindow (optional).
System requirements: Macintosh System 7.0.1 or higher; 68040, 68030 (25 MHz or faster recommended), or PowerPC; 8MB memory (RAM), 4100K unused; 13" or larger monitor, 256 or more colors; double-speed or faster CD-ROM drive; printer (optional); TouchWindow (optional).
Product (702-1076) runs on either Windows or Macintosh compatible hardware.
Youngsters encounter four delightful activities which help them practice problem solving, addition, subtraction, multiplication, division, fractions, probability, and interpreting graphs and charts. An exploration mode and a question-and-answer mode are included; difficulty levels can be changed. Works well with individual students and small groups.
SUBJ: Mathematics--Software./ Software--Mathematics./ Geometry--Software./ Software--Geometry./ Probabilities--Software./ Software--Probabilities./ Problem solving--Software./ Software--Problem solving./ Interactive media.

510   Ph-3 4-6/9 $3.95   P   KB930
PALLAS, NORVIN. Calculator puzzles, tricks and games. Illus. by Joyce Behr. Dover ISBN 0-486-26670-2; In Canada: General, c1976, 1991. 96p. ill.
Includes index.

Learn to use your calculator and have fun, too. This describes basic functions but is more complicated than the title suggests. Aimed at kids who never get their fill of math.
SUBJ: Calculators--Problems, exercises, etc./ Mathematical recreations.

SRC 510   Ph-1 1-3 $11.95   OD KB931
PALMER, HAP. Math readiness--vocabulary and concepts (Sound recording cassette). Educational Activities AC 650, n.d. 1 sound cassette.
Lively music and action songs teach the concepts and vocabulary needed for an understanding of basic mathematics. Big, little, long, short, shorter, same, like, different, before, after, greater and less are some of the words explored for general vocabulary development and math readiness. Suggestions and variations for using the material appear on the inside of the album jacket.
Contents: Count-up, countdown; Just like yours; Movin' by numerals; Make a set; Drawing lines and dots; Show me the card--1; Clapping sets; Can you catch a set; How many ways; Show me the card--2.
SUBJ: Mathematics.

510   Ph-1 4-8/9 $17.95   T OD KB932
SMOOTHEY, MARION. Calculators. Illus. by Ann Baum. Marshall Cavendish ISBN 1-85435-777-8; In Canada: Marshall Cavendish, 1995. 64p. col. ill. (Let's investigate).
Includes glossary and index.
Begins with a few pages about non-electronic calculators and then proceeds to the electronic kinds; teaches how to key hop, keep running totals, and use functions. Directions make allowances for different calculators. Activities are sequenced according to difficulty and built on knowledge acquired from the preceding pages. Clean, attractive layout with a lot of information for self-directed learning.
SUBJ: Calculators--Problems, exercises, etc./ Mathematical recreations.

510   Ph-3 4-6/6 $22.89   L   KB933
VANCLEAVE, JANICE PRATT. Janice VanCleave's math for every kid: easy activities that make learning math fun. Illus. by Barbara Clark. Wiley ISBN 0-471-54693-3; In Canada: Wiley, 1991. 215p. ill. (Janice VanCleave's science for every kid).
Includes glossary and index.
Inviting activities covering math basics: measurement, graphing, and geometry. Measurement is given in both English and metric systems. Some black and white number-filled pages will scare off a few students, but for the person who loves math and wants more than a textbook offers, this is it. Teachers will be grateful for the supplemental material.
SUBJ: Mathematics.

510   Ph-3 4-1/7 $18.95   T   KB934
ZEMAN, ANNE. Everything you need to know about math homework. By Anne Zeman and Kate Kelly. Scholastic ISBN 0-590-49358-2; In Canada: Scholastic, 1994. 136p. col. ill. (Scholastic homework reference series).
"Irving Place Press book."
"Scholastic Reference."
Includes index.
A practical inclusion as a source for quick answers to math questions, despite its drawbacks. Readers may need help in translating graphics and explanations into meaningful learning. Use of the table of contents is limited because page numbers are only given for main topics. The listed subtopics must be cross-referenced in the index. Some charts (slang words for money p.110 and bigger than a billion p.11) could inspire students to independent learning.
SUBJ: Mathematics./ Homework.

VCR 511   Ph-1 5-A   FREE   OD KB935
CHALLENGE OF THE UNKNOWN (Videocassette). American Association for the Advancement of Science/dist. by Karol Media, 1986. 7 programs on 1/2" VHS videocassette color.
Available for free loan to schools with permission to copy. Written requests only.
Includes teacher's guide.
Selectors' Choice, 16th ed.
The dual focus on the use of mathematics in everyday life and the seven steps toward problem solving is presented through lively examples ranging from orienteering to how to figure out if certain dinosaurs ran. The selection of illustrative applications is wide ranging and includes humor. The suggestions contained within the well-developed teacher's guide are directed to higher level thinking skills. Though each program is only about 20 minutes long, it is suggested for greater effect that discussion occur between each of the episodes. Contents: Situation: where am I (18min); Information: what do I know (21min); Restatement: how do I see it (19min); Outcomes: how do I get there (23min); Management: what do I do next (21min);

Estimation: am I close (21min); Argument: am I right (21min).
SUBJ: Mathematics./ Problem solving.

MCP 511   Ph-1 4-A $49.95   OD KB936
GRAPH ACTION (Microcomputer program). Tom Snyder Productions
ACT-D, 1996. 1 3.5" disk.
    Includes teacher's guide and reproducible worksheets.
    Version 1.0
    Network version ACT-NET-D available, $499.95.
    System requirements: Macintosh System 6.0.7 or higher; high density
disk drive; 1MB RAM; monochrome monitor.
    This math software tool provides an easy-to-use interface and a
writing option which allow youngsters to truly understand the
relationship of movement and graphing. Well designed teaching
activities integrate a number of language arts concepts. Works well
with individuals, small groups, or an entire class with the aid of a
large screen. Ideal for interdisciplinary studies.
    SUBJ: Mathematics--Graphic methods--Software./ Software--
Mathematics--Graphic methods./ Problem solving--Software./
Software--Problem solving.

CDR 511   Ph-1 4-A $99.95   OD KB937
GRAPH ACTION PLUS (CD-ROM). Tom Snyder Productions ACP-D,
1996. 1 CD-ROM color.
    Version 1.0.
    Includes teacher's guide.
    System requirements: Macintosh computer; double-speed CD-ROM
drive (or higher); System 7.0 or higher; QuickTime; color QuickDraw.
8MB Macintosh is recommended to run all three programs
simultaneously; individual programs may be run with less memory.
Combines the basics of distance/time graphing from GRAPH ACTION
with the software tools, ACTION ANALYZER and MULTI-VIEWER, so
students can build and view graphs of real-world motions. Provides an
easy-to-use interface and a writing option which allow students to
truly understand the relationship of movement and graphing. Well
designed teaching activities integrate a number of language arts
concepts. Works well with individuals, small groups, or an entire class
with the aid of a large screen. Ideal for interdisciplinary studies.
    SUBJ: Mathematics--Graphic methods--Software./ Software--
Mathematics--Graphic methods./ Problem solving--Software./
Software--Problem solving.

CDR 511   Ph-2 2-5 $59.95   OD KB938
LOGICAL JOURNEY OF THE ZOOMBINIS. School ed. (CD-ROM).
Broderbund 5120349, 1996. 1 CD-ROM color. (Active minds series).
    Includes user's guide, teacher's guide, troubleshooting guide and
overhead transparencies.
    System requirements: 33 MHz 486SX or faster; 8MB RAM for
Windows 3.1 and Windows 95; 2MB disk space available for
Windows 3.1, 3MB for Windows 95; double-speed CD-ROM drive or
faster; hard disk; Windows 3.1 or higher or Windows 95; QuickTime
2.0.3 for Windows 3.1, QuickTime 2.1 for Windows 95 (included on
this CD); MS/PC DOS 5.0 or higher with Windows 3.1; SuperVGA
(640x480, 256 colors); MPC-compliant sound device; mouse.
    System requirements: 25 MHz 68030 processor; 8-bit video support
(256 colors); 13" color monitor (640x480); 1MB disk space
available; 8MB RAM; hard disk; double-speed CD-ROM drive;
System 7.0.1 or higher; Sound Manager 3.1 (uses 96KB of hard disk
space--included on this CD); QuickTime 2.1 (uses 1056KB of hard
disk space--included on this CD).
    Product (5120349) runs on either Windows or Macintosh compatible
hardware.
    Students practice math problem solving and scientific reasoning skills
as they help the Zoombinis move to a new land. A variety of
activities which deal with pattern recognition, reasoning, observing,
inferring, and other skills are available. The program works well with
small groups or for an entire class with a projection device.
    SUBJ: Mathematics--Software./ Software--Mathematics./ Logic--
Software./ Software--Logic./ Problem solving--Software./ Software--
Problem solving./ Interactive media.

VCR 511   Ph-2 4-5 $90.00   OD KB939
PROBLEM SOLVING: USING GRAPHS (Videocassette). Agency for
Instructional Technology, 1985. 1/2" VHS videocassette color (15min).
(Math works).
    Includes teacher's guide.
    Determined to prove to their principal that the girls sports teams
deserve new uniforms, Lindsay and Katie find that different types of
graphs present their information clearly. Activities in the teacher's
guide reenforce which graph shows which data best. An appealing
presentation of important concepts.
    SUBJ: Graphs./ Problem solving.

MCP 511   Ph-1 3-A $59.95   OD KB940
PUZZLE TANKS: A GAME OF NUMBERS AND LOGIC (Microcomputer
program). Designed by Thomas C. O'Brien. Sunburst 6461, 1984. 3.5"
disk, 1 backup disk.
    Includes teacher's guide.
    Network versions available.
    Available on Macintosh CD-ROM (8472FG) and Windows CD-ROM
(8473FG).
    Also available Windows 3.1; IBM and Tandy 1000; and Apple II
family.
    System requirements: Macintosh family (2MB); hard drive or two
800K disk drives required.
    Develop math problem solving strategies. Attractive graphics, good
sound effects and levels of difficulty make this set helpful. The
curriculum oriented problem solving approach is welcomed.
    SUBJ: Mathematical recreations--Software./ Educational games--
Software./ Problem solving--Software./ Arithmetic--Software./
Software--Mathematical recreations./ Software--Educational games./
Software--Problem solving./ Software--Arithmetic.

511   Ph-2 A/7 $17.95   T   KB941
SMOOTHEY, MARION. Graphs. Illus. by Ann Baum. Marshall Cavendish
ISBN 1-85435-775-1, 1995. 64p. col. ill. (Let's investigate).
    Includes glossary and index.
    Begins by stating that "A graph is NOT a picture. It is a way of
representing two pieces of information in one place...." (p.16)
Proceeds to illustrate a wealth of information that can be conveyed
with dots and lines--from the simplest showing what happens to the
water level in a bathtub to a difficult family of parabolic curves.
Exercises require careful reading and experimentation; answers are
given in the back. For students who like to tinker with problems
independently.
    SUBJ: Graphic methods.

MCP 511   Ph-1 K-4 $79.95   OD KB942
STEARNS, PEGGY HEALY. Graph Club with Fizz and Martina
(Microcomputer program). Tom Snyder Productions GRP-T, 1993. 1
3.5" disk.
    Includes teacher's guide, activities guide, companion volume FIZZ
AND MARTINA'S INCREDIBLE NOT-FOR-PROFIT PET RESORT and
student portfolios.
    Also available for Windows, and AppleShare or Novell based
network versions.
    Also available in Spanish/English GRS-J, $129.95.
    System requirements: Macintosh, System 6.0.7 and higher; 1MB of
available RAM.
    Youngsters will make the transition from concrete to abstract as they
learn to create graphs/charts with manipulatives and then numbers.
The ease of use and ability to develop picture, bar, line, and circle
graphs as well as tables make the program fit a wide range of uses.
    SUBJ: Mathematics--Graphic methods--Software./ Software--
Mathematics--Graphic methods./ Problem solving--Software./
Software--Problem solving.

VCR 511.3   Ph-3 5-6 $90.00   OD KB943
PROBLEM SOLVING: USING DIAGRAMS AND MODELS
(Videocassette). Agency for Instructional Technology, 1985. 1/2" VHS
videocassette color (15min). (Math works).
    Includes teacher's guide.
    Putting together a swing set, touring an amusement park, planning
activities for a space shuttle flight, and setting out booths for a
carnival are all made easier with diagrams and models. While the
child actors are stilted, the variety of situations and pacing keep the
audience's attention.
    SUBJ: Problem solving./ Mathematics.

512   Ph-1 P-A/2 $16.95   T   KB944
ANNO, MASAICHIRO. Anno's mysterious multiplying jar. By Masaichiro
and Mitsumasa Anno. Illustrated by Mitsumasa Anno. Philomel ISBN
0-399-20951-4, 1983. unp. col. ill.
    Exposes the mind-boggling universe of factorials through first an
imaginary journey set inside a jar and secondly through specific
demonstrations using dots and equations. This creative introduction to
an often applied advanced mathematical concept is achieved with
singular clarity and beauty. A choice resource to share with a group.
    SUBJ: Factorials./ Mathematics.

513   Ph-1 P-2 $15.89   L   KB945
ANNO, MITSUMASA. Anno's counting book. Crowell/HarperCollins
ISBN 0-690-01288-8; In Canada: HarperCollins, 1977. 28p. col. ill.
    Selectors' Choice, 12th ed.
    Big book available (ISBN 0-06-443315-3, 1992).
    A charming and absorbing counting book, 0 - 12, which invites the
child to observe and classify, study and ponder. The lovely and

detailed illustrations show a landscape changing through the various times of day and the turning seasons, months and years, to say nothing of the interesting activities of the people and animals who enter the pictures, one-by-one, two-by-two, and so on.
SUBJ: Counting.

513   Ph-3 4-6/5 $15.95   T   KB946
BURNS, MARILYN. Math for smarty pants. Illus. by Martha Weston. Little, Brown ISBN 0-316-11738-2; In Canada: Little, Brown, 1982. 128p. ill. (Brown paper school book).
   Will lead the gifted math investigator up some devilish paths and into the realm of perfect numbers, looping, probability, logic, geometry, statistics and calculator queries. In a cartoon format, with chatty characters trying to out-whiz each other, deductive reasoning is stressed; answers are not easy to come by and strategy is not outlined.
SUBJ: Mathematics.

VCR 513   Ph-1 K-1 $45.95   OD   KB947
HOW MUCH IS A MILLION? (Videocassette). Hosted by LeVar Burton. GPN/WNED-TV 120, 1997. 1/2" VHS videocassette (29min). (Reading Rainbow).
   MATH IS EVERYWHERE series teacher's guide available separately, $17.00.
   Includes public performance rights.
   Closed captioned.
   After reading HOW MUCH IS A MILLION, LeVar Burton wonders just how much a million is! He wanders the streets of New York trying to comprehend the city's millions of residents, visits a Crayola factory where millions of crayons are manufactured, and arrives at Giants Stadium as the crew and concession vendors prepare for the gigantic crowd. Difficult numeric concepts are made more concrete through film footage and close-up views of Kellogg's whimsical illustrations.
SUBJ: Million (The number)./ Billion (The number)./ Trillion (The number)./ Number concept.

SRC 513   Ph-1 P-2 $9.98   OD   KB948
JENKINS, ELLA. Counting games and rhythms for the little ones, vol. 1 (Sound recording cassette). Smithsonian Folkways 45029, c1964, 1990. 1 sound cassette.
   Ella Jenkins leads children from Lake Meadows Nursery School in Chicago in folk songs, rhymes and activities that teach number concepts to preschoolers through second graders.
SUBJ: Counting.

VCR 513   Ph-3 4-5 $99.00   OD   KB949
MENTAL COMPUTATION: USING MENTAL COMPUTATION FOR MULTIPLICATION (Videocassette). Agency for Instructional Technology; In Canada; Kinetic Film Enterprises, 1987. 1/2" VHS videocassette color (15min). (Solve it).
   Includes teacher's guide.
   Taking inventory in a store, determining how much to purchase for a luncheon for a large group, and figuring up a customer's purchase when a power failure knocks out the cash register are used as examples of when and how to multiply in one's head. The movement from one example to another keeps students' attention and this can serve as an effective introduction to instruction. Price is an inhibitor.
SUBJ: Multiplication.

513   Ph-1 K-1/2 $15.93   L   KB950
SCHWARTZ, DAVID M. How much is a million? Illus. by Steven Kellogg. Lothrop, Lee & Shepard ISBN 0-688-04050-0, 1985. unp. col. ill.
   Big book available from Mulberry (ISBN 0-688-13630-3, 1994), $18.95.
   Adventure in the world of uncountable millions, billions and trillions with comparisons and drawings of children, goldfish and tiny stars. The author's note explains the calculations used to provide the analogies in the text proper. Written at a technical level, it probably will need to be explained by an adult. A book to enjoy aloud and quietly.
SUBJ: Million (The number)./ Billion (The number)./ Trillion (The number)./ Number concept.

MCP 513   Ph-1 4-A $59.95   OD   KB951
SEILER, BONNIE. How the west was one + three x four (Microcomputer program). Wings for Learning/Sunburst 3886, c1987, 1989. 3.5" disk, 1 backup disk.
   Includes teacher's guide.
   Network version available.
   Available on Macintosh CD-ROM (6905FG) and Windows (6906FG), $59.95.
   Also available for Windows 3.1 or higher; DOS and Apple II family.
   System requirements: Macintosh LC or better required (4 MB), hard drive required, color Macintosh recommended.

The game format allows students to practice mathematical skills as well as problem solving strategies. The goal is to be the first person to land exactly on fifty. Each player's turn allows for four operation symbols and three numbers. Youngsters may play against the computer or another person. The level of expertise for the computer may be determined: a hint option is also available.
SUBJ: Arithmetic--Software./ Problem solving--Software./ Software--Arithmetic./ Software--Problem solving.

513.2   Ph-1 3-6/2 $15.95   L   KB952
ADLER, DAVID A. Fraction fun. Illus. by Nancy Tobin. Holiday House ISBN 0-8234-1259-8, 1996. unp. col. ill.
   Play with a paper plate pizza or real money to learn about fractions--what numerator and denominator mean and how these tricky numbers can ensure that you get your fair share. Bright colors and clear instructions add up to success.
SUBJ: Fractions.

513.2   Ph-3 1-3/3 $15.95   L   KB953
BOWEN, BETSY. Gathering: a northwoods counting book. Little, Brown ISBN 0-316-10371-3; In Canada: Little, Brown, 1995. unp. col. ill.
   In spring, preparations for the zero degree temperatures of winter begin and continue until 12 inches of snow have fallen. Woodcuts and text offer information about the region and changing seasons, but are less successful as a counting book.
SUBJ: Natural history--Minnesota./ Country life--Minnesota./ Seasons./ Counting.

513.2   Ph-3 P-2/1 $14.95   T   KB954
BRUSCA, MARIA CRISTINA. Three friends: a counting book./Tres amigos: un cuento para contar. By Maria Cristina Brusca and Tona Wilson. Henry Holt ISBN 0-8050-3707-1; In Canada: Fitzhenry & Whiteside, 1995. unp. col. ill.
   This bilingual counting book with a wild West theme will provide little buckaroos with wild and woolly fun. Meet tumbleweeds, roadrunners, cactus, snakes, and the two hapless cowpokes who try to lasso them. Nice addition to cowboy units.
SUBJ: Counting./ Bilingual materials--Spanish./ Spanish language materials./ Cowboys--West (U.S.).

CDR 513.2   Ph-1 3-6 $59.95   OD   KB955
CALCULATING CREW. School version. (CD-ROM). Edmark/Harcourt Brace 702-1074, 1996. 1 CD-ROM color. (Mighty math).
   Version 1.01.
   Includes teacher's guide.
   System requirements: Windows 3.1, Windows 95 or later; 486, Pentium or better (33 MHz or faster recommended); hard disk with 2MB free (Windows 95) or 5MB free (Windows 3.1); 8MB memory (RAM); Super VGA graphics, 640x480, 256 or more colors; double-speed or faster CD-ROM drive; Windows-compatible sound card; Windows-compatible printer (optional); TouchWindow (optional).
   System requirements: Macintosh System 7.0.1 or higher; 68040, 68030 (25 MHz or faster recommended), or PowerPC; 8MB memory (RAM), 4100K unused; 13" or larger monitor, 256 or more colors; double-speed or faster CD-ROM drive; printer (optional); TouchWindow (optional).
   Product (702-1074) runs on either Windows or Macintosh compatible hardware.
   Youngsters encounter four delightful activities which help them practice problem solving, addition, subtraction, multiplication, division, money transactions, estimation, rounding, and 3-D geometry. An exploration mode and a question-and-answer mode are included; difficulty levels can be changed. Works well with individual students and small groups.
SUBJ: Arithmetic--Software./ Software--Arithmetic./ Problem solving--Software./ Software--Problem solving./ Interactive media.

513.2   Ph-3 K-3/2 $9.95   T   KB956
CHALLONER, JACK. Science book of numbers. Gulliver/Harcourt Brace Jovanovich ISBN 0-15-200623-0, 1992. 29p. col. ill. (Science book of).
   Construct manipulatives such as an abacus, a marble chute, and a digit dial to arrange and rearrange numerical patterns. No user will ever claim that math is dull. Teachers who need inexpensive teaching props will welcome this.
SUBJ: Number systems./ Counting./ Mathematical recreations.

513.2   Ph-2 P-1/2 $15.00   T   KB957
GOENNEL, HEIDI. Odds and evens: a numbers book. Tambourine ISBN 0-688-12918-8, 1994. unp. col. ill.
   Presents numbers 1-13 using familiar expressions such as a one horse town, two in the bush, three blind mice. Bright, graphic illustrations make beginner's counting fun. A wise adult will need to explain all the maxims. Useful for language arts as well as math classes.
SUBJ: Counting.

513.2   Ph-3 P-1/2 $14.95   L   KB958
HALSEY, MEGAN. 3 pandas planting. Bradbury ISBN 0-02-742035-3; In Canada: Maxwell Macmillan, 1994. unp. col. ill.
     Animals cavort while counting backwards from 12 to illustrate salient points of conservation such as recycling, tree planting, and collecting litter. The youngest readers will easily understand that taking care of the earth is everyone's job. For environmental studies.
     SUBJ: Counting./ Environmental protection.

513.2   Ph-2 P-2/3 $13.99   T   KB959
HARTMANN, WENDY. One sun rises: an African wildlife counting book. Illus. by Nicolaas Maritz. Dutton ISBN 0-525-45225-7, 1994. unp. col. ill.
     Ten African animals watch the sun rise; then another ten watch it set. Bold ethnic paintings make this a perfect complement to African and animal studies. Children will enjoy learning about kestrels, suricates, and hyenas along with the more mundane bats, lions, and moths. Includes notes on all the animals shown.
     SUBJ: Counting./ Zoology--Africa.

513.2   Ph-1 K-3/3 $13.89   L   KB960
HULME, JOY N. Sea squares. Illus. by Carol Schwartz. Hyperion ISBN 1-56282-080-X; In Canada: Hyperion, 1991. unp. col. ill.
     Marine animals cunningly introduce square numbers. Three clown fish swim by with a combination of nine stripes and four seals sun their sixteen flippery feet. Pictures can stand on their own, but when children are told the significance of the number combinations, they will spend hours pouring over the pages and pointing things out. More detailed information about the sea animals is given at the end of the book.
     SUBJ: Counting./ Multiplication./ Marine animals.

513.2   Ph-2 P-2/3 $13.89   L   KB961
HULME, JOY N. Sea sums. Illus. by Carol Schwartz. Hyperion ISBN 0-7868-2142-6; In Canada: Little, Brown, 1996. 31p. col. ill.
     Adding and subtracting appears naturally on a coral reef as sea creatures hunt and eat their prey. Rhyming text and oceanscape gouache paintings create an inviting story that can be read independently of the math lesson.
     SUBJ: Addition./ Subtraction./ Stories in rhyme.

CDR 513.2   Ph-2 1-3 $59.95   OD   KB962
JAMES DISCOVERS MATH. School ed. (CD-ROM). Broderbund 5270349, 1995. 1 CD-ROM color. (Active minds series).
     Includes user's guide, teacher's guide and set of 40 Attrilinks (TM).
     System requirements: Windows IBM or 100% compatible; 33MHz 386DX; 4MB RAM (8MB for Windows 95); hard disk with 4MB free; double-speed CD-ROM drive; Windows sound device with compatible drivers; Windows 3.1 with MS/PC DOS 5.0 or higher, or Windows 95; Quicktime for Windows 2.0 (version included on CD); SuperVGA monitor (640x480, 256 colors) with compatible drivers; mouse; monochrome or color printer (optional).
     System requirements: Macintosh 25MHz 68030 or faster; 4MB RAM with 2.5MB free; hard disk with 1MB free; double-speed CD-ROM drive; System 7.0.1 or higher; video support for 256 colors or shades of grey; 13" color or grey-scale monitor; Sound Manager 3.0 (uses 96KB of hard disk space--version included on CD); Quicktime 2.0 (uses 1,056KB of hard disk space--version included on CD); printer (optional).
     Product (5270349) runs on either Windows or Macintosh compatible hardware.
     Ten engaging activities and games introduce youngsters to the world of math through James' eyes. Shapes, numbers, patterns, telling time, measurement, and other concepts are covered. Excellent sound and animation hold student's attention. Some activities work well with the entire class.
     SUBJ: Arithmetic--Software./ Software--Arithmetic./ Mathematics--Software./ Software--Mathematics./ Mathematical recreations--Software./ Software--Mathematical recreations./ Interactive media.

513.2   Ph-2 2-4/2 $15.95   L   KB963
LEEDY, LOREEN. Fraction action. Holiday House ISBN 0-8234-1109-5, 1994. 32p. col. ill.
     The antics of an assortment of crocodiles, hens, cows, and dogs demonstrate fractions with a lemonade stand, a watermelon, and other goodies. Snappy dialogue and personable cartoon characters make this an appealing math book.
     SUBJ: Fractions./ Arithmetic.

513.2   Ph-2 K-3/2 $16.95   L   KB964
LEEDY, LOREEN. Mission: addition. Holiday House ISBN 0-8234-1307-1, 1997. unp. col. ill.
     Leedy's cartoon animals' antics come front and center to teach addition using familiar activities: shopping, bowling, and eating in a

restaurant. Number sentences, tallies, and pictures send the message that addition permeates our lives. Short stories can stand alone without a math lesson.
     SUBJ: Addition.

513.2   Ph-2 1-3/2 $15.95   L   KB965
LEEDY, LOREEN. 2 x 2 = boo!: a set of spooky multiplication stories. Holiday House ISBN 0-8234-1190-7, 1995. 32p. col. ill.
     Learn multiplication facts from zero to five with an assortment of ghosts, witches, bats, and pumpkins. The Halloween theme is a clever way to grab students' attention and hold it while readers absorb some math.
     SUBJ: Multiplication./ Halloween.

513.2   Ph-2 P-2/2 $15.88   L   KB966
LONG, LYNETTE. Domino addition. Charlesbridge ISBN 0-88106-879-9; In Canada: Monarch, 1996. unp. col. ill.
     Spanish edition available SUMEMOS CON EL DOMINO (ISBN 0-88106-909-4, 1997), $6.95.
     Black dominoes with white dots line up numerals 1 through 12. Readers are asked to add the spots and examine addition factors in eye-catching pages. This will be popular in math classes and at recess. Loan a set of dominoes when checking out the book!
     SUBJ: Addition./ Dominoes./ Spanish language materials.

FSS 513.2   Ph-2 K-2 $36.00   OD   KB967
MATH, MONEY, AND YOU (Sound filmstrip). National Geographic 30442, 1989. 2 filmstrips color, 2 sound cassettes.
     Includes teacher's guide.
     Canadian version available C30449, $72.00.
     "Introduces money, its value, and its uses." (CIP). Design using student participation is a plus as are the strong activity suggestions found in the teacher's guides. Valuable curriculum support for early grades and for special needs pupils.
     Contents: Count it out (65fr/16min); What does it cost? (64fr/15min).
     SUBJ: Counting./ Number games./ Money./ Arithmetic.

513.2   Ph-1 K-3/3 $15.95   L   KB968
MAZZOLA, FRANK. Counting is for the birds. Frank Mazzola, Jr. Charlesbridge ISBN 0-88106-951-5, 1997. unp. col. ill., map.
     Includes index.
     Count from one to 20 as various birds land on a swinging birdfeeder carefully guarded by a cat. Full-page illustrations of birds accompanied by rhyming text make this a joy for reading aloud and will convert even the youngest listener to bird watching. Migration patterns, food preferences, and other details are given in smaller print. Coloration, size proportions, and body shapes are presented true to life. Digital paintings created on a personal computer invite repeated viewings and will fascinate computer buffs.
     SUBJ: Birds./ Counting.

513.2   Ph-1 P-2/1 $14.95   L   KB969
MCMILLAN, BRUCE. Eating fractions. Cooked, written, drafted, and photo-illus. by Bruce McMillan. Scholastic ISBN 0-590-43770-4; In Canada: Scholastic, 1991. unp. col. ill.
     Two children, obviously enjoying themselves, divide up a variety of wholesome foods into 1/2s, 1/3s, and 1/4s to demonstrate fractional parts. Bright, large photographs fill the pages. Four recipes are included to encourage delicious math fun.
     SUBJ: Fractions.

513.2   Ph-1 P-A $18.93   L   KB970
MICKLETHWAIT, LUCY. I spy two eyes: numbers in art. Devised and selected by Lucy Micklethwait. Greenwillow ISBN 0-688-12642-1, 1993. unp. col. ill.
     View numerals 1 - 20 illustrated by masterpieces. Seven circles can be found in Kadinsky's "Swinging" while 20 angels float by in Botticelli's "Mystic Nativity." Here's a painless way to introduce famous artists to even the youngest students. Good choice to integrate fine arts with the curriculum.
     SUBJ: Counting./ Art appreciation.

CDR 513.2   Ph-1 P-2 $59.95   OD   KB971
MILLIE'S MATH HOUSE (CD-ROM). Edmark, 1995. 1 CD-ROM color. (Early learning house).
     Includes user's guide.
     Version 2.0.
     System requirements: Windows 3.1 (enhanced mode), Windows 95 or later; 4MB required (8MB highly recommended); CD-ROM drive (double-speed or faster recommended); 386DX/33 MHz required (486/33 MHz or better recommended); super VGA, 640x480 (256 colors, or more, required); hard disk with 2MB free; mouse; Windows-compatible sound-output device; Windows-compatible printer

(optional); microphone (optional); TouchWindow (optional).
System requirements: Macintosh: color Macintosh (256 colors required); 4MB (8MB recommended); CD-ROM drive (double-speed or faster recommended); System 7.0.1 or higher; 13" or larger monitor; printer (optional); microphone (optional); TouchWindow (optional).
Product runs on either Windows or Macintosh compatible hardware. The animation, graphics, and clear sound make this program a superb method for introducing preschoolers to the computer and math. Activities for seven different number concepts can be done in a question-and-answer or exploration mode. The synthesized voice instructions make adult help unnecessary.
SUBJ: Arithmetic--Software./ Software--Arithmetic./ Problem solving--Software./ Software--Problem solving./ Mathematical recreations--Software./ Software--Mathematical recreations./ Interactive media.

MCP 513.2   Ph-1 P-2 $49.95   OD KB972
MILLIE'S MATH HOUSE (Microcomputer program). Edmark, 1992. 4 3.5" disks. (Early learning house).
Includes teacher's guide.
Also available for Windows/DOS, $59.95.
Selectors' Choice, 19th ed.
System requirements: Macintosh Plus or later; Hard disk with 5.5 MB available during installation (System 6.0.7 or later: 1 MB RAM - black & white, 2 MB - color; System 7 or later: 2 MB RAM - black & white, 4 MB - color).
The animation, graphics, and clear sound make this program a superb method for introducing preschoolers to the computer and math. Activities for seven different number concepts can be done in a question-and-answer or exploration mode. The synthesized voice instructions make adult help unnecessary.
SUBJ: Arithmetic--Software./ Software--Arithmetic./ Problem solving--Software./ Software--Problem solving./ Mathematical recreations--Software./ Software--Mathematical recreations.

VCR 513.2   Ph-1 5-A $175.00   OD KB973
MR. MARFIL'S LAST WILL AND TESTAMENT (Videocassette). Human Relations Media 881-VS, 1991. 1/2" VHS videocassette color (39min). (Detective stories for math problem solving).
Includes 6 Student Clue Kits, and Teacher's Resource Book.
Mr. Marfil loved math games so he used his will to challenge his heir's math skills. Students have to solve four problems including square roots and percentages to get the numbers to his safe's combination. Challenging and intriguing to good mathematicians, but perhaps frustrating to those less skilled.
SUBJ: Mathematics./ Problem solving.

513.2   Ph-2 P-3/2 $14.89   L   KB974
MURPHY, STUART J. Too many kangaroo things to do! Illus. by Kevin O'Malley. HarperCollins ISBN 0-06-025884-5; In Canada: HarperCollins, 1996. 33p. col. ill. (MathStart).
Includes bibliography.
Kangaroo's friends are planning his surprise birthday party. Using multiplication, the animals bake a cake, make fruit punch, wrap presents, and decorate. Counting from 10 to 40 by tens is also part of the plot. Animal antics are fun, and the birthday theme threads the story together. Children will like working out the math pages with pretend or real objects that match the story items.
SUBJ: Multiplication./ Addition.

513.2   Ph-3 3-A/3 $16.95   T   KB975
OCKENGA, STARR. World of wonders: a trip through numbers. Photos by Starr Ockenga. Poem and painted backgrounds by Eileen Doolittle. Houghton Mifflin ISBN 0-395-48726-9, 1988. 48p. col. ill.
Includes bibliography.
Twelve collections of items related to a number are displayed in complexly composed photographs. Some of the items are easily associated, others require some thinking and a numbered key to each photograph is provided at the back of the book. The brief poems provides some clues but are virtually unnecessary--this is a visual puzzle.
SUBJ: Counting.

513.2   Ph-1 P-4/3 $14.95   L   KB976
OWENS, MARY BETH. Counting cranes. Little, Brown ISBN 0-316-67719-1; In Canada: Little, Brown, 1993. unp. col. ill.
One to fifteen whooping cranes follow seasonal patterns of mating, feeding, and migrating. Artistic renditions of marshes, shallows, frozen corn fields, and blustery skies speak of the beauty and dangers surrounding this great bird's life. Real-life crane counting began in 1941 when, due to human interference, crane population hit a low of 15. This extraordinary combination of math, ornithology, and artwork will enhance nature studies and environmental studies.
SUBJ: Counting./ Whooping cranes./ Cranes (Birds).

SRC 513.2   Ph-1 2-4 $11.95   OD KB977
PALMER, HAP. Singing multiplication tables (Sound recording cassette). By Hap and Penny Palmer. Educational Activities AC45-101R, 1971. 1 sound cassette.
Melodic jingles sung to swinging music, with rock, folk or jazz flavor encourage children to master, painlessly, the multiplication tables through 12 times 12. Each table is first sung twice with the correct answers and then sung again without the answers so the student can insert them. The final side of the series contains a quiz with mixed-up multiplication fact problems. Learning can be fun for both fast and slow achievers.
SUBJ: Multiplication.

VCR 513.2   Ph-1 5-A $175.00   OD KB978
PHANTOM OF THE BELL TOWER (Videocassette). Human Relations Media 880-VS, 1991. 1/2" VHS videocassette color (26min). (Detective stories for math problem solving).
Includes 6 Student Clue Kits, and Teacher's Resource Book.
Use math skills to solve the mystery of phantom bell-ringing at St. Barnabas Church. After viewing the story in part one, students are given maps, newspapers, and other clues to start their problem-solving process. Part two, with the solutions, can be viewed after students have tried it on their own. An intriguing and entertaining exercise for math classes.
SUBJ: Mathematics./ Problem solving.

VCR 513.2   Ph-2 3-5 $90.00   OD KB979
PROBLEM SOLVING: RECOGNIZING NECESSARY INFORMATION (Videocassette). Agency for Instructional Technology; In Canada: Kinetic Film Enterprises, 1982. 1/2" VHS videocassette color (15min). (It figures).
Includes teacher's guide.
A treasure hunt involves clues that include mathematical calculations and extraneous details. The live action scenario accented by an animated segment keeps the attention of young people and is a good introduction to skills that need to be brought together to solve word problems.
SUBJ: Problem solving./ Arithmetic.

VCR 513.2   Ph-3 5-6 $99.00   OD KB980
RATIO/PROPORTION/PERCENT: THE MEANING OF PERCENT (Videocassette). Agency for Instructional Technology; In Canada: Kinetic Film Enterpises, 1987. 1/2" VHS videocassette color (15min). (Solve it).
Includes teacher's guide.
Figuring out new prices for yard sale items reduced 5 to 50% provides the understanding of percentages. The child actors are fairly engaging even though somewhat stilted but the scenario does show viable concrete applications of the skill.
SUBJ: Percentage.

VCR 513.2   Ph-2 3-5 $90.00   OD KB981
RELATING FRACTIONS AND DECIMALS (Videocassette). Agency for Instructional Technology; In Canada: Kinetic Film Enterprises, 1982. 1/2" VHS videocassette color (14min). (It figures).
Includes teacher's guide.
Solving clues which require converting fractions to decimals in order to become a club member keeps David busy. The live action scenario augmented by an animated sequence reflecting a family feud between the Fractions and Decimals is attention holding. While designed to correlate with fourth grade math textbooks this can be used at other grade levels depending on need.
SUBJ: Word problems./ Problem solving./ Fractions./ Decimals./ Arithmetic.

513.2   Ph-2 P-1/3 $15.88   L   KB982
RYAN, PAM MUNOZ. Crayon counting book. By Pam Munoz Ryan and Jerry Pallotta. Illus. by Frank Mazzola, Jr. Charlesbridge ISBN 0-88106-955-8, 1996. unp. col. ill.
The youngest learner can relate crayons to counting beginning with a box of zero to ten; then proceeding in binary numbers from 12 to 24. Crayons appear in blushing pinks, rainbow formation, and other radiant hues. Exotic color names on the crayon labels add interest. Rhyming text reinforces the message that counting and coloring are fun.
SUBJ: Counting./ Color./ Crayons./ Stories in rhyme.

VCR 513.2   Ph-3 3-4 $90.00   OD KB983
USING FRACTIONS (Videocassette). Agency for Instructional Technology; In Canada: Kinetic Film Enterprises, 1982. 1/2" VHS videocassette color (14min). (It figures).
Includes teacher's guide.
Dividing up space in a camp bunk house and cutting a birthday cake into equal parts are the very real situations in which fractions are helpful. Well paced and mixing in a little humor this helps young

people see the use of fractions. Use as an introduction.
SUBJ: Problem solving./ Fractions./ Arithmetic.

VCR 513.2   Ph-1 A $19.95   OD KB984
VIEW FROM THE REAR TERRACE (Videocassette). Children's Television Workshop/dist. by GPN BL502, 1991. 1/2" VHS videocassette color (70min). (Mathnet mysteries).
Includes public performance rights.
Provides a first-class police show send-up while using mathematics skills. This MATHNET episode from Square One TV features mathematicians using percentages, combinatorics, pattern sequences, and interest rates. Strong motivator.
SUBJ: Mathematics./ Problem solving.

513.2   Ph-2 P-1 $15.90   L   KB985
YEKTAI, NIKI. Bears at the beach: counting 10 to 20. Millbrook Press ISBN 0-7613-0047-3, 1996. unp. col. ill.
"Lucas-Evans book."
Families of cartoon bears frolic in the sand, demonstrating numbers with sand castles, beach umbrellas, and popsicles. Children will have fun finger pointing and counting from 10 to 20.
SUBJ: Counting.

CDR 513.2   Ph-1 K-2 $59.95   OD KB986
ZOO ZILLIONS. School version (CD-ROM). Edmark/Harcourt Brace 702-1075, 1966. 1 CD-ROM color. (Mighty math).
Version 1.11.
Includes teacher's guide.
System requirements: Windows 3.1, Windows 95 or later; 486, Pentium or better (33 MHz or faster recommended); hard disk with 2MB free (Windows 95) or 5MB free (Windows 3.1); 8MB memory (RAM); Super VGA graphics, 640x480, 256 colors or more; double-speed or faster CD-ROM drive; Windows-compatible sound card; Windows-compatible printer (optional); TouchWindow (optional).
System requirements: System 7.0.1 or higher; 68040, 68030 (25 MHz or faster recommended), or PowerPC; 4MB memory (RAM), 1900K unused, 5MB for System 7.5 or later, 8MB highly recommended; 13" or larger monitor, 256 or more colors; double-speed or faster CD-ROM drive; printer (optional); TouchWindow (optional)
Product (702-1075) runs on either Windows or Macintosh compatible hardware.
Youngsters encounter five delightful activities which help them practice problem solving, addition, subtraction, money transactions, story problems, and simple 3-D geometry. An exploration mode and a question and answer mode are included; difficulty levels can be changed. Works well with individual students and small groups.
SUBJ: Arithmetic--Software./ Software--Arithmetic./ Problem solving--Software./ Software--Problem solving./ Interactive media.

513.4   Ph-1 P-4/3 $15.95   T   KB987
ANNO, MITSUMASA. Anno's magic seeds. Philomel ISBN 0-399-22538-2; In Canada: Putnam, 1995. unp. col. ill.
Selectors' Choice, 21st ed.
Available from the National Library Service for the Blind and Physically Handicapped on sound recording cassette RC 41329.
In this multilayered fable, Jack learns the dynamics of planting golden seeds (One seed is capable of keeping a person fed for an entire year!). Soon he begins to save, share, and sell his bounty. Mathematics is incorporated as one seed produces two fruits which become two seeds. Readers are encouraged to calculate as well as observe. Pair with Barry's RAJAH'S RICE for a lesson on mathematical progression. Magical.
SUBJ: Arithmetic./ Mathematical recreations.

513.5   Ph-3 K-4/6 $15.95   T   KB988
GEISERT, ARTHUR. Roman numerals I to MM./Numerabilia romana uno ad duo mila: liber de difficillimo computando numerum. Houghton Mifflin ISBN 0-395-74519-5, 1996. 32p. col. ill.
"Walter Lorraine books."
Geisert believes "The best way to learn Roman numerals is to use them" (p.xxii), and readers have to use a plethora of pigs to investigate I, V, X, L, C, D, and M. Humorous artwork combined with a foreign number system.
SUBJ: Roman numerals./ Counting.

513.5   Ph-2 P-1/2 $13.93   L   KB989
GIGANTI, JR., PAUL. Each orange had 8 slices: a counting book. Illus. by Donald Crews. Greenwillow ISBN 0-688-10429-0, 1992. unp. col. ill.
Big book available from Mulberry (ISBN 0-688-13116-6, 1994), $18.95. Includes study guide.
Pictures with pizzazz illustrate beginning counting and simple addition. For a child to share with an adult. Takes math to familiar surroundings and makes it enjoyable. (Parents' Shelf).
SUBJ: Counting./ Addition.

516   Ph-1 P-1 $13.95   L   KB990
HOBAN, TANA. Circles, triangles, and squares. Simon & Schuster ISBN 0-02-744830-4; In Canada: Distican, 1974. unp. ill.
In this wordless picture book, the young child is introduced to circles, triangles and squares through a series of strong, clear photographs of things with which he or she is familiar such as bubbles, windows, cut cookies. Useful also for a lesson in basic photography.
SUBJ: Circle./ Triangle./ Square./ Shape.

516   Ph-1 2-6 $15.93   L   KB991
HOBAN, TANA. Shapes, shapes, shapes. Greenwillow ISBN 0-688-05833-7, 1986. unp. col. ill.
Sparkling color photographs with layered composition provide valued experiences in observing and classifying shapes for experienced viewers.
SUBJ: Shape./ Circle./ Triangle./ Square.

516   Ph-1 P-2 $13.93   L   KB992
HOBAN, TANA. Spirals, curves, fanshapes and lines. Greenwillow ISBN 0-688-11229-3, 1992. unp. col. ill.
Hoban's photographs explore the lines and swirls surrounding us in dishes of noodles, sea shells, furniture, and more. A wordless book that forces us to look and observe. After sharing, have children bring their own examples of geometry to class.
SUBJ: Shape.

516   Ph-2 P-2 $13.95   L   KB993
MACDONALD, SUSE. Sea shapes. Harcourt Brace ISBN 0-15-200027-5; In Canada: Harcourt Brace c/o Canadian Manda, 1994. unp. col. ill.
"Gulliver books."
Stars, circles, hearts, and squares float about in colorful seas created from paper collages. Younger readers will spend hours engrossed in the pages figuring out how a square with an accompaniment of diamonds reworks itself into a catfish. Ends with twelve short paragraphs about the featured sea creatures for those who want the biological data. Use for shape recognition and preschool ocean units.
SUBJ: Shape./ Marine animals.

516   Ph-1 P-1 $13.95   L   KB994
REISS, JOHN J. Shapes. Bradbury ISBN 0-02-776190-8, c1974. 32p. ill.
Bright, colorful illustrations of familiar objects are used to introduce young children to both two- and three-dimensional geometric shapes. Two animal characters transform squares into cubes, triangles into pyramids and circles into spheres.
SUBJ: Shape./ Geometry.

VCR 516.2   Ph-3 4-A $125.00   OD KB995
GEOMETRY AND MEASUREMENT: MEASURING ANGLES (Videocassette). Agency for Instructional Technology; In Canada: Kenetic Film Enterprises, 1987. 1/2" VHS videocassette color (15min). (Solve it).
Includes teacher's guide.
Discover how to form and measure angles with dance movements and shooting pool used as examples. Further applications are shown by an architect and young people making a model. Excellent as an introduction to or review of studying angles although the cost is an inhibitor.
SUBJ: Angles (Geometry)./ Geometry.

VCR 519   Ph-2 3-5 $99.00   OD KB996
DECIDING HOW CLOSE TO MEASURE (Videocassette). Agency for Instructional Technology; In Canada: Kinetic Film Enterprises, 1982. 1/2" VHS videocassette color (14min). (It figures).
Includes teacher's guide.
Building a tree house cannot be done by the eye alone or just by casual measurement a group of children discover. While designed to coordinate with fourth grade math textbooks this application of the importance of measurement can be used across grade levels. The price does pose limitations.
SUBJ: Measurement./ Arithmetic./ Problem solving.

519.2   Ph-1 4-6/4 $14.95   T   KB997
CUSHMAN, JEAN. Do you wanna bet?: your chance to find out about probability. Illus. by Martha Weston. Clarion ISBN 0-395-56516-2, 1991. 102p. ill.
Includes bibliography and index.
Code breaking, birthdays, surveys, statistics and raffle tickets combine to test and explore the vagaries of probability. Demonstrates that luck and chance are encountered daily, and includes an intriguing approach to math and educated guessing. Introduce a few pages as whole class activities and watch everyone scramble for this book and beg for more.
SUBJ: Probabilities.

519.2   Ph-2 5-6/4 $10.98   L   KB998
WYLER, ROSE. Test your luck. By Rose Wyler and Mary Elting. Illus. by Patrick Girouard. Messner ISBN 0-671-74311-2, 1992. 64p. ill. (Math fun).
> Includes index.
> Games, tests, and teasers allow readers to expand on the contributions of luck and fate to daily events by testing math theories and formulas. Text is overly wordy but the topics such as prediction, probability, and psychics are mesmeric. Math achievers will find special delights and accomplishments.
> SUBJ: Probabilities./ Mathematical recreations.

VCR 519.5   Ph-3 4-A $99.00   OD KB999
STATISTICS: UNDERSTANDING MEAN, MEDIAN, AND MODE (Videocassette). Agency for Instructional Technology; In Canada: Kinetic Film Enterprises, 1987. 1/2" VHS videocassette color (15min). (Solve it).
> Includes teacher's manual.
> Finding himself delivering far more than the promised average number of loaves, a boy soon learns the difference between mean, median and mode as do a group of children trying to save their soccer field. Applications of the value of the midpoint measures is shown also in determining purchases of advertising space by a toy company. Well-developed and interesting, this serves as a good introduction and/or review although the cost is an inhibitor.
> SUBJ: Average./ Statistics./ Arithmetic.

520   Ph-3 A/10 $18.95   L   KC000
CAMP, CAROLE ANN. American astronomers: searchers and wonderers. Enslow ISBN 0-89490-631-3, 1996. 104p. ill. (Collective biographies).
> Includes index.
> Ten brief biographies of astronomers such as Maria Mitchell, Edwin Hubble, and Vera Rubin document the dedication and excitement of careers in science. Not all set out to study the heavens (some took circuitous routes), but all achieved success. Valuable in underscoring the roles of various women scientists; for inspiration and short reports. For women's studies.
> SUBJ: Astronomers./ Women astronomers.

520   Ph-2 3-A/8 $12.95   P   KC001
CAMPBELL, ANN. New York Public Library amazing space: a book of answers for kids. By Ann-Jeanette Campbell. Illus. by Jessica Wolk-Stanley. Wiley ISBN 0-471-14498-3; In Canada: Wiley, 1997. 186p. ill. (New York Public Library answer books for kids series).
> "Stonesong Press book."
> Includes chronology, glossary, bibliographies and index.
> A compilation of the New York Public Library's most common astronomy inquiries. Nine topical chapters describe the universe, stars, solar system, earth and moon, planets, and space exploration. Also contains charts, diagrams, and short paragraphs about Einstein's theory, mythology behind planet names, space tragedies, and more. Index allows use as a ready reference; but browsers will find much to learn. The real value is the concise, clear definitions that contain the most recent knowledge about the frontiers of space.
> SUBJ: Astronomy--Miscellanea./ Outer space--Miscellanea.

520   Ph-1 3-6/6 $16.95   T   KC002
COUPER, HEATHER. Space atlas. By Heather Couper and Nigel Henbest. Illus. by Luciano Corbella. Harcourt Brace Jovanovich ISBN 0-15-200598-6, 1992. 64p col illus and photos.
> Includes index.
> Oversized atlas brings readers up to date on the solar system, our moon, space exploration and colonization. Pages are filled with factual diagrams, photographs, facts and figure charts and text. Browsers and space enthusiasts alike will find hours of delight.
> SUBJ: Outer space./ Solar system./ Astronomy.

CDR 520   Ph-1 5-A $39.95   OD KC003
EYEWITNESS ENCYCLOPEDIA OF SPACE AND THE UNIVERSE (CD-ROM). DK Multimedia ISBN 0-7894-0881-3, 1996. 1 CD-ROM color.
> Also available for Macintosh (ISBN 0-7894-0886-4), $39.95.
> System requirements: IBM or compatible PC with 486DX/33MHz or above microprocessor; 4MB of RAM (8MB recommended), MPC-compatible double-speed CD-ROM drive and sound card; mouse; SVGA 256-color display; loudspeakers or headphones; and Microsoft Windows version 3.1 or later.
> A useful reference for quick information on the solar system, the space race, sky watching, important space scientists and astronauts, spacecraft, star clusters, and space history. The wealth of video, audio, and glossary entries makes the material easily accessible. Works well in a learning center.
> SUBJ: Solar system--Software./ Software--Solar System./ Astronomy--Software./ Software--Astronomy./ Interactive media.

520   Ph-1 3-A/11 $15.95   T   KC004
VISUAL DICTIONARY OF THE UNIVERSE. DK Publishing ISBN 1-56458-336-8, 1993. 64p. col. ill., maps. (Eyewitness visual dictionaries).
> Includes glossary and index.
> A kaleidoscope of heavenly views where each planet is peeled apart, like an orange, revealing its innermost secrets. A wealth of complex information is shared in the vivid, intelligent artwork that affirms this series' excellence. All inclusive index easily allows use as a ready reference. Will facilitate student understanding of astronomy, space exploration, and the Big Bang theory.
> SUBJ: Astronomy./ Solar system.

MCP 520   Ph-1 4-A $59.95   OD KC005
WHERE IN SPACE IS CARMEN SANDIEGO? (Microcomputer program). Broderbund, 1993. 4 3.5" disks.
> Includes teacher's guide and user's guide.
> Includes PETERSON FIRST GUIDES: ASTRONOMY, Houghton Mifflin (ISBN 0-395-46790-X, 1988).
> System requirements: IBM/Tandy and 100% compatibles. 16 MHz 386 or faster; 640K RAM and hard disk with 8 MB free space; MS/PC-DOS 3.1 or higher; VGA monitor card, VGA monitor; Mouse, keyboard; 1.44 MB 3.5" disk drive. To play digitized voices and sound effects: Sound Blaster, Sound Blaster Pro, Pro Audio Spectrum, Disney Sound Source, or PS/1 or Tandy computer equipped with support for digitized sound. To best hear musical scores: Sound Blaster, Sound Blaster Pro, Roland MT-32/CM-32L/LAPC-1, AdLib, or General MIDI sound devices recommended.
> System requirements: Macintosh System 6.0.7 or higher; 4MB RAM; 11MB free hard disk space; high-density disk drive; 256-color monitor.
> Like all of the Carmen Sandiego software, this program is designed so that students not only learn reference skills as they use PETERSON FIRST GUIDES: ASTRONOMY, but also learn about the solar system as they solve the Carmen mysteries. For use with individuals or small groups.
> SUBJ: Astronomy--Software./ Software--Astronomy./ Problem solving--Software./ Software--Problem solving.

522   Ph-3 A/7 $16.89   L   KC006
SCOTT, ELAINE. Adventure in space: the flight to fix the Hubble. Photos by Margaret Miller. Hyperion ISBN 0-7868-2031-4; In Canada: Little, Brown, 1995. 64p. col. ill.
> Includes index.
> Astronomy rocketed into the space age with the Hubble telescope; the problem was its mirror was too flat on one edge. Most wrote off the mission as a failure, but seven astronauts aboard the Endeavour turned it into a success story. Chronicles their journey into space to repair the telescope, replete with photographs of the astronauts and personal accounts of their courage. Will give inspiration and impetus to anyone considering a career in science. A true-life adventure story for reading aloud.
> SUBJ: Hubble Space Telescope./ Outer space--Exploration.

VCR 523   Ph-2 3-6 $49.95   OD KC007
MOON/OUTER SPACE (Videocassette). Disney Educational Productions 68A26VL00, 1994. 1/2" VHS videocassette color (52min). (Bill Nye the science guy: classroom edition).
> Includes teacher's guide.
> Includes public performance rights.
> 50 volume series also available for purchase as a set, 6P27VL00, $949.00.
> Closed captioned.
> Combines the latest graphic techniques and pop culture to create a palatable science lesson for young astronomers. Effective viewing assumes background knowledge and teacher preparation. Simple science experiments are demonstrated. Teacher's guide provides more experiment ideas. Good mix of entertainment and learning.
> SUBJ: Space sciences./ Astronomy./ Moon./ Experiments.

523.2   Ph-3 2-6/4 $14.95   L   KC008
COLE, JOANNA. Magic School Bus lost in the solar system. Illus. by Bruce Degen. Scholastic ISBN 0-590-41428-3, 1990. unp. col. ill.
> Spanish version available AUTOBUS MAGICO EN EL SISTEMA SOLAR (ISBN 0-590-46429-9, 1992).
> Ms. Frizzle's class is off again, this time to outer space. They make pit stops on the sun, moon and planets, learning a bus load of facts along the way. A must purchase for fans already hooked on the magic school bus series.
> SUBJ: Planets./ Solar system./ Astronomy./ Spanish language materials.

CDR 523.2　　　　　　Ph-1 5-A　　$99.95　　OD KC009
GREAT SOLAR SYSTEM RESCUE (CD-ROM). Tom Snyder
Productions/Chedd-Angier/MCET GSD-D, 1996. 1 CD-ROM color.
　　Version 2.0.
　　Includes teacher's guide and student reference booklets.
　　Also available for Windows, $99.95.
　　System requirements: QuickTime-capable Macintosh computer;
　　double-speed (or higher) CD-ROM drive; System 7.0 or higher; at
　　least 2MB of available RAM; minimum of 256 colors or 16
　　grayscales, thousands of colors are highly recommended, but not
　　required; 640x480 (or larger) monitor.
　　The four cooperative activities contained in this package introduce
　　students to the solar system, using scientific inquiry skills, and provide
　　practice in research skills. The package is easy to set up and use as
　　well as extremely motivating for students. Excellent for use with an
　　entire class or with small groups.
　　SUBJ: Solar system--Software./ Software--Solar System./ Planets--
　　Software./ Software--Planets./ Interactive media.

VD 523.2　　　　　　Ph-1 5-A　　$349.95　　OD KC010
GREAT SOLAR SYSTEM RESCUE (Videodisc). Tom Snyder Productions
ISBN 1-55998-299-3, 1992. 1 12" double-sided CAV videodisc color.
　　Includes teacher's guide, 28 student booklets, reproducible masters,
　　and student worksheets.
　　Software available GSSS-D $49.95.
　　Selectors' Choice, 19th ed.
　　System requirements: Monitor (large video monitor for whole-class
　　viewing), videodisc player (Hitachi 9500, 9550, 9600; Philips VP406
　　(PAL); Pioneer 2200, 4100 (PAL), 4200, 8000; Pioneer LDV 6000,
　　Pioneer 6000, 6000A, 6010A; Sony 1000A, 1200, 1450, 1500,
　　1500 (PAL), 1550, 2000, 3600); bar code reader (optional but
　　recommended).
　　The four cooperative activities contained in this package introduce
　　students to the solar system, using scientific inquiry skills, and provides
　　practice in research skills. The package is easy to set up and use as
　　well as extremely motivating for students. Excellent for use with an
　　entire class or with small groups.
　　SUBJ: Solar system./ Planets./ Interactive media.

VCR 523.2　　　　　　Ph-2 3-6　　$69.95　　OD KC011
JOURNEY THROUGH THE SOLAR SYSTEM (Videocassette). Knowledge
Unlimited 4672VD, 1991. 1/2" VHS videocassette color (15min).
　　Includes Teacher's Guide.
　　Closed-captioned videocassette available 4672VDCC, $55.00.
　　This short trip explores our solar system, highlighting special features
　　and wonders indigenous to each of the nine planets. Excellent pictures
　　and narration impart a wealth of information without overwhelming
　　the audience. Use as a review, for independent study, or to check out
　　for home viewing.
　　SUBJ: Solar system.

523.2　　　　　　Ph-1 1-6/3　　$15.95　　L　KC012
LEEDY, LOREEN. Postcards from Pluto: a tour of the solar system.
Holiday House ISBN 0-8234-1000-5, 1993. unp. col. ill.
　　Selectors' Choice, 20th ed.
　　Blast off for the solar system with a group of young astronauts
　　guided by a robot. The space explorers send witty, fact-filled
　　dispatches back to Earth describing the sights. Example: the postcard
　　sent from Venus has Botticelli's Venus as a stamp and is addressed to
　　Cupid City. The postcard format is engagingly effective and could
　　easily act as inspiration for other research and creative writing
　　assignments.
　　SUBJ: Solar system./ Planets.

CDR 523.2　　　　　　Ph-1 4-A　　$39.95　　OD KC013
MOHL, ROBERT. Planetary taxi (CD-ROM). By Robert Mohl and Margo
Nanny. Voyager ISBN 1-55940-626-7, 1993. 1 CD-ROM color. (Visual
almanac series).
　　Includes user's guide.
　　System requirements: Any color-capable Macintosh with a 13"
　　monitor; System 6.0.7; 2500K of available RAM; CD-ROM drive
　　(double-speed recommended).
　　System requirements: 486SX-25 or higher CPU, 640x480 256-color
　　display (accelerator recommended), 8MB RAM, MPC2-compatible
　　CD-ROM drive; sound card with speakers or headphones; Microsoft
　　Windows 3.1; MS-DOS 5.0 or later.
　　Product (ISBN 1-55940-626-7) runs on either Macintosh or Windows
　　compatible hardware.
　　Filled with excellent information, this program takes students on a tour
　　of the solar system as they pick up passengers, who provide hints
　　about where they wish to visit. Reference options are also included.
　　Works well with the entire class on a large screen or as a learning
　　center.
　　SUBJ: Solar system--Software./ Software--Solar System./
　　Astronomy--Software./ Software--Astronomy./ Interactive media.

CDR 523.2　　　　　　Ph-1 2-5　　$44.95　　OD KC014
SCHOLASTIC'S THE MAGIC SCHOOL BUS EXPLORES THE SOLAR
SYSTEM. Academic ed. (CD-ROM). Microsoft/Scholastic ISBN
1-57231-075-8; In Canada: Microsoft Canada, 1994. 1 CD-ROM color.
(Scholastic's the Magic School Bus explores).
　　Includes user's guide, teacher's guide and activity cards.
　　Version 1.00.
　　System requirements: Multimedia PC or compatible with a 486SX or
　　higher microprocessor, 25 MHz (33 MHz recommended), 4MB of
　　RAM (8MB recommended), at least 5MB of available hard-disk
　　space, doublespeed CD-ROM drive, 8-bit audio board (16-bit
　　suggested), and SVGA display capable of 256 colors (local bus
　　video recommended); MS-DOS operating system version 5.0 or later;
　　Microsoft Windows operating system version 3.1 or later; Microsoft
　　Mouse or compatable pointing device; headphones or speakers.
　　The whimsical Ms. Frizzle of Scholastic's book series takes users of
　　this CD-ROM throughout the solar system. NASA videos, science
　　experiments, games, multimedia reports, and planetary information are
　　available. Excellent learning center or small group activity.
　　SUBJ: Solar system--Software./ Software--Solar System./ Planets--
　　Software./ Software--Planets./ Interactive media.

523.2　　　　　　Ph-1 4-8/7　　$19.93　　L　KC015
SIMON, SEYMOUR. Our solar system. Morrow ISBN 0-688-09993-9,
1992. 64p. col. ill.
　　Includes index.
　　Wander through our solar system to visit nine planets, asteroids,
　　moons, and comets that orbit the sun. Astonishing photographs
　　coupled with the latest scientific information from satellites produce
　　exciting revelations and make this a powerful statement for continued
　　space exploration. Documents amazing discoveries that have been
　　made since Galileo first viewed the heavens. Leaves readers with a
　　sense of awe and wonder as to what still lies beyond.
　　SUBJ: Solar system./ Planets.

PIC 523.2　　　　　　Ph-1 4-A　　$9.95　　OD KC016
SOLAR SYSTEM (Picture). Hansen Planetarium, 1990. 1 study print color
(38"x26").
　　If you plan to purchase any scientific poster, this is it! Features a
　　large drawing of the orbiting planets in relative distances from the
　　sun. Along the bottom, blocks depict relative orbits, comets and
　　asteroids, Earth's placement in the Milky Way, and planets' sizes.
　　Includes brief descriptions of each planet and the sun, comparison
　　chart of known moons, and a chart with figures on the planets' orbits,
　　gravities, temperatures, atmospheres, and more. Students will absorb
　　a year's worth of information.
　　SUBJ: Solar system./ Planets.

VCR 523.2　　　　　　Ph-3 4-6　　$80.00　　KC017
SUN, EARTH, MOON (Videocassette). National Geographic 51727,
1995. 1/2" VHS videocassette color (20min).
　　Includes teacher's guide.
　　Closed captioned.
　　Using balloons, lighted globes, and a video camera, a teacher
　　explains the relative size of the three heavenly bodies, reasons for
　　seasonal changes, and phases of the moon. Also explains the
　　importance of gravity and a solar eclipse. To reinforce learning, the
　　classroom teacher should encourage students to carry out the same
　　activities under direction. Personalized approach has a lot of impact
　　and appeal; best used in small increments.
　　SUBJ: Solar system./ Sun./ Moon./ Earth.

VCR 523.2　　　　　　Ph-2 5-A　　$89.00　　OD KC018
WHAT'S OUT THERE?: OUR SOLAR SYSTEM AND BEYOND
(Videocassette). Rainbow Educational RB8330, 1997. 1/2" VHS
videocassette color (25min).
　　Includes teacher's guide.
　　Includes public performance rights.
　　Photographs taken from the Mariner and Voyager satellites exhibit
　　the advanced knowledge recently acquired about the sun, planets,
　　and moon. Although the narrative may need additional explanation,
　　the meaningful description and the photographs make this colorful
　　video valuable for individual and classroom use.
　　SUBJ: Solar system./ Astronomy.

523.3　　　　　　Ph-1 K-6/4　　$15.95　　L　KC019
GIBBONS, GAIL. Moon book. Holiday House ISBN 0-8234-1297-0,
1997. unp. col. ill.
　　Includes chronology.
　　Selectors' Choice, 21st ed.
　　Explains the moon's geology, exploration, and eclipses with minimum
　　text and large, colorful illustrations that captivate and inform.
　　Excellent diagrams of phases and orbit. Even the youngest listeners
　　will want to take out the binoculars and moon gaze. Final three

pages list milestones, stories, and facts. Enlightening both for beginners and seasoned observers.
SUBJ: Moon.

523.3   Ph-3 4-6/4 $13.95   L   KC020
KRUPP, E. C. Moon and you. Illus. by Robin Rector Krupp. Macmillan ISBN 0-02-751142-1; In Canada: Maxwell Macmillan, 1993. 48p. ill.
Learn moon facts, moon legends, and how people observed celestial cycles and organized their lives around lunar calendars. Discusses the dynamics of waxing, waning, eclipse, and the moon's geology. Fantastic, detailed black and white illustrations (including a full-page werewolf) have power to teach and entertain. Includes beliefs and folklore for multicultural studies.
SUBJ: Moon.

523.3   Ph-2 K-4/4 $14.95   L   KC021
SIMON, SEYMOUR. Moon. Four Winds/Macmillan ISBN 0-02-782840-9, 1984. unp. ill.
Summarizes knowledge of the moon's weather, temperature, appearance and questions about its origin based on the Apollo expeditions. Large black and white photographs enhance this title.
SUBJ: Moon.

523.4   Ph-1 3-6/7 $15.95   L   KC022
APFEL, NECIA H. Voyager to the planets. Clarion ISBN 0-395-55209-5, 1991. 48p. col. ill.
Includes index and bibliography.
Selectors' Choice, 18th ed.
Wondrous pictures and clear text follow the trail blazing Voyager II as it treks off into space for rendezvous with Jupiter, Saturn, Uranus and Neptune. Amazingly, when Voyager needs help due to technical breakdowns and malfunctioning equipment, scientists are able to respond across billions of miles. If you purchase only one new astronomy book, get this one!
SUBJ: Voyager Project./ Outer space--Exploration./ Planets--Exploration.

523.4   Ph-1 2-4/4 $14.89   L   KC023
BRANLEY, FRANKLYN M. Planets in our solar system. Rev. ed. Illus. by Don Madden. Crowell/HarperCollins ISBN 0-690-04581-6; In Canada: HarperCollins, 1987. 34p. col. ill.
Excellent, elementary introduction to solar system. Includes asteroids, comets, and the nine planets - their size and distance relationships, and directions for building a scale model solar system. Actual photographs, cartoons, diagrams, and charts make a lively, readable format.
SUBJ: Planets./ Solar system.

523.4   Ph-2 4-8/11 $17.95   T   KC024
BURROWS, WILLIAM E. Mission to deep space: Voyagers' journey of discovery. W. H. Freeman ISBN 0-7167-6500-4, 1993. 80p. col. ill.
"Scientific American books for young readers."
Includes glossary, index and bibliography.
Summarizes the two Voyager missions, planet by planet; dividing information into what scientists knew and what they learned. Good explanations of Voyager's construction and scientific instruments. Will bring outer space collections up-to-date.
SUBJ: Voyager Project./ Planets--Exploration./ Outer space--Exploration.

523.4   Ph-2 2-4/4 $15.95   L   KC025
GIBBONS, GAIL. Planets. Holiday House ISBN 0-8234-1040-4, 1993. unp. col. ill.
Here's a book for the youngest star gazers who want to know the names and characteristics of the planets. Each planet is given a doublespread of salient facts and large drawings. Also useful for reluctant readers.
SUBJ: Planets.

523.4   Ph-2 A/9 $14.95   T   KC026
HARRIS, ALAN W. Great Voyager adventure: a guided tour through the solar system. By Alan Harris and Paul Weissman. Messner ISBN 0-671-72539-4, 1990. 79p. col. ill.
Includes glossary and index.
Summarizes and interprets the data gathered by both Voyager explorations and highlights this wealth of information with outstanding satellite photographs, diagrams and charts. A carefully executed, fact-filled presentation guaranteed to bring astronomy buffs up to date.
SUBJ: Voyager Project./ Planets--Exploration./ Outer space--Exploration.

PIC 523.4   Ph-3 4-6 $14.95   KC027
KERROD, ROBIN. Story of space exploration (Picture). Illus. by Ron Jobson and Guy Smith. Lodestar/Dutton ISBN 0-525-67487-X; In Canada: McClelland & Stewart, 1994. 1 wall chart color (11' x 17" folded to 12" x 17").
An 11 section wall chart displays lunar explorations and missions to Mercury, Mars, Jupiter, Saturn, Neptune, Uranus and Pluto. Each space craft is shown alongside the planet it explored and data it gathered. Clever wall reference for science classrooms.
SUBJ: Planets--Exploration./ Outer space--Exploration./ Space probes.

523.4   Ph-1 4-6/6 $20.00   T   KC028
LAUBER, PATRICIA. Journey to the planets. 4th ed. Crown ISBN 0-517-59029-8, 1993. 90p. ill.
Includes index.
Selectors' Choice, 14th ed.
The planets and moons of our solar system reveal themselves through deft text and photography. Discussions of atmosphere, climate, and origins; examinations of present and past theories; and questions postulated for future enquiry will both inspire readers and enhance understanding. Updated to include data from the Voyager 2 missions.
SUBJ: Planets.

PIC 523.4   Ph-3 3-6 $32.95   OD KC029
PLANETS (Picture). Knowledge Unlimited 7012P, 1990. 9 study prints color (11"x17").
Includes teacher's guide.
Each of the nine planets is shown in a large color photograph accompanied by a few paragraphs of text explaining its position in the solar system and its physical characteristics. Bottom diagram visually displays its orbit in relation to the entire group of planets. With these posted for a few weeks, the whole class will absorb some astronomy.
SUBJ: Planets.

523.4   Ph-1 3-6/7 $14.00   T   KC030
RIDE, SALLY. Voyager: an adventure to the edge of the solar system. By Sally Ride and Tam O'Shaughnessy. Crown ISBN 0-517-58157-4, 1992. 36p. col. ill. (Face to face with science).
Includes index.
Selectors' Choice, 19th ed.
Available from the National Library Service for the Blind and Physically Handicapped on sound recording cassette RC 40093.
Blast off with Voyagers 1 and 2 to explore the outer planets. Outstanding color photographs and discerning text bring the encounters with Jupiter, Saturn, Uranus, and Neptune to life. As each planet reveals newly discovered wonders, orderly diagrams and drawings highlight the problems and build understanding. An excellent testimony to the challenge and excitement of space exploration.
SUBJ: Voyager Project./ Planets--Exploration./ Outer space--Exploration.

523.4   Ph-2 2-5/5 $14.95   L   KC031
ROBINSON, FAY. Space probes to the planets. Whitman ISBN 0-8075-7548-8; In Canada: General Publishing, 1993. unp. col. ill.
Fascinating photographs illustrate what has been learned from space probes and the uniqueness of each planet in the solar system. Clear text makes information easily accessible. An attractive addition, up-to-date and on target for its audience.
SUBJ: Planets./ Space probes.

523.41   Ph-1 3-6/7 $13.93   L   KC032
SIMON, SEYMOUR. Mercury. Morrow ISBN 0-688-10545-9, 1992. unp. col. ill.
Explores the beautiful and mysterious world of Mercury. Includes up-to-date, clearly explained information with photos from the Mariner 10 space probe.
SUBJ: Mercury (Planet)./ Project Mariner.

523.42   Ph-3 4-6/8 $17.71   L   KC033
SCHLOSS, MURIEL. Venus. Watts ISBN 0-531-20019-1; In Canada: Watts, 1991. 63p. col. ill. (First book).
Includes glossary, bibliography and index.
Explains the peculiarities of Earth's sister planet, Venus - the runaway greenhouse. When all the new data from the 1990 Magellan flyby is interpreted, more puzzles should be solved. Perhaps we will even glean clues to stop environmental damage on Earth. For collections that need updated information on Venus.
SUBJ: Venus (Planet).

523.42   Ph-1 3-6/8 $14.93   L   KC034
SIMON, SEYMOUR. Venus. Morrow ISBN 0-688-10543-2, 1992. unp. col. ill.

Recent space probes revealed a world where it rains sulfuric acid and the temperature reaches 900 degrees F within an atmosphere of carbon dioxide. These facts about Venus are illustrated and explained with clarity and beauty to both delight and inform.
SUBJ: Venus (Planet).

523.43   Ph-1 4-A/8 $15.93   L   KC035
SIMON, SEYMOUR. Mars. Morrow ISBN 0-688-06585-6, 1987. unp. col. ill.
Startling photographs in an oversized book reveal the harsh beauty of this planet. Four Mariner and two Viking spacecrafts have sent photographs of frosty scenes and red deserts. Earthling readers can travel to the red orb named for the Roman god of war and learn more than past legions of scientists even suspected.
SUBJ: Mars (Planet)./ Planets.

523.44   Ph-2 6-8/6 $16.95   L   KC036
POYNTER, MARGARET. Killer asteroids. Enslow ISBN 0-89490-616-X, 1996. 48p. col. ill., map. (Weird and wacky science).
Includes glossary, bibliography and index.
Presents how the Alvarez father and son team found the site of a killer asteroid that may explain dinosaur extinction, measures scientists might take to outwit a doomsday rock, and how you can view the greatest shows in outer space. Lively style paired with lots of color photographs keep readers interested.
SUBJ: Asteroids./ Catastrophes (Geology).

523.44   Ph-3 A/8 $16.90   L   KC037
VOGT, GREGORY. Search for the killer asteroid. Millbrook ISBN 1-56294-448-7, 1994. 71p. col. ill., map.
Includes glossary, bibliography and index.
Documents how scientific sleuths found the impact crater which verifies that a giant asteroid crashed into earth 65 million years ago and changed our planet forever. Explores strategies that could be employed against a killer asteroid occurring today. For avid space buffs. Parts will make theatrical text for reading aloud when discussing dinosaur extinction.
SUBJ: Asteroids./ Catastrophes (Geology).

523.45   Ph-1 3-6/7 $16.00   T   KC038
SIMON, SEYMOUR. Jupiter. Morrow ISBN 0-688-05796-9, 1985. unp. col. ill.
Spacecraft photography and precise writing reveal some of Jupiter's mysteries and most recent discoveries such as a thin ring surrounding the planet. Here is the most up-to-date, readable book about this solar system giant.
SUBJ: Jupiter (Planet)./ Planets.

523.46   Ph-1 3-6/6 $15.93   L   KC039
SIMON, SEYMOUR. Saturn. Morrow ISBN 0-688-05799-3, 1985. unp. col. ill.
Awesome, beautiful Saturn dazzles with photographs and perfectly matched text. A book to inspire, share aloud and learn from; the most up-to-date, appealing book on the ringed planet.
SUBJ: Saturn (Planet)./ Planets.

523.47   Ph-1 4-6/6 $12.93   L   KC040
SIMON, SEYMOUR. Uranus. Morrow ISBN 0-688-06583-X, 1987. unp. col. ill.
Visit Uranus and its moon--one of which, Miranda, is the "oddest mixture of surfaces ever found in the Solar System" (p24). While less substantial than other planet books by Simon because less is known about this faraway orb, it is still an absorbing and visually stunning presentation.
SUBJ: Uranus (Planet)./ Planets.

523.48   Ph-2 4-6/8 $13.88   L   KC041
SIMON, SEYMOUR. Neptune. Morrow ISBN 0-688-09632-8, 1991. unp. col. ill.
Geysers of nitrogen, clouds of methane, and slushy ammonia all make up some of the exotic environments of Neptune and its moon Triton. Superb satellite photography coupled with clear text give an amazing up-to-date view of a world almost unknown before the 1989 Voyager 2 flyby.
SUBJ: Neptune (Planet).

PIC 523.5   Ph-2 4-A $9.95   OD KC042
METEORITES (Picture). Bethany Sciences, 1991. 1 study print color (22 1/2"x29").
Meteorites hold secrets to the origin and evolution of the universe and provide physical evidence for scientific study and discovery. Poster discusses stone, iron, and stony-iron meteorites with a brief mention of tektites. Excellent color and layout make this a winner for the science classroom.
SUBJ: Meteorites.

523.6   Ph-3 4-6/7 $14.93   L   KC043
SIMON, SEYMOUR. Comets, meteors, and asteroids. Morrow ISBN 0-688-12710-X, 1994. unp. col. ill.
Explores the differences between these three heavenly objects, cites examples of their occurrences, and gives the latest scientific data. Full-page color photographs dissect comets, meteors, and asteroids and testify to the never-ending puzzles of space research.
SUBJ: Comets./ Meteors./ Asteroids.

523.7   Ph-3 1-3/5 $12.40   L   KC044
BENDICK, JEANNE. Sun: our very own star. Illus. by Mike Roffe. Millbrook Press ISBN 1-878841-02-5, 1991. 32p. col. ill. (Early bird).
Includes index.
Introduces the sun's surface, solar winds, and eclipses among other topics. Science terminology is integrated throughout. Will read well aloud to younger students.
SUBJ: Sun./ Solar system./ Stars.

523.7   Ph-3 P-2/2 $14.95   L   KC045
GIBBONS, GAIL. Sun up, sun down. Harcourt Brace Jovanovich ISBN 0-15-282781-1, 1983. unp. col. ill.
Available from National Library Service for the Blind and Physically Handicapped in Braille BR06110 and on sound recording cassette RC22321.
Exploding with color, this title presents a young girl's realization about the life-giving nature of the sun. A choice to share with a group of young children.
SUBJ: Sun.

523.7   Ph-1 P-A/7 $17.00   T   KC046
SIMON, SEYMOUR. Sun. Morrow ISBN 0-688-05857-4, 1986. unp. col. ill.
The sun's heat and light make our life possible. Amazing, dramatic photographs reveal what is inside, sunspot eruptions, magnetic storms and flashing prominences. Beautiful book to be shared across grade levels.
SUBJ: Sun.

523.8   Ph-3 A/10 $16.95   T   KC047
APFEL, NECIA H. Orion, the Hunter. Clarion ISBN 0-395-68962-7, 1995. col. ill.
Includes index.
Amazing satellite and Hubble Space Telescope photographs let readers travel through the constellation Orion and view its wonders: six blue-white supergiants, Betelgeuse (a red supergiant), the Horsehead Nebula, and the Giant Molecular Cloud. Orion is easily found in the winter sky and presents perfect learning opportunities to young stargazers. Explains in detail what is known, how today's scientists continue to unravel new mysteries, and what can be learned about the universe from the birth and evolution of stars.
SUBJ: Orion (Constellation)./ Stars--Formation.

523.8   Ph-1 1-4/2 $12.00   L   KC048
BERGER, MELVIN. Where are the stars during the day?: a book about stars. By Melvin and Gilda Berger. Illus. by Blanche Sims. Ideals ISBN 0-8249-8644-X; In Canada: Ideals, 1993. 48p. col. ill. (Discovery readers).
Includes index.
A beginning reader's book packed with information about the sun, Alpha Centauri, hydrogen, planets, and constellations. Will encourage readers to run outside to learn and observe. Perfect science that will wet primary inquisitiveness.
SUBJ: Astronomy./ Solar system.

523.8   Ph-3 K-2/4 $14.95   L   KC049
GIBBONS, GAIL. Stargazers. Holiday House ISBN 0-8234-0983-X, 1992. unp. col. ill.
Includes chronology.
Step outside and view the night sky with a family of four stargazers. Explains why stars twinkle, how constellations move, and the equipment astronomers use. Provides basic answers to questions about stars for anyone unfamiliar with the topic.
SUBJ: Stars./ Constellations./ Astronomy.

523.8   Ph-1 1-6/4 $13.93   L   KC050
KRUPP, E. C. Big dipper and you. Illustrated by Robin Rector Krupp. Morrow ISBN 0-688-07192-9, 1989. 48p. ill.
Full pages of black and white art work with the integrated text to explain the dipper, how it has changed and is changing and how other cultures view this same star pattern. The clear explanations of the earth's rotation and travel around the sun make parts of the book superb read alouds for primary students.
SUBJ: Ursa Major./ Constellations./ Polestar./ Stars.

PIC 523.8   Ph-2 3-A $12.95   OD KC051
MAP OF THE UNIVERSE: THE NORTHERN HEMISPHERE (Picture).
Celestial Arts/dist. by Tricycle Press ISBN 0-89087-309-7, 1980. 1 study
print color (35" x 35").
> Includes teacher's guide.
> A guide to the heavens showing all of the constellations glows with
> phosphorescent ink that can be recharged with exposure to light. Four
> corners are packed with information on stars, the solar system, and
> galaxies. Booklet includes star tables and gives brief background
> information. "The more you look...the more you will discover."
> (p.13) With this on the classroom wall, students will be motivated to
> seek out astronomy books. Also useful with mythology units.
> SUBJ: Constellations./ Zodiac./ Stars./ Astronomy.

523.8   Ph-1 4-6/6 $16.95   T KC052
REY, H. A. Find the constellations. Rev. ed. Houghton Mifflin ISBN
0-395-24509-5, 1976. 72p. col. ill.
> Includes glossary, bibliography and index.
> The clear, informal, lively text helps the reader know how to
> recognize the stars and find the constellations that one can see in the
> middle and Northern United States. Can be used indoors and
> outdoors all year round. Includes Planet-finder for the years 1976-
> 1985.
> SUBJ: Stars./ Constellations.

523.8   Ph-2 4-6/8 $16.95   T KC053
REY, H. A. Stars: a new way to see them. Houghton Mifflin ISBN
0-395-08121-1, c1967. 160p. col. ill.
> Includes glossary and index.
> Enlarged world-wide edition.
> Line drawings and charts which relate the stars and constellations to
> mythical characters show how to find them at any time and from any
> place on earth. The last part, somewhat more difficult, explains
> eclipses, phases of the moon, procession of the equinox, etc. AAAS.
> SUBJ: Stars.

523.8   Ph-1 4-6/6 $15.88   L KC054
SIMON, SEYMOUR. Stars. Morrow ISBN 0-688-05856-6, 1986. unp.
col. ill.
> Luminous photographs of constellations, star clusters and galaxies give
> clues to how stars begin, grow and die. Text discusses the frontiers of
> astronomy without overwhelming the reader. Book will be useful on
> several levels to expand knowledge and heighten wonder.
> SUBJ: Stars.

VCR 523.8   Ph-2 3-6 $99.00   OD KC055
STARS AND CONSTELLATIONS (Videocassette). National Geographic
51582, 1993. 1/2" VHS videocassette color (25min).
> Includes teacher's guide.
> From a city rooftop, two likeable girls view the night sky, finding
> constellations with star maps and flashlights. Talks about our sun
> being a star, nebulae (star nurseries), the birth and death of stars,
> and the fusion that keeps them burning. Discusses galaxies,
> computerized astronomy, and how cultures have given different names
> to the same constellations. Good blend of casualness and lecture
> brings astronomy to a user friendly level that should interest students
> in stargazing. Perfect to wrap up a science unit or to use during
> hobby week. Lend this one for home use and family viewing.
> SUBJ: Stars./ Constellations./ Astronomy.

523.8   Ph-3 P-2/2 $11.98   L KC056
WYLER, ROSE. Starry sky. Messner ISBN 0-671-66345-3, 1989. 32p.
col. ill. (Outdoor science book).
> Chart the Big Dipper inside an umbrella. This and other simple
> experiments teach movement of stars and planets. Oversized, basic
> text with lots of color appeals to primary teachers and their students.
> SUBJ: Astronomy./ Sky.

525   Ph-2 K-2/3 $14.89   L KC057
BRANLEY, FRANKLYN M. Sunshine makes the season. Rev. ed.
Illustrated by Shelley Freshman. Crowell/HarperCollins ISBN 0-690-
04482-8; In Canada: HarperCollins, 1985. 33p. col. ill. (Let's-read-and-
find-out science book).
> Available from National Library Service for the Blind and Physically
> Handicapped in Braille BR03037.
> An easy to read account of why the seasons change around the year
> and around the globe and why days are not always the same length.
> SUBJ: Seasons./ Day.

525   Ph-3 4-5/4 $15.27   L KC058
FRADIN, DENNIS B. Earth. Childrens Press ISBN 0-516-01172-3; In
Canada: Childrens Press, 1989. 48p. col. ill. (New true book).
> Includes glossary and index.
> Includes an introductory discussion of the solar system and then

proceeds to reveal Earth's movements, size, insides and temperatures.
The last chapter cautions against environmental pollution. A good
choice for upper grade, poorer readers.
> SUBJ: Earth.

525   Ph-1 P-4/5 $15.95   L KC059
GIBBONS, GAIL. Reasons for seasons. Holiday House ISBN 0-8234-
1174-5, 1995. unp. col. ill.
> Concepts of earth's rotations, seasonal patterns, and hemispheric
> differences are carefully explained and graphically illustrated in this
> superior book. Five pages are devoted to each season in the
> Northern Hemisphere--highlighting plant, animal, and human activities.
> Solid science accessible to the youngest student. Larger size makes it
> perfect for reading aloud.
> SUBJ: Seasons.

525   Ph-1 K-3/2 $4.95   P KC060
LAUBER, PATRICIA. How we learned the earth is round. Illus. by Megan
Lloyd. HarperCollins ISBN 0-06-445109-7, c1990, 1992. 32p. col. ill.
(Let's-read-and-find-out science book).
> Relates how people once believed the earth was flat, how the Greeks
> discovered otherwise and what Columbus accomplished. Includes a
> prove-it-yourself experiment. Perfect for sharing aloud around
> October 12th.
> SUBJ: Earth.

VCR 525   Ph-3 2-4 $89.00   OD KC061
MAGICAL MOTHER NATURE: THE FOUR SEASONS (Videocassette).
Rainbow Educational Video RB845, 1989. 1/2" VHS videocassette color
(18min).
> Includes teacher's guide.
> From the first buds of spring to the snows of winter, each season has
> its own physical characteristics, activities, and holidays. This full action
> video relates science to culture with examples easily understood by
> children.
> SUBJ: Seasons./ Spring./ Summer./ Autumn./ Winter.

525   Ph-1 2-8/7 $15.99   L KC062
RIDE, SALLY. Third planet: exploring the earth from space. By Sally Ride
and Tam O'Shaughnessy. Crown ISBN 0-517-59362-9, 1994. 48p. col.
ill., maps.
> Includes index.
> On a global scale see: sea ice, hurricanes, and a shroud of volcanic
> dust. Infrared instruments that measure temperature and color-
> enhanced, time-lapse photography show completely alien views of the
> familiar. As human growth increased, earth suffered exponentially
> from pollution, vegetation destruction, and natural resource depletion.
> However, "We are finally beginning to understand our home planet
> and how we are affecting it." (p.46) Even very young students will
> comprehend population densities when shown the night views of
> electric lights, and environmental concerns become self-evident in
> photographs of oil field and rain forest fires. Useful in all
> environmental studies classes.
> SUBJ: Earth./ Astronomy./ Astronautics.

FSS 525   Ph-2 K-2 $62.00   OD KC063
SEASONS. Rev. ed. (Sound filmstrip). National Geographic 30996,
c1975, 1993. 5 filmstrips color, 5 sound cassettes.
> Shows how plants and animals change throughout the four seasons,
> focusing on seasonal changes that children can observe. Stresses
> regional differences in seasons.
> Contents: The changing seasons (41fr/10min); Spring (47fr/12min);
> Summer (47fr/12min); Autumn (42fr/14min); Winter (45fr/10min).
> SUBJ: Spring./ Summer./ Autumn./ Winter./ Seasons./ Animals--
> Habits and behavior./ Plants.

526   Ph-1 K-6/6 $6.95   P KC064
CHAPMAN, GILLIAN. Maps and mazes: a first guide to mapmaking. By
Gillian Chapman and Pam Robson. Millbrook ISBN 1-56294-715-X,
1993. 32p. col. ill., maps.
> Includes glossary.
> An eclectic meld of old and new ideas to help unravel the language
> of maps. Vivid illustrations direct the reader in creating games,
> colorful 3-D maps, grids, and mazes to make discovery fun and
> rewarding. Try designing a story map game, a pebble map, an
> informational map using grocery store food labels, or a shell and stick
> map of a group of islands. Every student and teacher will find several
> easy-to-use ideas that they will want to experiment with immediately.
> Perfect for social studies reports and scout projects. Art teachers
> interested in integrating art into the curriculum will also find this
> useful.
> SUBJ: Map drawing.

526 Ph-3 A/12 $17.95 T KC065
LA PIERRE, YVETTE. Mapping a changing world. Edited by Nancy Kober. Lickle Publishing/dist. by PRI ISBN 0-9650308-4-9, 1996. 80p. col. ill., maps.
Beginning with a Babylonian stone tablet and closing with a NASA photograph, pages detail mapmaking history and evolution while illustrating how different times and cultures presented their worlds on paper. Replete with historical reproductions, engaging anecdotes, and cultural information, this advanced study might inspire nascent cartographers and collectors. For multicultural studies and world history classes.
SUBJ: Cartography./ Maps.

MCP 526 Ph-1 1-5 $79.95 OD KC066
NEIGHBORHOOD MAPMACHINE (Microcomputer program). Tom Snyder Productions NEI-D, 1997. 4 3.5" disks.
Version 1.0.
Includes teacher's guide.
Also available in Windows disks and Macintosh/Windows CD-ROM, $79.95.
System requirements: Macintosh computer with System 7 or better; 2MB of available RAM; 9MB of free hard disk space; 640x480 color monitor.
Easy-to-use software tool which helps youngsters not only make maps, but also develop map reading skills. A wide range of options are included as well as the ability to make a mystery challenge where youngsters find a secret place hidden on the student created map. Excellent tool for the entire class when used with a projection device.
SUBJ: Maps--Software./ Software--Maps./ Map drawing--Software./ Software--Map drawing./ Interactive media.

529 Ph-1 4-6/6 $13.95 T KC067
BRANLEY, FRANKLYN M. Keeping time: from the beginning and into the 21st century. Illus. by Jill Weber. Houghton Mifflin ISBN 0-395-47777-8, 1993. 105p. ill.
Includes bibliography and index.
Filled with activities to make timekeeping interesting: build a water alarm clock, find out how weekdays were named, cross the international date line in seventeen short chapters. Integrate into language arts (word origins), social studies (Egyptian and Babylonian systems), math (minutes, seconds), and science (time and space travel) via the excellent index. Everything you need to know about clocks and calendars.
SUBJ: Time./ Clocks and watches./ Calendars.

529 Ph-2 4-6/6 $11.95 P KC068
BURNS, MARILYN. This book is about time. Illus. by Martha Weston. Little, Brown ISBN 0-316-11750-1; In Canada: Little, Brown, 1978. 127p. ill. (Brown paper school book).
Historical information on time, timepieces, the Mayan and Egyptian calendars, time zones, and the international date line followed by experiments and projects reinforcing such concepts as reaction time, waking-up schedules, a second, and blooming time in nature. For teachers and students.
SUBJ: Time.

529 Ph-2 3-6/6 $14.40 L KC069
CHAPMAN, GILLIAN. Exploring time. By Gillian Chapman and Pam Robson. Photos by Rupert Horrox. Millbrook ISBN 1-56294-559-9, 1995. 32p. col. ill., map.
Originally published in Great Britain by Simon & Schuster, 1994.
Includes glossary and index.
Begin with once upon a time and make a daily activity chart, a family tree, solar and lunar calendars, and a time capsule. The activities will help children learn how all animals and plants have their own body clocks and how people have tried keeping track of time. Aside from science and math classes, this could be used in January at the beginning of a new calendar year. Students will need help with directions and materials to achieve the colorfully illustrated results.
SUBJ: Time.

529 Ph-2 4-6/8 $14.95 T KC070
GANERI, ANITA. Story of time and clocks. Oxford University Press ISBN 0-19-521326-2, 1996. 30p. col. ill., maps. (Signs of the times).
Includes chronology, glossary, and index.
Brief text and lots of pictures mark the history of timekeeping and timepieces from 4,000-year-old shadow clocks to today's atomic ones. Describes the differences in the religious calendars of the Hindu, Jewish, and Islamic faiths and the creation of time zones. Use when discussing moveable feasts, cultural differences, and the new year.
SUBJ: Time./ Clocks and watches./ Calendars.

SRC 529 Ph-2 P-1 $10.95 OD KC071
JAMES, DIXIE L. Singing calendar (Sound recording cassette). By Dixie L. James and Linda C. Becht. Kimbo KIM 1010C, 1984. 1 sound cassette.
Includes guide.
Each month has its own song and mini activities to enjoy; an excellent way to appreciate seasonal differences and insure learning. The lyrics are fairly simple and the music is not outstanding, but primary teachers will have plenty of use for this album.
SUBJ: Calendars--Songs and music./ Seasons--Songs.

529 Ph-1 K-3/2 $14.95 T KC072
LLEWELLYN, CLAIRE. My first book of time. DK Publishing ISBN 1-879431-78-5, 1992. 32p. col. ill.
Includes glossary.
From days to months and years, time goes by, often unnoticed. Bright colors in an oversized book along with a fold-out play clock help readers see how time's passage means changes in plants, animals, and people. Also includes background on timekeeping devices and some activities. High point is the instructions for telling time. A valuable addition.
SUBJ: Time./ Clocks and watches./ Toy and movable books.

529 Ph-2 4-A/8 $12.95 P KC073
SMITH, A. G. What time is it? Stoddart ISBN 0-7737-5525-X; In Canada: Stoddart, 1992. 86p. ill., maps.
Includes glossary.
From a giant structure such as Stonehenge to a small pocket watch, the author traces how we strive to keep chronological measurement. Demonstrates that there are various cultural and mercurial concepts of time. Large format and black and white line drawings validate and expand the text. A wealth of information to insert in social studies lessons or cultivate budding mechanics.
SUBJ: Time measurements./ Calendars./ Clocks and watches.

VCR 529 Ph-2 2-3 $89.00 OD KC074
TICK TOCK: ALL ABOUT THE CLOCK (Videocassette). Rainbow Educational RB858, 1992. 1/2" VHS videocassette color (16min).
Includes teacher's guide.
This three-part lesson in telling time discusses varieties of clocks, the terms used to say the time indicated on the clock, and briefly surveys early types of clocks. Digital clocks are covered quickly, and the emphasis is on the clock face with hands as early grade children hear and then drill time telling concepts and appear in vignettes demonstrating various times of day. Since the clear and attractive presentation covers a substantial amount of material, teachers might choose to use the film in parts. Useful teacher's guide includes review questions and activities along with the full script.
SUBJ: Time./ Clocks and watches.

CDR 529 Ph-1 P-3 $59.95 OD KC075
TRUDY'S TIME AND PLACE HOUSE. School version (CD-ROM). Edmark 1083, 1995. 1 CD-ROM color. (Early learning house).
Includes teacher's guide.
Version 1.0.
ALA notable computer software, 1996.
Selectors' Choice, 21st ed.
System requirements: Color Macintosh (256 colors required); 4MB RAM (8MB recommended); CD-ROM drive (doublespeed or faster recommended); System 7.0.1 or higher; 13" or larger monitor; printer (optional); TouchWindow (optional).
System requirements: Windows 3.1 (enhanced mode), Windows 95 or later; 4MB RAM required (8MB highly recommended); CD-ROM drive (doublespeed or faster recommended); 386DX/33 MHz required (486/33 MHz or better recommended); Super VGA, 640x480 (256 colors, or more, required); hard disk with 2MB free; mouse; Windows-compatible sound-output device; Windows-compatible printer (optional); TouchWindow (optional).
Product (1083) runs on either Macintosh or Windows compatible hardware.
Map skills and telling time activities are excellently presented. Analog and digital time options are available. Direction finding, using symbols to make a map, dealing with a globe and a world map, as well as understanding the passage of time on a calendar are concepts that are introduced. Superb voice options make the program usable by limited readers.
SUBJ: Time--Software./ Software--Time./ Maps--Software./ Software--Maps./ Geography--Software./ Software--Geography./ Interactive media.

530 Ph-3 2-5/3 $9.95 T KC076
ARDLEY, NEIL. Science book of sound. Gulliver/Harcourt Brace Jovanovich ISBN 0-15-200579-X, 1991. 29p col photos.
Brightly colored illustrated projects allow children to explore the

principles of sound by constructing a plastic drum, simple shakers, a rubber band guitar, bottle pipes and more. Will motivate the least scientifically inclined students to experiment and have some fun.
SUBJ: Sound--Experiments./ Music--Acoustics and physics./ Experiments.

530   Ph-3 4-8/7 $14.95   T   KC077
CASH, TERRY. 101 physics tricks: fun experiments with everyday materials. Sterling ISBN 0-8069-8786-3; In Canada: Sterling c/o Canadian Manda, 1993. 104p. col. ill.
Previously published as FUN WITH PHYSICS, Simon & Schuster, 1991.
Includes index.
Presents a series of one and two page experiments using everyday materials to explain natural energy and chemical forces. Well illustrated and carefully detailed. For maximum impact use as an adjunct to science lessons.
SUBJ: Physics./ Physics--Experiments./ Experiments./ Scientific recreations.

530   Ph-2 4-A/9 $15.95   T   KC078
COOPER, CHRISTOPHER. Matter. DK Publishing ISBN 1-879431-88-2, 1992. 64p. col. ill. (Eyewitness science).
Includes index.
Stunning photographs and brief text examine the properties of various types of matter. A two-page spread presents each topic such as conservation of matter, changes of state, radioactivity, and carbon rings and chains. A brief introduction to complex subject matter.
SUBJ: Matter./ Atoms./ Molecules.

530   Ph-1 2-6/6 $9.95   P   KC079
KANER, ETTA. Balloon science. Illus. by Louise Phillips. Addison-Wesley ISBN 0-201-52378-7; In Canada: Kids Can Press, 1989. 96p. ill.
Includes a packet of balloons and an index.
Learn principles of science with tricks, experiments and challenges using balloons. Every elementary science teacher will want to use this fine blend of fun and learning.
SUBJ: Balloons--Experiments./ Experiments./ Science--Experiments.

VCR 530   Ph-2 3-6 $49.95   OD KC080
SOUND/LIGHT AND COLOR (Videocassette). Disney Educational Productions 68A30VL00, 1994. 1/2" VHS videocassette color (52min). (Bill Nye the science guy: classroom edition).
Includes teacher's guide.
Includes public performace rights.
50 volume series also available for purchase as a set, 6P27VL00, $949.00.
Closed captioned.
Sound segment uses MTV mix of color montage, action, and experiments to prove that sound travels in waves and the ear is the perfect shape to capture vibrations. Lots of noise, music, and sound effects keep viewers interested and learning. Light and color segment demonstrates how a prism breaks apart the light spectrum and explains why objects are different colors. Also includes a short discussion of neon and laser light. Teacher's guide adds a few more hands-on experiments.
SUBJ: Sound./ Light./ Color./ Experiments.

530   Ph-2 5-A/7 $14.93   L   KC081
ZUBROWSKI, BERNIE. Making waves: finding out about rhythmic motion. Illus. by Roy Doty. Morrow ISBN 0-688-11787-2, 1994. 96p. ill. (Boston Children's Museum activity book).
Provides hours of scientific fun while demonstrating what gives waves their shapes and patterns. Includes instructions for building a test tank of Plexiglas and Plasticine or a wave generator from a 12 volt electric motor, batteries, Popsicle sticks, and rubber bands, and for creating soap film waves and waves in solids. Validates the progression from investigation and observation towards controlling variables and applying findings to other situations. Encourages students to think and discover for themselves. Most readers will need adult help, but once started, students will easily solo.
SUBJ: Waves--Experiments./ Experiments.

530.1   Ph-1 4-A/7 $14.95   L   KC082
DARLING, DAVID J. Could you ever build a time machine? Dillon ISBN 0-87518-456-1, 1991. 60p. col. ill.
Includes glossary and index.
A serious discussion of fantasies outlines baffling problems such as Einstein's time slowing effect and Hawking & Penrose's wormholes and white holes. Here is a chance for young astronauts to learn how theorists and researchers approach time travel. Clear text, good illustrations and informal presentation will keep readers turning the pages.
SUBJ: Time./ Time travel.

VCR 530.4   Ph-3 3-6 $79.00   OD KC083
SOLID, LIQUID, GAS (Videocassette). National Geographic 51205, 1986. 1/2" VHS videocassette (15min).
Includes teacher's guide.
Experiments and demonstrations with solids, liquids and gases lead to discovery of the characteristics of each form of matter and the methods by which they change. The activities are commonplace but the presentation is entertaining and well-paced, which makes it a good introduction to the study of matter where need warrants.
SUBJ: Physics./ Matter--Properties.

VCR 530.4   Ph-2 4-6 $89.00   OD KC084
SOLIDS, LIQUIDS AND GASES (Videocassette). Rainbow Educational RB8179, 1994. 1/2" VHS videocassette color (20min).
Includes teacher's guide and reproducibles.
Includes public performance rights.
Illustrates the differences between the three states of matter and how matter can undergo phase changes using photography, animation, and simple experiments (easily replicated in the classroom). Clear and informative, but it will be best shown in segments with time out for discussions.
SUBJ: Physics./ Matter.

530.4   Ph-3 4-6/8 $7.95   P   KC085
ZUBROWSKI, BERNIE. Bubbles. Illus. by Joan Drescher. Little, Brown ISBN 0-316-98881-2; In Canada: Little, Brown, 1979. 64p. col. ill. (Boston Children's Museum activity book).
Descriptions of very easy experiments used successfully at Boston's Children's Museum, which require simple equipment and may be performed for the fun of investigation and to create gigantic bubbles and bubble sculptures. Also for use by teachers of younger students.
SUBJ: Bubbles./ Experiments./ Physics--Experiments.

530.8   Ph-2 5-6/6 $17.00   L   KC086
MARKLE, SANDRA. Measuring up!: experiments, puzzles, and games exploring measurement. Atheneum ISBN 0-689-31904-5; In Canada: Distican, 1995. 44p. col. ill.
Includes index.
Using familiar athletes, recipes, and consumer economics, Markle poses problems and solutions to which young people will relate. Weighing toilet paper, measuring temperature, or learning how to keep a cup of tea hot allow the reader to experiment, control variables, and record results. Clever challenges will produce thoughtful results. Use to enhance science lessons, for independent study, or for enrichment.
SUBJ: Physical measurements--Experiments./ Experiments./ Scientific recreations.

530.8   Ph-3 K-2/2 $13.95   L   KC087
WELLS, ROBERT E. Is a blue whale the biggest thing there is? Whitman ISBN 0-8075-3655-5; In Canada: General, 1993. unp. col. ill.
Manipulates huge numbers to delight children who are forever concerned with "how big?" Begins by comparing whales to Mount Everest and ends by comparing the Milky Way to the universe. Introduces a rich vocabulary along with new concepts to the younger set. Proof that facts and figures are pure pleasure.
SUBJ: Size./ Number concept.

531   Ph-1 A/7 $13.95   L   KC088
ADKINS, JAN. Moving heavy things. Houghton Mifflin ISBN 0-395-29206-9, 1980. 47p. ill.
New York Academy of Sciences Children's Science Book Award.
Covers broadly and scientifically the art of moving heavy objects using traditional methods as well as imaginative, ingenious ideas for reducing friction and multiplying strength to accomplish the job. Good illustrations, often humorous, enhance the text. For the able reader.
SUBJ: Mechanics./ Force and energy./ Motion.

531   Ph-3 K-3/2 $9.95   T   KC089
ARDLEY, NEIL. Science book of gravity. Gulliver/Harcourt Brace Jovanovich ISBN 0-15-200621-4, 1992. 29p. col. ill. (Science book of).
Science experiments using common household objects explore the principles of gravity. Easy-to-read directions will appeal to primary grade students.
SUBJ: Gravity--Experiments./ Experiments.

531   Ph-3 K-3/2 $9.95   T   KC090
ARDLEY, NEIL. Science book of motion. Gulliver/Harcourt Brace Jovanovich ISBN 0-15-200622-2, 1992. 29p. col. ill. (Science book of).
Step-by-step experiments demonstrate basic principles of motion. Photographs and easy-to-follow directions make the experiments accessible to the youngest scientists.
SUBJ: Motion--Experiments./ Experiments.

531 Ph-3 2-4/4 $9.95 T KC091
ARDLEY, NEIL. Science book of water. Gulliver/Harcourt Brace
Jovanovich ISBN 0-15-200575-7, 1991. 29p. col. ill.
Series of eleven easy-to-do experiments that will help primary students
explore water's properties. Colorful and enticing.
SUBJ: Water--Experiments./ Experiments./ Science--Experiments.

531 Ph-2 4-6/5 $13.00 T KC092
COBB, VICKI. Why doesn't the earth fall up? Illustrated by Ted Enik.
Lodestar/Dutton ISBN 0-525-67253-2; In Canada: Fitzhenry &
Whiteside, 1988. 40p. ill.
Includes index.
This introduction to the scientific principles of gravity, centrifugal force
and Newton's Laws of Motion encourages questioning and exploring.
Cartoons of irreverent kids add to the snappy presentation. While the
work lacks a conclusion, teachers can use the nine questions for brain
storming or as a stimulus for independent research.
SUBJ: Motion./ Questions and answers./ Gravity./ Force and
energy.

531 Ph-2 4-A/5 $10.95 P KC093
DOHERTY, PAUL. Cool hot rod and other electrifying experiments on
energy and matter. By Paul Doherty, Don Rathjen and the Exploratorium
Teacher Institute. Wiley ISBN 0-471-11518-5; In Canada: Wiley, 1996.
100p. ill. (Exploratorium science snackbook series).
Includes index.
Explore basic principles related to heat and other forms of energy
through hands-on activities originally designed for a science museum.
Tasks vary from the simple to the complex (some require adult
assistance). Each provides a materials list and time required.
SUBJ: Force and energy--Experiments./ Experiments.

531 Ph-2 4-A/5 $10.95 P KC094
DOHERTY, PAUL. Spinning blackboard and other dynamic experiments
on force and motion. By Paul Doherty, Don Rathjen and the
Exploratorium Teacher Institute. Wiley ISBN 0-471-11514-2; In Canada:
Wiley, 1996. 112p. ill. (Exploratorium science snackbook series).
Includes index.
Over 20 brief experiments with homemade devices that explore the
principles of dynamics. Each activity includes: a list of materials, time
frame, diagrams, and an explanation of what's happening ranging
from the simple (giant bubble blowing) to the complex (Reuleaux
triangle nonround roller). Projects were originally designed for hands-
on museum exhibits and transfer easily to the classroom and home.
Adult help will be needed.
SUBJ: Mechanics--Experiments./ Experiments.

531 Ph-2 4-A/7 $15.95 T KC095
LAFFERTY, PETER. Force and motion. DK Publishing ISBN 1-879431-85-
8, 1992. 64p. col. ill. (Eyewitness science).
Includes index.
Extraordinary photographs of intricate equipment, models, and
instruments visually convey force and motion. Presents 29 topics, each
with a two-page spread, beginning with simple machines and ending
with Einstein's gravity. This is a book to dip into again and again for
inspiration and discovery. Reading in isolation becomes a trivia
exercise. Combining it with good teaching will guarantee success.
SUBJ: Force and energy.

VCR 531 Ph-2 5-A $89.00 OD KC096
LET'S MOVE IT: NEWTON'S LAWS OF MOTION (Videocassette).
Rainbow RB806, 1987. 1/2" VHS videocassette color (15min).
Sir Isaac Newton's discoveries about movement and motion are
explained using children and adults to demonstrate examples of the
actions for movement for each law. The laws are listed on the screen
at the beginning and end of the film and vocabulary words are
defined as they are introduced. This colorful, fast-paced video should
be useful for introducing and explaining movement and motion.
SUBJ: Motion./ Force and energy./ Physics.

VCR 531 Ph-1 4-6 $89.00 OD KC097
PUSH AND PULL: SIMPLE MACHINES AT WORK (Videocassette).
Rainbow Educational Video RB852, 1990. 1/2" VHS videocassette color
(22min).
Includes teacher's guide.
Can play be work? Yes, when you think of work as moving something
over a distance, such as one child pulling another in a wagon.
Playground and schoolroom settings provide familiar examples of
simple and complex machines, force, resistance, fulcrums, levers,
pulleys, and inclined planes.
SUBJ: Machinery./ Mechanics./ Force and energy.

VCR 531 Ph-2 5-6 $79.00 OD KC098
SIMPLE MACHINE (Videocassette). National Geographic 51570, 1993.
1/2" VHS videocassette color (20min).
Includes teacher's guide.
Interesting examples of work, play, and rescue demonstrate the
principles of simple machines invented thousands of years ago. The
inclined plane, lever, wheel and axle are the basis of screws, pulleys,
wedges, and much more complicated tools and inventions
demonstrated here in the pulling, pushing, and lifting work of
agriculture, boating, mountain climbing, and other efforts both
ordinary and dramatic. Appealing photographs and clear diagrams
and explanations offer good instruction on this fundamental topic.
SUBJ: Simple machines./ Machinery./ Mechanics./ Force and energy.

VCR 531 Ph-2 5-6 $79.00 OD KC099
SIMPLE MACHINES: USING MECHANICAL ADVANTAGE
(Videocassette). Society for Visual Education 95534-HAVT, 1992. 1/2"
VHS videocassette color (17min).
Includes teacher's manual and 12 skill sheets.
Several children explain and demonstrate the standard set of simple
machines: lever, wheel and axle, pulley, inclined plane and wedge.
The attractive presentation defines work; explains the roles of
resistance, fulcrum, and force; states the trade-offs between power
and speed; and introduces the idea of mechanical advantage. An
interesting variety of everyday implements, tools, and machines are
used to demonstrate this basic lesson in simple machines and how
they are combined to make complex machines.
SUBJ: Simple machines./ Machinery./ Mechanics./ Force and energy.

531 Ph-1 3-6/5 $14.95 L KC100
SKURZYNSKI, GLORIA. Zero gravity. Bradbury ISBN 0-02-782925-1; In
Canada: Maxwell Macmillan, 1994. 32p. col. ill.
Includes glossary and index.
Documents that "floating is so extraordinary." (p.28) Here's a
close-up look at weightlessness, centrifugal effect, and zero-g.
Astronauts working and living in space demonstrate to earthbound
mortals how it's done. Photographs of space shuttle astronauts doing
their special version of "this end up" entice beginners to learn more
about gravity. Clearly written and well-illustrated, this is a gem for
beginning physics.
SUBJ: Gravity./ Weightlessness./ Astronautics.

532 Ph-3 K-3/4 $17.50 L KC101
MURPHY, BRYAN. Experiment with water. Lerner ISBN 0-8225-2453-8,
1991. 32p. col. ill. (Science experiments).
Includes glossary and index.
Simple experiments demonstrate the basic properties of water
including water pressure, volume, evaporation, and condensation.
Visually attractive, the book will serve both independent learners and
small groups.
SUBJ: Water--Experiments./ Experiments.

533 Ph-2 4-6/4 $9.95 T KC102
ARDLEY, NEIL. Science book of air. Gulliver/Harcourt Brace Jovanovich
ISBN 0-15-200578-1, 1991. 29p. col. ill.
Encourages students to examine the properties of air, hands-on, by
using balloons, a lighted candle, a toy parachute and more. All
directions are given on two facing pages with plenty of illustrations to
insure success. For teachers who demand student-involved learning.
SUBJ: Air--Experiments./ Flight--Experiments./ Experiments./ Science-
-Experiments.

534 Ph-3 6-A/8 $13.95 L KC103
DARLING, DAVID J. Sounds interesting: the science of acoustics. Dillon
ISBN 0-87518-477-4; In Canada: Maxwell Macmillan, 1991. 59p. col. ill.
(Experiment!).
Includes glossary and index.
Attractive layout and color invite readers to learn (hands-on) about
sound waves, pitch, volume, and more. Offers some interesting
avenues to follow for science fair projects and independent
investigations. Contains many activities that will enrich science lessons.
SUBJ: Acoustics--Experiments./ Sound--Experiments./ Experiments.

CDR 534 Ph-1 4-A $54.95 OD KC104
SCIENCE IN YOUR EAR (CD-ROM). MECC/Learning Company CD-663,
1996. 1 CD-ROM color.
Version 1.0.
Includes teacher's guide.
Also available in Macintosh (MC263) and Windows (MW463) disks,
$49.95.
System requirements: Macintosh 68030 required (LC III or greater);
System 7.1 or later; 8MB RAM; 13" or larger color display required
(640x480, 256 colors); hard-disk space; double-speed CD-ROM
drive; microphone; headphones and speakers recommended.

System requirements: 486 MHz or higher processor; Microsoft
Windows 3.1 or higher; 256-color SVGA display; 8MB RAM;
Windows-compatible mouse; hard-disk space; double-speed CD-ROM
drive; Sound Blaster sound card; microphone and speakers;
headphones recommended.
Product (CD-663) runs on either Windows or Macintosh compatible
hardware.
Students explore the world of sound and hearing as they use this
program. Hands-on and simulated experiments with various forms of
waves, human hearing, and musical instruments provide practice with
using the scientific method. Works well with small groups or for the
entire class with a projection device.
SUBJ: Sound--Software./ Software--Sound./ Hearing--Software./
Software--Hearing./ Music--Acoustics and physics--Software./
Software--Music--Acoustics and physics./ Interactive media.

535   Ph-2 K-3/6 $9.95   T   KC105
ARDLEY, NEIL. Science book of light. Gulliver/Harcourt Brace
Jovanovich ISBN 0-15-200577-3, 1991. 29p. col. ill.
Urges young readers to experiment and learn by building a periscope,
kaleidoscope and box camera along with seven simpler projects. Clear
directions and illustrations insure success. Very young children will
need adult assistance but this does not lessen this book's appeal.
SUBJ: Light--Experiments./ Experiments.

CE 535   Ph-2 K-2/2 $14.89   L   KC106
BULLA, CLYDE ROBERT. What makes a shadow? Rev. ed. Illus. by June
Otani. HarperCollins ISBN 0-06-022916-0; In Canada: HarperCollins,
1994. 32p. col. ill. (Let's-read-and-find-out science book).
Read-along kit available from HarperCollins Audio (ISBN 0-69470-
081-9, 1996). 1 paperback book, 1 sound cassette (5min), $7.95.
Describes things that make shadows and why. Also shows how to
make shadow pictures.
SUBJ: Shadows.

535   Ph-2 4-A/7 $15.95   T   KC107
BURNIE, DAVID. Light. DK Publishing ISBN 1-879431-79-3, 1992. 64p.
col. ill. (Eyewitness science).
Includes index.
Various properties of light are presented with brief text and
fascinating photographs. Explores basic principles such as color,
reflection, and refraction as well as inventions that incorporate light
such as cameras, lasers, and holograms. Useful as a browsing book.
Students will need more detailed matter for reports.
SUBJ: Light.

535   Ph-3 2-6/7 $14.89   L   KC108
COBB, VICKI. Light action!: amazing experiments with optics. By Vicki
Cobb and Josh Cobb. Illus. by Theo Cobb. HarperCollins ISBN 0-06-
021437-6; In Canada: HarperCollins, 1993. 198p. ill.
Includes index.
Create a mirage without a desert or flash a ghost on a wall! Here are
activities that investigate and demystify the properties of light.
Carefully written chapters examine refraction, light waves, color, and
polarization. An upbeat book to be used across several grades.
SUBJ: Optics./ Light./ Science--Experiments.

535   Ph-3 6-A/8 $13.95   L   KC109
DARLING, DAVID J. Making light work: the science of optics. Dillon
ISBN 0-87518-476-6; In Canada: Maxwell MacMillan, 1991. 58p. col.
ill. (Experiment!).
Includes glossary and index.
The principles of optics and light are explained through experiments
which reinforce the concepts presented in the text. Explores everyday
phenomena such as shadows and rainbows as well as applications in
technology such as fiber optics and lasers.
SUBJ: Optics--Experiments./ Light--Experiments./ Experiments.

535   Ph-2 4-A/5 $10.95   P   KC110
DOHERTY, PAUL. Magic wand and other bright experiments on light
and color. By Paul Doherty, Don Rathjen and the Exploratorium Teacher
Institute. Wiley ISBN 0-471-11515-0; In Canada: Wiley, 1995. 125p. ill.
(Exploratorium science snackbook series).
Includes index.
Activities originally designed for a hands-on science museum will pique
curiosity and produce learning. Simple experiments demonstrate basic
science principles about light and color. Includes materials list and time
required. Some adult help will be needed.
SUBJ: Light--Experiments./ Color--Experiments./ Experiments.

535   Ph-1 1-3/5 $14.89   L   KC111
GOOR, RON. Shadows: here, there, and everywhere. By Ron and
Nancy Goor. Crowell/HarperCollins ISBN 0-690-04133-0; In Canada:
HarperCollins, 1981. 47p. ill.

Selectors' Choice, 14th ed.
Picture perfect photographs communicate texture, size, and shape of
everyday shadows. Sunlight and flashlight maneuvers insure observing
fun and increased awareness of surroundings.
SUBJ: Shadows.

535   Ph-1 P-6 $12.88   L   KC112
HOBAN, TANA. Shadows and reflections. Greenwillow ISBN 0-688-
07090-6, 1990. unp. col. ill.
Ubiquitous patterns and shapes evolve around commonplace scenes as
Hoban's photographs open our eyes to the beauty of the ordinary.
For units on light, sensory awareness and imagination.
SUBJ: Shadows--Pictorial works./ Reflections--Pictorial works.

535   Ph-1 1-6/4 $17.00   T   KC113
LAUBER, PATRICIA. What do you see and how do you see it?:
exploring light, color, and vision. Photos by Leonard Lessin. Crown ISBN
0-517-59390-4, 1994. 48p. col. ill.
Includes index.
Selectors' Choice, 20th ed.
Why do some people wear glasses? Are there colors we cannot see?
What's a superbounce image? Learn these answers along with
understanding the human eye, lenses, mirrors, and visible and invisible
spectrums. All are carefully explained in pithy text and many eye-
catching illustrations. Clean layout and large format add to the
success of this presentation which will add depth to all units on vision
and the senses.
SUBJ: Light./ Vision./ Color./ Senses and sensation.

535   Ph-2 3-5/6 $9.95   T   KC114
SIMON, SEYMOUR. Mirror magic. Illus. by Anni Matsick. Bell Books/
Boyds Mills ISBN 1-878093-07-X, 1991. 47p col illus.
Includes index.
A hands-on science book which includes experiments on mirror
writing, constructing a "corner cube" mirror, a periscope, and a
kaleidoscope. Concept of mirror image is explained in detail. New
color illustrations for this edition are certain to sustain reader interest.
SUBJ: Mirrors./ Science--Experiments.

535   Ph-2 4-6/5 $12.93   L   KC115
SIMON, SEYMOUR. Optical illusion book. Illustrated by Constance
Ftera. Morrow ISBN 0-688-03255-9, c1976, 1984. 78p. ill.
Includes index.
Explores the possible causes for the reasons the human eye can be
tricked into seeing things differently than they really are. Profusely
illustrated and provides simple experiments for children to try. A title
which crosses the art and science disciplines.
SUBJ: Eye./ Optical illusions./ Experiments./ Physics--Experiments.

535   Ph-3 5-6/8 $13.93   L   KC116
ZUBROWSKI, BERNIE. Mirrors: finding out about the properties of light.
Illus. by Roy Doty. Morrow ISBN 0-688-10592-0, 1992. 96p. ill. (Boston
Children's Museum activity book).
Have fun making mirror monsters, a copying device, or optical
illusions using this activity book that explores the properties of plane,
transparent, and curved mirrors. Materials are easy to come by,
directions are carefully written, and success is guaranteed. Makes
learning magic.
SUBJ: Mirrors--Experiments./ Light--Experiments./ Experiments.

535   Ph-2 4-8/7 $15.93   L   KC117
ZUBROWSKI, BERNIE. Shadow play: making pictures with light and
lenses. Illus. by Roy Doty. Morrow ISBN 0-688-13210-3, 1995. 112p. ill.
(Boston Children's Museum activity book).
A hands-on book to investigate the properties and peculiarities of
light and shadow begins by making shadows with sun and artificial
light, moves to construction of shadow boxes and box cameras, and
concludes with experiments using disposable cameras. All instructions
are carefully illustrated and explained. With an enthusiastic adult to
lead the way, young readers will clamor to try things "by
themselves." Great contribution to meaningful learning.
SUBJ: Shadows--Experiments./ Photography--Lighting--Experiments./
Experiments.

535.6   Ph-3 4-6/4 $9.95   T   KC118
ARDLEY, NEIL. Science book of color. Gulliver/Harcourt Brace
Jovanovich ISBN 0-15-200576-5, 1991. 29p. col. ill.
Experiments with water, paints and inks examine color and
demonstrate how we can fool the eye. Includes fabric dying and
paper marbling. Photos show each step and insure success. Younger
children may need assistance.
SUBJ: Color--Experiments./ Science--Experiments./ Experiments.

VCR 535.6   Ph-3 3-6 $69.00   OD KC119
COLOR: LIGHT FANTASTIC (Videocassette). National Geographic
51314, 1988. 1/2″ VHS videocassette color (17min).
   Includes Teacher's Guide.
   Demonstrates how colors in our surroundings separate white light into
   the visible color spectrum. Also introduces ultraviolet and infrared
   spectrums and distinguishes between light colors and paint (or
   pigment) colors. Useful to introduce color theory and presents simple
   class experiments that test the theory.
   SUBJ: Color./ Light.

535.6   Ph-1 4-8/8 $15.89   L   KC120
DEWEY, ARIANE. Naming colors. HarperCollins ISBN 0-06-021292-6; In
Canada: HarperCollins, 1995. 48p. col. ill., maps.
   Includes index.
   How did colors get their names? This book tells both the linguistic and
   serendipitous nature of fuchsia, ocher, magenta, and many, many
   more. Names are derived from places, things, foods, jewels, wines,
   and plants. Author gives historic references as far back as ancient
   Egypt coupled with linguistic underpinnings. Artwork renders indelible
   images to words like chocolate illustrated with Montezuma sipping
   from a gold cup. The section on spicy colors is perfect for Columbus
   Day. Index of color words is illustrated with bands of color. Useful
   for art, language, and social studies activities.
   SUBJ: Color./ English language--Etymology.

535.6   Ph-1 K-3/2 $10.95   T   KC121
GOLDSEN, LOUISE. Colors. [This edition American text by Louise
Goldsen.] Created by Gallimard Jeunesse and Pascale de Bourgoing.
Illus. by P. M. Valet and Sylvaine Perols. Scholastic ISBN 0-590-45236-
3; In Canada: Scholastic, 1991. unp. col. ill.(spiral bound). (First
discovery book).
   "Cartwheel books."
   Originally published in France, LA COULEUR, 1989.
   Basic and mixed colors are taught through an appealing use of plastic
   overlays in this small glossy volume. Each color is presented then
   overlays mix colors on images of plants and animals. The effects of
   white, black, and gray and a simple example of illusions created by
   color contrasts completes the inviting lesson. Useful for preschoolers,
   but the sophisticated presentation will be enjoyed by older students as
   well.
   SUBJ: Color.

535.6   Ph-2 P-1 $15.93   L   KC122
HOBAN, TANA. Colors everywhere. Greenwillow ISBN 0-688-12763-0,
1995. unp. col. ill.
   Learn primary colors along with subtle hues; exuberant photographs
   open the eyes to everyday beauty. A strip of color bands runs
   alongside each picture, helping young readers to match colors and
   identify them both independently and in context. A book to be used
   again and again. Make certain the art teacher knows about this one.
   SUBJ: Color--Pictorial works.

535.6   Ph-1 P-K $14.93   L   KC123
HOBAN, TANA. Of colors and things. Greenwillow ISBN 0-688-07535-
5, 1989. unp. col. ill.
   Selectors' Choice, 17th ed.
   Brilliantly clear and sharp photographs introduce things that are
   yellow, red, green, orange, blue, gray, brown, and black. Useful for
   a range of activities from identification of objects to a guide for
   creating scenes featuring individual or combined colors.
   SUBJ: Color.

535.6   Ph-3 P-1 $14.93   L   KC124
MCMILLAN, BRUCE. Growing colors. Lothrop, Lee & Shepard ISBN
0-688-07845-1, 1988. 32p. col. ill.
   Full page photographs of vegetables and fruits explode with color to
   teach about nature, food and hue.
   SUBJ: Color./ Vegetables./ Fruit.

535.6   Ph-1 1-6/5 $14.95   L   KC125
WESTRAY, KATHLEEN. Color sampler. Ticknor & Fields ISBN 0-395-
65940-X, 1993. unp. col. ill.
   Selectors' Choice, 20th ed.
   Color surrounds us--it is commonplace yet (when we look closer) it is
   complex. From twelve color wheel hues, we get hundreds of other
   colors that dance different tunes in different backgrounds and
   intensities. "The variety of color is endless..." (last p.) Patchwork
   quilt patterns are used to explain primary, secondary, and
   intermediate colors as well as complimentary colors and shades of
   color. Use across grade levels to enrich sensory experiences, assist art
   lessons, or simply enjoy. Give everyone a pack of crayons to check
   his own color findings.
   SUBJ: Color.

536   Ph-3 K-3/2 $9.95   T   KC126
ARDLEY, NEIL. Science book of hot and cold. Gulliver/Harcourt Brace
Jovanovich ISBN 0-15-200612-5, 1992. 29p. col. ill. (Science book of).
   Explore temperature by building a simple thermometer or cleaning up
   dirty water. These and 11 other easy-to-do activities allow young
   children to have fun learning. Colorful illustrations and the use of
   commonplace materials insure success. Primary teachers should love it.
   SUBJ: Heat--Experiments./ Cold--Experiments./ Experiments.

VCR 536   Ph-1 3-A $49.00   OD KC127
GOLDSMITH, SIDNEY. Man who loved machines (Videocassette).
National Film Board of Canada/dist. by Bullfrog Films, 1983. 1/2″ VHS
videocassette color (9min).
   Includes teacher's guide.
   Selectors' Choice, 15th ed.
   Driving his car to exercise his dog, building a perpetual motion
   machine to hammer nails, using a jackhammer to drill holes are all
   part of Mr. Battersby's failure to match appropriate energy resources
   to the task at hand. Superior animation and well paced script present
   a creative introduction to entropy, the second law of thermodynamics,
   that is certain to stimulate discussion and thinking.
   SUBJ: Entropy./ Thermodynamics./ Energy conservation.

VCR 536   Ph-3 5-6 $89.00   OD KC128
HEAT, TEMPERATURE AND ENERGY (Videocassette). Rainbow
Educational RB8229, 1995. 1/2″ VHS videocassette color (23min).
   Includes teacher's guide and reproducible.
   Includes public performance rights.
   Demonstrates how the constant motion of molecules creates thermal
   energy. Then explores the flow of this energy and how it can be
   converted into heat. While depicting the various characteristics of
   temperature and heat, it describes the differences between the Celcius
   and Fahrenheit scales. The use of calories as a measurement of heat
   and the concept of insulation are explained. A brief introduction to
   solar energy rounds out this overview of heat sources. For
   environmental studies.
   SUBJ: Heat./ Temperature./ Force and energy.

537   Ph-3 2-5/3 $9.95   T   KC129
ARDLEY, NEIL. Science book of electricity. Gulliver/Harcourt Brace
Jovanovich ISBN 0-15-200583-8, 1991. 29p. col. ill.
   Numbered step-by-step directions and full-color photographs present
   simple activities which explore basic concepts of electricity. Clear,
   uncluttered layout encourages young scientists to experiment with
   static electricity, simple circuits, switches, and circuit boards.
   SUBJ: Electricity--Experiments./ Experiments.

537   Ph-2 K-3/5 $15.89   L   KC130
BERGER, MELVIN. Switch on, switch off. Illus. by Carolyn Croll.
Crowell/HarperCollins ISBN 0-690-04786-X; In Canada: HarperCollins,
1989. 32p. col. ill. (Let's-read-and-find-out science book).
   Begin by making a small electrical generator with wind, a magnet and
   compass; proceed to understand how power plants create and
   distribute electricity to us. Interesting illustrations and active text make
   this a perfect read-aloud for the target audience.
   SUBJ: Electricity.

537   Ph-2 5-6/11 $22.80   L   KC131
HOOPER, TONY. Electricity. Raintree Steck-Vaughn ISBN 0-8114-2334-
4, 1994. 48p. col. ill. (Breakthrough).
   Includes chronology, glossary, bibliography and index.
   Chronologically traces the history of electrical discoveries from the
   early seventeen hundreds to theories about future superconductors.
   Important for demonstrating the continual building of a scientific body
   of knowledge. Will give all readers, especially those who are
   convinced they cannot absorb the intricateness of electricity, some
   scientific understanding.
   SUBJ: Electricity.

VCR 537   Ph-3 3-6 $175.00   OD KC132
JUNIOR ELECTRICIAN (Videocassette). United Learning 863-V, 1991. 4
1/2″ VHS videocassettes color.
   Includes teacher's guide and 25 work sheets.
   Introduces electricity and magnetism in four interrelated videos that
   depict students experimenting with ordinary objects and science
   equipment. Explains household current, power plant production, and
   the safe use of electricity. Lesson plans, work sheets, and suggested
   follow-up activities round out the three to four week unit. Helpful
   where schools have few hands-on materials; reinforces and reviews
   text book and lab experiences.
   Contents: 1. Static charges (10min); 2. Magnetism (10min); 3. Current
   electricity (10min); 4. Our electrical world (10min).
   SUBJ: Electric engineering./ Electricity./ Electric currents./ Magnetism.

537 Ph-1 3-6/7 $13.95 L KC133
MARKLE, SANDRA. Power up: experiments, puzzles, and games
exploring electricity. Atheneum ISBN 0-689-31442-6; In Canada: Collier
Macmillan, 1989. 40p. ill.
> Includes index.
> Selectors' Choice, 18th ed.
> Discover how batteries, circuits and fuses work; build your own
> flashlight, test for conductivity and learn about electricity hands-on by
> experimenting with household items. Clean, clear layout of diagrams
> and directions insure success. Just the correct amount of information
> to set young discoverers thinking and learning with enthusiasm.
> SUBJ: Electricity--Experiments./ Experiments.

537 Ph-2 4-A/9 $15.95 T KC134
PARKER, STEVE. Electricity. DK Publishing ISBN 1-879431-82-3, 1992.
64p. col. ill. (Eyewitness science).
> Includes index.
> Explores the discovery and uses of electricity while explaining its
> properties. Intriguing photographs which are sure to catch the interest
> of browsers and text introduce various electrical devices and their
> inventors. Report writers will need additional sources.
> SUBJ: Electricity./ Electric power.

537.6 Ph-3 5-A/7 $13.85 L KC135
ASIMOV, ISAAC. How did we find out about superconductivity? Illus. by
Erika Kors. Walker ISBN 0-8027-6778-8, 1988. 64p. ill. (How did we
find out).
> Includes index.
> Available from National Library Service for the Blind and Physically
> Handicapped on sound recording cassette RC30810.
> Details the scientific methods used in the search for absolute zero, the
> lowest possible temperature. Serendipitously it was discovered that
> superconductivity (electrical conductivity without resistance) was
> possible at temperatures above absolute zero. Timely reading, this
> ends with predictions about how this newest energy source could alter
> our lives.
> SUBJ: Superconductivity.

538 Ph-3 2-5/2 $9.95 T KC136
ARDLEY, NEIL. Science book of magnets. Gulliver/Harcourt Brace
Jovanovich ISBN 0-15-200581-1, 1991. 29p. col. ill.
> Clear, full-color photographs and easy-to-follow directions depict
> activities using bar magnets, horseshoe magnets, and electric magnets.
> Sidebars of information relate how magnetic principles are used in
> science and industry.
> SUBJ: Magnets--Experiments./ Experiments.

538 Ph-2 4-8/6 $19.90 L KC137
SHEPHERD, DONNA WALSH. Auroras: light shows in the night sky.
Watts ISBN 0-531-20181-3; In Canada: Nelson, 1995. 63p. col. ill.,
maps. (First book).
> Includes glossary, bibliography and index.
> Awesome curtains of light floating in the night skies have perplexed
> and amazed mankind for centuries. Now scientists tell us the aurora
> phenomena is "as natural as ... the air we breath." (p.19) Explains
> what causes the auroras, how solar storms change the earth's
> magnetic fields, different aurora colors and types, and where the best
> views are. A combination of inspiration and science that will satisfy
> the curious.
> SUBJ: Auroras.

538 Ph-3 6-A/7 $18.95 L KC138
SOUZA, D. M. Northern lights. Carolrhoda ISBN 0-87614-799-6, 1994.
48p. col. ill., maps. (Nature in action).
> Includes glossary and index.
> Describes how the aurora borealis received its name, what causes this
> light display, why it shines with different colors, and where to see it.
> Using familiar comparisons such as static electricity in clothes with
> wonderful photographs and diagrams, the book succinctly explains
> this complex phenomena. All the newest scientific findings are
> presented sequentially for effective learning.
> SUBJ: Auroras.

539.7 Ph-3 6-A/8 $21.50 L KC139
PFLAUM, ROSALYND. Marie Curie and her daughter Irene. Lerner ISBN
0-8225-4915-8, 1993. 144p. ill.
> Includes bibliography and index.
> Marie's extraordinary devotion to research and her daughter's equal
> dedication to the work her parents had begun are a story of
> teamwork in the sciences which can't be rivaled. Book shows the
> intimate relationship of Marie and Irene, their contributions to science,
> and how the health of both women was destroyed by their work with
> radium. For the advanced reader and for inclusion in career, women's
> studies, and science units.

SUBJ: Curie, Marie./ Joliot-Curie, Irene./ Radioactivity--History./
Chemists./ Physicists./ Women scientists.

539.7 Ph-1 3-6/5 $13.95 L KC140
WELLS, ROBERT E. What's smaller than a pygmy shrew? Whitman ISBN
0-8075-8837-7; In Canada: General, 1995. unp. col. ill.
> Includes glossary.
> Answers the question "How small can you get?" with deceptively
> simple comparisons between a pygmy shrew and toadstools. Objects
> become progressively smaller until elementary particles: electrons,
> protons, neutrons, and quarks! Clever way of conveying the mysteries
> of the molecular.
> SUBJ: Atoms./ Size.

546 Ph-3 K-2/5 $15.93 L KC141
WALPOLE, BRENDA. Water. Photos by Ed Barber. Garrett ISBN
0-944483-72-0, 1990. 25p. col. ill. (Threads).
> Includes index.
> Brightly colored pages document the importance of water in our lives.
> In addition to the obvious, the text gives a brief introduction to water
> and sewage treatment plants. Use in conjunction with the MAGIC
> SCHOOL BUS AT THE WATERWORKS.
> SUBJ: Water./ Water--Experiments./ Experiments.

546 Ph-1 K-6/6 $16.95 L KC142
WICK, WALTER. Drop of water: a book of science and wonder.
Scholastic ISBN 0-590-22197-3; In Canada: Scholastic, 1997. 40p. col.
ill.
> Selectors' Choice, 21st ed.
> Wonders are revealed in pristine photographs and pithy text. The
> many states of water are viewed as ice, steam, frost, dew, and liquid
> and are transformed into bubbles and rainbows. Provides experiments
> for condensation and evaporation, surface tension, capillary attraction,
> and more. Use when contemplating clouds, snow, or a droplet. Expert
> science at all levels: kindergartners will enjoy seeing molecules in
> motion while older children can make clouds. A gem of a book.
> SUBJ: Water./ Water--Experiments./ Experiments.

548 Ph-3 P-2/5 $17.50 L KC143
MAKI, CHU. Snowflakes, sugar, and salt: crystals up close. Photos by
Isamu Sekido. Lerner ISBN 0-8225-2903-3, 1993. 24p. col. ill. (Science
all around you).
> Includes glossary.
> An exciting world of crystals opens up for the young learner who has
> access to magnifying glasses and a helpful adult. Captivating
> photographs illustrate natural beauty and demonstrate how to grow
> several types of crystals. Large format and colorful photographs
> insure success.
> SUBJ: Crystals.

549 Ph-1 A/10 $29.95 T KC144
PELLANT, CHRIS. Eyewitness handbook of rocks and minerals. Photos by
Harry Taylor. DK Publishing ISBN 1-56458-033-4, 1992. 256p. col. ill.
(Eyewitness handbooks).
> Includes glossary and index.
> Selectors' Choice, 19th ed.
> Precisely illustrated and organized field guide gives the following
> information for minerals: group composition, hardness, specific gravity,
> cleavage, and fracture; for rocks: group origin, grain size, crystal
> shape (igneous), classification, occurence (igneous), temperature
> (metamorphic), and fossils (sedimentary). Detailed illustrations give
> true colors including vagaries such as luster, mineral deposits in rocks,
> and secondary crystalline formations. Ancillary topics include
> equipment, collection organization, rock formation cycles, mineral
> identification table, and more. A superior book. Purchase two copies,
> one for reference and one for circulation.
> SUBJ: Rocks./ Minerals./ Mineralogy--Handbooks, manuals, etc.

550 Ph-1 4-A/8 $16.95 L KC145
ENGLISH, JUNE A. Mission: Earth: voyage to the home planet. By June
A. English and Thomas D. Jones. Scholastic ISBN 0-590-48571-7; In
Canada: Scholastic, 1996. 42p. col. ill.
> Includes index.
> Astronaut Tom Jones chronicles his eleven day trip into space on
> Endeavour in 1994. The mission photographed Earth with new
> imaging technology--special cameras and Space Radar Lab 2--that
> created three-dimensional maps which "make sense of some of the
> environmental problems of our planet." (p. 40) Radar images of
> cities, rain forests, volcanoes, and water are integrated with the text
> enabling readers to understand the complexities of environmental
> problems. This riveting first-person account brings the excitement of
> space exploration and the concerns of environmental scientists
> together. Create a "you are there" scenario in the classroom by
> reading each day's account aloud. Compare the new maps with ones

in older reference books. For environmental studies.
SUBJ: Earth sciences--Remote sensing./ Astronautics in earth sciences.

550 Ph-2 3-6/6 $14.93 L KC146
GIBBONS, GAIL. Planet Earth/inside out. Morrow ISBN 0-688-09681-6, 1995. unp. col. ill., maps.
Gibbon's artwork examines four layers of our planet while text discusses the movement of tectonic plates that result in earthquakes and volcanic activity. Brief information is given on geological shaping and rock categories. Useful information presented in an attractive format is especially helpful to reluctant readers.
SUBJ: Earth.

550 Ph-2 1-3/3 $14.89 L KC147
LAUBER, PATRICIA. You're aboard spaceship Earth. Illus. by Holly Keller. HarperCollins ISBN 0-06-024408-9; In Canada: HarperCollins, 1996. 32p. col. ill. (Let's-read-and-find-out science book).
Everything needed for life is aboard spaceship Earth: food, oxygen, and water. Our resources are renewed through the water, oxygen, and carbon cycles. Book sows the seeds of environmental awareness early, so that readers will appreciate and take care of the Earth. For environmental studies.
SUBJ: Earth./ Life (Biology).

550 Ph-3 4-6/9 $13.50 P KC148
MARKLE, SANDRA. Digging deeper: investigations into rocks, shocks, quakes, and other earthly matters. Lothrop, Lee & Shepard ISBN 0-688-805987-2, 1987. 120p. ill.
Includes glossary and index.
The geology of plate tetonics, crystal formation and the rock cycle is explained through an assortment of tables, facts, and experiments. The various activities, placed throughout the book, enhance and expand the elementary science curriculum.
SUBJ: Geology.

CDR 550 Ph-1 4-A $44.95 OD KC149
SCHOLASTIC'S THE MAGIC SCHOOL BUS EXPLORES INSIDE THE EARTH. School ed. (CD-ROM). Microsoft ISBN 1-57231-261-0; In Canada: Microsoft Canada, 1996. 1 CD-ROM color. (Scholastic's the Magic School Bus explores).
Version 1.00.
Includes user's guide and teacher's guide.
System requirements: Multimedia PC with a 486SX/25 MHz or higher processor; MS-DOS operating system version 5.0 or later with Windows version 3.1 or later, Windows 95, or Windows NT 3.51; 4MB of RAM (8MB recommended) for Windows 3.1 or later, 8MB of RAM for Windows 95, 12MB of RAM for Windows NT 3.51; 5MB of available hard-disk space; Double-speed or faster CD-ROM drive; SVGA 256-color display monitor; 8-bit sound board (16-bit recommended); Headphone or speakers; Microsoft Mouse or compatible pointing device.
Youngsters will learn a great deal about geology as they join Ms. Frizzle's class in yet another Magic School Bus adventure. The task is to rescue the rocks missing from Arnold's collection. Student multimedia reports, experiments, rock collection, and transformation activities will be encountered as students gather the missing rocks.
SUBJ: Geology--Software./ Software--Geology./ Earth sciences--Software./ Software--Earth sciences./ Interactive media.

VD 550 Ph-3 4-A $325.00 OD KC150
STV: RESTLESS EARTH (Videodisc). National Geographic 81510, 1992. 1 CAV videodisc, 2 3.5" disks with HyperCard.
Includes user's guide with barcodes; and map.
Interactive.
System requirements: TV monitor, videodisc player: Pioneer, LD-V2200, 4200, 6000 series, or 8000, CLD-V2400, 4400; or Sony LDP-1200, 1500, 1550, or 2000. Macintosh with at least 1M RAM (2M RAM strongly recommended) for System 6.0.5 or higher, or at least 2.5M RAM for System 7.0 or higher, corresponding Hypercard 2.0v2 or higher, a 3.25" disk drive, and a hard drive. RS232 interface cable to connect videodisc player to computer. Printer (optional).
Plate tectonics, plate movement, and studies of earthquakes come alive with this interactive video package. A glossary, a limited number of print resources, a multimedia presentation tool, and a series of interactive video lessons are included. Works well with small groups or an entire class.
SUBJ: Volcanoes./ Earthquakes./ Plate tectonics./ Earth sciences./ Geology.

550 Ph-1 1-A/9 $15.95 T KC151
VISUAL DICTIONARY OF THE EARTH. DK Publishing ISBN 1-56458-335-X, 1993. 64p. col. ill., maps. (Eyewitness visual dictionaries).
Includes glossary and index.

Selectors' Choice, 20th ed.
If a picture is worth a thousand words, these are worth a billion! Dramatic diagrams and cut-away drawings allow "never seen before" views of earth's dynamics. A hurricane is dissected, the ocean floor laid bare, and global wind systems unraveled. The marvels of our planet are alluring even to a disinterested viewer. A mind-expanding book to use at all grade levels.
SUBJ: Earth sciences./ Geology.

551 Ph-1 2-4/3 $14.95 T KC152
COLE, JOANNA. Magic School Bus inside the earth. Illustrated by Bruce Degen. Scholastic ISBN 0-590-40759-7, 1987. 40p. col. ill.
Spanish edition available EL AUTOBUS MAGICO EN EL INTERIOR DE LA TIERRA (ISBN 0-590-46342-X, 1993), $4.95
Ms. Frazzle takes her class on a field trip to the inner depths of the earth to examine rocks and teach geology. The unusual cartoon format coupled with an off-handed blend of fact and fiction will intrigue young readers. The author does provide a lively explanation, in dialog form, that distinguishes between fact and embellishment. Best for individual use.
SUBJ: Earth--Internal structure./ Geology.

VCR 551 Ph-3 3-5 $89.00 OD KC153
OUR CHANGING EARTH (Videocassette). Written and produced by Peter Cochran. Rainbow Educational Video RB856, 1991. 1/2" VHS videocassette color (24min).
Includes teacher's guide.
Introduces the concept of one continent (Pangaea), continental drift, plate tectonics, volcanoes, and earthquakes and demonstrates how the earth is still changing and rearranging itself right up to the present. Dramatic changes are enhanced by video photography, insuring a basic understanding of elementary geology.
SUBJ: Earth sciences./ Geology./ Plate tectonics.

CE 551.1 Ph-1 2-4/6 $4.95 P KC154
MCNULTY, FAITH. How to dig a hole to the other side of the world. Illus. by Marc Simont. HarperCollins ISBN 0-06-443218-1; In Canada: HarperCollins, c1979, 1990. 32p. col. ill.
Selectors' Choice, 13th ed.
Read-along kit available from Live Oak (ISBN 0-87499-234-6, 1991). 1 hardcover book, 1 sound cassette (13min), $22.95.
Describes an imaginary trip 8,000 miles through the earth with simple, clear, and accurate information of the various layers and conditions which will be encountered. The detailed illustrations provide further information on the steps and equipment needed to assure the success of the journey.
SUBJ: Earth--Internal structure.

551.1 Ph-3 A/7 $15.93 L KC155
SATTLER, HELEN RONEY. Our patchwork planet: the story of plate tectonics. Illus. by Giulio Maestro. Lothrop, Lee & Shepard ISBN 0-688-09313-2, 1995. 48p. col. ill., maps.
Includes bibliography and index.
Seismologists, geologists, geophysicists, and oceanographers are all studying plate movements, and yet we still do not know exactly how earthquakes and volcanoes operate nor can we predict disasters. Sattler's informative text coupled with Maestro's maps and diagrams takes the reader to the frontiers of science. Introduces many new scientific concepts such as "...plates are moved by convection currents in the asthenosphere." (p.13) Definitely for advanced students; beneficial to teachers. For collections that need the latest information on plate tectonics.
SUBJ: Plate tectonics./ Continental drift./ Geology.

551.2 Ph-1 4-A/7 $19.95 L KC156
JACOBS, LINDA. Letting off steam. Carolrhoda ISBN 0-87614-300-1, 1989. 47p. col. ill. (Carolrhoda earth watch book).
Includes glossary and index.
Fascinating look at the geothermal energy of geysers, fumaroles, hot springs and mud pots accompanied by striking photos of bubbling landscapes. Useful for all energy and conservation studies. Even the most jaded learner will discover something interesting.
SUBJ: Geothermal engineering./ Steam.

551.21 Ph-3 4-6/7 $19.90 L KC157
LAMPTON, CHRISTOPHER. Volcano. Millbrook ISBN 1-56294-028-7, 1991. 64p. col. ill., maps. (Disaster!).
Includes glossary, bibliography and index.
The havoc of eruptions and the benefits of this natural geologic force are carefully presented in 12 thoughtful chapters and some interesting photographs. Informative and enjoyable reading.
SUBJ: Volcanoes./ Geology./ Earth--Crust./ Mountains.

NONFICTION

CE 551.21   Ph-1 P-A/6 $16.95 T KC158
LAUBER, PATRICIA. Volcano: the eruption and healing of Mount St.
Helens. Bradbury ISBN 0-02-754500-8; In Canada: Maxwell Macmillan,
1986. 60p. col. ill.
    Includes index.
    Newbery Honor Book.
    Selectors' Choice, 16th ed.
    Rather than demons of destruction, volcanoes are presented as
    builders of land and makers of soil. How life returns and gains
    footholds on the North side of Mt. St. Helens is the focus of the
    informative text and marvelous photographs. Documenting the saying
    that time is a healer of wounds, this is a unique presentation on an
    often hackneyed subject.
    SUBJ: Saint Helens, Mount (Wash.)--Eruption, 1980./ Volcanoes.

551.21   Ph-1 3-6/6 $15.88 L KC159
SIMON, SEYMOUR. Volcanoes. Morrow ISBN 0-688-07412-X, 1988.
unp. col. ill.
    Illustrates four types of volcanoes; explains what causes eruptions and
    how lava enriches the soil. Beautiful photographs highlight Hawaii,
    Mt. Rainier and Mt. St. Helens. Introduces a wealth of vocabulary
    and is an excellent read aloud; a must addition to this popular topic.
    SUBJ: Volcanoes.

551.21   Ph-3 3-6/7 $15.99 L KC160
VAN ROSE, SUSANNA. Volcano and earthquake. Photos by James
Stevenson. Knopf ISBN 0-679-91685-7, 1992. 64p. col. ill. (Eyewitness
books).
    "Dorling Kindersley book.
    Includes index.
    Awesome geophysical power unfolds in the dramatic pictures of fiery
    rocks, Pompeii's ruins, and devastated landscapes. Gives information
    on plate tectonics, sea floor spreading, volcanologists, and outer
    space volcanoes. Inviting pages will keep readers coming back for
    more.
    SUBJ: Volcanoes./ Earthquakes.

551.22   Ph-3 2-4/4 $14.89 L KC161
BRANLEY, FRANKLYN M. Earthquakes. Illustrated by Richard Rosenblum.
Crowell/HarperCollins ISBN 0-690-04663-4, 1990. 32p. col. ill. (Let's-
read-and-find-out science book).
    Danger and destruction are downplayed as Branley explains seismic
    waves, continental drift, and fault lines. Useful for reading aloud; your
    primary audience will be fascinated.
    SUBJ: Earthquakes.

551.22   Ph-3 5-6/7 $5.95 P KC162
LAMPTON, CHRISTOPHER. Earthquake. Millbrook ISBN 1-56294-777-X,
1991. 64p. col. ill., maps. (Disaster!).
    Includes glossary, bibliography and index.
    The devastation and terror of earthquakes are documented and
    illustrated with dramatic pictures from the 1989 San Francisco quake.
    Text examines plate tectonics, earthquake detection, and prediction.
    Gives up-to-date information on this awesome natural force.
    SUBJ: Earthquakes.

551.22   Ph-3 3-6/7 $14.88 L KC163
SIMON, SEYMOUR. Earthquakes. Morrow ISBN 0-688-09634-4, 1991.
unp col photos and illus.
    Full-color pages document the awesome power of earthquakes
    including the 1989 San Francisco quake. Discusses plate tectonics,
    seismography, San Andreas Fault and the Richter Scale.
    SUBJ: Earthquakes.

VCR 551.3   Ph-3 5-A $99.00 OD KC164
GLACIERS: ICE ON THE MOVE (Videocassette). National Geographic
51636, 1994. 1/2" VHS videocassette color (27min).
    Includes teacher's guide.
    Dramatic cinematography follows glaciers and the glaciologists who
    study them. "Students will observe how glaciers form and move, how
    they alter the landscape, and how they affect the lives of people..."
    (Teacher's guide) Glacial changes have wide-ranging influences on
    our entire planet. Use while studying climate, evolution of land
    masses, and Alaska.
    SUBJ: Glaciers.

551.3   Ph-1 3-6/7 $16.00 T KC165
SIMON, SEYMOUR. Icebergs and glaciers. Morrow ISBN 0-688-06186-
9, 1987. unp. col. ill.
    Selectors' Choice, 16th ed.
    The excitement and grandeur of a frozen world come alive in this
    oversized, richly illustrated book which "Explains how different types
    of glaciers and icebergs are formed, how they move, and how they
    affect life on earth." (Jacket) Simon is at his best.
    SUBJ: Glaciers./ Icebergs.

551.4   Ph-1 K-6/6 $14.95 L KC166
GIBBONS, GAIL. Caves and caverns. Harcourt Brace ISBN 0-15-
226820-0; In Canada: Harcourt Brace c/o Canadian Manda, 1993. unp.
col. ill.
    Includes directory.
    Explores underground limestone caves, sea and lava caves, and ice
    caves. Carefully diagrams limestone cave formation and the creation
    of stalactites and stalagmites. Introduces the speleologists who are
    cave experts. Last page lists supplies, caving rules, and famous
    caverns open to tourists. Useful to classes that have field trip access
    to this environment. Will also interest students playing fantasy video
    games where caves are often featured as game settings.
    SUBJ: Caves.

551.4   Ph-1 1-5/7 $13.88 L KC167
SIMON, SEYMOUR. Deserts. Morrow ISBN 0-688-07416-2, 1990. unp.
col. ill.
    View desert landscapes and learn what makes them very unusual
    habitats. Focus is mainly on U.S. sites; wonderful pictures and concise
    text make this a perfect choice for reading aloud in the primary
    grades.
    SUBJ: Deserts.

551.4   Ph-3 4-6/7 $14.93 L KC168
SIMON, SEYMOUR. Mountains. Morrow ISBN 0-688-11041-X, 1994.
unp. col. ill., map.
    Precise text and spectacular photography present views of mountain
    chains from space, the effects of tectonic plates, and four basic kinds
    of mountains and their role in climatic changes. From storing water to
    creating recreational wonderlands, mountains are a vital part of our
    geography.
    SUBJ: Mountains.

551.4   Ph-3 4-6/7 $17.27 L KC169
WOOD, JENNY. Caves: an underground wonderland. Gareth Stevens
ISBN 0-8368-0469-4; In Canada: Saunders, 1991. 32p. col. ill.
(Wonderworks of nature).
    Includes glossary and index.
    Describes cave formation, systems and explorations. Touches on cave
    wildlife and the discovery of the Lascaux Cave murals. Oversized with
    many illustrations to keep poorer readers interested.
    SUBJ: Caves.

551.43   Ph-2 2-4/4 $14.95 L KC170
ZOEHFELD, KATHLEEN WEIDNER. How mountains are made. Illus. by
James Graham Hale. HarperCollins ISBN 0-06-024510-7; In Canada:
HarperCollins, 1995. 32p. col. ill., maps. (Let's-read-and-find-out science
book).
    Cartoon characters add to the fun as diagrams illustrate how the
    lithosphere is broken into plates, volcanoes erupt, and land rises to
    make mountains that, in turn, get worn down through the years.
    Perfect match of text and illustrations for young mountaineers.
    SUBJ: Mountains./ Geology.

551.44   Ph-3 5-6/6 $15.95 T KC171
BENDICK, JEANNE. Caves!: underground worlds. Illus. by Todd
Telander. Henry Holt ISBN 0-8050-2764-5; In Canada: Fitzhenry &
Whiteside, 1995. 74p. ill. (some col.). (Redfeather book).
    Includes glossary and index.
    Seven short chapters discuss cave formations, features, and
    discoveries worldwide. Illustrated with photographs and diagrams to
    highlight text. Basic information with interesting historical background
    such as Baron Valvasor's imaginative travel writings, Stephen Bishop,
    a slave, who explored and mapped Mammoth Cave, and Lascaux's
    prehistoric murals. Good addition for geology studies.
    SUBJ: Caves.

551.46   Ph-1 4-6/7 $18.90 L KC172
FLEISHER, PAUL. Our oceans: experiments and activities in marine
science. Illus. by Patricia A. Keeler. Millbrook ISBN 1-56294-575-0,
1995. 80p. ill. (some col.).
    Includes bibliography and index.
    A hands-on approach to learning about ocean chemistry, tidal
    changes, global climate, and more. Simple activities such as floating
    an egg midway in a stratified water solution will pique curiosity.
    Nascent marine scientists will be sold on a career, and all visits to the
    seashore will be enriched. Perfect for oceanography units and a must
    purchase for coastal schools.
    SUBJ: Oceanography--Experiments./ Experiments.

551.46   Ph-2 4-A/6 $19.95 T KC173
GANERI, ANITA. Oceans atlas. Illus. by Luciano Corbella. DK Publishing
ISBN 1-56458-475-5, 1994. 64p. col. ill., maps.
    Includes index.

The wonders of oceanography are explained in lavish art work including maps, diagrams, and cutaway drawings. Every vignette is carefully captioned and placed for maximum learning. Will be referred to again and again. Helpful in discussing environmental concerns, social studies, and marine life.
SUBJ: Ocean./ Oceanography./ Marine resources.

551.46 Ph-2 2-6/7 $20.99 L KC174
MACQUITTY, MIRANDA. Ocean. Photos by Frank Greenaway. Knopf ISBN 0-679-97331-1, 1995. 64p. col. ill., maps. (Eyewitness books).
"Dorling Kindersley book."
"Borzoi book."
Includes index.
The amazing beauty of worldwide oceans is presented in typical Eyewitness format. Two-page subject treatment examines life on the surface, in the twilight zone, and in the darkest depths. Along with a parade of aquatic life, coverage includes: waves and weather, oil and gas explorations, pollution, diving equipment, and ocean products. A good addition to ocean studies.
SUBJ: Marine biology./ Ocean.

551.46 Ph-2 4-A/8 $17.00 L KC175
MARKLE, SANDRA. Pioneering ocean depths. Atheneum ISBN 0-689-31823-5; In Canada: Distican, 1995. 48p. col. ill., maps.
Includes index.
Text and pictures explain how scientists map the ocean floor with sound waves; collect deep sea animals; and conduct high sea prospecting for oil, gas, and minerals. Features easy experiments that explore these subjects. Since 95 percent of the sea floor still needs to be mapped, there is good reason to choose marine biology as a career. Includes up-to-date information on latest technology and advances in marine science. For career studies.
SUBJ: Underwater exploration./ Oceanography.

551.46 Ph-1 5-A/5 $13.89 L KC176
SIMON, SEYMOUR. How to be an ocean scientist in your own home. Illustrated by David A. Carter. Lippincott/HarperCollins ISBN 0-397-32292-5; In Canada: HarperCollins, 1988. 136p. ill.
Includes bibliography and index.
Available from National Library Service for the Blind and Physically Handicapped on sound recording cassette RC31179.
Over twenty simple experiments investigate the properties of sea-water, ocean currents, waves and sediments. Most can be done with homemade saltwater (using either table salt or saltwater aquarium crystals, requirements vary). Contains excellent directions for setting up and maintaining a saltwater aquarium. While especially useful in communities bordering the ocean, the book has broad based appeal and is an excellent way to raise consciousness about ocean pollution as well as making learning enjoyable.
SUBJ: Oceanography--Experiments./ Experiments.

551.46 Ph-2 3-6/7 $13.88 L KC177
SIMON, SEYMOUR. Oceans. Morrow ISBN 0-688-09454-6, 1990. unp. col. ill.
An awe-inspiring look at the ocean using computer-generated maps to highlight ocean currents, temperatures, and geology. Also includes diagrams, photographs, and discussions of tides and waves. A fascinating look at seventy percent of our planet's surface.
SUBJ: Ocean.

551.46 Ph-2 3-6/8 $27.95 T KC178
VANCLEAVE, JANICE PRATT. Janice VanCleave's oceans for every kid: easy activities that make learning science fun. By Janice VanCleave. Wiley ISBN 0-471-12454-0; In Canada: Wiley, 1996. 245p. ill., maps. (Janice VanCleave's science for every kid).
Includes glossary, bibliography and index.
How deep is the ocean? How do oceans affect weather? How can fish hear without ears? Find out by experimenting in and out of the water. Twenty-five activities begin with a paragraph or two of "what you need to know," followed by "let's think it through" (using charts and drawings), and lead to purposeful activities. Required materials are easy to obtain and procedures are carefully itemized. Children will need little supervision to attain safe, satisfactory results. Information on ocean pollution will fit with environmental studies.
SUBJ: Oceanography--Experiments./ Experiments.

551.46 Ph-3 4-6/7 $14.99 T KC179
WATERS, JOHN F. Deep-sea vents: living worlds without sun. Cobblehill/Dutton ISBN 0-525-65145-4, 1994. 48p. col. ill.
Includes index.
Dive to the frontier of ocean science to discover hydrothermal vents and creatures that create energy from chemicals (rather than from the sun). Presents the newest revelations in oceanography...what these creatures are, and how they were discovered. Attests to the fact:

there is new news in science.
SUBJ: Hydrothermal vents./ Oceanography./ Marine biology.

551.47 Ph-3 3-6/5 $17.50 L KC180
SOUZA, D. M. Powerful waves. Carolrhoda ISBN 0-87614-661-2, 1992. 48p. col. ill. (Nature in action).
Includes glossary.
Photographs of tsunamis' havoc make this presentation on wave movement, formation, and destruction a page turner. Useful for ocean studies, but should also receive plenty of independent student use because of topic's high appeal.
SUBJ: Ocean waves./ Tsunamis.

551.48 Ph-2 P-2 $14.95 T KC181
HATHORN, LIBBY. Wonder thing. Illus. by Peter Gouldthorpe. Houghton Mifflin ISBN 0-395-71541-5, 1996. unp. col. ill.
Full-page linoleum-block prints dispense clues as readers seek the riddle's answer: the wonder thing is water--earth's life-sustaining element. Readers see where water is found and how we use and abuse it. Combination of poetic text and boldly colored illustrations is certain to delight while teaching.
SUBJ: Water.

551.48 Ph-3 4-5/6 $15.27 L KC182
HENDERSON, KATHY. Great Lakes. Childrens Press ISBN 0-516-01163-4; In Canada: Childrens Press, 1989. 48p. col. ill. (New true book).
Includes glossary and index.
Contains information on the Great Lakes' formation, exploration and development. Useful for social studies units on the Great Lakes states. Information is minimal, pictures are interesting.
SUBJ: Great Lakes.

551.48 Ph-1 3-6/6 $16.00 T KC183
HISCOCK, BRUCE. Big rivers: the Missouri, the Mississipi, and the Ohio. Atheneum ISBN 0-689-80871-2; In Canada: Distican, 1997. unp. col. ill., maps.
Details the havoc caused by the Great Flood of 1993. Beginning with a few levees built in the 1800s, river control today means "hundreds of dams and thousands of miles of levees." In spite of this and millions of sandbags, the waters raged and roared to the sea. An important historical, ecological, and scientific account of the Mississippi River Valley. "We have gained control (but not mastery)...." (Author's note) Realistic watercolors aid understanding. For environmental studies.
SUBJ: Floods--Mississippi River Valley.

551.48 Ph-3 4-6/7 $19.95 L KC184
WALKER, SALLY M. Water up, water down: the hydrologic cycle. Carolrhoda ISBN 0-87614-695-7, 1992. 47p. col. ill. (Carolrhoda earth watch book).
Includes glossary and index.
Discusses ground and ocean water, humidity, dew point, condensation, what hydrologists study, and how pesticides and acid rain pollute water. Text is well-illustrated with pictures, charts, and diagrams, but information is not grouped in chapters. Topics merge together making understanding more work. Utilitarian title for science reports and environmental studies.
SUBJ: Hydrologic cycle./ Water.

551.5 Ph-3 K-3/3 $9.95 T KC185
ARDLEY, NEIL. Science book of weather. Gulliver/Harcourt Brace Jovanovich ISBN 0-15-200624-9, 1992. 29p. col. ill. (Science book of).
Simple science experiments demonstrate a variety of weather concepts including humidity, air pressure, wind, and rain. Use of common household objects makes the experiments easy to conduct. Useful for small learning groups or individuals in primary classrooms.
SUBJ: Weather--Experiments./ Experiments.

VCR 551.5 Ph-3 5-6 $99.00 OD KC186
ATMOSPHERE: ON THE AIR (Videocassette). National Geographic 51580, 1993. 1/2" VHS videocassette color (25min).
Includes teacher's guide.
Adolescents host questions and answers about science via a radio call-in show. Narrators expound on atmospheric layers, ozone build-up, and weather patterns. The format is engaging and will hold class attention. Most beneficial when used for reinforcement after concepts have been taught and absorbed.
SUBJ: Atmosphere./ Weather./ Meteorology.

551.5 Ph-3 K-5/2 $12.00 L KC187
BERGER, MELVIN. How's the weather?: a look at weather and how it changes. By Melvin and Gilda Berger. Illus. by John Emil Cymerman. Ideals ISBN 0-8249-8641-5; In Canada: Ideals/dist. by Vanwell, 1993. 48p. col. ill., maps. (Discovery readers).

Includes index.

Look at the sky to view and predict the weather with this beginning reader. Identifies clouds; cautions about lightning, hurricanes, and tornadoes; and includes brief, simple experiments. Especially suited for reluctant readers needing meteorology resources.
SUBJ: Weather./ Meteorology.

551.5   Ph-2 K-3/2 $15.89   L   KC188
BRANLEY, FRANKLYN M. Rain and hail. Rev. ed. Illus. by Harriett Barton. Crowell/HarperCollins ISBN 0-690-04353-8, 1983. 39p. col. ill. (Let's-read-and-find-out science book).

Coming from clouds, rain droplets are the ultimate result of an accumulation of water vapor. Simple text and new attractive illustrations present the cycle effectively for the young reader.
SUBJ: Rain and rainfall./ Hail.

551.5   Ph-2 P-2/6 $15.00   L   KC189
CASEY, DENISE. Weather everywhere. Photos by Jackie Gilmore. Macmillan ISBN 0-02-717777-7; In Canada: Distican, 1995. 36p. col. ill. Includes glossary.

Nature photographs and sparse text explain why it is hot in summer and cold in winter; how wind blows around the world; and how water is constantly changing. Weather phenomena are easily observed in the young child's world and can be seized upon as teaching moments to build scientific inquiry and appreciation of our environment.
SUBJ: Weather.

551.5   Ph-3 P-2/2 $13.89   L   KC190
DORROS, ARTHUR. Feel the wind. Crowell/HarperCollins ISBN 0-690-04741-X; In Canada: HarperCollins, 1989. 30p. col. ill. (Let's-read-and-find-out science book).

Wind affects weather, supplies energy and sometimes creates problems. Includes instructions for a simple weather vane. Attractive illustrations make this especially useful for teachers of young children.
SUBJ: Winds.

551.5   Ph-3 A/10 $23.95   L   KC191
JOHNSON, REBECCA L. Investigating the ozone hole. Lerner ISBN 0-8225-1574-1, 1993. 112p. col. ill., maps.
Includes glossary and index.

The destruction of the ozone layer is a fact verified by scientists working in Antarctica. How depletion was traced to chlorofluorocarbons, what's at risk, and what can be done about it create a scientific conundrum effecting all of us. For older, scientifically minded students. For environmental studies.
SUBJ: Ozone layer./ Ozone layer depletion./ Man--Influence on nature.

551.5   Ph-3 P-2/4 $16.00   L   KC192
PLUCKROSE, HENRY. Weather. Childrens Press ISBN 0-516-08123-3; In Canada: Childrens Press, 1994. 32p. col. ill. (Walkabout).
Includes index.

Clouds sail by and release water and snow. Wind whips the landscape, and forecasters help us decide whether to work or play outside. We cannot control it, so we must learn to live with whatever weather comes our way. Use as an introduction to seasonal units.
SUBJ: Weather./ Meteorology.

551.5   Ph-1 3-6/7 $14.93   L   KC193
SIMON, SEYMOUR. Weather. Morrow ISBN 0-688-10547-5, 1993. unp. col. ill.

Delineates weather complexities by explaining the interplay of earth's rotation, wind belts, landforms, and differently heated air mases. With lucid text and brilliant photography, Simon presents daily phenomena and attunes the reader to natural wonders that are often taken for granted. "...we can be sure of only two things about the weather: We're going to have it and it's going to change." (last page)
SUBJ: Weather./ Meteorology.

VCR 551.5   Ph-2 4-6 $79.00   OD KC194
TELLING THE WEATHER (Videocassette). National Geographic 50595, 1996. 1/2" VHS videocassette color (25min).
Includes teacher's guide.
Closed captioned.

Computers, radar, and satellites are the new weather mix--allowing meteorologists to create simulation models. The brave new world of forecasting is illustrated with pictures from space shuttle cameras and hand held video recorders. Gives basic information on cloud types, hurricane and tornado dynamics, and the interaction of weather fronts. Fast moving with no review or summary; best viewed as segments in tandem with textbook.
SUBJ: Weather./ Meteorology./ Weather forecasting.

CE 551.55   Ph-2 1-3/2 $14.89   L   KC195
BRANLEY, FRANKLYN M. Flash, crash, rumble and roll. Rev. ed. By Barbara and Ed Emberley. Crowell/HarperCollins ISBN 0-690-04425-9; In Canada: HarperCollins, 1985. 31p. col. ill. (Let's-read-and-find-out science book).

Available from National Library Service for the Blind and Physically Handicapped in Braille BR06146.
Read-along kit available from HarperCollins ISBN 0-694-00200-3, 1987. 1 paperback book, 1 sound cassette (13min), $7.95.
Afraid of thunder and lightning? Here's a simply but clearly written explanation of its causes. The revised edition has significantly improved illustrations.
SUBJ: Lightning./ Rain and rainfall./ Thunderstorms.

551.55   Ph-2 P-4/3 $13.89   L   KC196
BRANLEY, FRANKLYN M. Tornado alert. Illus. by Giulio Maestro. Crowell/HarperCollins ISBN 0-690-04688-X; In Canada: HarperCollins, 1988. 32p. col. ill. (Let's-read-and-find-out science book).

Explains what a tornado is, how it is formed and how it can destroy. Describes indoor and outdoor safety procedures. Excellent for discussion of hazardous weather, examines danger without panic and hype.
SUBJ: Tornadoes.

551.55   Ph-2 2-4/4 $14.95   L   KC197
COLE, JOANNA. Magic School Bus inside a hurricane. Illus. by Bruce Degen. Scholastic ISBN 0-590-44686-X; In Canada: Scholastic, 1995. unp. col. ill.

Spanish version available EL AUTOBUS MAGICO DENTRO DE UN HURACAN (ISBN 0-590-94365-0, 1996).
Ms. Frizzle's class is in for a rip-roaring treat as it travels through a hurricane to learn weather dynamics. Riding in the yellow school bus, a balloon, and a research plane, the class continues its adventures. Packed with cartoon drawings and sidebars, this newest installment will keep students reading and learning. Useful in all weather units and perfect for reading aloud during hurricane season, it should help put irrational fear aside.
SUBJ: Hurricanes./ Weather./ Meteorology./ Spanish language materials.

551.55   Ph-1 4-6/6 $14.95   L   KC198
HISCOCK, BRUCE. Big storm. Atheneum ISBN 0-689-31770-0; In Canada: Maxwell Macmillan, 1993. unp. col. ill., maps.
Selectors' Choice, 20th ed.
Follows a March and April, 1982 storm that wreaked havoc with high winds and heavy rains beginning in California and sweeping across the entire United States. "...One of the most powerful spring storms ever recorded." (front flap) Carefully exposes the dynamics of worldwide weather patterns, illustrating meteorologists feeding their computers and forecasting with radar screens. Retells the tale as the storm hopscotchs across the continent. No weather unit will suffer the doldrums as both science and geography are introduced when reading aloud this fascinating account. A must addition no matter how big the meteorology collection is.
SUBJ: Storms./ Weather.

551.55   Ph-3 2-6/3 $3.50   P   KC199
HOPPING, LORRAINE JEAN. Wild weather. Tornadoes! Illus. by Jody Wheeler. Scholastic ISBN 0-590-46338-1; In Canada: Scholastic, 1994. 48p. col. ill., map. (Hello reader!).
"Cartwheel books."
Tells the story of a Texas tornado chaser who meets danger head on in the name of science. Storm Centers have been able to save lives by quickly issuing weather warnings based upon the work of people like Tim Marshall. Readers will enjoy this true account of an unbelievably exciting job. High interest topic with low reading level will appeal to reluctant readers.
SUBJ: Tornadoes.

551.55   Ph-1 4-7/8 $19.95   L   KC200
KAHL, JONATHAN D. Storm warning: tornadoes and hurricanes. Lerner ISBN 0-8225-2527-5, 1993. 64p. col. ill. (How's the weather?).
Includes glossary and index.
This book is a one-stop information source on disastrous weather. Tornadoes and hurricanes fascinate all readers because of their destructive force and random touchdowns. Book provides background material on weather patterns, prediction, and damage--including Hurricane Andrew. Includes directions for making a tornado in a bottle.
SUBJ: Tornadoes./ Hurricanes.

551.55   Ph-3 3-6/6 $17.50   L   KC201
KRAMER, STEPHEN P. Tornado. Carolrhoda ISBN 0-87614-660-4, 1992. 48p. col. ill., maps. (Nature in action).

Includes glossary.
Amazing full-color photographs add an element of drama to the unusual facts, anecdotes, and personal accounts which describe tornadoes. Concise text includes information about different types of storms and their formation as well as safety guidelines. Good for reports and browsing.
SUBJ: Tornadoes.

551.55   Ph-3 4-6/7 $13.40   L   KC202
LAMPTON, CHRISTOPHER. Hurricane. Millbrook ISBN 1-56294-030-9, 1991. 64p. col. ill. (Disaster!).
Includes glossary, bibliography and index.
Describes hurricane formation and destruction even-handedly by reporting on headline making storms. Shows how weather instruments gather and track information while trying to determine a storm's direction and force. Concludes with precautions in case of a hurricane emergency or evacuation. A sizable amount of information useful for meteorology units.
SUBJ: Hurricanes./ Typhoons./ Meteorology./ Storms.

551.55   Ph-1 3-6/6 $16.95   L   KC203
LAUBER, PATRICIA. Hurricanes: Earth's mightiest storms. Scholastic ISBN 0-590-47406-5; In Canada: Scholastic, 1996. 64p. col. ill., maps.
Selectors' Choice, 21st ed.
Using an unpredicted and unnamed 1938 hurricane as an example, detailed, graphic descriptions of the forces of nature unleashed by hurricanes and their devastating effects on people, property, and ecological systems will fascinate and enlighten readers. Clear, lucid explanations combine with photographs, maps, diagrams, and satellite pictures and provide information on many aspects of these destructive storms. Use for interdisciplinary units in science and social studies.
SUBJ: Hurricanes./ Storms./ Meteorology.

551.55   Ph-2 2-4/3 $11.99   L   KC204
PENNER, LUCILLE RECHT. Twisters! Illus. by Kazushige Nitta. Random House ISBN 0-679-98271-X; In Canada: Random House, 1996. unp. col. ill., map. (Step into reading).
Reports on the formation, speed, and destruction of killer tornadoes and hurricanes; how forecasters track storms; and what to do for personal protection. An easy-to-read rendition of a popular science topic.
SUBJ: Tornadoes./ Hurricanes.

551.55   Ph-2 2-6/7 $14.93   L   KC205
SIMON, SEYMOUR. Storms. Morrow ISBN 0-688-07414-6, 1989. unp. col. ill.
The beauty and ferocity of electrical storms is fully documented with rich color photographs. Text is efficient and authoritative. Dovetails with elementary and primary units on weather.
SUBJ: Storms.

551.55   Ph-2 4-6/7 $19.95   L   KC206
SOUZA, D. M. Hurricanes. Carolrhoda ISBN 0-87614-861-5, 1996. 48p. col. ill., map. (Nature in action).
Includes glossary and index.
Begins by explaining how a hurricane forms, moves, and destroys. Discusses research, forecasting, and safety. Every page has generous color photographs. Sensationalism is kept to a minimum while destructive forces are illustrated by statistics and reports of historic storms (Camille, Andrew, Hugo). An even-handed presentation of exciting science.
SUBJ: Hurricanes./ Storms./ Meteorology.

551.56   Ph-3 4-6/9 $19.95   L   KC207
KAHL, JONATHAN D. Thunderbolt: learning about lightning. Lerner ISBN 0-8225-2528-3, 1993. 56p. col. ill. (How's the weather?).
Includes glossary and index.
Explains what scientists do and do not know about the awesome force of lightning. Takes readers through the cycle of an electrical storm and the anatomy of a flash. Discusses ongoing research and safety. Good illustrations and concise text make this a useful addition for both meteorology and electricity units.
SUBJ: Lightning./ Thunderstorms.

551.57   Ph-3 5-A/9 $17.95   L   KC208
BIANCHI, JOHN. Snow: learning for the fun of it. By John Bianchi and Frank B. Edwards. Bungalo Books/dist. by Firefly ISBN 0-921285-15-9; In Canada: Bungalo Books/dist. by Firefly, 1992. 48p. col. ill.
Includes index.
A flurry of facts for a snowy day, this reveals the intricateness of snow crystals, discusses icebergs, glaciers, snow travel, the Inuit, and northern animals. Capsules of facts such as a survival story and the Iditarod race are logically placed throughout the text. Wintery information in an attractive package students will pick up and read.
SUBJ: Snow.

551.57   Ph-3 P-K/2 $10.89   L   KC209
BRANDT, KEITH. What makes it rain? The story of a raindrop. Illus. by Yoshi Miyake. Troll ISBN 0-89375-582-6, 1982. 32p. col. ill.
Simple introduction to water cycle, attractively illustrated in watercolors.
SUBJ: Rain and rainfall./ Water./ Hydrologic cycle.

551.57   Ph-2 K-1/2 $4.95   P   KC210
BRANLEY, FRANKLYN M. Snow is falling. Rev. ed. Illus. by Holly Keller. Crowell/HarperCollins ISBN 0-06-445058-9; In Canada: HarperCollins, 1986. 32p. col. ill. (Let's-read-and-find-out science book).
Available from National Library Service for the Blind and Physically Handicapped on sound recording disc RD06301.
Provides answers to questions like "What good is snow? Is it good for plants? Is it good for animals?"
SUBJ: Nature study./ Snow.

551.57   Ph-1 3-6/A $4.95   P   KC211
DAY, JOHN A. Peterson first guide to clouds and weather. By John A. Day and Vincent J. Schaefer. Houghton Mifflin ISBN 0-395-56268-6, 1991. 128p. col. ill. (Peterson first guide).
Includes index.
Most take the sky overhead for granted. The observant know it is always changing, the educated will be able to read its patterns. Here is a pocket-sized guide to cloud types and phenomena such as halos, rainbows, and coronas along with an explanation of the water cycle and weather maps. For quick reference, weather units, and nature field trips.
SUBJ: Clouds./ Weather.

551.57   Ph-3 4-6/7 $19.95   L   KC212
KAHL, JONATHAN D. Wet weather: rain showers and snowfall. Lerner ISBN 0-8225-2526-7, 1992. 64p. col. ill. (How's the weather?).
Includes glossary and index.
Explains the water cycle, the formation of clouds, and the various types of precipitation. Useful for independent reading as well as reports.
SUBJ: Precipitation (Meteorology)./ Rain and rainfall./ Snow./ Weather.

551.57   Ph-3 3-6/6 $12.95   L   KC213
KRAMER, STEPHEN P. Avalanche. Photos by Patrick Cone. Carolrhoda ISBN 0-87614-422-9, 1991. 48p. col. ill. (Nature in action).
Includes glossary.
Talks of the causes and effects of giant mountain snowslides-- avalanches. Explains where they are likely to occur, how explosives are used to keep slopes safe, and avalanche rescue work. Interesting photographs are on every page. Use in weather and disaster units and when studying the Pacific Mountain states.
SUBJ: Avalanches.

551.57   Ph-3 P-2/6 $14.99   L   KC214
MARKLE, SANDRA. Rainy day. Illus. by Cathy Johnson. Orchard ISBN 0-531-08576-7, 1993. unp. col. ill.
A young child buttons up in a yellow slicker and observes changes caused by the rain: movement of earthworms, a soggy cardboard box, and finally a rainbow. Outside or inside a rainy day is magical. Watercolor illustrations harmonize with text that can be used as a spring adventure story. For reading aloud.
SUBJ: Rain and rainfall.

551.57   Ph-3 3-6/7 $17.71   L   KC215
STEELE, PHILIP. Rain: causes and effects. Watts ISBN 0-531-10989-5; In Canada: Watts, 1991. 32p. col. ill. (Weather watch).
Includes glossary and index.
Attractive illustrations are arranged around eleven chapter headings to give information on rain, such as how it affects the landscape and the lives of people and animals. Uses current meteorological terms and includes a couple of very easy experiments. Will be useful for elementary weather units.
SUBJ: Rain and rainfall.

551.57   Ph-3 3-6/7 $17.71   L   KC216
STEELE, PHILIP. Snow: causes and effects. Watts ISBN 0-531-10990-9; In Canada: Watts, 1991. 32p. col. ill. (Weather watch).
Includes glossary and index.
Explains snowfalls worldwide with two page chapters, attractive illustrations, weather terminology and a couple of easy experiments. Useful for collections where this topic is in demand.
SUBJ: Snow.

551.6   Ph-2 3-A/7 $17.95   T   KC217
DICKINSON, TERENCE. Exploring the sky by day: the equinox guide to weather and the atmosphere. Camden House/dist. by Firefly ISBN

0-920656-73-0; In Canada: Camden House/dist. by Firefly, 1988. 72p. col. ill.
Includes bibliography and index.
Superior illustrations and well written text yield a mother lode of weather information. Contains 29 subjects such as: clouds, wind, climate zones and precipitation but does not mention changing weather patterns or the greenhouse effect. Teachers can pick and choose topics to read aloud or assign for independent research from this attractive supplement to all weather units.
SUBJ: Weather.

551.6   Ph-2 K-4/4 $14.95   L   KC218
GIBBONS, GAIL. Weather words and what they mean. Holiday House ISBN 0-8234-0805-1, 1990. unp. col. ill.
Introduces temperature, air pressure, moisture and wind in a brightly colored cartoon format. Because the title conveys a lot of information, it is useful when reviewing and summing up weather units.
SUBJ: Weather--Terminology./ Meteorology--Terminology.

551.6   Ph-3 4-6/6 $19.95   L   KC219
KAHL, JONATHAN D. Weatherwise: learning about the weather. Lerner ISBN 0-8225-2525-9, 1992. 64p. col. ill. (How's the weather?).
Includes glossary and index.
Become "weatherwise" by learning to read a weather map, finding out what makes the wind blow, and appreciating other aspects of meteorology. Diagrams and photographs enhance the text and aid understanding of weather information. Organized in five chapters that can be read independently for reference and research reports. Not dazzling but an on-target, thorough presentation.
SUBJ: Weather.

551.6   Ph-2 5-A/7 $16.95   T   KC220
MCMILLAN, BRUCE. Weather sky. Farrar, Straus & Giroux ISBN 0-374-38261-1; In Canada: HarperCollins, 1991. 40p. col. ill.
Includes glossary and index.
Sequences cloud photographs to explain what happens as weather fronts move in, storms erupt and temperatures change. Each cloud formation is matched with a b&w chart showing cloud heights and relative altitudes. A succinct way of explaining atmospheric happenings. For science enrichment and photography clubs.
SUBJ: Weather./ Clouds.

551.6   Ph-3 P-1/2 $13.88   L   KC221
ROGERS, PAUL. What will the weather be like today? Illus. by Kazuko. Greenwillow ISBN 0-688-08951-8, 1990. unp. col. ill.
Bright colored paper collages fill the pages while the rhyming text canvasses weather variations. An exuberant picture book for all to enjoy.
SUBJ: Weather.

551.6   Ph-2 3-6/6 $8.98   P   KC222
WYATT, VALERIE. Weather watch. Illustrated by Pat Cupples. Addison-Wesley ISBN 0-201-15404-8; In Canada: Addison-Wesley, 1990. 95p. ill.
Includes index.
Twenty-four hands-on projects that help make sense of the weather. Includes directions for a cloud chamber and for testing the pollution of snow. A perfect book to enrich elementary weather units; enticing enough for independent use.
SUBJ: Weather./ Science--Experiments.

VCR 551.6   Ph-1 2-A $99.00   OD KC223
3-2-1 CONTACT: EXPLORING WEATHER, CLIMATE AND SEASONS (Videocassette). Children's Television Workshop/Guidance Associates 27022, 1988. 1/2" VHS videocassette color.
Includes program guide.
Animation and live-action are combined to explore different aspects of weather, climate and seasons. Terms are explained within the narratives which often incorporate conversations between children and scientists. The guide contains related experiments and activities. Contents: What makes the weather (7min); Studying lightning (7min); Investigating climate (6min); Adapting to the climate (13min); Adapting to the seasons--migration (7min); Adapting to the seasons--hibernating (10min).
SUBJ: Weather./ Animals--Habits and behavior./ Climate./ Adaptation (Biology).

551.63   Ph-2 2-4/7 $13.95   L   KC224
GIBBONS, GAIL. Weather forecasting. Four Winds/Macmillan ISBN 0-02-737250-2; In Canada: Collier Macmillan, 1987. unp. col. ill.
Follows the daily activities of weather forecasters as they read their instruments, communicate with one another, and broadcast their findings during a variety of weather conditions. Bright, flat cartoon-style illustrations in varied blocks and an accompanying text explain

aspects of weather equipment and human activity in simplified, sometimes sketchy, but coherent terms. An ambitious and attractive attempt to complement other sources on weather.
SUBJ: Meteorological stations./ Weather forecasting.

552   Ph-1 3-6 $17.95   T   KC225
CHESTERMAN, CHARLES W. Audubon Society field guide to North American rocks and minerals. Knopf ISBN 0-394-50269-8; In Canada: Random House, 1978. 850p. col. ill. (Audubon Society field guides).
Includes glossary, bibliography and index.
An excellent guide organized for the amateur. Minerals and rocks are identified in separate sections by the same basic technique: a thumb tab index guides the user by shape and color to a section of color photographs where the specimen can be identified, and thence to a detailed written description. Because of subject matter more difficult to use than other Audubon guides. Students will need help to determine such identification factors as cleavage and streaking. Pocket size, handy for field trips.
A duplicate copy is recommended for Reference collection.
SUBJ: Rocks./ Minerals./ Mineralogy--Handbooks, manuals, etc.

552   Ph-1 K-3/2 $14.95   L   KC226
DE PAOLA, TOMIE. Quicksand book. Holiday House ISBN 0-8234-0291-6, c1977. 32p. col. ill.
Spanish edition available EL LIBRO DE LAS ARENA MOVEDIZAS (ISBN 0-8234-1056-9, 1993).
Picture book format presents facts and fiction about quicksand through the eyes of Jungle Girl and Jungle Boy who rescues Girl from quicksand only to find himself in the same predicament. Humorous text and engaging illustrations make this a fun to learn book.
SUBJ: Quicksand.

VCR 552   Ph-1 5-A $89.00   OD KC227
ROCKS AND MINERALS: THE HARD FACTS (Videocassette). Rainbow Educational Video RB805, 1987. 1/2" VHS videocassette color (15min).
Includes teacher's guide.
Tests for identifying minerals and the explanation of how rocks are formed make this descriptive, well-paced film valuable for teaching about geology.
SUBJ: Rocks./ Minerals.

552   Ph-2 4-6/8 $9.95   P   KC228
VANCLEAVE, JANICE PRATT. Janice VanCleave's rocks and minerals: mind-boggling experiments you can turn into science fair projects. By Janice VanCleave. Illus. by Doris Ettlinger. Wiley ISBN 0-471-10269-5; In Canada: Wiley, 1996. 90p. ill. (Janice VanCleave's spectacular science projects).
Includes bibliography, directories, glossary and index.
Twenty ideas and activities incorporate a handy resource--rocks. Features tips on labeling a mineral collection, building paper models of crystals, and investigating properties. Turning the ideas into worthwhile science projects will take more reading and research, but this offers both a jumping-off place and worthwhile independent study.
SUBJ: Rocks--Experiments./ Minerals--Experiments./ Science projects./ Experiments.

553.4   Ph-1 4-8/7 $14.89   L   KC229
MELTZER, MILTON. Gold: the true story of why people search for it, mine it, trade it, steal it, mint it, hoard it, shape it, wear it, fight and kill for it. HarperCollins ISBN 0-06-022984-5; In Canada: HarperCollins, 1993. 167p. ill.
Includes bibliography and index.
A worldwide trek following gold lust through history beginning with Alexander the Great describes the minting of coins, African empires built on nugget wealth, and the American, Canadian, and Australian gold rushes. Details mining, trading, conquering, and destruction that left a violent wake of slaves, outlaws, and displaced peoples. Carefully researched and documented, the hallmark of excellent writing will be a perfect fit with units on American exploration, immigration, and politics.
SUBJ: Gold.

553.6   Ph-1 K-5/4 $15.93   L   KC230
DIXON, ANNABELLE. Clay. Photos by Ed Barber. Garrett ISBN 0-944483-69-0, 1990. 25p. col. ill. (Threads).
Includes index.
You can roll it, shape it and now read about how clay is dug, formed and used. Young children learning the delights of this pliable art material will be amazed to see grown-ups crafting clay and putting it to use. Pictures and hands-on activities insure a captive audience. Read aloud to younger children.
SUBJ: Clay./ Pottery craft.

553.7   Ph-3 P-2/2 $13.93   L   KC231
FOWLER, ALLAN. It could still be water. Childrens Press ISBN 0-516-06003-1; In Canada: Childrens Press, 1992. 32p. col. ill. (Rookie read-about science).
Includes index.
Spanish version available Y AUN PODRIA SER AGUA (ISBN 0-516-36003-5, 1993).
Lively pictures and minimum text show water as ice, steam, fog, and liquid. New readers will enjoy the experience of independently reading real science.
SUBJ: Water.

560   Ph-2 A/9 $18.95   L   KC232
AASENG, NATHAN. American dinosaur hunters. Enslow ISBN 0-89490-710-7, 1996. 112p. ill. (Collective biographies).
Includes bibliography and index.
Ten short biographies begin in 1835 with Edward Hitchcock investigating fossil tracks in the Connecticut Valley. Final pages examine Jack Horner's 1978 discovery of dinosaur eggs and the resulting proof that duckbills mothered their offspring. Interim detective work by others such as Joseph Leidy, O. C. Marsh, Charles Sternberg, and Robert Bakker fill in the blanks and show how knowledge about these extinct creatures is gathered. Advanced reading for dinosaur fans who have read nonstop about dinosaurs since kindergarten. Valuable addition to career studies for stressing the integrity and hard work necessary for a scientific career.
SUBJ: Paleontologists.

560   Ph-2 1-3/2 $15.89   L   KC233
ALIKI. Fossils tell of long ago. Rev. ed. Crowell/HarperCollins ISBN 0-690-04829-7, 1990. 32p. col. ill. (Let's-read-and-find-out science book).
Available from National Library Service for the Blind and Physically Handicapped as talking book TB04785.
All about fossils--what they are, how they are found and what they tell us about the past. Simply and lucidly written for beginning readers.
SUBJ: Fossils.

560   Ph-2 4-6/7 $12.95   P   KC234
BENTON, MICHAEL. Dinosaur and other prehistoric animal factfinder. Kingfisher ISBN 1-85697-802-8, 1992. 256p. col. ill.
Includes directory, glossary and index.
A dino dictionary. Each page includes a drawing, phonetic pronunciation, place of discovery, relative size, and color-keyed ribbons giving time periods in millions of years. Good use of tables, diagrams, and graphics condenses information and makes it easily consumable at a glance. Especially helpful for those who want to sound erudite during dinosaur discussions.
SUBJ: Dinosaurs--Dictionaries./ Prehistoric animals--Dictionaries.

560   Ph-3 3-6/5 $15.95   L   KC235
HENDERSON, DOUGLAS. Dinosaur tree. Bradbury ISBN 0-02-743547-4; In Canada: Maxwell Macmillan, 1994. 33p. col. ill., map.
Includes glossary/index.
Presents the biography of a Triassic conifer that now resides as a petrified log in the Arizona Painted Desert. Although the text is pure conjecture, it is based on scientific research and informed guesswork. This is how it could have happened. Will add dimension to all prehistory units; useful when discussing fossilization.
SUBJ: Plants, Fossil./ Dinosaurs.

560   Ph-1 4-6/6 $16.95   L   KC236
LAUBER, PATRICIA. Dinosaurs walked here and other stories fossils tell. Bradbury ISBN 0-02-754510-5; In Canada: Collier Macmillan, 1987. 56p. col. ill.
Includes index.
Available from National Library Service for the Blind and Physically Handicapped in Braille BR7605.
This beautiful book, filled with colored photographs, explains how fossils: shells, bones, prints, eggs, tracks, help scientists to resurrect and discover the past - extinct animals, different climates and compulsory adaptations. Documents successfully the view of the prehistoric world gained with the aid of fossils.
SUBJ: Fossils./ Paleontology./ Geology.

560   Ph-2 4-A/9 $15.99   L   KC237
TAYLOR, PAUL D. Fossil. Knopf ISBN 0-679-90440-9, 1990. 63p. col. ill. (Eyewitness books).
Includes index.
A superior examination of fossil remains - both those formed from actual plant and animal parts and those traces left in bogs, tar, and amber. There is something to learn on every page of dazzling illustrations. Especially useful in the classroom since few teachers have

access to actual fossils.
SUBJ: Fossils./ Paleontology.

560   Ph-3 4-6 $17.95   T   KC238
THOMPSON, IDA. Audubon Society field guide to North American fossils. Knopf ISBN 0-394-52412-8, 1982. 846p. col. ill. (Audubon Society field guides).
Includes index.
Defining fossils as "the remains of ancient life that have been buried in the earth or under the sea for anywhere from thousands of years to hundreds of millions of years" (p.12), this exemplary guidebook identifies those commonly found on some part of the North American continent. Very well organized and easy to use, this will be a useful resource on field trips.
A duplicate copy for the reference collection is recommended.
SUBJ: Fossils./ Fossils--Handbooks, manuals, etc.

560   Ph-2 3-6/6 $14.95   T   KC239
TROLL, RAY. Raptors, fossils, fins, and fangs: a prehistoric creature feature. By Ray Troll and Brad Matsen. Tricycle Press ISBN 1-883672-41-4, 1996. 32p. col. ill.
Includes chronology and index.
Wry humor and florescent paintings combine with clear text to bring swimming, squirming, unfamiliar prehistoric creatures front and center. Features bizarre sharks equipped with buzzsaw teeth, Leedsichthys, a fish as big as a house, and more. Bar graphs of million year periods run across the bottom of each page to help readers reach back into "great-times-a-gazillion."
SUBJ: Prehistoric animals./ Fossils.

566   Ph-2 3-6/8 $14.95   L   KC240
ARNOLD, CAROLINE. Dinosaurs down under and other fossils from Australia. Photos by Richard Hewett. Clarion ISBN 0-89919-814-7, 1990. 48p. col. ill.
Includes index.
Travel through an Australian fossil exhibit as it is transported to and set up in Los Angeles. The awe and fascination felt viewing prehistoric life is perfectly captured on the printed pages. A superior addition to this topic, valuable also because of behind-the-scenes museum workings.
SUBJ: Dinosaurs--Australia./ Paleontology--Australia./ Museum techniques.

566   Ph-3 P-3/5 $14.95   L   KC241
GIBBONS, GAIL. Prehistoric animals. Holiday House ISBN 0-8234-0707-1, 1988. unp. col. ill.
Some unusual animals such as Moropus, Baluchitherium, and Glyptodon, march across brightly colored pages in picture book format. Read aloud to the youngest prehistoric fans.
SUBJ: Prehistoric animals./ Vertebrates, Fossil.

CE 567.9   Ph-1 2-4/4 $13.89   L   KC242
ALIKI. My visit to the dinosaurs. Rev. ed. Crowell/HarperCollins ISBN 0-690-04423-2, c1969, 1985. 32p. col. ill. (Let's-read-and-find-out science book).
Read-along kit available from HarperCollins 0-694-00201-1, 1985. 1 cassette (12min), 1 paperback book, $7.95.
Big book available HarperCollins (ISBN 0-06-443350-1, 1994).
A young boy visits a museum with his father and sister. He meets some of the beasts that walked the earth millions of years ago. He discovers dinosaurs with horns, some that ate plants and some that ate meat. He sees one with sixteen hundred teeth as well as the fiercest of all dinosaurs, Tyrannosaurus Rex.
SUBJ: Dinosaurs./ Fossils.

567.9   Ph-1 3-6/8 $14.95   L   KC243
ARNOLD, CAROLINE. Dinosaurs all around: an artist's view of the prehistoric world. Photos by Richard Hewett. Clarion ISBN 0-395-62363-4, 1993. 48p. col. ill.
Includes index.
Selectors' Choice, 19th ed.
Stephen and Sylvia Czerkas are sculptors specializing in the creation of museum dinosaur models. By studying fossils, bones, and skin impressions, the artists are able to sculpture life-sized models which help people learn about and appreciate extinct animals. Photographs document a dazzling array of horns, teeth, and claws. Text explains the painstaking research and work behind construction. Book breathes life into its prehistoric subjects and encapsulates an exciting artistic career. Students will be inspired to experiment with their own models.
SUBJ: Dinosaurs--Models--Design and construction./ Dinosaurs.

567.9   Ph-3 2-4/5 $14.89   L   KC244
BRANLEY, FRANKLYN M. What happened to the dinosaurs? Illus. by Marc Simont. HarperCollins ISBN 0-690-04749-5, 1989. 32p. col. ill.

(Let's-read-and-find-out science book).
A brief look at several extinction theories with more attention paid to comet bombardment and a possible Nemesis star, a twin to our sun. The format design makes this especially useful for the older reluctant reader.
SUBJ: Dinosaurs./ Extinction (Biology).

567.9   Ph-2 2-4/3 $14.95   L   KC245
COLE, JOANNA. Magic School Bus in the time of the dinosaurs. Illus. by Bruce Degen. Scholastic ISBN 0-590-44688-6; In Canada: Scholastic, 1994. unp. col. ill.
Spanish edition EL AUTOBUS MAGICO EN TIEMPOS DE LOS DINOSAURIOS (ISBN 0-590-67702-0, 1995).
Hop aboard with Ms. Frizzle and friends to look for Maiasaura nests, learn about Triassic plants, and observe some tyrannosaurs. Students banter in cartoon balloons; charts and diagrams give capsule information. Popular and appealing, the series lets young people know they can learn exciting science even if they don't possess a time machine.
SUBJ: Dinosaurs./ Spanish language materials.

VCR 567.9   Ph-3 2-5 $25.00   OD   KC246
DEBECK, SUSAN. Dinosaurs! (Videocassette). Written and produced by Susan DeBeck. DeBeck Educational Video; In Canada: DeBeck Educational Video, 1989. 1/2" VHS videocassette color (15min).
Includes teacher's guide.
Includes public performance rights.
Closed captioned.
Children tour the dinosaur exhibit at the Tyrrell Museum in Drumheller, Alberta, Canada, to see life-size skeletons and drawings. A museum paleontologist gives a brief talk followed by a question and answer period. An enjoyable armchair field trip on an ever popular topic.
SUBJ: Dinosaurs./ Paleontology./ Fossils.

VCR 567.9   Ph-2 3-A $55.00   OD   KC247
DIGGING DINOSAURS (Videocassette). Centre Productions/Clearvue/eav CHV V318, 1986. 1/2" VHS videocassette color (12min).
Conveys the excitement of hunting for dinosaur fossils as well as demonstrating the steps necessary to reconstruct a dinosaur skeleton. This high interest subject is presented fairly thoroughly, though no mention is made of how the placement of bones is known for constructing the skeleton. Parallels and overlaps Aliki's Digging Up Dinosaurs.
SUBJ: Dinosaurs./ Fossils./ Paleontology.

567.9   Ph-1 1-6/5 $14.95   L   KC248
DODSON, PETER. Alphabet of dinosaurs. Illus. by Wayne D. Barlowe and Michael Meaker. Scholastic ISBN 0-590-46486-8; In Canada: Scholastic, 1995. unp. col. ill.
"Byron Preiss Visual Publications, Inc. book."
Includes glossary.
Twenty-six diverse dinosaurs march in splendor across pages which can be read at different levels. Each full-page, colored dinosaur illustration is accompanied by large-print text (of one to three sentences), a pencil sketch of its skull, and a brief aside about its anatomy. Glossary lists the meaning of each creature's name, its length, what it ate, when it lived, and where fossils were found. Thoughtful, creative approach that is information packed yet easily accessible to the youngest dinosaur lover.
SUBJ: Dinosaurs.

CE 567.9   Ph-2 P-2/4 $14.95   T   KC249
GIBBONS, GAIL. Dinosaurs. Holiday House ISBN 0-8234-0657-1, 1987. unp. col. ill.
Includes appendix "Dinosaur Footprints".
Read-along kit available from Listening Library FTR132 (ISBN 0-8072-0159-6, 1988). 1 paperback book, 1 sound cassette (11min) $15.98.
Brightly colored and stylized illustrations form the backdrop for this simple presentation of 14 types of dinosaurs. Featuring pronunciation guides for the technical terms and dinosaur names on the page, this also includes possible explanations for their extinction, and will prove appealing to the younger set.
SUBJ: Dinosaurs.

567.9   Ph-2 2-6/6 $14.95   T   KC250
KUROKAWA, MITSUHIRO. Dinosaur Valley. Chronicle ISBN 0-8118-0257-4, 1992. 49p. col. ill.
Includes glossary.
Travel back 70 million years to see Orodromeus, a small plant eating dinosaur, raise and protect her brood. Vibrant settings conjure prehistoric times and relate new knowledge of fast moving animals that traveled in packs and cared for their young. Foldout pages at the end of the book depict an excavation site stressing that scientific

knowledge is an ongoing quest. Text works at two levels with additional information presented for older readers. Top-notch presentation for independent readers and for reading aloud to younger children.
SUBJ: Dinosaurs.

567.9   Ph-2 4-A/6 $17.00   T   KC251
LAUBER, PATRICIA. How dinosaurs came to be. Illus. by Douglas Henderson. Simon & Schuster ISBN 0-689-80531-4; In Canada: Distican, 1996. 48p. col. ill., maps.
Includes index.
Go far back in time to learn about Coelophysis (a 50 pound early dinosaur), Cacops (a small amphibian), and Thrinaxodon (an advanced therapsid). Some were ancestors to later dinosaurs, some to mammals. Factual text combines with perfect illustrations in this presentation of the latest palentological findings. Latin terms are given phonetic spellings in the complete index. Certain to inform and captivate. Not a "basic" book, but a great addition to dinosauria.
SUBJ: Dinosaurs./ Prehistoric animals./ Evolution.

567.9   Ph-2 3-6/5 $15.95   L   KC252
LAUBER, PATRICIA. Living with dinosaurs. Illus. by Douglas Henderson. Bradbury ISBN 0-02-754521-0; In Canada: Collier Macmillan, 1991. 48p. col. ill.
Includes "Index and Pronunciations."
Available from the National Library Service for the Blind and Physically Handicapped on sound recording cassette RC 36400.
Travel back in time 75 million years to tour prehistoric Montana. See extinct reptiles, sea creatures and birds that neither walk nor fly. Recent scientific discoveries and imaginative artwork lay open a world no human eye has ever seen. A good addition to dinosauria by a well-known authority.
SUBJ: Dinosaurs.

567.9   Ph-1 P-A/7 $16.95   L   KC253
LAUBER, PATRICIA. News about dinosaurs. Illustrated by Gregory S. Paul, John Gurche, and Robert T. Bakker. Bradbury ISBN 0-02-754520-2; In Canada: Collier Macmillan, 1989. 48p. col. ill.
Includes pronunciation guide and index.
Selectors' Choice, 17th ed.
Available from the National Library Service for the Blind and Physically Handicapped on sound recording cassette RC34416.
Updates information and dispels misconceptions about dinosaurs. The discovery of four new dinosaurs, the different gaits dinosaurs had, the right head for the Brontosaurus, the fact that dinosaurs lived in herds, the ways dinosaurs cared for their young are all included. Set in an attractive and easy to read design with striking, large, active illustrations this will be in constant circulation.
SUBJ: Dinosaurs.

567.9   Ph-2 4-6/6 $19.95   T   KC254
LESSEM, DON. Dinosaur worlds: new dinosaurs, new discoveries. Boyds Mills ISBN 1-56397-597-1; In Canada: McClelland & Stewart, 1996. 192p. col. ill., maps.
Includes bibliographies, glossary and index.
Information packed with graphics, sidebars, and illustrations to satiate any and all dinosaur lovers. Maps worldwide excavations and discoveries paying attention to climate and geological factors as they relate to evolution, habitat, and extinction. A book to browse and read that tickles the imagination.
SUBJ: Dinosaurs./ Paleontology.

567.9   Ph-1 5-6/9 $12.95   T   KC255
LINDSAY, WILLIAM. Tyrannosaurus. DK Publishing ISBN 1-56458-124-1, 1992. 29p. col. ill.
At head of title: American Museum of Natural History.
Includes directory, glossary and index.
Bold photographs and interesting information about studying and digging for dinosaurs fill a large slim volume. Heavily illustrated pages cover many aspects of the physiology and behavior of Tyrannosaurus. Includes fine views of the work in reconstructing dinosaurs. The copious facts and explanations along with the great pictures will please dinosaur buffs of all ages, and older children should also find the information on scientific work interesting.
SUBJ: Tyrannosaurus rex./ Dinosaurs./ Fossils./ Paleontology.

CDR 567.9   Ph-1 2-A $29.95   OD   KC256
MICROSOFT DINOSAURS: EXPLORE THE INCREDIBLE WORLD OF PREHISTORIC CREATURES. Academic ed. (CD-ROM). Microsoft ISBN 1-57231-018-9; In Canada: Microsoft Canada, 1994. 1 CD-ROM color. (Exploration series).
Includes user's guide and teacher's guide.
Version 1.00.
Also available for Macintosh (ISBN 1-57231-019-7), $29.95.

ALA notable computer software, 1995.
System requirements: Multimedia PC or compatible with a 386SX or higher microprocessor; 4MB of RAM; at least 2.5MB of available hard-disk space; CD-ROM drive; audio board; and VGA display (for 16-color support) or VGA+ display (for full 256-color support); MS-DOS operating system version 3.1 or later; Microsoft Windows operating system version 3.1 or later; Microsoft Mouse or compatible pointing device; headphones or speakers.
Over 200 articles, fact cards on over 80 dinosaurs, and information about the world of the dinosaurs are included in this reference tool. Access is provided via geographical region, timeline, dinosaur family, and an A-to-Z listing. Ease of use makes this work well as an independent research tool, learning center, or small group activity.
SUBJ: Dinosaurs--Software./ Software--Dinosaurs./ Interactive media.

567.9   Ph-2 K-4/7 $15.00   L   KC257
MOST, BERNARD. Dinosaur questions. Harcourt Brace ISBN 0-15-292885-5; In Canada: Harcourt Brace c/o Canadian Manda, 1995. unp. col. ill.
Each page poses a popular question (What did dinosaurs eat? What color were they? How much did they weigh?) that is illustrated with a large fanciful cartoon (five dinosaurs sitting at a table using forks and plates) and answered with five or six lines of carefully written text. A very appealing picture book that is packed with accurate information for all dinosaur lovers, but especially for the youngest. A good complement to Most's earlier work HOW BIG WERE THE DINOSAURS?
SUBJ: Dinosaurs./ Questions and answers.

567.9   Ph-2 3-A/7 $15.99   L   KC258
NORMAN, DAVID. Dinosaur. By David Norman and Angela Milner. Photos by Colin Keates. Knopf ISBN 0-394-92253-0, 1989. 64p. col. ill. (Eyewitness books).
Includes index.
Close-ups of fossil bones, claws, eggs, and prints march across the pages. Topics include dinosaur discovery, birth and growth, extinction and myths. Children will delight in the pictures. Every reader is certain to learn something...browsers welcome.
SUBJ: Dinosaurs.

567.9   Ph-3 K-2/4 $6.95   T   KC259
ROYSTON, ANGELA. Dinosaurs. Photos by Colin Keates. Illus. by Jane Cradock-Watson and Dave Hopkins. Aladdin/Macmillan ISBN 0-689-71518-8, 1991. 21p. col. ill. (Eye openers).
Introduces eight dinosaurs each with its own two-page spread with minimal text and lifelike drawings. Perfect for beginners.
SUBJ: Dinosaurs.

567.9   Ph-2 3-6/8 $15.00   T   KC260
SATTLER, HELEN RONEY. Stegosaurs: the solar-powered dinosaurs. Illus. by Turi MacCombie. Lothrop, Lee & Shepard ISBN 0-688-10055-4, 1992. 32p. col. ill., map.
Includes index and bibliography.
Theorizes that bony plates running down the back of stegosaurs regulated body heat. Discusses where nine obscure relatives were found, their similarities, and life spans. Includes lively illustrations with presentation of new data for young people to devour.
SUBJ: Stegosaurus./ Dinosaurs.

567.9   Ph-2 3-6/8 $13.93   L   KC261
SATTLER, HELEN RONEY. Tyrannosaurus rex and its kin: the Mesozoic monsters. Illus. by Joyce Powzyk. Lothrop, Lee & Shepard ISBN 0-688-07748-X, 1989. 48p. col. ill.
Includes bibliography, glossary and index.
Introduces members of the tyrannosaurus family and details the latest scientific findings and theories. Illustrations include skeletal drawings and full page color renditions. Fossil footprints document acts such as whether or not dinosaurs traveled in packs, could swim, or had speed. Attractive and informative, this book will help to bring dinosaur collections up to date.
SUBJ: Tyrannosaurus rex./ Allosaurus./ Dinosaurs.

567.9   Ph-1 3-6/5 $14.95   L   KC262
SCHLEIN, MIRIAM. Discovering dinosaur babies. Illus. by Margaret Colbert. Four Winds/Macmillan ISBN 0-02-778091-0; In Canada: Collier Macmillan, 1991. 40p. col. ill.
Includes bibliography and index.
Selectors' Choice, 18th ed.
Readers get a double treat here learning about the newest fossil finds and discovering how paleontologists read eggs, embryos and nesting grounds to develop theories from 73 million year old evidence. This is a superior presentation of a spellbinding topic with the extra allure of birth and babyhood. It is hard to put down without finishing.
SUBJ: Dinosaurs./ Animals--Infancy./ Fossils.

CDR 567.9   Ph-1 1-4 $44.95   OD KC263
SCHOLASTIC'S MAGIC SCHOOL BUS EXPLORES IN THE AGE OF DINOSAURS. School ed. (CD-ROM). Microsoft ISBN 1-57231-476-1; In Canada: Microsoft Canada, 1996. 1 CD-ROM color. (Scholastic's the Magic School Bus explores).
Version 1.0.
Includes teacher's guide and user's guide.
Closed captioned.
System requirements: Multimedia PC with 486SX/33 MHz or higher processor; Microsoft Windows 95 operating system or Windows NT Workstation version 3.51 or later; 8MB of memory (RAM) for Windows 95, 12MB of memory for Windows NT; 6MB of available hard-disk space; double-speed CD-ROM drive or faster; super VGA, 256-color monitor; Microsoft Mouse or compatible pointing device; 8-bit sound card (16-bit recommended); headphones or speakers.
Students join Ms. Frizzle's class as they travel via the well-known Magic School Bus into the world of dinosaurs. Travels include seven sites in three Mesozoic time periods, eight activities, over 20 multimedia reports as well as seven educational games. Works well with small groups or as a learning center.
SUBJ: Dinosaurs--Software./ Software--Dinosaurs./ Interactive media.

567.9   Ph-2 4-8/7 $21.40   L   KC264
SENIOR, KATHRYN. X-ray picture book of dinosaurs and other prehistoric creatures. Illus. by Carolyn Scrace. Created and designed by David Salariya. Watts ISBN 0-531-14352-X; In Canada: Nelson, 1995. 48p. col. ill. (X-ray picture book).
Includes glossary and index.
Amazing cutaway drawings lay bear the flesh and bones of dinosaurs, revealing skeletons, muscles, and digestive and reproductive systems. Some of the pages to pore over are bloodthirsty, but all are wonderful. Students will learn that creatures are complex systems and that many have the same parts which often look alike when the skin is peeled away! A unique book based on the hypotheses of paleontologists.
SUBJ: Dinosaurs--Anatomy./ Prehistoric animals--Anatomy.

567.9   Ph-2 4-6/6 $13.95   L   KC265
SIMON, SEYMOUR. Largest dinosaurs. Illus. by Pamela Carroll. Macmillan ISBN 0-02-782910-3; In Canada: Collier Macmillan, 1986. 32p. ill.
Includes index.
Appraises six sauropods, the dinosaur giants. Focuses on new clues to prehistoric puzzles such as dinosaur appearance and habitat. Stresses the invaluable role of on-going research and discovery. Drawings augment the text. An attractive book for collections needing to update this topic.
SUBJ: Dinosaurs.

567.9   Ph-2 K-6/9 $17.90   L   KC266
UNWIN, DAVID. New book of dinosaurs. Consultant, Michael Benton. Illus. by Richard Rockwood...[et al.]. Copper Beech ISBN 0-7613-0568-8, 1997. 32p. col. ill., maps.
Includes glossary, chronology and index.
As scientists continue to disagree about dinosaur biology, it is important to keep up with the newest theories. This book discusses salient questions: Can we extract dinosaur DNA? How did dinosaurs manage to live in polar regions? and What caused extinction? As more remains are discovered (the latest Sauropods from Madagascar, the nearly complete Alxasaurus skeleton from Asia) and pieced together, our knowledge grows. Large size book has wonderful illustrations and enough extraneous facts (there is a dino under FBI arrest) to please fans of all ages.
SUBJ: Dinosaurs.

567.9   Ph-1 3-A/8 $15.99   L   KC267
VISUAL DICTIONARY OF DINOSAURS. DK PUblishing ISBN 1-56458-188-8, 1993. 64p. col. ill. (Eyewitness visual dictionaries).
Includes index.
Precisely labeled skeletons, models, and cutaway drawings cover every page of this oversized book documenting the strangeness and power of extinct dinosaurs. A specialized, scientific vocabulary is made easily accessible to the novice. Here is a subject that never grows stale invigorated by a brand new visual presentation. No matter how many dinosaur books are in your collection, this is a must purchase.
SUBJ: Dinosaurs.

569   Ph-1 1-3/4 $14.89   L   KC268
ALIKI. Wild and woolly mammoths. Rev. ed. HarperCollins ISBN 0-06-026277-X; In Canada: HarperCollins, 1996. 32p. col. ill.
Available from National Library Service for the Blind and Physically Handicapped on sound recording cassette RC12197.
Easy-to-read text and engaging pictures describe the huge beasts

which roamed the earth thousands of years ago during the last Ice
Age--the woolly mammoths.
SUBJ: Woolly mammoth./ Mammoths./ Prehistoric animals./
Paleontology.

569.9   Ph-1 4-A/8 $15.95   L   KC269
SATTLER, HELEN RONEY. Hominids: a look back at our ancestors. Illus.
by Christopher Santoro. Lothrop, Lee & Shepard ISBN 0-688-06061-7,
1988. 125p. ill.
Includes bibliography and index.
Selectors' Choice, 17th ed.
Garnered from interpretations of fossil records, the latest knowledge
shows how the genera Australopithecus and Homo have evolved
through five million years. Text is illuminated on nearly every page
with maps, diagrams and drawings. This extraction of
paleoanthropological research will stand as a classic for years.
SUBJ: Prehistoric peoples./ Fossil man.

570   Ph-3 P-4/8 $24.95   L   KC270
VANCLEAVE, JANICE PRATT. Biology for every kid: 101 easy
experiments that really work. By Janice VanCleave. Wiley ISBN 0-471-
51048-3; In Canada: Wiley, 1989. 224p. ill. (Janice VanCleave's science
for every kid).
Includes glossary and index.
101 experiments (using elementary equipment) examine plants,
animals and the human body. All are illustrated and directions are
limited to one page of text. The botany section will be especially
useful to primary teachers. Activities are quick, interesting and
appealing.
SUBJ: Biology--Experiments./ Experiments.

571   Ph-2 4-6/7 $9.95   P   KC271
SOUCIE, GARY. What's the difference between apes and monkeys and
other living things? Illus. by Jeff Domm. Wiley ISBN 0-471-08625-8; In
Canada: Wiley, 1995. 88p. ill. (What's the difference).
Includes glossary and index.
Describes the differences between commonly confused plants and
animals. Includes such familiar pairs as rabbits and hares, newts and
salamanders, butterflies and moths, pollen and spores, mosses and
lichens, and blossoms and flowers. Helps readers understand that
even small distinctions are important to scientists.
SUBJ: Animals--Miscellanea./ Plants--Miscellanea./ Questions and
answers.

571.1   Ph-1 3-5/7 $15.00   T   KC272
MACHOTKA, HANA. Terrific tails. Morrow ISBN 0-688-04562-6, 1994.
unp. col. ill.
Tails useful in swimming, signaling, and balancing are featured in this
simple guessing game. A clue and striking close-up photographs of
each tail are followed by a full-page view of the entire animal,
including a crocodile, peacock, horse, wallaby, dog, beaver, and
snow leopard. Concluding pages of facts and thought-provoking
questions about the structure and uses of tails round out the inviting
scheme. Fine fare for individual reading and group use.
SUBJ: Tail./ Animals--Habits and behavior.

571.2   Ph-3 K-3/3 $9.95   T   KC273
ARDLEY, NEIL. Science book of things that grow. Gulliver/Harcourt
Brace Jovanovich ISBN 0-15-200586-2, 1991. 29p. col. ill. (Science
book of).
Bright, large illustrations direct readers through various botany
activities such as growing mold, inflating a balloon with yeast, and
taking plant cuttings. Full of wonderful experiments that allow the
curious to achieve success.
SUBJ: Growth (Plants)--Experiments./ Experiments.

VCR 571.6   Ph-2 5-6 $99.00   OD KC274
CELL DIVISION (Videocassette). Rainbow Educational RB8231, 1995.
1/2" VHS videocassette color (17min). (Cell series).
Includes teacher's guide and reproducibles.
Includes public performance rights.
Discusses the human reproduction process and how chromosones and
genes become a newborn's inheritance. Mitosis and meiosis are
carefully dissected and illustrated with microscopic photography and
animated drawings. Tightly organized with no superfluous outtakes.
Preview before showing; subject matter will need to be taught and
reviewed prior to viewing.
SUBJ: Cells./ Genetics./ Reproduction.

VCR 571.6   Ph-2 5-6 $99.00   OD KC275
DISCOVERING THE CELL (Videocassette). National Geographic 51517,
1992. 1/2" VHS videocassette color (15min).
Includes teacher's guide.
Beginning with an overview of microscope development and the

discovery of cells, this video reveals cell components in motion using
the latest microscope technology and the scanning electron
microscope. Stunning images explain basic cell structures and viewers
see mitosis and meiosis. Use to introduce and review cell biology or
for independent study and research.
SUBJ: Cells./ Microscope and microscopy.

571.8   Ph-3 P-2/4 $11.95   T   KC276
KUHN, DWIGHT. My first book of nature: how living things grow.
Scholastic ISBN 0-590-45502-8; In Canada: Scholastic, 1993. 61p. col.
ill. (Cartwheel learning bookshelf).
"Cartwheel books."
Twenty-four familiar animals (along with a few plants) are shown as
newborns and in various stages of growth. All are represented by at
least four large colored photographs. Book ends by comparing how
humans fit into the animal kingdom. Young students will continue to
pour over the illustrations long after hearing the book read aloud.
Use to discuss growth and change, animals, and families.
SUBJ: Growth.

572   Ph-3 6-A/9 $11.95   T   KC277
ASIMOV, ISAAC. How did we find out about photosynthesis? Illus. by
Erika Kors. Walker ISBN 0-8027-6899-7; In Canada: Thomas Allen,
1989. 64p. ill. (How did we find out).
Includes index.
Available from the National Library Service for the Blind and
Physically Handicapped RC35254.
Traces the scientific discoveries, centered on oxygen, light and
chlorophyll, that led to a gradual understanding of photosynthesis. A
technical presentation, probably more than the average elementary
student wants but excellent and carefully paced to insure learning.
SUBJ: Photosynthesis.

572.8   Ph-3 5-A/6 $19.95   T   KC278
ARONSON, BILLY. They came from DNA. Illus. by Danny O'Leary. W.
H. Freeman ISBN 0-7167-9006-8, 1993. 80p. col. ill. (Mysteries of
science).
"Scientific American books for young readers."
Includes glossary, index and bibliography.
A space alien, Skreeg, is sent to an earth dump to unravel the secrets
of DNA. Skreeg also wanders over to a school library for clarification
of the finer points of genetic engineering gleaned from trashed cereal
boxes, newspapers, and a rock concert poster. The wacky premise
and cartoon characters have appeal, but they often overshadow the
science. For advanced students who have had prior exposure to
genetics.
SUBJ: DNA./ Genetics.

572.8   Ph-3 5-6/7 $17.50   L   KC279
BALKWILL, FRANCES R. DNA is here to stay. By Fran Balkwill. Illus. by
Mic Rolph. Carolrhoda ISBN 0-87614-763-5, 1993. 32p. col. ill.
In an effort to bring complex biological processes down to an
elementary level, colorful cartoons are used to explain DNA zipping
apart and replicating. Illustrates the gene recipes of adenine, thymine,
cytosine, and guanine. Mitosis is explained but not labeled. Leaves
out meiosis and any discussion of the genetic effects of fertilization.
Could be helpful to simplify the introduction to cellular biology.
Limited by a lack of a glossary or index.
SUBJ: DNA.

573.2   Ph-2 3-5/6 $14.93   L   KC280
MACHOTKA, HANA. Breathtaking noses. Morrow ISBN 0-688-09527-5,
1992. unp. col. ill.
Companion volume to WHAT NEAT FEET, 1991.
Full-page photographs of several different animals are used in a
guessing game to introduce facts about the many ways noses help
animals survive. The powerful digging nose of the pig, the orange bill
of a swan, and the long, closed nostrils of a camel are among the
intriguing views which are each followed by a page of text and a
photograph of the whole animal. Some noses don't breathe or smell,
but each is used is some important way to locate food, sense
enemies, or even communicate. This enjoyable lesson, which
encourages thoughtful observation, makes a pleasant browsing or
booktalking item.
SUBJ: Nose./ Animals--Physiology./ Animals--Miscellanea.

573.6   Ph-1 P-3/2 $11.95   T   KC281
GOLDSEN, LOUISE. Egg. [This edition American text by Louise
Goldsen.] Created by Gallimard Jeunesse and Pascale de Bourgoing.
Illus. by Rene Mettler. Scholastic ISBN 0-590-45266-5; In Canada:
Scholastic, 1992. unp. col. ill. (spiral bound). (First discovery book).
"Cartwheel books."
Originally published in France, L'OEUF, 1989.
This appealing first lesson in embryology begins with the development

of a chick explained through the use of plastic overlays. The simple text on glossy pages introduces several more birds and other egg laying animals. The attractive format provides an enjoyable introduction to this basic and ever interesting subject.
SUBJ: Eggs.

573.6   Ph-2 P-K $13.95   T   KC282
HELLER, RUTH. Chickens aren't the only ones. Grosset & Dunlap ISBN 0-448-01872-1, 1981. unp. col. ill.
Spanish version available LAS GALLINAS NO SON LAS UNICAS (ISBN 0-448-40586-5, 1992).
Colorful pages and loosely rhymed text introduce the various classes of animals which lay eggs as a means of reproduction. Plentiful examples amply illustrate the single concept in a warm, handsome presentation of a very basic and important idea for younger children.
SUBJ: Reproduction./ Spanish language materials.

VCR 573.7   Ph-3 5-6 $69.00   OD KC283
HOW ANIMALS MOVE (Videocassette). National Geographic 51368, 1989. 1/2" VHS videocassette color (15min). (Exploring the animal kingdom).
Includes teacher's guide.
Closed captioned.
Animals lope, fly, swim, slither and move in multitudinous ways in this handsome survey. The text ranges loosely over ideas why and how animals move, and numerous species are shown briefly as examples. Though the topical theme is not strongly structured, the animals in motion are lovely and intriguing, and the bits of information could be used to stimulate observation and introduce units on animals.
SUBJ: Animals--Physiology./ Animal locomotion.

VCR 573.7   Ph-2 5-A $52.95   OD KC284
LOCOMOTION (Videocassette). Carolina Biological Supply 49-2100-V, 1986. 1/2" VHS videocassette color (30min). (Biovideo series).
Includes teacher's guide.
Invertebrates and vertebrates all move but differently. Fascinating live action and animated sequences show how each animal group has adapted locomotion. Moderate pacing and clear details make this a useful explanation of the movement of animals.
SUBJ: Animal locomotion.

573.7   Ph-1 5-6/8 $20.99   L   KC285
PARKER, STEVE. Skeleton. Photos by Philip Dowell. Knopf ISBN 0-394-99620-8, 1988. 64p. col. ill. (Eyewitness books).
Includes index.
A great variety of skeletons--human, animal, and the exoskeletons of water creatures--appear in the intriguing photographs and drawings of this large, flat volume. Following explanations of the whole skeleton of humans, selected mammals, birds and fish, brief sections of text and numerous captions describe and compare specific segments of skeletons: skulls, teeth, backbones, arms and wings, legs and feet. Informative and fascinating, this will be a popular browsing item and useful for reports and science projects.
SUBJ: Skeleton./ Bones./ Anatomy, Comparative.

573.7   Ph-2 4-A/8 $16.95   T   KC286
VISUAL DICTIONARY OF THE SKELETON. DK Publishing ISBN 0-7894-0135-5, 1995. 64p. col. ill. (Eyewitness visual dictionaries).
"Dorling Kindersley book."
Includes index.
Copious drawings and diagrams offer detailed views of the supporting structures of many vertebrates, invertebrates, and even plants. The oversize volume of busy entries includes some difficult, brief text and inadequate explanations in many instances, but readers will pore over the many fascinating layouts on humans and other mammals, fish, amphibians, reptiles, birds, insects, and more. The short discussion of endoskeletons and exoskeletons and sections comparing features of humans with those of other animals are useful components of this detailed introduction which will find many uses.
SUBJ: Skeleton./ Bones./ Anatomy, Comparative.

574.5   Ph-1 3-6/6 $12.95   T   KC287
COBB, VICKI. This place is wet. Illus. by Barbara Lavallee. Walker ISBN 0-8027-6880-6; In Canada: Thomas Allen, 1989. unp. col. ill. (Imagine living here).
Visit the Amazon rainforest to experience an environment that produces plants like the strangler fig and animals like the sloth. Text is enlivened with colorful art work that testifies to nature's wealth found in this wonderous place. Use in both science and social studies to show why vigilance and conservation are everyone's concern.
SUBJ: Amazon River Region--Description and travel./ Rain forest ecology--Amazon River Region--Brazil./ Brazil--Description and travel.

576.5   Ph-1 4-8/6 $17.50   L   KC288
BALKWILL, FRANCES R. Amazing schemes within your genes. By Dr. Fran Balkwill. Illus. by Mic Rolph. Carolrhoda ISBN 0-87614-804-6, 1993. 32p. col. ill.
Though five billion humans inhabit the earth, none of us looks or acts the same. How can that be? The secret is locked in our genes. Scientists have revealed a world of chromosomes, DNA, and heredity; this book makes the information accessible. Touches on cystic fibrosis and sickle-cell anemia. Can easily step out of biology classes into discussions of ethnocentricity and culture. For multicultural studies.
SUBJ: Genetics.

576.5   Ph-3 5-6/9 $22.80   L   KC289
HOOPER, TONY. Genetics. Raintree Steck-Vaughn ISBN 0-8114-2332-8, 1994. 48p. col. ill., map. (Breakthrough).
Includes chronology, glossary, bibliographies and index.
Presents a historical overview of the source of genetics, including the theories of Darwin, Mendel, and Bateson. Contemporary theories and practices are explored with a brief mention of the moral issues involved in genetic engineering.
SUBJ: Genetics.

576.8   Ph-1 3-4/5 $13.89   L   KC290
COLE, JOANNA. Evolution. Illus. by Aliki. Crowell/HarperCollins ISBN 0-690-04598-0; In Canada: HarperCollins, 1987. 31p col illus. (Let's-read-and-find-out science book).
Sketches the discovery and study of fossils and the development of one-celled organism into increasingly complex animals and plants. Colorful childlike drawings and helpful charts of the various evolutionary time periods and the developmental stages of Homo Sapiens accompany the clear, simple text. This is a lucid explanation of this complex and fascinating topic.
SUBJ: Evolution./ Fossils.

576.8   Ph-3 A/7 $14.95   L   KC291
DARLING, DAVID J. Could you ever meet an alien? Dillon ISBN 0-87518-447-2, 1990. 60p. col. ill.
Includes glossary and index.
Analyzes what makes a hospitable environment for life as we know it. Traces the search for extraterrestrial life including Drake's equation for estimating the instances of extraterrestrial intelligence. Presents tantalizing ideas such as the creation of a "Dyson sphere" to trap the sun's energy and the conjecture that artificial beings might replace humans. A levelheaded presentation of an out-of-this-world topic with attention grabbing illustrations. Advanced readers and thinkers will devour the pages.
SUBJ: Life on other planets./ Extraterrestrial beings.

576.8   Ph-1 A/11 $15.95   L   KC292
GALLANT, ROY A. Before the sun dies: the story of evolution. Macmillan ISBN 0-02-735771-6; In Canada: Collier Macmillan, 1989. 131p.
Includes glossary and bibliography.
A definitive, careful examination of the fossil record detailing how evolutionary scientists work to interpret earth's cosmic history, cell development, and the emergence of homo sapiens. Includes the latest discoveries and scientific efforts. A superior book of value.
SUBJ: Evolution.

SRC 577   Ph-2 1-3 $10.95   OD KC293
AXELROD, GERRY. Songs of nature and environment (Sound recording cassette). By Gerry Axelrod and Robert Macklin. Smithsonian Folkways 7605, 1978. 1 sound cassette (40min).
Includes song sheet.
The importance of the world of nature expressed in folktype songs, some fanciful and some factual, about little and endangered species, naming the nine plants, and just enjoying the flowers.
SUBJ: Ecology--Songs and music./ Nature study--Songs and music./ Science--Songs and music.

577   Ph-3 2-4/5 $12.90   L   KC294
JOHNSON, KIPCHAK. Worm's eye view: make your own wildlife refuge. Illustrated by Thompson Yardley. Millbrook Press ISBN 1-878841-30-0, 1991. 40p. col. ill. (Lighter look).
Includes index.
Advises children to look around a yard or field, collect small animals, experiment with homemade habitats and learn. Stresses the need to guard the environment and appreciate natural surroundings.
SUBJ: Ecology./ Wildlife attracting./ Animals.

577   Ph-2 K-3/2 $14.89   L   KC295
LAUBER, PATRICIA. Who eats what?: food chains and food webs. Illus. by Holly Keller. HarperCollins ISBN 0-06-022982-9; In Canada: HarperCollins, 1995. 32p. col. ill. (Let's-read-and-find-out science book).

Whether an animal is at the top or the bottom of the food chain, its energy consumption can be traced, and any break in the chain's linkage will have wide ranging (often quite surprising) effects. Lots of color and pithy text present scientific concepts clearly. For environmental studies.
SUBJ: Food chains (Ecology)./ Ecology.

577 Ph-1 A $18.95 P KC296
MCCONNAUGHEY, BAYARD H. Pacific coast. By Bayard H. and Evelyn McConnaughey. Knopf ISBN 0-394-73130-1; In Canada: Random House, 1985. 633p. col. ill. (Audubon Society nature guides).
Includes glossary, bibliography and index.
Explore the flora and fauna of distinct types of ecological areas: the coasts, forests, grasslands, deserts, wetlands through these carefully researched and well organized field trip guides. Each title in the series includes habitat essays, color plates, species descriptions, and appendices. Choice of title(s) most appropriate to specific locations is recommended and duplicate copies are suggested for reference collection.
SUBJ: Natural history--Guides./ Seashore ecology--Guides.

SRC 577 Ph-2 P-2 $7.95 KC297
SUZUKI, DAVID. Connections: finding out about the environment (Sound recording cassette). Panda Books ISBN 0-7736-7357-1; In Canada: General, 1990. 1 paperback book, 1 sound cassette (45min).
Includes teacher's guide with lyrics.
Ten catchy tunes reinforce our connections to nature. "Watercycle polka" has the rain falling down, going up, and repeating the cycle. Songs could be pantomimed or choreographed to celebrate the completion of a science unit as well as to aid learning. Other topics include: earthworms, trees, and monarch butterflies. For environmental studies.
SUBJ: Ecology--Songs and music./ Environment--Songs and music.

CDR 577 Ph-3 6-A $249.00 OD KC298
VARIATIONS IN LIFE SCIENCE INVESTIGATIONS (CD-ROM). Learning in Motion 116-100-B, 1996. 1 CD-ROM color, 2 3.5" disks.
Version 2.0.
Includes teacher's guide.
System requirements: Macintosh System 7 or greater; color monitor; 4MB free RAM, accelerated for the Power PC; CD-ROM drive; 3.5" disk drive.
Twelve topics such as cells and microscopes, hormones, and genetics, each with two activities, are included. Users gain in-depth knowledge via the video, graphing tools, and questions asked. Works well in small groups or with an entire class.
SUBJ: Life (Biology)--Software./ Software--Life (Biology)./ Biology--Software./ Software--Biology.

VCR 577 Ph-3 4-6 $119.95 OD KC299
WHAT ARE ECOSYSTEMS? (Videocassette). Troll VW002, 1975. 1/2" VHS videocassette color (75min).
Describes and explains the structure, operation and the possibility of destruction of the major ecosystems. Compares the man-made ecosystem of the city to natural ecosystems, pointing out the reasons for the malfunction of the urban system.
Contents: The pond ecosystem; The stream ecosystem; Saltmarsh and seashore ecosystems; The forest ecosystem; Human urban ecosystem; Comparing the city to natural ecosystems.
SUBJ: Ecology./ Marine ecology./ Marshes./ Seashore./ Forest ecology./ Human ecology./ Cities and towns.

VCR 577 Ph-2 3-6 $39.95 KC300
WORLD PATROL KIDS. Earth tunes for kids (Videocassette). Kids Shop/Benjamin Goldstein Productions TKS101 ISBN 1-884629-12-1, 1994. 1/2" VHS videocassette color (30min).
Sound recording cassette available from Filmus/Kids Shop (ISBN 1-884629-10-5, 1995). 1 sound cassette (40min), $12.98. Includes lyrics.
Compact disc available from Filmus/Kids Shop (ISBN 1-884629-07-5, 1995). 1 compact disc (40min), $14.95. Includes lyrics.
The combination of delightfully zany youngsters and peppy songs about a variety of ecological issues makes this a winner. The songs can enrich social studies and science units on endangered species, recycling, and animal rights. The enthusiasm of the young singers is infectious. For environmental studies.
SUBJ: Ecology./ Environmental protection.

577 Ph-2 1-3/2 $14.89 L KC301
ZOEHFELD, KATHLEEN WEIDNER. What's alive? Illus. by Nadine Bernard Westcott. HarperCollins ISBN 0-06-023444-X; In Canada: HarperCollins, 1995. 32p. col. ill. (Let's-read-and-find-out science book).
A young girl explores the properties of plants and animals to show what life entails. Colorful and easy to understand, the book is a nice

addition to beginning science.
SUBJ: Life (Biology)./ Biology.

577.1 Ph-3 K-3/3 $13.89 L KC302
COBB, VICKI. Lots of rot. Illus. by Brian Schatell. Lippincott/HarperCollins ISBN 0-397-31939-8; In Canada: HarperCollins, 1981. 35p. col. ill.
Includes glossary.
Rotting is interesting. This book proves its point explaining and investigating decay with a series of experiments involving mold, bacteria and mildew.
SUBJ: Biodegradation./ Microbiology.

577.1 Ph-2 4-6/10 $15.00 P KC303
EMORY, JERRY. Dirty, rotten, dead? Illus. by T. Taylor Bruce. Gulliver Green/Harcourt Brace ISBN 0-15-200695-8; In Canada: Harcourt Brace c/o Canadian Manda, 1996. 48p. col. ill.
"Greenpatch book."
Includes bibliography, directory, glossary and index.
An oversized book with great illustrations that yield close-up views of death and decay in the soil and water, on skin, and finally of human life. Discusses: what pollutes, what happens at a mortuary, and what real kids are doing to care for planet earth. Large pictures and cutaway diagrams involve readers. Many simple activities, like composting and testing water quality, can be adopted for classroom learning. Biology teachers will love the pages on human parasites, healing of wounds, and legal death.
SUBJ: Biodegradation./ Biogeochemical cycles./ Death.

577.1 Ph-2 1-3/3 $15.90 L KC304
RING, ELIZABETH. What rot!: nature's mighty recycler. Photos by Dwight Kuhn. Millbrook ISBN 1-56294-671-4, 1996. unp. col. ill.
Includes glossary.
Beginning with an overripe Jack-o'-lantern, text and photographs introduce readers to mold, fungi, beetles, earthworms, and other components of the rotting cycle. Interesting pictures ensure that readers will want to know more. Perfect in combination with Vicki Cobb's LOTS OF ROT. For environmental studies.
SUBJ: Biodegradation./ Ecology.

577.2 Ph-1 A/8 $16.00 L KC305
PRINGLE, LAURENCE P. Fire in the forest: a cycle of growth and renewal. By Laurence Pringle. Illus. by Bob Marstall. Atheneum ISBN 0-689-80394-X; In Canada: Distican, 1995. unp. col. ill.
Includes bibliography.
Details the changes and rebirth after a forest fire, citing examples from the 1988 Yellowstone National Park firestorm. Park biologists have recorded plant and animal population recoveries and ensuing competition for soil nutrients. Dramatic two-page paintings are set between pages of text. Fire ecology is a complex phenomenon, and the authoritative text is best for reading aloud to students. Use with environmental studies on ecosystems, trees, and food chains.
SUBJ: Fire ecology./ Forest fires./ Forest ecology./ Ecology./ Yellowstone National Park.

577.2 Ph-2 4-6/8 $19.95 L KC306
STAUB, FRANK J. Yellowstone's cycle of fire. Carolrhoda ISBN 0-87614-778-3, 1993. 47p. col. ill. (Carolrhoda earth watch book).
Includes glossary and index.
Demystifies fire ecology by examining the fire and aftermath of Yellowstone's 1988 summer. The forest burn released a sudden wealth of minerals and nutrients. How this nutrient recycling effected the plant and animal life, fostered biodiversity, and is the precursor to regrowth makes interesting reading. A book for environmental studies that increases understanding of the balance of nature.
SUBJ: Forest fires--Yellowstone National Park./ Fire ecology./ Ecology./ Yellowstone National Park./ National parks and reserves.

VCR 577.27 Ph-2 3-6 $39.95 OD KC307
OUR ENDANGERED EARTH (Videocassette). Knowledge Unlimited 5870VD, 1990. 1/2" VHS videocassette color (18min).
Includes discussion guide.
This global view of land, water and air pollution illustrates rain forest destruction, desert encroachment, industrial and agricultural toxic waste, population growth and poverty - confirming that earth's life support systems are at grave risk. Ends on a positive note by encouraging recycling and conservation. The riveting photography and factual approach will shake the complacency of any viewer who continues to believe that it's not their problem.
SUBJ: Pollution./ Conservation of natural resources.

VCR 577.3 Ph-3 4-6 $99.00 OD KC308
ANCIENT FORESTS (Videocassette). National Geographic 51516, 1992. 1/2" VHS videocassette color (25min).

Includes teacher's guide.

Vividly demonstrates the wealth and diversity created by ancient forests. Shows how logging worked to devour our continent of trees and pushed animal populations to extinction because of our insatiable appetite for wood. Alaskan forests still have a chance of being saved if people act now and realize that trees are more valuable alive. A thoughtful, moving plea for action.

SUBJ: Forest ecology./ Forests and forestry.

VCR 577.3   Ph-3 P-3 $59.95   OD KC309
STOLTZ, WALKIN' JIM. Come walk with me (Videocassette). Wild Wind Records/dist. by Video Project COM-079-A, 1994. 1/2" VHS videocassette color (30min).

Every child will want to put on his walking shoes to join Jim Stoltz as he strums and sings his way along a Montana mountain trail learning about creatures and plants with a group of children. Catchy tunes such as "If I were a tree" and "Wild things need wild places" will have the whole class singing and celebrating nature's beauty. A wonderful way to foster awareness of nature. For environmental studies.

SUBJ: Forest ecology--Songs and music./ Forest animals--Songs and music./ Ecology--Songs and music.

577.3   Ph-3 4-6/9 $22.60   L OD KC310
STONE, LYNN M. Temperate forests. Rourke ISBN 0-86592-439-2, 1989. 48p. col. ill. (Ecozones).

Includes glossary and index.

Hike through the great North American woods to meet natural wonders. Introduces forest types, how they grow, plants, animals and conservation. Use when studying food chains and habitats.

SUBJ: Forest ecology./ Forests and forestry./ Ecology.

577.3   Ph-3 3-5/6 $15.00   L KC311
THORNHILL, JAN. Tree in a forest. Simon & Schuster ISBN 0-671-75901-9; In Canada: Greey de Pencier, 1992. unp. col. ill.

Follows a maple tree through 210 years of growth and environmental changes as it shelters animals, provides sap for syrup, and finally decomposes. Drawings are filled with details for the careful observer. A good read-aloud for older students.

SUBJ: Maple./ Trees./ Forest ecology./ Ecology.

577.3   Ph-3 K-4/6 $13.93   L KC312
TRESSELT, ALVIN. Gift of the tree. Illus. by Henri Sorensen. Lothrop, Lee & Shepard ISBN 0-688-10685-4, c1972, 1992. unp. col. ill.

Available from the National Library Service for the Blind and Physically Handicapped on sound recording cassette RC 40171.

When a hundred-year-old oak tree dies, it becomes a shelter for scurrying animals as it eventually decays and enriches the soil. Oversized full-page paintings capture the tree's life and death along with the activities of forest creatures and plants. Thoughtful addition to forest ecology.

SUBJ: Oak./ Forest ecology./ Ecology./ Trees.

577.3   Ph-1 A $19.00   P KC313
WHITNEY, STEPHEN. Western forests. Knopf ISBN 0-394-73127-1; In Canada: Random House, 1985. 670p. col. ill. (Audubon Society nature guides).

Includes glossary, bibliography and index.

Explore the flora and fauna of distinct types of ecological areas through these carefully researched and well organized field guides. Each title in the series includes habitat essays, color plates, species descriptions and appendices. Recommend that titles of regional interest be purchased as well as duplicate copies for reference collection.

SUBJ: Natural history--Guides./ Forest ecology--Guides.

MCP 577.34   Ph-2 3-A $59.95   OD KC314
FIELD TRIP TO THE RAINFOREST (Microcomputer program). Sunburst 6380, 1991. 2 5.25" program disks, 2 data disks.

Includes Tropical Rainforests booklet and teacher's guide.

Also available for Windows 3.1 or higher and Apple II family.

System requirements: Macintosh family (2MB), hard drive required for color version, hard drive or two disk drives required for black-and-white version. Color Macintosh recommended.

This discovery learning tool takes youngsters on a self-guided tour of a rainforest. Databases of 49 animals and 21 plants are available. Sixteen activities have the student determine the food chain for a set of rainforest inhabitants. Works well with individuals, small groups, or an entire class.

SUBJ: Rain forests--Software./ Software--Rain forests./ Rain forest ecology--Software./ Software--Rain forest ecology./ Food chains (Ecology)--Software./ Software--Food chains (Ecology).

577.34   Ph-3 4-6/6 $14.89   L KC315
GEORGE, JEAN CRAIGHEAD. One day in the tropical rain forest. Illustrated by Gary Allen. Crowell/HarperCollins ISBN 0-690-04769-X, 1990. 56p. ill.

Includes bibliography and index.

In hourly increments, the destruction of the rain forest is related by a young boy, Tepui, who miraculously staves off death by finding a nameless butterfly. Sentimental and contrived but valuable for descriptions of the relentless bulldozers; such paragraphs are perfect to read aloud during discussions of environmental pillage.

SUBJ: Rain forest ecology./ Jungle ecology./ Ecology.

577.34   Ph-1 2-6/5 $14.93   L KC316
GIBBONS, GAIL. Nature's green umbrella: tropical rain forests. Morrow ISBN 0-688-12354-6, 1994. unp. col. ill., maps.

Rain forests reveal their lush ecosystems. The emergents, canopy, understory, and forest floor animals parade in labeled, watercolored greenery. Habitat plunder is covered. The final pages illustrate different types of rain forests. Demand for intelligent books on this tropical topic make this a must purchase.

SUBJ: Rain forest ecology./ Ecology./ Rain forests.

577.34   Ph-3 K-3/3 $14.95   L KC317
GILLILAND, JUDITH HEIDE. River. Illus. by Joyce Powzyk. Clarion ISBN 0-395-55963-4, 1993. unp. col. ill., map.

Float down the mightiest river on earth into a rain forest world to meet unfamiliar animals and plants. Full-page watercolor drawings entice young readers. The cadence of the text effectively imparts a sense of place... so lush, so different. Use in animal, rain forest, river, and environmental studies.

SUBJ: Rain forests./ Amazon River./ Natural history--Amazon River Region.

577.34   Ph-1 3-6/7 $16.00   L KC318
GOODMAN, SUSAN E. Bats, bugs, and biodiversity: adventures in the Amazonian rain forest. Photos by Michael J. Doolittle. Atheneum ISBN 0-689-31943-6; In Canada: Distican, 1995. 46p. col. ill.

Includes glossary, bibliography and directory.

Selectors' Choice, 20th ed.

Join a group of Michigan seventh and eighth graders as they troop through the Amazon rain forest to experience an exotic culture. Children deal with insect bites, outdoor toilets, lack of electricity, and wildlife. They trade T-shirts for blow guns and ruminate about the consequences of saving a sloth from the cooking pot. Stateside, they share their adventures and awareness in assemblies and outreach programs. Back pages list sources for children's rain forest workshops. An inspiring journey for environmental and multicultural studies.

SUBJ: Rain forest ecology--Amazon River Region./ Ecology--Amazon River Region.

577.34   Ph-3 2-6/7 $18.00   T KC319
LESSEM, DON. Inside the amazing Amazon. Illus. by Michael Rothman. Crown ISBN 0-517-59490-0, 1995. unp. col. ill., map.

Includes glossary and directory.

Wonderful foldout paintings show the complexity and beauty of the Amazon rainforest. Children will pore over the pages, matching names and outlines shown in black and white to the colored pages. Illustrates the forest floor, understory, canopy, and emergent layer. A new view of one of the richest places on earth. Good accompaniment to environmental studies. Gatefold pages may limit usefulness.

SUBJ: Rain forests--Amazon River Region./ Rain forest ecology--Amazon River Region./ Ecology.

CDR 577.34   Ph-2 K-3 $14.95   OD KC320
LET'S EXPLORE THE JUNGLE WITH BUZZY THE KNOWLEDGE BUG (CD-ROM). Humongous Entertainment ISBN 1-886646-30-9, 1995. 1 CD-ROM color. (Junior field trips).

Includes user's guide and activity book.

System requirements: Windows IBM PC or 100% compatible; 33MHz 486 with 8MB of RAM; SVGA (640x480, 256-color) graphics; Windows 3.1 or higher; sound card; double-speed CD-ROM drive.

System requirements: Macintosh minimum 25MHz 68040 or Power PC with 8MB RAM; 640x480, 256-color; double-speed CD-ROM drive; System 7.0 or higher.

Product (ISBN 1-886646-30-9) runs on either Windows or Macintosh compatible hardware.

Youngsters can explore jungles in Asia, Africa, and the Amazon with this program. Information about animals, plants, and the environment is available as students explore and play the five activities. The excellent sound makes the program usable by limited readers. For environmental studies.

SUBJ: Jungles--Software./ Software--Jungles./ Rain forests--Software./ Software--Rain forests./ Interactive media.

577.34   Ph-2 3-6/7 $32.83   L   KC321
LEWINGTON, ANNA. Atlas of rain forests. Raintree Steck-Vaughn ISBN 0-8172-4756-4, 1997. 96p. col. ill., maps.
> Includes glossary, directory, bibliographies, filmography and index. Identifies both tropical and temperate rain forests worldwide, with regional and feature maps. Explores the diversity of plant and animal life, habitat threats, and conservation measures such as the reforestation of Vietnam. Eye-catching photographs add to text. For environmental studies.
> SUBJ: Rain forest ecology./ Atlases.

577.34   Ph-3 K-6/7 $14.95   T   KC322
PRATT, KRISTIN JOY. Walk in the rainforest. Dawn Publications ISBN 1-878265-99-7, 1992. 31p. col. ill.
> Available in Spanish UN PASEO POR EL BOSQUE LIUVIO (Dawn Publications, ISBN 1-883220-02-5, 1993).
> An alphabetical introduction to the rare rainforest flora and fauna. Younger students will turn pages to view the exotic pictures and will pick up unusual names; older students will stop to read the informational paragraphs. Encourage all readers to learn the pages that illustrate the initials of their names.
> SUBJ: Rain forests./ Rain forest ecology./ Ecology./ Alphabet./ Bilingual materials--Spanish./ Spanish language materials.

CDR 577.34   Ph-1 5-A $199.95   OD KC323
RAINFOREST RESEARCHERS (CD-ROM). Tom Snyder Productions RAI-D, 1996. 1 CD-ROM color.
> Includes teacher's guide, introductory videocassette, worksheets and student reference books.
> System requirements: At least a Macintosh LC II (68030 processor) or higher or Macintosh Power PC; System 7.1 or later; 5MB RAM, 8MB RAM for Power PC; 640x480 display, thousands of colors recommended, (minimum of 256 colors); hard disk; VCR and monitor (optional); speakers (optional).
> System requirements: IBM-compatible 486 or higher with sound card; Windows 3.1 or Windows 95; 8MB RAM; 640x480 display, thousands of colors recommended (256 colors minimum); hard disk; VCR or monitor (optional); speakers (optional).
> Product (RAI-D) runs on either Macintosh or Windows compatible hardware.
> Students take on the role of nature detectives to solve ecological mysteries of disappearing fruit or identifying a plant sample found by a scientist who kept incomplete notes. Excellent visuals and QuickTime movies shot on location in Indonesia are included. The cooperative learning aspects of the activities make the program work well with an entire classroom or small groups. For environmental studies.
> SUBJ: Rain forest ecology--Software./ Software--Rain forest ecology./ Rain forests--Software./ Software--Rain forests./ Problem solving--Software./ Software--Problem solving./ Interactive media.

VCR 577.34   Ph-2 5-A $39.95   KC324
RAINFOREST (Videocassette). Schlessinger Video N6629 ISBN 1-879151-49-9, 1993. 1/2" VHS videocassette color (30min). (Earth at risk environmental video series).
> Includes public performance rights.
> Closed captioned.
> Kevin Seal narrates three interwoven segments: vivid coverage of the landscape and what logging and deforestation are doing, satellite images interpreted to show the resulting effects on climate and landscape, and students conducting zoo studies to document animal behaviors and prepare for environmental careers. Mentions that underdeveloped countries need to exploit their natural resources to pay off debt and feed their population, but this important concept is left dangling without any investigating or hypothesizing of possible solutions. Viewers are urged to take an activist environmental role. Somewhat disjointed, but there are clear stopping places for review and discussion. For environmental studies.
> SUBJ: Rain forest ecology./ Ecology./ Man--Influence on nature.

CDR 577.34   Ph-1 6-A $34.95   OD KC325
SCHOLASTIC'S THE MAGIC SCHOOL BUS EXPLORES THE RAINFOREST. School ed. (CD-ROM). Microsoft ISBN 1-57231-577-6; In Canada: Microsoft Canada, 1997. 1 CD-ROM color. (Scholastic's the Magic School Bus explores).
> Version 1.0.
> Includes user's guide and teacher's guide.
> Closed captioned.
> System requirements: Multimedia PC with 486SX/33 MHz or higher processor; Microsoft Windows 95 operating system or Microsoft Windows NT Workstation operating system version 3.51 or later; 8MB of RAM for Windows 95, 12MB for Windows NT Workstation; 6MB of available hard-disk space; double-speed or faster CD-ROM drive; Super VGA, 256-color monitor; Microsoft Mouse or compatible pointing device; 16-bit sound card; headphones or speakers.

In another addition to the Magic School Bus series, Ms. Frizzle's students learn a great deal about the rainforest and ecology as they travel through the Costa Rican rainforest. Activities are plentiful and challenging. Program works well with individual students, small groups, or as a learning center with multiple visits. For environmental studies.
> SUBJ: Rain forest ecology--Costa Rica--Software./ Software--Rain forest ecology--Costa Rica./ Rain forests--Costa Rica--Software./ Software--Rain forests--Costa Rica./ Interactive media.

577.34   Ph-3 4-6/6 $13.95   L   KC326
SIY, ALEXANDRA. Brazilian rain forest. Dillon ISBN 0-87518-470-7; In Canada: Maxwell Macmillan, 1992. 80p col illus and photos. (Circle of life).
> Includes activity pages, directory, glossary, appendix and index. Describes rainforest geography and biodiversity while sounding the alarm against destruction and extinction caused by high demand for wood, beef and short term profits. Gives specific information about one rainforest that must be saved, and side-steps third world politics and poverty. Use with environmental studies and South American social studies.
> SUBJ: Rain forests./ Rain forest ecology./ Ecology.

VD 577.34   Ph-3 4-A $325.00   OD KC327
STV: RAIN FOREST (Videodisc). National Geographic 81500, 1991. 1 CAV videodisc, 2 3.5" disks w/HyperCard, 1 computer/videodisc cable.
> Includes User's Guide and Barcodes.
> Interactive.
> System requirements: Macintosh computer with at least 2 megabytes of RAM, system version 6.0.5 or higher, 3.5" disk drive, hard disk and mouse; HyperCard 2.0v2 or higher; videodisc player (Pioneer LD-V2200, 4200, 6000 series, or 8000; Sony LDP-1200, 1500, 1550, 2000; or almost any player equipped with RS-232 port); TV video monitor with audio and video cables: printer (optional).
> This program introduces youngsters to rain forests and concentrates on the one in Costa Rica. Youngsters learn about the plants and animals found in each layer of the forest. Economic considerations which are leading to the destruction of rain forests are also discussed. The software which accompanies this interactive video package includes a presentation maker which allows youngsters and teachers to create their own multimedia reports. The program works very well with an entire class or with small groups.
> SUBJ: Rain forests--Software./ Rain forest ecology--Software./ Software--Rain forests./ Software--Rain forest ecology./ Interactive media.

577.34   Ph-1 K-4/6 $14.95   T   KC328
WILLOW, DIANE. At home in the rain forest. Illus. by Laura Jacques. Charlesbridge ISBN 0-88106-485-8, 1991. unp. col. ill.
> Spanish edition available DENTRO DE LA SELVA TROPICAL (ISBN 0-88106-641-9, 1993), $15.88.
> A luxurious journey through five layers of vegetation unfolds a colorful array of rain forest animals and their special niches. Unfamiliar animals and plants are carefully indentified in offside drawings. Does not mention the problems of destruction. Useful across grade levels to illustrate this rich habitat.
> SUBJ: Rain forests./ Rain forest ecology./ Ecology.

577.34   Ph-3 K-3/4 $14.95   L   KC329
YOLEN, JANE. Welcome to the green house. Illus. by Laura Regan. Putnam ISBN 0-399-22335-5; In Canada: Putnam, 1993. unp. col. ill.
> Poetic text discloses the hot, green rainforest as a world of lush growth, unfamiliar animals, and exotic sounds. Young children will be captivated by the drawings and spellbound by the cadence when this is read aloud. Afterwards, try acting out animal sounds and movements just for the fun of it. Testifies to the beauty and diversity of this environment.
> SUBJ: Rain forests./ Rain forest ecology./ Ecology.

577.4   Ph-1 A $16.95   P   KC330
BROWN, LAUREN. Grasslands. Knopf ISBN 0-394-73121-2; In Canada: Random House, 1985. 606p. col. ill. (Audubon Society nature guides).
> Includes glossary, bibliography and index.
> Explore the flora and fauna of distinct types of ecological areas through these carefully researched and well organized field guides. Each title in the series includes habitat essays, color plates, species descriptions and appendices. Recommend that titles of regional interest be purchased as well as duplicate copies for reference collection.
> SUBJ: Natural history--Guides./ Grassland ecology--Guides.

577.4   Ph-3 3-6/4 $15.27   L   KC331
ROWAN, JAMES P. Prairies and grasslands. Childrens Press ISBN 0-516-01706-3; In Canada: Childrens Press, 1983. 45p. col. ill. (New

true book).
Includes glossary and index.
Introduces African, North and South American prairie wildlife and people. Final chapter stresses protection of habitat. Useful for elementary social studies.
SUBJ: Prairie ecology./ Grassland ecology./ Ecology.

577.4 Ph-3 4-6/7 $19.95 L KC332
STAUB, FRANK J. America's prairies. Carolrhoda ISBN 0-87614-781-3, 1994. 47p. col. ill., maps. (Carolrhoda earth watch book).
Includes glossary and index.
Presents the effects of sodbusters, droughts, and irrigation on the expanse of grass that "once covered a fifth of North America" (p.6). As the stresses of human intervention occur, conservationists fight to preserve our unique American heritage. Will enhance units on westward expansion and environmental studies.
SUBJ: Prairies./ Prairie ecology./ Man--Influence on nature.

VCR 577.4 Ph-2 3-A $99.00 OD KC333
TALL GRASS PRAIRIE: AN AMERICAN STORY (Videocassette).
National Geographic 52669, 1997. 1/2" VHS videocassette color (29min).
Includes teacher's guide.
Closed captioned.
Dramatic footage of the red buffalo (prairie fire) opens this tale of the buffalo and Native American interdependence, the hunting, and the conservation effort to save an endangered species on the verge of extinction. Since the prairie is part of our heritage, this is important in documenting how man has reduced a vibrant ecosystem to scraps of tall grass. Use with environmental studies, social studies, geography, and books such as the Little House series.
SUBJ: Prairies./ Prairie ecology./ Grassland ecology./ Man--Influence on nature./ Buffaloes.

577.5 Ph-2 3-5/4 $15.95 T KC334
GODKIN, CELIA. Wolf Island. W. H. Freeman ISBN 0-7167-6513-6; In Canada: Fitzhenry & Whiteside, 1993. 36p. col. ill.
"Scientific American books for young readers."
When wolves accidentally leave their island home, deer multiply and eat up the vegetation, leaving smaller animals to suffer. Balance is restored when the wolves return. Demonstrates the food chain, animals' need to survive, and how each species' well-being is interconnected. For environmental studies.
SUBJ: Island ecology./ Ecology./ Food chains (Ecology).

577.5 Ph-1 4-A/7 $13.95 T KC335
HISCOCK, BRUCE. Tundra, the Arctic land. Atheneum ISBN 0-689-31219-9; In Canada: Collier Macmillan, 1986. 135p. ill.
Includes glossary, bibliography and index.
Selectors' Choice, 16th ed.
Come on a guided tour of the northernmost land in the world. Learn about the workings of permafrost, the efficient ground-hugging flora, and the diverse population of fauna--all with their unique adaptations to this hostile environment. Here is a sensitive naturalist's loving account of an unlovable (to most of us) land.
SUBJ: Tundra./ Tundra ecology./ Ecology.

577.5 Ph-2 5-6/7 $14.99 L KC336
LAVIES, BIANCA. Compost critters. Text and photos by Bianca Lavies. Dutton ISBN 0-525-44763-6, 1993. unp. col. ill.
Garbage becomes an interesting science lesson as microphotographs show how small creatures cause the decay of a compost heap into rich humus for nurturing the garden. Bacteria, molds, fungi, mites, springtails, sow bugs, worms, nematodes, millipedes, and snails are all shown in vividly enlarged views, and their interrelationships and winter nesting habits are explained. As part of her exercise in ecology, Lavies planted tomatoes and beans around the compost pile with very impressive results. Simple instructions encourage readers to try composting.
SUBJ: Compost./ Soil biology./ Soil ecology./ Ecology.

577.5 Ph-3 6-A/6 $13.95 L KC337
SIY, ALEXANDRA. Arctic National Wildlife Refuge. Dillon ISBN 0-87518-468-5; In Canada: Maxwell Macmillan, 1991. 80p. col. ill., map.
Includes directory, glossary and index.
Visit the Arctic tundra where a wildlife refuge covers over 19 million acres in northeastern Alaska. Here an untouched ecosystem is threatened by oil development. Examines how plants, animals, and humans live in a harsh environment and presents arguments for and against drilling. Important for Alaskan and environmental studies.
SUBJ: Natural history--Alaska./ Tundra ecology./ Ecology./ Arctic National Wildlife Refuge (Alaska).

577.54 Ph-1 A $19.00 P KC338
MACMAHON, JAMES. Deserts. Knopf ISBN 0-394-73139-5; In Canada: Random House, 1985. 638p. col. ill. (Audubon Society nature guides).
Includes glossary, bibliography and index.
Explore the flora and fauna of distinct types of ecological areas through these carefully researched and well organized field guides. Each title in the series includes habitat essays, color plates, species descriptions and appendices. Recommend that titles of regional interest be purchased as well as duplicate copies for reference collection.
SUBJ: Natural history--Guides./ Desert ecology--Guides.

577.6 Ph-3 5-6/7 $14.95 L KC339
CRAIGHEAD, CHARLES. Eagle and the river. Photos by Tom Mangelsen. Macmillan ISBN 0-02-762265-7; In Canada: Maxwell Macmillan, 1994. unp. col. ill.
Wyoming's Snake River in winter is a bold backdrop for the eagle and other animals featured in lovely photographs and brief text. The flying and hunting behavior of the eagle are threaded throughout the photo-essay, which introduces elk, mule deer, ermine, and a variety of other mammals and birds living in the snowy landscape around the unfrozen river. This brief, appreciative introduction to animals sharing a habitat offers inviting browsing and a nice starting point for units on winter.
SUBJ: Stream animals--Snake River (Wyo.-Wash.)./ Bald eagle--Snake River (Wyo.-Wash.)./ Snake River (Wyo.-Wash.).

577.63 Ph-3 1-6/7 $15.99 L KC340
PARKER, STEVE. Pond and river. Knopf ISBN 0-394-99615-1, 1988. 64p. col. ill. (Eyewitness books).
Includes index.
No matter the season freshwater ponds and streams teem with life as these picture filled pages clearly show. Chapters include information on seasonal changes, fish, waterfowl, plants, the salt marsh and more. May be used at all grade levels and is especially useful for ecology units and during preparation for field trips.
SUBJ: Pond ecology./ Stream ecology.

577.68 Ph-3 K-3/7 $15.99 T KC341
LAVIES, BIANCA. Mangrove wilderness: nature's nursery. Text and photos by Bianca Lavies. Dutton ISBN 0-525-45186-2, 1994. unp. col. ill.
Mangrove "is an odd looking tree that seems to stand on stilts, and it grows ... in salt water." (p.2) A close-up look at Florida's red mangrove tree reveals the aquatic creatures that swim among its roots, a rat snake sunning itself on a branch, and a pelican's nest at the tip-top. Readers will meet a host of new animals in a wide rambling food chain. For environmental studies.
SUBJ: Swamp ecology./ Ecology./ Red mangrove swamps.

577.68 Ph-2 P-2/3 $14.95 L KC342
LUENN, NANCY. Squish!: a wetland walk. Illus. by Ronald Himler. Atheneum ISBN 0-689-31842-1; In Canada: Maxwell Macmillan, 1994. unp. col. ill.
Listen, touch, and smell the wetland world with a young boy and his grandfather as they explore a wetland throughout the seasons. Affirms wetlands as wildlife habitats, filters of pollution, and places of reverential beauty. For environmental studies.
SUBJ: Wetlands./ Wetland ecology./ Ecology.

VCR 577.68 Ph-3 2-4 $275.00 OD KC343
MARSH: NATURE'S NURSERY (Videocassette). Beacon Films/Altschul Group 8451, 1988. 1/2" VHS videocassette color (14min).
Includes public performance rights.
On a nature walk with David Suzuki, children find and learn about toads, leeches, snakes, and ducklings. The marsh comes alive in this overview of its inhabitants.
SUBJ: Marshes./ Nature study.

VCR 577.68 Ph-3 4-6 $79.95 KC344
OUR WONDERFUL WETLANDS (Videocassette). United Learning 10210V ISBN 1-56007-360-8, 1993. 1/2" VHS videocassette color (11min).
Includes teacher's guide.
Gives an overview of bogs, swamps, and salt marshes. Explains how wetlands provide a habitat for a huge variety of wildlife while filtering water as it enters rivers and streams. Touches on environmental concerns and the need to protect this unique resource. For environmental studies.
SUBJ: Wetlands./ Wetland ecology./ Ecology./ Environmental protection.

577.69   Ph-1 A $19.00   P   KC345
AMOS, WILLIAM H. Atlantic and Gulf coasts. By William H. and Steven
H. Amos. Knopf ISBN 0-394-73109-3; In Canada: Random House, 1985.
670p. col. ill. (Audubon Society nature guides).
  Includes glossary, bibliography and index.
  Explore the flora and fauna of distinct types of ecological areas
  through these carefully researched and well organized field guides.
  Each title in the series includes habitat essays, color plates, species
  descriptions and appendices. Recommend that titles of regional
  interest be purchased as well as duplicate copies for reference
  collection.
  SUBJ: Natural history--Guides./ Seashore ecology--Guides.

VCR 577.69   Ph-1 5-A $150.00   OD KC346
INTERTIDAL ZONE (Videocassette). National Film Board of Canada/
Bullfrog Films ISBN 0-7722-0384-9, c1985, 1986. 1/2" VHS
videocassette color (17min).
  Includes teacher's guide.
  Examines the plants and animals living in the narrow area of seashore
  covered by the tide twice daily. Focuses on adaptation required by
  the environment, the zonal food chain, dangers posed by predators
  and touches on the effects of pollution. Attractive and moderately
  paced, this is a good introduction to the study of this ecosystem and
  ideal to use before a field trip to the seashore.
  SUBJ: Seashore biology./ Seashore ecology.

577.69   Ph-3 P-2/4 $16.00   L   KC347
PLUCKROSE, HENRY. Seashore. Childrens Press ISBN 0-516-08120-9; In
Canada: Childrens Press, 1994. 32p. col. ill. (Walkabout).
  Includes index.
  Stroll through seaweed pools and sandy shorelines to discover the
  amazing variety of life at the beach. Swimming, fishing, and boating
  are bonuses. Lots of color on each page will open a child's eye to
  beauty. Use at the beginning of summer vacation.
  SUBJ: Seashore biology.

577.69   Ph-2 3-6/5 $15.40   L   KC348
SHAHAN, SHERRY. Barnacles eat with their feet: delicious facts about
the tide pool food chain. Text and photos by Sherry Shahan. Millbrook
ISBN 1-56294-922-5, 1996. 32p. col. ill.
  Includes glossary and index.
  Pull on boots to walk around in a tide pool where ocean water
  collects to create homes for some very unusual creatures: anemones,
  sea stars, tube-building worms, and more. Some are not too fussy
  about their food, a hermit crab with six pairs of mouthparts will eat
  just about anything, while others specialize. A photograph of each
  animal is accompanied with brief text. Useful before field trips and for
  ocean units and environmental studies.
  SUBJ: Tide pool ecology./ Food chains (Ecology)./ Ecology.

CDR 577.7   Ph-2 3-A $99.95   OD KC349
GREAT OCEAN RESCUE (CD-ROM). Tom Snyder Productions/Chedd-
Angier/MCET OCD-D, 1996. 1 CD-ROM color.
  Version 2.0.
  Includes teacher's guide and student reference booklets.
  Also available for Windows, $99.95.
  System requirements: QuickTime-capable Macintosh computer;
  double-speed (or higher) CD-ROM drive; System 7.0 or higher; 2MB
  (minimum) of available RAM; 256 colors or 16 grayscales (minimum),
  thousands of colors are highly recommended, but not required;
  640x480 (or larger) monitor.
  Activity oriented interactive CD invites youngsters to learn about the
  ocean as well as related topics in earth, life, and environmental
  sciences. Four adventures engage students in cooperative activities as
  they practice group problem solving. For environmental studies.
  SUBJ: Ocean--Software./ Software--Ocean./ Marine ecology--
  Software./ Software--Marine ecology./ Environmental protection--
  Software./ Software--Environmental protection./ Interactive media.

VD 577.7   Ph-2 3-A $349.95   OD KC350
GREAT OCEAN RESCUE (Videodisc). Tom Snyder Productions GOR-D,
1992. 1 12" double-sided CAV videodisc color.
  Includes teacher's guide, 28 student booklets, reproducible masters,
  and student worksheets.
  Software available GORS-D $49.95.
  System requirements: Monitor (large video monitor for whole-class
  viewing), videodisc player (Hitachi 9500, 9550, 9600; Panasonic
  LX150; Philips VP 406 (PAL); Pioneer 2200, 2400, 4100 (PAL),
  4200, 4400, 8000; Pioneer LDV6000-Pioneer 6000, 6000A, 6010A;
  Sony 1000A, 1200, 1450, 1500, 1500 (PAL), 1550, 2000, 3600,
  MDP 1100); bar code reader (optional but recommended).
  Activity oriented interactive disc invites youngsters to learn about the
  ocean as well as related topics in earth, life, and environmental
  sciences. Four adventures engage students in cooperative activities as
  they practice group problem solving. Second side contains a library of
  film and stills designed to help with research and student-created
  reports. For enviromental studies.
  SUBJ: Ocean./ Marine ecology./ Environmental protection./
  Interactive media.

577.7   Ph-1 5-6/7 $16.00   T   KC351
PRINGLE, LAURENCE P. Coral reefs: Earth's undersea treasures. By
Laurence Pringle. Simon & Schuster ISBN 0-689-80286-2; In Canada:
Distican, 1995. 45p. col. ill., map.
  Includes glossary and index.
  Selectors' Choice, 20th ed.
  Coral reefs, fascinating in their structure and the colorful variety of
  plants and animals they support, are beautifully introduced in clear
  text and striking photographs. Pringle discusses the structure and
  behavior of coral polyps, the nutritious ecosystem of the
  interdependent animals, the human benefits of coral reefs, and the
  vulnerability and threatened state of coral reefs worldwide. This
  outstanding presentation of this complex habitat should be widely
  useful for personal enjoyment, booktalking, and teaching. For
  environmental studies.
  SUBJ: Coral reef ecology./ Ecology.

577.7   Ph-3 4-6/7 $13.95   L   KC352
SIY, ALEXANDRA. Great Astrolabe Reef. Dillon ISBN 0-87518-499-5; In
Canada: Maxwell Macmillan, 1992. 80p col illus and photos. (Circle of
life).
  Includes "Activity Pages", appendix, glossary and index.
  Travel to Fiji to discover a three million-year-old barrier reef that
  stretches 25 nautical miles. Life on the reef is a constant struggle for
  survival yet food webs and the ecosystem remain clean and healthy.
  Scientists and divers who have been discovering unknown species and
  chemicals for medicines are concerned about reef destruction and
  overfishing. Use with global environmental units and ocean studies.
  SUBJ: Coral reef ecology./ Ecology./ Corals./ Coral reef biology./
  Great Astrolabe Reef (Fiji).

577.7   Ph-3 3-6/7 $12.95   T   KC353
WU, NORBERT. Beneath the waves: exploring the hidden world of the
kelp forest. Chronicle ISBN 0-87701-835-9, 1992. 39p. col. ill., map.
  Includes glossary and index.
  Dive deep into the ocean kelp forests that grow along coastlines
  worldwide. Their "beauty and bounty...is far richer than most people
  know." (p2) Pictures and text highlight the forests' variety of wildlife.
  Only briefly touches on environmental dangers being thrust upon this
  habitat. Perfect for wildlife and ocean units.
  SUBJ: Kelp bed ecology./ Marine animals.

577.7   Ph-2 4-6/8 $16.00   T   KC354
WU, NORBERT. City under the sea: life in a coral reef. Atheneum ISBN
0-689-31896-0; In Canada: Distican, 1996. 28p. col. ill.
  "Like a city, the coral reef has places to live, to socialize, and even
  to get haircuts and manicures." (p.11) Using the travels of a green
  sea turtle as a unifying element, text and photographs expand on
  symbiosis, predators, and food chains in this dazzling underwater
  world that very few people will actually visit. For environmental
  studies.
  SUBJ: Coral reef ecology./ Coral reefs and islands.

VCR 577.8   Ph-2 4-6 $59.95   OD KC355
TREE: A LIVING COMMUNITY (Videocassette). SVE/Churchill Media
C80390-HAVT, 1988. 1/2" VHS videocassette color (11min).
  Includes discussion guide.
  Adaptation of original film, The Tree.
  Sitting under a tree, a girl learns about the symbiotic relationship
  between the tree and the creatures that live in and around it.
  Concepts are explained through narrated live-action and animation.
  SUBJ: Trees./ Symbiosis./ Ecology.

PIC 578   Ph-3 6-A $99.95   OD KC356
REALMS OF LIFE (Picture). Carolina Biological Supply Company P7-57-
1510, 1996. 6 wall charts, color (38"x50").
  Also available as individual wall charts, $19.95 each.
  Based on the Five Kingdoms Classification System, these study aids
  give an attractive overview of the diversity of organisms. Full-color
  illustrations depict representative organisms, and each chart lists
  characteristics of the kingdom. An additional chart on viruses is
  illustrated with fascinating, computer-enhanced electron micrographs.
  Provides useful views of both familiar and microscopic forms of life.
  Contents: Kingdom animalia -- Kingdom plantae -- Kingdom protista --
  Kingdom monera -- Kingdom fungi -- Viruses.
  SUBJ: Biology--Classification./ Microorganisms./ Plants./ Animals./
  Viruses.

VCR 578.6   Ph-2 3-6 $79.00   OD KC357
HOW PLANTS ARE USED (Videocassette). National Geographic 51456, 1991. 1/2" VHS videocassette color (15min). (Kingdom of plants).
     Includes teacher's guide.
     Gives an eye-opening view of the plants that provide lumber, textiles, coal and medicines. Emphasizes that our existence is dependent upon plants and correct forest management. An excellent addition to primary botany.
     SUBJ: Plants./ Botany.

578.7   Ph-2 2-6/7 $16.95   L   KC358
DUNCAN, BEVERLY K. Explore the wild: a nature search-and-find book. HarperCollins ISBN 0-06-023597-7; In Canada: HarperCollins, 1996. 48p. col. ill., map.
     Includes glossary.
     Animals and plants are shown in different biomes: desert, grassland, tundra, the Arctic, undersea, and more. The subjects are first presented by themselves with a minimum of descriptive text; then a two page mural invites readers to find the animals and plants that they have just seen. Even nonreaders will enjoy the hide-and-seek pictures. For environmental studies.
     SUBJ: Habitat (Ecology)./ Natural history./ Ecology.

578.7   Ph-1 2-A/8 $17.95   T   KC359
ORR, RICHARD. Richard Orr's nature cross-sections. Illustrated by Richard Orr. Written by Moira Butterfield. DK Publishing ISBN 0-7894-0147-9, 1995. 30p. col. ill.
     Includes index.
     Orr's 12 amazing cutaway drawings, including a termite city, a tide pool, and a beaver lodge, delight and inform. Paper engineering allows the two-page foldout of Arctic life to expand to 20 by 27 inches! The longitudinal rain forest illustrates the massive layering of wildlife. Testimony to the beauty of nature; a book to pore over. For environmental studies.
     SUBJ: Habitat (Ecology)./ Ecology.

578.75   Ph-3 P-2/4 $16.60   L   KC360
PLUCKROSE, HENRY. Under the ground. Childrens Press ISBN 0-516-08122-5; In Canada: Childrens Press, 1994. 32p. col. ill. (Walkabout).
     Includes index.
     Cutaway photographs illustrate the action underground as animals burrow, vegetables grow, and roots branch. Also includes pages on caverns, mines, and tunnels. Use for environmental studies to encourage awareness of a "hidden" environment.
     SUBJ: Underground animals./ Soil animals./ Tunnels./ Soil ecology.

578.754   Ph-2 4-6/7 $19.95   L   KC361
ARNOLD, CAROLINE. Watching desert wildlife. Photos by Arthur Arnold. Carolrhoda ISBN 0-87614-841-0, 1994. 48p. col. ill., map. (Carolrhoda nature watch book).
     Includes glossary and index.
     A guided tour through world deserts allowing plenty of time to observe plants and animals that thrive in this harsh habitat. Color filled pages sustain interest. Arnold has done a good job of differentiating deserts geographically and making a strong case for preservation and survival. For environmental studies.
     SUBJ: Desert biology./ Deserts.

578.754   Ph-1 4-6/5 $14.95   L   KC362
BAYLOR, BYRD. Desert is theirs. Illus. by Peter Parnall. Scribner's ISBN 0-684-14266-X, c1975. unp. col. ill.
     Caldecott Honor Book.
     Selectors' Choice, 10th ed.
     The lyrical text speaks of the intimate relationship between Desert People and their land which they joyfully share with the hawks, deer and pack rats, the hard skinny plants and even the weeds. "A weed may wait three years to bloom/Just so it blooms sometime..." Peter Parnall's brightly colored line drawings are in perfect harmony with the text. Read aloud.
     SUBJ: Deserts.

578.754   Ph-2 K-3/4 $15.95   L   KC363
GIBBONS, GAIL. Deserts. Holiday House ISBN 0-8234-1276-8, 1996. unp. col. ill., maps.
     Introduces rocky and sandy generic deserts along with the plants, animals, and humans that live in them. Gibbons' hallmark, full-page illustrations are carefully drawn and labeled. Packed with information for nonreaders.
     SUBJ: Deserts.

578.754   Ph-2 4-6/7 $20.99   L   KC364
MACQUITTY, MIRANDA. Desert. Photos by Alan Hills and Frank Greenaway. Knopf ISBN 0-679-96003-1, 1994. 64p. col. ill., map. (Eyewitness books).

"Dorling Kindersley book."
"Borzoi book."
Includes index.
Depicts the fauna, flora, and accoutrements of desert life worldwide. Photography is outstanding; display is typical of Eyewitness books. An intriguing browser.
SUBJ: Deserts./ Man--Influence of environment.

578.754   Ph-1 2-A/10 $15.95   P   KC365
WALLACE, MARIANNE D. America's deserts: guide to plants and animals. Fulcrum Kids ISBN 1-55591-268-0, 1996. 48p. col. ill., maps.
     Includes glossary, directory and index.
     Learn about belly flowers, the patchnose snake, and a beavertail cactus while poring over the realistic, labeled drawings of common plants and animals from the Sonoran, Mojave, Chihuahuan, and Great Basin desert regions. Includes state maps, resource list, and common and scientific names. Fact filled and carefully illustrated, this is perfect for inclusion in social studies and environmental studies of the Southwest.
     SUBJ: Desert plants./ Desert animals./ Deserts.

578.769   Ph-2 1-4/4 $11.95   T   KC366
COHAT, ELISABETH. Seashore. Created by Gallimard Jeunesse and Elisabeth Cohat. Illus. by Pierre de Hugo. Scholastic ISBN 0-590-20303-7; In Canada: Scholastic, 1995. unp. col. ill. (spiral bound). (First discovery book).
     "Cartwheel books."
     Originally published in France, LE BORD DE LA MER, 1990.
     Colorful views of animals living at the seashore and under the sea appear in an appealing small volume. Glossy pages with plastic overlays show exterior and inside views of animals and their homes--crabs, mollusks, lobsters, and other denizens of the deep are all labeled and described very briefly. This is an attractive item that children will pore over and a nice introduction to ocean animals.
     SUBJ: Seashore animals./ Seashore biology.

578.77   Ph-1 A/10 $10.70   P   KC367
CARSON, RACHEL. Edge of the sea. Illustrated by Bob Hines. Houghton Mifflin ISBN 0-395-28519-4, c1955. 276p. ill.
     Available from National Library Service for the Blind and Physically Handicapped in Braille BR03811 and on sound recording cassette RC17779.
     An outstanding scientist and writer describes the three types of coastal habitats: the Rocky Shore, The Rim of sand, and Coral Coast. Illustrations of the Atlantic Coast line accompany text.
     SUBJ: Marine biology.

MCP 578.77   Ph-2 3-A $59.95   OD KC368
FIELD TRIP INTO THE SEA (Microcomputer program). Sunburst 6480, 1992. 2 3.5" disks.
     Includes THE KELP FOREST, Blake (ISBN 0-918303-21-4, 1990).
     Includes teacher's guide.
     Also available in Macintosh monochrome version.
     Also available on Apple II computers with 128K of memory.
     System requirements: Macintosh computer with 2MB RAM; system 6.0 or higher; hard drive and color monitor required.
     This discovery learning tool takes users on a self-guided trip of the sea. Databases of 23 sea views, 76 organisms, and 36 food chains are included. Fourteen guided activities help adults channel students through their exploration. Works well with small groups or individuals.
     SUBJ: Marine biology--Software./ Software--Marine biology./ Marine ecology--Software./ Software--Marine ecology.

CDR 578.77   Ph-1 2-A $44.95   OD KC369
SCHOLASTIC'S THE MAGIC SCHOOL BUS EXPLORES THE OCEAN. Teacher ed. (CD-ROM). Microsoft ISBN 1-57231-166-5; In Canada: Microsoft, 1995. 1 CD-ROM color. (Scholastic's the Magic School Bus explores).
     Version 1.00.
     Includes user's guide and teacher's guide.
     System requirements: Multimedia PC with a 486SX/25 MHz or higher processor; either MS-DOS operating system version 5.0 or later with Windows version 3.1 or later, or Windows 95; 4MB of RAM (8MB recommended); 5MB of available hard-disk space; double-speed CD-ROM drive; Super VGA display capable of 256 colors; 8-bit sound board (16-bit recommended); headphones or speakers; Microsoft Mouse or compatible pointing device.
     Users join the whimsical Ms. Frizzle and her class as they explore the various ocean zones. Experiments, activities, games, and reports are included. Works well with small groups or an entire class.
     SUBJ: Ocean--Software./ Software--Ocean./ Marine animals--Software./ Software--Marine animals./ Interactive media.

578.77   Ph-3 4-6/7 $16.95   L   KC370
SWANSON, DIANE. Safari beneath the sea: the wonder world of the
North Pacific coast. Photos by the Royal British Columbia Museum.
Sierra Club ISBN 0-87156-415-7; In Canada: Whitecap Books, 1994.
58p. col. ill.
> Includes index.
> The cold North Pacific is a hospitable habitat to a variety of unusual
> marine life: sea pens, octopuses, sponges, blue whales, and more.
> Wondrous photographs of startling wildlife document the sea's
> beauty. Will appeal to all students seeking the weirdest, biggest, and
> oddest looking creatures. Not a definitive text on marine life, rather a
> window into a strange environment. Use when studying the Pacific
> states, with oceanology units, and for environmental studies.
> SUBJ: Marine biology--Northwest, Pacific./ Marine animals./ Marine
> plants.

VCR 578.77   Ph-3 4-6 $39.95   OD KC371
WORLDS BELOW (Videocassette). Narrated by Dr. Sylvia Earle. Sea
Studios ISBN 09616824-2-6, 1988. 1/2" VHS videocassette color
(21min).
> Includes activity guide.
> Companion videocassette to WORLD ALIVE, Sea Studios, 1990.
> Includes public performance rights.
> This non-narrated film uses majestic music and underwater
> photography to provide a lingering view of sea animals and plants.
> Birds atop the water, sea lions, crabs, fish, anemones and other
> species move through the ocean bottom terrain in beautifully
> orchestrated sequences. The view here is esthetic, evocative, and slow
> moving. Use creatively to stimulate discussion, writing, or further
> investigation and study of ocean life and ecology.
> SUBJ: Marine animals./ Marine plants.

579   Ph-1 6-A/8 $16.00   T   KC372
LOEWER, H. PETER. Pond water zoo: an introduction to microscopic life.
By Peter Loewer. Illus. by Jean Jenkins. Atheneum ISBN 0-689-31736-0;
In Canada: Distican, 1996. 90p. ill.
> Includes glossary, bibliography and index.
> Whip out the microscope and head over to the nearest pond; learn
> about monera and protists along with rotifers and arthropods--life
> swimming in and on the water. Includes instructions on keeping a
> private zoo (with such exotica as water bears), making slides, and
> using the microscope. Large drawings ensure successful identifications.
> Once introduced, this book will not stay on the shelf.
> SUBJ: Freshwater biology./ Microorganisms./ Pond ecology./
> Ecology.

VCR 579   Ph-3 4-8 $225.00   OD KC373
MICROORGANISMS: THE INVISIBLE WORLD (Videocassette). Pyramid
Media 6353 ISBN 1-55981-483-7, 1995. 1/2" VHS videocassette color
(12min).
> Microscopic close-ups of one celled animals such as a amoebae and
> paramecia along with bacteria and viruses bring these hidden
> creatures into the classroom. Students will understand what
> multiplication by division means and how retro viruses are different
> from the common cold virus. Live action footage is supplemented by
> drawings that explain or elaborate salient points.
> SUBJ: Microorganisms./ Microscope and microscopy.

579   Ph-2 A/11 $16.98   L   KC374
SILVERSTEIN, ALVIN. Monerans and protists. By Alvin, Virginia, and
Robert Silverstein. Twenty-First Century ISBN 0-8050-3521-4; In Canada:
Fitzhenry & Whiteside, 1996. 64p. col. ill. (Kingdoms of life).
> Includes glossary and index.
> Explains two kingdoms on life's borderline and the difficulty science
> has in assigning exact labels to creatures which have both plantlike
> and animal-like characteristics. Well illustrated chapters discuss viruses,
> bacteria, diatoms, algae, and more, highlighting their interdependence
> and interaction with other life forms. A clear presentation of difficult
> material. Probably more than the average student wants to know, but
> enticing to the independent learner.
> SUBJ: Microbiology./ Microorganisms.

579   Ph-1 3-8/7 $15.00   T   KC375
SNEDDEN, ROBERT. Yuck!: a big book of little horrors. Photos by
Science Photo Library. Simon & Schuster ISBN 0-689-80676-0, 1996.
unp. col. ill.
> Using a monster theme, the author produces weird, devilish
> micromarvels magnified out of reality. Close-ups of buttered toast,
> flower parts, Post-it notes, and compact discs document an unknown
> universe that only the microscope can uncover. Each subject is given a
> foldout page that reveals its true identity. Wonderful color, terrific
> subject matter, and interesting science make a champion combination.
> SUBJ: Microscope and microscopy.

579   Ph-1 3-A/7 $16.00   L   KC376
TOMB, HOWARD. MicroAliens: dazzling journeys with an electron
microscope. By Howard Tomb and Dennis Kunkel. Illus. by Tracy
Dockray. Farrar, Straus & Giroux ISBN 0-374-34960-6; In Canada:
HarperCollins, 1993. 79p. ill.
> Includes bibliography.
> Using new technology, scientists continue to discover unbelievable
> wonders in the microscopic world. Subjects vary from bees to dust
> mites and from pollen to feathers while exploring watery
> environments, the backyard, inside a house, and inside and outside
> the human body. Readers will be mesmerized by these startling
> electron microscope photographs (necessarily in black & white) and
> enjoy conjuring up personal incredible journeys. Practical to use for
> biology and anatomy classes as well as art classes.
> SUBJ: Microscope and microscopy.

579.2   Ph-3 5-A/8 $15.95   L   KC377
FACKLAM, HOWARD. Viruses. By Howard and Margery Facklam.
Twenty-First Century ISBN 0-8050-2856-0; In Canada: Fitzhenry &
Whiteside, 1994. 64p. col. ill. (Invaders).
> Includes glossary, bibliography and index.
> Illustrates how tiny viral invaders package and execute their deadly
> punch. Virus biology is explained along with the history of discovery,
> grisly epidemics, and mutations. Valuable for information on HIV and
> AIDS.
> SUBJ: Viruses./ Virus diseases./ Diseases.

579.3   Ph-3 5-A/9 $15.95   L   KC378
FACKLAM, HOWARD. Bacteria. By Howard and Margery Facklam.
Twenty-First Century ISBN 0-8050-2857-9; In Canada: Fitzhenry &
Whiteside, 1994. 64p. col. ill. (Invaders).
> Includes glossary, bibliography and index.
> Documents that bacteria are omnipresent, even 8,000 feet
> underwater. Describes how organisms are harnessed to treat sewage,
> produce macrofibers, and process food. Also includes explanations of
> genetic engineering: treating humans with growth hormones, making
> insulin, and solving agricultural problems. Valuable for informing
> future citizens of "the brave new world." Useful in all discussions of
> environmental studies, current medical breakthroughs, and
> consciousness raising.
> SUBJ: Bacteria./ Microbiology.

VCR 579.4   Ph-2 5-6 $49.00   OD KC379
SMALLER THAN THE EYE CAN SEE (Videocassette). Insights Visual
Productions 304, 1989. 1/2" VHS videocassette color (14min).
> Includes teacher's guide.
> The amoeba, paramecium and hydra come to life under the
> microscope. This is a good introduction to microorganisms and how
> they move, eat and reproduce. Useful for classrooms with and without
> microscopes.
> SUBJ: Microorganisms./ Microscope and microscopy.

579.5   Ph-2 4-8/8 $16.98   L   KC380
SILVERSTEIN, ALVIN. Fungi. By Alvin, Virginia, and Robert Silverstein.
Twenty-First Century ISBN 0-8050-3520-6; In Canada: Fitzhenry &
Whiteside, 1996. 64p. col. ill. (Kingdoms of life).
> Includes glossary and index.
> Presents all the fungi fit to print: prime slime, black molds, orphans,
> fairy rings, and more. Eleven chapters demystify these
> underappreciated life forms that inhabit the kingdom below plants.
> Grow some molds and mildew or saute some mushrooms to
> popularize this information-packed book.
> SUBJ: Fungi.

579.6   Ph-1 3-A/6 $16.95   T   KC381
ARNOLD, KATYA. Katya's book of mushrooms. By Katya Arnold with
Sam Swope. Illus. by Katya Arnold. Henry Holt ISBN 0-8050-4136-2; In
Canada: Fitzhenry & Whiteside, 1997. 45p. col. ill.
> Includes glossary, bibliography and index.
> Selectors' Choice, 21st ed.
> Exuberantly written by an avowed mushroom lover/hunter, this book
> will inspire all readers to take a careful, closer look at fungi. "I am
> amazed by how clean and perfectly shaped they are, a true art of
> nature. They are wonderful to hold." (p.8) Joyful illustrations
> accompany directions on identifying and locating morsels such as King
> Boletes, Polypores, and Destroying Angels. Author continually cautions
> about not eating what is not positively identified and stresses the
> need to use good guidebooks. Enthusiasm for the subject is
> contagious.
> SUBJ: Mushrooms.

579.6   Ph-3 K-2/2 $9.98   L   KC382
WATTS, BARRIE. Mushroom. Silver Burdett ISBN 0-3820-9287-2, 1986.
24p. col. ill. (Stopwatch books).

Includes index.
Colorful photographs of growing mushrooms document this plant's idiosyncrasies. Vocabulary words: gill, spore, button, cap, and thread, are aptly presented so the youngest child will learn. Presentation is basic but does not talk down.
SUBJ: Mushrooms.

580   Ph-2 3-A/7 $15.00 T KC383
BURNIE, DAVID. Plant. Photos by Andrew McRobb, Karl Shone, and Dave King. Knopf ISBN 0-394-82252-8, 1989. 64p. col. ill. (Eyewitness books).
Includes index.
The magical world of plants and flowers unfolds with dramatic color photographs parading across every page. Discusses pollination, adaptation, and more. Will be useful for all levels of horticulture study.
SUBJ: Plants.

580   Ph-2 P-4/5 $13.95 T KC384
DIETL, ULLA. Plant-and-grow project book. Sterling ISBN 0-8069-0456-9; In Canada: Sterling c/o Canadian Manda, 1993. 48p. col. ill.
Includes index.
Grow corn and cotton on a window sill; or, better yet, sprout your initials on cotton with cress seeds. Illustrates a variety of easy-to-grow plants and seeds that children can successfully cultivate. Growing inexpensive seeds in the classroom can become part of writing, math, science, and art activities. Younger gardeners will need help with the wordy text.
SUBJ: Botany--Experiments./ Plants--Experiments./ Seeds--Experiments./ Botany projects./ Science projects./ Experiments.

580   Ph-1 A/7 $17.95 L KC385
DOW, LESLEY. Incredible plants. Consulting editor: Dr. Roger Carolin. Nature Company/Time-Life Books ISBN 0-7835-4799-4, 1997. 64p. col. ill., maps. (Nature Company discoveries library).
Includes glossary and index.
Lush view of botany with a center fold-out of the rainforest. Explains the plant kingdom, different habitats, and human exploitation. Oversized pages are replete with information about oddities such as bizarre never-ending leaves and scientific concepts such as cross fertilization. Good for browsing and useful for all plant and habitat discussions. For environmental studies.
SUBJ: Plants.

VCR 580 Ph-2 4-6 $150.00 OD KC386
FLOWER TO SEED (Videocassette). Churchill Films, 1985. 1/2" VHS videocassette color (9min).
Time-lapse photography, labeled still photographs, and animation are used to show pollination and fertilization on a cherry tree which leads to fruit and seeds. Attractive photography, good pace, and appropriate narration make this a good choice for botany units.
SUBJ: Botany.

580   Ph-2 P-2/1 $15.89 L KC387
JORDAN, HELENE J. How a seed grows. Rev. ed. Illus. by Loretta Krupinski. HarperCollins ISBN 0-06-020185-1; In Canada: HarperCollins, 1992. 31p. col. ill. (Let's-read-and-find-out science book).
Spanish edition COMO CRECE UNA SEMILLA available from Harper Arco Iris (ISBN 0-06-445145-3, 1996).
Simple experiments with seeds planted inside soil filled eggshells lead children to discover how seeds germinate, form roots and shoots, and finally emerge as recognizable plants. A must accompaniment to spring planting.
SUBJ: Seeds./ Spanish language materials.

580   Ph-3 A/7 $13.93 L KC388
LERNER, CAROL. Plant families. Morrow ISBN 0-688-07882-6, 1989. 32p. col. ill.
Includes glossary.
Presents twelve common plant families (species grouped together because of likenesses); explains their characteristics; and includes a life-sized botanical illustration on facing pages. This beautiful, specialized book encourages careful observance of nature and may spur interest in botanical science.
SUBJ: Plants--Identification./ Botany.

580   Ph-2 2-4/6 $19.95 L KC389
OVERBECK, CYNTHIA. How seeds travel. Photos by Shabo Hani. Lerner ISBN 0-8225-1474-5, 1982. 48p. col. ill. (Lerner natural science book).
Includes glossary and index.
Explains plant fertilization and investigates seed dispersal by "wings," hairs, water, barbs, animals and splitting pods. Many colorful illustrations of all the plants analyzed.
SUBJ: Seeds--Dispersal./ Plants--Reproduction.

VCR 580 Ph-3 4-A $149.00 OD KC390
PLANTS: ANGIOSPERMS (Videocassette). Yellow Brick Road/dist. by Human Relations Media 5140-VS, 1990. 1/2" VHS videocassette color (29min). (Biology live!).
Includes teacher's guide.
Covers most aspects of elementary botany by reviewing the world of flowering plants, the source of all our grains, fruits, vegetables and nuts. Animation helps explain fertilization, the differences between monocots and dicots, and annuals, biennials and perennials. Viewing time should be halved with time allowed for discussion and reinforcement.
SUBJ: Botany./ Plants.

580   Ph-1 4-6/6 $13.95 T KC391
RAHN, JOAN ELMA. Plants up close. Houghton Mifflin ISBN 0-395-31677-4, 1981. 119p. ill.
The physical characteristics of the tulip, the sugar maple, the butternut squash, the sunflower, and the Rose of Sharon are examined to show how they contribute to the plants continuing growth. The format of the book is excellent, with the descriptive text placed opposite the clarifying photographs.
SUBJ: Plants./ Botany.

580   Ph-2 5-A/7 $16.98 L KC392
SILVERSTEIN, ALVIN. Plants. By Dr. Alvin, Virginia, and Robert Silverstein. Twenty-First Century ISBN 0-8050-3519-2; In Canada: Fitzhenry & Whiteside, 1996. 64p. col. ill. (Kingdoms of life).
Includes glossary and index.
Twelve chapters cover the plant kingdom, evolution, reproduction, pharmacology, and more; information goes beyond a text book presentation. Book would have benefited from the inclusion of "hands on" activities. For research and reports.
SUBJ: Plants./ Botany.

580   Ph-1 3-8/8 $15.95 T KC393
TAYLOR, BARBARA. Incredible plants. DK Publishing ISBN 0-7894-1505-4, 1997. 44p. col. ill. (Inside guides).
Includes glossary and index.
Seventeen doublespread illustrations expose plant secrets with amazing three-dimensional models that show the internal structures of plants and cutaway drawings that reveal pollination, seed production, fungal anatomy, and symbiotic relationships. Documents the diversity of plants and their dramatic adaptive abilities from water storage to defense. Useful in any and all plant studies.
SUBJ: Plants./ Botany.

580   Ph-1 P-A/A $14.95 T KC394
VISUAL DICTIONARY OF PLANTS. DK Publishing ISBN 1-56458-016-4, 1992. 64p. col. ill. (Eyewitness visual dictionaries).
Includes index.
Selectors' Choice, 19th ed.
All the intricateness and diversification of the plant kingdom are revealed in cut-away pictures, micrographs of cross sections, drawings of plant cells, and beautiful nature photographs. Strangers such as epiphytic and parasitic plants are demystified while common leaves are shown to be exotically varied. Pictures are carefully labeled and artistically arranged. Young readers can dip in and read what interests them. Science teachers can discuss wetlands, flowering plants, plant classification, structure, and growth. When it is impossible to demonstrate with live plant material, this is the next best thing to use; the large format can be seen from the back of the class.
SUBJ: Plants./ Botany--Anatomy.

VCR 580 Ph-3 3-6 $79.00 OD KC395
WHAT IS A PLANT? (Videocassette). National Geographic 51453, 1991. 1/2" VHS videocassette color (15min). (Kingdom of plants).
Includes teacher's guide.
Introduces plant physiology and reproduction using common and uncommon plants. Uses animation to explain photosynthesis. Discusses ferns, leaf veins, and pollination along with special environmental adaptations.
SUBJ: Plants./ Plants--Reproduction./ Photosynthesis./ Botany.

VCR 580 Ph-2 K-3 $79.95 OD KC396
WONDERS OF GROWING PLANTS. 3rd ed. (Videocassette). Churchill Media/SVE C80429-HAVT ISBN 0-7932-3070-5, 1992. 1/2" VHS videocassette color (12min). (Wonders of discovery series).
Includes teacher's guide.
Includes public performance rights.
Also available in CAV videodisc format (C80429-LASR), $99.95.
Through time-lapse photography, a teacher and her class watch bean plants grow and learn how plants reproduce from seeds, stems, and leaves. Snappy songs and upbeat students both entertain and teach.
SUBJ: Plants./ Botany.

NONFICTION

581.4   Ph-2 A/9 $24.95 T KC397
CAPON, BRIAN. Plant survival: adapting to a hostile world. Timber Press ISBN 0-88192-283-8, 1994. 132p. col. ill.
> Includes glossary and index.
> Good overview of plant survival tactics in various habitats including forests, tundras, jungles, deserts, and underwater. Since plants cannot get up and walk away from hostile conditions, adaptation is the answer to their problems. "During their long occupation of our planet, plants have had plenty of practice in coping with environmental crises." (p.125) Detailed information and pastel drawings impart latest botanical findings. Salient points are summed up at the end of each chapter. Useful for environmental studies when studying biomes (especially the pages on leaf changes in the deciduous forest) and the necessity of biodiversity.
> SUBJ: Plants./ Adaptation (Biology)./ Ecology.

581.4   Ph-2 K-3/4 $14.95 L KC398
GIBBONS, GAIL. From seed to plant. Holiday House ISBN 0-8234-0872-8, 1991. unp. col. ill.
> Precise explanations of pollination, germination and seed dispersal enlivened with full page illustrations perfectly in tune with the text. Good fit with primary plant studies.
> SUBJ: Seeds./ Germination./ Plants.

581.4   Ph-2 4-6/9 $19.95 L KC399
JOHNSON, SYLVIA A. How leaves change. Photos by Yuko Sato. Lerner ISBN 0-8225-1483-4, 1986. 48p. col. ill. (Lerner natural science book).
> Includes glossary and index.
> Clear, colorful illustrations complement a well-written text which explores the growth of leaves and the autumn transformation of deciduous trees. An important addition to any elementary Fall unit.
> SUBJ: Leaves./ Fall foliage./ Seasons.

CE 581.4   Ph-1 P-4/2 $14.89 L KC400
MAESTRO, BETSY. Why do leaves change color? Illus. by Loretta Krupinski. HarperCollins ISBN 0-06-022874-1; In Canada: HarperCollins, 1994. 32p. col. ill. (Let's-read-and-find-out science book).
> Includes directory.
> Read-along kit available from HarperChildren's Audio (ISBN 0-69470-080-0, 1996). 1 paperback book, 1 sound cassette (10min), $7.95.
> Includes information on chlorophyll loss, leaf pigments made from extra stored sugars, and changes due to weather and light factors. Does not explain how leaves fall from trees. Provides useful instructions for leaf rubbings and pressings. Use with all autumn units and tree studies.
> SUBJ: Leaves./ Fall foliage.

VCR 581.4   Ph-3 K-3 $79.00 OD KC401
WHAT IS A LEAF? (Videocassette). National Geographic 51454, 1991. 1/2" VHS videocassette color (15min). (Kingdom of plants).
> Includes Teacher's Guide.
> Through animation and natural photography, students see that a leaf's job is photosynthesis. Brief but informative; for botany collections that need this format.
> SUBJ: Leaves./ Photosynthesis.

581.6   Ph-2 4-8/7 $16.95 T KC402
FORSYTH, ADRIAN. How monkeys make chocolate: foods and medicines from the rainforest. Owl Books/dist. by Firefly ISBN 1-895688-45-0; In Canada: Greey de Pencier/dist. by Firefly, 1995. 48p. col. ill.
> Includes index.
> Illustrates connections between rainforest people, plants, and animals, demonstrating that there is much to learn about undiscovered natural chemicals hiding in tropical plants. Perfect for extending rainforest lessons for independent learners who have mastered the basics. Coverage of chocolate, spices, and nuts will add interest to all nutrition and social studies units.
> SUBJ: Wild plants, Edible./ Medicinal plants.

581.6   Ph-3 4-A/6 $12.95 T KC403
LERNER, CAROL. Moonseed and mistletoe: a book of poisonous wild plants. Morrow ISBN 0-688-07307-7, 1988. 30p. col. ill.
> Includes index.
> Reviews common poisonous plants illustrated with colored botanical drawings. Students would probably do better with a plant field guide but there is something attractive about having all the baddies in one place.
> SUBJ: Poisonous plants.

581.6   Ph-2 5-6/9 $14.93 L KC404
LERNER, CAROL. Plants that make you sniffle and sneeze. Morrow ISBN 0-688-11490-3, 1993. 32p. col. ill.
> Includes bibliography and index.
> The three major groups of plants which are the culprits in causing hay fever--grasses, weeds, and trees and bushes--are examined in this handsome and informative discussion. Fine botanical drawings in delicate color accompany the well-organized introduction to pollen production and the ways pollen becomes airborne. The slim, attractive volume is a solid presentation on plant structures and propagation as well as an interesting account of allergies.
> SUBJ: Hay-fever plants./ Pollen./ Hay fever./ Allergy.

582.13   Ph-2 3-5/5 $15.95 L KC405
KELLY, M. A. Child's book of wildflowers. Illus. by Joyce Powzyk. Four Winds/Macmillan ISBN 0-02-750142-6; In Canada: Maxwell Macmillan, 1992. unp. col. ill.
> Depicts two dozen common wildflowers from black-eyed Susan to wild rose giving Latin and variant names, blooming time, size, habitat, and close to full-size color drawings. Use in the classroom to identify plants such as Queen Anne's lace that frequently appear in stories and to generate new collectors and flower lovers.
> SUBJ: Wild flowers.

582.13   Ph-3 3-6/8 $18.43 L KC406
LANDAU, ELAINE. State flowers: including the Commonwealth of Puerto Rico. Watts ISBN 0-531-20059-0; In Canada: Watts, 1992. 64p. col. ill.
> Includes glossary, bibliography and index.
> State flowers march across the pages in alphabetical order by their states. Information includes botanical name, habitat, and date of offical adoption along with occasional historic facts. All plants are not given equal coverage, and some are very shortchanged. Unfortunately, since no information is given on height or growth habits, it is impossible to realize the differences among the plants. A special interest purchase.
> SUBJ: State flowers./ Flowers./ Emblems, State.

582.13   Ph-1 3-6 $17.95 T KC407
NIERING, WILLIAM A. Audubon Society field guide to North American wildflowers, Eastern Region. By William A. Niering and Nancy Olmstead. Knopf ISBN 0-394-50432-1; In Canada: Random House, 1979. 887p. col. ill. (Audubon Society field guides).
> Includes glossary and index.
> This excellent guide for beginners covers the continent with the Rocky Mountains as dividing line. The user identifies a specimen first by color, then by sub-group of shape, thus locating a color photograph of the flower and a page reference for the full text description. More than seven hundred photographs are provided. Indexed by common and scientific names. Designed for easy carrying. A duplicate copy is recommended for the reference collection.
> SUBJ: Wild flowers.

582.13   Ph-1 3-6 $17.95 T KC408
SPELLENBERG, RICHARD. Audubon Society field guide to North American wildflowers, Western Region. Knopf ISBN 0-394-50431-3; In Canada: Random House, 1979. 883p. col. ill. (Audubon Society field guides).
> Includes glossary and index.
> This excellent guide for beginners covers the continent west of the Rocky Mountains. The user identifies a specimen first by color, then by sub-group of shape, thus locating a color photograph of the flower and a page reference for the full text description. More than seven hundred photographs are provided. Indexed by common and scientific names. Designed for easy carrying. A duplicate copy is recommended for the reference collection.
> SUBJ: Wild flowers.

582.16   Ph-2 K-6/7 $15.99 L KC409
BURNIE, DAVID. Tree. Photos by Peter Chadwick. Knopf ISBN 0-394-99617-8, 1988. 64p. col. ill. (Eyewitness books).
> Includes index.
> Spanish version EL ARBOL available from Santillana (ISBN 84-372-3708-4, 1995).
> "Discover the life of a tree in close-up--from tiny seed to forest giant to woody skeleton" (cover). Even though the information will be over the heads of many primary graders, the wonderful pictures testify to the nature of broadleaves, conifers, and palms. Use as a classroom field guide to match the real thing to its picture.
> SUBJ: Trees./ Spanish language materials.

PIC 582.16   Ph-3 2-6 $70.00 OD KC410
CHRISTIANSEN, CANDACE. Sky tree portfolio: science and art (Picture). By Candace Christiansen and Thomas Locker. Sky Tree Press, 1995. 14 study prints color (16"x20").
> A unique combination of text and art prints documents natural beauty. Illustrations from HarperCollin's book, SKY TREE, are separately packaged in a portfolio of 14 prints. The artwork depicts

one tree's relationship to its surroundings, seasonal and nocturnal changes, and natural beauty. Each print lists discussion questions to involve student's emotional response as well as to convey scientific learning such as the importance of the replenishment of oxygen to the atmosphere. Try discussing one painting at a time and then posting each side by side to create a panorama of natural phenomena. Aside from science and art classes, the duo would enhance the reading of WALK TWO MOONS in which the heroine is mystically bonded to trees. Mary Lynn Woods' companion study guide, SKY TREE PORTFOLIO GUIDE, outlines various art and science related activities, with step-by-step directions, which expand the uses of the portfolio. Especially valuable for the urban audience which is often divorced from nature. For environmental studies.
Companion book for the portfolio is SKY TREE: SEEING SCIENCE THROUGH ART (HarperCollins ISBN 0-06-024884-X, 1995, $15.89).
SUBJ: Trees./ Seasons./ Art and science./ Art appreciation.

582.16   Ph-3 5-8/9 $16.95   T   KC411
DOWDEN, ANNE OPHELIA. Blossom on the bough: a book of trees. Ticknor & Fields ISBN 0-395-68375-0, c1975, 1994. 71p. col. ill., map. Includes index.
Here is a parade of majestic plants that we often stroll right by and take for granted. Dowden's superb botanical illustrations explore trees from the Northeast to California, giving close-up views of 50 trees--leaves, seeds, flowers, fruits, and branches. Especially appropriate for advanced students.
SUBJ: Trees./ Forests and forestry.

582.16   Ph-3 P-1/4 $14.95   L   KC412
EHLERT, LOIS. Red leaf, yellow leaf. Harcourt Brace Jovanovich ISBN 0-15-266197-2; In Canada: Harcourt Brace c/o Canadian Manda, 1991. unp. col. ill.
Cutouts and collages bring a sugar maple tree to life. Minimum text and vibrant pages make it a surefire hit among primary dendrologists. Welcome addition to fall leaf units.
SUBJ: Trees.

582.16   Ph-2 1-4/2 $13.95   L   KC413
HALL, ZOE. Apple pie tree. Illus. by Shari Halpern. Blue Sky Press/Scholastic ISBN 0-590-62382-6; In Canada: Scholastic, 1996. unp. col. ill.
Bright cut-paper collages and simple text explain how an apple tree blossoms and yields fruit. Pie recipe is included. Use with tree, nutrition, or seasonal units.
SUBJ: Apples./ Cookery--Apples./ Fruit trees./ Pollination by insects.

582.16   Ph-1 1-5/6 $13.95   L   KC414
HISCOCK, BRUCE. Big tree. Atheneum ISBN 0-689-31598-8; In Canada: Collier Macmillan, 1991. unp. col. ill.
A combination of fact and fiction traces the events during the growth of a 200-year-old sugar maple. Readers see how the seedling sprouted in Revolutionary War times, shaded a pioneer's home in the 1800s, and is now spreading its branches over a 1990s family reunion picnic. Enhances understanding of the passage of time and intimately relates nature to human history.
SUBJ: Trees--Life cycle.

582.16   Ph-3 3-6/6 $8.95   P   KC415
JORGENSON, LISA. Grand trees of America: our state and champion trees. Roberts Rinehart ISBN 1-879373-15-7, 1992. 120p. ill.
Each state's official tree is illustrated in full view with smaller drawings of its leaves, flowers, fruit, nuts, and cones. Descriptions are given for leaves, flowers, bark and shape along with statistics for height and diameter and year of designation. Special information is listed for championship trees including how to go about nominating a tree for this status. Topic is thoroughly covered, and book offers original input to the study of fall leaves and trees. For state reports as well as tree units.
SUBJ: Trees.

CE 582.16   Ph-3 P-2/3 $14.89   L   KC416
LAUBER, PATRICIA. Be a friend to trees. Illus. by Holly Keller. HarperCollins ISBN 0-06-021529-1; In Canada: HarperCollins, 1994. 32p. col. ill. (Let's-read-and-find-out science book).
Read-along kit available from HarperChildren's Audio (ISBN 0-69470-047-9, 1996). 1 paperback book, 1 sound cassette (9min), $7.95.
An introduction to trees that documents their value. Touches on conservation, wood products, and animal needs. Use to supplement units about autumn and for environmental studies.
SUBJ: Trees.

582.16   Ph-1 3-6 $18.00   T   KC417
LITTLE, JR., ELBERT L. Audubon Society field guide to North American trees, Eastern Region. Photos by Sonja Bullaty, et al. Knopf ISBN 0-394-50760-6; In Canada: Random House, 1980. 714p. col. ill. Includes glossary and index.
This splendid guide for the beginner, along with the author's companion volume AUDUBON SOCIETY FIELD GUIDE TO NORTH AMERICAN TREES, WESTERN REGION (ISBN 0-394-50761-4), covers the continent with the Rocky Mountains as the dividing line. Four keys are provided for tree identification: leaf, flower, fruit and cones, autumn leaf color--with color photographs of each applicable characteristic. The photographs arranged by family. Index includes both common and scientific names. Format is designed for easy carrying. A duplicate copy is recommended for the reference collection.
SUBJ: Trees--Identification./ Trees--North America.

582.16   Ph-3 K-2/4 $13.89   L   KC418
MAESTRO, BETSY. How do apples grow? Illus. by Giulio Maestro. HarperCollins ISBN 0-06-020056-1; In Canada: HarperCollins, 1992. 32p. col. ill. (Let's-read-and-find-out science book).
Watch an apple tree bud and unfold into an abundance of blossoms which are fertilized and then form fruit. Flower parts and the pollination process are accurately drawn and explained. Use for units on trees, flowers, and fruit especially during fall apple-eating time.
SUBJ: Apples./ Plants--Development.

582.16   Ph-2 3-6/6 $15.95   L   KC419
MARKLE, SANDRA. Outside and inside trees. Bradbury ISBN 0-02-762313-0; In Canada: Maxwell Macmillan, 1993. 40p. col. ill. Includes glossary/index.
Nature photographs side-by-side with color-enhanced, magnified details show the reader unique views of tree bark, roots, buds, and leaves while educating about biology. Comprehensive, sequential presentation is attractive and interesting enough to read for enjoyment as well as a science assignment. Offers a lot of science despite its picture book appearance.
SUBJ: Trees.

582.16   Ph-2 P-2/3 $14.95   L   KC420
OPPENHEIM, JOANNE. Have you seen trees? Illus. by Jean and Mou-sien Tseng. Scholastic ISBN 0-590-46691-7; In Canada: Scholastic, 1995. unp. col. ill.
Rhythmic, rhyming text calls all readers to witness the beauty of trees through seasonal changes. Introduces diverse vocabulary: bole, ironwood, chokecherry, and more. Final pages list 16 familiar trees, picturing both a leaf and the mature plant. For reading aloud.
SUBJ: Trees./ Seasons.

582.16   Ph-2 3-6/3 $14.89   L   KC421
PINE, JONATHAN. Trees. Illus. by Ken Joudrey. HarperCollins ISBN 0-06-021469-4; In Canada: HarperCollins, 1995. 48p. ill. (HarperCollins nature study book).
Close-up look at seven familiar trees will nurture young tree lovers. Each tree is given three pages of text and one full page illustration. Use "Pine for evergreen" at Christmas and "Willow can come home with you" with WIND IN THE WILLOWS. Final pages discuss roots and leaves.
SUBJ: Trees.

582.16   Ph-3 P-2/4 $15.93   L   KC422
PLUCKROSE, HENRY. Trees. Childrens Press ISBN 0-516-08121-7; In Canada: Childrens Press, 1994. 32p. col. ill. (Walkabout).
Includes index.
Picture-packed pages show tree varieties, fruits, products, and beauty. Text is minimal. Readers will learn how to observe and value the trees that surround them.
SUBJ: Trees.

582.16   Ph-2 3-6/6 $14.95   T   KC423
RUSSO, MONICA. Tree almanac: a year-round activity guide. Photos by Kevin Byron. Sterling ISBN 0-8069-1252-9; In Canada: Sterling/dist. by Canadian Manda, 1993. 128p. ill. (some col.).
Includes glossary and index.
View trees throughout the four seasons while learning about their physiology, habitats, and use. Encourages readers to observe, collect, and experiment while fostering a love of nature. Use in December to talk about Christmas tree farms or late in summer while harvesting fruit and nuts. Includes activities throughout the year.
SUBJ: Trees./ Seasons./ Handicraft.

582.16   Ph-3 2-6 $20.00   T OD KC424
WOODS, MARY LYNN. Sky tree portfolio guide: an interdisciplinary environmental curriculum. Illus. by Audrey Matteson and Faith Matteson-

Shores. Heritage Education Foundation, 1995. 40p. ill. (spiral bound). (Partners with the earth curriculum).
Includes bibliographies.
SUBJ: Trees./ Seasons./ Art and science./ Art appreciation.

583   Ph-2 5-8/6 $16.95   L   KC425
AASENG, NATHAN. Meat-eating plants. Enslow ISBN 0-89490-617-8, 1996. 48p. col. ill. (Weird and wacky science).
Includes glossary, bibliography and index.
Meet green monster killer fungi and other carnivorous plants that amaze and delight. In the quest for survival, plants grow bladders, spew poison, and spring traps while anchored in the ground! Try growing a sundew or Venus's-flytrap in the classroom to prove fact is stranger than fiction. Excellent photographs and lots of information coupled with scientific vocabulary make this a good recommendation for gifted students.
SUBJ: Carnivorous plants.

583   Ph-2 K-2/2 $9.98   L   KC426
BACK, CHRISTINE. Bean and plant. Photos by Barrie Watts. Silver Burdett ISBN 0-3820-9286-4, 1986. 24p. col. ill. (Stopwatch books).
Includes index.
Photographs and spare text trace the development of green beans from seeds to food. Because these seeds are so easy to germinate in the classroom, this book is especially useful for hands-on primary science. Could be interwoven with lessons on nutrition.
SUBJ: Beans--Development.

583   Ph-1 2-6/6 $15.95   L   KC427
BASH, BARBARA. Desert giant: the world of the saguaro cactus. Sierra Club/Little, Brown ISBN 0-316-08301-1; In Canada: Little, Brown, 1989. unp. col. ill. (Tree tales).
Focuses on the interrelationships of the cactus and desert dwellers. Beautiful illustrations make this strange giant plant come alive for every reader. Excellent for sharing aloud with primary students and a must for the study of food chains and the southwest desert.
SUBJ: Saguaro./ Cactus./ Desert ecology./ Ecology.

583   Ph-1 4-6/7 $19.95   L   KC428
JOHNSON, SYLVIA A. Morning glories. Photos by Yuko Sato. Lerner ISBN 0-8225-1462-1, 1985. 48p. col. ill. (Lerner natural science book).
Includes glossary and index.
Plant growth and development unfolds through vivid photographs and fine text via an examination of this often overlooked flower. Perfect for a read-aloud while students plant seeds, measure growth and gain first hand experience.
SUBJ: Morning glories./ Plants--Development./ Experiments.

583   Ph-3 5-6/7 $14.93   L   KC429
LERNER, CAROL. Cactus. Morrow ISBN 0-688-09637-9, 1992. 32p. col. ill.
Includes glossary and index.
This detailed examination of cacti has superior botanical drawings and explains the three subfamilies, how the plants work and reproduce, and where they grow. Develops a sensitivity to an often endangered plant. For students who might like cactus raising as a hobby and for libraries in the Southwest where cacti are common.
SUBJ: Cactus.

583   Ph-2 1-4/5 $13.89   L   KC430
LUCHT, IRMGARD. Red poppy. Translated by Frank Jacoby-Nelson. Hyperion ISBN 0-7868-2043-8, 1995. 27p. col. ill.
The poetry and lushness of a red field poppy's life cycle unfold in a closeup look at this accessible plant. Handsome illustrations reveal growth, pollination, and seed production. Will enhance all botany classes. Since the red poppy is a symbol of Memorial Day, it is an excellent choice for study.
SUBJ: Poppies./ Plants--Development.

583   Ph-2 1-6/6 $11.90   L   KC431
NIELSEN, NANCY J. Carnivorous plants. Watts ISBN 0-531-20056-6; In Canada: Watts, 1992. 63p. col. ill. (First book).
Includes directories, bibliography and index.
Highlights five plants: Venus's-flytrap, bladderworts, sundews, butterworts, and pitcher plants. Text explains their habits and environments then gives directions for growing along with a list of suppliers. Readers cannot help but become hooked on these plants that eat animals!
SUBJ: Carnivorous plants.

583   Ph-1 3-5/6 $19.95   L   KC432
OVERBECK, CYNTHIA. Carnivorous plants. Photos by Kiyoshi Shimizu. Lerner ISBN 0-8225-1470-2, 1982. 48p. col. ill. (Lerner natural science book).
Includes glossary and index.
Selectors' Choice, 14th ed.
Close-ups of the Venus flytrap, sundew, waterwheel, bladderwort, and pitcher plants take the reader into an exotic world where dazzling plants are equipped to kill. Wonderful pictures.
SUBJ: Carnivorous plants./ Plants.

583   Ph-3 2-6/6 $14.95   L   KC433
WEXLER, JEROME. Queen Anne's lace. Whitman ISBN 0-8075-6710-8; In Canada: General, 1994. 32p. col. ill.
The beautiful, abundant wildflower grows just about everywhere in Canada and the northern United States because of its ability to adapt to "various environmental conditions" (p. 7). A perfect classroom plant for dissection, especially in the fall when the "dead" seed heads will open and close depending upon water conditions. Close-up photography traces plant development. Couple with hands-on discovery to create many wildflower enthusiasts.
SUBJ: Queen Anne's lace./ Flowers.

583   Ph-2 3-6/7 $19.95   L   KC434
WINNER, CHERIE. Sunflower family. Photos by Sherry Shahan. Carolrhoda ISBN 1-57505-007-2, 1996. 48p. col. ill. (Carolrhoda nature watch book).
Includes glossary and index.
Learn about several species of the composite family, plant growth, seed production and dispersal, habitats, and usefulness. Along with sunflowers common plants such as ragweed, dandelion, and chicory are included. Good photographs accompany carefully developed text. Useful for botany study because these plants are easily found throughout town and country.
SUBJ: Composites (Plants)./ Sunflowers.

585   Ph-3 3-6/7 $16.95   L   KC435
BASH, BARBARA. Ancient ones: the world of the old-growth Douglas fir. Sierra Club ISBN 0-87156-561-7; In Canada: Sierra Club, 1994. unp. col. ill. (Tree tales).
Illustrates the drama of the Douglas fir--the seeds of which can only germinate in the aftermath of a forest fire, when sunlight is admitted to the forest floor. One of earth's largest living plants, it is home to a variety of wildlife, some only microscopic. Use in all forest studies, but especially when discussing the Pacific Northwest. For environmental studies.
SUBJ: Douglas fir./ Old growth forests./ Forest ecology.

585   Ph-2 3-6/7 $19.95   L   KC436
FISCHER-NAGEL, HEIDEROSE. Fir trees. By Heiderose and Andreas Fischer-Nagel. Carolrhoda ISBN 0-87614-340-0, 1989. 47p. col. ill. (Carolrhoda nature watch book).
Includes glossary and index.
Learn about conifers--where they grow, how they reproduce and what they contribute to the earth. Wonderful photographs document the majesty of these forest giants. An excellent book to use when studying plant reproduction and forest ecology. Also valuable for environmental studies such as air pollution, acid rain, and recycling. Be sure to share this aloud during Arbor Day.
SUBJ: Fir./ Trees./ Forest ecology./ Ecology.

585   Ph-2 K-3/3 $14.95   T   KC437
REED-JONES, CAROL. Tree in the ancient forest. Illus. by Christopher Canyon. Dawn Publications ISBN 1-883220-32-7; In Canada: Raincoast, 1995. unp. col. ill.
Employing the pattern from "This is the House that Jack Built," cumulative text celebrates the world of the ancient forest, using a Douglas fir and its inhabitants: truffles, voles, owls, squirrels, etc. Predictable text teaches sophisticated concepts of interdependence and food webs in a completely accessible context. After reading aloud, try creating a similar pattern story based on local flora and fauna. A fine meld of literature and science for primary students for environmental studies.
SUBJ: Douglas fir./ Old growth forests./ Forest ecology.

588   Ph-2 6/8 $19.95   L   KC438
JOHNSON, SYLVIA A. Mosses. Photos by Masana Izawa. Lerner ISBN 0-8225-1482-6, 1983. 48p. col. ill. (Lerner natural science book).
Includes glossary and index.
Reproducing through spores or vegetative propagation, mosses and liverworts are atypical though fairly common plants that flourish in damp environments. Detailing the reproduction processes in text and attractive color photographs, this title also documents these plants role in the ecological chain.
SUBJ: Mosses.

CDR 590   Ph-1 4-A $49.95   OD KC439
ANIMAL PLANET (CD-ROM). Discovery Channel Multimedia ISBN
1-56331-262-X, 1996. 1 CD-ROM color.
> Version 1.0.
> Includes user's guide.
> System requirements: Windows 3.1 or Windows 95 (includes 16-bit
> and 32-bit versions); 486 50MHz or faster; 8MB of RAM (16MB
> preferred); double-speed CD-ROM drive; Windows compatible sound
> card; mouse; SVGA monitor (256 colors); MS/PC DOS 3.1; hard
> drive (16MB free).
> This compendium of over 1,100 life forms presents basic information
> on habitats, food, enemies, and location in the world as well as a
> number of cross references. Features include a search engine, a note
> taking pad, a report writer, and BioWeb, a set of Internet links to
> pre-screened animal web sites. Works well with small groups, as a
> learning center, or the report writer can be used with an entire class.
> For environmental studies.
> SUBJ: Animals--Software./ Software--Animals./ Interactive media.

VCR 590.73   Ph-2 2-5 $14.95   KC440
BIG ZOO (Videocassette). VanDerKloot Film & Television/Little
Mammoth Media, 1995. 1/2" VHS videocassette color (45min).
> Includes public performance rights.
> Zoo animals, functions, and workers appear as a child narrates and
> other young children visit the Baltimore Zoo. Animal behaviors, diets,
> and habitats are briefly mentioned; and keepers, caretakers, and
> veterinarians are seen interacting with the animals and working behind
> the scenes. A concluding quiz reviews some of the animals visited. The
> quick skim of many animals and facts provides a good introduction to
> how zoos work and the particular needs of many animals.
> SUBJ: Zoos./ Zoo animals.

CE 590.73   Ph-1 K-2/4 $5.95   P   KC441
GIBBONS, GAIL. Zoo. HarperCollins ISBN 0-06-446096-7, 1991. unp.
col. ill.
> Sound filmstrip available from Live Oak Media (ISBN 0-87499-098-
> X), 60fr color, 1 sound cassette (8min), guide. $32.95.
> Read-along kit available from Live Oak Media (ISBN 0-87499-211-
> 7). 1 hardback book, 1 sound cassette (10min), $22.95.
> Provides a behind-the-scenes tour of a zoo showing the tasks
> performed by many different zoo workers. Numerous small, colorful
> pictures and an economical text describe the work of vendors, animal
> keepers, and the veterinarian. The care and feeding of the animals,
> the creation of new exhibits, and the work of zoos in animal
> conservation are among the many topics covered in this attractive
> introduction.
> SUBJ: Zoos.

590.73   Ph-1 P-2/3 $13.88   L   KC442
ORMEROD, JAN. When we went to the zoo. Lothrop, Lee & Shepard
ISBN 0-688-09879-7, 1991. unp. col. ill.
> Two children visit the zoo with their father, and the animals they see
> appear in both the center scene and handsome wide border frames.
> Gibbons, pelicans, elephants, otters, orangutangs, penguins, sea lions,
> and giraffes are among the animals observed in this pleasant picture
> book. A map of the zoo on the endpapers begins and ends the
> sunny, absorbing exploration.
> SUBJ: Zoos./ Zoo animals.

590.75   Ph-1 3-A/7 $14.93   L   KC443
CUTCHINS, JUDY. Are those animals real?: how museums prepare
wildlife exhibits. Rev. & updated ed. By Judy Cutchins and Ginny
Johnston. Morrow ISBN 0-688-12855-6, 1995. 40p. col. ill.
> Includes glossary and index.
> Gain an insider's view of how museums create wildlife replicas. With
> 40 full-color photographs, it offers greater appreciation of the artistic
> effort and taxidermy skills needed to prepare the most naturalistic
> displays. Wonderful to use with a group in conjunction with museum
> field trips and career studies.
> SUBJ: Taxidermy./ Museum techniques./ Zoological models.

CDR 591   Ph-2 K-3 $29.95   OD KC444
AMAZING ANIMALS (CD-ROM). DK Multimedia ISBN 0-7894-1718-9,
1997. 1 CD-ROM color.
> System requirements: Windows 3.1X or 95; 486DX/33MHz CPU;
> 8MB RAM (12MB recommended for Windows 95); 640x480 pixels,
> 256 colors (16-bit colors preferred); double-speed CD-ROM drive;
> 11MB available hard drive space; 8-bit sound card; loudspeakers or
> headphones; mouse.
> System requirements: Macintosh System 7.0+; 68LC040 25MHz CPU;
> 8MB RAM (12MB required for System 7.5+, and for PowerPC);
> 640x480 pixels, 256 colors (thousands of colors preferred); double-
> speed CD-ROM drive; 4MB available hard drive space; 8-bit audio;
> loudspeakers or headphones; mouse

Product (ISBN 0-7894-1718-9) runs on either Windows or Macintosh
compatible hardware.
> A toy box filled with options to match animals and facts, gather
> information from the expert book, take a photo safari, visit animal
> Internet sites, play a number of games, assemble masks, and design
> stationary are included in this CD. The ease of use makes the
> program work well with limited readers. Youngsters will enjoy this in a
> learning center or individual environment.
> SUBJ: Animals--Software./ Software--Animals./ Interactive media.

591   Ph-2 4-6/5 $11.95   L   KC445
CREAGH, CARSON. Things with wings. Time Life ISBN 0-7835-4838-9,
1996. 32p. col. ill. (Nature Company young discoveries library).
> "Weldon Owen Production."
> Insects, birds and mammals appear in this quick, colorful survey.
> Illustrations dominate the page while short entries briefly discuss the
> bodies and behavior of ladybugs, bees, fireflies, butterflies,
> hummingbirds, raptors, penguins, and bats. Also introduces winged
> birds that don't fly, animals that fly without wings, and prehistoric
> flying animals. A pleasant, but superficial, introduction to set readers
> thinking.
> SUBJ: Animals./ Animal flight./ Wings.

591   Ph-1 5-6/7 $17.00   L   KC446
FEW, ROGER. Macmillan animal encyclopedia for children. Macmillan
ISBN 0-02-762425-0; In Canada: Maxwell Macmillan, 1991. 120p. col.
ill., maps.
> Includes glossary and index.
> Which animals live in the tundra, in coniferous forests, in the
> grasslands of the world? Nine chapters define major habitats, showing
> where they occur on a world map, and then survey types of animals
> with selected species introduced in small photographs and brief
> captions. Copious bits of information develop very good profiles of
> the wildlife in these standard geographic regions while many different
> individual animals can be located through the index.
> SUBJ: Animals--Encyclopedias.

591   Ph-2 3-6/6 $14.00   T   KC447
GANERI, ANITA. Creature features. Illus. by Steve Fricker. Simon &
Schuster ISBN 0-689-81186-1; In Canada: Distican, 1997. 30p. col. ill.
(How it works).
> Includes index.
> Zany diagrams and simple captions explain the special body functions
> of ten animals. Smaller realistic diagrams accompany the larger views
> featuring the hardware of cows, chickens, snakes, spiders, kangaroos,
> elephants, octopuses, tortoises, bats, and hummingbirds. An opening
> doublespread introduces the major groups of vertebrates and
> invertebrates, and there's a concluding set of animal trivia. The
> humorous approach and common sense information make this
> entertaining and useful. Includes a poster which is easily detached.
> SUBJ: Animals--Miscellanea./ Animals--Physiology.

591   Ph-1 P-K $15.93   L   KC448
HOBAN, TANA. Children's zoo. Greenwillow ISBN 0-688-05204-5,
1985. unp. col. ill.
> Vivid portrayals of eleven zoo animals in a handsome album of
> photographs. Pictures are effectively framed in white on black pages
> and accompanied by key words describing each animal and giving its
> name (PENGUIN, black, white, waddles; SEAL, sleek, black, swims).
> A final page providing a chart of additional information on where
> each animal comes from, where it lives and what it eats rounds out a
> striking exercise in observation for young viewers.
> SUBJ: Animals.

591   Ph-2 K-4/3 $14.95   T   KC449
JENKINS, STEVE. Biggest, strongest, fastest. Ticknor & Fields ISBN
0-395-69701-8, 1995. unp. col. ill.
> Includes bibliography.
> Fleas and snakes, hummingbirds, and sun jellyfish are among the
> largest, strongest, smallest, and fastest animals shown in the
> handsome cut-paper collages of this collection of miscellaneous facts.
> The featured animal spreads across a lovely scene filling the double-
> page spread; a single sentence explains the animal's distinctive feature
> on one page, while the other page includes two or three facts and a
> small diagram comparing the animal's size to that of a human. A
> table of added facts at the back of the book rounds out a book that
> will work well for reading aloud or personal enjoyment by animal
> fans.
> SUBJ: Animals--Miscellanea.

591   Ph-3 5-6/8 $14.95   T   KC450
LACEY, ELIZABETH A. What's the difference?: a guide to some familiar
animal look-alikes. Illus. by Robert Shetterly. Clarion ISBN 0-395-56182-
5, 1993. 70p. ill.

Includes glossary, bibliography and index.
Alligator or crocodile? Bison or buffalo? Tortoise or turtle? Seven essays illustrated with vigorous, useful pen and ink drawings describe the similarities and differences in physical characteristics and behavior of pairs of animals which are similar in appearance. Short, informative and somewhat difficult introductions offer enjoyable reading to children with a serious interest in animals.
SUBJ: Animals./ Zoology.

591   Ph-2 4-6/6 $12.95   T   KC451
LONG, MATTHEW. Any bear can wear glasses: the spectacled bear and other curious creatures. By Matthew Long and Thomas Long. Illus. by Sylvia Long. Chronicle ISBN 0-8118-0809-2; In Canada: Raincoast, 1995. unp. col. ill.
Includes glossary.
"Any fox can travel...but there's only one flying fox" in this compendium of oddly named animals. Humorous color drawings make playful use of the animal's name while a facing page has an attractive realistic drawing and several paragraphs of information about the animal's body and behavior. Eleven entries include the spectacled bear, frilled lizard, ringtail cat, fiddler crab, and others. Children will enjoy the wordplay and the assortment of familiar and exotic animals in this nice presentation on animal observation, which could also be used to spark creative writing activities. Many of the animals are endangered species, making it suitable for environmental studies.
SUBJ: Endangered species./ Rare animals.

591   Ph-1 P-2/1 $15.00   L   KC452
MACDONALD, SUSE. Peck slither and slide. Gulliver/Harcourt Brace ISBN 0-15-200079-8; In Canada: Harcourt Brace c/o Canadian Manda, 1997. unp. col. ill.
Selectors' Choice, 21st ed.
Handsome tissue paper collages and action verbs in bold letters create an inviting guessing game to introduce ten wild animals. Penguins slide, beavers build, flamingos wade, snakes slither. The verb and a few visual clues appear on the first doublespread, the following sequence names and shows the full figures of the animals, and the concluding pages offer a paragraph of facts for each animal. The handsome pages will work beautifully for story hour audiences, and a wide age range will enjoy the guessing game in this imaginative introduction to fairly familiar wild animals.
SUBJ: Animals--Miscellanea./ Picture puzzles./ English language--Verb.

591   Ph-2 4-A/9 $17.99   L   KC453
MARTIN, JAMES. Living fossils: animals that have withstood the test of time. Illus. by Janet Hamlin. Crown ISBN 0-517-59867-1; In Canada: Random House, 1997. 48p. col. ill.
Includes index.
Meet the horseshoe crab, an arthropod that has been around for the past 300 million years or the nautilus, a cephalopod that has lived in the sea for 500 million years. What are the secrets of survival for these and other creatures with ancient lineage? Wonderful pictures and interesting text make this a page turner for even the least scientifically inclined. Lots of material for reading aloud. Make sure to booktalk this one.
SUBJ: Living fossils.

591   Ph-2 P-5/5 $14.95   T   KC454
POWELL, CONSIE. Bold carnivore: an alphabet of predators. Roberts Rinehart ISBN 1-57098-023-3; In Canada: Publisher Group West, 1995. unp. col. ill.
Includes glossary.
Striking paintings introduce 26 animals, each in its own habitat and surrounded by the animals it eats. The elf owl, fisher, grass spider, hawk, and others appear in handsome poses framed by insets depicting their possible prey. A brief statement describes each animal's eating or hunting habits, an introduction states how the food chain works, and the final page is a key naming all animals shown in each entry. The sumptuous survey, organized around the alphabetic scheme, offers many possibilities for personal enjoyment and science lessons on predators and habitats. For environmental studies.
SUBJ: Animals./ Alphabet.

591   Ph-1 P-2 $16.00   P   KC455
THORNHILL, JAN. Wildlife 1 2 3: a nature counting book. Simon & Schuster ISBN 0-671-67926-0, 1989. unp. col. ill.
Includes "Nature notes".
Lovely paintings, decoratively framed, depict numbered assemblages of animals from 1/One Panda to 1,000/One Thousand Tadpoles. The counting scheme (1-20, 25, 50, 100, 1000) is reinforced by incorporating in the frames the same number of animals shown in the larger scenes; the animals reappear in two final pyramids, and a concluding doublespread provides an added paragraph of information

on each animal for adult reading. Very appealing as a lesson in counting, an introduction to the animals, or enjoyable browsing.
SUBJ: Animals./ Counting.

591   Ph-2 P-2/3 $15.95   L   KC456
WADSWORTH, GINGER. One on a web: counting animals at home. Illus. by James M. Needham. Charlesbridge ISBN 0-88106-971-X, 1997. unp. col. ill.
Three baby robins in their nest are among the 20 domestic and wild animals appearing in this pleasant counting scheme. The picture layout with full or double-page gouache scenes includes a three part block of text for each animal: a bold numeral, an introductory sentence in large type naming the number and animal, and a descriptive paragraph of simple text. The design allows the numbers and simple statements to be used with younger children while young readers will go on to use the simple text.
SUBJ: Animals./ Counting.

CE 591   Ph-3 P-3 $5.95   T   KC457
100 WORDS ABOUT ANIMALS. Illus. by Richard Brown. Gulliver/ Harcourt Brace Jovanovich ISBN 0-15-200550-1, 1987. unp. col. ill.
Also available in Spanish MUCHAS PALABRAS SOBRE ANIMALES (ISBN 0-15-200531-5, 1987).
Read-along kit available from Live Oak (ISBN 0-87499-183-8, 1990) 1 hardbound book, 1 sound cassette (9min), $22.95.
Depicts 100 animals, grouping them by habitat (farm, prairie and desert, grasslands, shore, mountains, etc.). Each group is shown in a double-page spread, the only text consisting of the names of the animals in dark, bold letters. Prepared as a mass market title with a glossy board cover and slightly crude art work, this has homely appeal as a vocabulary building device and a simple lesson in natural history.
SUBJ: Animals--Pictorial works./ Spanish language materials.

591.3   Ph-2 K-2/4 $11.00   L   KC458
GREENWAY, SHIRLEY. Whose baby am I? Photos by Oxford Scientific Films. Ideals ISBN 0-8249-8577-X; In Canada: Ideals/dist. by Vanwell, 1992. 32p. col. ill. (Animals Q & A).
Includes index.
Cygnets, fawns, pups, and tadpoles are among baby animals which have different names than their parents. This simple survey uses small color photographs, a question-and-answer scheme, and very brief text to introduce 12 species. Uneven in execution but a useful simple lesson.
SUBJ: Animals--Infancy./ Animals--Miscellanea.

591.3   Ph-2 3-5/6 $15.89   L   KC459
SIMON, SEYMOUR. Wild babies. HarperCollins ISBN 0-06-023034-7; In Canada: HarperCollins, 1997. unp. col. ill.
Beautiful full-page photographs of 13 animal mothers and babies accompany a brief discussion of the way each species cares for its young. Explains the size and early capabilities of each animal and the length of time--if any--it will stay with its mother. The animals include marsupials, penguins, polar bears, baboons, frogs, alligators, and more. The attractive album is an appealing browsing item and useful for introducing the variety of animal family arrangements.
SUBJ: Animals--Infancy./ Parental behavior in animals.

VCR 591.4   Ph-2 3-5 $12.98   KC460
ANIMAL WEAPONS (Videocassette). DK Vision/Partridge Films ISBN 0-7894-1959-9, 1996. 1/2" VHS videocassette color (30min). (Amazing animals).
Closed captioned.
Henry the Lizard explores animal defenses from the familiar, porcupine's quills, to the exotic, acid-squirting termites. 3-D animation and live action photography are effectively combined in this production originally produced for television.
SUBJ: Animal weapons./ Animals--Habits and behavior.

591.4   Ph-2 K-2/4 $11.00   L   KC461
GREENWAY, SHIRLEY. Can you see me? Photos by Oxford Scientific Films. Ideals ISBN 0-8249-8575-3; In Canada: Ideals/dist. by Vanwell, 1992. 32p. col. ill. (Animals Q & A).
Includes index.
Photographs of various animals which are hard to see in their natural surroundings accompany simple questions and answers on how appearance aids survival. Spiders, stick insects, frogs, lions, birds, and other animals are seen in two-page or four-page sequences which include very brief text. The small volume is a good introduction to the idea of animal camouflage and a nice lesson in observation.
SUBJ: Camouflage (Biology).

591.4   Ph-1 2-5/5 $14.95   T   KC462
JOHNSON, JINNY. How big is a whale? Illus. by Michael Woods. Rand McNally ISBN 0-528-83729-X, 1995. 30p. col. ill. (Rand McNally for kids).
> "Marshall Edition."
> Includes index.
> Relative sizes of assorted insects, birds, reptiles, and mammals receive intriguing comparisons in the well planned drawings of this large flat presentation. Whales, tarantulas, giraffes, elephants, and butterflies are among the creatures whose size is explained in captions and short bits of text. Some scenes feature large and small examples together while other views show shadowy forms of humans and smaller animals imposed on the body of the featured animal to dramatically convey the sense of size. An attractive lesson in the concept of size.
> SUBJ: Size./ Animals.

VCR 591.4   Ph-2 3-6 $79.00   KC463
WHERE DO ANIMALS GO IN WINTER? (Videocassette). National Geographic 51743, 1995. 1/2" VHS videocassette color (15min).
> Includes teacher's guide.
> Closed captioned.
> Animals gather and store food. Some migrate, others build hives or hibernate in caves, while still others move to lower ground. Eventually the spring sun warms the earth, and the cycle of seasons begins once again. National Geographic's hallmark photography insures that viewers will acquire an appreciation and understanding of animal survival.
> SUBJ: Animals--Habits and behavior./ Adaptation (Biology)./ Winter.

CDR 591.47   Ph-2 4-A $39.95   OD KC464
ALEXANDER, R. MCNEILL. How animals move (CD-ROM). Discovery Channel Multimedia/Maris Multimedia ISBN 1-563331-218-2, 1995. 1 CD-ROM color.
> Includes user's guide.
> System requirements: IBM and compatibles: IBM compatible 386SX or higher processor; double-speed CD-ROM drive; 256 color VGA display monitor with "Thousands" color display recommended; 4MB of RAM with at least 2.5MB free (8MB recommended); Microsoft Windows 3.1 and MS-DOS 3.3 or higher; QuickTime for Windows 2.0 or above; Adlib and SoundBlaster compatible.
> System requirements: Macintosh: LCII and above; Performa, Centris and Quadra families; double-speed CD-ROM drive; System 7.0 or above; 4MB of RAM with at least 2.5MB free (8MB recommended); QuickTime 2.0 or above; 13" or larger color monitor with "Thousands" color display recommended.
> System requirements: PowerMac: 6100 with System 7.1.2 or above; 8MB of RAM; double-speed CD-ROM drive; 13" color monitor or larger with "Thousands" color display recommended; QuickTime 2.0 or above.
> Product (ISBN 1-563331-218-2) runs on either Windows or Macintosh compatible hardware.
> Over 250 superb multimedia clips explain the various ways animals can move including flying, climbing, jumping, and swimming. Complex vocabulary may need to be explained. Sixteen games reinforce the concepts. Works well with an entire class or with small groups.
> SUBJ: Animal locomotion--Software./ Software--Animal locomotion./ Animals--Physiology--Software./ Software--Animals--Physiology./ Biomechanics--Software./ Software--Biomechanics./ Interactive media.

591.47   Ph-2 2-4/6 $12.95   L   KC465
ARNOSKY, JIM. I see animals hiding. Scholastic ISBN 0-590-48143-6; In Canada: Scholastic, 1995. unp. col. ill.
> Soft paintings and simple text demonstrate how a variety of animals use camouflage techniques. Depicts how protective coloration and seasonal changes of color help birds, mammals, reptiles, and fish hide from their enemies. The simple lesson invites children to observe the natural world.
> SUBJ: Camouflage (Biology).

591.47   Ph-2 P-2/3 $14.95   L   KC466
RILEY, LINDA CAPUS. Elephants swim. Illus. by Steve Jenkins. Houghton Mifflin ISBN 0-395-73654-4, 1995. unp. col. ill.
> Pleasant collage illustrations and simple rhymed text show many animals as they spend time in or under water. "Hippos sink to the bottom to sleep./Wildebeests wade where the water's not deep." The picture book presentation, softly shaded and handsomely textured, ends with a swimming human and a small paragraph of facts about each of the animals. Simple, appealing views of the animals make this a nice choice for reading aloud to a group, and teachers of younger children will find good opportunities for discussing animal life.
> SUBJ: Animal swimming./ Animals--Habits and behavior.

591.47   Ph-2 4-6/6 $11.99   L   KC467
SOWLER, SANDIE. Amazing armored animals. Photos. by Jerry Young and Jane Burton. Knopf ISBN 0-679-92767-0, 1992. 29p. col. ill. (Eyewitness juniors).
> Includes index.
> Spanish version available from Bruno ASOMBROSOS ANIMALES ACORAZADOS (ISBN 84-216-2576-4, 1995).
> An attractive variety of shelled, spiny, and tough- skinned species illustrates this interesting introduction to animal defenses. Mammals, fish, insects, crustaceans, and reptiles of many sorts appear in large and small photographs and drawings accompanied by short annotations. The information is sketchy, but diverse, and the presentation is appealing.
> SUBJ: Armored animals./ Animal defenses./ Spanish language materials.

591.47   Ph-2 2-5/2 $18.95   L   KC468
YAMASHITA, KEIKO. Paws, wings, and hooves: mammals on the move. Photos by Isamu Sekido. Lerner ISBN 0-8225-2901-7, 1993. 24p. col. ill. (Science all around you).
> Includes glossary.
> Close-up views of "hands" and "feet" demonstrate similarities and differences among a variety of mammals. A guessing game format shows a paw with just a hint of information; the turned page shows the entire animal with a short explanation about the structure and use of its hooves, paws, flippers, or wings. Includes the elephant, horse, cow, rhinoceros, bear, cat, dog, mole, seal, chimpanzee, and bat. Informative introduction to the bodies and behavior of mammals is also a nice browsing item and a good device for encouraging observation.
> SUBJ: Animal locomotion.

VCR 591.5   Ph-2 3-5 $12.98   KC469
ANIMAL APPETITES (Videocassette). DK Vision/Partridge Films ISBN 0-7894-1960-2, 1996. 1/2" VHS videocassette color (30min). (Amazing animals).
> Closed captioned.
> A lively look at eating habits explores a variety of animal appetites-- carnivorous, herbivorous, and omnivorous. Produced in magazine format for television, the film footage effectively combines animated scenes with live action photography. In addition to being a solid introduction to animal habits, this is a good discussion starter about personal eating habits and nutrition.
> SUBJ: Animals--Food habits.

VCR 591.5   Ph-2 3-5 $12.98   KC470
ANIMAL JOURNEYS (Videocassette). DK Vision/Partridge Films ISBN 0-7894-1955-6, 1996. 1/2" VHS videocassette color (30min). (Amazing animals).
> Closed captioned.
> Exotic and familiar animals from many regions of the world demonstrate behaviors that enable them to grow, care for their young, and survive. Animated sequences intercut with live action photography as Henry the Lizard converses with the narrator. Playful dialogue and informative narration restate the featured ideas of travel, eating, protective tactics, etc. as a great variety of mammals, insects, birds, reptiles, and fish briefly appear in their natural habitats. Produced for television, the magazine format with joking interludes is a familiar form which many children will enjoy, and the information content is substantial enough to introduce discussion in classrooms.
> SUBJ: Animals--Habits and behavior./ Animal locomotion.

591.5   Ph-1 2-5/4 $13.00   T   KC471
ARNOSKY, JIM. Crinkleroot's guide to knowing animal habitats. Simon & Schuster ISBN 0-689-80583-7; In Canada: Distican, 1997. unp. col. ill.
> Crinkleroot, the venerable outdoorsman, leads the reader on a compact tour of wetlands, woodlands, grasslands, and drylands. A sensible definition of a habitat introduces the cheerful tour on foot, by canoe, and in a jeep. Plentiful small watercolor drawings of animals and plants fill the sunny scenes. The masterful blend of information and the humorous main character provides enjoyable reading and effective definitions of these major habitats. For environmental studies.
> SUBJ: Habitat (Ecology).

VCR 591.5   Ph-3 2-6 $69.00   OD KC472
EAGLE AND THE SNAKE (Videocassette). National Geographic 51784, 1993. 1/2" VHS videocassette color (16min).
> Includes teacher's guide.
> Also available in Spanish (51765, $69.00).
> Closed captioned.
> Hundreds of sea snakes rendezvous on an island in the South China Sea and are sometimes met by a fearsome enemy, the white-bellied sea eagle. Magnificent photography of swimming snakes, slithering mating, and midair acrobatic eagles capturing snakes will enthrall

viewers. An intimate look at the interplay between predator and prey.
SUBJ: Predation (Biology)./ Predatory animals./ Animals--Habits and behavior.

591.5   Ph-2 P-2/6 $14.95   T   KC473
FELDMAN, EVE B. Animals don't wear pajamas: a book about sleeping. Illus. by Mary Beth Owens. Henry Holt ISBN 0-8050-1710-0; In Canada: Fitzhenry & Whiteside, 1992. unp. col. ill.
     Human and animal sleep habits are seen in this pleasant picture book discussion. Soft impressionistic paintings and simple text describe sleep places, coverings, and parental care of the young in many settings. The miscellaneous assortment of animals is appealing, and concluding pages add a few more facts about each animal. For reading aloud.
     SUBJ: Animals--Sleep behavior./ Animals--Habits and behavior.

VCR 591.5   Ph-2 4-6 $275.00   OD KC474
INSTINCTS IN ANIMALS (Videocassette). Produced by Maslowski Wildlife Productions. Altschul Group Corporation J4543, 1996. 1/2" VHS videocassette color (14min). (Concepts in nature series).
     Includes teacher's guide.
     Includes public performance rights.
     A spider spins, birds sing, ground squirrels dig, and brown bears fish for salmon--some behaviors that are instinctive and some that are learned. Attractive photography follows the life activities of many species as the narrator explains how inherited behavior helps animals survive and how some instinctive behavior is further developed into skills through learning. Human learning and instinct are mentioned briefly to conclude this well constructed introduction to this fundamental principle of behavior.
     SUBJ: Instinct./ Animals--Habits and behavior.

591.5   Ph-2 3-4/4 $19.90   L   KC475
KUDLINSKI, KATHLEEN V. Animal tracks and traces. Illus. by Mary Morgan. Watts ISBN 0-531-10742-6; In Canada: Watts, 1991. 48p. col. ill.
     Includes glossary and index.
     Children are invited to observe evidence of the activity of wild animals by finding tracks, feathers, fur, and nests of birds and small animals. A few puzzles are included as well as instructions for setting up an ant farm in a jar and capturing spider webs with the help of spray paint. The illustrations are not very sophisticated, but the book is useful as an adjunct to the active observation of nature.
     SUBJ: Animal tracks./ Animals--Habits and behavior.

591.5   Ph-1 A/8 $24.95   T   KC476
MURIE, OLAUS J. Field guide to animal tracks. 2nd ed. Houghton Mifflin ISBN 0-395-19978-6, 1974. 374p. ill. (Peterson field guide series).
     Includes bibliography and index.
     The physical descriptions and area of habitation of the mammal, bird, reptile or insect are included with the drawings of the foot tracks and running track patterns. The definitive title on animal tracks--essential for nature buffs or fans.
     SUBJ: Animals--Habits and behavior./ Zoology--North America./ Zoology--Central America./ Tracking and trailing.

VCR 591.5   Ph-2 3-5 $12.98   KC477
NIGHTTIME ANIMALS (Videocassette). DK Vision/Partridge Films ISBN 0-7894-1956-4, 1996. 1/2" VHS videocassette color (30min). (Amazing animals).
     Closed captioned.
     Nocturnal animals of many types search for food and protect themselves and their young from predators in this fast paced presentation featuring the jokes and questions of Henry Lizard. Bats, rats, owls, and worms are among the species seen in brief vignettes interspersed with cartoons while a narrator explains the special ways they use sight and sound to locate food. The familiar series format offers a useful introduction to animals of the night.
     SUBJ: Nocturnal animals./ Animals--Habits and behavior.

591.5   Ph-2 P-2/5 $16.95   L   KC478
THORNHILL, JAN. Wild in the city. Sierra Club ISBN 0-87156-910-8; In Canada: Greey de Pencier, 1996. unp. col. ill.
     Large, detailed paintings and text introduce the daily life of raccoons, squirrels, a skunk, birds, and other wild animals that pass through a child's backyard in the city. Interesting visual perspectives from the animals' points of view are a nice extension of the short descriptive narrative, and both will invite children to be more observant and to talk about animals they may have seen. Concluding pages list quick facts about the animals. A nice item for reading aloud, browsing enjoyment, or introducing natural science.
     SUBJ: Animals--Habitations./ City and town life.

591.5   Ph-3 4-6/5 $15.00   L   KC479
WHAYNE, SUSANNE SANTORO. Night creatures. Illus. by Steven Schindler. Simon & Schuster ISBN 0-671-73395-8; In Canada: Simon & Schuster, 1993. 47p. col. ill.
     Includes index.
     Bold drawings in dark tones introduce familiar and exotic animals which are active at night. Blocks of text offer a bit of information about the behavior of each animal, and the large pages are laid out according to terrain beginning with the local neighborhood and moving on to the skies, northern forests, African Savanna, tropical rain forests, the desert, and the ocean. A pleasant browsing item, this oversize volume might stimulate discussion or further reading about different animals or habitats or about the night.
     SUBJ: Nocturnal animals.

VCR 591.5   Ph-3 4-6 $39.95   OD KC480
WORLD ALIVE (Videocassette). Narrated by James Earl Jones. Musical score by Kit Walker. Sea Studios ISBN 0-9616824-6-9, 1990. 1/2" VHS videocassette color (25min).
     Includes teacher's guide.
     Companion videocassette to WORLDS BELOW, Sea Studios, 1988.
     Includes public performance rights.
     Many species of wild animals in their natural habitat--underwater, high in trees, in African plains--illustrate birth, feeding, and movement in this leisurely look at earth's diversity. There is a brief, rather majestic narrative stating some themes, but it is the beautiful photographs of birds, reptiles, insects, and mammals which are intriguing. The slow moving film is an aesthetic appreciation providing enjoyable viewing and useful for stimulating discussion or introducing study of natural history.
     SUBJ: Animals--Habits and behavior./ Animal locomotion.

591.5   Ph-1 P-1 $14.89   L   KC481
ZOLOTOW, CHARLOTTE. Sleepy book. Illus. by Ilse Plume. HarperCollins ISBN 0-06-026968-5; In Canada: HarperCollins, c1958, 1988. unp. col. ill.
     Curled up in a cave, standing in a field or stall, standing on one leg are among the ways animals sleep. The bare bones poetic text is paired in this new edition with effective full-color, full-page pencil drawings.
     SUBJ: Animals--Habits and behavior./ Sleep.

591.56   Ph-2 K-2/2 $14.89   L   KC482
BANCROFT, HENRIETTA. Animals in winter. Rev. ed. By Henrietta Bancroft and Richard G. Van Gelder. Illus. by Helen K. Davie. HarperCollins ISBN 0-06-027158-2; In Canada: HarperCollins, 1997. unp. col. ill. (Let's-read-and-find-out science book).
     Some animals travel away from the winter cold, some sleep, some live on stored food supplies, and others must continue to hunt for food. Simple explanations and watercolor scenes depict familiar and a few unusual animals as they migrate, hibernate, or otherwise cope with snowy conditions. The red fox on the jacket invites a look at this basic lesson on the winter season.
     SUBJ: Animals--Habits and behavior./ Winter.

591.56   Ph-3 A/9 $8.95   T   KC483
BROOKS, BRUCE. Nature by design. Farrar, Straus & Giroux ISBN 0-374-35495-2; In Canada: HarperCollins, 1991. 74p. col. ill. (Knowing nature).
     Includes glossary and index.
     Bruce Brooks makes many personal observations in these thoughtful essays on animal architecture, which are illustrated with a selection of beautiful photographs. An introductory chapter on the craftsmanship of animals is followed by discussions of animals that secrete their building materials, animals that dig their habitations, animals that gather up items from their environments to build nests, and a final chapter on animal intelligence. This personable presentation is filled with admiration for nature and will be most appreciated by capable readers of nonfiction.
     SUBJ: Animals--Habitations.

SRC 591.59   Ph-2 3-6 $12.95   OD KC484
ELLIOTT, LANG. Guide to night sounds (Sound recording cassette). NatureSound Studio/NorthWord Press 2654 ISBN 1-878194-03-8, 1992. 1 sound cassette (63min).
     Includes guide.
     Compact disc available 2655, 1992. 1 compact disc (63min), $16.95.
     Birds, insects, frogs, coyotes, and other mammals fill the night with a great variety of sounds which are recorded and discussed here. Narrator briefly introduces familiar and less well known animals, and each is heard for a short time. The call of the loon, mating cries of porcupines, the plaintive moans of baby otters, the hooting of several owls, and the peeps and croaks of a host of frogs and toads are

among the sounds included. Guidebook is a particularly helpful feature with a good sketch by Cynthia J. Page and a bit of factual information for each animal.
SUBJ: Animal sounds./ Nocturnal animals.

591.59   Ph-2 P-K $15.00   L   KC485
WOOD, JAKKI. Jakki Wood's animal hullabaloo: a wildlife noisy book. Simon & Schuster ISBN 0-689-80301-X, 1995. unp. col. ill.
Farm animals and wild animals make a great profusion of different sounds in this cheerful survey. Watercolor scenes feature groups of animals that live in similar environs--wild cats, varied monkeys, and crocodiles with snakes and a rhinoceros. Animal sounds are the only text, and an endpaper picture glossary names all the animals. Young children will enjoy the pandemonium, learning the sounds, and meeting the animals.
SUBJ: Animal sounds.

VCR 591.68   Ph-1 4-6 $99.00   OD KC486
ENDANGERED ANIMALS: SURVIVORS ON THE BRINK (Videocassette). National Geographic 52668, 1997. 1/2" VHS videocassette color (25min).
Includes teacher's guide.
Includes public performance rights.
Closed captioned.
Five endangered species are investigated by a Hollywood style detective hired by a concerned student. The gimmick of tough investigator and theme music lightens an informative and sometimes graphic case featuring the peregrine falcon, orangutan, manatee, American burying beetle, and the African black rhino. Human perpetrators of the crime include poachers, users of insecticides, other polluters, loggers, and speedboat operators who radically hasten nature's slower pace of extinction. A group of Minnesota students studying deformed frogs make this an up-to-date account encouraging viewer participation in further investigation and protective efforts. For environmental studies.
SUBJ: Rare animals./ Endangered species./ Man--Influence on nature.

VCR 591.68   Ph-3 4-6 $149.00   OD KC487
ENDANGERED SPECIES (Videocassette). Society for Visual Education 95538-HAVT, 1991. 2 1/2" VHS videocassettes color. (SVE basic skill booster).
Includes teacher's manual and 24 skill sheets.
Presents endangered animals of the land, sea and air, explaining how habitats are ruined and wildlife threatened to the point of extinction by human "progress." Outstanding color photography delivers the message that each of us must exert whatever effort possible to solve very large environmental problems. Will be useful with ecosystem studies, conservation and all enviromental and recycling activities.
Contents: Understanding the problem (16min); Endangered land animals (21min); Endangered water animals (18min); Endangered animals of the air (21min).
SUBJ: Endangered species./ Rare animals./ Wildlife conservation./ Rare and endangered species.

591.68   Ph-2 5-6/7 $15.95   L   KC488
FACKLAM, MARGERY. And then there was one: the mysteries of extinction. Illus. by Pamela Johnson. Sierra Club/Little, Brown ISBN 0-316-25984-5; In Canada: Little, Brown, 1990. 56p. ill.
"Lucas Evans book."
Includes index.
Many animals which have become extinct and others very near extinction appear in these informative essays about human and natural forces causing the world's creatures to disappear. Soft pencil drawings accompany the discussion which covers special problems of the Galapagos Islands, animal ways of adaptation, the greed of hunters, and how humans have upset nature's balance by transplanting animals. This thoughtful and thought provoking volume lends understanding to the critical worldwide problem of rapid extinction. For environmental studies.
SUBJ: Extinct animals./ Rare animals./ Wildlife conservation./ Man--Influence on nature.

591.68   Ph-2 5-6/8 $22.70   L   KC489
MAYNARD, THANE. Saving endangered mammals: a field guide to some of the earth's rarest animals. Watts ISBN 0-531-11076-1; In Canada: Watts, 1992. 59p. col. ill., maps. (Cincinnati Zoo book).
Includes glossary, directory, bibliography and index.
Available from the National Library Service for the Blind and Physically Handicapped on sound recording cassette RC 38107.
Handsome full-page photographs each paired with a full page of information introduce 28 mammals endangered in various parts of the world. Entries include vital statistics, a small map indicating range, and several paragraphs about factors endangering the animals and efforts to conserve it. This attractive survey offers interesting browsing as

well as useful information. For environmental studies.
SUBJ: Rare animals./ Mammals./ Wildlife conservation.

CDR 591.68   Ph-2 4-A $29.95   OD KC490
MICROSOFT DANGEROUS CREATURES: EXPLORE THE ENDANGERED WORLD OF WILDLIFE. Academic ed. (CD-ROM). Microsoft ISBN 1-57231-022-7; In Canada: Microsoft Canada, 1994. 1 CD-ROM color. (Exploration series).
Includes user's guide and teacher's guide.
Version 1.00.
Also available for Macintosh (ISBN 1-57231-023-5), $29.95.
System requirements: Multimedia PC or compatible with a 386SX or higher microprocessor, 4MB of RAM, at least 2.5MB of hard-disk space, CD-ROM drive, audio board, and VGA display (for 16-color support) or VGA+ display (for full 256-color); MS-DOS operating system version 3.1 or later; Microsoft Windows operating system version 3.1 or later; Microsoft Mouse or compatible pointing device; headphones or speakers.
This multimedia look at animals includes over 100 articles and 1,000 pictures including 100 narrated videos. Brief information makes the program usable as a reference tool. Interactive articles and activities make this CD-ROM useful in a learning center environment and as a secondary resource. For environmental studies.
SUBJ: Rare animals--Software./ Software--Rare animals./ Animals--Habitats and behavior--Software./ Software--Animals--Habitats and behavior./ Interactive media.

591.68   Ph-3 5-6/7 $16.95   T   KC491
POLLOCK, STEVE. Atlas of endangered animals. Facts On File ISBN 0-8160-2856-7; In Canada: Facts On File, 1993. 64p. col. ill., maps.
Includes glossary, directory and indexes.
Brief entries introduce a few of the endangered animals of many regions of the earth. An informative full-page map of each region is accompanied by one to three pages of text and photographs sketching the status of each featured animal, type of threat, and some statistics and discussion. Coverage is very spotty for some countries and regions, but the layout of the geographical survey works pretty well as a resource for reports.
SUBJ: Rare animals./ Wildlife conservation.

VCR 591.73   Ph-3 1-4 $79.00   OD KC492
WILD, WONDERFUL ANIMALS IN THE WOODS (Videocassette). National Geographic 50588, 1996. 1/2" VHS videocassette color (17min). (Unlovables).
Includes teacher's guide.
An amazing, yet informative view of a group of forest unlovables including bats, mosquitoes, and snakes. Despite the light tone, there are many topics that will enrich a science unit on animals, including adaptation, the forest food chain, homes, and survival. For environmental studies.
SUBJ: Forest animals./ Animals./ Animals--Habitations.

591.734   Ph-2 P-2/4 $6.95   T   KC493
ROYSTON, ANGELA. Jungle animals. Photos by Philip Dowell. Illus. by Martine Blaney and Dave Hopkins. Aladdin/Macmillan ISBN 0-689-71519-6, 1991. 21p. col. ill. (Eye openers).
"Dorling Kindersley book."
Eight animals appear in bold photographs dominating this simple survey. Bits of wooden text describe the animals briefly, and the central photograph of each animal is also accompanied by a few small labeled sketches. Featured animals are a monkey, jaguar, tree frog, crocodile, orangutan, toucan, iguana, and sloth. The minimal text and uncluttered pages work adequately as simple nonfiction for young children.
SUBJ: Jungle animals.

591.75   Ph-3 4-6/6 $12.95   P   KC494
SWANSON, DIANE. Coyotes in the crosswalk: true tales of animal life in the wilds...of the city! Illus. by Douglas Penhale. Voyageur Press ISBN 0-89658-272-8; In Canada: Whitecap Books, 1995. 71p. ill.
Includes index.
Raccoons, coyotes, peregrine falcons, and even skunks are among the ten wild animals whose city lives are introduced in this pleasant paperback. Brief chapters of text and pen and ink drawings describe each animal's physical characteristics and life cycle and explain how the animal adapts its behavior to survive in the city. This should be enjoyed by children who are fond of animals and will be useful for nature lessons in urban schools. Use to introduce the urban ecosystem in environmental studies units.
SUBJ: Urban animals./ Animals--Habits and behavior.

591.77   Ph-1 2-4/5 $14.95   L   KC495
COLE, JOANNA. Magic School Bus on the ocean floor. Illus. by Bruce Degen. Scholastic ISBN 0-590-41430-5; In Canada: Scholastic, 1992.

unp. col. ill.
Spanish version available AUTOBUS MAGICO EN EL FONDO DEL MAR (ISBN 0-590-47506-1, 1994).
Miss Frizzle takes her class on a learning expedition through the regions of ocean terrain in a cheerful, busy cartoon presentation. The school bus turns into a submarine, then a submersible, a glass-bottom boat, and finally a surfboard taking teacher, students, and Lenny the Lifeguard to explore the geography and plant and animal life of the intertidal zone, the continental shelf, the deep ocean floor, hot water vents, and a coral reef. The teacher's explanations, numerous labeled sketches, and short essays by the children provide an informative and enjoyable introduction to the ocean depths.
SUBJ: Ocean./ Marine animals./ Spanish language materials.

591.9   Ph-2 5-6/8 $19.40   L   KC496
LAMBERT, DAVID. Children's animal atlas: how animals have evolved, where they live today, why so many are in danger. Millbrook ISBN 1-56294-167-4, 1992. 95p. col. ill., maps.
"Quarto book."
Includes glossary and index.
This large busy jumble of photographs, charts, maps, bits of text, and framed insets explains how animals live together in particular habitats around the world. The many topics include coniferous forests, steppe animals, lakes and marshes, mangrove swamps, frozen oceans, animal travel, aspects of animal history, and much more. Evolution of animal life, adaptation, and conservation problems are all covered in the wide ranging discussion which will provide information for many aspects of animal study and environmental studies.
SUBJ: Animals--Migration--Maps.

591.96   Ph-2 5-6/10 $15.89   L   KC497
LINDBLAD, LISA. Serengeti migration: Africa's animals on the move. Photos by Sven-Olof Lindblad. Hyperion ISBN 1-56282-669-7; In Canada: Little, Brown, 1994. 40p. col. ill., maps.
Includes glossary.
Each year vast herds of zebras and wildebeests migrate together in a great loop through East Africa's Serengeti National Park. This photographic album follows their journey through varied terrain and introduces many other animals they encounter. Though fragmented, this is an interesting introduction to both the ecology of Serengeti and the survival problems of many African animals. For environmental studies.
SUBJ: Gnus--Migration./ Zebras--Migration./ Serengeti National Park (Tanzania)./ National parks and reserves--Tanzania./ Animals--Migration.

591.97   Ph-2 P-2/3 $14.95   L   KC498
THORNHILL, JAN. Wildlife A-B-C: a nature alphabet book. Simon & Schuster ISBN 0-671-67925-2; In Canada: Greey de Pencier, 1990. unp. col. ill.
Includes "Nature Notes."
Pleasantly framed drawings by a Canadian illustrator and simple rhymes set in a large flat volume introduce a variety of animals. The busy scenes provide much to see; the featured animals are repeated in enticing decorative borders around the pictures. Plentiful white space and large print encourage independent reading, and a concluding set of nature notes provides added factual information. An attractive browsing volume with versatile possibilities for use.
SUBJ: Animals./ Zoology--North America./ Alphabet.

591.981   Ph-1 K-5/3 $15.93   L   KC499
DARLING, KATHY. Amazon ABC. Photos by Tara Darling. Lothrop, Lee & Shepard ISBN 0-688-13779-2, 1996. unp. col. ill., map.
Insects, mammals, birds, and reptiles are presented in a vivid alphabet of photographs to introduce the variety of life in the Amazon Rain Forest. Phonetic pronunciation is often provided, and lower case and capital letters along with labels appear in red letters on a green background. The featured animals are each explained in a paragraph of information at the back of the book along with an introduction to the three layers of rain forest habitat. An attractive, bright volume with many uses as an alphabet book, survey of interesting animals, and lesson on rain forest life. For environmental studies.
SUBJ: Zoology--Amazon River Region./ Alphabet./ Rain forest animals.

591.998   Ph-2 1-3/4 $4.95   P   KC500
COWCHER, HELEN. Antarctica. Farrar, Straus & Giroux ISBN 0-374-40371-6, 1990. unp. col. ill.
Available in Spanish ANTARTIDA (ISBN 0-374-30370-3, 1993).
Beautiful paintings on doublespread pages and brief text introduce the Antarctic environment of the Emperor and Adelie penguins and the Weddell seals. The sketchy narrative tends to focus on enemies-- the leopard seal, skuas which in this case destroy all of the Adelie eggs, and most persistently, humans; the Emperors are shown

successfully hatching and rearing their young, though little detail on physical characteristics or behavior is actually provided. The final message on human endangerment is somewhat obliquely stated but sobering, and the wonderfully evocative scenes will need to be augmented with more specific factual information.
SUBJ: Animals--Antarctica.

591.998   Ph-2 4-6/8 $17.95   L   KC501
KALMAN, BOBBIE. Arctic animals. Crabtree ISBN 0-86505-145-3; In Canada: Crabtree, 1988. 56p. col. ill. (Arctic world).
Includes glossary and index.
To survive the bitter cold of the Arctic winter 25 animal species have to adapt to the harsh environment. Bits of text and plentiful color photographs describe behavior and raising of the young by various mammals, birds, fish, and even insects; there are also brief essays on ways animals keep warm, the Arctic food chain, and ecology. Though the information is sketchy, this is an attractive, slim introduction useful for the variety of animals covered.
SUBJ: Animal ecology--Arctic regions./ Zoology--Arctic regions.

592   Ph-3 A/12 $8.95   P   KC502
APPELHOF, MARY. Worms eat my garbage. Illustrated by Mary Frances Fenton. Flower Press ISBN 0-942256-03-4, 1982. 100p. ill.
Includes bibliography and index.
Provides thorough instructions for raising earthworms and establishing a vermicomposting system. Among the many practical topics covered in readable text and congenial drawings are: the recycling of food wastes, establishing a personal philosophy of energy use, and money making and saving uses of earthworms to produce fertilizer, fishing bait, and waste disposal. An informative guide with many uses for science projects, ecology units, and the hobbyist or gardener.
SUBJ: Earthworms./ Recycling (Waste).

592   Ph-2 5-6/8 $15.95   T   KC503
DORIS, ELLEN. Invertebrate zoology. Produced in association with the Children's School of Science, Woods Hole, Mass. Photos by Len Rubenstein. Thames & Hudson ISBN 0-500-19005-4, 1993. 64p. col. ill. (Real kids real science books).
Includes directory and glossary.
Instructions for finding and observing many different species of worms, mollusks, arthropods, and other invertebrates are given in brief bits of text and plentiful, small photographs with captions. The slim, busy volume offers information on scientific classification, physical characteristics, and simple projects. Many intriguing views of the animals, technical details about taxonomy, and information about ordering specimen animals are included in this multifaceted lesson.
SUBJ: Invertebrates./ Zoology.

592   Ph-2 5-6/9 $13.95   L   KC504
HALTON, CHERYL M. Those amazing leeches. Dillon ISBN 0-87518-408-1, 1989. 120p. col. ill.
Includes appendices, glossary, bibliography and index.
Related to the common earthworm, the blood drinking leech is both a serious pest and a performer of medical miracles. Color photographs and line drawings accompany a quite absorbing account of the history, physical characteristics, problems encountered by soldiers in various wars, current types of research, the production process of leech farms, and contemporary medical uses, particularly in surgical procedures and the clean up of blood clots. Instructions for keeping leeches for observation, suggested science projects, and a list of suppliers round out a thorough introduction to a genuinely intriguing animal. This is good material for science assignments, booktalks, and nonfiction readers.
SUBJ: Leeches.

592   Ph-2 5-6/7 $19.90   L   KC505
LABONTE, GAIL. Leeches, lampreys, and other cold-blooded bloodsuckers. Watts ISBN 0-531-20027-2; In Canada: Watts, 1991. 64p. ill. (some col.). (First book).
Includes bibliography and index.
This interesting introduction to bloodsucking animals explains how they feed and grow and how they have even affected history through spreading disease. In addition to leeches and lampreys, the discussion covers ticks, lice, mosquitoes, fleas, and certain flies; well chosen photographs accompany the informative text. The subject has a macabre appeal, and the undramatized discussion thoughtfully emphasizes ecology and history as well as the behavior and physical characteristics of particular animals.
SUBJ: Bloodsucking animals.

592   Ph-2 4-6/4 $15.95   L   KC506
PASCOE, ELAINE. Earthworms. Photos by Dwight Kuhn. Blackbirch ISBN 1-56711-177-7, 1997. 48p. col. ill. (Nature close-up).
Includes glossary, directory, bibliography and index.

Earthworms are "important members of the natural clean-up squad that disposes of dead plant and animal matter, breaking it down and returning it to the soil." Informative text and sidebars, abundantly illustrated, explain the ecological role of earthworms, describe their physiology, and outline how to care for and observe earthworms in captivity. Suggested experiments for observation make this a useful handbook for budding naturalists or for science projects for environmental studies.
SUBJ: Earthworms./ Earthworms--Experiments./ Experiments.

VCR 592   Ph-3 3-6 $175.00   OD KC507
RECYCLING WITH WORMS (Videocassette). East-West Food for All Foundation/dist. by Bullfrog Films ISBN 1-56029-652-6, 1995. 1/2" VHS videocassette color (12min).
Includes study guide.
Includes public performance rights.
Enjoyable film techniques and young narrators demonstrate how worms can be used to recycle organic garbage in classrooms, homes, and work places. A girl explains contemporary problems with disposing garbage through landfills, burning, and recycling, then meets with her friend Simon in his small apartment where she helps him set up a worm bin for composting his kitchen and table waste. Useful for classroom lessons on environmental studies, this will also be interesting to families wanting to be more actively involved in recycling. The concept could also be used as a science project for a science fair.
SUBJ: Earthworms./ Worms./ Recycling (Waste)./ Compost.

593.4   Ph-2 1-3/2 $14.89   L   KC508
ESBENSEN, BARBARA JUSTER. Sponges are skeletons. Illus. by Holly Keller. HarperCollins ISBN 0-06-021037-0; In Canada: HarperCollins, 1993. 32p. col. ill. (Let's-read-and-find-out science book).
"Your bath sponge has many relatives under the sea." (p. 20) Pleasant color drawings with bits of humor accompany the simple explanations of the physical characteristics and varieties of sponges and the way that sponges are harvested and treated for human use; brief mention is made of synthetic sponges. Nicely thought provoking in describing the natural origins of a common object, this will make enjoyable reading as well as interesting science material.
SUBJ: Sponges.

593.5   Ph-2 3-5/4 $14.95   L   KC509
KITE, PATRICIA. Down in the sea: the jellyfish. Whitman ISBN 0-8075-1712-7; In Canada: General, 1993. unp. col. ill.
Splendid photographs depict a colorful variety of "jiggly jellyfish" as a simple text describes the body parts and behavior of this stinging water creature. Tentacles, movement, and eating are very briefly discussed, and a one-page diagram with no explanation offers a confusing presentation of reproduction and structure. Skimpy explanations are offset by the visual appeal, providing a useful introduction to this commonly encountered and intriguing animal.
SUBJ: Jellyfishes.

594   Ph-1 4-6/7 $19.95   L   KC510
BUHOLZER, THERES. Life of the snail. Carolrhoda ISBN 0-87614-246-3, 1987. 47p. col. ill. (Carolrhoda nature watch book).
Includes glossary and index.
Follows three snail species through a year's time, and covers physical characteristics, behavior, mating, egg laying, and estivation and hibernation. Excellent color photographs highlight the beauty and intriguing details of this very common mollusk, and the text encourages patient observation of wildlife. A fine account of a life cycle that is appealing and interesting as well as informative.
SUBJ: Snails.

594   Ph-2 4-5/7 $15.00   L   KC511
FLORIAN, DOUGLAS. Discovering seashells. Scribner's ISBN 0-684-18740-X; In Canada: Collier Macmillan, 1986. unp. col. ill. (Discovering books).
Discusses various families of mollusks and the ocean provinces in which they are found. The information on characteristics of the shells is miscellaneous and brief, but the emphasis on groupings and similarities will encourage observation and collecting of shells. Attractive watercolor paintings in warm, sandy tones are simple and informative illustrations of this appealing subject.
SUBJ: Shells.

594   Ph-1 4-6/7 $19.95   L   KC512
JOHNSON, SYLVIA A. Snails. Photos by Modoki Masuda. Lerner ISBN 0-8225-1475-3, 1982. 48p. col. ill. (Lerner natural science book).
Includes glossary and index.
Splendid photographs and lucid text describe the physiology and life cycle of land snails and introduce a few of the highly varied marine species. The fine pictures of young snails hatching are particularly unusual and make this an excellent first source.
SUBJ: Snails.

594   Ph-2 3-5/4 $14.95   L   KC513
KITE, PATRICIA. Down in the sea: the octopus. Whitman ISBN 0-8075-1715-1; In Canada: General, 1993. unp. col. ill.
Underwater views depict the movement, hunting, and egg laying of octopi while a brief text explains how the soft body and tentacles work. A final page of facts adds a bit more information to the simple introduction. Striking photographs are appealing and informative.
SUBJ: Octopus.

594   Ph-2 1-3/4 $14.89   L   KC514
LAUBER, PATRICIA. Octopus is amazing. Illus. by Holly Keller. HarperCollins ISBN 0-690-04803-3, 1990. 32p. col. ill. (Let's-read-and-find-out science book).
Cheerful watercolor scenes and simple narrative introduce physical characteristics and behavior of the common octopus. Octopus dens, color changes, locomotion, hunting and eating, dispersing "ink," and laying and hatching eggs are the major topics covered. A bit sketchy (the male octopus is not discussed), this is still pleasant reading about an intriguing animal.
SUBJ: Octopus.

594   Ph-2 2-4/2 $9.95   L   KC515
OLESEN, JENS. Snail. Photos by Bo Jarner. Silver Burdett ISBN 0-3820-9289-9, 1986. 24p. col. ill. (Stopwatch books).
Includes index.
Examines the physiology and life cycle of the snail in simple text and excellent color photographs. Each page covers a different topic: eating, egg laying, growth of the young snail, etc., in general terms; a small drawing or photograph appears on the page of print with a facing full-page photograph. A final page asks the student to review main points of the book, which is most notable for the visual information.
SUBJ: Snails.

594   Ph-2 3-6 $19.00   T   KC516
REHDER, HARALD A. Audubon Society field guide to North American seashells. Photos by James H. Carmichael, Jr. Knopf ISBN 0-394-51913-2; In Canada: Random House, 1981. 894p. col. ill. (Audubon Society field guides).
Includes index, appendices and glossary.
A fine guide for amateurs. A simple visual key uses shape and color photographs to identify seashells and living mollusks. Photographs are keyed to detailed written descriptions giving habitat and range. 705 identification photographs. Pocket-size, handy for field trips. A duplicate copy in the reference collection is recommended.
SUBJ: Shells.

594   Ph-2 P-1/2 $14.89   L   KC517
ZOEHFELD, KATHLEEN WEIDNER. What lives in a shell? Illus. by Helen Davie. HarperCollins ISBN 0-06-022999-3; In Canada: HarperCollins, 1994. 32p. col. ill. (Let's-read-and-find-out science book).
Very simple explanations and nice watercolors tell how land animals--snails, turtles, and crabs and varieties of water animals--snails, clams, and oysters live in their shells. The longest segments focus on the land snail and the hermit crab, and the emphasis is on the shell as a protective home rather than biology or how the animal makes the shell. The pleasant introduction is simple enough for early independent reading and for reading aloud to nursery school children.
SUBJ: Shells./ Body covering (Anatomy)./ Animal defenses.

595.3   Ph-1 5-6/7 $15.99   T   KC518
CERULLO, MARY M. Lobsters: gangsters of the sea. Photos by Jeffrey L. Rotman. Cobblehill/Dutton ISBN 0-525-65153-5, 1994. 56p. col. ill.
Includes bibliography and index.
Two worlds--the underwater life of lobsters and the work of lobstermen--are viewed in fine photographs and interesting text. The intriguing bodies and aggressive, territorial behavior of lobsters are explained, and the discussion goes on to the equipment and tasks on lobster boats, the studies of scientists, and the regulations protecting lobsters. The close-up views of the lobsters and the writing are exceptional, making this a fine choice for reading and information.
SUBJ: Lobsters.

595.3   Ph-1 5-6/4 $19.95   L   KC519
HOLLING, HOLLING CLANCY. Pagoo. Illustrated by the author and Lucille Webster Holling. Houghton Mifflin ISBN 0-395-06826-6, 1957. 86p. col. ill.
Available from National Library Service for the Blind and Physically Handicapped on sound recording cassette RC12680.
"The habits of a hermit crab and numerous other tide pool creatures are portrayed through a fascinating text combined with vivid artwork." AAAS.
SUBJ: Crabs./ Marine animals.

NONFICTION

595.3   Ph-2 4-6/7 $19.95   L   KC520
JOHNSON, SYLVIA A. Crabs. Photos by Atsushi Sakurai. Lerner ISBN
0-8225-1471-0, 1982. 48p. col. ill. (Lerner natural science book).
     Includes glossary and index.
     The interesting body parts of the crab, the stages of its life cycle, and
the process of molting are among the topics discussed and shown in
the fine color photographs. Though emphasis is on the commonly
encountered shore crab, numerous other species are pictured.
     SUBJ: Crabs.

595.3   Ph-3 A/7 $19.95   L   KC521
JOHNSON, SYLVIA A. Hermit crabs. Photos by Kazunari Kawashima.
Lerner ISBN 0-8225-1488-5, 1989. 47p. col. ill. (Lerner natural science
book).
     Includes glossary and index.
     Hermit crabs are somewhat mysterious since they live in such a
diversity of borrowed homes; here a detailed text and a multitude of
selected photographs bring them to light. The ecology of the seashore
habitat is examined, and the physical characteristics, behavior,
feeding, molting, and selection of new homes, egg laying, and
protection from enemies are all explained. This is a complex
introduction best suited to the use of serious students interested in
unusual animals or shore species.
     SUBJ: Hermit crabs.

595.3   Ph-1 P-1/3 $15.99   L   KC522
MCDONALD, MEGAN. Is this a house for hermit crab? Illus. by S. D.
Schindler. Orchard ISBN 0-531-08455-8, 1990. unp. col. ill.
     A hermit crab, grown too large for his borrowed shell, sets out along
the beach and tries on many inappropriate items before solving his
problem. Fine pastel drawings enhance the natural tones of sand and
water as the simple narrative uses a repetitive scheme to move the
crab from tin can to driftwood to fish net and other objects until he is
washed back to sea and finally encounters an empty sea snail shell
that is a perfect fit. The spaciously set, attractively textured pictures
and good read aloud text make this a fine first lesson in seashore
ecology or the housing problems of this unusual animal.
     SUBJ: Hermit crabs.

VCR 595.4   Ph-2 5-6 $79.00   OD KC523
BITE OF THE BLACK WIDOW (Videocassette). National Geographic
51633, 1994. 1/2" VHS videocassette color (20min).
     Includes teacher's guide.
     Black widow spiders are seen as "graceful, gorgeous, and deadly,"
in this discussion of their life cycle and the effects of their powerful
poison on humans. Close-up photographs of the spider's web, mating,
and egg laying are intriguing: and the real-life suffering of bite victims
is scary. A particularly interesting sequence depicts a family raising
black widow spiders to extract the venom for the antivenin used to
treat people who have been bitten.
     SUBJ: Black widow spider./ Spiders.

595.4   Ph-2 5-6/7 $13.95   L   KC524
DAY, NANCY. Horseshoe crab. Dillon ISBN 0-87518-545-2; In Canada:
Maxwell Macmillan, 1992. 60p. col. ill. (Dillon remarkable animals
book).
     Includes directory, glossary and index.
     This large arthropod--not a true crab--has changed very little since
prehistoric times and is still commonly seen in the eastern United
States. The informative discussion accompanied by very good
photographs covers physical characteristics, history, reproduction,
development of the young, the animal's unusual blue blood, and its
value to human medicine. The story of this odd animal is genuinely
interesting, and children should be especially intrigued that the
horseshoe crab was a contemporary of the dinosaurs.
     SUBJ: Horseshoe crabs.

595.4   Ph-2 1-3/4 $15.95   L   KC525
GIBBONS, GAIL. Spiders. Holiday House ISBN 0-8234-1006-4, 1993.
unp. col. ill.
     Simple text and colorful drawings introduce the physical traits of
spiders and the types of webs they weave. Each framed page
includes a bold, labeled scene and a short explanation of a particular
topic. Includes differences between insects and spiders, hatching and
growth of spiderlings, hunting behavior, and characteristics of
particular species. The easy-to-read presentation is a useful sketch of
the ever interesting arachnid.
     SUBJ: Spiders.

595.4   Ph-2 3-5/5 $16.95   L   KC526
KALMAN, BOBBIE. Web weavers and other spiders. Crabtree ISBN
0-86505-632-3; In Canada: Crabtree, 1997. 32p. col. ill. (Crabapples).
     Includes glossary and index.
     Many aspects of spider bodies and behavior are presented in short

topical sections with a good selection of large and small photographs.
Differences between spiders and insects and among spider species are
explained, and the discussion also covers webs, hunting, eating,
babies, molting, enemies, protective strategies, and spiders and
humans. The clear and logical explanations provide a good
introduction to spider life.
     SUBJ: Spiders.

595.4   Ph-2 5-6/7 $13.95   L   KC527
LABONTE, GAIL. Tarantula. Dillon ISBN 0-87518-452-9, 1991. 58p. col.
ill. (Dillon remarkable animals book).
     Includes glossary and index.
     Intriguing for their size, appearance, eating habits, and longevity,
tarantulas also make satisfactory pets - which has helped bring some
species to near extinction. Interesting facts about physiology and
behavior are conveyed here in a useful discussion which sometimes
falls short in details provided; magnified photographs provide
dramatic detail but sometimes distort true proportions. Though there is
a tendency to sensationalize through descriptive terms and pictures,
the book does provide a fair and interesting introduction.
     SUBJ: Tarantulas./ Spiders.

595.4   Ph-1 5-6/4 $17.00   L   KC528
MARKLE, SANDRA. Outside and inside spiders. Bradbury ISBN 0-02-
762314-9; In Canada: Maxwell Macmillan, 1994. 40p. col. ill.
     Includes glossary/index.
     Spider bodies and spider webs are examined in unusual detail in
handsome magnified photographs and an informative essay text.
Microphotography reveals the inner organs as well as the spinning
process, eating, and the laying and hatching of eggs. Hunting,
digestion, and vision and other senses are among topics described.
Close-up views will intrigue many readers and should encourage
personal observation and respect for the often feared spider.
     SUBJ: Spiders.

595.4   Ph-2 2-6/6 $11.99   L   KC529
PARSONS, ALEXANDRA. Amazing spiders. Photos by Jerry Young.
Knopf ISBN 0-679-90226-0, 1990. 29p. col. ill. (Eyewitness juniors).
     Includes index.
     Dramatic photographs are the focus of this quick assemblage of brief
facts and anecdotes about spiders. Double spread segments provide
sketchy information and bits and pieces of text and drawings around
a central large photograph, which is often caught in the center
margin. Actual sizes are never stated, making all species seem much
larger than life, but browsers will be attracted by the subject matter.
     SUBJ: Spiders.

595.4   Ph-2 5-6/8 $15.95   L   KC530
PRINGLE, LAURENCE P. Scorpion man: exploring the world of
scorpions. By Laurence Pringle. Photos by Gary A. Polis. Scribner's ISBN
0-684-19560-7; In Canada: Maxwell Macmillan, 1994. 42p. col. ill.
     Includes bibliography and index.
     Interesting close-up views of scorpions follow the life cycle of the
venomous insect in this story of the work done by a wildlife scientist.
Pringle combines the real-life account with plentiful information on the
animal. A useful introduction to scorpions, this will also be a good
choice in career studies for children interested in science careers.
     SUBJ: Scorpions./ Polis, Gary A./ Biologists.

595.4   Ph-2 4-6/6 $19.95   L   KC531
SCHNIEPER, CLAUDIA. Amazing spiders. Photos by Max Meier.
Carolrhoda ISBN 0-87614-342-7, 1989. 48p. col. ill. (Carolrhoda nature
watch book).
     Includes glossary and index.
     Larger than life color photographs provide close-up views of many
species in this informative introduction to spider physiology and
behavior. The continuous essay text examines spider classification,
physical characteristics and coloration, eating habits, variations in web
spinning, molting, mating, and hatching of the young. The actual sizes
are stated, but the enlarged views tend to distort and overdramatize;
children will be intrigued by the "monstrous" views, and the
presentation is informative.
     SUBJ: Spiders.

VCR 595.4   Ph-2 4-6 $225.00   OD KC532
SPIDER SURVIVAL (Videocassette). Pyramid Media 06348 ISBN
1-55981-244-3, 1991. 1/2" VHS videocassette color (12min).
     Includes teacher's guide.
     Close-up views of spiders spinning their webs and capturing and
eating their prey demonstrate how this common predator plays its
role in the food chain. Diagrams and photographs explain the
arachnid body parts and the structure of webs. Includes segments on
nest building, the growth of spiderlings, and the unusual homes of
trap-door and underwater species. Children will be fascinated by the

speed and skill of the spiders in this attractive introduction.
SUBJ: Spiders.

VCR 595.4   Ph-3 6-A $52.95   OD KC533
WEAVE AND SPIN (Videocassette). Carolina Biological Supply 49-2460-V, 1986. 1/2" VHS videocassette color (13min).
    Includes teacher's manual.
    The spinning of spider webs and the uses of the webs as egg covers and snares are discussed in this interesting film which should be useful for research or advanced study of spiders. The teacher's manual contains suggested uses of video, related discussion questions and bibliography.
    SUBJ: Spiders.

595.7   Ph-2 2-4/4 $15.95   L   KC534
BERNHARD, EMERY. Dragonfly. Illus. by Durga Bernhard. Holiday House ISBN 0-8234-1033-1, 1993. unp. col. ill.
    Includes glossary.
    Follows the history, stages of growth, and flying and eating behavior of the colorful dragonfly. Various species are identified, and body parts, the stages of metamorphosis, and the significance of dragonflies in various cultures are explained. Attractive, framed paintings in soft, deep shades--predominantly blue, green, rust--complement the informative, short text. Useful introduction to the common, appealing insect.
    SUBJ: Dragonflies.

VCR 595.7   Ph-3 4-6 $149.00   OD KC535
CICADAS: THE 17-YEAR INVASION (Videocassette). Beacon Films/Alschul Group 8661CP-047, 1993. 1/2" VHS videocassette color (15min). (World of nature).
    Cicada nymphs emerge from their long underground sojourn and swarm in trees for their final transformation into adult insects. Careful photography follows the nymphs as they struggle through grass and across pavement to the trees where they labor to break out of their skins into vulnerable adult bodies. Shows homeowners shielding their trees, a zoologist who comes to study the event, and animals and humans disposing of the piles of unsuccessful nymphs that fall to the ground, unable to complete the process. Fascinating life cycle that will be especially appreciated during the rare times the cicadas emerge.
    SUBJ: Cicada./ Insects.

595.7   Ph-1 5-6/7 $16.00   T   KC536
COLE, JOANNA. Insect's body. Photos by Jerome Wexler and Raymond A. Mendez. Morrow ISBN 0-688-02771-7, 1984. 48p. ill.
    Examines in close detail the physiology of a house cricket with the purpose of showing the physical parts of all insects and particularly those features which enable these small animals to survive. Intriguing photographs provide remarkably close views and are expanded by plentiful diagrams to illustrate the well-organized text. An excellent introduction to a familiar species and to basic principles of insect life.
    SUBJ: Crickets.

595.7   Ph-1 K-2/3 $5.95   P   KC537
DALLINGER, JANE. Grasshoppers. Photos by Yuko Sato. Lerner ISBN 0-8225-9568-0, c1981, 1990. 48p. col. ill.
    Includes glossary and index.
    A detailed account in both text and color photographs of life cycle of grasshoppers. Their role in the food chain is clearly presented as well as need to control grasshopper populations.
    SUBJ: Grasshoppers.

595.7   Ph-2 K-3/4 $11.95   T   KC538
GOLDSEN, LOUISE. Ladybug and other insects. [This edition American text by Louise Goldsen.] Created by Gallimard Jeunesse and Pascale de Bourgoing. Illus. by Sylvie Perols. Scholastic ISBN 0-590-45235-5; In Canada: Scholastic, 1991. unp. col. ill. (spiral bound). (First discovery book).
    "Cartwheel books."
    Originally published in France, LA COCCINELLE, 1989.
    Ladybugs offer an attractive example of the insect life cycle as seen here through appealing plastic overlays. A good variety of ladybugs appear, there is a confusing mention of the three body segments of insects and a better discussion of metamorphosis, and finally a gallery of other beetles and a few assorted insects are presented. The overlay device is an inviting gimmick, and the small glossy volume is a fair introduction to insect life.
    SUBJ: Ladybugs./ Insects.

595.7   Ph-1 4-6/6 $14.95   L   KC539
GOOR, RON. Insect metamorphosis from egg to adult. By Ron and Nancy Goor. Atheneum ISBN 0-689-31445-0; In Canada: Collier Macmillan, 1990. 26p. col. ill.
    Includes index.

The impressive hickory horned devil caterpillar is followed from egg through several moltings as a caterpillar to its change to pupa and final emergence as a butterfly, while praying mantids, dragonflies, and cicadas are shown in the simpler cycle of incomplete metamorphosis. This is a first-rate introduction to this important principle and some of its variations. Its well focused text and lovely color photographs make it quite useful for the study of insects.
    SUBJ: Insects--Metamorphosis.

595.7   Ph-2 4-6/7 $9.95   P   KC540
HICKMAN, PAMELA M. Bugwise: thirty incredible insect investigations and arachnid activities. Illus. by Judie Shore. Addison-Wesley ISBN 0-201-57074-2; In Canada: Kids Can Press, c1990, 1991. 96p. ill.
    Plentiful bits of factual information and a good variety of experiments for observing insects and arachnids are combined in this appealing paperback. Eating, body changes, sounds, homes and much more are described along with instructions for locating and observing insects and other creatures that live underwater, in soil, and in shrubbery or other locations. The numerous pencil drawings are occasionally confusing in their portrayal of species, but the volume carefully employs the miscellany approach to convey an impressive amount of information.
    SUBJ: Insects./ Spiders.

VCR 595.7   Ph-1 2-6 $49.00   OD KC541
INSECTS (Videocassette). National Geographic 51099, c1979, 1986. 1/2" VHS videocassette color (12min).
    Includes teacher's guide.
    Insects come in all sizes, shapes and colors, yet they have many characteristics in common as illustrated with the fly, the metamorphosis of the Monarch butterfly, and life inside a beehive. This interesting, well-paced video offers a good explanation of the characteristics of insects.
    SUBJ: Fly (Insect)./ Insects./ Monarch butterfly./ Butterflies./ Bees.

595.7   Ph-2 5-6/7 $19.95   T   KC542
JOHNSON, JINNY. Simon and Schuster children's guide to insects and spiders. Simon & Schuster ISBN 0-689-81163-2, 1996. 80p. col. ill.
    Includes glossary and index.
    This large catalog introduces a generous variety of species in seven families of insects and briefly covers spiders and a few other arachnids. Introductory discussion on the bodies and history of insects and spiders is followed by colorful photographs and information about each family with several pages of brief entries on the selected species. The plentiful pictures and well structured presentation make this useful as a quick information source or for more in-depth study and reports.
    SUBJ: Insects./ Spiders.

595.7   Ph-3 A/7 $19.95   L   KC543
JOHNSON, SYLVIA A. Water insects. Photos by Modoki Masuda. Lerner ISBN 0-8225-1489-3, 1989. 48p. col. ill. (Lerner natural science book).
    Includes glossary and index.
    Colorful photographs and carefully developed text introduce a variety of beetles and bugs which spend most of their lives in water. Titled sections of text and photo captions describe physical characteristics, hunting and feeding behavior, the differing stages of the two types of life cycles, egg laying and development of the young, the flying of some species, and hibernation. A book for serious readers, this augments information available on insects and on the underwater environment.
    SUBJ: Insects, Aquatic.

595.7   Ph-1 5-6/8 $4.95   P   KC544
LEAHY, CHRISTOPHER W. Peterson first guide to insects of North America. Houghton Mifflin ISBN 0-395-35640-7, 1987. 128p. col. ill. (Peterson first guide).
    Includes index.
    Selectors' Choice, 17th ed.
    This attractive small guide is an adaptation of Donald J. Borror's "A Field Guide to the Insects" (1970). Beginning with an introductory explanation of insect life stages and a chart of the major insect orders, the informative entries are arranged by group and accompanied by facing pages of fine drawings. A handy compendium for field use, this also provides good browsing and reading.
    SUBJ: Insects--Identification.

595.7   Ph-2 5-6/8 $20.99   L   KC545
MOUND, LAURENCE. Insect. Knopf ISBN 0-679-90441-7, 1990. 63p. col. ill. (Eyewitness books).
    Includes index.
    Fascinating detail about many aspects of insect bodies and behavior is conveyed in this large, highly pictorial volume. Two-page topical

sections cover specific insects and such subjects as camouflage, metamorphosis, insects under water, and insect architects. Each entry includes a short segment of text, enlarged and actual size drawings, and informative captions. This suffers more from distortion through magnification than some volumes in the series, but it's a highly informative compendium.
SUBJ: Insects.

SRC 595.7   Ph-3 P-2 $10.95   OD KC546
MURPHY, JANE. Songs about insects, bugs and squiggly things (Sound recording cassette). Kimbo KIM 9127C ISBN 1-56346-033-5, 1993. 1 sound cassette (32min).
Includes lyrics.
Compact disc available KIM 9127CD, 1993. 1 compact disc (32min), $14.95.
Clever, witty lyrics about spiders, bees, crickets, and a variety of bugs. The peppy songs are delivered by the clear voices of children and an adult. Excellent for enriching nature studies.
SUBJ: Insects--Songs and music.

595.7   Ph-2 4-5/6 $15.93   L   KC547
PARKER, NANCY WINSLOW. Bugs. By Nancy Winslow Parker and Joan Richards Wright. Illustrated by Nancy Winslow Parker. Greenwillow ISBN 0-688-06624-0, 1987. 40p. col. ill.
Includes glossary and bibliography.
Bold diagrams and bits of humor highlight this colorful catalog of common insects. A full-page cartoon with rhyming question and answer faces each one page entry which includes a well labelled drawing, common and scientific names, and a paragraph of information on behavior and habitat. A concluding picture glossary graphically explains principles of metamorphosis, body structure, growth and reproduction. Unfortunately the book appears to be for a younger audience than it is.
SUBJ: Insects.

595.7   Ph-2 4-6/6 $13.95   L   KC548
SNEDDEN, ROBERT. What is an insect? Illus. by Adrian Lascom. Photos by Oxford Scientific Films. Sierra Club ISBN 0-87156-540-4; In Canada: Little, Brown, 1993. 32p. col. ill.
Includes glossary and index.
Plentiful photographs of different species demonstrate the body parts and behavior which set insects apart from other animals. Topical bits of text describe outer bodies, internal organs, metamorphosis, egg laying, the various senses, feeding, defenses, and types of movement. Brief, clear, and attractive, this quick skim is a good introduction to further study of insects.
SUBJ: Insects.

595.7   Ph-2 4-6/6 $11.95   L   KC549
STEELE, PHILIP. Insects. Crestwood House ISBN 0-89686-581-9; In Canada: Collier Macmillan, 1991. 32p. col. ill. (Pocket facts).
Includes index.
Basic principles of insect anatomy and behavior are presented in a small thin volume consisting of short, topical entries and numerous small photographs and drawings. A bit of history, the standard definition of "insect," senses and body parts, metamorphosis, social behavior, plant eating, hunting of prey, coloration, stinging, communication, and many more topics are covered. The illustrations are only adequate, but many insects are included, and this is good basic information quickly presented.
SUBJ: Insects--Miscellanea.

595.7   Ph-2 4-6/5 $27.95   L   KC550
SUZUKI, DAVID. Looking at insects. By David Suzuki with Barbara Hehner. Wiley ISBN 0-471-54747-6; In Canada: Stoddart Publishing, 1992. 96p. ill. (David Suzuki's looking at).
Includes index.
Collect and observe cocoons, aphids, ants, and mealworms to understand why we need these unheralded creatures. Includes activities such as constructing a magnifying insect cage, making clover honey, and preserving an orb web. Students doing reports and projects can pick and choose among the pages. Insures participatory learning.
SUBJ: Insects.

595.76   Ph-1 5-6/9 $19.95   L   KC551
FISCHER-NAGEL, HEIDEROSE. Life of the ladybug. By Heiderose and Andreas Fischer-Nagel. Carolrhoda ISBN 0-87614-240-4, 1986. 48p. col. ill. (Carolrhoda nature watch book).
Includes glossary.
Follows the life cycle of the ladybug from mating through egg laying and the development of the larva through the stages of metamorphosis into an adult insect. Fine color photographs provide intriguing close-up views, and there is information about physical

characteristics, behavior, habitat, and the coloration of various species. An attractive introduction to this handsome and popular insect.
SUBJ: Ladybugs.

595.76   Ph-2 P-2/4 $4.95   P   KC552
HAWES, JUDY. Fireflies in the night. Rev. ed. Illus. by Ellen Alexander. HarperCollins ISBN 0-06-445101-1; In Canada: HarperCollins, c1991. 32p. col. ill. (Let's-read-and-find-out science book).
A child captures fireflies in a jar and learns about the cool light these popular insects produce. The picture book format, pleasantly shaded in nighttime greens and blues, briefly describes the firefly's body and includes bits of anecdotal history about human use of fireflies for light. Simple presentation is sketchy in scientific information but offers an adequate introduction for young independent readers or for reading aloud.
SUBJ: Fireflies.

595.76   Ph-3 A/10 $19.95   L   KC553
JOHNSON, SYLVIA A. Fireflies. Photos by Satoshi Kuribayashi. Lerner ISBN 0-8225-1485-0, 1986. 47p. col. ill. (Lerner natural science book).
Includes glossary and index.
Explains the life cycle of a typical firefly species from mating through egg laying, the hatching of the larva, growth and molting, the changes through metamorphosis into a pupa and finally the adult beetle; the process of bioluminescence is also explained. Magnified photographs detailing the physiology, feeding habits, and life stages accompany the uneven text, which is occasionally quite difficult. A useful introduction to a common insect and to the principles and processes of bioluminescence and metamorphosis for advanced readers.
SUBJ: Fireflies.

595.76   Ph-1 A/11 $19.95   L   KC554
JOHNSON, SYLVIA A. Ladybugs. Photos by Yuko Sato. Lerner ISBN 0-8225-1481-8, 1983. 48p. col. ill. (Lerner natural science book).
Includes glossary and index.
Describes the life cycle, physiological structure, process of metamorphosis, behavior, variation of species, protection against enemies, dietary habits and benefits to man of the small beetle commonly known as ladybug. Very handsome color photographs and thoughtfully prepared text make an exemplary volume on insect life.
SUBJ: Ladybugs./ Beetles.

595.76   Ph-2 3-5/4 $9.98   L   KC555
WATTS, BARRIE. Ladybug. Silver Burdett ISBN 0-382-09437-9, 1987. 25p. col. ill. (Stopwatch books).
Includes index.
Magnified photographs follow ladybugs through the stages of metamorphosis: egg, larva, pupa, adult. A simple text explains the characteristics of each stage, and labelled drawings are included along with full-page color photographs. A large print sentence, intended for less skilled readers, heads the longer text on each page; though the device will not be readily evident to children the book is a good introduction to this familiar insect.
SUBJ: Ladybugs.

595.77   Ph-1 5-6/7 $19.95   L   KC556
FISCHER-NAGEL, HEIDEROSE. Housefly. By Heiderose and Andreas Fischer-Nagel. Carolrhoda ISBN 0-87614-374-5, 1990. 48p. col. ill. (Carolrhoda nature watch book).
Includes glossary and index.
Seldom does the ubiquitous housefly appear so attractive as in the bold, magnified photographs of this informative presentation. The continuous essay text describes the compound eyes, the other senses, eating, mating and egg laying, the stages of metamorphosis, the process of diapause, similarity to related species, and the ecological role of flies. This careful examination demands attentive reading and should stimulate the reader to further personal observation of this common insect.
SUBJ: Housefly./ Flies.

595.78   Ph-2 3-5/5 $13.00   T   KC557
ARNOSKY, JIM. Crinkleroot's guide to knowing butterflies and moths. Simon & Schuster ISBN 0-689-80587-X; In Canada: Distican, 1996. 32p. col. ill.
Crinkleroot, the elderly naturalist, takes readers on a forest walk and introduces many species of butterflies and moths. Pen and watercolor views blend humor in the figure of Crinkleroot with science in the clear, brief explanations and accurate, life-size drawings of the insects. An effective and congenial introduction for nonfiction readers, backyard naturalists, and students doing reports.
SUBJ: Butterflies./ Moths.

VCR 595.78   Ph-3 5-6 $225.00   OD KC558
BUTTERFLIES (Videocassette). Moody Institute of Science/dist. by Pyramid Media 06344, 1990. 1/2" VHS videocassette color (15min).
Includes Teacher's Guide.
Many lovely species illustrate the body structure and complex life cycle of the butterfly. The narration covers classification of butterflies as Lepidoptera, assorted statistics, differences between moths and butterflies, stages of metamorphosis of a zebra longwing, and a close-up examination of body parts. An excellent introduction, this will be useful where the life cycle of butterflies is included in the science curriculum of upper grades.
SUBJ: Butterflies.

595.78   Ph-1 4-6/6 $15.95   L   KC559
FACKLAM, MARGERY. Creepy, crawly caterpillars. Illus. by Paul Facklam. Little, Brown ISBN 0-316-27391-0; In Canada: Little, Brown, 1996. 32p. col. ill.
Includes glossary.
Bold drawings introduce 13 caterpillars. The attractive and useful format pairs a full-page portrait of the caterpillar with a page of text describing physical characteristics and behavior while a band along the bottom sketches each stage of the life cycle from egg to adult. The thoughtfully constructed volume is an informative lesson on metamorphosis as well as a good introduction to the assorted caterpillars.
SUBJ: Caterpillars./ Metamorphosis.

595.78   Ph-1 K-2/4 $15.95   L   KC560
GIBBONS, GAIL. Monarch butterfly. Holiday House ISBN 0-8234-0773-X, 1989. unp. col. ill.
Warm, colorful drawings and simple text follow the life stages of this familiar species from the egg laid on a milkweed plant to the hatching and growth of the caterpillar, its change to a chrysalis, and the emerging of the butterfly. Yellow bordered pages frame well structured scenes which include scientific names with phonetic division of the words superimposed on some of the pictures. Though these labels may occasionally confuse the reader this is a nice full explanation of the life cycle including both the process of metamorphosis and the migration behavior of this common butterfly.
SUBJ: Monarch butterfly./ Butterflies.

595.78   Ph-1 K-2/2 $14.89   L   KC561
HEILIGMAN, DEBORAH. From caterpillar to butterfly. Illus. by Bari Weissman. HarperCollins ISBN 0-06-024268-X; In Canada: HarperCollins, 1996. 32p. col. ill. (Let's-read-and-find-out science book).
Includes directory.
Children in a classroom watch a caterpillar in a jar, observing its growth, molting, and emergence as a butterfly. Cheerful full-page scenes of classroom and animal life and simple explanations provide a nice firsthand lesson on the process of metamorphosis. A pleasant accompaniment for this common classroom event.
SUBJ: Butterflies--Metamorphosis./ Metamorphosis./ Caterpillars.

595.78   Ph-2 5-6/7 $15.99   L   KC562
LAVIES, BIANCA. Monarch butterflies: mysterious travelers. Text and photos by Bianca Lavies. Dutton ISBN 0-525-44905-1, 1992. unp. col. ill.
Masses of monarchs hibernating in Mexico are the focus of this attractive photo essay which describes the work of scientist Fred Urquhart in solving the mystery of this migrating butterfly's winter location. The book begins with life cycle information before moving on to the famous discovery. Beautiful, recent photographs and the lack of information about dates suggest that the discovery was recent, which is far from correct. In spite of the omission, the handsome volume is an informative presentation on this widely known butterfly.
SUBJ: Monarch butterfly./ Butterflies.

595.78   Ph-2 4-6/6 $15.95   L   KC563
PASCOE, ELAINE. Butterflies and moths. Photos by Dwight Kuhn. Blackbirch ISBN 1-56711-180-7, 1997. 48p. col. ill. (Nature close-up).
Includes glossary, directory, bibliography and index.
Butterflies, moths, and caterpillars of many species illustrate an informative discussion of their physical characteristics and life cycle. A major portion of the book explains how to collect and observe caterpillars, eggs, pupae, and butterflies. Practical advice on capture and care of specimens includes thorough instructions for setting up simple housing, providing food, and careful handling of the insects. Useful material for science projects.
SUBJ: Butterflies./ Moths./ Butterflies--Experiments./ Moths--Experiments./ Experiments.

595.78   Ph-2 5-6/6 $19.99   L   KC564
PRINGLE, LAURENCE P. Extraordinary life: the story of a monarch butterfly. by Laurence Pringle. Illus. by Bob Marstall. Orchard ISBN 0-531-33002-8, 1997. 64p. col. ill., maps.
Includes bibliography and index.
From a Massachusetts hay field to a mountain in Mexico, this handsome, slim volume uses attractive paintings to follow a particular monarch butterfly through its unusually long migration. The stages of metamorphosis, animal predators, the capture of monarchs and tagging them for study, the life of the monarch through each season, the rigors of the journey, and advice on raising monarchs in captivity are explained in informative text and captions. The large, flat volume provides many scientific explanations as well as a close-up sense of the life experiences of the insect, making it useful for both information and reading enjoyment.
SUBJ: Monarch butterfly./ Butterflies.

595.78   Ph-1 P-2/5 $15.95   L   KC565
REIDEL, MARLENE. From egg to butterfly. Carolrhoda ISBN 0-87614-153-X, 1981. 24p. col. ill. (Carolrhoda start to finish book).
Attractive full-color paintings and simple informative text introduce the concept of metamorphosis and describe the stages in the life cycle of the butterfly. The reading level is not nearly as difficult as indicated--certain longer words are used repeatedly (caterpillar, butterfly, chrysalis, metamorphosis). The small format is pleasing, manageable, and informative.
SUBJ: Butterflies--Metamorphosis./ Insects--Metamorphosis.

CE 595.78   Ph-2 2-4/4 $3.50   P   KC566
SABIN, LOUIS. Amazing world of butterflies and moths. Illus. by Jean Helmer. Troll ISBN 0-89375-561-3, 1982. 32p. col. ill.
Read-along kit available from Troll MA051, 1983. 1 sound cassette (13min) 5 paperback books, guide, $28.95.
Attractive colored drawings and simple text introduce the physical characteristics, behavior and life cycle of butterflies and moths and briefly describe a few particular species. The differences between moths and butterflies are explained, and a variety of caterpillars are also presented in this informative survey for young readers.
SUBJ: Butterflies./ Moths.

595.78   Ph-2 3-6/6 $15.95   L   KC567
SANDVED, KJELL BLOCH. Butterfly alphabet. By Kjell B. Sandved. Scholastic ISBN 0-590-48003-0; In Canada: Scholastic, 1996. unp. col. ill.
Stunning microscopic photographs reveal the forms of letters in the colorful wings of 26 butterflies. A short poetic phrase emphasizing the featured letter and a small, natural photograph are handsomely arranged to face the full-page magnified wing. A page of commentary on butterfly variations and a key which lists brief facts and locale of each species conclude the book. A bit sentimental, this is both a beautiful visual exercise and a magnificent introduction to the variety and beauty of moths and butterflies.
SUBJ: Butterflies./ Moths./ Alphabet.

595.78   Ph-2 2-4/4 $9.95   L   KC568
WATTS, BARRIE. Butterfly and caterpillar. Silver Burdett ISBN 0-3820-9282-1, 1985. 24p. col. ill. (Stopwatch books).
Includes index.
Follows the life cycle of a cabbage butterfly from mating and egg laying through hatching of eggs, growth of the caterpillar, the change into a chrysalis, and the emergence of a new butterfly. A page of text with a bold print heading and smaller print for the explanation contains a small drawing or photograph and always faces an excellent full-page color photograph. Primarily a pictorial introduction, this is an attractive introduction to this complex life cycle.
SUBJ: Butterflies./ Caterpillars./ Metamorphosis.

595.78   Ph-3 A/10 $20.99   L   KC569
WHALLEY, PAUL. Butterfly and moth. Photos by Colin Keates and David King. Knopf ISBN 0-394-99618-6, 1988. 64p. col. ill. (Eyewitness books).
Includes index.
Bold illustrations depict the life cycle and physiology of butterflies and moths and introduce an impressive variety of species in this striking oversize volume. Short segments of difficult text and numerous captions cover numerous topics: differences between butterflies and moths, courtship and egg laying, the four stages of development, migration and hibernation, camouflage and more. Some of the magnified photographs are over-exaggerated, and the format is very busy, but the international scope and broad coverage are attractive and useful.
SUBJ: Butterflies./ Moths.

595.79   Ph-2 2-4/2 $15.95   L   KC570
COLE, JOANNA. Magic School Bus inside a beehive. Illus. by Bruce Degen. Scholastic ISBN 0-590-44684-3; In Canada: Scholastic, 1996. 48p. col. ill.

Ms. Frizzle drives her class into a bee hive, sprays everyone with a bee pheromone, and gives orders to make wax hexagonal cells. Her students also feed larvae, help defend against a bear attack, and make a beeline out of there on the magic yellow bus. Unbelievable antics reveal hive secrets. Use in combination with a realistic bee book for dynamite teaching and learning.
SUBJ: Honeybee./ Bees./ Beehives./ Honey.

595.79   Ph-1 1-4/4 $15.89   L   KC571
DORROS, ARTHUR. Ant cities. Crowell/HarperCollins ISBN 0-690-04570-0; In Canada: HarperCollins, 1987. 28p. col. ill. (Let's-read-and-find-out science book).
Spanish version CIUDADES DE HORMIGAS available from Harper Arco Iris (ISBN 0-06-025360-6, 1995).
Diagrams the layout of tunnel systems built by harvester ants and describes the responsibilities of the queen, the males, and the workers. Simple text and attractive crayon drawings explain anthills, the life cycle, care of the eggs, larvae, and pupae and also introduce various species of ants and their different eating habits. A one-page set of instructions for constructing an "ant-farm" in a jar rounds out an informative introduction by inviting children to engage in further observation.
SUBJ: Ants--Habits and behavior./ Spanish language materials.

595.79   Ph-1 4-6/7 $7.95   P   KC572
FISCHER-NAGEL, HEIDEROSE. Life of the honeybee. By Heiderose and Andreas Fischer-Nagel. Carolrhoda ISBN 0-87614-470-9, 1986. 47p. col. ill. (Carolrhoda nature watch book).
Includes glossary.
Remarkable color photographs follow the stages of development of honeybees and the tasks of the worker bees inside the hive and out among the trees and flowers as they gather pollen and nectar. The stages of metamorphosis, dealing with other insects that invade the hive, maintenance and construction of the honeycomb, and the swarming of bees to establish a new hive are among the topics covered in numerous pictures and straightforward text. Though an index would have been helpful, the careful development of this close-up view makes this a first choice for information on this important insect.
SUBJ: Honeybee./ Bees.

595.79   Ph-1 3-5/6 $15.93   L   KC573
GIBBONS, GAIL. Honey makers. Morrow ISBN 0-688-11387-7, 1997. unp. col. ill.
Both bees and beekeepers share the work in this carefully drawn, detailed explanation of making honey. Bright, well labelled drawings and framed text explain the bodies and life cycle of bees, the many tasks performed by worker bees, and foraging for nectar and its conversion to honey. Final section of the book describes the structure of wooden beehives, the colleciton of honey, and the beekeeper's month-by-month cycle of tasks through the year. The cheerful presentation and clear explanations offer a very solid introduction to the honeybee's life cycle and social behavior as well as the production of honey.
SUBJ: Honeybee./ Bees./ Bee culture./ Honey.

595.79   Ph-1 5-6/8 $19.95   L   KC574
JOHNSON, SYLVIA A. Wasps. Photos by Hiroshi Ogawa. Lerner ISBN 0-8225-1460-5, 1984. 48p. col. ill. (Lerner natural science book).
Includes glossary and index.
Follows the life cycle of the polistes wasp, describing the physical characteristics and behavior in food gathering, nest building, and caring for the young. The informative text and outstanding color photographs also explain the process of metamorphosis and the roles assigned to different members in communities of social insects. An excellent source for serious students and attractive browsing material as well.
SUBJ: Wasps./ Insect societies.

VCR 595.79   Ph-3 3-6 $49.00   OD KC575
LIFE CYCLE OF THE HONEYBEE (Videocassette). Produced by National Geographic in conjunction with Oxford Scientific Films. National Geographic 51124, c1976, 1986. 1/2" VHS videocassette color (12min). (Bio-science series).
Up to 70,000 honey bees inhabit a hive, and living in an advanced social structure, perform their specific functions. Straight-forward narrative and striking photography show each type of bee: queen, drone, attendant, and forager workers performing tasks. A useful adjunct to animal studies curriculum.
SUBJ: Honeybee.

595.79   Ph-1 4-6/6 $13.95   T   KC576
MICUCCI, CHARLES. Life and times of the honeybee. Ticknor & Fields ISBN 0-395-65968-X, 1995. 32p. col. ill.

Cheerful bits of information and plentiful drawings present many aspects of bee life and the production of honey. The slim volume includes doublespread pages on many topics: explaining bee anatomy, caring for the hive, tending the young, and making honey. Human activities as beekeepers are also explained. Enlarged drawings are striking, and the copious smaller sketches and captions are absorbing and useful in this versatile book.
SUBJ: Honeybee./ Bee culture./ Honey.

595.79   Ph-2 4-6/7 $19.95   L   KC577
OVERBECK, CYNTHIA. Ants. Photos by Satoshi Kuribayashi. Lerner ISBN 0-8225-1468-0, 1982. 48p. col. ill. (Lerner natural science book).
Includes glossary and index.
Color photographs provide fascinating close-up views of ants about their daily tasks, and a simple, straightforward text describes physiology, appearance of certain species, behavior and roles of the soldier, worker, and queen ants. A good introduction to ants and the life of social insects.
SUBJ: Ants.

595.79   Ph-2 A/8 $13.93   L   KC578
PRINGLE, LAURENCE P. Killer bees. Rev. ed. By Laurence Pringle. Morrow ISBN 0-688-09524-0, 1990. 56p. ill.
Includes glossary, bibliography and index.
Revised edition of: HERE COME THE KILLER BEES, c1986.
Laurence Pringle recounts the 1990 arrival in Texas of the dreaded African bees after more than thirty years of swarming northward through Latin America. Solid chapters of text, illustrated with black and white photographs cover history, behavior, efforts to control this worrisome insect, and possible future effects on bee keeping in the United States. An informative presentation on the species, this also demonstrates the folly of transplanting some animals from one continent to another.
SUBJ: Africanized honeybee./ Bees.

CE 595.79   Ph-1 2-4/2 $3.50   P   KC579
SABIN, FRANCENE. Amazing world of ants. Illus. by Eulala Conner. Troll ISBN 0-89375-559-1, 1982. 32p. col. ill.
Read-along kit from Troll MA053, 1983. 1 sound cassette (14min), 6 paperback books, guide. $39.70.
Provides basic information about the physical characteristics and social behavior of ants in a clear, simple text and pleasant colored drawings. Illustrations include diagrams of anatomy and the four typical members of an ant colony; queen, drone, soldier and worker as well as pictures of some particularly interesting types of species (weaver ants, leaf-cutters, honey ants, etc.). A useful and attractive introduction to a familiar insect.
SUBJ: Ants.

596   Ph-1 5-6/7 $7.95   P   KC580
ARNOSKY, JIM. Secrets of a wildlife watcher. Morrow ISBN 0-688-10531-9, c1983, 1991. 64p. col. ill.
Selectors' Choice, 15th ed.
Invites children to observe animals in their natural habitat, to develop techniques of locating animals, to sharpen observation skills and to record animal sightings and behavior in a personal journal. Anecdotes and attractive drawings of numerous species convey considerable information about animal behavior and physiology in a comfortable volume appealing to young naturalists and useful for teaching purposes and outdoor projects.
SUBJ: Nature study.

596   Ph-3 A/9 $16.98   L   KC581
SILVERSTEIN, ALVIN. Vertebrates. By Dr. Alvin, Virginia, and Robert Silverstein. Twenty-First Century ISBN 0-8050-3517-6; In Canada: Fritzhenry & Whiteside, 1996. 64p. col. ill. (Kingdoms of life).
Includes glossary and index.
This solid discussion of how different classes of vertebrate animals developed begins with a description of the classification scheme for plants and animals. Following an explanation of animal development, chapters are devoted to fish, reptiles and amphibians, birds, and several categories of mammals. The highly informative, slim volume offers a useful introduction to animal classification and evolution for serious science students.
SUBJ: Vertebrates.

597   Ph-1 2-4/5 $14.89   L   KC582
ALIKI. My visit to the aquarium. HarperCollins ISBN 0-06-021459-7; In Canada: HarperCollins, 1993. unp. col. ill.
A family's visit to a large aquarium becomes a colorful introduction to the fish and other animals living in the various types of habitats. Large views of the busy aquarium introduce each exhibit, and labeled drawings accompany explanations of life in tide pools, coastal streams, coral reefs, deep seas, and rivers. The young narrator's

enthusiasm for the aquarium and the attractive pictures will be enjoyed by readers before or after an aquarium visit. Concluding note is a thought-provoking reminder for environmental studies units that all the animals are endangered and need everyone's support.
SUBJ: Aquariums, Public./ Aquatic biology./ Marine animals./ Freshwater animals.

597   Ph-2   A/11 $19.00   T   KC583
AUDUBON SOCIETY FIELD GUIDE TO NORTH AMERICAN FISHES, WHALES AND DOLPHINS. Knopf ISBN 0-394-53405-0; In Canada: Random House, 1983. 848p. col. ill. (Audubon Society field guides).
Includes index.
Identifies through shape and color classifications over 500 species of marine and freshwater fish and all types of whales, dolphins, and porpoises native to North America. Detailed information is presented on physical characteristics, habitat, and range. A useful information source. A duplicate copy is recommended for the reference collection.
SUBJ: Fishes./ Whales./ Dolphins./ Porpoises.

597   Ph-1 5-6/7 $20.99   L   KC584
PARKER, STEVE. Fish. Photos by David King and Colin Keates. Knopf ISBN 0-679-90439-5, 1990. 63p. col. ill. (Eyewitness books).
Includes index.
Spanish version LOS PECES available from Santillana (ISBN 84-372-3729-7, 1995).
A wealth of information appears in this well constructed, highly pictorial volume. Topical presentations on double spread pages of short text, informative captions, and intriguing photographs and drawings cover many subjects: skeletal systems, early fishes, feeding, swimming, care of the young, dealing with enemies, snakes of the sea, and more. An absorbing introduction useful for reports and appealing as recreational reading.
SUBJ: Fishes./ Spanish language materials.

597   Ph-1 K-3/3 $14.89   L   KC585
PFEFFER, WENDY. What's it like to be a fish? Illus. by Holly Keller. HarperCollins ISBN 0-06-024429-1; In Canada: HarperCollins, 1996. 32p. col. ill. (Let's-read-and-find-out science book).
A pet goldfish is the focus of clear explanations of how fish breathe, swim, eat, and otherwise manage underwater life. As the senses, physical characteristics, and behavior of the goldfish are explained, they are compared to fish in the wild and to human beings. Pleasant watercolor views capture the experiences of the pet owner and the fish, and there are instructions for setting up a fishbowl. The attractive and lucid presentation will be widely enjoyed.
SUBJ: Fishes./ Pets.

597   Ph-2 4-6/8 $15.99   L   KC586
ROTHAUS, DON. Moray eels. By Don P. Rothaus. Child's World ISBN 1-56766-187-4, 1996. 32p. col. ill. (Naturebooks).
Includes index.
This brief introduction with striking photographs explains the appearance and size of various species of eels and the behavior and life cycle of this long fish. The history of the moray, its hunting and eating habits, the hatching of larvae, and the symbiotic partnerships with cleaning shrimp and wrasse are included. Human fascination with the moray concludes the discussion, and the full-page views will be a ready lure for browsers.
SUBJ: Morays.

597   Ph-1 P $7.50   P   KC587
WILDSMITH, BRIAN. Fishes. Oxford ISBN 0-19-272151-8, 1985. unp. col. ill.
Selectors' Choice, 15th ed.
A cluster of porcupine fish...a hover of trout...a party of rainbow fish...a battery of barracuda...and thirteen more groupings of glowing fishes. Wildsmith's album, formerly out of print, makes rich use of color and language to introduce these denizens of the deep to young viewers.
SUBJ: Fishes.

597   Ph-2 1-6/3 $6.95   P   KC588
WU, NORBERT. Fish faces. Henry Holt ISBN 0-8050-5347-6; In Canada: Fitzhenry & Whiteside, c1993, 1997. unp. col. ill.
"Spotted fish, dotted fish/Fish with lines and stripes and waves/Fish with spikes and spines and branches" appear in small vignettes and large underwater scenes which provide a striking introduction to the variety of tropical fish. Simple text is a commentary on the colorful photographs. Final page lists names of each of the fish.
SUBJ: Fishes./ Marine biology.

VCR 597.3   Ph-3 2-4 $49.00   OD KC589
ABOUT SHARKS (Videocassette). National Geographic 51000, 1981. 1/2" VHS videocassette color (12min).

The over 300 different varieties of sharks dwell in a variety of waters and are noted for unique physical characteristics. Well paced narration and attractive photography explore introductory information about habits and behavior and physiological traits of these feared fish.
SUBJ: Sharks.

597.3   Ph-2 4-6/7 $15.95   L   KC590
ARNOLD, CAROLINE. Watch out for sharks! Photos by Richard Hewett. Clarion ISBN 0-395-57560-5, 1991. 48p. col. ill.
Includes index and bibliography.
Several shark species serve as examples in this discussion of shark bodies and behavior. Based on an excellent touring museum exhibition organized in Los Angeles, the text is very informative. Excellent photographs of the exhibited sharks occasionally include human viewers reminding the reader that these are not actually live animals. Good information but less dramatic than documentary works of live sharks in their natural habitats.
SUBJ: Sharks.

597.3   Ph-2 4-6/7 $5.95   P   KC591
CARRICK, CAROL. Sand tiger shark. Illus. by Donald Carrick. Clarion ISBN 0-395-59701-3, c1977. 32p. col. ill.
In the subdued underwater world, we are eyewitnesses to the life cycle of the sand tiger shark. The blue-green watercolors give a feeling of this environment and this recently popular animal. Hunting, eating and grouping habits are described. The shark's life ends in an exciting feeding frenzy. A good book to satisfy current requests for books on this animal.
SUBJ: Sharks./ Sand tiger shark.

597.3   Ph-2 1-3/2 $11.99   L   KC592
COLE, JOANNA. Hungry, hungry sharks. Illustrated by Patricia Wynne. Random House ISBN 0-394-97471-9; In Canada: Random House, 1986. 46p. col. ill. (Step into reading).
Concentrating on simple descriptions of shark behavior, this elementary introduction mentions the long history of sharks, discusses comparative sizes, and shows members of several species. Short sentences with simplified text and pleasant drawings do not heavily emphasize the eating habits of sharks, and there is discussion of human efforts to study sharks. Though a sketchy overview, this thin volume adequately provides information at a simpler level than most other books on this popular subject.
SUBJ: Sharks.

597.3   Ph-1 P-3/3 $15.95   L   KC593
GIBBONS, GAIL. Sharks. Holiday House ISBN 0-8234-0960-0, 1992. unp. col. ill.
Simple text and effective drawings cover the general characteristics of sharks and introduce eleven different species. Shark bodies and senses, teeth, history, live birth and egg laying, varied sizes and eating habits, and different degrees of ferocity are briefly discussed. This is a sketchy but attractive survey sure to be popular with beginning readers.
SUBJ: Sharks.

597.3   Ph-1 4-6/5 $16.00   T   KC594
MARKLE, SANDRA. Outside and inside sharks. Atheneum ISBN 0-689-80348-6; In Canada: Distican, 1996. 40p. col. ill.
Includes glossary/index.
Shark senses and other bodily features are examined in well chosen photographs and clear, well shaped text. Includes many views of the internal organs as well as external views of assorted species. Explains how the shark's body is well adapted for its predator life underwater. Fascinating as personal reading or as an excellent introduction to the ever interesting animal.
SUBJ: Sharks.

597.3   Ph-1 5-6/7 $15.95   T   KC595
SIMON, SEYMOUR. Sharks. HarperCollins ISBN 0-06-023029-0; In Canada: HarperCollins, 1995. unp. col. ill.
Shark bodies and behavior are explained in a lucid, smooth discussion accompanied by striking full-page photographs. Simon begins with the premise that sharks have been stigmatized through endless sensationalized treatment, and he proceeds with an objective and informative discussion of physical characteristics, each of the senses, variety among species, eating preferences, and different types of birth. The handsome book is an appealing, excellent introduction to this impressive animal.
SUBJ: Sharks.

597.5   Ph-2 P-A/3 $14.93   L   KC596
COLE, JOANNA. Fish hatches. By Joanna Cole and Jerome Wexler. Morrow ISBN 0-688-32153-4, c1978. 39p. ill.

A collection of photographs that show the development of a trout embryo in the egg and follow its growth to maturity; how a fish swims, breathes, and the way its senses work are all examined. Adds to study of animal birth and life.
SUBJ: Trout./ Fishes.

597.5   Ph-2 5-6/7 $13.95   L   KC597
HALTON, CHERYL M. Those amazing eels. Dillon ISBN 0-87518-431-6, 1990. 96p. col. ill.
Includes bibliography, glossary, index and appendices.
Eels continue to be truly amazing to scientists for their long, complex metamorphosis which includes lengthy journeys between the Sargasso Sea and freshwater locations all over America and Europe. This competent account describes the eel's history, the slow work of scientists in discovering its life cycle, various species of eels and other eel-like species, and eel farms and fisheries. Instructions for building an eel trap and recipes are included. A very good introduction to this unusual animal.
SUBJ: Eels.

597.8   Ph-2 2-5/6 $15.95   L   KC598
BERNHARD, EMERY. Salamanders. Illus. by Durga Bernhard. Holiday House ISBN 0-8234-1148-6, 1995. unp. col. ill.
Includes glossary.
Colorful drawings of many species illustrate this attractive introduction to the land and water life of salamanders. Short text below framed pictures explains the life of amphibians, mating and egg laying, stages of growth, feeding, physical characteristics of particular species, and a bit of history. The names and the prehistoric appearance of many of these animals are intriguing. Useful, well-crafted life cycle presentation.
SUBJ: Salamanders.

597.8   Ph-3 5-6/9 $20.99   L   KC599
CLARKE, BARRY. Amphibian. Photos by Geoff Brightling and Frank Greenaway. Knopf ISBN 0-679-93879-6, 1993. 64p. col. ill. (Eyewitness books).
"Dorling Kindersley book."
Includes index.
Bold, busy pages often exaggerate the bodies of frogs, toads, newts, and salamanders in this profusion of information bits. Topical pages describe history, skeletons, egg laying, metamorphosis, unique characteristics of particular animals, and numerous other subjects. Sometimes dark and cluttered, this is a substantial compendium of standard and less familiar information.
SUBJ: Amphibians.

597.8   Ph-1 P-A/6 $15.93   L   KC600
COLE, JOANNA. Frog's body. Photos by Jerome Wexler. Morrow ISBN 0-688-32228-X, 1980. 47p. col. ill.
Photographs and drawings combine with the lucid text to describe the physical characteristics and anatomy of frogs.
SUBJ: Frogs--Anatomy.

597.8   Ph-2 3-5/5 $19.99   L   KC601
GERHOLDT, JAMES E. Frogs. Abdo & Daughters ISBN 1-56239-310-3, 1994. 24p. col. ill. (Amazing amphibians).
Includes glossary and index.
A colorful variety of frogs appear in this brief introduction to the physical characteristics and habits of the popular amphibian. Short bits of text discuss sizes, shapes, colors, habitats, senses, defenses, food, and babies. The wooden style and uneven photographs are a detriment, but the subject appeal will carry the book, and there's sufficient material for reports.
SUBJ: Frogs.

597.8   Ph-3 3-5/5 $19.99   L   KC602
GERHOLDT, JAMES E. Tree frogs. Abdo & Daughters ISBN 1-56239-311-1, 1994. 23p. col. ill. (Amazing amphibians).
Includes glossary and index.
Brief bits of text and useful color photographs introduce an interesting variety of tree frogs. The slim presentation covers sizes, shapes, colors, habitats, senses, defenses, food, and babies. Useful where science units cover tree frogs.
SUBJ: Tree frogs./ Frogs.

597.8   Ph-1 K-3/3 $15.95   L   KC603
GIBBONS, GAIL. Frogs. Holiday House ISBN 0-8234-1052-8, 1993. unp. col. ill.
Pleasant, informative drawings and simple text follow the frog life cycle from the hatching of eggs to the transformation of tadpoles into frogs. Bands of explanation run below the framed scenes, and occasional labels identify body parts. Characteristics of amphibians, eating, swimming, enemies, hibernation, and differences between frogs

and toads are all explained. Enjoyable reading and useful teaching material.
SUBJ: Frogs.

597.8   Ph-2 5-6/7 $19.95   L   KC604
JOHNSON, SYLVIA A. Tree frogs. Photos by Modoki Masuda. Lerner ISBN 0-8225-1467-2, 1986. 48p. col. ill. (Lerner natural science book).
Includes glossary and index.
Describes some of the physical characteristics of tree frogs along with their life cycle, metamorphosis, hibernation and behavior. Attractive color photographs accompany a text that is sometimes sketchy and is more difficult than the reading level suggests. Photographic sequences of tadpoles and very young frogs are very effective in this attractive work on an inherently appealing subject.
SUBJ: Tree frogs./ Frogs.

597.8   Ph-2 4-6/6 $11.95   T   KC605
JULIVERT, ANGELS. Fascinating world of frogs and toads. Barron's ISBN 0-8120-6345-7, 1993. 31p. col. ill.
Includes glossary and index.
Originally published in Spanish, EL FASCINANTE MUNDO DE LAS RANAS Y LAS SAPOS, 1993.
Many different species appear in this detailed introduction to the life cycle and behavior of frogs and toads. The slim paperback volume is arranged in topical sections, heavily illustrated with realistic paintings, covering differences between the two animals, mating and egg laying, metamorphosis, eating, camouflage, and life in trees and underground. A useful source for reports and personal reading.
SUBJ: Frogs./ Toads.

597.8   Ph-2 5-6/7 $14.93   L   KC606
PARKER, NANCY WINSLOW. Frogs, toads, lizards and salamanders. By Nancy Winslow Parker and Joan Richards Wright. Illustrated by Nancy Winslow Parker. Greenwillow ISBN 0-688-08681-0, 1990. 48p. col. ill.
Includes glossaries, range maps, and scientific classification.
Includes bibliography and index.
Each entry in this colorful dictionary of 16 amphibian and reptilean species begins with a rhymed cartoon. "Onto Patty's pie a la mode/ hopped a large American Toad," features a picnic, labelled pictures of the toad and several sentences describing aspects of the animal's behavior. The book concludes with a picture glossary of the growth of frogs and toads, the anatomy of frogs and lizards, and the scale patterns of salamanders.
SUBJ: Frogs./ Toads./ Lizards./ Salamanders.

597.8   Ph-2 4-6/4 $16.85   L   KC607
PATENT, DOROTHY HINSHAW. Flashy fantastic rain forest frogs. Illus. by Kendahl Jan Jubb. Walker ISBN 0-8027-8616-2; In Canada: Thomas Allen, 1997. 32p. col. ill.
Includes index.
Bold illustrations and short, clear text introduce several of the colorful frog species that are at home on the floor or in the tree tops of rainforests. Patent explains how these frogs live and protect themselves, ways they tend to their eggs and young, and dangers effecting their survival in the contemporary world. An attractive browsing item as well as useful information on frogs and rainforest life. For environmental studies.
SUBJ: Frogs./ Rain forest animals.

CE 597.8   Ph-2 K-2/2 $14.89   L   KC608
PFEFFER, WENDY. From tadpole to frog. Illus. by Holly Keller. HarperCollins ISBN 0-06-023117-3; In Canada: HarperCollins, 1994. unp. col. ill. (Let's-read-and-find-out science book).
Read-along kit available from HarperChildren's Audio (ISBN 0-69470-046-0, 1996). 1 paperback book, 1 sound cassette (8min), $7.95.
Winter brings hibernation to the frog pond, and spring is the season for mating and egg laying in this simple explanation of the bullfrog's life cycle. Watercolor scenes and simple text describe the long metamorphosis of tadpoles, which must also survive winter before they complete the transformation to adult bullfrogs. A pleasant book to read, this is not quite as clear as some in showing the process of change but will serve to introduce this important life cycle.
SUBJ: Frogs./ Tadpoles./ Animals--Infancy.

VCR 597.8   Ph-2 5-6 $99.00   OD   KC609
SALAMANDERS (Videocassette). With David Suzuki. Canadian Broadcasting Corp./dist. by Wombat Productions 9210, 1985. 1/2" VHS videocassette color (11min).
Sensitive to environmental changes, salamanders have adapted to a variety of surroundings throughout history. Close-up photography and narrative trace the life cycle of these amphibians, the threat posed to their survival by pollution, and the animal's capability to evolve in response to these factors.
SUBJ: Salamanders./ Man--Influence on nature./ Evolution.

VCR 597.8   Ph-2 3-6 $69.00   OD KC610
TADPOLES AND FROGS (Videocassette). National Geographic 51218, c1979, 1986. 1/2" VHS videocassette color (11min).
A student's diary logs the stages of development from round egg to bean shaped egg, to tadpole, to tadpole with back legs, to tadpole with front and back legs, and to frog. The presentation of metamorphosis in two species illustrates the differences in the rate of change.
SUBJ: Frogs./ Metamorphosis.

597.8   Ph-3 A/7 $19.95   L   KC611
WINNER, CHERIE. Salamanders. Carolrhoda ISBN 0-87614-757-0, 1993. 48p. col. ill. (Carolrhoda nature watch book).
Includes glossary and index.
Many salamander species appear in color photographs and will attract readers to this informative survey. The dense text examines many aspects of behavior, physical characteristics, reproduction, metamorphosis, and migration of aquatic and terrestrial salamanders. The substantial discussion will best serve skilled readers with a serious interest in this common and diverse amphibian.
SUBJ: Salamanders.

VCR 597.9   Ph-2 5-6 $99.00   OD KC612
AMPHIBIANS AND REPTILES (Videocassette). National Geographic 50591, 1996. 1/2" VHS videocassette color (25min). (Animal classes).
Includes teacher's guide.
Closed captioned.
Childrens' classroom reports form the well organized narration that accompanies live-action photography and animated scenes of amphibians and reptiles. Good questions by unseen classmates introduce key topics to define significant physical characteristics and behavior, and main points are listed and reviewed. Featuring a nice variety of species, this congenial and informative introduction is an excellent science lesson.
SUBJ: Amphibians./ Reptiles.

597.9   Ph-2 3-6/8 $18.95   L   KC613
CREAGH, CARSON. Reptiles. Allen E. Geer, Consulting Editor. Nature Company/Time-Life Books ISBN 0-8094-9247-4, 1996. 64p. col. ill. (Nature Company discoveries library).
"Weldon Owen Production."
Includes glossary and index.
Bold photographs and drawings fill the large pages of this colorful compendium. Topical entries include short, sometimes difficult paragraphs of text, captions, and boxed facts on many aspects of physiology and behavior of crocodilians, lizards, turtles, tortoises, and snakes. Some of the pictures sensationalize these ever popular animals, and some entries give scant information while others are informative. Above all this big book will have great browsing appeal.
SUBJ: Reptiles.

VCR 597.9   Ph-2 2-4 $5.99   OD KC614
EXPLORING THE WORLD OF REPTILES (Videocassette). Video Treasures ISBN 1-55529-703-X, 1992. 1/2" VHS videocassette color (30min). (Shamu and you).
Includes activity booklet.
Close-up views at Sea World in Busch Gardens of many different animals in natural settings demonstrate aspects of reptile bodies and behavior. Sporadic observations by children intercut with views of snakes, turtles, crocodiles, lizards, and others while an enthusiastic narrator offers facts and explanations of hunting and eating, movement, color, camouflage, use of tongues, size, dangers, and special traits of particular animals. Questions and answers between the narrator and children and other show business effects may be obtrusive.
SUBJ: Reptiles.

597.9   Ph-2 5-6/6 $14.93   L   KC615
JOHNSTON, GINNY. Scaly babies: reptiles growing up. By Ginny Johnston and Judy Cutchins. Morrow ISBN 0-688-07306-9, 1988. 40p. col. ill.
Includes glossary and index.
Concentrating on those reptiles which hatch from eggs, this introduces newly hatched snakes, lizards, turtles and crocodiles. A short chapter devoted to each group discusses eggs and hatching and aspects of physiology and behavior; color photographs of many different species extend the information. Developed by museum staff, the text is somewhat challenging and miscellaneous, but the slim volume and the subject matter will appeal widely.
SUBJ: Reptiles.

597.9   Ph-2 4-6/5 $11.95   L   KC616
LAMPRELL, KLAY. Scaly things. Time Life ISBN 0-7835-4842-7, 1996. 32p. col. ill. (Nature Company young discoveries library).

"Weldon Owen Production."
Reptiles, fish, and even a few mammals that have scaly bodies appear in short, colorful entries that touch briefly on some of their physical characteristics and ways of life. Illustrations have short captions and accompany a few sentences of text introducing turtles and tortoises, crocodilians, chameleons, a variety of lizards and snakes, fish, and the pangolin. The sketchy information offers an interesting introduction, and the good views of familiar and exotic species will attract browsers.
SUBJ: Scales (Reptiles)./ Body covering (Anatomy).

597.92   Ph-1 2-4/6 $15.95   L   KC617
GIBBONS, GAIL. Sea turtles. Holiday House ISBN 0-8234-1191-5, 1995. unp. col. ill.
Pleasant framed paintings and informative bands of text demonstrate the physical characteristics and interesting reproductive cycle of sea turtles. The long history of sea turtles, the eight different species, the use of senses, swimming, eating, the exodus from the sea for nesting, the return of hatchlings to the sea, conservation problems, and differences between sea and land turtles are all explained. An attractive and substantial picture book presentation, this will be used for pleasure reading and various teaching units including environmental studies.
SUBJ: Sea turtles./ Turtles.

597.92   Ph-2 1-3/3 $15.95   T   KC618
GUIBERSON, BRENDA Z. Into the sea. Illus. by Alix Berenzy. Henry Holt ISBN 0-8050-2263-5; In Canada: Fitzhenry & Whiteside, 1996. unp. col. ill.
Handsome, luminous paintings follow a newly hatched sea turtle as she leaves the nest and experiences several years of growth and adventure in the world's oceans. The picture book presentation relates the biography of a particular animal to demonstrate the enemies and pollution dangers encountered by sea turtles, rudiments of ocean ecology, and the long, interesting life cycle which comes full circle as the turtle returns to her birthplace in adulthood to lay her own eggs. An effective introduction that will lead to some of the fuller photographic accounts of the large and long-lived sea turtle. For environmental studies.
SUBJ: Sea turtles./ Turtles.

597.92   Ph-1 5-6/6 $17.95   L   KC619
HOLLING, HOLLING CLANCY. Minn of the Mississippi. Houghton Mifflin ISBN 0-395-17578-X, c1951. 85p. ill.
Newbery Honor Book.
Available from National Library Service for the Blind and Physically Handicapped in Braille BR01848.
The adventures of a snapping turtle as it travels from the headwaters to the mouth of the Mississippi.
SUBJ: Mississippi River./ Turtles.

597.92   Ph-2 P-2/4 $12.99   T   KC620
KUHN, DWIGHT. Turtle's day. Photos by Dwight Kuhn. Text by Ron Hirschi. Cobblehill/Dutton ISBN 0-525-65172-1, 1994. unp. col. ill.
An eastern box turtle, seen in lovely full-page photographs, demonstrates a few aspects of turtle life in this simple introduction. Pictures and brief text explain some of the turtle's eating habits, encounters with other animals, the protection of her shell, and dangers she faces. A final page of discussion emphasizes modern survival problems and differences between land and sea turtles. Not a true life cycle, this is a pleasant encounter to an intriguing animal for enjoyment by younger readers.
SUBJ: Box turtle./ Turtles.

597.92   Ph-3 P-K/1 $11.95   L   KC621
PALAZZO-CRAIG, JANET. Turtles. By Janet Craig. Illus. by Kathie Kelleher. Troll ISBN 0-89375-664-4, 1982. 32p. col. ill. (Now I know).
Colorful paintings and simple text introduce the idea of variety of species and habitat among turtles. Brief mention of physical characteristics and diet is also made, and the hatching of eggs is described in an appealing presentation for the very young.
SUBJ: Turtles.

597.92   Ph-2 5-6/7 $13.95   L   KC622
SCHAFER, SUSAN. Galapagos tortoise. Dillon ISBN 0-87518-544-4; In Canada: Maxwell Macmillan, 1992. 64p. col. ill., map. (Dillon remarkable animals book).
Includes directory, glossary and index.
Extensive information about the history and bodies of turtles and tortoises is included in this introduction to the huge tortoises unique to the Galapagos Islands. Five chapters of text, accompanied by attractive photographs, a map, and diagrams of the interior structure of turtles, discuss the huge dome tortoises and the smaller saddlebacks and describe social behavior and conservation problems.

Attractive and substantial introduction.
SUBJ: Galapagos tortoise./ Turtles.

VCR 597.92   Ph-2 4-6 $245.00   KC623
TALKING ABOUT SEA TURTLES (Videocassette). Georgia Department of Natural Resources/dist. by New Dimension Media ISBN 1-56353-162-3, 1992. 1/2" VHS videocassette color (12min).
Includes study guide.
Remarkable photography follows a loggerhead turtle as she comes out of the sea, makes her laborious trip across a Georgia beach, and lays her eggs. Video recording and brief, straightforward narrative follow the turtle's return to the sea and the emergence of the young turtles as they hatch and make their way into the sea. The second half of the film explains human activities endangering the turtles and ways young people can be helpful. The intriguing close-up views are an exceptional introduction to the interesting life cycle of this sea animal. For environmental studies.
SUBJ: Loggerhead turtle./ Sea turtles./ Turtles./ Man--Influence on nature./ Wildlife conservation.

VCR 597.92   Ph-1 3-6 $99.00   KC624
VOYAGE OF THE LOGGERHEAD (Videocassette). National Geographic 51737, 1995. 1/2" VHS videocassette color (25min).
Includes teacher's guide.
Closed captioned.
Remarkable underwater photography follows a baby loggerhead turtle through her first year of life in the ocean habitat. Depicts the long swim to the deep waters, lodging in sargassum--a great raft of water plants, eating of jellyfish, escape from sharks and other predators, and dangerous encounters with human garbage caught in the sea. The strong message about human damage to the ocean ecosystem finally overshadows the life cycle information, but the outstanding views of the many animals and the garbage endangering them are fascinating lessons that deserve wide use. For environmental studies.
SUBJ: Loggerhead turtle./ Sea turtles./ Turtles./ Marine ecology./ Man--Influence on nature.

597.95   Ph-1 4-6/7 $15.93   L   KC625
DARLING, KATHY. Komodo dragon: on location. Photos by Tara Darling. Lothrop, Lee & Shepard ISBN 0-688-13777-6; In Canada: Hearst Book Group, 1997. 40p. col. ill. (On location).
Includes index.
Indonesia's giant lizards appear in impressive close-ups in this photo-essay of their physical characteristics and behavior. The author and photographer recount their experiences while visiting the endangered species on Komodo Island and develop an informative account of the meat-eating lizard's history, skin, teeth, senses, movement, hunting, eating, mating, and egg laying. The prehistoric looking reptile will have great appeal for many readers, and the book is an apt choice for booktalking or information use. For environmental studies.
SUBJ: Komodo dragon./ Lizards.

597.95   Ph-1 5-6/7 $17.27   L   KC626
LINDLEY, MIKE. Lizard in the jungle. Oxford Scientific Films/Gareth Stevens ISBN 1-55532-303-0, 1988. 32p. col. ill. (Animal habitats).
Includes glossary/index.
Numerous species appear in small, attractive photographs to illustrate this informative introduction to the physiology and life cycle of lizards. Each doublespread page is devoted to a topic: lizards around the world, eyes, camouflage, eggs, laying, enemies, etc. Neither text nor captions indicates size of the pictured animals, which sometimes appear to be unnaturally large, but the subject is intriguing, and the book should attract many readers.
SUBJ: Lizards.

597.95   Ph-2 4-6/7 $15.99   L   KC627
PATTON, DON. Iguanas. Child's World ISBN 1-56766-190-4, 1996. 32p. col. ill. (Naturebooks).
Includes index.
The prehistoric appearance of many iguanas is handsomely portrayed in the full-page photographs of this slim introduction. Their range in size, appearance, and location is mentioned along with some discussion of eating, drinking, egg laying, self defense, differences between desert and marine iguanas, and human consumption of the lizards. Though the information is a bit sketchy, the striking pictures will readily attract readers interested in reptiles or unusual animals.
SUBJ: Iguanas.

597.95   Ph-2 1-3/5 $13.88   L   KC628
RYDER, JOANNE. Lizard in the sun. Illus. by Michael Rothman. Morrow ISBN 0-688-07173-2, 1990. unp. col. ill. (Just for a day).
A boy is transformed into a lean, green lizard and experiences a day of napping in the sun, hiding among the leaves, and snapping up

food in this pleasant picture book. The simple text and bold double spread paintings convey the natural habitat, physical characteristics, and behavior of the lizard in a generalized rather than specifically factual manner. Not all readers will like the imaginative, experimental approach, but it should work well in literature based teaching units, for inviting discussion and observation, and as an introduction to further study of lizards.
SUBJ: Chameleons./ Lizards.

597.95   Ph-2 5-6/5 $5.95   P   KC629
SCHAFER, SUSAN. Komodo dragon. Dillon ISBN 0-38239-607-3, c1992, 1996. 60p. col. ill. (Dillon remarkable animals book).
Includes directory, glossary and index.
Now endangered, the world's largest lizard lives on just a few islands in Indonesia. This informative discussion of the Komodo dragon's physical characteristics, behavior, history, and life cycle is accompanied by a good selection of color photographs. A well-crafted presentation on an exotic animal whose large size and predatory behavior appeal to children.
SUBJ: Komodo dragon.

597.95   Ph-2 5-6/7 $19.95   L   KC630
SCHNIEPER, CLAUDIA. Chameleons. Photos by Max Meier. Carolrhoda ISBN 0-87614-341-9, 1989. 47p. col. ill. (Carolrhoda nature watch book).
Includes glossary and index.
Available from the National Library Service for the Blind and Physically Handicapped on sound recording cassette RC34340.
Able to look in different directions at the same time, use their tongues as weapons and change colors as well as show a wide variety of appearance among species, the chameleon is seen here in striking photographs. The information and somewhat difficult text describes unique physical details, behavior, feeding, breeding, and the movement of pigment which causes color change. Since size of particular species is not usually given, the enlarged photographs highly dramatize the animals, but this is a very good discussion of uncommonly interesting lizards.
SUBJ: Chameleons./ Lizards.

597.95   Ph-2 4-6/6 $19.95   L   KC631
SOUZA, D. M. Catch me if you can. Carolrhoda ISBN 0-87614-713-9, 1992. 40p. col. ill. (Creatures all around us).
Includes glossary and index.
Small color photographs and half pages of text describe the bodies and behaviors of an interesting variety of lizards. Discussion ranges quickly and smoothly over many topics: eating, reproduction, color changing, horns and scales, loss and new growth of tails, protection from enemies, and hibernation.
SUBJ: Lizards.

597.96   Ph-1 5-6/7 $13.88   L   KC632
ARNOLD, CAROLINE. Snake. Photos by Richard Hewett. Morrow ISBN 0-688-09410-4, 1991. 48p col photos. (Baby zoo animals).
Includes index.
Boas, pythons, and other snake species owned by the Los Angeles Zoo appear in colorful photographs accompanying an informative discussion of snake bodies and behavior. Zoo keepers and children are seen handling some snakes, and snake life in their natural habitat is also covered as the author describes eating, egg laying, size, color, and special physical characteristics. The photographs are appealing, and the well written text includes some intriguing bits along with standard information.
SUBJ: Snakes.

597.96   Ph-2 2-4/2 $19.00   L   KC633
BROEKEL, RAY. Snakes. Childrens Press ISBN 0-516-01649-0; In Canada: Childrens Press, 1982. 45p. col. ill. (New true book).
Includes glossary and index.
Describes some of the basic physical characteristics and behaviors of snakes: scales, tongues, fangs, size, hatching or birthing of young snakes, eating, hunting, dealing with enemies. The plentiful color photographs of numerous species will attract many young readers. Sketchy but useful as an elementary survey of a popular subject.
SUBJ: Snakes.

597.96   Ph-2 4-6/4 $17.95   T   KC634
DEWEY, JENNIFER OWINGS. Rattlesnake dance: true tales, mysteries, and rattlesnake ceremonies. Boyds Mills ISBN 1-56397-247-6; In Canada: McClelland & Stewart, 1997. 48p. col. ill., map.
Three personal experiences with rattlesnakes intertwine with facts and Native American lore in this thin, oversized volume. Soft color pencil drawings follow the author's stories of how she was bitten by a rattlesnake as a child and then saw first a Hopi snake ceremony and later the combat ritual of two male rattlesnakes. Framed insets

provide bits of information on the snake's body, senses, and behavior. The large size of the book is awkward, but snake fans should be fascinated by the true stories.
SUBJ: Rattlesnakes./ Snakes./ Hopi Indians--Social life and customs./ Indians of North America--Social life and customs./ Dewey, Jennifer Owings./ Women authors, American.

VCR 597.96   Ph-2 5-6 $9.95   OD KC635
FASCINATING WORLD OF SNAKES (Videocassette). Stoney-Wolf Productions/dist. by Video Enterprise 55002, 1996. 1/2" VHS videocassette color (35min). (Fascinating world of).
Venomous and nonpoisonous snakes of many species appear in this informative survey. An overview of physical characteristics, behavior as predators, and hibernation is followed by a lengthy view of each family of poisonous snakes found in North America and a few that are not venomous. Discusses distinguishing markings, distribution, and food preferences of each species. A cautionary discussion of human interactions with snakes concludes the useful presentation which children will enjoy for the live action views of the ever intriguing reptile.
SUBJ: Snakes.

597.96   Ph-3 4-6/4 $14.95   L   KC636
GROSS, RUTH BELOV. Snakes. Rev. ed. Four Winds/Macmillan ISBN 0-02-737022-4; In Canada: Collier Macmillan, 1990. 63p. ill. (some col.).
Includes index.
This two-part introduction features several short chapters on snake physiology and behavior followed by an album of captioned photographs. Part one briefly covers discussions on baby snakes, shedding, eating, capturing prey, enemies, moving around, and keeping warm; while part two provides twenty-three color portraits with captions describing each species. In spite of awkward construction, the book offers good information in a volume that is easy to read without appearing to be for younger children.
SUBJ: Snakes.

597.96   Ph-1 2-4/3 $14.89   L   KC637
LAUBER, PATRICIA. Snakes are hunters. Illus. by Holly Keller. Crowell/HarperCollins ISBN 0-690-04630-8, 1988. 32p. col. ill. (Let's-read-and-find-out science book).
Many different species of snakes appear in this cheerful looking introduction. The clear, informative text explains the physical characteristics of snakes and the behavior of these animals as hunters. The shedding of skin, laying of eggs, hibernating and snakes in the zoo and in the wild are all discussed in a sure to please volume.
SUBJ: Snakes.

597.96   Ph-1 4-6/7 $15.99   L   KC638
LAVIES, BIANCA. Gathering of garter snakes. Dutton ISBN 0-525-45099-8, 1993. unp. col. ill.
Available from the National Library Service for the Blind and Physically Handicapped on sound recording cassette RC 38580.
Red-sided garter snakes swarm in large masses in the Canadian lime pits. Excellent photographs follow their hibernation, eating, mating, birth, and migration as they move from their winter stay in underground caverns to the marshes where they have a spring food supply. Children will be fascinated by the close-up views, and the text provides an interesting introduction to snake life.
SUBJ: Garter snakes./ Snakes.

597.96   Ph-2 2-6/6 $12.95   T   KC639
LING, MARY. Snake book. Written and edited by Mary Ling and Mary Atkinson. Photos by Frank Greenaway and Dave King. DK Publishing ISBN 0-7894-1526-7, 1997. unp. col. ill.
Bold photographs of 12 snakes from around the world fill the large pages of this slim introduction. Brief text in graduated type size mentions some aspects of the featured snake's physiology and behavior with a final page adding short facts on location, food, methods of hunting, and maximum length of each species. A super long view of the reticulated python fills doublespread fold-out pages in the center of the book. The dramatized approach distorts the actual dimensions of the snakes, but children will be fascinated with the large, close-up views.
SUBJ: Snakes.

597.96   Ph-1 3-5/6 $14.95   L   KC640
MAESTRO, BETSY. Take a look at snakes. Illus. by Giulio Maestro. Scholastic ISBN 0-590-44935-4; In Canada: Scholastic, 1992. 40p. col. ill.
Fine color drawings depict the internal structure of snakes, their movement, growth, eating habits, and other behavior. A clear succinct text accompanies pleasant, picture-filled pages showing assorted species to demonstrate basic facts and principles. Attractive, inviting

overview which is fun to browse.
SUBJ: Snakes.

597.96   Ph-1 4-6/4 $16.00   L   KC641
MARKLE, SANDRA. Outside and inside snakes. Macmillan ISBN 0-02-762315-7; In Canada: Distican, 1995. 40p. col. ill.
Includes glossary/index.
Fine photographs of many different types of snakes and interesting text explain the physical characteristics special to this reptile. Scales and senses, mouths and tongues, catching prey and eating, skeletons and movement are among the featured topics. In addition to the many colorful views of snakes at rest and in action, there are clear informative views of internal organs and the inside of a snake's mouth. This exquisite volume, among the most attractive ever done on this popular animal, is sure to be widely enjoyed by children.
SUBJ: Snakes.

597.96   Ph-1 2-6/5 $9.99   P   KC642
PARSONS, ALEXANDRA. Amazing snakes. Photos by Jerry Young. Knopf ISBN 0-679-80225-8, 1990. 29p. col. ill. (Eyewitness juniors).
Includes index.
Bold photographs and interesting facts and anecdotes introduce nine species of snakes. The book is an attractive survey organized in double spread segments that are well designed, placing smaller photographs, drawings, and short segments of text around a large picture of the featured snake. A fine browsing item, this will appeal to a wide spectrum of readers.
SUBJ: Snakes.

597.96   Ph-1 4-6/6 $15.89   L   KC643
SIMON, SEYMOUR. Snakes. HarperCollins ISBN 0-06-022530-0; In Canada: HarperCollins, 1992. unp col photos.
Bold photographs of several kinds of snakes accompany an informative essay describing snake bodies and behavior. A snake's skin, its movement, use of senses, eating behavior, egg laying, and dealing with enemies are discussed in a well developed overview using many specific species as examples. An exceptionally handsome book on this intriguing animal.
SUBJ: Snakes.

598   Ph-2 2-5/6 $15.00   L   KC644
ARNOSKY, JIM. Crinkleroot's guide to knowing the birds. Bradbury ISBN 0-02-705857-3; In Canada: Maxwell Macmillan, 1992. 32p. col. ill.
Includes index.
Cheerful old Crinkleroot takes the reader on a birdwatching walk through the woods, explaining aspects of bird life in a cartoon presentation featuring attractive sketches of many common birds. Soft watercolors fill the pages with labeled details, and Crinkleroot briefly explains male/female differences, types of nests, care of young, wintering habits, and how to attract birds to one's yard. Simple lesson identifies various species and encourages appreciation and observation of birds.
SUBJ: Birds.

598   Ph-2 P-2/3 $14.00   L   KC645
ARNOSKY, JIM. Crinkleroot's 25 birds every child should know. Bradbury ISBN 0-02-705859-X; In Canada: Maxwell Macmillan, 1993. unp. col. ill.
Watercolor portraits labeled in large letters provide an attractive lesson in naming a variety of birds. Crinkleroot, an elderly naturalist, states a few ideas about the feathers and bodies of birds as an introduction. The penguin, loon, swan, pelican, egret, vulture, eagle, turkey, chicken, parrot, ostrich, and hummingbird are among the featured birds. The simple scheme of attractive drawings in plentiful white space is an appealing introduction for young children.
SUBJ: Birds.

VCR 598   Ph-2 2-6 $89.95   OD KC646
BIRDS IN THE CITY: A FIRST FILM. 2ND ED. (Videocassette). BFA/Phoenix Films 72148, 1992. 1/2" VHS videocassette color (12min).
Originally published as BIRDS.
Provides an overview of the physiology and habits and behavior of a variety of birds. Striking photography and pleasant narration are companioned by a particularly appropriate background score. Useful as an introduction.
SUBJ: Birds.

598   Ph-1 3-6/7 $19.00   T   KC647
BULL, JOHN. Audubon Society field guide to North American birds--Eastern Region. By John Bull and John Farrand. Random House ISBN 0-679-42852-6; In Canada: Random House, 1994. 775p. col. ill. (Audubon Society field guides).
Includes glossary and index.
This admirable guide for the beginning birdwatcher, covers the

eastern area of the continent with the Rocky Mountains as the dividing point. A table of birds classified by shape and a section of color photographs with color key allow the amateur to begin with an easily identifiable characteristic. These graphics are cross-indexed to the text where entries are classified by habitat. A habitat key makes it easy for teacher and students to prepare for field trips. A general index includes both common and scientific names. Format is designed for easy carrying. A duplicate copy is recommended for the reference collection.
SUBJ: Birds--North America.

598   Ph-1 A/9 $19.00 T KC648
BURNIE, DAVID. Bird. Knopf ISBN 0-394-89619-X, 1988. 64p. col. ill. (Eyewitness books).
Include index.
Fascinating details of birds' feathers, bodies, nests, and hatching and raising of the young are depicted in numerous color photographs in this attractive oversize volume. Brief bits of text and the plentiful captions are often difficult, but the great variety of species from all over the world, and the informative detail about evolution, physiology, behavior, flight, and means of attracting birds for close-up viewing make this very useful. The wealth of detail in the busy presentation should spark interest in birdwatching or feather collecting, and self motivated students may find it useful in developing science projects.
SUBJ: Birds.

598   Ph-2 P-2/2 $19.00 L KC649
FRISKEY, MARGARET. Birds we know. Childrens Press ISBN 0-516-01609-1; In Canada: Childens Press, 1981. 48p. col. ill. (New true book).
Includes glossary and index.
Color photographs of many species and various eggs and nests are an informative accompaniment to a simple text introducing the physical characteristics, behavior, and life cycle of birds. A useful source of information for younger readers.
SUBJ: Birds./ Birds--Habits and behavior.

598   Ph-2 4-6/6 $9.95 P KC650
HICKMAN, PAMELA M. Birdwise: forty fun feats for finding out about our feathered friends. Illus. by Judie Shore. Addison-Wesley ISBN 0-201-51757-4; In Canada: Kids Can Press, 1988. 96p. ill.
Includes index.
This busy paperback compendium makes good use of the miscellany approach to explain many principles of bird bodies and behavior and to provide instructions for attracting and observing birds. Plentiful pencil drawings accompany discussions of flight, communication, vision, nests, migration and much more; the activities include building bird feeders and houses, constructing blinds, and photographing and drawing birds. The simple paperback format has child appeal and is chock-full of interesting information.
SUBJ: Birds.

598   Ph-2 3-5/5 $18.60 L KC651
KLEIN, TOM. Loon magic for kids. Gareth Stevens ISBN 0-8368-0402-3; In Canada: Saunders, c1989, 1991. 48p. col. ill. (Animal magic for kids).
Includes directory and "New Words" index.
Handsome photographs depict the common loon in this simple survey of its life cycle. The loon habitat, communication through its notable call and water dances, eating, nesting, and rearing of the young are all described, and there are distribution maps and nice pictures of less well known loon species. An added page of facts for parents to use with children and addresses of loon preservation organizations round out an attractive sketch of this striking species.
SUBJ: Loons.

598   Ph-2 2-4/4 $11.95 T KC652
KRULIK, NANCY E. Birds. [This edition American text by Nancy Krulik.] Created by Gallimard Jeunesse, Claude Delafosse and Rene Mettler. Illus. by Rene Mettler. Scholastic ISBN 0-590-46367-5; In Canada: Scholastic, 1993. unp. col. ill. (spiral bound). (First discovery book).
"Cartwheel books."
Originally published in France, L'OISEAU, 1990.
Shiny pages with plastic overlays offer an intriguing introduction to the physical characteristics and behavior of birds. Colorful images, some on white pages and others set in fully drawn scenes, depict many species to demonstrate body features, eating, nesting, and protection from enemies. A quick smattering of material, nicely done, with overlays providing appeal.
SUBJ: Birds.

598   Ph-1 4-6/8 $22.10 L KC653
LANDAU, ELAINE. State birds: including the Commonwealth of Puerto Rico. Watts ISBN 0-531-20058-2; In Canada: Watts, 1992. 63p. col. ill.
Includes bibliography and index.
Single-page entries for each of the states feature a color photograph and several sentences of information about the state bird. Different pictures are provided for birds chosen by several states--the first entry gives the basic description with brief facts added each time the bird appears. Index entries of the useful compendium tell which state or states each bird represents.
SUBJ: State birds./ Birds./ Emblems, State.

598   Ph-1 5-6/7 $15.93 L KC654
LERNER, CAROL. Backyard birds of summer. Morrow ISBN 0-688-13601-X, 1996. 48p. col. ill., maps.
Includes bibliography, directory and index.
Ten varieties of migrating birds that might be attracted to backyard feeders and bird houses appear in this handsome, informative discussion of bird life. Carol Lerner's fine paintings depict male and female birds and sometimes related species, and the double-page entries each include a map and interesting discussion of the bird's physical characteristics, behavior, and particular life patterns. Several pages describe the construction and care of feeders and houses and other aspects of backyard viewing to round out this attractive and useful introduction.
SUBJ: Birds--Attracting./ Birds--Habits and behavior./ Birds--North America.

598   Ph-1 4-6/5 $16.95 L KC655
MARKLE, SANDRA. Outside and inside birds. Bradbury ISBN 0-02-762312-2; In Canada: Maxwell Macmillan, 1994. 40p. col. ill.
Includes glossary/index.
Selectors' Choice, 20th ed.
Feathers, bones, beaks, and internal organs equip birds in special ways which are explained in clear, crisp text and fascinating photographs and x-ray views. Many different birds are featured, demonstrating flight, the structure of feathers and wings, the skeleton and composition of bones, feeding of the young, the production of eggs, the working of the gizzard, and more. Beautiful and informative, this is an appealing science lesson that develops understanding and encourages further observation.
SUBJ: Birds.

598   Ph-2 4-6/4 $12.95 L KC656
MORRISON, SUSAN DUDLEY. Passenger pigeon. Crestwood House/ Macmillan ISBN 0-89686-457-X; In Canada: Collier Macmillan, 1989. 48p. col. ill. (Gone forever).
Includes glossary/index.
Impressive for its size and large numbers, the now extinct passenger pigeon continues to be a prime example of human destruction of wildlife. In simple but substantial text, drawings, and color photographs of museum specimens, this provides good information on the history, physical characteristics, behavior, comparisons with surviving species, causes of extinction, and belated efforts to save this bird. Children who like reading about animals will enjoy this, and it provides a thorough profile of the long extinct bird.
SUBJ: Passenger pigeons./ Extinct birds.

598   Ph-2 5-6/5 $13.95 L KC657
O'CONNOR, KAREN. Herring gull. Dillon ISBN 0-87518-506-1; In Canada: Maxwell Macmillan, 1992. 60p. col. ill. (Dillon remarkable animals book).
Includes glossary and index.
Family life and history of the very common white and gray herring gull are seen at close range in this useful discussion. Three chapters of text explain wings and bills, scavenging, mating and nesting, care of the young, related species, life in the colony, and overpopulation. Many of the photographs are excellent, but a few seem to contradict what is said in the text about color and markings. Interesting glimpse into the private lives of these familiar birds with plentiful information for reports.
SUBJ: Herring gulls./ Gulls.

598   Ph-2 3-6/5 $9.99 P KC658
PARSONS, ALEXANDRA. Amazing birds. Photos by Jerry Young. Knopf ISBN 0-679-80223-1, 1990. 29p. col. ill. (Eyewitness juniors).
Includes index.
This attractive introduction to bird bodies and behavior features several interesting species in striking photographs and brief bits of text. The double spread segments feature penguins, swans, peacocks, ostriches and hummingbirds. An opening summary of bird characteristics and a concluding explanation of how birds fly rounds out the short, interesting, yet sketchy survey.
SUBJ: Birds.

598   Ph-2 4-6/7 $24.95   T   KC659
PETERSON, ROGER TORY. Field guide to the birds: a completely new guide to all birds of eastern and central North America. 4th ed. Maps by Virginia Marie Peterson. Houghton Mifflin ISBN 0-395-26621-1, 1980. 384p. col. ill. (Peterson field guide series).
> Includes index.
> A new format for this edition of the standard handbook places the description of each species opposite its illustration. All birds whether native or accidental or introduced species are shown in color. Color coded range maps are appended for each species.
> SUBJ: Birds--North America.

598   Ph-2 4-6/7 $22.95   T   KC660
PETERSON, ROGER TORY. Field guide to western birds. 3rd ed. Sponsored by the National Audubon Society and National Wildlife Federation. Houghton Mifflin ISBN 0-395-51749-4, 1990. 432p. col. ill. (Peterson field guide series).
> Offers a description of all species of birds found in North America west of the 100th meridian, with a section on the birds of the Hawaiian Islands.
> SUBJ: Birds--North America.

598   Ph-2 P-2/2 $15.95   L   KC661
REIDEL, MARLENE. From egg to bird. Carolrhoda ISBN 0-87614-159-9, 1981. 24p. col. ill. (Carolrhoda start to finish book).
> A simple explanation of the life cycle of birds in a brief text and attractive watercolor drawings of a nesting pair of birds and their young. The illustrations include a page diagraming the yolk and developing bird inside the egg and another showing the hatching process. The pleasing small format will serve as a picture book for pre-school children as well as a good introduction to a basic science concept for beginning readers.
> SUBJ: Birds--Development.

598   Ph-2 K-2/4 $14.00   L   KC662
ROCKWELL, ANNE F. Our yard is full of birds. By Anne Rockwell. Illus. by Lizzy Rockwell. Macmillan ISBN 0-02-777273-X; In Canada: Maxwell Macmillan, 1992. unp. col. ill.
> Simple text and full-page paintings introduce a host of common birds a child might encounter. "The phoebe sits on the stone wall by the garden and wags its tail at me. A wren lives in the little birdhouse my father helped me build." A pleasant scheme for teaching younger children to observe, appreciate, and identify the birds around them.
> SUBJ: Birds.

598   Ph-1 3-6 $12.00   P   KC663
SCHUTZ, WALTER E. How to attract, house and feed birds. Bruce Publishing ISBN 0-02-011910-0, c1974. 196p. ill.
> Available from National Library Service for the Blind and Physically Handicapped on sound recording cassette RC18852.
> This new revised edition adds useful information on bird watching, nesting habits, recipes for providing food, and methods for providing water, to the hard core of practical information on construction: designs, required materials and diagrams for making many kinds of bird baths, bird houses and feeders. Useful for shop and nature classes and in camp and club activities.
> SUBJ: Birds--Attracting./ Bird houses.

598   Ph-2 K-2/1 $14.95   T   KC664
SILL, CATHRYN. About birds: a guide for children. Illus. by John Sill. Peachtree ISBN 1-56145-028-6, 1991. unp. col. ill.
> Brief statements and simple attractive paintings express basic facts about birds. Different bird species demonstrate nest building, movement, eating, and size; picture labels name the birds, and a concluding set of page notes offers a small bit of information about each bird. Information is minimal, but the pleasant volume offers a very simple introduction to bird life.
> SUBJ: Birds.

598   Ph-2 4-6/6 $13.95   L   KC665
SNEDDEN, ROBERT. What is a bird? Illus. by Adrian Lascom. Photos by Oxford Scientific Films. Sierra Club ISBN 0-87156-539-0; In Canada: Little, Brown, 1993. 32p. col. ill.
> Includes glossary and index.
> Feathers, beaks, and wings along with other topics are described in brief sections of text and numerous photographs featuring many species. Flying, eggs, and songs and calls are briefly discussed. Omits basic topics such as migration, but is an attractive introduction to the traits distinguishing birds from other animals. Busy, informative volume is attractive, nicely organized, and useful for reports.
> SUBJ: Birds.

VCR 598   Ph-1 2-5 $275.00   OD KC666
SPRING (Videocassette). Produced by Steve Maslowski. Journal Films/ dist. by Altschul Group Corporation J4933, 1994. 1/2" VHS videocassette color (14min). (Through the seasons with birds).
> Includes teacher's guide.
> Includes public performance rights.
> Migrating birds return north as snow melts. Soon they stake out territory for hunting and nesting, sing and strut their courtship rituals, build nests, and lay eggs. Lovely close-up photography depicts many species as the narrator names some of the birds and describes these major activities of their springtime life. Viewers of all ages will be intrigued at the personal views of these colorful, busy creatures, and the piece will serve for family viewing as well as classroom units on birds and the seasons.
> SUBJ: Birds--North America./ Birds--Habits and behavior./ Spring.

598   Ph-2 4-5/5 $10.95   P   KC667
SWANSON, DIANE. Sky dancers: the amazing world of North American birds. Illus. by Douglas Penhale. Voyageur Press ISBN 0-89658-319-8; In Canada; Whitecap Books, 1995. 80p. ill.
> Includes index.
> Ten bird species--including hummingbirds, swans, puffins and hawks-- are introduced in short readable chapters and pen and ink drawings in this large, thin paperback. The author chooses well in discussing behavior, physical characteristics, and conservation problems special to each bird. Boxed inserts add odd bits of facts and anecdotes to the discussion. Though a bit dull in appearance, this book is useful and interesting for teaching about these birds.
> SUBJ: Birds--North America.

598   Ph-1 3-6/7 $19.00   T   KC668
UDVARDY, MIKLOS D.F. Audubon Society field guide to North American birds--Western Region. Random House ISBN 0-679-42851-8; In Canada: Random House, 1977. 773p. col. ill. (Audubon Society field guides).
> Includes glossary and index.
> This admirable guide for the beginning birdwatcher covers the western area of the continent with the Rocky Mountains as the dividing point. A table of birds classified by shape and a section of color photographs with color key allow the amateur to begin with an easily identifiable characteristic. These graphics are cross-indexed to the text where entries are classified by habitat. A habitat key makes it easy for teacher and students to prepare for field trips. A general index includes both common and scientific names. Format is designed for easy carrying. A duplicate copy is recommended for the reference section.
> SUBJ: Birds--North America.

VCR 598   Ph-1 2-5 $275.00   OD KC669
WINTER (Videocassette). Produced by Steve Maslowski. Journal Films/ dist. by Altschul Group Corporation J4934, 1994. 1/2" VHS videocassette color (14min). (Through the seasons with birds).
> Includes teacher's guide.
> Includes public performance rights.
> Winter is the season of struggle for nonmigrating birds that spend cold, snowy days hunting and searching for food in woods and fields and at bird feeders. Impressive photography follows many species as they forage and sweep down from the sky after prey while the narrator explains how feathers and skin insulate birds from cold and wet conditions and how their seasonal diet provides extra energy. Bird enthusiasts of all ages will enjoy the close-up views. For home use or as a classroom introduction to birds or the season of winter.
> SUBJ: Birds--North America./ Birds--Habits and behavior./ Winter.

598.147   Ph-2 5-6/6 $14.95   L   KC670
O'CONNOR, KAREN. Feather book. Dillon ISBN 0-87518-445-6, 1990. 59p. col. ill.
> "A single wing feather is made up of more than a million parts." (p.5). The intricacies of feather construction and color, the function of feathers in flight, the processes of molting and preening, and unusual feather formations on exotic species are discussed in this informative book. The interesting material is potentially useful for a variety of teaching and booktalking purposes.
> SUBJ: Feathers./ Birds.

598.147   Ph-1 5-6/6 $15.99   T   KC671
PATENT, DOROTHY HINSHAW. Feathers. Photos. by William Munoz. Cobblehill/Dutton ISBN 0-525-65081-4, 1992. 64p. col. ill.
> Includes index.
> Feathers are amazing in their intricacy and usefulness making birds "the most successful and varied of all animals with backbones." The structure of feathers, color, growth, function in flight, use for camouflage and attracting a mate, and much more are explained and illustrated in beautiful photographs of many species. Beautifully written

and highly informative, this offers absorbing reading.
SUBJ: Feathers./ Birds.

598.156   Ph-1 3-6/7 $5.95   P   KC672
BASH, BARBARA. Urban roosts: where birds nest in the city. Sierra
Club/Little, Brown ISBN 0-316-08312-7; In Canada: Little, Brown, 1990.
unp. col. ill.
Selectors' Choice, 18th ed.
"Cars and trucks lumber noisily over big city bridges. But underneath,
hidden among the beams and girders, peregrine falcons have found a
home." (text). Brief explanations and handsome drawings in many
doublespread scenes and vignettes survey a variety of birds and their
unusual nesting sites--stoplights, neon signs, the undersides of bridges
and elevated train tracks, etc. An exceptionally attractive picture book
exploration of the everyday world.
SUBJ: Birds--Eggs and nests./ Urban animals.

598.156   Ph-2 3-4/2 $14.89   L   KC673
GANS, ROMA. How do birds find their way? Illus. by Paul Mirocha.
HarperCollins ISBN 0-06-020225-4; In Canada: HarperCollins, 1996.
32p. col. ill., maps. (Let's-read-and-find-out science book).
Answers to the mysteries of bird migration give the reader much to
admire and ponder in this attractive discussion. The long, seasonal
flights of many species are diagrammed in pleasant scenes, and the
author considers how waterways, the earth's magnetic field, the sun
and stars all aid birds during their flights in all sorts of weather.
Seasons, science, and nature come together nicely in a thoughtful
presentation.
SUBJ: Birds--Migration.

598.176   Ph-1 4-6/6 $16.00   T   KC674
ARNOSKY, JIM. Watching water birds. National Geographic ISBN
0-7922-7073-8, 1997. unp. col. ill.
Seven types of birds appear in fresh and salt water, on land, and in
the air to demonstrate how different designs of body parts serve a
particular way of life. Lovely paintings, some of them full-size,
accompany conversational text which combines information about
each bird with practical advice on watching and learning firsthand
about birds. The species or groups include loons and grebes,
mergansers, mallards, wood ducks, Canada geese, gulls, and herons.
The inviting, slim volume will be enjoyed for nonfiction reading as well
as natural history lessons. For reading aloud.
SUBJ: Water birds./ Birds.

598.176   Ph-1 5-6/6 $18.95   T   KC675
BROWN, MARY BARRETT. Wings along the waterway. Orchard ISBN
0-531-05981-2, 1992. 80p. col. ill.
Includes bibliography and index.
Available from the National Library Service for the Blind and
Physically Handicapped on sound recording cassette RC 37680.
Beautiful paintings of 20 species of water birds accompany short
essays describing each animal's special behavior and raising of its
young. The text creates a good sense of how the birds interact with
their particular environment, and physical characteristics of adult and
juvenile birds are well conveyed in the fine pictures; the American
coot, osprey, wood stork, roseate spoonbill and several herons are
among the birds introduced. The handsome oversize volume is a very
appreciative exploration of natural history.
SUBJ: Water birds./ Birds.

598.3   Ph-2 K-4/3 $15.95   L   KC676
GIBBONS, GAIL. Gulls...gulls...gulls... Holiday House ISBN 0-8234-
1323-3, 1997. unp. col. ill., map.
Full-page scenes and smaller vignettes follow the daily life and life
cycle of the common herring gull. The cheerful views and clear
explanations describe physical characteristics, habitat, molting, eating,
care and growth of the young, migration, the ecological contribution
of gulls, and several other gull species. The attractive volume provides
a useful introduction to this familiar bird.
SUBJ: Gulls.

598.3   Ph-1 2-4/5 $14.89   L   KC677
GIBBONS, GAIL. Puffins are back! HarperCollins ISBN 0-06-021604-2;
In Canada: HarperCollins, 1991. unp. col. ill.
Pleasing watercolors follow the annual return of puffins to a Maine
island where they prepare their nests and raise their young. A simple
straightforward text explains the work of scientists in bringing the
birds back to Maine after their disappearance from U.S. waters and
in continuing to study the growing population of birds. The colorful
waterbirds are an intriguing species, and Gibbons' well crafted
introduction to them will be widely enjoyed.
SUBJ: Puffins.

598.3   Ph-1 1-3/6 $14.95   T   KC678
MCMILLAN, BRUCE. Nights of the pufflings. Houghton Mifflin ISBN
0-395-70810-9, 1995. 32p. col. ill.
Includes bibliography.
Iceland is the setting of this attractive bird rescue story. Appealing
photographs and essay text follow an annual event as puffins go
through their summer nesting and local children watch for the baby
birds to emerge from the nesting burrows for their first flight out to
sea. Many of the pufflings lose their way on this special night, placing
them in danger until the children catch them and release them into the
ocean in a satisfying conclusion. For environmental studies.
SUBJ: Puffins./ Zoology--Iceland.

598.3   Ph-3 4-6/7 $15.99   L   KC679
PATTON, DON. Flamingos. Child's World ISBN 1-56766-184-X, 1996.
32p. col. ill. (Naturebooks).
Includes index.
Flamingos are introduced in a sketchy text and handsome full-page
photographs which capture their intriguing appearance and depict
hugh numbers flocking together. The countries where various species
live are mentioned, though not all the birds are shown. Feeding,
mating rituals, hatching and care of chicks, and human encroachment
on the birds' habitats are discussed. The serviceable, attractive volume
will be useful for curriculum units on bird life and environmental
studies and where there's interest in exotic species.
SUBJ: Flamingos.

598.4   Ph-1 3-5/6 $15.95   L   KC680
ESBENSEN, BARBARA JUSTER. Great Northern diver: the loon. Illus. by
Mary Barrett Brown. Little, Brown ISBN 0-316-24954-8; In Canada:
Little, Brown, 1990. unp. col. ill.
Available from the National Library Service for the Blind and
Physically Handicapped on sound recording cassette RC34713.
Handsome paintings follow the progress of a pair of loons as they
return to their northern home for the summer, build a nest, raise their
chick, and begin the fall migration. The text provides an informative
explanation of the loon's primitive body features, the variety of
distinctive calls, behavior in defending territory, and encounters with
predators. An exceptionally well crafted life cycle picture book which
should serve a variety of reading and information uses.
SUBJ: Loons.

598.4   Ph-2 5-6/7 $19.95   L   KC681
JOHNSON, SYLVIA A. Albatrosses of Midway Island. Photos by Frans
Lanting. Carolrhoda ISBN 0-87614-391-5, 1990. 47p. col. ill.
(Carolrhoda nature watch book).
Includes glossary and index.
Gliding on their long narrow wings, albatrosses are a familiar sight
over many of the world's oceans. Beautiful color photographs and an
informative essay text describe the physical characteristics of these
large sea birds and the care and growth of the young in a breeding
colony on Midway Island. One of many fine life cycle books by this
capable author, this handsome book is an excellent introduction to an
impressive species.
SUBJ: Laysan albatross./ Albatrosses.

598.4   Ph-1 5-6/8 $14.95   L   KC682
PATENT, DOROTHY HINSHAW. Pelicans. Photos by William Munoz.
Clarion ISBN 0-395-57224-X, 1992. 64p. col. ill.
Includes bibliography and index.
Brown pelicans and white pelicans and a few relatives from around
the world appear in this attractive and informative life cycle. Excellent
photographs and four well-developed chapters describe shared
physical characteristics, behavior particular to brown pelican families
as they mate and rear their young, life in white pelican breeding
colonies, and problems of endangerment. Useful as a resource as well
as interesting reading.
SUBJ: Pelicans.

598.4   Ph-2 1-3/2 $12.95   L   KC683
SELSAM, MILLICENT E. First look at ducks, geese, and swans. By
Millicent E. Selsam and Joyce Hunt. Illus. by Harriett Springer. Walker
ISBN 0-8027-6976-4; In Canada: Thomas Allen, 1990. 32p. ill. (First
look at).
Differences in size, necks, markings and flying and diving distinguish
these common waterbirds from one another. The simple lesson in
observation includes soft pencil drawings, using many species as
examples of the basic principles stated in the easy-to-read text.
Intended as a very basic lesson in animal classification, this should
complement other materials on these common birds.
SUBJ: Ducks./ Geese./ Swans.

598.4 Ph-1 5-6/6 $13.95 L KC684
STONE, LYNN M. Pelican. Dillon ISBN 0-87518-430-8, 1990. 60p. col.
ill. (Dillon remarkable animals book).
Includes glossary and index.
Both brown and white pelicans appear in this informative survey of
the large bird's life cycle and behavior. A preliminary page of facts
introduces four chapters discussing flying and fishing, physical
characteristics, differences between the species, habitat, seasonal
changes in plumage, nesting, rearing of the young, and problems
created by humans. Some of the photographs are quite striking, and
the thorough discussion of this intriguing animal is useful.
SUBJ: Pelicans.

PIC 598.47 Ph-2 4-6 $9.95 OD KC685
CHESTER, JONATHAN. Penguins of the Antarctic (Picture). Celestial
Arts/dist. by Tricycle Press, 1995. 1 study print color (23" x 35").
This large display offers a multifaceted introduction to Adelie,
chinstrap, emperor, and gentoo penguins. Blocks of text, a map, large
and small portraits of the penguins, and small scenes of the birds in
their habitat describe aspects of survival and rearing the young. An
attractive browsing item for classroom or library walls.
SUBJ: Penguins.

PIC 598.47 Ph-3 3-6 $9.98 OD KC686
CHESTER, JONATHAN. Penguins of the world (Picture). Celestial Arts/
dist. by Tricycle Press, 1995. 1 study print color (23" x 35").
Attractive photographs introduce each of the penguin species. Labeled
images of adult and young penguins, pictured as individuals and in
groups, vary in size and are scattered on the white page. No written
information is provided, but a table of scientific names and groupings
with mean sizes runs along the bottom. The appealing animals make
this an attractive introduction for classroom or library walls though the
information is limited.
SUBJ: Penguins.

598.47 Ph-2 P-1/2 $7.95 T KC687
FLETCHER, NEIL. Penguin. Photos by Neil Fletcher. DK Publishing ISBN
1-56458-312-0, 1993. 21p. col. ill. (See how they grow).
This simple, busy life cycle follows the growth of a young King
penguin from the day of hatching until it is an adult with a chick of its
own. Photographed figures without backgrounds are scattered across
white pages with simple sentences of text. Small sketches of penguin
life move across narrow borders at the tops and bottoms of pages; a
final doublespread page reviews the penguin's stages of growth from
homely babyhood to handsome adulthood. A useful introduction to
this interesting bird.
SUBJ: Penguins./ Animals--Infancy.

598.47 Ph-1 1-4/4 $6.95 P KC688
FONTANEL, BEATRICE. Penguin: a funny bird. Photos by Andre Fatras
and Yves Cherel. Charlesbridge ISBN 0-88106-426-2, 1992. 27p. col. ill.
(Animal close-ups).
Impressive overhead views show the hundreds of thousands of king
penguins in a nesting colony, and close-up pictures follow the care of
eggs and the growth of young penguins. Simple text and picture
captions describe behavior and physical characteristics, and the fine
photographs offer a nice record of the slow growth of the homely
brown chicks to handsome adulthood. A most attractive introduction
to the king penguin, this also pictures a few related species.
SUBJ: Penguins.

598.47 Ph-1 5-6/5 $15.95 L KC689
PATENT, DOROTHY HINSHAW. Looking at penguins. Photos by
Graham Robertson. Holiday House ISBN 0-8234-1037-4, 1993. 40p.
col. ill.
Includes index.
Four chapters of text and very nice photographs introduce several
species of penguins and explain the life of those living in Antarctica.
The clear, interesting text focuses on physical characteristics, different
groups and species, and threats to survival. One longer chapter
follows emperor penguins as they rear their young. The handsome,
slim volume is an informative survey of these appealing birds. For
environmental studies.
SUBJ: Penguins.

598.5 Ph-1 5-6/7 $19.95 L KC690
ARNOLD, CAROLINE. Ostriches and other flightless birds. Photos by
Richard Hewett. Carolrhoda ISBN 0-87614-377-X, 1990. 47p. col. ill.
(Carolrhoda nature watch book).
Includes glossary and index.
Ostriches and their five cousins (rheas, cassowaries, emus, kiwis, and
tinamous) are introduced in splendid color photographs and an
informative text. The discussion covers history, size, physical
characteristics, egg laying and brooding, early days of the young,

and life of family groups. A helpful distribution map locating the
various birds appears early in the book, which is a first rate
presentation of these intriguing animals.
SUBJ: Ostriches./ Kiwis./ Cassowaries./ Emus./ Tinamou./ Ratites.

598.5 Ph-2 5-6/7 $21.00 L KC691
BASKIN-SALZBERG, ANITA. Flightless birds. By Anita Baskin-Salzberg
and Allen Salzberg. Watts ISBN 0-531-20117-1, 1993. 64p. col. ill.,
maps. (First book).
Includes bibliography, glossary and index.
All birds have feathers, but not all birds can fly. Informative chapters
of text include substantial charts, adequate photographs, and maps.
The author explains physical differences between birds that fly and
those that don't, introduces some extinct birds, talks about
conservation problems and the future of flightless birds, and
describes ostriches, emus, rheas, cassowaries, kiwis, and penguins. The
presentation is rather dull, but provides a useful discussion of this
important category of birds. For environmental studies.
SUBJ: Flightless birds./ Birds.

598.6 Ph-1 K-3/2 $9.95 L KC692
BACK, CHRISTINE. Chicken and egg. By Christine Back and Jens Olesen.
Photos by Bo Jarner. Silver Burdett ISBN 0-3820-9284-8, 1986. 24p.
col. ill. (Stopwatch books).
Includes index.
Shows the stages of development of the chick embryo inside the egg
from the laying of the egg until the chick hatches and dries out to
become the familiar ball of fluff. Clear cutaway photographs and line
drawings are accompanied by a two layered text--a single line in
darker print can be used with younger children, and a more detailed
explanation follows on each page. An attractive introduction to an
ever useful and appealing subject.
SUBJ: Chick embryo./ Reproduction./ Eggs.

VCR 598.6 Ph-2 5-A $49.00 OD KC693
CHICK EMBRYOLOGY (Videocassette). National Geographic 51034,
c1974, 1986. 1/2" VHS videocassette color (12min). (Bio-science
series).
Includes teacher's guide.
The development of a chicken embryo from its beginning until after
hatching is viewed through a window in an egg. Although there is
little change during the first week, the heartbeat is highly visible, and
this video can be effectively paired with books on the same subject
for individual research.
SUBJ: Chickens./ Embryology./ Eggs.

598.6 Ph-1 P-2/3 $14.93 L KC694
COLE, JOANNA. Chick hatches. Photos by Jerome Wexler. Morrow
ISBN 0-688-32087-2, 1977. 47p.
Selectors' Choice, 11th ed.
A superb primary science book that holds interest, evokes excitement
and imparts a great deal of information to young readers. Large,
close-up photographs of the developmental stages of a chick embryo
are linked with an easily read, clear and simple text.
SUBJ: Chickens./ Embryology./ Reproduction./ Eggs.

598.6 Ph-2 4-6/8 $19.95 L KC695
JOHNSON, SYLVIA A. Inside an egg. Photos by Kiyoshi Shimizu. Lerner
ISBN 0-8225-1472-9, 1982. 48p. col. ill. (Lerner natural science book).
Includes glossary and index.
Full-color microphotographs, detailed diagrams, and clearly written
text follow the stages of development of a chick embryo from
fertilization to hatching. A good introduction to an ever fascinating
subject, and a lucid explanation of the principles and processes of
embryology.
SUBJ: Chick embryo./ Eggs.

598.6 Ph-2 4-6/4 $19.00 L KC696
NOFSINGER, RAY. Pigeons and doves. By Ray Nofsinger and Jim
Hargrove. Childrens Press ISBN 0-516-02196-6; In Canada: Childrens
Press, 1992. 47p. col. ill. (New true book).
Includes glossary and index.
Short chapters of text and small color photographs describe pigeons
and doves of many countries; physical characteristics; raising of
young; and the care, training, and racing of homing pigeons. Useful
account for children who like pigeons and wish to raise them.
SUBJ: Pigeons./ Homing pigeons.

598.6 Ph-1 5-6/7 $14.95 L KC697
PATENT, DOROTHY HINSHAW. Wild turkey, tame turkey. Photos by
William Munoz. Clarion ISBN 0-89919-704-3, 1989. 57p. col. ill.
Includes index.
Available from the National Library Service for the Blind and
Physically Handicapped on sound recording cassette RC34496.

Handsome wild turkeys are the main focus of this interesting history, and the raising of domestic turkeys for the meat market is also described. Excellent color photographs and six chapters of text discuss the differences in physical characteristics and behavior in wild and domesticated turkeys, the rearing of young in the wild, the mass care of the commercial birds, and the near extinction and recovery of wild turkeys. Obviously useful for Thanksgiving reports, this informative account of the notable American bird deserves year round reading.
SUBJ: Wild turkeys./ Turkeys.

598.6 Ph-2 P-2/2 $14.89 L KC698
SELSAM, MILLICENT E. Egg to chick. Rev. ed. Illus. by Barbara Wolff. HarperCollins ISBN 0-06-025290-1, 1970. 63p. col. ill. (Science I can read book).
Gay, picture-book introduction to the development of the chick from the time the egg is laid to its hatching. Supplemented by a ten-page photographic section showing a chick actually pecking its way out of the egg, and standing beside the broken shell.
SUBJ: Birds./ Embryology./ Poultry.

VCR 598.6 Ph-3 4-6 $99.00 OD KC699
TURKEYS IN THE WILD (Videocassette). Berlet Films, 1991. 1/2" VHS videocassette color (20min). (Great animal stories).
Wild turkey toms strut their stuff in spring mating rituals and females guard their nests and raise the young in this documentary account. A particular hen with her 13 chicks is an appealing focus for part of the film, and the unusual warty face of the tom is also featured. Film shows both the permitted hunting and the efforts of a management crew to capture some of the birds for transfer to a less populated woods. Useful for discussion of habitat and wildlife survival as well as introducing the real bird which is only legendary to most children.
SUBJ: Wild turkeys./ Turkeys.

598.7 Ph-2 3-5/6 $15.95 L OD KC700
MURRAY, PETER. Hummingbirds. Child's World ISBN 1-56766-011-8, 1993. 32p. col. ill. (Naturebooks).
Includes index.
Fine full-page photographs and essay text introduce the behavior and life cycle of these tiny, colorful birds. Several species appear flying, feeding, and tending their young while the text briefly explains migration, mating, nest building, the state of torpor, and the role of the birds in pollinating plants. An appealing quick sketch which encourages children to observe hummingbird activity firsthand.
SUBJ: Hummingbirds.

598.7 Ph-2 3-5/7 $15.99 L OD KC701
MURRAY, PETER. Parrots. Child's World ISBN 1-56766-015-0, 1993. 32p. col. ill. (Naturebooks).
Includes index.
Brilliant colors mark the several species of parrots illustrating this quick introduction to the tropical birds. The essay text facing each full-page photograph sketches information about physical characteristics, eating, enemies, and the care of baby birds (seen in an intriguing photograph). Though the information is not very extensive, the attractive photographs are very inviting, and children will enjoy reading about the natural life of this animal usually only seen in captivity.
SUBJ: Parrots.

598.7 Ph-1 3-6/6 $15.93 L KC702
PATENT, DOROTHY HINSHAW. Quetzal: sacred bird of the cloud forest. Illus. by Neil Waldman. Morrow ISBN 0-688-12663-4, 1996. 40p. col. ill., map.
Includes bibliography and index.
The quetzal is the centerpiece for an examination of scientific, cultural, and historical aspects of Mexico and Central America, with emphasis on Olmec, Toltec, Mayan, and Aztec civilizations. Softly focused, full-color pencil illustrations picture the quetzal, events, artifacts, and symbols. Use for multicultural studies and interdisciplinary units in science and social studies.
SUBJ: Quetzals./ Indians of Mexico--History./ Indians of Central America--History./ Quetzalcoatl (Aztec deity).

598.7 Ph-1 5-6/5 $14.00 T KC703
TYRRELL, ESTHER QUESADA. Hummingbirds: jewels in the sky. Photos by Robert A. Tyrrell. Crown ISBN 0-517-58390-9, 1992. 36p. col. ill.
Includes index.
Numerous species of these colorful little birds appear in fine photographs accompanying an informative essay on appearance and behavior. Topics discussed include physical characteristics, coloring, flight, feeding, protection from enemies, and mating; a particularly intriguing sequence covers the laying and incubating of eggs and care of the young. This fine introduction to an appealing animal concludes

with a concise description of each of the 16 species which nest in the United States.
SUBJ: Hummingbirds.

598.8 Ph-1 4-6/7 $19.95 L KC704
ARNOLD, CAROLINE. House sparrows everywhere. Photos by Richard R. Hewett. Carolrhoda ISBN 0-87614-696-5, 1992. 47p. col. ill. (Carolrhoda nature watch book).
Includes glossary and index.
Close-up views of sparrows hatching and growing to adulthood offer an unusual glimpse of this very ordinary animal. The informative essay text and attractive photographs describe history, physical characteristics, mating, nest building, and many other aspects of sparrow behavior. This attractive life cycle invites readers to become more attentive observers of familiar animals.
SUBJ: English sparrow./ Sparrows.

598.8 Ph-1 K-2/2 $14.89 L KC705
JENKINS, PRISCILLA BELZ. Nest full of eggs. Illus. by Lizzy Rockwell. HarperCollins ISBN 0-06-023442-3; In Canada: HarperCollins, 1995. 32p. col. ill. (Let's-read-and-find-out science book).
A pair of robins build their springtime nest and care for their new family as a boy and girl observe and learn about eggs, nests, and feathers. The pleasant picture book presentation provides good views of the growing birds, informative diagrams following the stages of embryo development, and illustrations of various bird feathers and nests. The simple, well-structured introduction to bird life should encourage backyard observation and be useful for science lessons.
SUBJ: Robins./ Eggs./ Birds--Habits and behavior./ Birds.

598.8 Ph-2 2-5/2 $9.95 L KC706
WATTS, BARRIE. Birds' nest. Silver Burdett ISBN 0-382-09439-5, 1986. 25p. col. ill. (Stopwatch books).
Includes index.
Short text and fine color photographs follow the growth of a nest of blue titmice as their parents care for them in a nesting box. A few drawings supplement the photographs, which depict the nest building, egg laying, incubation by the mother, and endless feeding of the young as they grow. Similar in content to many bird life cycles, this doesn't show the hatching but the closeup views are intriguing, and it's a good simple introduction to this always intriguing subject.
SUBJ: Blue tit./ Birds.

598.8 Ph-2 K-3/5 $15.95 T KC707
WILLIS, NANCY CAROL. Robins in your backyard. Cucumber Island Storytellers ISBN 1-887813-21-7, 1996. 32p. col. ill.
Includes glossary/index and chronology.
Pleasant full-color, colored pencil drawings follow the nesting habits of robins and the growth of the young birds. Simple text describes the spring migration, nest building, hatching, and protection and feeding of the young. The large picture book presentation includes a good cutaway diagram of the embryo in the egg and follows the body changes as the babies grow to adulthood. Concluding information on dealing with injured or orphaned birds completes the attractive life cycle of the familiar bird.
SUBJ: Robins./ Birds--Habits and behavior.

598.9 Ph-1 4-6/7 $6.95 P KC708
ARNOLD, CAROLINE. Saving the peregrine falcon. Photos by Richard Hewett. Carolrhoda ISBN 0-87614-523-3, 1990. 48p. col. ill. (Carolrhoda nature watch book).
Includes glossary.
Selectors' Choice, 15th ed.
Follows the efforts of scientists to save this endangered species by repairing fragile eggs which cannot survive in the wild, hatching them, raising the chicks and releasing the grown birds back into the wild. Fine color photographs and informative essay convey the intricate details of the rescue process and the growth of the powerful, handsome birds. An important presentation which will appeal for personal reading as well as classroom needs.
SUBJ: Peregrine falcon./ Falcons./ Birds--Protection.

598.9 Ph-1 2-5/4 $15.95 L KC709
ARNOSKY, JIM. All about owls. Scholastic ISBN 0-590-46790-5; In Canada: Scholastic, 1995. unp. col. ill.
Selectors' Choice, 21st ed.
Owls of several species and habitats demonstrate the physical characteristics and behavior of this nocturnal hunter in energetic watercolors and short clear text. Doublespread rectangular pages in many shadings provide close-up views with useful small sketches and good explanations of body structure, eyes, calls, nesting, hunting, and eating. An appealing, informative introduction that should be widely enjoyed.
SUBJ: Owls.

598.9   Ph-1 3-6/6 $15.95   L   KC710
BERNHARD, EMERY. Eagles: lions of the sky. Illus. by Durga Bernhard.
Holiday House ISBN 0-8234-1105-2, 1994. unp. col. ill.
    Includes glossary.
    Striking illustrations and clear essay text describe the hunting behavior
and physical characteristics of eagles. Set against muted landscapes,
bold figures of many of the world's eagle species accompany the
discussion of the four major eagle groups, courtship and mating, care
of the young, the ecological role of eagles, and conservation
problems. An informative and appealing introduction useful for
environmental studies reports and interesting as nonfiction reading.
    SUBJ: Eagles.

598.9   Ph-2 5-6/5 $21.00   L   KC711
BROWN, FERN G. Owls. Watts ISBN 0-531-20008-6; In Canada:
Watts, 1991. 63p. col. ill. (First book).
    Includes glossary, bibliography, directory and index.
    Several species of owl illustrate the varied appearance of this
interesting bird, while five short chapters discuss aspects of history,
behavior, and physiology. Owl eyes, talons, feathers, eating habits,
and rearing of the young are discussed; a few particular species are
described, and there is a short list of suggested activities for
observing owls. The attractive color photographs are not always well
meshed with the text, and some information is sketchy, but the book
is an adequate introduction to owls.
    SUBJ: Owls.

VCR 598.9   Ph-2 4-6 $49.00   OD KC712
CRICKET, TIGLET AND FRIENDS (Videocassette). Young Naturalist
Foundation/Bullfrog Films, 1984. 1/2" VHS videocassette color (9min).
    Filmed at the Owl Rehabilitation Centre in Ontario, Canada; viewers
learn how injured burrowing, screech, and horned owls are cared for
and the practices that are followed so that they can be released back
into the wild. Some of the feeding procedures may be minorly
upsetting but the respect shown for the animals is very real. A useful
adjunct to owl studies and/or wildlife rehabilitation efforts.
    SUBJ: Wildlife rescue./ Owls.

598.9   Ph-1 4-6/5 $19.95   L   KC713
EPPLE, WOLFGANG. Barn owls. Photos by Manfred Rogl. Carolrhoda
ISBN 0-87614-742-2, 1992. 48p. col. ill. (Carolrhoda nature watch
book).
    Includes glossary and index.
    Barn owls are common in many parts of the world though their
nocturnal life keeps them hidden from view. This informative essay
with wonderful close-up photographs explains the owl's physiology
and behavior quite thoroughly as it follows one pair of owls as they
mate and raise their brood. The growth of the young owls is
fascinating, and this first-rate life cycle provides an outstanding
introduction to barn owls and owl life in general.
    SUBJ: Barn owl./ Owls.

598.9   Ph-2 5-6/6 $18.60   L   KC714
GIECK, CHARLENE. Bald eagle magic for kids. Photos by Tom and Pat
Leeson, and Bob Baldwin. Gareth Stevens ISBN 0-8368-0761-8; In
Canada: Saunders, 1991. 48p. col. ill. (Animal magic for kids).
    At head of title: Bald eagles.
    Includes glossary.
    Bald eagle family life is the focus of this slim introduction to the life
cycle of this impressive bird. Physical features, nest building, flight,
eating habits, egg laying, and care of the young are briefly
described. Photographs offer some remarkable views of life in the
nest and the young birds' stages of growth. Useful item for reports
includes several intriguing pictues.
    SUBJ: Bald eagle./ Eagles.

598.9   Ph-2 5-6/6 $19.93   L   KC715
KAPPELER, MARKUS. Owls. Gareth Stevens ISBN 0-8368-0687-5; In
Canada: Saunders, 1991. 48p. col. ill., map. (Animal families).
    Includes glossary, bibliography, directory and index.
    Two dozen owl species from around the world demonstrate the
diversity of this bird family. Double-page entries discuss particular
features, behavior, and habitat and include attractive photographs.
Introductory and concluding pages give added information on history
and scientific classification. A species only discovered in the 1970s is
an interesting point in this useful compendium on a bird intriguing to
many readers.
    SUBJ: Owls.

598.9   Ph-2 4-6/6 $14.95   L   KC716
PATENT, DOROTHY HINSHAW. Eagles of America. Photos by William
Munoz. Holiday House ISBN 0-8234-1198-2, 1995. 40p. col. ill.
    Includes index.
    Bald eagles and golden eagles are seen in flight, raising their young,

and being rescued in this quick introduction. Short chapters explain
differences between the two birds, their history as endangered
species, physical characteristics and behavior, and rehabilitation and
release of injured birds. Useful for reports on these impressive species
and on animal conservation. For environmental studies.
    SUBJ: Bald eagle./ Golden eagle./ Eagles.

598.9   Ph-3 A/7 $14.95   L   KC717
PATENT, DOROTHY HINSHAW. Ospreys. Photos by William Munoz.
Clarion ISBN 0-395-63391-5, 1993. 63p. col. ill.
    Includes bibliography and index.
    Chronicles the magnificent osprey, a world traveling marine animal,
who nests on four continents and winters in the tropics. Hunters,
pollution, and habitat destruction have all taken their toll on the birds,
but scientific knowledge and legal protection have helped it survive.
An in-depth wildlife study for birders of all ages.
    SUBJ: Ospreys.

598.9   Ph-1 5-6/7 $15.95   L   KC718
PATENT, DOROTHY HINSHAW. Where the bald eagles gather. Photos
by William Munoz. Clarion ISBN 0-89919-230-0, 1984. 56p. ill.
    Includes index.
    Gathering annually at Glacier National Park to feast on the spawning
kokanee salmon, the American bald eagle has given scientists the
opportunity to study their life cycle, hunting behavior, and survival
problems. The black and white photographs are excellent by and
large, and the well organized text provides an informative, skillfully
presented account of the current state of our national bird.
    SUBJ: Bald eagle./ Eagles./ Glacier National Park (Mont.).

598.9   Ph-1 5-6/6 $15.95   T   KC719
SATTLER, HELEN RONEY. Book of North American owls. Illus. by Jean
Day Zallinger. Clarion ISBN 0-395-60524-5, 1995. 64p. col. ill., maps.
    Includes bibliography and index.
    Twenty-one species of owls found in the United States, from the small
pygmy and elf owls to the impressive snowy and great gray owls, are
featured in excellent drawings and informative text. Describes physical
characteristics of owls, their behavior as predators, courtship and
nesting, care of the young, and the future of owls. The second half of
the book is an owl glossary with a full page devoted to a portrait
and specific facts about each species. This fine overview is an
excellent basic source on a bird that has been intriguing to humans,
but elusive because of its nocturnal life and camouflage coloration.
For environmental studies.
    SUBJ: Owls.

599   Ph-1 4-6/6 $4.95   P   KC720
ALDEN, PETER. Peterson first guide to mammals of North America.
Houghton Mifflin ISBN 0-395-42767-3, 1987. 128p. col. ill. (Peterson
first guide).
    Includes index.
    This reworking of William H. Burt's A FIELD GUIDE TO MAMMALS
(3rd. ed., 1976) simplifies the entries and sets them in a new
attractive format. The mammals are grouped by family with a very
short paragraph of information about each; the fine drawings, mostly
in color, occasionally include the animal's tracks or a small scene
showing the habitat. All pictures face the relevant entries for ease of
use as an identification guide, and children will enjoy the book's small
size and the interesting array of related species.
    SUBJ: Mammals--Identification.

599   Ph-3 A/7 $9.00   T   KC721
HILLER, ILO. Introducing mammals to young naturalists: from Texas Parks
& Wildlife Magazine. Texas A&M University Press ISBN 0-89096-427-0,
1990. 111p. col. ill. (Louise Lindsey Merrick Texas environment series).
    Includes index.
    Eleven attractive accounts of the physical characteristics and behavior
of particular mammals are combined with a variety of activities to
encourage animal observation. Originally published as magazine
articles, the readable text and handsome photographs cover red
foxes, bobcats, javelinas, porcupines and more; instructions are given
for collecting plaster casts of tracks, constructing a pantograph for
drawing enlarged pictures of animals, and making dough ornaments.
Substantial material for reports and a pleasing flat volume for
recreational reading.
    SUBJ: Mammals.

599   Ph-2 5-6/7 $16.95   L   KC722
KNIGHT, LINSAY. Sierra Club book of great mammals. Sierra Club
ISBN 0-87156-507-2, 1992. 68p. col. ill.
    Includes glossary and index.
    Short essays and numerous photographs introduce aspects of mammal
classification and history as well as the physical characteristics and
behavior of selected mammals. The 19 entries, each two or four

pages, cover a single animal or groups of animals commonly associated with one another such as whales and dolphins, and bears and pandas. Includes a chart of the orders in the Mammalia class. Useful for introducing mammal life and the particular animals.
SUBJ: Mammals.

VCR 599   Ph-1 5-6 $12.95   KC723
MAMMAL (Videocassette). Narrated by Martin Sheen. DK Vision/BBC Worldwide Americas ISBN 0-7894-0723-X, 1996. 1/2" VHS videocassette color (35min). (Eyewitness videos).
Closed captioned.
Numerous species appear in short vignettes to demonstrate many physical and behavioral characteristics of mammals. The complex narrative employs wordplay and compares humans to other animals as it ranges over many concepts: body flexibility, mammary glands and suckling, varieties of outer coats, gestation periods, development of bodies and senses, communication, social behavior, and mammals in human mythology. Visuals vary, interspersing old movie clips and views of animals against a bare white backdrop and in natural habitats. The wide range of ideas and information will most appeal to older viewers for personal enjoyment or classroom science lessons. A short concluding segment on the filmmaking techniques might be useful in discussions of visual literacy.
SUBJ: Mammals.

VCR 599   Ph-2 1-5 $9.95   OD KC724
NATURE'S NEWBORN: BEAR, BIGHORN SHEEP, MOUNTAIN GOATS (Videocassette). Stoney-Wolf Productions/dist. by Video Enterprise 50053, 1994. 1/2" VHS videocassette color (30min). (Nature's newborn).
Bighorn lambs, mountain goat kids, and black bear cubs romp through summer under their mothers' watchful eyes in various regions of the Rocky Mountains. The narrative briefly sketches the life of each animal over the four seasons. The information is cursory, but the view of each animal in its natural habitat will have wide appeal, and the three part structure adds versatility.
SUBJ: Animals--Infancy./ Bears./ Bighorn sheep./ Rocky Mountain goat.

599   Ph-1 4-6/7 $20.99   L   KC725
PARKER, STEVE. Mammal. Photos by Jane Burton and Dave King. Knopf ISBN 0-394-92258-1, 1989. 64p. col. ill. (Eyewitness books).
Includes index.
Fascinating views of small mammals and comparisons of the bones of a great variety of animals are the focus of this colorful introduction. Brief bits of discussion, informative captions, and copious drawings and photographs survey many topics: the classification and evolution of mammals, birth and care for the young, skeletal structure, feeding behavior, play, grooming, life underground, tracks, and more. There's an emphasis on cats, squirrels, chimps, and mice, but a liberal sprinkling of other examples and clear explanations of principles along with the appealing visual material make this an absorbing item.
SUBJ: Mammals.

599   Ph-2 2-6/6 $11.99   L   KC726
PARSONS, ALEXANDRA. Amazing mammals. Photos by Jerry Young. Knopf ISBN 0-679-90224-4, 1990. 29p. col. ill. (Eyewitness juniors).
Includes index.
Brief bits of fact and illustrations surround a bold central photograph of a featured mammal in this quick survey. Double spread segments feature the elephant, camel, fox, fruit bat, sloth, otter, squirrel monkey, porcupine and tiger. Superficial but interesting, the presentation concludes with a nice chart comparing these species and humans in number of babies, time of gestation, and period during which babies need mother's milk.
SUBJ: Mammals.

599   Ph-1 4-6/6 $14.99   T   KC727
PATENT, DOROTHY HINSHAW. Why mammals have fur. Photos by William Munoz. Cobblehill/Dutton ISBN 0-525-65141-1, 1995. 26p. col. ill.
Includes index.
Fur and other forms of hair are a major characteristic of most mammals, and this slim volume explains how hair warms animals and protects them from their enemies and their environment. Short chapters of text and an appealing assortment of original photographs explain the physical properties of hair, different types of fur, molting, fur color, and more. Informative and interesting presentation makes this a good choice for nonfiction readers and for study units on mammals or animal survival.
SUBJ: Mammals./ Fur./ Hair.

599   Ph-2 P-3/2 $14.95   L   KC728
SELSAM, MILLICENT E. Keep looking. By Millicent E. Selsam and Joyce Hunt. Illus. by Normand Chartier. Macmillan ISBN 0-02-781840-3; In Canada: Collier Macmillan, 1989. 32p. col. ill.
A snow covered landscape in stunning watercolor double-page spread illustrations show the wildlife found near a country home. The simple text helps young people see animal adaptations to seasonal changes. Share with a small group.
SUBJ: Winter./ Animals--Habits and behavior./ Wildlife watching.

599   Ph-1 5-6/6 $16.95   T   KC729
SIERRA CLUB BOOK OF SMALL MAMMALS. Sierra Club ISBN 0-87156-525-0, 1993. 68p. col. ill.
Includes glossary and index.
Pigs and peccaries, bats, rodents, and many other animals appear in this large informative presentation. Short, heavily illustrated entries treat broad topics and specific animals in the three mammal groups-- monotremes, marsupials, and placental. Coverage is sometimes sketchy, but this is often clear and informative and works well as a quick reference source.
SUBJ: Mammals.

599.097   Ph-1 3-6 $19.00   T   KC730
WHITAKER, JOHN O. Audubon Society field guide to North American mammals. Rev. & expanded. Random House ISBN 0-679-44631-1; In Canada: Random House, 1996. 743p. col. ill. (Audubon Society field guides).
Includes index.
A fine guide for amateurs. A thumb tab index guides the user by the mammal's shape to a section of color photographs where the specimen can be identified and thence to a detailed written description of its habitat, range and characteristics. A track guide is also included so that animal tracks can be identfed. Pocket size, handy for field trips. A duplicate copy is recommended for the reference collection.
SUBJ: Mammals--North America.

599.17   Ph-1 K-4/2 $14.89   L   KC731
DUNPHY, MADELEINE. Here is the Arctic winter. Illus. by Alan James Robinson. Hyperion ISBN 1-56282-337-X, 1993. unp. col. ill.
Using the cumulative pattern of THE HOUSE THAT JACK BUILT, text enumerates Artic life: whales, wolves, sea ice, northern lights, and more. Blue and black illustrations shimmer in the icy cold. Young readers will learn that this bleak and unique landscape is most definitely alive and that each animal has a place in the chain of life.
SUBJ: Zoology--Arctic regions./ Winter.

599.17   Ph-1 5-6/3 $14.00   L   KC732
MATTHEWS, DOWNS. Arctic summer. Photos by Dan Guravich. Simon & Schuster ISBN 0-671-79539-2; In Canada: Simon & Schuster, 1993. unp. col. ill.
Arctic animals, plants, and terrain appear in a beautiful compendium of photographs and brief explanations. Summer is a time of raising young, changing appearance, traveling, and stocking up on food; lemmings, ptarmigan, red foxes, ermine, polar bears, harp seals, muskoxen, and beluga whales are among the species introduced. The smoothly blended introduction to seasons, animals and plant relationships, and the Arctic world is an appealing, versatile volume.
SUBJ: Zoology--Arctic regions.

599.2   Ph-1 4-6/8 $5.95   P   KC733
ARNOLD, CAROLINE. Koala. Photos by Richard Hewett. Morrow ISBN 0-688-11503-9, c1987, 1992. 48p. col. ill. (Baby zoo animals).
Describes the physical characteristics and behavior of koalas along with the rearing of a particular young female who is ultimately selected for shipment from an Australian preserve to the San Francisco Zoo. Exceptionally fine color photographs and a deftly woven text provide an informative introduction to this appealing marsupial. An attractive choice for animal fans and science reports.
SUBJ: Koala.

599.2   Ph-1 4-6/8 $12.95   T   KC734
BURT, DENISE. Birth of a koala. Photos by Neil McLeod. Buttercup/dist. by Australian Book Source ISBN 0-944176-02-X, 1986. unp. col. ill.
Readers of all ages will be drawn to the ready appeal of the koala mothers and babies featured in this slim, informative introduction. Fine color photographs and clearly stated text cover aspects of physiology, behavior, protection of the species, and the various stages of development of young koalas from the months spent in the pouch to near adulthood. This attractive presentation of one of Australia's most endearing marsupials is an excellent item for both browsing and information.
SUBJ: Koala.

599.2   Ph-3 5-6/6 $15.93   L   KC735
DARLING, KATHY. Tasmanian devil: on location. Photos by Tara
Darling. Lothrop, Lee & Shepard ISBN 0-688-09727-8, 1992. 40p. col.
ill. (On location).
   Includes index.
   Small but fierce, the little-known Tasmanian devil is a nighttime
predator and scavenger introduced here in an attractive photo essay.
Color pictures and informative text examine teeth, claws, and other
physical characteristics of the fierce marsupial along with care of
young, fighting, eating, use of smell and scent, and history of the
species. Children who like rare or exotic animals will find this
interesting.
   SUBJ: Tasmanian devil.

VCR 599.2   Ph-3 5-6 $195.00   OD KC736
KOALAS: THE BARE FACTS (Videocassette). Bullfrog Films ISBN
1-56029-511-2, 1993. 1/2" VHS videocassette color (51min).
   Includes public performance rights.
   Chronicles the survival problems of koalas as their environment
disappears and environmentalists' efforts to save the endangered
animal. The film shows scenes of the animal in its natural habitat and
interacting with humans with a fine sequence on birth and
development. Part two includes troubling views of diseased animals
and reiterates much material covered in part one. Valuable in
addressing the problems of animal conservation with mature students.
For environmental studies.
   SUBJ: Koala.

599.2   Ph-1 2-5/4 $14.93   L   KC737
RYDEN, HOPE. Joey: the story of a baby kangaroo. Tambourine ISBN
0-688-12745-2, 1994. unp. col. ill.
   Fine photographs and a brief essay text follow the daily activities of
a mother kangaroo and her growing joey in their natural Australian
habitat. Many other animals are also introduced as the joey plays,
naps, grooms himself, eats, and practices fighting with his mother and
a nearly grown sibling. Two pages of added information and a
pronunciation guide to animal names conclude this appealing browsing
item and nonfiction reading choice.
   SUBJ: Kangaroos./ Animals--Infancy.

599.2   Ph-2 3-5/3 $16.95   L   KC738
SOTZEK, HANNELORE. Koala is not a bear! By Hannelore Sotzek and
Bobbie Kalman. Crabtree ISBN 0-86505-639-0; In Canada: Crabtree,
1997. 32p. col. ill., map. (Crabapples).
   "Bobbie Kalman book."
   Includes glossary and index.
   Koalas appear in attractive photographs demonstrating how they live
high in Australian treetops. The simple discussion explains how koalas
fit into the marsupial family, physical characteristics, eating, clumsy
movement on the ground, loss of habitat, and human efforts to
protect koalas. Children will enjoy the many photographs, and the
serviceable text will be useful for reports. For environmental studies.
   SUBJ: Koala.

599.3   Ph-2 4-6/9 $15.95   L OD KC739
PATTON, DON. Armadillos. Child's World ISBN 1-56766-182-3, 1996.
32p. col. ill. (Naturebooks).
   Includes index.
   Striking photographs of this small armored mammal fill the slim
introduction to its physical characteristics and life cycle. Brief
discussion covers history, eating, burrowing, birth and care of the
young, defense against predators, and human use of armadillo meat
and hides. The animal's unusual appearance will attract readers, and
this will be particularly useful in regions of the Southwest.
   SUBJ: Armadillos.

599.3   Ph-2 5-6/7 $13.95   L   KC740
PEMBLETON, SELIESA. Armadillo. Dillon ISBN 0-87518-507-X; In
Canada: Maxwell Macmillan, 1992. 60p. col. ill. (Dillon remarkable
animals book).
   Includes glossary and index.
   As the nine-banded armadillo moves further into the United States,
more children are becoming aware of this strange burrowing mammal
with its hard shell and substantial claws. Short chapters of text and
good color photographs describe physiology, care of the young,
winter behavior, and a variety of species. Children who enjoy unusual
animals will be well-served by this useful introduction.
   SUBJ: Armadillos.

599.3   Ph-2 5-6/7 $19.95   L   KC741
STUART, DEE. Astonishing armadillo. Carolrhoda ISBN 0-87614-769-4,
1993. 48p. col. ill., maps. (Carolrhoda nature watch book).
   Includes glossary and index.
   Fine photographs and an informative essay text describe the history,

physical characteristics, and behavior of the hardy nine-banded
armadillo. Burrowing and nesting habits, the regular formation of
quadruplets, rearing of young, feeding migration into wider ranges,
and adaptability are among the topics covered. Interesting
presentation on an animal which is very familiar in some southern
states but exotic for readers in most locations.
   SUBJ: Armadillos.

599.35   Ph-2 P-K/2 $12.88   L   KC742
ARNOSKY, JIM. Come out, muskrats. Lothrop, Lee & Shepard ISBN
0-688-05458-7, 1989. unp. col. ill.
   Warm, sunny pictures follow the late day emergence of a pair of
muskrats, who swim around the pond, play, groom themselves and
swim again into the night. This very simple picture book conveys a
pleasant sense of the muskrat's pond life through minimal text and
beautifully painted scenes of plants, other animals, the surrounding
farm and hills, the setting sun and emerging night. The book is a
gentle read aloud and a simple nature lesson which could be
expanded with discussion and other materials for teaching purposes.
   SUBJ: Muskrats.

599.35   Ph-1 4-6/6 $19.95   L   KC743
FISCHER-NAGEL, HEIDEROSE. Look through the mouse hole. By
Heiderose and Andreas Fischer-Nagel. Carolrhoda ISBN 0-87614-326-5,
1989. 47p. col. ill. (Carolrhoda nature watch book).
   Includes glossary and index.
   Fascinating photographs of a pair of house mice building their nest
and caring for their young accompany an informative discussion of
the behavior and life cycle of this familiar little rodent. The birth and
growth of the baby mice is most interesting, and the presentation also
covers eating habits, enemies, and a variety of species of mice. The
exceptional close-up view of the normally elusive mice will be widely
enjoyed.
   SUBJ: Mice.

599.35   Ph-2 4-6/7 $19.95   L   KC744
JARROW, GAIL. Naked mole-rats. By Gail Jarrow and Paul Sherman.
Carolrhoda ISBN 0-87614-995-6, 1996. 48p. col. ill., map. (Carolrhoda
nature watch book).
   Includes glossary and index.
   Naked mole-rats are African desert animals intriguing in their homely,
ungainly appearance and unusual in having physical characteristics of
mammals, the temperature system of reptiles, and the community
behavior of social insects. This informative life cycle, illustrated with
plentiful, excellent photographs, follows the animals through many
aspects of life in their underground burrows. Will appeal to readers
who like exotic animals, and the material would also be interesting for
units on desert habitats.
   SUBJ: Naked mole rat./ Rodents.

599.35   Ph-2 1-4/6 $15.99   L OD KC745
MURRAY, PETER. Porcupines. Child's World ISBN 1-56766-019-3, 1994.
32p. col. ill. (Naturebooks).
   Includes index.
   Full-page photographs and informative explanations make up this
picture book introduction to the bristly porcupine. The text describes
physical characteristics, behavior, diet, the structure and use of the
quills, care of the young, and a few porcupine species from other
parts of the world. The attractive, slim book will appeal to browsers,
and the nicely constructed text will serve for reading aloud.
   SUBJ: Porcupines.

599.35   Ph-2 1-3/8 $14.95   L   KC746
PEET, BILL. Capyboppy. Houghton Mifflin ISBN 0-395-24378-5, c1966.
62p. ill.
   A delightful story of a very odd pet, the capybara, a rodent, which
will soon grow to weigh 200 pounds and be hard to handle. The
author took one into his home and then the fun began. The
illustrations are very good and very funny.
   SUBJ: Capybaras.

599.35   Ph-1 5-6/6 $13.95   L   KC747
SHERROW, VICTORIA. Porcupine. Dillon ISBN 0-87518-442-1, 1991.
59p. col. ill. (Dillon remarkable animals book).
   Includes "Facts about the Porcupine," glossary and index.
   Attractive photographs of several porcupine species from around the
world accompany this informative introduction to these tree-climbing
herbivorous animals. The porcupine's history, physical characteristics,
behavior, preparations for lean winter months, raising of young, and
dealing with enemies are discussed. A table of facts introduces the
inviting presentation.
   SUBJ: North American porcupine./ Porcupines.

599.35   Ph-2 2-4/2 $9.95   L   KC748
WATTS, BARRIE. Hamster. Silver Burdett ISBN 0-3820-9281-3, 1986.
24p. col. ill. (Stopwatch books).
Includes index.
Follows the life cycle of a hamster litter in simple text and attractive
color photographs. Mating, nest-building, care of the newborn
through the stages of their growth to adulthood, and eating habits
are all described, and a final page recaps selected pictures, asking
the reader to remember and retell the appropriate parts of the story.
Though sketchy in some respects, this is an attractive introduction to a
naturally appealing animal.
SUBJ: Hamsters.

599.36   Ph-2 4-5/4 $3.95   P   KC749
ARNOLD, CAROLINE. Prairie dogs. Illus. by Jean Cassels. Scholastic
ISBN 0-590-46946-0; In Canada: Scholastic, 1993. 31p. col. ill.
Includes index and bibliography.
Informative text and pleasant drawings explain the physical
characteristics and life cycle of prairie dogs. Describes differences
between black-tailed and white-tailed prairie dogs, the defending of
territory, building of burrows, organization of social groups, care of
the young, and dangers from predators. It looks fictionalized but is a
good nonfiction introduction to this now diminishing rodent.
SUBJ: Prairie dogs.

VCR 599.36   Ph-2 3-6 $89.00   OD KC750
CHIPMUNK (Videocassette). TVOntario 320206, 1988. 1 1/2" VHS
videocassette color (24min). (Nature watch).
Teacher's Guide available for $3.45.
Three young chipmunks emerging cautiously from the underground
nest bring to a close a year in the life of a female chipmunk who is
followed through the seasons. The solitary chipmunk becomes a
monotonous if attractive figure, but there are threats of danger which
become dramatic as well as lovely views of the habitat. The sounds of
the anxious chipmunk and other animals in her world round out a
pleasant animal life cycle story useful for a broad range of audiences.
SUBJ: Chipmunks./ Animals--Habits and behavior.

599.36   Ph-2 4-6/4 $19.00   L   KC751
LEPTHIEN, EMILIE U. Squirrels. Childrens Press ISBN 0-516-01947-3; In
Canada: Childrens Press, 1992. 48p. col. ill. (New true book).
Includes glossary and index.
Many different animals belonging to the squirrel family are included in
this slim, informative discussion. Short chapters and color photographs
cover physical features, climbing, eating, nesting, care of the young,
molting, winter behavior, differences between ground squirrels and
tree squirrels, and human threats to survival. The simple narrative
provides both useful material and interesting views of this common
animal and its cousins.
SUBJ: Squirrels.

599.36   Ph-3 3-4/4 $19.00   L   KC752
LEPTHIEN, EMILIE U. Woodchucks. Childrens Press ISBN 0-516-01140-5;
In Canada: Childrens Press, 1992. 48p. ill. (some col.). (New true book).
Includes glossary and index.
Woodchucks, ground burrowing relatives of squirrels, are introduced
in short chapters of text and many small photographs. Physical
characteristics, hibernation, related animals, and various celebrations
of Groundhog Day are discussed. Some of the information is quite
sketchy, but this utilitarian volume will be useful in collections lacking
material on the subject.
SUBJ: Marmots./ Woodchucks.

599.36   Ph-2 1-5/5 $15.95   L OD KC753
MCDONALD, MARY ANN. Flying squirrels. Child's World ISBN
1-56766-058-4, 1993. 32p. col. ill. (Naturebooks).
Includes index.
Energetic and nocturnal, these swift gliders of the squirrel family
appear in fine color photographs with an essay text explaining their
activities. Simple explanations cover movement, senses, sounds, eating,
enemies, nesting, and growth of the young. Suggestions for observing
flying squirrels conclude the attractive introduction to this seldom seen
animal.
SUBJ: Flying squirrels./ Squirrels.

599.37   Ph-2 3-5/5 $19.00   L   KC754
LEPTHIEN, EMILIE U. Beavers. Childrens Press ISBN 0-516-01131-6; In
Canada: Childrens Press, 1992. 48p. col. ill. (New true book).
Includes glossary and index.
Beaver dams and lodges along with many other topics are introduced
in short chapters of text and color photographs. Basic facts about
teeth, tails, and other physical characteristics along with mating, care
of the young, life on land and underwater, and human threats to
survival are all described in sketchy but informative explanation. A

slim, useful introduction to this interesting water dwelling mammal.
SUBJ: Beavers.

599.37   Ph-2 K-2/4 $14.95   T   KC755
WALLACE, KAREN. Think of a beaver. Illus. by Mick Manning.
Candlewick ISBN 1-56402-179-3; In Canada: Douglas & McIntyre, 1993.
unp. col. ill. (Read and wonder).
A beaver family's life through the seasons is portrayed in short
descriptive text and captioned watercolor sketches. The crude,
congenial drawings follow swimming and building activities and life
inside the beaver lodge while the text describes the environment,
physical characteristics, eating, and family behavior. The cheery tone
and emphasis on how this animal is suited to its environment make
this an appealing life cycle for reading aloud or independent reading.
SUBJ: Beavers.

599.4   Ph-2 5-6/7 $19.99   L   KC756
ACKERMAN, DIANE. Bats: shadows in the night. Photos by Merlin
Tuttle. Crown ISBN 0-517-70920-1; In Canada: Random House, 1997.
32p. col. ill.
Includes index.
Fine photographs of many bat species accompany the author's
account of trips she and the photographer made to observe bats. The
somewhat gushy prose is most interesting when it moves from the
personal detail to explain the physical characteristics of the bats. The
captions and occasional text insets add further factual explanations.
Many readers will skip over the text to enjoy the photographs. The
enthusiastic presentation introduces naturalists at work as well as
offering considerable information on bats.
SUBJ: Bats.

599.4   Ph-2 4-6/7 $15.93   L   KC757
ARNOLD, CAROLINE. Bat. Photos by Richard Hewett. Morrow ISBN
0-688-13727-X, 1996. 48p. col. ill. (Baby animal series).
Includes directory and index.
Humans and bats often interact in the photographs of this life study
of the ever intriguing flying mammal. Many aspects of bat life and
history are explained in topical segments: physical characteristics,
variety of species, scientific classification, eating habits, rearing of the
young, false beliefs of humans, echolocation, enemies, endangerment,
and more. The solid presentation is an attractive and useful source on
a subject always in demand. For environmental studies.
SUBJ: Bats.

599.4   Ph-2 1-3/5 $16.95   L   KC758
BASH, BARBARA. Shadows of night: the hidden world of the Little
Brown Bat. Sierra Club ISBN 0-87156-562-5; In Canada: Sierra Club,
1993. unp. col. ill.
Doublespread paintings depict the life of a female brown bat as she
joins a maternity colony of bats in a barn and gives birth to her
baby. Black or white type set against deep-hued pages tells about the
bats' wing structure, use of echolocation, hunting and eating habits,
care of the young, late summer swarming, and hibernation.
Concluding white pages provide added facts and sketches of other
bat species in this pleasant introduction to the common small bat.
SUBJ: Little brown bat./ Bats.

599.4   Ph-1 1-3/4 $14.89   L   KC759
EARLE, ANN. Zipping, zapping, zooming bats. Illus. by Henry Cole.
HarperCollins ISBN 0-06-023480-6; In Canada: HarperCollins, 1995.
32p. col. ill. (Let's-read-and-find-out science book).
Includes directory.
"A little brown bat can catch 150 mosquitoes in 15 minutes." (p.8)
Children are invited to observe and understand how bats are
structured, how they hunt and use echolocation to find their way
around, and how they care for their young in this informative
introduction. Attractive illustrations and simple text invite browsing,
reading aloud, independent reading, and use in reports.
SUBJ: Bats.

599.4   Ph-1 4-6/9 $19.95   L   KC760
JOHNSON, SYLVIA A. Bats. Photos by Modiki Masuda. Lerner ISBN
0-8225-1461-3, 1985. 47p. col. ill. (Lerner natural science book).
Includes glossary and index.
Concentrating on the horseshoe bat, this handsome and informative
introduction to bat behavior and physiology mentions several other
species as well. The essay text, organized into a few long sections,
and amazingly detailed photographs cover structure of the wings and
body, eating habits, raising of the young, hibernation, and many
other aspects of bat life. The coverage on baby bats is exceptional
among children's books, and the colorful and informative presentation
will appeal to a wide age span of readers.
SUBJ: Bats.

599.4   Ph-2 1-4/6 $14.95   L   KC761
MAESTRO, BETSY. Bats: night fliers. Illus. by Giulio Maestro. Scholastic
ISBN 0-590-46150-8; In Canada: Scholastic, 1994. 32p. col. ill., map.
   Bats of many species appear in attractive watercolor illustrations, and
   a clear text explains their behavior and unusual physical
   characteristics. Structure of the wings, flying, echolocation, roosting,
   hygiene, care of the young, migration, and differences between
   megabats and microbats are all covered in the pleasant picture book
   presentation. A good, basic introduction to this populous and unusual
   looking animal.
   SUBJ: Bats.

599.4   Ph-2 5-A/9 $14.95   T   KC762
PRINGLE, LAURENCE P. Batman: exploring the world of bats. By
Laurence Pringle. Photos by Merlin D. Tuttle. Scribner's ISBN 0-684-
19232-2; In Canada: Collier Macmillan, 1991. 42p. col. ill.
   Includes bibliography and index.
   Part biography and part natural history, this thoughtful account
   explains the career history of naturalist/photographer Merlin Tuttle
   and his work on behalf of endangered bat species. Tuttle has done
   research, photography, and conservation efforts in assorted countries
   and regions of the United States; his exquisite photographs are
   intriguing, and his life story and the information about bats are
   equally absorbing. An outstanding introduction to contemporary work
   in natural science.
   SUBJ: Tuttle, Merlin D./ Bats.

599.4   Ph-2 5-6/8 $19.95   L   KC763
STUART, DEE. Bats: mysterious flyers of the night. Carolrhoda ISBN
0-87614-814-3, 1994. 47p. col. ill.
   "Carolrhoda nature watch book."
   Includes glossary, directory and index.
   Photographs of many species illustrate the intriguing variety of faces
   and wing structures of this populous order of mammals. Informative
   chapters explain the differences between Megachiroptera and
   Microchiroptera and go on to discuss physical characteristics, night
   flight, eating habits, migration, birth and care of the young, ways
   human activity is beginning to deplete bat populations, and the
   ecological importance of bats as pollinators of the world's plants and
   consumers of amazing quantities of insects. Close-up photography, at
   times, makes the animals seem larger than their true size. For
   environmental studies.
   SUBJ: Bats.

599.5   Ph-1 4-6/7 $14.93   L   KC764
ARNOLD, CAROLINE. Killer whale. Photos by Richard Hewett. Morrow
ISBN 0-688-12030-X, 1994. 48p. col. ill. (Baby zoo animals).
   Includes index.
   Killer whales are shown interacting with human trainers at marine
   parks and swimming at sea in this handsome photo-essay. Good
   explanations of physical characteristics--particularly the various senses
   and the flukes, fins and flippers--are provided. Other topics include
   eating, rearing of the young, social groupings, human threats, and
   training for performance. Close-up views will attract browsers, and
   the thoughtful presentation is an excellent introduction to the species.
   SUBJ: Killer whale./ Whales./ Killer whale--Training./ Captive wild
   animals.

599.5   Ph-3 3-5/4 $17.50   L   KC765
BEHRENS, JUNE. Whales of the world. Childrens Press ISBN 0-516-
08877-7; In Canada: Childrens Press, 1987. 45p. col. ill.
   Major whale species, including dolphins and porpoises appear here in
   their natural habitat and in captivity. The brief discussion covers
   physical characteristics, feeding habits, migration, intelligence, and
   brief references to human exploration. A sketchy introduction, this will
   be useful where more material is needed.
   SUBJ: Whales.

599.5   Ph-2 2-4/4 $17.50   L   KC766
BEHRENS, JUNE. Whalewatch. Photos collected by John Olguin.
Childrens Press ISBN 0-516-08873-4; In Canada: Childrens Press, 1978.
30p. col. ill. (Golden gate junior book).
   The annual winter migration of California gray whales is watched by
   boatloads of school children. Information about these whales is
   imparted through the text and the color photographs.
   SUBJ: Whales.

599.5   Ph-1 K-4/3 $15.99   T   KC767
DAVIES, NICOLA. Big blue whale. Illus. by Nick Maland. Candlewick
ISBN 1-56402-895-X; In Canada: Candlewick/dist. by Douglas &
McIntyre, 1997. unp. col. ill.
   Includes index.
   Imaginative, softly washed pen drawings and a short conversational
   essay explain the way of life of earth's largest creature. Comic human

figures appearing with the more realistic animals lend humor, and
captions add bits of fact as the text describes size, physical
characteristics, the eating of krill, migration, birth of the young, and
humming. Clever touches in pictures and text make this attractive for
reading aloud, browsing, and nonfiction reading.
   SUBJ: Blue whale./ Whales.

599.5   Ph-2 1-3/2 $14.89   L   KC768
ESBENSEN, BARBARA JUSTER. Baby whales drink milk. Illus. by
Lambert Davis. HarperCollins ISBN 0-06-021552-6; In Canada:
HarperCollins, 1994. 32p. col. ill., map. (Let's-read-and-find-out science
book).
   Includes directory.
   A humpback whale and her calf are followed through the year with
   simple explanations of their various characteristics as mammals.
   Pleasant paintings of underwater scenes illustrate the discussion of
   breathing and spouting, eating, migrating, size, physical
   characteristics, sounds, and warm-bloodedness. Closing pages depict
   various other whale species. Useful and informative introduction for
   younger readers.
   SUBJ: Humpback whale./ Whales./ Mammals.

599.5   Ph-2 K-4/3 $15.95   L   KC769
GIBBONS, GAIL. Whales. Holiday House ISBN 0-8234-0900-7, 1991.
unp. col. ill.
   An easy-to-read book that packs a wallop of information. Gibbons'
   watercolors and brief text present the world of whales, their habits
   and habitats. Phonetic pronunciation is unobtrusively included. Will
   appeal across grade levels and each rereading insures more learning.
   SUBJ: Whales.

CDR 599.5   Ph-1 3-A $39.95   OD KC770
IN THE COMPANY OF WHALES (CD-ROM). Discovery Channel
Multimedia ISBN 1-56331-320-0, 1993. 1 CD-ROM color.
   Includes user's guide.
   Also available for Macintosh (ISBN 1-56331-321-9), $39.95.
   System requirements for Windows: Multimedia PC or equivalent
   (includes 386SX or higher processer, 4MB of RAM, hard drive, CD-
   ROM drive, audio board, mouse and VGA display (256 colors);
   MS-DOS or PC-DOS operating system version 3.1 or later; Microsoft
   Windows graphical environment version 3.1 or later; MS-DOS CD-
   ROM Extensions (MSCDEX) version 2.2 or later.
   A complete look at the world of whales, this CD-ROM contains 45
   minutes of video, an ask-the-experts section, and over 200
   photographs. Navigation is logical and easy. Works well as a
   learning station or on a large monitor with an entire class.
   SUBJ: Whales--Software./ Software--Whales./ Interactive media.

599.5   Ph-1 5-6/6 $17.96   T   KC771
KALMAN, BOBBIE. Arctic whales and whaling. By Bobbie Kalman and
Ken Faris. Crabtree ISBN 0-86505-146-1, 1988. 55p. col. ill. (Arctic
world).
   Includes glossary and index.
   Whales, whaling boats and tools, and the work of whaling as it is still
   practiced by Arctic peoples are the subject of this attractive
   magazine-like presentation. Short sections of text and numerous
   photographs along with some drawings and charts discuss the various
   whale species, the importance of weather, life in the whaling camp,
   and many of the tasks involved in capturing the whales and preparing
   the meat and blubber for use. The documenting of the history and
   present life of the Inuit people is even more interesting than the
   whales!
   SUBJ: Whales--Arctic regions./ Whaling--Arctic regions./ Whaling--
   Arctic regions--History.

599.5   Ph-2 3-5/7 $12.00   L   KC772
KIM, MELISSA. Blue whale. Illus. by Shirley Felts. Ideals Children's Books
ISBN 0-8249-8628-8; In Canada: Ideals Children's Books/dist. by
Vanwell, 1993. 32p. col. ill., maps. (Creature club).
   Includes index.
   Questions about the large bodies of blue whales and their
   endangered status head the attractive busy pages of brief
   explanations and watercolor drawings in this large, slim book. Other
   species of great whales are briefly covered in the discussion of size,
   physical characteristics, eating, migration, history of whaling, and use
   of whale products today. The two-page topical format lends itself to
   browsing. Strong conservation theme encourages children to think
   about ways they can help protect endangered animals. For
   environmental studies.
   SUBJ: Blue whale./ Whales.

599.5   Ph-2 4-5/4 $6.95   P   KC773
LAUBER, PATRICIA. Great whales: the gentle giants. Illus. by Pieter
Folkens. Henry Holt ISBN 0-8050-2894-3; In Canada: Fitzhenry &

Whiteside, 1993. 64p. ill. (some col.). (Redfeather book).
Includes index.
Different species of whales, discoveries by scientists, and some history of whaling are discussed in this small pleasant volume. Photographs in color and black and white and informative drawings accompany the five readable chapters which include a final ancedotal account of men saving two stranded whales trapped in ice. A useful introduction to whale physiology, behavior, and conservation, this is also good reading for children who enjoy nonfiction.
SUBJ: Whales.

599.5   Ph-2 1-3/2 $3.99   P   KC774
MILTON, JOYCE. Whales: the gentle giants. Illus. by Alton Langford. Random House ISBN 0-394-89809-5; In Canada: Random House, 1989. 48p. col. ill. (Step into reading).
An easy-to-read text introduces several species of whales and discusses their eating habits, behavior, and young rearing practices. Migration, a bit of whaling history, and the currently popular whale watching activity are also discussed and pictured in softly colored drawings. While a little sketchy about some aspects of the life cycle this is a pleasant presentation for beginning readers.
SUBJ: Whales.

599.5   Ph-2 4-6/6 $15.95   L   KC775
PATENT, DOROTHY HINSHAW. Killer whales. Photos by John K.B. Ford. Holiday House ISBN 0-8234-0999-6, 1993. 32p. col. ill.
Includes index.
Handsome views of individual killer whales and groups feeding, playing, and traveling together accompany a simple essay which explains how scientists are studying this well-known yet elusive animal. Physical characteristics, feeding, breathing, care of the young, and communication are among the topics covered. This well crafted introduction will attract browsers and nonfiction readers as well as supply report material.
SUBJ: Killer whale./ Whales.

599.5   Ph-2 5-6/11   17.00   T   KC776
PRINGLE, LAURENCE P. Dolphin man: exploring the world of dolphins. By Laurence Pringle. Photos by Randall S. Wells and Dolphin Biology Research Institute. Atheneum ISBN 0-689-80299-4; In Canada: Distican, 1995. 42p. col. ill., map.
Includes bibliography and index.
Randy Wells, a marine biologist studying bottlenose dolphins in Florida's Sarasota Bay, had a strong childhood interest in ocean life leading to his life's work. Accompanied by attractive photographs, short chapters of text interweave information about Randy's career and the work of animal trainers and scientists with explanations of dolphin life. The slim volume works nicely as biography, science, or career studies material.
SUBJ: Dolphins./ Zoologists./ Wells, Randall S.

599.51   Ph-2 5-6/6 $16.89   L   KC777
SIMON, SEYMOUR. Whales. Crowell/HarperCollins ISBN 0-690-04758-4, 1989. unp. col. ill.
Assorted whale species are introduced briefly in an essay text and inky blue photographs. General information about size, physical characteristics and behavior is followed by some particular discussion of selected toothed and baleen whales. Somewhat sketchy and repetitive, this has many photographs which inadequately illustrate the specific whales, but the format is generally attractive, and this is an acceptable overview.
SUBJ: Whales.

599.53   Ph-2 K-2/2 $3.75   P   KC778
MORRIS, ROBERT A. Dolphin. Illus. by Mamoru Funai. HarperCollins ISBN 0-06-444043-5; In Canada: HarperCollins, c1975. 62p. col. ill. (I can read book).
Available from National Library Service for the Blind and Physically Handicapped in Braille BR03335.
Relates through simple text and pleasant green and blue watercolors the birth and early life of a dolphin. While the prose is somewhat choppy, it is neither cute nor heavily anthropomorphized. Well constructed and useful as elementary science information or easy-to-read materials.
SUBJ: Dolphins.

599.55   Ph-2 5-6/7 $14.88   L   KC779
DARLING, KATHY. Manatee: on location. Photos by Tara Darling. Lothrop, Lee & Shepard ISBN 0-688-09031-1, 1991. 48p. col. ill.
Includes index.
Gentle in nature and homely in appearance, the large underwater cousin of the elephant is seen here in Florida's Crystal River Wildlife Refuge. The text has many gaps but ranges over aspects of physiology, behavior, raising of young, and causes of endangerment;

handsome photographs, often full-page, add appeal. This is a readable introduction to this endangered and unusual water mammal, which in the United States is found only in Florida.
SUBJ: Manatees./ Rare animals.

599.55   Ph-2 1-3/2 $14.85   L   KC780
JACOBS, FRANCINE. Sam the sea cow. Illus. by Laura Kelly. Walker ISBN 0-8027-8147-0; In Canada: Thomas Allen, 1991. 48p. col. ill.
Includes directory.
Originally published as SEWER SAM, THE SEA COW, 1979.
Simple text and paintings follow the life experiences of a young manatee during his first year of life in Southern Florida. The story chapters effectively convey information about the history, physical characteristics, behavior, habitat, and conservation problems of this homely water mammal. Young Sam suffers entrapment by a man-made obstacle and is rescued by Seaquarium workers in a plausible account which will serve for reading aloud or independent reading.
SUBJ: Manatees.

599.55   Ph-3 5-6/7 $19.00   L   KC781
LEPTHIEN, EMILIE U. Manatees. Childrens Press ISBN 0-516-01114-6; In Canada: Childrens Press, 1991. 48p. col. ill. (New true book).
Includes glossary and index.
Manatees are underwater grazers long ago descended from an ancestor shared with elephants and having a variety of interesting physical characteristics. This small utilitarian volume has a wooden but informative text which describes related species and many aspects of physiology and behavior. Found only in Florida in the United States and appealing in its homeliness, the manatee serves as a useful example of the problems of endangered animals.
SUBJ: Manatees.

VCR 599.55   Ph-1 5-6 $19.95   OD KC782
MANATEES: RED ALERT (Videocassette). Kurtis Prod., Ltd. and The Chicago Prod. Center/WTTW/dist. by Public Media Video ISBN 0-7800-1890-7, 1996. 1/2" VHS videocassette color (60min).
Includes public performance rights.
When an alarming number of Florida's endangered manatees died in the summer of 1996, scientists from around the world joined efforts to study the dead animals and the live manatees to solve this scientific mystery. Dramatic scenes of the dead manatees and humans interacting with the huge, gentle mammals document the work of scientists and the urgency of solving conservation problems. An episode from the public television series THE NEW EXPLORERS with journalist Bill Kurtis, the substantial account is a fascinating story as well as a multifaceted lesson that will be enjoyed for classroom use and family and individual viewing. For environmental studies.
SUBJ: Manatees./ Rare animals./ Endangered species.

VCR 599.55   Ph-3 2-6 $275.00   OD KC783
SAVING THE MANATEE (Videocassette). TVOntario/dist. by Beacon Films/Altschul Group 8641, 1993. 1/2" VHS videocassette color (15min). (World of nature).
Meet the manatee, or sea cow, an air breathing, vegetarian mammal that lives in Florida's rivers and coastal waters and has some features similar to elephants. Manatees can walk underwater on their flippers and have no natural enemies, but motor boats and fishing nets have endangered their lives. Florida has set up a special manatee hospital to nurse the injured. Children will love this unique species and their Florida companions: the ibis, brown pelican, and alligator. Narrated by a young boy, the video will appeal to a wide audience. For environmental studies.
SUBJ: Manatees./ Rare animals./ Endangered species.

599.63   Ph-1 4-6/7 $14.93   L   KC784
ARNOLD, CAROLINE. Camel. Photos by Richard Hewett. Morrow ISBN 0-688-09499-6, 1992. 48p col photos. (Baby zoo animals).
Includes index.
A young bactrian camel and his parents are the appealing subjects of this photo essay on this homely animal's physiology and behavior. The fine photographs provide exceptionally clear views of the camel's coat and features, and the text offers an interesting fund of information on the history and body of the shaggy two-humped camel. An excellent life cycle which is both useful and a good reading choice.
SUBJ: Camels.

599.63   Ph-1 4-6/7 $5.95   P   KC785
ARNOLD, CAROLINE. Hippo. Photos by Richard Hewett. Morrow ISBN 0-688-11697-3, c1989, 1992. 48p. col. ill. (Baby zoo animals).
Includes index.
Hippopotamuses' life in zoos and in the wild are described in this attractive photo-essay. Handsome pictures are accompanied by a well developed text which follows the birth and early months of life of a young hippo at the San Francisco Zoo, inter-cutting broader

explanations of hippo physiology, behavior, and diet. Always intriguing for its huge size and unusual appearance, the hippo is well served in this competent introduction.
SUBJ: Hippopotamus.

599.63 Ph-1 5-6/9 $19.95 L KC786
NICHOLSON, DARREL. Wild boars. Photos by Craig Blacklock. Carolrhoda ISBN 0-87614-308-7, 1987. 47p. col. ill. (Carolrhoda nature watch book).
Includes glossary and index.
Examines the physical characteristics and behavior of the impressive Eurasian wild boar which ranges in California, New Hampshire, and some of the Southeastern states. Excellent color photographs and informative text document foraging and eating habits, fighting among males, nest building, care of the young, and impact of seasonal changes on these somewhat smaller relatives of the more familiar domestic pig. An attractive and interesting documentary introducing this hardy yet little known species.
SUBJ: Wild boar./ Pigs.

599.63 Ph-3 4-6/8 $15.95 L OD KC787
ROTHAUS, DON. Warthogs. By Don P. Rothaus. Child's World ISBN 1-56766-185-8, 1995. 32p. col. ill. (Naturebooks).
Includes index.
The homely countenance of this African pig fills handsome full-page photographs which accompany the slim volume of the animal's history and life cycle. The sketchy discussion covers history, physical characteristics, eating, family life, and self defense. An appealing item for study of African wildlife or to attract browsers who like exotic animals.
SUBJ: Warthog.

599.638 Ph-2 3-5/7 $16.95 L KC788
KALMAN, BOBBIE. Giraffes. By Bobbie Kalman and Greg Nickles. Crabtree ISBN 0-86505-641-2; In Canada: Crabtree, 1997. 32p. col. ill., map. (Crabapples).
Includes glossary and index.
Giraffes in their natural habitat appear in small and large photographs illustrating a simple discussion of the animal's body and behavior. The giraffe's physical characteristics, eating habits, movement, and problems with predators are covered. Pictures show a mother giraffe giving birth and the different spot patterns of the various species. The photographs are very uneven in quality and the format crowded, but it's a useful introduction to this popular animal.
SUBJ: Giraffes.

599.638 Ph-1 5-6/8 $15.95 L KC789
SATTLER, HELEN RONEY. Giraffes, the sentinels of the savannas. Illus. by Christopher Santoro. Lothrop, Lee & Shepard ISBN 0-688-08284-X, 1989. 80p. ill.
Includes bibliography and index.
Selectors' Choice, 19th ed.
Giraffes provide a special lookout service that benefits other animals in their habitat. This exceptionally attractive volume combines personal observation and research to explain history, scientific classification, physiology, birth and rearing of the young, logistics of eating and drinking, defense capabilities and future prospects as man encroaches on the habitat. Fine drawings add to the book's appeal, and there's a glossary of the nine giraffe sub-species, their cousin the okapi, and many of the extinct predecessors along with a distribution map, a geological timetable, and a classification chart. Ideal for reports as well as personal interest.
SUBJ: Giraffes.

599.64 Ph-1 5-6/7 $19.95 L KC790
BERMAN, RUTH. American bison. Photos by Cheryl Walsh Bellville. Carolrhoda ISBN 0-87614-697-3, 1992. 48p. col. ill., map. (Carolrhoda nature watch book).
Includes glossary and index.
Bison are becoming more familiar as they recover from their endangered status, and this informative photo essay offers excellent close-up views. Physical characteristics, migration, herd behavior, shedding of winter coats, birth, care of the young, and history are discussed. As America's largest land animal, the bison is interesting for many reasons, and libraries will find social studies as well as natural history uses for this fine volume.
SUBJ: Bison.

599.64 Ph-2 3-5/5 $15.27 L KC791
LEPTHIEN, EMILIE U. Buffalo. Childrens Press ISBN 0-516-01161-8; In Canada: Childrens Press, 1989. 45p. col. ill. (New true book).
Includes glossary and index.
Buffalo, once numbering in the millions, were nearly extinct by 1900, and this short history recounts the hunting by white men and Indians

and the eventual efforts to bring the buffalo back. Small color photographs accompany the chronological account, which also describes physical characteristics and behavior. The small volume looks utilitarian, but it contains a good straightforward history of this animal so important in American history.
SUBJ: Bison.

599.64 Ph-2 1-3/2 $11.85 L KC792
SELSAM, MILLICENT E. First look at animals with horns. By Millicent E. Selsam and Joyce Hunt. Illus. by Harriett Springer. Walker ISBN 0-8027-6872-5; In Canada: Thomas Allen, 1989. 32p. ill. (First look at).
"Horns can be big or tiny, straight or twisted, smooth or bumpy." Selsam's simple lesson in animal observation and classification discusses the structure of horns and the types of animals (cattle, goats, sheep, antelopes) that have them; she also explains how tusks and antlers differ from horns. Soft gray pictures showing an interesting array of animals rounds out this good lesson in scientific principle.
SUBJ: Bovidae./ Cervidae./ Horns.

599.64 Ph-3 3-5/2 $18.95 L KC793
STAUB, FRANK J. Mountain goats. Text and photos by Frank Staub. Lerner ISBN 0-8225-3000-7, 1994. 48p. col. ill., map. (Early bird nature books).
Includes glossary and index.
Short chapters of text and attractive photographs follow the lives of adult mountain goats and kids in their high, rocky terrain. Physical characteristics, eating, shedding, raising of the young, social life, and enemies all get brief coverage. The short picture captions are either obvious questions or reiterations of text. Two pages of notes for adults give teaching pointers to round out a pretty mundane introduction to this appealing animal.
SUBJ: Rocky Mountain goat.

599.65 Ph-2 5-6/8 $19.95 L KC794
ARNOLD, CAROLINE. Tule elk. Photos by Richard Hewett. Carolrhoda ISBN 0-87614-343-5, 1989. 47p. col. ill. (Carolrhoda nature watch book).
Includes glossary and index.
Smallest of the three American elk species, the tule elk lives only in California though its physiology and life cycle are similar to Roosevelt and Rocky Mountain elk. Splendid color photographs and informative text describe the history (including near extinction), behavior, raising of the young, growth and shedding of antlers and more. The magnificent physiology will appeal to animal lovers, and the strong theme of conservation efforts will make this useful in a variety of ways.
SUBJ: Tule elk./ Elk.

599.65 Ph-3 4-5/5 $13.00 T KC795
BARE, COLLEEN STANLEY. Never grab a deer by the ear. Cobblehill/Dutton ISBN 0-525-65112-8, 1993. 32p. col. ill.
Includes index.
Mule deer and whitetails, the only native Americans in the deer family, appear in numerous small photographs with brief explanations of physical characteristics and behavior. The bits of text on each page describe the life cycle, changes in coat, growth of antlers, eating habits, enemies, and how these deer are classified. The pictures and layout are not very enticing, but the book offers good basic explanations to introduce these commonly known animals.
SUBJ: Deer./ White-tailed deer./ Mule deer.

599.65 Ph-2 4-5/7 $15.95 L KC796
BERNHARD, EMERY. Reindeer. Illus. by Durga Bernhard. Holiday House ISBN 0-8234-1097-8, 1994. unp. col. ill.
Includes glossary.
Follows reindeer herds through the year as they migrate, feed, grow and use their horns, and raise their young. A fairly difficult text belies the simple appearance, but it's an attractive presentation of the animal's physical characteristics and the cycle of nature in far northern habitats. A bit of the history of human use of reindeer concludes this informative introduction.
SUBJ: Reindeer.

599.65 Ph-2 4-5/8 $13.95 L KC797
HARRIS, LORLE. Caribou. Dillon ISBN 0-87518-391-3, 1988. 60p. col. ill. (Dillon remarkable animals book).
Includes glossary and index.
Handsome photographs and informative text mark this introduction to these impressive northern animals. The four varieties of caribou (barren-ground, woodland and Peary's caribou and reindeer) are included, and four short chapters discuss history, physical characteristics, the growth and use of antlers, life throughout the year, enemies, and adaptation. A useful listing of facts precedes the text of

this appealing life cycle.
SUBJ: Caribou.

599.65   Ph-2 4-6/5 $20.00   L   KC798
LEPTHIEN, EMILIE U. Elk. Childrens Press ISBN 0-516-01063-8; In
Canada: Childrens Press, 1994. 48p. col. ill. (New true book).
    Includes glossary and index.
    Short chapters of text accompanied by small photographs describe
the physical characteristics and behaviors of the four subspecies of
American elk. Size, senses, hooves, stomach pouches and eating,
antlers, mating and rearing of calves, population problems, and
refuges are all discussed. Useful source for libraries where elk are
familiar or studied in the curriculum.
    SUBJ: Elk.

VCR 599.65   Ph-3 3-6 $9.95   OD   KC799
NATURE'S NEWBORN: ELK, MOOSE, DEER (Videocassette). Stoney-
Wolf Productions/dist. by Video Enterprise 50052, 1994. 1/2" VHS
videocassette color (30min). (Nature's newborn).
    Three impressive species each care for their young through the four
seasons of the year in their Rocky Mountain habitat. Each youngster
is seen soon after birth, and the separate segments of film devoted to
each animal follow adults and young as they eat, play, rest, deal with
predators, spar during mating season, and forage in winter. The
handsome natural setting and good wildlife photography offer a
pleasant introduction to the life cycle of these somewhat similar
animals.
    SUBJ: Animals--Infancy./ Elk./ Moose./ Deer.

599.65   Ph-2 3-6/6 $18.00   L   KC800
PETERSEN, DAVID. Moose. Childrens Press ISBN 0-516-01069-7; In
Canada: Childrens Press, 1994. 48p. col. ill. (New true book).
    Includes glossary and index.
    Homely and huge, the once plentiful moose can still be seen in several
northern states. This congenial introduction, presented in brief chapters
with good photographs, describes physical characteristics, eating, care
of the young, antlers, communication, and survival problems. The
small, slim volume is a useful introduction to "the third largest wild
animal in North America."
    SUBJ: Moose.

599.66   Ph-1 4-6/7 $15.93   L   KC801
ARNOLD, CAROLINE. Rhino. Photos by Richard Hewett with additonal
photos by Arthur P. Arnold. Morrow ISBN 0-688-12695-2, 1995. 48p.
col. ill.
    Includes index.
    Shimba, a young rhinoceros born in a Scottish zoo, is the focus of
this handsome introduction to rhinos in the wild and in captivity. Fine
photographs feature various animals in intriguing close-up views as
the author discusses history, many physical characteristics, eating, and
social behavior. The carefully crafted presentation about a fascinating
endangered species is appealing as information and for personal
enjoyment. For environmental studies.
    SUBJ: Rhinoceroses.

599.66   Ph-2 5-6/7 $22.10   L   KC802
MAYNARD, THANE. Rhino comes to America. Watts ISBN 0-531-
11173-3; In Canada: Nelson Canada, 1993. 43p. col. ill., map.
(Cincinnati Zoo book).
    Includes glossary, bibliographies and index.
    A special program in United States zoos seeks to breed the Sumatran
rhinoceros, now seriously endangered as rain forests in Asia
disappear. This large, slim volume with ample photographs and a
rather difficult text explains the history and physical characteristics of
the rhino and the process of trapping and shipping the elusive animal.
Discussion of both the rhinoceros and the conservation program is
brief, but interesting. Concludes with a succinct lesson on the global
impact of the rapidly growing human population. For environmental
studies.
    SUBJ: Bagus (Rhinoceros)./ Sumatran rhinoceros./ Rhinoceroses./
Rare animals./ Wildlife conservation.

599.66   Ph-2 4-6/7 $19.95   L   KC803
WALKER, SALLY M. Rhinos. Photos by Gerry Ellis. Carolrhoda ISBN
1-57505-008-0, 1996. 48p. col. ill., map. (Carolrhoda nature watch
book).
    Includes directory, glossary and index.
    Five rhinoceros species, each endangered, are all that remain of this
once widespread animal. This attractive book describes their lives in
zoos and their natural habitats, emphasizing black rhinos and white
rhinos. Excellent photographs and clear text cover history, physical
characteristics, behavior, care of the young, and conservation
problems. Children will be intrigued by this homely animal. Will serve
well for environmental studies, science lessons, and reports and will

also be enjoyed for personal reading.
    SUBJ: Rhinoceroses.

599.665   Ph-1 5-6/8 $13.95   T   KC804
ARNOLD, CAROLINE. Zebra. Photos by Richard Hewett. Morrow ISBN
0-688-07067-1, 1987. 48p. col. ill. (Baby zoo animals).
    Includes index.
    Fine color photographs accompany this appealing and informative
account of zebra behavior and life cycle. The camera follows a
particular baby zebra and the herd in which he lives in a New Jersey
animal park. Reference is made to zebra life in the wild and the essay
text points out the survival problems of this handsome species. The
book will attract browsers as well as children who need or want the
information.
    SUBJ: Zebras./ Six Flags Great Adventure Safari Park (N.J.).

599.665   Ph-1 4-6/7 $15.00   T   KC805
COLE, JOANNA. Horse's body. Photos by Jerome Wexler. Morrow
ISBN 0-688-00362-1, 1981. 45p. ill.
    Selectors' Choice, 13th ed.
    Focusing on the physiology of the horse, outstanding photographs,
clear diagrams and straightforward text show why the horse's "body
seems to have been designed especially to run."
    SUBJ: Horses.

599.665   Ph-2 K-3/4 $12.95   T   KC806
HONDA, TETSUYA. Wild horse winter. Chronicle ISBN 0-8118-0251-5;
In Canada: Raincoast, 1992. unp. col. ill.
    Bold paintings follow a wild colt through a bitter storm during his first
winter. The simple fictionalized text, based on the real experiences of
wild horses in Japan, explains how the horses are caught under the
snow while trekking through the forest in search of food, which they
eventually find when they reach a salt marsh at the edge of the sea.
The final gallop of the horses along the shore is reminiscent of the
wild horses on the eastern coast of the United States. Concluding
note sketches the history of the Japanese horses.
    SUBJ: Wild horses./ Horses./ Winter.

599.665   Ph-2 3-5/4 $19.00   L   KC807
LEPTHIEN, EMILIE U. Zebras. Childrens Press ISBN 0-516-01072-7; In
Canada: Childrens Press, 1994. 48p. col. ill. (New true book).
    Includes glossary and index.
    Effective displays of zebra stripes appear in small photographs
accompanying this informative discussion of the physical
characteristics, behaviors, and habitats of the three zebra species. The
zebra's relationship to the horse, stripe and color variations, running,
grazing, grooming, herd groupings, raising of foals, and survival
tactics and problems are explained in the brief chapters. This
introduction to these intriguing endangered animals will be useful for
reports and environmental studies.
    SUBJ: Zebras.

599.67   Ph-1 5-6/9 $15.00   T   KC808
ARNOLD, CAROLINE. Elephant. Photos by Richard Hewett. Morrow
ISBN 0-688-11344-3, 1993. 48p. col. ill. (Baby zoo animals).
    Includes index.
    African and Asian elephants living in a wild animal park are featured
in attractive close-up photographs and well-crafted text explaining
their physical characteristics and behavior. Trunks, teeth, skin, and feet
are examined; child care, eating, and need for water are discussed.
Concludes with a sobering explanation of the seriously endangered
status of elephants today. This is a first-rate introduction to an
appealing and impressive animal. For environmental studies.
    SUBJ: Elephants.

VCR 599.67   Ph-3 3-5 $50.00   OD   KC809
ELEPHANT DIARY (Videocassette). Direct Cinema ISBN 1-55974-335-2,
1990. 1/2" VHS videocassette color (15min).
    Two boys, an African and the son of a white conservationist, rescue a
baby elephant trapped by poachers and lead it off through the
African countryside in search of an elephant herd to adopt the
orphan. The dreamlike odyssey, told almost entirely without words, is
set among fabulous views of wild animals in their native habitat. The
lessons about poaching and ivory sales are effectively conveyed,
though there are also unfortunate innuendos in the juxtaposition of
black and white characters.
    SUBJ: Elephants./ Wildlife rescue./ Wildlife conservation.

599.67   Ph-2 5-6/8 $16.95   L   KC810
GRACE, ERIC S. Elephants. Illus. by Dorothy Siemens. Sierra Club ISBN
0-87156-538-2; In Canada: Key Porter, 1993. 64p. col. ill., map. (Sierra
Club wildlife library).
    Includes index.
    Elephant history, anatomy, and family life are among topics covered

in this large, attractive book. Fine photographs and doublespread drawings accompany the topical sections of text. The informative presentation examines differences between Asian and African elephants, effects of elephants on the environment, poaching and other human threats, care of the young, and much more. A substantial information source, this will also be enjoyable reading for animal fans. For environmental studies.
SUBJ: Elephants.

599.67   Ph-2 5-6/8 $19.95   L   KC811
MACMILLAN, DIANNE. Elephants: our last land giants. Carolrhoda ISBN 0-87614-770-8, 1993. 48p. col. ill., map. (Carolrhoda nature watch book).
Includes glossary and index.
This pleasant photo essay describes the bodies and behaviors of African and Asian elephants and also explains their serious survival problems in the modern world. Selected color photographs feature elephants in the wild and in captivity; the text describes mating, rearing the young, and many physical features. A good solid introduction to this massive mammal. For environmental studies.
SUBJ: Elephants.

599.67   Ph-2 K-4/6 $17.00   T   KC812
MOSS, CYNTHIA. Little big ears; the story of Ely. Photos by Martyn Colbeck. Simon & Schuster ISBN 0-689-80031-2; In Canada: Distican, 1997. unp. col. ill.
Includes directory.
Simple narrative and handsome photographs document the first year of life of a young elephant born in Kenya's wildlife park, Amboseli. The account, adapted from documentary films shown on television, features Ely's early physical problems, the family life of the elephants, and a drought which threatened the lives of many elephants. Capably told by an authority on the subject, this pleasant story provides interesting detail and an informative introduction to the social behavior and life cycle of elephants.
SUBJ: African elephant./ Elephants.

599.67   Ph-1 4-6/6 $14.95   L   KC813
PATENT, DOROTHY HINSHAW. African elephants: giants of the land. Photos by Oria Douglas-Hamilton. Holiday House ISBN 0-8234-0911-2, 1991. 40p col photos.
Includes index.
Elephant communication, family life and poaching for ivory are examined in a clear informative discussion accompanied by fine photographs. The author describes many aspects of elephant anatomy and behavior, feeding, dealing with enemies, mating, rearing of young, and the effect elephants have on their habitat. This excellent life cycle book updates previous information on elephant communication.
SUBJ: African elephant./ Elephants.

VCR 599.67   Ph-2 5-6 $275.00   OD   KC814
PLIGHT OF THE ASIAN ELEPHANT (Videocassette). Produced by TVOntario. Beacon Films/dist. by Altschul Group Corporation B8659, 1993. 1/2" VHS videocassette color (15min). (World of nature).
Includes public performance rights.
Asian elephant families are viewed at close range as they forage through the diminishing rainforests of Thailand and through less forested regions during the night. This well paced discussion examines the differences between Asian and African elephants, explains life in their natural habitat, and describes the training of young elephants for work in logging, circuses, transport, and sports. A thoughtful introduction to an interesting endangered species and the human economic needs that are destroying its habitat, this will be useful on various levels for personal enjoyment and classroom discussion. For environmental studies.
SUBJ: Asiatic elephant./ Elephants.

599.67   Ph-1 4-6/7 $20.99   L   KC815
REDMOND, IAN. Elephant. Photos by Dave King. Knopf ISBN 0-679-93880-X, 1993. 64p. col. ill. (Eyewitness books).
Includes index.
Elephant bodies, behavior, and history are detailed in copious illustrations and bits of text. The attractive, interesting volume describes related species, physiology, reproduction, diet, elephants in art, war, and entertainment, and much more. Informative volume skims the surface of what there is to know about the interesting pachyderm, but it's an appealing compendium.
SUBJ: Elephants.

599.67   Ph-2 4-6/6 $16.85   L   KC816
SCHMIDT, JEREMY. In the village of the elephants. Photos by Ted Wood. Walker ISBN 0-8027-8227-2; In Canada: Thomas Allen, 1994. unp. col. ill., map.

A boy in a village of southern India trains to be a mahout (elephant handler) in this interesting photodocumentary of a people who depend on the work of elephants for their livelihood. The large, slim volume is a handsome presentation of the daily care given the elephants as well as the various tasks the elephants perform. The respectful view of the animals and the traditional way of life make this an intriguing account for personal reading, booktalking, and use with both science and social studies units. For multicultural studies.
SUBJ: Elephants./ India--Social life and customs.

599.75   Ph-1 5-6/9 $15.93   L   KC817
ARNOLD, CAROLINE. Cheetah. Photos by Richard Hewett. Morrow ISBN 0-688-08144-4, 1989. 48p. col. ill. (Baby zoo animals).
Includes index.
Now found only in limited areas of Africa and in captivity, the elegant cheetah is described here as it lives in its wild habitat and in an Oregon wildlife park. Appealing color photographs and a continuous essay text range over many topics--physical markings, history, hunting behavior, rearing of the young, genetic weakness as the species declines, and more. Sometimes sketchy, the handsome volume is an absorbing introduction to the species and includes thoughtful emphasis on the necessity for conserving wildlife.
SUBJ: Cheetahs./ Rare animals.

599.75   Ph-1 4-6/6 $14.93   L   KC818
COLE, JOANNA. Cat's body. Photos by Jerome Wexler. Morrow ISBN 0-688-01054-7, 1982. 48p. ill.
Cats, though now domesticated, are hunters. Numerous physical characteristics which enable them to stalk and capture prey are examined in this attractive photo-essay which looks at the spine, body structure, paws, teeth, whiskers, ears, fur and several aspects of behavior. The book is actually an exercise in observation which will enable the reader to view this popular animal in a more informed and appreciative manner.
SUBJ: Cats./ Predatory animals.

599.75   Ph-1 1-4/5 $6.95   P   KC819
DUPONT, PHILIPPE. Cheetah: fast as lightning. By Philippe Dupont and Valerie Tracqui. Charlesbridge ISBN 0-88106-425-4, 1992. 27p. col. ill. (Animal close-ups).
Striking photographs and simple explanations follow a mother cheetah and her four cubs as the young animals grow to adulthood in the grasslands of Africa. The mother's hunting efforts and the stages of growth of the cubs are beautifully documented in the slim, attractive paperback. Concluding pages introduce the other four members of the spotted cat family and mention problems of survival caused by other animals and tourists. A beautiful introduction to this handsome hunter that makes an attractive reading item as well as a useful source of information.
SUBJ: Cheetahs.

CDR 599.75   Ph-2 3-A $29.95   OD   KC820
EYEWITNESS VIRTUAL REALITY: CAT (CD-ROM). DK Multimedia ISBN 0-7894-0291-2, 1995. 1 CD-ROM color. (Eyewitness virtual reality).
Also available for Macintosh (ISBN 0-7894-0295-5), $29.95.
System requirements: IBM or compatible PC, with 486SX/25MHz or higher microprocessor; 4MB of RAM, MPC-compatible doublespeed CD-ROM drive and sound card, mouse, SVGA 256-color display, and loudspeakers or headphones; Microsoft Windows version 3.1 or later.
Concise information, aided by the use of multimedia, is available on the entire world of the cat family. Navigation is standard; information may be advanced for limited readers. Use as an additional resource after purchasing more general purpose research tools.
SUBJ: Felidae--Software./ Software--Felidae./ Cats--Software./ Software--Cats./ Interactive media.

599.75   Ph-2 K-3/3 $15.95   L   KC821
GIBBONS, GAIL. Cats. Holiday House ISBN 0-8234-1253-9, 1996. unp. col. ill.
Crude sketches of many varieties of cats and straightforward explanations cover characteristics and behavior and care of pet cats in a colorful, flat guide. Labels name each breed as they demonstrate brief discussion of history, cats as hunters, each of the senses, sounds and other communication, fur, sleeping, care and growth of kittens, and pet shows. Cat fans and young pet owners will enjoy the quick, but informative and practical, discussion.
SUBJ: Cats./ Felidae./ Pets.

599.75   Ph-2 5-6/7 $19.93   L   KC822
KAPPELER, MARKUS. Big cats. Gareth Stevens ISBN 0-8368-0685-9; In Canada: Saunders, 1991. 48p. col. ill., map. (Animal families).
Includes glossary, bibliography, directory and index.
Useful survey provides details of the history and behavior of six species commonly known as big cats. A discussion of common

physical characteristics is followed by short chapters on the tiger, lion, leopard, jaguar, snow leopard, and cheetah; inset tables of facts and captioned color photographs accompany the substantial discussion. Text is rather difficult and the format utilitarian, but this provides good coverage on this appealing animal family.
SUBJ: Panthera./ Cats.

599.75   Ph-3 5-6/6 $17.95   T   KC823
LUMPKIN, SUSAN. Big cats. Facts On File ISBN 0-8160-2847-8; In Canada: Facts On File, 1993. 68p. col. ill. (Great creatures of the world).
Includes glossary and index.
Facts and colorful photographs fill this oversize slim volume of information about the seven large cat species. Several topical segments discuss some common characteristics of the cats (history, hunting, communication, man-eating behavior, conservation, and zoos). Separate sections cover lions, tigers, leopards, jaguars, cheetahs, pumas, and snow leopards. A good fund of interesting information in a rather difficult presentation for libraries needing added material.
SUBJ: Felidae./ Cats.

599.75   Ph-3 5-6/8 $17.95   T   KC824
LUMPKIN, SUSAN. Small cats. Facts On File ISBN 0-8160-2848-6, 1993. 68p. col. ill., maps. (Great creatures of the world).
Includes glossary and index.
Cat fans will find a wealth of information about small wild cat species around the world in this large, slim volume. Two-page topical segments include copious photographs of bobcats, lynxes, ocelots, and many lesser known cats. In addition to particular animals, entries cover history, body structure, domestication, cats in zoos, and conservation problems. The text is sometimes difficult, but the subject and the appealing pictures will be enjoyed by many children.
SUBJ: Felidae./ Cats.

599.75   Ph-1 4-6/5 $16.00   T   KC825
RYDEN, HOPE. Your cat's wild cousins. Lodestar/Dutton ISBN 0-525-67354-7; In Canada: McClelland & Stewart, 1991. 48p. col. ill.
Includes index.
Selectors' Choice, 19th ed.
African wildcats, cheetahs, ocelots, and pumas are among the 18 species compared to domestic cats in a very attractive presentation. Each animal is featured in a doublespread page of color photographs and brief text describing selected physical characteristics and behavior traits. Small photographs of the author's pet cat, juxtaposed in each spread, are beautifully composed to demonstrate similarities. The book is an informative, handsome introduction to Felidae and a thoughtful lesson in observation.
SUBJ: Cats./ Felidae.

599.75   Ph-2 4-6/6 $16.95   L   KC826
SIMON, SEYMOUR. Big cats. HarperCollins ISBN 0-06-021647-6; In Canada: HarperCollins, 1991. unp. col. ill.
Seven big wild cats appear in striking photographs which accompany a brief overview of the physical characteristics and behavior of these imposing predators. Lions, tigers, leopards, jaguars, pumas, cheetahs and snow leopards are dicussed, with emphasis on size, hunting, roaring and purring, and care of the young. The spacious layout and the animals are very appealing, and the economical text packs in considerable information.
SUBJ: Felidae./ Cats.

599.756   Ph-1 1-3/6 $14.95   T   KC827
COWCHER, HELEN. Tigress. Farrar, Straus & Giroux ISBN 0-374-37567-4, 1991. unp. col. ill.
Selectors' Choice, 19th ed.
Available in Spanish LA TIGRESA (ISBN 0-374-47779-5, 1993).
Stunning paintings depict the realistic story of a tigress who escapes from a game reserve and kills animals belonging to herdsmen. An understanding sanctuary ranger meets with the angry herdsmen around their campfire; together the men develop a plan to frighten the tigress back into protected territory. The handsome view of India is intriguing, and the story effectively balances the two points of view about killing or saving the tigress.
SUBJ: Tigers./ Wildlife conservation.

599.757   Ph-2 5-6/7 $15.93   L   KC828
ARNOLD, CAROLINE. Lion. Photos by Richard Hewett. Morrow ISBN 0-688-12693-6, 1995. 48p. col. ill.
Includes index.
Lion families in an Oregon wildlife park are the focus of an informative survey of the large cat's history, behavior, and life cycle. Close-up views of individual animals demonstrate many physical characteristics and the life of family members and the pride while

double columned text offers substantial information on history, life cycle, the lion as predator, and social behavior. Less striking than some work by this author and photographer team, this is a solid account of an impressive animal.
SUBJ: Lions.

599.757   Ph-2 3-5/5 $15.99   L   KC829
GOUCK, MAURA. Mountain lions. Child's World ISBN 1-56766-057-6, 1993. 32p. col. ill. (Naturebooks).
Includes index.
Handsome photographs and simple text introduce the powerful body of the mountain lion and it's hunting habits. The essay text gives broad explanations of the life cycle, eating habits, and conservation problems. The striking yet sketchy account will appeal to many readers, who may need to go on to other sources for more complete information.
SUBJ: Pumas.

599.757   Ph-1 3-6/6 $8.95   P   KC830
HOFER, ANGELIKA. Lion family book. Translated by Patricia Crampton. Photos by Gunter Ziesler. North-South Books ISBN 1-55858-502-8; In Canada: North-South Books/dist. by Vanwell, 1995. unp. col. ill. (Animal family series).
Originally published by Picture Book Studio, 1988.
Set in the "Masai Mara" Nature Reserve in the African plains, this attractive photo-documentary follows the life of a pride of lions for nearly a year. The short continuous text focuses on aspects of lion behavior and information about the habitat, while the splendid photographs concentrate particularly on a mother and her three cubs. The playful and affectionate relationships of the family members, the hunting activities of the females, and the role of other animals sharing this environment are viewed with remarkable clarity and closeness in this fine introduction.
SUBJ: Lions.

599.76   Ph-2 P-2/3 $4.95   P   KC831
ARNOSKY, JIM. Raccoons and ripe corn. Lothrop, Lee & Shepard ISBN 0-688-10489-4, c1987, 1991. unp. col. ill.
Depicts the autumn night's raid of a cornfield by a mother raccoon and her two kits. Softly colored full-page drawings and minimal text encourage leisurely viewing of leaves buffeted by the wind, the ripe corn, and the busy raccoons. A pleasant item for seasonal reading and a cursory but good introduction to the behavior of raccoons.
SUBJ: Raccoons.

599.769   Ph-2 K-2/2 $14.95   L   KC832
ARNOSKY, JIM. Otters under water. Putnam ISBN 0-399-22339-8; In Canada: Putnam, 1992. unp. col. ill.
Mother otter watches from the shore as her two babies swim through the pond observing other animals and catching fish. A very brief text accompanies broadly sketched double-spread scenes in sunny pastels. The information is minimal, but the attractive picture book presentation offers a pleasant introduction to the species.
SUBJ: Otters.

599.77   Ph-2 5-6/6 $14.95   L   KC833
PRINGLE, LAURENCE P. Jackal woman: exploring the world of jackals. By Laurence Pringle. Photos by Patricia D. Moehlman. Scribner's ISBN 0-684-19435-X; In Canada: Maxwell Macmillan, 1993. 42p. col. ill.
Includes bibliography and index.
On the Serengeti Plain of Tanzania, an American scientist has spent many years studying jackals. This account blends biography with interesting animal photographs taken by the scientist and explanations of what she has learned about the jackals. Though not as lively as some of the books Pringle has done in the past, this is useful in portraying a woman scientist and in describing African wildlife. For career studies, women's studies, and environmental studies.
SUBJ: Jackals./ Moehlman, Patricia Des Roses./ Zoologists./ Women scientists.

599.773   Ph-1 5-6/7 $17.85   L   KC834
BRANDENBURG, JIM. To the top of the world: adventures with arctic wolves. Edited by JoAnn Bren Guernsey. Walker ISBN 0-8027-8220-5; In Canada: Thomas Allen, 1993. 44p. col. ill.
Stunning close-up views of an Arctic wolf family accompany this personal account of a wildlife photographer as he tells about the wolves and his experiences with them. Many aspects of wolf play, hunting, care for the young, and other social behaviors are described. This first-rate account of animals in their natural habitat is informative and unusually interesting, sure to please nonfiction readers.
SUBJ: Wolves./ Animal ecology--Arctic regions.

599.773   Ph-3 5-6/6 $14.89 L KC835
GEORGE, JEAN CRAIGHEAD. Moon of the gray wolves. New ed. Illus. by Sal Catalano. HarperCollins ISBN 0-06-022443-6; In Canada: HarperCollins, 1991. 48p. col. ill. (Thirteen moons).
    Includes bibliography and index.
    A small pack of Alaskan wolves which includes five pups just reaching adulthood is followed through their nightly hunting and journeying in early winter. Jean Craighead George skillfully uses a fictionalized account to depict the skill and personalities of the wolves and their encounters with other animals sharing their habitat. Several fairly realistic paintings accompany the well rendered account. Offers good insight into the world of this perennially appealing animal though it is not as attractive as several documentary style accounts.
    SUBJ: Wolves--Alaska.

599.773   Ph-1 6/10 $23.95 L KC836
JOHNSON, SYLVIA A. Wolf pack: tracking wolves in the wild. By Sylvia A. Johnson and Alice Aamodt. Lerner ISBN 0-8225-1577-6, 1985. 96p. col. ill. (Discovery).
    Includes glossary and index.
    Available in Spanish LA MANADA DE LOBOS: SIGUIENDO LAS HUELLAS DE LOS LOBOS EN SU ENTORNO NATURAL (ISBN 0-8225-2007-9, 1993).
    Long feared and detested as predators, wolves are now the object of conservation and study. Handsome color photographs and diagrams are used effectively to show structure of the pack, the history of the species, and the physiology and behavior of the animals, this substantial presentation should find a wider audience than its reading level indicates.
    SUBJ: Wolves.

599.773   Ph-1 5-6/7 $17.95 L KC837
LAWRENCE, R. D. Wolves. Sierra Club/Little, Brown ISBN 0-316-51676-7; In Canada: Key Porter, 1990. 64p. col. ill. (Sierra Club wildlife library).
    Includes index.
    Gray and red wolves are featured in this attractive discussion of wolf physiology and behavior. Appealing photographs, useful drawings, and informative text cover raising of the young, hunting, senses and other body features, social behavior, and environmental considerations of Arctic wolves and related species of the United States and Canada. The tall - though not oversized - volume is an excellent information source that should also be popular.
    SUBJ: Wolves.

599.773   Ph-3 2-4/5 $19.00 L KC838
LEPTHIEN, EMILIE U. Wolves. Childrens Press ISBN 0-516-01129-4; In Canada: Childrens Press, 1991. 48p. col. ill. (New true book).
    Includes glossary and index.
    Wolf pups and adult wolves of different species appear in small photographs accompanying a simple discussion of wolf history, physical characteristics, behavior, and conservation. Wolf packs, wolves and people, rearing of the young, adaptations to climate, and communication are among many topics covered in short chapters. The small, utilitarian volume is a useful introduction to this ever popular animal.
    SUBJ: Wolves.

599.773   Ph-1 5-6/8 $15.95 T KC839
PATENT, DOROTHY HINSHAW. Gray wolf, red wolf. Photos by William Munoz. Clarion ISBN 0-89919-863-5, 1990. 64p. col. ill.
    Includes index, and Selected List of Addresses for Wolf Information.
    Fine photographs and an interesting discussion examine the behavior of wolves and the history of these animals in North America. Four chapters cover the social interactions of wolves, communicaton, hunting, rearing of the young, physiology, loss of habitat, human hatred of wolves, scientific studies, and conservation efforts. The photographs reveal an astonishing variety of appearance of individual wolves, and the book is both appealing and absorbing.
    SUBJ: Wolves./ Rare animals./ Wildlife conservation.

599.773   Ph-1 4-6/7 $15.89 L KC840
SIMON, SEYMOUR. Wolves. HarperCollins ISBN 0-06-022534-3; In Canada: HarperCollins, 1993. unp. col. ill.
    Stunning full-page photographs pull the reader into an engaging photo-essay explaining wolf behavior. Discusses human fear of wolves, physical characteristics, hunting, howling, organization of wolf packs, and care of the young. Readers of all ages will linger over the pictures and come away with understanding and respect for this handsome carnivore.
    SUBJ: Wolves.

599.773   Ph-2 5-6/5 $19.93 L KC841
WOLPERT, TOM. Wolf magic for kids. Gareth Stevens ISBN 0-8368-0662-X; In Canada: Saunders, c1990, 1991. 48p. col. ill. (Animal magic for kids).
    Includes glossary.
    Gray wolves of many shades are seen in attractive photographs accompanied by a discussion of physical characteristics and behavior. There is an emphasis on care of the young, social organization, and life through the seasons; eating and hunting are described but not shown specifically in the pictures. The text is serviceable and the views of this intriguing animal are appealing.
    SUBJ: Wolves.

599.775   Ph-2 3-5/4 $6.95 P KC842
HAVARD, CHRISTIAN. Fox: playful prowler. Photos by Jacana [et al.]. Charlesbridge ISBN 0-88106-434-3; In Canada: Monarch, 1995. 27p. col. ill. (Animal close-ups).
    Originally published: LE RENARD, RODEUR SOLITAIRE, Editions Milan, 1992.
    Quick red foxes pounce and play as they hunt and care for their young in this slim, appealing introduction. Excellent photographs follow the foxes through the seasons, and a clear text explains their physical characteristics and behavior. Added pages of facts include an introduction to related species.
    SUBJ: Foxes./ Red fox.

599.775   Ph-2 4-5/5 $15.95 T KC843
MASON, CHERIE. Wild fox: a true story. Illus. by Jo Ellen McAllister Stammen. Down East ISBN 0-89272-319-X, 1993. 32p. col. ill.
    A simple, gentle story, illustrated with soft drawings, intertwines the author's real-life story of befriending a wild fox with explanations of the physical characteristics and behavior of the red fox. The firsthand account is both intriguing and respectful of the wild nature of the animal--it's good nonfiction reading.
    SUBJ: Red fox./ Foxes.

599.775   Ph-1 4-6/8 $19.95 L KC844
SCHNIEPER, CLAUDIA. On the trail of the fox. Photos by Felix Labhardt. Carolrhoda ISBN 0-87614-287-0, 1986. 47p. col. ill. (Carolrhoda nature watch book).
    Includes glossary and index.
    Using a special blind in a game preserve, the photographer has had the unusual opportunity of following life inside the den of a red fox vixen as she cares for her litter. The photographic account of the affectionate behavior of the foxes and the account of their lives through the seasons is quite absorbing as described in this excellent photo-essay. Though foxes are mistrusted for their cleverness and thievery, this respectful account demonstrates their beauty, sharp use of senses and instincts, and their adaptability.
    SUBJ: Red fox./ Foxes.

599.776   Ph-1 4-6/7 $15.93 L KC845
ARNOLD, CAROLINE. Fox. Photos by Richard Hewett. Morrow ISBN 0-688-13729-6, 1996. 48p. col. ill. (Baby zoo animals).
    Includes index.
    Handsome photographs of the small kit fox and related foxes of North America draw the reader to an informative discussion. Profiles of several species are followed by sections devoted to history, characteristics common to the dog family, foxes as predators, burrows, family life, communication, and enemies. The appealing book will find many uses for science reports and reading enjoyment.
    SUBJ: Foxes.

599.776   Ph-2 3-6/7 $17.88 L KC846
LAUKEL, HANS GEROLD. Desert fox family book. Translated by Rosemary Lanning. North-South Books ISBN 1-55858-580-X; In Canada: North-South Books./dist. by Vanwell, 1996. unp. col. ill. (Animal family series).
    "Michael Neugebauer book."
    Lovely photographs and personable text follow the lives of a desert fox family in the Sahara. The tiny fennecs and other animals sharing their dramatic habitat are very appealing--particularly as they raise their cubs. The author, a skilled photographer whose hobby is wildlife study, has captured views of North Africa and of this smallest of all the wild dogs that offer many possibilities for use with animal studies and units on desert life. For environmental studies.
    SUBJ: Fennec./ Foxes.

599.776   Ph-1 4-6/4 $16.00 L KC847
MATTHEWS, DOWNS. Arctic foxes. Photos by Dan Guravich and Nikita Ovsyanikov. Simon & Schuster ISBN 0-689-80284-6; In Canada: Distican, 1995. unp. col. ill.
    Arctic foxes present an intriguing contrast in their winter white and summer brown coats in this attractive life cycle. Appealing

photographs and informative essay introduce the habitat, physical characteristics, and seasonal activities of the foxes as they play, hunt, molt, and care for their young. The slim, handsome introduction will please animal fans and nonfiction readers, and it's a useful source on Arctic life.
SUBJ: Arctic fox./ Foxes.

599.78 Ph-2 K-2/2 $13.85 L KC848
BRENNER, BARBARA. Two orphan cubs. By Barbara Brenner and May Garelick. Illus. by Erika Kors. Walker ISBN 0-8027-6869-5; In Canada: Thomas Allen, 1989. unp. col. ill.
Soft charcoal and wash illustrations follow the simple story of a pair of black bear cubs and the efforts of a wildlife scientist to place them with an adoptive mother when they become orphaned. The text describes the first months of the cubs life during the winter hibernation, the mother's venturing out of the den in spring and her failure to return, and the successful adoption effort. An effective use of the picture book format to tell a true-to-life nature story for the youngest grades.
SUBJ: Black bear./ Bears.

599.78 Ph-2 4-5/5 $18.60 L KC849
FAIR, JEFF. Black bear magic for kids. Photos by Lynn Rogers. Gareth Stevens ISBN 0-8368-0760-X; In Canada: Saunders, 1991. 48p. col. ill. (Animal magic for kids).
At head of title: Black bears.
Includes glossary.
A quick sketch of black bear life through the year is conveyed in brief discussion and attractive photographs. In addition to physical characteristics, growth of the young, aspects of behavior, and hibernation, the text touches briefly on the work of naturalist Lynn Rogers. Slim volume is cursory, and the bears are appealing.
SUBJ: Black bear./ Bears.

599.78 Ph-2 P/1 $12.95 T KC850
MORRIS, JACKIE. Bears, bears, and more bears. Barron's ISBN 0-8120-6516-6; In Canada: Barron's, 1995. unp. col. ill.
Previously published as JUST BEARS, 1995.
Pleasant watercolors depict a variety of bears as a brief text offers the simplest explanations of their way of life. Eating, swimming and hibernating are among the activities of black, brown, and polar bears and pandas; there's even a non-bear koala and a teddy bear. Added facts about each bear are printed on the endpapers.
SUBJ: Bears.

599.78 Ph-2 5-6/6 $15.95 L KC851
PATENT, DOROTHY HINSHAW. Looking at bears. Photos by William Munoz. Holiday House ISBN 0-8234-1139-7, 1994. 40p. col. ill.
Includes index.
Bears of assorted species from all over the world appear in this discussion of bear life. Short chapters of text, accompanied by excellent photographs, compare various species as the author describes history, physical characteristics, and behavior as well as serious survival problems bears are facing throughout the world. A chapter on the bears of America is part of the well organized presentation, useful as an introduction and survey of this impressive mammal. For environmental studies.
SUBJ: Bears.

599.78 Ph-1 5-6/7 $13.95 L KC852
PRINGLE, LAURENCE P. Bearman: exploring the world of black bears. By Laurence Pringle. Photos by Lynn Rogers. Scribner's ISBN 0-684-19094-X; In Canada: Collier Macmillan, 1989. 42p. col. ill.
Includes bibliography and index.
Selectors' Choice, 19th ed.
Lynn Rogers, a U.S. Forest Service biologist, has spent many years studying black bears as they travel, rear their young, and hibernate in the Minnesota woods. The discussion in this interesting account blends information about a life committed to a fascinating type of work and the discoveries made about the behavior of the bears. An exceptionally good collaboration, this is attractive as a personal reading choice and as an information source on this often feared species and on careers in natural history.
SUBJ: Black bear./ Bears.

599.78 Ph-2 2-4/2 $19.00 L KC853
ROSENTHAL, MARK. Bears. Childrens Press ISBN 0-516-01675-X; In Canada: Childrens Press, 1983. 45p. col. ill. (New true book).
Includes glossary and index.
Describes the general physical characteristics and behavior of bears and introduces each of the major species. Conservation problems and human dangers and responsibilities are also discussed. A simple, attractive presentation of a popular animal.
SUBJ: Bears.

599.78 Ph-3 5-6/7 $19.93 L KC854
SCHMIDT, ANNEMARIE. Bears and their forest cousins. By Annemarie and Christian R. Schmidt. Gareth Stevens ISBN 0-8368-0684-0; In Canada: Saunders, 1991. 48p. col. ill., map. (Animal families).
Includes glossary, bibliography, directory and index.
Short entries accompanied by good photographs introduce 22 members of the brown bear, black bear, panda, and racoon families as well as the koala. The single page of text devoted to each animal states the typical range of weight and length and briefly describes aspects of history, physical characteristics, and behavior. Though the information is brief, it's interesting and useful in providing a quick sketch of the specific animals.
SUBJ: Bears./ Procyonidae./ Pandas.

599.78 Ph-3 5-6/5 $14.00 T KC855
SCHWARTZ, ALVIN. Fat man in a fur coat and other bear stories. Illus. by David Christiana. Farrar, Straus & Giroux ISBN 0-374-32291-0; In Canada: HarperCollins, 1984. 167p.
Includes bibliography, notes and sources.
Available from National Library Service for the Blind and Physically Handicapped on sound recording cassette RC22090.
Presenting collected lore about bears, Schwartz entertains and informs. An excellent collection for sharing in science class or when reading folklore.
SUBJ: Bears.

VCR 599.78 Ph-3 4-A $49.00 OD KC856
SLEEPING BEARS (Videocassette). Bullfrog Films, 1986. 1/2" VHS videocassette color (8min). (OWL discovery film).
Includes teacher's guide.
Two delightful baby bears are examined and measured on a visit to the den of black bears during hibernation to illustrate techniques used by research biologists in studying habits of the bears. The interesting, fast-paced film augmented with activities from teacher's guide enhances the study of mammals.
SUBJ: Bears.

599.78 Ph-2 5-A/7 $14.95 L KC857
STIRLING, IAN. Bears. Photos by Aubrey Lang. Sierra Club/Little, Brown ISBN 0-87156-574-9; In Canada: Key Porter Books Ltd., 1992. 64p. ill. (some col.) (Sierra Club wildlife library).
Includes index.
This handsome introduction describes the world's eight bear species and discusses the history, classification, and conservation of bears. Topical chapters cover physical characteristics of bears, eating habits, communication, hibernation, rearing of the young, and the future outlook for bears. Numerous color photographs, a few drawings, diagrams, and maps are included. Plentiful factual material is sprinkled through longer discussion. Most useful for readers with a serious interest in the subject.
SUBJ: Bears.

599.784 Ph-2 5-6/7 $13.95 L KC858
CALABRO, MARIAN. Operation grizzly bear. Four Winds/Macmillan ISBN 0-02-716241-9; In Canada: Collier Macmillan, 1989. 118p. ill.
Includes bibliography and index.
Frank and John Craighead studied grizzlies for many years in Yellowstone National Park, developing techniques for tracking the bears through their terrain and in their dens. The substantial text recounts biographical information about these dedicated naturalists, details of their exploration of bear life, and considerable information about grizzlies. Dull photographs detract from the book's visual appeal, but the content is informative and should serve as inspiration for budding natural scientists.
SUBJ: Grizzly bear./ Bears./ Craighead, John J./ Craighead, Frank C./ Yellowstone National Park.

599.784 Ph-2 4-6/6 $16.95 T KC859
HOSHINO, MICHIO. Grizzly bear family book. Translated by Karen Colligan-Taylor. North-South Books ISBN 1-55858-350-5; In Canada: North-South Books, 1994. unp. col. ill. (Animal family series).
"Michael Neugebauer book."
Grizzly bears are viewed at close range in their Alaskan habitat as the author explains his experiences observing them. The essay text focuses especially on behavior and caring for the young with many interesting firsthand observations and fine photographs. A very good introduction to the species, this is an attractive choice for readers who enjoy wildlife.
SUBJ: Grizzly bear./ Bears./ Natural history--Alaska.

599.784 Ph-2 5-6/8 $13.95 L KC860
PATENT, DOROTHY HINSHAW. Way of the grizzly. Photos by William Munoz. Clarion ISBN 0-89919-383-8, 1987. 65p. ill.
Includes index.

After comparing members of the bear family, the grizzly becomes the focus of this detailed study which covers its physiology, habits and behavior, and the threat to its survival. The well organized text is augmented with captioned black and white photographs. Useful for reports on the animal and/or conservation studies.
SUBJ: Grizzly bear./ Bears./ Wildlife conservation.

599.784 Ph-2 5-6/6 $19.95 L KC861
STONE, LYNN M. Grizzlies. Carolrhoda ISBN 0-87614-800-3, 1993. 47p. col. ill., map. (Carolrhoda nature watch book).
Includes directory, glossary and index.
Solid information and attractive photographs examine grizzly bear life through the seasons of the year. A continuous essay text explains size, physical characteristics, eating, hibernation, and rearing of the young. A solid source for advanced readers, this has many appealing scenes to attract browsers.
SUBJ: Grizzly bear./ Brown bear./ Bears.

599.786 Ph-2 4-6/4 $8.95 P KC862
LARSEN, THOR. Polar bear family book. By Thor Larsen and Sybille Kalas. North-South Books ISBN 1-55858-613-X; In Canada: North-South Books/dist. by Vanwell, 1996. unp. col. ill. (Animal family series).
"Michael Neugebauer book."
Depicts polar bear life through the Arctic year in attractive photographs and informative text. Physical characteristics and hunting and eating behavior are followed by an account of a particular mother building her den and emerging in spring with her two cubs. The appealing bears and the interesting views of the terrain and other animals sharing the Arctic habitat make this attractive for personal reading and useful for classroom units on this region.
SUBJ: Polar bear./ Bears.

599.786 Ph-2 2-4/5 $19.00 L KC863
LEPTHIEN, EMILIE U. Polar bears. Childrens Press ISBN 0-516-01127-8; In Canada: Childrens Press, 1991. 48p. col. ill. (New true book).
Includes glossary and index.
Many small photographs of polar bears in their Arctic home accompany a simple text describing the bears' bodies and behavior. Topics covered include walking, swimming, hunting, care of cubs, and conservation activities. Text is wooden and the series format utilitarian, but this is a useful and attractive introduction to the polar bear and the Arctic environment.
SUBJ: Polar bear./ Bears.

VCR 599.786 Ph-3 4-A $49.00 OD KC864
POLAR BEARS (Videocassette). Bullfrog Films, 1986. 1/2" VHS videocassette color (11min). (OWL discovery film).
Techniques for studying wild animals are explained as a biologist demonstrates and explains to two students his study of the polar bear. With fascinating footage of tranquilizing a polar bear and laboratory explanation, this fast-paced video augmented with activities from teacher's guide is useful in the study of mammals.
SUBJ: Polar bear./ Bears.

599.786 Ph-2 3-5/4 $6.95 P KC865
TRACQUI, VALERIE. Polar bear: master of the ice. Charlesbridge ISBN 0-88106-432-7; In Canada: Monarch, 1994. 27p. col. ill., map. (Animal close-ups).
Originally published: L'OURS BLANC, SEIGNEUR DE LA BANQUISE, Editions Milan, 1991.
Polar bears and other animals sharing their Arctic habitat appear in lovely captioned photographs with brief text describing the bears' life cycle. Most pages have a single column of text explaining the activities of a mother and her cubs while three quarters of the spread contains a pleasing array of pictures. Added pages of facts about polar bears and other bear species are included. A useful introduction to the species and to Arctic wildlife, this is also a nice pleasure reading choice.
SUBJ: Polar bear./ Bears./ Wildlife conservation.

599.789 Ph-1 4-6/7 $14.93 L KC866
ARNOLD, CAROLINE. Panda. Photos by Richard Hewett. Morrow ISBN 0-688-09497-X, 1992. 48p col photos. (Baby zoo animals).
Includes index.
Mexico City's Chapultepec Zoo is home to the young panda and his mother featured in this attractive life cycle. Not very much is known about the reclusive and endangered panda, and the discussion emphasizes behavior and zoo care of the animal along with some history and description of physical characteristics. The panda's popularity assures heavy use of this well written presentation.
SUBJ: Giant panda./ Pandas.

599.79 Ph-1 4-6/6 $14.93 L KC867
ARNOLD, CAROLINE. Sea lion. Photos by Richard Hewett. Morrow ISBN 0-688-12028-8, 1994. 48p. col. ill. (Baby zoo animals).
Includes index.
California sea lions are increasingly injured and losing their food supply due to human behavior, and this fine photo-essay explains the work of marine animal centers in restoring the health of rescued seals and returning them to their wild habitat. Emphasis is on the physical characteristics enabling the seals to live as amphibians, on rearing of the young, and on behavior in their natural environment. The close-up photographs and informative text offer a first-rate view of this versatile sea mammal. For environmental studies.
SUBJ: California sea lion./ Sea lions./ Wildlife rescue.

599.79 Ph-1 5-6/6 $14.95 T KC868
DARLING, KATHY. Walrus: on location. Photos by Tara Darling. Lothrop, Lee & Shepard ISBN 0-688-09032-X, 1991. 48p. col. ill. (On location).
Includes "Walrus Facts", and index.
Huge herds of Pacific walrus bulls in their Alaskan summer grounds are presented in magnificent photographs and several chapters of interesting text. Little is apparently known about the nursery herds of females and calves, but the author discusses aspects related to all the animals: physical characteristics suiting them for cold waters, uses of the tusks, eating, migration, swimming, songs and other sounds, and depletion of the species. This first rate life cycle offers interesting reading, providing many appealing views of the homely walrus.
SUBJ: Walruses.

599.79 Ph-1 5-6/7 $19.95 L KC869
JOHNSON, SYLVIA A. Elephant seals. Photos by Frans Lanting. Lerner ISBN 0-8225-1487-7, 1989. 48p. col. ill. (Lerner natural science book).
Includes glossary and index.
Fine color photographs document the life of elephant seals as they come ashore on a California island to molt and mate and raise their young. An informative text explains physiology (only the males have the strange looking proboscis), fighting among the males for dominance, the rise of the species from near extinction, and family life. The close-up views of great masses of seals and of many individuals are quite intriguing, and the book should attract browsers and provide useful information.
SUBJ: Northern elephant seal./ Seals (Animals).

599.79 Ph-1 4-6/3 $17.00 T KC870
MATTHEWS, DOWNS. Harp seal pups. Photos by Dan Guravich. Simon & Schuster ISBN 0-689-80014-2; In Canada: Distican, 1997. unp. col. ill., map.
Fine photographs and essay text follow nursery life of harp seals in their Arctic home. The inviting close-up views of a newborn seal and her mother and neighboring seals during a few spring weeks accompanies the explanations of physical characteristics and behavior. A very appealing choice for personal reading and an impressive introduction to the Arctic world.
SUBJ: Harp seal./ Seals (Animals).

599.79 Ph-2 3-5/3 $15.95 L OD KC871
ROTTER, CHARLES. Walruses. Child's World ISBN 0-89565-841-0, 1993. unp. col. ill. (Naturebooks).
Walrus herds and individual walruses are viewed in their natural habitat in this short introduction to the life cycle of the burly Arctic mammal. Use of tusks, physical characteristics, migration, care of the young, and enemies are discussed in the essay text, while photographs include appealing close-up views and interesting aerial shots of large numbers of animals herded together. An inviting overview of this homely creature.
SUBJ: Walruses.

VCR 599.79 Ph-2 3-6 $99.00 OD KC872
SEA ANIMALS ASHORE (Videocassette). Berlet Films & Video, 1996. 1/2" VHS videocassette color (20min). (Great animal stories).
Includes teacher's guide.
Includes public performance rights.
Seals, sea lions, and walruses come ashore to give birth, care for their young, and mate before heading back to sea. The camera follows swimming animals, mothers and pups, and the fighting bulls as they protect their harems while the narrator explains physical characteristics and behavior. The elephant and fur seals will intrigue children, and the piece will be useful where water mammals are studied.
SUBJ: Seals (Animals)./ Sea lions./ Walruses./ Animals--Habits and behavior.

KIT 599.8   Ph-2 2-4 $19.95   KC873
NAGDA, ANN WHITEHEAD. Canopy crossing: a story of an Atlantic rainforest (Kit). Illus. by Thomas Buchs. Narrated by Randy Kaye. Soundprints/Nature Conservancy ISBN 1-56899-452-4; In Canada: Soundprints/dist. by Canadian Manda, 1997. 1 hardback book, 1 sound cassette (11min).
> Teacher's guide available upon request.
> A black-faced lion tamarin lives out his day in this picture book presentation of life in a Brazilian rainforest. Lush paintings and descriptive text explain details of the setting and activities and interactions of the forest animals while focusing on the lone tamarin's search for food, his brush with a predator, and his search for a group or a mate to provide company and safety. The pleasant, recorded narration of the book text is set against a music track and animal sounds. An attractive package to introduce the tamarin and rainforest ecology. For environmental studies.
> SUBJ: Tamarins./ Monkeys./ Rain forest animals.

599.884   Ph-2 5-6/7 $6.95   P   KC874
BURGEL, PAUL HERMANN. Gorillas. By Paul Hermann Burgel and Manfred Hartwig. Carolrhoda ISBN 0-87614-612-4, 1993. 48p. col. ill., maps. (Carolrhoda nature watch book).
> Includes glossary, directory, and index.
> Gorillas are seen at close range in mountain parklands of Zaire and Rwanda. The informative text and handsome photographs offer a solid introduction to the behavior of the mountain gorilla. Zoo animals are used to depict a mother's care of her infant, lowland gorillas and other related species are introduced, and there is good discussion of conservation problems and activities. Attractive volume on an intriguing animal for the serious reader.
> SUBJ: Gorilla.

599.884   Ph-2 4-5/8 $12.00   L   KC875
KIM, MELISSA. Mountain gorilla. Illus. by Ann Strugnell. Ideals Children's Books ISBN 0-8249-8629-6; In Canada: Ideals Children's Books/dist. by Vanwell, 1993. 32p. col. ill., map. (Creature club).
> Includes directory and index.
> Explains how the mountain gorilla is endangered by human destruction of the world's forests and how this same destruction of habitat also hurts humans. Soft crayon drawings illustrate explanations of gorilla life and the forest environment. Well-organized topics include differences among gorilla species, the structures of forests in different zones, a simulated tour to view gorillas in Africa, and suggested conservation activities. Provides good emphasis on scientific observation and useful lessons in environmental studies and gorilla behavior.
> SUBJ: Gorilla./ Endangered species./ Wildlife conservation.

VCR 599.884   Ph-2 4-6 $275.00   OD KC876
MOUNTAIN GORILLAS: GENTLE GIANTS (Videocassette). Produced by TVOntario. Beacon Films/dist. by Altschul Group Corporation B8642, 1993. 1/2" VHS videocassette color (15min). (World of nature).
> Includes public performance rights.
> Gorillas at home in the mountains of Central Africa display fascinating social behavior. One interesting sequence shows the gorillas reacting to a Japanese scientist who is studying them, but, for the most part, the animals are undisturbed by enemies or intruders as they eat, play, occasionally fight, and communicate through a great variety of grunts and affectionate touches. Not a complete life cycle, this will be appealing for viewers of all ages because of the playfulness of the babies, children, and adults as they range through their diminishing habitat. For environmental studies.
> SUBJ: Gorilla./ Wildlife conservation.

599.884   Ph-2 3-5/6 $14.95   T   KC877
PATTERSON, FRANCINE. Koko's kitten. Photos by Ronald H. Cohn. Scholastic ISBN 0-590-40952-2, 1985. unp. col. ill.
> Available from National Library Service for the Blind and Physically Handicapped in Braille BR06430.
> Depicts the real life story of Koko, a gorilla trained in sign language, and her experience in caring for a pet kitten. Large color photographs, slick in appearance, and simple narrative record this unusual story of a normally wild animal reared in human circumstances for research purposes. Though the ethics of the situation will be questionable to some, studies of animals making "pets" of other species are just emerging and seem likely to provide us with interesting insights into animal behavior.
> SUBJ: Koko (Gorilla)./ Gorilla./ Human-animal communication.

599.885   Ph-1 4-6/6 $8.95   P   KC878
GOODALL, JANE. Chimpanzee family book. Photos by Michael Neugebauer. North-South Books ISBN 1-55858-803-5, 1997. unp. col. ill.
> Tracking a chimpanzee and her baby through Tanzania's Gombe

National Park gives Goodall the opportunity to describe her observations of daily life among these animals. Neugebauer's handsome color photographs, accompanying the readable essay text, clearly demonstrate the various personalities and activities of several adult chimps and their young. A fine blend of information about the work of naturalists and this sociable animal, this very appealing presentation should serve a wide variety of reading interests.
> SUBJ: Chimpanzees./ Gombe National Park (Tanzania)./ Goodall, Jane.

599.9   Ph-2 2-4/5 $14.95   L   KC879
CARRICK, CAROL. Two very little sisters. Illus. by Erika Weihs. Clarion ISBN 0-395-60927-5, 1993. 31p. col. ill.
> The two very little sisters Lucy and Sarah Adams were midgets who proved that in spite of their size they could make their own way as entertainers and innkeepers. Appealing drawings show the sisters in their varied roles. Useful in units on persons with disabilities.
> SUBJ: Midgets./ Adams, Lucy./ Adams, Sarah.

600   Ph-1 4-A/6 $20.00   T   KC880
BIESTY, STEPHEN. Stephen Biesty's incredible cross-sections. Illus. by Stephen Biesty. Written by Richard Platt. Knopf ISBN 0-679-81411-6, 1992. 48p. col. ill.
> "Dorling Kindersley book."
> Includes index.
> Spanish version DEL INTERIOR DE LAS COSAS available from Santillana (ISBN 84-372-4524-9, 1995).
> Cutaway illustrations reveal the innards of such diverse structures as the jumbo jet, medieval castle, ocean liner, space shuttle, and steam train. Detailed, authentic drawings and fascinating facts will captivate inquisitive students and offer background information for reports.
> SUBJ: Technology./ Interior architecture./ Architecture./ Spanish language materials.

600   Ph-2 A/11 $29.95   T   KC881
MACAULAY, DAVID. Way things work. Houghton Mifflin ISBN 0-395-42857-2, 1988. 384p. col. ill.
> Includes glossary and index.
> Hundreds of machines and mechanical principles are examined in exaggerated diagrams and short, densely stated explanations. Juxtaposes humorous segments featuring woolly mammoths with the technical material, and small cartoons featuring angels are a running motif on the busy pages. This heavy volume will appeal largely to adult admirers of Macaulay, and gifted and talented students will like the humor and the ideas.
> SUBJ: Technology.

CDR 600   Ph-1 3-A $39.95   OD KC882
MACAULAY, DAVID. Way things work (CD-ROM). DK Multimedia ISBN 0-7894-1253-5, 1996. 1 CD-ROM color.
> Version 2.0.
> System requirements: Multimedia PC with 486DX/33MHz or higher microprocessor, 8MB RAM (12MB recommended for Windows 95); MPC-compatible double-speed CD-ROM drive and sound card; mouse; SVGA 256 color display (16-bit color preferred); loudspeakers or headphones; Windows 3.1x or Windows 95.
> System requirements: Macintosh 68LC040 25MHz computer or above, that supports a 640x480 pixel monitor displaying 256 colors (thousands of colors preferred); 8MB RAM; double-speed CD-ROM drive; System 7.0 or later.
> Product (ISBN 0-7894-1253-5) runs on either Windows or Macintosh compatible hardware.
> Excellent multimedia rendition of the print version. Youngsters are delighted with the interactive machines, the explanatory movies, and the interrelated explanations. A wealth of science is gathered as students wander through the information. The addition of an exclusive Internet link to MAMMOTH.NET, an Internet magazine for young inventors, makes this CD even more appealing. Works well with small groups.
> SUBJ: Technology--Software./ Software--Technology./ Interactive media.

603   Ph-3 3-6/5 $12.95   T   KC883
HOW THINGS WORK. Scholastic ISBN 0-590-47529-0; In Canada: Scholastic, 1995. 93p. col. ill. (Scholastic first encyclopedia).
> "Scholastic Reference."
> Includes glossary and index.
> Explains 35 topics from airplanes to wheels in a doublespread format with lots of illustrations and diagrams. While explanations are necessarily simplified (e.g. television pictures are changed into sound vibrations, changed to radio waves, and picked up by your antenna, pp 78-79), the information is satisfactory for young students who want answers that make sense. The wide variety of topics makes this useful in science, social studies, art, and music classes. Fine to

stimulate a browser's curiosity.
SUBJ: Technology--Encyclopedias.

608   Ph-2   A/10 $8.95   P   KC884
CANEY, STEVEN. Steven Caney's invention book. Workman ISBN
0-89480-076-0; In Canada: Saunders, 1985. 207p. ill.
Includes index.
Frisbees, band-aids and chocolate chip cookies are among the 25
familiar items viewed as inventing activities. By focusing on the
inventing process: ideas, research, design steps, copyright, this
entertaining work is also practical. Unfortunately it is difficult to read
and the quality of the photographs is not outstanding; still and all it is
a unique work and motivated advanced students have responded
favorably.
SUBJ: Inventions.

608   Ph-1   5-6/8 $24.95   T   KC885
CARROW, ROBERT S. Put a fan in your hat!: inventions, contraptions,
and gadgets kids can build. Illus. by Rick Brown. Learning Triangle
Press/McGraw-Hill ISBN 0-07-011657-1, 1997. 139p. ill.
Includes glossary, directory and index.
Ten characteristics of inventors and instructions for making a battery
and an engine introduce nine inventive electronic gadgets. Each
project incorporates interesting bits of history and science, describes
the problem and possible solutions, lists materials and procedures, and
raises questions for further investigation. Fountains, shoe shiners,
automatic fish feeders, and an ice cream cone rotater are among the
gizmos. Humor and plentiful, practical instructions should strike a
spark with readers who enjoy making things as a hobby or for
science projects.
SUBJ: Inventions.

VCR 608   Ph-2   3-A $89.00   OD   KC886
INVENT IT! (Videocassette). Insights Visual Productions 401, 1988. 1/2"
VHS videocassette color (28min).
Includes teacher's guide.
"Anyone can be an inventor" (Intro.), even children in elementary
school. This describes the creative process of invention and illustrates
it with clever and intriguing inventions of students and adults. Can be
used to encourage participation in "invention conventions" and
science fairs.
SUBJ: Inventions.

CDR 608   Ph-1   5-A $39.95   OD   KC887
INVENTION STUDIO (CD-ROM). Discovery Channel Multimedia ISBN
1-56331-260-3, 1996. 1 CD-ROM color.
Version 1.0.
Includes user's guide.
Also available in Macintosh, $39.95.
System requirements: Windows 3.1 or Windows 95 (includes 16-bit
and 32-bit versions); 486-50 or higher; 8MB of RAM (16MB
recommended) double-speed CD-ROM drive; Windows compatible
audio board; mouse; SVGA display (at least 256 colors), MS-DOS
version 3.1 or higher; hard drive (8MB free); MSCDEX version 2.2 or
later.
Inspired by the television series, this program challenges youngsters to
build a variety of machines. Options for brainstorming a new
invention, a journal to keep track of discoveries, a section to research
past inventions, a machine shop to learn principles of science, a
garage for building, a testing ground, and a patent office make the
invention experience real. Excellent for learning centers or structured
science activities.
SUBJ: Inventions--Software./ Software--Inventions./ Thought and
thinking--Software./ Software--Thought and thinking./ Interactive
media.

608   Ph-1   5-6/7 $11.95   T   KC888
TAYLOR, BARBARA. Be an inventor. Harcourt Brace Jovanovich ISBN
0-15-205950-4, 1987. 74p. ill. (Weekly reader presents).
Includes bibliography.
Practical advice on how to develop ideas and sell inventions along
with many accounts of successful inventors makes this a handy guide
for developing creative projects. Copious photographs and examples,
an emphasis on inventions by young people, and plentiful advice on
problem solving are all included here. This is useful and entertaining
as well, offering good material for hobbyists, and those interested in
inventors fairs or science projects.
SUBJ: Inventions.

609   Ph-2   A/9 $19.95   T   KC889
AASENG, NATHAN. Twentieth-century inventors. Facts On File ISBN
0-8160-2485-5; In Canada: Facts On File, 1991. 132p. ill. (American
profiles).
Includes chronologies, bibliographies and index.

Ten inventors whose work profoundly effected manufacturing, human
health, and many aspects of science and daily life are each introduced
in a detailed chapter. Featured inventions are the airplane, rocket,
cyclotron, computer, transistor, laser, implantable pacemaker, plastic,
television, and xerography. Discussion includes bits of personal history
along with details of the development of the particular invention.
Small photographs, a chronology, and a bibliography are included in
each chapter. The milestone stature of the inventions makes the
volume useful, and capable readers with a strong interest in science
will find these life stories interesting, too.
SUBJ: Inventors.

609   Ph-2   A/10 $13.95   T   KC890
HASKINS, JAMES. Outward dreams: black inventors and their
inventions. Walker ISBN 0-8027-6993-4; In Canada: Thomas Allen,
1991. 101p. ill.
Includes bibliography and index.
Informative chapters describe the inventions of some well-known men
and women and others relatively unknown. Accounts provide
interesting social history as well as specific information on the
particular work of these inventors including Benjamin Banneker, Elijah
McCoy, Madame C.J. Walker, and others. Appendix lists numerous
other black inventors and their inventions. For African-American
studies as well as science units.
SUBJ: Inventors./ Afro-Americans--Biography.

609   Ph-3   6-A/7 $15.95   L   KC891
HAYDEN, ROBERT C. 9 African-American inventors. Rev. and expanded
ed. Illus. by Richard Loehle. Twenty-First Century/Henry Holt ISBN
0-8050-2133-7, 1992. 169p. ill. (Achievers: African Americans in science
& tech.).
Includes appendixes and index.
From devising a gas mask and a shoe sewing machine to inventing an
illusion transmitter, African Americans have been important
contributors to improving the world. This collection of biographies will
introduce a new field of role models for study as students discover
that African Americans have consistently been part of that rare group
of people who see new ways to carry out familiar tasks.
SUBJ: Inventors./ Afro-Americans--Biography.

609   Ph-2   3-5/4 $3.99   P   KC892
HUDSON, WADE. Five notable inventors. Illus. by Ron Garnett.
Scholastic ISBN 0-590-48033-2; In Canada: Scholastic, 1995. 48p. ill.
(some col.). (Great Black heroes).
"Hello reader!"
"Cartwheel books."
Short chapters of simple text illustrated with paintings and
photographs explain five important inventing careers of the early
twentieth century. The African-American inventors and their major
contributions are: Jan Ernst Matzeliger (the shoe lasting machine),
Elijah McCoy (a lubricating device for locomotives), Granville T.
Woods (overhead electric lines for trains), Madam C. J. Walker (hair
care products), and Garret A. Morgan (gas masks and stop lights).
The wooden, controlled writing keeps the reading level manageable,
and children will find the inventions interesting and the book useful for
reports. For multicultural studies.
SUBJ: Inventors./ Afro-Americans--Biography.

VCR 609   Ph-2   5-6 $99.00   KC893
INVENTORS AND INVENTIONS (Videocassette). National Geographic
51725, 1995. 1/2" VHS videocassette color (25min).
Includes teacher's guide.
Closed captioned.
Inventors of all ages, working alone and in teams, explain the process
of inventing things to solve problems, to improve existing products,
and for the fun of being creative. The planning and experimentation
involved in inventing, getting a patent and marketing a product,
companies developing new items, an inventors' expo, and a survey of
recent inventions are all described. Good use of the ideas and
inventions of young people adds appeal to this thoughtful discussion
of the problem solving and creativity which are invention.
SUBJ: Inventors./ Inventions.

609   Ph-2   4-6/12 $18.95   L   KC894
JEFFREY, LAURA S. American inventors of the 20th century. Enslow
ISBN 0-89490-632-1, 1996. 112p. ill. (Collective biographies).
Includes index.
Compact disc players, microchips, and life saving medicines are
among the inventions created by the ten men and women described in
these short biographies. Some of these modern inventors achieved
fame and fortune, but others gained only the satisfaction of creating
something unique. Useful for reports, the book's real value is the
encouragement of children who enjoy inventing.
SUBJ: Inventors./ Inventions--History--20th century./ Women
inventors.

609   Ph-1 4-A/9 $16.95   T   KC895
JONES, CHARLOTTE FOLTZ. Accidents may happen. Illus. by John O'Brien. Delacorte ISBN 0-385-32162-7; In Canada: Bantam Doubleday Dell, 1996. 86p. ill.
Includes directory, bibliography and index.
Serendipitous events produce irreplaceable results such as masonite board, rayon, and dynamite. Eight chapters explore foods, Mother Goose rhymes, medicine, and science to prove that truth is stranger than fiction. Useful for encouraging inventive thinking and creative problem solving. Final pages mention summer camps and the United States Patent and Trademark Office's Project XL. Use with science, health, social studies, and gifted classes.
SUBJ: Inventions./ Technological innovations./ Discoveries in science./ History, Modern--Miscellanea.

609   Ph-2 5-A/9 $23.95   T   KC896
LOMASK, MILTON. Great lives: invention and technology. Scribner's ISBN 0-684-19106-7; In Canada: Maxwell Macmillan, 1991. 262p. ill. (Great lives).
Includes chronology, bibliography and index.
"Brief life stories of 27 persons whose inventions or discoveries have altered the environment to a marked degree." (Foreword) Comprehensive chronology and bibliography. Excellent source for brief reports.
SUBJ: Inventors./ Inventions.

609   Ph-1 5-6/7 $19.95   T   KC897
NOONAN, JON. Nineteenth-century inventors. Facts on File ISBN 0-8160-2480-4; In Canada: Facts on File, 1992. 114p. ill. (American profiles).
Includes bibliographies and index.
The eight inventors introduced in these interesting biographies include Robert Fulton, Samuel F. B. Morse, Charles Goodyear, Cyrus Hall McCormick, George Westinghouse, Thomas Alva Edison, Alexander Graham Bell, and Herman Hollerith. Each well-written account covers the life, times, and work of the individual and includes photographs, a chronology, and a bibliography of other biographies. Though most of the inventors have been amply covered elsewhere, this informative book offers interesting reading.
SUBJ: Inventors./ Inventions./ Fulton, Robert./ Morse, Samuel./ Goodyear, Charles./ McCormick, Cyrus./ Westinghouse, George./ Edison, Thomas Alva./ Bell, Alexander Graham./ Hollerith, Herman.

VCR 609   Ph-2 3-5 $99.00   OD KC898
STORIES OF INVENTION AND INGENUITY. VOL. 1 (Videocassette). Written and produced by Harriet Fier and Stephen Mantell. FM Productions/dist. by New Castle Communications ISBN 1-885285-40-X, 1995. 1/2" VHS videocassette color (30min). (American discovery).
Includes teacher's guide.
Includes public performance rights.
Classroom discussion intercuts with brief explanations of selected inventions to emphasize ways human imagination has solved practical problems, changing life for millions of people. Teacher and children discuss the importance of imagination, brainstorming, and collaboration. Well constructed sketches with historical and contemporary scenes introduce a diverse variety of inventions from cornflakes and Band-Aids to baby carriages, vulcanized rubber, and rockets. The children briefly describe their own inventions, rounding out a congenial presentation useful for introducing the process and history of invention and stimulating the work of young inventors.
STORIES OF INVENTION AND INGENUITY. VOL. 2 (Videocassette) (ISBN 1-885285-41-8, 1995). 1/2 VHS videocassette color (30min), $99.00.
CONTENTS: v1: Clothing, Food, Home, and Work -- v2: Transportation, Communication, Health and Safety, and Recreation.
SUBJ: Inventions./ Technological innovations.

610.69   Ph-2 5-6/6 $17.95   L   KC899
CROFFORD, EMILY. Frontier surgeons: a story about the Mayo Brothers. Illus. by Karen Ritz. Carolrhoda ISBN 0-87614-381-8, 1989. 56p. ill. (Carolrhoda creative minds book).
Includes bibliography.
Trained while they were young boys to assist in operations and care for the ill, Will and Charles Mayo became skilled surgeons and innovators in health care. Their hospital in Rochester, Minnesota, became world renowned and a training place for numerous physicians in the early 1900s. Combining adventure and early medical practices, this biography will provide motivational reading in addition to history.
SUBJ: Physicians./ Mayo, Charles Horace./ Mayo, William James.

610.69   Ph-3 5-6/8 $15.95   L   KC900
HAYDEN, ROBERT C. 11 African-American doctors. Rev. and expanded ed. Illus. by Richard Loehle. Twenty-First Century ISBN 0-8050-2135-3, 1992. 206p. ill. (Achievers: African Americans in science & tech.).

Includes index.
These 11 men and women of the twentieth century all made significant contributions to medicine while also struggling with problems of racial discrimination. Each account is illustrated with a well-drawn portrait and begins with a medical episode, then disucsses early life, education, and varied aspects of career and life always with a clear view of the particular accomplishments which had widespread importance. This reissue continues to be a fine compendium of social history and important achievements in the medical field.
SUBJ: Physicians./ Afro-Americans--Biography.

610.69   Ph-1 P-K/4 $15.00   L   KC901
KUKLIN, SUSAN. When I see my doctor. Bradbury ISBN 0-02-751232-0, 1988. unp. col. ill.
Documents a four-year-old child's visit to a pediatrician for his annual checkup. The text is narrated from the child's point of view, the medical staff are obviously gentle and caring, and the excellent color photographs picture each of the instruments used and follow all the procedures of the examination. The natural behavior of the appealing little boy lends a very reassuring quality to this useful introduction.
SUBJ: Medical care.

611   Ph-3 5-6/7 $16.95   T   KC902
FORNARI, GIULIANO. Inside the body: a lift-the-flap book. Illus. by Giuliano Fornari. Text by Anita Ganeri. DK Publishing ISBN 0-7894-0999-2, 1996. unp. col. ill.
This rectangular volume, which is hole-punched for hanging on a wall, opens lengthwise to reveal large diagrams of the human body with numerous flaps which lift to reveal bones, muscles, the circulatory system, and internal organs. Captions running on either side of the diagrams briefly explain aspects of the body's major systems. Unaccountably, only a female body is shown; and though there's a clever fold-out showing a fetus at several stages of development, there are limited explanations of reproductive organs. Children will love the detailed body views and the flaps, which will be subject to early damage, but do provide informative views of this ever interesting subject.
SUBJ: Human anatomy./ Body, Human./ Toy and movable books.

611   Ph-2 3-6/6 $14.00   T   KC903
GANERI, ANITA. Funny bones. Illus. by Steve Fricker and John Holder. Simon & Schuster ISBN 0-689-81187-X; In Canada: Distican, 1997. 30p. col. ill. (How it works).
Includes index.
Body mechanics and plumbing receive a humorous look in copious drawings and diagrams introducing the major organs and systems. Breezy, common sense explanations along with scientific and comic views map the brain and its whizzing electrical signals and lay out the nuts and bolts of all other body works except the reproductive organs and the glandular system. The humor and clarity will attract browsers and lead to an easy understanding of how the human body operates. Includes a poster which is easily detached.
SUBJ: Body, Human./ Human physiology.

611   Ph-2 5-6/5 $8.95   P   KC904
GRYSKI, CAMILLA. Hands on, thumbs up: secret handshakes, fingerprints, sign languages, and more handy ways to have fun with hands. Illus. by Pat Cupples. Addison-Wesley ISBN 0-201-56756-3; In Canada: Kids Can Press, 1993. 112p. ill.
Includes bibliography and index.
Science, signals, and sayings are among the many bits of information presented in this homely compendium of facts and entertainment. Doublespread pages of text and crude drawings explore such topics as skin, senses, fingerprints, left handedness, movement, shadowplay, mime, and several forms of sign language. Stories, riddles, cartoons, and puzzles are inserted for added appeal in the enjoyable miscellany.
SUBJ: Hand./ Sign language./ Amusements.

611   Ph-2 A/7 $19.95   T   KC905
PARKER, STEVE. Body atlas. Illus. by Giuliano Fornari. DK Publishing ISBN 1-56458-224-8, 1993. 64p. col. ill.
Includes index.
Plentiful detail in pictures and captions fills the large pages of this oversize volume. Large technical drawings and small computer-enhanced photographs accompany small bits of text, providing an extensive visual study of body organs and systems. Serious readers will find a wealth of information.
SUBJ: Human anatomy./ Body, Human.

611   Ph-2 4-6/7 $11.95   L   KC906
RICHARDSON, JAMES. Science dictionary of the human body. Illus. by Gil Hung. Troll ISBN 0-8167-2523-3, 1992. 48p. col. ill.

Small sketches accompany many of the short definitions which give a quick introduction to many workings of the human body. Common words (brain, pelvis, wrist) and more technical terms (amino acids, nephron, synapse) are included. Useful for specific information, and some children will enjoy reading it as a miscellany.
SUBJ: Body, Human--Dictionaries./ Human anatomy--Dictionaries.

611   Ph-1 4-6/8 $16.95   T   KC907
VISUAL DICTIONARY OF THE HUMAN BODY. DK Publishing ISBN 1-879431-18-1, 1991. 64p. col. ill. (Eyewitness visual dictionaries).
Includes index.
Vivid diagrams full of detail fill large pages with compelling internal views of the body's organs and systems. A brief, lucid introduction to each topic and an occasional caption are the only text. Copious labels accompany realistic and magnified photographs and drawings; bones, cells, skin and hair, the nervous system, hands, feet, and the reproductive system are among the 25 topical segments. Children will pore over the intriguing visual presentations of human anatomy and the unusual terms, and both students and teachers will find many uses for this informative survey.
SUBJ: Body, Human./ Human anatomy.

611   Ph-2 5-6/6 $18.90   L   KC908
WALKER, RICHARD. Children's atlas of the human body: actual size bones, muscles, and organs in full color. Millbrook ISBN 1-56294-503-3, 1994. 63p. col. ill.
"Quarto book."
Includes glossary, index and life-size human anatomy chart.
Detailed diagrams and photographs along with numerous bits of information introduce the major systems and specific organs of the human body. Some of the brief text segments are conversational, some fairly technical, and others too sketchy. Some of the pictures offer intriguing and even life-size views while the distorted perspectives of some items are confusing. Children will enjoy the copious compendium of facts about the body, and overall it's a useful information source on a heavily studied subject.
SUBJ: Human anatomy./ Body, Human.

KIT 611   Ph-2 1-3 $41.00   OD KC909
YOUR TEETH (Kit). National Geographic 30323, 1987. 1 sound casssette, 30 ill. booklets, 6 activity sheets. (Wonders of learning).
Includes teacher's guide.
Describes the functions of teeth in animals and humans, the number and placement of teeth, and simple steps in dental hygiene. The small read-along booklets feature a pleasant variety of color photographs and short segments of text in brief sentences. A utilitarian overview, this supples useful teaching material on a subject which is currently not well covered for this age group.
SUBJ: Teeth.

612   Ph-2 P-2/2 $14.89   L   KC910
ALIKI. My feet. Crowell/HarperCollins ISBN 0-690-04815-7, 1990. 32p. col. ill. (Let's-read-and-find-out science book).
Simple facts about feet and footwear and many busy activities featuring feet fill this simple, cheerful discussion. A multi-racial cast of children demonstrate the parts of the foot, comparative foot sizes among children and adults, and the use of feet in many movements and forms of play. A bit of humor and a text manageable by young independent readers make this an attractive little volume with many uses.
SUBJ: Foot.

612   Ph-2 P-2/2 $14.89   L   KC911
ALIKI. My hands. Rev. ed. Crowell/HarperCollins ISBN 0-690-04880-7, 1990. 32p. col. ill. (Let's-read-and-find-out science book).
A multi-racial group of children demonstrate the many ways hands are useful. Simple text and cheerful line drawings name the fingers; observe the uses of thumbs, fingers and palms; point out differences in size and appearance of the hands of different people; and depict many hands busy at work and play. More an invitation to observe this important body part than a factual discussion, this should prompt nice discussion with young listeners and readers.
SUBJ: Hand.

612   Ph-1 4-6/4 $11.95   P   KC912
ALLISON, LINDA. Blood and guts: a working guide to your own insides. Assisted by David Katz. Little, Brown ISBN 0-316-03443-6, c1976. 127p. ill. (Brown paper school book).
A refreshing and fun look at the parts of the human body. They are all described in text and stories and there are experiments and projects explained to discover how our parts function. Many humorous cartoons illustrate the experiments and descriptions. A real up-tempo book that will appeal to many students.
SUBJ: Physiology./ Human anatomy.

612   Ph-2 4-6/5 $15.00   P   KC913
BOOTH, JERRY. You animal! Illus. by Nancy King. Gulliver Green/Harcourt Brace ISBN 0-15-200696-6; In Canada: Harcourt Brace c/o Canadian Manda, 1996. 48p. col. ill.
"Greenpatch book."
Includes bibliographies, directories and glossary.
This tall, thin paperback introduces many interesting animals, explaining how they resemble and differ from humans in their bodies, senses, eating, and movements. Beginning with one celled animals and moving on to elephants, orangutans, sharks, and more, the double-page entries include substantial engaging text, attractive watercolor views of the animals, informative sketches, and occasional profiles of "Greenpatch Kids" working on conservation projects. The book promotes membership in the publisher's nature club, but apart from this commercial ploy, there are many fascinating lessons for personal enjoyment, classroom use, and scout and group projects. For environmental studies. (Parents' Shelf).
SUBJ: Body, Human./ Animals--Physiology.

612   Ph-2 3-5/5 $15.00   T   KC914
BRUUN, RUTH DOWLING. Brain--what it is, what it does. By Ruth Dowling Bruun and Bertel Bruun. Illustrated by Peter Bruun. Greenwillow ISBN 0-688-08453-2, 1989. 63p. col. ill. (Greenwillow read-alone).
Includes glossary.
Short chapters sprinkled with line drawings describe the physical components of the brain and how this organ works when we're awake and asleep. The small volume size, the brief, uneven lines of text and diagrams and humorous figures highlighted in orange offer an inviting, quick introduction to the brain's structure, brain differences among animals, thinking and feelings, sleep and dreams, and the importance of good health practices. Though sketchy in many explanations this is an adequate overview.
SUBJ: Brain.

612   Ph-1 5-6/7 $12.88   L   KC915
COLE, JOANNA. Human body: how we evolved. Illustrated by Walter Gaffney-Kessell and Juan Carlos Barberis. Morrow ISBN 0-688-06720-4, 1987. 63p. ill.
Includes index.
Selectors' Choice, 17th ed.
Describes the ways the human body differs from that of other primate species and explains the evolution of homo sapiens. The carefully constructed text gives logical, intriguing explanations of how the human hand, foot, pelvis, and especially the brain have led to the use of tools, problem solving, and the development of culture. Abundant pencil drawings and diagrams illustrate a most informative introduction to the history of homo sapiens as it developed to its present stage.
SUBJ: Prehistoric peoples./ Evolution.

612   Ph-1 2-5/5 $14.95   L   KC916
COLE, JOANNA. Magic School Bus inside the human body. Illus. by Bruce Degen. Scholastic ISBN 0-590-41426-7, 1989. unp. col. ill.
Selectors' Choice, 17th ed.
Spanish version available AUTOBUS MAGICO EN EL CUERPO HUMANO (ISBN 0-590-46428-0, 1990).
Mrs. Frizzle and her class take a humorous and informative trip through the human body on their magic school bus. The busy, comic format is packed with bits and pieces of information about the various organs and systems of the body, and the book concludes with a class drawing project and a true and false test. This highly amusing approach will be enjoyed both as recreational reading and as a useful introduction to human physiology.
SUBJ: Body, Human./ Spanish language materials.

VCR 612   Ph-3 P-2 $89.00   OD KC917
FABULOUS FIVE: OUR SENSES (Videocassette). Rainbow Educational RB846, 1989. 1/2" VHS videocassette color (20min).
Includes teacher's guide.
Tasting, touching, smelling, seeing and hearing are shown as ways to know the world. Pleasantly paced, effectively narrated and involving the audience, this is an appealing introduction to a unit of study.
SUBJ: Senses and sensation./ Taste./ Touch./ Smell./ Hearing./ Vision.

612   Ph-3 5-6/6 $9.93   P   KC918
GABB, MICHAEL. Human body. Illus. by Chris Forsey...[et al.]. Kingfisher ISBN 1-85697-812-5, c1991, 1992. 48p. col. ill. (World around us).
Includes glossary and index.
Originally published: Warwick Press, 1991.
This slim paperback volume offers heavily illustrated two-page introductions to many organs and systems of the body. Cells, muscles, bones, the respiratory system, and reproduction are among topics covered in colorful flat drawings, picture captions, and a few paragraphs of text. An adequate introduction for libraries needing

additional material.
SUBJ: Body, Human./ Human physiology.

612   Ph-2 5-6/8 $22.83   L   KC919
GANERI, ANITA. What's inside us? Raintree Steck-Vaughn ISBN
0-8114-3885-6, 1995. 41p. col. ill. (How do we know).
Includes glossary and index.
Numerous drawings and bits of text explain fundamental operations
of the body and also introduce related discoveries of well-known
scientists. Blood, the brain, hormones, X-rays, the digestive system,
and nutrition are among many topics introduced in informative two-
page entries, which include diagrams, photographs, and drawings.
Useful starting point for units on the human body and on scientific
discovery.
SUBJ: Body, Human./ Human physiology.

VCR 612   Ph-2 5-6 $89.00   OD   KC920
LOOK WHO'S GROWING UP (Videocassette). Rainbow Educational
RB8286, 1997. 1/2" VHS videocassette color (24min).
Includes teacher's guide.
Includes public performance rights.
Steve and Beth, juniors in high school, comfortably explain the many
body changes associated with puberty and give advice on body care
and decision making. The back and forth commentary is interjected
with diagrams and vignettes of other young people, moves on to a
quiz on body changes and sexuality, and discusses emotional changes
caused by hormones. The frank discussion and realistic concerns of
young people offer a good introduction to puberty for classroom
sessions or family use. (Parents' Shelf).
SUBJ: Body, Human./ Human anatomy./ Growth./ Puberty.

612   Ph-2 4-6/4 $15.95   L   KC921
MARKLE, SANDRA. Outside and inside you. Bradbury ISBN 0-02-
762311-4; In Canada: Collier Macmillan, 1991. 39p. ill. (some col.).
Includes glossary/index.
Vivid computer-enhanced photographs and a few x-rays offer
intriguing views of skin, bones and numerous organs in this colorful
photo-essay. Intended as a kind of introductory survey of body parts,
the colloquial text comments on the skin, eyes, ears, heart and blood,
kidneys and bladder, stomach and intestinal tract. Some explanations
are sketchy, but the attractive layout and inner views of the body
should pique interest.
SUBJ: Body, Human./ Human anatomy.

612   Ph-2 1-4/2 $8.95   T   KC922
MY BODY. DK Publishing ISBN 1-879431-07-6, 1991. 17p. col. ill.
(What's inside?).
Cutaway views of photographs of children display simple colorful
drawings with cursory explanations of how some body organs and
systems work. The skeleton, eyes, ears, heart and lungs, stomach, legs
and arms, and hands are all quickly viewed from both the ouside and
the inside with information provided in numerous captions. Inconsistent
in supplying specific terms and adequate explanations, however, this is
an attractive presentation which will intrigue children.
SUBJ: Human anatomy./ Human physiology./ Body, Human.

612   Ph-2 A/6 $12.95   T   KC923
PARKER, STEVE. Body and how it works. Illus. by Giovanni Caselli,
Giuliano Fornari and Sergio. DK Publishing ISBN 1-879431-95-5, 1992.
64p. col. ill. (See & explore library).
Includes glossary and index.
Each of the body's systems and major organs appears in bold,
detailed drawings accompanied by informative discussion. Captions
and short segments of text offer numerous bits of information and
generally clear explanations of the structure and functions of the
body. Browsers and nonfiction readers as well as students doing
reports should find good material here.
SUBJ: Body, Human./ Human physiology.

612   Ph-3 P-1/2 $14.95   L   KC924
ROTNER, SHELLEY. Faces. By Shelley Rotner and Ken Kreisler. Photos
by Shelley Rotner. Macmillan ISBN 0-02-777887-8; In Canada: Maxwell
Macmillan, 1994. unp. col. ill.
Close-ups of smiling, talking, and upset faces show that the human
face is capable of mirroring emotions. Helpful for identifying facial
characteristics and discovering that we are alike while looking quite
different. Useful for multicultural studies.
SUBJ: Face./ Similarity (Psychology)./ Individuality.

CDR 612   Ph-1 2-A $44.95   OD   KC925
SCHOLASTIC'S THE MAGIC SCHOOL BUS EXPLORES THE HUMAN
BODY. School ed. (CD-ROM). Microsoft ISBN 1-57231-074-X; In
Canada: Microsoft Canada, 1995. 1 CD-ROM color. (Scholastic's the
Magic School Bus explores).

Version 1.00.
Includes user's guide, activity guide and activity cards.
System requirements: Multimedia PC with a 486SX/25 MHz or higher
processor; either MS-DOS operating system version 5.0 or later with
Windows version 3.1 or later, Windows 95, or Windows NT 3.51;
4MB of RAM (8MB recommended) for Windows 3.1 or later, 8MB
of RAM for Windows 95, 12MB of RAM for Windows NT 3.51;
5MB of available hard-disk space; double-speed or faster CD-ROM
drive; SVGA 256-color display monitor; 8-bit sound board (16-bit
recommended); headphones or speakers; Microsoft Mouse or
compatible pointing device.
System requirements: Macintosh LC 550 or higher with color monitor;
System 7.1 or later; 8MB of RAM; 8MB of available hard-disk space;
double-speed CD-ROM drive; printer (optional); Network compatible
with System 7.1 or later (optional).
Product (ISBN 1-57231-074-X) runs on either Windows or Macintosh
compatible hardware.
Users explore classmate Arnold's body on this field trip. Visit the 12
body parts, 12 science experiments, 12 games, and multiple fact
sheets and student reports. Good for use with small groups, as a
learning center, or with an entire class.
SUBJ: Body, Human--Software./ Software--Body, Human./ Interactive
media.

VD 612   Ph-3 4-A $877.50   OD   KC926
STV: HUMAN BODY (Videodisc). National Geographic 81530, 1992. 3
CAV videodiscs, 6 3.5" disks.
Includes user's guides.
Level III interactive with barcodes.
Also available as Level I, $225.00 each volume or $607.50 for the
three-volume series.
System requirements: Macintosh 2MB of RAM and System version
6.0.5 or higher, or at least 2.5MB of RAM and System 7.0 or higher;
3.5" disk drive; hard disk; and mouse. HyperCard version 2.0v2 or
higher. Videodisc player (Pioneer LD-V2200, 4200, 6000 series,
8000, or CLD-V2400 or 4400; Sony LDP-1200, 1500, or 1550.
Other players with an RS-232 port may also work with STV.). TV or
video monitor and appropriate audio and video cables. RS-232
interface cable to connect the videodisc player to the computer.
Printer (optional).
This three volume series introduces the user to the many systems of
the human body via superb video which can be controlled by a
computer. The HyperCard stacks which accompany the discs provide
preview and review questions, a glossary, and a set of printed and
visual resources. A presenter option allows for teachers and students
to easily create their own hypermedia reports. Works well with an
entire class or with small groups.
Contents: v1: Circulatory, respiratory, and digestive systems; v2:
Muscular, skeletal, and nervous systems; v3: Immune and reproductive
systems.
SUBJ: Body, Human--Software./ Software--Body, Human./ Human
physiology--Software./ Software--Human physiology./ Human
anatomy--Software./ Software--Human anatomy./ Interactive media.

CDR 612   Ph-2 4-A $39.95   OD   KC927
ULTIMATE HUMAN BODY (CD-ROM). DK Multimedia ISBN 0-7894-
1204-7, 1996. 1 CD-ROM color.
Version 2.0.
Also available for Macintosh (ISBN 0-7894-1208-X, $39.95) and
Windows MMX (ISBN 0-7894-1868-1, $39.95).
System requirements: Windows 3.1X or 95; 486DX/33MHz CPU;
8MB RAM (12MB recommended for Windows 95); 640x480 pixels,
256 colors (16-bit colors preferred); double-speed CD-ROM drive;
22MB available hard drive space; 8-bit sound card; loudspeakers or
headphones; mouse
This updated version of a multimedia introduction to the human body
provides a wealth of information. Youngsters will enjoy the ability to
dissect the body. The addition of voice annotations and an Internet
web site, BODY ONLINE HEALTH CLUB, a magazine of health-
related issues which is accessed exclusively from the CD, makes the
program even more useful than the first edition.
SUBJ: Body, Human--Software./ Software--Body, Human./ Human
physiology--Software./ Software--Human physiology./ Human
anatomy--Software./ Software--Human anatomy./ Interactive media.

612   Ph-2 5-6/8 $27.95   T   KC928
VANCLEAVE, JANICE PRATT. Janice VanCleave's the human body for
every kid: easy activities that make learning science fun. By Janice
VanCleave. Illus. by Laurel Aiello. Wiley ISBN 0-471-02413-9; In
Canada: Wiley, 1995. 223p. ill. (Janice VanCleave's science for every
kid).
Includes glossary and index.
Numerous simple experiments, illustrated with small cartoons and
diagrams, demonstrate how the brain, different senses, skin, joints,

muscles, and many of the body's systems work. Short chapters begin with informative explanations about the featured body parts, offer instructions for an activity with questions to guide observations, and provide some answers. The short demonstrations, which can be used for fun or as a jumping off point for science projects, are an entertaining introduction to the science of the human body.
SUBJ: Human physiology--Experiments./ Body, Human--Experiments./ Experiments.

612 Ph-2 P-K/2 $14.95 T KC929
WHAT IS A BELLYBUTTON?: FIRST QUESTIONS AND ANSWERS ABOUT THE HUMAN BODY. Time-Life for Children ISBN 0-7835-0854-9; In Canada: Time-Life for Children/dist. by Gage., 1993. unp. col. ill. (Library of first questions and answers.).
Energetic crayon cartoon sketches of young children fill large pages of simple explanations about skin, bone, senses, and other aspects of the human body. Breathing and sneezing, muscles and assorted body parts, and going to the doctor are among the numerous topics introduced in brief text and varied amounts of visual detail. Some of the explanations work better than others, but parents and teachers will find entries useful in providing simple information and laying the groundwork for further exploration of these topics. (Parents' Shelf).
SUBJ: Body, Human./ Human physiology./ Questions and answers.

CDR 612 Ph-1 2-6 $59.95 OD KC930
WHAT IS A BELLYBUTTON?: FUN AND INTERACTIVE QUESTIONS AND ANSWERS ABOUT THE HUMAN BODY (CD-ROM). IVI Publishing/dist. by Time-Life Education; In Canada: IVI Publishing/dist. by Gage, 1994. 1 CD-ROM color.
Also available in Macintosh version.
System requirements: Windows 386SX IBM compatible PC (25MHz or better); hard disk with at least 4MB free space; 4MB of RAM; Windows 3.1 or higher; double-speed CD-ROM drive; 256 color VGA card or better (640x480 resolution); sound card; mouse.
Whimsical characters Baxter and Elizabeth provide answers to questions about the human body that many youngsters have. In addition to three ways to navigate through the story, there are a number of instructional games. Since the entire text is spoken, the information is accessible to nonreaders.
SUBJ: Body, Human--Software./ Software--Body, Human./ Human physiology--Software./ Software--Human physiology./ Questions and answers--Software./ Software--Questions and answers.

VCR 612 Ph-2 5-6 $79.00 OD KC931
YOUR BODY: CIRCULATORY AND RESPIRATORY SYSTEMS (Videocassette). National Geographic 51611, 1988. 1/2" VHS videocassette color (19min). (Human body).
Includes teacher's guide.
Closed captioned.
A teacher and his class examine a model of the human body and perform simple experiments to demonstrate the flow of blood carrying nutrients throughout the body and returning with wastes to the kidneys and heart. A narrator explains the small parts of the systems; scenes of children in athletic activities demonstrate the varied paces of circulation and respiration; views of the actual heart and lungs show the connection of the two systems. Useful introduction to this major set of bodily functions.
SUBJ: Circulatory system./ Heart./ Blood--Circulation./ Respiratory system./ Lungs./ Human anatomy.

612.1 Ph-1 4-6/6 $14.89 L KC932
COLE, JOANNA. Cuts, breaks, bruises and burns: how your body heals. Illus. by True Kelley. Crowell/HarperCollins ISBN 0-690-04438-0; In Canada: HarperCollins, 1985. 47p. col. ill.
Includes index.
Explains how blood cells and bone and tissue cells function in repairing the damage done by scrapes, burns, cuts, bumps, broken bones, and other minor injuries. The text covers each type of injury with clarity and without the use of technical terms and is accompanied by humorous drawings and simple diagrams. A list of sensible suggestions about first-aid concludes this sprightly, to-the-point and reassuring introduction to the fascinating topic of how the body heals itself.
SUBJ: Wound healing./ Blood cells.

612.1 Ph-2 5-6/8 $20.60 L KC933
PARKER, STEVE. Heart and blood. Rev. ed. Watts ISBN 0-531-10711-6, 1989. 48p. col. ill. (Human body).
Includes glossary and index.
Outlines the organs and cells of the circulatory system, describing the functions of the heart, arteries, veins, capillaries, lymphatic system and spleen. Numerous colorful diagrams and fact filled text also discuss the components of blood, ways the body fights disease, health problems related to the heart and heart transplants. Though dry in

tone, this serves as a useful introduction for older students.
SUBJ: Heart./ Blood./ Blood--Circulation.

612.1 Ph-2 5-6/8 $20.60 L KC934
PARKER, STEVE. Lungs and breathing. Rev. ed. Watts ISBN 0-531-10710-8, 1989. 48p. col. ill. (Human body).
Includes glossary and index.
Many aspects of respiration and the relationship of the lungs to other organs and body parts involved in breathing, speaking, and circulation of oxygen through the body are discussed in technical detail and illustrated with colorful diagrams and photographs. Two page topical sections discuss the nose and throat, the rib cage, the bronchial tree, the role of the brain in breathing, smoking, swallowing, respiratory illnesses and much more. The detail of definitions, diagrams and captions comprises quite substantial information.
SUBJ: Respiratory system.

612.1 Ph-2 5-6/6 $12.50 L KC935
SAUNDERSON, JANE. Heart and lungs. Illus. by Andrew Farmer and Robina Green. Troll ISBN 0-8167-2096-7, 1992. 32p. col. ill. (You and your body).
Includes glossary and index.
Bold diagrams, numerous captions, and short sections of text explain the body organs which supply oxygen to the body. Two-page topical presentations describe the physiology of the nose, lungs, heart, circulatory systems, and blood. The slim compendium offers a good beginning on these technical topics.
SUBJ: Cardiopulmonary system./ Heart./ Lungs.

612.1 Ph-1 K-2/2 $4.95 P KC936
SHOWERS, PAUL. Drop of blood. Rev. ed. Illus. by Don Madden. Crowell/HarperCollins ISBN 0-06-445090-2; In Canada: HarperCollins, 1989. 33p. col. ill. (Let's-read-and-find-out science book).
Available from National Library Service for the Blind and Physically Handicapped as talking book TB02381.
This simple introduction describes the basic components of blood and the way blood carries oxygen and nutrients through the body. The simple text and full-page drawings tell about red and white cells and platelets, the amounts of blood in persons of different ages, and the role of blood in fighting disease and clotting to cover wounds. Though sketchy, it's a cheerful and straightforward biology lesson.
SUBJ: Blood.

612.1 Ph-1 5-A/6 $15.93 L KC937
SIMON, SEYMOUR. Heart: our circulatory system. Morrow ISBN 0-688-11408-3, 1996. unp. col. ill.
Vividly enhanced photographs and essay text explain the components of blood and its travels through the heart and circulatory system. Explanations of the technical details of the structure and function of the heart, lungs, lymphatic system, and body tissues of this complex network are clearly stated, but also demand attentive reading. The handsome book with its many bold micrographs and drawings is a solid source of information for older students.
SUBJ: Circulatory system./ Heart./ Blood--Circulation.

VCR 612.2 Ph-2 5-6 $89.00 OD KC938
BREATH OF LIFE: OUR RESPIRATORY SYSTEM (Videocassette). Rainbow Educational RB860, 1992. 1/2" VHS videocassette color (22min).
Includes teacher's guide.
Like all living creatures, humans depend on respiration to acquire oxygen for energy and to dispose of carbon dioxide waste. Using photographs of children working and playing, magnified views of body cells and organs, and plentiful diagrams, this thoughtful presentation explains the functions of the brain, blood, and respiratory organs; suggests simple experiments demonstrating respiration; and describes respiratory problems caused by illness, smoking, and air pollution. A review of the main points sums up the careful lesson which is clear but demands attentive viewing.
SUBJ: Respiratory system./ Respiration.

VCR 612.3 Ph-2 5-6 $79.00 OD KC939
DIGESTIVE SYSTEM (Videocassette). National Geographic 51614, 1994. 1/2" VHS videocassette color (18min). (Human body).
Includes teacher's guide.
Fascinating live-action photographs of the internal organs of the body accompany views of a science teacher demonstrating each part of the digestive process. The film occasionally shows friends gathered for Thanksgiving dinner as the work of the mouth, esophagus, pancreas, liver, stomach, and intestines are explained. A particularly interesting experiment with hamburgers and soccer balls which demonstrates the work of the stomach is included. Emphasis on a balanced diet runs through this practical and interesting introduction.
SUBJ: Digestive system./ Nutrition.

612.3   Ph-2 5-6/8 $20.60   L   KC940
PARKER, STEVE. Food and digestion. Rev. ed. Watts ISBN 0-531-14027-X, 1990. 48p. col. ill. (Human body).
     Includes glossary and index.
     The value and characteristics of various food groups and the structure and functions of the organs of the digestive system are described in detail and illustrated with colorful diagrams. Useful for assignments in biology and health/nutrition.
     SUBJ: Nutrition./ Digestive system.

612.3   Ph-1 4-6/6 $15.95   L   KC941
PATENT, DOROTHY HINSHAW. Nutrition: what's in the food we eat. Photos by William Munoz. Holiday House ISBN 0-8234-0968-6, 1992. 40p. col. ill.
     Includes glossary and index.
     Carbohydrates, proteins, fats, and vitamins and minerals each provide energy and help the body to grown and renew itself. Short chapters of text and attractive photographs of foods and children offer a clear introduction to the nutrient groups. Concludes with a recipe for baking soft pretzels, the food guide pyramid, and a chart of fat and calorie contents of selected foods. Attractive introduction to nutrition--useful as information and encouragement for developing sensible eating habits.
     SUBJ: Nutrition.

612.3   Ph-1 K-2/3 $14.89   L   KC942
SHOWERS, PAUL. What happens to a hamburger? Rev. ed. Illus. by Anne Rockwell. Crowell/HarperCollins ISBN 0-690-04427-5, 1985. 32p. col. ill. (Let's-read-and-find-out science book).
     Details how the body turns milk, bacon, scrambled eggs and candy bars into bone, muscles and energy. The inclusion of simple experiments help make the process of digestion clear. The revised edition has significantly improved illustrations, making it worthy to be shared with a group of young children.
     SUBJ: Digestion.

612.6   Ph-2 P-1/2 $15.89   L   KC943
ALIKI. I'm growing! HarperCollins ISBN 0-06-020245-9; In Canada: HarperCollins, 1992. 32p. col. ill. (Let's-read-and-find-out science book).
     Suddenly all of a child's clothes no longer fit, and he learns simple facts about growth. The first-person narrative and flat, cheerful drawings of an almond-eyed, dark-skinned child review the child's changes in size since babyhood and explain that skin and internal organs grow as the body becomes larger, new teeth appear, nails and hair never stop growing, children grow at individual rates and stop growing at different times, and food provides the energy needed to work and grow. A pleasant introductory lesson.
     SUBJ: Growth.

VCR 612.6   Ph-2 5-6 $99.95   OD KC944
BOY TO MAN. 3rd ed. (Videocassette). SVE/Churchill Media ISBN 0-7932-2685-6, 1992. 1/2" VHS videocassette color (20min).
     Includes teacher's guide.
     A nice mix of kids interact quite naturally as a featured boy experiences concerns about his changing interest in girls and the changes that are happening and not happening with his body. The narrative voice, that of an older boy looking back with help from an older brother and a pregnant aunt, explains erections and wet dreams, masturbation as common behavior, the role of the pituitary gland, and development of the male and female reproductive organs. The frank, comfortable tone and humorous touches should be useful in initiating discussion. A good introduction to adolescence which ends with a brief message about not rushing into sex.
     SUBJ: Puberty./ Sex instruction./ Reproduction.

612.6   Ph-1 K-3/4 $14.93   L   KC945
COLE, JOANNA. How you were born. Rev. and expanded ed. Photos by Margaret Miller. Morrow ISBN 0-688-12060-1, 1993. 48p. col. ill.
     Includes bibliography.
     Appealing photographs of babies in a variety of families accompany simple, clear explanations of the development of the fetus and the birth of a baby. Several Lennart Nilsson photographs of the unborn baby are included, and diagrams provide greater detail of the stages of development and birth. Introductory remarks offer guidance to parents and a bibliography of other sources for their use. (Parents' Shelf).
     SUBJ: Pregnancy./ Childbirth./ Babies.

VCR 612.6   Ph-2 6 $99.95   OD KC946
FEELINGS: INSIDE, OUTSIDE, UPSIDE DOWN (Videocassette). Sunburst Communications 2366, 1992. 1/2" VHS videocassette color (19min).
     Includes teacher's guide.
     Several young teens enact situations with family and friends which demonstrate the ups-and-downs of their feelings about changing bodies, relationships with parents, and developing interests in the opposite sex. An attractive teen narrator comments on the normal developments among adolescents and the way both young people and parents give mixed messages to each other. These pleasant scenarios of middle-class black and Caucasian youth are natural and realistic, offer sensible information, and provide useful opportunities for developing discussion in human growth classes.
     SUBJ: Puberty./ Sex instruction./ Human anatomy.

612.6   Ph-1 5-6/7 $9.95   P   KC947
GARDNER-LOULAN, JOANN. Period: revised and updated with a parents' guide. By JoAnn Gardner-Loulan, Bonnie Lopex and Marcia Quackenbush. Illustrated by Marcia Quackenbush. Volcano ISBN 0-912078-88-X, 1991. 98p. ill.
     Includes Parents' Guide.
     Straightforward text and accurate pen and ink illustrations provide explicit information about the menstrual cycle and pelvic examinations in a manner designed to dispel confusion and misinformation. The emphasis on individuals different responses and reactions provide excellent and sensitive guidance.
     SUBJ: Menstruation./ Spanish language materials.

612.6   Ph-2 P/2 $5.95   P   KC948
GIRARD, LINDA WALVOORD. You were born on your very first birthday. Illus. by Christa Kieffer. Whitman ISBN 0-8075-9456-3; In Canada: General, 1982. unp. ill. (some col.).
     Simple information on the growth of the human fetus in the mother's body and the time of being born from the warm, watery womb into the outside world and the warmth of family. Text and watercolor pictures describe how these events are experienced by the baby and the mother and father. A nice explanation for the preschool child-- accurate and reassuring but not overwhelming in technical detail--this can be supplemented with more complete descriptions of intercourse and conception as the child is ready for them.
     SUBJ: Babies./ Reproduction.

612.6   Ph-1 5-6/6 $19.95   T   KC949
HARRIS, ROBIE H. It's perfectly normal: a book about changing bodies, growing up, sex, and sexual health. Illus. by Michael Emberley. Candlewick ISBN 1-56402-199-8; In Canada: Candlewick/dist. by Douglas & McIntyre, 1994. 89p. col. ill.
     Includes index.
     Frank explanations of body changes and many aspects of sexuality along with copious drawings fill this informative compendium. Puberty, the outsides and insides of female and male bodies, families and babies, planning and decision making, sexual health, and the emotions and physical intricacies of sex are discussed in clear detail. The humorous drawings include human bodies in many shapes and sizes and comic asides between a bird and a bee. The unabashed treatment and variety of topics will make this a popular source among older children and young adolescents. (Parents' Shelf).
     SUBJ: Sex instruction./ Puberty./ Human anatomy./ Reproduction./ Growth.

VCR 612.6   Ph-1 2-5 $79.95   OD KC950
HUMAN AND ANIMAL BEGINNINGS. 3rd ed (Videocassette). SVE/Churchill Media C81003-HAVT, 1990. 1/2" VHS videocassette color (14min).
     Includes guide.
     Also available in Spanish C81003-HAVT-SP, 1/2" VHS videocassette color (14min), $89.95.
     Young humans and animals all begin life as a single cell egg though humans especially need the care and love of families to grow. This simple explanation of babies and birth begins with a survey of young animals and humans. Then it briefly explores child development before using photography and drawings to show the growth of the fetus and the process of birth. Lovely photography and a reassuring tone make this a comfortable introduction to human reproduction which avoids the subject of sexuality--the origin of sperm and means for transferring them are not explained.
     SUBJ: Childbirth./ Child development.

VCR 612.6   Ph-2 5-6 $99.95   OD KC951
LOOKING GOOD, FEELING GOOD (Videocassette). Sunburst Communicatons 2461 ISBN 0-7805-4146-4, 1994. 1/2" VHS videocassette color (17min).
     Includes teacher's guide.
     Four young teens demonstrate sensible decisions in taking charge of one's own health and hygiene during puberty. Emphasizes caring for skin, hair, and teeth; knowing the food pyramid, reading labels, and avoiding fat; and exercising in simple, upbeat terms. The congenial narrators and basic wisdom make an attractive package for introducing health units, especially for young people who need help

with personal hygiene.
SUBJ: Puberty./ Health./ Physical fitness./ Nutrition.

612.6   Ph-1 5-6/9 $18.95   T   KC952
MADARAS, LYNDA. What's happening to my body? Book for girls. Rev.
ed. By Lynda and Area Madaras. Newmarket/dist. by Scribner's ISBN
1-557-04001-X, 1983. 191p. ill.
Includes bibliography.
Provides detailed explanations of female physiological changes, the
reproductive cycle, human sexuality, personal hygiene, and male
puberty. The language and rough line drawings are specific and
graphic, and the text also responds to questions asked by teens and
preteens in sex education classes taught by the author. A thorough,
informative guide for adolescents, families, classes.
SUBJ: Puberty./ Menstruation./ Sex instruction.

VCR 612.6   Ph-2 5-6 $99.95   OD KC953
NEW, IMPROVED ME: UNDERSTANDING BODY CHANGES
(Videocassette). Sunburst Communications 2339, 1991. 1/2" VHS
videocassette color.
Includes teacher's guide.
A multiracial cast of kids interacts with each other and family
members in sketches demonstrating their concerns over body changes
during puberty while young adult narrators explain the physical,
emotional, and social occurrences. Emphasis is on the normality of
different paces of individual development, and standard information is
explained with reassuring ease. The two part structure of the film
offers assorted uses of the material.
Contents: Part 1: Boy into man (12min); Part 2: Girl into woman
(13min).
SUBJ: Puberty./ Growth./ Sex instruction./ Human anatomy./ Boys./
Girls.

612.6   Ph-2 K-3/5 $14.95   T   KC954
PEARSE, PATRICIA. See how you grow. Barron's ISBN 0-8120-5936-0,
1988. unp. col. ill.
This "lift-the-flap body book" shows how babies develop before
birth and during their first year, and how children grow and change.
Flaps are used to uncover the mother's tummy and in several nice
ways to reveal the growing of an older child in the family, and there
is a fairly solid text providing simple explanations of cells, diet,
growth of nails and hair, heredity, and physical change. A nice
conclusion introduces the grandmother in the featured family, rounding
out a presentation that is adequately drawn and well structured,
taking the usual "where babies come from" episode into a much
larger context.
SUBJ: Child development./ Pregnancy.

612.6   Ph-2 2-5/6 $13.90   L   KC955
SANDEMAN, ANNA. Babies. Illus. by Ian Thompson. Copper Beech
ISBN 0-7613-0478-9, 1996. 31p. col. ill. (Body books).
Includes glossary and index.
Photographs and drawings floating on white pages accompany a
short text sketching the development of the fetus and the growth of
babies and children. Muscles, body shapes, the senses, speech, and
eating are parts of the growing process depicted. Talks about
conception, mentions genetic heritage, includes several ever fascinating
in utero photographs, but does not describe birth. The brief
introduction to human growth will be enjoyed by children who like
reading about babies and will be useful in early lessons on the human
body.
SUBJ: Pregnancy./ Babies./ Growth.

VCR 612.6   Ph-2 6 $295.00   OD KC956
SEXUALITY (Videocassette). International Marketing Exchange/dist. by
Altschul Group, 1995. 1/2" VHS videocassette color (16min).
(Conquering the media maze).
Includes teacher's guide.
Includes public performance rights.
A group of young adolescents discuss how magazine and television
ads glamorize sex. The discussion leads to talking about sexual
responsibility, sexual stereotyping, and personal ways to respond to
images in the media. The attractive, natural cast of preteens presents
a very comfortable approach both for classes in sex education and
lessons on media and advertising.
SUBJ: Sex instruction./ Sex in mass media./ Mass media--Influence.

VCR 612.6   Ph-2 5-6 $99.95   OD KC957
THEN ONE YEAR. 2ND ED. (Videocassette). SVE/Churchill Media
C80480-HAVT ISBN 0-7932-2695-3, 1992. 1/2" VHS videocassette
color (24min).
Includes teacher's guide.
A group of classmates begin to experience changes in size and
growth and feelings as they interact in and out of school. A boy and

a girl reminisce about that year as the film introduces the changes of
puberty--growth spurts, acne, perspiration, erections, wet dreams,
menstruation, masturbation, external changes, and development of
reproductive organs. An older brother and grown-up sister are
convenient sources of reassurance. Clear explanations and diagrams
augment the well acted scenes depicting the changing social situations
as boys and girls awkwardly begin to notice each other.
SUBJ: Puberty./ Growth./ Human anatomy.

612.7   Ph-2 5-6/7 $20.60   L   KC958
PARKER, STEVE. Skeleton and movement. Rev. ed. Watts ISBN 0-531-
10709-4, 1989. 48p. col. ill. (Human body).
Includes glossary and index.
Numerous color drawings and compact text detail the parts and
relationships of the human skeletal and muscular systems. The graphics
and definitions will both appeal to browsers and provide necessary
information for class assignments even though some explanations are
overly terse and some drawings incomplete or ambiguous.
SUBJ: Skeleton./ Muscles.

612.7   Ph-2 5-6/5 $12.50   L   KC959
SAUNDERSON, JANE. Muscles and bones. Illus. by Andrew Farmer and
Robina Green. Troll ISBN 0-8167-2088-6, 1992. 32p. col. ill. (You and
your body).
Includes glossary and index.
Groups of bones and muscles as well as the entire human skeleton
appear in vivid diagrams accompanying short clear discussions of the
makeup and functions of these important body parts. Two-page
topical segments discuss movement, the role of joints, groups of
bones, and the muscles in the face, trunk, arms and hands, and legs
and feet. A good introduction to the skeletal system.
SUBJ: Skeleton./ Bones./ Muscles.

612.7   Ph-3 K-2/2 $14.89   L   KC960
SHOWERS, PAUL. Your skin and mine. Rev. ed. Illus. by Kathleen
Kuchera. HarperCollins ISBN 0-06-022523-8; In Canada: HarperCollins,
1991. 32p. col. ill. (Let's-read-and-find-out science book).
Four young classmates with varied shades of skin learn about the
functions of skin. Simple explanations of hair follicles, fingerprints,
dermis and epidermis, melanin, and injuries and healing are
demonstrated in congenial everyday settings. This revision of an old
standby loses some of its energy and is too sketchy in its
explanations, but it's still an adequate introduction to this important
organ of the body.
SUBJ: Skin.

VCR 612.7   Ph-2 5-6 $79.00   OD KC961
YOUR BODY: MUSCULAR AND SKELETAL SYSTEMS (Videocassette).
National Geographic 51612, 1994. 1/2" VHS videocassette color
(16min). (Human body).
Includes teacher's guide.
Closed captioned.
Dancers and children performing athletic activities illustrate body
movement in scenes with informative demonstrations of bones,
muscles, ligaments, tendons, and joints. A narrator and a teacher
explain the composition and work of these parts of the skeletal and
muscular systems while students work with the bones of an actual
skeleton and participate in assorted experiments. The congenial lesson
explains many interesting facts about the growth and movement of
the human body.
SUBJ: Muscles./ Bones./ Skeleton./ Human anatomy.

612.8   Ph-2 K-2/2 $14.89   L   KC962
ALIKI. My five senses. Rev. ed. Crowell/HarperCollins ISBN 0-690-
04794-0, 1989. 32p. col. ill. (Let's-read-and-find-out science book).
Spanish version MIS CINCO SENTIDOS. ED. REV. available from
Harper Arco Iris (ISBN 0-06-025358-4, 1995).
Eating, playing, and many other daily experiences engage a child's
five senses in this simple, pleasant introduction. A brown-skinned,
doe-eyed child names each sense. ("I can taste! I taste with my
tongue.") and then recounts more ways he uses each sense to know
about the world. The line drawings set in soft colors are cheerful, the
reiteration of basic concepts forms a useful lesson, and this is simpler
than many books in the series.
SUBJ: Senses and sensation./ Spanish language materials.

612.8   Ph-1 1-3/2 $14.89   L   KC963
BERGER, MELVIN. Why I cough, sneeze, shiver, hiccup, and yawn. Illus.
by Holly Keller. Crowell/HarperCollins ISBN 0-690-04254-X; In Canada:
HarperCollins, 1983. 34p. col. ill. (Let's-read-and-find-out science book).
Available from National Library Service for the Blind and Physically
Handicapped on sound recording cassette RC23163.
A rudimentary explanation of the nervous system and the involuntary
movements (reflexes) of the body which includes simple exercises in

observation. The simple readable text and warmly humorous drawings provide enjoyable material for shared or independent reading and an interesting lesson in physiology.
SUBJ: Reflexes.

VCR 612.8   Ph-3 3-5 $245.00   OD KC964
EYES: BRIGHT AND SAFE. REV. ED. (Videocassette). Alfred Higgins Productions, 1997. 1/2" VHS videocassette color (15min).
Includes teacher's guide.
A rap musician sets a rhythmic beat to introduce a simple and informative lesson on the structure of the human eye. A doctor uses a medical model and close-up photographs to explain the cornea, iris, lens, and optical nerves along with the functions of tear ducts, eyebrows, and eyelashes. Final segment shows the use of glasses for improving vision and safety measures. Well-structured, clear presentation.
SUBJ: Eye./ Vision./ Senses and sensation.

612.8   Ph-2 5-6/6 $12.50   L   KC965
JEDROSZ, ALEKSANDER. Eyes. Illus. by Andrew Farmer and Robina Green. Troll ISBN 0-8167-2094-0, 1992. 32p. col. ill. (You and your body).
Includes glossary and index.
Parts of the eye, the process of vision, and the viewing of color are explained in bold diagrams and short pages of text. Clear explanations of physiology, the functions of light rays and lenses in creating images, optical illusions, and eye problems are offered in the two-page topical sections. A good introduction to the technicalities of vision.
SUBJ: Eye./ Vision.

612.8   Ph-2 5-6/6 $12.50   L   KC966
MATHERS, DOUGLAS. Brain. Illus. by Andrew Farmer and Robina Green. Troll ISBN 0-8167-2090-8, 1992. 32p. col. ill. (You and your body).
Includes glossary and index.
Senses, thinking, memory, movement, sleep, and other complexities of human capabilities controlled by the brain are explained in this thin colorful volume. Topical sections offer brief explanations of the history of ideas about the brain, the parts of the brain, the way messages are transmitted to and from the brain, and other aspects of sensory and thinking operations. Practical introduction to the brain and nervous system will interest many children and provide useful teaching material.
SUBJ: Brain./ Nervous system.

612.8   Ph-2 5-6/6 $12.50   L   KC967
MATHERS, DOUGLAS. Ears. Illus. by Andrew Farmer and Robina Green. Troll ISBN 0-8167-2092-4, 1992. 32p. col. ill. (You and your body).
Includes glossary and index.
Colorful diagrams accompany brief and somewhat technical explanations of the parts of the ear, the way sound is received and understood, and the sense of balance. The double-page topical format includes short columns of text and informative discussion that is more difficult than the appearance of the slim volume suggests. The factual presentation will be useful in collections where curriculum demand on the subject is heavy.
SUBJ: Ear./ Hearing.

612.8   Ph-1 P-2 $15.95   L   KC968
MCMILLAN, BRUCE. Sense suspense: a guessing game for the five senses. Scholastic ISBN 0-590-47904-0; In Canada: Scholastic, 1994. unp. col. ill., map.
Sunshine permeates full-page pictures from the Caribbean island of Culebra which tempt readers to match symbols for the five senses with objects such as a lollipop, conch shell, pineapple, and more. Text, in both English and Spanish (with pronunciation), is confined to the back pages. A concept book for multicultural studies that guarantees enjoyment and learning while expanding horizons.
SUBJ: Senses and sensation./ Bilingual materials--Spanish./ Spanish language materials.

612.8   Ph-2 P-1/2 $16.00   L   KC969
MILLER, MARGARET. My five senses. Simon & Schuster ISBN 0-671-79168-0; In Canada: Simon & Schuster, 1994. unp. col. ill.
Spanish version available MIS CINCO SENTIDOS from Harper Arco Iris (ISBN 0-06-025358-4, 1995).
Appealing young children tell about experiences with each of the senses. Attractive photographs depict pleasant and some not so pleasant tastes, smells, sounds, sights, and textures in a very simple picture book introduction to how senses help us "enjoy our world." Useful first lesson on the senses and for reading aloud.
SUBJ: Senses and sensation./ Spanish language materials.

VCR 612.8   Ph-2 5-6 $79.00   OD KC970
NERVOUS SYSTEM (Videocassette). National Geographic 51613, 1994. 1/2" VHS videocassette color (16min). (Human body).
Includes teacher's guide.
Live-action scenes of children at work and play intercut with medical photography and assorted models to explain the operation of the nervous system. The transmission of messages through neurons and nerves, parts of the brain, the difference between voluntary and involuntary actions, and the importance of practice and repetition are among the many topics explained and demonstrated. An attractive array of real-life activities demonstrating sensory activity and clear scientific explanations provide an interesting introduction to the operation of the human body.
SUBJ: Nervous system./ Brain./ Physiology.

612.8   Ph-2 5-6/8 $20.60   L   KC971
PARKER, STEVE. Ear and hearing. Rev. ed. Watts ISBN 0-531-10712-4, 1989. 40p. col. ill. (Human body).
This detailed discussion covers the physiology of the ear, the intricacies of brain/ear relationships in hearing and understanding sounds, and the function of the ear in the sense of balance. Two page topical segments are accompanied by photographs, colorful drawings and diagrams, and small sidebars of added information. The discussion is technical and somewhat dry, but the thorough coverage will serve the needs of older and advanced students.
SUBJ: Ear./ Hearing.

612.8   Ph-3 A/8 $20.60   L   KC972
PARKER, STEVE. Eye and seeing. Rev. ed. Watts ISBN 0-531-10654-3, 1989. 48p. col. ill. (Human body).
Includes glossary and index.
Colorful and informative, this slim collection of two page entries explains aspects of eye physiology and ways the eye utilizes light to register visual images. The eye is likened to a camera, the plentiful diagrams and photographs and tightly structured explanations cover the lense, retina, rods and cones, focus, eye movement, connection of eye and brain, vision defects, color blindness, mixing colors and more. Side bars, insets, and occasional exercises to demonstrate principles add miscellaneous facts to the main line of discussion which is technical but generally clear.
SUBJ: Vision./ Eye./ Physiology.

612.8   Ph-1 P-1/1 $6.95   P   KC973
PARRAMON, J. M. Hearing. By J.M. Parramon and J.J. Puig. Illus. by Maria Rius. Barron's ISBN 0-8120-3563-1; In Canada: Barron's, 1985. unp. col. ill. (Five senses).
Also available in Spanish, EL OIDO (ISBN 0-8120-3606-9, 1985).
Colorful light-hearted pictures follow a boy and girl into several situations where sounds are heard (birds, children singing, the beach, trains passing, talking on the telephone); each page is washed with aureoles representing sound waves. The simple picture book inviting observation is concluded with a page of scientific information on the process of hearing and a full diagram of the ear for parents or teachers to use with children. An attractive and imaginative introduction to a scientific concept at the simplest level done in a quality paperback format.
SUBJ: Hearing./ Ear./ Senses and sensation./ Spanish language materials.

612.8   Ph-2 P-1/1 $6.95   P   KC974
PARRAMON, J. M. Sight. By J.M. Parramon and J.J. Puig. Illus. by Maria Rius. Barron's ISBN 0-8120-3564-X; In Canada: Barron's, 1985. unp. col. ill. (Five senses).
Also available in Spanish, LA VISTA (ISBN 0-8120-3605-0, 1985).
Looking and seeing are presented in the pleasant activities of several children--watching a turtle, looking at a rainbow, reading books. Attractive color drawings in a sturdy paperback, picture book format are followed by four pages of more technical text and drawings intended for use by adults with children. An appealing introduction at a very elementary level.
SUBJ: Vision./ Eye./ Senses and sensation./ Spanish language materials.

612.8   Ph-2 P-1/2 $6.95   P   KC975
PARRAMON, J. M. Taste. By J.M. Parramon and J.J. Puig. Illus. by Maria Rius. Barron's ISBN 0-8120-3566-6; In Canada: Barron's, 1985. unp. col. ill. (Five senses).
Also available in Spanish, EL GUSTO (ISBN 0-8120-3608-5, 1985).
Uses an attractive and gently humorous picture book format to describe numerous taste experiences shared by children and sometimes by their pets. Enjoyable scenes are set at the kitchen table, in a pastry shop, at the beach, in an orchard. The simple introduction to tastes concludes with a page of scientific text and a colorful diagram of the tongue charting the different groupings of taste buds.
SUBJ: Taste./ Senses and sensation./ Spanish language materials.

NONFICTION

612.8 Ph-2 P-1/2 $6.95 P KC976
PARRAMON, J. M. Touch. By J.M. Parramon and J.J. Puig. Illus. by Maria Rius. Barron's ISBN 0-8120-3567-4; In Canada: Barron's, 1985. unp. col. ill. (Five senses).
Also available in Spanish, EL TACTO (ISBN 0-8120-3609-3, 1985). Provides a sunny collection of children in numerous daily situations in which they feel different sensations--cold snow, wet bath water, a soft mattress, smooth ice. The colorful picture book listing of "touch" experiences is followed by four pages of text describing rather complex information about the skin and nervous system--this section is to be used as desired by an adult. An attractive beginning science paperback--the appealing pictures can stimulate discussion and observation, and many children will be fascinated by the ideas and words in the final section.
SUBJ: Touch./ Senses and sensation./ Spanish language materials.

612.8 Ph-2 1-3/4 $13.95 T KC977
ROYSTON, ANGELA. Senses: a lift-the-flap body book. Illus. by Edwina Riddell. Barron's ISBN 0-8120-6272-8; In Canada: Barron's, 1993. unp. col. ill.
Watercolor illustrations of children include flaps which cover eyes, nose and ears and lift to reveal the internal parts and the route of signals to the brain. Simple explanations and suggested experiments invite personal observations, and the author emphasizes ways the senses operate simultaneously. Simple commonsense explanations (without scientific terms) and the flap device are an engaging introduction for younger viewers and readers.
SUBJ: Senses and sensation.

612.8 Ph-2 P-1/2 $15.89 L KC978
SHOWERS, PAUL. Look at your eyes. Rev. ed. Illus. by True Kelley. HarperCollins ISBN 0-06-020189-4; In Canada: HarperCollins, 1992. 32p. col. ill. (Let's-read-and-find-out science book).
Begins with a child's observation of his eyes while making silly faces in the mirror and continues to explain what he learns about parts of the eye from his aunt, an eye doctor. Children are invited to do their own simple observations of how eyes move and how the pupil changes size to let in light. Brief mention of eye color and the function of eyelids and lashes in protecting eyes are also included. Cheerful picture book offers a pleasant beginning lesson.
SUBJ: Eye./ Vision./ Senses and sensation.

612.8 Ph-2 K-2/3 $19.98 L KC979
SHOWERS, PAUL. Sleep is for everyone. Newly illustrated ed. Illus. by Wendy Watson. HarperCollins ISBN 0-06-025393-2; In Canada: HarperCollins, 1997. 32p. col. ill. (Let's-read-and-find-out science book).
Available from National Library Service for the Blind and Physically Handicapped in Braille BRA13513 and on sound recording cassette RC09178.
Colorful collage scenes follow simple explanations of the sleep habits of humans and animals. Sleep needs change as humans grow to adulthood, but all people need rest for their bodies and brains--though the brain still works in dreams during sleep. An inviting conclusion follows a child through a bedtime ritual in this congenial first lesson on the importance of sleep.
SUBJ: Sleep.

612.8 Ph-1 5-6/6 $15.93 L KC980
SIMON, SEYMOUR. Brain: our nervous system. Morrow ISBN 0-688-14641-4; In Canada: Hearst Book Group, 1997. unp. col. ill.
Vivid photographs--both realistic and computer enhanced--illustrate an essay text depicting the functions of each region of the brain. Simon explains some of the different scans doctors use to view the brain, and the lucid presentation of nerve cells and other brain tissue and operations is an intriguing introduction to the human body's control system. The handsome volume should find many uses for booktalking, browsing, nonfiction reading, and information.
SUBJ: Nervous system./ Brain.

612.8 Ph-1 5-6/8 $15.00 T KC981
STAFFORD, PATRICIA. Your two brains. Illus. by Linda Tunney. Atheneum ISBN 0-689-31142-7; In Canada: Collier Macmillan, 1986. 75p. ill.
Includes glossary, bibliography and index.
Explains various functions of the left and right hemispheres of the brain and discoveries scientists have made about human creativity and learning. The readable text describes the physiology of the brain and provides simple exercises in observation for children, suggesting that individuals can understand and even strengthen their own mental and creative capacities. An informative introduction to widely held current theory, this is more in-depth treatment of a subject covered much more briefly in most other sources for this age group.
SUBJ: Brain--Localization of function./ Intellect.

613 Ph-1 K-3/5 $15.95 L KC982
BROWN, LAURENE KRASNY. Dinosaurs alive and well! a guide to good health. By Laurie Krasny Brown and Marc Tolon Brown. Joy Street/Little, Brown ISBN 0-316-10998-3; In Canada: Little, Brown, 1990. 32p. col. ill.
A jolly cast of dinosaur families demonstrate sensible diet, exercise, hygiene and health practices. The cartoon format also covers human relations advice - making friends, dealing with feelings, the need for rest and recreation. A pleasant guide for healthy living which presents mundane lessons in an enjoyable format.
SUBJ: Children--Care and hygiene.

SRC 613 Ph-2 1-3 $10.95 OD KC983
GALLINA, JILL. Feelin' good (Sound recording cassette). Smithsonian Folkways 7450, 1981. 1 sound cassette.
Ten songs with simple though somewhat contrived and didactic lyrics encourage exercise, hygiene, nutrition, and a positive attitude about self and others. Catchy tunes, folk style, for drum, bass, guitar and keyboards have an infectious beat which sets feet tapping and the body into motion. Children will enjoy the music and adults will find the material attractive for a wide range of teaching purposes.
SUBJ: Physical fitness.

VCR 613.2 Ph-1 3-6 $99.95 OD KC984
JANEY JUNKFOOD'S FRESH ADVENTURE (Videocassette). Sunburst 2407-03 ISBN 0-7805-4091-3, 1992. 1/2" VHS videocassette color (28min).
Includes teacher's guide and reproducible worksheets.
Janey and her teammates perform juggling feats and discuss with their attractive coach eating habits that would make them champions. The group discussions are reinforced with pop music and humorous TV set presentations as they examine breakfast and lunch foods; snacks; and the salt, sugar, fat, and additives contained in favorite foods. The cheerful routines of the appealing cast provide enjoyable demonstrations to spark discussion and provoke thinking about healthy food choices.
SUBJ: Nutrition./ Diet.

613.2 Ph-2 5-A/7 $10.89 L KC985
KARLSBERG, ELIZABETH. Eating pretty. Illus. by Donald Richey. Troll ISBN 0-8167-2001-0, 1991. 121p. ill. (Smart talk).
Addressed to teenage girls, this practical discussion provides sensible information on numerous aspects of nutrition and fitness. Ten chapters discuss the effects of diet on appearance and health, sensible eating for weight loss, planning nutritional balance, dealing with junk food and sugar, and more. Includes recipes and current wisdom on smart eating practices.
SUBJ: Nutrition./ Diet.

VCR 613.2 Ph-3 3-5 $89.00 OD KC986
MY BODY, MY BUDDY: HEALTHY FOOD (Videocassette). Rainbow Educational RB8176, 1993. 1/2" VHS videocassette color (16min).
Includes teacher's guide.
Buddy, an attractive young African-American man explains to two friends why eating a sensible assortment of foods is important. Buddy and a talking picture of himself are then seen inside a library chatting back and forth about the need for good nutrition, the food groups in the nutritional pyramid, and the value of balanced meals every day. A simple, appealing lesson in personal nutrition useful for introducing discussions in health units or for individual viewing.
SUBJ: Nutrition./ Health./ Food.

VCR 613.2 Ph-2 5-6 $189.00 OD KC987
NUTRITION TO GROW ON (Videocassette). Human Relations Media 840-VSD, 1988. 1/2" VHS videocassette color (30min).
Includes Teacher's Guide.
The preteen growth spurt can be dramatic. Good food choices are important, no matter what body type is involved. This live-action video, interspersed with animation counsels kids about this period in their development.
Contents: Part I: Food and your body (15min); Part II: Choosing the right way for you.
SUBJ: Nutrition./ Growth.

VCR 613.7 Ph-3 3-5 $89.00 OD KC988
MY BODY, MY BUDDY: HEALTHY FUN (Videocassette). Rainbow Educational RB8175, 1993. 1/2" VHS videocassette color (15min).
Includes teacher's guide.
Simple ideas about how play builds a healthy body are explained in a congenial dialogue between a young man and a video image of himself. Beginning with an after school encounter with two children, Buddy and his alter-ego explain the importance of physical play and exercise for good growth and strength, the significance of proper rest, and the need for attention to safety in play. The pleasant lesson

237

in taking care of your body is an effective presentation of a basic principle of personal health.
SUBJ: Exercise./ Physical fitness.

613.7 Ph-1 3-5/6 $12.50 L KC989
PAIGE, DAVID. Day in the life of a sports therapist. Photos by Roger Ruhlin. Troll ISBN 0-8167-0099-0, 1985. 32p. col. ill. (Day in the life of).
Describes the daily tasks of a therapist as he trains, treats, and supervises the workouts, injuries, and diets of a team of football players. A slim volume of colorful pictures and brief text documents this important but often unnoticed job in the sports field. Though there is no information on the training and education requirements, this is a useful introduction to an interesting career and a very effective lesson in team efforts.
SUBJ: Sports medicine./ Physical fitness./ Occupations.

SRC 613.7 Ph-1 K-6 $10.95 OD KC990
ROCK 'N ROLL FITNESS FUN (Sound recording cassette). Kimbo 9115C, 1989. 1 sound cassette (34min).
Activity guide included.
Compact disc available KIM 9115CD. 1 compact disc (34min), $14.95, guide.
A rock 'n roll beat accompanies stretching and bending exercises, kicking and hopping and low aerobic exercises. The second side has no narrative cues and the rhythmic beat can accompany a variety of aerobic activities, such as walking, jogging, and dancing. Good for physical education classes, as well as regular class fitness exercise.
SUBJ: Physical fitness./ Aerobics.

SRC 613.7 Ph-3 P-3 $10.95 OD KC991
STEWART, GEORGIANA. Good morning exercises for kids (Sound recording cassette). Kimbo KIM 9098C, 1987. 1 sound cassette.
Includes guide.
Supplies a simple set of exercises, ranging from stretches through arm swings, knee bends, marches and dances, sit-ups and jumping. Special lyrics for familiar songs on a morning theme ("Carolina in the Morning," "Red Red Robin," "Oh, What a Beautiful Morning," etc.) call out instructions and include choruses sung by children; each side ends with a cool-down bend of breathing and stretching exercises. An easy paced and explained routine for teachers who need additional material that is less complex than many aerobic recordings.
SUBJ: Physical fitness.

VCR 613.8 Ph-1 5-A $39.95 OD KC992
ALPHABETTER ANSWER (Videocassette). Baylor University Medical Center/ dist. by Select Media, 1989. 1/2" VHS videocassette color (31min).
A fifth grade class prepares a play for a drug education program, and in the process the children's circumstances in school and at home reveal some troubled situations. The teacher here is a wonderful model, and the variety of families--affluent, struggling, supportive, harsh--are very realistic. The film allows the viewer to observe and think about the people, offering many issues for discussion by children, parent groups, and teachers.
SUBJ: Drug abuse--Prevention.

VCR 613.8 Ph-2 4-6 $299.00 OD KC993
ARMSTRONG, TIM. Dog who dared (Videocassette). By Tim Armstrong and Randall Frederick. Pyramid Media 01343, 1993. 1/2" VHS videocassette color (25min).
A clever dog leads three boys on a merry chase as one friend tries to coerce the others into trying alcohol and drugs. Narrator, Jonathan Winters, voices the dog's thoughts as he employs many strategies to destroy contraband marijuana and lead the children to books on drugs at the library and to an antidrug rally where a sports star is speaking. A little far-fetched, but the humor offers an enjoyable coating to a sensible examination of peer pressure and drug use that should be a good discussion starter.
SUBJ: Drugs./ Drug abuse--Prevention./ Alcohol./ Alcohol abuse--Prevention.

VCR 613.8 Ph-2 5-6 $79.95 OD KC994
DRUG DANGER: EASY TO START, HARD TO STOP (Videocassette). Rainbow Educational RB8144, 1992. 1/2" VHS videocassette color (12min).
Includes teacher's guide.
What influences our decision to use or not use drugs, and what information helps us to make sensible decisions about smoking, drinking, or using other drugs? A straightforward narration explains ways we are influenced by advertising and by what occurs in the home and the neighborhood; vignettes of young adolescents and preadolescents in many settings and some simple animation go on to

show the effects of drugs on the body, the steps of addiction, and some ways real kids have found to say no. Realistic and sensible lesson in social factors could prompt good discussion of ways of dealing with problems and of countering pressures from friends.
SUBJ: Drugs./ Drug abuse./ Smoking./ Alcoholism.

VCR 613.8 Ph-3 6-A $99.95 OD KC995
DRUGS, YOUR FRIENDS, AND YOU: HANDLING PEER PRESSURE (Videocassette). Sunburst Communications 2254, 1988. 1/2" VHS videocassette color.
Situations show young people urged by friends to drink alcohol and smoke marijuana against their own inclinations and provides strategies to help resist pressure. Structured to encourage discussion by the posing of questions and breaks in the action, this is well designed and carefully delineates the steps leading to individual assertiveness. Although the acting is somewhat stilted, the scenarios are realistic. Price may present problems at the building level, but this would be a good district level purchase.
Contents: Standing up for yourself (12min); How to say no (12min).
SUBJ: Decision making./ Drug abuse--Prevention./ Assertiveness (Psychology).

VCR 613.8 Ph-2 A $85.00 OD KC996
HOW TO JUST SAY NO TO DRUGS (Sound filmstrip). Learning Tree LT363, 1987. 1/2" VHS videocassette color.
Includes teacher's guide.
Emphasizes the importance of individual responsibility in making decisions about drugs and solving personal problems. A positive, realistic address by a narrator speaks to young people on the realities of peer pressure, the problems caused by drugs, and strategies of dealing with boredom, depression, improved communication, and setting life goals. Teenagers using drugs, experiencing the downside, and interacting in groups are shown in an account that is straightforward, sensible, and not condescending or preachy.
Contents: A Let's look at the problem (9min), Getting ready to just say no (9min).
SUBJ: Drugs./ Drug abuse.

VCR 613.8 Ph-2 K-6 $99.95 OD KC997
JUST FOR ME (Videocassette). Agency for Instructional Technology 336-WS, 1992. 7 1/2" VHS videocassettes color.
Includes teacher's guide, facilitator's guide and peer helper handbook. Closed captioned.
Spanish edition available, SOLO PARA MI 336SWS, 1992. 7 1/2" VHS videocassettes color, $99.95.
"Drug use affects every child and every community." Acting on the premise that it is better to prevent alcohol and drug use than to stop it once it begins, this program instructs primary students in the fine skills of rational thinking and decision making. Six different videos (with culturally diverse family settings) explore making decisions and the resulting consequences. Live action of typical situations is integrated with animated sequences which hold attention and reinforce the message that young people can make responsible choices. Parent and teacher video coaches and demonstrates extension activities (such as use of peer helpers) that enhance learning. Valid framework for a successful drug prevention program.
v1 - Who are you? (Self-concept) (15min); v2 - My choice (Decision making) (15min); v3 - The real me (Peer pressure and support) (14min); v4 - I do care (Social responsibility) (14min); v5 - My family, my self (Relationships with family and friends) (14min); v6 - I don't buy it (Influence of the media)! (15min); Using JUST FOR ME (26min).
SUBJ: Drug abuse--Prevention./ Alcohol abuse--Prevention./ Decision making./ Conduct of life./ Spanish language materials.

VCR 613.8 Ph-1 1-3 $59.95 OD KC998
LET'S TALK ABOUT DRUGS (Videocassette). Sunburst Communicatons 2427 ISBN 0-7805-4112-X, 1994. 1/2" VHS videocassette color (16min).
Includes teacher's guide and seven student worksheets.
Simple explanations about keeping healthy and happy by avoiding cigarettes, caffeine, alcohol, and casual use of medicine are offered in a well-paced mix of narrative, realistic family scenes, and a children's chorus. Young Margaret learns that it's acceptable to ask her grandmother to refrain from smoking, and the narrator follows other events to examine substance issues arising in everyday situations. The short vignettes and explanations are clear and relevant to the real experiences of children and provide a very congenial vehicle for initiating discussion with younger children.
SUBJ: Drugs./ Drug abuse./ Alcohol./ Smoking.

613.8 Ph-2 5-6/7 $13.98 L KC999
MADISON, ARNOLD. Drugs and you. Rev. ed. Messner ISBN 0-671-69147-3, 1990. 114p. ill.

Includes glossary and index.
Selectors' Choice, 7th ed.
This sensible discussion begins with a realistic classroom situation and moves on to survey legal with illegal drugs and a concluding discussion of personal choice in drug use. Anecdotal accounts and well chosen photographs add immediacy, and there are quickly sketched explanations of the origins of particular drugs, physical and emotional effects, and the many problems of addiction. An informative introduction for reports, personal interest, and discussion.
SUBJ: Drug abuse./ Drugs.

MCP 613.8   Ph-1 4-A $149.95   OD KD000
SUBSTANCE ABUSE (Microcomputer program). Tom Snyder Productions SUB-A, 1992. 2 3.5" disks. (Decisions, decisions).
Version 2.0.
Includes teacher's guide and student reference books.
Also available for Apple II and MS-DOS.
Also available for Macintosh and MS-DOS network versions: AppleShare or Novell based.
System requirements: Macintosh black and white version will run on all Macintosh computers with at least 1MB of internal memory and an 800K (or more) internal disk drive. Macintosh color version will run on all color Macintosh computers with at least 2MB of internal memory and a 1.4MB internal disk drive.
Based on the popular and useful Decisions, Decisions model, this simulation places students in the role of deciding what to do when a friend has a drug problem. Realistic and thought provoking, the activity works with either the entire class or small groups.
SUBJ: Drug abuse--Software./ Software--Drug abuse./ Drugs--Software./ Software--Drugs.

VCR 613.8   Ph-2 4-6 $295.00   OD KD001
SUBSTANCE ABUSE (Videocassette). International Marketing Exchange/dist. by Altschul Group, 1995. 1/2" VHS videocassette color (16min). (Conquering the media maze).
Includes teacher's guide.
Includes public performance rights.
How can kids deal with the loaded messages glamorizing alcohol and cigarettes in print and television advertising and in movies? Boy and girl narrators raise questions, assorted clips are shown, and an articulate group of kids discuss media manipulation and ways to evaluate what one views. The natural behavior of the participating children is appealing, and their comments should spark good discussion about both advertising and substance abuse.
SUBJ: Drug abuse--Prevention./ Drugs./ Mass media--Influence.

613.81   Ph-2 1-3/5 $11.88   L   KD002
SEIXAS, JUDITH S. Alcohol--what it is, what it does. Illus. by Tom Huffman. Greenwillow ISBN 0-688-84080-9, c1977. 56p. ill. (Greenwillow read-alone).
Through bright cartoon illustrations, facts about alcohol: What it is, where it can be found and its effects on the mind and body are introduced. Straightforward information with no sermonizing in an easy-to-read format.
SUBJ: Alcohol./ Alcoholism.

VCR 613.81   Ph-2 5-6 $169.00   OD KD003
WHAT'S WRONG WITH BEER? (Videocassette). Human Relations Media 958 ISBN 1-55548-558-8, 1992. 1/2" VHS videocassette color (24min).
Includes teacher's guide.
Two scenarios feature groups of diverse friends who have mixed feelings about drinking. Realistic situations show peer pressure, older friends' and siblings' drinking habits, personal hesitations, and ways to say "no" without losing friends. An older teenager explains problems caused by alcohol and raises discussion questions for viewers. Pauses for discussion are well placed and should offer comfortable opportunities for teachers and other group leaders to explore issues.
SUBJ: Alcohol./ Drug abuse.

VCR 613.85   Ph-2 5-6 $200.00   OD KD004
BILAL'S DREAM (Videocassette). Durrin Productions, 1990. 1/2" VHS videocassette color (12min).
Includes public performance rights.
Bilal falls asleep during a boring school assembly on smoking and leads a lively young rap group around the auditorium and into a courtroom where adolescent smokers are on trial. The young teenage judge sends all plaintiffs either to the smoking line or the clean air room, and the reiterated rap routines are infectious. This polished production should be very effective in conveying understanding about why people smoke, the addictive nature of nicotine, and the wisdom of not smoking.
SUBJ: Smoking.

VCR 613.85   Ph-2 3-5 $39.95   OD KD005
DUSTY THE DRAGON TALKS TO DR. MARGIE HOGAN ABOUT TOBACCO (Videocassette). ETR Associates/Network Publications, 1990. 1/2" VHS videocassette color (12min).
Animated figures interact with a human doctor in a courtroom scene where she puts smoking on trial to expose the bad influences of Nicky Teen and his gang, The Pack. Witnesses include Handsome Heart and the Lungs along with members of The Pack, who explain why they decided to smoke. The obvious lessons are made quite palatable in a scheme that should catch the attention of young viewers.
SUBJ: Smoking./ Tobacco--Physiological effect./ Health.

VCR 613.85   Ph-2 5-6 $159.00   OD KD006
SMOKE SIGNALS (Videocassette). Disney Educational Productions 68006, 1995. 1/2" VHS videocassette color (18min).
Includes teacher's guide.
Includes public performance rights.
On his thirteenth birthday, Joey's friend talks him into smoking in a scenario that plays out pretty naturally. Though Joey's skeptical about the idea at first, he smokes a cigarette and becomes a habitual smoker. He then finds himself in the aggravating situation of nightmarishly reliving his birthday over and over again with events speeding up as he becomes more involved with cigarettes. Joey's tension is managed to good comic effect, allowing viewers to think about several implications of the smoking decision without a sense of the didactic, and there's a nice positive ending.
SUBJ: Smoking.

VCR 613.85   Ph-1 5-6 $130.00   OD KD007
TOBACCO ACTION CURRICULUM: THE YOUNG AND THE BREATHLESS (Videocassette). Developed by Project 4-Health, University of California. Human Relations Media LG-979-VSD, 1991. 1/2" VHS videocassette color (18min).
Includes teacher's guide and reproducible masters.
This two part kit--video and activity handbook--encourages young people to explore decision making and health and social issues related to smoking and tobacco use. The video features an attractive variety of younger and middle teens discussing personal experiences as smokers and non-smokers, and the looseleaf handbook includes numerous suggestions for discussion, study, and social action by young people, teachers, and parents. The multifaceted approach effectively conveys the personal experience of addiction and includes addresses for numerous information resources. A substantial package that should be widely useful.
SUBJ: Smoking./ Tobacco.

VCR 613.85   Ph-2 4-6 $249.00   OD KD008
TOBACCO FREE YOU AND ME (Videocassette). Durrin Productions, 1994. 1/2" VHS videocassette color (19min).
A two part presentation features an outspoken group of children who discuss cigarette advertising and other aspects of tobacco use with their teacher. They then head out to the streets to start their own investigation and antismoking campaign. Their experiences with shopkeepers who do and who don't sell them cigarettes are interesting. The congenial kids should strike a chord with viewers, and the true-to-life situations will provoke thinking and discussion. Advertising directed towards kids, secondhand smoke, smokeless tobacco, and long term health hazards are among the topics covered.
SUBJ: Smoking./ Tobacco.

VCR 613.85   Ph-2 5-6 $79.95   OD KD009
TROUBLE WITH TOBACCO (Videocassette). Rainbow Educational RB8273, 1996. 1/2" VHS videocassette color (14min).
Includes teacher's guide and reproducible.
Includes public performance rights.
As preteen friends gather to smoke cigarettes, a narrator begins to explain why kids choose to smoke. He explains the harmful ingredients in cigarettes, the many negative effects of tobacco use, the similar problems with snuff and chewing tobacco, and the likelihood of addiction. Though the effects seem to happen here mainly to old people, there's plenty to prompt discussion among upper grade students.
SUBJ: Smoking./ Tobacco.

614.4   Ph-2 A/11 $14.89   L   KD010
GIBLIN, JAMES CROSS. When plague strikes: the Black Death, smallpox, AIDS. Woodcuts by David Frampton. HarperCollins ISBN 0-06-025864-0; In Canada: HarperCollins, 1995. 212p. ill.
Includes bibliographies and index.
These three contagious diseases spread fear and death and challenged doctors and scientists to hard work and discovery. This interesting, in-depth history of the worldwide and personal consequences of each disease is thoughtful and informative. The

substantial text, illustrated with three large woodcuts, will be most enjoyed by mature readers with a serious interest in history or medical discovery.
SUBJ: Plague--History./ Smallpox--History./ AIDS (Disease)--History./ Epidemics--History./ Diseases--History.

615.9 Ph-2 3-6/5 $5.95 P KD011
SKIDMORE, STEVE. Poison! beware! be an ace poison spotter. Illus. by Thompson Yardley. Millbrook Press ISBN 1-878841-41-6, 1991. 40p. col. ill. (Lighter look).
Includes index.
Poisons from many sources--household products, plants, animals, germs, food additives, tobacco, drugs--are introduced in a quick, bright survey. Busy pages of small pictures and short facts describe poisonous substances and their effects and provide sensible first-aid advice. Bits of humor lighten the serious message that poisons all around us must be taken seriously.
SUBJ: Poisons.

616 Ph-3 A/10 $19.60 L KD012
NOURSE, ALAN E. Virus invaders. Watts ISBN 0-531-12511-4; In Canada: Watts, 1992. 96p. ill. (Venture book).
Includes glossary, bibliography and index.
Complexities of virus behavior and research are detailed in an informative and inadequately illustrated discussion. The text is difficult but lucid in explaining how viruses were discovered, how they operate in the body, diseases they cause, and recent research activity. Muddy, dark photographs are not useful or interesting. Thorough introduction to this important body of organisms for advanced students.
SUBJ: Viruses./ Virus diseases.

VCR 616 Ph-3 A $99.00 OD KD013
VIRUS! (Videocassette). National Geographic 51618, 1994. 1/2" VHS videocassette color (25min).
Includes teacher's guide.
This thought-provoking discussion explains how viruses work, how they have altered people's lives and even the course of history, and how scientists study them. Computer models and microphotographs show many structures of viruses. Doctors and researchers explain how viruses reproduce, how the body's immune system fights them, the importance of vaccines, and why viruses are so difficult to conquer. Hospital and lab scenes along with the discussion emphasize the urgent need for studying viruses. Useful for science projects and career studies.
SUBJ: Viruses./ Virus diseases.

VCR 616.07 Ph-2 4-5 $59.95 OD KD014
IMMUNE SYSTEM: OUR INTERNAL DEFENDER (Videocassette). Marshmedia 9366, 1991. 1/2" VHS videocassette color (10min).
Includes teacher's guide.
Photographs of children and animated sequences depicting specialized cells in the immune system accompany this basic introduction to the human body's defense against bacteria and viruses. The presentation explains how harmful particles get inside the body; defines phagocytes, T cells, and B cells; discusses various ways the body acquires immunity; and briefly describes how the HIV virus destroys T cells. A good springboard for discussion and reading of more in-depth material on this important function of the body.
SUBJ: Immunity./ Immunology./ Bacteria./ Viruses.

616.2 Ph-2 5-6/7 $12.95 L KD015
OSTROW, WILLIAM. All about asthma. By William and Vivian Ostrow. Illus. by Blanche Sims. Whitman ISBN 0-8075-0276-6; In Canada: General, 1989. 39p. col. ill.
Asthma causes and treatments are described in considerable detail by a boy who experiences this common ailment. The first person narrative discusses the symptoms and panic of asthma attacks, triggers of attacks, and common myths about asthma. Humorous line drawings washed with a single color lighten the tone of the practical discussion which should be useful to families newly experiencing childhood asthma and informative for classmates.
SUBJ: Asthma./ Children's writings.

616.2 Ph-3 A/10 $11.98 L KD016
STEDMAN, NANCY. Common cold and influenza. Illustrated by Michael Reingold. Messner ISBN 0-671-60022-2, 1986. 64p. ill. (some col.).
Includes glossary and index.
Provides in-depth discussion of the behavior and effects of the many viruses which cause colds and influenza. The substantial text accompanied by helpful diagrams (some in color) describes how these organisms affect the organs and tissues, how the body fights back, and the history of medical efforts in fighting these diseases. Though this has more information than many readers will care to know, it will be very useful for students interested in serious reading and research.
SUBJ: Influenza./ Cold (Disease).

616.4 Ph-2 K-2/2 $12.95 L KD017
PIRNER, CONNIE WHITE. Even little kids get diabetes. Illus. by Nadine Bernard Westcott. Whitman ISBN 0-8075-2158-2; In Canada: General, 1991. unp. col. ill.
A little girl describes her experiences with the symptoms and treatment of diabetes. Accompanied by picture book illustrations, the simple first-person narrative recounts going to the hospital, daily blood checks and insulin shots, the need to avoid sugar, occasional problems, and family worries; a final page of sensible advice is directed to parents. Explanations are sketchy, but the honest admission of frustrations and the reassuring tone should help young children understand the diabetic child and also prompt recognition by children with this or other chronic illnesses.
SUBJ: Diabetes.

616.4 Ph-2 A/9 $13.98 L KD018
TIGER, STEVEN. Diabetes. Illustrated by Michael Reingold. Messner ISBN 0-671-63273-6, 1987. 63p. ill. (some col.).
Includes glossary and index.
Examines the causes, symptoms, physiology, and treatment of different forms of diabetes in a detailed, clinical discussion. The double columned text is clear, systematic, and thorough and is illustrated with diagrams in black and white and color. Although the format is "textbooky" this is an informative, objective source for the serious student and an excellent explanation of this common disease.
SUBJ: Diabetes.

VCR 616.86 Ph-3 5-6 $79.95 OD KD019
DRUG DANGER: IN THE BODY (Videocassette). Rainbow Educational RB8145, 1992. 1/2" VHS videocassette color (12min).
Includes teacher's guide.
Occasional scenes of young people socializing intercut with straightforward narration describing various types of body damage caused by tobacco, marijuana, and alcohol. Colorful animated diagrams illustrate the effect of these substances on the brain, heart, lungs, stomach, and other organs with an explanation of how these addictive substances act as gateway drugs. Sensible, dispassionate presentation can be used as a springboard to discussion and other related teaching activities.
SUBJ: Drug abuse./ Drugs./ Smoking./ Alcoholism.

616.89 Ph-2 5-6/9 $12.93 L KD020
DINNER, SHERRY H. Nothing to be ashamed of: growing up with mental illness in your family. Lothrop, Lee & Shepard ISBN 0-688-08482-6, 1989. 212p.
Includes glossary, bibliography and index.
A child psychologist provides informative explanations of common mental illnesses and reassuring advice for coping with the fears and stresses felt by the family. Chapters cover schizophrenia, mood disorders, phobias, posttraumatic stress disorders, Alzheimer's disease, and eating disorders. Typical cases are described, and advice on selecting a support group round out the practical presentation.
SUBJ: Mentally ill--Family relationships./ Mental illness.

616.9 Ph-1 1-3/5 $14.95 L KD021
BERGER, MELVIN. Germs make me sick! Rev. ed. Illus. by Marylin Hafner. HarperCollins ISBN 0-06-024250-7; In Canada: HarperCollins, 1995. 32p. col. ill. (Let's-read-and-find-out science book).
Amusing scenes of children and their pets demonstrate how viruses and bacteria affect the body. Thoughtful, clear text and plentiful diagrams explain the appearance and behavior of bacteria and viruses, ways they enter the body, different defenses of the body, and methods doctors use to treat types of sickness. There's a final list of healthy practices. The well-developed, sprightly lesson is interesting reading and useful science material.
SUBJ: Bacteria./ Viruses.

VCR 616.9 Ph-2 5-6 $79.95 OD KD022
COMMUNICABLE DISEASES (Videocassette). SVE/Churchill Media C80395-HAVT, 1992. 1/2" VHS videocassette color (13min).
Includes teacher's guide.
A girl visiting a scientist in his laboratory learns about the four types of organisms which cause sickness. Viruses, bacteria, parasites, and fungi are the topics of conversation and microscopic viewing while an unseen narrator explains the appearance of each, how they are transmitted, and the types of illnesses caused. Very general comments are made about taking care of the body to maintain good health. The sensible, well-organized presentation is a useful introduction for health or biology units.
SUBJ: Communicable diseases./ Diseases.

VCR 616.97 Ph-2 5-6 $295.00 OD KD023
A IS FOR AIDS (Videocassette). Perennial Education/Altschul Group 7487, 1992. 1/2" VHS videocassette color (15min).

Includes public performance rights.

Andy Answer, an animated dog, leads three children into a television odyssey in which they visit children who have AIDS, talk with a doctor, and see the battle between cells and virus in the body's immune system. Basic facts about the widespread occurrence of the disease, the activities which spread AIDS, and the common misconceptions about the disease are covered in a non-threatening manner. The children are a bit naive and the television gimmick a little simplistic but the presentation may serve as a useful introduction to discussion and further study.
SUBJ: AIDS (Disease).

VCR 616.97   Ph-2 5-6 $225.00   OD KD024
ABC'S OF AIDS: THE COACH APPROACH (Videocassette). Select Media, 1991. 1/2" VHS videocassette color (14min).
Includes public performance rights.
Several upbeat episodes explore realistic dilemmas young people face in dealing with peers and risky behavior. The multiracial cast features a young African-American man who appears to coach a younger boy at several intervals of his adolescence. The coach's advice to "find out what's going on, think of other things to do, and leave the door open" is thought provoking. Simple and to the point in delineating drugs and sex as the cause of AIDS among adolescents, this short piece will best be used as a discussion starter.
SUBJ: AIDS (Disease).

VCR 616.97   Ph-2 K-2 $69.95   OD KD025
COME SIT BY ME: AIDS EDUCATION (Videocassette). Pied Piper/AIMS Multimedia 8438, 1992. 1/2" VHS videocassette color (8min).
Includes teacher's guide.
When a little girl expresses concern about her new classmate Nicholas, her physician mother explains his illness, AIDS. Depicts a meeting of concerned parents which results in a peaceful resolution. A child narrator and still pictures offer a reassuring lesson which concludes with a reminder of all the ways you "can't" catch AIDS. The static production, despite limitations, offers a nice opportunity for group sharing and discussion of age appropriate information.
SUBJ: AIDS (Disease)./ HIV infections.

VCR 616.97   Ph-1 4-6 $40.00   KD026
CONVERSATION WITH MAGIC (Videocassette). Hosts: Linda Ellerbee, Magic Johnson. Barr Films V258V ISBN 0-7823-0257-2, 1992. 1/2" VHS videocassette color (26min).
Includes teacher's guide.
Also available in Spanish.
Closed captioned.
Magic Johnson and children of various ages hold a very straightforward conversation about the differences between HIV and AIDS, the ways HIV is transmitted, and the importance of empathy for those who are infected. Magic is positive while some of the children are very poignant--one boy has a grown brother with AIDS, and two little girls were born with HIV. Children in the group ask natural questions, and the discussion deals honestly, but briefly, with common fears and the risks involved in doing drugs or engaging in unprotected sex.
SUBJ: AIDS (Disease)./ HIV infections.

VCR 616.97   Ph-2 5-6 $250.00   OD KD027
DOUBLE DUTCH--DOUBLE JEOPARDY (Videocassette). Durrin Productions, 1990. 1/2" VHS videocassette color (20min).
Includes public performance rights.
A lively school class engages in dialogue with a young man who is infected with AIDS. The discussion is frank and simple--the children ask many good questions; the conversation is intercut by segments in which they do rap scenes on the playground, cautioning viewers against the double jeopardy of drugs and unprotected sex. The obvious lessons are very comfortably conveyed by the children in this serious but upbeat discussion.
SUBJ: AIDS (Disease).

616.97   Ph-2 A/8 $21.00   L   KD028
GREENBERG, LORNA. AIDS: how it works in the body. Watts ISBN 0-531-20074-4; In Canada: Watts, 1992. 64p. col. ill. (First book).
Includes glossary, bibliography, directory and index.
This extensive discussion of the immune system explains how HIV particles interact with body cells. The clear, lucid technical material is illustrated primarily with computer-enhanced microphotographs; methods of spreading the disease are mentioned briefly in the middle of the book. The scientific approach complements other materials which focus more strongly on the human experience of AIDS.
SUBJ: AIDS (Disease)./ HIV infections.

616.97   Ph-2 2-4/7 $15.95   T   KD029
HAUSHERR, ROSMARIE. Children and the AIDS virus: a book for children, parents, and teachers. Clarion ISBN 0-89919-834-1, 1989. 48p. ill.
Includes bibliography and index.
Viruses cause colds, measles, mumps, chicken pox and AIDS. This two level (one for children/one for adults) photographic essay explains the ways in which the virus is and isn't transmitted and focuses on two infected children. Listings of health care precautions and resources for further information conclude this work which will be a useful adjunct to the health curriculum.
SUBJ: AIDS (Disease).

616.97   Ph-2 5-6/8 $14.85   L   KD030
HYDE, MARGARET O. Know about AIDS. 3rd ed. By Margaret O. Hyde and Elizabeth H. Forsyth. Illustrated by Debora Weber. Walker ISBN 0-8027-8346-5; In Canada: Thomas Allen, 1994. 102p. ill. (Know about).
Includes bibliography and index.
Short chapters describe the origins and effects of the disease, who gets it, how it is transmitted, research, treatment and growing concerns over costs and ethical issues. The text is dry; incorporating utilitarian cases and using conservative estimates. The information will be useful for reports but not particularly helpful for stimulating discussion.
SUBJ: AIDS (Disease).

VCR 616.97   Ph-1 5-6 $119.00   OD KD031
LET'S TALK ABOUT AIDS! (Videocassette). Human Relations Media 957-VSD ISBN 1-55548-556-1, 1992. 1/2" VHS videocassette color (14min).
Includes teacher's guide.
An attractive cast of children perform a dance and talk about AIDS with a social worker after they view a video introducing children with AIDS. Led by a young narrator, the scenes cut back and forth asking questions, exploring common misconceptions, and reiterating basic information about the AIDS virus. Intended to develop understanding and tolerance towards young victims of AIDS as well as to teach sensible behavior, this is down to earth and comfortable, frank and humorous. Excellent opportunity to initiate further discussion with children.
SUBJ: AIDS (Disease).

VCR 616.97   Ph-1 6-A $125.00   OD KD032
PROTECT YOURSELF: HIV/AIDS EDUCATION PROGRAM (Videocassette). United Learning 10088V, 1992. 1/2" VHS videocassette color (46min).
Includes teacher's guide and blackline masters.
A savvy AIDS educator leads a class of children through a frank, effective discussion of AIDS/HIV and a humorous, down-to-earth lesson on the way the epidemic has occurred through unsafe sexual practices. The film has a three-part structure with an introductory plea to parents for preadolescent sex education presented by actress Audrey Hepburn; two long classroom segments are intercut with flashbacks to the home lives of four students worried about dangerous situations involving family members. The featured teacher is an outstanding model; some adults will laud the sexual realities, and others will be uncomfortable; the final sensible message is that refraining from sex is a sensible option and protected sex a lifesaving necessity.
SUBJ: AIDS (Disease)./ HIV infections.

616.97   Ph-2 3-5/6 $12.88   L   KD033
SEIXAS, JUDITH S. Allergies - what they are, what they do. Illus. by Tom Huffman. Greenwillow ISBN 0-688-08877-5, 1991. 56p. col. ill. (Greenwillow read-alone).
Food, animals, air, chemicals, plants, fabrics and metals are all cited here as causes of allergies, and the quick survey sketches symptoms and methods of diagnosis and treatment. The economical text is embellished with small, cartoon-style drawings and explains the various allergies, a bit of medical history, and common treatments. The text is not as simple as the series name suggests, but the format is inviting to children with reading difficulties, and the information is a good introduction to this very common problem.
SUBJ: Allergy.

616.99   Ph-3 A/9 $16.95   L   KD034
YOUNT, LISA. Cancer. Lucent ISBN 1-56006-125-1, 1991. 112p. ill. (Overview).
Includes glossary, bibliography and index.
In-depth explanations cover the nature of cancerous cells and the causes, detection, and treatment of cancer. The discussion, technical but clear, covers many types of cancers and research. Poorly printed gray photographs include unsettling, graphic views of tumors and

enlarged pictures of cells. Substantial presentation provides good information for the capable reader.
SUBJ: Cancer.

617   Ph-2 A/9 $15.95   T   KD035
FACKLAM, MARGERY. Spare parts for people. By Margery and Howard Facklam. Harcourt Brace Jovanovich ISBN 0-15-277410-6, 1987. 143p. ill.
Includes glossary, bibliography and index.
Organ transplants, computers and electronics, and neurological experiments are among the many remarkable accomplishments of modern medical technology. Readable text and a useful selection of photographs describe fascinating procedures now used to replace or regenerate defective body parts--hearts, kidneys, bones, skin, and even portions of the brain. Final questions on how bionic man may become round out an informative introduction for older and advanced students.
SUBJ: Artificial organs./ Implants, Artificial./ Transplantation of organs, tissues, etc./ Prosthesis.

VCR 617.6   Ph-3 1-3 $99.00   OD KD036
GOOFY OVER DENTAL HEALTH (Videocassette). Disney Educational Productions 68287, 1991. 1/2" VHS videocassette color (13min).
Includes teacher's guide.
A boy meets cartoon character Goofy in a dream and learns basic practices of caring for his teeth. Animated sequences highlight the live-action presentation in which a dentist discusses the growth of permanent teeth, the importance of healthy snack habits, how to brush and floss, and the importance of fluoride. A simple, pleasant lesson in dental hygiene.
SUBJ: Teeth--Care and hygiene./ Dental care./ Dentists.

617.6   Ph-1 P-1/2 $14.93   L   KD037
ROCKWELL, HARLOW. My dentist. Greenwillow ISBN 0-688-84004-3, 1975. unp. col. ill.
Available from National Library Service for the Blind and Physically Handicapped in Braille BR03232.
A young female patient describes her first visit to the dentist, including his tools and procedures. The spare text is accompanied by large neat drawings. A comfortable atmosphere is created which will be good for young children. A companion to MY DOCTOR.
SUBJ: Dentists.

618.92   Ph-2 K-3/2 $12.95   L   KD038
COLLINS, PAT LOWERY. Waiting for baby Joe. Photos by Joan Whinham Dunn. Whitman ISBN 0-8075-8625-0; In Canada: General, 1990. unp. ill.
This realistic story follows a family's first anxious weeks after the birth of a premature baby. The simple text and competent photographs follow the experience of Missy, who is perhaps five years old, as she wakes in the night to learn of her new brother's early birth. There is a visit to Joe in his isolette, the weeks of waiting for him to recover from heart surgery, and his eventual arrival home. Missy's feelings are well portrayed, the simple explanations are just right, and the book nicely extends the body of literature on new babies.
SUBJ: Babies./ Brothers and sisters.

618.92   Ph-2 3-5/5 $14.95   L   KD039
EMMERT, MICHELLE. I'm the big sister now. Illus. by Gail Owens. Whitman ISBN 0-8075-3458-7; In Canada: General, 1989. unp. col. ill.
Emphasizing the love a family feels for a child severely handicapped with cerebral palsy, this slim account describes daily life as family members care for Amy and include her in many family activities. Narrated in the first person by Amy's younger sister and accompanied by full-page pastel illustrations, the text discusses the cause of cerebral palsy, Amy's serious incapacity, her poor health and small size, her congenial response to people, and caring efforts by family members and friends. In places the book is sentimental and unrealistic, but the open discussion of the severe problems associated with this fairly common condition will be useful to some libraries.
SUBJ: Cerebral palsy./ Physically handicapped.

618.92   Ph-3 K-2/2 $16.95   T   KD040
KOPLOW, LESLEY. Tanya and the Tobo Man/Tanya y el Hombre Tobo: a story in English and Spanish for children entering therapy Illus. by Eric Velasquez. Magination Press ISBN 0-945354-34-7; In Canada: dist. by Book Center, 1991. unp. ill.
This black and white picture book tells how a therapist helps Tanya overcome her fears of the imaginary Tobo Man. The dual language text is valuable, and the homely, didactic book is as useful for parents as it is for preparing children for seeing a therapist and for dealing with fearful and angry feelings. (Parents' Shelf.)
SUBJ: Psychotherapy./ Fear./ Spanish language materials./ Bilingual materials--Spanish.

618.92   Ph-2 5-6/7 $19.95   P   KD041
QUINN, PATRICIA O. Putting on the brakes: young people's guide to understanding attention deficit hyperactivity disorder (ADHD). By Patricia O. Quinn and Judith M. Stern. Illus. by Michael Chesworth. Magination Press ISBN 0-945354-32-0; In Canada: dist. by Book Center, 1991. 64p. ill.
Includes glossary.
Clear explanations introduce the symptoms and treatment of ADHD. Plentiful advice is offered to encourage children in managing school work and everyday tasks. The honesty and reassurance will be helpful to families, teachers, and children troubled by this frustrating disorder as well as other children.
SUBJ: Attention deficit disorders./ Hyperactive child syndrome.

VCR 621.31   Ph-1 4-A $89.00   OD KD042
HOT LINE: ALL ABOUT ELECTRICITY (Videocassette). Rainbow Educational Video RB802, 1987. 1/2" VHS videocassette color (15min).
Includes teacher's guide.
From static electricity to power plants, this fast-paced film defines and demonstrates electricity, its charges and circuits, in an interesting manner useful for science classes or projects. The guide provides additional experiments.
SUBJ: Electricity./ Electric circuits./ Electricity--Experiments.

VCR 621.32   Ph-3 1-3 $34.95   OD KD043
LIGHT BULBS (Videocassette). TVOntario/dist. by Films for the Humanities, 1991. 1/2" VHS videocassette color (10min). (Here's how!).
Viewers visit a light bulb factory for a step-by-step introduction to the manufacture of light bulbs. The assembly line process is shown in good detail and explained in a simple narrative. The information is interrupted by stage business from the television series--conversations among a talking balloon and a mouse and a little girl--but the information is fairly interesting.
SUBJ: Electric lamps./ Electric lighting./ Lighting.

621.38   Ph-1 A/8 $17.00   L   KD044
SKURZYNSKI, GLORIA. Get the message: telecommunications in your high-tech world. Bradbury ISBN 0-02-778071-6; In Canada: Maxwell Macmillan, 1993. 64p. col ill. (Your high-tech world).
Includes glossary and index.
Marvelous photographs of the inner workings of the technology behind cellular phones and satellite systems accompany interesting explanations of modern telephone communications. Begins with familiar examples of car phones, telefacsimile transmissions, and even videophones and goes on to clear discussion of the science of sound, electricity, and light and of the technology of microwaves, underwater cables, and fiber optics. The engaging view of what makes telecommunications work will be interesting for many readers and will inspire some to do further investigation.
SUBJ: Telephone./ Telecommunication./ Communication.

621.381   Ph-3 A/9 $11.95   T   KD045
ASIMOV, ISAAC. How did we find out about microwaves? Illus. by Erika Kors. Walker ISBN 0-8027-6837-7; In Canada: Thomas Allen, 1989. 63p. ill. (How did we find out).
Includes index.
Available from National Library Service for the Blind and Physically Handicapped on sound recording cassette RC31182.
Discusses the many waves passing through the atmosphere--light, sound, radio, electromagnetic--and tells the history of many related scientific discoveries that led to our understanding of microwaves. Arranged in chronological order, the text is readable and informative and illustrated with occasional gray wash pictures. Useful for readers who enjoy learning about the history of science, this is not a direct explanation of how microwaves function.
SUBJ: Microwaves.

621.39   Ph-3 4-6/7 $12.95   L OD KD046
GREENBERG, KEITH ELLIOT. Steven Jobs and Stephen Wozniak: creating the Apple computer. Illus. by James Spence. Blackbirch ISBN 1-56711-086-X, 1994. 48p. col. ill. (Partners).
Includes glossary, bibliography and index.
Two loners met over their interests in inventing and electronics, and their common interests developed into the creation of the Apple computer. Their desire to make computers available for everyone produced one of the success stories of the 80s.
SUBJ: Jobs, Steven./ Wozniak, Stephen Gary./ Computer engineers./ Apple Computer, Inc.

621.43   Ph-2 5-6/10 $17.99   L   KD047
MAURER, RICHARD. Rocket!: how a toy launched the space age. Crown ISBN 0-517-59629-6; In Canada: Random House, 1995. 64p. ill. (some col.).
Includes bibliography, directory and index.

The principles of rocket science and Robert Goddard's work in developing rockets intertwine in well crafted text and a fine assortment of photographs. The text, sidebars, and captions discuss how the use and understanding of rockets has evolved and include directions for experiments and building model rockets for further discovery. The lucid, thorough science and the life story are challenging, but absorbing fare, for students, teachers, and nonfiction readers. Goddard's boyhood reading of science fiction should fascinate some children.
SUBJ: Rocketry--History./ Goddard, Robert Hutchings.

621.47 Ph-3 2-4/7 $6.95 P KD048
HILLERMAN, ANNE. Done in the sun, solar projects for children. Illustrated by Mina Yamashita. Sunstone Press ISBN 0-86534-018-8, 1983. 31p. ill.
Includes bibliography.
Uses simple, enjoyable experiments to demonstrate the sun's usefulness as an energy source in printing images on paper and the skin (a sun "tattoo"), drying fruit, cooking hot dogs, telling time, and more. Clear directions, simple drawings, short anecdotes about three children performing the experiments, and a useful bibliography on sun power and study make this attractive for teachers and group leaders looking for educational activities.
SUBJ: Solar energy--Experiments./ Sun./ Experiments./ Handicraft.

621.48 Ph-2 5-A/11 $21.50 L KD049
WILCOX, CHARLOTTE. Powerhouse: inside a nuclear power plant. Photos by Jerry Boucher. Carolrhoda ISBN 0-87614-945-X, 1996. 48p. col. ill.
Includes glossary and index.
Nuclear reactors may yet be an efficient choice for generating the electricity Americans use in great quantities. This informative discussion, amply illustrated with photographs and diagrams, explains the atomic basis for nuclear energy, the construction of nuclear power plants, the workings of the reactor and control room, problems of storing nuclear wastes, accidents that have caused a decline in the use of nuclear plants, and possible future modifications. A solid, evenhanded presentation, this is a good introduction to nuclear power for older students. For environmental studies.
SUBJ: Nuclear power plants./ Power resources.

621.8 Ph-3 4-6/4 $9.95 T KD050
ARDLEY, NEIL. Science book of machines. Harcourt Brace Jovanovich ISBN 0-15-200613-3, 1992. 29p. col. ill.
"Gulliver books."
Simple gadgets made of cardboard boxes and othe common materials illustrate the principles of the pulley, lever, fulcrum, and other simple machines which are the basis for more complicated technology. Doublespread pages present a series of small photographs and fairly clear instructions along with superficial explanations of the principles involved. Children who enjoy making things will have fun with the toy-like mechanisms to demonstrate force, hydraulic lift, pulleys, etc. which also could be the basis for further development into science projects.
SUBJ: Simple machines--Experiments./ Machinery--Experiments./ Experiments.

621.8 Ph-2 K-4/6 $6.95 P KD051
ROBBINS, KEN. Power machines. Henry Holt ISBN 0-8050-5297-6; In Canada: Fitzhenry & Whiteside, c1993, 1997. unp. col. ill.
Payloaders, forklifts, concrete crushers, and tree spades are among the power machines featured in this excellent album. Hand-tinted photographs lend the machines a weathered look, and boldly printed action verbs head the brief descriptions of the work of each machine. Attractive survey provides a thoughtful introduction to these ever intriguing, giant pieces of equipment.
SUBJ: Machinery.

621.8 Ph-1 K-2/3 $13.95 L KD052
ROCKWELL, ANNE F. Machines. By Anne and Harlow Rockwell. Macmillan ISBN 0-02-777520-8, c1972. unp. col. ill.
Colorful full-page pictures introduce the classification of simple machines, and describe the lever, the pulley and the wheel. Bold print and watercolor paintings enhance the usefulness of this simple book.
SUBJ: Machinery.

621.8 Ph-1 P-2/3 $13.95 L KD053
ROTNER, SHELLEY. Wheels around. Houghton Mifflin ISBN 0-395-71815-5, 1995. unp. col. ill.
Selectors' Choice, 21st ed.
Bold photographs and spare text introduce an appealing variety of wheeled vehicles which "help us to work and play in many different ways." Wagons, wheelbarrows, skateboards, bicycles, baby strollers, wheelchairs, and a host of buses, trucks, and tractors are among the

attractive array of featured machines running on wheels--huge and small. Particularly nice book design will attract young truck fans and serve beautifully as versatile teaching material.
SUBJ: Wheels.

621.8 Ph-1 5-6/8 $11.93 L KD054
ZUBROWSKI, BERNIE. Wheels at work: building and experimenting with models of machines. Illus. by Roy Doty. Morrow ISBN 0-688-06348-9, 1986. 112p. ill. (Boston Children's Museum activity book).
Paper cups, milk cartons and other easily found objects are materials for a variety of models and experiments demonstrating gears, wheels and pulleys. Explanations of the principles and history of windmills, paddlewheels and other machines and contraptions accompany detailed instructions and plentiful diagrams. An inviting collection of projects in an agreeably homely format, this will be welcome material for science fairs or children who enjoy making things.
SUBJ: Machinery--Models./ Machinery--Experiments./ Models and modelmaking./ Experiments./ Science--Experiments.

621.9 Ph-1 P-K/2 $15.95 L KD055
GIBBONS, GAIL. Tool book. Holiday House ISBN 0-8234-0444-7, 1982. unp. col. ill.
Tools for building and many other kinds of work are grouped by function--measuring, cutting, shaping, pounding, and more. A minimal text and clear drawings in bright, primary colors introduce a wide variety of common and less familiar tools, each labeled and shown in use. An attractive concept book for teaching purposes and a picture book with sure child appeal.
SUBJ: Tools./ Building.

621.9 Ph-2 P-2/2 $15.93 L KD056
MORRIS, ANN. Tools. Photos by Ken Heyman. Lothrop, Lee & Shepard ISBN 0-688-10171-2, 1992. 32p. col. ill., map.
Includes index.
People from many countries demonstrate tools for cutting, cleaning, farming, eating, mending, and many other useful activities. Attractive photographs and very simple text introduce tools as universal implements. Includes brief notes that identify the country and activity featured in each picture. World map is the final piece in a thoughtful concept book which is also a nice lesson for multicultural studies.
SUBJ: Tools./ Implements, utensils, etc.

621.9 Ph-1 P-K/3 $3.95 P KD057
ROCKWELL, ANNE F. Toolbox. By Anne and Harlow Rockwell. Aladdin ISBN 0-689-71382-7, 1990. unp. col. ill.
Available from National Library Service for the Blind and Physically Handicapped in Braille BR02583.
Handsome, realistic paintings, usually of one object to a page, and a simple, brief text depict the tools found in the average toolbox and tell what each does. Attractive and appealing as well as useful.
SUBJ: Tools.

622 Ph-1 4-6/8 $16.95 T KD058
DEEM, JAMES M. How to hunt buried treasure. Illus. by True Kelley. Houghton Mifflin ISBN 0-395-58799-9, 1992. 192p. ill.
Includes bibliographies and index.
Selectors' Choice, 19th ed.
Tips for seeking several categories of buried treasure include many anecdotes and puzzles along with practical instructions. Humorous drawings accompany chapters discussing lost, hidden, and criminal treasures; historical information and artifacts; fossils; childhood belongings; legal aspects of ownership; and search and research techniques. The subject has widespread appeal, and the book is enjoyable and informative.
SUBJ: Buried treasure.

CE 623 Ph-1 A/9 $16.95 L KD059
MACAULAY, DAVID. Castle. Houghton Mifflin ISBN 0-395-25784-0, 1977. 74p. ill.
Caldecott Honor Book.
Selectors' Choice, 12th ed.
A beautiful combination of illustrations and text tells the story of the building and defense of a castle in 13th century Wales. The author's careful research is evident in the detail with which he explains the building of the fortification, the town and area population. Lovers of castles, fairy tales, fortifications, battles, and previous Macaulay books are sure to enjoy this title.
SUBJ: Castles./ Fortification.

623.7 Ph-2 4-6/8 $6.95 P KD060
CHASEMORE, RICHARD. Tanks. Illus. by Richard Chasemore. Written by Ian Harvey. DK Publishing ISBN 0-7894-0768-X, 1996. 30p. col. ill. (Look inside cross-sections).
Includes glossary and index.

Copious details of tank design and history appear in cutaway drawings, labels, captions, and small blips of text. Tanks of World War I and World War II predominate with a quick look at contemporary tanks used in the 1991 Gulf War. An impressive amount of information about the many uses of tanks as heavy duty machinery combines with bits of world and military history. The wealth of facts on this seldom discussed vehicle will intrigue readers interested in weapons, heavy machines, and war.
SUBJ: Tanks (Military science)./ Military weapons./ Vehicles, Military.

623.7   Ph-2 4-6/8 $6.95   P   KD061
JENSSEN, HANS. Jets. Illus. by Hans Jenssen. Written by Moira Butterfield. DK Publishing ISBN 0-7894-0767-1, 1996. 30p. col. ill. (Look inside cross-sections).
Includes glossary and index.
Ten military aircraft appear in the extensive detail of cutaway drawings, labels, captions, and bits of text. The copious barrage of facts and technical data covers plane parts, weaponry, design considerations, and many other aspects of history, use, and performance. Difficult at times and also unsatisfactory in visual clarity, this ambitious pastiche will appeal to readers with specialized interest in mechanics.
SUBJ: Jet planes, Military./ Airplanes, Military.

623.8   Ph-2 P-1 $14.93   L   KD062
CREWS, DONALD. Harbor. Greenwillow ISBN 0-688-00862-3, 1982. unp. col. ill.
Clean, colorful drawings and minimal text introduce the boats, ships and activity of a busy harbor. The body of the book focuses on the liners, freighters, tugboats, barges, etc. moving against a softly colored city skyline while the final page, called "Ship Shapes," presents a labelled black silhouette of each.
SUBJ: Harbors./ Boats and boating.

623.8   Ph-1 5-6/7 $20.99   L   KD063
KENTLEY, ERIC. Boat. Knopf ISBN 0-679-91678-4, 1992. 64p. col. ill. (Eyewitness books).
"Dorling Kindersley book."
Includes index.
Boats and ships from many periods and places appear in striking pictures demonstrating a great variety of designs and uses. Bits of text and informative captions introduce sailing vessels, rafts, luxury liners, merchant ships, steamships, paddle wheelers, various building techniques, and much more. An absorbing survey in a colorful, appealing volume.
SUBJ: Ships--History./ Boats and boating--History.

623.8   Ph-2 3-5/5 $7.99   P   KD064
LINCOLN, MARGARETTE. Amazing boats. Photos by Mike Dunning and Ray Moller. Knopf ISBN 0-679-82770-6, 1992. 29p. col. ill. (Eyewitness juniors).
Includes index.
Eye-catching photographs of featured boats and ships will draw browsers to this slim survey. Small sketches and picture captions convey miscellaneous bits of information about historic and contemporary vessels from various countries and briefly describe the form and function of canoes and rafts, steamships, fishing boats, rowboats, sailboats, life boats, gondolas, motorboats, working boats, and houseboats. Inadequate definitions and explanations, but an appealing presentation.
SUBJ: Boats and boating--History.

623.8   Ph-2 4-6/6 $11.95   L   KD065
STEELE, PHILIP. Boats. Crestwood House ISBN 0-89686-522-3; In Canada: Collier Macmillan, 1991. 32p. col. ill. (Pocket facts).
Includes index.
Many types of ships and smaller boats appear in this small quick survey which includes a bit of history and sketchy information on construction while focusing on the many different uses of ships. Vessels from different countries are shown in small, adequate photographs, and information is presented in numerous short entries. Explanations are clear though superficial, and the value of this small volume is in the number and variety of craft depicted.
SUBJ: Boats and boating./ Ships.

VCR 624   Ph-2 5-6 $49.95   OD KD066
BRIDGES (Videocassette). Kaw Valley Films & Video ISBN 1-56126-047-9, 1988. 1/2" VHS videocassette color (22min).
Includes discussion questions.
Viewed from various perspectives, the numerous bridges seen in use provide a dramatic sense of the scale and design of these ever interesting structures. In addition to describing four basic types of bridges (beam, arch, suspension, pontoon), this looks briefly at the history of bridges, the capabilities of different materials used in

construction, bridge maintenance, and the removal of unwanted bridges. The film covers considerable information quickly and might be best used in conjunction with books on the subject.
SUBJ: Bridges.

624   Ph-3 5-6/8 $14.95   L   KD067
DOHERTY, CRAIG A. Golden Gate Bridge. By Craig A. Doherty and Katherine M. Doherty. Blackbirch ISBN 1-56711-106-8, 1995. 48p. ill. (some col.), map. (Building America).
Includes glossary, chronology, bibliography and index.
It took great effort to plan, raise the money, and then construct this famous bridge. Four short chapters of text describe the background of the Depression years, some of the politics, and the work of construction. A fairly good assortment of small black and white and color photographs add some perspective on the enormity of the task. This is a handy, slim, utilitarian volume that will serve regional interests and provide useful material for some curriculum purposes elsewhere.
SUBJ: Golden Gate Bridge (San Francisco, Calif.)./ Bridges.

624   Ph-1 5-6/5 $18.95   T   KD068
MANN, ELIZABETH. Brooklyn Bridge. Illus. by Alan Witschonke. Mikaya Press/dist. by Firefly ISBN 0-9650493-0-2; In Canada: Mikaya Press/dist. by Firefly, 1996. 48p. col. ill. (Wonders of the world book).
Includes index.
Selectors' Choice, 21st ed.
John Roebling's dream of building a great suspension bridge over the East River from Brooklyn to lower Manhattan is the focus of this detailed discussion of how the bridge was constructed. Roebling's son Washington and wife Emily also receive their share of credit. The presentation in text, sidebars, historical photographs, and diagrams and original paintings by the illustrator explain the hazards of work in the underwater caissons to anchor the towers and the challenge of stringing the cable high above the bridge. The book combines an interesting human story with the science of bridge building, making it a versatile item for pleasure reading as well as science and social studies units.
SUBJ: Bridges./ Brooklyn Bridge (New York, N.Y.)--History./ Roebling, John Augustus./ Roebling, Washington Augustus./ Engineers.

624.1   Ph-2 K-2/2 $5.95   P   KD069
GIBBONS, GAIL. Tunnels. Holiday House ISBN 0-8234-0670-9, c1984, 1987. unp. col. ill.
Demonstrates the processes and steps in the construction and use of various types of tunnels by animals and humans in simple text and bright attractive drawings. The very spare, though very attractive presentation does have some problems because of its simplistic nature e.g. sometimes confusing diagrams, and lack of certain information. The abundance of vehicles, and the colorful diagrams of subway, mining, highway, water, and traffic tunnels merit the title's use in book talks.
SUBJ: Tunnels.

624.1   Ph-3 A/10 $16.95   T   KD070
MACAULAY, DAVID. Underground. Houghton Mifflin ISBN 0-395-24739-X, 1976. 109p. col. ill.
Profusely illustrated in same style used in author's Newbery Honor Book, CATHEDRAL (Houghton Mifflin, 1973), this publication concentrates on the subject of a city's various kinds of underground systems--kinds of pilings, foundations, water, sewage, drainage, and the like. More complex than the earlier titles, this one will still be of interest to mature readers and to students avid in their interest in technological matters.
SUBJ: Underground utility lines./ Cities and towns.

VCR 624.1   Ph-2 5-6 $49.95   OD KD071
TUNNELS (Videocassette). Kaw Valley Films & Video, 1987. 1/2" VHS videocassette color (19min).
Includes teacher's guide.
Includes public performance rights.
Tunnels as practical constructions for animals and humans have a long history, and this thoughtful examination explains how tunnels are constructed in both rocky and soft ground. Explanations of modern tunnel building follow the steps of excavating in the different types of terrain and the construction of the shield and tunnel lining. The importance of tunnels in transportation systems is explained in an informative view that should be interesting for personal viewing as well as classroom units.
SUBJ: Tunnels./ Engineering.

625.1   Ph-2 5-6/8 $20.99   L   KD072
COILEY, JOHN. Train. Photos by Mike Dunning. Knopf ISBN 0-679-91684-9, 1992. 64p. col. ill. (Eyewitness books).

"Dorling Kindersley book."
Includes index.
Vivid photographs, numerous drawings, and bits of text cover many aspects of railroad history. Topical pages describe early railroads, steam engines, the building of railroads, the laying of tracks, freight trains, luxury passenger trains, diesel and electric trains, future trains, and more. The international scope gives little attention to American trains, but the book is an informative and sumptuous browsing item.
SUBJ: Railroads--Trains.

625.1 Ph-3 1-3/3 $15.95 L KD073
GIBBONS, GAIL. Trains. Holiday House ISBN 0-8234-0640-7, 1987. unp. col. ill.
Passenger trains and freight trains, steam, diesel, and electric engines are presented in colorful, detailed illustrations and diagrams. Somewhat disorganized and overly sketchy, this still will please train buffs who've moved beyond "Freight Train."
SUBJ: Railroads--Trains.

625.1 Ph-2 4-6/6 $14.95 L KD074
GUNNING, THOMAS G. Dream trains. Dillon ISBN 0-87518-558-4; In Canada: Maxwell Macmillan, 1992. 71p. col. ill.
Includes chronology, glossary and index.
Electricity, computers, and sleek design are bringing new comfort and speed to railway travel in different parts of the world. Several chapters in a slim volume describe efficient modern trains which hang in magnetic suspension over rails built above highways or whiz through underwater tunnels in European countries, Japan, and the United States. Sketchy explanations and photographs provide just an introductory glimpse of these exciting vehicles of the present and future.
SUBJ: Railroads--Trains.

625.1 Ph-2 K-2/2 $15.99 T KD075
MAGEE, DOUG. All aboard ABC. By Doug Magee and Robert Newman. Cobblehill/Dutton ISBN 0-525-65036-9; In Canada: Fitzhenry & Whiteside, 1990. unp. col. ill.
An album of color photographs arranged in an alphabetical scheme introduces many aspects of trains. Airbrakes, boxcars, and couplers...different types of freight cars...a junction, roadbed, switch and vents are among the items mentioned in simple lines of text, while each page carries the designated letter in red upper and lower case figures. Young train fans will enjoy the many nice scenes, and beginning readers will be able to manage much of the text.
SUBJ: Alphabet./ Railroads--Trains.

VCR 625.2 Ph-3 3-4 $14.95 KD076
LET ME TELL YOU ALL ABOUT TRAINS (Videocassette). Traditional Images, 1993. 1/2" VHS videocassette color (30min). (Let me tell you...).
Includes public performance rights.
Trains old and new, the various jobs they do, and the people who run them are introduced in well-chosen clips of film. Passenger trains in their heyday, the variety of boxcars and freight, the traditional functions of the caboose, the advent of the modern "bullet" trains, and the vast computerized control centers are among the interesting topics. The faded look of the photography and the "young" tone of the film are slight drawbacks, but the multifaceted and appreciative view of trains is interesting and informative for pleasure viewing or study.
SUBJ: Railroads--Trains.

VCR 625.2 Ph-2 2-4 $135.00 KD077
TRAINS (Videocassette). Film Ideas TRN-31 ISBN 1-57557-021-1, 1995. 1/2" VHS videocassette color (13min). (Transportation series).
Includes public performance rights.
Many different trains appear in live photography and colorful drawings to explain how this form of transportation carries people and all kinds of freight. A simple, informative narrative tells how trains work, a bit of history, and the use of steam and diesel engines. Highlights the different types of cars used on freight and passenger trains, and a final segment introduces subway trains. Young train fans will enjoy the variety of engines and cars, and the well organized presentation will be very useful for classroom lessons on trains and transportation.
SUBJ: Railroads--Trains.

625.7 Ph-1 1-3/4 $14.89 L KD078
GIBBONS, GAIL. New road! Crowell/HarperCollins ISBN 0-690-04343-0, 1983. unp. col. ill.
Illustrates in small, bright pictures and simple text the machines and processes used to construct highways. Trucks and machines are all labelled and shown at work, while the text emphasis is on the planning and construction steps to make the road rather than on the

machinery. A useful and attractive introduction likely to be pored over by young readers and prereaders.
SUBJ: Road construction.

628.1 Ph-1 2-3/4 $14.95 L KD079
COLE, JOANNA. Magic School Bus at the waterworks. Illus. by Bruce Degen. Scholastic ISBN 0-590-43739-9, 1986. 40p. col. ill.
Includes author's notes.
Selectors' Choice, 16th ed.
Big book available (ISBN 0-590-72488-6, 1986).
Spanish version available AUTOBUS MAGICO VIAJA POR EL AGUA (ISBN 0-590-464272, 1992).
Ms. Frizzle may be strange but she's one great teacher. A class field trip to the city water works is a hilarious affair with a jaunt (bus and all) through clouds, into rain drops and down to the water works where the children learn first hand the source of their water, how it's purified and how it gets from the reservoir to their bathroom. The illustrations and text work perfectly together combining fantasy with fact and showing that acquiring scientific knowledge can be lots of fun.
SUBJ: Water treatment plants./ Spanish language materials.

628.3 Ph-2 5-6/10 $21.50 L KD080
COOMBS, KAREN MUELLER. Flush!: treating wastewater. Photos by Jerry Boucher. Carolrhoda ISBN 0-87614-879-8, 1995. 56p. col. ill.
Includes glossary and index.
Clear explanations and good photographs follow the path of waste water from the time it leaves a house until it is clean enough to flow back into a natural waterway. A bit of history is followed by information on septic tanks and sewers, screening and grit chambers, sedimentation and sludge, aeration, and disinfection. Includes explanations of algae problems in waterways and uses of reclaimed water, but problems of industrial pollution of water are mentioned only briefly. Interesting statistics and practical suggestions for water conservation conclude this clear, well organized examination of water resources. For environmental studies.
SUBJ: Sewage disposal.

628.4 Ph-1 4-6/7 $16.00 L KD081
BANG, MOLLY. Chattanooga sludge. Gulliver Green/Harcourt Brace ISBN 0-15-216345-X; In Canada: Harcourt Brace c/o Canadian Manda, 1996. unp. col. ill.
Richly constructed collage scenes and humorous sketches explain the true-to-life story of a scientist's work in using bacteria to clean up poisonous waterways. A brief sketch of how the Chattanooga Creek developed over eons and became poisoned by modern industry precedes the explanations of a congenial biologist who constructed an impressive experiment using tanks of bacteria-laden water to break down the chemicals in the sludge. The imaginative format combines well with serious science to create an absorbing lesson about toxic wastes, recycling, and the structure of living organisms. For environmental studies.
SUBJ: Pollution./ Recycling (Waste)./ Environmental protection./ Man--Influence on nature.

VCR 628.4 Ph-2 5-6 $99.00 OD KD082
RECYCLING: THE ENDLESS CIRCLE (Videocassette). National Geographic 51514, 1992. 1/2" VHS videocassette color (23min).
Includes teacher's guide.
Monumental amounts of trash flow into landfills, incinerators, and recycling plants in this multifaceted tour. The thought-provoking discussion explains the heavy use of energy and raw materials in manufacturing and shows many of the steps at different recycling plants. The many ideas covered require attentive viewing and offer good possibilities for discussion and further investigation.
SUBJ: Recycling (Waste)./ Refuse and refuse disposal.

628.4 Ph-1 2-3/3 $14.89 L KD083
SHOWERS, PAUL. Where does the garbage go? Rev. ed. Illus. by Randy Chewning. HarperCollins ISBN 0-06-021057-5; In Canada: HarperCollins, 1994. 32p. col. ill. (Let's-read-and-find-out science book).
A school class learns about landfills, incinerators, and recycling plants in a clear, cheerful introduction to contemporary methods of trash and garbage disposal. Colorful cartoon scenes and diagrams explain how the various methods work and emphasize the need for everyone to recycle. A practical item for teaching, this will also be informative and thought provoking for family use. For environmental studies.
SUBJ: Refuse and refuse disposal./ Recycling (Waste).

628.5 Ph-2 5-6/7 $17.95 L KD084
RYBOLT, THOMAS R. Environmental experiments about air. By Thomas R. Rybolt and Robert C. Mebane. Enslow ISBN 0-89490-409-4, 1993. 96p. ill. (Science experiments for young people).
Includes index.

Simple experiments demonstrate the composition of air and the effects of natural phenomena and human activity on both the air we breathe and the more cosmic ranges of earth's atmosphere. Oxygen, ozone, thermal inversions, solar energy, the greenhouse effect, dust and smoke, and many aspects of pollution are all subjects. Each experiment is titled with a specific question and includes a materials list, procedures, observation questions, discussion of results, and simple line drawings. Information on any topic is limited but useful, and the experiments should aid understanding of these timely topics. For environmental studies.
SUBJ: Air--Experiments./ Air--Pollution--Experiments./ Greenhouse effect, Atmospheric--Experiments./ Experiments.

628.9   Ph-3 4-5/6 $21.50   L   KD085
BOUCHER, JERRY. Fire truck nuts and bolts. Carolrhoda ISBN 0-87614-783-X, 1993. 40p. col. ill.
A brief essay text and plentiful photographs explain the many tasks involved in the design and building of a pumper fire engine. After an ordinary truck chassis is delivered, workers develop plans, mount hardware, cut metal sheets, and paint the newly created parts. The pictures do not adequately capture the construction process, causing some confusion, but the subject is so intriguing that serious readers will stick with it.
SUBJ: Fire engines--Design and construction./ Trucks.

628.9   Ph-1 P-2/4 $14.89   L   KD086
GIBBONS, GAIL. Fire! Fire! Crowell/HarperCollins ISBN 0-690-04416-X, 1984. unp. col. ill.
Available from National Library Service for the Blind and Physically Handicapped on sound recording cassette RC23455.
Explains how firefighters fight fires in the city, in the country, in the forest, and on the waterfront. Bright, busy pictures provide details and action, and the book concludes with illustrated lists of additional equipment, fire prevention tips, and instructions for safely exiting a building in case of fire. A colorful, inviting addition on a popular subject.
SUBJ: Fire extinction./ Fire fighters.

628.9   Ph-1 K-3/5 $15.00   L   KD087
KUKLIN, SUSAN. Fighting fires. Bradbury ISBN 0-02-751238-X; In Canada: Maxwell Macmillan, 1993. unp. col. ill.
Firefighters at work are the focus of color photographs and informative text explaining equipment and tasks. Trucks, clothing, rescue operations, and dealing with smoke are described. Final page lists fire prevention and safety rules. Many children enjoy reading about this subject, and the book offers a good introduction to this important line of work. For career units.
SUBJ: Fire fighters./ Fire extinction.

628.9   Ph-1 P/3 $13.99   L   KD088
ROCKWELL, ANNE F. Fire engines. By Anne Rockwell. Dutton ISBN 0-525-44259-6; In Canada: Fitzhenry & Whiteside, 1986. 24p. col. ill.
Shows several types of fire trucks and other vehicles which assist in fighting fires--the firehouse, ambulance, the fire chief's car, and fireboats. Set as a slight story of a family of Dalmations in human guise, the book features colorful full-page pictures of the fire trucks so popular with young children.
SUBJ: Fire engines./ Fire fighters.

629.04   Ph-2 P-2/4 $4.99   P   KD089
RADFORD, DEREK. Cargo machines and what they do. Candlewick ISBN 1-56402-434-2, 1992. unp. col. ill.
Colorful drawings and simple labels and explanations introduce huge trucks and cranes which lift and transport heavy loads. Doublepage scenes depict a cast of uniformed bears loading and operating a cargo plane, log loader, sea cargo, gasoline tanker, dump trucks, car transporter, circus truck, snow vehicles, low bed, garbage truck, space vehicles, and a fire engine. The space vehicles and fire engines are poorly presented, but young children will generally relish the clear presentation on this ever popular topic.
SUBJ: Cargo handling--Equipment./ Machinery.

629.13   Ph-3 6-A/10 $21.50   L   KD090
BRIGGS, CAROLE S. At the controls: women in aviation. Lerner ISBN 0-8225-1593-8, 1991. 72p. ill. (some col.).
Includes index.
Following a brief history of the Ninety-Nines, a group of women pilots, are biographies of women who have excelled and won recognition for women in aviation.
SUBJ: Women air pilots./ Air pilots.

629.13   Ph-1 1-4/2 $14.95   L   KD091
BURLEIGH, ROBERT. Flight: the journey of Charles Lindbergh. Illus. by Mike Wimmer. Philomel ISBN 0-399-22272-3; In Canada: Putnam, 1991.
unp. col. ill.
Available from the National Library Service for the Blind and Physically Handicapped on sound recording cassette RC 36557.
Spare, descriptive text set against dramatic doublespread paintings re-creates Charles Lindbergh's historic thirty-three and a half hour flight from New York to Paris. Without a radio or parachute and with an extra fuel tank blocking his view, Lindbergh flew through fog, ice, and darkness, while battling the need for sleep, often uncertain of his course. The strong, deeply hued and detailed pictures bring this famous adventure to life in a handsome, satisfying picture book for readers of all ages.
SUBJ: Lindbergh, Charles A./ Air pilots./ Transatlantic flights.

629.13   Ph-1 4-6/3 $5.95   P   KD092
BURLEIGH, ROBERT. Flight: the journey of Charles Lindbergh. Illus. by Mike Wimmer. Introduction by Jean Fritz. PaperStar ISBN 0-698-11425-6; In Canada: Putnam, 1991. unp. col. ill.
Skillful paintings and terse text follow Charles Lindbergh's 1927 flight from New York to Paris. The handsome picture book presentation, incorporating short quotes from Lindbergh's diary, provides a fine over-the-shoulder, firsthand sense of the pilot's struggle to stay awake, his encounter with fog, and other details of his lonely journey. This riveting account should be enjoyed by readers of many ages as a great adventure or as an introduction to longer works on Lindbergh.
SUBJ: Air pilots./ Transatlantic flights./ Lindbergh, Charles A.

629.13   Ph-2 P-1 $14.88   L   KD093
CREWS, DONALD. Flying. Greenwillow ISBN 0-688-04319-4, 1986. unp. col. ill.
Follows the flight of a plane as it takes off, flies over the airport, highways, rivers, cities, countryside, mountains, into the clouds, above the clouds, heads down again, and lands. Bright, simple pictures of a red and white plane and simplified views and minimal, bold-faced text introduce the young child to the view below as a plane moves through its flight.
SUBJ: Flight./ Airplanes.

629.13   Ph-1 A/7 $18.95   L   KD094
FREEDMAN, RUSSELL. Wright brothers: how they invented the airplane. Holiday House ISBN 0-8234-0875-2, 1991. 129p. ill.
Includes bibliography and index.
Newbery Honor Book.
Selectors' Choice, 19th ed.
Available from the National Library Service for the Blind and Physically Handicapped on sound recording cassette RC34862.
Orville and Wilbur Wright were photographers as well as inventors, and a beautiful selection of their photographs illustrate this interesting presentation of their work in developing the airplane. Freedman writes about the lives of the Wrights and the earlier history of attempts at flight. Exceptionally informative and attractive, this provides a fresh examination of these important achievements which truly launched the age of flight.
SUBJ: Wright, Orville./ Wright, Wilbur./ Aeronautics--Biography.

629.13   Ph-1 K-2/2 $14.95   L   KD095
GIBBONS, GAIL. Flying. Holiday House ISBN 0-8234-0599-0, 1986. unp. col. ill.
Presents a sketchy history of flying vehicles and a bright album of various aircraft in use today. A brief text describes the uses of balloons, gliders, blimps, helicopters, jets, rockets, and space shuttles, which are all shown in colorful, flat pictures. A short chronology of famous flights concludes a sprightly introduction that is sure to please.
SUBJ: Aeronautics--History./ Flight--History.

629.13   Ph-2 1-3/1 $15.96   L   KD096
MARQUARDT, MAX. Wilbur and Orville and the flying machine. Illustrated by Mike Eagle. Raintree ISBN 0-8172-3530-2, 1989. 30p. col. ill. (Real readers).
Wilbur and Orville Wright turn their childhood interest in kits and other flying toys into the first successful airplane in this simple story of their life and work. Developed specifically for early independent reading, the easy-to-read text is cheerfully illustrated with scenes conveying a good sense of the late 19th century life and the work of the Wrights. Sketchy and sometimes wooden, this is an acceptable overview and one of the better items in a marginal series.
SUBJ: Wright, Wilbur./ Wright, Orville./ Aeronautics--Biography.

VCR 629.13   Ph-2 2-4 $39.95   OD   KD097
OTHER THINGS THAT FLY (Videocassette). Films for the Humanities 4850, 1994. 1/2" VHS videocassette color (15min). (Look up).
Closed captioned.
A group of children observe three flying crafts--helicopters, kites, and hang gliders--and then make their own projects to demonstrate basic principles of flight. Cheerful lyrics and the gimmicky use of a robot

woman and a small animated creature representing imagination help the children to ask questions about things that fly. Attractive live-action photography and diagrams explain the basic premises of lift, thrust, and thermal action. The presentation assumes further discussion and reading, and the suggested craft and writing projects are inviting opportunities for learning.
SUBJ: Flight.

CE 629.13 Ph-1 K-2/4 $14.95 L KD098
PROVENSEN, ALICE. Glorious flight: across the channel with Louis Bleriot. By Alice and Martin Provensn. Viking ISBN 0-670-34259-9; In Canada: Penguin, 1983. 39p. col. ill.
Caldecott Medal Award.
Selectors' Choice, 15th ed.
Read-along kit available from Live Oak (ISBN 0-87499-062-9). 1 hardback book, 1 sound cassette (8min), $37.95.
VHS videocassette available from Live Oak Media ISBN 0-87499-056-4 (11min), $34.95.
Persisting despite repeated failures Louis Bleriot finally achieved success and after six years of effort flew his eleventh aircraft across the English Channel in 1909. The simple text has a somewhat European construction and flavor well suited to the subtly designed richly detailed paintings which feature shifts in perspective between earth and plane. Sumptious story and history to be shared with a group.
SUBJ: Bleriot, Louis./ Air pilots./ Airplanes--Design and construction.

629.13 Ph-3 5-6/6 $12.95 L OD KD099
ROZAKIS, LAURIE. Dick Rutan and Jeana Yeager: flying non-stop around the world. Illus. by Jerry Harston. Blackbirch ISBN 1-56711-087-8, 1994. 48p. col. ill. (Partners).
Includes chronology, glossary, bibliography and index.
Nine days and nights to fly around the world without stopping or refueling! This is the amazing feat accomplished by Rutan and Yeager in 1986. Many drawings show the plane and the daring pair planning and executing their flight.
SUBJ: Voyager (Airplane)./ Rutan, Dick./ Yeager, Jeana./ Flights around the world.

629.13 Ph-2 4-6/6 $11.95 L KD100
STEELE, PHILIP. Planes. Crestwood House ISBN 0-89686-524-X; In Canada: Collier Macmillan, 1991. 32p. ill. (some col.). (Pocket facts).
Includes index.
This small volume offers an orderly progression of brief explanations of flight principles, plane design and construction, and the use of planes in transporting people and freight. Simple diagrams and adequate photographs illustrate the many short topics which include the tasks of flight and maintenance crews, the activities at airports and in air control towers, and future design of planes. A double page of miscellany concludes the serviceable introduction to aircraft.
SUBJ: Airplanes.

629.13 Ph-2 3-6/6 $14.99 T KD101
VAN METER, VICKI. Taking flight: my story. With Dan Gutman. Viking ISBN 0-670-86260-6; In Canada: Penguin, 1995. 134p. ill. (some col.), maps.
Available from the National Library Service for the Blind and Physically Handicapped on sound recording cassette RC 42431.
Vicki describes her decision to take flying lessons, her perseverance, her goals to fly across the United States and the Atlantic, and her acceptance of the role as the youngest pilot to accomplish both these feats. Much humor and insight into how a youngster can reach what to many seem impossible goals.
SUBJ: Air pilots./ Women air pilots./ Van Meter, Vicki./ Children's writings.

629.13 Ph-2 4-6/6 $15.95 T KD102
WEISS, HARVEY. Strange and wonderful aircraft. Houghton Mifflin ISBN 0-395-68716-0, 1995. 64p. ill.
Early contraptions leading to the Wright brothers' successful flight appear in attractive prints, original cartoons, and early photographs. Gives an especially clear account of how humans finally began to understand the principles of aerodynamics. The readable, attractive history of flying experiments is handsomely assembled with effective use of blue to enliven the black and white format. Simple experiments are suggested to readers along the way. A fine introduction which should satisfy a wide audience of readers and encourage many to find out more.
SUBJ: Flight--History./ Airplanes--History.

629.132 Ph-2 A/8 $17.95 T KD103
LINDBLOM, STEVEN. Fly the hot ones. Houghton Mifflin ISBN 0-395-51075-9, 1991. 102p. ill. (some col.).
Author/pilot Lindblom introduces eight assorted aircraft that stretch

the limits of flight in particular ways. Using a "you are there" approach, he describes the actual experience of flying the Pitts S-2B Aerobatic Biplane, the P-51D Mustang, the Janus Sailplane, and others; black and white photographs along with a color inset and numerous crude sketches complement the text. Written by a real flying enthusiast, this includes ample encouragement for readers who dream of becoming pilots.
SUBJ: Airplanes--Piloting.

629.133 Ph-2 4-6/8 $21.20 L KD104
BARRETT, NORMAN S. Flying machines. By Norman Barrett. Watts ISBN 0-531-14301-5; In Canada: Nelson, 1994. 48p. col. ill. (Visual guides).
Includes index.
Plentiful drawings, photographs, and diagrams fill the short entries of this survey of historical and contemporary aircraft. One long section is devoted to airliners, and shorter units cover design elements and flight principles of helicopters, rocket planes, hot air balloons, airships, and space shuttles. Record breaking flights, famous firsts, and other miscellaneous bits are included. Pictorial elements and explanations could both be more clearly done, but the variety and detail will please many readers intrigued by planes.
SUBJ: Airplanes./ Flight.

629.133 Ph-1 4-6/7 $9.50 L KD105
BELLVILLE, CHERYL WALSH. Airplane book. Carolrhoda ISBN 0-87614-686-8, 1991. 48p. col. ill.
Includes glossary and index.
Historical and contemporary photographs are the handsome focus of this survey of the history and principles of flight and of the features of many different planes. The author weaves easily through a knowledgeable commentary about the experiences of pilots and an appealing array of aircraft from the early gliders to contemporary experimental models. Attractive album offers an excellent overview of planes and flight.
SUBJ: Airplanes.

629.133 Ph-3 3-6/5 $13.00 T KD106
BROWNE, GERARD. Aircraft: lift-the-flap book. Illus. by Gerard Browne. Lodestar/Dutton ISBN 0-525-67351-2, 1992. unp. col. ill.
Flaps lift to reveal the frames, engines, and inner compartments of the eight contemporary and futuristic aircraft pictured in this brief survey. A small passenger plane, passenger jet, supersonic jet, helicopter, transport aircraft, jet fighter, new passenger planes, and space planes are described in single pages of text facing the large "flapped" pictures and other small sketches. A perishable but appealing item which offers a sensible introduction to the design and structure of aircraft.
SUBJ: Airplanes./ Toy and movable books.

629.133 Ph-2 5-6/8 $14.95 L KD107
CURLEE, LYNN. Ships of the air. Houghton Mifflin ISBN 0-395-69338-1, 1996. 32p. col. ill.
Includes bibliography.
Three centuries of hot-air and hydrogen balloons and dirigibles for military use, pleasure, polar exploration, and passenger transportation are introduced in a slim, informative history. Several attractive paintings illustrate the account, but this is a text-dominated presentation which focuses on such highlights as the work of the Montgolfiers, Von Zeppelin, and several other inventors; the explosion of the Hindenburg and many other airship accidents; and the current resurgence of interest in balloons. A careful, interesting introduction, this will be especially enjoyed by nonfiction readers and aircraft fans.
SUBJ: Airships--History./ Hot air balloons--History.

629.133 Ph-1 1-3/4 $4.95 P KD108
GIBBONS, GAIL. Catch the wind!: all about kites. Little, Brown ISBN 0-316-30996-6; In Canada: Little, Brown, 1989. unp. col. ill.
Sam and Katie visit Ike's Kite Shop, learn about different types of kites, and choose kites to fly in a festival. Gibbons uses bright flat pictures and a simple story to convey considerable information about the history and design of kites and practical pointers on flying them. An attractive introduction to the subject and also a pleasant choice for nonfiction reading.
SUBJ: Kites.

629.133 Ph-2 5-6/7 $14.95 L KD109
GUNNING, THOMAS G. Dream planes. Dillon ISBN 0-87518-556-8; In Canada: Maxwell Macmillan, 1992. 72p. col. ill.
Includes chronology and index.
Sleek, fast, and unusual aircraft along with their designers and pilots appear in photographs and discussion of recent designs and future possibilities. Chapters discuss several types of aircraft--business and personal planes, airliners, war planes, vertical-lift planes--and future

sources of power. A good combination of factual information and informed speculation for readers with a serious interest in planes.
SUBJ: Airplanes./ Aeronautics.

629.133 Ph-3 4-6/6 $11.44 L KD110
KERROD, ROBIN. Amazing flying machines. Photos. by Mike Dunning. Knopf ISBN 0-679-92765-4, 1992. 29p. col. ill. (Eyewitness juniors).
Includes index.
Gliders, hot air balloons, biplanes, jets, and seaplanes are among the many aircraft featured in photographs, drawings, and bits of discussion. There's a bit of history, mechanics, principles of flight, and recent developments--all brushed over quickly in picture captions. The sketchy miscellany provides a skimpy overview and an attractive browsing item.
SUBJ: Airplanes--History./ Flight--History.

VCR 629.133 Ph-3 4-5 $14.95 KD111
LET ME TELL YOU ALL ABOUT PLANES (Videocassette). Traditional Images, 1994. 1/2" VHS videocassette color (60min). (Let me tell you...).
Includes public performance rights.
Two children learn about the history of human flight and the principles of flight while touring a local airfield with their grandfather. Grandfather's clear, leisurely narration is accompanied by interesting film segments of historical and modern aircraft. The film's length makes it a good choice for home viewing, but it could be shown in segments for classroom use.
SUBJ: Airplanes./ Airplanes--History./ Flight--History.

629.133 Ph-2 3-6 $14.89 L KD112
SIEBERT, DIANE. Plane song. Illus. by Vincent Nasta. HarperCollins ISBN 0-06-021467-8; In Canada: HarperCollins, 1993. unp. col. ill.
Jumbo jets, firefighting planes, planes for dusting farmers' crops, and many other aircraft soar through bold oil paintings in a poetic survey. The distinctive introduction employs sparce poetry and striking art to pay an appreciative tribute to the different types of work accomplished by planes and their pilots. A fine accompaniment to a variety of study units on transportation and work, this will be widely enjoyed for browsing, reading aloud, and booktalking.
SUBJ: Airplanes./ Stories in rhyme.

629.133 Ph-2 3-5/6 $12.95 L KD113
SIMON, SEYMOUR. Paper airplane book. Illus. by Byron Barton. Viking ISBN 0-670-53797-7, c1971. 48p. ill.
Fly plain and fancy paper airplanes while you learn what keeps them up, through simple scientific experiments and explanations of concepts and terms.
SUBJ: Airplanes--Models./ Paper work.

629.222 Ph-2 5-6/8 $11.85 L KD114
FORD, BARBARA. Automobile. Walker ISBN 0-8027-6725-7; In Canada: Thomas Allen, 1987. 57p. ill. (Inventions that changed our lives).
Includes index.
Discusses the historical development of the automobile, its social impact through the decades, and recent efforts to improve the safety and efficiency of cars. Six informative chapters and an interesting selection of photographs begin with the intriguing bicycle-like vehicles developed by Benz and Daimler in the late 1800s and move through the career of Henry Ford, early automobile races, the development of motels and national parks as adjuncts to automobile travel, and much more. The small volume is a bit drab in appearance and has several noted errors, but the subject matter is appealing.
SUBJ: Automobiles.

629.222 Ph-2 P/1 $4.99 P KD115
ROCKWELL, ANNE F. Cars. By Anne Rockwell. Penguin ISBN 0-14-054741-X, 1992. unp. col. ill.
Notes a few salient points about automobiles--they are fast, slow, new, old, big, small--and depicts a variety of them in flat, bright, happy illustrations. All of the drivers, passengers, and other characters in the busy scenes are dogs in human dress. Cute in tone and slight on content, the attractive picture book format will please very young car buffs.
SUBJ: Automobiles.

629.222 Ph-2 P-2/2 $6.95 T KD116
ROYSTON, ANGELA. Cars. Photos by Tim Ridley. Illus. by Jane Cradock-Watson and Dave Hopkins. Aladdin/Macmillan ISBN 0-689-71517-X, 1991. 21p. col. ill. (Eye openers).
"Dorling Kindersley book."
Vivid views of cars dominate the pages of this small survey. Each doublespread entry includes brief, simple statements about the featured car, one big bright photograph, and small labeled drawings of common car parts. Cars include a hatchback, sedan, convertible,

sports car, racing car, vintage car, jeep, and police car. Young car fans will enjoy this cheerful looking introduction.
SUBJ: Automobiles.

629.224 Ph-1 P-1/1 $14.89 L KD117
GIBBONS, GAIL. Trucks. Crowell/HarperCollins ISBN 0-690-04119-5, 1981. unp. col. ill.
Numerous bright, clear drawings of trucks at work will delight many a child. A minimal text mentions the type of work done by each group of trucks, and near each vehicle is a red label indicating it's generic name (vendor truck, straight truck, tank truck, and many, many more). The comfortable small size of the book, the care for detail, and the inherent appeal of the subject guarantee ready popularity.
SUBJ: Trucks.

629.224 Ph-2 2-3/3 $14.95 L KD118
HORENSTEIN, HENRY. Sam goes trucking. Houghton Mifflin ISBN 0-395-44313-X, 1989. 39p. col. ill.
Young Sam is thrilled to spend the day with his father in Dad's big 16 wheeler Mack truck. The text is factual and nearly full-page color photographs give young truck fans every detail of trucking from hitching the trailer to the cab to CB radios.
SUBJ: Truck driving.

629.224 Ph-1 K-5/4 $14.99 L KD119
MARSTON, HOPE IRVIN. Big rigs. Rev. and updated ed. Cobblehill/Dutton ISBN 0-525-65123-3, 1993. unp. col. ill.
Includes glossary.
With exceptionally well-chosen photographs, this appealing survey describes the parts of big trucks and introduces assorted trailers designed for different types of loads. The clear, simple text explains the interiors and shapes of cabs and gives a brief overview of the hitching mechanism and engine. Most of the book focuses on a generous assortment of trucks with a section devoted to the emblems and grills of the most frequently seen tractors. Glossary of CB radio terms rounds out a thoughtful presentation sure to satisfy truck enthusiasts. Not overly technical, but nicely informative.
SUBJ: Tractor trailers./ Trucks.

CDR 629.225 Ph-2 K-3 $39.95 OD KD120
BIG JOB (CD-ROM). Discovery Channel Multimedia ISBN 1-56331-214-X, 1995. 1 CD-ROM color.
Includes user's guide.
System requirements: Windows 3.1 or Windows 95; 486SX or higher; 4MB of RAM (8MB recommended); double speed CD-ROM drive; Windows compatible audio board; mouse; VGA display (256 colors); MS-DOS version 3.3 or higher; MSCDEX version 2.2 or later.
System requirements: Macintosh Performa, Centris, Quadra, or PowerMac series computer; System 7.0 or later; doublespeed CD-ROM drive; 4MB of RAM (8MB recommended); color monitor with at least 256 colors.
Product (1-56331-214-X) runs on either Macintosh or Windows compatible hardware.
Community helper learning centers will be enriched by this CD-ROM. Interactive tours, construction options, and information are available for the jobs of farmer, firefighter, and construction worker. Excellent sound and directions allow the program to be used by limited readers. Use in conjunction with career studies in primary grades.
SUBJ: Construction equipment--Software./ Software--Construction equipment./ Trucks--Software./ Software--Trucks./ Interactive media.

629.225 Ph-2 K-2/5 $4.95 P KD121
DIGGERS AND DUMPERS. Snapshot ISBN 1-56458-731-2, 1994. 32p. col. ill.
Bold photographs on white pages and brief explanations introduce a fine variety of forklifts, bulldozers, excavators, and other giant vehicles. Each entry names the equipment, its major features, and its functions. An attractive survey and introduction for young truck fans.
SUBJ: Earthmoving machinery./ Construction equipment.

629.225 Ph-1 P-2 $14.93 L KD122
HOBAN, TANA. Dig, drill, dump, fill. Greenwillow ISBN 0-688-84016-7, 1975. 32p. ill.
A photographic essay on large, heavy duty machines by this renowned photographer. The "on the job" action shots will be a big hit with young students. The book is wordless, with the exception of a pictorial glossary.
SUBJ: Earthmoving machinery--Pictorial works./ Construction equipment--Pictorial works./ Machinery--Pictorial works.

629.225 Ph-2 P-2/4 $7.95 T KD123
ROYSTON, ANGELA. Diggers and dump trucks. Photos by Tim Ridley. Illus. by Jane Cradock-Watson and Dave Hopkins. Aladdin/Macmillan ISBN 0-689-71516-1, 1991. 21p. col. ill. (Eye openers).

"Dorling Kindersley book."
Bold photographs of big trucks dominate the pages of this small volume. A few sentences of information and several small labeled sketches fill each double-page entry, introducing a bulldozer, excavator, tilting dumper, backhoe, dump truck, forklift, tunneling loader, and giant dump truck. Simple survey appealing to young truck fans.
SUBJ: Earthmoving machinery.

629.227   Ph-1 2-5/3 $15.95   L   KD124
GIBBONS, GAIL. Bicycle book. Holiday House ISBN 0-8234-1199-0, 1995. unp. col. ill.
Plentiful facts on bicycle history, mechanics, and riding accompany cheerful drawings in this simple introduction. The variety of bikes and the labeled diagrams are especially useful, and there are safety rules and tips on bicycle care. A practical and interesting guide to bicycle ownership and use.
SUBJ: Bicycles and bicycling./ Bicycles and bicycling--Safety measures.

629.227   Ph-1 5-6/6 $15.99   T   KD125
HAUTZIG, DAVID. Pedal power: how a mountain bike is made. Lodestar/Dutton ISBN 0-525-67508-6; In Canada: McClelland & Stewart, 1996. 31p. col. ill.
Includes index.
This visit to a bicycle factory explains the construction and importance of the many parts of the familiar mountain bikes most people ride today. Informative text and color photographs follow the work of many people through the stages of manufacturing. Concludes with tips on purchasing a bike and riding safety. The details of bicycle mechanics will interest a wide variety of bike riders.
SUBJ: Bicycles and bicycling.

629.227   Ph-1 3-5/6 $7.99   P   KD126
LORD, TREVOR. Amazing bikes. Photos by Peter Downs. Knopf ISBN 0-679-82772-2, 1992. 29p. col. ill. (Eyewitness juniors).
Includes index.
Bicycles and motorbikes of many eras and countries appear in large clear photographs and numerous small sketches in an appealing survey of this popular vehicle. Picture captions provide assorted bits of information about historical bikes, sports models, unusual designs, and bikes used for work and pleasure in different parts of the world. Attractive introduction and overview for bike enthusiasts.
SUBJ: Bicycles and bicycling--History./ Motorcycles--History.

VCR 629.27   Ph-1 K-6 $49.95   OD   KD127
SEAT BELTS ARE FOR KIDS TOO (Videocassette). AIMS Media 9921, 1987. 1/2" VHS videocassette color (10min). (Adventures of safety frog).
Includes discussion guide.
Delightful, fast-paced, and colorful, this video stars the Schiefilly Puppets in "The Adventures of Safety Frog" which presents poignant evidence for wearing seatbelts. Explains the dangers of jumping, arguing, throwing a ball, etc. in a moving automobile, interspersed with film of dummies in test crashes. Ear-and-eye-catching explanations follow of how to buckle baby, big kids and adults into their seatbelts for safe travel. Cost may be a problem, but this video cuts across grade levels in appeal and is well done.
SUBJ: Safety education.

629.28   Ph-1 P-2/3 $4.95   P   KD128
FLORIAN, DOUGLAS. Auto mechanic. Mulberry ISBN 0-688-13104-2, 1994. unp. col. ill. (How we work).
Effective watercolor scenes follow many tasks of an auto mechanic, naming parts of the automobile engine and tools that are used. The very brief text is specific but limited to naming activities and objects without further explanation. The simplicity of this introduction will be very satisfying to younger children who love cars and machines.
SUBJ: Automobile mechanics./ Occupations.

629.28   Ph-1 K-3/4 $15.89   L   KD129
GIBBONS, GAIL. Fill it up! All about service stations. Crowell/HarperCollins ISBN 0-690-04440-2, 1985. unp. col. ill.
Gas pumps, auto mechanics, and tire repair are explained in simple text and bright, detailed pictures. The attractive introduction describes the work of the service station crew, the many needs of the customers, and the machinery and tools needed for many jobs. The subject and cheerful presentation will appeal to a wide range of beginning readers and even prereaders.
SUBJ: Automobiles--Service stations.

629.4   Ph-3 A/8 $14.00   L   KD130
KETTELKAMP, LARRY. Living in space. Morrow ISBN 0-688-10018-X, 1993. 104p. ill.
Includes index.

History of American space exploration and speculation about future efforts to explore Mars are a major focus in this discussion of the working and living conditions experienced by astronauts. Three lengthy, solid chapters illustrated with overly dark photographs cover early years of the space movement, life and work experienced on American and Soviet flights, and the future. Serious readers will find plentiful information.
SUBJ: Space stations./ Space shuttles./ Outer space--Exploration.

629.43   Ph-2 P-3/6 $15.88   L   KD131
COLE, NORMA. Blast off!: a space counting book. Illus. by Marshall Peck III. Charlesbridge ISBN 0-88106-493-9, 1994. unp. col. ill.
Rocket to adventure: first count from one to twenty ("one, two buckle your astronaut shoe...") while zooming among the planets; then count backward from ten to zero to head home. Colorful pages depict child astronauts, a rocket ship, and outer space along with objects to finger count (e.g. 11 small meteors for that numeral). Science information is set apart in white blocks along the bottom of each page for more experienced readers. A creative match of space travel with counting.
SUBJ: Outer space--Exploration./ Solar system./ Counting.

629.43   Ph-2 A/10 $15.90   L   KD132
VOGT, GREGORY. Viking and the Mars landing. Millbrook ISBN 1-878841-32-7, 1991. 112p. ill. (some col.). (Missions in space).
Includes glossary, bibliography and index.
Mars is the site of planned future exploration and a longtime object of human fascination--both subjects of this informative discussion. The author describes historical speculations about the planet and its geographical characteristics, concentrating most fully on a detailed account of the Mariner and Viking probes of the 1970s. Striking pictures from these voyages are among the well chosen photographs illustrating the pleasing narrow volume.
SUBJ: Mars (Planet)./ Viking Mars Program./ Space flight to Mars.

VCR 629.43   Ph-2 5-8 $99.00   OD   KD133
WHAT WE LEARN ABOUT EARTH FROM SPACE (Videocassette). National Geographic 50596, 1995. 1/2" VHS videocassette color (25min).
Includes teacher's guide.
Closed captioned.
Satellites are invisible workers predicting weather, scanning the results of catastrophic floods and fires, and giving us the top-down look at the earth--connecting what happens globally to what occurs locally. Combines computer screen graphics with nature photography and clear narration to give a comprehensive view of satellite data collection in meteorology, geology, hydrology, and oceanography. Use in weather and environmental studies units and while studying the interdependence of earth's natural systems.
SUBJ: Artificial satellites./ Outer space--Exploration.

VCR 629.44   Ph-1 5-6 $29.95   OD   KD134
DREAM IS ALIVE: A WINDOW SEAT ON THE SPACE SHUTTLE (Videocassette). Narrated by Walter Cronkite. Finley-Holiday V147, 1985. 1/2" VHS videocassette color (37min).
This fine documentary captures the drama of liftoff and explains the many types of work to prepare the space shuttle for flight and the details of astronaut life. Adapted from the giant screen IMAX format, this is an impressive view even on the small screen. Walking and working in outer space are among many intriguing moments on this round-trip journey.
SUBJ: Space shuttles./ Astronauts.

629.45   Ph-2 4-5/7 $10.79   L   KD135
ALSTON, EDITH. Space camp. Photos by Michael Plunkett. Troll ISBN 0-8167-1743-5, 1990. 32p. col. ill. (Let's visit).
At the Space and Rocket Center in Huntsville, Alabama, boys and girls experience the training routine of astronauts. Space camp activities are described in a continuous essay text and interesting color photographs which follow campers through the intriguing processes of becoming accustomed to weightlessness, donning space suits, and simulating a space shuttle flight; pictures and explanations of the recorded narrator implies a younger audience than is actually the case, but the book presents an inviting introduction to space travel, and some teachers and students will like the read-along feature.
SUBJ: Astronautics./ Space and Rocket Center (Huntsville, Ala.).

629.45   Ph-1 3-6/8 $18.95   T   KD136
BURNS, KHEPHRA. Black stars in orbit: NASA'S African American astronauts. By Khephra Burns and William Miles. Gulliver/Harcourt Brace ISBN 0-15-200432-7; In Canada: Harcourt Brace c/o Canadian Manda, 1995. 72p. ill.
Includes index.
The struggle of African-American pilots to be admitted to any of the

aviation branches of the American armed forces is graphically recalled in this book which is an offshoot of a television documentary. The accomplishments of African-American astronauts and the African-American contributions behind the scenes in the space program are detailed. Oversized and filled with clear photographs--this is a monument to another chapter in African-American history. Recommended for all collections. For multicultural studies.
SUBJ: Astronauts./ Afro-Americans--Biography.

629.45   Ph-1 5-6/9 $16.00   T   KD137
MAZE, STEPHANIE. I want to be... an astronaut. Creator/producer, Stephanie Maze; writer and educational consultant, Catherine O'Neill Grace. Harcourt Brace ISBN 0-15-201300-8; In Canada: Harcourt Brace c/o Canadian Manda, 1997. 48p. col. ill. (I want to be... book series).
"Maze Productions book."
Includes directory.
Men and women of many backgrounds are depicted as they train to be astronauts and travel and work in space. Plentiful photographs and informative text cover highlights of history, life aboard spacecraft, international cooperation, tasks done by both astronauts and support staff, and ways young people can investigate this complex field of work. A versatile book that's an attractive choice for personal reading and useful for class projects in career studies or the broader field of space exploration.
SUBJ: Astronautics--Vocational guidance./ Astronauts./ Occupations./ Vocational guidance.

629.45   Ph-1 4-6/7 $17.00   L   KD138
RIDE, SALLY. To space and back. By Sally Ride with Susan Okie. Lothrop, Lee & Shepard ISBN 0-688-06159-1, 1986. 96p. col. ill.
Includes glossary and index.
Describes the daily activities of the astronauts as they travel on the space shuttle. Outstanding color photographs in an oversize format accompany Sally Ride's first-person account of the problems and advantages of weightlessness, meal preparation and housekeeping, sleeping, dressing, personal hygiene, and work performed inside and outside the craft. Far more attractive and immediate than the many other books which have covered this intriguing subject.
SUBJ: Space flight./ Space shuttles.

629.47   Ph-1 5-6/9 $21.50   L   KD139
BERLINER, DON. Living in space. Lerner ISBN 0-8225-1599-7, 1993. 64p. ill. (some col.).
Includes directory and index.
Informative text and photographs discuss the details of daily living of cosmonauts and astronauts in space. With emphasis on how things have changed and why particular items are important, the author discusses food, clothing, hygiene, staying healthy, getting along together, efforts to design more livable spacecraft, and safety and maintenance practices. This thoughtful presentation is timely and interesting reading material.
SUBJ: Space stations./ Manned space flight.

629.47   Ph-3 3-5/3 $5.95   P   KD140
BLOCKSMA, MARY. Easy-to-make spaceships that really fly. By Mary and Dewey Blocksma. Illustrated by Marisabina Russo. Simon & Schuster ISBN 0-671-66302-X; In Canada: Simon & Schuster, 1983. 40p. ill.
Construct simple, fanciful flying toys from paper plates, styrofoam cups, and drinking straws. Clear instructions and line drawings present quick projects for individual use or group activity.
SUBJ: Space ships--Models.

629.8   Ph-2 5-6/8 $15.95   T   KD141
SKURZYNSKI, GLORIA. Robots: your high-tech world. Bradbury ISBN 0-02-782917-0; In Canada: Collier Macmillan, 1990. 64p. col. ill. (Your high-tech world).
Includes index.
Robot capabilities in industry, medicine, entertainment, and exploration undersea and in outer space are among the topics examined here. The text also discusses robot history, the impact of computer technology, and robot assistants for the disabled; well chosen photographs depict aspects of robot design and robots at work. An excellent presentation for capable readers.
SUBJ: Robots./ Robotics.

VCR 630   Ph-3 3-A $89.00   OD KD142
DOWN ON THE FARM: YESTERDAY AND TODAY (Videocassette). Rainbow Educational Video RB110, 1987. 1/2" VHS videocassette color (18min).
Includes teacher's guide.
Modern farming is contrasted with farming 200 years ago in this moderately-paced film which may be useful for teaching about farms in either social studies or science. The guide provides additional activities.
SUBJ: Farms./ Agribusiness.

630   Ph-1 K-3/2 $14.95   L   KD143
GIBBONS, GAIL. Farming. Holiday House ISBN 0-8234-0682-2, 1988. unp. col. ill.
Colorful pages are filled with details of farm life through the seasons. The work of farms is featured as the short text and picture captions and labels are all organized around the indoor and outdoor chores of caring for the many animals, cultivating crops, and working in the house and barn. A final section shows different types of farms--dairy, eggs and poultry, grain, fruit, vegetable, cattle--to round out a simple, appealing introduction.
SUBJ: Farms./ Farm life.

VCR 630   Ph-1 1-6 $14.95   KD144
LET'S GO TO THE FARM (Videocassette). With Mac Parker. Vermont Story Works ISBN 1-885958-00-5, 1994. 1/2" VHS videocassette color (60min).
ALA notable video, 1995.
Vermont farm life through the seasons featuring many forms of work and play is shown in detail and narrated by the farm's hired man. The fine view of animals, machines, and family members includes many events: care of the cows, collecting milk, maple sugaring, plowing and planting, harvesting of trees and farm crops, preparing animal feed, attending the county fair, gathering pumpkins, and more. The leisurely examination can be enjoyed in full for personal viewing or in segments for classroom use, and the appreciative tone, bit of playfulness, and well chosen detail invite viewers to actually visit a farm.
SUBJ: Farms./ Farm life--Vermont./ Agriculture.

630.973   Ph-2 5-6/8 $18.95   T   KD145
ANDERSON, JOAN. American family farm. Photos by George Ancona. Harcourt Brace Jovanovich ISBN 0-15-203025-5, 1989. unp. ill.
Farm families in Massachusetts, Georgia, and Iowa illustrate the way of life on a family farm. Hard work, personal commitment, and cooperative arrangements play key roles for these families. Ancona's black and white photographs document the people, their chores and the ultimate products (milk, chickens, grain). Useful for units on agriculture, career choices or family life.
SUBJ: Farm life./ Agriculture./ Vocational guidance--Farming./ Farmers./ Farming--Vocational guidance.

631.3   Ph-1 K-2/2 $14.95   L   KD146
BROWN, CRAIG. Tractor. Greenwillow ISBN 0-688-10500-9, 1995. unp. col. ill.
Includes glossary.
Spacious, soft paintings follow a tractor as it tows several attachments to prepare the soil, plant the seed, and harvest a corn crop. Minimal text introduces farm equipment while the illustrations follow the progress of the field and life on the farm. Concluding pages briefly explain the use of each attachment in a picture glossary. The pleasant, appreciative view of farm work and the strong focus on the tractor make a quite-versatile item for browsing, reading aloud, and teaching.
SUBJ: Tractors./ Corn./ Farm life.

631.3   Ph-3 4-6/6 $4.95   P   KD147
BUSHEY, JERRY. Farming the land, modern farmers and their machines. Carolrhoda ISBN 0-87614-493-8, 1987. 40p. col. ill.
Includes glossary.
This colorful catalog of farm machines--many of them intriguing giants--surveys various farming tasks. The color photographs are variable in quality, and explanations are sometimes superficial in discussing an interesting variety of tractors, mowers, rakes, weedspraying machines, balers, choppers, combines, etc. Though uneven, the book is informative, and the subject very appealing for truck and machine fans.
SUBJ: Agriculture./ Agricultural machinery.

631.4   Ph-1 4-6/6 $6.95   P   KD148
BOURGEOIS, PAULETTE. Amazing dirt book. Written by Paulette Bourgeois with Valerie Wyatt. Illus. by Craig Terlson. Addison-Wesley ISBN 0-201-55096-2; In Canada: Kids Can Press, 1990. 80p. ill.
Includes glossary and index.
Dirt is complex and interesting stuff in this thoughtful survey of dust, soil, sand, and mud. Homely drawings and informative, quick paced text explain how soap works, the origins and make-up of dirt, tunnels, dirt homes for animals and people, burial practices, archaeology, gardens, and more. Practical instructions for activities and experiments round out this multifaceted examination.
SUBJ: Soils.

633.1   Ph-1 K-3/3 $14.89   L   KD149
ALIKI. Corn is maize: the gift of the Indians. Crowell/HarperCollins ISBN 0-690-00975-5, c1976. 33p. col. ill. (Let's-read-and-find-out science

book).

New York Academy of Sciences Children's Science Book Award.
An engaging description of the important aspects of maize, an important world food source. The author's characteristic illustrations depict native Americans planting, harvesting, preparing and storing corn. The evolution of corn, how it grows and is pollinated, and how it saved the Pilgrims, are told in a simple, informative text. An excellent book for social studies, science and history.
SUBJ: Corn./ Indians of North America--Food.

633.1   Ph-3 4-5/7 $14.95   T   KD150
BIAL, RAYMOND. Corn belt harvest. Houghton Mifflin ISBN 0-395-56234-1, 1991. 48p. col. ill.
Includes bibliography.
Attractive photographs of the machines used in planting and harvesting corn and the operations at corn elevators offer a nice introduction to farm technology. The essay text is difficult at times and sketchy in its explanations of the corn plant and corn products. Capable readers may find this useful as information, but the machines in the photographs provide the most appeal.
SUBJ: Corn.

633.1   Ph-2 5-6/7 $19.95   L   KD151
JOHNSON, SYLVIA A. Wheat. Photos by Masaharu Suzuki. Lerner ISBN 0-8225-1490-7, 1990. 48p. col. ill. (Lerner natural science book).
Includes glossary and index.
Adapted from THE LIFE OF THE WHEAT PLANT by Masaharu Suzuki.
Magnified photographs and detailed explanations convey the intricate composition of the wheat grain and show how it forms the world's major food crop. Fertilization, pollination, and growth stages of the plant are depicted as well as the agricultural tasks of planting, harvesting, and milling this important grain. The thorough lesson in plant growth is set in a handsome slim volume that will have lasting value.
SUBJ: Wheat.

633.1   Ph-1 3-5/4 $15.93   L   KD152
THOMSON, RUTH. Rice. Photos by Prodeepta Das. Garrett ISBN 0-944483-71-2, 1990. 25p. col. ill. (Threads).
Includes index.
This useful survey shows how rice is grown and how it is prepared by people of various cultures. The slim volume, filled with color photographs and drawings, and short topical segments, introduces varieties of rice and the growing and harvesting of rice, and gives instructions for simple experiments and recipes. Intelligently designed to demonstrate both the origin and usefulness of a common item and its shared value around the world, this is a versatile book.
SUBJ: Rice./ Cookery--Rice.

633.2   Ph-1 K-3/5 $15.95   L   KD153
GEISERT, BONNIE. Haystack. By Bonnie and Arthur Geisert. Illus. by Arthur Geisert. Houghton Mifflin ISBN 0-395-69722-0, 1995. 32p. col. ill.
Selectors' Choice, 20th ed.
Absorbing views of farm life appear in softly colored, detailed etchings, while simple text explains the work of building a traditional haystack which provides food and shelter for farm animals over many months. A tractor cuts the hay and rolls it into windrows which are then gathered and stacked by the whole family into one great framed piled. Cattle and pigs eat the hay through fall and winter and share it with their piglets and calves in spring. The haystack is an ingenious arrangement, and the profusion of tiny animals and details of the farm are very appealing in this nice explanation and tribute to farms.
SUBJ: Hay./ Farm life.

633.6   Ph-3 5-6/7 $19.95   L   KD154
BURNS, DIANE L. Sugaring season: making maple syrup. Photos by Cheryl Walsh Bellville. Carolrhoda ISBN 0-87614-420-2, 1990. 48p. col. ill.
Includes glossary.
Available from the National Library Service for the Blind and Physically Handicapped on sound recording cassette RC34394.
This step-by-step report on the gathering of sap from maple trees and the production of maple syrup follows the process at a particular maple grove, or sugar bush, in an unspecified location. Short, detailed sections of text and numerous photographs explain the preparation of buildings and equipment, the tapping of the trees, the collecting and cooking of the sap, grading and packaging of syrup, and the conclusion of the brief season. The explanations of equipment and the many tasks involved in sugaring as well as comparison of traditional with contemporary methods demystifies romantic notions about the legendary enterprise, providing almost more detail than most readers will want.
SUBJ: Maple syrup.

CE 633.6   Ph-1 4-6/9 $13.95   L   KD155
LASKY, KATHRYN. Sugaring time. Photos by Christopher G. Knight. Macmillan ISBN 0-02-751680-6; In Canada: Collier Macmillan, 1983. unp. ill.
Newbery Honor book.
Videocassette available from SRA/McGraw-Hill 87-509281, 1989. 1/2" VHS enhanced videocassette with sound effects (22min), $39.00.
Maple syrup is as American as apple pie. The hard work and the pleasure of collecting the sap and converting it into syrup for the table are depicted in a photo-essay which follows a Vermont farm family through the various processes. Attractive material for social studies, seasonal units, and children who enjoy reading about real people and for library programs.
SUBJ: Maple sugar./ Maple syrup.

VCR 634   Ph-2 3-5 $35.00   OD KD156
APPLES (Videocassette). Written and produced by Susan DeBeck. DeBeck Educational Video; In Canada: DeBeck Educational Video, 1996. 1/2" VHS videocassette color (30min).
Includes teacher's guide.
Includes public performance rights.
Closed captioned.
Apple history, agriculture, harvesting, and cookery appear in a sprightly array of segments which can be used as a whole or separately. Still illustrations of Johnny Appleseed are followed by a historical reenactment of Hannah McIntosh who gives an interesting demonstration of making apple dolls. Contemporary children view apple cells through an electron microscope, visit an orchard, learn the history of several apple varieties and how to plant seeds, watch the pressing of apple juice, and bake an apple pie. Though the narrator talks down a bit for the level of content, this will be widely useful in the many regions where apples are grown.
SUBJ: Apples.

634   Ph-2 5-6/7 $19.95   L   KD157
BURNS, DIANE L. Cranberries: fruit of the bogs. Photos by Cheryl Walsh Bellville. Carolrhoda ISBN 0-87614-822-4, 1994. 48p. col. ill., map.
Includes glossary and index.
Two cranberry farms, one in Wisconsin and one in Massachusetts, are scenes for this informative account of the planting, care, and harvest of this colorful crop native to cool northern climates. Attractive photographs and detailed text explain history, preparation of land, planting, sprinkling and weeding, use of bees, machinery, wet and dry harvesting, and processing of the gathered berries. The carefully developed explanations are useful for reports and will be especially appreciated in states where cranberries grow.
SUBJ: Cranberries.

VCR 634   Ph-2 3-5 $35.00   OD KD158
CRANBERRY BOUNCE (Videocassette). DeBeck Educational Video, 1991. 1/2" VHS videocassette color (30min).
Includes teacher's guide.
Includes public performance rights.
Closed captioned.
This bouncy ramble through a family owned cranberry farm examines the development and care of the plant through the seasons. The meandering, upbeat presentation focuses on the children of the farm and offers many lessons: history of the plant, botanical parts, the role of bees, the origin and composition of peat bogs, wintering, harvesting, the bouncing of the berries through a conveyor frame to determine quality, and the preparation of popular foods. The teacher's guide and the film, used as a whole or in part, offer a diversity of learning opportunities about this native fruit.
SUBJ: Cranberries.

634   Ph-1 P-3/2 $10.95   T   KD159
GOLDSEN, LOUISE. Fruit. [This edition American text by Louise Goldsen.] Created by Gallimard Jeunesse and Pascale de Bourgoing. Illus. by P. M. Valet. Scholastic ISBN 0-590-45233-9; In Canada: Scholastic, 1992. unp. col. ill.(spiral bound). (First discovery book).
"Cartwheel books."
Originally published in France, LA POMME ET D'AUTRES FRUITS, 1989.
Apples are viewed from the outside and the inside through the use of appealing plastic overlays which also introduce other fruits. The growth cycle, different sorts of seeds, and a fine variety of fruits are surveyed in very simple lines of text and bright, clear pictures on thick glossy pages. The game of discovery will make this very popular with children, and the attractive presentation of the fruits makes a useful teaching item.
SUBJ: Fruit.

634   Ph-1 4-5/6 $14.95   L   KD160
JASPERSOHN, WILLIAM. Cranberries. Houghton Mifflin ISBN 0-395-52098-3, 1991. 32p. col. ill.
Beautiful red berries gathered for harvest make inviting endpapers for this photo-essay on one of America's few native fruits. Beginning with the late spring blossoms, photographs and short text explain two ways of harvesting along with steps in sorting and packing the berries for shipment. The raking of the berries is an unusual process, and the book could be used in units on food, agriculture or seasonal activities.
SUBJ: Cranberries.

634   Ph-1 4-6/9 $19.95   L   KD161
JOHNSON, SYLVIA A. Apple trees. Photos by Hiroo Koike. Lerner ISBN 0-8225-1479-6, 1983. 48p. col. ill. (Lerner natural science book).
Includes glossary and index.
Discusses the stages of growth, physical characteristics, and harvesting of apples. The slim format includes a well organized essay and attractive color photographs which convey a considerable amount of information about the development of the blossoms into fruit and introduce several varieties of apple.
SUBJ: Apples./ Fruit./ Fruit trees.

634   Ph-2 3-5/5 $13.99   L   KD162
MICUCCI, CHARLES. Life and times of the apple. Orchard ISBN 0-531-08539-2, 1992. 32p. col. ill.
Apple facts and miscellany are explained in short bits of text and plentiful small drawings. Attractive doublespread pages cover some technical topics such as cross fertilization, grafting of trees, parts of the blossom, bees and pollination, and stages of apple growth as well as interesting facts about the harvest, uses, varieties, and history of apples. Sometimes sketchy, but also humorous and detailed, this offers enjoyable browsing and facts not found in other books on this popular fruit.
SUBJ: Apples.

634   Ph-1 5-6/7 $19.95   L   KD163
SCHNIEPER, CLAUDIA. Apple tree through the year. Photos by Othmar Baumli. Carolrhoda ISBN 0-87614-248-X, c1982, 1987. 48p. col. ill. (Carolrhoda nature watch book).
Includes glossary and index.
Follows the growth cycle of apple trees throughout the year in a very attractive photo-essay presentation. Several apple varieties are shown, and the discussion covers both the botanical aspects of apple trees as well as aspects of cultivation, including problems with insects and other pests, the importance of bees for pollination, grafting and harvesting. An informative and appealing look at the origins of this widely enjoyed fruit.
SUBJ: Apples./ Apples--Ecology./ Ecology./ Orchards.

634.9   Ph-2 4-6/6 $15.95   L   KD164
ADAMS, PETER. Early loggers and the sawmill. Crabtree ISBN 0-86505-005-8; In Canada: Crabtree, 1981. 63p. ill. (Early settler life).
Includes glossary and index.
"Every pioneer was a logger and a lumberman." Life in families and logging camps, the work of logging, and numerous wooden buildings are described in detail and pictured in plentiful early photographs and prints. An informative introduction to this important component of our social and economic history.
SUBJ: Lumber and lumbering--History./ Sawmills--History./ Logging--History.

634.9   Ph-1 4-6/6 $9.95   P   OD KD165
KURELEK, WILLIAM. Lumberjack. Tundra ISBN 0-88776-052-X; In Canada: Tundra, 1974. unp. col. ill.
Earthy paintings and informative entries describe the daily life and work activities of traditional lumberjacks in the Canadian bush. Writing and painting his own experience, Kurelek explains the tools and techniques of lumbering as well as personal activities--eating, personal hygiene, recreation. The introduction provides a good biography of the author, and his recollection of lumber camp days is a fine choice for booktalking and nonfiction readers. Useful information on lumbering for science or social studies.
SUBJ: Lumber and lumbering--Canada./ Lumber camps./ Canada--Social life and customs./ Kurelek, William.

635   Ph-2 P-K/3 $15.90   L   KD166
GLASER, LINDA. Compost!: growing gardens from your garbage. Illus. by Anca Hariton. Millbrook ISBN 1-56294-659-5, 1996. unp. col. ill.
Pretty watercolors follow a family's daily activities as they add food and plant scraps to their compost pile. A young girl narrates the simple text explaining how the compost decays and is finally worked into the garden soil. Concluding pages for adults add further explanations of composting. Details of plant and animal life framing each page invite leisurely viewing. This cheerful lesson in recycling and gardening offers attractive materials for family and class use. For environmental studies.
SUBJ: Compost./ Gardening.

635   Ph-2 3-5/6 $12.95   P   KD167
HART, AVERY. Kids garden!: the anytime, anyplace guide to sowing and growing fun. By Avery Hart and Paul Mantell. Illus. by Loretta Braren and Jennie Chien. Williamson ISBN 0-913589-90-X; In Canada: Williamson/dist. by Fitzhenry & Whiteside, 1996. 158p. ill.
"Williamson Kids Can! book."
Includes index.
A bean-pole tepee, plants to repel fleas, and good things to eat are among the many indoor and outdoor projects included in this handy, quick compendium. Crude line drawings and brief instructions cover a wide variety of topics: tools and soil, seeds and bulbs, shade plants, experiments, cactus gardens, gifts, composting, insect pests, recipes, and more. A useful collection for hobby use, science projects, and group activities.
SUBJ: Gardening./ Indoor gardening.

635   Ph-3 5-6/7 $15.95   L   KD168
HUFF, BARBARA A. Greening the city streets: the story of community gardens. Photos by Peter Ziebel. Clarion ISBN 0-89919-741-8, 1990. 61p. col. ill.
Includes bibliography and index.
Community gardens in New York City are the focus for this discussion of how children and adults are improving city neighborhoods through gardening in vacant lots. Six chapters of text accompanied by attractive photographs talk about the history of community gardens, the gardening process, the use of common space for social activities and community theater, and New York's annual Harvest Fair. This looks at an interesting community activity which provides ecological, social and economic benefits.
SUBJ: Community gardens--New York (N.Y.)./ Gardening.

635   Ph-2 1-4/4 $14.00   L   KD169
KING, ELIZABETH. Pumpkin patch. Dutton ISBN 0-525-44640-0, 1990. unp. col. ill.
This brief photo-essay follows the planting and growth of pumpkins in the fields, their harvest and sale, and their uses to celebrate Halloween. The text is sketchy but many of the color photos are luscious views of this special vegetable. A very handy item for seasonal use.
SUBJ: Pumpkin.

635   Ph-2 4-5/5 $7.95   T   KD170
KUHN, DWIGHT. More than just a vegetable garden. Silver Press/Silver Burdett ISBN 0-671-69645-9, 1990. 40p. col. ill.
Includes glossary and index.
Observe and understand the development of seeds into plants and the interrelationships of plants and animals in this look at garden ecology. Instructions for starting a garden by transplanting seedlings or by planting seeds directly outdoors conclude an introduction that is sketchy and eclectic but pleasant.
SUBJ: Vegetable gardening./ Gardening./ Garden ecology./ Ecology.

VCR 635   Ph-1 1-6 $14.95   OD KD171
LOOK WHAT I GREW: WINDOWSILL GARDENS (Videocassette). Intervideo/dist. by Vermont Story Works IVI 3456 ISBN 1-883784-01-8, 1993. 1/2" VHS videocassette color (45min). (On my own adventure).
Includes bibliography.
Includes public performance rights.
Selectors' Choice, 21st ed.
Plants to grow in water or soil in various containers found around the house or easily acquired are enjoyable projects for fun, for eating, and for learning science. A pleasant narrator, occasionally joined by children, explains how to care for plants, do experiments and crafts, grow your own salad, record plant observations in a journal, set up terrariums, and more. Food, flowers, and craft projects will interest children of many ages and will be enjoyed for home use, classroom activities, scout and other group projects, and as a basis for science experiments. (Parents' Shelf).
SUBJ: Gardening./ Science--Experiments./ Experiments.

635   Ph-1 2-4/2 $9.98   L   KD172
WATTS, BARRIE. Potato. Silver Burdett ISBN 0-382-09527-8, 1987. 25p. col. ill. (Stopwatch books).
Includes index.
Potatoes growing on their underground stems are followed through all the stages of their growth in excellent color photographs. A simple text describes the shoots emerging from a whole potato, which diminishes as the shoot sprouts leaves, a root system develops, flowers bloom and produce seeds, and finally several new potatoes

begin to appear. A few informative line drawings augment the full page photographs of a very attractive introduction to this common yet unusual vegetable.
SUBJ: Potatoes.

635.9   Ph-2 3-5/6 $11.95   T   KD173
BJORK, CHRISTINA. Linnea's windowsill garden. By Christina Bjork and Lena Anderson. Translated by Joan Landin. R & S Books/dist. by Farrar, Straus & Giroux ISBN 91-29-59064-7; I Canada: Watts, c1978, 1988. 59p. col. ill.
Cheerful instructions for growing potted plants from seeds, bulbs, and cuttings also discuss many aspects of plant care. A small girl is the gardener, narrating the explanations for potting, watering, feeding, and re-potting plants, identifying insect pests, salvaging seeds and other growing portions from common foods, and other interesting information about plants and experiments and projects. Though the book appears young for the most likely audience, the activities offer fine material for youngsters with a green thumb, for rainy day entertainment, simple science projects, and a variety of group and individual uses.
SUBJ: Indoor gardening.

635.9   Ph-1 1-4/4 $13.99   L   KD174
KING, ELIZABETH. Backyard sunflower. Story and photos by Elizabeth King. Dutton ISBN 0-525-45082-3, 1993. unp. col. ill.
Samantha plants a sunflower which soon grows to be tall and golden and filled with seeds. Handsome photo essay explains the growth and structure of the plant and the uses of the seeds for food and oil. Photographs provide exceptional views of this tall, sturdy plant in an appealing, slim volume.
SUBJ: Sunflowers.

635.9   Ph-2 4-5/6 $15.98   L   KD175
KUHN, DWIGHT. More than just a flower garden. Silver Press/Silver Burdett ISBN 0-671-69642-4, 1990. 40p. col. ill.
Includes glossary and index.
Flowers, shown here in lovely photographs, are an important stage of a plant's growth. Close-up and magnified pictures explain their structure, functions, processes and stages in brief terms. The effects of animals in the garden is also discussed. A concluding set of instructions for planting and observing flowers in a garden completes the appreciative lesson in plant ecology.
SUBJ: Flowers./ Flower gardening./ Garden ecology./ Ecology.

635.9   Ph-2 3-5/4 $15.40   L   KD176
VAN HAGE, MARY AN. Little green thumbs. Illus. by Bettina Paterson. Photos by Lucy Tizard. Millbrook ISBN 1-56294-270-0, 1996. 32p. col. ill.
Originally published in Great Britain, Macdonald Young Books, 1995. Busy pages explain how to grow sunflowers, baby tomatoes, pumpkins, succulents, a Venus's-flytrap, and other indoor and outdoor plants. Detailed instructions for planting, plant care, and transplanting are provided. There's a good variety of enjoyable projects: grass head figures, egg carton arrangements, growing bulbs, miniature gardens, and more. Useful for family sharing, in classrooms, or with scouts and other groups. (Parents' Shelf)
SUBJ: Indoor gardening./ Handicraft.

636   Ph-1 P-2/3 $4.99   P   KD177
BARE, COLLEEN STANLEY. Guinea pigs don't read books. Penguin ISBN 0-14-054995-1, c1985, 1993. 28p. col. ill.
Points out the behavior traits of guinea pigs--who chew and sniffle and squeak and make affectionate pets. Appealing color photographs accompanying a minimal text show the attractive variety of color and appearances of this small friendly animal. A fine introduction for browsing, reading aloud and independent reading.
SUBJ: Guinea pigs./ Pets.

636   Ph-1 3-6/6 $9.95   T   KD178
EVANS, MARK. Guinea pigs. DK Publishing ISBN 1-56458-125-X, 1992. 45p. col. ill. (ASPCA pet care guides for kids).
Includes index.
Practical advice on selecting and caring for a pet guinea pig is offered in clear explanations and plentiful small photographs sprinkled liberally across each page. Guinea pigs in the wild, types of guinea pigs, preparing a home, feeding, grooming, cleaning the hutch, health care, understanding guinea pigs, and having babies are among the many topics presented in short bits of text and captions. Clarity and detail of instructions make this a very useful introduction and handbook.
SUBJ: Guinea pigs./ Pets.

636   Ph-1 3-6/4 $9.95   T   KD179
EVANS, MARK. Rabbit. DK Publishing ISBN 1-56458-128-4, 1992. 45p. col. ill. (ASPCA pet care guides for kids).
Includes index.
Rabbits in many shapes and sizes illustrate this practical, attractive guide to selecting and caring for a pet rabbit. Short bits of text and captions along with the numerous small photographs describe rabbits in the wild, various breeds, appropriate cages and equipment, feeding, grooming, health care, caring for rabbits indoors and outdoors, and other topics. The slim, colorful book is detailed and clear--a useful handbook for prospective and new rabbit owners.
SUBJ: Rabbits./ Pets.

636   Ph-3 P-2/2 $6.95   T   KD180
FARM ANIMALS. Photos by Philip Dowell and Michael Dunning. Aladdin/Macmillan ISBN 0-689-71403-3, 1991. 21p. col. ill. (Eye openers).
Most of the eight domestic animals featured in this simple survey appear with appealing babies. The animal figures in white space dominate the pages, which are busy with several small drawings and a few sentences providing sketchy information. Slight in content, this will serve where there's a need for added material on the subject.
SUBJ: Domestic animals.

636   Ph-2 4-6/6 $19.95   L   KD181
HANSEN, ELVIG. Guinea pigs. Carolrhoda ISBN 0-87614-681-7, 1992. 48p col photos. (Carolrhoda nature watch book).
Includes glossary and index.
The birth of a pair of guinea pigs and their first several weeks of life are conveyed in lovely photographs and informative text. The author carefully explains maternal care, feeding, physical characteristics, and differences between various breeds. The inviting presentation encourages pet ownership and offers an excellent introduction to this appealing rodent.
SUBJ: Guinea pigs./ Pets.

636   Ph-1 5-6/10 $19.95   L   KD182
JOHNSON, SYLVIA A. Ferrets. Carolrhoda ISBN 1-57505-014-5, 1997. 48p. col. ill. (Carolrhoda nature watch book).
Includes glossary and index.
This attractive guide to the selection and care of pet ferrets also provides interesting information on wild ferrets and the history of the domesticated animals. Numerous photographs and informative text describe the differences between ferret species, the advantages and disadvantages of ferrets as pets, many aspects of caring for them, the breeding of ferrets, and care of the kits. The growing popularity of ferrets as pets assures heavy use of this practical and appealing volume.
SUBJ: Ferret./ Ferrets as pets./ Pets.

636   Ph-2 K-4/3 $14.95   T   KD183
KING-SMITH, DICK. I love guinea pigs. Illus. by Anita Jeram. Candlewick ISBN 1-56402-389-3; In Canada: Candlewick/dist. by Douglas & McIntyre, 1995. unp. col. ill. (Read and wonder).
Available from the National Library Service for the Blind and Physically Handicapped on sound recording cassette RC 41435. Humorous sketches introduce a great variety of guinea pigs as the author explains a bit of their history, physical characteristics, and the qualities that make them good pets. Small, softly colored pictures scatter across the pages as a simple text describes the feeding and handling of guinea pigs, their various sounds, the birth and growth of babies, and more. An enthusiastic and useful introduction to this popular rodent.
SUBJ: Guinea pigs./ Pets.

636   Ph-2 3-5/6 $4.95   P   KD184
PIERS, HELEN. Taking care of your gerbils. Barron's ISBN 0-8120-1369-7; In Canada: Barron's, 1993. 32p. col. ill. (Young pet owner's guide).
Includes bibliography and index.
Many small photographs of gerbils and their equipment scatter across the pages of practical advice on selecting and caring for these small pets. Equipping cages or soil filled tanks, handling the animals, feeding, breeding, and health problems are discussed in small bits of text, captions, and boxed inserts. Slim useful paperback teaches responsible pet care. Handy guide for children and families as well as classrooms.
SUBJ: Gerbils as pets./ Pets.

636   Ph-1 P-K/1 $14.93   L   KD185
TAFURI, NANCY. Spots, feathers, and curly tails. Greenwillow ISBN 0-688-07537-1, 1988. unp. col. ill.
Combines a puzzle aspect and an easy question and answer game with a tour of a country farm. A brief question printed in large letters is faced on the opposite page by a picture of part of an unidentified

object, then on turning the page the children see a large doublespread of a farm animal and the answer to the question. A simple but striking book with great appeal to preschoolers and kindergarteners who love to shout out the answers to the questions.
SUBJ: Domestic animals./ Questions and answers.

636　　　　Ph-1 4-6/7　$14.95　L　KD186
WEXLER, JEROME. Pet gerbils. Whitman ISBN 0-8075-6523-7; In Canada: General, 1990. 48p. col. ill.
Includes index.
This attractive guide offers plenty of practical instruction for selecting, caring for, and breeding gerbils. Wexler's style is conversational, interjecting reports on the behavior of his own gerbils as he explains cage maintenance, feeding, health problems, training, mating, and the development of the babies; small photographs are scattered throughout the text, and there are a few very appealing full-page pictures. A handy, slim volume with first-rate information on pet care, this concludes with advice on photographing animals.
SUBJ: Gerbils as pets./ Pets.

636　　　　Ph-1 4-6/7　$14.95　L　KD187
WEXLER, JEROME. Pet hamsters. Text and photos by Jerome Wexler. Whitman ISBN 0-8075-6525-3; In Canada: General, 1992. 48p. col. ill.
Includes index.
Sensible and thorough instructions on selecting, housing, feeding, and training hamsters appear in a slim volume well illustrated with photographs. Includes a day-by-day account of the growth of a litter of newborn hamsters. Practical and appealing introduction to this common pet.
SUBJ: Hamsters./ Pets.

VCR 636.008　　　Ph-2 3-6　$14.99　　KD188
AMAZING ANIMALS (Videocassette). Narrated by Jack Hanna. Ingle Productions/Time-Life Video V670-10 ISBN 0-7835-8265-X, 1994. 1/2" VHS videocassette color (39min). (Zoo life with Jack Hanna).
Animal trainers and zoo specialists explain the senses and adaptation of numerous animals in this congenial visit to animal exhibits in several states. A zoo director narrates, handling a great variety of birds, mammals, and reptiles as he and the other animal experts explain each animal's capabilities and behavior. The pleasant survey is an interesting introduction to animal senses and the work of zoos. For career studies.
SUBJ: Zoo animals./ Zoos.

636.08　　　Ph-1 1-4/6　$14.95　L　KD189
ARNOLD, CAROLINE. Pets without homes. Photos by Richard Hewett. Clarion ISBN 0-89919-191-6, 1983. 46p. ill.
Follows the experiences of a lost dog and the animal control officer who finds him as a means of describing the procedures of animal shelters. Medical treatment, daily care, neglect of pets, overpopulation, and adoption (or lack of it) by new owners are all explained in a slim, pleasant photo-essay. Suitable for reading aloud, this is a straightforward, honest discussion of a subject of great interest and importance to children.
SUBJ: Animals--Treatment./ Pets.

636.088　　　Ph-2 5-6/6　$19.99　L　KD190
DOLPHINS. Raintree ISBN 0-8172-3085-8, 1988. 64p col photos. (Science and its secrets).
Includes glossary and index.
Dolphins in captivity are the focus of this selection of color photographs and explanations of many aspects of dolphin behavior, care and training and physical characteristics. The slim oversize format contains doublespread presentations on many aspects of physiology, sonar training, intelligence, and more. Discussion of marine parks where dolphins may be viewed in Europe and the United States round out an attractive and informative source.
SUBJ: Dolphins--Training.

VCR 636.088　　Ph-1 3-5　$14.95　　KD191
PAWS, CLAWS, FEATHERS AND FINS (Videocassette). KIDVIDZ ISBN 0-843136-83-9, 1993. 1/2" VHS videocassette color (30min).
Includes activity guide.
Several children share their experiences of caring for and enjoying different types of pets, demonstrating responsible pet ownership. Cats, fish, birds, dogs, horses, and several small animals are featured. Children explain how to decide on the appropriate pet, costs and time involved, and the many responsibilities of feeding, grooming, and training pets as well as common health problems. This attractive discussion is an especially helpful item for families considering pet ownership. (Parents' Shelf).
SUBJ: Pets.

636.088　　　Ph-2 5-6/7　$13.95　T　KD192
SQUIRE, ANN. 101 questions and answers about pets and people. Illllustrated by G. Brian Karas. Macmillan ISBN 0-02-786580-0; In Canada: Collier Macmillan, 1988. 85p b&w illus.
Includes index.
Why are there so many Egyptian statues in the shape of cats, and do animals ever have pets? Short entries provide well known and unusual bits of information about the behavior and bodies of familiar animals with the concluding set of questions covering ways that animals help people. A pleasant layout with wide margins and occasional small drawings and well written text providing an engaging volume for book talks, nonfiction readers, and miscellany fans.
SUBJ: Pets--Miscellanea./ Questions and answers.

636.088　　　Ph-2 K-3/2　$5.99　P　KD193
ZIEFERT, HARRIET. Let's get a pet. Illus. by Mavis Smith. Penguin ISBN 0-14-054808-4; In Canada: Penguin, c1993, 1996. 32p. col. ill.
Pleasant cartoon drawings and simple text describe the many practical questions to consider in deciding on a suitable pet. Aspects of caring for cats, dogs, mice, rats, fish, rabbits, birds, and guinea pigs are considered--housing, feeding, daily care, and particular advantages and disadvantages. Children will find this useful reading to guide their thinking about a first pet.
SUBJ: Pets.

636.089　　　Ph-1 P-2/2　$13.95　L　KD194
GIBBONS, GAIL. Say woof!: the day of a country veterinarian. Macmillan ISBN 0-02-736781-9; In Canada: Maxwell Macmillan, 1992. unp. col. ill.
A busy veterinarian sees a great variety of pets, farm animals, and wild creatures in his office and on visits to farms and homes. Simple text and cheerful line drawings briefly describe each animal's problem and treatment, and short descriptions of the doctor's tools are printed right in the pictures. Basic rules of pet care conclude the clear, pleasant introduction to the work of this popular "helper."
SUBJ: Veterinary medicine./ Veterinarians./ Occupations.

636.089　　　Ph-1 5-6/9　$16.00　T　KD195
MAZE, STEPHANIE. I want to be... a veterinarian. Creator/producer, Stephane Maze; writer and educational consultant, Catherine O'Neill Grace. Harcourt Brace ISBN 0-15-201296-6; In Canada: Harcourt Brace c/o Canadian Manda., 1997. 48p. col. ill. (I want to be... book series).
"Maze Productions book."
Includes directory.
Veterinarians and other animal care workers are depicted in many settings as they care for pets, farm and zoo animals, and wild creatures. Numerous photographs and engaging text incorporate children and suggest ways to investigate this type of work. A wide variety of humans and animals are featured to explain the many types of work veterinarians do and how they prepare for their careers. The true-life stories of animal rescue and care are intriguing, and there's good information for career studies.
SUBJ: Veterinarians./ Occupations.

CE 636.089　　Ph-2 2-5/6　$11.79　L　KD196
PAIGE, DAVID. Day in the life of a zoo veterinarian. Photos by Michael Mauney. Troll ISBN 0-8167-0095-8, 1985. 32p. col. ill. (Day in the life of).
Follows a young woman veterinarian through her day's work in Chicago's Lincoln Park Zoo. Attractive photographs show a wide variety of animals having routine check-ups, dental work, and more serious surgical treatment involving elaborate preparation. Lacking any discussion of how one becomes a veterinarian, this will not work so well as career material but will be highly appealing to children who are fascinated by veterinary work and zoos.
SUBJ: Veterinarians./ Zoos./ Women veterinarians./ Occupations.

636.1　　　Ph-3 5-6/6　$15.95　L　KD197
ANCONA, GEORGE. Man and mustang. Photos and text by George Ancona. Macmillan ISBN 0-02-700802-9; In Canada: Maxwell Macmillan, 1992. unp. ill.
Includes directory.
As legally protected mustangs flourish in the Southwest, the United States Bureau of Land Management rounds up some of the horses, breaks them in, and offers them for adoption. This wooden photo documentary follows the roundup, the transport of the mustangs to a state penitentiary where the taming process is conducted by inmates, and a family's adoption of a horse. Useful list of adoption agencies rounds out a dull, but informative, presentation on an appealing topic.
SUBJ: United States. Bureau of Land Management. Adopt-A-Horse or Burro./ Wild horse adoption./ Mustang./ Wildlife conservation.

636.1   Ph-2 4-6/7 $24.21   T   KD198
BUDD, JACKIE. Horses. Kingfisher/dist. by Raintree Steck-Vaughn ISBN 1-85697-566-5, 1995. 64p. col. ill., maps.
Includes glossary, index and directory.
Numerous facts about the history and riding of horses fill this oversize volume. Two-page segments with drawings, photographs, captions, and bits of text discuss the various breeds of horses, equipment for riding and horse care, the equipping of stables, and numerous historical and modern day riding events. Horse lovers will pore over instructions for grooming and riding horses as well as the many other nuggets of information in the busy compendium.
SUBJ: Horses.

636.1   Ph-1 4-6/8 $15.99   L   KD199
CLUTTON-BROCK, JULIET. Horses. Knopf ISBN 0-679-91681-4, 1992. 63p b&w and col illus and photos. (Eyewitness books).
Includes index.
Spanish version CABALLOS available from Santillana (ISBN 84-372-3766-1, 1995).
A grand variety of horses and related animals appear in this heavily illustrated survey of the history and uses of this popular animal. Topical doublespread pages of brief discussion and copious photographs and drawings describe equipment, breeds, bones, sporting horses, the age of chivalry and many other subjects. The handsome pictures and wide range of information are an irresistible compendium which will enthrall horse fans.
SUBJ: Horses./ Horse breeds./ Spanish language materials.

636.1   Ph-3 5-6/6 $14.95   P   KD200
HAAS, JESSIE. Safe horse, safe rider: a young rider's guide to responsible horsekeeping. Storey Communications ISBN 0-88266-700-9; In Canada: HarperCollins, 1994. 152p. ill.
Includes directories, bibliography and index.
This large, flat handbook provides extensive information about caring for horses and training for competitive riding events. Detailed text and black and white photographs explain many aspects of horse behavior, equipment for horse and rider, approaching and riding horses, selecting good boarding and teaching facilities, transporting animals, and much more. A useful compendium for very serious young horse owners.
SUBJ: Horses./ Horsemanship.

636.1   Ph-1 3-6/5 $19.95   L   KD201
ISENBART, HANS-HEINRICH. Birth of a foal. Photos by Thomas David. Carolrhoda ISBN 0-87614-239-0, 1986. 48p. col. ill. (Carolrhoda nature watch book).
Includes glossary.
Documenting the birth of a foal and his first few hours of life, this short informative essay makes excellent use of color photographs. Two pages of diagrams on the development of the foal fetus and the birth of a foal, along with a glossary, follow the many appealing pictures of the foal and his mother and other horses in the herd. A fine presentation on a highly popular subject, this will receive very heavy use by children of all ages.
SUBJ: Horses./ Animals--Infancy.

636.1   Ph-2 5-6/7 $14.89   L   KD202
MELTZER, MILTON. Hold your horses: a feedbag full of fact and fable. HarperCollins ISBN 0-06-024478-X; In Canada: HarperCollins, 1995. 133p. ill.
Includes bibliography and index.
Several chapters explore the uses of horses at various times in history. Small photographs, prints, and drawings accompany informative discussions of prehistoric times, ancient civilizations, the age of knights, the American Civil War and westward movement, Native American life, the golden age of cowboys, modern work horses, racetrack thoroughbreds, and folklore. This handsome, well-documented compendium is an attractive choice for nonfiction readers as well as a useful item for reports.
SUBJ: Horses.

636.1   Ph-1 4-6/7 $14.95   L   KD203
PATENT, DOROTHY HINSHAW. Appaloosa horses. Photos by William Munoz. Holiday House ISBN 0-8234-0706-3, 1988. 74p. ill.
Includes glossary, index and directory of organizations.
Favored by the Nez Perce and Palouse Indians, the Appaloosa remains a popular and distinctive breed. Their history, physical characteristics and breeding along with activities of Appaloosa horse clubs are described in an informative text and plentiful, attractive illustrations. This is a handy volume likely to see long and heavy use by horse fans.
SUBJ: Appaloosa horse./ Horses.

636.1   Ph-3 1-3/4 $13.27   L   KD204
POSELL, ELSA. Horses. Childrens Press ISBN 0-516-01623-7; In Canada: Childrens Press, 1981. 48p. col. ill. (New true book).
Includes glossary and index.
Physical characteristics of horses and ponies, history of horses in America, the use and care of horses are introduced in short chapters and small but attractive color photographs. Though the book looks and reads like a school reader, children in the early grades will be attracted by the subject.
SUBJ: Horses.

636.1   Ph-2 4-5/6 $17.80   L   KD205
STEWART, GAIL B. Appaloosa horse. Photos by William Munoz. Capstone ISBN 1-56065-243-8, 1995. 47p. col. ill. (Learning about horses).
Includes glossary, bibliography, directory and index.
This small book with numerous photographs sketches the history, physical characteristics, and behavior of the horses brought to America by Spanish explorers. Short chapters explain how the horses were once used by the Nez Perces then taken from them and later allowed to become almost extinct. The information is thin, but interesting, and the appeal of the horses survives the wooden writing and series format.
SUBJ: Appaloosa horse./ Horses.

636.1   Ph-2 4-6/5 $17.80   L   KD206
STEWART, GAIL B. Arabian horse. Photos by William Munoz. Capstone ISBN 1-56065-244-6, 1995. 48p. col. ill. (Learning about horses).
Includes glossary, bibliography, directory and index.
Brief chapters describe the history, physical characteristics, and current day uses of Arabian horses. The small, slim volume includes attractive photographs of Arabians in action and at rest, and the discussion is preceded by two pages of quick facts. The series is utilitarian, but the subject will readily attract readers.
SUBJ: Arabian horse./ Horses.

636.1   Ph-2 4-6/5 $17.80   L   KD207
STEWART, GAIL B. Quarter horse. Photos by William Munoz. Capstone ISBN 1-56065-242-X, 1995. 48p. col. ill. (Learning about horses).
Includes glossary, bibliography, directory and index.
A slim, series volume, this sketches the history, distinctive characteristics, and uses of the quarter horse. Short chapters and adequate photographs give a cursory account that will be primarily of interest to the dedicated horse fans.
SUBJ: Quarter horse./ Horses.

636.1   Ph-2 4-6/5 $17.80   L   KD208
STEWART, GAIL B. Thoroughbred horse: born to run. Photos by Ron Colbroth. Capstone ISBN 1-56065-245-4, 1995. 48p. col. ill. (Learning about horses).
Includes glossary, bibliography, directory and index.
Thoroughbreds are a fairly new breed, and this slim volume explains how certain English and Arabian horses were used to develop these popular race horses. Brief chapters of text and nice photographs discuss history, physical characteristics, and ways this horse is used. Two pages of added facts precede the opening chapter. Though the writing and book design are clumsy, children will be attracted by the animals.
SUBJ: Thoroughbred horse./ Race horses./ Horses.

636.1   Ph-2 5-A/7 $15.95   T   KD209
VISUAL DICTIONARY OF THE HORSE. DK Publishing ISBN 1-56458-504-2, 1994. 64p. col. ill. (Eyewitness visual dictionaries).
Includes glossary and index.
Two-page spreads of brief text and a profusion of labeled illustrations and drawings provide unusual detail about the anatomy of horses, the many breeds from around the world, and the uses of horses for sporting events and field work. Despite the difficult reading level and European emphasis, horse fans will delight in all the detail.
SUBJ: Horses./ Horses--Anatomy.

636.2   Ph-1 5-6/7 $12.88   L   KD210
ARNOLD, CAROLINE. Llama. Photos by Richard Hewett. Morrow ISBN 0-688-07541-X, 1988. 48p. col. ill. (Baby zoo animals).
Includes index.
Lovely color photographs and an informative text readily reveal the appealing and practical nature of llamas. The book follows the early weeks of life of a baby llama in a California herd and also describes related species, physiology, behavior of the herd, llamas as pack animals and a source of wool, and the events at a llama show. Llamas are growing rapidly in number in North America, and this attractive introduction is sure to enhance their popularity.
SUBJ: Llamas.

636.2   Ph-2 4-5/4 $3.95   P   KD211
ARNOLD, CAROLINE. Reindeer. Illus. by Pamela Johnson. Scholastic
ISBN 0-590-46943-6; In Canada: Scholastic, 1993. 32p. col. ill. map.
Includes index and bibliography.
Reindeer and the life of reindeer herders are explained in this slim,
attractively illustrated paperback. Though the book has the look of
fiction, the text provides straightforward information on the reindeer
life cycle, differences between the captive reindeer and their wild
caribou cousins, rearing of the young, use of antlers, and the seasonal
trek to pastures. Invites personal reading and will be useful where
curriculum covers the cold northern lands.
SUBJ: Reindeer.

VCR 636.2   Ph-2 1-3 $49.95   KD212
COWS! 2ND ED. (Videocassette). Churchill Media ISBN 0-7932-3345-3,
1995. 1/2" VHS videocassette color (9min).
Includes teacher's guide.
When a farm girl visits a herd of cows, she sees a newborn calf as it
struggles to its feet and makes its first search for milk. A narrator
explains simple facts about cows' responses to people, cud chewing
and the stomach system, machine milking, and calves' instinct for
standing soon after birth. Information is sketchy and will need to be
augmented, but it's a pleasant introduction.
SUBJ: Cows./ Milk./ Dairying.

VCR 636.2   Ph-2 3-5 $49.00   OD KD213
DAIRY FARM (Videocassette). TVOntario/dist. by Films for the
Humanities, 1991. 1/2" VHS videocassette color (10min). (Take a look
2).
Teacher's guide available for $3.45.
A child leads a tour of a family dairy farm pointing out a new-born
calf and explaining the care of the cows and the use of milking
machinery. The use of computers to record the eating habits of each
cow, the testing of milk before it is collected into a tank truck, and a
brief explanation of the operations of a milk processing plant are
explained. A quick look at the growing and storing of food for the
cows is the concluding segment of this sketchy but interesting
introduction to milk production.
SUBJ: Dairying./ Farm life./ Dairy cattle./ Milk.

636.2   Ph-1 P-4/2 $15.95   L   KD214
OLDER, JULES. Cow. Illus. by Lyn Severance. Charlesbridge ISBN
0-88106-957-4, 1997. unp. col. ill., maps.
Bright, flat drawings and cheerful text explain the bodies and milk
producing capabilities of cows. Ten sections of text include personal
quips and sensible explanations of a cow's daily life, stomach system,
major breeds, a digression into ice cream sundaes, the birth of calves,
and miscellaneous facts about cows and milk. The humorous patter
and choice of details will amuse and inform readers of all ages.
SUBJ: Cows./ Dairy cattle.

636.5   Ph-2 K-2/2 $5.99   P   KD215
WALLACE, KAREN. My hen is dancing. Illus. by Anita Jeram.
Candlewick ISBN 1-56402-961-1; In Canada: Candlewick/dist. by
Douglas & McIntrye, c1994, 1996. unp. col. ill. (Read and wonder).
A hen's life in the barnyard is described in pleasantly detailed
sketches and simple explanations. The hen's body, eating and sleeping
habits, home in the henhouse, egglaying, and care of chicks are
among topics covered in this nonfiction picture book. Nice material
for primary units on farm life, reading aloud, or beginning readers.
SUBJ: Chickens.

636.7   Ph-1 3-6/2 $15.95   L   KD216
CALMENSON, STEPHANIE. Rosie, a visiting dog's story. Photos by
Justin Sutcliffe. Clarion ISBN 0-395-65477-7, 1994. 47p. col. ill.
Rosie is a beguiling, longhaired black and white Tibetan terrier who is
trained to visit patients of all ages in hospitals and nursing homes.
The appealing photo-documentary shows Rosie attending puppy
kindergarten and then follows her later training, her preparations to
go visiting, and many visits made to children and disabled and elderly
persons. An interesting and heartwarming account of the care and
training of dogs for this special purpose, the book is also a nice
personal introduction to Stephanie Calmenson, author of many
children's books.
SUBJ: Dogs--Training./ Human-animal relationships.

636.7   Ph-2 A/8 $15.99   L   KD217
CLUTTON-BROCK, JULIET. Dog. Knopf/Dorling Kindersley ISBN 0-679-
91459-5, 1991. 64p col illus and photos. (Eyewitness books).
Includes index.
Plentiful pictures and bits of text survey the physical characteristics
and history of wild and domestic dogs. Senses, care of the young,
wolves and foxes, and the various types of dogs are among the
many topics covered. A good browsing compendium--the variety of

animals makes up for difficult text and uneven photographs in a
volume not up to the best standards of this series.
SUBJ: Dogs./ Dog breeds./ Working dogs.

636.7   Ph-1 P-2/2 $13.88   L   KD218
COLE, JOANNA. My puppy is born. Rev. and expanded ed. Photos by
Margaret Miller. Morrow ISBN 0-688-09771-5, 1991. unp col photos.
A Norfolk terrier and her five offspring are the attractive subjects of
this simple introduction to the birth and growth of puppies. The
account is narrated by the little girl who has selected one of the
puppies to be her own; she describes in simple terms the birth process
and the physical characteristics and behavior of the puppies until they
are eight weeks old and ready to leave their mother. The fine color
photographs are absorbing, and the clearly stated text is manageable
for beginning readers.
SUBJ: Dogs./ Animals--Infancy.

VCR 636.7   Ph-2 3-6 $12.95   KD219
DOG (Videocassette). Narrated by Martin Sheen. DK Vision ISBN
1-56458-916-1, 1994. 1/2" VHS videocassette color (35min).
(Eyewitness natural world).
Closed captioned.
Many species of wild and domestic dogs demonstrate the physical
characteristics that enable this animal to survive. A stark white
museum setting with domestic dogs and animal skeletons blends into
many live action scenes featuring wild dog species hunting and
communicating as well as contemporary dogs working and interacting
with humans. The shifting scene is occasionally confusing, but the
presentation is informative and the animals are very appealing.
SUBJ: Dogs.

636.7   Ph-2 5-6/6 $15.93   L   KD220
KAPPELER, MARKUS. Dogs: wild and domestic. Gareth Stevens ISBN
0-8368-0686-7; In Canada: Saunders, 1991. 48p. col. ill., map. (Animal
families).
Includes glossary, bibliography, directory and index.
African hunting dogs, fennecs, maned wolves, and bush dogs are
among several wild cousins of domestic dogs appearing in this brief,
informative survey. A discussion of the history and characteristics of
pet dogs precedes the single page entries featuring attractive color
photographs and commentaries on the wild dogs. The emphasis on
unusual animals is intriguing and creates a good sense of the diversity
among members of the dog family.
SUBJ: Dogs./ Dog breeds.

636.7   Ph-2 5-6/7 $12.95   L   KD221
SILVERSTEIN, ALVIN. Dogs: all about them. By Alvin and Virginia B.
Silverstein. Introduction by John C. McLoughlin. Lothrop, Lee & Shepard
ISBN 0-688-04805-6, 1986. 256p b&w photos.
Includes bibliography and index.
Examines numerous aspects of the history of the dog family, the use
and care of dogs as pets, and characteristics of selected breeds. The
substantial and informative text is accompanied by a utilitarian
selection of photographs and a useful bibliography. Though somewhat
mundane in appearance, this is a very well developed discussion
containing many interesting bits of information.
SUBJ: Dogs.

636.7   Ph-3 5-6/7 $14.95   L   KD222
SQUIRE, ANN. Understanding man's best friend: why dogs look and act
the way they do. Macmillan ISBN 0-02-786590-8; In Canada: Maxwell
Macmillan, 1991. 119p. ill.
Includes index.
Human uses of dogs for hunting, fighting, working, and
companionship are explored in this informative history. The dogs'
descent from wolves and the development of specialized breeds are
discussed in well-written chapters accompanied by poorly produced
photographs. A list of dog breeds and their original roles concludes a
useful account for serious dog fans.
SUBJ: Dogs--History./ Dog breeds./ Dogs--Habits and behavior.

636.7   Ph-2 1-3/2 $3.99   P   KD223
STANDIFORD, NATALIE. Bravest dog ever: the true story of Balto. Illus.
by Donald Cook. Random House ISBN 0-394-99695-X; In Canada:
Random House, 1989. 48p. col. ill. (Step into reading).
The heroic efforts of an Alaskan sled dog brought medicine to people
suffering from an outbreak of diptheria in Nome, Alaska in 1925. The
simple text has some unfamiliar words, but is a heartwarming tale
accompanied by pleasant pastel drawings. Worthwhile and interesting
reading material and a good introduction to both sled dogs and the
idea of animal heroes. For beginning readers.
SUBJ: Balto (Dog)./ Sled dogs./ Dogs./ Diphtheria--Alaska--Nome./
Alaska--History.

636.7   Ph-2 5-A $15.00   P   KD224
TAYLOR, DAVID. You and your dog. Knopf ISBN 0-394-72983-8; In
Canada: Random House, 1986. 288p. ill. (some col.).
> Includes index.
> Provides substantial, detailed information on the history, selection, and
> care of dogs. Very extensive in scope and very attractive in
> appearance, this will serve as a fine resource for reports as well as
> providing excellent guidance to both neophyte and experienced dog
> owners.
> SUBJ: Dogs./ Pets.

VCR 636.7   Ph-2 P-6 $14.95   KD225
WAGGING TAILS: THE DOG AND PUPPY MUSIC VIDEO
(Videocassette). Forney Miller Film & Video/dist. by New Market Sales,
1994. 1/2" VHS videocassette color (30min). (Children's adventure
videos).
> Dogs and puppies of many varieties romp and play with many
> different children in this cheerful celebration of this well loved pet. A
> medley of simple songs sung by an adult vocalist and children forms
> the soundtrack, mentioning pet sizes and some of their characteristics
> as the animals show affection, have baths, and perform simple tricks.
> Ostensibly designed to encourage children's observation of dogs, the
> film is really just a fine opportunity to enjoy dogs in all their diversity.
> SUBJ: Dogs.

636.73   Ph-2 3-6/5 $13.99   T   KD226
PATENT, DOROTHY HINSHAW. Hugger to the rescue. Photos by
William Munoz. Cobblehill/Dutton ISBN 0-525-65161-6, 1994. 32p. col.
ill.
> Friendly Newfoundland dogs of various ages are shown training for
> search and rescue work on land and in snow and water. The essay
> text and numerous photographs follow a Montana family as they
> train their dogs in different seasons and settings, including harnessing
> them for suspension from helicopters and riding in ski lifts and rescue
> rafts. This short, attractive account of dogs at work is a welcome
> addition on an ever interesting subject.
> SUBJ: Rescue dogs./ Search dogs./ Newfoundland dog./ Rescue
> work.

636.737   Ph-2 A/8 $15.00   T   KD227
ANCONA, GEORGE. Sheep dog. Lothrop, Lee & Shepard ISBN 0-688-
04118-3, 1985. unp. ill.
> Includes bibliography.
> Describes the various breeds of dogs used to guard and herd sheep,
> focusing on European breeds which are being used experimentally by
> American ranchers. Handsome photographs of nearly a dozen
> unfamiliar dogs--Shar Planinetz, Great Pyrenees, Maremma, etc. form
> the nucleus of an album presentation which also discusses the work
> styles and training of the dogs and the problems of wild predators
> for sheep farmers. Though the discussion is esoteric for most children,
> the pictures will attract browsers, and the unusual information on
> behavior will appeal to very serious dog fans.
> SUBJ: Sheep dogs./ Working dogs./ Dogs./ Sheep ranches.

636.752   Ph-2 2-5/5 $14.00   T   KD228
JONES, ROBERT F. Jake: a Labrador puppy at work and play. Photos
by Bill Eppridge. Farrar, Straus & Giroux ISBN 0-374-33655-5; In
Canada: HarperCollins, 1992. unp. col. ill.
> This appealing photo essay documents Jake's first year of life and
> simply explains the steps in obedience and retrieval training. Depicts
> Jake interacting with other animals and becoming fast friends with an
> older Labrador who helps train him. The competent photographs are
> modest and attractive and explanations of dog care and training are
> useful and interesting.
> SUBJ: Labrador retriever./ Dogs--Training.

636.8   Ph-2 K-3/2 $13.99   T   KD229
BARE, COLLEEN STANLEY. Toby the tabby kitten. Cobblehill/Dutton
ISBN 0-525-65211-6, 1995. 32p. col. ill.
> Includes index.
> Toby, a Manx kitten, appears in attractive photographs which follow
> his activities and growth during the first few months of life. The simple
> text introduces Toby's owner, Sara, and explains how she cares for
> him as well as describes his physical characteristics, and how he eats,
> sees, plays, and climbs. A final page adds explanation of the cat
> family's history. An appealing introduction to kittens as pets, this will
> be nice for reading aloud or independent reading.
> SUBJ: Manx cat./ Cats./ Pets./ Animals--Infancy.

636.8   Ph-1 P-1/2 $14.93   L   KD230
COLE, JOANNA. My new kitten. Photos by Margaret Miller. Morrow
ISBN 0-688-12902-1, 1995. unp. col. ill.
> A little girl explains the birth and growth of kittens during the first
> two months of their lives in a very attractive photo-essay. The child

visits the soft grey kittens at her aunt's house, waiting patiently for
the day she can choose her own kitten and take him home. Simple
explanations provide a brief account of the growth and care of
kittens, but the fine pictures are the irresistible feature of the book.
SUBJ: Cats./ Pets./ Animals--Infancy.

636.8   Ph-1 K-2/2 $14.95   L   KD231
DE PAOLA, TOMIE. Kids' cat book. Holiday House ISBN 0-8234-0365-
3, 1979. unp. col. ill.
> Appendix: "Some interesting cat facts."
> While choosing a free kitten from Granny Twinkle, Patrick becomes
> an expert in the history, love, care and breeds of cats. The touches of
> humor and watercolor illustrations combine to make this informational
> book an addition to read-aloud time.
> SUBJ: Cats.

636.8   Ph-1 P-1/1 $5.99   P   KD232
EISLER, COLIN. Cats know best. Illus. by Lesley Anne Ivory. Dial ISBN
0-8037-1139-5; In Canada: Fitzhenry & Whiteside, 1988. unp. col. ill.
> Cats and kittens and more cats play and hunt and explore in lovely
> detailed indoor and outdoor scenes. A simple picture book text
> describes the basic behavior traits of cats in keeping warm and cool,
> finding food, raising their young, grooming and more; the variety of
> realistic cats and the clever incorporation of cat motifs in page
> borders and room furnishings delight the eye and convey the essential
> nature of cats to perfection. A warm, colorful tribute to a favorite
> animal, this is a fine choice for reading aloud and lingering enjoyment.
> SUBJ: Cats.

636.8   Ph-2 K-4/2 $14.95   T   KD233
HIRSCHI, RON. What is a cat? Photos by Linda Quartman Younker.
Walker ISBN 0-8027-8122-5; In Canada: Thomas Allen, 1991. unp. col.
ill.
> Cats and kittens of many colors appear in the attractive photographs
> of this brief appreciative introduction to cat behavior. A simple,
> almost poetic text describes cats enjoying the sun, their morning milk,
> jumping, and playing with each other or the children who own them.
> A few bits of advice on caring for pet cats concludes this short album
> which will be most enjoyed for the appealing pictures.
> SUBJ: Cats.

636.8   Ph-2 P-K/4 $13.95   L   KD234
KUKLIN, SUSAN. Taking my cat to the vet. Bradbury ISBN 0-02-
751233-9; In Canada: Collier Macmillan, 1988. unp. col. ill.
> Young Ben explains all the procedures the vet uses in doing a routine
> examination of his cat, Willa. Attractive photographs show Ben
> watching the vet and helping her handle the cat. The slightly precious
> tone of the first person narrative and the very young age of the
> featured child will deter primary grade children who would otherwise
> be a likely audience, but the book is a useful first lesson in pet care.
> SUBJ: Cats--Diseases./ Veterinary hospitals./ Veterinary medicine.

636.8   Ph-2 5-A $13.00   P   KD235
TAYLOR, DAVID. You and your cat. Knopf ISBN 0-394-72984-6; In
Canada: Random House, 1986. 288p. ill. (some col.).
> Includes index.
> Offers a wealth of information on the history and physiology of cats,
> the characteristics of many breeds, and numerous aspects of caring
> for cats as pets. Appealing photographs and many drawings and
> charts accompany the detailed text organized in handbook form. Cat
> owners will find the sections on care of pets, breeding, training and
> showing of cats very useful, while other students will focus on the
> extensive information.
> SUBJ: Cats.

637   Ph-1 1-3/2 $13.89   L   KD236
ALIKI. Milk from cow to carton. Rev. ed. HarperCollins ISBN 0-06-
020435-4; In Canada: HarperCollins, 1992. 32p. col. ill. (Let's-read-and-
find-out science book).
> Cheerful drawings and simple text follow two children as they visit a
> farm and a dairy to learn about cows and the preparation of milk for
> the market. Clear, informative explanations describe a cow's body,
> milking by hand and machine, the transporting and processing of milk,
> varieties of milk and milk products, and the making of cheese.
> Instructions for making butter from cream at home round out this
> attractive presentation on this basic food.
> SUBJ: Dairying./ Milk./ Cows.

637   Ph-1 K-3/4 $13.932.8 L   KD237
CARRICK, DONALD. Milk. Greenwillow ISBN 0-688-04823-4, 1985.
unp. col. ill.
> Selectors' Choice, 16th ed.
> Beginning with cows in the pasture, this simple narrative describes the
> steps in milk at the dairy, packaging it and transporting it to the

supermarket. Clear, full-color pictures are warmly realistic in portraying the basic processes through which we receive this essential food. Appealing enough to be used as a picture book, this elementary lesson will serve widely for pleasure reading and a variety of teaching purposes.
SUBJ: Milk./ Dairying.

637   Ph-3 K-2/2 $12.60   L   KD238
FOWLER, ALLAN. Thanks to cows. Childrens Press ISBN 0-516-04924-0; In Canada: Childrens Press, 1992. 32p. col. ill. (Rookie read-about science).
Includes glossary and index.
Big book available (ISBN 0-516-49625-5, 1992).
Simple facts about cows and the production of milk and other dairy products appear in a small easy-to-read volume. Color photographs accompanying short sentences depict cows at rest and eating, and milking by hand and machine; text briefly mentions foods produced at the dairy plant. A picture glossary concludes the utilitarian introduction to this important animal and food group.
SUBJ: Dairying./ Milk./ Cows.

637   Ph-1 K-3/6 $13.95   L   KD239
GIBBONS, GAIL. Milk makers. Macmillan ISBN 0-02-736640-5, 1985. 32p. col. ill.
Available from National Library Service for the Blind and Physically Handicapped in Braille BR06116.
Surveys the steps in milk production from the physiology of cows through the milking machine, transport to the dairy, pasteurization, packaging, transport to the supermarket, and final consumption at home. The bright drawings include several informative diagrams including comparisons of cow species, the cow's internal organs, various machines, and a full page chart of common milk products. An attractive nonfiction read-aloud which will provide appealing recreational reading and superb teaching material.
SUBJ: Dairying./ Dairy cattle./ Milk./ Cows.

638   Ph-2 5-6/6 $16.95   T   KD240
JOHNSON, SYLVIA A. Beekeeper's year. Photos by Nick Von Ohlen. Little, Brown ISBN 0-316-46745-6; In Canada: Little, Brown, 1994. 32p. col. ill.
Includes glossary.
A careful introduction to beekeeping describes both the human work of the beekeeper and the work of the bees in the hives. Small clear photographs featuring a Minnesota beekeeper accompany the discussion of how hives are structured, tools and clothing, how queens are secured and placed, swarming, the seasonal cycle of human work and bee life, and the gathering of honey. Particularly useful where study units on bees include field trips to science museums or apiaries and where beekeeping is practiced as a hobby.
SUBJ: Bee culture./ Honeybee.

638   Ph-1 4-6/8 $5.95   P   KD241
JOHNSON, SYLVIA A. Silkworms. Photos by Isao Kishida. Lerner ISBN 0-8225-9557-5, 1982. 48p. col. ill. (Lerner natural science book).
Includes glossary and index.
Fine color photographs and informative text introduce in detail the stages of development of silkworms from the hatching of eggs through the larval and pupa stages to the final marvelous transformation into moths. The spinning of the valuable silk cocoons is discussed as are the evolutionary changes which have occurred as this insect has become dependent on man for its existence. While perhaps of more specialized interest, the principles discussed apply widely to moths and butterflies.
SUBJ: Silkworms./ Moths.

638   Ph-2 4-5/6 $11.79   L   KD242
MICHELS, PENNY. Day in the life of a beekeeper. Photos by John Halpern. Troll ISBN 0-8167-2206-4, 1990. 32p. col. ill. (Day in the life of).
A child visits a beekeeper who explains how he cares for the bees in his hives and how he separates honey from the comb. The photo-documentary follows the two as they don the necessary garments, light a smoker, lift out the combs and work the extractor; a most interesting sequence follows the preparation of a box of bees for shipping to another beekeeper. The visit device is a bit intrusive, but the handling of the bees and the necessary effort of bees and humans to produce honey are quite interesting.
SUBJ: Beekeepers./ Bee culture./ Occupations.

639.2   Ph-2 4-5/6 $15.95   L   KD243
CARRICK, CAROL. Whaling days. Woodcuts by David Frampton. Clarion ISBN 0-395-50948-3, 1993. 40p. ill.
Includes glossary, bibliography and index.
Available from the National Library Service for the Blind and

Physically Handicapped on sound recording cassette RC 38188. This history of whaling uses striking woodcut scenes and short descriptive text to explain the work of eighteenth and nineteenth century sailors in hunting and killing whales. The slim volume explains earlier history, the physical characteristics of whales, life aboard ship, the cutting of the dead whales in preparation for market, and twentieth century developments as whaling continues to be controversial. Handsome picture book format may be a drawback with the older children who can manage the text, but the presentation offers an excellent introduction which could stimulate group discussion or further study.
SUBJ: Whaling./ Whales.

639.2   Ph-1 1-3/5 $14.93   L   KD244
FLORIAN, DOUGLAS. Fisher. Greenwillow ISBN 0-688-13130-1, 1994. unp. col. ill. (How we work).
Follows a busy fisherman from dawn until late at night. Simple watercolor illustrations and matter-of-fact text impart basic information, naming objects and explaining their use. Valuable in "goods and services" and career awareness units.
SUBJ: Fishers./ Fishing./ Occupations.

639.2   Ph-3 A/9 $11.95   P   KD245
JENSON, L. B. Fishermen of Nova Scotia. Petheric ISBN 0-919380-33-6; In Canada: Petheric, 1980. 114p. ill., maps.
Generously illustrated with fine pen drawings of the ships, tools, animals (fish, whales, seals, birds) and buildings, the informative text, presented in short sections, relates the history of Nova Scotia's fishing industry from 570 AD to the present. The handlettered text is difficult to read but the title will prove very appealing for children who love detail and an excellent resource for advanced students.
SUBJ: Nova Scotia (Canada)./ Fisheries.

639.3   Ph-2 4-6/7 $15.95   L   KD246
ANCONA, GEORGE. Aquarium book. Written and photographed by George Ancona. Clarion ISBN 0-89919-655-1, 1991. 47p. col. ill.
Includes index and directory.
Aquarium animals and workers star in this striking photo essay. Four well-known aquariums are featured in a discussion covering the purposes and complexities of aquarium exhibits which house a great variety of marine mammals, exotic fish, reptiles, plants, and birds. This quick glimpse into underwater life and behind the scenes aquarium operations offers a good introduction to animal related careers as well.
SUBJ: Aquariums, Public.

639.3   Ph-1 5-6/9 $4.95   P   KD247
BRAEMER, HELGA. Tropical fish: a complete pet owner's manual. By Helga Braemer and Ines Scheurmann. Translated by Waltraut Riave. Illus. by Fritz W. Kohler. Barron's ISBN 0-8120-2686-1, 1983. 80p col photos and b&w illus. (Pet care).
Includes bibliography and index.
Provides thorough instructions on equipping and maintaining aquariums and selecting and caring for tropical fish. The clear, detailed text accompanied by handsome photographs and helpful diagrams is set in an attractive small format. A first rate guide for beginning and more experienced aquarists.
SUBJ: Tropical fish./ Aquariums./ Aquarium fishes.

639.3   Ph-2 4-6/6 $16.95   L   KD248
CONE, MOLLY. Come back, salmon: how a group of dedicated kids adopted Pigeon Creek and brought it back to life. Photos. by Sidnee Wheelwright. Sierra Club/Little, Brown ISBN 0-87156-572-2, 1992. 48p b&w illus, b&w and col photos.
Includes glossary and index.
Available from the National Library Service for the Blind and Physically Handicapped on sound recording cassette RC 37613.
Enterprising children and their teachers clean up a creek and re-introduce salmon to its waters in this true story of an outstanding conservation effort. Chapters of text discuss the history of the creek, its pollution, activities of the school classes, and many aspects of the salmon's complex life cycle. Sidebars of added information include helpful diagrams while attractive photographs add information and appeal. An inspiring example of creative teaching, this offers useful information on salmon and on ecology.
SUBJ: Fish habitat improvement./ Salmon./ Environmental protection./ Jackson Elementary School (Everett, Wash.)

639.3   Ph-2 A/9 $5.50   P   KD249
GRIEHL, KLAUS. Snakes: giant snakes and non-venomous snakes in the terrarium. Barron's ISBN 0-8120-2813-9, 1984. 80p. col. ill. (Pet care).
Includes bibliography and index.
Provides detailed information on selecting and caring for pet snakes, including the equipping of the terrarium, breeding snakes, providing

live food, setting up conditions for hibernation, and preventing illness and infection. Numerous helpful diagrams are provided, and there are handsome color photographs and detailed physical description of many species of small and large snakes. The attractive, highly informative slim volume will serve as a general source on snakes as well as a manual on pet care.
SUBJ: Snakes as pets./ Pets.

639.3 Ph-1 5-6/9 $4.95 P KD250
WILKE, HARTMUT. Turtles: everything about purchase, care, nutrition and diseases. Translated by Rita and Robert Kimber. Illus. by Fritz W. Kohler. Barron's ISBN 0-8120-2631-4, 1983. 75p b&w illus col photos. (Pet care.)
Includes index.
Explains the physical characteristics of different turtle species, numerous aspects of turtle physiology and behavior, the construction of terrariums to appropriately house turtles, and the care and breeding of turtles in captivity. The fine color photographs and line drawings and the thoroughness of the text along with the inherent appeal of the subject to children make this an excellent information source for both pet owners and animal lovers who will never undertake the rather difficult challenge of a turtle pet.
SUBJ: Turtles as pets./ Pets.

639.9 Ph-1 5-6/8 $17.95 L KD251
ARNOLD, CAROLINE. On the brink of extinction: the California condor. Photos by Michael Wallace. Gulliver/Harcourt Brace Jovanovich ISBN 0-15-257990-7; In Canada: Harcourt Brace Jovanovich, 1993. 48p. col. ill.
Includes index.
Available from the National Library Service for the Blind and Physically Handicapped on sound recording cassette RC 37849.
Impressive views of the enormous condor in captivity and in the wild accompany detailed discussion of the endangered bird's life cycle and human efforts to save the condor from extinction. The fine photographs follow the birth and growth of the young, the use of hand puppets to simulate the parent birds, and the preparation of the birds to live in the wild. The book ends on an uncertain note since re-establishing the birds has not yet truly succeeded, but the interesting and empathetic discussion offers excellent information about current efforts to manage endangered species.
SUBJ: California condor./ Condors./ Rare birds./ Wildlife conservation.

639.9 Ph-1 4-6/7 $16.95 T KD252
DEWEY, JENNIFER OWINGS. Wildlife rescue: the work of Dr. Kathleen Ramsay. Photos by Don MacCarter. Boyds Mills/dist. by St. Martin's ISBN 1-56397-045-7; In Canada: Boyds Mills/dist. by McClelland & Stewart, 1994. 64p. col. ill.
Dramatic episodes of injured animals cared for in a New Mexico veterinary center will fascinate animal lovers of all ages. Dr. Ramsay is seen performing many surgeries, and her staff care for sick and injured birds and mammals of all sizes. The care of orphaned baby animals and the return of healed animals to their wild habitats are also describred in the slim book. Attractive introduction to the work of a veterinarian and to the rescue of wild animals is useful for environmental studies and career studies. Fine choice for personal reading enjoyment and book talking.
SUBJ: Wildlife rescue./ Ramsay, Kathleen./ Women veterinarians.

639.9 Ph-1 1-4/3 $15.95 T KD253
FLEMING, DENISE. Where once there was a wood. Henry Holt ISBN 0-8050-3761-6; In Canada: Fitzhenry & Whiteside, 1996. unp. col. ill.
Includes directory and bibliography.
In this thoughtful introduction to ecology, poetic lines of text and attractive handmade paper collages describe the once-upon-a-time natural world of plants and animals that has been replaced by houses. The birds, berries, ferns, snakes, and other inhabitants of woodland and meadow are a satisfying entourage, ending abruptly at the final scene of houses. Several concluding pages explain how to turn a yard into a backyard habitat inviting to wildlife. This is a lovely item for reading aloud as a story, a science lesson, or an introduction to nature projects. For environmental studies.
SUBJ: Wildlife attracting./ Wildlife conservation./ Man--Influence on nature.

639.9 Ph-1 5-6/7 $15.99 T KD254
JOHNSON, SYLVIA A. Raptor rescue!: an eagle flies free. Photos by Ron Winch. Dutton ISBN 0-525-45301-6, 1995. 32p. col. ill.
Selectors' Choice, 21st ed.
An injured bald eagle receives treatment at a Minnesota raptor center and later is prepared for release into the wild in this handsome photo-essay. Three strands intertwine in the presentation: raptor life and dangers, the diagnosis and care of this particular bird, and the

work of wildlife centers in protecting the wild existence of animals. As an added bonus, the doctor and many of her assistants are women. Useful as material on endangered species and career studies, this will be widely enjoyed by animal fans. For environmental studies.
SUBJ: Bald eagle--Wounds and injuries--Treatment./ Birds of prey--Wounds and injuries--Treatment.

639.9 Ph-2 K-2/4 $13.93 L KD255
KOCH, MICHELLE. World water watch. Greenwillow ISBN 0-688-11465-2, 1993. unp. col. ill.
Six endangered animals appear in an appeal to keep the world's ocean waters clean and its wildlife safe. Four-page segments illustrated in simple, naive style watercolors describe animals living in different parts of the world with comments on what is harming them. Animals include the sea otter, green sea turtle, penguin, fur seal, polar bear, and humpback whale. Final page of notes adds a bit of information about other countries where each animal lives, rounding out an attractive picture book and sobering early lesson in wildlife protection.
SUBJ: Rare animals./ Wildlife conservation./ Man--Influence on nature.

639.9 Ph-2 A/6 $23.95 L KD256
NIRGIOTIS, NICHOLAS. No more dodos: how zoos help endangered wildlife. By Nicholas Nirgiotis and Theodore Nirgiotis. Lerner ISBN 0-8225-2856-8, 1996. 112p. col. ill.
Includes directory, glossary, bibliography and index.
Seven essays focus on various animals and zoo efforts to examine worldwide problems in conservation. Examples of extinction, the web of life, zoo breeding programs, advances in cryopreservation, genetic studies, and more are explained in the thoughtful, informative text accompanied by attractive small photographs. The difficult, but interesting, text will best serve very capable readers interested in animal science or ecology. For environmental studies.
SUBJ: Wildlife conservation./ Endangered species./ Wildlife reintroduction.

639.9 Ph-1 5-6/7 $15.95 T KD257
PATENT, DOROTHY HINSHAW. Where the wild horses roam. Photos by William Munoz. Clarion ISBN 0-89919-507-5, 1989. 71p. col. ill.
Includes index.
Wild horses, rapidly increasing in numbers in 10 western states, are introduced in an informative text and handsome color photographs. After describing the history and behavior of the animals, the author focuses strongly on the problems of overpopulation and human efforts to control the number of horses grazing on public lands. A list of agencies concerned with protection and adoption of horses concludes a fine presentation on a highly appealing subject.
SUBJ: Wild horses./ Horses./ Wildlife management.

639.9 Ph-1 A/9 $14.95 L KD258
PATENT, DOROTHY HINSHAW. Whooping crane: a comeback story. Photos by William Munoz. Clarion ISBN 0-89919-455-9, 1988. 88p. col. ill.
Includes index.
Available from National Library Service for the Blind and Physically Handicapped on sound recording cassette RC30532.
Both the whooping cranes and their comeback from near extinction are impressive, and they receive careful treatment in this handsome volume. The informative text covers the bird's life cycle and very interesting aspects of the work of scientists in protecting and nurturing the handsome species. Fine photographs in color and black and white are both appealing and informative, and the book cautions that the successful return of the cranes is still very tentative and requires further human diligence.
SUBJ: Whooping cranes./ Rare birds./ Birds--Protection./ Wildlife conservation.

VCR 640 Ph-3 2-4 $99.95 OD KD259
HOME ALONE: YOU'RE IN CHARGE (Videocassette). Sunburst Communications 2363, 1991. 1/2" VHS videocassette color (12min).
Includes teacher's guide and 8 reproducible activity sheets.
Discusses safety concerns such as not opening the door to strangers, using kitchen appliances only with permission, answering the telephone without letting the caller know you are alone, having emergency telephone numbers handy, and posting your home address. Most latchkey students will have had this training from their parents, but it never hurts to review and reinforce. Also discusses what to do with all the waiting time: starting a hobby such as stamp or baseball card collecting, reading, playing board games, and getting involved in art and science projects.
SUBJ: Latchkey children./ Life skills./ Self-reliance./ Children of working parents.

VCR 640   Ph-2 4-6 $80.00   KD260
HOME ON YOUR OWN (Videocassette). National Geographic 51600, 1994. 1/2" VHS videocassette color (18min).
Includes teacher's guide.
Closed captioned.
Young teen reporters do a television piece, interviewing children and adults about safe practices for staying home alone after school. Key safety, the route home, arriving home, use of a contact person, smart practices in answering the phone and the door, and useful ways of spending time alone are demonstrated by an attractive selection of children and assorted community workers including a police officer and a firefighter. The upbeat tone and sensible advice will be useful for parents as well as children. (Parents' Shelf).
SUBJ: Latchkey children./ Children of working parents./ Life skills./ Self-reliance./ Safety.

VCR 640   Ph-1 5-6 $125.00   OD KD261
LATCHKEY CHILDREN: WHEN YOU'RE IN CHARGE (Videocassette). Learning Tree LT355, 1986. 1/2" VHS videocassette color.
Includes teacher's guide.
Provides practical, common sense advice on setting house rules, scheduling chores, cooking and nutrition, answering the door and phone, handling fire and first aid emergencies, and developing personal interests and study habits. An attractive variety of boys and girls are shown in realistic situations, and occasionally children narrate small instances of their own experiences. A useful, attractive and reassuring guide to accepting responsibility.
Contents: Judgement and personal responsibilities (9min); Taking care of yourself (9min); Handling emergencies (9min); Making the most of your time (9min).
SUBJ: Children of working parents./ Self-reliance./ Life skills./ Latchkey children.

640   Ph-2 5-6/8 $12.95   L   KD262
SCHMITT, LOIS. Smart spending: a young consumer's guide. Scribner's ISBN 0-684-19035-4; In Canada: Collier Macmillan, 1989. 95p.
Includes index.
True to life examples illustrate practical advice on how to protect yourself from losing money on poor merchandise and bad advertising. The instructive text discusses money management, advertising hype, fraudulent sales schemes, labels and warranties, dealing with mail order problems, product safety, food and diet information and methods of effective complaining. Unfortunately dull in appearance this is useful consumer information that will be interesting to individuals and could well be used in class discussions.
SUBJ: Consumer education.

VCR 640.83   Ph-1 P-K $19.95   KD263
PRESCHOOL POWER!: JACKET FLIPS AND OTHER TIPS (Videocassette). Concept Associates ISBN 1-56319-007-9, 1991. 1/2" VHS videocassette color (30min). (Preschool power!).
Selectors' Choice, 19th ed.
An attractive cast of preschool children demonstrate many simple skills involved in personal hygiene, getting dressed, preparing food, playing, cleanup chores, and pet care. Numerous unlinked segments make up each film with a soundtrack filled with upbeat songs and occasional lines spoken by the children; viewers are encouraged to join in on occasion and many enjoyable projects are demonstrated. The appealing lessons in life skills encourage not only cleanliness, responsibility, and good nutrition but also playfulness and imagination. Additional videos in this series are: MORE PRESCHOOL POWER! ISBN 1-56319-014-1, 1991, (30min); PRESCHOOL POWER 3! ISBN 1-56319-017-6, 1992, (31min); and EVEN MORE PRESCHOOL POWER ISBN 1-56319-019-2, 1993, (31min).
SUBJ: Life skills./ Self-reliance./ Cleanliness.

641.3   Ph-1 5-6/7 $6.95   P   KD264
BOURGEOIS, PAULETTE. Amazing apple book. Illus. by Linda Hendry. Addison-Wesley ISBN 0-201-52333-7, 1990. 63p. ill.
Includes glossary and index.
History, crafts, recipes, and many miscellaneous subjects are treated in this appealing paperback. There's information on growing apples, advice on selecting and storing them, games to play, and much more along with humorous drawings and diagrams. The well chosen topics and brisk clear style offer many possiblities for use.
SUBJ: Apples.

641.3   Ph-2 4-6/7 $17.50   L   KD265
ERLBACH, ARLENE. Peanut butter. Lerner ISBN 0-8225-2387-6, 1994. 48p. col. ill. (How it's made).
Includes glossary and index.
Peanut butter facts and recipes accompany explanations of how peanuts are grown and the many steps of processing peanut butter. Small color photographs and bits of inserted miscellany break up the factual discussion. Provides an adequate overview of the manufacture of peanut butter as well as the production and treatment of raw peanuts. Explanations of the nutritional values of peanut butter, instructions for making peanut butter at home, and a good assortment of recipes add appeal to the small volume.
SUBJ: Peanut butter./ Peanuts.

641.3   Ph-2 K-2/2 $14.95   L   KD266
HAUSHERR, ROSMARIE. What food is this? Scholastic ISBN 0-590-46583-X; In Canada: Scholastic, 1994. 40p. ill. (some col.).
Includes glossary.
Questions about the origins of different foods accompany color photographs of a multiethnic cast of children. "What sweet food grows on a thorny bush?" "What food looks like colored gravel?" Explanations of how the foods are produced are illustrated with black and white photographs on pages following the questions. An inviting scheme for beginning discussion or for an informative picture book. Includes explanation of the USDA food pyramid and nutrition suggestions for parents. (Parents' Shelf).
SUBJ: Food./ Questions and answers.

641.3   Ph-2 5-6/6 $14.99   T   KD267
KING, ELIZABETH. Chile fever: a celebration of peppers. Story and photos by Elizabeth King. Dutton ISBN 0-525-45255-9, 1995. unp. col. ill.
Over 3,000 varieties of chile peppers grow worldwide, but this attractive introduction focuses on New Mexico-type chiles grown and celebrated in the town of Hatch. Photographs and text explain the history of the plant, how peppers are grown and harvested, ways different cultures prepare peppers, drying and roasting, the stringing of the popular ristras, and events at the annual Hatch Chile Festival. As this colorful food has become increasingly familiar, many children will enjoy reading about its production and use.
SUBJ: Hot peppers./ Hatch Chile Festival, Hatch, N.M./ Hatch (N.M.)--Social life and customs.

641.3   Ph-1 3-6/11 $15.95   L   KD268
MICUCCI, CHARLES. Life and times of the peanut. Houghton Mifflin ISBN 0-395-72289-6, 1997. 32p. col. ill., map.
Includes bibliography.
Selectors' Choice, 21st ed.
Humor and facts abound in the copious small drawings and topical entries discussing the history, growth, and many uses of this well-known legume. The peanut plant, peanut agriculture, the amazing range of peanut products, the making and uses of peanut butter, and the work of George Washington Carver are among the many topics in the cheerful, information-packed presentation. Useful as science, this will be widely enjoyed for personal reading.
SUBJ: Peanuts.

641.5   Ph-1 3-6 $15.95   T   KD269
COLEN, KIMBERLY. Peas and honey: recipes for kids (with a pinch of poetry). Illus. by Mandy Victor. Wordsong/Boyds Mills ISBN 1-56397-062-7; In Canada: McClelland & Stewart, 1995. 64p. col. ill.
Includes indexes.
Poems and useful bits of information accompany a variety of recipes in this attractive celebration of food to entice beginning cooks. Sensible safety tips and pleasant watercolor scenes in a small, manageable volume frame clear instructions in nearly 20 recipes for breakfast dishes, sandwiches, and all sorts of foods for lunch and dinner. Invites browsing and encourages appreciation of food--most novice cooks should find success here.
SUBJ: Cookery./ Food--Poetry./ Poetry.

641.5   Ph-2 K-2/5 $13.93   L   KD270
FLORIAN, DOUGLAS. Chef. Greenwillow ISBN 0-688-11109-2, 1992. unp. col. ill. (How we work).
Simple explanations and colorful pictures follow the many tasks of a chef and her staff as they work through the day preparing for the restaurant's dinner hour. Early day shopping, menu planning, and meat, vegetable, and dessert preparation are described. The author explains that chefs also work in schools, hospitals, and other places where many people eat. Effective introduction to this type of work concludes with a page of labelled pictures of the chef's tools.
SUBJ: Cooks./ Cookery./ Occupations.

641.5   Ph-1 3-6 $12.99   T   KD271
GORDON, LYNN. Messipes: a microwave cookbook of deliciously messy masterpieces. Illus. by Susan Synarski. Random House ISBN 0-679-87426-7; In Canada: Random House, 1996. 46p. col. ill. (spiral bound). "Spark! production."
Holy guacamole! Kids and parents will enjoy this inviting introduction to quick cookery featuring fresh and packaged foods. The format is an attention grabber--small, spiral bound, sandwich shaped book with

shiny pages. Practical recipes include safety instructions and cover an attractive array of snacks, main dish sandwiches, soups, salads, and miscellany. This will be especially enjoyed by children who must be responsible for meal preparation.
SUBJ: Cookery./ Microwave cookery.

641.5   Ph-1 P-3 $15.95   T   KD272
KATZEN, MOLLIE. Pretend soup and other real recipes: a cookbook for preschoolers and up. By Mollie Katzen and Ann Henderson. Illus. by Mollie Katzen. Tricycle Press ISBN 1-883672-06-6, 1994. 95p. col. ill.
Manageable child-tested recipes, plentiful advice to parents, and dual instructions in printed detail and pictographs are designed to enable young children to participate fully in food preparation. The nineteen recipes include soups, salads, popovers, muffins, sandwiches, and beverages, with an emphasis on fresh fruits and vegetables. Sharp knives and stoves are left to adult assistants while the major tasks of combining ingredients, slicing with a table knife, stirring, spreading, turning, and timing the cooking are tasks for the child. The practical, attractive volume is a treasure for parents, preschool teachers, and young cooks eager to work in the kitchen. (Parents' Shelf).
SUBJ: Cookery.

641.5   Ph-1 5-6 $13.95   P   KD273
KENDA, MARGARET. Cooking wizardry for kids. By Margaret Kenda and Phyllis S. Williams. Barron's ISBN 0-8120-4409-6, 1990. 314p. col. ill.
Includes index.
Each recipe is treated as a project in this clever combination of recipes, science experiments and bits of folklore. There are some 200 recipes for all kinds of foods, and the object is to learn about chemical processes and properties of foods; instructions for assembling several types of cooking mixes with related recipes is a particularly nice feature. This fat spiral bound volume offers an appealing blend of good reading, cooking, science, and enjoyment of food.
SUBJ: Science--Experiments./ Experiments./ Cookery.

641.5   Ph-2 5-6/7 $11.95   T   KD274
MACDONALD, KATE. Anne of Green Gables cookbook. Illustrated by Barbara DiLella. Oxford ISBN 0-19-540496-3, 1986. 48p. ill. (some col.)
Provides contemporary recipes for dishes mentioned in various books in the "Anne of Green Gables" series; the 25 recipes range from a simple lettuce salad through many tea goodies and saucy chicken and creamy vegetable soup. Preliminary information on cooking techniques and terms is included as are appropriate quotes and simply drawn, pleasant scenes from the novels. An enjoyable tie-in for cooking fans and a fine choice for book talks.
SUBJ: Cookery.

641.5   Ph-2 A/11 $13.95   L   KD275
PERL, LILA. Hunter's stew and hangtown fry: what pioneer America ate and why. Illus. by Richard Cuffari. Clarion ISBN 0-395-28922-X, c1977. 156p. ill.
An excellent book on history and food. The author describes the cultural situation of five sections of pioneer America and gives twenty representative recipes of the peoples (many of them immigrants) and the geographical areas. An excellent source of unusual information for history and food/nutrition classroom units. A follow-up title to the author's SLUMPS, GRUNTS AND SNICKERDOODLES.
SUBJ: Cookery./ Frontier and pioneer life./ Food supply--History.

641.5   Ph-1 A/9 $14.45   L   KD276
PERL, LILA. Slumps, grunts, and snickerdoodles: what Colonial America ate and why. Illus. by Richard Cuffari. Clarion ISBN 0-395-28923-8, 1975. 125p. ill.
Available from National Library Service for the Blind and Physically Handicapped in Braille BR03185.
A different cookbook that describes some of the history, culture and geography that contributed to the early colonists' culinary favorites. With a few modifications, we are given thirteen recipes that helped sustain these hardy pioneers. This book is an interesting way to expand a classroom history unit.
SUBJ: Cookery./ United States--Social life and customs--To 1775.

641.5   Ph-2 5-6 $14.95   P   KD277
REX-JOHNSON, BRAIDEN. That's fresh!: seasonal recipes for young cooks. By Braiden Rex-Johnson and David C. Wasson. Illus. by Spencer Johnson. Sasquatch Books ISBN 1-57061-017-7; In Canada: Raincoast, 1995. 95p. ill.
Includes index.
Practical explanations of many fresh foods and their preparation accompany a varied assortment of recipes for each of the four seasons. Advice on shopping or picking foods, cooking techniques,

and variations of ingredients offers interesting reading, and the recipes reflect contemporary food choices resulting from the international mix of our population. Serious cooks of all ages will enjoy the discussion and the flavorful array of meats, soups, breads, dips, and other dishes.
SUBJ: Cookery, American.

641.5   Ph-2 4-6 $14.65   L   KD278
RITCHIE, DOREEN. Kid's cuisine. Edited by Janet Stewart. Illustrated by Rick Rowden, et al. Durkin Hayes ISBN 0-88625-186-9, 1988. 48p. col. ill.
Includes glossary.
Good humored drawings of young cooks are sprinkled through this paperback compendium of recipes for each of the three meals plus snacks and desserts. Recipes are set in color blocks resembling recipe cards, and there's a drawing of each completed dish; nearly all of the dishes are fairly well-known, and the directions are clear and uncomplicated. This is a congenial and practical guide with just enough advice to make children comfortable with assorted cooking techniques and foods.
SUBJ: Cookery.

641.5   Ph-2 P/3 $13.95   L   KD279
ROCKWELL, ANNE F. Pots and pans. By Anne Rockwell. Illus. by Lizzy Rockwell. Macmillan ISBN 0-02-777631-X; In Canada: Maxwell Macmillan, 1993. unp. col. ill.
"Look what's in our kitchen--it is full of lots and lots of pots and pans and lots of other things" begins this simple kitchen tour. Large clear drawings name numerous cooking pans and other kitchen implements. The little boy and girl who enter the kitchen at the beginning are seen again at the end playing with the whole profusion of pots. The congenial exercise speaks to a universal pastime of young children.
SUBJ: Kitchen utensils.

641.5   Ph-2 A $19.95   T   KD280
SCOBEY, JOAN. Fannie Farmer junior cookbook. New and rev. ed. Illus. by Patience Brewster. Little, Brown ISBN 0-316-77624-6; In Canada: Little, Brown, 1993. 280p. ill.
Includes index.
This full-scale cookbook, containing substantial sections on food categories from soups to dessert sauces and drinks, is a fine handbook for serious cooks. Introductory sections on tools, cooking techniques, safety, and menu planning are followed by recipes for eleven food groups, including meat and fish, pasta and grains, cakes and pies. Clear instructions on shopping for ingredients and preparation of a wide variety of foods make this very useful for children and adults.
SUBJ: Cookery.

641.5   Ph-1 1-4 $4.95   P   KD281
SUPRANER, ROBYN. Quick and easy cookbook. Illus. by Renzo Barto. Troll ISBN 0-89586-342-1, c1981, 1985. 48p. col. ill.
"Some hints and rules:" p4-5.
Includes metric conversion table.
Twenty-one simple recipes for the very young chef featuring carefully explained instructions and colorful cartoon artwork. Whipped cream, homemade applesauce, egg salad, and hamburger heroes are some included.
SUBJ: Cookery.

641.5   Ph-3 4-6/9 $16.95   T   KD282
WALKER, BARBARA MUHS. Little House cookbook: frontier foods from Laura Ingalls Wilder's classic stories. New ed. Illus. by Garth Williams. HarperCollins ISBN 0-06-026418-7; In Canada: HarperCollins, 1995. 240p. ill.
Includes glossary, metric conversion table, bibliography and index.
Selectors' Choice, 13th ed.
Available from National Library Service for the Blind and Physically Handicapped on sound recording cassette RC18894.
Quotations from the original books describing foods set the framework for this collection of recipes similar to the ones that might well have been use by the Ingalls family. Excellent source material for use in social studies units as well as for family sharing and/or classroom experiences.
SUBJ: Cookery, American--History./ Wilder, Laura Ingalls./ Frontier and pioneer life.

641.5   Ph-2 4-6 $19.95   T   KD283
ZALBEN, JANE BRESKIN. Beni's family cookbook for the Jewish holidays. Forward by Joan Nathan. Henry Holt ISBN 0-8050-3735-7; In Canada: Fitzhenry & Whiteside, 1996. 91p. col. ill.
Includes index.
Beni, a badger, and his numerous relatives appear in small pretty

pictures and introduce each of several recipes for foods enjoyed during 11 Jewish holy days. The clear, straightforward recipes for breads, soups, main dishes, and desserts include dairy, meat, and pareve ingredients. Some of the foods are commonly enjoyed for most of the year while others are especially associated with a particular holiday. The animal characters suggest a young audience, but the book is a pleasant, substantial compendium that will be enjoyed for family cooking and as an introduction to the Jewish holidays. Recipes will require adult assistance.
SUBJ: Cookery, Jewish./ Fasts and feasts--Judaism./ Literary cookbooks.

641.59   Ph-1 5-6/5 $19.95   L   KD284
BRADY, APRIL A. Kwanzaa karamu: cooking and crafts for a Kwanzaa feast. Illus. by Barbara Knutson. Photos by Robert L. and Diane Wolfe. Carolrhoda ISBN 0-87614-842-9, 1995. 64p. col. ill.
Includes glossary and index.
Selectors' Choice, 20th ed.
Customs of celebrating Kwanzaa introduce a pleasing variety of recipes and instructions for a few simple craft projects. The history of the Kwanzaa festival in the United States and statements of the seven principles form the setting. Emphasis is on the sharing of good food with useful instructions on cooking, attractive color photographs, and a delectable assortment of dishes from the United States, the Caribbean, and Africa. Older children who enjoy cooking will find manageable recipes to use throughout the year. For multicultural studies.
SUBJ: Afro-American cookery./ Kwanzaa./ Cookery./ Kwanzaa decorations./ Handicraft.

641.59   Ph-2 3-5 $12.95   P   KD285
COOK, DEANNA F. Kids' multicultural cookbook: food and fun around the world. Illus. by Michael P. Kline. Williamson ISBN 0-913589-91-8, 1995. 159p. ill., maps.
"Williamson Kids Can! book."
Includes index.
Bits of information about daily life, common foods, special holidays, and children's play along with simple recipes from many countries fill this congenial broad volume. Useful introductory instructions on food preparation are included. Includes small photographs of children and suggestions for crafts and special food sharing events. Recipes vary in difficulty, are sometimes very Americanized, and include many fruit drinks along with a few main dishes, breads, and desserts. Though this is not the most authentic presentation of the foods, many of the activities will work well with children, and the worldwide scope serves the ever present interest in multicultural studies.
SUBJ: Cookery, International./ Manners and customs.

641.59   Ph-1 4-6/8 $18.95   L   KD286
CORONADA, ROSA. Cooking the Mexican way. Lerner ISBN 0-8225-0907-5, 1982. 47p. ill. (some col.), map. (Easy menu ethnic cookbooks).
Includes index.
Each book in this attractive series offers well-organized information on the geography and life in a particular country, menus for several meals and recipes for approximately twenty dishes. Useful material for social studies, cooking buffs, multicultural studies, or children interested in learning about their own ethnic backgrounds. Handsome color photographs and line drawings include a map, a cultural scene, most of the completed dishes, and some of the cooking utensils and ingredients.
Others in the series are: Bisignano, Alpohonse, COOKING THE ITALIAN WAY (ISBN 0-8225-0906-7, 1982); Waldee, Lynne Marie, COOKING THE FRENCH WAY (ISBN 0-8225-0904-0, 1982); Munsen, Sylvia, COOKING THE NORWEGIAN WAY (ISBN 0-8225-0901-6, 1982, OPC); Weston, Reiko, COOKING THE JAPANESE WAY (ISBN 0-8225-0905-9, 1983); Zamojska-Hutchins, Danuta, COOKING THE POLISH WAY (ISBN 0-8225-0909-1, 1984); Villios, Lynne, COOKING THE GREEK WAY (ISBN 0-8225-0910-5, 1984); Plotkin, Gregory, COOKING THE RUSSIAN WAY (ISBN 0-8225-0915-6, 1986); Hargittai, Magdolna, COOKING THE HUNGARIAN WAY (ISBN 0-8225-0916-4, 1986); Harrison, Supenn, COOKING THE THAI WAY (ISBN 0-8225-0917-2, 1986); Bacon, Josephine, COOKING THE ISRAELI WAY (ISBN 0-8225-0912-1, 1986); Amari, Suad, COOKING THE LEBANESE WAY (ISBN 0-8225-0913-X, 1985); Nguyen, Chi, COOKING THE VIETNAMESE WAY (ISBN 0-8225-0914-8, 1985); Madavan, Jay, COOKING THE INDIAN WAY (ISBN 0-8225-0911-3, 1985); Parnell, Helga, COOKING THE GERMAN WAY (ISBN 0-8225-0918-0, 1988); Kaufman, Cheryl Davidson, COOKING THE CARIBBEAN WAY (ISBN 0-8225-0920-2, 1988); Nabwire, Constance, COOKING THE AFRICAN WAY (ISBN 0-8225-0919-9, 1988); Chung, Okwha and Judy Monroe, COOKING THE KOREAN WAY (ISBN 0-8225-0921-0, 1988); and Hughes, Helga, COOKING THE IRISH WAY (ISBN 0-8225-0931-8, 1996).
SUBJ: Cookery, International.

641.59   Ph-2 5-6/7 $16.95   T OD KD287
MACK-WILLIAMS, KIBIBI. Food and our history. Rourke ISBN 1-57103-033-6, 1995. 48p. col. ill. (African American life).
Includes glossary, bibliography and index.
African food traditions and the American and European foods eaten by slaves are examined as influences still evident in African-American life. The slim volume includes historical prints, photographs, recipes, and explanations of soul food and foods associated with holiday celebrations. Though dry in tone, the subject and information are both interesting and useful for multicultural studies and browsing.
SUBJ: Afro-American cookery--History./ Cookery, American./ Afro-Americans--History.

641.59   Ph-2 4-5 $6.95   P OD KD288
WIKLER, MADELINE. Miracle meals, eight nights of food 'n fun for Chanukah. By Madeline Wikler and Judyth Groner. Illustrated by Chari Radin. Kar-Ben Copies ISBN 0-930494-71-7, 1987. 64p. ill.
Miracles have little to do with this straightforward cookbook which should be useful at Chanukah and throughout the year. Clear, simple recipes for a variety of soups, latkes, dairy and meat dishes, desserts and beverages include both uninteresting choices using packaged foods and simplified versions of more complex recipes. The story of Chanukah, a few Chanukah games, sprightly drawings of children, general working instructions, and symbols indicating level of difficulty and meat/dairy/parve dishes are all included in the slim, attractive book.
SUBJ: Hanukkah cookery./ Hanukkah.

641.6   Ph-2 P-2/2 $14.95   L   KD289
BROWN, LAURENE KRASNY. Vegetable show. By Laurie Krasny Brown. Little, Brown ISBN 0-316-11363-8; In Canada: Little, Brown, 1995. unp. col. ill.
Includes music and glossary.
Mr. B. A. Dilly and a silly cast of vegetable performers present "Vegetable Vaudeville...the Greatest, Greenest Show on Earth." Busy collages feature Mr. String Beanie, the Wee Peas of the Vine County School, Bud the Spud, and other zany characters who dance, sing, and tell jokes and riddles in an energetic and enjoyable tribute to vegetables. The fun romp concludes with a page of simple facts about each of the vegetables. An amusing introduction to the characters on the endpapers rounds out an upbeat show that will make children giggle. A very palatable introduction for beginning readers and reading aloud.
SUBJ: Vegetables./ Nutrition.

641.6   Ph-2 2-4/6 $15.95   L   KD290
DE PAOLA, TOMIE. Popcorn book. Holiday House ISBN 0-8234-0314-9, c1978. 32p. col. ill.
Spanish edition available EL LIBRO DE LAS PALOMITAS DE MAIZ (ISBN 0-8234-1058-7, 1993).
A skillful author manages to incorporate interesting facts and have a humorous story existing at the same time without the confusion one might expect. One twin brother reads about the history, varieties, uses and legends of popcorn from the encyclopedia while the other twin cooks a whopping amount. Two recipes conclude the book.
SUBJ: Popcorn.

641.8   Ph-2 4-6/6 $18.60   L   KD291
BADT, KARIN LUISA. Pass the bread! Childrens Press ISBN 0-516-08191-8; In Canada: Childrens Press, 1995. 32p. col. ill. (World of difference).
Includes glossary and index.
Depicts and describes the breads of various cultures worldwide. Emphasis is on the role of climate in determining types of grain used in preparing bread. Valuable in discussion of similarities and differences. For multicultural studies.
SUBJ: Bread.

641.8   Ph-2 3-4/2 $15.96   L   KD292
MARTINO, TERESA. Pizza! Illus. by Brigid Faranda. Raintree ISBN 0-8172-3533-7, 1989. 30p. col. ill. (Real readers).
Pizza fit for a queen required something special, so cheese was added to what were then traditional toppings of basil and tomatoes-- or so this story goes. Though undocumented, this simple history of pizza in Italy and the United States describes a probable evolution which is illustrated in full-page line drawings brightly accented with red, green, and golden yellow. The Italian names will be difficult for young readers, but the book is attractive and concludes with a page suggesting teaching reinforcement activities for parents.
SUBJ: Pizza.

641.8   Ph-2 K-2/2 $14.93   L   KD293
MORRIS, ANN. Bread, bread, bread. Photos by Ken Heyman. Lothrop, Lee & Shepard ISBN 0-688-06335-7, 1989. 29p. col. ill.

Includes index.
Handsome photographs and simple text introduce many forms of bread eaten in countries around the world. A somewhat playful narrative follows the pictures which show the eating of bread in many settings as well as the making and selling of bread in different cultures. A pictorial index recaps the book, adding some factual identification of the country and type of bread shown on each of the pages of this attractive celebration of one of the world's most commonly known foods.
SUBJ: Bread.

643   Ph-2 5-6/5 $15.00   L   KD294
COLMAN, PENNY. Toilets, bathtubs, sinks, and sewers: a history of the bathroom. Atheneum ISBN 0-689-31894-4; In Canada: Maxwell Macmillan, 1994. 70p. ill.
Includes bibliography and index.
Modern bathroom fixtures have a long history through many of the world's cultures as this interesting survey of human sanitation aptly explains. The informative discussion ranges over many topics: problems in securing water, bathing practices, and ancient and futuristic designs of tubs and toilets. Prints and photographs are unfortunately a bit too grey. Interesting social history as well as a useful explanation of sewers and bathroom technology.
SUBJ: Bathrooms--History./ Toilets--History./ Bathtubs--History./ Sanitation--History.

643   Ph-3 4-5/5 $15.95   L   KD295
KALMAN, BOBBIE. Kitchen. Crabtree ISBN 0-86505-484-3; In Canada: Crabtree, 1990. 32p. col. ill. (Historic communities).
Includes glossary and index.
Drawings and photographs of kitchens in historic communities demonstrate the utensils and techniques which early settlers used in preparing food. Short bits of text and picture captions explain early fireplaces and ovens, bread baking, food drying, pots and implements, making butter, and other assorted tasks. Utilitarian volume offers good material for social studies units.
SUBJ: Kitchen utensils./ Cookery./ Frontier and pioneer life.

645   Ph-2 P-3 $6.95   L   KD296
100 WORDS ABOUT MY HOUSE. Illus. by Richard Brown. Gulliver/Harcourt Brace Jovanovich ISBN 0-15-200552-8, 1988. unp. col. ill.
Also available in Spanish MUCHAS PALABRAS SOBRE MI CASA (ISBN 0-15-200532-3, 1987).
Busy scenes of different rooms in the house, the garage, and the backyard feature bold lower case print naming many objects. The Spanish version includes the English translations in smaller print, but there is no pronunciation guide for Spanish so that novice readers will have a mistaken sense of some terms. The colorful picture book format depicting people of varied ages and races and the categorizing scheme make these useful tools for expanding reading and vocabulary skills in a variety of ways.
SUBJ: House furnishings--Pictorial works./ Vocabulary./ Spanish language materials.

646.2   Ph-2 3-5/3 $13.89   L   KD297
HOFFMAN, CHRISTINE. Sewing by hand. Illus. by Harriett Barton. HarperCollins ISBN 0-06-021147-4; In Canada: HarperCollins, 1994. 32p. col. ill.
Cheerful drawings and step-by-step instructions explain how to sew several variations of three simple projects--a pillow, beanbag, and doll. Large, clear sketches identify basic sewing tools and materials and demonstrate cutting, sewing, and assembling each item. Finished pieces are crude, but appealing. Useful introduction for individual children and a nice springboard for classes, scout troups, and other groups looking for easy craft ideas.
SUBJ: Sewing./ Handicraft.

646.4   Ph-1 P-A/4 $13.95   L   KD298
CHERNOFF, GOLDIE TAUB. Easy costumes you don't have to sew. Costumes designed and illustrated by Margaret A. Hartelius. Four Winds/Macmillan ISBN 0-02-718230-4, c1975. 41p. col. ill.
Using these simple ideas and directions, one can easily and quickly construct a variety of temporary costumes for plays and parties from old sheets, bags, cardboard, and pleated paper. Illustrated with diagrams and two-color sketches.
SUBJ: Costume./ Paper work.

CE 646.4   Ph-1 P-2/3 $5.95   P   KD299
DE PAOLA, TOMIE. Charlie needs a cloak. Prentice-Hall ISBN 0-671-66467-0, 1982. unp. col. ill.
Also available as animated 1/2" VHS videocassette (8min) Weston Woods MPV167, $60.00.
Available from National Library Service for the Blind and Physically Handicapped in Braille BR02770.

Charlie the shepherd's tattered coat needs replacing so he shears the sheep, washes, cards and spins the wool, weaves and dyes the cloth, and sews a beautiful new red cloak. Facts are presented with delightful humor as the illustrations picture amusing sub-plots involving the expressions and activities of the sheep and a small mouse.
SUBJ: Clothing and dress./ Wool.

646.4   Ph-1 4-6/2 $11.95   T   KD300
HERSHBERGER, PRISCILLA. Make costumes!: for creative play. North Light ISBN 0-89134-450-0, 1992. 48p. col. ill. (Art and activities for kids).
Practical ideas and instructions for creating various parts of costumes appear in a clear, colorful guide. Tops, bottoms, capes, boots, animal heads, headgear, and many specific characters--angels, robots, wizards, etc.--are featured in brief text and plentiful photographs. Specific instructions are given for some items, and the pictures offer inspiration. A useful primer of attractive and simple outfits for plays, parties, and Halloween.
SUBJ: Costume./ Handicraft.

VCR 646.7   Ph-2 2-4 $89.00   OD KD301
MY BODY, MY BUDDY: HEALTHY HABITS (Videocassette). Rainbow Educational RB8174, 1993. 1/2" VHS videocassette color (15min).
Includes teacher's guide.
Personal hygiene, sensible eating, exercise, and safety are introduced by a pleasant young man who converses with his alter ego, seen as a talking photograph of himself. Stresses personal responsibility for taking care of the body including good habits, regular visits to the dentist and doctor, and steering clear of unhealthy substances. The simple, upbeat lesson is reviewed in a concluding discussion among the narrator and a young boy and girl. Useful as a discussion starter on health and nutrition.
SUBJ: Grooming./ Health./ Physical fitness./ Safety.

649   Ph-2 5-6/6 $16.95   T   KD302
BARKIN, CAROL. New complete babysitter's handbook. By Carol Barkin and Elizabeth James. Illus. by Martha Weston. Clarion ISBN 0-395-66557-4, 1995. 164p. ill.
Includes index.
Available from the National Library Service for the Blind and Physically Handicapped on sound recording cassette RC 42750.
Practical advice about preparing for babysitting jobs and caring for young children fills this small, sturdy compendium, which would fit beautifully in one's backpack of supplies. Covers numerous topics such as finding jobs, getting information from parents, age-appropriate play, feeding and bathing of young children, and dealing with many small problems as well as true emergencies. Thorough and thoughtful, this is nicely focused on helping new babysitters to make their work professional.
SUBJ: Babysitters--Handbooks, manuals, etc.

649   Ph-2 2-5/2 $19.95   T   KD303
LURIE, JON. Allison's story: a book about homeschooling. Photos by Rebecca Dallinger. Lerner ISBN 0-8225-2579-8, 1996. 40p. col. ill. (Meeting the challenge).
Includes bibliographies.
Third grader Allison describes her family's daily activities as her father and mother teach her many topics and skills. The supportive family structure, the flexibility, Allison's occasional frustrations, her opportunities to select things she wants to learn, and information about her extracurricular activities convey a positive picture for children whose families may be considering homeschooling. A concluding section for parents on the history and practice of homeschooling rounds out the honest, informative account. (Parents' Shelf).
SUBJ: Home schooling.

VCR 649   Ph-3 5-A $89.95   OD KD304
SUPER SITTERS: A TRAINING COURSE (Videocassette). Developed by Dr. Lee Salk and Jay Livitin. United Learning 513V, 1988. 1/2" VHS videocassette color (30min), 16 blackline masters.
Includes teacher's guide.
Set into 5 sessions, this highly structured course for prospective sitters incorporates video segments, guided discussions, and masters for personal and safety information. While not strictly tied to the curriculum, this well developed program will be useful for many upper grade students and can be linked with family life/health studies.
SUBJ: Babysitters--Handbooks, manuals, etc.

650.1   Ph-2 5-6/7 $11.93   L   KD305
BARKIN, CAROL. Jobs for kids: the guide to having fun and making money. By Carol Barkin and Elizabeth James. Illus. by Roy Doty. Lothrop, Lee & Shepard ISBN 0-688-09324-8, 1990. 113p. ill.
Includes index.

Practical points for selecting a type of work and finding opportunities to work will appeal to older children who wish to earn their own money. General instructions for preparing for work and promoting one's services are followed by chapters on several job categories: child care; pet care; yard, house and car care; gofers and party aides; teaching and tutoring; paperwork; selling things you make; working for your parents' business. Useful in its specific advice and in helping young people to identify a good range of possibilities.
SUBJ: Work./ Business enterprises./ Finance, Personal./ Moneymaking projects.

VCR 650.1   Ph-2 3-5 $195.00   OD KD306
NOEL'S LEMONADE STAND (UJAMAA) (Videocassette). Beacon Films/Altschul Group 8156, 1982. 1/2" VHS videocassette color (9min). (Nguzo Saba folklore series).
Includes public performance rights.
Noel demonstrates how a city kid succeeds in the lemonade business by enlisting the help of many neighbors who supply goodies to expand his product line. The simple lesson in the economics of a cooperative effort is depicted in pleasant roughly drawn animation resembling torn-paper collage. Adapting a set of ideals from the Swahili, this semirealistic piece is, in fact, a nice introduction to the ideals of cooperation and responsibility. The experience of a child who wants a "real job" will be familiar to many viewers.
SUBJ: Business enterprises./ Entrepreneurship./ Interpersonal relations.

650.1   Ph-2 5-6/6 $8.95   P KD307
THOMPSON, TERRI. Biz kids' guide to success: money-making ideas for young entrepreneurs. Illus. by Shannon Keegan. Barron's ISBN 0-8120-4831-8, 1992. 92p. col. ill.
Includes directory and glossary.
Practical advice for starting and managing one's own business accompanies true stories of young entrepreneurs. Determining one's service and market, use of computers, marketing, record keeping, and legal issues are among the topics. The slim paperback is a fine source for enterprising readers.
SUBJ: Moneymaking projects./ Business enterprises./ Entrepreneurship.

652   Ph-2 5-6/8 $3.50   P KD308
GARDNER, MARTIN. Codes, ciphers and secret writing. Dover ISBN 0-486-24761-9, c1972, 1984. 96p.
Includes bibliography.
Includes a wide range of codes, from transportation ciphers (moving letters) through easy and difficult substitution ciphers, hard-to-break polyalphabetic ciphers, simple code machines, invisible writing, to such unusual codes as the knot cycle and the playing card code. A fascinating account of the uses of cryptography and the workings of many code systems is accompanied by plentiful instructive diagrams. Though falling short of discussing computer codes, this is a welcome reissue on a subject that is challenging and intriguing.
SUBJ: Cryptography./ Ciphers.

652   Ph-2 A/7 $12.95   T KD309
JANECZKO, PAUL B. Loads of codes and secret ciphers. Macmillan ISBN 0-02-747810-6; In Canada: Collier Macmillan, 1984. 108p b&w illus.
Includes appendices and index.
Provides detailed explanations of the construction of code books and systems similar in nature to those used by national and international agencies concerned with secret information. Definitions, instructions, examples and exercises are given along with historical accounts and mention of special alphabets and such communication codes as braille. Absorbing and applying the directions will require patience, but the subject is challenging and intriguing.
SUBJ: Cryptography./ Ciphers.

MCP 652.3   Ph-1 4-A $49.95   OD KD310
MAVIS BEACON TEACHES TYPING! (Microcomputer program). Software Toolworks/MindScape 112002, 1987. 1 3.5" disk.
Version 4.0
Includes guide.
Also available on CD-ROM, MS-DOS/Windows.
Version 2.0 available for Macintosh.
System requirements: Windows; IBM PC 386 33MHz (486 33MHz recommended); 8Mb RAM or greater; Windows 3.1 (Enhanced mode); MS-DOS 5.0 or higher; Supports Windows 95; SVGA 640 x 480, 256 colors; Windows compatible mouse.
Based upon artificial intelligence which allows for customizing practice sessions, this typing tutor is one of the best available. Passages from GUINNESS BOOK OF WORLD RECORDS, classical literature, and riddles keep student attention. Word processor typewriter mode is available. Guide hands, arcade-like game practice, and musical tempo typing are all included.

SUBJ: Typewriting--Software./ Software--Typewriting./ Keyboarding--Software./ Software--Keyboarding.

652.3   Ph-2 4-6 $6.95   P KD311
MOUNTFORD, CHRISTINE. Kids can type too! Barrons ISBN 0-8120-3780-4, c1985, 1987. 30p. col. ill.
Uses the system of color coding the typewriter keys and the fingernails to teach typing quickly. The attractive spiral-bound book provides 22 exercises moving progressively and swiftly through the keys for each finger; colorful cartoon figures reinforce the instructions. A useful preface on keyboards of typewriters and computers is addressed to the teacher or parent, and the small volume stands up for easy use by the student.
SUBJ: Typewriting./ Data processing--Keyboarding.

MCP 652.3   Ph-1 2-A $99.95   OD KD312
TYPE TO LEARN: A NEW APPROACH TO KEYBOARDING (Microcomputer program). Sunburst 149002, 1986. 2 5.25" disks, 2 backup disks.
Includes teacher's guide.
Also available on Apple 5.25" disks (1490FG).
Available on eMate Macintosh/Windows CD-ROM, Macintosh 2.0--disks (6830FG) or CD-ROM (6831FG), Windows--CD-ROM (6809FG) or disk (6604).
System requirements: 64K Apple II family.
Also available for 128K IBM PC or PCjr, 1728 (Color graphics card required); IBN PS/2 Model 25; 256K Tandy 1000, 1737; and Macintosh 1M family.
Well-structured and paced tutorials are reinforced by games making this one of the best keyboarding programs available. The provision of teaching materials which mesh the typing activities with the language arts curriculum is a distinct plus.
SUBJ: Typewriting--Software./ Software--Typewriting.

MCP 658   Ph-1 2-5 $49.95   OD KD313
CLASSROOM STOREWORKS (Microcomputer program). Tom Snyder Productions CSW-D, 1997. 2 3.5" disks.
Version 1.0.
Includes teacher's guide.
Also available for Windows, $49.95.
Optional money kit available, CSW-MK-D, $29.95.
System requirements: Macintosh computer with System 7 or higher; a 256-color monitor with at least a 640x480 resolution; 4MB of available RAM (memory); printer (optional); play money and a cash drawer (optional).
This program provides the record keeping necessary for students to easily run their own store. Job descriptions, product information, and a cash register are all included. Options to check inventory and order more supplies are also available. Easy-to-use and works without much adult intervention at upper grade levels.
SUBJ: Business enterprises--Software./ Software--Business enterprises./ Entrepreneurship--Software./ Software--Entrepreneurship./ Interactive media.

VCR 658   Ph-2 3-6 $88.95   OD KD314
SMACKERS: ELEMENTARY ENTREPRENEURS (Videocassette). Media Projects and KTVT ISBN 1-880898-10-1, 1991. 1/2" VHS videocassette color (11min).
Includes teacher's guide.
A class of elementary school children explain how they started a business to raise money for a new trophy case. The children explain the steps in starting and running the business: identifying a product, investigating costs, borrowing money, setting up an assembly line, advertising, selling, problem solving, and accomplishing the goal. Demonstrates simple economic principles of entrepreneurship and offers a nice model for designing a fund-raising project.
SUBJ: Fund raising./ Business enterprises./ Moneymaking projects./ Entrepreneurship.

658.4   Ph-2 5-6/7 $18.95   L KD315
JEFFREY, LAURA S. Great American businesswomen. Enslow ISBN 0-89490-706-9, 1996. 112p. ill. (Collective biographies).
Includes index.
Short profiles of ten women describe an interesting variety of careers and contributions to American business. Banker Maggie Walker, entrepreneur Madam C. J. Walker, aircraft executive Olive Ann Beech, Barbie creator Ruth Handler, publisher Katherine Graham, modeling agency founder Eileen Ford, presidential adviser Alice Rivlin, Wall Street wizard Elaine Garzarelli, talk show star Oprah Winfrey, and cookie magnate Debbi Fields are the featured cast. More utilitarian than appealing, the book offers good glimpses at the world of work and the accomplishments of women through these well chosen careers. For career studies and women's studies.
SUBJ: Businesswomen./ Women executives.

VCR 659.14   Ph-1 2-5 $19.95   OD KD316
BUY ME THAT! A KID'S SURVIVAL GUIDE TO TV ADVERTISING
(Videocassette). Films, Inc./dist. by Public Media 410024 ISBN 0-7800-
0504-X, 1990. 1/2" VHS videocassette color (28min).
  Includes discussion guide.
  Includes public performance rights.
  This sprightly look at commercials features many familiar products,
behind-the-scenes views of photography techniques, and the reactions
of children who have had bad experiences with the advertised goods.
The quick pacing, energetic narrator, and attractive cast of children
offer thought-provoking consumer lessons around such issues as
misleading advertising, 900 numbers, kids' clubs, celebrity
endorsements, hidden commercials in movies and video games, prize
offers, brand loyalty, and more. The presentations should easily
prompt discussion by children and offer valuable material for units on
consumer education.
  BUY ME THAT, TOO! is available from Ambrose Video, 1992. 1/2"
VHS videocassette color (30min), $79.95.
  BUY ME THAT 3!: A KID'S GUIDE TO FOOD ADVERTISING is
available from Films, Inc./dist. by Public Media 410028 (ISBN
0-7880-1347-6, 1993). 1/2" VHS videocassette color (29min),
$19.95.
  SUBJ: Consumer education./ Commercials--Television./ Advertising--
Television./ Advertising, Truth in.

662   Ph-2 5-6/6 $15.89   L   KD317
KUKLIN, SUSAN. Fireworks: the science, the art, and the magic.
Hyperion ISBN 0-7868-2082-9, 1996. unp. col. ill.
  Behind the scenes views follow the work of the Grucci family as they
create their well-known fireworks displays. Detailed explanations and
photographs of the construction and artistry of fireworks describe
their materials, packing and transporting, mounting the components in
the ground and on frames, safety precautions and teamwork, assorted
pieces as they explode into display, a bit of history of fireworks, and
added notes on the Grucci family. Inherently interesting subject will be
especially enjoyed by nonfiction readers.
  SUBJ: Fireworks./ Grucci family.

VCR 664   Ph-2 2-5 $34.95   OD KD318
CHEWING GUM (Videocassette). TVOntario/dist. by Films for the
Humanities, 1991. 1/2" VHS videocassette color (10min). (Here's how!).
  Teacher's Guide available for $3.45.
  A quick tour of a chewing gum factory reveals some of the
ingredients and the processes of mixing, rolling, cutting, and
packaging this popular product. Produced for television, this includes
some rather contrived segments of conversation between an animated
balloon, a live mouse, and a girl in a classroom. Though the scheme
is hokey, the factory scenes are intriguing and could stimulate further
investigation of this surefire subject.
  SUBJ: Chewing gum.

664   Ph-3 3-4/7 $10.79   L   KD319
COREY, MELINDA. Spaghetti factory. Photos by Donald N. Emmerich.
Troll ISBN 0-8167-1741-9, 1990. 32p. col. ill. (Let's visit).
  Pasta, in all its forms: spaghetti, lasagne, macaroni, rigatoni, ditali,
sea shell, spirals, etc., is a favorite food and this quick survey shows
how it's made and ways it is prepared for the table. The tape
narration is pleasant but the book suffers from sketchy explanations
and often mediocre photographs. Still, pasta and manufacturing are
interesting to young people and this can be used in units on nutrition
as well as manufacturing.
  SUBJ: Pasta products./ Manufactures.

664   Ph-2 3-5/8 $14.95   L   KD320
JASPERSOHN, WILLIAM. Cookies. Macmillan ISBN 0-02-747822-X; In
Canada: Maxwell Macmillan, 1993. unp. ill.
  Famous Amos Chocolate Chip Cookies are baked in enormous
quantities at the bakery plant appearing in this photo essay.
Photographs and text introduce Wally Amos and describe the milling
of flour and the manufacture of chocolate chips before going on to
the several steps of storing ingredients, preparing the dough,
stamping out the cookies, and baking, inspecting, packing, and
shipping them. The factory view is not always clearly conveyed, but
this offers a good lesson in how this favorite food is made
commercially.
  SUBJ: Famous Amos Chocolate Chip Cookie Corporation./ Cookie
industry./ Chocolate chip cookies.

VCR 664   Ph-2 2-4 $34.95   OD KD321
SOUP (Videocassette). TVOntario/dist. by Films for the Humanities,
1991. 1/2" VHS videocassette color (10min). (Here's how!).
  Teacher's guide available for $3.45.
  Vegetable soup is being made and canned during this visit to a
Campbell plant. Various ingredients are chopped and sorted by

humans and machines with frequent inspections and washings as
vegetables move along conveyor belts. Then a great vacuum pump
pushes them to another floor of the factory for cooking in huge vats.
The talking mouse and balloon are intrusive, but this is an intriguing
view of the food canning industry.
  SUBJ: Food industry and trade.

664   Ph-2 5-6/6 $12.95   L   KD322
YOUNG, ROBERT. Chewing gum book. Dillon ISBN 0-87518-401-4,
1989. 72p. ill.
  Includes index.
  Mexican General Santa Anna's surprising role in introducing modern
chewing gum to the United States is part of this interesting account of
the long history, manufacture, and use of this well known commodity.
Adequate photographs of factory processes, various brands through
the years, and collectors' cards accompany short chapters of text,
each concluding with a "Facts to Stick in Your Mind" section for
trivia buffs. A discussion of the advantages and disadvantages of
gum chewing and a concluding time line round out a presentation that
is informative and good material for book talks and nonfiction
readers.
  SUBJ: Chewing gum.

666   Ph-2 3-6/7 $14.95   L OD KD323
FISHER, LEONARD EVERETT. Glassmakers. Benchmark Books/Marshall
Cavendish ISBN 0-7614-0477-5, 1997. 43p. ill. (Colonial craftsmen).
  Originally published by Franklin Watts, 1964.
  Includes glossary and index.
  Explores the history of glassmaking in Colonial America including
materials used and methods of production.
  SUBJ: Glass manufacture./ United States--History--Colonial period, ca.
1600-1775.

666   Ph-3 5-6/9 $14.95   T   KD324
PATERSON, ALAN J. How glass is made. Facts on File ISBN 0-8160-
0038-7, 1985. 32p. col. ill.
  Includes glossary and index.
  Surveys the techniques of glassmaking--both by hand and in
factories--in an informative, colorfully illustrated, flat oversize volume.
Glass containers, blown glass, sheet glass, stained glass, glass fiber
and more are described with numerous interesting photographs and
helpful diagrams. Though unfortunately British in focus with omissions
of famous American glass types, the many processes covered here are
very interesting and very attractively presented.
  SUBJ: Glass manufacture.

VCR 667   Ph-3 5-6 $29.95   OD KD325
PAINT (Videocassette). Kaw Valley Films & Video, 1984. 1/2" VHS
videocassette color (14min).
  Includes teacher's guide.
  Includes public performance rights.
  Paint is a universal product, which most viewers will need to choose
and use sometime for artistic efforts, to protect the surface of a host
of everyday objects, or even for cosmetic purposes. This well
structured lesson begins with a bit of art history and explains the
many other industrial and practical uses of paint and its basic
ingredients and manufacture. Concluding with a survey of different
implements for applying paint, the thoughtful introduction might be
useful to introduce discussions and study units in art, science, or even
industrial arts.
  SUBJ: Paint./ Manufactures.

VCR 668   Ph-2 5-6 $29.95   OD KD326
SOAP (Videocassette). Kaw Valley Films & Video, 1984. 1/2" VHS
videocassette color (13min).
  Includes teacher's guide.
  Includes public performance rights.
  Soap cleans humans, dogs, clothes, cars, and a great many other
things in this informative lesson about its history, use, and
manufacture. The smoothly constructed survey explains the ingredients
of soap, how it works to remove dirt, its importance in human
hygiene and sanitation, the differences between soap and detergent,
and many other topics. Especially interesting for its views of social
history and the manufacture of soap, this should be useful in both
science and social studies units.
  SUBJ: Soap./ Manufactures.

668.4   Ph-2 3-5/5 $15.93   L   KD327
CASH, TERRY. Plastics. Photos by Ed Barber. Garrett ISBN 0-944483-
70-4, 1990. 25p. col. ill. (Threads).
  Includes index.
  This useful survey encourages children to collect plastic objects and
test out their properties and explains how various forms of plastic are
manufactured. Brief and colorful topical segments cover plastic bags,

different types of molded containers, rods and tubes and plastic based clothing fibers. Simple experiments include some that will demonstrate conservation problems caused by plastics. A quickly sketched but informative introduction to the origins and usefulness of this widely used material.
SUBJ: Plastics./ Plastics--Experiments./ Experiments.

670   Ph-2 K-5/7 $12.95   T   KD328
JONES, GEORGE. My first book of how things are made: crayons, jeans, peanut butter, guitars, and more. Scholastic ISBN 0-590-48004-9; In Canada: Scholastic, 1995. 64p. col. ill. (Cartwheel learning bookshelf). "Cartwheel books."
Step-by-step explanations in a thin photographic volume follow the manufacturing of crayons, peanut butter, grape jelly, footballs, orange juice, blue jeans, guitars, and books. Though some explanations are sketchy, the material can be understood even by younger children. It will be useful in curriculum units on the origins of things and also in preparation for some field trips.
SUBJ: Manufactures.

674   Ph-2 P-2/2 $10.95   L   KD329
MITGUTSCH, ALI. From tree to table. Carolrhoda ISBN 0-87614-165-3, 1981. 24p. col. ill. (Carolrhoda start to finish book).
Brightly colored pictures and brief text in a small format describe in simplified terms the processes by which a tree becomes lumber and then furniture. Finally a new tree is planted to begin the cycle again. An attractive lesson about familiar items for younger readers.
SUBJ: Furniture making.

VCR 674   Ph-2 5-6 $29.95   OD KD330
WOOD (Videocassette). Kaw Valley Films & Video, 1985. 1/2" VHS videocassette color (17min).
Includes teacher's guide.
Includes public performance rights.
Wood, a valuable and fabulous resource, is shown in historical and modern uses for artistry, shelter, furniture, and transportation. The intelligent lesson about history, uses, and manufacturing includes substantial discussion of logging, forestry, fires and other threats to forests, and the need to care for forests as a renewable resource. The fine photography and choice of scenes are enjoyable, and the thoughtful content offers varied opportunities for introducing discussions of social history, conservation, and origins of common products. For environmental studies.
SUBJ: Wood./ Manufactures.

675   Ph-3 5-6/7 $5.95   P   KD331
FISHER, LEONARD EVERETT. Tanners. Godine ISBN 0-87923-609-4, c1966, 1986. 43p. ill. (Colonial American craftsmen).
Includes glossary and index.
Discusses the strenuous work of tanning animal hides into leather as this was practiced in the American colonies. The history of leather making in the ancient world and then in the first American settlements is sketched in quickly, and handsome scratchboard pictures and essay text concentrate on the techniques involved in this messy but valuable industry. An interesting account of a seldom covered aspect of U.S. history.
SUBJ: Leather--History.

676   Ph-1 5-6/6 $6.95   P   KD332
BOURGEOIS, PAULETTE. Amazing paper book. Illus. by Linda Hendry. Addison-Wesley ISBN 0-201-52377-9, 1989. 80p. ill.
Includes glossary and index.
Tall tales, experiments, and tricks combine with factual information about the history, manufacture and uses of paper. Cartoon-style pictures and diagrams extend the fun and the information; topics range from the printing of money to instructions for making handmade paper and much more. The congenial paperback volume suggests a wide variety of uses.
SUBJ: Paper./ Papermaking.

676   Ph-2 3-5/6 $15.93   L   KD333
DIXON, ANNABELLE. Paper. Photos by Ed Barber. Garrett ISBN 1-56074-003-5, 1991. 25p. col. ill. (Threads).
Includes index.
Slim discussion examines types of paper and then explains how wood chips and recycled paper are manufactured into large rolls of new paper. Text and photographs offer a simplified explanation of the technical processes and then present a short description of handmade paper and more extensive explanations of how children can make paper. Effectively demonstrates the making of this common product. Papermaking instructions offer many craft possibilities in addition to use for science teaching.
SUBJ: Paper.

VCR 676   Ph-2 5-6 $29.95   OD KD334
PAPER (Videocassette). Kaw Valley Films & Video, 1986. 1/2" VHS videocassette color (13min).
Includes teacher's guide.
Includes public performance rights.
Paper--that versatile and useful product--is also a fundamental tool of human civilization. This well crafted examination explores many aspects of history, uses, manufacturing, and environmental issues and provides an interesting, informative, and thought provoking lesson. Enjoyable for personal viewing, this should also prove useful for introducing classroom units on origins of common products, social history, and environmental studies.
SUBJ: Paper./ Papermaking./ Manufactures.

677   Ph-2 4-6/4 $16.00   L   KD335
KEELER, PATRICIA A. Unraveling fibers. By Patricia A. Keeler and Francis X. McCall, Jr. Atheneum ISBN 0-689-31777-8; In Canada: Distican, 1995. 36p. col. ill.
Includes index.
Interesting entries explain how plant and animal fibers and several man-made fibers are made into cloth. Presentations include clear explanations and well chosen photographs and drawings to show the origins of the fibers and the technology used to prepare them and convert them into cloth. Plant fibers include flax, cotton, and jute; wool, llama, alpaca, angora, mohair, cashmere, and silk derive from animals; and rayon, polyester, and Kevlar (bulletproof and flameproof) are made by man. Excellent introduction to these universal and basic products.
SUBJ: Fibers./ Textiles./ Clothing trade.

677   Ph-2 A/9 $15.95   T   KD336
MACAULAY, DAVID. Mill. Houghton Mifflin ISBN 0-395-34830-7, 1983. 128p. ill.
Includes glossary.
Available from National Library Service for the Blind and Physically Handicapped on sound recording cassette RC21616.
Focusing on four New England cotton mills of the 19th century, this detailed account covers the planning, construction and operation of the mills along with bits of personal history of mill owners and laborers. Considerable technical material is conveyed in a detailed narrative likely to make this fine book heavy going for many children though the copious, finely rendered pen drawings are a definite asset. Attractive browsing fare for machinery buffs and useful source material for history units.
SUBJ: Textile factories--History.

678   Ph-2 5-6/9 $10.95   T   KD337
COSNER, SHAARON. Rubber. Walker ISBN 0-8027-6653-6; In Canada: Wiley, 1986. 56p. ill. (Inventions that changed our lives).
Includes index.
Examines the history, manufacture and uses of rubber from the long-ago "miracle gum" of the Latin American Indians to the protective shields on space-age rockets. The informative text and photographs make up an attractive small volume with a readable narrative of the work of Goodyear and other inventors. A useful source on social history and a major invention and an interesting item for nonfiction readers.
SUBJ: Rubber.

680   Ph-3 4-5/6 $15.95   L   KD338
KALMAN, BOBBIE. Colonial crafts. Crabtree ISBN 0-86505-490-8; In Canada: Crabtree, 1992. 32p. col. ill. (Historic communities).
Includes glossary and index.
Photographs taken at Colonial Williamsburg illustrate the work of a wide variety of colonial craftspeople. Brief sections of text and picture captions describe the processes of making wheels, paper, furniture, wigs, guns, metal objects, and many other things. Apprenticeship system is also explained. Though superficial, this is an adequate introduction to many specific tasks, providing useful information about life in Colonial America. For social studies as well as art classes.
SUBJ: Artisans--History./ Frontier and pioneer life.

680   Ph-3 5-6/8 $20.30   L   KD339
STEVENS, BERNADINE S. Colonial American craftspeople. Watts ISBN 0-531-12536-X; In Canada: Nelson, 1993. 128p. ill., map. (Colonial America).
Includes glossary, bibliographies and index.
Iron, guns, books, and ladies' hats are among the products made by master craftspeople and apprentices in sixteenth and seventeenth century America. An introduction to life in the apprenticeship system is followed by chapters describing many different trades involved in the early manufacture of wood products, buildings, metal objects, clothing, and leather goods. Selected drawings and prints illustrate the discussion. A serviceable handbook for social studies units.

SUBJ: Handicraft--History./ Artisans--History./ Occupations--History./ United States--Social life and customs--To 1775.

684 Ph-2 5-6/4 $3.95 P KD340
LEAVITT, JEROME. Easy carpentry projects for children. Illustrated by Margrete Cunningham. Dover ISBN 0-486-25057-1, c1959, 1986. 91p. ill.
Easy step-by-step instructions with clear diagrams and illustrations introduce the novice to the proper use of tools in making fifteen simple objects of wood.
SUBJ: Woodwork./ Carpentry.

684 Ph-2 5-A $14.95 P KD341
MCGUIRE, KEVIN. Woodworking for kids: 40 fabulous, fun and useful things for kids to make. Sterling/Lark ISBN 0-8069-0430-5; In Canada: Sterling c/o Canadian Manda, 1993. 161p. col. ill.
Includes index.
Substantial information on tools and techniques of woodworking along with detailed instructions for numerous projects is included in this practical handbook. Safety and the assistance of adults is emphasized. Clear advice on setting up a workshop and building more than thirty objects including a tool chest, a bike rack, adjustable stilts, and other useful and appealing items. Detailed instructions and plentiful photographs will encourage young builders to develop a serious interest and skills. Solid presentation will be appreciated by adult hobbyists and scout leaders. (Parents' Shelf).
SUBJ: Woodwork./ Handicraft.

684 Ph-2 4-6/8 $12.95 P KD342
WALKER, LESTER. Carpentry for children. Overlook/Viking ISBN 0-87951-990-8, 1985. 208p. ill.
Well organized directions are provided for the selection and use of tools, building a workshop, and constructing several projects ranging in difficulty from a simple block set to a fairly complex coaster car. Projects are arranged by length of time required to complete them (one day, week-end, one week) and are illustrated with diagrams for cutting and assembling and photographs of children building each item. The tools and materials are not inexpensive and some adult supervision and assistance may be needed, but the instructions and advice are clear and practical.
SUBJ: Carpentry.

684.1 Ph-2 3-6/7 $14.95 L OD KD343
FISHER, LEONARD EVERETT. Cabinetmakers. Benchmark Books/Marshall Cavendish ISBN 0-7614-0479-1, 1997. 47p. ill. (Colonial craftsmen).
Originally published by Franklin Watts, 1966.
Includes index.
Many pieces of furniture made by colonial cabinetmakers are still in use today, two hundred years later. Describes and illustrates the work of the craftsmen; their tools; their methods; their designs and finishes; and the many native woods they used, such as walnut, chestnut, beech, pear, gum, apple, sycamore, cherry, cedar, pine, and tulip.
SUBJ: Cabinetwork./ Cabinetmakers./ Furniture--United States./ United States--History--Colonial period, ca. 1600-1775.

685 Ph-1 5-6/6 $14.95 L KD344
YOUNG, ROBERT. Sneakers: the shoes we choose! Dillon ISBN 0-87518-460-X, 1991. 64p. col. ill.
Includes glossary and index.
Since 1873 they've been called sneakers, and this look at their history and manufacture provides fascinating statistics about their growing popularity. Six short chapters illustrated with well chosen photographs cover milestones in sneaker development, processes of designing and making sneakers, growing problems of sneaker-related crime, and interesting bits of miscellany. A sneaker time-line and addresses of organizations and manufacturers conclude the attractive presentation.
SUBJ: Sneakers./ Shoes.

686 Ph-1 K-3/3 $13.89 L KD345
ALIKI. How a book is made. Crowell/HarperCollins ISBN 0-690-04498-4, 1986. 32p. col. ill.
Available in Spanish COMO SE HACE UN LIBRO (Juventud ISBN 84-261-2400-3, 1989).
Depicts the many stages of writing, editing, manufacturing and selling books. Colorful cartoon drawings featuring cats in all the human roles explain step-by-step many technical aspects, following the book from typewriter and paintbrush all the way to the reader's nighttime enjoyment. Though a bit precious in the use of animals, the information is detailed and absorbing for the primary grades.
SUBJ: Books./ Book industries and trade./ Publishers and publishing./ Printing.

686.2 Ph-1 3-5/5 $15.95 L KD346
KRENSKY, STEPHEN. Breaking into print: before and after the invention of the printing press. Illus. by Bonnie Christensen. Little, Brown ISBN 0-316-50376-2; In Canada: Little, Brown, 1996. unp. col. ill.
Includes chronology.
Wood engravings, painted and accented by elegant frames, depict events as a brief, well focused text describes how the invention of paper and the printing press changed human society. Added facts in the page margins introduce key figures in history and explanations of how early printing worked. The handsome book is both spare and substantial and will find many applications for interdisciplinary studies including science, social studies, and language arts.
SUBJ: Printing--History./ Books and reading--History.

MCP 686.2 Ph-1 2-A $129.95 OD KD347
WRITING CENTER (Microcomputer program). Learning Company 11080, 1991. 3 3.5" disks.
Includes user's guide, "Getting it all Together: a Guide to Writing a Report", and a ready reference card.
Also available in school versions.
Also available on CD-ROM.
Also available in Spanish/English THE BILINGUAL WRITING CENTER 12090, $229.95.
System requirements: All Macintosh computers (except Macintosh 128K and 512K computers) equipped with a hard disk drive (with 3,200K available), 1MB of RAM, and System 6.0 or higher; with ImageWriter I and II; LaserWriter Plus, IISC, IINT, and IINTX; StyleWriter; HP DeskWriter and PaintWriter XL.
Students are introduced to the world of desktop publishing with this program. Over 200 pictures are included for use. Templates for reports and newsletters are included; custom layout features allow for up to 3 columns of text on one page. The built-in word processor follows standard conventions.
STUDENT WRITING CENTER FOR WINDOWS (Microcomputer program). System requirements: IBM and compatibles; 80386 or better, 2MB RAM; (4MB RAM recommended); hard disk (with 8MB free); Windows 3.1 or greater; DOS 3.1 or greater; SVGA, VGA, XGA; all Windows-compatible printers.
SUBJ: Desktop publishing--Software./ Software--Desktop publishing.

VD 687 Ph-3 5-A $249.95 OD KD348
MINDS-ON SCIENCE: FOR PROFIT, FOR PLANET (Videodisc). Smithsonian Institution/Tom Snyder Productions PRF-J, 1995. 1 12" CAV single-sided videodisc color. (Minds-on science).
Includes teacher's guide and student portfolios.
Level I interactive with barcodes.
Optional 3.5" Macintosh or Windows software (Level III interactive) available, $49.95.
System requirements (Level I): CAV videodisc player with monitor (large video monitor for whole-class viewing recommended).
System requirements for optional Macintosh (Level III): Macintosh computer (LC series or better); System 7.0 or later; QuickTime system extension; 4MB RAM; hard disk with at least 4MB free space; 256 (8-bit) color monitor.
This cooperative learning activity allows youngsters to take on the role of CEO for a clothing manufacturer. Various scenarios allow for making money, being responsible citizens of the planet, and doing what is best for safety. Assessment strategies and various extended activities are included. Excellent for large groups. Useful for environmental studies.
SUBJ: Clothing trade./ Manufactures./ Science--Moral and ethical aspects./ Manufacturing processes--Environmental aspects./ Man--Influence on nature./ Interactive media.

VCR 688.6 Ph-2 2-6 $24.95 OD KD349
HOW TO BUILD CHAMPION PINEWOOD CARS (Videocassette). Leapfrog Productions, 1995. 1/2" VHS videocassette color (45min).
Includes public performance rights.
Step-by-step instructions for designing, constructing, and racing pinewood model cars are demonstrated by a father and son. Detailed explanations cover racing regulations, supplies, use of tools, safety measures, the design steps that improve speed, and many other aspects of design, building, and race preparation. The practical information and good views of many models in actual races will appeal to Cub Scouts interested in derby races, other young model car fans, scout leaders, and parents. (Parents' Shelf).
SUBJ: Coaster cars./ Soap box derbies.

688.7 Ph-1 4-6/6 $15.89 L KD350
KUKLIN, SUSAN. From head to toe: how a doll is made. Hyperion ISBN 1-56282-667-0, 1994. unp. col. ill.
Many people work to manufacture the lovely doll named Autumn which is featured in this photo-essay explaining how a favorite toy is made. Clear pictures and short pages of text introduce the workers

who design the doll, make various body parts and clothes, arrange the hair, and dress and finish the final figure. Children who collect dolls will be especially fascinated by this interesting, attractive discussion.
SUBJ: Dollmaking./ Alexander Doll Company.

688.7   Ph-2 K-2/3 $10.95   T   KD351
MORRIS, ANN. How teddy bears are made: a visit to the Vermont Teddy Bear factory. Photos by Ken Heyman. Scholastic ISBN 0-590-47152-X; In Canada: Scholastic, 1994. unp. col. ill.
"Cartwheel books."
Attractive photographs follow a small group of children as they visit a factory and learn how teddy bears are made. A simple text gives skimpy explanations about the actual manufacture of the bears and goes on to explain how they are dressed and packed for shipping. This skips over some of the more interesting steps and doesn't answer many questions, but it's a nice peek at how this favorite toy is made.
SUBJ: Teddy bears./ Toys--Design and construction.

688.7   Ph-2 K-2/2 $8.95   T   KD352
TOYS. DK Publishing ISBN 1-879431-08-4, 1991. 17p. col. ill. (What's inside?).
Bright photographs and cutaway drawings depict the inner workings of several attractive toys: an antique bear, rubber band airplane, jack-in-the-box, dolls' house, robot, kaleidoscope, baby doll, and party favor. Simple explanations are placed as captions sprinkled around the inside and outside views on facing pages. Pleasant exploration of familiar objects will intrigue young readers.
SUBJ: Toys--Design and construction.

688.7   Ph-3 5-6/6 $13.95   L   KD353
YOUNG, ROBERT. Dolls. Dillon ISBN 0-87518-517-7; In Canada: Maxwell Macmillan, 1992. 71p. col. ill. (Collectibles).
Includes chronology, directory, glossary and index.
Dolls from various times and places appear in this slim survey of doll history. Short informative chapters and color photographs in a utilitarian volume discuss the popularity of dolls as toys and collectors' items, their use as ritual objects in some cultures, famous American dolls (Raggedy Ann, Shirley Temple, Barbie), doll manufacture, doll hospitals, and the care and collecting of dolls. Most readers will wish for even more pictures, but the serviceable treatment includes interesting information.
SUBJ: Dolls.

688.7   Ph-3 5-6/6 $13.95   L   KD354
YOUNG, ROBERT. Teddy bears. Dillon ISBN 0-87518-520-7; In Canada: Maxwell Macmillan, 1992. 63p. col. ill. (Collectibles).
Includes chronology, directory, glossary and index.
Teddy bears as popular toys and collectors' items appear in a modest selection of photographs to accompany a slim discussion of teddy bear history and manufacture. The apocryphal story of Teddy Roosevelt's refusal to shoot a bear is included. Also describes ways that police, hospitals, and other agencies use teddy bears to bring comfort to children and adults in difficult situations.
SUBJ: Teddy bears.

690   Ph-1 P-2/2 $14.93   L   KD355
BARTON, BYRON. Building a house. Greenwillow ISBN 0-688-84291-7, 1981. unp. col. ill.
A simple, informative description of how a house is constructed. Brightly colored full-page illustrations make this useful for group discussion and sharing.
SUBJ: House construction.

690   Ph-1 K-3/6 $14.95   L   KD356
GIBBONS, GAIL. Up goes the skyscraper! Four Winds/Macmillan ISBN 0-02-736780-0, 1986. unp. col. ill.
Follows the construction of a skyscraper from the planning by architects, the excavation, the building of the superstructure, the topping off, and the finishing of the exterior and interior. Bright, clear pictures and diagrams and short, direct explanations of text and captions are set in a slim, tall format befitting the subject. An informative and appealing account for sidewalk superintendants of all ages.
SUBJ: Skyscrapers./ Building.

CE 690   Ph-1 A/10 $14.95   T   KD357
MACAULAY, DAVID. Pyramid. Houghton Mifflin ISBN 0-395-21407-6, 1975. 80p. ill.
Selectors' Choice, 10th ed.
Videocassette available from PBS Video PYRM-000H-FCL7, 1988. 1/2" VHS videocassette color (60min), $49.95. Includes teacher's guide.
Visually intriguing line drawings, diagrams, and well constructed text

detail the building of a typical pyramid and explain the process of mummification and the role of the pyramids in Egyptian society. A handsome presentation of a subject highly appealing to children, this fine book offers numerous possibilities for use in science, history and art units as well as recreational reading.
SUBJ: Building./ Pyramids--Egypt./ Egypt--Civilization.

690   Ph-3 A/10 $14.95   T   KD358
MICHAEL, DUNCAN. How skyscrapers are made. Facts on File ISBN 0-8160-1692-5, 1987. 32p. col. ill. (How it is made).
Includes index.
Skyscrapers in several countries are the focus of this quick, attractive introduction to the construction and design of tall buildings. Plentiful, clear color photographs and diagrams illustrate short, difficult sections of text discussing structure problems, stages of construction and materials used; a concluding segment provides data on great skyscrapers in different parts of the world. Though some of the explanations are sketchy and inadequate, the fine photographs, interesting bits of information, and innate appeal of the subject make this a worthwhile inclusion in larger collections.
SUBJ: Skyscrapers.

690   Ph-2 4-A/7 $18.99   L   KD359
PUTNAM, JAMES. Pyramid. Photos by Geoff Brightling and Peter Hayman. Knopf ISBN 0-679-96170-4, 1994. 64p. col. ill., maps. (Eyewitness books).
"Dorling Kindersley book."
"Borzoi book."
Includes index.
Describes pyramids in Egyptian, Nubian, and New World cultures as it provides details in the manner for which Eyewitness books are well-known. Final pages examine use of pyramids in today's buildings, money, and art. Great for browsing and curriculum support.
SUBJ: Pyramids--Egypt./ Pyramids--Sudan./ Pyramids--Central America./ Pyramids--Mexico./ Building.

690   Ph-2 5-6/7 $20.99   L   KD360
WILKINSON, PHILIP. Building. Photos by Dave King and Geoff Dann. Knopf ISBN 0-679-97256-0, 1995. 64p. col. ill. (Eyewitness books).
"Dorling Kindersley book."
"Borzoi book."
Includes index.
An attractive assortment of architectural details from many historical periods and places appear in this picture survey of buildings and construction materials. The principles of construction, roofs, balconies, wood, stained glass, and tiles are among the many topics covered in double-page spreads. Emphasis is on decorative and unusual buildings; modern buildings and materials are not really covered. Many interesting snippets of information, intriguing buildings, and artistic details make this a fine browsing item.
SUBJ: Structual engineering./ House construction./ Building materials.

693   Ph-1 2-6/7 $15.95   L   KD361
ROUNDS, GLEN. Sod houses on the Great Plains. Holiday House ISBN 0-8234-1162-1, 1995. unp. col. ill.
Selectors' Choice, 20th ed.
Available from the National Library Service for the Blind and Physically Handicapped on sound recording cassette RC 41493.
Life was inconvenient and gritty on the unsettled prairie, and Glen Rounds' spare, humorous drawings depict the process of constructing sod houses and the hardships of daily battles with weather, animals, and the heavy dust. Brief text explains how the building was done and the disadvantages and advantages of living in the soddies. The tongue-in-cheek view evokes a real sense of time and place, and readers of all ages will enjoy this informative glimpse into the prairie homes.
SUBJ: Sod houses./ Frontier and pioneer life--Great Plains.

CE 694   Ph-2 4-6/7 $11.79   L   KD362
MARTIN, JOHN HARDING. Day in the life of a carpenter. Troll ISBN 0-8167-0093-1, 1985. 32p. col. ill. (Day in the life of).
Follows a cabinetmaker as he receives an order in his shop, goes to the lumber yard and hardware store for materials, and then measures, cuts, assembles, and finishes this piece of furniture. Good color photographs and simple narrative describe the planning and care in doing the project, the tools used, and the processes involved. A useful explanation of how furniture is made and of the business and craft aspects of work as a cabinetmaker.
SUBJ: Carpentry./ Occupations.

700   Ph-3 5-A/6 $25.00   T   KD363
ISAACSON, PHILIP. Short walk around the Pyramids and through the world of art. Knopf ISBN 0-679-81523-6; In Canada: Random House, 1993. 120p. col. ill.

"Borzoi book."
Includes index.
Provides information on various aspects of art--form, sculpture, color, images, and photography. Enrichment for art classes, social studies, and language arts.
SUBJ: Art.

701   Ph-2 5-6/7 $18.99   T   KD364
DAVIDSON, ROSEMARY. Take a look: an introduction to the experience of art. Viking ISBN 0-670-84478-0; In Canada: Penguin, 1994. 128p. col. ill.
Includes chronology, glossary, bibliography and index.
A panoramic view of art touches upon many cultures and many historical periods. Photographs and reproductions cover a plethora of subjects, with fascinating information on a shaman's mask, Picasso's "Guernica," totem poles, the Bayeux Tapestry, and computer graphics. This overview will appeal to browsers and can offer answers to endless trivia questions. Coverage of both Eastern and Western art makes it suitable for multicultural studies.
SUBJ: Art./ Art--Technique./ Art appreciation.

VCR 701   Ph-3 4-A $142.15   OD KD365
LOOKING AT ART (Videocassette). SRA/McGraw-Hill 87-004827, 1992. 1/2" VHS videocassette color. (Educational Dimensions).
Includes teacher's guide.
A group of students tour an art museum, study the techniques and elements of art, and come to an understanding of basic styles in this live action video.
Contents: Part 1: The viewer (14min); Part 2: Elements of art (15min).
SUBJ: Art appreciation./ Art--Study and teaching.

701   Ph-1 P-1 $16.95   T   KD366
MICKLETHWAIT, LUCY. Child's book of art: great pictures, first words. Selected by Lucy Micklethwait. DK Publishing ISBN 1-56458-203-5, 1993. 64p. col. ill.
Includes index.
Introduces the youngest child to well-known works of art which illustrate basic concepts such as numbers, shapes, and opposites. The pictures reflect the history of art, covering many periods, and can be used as any picture book--to provoke discussion, to appreciate paintings, and to expand vocabulary and general knowledge.
SUBJ: Art appreciation./ Vocabulary.

VCR 701   Ph-2 1-4 $19.95   KD367
POLISAR, BARRY LOUIS. Barry's scrapbook: a window into art (Videocassette). ALA Video/Library Video Network 10142B ISBN 1-56641-014-2, 1994. 1/2" VHS videocassette color (42min).
Closed captioned.
A museum tour presents an overview of various aspects of art, including mosaics, collage, masks, and illustrations to a class of youngsters. Includes talks by professional artists and directions for making art projects. Artists, teachers, and students come from different ethnic groups and reflect the diversity that is America today. Can be divided into segments to use as brief lessons for students with short attention spans.
SUBJ: Art./ Art appreciation.

CDR 701   Ph-1 2-A $39.95   OD KD368
WITH OPEN EYES: IMAGES FROM THE ART INSTITUTE OF CHICAGO (CD-ROM). Voyager ISBN 1-55940-446-9, 1995. 1 CD-ROM color.
Includes user's guide.
System requirements: Any color Macintosh (25/MHz 68030 or better recommended); System 7; 13" (640x480 resolution) or larger display; at least 8MB RAM installed (5,000K free); double-speed CD-ROM drive.
System requirements: 486SX-33 or higher processor; 640x480, 256-color display; 8MB RAM; MPC2-compatible CD-ROM drive; sound card with speakers or headphones; Microsoft Windows 3.1.
Product (ISBN 1-55940-446-9) runs on either Macintosh or Windows compatible hardware.
Includes images of over 200 pieces from the Art Institute of Chicago. Youngsters can view details of the art, hear its history, view the art in specific geographic areas or time periods, create an individual scrapbook and slide show or strengthen visual skills by deciding what has been changed from the original. Works well with a projection device for use with an entire class or as a learning center.
SUBJ: Art appreciation--Software./ Software--Art appreciation./ Art--Study and teaching--Software./ Software--Art--Study and teaching./ Interactive media.

701.1   Ph-1 3-6/5 $13.95   T   KD369
BLIZZARD, GLADYS S. Come look with me: world of play. Lickle Publishing/dist. by PRI ISBN 1-56566-031-5, 1993. 32p. col. ill. (Come

look with me).
Twelve works of art are paired with stimulating questions to encourage discussion. Featured are paintings, prints, and sculpture with the theme of people at play by such artists as Red Grooms, Diego Rivera, and Pieter Bruegel. Explores the world of art in an innovative, creative manner fostering an appreciation for fine art.
SUBJ: Art appreciation./ Games in art.

702.8   Ph-2 2-6/4 $11.95   T   KD370
SOLGA, KIM. Paint! North Light ISBN 0-89134-383-0, 1991. 48p. col. ill. (Art and activities for kids).
Step-by-step instructions for 11 painting projects include painting in pointillism style, glass art, and watercolor batik.
SUBJ: Painting--Technique.

VCR 704   Ph-2 4-A $199.00   OD KD371
AFRICAN AMERICAN ART: PAST AND PRESENT (Videocassette). Reading & O'Reilly V-92, 1992. 3 1/2" VHS videocassettes color (90min).
Includes teacher's guide.
A comprehensive and historical view of African-American art and culture is revealed through paintings, sculptures, crafts, and photographs. Each brief unit can be used in a class period and covers such subjects as African art, quilting, wrought ironwork, and fine art. An excellent addition to multicultural studies.
SUBJ: Afro-American art./ Afro-American artists./ Art, African.

704.9   Ph-1 4-A/7 $18.95   L   KD372
MACCLINTOCK, DORCAS. Animals observed: a look at animals in art. Scribner's ISBN 0-684-19323-X; In Canada: Maxwell Macmillan, 1993. 56p. col. ill.
Includes index.
A fascinating view of animals as they are depicted in paintings, sculpture, and drawings. Includes such animals as antelopes, aardvarks, raccoons, and rhinoceros. The artistic creation is explained, and biographical information on the artist is included. Fosters art appreciation as well as love of animals.
SUBJ: Animals in art./ Art appreciation.

704.9   Ph-2 4-A/7 $14.95   T   KD373
MCHUGH, CHRISTOPHER. Animals. Thomson Learning ISBN 1-56847-025-8, 1993. 32p. col. ill. (Discovering art).
"Wayland book."
Includes glossary, bibliography and index.
Presents animals as they are portrayed in art by a variety of artists including Rousseau, Brueghel, and Picasso. A fascinating amalgam of art and animals useful for interdisciplinary studies.
SUBJ: Animals in art./ Art appreciation.

704.9   Ph-2 4-A/7 $14.95   T   KD374
MCHUGH, CHRISTOPHER. Faces. Thomson Learning ISBN 1-56847-071-1, 1993. 32p. col. ill. (Discovering art).
"Wayland book."
Includes glossary, bibliography and index.
Faces as depicted in many kinds of art from all sorts of materials are revealed with such examples as stone figures from ancient Mexico, gold masks from Egyptian coffins, and bronze heads from ancient Greece. Portraits from such diverse modern artists as Klee, Picasso, and Warhol mirror influences of earlier times, yet reflect the contemporary world.
SUBJ: Face in art./ Art appreciation.

704.9   Ph-2 4-A/7 $14.95   T   KD375
MCHUGH, CHRISTOPHER. Water. Thomson Learning ISBN 1-56847-024-X, 1993. 32p. col. ill. (Discovering art).
"Wayland book."
Includes glossary, bibliography and index.
A survey which shows how artists have depicted the seas, rivers, and waterways. Includes a wide variety of artists such as Monet, Morisot, Klee, and Hockney. Helps to develop an appreciation for art of many cultures.
SUBJ: Water in art./ Art appreciation.

708   Ph-3 2-A/7 $12.95   P   KD376
RICHARDSON, JOY. Inside the museum: a children's guide to the Metropolitan Museum of Art. Abrams ISBN 0-8109-2561-3, 1993. 72p. col. ill.
A fascinating, behind-the-scenes glimpse of an art museum. For those interested in the Metropolitan Museum of Art, this is a feast of facts and trivia. Much of the information presented here is applicable to any large museum and can increase interest in museum visits.
SUBJ: Museums./ Metropolitan Museum of Art (New York, N.Y.)

709.2   Ph-1 4-A/8 $22.80   L   KD377
CUSH, CATHIE. Artists who created great works. Raintree Steck-Vaughn ISBN 0-8114-4933-5, 1995. 48p. col. ill. (20 events).
> Includes glossary, bibliography and index.
> Brief biographies of noted artists with information on the times in which they lived and the art movements in which they participated. Includes sculptors Rodin and Henry Moore, architect Christopher Wren, photographer Ansel Adams, and painters from Rembrandt to Georgia O'Keeffe. Excellent for reports.
> SUBJ: Artists./ Women artists./ Art appreciation.

709.2   Ph-2 6-A/12 $22.50   T   KD378
DI CAGNO, GABRIELLA. Michelangelo. Illus. by Simone Boni and L.R. Galante. Peter Bedrick ISBN 0-87226-319-3, 1996. 64p. col. ill. (Masters of art).
> Includes chronology and index.
> While focusing on the sculptures and paintings of the great Michelangelo, this explores the world of the Renaissance with information and pictures of the architecture, fortifications, theater, and art. Excellent for reports. A beautiful book about a glorious time in history.
> SUBJ: Artists./ Michelangelo Buonarroti./ Art, Renaissance./ Art appreciation.

709.2   Ph-2 4-6/6 $16.99   L   KD379
RINGGOLD, FAITH. Talking to Faith Ringgold. By Faith Ringgold, Linda Freeman and Nancy Roucher. Crown ISBN 0-517-70914-7, 1996. 48p. col. ill.
> Includes bibliography, filmography and index.
> Inspiring discussion by Ringgold of the influences in her life which have prompted her to work in textiles and to persist until she gained recognition. Contains numerous suggestions for activities for students to interact with Ringgold's writings. For multicultural studies and art classes.
> SUBJ: Artists./ Ringgold, Faith./ Afro-Americans--Biography./ Women artists./ Art appreciation.

709.2   Ph-3 4-A/6 $18.95   L   KD380
SILLS, LESLIE. Visions: stories about women artists. Whitman ISBN 0-8075-8491-6, 1993. 63p. col. ill.
> Includes bibliography.
> Explores the lives and works of four women artists--Mary Cassatt, Leonora Carrington, Betye Saar, and Mary Frank. A fine addition to multicultural and women's studies. Excellent for reports.
> SUBJ: Women artists./ Artists.

VCR 709.73   Ph-3 4-A $144.00   OD   KD381
AMERICAN ART AND ARCHITECTURE (Videocassette). Alarion 803V, 1991. 1/2" VHS videocassettes color, workbook, poster. (History through art and architecture).
> Includes teacher's guide.
> Focuses on American history and culture from pre-colonial time to the present. Explores paintings and sculptures which reflect the changing interests of American society. Also traces architecture from adobe "condos" of the Anasazi Indians to log cabins of early settlers through to today's skyscrapers. Excellent for gifted students working on interdisciplinary projects.
> Contents: Part I: From the condos of the Anasazi to Jefferson (35min); Part II: American history through painting and sculpture from precolonial to today (60min).
> SUBJ: Art, American--History./ Architecture--History./ Art appreciation.

720   Ph-1 4-A/8 $11.95   T   KD382
CASELLI, GIOVANNI. Wonders of the world. DK Publishing ISBN 1-56458-145-4, 1992. 64p. col. ill. (See & explore library).
> Includes index.
> The seven wonders of the world are described with comparisons made between ancient and modern edifices. Excellent reference source for reports on this often researched topic. Information is presented clearly and graphically.
> SUBJ: Seven Wonders of the World./ Architecture.

720   Ph-2 3-6/7 $13.95   T   KD383
DUNN, ANDREW. Skyscrapers. Thomson Learning ISBN 1-56847-027-4, 1993. 32p. col. ill. (Structures).
> "Wayland book."
> Includes glossary, bibliography and index.
> Provides information on how skyscrapers are built, the advantages and drawbacks of these tall buildings, and the limits of this technology. Photographs of skyscrapers around the world are particularly stunning.
> SUBJ: Skyscrapers.

720   Ph-1 4-A/9 $22.80   L   KD384
SINGER, DONNA. Structures that changed the way the world looked. Raintree Steck-Vaughn ISBN 0-8114-4937-8, 1995. 48p. col. ill., maps. (20 events).
> Includes glossary, bibliography and index.
> Information on 20 significant structures including the Great Pyramid, the Great Wall of China, the Anasazi Cliff Dwellings, the Eiffel Tower, and the English Channel Tunnel. Filled with fascinating facts for reports.
> SUBJ: Architecture./ Monuments.

720   Ph-1 4-A/9 $16.95   T   KD385
WILKINSON, PHILIP. Amazing buildings. Illus. by Paolo Donati and Studio Illibill. DK Publishing ISBN 1-56458-234-5, 1993. 48p. col. ill.
> Includes index.
> A fascinating view of the internal construction of 21 famous edifices, including the Statue of Liberty, a Mayan pyramid, and Versailles. This stimulating introduction is filled with historical information and will enliven reports. Browsers, as well as architecture buffs, will be captivated by this beautifully illustrated work.
> SUBJ: Buildings.

720.9   Ph-1 4-6/12 $15.00   L   KD386
LYNCH, ANNE. Great buildings. Nature Company/Time-Life Books ISBN 0-8094-9371-3, 1996. 64p. col. ill., map. (Nature Company discoveries library).
> "Weldon Owen production."
> Includes glossary and index.
> An historical, international survey of the great architectural constructions of man, including the ancient pyramids of Egypt and Mexico, the Roman Colosseum, the Great Wall of China, Taj Mahal, the Palace of Versailles, Notre Dame Cathedral, the Alhambra, and the Sydney Opera House. An informative and fascinating overview with sufficient facts for reports and excellent illustrations for browsers.
> SUBJ: Historic buildings./ Architecture--History.

725   Ph-2 2-4/6 $14.93   L   KD387
ZELVER, PATRICIA. Wonderful Towers of Watts. Illus. by Frane Lessac. Tambourine ISBN 0-688-12650-2, 1994. unp. col. ill.
> A stirring description of the creation of the unusual Watts Towers outside of Los Angeles. This true story reflects the dreams of a poor Italian laborer who without architectural training built the towers which are still a part of the Watts neighborhood.
> SUBJ: Simon Rodia's Towers (Watts, Los Angeles, Calif.)./ Los Angeles (Calif.)--Buildings, structures, etc.

726   Ph-3 5-6/6 $15.95   T   KD388
MACAULAY, DAVID. Cathedral: the story of its construction. Houghton Mifflin ISBN 0-395-17513-5, c1973. 77p. ill.
> Caldecott Honor Book.
> Selectors' Choice, 9th ed.
> The construction of a French Gothic cathedral from the ground-breaking to completion is described in lucid, detailed text with profuse and striking pen-and-ink illustrations. Each craftsman's job is presented along with drawings of his tools. The construction of the soaring, vaulting buttresses and columns becomes clear, along with the casting of the bells and stained glass production. The awe-inspiring Gothic cathedral is fittingly presented in a masterpiece of a volume. Glossary.
> SUBJ: Cathedrals./ Architecture, Gothic.

VCR 726   Ph-3 6-A $49.95   OD   KD389
MACAULAY, DAVID. Cathedral (Videocassette). PBS Video CADL-000-FCL7, 1986. 1/2" VHS videocassette color (25min).
> Includes teacher's guide.
> This animated interpretation of Macaulay's book of the same name is excerpted from the PBS presentation and serves as an effective resource for studies of the Middle Ages.
> SUBJ: Cathedrals./ Middle Ages.

726   Ph-3 6-A/9 $17.95   T   KD390
MACDONALD, FIONA. Medieval cathedral. Illus. by John James. Bedrick ISBN 0-87226-350-9, 1991. 48p col illus. (Inside story).
> Includes glossary and index.
> Traces the construction of medieval cathedrals from the selection of the site through the actual construction. Includes information on the daily life of the workers, the monks, the pilgrims and the craftsmen. Excellent for reports, with good illustrations.
> SUBJ: Cathedrals./ Civilization, Medieval.

726   Ph-1 4-A/10 $17.95   L   KD391
MACDONALD, FIONA. 16th century mosque. Illus. by Mark Bergin. Peter Bedrick ISBN 0-87226-310-X, 1994. 48p. col. ill., maps. (Inside story).

Includes glossary, chronology and index.
Describes the magnificent houses of worship so representative of the Islamic faith. Includes information on the elaborate architectural features; lives of the construction workers; and work of the craftsmen who carved the stone, made the tiles, and wove the rugs. An excellent component of the study of Islamic history.
SUBJ: Mosques./ Islam.

726.6   Ph-2 5-6/7 $14.93   L   KD392
ANCONA, GEORGE. Cutters, carvers and the cathedral. Lothrop, Lee & Shepard ISBN 0-688-12057-1, 1995. unp. col. ill.
Includes glossary.
Stone quarries and stone carvers join forces with computers as craftsmen continue the long project of building the Cathedral of St. John the Divine in New York City. Excellent photographs and short explanations follow the work of assorted individuals in preparing the stone, carving, and mounting the carved blocks on the impressive facade of the cathedral. Useful for units about buildings and construction and about earlier cathedrals and architecture.
SUBJ: Cathedrals./ Stone cutters./ Stone carvers./ Cathedral of St. John the Divine (New York, N.Y.).

728   Ph-2 1-3/2 $14.95   L   KD393
DORROS, ARTHUR. This is my house. Scholastic ISBN 0-590-45302-5; In Canada: Scholastic, 1992. unp. col. ill.
Also available in Spanish, ESTA ES MI CASA (ISBN 0-590-49444-9, 1993).
Illustrates the types of houses people inhabit in many countries of the world. On each page, the words "This is my house" are translated into the native language of the country depicted. A good introduction to units on houses for multicultural studies.
SUBJ: Dwellings./ Architecture./ Spanish language materials.

728   Ph-2 2-4/6 $13.93   L   KD394
MORRIS, ANN. Houses and homes. Photos by Ken Heyman. Lothrop, Lee & Shepard ISBN 0-688-10169-0, 1992. 32p. col. ill.
Includes index.
Depicts homes, large and small, in many parts of the world. A picture "index" serves as a key to the location of the homes and tells a bit about construction techniques or specialized features. Useful social studies support on several levels.
SUBJ: Dwellings.

728   Ph-1 4-A/9 $16.95   T   KD395
VENTURA, PIERO. Houses: structures, methods, and ways of living. With the collaboration of Max Casalini, Pierluigi Longo, and Marisa Murgo Ventura. Houghton Mifflin ISBN 0-395-66792-5, 1993. 64p. col. ill.
Includes glossary.
Traces the history of abodes from caves to castles, chateaus, and apartment houses. Humorous illustrations illuminate the fascinating text. Excellent for reports.
SUBJ: Dwellings--History./ Architecture, Domestic--History.

728   Ph-2 4-6/6 $18.60   L   KD396
WHITE, SYLVIA. Welcome home! Childrens Press ISBN 0-516-08193-4; In Canada: Childrens Press, 1995. 32p. col. ill. (World of difference).
Includes glossary and index.
Describes housing around the world, emphasizing the impact of climate and resources on the favored modes of construction. Color photographs make for an appealing browser; the text tags along but is nonetheless useful. Helpful curriculum support for multicultural studies and social studies.
SUBJ: Dwellings.

730   Ph-3 3-6/6 $16.95   L   KD397
GARDNER, JANE MYLUM. Henry Moore: from bones and stones to sketches and sculptures. Four Winds ISBN 0-02-735812-7; In Canada: Maxwell Macmillan, 1993. 32p. ill.
A glimpse into the life and work of one of the twentieth century's greatest sculptors, Henry Moore. Explores the creative process that resulted in his works that reflect dignity and grandeur.
SUBJ: Moore, Henry./ Sculptors.

730   Ph-2 4-6/9 $25.69   L   KD398
HESLEWOOD, JULIET. History of Western sculpture: a young person's guide. Raintree Steck-Vaughn ISBN 0-8172-4001-2, 1996. 64p. col. ill., map.
Includes glossary, bibliography and index.
An overview of Western sculpture from the temples of Greece and Rome to the changing forms representing the twentieth century. Explains sculpture in its many forms with clear text and profuse pictures.
SUBJ: Sculpture--History.

730   Ph-1 4-A/9 $19.95   L   KD399
ROMEI, FRANCESCA. Story of sculpture. Illus. by Giacinto Gaudenzi. Peter Bedrick ISBN 0-87226-316-9, 1995. 64p. col. ill., maps. (Masters of art).
Includes index.
The history of sculpture is presented with three-dimensional, detailed illustrations and fascinating background information. Includes sections on the Stone Age, ancient Greece and Rome, the Baroque, and the sculpture of Asia, Africa, and the Americas. An opulent, powerful work suitable for reports and a treat for browsers.
SUBJ: Sculpture./ Art appreciation.

735   Ph-2 5-6/7 $14.95   L   KD400
FISHER, LEONARD EVERETT. Statue of Liberty. Holiday House ISBN 0-8234-0586-9, 1985. 64p. ill.
Includes index.
Chronicles the history of the Statue of Liberty from its inception to its completion and dedication in 1886. Illustrated with period photographs and occasional artwork by the author. Use in patriotic units, in the study of immigration, and in units on national monuments.
SUBJ: Statue of Liberty (New York, N.Y.)./ National monuments./ Statues.

735   Ph-2 P-3/6 $16.93   L   KD401
MAESTRO, BETSY. Story of the Statue of Liberty. By Betsy and Giulio Maestro. Lothrop, Lee & Shepard ISBN 0-688-05774-8, 1986. unp. col. ill.
Includes appendices.
Follow the planning and building of the Statue of Liberty through active color illustrations and sparse text. While the narrative is simple, it has been written in an engaging manner and is amplified by the appendices which include statistics and a chronology. This is the title of choice for younger children.
SUBJ: Statue of Liberty (New York, N.Y.)./ National monuments./ Statues.

VCR 736   Ph-1 3-6 $89.95   OD KD402
HOW TO FOLD A PAPER CRANE (Videocassette). Informed Democracy ISBN 1-879368-01-3, 1994. 1/2" VHS videocassette color (30min).
Includes teacher's guide and origami paper.
An easy-to-follow presentation for teaching the art form of origami, which develops listening and motor skills. Explicit instructions are given by offscreen narration while a pair of gloved hands gracefully creates the paper cranes. This companion piece to SADAKO AND THE THOUSAND PAPER CRANES begins with a history of Sadako, the girl who contracted leukemia from the atomic bomb fallout, and tells of the Children's Monument which she inspired in Hiroshima's Peace Park. Can be utilized in art classes, math units, conflict resolution units, and multicultural studies.
SUBJ: Origami./ Paper work./ Handicraft.

736   Ph-2 3-6 $6.95   P   KD403
SMOLINSKI, JILL. Holiday origami. Illus. by Mary Ann Fraser. Photos by Ann Bogart. Lowell House Juvenile/Contemporary Books ISBN 1-56565-359-9, 1995. 32p. col. ill.
A variety of origami craft projects designed to enhance holiday celebrations. Make a secret pocket valentine, a Thanksgiving turkey basket, and a Hanukkah dreidel. Encourages dexterity and creativity.
SUBJ: Origami./ Holiday decorations./ Paper work./ Handicraft.

736   Ph-3 4-6/4 $7.95   P   KD404
TEMKO, FLORENCE. Origami for beginners: the creative world of paperfolding. Tuttle ISBN 0-8048-1688-3, 1991. 48p. col. ill.
Includes index.
Step-by-step directions for paperfolding greeting cards, cats, sharks, flower arrangements, and tropical fish. Includes suggestions for using origami in the classroom.
SUBJ: Origami.

741.2   Ph-2 2-6/4 $11.95   T   KD405
SOLGA, KIM. Draw! North Light ISBN 0-89134-385-7, 1991. 48p. col. ill. (Art and activities for kids).
Basic principles of art are incorporated into drawing projects that also foster creativity. Includes clear, step-by-step instructions for 3-D drawings, flip books, and experimenting with tools and techniques.
SUBJ: Drawing--Technique.

741.2   Ph-2 3-6/6 $14.95   T   KD406
WELTON, JUDE. Drawing: a young artist's guide. Produced in association with the Tate Gallery; Colin Grigg, Consultant. DK Publishing ISBN 1-56458-676-6, 1994. 45p. col. ill. (Young artist).
Includes index.
Introduces such drawing techniques as light and shade, pattern and texture, near and far, scratching and tracing. A variety of creative

projects help young artists appreciate the many skills involved in drawing.
SUBJ: Drawing--Technique.

VCR 741.5   Ph-2 4-A $175.00   OD KD407
ANIMATION FOR KIDS: HOW TO MAKE YOUR CARTOON MOVE! (Videocassette). Bullfrog Films S0055 ISBN 1-56029-582-1, 1994. 1/2" VHS videocassette color (12min).
Includes teacher's guide.
Five children introduce the world of animation through such simple projects as flipbooks, spinning disks, and spinning drums. Readily available supplies and easy-to-follow directions help the artistic novice succeed. In addition to fostering creativity, the projects encourage the observation of optical illusions, increase depth perception, and teach the scientific principles inherent in modern motion picture technology.
SUBJ: Cartooning./ Animation (Cinematography)./ Drawing--Technique.

VCR 741.5   Ph-2 3-6 $24.95   OD KD408
ARTELL, MIKE. Basic cartooning with Mike Artell (Videocassette). Video Specialties, 1995. 1/2" VHS videocassette color (60min).
Includes public performance rights.
Easy directions turn everyone into an artist. Using basic shapes, illustrator Mike Artell makes cartooning fun and very simple. Create a caterpillar, a robot, and a "flip" book of funny faces. Will delight all budding cartoonists.
SUBJ: Cartooning./ Drawing--Technique.

741.5   Ph-3 4-6/6 $15.95   L   KD409
AVI. City of light, city of dark: a comic-book novel. Illus. by Brian Floca. Orchard ISBN 0-531-08650-X, 1993. 192p. ill.
"Richard Jackson book."
A comic-book novel relates the adventures of a particular transit token which has the power to prevent the Kurbs from freezing the city. A combination of myth and magic, the action-packed plot and the comic-book format will appeal to both reluctant and advanced readers.
SUBJ: Fantasy./ Cartoons and comics.

741.5   Ph-3 3-6/5 $16.95   T   KD410
LIGHTFOOT, MARGE. Cartooning for kids. Owl/dist. by Firefly ISBN 1-895688-03-5; In Canada: Greey de Pencier/Owl/dist. by Firefly, 1993. 64p. col. ill.
Instructions for creating cartoons whether drawing people or animals.
SUBJ: Cartooning./ Drawing--Technique.

741.6   Ph-3 5-6/7 $19.95   T   KD411
BIESTY, STEPHEN. Stephen Biesty's incredible explosions. Illus. by Stephen Biesty. Text by Richard Platt. DK Publishing ISBN 0-7894-1024-9, 1996. 32p. col. ill.
Includes index.
Stephen Biesty offers voluminous detail in large, intricate cross sections of a dozen highly varied settings. Copious labels and brief captions accompany all the visual minutiae of a steam tractor, firefighters at work in a highrise building, space station, airport, windmill, layers of history beneath a city, Antarctic base, movie studio, Venice, London's Tower Bridge, the human body, and the Grand Canyon. Visually overwhelming at times, this offers intriguing perspectives that will appeal to Stephen Biesty fans and readers who love detail and miscellany.
SUBJ: Drawing./ Graphic arts.

741.6   Ph-2 3-6/7 $12.90   L   KD412
CHAPMAN, GILLIAN. Making books. By Gillian Chapman and Pam Robson. Millbrook ISBN 1-56294-154-2, 1992. 32p. col. ill.
Step-by-step directions for making and designing a variety of books. Projects range from simple booklets to more sophisticated portfolios incorporating special effects.
SUBJ: Bookbinding./ Books.

741.6   Ph-1 K-6 $23.00   L   KD413
MAXFIELD PARRISH: A TREASURY OF ART AND CHILDREN'S LITERATURE. Compiled by Alma Gilbert. Illus. by Maxfield Parrish. Atheneum ISBN 0-689-80300-1; In Canada: Distican, 1995. 88p. col. ill.
Includes index.
The glowing paintings of the great illustrator Maxfield Parrish add distinction to a variety of literary forms--Mother Goose rhymes, fairy tales, Greek myths, and tales from the Arabian Nights. A wonderful vehicle for appreciating art. For reading aloud.
SUBJ: Parrish, Maxfield./ Artists./ Illustrators./ Literature--Collections.

742   Ph-3 5-A/7 $8.95   P   KD414
DUBOSQUE, DOUG. Learn to draw 3-D. Peel Productions ISBN 0-939217-17-1, 1992. 80p. ill. (Learn to draw).

Easy-to-follow, step-by-step directions teach the concept of perspective drawing. Good for advanced art students.
SUBJ: Perspective./ Drawing--Technique.

743   Ph-2 4-6 $8.00   P   KD415
AMES, LEE J. Draw 50 cars, trucks, and motorcycles. Doubleday ISBN 0-385-24639-0, 1986. unp. col. ill. (Draw 50).
Automotive and racing enthusiasts will enjoy trying to illustrate a variety of dragsters, bikes, cars, and trucks. Step-by-step directions help the novice artist.
SUBJ: Drawing--Technique./ Motor vehicles in art./ Drawing books.

743   Ph-3 4-6 $8.00   P   KD416
AMES, LEE J. Draw 50 horses. Bantam Doubleday Dell ISBN 0-385-17642-2; In Canada: Bantam, 1986. unp. col. ill. (Draw 50).
Step by step examples for developing a sequential method of drawing and sharpening observation skills.
Other similar titles include: DRAW 50 DOGS (ISBN 0-385-15681-7, 1986); DRAW 50 DINOSAURS (ISBN 0-385-19520-6, 1985); DRAW 50 BOATS, SHIPS, TRUCKS AND TRAINS (ISBN 0-385-23630-1, 1987); DRAW 50 ANIMALS (ISBN 0-385-19519-2, 1974); DRAW 50 AIRPLANES, AIRCRAFT & SPACECRAFT (ISBN 0-385-23629-8, 1987); DRAW 50 SHARKS, WHALES AND OTHER SEA CREATURES (ISBN 0-385-24628-5, 1989, OPC); DRAW 50 BEASTIES AND YUGGLIES AND TURNOVER UGLIES AND THINGS THAT GO BUMP IN THE NIGHT (ISBN 0-385-26767-3, 1990).
SUBJ: Drawing books./ Drawing--Technique.

743   Ph-2 4-A/5 $8.95   P   KD417
DUBOSQUE, DOUG. Draw! cars. Rev. ed. Peel Productions ISBN 0-93-921729-5, 1997. 79p. ill.
Step-by-step instructions for drawing a variety of favorite cars such as the Porsche, Ferrari, Dodge Stealth, and Lamborghini. Gives basic information on drawing and sharpens observation skills. Car lovers will enjoy browsing as well as drawing.
SUBJ: Automobiles in art./ Drawing--Technique.

743   Ph-3 5-A/3 $18.60   L   KD418
SANCHEZ SANCHEZ, ISIDRO. Drawing dinosaurs. By Isidro Sanchez. Illus. by Vicenc Ballestar. Photos by Juan Carlos Martinez. Gareth Stevens ISBN 0-8368-1519-X; In Canada: Saunders, 1996. 32p. col. ill. (Draw, model, and paint).
Originally published in Spain as DIBUJA DINOSAURIOS, Ediciones Este, S.A., 1994.
Includes glossary, bibliography/filmography and index.
Provides step-by-step instructions for drawing dinosaurs using colored pencils. For the experienced artist who has mastered the Ames books, this demonstrates techniques of shading, darkening, etc. Inserts list basic facts about the depicted dinosaurs.
SUBJ: Colored pencil drawing--Technique./ Drawing--Technique./ Dinosaurs in art./ Dinosaurs.

743   Ph-3 5-A/3 $18.60   L   KD419
SANCHEZ SANCHEZ, ISIDRO. Painting and coloring dinosaurs. By Isidro Sanchez. Illus. by Vicenc Ballestar. Photos by Juan Carlos Martinez. Gareth Stevens ISBN 0-8368-1517-3; In Canada: Saunders, 1996. 32p. col. ill. (Draw, model, and paint).
Originally published in Spain as PINTA DINOSAURIOS, Ediciones Este, S.A., 1994.
Includes glossary, bibliography/filmography and index.
Describes shading, darkening, outlining, and other coloring techniques using felt tip pens, crayons, and tempera paints. Assumes the artist has already mastered the basic drawing techniques required to draw the dinosaur outlines. Inserts provide basic information about the depicted dinosaurs.
SUBJ: Painting--Technique./ Drawing--Technique./ Dinosaurs in art./ Dinosaurs.

745   Ph-2 P-3/1 $12.95   T   KD420
FOLK ART COUNTING BOOK. Based on a concept originated by Florence Cassen Mayers. Developed by Amy Watson and the staff of the Abby Aldrich Rockefeller Folk Art Center. Colonial Williamsburg Foundation, in association with Abrams ISBN 0-8109-3306-3, 1992. unp. col. ill.
American folk art of the eighteenth, nineteenth, and twentieth centuries illustrates an enchanting counting book designed to stimulate visual and cognitive senses and enhance young children's appreciation of folk art. Images are from the Abby Aldrich Rockefeller Folk Art Center in Williamsburg, Virginia.
SUBJ: Folk art./ Counting./ Abby Aldrich Rockefeller Folk Art Center.

VCR 745   Ph-3 5-A $83.00   OD KD421
MEXICAN FOLK ART (Videocassette). American School Publishers/SRA 87-005395 ISBN 0-383-05395-1, 1992. 1/2" VHS videocassette color

(22min). (Art explorations).
Includes guide.
An introduction to the variety of Mexican folk art, focusing on four categories: utilitarian, ceremonial, play and fantasy, and decoration. Guide describes creative activities for students and review questions. A colorful, dramatic addition to Mexican studies and multicultural lessons.
SUBJ: Folk art, Mexican./ Art, Mexican.

745   Ph-2 4-6/7 $21.50   L   KD422
TEMKO, FLORENCE. Traditional crafts from Africa. Illus. by Randall Gooch. Photos by Robert L. and Diane Wolfe. Lerner ISBN 0-8225-2936-X, 1996. 64p. col. ill., maps. (Culture crafts).
Includes glossary, bibliographies and index.
Offers directions for creating a variety of African crafts such as Senufo mud painting, Asante adrinka stamping, and the kigogo game. Can be used to enrich African studies and can be an interesting component of multicultural and interdisciplinary studies.
SUBJ: Handicraft--Africa.

MCP 745.4   Ph-1 2-A $56.95   OD KD423
KID CAD (Microcomputer program). Davidson & Associates/dist. by Educational Resources, 1993. 3 3.5" high density disks.
Includes teacher's guide, user's guide and reproducible student worksheets.
Also available in CD-ROM (162), $79.95.
System requirements: IBM or IBM-compatible computer; Microsoft Windows 3.1 (enhanced mode); an 80386 (or above) processor with 4MB of memory; a hard disk with at least 9MB of free space; a Sound Blaster-compatible sound card (recommended).
An easy-to-use computer-aided design program which introduces youngsters to the concepts of 3-D drawing. A camera feature allows the creator to zoom in or out on an object plus observe it from a number of angles. Premade scenes from a city, town, and farm are also available as a background or starting point.
SUBJ: Design--Software./ Software--Design./ Drawing--Technique--Software./ Software--Drawing--Technique.

745.5   Ph-1 A $7.95   P   KD424
BLAKEY, NANCY. Mudpies activity book: recipes for invention. Tricycle Press ISBN 1-883672-19-8, c1989, 1993. 132p. ill.
Includes index.
Simple science experiments, crafts, cooking, holiday projects, and indoor and outdoor activities fill this volume of advice to parents. Some projects--explained in practical terms and simple sketches--require parental supervision while others allow children to independently explore their creative interests. Activities tend to be imaginative, resourceful, and enjoyable for a variety of ages. The range of activities will be much appreciated by many adults looking for activities to use with individual children or groups. (Parents' Shelf). Additional activities can be found in MORE MUDPIES: 101 ALTERNATIVES TO TELEVISION (ISBN 1-883672-11-2, 1994).
SUBJ: Handicraft./ Science--Experiments./ Experiments.

745.5   Ph-3 K-4 $12.95   P   KD425
CARLSON, LAURIE. EcoArt!: earth-friendly art and craft experiences for 3-to 9-year olds. Illus. by Loretta Trezzo Braren. Williamson ISBN 0-913589-68-3; In Canada: Williamson/dist. by Fitzhenry & Whiteside, 1993. 157p. ill.
"Williamson Kids Can! book."
Includes index.
A plethora of arts and crafts projects that are environmentally sound, using recycled and natural materials. Includes the creation of seed mosaic wreaths, dried flowers, and pastes and paints.
SUBJ: Handicraft./ Nature craft./ Recycling (Waste).

745.5   Ph-2 4-A/7 $17.71   L   KD426
CORWIN, JUDITH HOFFMAN. Asian crafts. Watts ISBN 0-531-11013-3; In Canada: Watts, 1992. 48p. col. ill.
Includes index.
A potpourri of craft ideas from such Asian countries as Sri Lanka, Malaysia, and China; recipes from Russia and Lebanon; and toys and games of India and Thailand. Useful for enrichment of the social studies curriculum and for multicultural units.
SUBJ: Handicraft--Asia./ Toy making./ Cookery./ Asia--Social life and customs.

745.5   Ph-2 4-A/5 $17.71   L   KD427
CORWIN, JUDITH HOFFMAN. Latin American and Caribbean crafts. Watts ISBN 0-531-11014-1; In Canada: Watts, 1992. 48p. col. ill.
Includes index.
An assortment of Latin American and Caribbean crafts and recipes that are excellent for enriching social studies units and multicultural curriculum.

SUBJ: Handicraft--Latin America./ Handicraft--Caribbean Area./ Cookery, Latin American./ Cookery, Caribbean.

745.5   Ph-3 4-8/6 $21.95   T   KD428
DIEHN, GWEN. Kid style nature crafts: 50 terrific things to make with nature's materials. By Gwen Diehn and Terry Krautwurst. Photos by Richard Babb. Illus. by Gwen Diehn and Chris Colando. Sterling/Lark ISBN 0-8069-0996-X; In Canada: Sterling c/o Canadian Manda, 1995. 144p. col. ill.
Includes index.
Here is a surefire way to nurture an appreciation and awe of nature's bounty and to have some fun during all four seasons. Most craft projects will need some adult guidance, but material lists are inclusive and the directions are concise and well illustrated. Children can make grass mats, willow whistles, a lotus keepsake book, and even a piece of indoor twig furniture. An excellent resource for scout and 4-H leaders. (Parents' Shelf).
SUBJ: Nature craft./ Handicraft.

745.5   Ph-3 4-6/6 $19.95   T   KD429
DIEHN, GWEN. Nature crafts for kids. By Gwen Diehn and Terry Krautwurst. Sterling ISBN 0-8069-8372-8; In Canada: Sterling c/o Canadian Manda, 1992. 144p. col. ill.
"Sterling/Lark book."
Includes index.
Offers directions for making 50 outdoor craft projects using natural materials such as sand, flowers, shells, and twigs. The projects are arranged according to each season and result in the creation of leaf prints, pinch pots, and evergreen garlands. Includes some more involved projects which will require adult help. Useful for environmental studies projects.
SUBJ: Nature craft./ Handicraft.

745.5   Ph-2 4-A/8 $15.95   L   KD430
KALMAN, BOBBIE. Early artisans. Crabtree ISBN 0-86505-023-6; In Canada: Crabtree, 1983. 64p. ill. (Early settler life).
Delineates the work done by such early artisans as the shoemaker, glass blower, village smithy, and harness maker. Photographs from Williamsburg and sepia illustrations make this highly pictorial view of early settler life valuable for social studies units.
SUBJ: Handicraft--History--18th century./ Handicraft--History--19th century.

745.5   Ph-3 3-6/6 $15.95   L   KD431
KALMAN, BOBBIE. Home crafts. Crabtree ISBN 0-86505-485-1; In Canada: Crabtree, 1990. 32p. col. ill. (Historic communities).
Includes glossary and index.
A historical view of crafts produced by the pioneers for their daily use as they dipped candles, made soap, and wove rugs. Useful for social studies and art classes.
SUBJ: Handicraft./ Frontier and pioneer life.

745.5   Ph-2 3-5/6 $17.95   L   KD432
KALMAN, BOBBIE. Pioneer projects. Photos by Marc Crabtree. Illus. by Barbara Bedell. Crabtree ISBN 0-86505-437-1; In Canada: Crabtree, 1997. 32p. col. ill. (Historic communities).
Includes index and glossary.
Students learn about pioneer life as they pursue a variety of crafts and projects including decoupage, cornhusk dolls, and stitched story squares. Excellent enrichment activities for social studies.
SUBJ: Handicraft./ Frontier and pioneer life.

VCR 745.5   Ph-2 3-6 $14.95   OD KD433
LOOK WHAT I MADE: PAPER, PLAYTHINGS AND GIFTS (Videocassette). Intervideo/dist. by Vermont Story Works IVI 1234 ISBN 1-883784-00-X, 1993. 1/2" VHS videocassette color (45min). (On my own adventure).
Includes public performance rights.
A lively and colorful craft demonstration that includes easy-to-follow directions for making pinatas, paper flowers, and party hats. The project materials are few and easy to find. Fun for activities in the classroom and at home. (Parents' Shelf).
SUBJ: Paper work./ Handicraft.

745.5   Ph-3 3-5 $12.95   P   KD434
SABBETH, CAROL. Kids' computer creations: using your computer for art and craft fun. Illus. by Loretta Trezzo Braren. Williamson ISBN 0-913589-92-6; In Canada: Williamson/dist. by Fitzhenry & Whiteside, 1995. 158p. ill.
"Williamson Kids Can! book."
Includes index.
Lots of ideas for creating arts and crafts on the computer are interspersed with a plethora of facts about computers. Projects can be done at home or at school. (Parents' Shelf).
SUBJ: Computer art./ Handicraft.

745.5   Ph-1 4-6/6 $4.95   P   KD435
SATTLER, HELEN RONEY. Recipes for art and craft material. Newly rev. New illus. by Marti Shohet. Beech Tree ISBN 0-688-13199-9, c1973, 1994. 128p. ill.
> Available from National Library Service for the Blind and Physically Handicapped in Braille BR02437 and on sound recording cassette RC08861.
> A volume that brings together all the instructions for making pastes, modeling compounds, papier-mache, inks, casting compounds and paints and gives clear, precise directions. Sattler gives general hints and has a page with the advice that children should be supervised while making these concoctions. The index and detailed table of contents makes this perfect for ready reference.
> SUBJ: Handicraft--Equipment and supplies./ Artists' materials.

745.5   Ph-2 3-6/7 $12.95   T   KD436
SIRETT, DAWN. My first paint book. DK Publishing ISBN 1-56458-466-6, 1994. 48p. col. ill.
> An easy-to-follow, colorful format with large pictures gives step-by-step instructions for creating painted T-shirts, marbled paper, painted bottles, and stenciled art boxes. The projects often need adult help, but the directions are simple, and the results can be smashing.
> SUBJ: Painting--Technique./ Handicraft.

745.5   Ph-2 3-6/5 $21.50   L   KD437
SWAIN, GWENYTH. Bookworks: making books by hand. By Gwenyth Swain with Minnesota Center for Book Arts. Illus. by Jennifer Hagerman. Photos by Andy King. Carolrhoda ISBN 0-87614-858-5, 1995. 64p. col. ill.
> Includes glossary, bibliographies, directory and index.
> Directions for making different kinds of books such as pop-ups, sewn books, and bound up the side books. Includes information on finding your own story, making your own paper, printing, and illustrating. Could be the basis for exciting interdisciplinary projects incorporating creative writing skills and art activities.
> SUBJ: Books./ Book design./ Handicraft.

745.5   Ph-2 3-6/5 $21.50   L   KD438
TEMKO, FLORENCE. Traditional crafts from Mexico and Central America. Illus. by Randall Gooch. Photos by Robert L. and Diane Wolfe. Lerner ISBN 0-8225-2935-1, 1996. 64p. col. ill., map. (Culture crafts).
> Includes glossary, bibliography and index.
> Offers easy-to-follow directions for the construction of eight Latin American crafts including Guatemalan weaving, Mexican Day of the Dead skeletons, and Trees of Life. A good resource for teachers desiring to add a multicultural component to studies.
> SUBJ: Handicraft--Mexico./ Handicraft--Central America.

745.5   Ph-2 4-A/8 $17.00   L   KD439
WRIGHT, RACHEL. Knights: facts, things to make, activities. Watts ISBN 0-531-14163-2; In Canada: Watts, 1991. 32p. col. ill. (Craft topics).
> Includes glossary, bibliography and index.
> Discusses feudalism, chivalry, armor, and castles and is accompanied by craft projects creating cardboard castles, stained glass windows, and coats of arms. Good for enriching social studies units.
> SUBJ: Handicraft./ Knights and knighthood.

745.54   Ph-3 2-6/6 $19.95   T   KD440
FIAROTTA, PHYLLIS. Papercrafts around the world. By Phyllis Fiarotta and Noel Fiarotta. Sterling ISBN 0-8069-3990-7; In Canada: Sterling c/o Canadian Manda, 1996. 96p. col. ill.
> Includes index.
> Provides instructions for creating paper crafts from many countries. Students may require adult assistance with directions. These international folk art projects can be used to enrich multicultural studies.
> SUBJ: Paper work./ Handicraft.

745.54   Ph-2 K-2/3 $18.95   L   KD441
LYNN, SARA. Play with paper. By Sara Lynn and Diane James. Carolrhoda ISBN 0-87614-754-6, 1993. unp. col. ill.
> Easy directions for creating paper crafts. Colorful pictures illustrate the masks, flowers, and beads that the youngest children will enjoy making.
> SUBJ: Paper work./ Handicraft.

745.58   Ph-2 K-3/5 $15.40   L   KD442
ROSS, KATHY. Every day is Earth Day: a craft book. Illus. by Sharon Lane Holm. Millbrook ISBN 1-56294-490-8, 1995. 47p. col. ill. (Holiday crafts for kids).
> Twenty easy craft projects, using everyday materials, can be integrated into Earth Day celebrations. Emphasis is placed on recycling, pollution, and endangered species. Good for enriching environmental studies.
> SUBJ: Handicraft./ Recycling (Waste)./ Earth Day.

745.592   Ph-2 2-5/3 $19.95   T   KD443
BUETTER, BARBARA MACDONALD. Simple puppets from everyday materials. Sterling ISBN 1-89556-905-2; In Canada: Sterling c/o Canadian Manda, 1997. 80p. col. ill.
> "Sterling/Tamos book."
> Includes directory and index.
> A colorful, lively format leads readers through easy-to-follow directions for making accordian caterpillars, paper bag puppets, and marionettes. Using such everyday materials as popsicle sticks, toilet paper tubes, wooden spoons, juice cans, cereal boxes, and tube socks, ingenious puppets can be created. Fun for creating puppet shows or for classroom crafts.
> SUBJ: Puppet making./ Handicraft.

745.592   Ph-2 3-5/5 $9.95   T   KD444
BULLOCH, IVAN. I want to be a puppeteer. By Ivan Bulloch and Diane James. World Book/Two-Can ISBN 0-7166-1743-9, 1996. 32p. col. ill. (I want to be).
> Includes index.
> Basic, easy-to-follow directions for making a variety of puppets includes finger puppets, sock and glove puppets, shadow puppets, and traditional marionettes. Useful for students and teachers in creating puppet theater.
> SUBJ: Puppets./ Puppet making./ Puppet theater./ Handicraft.

745.592   Ph-2 3-6/7 $13.90   L   KD445
CRAFTS FOR PLAY. Edited by Caroline Bingham and Karen Foster. Millbrook ISBN 1-56294-096-1, 1993. 48p. col. ill. (Millbrook arts library).
> Includes index.
> Examines the dolls, toys, games, and puzzles of many cultures. Includes information to create simple projects. Can be used to enrich multicultural studies.
> SUBJ: Toy making./ Handicraft.

VCR 745.592   Ph-1 K-6 $29.95   OD KD446
MAKING AND USING PUPPETS IN THE PRIMARY GRADES (Videocassette). By Susan Barthel, Bruce Chesse and the Oregon Puppet Theatre. Puppet Concepts ISBN 0-96-28-355-2-8, 1992. 1/2" VHS videocassette color (28min).
> Includes teacher's guide.
> Clear instructions are accompanied by lively music as students actually follow the directions to make puppets. Projects are easy and the supplies are simple. Lots of fun activities here.
> SUBJ: Puppets./ Puppet making./ Puppet theater./ Handicraft.

745.592   Ph-3 3-6/3 $18.60   L   KD447
SANCHEZ SANCHEZ, ISIDRO. Dragons and prehistoric monsters. By Isidro Sanchez. Models by Roser Pinol. Photos by Juan Carlos Martinez. Gareth Stevens ISBN 0-8368-1521-1; In Canada: Saunders, 1996. 32p. col. ill. (Draw, model, and paint).
> Originally published in Spain as DRAGONES Y MONSTRUOS PREHISTORICOS, Ediciones Este, S.A., 1995.
> Includes glossary, bibliography/filmography and index.
> Instructions for using various materials including clay, plaster of paris, and papier-mache to create three-dimensional models of dragons and prehistoric creatures such as a pterodactyl and a woolly mammoth. Some instructions may require adult interpretation.
> SUBJ: Sculpture./ Dragons in art./ Monsters in art./ Handicraft.

745.592   Ph-3 3-6/3 $18.60   L   KD448
SANCHEZ SANCHEZ, ISIDRO. Modeling dinosaurs. By Isidro Sanchez. Models by Roser Pinol. Photos by Juan Carlos Martinez. Gareth Stevens ISBN 0-8368-1518-1; In Canada: Saunders, 1996. 32p. col. ill. (Draw, model, and paint).
> Originally published in Spain as MODELA DINOSAURIOS, Ediciones Este, S.A., 1994.
> Includes glossary, bibliography/filmography and index.
> Instructions for making dinosaur models incorporate a variety of media including plaster of paris, modeling clay, and papier-mache. Some directions may require adult interpretation. Inserts provide basic facts about the depicted dinosaurs.
> SUBJ: Modeling./ Handicraft./ Dinosaurs in art.

745.592   Ph-3 3-6/3 $18.60   L   KD449
SANCHEZ SANCHEZ, ISIDRO. Monsters and extraterrestrials. By Isidro Sanchez. Models by Elisabet Morgui. Photos by Juan Carlos Martinez. Gareth Stevens ISBN 0-8368-1520-3; In Canada: Saunders, 1996. 32p. col. ill. (Draw, model, and paint).
> Originally published in Spain as MONSTRUOS Y EXTRATERRESTRES, Ediciones Este, S.A., 1995.
> Includes glossary, bibliography/filmography and index.
> Provides instructions for creating a variety of monsters out of modeling clay. Adult help is often needed, so these are not

independent projects. The instructions are not always easy to follow, but the results will be very satisfying. Will be popular at Halloween. Additonal projects with monstrous results can be found in DREADFUL CREATURES (ISBN 0-8368-1522-X, 1996).
SUBJ: Modeling./ Handicraft./ Monsters in art.

745.594   Ph-1 3-6/6 $16.95   L   KD450
ANCONA, GEORGE. Pinata maker./El Pinatero. Harcourt Brace ISBN 0-15-261875-9; In Canada: Harcourt Brace c/o Canadian Manda, 1994. unp. col. ill.
Follows the working day of a Mexican craftsman, a seventy-seven-year-old pinata worker. Told in English and Spanish, the story reveals much about life in a Mexican village. Excellent for enriching social studies and Spanish language classes. For multicultural studies.
SUBJ: Paper work./ Pinatas./ Spanish language materials./ Bilingual materials--Spanish.

745.594   Ph-2 3-6/7 $13.90   L   KD451
CRAFTS FOR DECORATION. Edited by Caroline Bingham and Karen Foster. Millbrook ISBN 1-56294-098-8, 1993. 48p. col. ill. (Millbrook arts library).
Includes index.
Examines the methods used by many cultures to create decorations using color, natural fabrics, and textures. Includes batik, embroidery, bead work, and enamel. Use to enrich multicultural units.
SUBJ: Handicraft./ Decoration and ornament.

745.594   Ph-3 3-5 $15.90   L   KD452
ROSS, KATHY. Crafts for Christmas. Illus. by Sharon Lane Holm. Millbrook ISBN 1-56294-536-X, 1995. 47p. col. ill. (Holiday crafts for kids).
Glitter ornaments, grass wreaths, Santa door decorations, and reindeer treat bags will enrich the Christmas experience for many younsters. With adult supervision, projects would be suitable for primary students.
SUBJ: Christmas decorations./ Handicraft.

745.594   Ph-3 3-5 $15.90   L   KD453
ROSS, KATHY. Crafts for Easter. Illus. by Sharon Lane Holm. Millbrook ISBN 1-56294-918-7, 1995. 47p. col. ill. (Holiday crafts for kids).
Easy-to-follow instructions to create imaginative Easter baskets, party hats, and cards. With adult assistance, primary students could use for projects at holiday time.
SUBJ: Easter decorations./ Handicraft.

745.594   Ph-3 3-5 $15.40   L   KD454
ROSS, KATHY. Crafts for Halloween. Illus. by Sharon Lane Holm. Millbrook ISBN 1-56294-411-8, 1994. 47p. col. ill. (Holiday crafts for kids).
A plethora of easy projects for the celebration of Halloween. Includes instructions for owl message can, spiderwebs, and a bat out of stuffed socks. Made out of everyday objects, the crafts can be used as party favors as well.
SUBJ: Halloween decorations./ Handicraft.

745.594   Ph-2 3-6 $15.90   L   KD455
ROSS, KATHY. Crafts for Hanukkah. Illus. by Sharon Lane Holm. Millbrook ISBN 1-56294-919-5, 1996. 48p. col. ill. (Holiday crafts for kids).
Step-by-step instructions for a variety of projects that can be used as gifts, games, and decorations to celebrate the holiday season. Directions are easy to follow and everyday materials are used.
SUBJ: Hanukkah decorations./ Handicraft.

745.594   Ph-3 3-6 $15.40   L   KD456
ROSS, KATHY. Crafts for Kwanzaa. Illus. by Sharon Lane Holm. Millbrook ISBN 1-56294-412-6, 1994. 47p. col. ill. (Holiday crafts for kids).
Twenty simple craft projects including games, flags, greeting cards, and wrapping paper are designed to celebrate the holiday of Kwanzaa which honors the African roots of African Americans. For multicultural studies.
SUBJ: Kwanzaa./ Kwanzaa decorations./ Handicraft.

745.594   Ph-3 3-5 $15.90   L   KD457
ROSS, KATHY. Crafts for Thanksgiving. Illus. by Sharon Lane Holm. Millbrook ISBN 1-56294-535-1, 1995. 47p. col. ill. (Holiday crafts for kids).
A variety of holiday crafts that will enrich Thanksgiving celebrations in school and at home. Directions are easy to follow, and many of them can be done independently. Useful when additional holiday activities are needed.
SUBJ: Thanksgiving decorations./ Handicraft.

745.594   Ph-2 1-6/6 $15.95   L   KD458
SMITH, DEBBIE. Holidays and festivals activities. Crabtree ISBN 0-86505-121-6; In Canada: Crabtree, 1994. 62p. col. ill. (Holidays and festivals series).
Includes index.
A compilation of independent, partner, and group activities devoted to multicultural holiday celebrations. Includes choice games, recipes, and captivating information on celebratory rituals around the world. Valuable for incorporation into multicultural studies.
SUBJ: Handicraft./ Holidays./ Festivals.

745.594   Ph-1 1-5/5 $11.95   T   KD459
SOLGA, KIM. Make cards! North Light ISBN 0-89134-481-0, 1992. 48p. col. ill. (Art and activities for kids).
Twenty-one easy-to-follow projects result in the creation of imaginative greeting cards. Budding artists will learn composition, design, color, and texture while engineering a delightful variety of cards for all occasions.
SUBJ: Greeting cards./ Handicraft.

745.594   Ph-2 3-6 $12.95   T   KD460
WILKES, ANGELA. My first Christmas activity book. DK Publishing ISBN 1-56458-674-X, 1994. 48p. col. ill.
Brightly colored photographs give step-by-step instructions for creating a variety of Christmas goodies from cookies and truffles to wreaths, cards, and wrapping paper. The directions are clear and make everything seem so easy. Good for home and school projects.
SUBJ: Christmas decorations./ Handicraft./ Christmas cookery.

VCR 746.46   Ph-2 5-A $49.95   OD   KD461
FAITH RINGGOLD PAINTS CROWN HEIGHTS (Videocassette). L & S Video ISBN 1-882660-07-2, 1995. 1/2" VHS videocassette color (28min). (African American artists).
Faith Ringgold creates a quilt which depicts folktales from the major groups of immigrants who have lived in the Crown Heights section of Brooklyn. This is a remarkable tape as it weaves folklore, painting, and cultural history into a whole. Its primary use is to prompt groups to collect local history about the area in which they live; but it also brings Ringgold into the classroom as a vibrant artist. Inspiration for creative writing classes and for multicultural studies.
SUBJ: Quiltmakers./ Ringgold, Faith./ Women artists./ Afro-American artists./ Afro-Americans--Biography./ Brooklyn (New York, N.Y.)--Folklore.

746.46   Ph-3 3-6/7 $16.00   L   KD462
PAUL, ANN WHITFORD. Seasons sewn: a year in patchwork. Illus. by Michael McCurdy. Browndeer/Harcourt Brace ISBN 0-15-276918-8; In Canada: Harcourt Brace c/o Canadian Manda, 1996. unp. col. ill.
Includes bibliography.
An informative perspective on frontier and pioneer life as reflected in the changing seasons and in the patchwork quilt patterns that symbolized daily life and rituals. An interesting addition to American history studies.
SUBJ: Patchwork./ Quilts./ Frontier and pioneer life.

749   Ph-1 4-A/7 $14.89   L   KD463
GIBLIN, JAMES CROSS. Be seated: a book about chairs. HarperCollins ISBN 0-06-021538-0; In Canada: HarperCollins, 1993. 136p. ill.
Includes bibliography and index.
Available from the National Library Service for the Blind and Physically Handicapped on sound recording cassette RC 38930.
Traces the history, development, and social significance of the chair in many cultures and many times. Comprehensive and fascinating for browsing and reports.
SUBJ: Chairs.

750   Ph-3 1-2/4 $14.00   T   KD464
FLORIAN, DOUGLAS. Painter. Greenwillow ISBN 0-688-11872-0, 1993. unp. col. ill. (How we work).
Easy text explains the ways an artist paints--his feelings, his observations, his imagination. Includes the various materials used by painters. An enrichment tool for art appreciation and career studies for the very young.
SUBJ: Art./ Artists./ Occupations.

750   Ph-2 K-2/3 $18.95   L   KD465
LYNN, SARA. Play with paint. By Sara Lynn and Diane James. Carolrhoda ISBN 0-87614-755-4, 1993. unp. col. ill.
Offers instructions for a variety of activities using paint such as stencils, prints, and painted eggs. Colorful pictures illustrate the directions.
SUBJ: Paint./ Stencil work./ Printing.

750   Ph-2 K-2/2 $9.95   T   KD466
MICKLETHWAIT, LUCY. Spot a cat. DK Publishing ISBN 0-7894-0144-4,
1995. unp. col. ill.
"Dorling Kindersley book."
In this introduction to famous paintings, the youngest reader is asked
to find a cat in each one. An innovative way to encourage
observation while making great art familiar. Clearly reproduced
paintings in a variety of styles provide the feline hunt.
SUBJ: Cats in art./ Painting./ Art appreciation.

750   Ph-2 K-2/1 $9.95   T   KD467
MICKLETHWAIT, LUCY. Spot a dog. DK Publishing ISBN 0-7894-0145-
2, 1995. unp. col. ill.
"Dorling Kindersley book."
In this introduction to famous paintings, the youngest reader is asked
to find a dog in each one. An innovative way to encourage
observation while making great art familiar. Clearly reproduced
paintings from a variety of periods provide the canine search.
SUBJ: Dogs in art./ Painting./ Art appreciation.

CDR 750.28   Ph-1 P-A $69.95   OD KD468
KID PIX STUDIO (CD-ROM). Broderbund, 1994. 1 CD-ROM color.
Includes teacher's guide.
Also available for Windows.
System requirements: Macintosh and Power Macintosh; System 7.0.1
or higher; 20MHz 68030 processor faster; Power Macintosh; 4MB
RAM; 2.5MB free; requires 14MB hard disk space; double-speed
CD-ROM drive or faster required; monitor: 13 inch or larger color,
256 colors; works with most popular Macintosh compatible printers
(monochrome and color).
System requirements: Windows 3.1 or Windows 95; 33MHz 386 or
faster for Windows 3.1, 486 or faster for Windows 95; 4MB RAM
for Windows 3.1; 8MB RAM for Windows 95; requires 16MB hard
disk space; double-speed CD-ROM drive or faster required; SVGA
monitor/display card 640x480, 256 colors; Windows compatible
sound device; works with most popular printers (monochrome and
color) supported by Windows.
Product runs on either Macintosh or Windows compatible hardware.
This updates the classic KID PIX and KID PIX COMPANION programs
with options for more animations, slide shows, and QuickTime movies.
Students can create a digital puppet show or multimedia productions
integrating animation, special effects, photos, music, and sound. The
same easy-to-use interface remains. Excellent tool for student
creativity.
SUBJ: Art--Software./ Software--Art./ Painting--Technique--Software./
Software--Painting--Technique./ Spanish language materials--
Software./ Software--Spanish language materials./ Bilingual
materials--Spanish--Software./ Software--Bilingual materials--Spanish./
Interactive media.

MCP 750.28   Ph-1 P-A $49.95   OD KD469
NEW KID PIX. School version (Microcomputer program). Broderbund,
1996. 2 sets of 3.5" disks.
Formerly KID PIX and KID PIX COMPANION.
Includes teacher's guide, user's guide and troubleshooting guide.
Also available for Windows.
System requirements: Macintosh System 7.0.1 or higher; 25 MHz
68030 processor or faster; 4MB RAM, 2.5MB free; 9-14MB hard-
disk space; high-density floppy drive; 13" monitor or larger, 256
colors.
Both Macintosh and Windows versions contain program disks which
will run on older equipment.
This paint program opens many new horizons for young computer
users. A stamp feature as well as a number of different paint brush
strokes make artistic creation bloom. In addition, sounds can be
added to student productions. Excellent tool for student creativity.
SUBJ: Art--Software./ Software--Art./ Painting--Technique--Software./
Software--Painting--Technique./ Spanish language materials--
Software./ Software--Spanish language materials./ Bilingual
materials--Spanish--Software./ Software--Bilingual materials--Spanish./
Interactive media.

751.4   Ph-3 5-6/8 $14.95   T   KD470
WATERS, ELIZABETH. Painting: a young artist's guide. By Elizabeth
Waters and Annie Harris. DK Publishing ISBN 1-56458-348-1, 1993.
45p. col. ill. (Young artist).
Includes index.
Provides techniques for mixing colors, choosing brushes and papers,
and painting light and shadow. Includes activities for sketching ideas,
combining shapes in painting, seeing patterns in nature, and painting
portraits. An excellent guide for budding artists.
SUBJ: Painting--Technique.

757   Ph-2 3-6/7 $16.00   L   KD471
RICHMOND, ROBIN. Story in a picture: children in art. Ideals ISBN
0-8249-8588-5; In Canada: Ideals, 1992. 48p. col. ill. (Story in a
picture).
Includes index.
An excellent selection of paintings depicting the lives and activities of
children. Includes the works of Renoir, Gauguin, and Van Gogh.
Encourages young readers to increase their powers of observation
and to focus on artistic techniques and styles.
SUBJ: Children in art./ Painting--History./ Art appreciation.

757   Ph-3 5-A/7 $14.89   L   KD472
ROALF, PEGGY. Families. Hyperion ISBN 1-56282-088-5, 1992. 48p.
col. ill. (Looking at paintings).
"Jacques Lowe Visual Arts projects book."
Includes glossary and index.
Eighteen paintings, formal portraits as well as scenes of everyday
family activities, present the family as viewed by numerous artists.
Various methods and techniques used to create the paintings from
different periods are explained in the text. Useful for art history
classes.
SUBJ: Family in art./ Painting--History./ Art appreciation.

758   Ph-1 P-2/2 $18.93   L   KD473
MICKLETHWAIT, LUCY. I spy a freight train: transportation in art.
Devised and selected by Lucy Micklethwait. Greenwillow ISBN 0-688-
14701-1, 1996. unp. col. ill.
A fascinating way to encourage art appreciation through games.
Visual skills are enhanced, and discussions can strengthen verbal skills
and broaden tastes.
SUBJ: Transportation in art./ Art appreciation.

758   Ph-1 P-2/2 $18.93   L   KD474
MICKLETHWAIT, LUCY. I spy a lion: animals in art. Devised and selected
by Lucy Micklethwait. Greenwillow ISBN 0-688-13231-6, 1994. unp. col.
ill.
Powers of observation are sharpened as 20 paintings by such varied
artists as Titian, Holbein, Rousseau, and Picasso are searched carefully
to reveal a specific animal. Familiarizes youngsters with great works
of art, and fosters oral communication.
SUBJ: Animals in art./ Art appreciation.

758   Ph-3 4-A/7 $16.00   L   KD475
RICHMOND, ROBIN. Story in a picture: animals in art. Ideals ISBN
0-8249-8626-1; In Canada: Ideals, 1993. 48p. col. ill. (Story in a
picture).
Includes index.
Paintings which portray animals are analyzed with information on the
artists' biographies, techniques, and the history of the times. Beautiful
reproductions introduce the work of such great artists as Picasso,
Chagall, and Rousseau. Excellent for enrichment of the art curriculum
as well as for reports.
SUBJ: Animals in art./ Painting./ Art appreciation.

758   Ph-3 5-A/8 $14.89   L   KD476
ROALF, PEGGY. Cats. Hyperion ISBN 1-56282-092-3, 1992. 48p. col.
ill. (Looking at paintings).
"Jacques Lowe Visual Arts projects book."
Includes glossary and index.
Cats are presented in a variety of artistic styles from a facsimile of an
Egyptian wall hanging to a stylized painting by Paul Klee. Text
explores the techniques used to create the 19 feline portraits. Popular
subject and high quality reproductions will invite browsers.
SUBJ: Cats in art./ Painting--History./ Art appreciation.

758   Ph-3 5-A/8 $14.89   L   KD477
ROALF, PEGGY. Circus. Hyperion ISBN 1-56282-304-3, 1993. 48p. col.
ill. (Looking at paintings).
"Jacques Lowe Visual Arts projects book."
Includes glossary and index.
The circus is interpreted by 19 artists who lived in different periods
and used a variety of art styles and techniques. Text explains the
materials and methods used to create the paintings. Attractive design
and high interest topic will appeal to browsers as well as art students.
SUBJ: Circus in art./ Painting--History./ Art appreciation.

758   Ph-3 5-A/7 $14.89   L   KD478
ROALF, PEGGY. Dancers. Hyperion ISBN 1-56282-090-7, 1992. 48p.
col. ill. (Looking at paintings).
"Jacques Lowe Visual Arts projects book."
Includes glossary and index.
Nineteen full-color reproductions from many periods capture the fluid
movements of dance. Text explains the cultural importance of dance
as well as the techniques used to create the paintings. An attractive

book useful for art history as well as dance history.
SUBJ: Dancers in art./ Dancing in art./ Painting--History./ Art appreciation.

758 Ph-3 5-A/8 $14.89 L KD479
ROALF, PEGGY. Flowers. Hyperion ISBN 1-56282-359-0, 1993. 48p. col. ill. (Looking at paintings).
"Jacques Lowe Visual Arts project book."
Includes glossary and index.
Nineteen high quality art reproductions depict the world of flowers as seen through the eyes of artists. Arranged chronologically, the full-page illustrations show a variety of styles and periods. Text explores the techniques and materials used while providing a brief social history of the period. Useful for art history as well as browsing.
SUBJ: Flowers in art./ Painting--History./ Art appreciation.

758 Ph-3 5-A/8 $14.89 L KD480
ROALF, PEGGY. Horses. Hyperion ISBN 1-56282-306-X, 1992. 48p. col. ill. (Looking at paintings).
"Jacques Lowe Visual Arts Projects book."
Includes glossary and index.
From the cave drawings of early man to the present, horses have fascinated artists and have been the subject of more paintings than any other animal. This overview of the depiction of the horse in art includes 19 examples from various periods. Text explains the techniques and methods used while giving brief factual information about the artists.
SUBJ: Horses in art./ Painting--History./ Art appreciation.

758 Ph-3 5-A/8 $14.89 L KD481
ROALF, PEGGY. Landscapes. Hyperion ISBN 1-56282-302-7, 1992. 48p. col. ill. (Looking at paintings).
"Jacques Lowe Visual Arts Projects book."
Includes glossary and index.
Nineteen landscapes by artists from various periods provide a unique look at 2,000 years of art history. Text explores techniques and styles of the different painters while giving brief biographical glimpses of their lives.
SUBJ: Landscape in art./ Painting--History./ Art appreciation.

758 Ph-3 5-A/7 $14.89 L KD482
ROALF, PEGGY. Seascapes. Hyperion ISBN 1-56282-094-X, 1992. 48p. col. ill. (Looking at paintings).
"Jacques Lowe Visual Arts projects book."
Includes glossary and index.
Seascapes are presented from the point of view of many different artists with various styles. Nineteen full-color reproductions depict the ever changing moods of the sea as painted by such artists as Monet, Winslow Homer, and Picasso. Text discusses the techniques used by the various artists. Good for art history as well as browsing.
SUBJ: Sea in art./ Marine painting./ Painting--History./ Art appreciation.

759 Ph-2 4-6/8 $25.69 L KD483
HESLEWOOD, JULIET. History of Western painting: a young person's guide. Raintree Steck-Vaughn ISBN 0-8172-4000-4, 1996. 64p. col. ill.
Includes glossary, bibliography and index.
An overview of Western art traces developments from the ancient world, through the Renaissance, and on to the modern world. Attractive browser offers information on major artists with reproductions of some of their greatest paintings.
SUBJ: Painting--History.

759 Ph-1 P-2/2 $19.00 L KD484
MICKLETHWAIT, LUCY. I spy: an alphabet in art. Devised and selected by Lucy Micklethwait. Greenwillow ISBN 0-688-11679-5, 1992. unp. col. ill.
Includes index.
Selectors' Choice, 19th ed.
An ingenious introduction to the world of art through twenty-six great paintings, each containing objects from A-Z. An examination of the paintings of Goya, Chagall, Miro, Renoir, and others will provoke dicussion, sharpen observation skills, and provide a familiarity with fine art.
SUBJ: Art appreciation./ Alphabet.

759.05 Ph-3 6-A/9 $19.95 T KD485
SALVI, FRANCESCO. Impressionists: the origins of modern painting. Illus. by L. R. Galante and Andrea Ricciardi. Peter Bedrick ISBN 0-87226-314-2, 1994. 64p. col. ill., maps (Masters of art).
Includes chronology, directory and indexes.
Profusely illustrated exploration of the artistic movement known as Impressionism includes information on the artists' lives, key dates, descriptions of life in Paris, and a directory of museums and

collections. For the mature student. Excellent for reports.
SUBJ: Impressionism (Art)./ Art, Modern--19th century./ Art, Modern--20th century./ Artists./ Art appreciation.

759.1 Ph-3 5-A/7 $16.95 L KD486
SILLS, LESLIE. Inspirations: stories about women artists. Whitman ISBN 0-8075-3649-0, 1989. 55p. ill. (some col.).
Includes bibliography.
Profiles four diverse women artists as they conquer obstacles to achieve their artistic vision. Includes Georgia O'Keefe, who immortalized the New Mexican desert; Mexican Frida Kahlo, known for her detailed family portraits; Alice Neel who created soul searing portraits that revealed the inner life of her subjects; and contemporary black artist Faith Ringgold, author of TAR BEACH, who reveals the faces of Harlem on quilts, dolls, and masks. Excellent for art enrichment activities and women's studies.
SUBJ: Women artists./ Artists.

VCR 759.13 Ph-3 5-A $49.95 KD487
JACOB LAWRENCE: THE GLORY OF EXPRESSION (Videocassette). Narrated by Ossie Davis. L & S Video ISBN 1-882660-04-8, 1995. 1/2" VHS videocassette color (28min). (African American artists).
Jacob Lawrence explains his painting techniques while working on a new project. He also gives insight into his roots and his need to portray some of the life stories of individuals (e.g., Harriet Tubman) who were leaders in the African-American search for freedom. Inspiring tape for use in multicultural studies and art units.
SUBJ: Painting, American./ Lawrence, Jacob./ Artists./ Afro-American artists./ Art appreciation./ Afro-Americans in art./ Afro-Americans--Biography.

759.13 Ph-1 K-5/7 $22.89 L KD488
LAWRENCE, JACOB. Great migration: an American story. Paintings by Jacob Lawrence with a poem in appreciation by Walter Dean Myers. HarperCollins ISBN 0-06-023038-X; In Canada: HarperCollins, 1993. unp. col. ill.
Selectors' Choice, 20th ed.
Dramatic paintings evoke the struggle of African Americans for a better life. Their heroism and courage are revealed as they migrate from the rural South to the industrial North despite the violence often whirling around them. Interesting amalgam of art and history which is an inspiring component for multicultural studies.
SUBJ: Afro-Americans in art./ Painting, American./ Afro-Americans--History.

759.13 Ph-3 5-A/7 $11.99 P KD489
MUHLBERGER, RICHARD. What makes a Cassatt a Cassatt? Metropolitan Museum of Art/Viking ISBN 0-670-85742-4; In Canada: Penguin, 1994. 48p. col. ill. (What makes a...a...?).
Examines 12 of the paintings of Mary Cassatt in detail, with information about her life, her studies, and her techniques. Excellent for integration into art lessons.
SUBJ: Painting, American./ Art appreciation./ Cassatt, Mary./ Women artists.

759.4 Ph-2 4-A/12 $19.95 T KD490
LORIA, STEFANO. Pablo Picasso. Illus. by Simone Boni and L. R. Galante. Peter Bedrick ISBN 0-87226-318-5, 1995. 64p. col. ill. (Masters of art).
Includes chronology and indexes.
Traces Picasso's career with excellent reproductions, photographs, and drawings of the artist at work. A wonderful book for browsing and using as an introduction to the art of Picasso.
SUBJ: Painting, French./ Picasso, Pablo./ Artists./ Art appreciation.

759.4 Ph-3 5-A/7 $9.95 P KD491
MUHLBERGER, RICHARD. What makes a Degas a Degas? Metropolitan Museum of Art/Viking ISBN 0-670-85205-8; In Canada: Penguin, 1993. 48p. col. ill. (What makes a...a...?).
Discusses the uniqueness of the work of Degas, exploring his style, use of color, composition, and subject matter. Includes biographical information and reproductions of twelve of his paintings. Excellent for use with gifted students.
SUBJ: Painting, French./ Art appreciation./ Degas, Edgar./ Artists.

759.4 Ph-3 5-A/7 $9.95 P KD492
MUHLBERGER, RICHARD. What makes a Monet a Monet? Metropolitan Museum of Art/Viking ISBN 0-670-85200-7; In Canada: Penguin, 1993. 48p. col. ill. (What makes a...a...?).
Monet, one of the French Impressionists, is introduced in a brief biographical sketch with reproductions of twelve of his works. His repeated use of water and flowers as subjects is explored as well as his use of color and vertical and horizontal perspective.
SUBJ: Painting, French./ Art appreciation./ Monet, Claude./ Artists.

759.4   Ph-3 5-A/7 $11.99   P   KD493
MUHLBERGER, RICHARD. What makes a Picasso a Picasso?
Metropolitan Museum of Art/Viking ISBN 0-670-85741-6; In Canada:
Penguin, 1994. 48p. col. ill. (What makes a...a...?).
> Examines the life and works of one of the greatest twentieth century
> artists, Picasso. Details the various artistic periods through which he
> evolved and the techniques he developed. For the mature reader.
> SUBJ: Painting, French./ Art appreciation./ Picasso, Pablo./ Artists./
> Painting, Modern--20th century--France.

759.5   Ph-2 4-A/9 $19.95   L   KD494
CORRAIN, LUCIA. Giotto and medieval art: the lives and works of the
medieval artists. Illus. by Sergio with the assistance of Andrea Ricciardi.
Peter Bedrick ISBN 0-87226-315-0, 1995. 64p. col. ill., maps. (Masters
of art).
> Includes chronology and index.
> A lavishly illustrated view of medieval Europe features the life and
> works of Giotto, one of the most innovative artists of his time.
> SUBJ: Art, Medieval./ Giotto./ Artists./ Art appreciation.

759.5   Ph-3 6-A/6 $19.95   T   KD495
MCLANATHAN, RICHARD. Leonardo da Vinci. Abrams ISBN 0-8109-
1256-2, 1990. 92p. col. ill. (First impressions).
> Explores the many facets of Leonardo's genius as an artist, scientist,
> inventor, and musician with full-color reproductions of some of his
> most famous paintings. Excellent for gifted students.
> SUBJ: Painting, Italian./ Artists./ Leonardo, da Vinci./ Art
> appreciation.

759.5   Ph-3 5-A/7 $11.99   P   KD496
MUHLBERGER, RICHARD. What makes a Leonardo a Leonardo?
Metropolitan Museum of Art/Viking ISBN 0-670-85744-0; In Canada:
Penguin, 1994. 48p. col. ill. (What makes a...a...?).
> Examines 12 of Leonardo's paintings, with information on his painting
> techniques, his choice of subjects, and the qualities that make his art
> unique. For the advanced student.
> SUBJ: Painting, Italian./ Art appreciation./ Leonardo, da Vinci./
> Artists.

759.5   Ph-3 5-A/7 $9.95   P   KD497
MUHLBERGER, RICHARD. What makes a Raphael a Raphael?
Metropolitan Museum of Art/Viking ISBN 0-670-85204-X; In Canada:
Penguin, 1993. 48p. col. ill. (What makes a...a...?).
> Twelve of Raphael's works are explored in detail, examining style,
> composition, color, and subject matter. Includes brief biographical
> information.
> SUBJ: Painting, Italian./ Art appreciation./ Raphael Sanzio./ Artists.

759.6   Ph-3 5-A/7 $11.99   P   KD498
MUHLBERGER, RICHARD. What makes a Goya a Goya? Metropolitan
Museum of Art/Viking ISBN 0-670-85743-2; In Canada: Penguin, 1994.
48p. col. ill. (What makes a...a...?).
> Explores the artistic techniques employed by Goya in 12 of his
> paintings. Offers biographical information as well as information on
> other Spanish artists. An excellent analysis of Goya's work.
> SUBJ: Painting, Spanish./ Art appreciation./ Goya, Francisco./
> Artists.

759.9492   Ph-2 6-A/12 $19.95   T   KD499
CRISPINO, ENRICA. Van Gogh. Illus. by Simone Boni...[et al.]. Peter
Bedrick ISBN 0-87226-525-0, 1996. 64p. col. ill., maps. (Masters of
art).
> Includes chronology and index.
> Explores the career of Vincent Van Gogh, emphasizing his greatest
> works, his troubled life, and the artistic techniques he employed.
> Includes information on France during the Belle Epoque when
> Toulouse-Lautrec, Matisse, and Cezanne were painting. A beautiful
> book for browsers, as well as for reports.
> SUBJ: Painting, Dutch./ Painting, Modern--19th century--Netherlands./
> Gogh, Vincent van./ Artists./ Art appreciation.

759.9492   Ph-3 5-A/7 $9.95   P   KD500
MUHLBERGER, RICHARD. What makes a Rembrandt a Rembrandt?
Metropolitan Museum of Art/Viking ISBN 0-670-85199-X; In Canada:
Penguin, 1993. 48p. col. ill. (What makes a...a...?).
> Explores twelve works of Rembrandt while providing brief
> biographical information. Examines his attention to detail, his use of
> light and shadow, and the informal poses of his subjects who were
> often dressed in elaborate costumes.
> SUBJ: Painting, Dutch./ Art appreciation./ Rembrandt Harmenszoon
> van Rijn./ Artists.

759.9492   Ph-2 4-A/12 $19.95   T   KD501
PESCIO, CLAUDIO. Rembrandt and seventeenth-century Holland. Illus. by
Sergio. Peter Bedrick ISBN 0-87226-317-7, 1995. 64p. col. ill., maps.
(Masters of art).
> Includes chronology and indexes.
> Introduces Rembrandt with an in-depth look at his life and times,
> artistic influences, and techniques. Beautiful reproductions of his
> paintings reveal the stories behind his great works.
> SUBJ: Painting, Dutch./ Rembrandt Harmenszoon van Rijn./ Art
> appreciation./ Artists./ Netherlands--Civilization--17th Century.

759.9493   Ph-3 5-A/8 $9.95   P   KD502
MUHLBERGER, RICHARD. What makes a Bruegel a Bruegel?
Metropolitan Museum of Art/Viking ISBN 0-670-85203-1; In Canada:
Penguin, 1993. 48p. col. ill. (What makes a...a...?).
> Explores the unique style of Bruegel. Examines his unusual points of
> view, his concealed references to Greek myths, and the minute details
> which make his work so recognizable. Includes brief biographical
> information and reproductions of twelve of his paintings.
> SUBJ: Painting, Flemish./ Art appreciation./ Bruegel, Pieter./ Artists.

760   Ph-2 3-6/7 $13.89   L   KD503
FLEISCHMAN, PAUL. Copier creations: using copy machines to make
decals, silhouettes, flip books, films, and much more! Illus. by David Cain.
HarperCollins ISBN 0-06-021053-2; In Canada: HarperCollins, 1993.
122p. ill.
> Includes bibliography.
> Instructions for using copy machines to create stationery, flip books,
> decals, puzzles, and films. Creative and artistic projects progress from
> the simple to the more involved.
> SUBJ: Copy art.

760   Ph-2 P-6/4 $11.95   T   KD504
SOLGA, KIM. Make prints! North Light ISBN 0-89134-384-9, 1991.
48p. col. ill. (Art and activities for kids).
> Create a variety of prints using vegetables, soap, and your own
> fingers! Easy-to-follow directions and sharp photographs clearly
> explain printing techniques which will appeal to a wide range of
> interests and abilities.
> SUBJ: Prints--Technique.

769   Ph-2 4-A/7 $14.90   L   KD505
OWENS, THOMAS S. Collecting baseball cards. Millbrook ISBN
1-56294-254-9, 1993. 80p. col. ill.
> Includes directory, glossary and index.
> An overview of baseball card collecting stresses such practicalities as
> building a collection, preserving and finding cards, and the hurdles
> and errors implicit in this hobby.
> SUBJ: Baseball cards--Collectors and collecting.

769.5   Ph-2 3-6/11 $14.89   L   KD506
PARKER, NANCY WINSLOW. Money, money, money: the meaning of
the art and symbols on United States paper currency. HarperCollins ISBN
0-06-023412-1; In Canada: HarperCollins, 1995. 32p. col. ill., map.
> Includes index.
> Offers information on the meaning of the art and symbols on United
> States paper currency, including brief biographies of the historical
> personages who appear on paper bills and descriptions of the
> historical buildings and other symbols. Discusses the engraving,
> printing, and the counterfeiting of currency. Fascinating for browsing
> and useful for reports.
> SUBJ: Paper money--History./ Money--History./ Signs and symbols--
> History.

769.56   Ph-2 1-3/2 $12.95   L   KD507
ANSARY, MIR TAMIM. Stamps. Rigby ISBN 1-57572-113-9, 1997.
24p. col. ill. (Cool collections).
> Includes glossary, index and bibliography.
> A basic introduction to stamp collecting for very beginning readers.
> SUBJ: Stamp collecting.

769.56   Ph-2 4-6/8 $16.90   L   KD508
GRANGER, NEILL. Stamp collecting. Edited by Brenda Ralph Lewis.
Millbrook ISBN 1-56294-399-5, 1994. 93p. col. ill., maps. (First guide).
"Quarto book."
> Includes glossary and index.
> A colorful, comprehensive look at stamps, which includes information
> on the postal service, building a collection, famous collectors, and
> displaying stamps. The brightly illustrated format will invite collectors
> and browsers alike.
> SUBJ: Postage stamps--Collectors and collecting.

770 Ph-3 5-6/10 $19.95 L KD509
CZECH, KENNETH P. Snapshot: America discovers the camera. Lerner ISBN 0-8225-1736-1, 1996. 88p. ill. (People's history).
    Includes bibliography and index.
    A historical recounting of the invention of the camera and its development and popularity. Includes many old photographs that reveal much about America of long ago. Excellent for reports as well as fun for browsers.
    SUBJ: Photography--History.

770 Ph-3 5-6/12 $16.99 T KD510
SULLIVAN, GEORGE. Black artists in photography, 1840-1940. Cobblehill/Dutton ISBN 0-525-65208-6; In Canada: McClelland & Stewart, 1996. 104p. ill.
    Includes bibliography and index.
    Provides insights into the work of African-American professional photographers from the mid-nineteenth to the mid-twentieth century. An important addition to multicultural studies.
    SUBJ: Photographers./ Afro-Americans--Biography./ Photography--History.

770 Ph-1 K-6/5 $13.95 T KD511
TUCKER, JEAN S. Come look with me: discovering photographs with children. Lickle Publishing/dist. by PRI ISBN 1-56566-062-5, 1994. 32p. ill. (some col.). (Come look with me).
    Includes bibliography.
    Twelve superb photographs of children are accompanied by questions designed to provoke discussion and by brief text explaining the creative process involved in each photograph. Includes Alfred Eisenstaedt's memorable "Drum major and children" and Mathew Brady's formal daguerreotype of a father and son. An outstanding introduction to photography for individual as well as classroom use.
    SUBJ: Photography, artistic./ Art appreciation.

771 Ph-1 2-4/5 $14.95 L KD512
GIBBONS, GAIL. Click!: a book about cameras and taking pictures. Little, Brown ISBN 0-316-30976-1; In Canada: Little, Brown, 1997. unp. col. ill.
    Explains the parts of a camera, how to take a picture, and how to select a subject. The illustrations are colorful cartoons which enhance the information. Simple language and a plethora of helpful hints will make this a delightful choice for novice photographers.
    SUBJ: Cameras./ Photography.

771 Ph-2 3-6/3 $12.95 T KD513
KING, DAVE. My first photography book. DK Publishing ISBN 1-56458-673-1, 1994. 48p. col. ill.
    Includes glossary.
    Offers tips on how to take creative pictures with a simple automatic or disposable camera. Projects include making a pinhole camera, cropping and enlarging, special effects, close-ups, photo montages, panoramas, and collages. Inventive ideas with easy-to-follow directions.
    SUBJ: Photography./ Handicraft.

771 Ph-3 5-A/7 $16.90 L KD514
PHOTOGRAPHY. Edited by Jonathan Hilton and Barrie Watts. Millbrook ISBN 1-56294-398-7, 1994. 93p. col. ill. (First guide).
    "Quarto book."
    Includes directory, glossary and index.
    Introduces different kinds of cameras, gives information on composition of pictures and developing film, and offers many tips on how to take a good photograph.
    SUBJ: Photography.

778.5 Ph-2 5-A/6 $19.95 T KD515
ANDERSEN, YVONNE. Make your own animated movies and videotapes. Little, Brown ISBN 0-316-03941-1; In Canada: Little, Brown, 1991. 176p. ill.
    Includes appendix and index.
    Updated, expanded ed. of: MAKE YOUR OWN ANIMATED MOVIES, 1st ed, 1970.
    Offers techniques for creating animated movies with emphasis on use of equipment, types of shots, special effects, editing and sound tracks. A must for all schools that are into moviemaking and need clear, concise information.
    SUBJ: Cinematography./ Animation (Cinematography)./ Amateur motion pictures.

779 Ph-2 P-K $15.93 L KD516
HOBAN, TANA. Look book. Greenwillow ISBN 0-688-14972-3; In Canada: Hearst Book Group., 1997. unp. col. ill.
    Peek through a die-cut hole to examine full-color nature photographs. Encourages observation and articulation, creating a guessing game for

storytimes.
    SUBJ: Nature photography./ Photography./ Toy and movable books./ Visual perception.

VCR 780 Ph-2 1-6 $30.00 OD KD517
AMERICAN IN PARIS: GERSHWIN (Videocassette). Clearvue/EAV 7VH-7412, 1993. 1/2" VHS videocassette color (19min).
    Includes teacher's guide.
    Scenes of Paris accompany Gershwin's paean to the "City of lights." As students view the famous monuments and avenues, they will develop appreciation for the places that inspired Gershwin's glorious music. Can be used for music appreciation and for introductory French classes.
    SUBJ: Gershwin, George./ Composers./ Paris (France)--Description.

BA 780 Ph-2 5-A/8 $24.95 KD518
ARDLEY, NEIL. Young person's guide to music. Music by Poul Ruders. In association with the BBC Symphony Orchestra conducted by Andrew Davis. DK Publishing ISBN 0-7894-0313-7, 1995. 88p. ill., 1 compact disc (60min).
    Includes chronologies, glossary and index.
    An accessible presentation explains how music is made as well as the history of classical music. Excellent photographs show the various instruments. The historical overview delineates the music of many periods and provides an index of classical composers. Excellent for reports, especially for advanced students.
    SUBJ: Music--Study and teaching./ Orchestra./ Music--History and criticism.

VCR 780 Ph-3 3-A $29.95 KD519
HOW TO READ MUSIC. 2ND ED. (Videocassette). Allied Video 0795 ISBN 1-56913-034-5, 1994. 1/2" VHS videocassette color (20min). (Assistant professor).
    A lively presentation teaches musical understanding through the use of animated graphics. Explains the musical scale, the treble and bass staffs, pitch, and notation. An excellent aid for teaching basic music concepts.
    SUBJ: Music--Study and teaching./ Musical meter and rhythm.

780 Ph-2 5-A/6 $18.95 T KD520
KRULL, KATHLEEN. Lives of the musicians: good times, bad times (and what the neighbors thought). Illus. by Kathryn Hewitt. Harcourt Brace Jovanovich ISBN 0-15-248010-2; In Canada: Harcourt Brace c/o Canadian Manda, 1993. 96p. col. ill.
    Includes glossary, index and bibliography.
    Available from the National Library Service for the Blind and Physically Handicapped on sound recording cassette RC 37607.
    Twenty composers, Europeans and Americans, males and females, are discussed briefly. The sections contain some well-known facts and some little known items which make the person come alive. A humorous and informative presentation to enliven music programs.
    SUBJ: Musicians.

780 Ph-1 4-6/11 $16.89 L KD521
MEDEARIS, ANGELA SHELF. Music. By Angela Shelf Medearis and Michael R. Medearis. Twenty-First Century ISBN 0-8050-4482-5; In Canada: Fitzhenry & Whiteside, 1997. 80p. ill. (some col.). (African-American arts).
    Includes bibliography and index.
    Explores the development of African-American music from the rhythm and instrumentation of Africa through minstrel shows, ragtime, jazz, and gospel to rhythm and blues, soul, and rap. Excellent for reports. For multicultural studies.
    SUBJ: Afro-Americans--Music--History and criticism./ Popular music--History and criticism.

VCR 780 Ph-2 K-2 $34.95 OD KD522
METER (Videocassette). Films for the Humanities & Sciences FFH 4739, 1994. 1/2" VHS videocassette color (15min). (Music box).
    Includes public performance rights.
    A lively presentation about strong beats and weak beats. Uses music and dancing to help explain accents. Encourages audience participation.
    SUBJ: Musical meter and rhythm./ Music--Study and teaching.

VCR 780 Ph-2 K-2 $34.95 OD KD523
PITCH (Videocassette). Films for the Humanities & Sciences FFH 4740, 1994. 1/2" VHS videocassette color (15min). (Music box).
    Includes public performance rights.
    Teaches musical sounds using experiments, questions, and riddles--all designed to encourage audience participation. A highly entertaining presentation of a simple musical concept.
    SUBJ: Music--Acoustics and physics./ Music--Study and teaching.

780   Ph-2 3-6/8 $19.95   L   KD524
REDIGER, PAT. Great African Americans in music. Crabtree ISBN
0-86505-800-8; In Canada: Crabtree, 1996. 64p. col. ill. (Outstanding
African Americans).
  Includes index.
  Brief biographies of such great musicians as Ella Fitzgerald, Stevie
  Wonder, Aretha Franklin, and Whitney Houston. Emphasizes the
  development of musical skills, overcoming obstacles, and
  accomplishments. Useful for reports. For multicultural studies.
  SUBJ: Musicians./ Afro-Americans--Biography./ Women musicians.

CDR 780   Ph-2 4-A $54.95   OD KD525
WINTER, ROBERT. Microsoft composer collection (CD-ROM). By Robert
Winter and Alan Rich with The Voyager Company. Microsoft ISBN
1-57231-082-0; In Canada: Microsoft Canada, 1994. 3 CD-ROMs color.
Version 1.00.
  Includes user's guides.
  Also available as individual CD-ROM products, $29.95 each.
  System requirements: Multimedia PC with a 386SX or higher
  microprocessor; 4MB of memory; 5MB hard-disk space; CD-ROM
  drive; audio board; VGA or SVGA monitor (256-color display
  recommended); MS-DOS operating system version 3.1 or later;
  Microsoft Windows operating system version 3.1 or later; Microsoft
  Mouse or compatible pointing device; headphone or speakers.
  Multimedia examines the works of three composers, including not only
  their music but also the ability to look at their compositions in-depth.
  Sections on the composers' inspirations, the world at that time, key
  instruments and musical ensembles, and composition theories make
  these very useful classroom tools. Music teachers will find they work
  well with an entire class; classroom teachers will find them useful as
  learning centers. Discs may also be played as audio compact discs.
  Microsoft multimedia Beethoven -- Microsoft multimedia Mozart --
  Microsoft multimedia Schubert.
  SUBJ: Composers--Software./ Software--Composers./ Music
  appreciation--Software./ Software--Music appreciation./ Music--
  Theory--Software./ Software--Music--Theory./ Beethoven, Ludwig
  van--Software./ Software--Beethoven, Ludwig van./ Mozart,
  Wolfgang Amadeus--Software./ Software--Mozart, Wolfgang
  Amadeus./ Schubert, Franz--Software./ Software--Schubert, Franz./
  Interactive media.

780   Ph-2 3-6/7 $16.95   L OD KD526
WOODYARD, SHAWN. Music and song. Rourke ISBN 1-57103-029-8,
1995. 48p. col. ill. (African American life).
  Includes glossary, bibliography and index.
  An overview of African-American music with concise chapters
  revealing the origins of the music and its development into blues,
  gospel, ragtime, jazz, soul, and rap. Good source for reports for
  reluctant readers. For multicultural studies.
  SUBJ: Afro-Americans--Music--History and criticism./ Music--History
  and criticism.

782   Ph-2 4-6/7 $19.97   L   KD527
SHIPTON, ALYN. Singing. Raintree Steck-Vaughn ISBN 0-8114-2315-8,
1994. 32p. col. ill. (Exploring music).
  Includes glossary and index.
  A good blend of text and illustrations explains the role of the human
  voice in music. Includes information on such varied presentations as
  cantatas, operas, musicals, jazz, and rock video. Scrutinizes the
  technology used in the modern recording studio.
  SUBJ: Vocal music--History./ Singing--History./ Sound--Recording and
  reproducing.

CD 782.1   Ph-2 2-6 $14.95   OD KD528
BROADWAY KIDS SING BROADWAY (Compact disc). With special
guest Petula Clark. IDOC Productions ILM 7245D, 1994. 1 compact disc
(53min).
  Sound recording cassette available ILM 7245C, 1994. 1 sound
  cassette (53min), $9.95.
  Young exuberant voices render songs from such Broadway shows as
  "Annie," "Gypsy," and "Oliver," as well as a Rodgers and
  Hammerstein medley. A joyful introduction to the American musical
  theater.
  SUBJ: Songs./ Musicals.

SRC 782.1   Ph-1 P-3 $9.95   KD529
CHILD'S CELEBRATION OF SHOWTUNES (Sound recording cassette).
Music for Little People 2390 ISBN 1-877737-99-2, 1992. 1 sound
cassette (38min).
  Compact disc available D2390, 1992. 1 compact disc (38min),
  $15.95.
  A celebration of musical theater with exuberant selections designed to
  encourage audience participation. The original casts offer rousing
  renditions of "Do re mi," "Getting to know you," and "I'm

flying."
  SUBJ: Songs./ Musicals.

782.1   Ph-2 4-A/6 $16.95   T   KD530
PRICE, LEONTYNE. Aida. Illustrated by Leo and Diane Dillon. Gulliver/
Harcourt Brace Jovanovich ISBN 0-15-200405-X, 1990. unp. col. ill.
  Ethiopian princess Aida is captured by Egyptian soldiers and forced
  into slavery. When she falls in love with the leader of the Egyptian
  army - the enemy of her people - her loyalty and honor are at stake.
  This great love story, the basis for the opera "Aida", is told with
  emotional intensity, accompanied by darkly dramatic, stunning
  paintings. Accompanied by some of the operatic music, this book
  would be an exciting experience.
  SUBJ: Verdi, Giuseppe./ Aida (Opera)./ Operas--Stories, plots, etc.

SRC 782.1   Ph-1 K-A $9.98   OD KD531
RODGERS, RICHARD. Sound of music. Selections. 2nd ed. (Sound
recording cassette). Sound of music: an original cast soundtrack from the
motion picture. Music by Richard Rodgers. Lyrics by Oscar Hammerstein.
RCA OK1001, 1965. 1 sound cassette.
  When a music-loving postulant from Nonnberg Abbey becomes
  governess to seven rigidly brought up children, her natural warmth
  and wisdom help transform her charges into confident, confident
  individuals. The music from the motion picture features Julie Andrews
  and Christopher Plummer in the starring roles.
  SUBJ: Musical revues, comedies, etc./ Trapp family.

782.25   Ph-2 K-6 $14.95   L   KD532
WHAT A MORNING! THE CHRISTMAS STORY IN BLACK SPIRITUALS.
Selected and edited by John Langstaff. Illus. by Ashley Bryan. McElderry
ISBN 0-689-50422-5; In Canada: Collier Macmillan, 1987. unp. col. ill.
  Coretta Scott King Honor Book.
  Five spirituals ranging "from a mother's simple lullaby to an angel's
  clarion declaration" retell the story of Christ's birth. Striking full color
  illustrations and musical notation round out a satisfying addition to
  celebrating the holiday.
  SUBJ: Jesus Christ--Nativity--Songs and music./ Spirituals (Songs)./
  Christmas music.

782.28   Ph-3 K-2 $13.95   L   KD533
FRIENDLY BEASTS: A TRADITIONAL CHRISTMAS CAROL. Illus. by
Sarah Chamberlain. Dutton ISBN 0-525-44773-3, 1991. unp. col. ill.
  A beautifully illustrated version of the old English Christmas carol tells
  the story of the Nativity.
  SUBJ: Carols, English./ Christmas music./ Folk songs--Great Britain.

782.28   Ph-3 K-6 $17.00   T   KD534
HARK! THE HERALD ANGELS SING. Music arranged by Barrie Carson
Turner. Illus. with paintings from the National Gallery, London. Simon &
Schuster ISBN 0-671-87146-3; In Canada: Simon & Schuster, 1993.
45p. col. ill.
  Includes index.
  A collection of Christmas carols, both traditional and modern, is
  accompanied by the paintings of such artists as Brueghel, Botticelli,
  and Fra Angelico. Includes such favorites as "O Christmas tree,"
  "Deck the hall," and "Hark! The herald angels sing." Great
  resource for art appreciation.
  SUBJ: Carols./ Christmas music.

SRC 782.28   Ph-2 P-3 $10.95   OD KD535
RAFFI. Raffi's Christmas album (Sound recording cassette). With Ken
Whitely. Kimbo 8116C; In Canada: Shoreline Records, 1983. 1 sound
cassette (31min).
  Presents 15 popular Christmas songs such as "Rudolph the Red-
  Nosed Reindeer," "We Wish You a Merry Christmas," and "Frosty
  the Snowman." Particularly recommended for its inclusion of
  unreligious songs, this should be popular and practicable in most
  collections.
  SUBJ: Christmas music.

782.28   Ph-3 5-A $15.95   L   KD536
SILVERMAN, JERRY. Christmas songs. Chelsea House ISBN 0-7910-
1832-6, 1993. 64p. ill. (Traditional Black music).
  Includes indexes.
  The birth of a savior had a dual meaning for African-Americans who
  sought both personal and spiritual freedom. These parallel meanings
  are reflected in the Christmas carols from the African-American
  tradition. Joyous collection for holiday celebrations and multicultural
  studies.
  SUBJ: Christmas music./ Carols./ Afro-Americans--Songs and music.

782.28   Ph-1 P-A $14.95   T   KD537
TWELVE DAYS OF CHRISTMAS. Illus. by Jan Brett. Putnam ISBN
0-396-08821-X; In Canada: Putnam, 1986. unp. col. ill.

Delights the senses with brightly colored nostalgic illustrations of Christmases gone by. Includes the music to the famous carol, an historical note on the derivation of the song, and the greeting "Merry Christmas" in eleven languages. Wonderful to use as a counting song, or as an exhuberant round to mark the holiday season.
SUBJ: Folk songs--England./ Christmas music.

782.28   Ph-2 P-A $14.95   L   KD538
TWELVE DAYS OF CHRISTMAS. Illus. by John O'Brien. Boyds Mills/ dist. by St. Martin's Press ISBN 1-56397-142-9; In Canada: McCelland & Stewart, 1993. unp. col. ill.
An engaging, refreshing version of the traditional song. The high-spirited truelove wreaks havoc as she turns 12 peaceful days into hilarious, chaotic happenings. Will provoke guffaws.
SUBJ: Christmas music./ Folk songs--England.

782.28   Ph-1 K-3 $5.95   P   KD539
TWELVE DAYS OF CHRISTMAS. Illus. by Brian Wildsmith. Millbrook ISBN 1-56294-907-1, 1995. unp. col. ill.
Originally published by Oxford University Press, 1972.
Dazzling, brilliantly colored illustrations invigorate the Old English folk song. A splendid, artistic creation.
SUBJ: Folk songs--England./ Christmas music.

VCR 782.28   Ph-1 P-A $49.95   OD   KD540
TWELVE DAYS OF CHRISTMAS (Videocassette). Weston Woods HMPV121V, 1990. 1/2" VHS videocassette color (6min).
Includes picture-cued text booklet.
Based on the book of the same title, with illustrations by Robert Broomfield.
SUBJ: Folk songs--England./ Carols./ Christmas music.

782.28   Ph-1 K-2 $15.95   L   KD541
TYRRELL, FRANCES. Woodland Christmas: twelve days of Christmas in the North Woods. Scholastic ISBN 0-590-86367-3; In Canada: Scholastic, 1996. unp. col. ill.
The traditional twelve day Christmas carol is extended through the illustrations which feature wild animals. The true love is a bear elegantly dressed, and the numbered gifts are wild animals identified in the front of the book. Snowy and stylish, the book's design and brilliant watercolor illustrations offer a superb choice for the holiday.
SUBJ: Folk songs--England./ Christmas music./ Twelve days of Christmas (English folk song).

784.19   Ph-3 3-6/6 $18.60   L   KD542
CORBETT, SARA. Shake, rattle, and strum. Childrens Press ISBN 0-516-08194-2; In Canada: Childrens Press, 1995. 32p. col. ill. (World of difference).
Includes glossary and index.
An overview of many musical instruments from around the world. Profusely illustrated with quality photographs, it contains many interesting facts. Fine for integrating into music curriculum and multicultural studies.
SUBJ: Musical instruments.

784.192   Ph-2 2-4/2 $12.95   T   KD543
DREW, HELEN. My first music book. Dorling Kindersley ISBN 1-56458-215-9, 1993. 48p. col. ill.
Step-by-step photographs accompanied by clear instructions tell how to make such musical instruments as maracas, drums, and xylophones. Easy and fun activities for an amateur orchestra.
SUBJ: Musical instruments--Construction.

784.2   Ph-1 4-6/8 $16.90   L   KD544
BLACKWOOD, ALAN. Orchestra: an introduction to the world of classical music. Millbrook ISBN 1-56294-202-6, 1993. 92p. col. ill.
Includes glossary and index.
Delineates the history of the orchestra with information on the great classical composers, conductors, and the instruments. Includes a day in the life of an orchestra. A clear, comprehensive introduction to the orchestra which contains a wealth of factual information for reports.
SUBJ: Orchestra./ Musical instruments.

BA 784.2   Ph-2 4-6/10 $25.00   T   KD545
GANERI, ANITA. Young person's guide to the orchestra: Benjamin Britten's composition on CD. Narrated by Ben Kingsley. Illus. by Alex Yan. Harcourt Brace ISBN 0-15-201304-0; In Canada: Harcourt Brace c/o Canadian Manda, 1996. 56p. col. ill., map, 1 compact disc (29min).
First published in Great Britain, Pavilion Books, 1996.
Includes index and glossary.
Accompanying compact disc also includes THE SORCERER'S APPRENTICE by Paul Dukas.
Describes the four sections of an orchestra, using colorful photographs

and an easy-to-follow format. The accompanying compact disc offers Benjamin Britten's introduction to classical music, a set of variations for the orchestral families. Informative and enriching for the advanced student.
SUBJ: Orchestra./ Musical instruments./ Music appreciation.

BA 786.2   Ph-2 4-6/12 $25.00   KD546
TURNER, BARRIE CARSON. Living piano. Knopf/EMI ISBN 0-679-88180-8; In Canada: Random House, 1996. 48p. ill. (some col.), 1 compact disc (60min). (Living music series).
"Borzoi book."
Includes index.
Combines recordings of ten great piano compositions with historical information about the instrument and biographical information about the composers. Profiles of the composers are keyed to the tracks on the CD enabling piano students to easily locate musical selections. Enrichment for advanced music classes.
SUBJ: Piano./ Keyboard instruments./ Music appreciation.

786.8   Ph-2 4-6/7 $19.97   L   KD547
SHIPTON, ALYN. Percussion. Raintree Steck-Vaughn ISBN 0-8114-2316-6, 1994. 32p. col. ill. (Exploring music).
Includes glossary and index.
Introduces a variety of percussion instruments including drums, cymbals, xylophones, and timpani and discusses how they are played. A cogent text and a plethora of pictures convey the use of percussion instruments used around the world. Descriptions of maracas, gamelan orchestras, and steel bands will be useful for multicultural studies.
SUBJ: Percussion instruments.

787   Ph-2 4-6/7 $19.97   L   KD548
SHIPTON, ALYN. Strings. Raintree Steck-Vaughn ISBN 0-8114-2320-4, 1994. 32p. col. ill. (Exploring music).
Includes glossary and index.
Focuses on the string instruments, with information on the history and the parts of a bowed instrument. Drawings and photos illustrate the violin, cello, harp, guitar, and lute. Excellent for use in writing reports and for supplementing the music curriculum.
SUBJ: Stringed instruments.

BA 787.2   Ph-2 4-6/12 $25.00   KD549
TURNER, BARRIE CARSON. Living violin. Knopf/EMI ISBN 0-679-88177-8; In Canada: Random House, 1996. 48p. ill. (some col.), 1 compact disc (60min). (Living music series).
"Borzoi book."
Includes index.
Focuses on ten great violin compositions which are presented on the accompanying audio CD. Brief biographies of the composers in the text are keyed to the tracks on the CD. Includes information about the origins and construction of the violin and its role in the orchestra. Excellent introduction to classical music that can be used to enrich studies for advanced students.
SUBJ: Violin./ Stringed instruments./ Music appreciation.

788.2   Ph-2 4-6/7 $19.97   L   KD550
SHIPTON, ALYN. Woodwinds. Raintree Steck-Vaughn ISBN 0-8114-2319-0, 1994. 32p. col. ill. (Exploring music).
Includes glossary and index.
A colorful, pictorial format explores the history of woodwinds and gives information on how to play such instruments as the flute, recorder, clarinet, saxophone, and oboe. Excellent, uncluttered format.
SUBJ: Woodwind instruments.

BA 788.3   Ph-2 4-6/11 $25.00   KD551
TURNER, BARRIE CARSON. Living flute. Knopf/EMI ISBN 0-679-88178-6; In Canada: Random House, 1996. 48p. ill. (some col.), 1 compact disc (60min). (Living music series).
"Borzoi book."
Includes index.
Features ten great compositions for the flute along with the history and origins of the instrument and biographical information about the composers. Sections of the book are keyed to tracks on the CD for easy access. An attractive package to enrich music classes and inspire young flutists.
SUBJ: Flute./ Wind instruments./ Music appreciation.

BA 788.6   Ph-2 4-6/12 $25.00   KD552
TURNER, BARRIE CARSON. Living clarinet. Knopf/EMI ISBN 0-679-88179-4; In Canada: Random House, 1996. 48p. ill. (some col.), 1 compact disc (60min). (Living music series).
"Borzoi book."
Includes index.
Presents ten great compositions for the clarinet along with biographical information about the composers, historical information

about the clarinet's origins, details about the construction of the instrument, and a description of its role in the orchestra. Sections in the book are keyed to tracks on the CD for easy access. Enrichment material for music classes.
SUBJ: Clarinet./ Wind instruments./ Music appreciation.

788.9   Ph-3 4-A/7 $19.97   L   KD553
SHIPTON, ALYN. Brass. Raintree Steck-Vaughn ISBN 0-8114-2317-4, 1994. 32p. col. ill. (Exploring music).
Includes glossary and index.
An introduction to the brass section of an orchestra which includes such instruments as tuba, and French horn. Excellent for reports.
SUBJ: Brass instruments.

789.2   Ph-2 K-6 $14.95   L   KD554
ALL NIGHT, ALL DAY: A CHILD'S FIRST BOOK OF AFRICAN-AMERICAN SPIRITUALS. Selected and illustrated by Ashley Bryan. Atheneum ISBN 0-689-31662-3; In Canada: Collier Macmillan, 1991. 48p. col. ill.
Includes musical scores.
Coretta Scott King Honor Book.
A songbook containing the lyrics, piano accompaniments and guitar chords of twenty spirituals. Many of these Afican-American spirituals are well known, such as "All Night, All Day," "When the Saints Come Marching In," and "He's Got the Whole World In His Hands." Warm, vividly colored illustrations capture the spirit of these lively songs.
SUBJ: Spirituals (Songs)./ Afro-Americans--Songs and music.

CD 789.2   Ph-1 K-6 $13.98   OD KD555
AMERICAN MELODY SAMPLER (Compact disc). American Melody AM-CD-5501, 1994. 1 compact disc (44min).
Sound ecording cassette available AM-C-501, 1994. a sound cassette (44min), $9.98.
An excellent collection of American folk songs that every child should know. Includes "Shenandoah," "On top of Old Smoky," and "One wide river." Wonderful for singalongs.
SUBJ: Songs./ Folk songs--United States.

789.2   Ph-1 P-3 $13.95   L   KD556
ARROZ CON LECHE: POPULAR SONGS AND RHYMES FROM LATIN AMERICA. Selected and illustrated by Lulu Delacre. English lyrics by Elena Paz. Musical arrangements by Ana-Maria Rosada. Scholastic ISBN 0-590-41887-4, 1989. 32p. col. ill.
The lyrics for a dozen songs and folkgames from Puerto Rico, Mexico and Argentina are presented in both Spanish and English. Directions for the games are included and the musical notations for the melody lines are grouped in the back with a recapitulation of the lyrics. Attractive watercolor illustrations round out this useful book for FLES programs.
SUBJ: Folk songs--Latin America./ Spanish language materials./ Bilingual materials--Spanish.

789.2   Ph-2 P-2 $16.00   L   KD557
BANGS, EDWARD. Yankee Doodle. 2nd ed. Illus. by Steven Kellogg. Simon & Schuster ISBN 0-689-80158-0; In Canada: Distican, c1976, 1996. unp. col. ill.
Exuberant, humorous, detailed illustrations catch the patriotic spirit of the American Revolution in this masterful interpretation of the well-known song. Author's note describes the song's history.
SUBJ: Songs--United States./ United States--History--Revolution, 1775-1783--Songs and music.

789.2   Ph-2 K-3 $14.95   L   KD558
BATES, KATHARINE LEE. America the beautiful. Illus. by Neil Waldman. Atheneum ISBN 0-689-31861-8; In Canada: Maxwell Macmillan, 1993. unp. col. ill.
Includes music.
The familiar patriotic song, a celebration of the glories of America, is accompanied by inspiring paintings of such magnificent wonders as Niagara Falls, the Grand Tetons, and the Grand Canyon.
SUBJ: National songs--United States./ United States--History--Songs and music.

SRC 789.2   Ph-3 K-6 $9.98   OD KD559
CALLINAN, TOM. Let's clean up our act: songs for the earth (Sound recording cassette). By Tom Callinan and Ann Shapiro. American Melody AM 106C, 1989. 1 sound cassette (47min).
Includes booklet with lyrics, glossary, and resource guide.
A devastatingly funny, right-on-target view of environmental issues including such irreverent songs as "Pollution", "Garbage Blues", and "Let's Clean Up Our Act." The accompanying booklet offers activities to start us cleaning up the Earth.
SUBJ: Ecology--Songs and music./ Songs.

SRC 789.2   Ph-1 4-A $19.95   OD KD560
COWBOY SONGS (Sound recording cassette). Narrated and sung by Keith and Rusty McNeil. WEM Records 601C, 1992. 2 sound cassettes (180min). (American history through folksong).
Includes teacher's guide.
The golden age of the cowboy is revealed through a combination of excellent historical narration and 50 songs. The Western experience comes alive. Excellent for enriching social studies lessons.
SUBJ: West (U.S.)--History--Songs and music./ Folk songs--United States./ Cowboys--Songs and music.

789.2   Ph-2 K-3 $16.99   T   KD561
DE COLORES AND OTHER LATIN-AMERICAN FOLK SONGS FOR CHILDREN. Selected, arranged, and translated by Jose-Luis Orozco. Illus. by Elisa Kleven. Dutton ISBN 0-525-45260-5, 1994. 56p. col. ill.
Includes index.
A collection of 27 Latin-American folk songs is accompanied by musical arrangements for piano, voice, and guitar. Includes background notes and suggestions for recipes, sing-alongs, and games. Lyrics are offered in Spanish and English. The illustrations are vivid and joyous. Excellent for multicultural studies.
SUBJ: Folk songs, Spanish--Latin America./ Songs, Spanish--Latin America./ Spanish language materials./ Bilingual materials--Spanish.

SRC 789.2   Ph-3 K-5 $9.95   OD KD562
FAMILY FOLK FESTIVAL: A MULTI-CULTURAL SING-ALONG (Sound recording cassette). Music for Little People 2105, 1990. 1 sound cassette (40min).
Includes lyrics.
A sing-along features such musicians as Pete Seeger, the Smothers Brothers, Taj Mahal, and John McCutcheon performing songs from many cultures. Includes such diverse songs as "El gallo pinto," "Puff the Magic Dragon," and "Ise Oluwa." Good for multicultural enrichment.
SUBJ: Folk songs./ Culture--Songs and music.

SRC 789.2   Ph-3 K-6 $8.50   OD KD563
FISH THAT'S A SONG: SONGS AND STORIES FOR CHILDREN (Sound recording cassette). Smithsonian/Folkways SF 45037, 1990. 1 sound cassette (40min).
38-page illustrated, descriptive booklet with lyrics available separately for $2.00.
Classic folk songs are delivered by some of the great folk artists including Woody Guthrie and Pete Seeger. Rousing renditions of 19 songs encourage audience participation. Listeners won't be able to resist clapping and singing along.
SUBJ: Songs./ Folk songs.

789.2   Ph-3 2-A $24.95   T   KD564
GO IN AND OUT THE WINDOW: AN ILLUSTRATED SONGBOOK FOR YOUNG PEOPLE. Music arranged and edited by Dan Fox. Metropolitan Museum of Art/Henry Holt ISBN 0-8050-0628-1; In Canada: Fitzhenry & Whiteside, 1987. 144p. col. ill.
Couples classic childhood songs with treasures from the Metropolitan Museum of Art. A splendid offering replete with fascinating historical information on paintings, objets d'art, and musical instruments.
SUBJ: Songs.

SRC 789.2   Ph-2 K-2 $9.98   KD565
GORDH, BILL. Morning, noon and nighttime tales (Sound recording cassette). Lingonberry Music/dist. by Silo LB103, 1993. 1 sound cassette (46min).
ALA notable recording, 1994.
Hilarious combination of narration, music, and sound effects is certain to provoke guffaws. For multicultural studies.
SUBJ: Short stories./ Songs./ Culture--Songs and music.

789.2   Ph-2 1-3/2 $15.95   L   KD566
GRAHAM, STEVE. Dear old Donegal. Words and music by Steve Graham. Illus. by John O'Brien. Clarion ISBN 0-395-68187-1, 1996. 32p. col. ill., map.
A prosperous Irish immigrant returns to Ireland to celebrate with extended family and friends. The words of the 1940s song, printed on the endpapers, serve as the text for the book. Green predominates in the illustrations which depict an idealized Irish countryside. Offers flavor and fun for units on immigration and Ireland and St. Patrick's Day celebrations.
SUBJ: Ireland--Songs and music./ Songs.

CD 789.2   Ph-3 P-1 $15.00   OD KD567
GUTHRIE, WOODY. Nursery days (Compact disc). Smithsonian Folkways Records, 1992. 1 compact disc (41min).
Includes lyrics.
Sixteen original songs are performed by Woody Guthrie. His country

twang is easy to understand, and the songs invite movement and acting.
SUBJ: Folk songs.

CD 789.2   Ph-2 2-6 $15.00   OD KD568
HINOJOSA, TISH. Cada nino./Every child (Compact disc). Rounder Records CD 8032 ISBN 1-886767-10-6, 1996. 1 compact disc (37min).
Includes lyrics.
ALA notable recording, 1997.
Sound recording cassette available C8032 (ISBN 1-886767-11-4, 1995). 1 sound cassette (37min), $9.98.
A bilingual collection of original songs sung by the singer/songwriter. Her voice is clear, her message thoughtful. Can be used to enrich multicultural studies, in Spanish classes, and with Spanish speaking children as they learn English.
SUBJ: Songs./ Spanish language materials./ Bilingual materials--Spanish.

SRC 789.2   Ph-2 K-4 $9.98   KD569
HOLT, DAVID. Grandfather's greatest hits (Sound recording cassette). High Windy Audio HW 1251 ISBN 0-942303-26-1, 1991. 1 sound cassette (29min).
Compact disc available HW 1251-D, 1991. 1 compact disc (29min), $15.98.
Spirited interpretation of such classic mountain music as "John Henry," "Wabash Cannonball," and "Dixie." Useful to integrate into the social studies curriculum.
SUBJ: Folk songs--United States./ Bluegrass music--United States.

SRC 789.2   Ph-1 2-4 $9.98   KD570
HOLT, DAVID. I got a bullfrog: folksongs for the fun of it (Sound recording cassette). High Windy Audio HW 1255 ISBN 0-942303-33-4, 1994. 1 sound cassette (36min).
Includes lyrics.
ALA notable recording, 1995.
Compact disc available HW 1255-D, 1994. 1 compact disc (36min), $15.98.
A lively collection of great American folksongs includes "The cat came back," "Ain't no bugs on me," and other traditional songs. Holt's rambunctious renditions are full of fun and a lively way to introduce folksongs.
SUBJ: Folk songs--United States.

CE 789.2   Ph-2 K-6 $15.95   L KD571
HOW SWEET THE SOUND: AFRICAN-AMERICAN SONGS FOR CHILDREN. Selected by Wade and Cheryl Hudson. Illus. by Floyd Cooper. Scholastic ISBN 0-590-48030-8; In Canada: Scholastic, 1995. 48p. col. ill.
Includes music, lyrics, bibliography and index.
Read-along kit available from Just Us Books/Scholastic (ISBN 0-590-96911-0, 1995). 1 paperback book, 1 sound cassette (66min), $9.95.
A poignant glimpse into African-American history is reflected in this collection of spirituals, gospel hymns, jazz tunes, traditional songs, and contemporary music. Includes such well-known songs as "Kum ba ya," "Take the 'A' train," and "Get on board, little children." The accompanying paintings are evocative of the joys and sorrows of the African-American experience. For multicultural studies.
SUBJ: Songs./ Afro-Americans--Songs and music.

SRC 789.2   Ph-1 K-6 $9.50   OD KD572
JENKINS, ELLA. African-American folk songs and rhythms (Sound recording cassette). With Ella Jenkins and the Goodwill Spiritual Choir. Smithsonian Folkways SF 45003, c1960, 1992. 1 sound recording cassette (42min).
Includes lyrics.
A collection of traditional African-American songs emphasizes spirituals but also includes humorous chants, civil rights anthems, and inspirational songs.
SUBJ: Folk songs--United States./ Afro-Americans--Songs and music./ Spirituals (Songs)./ Songs.

SRC 789.2   Ph-1 K-3 $8.50   KD573
JENKINS, ELLA. Jambo and other call and response songs and chants (Sound recording cassette). Smithsonian Folkways C-SF 45017, 1990. 1 sound cassette (32min).
Originally published by Folkways (FC 7661), 1974.
Includes lyrics.
An enthusiastic collection of African call and response songs for audience participation. Swahili words and numbers are taught as the children are urged to echo Ella Jenkins' clear voice and follow her crisp directions. Excellent for inclusion in multicultural studies.
SUBJ: Songs./ Folk songs--Africa./ Culture--Songs and music.

SRC 789.2   Ph-2 K-A $9.98   OD KD574
JENKINS, ELLA. Long time to freedom (Sound recording cassette). Smithsonian Folkways SF 45034, c1969, 1992. 1 sound cassette (48min).
A spirited collection of African-American folk songs on the theme of freedom. Includes gospel songs, spirituals, work songs, and blues. Excellent for multicultural studies.
SUBJ: Folk songs--United States./ Afro-Americans--Songs and music./ Civil rights--Songs and music.

SRC 789.2   Ph-2 K-2 $9.50   OD KD575
JENKINS, ELLA. Songs and rhythms from near and far (Sound recording cassette). Smithsonian Folkways SF 45033, c1964, 1992. 1 sound cassette (37min).
Includes lyrics.
Compact disc available SF 45033. 1 compact disc (37min), $14.95.
A collection of international songs, many written by Ella Jenkins. Some traditional ones such as "Let my people go," and "Joshua fit the Battle of Jericho," and a selection of dance tunes from many lands are all rendered by Ella Jenkins' clear, easy-to-understand voice and gentle music.
SUBJ: Songs./ Folk songs./ Culture--Songs and music.

CD 789.2   Ph-1 K-2 $13.00   OD KD576
JENKINS, ELLA. Travellin' with Ella Jenkins: a bilingual journey (Compact disc). Smithsonian Folkways CD SF 45009, 1989. 1 compact disc (28min).
Originally published by Folkways (FH 7640), 1979.
Includes lyrics.
Sound recording cassette available CS F 45009. 1 sound cassette (28min), $8.50.
A multicultural journey through songs in which children's voices repeat phrases and sing along. Includes Arabic, Hebrew, Spanish, and Australian songs as well as greetings and thank you in many languages. Jenkins has a voice that is at once commanding and clear, and this collection will be well used for multicultural studies.
SUBJ: Folk songs./ Culture--Songs and music./ Bilingual materials.

CD 789.2   Ph-2 1-6 $14.00   OD KD577
JENKINS, ELLA. We are America's children (Compact disc). With the Raymond School Children's Choir and the Glen Ellyn Chidren's Chorus. Smithsonian/Folkways CD SF 45006, 1989. 1 compact disc (24min).
Includes lyrics.
Originally published by Folkways FC7666, 1976.
Sound recording cassette available C SF 45006, 1989. 1 sound cassette (24min), $8.50.
These songs of freedom help students become more acquainted with Native American and African-American cultures. Repetition encourages audience participation, and the themes promote patriotic attitudes for all Americans. Enrichment for multicultural studies.
SUBJ: Folk songs--United States./ United States--History--Songs and music.

SRC 789.2   Ph-3 K-6 $9.98   KD578
JUNIPER TREE AND OTHER SONGS (Sound recording cassette). American Melody AM-C-115 ISBN 1-879305-17-8, 1994. 1 sound cassette (36min).
A peppy rendition of traditional and contemporary folk songs, including such old favorites "Clementine" and "Mairzy doats." The lively music is enhanced by the sounds of the guitar, banjo, mandolin, fiddle, and harmonica.
SUBJ: Songs./ Folk songs.

CE 789.2   Ph-3 P-3 $14.95   T KD579
LANGSTAFF, JOHN. Frog went a-courtin'. Retold by John Langstaff. Illus. by Feodor Rojankovsky. Harcourt Brace Jovanovich ISBN 0-15-230214-X, c1955. unp. col. ill.
Caldecott Medal Award.
Videocassette available from Weston Woods HMPV28V. 1/2" VHS videocasssette color (12min), $39.00.
Read-along kit available from Weston Woods HB28. 1 hardcover book, 1 sound cassette (13min), $12.95.
Useful as both story telling and singing material is the colorfully illustrated familiar ballad of Frog who courts Mistress Mouse.
SUBJ: Animals--Songs and music.

789.2   Ph-2 K-3 $4.99   P KD580
LAS NAVIDADES: POPULAR CHRISTMAS SONGS FROM LATIN AMERICA. Selected and illustrated by Lulu Delacre. Scholastic ISBN 0-590-43549-3, 1990. 32p. col. ill.
Includes lyrics and musical arrangements.
Popular Christmas songs from Latin America and colorful illustrations reveal the Hispanic culture's lively celebrations. This bilingual collection will have many uses--at holiday time, as part of Social Studies units,

and as a basis for cultural enrichment activities.
SUBJ: Bilingual materials--Spanish./ Folk songs, Spanish--Latin
America./ Christmas music./ Spanish language materials.

SRC 789.2 Ph-2 P-3 $9.50 OD KD581
MCCUTCHEON, JOHN. Family garden (Sound recording cassette).
Rounder Records RO 8026, 1993. 1 sound recording cassette (53min).
  Includes lyrics.
  ALA notable recording, 1994.
  Thirteen original songs discuss such diverse topics as the tooth fairy,
  adoption, phobias, and the joys of family life. The music ranges from
  blues and rock to Caribbean and Cajun styles and encourages
  audience participation.
  SUBJ: Songs.

SRC 789.2 Ph-3 K-6 $10.95 OD KD582
PATRIOTIC SONGS AND MARCHES (Sound recording cassette). Kimbo
KIM 9125C, 1991. 1 sound cassette (32min).
  Includes lyrics.
  Compact disc available KIM 9125CD, 1991. 1 compact disc (32min),
  $14.95.
  Peppy instrumental and vocal renditions of 18 well-known patriotic
  songs and marches including "America the beautiful," "Pomp and
  circumstance," and "Battle hymn of the Republic." Sung by a male
  and a female vocalist along with two children giving the aura of a
  family's clear, optimistic voices.
  SUBJ: National songs./ Marches.

CD 789.2 Ph-2 P-3 $9.98 OD KD583
PETER, PAUL & MARY. Peter, Paul and Mommy, too (Compact disc).
Warner Brothers 9 45216-2 ISBN 1-880528-15-0, 1993. 1 compact disc
(52min).
  Includes lyrics.
  ALA notable recording, 1994.
  This eclectic collection includes some of Peter, Paul, and Mary's
  classics such as "Puff, the magic dragon," and "We shall
  overcome;" African and Spanish folk songs; and such oldies as "I
  know an old lady who swallowed a fly." A nostalgic, beautifully
  rendered group of songs.
  SUBJ: Folk songs./ Culture--Songs and music.

789.2 Ph-2 P-1/2 $16.95 L KD584
POLLITOS DICEN: JUEGOS, RIMAS Y CANCIONES INFANTILES DE
PAISES DE HABLA HISPANA./THE BABY CHICKS SING: TRADITIONAL
GAMES, NURSERY RHYMES, AND SONGS FROM SPANISH-
SPEAKING COUNTRIES. Collected and adapted by Nancy Abraham
Hall and Jill Syverson-Stork. Illus. by Kay Chorao. Little, Brown ISBN
0-316-34010-3; In Canada: Little, Brown, 1994. 32p. col. ill.
  A collection of nursery rhymes, games, and songs from Spanish-
  speaking countries with energetic watercolor illustrations. The lyrics
  are given in English and Spanish with basic music. This attractive book
  will be useful in classes where children are being introduced to either
  Spanish or English. For multicultural studies.
  SUBJ: Songs--Spain./ Songs--Latin America./ Nursery rhymes./
  Spanish language materials./ Bilingual materials--Spanish.

CD 789.2 Ph-1 P-A $9.98 OD KD585
RAINBOW SIGN (Compact disc). Rounder Records CD 8025, 1992. 1
compact disc (60min).
  Includes lyrics.
  Songs from many cultures are performed by a group of
  internationally renowned artists including Sweet Honey in the Rock,
  Jose-Luis Orozco, John McCutcheon, and Flor de Cana. "Unite
  children" features the Children of Selma. Profits from the recording
  benefit "Barriers & Bridges" a program of Grassroots Leadership
  designed to promote racial harmony. Outstanding addition to
  multicultual studies.
  SUBJ: Folk songs./ Culture--Songs and music.

789.2 Ph-2 K-3 $14.95 L KD586
ROUNDS, GLEN. I know an old lady who swallowed a fly. Holiday
House ISBN 0-8234-0814-0, 1990. unp. col. ill.
  Whimsical and outlandish poster paint illustrations accompany the text
  of this favorite nonsense song. The musical notation is not included
  but most children know the melody and will sing with relish when this
  is shared with a large group.
  SUBJ: Nonsense verses.

789.2 Ph-3 2-5 $15.95 L KD587
SEEGER, PETE. Abiyoyo: based on a South African lullaby and folk
story. Illustrated by Michael Hays. Macmillan ISBN 0-02-781490-4; In
Canada: Collier Macmillan, 1986. unp col illus.
  Available from National Library Service for the Blind and Physically
  Handicapped in Braille BR07103.

Banished from their town for making mischief, a young boy and his
father return triumphantly when they devise a plan to make the evil
giant Abiyoyo disappear. Loosely based on a South African folktale
and lullaby, this version features stunning full color oil on linen
paintings and would be effective shared with a group in combination
with Seeger's recording.
SUBJ: Folk songs--South Africa./ Magicians--Folklore./ Giants--
Folklore.

VCR 789.2 Ph-2 K-3 $14.98 KD588
SEEGER, PETE. Pete Seeger's family concert (Videocassette). Sony
Wonder LV-49550, 1992. 1/2" VHS videocassette color (45min).
  A combination of folk songs and a message--think globally, act
  locally. Seeger, an environmentalist who promotes the clean up of
  America's polluted waterways, invites children at a concert on the
  banks of the Hudson River to sing along to 12 folk songs. Includes
  "Skip to my Lou." Excellent music resource as well as for
  environmental studies.
  SUBJ: Folk songs./ Environmental protection--Songs and music.

SRC 789.2 Ph-2 K-3 $8.50 OD KD589
SEEGER, PETE. Song and play time (Sound recording cassette).
Smithsonian/Folkways C-SF 45023, 1990. 1 sound cassette (38min).
  Originally published by Folkways (FC 7526), 1960.
  Includes lyrics.
  An additional collection of familiar and not-so-familiar folk songs
  including "Go In and Out the Window" and "Skip to My Lou."
  Songs encourage audience participation and creative movement.
  SUBJ: Folk songs./ Songs.

789.2 Ph-3 5-A $15.95 L KD590
SILVERMAN, JERRY. African roots. Chelsea House ISBN 0-7910-1828-8,
1994. 64p. ill. (Traditional Black music).
  Includes indexes.
  Traditional and contemporary music of sub-Saharan Africa is closely
  linked with African-American musical forms. This collection of 28
  songs explores the connections. Notes and captioned photographs
  provide supplemental information. For multicultural studies.
  SUBJ: Folk songs, English--Africa./ Folk music--Africa./ Blacks--Africa-
  -Music.

789.2 Ph-3 5-A $15.95 L KD591
SILVERMAN, JERRY. Children's songs. Chelsea House ISBN 0-7910-
1831-8, 1993. 64p. ill. (Traditional Black music).
  Includes indexes.
  A musical look at the world of the African-American child presents 30
  songs including the familiar "Oh, John the rabbit," "Miss Mary
  Mack," and "One more river." Many of the play songs, rooted in
  the call-and-response songs of long-ago Africa, invite audience
  participation. For multicultural studies.
  SUBJ: Songs./ Afro-Americans--Songs and music.

789.2 Ph-3 5-A $15.95 L KD592
SILVERMAN, JERRY. Slave songs. Chelsea House ISBN 0-7910-1837-7,
1994. 64p. ill. (Traditional Black music).
  Includes indexes.
  A collection of slave songs--spirituals, work chants, hymns, ballads,
  protest songs, minstrel songs, and humorous ditties--provides an
  authentic view of African-Americans in the preCivil War South. Many
  familiar songs such as "Michael, row the boat ashore," "Jim along
  Josey," and "Go down, Moses" are included. Unique resource for
  social studies and multicultural studies.
  SUBJ: Afro-Americans--Songs and music./ Folk songs--United States./
  Slaves--Songs and music.

789.2 Ph-3 5-A $15.95 L KD593
SILVERMAN, JERRY. Songs of protest and civil rights. Chelsea House
ISBN 0-7910-1827-X, 1992. 64p. ill. (Traditional Black music).
  Includes indexes.
  Illustrated songbook of traditional African-American folk songs with
  piano arrangements, lyrics, and notes which place the songs in their
  historical perspective. An excellent addition to music, social studies,
  and multicultural studies.
  SUBJ: Afro-Americans--Civil rights--Songs and music./ Civil rights
  movements--Songs and music./ Protest songs./ Spirituals (Songs)./
  Songs.

789.2 Ph-2 P-2/2 $13.95 L KD594
SLAVIN, BILL. Cat came back: a traditional song. Illustrated by Bill
Slavin. Whitman ISBN 0-8075-1097-1; In Canada: Kids Can Press, 1992.
unp. col. ill.
  The repetitiveness of this traditional song will engage youngsters as
  they repeat "The cat came back." The illustrations are as warm and
  witty as the lyrics and are certain to provoke laughter as well as

participation.
SUBJ: Folk songs./ Cats--Songs and music.

SRC 789.2 Ph-2 K-3 $11.95 OD KD595
SLONECKI, CATHERINE. Children's songs around the world (Sound recording cassette). Educational Activities AC 56, 1989. 1 sound cassette (25min).
Includes teacher's guide with lyrics.
Compact disc available from Educational Activities CD 56, 1989. 1 compact disc (25min), $14.95.
An engaging danceable collection of popular songs from around the world. Offers dance movements to accompany such favorites as "Cielito Lindo," "Jamaica farewell," and "Waltzing Matilda." Provides enrichment for multicultural studies.
SUBJ: Folk songs./ Culture--Songs and music.

789.2 Ph-1 1-6 $18.99 T KD596
SONGS FOR SURVIVAL: SONGS AND CHANTS FROM TRIBAL PEOPLES AROUND THE WORLD. Compiled by Nikki Siegen-Smith. Illus. by Bernard Lodge. Dutton ISBN 0-525-45564-7, 1996. 80p. col. ill.
Includes directory and index.
Selectors' Choice, 21st ed.
A collection of tribal songs and chants from around the world includes music of the Indians of the Americas, the Aborigines of Australasia, and many of the peoples of Asia and Africa. The songs are joyful, affirmative, and life enhancing. Excellent for use in multicultural studies.
SUBJ: Folk songs./ Culture--Songs and music.

789.2 Ph-2 2-A $19.95 L KD597
SONGS OF THE WILD WEST. Commentary by Alan Axelrod. Arrangements by Dan Fox. Metropolitan Museum of Art and the Buffalo Bill Historical Center. Metropolitan Museum of Art/Simon & Schuster ISBN 0-671-74775-4, 1991. 128p b&w and col prints.
Includes indexes.
The classic ballads of the Old West are coupled with works of art from that period. The confluence of cultures--Spanish and Native American, the hard life of the cowboy, railroad workers, gold miners, and sodbusters--all combine to present a vivid picture of westward expansion. An excellent interdisciplinary tool for music, social studies and art studies.
SUBJ: Cowboys--Songs and music./ Folk music--West (U.S.)./ Folk songs, English--West (U.S.).

789.2 Ph-3 4-A/6 $12.90 L KD598
ST. PIERRE, STEPHANIE. Our national anthem. Millbrook ISBN 1-56294-106-2, 1992. 48p. col. ill., maps. (I know America).
Includes chronology, bibliography and index.
Traces the history of the national anthem. Good for use in reports.
SUBJ: Star-spangled banner (Song)./ National songs--United States.

SRC 789.2 Ph-2 K-2 $9.95 KD599
SUNSERI, MARYLEE. Rhythm of the rocks: a multicultural musical journey (Sound recording cassette). By MaryLee and Nancy. Friends Street Music/BMI and Piper Grove Music FS106, 1993. 1 sound cassette (35min).
Includes lyrics.
ALA notable recording, 1994.
Compact disc available (ISBN 1-885430-11-6, 1996) 1 compact disc (35min), $15.95.
A collection of multicultural songs represents varied cultures including Morocco, Australia, Japan, Italy, and Vietnam. The songs are bouncy and danceable. Vocal renditions utilize instruments such as dulcimer, waterphone, and Romanian panpipes, as well as more conventional instruments. Good for integrating into multicultural studies.
SUBJ: Songs./ Culture--Songs and music.

789.2 Ph-2 K-2 $7.95 P OD KD600
SUNSERI, MARYLEE. Rhythm of the rocks songbook: a multicultural musical journey... By MaryLee and Nancy. Friends Street Music/Piper Grove Music ISBN 1-885430-01-9, 1994. 35p. ill.
A collection of multicultural songs represents varied cultures including Morocco, Australia, Japan, Italy, and Vietnam. The songs are bouncy and danceable. Good for integrating into multicultural studies.
SUBJ: Songs./ Culture--Songs and music.

SRC 789.2 Ph-2 3-6 $9.98 OD KD601
SWEET HONEY IN THE ROCK: ALL FOR FREEDOM (Sound recording cassette). Music for Little People MLP 2230, 1989. 1 sound cassette (55min).
Includes lyrics.
Available on Compact disc D2230, $12.98.
This quintet of African-American female singers join with elementary school students to render a collection of traditional and new songs

including such West African songs as "Cumbayah" and "Ise Oluwa" and songs made famous by Bessie Jones and "Leadbelly" Ledbetter. A stirring collection that can be an integral part of intercultural studies.
SUBJ: Afro-Americans--Songs and music./ Folk songs--Africa.

789.2 Ph-1 P-1 $12.95 T KD602
THIS OLD MAN. Illus. by Carol Jones. Houghton Mifflin ISBN 0-395-54699-0, 1990. unp. col. ill.
Includes music and lyrics.
Selectors' Choice, 18th ed.
Young readers peep into a hole in the middle of each page as they guess what the Old Man will play nicknack next. The familiar old song is accompanied by warm, detailed, enchanting pictures.
SUBJ: Songs./ Counting./ Stories in rhyme.

SRC 789.3 Ph-3 K-6 $10.95 OD KD603
ALL-TIME FAVORITE DANCES (Sound recording cassette). Kimbo KIM 9126C, 1991. 1 sound cassette (36min).
Includes lyrics and guide.
Videocassette available KV 100V, 1993. 1/2" VHS videocassette color (34min), $19.95.
Compact disc available 9126CD, 1991. 1 compact disc (36min), $14.95.
Spanish edition BAILES FAVORITOS TODS LOS TIEMPOS available KMS 9126C, 1991. 1 sound cassette (36min), $10.95.
Favorite traditional and modern dances are given a lively treatment. Includes the twist, the hora, the Mexican hat dance, and the conga. Directions for the dance steps are given. Use for exercise classes and for creative movement activities.
SUBJ: Dance music./ Dancing./ Singing games./ Songs.

SRC 789.3 Ph-2 1-5 $11.00 OD KD604
ALSOP, PETER. Plugging away (Sound recording cassette). Moose School Productions MS504, 1990. 1 sound cassette (46min).
Includes activity sheets and lyrics.
An exceptional, sensitive collection of songs airing pertinent issues from the perspectives of young people will provoke discussion on environmental concerns, physical disabilities, AIDS, and nuclear bombing. Although the subjects are frequently serious, the arrangements are peppy and the lyrics are fun.
SUBJ: Songs./ Current events--Songs and music.

SRC 789.3 Ph-3 K-6 $12.95 OD KD605
BARCHAS, SARAH. Pinata!: bilingual songs for children (Sound recording cassette). High Haven Music/dist. by Educational Record Center HI-101C, 1991. 1 sound cassette (40min).
Includes lyrics.
Compact disc available HI-101D, 1991. 1 compact disc (40min), $15.98.
A collection of songs sung in Spanish and English is accompanied by a songbook. Fun for sing-alongs in schools with Spanish speaking students, where Spanish is taught, or as an enrichment for multicultural studies.
SUBJ: Songs./ Spanish language materials./ Bilingual materials--Spanish.

SRC 789.3 Ph-3 K-2 $9.95 KD606
BARCHAS, SARAH. This old man/Este viejito (Sound recording cassette). By Sarah Barchas and "De Colores" Chorus. High Haven Music ISBN 0-9632621-9-X, 1997. 1 sound cassette (16min).
Includes lyrics.
A lively bilingual interpretation of the popular English folk song. Can be used for multicultural studies, or used with bilingual students.
SUBJ: Songs./ Spanish language materials./ Bilingual materials--Spanish.

SRC 789.3 Ph-3 K-2 $9.98 KD607
BETHIE. Bethie's really silly songs about animals (Sound recording cassette). Discovery Music/dist. by Silo DIS 94454C ISBN 1-881225-17-8, 1993. 1 sound cassette (32min). (Really silly series).
Fun songs about such denizens of the animal world as "Ivana the Iguana" and "Sam the Snake." Certain to please animal lovers.
SUBJ: Songs./ Humorous songs./ Animals--Songs and music.

SRC 789.3 Ph-1 P-3 $9.95 OD KD608
CHILD'S CELEBRATION OF SONG (Sound recording cassette). Music for Little People SRC2546 ISBN 1-877737-43-7, 1992. 1 sound recording cassette (42min).
Compact disc available D2546, 1992. 1 compact disc (42min), $15.95.
An eclectic group of singers including Pete Seeger; Peter, Paul and Mary; Judy Garland; James Taylor; and Paul Simon render an assorted collection of popular songs including "Over the rainbow,"

NONFICTION

"Puff the magic dragon," and "This old man." Excellent for singing aloud and for appreciating classic popular songs.
SUBJ: Songs.

SRC 789.3   Ph-2 P-1 $11.95   KD609
COLGATE, BRENDA. Silly Willy workout (Sound recording cassette). Educational Activities AC 548, 1994. 1 sound cassette (25min). (High energy fitness series).
"Fitness program for ages 2-10 years."
Includes lyrics.
Compact disc available CD 548, 1996. 1 compact disc (25min).
Exuberant childrens' voices extol the virtues of fitness. The songs promote movement, dancing, stretching, marching. A combination of joyous participation and easy-to-follow directions makes this an excellent exercise tape for the youngest.
SUBJ: Songs./ Physical fitness.

SRC 789.3   Ph-2 P-1 $9.95   OD KD610
EPSTEIN-KRAVIS, ANNA. Tot's tunes (Sound recording cassette). Anna Epstein-Kravis BR101, c1987, 1990. 1 sound cassette (30min).
Includes lyrics.
Eleven charming, delightful songs promote friendship and brotherhood and are rendered by a vocalist who has an endearing personality that comes through in her voice. A wonderful collection.
SUBJ: Songs./ Friendship--Songs and music.

789.3   Ph-2 P-2 $15.00   T   KD611
FARJEON, ELEANOR. Morning has broken. Illus. by Tim Ladwig. Eerdmans ISBN 0-8028-5127-4, 1996. unp. col. ill.
A young boy and his grandfather celebrate the dawn of a new day. A pictorial version of the popular song emphasizes the beauty and wonder of nature.
SUBJ: Morning--Songs and music./ Songs.

SRC 789.3   Ph-1 P-1 $10.95   OD KD612
GALLINA, JILL. A to Z, the animals and me (Sound recording cassette). By Jill and Michael Gallina. Kimbo KIM 9136C ISBN 1-56346-047-5, 1993. 1 sound cassette (33min).
Includes lyrics and guide.
Compact disc available KIM 9136CD, 1993. 1 compact disc (33min), $14.95.
Rousing music introduces creative movement activities that encourage lively audience participation, gross motor skills, and creative expression. Songs begin with "Aerobic armadillo," "Ballet dancing bear," and "Cat who clowns around," and continue all the way through the alphabet to "Zig-zagging zebra."
SUBJ: Alphabet--Songs and music./ Animals--Songs and music./ Singing games.

SRC 789.3   Ph-3 P-3 $9.98   OD KD613
GREEN CHILI JAM BAND. Magic bike (Sound recording cassette). Green Chili Jam/dist. by Squeaky Wheel GC001, 1991. 1 sound cassette (45min).
Includes lyrics.
Includes teacher's guide.
Fourteen songs encourage activities that will fit in with science, math, social studies, and language arts curricula. Includes "Trees," "Muscle shuffle," and "Language discrepancies."
SUBJ: Songs./ Singing games./ Handicraft.

SRC 789.3   Ph-2 P-2 $9.98   KD614
GREEN CHILI JAM BAND. Starfishing (Sound recording cassette). Green Chili Jam/dist. by Squeaky Wheel GC020 ISBN 0-9638680-1-2, 1993. 1 sound cassette (45min).
Includes lyrics.
ALA notable recording, 1994.
Compact disc available from Green Chili Jam/dist. by Squeaky Wheel (45min), $14.98.
Thirteen original songs designed to educate and to entertain. The bouncy music is accompanied by lyrics which extol the wonder of individual expression, joys of conquering phobias, and the pleasure of acquiring self-awareness.
SUBJ: Songs.

SRC 789.3   Ph-2 2-4 $10.00   OD KD615
HARLEY, BILL. Lunchroom tales: a natural history of the cafetorium (Sound recording cassette). Round River/Alcazar Productions RRR110C ISBN 1-878126-19-9, 1996. 1 sound cassette (55min).
Includes lyrics.
Compact disc available 110J, 1996. 1 compact disc (55min), $15.00.
Amusing lyrics and peppy music recall the elementary school experience. Songs extol friendship, bemoan procrastination, and recount the fun activity of sitting in the back of the bus.
SUBJ: Schools--Songs and music./ Humorous songs.

SRC 789.3   Ph-1 P-2 $11.95   OD KD616
HARTMANN, JACK. Let's read together and other songs for sharing and caring (Sound recording cassette). Educational Activities AC 648, 1991. 1 sound cassette (52min).
Includes teacher's guide and lyrics.
Fourteen songs encourage sharing and caring, reading, concern for the environment, library use, and self-confidence. Promotes discussion about feelings, dreams, hopes, and feeling needed. Good for singing along and promoting communication skills.
SUBJ: Songs./ Emotions--Songs and music.

SRC 789.3   Ph-2 K-5 $11.95   OD KD617
HARTMANN, JACK. Make a friend, be a friend: songs for growing up and growing together with friends (Sound recording cassette). Educational Activities AC 643, 1990. 1 sound cassette (35min).
Twelve lively, imaginative songs stress learning to play together with cooperation and friendship. The lyrics encourage positive social problem-solving and managing childhood stress through humor.
SUBJ: Friendship--Songs and music./ Songs.

VCR 789.3   Ph-1 K-4 $19.95   OD KD618
HARTMANN, JACK. One voice for children (Videocassette). Educational Activities VS055, 1993. 1/2" VHS videocassette color (30min).
Exuberant songs urge young people to be persistent as they follow their goals, to be aware of conservation and ecology, and to have an appreciative understanding of other generations. The music is infectious; the participants, some of whom have disabilities, are young children from multicultural backgrounds. Themes that are expounded encourage children to live positive, energetic, caring lives.
SUBJ: Songs./ Self-esteem--Songs and music.

SRC 789.3   Ph-2 3-6 $10.00   OD KD619
I'M GONNA LET IT SHINE: A GATHERING OF VOICES FOR FREEDOM (Sound recording cassette). Produced by Bill Harley. Round River Records RRR401, 1990. 1 sound cassette (53min).
Compact disc availablec 401, n.d. 1 compact disc (53min), $15.00.
A collection of activist songs reflecting the experiences and feelings of people who have participated in the civil rights movement. Includes such stirring songs as "We Shall Overcome," Hold on (Keep Your Eyes on the Prize)", and "If You Miss Me From the Back of the Bus." Excellent for enriching the social studies curriculum, for celebrations of Black History Month, and Martin Luther King's Birthday, and for understanding our multicultural society.
SUBJ: Songs./ Civil rights--Songs and music./ Afro-Americans--Songs and music.

SRC 789.3   Ph-3 K-3 $9.95   OD KD620
JACK, DAVID. Dance in your pants: great songs for little kids to dance to (Sound recording cassette). Words and music by Susan Jack Cooper and David Jack. Ta-Dum TD 2005 ISBN 0-942181-04-2, 1988. 1 sound cassette (23min).
Includes lyrics.
Lively music invites dancing. The songs have a good beat, and the lyrics are amusing.
SUBJ: Songs./ Humorous songs./ Dance music.

VCR 789.3   Ph-3 P-2 $14.95   OD KD621
JACK, DAVID. David Jack... live!: Makin' music, makin' friends (Videocassette). Lyrics by Susan Jack Cooper. Ta-Dum TD1225 ISBN 0-942181-06-9, 1991. 1/2" VHS videocassette color (40min).
Forty minutes of lively music certain to stir physical movement and enthusiasm in the youngest children. David Jack encourages singing along, clapping, and dancing participation.
SUBJ: Songs./ Humorous songs./ Dance music.

SRC 789.3   Ph-3 K-3 $9.95   OD KD622
JACK, DAVID. Gotta hop (Sound recording cassette). Lyrics by Susan Jack Cooper. Ta-Dum 2003 ISBN 0-942181-08-5, 1990. 1 sound cassette (30min).
Includes lyrics.
Catchy lyrics encourage physical movement and sing-along.
SUBJ: Songs./ Humorous songs./ Dance music./ Singing games.

SRC 789.3   Ph-1 P-K $10.95   OD KD623
JANIAK, WILLIAM. Basic skills for young children (Sound recording cassette). Kimbo KIM 9117C, c1980, 1990. 1 sound cassette (29min).
Includes activity guide and lyrics.
Young children can practice motor control, body identification, right/left discrimination, listening skills, directionality, and rymthmic awareness from these learning songs. Some of the songs introduce socialization skills, emotionalization, and encourage awareness and expression.
SUBJ: Songs.

CD 789.3 Ph-2 P-K $14.00 OD KD624
JENKINS, ELLA. And one and two and other songs for pre-school and primary children (Compact disc). Smithsonian/Folkways CD SF 45016, 1995. 1 compact disc (28min).
Includes lyrics.
Originally published by Folkways 7544, 1971.
Sound recording cassette available C SF 45016, 1990. 1 sound cassette (28min), $8.50.
A variety of songs teach counting and following directions and encourage creative movement, sharing, and singing along. A clear voice and easy-to-follow instructions ensure audience participation. Includes several Jewish holiday songs--"My little blue dredle" and the popular Chanukah song "Dredle, dredle, dredle."
SUBJ: Songs.

SRC 789.3 Ph-1 K-3 $8.50 OD KD625
JENKINS, ELLA. Call and response: rhythmic group singing (Sound recording cassette). Smithsonian/Folkways C-SF 45030, 1990. 1 sound cassette (27min).
Originally published by Folkways (FC 7638), 1957.
Includes lyrics.
A vibrant collection of African, Arabic, and American chain gang chants. Audience participation is encouraged, and many children will strive to lead the chants. Discourages shyness; promotes listening skills; and fosters an interest in many cultures. For multicultural studies.
SUBJ: Songs./ Folk songs./ Culture--Songs and music.

SRC 789.3 Ph-2 P-2 $9.98 OD KD626
JENKINS, ELLA. Come dance by the ocean (Sound recording cassette). Smithsonian Folkways 45014, 1991. 1 sound cassette (40min).
Compact disc available 45014CD, $15.00.
Ella Jenkins sings a group of songs about our world which promote improving the environment and enjoying different cultures, languages, and places. Includes notes about each song.
SUBJ: Songs./ Environmental protection--Songs and music./ Culture--Songs and music.

VCR 789.3 Ph-3 P-K $14.95 OD KD627
JENKINS, ELLA. Ella Jenkins live!: at the Smithsonian (Videocassette). Smithsonian Folkways 48002, 1991. 1/2" VHS videocassette color (30min).
Brings Ella Jenkins as a guest to your classroom as she leads a group of youngsters in audience participation songs such as "Once there was a king," "Miss Mary Mack," and "London Bridge."
SUBJ: Songs./ Singing games.

SRC 789.3 Ph-2 P-2 $8.50 OD KD628
JENKINS, ELLA. Growing up with Ella Jenkins: rhythms songs and rhymes (Sound recording cassette). Smithsonian Folkways C-SF 45032, 1990. 1 sound cassette (35min).
Originally published by Folkways (FC 7662), 1976.
Includes lyrics.
In a voice resonating with warmth and clarity, Ella Jenkins sings songs that are part of her childhood. Listeners are urged to participate and to sing along. Good choice for audience participation.
SUBJ: Songs./ Rhythm./ Dance music.

CD 789.3 Ph-2 K-2 $13.00 OD KD629
JENKINS, ELLA. Multicultural children's songs (Compact disc). Smithsonian/Folkways SF CD 45045, 1995. 1 compact disc (41min).
Sound recording cassette available C SF 45045, 1995. 1 sound cassette (41min), $8.50.
Selections from Ella Jenkins' previous albums are gathered in a lively collection for multicultural studies. The group of call and response chants and songs from Africa, Mexico, Australia, the United States, the Caribbean, and the Middle East invite creative movement and audience participation.
SUBJ: Songs./ Folk songs./ Culture--Songs and music.

SRC 789.3 Ph-2 P-K $9.98 OD KD630
JENKINS, ELLA. Rhythm and game songs for the little ones (Sound recording cassette). Smithsonian Folkways C-SF 45027, 1990. 1 sound cassette (25min).
Originally published by Folkways (FC 7680), 1964.
Includes lyrics.
Familiar songs and activities encourage physical activity, promote listening skills, and facilitate coordination. Includes "Teddy Bear," "Jack and Jill," and "Skip to My Lou." Good for creative movement and audience participation for the youngest children.
SUBJ: Songs./ Singing games.

CD 789.3 Ph-2 K-3 $14.00 OD KD631
JENKINS, ELLA. Songs children love to sing (Compact disc). Smithsonian/Folkways CD SF 45042, 1996. 1 compact disc (37min).

Includes lyrics.
Sound recording cassette available from Smithsonian/Folkways CS SF 45042, 1996. 1 sound cassette (37min), $8.50.
A variety of popular songs are clearly rendered, encouraging audience participation. Includes such diverse offerings as "This Old Man," "Tu Cantaras, yo cantare," and "Harmonica for Hanukkah."
SUBJ: Songs.

CD 789.3 Ph-2 K-2 $13.00 OD KD632
JENKINS, ELLA. This is rhythm (Compact disc). Smithsonian/Folkways CD SF 45028, 1994. 1 compact disc (40min).
Originally published by Folkways (FC 7652), 1981.
Includes lyrics.
Also available on sound recording cassette (C SF 45028), $8.50.
A variety of musical instruments such as the conga drum, bongos, tambourine, and cow bell are used to convey the essence of rhythm. The selection of songs from many lands is excellent for multicultural studies and for inviting audience participation.
SUBJ: Songs./ Rhythm.

SRC 789.3 Ph-3 P-2 $10.95 OD KD633
JENKINS, ELLA. You'll sing a song and I'll sing a song (Sound recording cassette). Smithsonian Folkways 45010, c1966, 1989. 1 sound cassette (33min).
Compact disc available CD SF 45010, 1989. 1 compact disc (33min), $15.00.
With a lively and enthusiastic style, this well-known folk music composer and teacher leads the Urban Gateways Children's Chorus in 12 songs. The songs include both original and traditional pieces, but all emphasize rhythm and encourage listener participation. Accompanying notes contain texts of the songs, descriptive material, and guides for teachers for coordinated activities.
Contents: You'll sing a song and I'll sing a song; Shabot Shalom; Cadima; This train; Did you feed my cow?; Miss Mary Mack; May-Ree Mack; Dulce Dulce; Maori Indian Battle Chant; I saw; Sitting in the sand; Guide me.
SUBJ: Songs.

SRC 789.3 Ph-3 K-6 $9.98 OD KD634
KEEP THE SPIRIT (Sound recording cassette). Tickle Tune Typhoon MLP428, 1989. 1 sound cassette (42min).
Includes lyrics.
A rousing rendition of such popular holiday tunes as "Jingle Bells," "Rudolph the Rednose Reindeer," and "Silent Night." Also includes one song called "Hanukkah."
SUBJ: Christmas music./ Holidays--Songs./ Songs.

SRC 789.3 Ph-2 P-2 $11.95 OD KD635
LATE LAST NIGHT (Sound recording cassette). Educational Activities AC 608, 1984. 1 sound cassette.
Compact disc available CD 608, n.d. 1 compact disc, $14.95.
Encourages spirited movement to such songs as "Wiggle in my Toe" and "Ants in my Pants" and provides quiet listening to such humorous songs as a paeon to peanut butter and an inquiry into the nature of the belly button.
SUBJ: Songs./ Humorous songs.

VCR 789.3 Ph-2 K-6 $14.95 KD636
LYRIC LANGUAGE: A BILINGUAL MUSIC PROGRAM: SPANISH/ENGLISH (Videocassette). Penton Overseas ISBN 1-56015-326-1, 1992. 1/2" VHS videocassette color (35min).
Animated Family Circus characters introduce each song as a group of children embark on a series of real-life adventures which are accompanied by Spanish/English subtitles. The children sing with great ebullience; the pictures are bright and amusing; and the Spanish/English translations are repeated sufficiently to enhance rapid learning. A fun enrichment activity for schools where Spanish is taught.
SUBJ: Songs./ Bilingual materials--Spanish./ Spanish language materials.

789.3 Ph-2 2-4/3 $15.95 L KD637
MCCUTCHEON, JOHN. Happy adoption day! Illus. by Julie Paschkis. Little, Brown ISBN 0-316-55455-3; In Canada: Little, Brown, 1996. unp. col. ill.
A celebration of adoption. One family welcomes a new addition and makes the newcomer feel loved and very special. Particularly of interest to adopted children.
SUBJ: Adoption--Songs and music./ Family life--Songs and music./ Songs.

CD 789.3 Ph-1 K-3 $15.00 OD KD638
MCCUTCHEON, JOHN. John McCutcheon's four seasons: wintersongs (Compact disc). Rounder Records 8038 ISBN 1-886767-06-8, 1995. 1

compact disc (44min).

ALA notable recording, 1996.

Also available on sound recording cassette (ISBN 1-886767-07-6, 1995), $9.98.

A rousing celebration of winter with songs both personal and universal extols the comfort of hot chocolate, the delight in ice skating, and the anticipation of the first snowfall. Can be used to enrich study of the seasons or to encourage listening for the sheer joy of the music.

SUBJ: Songs./ Winter--Songs.

789.3   Ph-2 K-2 $14.95   L   KD639
NORWORTH, JACK. Take me out to the ballgame. Original lyrics by Jack Norworth. Illus. by Alec Gillman. Four Winds ISBN 0-02-735991-3; In Canada: Maxwell Macmillan, 1992. unp. col. ill.

Includes bibliography.

A paean to the sport of baseball containing the original verses and music to this nostalgic song. Notes at the end of the book recount the glory days of Ebbets Field and the Brooklyn Dodgers. Young readers will enjoy the picture book format while older students will appreciate the baseball history in the afterword.

SUBJ: Baseball--Songs and music./ Songs.

SRC 789.3   Ph-2 K-4 $10.95   OD KD640
ON THE ROAD AGAIN (Sound recording cassette). Kimbo KIM 9129C, 1992. 1 sound cassette (35min).

Subtitle on container: More car songs.

Includes lyrics.

A collection of popular, often hilarious, songs which children will enjoy singing. Includes "Do your ears hang low," "On top of spaghetti," and "Be kind to your web-footed friends."

SUBJ: Songs./ Humorous songs./ Automobile travel--Songs and music.

SRC 789.3   Ph-1 P-K $11.95   OD KD641
PALMER, HAP. Can a cherry pie wave goodbye?: songs for learning through music and movement (Sound recording cassette). Hap-Pal Music/Educational Activities HP103, 1991. 1 sound cassette (35min).

Includes teacher's guide.

Also available on compact disc.

Thirteen songs encourage movement as children are invited to respond. Includes follow-up activities designed to stimulate mental aptitudes such as imagining, remembering, and classifying.

SUBJ: Songs./ Singing games.

SRC 789.3   Ph-1 P-2 $10.95   OD KD642
PALMER, HAP. Child's world of lullabies: multicultural songs for quiet times (Sound recording cassette). Sung by Hap Palmer and Penny Palmer. Hap Palmer Music/dist. by Educational Activities, 1993. 1 sound cassette (30min).

Includes lyrics.

Compact disc available, 1993. 1 compact disc (30min), $10.95.

Gentle songs for quiet times reflect a diversity of themes, cultures, and musical styles. Creates a loving, peaceful environment for singing and playing together with such multicultural songs as "A la nanita nana," "Chippewa lullaby," and "Dormite ninito." For multicultural studies.

SUBJ: Lullabies./ Culture--Songs and music.

VCR 789.3   Ph-1 P-1 $19.95   OD KD643
PALMER, HAP. Sammy and other songs from "Getting to know myself" (Videocassette). Educational Activities VS053, 1993. 1/2" VHS videocassette color (30min).

Encouraging movement and participation, these lively songs reinforce the learning of body parts, right and left discrimination, and opposites. An excellent combination of fun and learning.

SUBJ: Songs./ Physical fitness./ Singing games.

CD 789.3   Ph-1 P-2 $12.95   OD KD644
PALMER, HAP. So big: activity songs for little ones (Compact disc). Hap-Pal Music HP107CD678, 1994. 1 compact disc (60min).

Includes teacher's guide.

Rousing renditions of activity songs encourage creative movement, singing, and make-believe. Develops movement skills, teaches basic math and science concepts, and stimulates imaginative powers.

SUBJ: Songs./ Singing games.

VCR 789.3   Ph-1 P-2 $19.95   KD645
PALMER, HAP. Stepping out with Hap Palmer (Videocassette). Educational Activities VS 058, 1994. 1/2" VHS videocassette (25min).

Enchanting, enthusiastic youngsters move around--jumping, dancing, wiggling, running--to music that is alternately low key or lively. Emphasis is given to learning--time, numbers, shapes, and days of the week. Excellent vehicle for encouraging creative movement, exercise,

and following directions.

SUBJ: Songs./ Singing games.

VCR 789.3   Ph-2 P-2 $14.95   OD KD646
PETER COTTONTAIL: HOW HE GOT HIS HOP! (Videocasstte). Bogner Entertainment, 1993. 1/2" VHS videocassette color (30min). (Holiday classics).

Lively music, enchanting, colorful puppets by Jim Gamble, and a modern tale make this a program certain to encourage attentive listening.

SUBJ: Songs./ Puppet plays.

SRC 789.3   Ph-2 K-6 $12.00   OD KD647
POLANSKY, DAVID S. I like dessert (Sound recording cassette). Perfect Score Great American Music, 1987. 1 sound cassette (32min).

Includes lyrics.

Interprets the experiences of elementary school students with gusto. Scat singing, rap beat, the beltings of a blues singer, the voices of children bring to life such eternal problems as the slow preparation for school each morning while the lament, "why am I so shy," speaks to everyone. This lilting medley will be a favorite.

SUBJ: Songs.

CD 789.3   Ph-2 1-6 $14.95   OD KD648
POLISAR, BARRY LOUIS. Family concert (Compact disc). Rainbow Morning Music CD 5161 ISBN 0-938663-44-5, 1993. 1 compact disc (47min).

Sound recording cassette available (ISBN 0-938663-12-7, 1993). 1 sound cassette (47min).

A very funny collection of songs with such titles as "My brother threw-up on my stuffed toy bunny," "Don't put you finger up your nose," and "I wanna be a dog." Certain to produce guffaws.

SUBJ: Songs./ Humorous songs.

SRC 789.3   Ph-3 P-3 $9.95   KD649
POLISAR, BARRY LOUIS. Old dogs, new tricks (Sound recording cassette). Rainbow Morning Music 5181C ISBN 0-938663-17-8, 1993. 1 sound cassette (38min).

Compact disc available from Rainbow Morning Music (ISBN 0-938663-49-6, 1993 OD). 1 compact disc (38min), $14.95.

Appreciation of the peculiar habits of animals is rendered with a country twang. Certain to produce giggles at the mere thought of a three-toed, triple-eyed, double-jointed dinosaur.

SUBJ: Songs./ Humorous songs.

SRC 789.3   Ph-2 P $10.95   OD KD650
PRESCHOOL ACTION TIME (Sound recording cassette). By Carol Hammett. Kimbo KIM 9110C, 1988. 1 sound cassette (30min).

Includes activity guide.

Stretches bodies and exercises minds as pre-schoolers express themselves while listening to peppy renditions of 16 songs including "I'm a little teapot," "Where is Thumbkin," and "Dinosaur Visit."

SUBJ: Finger play./ Singing games.

SRC 789.3   Ph-3 P-K $10.95   OD KD651
PRESCHOOL PLAYTIME BAND (Sound recording cassette). Kimbo KIM 9099C, 1987. 1 sound cassette (30min).

Includes lyrics.

Starts the day with a combination of peppy songs to accompany stretching exercises. Fun to get the youngest students awake.

SUBJ: Songs./ Rhythm bands and orchestras.

SRC 789.3   Ph-2 P-5 $10.95   OD KD652
RAFFI. Rise and shine (Sound recording cassette). Kimbo KIM 8111C; In Canada: Shoreline Records, c1982. 1 sound cassette (31min).

Filled with joie de vivre, these 17 rhythmic renditions including "He's Got the Whole World", "Thumbelina," "Wheels on the Bus" in danceable, peppy arrangements are certain to inspire a love of singing and dancing among children.

SUBJ: Songs.

789.3   Ph-2 P-2 $5.99   P   KD653
RAFFI. Wheels on the bus. Illus. by Sylvie Wickstrom. Crown ISBN 0-517-57645-7, c1988, 1990. unp. col. ill. (Raffi songs to read).

All the sights and sounds of a bus ride around town with an assortment of strange passengers are incorporated in a rhythmic song with lots of repetition and amusing illustrations. Music is included.

SUBJ: Buses--Songs and music.

SRC 789.3   Ph-3 P-2 $11.50   OD KD654
ROGERS, SALLY. What can one little person do? (Sound recording cassette). Sally Rogers, 1992. 1 sound cassette (38min).

Includes lyrics.

Compact disc available 302J, 1992. 1 compact disc (38min), $15.00.

A collection of original songs about people who have made a difference in this world (e.g., Harriet Tubman, Martin Luther King, Jr., and Amelia Earhart). Extols the quest for peace, the Native Americans who welcomed Columbus, and the need for recycling. Can be used in social studies and science lessons as enrichment.
SUBJ: Songs./ Peace--Songs and music./ Human rights--Songs and music.

CD 789.3   Ph-2 K-6 $15.00   OD KD655
SAPP, JANE. We've all got stories: songs from the Dream Project (Compact disc). Rounder Kids CD 8035 ISBN 1-886767-12-2, 1996. 1 compact disc (57min).
Includes lyrics.
Sound recording cassette available C 8035 (ISBN 1-886767-13-0, 1996). 1 sound cassette (57min), $9.98.
A group of youngsters share their thoughts, feelings, and identities through music as their exuberant voices render such songs as "Let me be your friend" and "Everybody makes a difference." Can be integrated into multicultural studies.
SUBJ: Songs.

SRC 789.3   Ph-2 2-6 $6.00   OD KD656
SCHOOL RAP (Sound recording cassette). Sung by Dre & Ty and the Cold Crush Cru. Cascade Pass, 1990. 1 sound cassette (5min).
Includes lyrics.
Presents school in a positive light in a rap routine which will warm the hearts of most educators. Text accompanies recording. Use as a pattern for creative writing activities.
SUBJ: Songs./ Rap (Music)./ School--Songs and music.

CD 789.3   Ph-1 K-3 $12.98   OD KD657
SCRUGGS, JOE. Ants (Compact disc). Shadow Play Records & Video/ Educational Graphics Press SPD 108 ISBN 0-916123-34-0, 1994. 1 compact disc (30min).
Includes lyrics.
ALA notable recording, 1995.
Sound recording cassette available SPR 350, 1994. 1 sound cassette (30min), $9.95.
Disarming, thought-provoking lyrics reflect alternative ways of looking at the world. Includes such songs as "Rapunsel has a mohawk," "Different drum," and "Not fair." Excellent for promoting discussion on getting along together, and respect for those who march to the beat of a different drummer.
SUBJ: Songs.

SRC 789.3   Ph-2 K-4 $10.95   OD KD658
SKIERA-ZUCEK, LOIS. Save the animals, save the earth: songs about endangered animals and the earth (Sound recording cassette). Kimbo KIM 9124C, 1991. 1 sound cassette (29min).
Includes lyrics and guide.
A variety of music styles--rap, calypso, and country and western--presents 13 songs with lyrics designed to teach about conservation, endangered species, rainforests, and recycling. The messages are never heavy-handed, but sparkle with humor and are accompanied by lively, witty music. Excellent for enriching environmental studies units. Facts about the endangered animals mentioned in the songs are included in the lyrics sheet.
SUBJ: Songs./ Environmental protection--Songs and music./ Wildlife conservation--Songs and music.

SRC 789.3   Ph-1 P-K $10.95   OD KD659
STEWART, GEORGIANA. Pre-K hooray! (Sound recording cassette). Kimbo KIM 9134C, 1993. 1 sound cassette (32min).
Includes lyrics.
Lively music accompanies learning and physical activities. Such songs as "Alphabet stretch" and the "Color wheel dance" encourage creative movement and musical enjoyment and can be the focus of many happy playtimes.
SUBJ: Songs./ Rhythm./ Singing games.

SRC 789.3   Ph-1 P-K $10.95   OD KD660
STEWART, GEORGIANA. Preschool favorites (Sound recording cassette). Kimbo KIM 9122C, 1990. 1 sound cassette (28min).
Includes Activity Guide and lyrics.
Clear lyrics and peppy music inspire pre-schoolers to do the "Bean Bag Rock", "Mexican Hat Dance", and "Bendable, Stretchable". This lively collection of songs encourage rhythm and movement.
SUBJ: Songs./ Rhythm./ Singing games.

789.3   Ph-1 P-1 $14.95   L   KD661
TODAY IS MONDAY. Illus. by Eric Carle. Philomel ISBN 0-399-21966-8; In Canada: Putnam, 1993. unp. col. ill.
Eric Carle's exuberant animals stride boldly across the pages accompanied by the refrain of the popular song. Encourages readers

to repeat the words, learn the days of the week, and sing the song. Good for reading aloud.
SUBJ: Food--Songs and music./ Songs.

789.3   Ph-2 P-1/2 $18.60   L   KD662
TRAPANI, IZA. Itsy bitsy spider. Told and illus. by Iza Trapani. Gareth Stevens ISBN 0-8368-1550-5; In Canada: Saunders, 1996. 32p. col. ill.
First published by Whispering Coyote Press, 1993.
Extends the familiar nursery song with numerous extra verses in which the spider has a series of adventures until she finally rests in the sun. Attractive watercolor illustrations show the various predicaments of the spider. The new verses faithfully follow the well-known tune, and the music is included.
SUBJ: Spiders--Songs and music./ Songs.

SRC 789.3   Ph-2 K-3 $11.95   OD KD663
VALERI, MICHELE. Mi casa es su casa/my house is your house: a bi-lingual musical journey through Latin America (Sound recording cassette). Harper Audio ISBN 0-89845-175-2, 1991. 1 sound cassette (38min).
Subtitle on container: A Latin American musical journey.
Includes lyrics.
Learn Spanish words and customs and sing to lively salsas and sambas. Excellent for multicultural studies and just for fun sing-alongs.
SUBJ: Songs./ Latin America--Songs and music./ Spanish language materials./ Bilingual materials--Spanish.

SRC 789.3   Ph-2 K-4 $10.00   OD KD664
VAN MANENS. We recycle and other songs for Earth keepers (Sound recording cassette). People Records PR309, 1990. 1 sound cassette (30min).
Includes lyrics.
Inspiring songs about preserving our environment, peace, freedom, and getting along with each other. Excellent for provoking discussion as well as encouraging one to sing along. For environmental studies.
SUBJ: Songs./ Recycling (Waste)--Songs and music.

BA 789.3   Ph-3 P-2 $24.95   KD665
WEEKS, SARAH. Crocodile smile: 10 songs of the Earth as the animals see it. Written and sung by Sarah Weeks. Illus. by Lois Ehlert. HarperCollins ISBN 0-06-022867-9; In Canada: HarperCollins, 1994. 1 hardback book, 1 sound cassette (45min).
"Laura Geringer book."
Over 40 species, including many endangered animals, appear in these songs. Features a giant panda, an egret, a Galapagos tortoise, and a crocodile among others. Dramatic illustrations bring the animals to life. Ancillary material for environmental studies.
SUBJ: Animals--Songs and music./ Endangered species--Songs and music./ Songs.

SRC 789.3   Ph-2 K-3 $10.95   OD KD666
WEISSMAN, JACKIE. Joining hands with other lands: multicultural songs and games (Sound recording cassette). Kimbo 9130C, 1993. 1 sound cassette (40min).
Includes teacher's guide and lyrics.
Compact disc available 9130CD, 1994. 1 compact disc (40min), $14.95.
Lively audience participation songs encourage learning words from many languages and include many multicultural games and activities. Excellent for social studies units.
SUBJ: Songs./ Singing games./ Culture--Songs and music.

SRC 789.4   Ph-3 K-4 $9.95   OD KD667
BOOKER, CEDELLA MARLEY. Smilin' island of song (Sound recording cassette). Music for Little People SRC258 ISBN 1-877737-10-0, 1994. 1 sound cassette (40min).
Includes lyrics.
Compact disc available D258, 1993. 1 compact disc (40min), $15.95.
Native reggae and calypso songs of the West Indies all have a lively, rhythmic beat with titles such as "Tingalayo," "Ooey Gooey the silly worm," and "Jah wanna dance." Good for enriching multicultural studies and units on Jamaica.
SUBJ: Reggae music./ Calypso (Songs)./ Jamaica--Songs and music.

SRC 789.4   Ph-3 2-4 $9.95   OD KD668
HORSE SENSE FOR KIDS AND OTHER PEOPLE (Sound recording cassette). Music for Little People 239 ISBN 1-877737-91-7, 1992. 1 sound cassette (30min).
Includes lyrics.
Compact disc available D239, 1992. 1 compact disc (30min), $12.95.
Presents some familiar songs of the Old West, including "Red River Valley," "Turkey in the straw," and "The old Chisholm Trail." Authentic renditions good for incorporating into regional studies.
SUBJ: Cowboys--Songs and music./ West (U.S.)--Songs and music./ Folk songs--United States.

SRC 789.4   Ph-1 K-3 $9.00   OD KD669
REGGAE FOR KIDS: A COLLECTION OF MUSIC FOR KIDS OF ALL AGES! (Sound recording cassette). RAS Records RASCS 3095, 1992. 1 sound cassette (42min).
    Includes lyrics.
    Also available on compact disc RASCD 3095, 1992. 1 compact disc (42min), 12.00.
    Thirteen selections, including rock remakes and original and traditional songs, are arranged in Jamaican reggae style. Great for dancing, singing along, or just listening. Some of the songs have messages while others just exude joy. Good for use in multicultural studies.
    SUBJ: Songs./ Reggae music.

BA 789.4   Ph-2 K-3 $15.96   KD670
STANLEY, LEOTHA. Be a friend: the story of African American music in song, words and pictures. Illus. by Henry Hawkins. Zino Press ISBN 1-55933-153-4, 1994. 1 paperback book, 1 sound cassette (25min).
    An overview of African-American music touches upon spirituals, blues, jazz, gospel, and rap. Eight original songs reflect these musical styles and convey such positive messages as staying in school, being a friend, saying no to drugs, and fostering a good attitude. An easy-to-read introduction to African-American music history. For multicultural studies.
    SUBJ: Afro-Americans--Music--History and criticism./ Music--History and criticism.

789.43   Ph-3 5-A $15.95   P   KD671
SILVERMAN, JERRY. Blues. Chelsea House ISBN 0-7910-1846-6, 1994. 64p. ill. (Traditional Black music).
    Includes indexes.
    A songbook of 26 tunes explores the uniquely African-American music form--the blues. Comments and captioned photographs add historical context. For multicultural studies.
    SUBJ: Blues (Music)./ Songs./ Afro-Americans--Songs and music.

789.44   Ph-1 2-6/5 $14.95   T   KD672
JOHNSON, JAMES WELDON. Lift every voice and sing. Illus. by Elizabeth Catlett. Introduction by Jim Haskins. Walker ISBN 0-8027-8250-7; In Canada: Thomas Allen, 1993. unp. ill.
    Includes music.
    Written at the turn of the century, this well-known African-American anthem expresses the strength, tenacity, and dignity of their struggles for equal rights. The linocut illustrations are dramatic and evocative, depicting such strong, outstanding historical personalities as Harriet Tubman, Phyllis Wheatley, and Sojourner Truth. For multicultural studies.
    SUBJ: Afro-Americans--Songs and music./ Songs.

SRC 789.5   Ph-3 5-6 $10.95   OD KD673
HUGHES, LANGSTON. Story of jazz (Sound recording cassette). Smithsonian Folkways 7312, 1954. 1 sound cassette.
    A history of jazz from its African roots and the rhythms brought by slaves to the South to its many sounds today. Characteristics of jazz and the blues are demonstrated by past and present musical artists, including Jelly Roll Morton, Leadbelly, Bix Biederbecke, Duke Ellington, Dizzy Gillespie, Mary Lou Williams, and Louis Armstrong.
    SUBJ: Jazz--History.

CD 789.8   Ph-1 4-6 $14.98   OD KD674
BIBBIDI BOBBODI BACH (Compact disc). Delos International DE 3195, 1996. 1 compact disc (56min).
    Includes program notes.
    ALA notable recording, 1997.
    Sound recording cassette available CF 3195, 1996. 1 sound cassette (56min).
    The teaching of classical music is enhanced by incorporating familiar themes from Disney music performed in the style of such composers as Beethoven, Bach, and Pachelbel. A clever approach to introducing classical music to the uninitiated.
    SUBJ: Orchestral music./ Music appreciation.

SRC 789.8   Ph-1 P-3 $9.98   KD675
LOUCHARD, RIC. Hey, Ludwig!: classical piano solos for playful times (Sound recording cassette). Music for Little People 9 42537-4 ISBN 1-56628-015-X, 1993. 1 sound cassette (51min).
    Compact disc available D2839, 1993. 1 compact disc (51min), $12.95.
    Piano solos of seven master composers including Mozart, Bach, Beethoven, and Scott Joplin provide energetic music that is excellent for incorporating classical music into childrens' playtime activities. Useful to develope music appreciation.
    SUBJ: Piano music./ Music appreciation.

CE 789.8   Ph-3 P-3/4 $4.95   P   KD676
PROKOFIEV, SERGEI. Peter and the wolf. Translated by Maria Carlson. Illus. by Charles Mikolaycak. Penguin ISBN 0-14-050633-0, 1982. unp col illus.
    Vigorous, detailed, and richly colored illustrations combine with the straightforward text to retell the story of Peter who disobeys his grandfather and goes out into the meadow. When the wolf with malevolent orange eyes swallows the duck, Peter, with the help of the bird, captures him and in a truly triumphant procession conveys him to the zoo. Superb in its own right the book achieves still another dimension when read aloud against the background of the orchestral program music.
    SUBJ: Folklore--Soviet Union./ Soviet Union--Folklore./ Animals--Folklore./ Program music.

790   Ph-2 3-6/7 $9.95   P   KD677
BERGSTROM, JOAN M. All the best contests for kids, 1996-1997. 5th ed. By Joan M. Bergstrom and Craig Bergstrom. Tricycle Press ISBN 0-89815-451-0, 1996. 274p. ill.
    Includes directory, bibliographies and indexes.
    Engages children in a wealth of activities and encourages their desire to compete in contests devoted to writing, art, music, model airplanes, knitting, and photography as well as many other subjects. Encourages creativity and originality and includes something of interest for everyone. (Parents' Shelf)
    SUBJ: Contests./ Hobbies.

790.1   Ph-3 3-6/6 $15.95   T   KD678
DRAKE, JANE. Kids' summer handbook. By Jane Drake and Ann Love. Illus. by Heather Collins. Ticknor & Fields ISBN 0-395-68711-X, 1994. 207p. ill.
    Originally published THE KIDS COTTAGE BOOK, Kids Can Press Ltd., 1993.
    Includes index.
    A variety of projects planned to enrich summer days. Includes activities at the seashore, at camp, and for rainy days. (Parents' Shelf).
    SUBJ: Nature craft./ Handicraft./ Outdoor recreation.

790.1   Ph-2 1-3/2 $19.97   L   KD679
HANKIN, ROSIE. What was it like before television? Illus. by Diana Bowles. Steck-Vaughn ISBN 0-8114-5735-4, 1995. 32p. col. ill. (Read all about it).
    Includes index.
    An overview of the way life used to be before the advent of television. Good for encouraging oral discussion and for introducing intergenerational research projects that involve interviewing grandparents and community members about life during the first half of our century.
    SUBJ: Amusements--History./ Games--History./ Hobbies--History.

790.1   Ph-3 4-A/8 $15.95   T   KD680
KALMAN, BOBBIE. Early pleasures and pastimes. Crabtree ISBN 0-86505-025-2, 1983. 95p ill. (Early settler life).
    Includes glossary and index.
    Discusses the pleasures and joys of early settler life, with emphasis on holiday celebrations, indoor and outdoor projects, and the maintenance of family harmony. Detailed sepia illustrations combine with photographs and make this a nostalgic and fascinating look at life of long ago. Excellent for social studies reports.
    SUBJ: Recreation--History./ Amusements--History.

VCR 790.1   Ph-2 P-2 $9.98   KD681
LEWIS, SHARI. Get your teddy ready (Videocassette). A&M Video ISBN 0-945338-66-X, 1994. 1/2" VHS videocassette color (30min). (Lamb Chop's play-along!).
    Lamb Chop and her teddy bear, Mr. Bearly, invite children to bring their teddy bears for a rousing time with songs, stories, arts and crafts projects, and dancing. Delightful fun for audience participation.
    SUBJ: Songs./ Storytelling./ Handicraft.

791.3   Ph-3 4-6/6 $15.00   T   KD682
MCCLUNG, ROBERT M. Old Bet and the start of the American circus. Illus. by Laura Kelly. Morrow ISBN 0-688-10642-0, 1993. unp. col. ill.
    The American circus started with an Indian elephant named Old Bet. He toured many states and his fascinating story is told accompanied by illustrations. Good for browsing and reports.
    SUBJ: Old Bet (Elephant)./ Elephants./ Circus animals./ Circus--History.

791.43   Ph-2 4-6/8 $14.95   T   KD683
CROSS, ROBIN. Movie magic. Sterling ISBN 0-8069-1364-9; In Canada: Sterling c/o Canadian Manda, 1995. 62p. col. ill.
    Originally published in Great Britain by Simon & Schuster, 1994.

Includes index.

This tour of the film industry with myriad graphics reveals how special effects are created and how stunt people keep from getting hurt. These fascinating facts will be of great interest to movie buffs.
SUBJ: Motion pictures--Production and direction.

791.43   Ph-2 3-6/6 $15.95   T   KD684

DAHL, LUCY. James and the giant peach: the book and movie scrapbook. Designed by Molly Leach. Photos by Lucy Dahl. Disney Press ISBN 0-7868-3106-5; In Canada: Little, Brown, 1996. 57p. col. ill.

Lucy Dahl writes about her father's creation of the fantasy of "The Giant Peach," his young admirers, and how the book evolved into a film. Along the way, she pictures her father's childhood, its influence on his writings, and his warm response to his fans who wrote to him. Includes many behind-the-scenes photographs of the making of the film. Use with creative writing classes.
SUBJ: Motion pictures--Production and direction./ Dahl, Roald./ Authors, English./ Fathers and daughters.

791.43   Ph-2 4-6/9 $16.89   L   KD685

HAHN, DON. Animation magic: a behind-the-scenes look at how an animated film is made. Disney Press ISBN 0-7868-5041-8, 1996. 96p. col. ill.

Includes glossary and bibliography.

A behind-the-scenes exploration of the Disney creative process. Discusses animation techniques, revealing how artwork, story, music, and technology combine to create the popular Disney films.
SUBJ: Walt Disney Company./ Animated films.

791.45   Ph-2 3-6/4 $15.90   L   KD686

BENTLEY, NANCY. Young producer's video book: how to write, direct, and shoot your own video. By Nancy Bentley and Donna W. Guthrie. Illus. by Katy Keck Arnsteen. Millbrook ISBN 1-56294-566-1, 1995. 64p. col. ill.

Includes index.

Offers information on the steps necessary to produce a video with emphasis on how to research, write a script, plan a storyboard, tape, and edit. Excellent to use to incorporate video into research projects.
SUBJ: Video recordings--Production and direction.

792   Ph-2 4-6/7 $16.40   L   KD687

BENTLEY, NANCY. Putting on a play: the young playwright's guide to scripting, directing, and performing. By Nancy Bentley and Donna Guthrie. Illus. by Katy Keck Arnsteen. Millbrook ISBN 0-7613-0011-2, 1996. 64p. col. ill.

Includes index.

A step-by-step guide to finding a story, writing a script, and producing and performing a play. Includes lots of ideas for plays, readers' theater, and monologues. A good beginning for young dramatists.
SUBJ: Playwriting./ Theater--Production and direction.

792   Ph-2 3-5/5 $9.95   T   KD688

BULLOCH, IVAN. I want to be an actor. By Ivan Bulloch and Diane James. World Book/Two-Can ISBN 0-7166-1741-2, 1996. 32p. col. ill. (I want to be).

Includes index.

Colorful format with tips for actors includes voice exercises, body language, facial expressions, miming, costumes, props, and scenery. Great fun for the neophyte thespian.
SUBJ: Acting.

792   Ph-1 4-A/7 $17.95   L   KD689

MORLEY, JACQUELINE. Shakespeare's theater. Illus. by John James. Bedrick ISBN 0-87226-309-6, 1994. 48p. col. ill., map (Inside story).

Includes chronology, glossary and index.

Fascinating facts about life in England during the age of William Shakespeare. Traces the development of the Globe Theater with information on its construction, the players, the writers, the costumes, and the audience. Will enrich research projects and will be fun for browsers. A reconstructed Globe Theater opened in London in 1995.
SUBJ: Theaters--History./ Globe Theatre (Southwark, London, England)./ Shakespeare, William--Stage history.

VCR 792   Ph-3 K-2 $34.95   OD KD690

SHOW TIME (Videocassette). Films for the Humanities & Sciences FFH 4673, 1994. 1/2" VHS videocassette color (14min). (Art's place).

Includes public performance rights.

Reveals the many tasks involved in putting on a show. An interesting glimpse of backstage production offers incentives to create dramatic projects. A fun preamble to actual performances.
SUBJ: Stage props./ Scenery./ Costume.

VCR 792.8   Ph-3 3-6 $19.98   KD691

ALICE IN WONDERLAND IN DANCE (Videocassette). V.I.E.W Video 1211 ISBN 0-8030-1211-X, 1993. 1/2" VHS videocassette color (27min).

A dance fantasy, replete with colorful costumes and sets, introduces ballet to youngsters who have read Lewis Carroll's ALICE IN WONDERLAND and who can appreciate and identify such characters as the Cheshire Cat and the Mad Hatter. Excellent vehicle for infusing the literature curriculum with dance, theater, and acrobatics. Will be of interest to reluctant readers as well as aspiring balletomanes.
SUBJ: Ballet./ Ballet dancing.

792.8   Ph-1 3-6/8 $15.95   T   KD692

BUSSELL, DARCEY. Young dancer. By Darcey Bussell with Patricia Linton. DK Publishing ISBN 1-56458-468-2, 1994. 64p. col. ill.

Includes directory, glossary and index.

Profuse full-color photographs and brief text depict and explain the basic positions of ballet. Information is given on the history of dance, exercises to promote strength and lightness, mime and makeup, and the preparation involved for a performance. A beautiful introduction to dance for those who love to dance and those who wish to be part of an educated audience.
SUBJ: Ballet dancing.

CE 792.8   Ph-3 4-6/7 $14.95   T   KD693

FONTEYN, MARGOT. Swan Lake. Illus. by Trina Schart Hyman. Gulliver/Harcourt Brace Jovanovich ISBN 0-15-200600-1, 1989. unp. col. ill.

Read-along kit read by the author, music by P.I. Tchaikowsky, conducted by Andre Previn and performed by the London Symphony Orchestra, available from Harcourt Brace Jovanovich (ISBN 0-15-200602-8, 1991). 1 hardback book, 1 sound cassette (13min), $19.95.

The spell cast by an evil magician turns a princess and other young women into swans by day. The attempt to break the enchantment has been the focus of the well loved ballet and the narrative line incorporates many of the dance elements. Lush India ink, acrylic, and pastel illustrations enhance the romantic character of the plot which will be most enjoyed by ballet students.
SUBJ: Ballets--Stories, plots, etc./ Fairy tales./ Swan Lake (Ballet).

792.8   Ph-2 4-A/7 $14.95   L   KD694

GREGORY, CYNTHIA. Cynthia Gregory dances Swan Lake. Photos by Martha Swope. Simon & Schuster ISBN 0-671-68786-7; In Canada: Simon & Schuster, 1990. unp. ill. (some col.).

A glimpse into the day of a famous ballerina. Cynthia Gregory is followed as she works out, rehearses, is fitted for costumes, applies makeup, and then triumphantly dances "Swan Lake." Young ballet fans will enjoy the glamour and excitement that are part of this star's career.
SUBJ: Gregory, Cynthia./ Ballet dancers./ Swan Lake (Ballet).

792.8   Ph-3 1-5/7 $14.95   L   KD695

HOROSKO, MARIAN. Sleeping Beauty: the ballet story. Retold by Marian Horosko. Illus. by Todd L. W. Doney. Atheneum ISBN 0-689-31885-5; In Canada: Maxwell Macmillan, 1994. unp. col. ill.

Following each scene exactly, the story of the ballet is recounted with emphasis on Perrault's fairy tale as well as information on the scenery, musical accompaniment, and costumes. Ethereal illustrations capture the magic of the ballet. Lovely to read before seeing a performance.
SUBJ: Sleeping Beauty (Ballet)./ Ballets--Stories, plots, etc.

792.8   Ph-2 3-6/6 $19.99   L   KD696

MCCAUGHREAN, GERALDINE. Random House book of stories from the ballet. Retold by Geraldine McCaughrean. Illus. by Angela Barrett. Random House ISBN 0-679-97125-4; In Canada: Random House, 1994. 112p. col. ill.

Originally published as: THE ORCHARD BOOK OF STORIES FROM THE BALLET, Orchard, 1994.

Easy-to-read versions of ten well-known ballets, including "Swan Lake," "Petrouchka," and "Cinderella." Beautifully detailed period illustrations enrich the stories.
SUBJ: Ballets--Stories, plots, etc.

792.8   Ph-2 4-6/9 $13.99   T   KD697

SPATT, LESLIE E. Behind the scenes at the ballet: rehearsing and performing "The Sleeping Beauty." Viking ISBN 0-670-86162-6; In Canada: Penguin, 1995. 48p. col. ill.

Includes glossary and index.

The rigors of ballet are explored. Includes information on the rehearsals, costumes, makeup and scenery, all leading up to the performance of "The Sleeping Beauty." A beautiful book for browsing.
SUBJ: Ballet dancing./ Ballet dancers./ Sleeping Beauty (Ballet).

793   Ph-3 K-2/3 $14.93   L   KD698
COLE, JOANNA. Pin the tail on the donkey and other party games.
Compiled by Joanna Cole and Stephanie Calmenson. Illus. by Alan
Tiegreen. Morrow ISBN 0-688-11892-5, 1993. 48p. col. ill.
     Includes bibliography.
     Step-by-step instructions for classic party games such as "Musical
chairs," "Giant steps," and "Duck, duck, goose." Simple games to
use in classrooms as well as at home. (Parents' Shelf).
     SUBJ: Games./ Parties.

793   Ph-2 3-6 $20.00   L   KD699
COLE, JOANNA. Rain or shine activity book: fun things to make and
do. By Joanna Cole and Stephanie Calmenson. Illus. by Alan Tiegreen.
Morrow ISBN 0-688-12131-4; In Canada: Hearst Book Group, 1997.
192p. ill.
     Packed full of fun activities. Includes a variety of tongue twisters, card
games, riddles, jump rope rhymes, word games, brainteasers and
simple crafts.
     SUBJ: Amusements./ Games./ Handicraft.

VCR 793   Ph-2 P-1 $19.95   OD KD700
PALMER, HAP. Learning basic skills (Videocassette). Educational
Activities VS-005, 1986. 1/2" VHS videocassette color (25min).
     Includes song sheet and teacher's guide.
     Three humorous situations set into lively song and movement activities
are used to teach colors, numbers and letters. Young viewers can
participate with group shown on the videos if the necessary props
have been made. The songs have been selected from three earlier
Hap Palmer recordings, but the video is welcomed because of its easy
to use format.
     SUBJ: Color./ Number systems./ Alphabet.

793.2   Ph-3 3-6/5 $19.95   L   KD701
WEST, ROBIN. My very own Halloween: a book of cooking and crafts.
Illus. by Susan Slattery Burke. Photos by Robert L. and Diane Wolfe.
Carolrhoda ISBN 0-87614-725-2, 1993. 64p. col. ill. (My very own
holiday books).
     Includes glossary and index.
     Despite Halloween nomenclature, these classic recipes can be made
any season of the year. Easy-to-follow, tasty recipes fill a fun
cookbook interspersed with ghostly information and not-so-easy crafts.
     SUBJ: Halloween./ Cookery./ Parties.

VCR 793.3   Ph-3 K-2 $59.95   OD KD702
DANCE WITH US: A CREATIVE MOVEMENT VIDEO (Videocassette).
Sunburst 2468 ISBN 0-7805-4134-0, 1994. 1/2" VHS videocassette
color (25min).
     Includes teacher's guide.
     An introduction to creative movement will help students to increase
their motor skills, gain body coordination, and develop their creativity.
Six youngsters lead the exercises with exuberance and poise, worthy
of emulation.
     SUBJ: Dancing./ Motor ability./ Exercise.

SRC 793.3   Ph-3 3-6 $36.00   OD KD703
FOLK DANCES FOR CHILDREN (Sound recording cassette). Can-Ed
Media; In Canada: Can-Ed Media, 1985. 3 sound cassettes. (Folk
dances for children).
     Music and directions for folkdances from all over the world that will
be useful in extending social studies units or for physical education
classes.
     SUBJ: Folk dancing.

793.3   Ph-1 4-6/11 $16.98   L   KD704
MEDEARIS, ANGELA SHELF. Dance. By Angela Shelf Medearis and
Michael R. Medearis. Twenty-First Century ISBN 0-8050-4481-7; In
Canada: Fitzhenry & Whiteside, 1997. 80p. ill. (some col.). (African-
American arts).
     Includes bibliography and index.
     Traces the beginning of African-American dance from the expressive
dances of the slaves through the development of jazz, tap, and
ballet. Excellent for reports. Comprehensive, serious history for
multicultural studies.
     SUBJ: Afro-American dance--History./ Dance--History.

SRC 793.3   Ph-3 2-6 $10.95   OD KD705
STEWART, GEORGIANA. Folk dance fun: simple folk songs and dances
(Sound recording cassette). Kimbo KIM 7037C, 1984. 1 sound cassette.
     Encourages children to sing and dance along to popular folk songs
from many lands. Includes "Mexican Hat Dance," "Italian
Tarantella," "The Irish Jig," and "The American Virginia Reel." The
interior sleeve provides the directions for the dances and the lyrics for
the songs.
     SUBJ: Folk dancing.

793.4   Ph-3 P-K $13.88   L   KD706
COLE, JOANNA. Eentsy, weentsy spider: fingerplays and action rhymes.
Compiled by Joanna Cole and Stephanie Calmenson. Illus. by Alan
Tiegreen. Morrow ISBN 0-688-09439-2, 1991. 64p. col. ill.
     Includes music, bibliography and index.
     A delightful collection of 38 action rhymes and fingerplays with such
old favorites as "If you're happy and you know it," and "This old
man" as well as many less familiar ones. Fun for the youngest to
develop coordination as they learn to sing.
     SUBJ: Singing games./ Finger play.

793.4   Ph-1 P-1 $12.95   T   KD707
COOPER, KAY. Too many rabbits and other fingerplays about animals,
nature, weather, and the universe. Illus. by Judith Moffatt. Scholastic
ISBN 0-590-45564-8; In Canada: Scholastic, 1995. 46p. col. ill.
     "Cartwheel book."
     Wonderful fingerplays for the youngest set to help them appreciate
animals (rabbits, fireflies, frogs, owls, bears, and walrus), plants,
seasons, and weather. A joyful way to learn. Full-page cut-paper
illustrations add to the appeal. Scientific explanations are included
with each topic.
     SUBJ: Finger play./ Animals./ Botany./ Weather./ Astronomy.

VCR 793.4   Ph-2 P-K $19.95   OD KD708
HALLUM, ROSEMARY. Fingerplays and footplays (Videocassette). By
Rosemary Hallum and Henry "Buzz" Glass. Educational Activities VS
057, 1997. 1/2" VHS videocassette color (24min).
     Includes teacher's guide with lyrics.
     A multicultural group of teachers and students demonstrate nine fun-
filled activities that help develop coordination, concentration, and
listening skills. Audience participation activities that even the youngest
will enjoy.
     SUBJ: Finger play./ Singing games.

VCR 793.4   Ph-2 P-2 $9.98   KD709
LEWIS, SHARI. Let's play games (Videocassette). A&M Video ISBN
0-945338-65-1, 1994. 1/2" VHS videocassette color (30min). (Lamb
Chop's play-along!).
     Shari Lewis' peppy personality invites listeners to play along with
hilarious tunes and imaginative, educational activities. Filled with lively
songs and much enthusiasm. Will spark audience participation.
     SUBJ: Games./ Finger play./ Songs.

BA 793.4   Ph-3 P-1 $14.95   KD710
WEIMER, TONJA EVETTS. Fingerplays and action chants: volume 1:
animals. Pearce-Evetts Productions ISBN 0-936823-13-5, 1995. 1
paperback book, 1 sound cassette (20min).
     Sound recording cassette available (ISBN 0-936823-01-1, 1986). 1
sound cassette (20min), $8.95.
     Uses hand and small body movements to create amusing finger
games. Useful teaching device to encourage audience participation
and creative movement. (Parents' Shelf).
     FINGERPLAYS AND ACTION CHANTS, VOLUME 2 (ISBN
0-936823-14-3, 1996). 1 paperback book, 1 sound cassette (20min).
Also available on sound record cassette (ISBN 0-936823-03-8,
1986).
     SUBJ: Finger play./ Singing games./ Counting./ Nursery rhymes.

793.7   Ph-3 5-A $14.95   T   KD711
BLUM, RAYMOND. Mathemagic. Illus. by Jeff Sinclair. Sterling ISBN
0-8069-9783-4; In Canada: Sterling c/o Canadian Manda, 1997. 128p.
ill.
     Includes index.
     Tricks with calculators, cards, coins, and other devices to develop
memory and mathematical skills. For the fun loving, advanced student.
     SUBJ: Mathematical recreations.

793.7   Ph-3 3-6/6 $2.95   P   KD712
SACHAR, LOUIS. Sideways arithmetic from Wayside School. Apple/
Scholastic ISBN 0-590-45726-8, 1989. 89p.
     An amalgam of arithmetic and jokes purporting to be mathematics
lessons from the popular fictional Wayside School. Many of the
puzzles can be incorporated into traditional lessons for enrichment.
     SUBJ: Mathematical recreations.

793.7   Ph-2 4-A/4 $10.95   P   KD713
WYLER, ROSE. Math fun with a pocket calculator. By Rose Wyler and
Mary Elting. Illus. by G. Brian Karas. Messner ISBN 0-671-74309-0,
1992. 63p. ill. (Math fun).
     Includes index.
     Playing tricks and games with a pocket calculator can make you
appear to be a mathematical wizard.
     SUBJ: Mathematical recreations./ Calculators.

793.7   Ph-2 4-A/5 $5.95   P   KD714
WYLER, ROSE. Math fun with tricky lines and shapes. By Rose Wyler
and Mary Elting. Illus. by Paul Harvey. Messner ISBN 0-671-74316-3,
1992. 64p. ill. (Math fun).
> Includes index.
> Puzzles, games, and magic tricks which explore geometrical concepts.
> Fun to enrich math lessons or to fascinate puzzle fans.
> SUBJ: Mathematical recreations./ Geometry.

793.73   Ph-3 P-2 $12.95   L   KD715
WICK, WALTER. I spy Christmas: a book of picture riddles. Photos by
Walter Wick. Riddles by Jean Marzollo. Scholastic ISBN 0-590-45846-9;
In Canada: Scholastic, 1992. 37p. col. ill. (I spy books).
> "Cartwheel books."
> Search for hidden objects in these large photographs of Christmas
> items. Encourages the writing of rhyming picture riddles and other
> activities. Puzzle lovers will enjoy the challenge.
> SUBJ: Picture puzzles./ Christmas--Miscellanea.

793.73   Ph-3 K-3/3 $12.95   T   KD716
WICK, WALTER. I spy fantasy: a book of picture riddles. Photos by
Walter Wick. Riddles by Jean Marzollo. Scholastic ISBN 0-590-46295-4;
In Canada: Scholastic, 1994. 37p. col. ill. (I spy books).
> "Cartwheel books."
> A variety of objects are used in elaborate photographs to inspire
> rhyming, riddle making, visual creativity, and, of course, to create the
> challenge of the hunt for the "I Spy puzzles." Great fun for the
> reader as he/she tries to locate the well hidden objects.
> SUBJ: Picture puzzles.

793.73   Ph-3 K-3/3 $12.95   T   KD717
WICK, WALTER. I spy school days: a book of picture riddles. Photos by
Walter Wick. Riddles by Jean Marzollo. Scholastic ISBN 0-590-48135-5;
In Canada: Scholastic, 1995. 37p. col. ill. (I spy books).
> "Cartwheel books."
> Poring over these puzzles will increase powers of observation and
> provide many fun-filled moments. Encourages children to create their
> own riddles.
> SUBJ: Picture puzzles.

793.73   Ph-2 P-3/5 $12.95   T   KD718
WICK, WALTER. I spy spooky night: a book of picture riddles. Photos
by Walter Wick. Riddles by Jean Marzollo. Scholastic ISBN 0-590-
48137-1; In Canada: Scholastic, 1996. 35p. col. ill. (I spy books).
> "Cartwheel books."
> A search for hidden objects in each spooky picture will sharpen
> powers of observation. A challenge for all puzzle lovers.
> SUBJ: Picture puzzles.

793.734   Ph-3 3-6 $12.21   L   KD719
AGEE, JON. So many dynamos!: and other palindromes. Farrar Straus
Giroux ISBN 0-374-22473-0; In Canada: HarperCollins, 1994. unp. ill.
> More amazing and astounding palindromes--words, phrases, and
> sentences that read the same backward and forward. Challenging
> language pattern for creative writing activities.
> SUBJ: Palindromes.

793.734   Ph-2 1-4 $15.95   T   KD720
BOURKE, LINDA. Eye spy: a mysterious alphabet. Chronicle ISBN
0-87701-805-7, 1991. unp. col. ill.
> An unusual alphabet book in which a two-tiered guessing game is
> accompanied by glowing illustrations. Each doublespread presents a
> letter of the alphabet and a puzzle which contains a clue to the
> puzzle on the following page. Readers discover the answers through
> visual detective work. Fun picture puzzles useful to introduce the
> concepts of homonyms and homophones.
> SUBJ: Alphabet./ Word games.

793.734   Ph-2 3-6 $9.88   L   KD721
JUSTER, NORTON. Otter nonsense. Illus. by Michael Witte. Morrow
ISBN 0-688-12283-3, 1994. unp. col. ill. (Books of wonder).
> A delightful collection of outrageous animal puns is accompanied by
> hilarious illustrations. This small-sized book will enchant punsters.
> SUBJ: Animals--Wit and humor./ Puns and punning.

793.735   Ph-2 3-6 $12.95   T   KD722
ADLER, DAVID A. Calculator riddles. Illus. by Cynthia Fisher. Holiday
House ISBN 0-8234-1186-9, 1995. unp. ill.
> Provides delightful fun as answers to riddles are revealed while
> solving math problems on a calculator. After mastering the patterns,
> students will enjoy creating their own riddle problems.
> SUBJ: Calculators./ Riddles./ Mathematical recreations.

793.735   Ph-2 K-3 $14.95   L   KD723
ADLER, DAVID A. Easy math puzzles. Illus. by Cynthia Fisher. Holiday
House ISBN 0-8234-1283-0, 1997. unp. ill.
> Easy math puzzles that will enrich math lessons and will be fun for
> those who are not lovers of arithmetic.
> SUBJ: Riddles./ Mathematical recreations.

793.735   Ph-2 3-6 $12.95   T   KD724
ARTELL, MIKE. Wackiest nature riddles on earth. Sterling ISBN 0-8069-
1250-2; In Canada: Sterling c/o Canadian Manda, 1992. 96p. ill.
> Includes glossary and index.
> A collection of riddles devoted to ecological and environmental issues
> such as deserts, jungles, water, animals, and weather.
> SUBJ: Riddles./ Ecology--Wit and humor.

793.735   Ph-1 2-4 $19.95   L   KD725
BIXENMAN, JUDY. Dinosaur jokes. Written and compiled by Judy
Bixenman. Illus. by Viki Woodworth. Child's World ISBN 0-89565-728-7,
1991. 32p. col. ill.
> Silly jokes and ridiculous illustrations about dinosaurs will tickle the
> funny bone.
> SUBJ: Dinosaurs--Wit and humor./ Jokes./ Riddles.

793.735   Ph-2 3-6 $4.95   P   KD726
COLE, RONNY M. Zany knock knocks. Illus. by Rich Garramone.
Sterling ISBN 0-8069-8589-5; In Canada: dist. by Sterling c/o Canadian
Manda, 1993. 96p. ill.
> Includes index.
> An alphabetical arrangement of knock-knock jokes designed to tickle
> the funny bone.
> SUBJ: Knock-knock jokes./ Jokes.

793.735   Ph-3 2-5 $11.95   L   KD727
GORDON, JEFFIE ROSS. Hide and shriek: riddles about ghosts and
goblins. Illus. by Susan Slattery Burke. Lerner ISBN 0-8225-2336-1,
1991. unp. col. ill.
> Riddles about ghosts and goblins such as "What do witches do when
> they are tired? They stop for a spell."
> SUBJ: Ghosts--Wit and humor./ Riddles.

793.735   Ph-3 K-3 $11.99   T   KD728
HALL, KATY. Batty riddles. By Katy Hall and Lisa Eisenberg. Illus. by
Nicole Rubel. Dial ISBN 0-8037-1217-0, 1993. 48p. col. ill. (Dial easy-
to-read).
> Some riddles about bats are accompanied by delightfully funny full-
> page illustrations. "Why did the little bat use mouthwash?" "She
> had bat breath."
> SUBJ: Bats--Wit and humor./ Riddles.

793.735   Ph-2 2-4/5 $13.93   L   KD729
HARTMAN, VICTORIA. Silliest joke book ever. Illus. by R.W. Alley.
Lothrop, Lee & Shepard ISBN 0-688-10110-0, 1993. unp. col. ill.
> A plethora of wacky wordplays certain to cause laughter. (e.g.,
> "What bunny gives out parking tickets? Meter Rabbit.") Comical
> watercolor drawings add to the fun.
> SUBJ: Riddles./ Jokes.

793.735   Ph-2 2-4 $13.88   L   KD730
KESSLER, LEONARD. Old Turtle's 90 knock-knocks, jokes, and riddles.
Greenwillow ISBN 0-688-09586-0, 1991. 48p. col. ill.
> An amusing collection of knock-knocks, riddles and jokes,
> accompanied by silly, colorful illustrations of Old Turtle and his
> menagerie of cohorts.
> SUBJ: Knock-knock jokes./ Jokes./ Riddles./ Animals--Wit and humor.

793.735   Ph-3 3-A $12.95   P   KD731
LAUGHING TOGETHER: GIGGLES AND GRINS FROM AROUND THE
GLOBE. Compiled by Barbara K. Walker with everybody else's help.
Designed and illus. by Simms Taback. Free Spirit ISBN 0-915793-37-7,
c1977, 1992. 108p. ill.
> Includes index.
> An international collection of snickers and funnies, of goons and
> goofs, of tricks and teases collected from nearly 100 countries around
> the world. Compiled in cooperation with the United States Committee
> for the United Nations International Children's Emergency Fund
> (UNICEF), some of the original humor such as word play and puns
> are lost in translation. Fun resource for multicultural studies.
> SUBJ: Jokes./ Wit and humor.

793.735   Ph-2 2-5 $8.95   L   KD732
LEVINE, CAROLINE ANNE. Riddles to tell your cat. Illus. by Meyer
Seltzer. Whitman ISBN 0-8075-7006-0; In Canada: General Publishing,
1992. unp. col. ill.
> Funny feline jokes, riddles, and tales destined to be read joyously by

cat lovers.
SUBJ: Cats--Wit and humor./ Riddles./ Jokes.

793.735   Ph-3 3-6 $14.00   L   KD733
LIGHTNING INSIDE YOU AND OTHER NATIVE AMERICAN RIDDLES.
Edited by John Bierhorst. Illus. by Louise Brierley. Morrow ISBN 0-688-09582-8, 1992. 104p. ill.
Includes bibliography.
Traditional Native American riddles which deal with courtship, animals, the human body, things that grow, and things made to be used. Excellent resource material for multicultural studies.
SUBJ: Riddles./ Indians--Humor./ Indians--Folklore.

793.735   Ph-2 2-6 $14.89   L   KD734
MAESTRO, MARCO. Riddle City, USA!: a book of geography riddles. By Marco and Giulio Maestro. HarperCollins ISBN 0-06-023369-9; In Canada: HarperCollins, 1994. 64p. col. ill., map.
Riddles and geographical facts are combined to incite laughter and provide information. "How scared is the forest in Arizona?" "It's petrified."
SUBJ: Riddles./ United States--Geography--Miscellanea.

793.735   Ph-2 2-6 $8.95   L   KD735
MATHEWS, JUDITH. Oh, how waffle!: riddles you can eat. By Judith Mathews and Fay Robinson. Illus. by Carl Whiting. Whitman ISBN 0-8075-5907-5; In Canada: General Publishing, 1993. unp. col. ill.
Food oriented jokes and riddles will provoke guffaws from humor lovers (e.g., "What did the monster eat after its teeth were cleaned? The dentist.")
SUBJ: Riddles./ Jokes./ Eating customs--Wit and humor./ Food--Wit and humor.

793.735   Ph-2 3-6 $12.99   L   KD736
PHILLIPS, LOUIS. Keep 'em laughing: jokes to amuse and annoy your friends. Illus. by Michael Chesworth. Viking ISBN 0-670-86009-3; In Canada: Penguin, 1996. 60p. ill.
Some very funny jokes, knock-knocks, puns, and riddles designed to keep them rolling in the aisles.
SUBJ: Wit and humor./ Riddles./ Jokes.

793.735   Ph-2 3-6 $12.95   L   KD737
PLANET OF THE GRAPES: SHOW BIZ JOKES AND RIDDLES. Compiled by Charles Keller. Illus. by Mischa Richter. Pippin ISBN 0-945912-17-X, 1992. unp. ill.
A collection of show biz guffaws, "What's round, purple and orbits the sun? The Planet of the Grapes." Riddles refer to popular movies, television shows, sports, and other performing arts.
SUBJ: Performing arts--Wit and humor./ Jokes./ Riddles.

793.735   Ph-3 3-5 $13.95   L   KD738
RIDDLE-ME RHYMES. Selected by Myra Cohn Livingston. Illus. by Rebecca Perry. McElderry ISBN 0-689-50602-3; In Canada: Maxwell Macmillan, 1994. 90p. ill.
Includes indexes.
Culled from literature from around the world, these examples illustrate how timeless riddles are. For advanced readers who still delight in puzzles and mind-benders.
SUBJ: Riddles./ Poetry--Collections.

793.735   Ph-2 3-6 $13.50   L   KD739
SWANSON, JUNE. Summit up: riddles about mountains. Illus. by Susan Slattery Burke. Lerner ISBN 0-8225-2342-6, 1994. unp. col. ill. (You must be joking).
A small book filled with funny riddles about mountains is accompanied by amusing line drawings. Certain to provoke snickers from joke lovers.
SUBJ: Mountains--Wit and humor./ Riddles./ Jokes.

793.735   Ph-2 3-6 $12.95   L   KD740
TAKE ME TO YOUR LITER: SCIENCE AND MATH JOKES. Compiled by Charles Keller. Illus. by Gregory Filling. Pippin ISBN 0-945912-13-7, 1991. unp. ill.
Hilarious science and math jokes. Great fun for enlivening lessons or for browsing by joke lovers.
SUBJ: Science--Wit and humor./ Mathematics--Wit and humor./ Jokes./ Riddles.

793.735   Ph-3 2-4 $10.95   T   KD741
THALER, MIKE. Earth mirth: the ecology riddle book. Illus. by Rick Brown. W. H. Freeman ISBN 0-7167-6521-7, 1994. unp. col. ill.
"Scientific American books for young readers."
"Silly science."
Full-page illustrations highlight amusing riddles devoted to the Earth and its environment. Use to instill humor into environmental studies

units.
SUBJ: Ecology--Wit and humor./ Riddles./ Jokes.

793.735   Ph-1 2-4 $19.95   L   KD742
WOODWORTH, VIKI. Animal jokes. Compiled and illus. by Viki Woodworth. Child's World ISBN 0-89565-861-5, 1993. 31p. col. ill.
A collection of very funny animal jokes is accompanied by hilarious cartoon illustrations. Includes such groaners as "Why did one elephant hate his trip to Mexico?" "Because the airline sent his trunk to Spain."
SUBJ: Animals--Wit and humor./ Jokes./ Riddles.

793.735   Ph-1 2-4 $19.95   L   KD743
WOODWORTH, VIKI. Fairy tale jokes. Compiled and illus. by Viki Woodworth. Child's World ISBN 0-89565-862-3, 1993. 31p. col. ill.
The combination of ludicrous illustrations and amusing jokes about fairy-tale characters will produce howls of laughter. "What does the Big Bad Wolf eat in a restaurant?" "The waiter."
SUBJ: Fairy tales--Wit and humor./ Jokes./ Riddles.

793.8   Ph-2 4-6 $12.95   T   KD744
BROWN, DAVE. Amazing magic tricks. By Dave Brown and Paul Reeve. DK Publishing ISBN 1-56458-877-7, 1995. 48p. col. ill.
Large, colorful photographs illustrate 20 magic tricks. Directions are easy to follow and the equipment used is easily obtained. Great fun for budding magicians.
SUBJ: Magic tricks.

793.8   Ph-2 4-A/7 $13.95   L   KD745
COBB, VICKI. Bet you can!: science possibilities to fool you. By Vicki Cobb and Kathy Darling. Illus. by Stella Ormai. Lothrop, Lee & Shepard ISBN 0-688-09865-7, 1990. 112p. ill.
Includes index.
Scientific facts about the human body, matter, and energy help to solve over 60 puzzles. Although adult supervision is sometimes needed, these tricks are certain to amaze onlookers.
SUBJ: Science--Experiments./ Scientific recreations./ Experiments.

793.8   Ph-3 4-6/6 $14.00   L   KD746
COBB, VICKI. Wanna bet?: science challenges to fool you. By Vicki Cobb and Kathy Darling. Illus. by Meredith Johnson. Lothrop, Lee & Shepard ISBN 0-688-11213-7, 1993. 128p. ill.
Includes index.
Scientific tricks are described. Learn how to lose weight in one second or stop a spinning egg. Great for enlivening science lessons.
SUBJ: Scientific recreations./ Magic tricks.

793.8   Ph-2 3-6 $9.95   P   KD747
DAY, JON. Let's make magic. Illus. by Chris Fisher. Kingfisher ISBN 1-85697-806-0, 1992. 96p. col. ill.
The art of deception is inherent in the 11 magic tricks presented with step-by-step directions. Comic book style illustrations are fun and easy-to-follow.
SUBJ: Magic tricks.

793.8   Ph-3 4-A/6 $9.95   L   KD748
OXLADE, CHRIS. Science magic with air. Barron's ISBN 0-8120-6444-5; In Canada: Barron's, 1994. 30p. col. ill. (Science magic).
Includes glossary and index.
Eleven magic tricks based on the scientific principle that air can be squeezed, expanded, and moved around--thus becoming a prop in a magic show. Good for teachers who want to enliven science lessons and for motivated students who have the patience to prepare these tricks.
SUBJ: Magic tricks./ Air--Experiments./ Scientific recreations.

793.8   Ph-2 3-6/5 $9.95   T   KD749
OXLADE, CHRIS. Science magic with light. Barron's ISBN 0-8120-6445-3; In Canada: Barron's, 1994. 30p. col. ill. (Science magic).
First published in Great Britain, Watts, 1993.
Includes glossary and index.
Colorful pictures show young magicians conjuring up tricks based on light--refraction, reflection, and optical illusions. Directions are easy to follow, although adult help is often needed. Fun for science classes as well.
SUBJ: Magic tricks./ Light./ Scientific recreations.

793.8   Ph-2 3-6/6 $10.95   T   KD750
OXLADE, CHRIS. Science magic with magnets. Barron's ISBN 0-8120-6501-8; In Canada: Barron's, 1995. 30p. col. ill.
Includes glossary and index.
Create magnetic performances with mysterious magic tricks. Easy-to-follow pictorial directions explain how to perform the tricks and the science behind each one. Fun to use when teaching magnetism.
SUBJ: Magic tricks./ Magnets./ Scientific recreations.

793.8 Ph-2 3-6/5 $10.95 L KD751
OXLADE, CHRIS. Science magic with shapes and materials. Barron's ISBN 0-8120-6518-2; In Canada: Barron's, 1995. 30p. col. ill. (Science magic).
First published in Great Britain, Watts, 1994.
Includes glossary and index.
Ten magic tricks with easy-to-follow directions demonstrate the effects of freezing or boiling water and the use of friction. Fun projects that can be used in magic shows or in science lessons.
SUBJ: Magic tricks./ Form perception./ Scientific recreations.

VCR 793.8 Ph-3 3-6 $19.95 OD KD752
RAY, JOEL. Fun magic with things around the house (Videocassette). Video Specialties, 1995. 1/2" VHS videocassette color (30min).
"Laughing Boy Entertainment production."
Includes public performance rights.
Great magic tricks are revealed by Joel Ray, an unassuming professional magician. Props are easy to find around the house. Budding magicians will find this full of fun.
SUBJ: Magic tricks.

793.9 Ph-3 K-6 $8.95 T KD753
WEBB, PHILA H. Shadowgraphs anyone can make. By Phila H. Webb and Jane Corby. Running Press ISBN 1-56138-014-8, 1991. unp. ill.
For lovers of shadowplay, this is the ultimate book. The easy-to-follow directions first appeared in the 1927 classic edition. Creative performers will enjoy bringing animals and objects to life.
SUBJ: Shadow pictures.

CDR 794 Ph-1 3-A $39.95 OD KD754
STRATEGY CHALLENGES COLLECTION 1: AROUND THE WORLD. School version (CD-ROM). Edmark 702-1069, 1995. 1 CD-ROM color. (Strategy series).
Version 1.03.
Includes teacher's guide.
System requirements: System 7.0.1 or higher; 68040, 68030 (25 MHz or faster recommended), or PowerPC; 8MB memory (RAM), 4200K unused; 13" or larger monitor, 256 or more colors; double-speed or faster CD-ROM drive; TouchWindow (optional).
System requirements: Windows 3.1, Windows 95 or later; 486, Pentium or better (33 MHz or faster recommended); hard drive with 5MB free; 8MB memory (RAM); Super VGA graphics, 640x480, 256 colors; double-speed or faster CD-ROM drive; Windows-compatible sound card; TouchWindow (optional).
Product (702-1069) runs on either Windows or Macintosh compatible hardware.
Students can play one of three games--nine men's Morris, go-moku, and mancala--with this program. Each game has three levels of difficulty, and game progress can be saved for continuation at a later time. Users can play against either the computer or a friend. Excellent practice for critical thinking and problem solving skills.
SUBJ: Educational games--Software./ Software--Educational games./ Software--Problem solving./ Problem solving--Software./ Thought and thinking--Software./ Software--Thought and thinking./ Interactive media.

CDR 794 Ph-1 4-A $39.95 OD KD755
STRATEGY CHALLENGES COLLECTION 2: IN THE WILD. School version (CD-ROM). Edmark 702-1072, 1996. 1 CD-ROM color. (Strategy series).
Version 1.01.
Includes teacher's guide.
System requirements: Windows 3.1, Windows 95 or later; 486, Pentium or better (33 MHz or faster recommended); hard disk with 5MB free; 8MB memory (RAM); Super VGA graphics, 640x480, 256 colors; double-speed or faster CD-ROM drive; Windows-compatible sound card; TouchWindow (optional).
System requirements: System 7.0.1 or higher; 68040, 68030 (25 MHz or faster recommended), or PowerPC; 8MB memory (RAM), 4200K unused; 13" or larger monitor, 256 or more colors; double-speed or faster CD-ROM drive; TouchWindow (optional).
Product (702-1072) runs on either Windows or Macintosh compatible hardware.
Students can play one of three games--tablut, jungle chess, or surakarta--with this program. Each game has three levels of difficulty, and game progress can be saved for continuation at a later time. Users can play against either the computer or a friend. Excellent practice for critical thinking and problem solving skills.
SUBJ: Educational games--Software./ Software--Educational games./ Problem solving--Software./ Software--Problem solving./ Thought and thinking--Software./ Software--Thought and thinking./ Interactive media.

794.1 Ph-2 4-A/8 $14.95 T KD756
NOTTINGHAM, TED. Chess for children. By Ted Nottingham, Bob Wade and Al Lawrence. Sterling ISBN 0-8069-0452-6; In Canada: dist. by Sterling c/o Canadian Manda, 1993. 126p. ill.
Includes glossary and index.
A new way to teach chess, the Lincolnshire system, is employed to explain the rules and strategies of this international game. Captioned photographs illuminate the game while text clearly gives the rationale for every move. Thorough, easy-to-follow manual.
SUBJ: Chess.

794.8 Ph-3 3-6/8 $16.95 L KD757
SKURZYNSKI, GLORIA. Know the score: video games in your high-tech world. Bradbury ISBN 0-02-782922-7; In Canada: Maxwell Macmillan, 1994. 64p. col. ill. (Your high-tech world).
Includes glossary and index.
Describes how to develop a video game--from its inception to its maintenance. Conveys the creativity behind video games and the people who are involved in the design, production and marketing of the program. Good for browsing by computer buffs as well as for background information for reports. Use in career studies to introduce high-tech job opportunities.
SUBJ: Video games./ Games.

795.4 Ph-3 3-6/3 $14.93 L KD758
COLE, JOANNA. Crazy eights and other card games. By Joanna Cole and Stephanie Calmenson. Illus. by Alan Tiegreen. Morrow ISBN 0-688-12200-0, 1994. 76p. ill.
Includes bibliography.
Clear, step-by-step instructions introduce a variety of card games ranging from "Go fish" and "Old maid" to "Rummy" and "Poker." These twenty card games will provide activity for rainy days, sharpen memory skills, and serve as the basis for family fun.
SUBJ: Card games./ Games.

796 Ph-3 4-A/7 $17.71 L KD759
BROWN, FERN G. Special Olympics. Watts ISBN 0-531-20062-0; In Canada: Watts, 1992. 64p. col. ill. (First book).
Includes glossary and index.
Traces the history of the Special Olympics and explains the organization, volunteer programs, and goals of the competition.
SUBJ: Special Olympics.

796 Ph-2 4-6/9 $21.95 L KD760
DINN, SHEILA. Hearts of gold: a celebration of Special Olympics and its heroes. Foreword by Eunice Kennedy Shriver. Blackbirch ISBN 1-56711-163-7, 1996. 96p. col. ill.
Includes chronology, glossary, bibliography and index.
Focuses on the Special Olympics in which mentally and physically challenged athletes compete. Includes the history, various events, and information on the people whose efforts have made the Special Olympics a reality. For units on persons with disabilities.
SUBJ: Special Olympics./ Athletes./ Handicapped.

796 Ph-2 4-A/8 $15.00 T KD761
HAMMOND, TIM. Sports. Knopf ISBN 0-394-89616-5, 1988. 64p. col. ill. (Eyewitness books).
Includes index.
Offers a veritable fountain of facts on a variety of sports, such as the popular soccer, ice hockey, football, but also includes table tennis, pool, snooker, and the martial arts. Sports enthusiasts will find a wealth of information here, and the pictorial format with concise facts will tempt those who are not sports fans into some casual browsing.
SUBJ: Sports.

796 Ph-3 5-6/6 $14.98 L KD762
JENNINGS, JAY. Long shots: they beat the odds. Silver Burdett ISBN 0-382-24105-3, 1990. 58p. col. ill. (Sports triumphs).
Includes index.
Using bright dramatic photographs and smooth text, the author demonstrates to readers that height, illness, and physical handicaps can't hold back a gifted, determined athlete. The sports enthusiast will enjoy this book and gain understanding of how one can make it in a difficult field in spite of many problems.
SUBJ: Athletes./ New York Mets (Baseball team)./ Abbott, Jim./ Webb, Spud./ Rudolph, Wilma./ Muldowney, Shirley.

796 Ph-2 4-6/7 $17.98 L KD763
LINDOP, LAURIE. Athletes. Twenty-First Century ISBN 0-8050-4167-2; In Canada: Fitzhenry & Whiteside, 1996. 128p. col. ill. (Dynamic modern women).
Includes bibliography and index.
Ten brief biographies of famous women athletes who have succeeded despite many obstacles. Includes sprinter Florence Griffith Joyner,

golfer Nancy Lopez, tennis star Monica Seles, and skater Kristi Yamaguchi. Good for inspirational reading and for reports.
SUBJ: Athletes./ Women athletes.

796   Ph-1 4-6/12 $15.95 T KD764
MACY, SUE. Winning ways: a photohistory of American women in sports. Henry Holt ISBN 0-8050-4147-8; In Canada: Fitzhenry & Whiteside, 1996. 217p. ill.
Includes chronology, bibliography, directory and index.
A fascinating account of the struggle of American women to compete fully in sports. Captures the highlights and turning points in the lives of women athletes as they triumphed in their respective fields.
SUBJ: Women athletes--History./ Sports--History.

796   Ph-3 2-4/3 $3.99 P KD765
O'CONNOR, JIM. Comeback!: four true stories. Illus. by Jim Campbell. Random House ISBN 0-679-82661-1; In Canada: Random House, 1992. 48p. col. ill. (Step into reading).
Follows the careers of four superstar athletes: runner Wilma Rudolph, baseball pitcher Catfish Hunter, gymnast Bart Conner, and biker Greg LeMond as they fight valiantly to triumph over serious injuries and debilitating conditions.
SUBJ: Athletes--Wounds and injuries.

796.1   Ph-2 2-5 $11.88 L KD766
MISS MARY MACK AND OTHER CHILDREN'S STREET RHYMES. Compiled by Joanna Cole and Stephanie Calmenson. Illus. by Alan Tiegreen. Morrow ISBN 0-688-08330-7, 1990. 64p. ill.
Includes bibliography and index.
Traditional ball bouncing rhymes, teases, and taunts, collected from street games of yesteryear, but fun to apply today.
SUBJ: Games./ Nursery rhymes./ Jump rope rhymes./ Counting rhymes./ Poetry--Collections.

BA 796.1   Ph-2 K-4 $9.95 KD767
SHAKE IT TO THE ONE THAT YOU LOVE THE BEST: PLAY SONGS AND LULLABIES FROM BLACK MUSICAL TRADITIONS. Collected and adapted by Cheryl Warren Mattox. Warren-Mattox Productions/dist. by JTG of Nashville, 1989. 1 paperback book, 1 sound cassette (43min).
Paperback book available (ISBN 0-9623381-0-9, 1989), $6.95.
Twenty-six play songs and lullabies reflect the African-American experience. The accompanying book has outstanding illustrations which recreate everyday life using bold colors and page borders designed to represent African cloth patterns. An excellent addition to African-American studies and music appreciation lessons. Includes musical scores.
SUBJ: Singing games./ Lullabies./ Folk songs./ Afro-Americans--Songs and music.

SRC 796.1   Ph-2 P-2 $10.95 OD KD768
STEWART, GEORGIANA. Multicultural rhythm stick fun (Sound recording cassette). Kimbo KIM 9128C, 1992. 1 sound cassette (32min).
Includes activities and lyrics guide.
Compact disc available KIM 9128CD, 1992. 1 compact disc (32min), $14.95.
The music of various countries such as Puerto Rico, West Africa, and Israel form the background for a variety of movement activities using rhythm sticks. The movements can be accompanied by clapping hands when rhythm sticks are unavailable. Good for developing memory skills and coordination as well as an appreciation for the music of many cultures.
SUBJ: Singing games./ Rhythm./ Songs./ Ethnic groups--Music.

796.2   Ph-2 2-5/6 $17.90 L KD769
ERLBACH, ARLENE. Sidewalk games around the world. Illus. by Sharon Lane Holm. Millbrook ISBN 0-7613-0008-2, 1997. 64p. col. ill.
Includes index and bibliography.
Explains the rules for sidewalk games played by children in 26 countries. Background information on each country can be integrated into multicultural studies.
SUBJ: Games.

796.2   Ph-2 3-6/10 $15.93 L KD770
LANKFORD, MARY D. Jacks around the world. Illus. by Karen Dugan. Morrow ISBN 0-688-13708-3, 1996. 40p. col. ill., map.
Includes bibliography and index.
A lively collection of jacks type games as they are played in countries around the world, including Zimbabwe, New Zealand, and Brazil. Directions are clear and easy to follow. A good resource for teachers who want to enliven multicultural studies.
SUBJ: Jacks (Game)./ Games.

796.21   Ph-2 3-6/6 $15.95 T KD771
EDWARDS, CHRIS. Young inline skater. DK Publishing ISBN 0-7894-1124-5, 1996. 37p. col. ill.
Includes glossary, index and directory.
Colorful pictures and brief text introduce young people to the world of inline skating. Young rollerbladers learn about warm-up exercises, equipment, strokes and slides, stopping, turning, and falling safely. Fun for the neophyte and for the expert.
SUBJ: In-line skating.

796.21   Ph-2 3-6/6 $6.95 P KD772
MAYO, TERRY. Illustrated rules of in-line hockey. Illus. by Ned Butterfield. Ideals Children's Books ISBN 1-57102-064-0, 1996. 32p. col. ill.
Includes glossary.
An easy-to-follow format explains the rules, the players' positions, and sportsmanship involved in the game. A basic sports book good for hockey lovers and reluctant readers.
SUBJ: Roller hockey./ Hockey.

796.21   Ph-2 4-6/5 $13.99 T KD773
SULLIVAN, GEORGE. In-line skating: a complete guide for beginners. Cobblehill/Dutton ISBN 0-525-65124-1, 1993. 48p. col. ill.
Includes glossary.
A guide to the sport of the 90's--in-line skating. Discusses its appeal, selection of skates, safety equipment, techniques, and tips on skating smart. Fun for skaters and for those who dream of owning in-line skates someday.
SUBJ: In-line skating.

796.3   Ph-3 4-6/8 $13.95 L KD774
SANDELSON, ROBERT. Ball sports. Crestwood House ISBN 0-89686-664-5, 1991. 48p. col. ill.
Includes glossary, bibliography and index.
Focuses on the great teams that have competed in the Olympic Games in the ball sports of tennis, soccer, field hockey, handball, basketball, and volleyball. Covers both male and female athletes.
SUBJ: Ball games./ Olympics.

796.323   Ph-2 4-6/7 $14.95 L KD775
KELLY, J. Superstars of women's basketball. Chelsea House ISBN 0-7910-4389-4, 1997. 64p. ill. (Female sports stars).
Includes bibliography and index.
Discusses the perseverance and diligence of stars of women's basketball. Includes historical as well as contemporary players and mentions the new professional women's basketball leagues.
SUBJ: Basketball players./ Women basketball players.

796.323   Ph-2 3-6/4 $14.95 L KD776
KNAPP, RON. Top 10 basketball centers. Enslow ISBN 0-89490-515-5, 1994. 48p. col. ill. (Sports top 10).
Includes index.
Gives career statistics and brief biographies of ten top basketball centers. Not enough in-depth information for reports, but photographs and star quality will make it a delight for browsers and reluctant readers.
SUBJ: Basketball players.

796.323   Ph-2 3-6/4 $14.95 L KD777
KNAPP, RON. Top 10 basketball scorers. Enslow ISBN 0-89490-516-3, 1994. 48p. col. ill. (Sports top 10).
Includes index.
Brief biographies of some of the greatest basketball stars are accompanied by full-page color photographs and statistics. Great fun for browsers and reluctant readers.
SUBJ: Basketball players.

796.323   Ph-3 4-A $14.95 P KD778
MANLEY, MARTIN. Martin Manley's basketball heaven. Doubleday, 1987-. ill. annual.
Statistical and factual information on basketball teams and players. This annual has a wealth of information for all basketball devotees.
SUBJ: Basketball.

796.323   Ph-2 5-6/6 $16.95 T KD779
VANCIL, MARK. NBA basketball basics. Sterling ISBN 0-8069-0927-7; In Canada: Sterling c/o Canadian Manda, 1995. 128p. col. ill.
Includes glossary and index.
An official National Basketball Association guide to playing basketball presents practice sessions with sequential color snapshots and photographs of sports stars in action. A wealth of information for basketball fans. Appealing format with excellent photographs.
SUBJ: Basketball.

796.323 Ph-2 5-6/10 $19.95 L KD780
WILKER, JOSH. Harlem Globetrotters. Chelsea House ISBN 0-7910-2585-3, 1997. 133p. ill. (African-American achievers).
Includes chronology, bibliography and index.
Discusses the exciting brand of basketball practiced by the Harlem Globetrotters. Includes information on the history of the team, the great games in which they participated, and their stars. Emphasis is on the team as performers as well as players. For multicultural studies.
SUBJ: Harlem Globetrotters./ Basketball players./ Afro-Americans--Biography.

796.323 Ph-1 3-6/4 $21.34 L KD781
WITHERS, TOM. Basketball. Illus. by Art Seiden. Photos by Mary Pat Boron. Raintree Steck-Vaughn ISBN 0-8114-5779-6, 1994. 48p. col. ill. (How to play the all-star way).
"Arvid Knudsen book."
Includes glossary, bibliography and index.
Introduces the sport of basketball with information on physical conditioning, equipment, shooting, passing, dribbling, and team positions.
SUBJ: Basketball.

796.332 Ph-1 4-A/7 $13.95 L KD782
ANDERSON, DAVE. Story of football. Morrow ISBN 0-688-05634-2, 1985. 196p b&w photos.
Includes index.
Available from National Library Service for the Blind and Physically Handicapped in Braille BR06512.
Explores the world of football--its history, fundamentals, and exciting moments. This comprehensive account enthusiastically explains the popularity of this American spectacle.
SUBJ: Football--History.

796.332 Ph-2 3-6/4 $14.95 L KD783
LACE, WILLIAM W. Top 10 football quarterbacks. Enslow ISBN 0-89490-518-X, 1994. 48p. col. ill. (Sports top 10).
Includes index.
Provides brief biographies and statistics of ten well-know quarterbacks. Highlights contemporary as well as retired players. Browsing title for armchair quarterbacks and good for reluctant readers.
SUBJ: Football players./ National Football League.

796.332 Ph-2 3-6/4 $14.95 L KD784
LACE, WILLIAM W. Top 10 football rushers. Enslow ISBN 0-89490-519-8, 1994. 48p. col. ill. (Sports top 10).
Includes index.
Brief biographies of ten of the all-time great football stars are accompanied by full-page color photographs and statistics. High interest for browsers and reluctant readers.
SUBJ: Football players./ National Football League.

796.332 Ph-1 3-6/4 $21.34 L KD785
RAFFO, DAVE. Football. Illus. by Art Seiden. Photos by Cliff Ginsburg. Raintree Steck-Vaughn ISBN 0-8114-5780-X, 1994. 48p. col. ill. (How to play the all-star way).
"Arvid Knudsen book."
Includes glossary, bibliography and index.
How to play the game of football with information on playing positions, techinques for offense and defense, kicking, and tackling.
SUBJ: Football.

796.332 Ph-2 K-2/2 $14.95 T KD786
SAMPSON, MICHAEL. Football that won... Illus. by Ted Rand. Henry Holt ISBN 0-8050-3504-4; In Canada: Fitzhenry & Whiteside, 1996. unp. col. ill.
"Bill Martin book."
Incorporating the cumulative pattern that is used in THIS IS THE HOUSE THAT JACK BUILT tribute is paid to the exciting game of football. The predictable book will be excellent for reciting aloud, for increasing memory skills in young sports fans.
SUBJ: Super Bowl (Football game)./ Football.

796.332 Ph-1 4-6/6 $11.99 L KD787
SULLIVAN, GEORGE. All about football. Putnam ISBN 0-399-61227-0, 1987. 128p. ill.
Includes index.
Delineates the fundamentals of football, the rules to remember, the history of the game, and offers brief biographies of favorite players. This basic introduction is excellent for novices and the profuse black and white photos graphically clarify the text.
SUBJ: Football.

796.334 Ph-3 3-6/6 $18.00 L KD788
HOWARD, DALE E. Soccer stars. Childrens Press ISBN 0-516-08047-4; In Canada: Childrens Press, 1994. 48p. ill. (some col.). (World Cup soccer).
Includes glossary and index.
Brief biographies of international soccer greats. Fun for browsers and good for reports by sports fans.
SUBJ: Soccer players.

796.334 Ph-1 3-6/4 $21.34 L KD789
WILNER, BARRY. Soccer. Illus. by Art Seiden. Photos by the Photo Shoppe. Raintree Steck-Vaughn ISBN 0-8114-5777-X, 1994. 48p. col. ill. (How to play the all-star way).
"Arvid Knudsen book."
Includes directory, glossaries, bibliography and index.
An overview of the international sport of soccer. Emphasizes positions, playing skills, and techniques. Diagrams illustrate how to play the game. A good beginning for the novice.
SUBJ: Soccer.

796.342 Ph-2 3-6/7 $15.95 L KD790
HARRINGTON, DENIS J. Top 10 women tennis players. Enslow ISBN 0-89490-612-7, 1995. 48p. col. ill. (Sports top 10).
Includes index.
Brief sketches depict 10 top women tennis players chosen for their "shot-making abilities and colorful personalities." (p. 5) Contemporary superstars such as Monica Seles and Martina Navratilova are listed along with historical figures such as Althea Gibson, the first African-American woman to play championship level tennis. Interesting overview of an increasingly popular sport.
SUBJ: Women tennis players.

796.342 Ph-2 4-6/7 $14.95 L KD791
SCHWABACHER, MARTIN. Superstars of women's tennis. Chelsea House ISBN 0-7910-4393-2, 1997. 64p. ill. (Female sports stars).
Includes bibliography and index.
Discusses the vigor and tenacity of great women stars of the international tennis world. Includes Martina Navratilova, Steffi Graf, Monica Seles, and others, describing players personal lives as well as their sports accomplishments.
SUBJ: Tennis players./ Women tennis players.

796.352 Ph-2 4-6/7 $14.95 L KD792
WILNER, BARRY. Superstars of women's golf. Chelsea House ISBN 0-7910-4390-8, 1997. 64p. ill. (Female sports stars).
Includes bibliography and index.
Traces the advent of women into the male dominated world of golf. Includes Babe Didrikson Zaharias and Nancy Lopez.
SUBJ: Golfers./ Women athletes.

796.357 Ph-2 4-6/6 $15.99 T KD793
ANDERSON, JOAN. Batboy: an inside look at spring training. Photos by Matthew Cavanaugh. Lodestar/Dutton ISBN 0-525-67511-6; In Canada: McClelland & Stewart, 1996. unp. col. ill.
Includes glossary.
Follows thirteen-year-old Kenny Garibaldi, batboy for the San Francisco Giants, as he performs a variety of duties--delivering fan mail, cleaning shoes, sorting uniforms, etc. An engaging, highly pictorial behind-the-scenes view of the great game of baseball. Fans will identify with Kenny, and many will hope to emulate him.
SUBJ: Baseball.

796.357 Ph-2 4-A/7 $19.95 T KD794
BERLER, RON. Super book of baseball. Warner/Little, Brown ISBN 0-316-09240-1; In Canada: Little, Brown, 1991. 129p b&w and col photos.
Includes glossary.
A comprehensive survey of the history of baseball with emphasis on the origins and early years of the game, Hall of Fame players, the greatest teams, record holders, and World Series winners.
SUBJ: Baseball--History.

796.357 Ph-3 P-1/2 $5.95 P KD795
BLACKSTONE, MARGARET. This is baseball. Illus. by John O'Brien. Henry Holt ISBN 0-8050-5169-4; In Canada: Fitzhenry & Whiteside, c1993, 1997. unp. col. ill.
A very simple picture book covers the basics of baseball.
SUBJ: Baseball.

796.357 Ph-2 4-A/5 $14.95 L KD796
EGAN, TERRY. Macmillan book of baseball stories. By Terry Egan, Stan Friedmann and Mike Levine. Macmillan ISBN 0-02-733280-2; In Canada: Maxwell Macmillan, 1992. 127p. ill.
Sports stories about the eternal verities--winning and losing, right and

wrong, struggles and triumphs, and heroism. Retells incidents in the lives of such baseball legends as Lou Gehrig, Sandy Koufax, Ted Williams, and Roberto Clemente. Fun to read as an antidote to books of statistics and trivia, and excellent to use in reports on these great baseball personalities.
SUBJ: Baseball--Miscellanea.

796.357 Ph-3 4-6/6 $18.95 L KD797
GALT, MARGOT FORTUNATO. Up to the plate: the All American Girls Professional Baseball League. Lerner ISBN 0-8225-3326-X, 1995. 96p. ill. (Lerner's sports legacy series).
Includes index.
The chronicle of the All American Girls Professional Baseball League during World War II is accompanied by many excellent photographs. The story of these feisty athletes provides a fascinating glimpse into history. Incorporate into American history units as well as women's studies.
SUBJ: All-American Girls Professional Baseball League--History./ Women athletes./ Baseball--History.

796.357 Ph-1 3-6/6 $15.95 L KD798
GOLENBOCK, PETER. Teammates. Illus. by Paul Bacon. Gulliver/ Harcourt Brace Jovanovich ISBN 0-15-200603-6, 1990. unp. col. ill.
The stirring story of Jackie Robinson, the first black man to play on a Major League baseball team, the racial prejudices he endured, and the support he received from his white teammate, Pee Wee Reese. A poignant story of heroism and friendship.
SUBJ: Robinson, Jackie./ Reese, Pee Wee./ Baseball players./ Afro-Americans--Biography./ Race relations.

796.357 Ph-2 4-6/7 $9.95 P KD799
MACKAY, CLAIRE. Touching all the bases: baseball for kids of all ages. Illus. by Bill Slavin. Firefly ISBN 1-55209-000-0; In Canada: Scholastic, c1994, 1996. 96p. col. ill.
"Boardwalk book."
Includes glossary and index.
An endless array of fascinating facts about the great American pastime. Curious about the origin of the phrase "base stealing?" Want to know who was the first African-American player in major league baseball? It's all here. Baseball fans will find this great for browsing.
SUBJ: Baseball--Miscellanea.

796.357 Ph-2 4-6/7 $13.95 L KD800
MCKISSACK, PAT. Black diamond: the story of the Negro baseball leagues. By Patricia C. McKissack and Fredrick McKissack, Jr. Scholastic ISBN 0-590-45809-4; In Canada: Scholastic, 1994. 184p. ill.
Includes chronology, bibliography and index.
Coretta Scott King Author Honor book, 1995.
Delineates the trials, tribulations, and triumphs of the African-American baseball players who formed their own Negro leagues when segregation kept them out of major-league baseball. Some of the greatest ball players, Willie Mays and Hank Aaron, crossed over into the majors when desegregation took effect in 1947. An integral part of sports history for multicultural studies.
SUBJ: Negro leagues--History./ Baseball--History./ Afro-Americans--Biography.

796.357 Ph-2 3-6/3 $13.95 P KD801
PUCKETT, KIRBY. Kirby Puckett's baseball games. By Kirby Puckett and Andrew Gutelle. Illus. by Paul Meisel. Workman ISBN 0-7611-0155-1, 1996. 100p. ill.
Includes index and one "soft-hit" safety baseball.
Baseball fans will delight in this cluttered format of facts, games, drills, and exercises all designed to help children play better baseball. The accompanying baseball can be easily removed from the book without damaging either.
SUBJ: Baseball.

796.357 Ph-2 2-4/7 $14.93 L KD802
RITTER, LAWRENCE S. Leagues apart: the men and times of the Negro baseball leagues. Illus. by Richard Merkin. Morrow ISBN 0-688-13317-7, 1995. unp. col. ill.
Vivid illustrations illuminate the story of the history and players of the Negro baseball leagues. This story of sports and segregation will enrich multicultural studies and entice reluctant readers.
SUBJ: Negro leagues--History./ Baseball--History.

796.357 Ph-2 3-6/6 $6.95 P KD803
SUBLETT, ANNE. Illustrated rules of softball. Illus. by Patrick Kelley. Ideals Children's Books ISBN 1-57102-063-2, 1996. 32p. col. ill.
Includes glossary.
A basic guide to softball with information on the rules, the various positions, the techniques, and sportsmanship. Illustrations depict both

boys and girls playing ball. Good for reluctant readers.
SUBJ: Softball.

796.357 Ph-2 4-6/8 $18.00 T KD804
SULLIVAN, GEORGE. Glovemen: twenty-seven of baseball's greatest. Atheneum ISBN 0-689-31991-6; In Canada: Distican, 1996. 72p. ill. (some col.).
Companion to: SLUGGERS, 1991; and PITCHERS, 1994.
Brief biographies of 27 great fielders including Roberto Clemente, Joe DiMaggio, and Willie Mays. Fun reading for browsers and a good basis for reports.
SUBJ: Baseball players./ Fielding (Baseball).

796.357 Ph-2 5-A/6 $17.95 L KD805
SULLIVAN, GEORGE. Pitchers: twenty-seven of baseball's greatest. Atheneum ISBN 0-689-31825-1; In Canada: Maxwell Macmillan, 1994. 76p. ill.
Companion volume: SLUGGERS.
Includes index.
Brief biographies of some of the great pitchers of all time, including Bob Feller, Satchel Paige, Dizzy Dean, and Sandy Koufax. Baseball fans will use this for browsing and for reports.
SUBJ: Baseball players.

796.357 Ph-2 5-A/6 $16.95 L KD806
SULLIVAN, GEORGE. Sluggers: twenty-seven of baseball's greatest. Atheneum ISBN 0-689-31566-X; In Canada: Maxwell Macmillan, 1991. 74p b&w and col photos.
Includes "All-time Records" and index.
Brief biographies of twenty-seven of baseball's greatest hitters bring the sport of life. Baseball fans and good readers will like this one.
SUBJ: Baseball players.

796.357 Ph-2 3-6/4 $14.95 L KD807
SULLIVAN, MICHAEL JOHN. Top 10 baseball pitchers. Enslow ISBN 0-89490-520-1, 1994. 48p. col. ill. (Sports top 10).
Includes index.
Provides a brief look at ten baseball pitching greats from Cy Young to Satchel Paige to Roger Clemens. Includes biographical information, career statistics, and photographs. Good choice for browsers and reluctant readers.
SUBJ: Baseball players.

796.357 Ph-1 3-6/3 $21.34 L KD808
TEIRSTEIN, MARK ALAN. Baseball. Illus. by Art Seiden. Photos by Frank Becerra, Jr. Raintree Steck-Vaughn ISBN 0-8114-5776-1, 1994. 48p. col. ill. (How to play the all-star way).
"Arvid Knudsen book."
Includes glossaries, bibliography and index.
Brings the basics of baseball to life with information on how to play the game, positions, techniques and tips, batting and baserunning, and keeping score. Excellent introduction with good illustrations.
SUBJ: Baseball.

796.42 Ph-2 1-3/4 $17.28 L KD809
BAILEY, DONNA. Track and field. Steck-Vaughn ISBN 0-8114-2901-6, 1991. 33p. col. ill. (Sports world).
Includes index.
Depicts young athletes participating in track and field events such as high jumping, pole vaulting, and running hurdles. Large print and full-color photographs will appeal to older reluctant readers.
SUBJ: Track and field.

796.42 Ph-2 3-6/4 $21.34 L KD810
ROSENTHAL, BERT. Track and field. Illus. by Art Seiden. Photos by Jacob Brown and Victah Sailor. Raintree Steck-Vaughn ISBN 0-8114-5778-8, 1994. 48p. col. ill. (How to play the all-star way).
"Arvid Knudsen book."
Includes glossary, bibliography and index.
Explains the history, required training, and necessary equipment of track and field events. Includes information on sprinting, hurdling, relay racing, distance running, long jumping, and javelin throwing. Excellent full-color photographs convey the speed and excitement of the sport.
SUBJ: Track and field.

796.42 Ph-2 4-6/7 $13.95 L KD811
SANDELSON, ROBERT. Track athletics. Crestwood House ISBN 0-89686-671-8, 1991. 48p. col. ill. (Olympic sports).
Includes glossary, bibliography and index.
Features male and female track stars and their record breaking moments in Olympic Games.
SUBJ: Track and field./ Running./ Olympics.

796.42   Ph-2 3-6/8 $11.95   T   KD812
WARD, TONY. Field. Rigby ISBN 1-57572-038-8, 1996. 32p. col. ill.
(Olympic library).
  Includes glossary and index.
  An overview of Olympic field events, including track, discus throw,
  decathlon, high jump, hurdles, and pole vault. Good pictures and
  minimal text make this a winner.
  SUBJ: Track and field./ Jumping./ Olympics.

796.42   Ph-2 3-6/8 $12.00   T   KD813
WARD, TONY. Track. Rigby ISBN 1-57572-037-X, 1996. 32p. col. ill.
(Olympic library).
  Includes glossary and index.
  An overview of the races and champions of the Olympic track events.
  Colorful, picture-filled format provides information on training, making
  the grade, and getting to the top.
  SUBJ: Track and field./ Running races./ Olympics.

796.42   Ph-2 4-6/7 $14.95   L   KD814
WICKHAM, MARTHA. Superstars of women's track and field. Chelsea
House ISBN 0-7910-4394-0, 1997. 64p. ill. (Female sports stars).
  Includes bibliography and index.
  Celebrates the triumphs of some of the top women athletes in track
  and field events. Includes Florence Griffith Joyner, Jackie Joyner-
  Kersee, and Wilma Rudolph. Sports fans will empathize with their
  difficult lives and their courage to overcome all obstacles.
  SUBJ: Track and field athletes./ Women athletes.

796.44   Ph-2 4-6/7 $14.95   L   KD815
COHEN, JOEL H. Superstars of women's gymnastics. Chelsea House
ISBN 0-7910-4391-6, 1997. 64p. ill. (Female sports stars).
  Includes chronology, bibliography and index.
  Highlights the careers of great Olympic gymnasts including Olga
  Korbut, Nadia Comaneci, Mary Lou Retton, and Shannon Miller.
  SUBJ: Gymnasts./ Gymnastics./ Women athletes.

796.44   Ph-3 3-5/4 $13.95   T   KD816
KUKLIN, SUSAN. Going to my gymnastics class. Bradbury ISBN 0-02-
751236-3; In Canada: Collier Macmillan, 1991. unp. col. ill.
  Follows a young boy as he joyfully practices gymnastics.
  Accompanied by very clear, bright photos of elementary age students.
  SUBJ: Gymnastics.

796.44   Ph-2 3-6/6 $24.26   L   KD817
NORMILE, DWIGHT. Gymnastics. Introduction by Tatiana Gutsu. Illus.
by Dwight Normile. Photos by Eileen Langsley and Mary Pat Boron.
Raintree Steck-Vaughn ISBN 0-8114-6595-0, 1996. 48p. col. ill. (How to
play the all-star way).
  "Arvid Knudsen book."
  Includes glossary, bibliography and index.
  Covers the basics of gymnastics, including warm-up exercises,
  tumbling, bar skills, vaulting, balance beam, horse, and rings. Full-
  color photographs and diagrams offer a pictorial glimpse into the
  challenge of gymnastics.
  SUBJ: Gymnastics.

796.44   Ph-2 3-6/8 $11.95   T   KD818
READHEAD, LLOYD. Gymnastics. Rigby ISBN 1-57572-036-1, 1996.
32p. col. ill. (Olympic library).
  Includes glossary and index.
  A highly pictorial overview of gymnastic events, heroes, training,
  diets, and competitions. Colorful format will entice browsers as well as
  sports enthusiasts.
  SUBJ: Gymnastics./ Olympics.

796.48   Ph-3 4-6/11 $16.00   L   KD819
ANDERSON, DAVE. Story of the Olympics. Foreward by Carl Lewis.
Morrow ISBN 0-688-12954-4, 1996. 160p. ill.
  Includes index.
  Surveys the Olympic Games from their inception in 776 B.C. to
  present day, with exciting stories about such events as gymnastics,
  speed skating, and swimming. Written in an interesting style, it is
  useful where historical information on the Olympics is needed.
  SUBJ: Olympics--History.

796.48   Ph-2 P-2/4 $14.99   L   KD820
HENNESSY, B. G. Olympics! Illus. by Michael Chesworth. Viking ISBN
0-670-86522-2; In Canada: Penguin, 1996. unp. col. ill.
  A pictorial overview of the Olympics is designed for the youngest
  reader. Includes history, training, and events that make up the
  Olympic Games. Can be used during Winter and Summer Games as
  an introduction to the excitement of the Olympics.
  SUBJ: Olympics.

796.48   Ph-2 3-6/8 $11.95   T   KD821
TAMES, RICHARD. Ancient Olympics. Rigby ISBN 1-57572-034-5, 1996.
32p. col. ill., map. (Olympic library).
  Includes glossary and index.
  Offers information on the history, traditions, champions, and training
  involved in the Ancient Olympics. Can be used to enrich mythology
  units.
  SUBJ: Olympic games (Ancient).

796.48   Ph-2 3-6/8 $12.00   T   KD822
TAMES, RICHARD. Modern Olympics. Rigby ISBN 1-57572-035-3,
1996. 32p. ill. (some col.). (Olympic library).
  Includes glossary and index.
  Provides information on the history, politics, events, and globalization
  of the Olympics. Includes an overview of some of the athletes, the
  ceremonies, and the Olympic ideal. Good pictures, varied format, and
  minimal text will entice sports enthusiasts and reluctant readers.
  SUBJ: Olympics--History.

796.5   Ph-2 4-6/6 $16.95   T   KD823
MCMANNERS, HUGH. Outdoor adventure handbook. DK Publishing
ISBN 0-7894-1035-4, 1996. 64p. col. ill.
  Includes directory and index.
  A great outdoor adventure guide for families. Includes a wealth of
  information on camping experiences including proper clothing,
  messages and trails, using the sun and stars to navigate, observing
  animals and plants, and first aid. (Parents' Shelf).
  SUBJ: Outdoor recreation--Handbooks, manuals, etc./ Outdoor life--
  Handbooks, manuals, etc./ Camping--Handbooks, manuals, etc./
  Wilderness survival--Handbooks, manuals, etc.

796.5   Ph-1 5-A/6 $12.95   T   KD824
PAULSEN, GARY. Woodsong. Bradbury ISBN 0-02-770221-9; In
Canada: Maxwell Macmillan, 1990. 132p.
  Available from the National Library Service for the Blind and
  Physically Handicapped on sound recording cassette RC34757.
  Novelist Gary Paulsen writes about the beauty and drama of outdoor
  life. In this autobiography, he tells of competing in the Iditarod, the
  1180 mile dogsled race across Alaska. He evokes the glories and
  violence of nature and the need for humans to refrain from destroying
  it. A compelling voice for the preservation of nature in all its wonders.
  SUBJ: Outdoor life--Minnesota./ Sled dogs./ Sled dog racing./
  Paulsen, Gary.

796.54   Ph-3 4-A/6 $12.95   L   KD825
EVANS, JEREMY. Camping and survival. Crestwood House ISBN
0-89686-686-6; In Canada: Maxwell Macmillan, 1992. 48p. col. ill.
(Adventurers).
  Includes directory, glossary and index.
  Surviving in the wilderness is emphasized in this overview of camping
  with strategies for selecting equipment, choosing campsites, and
  cooking outdoors. Includes a great deal of fundamental facts to insure
  fun and safety while camping.
  SUBJ: Camping./ Wilderness survival./ Survival.

796.6   Ph-2 2-4/2 $17.28   L   KD826
BAILEY, DONNA. Cycling. Steck-Vaughn ISBN 0-8114-2855-9, 1990.
33p. col. ill. (Sports world).
  Includes index.
  A young boy learns to ride his new bike. Includes easy-to-read
  information on the Tour de France and BMX racers.
  SUBJ: Bicycles and bicycling.

796.6   Ph-2 3-6/6 $24.26   L   KD827
FRANCIS, JOHN. Bicycling. Introduction by Frank J. Torpey. Illus. by Art
Seiden. Photos by Gork and others. Raintree Steck-Vaughn ISBN
0-8114-6598-5, 1996. 48p. col. ill. (How to play the all-star way).
  "Arvid Knudsen book."
  Includes directories, glossary, bibliography and index.
  The sport of cycling is analyzed in its many aspects. Includes history,
  strategy, and safety rules.
  SUBJ: Bicycles and bicycling.

796.7   Ph-2 4-A/5 $12.95   L   KD828
CARSER, S. X. Motocross cycles. Capstone Press ISBN 1-56065-069-9,
1992. 48p. col. ill. (Cruisin').
  Includes glossary and index.
  Discusses the selection and use of motocross motorcycles. Explains
  techniques for riding while emphasizing safety. Includes many action
  photographs.
  SUBJ: Motocross.

796.7   Ph-3 4-A/4 $12.95   L   KD829
CONNOLLY, MAUREEN. Dragsters. Capstone Press ISBN 1-56065-074-5, 1992. 48p. col. ill. (Cruisin').
     Includes glossary and index.
     Describes drag races focusing on racing rules, different kinds of dragsters, and the capabilities of the cars themselves.
     SUBJ: Automobiles, Racing./ Drag racing.

796.7   Ph-2 5-6/6 $17.80   L   KD830
SMITH, JAY H. Most rugged all-terrain vehicles. Capstone ISBN 1-56065-218-7, 1995. 48p. col. ill. (Wheels).
     Includes glossary, bibliography and index.
     Colorful views of a variety of ATVs and riders accompany short informative chapters describing the vehicles along with riding techniques and competitive events. A you-are-there approach and the naming of local riders are part of the discussion of choosing a vehicle, safety procedures and gear, and preparation for riding in races. Though intended for young adults and utilitarian in text, this will have great appeal.
     SUBJ: All terrain vehicle racing./ Vehicles.

796.815   Ph-2 4-6/5 $15.95   L   KD831
GOEDECKE, CHRISTOPHER J. Wind warrior: the training of a Karate champion. Photos by Rosmarie Hausherr. Four Winds ISBN 0-02-736262-0; In Canada: Maxwell Macmillan, 1992. 64p. ill.
     Follows a thirteen-year-old boy as he trains for a karate tournament with black and white photographs illustrating every step of the way.
     SUBJ: Karate.

796.815   Ph-2 2-4/5 $15.99   T   KD832
MORRIS, ANN. Karate boy. Photos by David Katzenstein. Dutton ISBN 0-525-45337-7; In Canada: McClelland & Stewart, 1996. 32p. col. ill.
     Includes glossary.
     Spanish version available from Penguin Ediciones CHICO KARATEKA (ISBN 0-525-45588-4, 1996).
     Follows young David as he learns the sport of karate. A typical class with its procedures and activities is explored. Large pictures invite reluctant readers.
     SUBJ: Karate./ Spanish language materials.

796.815   Ph-2 3-6/6 $24.26   L   KD833
NARDI, THOMAS J. Karate and judo. By Thomas Nardi. Introduction by Leo T. Fong. Illus. by Art Seiden. Photos by Mary Pat Boron. Raintree Steck-Vaughn ISBN 0-8114-6597-7, 1996. 48p. col. ill. (How to play the all-star way).
     "Arvid Knudsen book."
     Includes directory, glossary, bibliography and index.
     Basic introduction to the martial arts of judo and karate includes history, philosophy, and techniques of self defense. Good for reports and for browsing.
     SUBJ: Karate./ Judo.

796.815   Ph-2 4-6/6 $19.95   L   KD834
QUEEN, J. ALLEN. Complete karate. Sterling ISBN 0-8069-8678-6; In Canada: dist. by Sterling c/o Canadian Manda, 1993. 191p. ill.
     Includes index.
     Large, clear, action photographs are found in abundance in this easy-to-follow introduction to karate. In addition to focusing on basic karate skills, it covers the history of the sport, the dress, and meditation. The students that demonstrate various stances are of different ages and sizes, girls as well as boys, and are from different ethnic backgrounds.
     SUBJ: Karate.

796.9   Ph-2 4-6/7 $13.95   L   KD835
SANDELSON, ROBERT. Ice sports. Crestwood House ISBN 0-89686-667-X, 1991. 48p. col. ill.
     Includes glossary, bibliography and index.
     A historical approach to the ice sports competitions in the Olympic Winter Games focuses on ice hockey, skating, and bobsledding. Excellent for use in research projects on the Olympics.
     SUBJ: Winter sports./ Olympics./ Winter Olympics.

796.91   Ph-2 4-6/7 $14.95   L   KD836
SMITH, POHLA. Superstars of women's figure skating. Chelsea House ISBN 0-7910-4392-4, 1997. 64p. ill. (Female sports stars).
     Includes chronology, bibliography and index.
     Traces the achievements of great women figure skating champions. Includes Kristi Yamaguchi, Oksana Baiul, and Katarina Witt. Stresses their determination and hard work.
     SUBJ: Ice skaters./ Women athletes.

796.93   Ph-2 5-A/7 $12.95   L   KD837
EVANS, JEREMY. Skiing. Crestwood House ISBN 0-89686-681-5; In Canada: Maxwell Macmillan, 1992. 48p. col. ill. (Adventurers).
     Includes directory, glossary and index.
     Provides information on the sport of skiing focusing on apparel, techniques, snow conditions, and competition.
     SUBJ: Skis and skiing.

796.962   Ph-2 4-6/6 $12.00   L   KD838
DUPLACEY, JAMES. Amazing forwards. Morrow ISBN 0-688-15024-1; In Canada: Kids Can Press, 1996. 40p. col. ill. (Hockey superstars).
     Brief biographies of many hockey superstars including Wayne Gretsky and Gordie Howe. Good for reluctant readers.
     SUBJ: Hockey players./ National Hockey League.

796.962   Ph-2 4-6/6 $5.95   P   KD839
DUPLACEY, JAMES. Great goalies. Morrow ISBN 0-688-15021-7; In Canada: Kids Can Press, 1996. 40p. col. ill. (Hockey superstars).
     Profiles some of the great goalkeepers of the National Hockey League including Tony Esposito, Curtis Joseph, and Glenn Hall. Lots of action photographs and little text make this appealing to reluctant readers who are sports fans.
     SUBJ: Hockey players./ National Hockey League.

796.962   Ph-2 4-6/6 $12.00   L   KD840
DUPLACEY, JAMES. Top rookies. Morrow ISBN 0-688-15022-5; In Canada: Kids Can Press, 1996. 40p. col. ill. (Hockey superstars).
     Focuses on the professional lives of 40 rookies in the National Hockey League. Includes colorful action photographs and many statistics. High appeal for reluctant readers.
     SUBJ: Hockey players./ National Hockey League.

796.962   Ph-1 3-6/4 $22.80   L   KD841
HARRIS, LISA. Hockey. Illus. by Art Seiden. Photos by Frank McGady. Raintree Steck-Vaughn ISBN 0-8114-5781-8, 1994. 48p. col. ill. (How to play the all-star way).
     "Arvid Knudsen book."
     Includes glossary, bibliography and index.
     Introduces the sport of hockey. A clear, easy-to-comprehend text accompanied by full-color photographs and informative diagrams explains the rules, positions, stick and skating skills, offensive and defensive strategies, and penalties. Excellent overview of the sport.
     SUBJ: Hockey.

796.962   Ph-3 4-6/5 $15.95   L   KD842
KNAPP, RON. Top 10 hockey scorers. Enslow ISBN 0-89490-517-1, 1994. 48p. col. ill. (Sports top 10).
     Includes index.
     Brief biogaphies of such hockey stars as Wayne Gretzky, Gordie Howe, and Bobby Orr. Emphasizes the international aspect of the sport.
     SUBJ: Hockey players./ Hockey--Records.

796.962   Ph-2 3-6/8 $12.95   L   KD843
LITKE, RONALD. Ice hockey. Rigby ISBN 1-57572-074-4, 1997. 32p. col. ill. (Successful sports).
     Icludes glossary and index.
     Surveys the sport of ice hockey with information on the rules, the famous players, the necessary skills, and the tactics involved in this popular sport.
     SUBJ: Hockey.

796.962   Ph-2 4-6/7 $12.00   L   KD844
MCFARLANE, BRIAN. Hockey for kids: heroes, tips, and facts. Illus. by Bill Slavin. Morrow ISBN 0-688-15026-8; In Canada: Kids Can Press, 1996. 64p. col. ill.
     Includes index.
     Highlights the game of ice hockey with information on equipment, a typical day in the life of a professional player, women in hockey, the Stanley Cup, and stars of the game. Colorful and easy-to-follow format is sure to please hockey fans.
     SUBJ: Hockey.

797.1   Ph-3 4-A/7 $12.95   L   KD845
EVANS, JEREMY. Whitewater kayaking. Crestwood House ISBN 0-89686-685-8, 1992. 48p. col. ill. (Adventurers).
     Includes directory, glossary and index.
     Provides comprehensive coverage of facts on kayaks with information on paddles, appropriate clothing, safety, techniques, and water conditions.
     SUBJ: Canoes and canoeing./ White-water canoeing./ Kayaks and kayaking.

797.2   Ph-2 2-4/2 $17.28   L   KD846
BAILEY, DONNA. Swimming. Steck-Vaughn ISBN 0-8114-2852-4, 1990.
33p. col. ill. (Sports world).
Includes index.
A young girl learns to swim. Information is given on other aspects of
water sports such as diving, snorkeling, scuba diving and surfing.
Attractive, easy reading for young or reluctant readers.
SUBJ: Swimming.

797.2   Ph-3 4-6/8 $14.60   L   KD847
MCDONALD, KENDALL. Divers. Garrett Educational ISBN 1-56074-
043-4, 1992. 32p. col. ill. (Living dangerously).
Includes glossary and index.
The excitement and danger of diving are discussed with focus on
deep-sea diving, science diving, and the problems encountered in the
sea including poisonous fishes and sharks.
SUBJ: Divers./ Diving, Submarine.

797.2   Ph-2 3-6/6 $15.95   T   KD848
ROUSE, JEFF. Young swimmer. DK Publishing ISBN 0-7894-1533-X,
1997. 37p. col. ill.
Includes glossary, index and directory.
An introduction to swimming includes the four main strokes,
competitions, and practical advice about water safety. Colorful
photographs offer step-by-step demonstrations of proper swimming
techniques. Great for browsing.
SUBJ: Swimming.

797.2   Ph-2 3-6/8 $11.95   T   KD849
VERRIER, JOHN. Swimming and diving. Rigby ISBN 1-57572-039-6,
1996. 32p. col. ill. (Olympic library).
Includes glossary and index.
An overview of the swimming and diving Olympic events includes
information on selection, competition, drug testing, and the heroes
and heroines who make the Olympics great.
SUBJ: Swimming./ Diving./ Olympics.

797.2   Ph-2 3-6/6 $24.26   L   KD850
WILNER, BARRY. Swimming. Introduction by Sam Freas. Illus. by Art
Seiden. Photos by Dan Helms and others. Raintree Steck-Vaughn ISBN
0-8114-6596-9, 1996. 48p. col. ill. (How to play the all-star way).
"Arvid Knudson book."
Includes directories, glossary, bibliography and index.
Introduces the world of competitive swimming. Includes the various
strokes, racing techniques, and rules for competition.
SUBJ: Swimming.

797.3   Ph-3 4-A/7 $12.95   L   KD851
WALKER, CHERYL. Waterskiing and kneeboarding. Capstone Press ISBN
1-56065-056-7, 1992. 48p. col. ill. (Action sports).
Includes directory, glossary and index.
An introduction to the sports of waterskiing and kneeboarding with
information on the history, equipment, challenges, and dangers that
are so much a part of the sports.
SUBJ: Water skiing./ Kneeboarding.

797.5   Ph-2 4-6/7 $19.95   L   KD852
BELLVILLE, CHERYL WALSH. Flying in a hot air balloon. Carolrhoda
ISBN 0-87614-750-3, 1993. 48p. col. ill.
Includes glossary and index.
Follows the flight of hot air balloons with information on how they fly
and how they gain and lose altitude. Bright, full-color photographs
reveal the pleasures of flying above the world in a hot air balloon.
SUBJ: Hot air balloons./ Ballooning.

797.5   Ph-3 2-5/7 $14.95   L   KD853
FINE, JOHN CHRISTOPHER. Free spirits in the sky. Text and photos by
John Christopher Fine. Atheneum ISBN 0-689-31705-0; In Canada:
Maxwell Macmillan, 1994. 32p. col. ill.
Includes index.
The fun of hot air ballooning is reflected in this brilliantly
photographed introduction to the sport. Includes information on the
history and science of flight as well as the contests and festivals that
attract balloonists.
SUBJ: Hot air balloons./ Ballooning.

798.2   Ph-2 3-5/2 $14.93   L   KD854
COLE, JOANNA. Riding Silver Star. Photos by Margaret Miller.
Morrow ISBN 0-688-13896-9, 1996. unp. col. ill.
Follows a young horseback rider as she prepares for a lesson and a
show. Large, colorful photographs depict the preparation, practice,
and hard work as well as the joy and pleasure of riding.
SUBJ: Horsemanship./ Show riding./ Horses.

798.2   Ph-2 4-A/6 $12.95   L   KD855
EVANS, JEREMY. Horseback riding. Crestwood House ISBN 0-89686-
683-1; In Canada: Maxwell Macmillan, 1992. 48p. col. ill. (Adventurers).
Includes directory, glossary and index.
The joys of horseback riding are revealed with sections on popular
breeds, putting on a saddle, changing pace, and safety. Contains bits
of information on many aspects of horsemanship.
SUBJ: Horsemanship./ Horses./ Ponies.

798.2   Ph-3 3-8/8 $15.95   T   KD856
GREEN, LUCINDA. Young rider. DK Publishing ISBN 1-56458-320-1,
1993. 64p. col ill.
Includes directory, glossary and index.
An introduction to the British equestrian world. Novice horseback
riders will enjoy browsing through this colorfully photographed guide
which is filled with instructions and techniques for young riders.
SUBJ: Horsemanship./ Ponies.

VCR 798.2   Ph-2 2-6 $12.95   KD857
LITTLE HORSE THAT COULD: THE CONNEMARA STALLION: ERIN GO
BRAGH (Videocassette). Dreams Come True Productions ISBN
0-9649755-1-3, 1996. 1/2" VHS videocassette color (60min).
Includes public performance rights.
A glimpse into the life of an Irish stallion, with emphasis on the care
and training involved in developing a champion. A heartwarming story
that will delight horse lovers.
SUBJ: Horsemanship./ Show riding./ Horses.

798.8   Ph-2 5-6/7 $14.95   L   KD858
CRISMAN, RUTH. Racing the Iditarod Trail. Dillon ISBN 0-87518-523-1;
In Canada: Maxwell Macmillan, 1993. 72p. col. ill.
Includes bibliography and index.
The rigors and excitement of the Iditarod sled dog race through
1,049 miles in Alaska are described. Includes history of the event and
a chart of winners. Excellent for use when Alaska is studied.
SUBJ: Iditarod Trail Sled Dog Race, Alaska./ Sled dog racing.

798.8   Ph-2 3-6/7 $15.00   T   KD859
PAULSEN, GARY. Puppies, dogs, and blue northers: reflections on being
raised by a pack of sled dogs. Harcourt Brace ISBN 0-15-292881-2; In
Canada: Harcourt Brace c/o Canadian Manda, 1996. 81p. col. ill.
Gary Paulsen is a dog musher and an experienced Iditarod racer. His
love of the sport is evident as he tells of the bond of survival that
grows between a driver and his dog in this moving essay. Excellent
for enrichment of Alaska and Iditarod studies as well as an unusual
complement to an author study of Paulsen.
SUBJ: Paulsen, Gary./ Mushers./ Sled dogs./ Sled dog racing./
Outdoor life--Minnesota.

798.8   Ph-2 4-6/7 $16.90   L   KD860
SHAHAN, SHERRY. Dashing through the snow: the story of the Jr.
Iditarod. Millbrook ISBN 0-7613-0208-5, 1997. 47p. col. ill., maps.
Includes glossary and index.
An action-filled history of the Jr. Iditarod, the annual dogsled race for
young people in Alaska. Includes information on dog care, equipment,
and technique. Good photographs make the race come alive.
Excellent for integration into Alaska studies.
SUBJ: Junior Iditarod Trail Sled Dog Race, Alaska./ Sled dog racing.

799.1   Ph-2 K-2/2 $17.28   L   KD861
BAILEY, DONNA. Fishing. Steck-Vaughn ISBN 0-8114-2851-6, 1990.
33p. col. ill. (Sports world).
Includes index.
A young fisherman learns from his father how to get a rod ready, to
cast, and to catch a fish. Full color photos and an easy-to-read text
reveal the pleasures of fishing and offer a view of commercial fishing.
SUBJ: Fishing./ Fisheries.

MCP 808   Ph-2 3-6 $129.00   OD KD862
BOOK EXCHANGE (Microcomputer program). Learning In Motion/Open
Court 112-000-B, 1996. 1 3.5" disk, 1 3.5" backup disk.
Version 1.0.
Includes teacher's guide.
System requirements: Macintosh or compatible System 7.0 or greater;
color monitor, 12" minimum, 256 colors; at least 2MB of free RAM.
This program allows readers to share views, questions, and general
analysis of their reading in an easy-to-use format. The database
resembles a card catalog environment and is designed for easy
sharing of student information. Excellent tool to introduce literary
criticism and have a classroom or school begin practicing this skill.
SUBJ: Literature--Criticism and interpretation--Software./ Software--
Literature--Criticism and interpretation./ Interactive media.

808   Ph-1 2-6/4 $15.40   L   KD863
GUTHRIE, DONNA. Young author's do-it-yourself book: how to write, illustrate, and produce your own book. By Donna Guthrie, Nancy Bentley, and Katy Keck Arnsteen. Illus. by Katy Keck Arnsteen. Millbrook ISBN 1-56294-350-2, 1994. 64p. col. ill.
> Put on an author's hat and begin with what you know or go wherever your imagination leads. Creating characters, settings, problems, and solutions with a beginning, middle, climax, and end is the name of this game. Careful explanations illustrated with colorful cartoons will encourage all students to forge ahead with research and/or creative writing projects. Also includes instructions for book construction. A must purchase; all language arts teachers will want to own a copy.
> SUBJ: Authorship./ Books./ Creative writing.

808   Ph-2 5-A/9 $14.95   T   KD864
STEVENS, CARLA. Book of your own: keeping a diary or journal. Clarion ISBN 0-89919-256-4, 1993. 100p.
> Includes bibliography and index.
> Information on how to start a journal or diary includes excerpts from diaries of ages past and from journals of famous people. Excellent for use in whole language projects.
> SUBJ: Diaries.

808   Ph-3 5-A/8 $13.95   T   KD865
TERBAN, MARVIN. It figures!: fun figures of speech. Illus. by Giulio Maestro. Clarion ISBN 0-395-61584-4, 1993. 61p. ill.
> Includes bibliography.
> Explores the use of such figures of speech as metaphors, onomatopoeia, alliteration, hyperbole, and personification. Accompanying illustrations are comic, and the text is often jocular, lending an air of levity to a subject that can be dry. Incorporate into language arts and creative writing classes.
> SUBJ: English language--Style./ Figures of speech.

808.06   Ph-2 2-4/2 $14.95   L   KD866
CHRISTELOW, EILEEN. What do authors do? Clarion ISBN 0-395-71124-X, 1995. 32p. col. ill.
> A picture book that describes how to create a picture book. From the gathering of ideas, through the writing experience, to finding a publisher--all concepts of the creative process are explored. Can inspire students to write and illustrate their own picture books. Use as an introductory activity prior to an author's visit or for career studies.
> SUBJ: Authorship./ Authors./ Illustrators.

808.06   Ph-2 3-6 $17.90   L   KD867
HULME, JOY N. How to write, recite, and delight in all kinds of poetry. By Joy N. Hulme and Donna W. Guthrie. Millbrook ISBN 1-56294-576-9, 1996. 96p. col. ill.
> Includes bibliography and index.
> An easy, appealing format invites budding poets to experiment with a variety of poetic forms and to recite and preserve their creations. Includes 70 poems written by young people and reproductions of great works of art. Delightful verses can be the basis for many poetry and creative writing lessons.
> SUBJ: Poetry--Authorship.

808.1   Ph-1 5-6/7 $15.89   L   KD868
LIVINGSTON, MYRA COHN. Poem-making: ways to begin writing poetry. HarperCollins ISBN 0-06-024020-2; In Canada: HarperCollins, 1991. 162p.
> Includes index.
> Examines the voices of poetry, sound and rhyme, figures of speech and more in a readable text supported by examples. A valuable handbook for students and a useful review resource for teachers.
> SUBJ: Poetry--Authorship./ Creative writing.

808.1   Ph-3 4-6/7 $11.90   L   KD869
RYAN, MARGARET. How to read and write poems. Watts ISBN 0-531-20043-4, 1991. 63p col and b&w photos. (First book).
> Includes bibliography and index.
> An overview of the study of poetry with emphasis on metaphors and similes, rhythm and rhyme. Good for teachers and students to use as an accompaniment to their understanding and writing of poetry.
> SUBJ: Poetry./ Creative writing.

808.6   Ph-3 3-6/7 $14.95   T   KD870
JAMES, ELIZABETH. Sincerely yours: how to write great letters. By Elizabeth James and Carol Barkin. Clarion ISBN 0-395-58831-6, 1993. 166p.
> Includes appendixes and index.
> A wealth of information on letter writing with advice on personal and business letters, decorating stationery, getting a pen pal and publishing a letter in a periodical.
> SUBJ: Letter writing.

808.8   Ph-3 K-3 $20.00   T   KD871
CHILDREN'S BOOK OF VIRTUES. Edited by William J. Bennett. Illus. by Michael Hague. Simon & Schuster ISBN 0-684-81353-X; In Canada: Distican, 1995. 112p. col. ill.
> Selections from: THE BOOK OF VIRTUES.
> Didactic selections from fables, folktales, poems, and legends teach the essentials of good character--courage, perseverance, responsibility, self-discipline, compassion, faith, honesty, loyalty, and friendship.
> SUBJ: Children's literature./ Conduct of life--Literary collections.

808.8   Ph-1 K-3 $15.00   L   KD872
DIANE GOODE'S BOOK OF SILLY STORIES AND SONGS. Collected and illus. by Diane Goode. Dutton ISBN 0-525-44967-1, 1992. 64p col illus.
> Includes source notes.
> A collection of foolish folktales and songs including "The Magic Pot" and "The Husband Who Was to Mind the House." The accompanying illustrations are properly silly and bring these multicultural characters to life. Wonderful for reading aloud.
> SUBJ: Folklore./ Songs.

808.8   Ph-3 3-6   FREE   P OD KD873
EXPECTATIONS. Braille Institute, 1948-. v. ill. annual.
> Provides access for blind children to current children's literature in braille with embossed illustrations and microfragrance labels. Schools, agencies, libraries and teachers may request a copy on official stationary.
> SUBJ: Blind--Books and reading./ Literature--Collections.

808.8   Ph-2 K-4 $16.95   L   KD874
GIVE A DOG A BONE: STORIES, POEMS, JOKES, AND RIDDLES ABOUT DOGS. Compiled by Joanna Cole and Stephanie Calmenson. Illus. by John Speirs. Scholastic ISBN 0-590-46374-8; In Canada: Scholastic, 1996. 90p. col. ill.
> Includes indexes.
> A delightful collection for dog lovers includes poems, jokes, stories, and riddles all about canine capers. Alternately sentimental, amusing, and loving, this paean to puppies is great for reading aloud.
> SUBJ: Dogs--Literary collections.

808.8   Ph-2 1-4 $23.99   T   KD875
MILLS, LAUREN A. Book of little folk: faery stories and poems from around the world. Collected, retold, and illus. by Lauren Mills. Dial ISBN 0-8037-1458-0; In Canada: McClelland & Stewart, 1997. 134p. col. ill.
> Includes bibliography and index.
> A wonderful collection of poems, short stories, folktales, and fairytales from a variety of cultures--all superb for reading aloud. Includes such favorites as "Thumbelina," "The elves and the shoemaker," and "Tom Thumb" as well as a host of unfamiliar little folk. Excellent for multicultural studies.
> SUBJ: Fairies--Literary collections.

TB 808.8   Ph-2 P-1 $15.95   OD KD876
PINDER, MIKE. People with one heart (Talking book). One Step Records OSR0435 ISBN 1-888057-05-X, 1996. 1 compact disc (61min).
> Talking book also available as sound cassette (ISBN 1-888057-01-7, 1996). 1 sound cassette (61min), $9.95.
> Seven stories about people who care deeply about those around them! Tales show that people should be loved for their deeds rather than their looks. Pinder reads in a quiet, relaxed manner and has as his background, music which is soothing. Useful for developing listening skills and stressing positive character traits.
> Contents: John Jeremy Colton -- I wish I were a butterfly -- The little blue ball -- Dream feather -- The gifts of Wali Dad -- Brother Eagle, Sister Sky -- Tsubu, the little snail.
> SUBJ: Literature--Collections./ Folklore.

TB 808.8   Ph-1 1-4 $15.95   OD KD877
PINDER, MIKE. Planet with one mind: stories from around the world for the child within us all (Talking book). One Step Records OSR0434 ISBN 1-888057-04-1, 1995. 1 compact disc (59min).
> ALA notable recording, 1997.
> Talking book also available as sound cassette (ISBN 1-888057-00-9, 1995). 1 sound cassette (59min), $9.95.
> Inspired by books as a child "to follow a path of peace, a path of truth," Mike Pinder gathered seven outstanding stories by Laurence Yep, Tomie De Paola, Richard Lewis, and others which he reverently read and accompanied with music of his own composing. The disc is a haunting creation and will inspire listeners to discover these wonderful books. For all collections.
> Contents: A spark in the dark -- The legend of the Indian paintbrush -- The Butterfly Boy -- Old Turtle -- The Rajah's rice -- Why the sky is far away -- All of you was singing.
> SUBJ: Literature--Collections./ Folklore.

808.8   Ph-2 P-2/3 $17.95   L   KD878
POLACCO, PATRICIA. Babushka's Mother Goose. Philomel ISBN 0-399-22747-4; In Canada: Putnam, 1995. 64p. col. ill.
A delightful treasury of rhymes and stories filled with rollicking good humor. Bold illustrations in Polacco's signature style are reminiscent of Rojankovsky. The anthology of original and traditional materials provides numerous selections for reading aloud and memorizing. Older students will enjoy comparing and contrasting with traditional Mother Goose rhymes.
SUBJ: American poetry./ Nursery rhymes--Adaptations.

808.8   Ph-2 P-3 $24.95   T   KD879
TREASURY OF CHILDREN'S LITERATURE. Edited by Armand Eisen. Houghton Mifflin ISBN 0-395-53349-X, 1992. 303p. col. ill.
"Ariel books."
This comprehensive anthology of children's literature includes Aesop's fables, fairy tales of Grimm and Andersen, traditional folk tales, Mother Goose rhymes, poetry of Robert Louis Stevenson and Clement C. Moore, American tall tales, and excerpts from classic novels such as PINOCCHIO and PETER PAN. Useful where individual copies of these literary favorites are unavailable and for introducing children to a wide range of literature. (Parents' Shelf).
SUBJ: Literature--Collections.

808.81   Ph-1 P-3 $18.95   T   KD880
CARLE, ERIC. Eric Carle's animals, animals. Compiled by Laura Whipple. Philomel ISBN 0-399-21744-4; In Canada: Putnam, 1989. 88p. col. ill.
Includes indices.
An inspired choice of poems accompany vivid, boldly conceived illustrations of a variety of animals. The poems range from the solemnity of the Bible, Carl Sandburg and D.H. Lawrence to the mirthful refrains of Judith Viorst and Ogden Nash, all bearing homage to wonders of animal life. The exuberant drawings exemplify the words of the African pygmy "everything lives, everything dances, everything sings."
SUBJ: Poetry--Collections./ Animals--Poetry.

808.81   Ph-1 K-3 $18.95   L   KD881
CARLE, ERIC. Eric Carle's dragons dragons and other creatures that never were. Compiled by Laura Whipple. Illus. by Eric Carle. Philomel ISBN 0-399-22105-0; In Canada: Putnam, 1991. 69p. col. ill.
Includes glossary and index.
Selectors' Choice, 19th ed.
A melange of mythological monsters are vividly and dramatically depicted and are accompanied by poems from such writers as X.J. Kennedy and Myra Cohn Livingston. A stunning amalgam which will fascinate readers of all ages.
SUBJ: Animals, Mythical--Poetry./ Poetry--Collections.

808.81   Ph-2 P-1 $17.95   L   KD882
DYER, JANE. Animal crackers: a delectable collection of pictures, poems, and lullabies for the very young. Little, Brown ISBN 0-316-19766-1; In Canada: Little, Brown, 1996. 64p. col. ill.
Includes index.
A celebration of the golden days of youth is reflected in a charming collection of Mother Goose rhymes, lullabies, and verses. Muted watercolor illustrations create a feeling of coziness and warmth.
SUBJ: Poetry--Collections./ Nursery rhymes./ Lullabies.

808.81   Ph-1 3-6 $16.95   L   KD883
EARTH IS PAINTED GREEN: A GARDEN OF POEMS ABOUT OUR PLANET. Edited by Barbara Brenner. Illus. by S. D. Schindler. Scholastic ISBN 0-590-45134-0; In Canada: Scholastic, 1994. 81p. col. ill.
"Byron Preiss book."
Includes indexes.
A celebratory work reveling in the glories of our green planet. Lillian Morrison's poem articulates the prevailing theme, "I can never get my fill of chlorophyll." Nearly 100 poems by such poets as X. J. Kennedy, Shel Silverstein, Eve Merriam, and Jack Prelutsky capture the botanical beauty of the earth. An excellent anthology with poems which can be enjoyed for themselves or incorporated into units on the seasons, science, and environmental studies.
SUBJ: Earth--Poetry./ Nature--Poetry./ Poetry--Collections.

808.81   Ph-2 P-1 $16.95   L   KD884
FROG INSIDE MY HAT: A FIRST BOOK OF POEMS. Compiled by Fay Robinson. Illus. by Cyd Moore. BridgeWater ISBN 0-8167-3129-2, 1993. 62p. col. ill.
Gentle verses capture the essence of childhood in poems about food, animals, and seasons. Poets include Jack Prelutsky, Arnold Lobel, A.A. Milne, and Eve Merriam. A good collection for the very young accompanied by delightfully funny, colorful illustrations.
SUBJ: Poetry--Collections.

808.81   Ph-3 2-6 $14.95   T   KD885
INNER CHIMES: POEMS ON POETRY. Selected by Bobbye S. Goldstein. Illus. by Jane Breskin Zalben. Wordsong/Boyds Mills ISBN 1-56397-040-6, 1992. 24p. col. ill.
An anthology of poems about poetry joyfully recounts the magic in its creation and reflects on the ideas, feelings, and words that are integral to the process. Can be used in creative writing classes on the appreciation and understanding of the writing of poetry.
SUBJ: Poetry--Collections.

808.81   Ph-2 4-6 $12.79   T   KD886
LITTLE BOOK OF LOVE. Selected by Caroline Walsh. Illus. by Susan Field. Kingfisher/dist. by Raintree Steck-Vaughn ISBN 1-85697-535-5, 1995. 60p. col. ill.
Includes index.
An enchanting anthology of poems and nursery rhymes about love. The great writers are here--Shakespeare, Browning, and Herrick, as well as amusing ditties such as Arnold Adoff's "Chocolate, Chocolate." A perfect treasure--charming, romantic, witty--for all those who have ever loved.
SUBJ: Love--Poetry./ Poetry--Collections.

808.81   Ph-1 1-4 $16.95   L   KD887
MY SONG IS BEAUTIFUL: POEMS AND PICTURES IN MANY VOICES. Selected by Mary Ann Hoberman. Little, Brown ISBN 0-316-36738-9; In Canada: Little, Brown, 1994. 32p. col. ill.
A collection of 14 poems, both poignant and triumphant, celebrates the exuberance of childhood. Illustrations utilize a variety of techniques, and they are representative of many cultures. A lovely introduction to poetry for multicultural studies.
SUBJ: Poetry--Collections.

808.81   Ph-1 A $14.89   L   KD888
PEELING THE ONION: AN ANTHOLOGY OF POEMS. Selected by Ruth Gordon. HarperCollins ISBN 0-06-021728-6; In Canada: HarperCollins, 1993. 94p.
"Charlotte Zolotow book."
Includes indexes.
An international collection of poetry about animals, family, seasons, and a variety of life experiences. The haunting poems are beautifully written and would be particularly meaningful for the mature reader.
SUBJ: Poetry--Collections.

808.81   Ph-2 P-K $18.00   L   KD889
SLEEP, BABY, SLEEP: LULLABIES AND NIGHT POEMS. Selected and illus. by Michael Hague. Morrow ISBN 0-688-10877-6, 1994. 80p. col. ill.
Includes musical arrangements.
Glowing illustrations bring to life a charming collection of lullabies and night poems.
SUBJ: Poetry--Collections./ Bedtime--Poetry./ Sleep--Poetry./ Night--Poetry./ Lullabies.

808.81   Ph-1 P-3 $16.95   L   KD890
SLEEP RHYMES AROUND THE WORLD. Edited by Jane Yolen. Illus. by 17 international artists. Wordsong/Boyds Mills ISBN 1-56397-243-3, 1994. 40p. col. ill.
Twenty-one lullabies from seventeen countries are rendered in both the original language and the English translation. International illustrators capture the essence of their various cultures in exquisite illustrations. The beautifully conceived collection is excellent for enriching multicultural studies.
SUBJ: Bedtime--Poetry./ Poetry--Collections./ Bilingual materials.

808.81   Ph-2 K-3 $18.95   T   KD891
TOMIE DE PAOLA'S BOOK OF POEMS. Selected and illustrated by Tomie De Paola. Putnam ISBN 0-399-21540-9; In Canada: Putnam, 1988. 96p. col. ill.
Includes index.
Full color illustrations illuminate a choice collection of 80 plus poems ranging from the works of classic poets such as William Blake and Lewis Carroll to the modern poets such as Jack Prelutsky and Judith Viorst. This potpourri contains something for everyone--all with a sense of humor or a sense of wonder.
SUBJ: Poetry--Collections.

808.81   Ph-2 2-5 $13.95   L   KD892
WIND IN THE LONG GRASS: A COLLECTION OF HAIKU. Edited by William J. Higginson. Illus. by Sandra Speidel. Simon & Schuster ISBN 0-671-67978-3; In Canada: Simon & Schuster, 1991. unp. col. ill.
Dreamy, evocative illustrations join with poems in haiku form written by poets from around the world. Will inspire budding poets as they write their own haiku.
SUBJ: Haiku./ Poetry--Collections.

808.86   Ph-2 3-6 $16.89   L   KD893
DEAR LAURA: LETTERS FROM CHILDREN TO LAURA INGALLS
WILDER. HarperCollins ISBN 0-06-026275-3; In Canada: HarperCollins,
1996. 152p. ill. (some col.).
Includes directory.
Includes over 100 of the letters and drawings sent to Laura Ingalls
Wilder by her admiring fans with photographs of the author and her
home. A list of the Little House sites and museums complete the book.
Use to encourage creative writing projects or correspondence with
favorite contemporary authors.
SUBJ: Wilder, Laura Ingalls--Correspondence./ Children's writings./
Books and reading./ Women authors, American--Correspondence.

808.88   Ph-3 3-6 $14.93   L   KD894
YOURS TILL BANANA SPLITS: 201 AUTOGRAPH RHYMES. Compiled
by Joanna Cole and Stephanie Calmenson. Illus. by Alan Tiegreen.
Morrow ISBN 0-688-13186-7, 1995. 64p. ill.
Includes bibliography.
An amusing anthology of autographs contains a witty collection of
insults, puns, jokes, and rhymes. For collections where autograph
books are part of the year-end tradition.
SUBJ: American poetry--Collections./ Humorous poetry--Collections./
Autograph verses.

809.3   Ph-3 3-6/8 $13.95   L   KD895
RAINEY, RICHARD. Monster factory. New Discovery ISBN 0-02-
775663-7; In Canada: Maxwell Macmillan, 1993. 128p. ill.
"Wordsmith book."
Includes bibliography and index.
Examines the lives and works of the authors of literature's most
famous monsters. Includes the real-life stories that formed the
backgrounds for Washington Irving's THE HEADLESS HORSEMAN,
Mary Shelley's FRANKENSTEIN, and Bram Stoker's DRACULA.
Enhances appreciation of this genre of literature.
SUBJ: Authors./ Monsters in literature./ Horror stories--History and
criticism.

810.8   Ph-1 3-A/7 $24.95   T   KD896
CHILDREN OF PROMISE: AFRICAN-AMERICAN LITERATURE AND ART
FOR YOUNG PEOPLE. Edited by Charles Sullivan. Abrams ISBN
0-8109-3170-2, 1991. 126p. ill. (some col.).
Includes bibliographical notes and index.
Selectors' Choice, 19th ed.
The African-American experience is reflected in art and literature. The
poetry, prose, historical photographs, and reproductions of paintings
and sculpture are stirring. A fine introduction to the achievements of
African-American authors. Superb component of multicultural studies.
SUBJ: Afro-Americans--Literary collections./ American literature--Afro-
American authors--Collections./ Art appreciation.

810.8   Ph-3 4-6 $14.50   T   KD897
CHRISTMAS GIF': AN ANTHOLOGY OF CHRISTMAS POEMS,
SONGS, AND STORIES WRITTEN BY AND ABOUT AFRICAN-
AMERICANS. Compiled by Charlemae Hill Rollins. Illus. by Ashley Bryan.
With a new introduction by Dr. Augusta Baker. Morrow ISBN 0-688-
11667-1, 1993. 106p. ill.
Includes indexes.
A reissue of the 1963 anthology with stories and poems by such
African-American writers as Langston Hughes, Paul Laurence Dunbar,
and Booker T. Washington. Some stories may seem dated, and others
have difficult dialect. Will be most effective when taught in historical
context. For multicultural studies.
SUBJ: Christmas--Literary collections./ Afro-Americans--Literary
collections.

810.8   Ph-3 K-A $6.99   P   KD898
DIANE GOODE'S AMERICAN CHRISTMAS. Selected and illustrated by
Diane Goode. Penguin ISBN 0-14-056254-0, 1997. 80p. col. ill.
The many splendored celebrations of Christmas are evoked in this
collection of familiar songs, poems, and stories. Includes such diverse
selections as the amusing poem "Mr. Willoughby's Christmas Tree,"
the popular song "Silver Bells," and the classic story "The Peterkins'
Christmas Tree."
SUBJ: Christmas--Literary collections./ Christmas--Poetry./ Christmas
music.

810.8   Ph-1 K-6 $39.95   L   KD899
FROM SEA TO SHINING SEA: A TREASURY OF AMERICAN
FOLKLORE AND FOLK SONGS. Compiled by Amy L. Cohn. Illus. by
eleven Caldecott Medal and four Caldecott Honor book artists: Molly
Bang...[et al.]. Scholastic ISBN 0-590-42868-3; In Canada: Scholastic,
1993. 399p. col. ill.
Includes glossary, bibliography, indexes, and chronology.
Selectors' Choice, 20th ed.

A compendium of Americana dramatizes the triumphs and tragedies
of our country as reflected in stories, songs, poetry, and speeches.
The stunning illustrations complement an extensive range of subjects
including Native American creation myths, Paul Revere's ride, the
horrors of slavery, the shame of Japanese American imprisonment
during World War II, and Martin Luther King, Jr.'s "I have a
dream" speech. A fine collection of folklore that can enrich the
curriculum, extend the breadth of knowledge about America, and
increase pride in and understanding of the multicultural heritage of the
United States. Essential for interdisciplinary curricula and multicultural
studies.
SUBJ: United States--Literary collections./ Folklore--United States--
Collections./ United States--Folklore--Collections./ Folk songs--United
States.

810.8   Ph-2 K-6 $4.95   P   KD900
HOME. Edited by Michael J. Rosen. HarperTrophy ISBN 0-06-443470-2;
In Canada: HarperCollins, 1992. unp. col. ill.
"Charlotte Zolotow book."
A collection of poems ranging from Virginia Hamilton's poignant
"Under the back porch" to a hilarious account of living in a
refrigerator by Arthur Yorinks. The illustrations can be as exuberant
as Aliki's vibrant and colorful concept of bedtime or as surrealistic as
the kitchen table drawn by Vladimir Radunsky. This outstanding,
varied collection is a project of SOS (Save Our Strength) to which
the authors and illustrators have donated their talents to provide aid
to the homeless. Students can write their own poems on the meaning
of home and on the plight of the homeless.
SUBJ: Homeless persons--Literary collections./ Literature--Collections.

810.8   Ph-1 P-2 $17.95   T   KD901
READY...SET...READ!: THE BEGINNING READER'S TREASURY.
Compiled by Joanna Cole and Stephanie Calmenson. Illus. by Anne
Burgess...[et al.]. Doubleday ISBN 0-385-41416-1; In Canada: Bantam
Doubleday Dell, 1990. 144p. col. ill.
Includes indexes.
An anthology of delightful stories, poems, and word games for
beginning readers. Includes such beloved characters as Minarik's
"Little Bear," Lobel's "Frog and Toad" and delightful poems by
Eve Merriam, David McCord, and Gwendolyn Brooks. An appealing
collection which will encourage a love of reading.
SUBJ: Literature--Collections.

810.8   Ph-2 K-2 $17.95   T   KD902
READY...SET...READ--AND LAUGH!: A FUNNY TREASURY FOR
BEGINNING READERS. Compiled by Joanna Cole and Stephanie
Calmenson. Doubleday ISBN 0-385-32119-8; In Canada: Bantam
Doubleday Dell, 1995. 144p. col. ill.
Companion to: READY...SET...READ!
Includes indexes.
Bright, amusing illustrations enliven a collection of stories, songs,
poems, and riddles. Includes the humorous reflections of such authors
as Jack Prelutsky, Peggy Parish, and Dr. Seuss.
SUBJ: Literature--Collections./ Humorous stories./ Humorous poetry.

810.8   Ph-2 5-A/7 $12.95   L   KD903
RISING VOICES: WRITINGS OF YOUNG NATIVE AMERICANS.
Selected by Arlene B. Hirschfelder and Beverly R. Singer. Scribner's
ISBN 0-684-19207-1; In Canada: Maxwell Macmillan, 1992. 115p.
Includes index.
Available from the National Library Service for the Blind and
Physically Handicapped on sound recording cassette RC 37035.
Young Native Americans speak of their identity, rituals, family, and
history in a collection of poems and essays. Excellent for
incorporation into multicultural studies and for research papers.
SUBJ: Indians of North America--Literary collections./ American
literature--Indian authors--Collections./ Youths' writings./ Children's
writings.

810.8   Ph-1 K-3 $18.95   L   KD904
SCARED SILLY! A BOOK FOR THE BRAVE. Compiled and illus. by Marc
Brown. Little, Brown ISBN 0-316-11360-3; In Canada: Little, Brown,
1994. 61p. col. ill.
Includes indexes.
An enchanting collection of poems, stories, songs, games, and
riddles--all designed to encourage laughing at one's fears. Illustrations
of some adorable witches and monsters are certain to captivate even
the most timid. For reading aloud at Halloween and throughout the
year.
SUBJ: Literature--Collections./ Supernatural--Literary collections./
Ghosts--Literary collections./ Monsters--Literary collections.

810.8   Ph-3 K-6 $9.50   P   KD905
TUN-TA-CA-TUN: MORE STORIES AND POEMS IN ENGLISH AND
SPANISH FOR CHILDREN. Edited by Sylvia Cavazos Pena. Illus. by
Narciso Pena. Arte Publico Press ISBN 0-934770-43-3, 1986. 191p. ill.
> Presents a compilation of stories and poems in English and Spanish.
> Useful for schools with ESL programs and for incorporation into
> multicultural studies.
> SUBJ: American literature--Collections./ Spanish literature--
> Collections./ Spanish language materials./ Bilingual materials--Spanish.

810.9   Ph-2 K-6/7 $19.95   T   KD906
CURRY, BARBARA K. Sweet words so brave: the story of African
American literature. By Barbara K. Curry and James Michael Brodie. Illus.
by Jerry Butler. Zino Press ISBN 1-55933-179-8, 1996. 64p. col. ill.
> Includes glossary and bibliography.
> A grandfather speaks to his granddaughter, revealing the history of
> African-American literature. Colorful, dramatic illustrations interspersed
> with black and white photographs tell about slave narratives, and the
> works of such well-known African American writers as Phillis
> Wheatley, Langston Hughes, Richard Wright, and Maya Angelou. A
> significant addition to multicultural studies.
> SUBJ: American literature--Afro-American authors--History and
> criticism.

811   Ph-3 4-6 $13.93   L   KD907
ADOFF, ARNOLD. All the colors of the race. Illus. by John Steptoe.
Lothrop, Lee & Shepard ISBN 0-688-00880-1, 1982. 56p. col. ill.
> Available from National Library Service for the Blind and Physically
> Handicapped on sound recording cassette RC23525.
> A young girl explores her feelings about herself vis-a-vis how she is
> perceived because one parent is black and one is white. A handsome
> and sensitive book.
> SUBJ: American poetry./ Family--Poetry./ Race awareness--Poetry.

811   Ph-2 P-A $3.95   P   KD908
ADOFF, ARNOLD. Eats. Illus. by Susan Russo. Lothrop, Lee & Shepard
ISBN 0-688-11695-7, c1979, 1992. unp. col. ill.
> Available from National Library Service for the Blind and Physically
> Handicapped in Braille BR04460.
> These hymns to gluttony glorify the delicious temptations of such
> treats as luscious, sinful chocolate "fudge and milk/ and german and
> sour cream/ light and dark and bitter sweet and/ even/ white/ you
> are no good/ for me/ you are no good/ you are so good." Fun for
> gourmands of all ages. Useful to stimulate the palate and creative
> writing as well.
> SUBJ: Food--Poetry./ American poetry.

811   Ph-3 1-2 $12.88   L   KD909
ADOFF, ARNOLD. Hard to be six. Illus. by Cheryl Hanna. Lothrop, Lee
& Shepard ISBN 0-688-09579-8, 1991. unp. col. ill.
> A six-year-old boy wants to grow up quickly, but is counselled to
> value patience by his grandmother. He is part of a warm, loving
> interracial family who participate in activities all children will
> recognize. A good read-aloud in blank verse with some rhyme.
> SUBJ: Growth--Poetry./ Family life--Poetry.

811   Ph-2 1-4 $14.95   L   KD910
ADOFF, ARNOLD. In for winter, out for spring. Illus. by Jerry Pinkney.
Harcourt Brace Jovanovich ISBN 0-15-238637-8, 1991. unp. col. ill.
> A celebration of family life chronicled through the seasons by a young
> black girl. Her love of nature is shared with her brother, parents, and
> grandmother as they view the quiet miracles of each changing season.
> Useful for incorporation into nature study.
> SUBJ: Seasons--Poetry./ Family life--Poetry./ American poetry.

811   Ph-1 K-4 $15.95   L   KD911
ADOFF, ARNOLD. Love letters. Illus. by Lisa Desimini. Blue Sky Press/
Scholastic ISBN 0-590-48478-8; In Canada: Scholastic, 1997. unp. col.
ill.
> Twenty enchanting love poems exhibit humor, joie de vivre, and
> delight in the human spirit. These romantic letters are written to
> teachers, to fellow classmates, to grandmothers, and, of course, to
> mother who is urged to "keep momming." A variety of collage and
> photography techniques are used to create unique illustrations. For
> Valentine's Day or any day.
> SUBJ: Love--Poetry./ American poetry.

VCR 811   Ph-2 P-2 $275.00   OD KD912
ALLIGATOR PIE (Videocassette). Beacon Films/Altschul Group 8516,
1993. 1/2" VHS videocassette color (48min).
> Includes public performance rights.
> Young Nicholas has wild adventures with a group of stuffed animals
> that come to life. Imaginative spoof based on the poems of Dennis
> Lee that combines live action, puppetry, and claymation.
> SUBJ: Nonsense verses./ Canadian poetry./ Imagination--Poetry.

811   Ph-1 3-A $19.93   L   KD913
ALTMAN, SUSAN. Followers of the North Star: rhymes about African
American heroes, heroines, and historical times. By Susan Altman and
Susan Lechner. Illus. by Byron Wooden. Childrens Press ISBN 0-516-
05151-2; In Canada: Childrens Press, 1993. 48p. col. ill. (Many voices,
one song).
> Extols African-American heroes and heroines as they battle slavery,
> prejudice, and poverty and fight for integration, civil rights, and a
> place in the American dream. Includes poems about such leaders as
> Benjamin Banneker, astronomer; Matthew Henson, explorer; Jackie
> Robinson, baseball player; Leontyne Price, opera star; Thurgood
> Marshall, Supreme Court justice; and Guion Bluford, Jr., astronaut. A
> moving, inspirational collection that can be used across the curriculum,
> integrating the African-American experience into every course of
> study. For multicultural studies.
> SUBJ: Afro-Americans--Poetry./ American poetry.

811   Ph-1 3-5 $15.95   L   KD914
ASKA, WARABE. Aska's sea creatures. Text by David Day. Doubleday
ISBN 0-385-32107-4; In Canada: Doubleday, 1994. unp. col. ill.
> Dramatic boldly colored paintings recreate the world of sea creatures.
> Lyrical poems describe the octopus, stingray, great white shark, and
> dolphin. An exquisite work of art to complement interdisciplinary units
> on ocean life.
> SUBJ: Marine animals--Poetry./ Canadian poetry.

811   Ph-3 P-1 $13.95   L   KD915
AYLESWORTH, JIM. Cat and the fiddle and more. Illus. by Richard Hull.
Atheneum ISBN 0-689-31715-8; In Canada: Maxwell Macmillan, 1992.
unp. col. ill.
> Nonsensical variations on the traditional Mother Goose rhyme about
> the cat and the fiddle are accompanied by equally ridiculous
> illustrations. Wonderful rhythm and detailed drawings will captivate
> the youngest readers.
> SUBJ: Nursery rhymes--Adaptations./ American poetry.

811   Ph-2 P-2 $15.00   T   KD916
BENJAMIN, ALAN. Nickel buys a rhyme. Illus. by Karen Lee Schmidt.
Morrow ISBN 0-688-06698-4, 1993. unp. col. ill.
> A collection of witty verses accompanied by charming, often hilarious
> illustrations. The short poems cover such popular subjects as animals,
> bellyaches, snobbery, friends, wishes, and the love of reading. An
> excellent introduction to the joys of poetry.
> SUBJ: American poetry.

811   Ph-3 K-6 $14.95   T   KD917
BORNSTEIN, HARRY. Night before Christmas: told in sign language: an
adaptation of the original poem "A visit from St. Nicholas" by Clement
C. Moore. By Harry Bornstein and Karen Luczak Saulnier. Illus. by
Stephen Marchesi. Sign drawings by Jan Skrobisz. Kendall Green ISBN
1-56368-020-3, 1994. unp. col. ill.
> Includes bibliography.
> Line drawings illustrating the sign language for each word present the
> familiar Christmas poem. Deaf and hearing impaired children and
> hearing students interested in signing will also find this a fascinating
> experience. Use as a supplement in units on persons with disabilities.
> SUBJ: Santa Claus--Poetry./ Christmas--Poetry./ American poetry./
> Narrative poetry./ Sign language.

811   Ph-2 P-2 $14.89   L   KD918
BROWN, MARGARET WISE. Under the sun and the moon and other
poems. Illus. by Tom Leonard. Hyperion ISBN 1-56282-355-8; In
Canada: Little, Brown, 1993. 33p. col. ill.
> Nineteen previously unpublished poems extol the joys of nature with
> emphasis on the changing of the seasons, insects, and animals. The
> illustrations are quiet and gentle and are perfect accompaniments to
> the imaginative poems.
> SUBJ: American poetry.

811   Ph-1 2-6 $15.95   L   KD919
BRUCHAC, JOSEPH. Thirteen moons on turtle's back: a Native American
year of moons. By Joseph Bruchac and Jonathan London. Illus. by
Thomas Locker. Philomel ISBN 0-399-22141-7; In Canada: Putnam,
1992. unp. col. ill.
> A collection of poems based on Native American legends recounts the
> wonders of the changing seasons. Dramatic, luminous oil paintings
> reveal the glories of nature and give life to moon stories from 13
> North American tribal nations. Excellent for integrating into
> multicultural units on Native Americans.
> SUBJ: Indians of North America--Folklore./ Indians of North
> America--Poetry./ American poetry./ Seasons--Poetry.

811   Ph-2 P-1 $14.00   T   KD920
CARLSTROM, NANCY WHITE. Who said boo?: Halloween poems for
the very young. Illus. by R. W. Alley. Simon & Schuster ISBN 0-689-
80308-7; In Canada: Distican, 1995. 32p. col. ill.
> A gentle glimpse into a gaggle of ghosts and goblins, haunted
> houses, and funny aspects of Halloween. Definitely will not frighten
> anyone.
> SUBJ: Halloween--Poetry./ American poetry.

811   Ph-3 3-6 $13.89   L   KD921
CASSEDY, SYLVIA. Zoomrimes: poems about things that go. Illus. by
Michele Chessare. HarperCollins ISBN 0-06-022633-1; In Canada:
HarperCollins, 1993. 51p. ill.
> Things that go--arks, dogsleds, unicycles--arranged in an alphabetic
> framework are the subjects of 26 poems. A variety of poetic forms
> are used and can be the basis for creative writing exercises.
> SUBJ: Transportation--Poetry./ American poetry.

811   Ph-3 3-6 $13.95   T   KD922
CIARDI, JOHN. Monster den: or look what happened at my house - and
to it. Illus. by Edward Gorey. Wordsong/Boyds Mills ISBN 1-878093-
35-5, c1966, 1991. 62p b&w illus.
> In this collection of nonsense verse, one of our most distinguished
> American poets and his illustrator present to us some of the monsters
> in his home--including his own children Benn, John L., and Myra.
> SUBJ: American poetry./ Humorous poetry.

811   Ph-3 3-5 $13.95   T   KD923
CIARDI, JOHN. You know who. Illus. by Edward Gorey. Wordsong/
Boyds Mills ISBN 1-878093-34-7, c1964, 1991. 63p. ill.
> Humorous poems about the problems of childhood--skinning knees,
> running away from home, and getting up late for school. Ciardi's
> poems are accompanied by Edward Gorey's delightfully funny
> drawings.
> SUBJ: American poetry./ Humorous poetry.

Kit 811   Ph-3 3-5 $24.90   OD   KD924
CIARDI, JOHN. You know who, John J. Plenty and Fiddler Dan, and
other poems (Kit). Spoken Arts SAC6692C, n.d. 1 hardback book, 1
sound cassette.
> Available from National Library Service for the Blind and Physically
> Handicapped as talking book TB01117.
> John Ciardi reads some of his most popular poetry for children,
> including About Eskimos and Why they wear pants, The king who
> saved himself from being saved, You know who, Fiddler Dan and
> John J. Plenty. A lively and whimsical collection, read with gusto and
> every proper nuance. Good technical production.
> SUBJ: Nonsense verses./ American poetry.

811   Ph-2 P-1 $14.95   T   KD925
CLIFTON, LUCILLE. Everett Anderson's Christmas coming. Illus. by Jan
Spivey Gilchrist. Henry Holt ISBN 0-8050-1549-3; In Canada: Fitzhenry
& Whiteside, 1991. unp. col. ill.
> Everett Anderson spends the five days before Christmas watching
> snow fall, window shopping, and decorating the tree while
> anticipating the holiday. Bright new illustrations framed in red
> accompany the verse in this seasonal choice originally published in
> 1971.
> SUBJ: Christmas--Poetry./ Apartment houses--Poetry./ Single-parent
> family--Poetry./ Afro-Americans--Poetry./ Stories in rhyme.

811   Ph-1 2-6 $11.99   L   KD926
CUMMINGS, E. E. Hist whist. Illus. by Deborah Kogan Ray. Crown
ISBN 0-517-57258-3, c1923, 1989. unp col illus.
> Dark, eerie illustrations capture the mystery of Halloween and the
> spirit of E.E. Cummings' classic poem of witches with warts on their
> noses and great green dancing devils. Certain to scare and delight
> the young readers. Great for reading out loud.
> SUBJ: Halloween--Poetry./ American poetry.

811   Ph-1 3-6 $20.60   L   KD927
CUMPIAN, CARLOS. Latino rainbow: poems about Latino Americans.
Illus. by Richard Leonard. Childrens Press ISBN 0-516-05153-9; In
Canada: Childrens Press, 1994. 47p. col. ill. (Many voices, one song).
> Includes glossary.
> Recounts the triumphs and tragedies of Hispanic history. Brief
> biographical poems about such luminaries as Joan Baez, Cesar
> Chavez, and Roberto Clemente provide vivid and dramatic insight into
> the Latin American heritage. Fine for choral reading and for
> supplementing multicultural studies.
> SUBJ: Hispanic Americans--Poetry./ American poetry.

811   Ph-3 4-6 $13.95   L   KD928
DAKOS, KALLI. Don't read this book, whatever you do!: more poems
about school. Illus. by G. Brian Karas. Four Winds ISBN 0-02-725582-4;
In Canada: Maxwell Macmillan, 1993. 64p. ill.
> A collection of poems examines elementary school life. Includes such
> subjects as best friends, spelling tests, and boring classes. A popular
> subject of great amusement to students.
> SUBJ: Schools--Poetry./ American poetry.

811   Ph-2 2-5 $12.95   L   KD929
DAKOS, KALLI. If you're not here, please raise your hand: poems about
school. Illus. by G. Brian Karas. Four Winds/Macmillan ISBN 0-02-
725581-6; In Canada: Collier Macmillan, 1990. 60p. ill.
> A collection of poems which perpetuate the pranks, pratfalls, and
> problems of elementary school students. Excuses, fear of failure, and
> the triumphs all ring of veracity.
> SUBJ: Schools--Poetry./ American poetry.

811   Ph-3 P-K $4.99   P   KD930
DEMING, A. G. Who is tapping at my window? Illus. by Monica
Wellington. Puffin Unicorn ISBN 0-14-054553-0; In Canada: Penguin,
c1988, 1994. unp. col. ill.
> Big book available (ISBN 0-14-080303-X, c1988, 1994), $17.99.
> An enchanting picture book in which a child speculates who is tapping
> at her window. The repetitive refrain and predictable story will
> encourage audience participation until listeners discover that it is the
> rain. For reading aloud.
> SUBJ: Rain--Poetry./ American poetry.

811   Ph-1 1-4 $13.95   L   KD931
DE REGNIERS, BEATRICE SCHENK. Way I feel--sometimes. Illus. by
Susan Meddaugh. Clarion/Houghton Mifflin ISBN 0-89919-647-0, 1988.
48p. col. ill.
> Expresses emotions common to children ranging from churlishness to
> cheerfulness in witty poems abetted by lively water color illustrations
> that accurately reflect the moods and vagaries of the young.
> SUBJ: Emotions--Poetry./ American poetry.

811   Ph-3 3-6 $17.95   T   KD932
DICKINSON, EMILY. Brighter garden. Collected by Karen Ackerman.
Illus. by Tasha Tudor. Philomel ISBN 0-399-21490-9; In Canada: Putnam,
1990. 63p. col. ill.
> The talents of Emily Dickinson and Tasha Tudor combine to create a
> gently beautiful amalgam of intensely personal, simple poetry and
> delicate watercolor paintings that evoke the change of seasons in a
> work of classic beauty.
> SUBJ: American poetry.

811   Ph-3 4-A $14.95   T   KD933
DICKINSON, EMILY. Poetry for young people. Edited by Frances
Schoonmaker Bolin. Illus. by Chi Chung. Sterling ISBN 0-8069-0635-9; In
Canada: Sterling c/o Canadian Manda, 1994. 48p. col. ill.
> "Magnolia Editions book."
> Includes bibliography and index.
> Emily Dickinson glorified the everyday world, finding magic in insects,
> the sunrise, and the warmth of snow. For the gifted student.
> SUBJ: American poetry.

811   Ph-1 4-6 $13.89   L   KD934
FLEISCHMAN, PAUL. Joyful noise: poems for two voices. Illus. by Eric
Beddows. HarperCollins ISBN 0-06-021853-3, 1988. 44p. ill.
> Newbery Medal.
> Selectors' Choice, 17th ed.
> Available from National Library Service for the Blind and Physically
> Handicapped on sound recording cassette RC28922.
> Guides the reader through the world of the insect with a poetic
> vocabulary that hauntingly re-creates the sounds and movements of a
> variety of insects. The poems are written to be read aloud by 2
> readers at once and they are excellent for encouraging dramatic
> expression while increasing the vocabulary and knowledge of insects.
> SUBJ: Insects--Poetry./ American poetry.

811   Ph-1 K-3 $14.95   L   KD935
FLORIAN, DOUGLAS. Beast feast. Poems and paintings by Douglas
Florian. Harcourt Brace ISBN 0-15-295178-4; In Canada: Harcourt Brace
c/o Canadian Manda, 1994. 48p. col. ill.
> This collection of amusing poems about a variety of beasts including
> the barracuda, the bat, and the boa serves as an excellent
> introduction to poetry. Humorous paintings are certain to provoke
> guffaws.
> SUBJ: Animals--Poetry./ Humorous poetry./ American poetry.

811   Ph-1 3-6 $15.95   T   KD936
FLORIAN, DOUGLAS. Bing bang boing. Poems and drawings by
Douglas Florian. Harcourt Brace ISBN 0-15-233770-9; In Canada:
Harcourt Brace c/o Canadian Manda, 1994. 144p. ill.
> Includes indexes.
> More than 170 nonsense verses are delightfully wicked, wily, and
> winsome. The titles reveal the world of children and their concerns--
> "They put me in the stupid class," School cafeteria," "I'm in the
> mood for mud," and "Little-naughty-nasty Ned." Wonderful
> addition to the study of poetry is bound to enliven any school day.
> SUBJ: American poetry./ Nonsense verses.

811   Ph-2 1-3 $15.00   L   KD937
FLORIAN, DOUGLAS. In the swim: poems and paintings. Harcourt Brace
ISBN 0-15-201307-5; In Canada: Harcourt Brace c/o Canadian Manda,
1997. 48p. col. ill.
> A collection of charming, witty poems about such denizens of the
> underwater world as sharks, manatees, and eels. The watercolor
> illustrations are fluid and inventive. A beautiful combination of simple
> rhymes and extraordinary paintings. Useful for integrating into studies
> of sea life.
> SUBJ: Marine animals--Poetry./ Humorous poetry./ American poetry.

811   Ph-2 4-6 $13.95   L   KD938
FLORIAN, DOUGLAS. Monster Motel: poems and paintings. Harcourt
Brace Jovanovich ISBN 0-15-255320-7; In Canada: Harcourt Brace
Jovanovich c/o Canadian Manda, 1993. unp. col. ill.
> The horribly horrid Monster Motel is home to the Brilly who munches
> traffic signs for lunch, the Bleen who is a mean and rotten ghoul, and
> the Slender Slimy Slatch. Comical illustrations and spirited wordplay
> introduce poetry in an imaginative manner.
> SUBJ: Monsters--Poetry./ American poetry.

811   Ph-2 1-4 $16.00   L   KD939
FLORIAN, DOUGLAS. On the wing: bird poems and paintings. Harcourt
Brace ISBN 0-15-200497-1; In Canada: Harcourt Brace c/o Canadian
Manda, 1996. 47p. col. ill.
> A bevy of birds is discussed in 21 delightfully whimsical watercolor
> illustrations and irreverent poems. The humor inherent in both words
> and pictures bring such birds as the rhinocerous hornbill, the
> roadrunner, and the royal spoonbill to life. Great fun for units on bird
> life.
> SUBJ: Birds--Poetry./ American poetry.

811   Ph-2 4-A $14.95   T   KD940
FROST, ROBERT. Poetry for young people. Edited by Gary D. Schmidt.
Illus. by Henri Sorensen. Sterling ISBN 0-8069-0633-2; In Canada:
Sterling c/o Canadian Manda, 1994. 48p. col. ill.
> "Magnolia Editions book."
> Includes index.
> A collection of 29 seasonal poems by one of America's greatest
> poets. Includes a brief biography of Frost, thought-provoking notes,
> and such favorites as "The road not taken," "Birches," and
> "Mending wall." Good collection for the gifted student.
> SUBJ: American poetry./ Seasons--Poetry.

811   Ph-3 P-A $13.00   L   KD941
FROST, ROBERT. Stopping by the woods on a snowy evening. Illus. by
Susan Jeffers. Dutton ISBN 0-525-40115-6, 1978. unp. col. ill.
> Double-page spreads muted in tone and gloriously detailed in soft
> pencil and watercolors illustrate Frost's familiar and well loved poem.
> SUBJ: Winter--Poetry./ American poetry.

811   Ph-2 3-6 $21.95   T   KD942
FROST, ROBERT. Swinger of birches: poems of Robert Frost for young
people. Introduction by Clifton Fadiman. Illus. by Peter Koeppen.
Stemmer House ISBN 0-916144-92-5, 1982. 80p. col. ill.
> Includes glossary.
> Directed toward young readers, this collection of Frost's most popular
> poems achieves new interest due to the pictorial presentation. The
> introduction and glossary are helpful. An enrichment for poetry units.
> SUBJ: American poetry.

811   Ph-2 5-6 $14.95   L   KD943
FROST, ROBERT. You come too: favorite poems for young readers.
Wood engravings by Thomas W. Nason. Henry Holt ISBN 0-8050-
0299-5; In Canada: Fitzhenry & Whiteside, c1959, 1987. 94p. ill.
> Available from National Library Service for the Blind and Physically
> Handicapped in Braille BRA07024.
> Fifty-one of the better-known poems of Robert Frost serve as an
> excellent introduction to his work when read to or by young people.
> SUBJ: Nature--Poetry./ American poetry.

811   Ph-3 P-1 $14.89   L   KD944
GHIGNA, CHARLES. Tickle Day: poems from Father Goose. Illus. by
Cyd Moore. Hyperion ISBN 0-7868-2010-1, 1994. 40p. col. ill.
> Charming verses celebrate the joys of nature. Imaginative concepts
> and illustrations will provoke smiles and giggles from the very
> youngest. Great for reading aloud.
> SUBJ: Nature--Poetry./ American poetry.

811   Ph-2 P-1/2 $14.95   L   KD945
GIOVANNI, NIKKI. Knoxville, Tennessee. Illus. by Larry Johnson.
Scholastic ISBN 0-590-47074-4; In Canada: Scholastic, 1994. unp. col.
ill.
> A gentle poem about childhood visits to beloved grandparents evokes
> summer memories of church picnics, homemade ice cream, and gospel
> music in the mind of an African-American girl. Warm, deeply colored
> illustrations reflect the joys of summer and of family life. For
> multicultural studies.
> SUBJ: Afro-Americans--Poetry./ Family life--Poetry./ Knoxville
> (Tenn.)--Poetry./ Summer--Poetry./ American poetry--Afro-American
> authors.

811   Ph-3 1-4 $3.50   P   KD946
GIOVANNI, NIKKI. Spin a soft black song. Rev. ed. Illus. by George
Martins. Farrar, Straus & Giroux ISBN 0-374-46469-3; In Canada:
HarperCollins, c1971, 1985. 57p b&w illus.
> Illuminates the experiences of black children with ingenuous wit and
> wisdom complimented by soft pencil drawings.
> SUBJ: Afro-Americans--Poetry./ American poetry--Afro-American
> authors.

811   Ph-3 4-6/7 $15.95   T   KD947
GRANFIELD, LINDA. In Flanders Fields: the story of the poem by John
McCrae. Illus. by Janet Wilson. Doubleday ISBN 0-385-32228-3; In
Canada: Lester Publishing, 1995. unp. col. ill.
> The history of the famous poem is a backdrop for historical
> information about World War I. Gives insight into the horrors and
> tragedies of that terrible war.
> SUBJ: McCrae, John. In Flanders fields./ World War, 1914-1918--
> Literature and the war./ War--Poetry.

811   Ph-1 K-6 $12.95   T   KD948
GREENFIELD, ELOISE. Nathaniel talking. Illus. by Jan Spivey Gilchrist.
Black Butterfly ISBN 0-86316-200-2, 1988. unp b&w illus.
> A collection of sensitive, thought-provoking poems articulated by a
> nine-year-old African-American child named Nathaniel B. Free. He
> ruminates on friendship, families, life, and death. He speaks to all
> children, but African-American children will identify with him and the
> pencil illustrations of Nathaniel and his pals.
> SUBJ: American poetry--Afro-American authors./ Family life--Poetry.

811   Ph-2 2-4 $14.93   L   KD949
GRIMES, NIKKI. Meet Danitra Brown. Illus. by Floyd Cooper. Lothrop,
Lee & Shepard ISBN 0-688-12074-1, 1994. unp. col. ill.
> Coretta Scott King Illustrator Honor book, 1995.
> Thirteen original poems offer a paean to friendship. Two young
> African-American girls reveal the closeness they feel for each other,
> the pride they take in each other's achievements, and the pain and
> joy they share. There is universality in the school and neighborhood
> experiences of these two urban youths. An excellent book to promote
> understanding and appreciation. For multicultural studies.
> SUBJ: Afro-Americans--Poetry./ City and town life--Poetry./
> Friendship--Poetry./ Single-parent family--Poetry./ American poetry.

811   Ph-2 P-3 $14.95   L   KD950
GUNNING, MONICA. Not a copper penny in me house: poems from
the Caribbean. Illus. by Frane Lessac. Wordsong/Boyds Mills ISBN
1-56397-050-3; In Canada: McClelland & Stewart, 1993. 31p. col. ill.
> The life of a Caribbean child is vividly revealed in poems about
> tropical hurricanes, classes under the trees, and markets in the village
> square. Primitive paintings in rich, vibrant colors convey the charms
> and hardships of Caribbean life. A lovely component for multicultural
> studies.
> SUBJ: Caribbean poetry (English)./ Caribbean Area--Poetry.

811   Ph-3 2-6 $13.95   T   KD951
HARRISON, DAVID L. Somebody catch my homework. Illus. by Betsy
Lewin. Wordsong/Boyds Mills ISBN 1-878093-87-8, 1993. 31p. col. ill.
> Lively poems about the agonies and ecstasies of the elementary
> school experience.
> SUBJ: American poetry./ Schools--Poetry.

811   Ph-2 P-1 $16.99   L   KD952
HO, MINFONG. Hush!: a Thai lullaby. Illus. by Holly Meade. Orchard
ISBN 0-531-08850-2, 1996. unp. col. ill.

Caldecott Honor book, 1997.
A mother asks all the animals to be quiet, so that baby can sleep. The gentle cut-paper illustrations, quiet tone, and whimsical ending make this excellent for reading aloud and for choral reading. Repetitive, lyrical text creates a predictable book which beginning readers will easily master. Thai setting makes it suitable for multicultural studies.
SUBJ: Thailand--Poetry./ Lullabies./ American poetry.

811   Ph-2 3-6 $14.95   T   KD953
HOPKINS, LEE BENNETT. Been to yesterdays: poems of a life. Illus. by Charlene Rendeiro. Wordsong/Boyds Mills ISBN 1-56397-467-3; In Canada: McClelland & Stewart, 1995. 64p. ill.
Includes index.
Bittersweet poems capture the chaotic thirteenth year in the life of Lee Bennett Hopkins. The divorce of his parents, a move to a new home, attendance at different schools--all serve to create a painful period, but his aspirations and dreams are never daunted. Useful for bibliotherapy.
SUBJ: Poets, American./ Youth--Poetry./ Hopkins, Lee Bennett.

811   Ph-1 4-6 $12.99   L   KD954
HUGHES, LANGSTON. Dream keeper and other poems, including seven additional poems. Illus. by Brian Pinkney. Knopf ISBN 0-679-94421-4; In Canada: Random House, 1994. 83p. ill.
A beautiful collection of 66 poems, songs, and blues reflects the African-American experience. Hughes' poetry embodies hopes, dreams, and universalities that are applicable to all people. An uplifting, triumphant edition. For multicultural studies.
SUBJ: Afro-Americans--Poetry./ American poetry--Afro-American authors.

811   Ph-2 3-6 $20.60   L   KD955
IZUKI, STEVEN. Believers in America: poems about Americans of Asian and Pacific islander descent. Illus. by Bill Fukuda McCoy. Childrens Press ISBN 0-516-05152-0; In Canada: Childrens Press, 1994. 48p. col. ill.
(Many voices, one song).
Includes glossary.
The Asian-American experience is conveyed in poems that tell of the tribulations of Chinese railroad workers, Filipino migrant workers, and Japanese Americans interned during World War II and of the triumphs of such outstanding contributors to American life as Senator Daniel Inouye, Congresswoman Patsy Mink, and Kristi Yamaguchi, Olympic ice skater. Poems are of mixed quality, but useful for multicultural studies.
SUBJ: Asian Americans--Poetry./ Pacific Islander Americans--Poetry./ American poetry.

811   Ph-1 K-3 $15.95   L   KD956
JOHNSON, JAMES WELDON. Creation. Illustrated by James E. Ransome. Holiday House ISBN 0-8234-1069-2, 1994. unp. col. ill.
Coretta Scott King Illustrator Award, 1995.
The biblical story of God's creation of the world was written by James Weldon Johnson in 1919. In this newly illustrated version, the free verse is enhanced by dramatic illustratons which inspire awe. An African-American storyteller is depicted carrying on the oral tradition to a group of attentive listeners. For multicultural studies.
SUBJ: Creation--Poetry./ American poetry--Afro-American authors./ Bible stories--O.T.

811   Ph-1 1-6 $15.95   L   KD957
JOHNSON, JAMES WELDON. Creation: a poem. Illus. by Carla Golembe. Little, Brown ISBN 0-316-46744-8; In Canada: Little, Brown, 1993. unp. col. ill.
In this retelling of the creation story, one can hear the preacher's voice as he dramatically describes the beginning of the world. Expressive text combines with colorful and triumphant illustrations to create a moving reading experience for multicultural studies.
SUBJ: Creation--Poetry./ American poetry--Afro-American authors./ Bible stories--O.T.

811   Ph-3 K-3 $15.99   L   KD958
JOHNSTON, TONY. My Mexico--Mexico mio. Illus. by F. John Sierra. Putnam ISBN 0-399-22275-8; In Canada: BeJo Sales, 1996. 36p. col. ill.
Includes glossary.
A bilingual approach to love of country. Mexico is depicted in soft, pale colors as if part of a loving dream. The poems reflect everyday life activities. Useful for studying Mexico and in schools where there are bilingual classes. For multicultural studies.
SUBJ: Mexico--Poetry./ Spanish language materials./ Bilingual materials--Spanish.

811   Ph-2 1-3 $14.95   T   KD959
KATZ, BOBBI. Could we be friends?: poems for pals. Illus. by Joung Un Kim. Mondo ISBN 1-57255-230-1; In Canada: Scholastic, 1997. 32p. col. ill.
A collection of poignant poems about friendship. Many of the mixed feelings inherent in the verses could be the basis for discussion of hurts, wounds, sibling rivalry, love of pets, and the sadness of illness. Use as a model for creative writing activities.
SUBJ: Friendship--Poetry./ American poetry.

811   Ph-2 1-6 $14.95   L   KD960
KENNEDY, X. J. Beasts of Bethlehem. Verse by X.J. Kennedy. Illus. by Michael McCurdy. McElderry ISBN 0-689-50561-2; In Canada: Maxwell Macmillan, 1992. 39p. col. ill.
According to folk legends, animals were blessed with the power of speech at the time of Christ's birth. Nineteen beasts speak in their own voices as they are witness to the Christmas miracle.
SUBJ: Jesus Christ--Nativity--Poetry./ Animals--Poetry./ Christmas--Poetry./ American poetry.

811   Ph-2 3-6 $12.95   T   KD961
KENNEDY, X. J. Brats. Illus. by James Watts. Atheneum ISBN 0-689-50392-X; In Canada: Maxwell Macmillan, 1986. 42p. ill.
"Margaret K. McElderry book."
A group of bratty kids devises such devilish deeds as hurling a can of smelly herring into the grade school furnace and drizzling antifreeze over the piano keys. Forty-two witty poems will arouse laughter.
SUBJ: Behavior--Poetry./ American poetry./ Humorous poetry.

811   Ph-3 3-6 $12.95   L   KD962
KENNEDY, X. J. Drat these brats! Illus. by James Watts. McElderry ISBN 0-689-50589-2; In Canada: Maxwell Macmillan, 1993. 44p. ill.
The bratty kids are back, more brash than ever, as they open cans of cola with their dad's dental drill and pour wax on railroad tracks. The 44 irreverent rhymes humorously describe disgusting demeanor.
SUBJ: Behavior--Poetry./ American poetry./ Humorous poetry.

811   Ph-2 4-6 $12.95   L   KD963
KENNEDY, X. J. Forgetful wishing well. Illus. by Monica Incisa. Atheneum ISBN 0-689-50317-2, 1985. 88p. ill.
Engages the intermediate reader with delightful poems touching on the challenges of growing up and the vagaries of family life, all with an abundance of verisimilitude.
SUBJ: American poetry.

811   Ph-2 3-6 $12.95   L   KD964
KENNEDY, X. J. Fresh brats. Illus. by James Watts. McElderry ISBN 0-689-50499-3; In Canada: Collier Macmillan, 1990. 44p. ill.
A bevy of brats devises the most diabolical of deeds from sealing the school doors with a welding torch to placing a dead mouse in newly baked bread. Forty-one brief rhymes are certain to provoke giggles and vicarious pleasure.
SUBJ: Humorous poetry./ American poetry./ Behavior--Poetry.

811   Ph-1 4-A $12.95   L   KD965
KENNEDY, X. J. Ghastlies, goops & pincushions. Illus. by Ron Barrett. McElderry ISBN 0-689-50477-2; In Canada: Collier Macmillan, 1989. 58p.
From gentle humor provoking chuckles to macabre nonsense provoking guffaws, X. J. Kennedy creates absurdly funny situations in his verses. Whether the poem relates to poor Will who's been swallowed by the vacuum cleaner or brother Peter who's tied to a parking meter, these hilarious portraits tickle the funny bone.
SUBJ: Humorous poetry./ American poetry.

811   Ph-3 4-A $2.95   P   KD966
KORMAN, GORDON. D- poems of Jeremy Bloom: a collection of poems about school, homework, and life (sort of). By Gordon Korman and Bernice Korman. Scholastic ISBN 0-590-44819-6; In Canada: Scholastic, 1992. 97p.
"Apple paperback."
A collection of amusing poems which reflect the problems of a typical young person. Includes such laments as "I can't clean my room," "Appeal for a raise in allowance," and "Negotiating bedtime."
SUBJ: Schools--Poetry./ Humorous poetry./ Canadian poetry.

811   Ph-2 P-3 $15.00   T   KD967
LANSKY, BRUCE. New adventures of Mother Goose: gentle rhymes for happy times. Created by Bruce Lansky. Illus. by Stephen Carpenter. Meadowbrook Press/dist. by Simon & Schuster ISBN 0-671-87288-5, 1993. 32p. col. ill.
A satiric, irreverent view of popular nursery rhymes. Contemporary twists have Little Miss Muffet scolding the spider and Mother Hubbard's dog ordering pizza by phone. Why wait for a bone?

Good patterns for creative writing, particularly with children who are already familiar with the traditional Mother Goose.
SUBJ: Nursery rhymes--Adaptations./ American poetry.

811   Ph-2 3-6 $12.00   T   KD968
LANSKY, BRUCE. You're invited to Bruce Lansky's poetry party! Illus. by Stephen Carpenter. Meadowbrook Press/dist. by Simon & Schuster ISBN 0-671-57303-9, 1996. 83p. ill.
Includes index.
Hilarious, irreverent poems about teachers, pets, parents, and siblings. Youngsters will identify with these feelings and will observe that these poems accurately reflect the human condition. Not great poetry, but a way to introduce poetry painlessly.
SUBJ: American poetry./ Humorous poetry.

811   Ph-3 K-3 $15.00   L   KD969
LAWRENCE, JACOB. Harriet and the Promised Land. Simon & Schuster ISBN 0-671-86673-7; In Canada: Simon & Schuster, 1993. unp. col. ill.
Harriet Tubman's dedication to saving her fellow slaves from tyranny is reflected in this verse. The road to freedom is a dramatic one, and its drama is reflected in the powerful paintings which accompany the poem. For multicultural studies.
SUBJ: Tubman, Harriet (Ross)--Poetry./ Afro-Americans--Poetry./ Slaves--Poetry.

811   Ph-1 K-3 $17.00   T   KD970
LEE, DENNIS. Dinosaur dinner (with a slice of alligator pie): favorite poems. Selected by Jack Prelutsky. Illus. by Debbie Tilley. Knopf ISBN 0-679-87009-1, 1997. unp. col. ill.
"Borzoi book."
A humorous collection of playful poems. Some of the titles reflect the joy of language, the love of rhyme. There is "Willoughby wallaby woo," "The dreadful doings of Jelly Belly," and "I eat kids yum yum!" Wonderful for reading aloud, they will provoke gales of laughter.
SUBJ: Humorous poetry./ Canadian poetry.

811   Ph-1 3-6 $15.00   L   KD971
LEWIS, J. PATRICK. Black swan/white crow: haiku. Woodcuts by Chris Manson. Atheneum ISBN 0-689-31899-5; In Canada: Distican, 1995. unp. col. ill.
Themes of nature permeate these 13 exquisitely formed haiku poems. Wood-cut prints echo the simplicity and beauty inherent in each poem. Excellent for introducing haiku. The stunning images in both the text and the illustrations will provide inspiration for creative writing classes.
SUBJ: Nature--Poetry./ American poetry./ Haiku.

811   Ph-3 P-3 $14.95   L   KD972
LEWIS, J. PATRICK. July is a mad mosquito. Illus. by Melanie W. Hall. Atheneum ISBN 0-689-31813-8; In Canada: Maxwell Macmillan, 1994. unp. col. ill.
Twelve short poems relate the sounds, sights, and activities associated with the months of the year. Brightly colored illustrations bring each month to life. Excellent for integrating poetry into lessons on the seasons.
SUBJ: Months--Poetry./ American poetry./ Nature--Poetry./ Seasons--Poetry.

811   Ph-1 K-3 $14.95   L   KD973
LINDBERGH, REEVE. Johnny Appleseed. Illus. by Kathy Jakobsen. Joy Street/Little, Brown ISBN 0-316-52618-5; In Canada: Little, Brown, 1990. unp. col. ill.
Describes in poetry the travels of John Chapman, known as Johnny Appleseed, a religious man who followed the settlers west planting apple trees everywhere he went. Folk art paintings including a few double-spread vistas show the American wilderness and the homes of the early settlers. The text is bordered with a quilt motif with small inserts filled with apples, apple blossoms, apple trees and even an apple pie. An extensive note about the life of Johnny Appleseed is included on the final page. Pure Americana useful throughout the curriculum especially during the Fall apple season.
SUBJ: Appleseed, Johnny--Poetry./ Stories in rhyme./ American poetry.

811   Ph-2 K-3 $15.95   L   KD974
LIVINGSTON, MYRA COHN. Abraham Lincoln: a man for all the people: a ballad. Illus. by Samuel Byrd. Holiday House ISBN 0-8234-1049-8, 1993. 32p. col. ill.
Recounts Lincoln's life story, emphasizing his heroism and courage. The narration is accompanied by full-color illustrations which vivify the history. Excellent for use at holiday time, for recitation purposes, and to enhance social studies lessons.
SUBJ: Lincoln, Abraham--Poetry./ Presidents--Poetry./ Narrative poetry./ American poetry.

811   Ph-2 3-6 $15.00   T   KD975
LIVINGSTON, MYRA COHN. Cricket never does: a collection of haiku and tanka. Illus. by Kees de Kiefte. McElderry ISBN 0-689-81123-3; In Canada: Distican, 1997. 42p. ill.
Includes index.
Sixty-seven sensitive haiku about the four seasons will encourage budding poets to write their own feelings and thoughts in this poetic style. For creative writing activities.
SUBJ: Seasons--Poetry./ Haiku./ Waka./ American poetry.

811   Ph-2 3-6 $16.95   L   KD976
LIVINGSTON, MYRA COHN. Festivals. Illus. by Leonard Everett Fisher. Holiday House ISBN 0-8234-1217-2, 1996. 32p. col. ill.
Includes glossary.
Simple, elegant poems describe festivals around the world. The starkly dramatic illustrations highlight 14 celebrations, such as Las Posadas, Chinese New Year, and Mardi Gras. A beautiful addition to multicultural studies.
SUBJ: Festivals--Poetry./ American poetry.

811   Ph-2 1-3 $15.95   L   KD977
LIVINGSTON, MYRA COHN. Keep on singing: a ballad of Marian Anderson. Illus. by Samuel Byrd. Holiday House ISBN 0-8234-1098-6, 1994. unp. col. ill.
A ballad extolling the triumphs and tribulations of the life of the great singer, Marian Anderson. For multicultural and women's studies.
SUBJ: Anderson, Marian--Poetry./ Afro-Americans--Poetry./ Narrative poetry./ American poetry./ Women musicians--Poetry.

811   Ph-2 K-2/4 $15.95   L   KD978
LIVINGSTON, MYRA COHN. Let freedom ring: a ballad of Martin Luther King, Jr. Illus. by Samuel Byrd. Holiday House ISBN 0-8234-0957-0, 1992. 32p col illus.
Martin Luther King's life and vision are told in ballad form emphasizing his desire for a peaceful world.
SUBJ: King, Martin Luther, Jr.--Poetry./ Afro-Americans--Poetry./ American poetry.

CE 811   Ph-3 P-A $16.99   T   KD979
LONGFELLOW, HENRY WADSWORTH. Hiawatha. Illus. by Susan Jeffers. Dial/Dutton ISBN 0-8037-0013-X, 1983. unp. col. ill.
Available from National Library Service for the Blind and Physically Handicapped on sound recording cassette RC22692 and in Braille BR06112.
Spanish version available HIAWATHA (ISBN 0-8037-1662-1, 1996).
Videocassette available from Weston Woods VC338V (ISBN 0-78820-701-6, 1995), 1/2" iconographic VHS videocassette color (11min), $60.00. Includes teacher's guide.
Presents the verses of the beloved epic poem that relate the childhood of Hiawatha with doublespread, finely detailed, colored pen drawings. The superior quality of the illustrations reinforces the rhythmic text. Recommended for reading aloud and for use in units relating to Indians of North America. For multicultural studies.
SUBJ: Indians of North America--Poetry./ Narrative poetry./ American poetry./ Spanish language materials.

CE 811   Ph-2 3-A $15.99   L   KD980
LONGFELLOW, HENRY WADSWORTH. Paul Revere's ride. Illus. by Ted Rand. Dutton ISBN 0-525-44610-9, 1990. unp. col. ill.
Videocassette available from SRA/McGraw-Hill 87-05093, 1992. 1/2" iconographic VHS videocassette color (8min), guide, $37.00. (Children's literature series).
Dark, ominous, beautiful illustrations capture the dangerous and exciting midnight ride of Paul Revere. Longfellow's words have never been more beautifully combined with art, and this rendition will enliven history lessons.
SUBJ: Revere, Paul--Poetry./ Lexington, Battle of, 1775--Poetry./ Narrative poetry./ American poetry./ Spanish language materials.

811   Ph-2 K-2/3 $2.50   P   KD981
MARZOLLO, JEAN. I'm tyrannosaurus!: a book of dinosaur rhymes. Illus. by Hans Wilhelm. Scholastic ISBN 0-590-44641-X; In Canada: Scholastic, 1993. unp. col. ill. (Read with me).
"Cartwheel books."
Simple poems and delightfully humorous illustrations will captivate young dinosaur fans. Use as a pattern for creative writing exercises.
SUBJ: American poetry./ Dinosaurs--Poetry.

811   Ph-1 P-A $14.95   L   KD982
MERRIAM, EVE. Halloween A B C. Illus. by Lane Smith. Macmillan ISBN 0-02-766870-3; In Canada: Collier Macmillan, 1987. unp. col. ill.
Sends shivers down the spine with 26 spooky Halloween poems, one for each letter of the alphabet. The vocabulary is both joyous and scary, and this collection is Merriam at her most virulent, venomous,

villainess best, as she darts "poison with a snaky smile."
SUBJ: Halloween--Poetry./ Alphabet.

811 Ph-2 P-1 $14.93 L KD983
MERRIAM, EVE. Higgle wiggle: happy rhymes. Poems by Eve Merriam.
Illus. by Hans Wilhelm. Morrow ISBN 0-688-11949-2, 1994. unp. col. ill.
 A joyous collection of upbeat verses about such subjects as food and
animals. A rhythmic introduction to poetry for the very young.
 SUBJ: American poetry.

811 Ph-2 3-A $14.00 L KD984
MERRIAM, EVE. Singing green: new and selected poems for all seasons.
Illus. by Kathleen Collins Howell. Morrow ISBN 0-688-11025-8, 1992.
102p b&w illus.
 Eve Merriam is at her best in this collection of some of her old and
many of her new poems, all filled with exuberance on a wide variety
of subjects.
 SUBJ: American poetry.

811 Ph-2 K-3 $16.00 T KD985
MICHELSON, RICHARD. Animals that ought to be: poems about
imaginary pets. Illus. by Leonard Baskin. Simon & Schuster ISBN 0-689-
80635-3; In Canada: Distican, 1996. 24p. col. ill.
 A menagerie of unusual animals inhabits poems about the Nightmare
Scarer who frightens away bad dreams, the Channel Changer who
presses "each button on his eighty-button belly," and the Talkback
Bat who answers back and shouts and screams. The accompanying
paintings are humorous, colorful, and weird. A delightfully funny
collection which will encourage creative writing.
 SUBJ: Animals--Poetry./ Imagination--Poetry./ American poetry.

811 Ph-2 K-3 $14.95 L KD986
MONSTER SOUP AND OTHER SPOOKY POEMS. Compiled by Dilys
Evans. Illus. by Jacqueline Rogers. Scholastic ISBN 0-590-45208-8; In
Canada: Scholastic, 1992. unp. col. ill.
 Spooky, scary, spirited verses about monsters, trolls, dragons, and
bats are designed to provoke fear and laughter. The illustrations are
detailed, droll, and imaginative. Hilarious for Halloween.
 SUBJ: Monsters--Poetry./ American poetry.

811 Ph-2 P-A $15.99 L KD987
MOORE, CLEMENT C. Grandma Moses Night before Christmas. Illus.
by Grandma Moses. Random House ISBN 0-679-91526-5; In Canada:
Random House, 1991. unp col illus.
 Grandma Moses' 1960 series of paintings, "The Night Before
Christmas" accompany Clement Moore's traditional holiday poem.
Moses' cozy, country atmosphere perfectly matches the warm, familial
poem.
 SUBJ: Santa Claus--Poetry./ Christmas--Poetry./ Narrative poetry./
American poetry.

811 Ph-1 P-A $14.45 T KD988
MOORE, CLEMENT C. Twas the night before Christmas: a visit from St.
Nicholas. Illus. by Jessie Willcox Smith. Houghton Mifflin ISBN 0-395-
06952-1, c1912, 1992. unp. col. ill.
 First published in 1912, this is the eightieth anniversary edition of
Moore's familiar poem with the famous illustrations by Jessie Willcox
Smith.
 SUBJ: Christmas--Poetry./ Santa Claus--Poetry./ Narrative poetry./
American poetry.

811 Ph-2 K-3 $14.95 T KD989
MORA, PAT. Desert is my mother./El desierto es mi madre. Illus. by
Daniel Lechon. Pinata Books ISBN 1-55885-121-6, 1994. unp. col. ill.
 A bilingual poem extols the desert as a provider of food, healing,
comfort, and life. Useful where bilingual materials are needed.
 SUBJ: Deserts--Poetry./ American poetry./ Spanish language
materials./ Bilingual materials--Spanish.

811 Ph-3 P-1 $14.95 L KD990
MORA, PAT. Listen to the desert/Oye al desierto. Illus. by Francisco X.
Mora. Clarion ISBN 0-395-67292-9, 1994. unp. col. ill.
 The natural world is revealed in this colorfully illustrated view of
desert life. The bilingual poem is excellent for reading aloud, reciting
in English and then in Spanish. Will enrich multicultural studies.
 SUBJ: Deserts--Poetry./ Animal sounds--Poetry./ American poetry./
Spanish language materials./ Bilingual materials--Spanish.

811 Ph-2 2-6 $15.00 T KD991
MOSS, JEFFREY. Butterfly jar. Illus. by Chris L. Demarest. Bantam ISBN
0-553-05704-9; In Canada: Bantam, 1989. 115p. ill.
 Witty, captivating poems that speak about life's problems--moving to
a new home, washing one's neck, and exhibiting bravery by going to
sleep without the night-light on. Wonderful for reading aloud and for

encouraging writing activities.
 SUBJ: American poetry.

811 Ph-1 K-6 $15.89 L KD992
MYERS, WALTER DEAN. Brown angels: an album of pictures and verse.
HarperCollins ISBN 0-06-022918-7; In Canada: HarperCollins, 1993.
unp. ill.
 An engaging collection of turn-of-the-century photographs of African-
American children is accompanied by moving poems. Photographs
recollect a time long gone by and reveal much about the clothing,
schooling, and lives of these children as they dress up for a
photograph or pose for a candid shot. Wonderful for provoking
discussion and integrating into social studies or multicultural studies
curricula.
 SUBJ: Afro-Americans--Poetry./ American poetry.

811 Ph-1 K-6 $15.89 L KD993
MYERS, WALTER DEAN. Glorious angels: a celebration of children.
HarperCollins ISBN 0-06-024823-8; In Canada: HarperCollins, 1995.
unp. ill.
 A collection of poems and antique photographs depict children of
many cultures. Excellent for encouraging children to use their own
photos and create their own poems. For multicultural studies and
creative writing activities.
 SUBJ: Children--Poetry./ American poetry.

811 Ph-2 3-6 $16.95 L KD994
MYERS, WALTER DEAN. Harlem: a poem. Illus. by Christopher Myers.
Scholastic ISBN 0-590-54340-7; In Canada: Scholastic, 1997. unp. col.
ill.
 Boldly dramatic collages throb with the life of Harlem and give
testimony to the significant contributions of the community. A
sophisticated poem to provoke discussion for multicultural studies.
 SUBJ: Afro-Americans--Poetry./ American poetry./ Harlem (New
York, N.Y.)--Poetry.

CDR 811 Ph-1 K-A $39.95 OD KD995
NEW KID ON THE BLOCK (CD-ROM). Broderbund ISBN 1-55790-806-
0, 1993. 1 CD-ROM, 1 paperback book. (Living books).
 Includes teacher's guide and MPC trouble shooting guide.
 Also available for Macintosh.
 System requirements: IBM/Tandy or 100% compatible 386SX or
higher with 4MB of RAM; Windows 3.1; MS/PC-DOS 3.3 or higher;
Super VGA (640 x 480, 256 colors); Sound Blaster or SB Pro and
100% compatible sound cards; Mouse; Hard drive; CD-ROM drive.
This interactive poetry collection provides youngsters of all ages an
entertaining look at the genre. The user can either have the poem
read or control the reading by clicking on individual lines. Entertaining
animations can be found by clicking on objects in the picture.
 SUBJ: Humorous poetry--Software./ Software--Humorous poetry./
American poetry--Software./ Software--American poetry./ Interactive
media.

811 Ph-2 P-2 $14.95 L KD996
NIKOLA-LISA, W. Bein' with you this way. Illus. by Michael Bryant. Lee
& Low ISBN 1-880000-05-9, 1994. unp. col. ill.
 Spanish version LA ALEGRIA DE SER TU Y YO available (ISBN
1-880000-35-0, 1996).
 Celebrates diversity with verses asserting that we are all the same
despite physical differences. Warm, colorful illustrations show the joy
of friends just hanging out together. For multicultural studies.
 SUBJ: Ethnic groups--Poetry./ Brotherliness--Poetry./ American
poetry./ Spanish language materials.

811 Ph-3 3-6 $19.95 T KD997
POE, EDGAR ALLAN. Annabel Lee. Illus. by Gilles Tibo. Tundra ISBN
0-88776-200-X; In Canada: Tundra/dist. by Univ. of Toronto Press,
1987. unp. col. ill.
 Also available in French (ISBN 0-88776-203-4).
 Lyric and romantic, Poe's classic poem about found and lost love is
interpreted in wistful, stylized, and luminously hued full paged
paintings. Fine for reading aloud.
 SUBJ: American poetry./ Narrative poetry./ French language
materials.

811 Ph-2 5-A $14.95 T KD998
POE, EDGAR ALLAN. Poetry for young people. Edited by Brod Bagert.
Illus. by Carolynn Cobleigh. Sterling ISBN 0-8069-0820-3; In Canada:
Sterling c/o Canadian Manda, 1995. 48p. col. ill.
 "Magnolia Editions book."
 Includes index.
 Poe's poetry and some of his prose are accompanied by dramatic
illustrations, helpful notes and definitions, and a brief biography.
 SUBJ: American poetry./ Short stories.

811 Ph-1 K-2 $14.95 T KD999
POLISAR, BARRY LOUIS. Peculiar zoo. Illus. by David Clark. Rainbow Morning Music ISBN 0-938663-14-3, 1993. unp. col. ill.
Includes glossary.
Hilarious illustrations accompany witty poems about such varied denizens of the animal world as warthogs, manatees, and armadillos. Perfect introduction to poetry for the youngest reader.
SUBJ: Animals--Poetry.

811 Ph-2 1-3 $13.88 L KE000
PRELUTSKY, JACK. Baby uggs are hatching. Illus. by James Stevenson. Greenwillow ISBN 0-688-00923-9, 1982. 32p. col. ill.
Selectors' Choice, 14th ed.
Available from National Library Service for the Blind and Physically Handicapped in Braille BR05455.
Slithery snitches and grubby grebbies and baby uggs lunge and lurch and sneeze and snooze through delectably delicious rhymes enhanced by marvelous monstrous illustrations. Wonderful for storytelling.
SUBJ: American poetry./ Humorous poetry.

811 Ph-2 K-2 $15.95 L KE001
PRELUTSKY, JACK. Beneath a blue umbrella. Illus. by Garth Williams. Greenwillow ISBN 0-688-06429-9, 1990. 64p. col. ill.
Brief, whimsical poems and beautiful, colorful illustrations combine to describe Anna Banana, Eleven Yellow Monkeys, and more. A delightful book, in the same vein as RIDE A PURPLE PELICAN, to be read aloud.
SUBJ: Humorous poetry./ American poetry.

811 Ph-1 2-4 $14.93 L KE002
PRELUTSKY, JACK. Dragons are singing tonight. Illus. by Peter Sis. Greenwillow ISBN 0-688-12511-5, 1993. 39p. col. ill.
Available from the National Library Service for the Blind and Physically Handicapped on sound recording cassette RC 39084.
Dreadful dragons lament their repulsive reputation, slither about on computer screens, and cavort in the bathtub. Alternately disconsolate, fearless, playful, and nasty, these dragons are depicted in captivating, detailed illustrations which exactly match the delightful dragon odes. Great for reading aloud.
SUBJ: Dragons--Poetry./ American poetry.

811 Ph-1 2-4 $13.88 L KE003
PRELUTSKY, JACK. Headless Horseman rides tonight: more poems to trouble your sleep. Illus. by Arnold Lobel. Greenwillow ISBN 0-688-84273-9, 1980. 38p. ill.
A dozen deadly creatures - the mummy, the banshee, the poltergeist, the sorceress - are here to make "you shiver and scream/ and hope it's all a dream/ as the zombie nears your bed." Splendid horrific rhymes for all seasons, but particularly effective for reading aloud at Halloween. The darkly dramatic illustrations fit the bone-chilling atmosphere.
SUBJ: Monsters--Poetry./ American poetry.

811 Ph-1 1-3 $13.88 L KE004
PRELUTSKY, JACK. It's Halloween. Illus. by Marylin Hafner. Greenwillow ISBN 0-688-84102-3, c1977. 56p. col. ill. (Greenwillow read-alone).
Available from National Library Service for the Blind and Physically Handicapped in Braille BR05459.
Halloween is more fun- than fright-filled when presented in these thirteen easy-to-read poems about jack-o-lanterns, haunted houses, ghosts and goblins. Colorful illustrations show friends enjoying the special day's activities.
SUBJ: Halloween--Poetry./ American poetry.

811 Ph-2 K-3 $14.93 L KE005
PRELUTSKY, JACK. It's snowing! It's snowing! Illus. by Jeanne Titherington. Greenwillow ISBN 0-688-01513-1, 1984. 47p. col. ill.
Relive the glories of winter in jolly verse that details dripping noses, wearing layers and layers of clothes, and snowball fights. An accurate assessment of the young child's perspective on the snowy season.
SUBJ: Winter--Poetry./ Snow--Poetry./ American poetry.

CE 811 Ph-2 1-3 $12.88 L KE006
PRELUTSKY, JACK. It's Thanksgiving. Illus. by Marylin Hafner. Greenwillow ISBN 0-688-00442-3, 1982. 48p. col. ill. (Greenwillow read-alone).
Available from National Library Service for the Blind and Physically Handicapped in Braille BR05451 and on sound recording cassette RC20097.
Every aspect of the Thanksgiving holiday from the familial warmth at Grandma's house to Daddy's roars while watching the football game on TV to the interminable turkey leftovers. An easy-to-read comic view of the holiday.
SUBJ: Thanksgiving Day--Poetry./ American poetry.

811 Ph-3 K-2 $16.00 T KE007
PRELUTSKY, JACK. It's Valentine's Day. Illus. by Yossi Abolafia. Greenwillow ISBN 0-688-02311-8, 1983. 48p. col. ill. (Greenwillow read-alone).
Humorously views the various emotions: guilt, embarrassment and joy, associated with Valentine's Day celebrations at school and home. On target for young people.
SUBJ: Valentine's Day--Poetry./ American poetry.

CE 811 Ph-1 K-4 $15.93 L KE008
PRELUTSKY, JACK. Monday's troll: poems. Illus. by Peter Sis. Greenwillow ISBN 0-688-14373-3, 1996. 39p. col. ill.
Selectors' Choice, 21st ed.
Talking book available from Listening Library FTR 175 (ISBN 0-8072-0240-1, 1996). 1 sound cassette (35min), $9.95.
Each of these 17 poems is told by such scary, unsavory supernatural creatures as Blizzard, a wizard; Underfoot, a troll; and a solitary yeti. Witty, restrained illustrations illuminate the delightful poems which resound with Prelutsky's enchanting wordplay and devious imagination. Fun for all seasons, but especially useful to enhance Halloween units.
SUBJ: American poetry./ Supernatural--Poetry.

811 Ph-2 2-5 $13.93 L KE009
PRELUTSKY, JACK. My parents think I'm sleeping. Illus. by Yossi Abolafia. Greenwillow ISBN 0-688-04019-5, 1985. 47p. col. ill.
Explores the non-sleeping vagaries of a young insomniac with great humor. This witty collection of poems describes the strange sounds, the longing for food, the scary shadows that confound the child who is wide awake at bedtime.
SUBJ: Sleep--Poetry./ American poetry.

CE 811 Ph-1 2-6 $14.93 L KE010
PRELUTSKY, JACK. New kid on the block. Illus. by James Stevenson. Greenwillow ISBN 0-688-02272-3, 1984. 159p. ill.
Selectors' Choice, 15th ed.
Talking book performed by the author from Listening Library FTR 115CX (ISBN 0-8072-0115-4, 1986). 1 sound cassette (40min) $9.98.
Available from National Library Service for the Blind and Physically Handicapped on sound recording cassette RC22791.
Introduces a variety of amusing creatures--yubbazubbies and gloopy gloppers and zooshers. These irreverent humorous poems reflect the world, as young people see it, with great accuracy. A wonderful beginning for a poetry unit.
SUBJ: Humorous poetry./ American poetry.

811 Ph-1 3-5 $13.93 L KE011
PRELUTSKY, JACK. Nightmares: poems to trouble your sleep. Illus. by Arnold Lobel. Greenwillow ISBN 0-688-84053-1, c1976. 38p. ill.
Selectors' Choice, 11th ed.
Available from National Library Service for the Blind and Physically Handicapped on sound recording cassette RC12764.
Written for dedicated monster-lovers, twelve startling cautionary poems describe the full gory horror of demons and witches, werewolves and vampires, ogres and ghouls--all visualized in ominous black line drawings.
SUBJ: Monsters--Poetry./ American poetry.

811 Ph-1 K-A $17.93 L KE012
PRELUTSKY, JACK. Pizza the size of the sun: poems. Illus. by James Stevenson. Greenwillow ISBN 0-688-13236-7, 1996. 159p. ill.
Includes indexes.
Selectors' Choice, 21st ed.
A collection of hilarious poems: some are backwards and can only be deciphered by holding them up to a mirror; some are innately zany as revealed in their equally zany titles--"Eyeballs for Sale," "My Gerbil Seemed Bedraggled," and "Do Not Approach an Emu." Wonderful for reading aloud and for bringing laughter into the classroom.
SUBJ: Humorous poetry./ American poetry.

811 Ph-2 1-3 $13.88 L KE013
PRELUTSKY, JACK. Rainy rainy Saturday. Illus. by Marylin Hafner. Greenwillow ISBN 0-688-84252-6, 1980. 47p. col. ill. (Greenwillow read-alone).
Fourteen short poems about the delights and despairs of a rainy day. The comforting warmth of family and friends, and the conflicting emotions of joy and sadness are explored.
SUBJ: Rain and rainfall--Poetry./ Humorous poetry./ American poetry.

811 Ph-1 P-3 $17.95 T KE014
PRELUTSKY, JACK. Ride a purple pelican. Illus. by Garth Williams. Greenwillow ISBN 0-688-04031-4, 1986. 64p. col. ill.
Available from National Library Service for the Blind and Physically Handicapped in Braille BR07101.

Creates a nursery world with imaginative nonsense rhymes punctuated by spellbinding rhythm. The wit in the poems extends to the enchanting illustrations containing a veritable menagerie of cunning creatures.
SUBJ: American poetry./ Nonsense verses./ Nursery rhymes--Adaptations.

CE 811   Ph-1 1-4 $14.88   L   KE015
PRELUTSKY, JACK. Rolling Harvey down the hill. Illus. by Victoria Chess. Greenwillow ISBN 0-688-84258-5, 1980. 30p. ill.
Talking book available from Listening Library FTR 167-1 (ISBN 0-8072-0217-7, 1993). 1 sound cassette (38min), $9.98.
Rhythmic cadences relate the adventures of a gang of small boys who hate girls, break windows, fight, and brag and cheat. Verisimilitude is achieved through the revelation of all the nasty traits so much a part of the world of children. Beyond laughing at the antics of the kids, the verses offer an opportunity for discussion of social behavior and an opportunity to participate in the amusing refrain of the title poem, when revenge is visited upon that glutton, that braggart--Harvey, and we see him "rolling, rolling, see him rolling down the hill".
SUBJ: Friendship--Poetry./ Humorous poetry./ American poetry.

TB 811   Ph-1 K-4 $9.98   OD KE016
PRELUTSKY, JACK. Something big has been here (Talking book). Listening Library FTR 147 CX ISBN 0-8072-0202-9, 1991. 1 sound cassette (23min).
Jack Prelutsky's enchanting poems are delivered by the author who has a repertoire of many hilarious voices. Can be used as a read-along with the book or as a delightful listening activity in the study of humorous poetry.
SUBJ: American poetry./ Humorous poetry.

CE 811   Ph-2 1-5 $4.95   P   KE017
PRELUTSKY, JACK. Tyrannosaurus was a beast: dinosaur poems. Illus. by Arnold Lobel. Mulberry ISBN 0-688-11569-1, c1988, 1992. 32p. col. ill.
Includes chronology.
Big book available (ISBN 0-688-12613-8, 1992), $18.95.
Read-along kit available from Listening Library FTR 169 (ISBN 0-8072-0226-6, 1988). 1 paperback book, 1 sound cassette (12min), $15.98.
Witty poems describe 14 kinds of dinosaurs. A good accompaniment to lessons on prehistoric life.
SUBJ: Dinosaurs--Poetry./ American poetry.

811   Ph-1 4-6 $14.95   T   KE018
SANDBURG, CARL. Poetry for young people. Edited by Frances Schoonmaker Bolin. Illus. by Steven Arcella. Sterling ISBN 0-8069-0818-1; In Canada: Sterling c/o Canadian Manda, 1995. 48p. col. ill.
"Magnolia Editions book."
Includes index.
Carl Sandburg, poet and wanderer, traveled throughout America, and these poems reflect his experiences. His use of free verse makes his work more understandable to young people. Definitions of unusual words and glowing illustrations combine to create a fine introduction to his poetry.
SUBJ: American poetry.

811   Ph-2 3-5 $15.93   L   KE019
SCHERTLE, ALICE. Advice for a frog. Illus. by Norman Green. Lothrop, Lee & Shepard ISBN 0-688-13487-4, 1995. unp. col. ill.
Includes glossary.
The witty, detailed illustrations of such animals as the toucan, iguana, and black rhino are accompanied by wry, poignantly honest poems. Can be used as a springboard for creative writing.
SUBJ: Animals--Poetry./ American poetry.

811   Ph-2 1-3 $14.95   L   KE020
SCHERTLE, ALICE. How now, brown cow? Illus. by Amanda Schaffer. Browndeer/Harcourt Brace ISBN 0-15-276648-0; In Canada: Harcourt Brace c/o Canadian Manda, 1994. unp. col. ill.
The cow is viewed alternately with warmth, compassion, irreverence, and wit. Certain to provoke guffaws as cows are driven in a convertible and as sweet brown cows give chocolate milk and a frisky white one provides vanilla milkshakes. Fun for bovine lovers.
SUBJ: Cows--Poetry./ American poetry.

811   Ph-2 P-1 $14.99   L   KE021
SCIESZKA, JON. Book that Jack wrote. Illus. by Daniel Adel. Viking ISBN 0-670-84330-X; In Canada: Penguin, 1994. unp. col. ill.
The familiar nursery rhyme is given a zany interpretation that begins where Jack writes a book instead of building a house. The cumulative story provides a chaotic view that will provoke laughter.
SUBJ: Nursery rhymes--Adaptations.

811   Ph-2 P-1/3 $13.95   L   KE022
SHAPIRO, ARNOLD. Mice squeak, we speak: a poem. By Arnold L. Shapiro. Illustrated by Tomie dePaola. Putnam ISBN 0-399-23202-8; In Canada: Putnam, 1997. unp. col. ill.
The animals purr, moo, and cluck while the children speak, say, and talk. An easy-to-read poem is accompanied by brightly colored portraits of the animals. The animal sounds will delight young listeners, and the predictable book is well suited for beginning readers.
SUBJ: Animal sounds--Poetry./ American poetry.

811   Ph-3 2-6 $4.95   P   KE023
SIEBERT, DIANE. Sierra. Illus. by Wendell Minor. HarperTrophy ISBN 0-06-443441-9; In Canada: HarperCollins, 1991. unp. col. ill.
"Trophy Picture Book."
The magnificent mountains of the Sierra Nevada, created millions of years ago and shaped by ice and time, are home to junipers and sequoia and numerous animals. The natural beauty and majesty of these mountains is presented in a compelling combination of poetry and large acrylic paintings suitable for sharing. Useful for interdisciplinary studies.
SUBJ: Sierra Nevada Mountains (California and Nevada)--Poetry./ Stories in rhyme.

811   Ph-1 P-A $16.89   L   KE024
SILVERSTEIN, SHEL. Falling up: poems and drawings. HarperCollins ISBN 0-06-024803-3; In Canada: HarperCollins, 1996. 175p. ill.
Includes index.
Selectors' Choice, 21st ed.
Available from the National Library Service for the Blind and Physically Handicapped on sound recording cassette RC 42824.
A poetic glance at the silly antics of some amusing characters such as Headphone Harold and his unfortunate demise, the reluctant camper sent off to Camp Wonderful, and the feckless foreman who demolishes the wrong house. The zany illustrations heighten the hilarity. Excellent for reading aloud and for encouraging young thespians in creative dramatics.
SUBJ: Humorous poetry./ American poetry.

811   Ph-1 P-A $15.89   L   KE025
SILVERSTEIN, SHEL. Light in the attic. HarperCollins ISBN 0-06-025674-5, 1981. 167p. ill.
Includes index.
Selectors' Choice, 14th ed.
Available from National Library Service for the Blind and Physically Handicapped in Braille BRA17511 and sound recording cassette RC17732.
A combination of whimsy and philosophy pervades this exuberant collection of poems that often reflect young people's most hidden feelings. The comedic black and white illustrations in this well designed book add to the appeal.
SUBJ: Humorous poetry./ American poetry.

811   Ph-1 P-A $16.89   L   KE026
SILVERSTEIN, SHEL. Where the sidewalk ends: the poems and drawings of Shel Silverstein. HarperCollins ISBN 0-06-025668-0, c1974. 166p. ill.
Available from National Library Service for the Blind and Physically Handicapped in Braille BR02970, and on sound recording cassette RC35732.
Rollicking verses with irreverent humor, lively rhythms, surprise endings, and a touch of truth are accompanied by the poet's own thoroughly appropriate ink drawings. Hilarious to read aloud, to perform, or to chuckle over, the poems will appeal to the upper primary grades for listening and older children for reading to an appreciative audience.
SUBJ: Humorous poetry./ American poetry.

811   Ph-2 3-6 $15.00   T   KE027
SINGER, MARILYN. All we needed to say: poems about school from Tanya and Sophie. Photos by Lorna Clark. Atheneum ISBN 0-689-80667-1; In Canada: Distican, 1996. unp. ill.
Poems which depict typical school days for two young girls are juxtaposed, showing the differences between the two friends. A good basis for creative writing and creative dramatics.
SUBJ: Schools--Poetry./ American poetry.

811   Ph-2 4-6 $17.00   T   KE028
SOTO, GARY. Canto familiar. Illus. by Annika Nelson. Harcourt Brace ISBN 0-15-200067-4; In Canada: Harcourt Brace c/o Canadian Manda, 1995. 79p. col. ill.
A collection of poems that echo the experiences of Mexican-American children. Excellent for reading aloud and for encouraging creative writing activities in which young people write about their own experiences. For multicultural studies.

SUBJ: Mexican Americans--Poetry./ American poetry./ Hispanic Americans--Poetry.

811   Ph-2 3-A $15.95   T   KE029
SOTO, GARY. Neighborhood odes: poems. Illus. by David Diaz. Harcourt Brace Jovanovich ISBN 0-15-256879-4; In Canada: Harcourt Brace Jovanovich c/o Canadian Manda, 1992. 68p. ill.
Includes glossary.
The joys of life in a Mexican-American neighborhood are celebrated. These childhood pleasures include memories of eating warm tortillas dripping with butter, and jumping in and out of the sprinkler and pounding the mushy grass in summertime. An excellent evocation of the Hispanic experience which demonstrates the universality of juvenile joys. For multicultural studies.
SUBJ: Hispanic Americans--Poetry./ Neighborhood--Poetry./ American poetry.

811   Ph-2 K-6 $9.00   T   KE030
STEIG, JEANNE. Consider the lemming. Illus. by William Steig. Farrar, Straus & Giroux ISBN 0-374-31536-1, 1988. unp. ill.
Selectors' Choice, 17th ed.
Available from National Library Service for the Blind and Physically Handicapped on sound recording cassette RC30509.
Reflects with playful spirit on the vagaries and pecadillos a variety of creatures--including man. The poet's sly wit is enhanced by William Steig's delightfully funny, insouciant drawings.
SUBJ: Animals--Poetry./ American poetry.

811   Ph-1 K-6 $14.89   L   KE031
THOMAS, JOYCE CAROL. Brown honey in broomwheat tea: poems. Illus. by Floyd Cooper. HarperCollins ISBN 0-06-021088-5; In Canada: HarperCollins, 1993. unp. col. ill.
Coretta Scott King Honor book, 1994.
Available from the National Library Service for the Blind and Physically Handicapped on sound recording cassette RC 40134.
Heartfelt poems and warm, loving illustrations describe the African-American family, encouraging pride in heritage, identity, and family ties. Perfect for multicultural studies and for introduction to poetry.
SUBJ: Afro-Americans--Poetry./ American poetry.

811   Ph-1 K-4 $14.89   L   KE032
THOMAS, JOYCE CAROL. Gingerbread days: poems. Illus. by Floyd Cooper. HarperCollins ISBN 0-06-023472-5; In Canada: HarperCollins, 1995. unp. col. ill.
"Joanna Cotler book."
A nostalgic celebration of love and family life and the passing of the seasons. These poems mirror a world that should exist for everyone. Will encourage discussion about values. Depiction of a close-knit African-American family is suitable for multicultural studies.
SUBJ: Afro-Americans--Poetry./ Family--Poetry./ American poetry./ Months--Poetry.

811   Ph-2 K-3 $13.95   L   KE033
TILLER, RUTH. Cinnamon, mint, and mothballs: a visit to Grandmother's house. Illus. by Aki Sogabe. Browndeer/Harcourt Brace ISBN 0-15-276617-0; In Canada: Harcourt Brace c/o Canadian Manda, 1993. unp. col. ill.
A charming, nostalgic story of a young girl's overnight stay at Grandmother's house. Recounted in haiku and accompanied by stunning woodcuts, the tale reflects warm memories of the visit.
SUBJ: Haiku./ Grandmothers--Poetry./ Bedtime--Poetry./ American poetry.

811   Ph-2 3-6 $14.95   L   KE034
TURNER, ANN. Moon for seasons. Illus. by Robert Noreika. Macmillan ISBN 0-02-789513-0; In Canada: Maxwell Macmillan, 1994. unp. col. ill.
Words are carefully chosen in these short poems that reflect the natural world and the change of seasons. The colorful illustrations are incredibly lovely and capture the essence of every verse.
SUBJ: Nature--Poetry./ Seasons--Poetry./ American poetry.

811   Ph-2 P-1 $16.00   T   KE035
UPDIKE, JOHN. Helpful alphabet of friendly objects: poems. Photos by David Updike. Knopf ISBN 0-679-84324-8; In Canada: Random House, 1995. unp. col. ill.
"Borzoi book."
Brief poems and colorful photographs depict everyday objects for each letter of the alphabet. Novelist John Updike has a charming way with words, and his son, photographer David Updike, has taken snapshots which will provoke discussion among the very young.
SUBJ: Alphabet./ American poetry.

811   Ph-3 2-5 $14.95   L   KE036
VIORST, JUDITH. Alphabet from Z to A: (with much confusion on the way). Illus. by Richard Hull. Atheneum ISBN 0-689-31768-9; In Canada: Maxwell Macmillan, 1994. unp. col. ill.
Many of the inconsistencies inherent in the English language are revealed in Viorst's clever, lively verses. The playful, detailed drawings offer clues to identify hidden objects. A charming, unusual alphabet book.
SUBJ: English language--Poetry./ American poetry./ Alphabet.

811   Ph-3 2-4 $14.95   L   KE037
VIORST, JUDITH. If I were in charge of the world and other worries. Illus. by Lynne Cherry. Atheneum ISBN 0-689-30863-9; In Canada: Collier Macmillan, 1981. 56p. ill.
Includes index.
Available from National Library Service for the Blind and Physically Handicapped on sound recording cassette RC19444.
A collection of poems about the voiced and unvoiced wishes, fears, and humiliations of childhood and its impatience with the adult world.
SUBJ: Humorous poetry./ American poetry.

811   Ph-2 2-4 $15.00   L   KE038
VIORST, JUDITH. Sad underwear and other complications: more poems for children and their parents. Illus. by Richard Hull. Atheneum ISBN 0-689-31929-0; In Canada: Distican, 1995. 78p. ill.
Companion volume to IF I WERE IN CHARGE OF THE WORLD AND OTHER WORRIES, Atheneum, 1981.
Includes index.
With her usual caustic wit, Viorst conveys, somewhat ruefully, life from a child's point of view--a complicated world where one worries about finding the bathroom on the first day of school, about trying to understand the difference between good manners and telling a lie, and about getting along without a dad.
SUBJ: Humorous poetry./ American poetry.

CE 811   Ph-3 P-3 $14.95   L   KE039
WESTCOTT, NADINE BERNARD. I know an old lady who swallowed a fly. Retold and illustrated by Nadine Bernard Westcott. Atlantic/Little, Brown ISBN 0-316-93128-4; In Canada: Little, Brown, 1980. unp. col. ill.
Includes music.
This rollicking interpretation of the classic nonsense tale is illustrated wildly and hilariously. A delight for reading aloud to children who can join in the amusing repetition.
SUBJ: Nonsense verses.

811   Ph-3 1-3 $13.93   L   KE040
WHITTIER, JOHN GREENLEAF. Barbara Frietchie. Illus. by Nancy Winslow Parker. Greenwillow ISBN 0-688-09830-4, 1992. 32p. col. ill., maps.
Includes glossary.
Colorful illustrations accompany the words of John Greenleaf Whittier's famous poem. Excellent for memorization and recitation. Historical, biographical, and military notes provide additional information which can easily be incorporated into social studies curriculum.
SUBJ: Fritchie, Barbara--Poetry./ United States--History--Civil War, 1861-1865--Poetry./ American poetry./ Narrative poetry.

811   Ph-2 2-5 $15.95   L   KE041
WILLARD, NANCY. Sorcerer's apprentice. Illus. by Leo and Diane Dillon. Blue Sky Press/Scholastic ISBN 0-590-47329-8; In Canada: Scholastic, 1993. unp. col. ill.
This cautionary tale about the misuse of magic is based on a poem by Goethe. Unlike in the Disney version, FANTASIA, the apprentice is a young woman whose adventures are depicted in exquisite, detailed, stylized illustrations. The dramatic, rhythmic verses are captivating and certain to hold interest.
SUBJ: Magicians--Poetry./ Magic--Poetry.

CE 811   Ph-2 5-A $14.95   L   KE042
WILLARD, NANCY. Visit to William Blake's inn: poems for innocent and experienced travelers. Illustrated by Alice and Martin Provensen. Harcourt Brace Jovanovich ISBN 0-15-293822-2, 1981. 44p. col. ill.
Newbery Medal Award.
Caldecott Honor Book.
Available from National Library Service for the Blind and Physically Handicapped in Braille BR05501 and on sound recording cassette RC19591.
A magnificently illustrated re-creation of 18th century London. Life at an imaginary inn run by William Blake is captured with lyrical cadences. A perfect choice to read aloud.
SUBJ: American poetry.

811   Ph-2 K-3 $13.95   L   KE043

WILMER, ISABEL. B is for Bethlehem: a Christmas alphabet. Illus. by Elisa Kleven. Dutton ISBN 0-525-44622-2, 1990. unp. col. ill.
Colorful collages reminiscent of the work of Chagall illustrate this joyous story of the birth of Jesus. This alphabet book is a beautiful amalgam of exquisite illustrations and graceful couplets.
SUBJ: Jesus Christ--Nativity--Poetry./ Christmas--Poetry./ Alphabet./ American poetry.

811   Ph-3 5-6 $13.95   L   KE044

WONG, JANET S. Good luck gold and other poems. McElderry ISBN 0-689-50617-1; In Canada: Maxwell Macmillan, 1994. 42p.
Thoughtful poems from the perspective of an Asian American reflect the author's desire to maintain her heritage and her strong familial ties while fitting in with American culture. Excellent for multicultural studies.
SUBJ: American poetry--Asian American authors.

811   Ph-3 5-A $15.00   T   KE045

WONG, JANET S. Suitcase of seaweed and other poems. McElderry ISBN 0-689-80788-0; In Canada: Distican, 1996. 42p.
Asian-American life is explored in a collection of poems that resonate with truth, humor, and bittersweet experience. For multicultural studies.
SUBJ: Asian Americans--Poetry./ Family life--Poetry./ American poetry./ American poetry--Asian American authors.

811   Ph-3 6-A $19.95   T   KE046

WOOD, NANCY. Spirit walker: poems. Illus. by Frank Howell. Doubleday ISBN 0-385-30927-9; In Canada: Bantam, 1993. 80p. col. ill.
Includes index.
The wisdom and spirituality of the Taos Indians are incorporated into haunting poems and dramatic paintings. Geared toward mature students. For multicultural studies.
SUBJ: Taos Indians--Poetry./ Indians of North America--Poetry./ American poetry.

811   Ph-3 K-3 $14.95   L   KE047

YOLEN, JANE. Animal fare: poems. Illus. by Janet Street. Harcourt Brace ISBN 0-15-203550-8; In Canada: Harcourt Brace c/o Canadian Manda, 1994. 32p. col. ill.
Hilarious nonsense poems about a group of fantastic animals including the "blimpanzee," "raggit," and "giraft." The wordplay is engaging, and the pictures are filled with mirth.
SUBJ: Animals, Mythical--Poetry./ Nonsense verses./ American poetry.

811   Ph-1 3-6 $16.00   L   KE048

YOLEN, JANE. Sacred places. Illus. by David Shannon. Harcourt Brace ISBN 0-15-269953-8; In Canada: Harcourt Brace c/o Canadian Manda, 1996. 40p. col. ill., map.
Includes glossary.
Haunting poems reveal the essence of 12 sacred sites and magical places. Includes The Wailing Wall in Jerusalem, the Christian Cathedrals of Europe, Mecca, the Oracle at Delphi, and Stonehenge. Brief informative notes explain the significance of each place and encourage further research. A wonderful amalgam of social studies, religion, and poetry.
SUBJ: Sacred space--Poetry./ American poetry.

811   Ph-1 4-6 $15.95   L   KE049

YOLEN, JANE. Sea watch: a book of poetry. Illus. by Ted Lewin. Philomel ISBN 0-399-22734-2; In Canada: BeJo Sales, 1996. unp. col. ill.
Beautifully alliterative poems are accompanied by lifelike watercolors which evoke such sea creatures as the grunion, the paper nautilus, and the sea otter. The poems are great for reading aloud, and the evocative paintings bring the sea world to life. Notes on the animals round out this excellent selection for interdisciplinary studies.
SUBJ: Marine animals--Poetry./ American poetry.

811   Ph-2 K-3 $14.95   L   KE050

YOLEN, JANE. Sip of Aesop. Illus. by Karen Barbour. Blue Sky Press/Scholastic ISBN 0-590-47895-8; In Canada: Scholastic, 1995. unp. col. ill.
Thirteen of Aesop's fables are retold in verse with boldly colored acrylic illustrations. Can be used to compare prose and poetry.
SUBJ: Fables./ Stories in rhyme.

811   Ph-2 2-6 $16.95   T   KE051

YOLEN, JANE. Water music: poems for children. Photos by Jason Stemple. Wordsong/Boyds Mills ISBN 1-56397-336-7; In Canada: McClelland & Stewart, 1995. 40p. col. ill.
Stunning photographs of ponds, rivers, oceans, and snow are matched with evocative poems about water, a basic element of life.
Can be integrated into science, environmental studies, and nature studies.
SUBJ: Water--Poetry./ Poetry.

811.008   Ph-2 K-2 $13.00   T   KE052

A. NONNY MOUSE WRITES AGAIN!: POEMS. Selected by Jack Prelutsky. Illus. by Marjorie Priceman. Knopf ISBN 0-679-83715-9; In Canada: Random House, 1993. unp. col. ill.
"Borzoi book."
A collection of witty, often irreverent poems accompanied by hilarious illustrations. Great for memorizing.
SUBJ: American poetry--Collections./ Anonymous writings.

811.008   Ph-2 3-6 $14.89   L   KE053

AT THE CRACK OF THE BAT: BASEBALL POEMS. Compiled by Lillian Morrison. Illus. by Steve Cieslawski. Hyperion ISBN 1-56282-177-6, 1992. 64p. col. ill.
Includes index.
An anthology of baseball poems about famous players such as Reggie Jackson and Roberto Clemente includes nostalgic and humorous moments in the great American pastime. Excellent for persuading sports addicts to get interested in poetry.
SUBJ: Baseball--Poetry./ American poetry--Collections.

811.008   Ph-1 3-6 $18.89   L   KE054

CELEBRATE AMERICA IN POETRY AND ART. Edited by Nora Panzer. Published in association with the National Museum of American Art, Smithsonian Institute. Hyperion ISBN 1-56282-665-4, 1994. 96p. col. ill.
Includes index.
Selectors' Choice, 20th ed.
An exquisite amalgam of poetry, history, and art celebrates 200 years of America's history with works from some of the greatest American artists. A beautifully conceived patriotic anthology to be treasured and used as the basis for infinite lessons and discussions in both the art and social studies curriculum.
SUBJ: United States--Poetry./ American poetry--Collections./ United States in art.

811.008   Ph-1 K-A $3.95   P   KE055

DRAGON POEMS. Compiled by John Foster. Illus. by Korky Paul. Oxford ISBN 0-19-916425-8; In Canada: Oxford, 1991. 32p. col. ill.
Twenty-three lively, irreverently funny poems recount the adventures of a myriad of dragons, those who breathe fire, those who breathe frost, all accompanied by deliciously wicked illustrations. The poets include Jack Prelutsky and X.J. Kennedy.
SUBJ: Dragons--Poetry./ American poetry--Collections.

811.008   Ph-1 3-6 $14.95   T   KE056

EXTRA INNINGS: BASEBALL POEMS. Selected by Lee Bennett Hopkins. Illus. by Scott Medlock. Harcourt Brace Jovanovich ISBN 0-15-226833-2; In Canada: Harcourt Brace c/o Canadian Manda, 1993. 40p. col. ill.
A fine anthology of 19 buoyant poems about the great American pastime is accompanied by exuberant, full-page paintings. The immortals of baseball are celebrated--Satch, DiMaggio, Robinson, and, of course, Mighty Casey. Little Leaguers, women umpires, and spectators are also covered in this sprightly amalgam of poetry and sports. Great to entice reluctant readers to poetry.
SUBJ: Baseball--Poetry./ American poetry--Collections.

811.008   Ph-2 K-3 $14.95   T   KE057

FAMILIES: POEMS CELEBRATING THE AFRICAN AMERICAN EXPERIENCE. Selected by Dorothy S. Strickland and Michael R. Strickland. Illus. by John Ward. Wordsong/Boyds Mills ISBN 1-56397-288-3; In Canada: McClelland & Stewart, 1994. 29p. col. ill.
Includes music and lyrics.
Examines the African-American family, exploring the values and diversity inherent in their heritage. Such poets as Gwendolyn Brooks, Lucille Clifton, and Nikki Giovanni convey a warm understanding of familial ups and downs. A valuable addition to multicultural studies.
SUBJ: Afro-Americans--Poetry--Collections./ Family life--Poetry./ American poetry--Collections.

811.008   Ph-1 K-5 $15.99   L   KE058

FOR LAUGHING OUT LOUD: POEMS TO TICKLE YOUR FUNNYBONE. Selected by Jack Prelutsky. Illus. by Marjorie Priceman. Knopf ISBN 0-394-92144-5; In Canada: Random House, 1991. 84p. col. ill.
Includes indexes.
Available from the National Library Service for the Blind and Physically Handicapped on sound recording cassette RC35067.
A truly funny anthology of poems by such humorists as Jack Prelutsky, Ogden Nash, X.J. Kennedy, and Shel Silverstein. Excellent for introducing poetry and for memorization.
SUBJ: American poetry--Collections./ Humorous poetry.

811.008 Ph-1 K-5 $16.99 L KE059
FOR LAUGHING OUT LOUDER: MORE POEMS TO TICKLE YOUR
FUNNYBONE. Selected by Jack Prelutsky. Illus. by Marjorie Priceman.
Knopf ISBN 0-679-97063-0; In Canada: Random House, 1995. 40p. col.
ill.
    "Borzoi book."
    Includes indexes.
    Selectors' Choice, 21st ed.
    Another hilarious collection of poems by such children's favorites as
    Myra Cohn Livingston, Margaret Mahy, and Jane Yolen. Fanciful,
    colorful illustrations perfectly capture the humor of the verse. Useful
    as a lively introduction to poetry and for memorization.
    SUBJ: American poetry--Collections./ Humorous poetry.

811.008 Ph-1 K-3 $13.89 L KE060
GOOD BOOKS, GOOD TIMES! Selected by Lee Bennett Hopkins.
Illustrated by Harvey Stevenson. HarperCollins ISBN 0-06-022528-9; In
Canada: HarperCollins, 1990. 31p. col. ill.
    Fourteen poems by a distinguished group of poets such as Jack
    Prelutsky, William Cole, and Arleen Fisher extol the joys of reading.
    To lose oneself in a book, or to find oneself; to read of adventures
    and dragons and nonsense - all through the lure of good books,
    good friends.
    SUBJ: Books and reading--Poetry./ American poetry--Collections.

811.008 Ph-3 K-6 $9.95 T KE061
GOOD MORNING TO YOU, VALENTINE: POEMS FOR VALENTINE'S
DAY. Selected by Lee Bennett Hopkins. Illus. by Tomie de Paola.
Wordsong/Boyds Mills ISBN 1-878093-59-2, c1976, 1993. 32p. ill.
    Includes index.
    Twenty-three poems for Valentine's Day including such poets as
    William Shakespeare, Shel Silverstein, and John Updike. De Paola's
    red and white illustrations add holiday spirit to the anthology.
    SUBJ: Valentine's Day--Poetry./ Poetry--Collections.

811.008 Ph-2 K-4 $13.95 L KE062
HALLOWEEN POEMS. Selected by Myra Cohn Livingston. Illus. by
Stephen Gammell. Holiday House ISBN 0-8234-0762-4, 1989. 32p. ill.
    Dramatically frightening b&w illustrations create a mood of horror for
    this anthology of 18 poems which celebrate the holiday of Halloween.
    Traditional favorites are mixed with the works of such contemporary
    poets as X.J. Kennedy and N.M. Bodecker.
    SUBJ: Halloween--Poetry./ American poetry--Collections.

811.008 Ph-2 2-6 $19.95 T KE063
HAND IN HAND: AN AMERICAN HISTORY THROUGH POETRY.
Collected by Lee Bennett Hopkins. Illus. by Peter M. Fiore. Simon &
Schuster ISBN 0-671-73315-X; In Canada: Simon & Schuster, 1994.
144p. col. ill., map.
    Includes indexes.
    An anthology of poems that reflects the American experience from
    the Pilgrims to the astronauts. Excellent for incorporating into the
    social studies curriculum and for encouraging memorization and
    dramatic expression. Adds a multicultural component to the study of
    poetry.
    SUBJ: United States--Poetry./ American poetry--Collections.

811.008 Ph-3 K-3 $13.89 L KE064
HOPKINS, LEE BENNETT. Weather: poems. Selected by Lee Bennett
Hopkins. Illus. by Melanie W. Hall. HarperCollins ISBN 0-06-021462-7;
In Canada: HarperCollins, 1994. 64p. col. ill. (I can read book).
    Includes index.
    An easy-to-read compendium of weather poems including Carl
    Sandburg's "Fog," Ogden Nash's "Winter morning," and Christina
    Rossetti's "Clouds."
    SUBJ: Weather--Poetry./ American poetry--Collections./ English
    poetry--Collections.

811.008 Ph-1 3-A $13.95 T KE065
I LIKE YOU, IF YOU LIKE ME: POEMS OF FRIENDSHIP. Selected and
edited by Myra Cohn Livingston. McElderry ISBN 0-689-50408-X; In
Canada: Collier Macmillan, 1987. 144p.
    Available from National Library Service for the Blind and Physically
    Handicapped on sound recording cassette RC26407.
    Examines the pathos, joy, poignancy, and hilarity of friendship in
    poems by such modern masters as Shel Silverstein and Eve Merriam.
    A wonderfully compassionate anthology certain to captivate readers
    with its joyous wisdom. Excellent for provoking discussion on the
    vagaries of friendship.
    SUBJ: Friendship--Poetry./ American poetry--Collections.

811.008 Ph-2 2-5 $15.95 L KE066
I THOUGHT I'D TAKE MY RAT TO SCHOOL: POEMS FOR
SEPTEMBER TO JUNE. Selected by Dorothy M. Kennedy. Illus. by Abby
Carter. Little, Brown ISBN 0-316-48893-3; In Canada: Little, Brown,
1993. 63p. ill.
    Includes indexes.
    An anthology devoted to the joys and terrors, the mischief and
    accomplishments, and the teachers and the homework that make up
    the universal experience of going to school. A wonderful introduction
    to poetry certain to provoke giggles as well as discussion.
    SUBJ: Schools--Poetry./ American poetry--Collections.

811.008 Ph-1 4-A $19.95 T KE067
IMAGINARY GARDENS: AMERICAN POETRY AND ART FOR YOUNG
PEOPLE. Edited by Charles Sullivan. Abrams ISBN 0-8109-1130-2,
1989. 111p. col. ill.
    A splendid melange of poetry and art which reflects the American
    experience. The words of Robert Frost, Carl Sandburg, Emily
    Dickinson and Bret Harte stand in juxtaposition with art by Mary
    Cassatt, Andrew Wyeth, Maurice Prendergast, and Roy Lichtenstein.
    Certain to provoke appreciation of America's greatness and diversity
    and enhance social studies lessons.
    SUBJ: American poetry--Collections./ Art appreciation.

811.008 Ph-2 3-6 $14.00 T KE068
KIDS PICK THE FUNNIEST POEMS. Compiled by Bruce Lansky.
Illustrated by Steve Carpenter. Meadowbrook/dist. by Simon & Schuster
ISBN 0-88166-149-X, 1991. 115p. ill.
    Includes indexes.
    A collection of humorous poems selected by children as their
    favorites. Subjects include parents, brothers and sisters, and school
    days. Includes such familiar poets as Shel Silverstein, Jack Prelutsky,
    and Judith Viorst. A sparkling anthology certain to provoke lots of
    laughs.
    SUBJ: Humorous poetry--Collections./ American poetry--Collections.

811.008 Ph-2 3-6 $13.95 T KE069
LOTS OF LIMERICKS. Selected by Myra Cohn Livingston. Illus. by
Rebecca Perry. McElderry ISBN 0-689-50531-0; In Canada: Maxwell
Macmillan, 1991. 131p. ill.
    Includes indexes.
    A comprehensive collection of 210 limericks by a wide range of poets
    including Lewis Carroll, Edward Lear, Jack Prelutsky, and X.J.
    Kennedy. The poems are arranged according to such subjects as
    holidays, peculiar people, and accidents. Although not highly pictorial,
    the book is engaging and a good source for poetry units.
    SUBJ: Limericks./ American poetry--Collections./ English poetry--
    Collections.

811.008 Ph-1 1-6 $12.95 T KE070
MAKE A JOYFUL SOUND: POEMS FOR CHILDREN BY AFRICAN-
AMERICAN POETS. Edited by Deborah Slier. Illus. by Cornelius Van
Wright and Ying-Hwa Hu. Checkerboard Press ISBN 1-56288-000-4,
1991. 104p b&w and col illus.
    Includes indexes.
    An anthology of poems written by such African-American poets as
    Langston Hughes, Gwendolyn Brooks, Abiodun Oyewole, and Dakari
    Kamau Hru. Illustrations depict the African-American experience.
    Although many of the poems have universal appeal, they will have
    special meaning for African-American children and will encourage
    pride in African-American history and achievements.
    SUBJ: Afro-Americans--Poetry--Collections./ American poetry--
    Collections./ American poetry--Afro-American authors--Collections./
    Race awareness--Poetry.

811.008 Ph-2 1-4 $17.00 T KE071
MARVELOUS MATH: A BOOK OF POEMS. Selected by Lee Bennett
Hopkins. Illus. by Karen Barbour. Simon & Schuster ISBN 0-689-80658-
2; In Canada: Distican, 1997. 32p. col. ill.
    Colorful, playful illustrations accompany 16 poems about math. A
    good way to integrate poetry into math lessons, thereby enriching
    both disciplines. For interdisciplinary studies.
    SUBJ: Mathematics--Poetry./ American poetry--Collections.

811.008 Ph-1 K-2 $17.99 L KE072
MAVOR, SALLEY. You and me: poems of friendship. Selected and illus.
by Salley Mavor. Orchard ISBN 0-531-33045-1, 1997. unp. col. ill.
    An anthology about the joys, sorrows, and fun inherent in keeping
    and losing friends. The poems by such writers as Judith Viorst and
    Jack Prelutsky are alternately joyous, wistful, and exuberant. The
    fabric relief artwork is very unusual and invites careful attention to the
    infinite detail.
    SUBJ: Friendship--Poetry./ American poetry--Collections.

811.008 Ph-1 1-4 $18.95 T KE073
NEVER TAKE A PIG TO LUNCH AND OTHER POEMS ABOUT THE
FUN OF EATING. Selected and illus. by Nadine Bernard Westcott.

Orchard ISBN 0-531-06834-X, 1994. 64p. col. ill.
"Melanie Kroupa book."
Includes indexes.
Available from the National Library Service for the Blind and
Physically Handicapped on sound recording cassette RC 39647.
Funny poems, limericks, and rhymes devoted to food foibles, hateful
food habits, messy food manners, and gleeful gluttony. Written by
such poets as Jack Prelutsky and X.J. Kennedy, this collection is a
tasty treat for those who are "constantly in the mood for food," to
quote Ogden Nash. Clever, colorful cartoon illustrations add to the
hilarity.
SUBJ: Food--Poetry./ American poetry--Collections./ English poetry--
Collections.

811.008   Ph-2 3-6 $16.00   L   KE074
OPENING DAYS: SPORTS POEMS. Selected by Lee Bennett Hopkins.
Illus. by Scott Medlock. Harcourt Brace ISBN 0-15-200270-7; In Canada:
Harcourt Brace c/o Canadian Manda, 1996. 37p. col. ill.
The thrill of participating in sports is conveyed in poems which give
insight into the disciplines of karate, long distance running, and tennis.
The colorful paintings bring the exuberance of skiing, ice skating, and
baseball to life. A wonderful introduction to poetry for reluctant
readers.
SUBJ: Sports--Poetry./ American poetry--Collections.

811.008   Ph-1 1-3 $14.95   L   KE075
PASS IT ON: AFRICAN-AMERICAN POETRY FOR CHILDREN. Selected
by Wade Hudson. Illus. by Floyd Cooper. Scholastic ISBN 0-590-45770-
5; In Canada: Scholastic, 1993. 32p. col. ill.
Moving poems by such African-American poets as Langston Hughes,
Nikki Giovanni, Paul Laurence Dunbar, and Gwendolyn Brooks are
accompanied by warm, glowing illustrations. Fine to use as enrichment
in multicultural studies.
SUBJ: American poetry--Afro-American authors--Collections./ Afro-
Americans--Poetry--Collections.

811.008   Ph-2 3-A $14.95   L   KE076
PLACE MY WORDS ARE LOOKING FOR: WHAT POETS SAY ABOUT
AND THROUGH THEIR WORK. Selected by Paul B. Janeczko. Bradbury
ISBN 0-02-747671-5; In Canada: Collier Macmillan, 1990. 150p. ill.
Includes index.
39 American poets, such as Jack Prelutsky, Eve Merriam, and
Gwendolyn Brooks are represented by their poetry and thoughts.
Pictures of the poets are accompanied by their words on how they
came to write that particular poem. An excellent enrichment to poetry
writing lessons.
SUBJ: American poetry--Collections./ Poets, American./ Poetry--
Authorship.

811.008   Ph-2 K-3 $13.95   L   KE077
POEMS FOR JEWISH HOLIDAYS. Selected by Myra Cohn Livingston.
Illus. by Lloyd Bloom. Holiday House ISBN 0-8234-0606-7, 1986. 32p.
ill.
Conveys the bittersweet quality of such Jewish holidays as Rosh
Hashanah and Hanukkah with poems which focus on a child's
perspective of the celebratory rituals.
SUBJ: Fasts and feasts--Judaism--Poetry./ American poetry--
Collections.

811.008   Ph-2 1-3 $13.95   L   KE078
RAINY DAY RHYMES. Selected by Gail Radley. Illus. by Ellen Kandoian.
Houghton Mifflin ISBN 0-395-59967-9, 1992. 48p col illus.
Includes index.
Seventeen delightful poems about mizzly, drizzly rain written by
familiar poets including Aileen Fisher, Robert Louis Stevenson and
Rachel Field. Poems are short, easy to understand and on a topic of
high interest to youngsters. Great for reading aloud.
SUBJ: Rain and rainfall--Poetry./ American poetry--Collections.

811.008   Ph-1 P-K $21.99   L   KE079
READ-ALOUD RHYMES FOR THE VERY YOUNG. Selected by Jack
Prelutsky. Illus. by Marc Brown. With an introduction by Jim Trelease.
Knopf ISBN 0-394-97218-X; In Canada: Random House, c1986. 98p.
col. ill.
"Borzoi book."
Includes indexes.
Available from National Library Service for the Blind and Physically
Handicapped on sound recording cassette RC25640.
Captivates the youngest listener with an inviting collection of over 200
rhymes, which are accompanied by softly colored, witty illustrations.
SUBJ: American poetry--Collections./ English poetry--Collections.

811.008   Ph-1 4-A $14.95   L   KE080
ROLL ALONG: POEMS ON WHEELS. Selected by Myra Cohn
Livingston. McElderry ISBN 0-689-50585-X; In Canada: Maxwell
Macmillan, 1993. 72p.
Includes indexes.
Contemporary poems about vehicles that roll--unicycles, buses, taxis,
motorcycles, trucks. The selections are current--"My mother drives the
mailtruck," fanciful--"The ice cream truck," and hilarious--"A driver
from Deering." The diverse authors in this anthology include N.M.
Bodecker, Karla Kuskin, and X.J. Kennedy. Encourages original poetry
writing about transportation and similar modern subjects.
SUBJ: Transportation--Poetry./ Vehicles--Poetry./ Wheels--Poetry./
American poetry--Collections.

811.008   Ph-2 4-6 $15.89   L   KE081
SLAM DUNK: BASKETBALL POEMS. Compiled by Lillian Morrison. Illus.
by Bill James. Hyperion ISBN 0-7868-2042-X; In Canada: Little, Brown,
1995. 64p. ill. (some col.).
Includes index.
Energetic poems and drawings capture the movement, excitement, and
artistry of basketball. Will entice sports lovers into poetry.
SUBJ: Basketball--Poetry./ American poetry--Collections.

811.008   Ph-2 2-6 $5.99   P   KE082
SNOW TOWARD EVENING: A YEAR IN A RIVER VALLEY: NATURE
POEMS. Selected by Josette Frank. Illus. by Thomas Locker. Puffin ISBN
0-14-055582-X, 1995. unp. col. ill.
A paean to nature created by the combination of Thomas Locker's
evocative paintings and 13 celebratory poems by such writers as John
Updike, Langston Hughes, and Edna St. Vincent Millay. Can be used
as an enriching addition to a study of the seasons.
SUBJ: American poetry--Collections./ English poetry--Collections./
Nature--Poetry./ Months--Poetry.

811.008   Ph-2 P-2 $14.89   L   KE083
SNUFFLES AND SNOUTS: POEMS. Selected by Laura Robb. Illus. by
Steven Kellogg. Dial ISBN 0-8037-1598-6, 1995. 40p. col. ill.
A paean to pigs--pigs who nap in squishy seep, pigs who cool off in
the muck and grime, pigs who wear wigs, pigs who dance jigs--all
cavort in comic illustrations which accompany the hilarious poems.
SUBJ: Pigs--Poetry./ American poetry--Collections./ English poetry--
Collections.

811.008   Ph-2 4-A $15.99   T   KE084
SOUL LOOKS BACK IN WONDER. Poems by Maya Angelou...[et al.].
Illus. by Tom Feelings. Dial ISBN 0-8037-1001-1, 1993. unp. col. ill.
Coretta Scott King Award, 1994.
The African-American spirit is extolled in dramatic and dynamic poems
by such poets as Maya Angelou, Langston Hughes, and Lucille
Clifton. The art work is beautiful and haunting, reflecting the joy and
challenge of being born African American. Excellent for multicultural
studies.
SUBJ: American poetry--Afro-American authors./ Afro-Americans--
Poetry--Collections.

811.008   Ph-1 4-8 $14.93   L   KE085
STAR WALK. Edited by Seymour Simon. Morrow ISBN 0-688-11888-7,
1995. unp. col. ill.
The mystery of the universe is explored in dramatic full-color
photographs and in exquisite, thought-provoking poems by such poets
as Whitman, Blake, and Thoreau. A distinguished book to treasure.
Use to form the basis for scientific speculation and discussion and to
encourage creative writing of poetry about the sky, stars, planets,
and heavens.
SUBJ: Outer space--Poetry./ Stars--Poetry./ American poetry./
English poetry.

811.008   Ph-2 P-2 $18.95   T   KE086
SUNFLAKES: POEMS FOR CHILDREN. Selected by Lilian Moore. Illus.
by Jan Ormerod. Clarion ISBN 0-395-58833-2, 1992. 96p. col. ill.
Includes indexes.
The universal experiences of childhood are explored in this anthology
of American poetry by such writers as Shel Silverstein, Eve Merriam,
Eloise Greenfield, Arnold Adoff, and Jack Prelutsky. Wonderful for
reading aloud and for introducing poetry to the very young.
SUBJ: American poetry--Collections.

811.008   Ph-3 6-A $22.50   T   KE087
TALKING TO THE SUN: AN ILLUSTRATED ANTHOLOGY OF POEMS
FOR YOUNG PEOPLE. Selected and introduced by Kenneth Koch and
Kate Farrell. Metropolitan Museum of Art/Henry Holt ISBN 0-8050-
0144-1, 1985. 112p. col. ill.
Includes appendix and index.
Combines reproductions of some elegant treasures owned by the

Metropolitan Museum of Art with an eclectic selection of poems. The juxtaposition of Matisse and Shakespeare, of Sandburg and Steichen is fascinating. This unique blend of art and poetry can inspire the creative, gifted student.
SUBJ: Poetry--Collections./ Art.

811.008　　　　Ph-2 3-6　$16.00　T　KE088
TEN-SECOND RAINSHOWERS: POEMS BY YOUNG PEOPLE. Compiled by Sandford Lyne. Illus. by Virginia Halstead. Simon & Schuster ISBN 0-689-80113-0; In Canada: Distican, 1996. 124p. col. ill. Includes index.
A collection of poems written by young people about childhood, family, challenges, nature, beauty, friendship, love, solitude, and spirit. Excellent for inspiring neophyte poets as they embark upon creative writing activities.
SUBJ: American poetry--Collections./ Children's writings./ Teenagers' writings.

811.008　　　　Ph-2 K-6　$13.95　L　KE089
THANKSGIVING POEMS. Selected by Myra Cohn Livingston. Illus. by Stephen Gammell. Holiday House ISBN 0-8234-0570-2, 1985. 32p. col. ill.
Available from National Library Service for the Blind and Physically Handicapped on sound recording cassette RC26292.
Evokes the essence and significance of the holiday in a diversified group of 16 poems. At times stirring, humorous, and religious, with dramatically handsome illustrations, this anthology lends itself to reading aloud and as a basis for holiday presentations.
SUBJ: Thanksgiving Day--Poetry./ Poetry--Collections.

811.008　　　　Ph-2 K-4　$17.95　T　KE090
ZOOFUL OF ANIMALS. Selected by William Cole. Illus. by Lynn Munsinger. Houghton Mifflin ISBN 0-395-52278-1, 1992. 88p. col. ill. Includes index.
A compilation of 40 witty, wise, wistful poems about personable porcupines, monstrous whales, and tall toucans all accompanied by hilarious illustrations is certain to provoke giggles.
SUBJ: Animals--Poetry./ American poetry--Collections./ English poetry--Collections.

812　　　　Ph-2 A-6　$3.99　P　KE091
DAVIS, OSSIE. Escape to freedom: a play about young Frederick Douglass. Puffin/Penguin ISBN 0-14-034355-5, c1976, 1990. 89p. Includes bibliography.
Coretta Scott King Award.
This drama about Frederick Douglass calls for seven characters: Frederick Douglass, black woman, black man, black child, white woman, white man, and white child. The roles (with the exception of Douglass) can be played either by this small group or a larger cast. Further flexibility is provided by the use of the simple stage effects and a larger group which can provide the singing (many spirituals) dancing and dialogue. The play is subject to a royalty but addresses are given.
SUBJ: Douglass, Frederick--Drama./ Afro-Americans--Drama./ Slavery--Drama./ Plays.

812　　　　Ph-3 3-6　$25.00　T　KE092
MACDONALD, MARGARET READ. Skit book: 101 skits from kids. Illustrated by Marie-Louise Scull. Linnet/Shoe String ISBN 0-208-02258-9, 1990. 147p.
Includes sources, bibliography and index.
A selection of simple skits which promote creativity. Few characters are needed and costumes and props are not essential. A good introduction to dramatics.
SUBJ: Plays./ Children's writings.

812　　　　Ph-2 4-A　$13.95　P　KE093
WINTHER, BARBARA. Plays from African tales: one-act, royalty-free dramatizations for young people, from stories and folktales of Africa. Plays, Inc. ISBN 0-8238-0296-5, 1992. 145p.
The stories and legends of Africa are dramatized in one-act, royalty-free plays. Production notes are included. Contains such folktales as "Anansi, the African spider" and "The monkey without a tail." Excellent for multicultural studies.
SUBJ: Folklore--Africa--Drama./ Africa--Folklore--Drama./ Africa--Drama./ Plays.

812.008　　　　Ph-2 3-6　$13.95　P　KE094
PLAYS FROM FAVORITE FOLK TALES. Edited by Sylvia Kamerman. Plays ISBN 0-8238-0280-9, 1987. 293p.
Anthologizes 25 one act adaptions of popular folktales including such favorites as Rumplestiltskin, Robin Hood, Rapunzel, and Stone Soup. Flexible cast sizes and minimum costume requirements make for easy staging.
SUBJ: Folklore--Drama./ Plays--Collections.

812.008　　　　Ph-2 4-6　$13.95　P　KE095
PLAYS OF BLACK AMERICANS: THE BLACK EXPERIENCE IN AMERICA, DRAMATIZED FOR YOUN PEOPLE. New expanded ed. Edited by Sylvia E. Kamerman. Plays Inc. ISBN 0-8238-0301-5, 1994. 154p.
Dramatizes the achievements of such great African Americans as Martin Luther King, Jr., Mary McLeod Bethune, and Harriet Tubman in a collection of plays, pantomimes, and choral readings. Particularly useful during Black History Month. For multicultural studies.
SUBJ: Afro-Americans--Drama./ Plays--Afro-American authors.

821　　　　Ph-1 1-4　$15.95　L　KE096
BLAKE, WILLIAM. Tyger. Illus. by Neil Waldman. Harcourt Brace ISBN 0-15-292375-6; In Canada: Harcourt Brace c/o Canadian Manda, 1993. unp. col. ill.
Selectors' Choice, 20th ed.
Stunning, boldly colored illustrations mark the drama, intensity, and magic of Blake's immortal poem. Excellent for memorization and for analysis by mature students.
SUBJ: Tigers--Poetry./ English poetry.

821　　　　Ph-3 K-2/3　$13.89　L　KE097
CARROLL, LEWIS. Jabberwocky. With illus. from the Disney Archives. Disney Press ISBN 1-56282-246-2, 1992. unp. col. ill. (Disney Archives).
Cartoon storyboards from the Disney Archives convey the humor and zaniness inherent in Lewis Carroll's famous poem. The action, cartoon format accompanying the silly words will delight young readers.
SUBJ: Nonsense verses./ English poetry.

SRC 821　　　　Ph-3 2-6　$20.95　OD KE098
CHILD'S GARDEN OF VERSES AND A POTPOURRI OF POETRY: AN INTRODUCTION TO GREAT POETS (Sound recording cassette). By Robert L. Stevenson...[et al.]. Audio Book Contractors, n.d. 2 sound cassettes.
Dramatizes the works of such poets as Stevenson, Wordsworth, Dickinson, and Coleridge. The narrator's voice is clear, rich and expressive, and the selection of poems is judicious. Contributes to an enriching of the poetry curriculum.
SUBJ: Poetry--Collections.

821　　　　Ph-2 4-6　$15.95　T　KE099
DE LA MARE, WALTER. Rhymes and verses: collected poems for children. Illus. by Ellinore Blaisdell. Henry Holt ISBN 0-8050-0847-0; In Canada: Fitzhenry & Whiteside, 1947. 344p.
Includes first line index.
Fosters youthful imagination with enchanting, fanciful, and often macabre poems. Wonderful for reading aloud.
SUBJ: English poetry.

821　　　　Ph-1 4-A　$12.95　T　KE100
ELIOT, T. S. Old possum's book of practical cats. Illus. by Edward Gorey. Harcourt Brace Jovanovich ISBN 0-15-168657-2, 1982. 56p. ill.
This edition of classic poems celebrating the inscrutable nature of cats is delightfully illustrated with black and white, tongue in cheek drawings. The masterful use of language should be shared by reading aloud.
SUBJ: Cats--Poetry./ English poetry.

821　　　　Ph-2 K-3　$12.89　L　KE101
FARJEON, ELEANOR. Cats sleep anywhere. Illus. by Anne Mortimer. HarperCollins ISBN 0-06-027335-6; In Canada: HarperCollins, 1996. unp. col. ill.
The classic poem is accompanied by exquisite illustrations. Feline fans will love this.
SUBJ: Cats--Poetry./ English poetry.

821　　　　Ph-2 P-2　$16.00　L　KE102
HUGHES, SHIRLEY. Rhymes for Annie Rose. Lothrop, Lee & Shepard ISBN 0-688-14220-6, 1995. unp. col. ill.
The everyday delights of a young girl's life are revealed in warm, lilting poems. The illustrations are loving reproductions of family life. A charming collection of rhymes for the nursery.
SUBJ: English poetry./ Children--Poetry./ Family life--Poetry.

821　　　　Ph-1 K-A　$14.95　T　KE103
LEAR, EDWARD. Daffy down dillies: silly limericks. Illus. by John O'Brien. Caroline House/Boyds Mills ISBN 1-56397-007-4, 1992. unp. col. ill.
An excellent sampling of Lear's limericks accompanied by divinely silly illustrations. This appealing amalgam can serve as an integral part of poetry studies of the limerick form as well as a wonderful book to read and enjoy.
SUBJ: Nonsense verses./ English poetry./ Limericks./ Humorous poetry.

821   Ph-2 K-3 $16.00   T   KE104

LEAR, EDWARD. Nonsense songs. Illus. by Bee Willey. McElderry ISBN 0-689-81369-4; In Canada: Distican, 1997. 32p. col. ill.

First published in London, England by Orion Children's Books, 1996. Wonderful for reading aloud, this version of some of Edward Lear's most infectious verses includes some of his favorite poems--"The Owl and the Pussycat," "The Pobble who has no toes," "The Jumblies," and "The Quangle Wangle's hat." Charming illustrations add to the fun.
SUBJ: Nonsense verses./ English poetry.

821   Ph-2 P-2 $13.00   T   KE105

LEAR, EDWARD. Owl and the Pussy-cat. Illus. by Ian Beck. Atheneum ISBN 0-689-81032-6; In Canada: Distican, 1996. unp. col. ill.

Originally published in Great Britain, Transworld Publishers, Inc., 1994.
In this version of Lear's well-known poem, captivating illustrations of witty landscapes and seascapes and irresistible animals bring to life the familiar tale of the Owl and the Pussy-cat who go to sea in their beautiful pea-green boat.
SUBJ: Nonsense verses./ Animals--Poetry./ English poetry.

821   Ph-2 3-6 $18.95   T   KE106

LEAR, EDWARD. Owl and the Pussy-cat and other nonsense poems. Selected and illus. by Michael Hague. North-South Books ISBN 1-55858-467-6; In Canada: North-South Books, 1995. 61p. col. ill.

Hilarious illustrations replete with the wit and verve that should accompany Lear's silly nonsense verses combine with poems gathered from Lear's various works to form a very funny and absurd collection.
SUBJ: Nonsense verses./ English poetry./ Humorous poetry./ Limericks.

821   Ph-3 K-3 $19.95   T   KE107

MCNAUGHTON, COLIN. Making friends with Frankenstein: a book of monstrous poems and pictures. Candlewick ISBN 1-56402-308-7; In Canada: Candlewick/dist. by Douglas & McIntyre, 1994. 93p. col. ill.

Includes index.
A wacky collection of rude rhymes, insidious insults, disgusting diatribes, and much monstrous mayhem. The vivid, irreverent vocabulary and hilarious illustrations will prove irresistible to all devotees of ghosts and spirits, mummies, and hideous, scary creatures. Good for reading aloud.
SUBJ: Monsters--Poetry./ English poetry.

821   Ph-3 P-2 $17.50   L   KE108

MILNE, A. A. World of Christopher Robin: the complete When we were very young and Now we are six. With decorations and new illlustrations in full color. Dutton ISBN 0-525-44448-3, c1958. 234p. col. ill.

Available from National Library Service for the Blind and Physically Handicapped in Braille BR02188, on sound recording cassette RC15330, and as talking book TB01125.
The complete "When we were very young" and "Now we are six" with some new illustrations.
SUBJ: English poetry.

821   Ph-2 2-4 $17.90   L   KE109

ROSEN, MICHAEL. Michael Rosen's ABC. Illus. by Bee Willey. Millbrook Press ISBN 1-56294-138-0, 1996. unp. col. ill.

First published in Great Britain, Macdonald Young Books, 1995.
A delightful combination of nonsense poems and hilarious illustrations. The rhymes employ alliteration in a most amusing manner. Great for reading aloud and for memorization.
SUBJ: Nonsense verses./ English poetry./ Alphabet./ Picture puzzles.

821   Ph-3 P-2 $18.95   T   KE110

STEVENSON, ROBERT LOUIS. Child's garden of verses. Illus. by Jessie Willcox Smith. Scribner's ISBN 0-684-20949-7, 1905. 124p. ill.

Available from National Library Service for the Blind and Physically Handicapped in Braille BR01428 and as talking book TB01125.
The long-lived and still beloved poems in this classic collection evoke the 19th-century England in which the author lived as a child. "My shadow" and "Bed in summer" are still as true as when they were first written.
SUBJ: English poetry.

821   Ph-3 P-K $14.93   L   KE111

TAYLOR, JANE. Twinkle, twinkle, little star. Illus. by Michael Hague. Morrow ISBN 0-688-11169-6, 1992. unp. col. ill.

"Books of wonder."
Vivid, detailed, colorful illustrations accompany this version of the classic poem which was first published in 1806.
SUBJ: Stars--Poetry./ English poetry.

821.008   Ph-1 P-2 $17.95   L   KE112

TALKING LIKE THE RAIN: A FIRST BOOK OF POEMS. Selected by X.J. and Dorothy M. Kennedy. Illus. by Jane Dyer. Little, Brown ISBN 0-316-48889-5; In Canada: Little, Brown, 1992. 96p col illus.

Includes indices.
A glorious collection of more than 100 contemporary and traditional poems representing many of the great poets--Wallace Stevens, Langston Hughes, Ogden Nash and Edward Lear. Charming, witty, tender watercolor illustrations enliven this distinguished anthology.
SUBJ: Poetry--Collections.

821.008   Ph-2 2-4 $21.36   T   KE113

WALKING THE BRIDGE OF YOUR NOSE. Selected by Michael Rosen. Illus. by Chloe Cheese. Kingfisher/dist. by Raintree Steck-Vaughn ISBN 1-85697-596-7, 1995. 61p. col. ill.

Includes index.
Witty, engaging froth filled with poems, rhymes, tongue twisters, word puzzles, tombstone tomfoolery, and silly patter. The exuberance and fun engendered by this collection will insure its popularity.
SUBJ: Nonsense verses./ Humorous poetry./ English poetry--Collections.

822.3   Ph-3 4-6/4 $16.89   L   KE114

COVILLE, BRUCE. William Shakespeare's A midsummer night's dream. Retold by Bruce Coville. Illus. by Dennis Nolan. Dial ISBN 0-8037-1785-7, 1996. unp. col. ill.

Shakespeare's tale is retold in simplified prose. The story of the magic forest inhabited by fairies and hobgoblins, intertwined with the romantic fate of two young couples is easy to understand and serves as a lively introduction to Shakespeare.
SUBJ: Shakespeare, William--Adaptations./ English literature.

822.3   Ph-3 A/9 $35.00   T   KE115

LAMB, CHARLES. Tales from Shakespeare. By Charles and Mary Lamb. Folger ISBN 0-918016-04-5, 1979. 363p. col. ill.

Available from National Library Service for the Blind and Physically Handicapped in Braille BRA09693 and on sound recording cassette RC24524.
The classic retelling of twenty of Shakespeare's plays is presented in a visually stunning oversized edition. The many and varied illustrations drawn from the collection of the world renowned Folger Shakespeare Library make this title outstanding. For the special reader.
SUBJ: Shakespeare, William--Adaptations./ English literature.

822.3   Ph-3 5-A/7 $16.99   T   KE116

ROSS, STEWART. Shakespeare and Macbeth: the story behind the play. Illustrated by Tony Karpinski and Victor Ambrus. Foreword by Kenneth Branagh. Viking ISBN 0-670-85629-0; In Canada: Penguin, 1994. 45p. col. ill.

Includes chronologies, index, and bibliography.
Recounts the background of Shakespeare's play, MACBETH, with information on how he conceived and wrote it. Emphasis is placed on Shakespeare's life, the Globe Theater, and the fascinating period of seventeenth century England. Gifted students will find this a valuable source of background material.
SUBJ: Shakespeare, William. Macbeth./ English literature--History./ Authors, English.

SRC 822.3   Ph-3 4-6 $14.95   OD   KE117

SHAKESPEARE FOR CHILDREN (Sound recording cassette). As told by Jim Weiss. Greathall Productions 1124-15 ISBN 1-882513-15-2, 1995. 1 sound cassette (60min).

Compact disc available 1124-015 (ISBN 1-882513-15-0, 1995). 1 compact disc (60min), $14.95.
Two of Shakespeare's plays, "A Midsummer Night's Dream" and "The Taming of the Shrew," are told with dramatic verve by an actor with a clear, easy-to-understand voice. Will appeal to students who learn more easily by listening, rather than reading. A good addition to Shakespearean studies.
SUBJ: Shakespeare, William--Adaptations./ English literature.

822.3   Ph-3 6-A $27.07   T   KE118

SOMETHING RICH AND STRANGE: A TREASURY OF SHAKESPEARE'S VERSE. Selected by Gina Pollinger. Illus. by Emma Chichester Clark. Kingfisher/dist. by Raintree Steck-Vaughn ISBN 1-85697-597-5, 1995. 96p. col. ill.

Includes indexes and glossary.
An illustrated anthology of familiar lines from Shakespeare's plays and sonnets serves as a useful introduction to the famous bard. For advanced students studying Shakespeare.
SUBJ: Shakespeare, William--Quotations./ Quotations.

828   Ph-2 P-A/8 $14.95   T   KE119
THOMAS, DYLAN. Child's Christmas in Wales. Illus. by Trina Schart
Hyman. Holiday House ISBN 0-8234-0565-6, 1985. 47p. ill. (some col.).
     Available from National Library Service for the Blind and Physically
Handicapped on sound recording cassette RC24355.
     From the anxiously awaited arrival of the postman, to the snow that
suddenly covered everything, to the fire at the Protheros on Christmas
Day, and to the descriptions of the useful and useless presents, this
lyrical presentation of Christmas at the turn of the century is a read-
aloud of exceptional merit. Hyman's illustrations are as richly textured
and vital as the text.
     SUBJ: Christmas--Wales.

CE 841   Ph-3 3-5 $16.95   T   KE120
CENDRARS, BLAISE. Shadow. Translated and illustrated by Marcia
Brown. Scribner's ISBN 0-684-17226-7; In Canada: Collier Macmillan,
1982. unp. col. ill.
     Caldecott Medal Award.
     Free verse form and full color stunning and eerie collage illustrations
present aspects of the African spectre of Shadow.
     SUBJ: Folklore--Africa.

860.9   Ph-1 5-A $19.95   L   KE121
TREE IS OLDER THAN YOU ARE: A BILINGUAL GATHERING OF
POEMS AND STORIES FROM MEXICO WITH PAINTINGS BY
MEXICAN ARTISTS. Selected by Naomi Shihab Nye. Simon & Schuster
ISBN 0-689-80297-8; In Canada: Distican, 1995. 112p. col. ill.
     Includes indexes.
     Selectors' Choice, 21st ed.
     An amalgam of haunting, imaginative artwork and insightful poems,
rendered in both English and Spanish, is blended to create an
outstanding anthology. Includes source notes on folktales and
biographical notes on contributors. Excellent for multicultural studies.
     SUBJ: Mexican literature--Collections./ Mexican poetry--Collections./
Spanish language materials./ Bilingual materials--Spanish.

861   Ph-2 1-3 $15.93   L   KE122
ADA, ALMA FLOR. Gathering the sun: an alphabet in Spanish and
English. English translation by Rosa Zubizarreta. Illus. by Simon Silva.
Lothrop, Lee & Shepard ISBN 0-688-13904-3; In Canada: Hearst Book
Group, 1997. unp. col. ill.
     Twenty-eight poems in Spanish and English about working in the
fields emphasize love of family, heritage, and the bounty of the
harvest. Sunny illustrations give the life of the migrant worker dignity
and respect. Useful for enriching units on farming and the Mexican-
American heritage. For multicultural studies.
     SUBJ: Hispanic American poetry (Spanish)./ Alphabet./ Agricultural
laborers--Poetry./ Spanish language materials./ Bilingual materials--
Spanish.

883   Ph-3 A/6 $9.95   P   KE123
COLUM, PADRAIC. Children's Homer: The Adventures of Odysseus and
Tale of Troy. Illus. by Willy Pogany. Macmillan ISBN 0-02-042520-1; In
Canada: Collier Macmillan, 1982. 247p. ill.
     Available from National Library Service for the Blind and Physically
Handicapped in Braille BRA11788.
     A welcomed reissue of the 1918 classic easy to read, literate retelling
of the heroic saga of ancient Greece. Based on Homer's Iliad and
Odyssey, the epic of the Trojan War and the wanderings of
Odysseus on his perilous journeys are recreated.
     SUBJ: Epic poetry--Paraphrases, tales, etc./ Odysseus (Greek
mythology)./ Trojan War.

883   Ph-2 2-5/5 $14.95   L   KE124
HUTTON, WARWICK. Trojan horse. Retold and illus. by Warwick
Hutton. McElderry ISBN 0-689-50542-6; In Canada: Maxwell Macmillan,
1992. unp. col. ill.
     Available from the National Library Service for the Blind and
Physically Handicapped on sound recording cassette RC 38259.
     The ancient tragedy of the Greek and Trojan War is retold with bold
dramatic illustrations which bring the myth to life.
     SUBJ: Trojan War./ Mythology, Greek.

883   Ph-1 3-6/5 $17.95   T   KE125
PHILIP, NEIL. Adventures of Odysseus. Illus. by Peter Malone. Orchard
ISBN 0-531-30000-5, 1997. 72p. col. ill., map.
     First published in Great Britian, Orion Children's Books, 1996.
     A dramatic retelling of the adventures of Odysseus. Accompanied by
fascinating, colorful illustrations, the thrilling text is perfect for reading
aloud and bringing these myths to life.
     SUBJ: Odysseus (Greek mythology)./ Mythology, Greek.

883   Ph-3 5-A/7 $10.95   P   KE126
PICARD, BARBARA LEONIE. Odyssey of Homer. Retold by Barbara
Leonie Picard. Illus. by Joan Kiddel-Monroe. Oxford ISBN 0-19-274146-
2; In Canada: Oxford, c1952, 1992. 272p., map. (Oxford myths and
legends).
     Picard's classic narrative retells Homer's epic poem about the
adventures of Odysseus on his ten year journey. Excellent enrichment
material for gifted students studying mythology.
     SUBJ: Odysseus (Greek mythology)./ Trojan War./ Epic poetry.

883   Ph-2 5-A/8 $19.95   T   KE127
SUTCLIFF, ROSEMARY. Black ships before Troy: the story of the Iliad.
Illus. by Alan Lee. Delacorte ISBN 0-385-31069-2, 1993. 128p. col. ill.
     Includes bibliography.
     A spirited retelling of the Trojan War makes the ancient stories of
Greece and Troy come alive. Detailed, evocative watercolors illustrate
the classic legend. Excellent for advanced readers.
     SUBJ: Trojan War./ Mythology, Greek.

883   Ph-2 5-A/7 $22.50   T   KE128
SUTCLIFF, ROSEMARY. Wanderings of Odysseus: the story of the
Odyssey. Illus. by Alan Lee. Delacorte ISBN 0-385-32205-4; In Canada:
Bantam Doubleday Dell, 1996. 119p. col. ill., map.
     First published in Great Britain by Frances Lincoln Limited, 1995.
     Dramatically recounts the adventures of Odysseus as he voyages
home from the Trojan War. Encounters with Cyclops and Circe
precede his journey's end at the long lost kingdom. For advanced
readers.
     SUBJ: Odysseus (Greek mythology)./ Mythology, Greek./ Epic
poetry.

883   Ph-3 3-6/8 $17.99   T   KE129
WILLIAMS, MARCIA. Iliad and the Odyssey. Retold and illus. by Marcia
Williams. Candlewick ISBN 0-7636-0053-9; In Canada: Candlewick/dist.
by Douglas & McIntyre, 1996. unp. col. ill.
     An enchanting comic-strip version of the Iliad and the Odyssey
incorporates humor and irreverence into the classic epics. This modern
retelling will attract reluctant readers and spur them on to reading the
real thing.
     SUBJ: Trojan War./ Odysseus (Greek mythology)./ Mythology,
Greek--Cartoons and comics./ Cartoons and comics.

892.1   Ph-1 4-6/4 $19.95   T   KE130
ZEMAN, LUDMILA. Gilgamesh the King. Retold and illus. by Ludmila
Zeman. Tundra ISBN 0-88776-283-2; In Canada: Tundra, 1992. unp.
col. ill.
     Also available in French ROI GILGAMESH (ISBN 0-88776-288-3,
1992), $19.95.
     Gilgamesh, part man and part god, is one of the first super heroes
described in legend. The handsomely illustrated retelling of his battle
with Enkidu, the wild man, and their ensuing friendship will introduce
readers to this classic material.
     SUBJ: Gilgamesh./ Epic poetry./ French language materials.

892.1   Ph-1 4-6/4 $19.95   T   KE131
ZEMAN, LUDMILA. Last quest of Gilgamesh. Retold and illus. by
Ludmila Zeman. Tundra ISBN 0-88776-328-6; In Canada: Tundra, 1995.
unp. col. ill.
     French edition DERNIERE QUETE DE GILGAMESH available (ISBN
0-88776-329-4, 1995).
     The final story in the re-creation of the great Gilgamesh epic. In this
quest, Gilgamesh is determined to learn the secret of immortality. He
travels far, never succumbing to the terrors and temptations along his
way. In the end, he learns that true immortality lies in the good he
accomplishes in his lifetime. An inspirational end to a powerful story.
A haunting tale for reading aloud.
     SUBJ: Gilgamesh./ Epic poetry./ French language materials.

892.1   Ph-1 4-6/4 $19.95   T   KE132
ZEMAN, LUDMILA. Revenge of Ishtar. Retold and illus. by Ludmila
Zeman. Tundra ISBN 0-88776-315-4; In Canada: Tundra, 1993. unp.
col. ill.
     Also available in French REVANCHE D'ISHTAR from Tundra (ISBN
0-88776-325-1, 1993), $19.95.
     The monster Humbaba brings havoc to Gilgamesh's peaceful kingdom.
When Gilgamesh and Enkidu destroy the fearsome monster, they incur
the rath of the goddess Ishtar. Based on the classic epic from ancient
Mesopotamia, this will serve as a corollary to studies of Greek and
Roman mythology or units on ancient civilizations.
     SUBJ: Ishtar./ Gilgamesh./ Epic poetry./ French language materials.

895   Ph-2 K-3 $15.00   T   KE133
MAPLES IN THE MIST: CHILDREN'S POEMS FROM THE TANG
DYNASTY. Translated by Minfong Ho. Illus. by Jean and Mou-sien

Tseng. Lothrop, Lee & Shepard ISBN 0-688-12044-X, 1996. unp. col. ill.
These brief classical poems for children written over 1,000 years ago during the Tang Dynasty in China have universal appeal. The simplicity of the poetry, the expression of love for nature, and the delicate illustrations make this a worthy edition for multicultural studies.
SUBJ: Chinese poetry--T'ang dynasty, 618-907./ Chinese language materials./ Bilingual materials--Chinese.

895.6   Ph-1 3-A $29.95   T   KE134
FESTIVAL IN MY HEART: POEMS BY JAPANESE CHILDREN. Selected and translated from the Japanese by Bruno Navasky. Abrams ISBN 0-8109-3314-4, 1993. 120p. col. ill.
Includes index.
Selectors' Choice, 20th ed.
A stunning amalgam of fine Japanese art and poems written by Japanese elementary schoolchildren. This unusual combination provides insight and perspective on Japanese culture. Excellent for social studies and multicultural studies on Asia.
SUBJ: Japanese poetry--Collections./ Children's writings.

895.6   Ph-1 2-6 $16.95   L   KE135
MADO, MICHIO. Animals: selected poems. Translated by the Empress Michiko of Japan. Decorations by Mitsumasa Anno. McElderry ISBN 0-689-50574-4; In Canada: Maxwell Macmillan, 1992. 47p. ill.
Twenty sensitive and delicate poems reflect the essence of animals, insects, and birds. Reverence for the natural world is revealed in the text which is presented in both Japanese and English. Incorporate into multicultural studies.
SUBJ: Animals--Poetry./ Japanese poetry./ Japanese language materials./ Bilingual materials--Japanese.

895.6   Ph-1 1-4/5 $16.00   T   KE136
SPIVAK, DAWNINE. Grass sandals: the travels of Basho. Illus. by Demi. Atheneum ISBN 0-689-80776-7; In Canada: Distican, 1997. unp. col. ill., map.
A retelling of the journeys of Basho, one of the best loved poets in the history of Japan. Includes samples of the haiku he wrote and provides a glimpse into the culture of Japan. Luminous illustrations drawn with colored ink and Oriental brushes depict figures that appear life-like on the page. Excellent for multicultural studies and for enriching lessons in haiku.
SUBJ: Matsuo, Basho./ Poets, Japanese./ Japan--Description and travel./ Haiku.

895.6   Ph-1 1-6 $16.00   L   KE137
SPRING: A HAIKU STORY. Selected by George Shannon. Illus. by Malcah Zeldis. Greenwillow ISBN 0-688-13888-8, 1996. unp. col. ill.
Selectors' Choice, 21st ed.
Fourteen haiku poems suggest the story of a spring walk. Vivid drawings encourage discussion about the season and the writing of original haiku poetry. Use as a springboard for creative writing activities.
SUBJ: Haiku./ Spring--Poetry./ Japanese poetry--Collections.

895.6   Ph-3 5-A $14.95   P   KE138
WAKAN, NAOMI. Haiku: one breath poetry. Pacific-Rim ISBN 0-921358-18-0, 1993. 72p. ill.
Includes bibliography and index.
Tells the history, inspiration, imagery, and rhythm of haiku. Particularly useful for teachers to create sequential lessons and for advanced students.
SUBJ: Haiku./ Poetics./ Creative writing./ Poetry--Study and teaching.

896   Ph-2 K-2 $14.95   T   KE139
OLALEYE, ISAAC. Distant talking drum: poems from Nigeria. Illus. by Frane Lessac. Wordsong/Boyds Mills ISBN 1-56397-095-3; In Canada: McClelland & Stewart, 1995. 33p. col. ill.
Available from the National Library Service for the Blind and Physically Handicapped on sound recording cassette RC 42915.
The simplicity and the rigors of daily life in a small Nigerian farming village are revealed in brief, childlike verses. Exquisite, full-page color illustrations are a perfect match for the playfulness apparent in the poems. An excellent addition to multicultural studies.
SUBJ: Nigerian poetry (English)./ Nigeria--Poetry./ Africa--Poetry.

897   Ph-2 4-6 $15.95   T   KE140
SONGS ARE THOUGHTS: POEMS OF THE INUIT. Edited with an introduction by Neil Philip. Illus. by Maryclare Foa. Orchard ISBN 0-531-06893-5, 1995. unp. col. ill.
Joyous poems of the Inuit of Canada and Alaska are accompanied by bright, expressive oil paintings. Will enrich Native American units and multicultural studies.
SUBJ: Eskimos--Poetry./ Indians of North America--Poetry.

897.008   Ph-3 2-6 $15.95   L   KE141
BIERHORST, JOHN. On the road of stars: Native American night poems and sleep charms. Selected by John Bierhorst. Illus. by Judy Pedersen. Macmillan ISBN 0-02-709735-8; In Canada: Maxwell Macmillan, 1994. unp. col. ill.
Includes glossary.
Over 50 Native American poems herald the coming of night and dreams. This insight into diverse cultures can be a source of enrichment in multicultural studies.
SUBJ: Night--Poetry./ Indian poetry--Collections./ Indians of North America--Magic.

MCP 902   Ph-1 K-A $79.95   OD   KE142
TIMELINER: HISTORY IN PERSPECTIVE (Microcomputer program). Tom Snyder Productions TIM-A ISBN 0-926891-64-2, 1986. 1 3.5" program disk, 1 backup disk.
Version 4.0.
Includes teacher's guide.
Network versions available.
BILINGUAL TIMELINER available for Macintosh or Windows, $129.95.
System requirements: Macintosh System 6.0.7 or higher.
Product (TIM-D) also available for Widows 3.1 or Windows 95.
This utility program facilitates the development of time lines on any subject. The easy-to-use format makes the program available to young students as well as teachers. Superb curriculum tool.
SUBJ: Chronology--Software./ Software--Chronology.

909   J609   Ph-3 3-6/10 $15.00   L   KE143
ROLAND-ENTWISTLE, THEODORE. More errata: another book of historical errors. Illus. by Hemesh Alles. Simon & Schuster ISBN 0-689-80170-X, 1995. unp. col. ill.
Published in Great Britain as EUREKA!, Templar Publishing, 1995.
Picture history for WHERE'S WALDO? fans. Detailed drawings of twelve historical settings such as an early 1900s kitchen, an 1880s census office, and a 1747 German music room invite the reader to discover ten anachronisms. (Answers are given with explanations.) Children will see how far technology and standards of living have advanced. Illustrations will appeal to all ages and may lead to independent learning.
SUBJ: Civilization--History./ Technology--History./ Picture puzzles.

909.07   Ph-2 5-A/7 $16.95   T   KE144
CASELLI, GIOVANNI. Middle Ages. Peter Bedrick ISBN 0-87226-176-X, 1988. 48p col illus. (History of everyday things).
Includes bibliography.
Examines life in the Middle Ages in text and pictures. A large format import, this work joins others in the "History of Everyday Things" series in focusing on ordinary objects and happenings. Appealing as a browser and display item, it also offers strong support of social studies units.
SUBJ: Civilization, Medieval.

910   Ph-2 4-6/7 $14.85   L   KE145
COOPER, KAY. Where in the world are you? a guide to looking at the world. Illus. by Justin Novak. Walker ISBN 0-8027-6913-6; In Canada: Thomas Allen, 1990. 95p.
Includes glossary and index.
Offers games, ideas, and activities designed to help the reader learn and use "the tools of geography." A no-nonsense glossary provides assistance. Use in support of social studies curriculum.
SUBJ: Geography.

910   Ph-1 2-6/10 $39.95   T   KE146
DK GEOGRAPHY OF THE WORLD. DK Publishing ISBN 0-7894-1004-4, 1996. 304p. col. ill., maps.
Includes glossary and indexes.
Organized first by continent with overview maps, then by region and/or country with other maps as appropriate, this resource presents a wide array of physical, social, and political information. Lavishly illustrated with photographs, maps, and graphic drawings and enhanced with fact boxes and leads to related information, it also contains a gazetteer index as well as a general index. A browser's delight, this will provide background and specific information for almost any country or area of the world.
SUBJ: Geography.

VCR 910   Ph-2 4-6 $99.00   OD   KE147
GEOGRAPHY: FIVE THEMES FOR PLANET EARTH (Videocassette). National Geographic 51515, 1992. 1/2" VHS videocassette color (21min).
Includes teacher's guide.
Explores the five themes of geography--location, place, human/environment interactions, movement, and regions. Presentation is low

key; educational design is strong. Use to give an overview of the subject and then schedule a second viewing to strenghten note taking skills.
SUBJ: Geography.

VCR 910   Ph-1 3-5 $89.00   OD KE148
GEOGRAPHY FOR EVERYONE (Videocassette). Rainbow Educational RB884, 1992. 1/2" VHS videocassette color (19min).
  Includes Teacher's Guide.
  Defines geography and introduces basic concepts of the subject. Strong in educational design and production quality. Particularly valuable as an individual knowledge-builder.
  SUBJ: Geography.

MCP 910   Ph-2 5-A $149.95   OD KE149
INTERNATIONAL INSPIRER (Microcomputer program). Tom Snyder Productions ISBN 1-55998-088-5, 1990. 1 5.25" program disk, backup disk.
  Version 4.0.
  Includes teacher's guide and 6 sets of 4 different student workbooks. Macintosh and Windows network versions: AppleShare or Novelle based.
  System requirements: Macintosh LC II or better; System 7.1 or higher; 4 megs of available RAM; 256-color 13" monitor or larger.
  System requirements: Windows 3.1 or higher; 8 megs of RAM; 256-color VGA monitor.
  Product (INT-B) runs on either Macintosh or Windows-compatible equiment.
  This geography game exposes students not only to geographical location but also demographic, economic, and political information about countries throughout the world. It can be used by a single student, small groups, or an entire class divided into two teams. Map reading and research skills are practiced.
  SUBJ: Geography--Software./ Maps--Software./ Software--Geography./ Software--Maps.

910   Ph-1 3-6 $15.89   L   KE150
KNOWLTON, JACK. Geography from A to Z: a picture glossary. Illus. by Harriett Barton. Crowell/HarperCollins ISBN 0-690-04618-9, 1988. 47p. col. ill.
  Describes the earth's features in cheerful fashion as it combines bold, colorful illustrations with definitions which bring a freshness to geographic terms ranging from words as simple as "bay" and "ocean" to the more sophisticated "seamount" with its sub entry "guyot." An additional strength is the book's use of comparisons in both illustrations and text. A solid knowledge-provider.
  SUBJ: Geography--Dictionaries.

910   Ph-2 1-4/4 $14.95   L   KE151
LEEDY, LOREEN. Blast off to Earth!: a look at geography. Holiday House ISBN 0-8234-0973-2, 1992. unp. col. ill.
  Humorously offers geographic basics--poles, the equator, continents, and oceans--as a group of young aliens on a field trip visit Earth. Information offered is slight, but the work's appeal to young readers is strong. Combine with other geography materials for a colorful display of the versatile resources on the subject.
  SUBJ: Geography./ Continents.

910   Ph-2 4-6/8 $15.99   L   KE152
MATTHEWS, RUPERT. Explorer. Photos by Jim Stevenson...[et al.]. Knopf ISBN 0-679-91460-9, 1991. 64p. col. ill., maps. (Eyewitness books).
  Includes index.
  Ranges from a Phoenician map through a cat-o'-nine-tails to a space traveler's food as the accoutrements of exploration are displayed. As with others in this justly popular series, there are curriculum possiblities as well as intriguing details for the individual reader.
  SUBJ: Discoveries in geography./ Explorers.

910   Ph-2 4-6/6 $11.00   P   KE153
ROSENTHAL, PAUL. Where on earth: a geografunny guide to the globe. Illus. by Marc Rosenthal. Knopf ISBN 0-679-80833-7; In Canada: Random House, 1992. 106p. col. ill., maps.
  Includes glossary and index.
  Makes use of lively, cartoon illustrations and a rather off-the-wall text to demonstrate how geographic differences on each continent have effected cultures and civilizations. High appeal for good readers and/or browsers.
  SUBJ: Geography.

910.4   Ph-3 2-4/7 $14.95   L   KE154
GIBBONS, GAIL. Pirates: robbers of the high seas. Little, Brown ISBN 0-316-30975-3; In Canada: Little, Brown, 1993. unp. col. ill., maps.
  Simple text and colorful illustrations skim the surface of this popular

subject. Attractive as a browser and useful as a jumping off spot for further study.
SUBJ: Pirates.

910.4   Ph-2 3-5/4 $14.93   L   KE155
KRUPP, ROBIN RECTOR. Let's go traveling. Morrow ISBN 0-688-08990-9, 1992. unp. col. ill.
  Includes timeline.
  Uses a collage technique, lots of detail, a diary and postcards to record a young girl's trip to famous, ancient sites located in France, England, Egypt, China, Mexico, and Peru. Though not an in-depth provider of information, this work serves well as a browser and will help some students find their way to further reading.
  SUBJ: Travel./ Voyages and travels./ Civilization, Ancient.

910.4   Ph-1 3-5/5 $16.95   L   KE156
MCCULLY, EMILY ARNOLD. Pirate queen. Putnam ISBN 0-399-22657-5; In Canada: Putnam, 1995. unp. col. ill., map.
  Grania O'Malley was born in 1530. Her talents were many, but above all she loved to sail. On her father's ship, she became famous for her bravery. As a wife, she fought beside her husband one day after the birth of a son. Her desire to control all of the Irish seas brought her into conflict with Elizabeth I. Based on legends, this female pirate's life is aptly related in a picture-book biography filled with "dashing" illustrations. For women's studies.
  SUBJ: Pirates./ O'Malley, Grace./ Ireland--History--1558-1603./ Women pirates.

910.4   Ph-2 4-A/7 $20.99   L   KE157
PLATT, RICHARD. Pirate. Photos by Tina Chambers. Knopf ISBN 0-679-97255-2, 1994. 64p. col. ill., maps. (Eyewitness books).
  "Dorling Kindersley book."
  "Borzoi book."
  Includes index.
  Presents the memorabilia of pirates, buccaneers, and privateers who in one form or another roved the seas for 5000 years preceding the Declaration of Paris in 1856. Useful as a browser and report resource.
  SUBJ: Pirates.

910.4   Ph-2 4-6/7 $16.95   L   KE158
SPEDDEN, DAISY CORNING STONE. Polar, the Titanic bear. Introduction by Leighton H. Coleman III. Illus. by Laurie McGaw. Little, Brown ISBN 0-316-80625-0; In Canada: Little, Brown, 1994. 64p. col. ill.
  "Madison Press book."
  Depicts the privileged life of the American rich early in the twentieth century and tells the story of the sinking of the TITANIC. Unusual approach combines period photographs with a narrative told in the voice of a Steiff bear purchased at F.A.O. Schwarz. Useful in period studies and of particular interest to TITANIC buffs.
  SUBJ: Titanic (Steamship)./ Shipwrecks./ Spedden, Daisy Corning Stone--Diaries.

910.4   Ph-1 2-5/7 $15.89   L   KE159
STANLEY, DIANE. True adventure of Daniel Hall. Dial ISBN 0-8037-1469-6, 1995. unp. col. ill., maps.
  Based on true events, this exciting account follows Daniel Hall through his service on a whaling ship under a cruel and physically abusive captain; his escape to the wilds of Siberia; his courage and determination in surviving illness, challenges of climate, and attacks by wolves; and his ultimate rescue and return home. Full-page color paintings and oval inserts with details and maps attractively illustrate the text. This true-life adventure will appeal to readers studying the whaling era and will be a good choice for reading aloud.
  SUBJ: Hall, Daniel Weston./ Adventure and adventurers./ Whaling.

910.4   Ph-2 3-6/7 $25.64   T   KE160
STEELE, PHILIP. Pirates. Kingfisher/dist. by Raintree Steck-Vaughn ISBN 0-7534-5052-6, 1997. 64p. col. ill., maps.
  Includes bibliographies, filmography, glossary and index.
  An overview of the world of piracy from Roman times to the present, with numerous sidebars and captions, provides information about personalities, ships, flags, treasures, and daily life. Illustrated with full-color drawings by a number of artists and with a few archival photographs. Students looking for background for reports or for general interest browsing will find this an appealing source.
  SUBJ: Pirates.

VCR 910.9   Ph-1 K-3 $99.00   OD KE161
BEING AN EXPLORER (Videocassette). Written and produced by Harriet Fier and Stephen Mantell. FM Productions/dist. by New Castle Communications 3031B ISBN 1-885285-44-2, 1996. 1/2" VHS videocassette color (30min). (American discovery).

Includes teacher's guide.

Includes public performance rights.

Excellent introduction to concepts of exploration in four sections: discussion with students about what they'd like to explore and what it takes to be an explorer; detailed look at the explorations of Lewis and Clark and contemporary Arctic explorers Will Steger and Julie Hanson; second grade exploration field trip modeling observation strategies; and a look at future possibilities for exploration. Good production values, high audience appeal for intended age group. Although long, pause points among sections allow for discussion and/or activities between segments. Numerous interdisciplinary connections for science, language arts and social studies.

SUBJ: Exploration./ Explorers.

VCR 910.9   Ph-1 4-6 $99.00   OD KE162

SCIENCE OF EXPLORATION (Videocassette). Written and produced by Harriet Fier and Stephen Mantell. FM Productions/dist. by New Castle Communications 3032B ISBN 1-885285-45-0, 1996. 1/2" VHS videocassette color (30min). (American discovery).

Includes teacher's guide.

Includes public performance rights.

A content-dense, student-centered production looks at concepts of exploration in four sections: discussion of what explorers do and how they might plan for an exploration; detailed look at the modern polar exploration of Will Steger, Julie Hanson, and a multicultural team of scientists; description of tools to assist in twenty-first century exploration with a brief recap of pioneers of exploration in aviation and space; and a model of the scientific process in conducting a tree census by a fifth grade class. Good production values and presentation of scientific concepts in an interesting, understandable context give this high audience and curriculum appeal. Numerous interdisciplinary connections for science, language arts, and social studies.

SUBJ: Exploration./ Explorers.

910.92 _JB_   Ph-1 5-6/7 $18.95   L   KE163

BLUMBERG, RHODA. Remarkable voyages of Captain Cook. Bradbury ISBN 0-02-711682-4; In Canada: Maxwell Macmillan, 1991. 137p. ill.

Includes bibliography and index.

Available from the National Library Service for the Blind and Physically Handicapped on sound recording cassette RC 38185. Describes the three voyages of Captain James Cook in the twelve years between 1768 and 1780. Quality of the writing is high; format is distinguished. Has potential for use as a nonfiction read-aloud.

SUBJ: Cook, James./ Explorers.

910.92   Ph-1 5-A/7 $17.95   T   KE164

FRITZ, JEAN. Around the world in 100 years: from Henry the Navigator to Magellan. Illus. by Anthony Bacon Venti. Putnam ISBN 0-399-22527-7; In Canada: Putnam, 1994. 128p. ill., maps.

Includes bibliography and index.

Available from the National Library Service for the Blind and Physically Handicapped on sound recording cassette RC 38972. Introduces the explorers of the fifteenth century and traces their journeys. Cheerful, well-written text is complemented by good-humored illustrations; endpapers depict the voyages of nine explorers. Has good potential for reading aloud.

SUBJ: Explorers./ Discoveries in geography.

912   Ph-1 3-5 $14.95   T   KE165

AROUND THE WORLD: AN ATLAS OF MAPS AND PICTURES. Rand McNally ISBN 0-528-83691-9, 1994. 80p. col. ill., maps.

"Rand McNally for kids."

Includes indexes.

Organized by continent, with overview maps identifying each country, its area, population, capital, languages, and flag. These are followed by clear, informative, specific country maps, factual information, and illustrations correlated to map locations. Basic overview atlas for research on specific countries and for social studies units.

SUBJ: Atlases.

912   Ph-3 1-3/2 $12.00   L   KE166

BERGER, MELVIN. Whole world in your hands: looking at maps. By Melvin and Gilda Berger. Illus. by Robert Quackenbush. Ideals ISBN 0-8249-8646-6; In Canada: Ideals., 1993. 48p. col. ill., maps. (Discovery readers).

Includes index.

Introduces map reading concepts using home-community-town progression. Text is mildly interactive with frequent questions which require use of illustrations. Particularly useful as follow-up to classroom teaching.

SUBJ: Maps.

912   Ph-1 K-3/5 $14.95   T   KE167

BOYLE, BILL. My first atlas. Illus. by Dave Hopkins. DK Publishing ISBN 1-56458-624-3, 1994. 45p. col. ill., maps.

Includes glossary and index.

Introduces the reader to the language of maps and to the countries and continents of the world. Endpapers display flags of 170 countries. Intriguing browser and useful one-to-one item.

SUBJ: Atlases.

VCR 912   Ph-1 3-6 $89.00   OD KE168

FINDING YOUR WAY: USING MAPS AND GLOBES (Videocassette). Rainbow Educational Video RB851, 1990. 1/2" VHS videocassette color (20min).

Includes Teacher's Guide.

Offers a thorough presentation of standard map and globe wisdom. Production quality is good and teacher's guide is unusually strong. Useful for class viewing or as an individual skill-builder.

SUBJ: Maps./ Globes.

912   Ph-1 2-5/7 $15.95   T   KE169

KNOWLTON, JACK. Maps and globes. Illus. by Harriett Barton. Crowell/HarperCollins ISBN 0-680-04457-7; In Canada: HarperCollins, 1985. 42p. col. ill.

Spanish edition MAPAS Y GLOBOS TERRAQUEOS available from Harper Arco Iris (ISBN 0-06-026224-9, 1996).

Explains how to read maps and globes; also includes a brief history of mapmaking. Appealing illustrations and handsome design add to the effectiveness of the book. Useful in support of map reading units.

SUBJ: Maps./ Globes./ Spanish language materials.

CDR 912   Ph-1 1-3 $29.95   OD KE170

MY FIRST AMAZING WORLD EXPLORER (CD-ROM). DK Multimedia ISBN 0-7894-0294-7, 1996. 1 CD-ROM color.

System requirements: Windows: IBM or compatible PC with 486SX/ 25 MHz or higher microprocessor; 4MB of RAM (8MB recommended); MPC-compatible doublespeed CD-ROM drive and sound card; mouse; SVGA 256-color display; loudspeakers or headphones; and Microsoft Windows version 3.1 or higher.

System requirements: Apple Macintosh computer with a 25MHz 68030 processor or above that supports a 640 x 480 pixel monitor displaying 256 colors; 6MB RAM (8MB recommended); a doublespeed CD-ROM drive; System 7.0 or later.

Product (ISBN 0-7894-0294-7) runs on either Windows or Macintosh compatible hardware.

Delightful introduction to maps and the world, this CD-ROM provides options for traveling throughout the world, searching for stickers, sending postcards, taking guided tours, and developing map making skills. The excellent narration makes the information accessible to limited readers. Works well as a learning center and with small groups or an entire class.

SUBJ: Geography--Software./ Software--Geography./ Maps--Software./ Software--Maps./ Interactive media.

912   Ph-2 2-4/3 $13.95   T   KE171

PICKERING, MEL. Picture reference atlas. World Book/Two-Can ISBN 0-7166-1745-5, 1996. 48p. col. ill., maps.

Includes index.

Introductory atlas with detailed instructions for reading and interpreting maps. Factfiles provide information on places in the world, and Fact Finders give students practice in using map grids to locate information. Colorful, double-page maps are clear, and geographic divisions are appropriate to show detail.

SUBJ: Atlases./ Geography.

912   Ph-1 K-1/1 $13.99   L   KE172

SWEENEY, JOAN. Me on the map. Illus. by Annette Cable. Crown ISBN 0-517-70096-4, 1996. unp. col. ill., maps.

A young girl begins with a map of her room and extends it to her house, street, town, state, country, world, and back again. Clear, bright illustrations help define concepts and provide a model for classroom activities. This very personal approach helps the youngest students to an understanding of basic locational concepts and beginning map skills. A welcome addition for social studies units.

SUBJ: Maps.

912   Ph-1 3-6/6 $14.95   T   KE173

WEISS, HARVEY. Maps: getting from here to there. Houghton Mifflin ISBN 0-395-56264-3, 1991. 64p. col. ill., maps.

"Discusses various aspects of maps including direction, distance, symbols, latitude and longitude, how maps are made, special purpose maps, and charts." (CIP). The introduction offers a demonstration of "increase in scope" which teachers can replicate as an effective classroom activity; illustrations are in a cartooned style. Valuable in support of curriculum and as a resource for individual students.

SUBJ: Maps.

CDR 912   Ph-1 3-6 $59.95   OD KE174
WHERE IN THE WORLD IS CARMEN SANDIEGO? JUNIOR
DETECTIVE EDITION (CD-ROM). Broderbund, 1994. 1 CD-ROM color.
Includes teacher's guide and BEGINNING GEOGRAPHY: HOW TO
USE A MAP.
System requirements: Macintosh and Power Macintosh; System 7.0.1
or higher; 25MHz 68030 processor or faster; Power Macintosh; 5MB
RAM; 3.5MB free; required 1MB hard sisk space; CD-ROM drive
required; 13" or larger monitor with 256 colors.
System requirements: Windows 3.1 or Windows 95; 33MHz 386DX
or faster required; 4MB RAM for Windows 3.1; 8MB RAM for
Windows 95; requires 1MB hard disk space; CD-ROM required;
SVGA monitor/display card 640x480, 256 colors; Windows
compatible sound device.
Product runs either on Macintosh or Windows compatible hardware.
This junior version of the classic Carmen Sandiego opens the world of
geography to even younger students. Digitized pictures and searches
based on clues such as agricultural products, geographical features,
landmarks, sports, and cultural events make the program challenging
and fun.
SUBJ: Geography--Software./ Software--Geography./ Problem
solving--Software./ Software--Problem solving.

CDR 912   Ph-1 3-A $59.95   OD KE175
WHERE IN THE WORLD IS CARMEN SANDIEGO? New ed. (CD-
ROM). Broderbund ISBN 1-57382-072-5, 1996. 2 CD-ROMs color, 1
paperback book.
Version 3.0.
Includes user's guide, troubleshooting guide and WORLD ALMANAC
AND BOOK OF FACTS.
Includes one Windows disc and one Macintosh disc.
System requirements: Windows 3.1 or Windows 95; 33MHz 486 or
faster processor (66MHz 486 recommended); 8MB RAM; 1MB hard-
disk space; double-speed or faster CD-ROM drive; SVGA monitor/
display card, 640x480, 256 colors, thousands of colors supported;
Windows compatible sound device.
System requirements: Macintosh and Power Macintosh native; System
7.0.1 or higher; 20MHz 68040 processor or faster, Power Macintosh;
8MB RAM, 4.4MB free; double-speed or faster
CD-ROM drive; 13" or larger color monitor, 256 colors, thousands
of colors supported on Power Macintosh.
This updated version of a popular classic still delights student. The
capers of Carmen are even more engaging with digitized pictures,
videos, and a database of information about countries which can be
easily accessed. This version of Carmen does not depend as heavily
on use of THE WORLD ALMANAC.
SUBJ: Geography--Software./ Software--Geography./ Problem
solving--Software./ Software--Problem solving.

912   Ph-1 4-6 $18.95   T   KE176
WRIGHT, DAVID. Facts on File children's atlas. By David and Jill
Wright. Facts on File ISBN 0-8160-3713-2, 1997. 96p. col. ill.
Includes index.
An attractive, beginning atlas provides detailed information on 30
separate nations and regions. Typical entry includes textual
information about an amazing fact, a stamp reflecting the country,
fact box, and some quiz/puzzle boxes. The instructions on use of the
index are excellent.
SUBJ: Atlases.

CDR 914   Ph-1 4-A $99.95   OD KE177
EUROPE INSPIRER (CD-ROM). Tom Snyder Productions EUR-D, 1997. 1
CD-ROM color.
Version 4.0.
Includes teacher's guide.
Also available in Macintosh or Windows disks, $99.95.
System requirements: Macintosh LC II (68030 processor or higher) or
Macintosh Power PC; System 7.1 or later; 4MB RAM available; 256-
color monitor, 640x480 monitor resolution or higher; double-speed or
higher CD-ROM drive.
System requirements: IBM-compatible 486 or higher processor;
Windows 3.1 or Windows 95; 8MB RAM; 256-color monitor,
640x480 monitor resolution or higher; double-speed or higher CD-
ROM drive.
Product (EUR-D) runs on either Macintosh or Windows compatible
hardware.
Youngsters not only gain geographic knowledge, but also practice
problem solving skills as they travel about Europe looking for a
variety of items. The scavenger hunt format works with the
cooperative learning techniques seen in all Tom Snyder software.
Great for use with small groups or an entire class.
SUBJ: Europe--Geography--Software./ Software--Europe--
Geography./ Maps--Software./ Software--Maps./ Problem solving--
Software./ Software--Problem solving.

916   *J960*   Ph-3 2-4/5 $14.99   L   KE178
ONYEFULU, IFEOMA. A is for Africa. Cobblehill/Dutton ISBN 0-525-
65147-0, 1993. unp. col. ill.
Employs an alphabetic approach to introduce twenty-six elements of
African life. Photographed in Nigeria, the work effectively presents
traditional village life. Useful supplementary resource, but too narrow
in focus to stand alone as a representation of life in Africa today. For
multicultural studies.
SUBJ: Africa./ Alphabet.

VCR 916.762   Ph-1 3-5 $49.95   OD KE179
KIDS EXPLORE KENYA (Videocassette). Learning Matters, 1990. 1/2"
VHS videocassette color (40min). (Where in the world).
Includes teacher's guide.
Public performance rights included.
Moves at a fast pace as five young friends head for Kenya on an
information safari. Culture, history, music, family life, and clothing are
introduced. Strong supplemental material.
SUBJ: Kenya--Description and travel./ Kenya--Social life and customs.

916.78   *J967*   Ph-2 3-6/4 $4.99   P   KE180
MARGOLIES, BARBARA A. Rehema's journey: a visit in Tanzania.
Scholastic ISBN 0-590-42847-0; In Canada: Scholastic, c1990. unp. col.
ill., map.
Includes glossary.
Follows nine-year-old Rehema as she travels with her father from her
rural mountain home to the wildlife area of Ngorongoro Crater.
Colorful photographs depict Rehema's first visit to a town and show
many of the people she meets and animals she sees on her trip.
Valuable as an awareness-expander. For multicultural studies.
SUBJ: Tanzania--Description and travel.

VCR 917   Ph-1 5-6 $69.00   OD KE181
ROCKY MOUNTAINS (Videocassette). National Geographic Society
51360, 1989. 1/2" VHS videocassette color (20min). (Physical
geography of North America).
Includes Teacher's Guide.
Explores the backbone of the North American continent in an
excellent presentation of the physical geography of the Rocky
Mountain region. Geology, landforms, plants and animals receive
attention. Brief teacher's guide gives synopsis, objectives, vocabulary,
and several activities.
Other videocassettes in the series include THE PACIFIC EDGE
(51358); THE WESTERN DRY LANDS (51361); THE CENTRAL
LOWLANDS (51363); THE NORTHLANDS (51362); and THE EAST
(51359).
SUBJ: Rocky Mountains Region./ Physical geography--North America.

CDR 917   Ph-1 3-A $59.95   OD KE182
WHERE IN THE U.S.A. IS CARMEN SANDIEGO? New ed. (CD-ROM).
Broderbund ISBN 1-57382-039-3, 1996. 1 CD-ROM color, 1 paperback
book.
Version 3.0.
Includes user's guide, troubleshooting guide and WORLD ALMANAC
OF THE U.S.A.
System requirements: Windows 3.1 or Windows 95; 33MHz 486 or
faster processor (66MHz 486 or faster recommended); 8MB RAM;
3MB hard-disk space; double-speed or faster CD-ROM drive; SVGA
monitor/display card, 640x480, 256 colors, thousands of colors
supported; Windows compatible sound device.
System requirements: Macintosh and Power Macintosh native; System
7.0.1 or higher; 20MHz 68040 processor or faster; 8MB RAM
(12MB RAM for Power Macintosh); 4.6MB free; 3MB hard-disk
space; double-speed or faster CD-ROM drive; 13" or larger color
monitor, 256 colors, thousands of colors supported on Power
Macintosh.
Product (ISBN 1-57382-039-3) runs on either Windows or Macintosh
compatible hardware.
This updated version of a popular classic still delights students. The
capers of Carmen are even more engaging with digitized pictures,
videos, and a database of information about states which can be
easily accessed. This version of Carmen does not depend as heavily
on the use of the almanac.
SUBJ: Geography--Software./ Software--Geography./ Problem
solving--Software./ Software--Problem solving./ United States--
Geography--Software./ Software--United States--Geography.

917.04   *J973.1*   Ph-1 2-6/8 $14.93   L   KE183
MAESTRO, BETSY. Discovery of the Americas. By Betsy and Giulio
Maestro. Lothrop, Lee & Shepard ISBN 0-688-06838-3, 1991. 48p. col.
ill.
Includes "Additonal Information" section.
Selectors' Choice, 18th ed.
Available from the National Library Service for the Blind and

Physically Handicapped on sound recording cassette RC 36461. Presents the story of the discovery and rediscovery of the Americas from earliest times on. Illustrations and text mesh with effective clarity; backmatter contains a table of dates, discussion of how the Americas were named, and more. A leader in the parade of books on Columbus and the Age of Exploration.
A companion volume, THE DISCOVERY OF THE AMERICAS: ACTIVITIES BOOK (ISBN 0-688-08590-3, 1992), $7.95 (pbk) includes more than 40 innovative classroom projects to be used in conjunction with the parent title.
SUBJ: America--Discovery and exploration.

917.04 Ph-1 2-6/7 $15.93 L KE184
MAESTRO, BETSY. Exploration and conquest: the Americas after Columbus: 1500 - 1620. By Betsy and Giulio Maestro. Lothrop, Lee & Shepard ISBN 0-688-09268-3, 1994. 48p. col. ill., maps.
Includes chronologies.
Describes European exploration of the New World. Picture book format, chronologies, and listing of explorers combine to create a valuable companion volume to the authors' THE DISCOVERY OF THE AMERICAS. Use for reading aloud and in support of period studies.
SUBJ: America--Discovery and exploration./ America--History--To 1810.

917.104 Ph-2 1-4/6 $13.95 L KE185
MANSON, AINSLIE. Dog came, too: a true story. Illus. by Ann Blades. McElderry ISBN 0-689-50567-1; In Canada: Douglas & McIntyre, 1993. unp. col. ill.
Tells of the large brown dog which accompanied explorer Alexander Mackenzie as he journeyed across Canada in 1793. The loss and recovery of the dog adds drama to the text which is based on Mackenzie's journal. Use in social studies, pet units, and for reading aloud.
SUBJ: Mackenzie, Alexander, Sir./ Dogs./ Overland journeys to the Pacific./ Explorers.

VCR 917.2 Ph-3 3-6 $49.95 OD KE186
KIDS EXPLORE MEXICO (Videocassette). Learning Matters, 1990. 1/2" VHS videocassette color (40min). (Where in the world).
Includes teacher's guide.
Public performance rights included.
Lively format involving neighborhood friends discovering the larger world though a pen pal provides the framework for general information on history, culture, and daily life of Mexico. Designed to be used in two segments. Useful supplementary material.
SUBJ: Mexico--Description and travel./ Mexico--Social life and customs.

917.2 Ph-1 2-4/6 $15.93 L KE187
KRUPP, ROBIN RECTOR. Let's go traveling in Mexico. Morrow ISBN 0-688-12368-6, 1996. unp. col. ill., maps.
Includes chronology.
Quetzalcoatl, the feathered serpent, is the guide on a year-long tour of Mexico, visiting cities, towns, jungles, seasides, and ancient sites as readers explore Mexico's diverse heritage and cultural traditions. Vibrant, richly detailed artwork picturing sites, artifacts, and traditions illustrate the text with Spanish translations, timelines, and vocabulary embedded in both text and illustrations, and small maps show relationships of the places visited. Use in multicultural studies as an overview to introduce students to many aspects of Mexican culture.
SUBJ: Mexico--Description and travel./ Mexico--Social life and customs./ Mexico--History.

VCR 917.3 Ph-3 4-6 $299.00 OD KE188
GEOGRAPHY OF THE UNITED STATES (Videocassette). Society for Visual Education 9551-HAVT, 1991. 2 1/2" VHS videocassettes color.
Includes teacher's guide and study prints.
Introduces concepts of regional geography and provides broad information about each of seven geographic regions of the United States. Though a script is not included, the teacher's guide does contain learning objectives and reproducible worksheets. Helpful in expanding awareness and in supplementing geographic study.
Contents: United States: a geographic overview (13min); Geography of the New England States (16min); ...Mid-Atlantic States (15min); ...Southern States (16min); ...South Central States (16min); ...North Central States (16min); ...Mountain States (16min); ...Pacific States (20min).
SUBJ: United States--Geography./ Geography.

VCR 917.3 Ph-3 4-6 $89.00 OD KE189
GEOGRAPHY OF THE U.S.A. (Videocassette). Rainbow Educational RB883, 1991. 1/2" VHS videocassette color (19min).
Includes Teacher's Guide.
Examines the geography of the United States comparing similarities

and differences while introducing six distinct regions of the nation. Coverage is somewhat superficial but program is strong overall. Useful in patriotic programming or in social studies units.
SUBJ: United States--Description and travel./ United States--Geography./ Geography.

MCP 917.3 Ph-2 5-A $99.95 OD KE190
NATIONAL INSPIRER (Microcomputer program). Tom Snyder Productions NAT-D, 1997. 2 3.5" disks.
Version 4.0.
Includes teacher's guide.
Also available in Windows disks, Macintosh or Windows network version disks, and Macintosh/Windows CD-ROM.
System requirements: Macintosh LC II (68030 processor) or higher, or Macintosh Power PC; System 7.1 or later; 4MB available RAM; 256 colors, 640x480 monitor resolution or higher; hard disk.
Geography skills are a must when using this game. Designed to work with an entire class and one computer, the teams travel throughout the United States seeking resources as well as population density, square area, and elevation information about each state. The ability to add data and custom categories has been added.
SUBJ: Educational games--Software./ Geography--Software./ Problem solving--Software./ Software--Educational games./ Software--Geography./ Software--Problem solving./ United States--Geography--Software./ Software--United States--Geography.

VCR 917.304 Ph-2 3-6 $49.95 OD KE191
KIDS EXPLORE AMERICA'S NATIONAL PARKS (Videocassette). Children's International Network/dist. by Learning Matters, 1991. 1/2" VHS videocassette color (40min). (Where in the world).
Includes teacher's guide.
Public performance rights included.
Features upbeat approach as a lively group of friends learn about national parks. Teacher's guide includes overview and follow-up questions; video is divided into two sections for ease in classroom use. Use as a discussion-starter or basis for writing activities.
SUBJ: National parks and reserves.

917.47 Ph-2 4-6/6 $15.95 T KE192
LOURIE, PETER. Hudson River: an adventure from the mountains to the sea. Caroline House ISBN 1-878093-01-0; In Canada: Caroline House/ Boyds Mills/dist. by McClelland & Stewart, 1992. 47p. col. ill., map.
Reports a 315-mile canoe trip from the headwaters of the Hudson River to its Manhattan outlet to the Atlantic. Captions and color photographs of varying value accompany the text. Useful in regional and environmental units.
SUBJ: Hudson River (N.Y. and N.J.)--Description and travel./ Canoes and canoeing.

917.53 Ph-2 4-6/7 $16.95 L KE193
CLIMO, SHIRLEY. City! Washington, D.C. Photos by George Ancona. Macmillan ISBN 0-02-719036-6; In Canada: Collier Macmillan, 1991. 60p. col. ill.
Includes index.
Provides a lively, quick-paced look at Washington, D.C. Color photographs, maps, history and lists of things to do and see are featured. Valuable in area studies and in units featuring patriotic symbols and historic buildings.
SUBJ: Washington (D.C.).

917.59 Ph-2 4-6/6 $14.89 L KE194
GIBBONS, GAIL. Sunken treasure. Crowell/HarperCollins ISBN 0-690-04736-3, 1988. 32p. col. ill.
Focuses on the search for "Nuestra Senora de Atocha" as it illustrates techniques in modern day treasure hunting. Final pages provide information about four other famous underwater searches and use picture panels to give a brief history of diving. Useful alone or in conjunction with Sullivan's TREASURE HUNT.
SUBJ: Nuestra Senora de Atocha (Ship)./ Underwater archaeology./ Buried treasure.

917.59 Ph-3 3-6/6 $15.95 L OD KE195
MURRAY, PETER. Everglades. Child's World ISBN 1-56766-012-6, 1993. 32p. col. ill. (Vision book).
Includes index.
Introduces the Everglades, a four million acre wetland teaming with wildlife. Half pages of text raise concerns for preservation as bright full-page photographs depict the unique plants and animals native to the biome. For environmental studies.
SUBJ: Natural history--Florida--Everglades./ Everglades (Fla.).

917.8 Ph-1 3-5/10 $8.95 P KE196
ANDERSON, WILLIAM. Little House guidebook. Photos by Leslie A. Kelly. HarperTrophy ISBN 0-06-446177-7; In Canada: HarperCollins,

1996. 96p. col. ill., maps.

Includes index.

Descriptions of and guides to each of the sites featured in Laura Ingalls Wilder's "Little House" series. Includes history, things to see and do when visiting, where to stay, and how to get there. Illustrated with many contemporary color photographs. Inviting adjunct to the series for curriculum studies, it will be useful for planning actual visits to Laura Ingalls Wilder country or for class activities. (Parents' Shelf).

SUBJ: Wilder, Laura Ingalls--Homes and haunts./ Authors, American--Homes and haunts./ Frontier and pioneer life--United States.

917.8   Ph-2 5-6/5 $15.00   T   KE197

KNIGHT, AMELIA STEWART. Way west: journal of a pioneer woman. Adapted and with an introduction by Lillian Schlissel. Illus. by Michael McCurdy. Simon & Schuster ISBN 0-671-72375-8; In Canada: Simon & Schuster, 1993. unp. col. ill.

Available from the National Library Service for the Blind and Physically Handicapped on sound recording cassette RC 40035.

Provides an adapted transcription of the 1853 diary of Amelia Stewart Knight written as she and her large family traveled west from Iowa to Oregon Territory. Bold, scratchboard illustrations accompany the text which offers a sense of the difficulties of the trip. Useful in period studies and to encourage journal keeping.

SUBJ: Overland journeys to the Pacific./ Knight, Amelia Stewart./ Pioneers./ Frontier and pioneer life./ Diaries./ Women pioneers.

917.8   Ph-1 3-6/6 $15.95   L   KE198

LASKY, KATHRYN. Searching for Laura Ingalls: a reader's journey. By Kathryn Lasky and Meribah Knight. Photos by Christopher G. Knight. Macmillan ISBN 0-02-751666-0; In Canada: Maxwell Macmillan, 1993. unp. col. ill.

Details a family's summer trip to the Midwestern locations where Laura Ingalls Wilder lived more than 100 years ago. Diary entries and skilled color photography capture both the events of the trip and historic sites. Of particular appeal to fans of the "Little House" books.

SUBJ: Frontier and pioneer life./ Voyages and travels./ Authors, American./ Wilder, Laura Ingalls.

917.8   Ph-2 4-6/7 $16.95   L   KE199

RUSSELL, MARION. Along the Santa Fe Trail: Marion Russell's own story. Adapted by Ginger Wadsworth. Illus. by James Watling. Whitman ISBN 0-8075-0295-2; In Canada: General, 1993. unp. col. ill., map.

Traces the story of seven-year-old Marion Russell's 1852 journey along the Santa Fe Trail. Watercolor illustrations and first-person text bring the hardships and pleasures of trail life into focus. Strong social studies support.

SUBJ: Frontier and pioneer life--Southwest, New./ Overland journeys to the Pacific./ Santa Fe Trail./ Russell, Marion Sloan.

VCR 917.804   Ph-3 4-6 $24.95   OD   KE200

AMERICA'S WESTERN NATIONAL PARKS (Videocassette). Finley-Holiday Films V131, 1990. 1/2" VHS videocassette color (60min). (National park & monument series).

Tours 28 national parks and monuments. Photography and script are prosaic but acceptable. Useful for armchair travels and in units on national parks.

SUBJ: National parks and reserves--Guides./ National monuments--Guides./ West (U.S.)--Description and travel--Guides.

917.804   Ph-1 4-6/7 $15.85   L   KE201

CLARK, WILLIAM. Off the map: the journals of Lewis and Clark. Edited by Peter and Connie Roop. Illus. by Tim Tanner. Walker ISBN 0-8027-8208-6; In Canada: Thomas Allen, 1993. 40p. col. ill.

Offers excerpts from the journals of Lewis and Clark as they met President Jefferson's 1803 charge to explore the Missouri River, to note the land and its flora and fauna, and to become acquainted with the Indians and their numbers. Journal entries selected (and reworked) by the editors are brief and readable. Use as the basis for interdisciplinary projects and for reading aloud.

SUBJ: Lewis and Clark Expedition (1804-1806)./ Lewis, Meriwether--Diaries./ Clark, William--Diaries./ Explorers--Diaries./ Diaries./ Lewis, Meriwether./ Clark, William.

917.804   Ph-2 A/9 $21.95   T   KE202

FREEDMAN, RUSSELL. Indian winter. Illus. by Karl Bodmer. Holiday House ISBN 0-8234-0930-9, 1992. 88p. col. ill., map.

Includes directory, bibliography and index.

"Relates the experiences of a German prince, his servant, and a young Swiss artist as they traveled through the Missouri River Valley in 1833 learning about the territory and its inhabitants and recording their impressions in words and pictures." (CIP) Impact of the combination of text and paintings is memorable. A satisfying afterword informs the reader of the lives of both Prince Maximilian

and Karl Bodmer after their American adventure.

SUBJ: Bodmer, Karl--Journeys--Missouri River Valley./ Wied, Maximilian, Prinz von--Journeys--Missouri River Valley./ Indians of North America--Missouri River Valley./ Missouri River Valley--Description and travel.

917.804   Ph-2 4-6/6 $16.95   L   KE203

KROLL, STEVEN. Lewis and Clark: explorers of the American West. Illus. by Richard Williams. Holiday House ISBN 0-8234-1034-X, 1994. 32p. col. ill., map.

Includes chronology and index.

Provides an introduction to Lewis' and Clark's journey in search of a water route across the North American continent. Colorful illustrations accompany the text; back matter includes an afterword and a chronology of the two year expedition. Strong support for the social studies curriculum.

SUBJ: Lewis and Clark Expedition (1804-1806)./ Lewis, Meriwether./ Clark, William./ Explorers./ West (U.S.)--Discovery and exploration.

VCR 917.804   Ph-3 5-6 $95.00   OD   KE204

LEWIS AND CLARK EXPEDITION (Videocassette). Delphi Productions/dist. by United Learning 1923V, 1992. 1/2" VHS videocassette color (20min). (Opening of the American West).

Includes teacher's guide.

Provides an overview of the Lewis and Clark expedition. Production quality is good with journal excerpts and historical reenactments featured. Useful in support of United States history studies.

SUBJ: Lewis and Clark Expedition (1804-1806)./ Lewis, Meriwether./ Clark, William./ Explorers./ West (U.S.)--Discovery and exploration.

917.804   Ph-1 3-6/7 $18.00   T   KE205

SCHANZER, ROSALYN. How we crossed the West: the adventures of Lewis and Clark. National Geographic ISBN 0-7922-3738-2, 1997. unp. col. ill.

Based on original sources, with brief, identified excerpts and quotes and other journal information, this traces the travels of Lewis and Clark from their agreement to form a partnership in the summer of 1803 through their departure from St. Louis in May, 1804 and their arrival at the Pacific Ocean in November, 1805. Illustrative paintings range from full page to small cameo, are well researched, and are done in the style of folk artists of the period. The lively, easy-to-follow combination of text and pictures makes an attractive addition to units on the Lewis and Clark Expedition.

SUBJ: Lewis and Clark Expedition (1804-1806)./ Lewis, Meriwether./ Clark, William.

917.804   Ph-3 5-6/5 $18.95   L   KE206

STEFOFF, REBECCA. Lewis and Clark. Chelsea Juniors ISBN 0-7910-1750-8, 1992. 80p. ill., map. (Junior world biographies).

Includes chronology, glossary and index.

Examines the lives and characters of the two explorers who successfully made their way across the Rockies to the Pacific coast, opening the Louisiana Territory. Black and white illustrations show the terrain and wildlife they saw on their trip.

SUBJ: Lewis, Meriwether./ Clark, William./ Explorers./ Lewis and Clark Expedition (1804-1806)./ West (U.S.)--Discovery and exploration.

917.94   Ph-2 1-5/7 $12.95   T   KE207

BROWN, TRICIA. City by the bay: a magical journey around San Francisco. Written by Tricia Brown and The Junior League of San Francisco. Illus. by Elisa Kleven. Chronicle ISBN 0-8118-0233-7; In Canada: Chronicle/dist. by Raincoast, 1993. unp. col. ill.

Includes glossary and directory.

Offers a colorfully exciting tour of San Francisco and provides an array of miscellaneous "infobits" about neighborhoods and sights of the city. Closing section suggests attractions to visit, listing locations and phone numbers. Great for armchair travelers and art lovers, and as the basis of student projects.

SUBJ: San Francisco (Calif.)--Description and travel--Guides.

917.94   Ph-3 5-6/6 $13.95   T   KE208

O'DELL, SCOTT. Cruise of the Arctic Star. Maps by Samuel Bryant. Houghton Mifflin ISBN 0-395-16034-0, c1973. 206p. ill.

Includes bibliography.

Describes adventures experienced by O'Dell, his wife and two crewmen as they voyage up the length of the California coast. Also serves as an informal history of California from San Diego to the Columbia River. Interwoven in the account is information on ecological, historical and nautical subjects. Includes maps of each area traversed; an index and a reading list are appended.

SUBJ: California--Description and travel./ Voyages and travels.

NONFICTION

VCR 917.98   Ph-2 3-6 $49.95   OD KE209
KIDS EXPLORE ALASKA (Videocassette). Learning Matters, 1990. 1/2"
VHS videocassette color (40min). (Where in the world).
> Includes teacher's guide.
> Public performance rights included.
> Lively quartet of neighborhood pals gathers information about Alaska
> in a fast-paced adventure. Part of an award-winning series, it is
> designed for use in two segments. Useful curriculum support.
> SUBJ: Alaska--Description and travel./ Alaska--Social life and
> customs.

917.98   *J 979.8*   Ph-2 4-6/6 $15.95   T   KE210
LOURIE, PETER. Yukon River: an adventure to the gold fields of the
Klondike. Caroline House/Boyds Mills ISBN 1-878093-90-8; In Canada:
Caroline House/Boyds Mills/dist. by McCelland & Stewart, 1992. 47p.
col. ill., map.
> Chronicles a 460-mile canoe journey retracing the trail of the gold
> miners who struggled through the Yukon Territory in the 1890s during
> the Klondike Gold Rush. Mood is reflective and photographs are
> interwoven with the text. A good companion for other Klondike titles.
> SUBJ: Yukon River (Yukon and Alaska)--Description and travel./
> Yukon River Valley (Yukon and Alaska)--Description and travel./
> Klondike River Valley (Yukon)--Gold discoveries./ Canoes and
> canoeing.

918.1   *VIDEO*   Ph-2 4-6/7 $14.00   L   KE211
ADVENTURE IN THE AMAZON. By the Cousteau Society. Simon &
Schuster ISBN 0-671-77071-3; In Canada: Simon & Schuster, 1992.
45p. col. ill., map.
> Recounts a Cousteau exploration of the Amazon with emphasis on the
> ecosystem and indigenous peoples. Absorbing photographs reveal
> unusual sights and balance difficult text. Browser and background-
> builder for social studies curriculum and environmental studies.
> SUBJ: Amazon River Region--Description and travel./ Natural history-
> -Amazon River Region./ Indians of South America--Amazon River
> Region./ Cousteau, Jacques Yves.

918.1   Ph-3 3-6/7 $15.95   L   KE212
MURRAY, PETER. Amazon. Child's World ISBN 1-56766-021-5, 1994.
32p. col. ill. (Vision book).
> Includes index.
> Brief half pages of text and bold, full-page photographs depict the
> remarkable wildlife and plants of the Amazon Region. Concerns about
> the deforestation of the rainforests are raised. Attractive introduction
> to the unique biome. For environmental studies.
> SUBJ: Amazon River./ Natural history--Amazon River Region.

VCR 919.8   Ph-2 4-6 $12.95   KE213
ARCTIC AND ANTARCTIC (Videocassette). Narrated by Martin Sheen.
DK Vision/BBC Worldwide Americas ISBN 0-7894-0725-6, 1996. 1/2"
VHS videocassette color (35min). (Eyewitness living earth).
> Closed captioned.
> Lively, engaging presentation explores elements of literature, folktales
> and fairy tales, cultural traditions, wildlife, and the environment in
> making comparisons between these two regions. Interesting facts and
> observations lead to many areas for further research and
> investigation. Post-program information on filmmaking techniques and
> computer-generated graphics for the Eyewitness Museum are also of
> interest.
> SUBJ: Polar regions./ Natural history--Polar regions.

919.8   Ph-2 4-6/6 $23.95   L   KE214
JOHNSON, REBECCA L. Braving the frozen frontier: women working in
Antarctica. Lerner ISBN 0-8225-2855-X, 1997. 112p. col. ill., map.
> Includes bibliography and index.
> Accounts of activities of women scientists, helicopter pilots, survival
> experts, communications officers, doctoral students, researchers,
> cartographers, and heavy equipment operators convey daily life in
> Antarctica and detail the scientific and ecological explorations taking
> place there. Full-color photographs illustrate the text. Use for women's
> studies and interdisciplinary units in science and social studies.
> SUBJ: Antarctica--Discovery and exploration./ Explorers./ Scientists./
> Women--Biography.

919.8   Ph-3 5-A/7 $24.95   L   KE215
JOHNSON, REBECCA L. Science on the ice: an Antarctic journal. Lerner
ISBN 0-8225-2852-5, 1995. 128p. col. ill., maps.
> Includes index.
> Details a modern day journey to Antarctica where the author spends
> time with researchers in biology, geology, and astrophysics. Color
> photographs support the rather difficult text. For large collections.
> SUBJ: Antarctica.

919.8   *J 998*   Ph-3 A/8 $15.95   L   KE216
MCMILLAN, BRUCE. Summer ice: life along the Antarctic Peninsula.
Houghton Mifflin ISBN 0-395-66561-2, 1995. 48p. col. ill., maps.
> Includes glossary, bibliography and index.
> The majestic and forbidding continent of Antarctica is home to
> penguins, whales, limpets, skuas, and algae. Animals cope with
> biological antifreeze, blubber, and earflaps. Amazing photographs
> (one shot was taken by the Discovery space shuttle) and detailed text
> offer up-to-date scientific information.
> SUBJ: Natural history--Antarctica./ Antarctica./ Zoology--Antarctic
> regions.

919.8   *J 508.97*   Ph-2 4-6/6 $17.00   L   KE217
PONCET, SALLY. Antarctic encounter: destination South Georgia. Photos
by Ben Osborne. Simon & Schuster ISBN 0-02-774905-3; In Canada:
Distican, 1995. 48p. col. ill., maps.
> Includes index.
> When you have parents who study bird populations on Antarctic
> islands, you have an extraordinary childhood! Meet three brothers
> who sail aboard a steel yacht in rough, cold seas for six months of
> the year. First person accounts of wildlife encounters with seals,
> penguins, and albatross make this captivating ecological travelogue a
> "must" for reading aloud for fun, adventure, zoology, and
> environmental studies.
> SUBJ: South Georgia Island--Description and travel./ Zoology--South
> Georgia Island./ Zoology--Antarctic regions.

919.8   *J 998*   Ph-1 4-6/6 $15.00   L   KE218
PRINGLE, LAURENCE P. Antarctica: the last unspoiled continent. By
Laurence Pringle. Simon & Schuster ISBN 0-671-73850-X; In Canada:
Simon & Schuster, 1992. 56p. col. ill., maps.
> Includes glossary and index.
> Examines the geology, climate, history and exploration of the White
> Continent whose name means "opposite the Arctic." Well-written
> text, fresh information, and excellent photographs add up to an
> unusually effective presentation. Useful in current events, science, and
> social studies activities.
> SUBJ: Antarctic regions.

919.8   *J 998*   Ph-2 5-6/6 $17.95   L   KE219
STEGER, WILL. Over the top of the world: explorer Will Steger's trek
across the Arctic. By Will Steger with Jon Bowermaster. Scholastic ISBN
0-590-84860-7; In Canada: Scholastic, 1997. 64p. col. ill.
> In 1994, Will Steger, an international team of explorers, and three
> teams of sled dogs crossed the Arctic Ocean in a four-month
> adventure during which they communicated daily with schools and
> individuals about the environment and conditions via the Internet. Full-
> color photographs and numerous sidebars add interest and detail to
> Steger's journal entries describing the exploration. For regional
> studies, units on exploration, and general interest.
> SUBJ: Steger, Will./ Arctic regions--Discovery and exploration./
> North Pole--Discovery and exploration./ Explorers./ Diaries.

919.8   *J 508.3*   Ph-2 3-6/7 $20.99   L   KE220
TAYLOR, BARBARA. Arctic and Antarctic. Photos by Geoff Brightling.
Knopf ISBN 0-679-97257-9, 1995. 64p. col. ill. (Eyewitness books).
> "Dorling Kindersley book."
> "Borzoi book."
> Includes index.
> The beauty and wildlife of the Arctic regions are accessible to the
> armchair traveler in this illustration-packed presentation that covers:
> climate, wildlife, seas, and survival. For any reader interested in
> zoology and the Poles. Nice complement to Alaskan studies and polar
> explorations.
> SUBJ: Zoology--Polar regions./ Animals--Habits and behavior./ Polar
> regions.

919.8   *J 998*   Ph-2 5-6/8 $21.50   L   KE221
WINCKLER, SUZANNE. Our endangered planet: Antarctica. By Suzanne
Winckler and Mary M. Rodgers. Lerner ISBN 0-8225-2506-2, 1992.
64p. col. ill., maps. (Our endangered planet).
> Includes directory, glossary and index.
> Available in Spanish NUESTRO PLANETA EN PELIGRO: LA
> ANTARTIDA (ISBN 0-8225-2006-0, 1993).
> Examines Antarctica's environment, wildlife, and issues in a call for
> protective actions. Photographs, drawings, sidebars, and addresses
> are all part of the package. Useful in both geography and
> environmental activities.
> SUBJ: Antarctic regions.

B AARON, H.   Ph-2 5-A/9 $18.95   L   KE222
RENNERT, RICHARD SCOTT. Henry Aaron. Introductory essay by
Coretta Scott King. Chelsea House ISBN 0-7910-1859-8, 1993. 127p. ill.
(Black Americans of achievement).

Includes chronology, bibliography and index.
Aaron's amazing feats are described in this well-illustrated story of a determined, steady achiever. Also covered are a brief history of baseball, the Negro leagues, and changing attitudes toward African-American athletes. For multicultural studies.
SUBJ: Aaron, Henry./ Baseball players./ Afro-Americans--Biography.

B ABBOTT, J.   Ph-2 4-5/6 $22.83   L   KE223
KRAMER, JON. Jim Abbott. Raintree Steck-Vaughn ISBN 0-8172-4119-1, 1996. 48p. col. ill. (Overcoming the odds).
Includes chronology, bibliography and index.
Born without a right hand, Jim Abbott as a youngster learned how to play all sports with the help of his dad. Today, he uses skills his father taught him to be one of the best pitchers in baseball. His ability to adapt and accept are covered as well as his feats. For units on persons with disabilities.
SUBJ: Abbott, Jim./ Baseball players./ Physically handicapped.

VCR B ABUBAKARI   Ph-3 5-6 $99.00   OD KE224
ABUBAKARI: THE EXPLORER KING OF MALI (Videocassette). All Media Productions, 1992. 1/2" VHS videocassette color (15min).
Includes teacher's guide and activity guide.
In the fourteenth century, Abubakari, king of Mali, outfitted two fleets of boats to explore the lands across the Atlantic Ocean. After the first fleet failed to return, he sailed with the second and perhaps reached the shores of South America. Story of great adventure and courage to be used in units studying explorers and African history. For multicultural studies.
SUBJ: Abubakari./ Explorers./ Kings, queens, rulers, etc.

B ADAMS, A.   Ph-2 3-6/7 $17.50   L   KE225
DUNLAP, JULIE. Eye on the wild: a story about Ansel Adams. Illus. by Kerry Maguire. Carolrhoda ISBN 0-87614-944-1, 1995. 64p. ill. (Carolrhoda creative minds book).
Includes bibliography.
Ansel Adams, torn between careers in music and photography, found that his camera expressed the beauty of nature which he discovered in Yosemite National Park. His photographs also awaken others to the need to preserve the natural wilderness of the United States. Adam's life story as a photographer and environmentalist is vital in units celebrating Earth Day. For environmental studies.
SUBJ: Adams, Ansel./ Photographers./ Environmentalists.

B ADAMS, J.Q.   Ph-3 3-5/6 $15.95   L   KE226
HARNESS, CHERYL. Young John Quincy. Bradbury ISBN 0-02-742644-0; In Canada: Maxwell Macmillan, 1994. unp. col. ill. maps.
Includes bibliography.
John Quincy Adams' closeness to his family is captured in this handsomely illustrated volume which incorporates much historical information into the pictures and maps. Attractive format will appeal to children and generate interest in this lesser-known president.
SUBJ: Adams, John Quincy--Childhood and youth./ Presidents./ United States--History--Revolution, 1775-1783--Biography.

CE B ADAMS, S.   Ph-2 3-5/7 $13.95   T   KE227
FRITZ, JEAN. Why don't you get a horse, Sam Adams? Illus. by Trina Schart Hyman. Coward-McCann/Putnam ISBN 0-698-20292-9; In Canada: Putnam, c1974. 47p. col. ill.
In the time when men wore ruffles on their shirts, rode horseback and swore allegiance to the King of England, Sam Adams did none of these. His clothes were so shabby that friends presented him with a wig, suit, and shoes for this first journey out of Massachusetts as a representative to Philadelphia in 1774. On his way to the Philadelphia Convention Sam finally did learn to ride--but he never changed his mind about the King of England.
SUBJ: Adams, Sam./ United States--History--Revolution, 1775-1783--Biography.

B ADDAMS, J.   Ph-3 4-6/5 $17.50   L   KE228
MCPHERSON, STEPHANIE SAMMARTINO. Peace and bread: the story of Jane Addams. Carolrhoda ISBN 0-87614-792-9, 1993. 96p. ill.
Includes bibliography and index.
From childhood into adulthood, Jane Addams firmly lived her belief that one must do everything possible to help less fortunate people. She created Hull House (a settlement house) in Chicago, fought for improved working conditions for children and factory workers, led peace and women's rights movements, and struggled to maintain freedom of speech in America. One of the remarkable women of the twentieth century to include in women's studies.
SUBJ: Addams, Jane./ Women social reformers./ Hull House (Chicago, Ill.)--History./ Social reformers.

B AGASSI, A.   Ph-2 4-5/7 $19.95   L   KE229
SAVAGE, JEFF. Andre Agassi: reaching the top--again. Lerner ISBN 0-8225-2894-0, 1997. 64p. col. ill.
Includes glossary and index.
Chronicles his father's drive to make Agassi a tennis star, his wild behavior as a teenager, his return to religion, and his struggles to stay at the top of his field. Insight into what has driven this willful man to the peak of his sport makes this book good reading for sports fans.
SUBJ: Agassi, Andre./ Tennis players.

B AIKMAN, T.   Ph-2 4-6/6 $19.95   L   KE230
DIPPOLD, JOEL. Troy Aikman: quick-draw quarterback. Lerner ISBN 0-8225-2880-0, 1994. 64p. ill. (some col.). (Achievers).
The Dallas Cowboys' amazing performance in the Super Bowl has largely been the result of the sterling play of their quarterback, Troy Aikman. This slim volume, filled with color photographs, tells of his struggles and numerous injuries. For football fans.
SUBJ: Aikman, Troy./ Football players.

B AILEY, A.   Ph-1 2-4/5 $13.89   L   KE231
PINKNEY, ANDREA DAVIS. Alvin Ailey. Illus. by J. Brian Pinkney. Hyperion ISBN 1-56282-414-7, 1993. unp. col. ill.
Ailey's first view of Katherine Dunham's dance troupe set his goals for life. His integrated, modern dance company interpreted the African-American cultural experience in a style which revolutionized American dance. In full-page scratchboard drawings, Brian Pinkney captures the rhythm and movement which filled Ailey's choreographies. Inspirational for young dancers. For multicultural studies.
SUBJ: Ailey, Alvin./ Dancers./ Choreography./ Afro-Americans--Biography.

B ALCOTT, L.   Ph-1 5-6/8 $2.95   P   KE232
MEIGS, CORNELIA. Invincible Louisa. Scholastic ISBN 0-590-44818-8; In Canada: Scholastic, 1933. 247p.
Newbery Award.
Available from National Library Service for the Blind and Physically Handicapped in Braille BR06305, on sound recording cassette RC23477, and as talking book TB04276.
Raised in an intellectually stimulating family, Louisa determined in her childhood to provide for them. Using the family as models, she produced a series of books which were avidly read by American girls.
SUBJ: Alcott, Louisa May./ Authors, American./ Women authors, American.

B ALI, M.   Ph-3 4-6/6 $13.95   L   KE233
MACHT, NORMAN L. Muhammad Ali. Chelsea House ISBN 0-7910-1760-5, 1994. 79p. ill. (Junior world biographies).
Includes bibliography, chronology, glossary and index.
Muhammad Ali's boyhood adventures which resulted in his amazing career in the ring are described in addition to his adult religious conversion and his many successful defenses of his boxing crown. Includes a good discussion of his present circumstances. For sports collections and multicultural studies.
SUBJ: Ali, Muhammad./ Boxers (Sports)./ Afro-Americans--Biography.

B ANASTASIIA   Ph-3 5-A/7 $17.95   T   KE234
BREWSTER, HUGH. Anastasia's album. Photos by Peter Christopher. Hyperion ISBN 0-7868-0292-8; In Canada: Madison Press, 1996. 64p. ill. (some col.), map.
"Hyperion/Madison Press book."
Includes glossary and bibliography.
As a child, Anastasia was a photographer. This picture-biography combines many of the photographs she took of her family with other pictures which show the royal residences and the activities of the princesses. The last days of the Romanovs are discussed as well as the mystery surrounding Anastasia. For units on Russian history.
SUBJ: Anastasiia Nikolaevna, Grand Duchess, daughter of Nicholas II, Emperor of Russia./ Princesses./ Russia--History--Biography.

B ANDERSEN, H.   Ph-2 3-5/8 $15.95   T   KE235
BRUST, BETH WAGNER. Amazing paper cuttings of Hans Christian Andersen. Ticknor & Fields ISBN 0-395-66787-9, 1994. 80p. ill.
Includes bibliography and index.
While he told stories, Hans Christian Andersen would cut out designs to entertain his listeners. Included with the discussion of his life are reproductions of some of the existing paper cuttings found in the Hans Christian Andersen Museum at Odense, Denmark.
SUBJ: Andersen, Hans Christian./ Authors, Danish.

B ANDERSON, M.   Ph-1 5-A/6 $14.95   L   KE236
FERRIS, JERI. What I had was singing: the story of Marian Anderson. Carolrhoda ISBN 0-87614-818-6, 1994. 96p. ill. (Trailblazers).
Includes bibliography and index.
The many difficulties Marian Anderson overcame in her drive to gain a singing career are explained. More importantly, the support of her family, the devotion of her fellow musicians, and the friendship of other fair-minded people are detailed. This balanced presentation will find a place in units on music, civil rights, multicultural studies, and women's studies. For mature readers.
SUBJ: Anderson, Marian./ Singers./ Afro-Americans--Biography./ Women singers.

B ANGELOU, M.   Ph-2 4-6/8 $14.99   T   KE237
PETTIT, JAYNE. Maya Angelou: journey of the heart. Lodestar/Dutton ISBN 0-525-67518-3; In Canada: McClelland & Stewart, 1996. 70p. ill. (Rainbow biography).
Includes chronology, bibliography and index.
Maya's turbulent childhood as she moved with her brother back and forth from her grandmother's, then to her mother's, and to other relatives' homes is described in addition to her struggles to gain recognition in many fields. Readers will know her as an author, poet, and playwright, but this book also explores her roles as a dancer, newspaper reporter, and movie star. A collection of photographs fill out the book. For multicultural studies and women's studies.
SUBJ: Angelou, Maya./ Authors, American./ Afro-Americans--Biography./ Women authors, American.

B APPLESEED, J.   Ph-1 2-4/6 $15.95   L   KE238
HODGES, MARGARET. True tale of Johnny Appleseed. Illus. by Kimberly Bulcken Root. Holiday House ISBN 0-8234-1282-2, 1997. unp. col. ill.
John Chapman's lonely trek across Pennsylvania, Ohio, and Indiana planting apple trees is lovingly related in this picture book biography. The soft hues of the drawings capture the beauty he spread on his journey. For reading aloud.
SUBJ: Appleseed, Johnny./ Apple growers./ Frontier and pioneer life.

VCR B APPLESEED, J.   Ph-2 2-5 $9.95   KE239
KUNSTLER, JAMES HOWARD. Johnny Appleseed (Videocassette). Told by Garrison Keillor. Music by Mark O'Connor. Illus. by Stan Olson. Rabbit Ears ISBN 1-56204-023-5, 1992. 1/2" VHS videocassette color (30min). (American heroes and legends).
"Family classics from the stars."
Several of John Chapman's adventures as he planted apple seeds during the 1800's in the new settlements in Ohio are quietly recited. Accompanying pictures show his strange garb and the landscape of the area he traversed. Not only a legend but also a bit of American history and the movement West.
SUBJ: Appleseed, Johnny./ Apple growers./ Frontier and pioneer life--Biography.

B APPLESEED, J.   Ph-2 5-6/8 $13.95   L   KE240
LAWLOR, LAURIE. Real Johnny Appleseed. Illus. by Mary Thompson. Whitman ISBN 0-8075-6909-7; In Canada: General, 1995. 63p. ill., map.
Includes bibliography and index.
Putting aside the folklore that surrounds Johnny Appleseed, the author searched areas of Pennysylvania and Ohio where he established nurseries to sell young apple trees to migrants moving West. She depicts a deeply religious, kindly, and courageous man. For social studies units on westward expansion.
SUBJ: Appleseed, Johnny./ Apple growers./ Frontier and pioneer life--Biography.

B ARMSTRONG, L.   Ph-2 2-4/6 $13.99   L   KE241
MEDEARIS, ANGELA SHELF. Little Louis and the jazz band: the story of Louis "Satchmo" Armstrong. Illus. by Anna Rich. Lodestar/Dutton ISBN 0-525-67424-1; In Canada: McClelland & Stewart, 1994. 42p. ill. (Rainbow biography).
Includes chronology, bibliographies and index.
Louis Armstrong was sent to reform school following a prank with a gun. At the school he gained the musical experience to start him on his way to becoming an internationally respected jazz musician. For music collections, African-American history units, and multicultural studies.
SUBJ: Armstrong, Louis./ Musicians./ Afro-Americans--Biography./ Jazz.

CE B ASHE, A.   Ph-3 2-3/6 $11.95   L   KE242
DEXTER, ROBIN. Young Arthur Ashe: brave champion. Illus. by R. W. Alley. Troll ISBN 0-8167-3772-X, 1996. 32p. col. ill. (Troll first-start biography).
Talking book available, 1996. 1 sound cassette (8min), $9.95.
Ashe's many contributions to sports and his dedication to his family are stressed in this picture-biography. Describes the climate of segregation in which he was raised and learned to play tennis. For multicultural studies.
SUBJ: Ashe, Arthur./ Tennis players./ Afro-Americans--Biography.

B ASHE, A.   Ph-2 3-5/7 $14.00   L   KE243
QUACKENBUSH, ROBERT. Arthur Ashe and his match with history. Simon & Schuster ISBN 0-671-86597-8; In Canada: Distican, 1994. 37p. ill.
Includes bibliography.
Arthur Ashe's childhood, devotion to sports, and his confidence in himself that helped him rise above racial and physical challenges are detailed in this slim biography. For multicultural studies.
SUBJ: Ashe, Arthur./ Tennis players./ Afro-Americans--Biography.

B AUNG SAN SUU   Ph-2 5-A/7 $23.95   L   KE244
STEWART, WHITNEY. Aung San Suu Kyi: fearless voice of Burma. Lerner ISBN 0-8225-4931-X, 1997. 128p. ill. (some col.).
Includes bibliography and index.
Suu Kyi received the Nobel Prize for peace in 1991. Unable to accept it herself because she was under house arrest in her own country, Burma, she became a world known and respected figure. The story of her remarkable ability to inspire and lead her people in spite of all her opposition has done to restrain her makes inspirational reading. For units on world affairs, multicultural studies, and women's studies.
SUBJ: Aung San Suu Kyi./ Politicians./ Women in politics./ Burma--Politics and government--1948-./ Burma--Politics and government--1988-.

VCR B AVI   Ph-3 5-6 $49.98   OD   KE245
TALK WITH AVI (Videocassette). Tim Podell Productions, 1995. 1/2" VHS videocassette color (22min). (Good conversation!).
Avi takes the viewer through his Rhode Island home which has provided settings for some of his writings. Some of his family's theater background, his reading disability, and the influence he felt being raised in a literary household are described. Could provide inspiration for children with learning disabilities.
SUBJ: Avi./ Authors, American./ Newbery Medal books.

B BACH, J.   Ph-3 2-4/2 $15.95   L   KE246
GREENE, CAROL. Johann Sebastian Bach: great man of music. Childrens Press ISBN 0-516-04251-3; In Canada: Childrens Press, 1992. 47p. ill. (some col.). (Rookie biography).
Includes chronology and index.
Brief introduction to the world in which Bach lived and produced great music. This copiously illustrated book will make the composer come alive for the young music student.
SUBJ: Bach, Johann Sebastian./ Composers.

B BAIUL, O.   Ph-2 3-6/4 $16.99   T   KE247
BAIUL, OKSANA. Oksana: my own story. As told to Heather Alexander. Random House ISBN 0-679-88382-7; In Canada: Random House, 1997. 46p. col. ill.
Includes directory.
Oksana tells of her early love of skating and ballet, the encouragement of her mother and grandparents, the loss of her family and the willingness of her coaches to rear and train her, and her move to the United States. A gold medal winner at the 1994 Olympic Games, she can serve as inspiration for young athletes.
SUBJ: Baiul, Oksana./ Ice skaters./ Women athletes.

VCR B BAKER, K.   Ph-2 2-5 $39.95   KE248
GET TO KNOW KEITH BAKER (Videocassette). Harcourt Brace ISBN 0-15-200107-7, 1994. 1/2" VHS videocassette color (21min). (Get to know...).
Includes teacher's guide.
Baker welcomes the viewer into his home where he works and to his excursions with children. He explains his sources of ideas for his books and how he makes mock-ups of future books. His enthusiasm for writing and illustrating is contagious. This film will be a great tool for creative writing activities, and some segments could be used with art classes.
SUBJ: Baker, Keith./ Authors, American./ Illustrators.

B BANNEKER, B.   Ph-2 4-6/6 $14.95   L   KE249
PINKNEY, ANDREA DAVIS. Dear Benjamin Banneker. Illus. by Brian Pinkney. Gulliver/Harcourt Brace ISBN 0-15-200417-3; In Canada: Harcourt Brace c/o Canadian Manda, 1994. unp. col. ill.
Available from the National Library Service for the Blind and Physically Handicapped on sound recording cassette RC 42505.
Benjamin Banneker's early love of numbers continued into his adult life as he became an astronomer, surveyor, and almanac compiler in spite

of the daily burden of cultivating an extensive farm. Troubled by the practice of slavery, Banneker, a free man, corresponded with Thomas Jefferson about his concerns. For multicultural studies.
SUBJ: Banneker, Benjamin./ Astronomers./ Almanacs--History./ Afro-Americans--Biography.

B BARTON, C. Ph-2 4-6/6 $18.95 L KE250
SONNEBORN, LIZ. Clara Barton. Chelsea House ISBN 0-7910-1565-3, 1992. 79p. ill. (Junior world biographies).
Includes chronology and glossary.
When Clara Barton didn't become principal of the school which she had founded, she turned to other fields to satisfy her need to serve. The Civil War brought out her leadership and determination. Her continued interest in helping people in desperate situations led to the founding of the American Red Cross. Background of the era is so carefully related, it makes this book invaluable in the study of the Civil War as well as women's studies.
SUBJ: Barton, Clara./ Nurses./ American National Red Cross.

B BAUM, L. Ph-3 4-6/4 $21.50 L KE251
CARPENTER, ANGELICA SHIRLEY. L. Frank Baum: royal historian of Oz. By Angelica Shirley Carpenter and Jean Shirley. Lerner ISBN 0-8225-4910-7, 1992. 144p. ill., maps.
Includes bibliographies and index.
Available from the National Library Service for the Blind and Physically Handicapped on sound recording cassette RC 38162. Frank Baum loved to tell stories to his son, and it was his family's enthusiasm for these tales which prompted him to begin a career in writing for children. The world's devotion to his work, especially the stories of Oz, led him to produce dramatic presentations of his stories. A good tool to introduce units on fantasy and creative writing.
SUBJ: Baum, L. Frank./ Authors, American.

B BERLIN, I. Ph-2 4-5/5 $14.95 L KE252
STREISSGUTH, TOM. Say it with music: a story about Irving Berlin. Illus. by Jennifer Hagerman. Carolrhoda ISBN 0-87614-810-0, 1994. 64p. ill. (Carolrhoda creative minds book).
Includes bibliography.
Emigrating from Russia as a young boy, Israel Baline was forced to find work and turned his talents of verse writing and singing into a career. Spirited description of Berlin's life and the era in which he flourished will be useful in music classes as well as social studies units on immigration.
SUBJ: Berlin, Irving./ Composers./ Jews--Biography.

B BERNSTEIN, L. Ph-2 5-A/7 $12.95 T KE253
HURWITZ, JOHANNA. Leonard Bernstein: a passion for music. Illus. by Sonia O. Lisker. Jewish Publication Society ISBN 0-8276-0501-3, 1993. 72p. ill. (JPS young biography).
Includes chronology, bibliography and index.
Leonard Bernstein's enthusiasms: composing, conducting, and playing the piano are all discussed in this biography of the first world-renowned conductor trained in America. Lenny's contributions which inspired youngsters to enjoy classical music are also described.
SUBJ: Bernstein, Leonard./ Musicians./ Composers./ Conductors (Music).

B BETHUNE, M. Ph-2 4-6/5 $15.93 L KE254
MCKISSACK, PAT. Mary McLeod Bethune. By Patricia C. and Fred McKissack. Childrens Press ISBN 0-516-06658-7; In Canada: Childrens Press, 1992. 32p. ill. (some col.). (Cornerstones of freedom).
Includes index.
Mary McLeod Bethune was determined to start a school for young African-American women. With the backing of supportive businessmen and the encouragement of many individuals including the president, she achieved her dream beyond what she had ever imagined possible. This brief biography gives good coverage of her life's achievements with a variety of photographs to support the text. Useful for both African-American studies and women's studies.
SUBJ: Bethune, Mary McLeod./ Teachers./ Afro-Americans--Biography./ Women educators./ Educators.

B BLAIR, B. Ph-2 4-6/6 $3.99 P KE255
DALY, WENDY. Bonnie Blair: power on ice. Random House ISBN 0-679-86997-2; In Canada: Random House, 1996. 91p. ill. (Bullseye biography).
An amazing five gold medals in the Olympics is a record. This recitation of Bonnie Blair's achievements tells not only of her dedication to speed skating, but also of the support that her family and town have continued to give her as she won her medals. A sports biography for readers interested in individual sports.
SUBJ: Blair, Bonnie./ Ice skaters./ Women athletes./ Speed skating.

B BLY, N. Ph-2 4-6/5 $12.40 L KE256
KENDALL, MARTHA E. Nellie Bly: reporter for the world. Millbrook ISBN 1-56294-061-9, 1992. 47p. col. ill. (Gateway biography).
Includes chronology, bibliography and index.
Nelly Bly began her career in investigative reporting by writing an expose of the conditions of an insane asylum for women. She continued to be an advocate for women as she reported on topics such as divorce, working conditions, and medical care. This overview of her career emphasizes her interests and concerns that led to her achievements rather than her childhood and family life. Photographs and a strong bibliography support the text.
SUBJ: Bly, Nellie./ Journalists./ Women journalists.

B BOLIVAR, S. Ph-2 3-4/5 $14.95 L KE257
ADLER, DAVID A. Picture book of Simon Bolivar. Illus. by Robert Casilla. Holiday House ISBN 0-8234-0927-9, 1992. unp col illus. (Picture book biography).
Includes chronology.
Bolivar dedicated his entire life to freeing Venezuela from Spain. Briefly told with handsome full-page illustrations, this introduces young readers to "The Liberator."
SUBJ: Bolivar, Simon./ Heads of state./ South America--History--Wars of Independence, 1806-1830./ Revolutionists.

B BONDS, B. Ph-3 4-6/3 $17.95 L KE258
SAVAGE, JEFF. Barry Bonds: Mr. Excitement. Lerner ISBN 0-8225-2889-4, 1997. 64p. col. ill. (Achievers).
Son of Bobby Bonds and godson of Willie Mays, Barry seemed destined to be a baseball player. This pictorial study examines the extra determination which this young athlete developed to make him the slugging hitter he is today. For sports enthusiasts.
SUBJ: Bonds, Barry./ Baseball players./ Afro-Americans--Biography.

VCR B BOONE, D. Ph-2 4-5 $195.00 OD KE259
DANIEL BOONE'S FINAL FRONTIER (Videocassette). Landmark Media, 1995. 1/2" VHS videocassette color (22min).
Includes study guide.
Includes public performance rights.
Boone's early life as a scout for the British, his role as a father, and his later years as a judge and steadying force in the community are presented. Also covers the daily life of his family as they harvest and store food, make cloth and candles, and entertain.
SUBJ: Boone, Daniel./ Frontier and pioneer life--Biography./ Pioneers.

CE B BOWDITCH, N. Ph-2 5-A/3 $14.45 T KE260
LATHAM, JEAN LEE. Carry on, Mr. Bowditch. Illustrated by John O'Hara Cosgrave II. Houghton Mifflin ISBN 0-395-06881-9, c1955. 251p. ill.
Newbery Medal Award.
Talking book available from SRA/McGraw-Hill 87-507907, 1971. $16.00.
About a seafaring boy who later wrote the American Practical Navigator, a book still in use.
SUBJ: Bowditch, Nathaniel./ Seamen./ Navigation--History.

B BRAILLE, L. Ph-2 2-3/3 $16.95 L KE261
ADLER, DAVID A. Picture book of Louis Braille. Illus. by John and Alexandra Wallner. Holiday House ISBN 0-8234-1291-1, 1997. unp. col. ill. (Picture book biography).
Includes chronology.
An accident when he was a child left Louis Braille blind. Sent to Paris to study at the National Institute of Blind Children, Louis spent the rest of his life there. As a teacher, he devised his code of six raised dots for reading and raphigraphy so that blind people could write to sighted ones. Final page depicts the alphabet and numbers in braille. For units on persons with disabilities.
SUBJ: Braille, Louis./ Teachers./ Blind--Biography./ Physically handicapped./ Braille.

B BRAILLE, L. Ph-1 3-5/6 $15.95 T KE262
FREEDMAN, RUSSELL. Out of darkness: the story of Louis Braille. Illus. by Kate Kiesler. Clarion ISBN 0-395-77516-7, 1997. 81p. ill.
Includes index.
Louis' early injury which resulted in blindness, his education at the Royal Institute of Blind Youth, and his development of a system of raised dots which enabled blind people to read are related with sympathy and warmth. The author has numerous biographies to his credit, and Braille's life is inspirational and insightful reading. For units on persons with disabilities.
SUBJ: Braille, Louis./ Blind--Biography./ Teachers./ Physically handicapped./ Braille.

B BROWN, J.   Ph-2 3-5/6 $4.95   P   KE263
COLLINS, JAMES L. John Brown and the fight against slavery. Millbrook ISBN 1-87884-172-6, 1991. 32p. ill. (Gateway civil rights).
    Includes chronology, bibliography and index.
    Discusses John Brown's role in the first uprisings to protest slavery as well as his plan to create a "freedman's republic" in Virginia and Maryland. Attractive selection of photographs and drawings adds life to the text.
    SUBJ: Brown, John./ Abolitionists.

B BROWN, J.   Ph-1 5-A/8 $15.95   T   KE264
COX, CLINTON. Fiery vision: the life and death of John Brown. Scholastic ISBN 0-590-47574-6; In Canada: Scholastic, 1997. 230p. ill.
    Includes bibliography and index.
    John Brown's compassion for slaves emerged early in his life, but a large family and business affairs kept him from active involvement. When he did determine to commit himself to helping Kansas become a free state, his commitment was complete for himself and his family. This detailed biography gives tremendous insight into the man and the times and explains fully how his actions showed the conviction of his belief that "There will be no peace in this land until slavery is done for." For mature readers. For multicultural studies.
    SUBJ: Brown, John./ Abolitionists.

B BROWN, M.   Ph-3 5-6/6 $14.88   L   KE265
BLOS, JOAN W. Heroine of the Titanic: a tale both true and otherwise of the life of Molly Brown. Illus. by Tennessee Dixon. Morrow ISBN 0-688-07547-9, 1991. unp col illus.
    The known facts of Molly Brown's life are embellished in this colorful (both text and illustrations) retelling of her life. Studies in western expansion and the sinking of the Titanic will find this book adds spark to the time.
    SUBJ: Brown, Margaret Tobin./ Titanic (Steamship)./ Voyages and travels.

VCR B BRYAN, A.   Ph-2 4-6 $85.00   OD KE266
MEET ASHLEY BRYAN: STORYTELLER, ARTIST, WRITER (Videocassette). SRA/McGraw-Hill 87-005010, 1992. 1/2" VHS videocassette color (23min). (Meet the author).
    Includes guide.
    Ashley Bryan's talents as a storyteller are displayed as well as many of his drawings and the toys and art objects which inspire his work. Tape may be used to introduce the author to students in fourth grade and beyond.
    SUBJ: Bryan, Ashley./ Authors, American./ Illustrators.

B BUFFALO BILL   Ph-2 5-6/6 $17.71   L   KE267
ROBISON, NANCY. Buffalo Bill. Watts ISBN 0-531-20007-8; In Canada: Watts, 1991. 64p. ill. (some col.). (First book).
    Includes bibliography and index.
    Bill Cody earned his nickname "Buffalo Bill" while hunting buffalo for railway workers to eat, but he is best remembered for his shows which incorporated many of the people he knew and told some of the exciting happenings in his life. Readers will gain information about the Pony Express, Indian scouting and the heroes of the West.
    SUBJ: Buffalo Bill./ West (U.S.)--Biography.

B BUNTING, E.   Ph-1 2-5/3 $13.95   T   KE268
BUNTING, EVE. Once upon a time. Photos by John Pezaris. Richard C. Owen ISBN 1-878450-59-X, 1995. 32p. col. ill. (Meet the author).
    In a simple text supplemented with numerous photographs, Eve Bunting tells of her childhood in Ireland, her migration to the United States, her subsequent development into a prominent children's author, and her hopes for the future of the world. Brief introduction to the popular author is suitable for author studies.
    SUBJ: Bunting, Eve./ Authors, American./ Authorship./ Women authors, American.

VCR B BUNTING, E.   Ph-1 4-6 $40.00   OD KE269
VISIT WITH EVE BUNTING (Videocassette). Houghton Mifflin-Clarion ISBN 0-395-59025-6, 1991. 1/2" VHS videocassette color (19min). (Author and artist series).
    Eve Bunting turned to writing when her children entered high school. She relates here her sources for her stories and how she writes in all kinds of situations. Motivational material for creative writing.
    SUBJ: Bunting, Eve./ Authors, American./ Women authors, American.

CE B BURGESS, A.   Ph-1 1-3/1 $14.95   L   KE270
ROOP, PETER. Keep the lights burning, Abbie. By Peter and Connie Roop. Illustrated by Peter E. Hanson. Carolrhoda ISBN 0-87614-275-7, 1985. 40p. col. ill.
    Read-along kit available from Live Oak Media (ISBN 0-87499-135-8, 1989). 1 hardcover book, 1 sound cassette (10min), $19.95.
    Leaving his daughter Abbie on Matinicus Rock to tend the lamps in the lighthouse, Captain Burgess intended to return to his family and his job within a few hours. However, a gigantic storm came up and Abbie was forced to become a lighthouse keeper. This is a tale of dedication, determination, and adventure and is an excellent choice as a "bridge" book.
    SUBJ: Burgess, Abbie./ Lighthouse keepers.

B BURROUGHS, J.   Ph-3 A/7 $16.95   T   KE271
WADSWORTH, GINGER. John Burroughs, the sage of Slabsides. Clarion ISBN 0-395-77830-1, 1997. 95p. ill.
    Includes directory, bibliographies and index.
    Burroughs' love of the outdoors was the core of his life, and he was able to capture it in essays. Teachers in the early twentieth century begged that his writings be read in classrooms. In this way, Burroughs brought natural science into the curriculum. For historical collections which explain the growth of conservation in the United States. For environmental studies.
    SUBJ: Burroughs, John./ Naturalists.

B BUSH, G.   Ph-2 5-6/8 $17.27   L   KE272
KENT, ZACHARY. George Bush: forty-first president of the United States. Childrens Press ISBN 0-516-01374-2; In Canada: Childrens Press, 1989. 100p. ill. (Encyclopedia of presidents).
    Includes chronology and index.
    At eighteen, George Bush was the youngest pilot in World War II. He continued this pursuit of being a leader until he won the presidency. Copious black and white photographs augment the text of this biography, which can be used to supplement social studies units on the 20th century.
    SUBJ: Bush, George Herbert./ Presidents.

VCR B BYARS, B.   Ph-3 4-6 $49.98   OD KE273
TALK WITH BETSY BYARS (Videocassette). Tim Podell Productions, 1995. 1/2" VHS videocassette color (20min). (Good conversation!).
    In this interview with a Newbery author, the viewer discovers the sources for her stories, her current interests which include restoration of antique airplanes, and her mode of writing. Useful to introduce Byars' numerous books and to encourage young writers.
    SUBJ: Byars, Betsy Cromer./ Authors, American./ Women authors, American./ Newbery Medal books.

B CALAMITY JANE   Ph-2 4-6/8 $14.95   T   KE274
FABER, DORIS. Calamity Jane: her life and her legend. Houghton Mifflin ISBN 0-395-56396-8, 1992. 62p. ill.
    Includes bibliographies and index.
    What was fact and what was fiction in the life of Calamity Jane (Martha Jane Cannary)? This book carefully separates the two and shows how folk heroes and heroines developed. For study of the West and women's studies.
    SUBJ: Calamity Jane./ Cowgirls./ West (U.S.)--Biography.

B CAMPANELLA, R   Ph-3 1-2/2 $16.60   L   KE275
GREENE, CAROL. Roy Campanella: major-league champion. Childrens Press ISBN 0-516-04261-0; In Canada: Childrens Press, 1994. 47p. ill. (some col.). (Rookie biography).
    Includes chronology and index.
    Roy Campanella has left his mark on baseball as one of the first African Americans to play in the major leagues. He is noted for his amazing battle with paralysis and his work with other people with disabilities. Full-page photographs capture the many facets of Roy's life, and simple text make his story accessible to beginning readers. For multicultural studies.
    SUBJ: Campanella, Roy./ Baseball players./ Afro-Americans--Biography.

B CARSON, B.   Ph-3 4-6/7 $22.83   L   KE276
SIMMONS, ALEX. Ben Carson. Raintree Steck-Vaughn ISBN 0-8172-3975-8, 1996. 48p. ill. (some col.). (Contemporary African Americans).
    Includes chronology, glossary, bibliography and index.
    Ben Carson is currently Chief of Pediatric Neurosurgery at Johns Hopkins Hospital in Baltimore, Maryland. His childhood struggles and his mother's determination that he and his brother get a good education are all chronicled as well as his amazing medical achievements. Motivational reading in addition to being useful in career units. For multicultural studies.
    SUBJ: Carson, Ben./ Neurosurgeons./ Physicians./ Afro-Americans--Biography.

B CARSON, K.   Ph-2 5-6/7 $15.95   L   KE277
SANFORD, WILLIAM R. Kit Carson: frontier scout. By William R. Sanford and Carl R. Green. Enslow ISBN 0-89490-650-X, 1996. 48p. ill., map. (Legendary heroes of the Wild West).
    Includes glossary, bibliography and index.
    Longing from childhood to hunt and trap, Kit Carson fulfilled his

dreams by accompanying traders and explorers to the West. His knowledge of the languages and the needs of the Native Americans earned him recognition and honors. This straightforward telling of Carson's life will assist students in gaining a knowledge of frontier life.
SUBJ: Carson, Kit./ Pioneers./ West (U.S.)--Biography.

B CARSON, R.   Ph-2 5-6/6 $14.95   L   KE278
RANSOM, CANDICE F. Listening to crickets: a story about Rachel Carson. Illus. by Shelly O. Haas. Carolrhoda ISBN 0-87614-727-9, 1993. 64p. ill. (Carolrhoda creative minds book).
Includes bibliography.
Raised in a family which cherished wild life, Carson found her writing was a way to reach people and raise their concern about their environment and the importance of preserving it. Her life and dedication makes inspiring reading.
SUBJ: Carson, Rachel./ Environmentalists./ Biologists./ Women biologists.

B CARTER, H.   Ph-2   A/9 $14.95   T   KE279
FORD, BARBARA. Howard Carter: searching for King Tut. Illus. by Janet Hamlin. W. H. Freeman ISBN 0-7167-6587-X, 1995. 63p. ill. (Science superstars).
"Scientific American books for young readers."
Includes index/glossary and bibliography.
Carter went to Egypt as an artist, but soon he became recognized as a competent scientist. He was sure that there were more treasures to be found in the Valley of the Kings. His final discovery of King Tut's tomb and the curse, which many believed followed his discovery, make exciting reading for young scientists.
SUBJ: Carter, Howard./ Tutankhamen, King of Egypt./ Egypt--Antiquities--Biography./ Archaeologists.

B CARTER, J.   Ph-3 5-6/7 $15.80   L   KE280
CARRIGAN, MELLONEE. Jimmy Carter: beyond the presidency. Childrens Press ISBN 0-516-04193-2; In Canada: Childrens Press, 1995. 32p. ill. (some col.). (Picture-story biographies).
Includes chronology and index.
Carter's unique role in today's world as peacemaker is stressed in this volume which also covers his childhood and presidency. Color and black and white photographs capture him in his varied roles: father, president, carpenter, and peanut farmer.
SUBJ: Carter, Jimmy./ Presidents.

VCR B CARVER, G.   Ph-3 5-A $89.00   OD   KE281
GEORGE WASHINGTON CARVER: A MAN OF VISION (Videocassette). United Learning 873V, 1990. 1/2" VHS videocassette color (26min).
Includes Instruction Guide.
Carver's simple lifestyle and dedication to enriching the lives of Southern farmers are emphasized in this depiction of his noble life. Multiple uses include: Black History month, career units and history of education in the United States.
SUBJ: Carver, George Washington./ Agriculturists./ Afro-Americans--Biography./ Educators./ Scientists.

B CARVER, G.   Ph-2 2-4/5 $13.25   L   KE282
MCLOONE, MARGO. George Washington Carver: a photo-illustrated biography. Bridgestone ISBN 1-56065-516-X, 1997. 24p. ill. (some col.). (Read and discover photo-illustrated biographies).
Includes chronology, glossary, bibliographies, directory and index.
Photographs and brief text show and tell Carver's devotion to science and his creative use of the peanut. His inspirational life fits into units on African-American history and agriculture. For multicultural studies.
SUBJ: Carver, George Washington./ Agriculturists./ Afro-Americans--Biography.

B CASSATT, M.   Ph-2 6-A/8 $19.95   T   KE283
MEYER, SUSAN E. Mary Cassatt. Abrams ISBN 0-8109-3154-0, 1990. 91p b&w and col illus, b&w photos. (First impressions).
Includes index of illustrations.
Traces the life and work of Mary Cassatt, the noted American painter. Emphasis is placed on the obstacles confronting a Victorian Age woman who tries to enter the art world. Lavishly pictorial, with reproductions of Cassatt's extraordinary paintings, this inspirational biography will be of particular interest to girls who can identify with the courage, tenacity and independence necessary to succeed in a male dominated field. Excellent for reports and for learning to appreciate art.
SUBJ: Cassatt, Mary./ Women artists./ Painting, American./ Art appreciation./ Artists.

B CHAGALL, M.   Ph-2 6-A/8 $19.95   T   KE284
GREENFELD, HOWARD. Marc Chagall. Abrams ISBN 0-8109-3152-4, 1990. 92p b&w and col illus. (First impressions).
Marc Chagall's life and work are discussed in this moving examination of the great Russian Jewish painter who traveled the world but always remained true to his Russian village heritage. Abundant reproductions of Chagall's paintings with their dreamlike quality, puzzling images, and animals that defy gravity and logic and fly through the air with joyful abandon are included. Excellent for art appreciation.
SUBJ: Chagall, Marc./ Artists--Soviet Union./ Painting, Russian./ Art appreciation.

B CHANG, W.   Ph-3 5-6/6 $17.95   L   KE285
RILEY, GAIL BLASSER. Wah Ming Chang: artist and master of special effects. Enslow ISBN 0-89490-639-9, 1995. 112p. ill. (Multicultural junior biographies).
Includes chronology, filmography, bibliography and index.
As a child, Wah was considered a prodigy because of his skills in drawing. As an adult, he worked at the Walt Disney Studios. At twenty-one, when he became ill with polio, he battled the illness and continued to make a mark in film and television. His range of work includes painting, sculpture, etching, and filmmaking. Though his name may not be recognizable to children, his work will be familiar--BAMBI, CLEOPATRA, FANTASIA, PINOCCHIO, PLANET OF THE APES, etc. For multicultural studies.
SUBJ: Chang, Wah./ Chinese Americans--Biography./ Artists./ Asian Americans--Biography.

B CHARLES, R.   Ph-2 5-A/8 $23.95   L   KE286
TURK, RUTH. Ray Charles: soul man. Lerner ISBN 0-8225-4928-X, 1996. 112p. ill. (some col.). (Newsmakers).
Includes discography, bibliography and index.
Ray Charles' amazing musical talents helped him to overcome loss of family, sight, and roots. He moved from city to city living hand to mouth until his style was recognized and he became a celebrity. For music classes, multicultural studies, and units on persons with disabilities.
SUBJ: Charles, Ray./ Singers./ Afro-Americans--Biography./ Blind--Biography.

B CHAVEZ, C.   Ph-2 4-5/6 $12.40   L   KE287
CEDENO, MARIA E. Cesar Chavez: labor leader. Millbrook ISBN 1-56294-280-8, 1993. 32p. ill. (some col.). (Hispanic heritage).
Includes chronology, bibliography and index.
Childhood experiences taught Chavez what it means to loose one's home, labor in the fields, and be discriminated against because of one's color. He dedicated his life to improving the lives of the Mexican-American people. For collections on contemporary problems and minorities.
SUBJ: Chavez, Cesar./ Labor leaders./ Migrant labor./ United Farm Workers--History./ Mexican Americans--Biography.

B CHINN, M.   Ph-3 5-A/8 $14.95   T   KE288
BUTTS, ELLEN R. May Chinn: the best medicine. By Ellen R. Butts and Joyce R. Schwartz. Illus. by Janet Hamlin. W. H. Freeman ISBN 0-7167-6589-6, 1995. 48p. ill. (Science superstars).
"Scientific American books for young readers."
Includes index/glossary and bibliography.
May Chinn's mother had a dream that her daughter get a good education. Accepted at Columbia University's Teachers College without finishing high school, May found her real interest was in science rather than music, the field in which she first began her studies. She became a leading doctor and cancer researcher while she continued her interest in music as Paul Robeson's accompanist. A motivational study for science students, multicultural studies, and women's studies.
SUBJ: Chinn, May Edward./ Physicians./ Women physicians./ Afro-Americans--Biography.

B CHISHOLM, S.   Ph-3 5-6/10 $19.90   L   KE289
POLLACK, JILL S. Shirley Chisholm. Watts ISBN 0-531-20168-6, 1994. 63p. ill. (some col.). (First book).
Includes bibliography and index.
Shirley's father was deeply interested in politics and social issues. He passed his passion on to his daughter who rose through the ranks of the Democratic Party to become the first African-American woman to serve in the House of Representatives. Well designed and highlighted with photographs. Useful for multicultural studies and women's studies.
SUBJ: Chisholm, Shirley./ Legislators./ Afro-Americans--Biography./ Women in politics.

NONFICTION

B CHURCHILL, W.   Ph-3 5-6/7 $13.95   L   KE290
DRIEMEN, J. E. Winston Churchill: an unbreakable spirit. Dillon ISBN 0-87518-434-0, 1990. 128p. ill. (People in focus).
     Includes appendix, bibliography and index.
     Churchill's education, military service, activities as a journalist, author, and parent are examined in addition to his years as Prime Minister of Great Britain in this detailed biography. Insightful discussions of World War I, the Boer War and rise of Hitler are included. For World War II buffs or for those intrigued by real life heroes.
     SUBJ: Churchill, Winston, Sir./ Prime ministers./ Great Britain--Politics and government--20th Century.

B CHURCHILL, W.   Ph-1 6-A/10 $17.95   L   KE291
SEVERANCE, JOHN B. Winston Churchill: soldier, statesman, artist. Clarion ISBN 0-395-69853-7, 1996. 144p. ill.
     Includes bibliography and index.
     Churchill's lonely childhood, daring escapades as a young man, his service as a political leader during World War I and II, and his lasting marriage are all vividly pictured. His remarkable skill with words, both written and oral, is also fully developed in the text. Added section called "Winston's Wit" brings the man alive for the reader. His long and active life makes this must reading for any unit on twentieth century history.
     SUBJ: Churchill, Winston, Sir./ Prime ministers./ Great Britain--History--20th Century.

B CLEARY, B.   Ph-2 5-6/7 $17.00   T   KE292
CLEARY, BEVERLY. Girl from Yamhill. Morrow ISBN 0-688-07800-1, 1988. 279p. ill.
     Drawing from remembered experiences, some funny, some dramatic and some heart breaking, Beverly Cleary tells of her family's struggles during the depression. Distinctly at variance with her usual style and carrying a fair amount of bitterness this appeals to the mature Cleary fan.
     SUBJ: Cleary, Beverly./ Authors, American./ Women authors, American.

B CLEMENTE, R.   Ph-2 2-4/2 $3.99   P   KE293
ENGEL, TRUDIE. We'll never forget you, Roberto Clemente. Scholastic ISBN 0-590-68881-2; In Canada: Scholastic, 1997. 107p. ill. (Scholastic biography).
     Includes glossaries.
     Clemente's early love of baseball, his arrival in the states, and his struggles to overcome discrimination are all related in a direct style well suited to beginning readers. Black and white photographs show him playing baseball and with his family. For multicultural studies.
     SUBJ: Clemente, Roberto./ Baseball players./ Puerto Rico--Biography.

B CLEMENTE, R.   Ph-3 5-A/7 $14.95   L   KE294
MACHT, NORMAN L. Roberto Clemente. Chelsea House ISBN 0-7910-1764-8, 1994. 79p. ill. (Junior world biographies).
     Includes bibliography, glossary, chronology and index.
     Spanish edition ROBERTO CLEMENTE available from Chelsea House (ISBN 0-7910-3105-5, 1995), $18.95.
     Clemente was never a favorite with the media. This book explains his drive to prove to all the world that a poor boy from Puerto Rico could be the best player in the major leagues. Frequent use of quotes reveal that he won his place through hustle and intelligence. For multicultural studies.
     SUBJ: Clemente, Roberto./ Baseball players./ Puerto Rico--Biography./ Spanish language materials.

B CLEOPATRA   Ph-1 4-6/6 $14.93   L   KE295
STANLEY, DIANE. Cleopatra. By Diane Stanley and Peter Vennema. Illus. by Diane Stanley. Morrow ISBN 0-688-10414-2, 1994. unp. col. ill., maps.
     Includes bibliography.
     Vividly follows Cleopatra through her tumultuous life. Egyptian practices which made her queen and wife of her brother, her relationships with Caesar and Mark Antony, and their deaths are explained. Provides understanding of this epic era in Roman and Egyptian history. Stunning illustrations depict dress and practices of the times. Pronunciation guide is provided.
     SUBJ: Cleopatra, Queen of Egypt./ Kings, queens, rulers, etc.

B CLINTON, B.   Ph-2 5-6/8 $14.90   L   KE296
CWIKLIK, ROBERT. Bill Clinton: president of the 90s. Rev. ed. Millbrook ISBN 0-7613-0129-1, 1997. 48p. col. ill. (Gateway biography).
     Includes chronology and index.
     Stating that Clinton was the first Democratic president since Franklin D. Roosevelt to be reelected, this study chronicles the events that brought him to a second term. An honest discussion of his relationship with his stepfather, reluctance to fight in Vietnam, and attempts to change medical coverage and to balance the budget makes the book

valuable for social studies units.
     SUBJ: Clinton, Bill./ Presidents.

B CLINTON, H.   Ph-2 4-6/9 $12.90   L   KE297
LEVERT, SUZANNE. Hillary Rodham Clinton, first lady. Millbrook ISBN 1-56294-432-0, 1994. 48p. ill. (some col.) (Gateway biography).
     Includes chronology, bibliography and index.
     Hillary Clinton's achievements in high school, college, and as a lawyer are delineated as well as her role as the first lady in Arkansas and Washington, D.C. Ample illustrations show her development into a mature leader.
     SUBJ: Clinton, Hillary Rodham./ First ladies.

B COBB, T.   Ph-2 2-4/4 $3.95   P   KE298
KRAMER, S. A. Ty Cobb: bad boy of baseball. Random House ISBN 0-679-87283-3; In Canada: Random House, 1995. 47p. ill. (Step into reading).
     Ty Cobb wanted to impress his father, whose untimely death prevented him from seeing Ty play in the major leagues. How Cobb earned his reputation for being ruthless, prejudiced, and lonely is amply explained. Will be attractive to reluctant readers.
     SUBJ: Cobb, Ty./ Baseball players.

B COLEMAN, B.   Ph-2 4-6/8 $19.95   L   KE299
HART, PHILIP S. Up in the air: the story of Bessie Coleman. Carolrhoda ISBN 0-87614-949-2, 1996. 80p. ill.
     Includes bibliography and index.
     Bessie Coleman longed to fly, but in the 1920s she could find no school in America which would grant her a license. Her trip to France, subsequent licensing, and her efforts to support herself through flying shows and exhibits are chronicled. Black and white photographs document the career of this amazing pilot. The author has also produced a film based on the life of Bessie Coleman. For multicultural studies and women's studies.
     SUBJ: Coleman, Bessie./ Air pilots./ Afro-Americans--Biography./ Women air pilots.

CE B COLUMBUS, C.   Ph-3 2-3/4 $14.95   L   KE300
ADLER, DAVID A. Picture book of Christopher Columbus. Illustrated by John C. and Alexandra Wallner. Holiday House ISBN 0-8234-0857-4, 1991. unp. col. ill. (Picture book biography).
     Includes "Important Dates".
     Read-along kit available from Live Oak Media: (ISBN 0-87499-263-X, 1992) 1 hardcover book, 1 sound cassette (12min), $22.95.
     Available in Spanish UN LIBRO ILUSTADO SOBRE CRISTOBAL COLON (ISBn 0-8234-0981-3, 1992).
     Columbus proposed sailing to the West instead of going eastward in the search for India. His remarkable perseverance and discoveries are touched upon in this brief discussion of his life. For beginning readers and holiday displays.
     SUBJ: Columbus, Christopher./ Explorers.

B COLUMBUS, C.   Ph-2 4-5/4 $13.95   L   KE301
ADLER, DAVID A. Christopher Columbus: great explorer. Illus. by Lyle Miller. Holiday House ISBN 0-8234-0895-7, 1991. 48p b&w illus. (First biography).
     Includes chronology and index.
     Columbus' childhood, early sailing experiences, his efforts to find backing for his trips of exploration and his voyages to America are all covered in this attractive presentation of his life. Useful for Columbus Day and exploration units or middle grade independent reading.
     SUBJ: Columbus, Christopher./ Explorers./ America--Discovery and exploration--Spanish.

B COLUMBUS, C.   Ph-2 4-5/5 $18.60   L   KE302
ASIMOV, ISAAC. Christopher Columbus: navigator to the New World. Gareth Stevens ISBN 0-8368-0556-9; In Canada: Saunders, 1991. 48p. col. ill., maps. (Isaac Asimov's pioneers of science and exploration).
     Includes chronology, glossary, bibliography, directory and index.
     Copiously illustrated and supplemented with maps and diagrams, this summary of Columbus' explorations will be useful in units on explorers and world history.
     SUBJ: Columbus, Christopher./ Explorers./ America--Discovery and exploration--Spanish.

CE B COLUMBUS, C.   Ph-2 4-6/6 $13.95   T   KE303
FRITZ, JEAN. Where do you think you're going, Christopher Columbus? Illus. by Margot Tomes. Putnam ISBN 0-399-20723-6; In Canada: Academic Press, 1980. 80p. col. ill.
     Includes index.
     Talking book read by Jean Fritz available from Weston Woods WW483C, 1982. 1 sound cassette (77min) $8.95.
     Available from National Library Service for the Blind and Physically

Handicapped on sound recording cassette RC19724.
Videocassette available from Weston Woods HMPV483V, 1991.
1/2" VHS videocassette color (32min), $39.95.
Christopher Columbus believed that there was a shorter route to the Indies than sailing around Africa. This biography tells of his efforts to prove his belief, his search for support and his exploration of Central America and the West Indies.
SUBJ: Columbus, Christopher./ Explorers./ America--Discovery and exploration--Spanish.

B COPLAND, A.   Ph-3 5-6/7 $17.20   L   KE304
VENEZIA, MIKE. Aaron Copland. Childrens Press ISBN 0-516-04538-5; In Canada: Childrens Press, 1995. 32p. col. ill. (Getting to know the world's greatest composers).
Aaron Copland's long outpouring of musical compositions that capture American life and spirit is presented in a slim volume illustrated with cartoons as well as photography of the musician.
SUBJ: Copland, Aaron./ Composers.

B COUSTEAU, J.   Ph-2 4-6/7 $14.95   L   KE305
REEF, CATHERINE. Jacques Cousteau: champion of the sea. Illus. by Larry Raymond. Twenty-First Century ISBN 0-8050-2114-0, 1992. 72p. ill. (Earth keepers).
Includes glossary and index.
Early interest in swimming and diving led Jacques Cousteau to devote his life to exploring and explaining the wonders of the undersea world. Line drawings show Cousteau at work and some of the sea wonders seen in his explorations. For ecology units.
SUBJ: Cousteau, Jacques Yves./ Oceanographers.

B CRANDALL, P.   Ph-2 6-A/6 $16.95   T   KE306
YATES, ELIZABETH. Prudence Crandall: woman of courage. 2nd ed. Boyds Mills ISBN 1-56397-391-X; In Canada: McClelland & Stewart, 1996. 238p.
Originally published by E.P. Dutton, 1955.
Prudence founded a school for African-American girls in the town of Canterbury, Connecticut in 1833. The town rose up against her, subjecting her to trials and imprisonment and all forms of abuse. Her courage before all this hatred makes a remarkable story which gives insight into the turmoil that preceded the Civil War. The book, for mature readers, will be useful for multicultural studies, women's studies, and United States history.
SUBJ: Crandall, Prudence./ Afro-Americans--Education--Connecticut./ Canterbury (Conn.)--History./ Abolitionists./ Women reformers.

B CRAZY HORSE   Ph-2 6-A/7 $19.95   T   KE307
FREEDMAN, RUSSELL. Life and death of Crazy Horse. Illus. by Amos Bad Heart Bull. Holiday House ISBN 0-8234-1219-9, 1996. 166p. ill., maps.
Includes chronology, bibliography and index.
Crazy Horse's lifetime spans the period of the vast migrations of people into the West. Leading the Sioux, he fought major battles with the United States Army to protect their hunting grounds. Augmented with maps and drawings by a Native American who recorded ceremonies and battles. Outstanding for its sympathetic portrayal of the Native American's defiance at Little Big Horn. For multicultural studies.
SUBJ: Crazy Horse./ Oglala Indians--Biography./ Indians of North America--Biography./ Fetterman Fight, Wyo., 1866./ Little Big Horn, Battle of the, 1876.

B CRAZY HORSE   Ph-3 A/9 $17.95   T   KE308
ST. GEORGE, JUDITH. Crazy Horse. Putnam ISBN 0-399-22667-2; In Canada: Putnam, 1994. 180p., maps.
Includes bibliography and index.
As the author relates the important events in the life of Crazy Horse, she incorporates much of the history of the period during which the Native Americans were being driven from their homelands and deprived of their food supply (the buffalo). Crazy Horse was a solemn, stoic individual who was faithful to his family and friends. This picture of a troubled time in American history is for mature readers who are serious students. For multicultural studies.
SUBJ: Crazy Horse./ Oglala Indians--Biography./ Indians of North America--Biography.

CE B CREWS, D.   Ph-1 K-2/2 $13.88   L   KE309
CREWS, DONALD. Bigmama's. Greenwillow ISBN 0-688-09951-3, 1991. unp. col. ill.
Selectors' Choice, 19th ed.
Videocassette available from Reading Adventures 1001. 1/2" VHS videocassette color (6min), $42.50.
Donald Crews vividly recalls through illustrations and text the joy of vacationing with his grandparents at their home in Florida.
Autobiography for the beginning reader.
SUBJ: Crews, Donald./ Authors, American./ Illustrators./ Family life./ Country life./ Afro-Americans--Biography.

B CROCKETT, D.   Ph-2 2-3/7 $15.95   L   KE310
ADLER, DAVID A. Picture book of Davy Crockett. Illus. by John and Alexandra Wallner. Holiday House ISBN 0-8234-1212-1, 1996. unp. col. ill. (Picture book biography).
Includes chronology.
Weaves quotes from Davy Crockett's autobiography with the numerous adventures that filled his life. While acknowledging the many tall tales that have grown up around this folk hero, the author stays with the known facts. Watercolor illustrations extend the text.
SUBJ: Crockett, Davy./ Pioneers./ Legislators./ United States. Congress. House--Biography.

B CURIE, M.   Ph-3 4-6/4 $17.95   L   KE311
POYNTER, MARGARET. Marie Curie: discoverer of radium. Enslow ISBN 0-89490-477-9, 1994. 128p. ill., maps. (Great minds of science).
Includes chronology, glossary, bibliography and index.
Maps, charts, and photographs augment this detailed narrative of Marie Curie's life and her impact on the scientific world. For science units and women's studies.
SUBJ: Curie, Marie./ Chemists./ Women chemists.

B DAHL, R.   Ph-1 5-6/6 $16.00   T   KE312
DAHL, ROALD. Boy: tales of childhood. Farrar, Straus & Giroux ISBN 0-374-37374-4, 1984. 160p. ill.
Available in large print from Windrush/dist. by Cornerstone (ISBN 1-85089-917-7, $ 13.95).
Being spanked for putting a dead mouse in a candy jar, careening around the countryside in a new car and nearly losing his nose, and becoming a competent toilet seat warmer are some of the adventures which Roald Dahl tells in this biography which covers his childhood and first job. The episodes can be read individually and in addition to introducing this well known author to students will give them insight into the English educational system in the 1920s.
GOING SOLO (ISBN 0-374-16503-3, 1986) (available from National Library Service for the Blind and Physically Handicapped on sound recording cassette RC25439) furthers Dahl's life through training and as a pilot during World War II.
SUBJ: Dahl, Roald./ Authors, English./ World War, 1939-1945--Personal narratives.

B DALI, S.   Ph-3 4-6/7 $15.00   L   KE313
VENEZIA, MIKE. Salvador Dali. Childrens Press ISBN 0-516-02296-2; In Canada: Childrens Press, 1993. 32p. col. ill. (Getting to know the world's greatest artists).
The impact of his childhood on Salvador Dali's work is discussed. Includes some of his best known paintings and an explanation of surrealism.
SUBJ: Dali, Salvador./ Artists./ Painting, Spanish./ Painting, Modern--Spain./ Art appreciation.

B DARWIN, C.   Ph-3 5-A/4 $17.95   L   KE314
ANDERSON, MARGARET JEAN. Charles Darwin: naturalist. By Margaret J. Anderson. Enslow ISBN 0-89490-476-0, 1994. 128p. ill., maps. (Great minds of science).
Includes chronology, glossary, bibliography and index.
Uncertain about a career, Charles Darwin opted to join a group mapping the coast of South America, so he could study the terrain they visited. The results of these explorations were published in books which stunned the scientific community in 1859 and formed the basis of the theory of evolution. For mature readers.
SUBJ: Darwin, Charles./ Naturalists.

B DARWIN, C.   Ph-3 5-8/8 $22.80   L   KE315
TWIST, CLINT. Charles Darwin: on the trail of evolution. Illus. by Brian Watson. Raintree Steck-Vaughn ISBN 0-8114-7256-6, 1994. 46p. col. ill., maps. (Beyond the horizons).
Includes glossary, bibliography and index.
On the first voyage, sail aboard the HMS Beagle for more than 36,000 miles of exploration and discovery. On the second voyage, learn how Darwin's intellect led him to formulate the theory of evolution. Historical background, interesting illustrations, and sound text document the astounding life of this scientific genius. Will complement any units on nineteenth century history.
SUBJ: Evolution./ Darwin, Charles./ Beagle Expedition (1831-1836)./ Naturalists.

B DEBUSSY, C.   Ph-3 6-A/9 $17.99   T   KE316
THOMPSON, WENDY. Claude Debussy. Viking ISBN 0-670-84482-9; In Canada: Penguin, 1993. 48p. col. ill. (Composer's world).
Includes index.
A recounting of Debussy's life and the external events which

prompted many of his compositions is complimented by a map, musical scores, drawings, and photographs of the major figures in his life. For music students and mature readers.
SUBJ: Debussy, Claude./ Composers.

B DEERE, J.　　　　Ph-2 5-6/6　$14.95　L　KE317
COLLINS, DAVID R. Pioneer plowmaker: a story about John Deere. Illustrated by Steve Michaels. Carolrhoda ISBN 0-87614-424-5, 1990. 63p. ill. (Carolrhoda creative minds book).
Includes bibliography.
As a boy, John Deere was fascinated by the blacksmith's forge and at seventeen he was apprenticed. His skills with repairing tools won him the praise and approval of farmers and started him on developing his own tools and farm implements. Another biography of the opening of the West through hard work and creativity. For career and history units.
SUBJ: Deere, John./ Industrialists./ Inventors./ Agricultural machinery industry--History.

B DEGAS, E.　　　　Ph-2 6-A/9　$19.95　T　KE318
MEYER, SUSAN E. Edgar Degas. Abrams ISBN 0-8109-3220-2, 1994. 92p. col. ill. (First impressions).
Includes index.
Discusses the life and work of the great French Impressionist painter, Edgar Degas. Unlike his contemporaries, Degas preferred to work indoors, immortalizing the world of ballet, of the racetrack, and of musicians. Reproductions of some of his greatest paintings are included.
SUBJ: Degas, Edgar./ Artists./ Painting, French.

B DEVERS, G.　　　　Ph-2 5-6/6　$22.83　L　KE319
GUTMAN, BILL. Gail Devers. Raintree Steck-Vaughn ISBN 0-8172-4122-1, 1996. 48p. col. ill. (Overcoming the odds).
Includes chronology, bibliography and index.
Gail won an award in track for her high school when she was the only one running and had no coach. She overcame Graves' disease although the treatment almost resulted in the amputation of her feet. She won a gold medal in the Olympics in 1992. In 1993 she was named United States Women's Athlete of the Year. Her amazing career is covered in a book in which readers can see what determination can bring to fruition. A biography for multicultural studies.
SUBJ: Devers, Gail./ Runners (Sports)./ Women athletes./ Afro-Americans--Biography./ Track and field athletes./ Graves' disease.

B DEWEY, J.　　　　Ph-2 3-4/4　$14.95　T　KE320
DEWEY, JENNIFER OWINGS. Cowgirl dreams: a western childhood. Boyds Mills ISBN 1-56397-377-4; In Canada: McClelland & Stewart, 1995. 141p. ill.
An autobiography of an author who spent her childhood in northern New Mexico. On the ranch she raised a pig, the runt of the litter, mingled with the Native Americans and Hispanics, and attempted to understand her father's problems with alcohol. While warm and humorous, the story is a study of parenting.
SUBJ: Dewey, Jennifer Owings./ New Mexico--Biography./ Ranch life./ Authors, American./ Women authors, American./ Illustrators./ Women illustrators.

B DICKENS, C.　　　　Ph-3 5-6/7　$14.93　L　KE321
STANLEY, DIANE. Charles Dickens: the man who had great expectations. By Diane Stanley and Peter Vennema. Morrow ISBN 0-688-09111-3, 1993. unp. col. ill., map.
Includes bibliography.
Describes the life and career of the nineteenth century British novelist. Stunning illustrations show the London Charles Dickens discovered as a child and so clearly described in his many books. For mature readers interested in authors of the classics.
SUBJ: Dickens, Charles./ Authors, English.

B DISNEY, W.　　　　Ph-2 4-6/8　$17.95　L　KE322
COLE, MICHAEL D. Walt Disney: creator of Mickey Mouse. Enslow ISBN 0-89490-694-1, 1996. 112p. ill. (People to know).
Includes chronology, bibliography and index.
Presents Disney's early search for a career in which he could express his artistic talents, his brother's continuing support, and the making of the early cartoons and films which launched him into leadership in the film industry. His devotion to his family and his demands for perfection are also covered. Students interested in filmmaking and animation will welcome this title.
SUBJ: Disney, Walt./ Motion pictures--Biography.

B DORRIS, M.　　　　Ph-3 6-A/7　$24.26　KE323
WEIL, ANN. Michael Dorris. Raintree Steck-Vaughn ISBN 0-8172-3994-4, 1997. 48p. ill. (some col.). (Contemporary Native Americans).

Includes chronology, glossary, bibliography and index.
Well-known for his advocacy for Native Americans and being a single father in the 1970's, Michael Dorris wrote fiction with his wife, Louise Erdrich, on Native American life. This slim biography will be useful when introducing his works during author studies. For multicultural studies.
SUBJ: Dorris, Michael./ Authors, American./ Indian authors./ Modoc Indians--Biography./ Indians of North America--Biography.

B DOUGLAS, M.　　　　Ph-3 4-5/6　$14.95　L　KE324
BRYANT, JENNIFER. Marjory Stoneman Douglas: voice of the Everglades. Illus. by Larry Raymond. Twenty-First Century/Henry Holt ISBN 0-8050-2113-2, 1992. 72p b&w illus. (Earth keepers).
Includes glossary and index.
Since 1948, Marjory Douglas has fought to preserve the Florida Everglades. Stressing the uniqueness of the area, she has saved the Everglades for wildlife conservation and the education of the American public. For Florida and science units.
SUBJ: Douglas, Marjory Stoneman/ Conservationists./ Everglades (Fla.)./ Women conservationists.

VCR B DOUGLASS, F.　　　　Ph-2 4-A　$39.95　KE325
FREDERICK DOUGLASS (Videocassette). Schlessinger Video 6602, 1992. 1/2" VHS videocassette b&w and color (30min). (Black Americans of achievement video collection).
Includes public performance rights.
Depicts the life of an amazingly courageous, determined man who gained education, freedom, and recognition and who inspired people to fight to overcome slavery. Essential for units on slavery, African-American history, and the Civil War.
SUBJ: Douglass, Frederick./ Afro-Americans--Biography./ Abolitionists.

B DOUGLASS, F.　　　　Ph-2 3-5/3　$18.60　L　KE326
WEINER, ERIC. Story of Frederick Douglass: voice of freedom. Illus. by Steven Parton. Gareth Stevens ISBN 0-8368-1464-9; In Canada: Saunders, 1996. 108p. ill. (Famous lives).
Originally published by Parachute Press, 1992.
Includes chronology, bibliography and index.
As a boy and young man, Douglass was beaten many times and witnessed brutality to other slaves. He was determined to learn to read in order to gain his freedom. When he finally escaped his cruel master, he turned to writing and speaking about the inhumanity of slavery. He became the true spokesperson for the slaves and is today recognized as one of the real leaders in the abolitionist movement. For multicultural studies.
SUBJ: Douglass, Frederick./ Abolitionists./ Afro-Americans--Biography.

B EARHART, A.　　　　Ph-2 3-4/5　$10.95　L　KE327
KERBY, MONA. Amelia Earhart: courage in the sky. Illustrated by Eileen McKeating. Viking/Penguin ISBN 0-670-83024-0; In Canada: Penguin, 1990. 57p b&w illus. (Women of our time).
Always pursuing outdoor and adventuresome activities, it was natural for Amelia to become interested in flying when there were few women who would venture into a plane. Developing from a discussion of her childhood escapades and family problems is a picture of a woman who was self-sufficient and willing to try what had never been done. For units on early aviation and women's studies.
SUBJ: Earhart, Amelia./ Air pilots./ Women air pilots.

B EARHART, A.　　　　Ph-2 2-4/7　$11.99　L　KE328
KULLING, MONICA. Vanished!: the mysterious disappearance of Amelia Earhart. Illus. by Ying-Hwa Hu and Cornelius Van Wright. Random House ISBN 0-679-97124-6; In Canada: Random House, 1996. 48p. ill. (some col.), maps. (Step into reading).
Discusses the many theories that have arisen since Amelia Earhart disappeared in 1939. Was she a spy? Was she captured by the Japanese? Is she still alive? For units on World War II, aviation, and women's studies.
SUBJ: Earhart, Amelia./ Air pilots./ Women air pilots.

B EARHART, A.　　　　Ph-1 4-6/12　$16.00　T　KE329
SZABO, CORINNE. Sky pioneer: a photobiography of Amelia Earhart. National Geographic/dist. by Publishers Group West ISBN 0-7922-3737-4, 1997. 63p. ill., maps.
Includes chronology, bibliography and index.
Dramatic photographs as much as the text tell the life of Amelia Earhart in this stunning book. Quotes from her writings give the reader the essence of her drive and courage. For aviation and women's studies.
SUBJ: Earhart, Amelia./ Air pilots./ Women air pilots.

B EDISON, T.   Ph-2 2-3/3 $15.95   L   KE330
ADLER, DAVID A. Picture book of Thomas Alva Edison. Illus. by John and Alexandra Wallner. Holiday House ISBN 0-8234-1246-6, 1996. unp. col. ill. (Picture book biography).
  Includes chronology.
  Edison's lack of interest in formal education, his early experiments which set a train on fire, his work on improving the telegraph, and later discoveries of electric light bulbs, the phonograph, and movie camera are all briefly described in a picture book biography.
  SUBJ: Edison, Thomas Alva./ Inventors.

B EDISON, T.   Ph-3 4-6/6 $14.95   L   KE331
MITCHELL, BARBARA. Wizard of sound: a story about Thomas Edison. Illus. by Hetty Mitchell. Carolrhoda ISBN 0-87614-445-8, 1991. 64p. ill. (Carolrhoda creative minds book).
  Includes bibliography.
  Describes Edison's numerous inventions and provides insight into his constant battle with hearing loss. Text can be an adjunct to units on electricity as well as motivational reading on lives of individuals with hearing impairments.
  SUBJ: Edison, Thomas Alva./ Inventors.

B EDMONDS, S.   Ph-3 6-A/7 $13.95   L   KE332
STEVENS, BRYNA. Frank Thompson: her Civil War story. Macmillan ISBN 0-02-788185-7; In Canada: Maxwell Macmillan, 1992. 144p. ill., map.
  Includes bibliography and index.
  Emma E. Edmonds fled from her home in Canada to the United States where she pursued a career in sales. She enlisted in the Union Army as a man and served as a nurse, spy, and postmaster. Much of the material is taken from her own writings. Will interest readers of spy stories and Civil War exploits.
  SUBJ: Edmonds, S. Emma E./ Spies./ United States--History--Civil War, 1861-1865--Secret service./ Women spies.

B EHLERT, L.   Ph-2 3-6/2 $13.95   T   KE333
EHLERT, LOIS. Under my nose. Photos by Carlo Ontal. Richard C. Owens ISBN 1-57274-027-2, 1996. 32p. col. ill., map. (Meet the author).
  Ehlert's spontaneous joy in her work of writing and illustrating books for children is captured in this brief biography. Explanations are given of how she develops a theme, and a mock-up of one of her books makes this a tool for introducing the making of books and creative writing activities.
  SUBJ: Ehlert, Lois./ Authors, American./ Illustrators./ Women authors, American.

B EINSTEIN, A.   Ph-3 5-A/6 $17.50   L   KE334
MCPHERSON, STEPHANIE SAMMARTINO. Ordinary genius: the story of Albert Einstein. Carolrhoda ISBN 0-87614-788-0, 1995. 95p. ill. (Trailblazers).
  Includes bibliography and index.
  The multifaceted Einstein is covered in this biography which shows his lifelong quest for answers in the scientific world, dedication to world peace, and love of family, children, and music. For mature readers.
  SUBJ: Einstein, Albert./ Physicists.

B EISENHOWER, D   Ph-1 5-6/6 $21.50   L   KE335
DARBY, JEAN. Dwight D. Eisenhower: a man called Ike. Lerner ISBN 0-8225-4900-X, 1989. 112p. ill. (Lerner biography).
  Includes appendix, glossary, bibliography and index.
  A man totally dedicated to his career and country is pictured in this book. Ike's rise in the military ranks, his masterful command of the forces during World War II, his resistance to the use of the Atom Bomb, and his presidency are covered in a text which is liberally supplemented with photographs and maps.
  SUBJ: Eisenhower, Dwight D./ Presidents.

B EISENREICH, J   Ph-2 3-5/6 $22.83   L   KE336
GUTMAN, BILL. Jim Eisenreich. Raintree Steck-Vaughn ISBN 0-8172-4120-5, 1996. 48p. col. ill. (Overcoming the odds).
  Includes chronology, bibliography and index.
  Tormented during his entire baseball career by tics and involuntary movements (Tourette's syndrome), Eisenreich fought successfully to gain understanding of his illness. The story of his ups and downs while establishing himself as a major league baseball player will encourage any child with similar problems. Useful in units on persons with disabilities.
  SUBJ: Eisenreich, Jim./ Baseball players./ Tourette syndrome.

B ELIZABETH I   Ph-3 6-A/7 $15.95   L   KE337
STANLEY, DIANE. Good Queen Bess: the story of Elizabeth I of England. By Diane Stanley and Peter Vennema. Illustrated by Diane Stanley. Four Winds/Macmillan ISBN 0-02-786810-9; In Canada: Collier Macmillan, 1990. unp. col. ill.
  Includes bibliography.
  Available from the National Library Service for the Blind and Physically Handicapped on sound recording cassette RC34679. Following violent conflict to name the ruler of England in the 1550s, Elizabeth I was placed on the throne. Her long reign brought peace, prosperity, explorations, and artistic achievements to her country. For the mature reader and units on courtly life.
  SUBJ: Elizabeth I, Queen of England./ Kings, queens, rulers, etc.

B ELLINGTON, D.   Ph-2 5-A/9 $18.95   L   KE338
OLD, WENDIE C. Duke Ellington: giant of jazz. Enslow ISBN 0-89490-691-7, 1996. 128p. ill. (African-American biographies).
  Includes chronology, bibliography and index.
  His family, his band, and his composing were equally important to Duke Ellington. What part each of these components played in his life and development are fully explained in this detailed biography. Valuable in music classes studying twentieth century music, social studies units on civil rights, and multicultural studies.
  SUBJ: Ellington, Duke./ Musicians./ Composers./ Afro-Americans--Biography.

B ERATOSTHENES   Ph-2 4-A/6 $16.95   L   KE339
LASKY, KATHRYN. Librarian who measured the earth. Illus. by Kevin Hawkes. Little, Brown ISBN 0-316-51526-4; In Canada: Little, Brown, 1994. 48p. col. ill.
  Includes bibliography.
  Curious as a boy about how the world worked, Eratosthenes was delighted to be named the librarian of the Alexandria Museum as a young man. There he pored over the scrolls dedicated to geography, and he determined to write his own text. Basic to this work was the need to measure the earth. How he did this is described in narration and diagram in this picture biography. For mature readers.
  SUBJ: Eratosthenes./ Geographers./ Earth.

B ESTEFAN, G.   Ph-3 5-6/6 $22.83   L   KE340
RODRIGUEZ, JANEL. Gloria Estefan. Raintree Steck-Vaughn ISBN 0-8172-3982-0, 1996. 48p. col. ill. (Contemporary Hispanic Americans).
  Includes chronology, glossary, bibliography and index.
  Estefan's remarkable rise to fame in the music industry as well as her recovery from a bus accident are the highlights of this portrait of a Cuban-American star. For multicultural studies and women's studies.
  SUBJ: Estefan, Gloria./ Singers./ Rock music./ Cuban Americans--Biography./ Women singers.

VCR B ESTEVANICO   Ph-3 5-6 $99.00   OD KE341
ESTEVANICO AND THE SEVEN CITIES OF GOLD (Videocassette). All Media Productions, 1992. 1/2" VHS videocassette color (20min).
  Includes teacher's guide and activity guide.
  Captured and forced into slavery, young Estevanico becomes a companion to a Spanish soldier and becomes one of the first Africans to explore southern United States and Mexico. His unusual talents with languages made him a unique figure in the early exploration of America. For units on exploration, African-American history, and multicultural studies.
  SUBJ: Estevanico./ Explorers./ America--Discovery and exploration--Spanish.

B FARNSWORTH, P   Ph-3 5-A/9 $21.50   L   KE342
MCPHERSON, STEPHANIE SAMMARTINO. TV's forgotten hero: the story of Philo Farnsworth. Carolrhoda ISBN 1-57505-017-X, 1996. 96p. ill.
  Includes bibliography and index.
  A relatively little known figure in the world of electronics whose importance to the development of television is basic. At the age of fourteen, Philo Farnsworth conceived the idea of electronic television. This summarizes the trials and disappointments as he developed his invention. Students will relate to the efforts of school children in Utah to have a statue of Farnsworth erected in the United States Capitol. Diagrams and black and white photographs show the evolution of the television.
  SUBJ: Farnsworth, Philo Taylor./ Television--History./ Inventors.

B FIELD, E.   Ph-3 2-4/4 $17.20   L   KE343
GREENE, CAROL. Eugene Field: the children's poet. Childrens Press ISBN 0-516-04259-9; In Canada: Childrens Press, 1994. 47p. ill. (some col.) (Rookie biography).
  Includes chronology and index.
  Eugene Field wrote for newspapers, but his joy in his family prompted him to compose poems for children. This is the area which gained him fame. A brief introduction to the poet.
  SUBJ: Field, Eugene./ Poets, American.

JB   **B FLEISCHMAN, S**   Ph-1 3-A/7 $16.00   L   KE344
FLEISCHMAN, SID. Abracadabra kid: a writer's life. Greenwillow ISBN 0-688-14859-X, 1996. 198p. ill.
> Fleischman's career as a magician as a youth gave him opportunities to travel and meet a wide variety of people. He later incorporated all these experiences and individuals into his fanciful tales which delight his readers. Also, his love of his family is evident in this autobiography which reads exactly like his books.
> SUBJ: Fleischman, Sid./ Authorship./ Authors, American.

Adult es. B   **B FLIPPER, H.**   Ph-3 4-6/9 $14.95   L   KE345
PFEIFER, KATHRYN BROWNE. Henry O. Flipper. Twenty-First Century ISBN 0-8050-2351-8; In Canada: Fitzhenry & Whiteside, 1993. 80p. ill. (African-American soldiers).
> Includes chronology, index and bibliography.
> In 1976 the Army Board for Correction of Military Records reversed Flipper's dishonorable discharge. The first African-American graduate of West Point was finally vindicated and recognized for his ground breaking achievement. For multicultural studies.
> SUBJ: Flipper, Henry Ossian./ Soldiers./ Afro-Americans--Biography.

JB   **B FORD, H.**   Ph-2 4-5/3 $14.95   L   KE346
MITCHELL, BARBARA. We'll race you, Henry: a story about Henry Ford. Illustrated by Kathy Haubrich. Carolrhoda ISBN 0-87614-291-9, 1986. 56p. ill. (Carolrhoda creative minds book).
> Born on a farm, Henry, a young man with "wheels in his head," moved to Detroit at an early age and devoted his life to inventing and producing "horseless carriages." Determined to produce a vehicle that would be purposeful and reliable, he persevered despite numerous setbacks. A good choice for social studies and career units.
> SUBJ: Ford, Henry./ Automobile industry and trade--Biography./ Inventors.

JB   **B FOREMAN, M.**   Ph-1 4-A/6 $16.95   L   KE347
FOREMAN, MICHAEL. War boy: a country childhood. Arcade/Little, Brown 1-55970-049-1, 1990. 92p. ill. (some col.).
> With remarkable clarity and humor, Michael Foreman tells of his life with his family in Britain during WW II. The illustrations show bomb shelters, gun emplacements and the ravages of war which will explain better than any text what war was like on the home-front.
> SUBJ: Foreman, Michael./ World War, 1939-1945--Great Britain./ World War, 1939-1945--Personal narratives

JB   **B FORTUNE, A.**   Ph-2 A/7 $15.00   L   KE348
YATES, ELIZABETH. Amos Fortune, free man. Illustrated by Nora S. Unwin. Dutton ISBN 0-525-25570-2, c1950. 181p. ill.
> Newbery Medal Award.
> Available from National Library Service for the Blind and Physically Handicapped on sound recording cassette RC23596, talking book TB01458 and in Braille BRA06930.
> Forty years after he was brought from Africa to the United States, this black slave was able to buy his freedom. He spent the rest of his life helping other slaves.
> SUBJ: Fortune, Amos./ Afro-Americans--Biography./ Slavery--Biography.

JB   **B FRANCIS, ST.**   Ph-3 3-5/5 $13.95   L   KE349
HODGES, MARGARET. Brother Francis and the friendly beasts. Illus. by Ted Lewin. Scribner's ISBN G-684-19173-3; In Canada: Maxwell Macmillan, 1991. unp. col. ill.
> Renouncing his family's wealth, Francis turned to a life of poverty and service to his fellow man and animals. Handsomely illustrated biography includes an explanation of the origins of the first Christmas creche.
> SUBJ: Francis of Assisi, Saint./ Saints.

J271   **B FRANCIS, ST.**   Ph-1 2-4/2 $20.00   T   KE350
WILDSMITH, BRIAN. Saint Francis. Eerdmans ISBN 0-8028-5123-1, 1996. unp. col. ill.
> First published by Oxford University Press, 1995.
> Born to luxury, Francis rejects worldly goods when his father takes him to court for stealing money to rebuild a church which God had called him to repair. His message of love for all God's creatures brings others to follow him. To enrich this telling of the saint's life, Wildsmith has created large paintings of the world of the twelfth century.
> SUBJ: Francis of Assisi, Saint./ Saints.

CE B FRANK, A.   Ph-2 3-4/5 $14.95   L   KE351
ADLER, DAVID A. Picture book of Anne Frank. Illus. by Karen Ritz. Holiday House ISBN 0-8234-1003-X, 1993. unp. col. ill. (Picture book biography).
> Includes chronology.
> Read-along kit available from Live Oak Media (ISBN 0-87499-346-6,

1995). 1 paperback book, 1 sound cassette (15min), $15.95.
> Basic introduction to the life endured by the Franks as they lived in hiding in Amsterdam during World War II. The drawings which show the rise of Hitler, the hiding place, and an internment camp will give the reader understanding when Anne Frank's diary is read.
> SUBJ: Frank, Anne./ Jews--Biography./ Holocaust, Jewish (1939-1945)--Netherlands--Amsterdam.

B FRANK, A.   Ph-1 4-6/6 $21.95   T   KE352
FRANK, ANNE. Diary of a young girl. Translated from the Dutch by B.M. Mooyaart-Doubleday. Introduction by Eleanor Roosevelt. Doubleday ISBN 0-385-04019-9, c1967. 308p.
> Available from National Library Service for the Blind and Physically Handicapped on sound recording cassette RC25864, in Braille BR00927, and as talking book TB00712, TB02506.
> The heroic Frank family is hidden away by friends in a hidden top floor of an office building in Amsterdam during the German occupation, 1942-1944. Anne's diary describes the daily problems, deprivations and unusual strengths as the eight inhabitants of the hidden room face hunger, boredom and finally death. A monumental book to come from the sufferings of World War II.
> SUBJ: Frank, Anne./ Netherlands--History--German occupation, 1940-1945./ World War, 1939-1945--Netherlands./ Jews--Persecutions./ Holocaust, Jewish (1939-1945)--Netherlands--Amsterdam--Personal narratives.

B FRANK, A.   Ph-1 6-A/7 $17.00   T   KE353
VAN DER ROL, RUUD. Anne Frank, beyond the diary: a photographic remembrance. By Ruud van der Rol and Rian Verhoeven in association with the Anne Frank House; translated by Tony Langham and Plym Peters. Viking ISBN 0-670-84932-4; In Canada: Penguin, 1993. 113p. ill. (some col.), maps.
> Includes chronology, bibliography and index.
> Otto Frank was an avid photographer. This spellbinding collection of photographs, diagrams, and maps retells the drama of the flight of Jews from Germany and their attempts to hide in Holland. Fascinating primary documentation of the Holocaust for development of units on World War II and creative writing.
> SUBJ: Frank, Anne./ Jews--Biography./ Holocaust, Jewish (1939-1945)--Netherlands--Amsterdam.

B FRANKLIN, B.   Ph-3 2-4/6 $11.95   P   KE354
D'AULAIRE, INGRI. Benjamin Franklin. By Ingri and Edgar Parin D'Aulaire. Doubleday ISBN 0-385-24103-8, c1950. 48p. col. ill.
> As a printer, inventor, scientist and statesman Benjamin Franklin made many important contributions to our history. The biography of one of America's favorite early leaders is told here in text and pictures.
> SUBJ: Franklin, Benjamin./ Statesmen./ Inventors./ United States--History--Colonial period, ca. 1600-1775--Biography.

CE B FRANKLIN, B.   Ph-1 5-6/7 $13.95   T   KE355
FRITZ, JEAN. What's the big idea, Ben Franklin? Illus. by Margot Tomes. Coward, McCann/Putnam ISBN 0-698-20365-8, c1976. 46p. ill.
> Talking book available from Weston Woods WW476C, 1977. 1 sound cassette (39min) $8.95.
> Available from National Library Service for the Blind and Physically Handicapped on sound recording cassette RC10461.
> Read-along kit available from Weston Woods, 1 hardcover book, 1 sound cassette (39min), $22.95.
> Videocassette available from Weston Woods HMPV476V, 1/2" VHS iconographic color (20min), $39.95.
> A warm, light-hearted account of the unforgettable American hero who was an inventor, scientist, writer, philosopher and a great statesman.
> SUBJ: Franklin, Benjamin./ Statesmen./ Inventors./ United States--History--Colonial period, ca. 1600-1775--Biography.

VCR B FREEDMAN, R.   Ph-3 5-A $88.00   OD KE356
MEET THE NEWBERY AUTHOR: RUSSELL FREEDMAN (Videocassette). SRA/McGraw-Hill 87-909996, 1991. 1/2" VHS videocassette color (20min). (Meet the Newbery author).
> Includes guide.
> Freedman sketches for the viewer how he became an author, how he selects a topic, researches it and finally puts it into book form. For advanced language arts classes.
> SUBJ: Freedman, Russell./ Authors, American.

B FREMONT, J.   Ph-2 5-6/4 $14.95   L   KE357
SANFORD, WILLIAM R. John C. Fremont: soldier and pathfinder. By William R. Sanford and Carl R. Green. Enslow ISBN 0-89490-649-6, 1996. 48p. ill., map. (Legendary heroes of the Wild West).
> Includes glossary, bibliography and index.
> Fremont's varied careers as an explorer, soldier, politician, and land developer are all explained in a slim book illustrated with prints. Of

value in units on the westward movement.
SUBJ: Fremont, John Charles./ Explorers./ Generals./ Presidential candidates.

VCR B FRITZ, J.   Ph-3 5-6 $49.98   OD KE358
TALK WITH JEAN FRITZ (Videocassette). Tim Podell Productions, 1993. 1/2″ VHS videocassette color (20min). (Good conversation!).
   Jean Fritz talks about her childhood in China, her experiences there when she returned recently, and also the process of doing research for her many biographies. Useful for introducing her to young readers and for units on writing.
   SUBJ: Fritz, Jean./ Authors, American./ Women authors, American.

B FULTON, R.   Ph-2 4-5/8 $18.95   L   KE359
BOWEN, ANDY RUSSELL. Head full of notions: a story about Robert Fulton. Illus. by Lisa Harvey. Carolrhoda ISBN 0-87614-876-3, 1997. 64p. ill. (Carolrhoda creative minds book).
   Includes bibliography and index.
   Fulton's many talents led him to painting, but his busy mind prompted him to turn to inventing. Traveling abroad, he developed a submarine for the French, but after his return to the United States, he produced the steamboat which opened up the navigation of the Mississippi River.
   SUBJ: Fulton, Robert./ Inventors./ Steamboats--History.

CE B GALILEO   Ph-2 3-6/6 $16.00   T   KE360
SIS, PETER. Starry messenger: a book depicting the life of a famous scientist, mathematician, astronomer, philosopher, physicist: Galileo Galilei. Farrar Straus Giroux ISBN 0-374-37191-1; In Canada: HarperCollins, 1996. unp. col. ill.
   "Francis Foster books."
   Caldecott Honor book, 1997.
   Talking book available from Recorded Books 95042 (ISBN 0-7887-0904-6, 1997). 1 sound cassette (15min), $10.00.
   Galileo's numerous activities in the world of science and mathematics are detailed in this pictorial biography. His difficulties in having his theories accepted and his perserverance in spite of imprisonment and blindness are all described. Sis' talent as an illustrator is shown in his detailed drawings.
   SUBJ: Galileo./ Scientists.

B GALLAUDET, T.   Ph-2 3-5/6 $17.50   L   KE361
BOWEN, ANDY RUSSELL. World of knowing: a story about Thomas Hopkins Gallaudet. Illus. by Elaine Wadsworth. Carolrhoda ISBN 0-87614-871-2, 1995. 64p. ill. (Carolrhoda creative minds book).
   Includes bibliography and index.
   Thomas Gallaudet's understanding of children with disabilities prompted him to found the first school for deaf persons in the United States. The development of sign language into a useful tool for his students is also described in his life story. Use in units about persons with disabilities and in conjunction with materials on the life of Helen Keller.
   SUBJ: Gallaudet, T. H. (Thomas Hopkins)./ Teachers of the deaf./ Deaf--Education.

B GANDHI, M.   Ph-1 3-6/8 $16.00   L   KE362
FISHER, LEONARD EVERETT. Gandhi. Atheneum ISBN 0-689-80337-0; In Canada: Distican, 1995. unp. ill., map.
   Includes chronology.
   Gandhi's development from a copy of a British gentleman to a political activist who valued intelligence and freedom is carefully traced in this picture-biography. A chronology and afterword make this useful for reports on the man and history of the 20th century. For multicultural studies.
   SUBJ: Gandhi, Mahatma./ Statesmen--India.

B GANDHI, M.   Ph-2 4-6/7 $13.95   L   KE363
LAZO, CAROLINE. Mahatma Gandhi. Dillon ISBN 0-87518-526-6; In Canada: Maxwell Macmillan, 1993. 64p. ill. (Peacemakers).
   Includes bibliography and index.
   Photographs show Gandhi in his many roles--peacemaker, family man, world leader, spinner, and humanitarian. How he developed his philosophy of self-discipline and peaceful force is fully explained and their impact on India and later the world is described. For mature readers.
   SUBJ: Gandhi, Mahatma./ Statesmen--India.

B GEHRIG, L.   Ph-2 5-A/7 $14.95   L   KE364
MACHT, NORMAN L. Lou Gehrig. Introduction by Jim Murray; senior consultant, Earl Weaver. Chelsea House ISBN 0-7910-1176-3, 1993. 64p. ill. (Baseball legends).
   Includes chronology, bibliography and index.
   The "Iron Horse" is known for his 2,130 consecutive games, but he is also remembered for his courageous battle against the disease that

took him out of the starting lineup. The study captures his shyness and good manners while depicting the amazing years that Gehrig played with the Yankees. For all sports fans.
   SUBJ: Gehrig, Lou./ Baseball players./ Amyotrophic lateral sclerosis.

CE B GEORGE III   Ph-3 5-6/7 $13.95   T   KE365
FRITZ, JEAN. Can't you make them behave, King George? Illus. by Tomie De Paola. Coward-McCann/Putnam ISBN 0-698-20315-1, c1977. 45p. ill.
   Talking book available from Weston Woods WW481C, 1977. 1 sound cassette (28min) $8.95.
   Entertaining story of George the Third, King of Great Britain, whose unreasonable taxes enraged the American colonists and whose actions precipitated the American Revolution. Delightful illustrations add zest to the text.
   SUBJ: George III, King of Great Britain./ Great Britain--Kings and rulers./ Great Britain--History--1714-1837--Biography.

B GEORGE, J.   Ph-1 4-6/4 $14.89   L   KE366
GEORGE, JEAN CRAIGHEAD. Tarantula in my purse and 172 other wild pets. HarperCollins ISBN 0-06-023627-2; In Canada: HarperCollins, 1996. 134p. ill.
   George's home was filled with pets of all kinds. The respected naturalist tells how she housed and loved them. A warm, humorous autobiography for animal lovers.
   SUBJ: George, Jean Craighead./ Naturalists./ Women naturalists./ Wild animals as pets.

B GERONIMO   Ph-2 5-6/12 $18.95   L   KE367
HERMANN, SPRING. Geronimo: Apache freedom fighter. Enslow ISBN 0-89490-864-2, 1997. 128p. ill. (Native American biographies).
   Includes chronology, glossary, bibliography and index.
   The sadness of Geronimo's life as his friends, wives, and children are killed by Mexicans and Americans is fully explored. These tragedies help explain his continuing warfare and discontent with reservation life. For multicultural studies.
   SUBJ: Geronimo, Apache Chief./ Apache Indians--Biography./ Indians of North America--Biography.

B GERSHWIN, G.   Ph-3 4-6/7 $17.20   L   KE368
VENEZIA, MIKE. George Gershwin. Childrens Press ISBN 0-516-04536-9; In Canada: Childrens Press, 1994. 32p. col. ill. (Getting to know the world's greatest composers).
   Brief text supplemented with cartoons, photographs, and reproductions of the Gershwins' artwork tells how George's early love of music developed into the talent which brought a new sound to American music. For music appreciation units.
   SUBJ: Gershwin, George./ Composers.

B GOGH, V.   Ph-2 4-6/7 $14.95   T   KE369
HARRISON, PETER. Vincent van Gogh. Sterling ISBN 0-8069-6156-2; In Canada: Sterling c/o Canadian Manda, 1996. 31p. col. ill., map. (Art for young people).
   Originally published in Great Britain as AN INTRODUCTION TO VINCENT VAN GOGH, Macdonald Young Books, 1995.
   Includes chronology, glossary and index.
   Discusses van Gogh's tortured life and passionate paintings with information on his times and the artistic techniques he employed. Excellent for reports and for browsing.
   SUBJ: Gogh, Vincent van./ Artists./ Painting, Dutch./ Art appreciation./ Painting, Modern--19th century--Netherlands.

B GOGH, V.   Ph-3 6-A/9 $10.95   L   KE370
HUGHES, ANDREW. Van Gogh. Barron's ISBN 0-8120-6462-3; In Canada: Barron's, 1994. 32p. col. ill. (Famous artists).
   First published in Great Britain by Watts Books, 1993.
   Includes chronology, glossary and indexes.
   In addition to facts about the artist, the book includes good reproductions of Van Gogh's works with explanations of his techniques. Insets explain scaling up, perspective, sketching, and other basic artistic terms which help the reader better understand the text. For advanced readers.
   SUBJ: Gogh, Vincent van./ Artists./ Painting, Dutch./ Painting, Modern--19th century--Netherlands./ Art appreciation.

B GOLDBERG, W.   Ph-2 4-6/7 $13.95   L   KE371
ADAMS, MARY AGNES. Whoopi Goldberg: from street to stardom. Dillon ISBN 0-87518-562-2; In Canada: Maxwell Macmillan, 1993. 64p. col. ill. (Taking part).
   Includes index.
   Whoopi Goldberg (Karen Johnson) reached the top of her career the hard way after being a welfare mother, a drug user, and divorced. Through it all she knew that she wanted to be an actress. Fans will find more to respect in her when they read this biography filled with

color photographs.
SUBJ: Goldberg, Whoopi./ Entertainers./ Actors and actresses./
Afro-Americans--Biography./ Women entertainers.

B GOODALL, J.   Ph-2 5-A/7 $18.95   L   KE372
MEACHUM, VIRGINIA. Jane Goodall: protector of chimpanzees. Enslow
ISBN 0-89490-827-8, 1997. 104p. ill. (People to know).
    Includes chronology, bibliography and index.
    A favorite toy chimpanzee and numerous books about animals
inspired Jane to be determined to find work with animals. Her
fortunate encounter with Dr. Leakey allowed her to pursue her
dreams. Her unique life studying chimpanzees in Africa is chronicled in
a book highlighted by photographs of Jane at work. For women's
studies.
    SUBJ: Goodall, Jane./ Chimpanzees./ Zoologists./ Women
zoologists.

B GORDON, J.   Ph-2 5-6/7 $14.95   L   KE373
BRINSTER, RICHARD. Jeff Gordon. Chelsea House ISBN 0-7910-4430-0,
1997. 64p. ill. (Race car legends).
    Includes chronology, bibliography and index.
    Gordon is known to racing fans as "The Kid." He raced midget cars
as a boy and was a champion in that sport. Few expected him,
however, to become the youngest driver to win the Daytona 500.
This detailed biography, filled with photographs, explains how he
climbed to the top.
    SUBJ: Gordon, Jeff./ Automobile racing drivers.

B GORE, A.   Ph-3 4-5/6 $12.90   L   KE374
STEFOFF, REBECCA. Al Gore, vice president. Millbrook ISBN 1-56294-
433-9, 1994. 47p. col. ill. (Gateway biography).
    Includes chronology, bibliography and index.
    As vice president, Al Gore has championed his own programs in
technology and ecology. This copiously illustrated text shows his
childhood and family life as well as his political career.
    SUBJ: Gore, Albert./ Vice-Presidents.

B GORMAN, R.C.   Ph-2 3-5/3 $17.95   L   KE375
HERMANN, SPRING. R.C. Gorman: Navajo artist. Enslow ISBN
0-89490-638-0, 1995. 104p. ill. (Multicultural junior biographies).
    Includes chronology, bibliography and index.
    Gorman, a Native American currently living in Taos, New Mexico, is
world known in artistic circles. His kindness to other creative people is
respected and admired. Use in units on Native Americans, multicultural
studies, and artists.
    SUBJ: Gorman, R. C./ Artists./ Navajo Indians--Biography./ Indians
of North America--Biography.

B GOYA, F.   Ph-3 4-5/6 $15.00   L   KE376
VENEZIA, MIKE. Francisco Goya. Childrens Press ISBN 0-516-02292-X;
In Canada: Childrens Press, 1991. 32p. col. ill. (Getting to know the
world's greatest artists).
    Goya's subjects are discussed in this brief text and the young reader
discovers why he painted children, bull fights, historical figures and
the horrors of war. This brief introduction will lead readers to find out
more about this great artist.
    SUBJ: Goya, Francisco./ Artists./ Painting, Spanish./ Art
appreciation.

B GRANT, U.   Ph-2 6-A/6 $18.98   L   KE377
RICKARBY, LAURA ANN. Ulysses S. Grant and the strategy of victory.
Silver Burdett ISBN 0-382-09944-3, 1991. 125p. ill. (some col.). (History
of the Civil War).
    Includes timetable, bibliography and index.
    Shunning aristocratic men at West Point, Grant was known for his
careless dress and shyness. These characteristics he carried with him
as he commanded the Union forces and became president. This
biography focuses on Grant's remarkable military skills and his
problems outside the army. For students interested in the battles of
the Civil War.
    SUBJ: Grant, Ulysses S./ Generals./ Presidents./ United States--
History--Civil War, 1861-1865.

VCR B GRANT, U.   Ph-3 6-A $19.95   KE378
ULYSSES S. GRANT (Videocassette). Atlas Video ISBN 0-945716-12-5,
1989. 1/2" VHS videocassette color (30min). (Civil War Generals).
    Study of Grant's many careers - shop clerk, general of the Union
Army and 18th president. For units on the Civil War and the
presidency.
    SUBJ: Grant, Ulysses S./ Generals./ Presidents./ United States--
History--Civil War, 1861-1865.

B GRETZKY, W.   Ph-2 3-6/7 $4.50   P   KE379
CHRISTOPHER, MATT. On the ice with...Wayne Gretzky. Little, Brown
ISBN 0-316-13789-8; In Canada: Little, Brown, 1997. 133p. ill. (Matt
Christopher sports biographies).
    Wayne Gretzky's love of ice hockey was encouraged by his parents
who turned their backyard into a rink for their son. Further proof of
their dedication to their son's career was shown when they allowed
him to live away from home with supportive fans, so that he could
play. His amazing rise to being a superstar is traced here in a
comprehensive study.
    SUBJ: Gretzky, Wayne./ Hockey players--Canada--Biography.

B GRIFFEY,K. JR   Ph-2 3-6/6 $4.50   P   KE380
CHRISTOPHER, MATT. At the plate with...Ken Griffey Jr. Little, Brown
ISBN 0-316-14233-6; In Canada: Little, Brown, 1997. 121p. ill. (Matt
Christopher sports biographies).
    Includes chronology.
    As a boy, Junior ran around the locker room while his father played
major league baseball. His talents led him to soon follow in his
father's footsteps. This detailed biography relates his failures as well
as his many successes as he led the Seattle Mariners to become one
of baseball's greatest teams.
    SUBJ: Griffey, Ken, Jr./ Baseball players./ Afro-Americans--
Biography.

B GRIFFEY,K. JR   Ph-2 4-5/4 $19.95   L   KE381
KRAMER, BARBARA. Ken Griffey Junior: all-around all-star. Lerner ISBN
0-8225-2887-8, 1996. 64p. col. ill. (Achievers).
    Junior grew up watching his dad play baseball and learning the rules
of the game from him. This colorful chronicle of Griffey's
achievements includes much of this family's devotion to each other.
For multicultural studies.
    SUBJ: Griffey, Ken, Jr./ Baseball players./ Afro-Americans--
Biography.

B GUTENBERG, J.   Ph-1 5-A/8 $14.95   T   KE382
FISHER, LEONARD EVERETT. Gutenberg. Macmillan ISBN 0-02-
735238-2; In Canada: Maxwell Macmillan, 1993. unp. ill., map.
    Includes chronology.
    Oversized black and white drawings show Gutenberg struggling to
develop his printing process and keep his business alive in spite of
court trials and other setbacks. Like Gutenberg's products, this is an
example of fine bookmaking.
    SUBJ: Gutenberg, Johann./ Printers./ Printing--History.

CE B HANCOCK, J.   Ph-2 5-6/7 $5.95   P   KE383
FRITZ, JEAN. Will you sign here, John Hancock? Illus. by Trina Schart
Hyman. Coward-McCann/Putnam ISBN 0-698-20308-9, c1976, 1997.
47p. col. ill.
    Talking book available from Weston Woods WW480C, 1977. 1
sound cassette (29min) $8.95.
    Available from National Library Service for the Blind and Physically
Handicapped on sound recording cassette RC11807.
    Follows the life of the first signer of the Declaration of Independence
from his boyhood through his governorship of Massachusetts, and
includes his many contributions to the new nation.
    SUBJ: Hancock, John./ Statesmen./ United States--History--
Revolution, 1775-1783--Biography.

B HARDAWAY, A.   Ph-2 3-5/6 $19.95   L   KE384
TOWNSEND, BRAD. Anfernee Hardaway: basketball's lucky penny.
Lerner ISBN 0-8225-3652-8, 1997. 64p. col. ill.
    Incudes glossary, index and directory.
    Poor grades in high school sometimes kept Anfernee from playing
basketball, and low college boards kept him off the courts when he
entered college. Yet this determined young man proved that he could
overcome these setbacks as he did the poverty into which he was
born. Hardaway is a true role model for students struggling against
great odds. Filled with action photographs. For multicultural studies.
    SUBJ: Hardaway, Anfernee./ Basketball players./ Afro-Americans--
Biography.

B HELLER, R.   Ph-2 4-6/2 $13.95   T   KE385
HELLER, RUTH. Fine lines. Photos by Michael Emery. Richard C. Owens
ISBN 1-878450-76-X, 1996. 32p. col. ill., map. (Meet the author).
    Ruth Heller's interest in art developed after her sons went to school
and she tried many fields. In the 70s she developed an idea for a
picture book which was published in the 80s. Since that time, her
efforts have been dedicated to producing fine illustrations. Her
techniques are explained in the text.
    SUBJ: Heller, Ruth./ Illustrators./ Illustration of books./ Women
illustrators.

CE B HENRY, P. Ph-1 5-6/7 $13.95 T KE386
FRITZ, JEAN. Where was Patrick Henry on the 29th of May? Illus. by Margot Tomes. Coward-McCann/Putnam ISBN 0-698-20307-0, c1975, 1982. 47p. col. ill.
Selectors' Choice, 19th ed.
Talking book available from Weston Woods WW477C, 1977. 1 sound cassette (29min) $8.95.
Available from National Library Service for the Blind and Physically Handicapped on sound recording cassette RC12490.
A colorful and human portrait of a Revolutionary War figure who was a man of many talents, but most important was his dedication and devotion to his country. Where was he on the 29th of May?
SUBJ: Henry, Patrick./ Statesmen./ United States--History--Colonial period, ca. 1600-1775--Biography.

B HENRY, PRINCE Ph-2 4-6/6 $14.95 T KE387
FISHER, LEONARD EVERETT. Prince Henry the Navigator. Macmillan ISBN 0-02-735231-5; In Canada: Collier Macmillan, 1990. unp. ill.
Portugal controlled the waterways in the 15th century, but to remain rich, she had to find a route to India. The young Prince Henry set out to do this by establishing a navigation school and sending out ships for exploration. Dramatic black and white drawings complement the text of this tale of the man who set out to chart the seas.
SUBJ: Henry the Navigator./ Explorers.

VCR B HENSON, M. Ph-3 5-A $39.95 KE388
MATTHEW HENSON (Videocassette). Schlessinger D6619 ISBN 1-879151-30-8, 1994. 1/2" VHS videocassette color (30min). (Black Americans of achievement video collection).
Based on the book MATTHEW HENSON, Chelsea House, (ISBN 1-55546-590-0, 1988).
Closed captioned.
Henson's explorations of the Arctic Region with Admiral Peary, their discovery of the North Pole, and his friendships with the indigenous population are depicted. For units on exploration, African-American history, and multicultural studies.
SUBJ: Henson, Matthew Alexander./ Explorers./ Afro-Americans--Biography.

B HIAWATHA Ph-2 5-6/7 $14.95 L KE389
FRADIN, DENNIS B. Hiawatha: messenger of peace. McElderry ISBN 0-689-50519-1; In Canada: Maxwell Macmillan, 1992. 40p. col. ill.
Includes bibliography and index.
Tormented by the warring he saw within his own tribe and neighboring tribes, Hiawatha devised a plan of council meetings to settle disputes. The Native-American efforts for self-government may have had lasting impact on the American government. A probing study which portrays Hiawatha as a creative leader. For mature readers.
SUBJ: Hiawatha./ Iroquois Indians--Biography./ Iroquois Indians--Tribal government.

B HILL, G. Ph-2 5-6/7 $14.40 L KE390
GUTMAN, BILL. Grant Hill: basketball's high flier. Millbrook ISBN 0-7613-0038-4, 1996. 48p. col. ill. (Millbrook sports world).
Includes chronology, bibliography, directory and index.
Hill's unexpected popularity with basketball fans is due to his ability, his determination to learn all facets of the sport, and his good character. Briefly mentions the professional football career of his father Calvin Hill.
SUBJ: Hill, Grant./ Basketball players./ Afro-Americans--Biography.

B HORNER, J. Ph-2 5-A/8 $4.95 P KE391
LESSEM, DON. Jack Horner: living with dinosaurs. Illus. by Janet Hamlin. W. H. Freeman ISBN 0-7167-6549-7, 1994. 48p. ill., map. (Science superstars).
"Scientific American books for young readers."
Includes index/glossary, directory and bibliography.
Available from the National Library Service for the Blind and Physically Handicapped on sound recording cassette RC39834.
As a young boy, Jack Horner began his search for dinosaur bones. Hampered in formal school studies because he was dyslexic, Horner never finished college. His dedication to paleontology, however, led him to become a leading expert in the field. Today, much of what we know about dinosaurs is the result of his efforts. For science students.
SUBJ: Horner, John R./ Paleontologists.

B HOUSTON, S. Ph-2 6/7 $13.95 T KE392
FRITZ, JEAN. Make way for Sam Houston. Illus. by Elise Primavera. Putnam ISBN 0-399-21303-1; In Canada: General, 1986. 109p. ill.
Selectors' Choice, 16th ed.
Available from National Library Service for the Blind and Physically Handicapped on sound recording cassette RC24715.
Assuming many roles in dress as well as actions during his lifetime,

Sam Houston was an adopted Indian, Indian advocate, Army officer, lawyer, governor, congressman, and one of the founding fathers of Texas. The many facets of this man's character and career are discussed here. For history classes as well as being an adventure story.
Includes bibliography and index.
SUBJ: Houston, Sam./ Governors./ Legislators./ Texas--History--To 1846.

B HUGHES, A. Ph-1 3-5/4 $14.89 L KE393
HOUSTON, GLORIA. My great-aunt Arizona. Illus. by Susan Condie Lamb. HarperCollins ISBN 0-06-022607-2; In Canada: HarperCollins, 1992. unp. col. ill.
Selectors' Choice, 19th ed.
This tribute to a teacher who influenced the author is the perfect picture book to introduce youngsters to the joys of teaching whether in a one-room schoolhouse or a modern building. Drawings enhance the simple text complementing the work.
SUBJ: Hughes, Arizona Houston./ Teachers.

B HUGHES, L. Ph-2 3-5/6 $15.95 L KE394
COOPER, FLOYD. Coming home: from the life of Langston Hughes. Philomel ISBN 0-399-22682-6; In Canada: Putnam, 1994. unp. col. ill.
Includes bibliography.
Hughes' childhood during which he lived at different times with his Granma, mother, father, and a foster family, the Reeds, is portrayed in text and large, comforting pictures. The effects of this lonely, varied existence showed in his verse and lifelong wonderings. This portrait of a lonely child can be used to explain segregation and its impact on children in African-American families. For multicultural studies.
SUBJ: Hughes, Langston--Childhood and youth./ Afro-Americans--Biography./ Poets, American.

B HUGHES, L. Ph-2 6-A/7 $16.00 L KE395
OSOFSKY, AUDREY. Free to dream: the making of a poet: Langston Hughes. Lothrop, Lee & Shepard ISBN 0-688-10606-4, 1996. 112p. ill.
Includes music.
Includes bibliography and index.
Langston Hughes' childhood of loneliness and neglect by his parents is covered as background to his amazing determination to be educated and write poetry. Well-chosen photographs and prints show the poet, his family, and the world in which he lived. The insightful biography of a poet who wrote for children as well as adults has value for author studies as well as multicultural studies.
SUBJ: Hughes, Langston./ Poets, American./ Afro-Americans--Biography.

B HURSTON, Z. Ph-1 6-A/6 $13.95 L KE396
LYONS, MARY E. Sorrow's kitchen: the life and folklore of Zora Neale Hurston. Scribner's ISBN 0-684-19198-9; In Canada: Collier Macmillan, 1990. 144p. ill.
Includes bibliographies and index.
By incorporating sections from Hurston's books, the author brings this determined woman vividly alive. Her childhood in Florida, trips to Haiti, Jamaica and other folklore gathering jaunts are discussed along with the role racial discrimination played in her life.
SUBJ: Hurston, Zora Neale./ Authors, American./ Afro-Americans--Biography./ Afro-American authors./ Women authors, American.

VCR B JACKSON, A. Ph-3 6-A $30.00 OD KE397
ANDREW JACKSON: THE PEOPLE'S PRESIDENT (Videocassette). Clearvue/EAV AH012-CV, 1990. 1/2" VHS videocassette color (15min). (American portraits).
Includes Teacher's Guide.
Jackson's role as advocate of the common man and his tragic family life are discussed in this video to give viewers a better understanding of his years as president. Film moves quickly and gives excellent coverage of the War of 1812 and the development of the Spoils System.
SUBJ: Jackson, Andrew./ Presidents.

B JACKSON, B. Ph-2 4-5/6 $22.83 L KE398
KRAMER, JON. Bo Jackson. Raintree Steck-Vaughn ISBN 0-8172-4123-X, 1996. 48p. col. ill. (Overcoming the odds).
Includes chronology, bibliography and index.
Jackson's amazing feats in baseball and football are chronicled with a tribute to his amazing comeback after a hip replacement. An inspirational book as well as a sports story. Color photographs show him in all aspects of his life. A biography for multicultural studies.
SUBJ: Jackson, Bo./ Football players./ Baseball players./ Afro-Americans--Biography.

B JACKSON, T.   Ph-1 5-A/8 $15.95   T   KE399
FRITZ, JEAN. Stonewall. Illus. by Stephen Gammell. Putnam ISBN 0-399-20698-1; In Canada: Longman, 1979. 152p. ill.
> Includes bibliography.
> Selectors' Choice, 13th ed.
> Available from National Library Service for the Blind and Physically Handicapped on sound recording cassette RC18386.
> Thomas Jackson's complex, contradictory personality (courageous, cruelly competitive, with an exaggerated attention to detail and fanatic devotion to goodness, self righteous) and his choice of a military career forged a hero, brilliant in battle, a great military leader in the tragic conflict of the Civil War.
> SUBJ: Jackson, Thomas./ United States--History--Civil War, 1861-1865--Biography./ United States--History--Civil War, 1861-1865--Campaigns./ Generals.

VCR B JACKSON, T.   Ph-3 6-A $19.95   KE400
STONEWALL JACKSON (Videocassette). Atlas Video ISBN 0-945716-11-7, 1989. 1/2" VHS videocassette color (30min). (Civil War Generals).
> Stressing Jackson's military genius, this presentation includes material on his idiosyncrasies and discussion of his death's impact on the outcome of the Civil War. For the history buff.
> SUBJ: Jackson, Thomas Jonathan./ United States--History--Civil War, 1861-1865--Biography./ Generals.

B JAMES, D.   Ph-2 5-A/6 $14.95   L   KE401
SUPER, NEIL. Daniel "Chappie" James. Twenty-First Century ISBN 0-8050-2138-8, 1992. 80p. ill. (African-American soldiers).
> Includes chronology, index and bibliography.
> Chappie James' record is an outstanding one. He fought in three wars, but his greatest battle was for civil rights and respect for the role of the African-American soldier in defending the United States. Well illustrated work equally valuable in units on World War II, the Korean War, the Vietnam War, and African-American history.
> SUBJ: James, Daniel./ Generals./ Afro-Americans--Biography.

B JAMES, J.   Ph-3 4-6/10 $14.95   L   KE402
WUKOVITS, JOHN F. Jesse James. By John Wukovits. Chelsea House ISBN 0-7910-3876-9, 1997. 64p. ill., map. (Legends of the West).
> Includes chronology, bibliography and index.
> A balanced presentation of his strengths and weaknesses explores James' career as a bank robber and killer. There is a clear explanation of how his service in the Confederate Army honed his skills as a guerrilla and scout. Illustrated by black and white photographs, the book explains a period of United States history which had been glamorized in the past in pulp fiction.
> SUBJ: James, Jesse./ Robbers and outlaws./ Frontier and pioneer life--West (U.S.)./ West (U.S.)--History.

B JEFFERSON, T.   Ph-2 2-3/5 $14.95   L   KE403
ADLER, DAVID A. Picture book of Thomas Jefferson. Illustrated by John and Alexandra Wallner. Holiday House ISBN 0-8234-0791-8, 1990. unp. col. ill. (Picture book biography).
> Double page spread full color pictures and scant text trace Jefferson's life. Distinctly on the light side, this picture biography is for upper primary graders.
> SUBJ: Jefferson, Thomas./ Presidents.

B JEFFERSON, T.   Ph-2 3-5/5 $16.95   L   KE404
GIBLIN, JAMES CROSS. Thomas Jefferson: a picture book biography. Illus. by Michael Dooling. Scholastic ISBN 0-590-44838-2; In Canada: Scholastic, 1994. 48p. col. ill.
> Includes chronology and index.
> Watercolors capture the countryside which Jefferson loved and the mansion which he created in this pictorial study of the major events in his life.
> SUBJ: Jefferson, Thomas./ Presidents.

B JEMISON, M.   Ph-3 5-A/8 $17.50   T   KE405
SEAVER, JAMES E. Captured by Indians: the life of Mary Jemison. Edited by Karen Zienert. Linnet ISBN 0-208-02368-2, 1995. 104p. ill., maps.
> Includes chronology, glossary, bibliography and directory.
> Mary Jemison was captured by a raiding party of Frenchmen and Shawnee after her family was killed. She adjusted to the Native American way of life and was befriended by several Seneca women. Mary later married a Delaware and had eight children. The abridgement of the original account omits Seaver's opinions and presents Mary's story without comment. Though a scholarly presentation, it will find a wide audience of interested children. For multicultural studies.
> SUBJ: Jemison, Mary./ Pioneers./ Indians of North America--Captivities./ Women pioneers.

B JOHNSON, L.   Ph-2 6-A/9 $17.25   L   KE406
FALKOF, LUCILLE. Lyndon B. Johnson, 36th president of the United states. Garrett ISBN 0-944483-20-8, 1989. 120p b&w photos. (Presidents of the United States).
> Includes bibliography and index.
> Covers Johnson's youth in Texas, his career in Congress, his ascension to the Presidency through tragedy, and the major points of his administration.
> SUBJ: Johnson, Lyndon B./ Presidents.

B JOPLIN, S.   Ph-3 A/8 $14.95   L   KE407
MITCHELL, BARBARA. Raggin', a story about Scott Joplin. Carolrhoda ISBN 0-87614-310-9, 1987. 55p. ill. (Carolrhoda creative minds book).
> Setting out to introduce people to music which incorporated African melodies, Joplin traveled from Texas to New York City. This biography shows that even when a man is graced with an abundance of musical talent, it takes great determination to become a major composer. A worthy addition to collections on American musicians.
> SUBJ: Joplin, Scott./ Composers./ Afro-Americans--Biography.

B JORDAN, B.   Ph-3 4-6/8 $22.83   L   KE408
PATRICK-WEXLER, DIANE. Barbara Jordan. Raintree Steck-Vaughn ISBN 0-8172-3976-6, 1996. 48p. ill. (some col.). (Contemporary African Americans).
> Includes chronology, glossary, bibliography and index.
> Barbara Jordan as a child felt great respect for her hardworking grandfather and also the pain of racial segregation. As an adult and political spokesperson, she continued her fight for the working people and for equal rights for all people. Illustrated with photographs which show her in many political settings. For multicultural studies and women's studies.
> SUBJ: Jordan, Barbara./ Legislators./ Afro-Americans--Biography./ Women in politics./ United States. Congress. House--Biography.

CE B JORDAN, M.   Ph-2 4-6/8 $4.50   P   KE409
CHRISTOPHER, MATT. On the court with...Michael Jordan. Little, Brown ISBN 0-316-13792-8; In Canada: Little, Brown, 1996. 128p. ill. (Matt Christopher sports biographies).
> Talking book available from Recorded Books 94944 (ISBN 0-7887-0794-9, 1997). 3 sound cassettes (180min), $26.00.
> Jordan's remarkable career and his ability to remain humble as he strives to improve are covered in this comprehensive biography. A section of black and white photographs shows the athlete's amazing jumping ability. For multicultural studies.
> SUBJ: Jordan, Michael./ Basketball players./ Afro-Americans--Biography.

B JORDAN, M.   Ph-2 4-6/8 $14.40   L   KE410
GUTMAN, BILL. Michael Jordan: basketball to baseball and back. Rev. ed. Millbrook ISBN 1-56294-924-1, 1995. 48p. col. ill. (Millbrook sports world).
> Includes chronology, bibliography, directory and index.
> Jordan's versatility and drive have made him one of the outstanding athletes of the 80s and 90s. This study of his childhood grief and successes, his devotion to his family, and his ability to put being a team player ahead of professional glory make this a book to inspire young athletes. Attractive layout includes many full-color photographs.
> SUBJ: Jordan, Michael./ Basketball players./ Afro-Americans--Biography.

B JORDAN, M.   Ph-1 4-6/7 $14.89   L   KE411
LIPSYTE, ROBERT. Michael Jordan: a life above the rim. HarperCollins ISBN 0-06-024235-3; In Canada: HarperCollins, 1994. 106p. ill. (Superstar lineup).
> Includes bibliography and index.
> Jordan's abilities are described vividly plus his dedication to his family, his advertising successes, and his interaction with other basketball stars by an author who writes with style and enthusiasm. Interwoven with the star's life is the history of basketball and the rise of the African-American athlete after World War II. For multicultural studies.
> SUBJ: Jordan, Michael./ Basketball players./ Afro-Americans--Biography.

B JOYNER-KERSEE   Ph-3 4-6/6 $4.95   P   KE412
COHEN, NEIL. Jackie Joyner-Kersee. Sports Illustrated for Kids/Little, Brown ISBN 0-316-15047-9; In Canada: Little, Brown, 1992. 124p col illus and photos.
> Includes glossary.
> Three d's mark Jackie Kersee's life--desire, dedication, and determination. Her struggles and successes are fully related in this biography which brings her to the time of the summer games in Spain. Motivational reading.
> SUBJ: Joyner-Kersee, Jacqueline./ Track and field athletes./ Afro-Americans--Biography./ Women athletes.

B KAIULANI   Ph-3 5-6/7 $16.95   L   KE413
STANLEY, FAY. Last princess: the story of Princess Kaiulani of Hawaii. Illus. by Diane Stanley. Four Winds/Macmillan ISBN 0-02-786785-4; In Canada: Collier Macmillan, 1991. 40p. col. ill.
  Includes bibliography.
  Bells rang out to announce Princess Ka'iulani's birth and although it seemed certain that one day she would rule over the Hawaiian Islands, the monarchy was abolished before she could take the throne. Her story is an adventure with a tragic ending. Useful for social studies units on Hawaii or changing governments.
  SUBJ: Kaiulani, Princess of Hawaii./ Princesses./ Hawaii--History.

B KEHRET, P.   Ph-2 2-5/5 $14.95   L   KE414
KEHRET, PEG. Small steps: the year I got polio. Whitman ISBN 0-8075-7457-0; In Canada: General, 1996. 179p. ill.
  Peg Schulze Kehret relates how she contracted polio and her treatments during her stay in a rehab facility. Her friends come vividly alive, and in an epilogue, she tells the reader how they fared in later life. This autobiography will inform readers about a fearful time for youngsters when polio wasn't controlled and left many disabled. Use to complement units on persons with disabilities.
  SUBJ: Kehret, Peg./ Authors, American./ Poliomyelitis--Patients--Rehabilitation./ Women authors, American.

VCR B KELLER, H.   Ph-1 4-6 $69.95   OD KE415
HELEN KELLER (Videocassette). Films for the Humanities 1837A, 1990. 1/2" VHS videocassette color (10min). (Against the odds).
  By using family photos, newsreel excerpts and material from Helen Keller's own writings, this video gives a full explanation of how she developed speech and became a leader in the women's rights movement. Useful to illustrate overcoming physical challenges or accomplishments of American women.
  SUBJ: Keller, Helen./ Blind--Biography./ Deaf--Biography./ Physically handicapped--Biography.

B KELLER, H.   Ph-3 6-A/8 $3.50   P   KE416
KELLER, HELEN. Story of my life. Bantam ISBN 0-553-21387-3; In Canada: Bantam, c1988, 1990. 225p.
  In her own words comes the story of Helen Keller's struggles to overcome blindness and deafness, and her relationship with her devoted teacher and friend, Anne Sullivan. For the advanced reader.
  SUBJ: Keller, Helen./ Physically handicapped--Biography./ Blind--Biography./ Deaf--Biography.

B KELLER, H.   Ph-2 1-2/1 $3.50   P   KE417
LUNDELL, MARGO. Girl named Helen Keller. Illus. by Irene Trivas. Scholastic ISBN 0-590-47963-6; In Canada: Scholastic, 1995. unp. col. ill. (Hello reader!).
  "Cartwheel books."
  Explains the illness which robbed Helen of sight and hearing, her struggles to understand hand signing, and her success when she learned the word "water." Inspirational.
  SUBJ: Keller, Helen./ Blind--Biography./ Deaf--Biography./ Physically handicapped--Biography.

B KENNEDY, J.   Ph-1 6-A/8 $18.00   T   KE418
HARRISON, BARBARA. Twilight struggle: the life of John Fitzgerald Kennedy. By Barbara Harrison and Daniel Terris. Lothrop, Lee & Shepard ISBN 0-688-08830-9, 1992. 159p. ill.
  Includes bibliographies, chronology and index.
  Kennedy's childhood, Navy experiences, marriage and family, and presidency are all detailed in this account which makes the man very human, pragmatic as well as idealistic. For mature readers.
  SUBJ: Kennedy, John Fitzgerald./ Presidents.

B KING, C.S.   Ph-2 3-5/3 $13.99   T   KE419
MEDEARIS, ANGELA SHELF. Dare to dream: Coretta Scott King and the civil rights movement. Illus. by Anna Rich. Lodestar/Dutton ISBN 0-525-67426-8; In Canada; McClelland & Stewart, 1994. 60p. ill. (Rainbow biography).
  Includes bibliographies and index.
  Available from the National Library Service for the Blind and Physically Handicapped on sound recording cassette RC 41326.
  A childhood filled with racial mistreatment prepared Coretta Scott to be a partner with Martin Luther King, Jr. in the battle to gain equality for African Americans. A sensitive retelling of Mrs. King's childhood, career aspirations, and role in the civil rights movement. For multicultural studies.
  SUBJ: King, Coretta Scott./ Civil rights workers./ Civil rights movements--History./ Afro-Americans--Biography./ Women civil rights workers.

CE B KING, M.L.   Ph-3 3-4/4 $14.95   L   KE420
ADLER, DAVID A. Picture book of Martin Luther King, Jr. Illustrated by Robert Casilla. Holiday House ISBN 0-8234-0770-5, 1989. unp. col. ill. (Picture book biography).
  Includes "Important dates."
  Available in Spanish UN LIBRO ILUSTRADO SOBRE MARTIN LUTHER KING, HIJO (ISBN 0-8234-0982-1, 1992).
  Videocassette available from Live Oak (ISBN 0-87499-164-1, 1990). 1/2" VHS videocassette color (10min), $37.95.
  Read-along kit available from Live Oak (ISBN 0-87499-166-8, 1990). 1 hardcover book, 1 sound cassette (9min), $19.95.
  Read-along kit available in Spanish UN LIBRO ILUSTRADO SOBRE MARTIN LUTHER KING, HIJO (ISBN 0-87499-297-4, 1993, Must order direct). 1 hardcover book, 1 sound cassette (14min), $22.50.
  The impact of childhood cruelty on King and his ability to rise above it in childhood and adult life are stressed in this amply illustrated text.
  SUBJ: King, Martin Luther, Jr./ Clergy./ Civil rights workers./ Afro-Americans--Biography.

B KING, M.L.   Ph-2 2-6/7 $15.93   L   KE421
BRAY, ROSEMARY L. Martin Luther King. Illus. by Malcah Zeldis. Greenwillow ISBN 0-688-13132-8, 1995. 48p. col. ill.
  Includes chronology.
  Folk artist Malcah Zeldis graphically pictures the major events in King's life so that readers can imagine themselves sharing in the events which shaped his and American history. The text develops concepts which clarify many of King's ideals and actions. In picture book format, but can be used on all levels. For multicultural studies.
  SUBJ: King, Martin Luther, Jr./ Civil rights workers./ Clergy./ Civil rights movements--History./ Afro-Americans--Biography.

B KING, M.L.   Ph-2 1-5/5 $14.95   L   KE422
MARZOLLO, JEAN. Happy Birthday, Martin Luther King. Illus. by J. Brian Pinkney. Scholastic ISBN 0-590-44065-9; In Canada: Scholastic, 1993. unp. col. ill.
  Simplicity is the keynote of this book. Dramatic illustrations capture the major events of King's life which are explained in an abbreviated text. For use in African-American history and civil rights units.
  SUBJ: King, Martin Luther, Jr./ Civil rights workers./ Afro-Americans--Biography.

B KING, M.L.   Ph-2 3-5/7 $18.99   L   KE423
RINGGOLD, FAITH. My dream of Martin Luther King. Crown ISBN 0-517-59977-5, 1995. unp. col. ill.
  Includes chronology and bibliography.
  The major events in Martin Luther King, Jr.'s life are related as if in a child's dream. The dream includes a hope that prejudices, hate, and ignorance can be replaced by hope, freedom, and love. The strength of the book lies in the illustrations which are more subdued (in keeping with the subject) than much of Ringgold's work. For multicultural studies.
  SUBJ: King, Martin Luther, Jr./ Civil rights workers./ Clergy./ Afro-Americans--Biography.

B KIPLING, R.   Ph-3 3-6/2 $17.20   L   KE424
GREENE, CAROL. Rudyard Kipling: author of the "Jungle books." Childrens Press ISBN 0-516-04266-1; In Canada: Childrens Press, 1994. 47p. ill. (some col.). (Rookie biography).
  Includes chronology and index.
  Briefly describes Kipling's troubled childhood, travels, and family which prompted many of his stories. Numerous photographs augment the text. Use to introduce the author's material in the library and classroom.
  SUBJ: Kipling, Rudyard./ Authors, English.

B KRONE, J.   Ph-2 5-6/5 $22.83   L   KE425
GUTMAN, BILL. Julie Krone. Raintree Steck-Vaughn ISBN 0-8172-4121-3, 1996. 48p. col. ill. (Overcoming the odds).
  Includes chronology, bibliography and index.
  Julie Krone's entire life has centered around horses. Her struggle to gain recognition in a male-dominated sport, setbacks due to injuries, and stunning recovery and return to racing are examined in a biography filled with color photographs.
  SUBJ: Krone, Julie./ Jockeys./ Women athletes.

B KUSKIN, K.   Ph-2 2-5/6 $13.95   T   KE426
KUSKIN, KARLA. Thoughts, pictures, and words. Photos by Nicholas Kuskin. Richard C. Owen ISBN 1-878450-41-7, 1995. 32p. col. ill., map. (Meet the author).
  A motivational autobiography to inspire young writers to follow Kuskin's way of finding ideas for her writings and illustrations. Photographs, taken by Kuskin's son, create the feeling that the reader has been personally invited into her home and inner thoughts.
  SUBJ: Kuskin, Karla./ Authors, American./ Authorship./ Women authors, American.

NONFICTION

B LANGE, D. Ph-2 5-A/7 $15.95 T KE427
TURNER, ROBYN. Dorothea Lange. By Robin Montana Turner. Little, Brown ISBN 0-316-85656-8; In Canada: Little, Brown, 1994. 32p. ill. (Portraits of women artists for children).
As a teenager, Lange was determined to be a photographer, and later she concentrated on portraits. Her portraits of people during the Depression and of migrant workers during the 30s and 40s have made her world renowned. A study of an individual who fought through problems and who focused the world's attention on great social problems. Useful for women's studies and both art and social studies classes.
SUBJ: Lange, Dorothea./ Photographers./ Women photographers.

B LAW, R. Ph-2 2-3/4 $13.95 L KE428
BROWN, DON. Ruth Law thrills a nation. Ticknor & Fields ISBN 0-395-66404-7, 1993. unp. col. ill.
Brief description of the first American woman to attempt to fly non-stop from Chicago to New York City in 1916. Sprightly pictures capture the humor and drama of her almost successful effort that broke existing flight records.
SUBJ: Law, Ruth./ Air pilots./ Women air pilots./ Cross-country flying.

B LEE, R. Ph-3 2-5/5 $15.95 L KE429
ADLER, DAVID A. Picture book of Robert E. Lee. Illus. by John and Alexandra Wallner. Holiday House ISBN 0-8234-1111-7, 1994. unp. col. ill. (Picture book biography).
Includes chronology.
Lee's character is shown through his early care for and devotion to his mother, his hatred of war, and his dedication to his men during the Civil War. For readers interested in major military figures.
SUBJ: Lee, Robert E./ Generals./ United States--History--Civil War, 1861-1865--Biography.

B LEE, R. Ph-3 4-5/6 $12.95 L KE430
KAVANAGH, JACK. Robert E. Lee. by Jack Kavanagh and Eugene C. Murdoch. Chelsea Juniors ISBN 0-7910-1768-0, 1995. 79p. ill. (Junior world biographies).
Includes bibliography, glossary, chronology and index.
Photographs of Lee and the men who served under him and of other scenes of the Civil War make this study of a distinguished general come alive.
SUBJ: Lee, Robert E./ Generals./ United States--History--Civil War, 1861-1865--Biography.

VCR B LEE, R. Ph-1 5-6 $19.95 KE431
ROBERT E. LEE (Videocassette). Atlas Video ISBN 0-945716-09-5, 1989. 1/2" VHS videocassette color (30min). (Civil War Generals).
By visiting Lee's homes and various Civil War battlefields, Lee's story is told quietly and respectfully. This historically sound video could be used in class units or viewed independently.
SUBJ: Lee, Robert E./ United States--History--Civil War, 1861-1865--Biography./ Generals.

B LEEUWENHOEK,A Ph-2 5-A/5 $18.95 L KE432
YOUNT, LISA. Antoni van Leeuwenhoek: first to see microscopic life. Enslow ISBN 0-89490-680-1, 1996. 128p. ill., map. (Great minds of science).
Includes chronology, glossary, bibliography and index.
Uneducated but with a great curiosity, Leeuwenhoek discovered many things for the first time: cells, microscopic animals, and sperm. His reporting of these findings earned him a place in the Royal Society of London and the respect of scientists. For mature science students.
SUBJ: Leeuwenhoek, Antoni van./ Biologists./ Microscopes./ Microscope and microscopy.

B LEMIEUX, M. Ph-3 4-6/9 $18.95 L KE433
HUGHES, MORGAN E. Mario Lemieux: beating the odds. Lerner ISBN 0-8225-2884-3, 1996. 64p. col. ill. (Achievers).
Mario is known as the comeback kid of ice hockey. This pictorial presentation of his life traces his childhood devotion to the sport, his ability to play in spite of great pain from injuries which he feels were unjustly caused by other players, and his battle against Hodgkin's disease. For hockey enthusiasts.
SUBJ: Lemieux, Mario./ Hockey players.

B LEONARDO Ph-3 4-6/7 $17.95 T KE434
PROVENSEN, ALICE. Leonardo da Vinci. By Alice and Martin Provensen. Viking ISBN 0-670-42384-X, 1984. unp. col. ill.
Astounding the world with his multifaceted genius, Leonardo da Vinci's major accomplishments as artist, engineer, astronomer are captured in this pop-up book. This delightful creation will tantalize students when placed on display in media centers or used in book talks and other programs.
SUBJ: Leonardo, da Vinci./ Inventors./ Artists.

B LEONARDO Ph-1 5-A/8 $15.93 L KE435
STANLEY, DIANE. Leonardo da Vinci. Morrow ISBN 0-688-10438-X, 1996. unp. col. ill.
Includes bibliographies.
The life of an illegitimate boy whose amazing curiosity and talents developed in spite of his lack of education is captured in text and detailed paintings. The author stresses the information drawn from Leonardo's notebooks and how science could have benefited if these writings had been published earlier. A book with multiple uses in art and science units.
SUBJ: Leonardo, da Vinci./ Artists./ Inventors./ Art appreciation.

B LESTER, H. Ph-1 2-5/2 $10.95 L KE436
LESTER, HELEN. Author: a true story. Houghton Mifflin ISBN 0-395-82744-2, 1997. 32p. col. ill.
"Walter Lorraine books."
A winsome little girl begins the story of how one determined teacher (who loved to write) became an author. Lester is frank in this brief autobiography about her failures (rejections) and her successes (published books). Her amusing self-portraits will delight struggling young authors. A book to inspire any creative writing project.
SUBJ: Lester, Helen./ Authors, American./ Women authors, American./ Authorship.

B LIN, M. Ph-2 4-6/10 $24.26 L KE437
LING, BETTINA. Maya Lin. Raintree Steck-Vaughn ISBN 0-8172-3992-8, 1997. 48p. col. ill. (Contemporary Asian Americans).
Includes chronology, glossary, bibliography and index.
Maya Lin designed the Vietnam Veterans Memorial as a project during her senior year at Yale University where she was studying sculpture and architecture. Her continuing contributions in creating memorials and sculptures make her a major name in today's art world.
SUBJ: Lin, Maya Ying./ Architects./ Sculptors./ Chinese Americans--Biography./ Women artists./ Artists.

VCR B LINCOLN, A. Ph-1 A $30.00 OD KE438
ABRAHAM LINCOLN: THE GREAT EMANCIPATOR (Videocassette). Clearvue/EAV AH013-VC, 1990. 1/2" VHS videocassette color (15min). (American portraits).
Includes Teacher's Guide.
Lincoln's origins, education, family joys and sadnesses are covered in addition to his years in the White House. A variety of actors read the text and give the presentation vitality. Many cartoons of the times show how the newspapers viewed his position with the public.
SUBJ: Lincoln, Abraham./ Presidents.

B LINCOLN, A. Ph-2 1-3/2 $7.99 L KE439
BRENNER, MARTHA. Abe Lincoln's hat. Illus. by Donald Cook. Random House ISBN 0-679-94977-1; In Canada: Random House, 1994. 48p. col. ill. (Step into reading).
Lincoln always stored important papers in his stovepipe hat. This slim story covers his entire life by citing times when the unconventional "paper keeper" was useful to Abe. For beginning readers.
SUBJ: Lincoln, Abraham./ Presidents.

CE B LINCOLN, A. Ph-1 3-4/4 $9.95 P KE440
D'AULAIRE, INGRI. Abraham Lincoln. By Ingri and Edgar Parin D'Aulaire. Dell ISBN 0-440-40690-0, c1957, 1993. unp. col. ill.
Caldecott Medal Award.
Available from National Library Service for the Blind and Physically Handicapped in Braille BR05871 and on sound recording cassette RC21812.
An illustrated life of Lincoln from his boyhood days in Kentucky to the end of the Civil War.
SUBJ: Lincoln, Abraham./ Presidents./ United States--History--Civil War, 1861-1865--Biography.

B LINCOLN, A. Ph-3 A/11 $16.95 T KE441
FREEDMAN, RUSSELL. Lincoln, a photobiography. Clarion ISBN 0-89919-380-3, 1987. 150p. ill.
Includes appendices and index.
Newbery Award.
Following a clear description of Lincoln's childhood and early political attempts is a vivid presentation of his years as a military leader as well as president of the U.S. Although not easy to read, this fluidly written text, amply illustrated with period photographs and art, is enthralling reading for skilled students and teachers as well as being a fine resource for history units.
SUBJ: Lincoln, Abraham./ Presidents./ United States--History--Civil War, 1861-1865--Biography.

B LINCOLN, A.　　　　Ph-1 2-4/5　$15.95　T　KE442
HARNESS, CHERYL. Young Abe Lincoln: the frontier days, 1809-1837.
National Geographic ISBN 0-7922-2713-1, 1996. unp. col. ill., maps.
　Includes bibliography.
　Attractive picture-book presentation of Lincoln's early years. In
　addition to full-page paintings of the Lincoln family and their activities,
　there are maps which show the locations of their homes and travels.
　The book highlights the major figures (family and friends) in Lincoln's
　life and will be good for reading aloud to celebrate his birthday.
　SUBJ: Lincoln, Abraham--Childhood and youth./ Presidents.

B LINCOLN, A.　　　　Ph-1 2-4/7　$18.00　T　KE443
HARNESS, CHERYL. Abe Lincoln goes to Washington 1837-1865.
National Geographic ISBN 0-7922-3736-6, 1997. unp. col. ill., maps.
　Includes bibliography.
　Traces the later years of Lincoln's life from his arrival in Springfield,
　Illinois to his untimely death. The large colorful paintings depict Abe
　courting Mary Todd and as a lawyer, a father, and a president.
　Maps show the country in 1858, 1861, 1863, and 1865 with
　important locations marked. The pictures capture much of the action
　making this book good for browsing as well as for reading aloud.
　SUBJ: Lincoln, Abraham./ Presidents.

B LINCOLN, A.　　　　Ph-2 1-3/4　$14.93　L　KE444
KUNHARDT, EDITH. Honest Abe. Illus. by Malcah Zeldis. Greenwillow
ISBN 0-688-11190-4, 1993. unp. col. ill.
　Includes chronology.
　All the major events of Lincoln's life are presented in large, childlike
　drawings and simple, direct text. For use in primary grades.
　SUBJ: Lincoln, Abraham./ Presidents.

VCR B LITTLE, J.　　　　Ph-2 5-6　$49.98　OD KE445
MIND'S EYE: JEAN LITTLE (Videocassette). School Services of Canada;
In Canada: School Services of Canada, 1996. 1/2" VHS videocassette
color (21min). (Meet the author/illustrator).
　Includes teacher's guide.
　Inspirational piece in which Jean Little talks about dealing with
　blindness and how the talking computer has enabled her to write her
　books more easily. Once children meet her as an individual, they will
　want to read everything she has written. Can be incorporated into
　units on persons with disabilities and creative writing.
　SUBJ: Little, Jean./ Authors, Canadian./ Women authors, Canadian./
　Blind--Biography.

VCR B LONGFELLOW, H　　　　Ph-2 5-A　$85.00　OD KE446
MEET THE AUTHOR: HENRY WADSWORTH LONGFELLOW
(Videocassette). SRA/McGraw-Hill 87-005418, 1992. 1/2" VHS
videocassette color (19min). (Meet the author).
　Includes teacher's guide.
　Taped at Longfellow's home, this video depicts major events in
　Longfellow's life and gives the background to the creation of poems
　like "Hiawatha" and "Paul Revere's ride." For poetry and creative
　writing units.
　SUBJ: Longfellow, Henry Wadsworth./ Poets, American.

B LOUIS, J.　　　　Ph-1 4-6/6　$14.00　T　KE447
LIPSYTE, ROBERT. Joe Louis: a champ for all America. HarperCollins
ISBN 0-06-023409-1; In Canada: HarperCollins, 1994. 92p. ill.
(Superstar lineup).
　Includes bibliography and index.
　Selectors' Choice, 20th ed.
　Joe Louis' mother hoped that her son would become a musician, but
　he used her money for lessons to go to a gym. Thus began his
　remarkable career as a boxer. The book discusses the era in which
　Louis broke color lines as well as boxing history. A book with multiple
　uses--African-American history, World War II units, sports history, and
　multicultural studies.
　SUBJ: Louis, Joe./ Boxers (Sports)./ Afro-Americans--Biography.

B LOW, J.　　　　Ph-2 3-6/7　$14.95　L　KE448
BROWN, FERN G. Daisy and the Girl Scouts: the story of Juliette
Gordon Low. Illus. by Marie DeJohn. Whitman ISBN 0-8075-1440-3; In
Canada: General, 1996. 111p. ill.
　Includes chronology and index.
　A disappointing marriage and hearing loss couldn't discourage this
　creative woman. She found in scouting an outlet for her artistic talents
　and love for young people. This title will be appealing to readers
　interested in major women of the early twentieth century as well as
　those involved in Girl Scouting and in units about persons with disabilities.
　Useful in women's studies and in units
　about persons with disabilities.
　SUBJ: Low, Juliette Gordon./ Girl Scouts of The United States of
　America--Biography./ Women--History./ Deaf--Biography.

B LUCAS, J.　　　　Ph-3 5-A/7　$22.83　L　KE449
SIMMONS, ALEX. John Lucas. Raintree Steck-Vaughn ISBN 0-8172-
3978-2, 1996. 48p. ill. (some col.). (Contemporary African Americans).
　Includes chronology, glossary, bibliography and index.
　John Lucas was a super basketball player in the 70s and 80s.
　However, he became dependent on drugs and alcohol until he was
　kicked off the Houston Rockets' basketball team in 1986. John's
　struggle to overcome his addictions, return as a coach to the sport he
　loves, and determination to help others surmount their problems
　makes him a role model for young people today. For multicultural
　studies and drug awareness units.
　SUBJ: Lucas, John (John H.)./ Basketball players./ Afro-Americans--
　Biography.

B LYON, G. E.　　　　Ph-2 4-5/4　$13.95　T　KE450
LYON, GEORGE ELLA. Wordful child. Photos by Ann W. Olson. Richard
C. Owen ISBN 1-57274-016-7, 1996. 32p. col. ill. (Meet the author).
　George Ella Lyon explains how she began to write when she was a
　youngster and how this early interest developed into a full-time
　profession. The text is full of color photographs. An inspirational book
　for use in creative writing activities.
　SUBJ: Lyon, George Ella./ Authors, American./ Women authors,
　American.

B MADDEN, J.　　　　Ph-2 5-A/7　$14.95　L　KE451
CHADWICK, BRUCE. John Madden. Introduction by Chuck Noll. Chelsea
House ISBN 0-7910-4399-1, 1997. 64p. ill. (Football legends).
　Includes chronology, bibliography and index.
　Madden's analysis of football plays is well known to television
　viewers. His early problems as a coach and his aversion to flying are
　not as well known, but are explored in this study of his amazing skills
　and warm personality. Illustrated with action photographs.
　SUBJ: Madden, John./ Football coaches./ Sportscasters.

B MADDUX, G.　　　　Ph-2 3-5/7　$4.50　P　KE452
CHRISTOPHER, MATT. On the mound with...Greg Maddux. Little, Brown
ISBN 0-316-14191-7; In Canada: Little, Brown, 1997. 121p. ill. (Matt
Christopher sports biographies).
　Includes chronology.
　Greg worked with his father and brother to become a baseball
　player, and his willingness to constantly improve his technique served
　him well when he joined a major league team. Greg's drive to join a
　winning team is also described. His success with the Atlanta Braves
　completes this story of one of the most outstanding of the ball
　players today.
　SUBJ: Maddux, Greg./ Baseball players.

B MADISON, J.　　　　Ph-1 5-A/8　$15.95　T　KE453
FRITZ, JEAN. Great little Madison. Illustrated with prints and engravings.
Putnam ISBN 0-399-21768-1; In Canada: Putnam, 1989. 159p. ill.
　Forced to remain quiet during many discussions because of his weak
　voice, Madison listened and didn't intervene until his thoughts would
　have impact on the situation. This finely developed book shows how
　often the "small" voice brought wisdom to the formation of the
　United States and leadership when England again tried to gain
　control of her "colonies."
　SUBJ: Madison, James./ Presidents./ United States--History--
　Constitutional period, 1789-1809--Biography.

B MAHY, M.　　　　Ph-3 2-4/6　$13.95　T　KE454
MAHY, MARGARET. My mysterious world. Photos by David Alexander.
Richard C. Owen ISBN 1-878450-58-1, 1995. 32p. col. ill., map. (Meet
the author).
　Margaret Mahy expresses her love of her country, New Zealand, and
　of her craft, writing, in a picture-autobiography which will prompt
　youngsters to discover her work. Worthwhile introduction to a
　children's author which may be used for instruction as well as
　pleasure reading.
　SUBJ: Mahy, Margaret./ Authors, New Zealand./ Authorship./
　Women authors, New Zealand.

B MALCOLM X　　　　Ph-3 5-6/6　$11.90　L　KE455
CWIKLIK, ROBERT. Malcolm X and black pride. Millbrook ISBN
1-56294-042-2, 1991. 28p b&w and col photos. (Gateway civil rights).
　Includes chronology, bibliography and index.
　The numerous tragedies of Malcolm X's life are detailed in this
　pictorial study. Also explained are the reasons for which he has
　become increasingly important in studies of African-American history.
　Excellent study of a controversial figure, useful for units on African-
　American history, civil rights movement and Islamic religion.
　SUBJ: Malcolm X./ Afro-Americans--Biography./ United States--Race
　relations./ Civil rights workers.

NONFICTION

B MALCOLM X   Ph-3 6-A/8 $13.95   L   KE456
MYERS, WALTER DEAN. Malcolm X: by any means necessary: a
biography. Scholastic ISBN 0-590-46484-1; In Canada: Scholastic, 1993.
210p. ill.
   Includes chronology, bibliography and index.
   Coretta Scott King Honor book, 1994.
   A troubled youth, a streetwise thief, a self-educated scholar, a
religious leader, and a respected spokesperson for African Americans
are all sides of Malcolm X which are carefully examined and studied
in this balanced biography by a talented author. For mature readers.
   SUBJ: Malcolm X./ Civil rights workers./ Afro-Americans--Biography.

B MANDELA, N.   Ph-1 3-6/7 $15.89   L   KE457
COOPER, FLOYD. Mandela: from the life of the South African
statesman. Philomel ISBN 0-399-22942-6; In Canada: Putnam, 1996.
unp. col. ill.
   Includes bibliography.
   Selectors' Choice, 21st ed.
   Mandela's early childhood which taught him to stand firm, to be fair,
and to be a leader sets the stage for the events of his later life. His
determination to gain an education, fight for civil rights, endure
imprisonment, and become the leading spokesperson in South Africa
is all related in a hushed, reverent text. The carefully crafted art work
is done in an oil wash on board. A monumental book! For
multicultural studies.
   SUBJ: Mandela, Nelson./ Civil rights workers./ Blacks--Biography./
South Africa--Race relations.

B MANKILLER, W.   Ph-2 2-3/4 $11.96   L   KE458
LOWERY, LINDA. Wilma Mankiller. Illus. by Janice Lee Porter.
Carolrhoda ISBN 0-87614-880-1, 1996. 56p. col. ill. (Carolrhoda on my
own book).
   Includes chronology.
   Wilma was raised on a farm among her Cherokee roots, but poverty
drove her family to San Francisco. Stirred by protests for Native
American rights, she returned to Oklahoma and devoted her efforts
to improving the lives of rural Cherokee. Forthright telling of the life
of a dedicated woman. Use for multicultural studies and women's
studies.
   SUBJ: Mankiller, Wilma Pearl./ Cherokee Indians--Biography./ Indians
of North America--Biography./ Indians of North America--Women.

B MARSALIS, W.   Ph-2 5-A/10 $24.26   L   KE459
ELLIS, VERONICA FREEMAN. Wynton Marsalis. Raintree Steck-Vaughn
ISBN 0-8172-3988-X, 1997. 48p. col. ill. (Contemporary African
Americans).
   Includes chronology, glossary, bibliography and index.
   Wynton learned early from his father the importance of practicing
and the many facets of music. He continues to share his love of music
with children through concerts and by visiting schools. Twice he has
won Grammy Awards in the same year for both jazz and classical
recordings. A true inspiration to music students. For multicultural
studies.
   SUBJ: Marsalis, Wynton./ Trumpet players./ Afro-Americans--
Biography./ Musicians./ Jazz musicians.

VCR B MARTIN, B.   Ph-3 3-4 $29.95   KE460
VISIT WITH BILL MARTIN, JR. (Videocassette). Henry Holt ISBN
0-8050-4712-3, 1996. 1/2" VHS videocassette color (26min).
   Includes teacher's guide.
   Bill Martin reads several of his books and then explains how he wrote
each work and the joy he receives from seeing a finished manuscript.
Unable to read until he entered college, he relates how persistence
finally paid off and the joy he gets from reading today. Inspiration
for reluctant readers.
   SUBJ: Martin, Bill, Jr./ Authors, American.

B MARTINEZ, M.   Ph-3 5-6/3 $13.95   T   KE461
KREISCHER, ELSIE KARR. Maria Montoya Martinez: master potter. Illus.
by Elsie Karr Kreischer and Roberta Sinnock. Pelican ISBN 1-56554-098-
0, 1995. 79p. ill.
   The development of Maria Martinez as a clay potter and reknowned
artist is fully explained with a summary of her life and devotion to the
people with whom she has shared her skills and life. For art units,
multicultural studies, and studies of Native Americans.
   SUBJ: Martinez, Maria Montoya./ Pueblo Indians--Biography./
Indians of North America--New Mexico--Biography./ Indians of North
America--Women.

B MCCOY, E.   Ph-3 4-6/7 $4.95   P   KE462
TOWLE, WENDY. Real McCoy: the life of an African-American inventor.
Illus. by Wil Clay. Scholastic ISBN 0-590-48102-9; In Canada:
Scholastic, c1993, 1995. unp. col. ill.
   Elijah McCoy was born in Canada and educated in Scotland. Yet the

free black man was unable to pursue his chosen field, engineering,
after the Civil War. He finally gained recognition for his ingenious
inventions used by the railroad and in the home. For multicultural
studies.
   SUBJ: McCoy, Elijah./ Inventors./ Afro-Americans--Biography.

B MEREDITH, J.   Ph-2 4-5/7 $12.90   L   KE463
ELISH, DAN. James Meredith and school desegregation. Millbrook ISBN
1-56294-379-0, 1994. 32p. ill. (some col.) (Gateway civil rights).
   Includes chronology, bibliography and index.
   Meredith's determined fight to enter the University of Mississippi is
pictured both in text and photographs. Informative reading about the
troubled times and the civil rights landmarks of the 1960s. For
multicultural studies.
   SUBJ: Meredith, James./ Afro-Americans--Biography./ Afro-
Americans--Education./ School integration./ Mississippi--Race
relations.

B MESSIER, M.   Ph-2 5-A/7 $18.95   L   KE464
SULLIVAN, MICHAEL JOHN. Mark Messier: star center. By Michael J.
Sullivan. Enslow ISBN 0-89490-801-4, 1997. 104p. ill. (Sports reports).
   Includes directory and index.
   Since joining the Rangers, Mark Messier has led his team to a
Stanley Cup. His team spirit and continuing efforts to bring excitement
to the game for his New York fans is related in a book filled with
black and white photographs.
   SUBJ: Messier, Mark./ Hockey players.

B MITCHELL, M.   Ph-3 4-5/6 $14.95   L   KE465
MCPHERSON, STEPHANIE SAMMARTINO. Rooftop astronomer: a
story about Maria Mitchell. Illus. by Hetty Mitchell. Carolrhoda ISBN
0-87614-410-5, 1990. 64p. ill. (Carolrhoda creative minds book).
   Includes bibliography.
   Encouraged by her father, Maria Mitchell studied the stars and
astounded the world by sighting a comet. Her successes continued as
she became an instructor in astronomy at Vassar College and a
spokesperson for women's rights. Include in science units and women's
studies.
   SUBJ: Mitchell, Maria./ Astronomers./ Women astronomers.

B MONET, C.   Ph-2 4-6/7 $14.95   T   KE466
HARRISON, PETER. Claude Monet. Sterling ISBN 0-8069-6158-9; In
Canada; Sterling c/o Canadian Manda, 1996. 31p. col. ill., map. (Art
for young people).
   Originally published in Great Britain as AN INTRODUCTION TO
CLAUDE MONET, Macdonald Young Books Ltd., 1995.
   Includes chronology, glossary and index.
   Offers a wealth of information on Monet's life, his work, and his
times. His most important paintings are explained and analyzed, so
that the art can be appreciated. Excellent for reports and to
encourage enjoyment of great art.
   SUBJ: Monet, Claude./ Artists./ Painting, French./ Art appreciation.

B MONTESSORI, M   Ph-3 4-6/6 $14.95   L   KE467
O'CONNOR, BARBARA. Mammolina: a story about Maria Montessori.
Illus. by Sara Campitelli. Carolrhoda ISBN 0-87614-743-0, 1993. 64p.
ill. (Carolrhoda creative minds book).
   Includes bibliography.
   Starting her career by working with retarded children, Maria later
established schools where children were allowed to learn in a
challenging, supportive atmosphere. Her methods rapidly spread to
other countries, and she became a leading figure in education in the
1900s. Use for units on teaching and for women's studies.
   SUBJ: Montessori, Maria./ Educators./ Montessori method of
education./ Women educators.

B MONTESSORI, M   Ph-2 A/9 $22.95   L   KE468
SHEPHARD, MARIE TENNENT. Maria Montessori: teacher of teachers.
Lerner ISBN 0-8225-4952-2, 1996. 112p. ill. (Lerner biography).
   Includes bibliography and index.
   Thorough, well documented biography of a determined pioneer in
medicine and education who has had a major influence on early
childhood education world-wide. Illustrated with black and white
photographs of varying quality. For advanced readers.
   SUBJ: Montessori, Maria./ Educators./ Women educators./
Montessori method of education.

B MONTGOMERY, L   Ph-2 5-A/6 $15.00   L   KE469
ANDRONIK, CATHERINE M. Kindred spirit: a biography of L. M.
Montgomery, creator of Anne of Green Gables. Atheneum ISBN 0-689-
31671-2, 1993. 160p. ill.
   Includes bibliography and index.
   Lucy M. Montgomery's life on Prince Edward Island at times caused
her heartaches as she longed to escape the burdens of caring for her

grandparents, but it also was the source of the material for the many books which she wrote. This Canadian author's life is relived in her works. This title will prompt readers to rediscover her books and will add background to understanding them.
SUBJ: Montgomery, Lucy M./ Authors, Canadian./ Women authors, Canadian.

VCR B MONTGOMERY, L Ph-3 6-A $39.98 OD KE470
LUCY MAUD MONTGOMERY: THREADS FROM THE QUILT (Videocassette). School Services of Canada/dist. by Delta Education TG-220-7920; In Canada: School Services of Canada, 1993. 1/2" VHS videocassette color (21min).
Includes teacher's guide.
A sympathetic interpretation of the early life of Lucy Montgomery and her experiences on Prince Edward Island which she later incorporated into her many books. For sensitive viewers.
SUBJ: Montgomery, Lucy M./ Authors, Canadian./ Women authors, Canadian.

VCR B MOST, B. Ph-3 2-3 $39.95 KE471
GET TO KNOW BERNARD MOST (Videocassette). Harcourt Brace ISBN 0-15-253159-9, 1993. 1/2" VHS videocassette color (20min). (Get to know...).
Includes teacher's guide.
Showing viewers where he finds ideas for his books, Bernard Most introduces most of his books to eager readers. Music and fantastic shots of youngsters make this a spirited introduction to a talented author/illustrator.
SUBJ: Most, Bernard./ Authors, American./ Illustrators.

B MOZART, W. Ph-2 2-3/6 $14.99 L KE472
ISADORA, RACHEL. Young Mozart. Viking ISBN 0-670-87120-6; In Canada: Penguin, 1997. unp. col. ill.
Mozart began to compose at the age of three, taught himself to play the violin, and was entertaining society when he was a child. This picture book biography depicts him as an appealing child and composer, but does not present his financial difficulties or his extended illness. For music units.
SUBJ: Mozart, Wolfgang Amadeus./ Composers.

B MUIR, J. Ph-2 5-6/4 $11.90 L KE473
NADEN, CORINNE J. John Muir: saving the wilderness. By Corinne J. Naden and Rose Blue. Millbrook ISBN 1-56294-110-0, 1992. 48p b&w illus, b&w and col photos. (Gateway green biography).
Includes timeline, bibliography and index.
Inventor, naturalist, conservationist, and presidential advisor--all these terms apply to John Muir. This well illustrated appreciation will inspire readers to value the national parks and our natural heritage.
SUBJ: Muir, John./ Conservationists./ Naturalists.

B MUSIAL, S. Ph-2 5-A/7 $14.95 L KE474
GRABOWSKI, JOHN. Stan Musial. Chelsea House ISBN 0-7910-1184-4, 1993. 64p. ill. (Baseball legends).
Includes chronology, bibliography and index.
Musial almost equaled Babe Ruth's feats on the baseball diamond. This well-written study of a shy, dedicated player explains why he is known as "a perfect knight." For mature readers.
SUBJ: Musial, Stan./ Baseball players.

B MYERS, W. Ph-2 5-6/6 $22.83 L KE475
PATRICK-WEXLER, DIANE. Walter Dean Myers. Raintree Steck-Vaughn ISBN 0-8172-3979-0, 1996. 48p. col. ill. (Contemporary African Americans).
Includes chronology, glossary, bibliography and index.
Myers' speech problem and his early childhood placement with foster parents are related to develop the reader's empathy for this popular author. Many of his books are described to create interest in his writings. For units on author studies, creative writing, and multicultural studies.
SUBJ: Myers, Walter Dean./ Authors, American./ Afro-Americans--Biography.

B NEWTON, I. Ph-2 6-A/7 $18.95 L KE476
ANDERSON, MARGARET JEAN. Isaac Newton: the greatest scientist of all time. By Margaret J. Anderson. Enslow ISBN 0-89490-681-X, 1996. 128p. ill., map. (Great minds of science).
Includes chronology, glossary, bibliography and index.
Newton's ability to observe and draw his own conclusions made him one of the greatest scientists of his age. He is respected for his work in mathematics, for his design of a reflecting telescope, and for his theory of gravity. Experiments to challenge the reader complete the book.
SUBJ: Newton, Isaac, Sir./ Scientists.

B NICE, M. Ph-2 3-5/9 $13.13 L KE477
DUNLAP, JULIE. Birds in the bushes: a story about Margaret Morse Nice. Illus. by Ralph L. Ramstad. Carolrhoda ISBN 1-57505-006-4, 1996. 64p. ill. (Carolrhoda creative minds book).
Includes bibliography and index.
Margaret Morse Nice began her study of birds as a youngster and found in college that research into the ways of birds was a field she loved. Her ability to coordinate her family, research, and publications made her an early role model for women. For environmental studies and women's studies.
SUBJ: Nice, Margaret Morse./ Ornithologists./ Women scientists.

B NIGHTINGALE Ph-2 2-4/3 $14.95 L KE478
ADLER, DAVID A. Picture book of Florence Nightingale. Illus. by John and Alexandra Wallner. Holiday House ISBN 0-8234-0965-1, 1992. unp. col. ill. (Picture book biography).
Includes chronology.
Florence Nightingale's driving determination to become a nurse and her remarkable leadership in improving care for the ill are covered in this pictorial biography. For early grades.
SUBJ: Nightingale, Florence./ Nurses.

VCR B OAKLEY, A. Ph-1 3-6 $11.99 OD KE479
ANNIE OAKLEY (Videocassette). Narrated by Keith Carradine. Music by Los Lobos. Illus. by Fred Warter. Rabbit Ears/Microleague Multimedia Inc. (MMI)/dist. by Ingram Library Services ISBN 157099978-3, 1997. 1/2" VHS videocassette color (30min).
Includes public performance rights.
The life story of Annie Oakley is told through the eyes of Will Rogers. Annie earned her living by being a sharpshooter and appearing in wild West shows around the world. Rogers emphasized her happy marriage, concern for others, and the hardships of being a performer. For units on the West or women's studies.
SUBJ: Oakley, Annie./ Sharpshooters./ Women entertainers.

B OAKLEY, A. Ph-2 5-6/8 $14.95 L KE480
WUKOVITS, JOHN F. Annie Oakley. By John Wukovits. Chelsea House ISBN 0-7910-3906-4, 1997. 64p. ill. (Legends of the West).
Includes chronology, bibliography and index.
Annie's childhood was beset with problems following her father's death. Her unique skill was shooting. This detailed picture of her life shows how this skill became her livelihood and brought her fame all over the world. Text is enhanced with good photographs of Annie and the people who filled her life. For mature readers interested in women's studies and "The West."
SUBJ: Oakley, Annie./ Sharpshooters./ Entertainers./ Women--West (U.S.)./ Frontier and pioneer life--West (U.S.).

B O'CONNOR, S. Ph-3 4-5/8 $13.95 L KE481
MACHT, NORMAN L. Sandra Day O'Connor. Chelsea House ISBN 0-7910-1756-7, 1992. 80p. ill. (Junior world biographies).
Includes bibliography, chronology, glossary and index.
O'Connor's search for an education often separated her from her family but never lessened her dedication to them. How she balanced the many facets of her life makes this good reading for readers puzzled by the complexities of seeking a career today.
SUBJ: O'Connor, Sandra Day./ United States. Supreme Court--Biography./ Judges./ Women judges.

B O'KEEFFE, G. Ph-2 2-3/2 $15.95 L KE482
LOWERY, LINDA. Georgia O'Keeffe. Illus. by Rochelle Draper. Carolrhoda ISBN 0-87614-860-7, 1996. 48p. col. ill. (Carolrhoda on my own book).
Includes chronology.
When Georgia O'Keeffe found bones in the desert of New Mexico, they prompted a great change in her paintings and techniques. This easy-to-read biography brings beginning readers insight into the works of an artist whose paintings are widely admired. The illustrations capture O'Keeffe's world in New Mexico and New York. For women's studies.
SUBJ: O'Keeffe, Georgia./ Artists./ Women artists./ Painting, American.

B OLAJUWON, H. Ph-3 4-5/6 $14.40 L KE483
GUTMAN, BILL. Hakeem Olajuwon: superstar center. Millbrook ISBN 1-56294-568-8, 1995. 48p. col. ill. (Millbrook sports world).
Includes chronology, bibliography, directory and index.
Coming from Nigeria, Hakeem found his place on the University of Houston's basketball team and with the Houston Rockets. His amazing career is covered with numerous black and white and color photographs.
SUBJ: Olajuwon, Hakeem./ Basketball players./ Blacks--Nigeria--Biography.

B ONASSIS, J.   Ph-2   A/7 $18.95   L   KE484
ANDERSON, CATHERINE CORLEY. Jackie Kennedy Onassis: woman of courage. Lerner ISBN 0-8225-2885-1, 1995. 88p. ill. (some col.). (Achievers).
> This much admired first lady is portrayed as a loving daughter to an alcoholic father, an adventurous reporter, a devoted mother, and an asset to her husband during his time as president. Numerous color photographs as well as black and white ones show her in her many roles.
> SUBJ: Onassis, Jacqueline Kennedy./ Kennedy, John Fitzgerald./ First ladies.

B O'NEAL, S.   Ph-2   4-5/6 $18.95   L   KE485
MACNOW, GLEN. Shaquille O'Neal: star center. Enslow ISBN 0-89490-656-9, 1996. 104p. ill. (Sports reports).
> Includes directory and index.
> Shaquille's amazing height caught the attention of a college coach when he was only thirteen. How this coach became a major force in his life, how his parents' code of ethics has molded him, and how he remains a friend to the underprivileged are all explained in a biography filled with action photographs. For multicultural studies.
> SUBJ: O'Neal, Shaquille./ Basketball players./ Afro-Americans--Biography.

B OWENS, J.   Ph-2   3-4/6 $14.95   L   KE486
ADLER, DAVID A. Picture book of Jesse Owens. Illus. by Robert Casilla. Holiday House ISBN 0-8234-0966-X, 1992. unp col illus. (Picture book biography).
> Includes chronology.
> Encouraged by a high school track coach who recognized his talents, Jesse Owens developed his running and jumping abilities to become an Olympic gold medal winner. Highlighted by attractive full-color drawings, this pictorial study will attract readers interested in sports and African-American history.
> SUBJ: Owens, Jesse./ Track and field athletes./ Runners (Sports)./ Afro-Americans--Biography.

B OWENS, J.   Ph-2   5-A/8 $18.95   L   KE487
JOSEPHSON, JUDITH PINKERTON. Jesse Owens: track and field legend. Russell L. Adams, Series consultant. Enslow ISBN 0-89490-812-X, 1997. 128p. ill. (African-American biographies).
> Includes chronology, bibliography and index.
> Covers Owens' impoverished childhood and his rise to fame with the help of his coaches and explains the reasons Hitler refused to shake his hand after his success at the Olympic Games in 1936. His struggles, in his later years, to support his family finish the book. For African-American history, multicultural studies, and units on the Olympics. For advanced students.
> SUBJ: Owens, Jesse./ Track and field athletes./ Afro-Americans--Biography.

B OZAWA, S.   Ph-3   4-5/6 $13.27   L   KE488
SIMON, CHARNAN. Seiji Ozawa: symphony conductor. Childrens Press ISBN 0-516-04182-7; In Canada: Childrens Press, 1992. 32p. ill. (Picture-story biographies).
> Includes chronology and index.
> Ozawa's success spanning two musical worlds--Asian and Western--is explained in this direct exploration of his life. Useful for music units and multicultural studies.
> SUBJ: Ozawa, Seiji./ Conductors (Music).

B PAIGE, S.   Ph-3   3-5/2 $12.95   L   KE489
MCKISSACK, PAT. Satchel Paige: the best arm in baseball. By Patricia and Fredrick McKissack. Illus. by Michael David Biegel. Enslow ISBN 0-89490-317-9, 1992. 32p b&w illus and photos. (Great African Americans).
> Includes glossary and index.
> Satchel Paige's entering the American League in 1948 was exceptional in many ways. He was the first African-American pitcher in the league and the oldest rookie. Brief history of a man with ability and humor destined to become a role model for African-American youths.
> SUBJ: Paige, Leroy./ Baseball players./ Afro-Americans--Biography.

B PARKS, R.   Ph-1   6-A/5 $17.00   T   KE490
PARKS, ROSA. Rosa Parks: my story. By Rosa Parks with Jim Haskins. Dial ISBN 0-8037-0673-1, 1992. 192p. ill.
> Includes chronology and index.
> Selectors' Choice, 19th ed.
> This insightful autobiography explains fully why Rosa Parks made history by not giving up her seat on a bus. Her own expressions of anger, frustration, fear, and determination will aid readers to better understand the civil rights movement. Mature readers will use this book as a stepping-stone to other books about the leaders in the

fight for equality.
> SUBJ: Parks, Rosa./ Civil rights workers./ Afro-Americans--Civil rights./ Afro-Americans--Biography./ Segregation./ Women civil rights workers.

B PARKS, R.   Ph-1   1-2/4 $12.89   L   KE491
PARKS, ROSA. I am Rosa Parks. By Rosa Parks with Jim Haskins. Illus. by Wil Clay. Dial ISBN 0-8037-1207-3; In Canada: McClelland & Stewart, 1997. 48p. col. ill. (Dial easy-to-read).
> Rosa Parks explains in simple language why she refused to give up her seat to a white person. She also describes the effects of the bus boycott and expresses her satisfaction that she was part of the civil rights movement. A stirring autobiography for multicultural studies and women's studies.
> SUBJ: Parks, Rosa./ Civil rights workers./ Afro-Americans--Biography.

B PATRICK, ST.   Ph-1   2-4/4 $15.95   L   KE492
DE PAOLA, TOMIE. Patrick: patron saint of Ireland. Holiday House ISBN 0-8234-0924-4, 1992. unp col illus.
> Patrick's childhood captivity, his reunion with his family and his decision to return to his homeland and establish the first Christian church in Ireland are all described in a simple text accompanied by many pictures. Includes some of the familiar legends which have grown up around the saint. Worthwhile addition for holiday and legends collections and curriculum in parochial schools.
> SUBJ: Patrick, Saint./ Saints.

B PEALE, C.   Ph-1   6-A/8 $16.00   T   KE493
WILSON, JANET. Ingenious Mr. Peale: painter, patriot and man of science. Illus. by Charles Willson Peale. Atheneum ISBN 0-689-31884-7; In Canada: Distican, 1996. 122p. ill.
> Includes bibliography and index.
> Peale's childhood was beset by poverty, and as a youth, he became an apprentice to a saddle maker. His continuing efforts to earn a living for his family resulted in such diverse occupations as a watchmaker, painter, soldier, and eventually a museum founder and developer. This amazing man's versatility is captured in a book filled with black and white reproductions of his paintings.
> SUBJ: Peale, Charles Willson./ Artists.

B PEET, B.   Ph-2   6-A/8 $16.95   T   KE494
PEET, BILL. Bill Peet: an autobiography. Houghton Mifflin ISBN 0-395-50932-7, 1989. 190p. ill.
> Caldecott Honor Book, 1990.
> Selectors' Choice, 19th ed.
> Available from National Library Service for the Blind and Physically Handicapped on sound recording cassette RC31287.
> Dedicated to drawing throughout his life, Bill Peet demonstrates the many avenues open to illustrators and the hard work and disappointments met in developing a reputation. The details of his career in the Disney studios presents insights on cartoons. Extensively illustrated this is for the discerning reader interested in authors, illustrators, and Disney films.
> SUBJ: Peet, Bill./ Authors, American./ Illustrators./ Walt Disney Company.

B PIAZZA, M.   Ph-2   4-6/7 $19.95   L   KE495
SAVAGE, JEFF. Mike Piazza: hard-hitting catcher. Lerner ISBN 0-8225-2895-9, 1997. 64p. ill. (some col.). (Achievers).
> Includes glossary and index.
> When Mike was overlooked by baseball scouts, Tommy Lasorda, as a favor to Mike's dad, had the Dodgers draft him on the sixty-second round. Mike, determined to make the fiftieth pay off, worked hard and turned himself into an outstanding ball player. This text can be used as motivational material as well as a good sports story.
> SUBJ: Piazza, Mike./ Baseball players.

B PICKETT, B.   Ph-1   2-5/7 $16.00   L   KE496
PINKNEY, ANDREA DAVIS. Bill Pickett: rodeo-ridin' cowboy. By Andrea D. Pinkney. Illus. by Brian Pinkney. Gulliver/Harcourt Brace ISBN 0-15-200100-X; In Canada: Harcourt Brace c/o Canadian Manda, 1996. unp. col. ill.
> Includes bibliography.
> When he was ten, Bill Pickett wrestled a steer to the ground by sinking his teeth into the animal's lip. He went on to become a cowhand and appeared in rodeos. His particular technique became known as "bulldogging." This legend comes alive in dramatic scratchboard renderings, hand-colored with oil paint. For units on the West, cowboys, African-American history and multicultural studies.
> SUBJ: Pickett, Bill./ Cowboys./ Afro-Americans--Biography.

B PIKE, Z.   Ph-3   5-6/8 $14.95   L   KE497
SANFORD, WILLIAM R. Zebulon Pike: explorer of the Southwest. By William R. Sanford and Carl R. Green. Enslow ISBN 0-89490-671-2,

1996. 48p. ill., map. (Legendary heroes of the Wild West).
Includes glossary, bibliography and index.
Pike never climbed the mountain named after him, but he did explore much of the Southwest when he was serving in the United States Army. He was seeking information about the Spaniards in the area. Later, he was killed during the War of 1812. For units on exploration and regional studies.
SUBJ: Pike, Zebulon Montgomery./ Explorers./ Southwest, New--Discovery and exploration./ West (U.S.)--Discovery and exploration.

B PIPPEN, S.   Ph-3 4-6/6 $19.95   L   KE498
SCHNAKENBERG, ROBERT. Scottie Pippen: reluctant superstar. Lerner ISBN 0-8225-3653-6, 1997. 64p. col. ill.
Includes glossary and index.
Pippen is best known for being part of a team dominated by Michael Jordon. This text shows that Pippen is a star in his own right. Illustrated with many photographs showing Scottie in action on the court and as a part of the Dream Team. For multicultural studies.
SUBJ: Pippen, Scottie./ Basketball players./ Afro-Americans--Biography.

B PIPPIN, H.   Ph-3 5-A/5 $15.95   L   KE499
LYONS, MARY E. Starting home: the story of Horace Pippin, painter. Scribner's ISBN 0-684-19534-8; In Canada: Maxwell Macmillan, 1993. 42p. col. ill.
Includes index.
Pippin's pencil always got him into trouble, but his ability to capture the world around him and the horrors of World War I made him one of the better known African-American artists of the twentieth century. Includes many illustrations of the artist's work. For multicultural studies.
SUBJ: Pippin, Horace./ Artists./ Afro-Americans--Biography./ Painting, American./ Painting, Modern--20th century./ Art appreciation.

B POCAHONTAS   Ph-1 5-6/6 $14.95   T   KE500
FRITZ, JEAN. Double life of Pocahontas. Illus. by Ed Young. Putnam ISBN 0-399-21016-4; In Canada: General, 1983. 96p. ill.
Includes map, notes, bibliography and index.
Selectors' Choice, 15th ed.
Available from National Library Service for the Blind and Physically Handicapped on sound recording cassette RC21795.
Torn between the life of her parents and friends, Pocahontas decides to wed John Rolfe, one of the early settlers of Virginia. Carefully written to present actions as probable interpretations based on known facts rather than the usual romantic pronouncements, this poignant telling of the Indian princess' life will give students understanding of the problems which existed between the first settlers and the Indians.
SUBJ: Pocahontas./ Indians of North America--Biography./ Smith, John./ Powhatan./ Jamestown (Va.)--History./ Virginia--History--Colonial period, ca. 1600-1775./ Indians of North America--Women.

VCR B POLACCO, P.   Ph-1 2-4 $39.95   OD KE501
POLACCO, PATRICIA. Dream keeper (Videocassette). Philomel/dist. by Berkley Publishing ISBN 0-399-22947-7; In Canada: Philomel/dist. by BeJo Sales, 1996. 1/2" VHS videocassette color (23min).
Includes public performance rights.
Selectors' Choice, 21st ed.
Reading from her books, Patricia Polacco explains how her parents and grandparents told stories to her as a child and how she incorporates them today into her popular picture books. She also relates how a teacher encouraged her to overcome her dyslexia and to go on to read extensively. Can be used to excite interest in Polacco's books, to inspire students with disabilities, and to support author studies.
SUBJ: Polacco, Patricia./ Women authors, American./ Women illustrators./ Learning disabilities--Biography.

B POWELL, C.   Ph-2 3-6/7 $14.90   L   KE502
BLUE, ROSE. Colin Powell: straight to the top. Updated ed. By Rose Blue and Corinne J. Naden. Millbrook ISBN 0-7613-0256-5, 1997. 48p. col. ill., map. (Gateway biography).
Includes chronology and index.
While serving in the ROTC, Colin Powell developed his interest in the Army and also became a determined student. His roles in Vietnam, Korea, Panama, Desert Storm, and Haiti show his dedication and competence. Will serve students seeking information about United States military leaders. For multicultural studies.
SUBJ: Powell, Colin L./ Generals./ Afro-Americans--Biography.

VCR B PRELUTSKY, J.   Ph-3 3-6 $85.00   OD KE503
MEET JACK PRELUTSKY (Videocassette). SRA/McGraw-Hill 87-05005, 1992. 1/2" VHS videocassette color (24min). (Meet the author).
Includes teacher's guide.

Jack Prelutsky discusses his life and work. When he performs before a group of students, their delight in his humorous poems is very evident. For units on poetry and humor.
SUBJ: Prelutsky, Jack./ Poets, American.

B REAGAN, R.   Ph-2 6-A/10 $18.95   L   KE504
JUDSON, KAREN. Ronald Reagan. Enslow ISBN 0-89490-835-9, 1997. 112p. ill. (United States presidents).
Includes chronology, bibliography, directory and index.
Concentrating on Reagan's traits which made him a good speaker and an able administrator, the author deals fairly with the problems which beset his administration. This title is not a survey discussion, but rather an in-depth coverage of his years in the White House. For mature readers.
SUBJ: Reagan, Ronald./ Presidents./ Actors and actresses.

VCR B REID BANKS, L   Ph-2 4-6 $49.98   OD KE505
TALK WITH LYNNE REID BANKS (Videocassette). Tim Podell Productions, 1995. 1/2" VHS videocassette color (23min). (Good conversation!).
Lynne Reid Banks discusses her experiences in other countries that have prompted her most popular books. She also explains the source for THE INDIAN IN THE CUPBOARD and her expectations for the motion picture.
SUBJ: Reid Banks, Lynne./ Authors, English./ Women authors, English.

B REISS, J.   Ph-2 5-6/5 $15.00   T   KE506
REISS, JOHANNA. Upstairs room. Crowell/HarperCollins ISBN 0-690-85127-8, c1972. 196p.
Newbery Honor Book.
Selectors' Choice, 8th ed.
The illness of Mrs. Reiss made the Reiss family remain in the small Dutch town of Winterswijk when the Germans attacked Holland. Soon it became evident to the family that to remain visible in the town would lead to imprisonment. Annie and her older sister Sini found concealment in a small farmhouse where the Dutch family ingeniously protected them even while German soldiers occupied the house. Peace enabled the Reiss family to find one another again. The book is Johanna Reiss' tribute to her "adopted" family who showed great courage and strength in difficult times.
In JOURNEY BACK (ISBN 0-06-447042-3, c1976, 1987)the de Leeuw family attempts to begin life again.
SUBJ: Reiss, Johanna./ Jews--Biography./ Jews--Netherlands./ World War, 1939-1945--Personal narratives.

B REMBRANDT   Ph-1 6-A/7 $18.95   T   KE507
SCHWARTZ, GARY. Rembrandt. Abrams ISBN 0-8109-3760-3, 1992. 92p. col. ill. (First impressions).
Includes index.
Reviews the life of Rembrandt with his glorious successes in the art world, his sad family life, the controversies surrounding his paintings, and his glorification of the lives of real people revealing their inner feelings, their very souls. A well balanced view of a very great artist.
SUBJ: Rembrandt Harmenszoon van Rijn./ Artists./ Painting, Dutch.

B REVERE, P.   Ph-2 2-4/5 $15.95   L   KE508
ADLER, DAVID A. Picture book of Paul Revere. Illus. by John and Alexandra Wallner. Holiday House ISBN 0-8234-1144-3, 1995. unp. col. ill. (Picture book biography).
Includes chronology.
Revere's activities during the Revolutionary War are detailed. Also depicts his devotion to his family and his creativity working in silver and other materials. This simplified story of his life will bring readers to the more detailed biographies written by Jean Fritz and Esther Forbes.
SUBJ: Revere, Paul./ United States--History--Revolution, 1775-1783--Biography./ Boston (Mass.)--History./ Statesmen.

B REVERE, P.   Ph-1 A/7 $14.95   L   KE509
FORBES, ESTHER. America's Paul Revere. Illustrated by Lynd Ward. Houghton Mifflin ISBN 0-395-24535-4, c1946. 46p col illus.
Available from National Library Service for the Blind and Physically Handicapped in Braille BR07383.
Biography of a patriot as seen against a backdrop of political unrest in pre-Revolutionary Boston. The famous midnight ride is dramatically told.
SUBJ: Revere, Paul./ United States--History--Revolution, 1775-1783--Biography./ Boston (Mass.)--History./ Statesmen.

CE B REVERE, P.   Ph-1 5-6/6 $13.95   T   KE510
FRITZ, JEAN. And then what happened, Paul Revere? Illus. by Margot Tomes. Coward-McCann/Putnam ISBN 0-698-20274-0, c1973. 45p. col. ill.

Selectors' Choice, 9th ed.
Talking book available from Weston Woods WW478C, 1977. 1 sound cassette (23min) $8.95.
Available from National Library Service for the Blind and Physically Handicapped on sound recording cassette RC25588.
Everyone knows about his famous ride but not everyone knows what an engaging fellow he was and perhaps the reader will be surprised to learn that when he wasn't galloping off somewhere with "his hat clapped to his head and his coattails flying" he was busy at home making silver spoons, teapots and cups, false teeth, and church bells, to say nothing of running a hardware store or building a foundry. The amusing illustrations add to the book's delight.
SUBJ: Revere, Paul./ Silversmithing./ Boston (Mass.)--History./ United States--History--Revolution, 1775-1783--Biography./ Statesmen.

B RINGGOLD, F.　　　　Ph-1 4-A/7　$15.95　L　KE511
TURNER, ROBYN. Faith Ringgold. By Robyn Montana Turner. Little, Brown ISBN 0-316-85652-5; In Canada: Little, Brown, 1993. 32p. col. ill. (Portraits of women artists for children).
Faith Ringgold decided to be an artist at a time when there were few woman artists and even fewer African-American women artists. An inclusive study of her art and the influences from her childhood and family which prompted much of her work. For art collections and for multicultural studies and women's studies.
SUBJ: Ringgold, Faith./ Artists./ Afro-Americans--Biography./ Art appreciation./ Women artists.

B RIPKEN, C.　　　　Ph-2 5-6/7　$14.95　L　KE512
CAMPBELL, JIM. Cal Ripken, Jr. Introduction by Jim Murray. Senior consultant, Earl Weaver. Chelsea House ISBN 0-7910-4380-0, 1997. 63p. ill. (Baseball legends).
Includes chronology, bibliography and index.
Cal Ripken did the impossible in 1995. He broke Lou Gehrig's record for consecutive games played in baseball. Devotion to the game and work habits of this "superstar" are explained in this narration of his career. Black and white photographs include family shots as well as Ripken in action.
SUBJ: Ripken, Cal, Jr./ Baseball players.

B RIVERA, D.　　　　Ph-3 5-6/7　$14.95　L　KE513
SHIRLEY, DAVID. Diego Rivera. Chelsea Juniors ISBN 0-7910-2292-7, 1995. 79p. ill. (Junior world biographies).
"Junior Hispanics of achievement book."
Includes bibliography, glossary, chronology and index.
Rivera's murals reflect Mexican life and the Mexican people so well that he has become an icon for his nation. The prints are in black and white limiting the appeal of this book. For multicultural studies.
SUBJ: Rivera, Diego./ Artists.

B ROBESON, P.　　　　Ph-2 2-5/2　$12.95　L　KE514
MCKISSACK, PAT. Paul Robeson: a voice to remember. By Patricia and Fredrick McKissack. Enslow ISBN 0-89490-310-1, 1992. 32p. ill. (Great African Americans).
Includes glossary and index.
The many problems faced by Paul Robeson as he struggled to overcome prejudice in the United States are clearly presented in this introductory biography. Slim volume is augmented by photographs. For African-American history, music and twentieth century history units.
SUBJ: Robeson, Paul./ Actors and actresses./ Singers./ Afro-Americans--Biography.

B ROBINSON, J.　　　　Ph-2 2-4/6　$15.95　L　KE515
ADLER, DAVID A. Picture book of Jackie Robinson. Illus. by Robert Casilla. Holiday House ISBN 0-8234-1122-2, 1994. unp. col. ill. (Picture book biography).
Includes chronology.
Jackie Robinson's problems as the first African-American athlete to play on a professional baseball team are told in a straightforward manner. Gives readers a good picture of the racial injustices of the late 1940s and early 1950s. For multicultural studies.
SUBJ: Robinson, Jackie./ Baseball players./ Afro-Americans--Biography.

B ROBINSON, J.　　　　Ph-2 5-6/6　$3.95　P　KE516
RUDEEN, KENNETH. Jackie Robinson. Illus. by Michael Hays. HarperTrophy ISBN 0-06-442042-6; In Canada: HarperCollins, 1996. 53p. ill. (Trophy chapter book).
The life story of a remarkable individual, the son of a Georgia sharecropper, who was the first African-American to play major-league baseball. In the beginning he had to endure insults, threats, and taunts from other players and even members of his own team until he proved to the world that he was the greatest, regardless of his color. For multicultural studies.

SUBJ: Robinson, Jackie./ Baseball players./ Afro-Americans--Biography.

B ROBINSON, J.　　　　Ph-2 4-6/6　$18.00　L　KE517
SANTELLA, ANDREW. Jackie Robinson breaks the color line. Children's Press ISBN 0-516-06637-4; In Canada: Grolier Ltd., 1996. 32p. ill. (Cornerstones of freedom).
Includes glossary, chronology and index.
Clearly defines the problems which Robinson faced when he became the first African-American player in the major leagues of baseball. Also discusses the problems Robinson encountered when he was in the service. Excellent photographs show this athlete as a boy, ball player, father, and civil rights activist. For African-American history units and multicultural studies.
SUBJ: Robinson, Jackie./ Baseball players./ Afro-Americans--Biography./ Discrimination in sports.

B ROBINSON, J.　　　　Ph-1 6-A/7　$15.95　L　KE518
WEIDHORN, MANFRED. Jackie Robinson. Atheneum ISBN 0-689-31644-5; In Canada: Maxwell Macmillan, 1993. 207p. ill.
Includes bibliography and index.
Jackie Robinson's amazing athletic abilities, his courage and determination, and his fight for recognition for African-Americans are all detailed in this study which fully describes the 1940s and 50s when he broke the color barrier in major league baseball. For mature readers interested in civil rights and multicultural studies.
SUBJ: Robinson, Jackie./ Baseball players./ Afro-Americans--Biography.

B ROGERS, W.　　　　Ph-2 1-3/2　$15.95　L　KE519
SCHOTT, JANE A. Will Rogers. Illus. by David Charles Brandon. Carolrhoda ISBN 0-87614-983-2, 1996. 48p. col. ill. (Carolrhoda on my own book).
Includes chronology and glossary.
Will Rogers won a special place in the hearts of Americans with his humor. This biography for young readers explores how he developed his humor, learned to rope steers, and became a stage performer. For multicultural studies and for units on humor, Native Americans, and the West.
SUBJ: Rogers, Will./ Entertainers./ Humorists.

B ROOSEVELT, E.　　　　Ph-1 4-5/7　$15.99　L　KE520
COONEY, BARBARA. Eleanor. Viking ISBN 0-670-86159-6; In Canada: Penguin, 1996. unp. col. ill.
Through pictures and text, Barbara Cooney describes Eleanor Roosevelt's early, lonely childhood and her struggle to develop her own personality. The confidence that she gained while studying in England is stressed. Cooney's drawings capture the elegance and strictness of the homes in which she lived as a youngster.
SUBJ: Roosevelt, Eleanor--Childhood and youth./ First ladies.

B ROOSEVELT, E.　　　　Ph-1 6-A/7　$17.95　T　KE521
FREEDMAN, RUSSELL. Eleanor Roosevelt: a life of discovery. Clarion ISBN 0-89919-862-7, 1993. 198p. ill.
Includes bibliography and index.
Newbery Honor book, 1994.
Following a detailed study of Eleanor Roosevelt's childhood, this sympathetic biography explains how she overcame her shyness and insecurities to become a teacher, writer, and diplomat. For mature readers wanting to better understand the woman who broke all the molds.
SUBJ: Roosevelt, Eleanor./ First ladies.

B ROOSEVELT, F.　　　　Ph-1 6-A/7　$16.95　T　KE522
FREEDMAN, RUSSELL. Franklin Delano Roosevelt. Clarion ISBN 0-89919-379-X, 1990. 200p. ill.
Includes index.
His education and family training prompted Franklin Roosevelt to seek political involvement soon after he became a lawyer. His illness and handicap didn't deter his continued battle for political office. This lavishly illustrated book pictures his attempts to bring prosperity and peace to his country. An in-depth study for mature readers seeking an understanding of World War II and the troubled 30s.
SUBJ: Roosevelt, Franklin Delano./ Presidents.

B ROOSEVELT, T.　　　　Ph-1 5-6/6　$15.95　T　KE523
FRITZ, JEAN. Bully for you, Teddy Roosevelt! Illus. by Mike Wimmer. Putnam ISBN 0-399-21769-X; In Canada: Putnam, 1991. 127p. ill.
Includes bibliography and index.
Available from the National Library Service for the Blind and Physically Handicapped on sound recording cassette RC34832.
Teddy learned as a child that determination could overcome many obstacles--weak vision, small stature, etc. This determination served him well when he sought political office, and his vigor as he

approached each new job won him the love of the American people. For history and conservation units.
SUBJ: Roosevelt, Theodore./ Presidents.

VCR B ROOSEVELT, T.   Ph-2 6-A $30.00   OD KE524
THEODORE ROOSEVELT: THE COWBOY PRESIDENT (Videocassette). Clearvue/EAV AH014-14, 1990. 1/2" VHS videocassette color (15min). (American portraits).
Includes Teacher's Guide.
The many facets of Roosevelt's life are covered in this lively video which uses numerous cartoons to show how Roosevelt looked to the public during his many years as a public servant.
SUBJ: Roosevelt, Theodore./ Presidents.

B ROOSEVELT, T.   Ph-2 5-A/7 $11.95   L   KE525
WHITELAW, NANCY. Theodore Roosevelt takes charge. Whitman ISBN 0-8075-7849-5, 1992. 192p b&w illus and photos.
Includes chronology, bibliography and index.
Available from the National Library Service for the Blind and Physically Handicapped on sound recording cassette RC 38465.
Overcoming sickness and a weak body, Teddy Roosevelt became a political figure known for his interest in preserving nature, championing the mistreated worker and bringing about changes in government and business. Roosevelt's long involvement with politics makes this title equally useful as a biography and a resource for history units.
SUBJ: Roosevelt, Theodore./ Presidents.

B ROSS, B.   Ph-3 3-4/6 $15.95   L   KE526
WALLNER, ALEXANDRA. Betsy Ross. Holiday House ISBN 0-8234-1071-4, 1994. unp. col. ill.
Trained as a girl to be a seamstress, Elizabeth Griscom Ross plied her trade as she worked with her husband in their upholstery shop. According to legend, it was there that George Washington asked her to design a flag for the newly formed United States of America. Colorful, full-page illustrations capture the area of Philadelphia in which Betsy lived and worked.
SUBJ: Ross, Betsy./ Revolutionaries./ Flags--United States./ Women revolutionaries.

B RUDOLPH, W.   Ph-1 3-5/7 $16.00   L   KE527
KRULL, KATHLEEN. Wilma unlimited: how Wilma Rudolph became the world's fastest woman. Illus. by David Diaz. Harcourt Brace ISBN 0-15-201267-2; In Canada: Harcourt Brace c/o Canadian Manda, 1996. unp. col. ill.
As a child Wilma Rudolph was sickly. When she was five, she had scarlet fever and polio. Fighting to get rid of the brace she wore, Wilma developed the determination and stamina which led her to the greatest victory of her life--three gold medals in the 1960 Olympics. The illustrations are a combination of acrylics, watercolors, and gouache and are set against background photographs also created by the artist, David Diaz, a Caldecott medal winner. For multicultural studies and women's studies.
SUBJ: Rudolph, Wilma./ Track and field athletes./ Afro-Americans--Biography./ Women athletes./ Runners (Sports).

B RUSSELL, C.   Ph-2 2-5/5 $15.00   L   KE528
WINTER, JEANETTE. Cowboy Charlie: the story of Charles M. Russell. Harcourt Brace ISBN 0-15-200857-8; In Canada: Harcourt Brace c/o Canadian Manda, 1995. unp. col. ill.
Charles Russell's experiences in the West which he incorporated in his paintings are described in this picture book biography. Illustrations done in acrylics capture the sweep of the frontier and the life of the prairies.
SUBJ: Russell, Charles M. (Charles Marion)./ Artists./ West (U.S.) in art.

B SACAGAWEA   Ph-1 5-6/6 $18.60   L   KE529
ROWLAND, DELLA. Story of Sacajawea: guide to Lewis and Clark. Illus. by Richard Leonard. Gareth Stevens ISBN 0-8368-1385-5; In Canada: Saunders, 1995. 104p. ill., map. (Famous lives).
Originally published by Parachute Press, 1989.
Includes chronology, bibliography and index.
Remaining close to known facts about Sacagawea, this presentation shows how her remarkable courage and wisdom enabled her to be leader, diplomat, and inspiration to the Lewis and Clark expedition. In addition to value in American history units, this title will fit into units on multicultural studies and women's studies.
SUBJ: Sacagawea./ Indians of North America--Biography./ Lewis and Clark Expedition (1804-1806)./ Shoshoni Indians--Biography./ Indians of North America--Women.

VCR B SACAGAWEA   Ph-1 2-5 $275.00   OD KE530
SACAJAWEA (Videocassette). FilmFair Communications/Altschul Group 6109, 1991. 1/2" VHS videocassette color (18min).
Includes teacher's guide.
Includes public performance rights.
All known facts about this Native American heroine are woven into a poetic, animated film which sustains interest from beginning to end. The low-key narration never interrupts the flow of the story. For multicultural studies.
SUBJ: Sacagawea./ Indians of North America--Biography./ Lewis and Clark Expedition (1804-1806)./ Shoshoni Indians--Biography./ Indians of North America--Women.

B SANDBURG, C.   Ph-2 4-6/6 $14.95   L   KE531
MITCHELL, BARBARA. Good morning, Mr. President: a story about Carl Sandburg. Illus. by Dane Collins. Carolrhoda ISBN 0-87614-329-X, 1988. 56p. ill. (Carolrhoda creative minds book).
Includes bibliography.
The time spent as a hobo wasn't wasted time for Carl Sandburg. As he mingled with these footloose men, he gathered their stories and songs to be incorporated later into poems and books. This biography also explains his fascination with Abraham Lincoln and how he became this Civil War president's biographer. Motivational reading for budding authors.
SUBJ: Sandburg, Carl./ Poets, American.

B SEAU, J.   Ph-2 5-A/10 $19.95   L   KE532
MORGAN, TERRI. Junior Seau: high-voltage linebacker. Lerner ISBN 0-8225-2896-7, 1997. 56p. col. ill.
Includes index.
Junior's family originally came from American Samoa located in the South Pacific Ocean. Junior's talents in sports were recognized early and encouraged by his family. Today he is a top defensive player and was twice named Linebacker of the Year by the NFL Players Association.
SUBJ: Seau, Junior./ Football players./ Samoan Americans--Biography.

B SELES, M.   Ph-2 4-6/10 $19.95   L   KE533
FEHR, KRISTIN SMITH. Monica Seles: returning champion. Lerner ISBN 0-8225-2899-1, 1997. 64p. col. ill.
Includes glossary and index.
Monica's grunts and groans are known to all sports enthusiasts. Explains why this young woman gives her all when she is on the tennis court, her flight from Yugoslavia, her conquest of fear and depression after a stabbing by a German fan of Steffi Graf, and her devotion to her family. Color photographs enliven the book.
SUBJ: Seles, Monica./ Tennis players./ Women athletes.

VCR B SENDAK, M.   Ph-2 4-A $49.95   OD KE534
SENDAK (Videocassette). Weston Woods L439, 1993. 1/2" VHS videocassette color (27min).
Maurice Sendak invites the viewer into his studio and explains fully the inspiration for his drawings, primarily his childhood and his family. His great joy, the operettas based on his stories, is also captured on the film. For large collections with adequate funding for material to introduce authors and illustrators to students.
SUBJ: Sendak, Maurice./ Authors, American./ Illustrators.

B SEQUOYAH   Ph-1 5-6/7 $14.89   L   KE535
KLAUSNER, JANET. Sequoyah's gift: a portrait of the Cherokee leader. With an afterword by Duane H. King. HarperCollins ISBN 0-06-021236-5; In Canada: HarperCollins, 1993. 111p. ill., map.
Includes directory, bibliography and index.
Sequoyah's many talents are carefully explored in this well-researched study. Describes his creation of an alphabet for the Cherokee language and his leadership during the troubled times when the Cherokee nation was forced to relocate. For multicultural studies.
SUBJ: Sequoyah./ Cherokee Indians--Biography./ Indians of North America--Biography.

B SERRA, J.   Ph-2 4-6/7 $19.93   L   KE536
WHITE, FLORENCE MEIMAN. Story of Junipero Serra: brave adventurer. Illus. by Stephen Marchesi. Gareth Stevens ISBN 0-8368-1460-6, 1996. 100p. ill. (Famous lives).
Originally published by Parachute Press, Inc. as a Yearling Biography, 1987.
Includes chronology, bibliography, filmography and index.
Describes the life of a dedicated Franciscan missionary who established the first nine missions in California and devoted his life to Native Americans. Sensitively told with a high degree of historical accuracy, the study is well suited for regional and multicultural studies.
SUBJ: Serra, Junipero./ Explorers./ Missionaries./ Indians of North America--Missions--California./ California--History--To 1846.

[handwritten: JB Chaka]

B SHAKA, KING   Ph-1 4-6/6 $15.93   L   KE537
STANLEY, DIANE. Shaka, king of the Zulus. By Diane Stanley and Peter Vennema. Illustrated by Diane Stanley. Morrow ISBN 0-688-07343-3, 1988. unp. col. ill.
  Includes bibliography.
  By defending her son, Shaka's mother becomes an outcast from her tribe and the young boy learns as a youth that he must defend himself. His skill in warfare soon singles him out as a born leader and he develops a formidable army of Zulu warriors. Stunning full page, full color drawings retell the life of this Zulu chief. For all Black History and Africa collections.
  SUBJ: Chaka, Zulu Chief./ Zulus--Biography.

B SHAKESPEARE   Ph-3 4-6/7 $14.93   L   KE538
STANLEY, DIANE. Bard of Avon: the story of William Shakespeare. By Diane Stanley and Peter Vennema. Illus. by Diane Stanley. Morrow ISBN 0-688-09109-1, 1992. unp. col. ill.
  Includes bibliography.
  The known facts of Shakespeare's life are told against a description of the development of the theater during the reigns of Queen Elizabeth I and King James I. Full-page illustrations show the interior of the theater and typical costumes of the era.
  SUBJ: Shakespeare, William./ Dramatists, English./ Poets, English.

B SHELLEY, K.   Ph-2 3-5/5 $14.89   L   KE539
SAN SOUCI, ROBERT D. Kate Shelley: bound for legend. Illus. by Max Ginsburg. Dial ISBN 0-8037-1290-1, 1995. unp. col. ill., map.
  Kate's heroism on the night of July 6th, 1881 as she battled through a storm to stop a train from crossing a washed-out bridge is vividly retold in this picture-book biography. The train had been stopped, but Kate's daring led rescuers to the site of a steam engine which had plunged off the broken bridge. A good, carefully researched addition to collections featuring strong female role models. For women's studies.
  SUBJ: Shelley, Kate./ Heroines./ Railroads--Accidents.

B SITTING BULL   Ph-2 3-4/5 $15.95   L   KE540
ADLER, DAVID A. Picture book of Sitting Bull. Illus. by Samuel Byrd. Holiday House ISBN 0-8234-1044-7, 1993. unp. col. ill. (Picture book biography).
  Includes chronology.
  Sitting Bull's many attempts to protect the Sioux and their way of life are described in text and pictures. Depicts his many roles as leader, warrior, showman, and prophet. Use in units on Native Americans, multicultural studies, and settlement of the West.
  SUBJ: Sitting Bull, Sioux Chief./ Dakota Indians--Biography./ Indians of North America--Great Plains--Biography.

B SITTING BULL   Ph-2 3-4/6 $15.95   L   KE541
BRUCHAC, JOSEPH. Boy called Slow: the true story of Sitting Bull. Illus. by Rocco Baviera. Philomel ISBN 0-399-22692-3; In Canada: Putnam, 1994. unp. col. ill., map.
  Using a picture book format, this retelling shows how Sitting Bull was able through daring and strength to gain his name. As a child he had been called "Slow" because of his mannerisms, but his actions as a youth proved this name to be inappropriate. Somber paintings show the life-style of the Lakota Indians. For multicultural studies.
  SUBJ: Sitting Bull, Sioux Chief./ Dakota Indians--Biography./ Indians of North America--Biography.

B SITTING BULL   Ph-2 5-A/6 $17.95   L   KE542
ST. GEORGE, JUDITH. To see with the heart: the life of Sitting Bull. Putnam ISBN 0-399-22930-2; In Canada: Putnam, 1996. 182p. maps.
  Includes bibliography and index.
  Several times in his life, Sitting Bull's heart ruled over his reason. This detailed telling of his life explains these times as well as the many times he showed his remarkable powers as war chief, hunter, and inspirational leader of the Hunkpapa tribe of the Sioux. In researching this book, the author examined many resources about the Sioux Indians and traveled the land occupied by Sitting Bull. For advanced readers who are exploring the history of Native Americans. For multicultural studies.
  SUBJ: Sitting Bull, Sioux Chief./ Dakota Indians--Biography./ Indians of North America--Biography./ Hunkpapa Indians--Biography.

B SMITH, E.   Ph-2 4-6/7 $19.95   L   KE543
THORNLEY, STEW. Emmitt Smith: relentless rusher. Lerner ISBN 0-8225-2897-5, 1997. 64p. col. ill.
  Includes index.
  Emmitt Smith's statistics after five NFL seasons (2 Super Bowl championships and 7,000 yards on the ground) are outstanding, but it is his personal devotion to the sport and his family which make him a star football player. For multicultural studies.
  SUBJ: Smith, Emmitt./ Football players./ Afro-Americans--Biography.

B SOUSA, J.   Ph-2 2-4/2 $4.95   P   KE544
GREENE, CAROL. John Philip Sousa: the march king. Childrens Press ISBN 0-516-44226-0; In Canada: Childrens Press, 1992. 47p. ill. (Rookie biography).
  Includes chronology and index.
  At thirteen, John Philip Sousa joined the Marines and their band! The remarkable dedication of this composer to music and his lifelong role in developing and leading bands are simply presented in this brief text with well selected photographs. For beginning readers.
  SUBJ: Sousa, John Philip./ Composers./ Musicians.

B SPIELBERG, S.   Ph-2 4-6/8 $18.95   L   KE545
MEACHUM, VIRGINIA. Steven Spielberg: Hollywood filmmaker. Enslow ISBN 0-89490-697-6, 1996. 112p. ill. (People to know).
  Includes chronology, bibliography and index.
  The unique way Spielberg entered the film industry is described along with the plots of many of his well-known films. For science fiction fans and students interested in filmmaking.
  SUBJ: Spielberg, Steven./ Motion picture producers and directors.

B SPIELBERG, S.   Ph-2 5-A/7 $21.50   L   KE546
POWERS, TOM. Steven Spielberg: master storyteller. Lerner ISBN 0-8225-4929-8, 1997. 128p. ill. (some col.). (Newsmakers).
  Includes filmography, bibliography and index.
  Spielberg's early fascination with filmmaking is covered along with descriptions of the many films which have made him a household name. Spielberg's recent business ventures are also described.
  SUBJ: Spielberg, Steven./ Motion picture producers and directors.

B SQUANTO   Ph-3 3/3 $2.75   P   KE547
BULLA, CLYDE ROBERT. Squanto: friend of the Pilgrims. Illustrated by Peter Burchard. Scholastic ISBN 0-590-44055-1; In Canada: Scholastic, c1954, 1982. 112p. ill. (Scholastic biography).
  His kindness to the Pilgrims and his trip to London resulted in Squanto becoming a vital link in New England. This simple story of the role of an Indian in caring for settlers has a place in units on settlers, holidays and American Indians.
  SUBJ: Squanto./ Thanksgiving Day./ Indians of North America--Massachusetts--Biography./ Pilgrims (New Plymouth Colony).

KIT B SQUANTO   Ph-1 2-6 $19.95   KE548
METAXAS, ERIC. Squanto and the first Thanksgiving (Kit). Illus. by Michael A. Donato. Read by Graham Greene. Rabbit Ears/dist. by Simon & Schuster ISBN 0-689-80234-X; In Canada: Distican, 1996. 1 hardback book, 1 sound cassette (25min).
  Tells the story of Squanto in memorable fashion as narration, distinguished visuals, and a woodwind score mesh effectively. Depicts the hardships of life in the New Plymouth colony and the hope that the first Thanksgiving represented. Use in units related to holidays, American heroes, early United States history, and Indians of North America. For multicultural studies.
  SUBJ: Squanto./ Thanksgiving Day./ Indians of North America--Massachusetts--Biography./ Pilgrims (New Plymouth Colony).

B STANTON, E.   Ph-1 3-6/5 $15.95   L   KE549
FRITZ, JEAN. You want women to vote, Lizzie Stanton? Illus. by DyAnne DiSalvo-Ryan. Putnam ISBN 0-399-22786-5; In Canada: Putnam, 1995. 88p. ill.
  Includes bibliography and index.
  Longing to be the boy that her father desperately wanted, Lizzie Stanton realized as a young woman that this was not possible and that women in general were denied the privileges granted to males. This lively retelling of her life describes her writings, lectures, and valiant battle to get women the right to vote. For women's studies.
  SUBJ: Stanton, Elizabeth Cady./ Feminists./ Women's rights--History./ Women--Suffrage--History.

B STEIFF, M.   Ph-2 2-3/2 $16.60   L   KE550
GREENE, CAROL. Margarete Steiff: toy maker. Childrens Press ISBN 0-516-04257-2; In Canada: Childrens Press, 1993. 47p. col. ill. (Rookie biography).
  Includes chronology and index.
  Margarete's parents worried about who would care for her because of her disability resulting from childhood polio. Instead she created a toy manufacturing industry which cared for her, her family, and the people of her village. Beginning readers will find Margarete Steiff an inspirational, creative person. For units on persons with disabilities.
  SUBJ: Steiff, Margarete./ Toymakers./ Physically handicapped--Biography./ Businesswomen.

B STEVENSON, J.   Ph-1 3-4/4 $13.93   L   KE551
STEVENSON, JAMES. When I was nine. Greenwillow ISBN 0-688-05943-0, 1986. unp. col. ill.
  Softly hued illustrations and simple but exuberant text recall life in

upstate New York in the 1930s. The entrancing autobiography serves as a fine model of the literary form for middle graders.
The magic of a vacation at the beach with loving grandparents is captured in JULY (ISBN 0-688-08823-6, 1990). When Stevenson was young, he found most things in life were fun--but some things weren't in FUN NO FUN (ISBN 0-688-11674-4, 1994).
In I HAD A LOT OF WISHES (ISBN 0-688-13706-7, 1995) simple text continues the author-artist's memories of his childhood as he recalls his childhood wishes.
SUBJ: Stevenson, James./ Authors, American./ Illustrators.

B STEVENSON, J.   Ph-1 K-3/2 $14.00   T   KE552
STEVENSON, JAMES. Don't you know there's a war on? Greenwillow ISBN 0-688-11383-4, 1992. unp. col. ill.
Available from the National Library Service for the Blind and Physically Handicapped on sound recording cassette RC 36431.
James Stevenson was a young boy during World War II, and this pictorial memoir captures his activities during the war years and his loneliness when his father and brother left home. An autobiography for the lower grades.
SUBJ: Stevenson, James./ Authors, American./ Illustrators./ World War, 1939-1945--United States.

B STEVENSON, J.   Ph-1 3-4/4 $12.88   L   KE553
STEVENSON, JAMES. Higher on the door. Greenwillow ISBN 0-688-06637-2, 1987. unp. col. ill.
Selectors' Choice, 16th ed.
In another nostalgic childhood reminiscence, the author "remembers what it was like growing up in a village, sometimes taking a train to New York City, and waiting to get older." (CIP)
SUBJ: Stevenson, James./ Authors, American./ Illustrators.

B STEVENSON, R.   Ph-3 2-4/4 $17.20   L   KE554
GREENE, CAROL. Robert Louis Stevenson: author of A CHILD'S GARDEN OF VERSES. Childrens Press ISBN 0-516-04265-3; In Canada: Childrens Press, 1994. 47p. ill. (some col.). (Rookie biography).
Includes chronology and index.
The sickly and overprotected childhood of Robert Louis Stevenson is pictured, so readers may better understand how his imagination developed and produced the poetry and stories which made him famous. Background reading for young readers being introduced to his verse.
SUBJ: Stevenson, Robert Louis./ Authors, Scottish.

VCR B STEVENSON, R.   Ph-1 5-6 $58.00   OD KE555
MEET THE AUTHOR: ROBERT LOUIS STEVENSON (Videocassette). SRA/McGraw-Hill 87-509245, 1989. 1/2" iconographic VHS videocassette color (18min). (Meet the author).
The creative years of Stevenson's life are seen through the eyes of his adopted son with skillful use of photographs and pictures of areas in which Stevenson lived. Can be used to introduce Stevenson's works or as a view of how books are created.
SUBJ: Stevenson, Robert Louis./ Authors, Scottish.

B STOWE, H.   Ph-2 6-A/7 $15.95   T   KE556
FRITZ, JEAN. Harriet Beecher Stowe and the Beecher preachers. Putnam ISBN 0-399-22666-4; In Canada: Putnam, 1994. 144p. ill.
Includes bibliography and index.
Harriet is only one of the Beecher family, boys and girls, whom her father molded (forced) into becoming ministers. The impact of her father's preferences for boys, her sincere devotion to stopping slavery, and her ability to provide financial stability for her family through writing are all investigated in this study of the Beecher clan. For mature readers interested in the era preceding and during the Civil War. For women's studies and multicultural studies.
SUBJ: Stowe, Harriet Beecher./ Authors, American./ Women authors, American./ Abolitionists./ Beecher family.

B STRAVINSKY, I   Ph-2 5-6/7 $19.50   L   KE557
VENEZIA, MIKE. Igor Stravinsky. Children's Press ISBN 0-516-20054-2; In Canada: Children's Press, 1996. 32p. col. ill. (Getting to know the world's greatest composers).
Stravinsky's best known compositions are for the ballet. He incorporated into his works his love of folklore and folk music. Cartoon reproductions of artwork and sketches expand the text and explain the events in the world which influenced his music. For music classes.
SUBJ: Stravinsky, Igor./ Composers.

B TCHAIKOVSKY,P   Ph-3 6-A/8 $17.99   T   KE558
THOMPSON, WENDY. Pyotr Ilyich Tchaikovsky. Viking ISBN 0-670-84476-4; In Canada: Penguin, 1993. 48p. col. ill. (Composer's world).
Includes glossary and index.
Tchaikovsky's troubled life is examined. Includes simple keyboard

arrangements for many of his outstanding works as well as a map of nineteenth-century Russia. For mature students interested in music and Russian history.
SUBJ: Tchaikovsky, Peter Ilych./ Composers.

B TECUMSEH   Ph-2 5-6/7 $19.92   L   KE559
CONNELL, KATE. These lands are ours: Tecumseh's fight for the Old Northwest. Illus. by Jan Naimo Jones. Raintree Steck-Vaughn ISBN 0-8114-7227-2, 1993. 96p. ill. (Stories of America).
Tecumseh foresaw the white settlers' invasion of the lands on which the Shawnee had lived and hunted. When treaties failed, he organized and led war parties to hold the lands. His death while serving with the British in 1812 brought an end to his courageous leadership and perhaps, allowed the continuing westward movement. An invaluable book for history units.
SUBJ: Tecumseh, Shawnee Chief./ Shawnee Indians--Biography./ Indians of North America--Biography.

VCR B TERBAN, M.   Ph-1 5-A $29.95   OD KE560
VISIT WITH MARVIN TERBAN (Videocassette). Houghton Mifflin-Clarion ISBN 0-395-60536-9, c1991, 1992. 1/2" VHS videocassette color (14min). (Author and artist series).
Selectors' Choice, 19th ed.
Marvin Terban's ideas for his books come from his efforts to make his classes exciting, and his rapport with students certainly comes across here. Teachers will enjoy watching this master teacher in action.
SUBJ: Terban, Marvin./ Authors, American./ Educators.

B TERESA,MOTHER   Ph-2 4-6/6 $6.95   P   KE561
JACOBS, WILLIAM JAY. Mother Teresa: helping the poor. Millbrook ISBN 1-87884-157-2, 1991. 47p. col. ill. (Gateway biography).
Includes chronology, bibliography and index.
Inspired by the teachings of her mother and her church, Agnes Bojaxhiu left her home in Albania and went to Calcutta, India to teach. There she established a new order of nuns to care for the poor and sick of India. Liberal use of photographs show the conditions in which Mother Teresa works.
SUBJ: Teresa, Mother./ Nuns./ Calcutta (India)--Biography./ Missionaries./ Missionaries of Charity.

B TERRELL, M.   Ph-3 3-6/2 $12.95   L   KE562
MCKISSACK, PAT. Mary Church Terrell: leader for equality. By Patricia and Fredrick McKissack. Illus. by Ned O. Enslow ISBN 0-89490-305-5, 1991. 32p b&w photos and illus. (Great African Americans).
Includes glossary and index.
Coming from a financially secure family, Mary used her position, education and influence to gain understanding for the inequalities facing her people. Mrs. Terrell is certainly a role model for girls interested in government and education. Freely illustrated and with an appendix of words introduced in the text.
SUBJ: Terrell, Mary Church./ Civil rights workers./ Afro-Americans--Biography./ Women civil rights workers.

B THOMAS, F.   Ph-2 3-5/6 $14.40   L   KE563
GUTMAN, BILL. Frank Thomas: power hitter. Millbrook ISBN 1-56294-569-6, 1996. 48p. col. ill. (Millbrook sports world).
Includes chronology, bibliography, directory and index.
Frank Thomas' life seems full of setbacks: the death of a baby sister, not being drafted out of high school, and being sent back to the minors. Each setback he turned into a positive achievement. This baseball player has the potential of being in Baseball's Hall of Fame, and this title explains his drive. Motivational reading for sports fans and multicultural studies.
SUBJ: Thomas, Frank./ Baseball players./ Afro-Americans--Biography.

B THOMPSON, S.   Ph-1 K-3/2 $12.89   L   KE564
LEVINSON, NANCY SMILER. Snowshoe Thompson. Illus. by Joan Sandin. HarperCollins ISBN 0-06-023802-X; In Canada: HarperCollins, 1992. 64p. col. ill., map. (I can read book).
John Thompson (a pioneer of skiing in America) makes a pair of skis and crosses the Sierra Nevada in winter to assure that the mail will be delivered. A bit of American folklore told through the eyes of a young boy who wants to send a letter to his dad on the other side of the mountain.
SUBJ: Thompson, Snowshoe./ Postal service--Letter carriers./ Pioneers./ Frontier and pioneer life--West (U.S.).

B THOREAU, H.   Ph-2 2-5/3 $12.40   L   KE565
RING, ELIZABETH. Henry David Thoreau: in step with nature. Millbrook ISBN 1-56294-258-1, 1993. 48p. col. ill. (Gateway green biography).
Includes chronology, bibliography and index.
Believing that a person might live differently from his neighbors, young Thoreau left his comfortable home to reside in a simple cabin beside Walden Pond outside Concord, Massachusetts. The writing he

did while living there has become a literary masterpiece. This poetic biography will inspire students to discover more about the man. Background for history and language arts units and for environmental studies.
SUBJ: Thoreau, Henry David./ Authors, American./ Naturalists.

B THORPE, J.   Ph-1 6-A/7 $13.89   L   KE566
LIPSYTE, ROBERT. Jim Thorpe: 20th-century jock. HarperCollins ISBN 0-06-022989-6; In Canada: HarperCollins. 103p. ill. (Superstar lineup).
Includes bibliography and index.
The many heartbreaks which filled Jim Thorpe's life are hauntingly portrayed in this full study of his life which concentrates on his formative years. Dispels the myth that the Olympic star gained his medals by chance. The fascinating episode of early Olympic history is useful for multicultural studies and recommended for mature readers.
SUBJ: Thorpe, Jim./ Athletes./ Indians of North America--Biography.

B TOLKIEN, J.   Ph-3 6-A/6 $15.95   L   KE567
COLLINS, DAVID R. J.R.R. Tolkien: master of fantasy. Illus. by William Heagy. Lerner ISBN 0-8225-4906-9, 1992. 112p. ill., maps.
Includes chronology, glossary, bibliographies and index.
The creation of the world of THE HOBBIT and the books which followed were labors of delight. This title explores the life of the creator of these modern classics. For advanced readers.
SUBJ: Tolkien, J.R.R. (John Ronald Reuel)./ Authors, English.

B TOULOUSE-LAUT   Ph-2 4-6/8 $17.20   L   KE568
VENEZIA, MIKE. Henri de Toulouse-Lautrec. Childrens Press ISBN 0-516-02283-0; In Canada: Childrens Press, 1995. 32p. col. ill. (Getting to know the world's greatest artists).
Stresses Toulouse-Lautrec's lifelong interest in drawing the animals, scenes, and people around him. Reproductions of his paintings, drawings, and posters are excellent and make this suitable for browsing as well as class assignments.
SUBJ: Toulouse-Lautrec, Henry de./ Artists./ Painting, French./ Art appreciation.

B TOUSSAINT   Ph-1 4-A/8 $16.00   T   KE569
LAWRENCE, JACOB. Toussaint L'Ouverture: the fight for Haiti's freedom. Paintings by Jacob Lawrence. Text by Walter Dean Myers. Simon & Schuster ISBN 0-689-80126-2; In Canada: Distican, 1996. unp. col. ill.
Jacob Lawrence explains in a preface his admiration for L'Ouverture who led the battle for Haiti's freedom. His paintings, stark and poignant, of this hero's life are augmented by a text which is equally dramatic. For all collections. For multicultural studies.
SUBJ: Toussaint L'Ouverture./ Haiti--History--Revolution, 1791-1804./ Revolutionaries./ Generals./ Blacks--Haiti--Biography.

B TREVINO, L.   Ph-2 5-6/6 $22.83   L   KE570
KRAMER, JON. Lee Trevino. Raintree Steck-Vaughn ISBN 0-8172-4124-8, 1996. 48p. col. ill. (Overcoming the odds).
Includes chronology, bibliography and index.
At the age of eight, Lee Trevino worked as a caddie. His natural ability, sense of humor, and willingness to work brought him into the top rank of golfers in the United States. Also covered are his setbacks--being struck by lightning, back surgery, and a broken thumb. Color photographs cover all aspects of his career. For multicultural studies.
SUBJ: Trevino, Lee./ Golfers./ Mexican Americans--Biography.

B TRUMAN, H.   Ph-2 5-A/9 $18.95   L   KE571
SCHUMAN, MICHAEL. Harry S. Truman. By Michael A. Schuman. Enslow ISBN 0-89490-833-2, 1997. 112p. ill. (United States presidents).
Includes chronology, directory, bibliographies and index.
Constantly struggling to find employment to support himself and his family, Truman was known for hard work, honesty, and dedication to the people he knew. This keen study of the evolution of this man who catapulted into the presidency shows how he grew in stature and became one of our most respected presidents. Numerous photographs and chronology round out this solid work.
SUBJ: Truman, Harry S./ Presidents.

B TRUTH, S.   Ph-2 2-5/6 $15.95   L   KE572
ADLER, DAVID A. Picture book of Sojourner Truth. Illus. by Gershom Griffith. Holiday House ISBN 0-8234-1072-2, 1994. unp. col. ill. (Picture book biography).
Includes chronology.
A brutal childhood, during which Isabella (Sojourner) belonged to many masters, strengthened her resolve to gain freedom for herself and her children. Stresses the firsts in her life--success in the courts, on the dais, and in print as a narrator of life under slavery. Full-page illustrations augment the text. For multicultural studies and women's studies.

SUBJ: Truth, Sojourner./ Abolitionists./ Reformers./ Afro-Americans--Biography./ Women reformers.

B TRUTH, S.   Ph-1 6-A/7 $13.95   L   KE573
MCKISSACK, PAT. Sojourner Truth: ain't I a woman? By Patricia C. and Fredrick McKissack. Scholastic ISBN 0-590-44690-8; In Canada: Scholastic, 1992. 186p. ill.
Includes bibliography and index.
Coretta Scott King Award Honor book, 1993.
The inspiring story of Sojourner Truth, the freed slave who became a staunch abolitionist and feminist, is supported by photographs and reproductions of historical documents. Her life is presented in the context of the period as the text introduces other notable figures of the time--Frederick Douglass, Harriet Beecher Stowe, William Lloyd Garrison, and others. Afterword provides biographical information of many of the famous people with whom she worked. Liberal use of quotes personalizes the work. For mature readers.
SUBJ: Truth, Sojourner./ Abolitionists./ Reformers./ Afro-Americans--Biography./ Women reformers.

B TUBMAN, H.   Ph-3 4-6/4 $11.90   L   KE574
ELISH, DAN. Harriet Tubman and the Underground Railroad. Millbrook ISBN 1-56294-273-5, 1993. 32p. col. ill. (Gateway civil rights).
Includes chronology, bibliography and index.
An overview of the life of Harriet Tubman, well-known for her role as a guide on the Underground Railroad. Includes information about her childhood as well as her later years as a women's rights suffragette. Photographs of Tubman augment the text. For African-American studies as well as social studies and women's studies.
SUBJ: Tubman, Harriet (Ross)./ Slavery--Biography./ Afro-Americans--Biography./ Underground railroad.

B TUBMAN, H.   Ph-2 A/7 $3.99   P   KE575
PETRY, ANN. Harriet Tubman: conductor on the Underground Railroad. Pocket Books ISBN 0-671-73146-7; In Canada: HarperCollins, c1955, 1996. 247p.
Includes index.
As a child Minty endured abuse in many forms. Beatings scarred her body, but didn't beat out her longing to be free. Her escape North and her ability to make friends in Philadelphia encouraged her to go back and lead others to freedom "guided only by the North Star." A scholarly work which includes many quotations from other leading figures in the Abolitionist movement. For history units and multicultural studies.
SUBJ: Tubman, Harriet (Ross)./ Slavery--Biography./ Afro-Americans--Biography./ Underground railroad.

VCR B TUBMAN, H.   Ph-2 4-A $99.00   OD KE576
STEAL AWAY: THE HARRIET TUBMAN STORY (Videocassette). National Geographic 52670, 1997. 1/2" VHS videocassette color (28min).
Includes teacher's guide.
Closed captioned.
A fictional character relates Harriet Tubman's life as she heard "Moses" tell it as they fled north to Canada. All of the additional material about slavery is based on historical documents. The enactments are well done, and this tape is a good addition to any discussion of African-American history. For multicultural studies.
SUBJ: Tubman, Harriet (Ross)./ Slavery--Biography./ Afro-Americans--Biography./ Underground railroad.

B TURNER, N.   Ph-3 5-6/6 $4.95   P   KE577
BARRETT, TRACY. Nat Turner and the slave revolt. Millbrook ISBN 1-56294-792-3, c1993, 1995. 32p. col. ill. (Gateway civil rights).
Includes chronology, bibliography and index.
Nat Turner's rebellion and death brought attention to the horrors of slavery. A variety of prints, drawings, and photographs explain the circumstances under which he lived and his impact upon history.
SUBJ: Turner, Nat./ Slavery--Biography./ Afro-Americans--Biography./ Southampton Insurrection, 1831.

B TUTANKHAMEN   Ph-1 2-4/3 $15.95   L   KE578
SABUDA, ROBERT. Tutankhamen's gift. Atheneum ISBN 0-689-31818-9; In Canada: Maxwell Macmillan, 1994. unp. col. ill.
Tutankhamen's brief life unfolds in colorful pictures which include his cats. Depicts how he gains the throne as a young boy and restores the splendor of the temples. Readers will appreciate his desire to bring back the glories of his father's reign. For units on Egypt and Egyptian art.
SUBJ: Tutankhamen, King of Egypt./ Kings, queens, rulers, etc.

B TWAIN, M.   Ph-1 6-A/8 $14.95   L   KE579
COX, CLINTON. Mark Twain: America's humorist, dreamer, prophet. Scholastic ISBN 0-590-45642-3; In Canada: Scholastic, 1995. 234p. ill.

Includes bibliography and index.
A fast paced anecdotal account of Twain's life as a river pilot, journalist, speaker, and author. The numerous excerpts from his letters and journals explore his prejudices, attempts to overcome them, and ability to laugh at man's foibles. For readers of Tom Sawyer or teachers explaining racial attitudes of the past.
SUBJ: Twain, Mark./ Authors, American./ Humorists.

B TWAIN, M.   Ph-1 6/8 $11.95   L   KE580
QUACKENBUSH, ROBERT. Mark Twain? What kind of name is that?: a story of Samuel Langhorne Clemens. Prentice-Hall ISBN 0-671-66294-5; In Canada: Prentice-Hall, 1984. 33p. ill.
Helping his older brother Orion print a newspaper convinced Samuel Clemens that journalism and story writing was the thing that he could do best. This humorous biography traces Clemens' travels on the Mississippi, through the western states and Europe. The book's primary use will be in Language Arts but will have value for career units.
SUBJ: Twain, Mark./ Authors, American./ Humorists.

B VALENTINE,ST.   Ph-2 4-6/4 $14.95   L   KE581
SABUDA, ROBERT. Saint Valentine. Retold and illus. by Robert Sabuda. Atheneum ISBN 0-689-31762-X; In Canada: Maxwell Macmillan, 1992. unp. col. ill.
Available from the National Library Service for the Blind and Physically Handicapped on sound recording cassette RC 37982.
A humble physician treats a blind child in Rome in the year 200. When he is sentenced to death because he is a Christian, his final gift to the child is signed "From your Valentine." Thus this legend is remembered at the time of Valentine's Day. Illustrated with dramatic mosaics. For holiday celebrations, units on saints, and art classes.
SUBJ: Valentine, Saint./ Saints.

B VERNE, J.   Ph-3 5-A/6 $14.85   L   KE582
TEETERS, PEGGY. Jules Verne: the man who invented tomorrow. Walker ISBN 0-8027-8191-8; In Canada: Thomas Allen & Son, 1992. 120p. ill.
Includes bibliography and index.
Available from the National Library Service for the Blind and Physically Handicapped on sound recording cassette RC 37657.
Defying his father's wishes that he become a lawyer, Verne continued his aspirations to be an author and his consuming interest in science. His books amazed his audiences in the nineteenth century and set the stage for science-fiction writing. For mature readers.
SUBJ: Verne, Jules./ Authors, French.

B WALKER, C.J.   Ph-3 4-6/7 $13.40   L   KE583
COLMAN, PENNY. Madam C.J. Walker: building a business empire. Millbrook ISBN 1-56294-338-3, 1994. 48p. ill. (some col.). (Gateway biography).
Includes chronology, bibliography and index.
Recognizing that there was a need for hair products for African-American women, Madam C.J. Walker produced such a cosmetic, manufactured it, trained a sales force, and became "America's first female self-made millionaire." Slim, inspirational volume for inclusion in multicultural studies and women's studies.
SUBJ: Walker, C.J., Madam./ Businesswomen./ Afro-Americans--Biography./ Cosmetics industry--History.

VCR B WALKER, C.J.   Ph-3 5-A $39.95   KE584
MADAM C.J. WALKER (Videocassette). Adapted from the book by Marian W. Taylor. Schlessinger Video D6610, 1992. 1/2" VHS videocassette color (30min). (Black Americans of achievement video collection).
Based on the book MADAM C.J. WALKER, Chelsea House, (ISBN 1-55546-615-X, 1991).
Closed captioned.
The amazing story of a young woman's rise from being a washerwoman to being one of America's leading businesswomen is related by historians and relatives. Augmented by numerous archival photographs. For multicultural studies and women's studies.
SUBJ: Walker, C.J., Madam./ Businesswomen./ Afro-Americans--Biography.

VCR B WASHINGTON, B   Ph-1 3-6 $14.95   KE585
BOOKER (Videocassette). WQED, Pittsburgh/dist. by Bonneville Worldwide Entertainment BWE 0035 ISBN 1-57742-035-7, 1983. 1/2" VHS videocassette color (58min). (Wonderworks family movie).
Includes public performance rights.
Closed captioned.
The early years of Booker T. Washington's life are dramatized in this film made originally for TV. Covers his longing to read, his family's relocation after the Civil War, and his attendance at a school for Negro children developed by members of his church. The acting is outstanding. One gains an understanding of how freed slaves were cheated because of their illiteracy and how difficult the Reconstruction years were. For multicultural studies.
SUBJ: Washington, Booker T./ Teachers./ Afro-Americans--Biography.

B WASHINGTON, B   Ph-2 4-6/5 $13.90   L   KE586
ROBERTS, JACK L. Booker T. Washington: educator and leader. Millbrook ISBN 1-56294-487-8, 1995. 32p. ill. (some col.). (Gateway civil rights).
Includes chronology, bibliography and index.
Booker T. Washington's role as an educator in the late 1890s and early 1900s is fairly examined in this brief summary of his life. The impact of his speeches and beliefs in a time of racial inequality has left a permanent mark on American history. Readers are asked to review their thinking about this leader when reading this text. For multicultural studies.
SUBJ: Washington, Booker T./ Teachers./ Afro-Americans--Biography.

B WASHINGTON, G   Ph-2 4-5/6 $13.95   L   KE587
ADLER, DAVID A. George Washington: father of our country. Illus. by Jacqueline Garrick. Holiday House ISBN 0-8234-0717-9, 1988. 48p. ill. (First biography).
Includes index.
Discovering in his youth that he enjoyed mathematics, George Washington became a surveyor first and then a soldier. The early skills aided him when he became the first general of the Continental Army. This slim book with black and white drawings is a good addition to social studies and holiday units.
SUBJ: Washington, George./ Presidents.

VCR B WASHINGTON, G   Ph-2 6-A $30.00   OD KE588
GEORGE WASHINGTON: THE FIRST (Videocassette). Clearvue/EAV AH011-CV, 1990. 1/2" VHS videocassette color (15min). (American portraits).
Includes Teacher's Guide.
By discussing how his contemporaries viewed him, this film allows the viewer to form his own opinion as to whether George Washington created the times in which he lived or was created by the times. Extensive use of pictures from the era. For social studies units or Washington's birthday.
SUBJ: Washington, George./ Presidents.

B WATSON, L.   Ph-2 4-6/7 $27.07   L   KE589
WATSON, LYALL. Warriors, warthogs, and wisdom: growing up in Africa. Illus. by Keith West. Kingfisher/dist. by Raintree Steck-Vaughn ISBN 0-7534-5066-6, 1997. 80p. ill., map.
Selectors' Choice, 21st ed.
The author's childhood in South Africa was filled with unique experiences. He raised a warthog as a pet, watched his grandmother rig up a contraption from his grandfather's pants to cure a sick saddlehill stork, and admired her for her creation "of crocodiles with four left hind feet." The author invites readers to "come soon" to Africa, and after reading this humorous autobiography, they will long to go. Useful for multicultural studies and for geography or nature study units.
SUBJ: Watson, Lyall--Childhood and youth./ South Africa--Biography.

B WEBBER, C.   Ph-2 5-6/7 $18.95   L   KE590
KNAPP, RON. Chris Webber: star forward. Enslow ISBN 0-89490-799-9, 1997. 104p. ill. (Sports reports).
Includes directory and index.
Webber's teenage years in a private school, his great role as part of the Fab Five at the University of Michigan, and his injuries as a Washington Bullet are described for the reader seeking insight into this star of the NBA. The photographs are black and white, but capture the action of Webber on the court.
SUBJ: Webber, Chris./ Basketball players./ Afro-Americans--Biography.

B WHEATLEY, P.   Ph-3 4-6/7 $14.95   L   KE591
SHERROW, VICTORIA. Phillis Wheatley. Chelsea Juniors ISBN 0-7910-1753-2, 1992. 80p. ill. (Junior world biographies).
Includes bibliography, chronology, glossary and index.
Wheatley was transported from Africa to America in 1761. Fortunately, she was purchased by a family which encouraged her poetic talent and cared for her fragile health. She was the second woman to be published in the United States, and the first African-American woman to see her verse in print. Prints show the Revolutionary War era in which she wrote. For multicultural studies and women's studies.
SUBJ: Wheatley, Phillis./ Poets, American./ Slaves./ Afro-Americans--Biography./ Women poets, American.

B WHISTLER, J. Ph-3 5-A/7 $19.95 T KE592
BERMAN, AVIS. James McNeil Whistler. Abrams ISBN 0-8109-3968-1, 1993. 92p. col. ill. (First impressions).
Includes index.
A biography of the great nineteenth century painter known for his landscapes, portraits, and innovative printmaking techniques. Beautiful reproductions reveal Whistler's fascination with Japanese art and scenes of London. Excellent for reports for good readers.
SUBJ: Whistler, James./ Artists./ Painting, American.

B WHITE, E.B. Ph-3 6-A/8 $13.95 L KE593
GHERMAN, BEVERLY. E.B. White: some writer! Atheneum ISBN 0-689-31672-0; In Canada: Maxwell Macmillan, 1992. 136p. ill.
Includes bibliography and index.
Available from the National Library Service for the Blind and Physically Handicapped on sound recording cassette RC 37490. Though a prolific writer for adults, E.B. White is probably best known for his books for children. This straightforward account of his life gives a balanced view of his childhood, marriage, work, and friendships while clearly showing how his love of nature influenced his writing. Photographs throughout the text add a personal touch. Detailed source notes complete the package. For advanced students who have enjoyed CHARLOTTE'S WEB.
SUBJ: White, E.B. (Elwyn Brooks)./ Authors, American.

B WHITE, R. Ph-3 5-A/5 $16.95 T KE594
WHITE, RYAN. Ryan White: my own story. By Ryan White and Ann Marie Cunningham. Dial ISBN 0-8037-0977-3, 1991. 277p. ill. (some col.).
Includes resources list.
Includes "Does AIDS Hurt?", Answers to Questions People Ask.
The tragedy of Ryan White's life was not that he was a hemophiliac who contacted AIDS from Factor, a blood product that helps blood to clot. The tragedy was the abuse he suffered from people in his home town when it was discovered that he was ill. A forthright telling of the crusade of one young man to educate a nation about AIDS.
SUBJ: White, Ryan./ AIDS (Disease)--Patients.

B WILDER, L. Ph-1 4-A/5 $22.95 L KE595
WADSWORTH, GINGER. Laura Ingalls Wilder: storyteller of the prairie. Lerner ISBN 0-8225-4950-6, 1997. 128p. ill., map.
Includes directory, bibliography and index.
The life in the Midwest which prompted Laura Wilder to write her classics, "The Little House" books, is fondly related in this biography which also tells of her close relationship with her daughter, Rose Wilder Lane. Numerous photographs and illustrations from her books highlight the major events in her life. For readers who want to know more about this beloved author.
SUBJ: Wilder, Laura Ingalls./ Authors, American./ Women authors, American./ Frontier and pioneer life.

B WILLIAMS, R. Ph-2 2-3/4 $14.89 L KE596
AVI. Finding Providence: the story of Roger Williams. Illus. by James Watling. HarperCollins ISBN 0-06-025294-4; In Canada: HarperCollins, 1997. 48p. col. ill. (I can read chapter book).
The events which drove Roger Williams from the Massachusetts Bay Colony are told through the eyes of his daughter, Mary. His trek through wintry storms until he found protection among the Narragansett Indians is also related. Text reads smoothly and the illustrations are well suited to the material. For units on the early settlement of America and the search for religious freedom.
SUBJ: Williams, Roger./ United States--History--Colonial period, ca. 1600-1775--Biography./ Reformers.

B WILSON, W. Ph-2 5-A/8 $17.27 L KE597
OSINSKI, ALICE. Woodrow Wilson: twenty-eighth President of the United States. Childrens Press ISBN 0-516-01367-X; In Canada: Childrens Press, 1989. 98p. ill. (Encyclopedia of presidents).
Includes chronology and index.
Wilson's development of his political beliefs and his talents to persuade people are described in this well illustrated biography. This title amplifies the history of the years preceding World War I and Wilson's impact on peace plans.
SUBJ: Wilson, Woodrow./ Presidents.

B WONG, B. Ph-2 3-5/4 $14.95 L KE598
SAY, ALLEN. El Chino. Houghton Mifflin ISBN 0-395-52023-1, 1990. 32p. ill. (some col.).
Determined to be an athlete, Bill Wong found that he was too short to become a star until he visited Spain and became a matador, a Chinese matador. The pictures are as distinguished as the text in this motivational book for minority students.
SUBJ: El Chino (Bong Way Wong)./ Bullfighters.

B WOOD, G. Ph-2 5-A/6 $15.95 L KE599
DUGGLEBY, JOHN. Artist in overalls: the life of Grant Wood. Chronicle ISBN 0-8118-1242-1; In Canada: Raincoast, 1995. 56p. col. ill., map.
Wood's childhood, his successes as a farmer and art teacher, and his contributions to the art world are described in a text which is augmented by fine reproductions of his artwork. A full explanation of the term "Regionalism" makes this a useful resource for art classes. Briefly explains how to draw a chicken to inspire young artists. For mature readers.
SUBJ: Wood, Grant./ Artists.

B WOODS, T. Ph-2 2-6/6 $11.99 L KE600
KRAMER, SYDELLE. Tiger Woods: golfing to greatness. By S. A. Kramer. Random House ISBN 0-679-98969-2; In Canada: Random House, 1997. 114p. col. ill.
Describes Tiger's natural abilities, his determination, and his parents' total dedication to developing his skills. Stresses Tiger's early years when he practiced with his father and learned discipline and how to handle disappointment. Will interest sports enthusiasts who are curious about this golfing sensation. For multicultural studies.
SUBJ: Woods, Tiger./ Golfers.

B WOODSON, C. Ph-2 3-6/2 $12.95 L KE601
MCKISSACK, PAT. Carter G. Woodson: the father of black history. By Patricia and Fredrick McKissack. Illus. by Ned O. Enslow ISBN 0-89490-309-8, 1991. 32p b&w photos and illus. (Great African Americans).
Includes glossary and index.
After gaining his own education, Carter Woodson became a leader in the instruction of his people and a writer of material which emphasized African-American history. His motto "never too late to learn" is as fitting today as when his father, a former slave, first said it. This is a vital addition for use during African-American History month.
SUBJ: Woodson, Carter Godwin./ Educators./ Historians./ Afro-Americans--Biography.

B WYETH, A. Ph-3 6-A/7 $19.95 T KE602
MERYMAN, RICHARD. Andrew Wyeth. Abrams ISBN 0-8109-3956-8, 1991. 92p b&w photos and b&w and col prints. (First impressions).
Includes index.
A look at one of America's most famous artists with emphasis on his family life and its great influence on his work. Includes information on his famous father, N.C. Wyeth, and the subjects of his paintings with (28 color plates). Use for art history or offer as a biography.
SUBJ: Wyeth, Andrew./ Artists./ Painting, American./ Painting, Modern--20th century./ Art appreciation.

B YAMAGUCHI, K. Ph-2 3-5/7 $13.95 L KE603
SAVAGE, JEFF. Kristi Yamaguchi: pure gold. Dillon ISBN 0-87518-583-5; In Canada: Maxwell Macmillan, 1993. 64p. col. ill. (Taking part).
Includes index.
Seeing skaters at a mall, Kristi started dreaming. A pictorial study examines her determination and the sacrifices of her family which made her dream a reality. Many colored photographs capture the winning smile and grace of the petite role model.
SUBJ: Yamaguchi, Kristi./ Ice skaters./ Japanese Americans--Biography./ Athletes./ Women athletes.

B YEP, L. Ph-1 5-A/7 $4.95 P KE604
YEP, LAURENCE. Lost garden. Beech Tree ISBN 0-688-13701-6, 1996. 117p. ill.
Originally published by Julian Messner, 1991.
Yep tells about his childhood and college years and explains how they have become his sources for his writings for children. His picture of the child who spans two cultures, belonging to neither, is memorable. For developing sensitivity to people from diverse cultures. For multicultural studies.
SUBJ: Yep, Laurence./ Authors, American./ Chinese Americans--Biography.

B YOUNG, B. Ph-3 5-6/8 $14.95 L KE605
SANFORD, WILLIAM R. Brigham Young: pioneer and Mormon leader. By William R. Sanford and Carl R. Green. Enslow ISBN 0-89490-672-0, 1996. 48p. ill., map. (Legendary heroes of the Wild West).
Includes glossary, bibliography and index.
As a young man, Brigham Young was attracted to the teachings of Joseph Smith. He soon became an apostle of the Mormon Church, and upon Smith's death, he was chosen as the church president. He was instrumental in leading the members westward to Salt Lake City and served as governor of the territory. Includes a brief explanation of plural marriages.
SUBJ: Young, Brigham./ Mormon Church--Presidents./ Church of Jesus Christ of Latter-Day Saints--Presidents.

B YOUNG, S.   Ph-2 3-5/8 $4.50   P   KE606
CHRISTOPHER, MATT. In the huddle with...Steve Young. Little, Brown
ISBN 0-316-13793-6; In Canada: Little, Brown, 1996. 131p. ill. (Matt
Christopher sports biographies).
> Young's patience and determination are explained in this biography
> which details how often this football superstar met frustration and
> overcame it. Includes a summary of his career's highlights.
> SUBJ: Young, Steve./ Football players.

B YOUNG, S.   Ph-2 4-6/7 $19.90   L   KE607
GUTMAN, BILL. Steve Young: NFL passing wizard. Millbrook ISBN
1-56294-184-4, 1996. 48p. col. ill. (Millbrook sports world).
> Includes chronology, bibliography, directory and index.
> Young's determination to become an outstanding football player in
> spite of being on poor teams and playing second fiddle to Joe
> Montana is fully described. His religious faith and continuation of
> postgraduate studies while playing on the 49ers make him an
> exceptional man.
> SUBJ: Young, Steve./ Football players.

B ZAHARIAS, B.   Ph-3 4-5/4 $11.95   L   KE608
SANFORD, WILLIAM R. Babe Didrikson Zaharias. By William R. Sanford
and Carl R. Green. Crestwood House ISBN 0-89686-736-6; In Canada:
Maxwell Macmillan, 1993. 48p. ill. (Sports immortals).
> Includes glossary, bibliography, and index.
> Babe's ability to star in a variety of sports: track, shot put, javelin,
> basketball, baseball, tennis, and finally golf has made her one of the
> most amazing athletes in the world. Briefly covers her achievements in
> text and photographs.
> SUBJ: Zaharias, Babe Didrikson./ Athletes./ Women athletes.

B ZHANG, S.   Ph-3 4-6/6 $19.95   T   KE609
ZHANG, SONG NAN. Little tiger in the Chinese night: an
autobiography in art. Tundra ISBN 0-88776-320-0; In Canada: Tundra.
48p. col. ill., map.
> Includes chronology.
> Graphic paintings capture various aspects of Zhang's life: his
> childhood in Shanghai; life under the Communists as an art student,
> coal miner, and fisherman; his marriage; his escape to Canada; and
> the emigration of his family to Canada. Insightful view of Chinese
> history for multicultural studies.
> SUBJ: Zhang, Song Nan./ Artists./ China--History--1949- .

929   J929.1   Ph-2 5-A/7 $9.95   P   KE610
WOLFMAN, IRA. Do people grow on family trees?: genealogy for kids
and other beginners: the official Ellis Island handbook. Foreword by Alex
Haley. Illus. by Michael Klein. Workman ISBN 0-89480-348-4; In
Canada: Thomas Allen, 1991. 179p. ill.
> Includes directories, bibliography and index.
> Encourages readers to use library research, interviews, and record
> searches to learn family history. Sample forms, pedigree charts, and
> important addresses are included. Particularly useful for those
> participating in a "European roots" search as emphasis is on those
> who entered the United States through Ellis Island.
> SUBJ: Genealogy.

929.4   Ph-1 K-3/2 $15.95   L   KE611
SANDERS, MARILYN. What's your name?: from Ariel to Zoe. Photos by
Marilyn Sanders. Text by Eve Sanders. Holiday House ISBN 0-8234-
1209-1, 1995. unp. col. ill.
> Presented in alphabetical order, 26 children from a broad range of
> cultures share personal information about themselves and their names:
> why those names were chosen for them, what they mean, nicknames,
> and how they feel about their names. Illustrated with full-page color
> photographs. Use for multicultural studies and as a model for creative
> writing activities.
> SUBJ: Names, Personal./ Alphabet.

VCR 929.9   Ph-2 4-6 $30.00   OD   KE612
ALABAMA TO WYOMING: FLAGS OF THE UNITED STATES
(Videocassette). City Island Entertainment/Ondeck Home Entertainment
CI 420, 1994. 1/2" VHS videocassette color (60min).
> Includes index and glossary.
> Includes public performance rights.
> Describes the flags of the 50 states and also provides additional
> information such as each state's bird, flower, tree, motto, slogan, and
> capital. Arrangement is alphabetic, and a fifteen-question quiz
> provides a closing challenge. Use as an alternate source for state fact
> information.
> SUBJ: Flags--United States--States--History./ Emblems, State.

929.9   Ph-1 4-6/8 $11.90   L   KE613
ARMBRUSTER, ANN. American flag. Watts ISBN 0-531-20045-0; In
Canada: Watts, 1991. 64p col and b&w photos and illus. (First book).

Includes appendix, bibliography and index.
Provides information on the history of the American flag. Particularly
notable features are chapters on the flag and the arts and the flag
and the Constitution; the appendix contains a discussion of flag
etiquette.
SUBJ: Flags--United States--History.

929.9   Ph-2 4-6/7 $18.43   L   KE614
BRANDT, SUE R. State flags: including the Commonwealth of Puerto
Rico. Watts ISBN 0-531-20001-9; In Canada: Watts, 1992. 63p. col. ill.
> Includes bibliography and index.
> Provides a straightforward explanation of the history, design, and
> significance of state flags. State mottoes and dates of admission also
> are included. Helpful for reports and as a quick-answer resource.
> SUBJ: Flags--United States--States--History.

VCR 929.9   Ph-3 1-4 $35.00   OD   KE615
CANADA'S MAPLE TREE: THE STORY OF THE COUNTRY'S EMBLEM
(Videocassette). Written and produced by Susan DeBeck. DeBeck
Educational Video; In Canada: DeBeck Educational Video, 1995. 1/2"
VHS videocassette color (30min).
> Includes teacher's guide.
> Includes public performance rights.
> Closed captioned.
> Vibrant, active video uses the variety of maple trees found in Canada
> to describe the maple sugaring process and growth cycle of trees, as
> well as to provide a history of the maple leaf as a Canadian symbol
> and to show differences in Canadian provinces. Excellent technical
> quality with suggestions for classroom activities in both video and
> teacher's guide. Will be useful for interdisciplinary studies combining
> science and social studies.
> SUBJ: Emblems, National--Canada./ Maple--Canada./ Canada--
> History.

929.9   Ph-1 5-A/8 $15.00   T   KE616
CRAMPTON, W. G. Flag. Knopf ISBN 0-394-82255-2, 1989. 63p. col.
ill. (Eyewitness books).
> Includes index.
> Photographs and careful drawings combine in this colorful, large
> format import which presents an intriguing examination of flags, their
> development and history. Part of the critically acclaimed Eyewitness
> series, this title will create in some readers a lifelong interest in flags.
> SUBJ: Flags.

929.9   J973.7   Ph-2 3-6/7 $15.95   L   KE617
FISHER, LEONARD EVERETT. Stars and Stripes: our national flag.
Holiday House ISBN 0-8234-1053-6, 1993. unp. col. ill.
> Uses bold, borderless pages to display fifteen flags of the United
> States with a brief note about each. Words of the Pledge of
> Allegiance add to the effectiveness of the graphic design. For
> patriotic holidays and study of national symbols.
> SUBJ: Flags--United States--History./ Pledge of Allegiance./ United
> States--History--Revolution, 1775-1783--Flags.

VCR 929.9   Ph-3 A $29.95   OD   KE618
FLAGS OF THE NATIONS (Videocassette). City Island Entertainment/
Ondeck Home Entertainment CI 419, 1993. 1/2" VHS videocassette
color (60min).
> Includes reference directory.
> Provides a businesslike description of the flags of more than 270
> countries. Arrangement is by continent; accompanying country list is
> keyed to an interactive flag locator and allows access to individual
> flags. For use in special projects or as part of an introduction to the
> study of a continent.
> SUBJ: Flags./ Geography.

929.9   Ph-2 5-6/8 $23.95   L   KE619
HABAN, RITA D. How proudly they wave: flags of the fifty states.
Lerner ISBN 0-8225-1799-X, 1989. 111p. col. ill.
> Includes glossary.
> From Alabama to Wyoming, the flags of each state of the United
> States receive attention. A two-page entry for each flag offers a
> color drawing, description of elements, and history of the adoption of
> the flag. A solid resource for information-seekers.
> SUBJ: Flags--United States--States--History.

PIC 930   Ph-2 4-6 $39.95   OD   KE620
ANCIENT CIVILIZATIONS (Picture). Knowledge Unlimited 7020P ISBN
1-55933-071-6, 1991. 10 study prints color (17"x22").
> Includes teacher's guide.
> Also available as individual posters, $7.95 each.
> Provides brief information about ten ancient civilizations. Each poster
> offers approximately 200 words of text, full-color illustration, and an
> inset showing geographic location; guide suggests several activities for

NONFICTION

each poster. Effective display item.
Contents: Sumerians -- Ancient Jews -- Greeks -- Egyptians -- Persians -- Roman Empire -- Ancient India -- Ancient China -- Mayans -- Incas.
SUBJ: Civilization, Ancient./ World history.

930 *JR930* Ph-2 4-6/10 $19.95 T KE621
MARTELL, HAZEL. Kingfisher book of the ancient world: from the Ice Age to the fall of Rome. By Hazel Mary Martell. Kingfisher/dist. by Raintree Steck-Vaughn ISBN 1-85697-565-7, 1995. 160p. col. ill., maps.
Includes glossaries, chronologies and index.
An overview of ancient civilizations, arranged geographically, discusses cultures that flourished from about 10,000 B.C. to 600 A.D. Illustrated with photographs and descriptions of artifacts, maps, and original drawings. Although there are no source notes or bibliography, students will find this a fascinating source for reports or browsing.
SUBJ: Civilization, Ancient./ Antiquities./ World history.

930 *JR930* Ph-2 4-6/8 $15.95 T KE622
VISUAL DICTIONARY OF ANCIENT CIVILIZATIONS. DK Publishing ISBN 1-56458-701-0, 1994. 64p. col. ill. (Eyewitness visual dictionaries).
Includes chronologies and index.
Serves as a finder's guide in naming the objects of ancient civilizations worldwide. Large-format, excellent timelines, and clear-cut photographs are characteristics of this Eyewitness book. Top-notch browsing resource.
SUBJ: Civilization, Ancient.

930.1 *J913* Ph-1 2-4/3 $14.89 L KE623
DUKE, KATE. Archaeologists dig for clues. HarperCollins ISBN 0-06-027057-8; In Canada: HarperCollins, 1997. 32p. col. ill. (Let's-read-and-find-out science book).
Three students accompany archeologist Sophie on a dig and find clues to life in the Archaic era in spear points, burned wood, pieces of bone, and other artifacts. Humorous cartoon drawings supplement written information and add detail and interest. This is a student-friendly source for exploring beginning concepts, vocabulary, and processes of archeological excavation.
SUBJ: Archaeology.

930.1 Ph-2 3-6/7 $16.95 L KE624
GOLDENSTERN, JOYCE. Lost cities. Enslow ISBN 0-89490-615-1, 1996. 48p. ill. (some col.), maps. (Weird and wacky science).
Includes glossary, chronology, bibliography and index.
Accounts of five archeological excavations and finds throughout the world: Bonampak, a Maya ruin in Mexico; Troy; Machu Picchu; two cities in the Indus Valley; and Pompeii and Herculaneum. Illustrated with photographs of artifacts and sites and small maps to put each site in geographical context. A readable resource for units on archaeology and ancient civilizations.
SUBJ: Cities and towns, Ancient./ Archaeology--History./ Civilization, Ancient.

930.1 Ph-1 4-6/9 $16.00 T KE625
JESPERSEN, JAMES. Mummies, dinosaurs, moon rocks: how we know how old things are. By James Jespersen and Jane Fitz-Randolph. Illus. by Bruce Hiscock. Atheneum ISBN 0-689-31848-0; In Canada: Distican, 1996. 92p. ill.
Includes glossary, bibliography and index.
Explains dating processes such as carbon 14, thermoluminescence, tree ring dating, and radioactive dating; and relates how they are used to date events and artifacts such as the eruption of Mt. Vesuvius, the prehistoric cave paintings at Lascaux, the Dead Sea Scrolls, skeletons, and space debris. Illustrated with clear, descriptive diagrams, drawings, and photographs. High appeal reading for interdisciplinary studies in science and history, and for general interest.
SUBJ: Archaeological dating./ Radioactive dating.

930.1 Ph-1 4-6/8 $16.89 L KE626
LAUBER, PATRICIA. Tales mummies tell. Crowell/HarperCollins ISBN 0-690-04389-9, 1985. 128p. ill.
Selectors' Choice, 15th ed.
Describes how people lived in other cultures a long time ago as evidenced by the tales their mummies tell. Details of carbon dating and analysis of research illustrate the information that can be gained through this study. The individual reader will be caught up in this subject which is also good support for the curriculum.
SUBJ: Mummies.

930.1 Ph-2 4-A/11 $18.99 L KE627
MCINTOSH, JANE. Archeology. By Dr. Jane McIntosh. Knopf ISBN 0-679-96572-6, 1994. 64p. col. ill. (Eyewitness books).
"Borzoi book."
Includes index.

Uses objects, cross sections, and distinctive displays to present techniques of archeology. An array of archeological finds ranging from an Egyptian doll through counterfeit coins fill the pages of this Eyewitness book. Intriguing browsing is available in this useful knowledge-expander.
SUBJ: Archaeology.

930.1 *J622.19* Ph-1 4-6/6 $14.00 T KE628
SCHWARTZ, ALVIN. Gold and silver, silver and gold. Illus. by David Christiana. Farrar, Straus & Giroux ISBN 0-374-32690-8; In Canada: HarperCollins, 1988. 128p. ill.
Includes notes, sources and bibliography.
Selectors' Choice, 17th ed.
Seeking, finding and losing treasure is the theme of these ten chapters relaying both true and folkloric accounts of troves of riches. Well paced narratives, attractive illustrations and, as always, Schwartz's fine documentation. Fine book talk material as well as independent reading fare.
SUBJ: Buried treasure.

931 Ph-2 4-A/10 $18.99 L KE629
COTTERELL, ARTHUR. Ancient China. Photos by Alan Hills and Geoff Brightling. Knopf ISBN 0-679-96167-4, 1994. 64p. col. ill., maps. (Eyewitness books).
"Borzoi book."
Includes index.
Presents objects of Chinese culture from the Shang dynasty of 1650 B.C. through the 1912 A.D. end of the empire. A valuable timeline provides a reference point for following pages which include familiar Eyewitness depiction of accoutrements of medicine, war, invention, and daily life in early China. Valuable background-builder and browser.
SUBJ: China--Civilization.

931 Ph-1 3-6/3 $14.95 L KE630
FISHER, LEONARD EVERETT. Great Wall of China. Macmillan ISBN 0-02-735220-X; In Canada: Collier Macmillan, 1986. 30p. ill.
Selectors' Choice, 16th ed.
Available from National Library Service for the Blind and Physically Handicapped on sound recording cassette RC25018.
Chronicles the building of the Great Wall of China. Unusually handsome illustrations by the famed author/artist mirror the massiveness of the wall itself in a work marked by quality of design and attention to detail. Suitable for use in book talks or as a read aloud, its reading level makes it accessible to a broad range of readers.
SUBJ: Great Wall of China (China)--History./ China--History--To 221 B.C.

931 *J509.51* Ph-2 4-6/6 $18.95 T KE631
WILLIAMS, SUZANNE. Made in China: ideas and inventions from Ancient China. Illus. by Andrea Fong. Pacific View Press ISBN 1-881896-14-5, 1996. 48p. ill. (some col.), map.
Includes chronology and index.
A look at many of the scientific discoveries and ideas contributed to the world by ancient Chinese culture, including such inventions as paper, silk, and porcelain; and technological advances in medicine, astronomy, warfare, and agriculture. Illustrated with paintings, drawings, and sketches. Use for units on ancient cultures and for multicultural studies.
SUBJ: China--Civilization./ Science--China--History./ Technology--China--History./ Inventions--China--History./ Science, Ancient.

932 Ph-2 4-6/7 $17.71 L KE632
BENDICK, JEANNE. Egyptian tombs. Watts ISBN 0-531-10462-1; In Canada: Watts, 1989. 64p. col. ill. (First book).
Includes glossary and index.
Examines early Egyptians' beliefs about death and describes construction of the pyramids and preparation of mummies. Readable text and neat, pleasing illustrations are pluses. Useful in study of ancient Egypt and Egyptians culture.
SUBJ: Tombs--Egypt./ Pyramids--Egypt./ Egypt--Antiquities.

932 Ph-2 5-6/8 $15.99 L KE633
HART, GEORGE. Ancient Egypt. Photos by Peter Hayman. Knopf ISBN 0-679-90742-4, 1990. 64p. col. ill. (Eyewitness books).
Includes index.
Spanish version EL ANTIGUO EGIPTO available from Santillana (ISBN 84-372-3742-4, n.d.).
Hundreds of handsomely photographed objects of ancient Egyptian life range across the pages of this large format work. Part of a popular series, this title will attract browsers and those more serious. Useful as a background builder.
SUBJ: Egypt--Civilization--To 332 B.C./ Spanish language materials.

932 Ph-3 4-6/7 $17.95 L OD KE634
KING, DAVID C. Egypt: ancient traditions, modern hopes. Benchmark Books/Marshall Cavendish ISBN 0-7614-0142-3, 1997. 64p. col. ill., maps. (Exploring cultures of the world).
Includes glossary, bibliography and index.
Discussion of the history, geography, culture, traditions, and religion of ancient and modern Egypt, with emphasis on contemporary life in cities, villages, and oases. Illustrated with color photographs. Students looking for detailed information for regional social studies reports will find this a useful resource.
SUBJ: Egypt.

932 Ph-2 4-6/6 $18.95 T KE635
MANN, ELIZABETH. Great Pyramid. Illus. by Laura Lo Turco. Mikaya Press/dist. by Firefly ISBN 0-9650493-1-0, 1996. 48p. col. ill., map. (Wonders of the world book).
Includes glossary and index.
A history of the building of the Great Pyramid at Giza shows the culture and beliefs of the ancient Egyptian civilization that produced it. Illustrations include paintings, photographs of ancient wall reliefs and statues, and large fold-out illustrations of the site. Use for units on ancient Egyptian history.
SUBJ: Great Pyramid (Egypt)./ Pyramids--Egypt./ Egypt--Antiquities./ Egypt--Civilization--To 332 B.C.

932 Ph-2 5-A/8 $14.95 L KE636
PERL, LILA. Mummies, tombs, and treasure: secrets of ancient Egypt. Illus. by Erika Weihs. Clarion ISBN 0-89919-407-9, 1987. 120p. ill.
Includes bibliography and index.
The customs and practices that came about because of ancient Egyptians' beliefs in a life after death are discussed. The information is substantial and the black and white photographs are useful, making this helpful for reports.
SUBJ: Mummies--Egypt./ Tombs--Egypt./ Egypt--Antiquities.

932 Ph-2 3-6/9 $15.95 T KE637
TRUMBLE, KELLY. Cat mummies. Illus. by Laszlo Kubinyi. Clarion 0-395-68707-1, 1996. 56p. col. ill.
Includes chronology, directory, glossary, bibliography and index.
Account of animal worship in ancient Egypt focuses on cats and the thousands of cat mummies discovered in Beni Hasan in the late nineteenth century. Illustrated with full-color drawings and includes chapter notes. An interesting aspect of Egyptian history for social studies units and for general interest in mummification.
SUBJ: Egypt--Antiquities./ Mummies./ Cats--Religious aspects.

937 Adult 930.12 Seba Ph-2 4-6/7 $14.95 T KE638
GETZ, DAVID. Frozen man. Illus. by Peter McCarty. Henry Holt ISBN 0-8050-3261-4; In Canada: Fitzhenry & Whiteside, 1994. 68p. ill. (some col.), map (Redfeather book).
Includes glossary, bibliography and index.
Describes the 1991 discovery in the Austro-Italian Alps of a body now determined to be more than 5,000 years old. Smoothly written narrative discusses the methods used to preserve and study the "Iceman." Strong glossary and bibliography are notable features. Solid science/social studies support.
SUBJ: Prehistoric peoples./ Copper Age./ Excavations (Archaeology).

937 Ph-2 5-6/8 $15.99 L KE639
JAMES, SIMON. Ancient Rome. Knopf ISBN 0-679-90741-6, 1990. 64p. col. ill. (Eyewitness books).
Includes index.
Spanish version LA ANTIGUA ROMA available from Santillana (ISBN 84-372-3745-9, n.d.).
Bronzes, artifacts, pottery, and more are splashed across the attractive pages of this photo-essay which examines ancient Rome. Browsers and history buffs will enjoy this attention-grabbing compilation. Useful as an awareness expander.
SUBJ: Rome--Antiquities./ Rome--Social life and customs./ Spanish language materials.

937 Ph-2 4-6/6 $14.99 L KE640
LESSEM, DON. Iceman. Crown ISBN 0-517-59597-4, 1994. 32p. col. ill., maps.
Includes index.
Reports the 1991 Alpine discovery of a frozen mummy dated at more than 5,000 years old. Text and illustrations describe the excavation and archeological study of the mummy dubbed the "Iceman" and his belongings. High interest material for browsing and project support.
SUBJ: Prehistoric peoples./ Copper Age./ Excavations (Archaeology).

937 Ph-2 4-6/7 $17.95 L KE641
MORLEY, JACQUELINE. Roman villa. Illus. by John James. Peter Bedrick ISBN 0-87226-360-6, 1992. 48p. col. ill. (Inside story).
Includes chronology, glossary and index.
Visits a country villa outside Rome in the first century A.D. A farming calendar, time chart, and intriguing cutaway drawings are high appeal features in this large format work. Use with other titles from this series for activities comparing ancient civilizations.
SUBJ: Country life--Rome./ Rome--Social life and customs.

937 J 930.12 Ph-1 3-5/4 $16.95 T KE642
TANAKA, SHELLEY. Discovering the Iceman: what was it like to find a 5,300-year-old mummy? Illus. by Laurie McGaw. Hyperion ISBN 0-7868-0284-7; In Canada: Madison Press, 1997. 48p. col. ill., map. (I was there).
"Hyperion/Madison Press book."
Includes chronology, glossary and bibliography.
An account of the discovery and examination of the body of a late Stone Age man in the Alps in 1991 details possible explanations of his life and the artifacts found with him. Illustrated with photographs, numerous informative sidebars, and artistic renderings of a hypothetical narrative of his last days. Comparative timeline adds to the usefulness of this resource for units on prehistoric times and for interdisciplinary science and social studies units.
SUBJ: Prehistoric peoples./ Copper Age.

938 J 722.8 Ph-2 4-6/7 $17.95 L KE643
MACDONALD, FIONA. Greek temple. By Fiona MacDonald and Mark Bergin. Peter Bedrick ISBN 0-87226-361-4, 1992. 48p. col. ill. (Inside story).
Includes glossary and index.
Features cutaway drawings to depict the construction and history of the Parthenon in ancient Greece. Text and captions add to the information mix. Of particular value in collections serving curricula which emphasize ancient civilizations.
SUBJ: Parthenon (Athens, Greece)./ Athens (Greece)--Antiquities.

940.1 Ph-2 5-A/9 $16.95 T KE644
CASELLI, GIOVANNI. Roman Empire and the Dark Ages. Peter Bedrick ISBN 0-911745-58-0, 1985. 48p col illus. (History of everyday things).
Includes chronology and bibliography.
Presents artifacts and costumes from pre-Roman Britain to the 14th century. "A history of people through the things they made," the detailed illustrations depict the objects of daily life with clarity and appeal. Though following the format of imported nonfiction series, the title does offer strong support for upper grade social studies curriculum.
SUBJ: Civilization, Ancient./ Civilization, Medieval./ Rome--Civilization.

940.1 Ph-2 3-6/6 $18.95 L KE645
CLEMENTS, GILLIAN. Truth about castles. Carolrhoda ISBN 0-87614-401-6, c1988, 1990. 40p. col. ill.
Includes glossary and index.
Dispenses castle lore with a light touch which features cheerful drawings and murmured asides. A glossary helps with unfamiliar words in this import originally published in Great Britain.
SUBJ: Castles./ Civilization, Medieval.

940.1 Ph-2 4-6/4 $17.71 L KE646
CORBIN, CAROLE LYNN. Knights. Watts ISBN 0-531-10692-6; In Canada: Watts, 1989. 64p. col. ill. (First book).
Includes bibliography and index.
Dispenses information about the training, equipment, and daily lives of knights of medieval times. Colorful drawings and photographs support the text. An easy reading level makes this title an accessible source for both reports and browsing.
SUBJ: Knights and knighthood./ Civilization, Medieval.

940.1 J 792.7 Ph-2 4-6/7 $14.99 L KE647
FRADON, DANA. King's fool: a book about medieval and renaissance fools. Dutton ISBN 0-525-45074-2, 1993. unp. col. ill.
Fact and fiction are combined in this hilarious recounting of the role played by fools and jesters in medieval life. Cartoon illustrations enliven the anecdotes in this informative resource. Useful for enrichment material as well as enjoyable reading for browsers.
SUBJ: Fools and jesters./ Civilization, Medieval./ Civilization, Renaissance.

940.1 Ph-2 4-A/7 $16.99 L KE648
GRAVETT, CHRISTOPHER. Knight. Photos by Geoff Dann. Knopf ISBN 0-679-93882-6, 1993. 64p. col. ill. (Eyewitness books).
"Dorling Kindersley book."
Includes index.
Displays the accoutrements of knighthood and discusses chivalric training, codes, and ceremonies. Photographs and drawings in the quality for which Eyewitness books are known offer a high-appeal

presentation for readers of all ages. Use in social studies, art, and literature support.
SUBJ: Knights and knighthood./ Civilization, Medieval.

940.1   Ph-3 4-6/8 $17.95   L   KE649
MACDONALD, FIONA. Medieval castle. Illus. by Mark Bergin. Peter Bedrick ISBN 0-87226-340-1, 1990. 48p. col. ill. (Inside story).
Includes glossary and index.
Provides a look at many aspects of castle life. Cutaway drawings, farming schedule, armor, and knight's training are among subjects presented in this appealing import. Good browser.
SUBJ: Castles./ Civilization, Medieval.

940.1   Ph-1 4-6/7 $24.21   T   KE650
STEELE, PHILIP. Castles. Kingfisher/dist. by Raintree Steck-Vaughn ISBN 1-85697-547-9, 1995. 64p. col. ill.
Includes chronology, glossary and index.
Each doublespread introduces some aspect of castle life, including castles in general, castle towns, defenses, life in the castle, and life under siege. Supplementary information and original illustrations add focus and detail, and some archival art is included. Although there is no bibliography and source notes are not included, this is well organized and readable and will serve as a resource for reports or satisfy general interest in the medieval period.
SUBJ: Castles./ Civilization, Medieval./ Fortification.

940.3   Ph-2 5-A/7 $27.40   L   KE651
DOLAN, EDWARD F. America in World War I. Millbrook Press ISBN 1-56294-522-X, 1996. 96p. ill., maps.
Includes bibliography and index.
Clear, readable, comprehensive account of causes, European circumstances before America's entry into the war, America's participation, and post-war events. Illustrated with archival photographs and graphics. Lack of adequate maps is a drawback. Will be useful for looking at many aspects of this period in a broader context.
SUBJ: World War, 1914-1918--United States.

940.3   Ph-2 A/7 $15.95   T   KE652
MARRIN, ALBERT. Yanks are coming: the United States in the First World War. Atheneum ISBN 0-689-31209-1, 1986. 248p. ill.
Includes bibliography and index.
Tells the story of U.S. participation in World War I. Black and white photographs and a smooth writing style with considerable detail add to the interest of the text. Useful as a read-aloud or for advanced students' research activities.
SUBJ: World War, 1914-1918--United States./ World War, 1914-1918--Campaigns.

940.3   Ph-2 4-6/8 $19.90   L   KE653
MCGOWEN, TOM. World War I. Watts ISBN 0-531-20149-X; In Canada: Nelson, 1993. 64p. ill. (some col.), maps. (First book).
Includes bibliography and index.
Offers a straightforward report of the military battles and political impact of World War I. Detailed maps and historical photographs accompany the text. Useful as a starter source on the subject.
SUBJ: World War, 1914-1918.

SRC 940.4   Ph-2 A $11.50   OD KE654
LIEBERMAN, SYD. Intrepid birdmen: the fighter pilots of World War I (Sound recording cassette). Syd Lieberman SL-106, 1993. 1 sound cassette (45min).
ALA notable recording, 1994.
Captures in moving fashion the life and times of the World War I pilot in the days when flying was new and the rules unwritten. Based on Smithsonian archives, presentation is filled with rarely mentioned information. For flight and military buffs.
SUBJ: World War, 1914-1918--Aerial operations./ Aeronautics, Military--History.

940.53   Ph-2 4-6/5 $15.95   L   KE655
ADLER, DAVID A. Hilde and Eli: children of the Holocaust. Illus. by Karen Ritz. Holiday House ISBN 0-8234-1091-9, 1994. unp. col. ill.
Tells of the brief lives of two young people killed in the Holocaust. Text is commendably straightforward and unemotional. Valuable background-builder.
SUBJ: Holocaust, Jewish (1939-1945)--Biography./ Jews--Biography./ Rosenzweig, Hilde./ Lax, Eli.

940.53   Ph-1 5-6/8 $10.95   P   KE656
ADLER, DAVID A. We remember the holocaust. Henry Holt ISBN 0-8050-3715-2; In Canada: Fitzhenry & Whiteside, c1989, 1995. 147p. ill.
Includes glossary, bibliography and index.

Available from the National Library Service for the Blind and Physically Handicapped on sound recording cassette RC34318.
Personal remembrances of survivors bring the horror of the Holocaust to life. Using brief, paragraph-long recollections and photographs taken of survivors during the period, the author builds a powerful portrait of the Holocaust. The chronology at the end documents events between 1933 and 1945. Valuable alone or in conjunction with other works, fiction or nonfiction, on the subject.
SUBJ: Holocaust, Jewish (1939-1945)./ Holocaust, Jewish (1939-1945)--Personal narratives./ World War, 1939-1945--Jews.

940.53   Ph-1 A/7 $15.95   T   KE657
GREENFELD, HOWARD. Hidden children. Ticknor & Fields ISBN 0-395-66074-2, 1993. 118p. ill.
Includes bibliography and index.
Available from the National Library Service for the Blind and Physically Handicapped on sound recording cassette RC 40001.
Gathers recollections of men and women who were forced by the Holocaust to live as hidden children. Photographs and first-person narratives are interwoven by a skillful text. Works well with other titles on the subject and stands strongly alone.
SUBJ: Holocaust, Jewish (1939-1945)./ Holocaust survivors./ Holocaust, Jewish (1939-1945)--Personal narratives.

940.53   Ph-1 5-6/4 $13.89   L   KE658
HAUTZIG, ESTHER. Endless steppe: growing up in Siberia. HarperCollins ISBN 0-690-04919-6; In Canada: HarperCollins, c1968. 243p.
Jane Addams Book Award.
Available from National Library Service for the Blind and Physically Handicapped on sound recording cassette RC24519 and talking book TB02535.
When she was 10 years old, Esther Rudomin and her family were declared "capitalists" by the Russians and deported to Siberia from their native Poland. This memorable account describes their five year stay in an impossible climate where obtaining food and shelter became a way of life.
SUBJ: World War, 1939-1945--Personal narratives./ Poles--Siberia.

940.53   Ph-2 A/7 $24.00   T   KE659
KRULL, KATHLEEN. V is for victory: America remembers World War II. Apple Soup/Knopf ISBN 0-679-86198-X; In Canada: Random House, 1995. 115p. ill. (some col.), map.
Includes chronology, bibliography and index.
Recalls life in the United States during World War II. A lively text supported by period photographs and memorabilia captures a distinctive time in the nation's history. Popular browser and useful trigger for specialized activities.
SUBJ: World War, 1939-1945--United States.

940.53   Ph-2 A/7 $19.95   L   KE660
MARX, TRISH. Echoes of World War II. Lerner ISBN 0-8225-4898-4, 1994. 96p. ill., maps.
First published in 1989 by Macdonald Children's Books, Hemel Hempstead, England.
Includes chronology and index.
"Presents the stories of six people... whose childhoods were shaped by their experiences during World War II." (CIP) Maps and photographs accompany text. Stands alone or in conjunction with an oral history project which captures recollections of the period.
SUBJ: World War, 1939-1945--Personal narratives./ World War, 1939-1945--Children.

940.53   Ph-1 5-A/7 $153.89   L   KE661
MELTZER, MILTON. Rescue: the story of how Gentiles saved Jews in the Holocaust. HarperCollins ISBN 0-06-024210-8; In Canada: HarperCollins, 1988. 168p. maps.
Includes bibliography and index.
Reports stories of Gentile assistance in the concentration camps, in the Netherlands, Belgium, Italy and other countries to Jews during the Holocaust. Maps pinpoint the geographical sites. Background information provided includes a brief history of anti-Semitism.
SUBJ: World War, 1939-1945--Jews--Rescue./ Holocaust, Jewish (1939-1945).

940.53   Ph-1 3-6/4 $15.95   T   KE662
MOCHIZUKI, KEN. Passage to freedom: the Sugihara story. Illus. by Dom Lee. Afterword by Hiroki Sugihara. Lee & Low ISBN 1-880000-49-0, 1997. unp. ill.
Selectors' Choice, 21st ed.
In 1940, the Japanese ambassador to Lithuania, despite refusal of his government for permission to do so, issued handwritten visas to thousands of Soviet Jews desperate to escape the Nazi onslaught. The muted tones of the illustrations complement the actions and feelings of the narrative. This moving account, told from the

perspective of the ambassador's five-year-old son, deserves a prominent place in Holocaust studies and as a wonderful example of how the actions of one person can make a difference.
SUBJ: Holocaust, Jewish (1939-1945)--Poland./ World War, 1939-1945--Jews--Rescue./ Righteous Gentiles in the Holocaust./ Sugihara, Chiune./ Diplomats--Japan--Biography.

940.53   Ph-3 5-A/7 $2.95   P   KE663
PETTIT, JAYNE. Place to hide. Scholastic ISBN 0-590-45353-X; In Canada: Scholastic, 1993. 114p. ill. (Scholastic biography).
Includes bibliography and index.
In the midst of the Holocaust, courageous individuals attempted to protect Jews who were fleeing from Nazi persecution. This collection portrays the Schindlers and Miep, Anne Frank's protector, as well as many lesser-known rescuers. For mature readers.
SUBJ: Holocaust, Jewish (1939-1945)--Personal narratives./ World War, 1939-1945--Jews--Rescue./ Righteous Gentiles in the Holocaust.

940.53 *Adult J940.5315*   Ph-1 A/8 $17.95   T   KE664
ROGASKY, BARBARA. Smoke and ashes: the story of the Holocaust. Holiday House ISBN 0-8234-0697-0, 1988. 187p. ill.
Includes bibliography and index.
Examines the background of anti-Semitism and events leading to the Holocaust and then vividly describes the nightmare of systematic extermination of more than six million European Jews. Final chapters deal with Jewish resistance and with slowness of British and American response to events. Useful for advanced students and as a valuable follow-up to Chaikin's "A nightmare in history."
SUBJ: Holocaust, Jewish (1939-1945).

940.53   Ph-1 A/6 $15.95   T   KE665
ROSENBERG, MAXINE B. Hiding to survive: stories of Jewish children rescued from the Holocaust. Clarion ISBN 0-395-65014-3, 1994. 166p. ill.
Includes glossary and bibliography.
Retraces the childhood of each of 14 Jewish children hidden from Nazi persecution during World War II. Individual accounts, told in first person, conclude with postscripts which comment on their feelings some fifty years later about having been a hidden child. Stands strongly on its own merit and also works well as a companion to THE HIDDEN CHILDREN by Howard Greenfeld.
SUBJ: Holocaust, Jewish (1939-1945)--Personal narratives./ Holocaust survivors./ Righteous Gentiles in the Holocaust./ Jews--Biography.

940.53   Ph-1 5-A/8 $15.99   L   KE666
STANLEY, JERRY. I am an American: a true story of Japanese internment. Crown ISBN 0-517-59787-X, 1994. 102p. ill., maps.
Includes index.
Tells of the World War II internment of Japanese and Japanese Americans living on the west coast of the United States. The narrative follows the experiences of Shiro Nomura, born in the United States and just completing high school in the 1940s; black and white photographs add an immediacy to the text. Strong social studies material for advanced students and for multicultural studies.
SUBJ: Japanese Americans--Evacuation and relocation, 1942-1945./ World War, 1939-1945--United States.

940.53   Ph-1 5-6/8 $16.95   T   KE667
TUNNELL, MICHAEL O. Children of Topaz: the story of a Japanese-American internment camp: based on a classroom diary. By Michael O. Tunnell and George W. Chilcoat. Holiday House ISBN 0-8234-1239-3, 1996. 74p. ill.
Includes bibliography and index.
Selectors' Choice, 21st ed.
Using excerpts from an illustrated class diary of Japanese-American third graders interned in Topaz during 1943, this moving account explores circumstances and issues and details everyday life in one of the internment camps during World War II. Reproductions of original diary pages and archival photographs illustrate the informative text. Advanced readers can pair this effectively with I AM AN AMERICAN: A TRUE STORY OF JAPANESE INTERNMENT by Jerry Stanley. For multicultural studies.
SUBJ: Japanese Americans--Evacuation and relocation, 1942-1945./ World War, 1939-1945--Children./ Central Utah Relocation Center./ Diaries.

940.54 53   Ph-2 5-6/7 $15.95   L   KE668
BALLARD, ROBERT D. Exploring the Bismarck. By Robert D. Ballard with Rick Archbold. Scholastic ISBN 0-590-44268-6; In Canada: Scholastic, 1991. 64p. col. ill., maps. (Time quest book).
"Scholastic/Madison Press book."
Includes glossary, chronology and bibliography.
The story of the sinking of the Bismarck in 1941 and the discovery of her wreckage in 1989 is recounted. Drawings, photographs, and

maps join in an effective package. Especially appealing to World War II naval enthusiasts.
SUBJ: Bismarck (Battleship)./ Shipwrecks./ World War, 1939-1945--Antiquities./ Underwater archaeology.

940.54   Ph-1 4-6/9 $21.00   L   KE669
DAILY, ROBERT. Code talkers: American Indians in World War II. Watts ISBN 0-531-20190-2; In Canada: Grolier Ltd., 1995. 63p. ill. (First book).
Includes bibliography and index.
An account of the activities of the Navaho Indian soldiers who used their native language and specially designed code words to communicate among Marine units in the Pacific during World War II, and thus prevented the Japanese from decoding intercepted messages. Sepia-toned photographs of the period appear throughout the text. For social studies units and multicultural studies and of general interest to World War II buffs.
SUBJ: World War, 1939-1945--Participation, Indian./ Cryptography./ Navajo Indians./ Indians of North America.

940.54   Ph-1 4-6/4 $15.95   T   KE670
KODAMA, TATSUHARU. Shin's tricycle. Illus. by Noriyuki Ando. English translation by Kazuko Hokumen-Jones. Walker ISBN 0-8027-8375-9; In Canada: Thomas Allen, 1995. unp. col. ill.
Makes a strong antiwar statement as a father movingly tells the story of his three-year-old son's death following the bombing of Hiroshima in August 1945. The boy's tricycle, now in the Hiroshima Peace Museum, serves as a poignant reminder of the tragedy of war. Valuable as a starter for discussions and writing activities and as a resource for units on conflict resolution.
SUBJ: Hiroshima-shi (Japan)--Bombardment, 1945./ Atomic bomb.

940.54 *adult*   Ph-1 4-6/7 $14.95   T   KE671
MARRIN, ALBERT. Victory in the Pacific. Atheneum ISBN 0-689-30948-1; In Canada: Collier Macmillan, 1983. 217p. ill.
Includes bibliography and index.
Describes the battles of World War II in the Pacific from the bombing of Pearl Harbor through the Japanese surrender. Includes diagrams of ships and submarines, description of how torpedoes and depth charges were aimed and many black/white photographs of people and events of this era. The war buff will find this a well chronicled account in an easy to read format.
SUBJ: World War, 1939-1945--Naval operations./ World War, 1939-1945--Pacific Ocean.

940.54   Ph-1 4-6/5 $16.00   T   KE672
MARUKI, TOSHI. Hiroshima no pika. Lothrop, Lee & Shepard ISBN 0-688-01297-3, 1982. unp. col. ill.
Batchelder Award, 1983.
Jane Addams Book Award.
Selectors' Choice, 14th ed.
Personal, pictorial account of a little girl and her parents who were eating breakfast at the time the atomic bomb was dropped on Hiroshima in 1945. Follows what happens to them for the next few days and describes later effects. Brilliant then subdued full page paintings express the mood and expand the text as they graphically detail the event that led to the end of the war with Japan. Leads to understanding the devastation of nuclear warfare.
SUBJ: Hiroshima-shi (Japan)--Bombardment, 1945./ World War, 1939-1945--Japan./ Atomic bomb.

940.54   Ph-2 4-6/8 $19.90   L   KE673
MCGOWEN, TOM. World War II. Watts ISBN 0-531-20150-3; In Canada: Nelson, 1993. 64p. ill. (some col.), maps. (First book).
Includes bibliography and index.
"Provides an overview of the military battles and political changes that occurred during World War II." (CIP) Includes historical photographs and detailed maps. For military buffs and twentieth century background.
SUBJ: World War, 1939-1945.

940.54   Ph-1 A/7 $15.89   L   KE674
MELTZER, MILTON. Never to forget: the Jews of the Holocaust. HarperCollins ISBN 0-06-024175-6, c1976. 217p. maps.
Includes bibliography.
Jane Addams Book Award.
Available from National Library Service for the Blind and Physically Handicapped on sound recording cassette RC10542.
The horrors of the Nazi systematic extermination while they ruled Europe, 1933-1945, is vividly told here. The brutality of the leaders, the apathy of the Christian nations and the fear that such a horror could sweep the world again are captured in the text. This book is necessary for today's youth in their understanding of the 1930's and 1940's.

NONFICTION

SUBJ: World War, 1939-1945--Jews./ Jews--Persecutions./ World War, 1939-1945--Underground movements./ Germany--Politics and government--1933-1945./ Holocaust, Jewish (1939-1945).

940.54 Ph-2 A/8 $17.50 L KE675
WHITMAN, SYLVIA. Uncle Sam wants you!: military men and women of World War II. Lerner ISBN 0-8225-1728-0, 1993. 80p. ill. (People's history).
Includes bibliography and index.
"Describes the experiences of men and women in the United States armed services during World War II, discussing such topics as the draft, boot camp, stateside duty, and combat in Europe and the Pacific." (CIP) Sepia photographs support the text. Use as background for an oral history project.
SUBJ: United States--Armed Forces--History--World War, 1939-1945./ World War, 1939-1945./ Soldiers.

941.081 Ph-3 3-6/7 $16.95 T KE676
WILSON, LAURA. Daily life in a Victorian house. Preservation Press, National Trust for Historic Preservation/dist. by Wiley ISBN 0-471-14377-4; In Canada: Wiley, 1993. 48p. col. ill., map.
Includes chronology, glossary, index and directory.
A compendium of life in the Victorian age, uses a middle class family as a model and includes discussions of meals, household activities, schooling, duties of servants, and other aspects of daily life. Illustrated with many full-color photographs of artifacts of the era. Use for background and examples of Victoriana and to provide context for children's literature in this historical time.
SUBJ: Great Britain--Social life and customs--19th century./ Great Britain--History--Victoria, 1837-1901./ Dwellings--Great Britain./ Family--Great Britain.

941.1 J 936.1 Ph-1 3-6/8 $15.95 L KE677
ARNOLD, CAROLINE. Stone Age farmers beside the sea: Scotland's prehistoric village of Skara Brae. Photos by Arthur P. Arnold. Clarion ISBN 0-395-77601-5, 1997. 48p. col. ill., maps.
Includes glossary and index.
In 1850, a fierce storm unearthed the remains of the prehistoric village of Skara Brae in Scotland's Orkney Islands, and their subsequent excavation, preservation, and details of what they reveal about long ago life are recounted here. Full-color photographs illustrate the text. For units on early civilization and for general interest.
SUBJ: Skara Brae Site (Scotland)./ Scotland--Antiquities./ Prehistoric peoples.

941.8 Ph-3 3-5/8 $24.00 L KE678
KENT, DEBORAH. Dublin. Childrens Press ISBN 0-516-20302-9; In Canada: Children's Press, 1997. 64p. col. ill., maps. (Cities of the world).
Includes chronology, glossary and index.
An interesting, detailed look at one of the major cities of the world emphasizes history; current political, social, and economic conditions; and information about the contemporary life of residents. Many bright, full-color photographs of people, places, and scenes capture the flavor of Dublin. For muticultural units and regional studies.
SUBJ: Dublin (Ireland).

942 Ph-1 3-6/7 $14.95 L KE679
FISHER, LEONARD EVERETT. Tower of London. Macmillan ISBN 0-02-735370-2, 1987. unp. ill.
Tells of thirteen episodes of British history which occurred in the Tower of London between the time of its completion in 1078 and the Great Fire of 1666. Black and white acrylic paintings of stony strength illustrate the text; small, colorful representations of the evolving Royal Arms of England appear on each two-paged section. Useful for display, for reading aloud, or for background awareness building.
SUBJ: Tower of London (London, England)./ London (England)--Buildings, structures, etc./ Great Britain--History--1066-1687.

942 Ph-1 2-6 $14.95 T KE680
GOODALL, JOHN S. Story of a castle. McElderry ISBN 0-689-50405-5, 1986. unp. col. ill.
Traces the happenings in a typical English castle from Norman times to modern day use as a tourist site. The quality of its illustrations and the appeal of its wordless, cut-page format will draw many readers; a forepage with written descriptive material aids in understanding. Particularly useful in stimulating creative activities or in understanding events in English life.
SUBJ: Great Britain--History./ Castles--History.

942.1 Ph-1 2-A $5.99 P KE681
MUNRO, ROXIE. Inside-outside book of London. Penguin ISBN 0-14-055810-1; In Canada: Fitzhenry & Whiteside, c1989, 1996. unp. col. ill. (Inside-outside).
Joins the author's city books about New York and Washington, D.C., as it depicts famous indoor and outdoor sights of London. Detailed drawings from unusual perspectives assure the continued freshness and eye appeal of this work by a prizewinning illustrator/author. Useful in study of buildings and art and also serves nicely as the cornerstone for study of important cities.
SUBJ: London (England)--Pictorial works.

942.1 Ph-3 3-5/8 $24.00 L KE682
STEIN, R. CONRAD. London. Children's Press ISBN 0-516-00351-8; In Canada: Children's Press, 1996. 64p. col. ill., maps. (Cities of the world).
Includes chronology, glossary and index.
An interesting, detailed look at one of the major cities of the world emphasizes history; current political, social, and economic conditions; and information about the contemporary life of residents. Many bright full-color photographs of people, places, and scenes capture the flavor of London. For multicultural units and regional studies.
SUBJ: London (England).

VCR 944 Ph-2 5-A $29.95 OD KE683
BONJOUR DE PARIS (Videocassette). Gessler Publishing 1320, 1988. 1/2" VHS videocassette color (45min). (Languages and lifestyles).
French version available BONJOUR DE PARIS 1319, 1988. 1/2" VHS videocassette color (45min). $29.95.
The sights and sounds of Paris today as well as some of its history are presented in this engaging and well paced film as a young teenager tours the city with her uncle. Previewing allows determination of break points if desired. Useful in country studies and in FLES programs.
SUBJ: Paris (France)--Description./ French language materials.

944 Ph-1 2-6/8 $15.00 L KE684
MUNRO, ROXIE. Inside-outside book of Paris. Dutton ISBN 0-525-44863-2, 1992. unp. col. ill. (Inside-outside).
Takes the reader on a stylized tour of Paris offering a sense of some of the well-known buildings and sights. Similar in approach to the author's books about London, New York, and Washington, this work also features unusual, fresh perspectives. Valuable in units on cities of the world or as the cornerstone for a group project in which students write and illustrate a book about their city or town.
SUBJ: Paris (France)--Pictorial works.

944 Ph-3 3-5/8 $24.00 L KE685
STEIN, R. CONRAD. Paris. Children's Press ISBN 0-516-20026-7; In Canada: Children's Press, 1996. 64p. col. ill., maps. (Cities of the world).
Includes chronology, glossary and index.
An interesting, detailed look at one of the major cities of the world emphasizes history; current political, social, and economic conditions; and information about the contemporary life of residents. Many bright, full-color photographs of people, places, and scenes capture the flavor of Paris. For multicultural units and regional studies.
SUBJ: Paris (France).

946 Ph-3 4-6/7 $17.95 L OD KE686
CHICOINE, STEPHEN. Spain: bridge between continents. Benchmark Books/Marshall Cavendish ISBN 0-7614-0143-1, 1997. 64p. col. ill., maps. (Exploring cultures of the world).
Includes glossary, bibliography and index.
Account of Spain's early history including Roman, Arab, and Muslim influences; geography; culture; and modern life, with attention to general government structure, education, arts, festivals, and holidays. Color photographs of people and places add interest. Use for regional units.
SUBJ: Spain.

946 J 970.01 Ph-2 5-6/8 $7.95 P KE687
FINKELSTEIN, NORMAN H. Other 1492: Jewish settlement in the new world. Morrow ISBN 0-688-11572-1, 1992. 100p. ill.
Includes bibliography and index.
Describes the causes and events of the expulsion of Jews from Spain in 1492 and traces the wanderings of Sephardic Jews in the years that followed. Final chapters detail the arrival in New Amsterdam almost two centuries later of a small group of descendants of Spanish Jews. Strong, well-written material for an interesting curriculum-related excursion.
SUBJ: Jews--Spain--History./ Sephardim--History./ Spain--Ethnic relations.

947 *FIC*   Ph-1 1-4/6 $18.60   L   KE688
BRESNICK-PERRY, ROSLYN. Leaving for America. Illus. by Mira
Reisberg. Children's Book Press ISBN 0-89239-105-7, 1992. 31p. col. ill.
Recounts memories of childhood in the small Russian Jewish village
where the author lived before coming to the United States in the
1920s. Warm anecdotes are supported by colorful, primitive
illustrations surrounded by borders which suggest display and
discussion possibilities. For reading aloud.
SUBJ: Bresnick-Perry, Roslyn./ Jews--Soviet Union./ Soviet Union--
Emigration and immigration./ United States--Emigration and
immigration.

947   Ph-2 5-A/7 $16.40   L   KE689
HARVEY, MILES. Fall of the Soviet Union. Childrens Press ISBN 0-516-
06694-3; In Canada: Childrens Press, 1995. 32p. col. ill., maps.
(Cornerstones of freedom).
Includes glossary, chronology and index.
Reviews history of the Union of Soviet Socialist Republics and
describes the role of Mikhail Gorbachev in providing the foundation
for change which led to the breakup of the Soviet Union. Closing
section briefly mentions later problems of Russia and other former
Soviet countries. Useful background information.
SUBJ: Soviet Union--History./ Former Soviet republics--History.

947 . 7   Ph-2 3-6/5 $14.95   L   KE690
KENDALL, RUSS. Russian girl: life in an old Russian town. Scholastic
ISBN 0-590-45789-6; In Canada: Scholastic, 1994. 40p. col. ill., map.
Visits a nine-year-old Russian girl in her home in Suzdal, 150 miles
east of Moscow. Handsome color photographs follow Olga's daily
routine. Afterword provides facts about Russia and a brief history.
Pleasing browser which has potential in a compare-and-contrast
activity.
SUBJ: Russia (Federation)--Social life and customs.

CE 947.084 *JB*   Ph-1 4-6/8 $16.00   T   KE691
SIEGAL, ARANKA. Upon the head of the goat: a childhood in Hungary
1939-1944. Farrar, Straus & Giroux ISBN 0-374-38059-7; In Canada:
McGraw-Hill Ryerson, 1981. 213p.
Newbery Honor Book.
Nine-year-old Piri retells the story of the slow and painful destruction
of her family and the Jewish community of Beregzasz under Hitler's
regime. From 1939 when war broke out along the Hungary/Ukraine
border through the spring of 1944 when Piri, her mother, her brother
Sandor and her sisters Iboya and Joli were loaded onto railroad cars
destined for Auschwitz, the effects of "the Holocaust and what it did
to young and old" (I. B. Singer) are poignantly portrayed.
SUBJ: Siegal, Aranka./ Holocaust, Jewish (1939-1945)--Personal
narratives./ World War, 1939-1945--Hungary.

947.086   Ph-2 4-6/8 $22.95   L   KE692
BUETTNER, DAN. Sovietrek: a journey by bicycle across Russia. Lerner
ISBN 0-8225-2950-5, 1994. 104p. col. ill., maps.
Includes glossary and index.
Available from the National Library Service for the Blind and
Physically Handicapped on sound recording cassette RC 41940.
Offers a first-person account of a United States-Russian cycling trip
which crossed the Ukraine and Russia in 1990. Color photographs
illustrate a lively travelog which serendipitously provides insight into
the people of the then-Soviet region. Of interest to travelers, cyclists,
and those interested in the world around them.
SUBJ: Russia, Southern--Description and travel.

948   Ph-2 4-6/7 $20.99   L   KE693
MARGESON, SUSAN M. Viking. Photos by Peter Anderson. Knopf
ISBN 0-679-96002-3, 1994. 64p. col. ill., maps. (Eyewitness books).
"Dorling Kindersley book."
"Borzoi book."
Includes index.
Presents Viking life through the objects of the civilization. Clear-cut
photography, realistic models, and fact-filled captions support the
brief text in this Eyewitness book. Valuable browser.
SUBJ: Vikings.

948   Ph-3 4-6/8 $19.95   L   KE694
PITKANEN, MATTI A. Grandchildren of the Vikings. By Matti A.
Pitkanen with Reijo Harkonen. Carolrhoda ISBN 0-87614-889-5, 1996.
48p. col. ill., maps. (World's children).
Includes glossary and index.
Describes the daily life, flora and fauna, climate, and other aspects of
life on the Faeroe Islands, Iceland, Gotland (the home of Pippi
Longstocking), the Aland Islands, and Lofoten, showing how some of
the traditions can be traced back to the days of Viking explorers.
Full-color photographs amplify the text. Use for multicultural studies,
regional studies, and as background for units on early exploration.

SUBJ: Vikings./ Iceland--Description and travel./ Islands--Scandinavia-
-Description and travel./ Family life--Iceland.

948.97   Ph-2 4-6/6 $14.95   L   KE695
LEWIN, TED. Reindeer people. Macmillan ISBN 0-02-757390-7; In
Canada: Maxwell Macmillan, 1994. unp. col. ill.
Records vignettes of Sami life--a sledge ride, camp life, a wedding,
northern lights, and always, the reindeer. Dazzling watercolors
illustrate a somewhat disorganzied text and capture moments in the
colorful way of life. Valuable as a background builder for multicultural
studies.
SUBJ: Sami (European people)./ Lapland.

948.97   Ph-2 3-6/6 $16.95   T   KE696
REYNOLDS, JAN. Far north: vanishing cultures. Harcourt Brace ISBN
0-15-227178-3, 1992. unp. col. ill. (Vanishing cultures).
Makes use of handsome color photographs and accompanying text to
record the vanishing culture of the Samis, reindeer herders in Finmark
in the Arctic Circle north of Sweden and Finland. Has potential for
use with other works by the same author to examine change in the
world of today.
SUBJ: Sami (European people)./ Finmark (Norway)--Social life and
customs./ Lapland.

949.12 *J551.42*   Ph-1 A/7 $15.89   L   KE697
LASKY, KATHRYN. Surtsey: the newest place on earth. Photos by
Christopher G. Knight. Hyperion ISBN 1-56282-301-9, 1992. 64p. col.
ill.
Includes index.
In November, 1963, a volcanic eruption added new land to our
planet--the Icelandic island of Surtsey. Text and photographs carefully
explain how this inhospitable lava mass metamorphosed to
accommodate plants and animals and why scientists followed every
development with relish and reverence. Excellent view of science taken
out of the laboratory. Quotations from the Icelandic epic, THE PROSE
EDDA, head each chapter and weave Norse mythology in and out of
reality. Perfect read-aloud for science and language arts classes in the
upper grades.
SUBJ: Surtsey (Iceland)./ Island ecology--Iceland--Surtsey./ Ecology--
Iceland--Surtsey.

949.6 *JB*   Ph-1 5-6/6 $13.93   L   KE698
KHERDIAN, DAVID. Road from home: the story of an Armenian girl.
Greenwillow ISBN 0-688-84205-4, 1979. 238p. ill.
Includes "Author's note".
Jane Addams Book Award.
Newbery Honor Book.
Veron Kherdian's story is told by her son who recounts the life of the
Armenians in Turkey and the wanderings of Veron and her family as
they are expelled from their prosperous home by the Turkish
overlords, persecuted in many ways, and finally forced forever from
their homeland. Veron's courage and determination to be educated
are climaxed when she leaves for America as a "mail-order bride."
A story similar to that of "The Holocaust" in cruelty and courage for
the special reader.
SUBJ: Kherdian, Veron./ Armenians--Turkey--Biography./ Armenian
massacres--1915-1923.

VCR 950   Ph-3 4-A $99.00   OD KE699
ASIA (Videocassette). National Geographic 51442, 1991. 1/2" VHS
videocassette color (25min). (Physical geography of the continents).
Includes Teacher's Guide.
Emphasizes the size of the Asian continent and the variety of its life
forms. Production quality is good; teacher's guide is slight.
Recommended as budget allows.
SUBJ: Physical geography--Asia./ Asia--Geography.

950   Ph-2 K-3/8 $16.99   L   KE700
CHIN-LEE, CYNTHIA. A is for Asia. Illus. by Yumi Heo. Orchard ISBN
0-531-33011-7, 1997. unp. col. ill.
A descriptive alphabet from a variety of Asian cultures including
Tibet, Indonesia, China, Vietnam, Burma, Korea, and Japan acquaints
readers with some traditional aspect of each area represented.
Colorful illustrations and a rendering of each alphabet word in its
Asian language make this an appealing model for a classroom activity
as well as a resource for multicultural studies.
SUBJ: Asia./ Alphabet.

950   Ph-1 4-6/6 $5.95   P   KE701
MAJOR, JOHN S. Silk Route: 7,000 miles of history. Illus. by Stephen
Fieser. HarperCollins ISBN 0-06-443468-0; In Canada: HarperCollins,
c1995, 1996. 32p. col. ill., map.
Travels the 7,000-mile Silk Route between the Chinese city of
Chang'an and Byzantium (Istanbul) in the eastern Mediterranean.

Vivid drawings bring to life ten major locations along the fabled trade route. Useful in economics, transportation, and geography units.
SUBJ: Silk Road--History./ Trade routes--Asia--History.

951.04 Ph-2 A/6 $15.95 T KE702
FRITZ, JEAN. China's long march: 6,000 miles of danger. Illus. by Yang Zhr Cheng. Putnam ISBN 0-399-21512-3, 1988. 124p. ill.
Includes bibliography and index.
Traces the 6,000 mile journey of Mao Zedong's First Front Army as it retreated from Nationalist forces and sought a base area in which it could safely expand. The well-known author makes liberal use of both secondary sources and interviews as she brings to life events of the year-long march which saw the Communist army group reduced from more than 90,000 men to about 20,000. A closing chapter compresses the history of Mao and the People's Republic of China in the 50 years following the Long March.
SUBJ: China--History--Long March, 1934-1935.

951.05 Ph-2 4-6/7 $15.95 T KE703
FRITZ, JEAN. China homecoming. Photos by Michael Fritz. Putnam ISBN 0-399-21182-9, 1985. 143p. ill. (some col.).
Includes bibliography.
Available from National Library Service for the Blind and Physically Handicapped on sound recording cassette RC23861.
Recounts the experiences of Jean Fritz as she revisited China after 55 years, noting changes brought about by political activities and the life style of the people today. Photographs taken by her husband illustrate this personalized travelogue. This sequel to HOMESICK: MY OWN STORY describes China and its culture today.
SUBJ: China--Description and travel./ Fritz, Jean.

951.7 Ph-2 4-6/7 $16.95 L KE704
REYNOLDS, JAN. Mongolia: vanishing cultures. Harcourt Brace ISBN 0-15-255312-6; In Canada: Harcourt Brace c/o Canadian Manda, 1994. unp. col. ill., map. (Vanishing cultures).
Visits a nomadic Mongolian family and records their daily life in a culture soon to change. Photographs of unusual quality provide a strong sense of place and expand the text. Strong support for multicultural studies.
SUBJ: Mongols--Social life and customs.

951.95 Ph-2 3-5/6 $9.95 P KE705
MCMAHON, PATRICIA. Chi-hoon: a Korean girl. Photos by Michael F. O'Brien. Caroline House/Boyds Mills ISBN 1-56397-720-6, c1993, 1998. 48p. col. ill.
Uses a day-by-day diary entry and outstanding photography to present a week in the life of an eight-year-old, middle-class Korean girl. Pronunciation assistance is provided throughout. Valuable as a browser and in support of curriculum units.
SUBJ: Korea (South).

CE 952 Ph-1 5-A/7 $15.00 T KE706
BLUMBERG, RHODA. Commodore Perry in the land of the Shogun. Lothrop, Lee & Shepard ISBN 0-688-03723-2, 1985. 144p. ill.
Includes appendices, bibliography and index.
Newbery Honor Book.
Available from National Library Service for the Blind and Physically Handicapped in Braille BR06429 and sound recording cassette RC23821.
Details the 1854 opening of Japan to the United States and the deft hand of Commodore Matthew Perry in the negotiations. Appendices include President Fillmore's letter to the emperor, listings of presents exchanged, and more. Superb design, lively and readable text, and appealing format hallmark this presentation which will be read for pleasure, for the quality of its writing and the freshness of its material.
SUBJ: United States Naval Expedition to Japan (1852-1854)./ United States--Foreign relations--Japan./ Japan--Foreign relations--United States./ Perry, Matthew Calbraith.

952 Ph-2 3-5/10 $24.26 L KE707
BORNOFF, NICHOLAS. Japan. By Nick Bornoff. Raintree Steck-Vaughn ISBN 0-8172-4786-6, 1997. 48p. col. ill., maps. (Country insights).
Includes glossary, bibliography, directory, filmography and index.
Compares life in an urban center and a rural town in Japan to show various aspects of life, including daily activities, employment, education, and recreation. Illustrated with color photographs. While it does not discuss political or social issues, it will be useful for report writers seeking basic information. For multicultural studies.
SUBJ: Japan.

VCR 952 Ph-3 3-6 $39.95 OD KE708
JAPAN: ASIA, VOLUME 2 (Videocassette). Ernst Interactive Media, 1993. 1/2" VHS videocassette color (20min). (Hello! From around the world!).
Describes the customs and daily routines of life in modern Japan. Script is upbeat, production quality is good. Visually similar to "country books" and useful in the same ways.
SUBJ: Japan./ Japan--Social life and customs.

952.1 Ph-3 3-5/8 $24.00 L KE709
KENT, DEBORAH. Tokyo. Children's Press ISBN 0-516-00354-2; In Canada: Children's Press, 1996. 64p. col. ill., maps. (Cities of the world).
Includes chronology, glossary and index.
An interesting, detailed look at one of the major cities of the world emphasizes history; current political, social, and economic conditions; and information about the contemporary life of residents. Many bright full-color photographs of people, places, and scenes capture the flavor of Tokyo. For multicultural units and regional studies.
SUBJ: Tokyo (Japan).

952.04 Ph-1 3-5/6 $15.95 L KE710
KUKLIN, SUSAN. Kodomo: children of Japan. Putnam ISBN 0-399-22613-3; In Canada: Putnam, 1995. 48p. col. ill.
Includes glossary.
Seven Japanese children from Hiroshima and Kyoto share things about themselves that each wanted readers in other countries to know, including school, wearing a traditional kimono, kendo and judo classes, calligraphy, the tea ceremony, and Japanese dance. Clear, bright color photographs accompany the text, and a brief description of each city and its history is included. Excellent examples of how modern and traditional attitudes combine in everyday life. Use for multicultural studies.
SUBJ: Japan--Social life and customs./ Japan.

954 Ph-3 4-6/6 $19.95 L KE711
HERMES, JULES. Children of India. Carolrhoda ISBN 0-87614-759-7, 1993. 48p. col. ill., map. (World's children).
Includes glossary and index.
Introduces India through vignettes describing the daily life of children in this country of 850 million people. Excellent photographs are a high point as an occasionally confusing text lags behind. Best use is as supplemental material. For multicultural studies.
SUBJ: India--Social life and customs./ Family life--India.

VCR 954.96 Ph-1 K-6 $14.99 OD KE712
HIMALAYAN ADVENTURE (Videocassette). Narrated by Jack Hanna. Ingle Productions/Time-Life Video V670-06 ISBN 0-7835-8261-7, 1994. 1/2" VHS videocassette color (40min). (Zoo life with Jack Hanna).
Includes public performance rights.
Travel to Nepal with Jack Hanna to see how a country reveres and preserves its rich cultural and natural heritage. Visit a wildlife preserve where endangered crocodiles are being saved. See how a baby elephant is both worshiped and trained. Climb to the temple home of 600 monkeys, and finally take a helicopter ride into the mountains to visit people who herd, milk, and live side-by-side with yaks. Stresses the harmony and productivity achieved when people work and live within the circle of nature. The love and respect for animals is evident in every frame. For environmental studies as well as geography units.
SUBJ: Natural history--Nepal./ Himalaya Mountains./ Zoology--Nepal.

954.96 Ph-2 3-5/6 $14.95 L KE713
MARGOLIES, BARBARA A. Kanu of Kathmandu: a journey in Nepal. Four Winds/Macmillan ISBN 0-02-762282-7; In Canada: Maxwell Macmillan, 1992. 35p. col. ill.
Joins middle-class, eight-year-old Kanu as he travels from Nepal's capital city of Kathmandu to small villages in the surrounding area. Color illustrations, a pronunciation key, and map endsheets are part of the package. Expands knowledge and supports the social studies curriculum.
SUBJ: Nepal--Social life and customs.

954.96 Ph-2 4-6/7 $16.95 T KE714
REYNOLDS, JAN. Himalaya: vanishing cultures. Harcourt Brace Jovanovich ISBN 0-15-234465-9; In Canada: Harcourt Brace c/o Canadian Manda, 1991. unp. col. ill., map. (Vanishing cultures).
Visits a Sherpa family high in the Himalaya and describes their lifeways in a changing cultural setting. Handsome photographs lift this effort far beyond the norm. Valuable awareness-builder for multicultural studies.
SUBJ: Himalaya Mountains Region--Social life and customs.

956.7044 Ph-2 6-A/6 $17.95 L KE715
KENT, ZACHARY. Persian Gulf War: "the mother of all battles." Enslow ISBN 0-89490-528-7, 1994. 128p. ill., maps. (American war).
Includes chronology, bibliography and index.

Available from the National Library Service for the Blind and Physically Handicapped on sound recording cassette RC 42892. Traces events of "The mother of all battles" from early CNN reporting of the retaliatory attack in January 1991 through Iraq's acceptance of the United Nations resolutions in early April 1991. Chronology, notes, and bibliography expand the text. Difficult but high-interest reading.
SUBJ: Persian Gulf War, 1991.

959.404   *J 973.04*   Ph-1 2-6/6 $14.95   T   KE716
CHA, DIA. Dia's story cloth. Stitched by Chue and Nhia Thao Cha. Compendium by Joyce Herold. Lee & Low/Denver Museum of Natural History. ISBN 1-880000-34-2, 1996. unp. col. ill.
Includes bibliography.
Selectors' Choice, 21st ed.
Using traditional Hmong needlework as the basis for a new folk art, story cloths were developed in refugee camps as a way to keep and transmit stories and experiences. This one recounts, in beautifully detailed and intricate embroidery, one family's search for freedom as they move from China in ancient days through days of war in Laos, refugee camps in Thailand, and arrival in America. Afterword provides much background information on the Hmong and their needlework traditions. For multicultural studies.
SUBJ: Hmong (Asian people)./ Hmong Americans./ Embroidery, Hmong.

959.7   Ph-2 5-6/7 $14.95   L   KE717
GARLAND, SHERRY. Vietnam: rebuilding a nation: Dillon ISBN 0-87518-422-7, 1990. 127p. ill. (some col.). (Discovering our heritage).
Includes glossary, bibliography and index.
Describes geography, history, traditions, religious observances, and modern political events of Vietnam. A small, significant portion of the text discusses Vietnamese in the United States; fact pages and glossary are other features. Valuable for reports and as an awareness-builder.
SUBJ: Vietnam.

959.7   Ph-2 5-6/7 $13.89   L   KE718
HUYNH, QUANG NHUONG. Land I lost: adventures of a boy in Vietnam. Illus. by Dinh Mai Vo. HarperCollins ISBN 0-06-024593-X; In Canada: HarperCollins, 1982. 115p. ill.
Available from National Library Service for the Blind and Physically Handicapped on sound recording cassette RC22179.
The author recalls, through a series of episodes, his life in a small Vietnamese village before the eruption of war. His relationship with the family's pet water buffalo, his escapades with his cousin, the myriad adventures with unusual animals, and most of all his very strong ties to a land and lifestyle now drastically changed are dramatically presented.
SUBJ: Huynh, Quang Nhuong./ Central Highlands (Vietnam)--Social life and customs./ Vietnam--Social life and customs.

959.7   Ph-1 1-3/7 $16.85   L   KE719
SCHMIDT, JEREMY. Two lands, one heart: an American boy's journey to his mother's Vietnam. By Jeremy Schmidt and Ted Wood. Photos by Ted Wood. Walker ISBN 0-8027-8358-9; In Canada: Thomas Allen, 1995. 44p. col. ill., maps.
An outstanding photo-essay follows seven-year-old TJ, a boy of mixed Vietnamese and American heritage, as he travels with his mother and aunt to visit the family that had been lost to them since the final days of the Vietnam War. Photographs and text work together to convey a sense of warm family relationships, the culture of the country, and everyday life on a family farm. Excellent resource for multicultural studies in early grades.
SUBJ: Vietnam--Description and travel./ Sharp, Timothy James--Journeys--Vietnam.

959.704   Ph-2 4-6/7 $17.30   L   KE720
KENT, DEBORAH. Vietnam Women's Memorial. Childrens Press ISBN 0-516-06698-6; In Canada: Childrens Press, 1995. 32p. ill. (some col.). (Cornerstones of freedom).
Includes glossary, chronology and index.
Describes the role of the approximately 13,000 American women who served in the Vietnam War, and traces efforts to establish the Vietnam Women's Memorial which was dedicated in 1993 on the grounds of the Vietnam Veterans Memorial in Washington, D.C. Use in units dealing with patriotic sites, in women's studies, and in discussion of the Vietnam War.
SUBJ: Vietnam Women's Memorial (Washington, D.C.)./ Vietnamese Conflict, 1961-1975--Women--United States./ United States--Armed Forces--Women.

959.704   Ph-3 5-6/6 $19.92   L   KE721
MYERS, WALTER DEAN. Place called heartbreak: a story of Vietnam. Illus. by Frederick Porter. Raintree Steck-Vaughn ISBN 0-8114-7237-X, 1993. 71p. ill., map. (Stories of America).
Tells the story of Fred V. Cherry, an African-American Air Force pilot who spent seven years imprisoned in North Vietnam. An afterword provides information and comment beyond the main text. Supplements other titles on the Vietnamese Conflict.
SUBJ: Vietnamese Conflict, 1961-1975--Prisoners and prisons, North Vietnam./ Cherry, Fred V./ Prisoners of war./ Afro-American air pilots.

959.9   Ph-3 3-6/8 $19.95   L   KE722
KINKADE, SHEILA. Children of the Philippines. Photos by Elaine Little. Carolrhoda ISBN 0-87614-993-X, 1996. 48p. col. ill., map. (World's children).
Includes index.
Children from several areas of the Philippine Islands share aspects of their daily life, history, and culture. Well-captioned photographs extend and enhance the text. Use for regional studies and for multicultural units.
SUBJ: Philippines--Social life and customs./ Family life--Philippines.

CDR 960   Ph-2 4-A $79.00   OD KE723
AFRICA TRAIL (CD-ROM). MECC CD-640 ISBN 0-7929-0904-6, 1995. 1 CD-ROM color.
Includes teacher's guide.
Version 1.01.
Also available on disk for Macintosh MC240 (ISBN 0-7929-0905-3) or Windows MW440 (ISBN 0-7929-0901-1), $69.00.
System requirements: Macintosh LC III or faster processor (68040 or PowerMac recommended); System 7.1 or later; 5MB RAM required (8MB RAM recommended); 13" or larger color display (640 x 480, 256-colors); hard disk; doublespeed CD-ROM drive.
System requirements: 486 or higher processor; Microsoft Windows 3.1 or higher, or Windows 95; 256 color SVGA display; 4MB RAM (8MB recommended for Windows 3.1 and required for Windows 95); doublespeed CD-ROM drive; Windows-compatible mouse; hard disk; Windows-compatible sound card.
Product (CD-640) runs on either Macintosh or Windows compatible hardware.
Youngsters take a challenging bike trek across Africa as they complete this simulation. Based on the OREGON TRAIL philosophy, choices about routes, supplies, companions, and the like influence progress and success. Multimedia additions, a journal feature, and good sound effects keep students' attention and allow for educational impact. Works well with small groups or an entire class.
SUBJ: Africa--Software./ Software--Africa./ Thought and thinking--Software./ Software--Thought and thinking./ Interactive media.

VCR 960   Ph-3 4-A $99.00   OD KE724
AFRICA (Videocassette). National Geographic 51440, 1991. 1/2" VHS videocassette color (25min). (Physical geography of the continents).
Includes Teacher's Guide.
Focuses on the physical geography of the second largest continent. Production quality is good; teacher's guide is slight. Valuable as curriculum support, this item is recommended as budget allows.
SUBJ: Physical geography--Africa./ Africa--Geography.

960   Ph-1 A/11 $17.95   L   KE725
CHIASSON, JOHN. African journey. Bradbury ISBN 0-02-718530-3, 1987. 55p. col. ill.
Selectors' Choice, 17th ed.
Emphasizes the impact of nature in shaping the lives of people in six areas of Africa. Quality of text and color photographs by the experienced photojournalist author is unusually high. Portions work well as a read aloud.
SUBJ: Africa--Description and travel./ Africa--Social life and customs./ Ethnology--Africa./ Man--Influence of environment--Africa.

960   *.04 Adult*   Ph-2 6-A/12 $15.95   L   KE726
KOSLOW, PHILIP. Yorubaland: the flowering of genius. Chelsea House ISBN 0-7910-3131-4, 1996. 64p. ill. (some col.), maps. (Kingdoms of Africa).
Includes chronology, bibliography, glossary and index.
Explores the ancient traditions and culture that existed in West Africa in present-day Nigeria. Illustrated with many examples of Yoruba art, it is well researched in terms of both history and oral tradition. Advanced readers will find this a useful resource on ancient cultures. For multicultural studies.
SUBJ: Yoruba (African people)./ Nigeria--History./ Africa--History./ Art, African.

960   Ph-1 4-6/6 $17.00   L   KE727

MUSGROVE, MARGARET. Ashanti to Zulu: African traditions. Illustrated by Leo and Diane Dillon. Dial ISBN 0-8037-0358-9, c1976. 28p. col. ill., map.

Caldecott Medal Award.

Handsome, full-page illustrations amplify brief texts about various African tribes and their customs. The richly colored pictures show the people in typical dress; their land; animals; and, in many instances, their homes. For multicultural studies.

SUBJ: Ethnology--Africa./ Africa--Social life and customs./ Alphabet.

960   Ph-2 1-4/5 $14.99   T   KE728

ONYEFULU, IFEOMA. Emeka's gift: an African counting story. Cobblehill/Dutton ISBN 0-525-65205-1, 1995. unp. col. ill., map.

Uses a counting book scheme to introduce items common to southern Nigerian life. Appealing color photographs lead the text. Use as a one-to-one read aloud for younger students. For multicultural studies.

SUBJ: Africa--Social life and customs./ Nigeria--Social life and customs./ Counting.

VCR 960   Ph-3 6-A $59.95   OD   KE729

ROOTS OF AFRICAN CIVILIZATION (Videocassette). Knowledge Unlimited ISBN 1-55933-205-0, 1996. 1/2" VHS videocassette color (25min).

Includes teacher's guide.

Closed captioned.

With a focus on West Africa, this video illustrates history with art and cultural artifacts and explores ancient culture, religion, art, and the slave trade. Contemporary experts in West African art, culture, and politics comment on aspects of the narration. Use in concert with print materials in social studies and multicultural studies units on the region and time period.

SUBJ: Africa./ Civilization, African./ Africa--History.

964   Ph-3 3-6/7 $19.95   L   KE730

HERMES, JULES. Children of Morocco. Carolrhoda ISBN 0-87614-857-7, 1995. 48p. col. ill., map. (World's children).

Includes index.

Supplies a series of one-page vignettes which introduce many of the lifeways of the children of Morocco. Color photographs add a sense of place and a fast fact box meets the needs of report-writers. Useful geography/social studies support for multicultural studies.

SUBJ: Morocco--Social life and customs./ Family life--Morocco.

966   Ph-3 3-6/6 $15.95   L OD   KE731

MURRAY, PETER. Sahara. Child's World ISBN 1-56766-023-1, 1994. 32p. col. ill. (Vision book).

Includes index.

Testifies to the beauty of the Sahara, a desert as large as the United States, with unique landforms, wildlife, and two million people. Modern encroachments cause ecological problems, and scientists worry that the sands are expanding. Text is on half pages set between full pages of color photographs which impart a true sense of unforgiving harshness. Use with African studies and environmental studies.

SUBJ: Sahara./ Deserts.

966   Ph-2 4-6/6 $16.95   T   KE732

REYNOLDS, JAN. Sahara: vanishing cultures. Harcourt Brace ISBN 0-15-269959-7; In Canada: Harcourt Brace c/o Canadian Manda, 1991. unp. col. ill., map. (Vanishing cultures).

Captures the windswept desert and the lifeways of the Tuaregs as the photographer/author records a nomadic culture vanishing under the pressure of modern transportation. Slight storyline follows a young boy as he joins his father on caravan, but it is the photographs which intrigue the reader. Good background-builder.

SUBJ: Tuaregs./ Sahara--Social life and customs.

966.1   Ph-3 4-6/6 $19.95   L   KE733

GOODSMITH, LAUREN. Children of Mauritania: days in the desert and by the river shore. Carolrhoda ISBN 0-87614-782-1, 1993. 56p. col. ill., map. (World's children).

Includes index.

Follows the lives of Fatimatou, a Moor living in the northern desert of Mauritania; the Hamadi, a Halpoular boy living in the south on the Senegal River. Handsome photographs typical of the World's children series enhance the text. Good supplemental support for multicultural studies.

SUBJ: Mauritania--Social life and customs./ Family life--Mauritania.

966.2   Ph-2 A/8 $7.95   P   KE734

MCKISSACK, PAT. Royal kingdoms of Ghana, Mali, and Songhay: life in medieval Africa. By Patricia and Fredrick McKissack. Henry Holt ISBN 0-8050-4259-8; In Canada: Fitzhenry & Whiteside, c1994, 1995. 142p.

ill., maps.

Includes chronology, bibliography and index.

Describes the medieval kingdoms of the Western Sudan as they rose and flourished between 500 and 1700 A.D. Text is thorough, evenhanded, and difficult enough to require determination. Assists in filling a good-sized gap in many collections.

SUBJ: Ghana Empire--History./ Mali Empire--History./ Songhay Empire--History./ Africa--History.

966.7   Ph-1 2-5/3 $18.99   L   KE735

ANGELOU, MAYA. Kofi and his magic. Photos by Margaret Courtney-Clarke. Designed by Alexander Isley Design. Clarkson Potter ISBN 0-517-70796-9; In Canada: Random House, 1996. unp. col. ill.

Selectors' Choice, 21st ed.

Poetic text, luminous photographs, and excellent graphic design combine to make an outstanding picture of life in Ashanti West Africa, seen through the eyes of seven-year-old Kofi. The magic of "I sit down, close my eyes, and open my mind" transports readers to various locales and provides an excellent model for classroom activities and personal reflection. Use for multicultural studies and interdisciplinary units in language arts and social studies.

SUBJ: Ashanti (African poeple)./ Ghana--Social life and customs./ Africa, West--Social life and customs.

966.9   Ph-2 6-A/9 $15.95   L   KE736

KOSLOW, PHILIP. Dahomey: the warrior kings. Chelsea House ISBN 0-7910-3137-3, 1997. 64p. ill. (some col.), maps. (Kingdoms of Africa).

Includes chronology, bibliography, glossary and index.

Explores the ancient traditions and culture that existed in West Africa in present-day Togo. Illustrated with many examples of Dahomey art, it is well researched in terms of both history and oral tradition. Advanced readers will find this a useful resource on ancient cultures. For multicultural studies.

SUBJ: Benin--History--To 1894./ Africa--History.

966.9   Ph-2 3-5/6 $15.00   T   KE737

ONYEFULU, IFEOMA. Ogbo: sharing life in an African village. Gulliver/Harcourt Brace ISBN 0-15-200498-X; In Canada: Harcourt Brace c/o Canadian Manda, 1996. unp. col. ill., map.

First published in Great Britain by Frances Lincoln Limited, 1996.

Obioma introduces readers to members of several ogbo, peer group associations that last a lifetime, in her village in Nigeria; and through the descriptions of their activities, a great deal is learned about culture and traditions. Colorful photographs show children and adults engaged in daily activities and traditional celebrations. For multicultural studies and discussion of community involvement.

SUBJ: Igbo (African people)--Social conditions./ Nigeria, Eastern--Social conditions./ Family life--Nigeria.

967.8   Ph-3 4-6/6 $13.95   L   KE738

PETERS, LISA WESTBERG. Serengeti. Crestwood House ISBN 0-89686-433-2; In Canada: Collier Macmillan, 1989. 48p. col. ill. (National parks).

Includes glossary and index.

The beauty and importance of the Serengeti are explored in this slender, colorful book. Text set into sections emphasizes the wild and exotic animal life and how Africa has evolved into a sea of people with pockets of wildlife. Information will tie in with studies of biomes, evolution, and animals. Independent readers will enjoy an armchair safari.

SUBJ: Serengeti National Park (Tanzania)./ National parks and reserves--Tanzania.

968   Ph-1 1-3/2 $16.00   T   KE739

ANGELOU, MAYA. My painted house, my friendly chicken, and me. Photos by Margaret Courtney-Clarke. Clarkson Potter ISBN 0-517-59667-9; In Canada: Random House, 1994. unp. col. ill.

A glimpse at the culture of a South African village is gleaned by following an eight-year-old Ndebele girl. Stunning photographs reveal the arts, crafts, customs, and daily life. Excellent for multicultural studies with the youngest audience.

SUBJ: South Africa--Social life and customs./ Art, Ndebele./ Art, African.

968.81   Ph-1 5-6/6 $16.95   T   KE740

BRANDENBURG, JIM. Sand and fog: adventures in Southern Africa. Edited by JoAnn Bren Guernsey. Walker ISBN 0-8027-8232-9; In Canada: Thomas Allen, 1994. 44p. col. ill., maps.

Striking photographs illustrate a wildlife photographer's experience in the Namib Desert and Etosha Pan of Namibia as well as his interactions with indigenous cultures and visits to the diamond mines of the Diamond Coast. Also describes adaptations of animals to this desert environment. Use for interdisciplinary units on Africa and environmental studies.

NONFICTION

SUBJ: Namibia--Description and travel./ Natural history--Namibia./ Africa--Description and travel.

970.01 *adult* — Ph-1 4-6/7 $17.00 T KE741
COLUMBUS, CHRISTOPHER. Log of Christopher Columbus' first voyage to America in the year 1492. Illustrated by John O'Hara Cosgrave, II. Linnet/Shoe String ISBN 0-208-02247-3, c1938, 1989. unp. ill.
Offers intriguing insight into Columbus' 1492 voyage as his log is copied in brief by one of his companions. A valuable primary source for teachers and students, this material is interesting in its own right as it captures touches of the tedium of the voyage and the apprehension of the unknown.
SUBJ: Columbus, Christopher./ America--Discovery and exploration./ Explorers./ Diaries.

970.01 — Ph-1 A/6 $19.95 L KE742
PELTA, KATHY. Discovering Christopher Columbus. Lerner ISBN 0-8225-4899-2, 1991. 112p. ill. (some col.), maps. (How history is invented).
Includes bibliography and index.
Available from the National Library Service for the Blind and Physically Handicapped on sound recording cassette RC35276. Discusses the variety of approaches historians have brought to the study of the life and accomplishments of Christopher Columbus. Text is rather difficult, but reasoning and exposition are clear. A valuable adjunct to the many materials about Columbus.
SUBJ: Columbus, Christopher./ Explorers./ America--Discovery and exploration--Spanish--Historiography.

970.01 — Ph-2 5-A/8 $16.95 T KE743
SATTLER, HELEN RONEY. Earliest Americans. Illus. by Jean Day Zallinger. Clarion ISBN 0-395-54996-5, 1993. 125p. ill., maps.
Includes chronology, bibliography and index.
Available from the National Library Service for the Blind and Physically Handicapped on sound recording cassette RC 37590. Examines the history of early man in America. Quality of writing and illustration is high; timeline and extensive bibliography are additional noteworthy features in this large format work. Useful research item for advanced students.
SUBJ: Indians--Origin./ America--Antiquities.

970.01 *JB* — Ph-2 5-A/7 $13.95 T KE744
YUE, CHARLOTTE. Christopher Columbus: how he did it. By Charlotte and David Yue. Houghton Mifflin ISBN 0-395-52100-9, 1992. 136p. ill.
Includes bibliographies and index.
Describes in detail the ships, instruments, and personnel which were a part of Columbus' "Great Enterprise." Skilled writing and careful black and white drawings make this a useful addition to any Columbus shelf.
SUBJ: America--Discovery and exploration--Spanish./ Columbus, Christopher.

CDR 970.04 — Ph-1 4-A $69.95 OD KE745
OREGON TRAIL II (CD-ROM). MECC CD744 ISBN 0-7929-0893-7, 1994. 1 CD-ROM color.
Includes teacher's guide.
Version 1.0.
System requirements: 68030-based Macintosh or Windows; (LC III or greater; 68040 or Power Macintosh recommended); 5 MB RAM (8 MB RAM recommended); System 7.1 or later; hard disk with 12 MB free space; 13-inch or larger color display (640x480, 256 colors); double-speed CD-ROM drive.
Product (CD-644) runs on either Macintosh or Windows compatible hardware.
Simulates traveling west on the Oregon, California, or Mormon trails. Pre-trip planning, day-to-day decisions, and life on the trail are fully explored. Works well with individual students or small groups. Teacher guidance is necessary for optimum educational meaning.
SUBJ: Overland journeys to the Pacific--Software./ Software--Overland journeys to the Pacific./ Frontier and pioneer life--Software./ Software--Frontier and pioneer life./ Oregon Trail--Software./ Software--Oregon Trail./ Interactive media.

970.1 *004* — Ph-2 6-A/9 $15.95 L KE746
ALLEN, PAULA GUNN. As long as the rivers flow: the stories of nine Native Americans. By Paula Gunn Allen and Patricia Clark Smith. Scholastic ISBN 0-590-47869-9; In Canada: Scholastic, 1996. 328p. ill.
Includes bibliography and index.
In-depth accounts of the lives and works of nine Native Americans weave much historical background and cultural information into the narratives, which include historical figures and contemporary personalities in the arts, literature, politics, and sports. A photograph or drawing of each illustrates the essays. Advanced readers will use these for multicultural studies, units on Native Americans, and biography assignments.

SUBJ: Indians of North America--Biography./ Indians of North America--Women.

970.1 *J 973.04* — Ph-2 5-6/7 $30.60 L KE747
AVERY, SUSAN. Extraordinary American Indians. By Susan Avery and Linda Skinner. Childrens Press ISBN 0-516-00583-9; In Canada: Childrens Press, 1992. 252p. ill., maps. (Extraordinary people).
Includes bibliography and index.
Offers brief accounts of the lives and contributions of more than 50 Native Americans from the eighteenth century through today. Emphasis is on each subject's accomplishments and cumulative effect of the work is powerful. Strong support for special projects.
SUBJ: Indians of North America--History./ Indians of North America--Biography.

970.1 *J970.4* — Ph-2 3-5/6 $13.95 L KE748
BAYLOR, BYRD. When clay sings. Illus. by Tom Bahti. Scribner's ISBN 0-684-18829-5, c1972, 1987. 32p. col. ill.
Caldecott Honor book.
Modern Indian children of the American Southwest often find bits of pottery made by their prehistoric ancestors in the desert near their homes. This book tells how the pottery was made and evokes a feeling for the Indian way of life of the past. Beautifully illustrated with line drawings which are derived from prehistoric Indian pottery and are arranged on brown, sepia, and beige paper. Suggested for supplementary reading in a study of Indian arts and crafts.
SUBJ: Indians of North America--Antiquities./ Pottery.

970.1 *004* — Ph-1 5-6/8 $17.95 L KE749
FREEDMAN, RUSSELL. Indian chiefs. Holiday House ISBN 0-8234-0625-3, 1987. 151p. ill.
Includes bibliography and index.
Selectors' Choice, 16th ed.
Illustrated by striking portraits, these full biographies tell the major happenings in the life of six American Indians. Covered also are the decisions made by the United States government concerning their relocation and ability to survive. Invaluable to units on the American West.
SUBJ: Indians of North America--Biography./ Red Cloud, Sioux Chief./ Satanta, Kiowa Chief./ Quanah Parker, Comanche Chief./ Washakie, Shoshoni Chief./ Joseph, Nez Perce Chief./ Sitting Bull, Sioux Chief.

970.1 *J 306* — Ph-1 2-6/6 $9.95 P KE750
MCLAIN, GARY. Indian way: learning to communicate with Mother Earth. Paintings by Gary McLain. Illus. by Michael Taylor. John Muir ISBN 0-945465-73-4, 1990. 103p. ill.
Includes bibliography.
Selectors' Choice, 21st ed.
Thirteen Northern Arapahoe stories, one for each full moon of the year, emphasize our relationship to Mother Earth and our responsibility for all living things. Grandfather Iron's tales provide life lessons with many applications for today's world. Symbolic paintings illustrate the stories, and pictures of daily activities accompany the section of suggestions for further activities. An attractive choice for reading aloud, for multicultural units, and for an interdisciplinary companion to environmental studies.
SUBJ: Indians of North America--Social life and customs./ Human ecology./ Ecology.

970.1 *3* — Ph-1 4-6/8 $20.99 L KE751
MURDOCH, DAVID H. North American Indian. Chief consultant, Stanley A. Freed. Photos by Lynton Gardiner. Knopf/American Museum of Natural History ISBN 0-679-96169-0, 1995. 64p. col. ill. (Eyewitness books).
"Dorling Kindersley book."
"Borzoi book."
Includes index.
Displays artifacts of North American Indian cultures. Arrangement is regional, period photographs and drawings that accompany text and cultural objects are presented in the familiar Eyewitness format. Appealing knowledge-expander for multicultural studies.
SUBJ: Indians of North America.

PIC 970.1 — Ph-1 4-6 $44.95 OD KE752
NATIVE AMERICAN CULTURES (Picture). Knowledge Unlimited 7024P ISBN 1-55933-098-8, 1992. 10 study prints color (17"x22").
Includes teacher's guide.
Also available as individual posters, $7.95 each.
Depicts ten geographical groupings of Native Americans. Focus of each poster is on food, clothing, tools, and physical artifacts; teacher's guide repeats poster text and offers student activities. Strong visual support for related curriculum areas and multicultural studies.

365

Contents: Northeast -- Southeast -- Plains -- Southwest -- Plateau -- Great Basin -- California -- Pacific Northwest -- Subarctic -- Arctic.
SUBJ: Indians of North America--History./ Indians of North America-- Social life and customs.

VCR 970.1   Ph-2 4-6 $369.00   OD KE753
NATIVE AMERICAN SERIES (Videocassette). Rainbow Educational RB886, 1993. 4 1/2" VHS videocassettes color.
Includes teacher's guides.
Depicts the daily life and customs of Native American groups prior to contact with European settlers. Presents the habitat, food, clothing, tools, weapons, art, economic system, and family structure of Native Americans from various regions in the United States. Technical quality is good. Guide includes script, discussion questions, and activities. For multicultural studies.
Contents: Native Americans: people of the Plains RB863 (24min); Native Americans: people of the forest RB864 (25min); Native Americans: people of the desert RB865 (24min); Native Americans: people of the Northwest Coast RB866 (23min).
SUBJ: Indians of North America--Social life and customs./ Indians of North America--History.

970.1   Ph-1 4-6/7 $24.89   L   KE754
TUNIS, EDWIN. Indians. Rev. ed. Crowell/HarperCollins ISBN 0-690-01283-7; In Canada: HarperCollins, 1979. 157p. ill.
Includes index.
Presents the habits and customs of the various Indian tribes of North America. Divided into nine major areas with emphasis on food, clothing, shelter, weapons, crafts and recreation.
SUBJ: Indians of North America.

970.1 *970.004*   Ph-1 4-6/10 $26.99   L   KE755
VIOLA, HERMAN J. North American Indians. Illus. by Bryn Barnard. Crown ISBN 0-517-59018-2; In Canada: Random House, 1996. 128p. col. ill., maps.
Includes chronology, glossary, and index.
Selectors' Choice, 21st ed.
Emphasizing the diversity of North American Indian cultures, this overview provides an attractive snapshot in time of people from eight regions at the moment of their first contact with Europeans. Each geographic section is introduced by a doublespread painting featuring various aspects of life, with additional paintings, maps, and drawings enhancing the text. Numerous sidebars encompass diverse aspects of historic life, and essays written by members of different tribes feature a discussion of contemporary issues. This handsome resource will serve students and teachers well for Native American studies, for units on comparative cultures, for multicultural studies, and for general interest reading.
SUBJ: Indians of North America--History./ Indians of North America-- Social life and customs.

CDR 970.1   Ph-1 4-A $29.95   OD KE756
500 NATIONS: STORIES OF THE NORTH AMERICAN INDIAN EXPERIENCE Academic ed. (CD-ROM). Microsoft/500 Nations Productions ISBN 1-57231-132-0; In Canada: Microsoft Canada, 1995. 1 CD-ROM color.
Includes user's guide and teacher's guide.
Version 1.00.
System requirements: multimedia PC with a 386SX/25 MHz or higher processor; 8MB of memory; at least 4MB of available hard-disk space; CD-ROM drive; sound board; Super VGA, 256-color display; MS-DOS operating system version 3.1 or later; Microsoft Windows operating system version 3.1 of later (including Windows 95); Microsoft Mouse or compatible pointing device; headphones or speakers.
Based on the miniseries hosted by Kevin Costner, this multimedia program provides a wealth of Native American stories and cultural information. Over 2,000 well researched images are available. The main menu provides access via a timeline, homelands, themes, and storytellers. Excellent reference tool and learning center mainstay. For multicultural studies.
SUBJ: Indians of North America--Software./ Software--Indians of North America./ Interactive media.

970.3   Ph-1 4-6/7 $19.90   L   KE757
ANDERSON, MADELYN KLEIN. Nez Perce. Watts ISBN 0-531-20063-9; In Canada: Nelson, 1994. 63p. ill. (some col.), maps. (First book).
WIND
Includes glossary, bibliography and index.
Treats ancient and recent history, culture, and traditions with dignity and respect. Illustrated with archival photographs and engravings. Portrayal of relationships and interactions with white settlers and missionaries will make this useful as historical background for discussion of current issues. For multicultural studies.
SUBJ: Nez Perce Indians./ Indians of North America.

970.3   Ph-2 5-6/8 $15.95   L   KE758
BEALER, ALEX W. Only the names remain: the Cherokees and the Trail of Tears. 2nd ed. Illus. by Kristina Rodanas. Little, Brown ISBN 0-316-08518-9; In Canada: Little, Brown, 1996. 79p. ill.
Includes index.
Describes the life of the Cherokees, their acceptance of the ways of the white settlers, and their willingness to become their allies. Tells of their great civilization in which they developed their own alphabet, a written constitution, and a national newspaper. Details how their alliance was broken by the white settlers when gold was discovered in Cherokee territory and depicts the forcible removal of the Cherokee from their land. Illustrated with contemporary drawings of artifacts. Use for Native American studies and multicultural studies.
SUBJ: Cherokee Indians--History./ Trail of Tears, 1838./ Indians of North America--Government relations.

970.3   Ph-3 1-4 $15.95   T   KE759
CLARK, ANN NOLAN. In my mother's house. Illus. by Velino Herrera. Viking Penguin ISBN 0-670-83917-5; In Canada: Penguin, c1941, 1991. 56p. ill.
Caldecott Honor Book.
Originally published in 1941, this reissued classic tells of daily life in the early 1900s in the Tesuque Pueblo near Santa Fe, New Mexico. Primitive black and white drawings are the illustrative staple though color is occasionally used.
SUBJ: Pueblo Indians./ Indians of North America.

970.3   Ph-2 4-6/7 $17.71   L   KE760
LANDAU, ELAINE. Cherokees. Watts ISBN 0-531-20066-3; In Canada: Watts, 1992. 61p. col. ill. (First book).
Includes glossary, bibliography and index.
Examines the history and culture of the Cherokee nation including present-day customs and living.
SUBJ: Cherokee Indians./ Indians of North America.

970.3   Ph-2 4-6/7 $17.71   L   KE761
MYERS, ARTHUR. Cheyenne. Watts ISBN 0-531-20069-8; In Canada: Watts, 1992. 63p. col. ill. (First book).
Includes glossary, bibliography and index.
Presents a brief overview of the customs, spiritual beliefs, and history of the Cheyenne people. Includes information about modern life and customs.
SUBJ: Cheyenne Indians./ Indians of North America.

970.3 *J979.50049*   Ph-1 4-6/9 $9.98   T   KE762
PRESS, PETRA. Indians of the Northwest: traditions, history, legends, and life. Courage Books ISBN 0-7624-0072-2, 1997. 64p. ill. (some col.), map. (Native Americans).
Adult
Includes chronology, glossary, bibliography and index.
An in-depth examination of the history, culture, traditions, and daily activities of the Northwest Indians focuses on the time frame prior to direct contact with European settlers, but includes a brief section on modern life. Illustrations include paintings, drawings, and photographs from Inuit, Tlingit, Chinook, Aleut, and other tribes of the region. Numerous sidebars, a world timeline, glossary, and bibliography add to the usefulness of this interesting, well-organized resource for Native American studies, early United States history, and multicultural studies.
SUBJ: Indians of North America--Northwest, Pacific--History./ Indians of North America--Northwest, Pacific--Social life and customs.

970.3   Ph-3 4-6/6 $17.71   L   KE763
QUIRI, PATRICIA RYON. Algonquians. Watts ISBN 0-531-20065-5; In Canada: Watts, 1992. 63p. col. ill. (First book).
Includes glossary, bibliography and index.
Provides a simple discussion of the daily life, crafts, and history of the Algonquians. A closing chapter examines the life of Algonquians today.
SUBJ: Algonquin Indians./ Indians of North America.

970.3   Ph-1 3-6/7 $16.90   L   KE764
SHERROW, VICTORIA. American Indian children of the past. Millbrook ISBN 0-7613-0033-3, 1997. 96p. ill.
Includes bibliographies and index.
This look at Native American life from the perspective of children includes comparative information about homes and villages, spirituality and legends, childhood, food, games and recreation, and coming-of-age for cultures of the Northeast Woodlands, Southeast, Southwest, Plains, Far West, and Northwest Coast. Illustrated with archival photographs. A high interest source of information for units on Native American cultures, American history, and multicultural studies.
SUBJ: Indians of North America.

970.3 *Adult 978.00497* Ph-1 4-6/8 $9.98 T KE765
SITA, LISA. Indians of the Great Plains: traditions, history, legends, and life. Courage Books ISBN 0-7624-0073-0, 1997. 64p. ill. (some col.), map. (Native Americans).
  Includes chronology, glossary, bibliography and index.
  An in-depth examination of the history, culture, traditions, and daily activities of the Plains Indians focuses on the time frame prior to direct contact with European settlers, but includes a brief section on modern life. Illustrations include paintings, drawings, and photographs from Pawnee, Blackfoot, Cheyenne, Mandan, and other tribes of the region. Numerous sidebars, a world timeline, glossary, and bibliography add to the usefulness of this interesting, well-organized resource for Native American studies, early United States history, and multicultural studies.
  SUBJ: Indians of North America--Great Plains--History./ Indians of North America--Great Plains--Social life and customs.

970.3 *974.00497* Ph-1 4-6/9 $9.98 T KE766
SITA, LISA. Indians of the Northeast: traditions, history, legends, and life. Courage Books ISBN 0-7624-0071-4, 1997. 64p. col. ill., maps. (Native Americans).
  Includes chronology, glossary, bibliography and index.
  An in-depth examination of the history, culture, traditions, and daily activities of the Northeast Indians focuses on the time frame prior to direct contact with European settlers, but includes a brief section on modern life. Illustrations include paintings, drawings, and photographs from Seneca, Mohawk, Iroquois, Chippewa, and other tribes of the region. Numerous sidebars, a world timeline, glossary, and bibliography add to the usefulness of this interesting, well-organized resource for Native American studies, early United States history, and multicultural studies.
  SUBJ: Indians of North America--Northeastern States--History./ Indians of North America--Northeastern States--Social life and customs.

970.3 *Adult 979.00497* Ph-1 4-6/9 $9.98 T KE767
SITA, LISA. Indians of the Southwest: traditions, history, legends, and life. Courage Books ISBN 0-7624-0070-6, 1997. 64p. col. ill., map. (Native Americans).
  Includes chronology, glossary, bibliography and index.
  An in-depth examination of the history, culture, traditions, and daily activities of the Southwest Indians focuses on the time frame prior to direct contact with European settlers, but includes a brief section on modern life. Illustrations include paintings, drawings, and photographs from Hopi, Anasazi, Zuni, Acoma, and other tribes of the region. Numerous sidebars, a world timeline, glossary, and bibliography add to the usefulness of this interesting, well-organized resource for Native American studies, early United States history, and multicultural studies.
  SUBJ: Indians of North America--Southwest, New--History./ Indians of North America--Southwest, New--Social life and customs.

970.3 Ph-2 4-6/5 $16.95 L KE768
SNEVE, VIRGINIA. Apaches. By Virginia Driving Hawk Sneve. Illus. by Ronald Himler. Holiday House ISBN 0-8234-1287-3, 1997. 32p. col. ill., map. (First Americans book).
  Describes the history, social customs, and differing roles of men, women, and children of the Apache Indians. Includes interactions with white settlers, life on the reservations, and current conditions on the reservation. Illustrated with paintings of events and cultural artifacts. Use with other titles in the "First Americans" series. For multicultural studies.
  SUBJ: Apache Indians./ Indians of North America--New Mexico.

970.3 Ph-2 4-6/5 $15.95 L KE769
SNEVE, VIRGINIA. Cherokees. By Virginia Driving Hawk Sneve. Illus. by Ronald Himler. Holiday House ISBN 0-8234-1214-8, 1996. 32p. col. ill., maps. (First Americans book).
  Includes index.
  Depicts Cherokee life and traditions before and after the coming of European settlers. Use with other titles in the First Americans series for comparisons of Native American cultures. For multicultural studies.
  SUBJ: Cherokee Indians./ Indians of North America.

970.3 Ph-2 4-6/6 $15.95 L KE770
SNEVE, VIRGINIA. Cheyennes. By Virginia Driving Hawk Sneve. Illus. by Ronald Himler. Holiday House ISBN 0-8234-1250-4, 1996. 32p. col. ill., maps. (First Americans book).
  Includes index.
  Describes the history, social customs, and differing roles of men, women and children of the Cheyenne Indians; and includes creation myths, interactions with white settlers, and current conditions on the reservation. Illustrated with paintings of events, maps, and cultural artifacts. For multicultural studies.
  SUBJ: Cheyenne Indians./ Indians of North America.

970.3 Ph-2 4-6/7 $15.95 L KE771
SNEVE, VIRGINIA. Hopis. By Virginia Driving Hawk Sneve. Illus. by Ronald Himler. Holiday House ISBN 0-8234-1194-X, 1995. 32p. col. ill., maps. (First Americans book).
  Includes index.
  Retells the creation myth and describes the pre-reservation culture of the Hopis. Final pages update the reader with mention of current Hopi life. Useful curriculum support. For multicultural studies.
  SUBJ: Hopi Indians./ Indians of North America.

970.3 Ph-2 4-6/5 $15.95 L KE772
SNEVE, VIRGINIA. Iroquois. By Virginia Driving Hawk Sneve. Illus. by Ronald Himler. Holiday House ISBN 0-8234-1163-X, 1995. 32p. col. ill., map. (First Americans book).
  Includes index.
  Recounts the history, beliefs, and daily patterns of the Iroquois tribes. Final pages mention the Iroquois of today, but major emphasis is on pre-nineteenth century lifeways. Joins other similar titles by the author in support of Native American units. For multicultural studies.
  SUBJ: Iroquois Indians./ Indians of North America.

970.3 Ph-2 4-6/6 $15.95 L KE773
SNEVE, VIRGINIA. Navajos. By Virginia Driving Hawk Sneve. Illus. by Ronald Himler. Holiday House ISBN 0-8234-1039-0, 1993. 32p. col. ill., map. (First Americans book).
  Includes index.
  Offers an overview of traditional lifeways of the Navajo people. Handsome illustrations are a plus; brevity of information about the Navajo of today is a negative. Joins the author's THE SIOUX in meeting a need for resources in this subject area.
  SUBJ: Navajo Indians./ Indians of North America--Southwest, New.

970.3 Ph-2 4-6/7 $15.95 L KE774
SNEVE, VIRGINIA. Nez Perce. By Virginia Driving Hawk Sneve. Illus. by Ronald Himler. Holiday House ISBN 0-8234-1090-0, 1994. 32p. col. ill., map. (First Americans book).
  Includes index.
  Provides simple information on traditional family life, clothing, food gathering, and cultural beliefs. Closing pages quote the words of Chief Joseph; only slight mention of today's Nez Perce is supplied. Support for social studies and multicultural studies.
  SUBJ: Nez Perce Indians./ Indians of North America.

970.3 Ph-2 4-6/7 $15.95 L KE775
SNEVE, VIRGINIA. Seminoles. By Virginia Driving Hawk Sneve. Illus. by Ronald Himler. Holiday House ISBN 0-8234-1112-5, 1994. 32p. col. ill., map. (First Americans book).
  Includes index.
  Describes the lifeways and history of the traditional Seminole. Closing pages discuss the Seminole of today. Useful with other titles in the "First Americans" series. For multicultural studies.
  SUBJ: Seminole Indians./ Indians of North America.

970.3 Ph-2 4-6/5 $15.95 L KE776
SNEVE, VIRGINIA. Sioux. By Virginia Driving Hawk Sneve. Illus. by Ronald Himler. Holiday House ISBN 0-8234-1017-X, 1993. 32p. col. ill., map. (First Americans book).
  Includes index.
  Depicts the traditional lifeways of the Sioux people discussing their beliefs and their history. Describes the various tribes of the Sioux nation, but only briefly mentions current conditions.
  SUBJ: Dakota Indians./ Indians of North America--Great Plains.

VCR 970.3 Ph-2 4-6 $40.00 OD KE777
WILK, BARBARA. Letter from an Apache: a true story (Videocassette). Centre Productions/Clearvue/eav CVH D028, 1983. 1/2" VHS videocassette color (12min).
  Selectors' Choice, 15th ed.
  Based on an actual letter written in 1905, this account of an Apache's early boyhood and the shock and trauma as the result of being captured by another tribe and sold away from his family is delivered in an understated yet moving manner. Stylistically primitive animation interspersed with authentic photographs is set against the calm narration and chanting background. A stunning experience that proved to be a superior discussion initiator.
  SUBJ: Apache Indians./ Indians of North America--Captivities.

970.3 *J 728* Ph-1 4-6/9 $13.95 T KE778
YUE, CHARLOTTE. Igloo. By Charlotte and David Yue. Houghton Mifflin ISBN 0-395-44613-9, 1988. 117p. ill.
  Includes bibliography and index.
  Selectors' Choice, 17th ed.
  Describes in intriguing detail how igloos are constructed and their role in the lives of the Eskimo people. Other portions of the work consider

that impact of the Arctic climate on Eskimo culture and final pages portray the changes occurring in the Eskimo world of today. The combination of scholarship, writing skill, and topic add up to valuable newcomer in a special group of outstanding titles by this author team.
SUBJ: Eskimos--Dwellings./ Igloos./ Indians of North America--Dwellings.

PIC 970.4   Ph-2 5-6 $24.95   OD KE779
CONTEMPORARY NATIVE AMERICANS (Picture). Knowledge Unlimited 7068PN ISBN 1-55933-187-9, 1995. 6 study prints color (17"x22").
Includes teacher's guide.
Also available as individual posters, $7.95 each.
The six posters in this informative series feature large photographs and brief biographical information about prominent contemporary Native Americans from varying cultures and fields. Teacher's Resource Guide contains augmented biographical information, activities, and bibliography for further reading. Visuals of excellent technical quality for contemporary multicultural studies and for exploring issues in the Native American struggle for cultural survival.
Contents: Sherman Alexie -- Ben Nighthorse Campbell -- Charlotte Black Elk -- Tim Giago -- Wilma Mankiller -- Maria Tallchief.
SUBJ: Indians of North America--Biography./ Indians of North America--Women.

970.444   *J 970.3*   Ph-2 4-6/5 $19.95 L KE780
PETERS, RUSSELL M. Clambake: a Wampanoag tradition. Photos by John Madama. Lerner ISBN 0-8225-2651-4, 1992. 48p col photos. (We are still here: Native Americans today).
Includes glossary, pronunciation guide and bibliography.
Combines color photographs and first-person narrative in an effective presentation of Wampanoag traditions of today.
SUBJ: Wampanoag Indians--Rites and ceremonies./ Indians of North America--Massachusetts--Rites and ceremonies./ Clambakes./ Peters, Steven.

970.466   *J 970.3*   Ph-3 6-A/7 $15.00 T KE781
HOIG, STAN. People of the sacred arrows: the Southern Cheyenne today. Cobblehill ISBN 0-525-65088-1, 1992. 130p. ill., map.
Includes bibliography and index.
Tells of the "background, beliefs, and past and present way of life of the Southern Cheyennes." (CIP) Black and white photographs accompany a workmanlike text. A strong addition to large or regional collections.
SUBJ: Cheyenne Indians./ Indians of North America--Social life and customs.

970.466   *J 970.3*   Ph-2 3-5/5 $15.95 L KE782
HOYT-GOLDSMITH, DIANE. Cherokee summer. Photos by Lawrence Migdale. Holiday House ISBN 0-8234-0995-3, 1993. 32p. col. ill., map.
Includes glossary and index.
Details the summer activities, modern and traditional, of ten-year-old Bridget, a young Cherokee living in Okay, Oklahoma. Color photographs of superior quality provide a sense of the terrain; an added plus is an informational section on the Trail of Tears. Valuable in a "how-we-live" unit or in a comparative activity using other books by the same author.
SUBJ: Cherokee Indians./ Indians of North America--Social life and customs.

970.475   *J 301.45*   Ph-2 4-6/7 $15.99 T KE783
KRULL, KATHLEEN. One nation, many tribes: how kids live in Milwaukee's Indian community. Photos by David Hautzig. Lodestar/ Dutton ISBN 0-525-67440-3; In Canada: McClelland & Stewart, 1995. 48p. col. ill., map. (World of my own).
Includes bibliography and index.
Reports the lifestyles of two Native American young people who attend the Milwaukee Indian Community School. Colorful photographs support the text; a well-chosen bibliography is a plus indicative of the general quality of this series. Useful in "how we live" units and regional units. For multicultural studies.
SUBJ: Indians of North America--Wisconsin--Social life and customs./ Indians of North America--History.

970.476   *J 970.3*   Ph-2 4-6/4 $19.95 L KE784
KING, SANDRA. Shannon: an Ojibway dancer. Photos by Catherine Whipple. Lerner ISBN 0-8225-2652-2, 1993. 48p. col. ill., map. (We are still here: Native Americans today).
Includes glossary and bibliography.
Describes the costume and dancing of young Ojibway fancy shawl and jingle dress dancers. Color photographs and a text which features thirteen-year-old Shannon Anderson trace preparations for the Mille Lacs powwow held each summer in Minnesota. Use alone or in combination with Ancona's POWWOW or other titles from the "We are still here" series for an effective display or cross-cultural activity.

For multicultural studies.
SUBJ: Ojibwa Indians--Dances./ Indians of North America--Minnesota--Dances./ Ojibwa Indians--Costume and adornment./ Indians of North America--Minnesota--Costume and adornment./ Powwows./ Indians of North America--Social life and customs.

970.476   *J 970.3*   Ph-2 4-6/6 $14.95 L KE785
REGGUINTI, GORDON. Sacred harvest: Ojibway wild rice gathering. Photos by Dale Kakkak. Lerner ISBN 0-8225-2650-6, 1992. 48p. col. ill. (We are still here: Native Americans today).
Includes glossary and bibliography.
The ritual of gathering wild rice, a sacred food of the Ojibway, is depicted through first-person narrative and colored photographs. A view of contemporary Native-American life useful for social studies units.
SUBJ: Ojibwa Indians--Social life and customs./ Indians of North America--Social life and customs./ Wild rice--Harvesting./ Jackson, Glen.

970.476   *J 970.3*   Ph-3 3-6/3 $6.95 P KE786
WITTSTOCK, LAURA WATERMAN. Ininatig's gift of sugar: traditional native sugarmaking. Lerner ISBN 0-8225-9642-3, c1993. 48p. col. ill., map. (We are still here: Native Americans today).
Includes glossary and bibliography.
"Describes how Indians have relied on the sugar maple tree...and tells how an Anishinabe Indian in Minnesota continues his people's traditions by teaching students to tap the trees and make maple sugar." (CIP) Color photographs appear on each page and a word list aids pronunciation. Particularly useful in building awareness of today's Native Americans.
SUBJ: Ojibwa Indians--Social life and customs./ Indians of North America--Minnesota--Social life and customs./ Maple sugar./ Maple syrup.

970.48   *J 978*   Ph-1 4-6/7 $18.95 L KE787
FREEDMAN, RUSSELL. Buffalo hunt. Holiday House ISBN 0-8234-0702-0, 1988. 52p. col. ill.
Includes index.
Selectors' Choice, 17th ed.
Chronicles the important role of the buffalo in the life of the Indians of the Great Plains. The lyrical quality of the text and the careful selection of reproductions of paintings of nineteenth century artist/adventurers mesh in creation of a book of unusual merit. Valuable on many fronts; read-aloud, curriculum support in several disciplines, individual growth and more.
SUBJ: Indians of North America--Great Plains./ Indians of North America--Great Plains--Hunting bison.

PIC 970.48   Ph-1 5-6 $79.00   OD KE788
INDIANS OF THE PLAINS (Picture). Documentary Photo Aids 90G, n.d. 46 study prints (11"x14").
An extensive collection of authentic photographs of the Plains Indians, showing their encampments, their homes and dress, traditions and customs, and lifestyles. With explanatory captions.
SUBJ: Indians of North America--Great Plains.

970.48   *J 970.3*   Ph-2 4-6/5 $19.95 L KE789
ROESSEL, MONTY. Kinaalda: a Navajo girl grows up. Text and photos by Monty Roessel. Lerner ISBN 0-8225-2655-7, 1993. 48p. col. ill., map. (We are still here: Native Americans today).
Includes glossary and bibliography.
Follows thirteen-year-old Celinda McKelvey as she participates in the Navajo coming-of-age ceremony. Effective color photographs accompany a well-written text which offers general cultural information in addition to description of Kinaalda. Useful in cross-cultural and "how we live" units. For multicultural studies.
SUBJ: Kinaalda (Navajo rite)./ Navajo Indians--Rites and ceremonies./ Indians of North America--Southwest, New--Rites and ceremonies.

970.488   *J 978.8*   Ph-2 5-6/8 $15.95 L KE790
ARNOLD, CAROLINE. Ancient cliff dwellers of Mesa Verde. Photos by Richard Hewett. Clarion ISBN 0-395-56241-4, 1992. 64p col photos.
Includes glossary and index.
Available from the National Library Service for the Blind and Physically Handicapped on sound recording cassette RC 36582.
Details the Anasazi way of life in the Four Corners region of the Southwest. The thorough text, supported by color photographs, discusses the history of the ancient people of the region and theories of their departure from Mesa Verde in the late 1200s. Valuable in study of Native Americans and in discussion of archeological techniques.
SUBJ: Pueblo Indians--Social life and customs./ Indians of North America--Southwest, New--Social life and customs./ Cliff dwellings--Southwest, New./ Mesa Verde National Park (Colo.).

970.489 *J 978.9*   Ph-1 2-4/6 $16.00   T   KE791
ANCONA, GEORGE. Earth daughter: Alicia of Acoma Pueblo. Simon & Schuster ISBN 0-689-80322-2; In Canada: Distican, 1995. unp. col. ill.
Includes glossary.
Photo-essay follows Alicia and her family through the traditional pottery making of the Acoma Pueblo in New Mexico. Striking photographs show details of everyday life and the process of making pottery from gathering clay to firing finished pieces. Use for multicultural studies and for a look at creative arts.
SUBJ: Acoma Indians--Social life and customs./ Indians of North America--Social life and customs./ Pottery craft./ Acoma Pueblo (N.M.)./ Histia, Alicia.

970.489 *J 970.3*   Ph-1 3-6/6 $15.95   L   KE792
HOYT-GOLDSMITH, DIANE. Pueblo storyteller. Photos by Lawrence Migdale. Holiday House ISBN 0-8234-0864-7, 1991. 28p. col. ill.
Includes glossary and index.
Ten-year-old April tells of her life in the Cochiti Pueblo near Sante Fe, New Mexico. Effective color photographs and pleasing design mesh with a text which provides on-the-spot assistance with Spanish and Indian words. An attractive awareness builder.
SUBJ: Cochiti Indians./ Cochiti Pueblo (N.M.)--Social life and customs./ Indians of North America--Southwest, New--Social life and customs.

970.489 *J 970.3*   Ph-2 4-6/5 $15.00   T   KE793
KEEGAN, MARCIA. Pueblo boy: growing up in two worlds. Cobblehill/Dutton ISBN 0-525-65060-1, 1991. unp. col. ill.
Depicts the daily life and customs of a boy growing up today at the San Ildefonso Pueblo in northern New Mexico. Color photographs showing the Green Corn Dance of the Corn Clan are particularly effective in this work which demonstrates the combination of old and new in the life of a ten-year-old Native American New Mexican.
SUBJ: Roybal, Timmy./ Pueblo Indians--Biography./ Pueblo Indians--Social life and customs./ Indians of North America--New Mexico--Biography./ Indians of North America--New Mexico--Social life and customs.

970.489 *J 978.9*   Ph-1 2-4/2 $14.99   T   KE794
MOTT, EVELYN CLARKE. Dancing rainbows: a Pueblo boy's story. Text and photos by Evelyn Clarke Mott. Cobblehill/Dutton ISBN 0-525-65216-7; In Canada: McClelland & Stewart, 1996. unp. col. ill.
Includes directory.
Andy Garcia and his grandson Curt demonstrate Tewa cultural beliefs, traditions, and dancing as they celebrate Feast Day together. Strong color photographs illustrate and amplify the informative text. Conveys a sense of contemporary Native American life. For multicultural studies.
SUBJ: Tewa Indians--Social life and customs./ Indians of North America--Social life and customs./ Tewa Indians--Dances./ Indians of North America--Dances.

970.489 *J 978.9*   Ph-2 4-6/6 $19.95   L   KE795
SWENTZELL, RINA. Children of clay: a family of Pueblo potters. Photos by Bill Steen. Lerner ISBN 0-8225-2654-9, 1992. 40p. col. ill. (We are still here: Native Americans today).
Includes glossary and bibliography.
Follows a Tewa Indian family of the Santa Clara Pueblo in northern New Mexico as they gather clay and create pottery in the age-old Pueblo tradition. Bibliography offers a listing of current children's books for further reading or quick displays. Strong potential for interdisciplinary use.
SUBJ: Tewa Indians--Social life and customs./ Indians of North America--Social life and customs./ Pottery craft./ Santa Clara Pueblo (N.M.).

970.489 *J 978.9*   Ph-2 5-6/6 $16.99   T   KE796
THOMSON, PEGGY. Katie Henio: Navajo sheepherder. Photos by Paul Conklin. Cobblehill/Dutton ISBN 0-525-65160-8, 1995. 51p. col. ill.
Examines the daily life of grandmotherly Katie Henio, weaver and sheepherder. Color photographs capture Henio's outdoor life on the Ramah Navajo reservation in west central New Mexico. Useful in "how we live" units and in regional and multicultural studies.
SUBJ: Henio, Katie./ Navajo Indians--Biography./ Indians of North America--Biography./ Indians of North America--Women./ Navajo Indians--Social life and customs./ Indians of North America--Social life and customs.

970.49 *E*   Ph-2 2-4 $15.00   T   KE797
TAPAHONSO, LUCI. Navajo ABC: a Dine alphabet book. By Luci Tapahonso and Eleanor Schick. Illus. by Eleanor Schick. Simon & Schuster ISBN 0-689-80316-8; In Canada: Distican, 1995. unp. col. ill.
Includes glossary.
Using both English and Dine words, 26 distinctly Navajo objects,

people, or places are presented. Each represents an important aspect of Dine life, and full-page pastel pencil drawings and glossary notes provide cultural context. Though upper and lower case letters are depicted, this is more useful as an introduction to contemporary Navajo life than as an alphabet book for letter recognition. For multicultural studies.
SUBJ: Navajo Indians./ Navajo language--Glossaries, vocabularies, etc./ Alphabet.

970.491 *J 970.3*   Ph-2 4-6/7 $15.95   L   KE798
HOYT-GOLDSMITH, DIANE. Apache rodeo. Photos by Lawrence Migdale. Holiday House ISBN 0-8234-1164-8, 1995. 32p. col. ill., map.
Includes directory, glossary and index.
Describes the life of ten-year-old Felecita on the Fort Apache reservation in Arizona. Color photographs strengthen a rather clumsy text which includes a depiction of rodeo activities as well as a two-paged description of the coming-of-age Sunrise Ceremony. Particularly useful for its portrayal of modern Apache life.
SUBJ: Apache Indians--Social life and customs./ Indians of North America--Southwest, New--Social life and customs./ Rodeos--Arizona./ Apache Indians--Rites and ceremonies./ Indians of North America--Southwest, New--Rites and ceremonies.

970.491 *J 970.3*   Ph-3 4-6/6 $19.95   L   KE799
ROESSEL, MONTY. Songs from the loom: a Navajo girl learns to weave. Text and photos by Monty Roessel. Lerner ISBN 0-8225-2657-3, 1995. 48p. col. ill., maps. (We are still here: Native Americans today).
Includes glossary and bibliography.
Examines the history and culture of the Dine as a grandmother teaches her granddaughter traditional Navajo weaving along with the stories and songs that make it a sacred art. For multicultural studies.
SUBJ: Navajo Indians--Social life and customs./ Navajo textile fabrics./ Hand weaving./ Navajo Indians--Folklore./ Indians of North America--Arizona--Folklore./ Folklore--Arizona./ Arizona--Folklore.

970.494 *J 970.3*   Ph-3 5-A/6 $7.95   P   KE800
NATIVE WAYS: CALIFORNIA INDIAN STORIES AND MEMORIES. Edited by Malcolm Margolin and Yolanda Montijo. Heyday Books ISBN 0-930588-73-8, 1995. 127p. ill., map.
Includes directory and index.
Authentic voices from many Native American cultures share memories and insights on aspects of modern and traditional life, including village ways, toys and games, basketry, hunting, and traditional stories. Well-defined sketches and photographs help make visual comparisions among cultures. Presentation of a variety of cultures from a specific geographic region will give students a sense of the diversity of Native American cultures and traditions. For multicultural studies.
SUBJ: Indians of North America--California./ Indians of North America--California--History./ Indians of North America--Social life and customs.

VCR 971   Ph-2 4-6 $199.00   OD   KE801
CANADA: PORTRAIT OF A NATION (Videocassette). Society for Visual Education 95544-HAVT, 1991. 2 1/2" VHS videocassettes color. (SVE basic skill booster).
Includes teacher's guide.
Surveys Canada's history and geography and then offers a more specific examination of each of four Canadian regions. Technical quality is excellent and accompanying teacher's guide contains objectives, scripts, and suggestions of activities to be used before and after viewing.
Contents: Exploring Canada (17min); The Atlantic provinces (16min); Ontario and Quebec (15min); The Prairie provinces (16min); British Columbia and the far north (19min).
SUBJ: Canada.

971   Ph-2 3-6/6 $14.95   L   KE802
HARRISON, TED. O Canada. Ticknor & Fields ISBN 0-395-66075-0; In Canada: Kids Can Press, 1993. unp. col. ill., map.
Includes music and lyrics.
Introduces and describes each of Canada's provinces and territories. Distinctive acrylic paintings and personalized text reveal the author's depth of feeling for his adopted land. Particularly useful for reading aloud as a complement to recommended nonprint resources.
SUBJ: Canada--Description and travel./ National songs--Canada.

971.004   Ph-1 2-A/4 $21.34   L   KE803
LITTLECHILD, GEORGE. This land is my land. Children's Book Press ISBN 0-89239-119-7, 1993. 31p. col. ill.
Offers a mix of autobiography, history, and powerful artwork as George Littlechild, a member of the Plains Cree Nation, describes experiences of Native Americans of North America, particularly in Canada. Photographs of the author's forebearers provide an

intriguing dedicatory page. Strong potential for interdisciplinary use and multicultural studies.
SUBJ: Indians of North America--Canada./ Littlechild, George./ Cree Indians--Biography.

971 Ph-3 5-A/7 $35.00 T KE804
LUNN, JANET. Story of Canada. By Janet Lunn and Christopher Moore. Illus. by Alan Daniel. Lester Publishing/Key Porter dist. by Children's Bookstore ISBN 1-895555-32-9; In Canada: Lester Publishing/Key Porter, 1992. 319p. col. ill., maps.
Includes chronology and index.
Celebrates the history, lore, and 125 years of Canada's nationhood in this large format, Canadian work. A useful chronology follows the colorfully illustrated text. Comprehensive coverage valuable in regional collections.
SUBJ: Canada./ Canada--History.

971 Ph-3 A/10 $19.00 T KE805
MALCOLM, ANDREW H. Land and people of Canada. HarperCollins ISBN 0-06-022494-0; In Canada: HarperCollins, 1991. 220p. ill. (Portraits of the nations).
Includes bibliography, filmography and index.
Offers a knowledgeable exposition of "the history, geography, people, culture, government, and economy of Canada." (CIP) Photographs are undistinguished, but quality of writing is high and unusually strong bibliographic comments lead the reader to additional resources. Useful in both general and regional collections. For advanced students.
SUBJ: Canada.

971 Ph-3 4-6/4 $17.20 L KE806
SCHEMENAUER, ELMA. Canada. Childrens Press ISBN 0-516-01065-4; In Canada: Childrens Press, 1994. 48p. col. ill., maps. (New true book).
Includes glossary and index.
Offers a generalized introduction to Canada. Reading level is a plus; lack of information is a negative. Regional purchase.
SUBJ: Canada.

VCR 971 Ph-3 4-6 $79.95 OD KE807
SHEENA AZAK OF CANADA (Videocassette). Rainbow Educational RB8224, 1995. 1/2" VHS videocassette color (15min). (Children of other lands).
Includes teacher's guide and reproducible.
Includes public performance rights.
A weekend in the life of Sheena and her family, contemporary Canadian Native Americans, help viewers to compare and contrast traditional customs and beliefs with aspects of modern life. Specific information and examples contribute to an understanding of cultural tradition, everyday activities, and how the two are connected. Use for multicultural and regional studies.
SUBJ: Indians of North America--Canada--Social life and customs./ Canada--Social life and customs.

VCR 971.01 Ph-3 A $39.95 OD KE808
CONFRONTING THE WILDERNESS (Videocassette). WNET/dist. by PBS Video ISBN 0-7936-0653-5, 1991. 1/2" VHS videocassette color (60min). (Land of the eagle).
Includes series study guide.
Combines dazzling photography and nature-centered script in an examination of the development by Europeans of Canada. Strong production values are a hallmark of the WNET and BBC television series of which this video is a part. Length mandates preview and decisions about pattern of use.
SUBJ: Canada--History--To 1763./ Indians of North America--Canada.

971.1 Ph-3 4-6/9 $18.95 L KE809
BOWERS, VIVIEN. British Columbia. Lerner ISBN 0-8225-2755-3, 1995. 76p. col. ill., maps. (Hello Canada).
Includes chronology, glossary and index.
Discusses the land, history, cultures, and people that comprise this diverse Canadian Province. Special interest pages with personal stories are interspersed throughout the text. Also contains Famous British Columbians illustrated with photos, Fast Facts, timeline, and pronunciation guide. The attractive format and layout will appeal to students and will be a useful resource for units on Canada.
SUBJ: British Columbia (Canada).

971.1 Ph-3 5-A/9 $27.40 L KE810
NANTON, ISABEL. British Columbia. Edited by Nancy Flight...[et al.]. Childrens Press ISBN 0-516-06619-6; In Canada: Grolier Limited, 1994. 144p. col. ill., maps. (Discover Canada).
Includes chronology and index.
Provides information about the land, people, history, government, and the modern day scene in the Pacific Province of Canada. Color

photographs enhance the text to which a solid fact section is appended. For medium and large regional collections.
SUBJ: British Columbia (Canada).

971.2 Ph-3 2-6/6 $19.95 T KE811
BANNATYNE-CUGNET, JO. Prairie alphabet. Illus. by Yvette Moore. Tundra ISBN 0-88776-292-1; In Canada: Tundra, 1992. unp. col. ill.
Stretches a bit to combine alliteration, objects beginning with named letter, and artwork depicting rural Canadian prairie life. "A--We auction our Aberdeen Angus at Agribition" to "Z--At zero degrees we cover zinnias and zucchini." Potential for social studies support in regional collections.
SUBJ: Prairies--Canada./ Farm life--Canada./ Alphabet.

971.2 Ph-2 4-6/4 $17.95 T KE812
BANNATYNE-CUGNET, JO. Prairie year. Illus. by Yvette Moore. Tundra Books ISBN 0-88776-334-0; In Canada: Tundra Books, 1994. 32p. col. ill.
Includes glossary.
Traces a year--January to December--of contemporary Canadian prairie life. Illustrations are distinguished, and the text provides vignettes of rural life. Use as a monthly read-aloud in a yearlong unit emphasizing Canada or develop a comparison and contrast activity with patterns of 150 years earlier as depicted in PIONEER SAMPLER. For reading aloud.
SUBJ: Prairies--Canada./ Farm life--Canada.

971.2 Ph-2 3-5/7 $14.95 T OD KE813
KURELEK, WILLIAM. Prairie boy's summer. Paintings and story by William Kurelek. Tundra ISBN 0-88776-058-9; In Canada: Tundra, 1975. 47p. col. ill.
Vividly recreates summer life on the prairie during the 1930's through a series of detailed vignettes. Each is accompanied by a rich primitive full color illustration.
SUBJ: Farm life--Canada./ Summer./ Prairies--Canada.

CE 971.2 Ph-2 3-6/7 $14.95 T OD KE814
KURELEK, WILLIAM. Prairie boy's winter. Paintings and story by William Kurelek. Tundra/c/o Houghton Mifflin ISBN 0-88776-022-8; In Canada: Tundra, c1973. unp. col. ill.
Selectors' Choice, 9th ed.
Depicts the harsh winter life on the prairies during the 1930's. The author tells the story of his own childhood through 20 brief flashbacks, each accompanied by a rich textured full-color painting.
SUBJ: Farm life--Canada./ Winter./ Prairies--Canada.

971.2 Ph-3 3-5/6 $9.95 P OD KE815
SYMONS, R. D. Grandfather Symons' homestead book. Western Producer Prairie Book ISBN 0-88833-082-0; In Canada: Western Producer Prairie Book, 1981. 80p. col. ill.
Includes index.
Describes daily activities of homesteaders in Canada's prairie provinces in the early 1900s. Colorful drawings enliven the text which describes jobs to be done each month. A lively look at this period especially useful in study of Canadian history.
SUBJ: Frontier and pioneer life--Canada./ Prairies--Canada.

971.27 Ph-3 5-A/8 $28.30 L KE816
EMMOND, KEN. Manitoba. Children's Press ISBN 0-516-06612-9; In Canada: Grolier, 1992. 128p. ill. (some col.). (Discover Canada).
Includes "Facts at a Glance," "Important Dates," "Important People," maps and index.
Provides information on the land, people, history and government, and modern day scene in the province of Manitoba. Color photographs support a text to which a strong fact section is appended. Useful regional material.
SUBJ: Manitoba (Canada).

971.3 Ph-3 4-6/10 $18.95 L KE817
BARNES, MICHAEL. Ontario. Lerner ISBN 0-8225-2754-5, 1995. 76p. col. ill., maps. (Hello Canada).
Includes chronology, glossary and index.
Discusses land, history, economy, and culture of this Canadian province. Includes Famous People from Ontario illustrated with photographs, Fast Facts, timeline, and pronunciation guide. The attractive format and layout will appeal to students. A useful resource for social studies units on Canada.
SUBJ: Ontario.

971.3 Ph-3 5-6/8 $9.95 P KE818
EDWARDS, FRANK B. Ottawa: a kid's eye view. By Frank B. Edwards and J. A. Kraulis. Bungalo/dist. by Firefly ISBN 0-921285-26-4; In Canada: Bungalo/dist. by Firefly, 1993. 72p. col. ill.
Includes index.

Features color photographs of dazzling quality depicting public buildings, parks, and institutions of Ottawa. Text is difficult but provides strong supporting information. Good choice for an armchair journey.
SUBJ: Ottawa (Ont.).

971.3   Ph-3 5-A/8 $28.30   L   KE819
MACKAY, KATHRYN. Ontario. Children's Press ISBN 0-516-06614-5; In Canada: Grolier, 1992. 144p. ill. (some col.). (Discover Canada).
Includes "Facts at a Glance," "Important Dates," "Important People," maps and index.
Introduces Ontario and offers information on the land, people, history and government, industry, environmental concerns, and culture of the province. Fact pages, timeline, and maps complete this useful book. A solid addition to regional collections on both sides of the Canadian-U.S. border.
SUBJ: Ontario.

971.5   Ph-3 5-A/9 $27.40   L   KE820
GANN, MARJORIE. New Brunswick. Childrens Press ISBN 0-516-06620-X; In Canada: Grolier Limited, 1995. 128p. col. ill., maps. (Discover Canada).
Includes chronology and index.
Examines the geography, history, economy, and government of Canada's only officially bilingual province. Color photographs add appeal for armchair travelers, and fast fact section provides quick answers. Use in regional collections both in Canada and the United States.
SUBJ: New Brunswick (Canada).

971.6   Ph-3 5-A/8 $28.30   L   KE821
LOTZ, JIM. Nova Scotia. Children's Press ISBN 0-516-06613-7; In Canada: Grolier, 1992. 128p. ill. (some col.). (Discover Canada).
Includes "Facts at a Glance," "Important Dates," "Important People," maps and index.
Offers an overview of the land, history, development, and modern day life-styles of the Canadian province. Color photographs provide a sense of place, while "Facts at a Glance" section serves report writers. A strong addition to regional collections.
SUBJ: Nova Scotia (Canada).

971.8   Ph-3 4-6/8 $18.95   L   KE822
JACKSON, LAWRENCE. Newfoundland and Labrador. Lerner ISBN 0-8225-2757-X, 1995. 72p. col. ill., maps. (Hello Canada).
Includes chronology, glossary and index.
Discusses land, history, economy, and culture of these Canadian provinces. Includes Famous People from Newfoundland and Labrador illustrated with photographs, Fast Facts, timeline, and pronunciation guide. The attractive format and layout will appeal to students. A useful resource for social studies units on Canada.
SUBJ: Newfoundland.

971.9   Ph-1 5-6/6 $6.95   P   KE823
COOPER, MICHAEL L. Klondike fever. By Michael Cooper. Clarion ISBN 0-395-54784-9, 1989. 80p. ill.
Includes bibliography and index.
Recreates the 1890s world of the three-year Klondike Gold Rush as it details events along the Dyea Trail through Chilkoot Pass, in rapidly growing Dawson, and in placer mining camps. Excellent black and white photographs tell stories themselves as they add to the effectiveness of the work. Use with Blumberg's book on the Gold Rush in California, Robert Service's poems, and Jack London's books.
SUBJ: Klondike River Valley (Yukon)--Gold discoveries./ Gold mines and mining--Klondike River Valley (Yukon)--History.

971.9   Ph-2 5-6/8 $27.50   L   KE824
HANCOCK, LYN. Northwest Territories. Childrens Press ISBN 0-516-06615-3; In Canada: Grolier Limited, 1993. 128p. col. ill., maps. (Discover Canada).
Includes chronology and index.
Introduces Canada's "outback" and supplies information on the land, people, history, and government and culture of this large province. Fact pages, timelines, and maps add further understanding. A useful addition to collections on both sides of the Canadian-United States border.
SUBJ: Northwest Territories.

971.9   Ph-3 4-6/7 $18.95   L   KE825
HANCOCK, LYN. Nunavut. Lerner ISBN 0-8225-2758-8, 1995. 76p. col. ill., maps. (Hello Canada).
Includes chronology, glossary and index.
Discusses land, history, economy, and culture of this newly created Arctic Canadian province. Includes Famous People from Nunavut illustrated with photographs, Fast Facts, timeline, and pronunciation guide. The attractive format and layout will appeal to students. A useful resource for social studies units on Canada and Native Americans.
SUBJ: Nunavut (N.W.T.)./ Inuit./ Eskimos.

PIC 971.9   Ph-2 A $27.50   OD KE826
KLONDIKE GOLD RUSH (Picture). Documentary Photo Aids 201C, n.d. 15 study prints, (11"x14").
Provides 15 black and white study prints with captions which tell of the Klondike Gold Rush of 1897-99. Useful for display purposes as well as for individual study, the prints supply an additional dimension when used with Ray's GOLD! THE KLONDIKE ADVENTURE or Cooper's KLONDIKE FEVER.
SUBJ: Klondike River Valley (Yukon)--Gold discoveries./ Gold mines and mining--Klondike River Valley (Yukon)--History.

971.9   Ph-2 3-6/6 $16.95   T   KE827
REYNOLDS, JAN. Frozen land: vanishing cultures. Harcourt Brace ISBN 0-15-238787-0; In Canada: Harcourt Brace c/o Canadian Manda, 1993. unp. col. ill., map. (Vanishing cultures).
Depicts a young girl as she learns the early ways of the Inuit. Outstanding photography captures the details of igloo-building, fishing, and the drum dance. Coordinate with the Yue's IGLOO and Hoyt-Goldsmith's ARCTIC HUNTER for a strong presentation of the traditional lifeways of the North. For multicultural studies.
SUBJ: Northwest Territories./ Eskimos--Northwest Territories.

972   Ph-2 5-6/7 $14.95   T   KE828
ARNOLD, CAROLINE. City of the gods: Mexico's ancient city of Teotihuacan. Photos by Richard Hewett. Clarion ISBN 0-395-66584-1, 1994. 48p. col. ill., map.
Includes glossary and index.
Explores the ruins of the ancient city of Teotihuacan, built nearly 2000 years ago and abandoned after 600 years. Religion, trade and commerce, and ceremonial structures receive attention in the text which includes pronunciation aids. Serves as a needed resource on the subject.
SUBJ: Teotihuacan Site (San Juan Teotihuacan, Mexico)./ Indians of Mexico--Antiquities./ Mexico--Antiquities.

972   Ph-1 4-6/9 $12.99   L   KE829
BAQUEDANO, ELIZABETH. Aztec, Inca and Maya. Photos by Michel Zabe. Knopf ISBN 0-679-93883-4, 1993. 64p. col. ill., maps. (Eyewitness books).
"Dorling Kindersley book."
"Borzoi book."
Includes index.
Portrays trading practices, cities, and cultures of ancient civilizations of Mesoamerica and South America. Skillful illustrations and worthwhile captions in the Eyewitness style create an outstanding resource. Browser and report source.
SUBJ: Aztecs./ Mayas./ Incas./ Indians of Mexico./ Indians of Central America./ Indians of South America.

972.08   Ph-2 5-A/11 $16.95   L   KE830
FROST, MARY PIERCE. Mexican Revolution. By Mary Pierce Frost and Susan Keegan. Lucent ISBN 1-56006-292-4, 1997. 128p. ill., maps. (World history series).
Includes chronology, bibliographies and index.
An account of the events leading up to, during, and following the Mexican Revolution begins with the election of Porfirio Diaz as president in 1876 and ends with the retirement of Lazaro Cardenas in 1940. Black and white photographs illustrate the text which is accompanied by timelines, brief sidebars, chapter notes, and bibliographies. Advance readers looking for in-depth information will find this a useful resource for Mexican history. For multicultural studies.
SUBJ: Mexico--History--Revolution, 1910-1920.

972   Ph-3 A/11 $20.50   L   KE831
IRIZARRY, CARMEN. Mexico. Rev. ed. Watts ISBN 0-531-14322-8; In Canada: Watts, 1994. 48p. ill. (some col.), maps.
Includes index.
Utilizes large format, expanded text, and colorful photography to provide more depth than often found in series books as it describes the land, population, lifestyle, economy, and role of government in Mexico. Four two-paged fact files use graphs to present information in an alternate fashion. Of value to report writers, use of several titles from the series has potential for side-by-side comparative work on countries.
SUBJ: Mexico.

972 Ph-2 3-5/7 $17.95 L OD KE832
KENT, DEBORAH. Mexico: rich in spirit and tradition. Benchmark Books/Marshall Cavendish ISBN 0-7614-0187-3, 1996. 64p. col. ill., maps. (Exploring cultures of the world).
Includes glossary, bibliography and index.
"Covers the geography, history, people, customs, and the arts of Mexico." (CIP) Illustrated with full-color photographs. Useful for reports and comparative multicultural studies.
SUBJ: Mexico.

972.01 Ph-2 5-6/7 $15.95 T KE833
MARRIN, ALBERT. Aztecs and Spaniards: Cortes and the conquest of Mexico. Atheneum ISBN 0-689-31176-1; In Canada: Collier Macmillan, 1986. 212p. ill.
Includes bibliography and index.
Available from National Library Service for the Blind and Physically Handicapped in Braille BRA06605.
Details the history and culture of the Aztecs, reports the clash between them and armies of Hernan Cortes, and tells of the Aztecs' ultimate defeat by the Spaniards. Based on reputable sources, this readable book includes illustrations redrawn from 16th century works. Some sections have potential for read-aloud use; good readers will use it for research.
SUBJ: Aztecs--History./ Indians of Mexico--History./ Mexico--History--Conquest, 1519-1540./ Cortes, Hernando./ America--Discovery and exploration--Spanish.

972 Ph-1 4-6/6 $16.95 T KE834
MATHEWS, SALLY SCHOFER. Sad Night: the story of an Aztec victory and a Spanish loss. Clarion ISBN 0-395-63035-5, 1994. unp. col. ill., map.
Selectors' Choice, 20th ed.
Presents a brief history of the Aztecs and vividly details the dramatic story of Montezuma and Cortes. Narrative is skilled and readable; illustrations after the Aztec style demand attention. Valuable in study of the Aztecs and for independent reading. For multicultural studies.
SUBJ: Mexico--History--Conquest, 1519-1540./ Aztecs--History./ Indians of Mexico--History.

972.03 Ph-2 5-A/11 $16.95 L KE835
MEXICAN WAR OF INDEPENDENCE. Lucent ISBN 1-56006-297-5, 1997. 112p. ill., maps. (World history series).
Includes chronology, glossary, bibliographies and index.
An account of the political, social, and economic struggle for Mexican independence includes background information from the early days of Spanish rule. Black and white photographs illustrate the text which is accompanied by timelines, brief sidebars, chapter notes, and bibliographies. Advanced readers looking for in-depth information will find this a useful resource for Mexican history. For multicultural studies.
SUBJ: Mexico--History--Wars of Independence, 1810-1821.

VCR 972 Ph-3 6-A $295.00 OD KE836
MEXICO: A CHANGING LAND. 3rd ed. (Videocassette). Alfred Higgins Productions, 1996. 1/2" VHS videocassette color (21min).
Includes teacher's guide.
Includes public performance rights.
A straightforward presentation of Mexico's historical and cultural heritage and traditions is contrasted with contemporary industry, agriculture, trade, art, and education. Emphasizes the changes currently underway to modernize and develop Mexico's role in a world economy. Use for multicultural and regional studies.
SUBJ: Mexico.

972.37 Ph-1 2-6/8 $16.95 T KE837
PRESILLA, MARICEL E. Life around the lake. By Maricel E. Presilla and Gloria Soto. Embroideries by the women of Lake Patzcuaro. Henry Holt ISBN 0-8050-3800-0; In Canada: Fitzhenry & Whiteside, 1996. unp. col. ill.
The daily life and culture of the Tarascan Indians who live on the shores of Lake Patzcuaro in Central Mexico are vividly portrayed in colorful, detailed embroideries made by the women of the village. Their concerns about pollution and other changes that threaten their traditional way of life are also addressed. Pair this with DIA'S STORY CLOTH for a comparison of two cultures expressed in the same art medium. An unusual selection for environmental studies, multicultural studies, and women's studies.
SUBJ: Tarasco Indians--Social life and customs./ Indians of Mexico--Social life and customs./ Embroidery, Mexican.

972 Ph-2 4-6/7 $17.71 L KE838
SHEPHERD, DONNA WALSH. Aztecs. Watts ISBN 0-531-20064-7; In Canada: Watts, 1992. 63p. col. ill. (First book).
Includes glossary, bibliography and index.
Traces the history of the Aztec Indians as it describes the religion and lifeways of this ancient people. Text is straightforward and workmanlike. Useful for background and curriculum support.
SUBJ: Aztecs./ Indians of Mexico.

972 Ph-2 4-6/8 $19.95 L KE839
STAUB, FRANK J. Children of the Sierra Madre. Text and photos by Frank Staub. Carolrhoda ISBN 0-87614-943-3, 1996. 48p. col. ill., map. (World's children).
Includes index.
A look at life in the Barrancas del Cobre, or Copper Canyon, region of northern Mexico as seen through the daily activities of the Tarahumara Indians, mestizo, and white Mexicans who live there. Fine, well-captioned photographs amplify the text. Use for multicultural studies and for comparisons among Native Americans in Mexico and the American Southwest.
SUBJ: Sierra Madre Occidental Region (Mexico)--Social life and customs./ Tarahumara Indians./ Indians of Mexico--Sierra Madre Occidental Region.

972 Ph-3 4-6/7 $19.95 L KE840
STAUB, FRANK J. Children of Yucatan. Text and photos by Frank Staub. Carolrhoda ISBN 0-87614-984-0, 1996. 48p. col. ill., map. (World's children).
Includes index.
A rich portrait of cultural and historical life in the Yucatan as seen through daily routines of Mayan and mestizo children. Full-color photographs show the children and their families in various activities and settings including archeological sites and other monuments. Use for multicultural studies and regional units.
SUBJ: Mayas--Social life and customs./ Indians of Mexico--Social life and customs./ Yucatan (Mexico: State)--Social life and customs./ Family life--Mexico.

VCR 972 Ph-3 5-A $79.95 OD KE841
SUEMI'S STORY: MY MODERN MAYAN HOME (Videocassette). Little Fort Media/dist. by United Learning 2047V, c1991. 1/2" VHS videocassette color (22min).
Includes teacher's guide.
Visits fourteen-year-old Suemi in her village in the Yucatan region of Mexico. Emphasis is on daily routine and lifestyle. Helpful background-builder.
SUBJ: Mayas--Social life and customs./ Indians of Mexico--Social life and customs./ Yucatan Peninsula.

972 Ph-3 5-6/7 $15.00 T KE842
WOOD, TIM. Aztecs. Viking ISBN 0-670-84492-6; In Canada: Penguin, 1992. 48p. col. ill., map. (See through history).
Includes chronology, glossary and index.
Describes Aztec history and customs in a large-format presentation which features see-through cutaways of homes and temples. Additional illustrative material includes a map, drawings, and photographs. Useful in large collections.
SUBJ: Aztecs./ Mexico--Civilization.

972.81 Ph-2 4-6/7 $11.90 L KE843
GREENE, JACQUELINE DEMBAR. Maya. Watts ISBN 0-531-20067-1; In Canada: Watts, 1992. 63p. col. ill. (First book).
Includes glossary, bibliography and index.
Examines life in the ancient civilization of the Maya. Photographs and an occasional drawing support the text. A solid curriculum enhancer.
SUBJ: Mayas./ Indians of Central America.

VCR 972.81 Ph-3 6-A $69.00 OD KE844
LOST CITY OF THE MAYA (Videocassette). National Geographic 52630, 1990. 1/2" VHS videocassette color (18min).
Includes teacher's guide.
Also available in Spanish (51756, $69.00).
Closed captioned.
Archeological excavation of the Mayan city of Dos Pilas reveals hieroglyphics, evidence of ritual bloodletting, human sacrifice, and militaristic expansionism before its abandonment. Use for regional studies and for units on Mayan civilization.
SUBJ: Mayas./ Indians of Central America./ Dos Pilas Site (Guatemala).

CDR 972.81 Ph-1 5-A $79.00 OD KE845
MAYAQUEST TRAIL (CD-ROM). MECC/Learning Company CD-645 ISBN 0-7929-0906-2, 1996. 1 CD-ROM color.
Version 1.1.
Includes teacher's guide.
System requirements: Windows 486 or higher; Microsoft Windows 3.1 or higher, including Windows 95; 256-color SVGA display; 4MB RAM (8MB RAM recommended for Windows 3.1 and required for

Windows 95); double-speed CD-ROM drive; 2MB free hard-disk space; Windows-compatible mouse; Windows-compatible sound card; Windows-compatible printer (optional).
System requirements: Macintosh 68030 required (LC III or greater); System 7.1 or later; 5MB RAM required (8MB RAM recommended); 13" or larger color display required (640x480, 256 colors); double-speed CD-ROM drive; 2MB free hard-disk space; Macintosh-compatible printer (optional).
Product CD-645 (ISBN 0-7929-0906-2) runs on either Macintosh or Windows compatible hardware.
This is a well developed simulation based on the spring expedition of the MayaQuest team. Exploration and adventure game options are available. A multimedia resource tool allows students to create projects and helps foster research skills. Works well with small groups.
SUBJ: Mayas--Software./ Software--Mayas./ Indians of Central America--Software./ Software--Indians of Central America./ Spanish language materials--Software./ Software--Spanish language materials./ Interactive media.

972.91 Ph-3 4-6/8 $19.95 L KE846
STAUB, FRANK J. Children of Cuba. Text and photos by Frank Staub. Carolrhoda ISBN 0-87614-989-1, 1996. 48p. col. ill., map. (World's children).
Includes index.
Discusses the history of Cuba as well as current economic, political, and social conditions. Full-color photographs show young people and others engaged in various activities and at places of cultural significance. Useful as a background builder as well as for student reports and multicultural studies.
SUBJ: Cuba--Social life and customs./ Family life--Cuba.

972.95 Ph-3 5-6/6 $26.60 L OD KE847
KENT, DEBORAH. Puerto Rico. Childrens Press ISBN 0-516-00498-0; In Canada: Childrens Press, 1992. 144p. col. ill., maps. (America the beautiful).
Includes chronology and index.
Available from the National Library Service for the Blind and Physically Handicapped on sound recording cassette RC34652.
Presents geography, history, government, economy, and cultural/recreational aspects of the commonwealth. Closing section includes maps, chronology, and pictures of persons tied to the history of Puerto Rico. Useful as background for current events and as an awareness-builder.
SUBJ: Puerto Rico.

973 Ph-2 4-6/7 $14.99 L KE848
BLASSINGAME, WYATT. Look-it-up book of presidents. Rev. ed. Random House ISBN 0-679-90353-4; In Canada: Random House, 1996. 160p. ill.
Includes index.
Presents in chronological order basic biographical information about each president through Clinton. The handy organization along with "The Presidents at a glance" make this useful for reports and/or informative reading.
SUBJ: Presidents./ United States--History.

973 Ph-2 5-6/7 $17.90 L KE849
BLUE, ROSE. White House kids. By Rose Blue and Corinne J. Naden. Millbrook ISBN 1-56294-447-9, 1995. 96p. ill. (some col.).
Includes chronology, bibliography and index.
Available from the National Library Service for the Blind and Physically Handicapped on sound recording cassette RC 42568.
Tells of the children and young people who have lived in the White House, providing a glimpse at the human side of the presidents. A chronology which lists all presidential children is appended to the main text. Useful for specialized reports and casual readers.
SUBJ: Children of presidents./ Presidents--Family./ White House (Washington, D.C.).

973 Ph-2 5-6/10 $18.95 L KE850
BREDESON, CARMEN. Presidential Medal of Freedom winners. Enslow ISBN 0-89490-705-0, 1996. 104p. ill. (Collective biographies).
Includes bibliography and index.
Brief biographies of ten of the more than 300 men and women who have made significant contributions to life in the United States and who have been honored with the nation's highest civilian award for their achievements. The profiled recipients represent diverse fields and cultural backgrounds, making the book suitable for multicultural studies and women's studies. Will add depth to study of twentieth century history.
SUBJ: United States--Biography./ Presidential Medal of Freedom.

973 .04 Ph-2 6-A/9 $15.99 T KE851
COOPER, MICHAEL L. Bound for the promised land.: the great black migration. Lodestar/Dutton ISBN 0-525-67476-4; In Canada: McClelland & Stewart, 1995. 85p. ill.
Includes bibliography and index.
The "Great Migration" of southern African-Americans to the north between 1915 and 1930 had significant social, economic, and political effects on both the North and South. Personal stories, readable narrative, and black and white photographs capture the essence of the period, which included both racial violence and the Harlem Renaissance. Advanced readers will use this for general interest in African-American history and for multicultural studies.
SUBJ: Afro-Americans--History--1877-1964./ Rural-urban migration./ Harlem Renaissance.

973 Ph-2 4-6/9 $6.99 P KE852
GORMLEY, BEATRICE. First Ladies: women who called the White House home. Scholastic ISBN 0-590-25518-5; In Canada: Scholastic, 1997. 96p. ill.
Brief biographical sketches of the lives of the First Ladies of the United States, including several who died before their husbands took office. Illustrated with black and white portraits and photographs. Useful background for reports and for women's studies.
SUBJ: First ladies.

VD 973 Ph-3 5-A $495.00 OD KE853
GTV: A GEOGRAPHIC PERSPECTIVE ON AMERICAN HISTORY (Videodisc). National Geographic 81120, c1990. 2 videodiscs, 3 3.5" disks, computer/videodisc cable.
Includes guide, wall map of U.S., timeline wall chart, barcodes.
Standard/Interactive.
Also available in Macintosh and IBM versions.
System requirements: Standard: monitor TV, videodisc player with audio and video cables. Interactive: Apple IIGS with 512M (works best with more); computer monitor, keyboard mouse, monitor TV; 2 3.5" disk drives; videodisc player with audio and video cables (for Level III Interative power must be Pioneer LD-V2000, 2200, 4200, 6000, 6000A; Sony LDP-1000 or 1200); printer (optional).
This package helps set the standards in interactive video. Teachers and students learn about American history with a geographic viewpoint. Video footage on topics from a pre-Columbian look at the American landscape to studies of the Lewis and Clark expedition to a segment on the information age are included. The tools are provided for using the videodisc and a barcode reader with an entire class or using the videodisc with a computer for an interactive lesson with individual students or small groups. The materials can also be used by students to create their own multimedia reports.
SUBJ: United States--History--Software./ Geography--Software./ Software--United States--History./ Software--Geography.

973 Ph-2 5-6/7 $18.99 L KE854
HAMANAKA, SHEILA. Journey: Japanese Americans, racism, and renewal. Painting and text by Sheila Hamanaka. Book designed by Steve Frederick. Orchard ISBN 0-531-08449-3, 1990. 39p. col. ill.
Includes index.
Dark, anguished artwork taken from the artist-author's 25-foot mural depicts the history of the treatment of Japanese-Americans in the United States. Major emphasis in this revealing, personalized work is on the relocation camps of the World War II era. Valuable in units dealing with human rights, prejudice, and twentieth century events.
SUBJ: Japanese--United States--History./ Japanese Americans--History.

973 J 923 Ph-2 6-A/9 $14.99 T KE855
JONES, REBECCA C. President has been shot!: true stories of the attacks on ten U.S. presidents. Dutton ISBN 0-525-45333-4; In Canada: McClelland & Stewart, 1996. 134p. ill.
Includes bibliography and index.
Thorough, interestingly detailed accounts of assassinations and attempts on lives of United States Presidents from Andrew Jackson to Ronald Reagan raise issues and identify unanswered questions. Illustrated with archival photographs and prints. This will be useful for extending the scope of social studies units on the United States from early 1800s to the present.
SUBJ: Presidents--Assassination./ Presidents--Assassination attempts.

973 Ph-3 A/9 $20.00 L KE856
LEINER, KATHERINE. First children: growing up in the White House. Illus. by Katie Keller. Tambourine ISBN 0-688-13341-X, 1996. 157p. ill. (some col.).
Includes chronology, and bibliography.
Vignettes of White House life from the perspective of presidential children, grandchildren, and other young residents combine everyday events with those of significance and include interesting historical

tidbits that today's readers will use to connect to their own experiences. Original portraits of 17 White House children are accompanied by archival and contemporary photographs and illustrations. Mature readers will find these lively accounts a good resource for adding detail to reports or for browsing.
SUBJ: Children of presidents./ Presidents--Family./ White House (Washington, D.C.).

973   Ph-1 5-6/9 $14.89   L   KE857
MELTZER, MILTON. Black Americans: a history in their own words 1619-1983. Crowell/HarperCollins ISBN 0-690-04418-6; In Canada: HarperCollins, 1984. 306p b&w illus.
Includes index.
Presents the history of black life in America through selections from letters, speeches, memoirs and testimonies. Based on primary resources, this account brings this segment of our history to life. This revised edition will be a more workable choice for the study of blacks in America.
SUBJ: Afro-Americans--History--Sources./ Race relations--Sources.

973, 0496 Adult   Ph-1 A/7 $17.89   L   KE858
MYERS, WALTER DEAN. Now is your time!: the African-American struggle for freedom. HarperCollins ISBN 0-06-024371-6; In Canada: HarperCollins, 1991. 292p. ill.
Includes bibliography and index.
Coretta Scott King Award, 1992.
Available from the National Library Service for the Blind and Physically Handicapped on sound recording cassette RC35154.
Presents a vivid story of the people whose lives made a difference in the African-American struggle for freedom. Portrays well-known figures such as Frederick Douglass as well as less familiar persons such as artist Meta Vaux Warrick. Photographs accompany the text. For advanced students.
SUBJ: Afro-Americans--History.

PIC 973   Ph-2 5-6 $29.00   OD KE859
OLD TIME AMERICA (Picture). Documentary Photo Aids 30G, n.d. 23 study prints, (11"x14").
Includes index.
Black and white photographs offer an early day American potpourri featuring schools, money, authors, and miscellaneous events, historic and otherwise. Of browsing interest, the set will see most of its use in support of student reports and on bulletin boards.
SUBJ: United States--History--Pictorial works./ United States--History--Miscellanea.

973   Ph-2 3-6/8 $24.95   L   KE860
PASCOE, ELAINE. First facts about the presidents. Blackbirch ISBN 1-56711-167-X, 1996. 112p. ill. (some col.). (First facts about...).
Includes chronology, bibliography and index.
Provides very brief information about each president with life statistics, overview of first lady and vice president, and administrative highlights. Full-color portraits and timelines complement the text. A useful starting place for reports and for general browsing.
SUBJ: Presidents./ Presidents--Pictorial works.

973   Ph-1 4-A/7 $21.95   T   KE861
PERL, LILA. It happened in America: true stories from the fifty states. Illus. by Ib Ohlsson. Henry Holt ISBN 0-8050-1719-4; In Canada: Fitzhenry & Whiteside, 1992. 288p. col. ill., maps.
Includes bibliography.
Pulls stories from the breadth of America's tradition as it provides a story for each of the 50 states. Preceding each story is a brief look at the history of the state. Good read-aloud, browser's pleasure, and teacher's delight.
SUBJ: United States--History.

973   Ph-1 3-6/9 $19.95   T   KE862
PROVENSEN, ALICE. My fellow Americans: a family album. Browndeer/Harcourt Brace ISBN 0-15-276642-1; In Canada: Harcourt Brace c/o Canadian Manda, 1995. 61p. col. ill.
Includes bibliography.
Brief quotes from and descriptions of over 500 Americans who have shaped the country's history in politics, science, the arts, religion, finance, education, sports, the military, and social reform are featured in full-color doublespreads. Provensen's distinctive illustrations include portraits, events, and places; and the endpapers form an American quilt. This colorful, sweeping look at the diversity of people from all walks of life who have made contributions to American society will be an appealing resource for American history units and for enjoyable browsing.
SUBJ: United States--History--Pictorial works./ Quotations.

973   J 325.2   Ph-2 4-6/4 $14.95   T   KE863
RAPPAPORT, DOREEN. Escape from slavery: five journeys to freedom. Illus. by Charles Lilly. HarperCollins ISBN 0-06-021631-X; In Canada: HarperCollins, 1991. 117p. ill.
Includes bibliography.
Details the stories of five black slaves who fled to freedom in pre-Civil War days. Fictionalized text is followed by a solid bibliography and an afterword which discusses resources. Useful for curriculum support, general reading, and read-aloud use.
SUBJ: Fugitive slaves./ Underground railroad.

973   Ph-2 5-A/8 $20.89   L   KE864
SANDLER, MARTIN W. Presidents. Introduction by James H. Billington, Librarian of Congress. HarperCollins ISBN 0-06-024535-2; In Canada: HarperCollins, 1995. 94p. ill. (some col.).
"Library of Congress book."
Includes index.
Combines informational tidbits and seldom seen photographs to provide a picture of the private and public lives of United States presidents and their families. A closing chapter depicts pets of the presidents. Great browser and useful report expander.
SUBJ: Presidents./ Presidents--Pictorial works./ United States--History--Pictorial works.

CDR 973   Ph-1 3-A $39.95   OD KE865
SKYTRIP AMERICA: AN INCREDIBLE RIDE THROUGH U.S. HISTORY. Teacher ed. (CD-ROM). Discovery Channel Multimedia/Human Code, Inc. ISBN 1-56331-368-5, 1996. 1 CD-ROM color.
Version 1.0.
Includes user's guide and teacher's guide.
Also available for Macintosh (ISBN 1-56331-360-X), $39.95.
System requirements: 486 33MHz or faster; 8MB of RAM; double-speed CD-ROM; Windows compatible sound card; mouse; VGA monitor (256 colors); MS/PC DOS 3.1; hard drive; Windows 3.1 or Windows 95.
A unique multimedia look at American history in which the user can fly across the country visiting any era or region he likes. Students can develop their own multimedia journals, experience the Old West, hear what life is like in America from various viewpoints, and play several games as they gather information. Works well in a learning center or with small groups.
SUBJ: United States--History--Software./ Software--United States--History./ Interactive media.

973.09   Ph-2 6-A/9 $24.95   T   KE866
SMITHSONIAN BOOK OF THE FIRST LADIES: THEIR LIVES, TIMES, AND ISSUES. Edited by Edith P. Mayo. Foreword by Hillary Rodham Clinton. Henry Holt ISBN 0-8050-1751-8; In Canada: Fitzhenry & Whiteside, 1996. 302p. ill. (some col.).
Includes bibliographies and index.
Biographical sketches of First Ladies of the United States interspersed with short essays on important issues of each era. Illustrated with portraits and photographs, some in color. Advanced readers will find this useful for biographical background, United States history units, and women's studies.
SUBJ: First ladies.

973   Ph-2 4-A/9 $27.40   L   KE867
STEIN, R. CONRAD. United States of America. Childrens Press ISBN 0-516-02623-2; In Canada: Childrens Press, 1994. 171p. col. ill., maps. (Enchantment of the world).
Includes chronology and index.
Provides information on history, geography, arts, and everyday life in the United States. Minifact section is strong, listing of "important people" verges on the stodgy. Useful social studies support.
SUBJ: United States.

VCR 973.1   Ph-3 A $69.95   OD KE868
GREAT ENCOUNTER (Videocassette). PBS Video ISBN 0-7936-0652-7, 1991. 1/2" VHS videocassette color (60min). (Land of the eagle).
Includes series study guide.
Captures the natural wonders found by European settlers as they arrived on North America's eastern coast and examines the interrelatedness of man and nature, settler and Native American. Superb nature footage moves through seasonal cycles and features eagle chicks and mating of blue crabs. Length requires preview for best utilization.
SUBJ: America--Discovery and exploration--English./ Indians of North America--History.

973.2   Ph-2 4-6/9 $16.90   L   KE869
BARRETT, TRACY. Growing up in colonial America. Millbrook ISBN 1-56294-578-5, 1995. 96p. ill. (American children).
Includes bibliographies and index.

Chronicles the daily life of children of European heritage in the New England and Virginia colonies, including household chores, education, religious training, and the contributions of children to making clothing, food, and other items necessary for survival. Illustrated with archival drawings and engravings. Provides an unusual and interesting perspective for units on Colonial America.
SUBJ: United States--Social life and customs--To 1775./ Children--United States--History--17th century./ Children--United States--History--18th century.

973.2   Ph-1 5-6/7 $19.89   L   KE870
BOWEN, GARY. Stranded at Plimoth Plantation, 1626. Words and woodcuts by Gary Bowen. Introduction by David Freeman Hawke. HarperCollins ISBN 0-06-022542-4; In Canada: HarperCollins, 1994. 81p. ill.
Selectors' Choice, 20th ed.
Captures the difficult existence at Plimoth Plantation six years after the arrival of the Pilgrims on the Mayflower. Using a journal format, the narrative unfolds in the words of a thirteen-year-old orphan marooned in the colony. Historical content and graphic quality are outstanding. Combines strong potential for reading aloud with usefulness as a social studies project trigger.
SUBJ: Pilgrims (New Plymouth Colony)./ Massachusetts--Social life and customs--To 1775./ Massachusetts--History--New Plymouth, 1620-1691./ Diaries.

973.2   Ph-2 4-6/5 $15.27   L   KE871
KENT, ZACHARY. Williamsburg. Childrens Press ISBN 0-516-04854-6; In Canada: Childrens Press, 1992. 32p. col. ill. (Cornerstones of freedom).
Includes index.
Traces the history of colonial Williamsburg and tells of its restoration during the twentieth century. Color photographs rather than illustrative drawings bring a new look to this addition to a widely known series. Use in curriculum support and in regional studies.
SUBJ: Williamsburg (Va.)--History./ United States--History--Colonial period, ca. 1600-1775.

973.2 *Adult*   Ph-2 5-6/8 $15.95   L   KE872
MARRIN, ALBERT. Struggle for a continent: the French and Indian wars 1690-1760. Atheneum ISBN 0-689-31313-6; In Canada: Collier Macmillan, 1987. 219p. ill.
Includes index and bibliography.
Details events and causes of the 70 years of struggle now known as the French and Indian Wars. The introductory section which examines the three groups involved in the wars is particularly strong. Of value as a research starter and a motivator of further study.
SUBJ: United States--History--French and Indian War, 1755-1763.

973.2   Ph-3 5-6/7 $16.98   L   KE873
OCHOA, GEORGE. Fall of Quebec and the French and Indian War. Silver Burdett ISBN 0-382-09954-0, 1990. 64p. ill. (some col.). (Turning points in American history).
Includes bibliography and index.
Reports background, events, and personalities of the French and Indian War. Includes maps, drawings, and photographs. Useful for report writers and as a textbook-expander.
SUBJ: United States--History--French and Indian War, 1755-1763.

973.2   Ph-1 4-6/7 $17.00   L   KE874
SEWALL, MARCIA. Thunder from the clear sky. Atheneum ISBN 0-689-31775-1; In Canada: Distican, 1995. 56p. col. ill.
Includes glossary and bibliography.
Experiences from the early days of settlement through the time of King Philip's War in 1675 are narrated from the perspectives of a Pilgrim settler and a Wampanoag. The misunderstandings that characterized the relationships between them are clearly shown. Details in the full-color, gouache illustrations have been as carefully researched as the text. Use with the companion books in this series, THE PILGRIMS OF PLIMOTH and PEOPLE OF THE BREAKING DAY for an engaging portrait of early colonial life.
SUBJ: King Philip's War, 1675-1676./ Wampanoag Indians--History./ Indians of North America--Massachusetts--History.

973.3   Ph-2 5-6/6 $16.00   L   KE875
BRENNER, BARBARA. If you were there in 1776. Bradbury ISBN 0-02-712322-7; In Canada: Maxwell Macmillan, 1994. 136p. ill., map.
Includes bibliography and index.
Describes events on both sides of the Atlantic at the time of the Revolutionary War, but major focus is on the American colonies. Black and white period illustrations add to this solid background-builder.
SUBJ: United States--Social life and customs--1775-1783./ United States. Declaration of Independence.

973.3   Ph-2 3-6/4 $11.95   L   KE876
BROWN, DROLLENE P. Sybil rides for independence. Illus. by Margot Apple. Whitman ISBN 0-8075-7684-0; In Canada: General, 1985. 48p. col. ill.
Tells the story of sixteen year old Sybil Ludington's 1777 ride to awaken and warn the minutemen of the British attack on Danbury. A factual report follows the fictionalized account of the nightlong adventure. Has potential as a read-aloud, although its easy reading level makes it accessible to many.
SUBJ: Ludington, Sybil./ Danbury (Conn.)--Burning by the British, 1775--Biography./ United States--History--Revolution, 1775-1783--Biography.

973.3   Ph-2 5-6/10 $5.00   P   KE877
DAVIS, BURKE. Black heroes of the American revolution. Foreward by Edward W. Brooke. Harcourt Brace ISBN 0-15-208561-0, 1976. 82p. ill. "Odyssey book."
Includes bibliography and index.
The many African-American men who served during the Revolutionary War as soldiers and spies are described. An index will aid students to find information about these heroes who are often given little attention in other texts. Useful for multicultural studies and for units on the American Revolution.
SUBJ: United States--History--Revolution, 1775-1783--Afro-Americans./ Afro-Americans--Biography.

VCR 973.3   Ph-1 5-A $89.95   OD   KE878
DECLARATION OF INDEPENDENCE (Videocassette). CBS News Production/dist. by BFA Educational Media 71720, 1976. 1/2" VHS videocassette color (9min). (Spirit of America).
In Philadelphia's Independence Hall, Charles Kuralt recreates the discussions and opinions of the representatives of the colonies who met to discuss freedom from England. Quoting from diaries and letters, Kuralt brings the drama of the scene to life. Effective for classes on government, group dynamics, or history.
SUBJ: United States. Declaration of Independence./ United States--History--Revolution, 1775-1783.

973.3   Ph-2 4-6/8 $19.90   L   KE879
DOLAN, EDWARD F. American revolution: how we fought the War of Independence. Millbrook ISBN 1-56294-521-1, 1995. 110p. ill., maps.
Includes bibliography and index.
Accounts of major Revolutionary War battles emphasize those in the North, beginning with a brief description of historical events that led to the confrontation at Lexington and Concord. Illustrated with archival paintings, engravings, and maps of significant military sites. High interest source for reports and general reading.
SUBJ: United States--History--Revolution, 1775-1783.

973.3 *J394.2*   Ph-1 3-5/8 $13.95   L   KE880
GIBLIN, JAMES CROSS. Fireworks, picnics, and flags. Illus. by Ursula Arndt. Clarion ISBN 0-89919-146-0, 1983. 90p. col. ill.
Includes index.
Available from National Library Service for the Blind and Physically Handicapped in Braille BR05516.
Highlights the historical events leading to the signing of the Declaration of Independence and the early celebrations of this day. Lively text and drawings explain the background of the nation's symbols of the flag, bald eagle, Liberty Bell and Uncle Sam. Will answer questions of why we have some symbols; useful for both social studies curriculum and holiday units.
SUBJ: Fourth of July.

973.3   Ph-2 4-6/7 $15.95   L   KE881
JOHNSON, NEIL. Battle of Lexington and Concord. Four Winds/Macmillan ISBN 0-02-747841-6; In Canada: Maxwell Macmillan, 1992. 40p col photos, b&w map.
Includes bibliography.
Recounts events of the first battle of the American Revolution. Color photographs of a recent reenactment capture the details of the day. Use with Longfellow's PAUL REVERE'S RIDE (Dutton, 1990) illustrated by Ted Rand for an effective memorable presentation.
SUBJ: Concord, Battle of, 1775./ Lexington, Battle of, 1775./ United States--History--Revolution, 1775-1783--Campaigns.

973.3   Ph-1 5-6/9 $15.95   L   KE882
MARRIN, ALBERT. War for independence: the story of the American Revolution. Atheneum ISBN 0-689-31390-X, 1988. 376p. ill.
Includes bibliography and index.
Examines causes of the American Revolution and tells of events and people of the time in a fresh, lively reportorial style. Maps, paintings, and prints support the text which has more depth than many titles offered in support of the upper elementary grade curriculum. Valuable as a read-aloud or as material for individual research.
SUBJ: United States--History--Revolution, 1775-1783.

973.3   Ph-1 5-6/8 $6.95   P   KE883
MELTZER, MILTON. American revolutionaries: a history in their own words--1750-1800. HarperCollins ISBN 0-06-446145-9; In Canada: HarperCollins, 1993. 210p. ill.
> Includes index.
> Uses excerpts from letters, journals, interviews, and other sources as it focuses on human aspects of the American Revolution. Explanatory sections set the scene for each group of materials and a sources note by the editor suggests additional items advanced students may wish to explore. A valuable resource for individual study or for teacher use in introducing topics related to the Revolution.
> SUBJ: United States--History--Revolution, 1775-1783./ United States--Social life and customs--1775-1783.

973.3   Ph-1 5-A/9 $15.95   T   KE884
MURPHY, JIM. Young patriot: the American Revolution as experienced by one boy. Clarion ISBN 0-395-60523-7, 1996. 101p. ill., maps.
> Includes bibliography, chronology and index.
> Joseph Plumb Martin was a soldier in the Revolutionary Army throughout the entire war. This book, quoting frequently from Martin's memoirs, not only covers many of the major battles, but also depicts the suffering and hardships he endured. The prints, chosen to fit the text, show the troops in action and the major leaders. Basic to any discussion of the Revolutionary War.
> SUBJ: United States--History--Revolution, 1775-1783--Campaigns./ Martin, Joseph Plumb./ Soldiers./ Connecticut--Revolution, 1775-1783--Campaigns.

973.3   *JB*   Ph-3 4-6/4 $14.95   L   KE885
ROOP, PETER. Buttons for General Washington. By Peter and Connie Roop. Illus. by Peter E. Hanson. Carolrhoda ISBN 0-87614-294-3, 1986. 48p. ill. (some col.).
> Available from National Library Service for the Blind and Physically Handicapped in Braille BR7398.
> A fictionalized account of fourteen year old John Darragh's delivery of coded messages to General Washington. An easy reading level and the age of the protagonist combine to make this a hi-lo possibility for students searching for American history supplemental material.
> SUBJ: Darragh, John./ Spies./ United States--History--Revolution, 1775-1783--Secret Service.

973.3   Ph-3 5-A/8 $17.50   T   KE886
SHERBURNE, ANDREW. Memoirs of Andrew Sherburne: patriot and privateer of the American Revolution. Edited by Karen Zeinert. Illus. by Seymour Fleishman. Linnet ISBN 0-208-02354-2, 1993. 96p. ill., maps.
> Includes glossary and bibliography.
> Chronicles Andrew Sherburne's experiences as a young American sailor during the time of the American Revolution. First-person narrative gives a simple, illuminating view of the difficult life at sea. Useful in support of American history studies.
> SUBJ: Sherburne, Andrew./ United States--History--Revolution, 1775-1783--Personal narratives./ Privateering./ Seamen.

973.3   Ph-2 5-A/7 $17.30   L   KE887
STEIN, R. CONRAD. Declaration of Independence. Childrens Press ISBN 0-516-06693-5; In Canada: Childrens Press, 1995. 32p. ill. (some col.). (Cornerstones of freedom).
> Includes glossary, chronology and index.
> Discusses the development of the Declaration of Independence which was drafted in 17 days by thirty-three-year-old Thomas Jefferson, who was delegated to do so by the Continental Congress in June 1776. Illustrations, a reproduction of Jefferson's handwritten draft, timeline, and glossary support the text. Strong social studies material.
> SUBJ: United States. Declaration of Independence./ United States--Politics and government--1775-1783.

VCR 973.3   Ph-1 4-6 $24.95   KE888
STORY OF A PATRIOT (Videocassette). Colonial Williamsburg Foundation/Barr Films, 1957. 1/2" VHS videocassette color (36min).
> Includes teacher's manual.
> Traces the critical events leading up to the American Revolution as they occurred between 1769 and 1776 in and near Williamsburg, Virginia. Though the focal character is representative rather than real, the events and settings are portrayed authentically and dramatically. Students need introduction to vocabulary before viewing.
> SUBJ: United States--History--Colonial period, ca. 1600-1775./ United States--History--Revolution, 1775-1783--Causes./ Williamsburg (Va.)--History.

973.3   Ph-1 5-6/10 $27.40   L   KE889
ZEINERT, KAREN. Those remarkable women of the American Revolution. Millbrook ISBN 1-56294-657-9, 1996. 96p. ill. (some col.).
> Includes chronology, bibliographies and index.
> "Examines the important contributions of various women, Patriot and Loyalist, to the American Revolution, on the battlefield, in the press, in the political arena, and in other areas, and shows how they challenged traditional female roles." (CIP) Portraits and engravings illustrate the text. For colonial history and women's studies.
> SUBJ: United States--History--Revolution, 1775-1783--Women./ Women--United States--History--18th century.

VCR 973.4   Ph-2 A $24.95   OD   KE890
INDEPENDENCE: BIRTH OF A FREE NATION (Videocassette). Narrated by E. G. Marshall. Starring Eli Wallach and Ken Howard. Finley-Holiday V62, 1976. 1/2" VHS videocassette color (28min). (Our national heritage).
> Recreates the nation's founding in 18th century Philadelphia. Quality is high in this award-winning production. Advanced concepts indicate use after introductory information has been provided to students.
> SUBJ: United States--Politics and government--1789-1797./ United States. Declaration of Independence./ United States--Constitution./ Philadelphia (Pa.)--History.

973.4   *E*   Ph-2 4-6 $14.00   L   KE891
LAWSON, ROBERT. They were strong and good. Viking ISBN 0-670-69949-7, c1940. unp. ill.
> Caldecott Medal Award.
> The author proudly tells about his four grandparents and his father and mother--all of whom were fine people even though they were not famous.
> SUBJ: Lawson family./ Frontier and pioneer life--Biography.

973.4   Ph-2 3-5/6 $13.95   L   KE892
REEF, CATHERINE. Monticello. Dillon ISBN 0-87518-472-3; In Canada: Maxwell Macmillan, 1991. 71p. col. ill. (Places in American history).
> Includes chronology, directory and index.
> Provides a history of Jefferson's Monticello and offers quite a bit of information about the nation's third president as well. Final chapters tell of the history of the home after Jefferson's death in 1826 and give visitor information. Useful in study of historic locations and in units emphasizing lives of United States presidents.
> SUBJ: Monticello (Va.)./ Jefferson, Thomas.

973.4   Ph-1 5-6/9 $26.00   T   KE893
TUNIS, EDWIN. Frontier living. Crowell/HarperCollins ISBN 0-690-01064-8, c1961. 168p. ill.
> Newbery Honor Book.
> Available from National Library Service for the Blind and Physically Handicapped as talking book TB02678.
> A companion volume to COLONIAL LIVING. Beginning in the Piedmont in the 1700s, moves westward with the pioneers and describes and illustrates every aspect of daily living. The detailed drawings are authentic reference sources in themselves.
> A duplicate copy in the REF collection is recommended.
> SUBJ: Frontier and pioneer life./ United States--Social life and customs--1783-1865.

973.5   *JB*   Ph-3 4-5/7 $14.95   L   KE894
QUACKENBUSH, ROBERT. James Madison and Dolley Madison and their times. Pippen ISBN 0-945912-18-8, 1992. 70p. col. ill.
> Madison's education, marriage to Dolley, and presidency are discussed, but the major emphasis is on his contributions to the writing of the Constitution. Full-page drawings and border cartoons add to the information supplied in the text.
> SUBJ: Madison, James./ Madison, Dolley./ Presidents./ First ladies.

973.5   Ph-2 4-A/8 $18.95   T   KE895
RUBEL, DAVID. United States in the 19th century. Scholastic Reference ISBN 0-590-72564-5; In Canada: Scholastic, 1996. 192p. ill. (some col.), maps. (Scholastic timelines).
> "Agincourt Press book."
> Includes glossary and index.
> Packed with information of significance and interest, this visual timeline is organized by era and includes politics, life, arts and entertainment, and science and technology as well as highlights of events, trends, and personalities. Amply illustrated with photographs, archival materials, graphics, and drawings; and extensively indexed. Provides background for study of nineteenth century American history and is an attractive general interest browser.
> SUBJ: United States--Civilization--19th century--Chronology./ United States--History--19th century--Chronology.

973.5   Ph-3 A/7 $16.90   L   KE896
TOYNTON, EVELYN. Growing up in America, 1830-1860. Millbrook ISBN 1-56294-453-3, 1995. 96p. ill.
> Includes bibliographies and index.
> Presents lives of different groups of children during the 1830-1860

time period, depicting children of New England, Plains, Sioux, homeless, and slave groups. Second section which describes activities at school, work, and play is rather pedantic. A resource for reports by advanced students.
SUBJ: United States--History--19th century--Children./ United States--Social life and customs--1783-1865.

973.7 Ph-2 A/9 $15.00 T KE897
BELLER, SUSAN PROVOST. To hold this ground: a desperate battle at Gettysburg. McElderry ISBN 0-689-50621-X; In Canada: Distican, 1995. 95p. ill., maps.
Includes bibliography and index.
Engrossing, detailed account focuses on two units, the 15th Alabama and the 20th Maine, in the struggle for Little Round Top at Gettysburg. Includes quotes from both colonels and soldiers in the line, well-captioned archival and contemporary photographs, and maps clearly showing battle positions. Will add depth and detail to Civil War studies for advanced students.
SUBJ: Gettysburg, Battle of, 1863./ United States--History--Civil War, 1861-1865--Campaigns.

973.7 Ph-2 4-6/4 $14.95 L KE898
BRILL, MARLENE TARG. Allen Jay and the Underground Railroad. Illus. by Janice Lee Porter. Carolrhoda ISBN 0-87614-776-7, 1993. 48p. col. ill.
Describes how eleven-year-old Allen Jay helps move a runaway slave to safety. The fictionalized text is based on an actual event which occurred in 1842. Good curriculum support with special potential for reading aloud.
SUBJ: Underground railroad./ Fugitive slaves./ Jay, Allen./ Quakers.

973.7 Ph-2 4-6/7 $17.71 L KE899
CARTER, ALDEN R. Battle of Gettysburg. Watts ISBN 0-531-10852-X; In Canada: Watts, 1990. 64p. ill. (some col.). (First book).
Includes bibliography and index.
"Describes the Confederate Army's northern campaign, its defeat at the Battle of Gettysburg, and the subsequent effect on the course of the Civil War." (CIP) The author's readable style meshes with charts, maps, photographs and drawings to effectively tell of a landmark event. Joins other recommended Gettysburg materials as a solid resource.
SUBJ: Gettysburg, Battle of, 1863./ United States--History--Civil War, 1861-1865--Campaigns.

973.7 Ph-1 4-6/8 $21.00 L KE900
CARTER, ALDEN R. Battle of the ironclads: the Monitor and the Merrimack. Watts ISBN 0-531-20091-4; In Canada: Nelson, 1993. 64p. ill. (some col.), maps. (First book).
Includes bibliography and index.
An exciting account of ironclads in the Civil War and their role in the fight for supremacy of the seas begins with the sinking of the Merrimack and other ships in Hampton Roads shipyard by the Union Navy early in the war and concludes with the final confrontation of the raised and restored Confederate Merrimack with the Union Monitor. Illustrated with photographs and engravings, some in color. Excellent resource for Civil War units, and for students with an interest in military history.
SUBJ: Monitor (Ironclad)./ Merrimack (Frigate)./ Hampton Roads (Va.), Battle of, 1862./ United States--History--Civil War, 1861-1865--Naval operations.

VCR 973.7 Ph-2 5-A $19.95 KE901
CIVIL WAR: THE FIERY TRIAL (Videocassette). Narrated by Edwin Newman. Music by Jon Carroll. Atlas Video ISBN 0-945716-00-1, 1988. 1/2" VHS videocassette color (35min). (Civil War).
Uses on-site photography, period music, and maps in depicting the broad sweep of the Civil War. Development of the subject is strong and quality is high. Particularly valuable for use with advanced students.
SUBJ: United States--History--Civil War, 1861-1865.

973.7 Ph-2 5-6/10 $19.95 L KE902
DAMON, DUANE. When this cruel war is over: the Civil War home front. Lerner ISBN 0-8225-1731-0, 1996. 88p. ill. (People's history).
Includes bibliography and index.
A look at the Civil War from the perspective of civilians, North and South. Photographs and illustrations are of uneven quality, there are no maps, and sources of quotes are not specifically cited. Despite these drawbacks, the civilian and home front points of view will add immediacy to units on the Civil War.
SUBJ: United States--History--Civil War, 1861-1865.

973.7 Ph-2 4-6/4 $14.95 L KE903
GAUCH, PATRICIA LEE. Thunder at Gettysburg. Illus. by Stephen Gammell. Putnam ISBN 0-399-22201-4; In Canada: Putnam, c1975, 1990. 46p. ill.
Based on Tillie Pierce Alleman's AT GETTYSBURG, Coward-McCann (1975).
Selectors' Choice, 10th ed.
Tillie Pierce was separated from her family at Gettysburg on July 1, 1863, and found herself in the middle of a battle which became the turning point of the Civil War. She tells of the realities of war as she lived them for three days.
SUBJ: Gettysburg, Battle of, 1863./ Alleman, Tillie Pierce./ United States--History--Civil War, 1861-1865--Campaigns.

VCR 973.7 Ph-3 5-A $29.95 OD KE904
GETTYSBURG (Videocassette). Osterlund/Regency Home Video CW-G 1001, 1987. 1/2" VHS videocassette color (40min). (Video history of the civil war).
Traces the strategies before and during the three day battle of the Union and Confederate armies. The mixture of live reenactment, archival photographs, paintings, and maps is vivid and well matched by the narration and sound effects. Previewing allows determination of break points which may be needed.
SUBJ: Gettysburg, Battle of, 1863./ United States--History--Civil War, 1861-1865.

973.7 Ph-2 5-6/8 $17.95 T KE905
GORRELL, GENA K. North Star to freedom: the story of the Underground Railroad. Foreword by Rosemary Brown. Delacorte ISBN 0-385-32319-0; In Canada: Stoddart, 1997. 168p. ill., map.
Includes chronology, bibliographies and index.
After a brief historical overview of slavery worldwide, the author explores the history of slavery in the United States from earliest colonial times through 1865, emphasizing the efforts of slaves to reach freedom in Canada and the struggle to build a new life upon arrival. Extensively captioned archival materials, source notes, bibliography, and suggested readings are included. Interesting well-written personal accounts make this a source that will appeal to students looking for in-depth information to accompany units on slavery. For multicultural studies.
SUBJ: Underground railroad./ Fugitive slaves./ Slavery.

973.7 Ph-1 4-6/6 $14.95 L KE906
LINCOLN, ABRAHAM. Gettysburg Address. Illus. by Michael McCurdy. Foreword by Garry Wills. Houghton Mifflin ISBN 0-395-69824-3, 1995. unp. ill.
Presents the complete text of Abraham Lincoln's remarks at the dedication of the cemetery at Gettysburg in 1863. Scratchboard illustrations convey the spirit of the memorable speech.
SUBJ: Lincoln, Abraham. Gettysburg address./ Lincoln, Abraham./ Presidents.

973.7 Ph-1 A/8 $22.95 T KE907
LINCOLN, IN HIS OWN WORDS. Edited by Milton Meltzer. Illus. by Stephen Alcorn. Harcourt Brace ISBN 0-15-245437-3; In Canada: Harcourt Brace c/o Canadian Manda, 1993. 226p. ill.
Includes chronology, bibliography and index.
"Combines background commentary with quotes from Lincoln's letters, speeches and public papers..." (CIP) Text is insightful; linocut illustrations, powerful. Useful reference with potential for reading aloud.
SUBJ: Lincoln, Abraham./ Presidents./ United States--History--Civil War, 1861-1865.

973.7 Ph-2 3-5/6 $4.95 P KE908
MOORE, KAY. ...If you lived at the time of the Civil War. Illus. by Anni Matsick. Scholastic ISBN 0-590-45422-6; In Canada: Scholastic, 1994. 64p. col. ill., map.
Contrasts everyday life in the North and the South during the Civil War. Question and answer format places this title in a special niche among Civil War materials. Supplemental support for social studies curriculum.
SUBJ: United States--History--Civil War, 1861-1865./ Questions and answers.

973.7 Ph-1 5-6/7 $15.95 T KE909
MURPHY, JIM. Boys' war: Confederate and Union soldiers talk about the Civil War. Clarion ISBN 0-89919-893-7, 1990. 110p. ill.
Includes bibliography and index.
Available from the National Library Service for the Blind and Physically Handicapped on sound recording cassette RC34876.
Offers a vivid picture of the lives of the underaged Confederate and Union soldiers who served in the Civil War. Text draws heavily from diary entries, journals, personal letters and photographs of the period.

A unique and valuable resource for social studies curriculum support and for history buffs.
SUBJ: United States--History--Civil War, 1861-1865--Personal narratives./ United States--History--Civil War, 1861-1865--Children.

973.7   Ph-1 5-A/7 $15.95   T   KE910
MURPHY, JIM. Long road to Gettysburg. Clarion ISBN 0-395-55965-0, 1992. 116p. ill., maps.
Includes bibliography and index.
"Describes the events of the Battle of Gettysburg in 1863 as seen through the eyes of two actual participants..." (CIP) Text, illustrated by photographs and drawings, is carefully written; a closing note tells of the life of the two men, a Confederate lieutenant and a Union soldier, after the Civil War. A strong background-builder.
SUBJ: Gettysburg, Battle of, 1863./ Lincoln, Abraham. Gettysburg address./ United States--History--Civil War, 1861-1865--Campaigns.

973.7   Ph-2 5-A/7 $16.00   L   KE911
RAY, DELIA. Behind the blue and gray: the soldier's life in the Civil War. Lodestar/Dutton ISBN 0-525-67333-4; In Canada: McClellan & Stewart, 1991. 102p. ill. (Young readers' history of the Civil War).
Includes glossary, bibliography and index.
Describes the experiences of individual soldiers, Confederate and Union, during the Civil War. Housing, training and daily detail receive particular attention in a text which features first-person accounts; archival photographs and pleasing design are pluses.
SUBJ: United States. Army--History--Civil War, 1861-1865./ Confederate States of America. Army--History./ United States--History--Civil War, 1861-1865.

PIC 973.8   Ph-2 4-6 $131.75   OD   KE912
AMERICAN HISTORY: GROWING PAINS (Picture). Shorewood Reproductions 5026, c1974. 15 art prints color (29"x22"). (Shorewood art programs for education).
Includes teacher's guide.
Also available mounted $146.75.
Fifteen reproductions which include Currier and Ives, Remington, Russell and Hansen as artists, concentrate on the westward movement in the United States during the second half of the 19th century. The study guide describes each reproduction and includes suggested ways they can be used in discussion. A list of suggested reading is appended.
SUBJ: United States--History--1865-1898--Pictorial works./ West (U.S.)--History--Pictorial works./ United States--Social life and customs--Pictorial works./ Frontier and pioneer life--Pictorial works./ Painting, American./ Prints, American.

973.8   *J970.4*   Ph-2 5-6/6 $9.95   P   KE913
GOBLE, PAUL. Brave Eagle's account of the Fetterman Fight, 21 December 1866. University of Nebraska Press ISBN 0-8032-7032-1, c1972, 1992. 61p. col. ill., maps.
Uses Native American sources to give an account of the 1866 battle in which Captain Fetterman's command of 82 men was wiped out. Works well in conjunction with Goble's RED HAWK'S ACCOUNT OF CUSTER'S LAST BATTLE.
SUBJ: Fetterman Fight, Wyo., 1866./ Red Cloud, Sioux Chief.

973.8   Ph-2 5-6/6 $9.95   P   KE914
GOBLE, PAUL. Red Hawk's account of Custer's last battle; the Battle of the Little Bighorn, 25 June 1876. University of Nebraska Press ISBN 0-8032-7033-X, c1969, 1992. 59p. col. ill.
Sound recording cassette available from Caedmon CDL51365, 1971. 1 sound cassette, $9.95.
Based on primary source material, this is a vivid retelling of the Battle of the Little Big Horn from the perspective of a young Sioux warrior. Rhythmic prose makes this a moving presentation of the savage and tragic battle and adds another perspective to units of study about native Americans.
SUBJ: Little Big Horn, Battle of the, 1876./ Custer, George Armstrong./ Cheyenne Indians./ Sioux Indians.

973.8   Ph-2 A/7 $14.95   T   KE915
MARRIN, ALBERT. Spanish-American War. Atheneum ISBN 0-689-31663-1; In Canada: Collier Macmillan, 1991. 192p. ill.
Includes bibliography and index.
Describes causes and events of the Spanish-American War in a smoothly written text which stands solidly beside the author's 1812: THE WAR NOBODY WON and WAR CLOUDS IN THE WEST. Portions are useful as a non-fiction read-aloud.
SUBJ: United States--History--War of 1898.

973.9   Ph-2 4-A/8 $16.95   T   KE916
RUBEL, DAVID. United States in the 20th century. Scholastic Reference ISBN 0-590-27134-2; In Canada: Scholastic, 1995. 192p. ill. (some col.)
(Scholastic timelines).
"Agincourt Press book."
Includes glossary and index.
Packed with information of significance and interest, this visual timeline is organized by era and includes politics, life, arts and entertainment, science and technology as well as highlights of events, trends, and personalities. Amply illustrated with photographs, archival materials, graphics, and drawings; and extensively indexed. Provides background for study of twentieth century American history and is an attractive general interest browser.
SUBJ: United States--Civilization--20th century--Chronology./ United States--History--20th century--Chronology.

PIC 973.917   Ph-3 5-6 $34.50   OD   KE917
DUST BOWL (Picture). Documentary Photo Aids 139G, n.d. 20 study prints (11"x14").
Authentic captioned photographs illustrating the dust storms, drought and depression that devastated Kansas, Oklahoma, Texas, New Mexico and Colorado in the 1930s.
SUBJ: United States--History--1933-1945.

973.917   Ph-2 4-6/7 $16.40   L   KE918
STEIN, R. CONRAD. Great Depression. Rev. ed. Childrens Press ISBN 0-516-06668-4; In Canada: Childrens Press, 1993. 32p. ill. (some col.). (Cornerstones of freedom).
Includes index.
Traces the ten-year-long depression of the 1930s when, at times, as much as 25% of the work force was unemployed. Period photographs support the text. Useful in study of the twentieth century.
SUBJ: Depressions--1929./ United States--History--1933-1945.

973.917   Ph-2 5-6/8 $17.50   L   KE919
WHITMAN, SYLVIA. V is for victory: the American home front during World War II. Lerner ISBN 0-8225-1727-2, 1993. 80p. ill. (People's history).
Includes bibliography and index.
Captures the American scene during World War II. Supporting photographs go beyond the ordinary and are a high point. Use as background for an oral history project or in conjunction with Hahn's STEPPING ON THE CRACKS.
SUBJ: World War, 1939-1945--United States.

973.92   Ph-1 4-6/7 $13.95   P   KE920
CANEY, STEVEN. Steven Caney's Kids' America. Illus. by Ginger Brown. Workman ISBN 0-911104-80-1, 1978. 414p.
Includes index.
Selectors' Choice, 12th ed.
Collection of craft and project ideas on interesting aspects of growing up in America. Includes how to make cheese, tell fortunes, search genealogy, make soap, dowse for water, dance to hustle and much, much more. An eleven page index provides easy access to many ideas.
SUBJ: United States--Social life and customs./ Handicraft./ Genealogy./ Amusements.

973.922   Ph-3 5-6/7 $15.27   L   KE921
STEIN, R. CONRAD. Assassination of John F. Kennedy. Childrens Press ISBN 0-516-06652-8; In Canada: Childrens Press, 1992. 32p. ill. (some col.). (Cornerstones of freedom).
Includes index.
Provides an overview of the events of the assassination of John F. Kennedy in November 1963. News photos accompany a text which describes the event and its aftermath. Useful to build awareness.
SUBJ: Kennedy, John Fitzgerald--Assassination./ Presidents--Assassination.

973.927   *J031.02*   Ph-3 4-6/7 $7.95   P   KE922
MARTINET, JEANNE. Year you were born, 1983. Compiled by Jeanne Martinet. Illus. by Judy Lanfredi. Tambourine ISBN 0-688-11077-0, 1992. unp. col. ill.
An assortment of events, humorous and historical, are presented in a day-by-day account of 1983--365 days of happenings directed to the children who were born that year. Step from here to an almanac to learn what was going on when parents and grandparents were born. Slyly teaches the importance of record keeping and historical inquiry. Fun for browsing and useful for social studies classes and scout badges.
More events in THE YEAR YOU WERE BORN, 1981 (ISBN 0-688-12874-2, 1994); THE YEAR YOU WERE BORN, 1982 (ISBN 0-688-12876-9, 1994); THE YEAR YOU WERE BORN, 1984 (ISBN 0-688-11080-0, 1992); THE YEAR YOU WERE BORN, 1985 (ISBN 0-688-11082-7, 1992); THE YEAR YOU WERE BORN, 1986 (ISBN 0-688-11969-7, 1993); THE YEAR YOU WERE BORN, 1987 (ISBN 0-688-11971-9, 1993); THE YEAR YOU WERE BORN, 1988 (ISBN 0-688-

13861-6, 1995); and THE YEAR YOU WERE BORN, 1989 (ISBN 0-688-14385-7, 1996).
SUBJ: United States--History--1969- --Chronology./ Calendars.

974 J975   Ph-2 4-6/9 $14.95   T   KE923
BIAL, RAYMOND. Mist over the mountains: Appalachia and its people. Houghton Mifflin ISBN 0-395-73569-6, 1997. 48p. col. ill.
Includes bibliography.
An account of regional history, early settlement, Cherokee resettlement, and culture interspersed with brief first person remembrances and experiences about traditions including religion, music, storytelling, and crafts. A diverse collection of full-color photographs picture many aspects of daily life. A welcome addition to regional studies and to provide general information to enhance American history units on early pioneers.
SUBJ: Appalachian Region./ Mountain life--Appalachian Region.

VCR 974   Ph-2 4-6 $275.00   OD KE924
MIDDLE ATLANTIC REGION: NEW YORK, NEW JERSEY, DELAWARE, MARYLAND, PENNSYLVANIA, DISTRICT OF COLUMBIA (Videocassette). Preview Media/dist. by Altschul Group J4939, 1996. 1/2" VHS videocassette color (20min). (U.S. geography from sea to shining sea).
Includes teacher's guide.
Includes public performance rights.
Examines geographic features, climate, and industrial, agricultural, commercial development of the Middle Atlantic States. Emphasizes how natural and man-made waterways contributed to development of this region as a transportation and industrial center. Excellent production values with clear, illustrative visuals.
SUBJ: Middle Atlantic States./ New York (State)./ New Jersey./ Delaware./ Maryland./ Pennsylvania./ Washington (D.C.).

974   Ph-1 3-6/6 $14.95   L   KE925
RYLANT, CYNTHIA. Appalachia: the voices of sleeping birds. Illus. by Barry Moser. Harcourt Brace Jovanovich ISBN 0-15-201605-8, 1991. unp. col. ill.
Text and handsome illustrations mesh to provide a strong sense of place in this evocation of Appalachia. Works well with LITTLEJIM; NO STAR NIGHTS; and additional Appalachian titles suggested in May 1991 "Book Links".
SUBJ: Appalachian Region, Southern--Description and travel./ Appalachian Region, Southern--Social life and customs.

974.1   Ph-2 4-6/8 $14.95   T   KE926
DEAN, JULIA. Year on Monhegan Island. Ticknor & Fields ISBN 0-395-66476-4, 1995. 48p. col. ill.
Available from the National Library Services for the Blind and Physically Handicapped on sound recording cassette RC 41682.
Shows the yearly cycle on a small island off the central coast of Maine from the solitude of winter with only 75 residents through the crowded times when day trippers and summer residents come ashore. Color photographs depict the people and places of the island. Useful in regional studies and in "how we live" units.
SUBJ: Monhegan Island (Me.)--Social life and customs.

974.1   Ph-3 4-6/7 $17.50   L   KE927
ENGFER, LEEANNE. Maine. Lerner ISBN 0-8225-2701-4, 1991. 72p. ill. (some col.). (Hello U.S.A.).
Includes pronunciation guide, glossary and index.
Fresh design, colorful photographs, fast facts, and timelines add up to an appealing "state" book. As with other state series, it is suggested that only state books of particular regional or curriculum interest be purchased.
SUBJ: Maine.

974.1   Ph-3 4-6/4 $24.00   L OD KE928
FRADIN, DENNIS B. Maine. By Dennis Brindell Fradin. Childrens Press ISBN 0-516-03819-2; In Canada: Childrens Press, 1994. 64p. col. ill., maps. (From sea to shining sea).
Includes chronology, glossary and index.
Introduces the people, history, cities, and geography of Maine. Famous people section mentions figures in politics, sports, and the arts. Purchase as needed as a regional acquisition.
SUBJ: Maine.

974.1   Ph-1 5-A/7 $14.95   T   KE929
MURPHY, JIM. Into the deep forest with Henry David Thoreau. Illus. by Kate Kiesler. Clarion ISBN 0-395-60522-9, 1995. 39p. col. ill.
Selectors' Choice, 20th ed.
Meshes entries from Thoreau's journals, line drawings, and oil paintings to tell of a trip through the Maine wilderness to Mount Ktaadn. A biographical introduction builds the reader's understanding of Thoreau. Valuable in its own right and in support of social studies,

environmental studies, and language arts curricula.
SUBJ: Katahdin, Mount, Region (Me.)--Description and travel./ Thoreau, Henry David--Diaries./ Natural history--Maine.

974.2   Ph-3 4-6/7 $17.50   L   KE930
BROWN, DOTTIE. New Hampshire. Lerner ISBN 0-8225-2730-8, 1993. 72p. col. ill., maps. (Hello U.S.A.).
Includes chronology, glossary and index.
Color photographs, fast facts, small format, and timeline add up to an appealing state book. Recommended for regional purchase.
SUBJ: New Hampshire.

974.2   Ph-2 5-6/9 $23.93   L   KE931
FRADIN, DENNIS B. New Hampshire Colony. Childrens Press ISBN 0-516-00388-7; In Canada: Childrens Press, 1988. 144p. ill. (Thirteen colonies).
Includes index.
Relates the history of the New Hampshire Colony from its earliest days through ratification of the Constitution in 1788. Eight brief biographical sketches accompany the text; colonial timeline, reproduction of historic documents, and early recipes further add to the value of this title. Useful for project support and as material to extend study beyond the textbook.
SUBJ: New Hampshire--History--Colonial period, ca. 1600-1775.

974.2   Ph-3 4-6/9 $26.60   L OD KE932
HEINRICHS, ANN. Rhode Island. Childrens Press ISBN 0-516-00485-9; In Canada: Childrens Press, 1990. 144p. col. ill. (America the beautiful).
Includes index.
Available from the National Library Service for the Blind and Physically Handicapped on sound recording cassette RC34613. Covers geography, history, government, economy, and cultural/recreational aspects of the state. Closing section includes maps, chronology, people profiles and state facts. Most effective purchasing pattern for this series is acquisition of regionally applicable titles.
SUBJ: Rhode Island.

974.3 508.74   Ph-3 A/6 $18.00   L   KE933
ARNOSKY, JIM. Nearer nature. Lothrop, Lee & Shepard ISBN 0-688-12213-2, 1996. 160p. ill.
Includes index.
Naturalist and artist, Jim Arnosky invites readers to wander the Vermont countryside in winter and spring to observe animals, tracks, and plants. Accounts of a fisher, porcupine fight, and a flock of crows signaling each other about food are close encounters that will make the reader wonder and reflect. Few have the luxury of wandering in wild country and observing nature. This account both nurtures and testifies that adventure is close at hand. For reading aloud as a seasonal almanac.
SUBJ: Natural history--Vermont./ Farm life--Vermont./ Vermont--Description and travel./ Arnosky, Jim.

974.3   Ph-3 4-6/4 $24.00   L OD KE934
FRADIN, DENNIS B. Vermont. Childrens Press ISBN 0-516-03845-1; In Canada: Childrens Press, 1993. 64p. col. ill., maps. (From sea to shining sea).
Includes glossary and index.
Introduces the cities, people, history, and landforms of Vermont. Famous people section mentions figures (some well-known and some obscure) in politics, sports, and arts. Purchase as needed as a regional acquisition.
SUBJ: Vermont.

974.4   Ph-1 2-4/7 $14.95   L   KE935
ANDERSON, JOAN. First Thanksgiving feast. Photos by George Ancona. Clarion ISBN 0-89919-287-4, 1984. unp. ill.
Recreates the first Thanksgiving feast celebrated by the Pilgrims in 1621. Excellent black/white photographs capture Pilgrim and Indian action at Plimoth Plantation. A meaningful look at the basis for Thanksgiving for holiday units and social studies curriculum.
SUBJ: Massachusetts--History--New Plymouth, 1620-1691./ Pilgrims (New Plymouth Colony)./ Thanksgiving Day.

974.4   Ph-3 5-6/7 $15.90   L   KE936
AVAKIAN, MONIQUE. Historical album of Massachusetts. Millbrook ISBN 1-56294-481-9, 1994. 64p. ill. (some col.), maps. (Historical albums).
Includes chronologies, bibliography, directory and index.
Traces the history of Massachusetts from early days through the present. Fast fact section is included. Suitable for regional purchase.
SUBJ: Massachusetts--History.

974.4   Ph-2 4-6/6 $14.95   L   KE937
CHERRY, LYNNE. River ran wild: an environmental history. Gulliver/ Harcourt Brace Jovanovich ISBN 0-15-200542-0, 1992. unp col illus.
Provides a 7000-year environmental history of the Nashua River and watershed as it relates events from the time of early Native Americans through mill days to the beginnings of ecological recovery. Effective border illustrations tell much of the story of citizens' efforts to restore the river while full-page watercolors offer a sense of place. Useful in support of environmental projects.
SUBJ: Nashua River (Mass. and N.H.)--History./ Man--Influence on nature./ Water--Pollution.

974.4   J973.2   Ph-1 4-6/7 $8.99   L   KE938
DAUGHERTY, JAMES. Landing of the Pilgrims. Random House ISBN 0-394-90302-1, c1950. 186p illus.
Account of the first three years of the Plymouth Colony which the Pilgrims founded in their determination to remain Englishmen and to worship God as they wished.
SUBJ: Pilgrims (New Plymouth Colony)./ Massachusetts--History.

VCR 974.4   Ph-3 4-6 $14.99   OD   KE939
FREEDOM TRAIL (Videocassette). VideoTours 1019, 1991. 1/2" VHS videocassette color (31min). (VideoTours history collection).
Takes a tourist's walking tour through Boston from the Commons to 15 other sites in the area. Serves to give a casual overview of historic locations and provides a sense of place valuable in support of curriculum activities. For large collections.
SUBJ: Boston (Mass.)--Description./ Boston (Mass.)--History.

CE 974.4   Ph-2 3-5/5 $13.95   T   KE940
FRITZ, JEAN. Who's that stepping on Plymouth Rock? Illus. by J.B. Handelsman. Coward-McCann/Putnam ISBN 0-698-20325-9, c1975. 30p. col. ill.
Talking book read by author available from Weston Woods WW484C, 1982. 1 sound cassette (23min) $8.95.
A clever and amusing story of Plymouth Rock from the time of the Pilgrims in 1620 to the present day. Includes the many places it has been located and reasons for its movement. A look not only at a symbol of our history but at the concerns of the people through the years.
SUBJ: Pilgrims (New Plymouth Colony).

974.4   J973.2   Ph-1 5-A/8 $10.95   P   KE941
MOURT'S RELATION. Homes in the wilderness: a pilgrim's journal of Plymouth Plantation in 1620. By William Bradford and others of the Mayflower company. Edited by Margaret Wise Brown. Illus. by Mary Wilson Stewart. Linnet ISBN 0-208-02269-4, c1939, 1988. 76p. ill., maps.
Originally published by W.R. Scott, 1939.
Includes glossary.
Adapted, with somewhat modernized text, from the journal commonly called "Mourt's Relation" first published in London in 1622 and believed to have been written by Governor Bradford and others of the Mayflower company, this captures the colonists difficult first winter in North America and provides important primary source material for students and teachers. Valuable also for reading aloud as journal entries from September - March or at Thanksgiving as a companion volume to Sewall's THE PILGRIMS OF PLIMOTH.
SUBJ: Pilgrims (New Plymouth Colony)./ Massachusetts--History--New Plymouth, 1620-1691./ Bradford, William./ Diaries.

VCR 974.4   Ph-2 4-6 $14.99   KE942
OLD STURBRIDGE VILLAGE (Videocassette). VideoTours 1010, 1989. 1/2" VHS videocassette color (30min). (VideoTours history collection).
Visits Old Sturbridge Village, living history replication of a rural community in the New England of the 1830s. Though modern visitors and tourists are evident, major emphasis is on early nineteenth century life. Good curriculum support with potential uses in social studies and language arts.
SUBJ: Old Sturbridge Village (Mass.)./ Massachusetts--Social life and customs./ City and town life--New England./ New England--Social life and customs.

974.4   Ph-2 1-3/2 $14.99   L   KE943
PENNER, LUCILLE RECHT. Pilgrims at Plymouth. Illus. by S. D. Schindler. Random House ISBN 0-679-93201-1; In Canada: Random House, 1996. 39p. col. ill. (Picture landmark books).
Includes index.
Describes the Mayflower voyage, early exploration of landfall, the first winter, and the culminating event that was the First Thanksgiving in language and format accessible to younger readers. Colorful illustrations are combined with main text and with interesting sidebar information. A good resource for early grades.
SUBJ: Pilgrims (New Plymouth Colony)./ Massachusetts--History--New Plymouth, 1620-1691.

974.4   Ph-1 3-6/7 $17.85   L   KE944
PILGRIM VOICES: OUR FIRST YEAR IN THE NEW WORLD. Edited by Connie and Peter Roop. Illus. by Shelley Prichett. Walker ISBN 0-8027-8315-5; In Canada: Thomas Allen, 1995. 48p. col. ill.
Includes glossary, bibliographies and index.
A fascinating, first-person account of the Pilgrims' first year of settlement, including preparations, hardships of the voyage, early exploration of the immediate area, relationships with the native population, the struggle for survival, and the celebration of the first harvest. Illustrated with full-page color paintings. Based on primary source diaries of William Bradford and a journal attributed to Bradford and Edward Winslow. Solid curriculum support for Thanksgiving units.
SUBJ: Pilgrims (New Plymouth Colony)./ Massachusetts--History--New Plymouth, 1620-1691./ Diaries.

974.4   Ph-1 3-6/10 $14.95   T   KE945
ROACH, MARILYNNE K. In the days of the Salem witchcraft trials. Houghton Mifflin ISBN 0-395-69704-2, 1996. 92p. ill., maps.
Includes bibliography and index.
Using primary sources, the author documents the life and times of New England settlers in 1692. Historical research reveals how people worshiped, worked, played, earned a living, and raised a family in a close-knit, observant society where everyone's contribution was vital. Details the contributions of all classes and highlights the lives of women who were expected to bear many children, keep house, obey their husbands, and prepare bodies for burial. Skillfully describes the context of the Salem witchcraft trials in which 19 people were condemned and executed for witchcraft. Read aloud to prove that history is not a dead topic.
SUBJ: Salem (Mass.)--History--Colonial period, ca. 1600-1775./ Witchcraft--Massachusetts--Salem./ Trials (Witchcraft)--Massachusetts--Salem.

974.4   Ph-3 4-6/7 $13.95   T   KE946
SAN SOUCI, ROBERT D. N.C. Wyeth's pilgrims. Illus. by N. C. Wyeth. Chronicle ISBN 0-87701-806-5; In Canada: Chronicle/dist. by Raincoast Books, 1991. unp. col. ill.
Handsome geese and romanticized Pilgrims and Native Americans grace the pages of this work based on a series of murals painted in lyric style in 1940 by N.C. Wyeth. An author's note provides important background information for teachers using this book in holiday, social studies, or art units.
SUBJ: Pilgrims (New Plymouth Colony)./ Pilgrims (New Plymouth Colony) in art./ Massachusetts--History--New Plymouth, 1620-1691.

CE 974.4   Ph-1 4-6/7 $15.95   L   KE947
SEWALL, MARCIA. Pilgrims of Plimoth. Atheneum ISBN 0-689-31250-4, 1986. 48p. col. ill.
Includes glossary.
Videocassette available from Weston Woods HFOV330V, 1990. 1/2" VHS videocassette color (26min), $39.95.
Presents the daily routine of life of the Mayflower settlers in the New World. The unusual quality of the illustrations and the stately dignity of the text, at times using 17th century quotations, make this work distinctive. For the classroom, the glossary (with words such as boulter and woad) can form the foundation for a language lesson and read-aloud and social studies opportunities abound.
SUBJ: Pilgrims (New Plymouth Colony)./ Massachusetts--Social life and customs--Colonial period, ca. 1600-1775.

974.4   Ph-1 3-5/6 $14.95   L   KE948
WATERS, KATE. Samuel Eaton's day: a day in the life of a Pilgrim boy. Photos by Russ Kendall. Scholastic ISBN 0-590-46311-X; In Canada: Scholastic, 1993. 40p. col. ill.
Includes glossary.
"...follows a young Pilgrim boy through a busy day during the summer harvest in 1627." (CIP) Pictures photographed at Plimoth Plantation's living history museum, period clothing, and text using the language of the time create a valuable learning tool. Use alone or with companion work SARAH MORTON'S DAY.
SUBJ: Pilgrims (New Plymouth Colony)./ Massachusetts--Social life and customs--Colonial period, ca. 1600-1775.

974.4   Ph-1 3-5/3 $12.95   L   KE949
WATERS, KATE. Sarah Morton's day: a day in the life of a Pilgrim girl. Photos by Russ Kendall. Scholastic ISBN 0-590-42634-6, 1989. 32p. col. ill.
Includes glossary.
Recreates a day in 1627 as it follows the footsteps of nine-year-old Sarah Morton. Using handsome photographs made at the Plimoth Plantation living history museum, the readable text in the style of English spoken then offers a gentle story line as Sarah helps with chores, enjoys a friend, and learns to adjust to changes in her family.

Strong support for the social studies curriculum.
SUBJ: Pilgrims (New Plymouth Colony)./ Massachusetts--Social life and customs--Colonial period, ca. 1600-1775.

974.4 Ph-1 3-5/2 $16.95 L KE950
WATERS, KATE. Tapenum's day: a Wampanoag Indian boy in pilgrim times. Photos by Russ Kendall. Scholastic ISBN 0-590-20237-5; In Canada: Scholastic, 1996. 40p. col. ill., map.
Includes glossary/index.
Follows Tapenum, a Wampanoag boy, as he seeks to strengthen his hunting and physical skills in hopes to be chosen for training as a warrior counselor. Photographed at Plimoth Plantation, a living history museum. Use with SARAH MORTON'S DAY and SAMUEL EATON'S DAY for a portrait of three aspects of life in the early Massachusetts Colony. For multicultural studies and Thanksgiving units.
SUBJ: Wampanoag Indians./ Indians of North America./ Pilgrims (New Plymouth Colony)./ Massachusetts--Social life and customs--To 1775.

974.5 Ph-2 5-6/7 $23.93 L KE951
FRADIN, DENNIS B. Rhode Island Colony. Childrens Press ISBN 0-516-00391-7; In Canada: Childrens Press, 1989. 159p. col. ill. (Thirteen colonies).
Includes index.
Relates the history of the Rhode Island Colony from its earliest days to its 1790 ratification of the Constitution. Seven biographical sketches accompany the text; colonial timeline and reproduction of historical documents add further value to this title. Useful project support.
SUBJ: Rhode Island--History--Colonial period, ca. 1600-1775./ Rhode Island--History--Revolution, 1775-1783.

974.6 Ph-3 4-6/4 $24.00 L OD KE952
FRADIN, DENNIS B. Connecticut. By Dennis Brindell Fradin and Judith Bloom Fradin. Childrens Press ISBN 0-516-03807-9; In Canada: Childrens Press, 1994. 64p. col. ill., maps. (From sea to shining sea).
Includes chronology, glossary and index.
Combines fast facts, trivia, easy-to-read text, and color photographs in a package appealing to elementary students in search of a "state book." The accompanying timeline has 37 entries with the most recent being 1991. Recommended for regional purchase.
SUBJ: Connecticut.

974.6 Ph-3 4-6/7 $15.90 L KE953
WILLS, CHARLES A. Historical album of Connecticut. Millbrook ISBN 1-56294-506-8, 1995. 64p. ill. (some col.), maps. (Historical albums).
Includes chronologies, bibliography, directory and index.
Offers an overview of the history of the Constitution State. Backmatter includes fast facts, timelines, personalities, and addresses for sources of additional information. Recommended for regional purchase.
SUBJ: Connecticut--History.

974.7 Ph-3 5-6/8 $15.90 L KE954
AVAKIAN, MONIQUE. Historical album of New York. By Monique Avakian and Carter Smith III. Millbrook ISBN 1-56294-005-8, 1993. 64p. ill. (some col.), maps. (Historical albums).
Includes chronology, bibliography and index.
Presents the history of New York from early days of European contact through the present. Fast fact section is included. Suitable for regional purchase when this type of state material is desired.
SUBJ: New York (State)--History.

974.7 Ph-3 4-6/3 $24.00 L OD KE955
FRADIN, DENNIS B. New York. By Dennis Brindell Fradin. Childrens Press ISBN 0-516-03832-X; In Canada: Childrens Press, 1993. 64p. col. ill., maps. (From sea to shining sea).
Includes chronology, glossary and index.
Provides fast facts, trivia, easy-to-read text, and color photographs in a package which meets the needs of a student in search of a "state book." The accompanying timeline supplies significant dates through 1993. Regional purchase.
SUBJ: New York (State).

974.7 Ph-2 5-6/8 $23.93 L KE956
FRADIN, DENNIS B. New York Colony. Childrens Press ISBN 0-516-00389-5; In Canada: Childrens Press, 1988. 159p. col. ill. (Thirteen colonies).
Includes index.
Relates the history of the New York colony from its earliest days through the 1790s when the capital of the nation was moved from New York City to Philadelphia. Nine brief biographical sketches accompany the text; reproductions of historic documents and a colonial timeline add further to its value. Useful for project support

and as material to extend study beyond the textbook.
SUBJ: New York (State)--History--Colonial period, ca. 1600-1775./ New York (State)--History--Revolution, 1775-1783./ New York (State)--Biography.

974.7 Ph-1 2-5/3 $15.95 L KE957
JAKOBSEN, KATHY. My New York. Little, Brown ISBN 0-316-45653-5; In Canada: Little, Brown, 1993. 32p. col. ill.
Combines a primitive illustrative style with a letter-to-a-friend premise to serve up a lively description of New York City's attractions. An appended guide provides additional information about places mentioned, and maps appear on the endpapers. Particularly enjoyable for armchair travelers and those who have been sightseeing in New York.
SUBJ: New York (N.Y.)./ Letters.

974.7 Ph-3 3-5/8 $24.00 L KE958
KENT, DEBORAH. New York City. Children's Press ISBN 0-516-20025-9; In Canada: Children's Press, 1996. 64p. col. ill., maps. (Cities of the world).
Includes chronology, glossary and index.
An interesting, detailed look at one of the major cities of the United States and of the world, emphasizes history; current political, social, and economic conditions; and information about the contemporary life of residents. Many bright, full-color photographs of people, places, and scenes capture the flavor of New York City. For multicultural units and regional studies.
SUBJ: New York (N.Y.).

974.8 Ph-2 5-6/7 $23.93 L KE959
FRADIN, DENNIS B. Pennsylvania Colony. Childrens Press ISBN 0-516-00390-9; In Canada: Childrens Press, 1988. 160p. col. ill. (Thirteen colonies).
Includes index.
Recounts the history of the Pennsylvania Colony from its earliest days through the ratification of the Constitution. Eight biographical sketches accompany the text; colonial timeline and reproductions of historic documents (including a pay scale for Washington's army) add further value to this title. Useful for project support and as material to extend study beyond the textbook.
SUBJ: Pennsylvania--History--Colonial period, ca. 1600-1775./ Pennsylvania--History--Revolution, 1775-1783.

974.8 Ph-3 4-6/7 $17.50 L KE960
SWAIN, GWENYTH. Pennsylvania. Lerner ISBN 0-8225-2727-8, 1994. 72p. col. ill., maps. (Hello U.S.A.).
Includes glossary and index.
Lively design, color photographs, fast facts, and minor mention of the famous and nearly famous add up to an appealing state book. Recommended if regionally appropriate.
SUBJ: Pennsylvania.

974.8 Ph-3 4-6/7 $16.40 L KE961
WILLS, CHARLES A. Historical album of Pennsylvania. Millbrook ISBN 1-56294-595-5, 1996. 64p. ill. (some col.), maps. (Historical albums).
Includes chronologies, bibliography, directory and index.
Richly detailed history of Pennsylvania from early Native American settlement to the present day focuses on political, cultural, and economic events. Illustrations include modern and historic photographs and reproductions of primary source documents and graphics. Gazetteer contains quick facts, timelines, and personalities. Recommended for regional studies.
SUBJ: Pennsylvania--History.

974.9 Ph-3 5-A/5 $9.95 P KE962
CHERIPKO, JAN. Voices of the river: adventures on the Delaware. Boyds Mills ISBN 1-56397-622-6; In Canada: McClelland & Stewart, 1996. 48p. col. ill., map.
Includes index.
Photo-essay documents the rigorous and sometimes hazardous canoe trip of fourteen-year-old Matthew and his author/photographer companion on a 215 mile, ten day journey on the Delaware River from Hancock, New York to Philadelphia. Useful for regional studies and for general interest adventure stories.
SUBJ: Delaware River (N.Y.-Del. and N.J.)--Description and travel./ Canoes and canoeing--Delaware River (N.Y.-Del. and N.J.).

974.9 Ph-2 5-6/7 $23.93 L KE963
FRADIN, DENNIS B. New Jersey Colony. Childrens Press ISBN 0-516-00395-X; In Canada: Childrens Press, 1991. 158p. col. ill. (Thirteen colonies).
Includes timeline and index.
Traces the history of the New Jersey colony from its earliest days to approval of the Constitution on December 18, 1787, at the Blazing Star Tavern in Trenton. A colonial timeline and biographical sketches

of early leaders add further value to the work.
SUBJ: New Jersey--History--Colonial period, ca. 1600-1775./ New Jersey--History--Colonial period, ca. 1600-1775--Biography./ New Jersey--History--Revolution, 1775-1783./ New Jersey--History--Revolution, 1775-1783--Biography.

974.9   Ph-3 4-6/5 $17.50   L   KE964
FREDEEN, CHARLES. New Jersey. Lerner ISBN 0-8225-2732-4, 1993. 72p. col. ill., maps. (Hello U.S.A.).
    Includes glossary and index.
    Lively design, colorful photographs, fast facts, information on the famous and near famous, and horizontal format add up to an appealing state book. Recommended if regionally appropriate.
    SUBJ: New Jersey.

974.9   Ph-3 4-6/7 $15.90   L   KE965
TOPPER, FRANK. Historical album of New Jersey. By Frank Topper and Charles A. Wills. Millbrook ISBN 1-56294-505-X, 1995. 64p. ill. (some col.), maps. (Historical albums).
    Includes chronologies, bibliography, directory and index.
    Supplies an overview of the history of the state whose motto is "Liberty and Prosperity." Back matter supplies addresses for sources of further information and offers sections with timelines, personalities, and fast facts. Recommended for regional purchase.
    SUBJ: New Jersey--History.

975   Ph-2 A/8 $15.95   L   KE966
KATZ, WILLIAM LOREN. Breaking the chains: African-American slave resistance. Atheneum ISBN 0-689-31493-0; In Canada: Maxwell Macmillan, 1990. 194p. ill.
    Includes bibliography and index.
    Describes slavery in the United States through the accounts of those held in bondage and the reports of others of the time. Advanced students will be interested in this look at an infrequently presented view of the nation's history. For multicultural studies.
    SUBJ: Slavery./ Antislavery movements./ United States--History--Civil War, 1861-1865--Afro-Americans.

975   Ph-1 4-A/6 $15.95   L   KE967
MCKISSACK, PAT. Christmas in the big house, Christmas in the quarters. By Patricia C. McKissack and Fredrick L. McKissack. Illus. by John Thompson. Scholastic ISBN 0-590-43027-0; In Canada: Scholastic, 1994. 68p. col. ill.
    Includes bibliography.
    Coretta Scott King Author Award, 1995.
    Available from the National Library Service for the Blind and Physically Handicapped on sound recording cassette RC 40586.
    Effectively chronicles events of the 1859 Christmas season in a Virginia plantation and its slave quarters. Parallel tracks compare and contrast celebrations and activities in the differing circumstances; handsome illustrations provide detail and insight. Useful in United States history units and multicultural studies at any time of the year.
    SUBJ: Plantation life--Southern States--History--19th century./ Christmas--Southern States--History--19th century./ Slaves--Social life and customs./ Southern States--Social life and customs--1775-1865.

975.1   Ph-3 4-6/3 $24.00 L OD KE968
FRADIN, DENNIS B. Delaware. By Dennis Brindell Fradin and Judith Bloom Fradin. Childrens Press ISBN 0-516-03808-7; In Canada: Childrens Press, 1994. 64p. col. ill., maps. (From sea to shining sea).
    Includes chronology, glossary and index.
    Introduces the people, history, cities, and geography of Delaware. Famous people section mentions figures in politics, sports, and the arts. Purchase as needed as a regional acquisition.
    SUBJ: Delaware.

975.2   Ph-3 4-6/3 $24.00 L OD KE969
FRADIN, DENNIS B. Maryland. By Dennis Brindell Fradin. Childrens Press ISBN 0-516-03820-6; In Canada: Childrens Press, 1994. 64p. col. ill., maps. (From sea to shining sea).
    Includes chronology, glossary and index.
    Introduces the people, history, cities, and geography of Maryland. Famous people section offers the briefest of information on figures in the arts and humanities, politics, and sports. Purchase as needed as a regional acquisition.
    SUBJ: Maryland.

975.3   Ph-2 5-6/8 $14.95   L   KE970
FISHER, LEONARD EVERETT. White House. Holiday House ISBN 0-8234-0774-8, 1989. 95p. ill.
    Includes index.
    Available from National Library Service for the Blind and Physically Handicapped on sound recording cassette RC31327.
    Traces the history of the White House from its earliest days through

the 1980s. Period photographs, drawings, and illustrations, all in black and white, give a sense of the structure and its inhabitants. Of value as a browser and in social studies and patriotic units.
    SUBJ: White House (Washington, D.C.)./ Presidents.

975.3   Ph-3 4-6/7 $17.50   L   KE971
JOHNSTON, JOYCE. Washington, D.C. Lerner ISBN 0-8225-2751-0, 1993. 72p. col. ill., maps. (Hello U.S.A.).
    Includes chronology, glossary and index.
    Color photographs, fast facts, small format, and timeline add up to an appealing introduction to the nation's capital. Recommended for use in social studies and regional geography activities.
    SUBJ: Washington (D.C.).

975.3   Ph-1 4-6/10 $21.00   L   KE972
QUIRI, PATRICIA RYON. White House. Watts ISBN 0-531-20221-6; In Canada: Grolier Ltd., 1996. 63p. col. ill., maps. (First book).
    Includes bibliographies and index.
    Describes the planning, construction, and subsequent renovations of the White House as well as its interior layout and design, along with many interesting facts about how some of the Presidents and First Ladies contributed to its history. Many photographs, some in color, show personalities and details. For United States history units, general interest, and as preparation for field trips.
    SUBJ: White House (Washington, D.C.)./ Presidents--United States./ Washington (D.C.)--Buildings, structures, etc.

975.3   Ph-3 4-6/9 $13.90   L   KE973
STEINS, RICHARD. Our national capital. Millbrook ISBN 1-56294-439-8, 1994. 48p. col. ill., maps. (I know America).
    Includes chronology, bibliography and index.
    Describes our capital city, its design, and its attractions. Emphasis is on governmental buildings and monuments, but theaters, museums, and parks also receive attention. Useful in patriotic units and for social studies support.
    SUBJ: Washington (D.C.)--History./ Washington (D.C.)--Guides.

975.4   Ph-1 4-6/6 $13.95   L   KE974
ANDERSON, JOAN. Pioneer children of Appalachia. Photos by George Ancona. Clarion ISBN 0-89919-440-0, 1986. unp. ill.
    Depicts with detail the life of a typical Appalachian family of the early 19th century. Photographed in a living history village the book features daily activities of young Elizabeth as she helps her family in the never ceasing effort required to survive in earlier times. Can be used as a source in developing an historical crafts unit or in building awareness of pioneer life.
    SUBJ: Frontier and pioneer life--Appalachian region./ Appalachian Region--Social life and customs./ West Virginia--Social life and customs.

975.4   Ph-3 4-6/7 $24.00   L   KE975
FRADIN, DENNIS B. West Virginia. By Dennis Brindell Fradin and Judith Bloom Fradin. Childrens Press ISBN 0-516-03848-6; In Canada: Childrens Press, 1994. 64p. col. ill., maps. (From sea to shining sea).
    Includes chronology, glossary and index.
    Introduces the cities, geography, history, and people of West Virginia. Closing section offers fast facts, trivia, and mention of famous West Virginians. For regional collections.
    SUBJ: West Virginia.

975.5   Ph-3 4-6/7 $16.90   L   KE976
COCKE, WILLIAM. Historical album of Virginia. Millbrook ISBN 1-56294-596-3, 1995. 64p. ill. (some col.), maps. (Historical albums).
    Includes chronologies, bibliography, directory and index.
    Richly detailed history of Virginia from early Native American settlement to the present day. Illustrations include modern and historic photographs and reproductions of primary source graphics. Gazetteer contains quick facts, timelines, and personalities. Lack of historical and contemporary maps are a drawback, but this will be useful for regional reports and studies of early colonies.
    SUBJ: Virginia--History.

975.5   Ph-2 A/10 $23.93   L   KE977
FRADIN, DENNIS B. Virginia Colony. Childrens Press ISBN 0-516-00387-9; In Canada: Childrens Press, 1986. 158p. ill. (Thirteen colonies).
    Includes chronology, bibliography and index.
    Recounts the history of the Virginia Colony from its earliest Indian settlement to the American Revolution. Eight brief biographical sketches accompany the text; colonial timeline, annotated bibliography, and reproduction of several documents further add to the value of this title. Useful for project support and as material to extend study beyond the textbook.
    SUBJ: Virginia--History--Colonial period, ca. 1600-1775./ Virginia--History--Revolution, 1775-1783.

975.5   Ph-2 5-A/7 $15.95   L   KE978

GOOR, RON. Williamsburg: cradle of the revolution. By Ron and Nancy Goor. Atheneum ISBN 0-689-31795-6; In Canada: Maxwell Macmillan, 1994. 90p. ill., maps.

Includes bibliography and index.

Explores the Williamsburg of the late 1700s, capturing everyday life as well as events preceding the American Revolution. Black and white photographs support a well-written, rather demanding text. Solid curriculum support.

SUBJ: Williamsburg (Va.)--Social life and customs./ Virginia--Politics and government--1775-1783.

975.5   Ph-2 2-4/3 $14.88   L   KE979

MILLS, PATRICIA. On an island in the bay. Text and photos by Patricia Mills. North-South Books ISBN 1-55858-334-3; In Canada: North-South Books/dist. by Vanwell, 1994. unp. col. ill.

Captures the water-tied life on islands in the Chesapeake Bay. Combine with Foster's PRIVATE WORLD OF SMITH ISLAND, Gibbon's SURROUNDED BY SEA, and Krull's BRIDGES TO CHANGE for a "how we live" activity. Useful in building knowledge of coastal regions.

SUBJ: Chesapeake Bay (Md. and Va.)./ Natural history--Chesapeake Bay (Md. and Va.)./ Islands.

VCR 975.5   Ph-2 4-6 $24.95   OD KE980

MOUNT VERNON: HOME OF GEORGE WASHINGTON (Videocassette). Finley-Holiday Films V115, 1989. 1/2" VHS videocassette color (30min). (Our national heritage).

Offers a tour of the handsome grounds and dwellings of Mount Vernon while providing information about George and Martha Washington and life in their Virginia home. Production design and quality are good. Useful in social studies and "historic buildings" units and as a general background-builder.

SUBJ: Washington, George./ Virginia--Buildings, structures, etc./ Mount Vernon (Va.).

975.5   Ph-3 4-6/6 $17.50   L   KE981

SIRVAITIS, KAREN. Virginia. Lerner ISBN 0-8225-2702-2, 1991. 72p. ill. (some col.). (Hello U.S.A.).

Includes pronunciation guide, glossary and index.

Fresh design, colorful photographs, fast facts, and timelines add up to an appealing "state" book. Recommended for special regional or curriculum interest.

SUBJ: Virginia.

975.6   Ph-2 5-6/7 $22.60   L   KE982

FRADIN, DENNIS B. North Carolina Colony. Childrens Press ISBN 0-516-00396-8; In Canada: Childrens Press, 1991. 160p. ill., maps. (Thirteen colonies).

Includes chronology and index.

Relates the history of the North Carolina colony from its earliest days through its approval of the United States Constitution in 1789. A timeline, biographical information, and sample documents add to the package. Solid curriculum support.

SUBJ: North Carolina--History--Colonial period. ca. 1600-1775.

975.6   Ph-3 4-6/7 $17.50   L   KE983

SCHULZ, ANDREA. North Carolina. Lerner ISBN 0-8225-2744-8, 1993. 72p. col. ill., maps. (Hello U.S.A.).

Includes chronology, glossary and index.

Combines fresh format, colorful photographs, and customary "state book" information in creating an attractive overview of the "Tar Heel State." Recommended for regional collections.

SUBJ: North Carolina.

975.7   Ph-3 4-6/5 $24.00   L OD KE984

FRADIN, DENNIS B. South Carolina. Childrens Press ISBN 0-516-03840-0; In Canada: Childrens Press, 1992. 64p. col. ill., maps. (From sea to shining sea).

Includes chronology, glossary and index.

Discusses the history, geography, economic base, and tourist attractions of South Carolina. Fast facts and famous people also receive attention. Recommended as a regional acquisition.

SUBJ: South Carolina.

975.7   Ph-2 A/7 $23.93   L   KE985

FRADIN, DENNIS B. South Carolina Colony. Children's Press ISBN 0-516-00397-6; In Canada: Children's Press, 1992. 160p. ill., maps. (Thirteen colonies).

Includes chronology and index.

Provides a history of the twelfth colony from the time of indigenous peoples through the American Revolution. Brief biographical sketches of major figures of the period are included as are a colonial timeline and reproductions of historical documents. A strong curriculum-

supporter.

SUBJ: South Carolina--History--Colonial period, ca. 1600-1775./ South Carolina--History--Revolution, 1775-1783.

975.7   Ph-3 4-6/6 $17.50   L   KE986

FREDEEN, CHARLES. South Carolina. Lerner ISBN 0-8225-2712-X, 1991. 72p. col. ill., map. (Hello U.S.A.).

Includes glossary and index.

Combines fresh format and color photographs with the usual "state book" information to offer an appealing resource. Recommended for regional collections.

SUBJ: South Carolina.

975.7   Ph-1 4-6/7 $15.99   T   KE987

KRULL, KATHLEEN. Bridges to change: how kids live on a South Carolina Sea Island. Photos by David Hautzig. Lodestar/Dutton ISBN 0-525-67441-1; In Canada: McClelland & Stewart, 1995. 46p. col. ill., map. (World of my own).

Includes bibliography and index.

Describes life on St. Helena, one of the Sea Islands off the coast of South Carolina. Well-written text offers information about the Gullah culture while maintaining interest in the ten-year-old children depicted. Valuable in "how we live" units, state studies, and multicultural studies.

SUBJ: St. Helena Island (S.C.)--Social life and customs./ Gullahs./ Afro-Americans--Social life and customs.

975.8   Ph-2 5-6/7 $23.93   L   KE988

FRADIN, DENNIS B. Georgia Colony. Childrens Press ISBN 0-516-00392-5; In Canada: Childrens Press, 1989. 143p. ill. (Thirteen colonies).

Includes timeline and index.

Presents the history of the Georgia Colony from its founding as a colony for debtors through its ratification of the Constitution in 1788. Six brief biographical sketches accompany the text; colonial timeline and reproductions of historical documents add further to its value. Useful for project starters.

SUBJ: Georgia--History--Colonial period, ca. 1600-1775.

975.8   Ph-3 4-6/7 $17.50   L   KE989

LADOUX, RITA C. Georgia. Lerner ISBN 0-8225-2703-0, 1991. 72p. ill. (some col.). (Hello U.S.A.).

Includes pronunciation guide, glossary and index.

Fresh design, colorful photographs, fast facts, and timelines add up to an appealing "state" book. Recommended for special regional collections or in areas where needed for curriculum support.

SUBJ: Georgia.

VCR 975.9   Ph-3 A $39.95   OD KE990

CONQUERING THE SWAMPS (Videocassette). PBS Video ISBN 0-7936-0654-3, 1991. 1/2" VHS videocassette color (60min). (Land of the eagle).

Includes series study guide.

Combines distinguished photography and a nature-centered script in an examination of early Spanish exploration and the subsequent development of Florida. Strong production values are characteristic of the series of which this video is a part. Length mandates preview and pre-class decisions about best patterns of use.

SUBJ: Florida--History./ America--Discovery and exploration--Spanish./ Indians of North America--Florida.

975.9   Ph-2 2-5/7 $14.95   L   KE991

GEORGE, JEAN CRAIGHEAD. Everglades. Illus. by Wendell Minor. HarperCollins ISBN 0-06-021229-2; In Canada: HarperCollins, 1995. unp. col. ill.

Available from the National Library Service for the Blind and Physically Handicapped on sound recording cassette RC 42052.

Describes the Everglades and the impact of environmental carelessness upon them. Appealing paintings by Wendell Minor depict regional birds and animals to good effect though details lack accuracy. Particularly useful in enviromental studies.

SUBJ: Everglades (Fla.)./ Natural history--Florida--Everglades./ Man--Influence on nature.

975.9   Ph-1 4-6/6 $9.95   P   KE992

LOURIE, PETER. Everglades: Buffalo Tiger and the river of grass. Boyds Mills ISBN 1-56397-702-8; In Canada: McClelland & Stewart, c1994, 1998. 47p. col. ill., map.

The author travels to the Everglades with a Miccosukee Indian guide, Buffalo Tiger, and experiences firsthand how a way of life and an entire ecosystem were irreversibly destroyed by overhunting, development, and pollution. Testifies to a loss of American heritage and pointedly cries for introspection and environmental awareness. Use in Florida units and multicultural and environmental studies.

SUBJ: Everglades (Fla.)./ Man--Influence on nature./ Indians of North America--Florida.

975.9   Ph-3 4-6/7 $17.50   L   KE993
SIRVAITIS, KAREN. Florida. Lerner ISBN 0-8225-2728-6, 1994. 72p. col. ill., maps. (Hello U.S.A.).
     Includes chronology, glossary and index.
     Fresh design, color photographs, fast facts, and timeline add up to an appealing look at the state. Recommended for regional purchase.
     SUBJ: Florida.

975.9   Ph-3 4-6/7 $15.90   L   KE994
WILLS, CHARLES A. Historical album of Florida. Millbrook ISBN 1-56294-480-0, 1994. 64p. ill. (some col.), maps. (Historical albums).
     Includes chronologies, bibliography, directory and index.
     Provides an overview of the history of the "Sunshine State." Back matter includes fast facts, timelines, personalities, and addresses for sources of additional information. Recommended for regional purchase.
     SUBJ: Florida--History.

VCR 976   Ph-3 3-5 $275.00   KE995
SOUTH CENTRAL REGION: TEXAS, NEW MEXICO, OKLAHOMA (Videocassette). Preview Media/dist. by Altschul Group J4937, 1995. 1/2" VHS videocassette color (20min). (U.S. geography from sea to shining sea).
     Includes teacher's guide.
     Includes public performance rights.
     Overview of the geography, history, economic development, and population of the South Central states serves as a brief introduction to the region. Clear narration and photographs highlight important facts while beautifully filmed video clips provide a sense of the region's vastness and unique landscape. For regional studies.
     SUBJ: Southwest, Old./ Texas./ Oklahoma./ New Mexico.

976.1   Ph-3 4-6/7 $17.50   L   KE996
BROWN, DOTTIE. Alabama. Lerner ISBN 0-8225-2741-3, 1994. 72p. col. ill., maps. (Hello U.S.A.).
     Includes chronology, glossary and index.
     Discusses history, geographic features, information on aspects of life today, and brief biographies of famous residents; includes a chapter on local efforts to protect the environment. Illustrated with photographs and other graphics. Useful for state reports and regional collections.
     SUBJ: Alabama.

MMK 976.1   Ph-3 5-A $37.00   OD KE997
OKLAHOMA LAND RUSH (Multimedia kit). Compiled by Sidney Theil. Jackdaws Publications ISBN 0-305-62081-9; In Canada: Clarke, Irwin, 1993. 11 exhibits, 5 broadsheets. (Jackdaws).
     Offers historical broadsheets and facsimiles of original documents related to the 1889 Oklahoma land rush when 100,000 persons surged into the territory to claim homestead land. Useful in preparing exhibits or for individual study.
     SUBJ: Oklahoma--History.

976.1   Ph-3 5-6/6 $16.40   L   KE998
STEIN, R. CONRAD. Montgomery bus boycott. Rev. ed. Childrens Press ISBN 0-516-06671-4; In Canada: Childrens Press, 1993. 32p. ill. (some col.). (Cornerstones of freedom).
     Includes index.
     Traces events of the 1955 boycott of segregated buses in Montgomery, Alabama. The role of Martin Luther King, Jr. receives attention as does the boycott's impact on Jim Crow laws nationwide. Of value for reports on post-1950 American events or in the study of the civil rights struggle. For multicultural studies.
     SUBJ: Segregation in transportation--Alabama--Montgomery./ Montgomery (Ala.)--Race relations./ Afro-Americans--Civil rights.

976.1   Ph-3 4-6/7 $16.40   L   KE999
WILLS, CHARLES A. Historical album of Alabama. Millbrook ISBN 1-56294-591-2, 1995. 64p. ill. (some col.), maps. (Historical albums).
     Includes chronologies, bibliography, directory and index.
     Richly detailed history of Alabama from early Native American settlement to the present day includes an in-depth discussion of events leading to and following the Civil War as well as the role of the state in civil rights struggles. Illustrated with modern and historic photographs and primary source graphics. Gazetteer contains quick facts, key events, and personalities. Recommended for regional studies.
     SUBJ: Alabama--History.

976.3   Ph-3 4-6/4 $24.00   L OD KF000
FRADIN, DENNIS B. Louisiana. By Dennis Brindell Fradin and Judith Bloom Fradin. Childrens Press ISBN 0-516-03818-4; In Canada: Childrens Press, 1995. 64p. col. ill., maps. (From sea to shining sea).
     Includes chronology, glossary and index.

Introduces the people, history, cities, and geography of Louisiana. Famous people section features figures in sports, politics, and the arts. Recommended for regional acquisition.
     SUBJ: Louisiana.

976.4   Ph-2 4-6/7 $17.71   L   KF001
CARTER, ALDEN R. Last stand at the Alamo. Watts ISBN 0-531-10888-0; In Canada: Watts, 1990. 64p. col. ill. (First book).
     Includes bibliography and index.
     Retells the traditional story of the Alamo in a smoothly written text set in the First Book series format. Action is balanced by background information and the result is a well-rounded treatment. Useful in support of the social studies curriculum and for activities planned around "best-known events in American history."
     SUBJ: Alamo (San Antonio, Tex.)--Siege, 1836./ Texas--History--To 1846.

976.4   Ph-1 4-6/10 $5.99   P   KF002
SULLIVAN, GEORGE. Alamo! Scholastic ISBN 0-590-50313-8; In Canada: Scholastic, 1997. 96p. ill., maps.
     Includes chronology, bibliography and index.
     Describes events leading up to and following the siege of the Alamo, recounting the early conflict over command between army regulars and volunteers, pleas to other army units for help, details of the final defeat of the garrison, aftermath of the battle, and acknowledging the role that Tejanos and Native Americans played as defenders of the Alamo. Illustrated with black and white photographs, graphics, and engravings. This will be interesting to history buffs as well as useful information for assignments.
     SUBJ: Alamo (San Antonio, Tex.)--Siege, 1836./ Texas--History--To 1846.

976.4   Ph-3 4-6/10 $19.95   T   KF003
TURNER, ROBYN. Texas traditions: the culture of the Lone Star State. By Robyn Montana Turner. Little, Brown ISBN 0-316-85675-4; In Canada: Little, Brown, 1996. 96p. col. ill., maps.
     Includes bibliography and index.
     The culture, history, geography, and personalities of Texas are depicted in a lavishly illustrated presentation. Many sidebars give additional information of interest. Use for regional studies or where there is general interest or curriculum emphasis on Texas.
     SUBJ: Texas.

976.4   Ph-3 4-6/7 $15.90   L   KF004
WILLS, CHARLES A. Historical album of Texas. Millbrook Press ISBN 1-56294-504-1, 1995. 64p. ill. (some col.), maps. (Historical albums).
     Includes chronologies, bibliography, directory and index.
     Offers an overview of the history of the "Lone Star State." Back matter includes fast facts, timelines, personalities, and addresses for more information. Recommended for regional purchase.
     SUBJ: Texas--History.

976.6   Ph-3 4-6/4 $24.00   L OD KF005
FRADIN, DENNIS B. Oklahoma. By Dennis Brindell Fradin and Judith Bloom Fradin. Childrens Press ISBN 0-516-03836-2; In Canada: Childrens Press, 1995. 64p. col. ill., maps. (From sea to shining sea).
     Includes chronology, glossary and index.
     Introduces the people, history, cities, and geography of Oklahoma. Famous people section mentions figures in politics, sports, and the arts. Purchase as needed as a regional acquisition.
     SUBJ: Oklahoma.

976.6   Ph-3 2-6/6 $15.93   L   KF006
LAMB, NANCY. One April morning: children remember the Oklahoma City bombing. By Nancy Lamb and children of Olkahoma City. Illus. by Floyd Cooper. Lothrop, Lee & Shepard ISBN 0-688-14724-0, 1996. unp. col. ill.
     In a series of insightful conversations, children from Oklahoma City share their thoughts and feelings, fears and anxieties in the devastating aftermath of the bombing of the Federal Building. Illustrations are softly focused and show both the anguish and the love portrayed in the text. Students may need the guidance of a sensitive adult to lead them through this very personal effort to understand and respond to tragedy.
     SUBJ: Oklahoma City Federal Building Bombing, Oklahoma City, Okla., 1995./ Psychic trauma.

976.7   Ph-3 4-6/7 $17.50   L   KF007
DI PIAZZA, DOMENICA. Arkansas. Lerner ISBN 0-8225-2742-1, 1994. 72p. col. ill., maps. (Hello U.S.A.).
     Includes chronology, glossary and index.
     Discusses history, geographic features, information on aspects of contemporary life, and brief biographies of famous residents; includes a chapter on local efforts to protect the environment. Illustrated with

photographs and other graphics. Useful for state reports and regional collections.
SUBJ: Arkansas.

976.7 Ph-3 4-6/4 $24.00 L OD KF008
FRADIN, DENNIS B. Arkansas. By Dennis Brindell Fradin and Judith Bloom Fradin. Childrens Press ISBN 0-516-03804-4; In Canada: Childrens Press, 1994. 64p. col. ill., maps. (From sea to shining sea).
Includes chronology, glossary and index.
Supplies fast facts, trivia, easy-to-read text, and color photographs in a package which meets the needs of a student in search of a "state book." The accompanying timeline has 40 entries with the most recent being 1992. Regional purchase.
SUBJ: Arkansas.

976.8 Ph-3 4-6/2 $24.00 L OD KF009
FRADIN, DENNIS B. Tennessee. Childrens Press ISBN 0-516-03842-7; In Canada: Childrens Press, 1992. 64p. col. ill., maps. (From sea to shining sea).
Includes chronology, glossary and index.
Discusses the history, geography, economic base, and tourist attractions of the Volunteer State. Fast facts and famous people also receive their due. Purchase recommended if regionally appropriate.
SUBJ: Tennessee.

976.9 Ph-3 4-6/6 $17.50 L KF010
BROWN, DOTTIE. Kentucky. Lerner ISBN 0-8225-2715-4, 1992. 72p. col. ill., maps. (Hello U.S.A.).
Includes glossary and index.
Fresh design, colorful photographs, fast facts, and a horizontal format add up to an appealing "state book." Recommended for regional collections.
SUBJ: Kentucky.

976.9 Ph-3 4-6/7 $15.90 L KF011
SMITH, ADAM. Historical album of Kentucky. By Adam Smith and Katherine Snow Smith. Millbrook ISBN 1-56294-507-6, 1995. 64p. ill. (some col.), maps. (Historical albums).
Includes chronologies, bibliography, directory and index.
Offers an overview of the history of the "Bluegrass State." Back matter includes fast facts, timelines, personalities, and addresses for sources of more information. Recommended for regional acquisition.
SUBJ: Kentucky--History.

VCR 977 Ph-3 A $95.00 OD KF012
RILEY, JOCELYN. Prairie cabin: a Norwegian pioneer woman's story (Videocassette). Written and produced by Jocelyn Riley. Her Own Words ISBN 1-877933-15-5, 1991. 1/2" VHS videocassette color (17min). (Women's history and literature media).
Resource guide available for $20.00.
Offers a sense of the challenges of nineteenth century pioneer life in the prairie midwest. Based on diaries and reminiscences of Norwegian immigrants, the first-person, fictionalized narrative uses music, furniture, and clothing of the times. Useful in social studies, regional studies, and writing and discussion activities.
SUBJ: Middle West--History./ Frontier and pioneer life--Middle West./ Women pioneers./ Norwegian Americans./ Diaries.

977.1 Ph-3 4-6/7 $16.40 L KF013
WILLS, CHARLES A. Historical album of Ohio. Millbrook ISBN 1-56294-593-9, 1996. 64p. ill. (some col.), maps. (Historical albums).
Includes chronologies, bibliography, directory and index.
Richly detailed history of Ohio from early Native American settlement to the present day focuses on political, cultural, and economic events. Illustrations include modern and historic photographs and reproductions of primary source documents and graphics. Gazetteer contains quick facts, timelines, and personalities. Recommended for regional studies.
SUBJ: Ohio--History.

977.2 Ph-3 4-6/3 $24.00 L OD KF014
FRADIN, DENNIS B. Indiana. By Dennis Brindell Fradin and Judith Bloom Fradin. Childrens Press ISBN 0-516-03814-1; In Canada: Childrens Press, 1994. 64p. col. ill., maps. (From sea to shining sea).
Includes chronology, glossary and index.
Presents the people, history, cities, and geography of Indiana. Famous people section mentions figures in politics, sports, and the arts. Purchase as needed as a regional acquisition.
SUBJ: Indiana.

977.3 Ph-2 A/7 $16.95 L KF015
MURPHY, JIM. Great fire. Scholastic ISBN 0-590-47267-4; In Canada: Scholastic, 1995. 144p. ill., maps.
Includes bibliography and index.

Newbery Honor book, 1996.
Depicts the Chicago tragedy of 1871 which began when a small fire started in the O'Learys' barn. Personal accounts, maps, drawings, and photographs join in providing a vivid sense of the event. High appeal for browsers and report writers.
SUBJ: Fires--Illinois--Chicago--History--19th century./ Chicago (Ill.)--History--To 1875.

977.3 Ph-3 4-6/7 $15.90 L KF016
WILLS, CHARLES A. Historical album of Illinois. Millbrook ISBN 1-56294-482-7, 1994. 64p. ill. (some col.), maps. (Historical albums).
Includes chronologies, bibliography, directory and index.
Presents an overview of the history of the state known as the "Land of Lincoln." Back matter supplies addresses for sources of additional information and contains sections with timelines, personalities, and fast facts. Recommended for regional purchase.
SUBJ: Illinois--History.

977.4 Ph-3 4-6/7 $17.50 L KF017
SIRVAITIS, KAREN. Michigan. Lerner ISBN 0-8225-2722-7, 1994. 72p. col. ill., maps. (Hello U.S.A.).
Includes chronology, glossary and index.
Joins colorful photographs and fresh format with typical "state book" fare to provide an appealing introduction to the "Wolverine State." Recommended for regional collections.
SUBJ: Michigan.

977.4 Ph-3 4-6/7 $23.40 L KF018
WILLS, CHARLES A. Historical album of Michigan. By Charles A. Wills. Millbrook ISBN 0-7613-0036-8, 1996. 64p. ill. (some col.), maps. (Historical albums).
Includes chronology, bibliography, directory and index.
Richly detailed history of Michigan from early Native American settlement to the present day. Illustrations include modern and historic photographs and reproductions of primary source graphics. Gazetteer contains quick facts, timelines, and personalities. For regional studies.
SUBJ: Michigan--History.

977.5 Ph-3 4-6/7 $17.50 L KF019
BRATVOLD, GRETCHEN. Wisconsin. Lerner ISBN 0-8225-2700-6, 1991. 72p. ill. (some col.). (Hello U.S.A.).
Includes pronunciation guide, glossary and index.
Fresh design, colorful photographs, fast facts, and timelines add up to an appealing "state" book. Recommended for special regional or curriculum interest.
SUBJ: Wisconsin.

977.6 Ph-3 5-6/7 $15.40 L KF020
CARLSON, JEFFREY D. Historical album of Minnesota. Millbrook ISBN 1-56294-006-6, 1993. 64p. ill. (some col.), maps. (Historical albums).
Includes chronology, bibliography, directory and index.
Traces the history of Minnesota from early days of European contact through the present. Fast fact section is included. Suitable for regional purchase when this type of state material is desired.
SUBJ: Minnesota--History.

977.6 Ph-3 4-6/3 $24.00 L OD KF021
FRADIN, DENNIS B. Minnesota. By Dennis Brindell Fradin and Judith Bloom Fradin. Childrens Press ISBN 0-516-03823-0; In Canada: Childrens Press, 1994. 64p. col. ill., maps. (From sea to shining sea).
Includes chronology, glossary and index.
Introduces the people, history, cities, and geography of Minnesota. Section featuring famous people includes figures in sports, the arts, and politics. Recommended for regional acquisition.
SUBJ: Minnesota.

977.7 Ph-3 5-6/8 $26.60 L OD KF022
KENT, DEBORAH. Iowa. Childrens Press ISBN 0-516-00461-1; In Canada: Childrens Press, 1991. 144p. ill. (some col.). (America the beautiful).
Includes maps and index.
Available from the National Library Service for the Blind and Physically Handicapped on sound cassette RC34629.
Part of an attractive but rather difficult "state books" series, this provides information about Iowa's history, geography, people, government, and more. Closing sections include state facts, brief biographical sketches of more interest to adults than to children, and maps. For regional collections.
SUBJ: Iowa.

977.8 Ph-3 4-6/4 $24.00 L OD KF023
FRADIN, DENNIS B. Missouri. By Dennis Brindell Fradin and Judith Bloom Fradin. Childrens Press ISBN 0-516-03825-7; In Canada: Childrens Press, 1994. 64p. col. ill., maps. (From sea to shining sea).

Includes chronology, glossary and index.
Combines fast facts, trivia, easy-to-read text and color photographs in a package which meets the needs of a student in search of a "state book." The accompanying timeline notes significant dates through 1993. Regional purchase.
SUBJ: Missouri.

VCR 978   Ph-3   A $59.95   OD KF024
ACROSS THE SEA OF GRASS (Videocassette). WNET/dist. by PBS Video ISBN 0-7936-0655-1, 1991. 1/2" VHS videocassette color (60min). (Land of the eagle).
Includes series study guide.
Meshes outstanding photography and a nature-centered script which follows the westward expansion of the United States. Length mandates preview and solid pre-class planning.
SUBJ: West (U.S.)--Discovery and exploration./ Indians of North America--West (U.S.).

978   Ph-2 3-5/6 $16.95   L   KF025
ANDERSON, JOAN. Cowboys: roundup on an American ranch. Photos by George Ancona. Scholastic ISBN 0-590-48424-9; In Canada: Scholastic, 1996. 48p. col. ill.
Includes glossary/index.
Photo-essay follows Leedro and Colter Eby, their parents, and hired hands as they meet the challenges of a modern-day cattle roundup. Will appeal to students who are interested in horses or Western living and may be used to discover similarities and differences in roundups of bygone eras.
SUBJ: Cowboys./ Ranch life--New Mexico./ New Mexico--Social life and customs./ Eby family.

978   Ph-2 4-6/7 $16.99   T   KF026
ASHABRANNER, BRENT. Strange and distant shore: Indians of the Great Plains in exile. Cobblehill/Dutton ISBN 0-525-65201-9; In Canada: McClelland & Stewart, 1996. 54p. ill. (some col.).
Includes bibliography and index.
Presents the remarkable story of 72 Plains Indian chiefs and warriors exiled to an old Spanish fort in Florida after the Red River War of 1875. They fought loneliness, isolation, and despair by producing thousands of paintings and drawings portraying a whole range of Native American life. Discusses issues of racism, education, and efforts at assimilation through the establishment of boarding schools. Illustrated with photographs of the exiles and other Native Americans in a variety of settings, some of the Fort Marion artwork, and other examples of Native American art. Use for multicultural studies, background on contemporary issues, and units covering the post-Civil War period.
SUBJ: Indians of North America--Great Plains--History./ Indian art--Florida./ Castillo de San Marcos National Monument (Saint Augustine, Fla.)--History.

978   Ph-2 4-6/8 $15.95   L   KF027
BIAL, RAYMOND. Frontier home. Houghton Mifflin ISBN 0-395-64046-6, 1993. 39p. col. ill.
Includes bibliography.
Describes the life of pioneer families, showing equipment, implements, and homes. Photographs used were taken at historic sites in Illinois.
SUBJ: Frontier and pioneer life./ West (U.S.)--Social life and customs.

VCR 978   Ph-3 5-6 $99.00   OD KF028
BLACK WEST (Videocassette). All Media Productions ISBN 1-882205-00-6, 1992. 1/2" VHS videocassette color (23min).
Includes teacher's guide and activity guide.
Introduces African-American cowboys, frontiersmen, outlaws, and sheriffs of the Old West. Graphic quality is a highlight of this overview narrated by artist (and former Harlem Globetrotter) Herschell Turner. Useful as an awareness-expander and as a trigger for further study.
SUBJ: West (U.S.)--Social life and customs./ Frontier and pioneer life--West (U.S.)./ Afro-Americans--West (U.S.)./ West (U.S.)--Biography./ Afro-Americans--Biography.

978   Ph-1 5-A/7 $15.95   L   KF029
FREEDMAN, RUSSELL. Cowboys of the wild west. Clarion ISBN 0-89919-301-3, 1985. 103p. ill.
Includes bibliography and index.
Selectors' Choice, 16th ed.
Provides a vivid look at the trail driving cowboy of the last part of the nineteenth century. Photographs taken on the open range and in cattle towns provide an opportunity to pursue detail and the readable text tells the history and examines the cowboy's daily life. Useful for individual projects and pursuit of student interests.
SUBJ: Cowboys--West (U.S.)./ Frontier and pioneer life--West (U.S.)./ West (U.S.)--Social life and customs.

978   Ph-2 5-A/8 $18.95   T   KF030
GRANFIELD, LINDA. Cowboy: an album. Ticknor & Fields ISBN 0-395-68430-7; In Canada: Douglas & McIntyre, 1994. 96p. ill. (some col.).
Includes bibliography and index.
Combines strong graphics with a thorough text which discusses the cowboy of history, cattle drives, end of the cattle boom, the cowboy myth, and today's cowboy. Scope includes Canadian cowboys as well as those in the United States. Useful for browsing and special projects.
SUBJ: Cowboys./ Cowboys--West (U.S.)./ Cowgirls.

978 J971.3   Ph-1 4-6/6 $18.95   T   KF031
GREENWOOD, BARBARA. Pioneer sampler: the daily life of a pioneer family in 1840. Illus. by Heather Collins. Ticknor & Fields ISBN 0-395-71540-7, 1995. 240p. ill.
Includes glossary and index.
Originally published in Canada as PIONEER SAMPLER: THE DAILY LIFE OF A CANADIAN FAMILY IN 1840, Kids Can Press, 1994.
Use fictional and factual material in providing informative, intriguing insight into North American pioneer life of the 1840s. Solid design, pencil drawings, and activities for today's child lift this effort above the average. Use for reading aloud and in support of social studies/crafts interdisciplinary activities.
SUBJ: Frontier and pioneer life--West (U.S.)./ West (U.S.)--Social life and customs.

978   Ph-2 4-6/10 $16.99   T   KF032
HERB, ANGELA M. Beyond the Mississippi: early westward expansion of the United States. Lodestar/Dutton ISBN 0-525-67503-5; In Canada: McClelland & Stewart, 1996. 138p. ill., map. (Young readers' history of the West).
Includes chronology, glossary, bibliography and index.
From the Lewis and Clark expeditions through the discovery of gold in California, this is a comprehensive account of early westward experiences of trappers, missionaries, explorers, and settlers. Illustrated with archival engravings, primary source items, boxed quotes, and photographs. Use for research, background, and accounts of everyday people who were part of the nation's westward expansion.
SUBJ: West (U.S.)--History--To 1848./ West (U.S.)--Discovery and exploration./ United States--Territorial expansion.

978   Ph-2 4-6/8 $16.98   L   KF033
HILTON, SUZANNE. Miners, merchants, and maids. Twenty-First Century ISBN 0-8050-2998-2; In Canada: Fitzhenry & Whiteside, 1995. 96p. ill. (some col.), maps. (Settling the West).
Includes bibliographies and index.
Presents interesting anecdotes and vignettes filled with well-documented first-person accounts of the experiences of men and women searching for mineral wealth, shopkeepers who traded for goods or gold dust, and women who set up boardinghouses and other accommodations for travelers, who became Harvey House "waiter girls," or who supported their families by taking in laundry. Some archival photographs accompany text. Inclusion of individuals from various cultures and some emphasis on the role of women in settling the West make this a resource for multicultural studies and women's studies.
SUBJ: West (U.S.)--History./ Mines and mineral resources--West (U.S.)--History--19th century./ Merchants--West (U.S.)--History--19th century./ Women--West (U.S.)--History--19th century.

VCR 978   Ph-2 4-6 $95.00   OD KF034
HOMESTEADING: 70 YEARS ON THE GREAT PLAINS, 1862-1932 (Videocassette). United Learning 10048V ISBN 1-56007-302-0, 1992. 1/2" VHS videocassette color (18min).
Includes teacher's guide.
Includes public performance rights.
Closed captioned.
Live action reenactments give the flavor of life on the plains from the movement west in the 1860s to the Dust Bowl of the 1930s, clearly showing the laborious processes previously required for everyday household and farming activities, the effects of mechanization and electrification, and briefly discussing the effects of settlement on Native American populations. Some primary source quotes and archival photographs are used. Use for units on the westward movement, agriculture, and women's studies.
SUBJ: Frontier and pioneer life--West (U.S.)./ West (U.S.)--History.

VCR 978   Ph-3   A $59.95   OD KF035
INTO THE SHINING MOUNTAINS (Videocassette). WNET/dist. by PBS Video ISBN 0-7936-0656-X, 1991. 1/2" VHS videocassette color (60min). (Land of the eagle).
Includes series study guide.
Takes a look at the varied terrain of the Rocky Mountains and

contrasts the views of old and new Americans toward this region. Strong production values are a feature of the series of which this video is a part. Length requires careful planning for effective use.
SUBJ: West (U.S.)--History./ Indians of North America--West (U.S.).

978   Ph-1 5-6/9 $18.00   T   KF036
KATZ, WILLIAM LOREN. Black women of the Old West. Atheneum ISBN 0-689-31944-4; In Canada: Distican, 1995. 84p. ill.
Includes bibliography and index.
Accounts of nineteenth century African-American women who played a part in abolition, expanding educational opportunities, community affairs, and westward expansion. Archival photographs depict the individual women, their families, and their surroundings. An excellent resource for an aspect of women's studies and the westward movement not often emphasized. For multicultural studies.
SUBJ: Afro-Americans--West (U.S.)./ Frontier and pioneer life--West (U.S.)./ Women pioneers.

978   Ph-2 A/6 $15.95   L   KF037
LAVENDER, DAVID SIEVERT. Santa Fe Trail. Holiday House ISBN 0-8234-1153-2, 1995. 64p. ill., map.
Includes index.
Chronicles commerce and travel on the 775-mile wagon trail to Santa Fe during the mid 1800s. Writing style is strong, and good readers will enjoy the detail supplied. Useful in transportation units and regional studies. For reading aloud.
SUBJ: Santa Fe Trail./ Frontier and pioneer life--Southwest, New./ Overland journeys to the Pacific.

978   Ph-2 5-6/6 $16.95   T   KF038
LAVENDER, DAVID SIEVERT. Snowbound: the tragic story of the Donner Party. By David Lavender. Holiday House ISBN 0-8234-1231-8, 1996. 87p. ill., maps.
Includes bibliography and index.
Narrative account of the ill-fated Donner party from the decision to go West from Illinois in the spring of 1846 to the final rescue of survivors in the late winter of 1847. Illustrated with archival photographs and drawings, the narrative raises questions and provokes discussion about reports of cannibalism and other events that are unlikely to ever be resolved. Students will find this a fascinating account which may lead to comparisons with the primary source account in ACROSS THE PLAINS IN THE DONNER PARTY.
SUBJ: Donner Party./ Overland journeys to the Pacific.

978   Ph-2 4-6/6 $14.59   L   KF039
MILLER, ROBERT H. Cowboys. Illus. by Richard Leonard. Silver Burdett ISBN 0-382-24079-0, 1991. 80p. ill. (Reflections of a Black cowboy).
Includes bibliography.
Told as legends, the five biographies in this collection tell of African-Americans who, following the Civil War, made their way West. As marshal, cowboy, mail rider or outlaw, they made a name in history. Incidents can be read individually or as a collection of "tall tales." Book two in this series continues with five tales of heroic black soldiers in THE BUFFALO SOLDIERS (ISBN 0-382-24080-4, 1991).
SUBJ: West (U.S.)--Social life and customs./ Cowboys./ Afro-Americans--Biography./ West (U.S.)--Biography.

978   Ph-1 4-A/8 $16.99   L   KF040
MURDOCH, DAVID H. Cowboy. Photos by Geoff Brightling. Knopf ISBN 0-679-94014-6, 1993. 64p. col. ill. (Eyewitness books).
"Borzoi book."
Includes index.
Examines with worldwide scope the life and accoutrements of the cowboy. Clear-cut photographic illustrations and accompanying text turn this high-appeal Eyewitness book into a true knowledge-expander. Useful for individual pleasure reading or in research projects.
SUBJ: Cowboys--West (U.S.)./ Cowboys./ Cowgirls.

978   Ph-2 5-6/7 $19.50   T   KF041
MURPHY, VIRGINIA REED. Across the plains in the Donner Party. With letters by James Reed. Edited by Karen Zeinert. Linnet ISBN 0-208-02404-2, 1996. 112p. ill., maps.
Includes chronologies and bibliographies.
Forty-five years after the horrific experience of the Donner party in attempting to cross the Sierras in the dead of winter, Virginia Reed Murphy wrote a memoir of the harrowing events as she remembered them. Accompanied by archival photographs of uneven clarity, this edited memoir is supplemented by letters written during the journey by James Reed, diary excerpts of Reed and another member of the group, and other original sources. Teachers and advanced readers looking for primary source materials documenting events in the westward movement will find this a fascinating and thought-provoking account.

SUBJ: Donner Party./ Murphy, Virginia Reed./ Overland journeys to the Pacific./ West (U.S.)--History.

978   Ph-2 A/12 $12.95   P   KF042
OVERLAND TO CALIFORNIA IN 1859: A GUIDE FOR WAGON TRAIN TRAVELERS. Compiled and edited by Louis M. Bloch Jr. Bloch and Co. ISBN 0-914276-04-2, 1983. 64p. ill.
Includes index.
Offers details from a handbook for overland travel written in 1859 in choosing a route to California, how to cross a river, camping, etc. This primary source material will put the reader at the scene. High reading level but valuable in curriculum support.
SUBJ: Overland journeys to the Pacific--Handbooks, manuals, etc./ California--History.

978   Ph-2 2-4/8 $16.85   L   KF043
PATENT, DOROTHY HINSHAW. West by covered wagon: retracing the pioneer trails. Photos by William Munoz. Walker ISBN 0-8027-8378-3; In Canada: Thomas Allen, 1995. 32p. col. ill., map.
Uses a contemporary Memorial Day event, the Westmont Wagoneers annual wagon trek through the Flatland Indian Reservation in Montana, to compare and contrast the experiences of early pioneers who traveled west with their families with life today. Photographs follow one family as they retrace one of the pioneer trails. A good resource for introducing younger students to the concepts of migration westward.
SUBJ: Overland journeys to the Pacific./ West (U.S.)--History--1848-1860.

PIC 978   Ph-2 5-6 $30.00   OD KF044
REAL COWBOYS (Picture). Documentary Photos Aids 11G, n.d. 20 b&w study prints (11"x14").
Authentic photographs, with captions, picture the cowboy as he really was, showing the hardships and loneliness of his life, the long cattle drives, his equipment and what he wore.
SUBJ: Cowboys.

978   Ph-1 5-6/9 $19.95   L   KF045
RITCHIE, DAVID. Frontier life. Chelsea House ISBN 0-7910-2842-9, 1996. 104p. ill. (some col.). (Life in America 100 years ago).
Includes bibliography and index.
Presents colorful accounts of high interest aspects of frontier life, including law and order, manners and customs, health and medicine, and sports and recreation. The excellent primary source photographs are a major strength, although their placement occasionally interferes with the flow of narrative. Use for reports and recreational reading.
SUBJ: Frontier and pioneer life--West (U.S.)./ West (U.S.)--History.

VCR 978   Ph-3 4-6 $95.00   OD KF046
ROCKY MOUNTAIN REGION OF THE UNITED STATES (Videocassette). United Learning 10061V ISBN 1-56007-337-3, 1993. 1/2" VHS videocassette color (18min).
Includes teacher's guide.
Includes public performance rights.
Straightforward, informative presentation of some of the diverse aspects of the region includes climate and geographic features, population centers, Native American populations, development of railroads, contemporary economic activities, and education. Combination of historical background and contemporary features will make this valuable for units on the Westward Movement as well as regional studies.
SUBJ: Rocky Mountains Region.

978   Ph-3 P-K/6 $14.95   L   KF047
ROUNDS, GLEN. Cowboys. Holiday House ISBN 0-8234-0867-1, 1991. unp col illus.
Describes a day in the life of a cowboy including saddling and riding a wild horse, rounding up stray cattle and an encounter with a rattlesnake. Expressive use of line and color in the illustrations lend drama and humor to this story best shared with young cowboy enthusiasts.
SUBJ: Cowboys.

978   Ph-1 4-6/8 $18.00   L   KF048
SCHLISSEL, LILLIAN. Black frontiers: a history of African American heroes in the Old West. Simon & Schuster ISBN 0-689-80285-4; In Canada: Distican, 1995. 80p. ill.
Includes bibliography, directory and index.
Covers many individuals, named and unnamed, who contributed to the settlement of the West and left their mark on farms and communities, including cowboys, homesteaders, Buffalo Soldiers, baseball players, bronco riders, miners, businessmen, and others. Illustrated with archival photographs and includes an excerpt from a "dime novel" showing an unusual friendship between two cowboys, Texas Jack and

his partner, Ebony Star. A good companion to BLACK WOMEN OF THE OLD WEST by William Loren Katz. For multicultural studies and units on pioneer days.
SUBJ: Afro-Americans--Biography./ West (U.S.)--Biography./ Cowboys./ Afro-American soldiers./ Frontier and pioneer life.

978   Ph-1 3-6/3 $14.95   L   KF049
SCOTT, ANN HERBERT. Cowboy country. Illus. by Ted Lewin. Clarion ISBN 0-395-57561-3, 1993. unp. col. ill.
Selectors' Choice, 20th ed.
Reports a young boy's pack trip with an "old buckaroo" who describes his life in cowboy country. Memorable watercolors illustrate the text and capture the world of today's ranch work.
SUBJ: Cowboys./ West (U.S.)--Social life and customs.

978   Ph-2 4-6/8 $16.90   L   KF050
STEFOFF, REBECCA. Children of the westward trail. Millbrook Press ISBN 1-56294-582-3, 1996. 96p. ill., map.
Includes bibliography and index.
Chronicle of westward migration interspersed with brief diary excerpts and recollections of many who were children at the time of their family's journey. Many period engravings illustrate the text. Gives a sense of the perils, hardships, and adventures faced by families in their search for a new life in Oregon and California.
SUBJ: Pioneers./ Frontier and pioneer life--West (U.S.)./ West (U.S.)--History./ Overland journeys to the Pacific.

978.02   Ph-2 4-6/7 $5.99   P   KF051
STEWART, GEORGE RIPPEY. Pioneers go west. By George R. Stewart. Random House ISBN 0-394-89180-5; In Canada: Random House, c1982, 1997. 152p. maps. (Landmark books).
Originally published as TO CALIFORNIA BY COVERED WAGON, Random House, 1954.
Describes the westward journey of a group of early pioneers traveling by covered wagon from Iowa to California in 1844. Based on the recollections of Moses Schallenberger who was seventeen at the time of the trip, the text recreates the difficulties and daily life of the journey. Has potential for reading aloud as a motivator for further study or as a high interest nonfiction title.
SUBJ: Overland journeys to the Pacific./ West (U.S.)--Description and travel--To 1848./ Frontier and pioneer life.

978   Ph-2 4-6/3 $15.95   L   KF052
WRIGHT, COURTNI C. Wagon train: a family goes West in 1865. Illus. by Gershom Griffith. Holiday House ISBN 0-8234-1152-4, 1995. unp. col. ill.
Details the westward trip of a Virginia family freed from slavery by the Civil War. Hunger, dust, and dangers are among their challenges before they reach California. Useful in study of the westward movement. For multicultural studies.
SUBJ: Overland journeys to the Pacific./ Frontier and pioneer life./ West (U.S.)--History--1860-1890./ Afro-Americans--History--1863-1877.

978.1   Ph-3 4-6/5 $17.50   L   KF053
FREDEEN, CHARLES. Kansas. Lerner ISBN 0-8225-2716-2, 1992. 72p. col. ill., maps. (Hello U.S.A.).
Includes glossary and index.
Fresh design, colorful photographs, fast facts, and a horizontal format add up to an appealing "state book." Recommended for regional collections.
SUBJ: Kansas.

978.1   Ph-3 4-6/9 $26.60   L OD KF054
KENT, ZACHARY. Kansas. Childrens Press ISBN 0-516-00462-X; In Canada: Childrens Press, 1990. 144p. col. ill. (America the beautiful).
Includes index.
Available from the National Library Service for the Blind and Physically Handicapped on sound cassette RC 34634.
Covers geography, history, government, economy, and cultural/recreational aspects of the state. Closing section includes maps, chronology, people profiles and state facts. Most effective purchasing pattern for this series is acquisition of regionally applicable titles.
SUBJ: Kansas.

978.2   Ph-3 4-6/7 $15.90   L   KF055
WILLS, CHARLES A. Historical album of Nebraska. Millbrook ISBN 1-56294-509-2, 1994. 64p. ill. (some col.), maps. (Historical albums).
Includes chronologies, bibliography, directory and index.
Supplies an overview of the history of the "Cornhusker State." Back matter includes timelines, fast facts, personalities, and addresses for sources of additional information. Recommended for regional purchase.
SUBJ: Nebraska--History.

978.3   Ph-3 4-6/7 $24.00   L OD KF056
FRADIN, DENNIS B. South Dakota. By Dennis Brindell Fradin and Judith Bloom Fradin. Childrens Press ISBN 0-516-03841-9; In Canada: Childrens Press, 1995. 64p. col. ill., maps. (From sea to shining sea).
Includes chronology, glossary and index.
Introduces the people, cities, history, and geography of South Dakota. Closing sections provide fast facts, trivia, and an introduction to famous South Dakotans. Suggested for regional purchase.
SUBJ: South Dakota.

978.4   Ph-3 4-6/3 $24.00   L OD KF057
FRADIN, DENNIS B. North Dakota. By Dennis Brindell Fradin and Judith Bloom Fradin. Childrens Press ISBN 0-516-03834-6; In Canada: Childrens Press, 1994. 64p. col. ill., maps. (From sea to shining sea).
Includes chronology, glossary and index.
Introduces the people, history, towns, and geography of North Dakota. Famous people section mentions figures (some less high profile) in politics, sports, and the arts. Purchase as needed as a regional acquisition.
SUBJ: North Dakota.

978.6   Ph-3 5-6/8 $26.60   L OD KF058
HEINRICHS, ANN. Montana. Childrens Press ISBN 0-516-00472-7; In Canada: Childrens Press, 1991. 144p. ill. (some col.). (America the beautiful).
Includes maps and index.
Available from the National Library Service for the Blind and Physically Handicapped on sound recording cassette RC34641.
Part of an attractive but rather difficult "state books" series, which presents information about the geography, history, government, economy, and recreational features of Montana. Fast fact seekers will welcome the back sections which include state facts, maps, chronology, and famous citizen profiles. Recommended as a regional acquisition.
SUBJ: Montana.

978.7   Ph-3 4-6/7 $17.50   L   KF059
FRISCH, CARLIENNE. Wyoming. Lerner ISBN 0-8225-2736-7, 1994. 72p. col. ill., maps. (Hello U.S.A.).
Includes glossary and index.
Lively design, color photographs, fast facts, and minor mention of the famous and borderline well-known add up to an appealing state book. Regional purchase.
SUBJ: Wyoming.

978.8   Ph-3 4-6/7 $17.50   L   KF060
BLEDSOE, SARA. Colorado. Lerner ISBN 0-8225-2750-2, 1993. 72p. col. ill., maps. (Hello U.S.A.).
Includes chronology, glossary and index.
Fresh design, color photographs, fast facts, and timeline add up to an appealing introduction to the state. Recommended for regional purchase.
SUBJ: Colorado.

978.8   Ph-3 3-6/3 $24.00   L OD KF061
FRADIN, DENNIS B. Colorado. By Dennis Brindell Fradin. Childrens Press ISBN 0-516-03806-0; In Canada: Childrens Press, 1993. 64p. col. ill., maps. (From sea to shining sea).
Includes chronology, glossary and index.
Presents the cities, people, history, and landforms of Colorado. Fast facts and famous people of the state also receive attention. Purchase recommended as a regional acquisition.
SUBJ: Colorado.

978.8   Ph-3 4-6/7 $16.40   L   KF062
WILLS, CHARLES A. Historical album of Colorado. Millbrook ISBN 1-56294-592-0, 1996. 64p. ill. (some col.), maps. (Historical albums).
Includes chronologies, bibliography, directory and index.
Richly detailed historical perspective of Colorado begins with prehistoric times and includes early settlement and exploration, early statehood, and current issues. Illustrations include paintings, photographs, and primary source materials. Lack of historical and contemporary maps is a drawback, but this will be useful for regional reports and studies of the American West.
SUBJ: Colorado--History.

979.01   Ph-1 4-6/6 $14.95   L   KF063
TRIMBLE, STEPHEN. Village of blue stone. Illus. by Jennifer Owings Dewey and Deborah Reade. Macmillan ISBN 0-02-789501-7; In Canada: Collier Macmillan, 1990. 58p. ill.
Includes bibliography, glossary and index.
Gently traces life in an Anasazi community some nine hundred years ago. Quality of text and detailed illustrations are significant plusses in this work which will serve as a companion to Bleeker's THE PUEBLO

INDIANS and Yue's THE PUEBLO. Valuable in units emphasizing Indian culture and as a nonfiction read-aloud choice.
SUBJ: Pueblo Indians--Social life and customs./ Indians of North America--Southwest, New--Social life and customs./ Cliff dwellings--Colorado./ Mesa Verde National Park (Colo.).

979.01   Ph-3 5-6/8 $10.95   T   KF064
WARREN, SCOTT. Cities in the sand: the ancient civilizations of the Southwest. Text and photos by Scott Warren. Chronicle ISBN 0-8118-0012-1; In Canada: Raincoast, 1992. 55p. col. ill., map.
Includes glossary and index.
Explores archeological ruins of the southwestern United States. Sidebars and interactive questions are pluses; difficulty of the text is a negative. Includes list of national parks and monuments where prehistoric ruins and rock art can be seen. Useful in units on Native Americans or on the Southwest.
SUBJ: Indians of North America--Southwest, New--Antiquities./ Pueblo Indians--Antiquities./ Hohokam culture./ Mogollon culture./ Southwest, New--Antiquities./ Archaeology.

979   J 970.3   Ph-1 5-6/8 $13.95   T   KF065
YUE, CHARLOTTE. Pueblo. By Charlotte and David Yue. Houghton Mifflin ISBN 0-395-38350-1, 1986. 117p. ill.
Includes bibliography and index.
Describes the structure of pueblo dwellings and the lifeways of the Indians who built and lived in them. Quality of text and drawing move this title above the average; other features of note are a list of further readings for students and a thorough bibliography which will be of value to teachers. Useful as an introduction to pueblo life or as a background for reports.
SUBJ: Pueblo Indians./ Indians of North America--Southwest, New.

979.1   E   Ph-2 P-3/3 $14.89   L   KF066
DUNPHY, MADELEINE. Here is the southwestern desert. Illus. by Anne Coe. Hyperion ISBN 0-7868-2038-1; In Canada: Little, Brown, 1995. unp. col. ill.
Includes directory.
A cumulative poem reveals Sonoran Desert wildlife from cactus to hawk, to lizard, ending with the hare. Lifelike acrylic paintings cover three-quarters of the doublespreads. Repetitive phrasing offers beginning readers meaningful science text. Excellent for reading aloud. For environmental studies.
SUBJ: Desert ecology--Sonoran Desert./ Sonoran Desert./ Ecology--Sonoran Desert.

979.1   Ph-3 4-6/7 $17.50   L   KF067
FILBIN, DAN. Arizona. Lerner ISBN 0-8225-2705-7, 1991. 72p. ill. (some col.). (Hello U.S.A.).
Includes glossary and index.
Fresh design, colorful photographs, fast facts, and timelines add up to an appealing "state" book. Recommended for special regional or curriculum interest.
SUBJ: Arizona.

979.1   Ph-2 3-5/6 $14.95   T   KF068
FRASER, MARY ANN. In search of the Grand Canyon. Henry Holt ISBN 0-8050-3495-1; In Canada: Fitzhenry & Whiteside, 1995. 70p. ill. (some col.), maps. (Redfeather book).
Includes bibliography and index.
Clearly written, dramatic account of John Wesley Powell's exploration of the Colorado River and the Grand Canyon in the 1860s. Illustrated with color photographs, graphics, maps, and status reports showing men, boats, and remaining supplies at various stages of the expedition. Use for regional studies, environmental units, and units on modern exploration and adventure.
SUBJ: Colorado River (Colo.-Mexico)--Discovery and exploration./ Grand Canyon (Ariz.)--Discovery and exploration./ Powell, John Wesley.

VCR 979.1   Ph-2 5-A $29.95   OD KF069
GRAND CANYON OF THE COLORADO (Videocassette). Kaw Valley Films & Video, 1983. 1/2" VHS videocassette color (18min).
Includes teacher's guide.
Includes public performance rights.
A visual exploration of the might and grandeur of the Grand Canyon includes a discussion of its formation and geology, differences in the North and South rim, a history of its exploration, scenes of rafting on the Colorado, and its present day National Park facilities. Contains primary source quotations from explorer John Wesley Powell and others. An excellent balance of historical and modern perspectives.
SUBJ: Grand Canyon National Park (Ariz.)./ National parks and reserves./ Colorado--Description and travel.

979.1   Ph-3 4-6/7 $26.60   L OD KF070
HEINRICHS, ANN. Arizona. Childrens Press ISBN 0-516-00449-2; In Canada: Childrens Press, 1991. 144p. col. ill. (America the beautiful).
Includes maps and index.
Available from the National Library Service for the Blind and Physically Handicapped on sound recording cassette RC34648.
Offers reliable, attractive coverage of geography, history, government, cultural and recreational features of the state. Closing sections include maps, state facts, chronology, and people profiles. Suggested as a regional acquisition.
SUBJ: Arizona.

VCR 979.1   Ph-3 A $39.95   OD KF071
LIVING ON THE EDGE (Videocassette). WNET/dist. by PBS Video ISBN 0-7936-0657-8, 1991. 1/2" VHS videocassette color (60min). (Land of the eagle).
Includes series study guide.
Focuses on the relationship of terrain, climate, and life in the Sonoran desert region of Arizona. Quality of photography is distinguished; script is politically correct from an environmentalist's point of view. Length and narrowness of approach mandate careful planning for effective use.
SUBJ: Arizona--History./ Indians of North America--Arizona.

979.1   J 574.9   Ph-2 3-5/7 $16.00   T   KF072
WRIGHT-FRIERSON, VIRGINIA. Desert scrapbook: dawn to dusk in the Sonoran Desert. Simon & Schuster ISBN 0-689-80678-7; In Canada: Distican, 1996. unp. col. ill.
Includes directory.
An artist shares her desert watercolors and drawings of the Sonoran Desert, revealing the beauty and struggle for survival in the dry heat. Use while studying deserts, particularly in California and Arizona. For environmental studies.
SUBJ: Sonoran Desert./ Desert animals./ Desert plants.

979.2   Ph-3 4-6/6 $17.50   L   KF073
SIRVAITIS, KAREN. Utah. Lerner ISBN 0-8225-2707-3, 1991. 72p. col. ill., map. (Hello U.S.A.).
Includes glossary, and index.
Fresh design, colorful photographs, fast facts, and a timeline add up to an appealing "state book." As suggested for other similar series, it is recommended that only titles of particular regional interest be purchased.
SUBJ: Utah.

979.3   Ph-3 4-6/9 $26.60   L OD KF074
LILLEGARD, DEE. Nevada. By Dee Lillegard and Wayne Stoker. Childrens Press ISBN 0-516-00474-3; In Canada: Childrens Press, 1990. 144p. col. ill. (America the beautiful).
Includes index.
Available from the National Library Services for the Blind and Physically Handicapped on sound recording cassette RC34636.
Covers geography, history, government, economy, and cultural/ recreational aspects of the state. Closing section includes maps, chronology, people profiles and state facts. Most effective purchasing pattern for this series is acquisition of regionally applicable titles.
SUBJ: Nevada.

979.4   Ph-3 4-6/9 $22.95   L OD KF075
ABBINK, EMILY. Missions of the Monterey Bay Area. Lerner ISBN 0-8225-1928-3, 1996. 80p. ill. (some col.), maps. (California missions).
Includes glossary, chronology and index.
Includes the missions of San Carlos Borromeo de Carmelo, San Juan Bautista, and Santa Cruz in an in-depth portrait describing life in Native American communities before the arrival of the Spaniards and the Franciscan mission builders, establishment and building of the missions, mission life and art, influence of the missions on regional Native Americans, and the missions in modern times. Illustrated with maps and extensively captioned photographs and graphics; contains many sidebars with focused information. Discussion of issues and presentation of conflicting interpretations of events will be useful in social studies units on California and Native American studies. For multicultural studies.
SUBJ: Missions--California./ California--History./ Costanoan Indians--Missions--California./ Indians of North America--Missions--California.

979.4   Ph-3 4-6/9 $22.95   L OD KF076
BEHRENS, JUNE. Missions of the central coast. Lerner ISBN 0-8225-1930-5, 1996. 80p. ill. (some col.), maps. (California missions).
Includes glossary, chronology and index.
Includes the missions of Santa Barbara, Santa Inez, and La Purisima Concepcion in an in-depth portrait describing life in Native American communities before the arrival of the Spaniards and the Franciscan mission builders, establishment and building of the missions, mission

life and art, influence of the missions on regional Native Americans, and the missions in modern times. Illustrated with maps and extensively captioned photographs and graphics; contains many sidebars with focused information. Discussion of issues and presentation of conflicting interpretations of events will be useful in social studies units on California and Native American studies. For multicultural studies.
SUBJ: Missions--California./ California--History./ Chumash Indians--Missions--California./ Indians of North America--Missions--California.

979.4   Ph-3 4-6/9 $22.95   L OD KF077
BROWER, PAULINE. Missions of the inland valleys. Lerner ISBN 0-8225-1929-1, 1997. 80p. col. ill., maps. (California missions).
Includes glossary, chronology and index.
Includes the missions of San Luis Obispo de Tolosa, San Miguel Arcangel, San Antonio de Padua, and Nuestra Senora de la Soledad in an in-depth portrait describing life in Native American communities before the arrival of the Spaniards and the Franciscan mission builders, establishment and building of the missions, mission life and art, influence of the missions on regional Native Americans, and the missions in modern times. Illustrated with maps and extensively captioned photographs and graphics; contains many sidebars with focused information. Discussion of issues and presentation of conflicting interpretations of events will be useful in social studies units on California and Native American studies. For multicultural studies.
SUBJ: Missions--California./ California--History./ Salinan Indians--Missions--California./ Chumash Indians--Missions--California./ Indians of North America--Missions--California.

PIC 979.4   Ph-3 5-6 $31.25   OD KF078
CALIFORNIA GOLD RUSH (Picture). Documentary Photo Aids 11G, n.d. 18 study prints (11"x14").
Authentic captioned photographs of the California gold rush of 1849, showing miners at work, Sutter's Mill, Marshall and Sutter, San Francisco Bay, mining equipment and other artifacts.
SUBJ: California--Gold discoveries./ Gold mines and mining--California--History--19th century.

MMK 979.4   Ph-2 5-A $37.00   OD KF079
CALIFORNIA GOLD RUSH: 1849 (Multimedia kit). Compiled by Andrew Bronin. Jackdaws Publications ISBN 0-305-62049-5; In Canada: Clarke, Irwin, 1991. 11 exhibits, 6 broadsheets. (Jackdaws).
Provides maps, broadsides, a menu, trail advice, and more from the gold rush days of the late 1840s in a collection of memorabilia valuable for exhibits, individual study, and reports. Curriculum implications are many and interdisciplinary in these materials which offer a glimpse of an earlier time.
SUBJ: California--Gold discoveries./ Gold mines and mining--California--History--19th century.

979.4   Ph-1 5-6/11 $16.95   L KF080
ITO, TOM. California gold rush. Lucent ISBN 1-56006-293-2, 1997. 112p. ill., maps. (World history series).
Includes chronology, bibliographies and index.
An in-depth, well-documented account of the California gold rush details personalities, the struggle to reach the goldfields, camp life, and mining operations. Archival illustrations, numerous primary source quotes, and sidebars add interest. An excellent resource for American history units and regional studies.
SUBJ: California--Gold discoveries./ Gold mines and mining--California--History--19th century.

979.4   Ph-2 4-6/6 $19.95   T KF081
KETCHUM, LIZA. Gold rush. With an introduction by Stephen Ives and Ken Brown. Little, Brown ISBN 0-316-59133-5; In Canada: Little, Brown, 1996. 118p. ill., map.
Includes bibliography and index.
A companion volume to the PBS television series, "The West," this contains lively first-person accounts of diverse aspects of the gold rush such as the effects on Native Americans and ranchers, perils of the journey to California either by sea or overland, difficulties and frustrations of life in the diggings, stories of the businessmen and women who made and lost fortunes supporting the miners, and daily lives of children and adults. Illustrated with photographs, engravings, and other archival information. Use for social studies units on the gold rush, westward expansion, and the immigrant experience.
SUBJ: California--Gold discoveries./ Gold mines and mining--California--History--19th century.

979.4   Ph-1 2-4/5 $14.00   T KF082
KRENSKY, STEPHEN. Striking it rich: the story of the California gold rush. Illus. by Anna DiVito. Simon & Schuster ISBN 0-689-80804-6; In Canada: Distican, 1996. 48p. col. ill., maps. (Ready-to-read).
A lively account of the rush to California for gold from 1848 to 1850

relates routes from the East, mining processes, and aspects of daily life in the gold fields. Illustrated with cheerful cartoons, this will appeal to independent readers looking for solid information, attractively presented. Use for social studies units on the gold rush and early California.
SUBJ: California--Gold discoveries./ California--History--1846-1850./ Gold mines and mining--History.

979.4   Ph-3 4-6/9 $22.95   L OD KF083
LEMKE, NANCY. Missions of the Southern Coast. Lerner ISBN 0-8225-1925-9, 1996. 80p. col. ill., maps. (California missions).
Includes glossary, chronology and index.
Presents the missions of San Diego de Alcala, San Luis Rey de Francia, and San Juan Capistrano in an in-depth portrait describing life in Native American communities before the arrival of the Spaniards and the Franciscan mission builders. Covers the establishment and building of the missions, mission life and art, influence of the missions on regional Native Americans, and the missions in modern times. Illustrated with maps and extensively captioned photographs and graphics; contains many sidebars with focused information. Discussion of issues and presentation of conflicting interpretations of events will be useful in social studies units on California and Native American studies. For multicultural studies.
SUBJ: Missions--California./ California--History./ Indians of North America--Missions--California.

979.4   Ph-3 4-6/9 $22.95   L OD KF084
MACMILLAN, DIANNE. Missions of the Los Angeles Area. Lerner ISBN 0-8225-1927-5, 1996. 80p. col. ill., maps. (California missions).
Includes glossary, chronology and index.
Presents the missions of San Gabriel Arcangel, San Fernando Rey de Espana, and San Buenaventura in an in-depth portrait describing life in Native American communities before the arrival of the Spaniards and the Franciscan mission builders. Covers the establishment and building of the missions, mission life and art, influence of the missions on regional Native Americans, and the missions in modern times. Illustrated with maps and extensively captioned photographs and graphics; contains many sidebars with focused information. Discussion of issues and presentation of conflicting interpretations of events will be useful in social studies units on California and Native American studies. For multicultural studies.
SUBJ: Missions--California./ California--History./ Chumash Indians--Missions--California./ Gabrielino Indians--Missions--California./ Indians of North America--Missions--California.

979.4   Ph-3 4-6/7 $17.50   L KF085
PELTA, KATHY. California. Lerner ISBN 0-8225-2738-3, 1994. 72p. col. ill., maps. (Hello U.S.A.).
Includes chronology, glossary and index.
Fresh design, color photographs, fast facts, and timeline add up to an appealing state book. Recommended for regional purchase.
SUBJ: California.

VCR 979.4   Ph-3 A $59.95   OD KF086
SEARCHING FOR PARADISE (Videocassette). WNET/dist. by PBS Video ISBN 0-7936-0659-4, 1991. 1/2" VHS videocassette color (60min). (Land of the eagle).
Includes series study guide.
Mixes distinguished photography and a nature-centered script to demonstrate how the discovery and settlement of California are a microcosm of the story of the entire continent. Strong production values are characteristic of the series of which this video is a part. Length mandates preview and pre-class decisions about best patterns of use.
SUBJ: California--History./ Indians of North America--California--History.

979.4   Ph-3 4-6/9 $22.95   L OD KF087
WHITE, TEKLA N. Missions of the San Francisco Bay Area. Lerner ISBN 0-8225-1926-7, 1996. 80p. col. ill., maps. (California missions).
Includes glossary, chronology and index.
Presents the missions of Santa Clara de Asis, San Jose de Guadalupe, San Francisco de Asis, San Rafael Arcangel, and San Francisco Solano in an in-depth portrait describing life in Native American communities before the arrival of the Spaniards and the Franciscan mission builders. Covers the establishment and building of the missions, mission life and art, influence of the missions on regional Native Americans, and the missions in modern times. Illustrated with maps and extensively captioned photographs and graphics; contains many sidebars with focused information. Discussion of issues and presentation of conflicting interpretations of events will be useful in social studies units on California and Native American studies. For multicultural studies.
SUBJ: Missions--California./ California--History./ Costanoan Indians--

Missions--California./ Miwok Indians--Missions--California./ Indians of North America--Missions--California.

979.4 Ph-3 4-6/7 $15.90 L KF088
WILLS, CHARLES A. Historical album of California. Millbrook ISBN 1-56294-479-7, 1994. 64p. ill. (some col.), maps. (Historical albums).
Includes chronologies, bibliography, directory and index.
Supplies an overview of the history of the state whose motto is "Eureka." Back matter includes addresses for sources of additional information, fast facts, timelines, and personalities. Recommended for regional purchase.
SUBJ: California--History.

979.5 Ph-3 4-6/4 $24.00 L OD KF089
FRADIN, DENNIS B. Oregon. By Dennis Brindell Fradin and Judith Bloom Fradin. Childrens Press ISBN 0-516-03837-0; In Canada: Childrens Press, 1995. 64p. col. ill., maps. (From sea to shining sea).
Includes chronology, glossary and index.
Introduces the people, history, cities, and geography of Oregon. Famous people section highlights figures in politics, sports, and the arts. Recommended for regional acquisition.
SUBJ: Oregon.

979.5 Ph-3 4-6/7 $16.40 L KF090
WILLS, CHARLES A. Historical album of Oregon. Millbrook ISBN 1-56294-594-7, 1995. 64p. ill. (some col.), maps. (Historical albums).
Includes chronologies, bibliography, directory and index.
Richly detailed historical perspective of Oregon begins with prehistoric times and includes early exploration and settlement, early statehood, and current issues. Illustrations include paintings, photographs, and primary source materials. Gazetteer contains quick facts, key events, and personalities. Useful for regional reports and studies of the American West.
SUBJ: Oregon--History.

979.6 Ph-3 4-6/9 $26.60 L OD KF091
KENT, ZACHARY. Idaho. Childrens Press ISBN 0-516-00458-1; In Canada: Childrens Press, 1990. 144p. col. ill. (America the beautiful).
Includes index.
Available from the National Library Service for the Blind and Physically Handicapped on sound recording cassette RS34643.
Covers geography, history, government, economy, and cultural/recreational aspects of the state. Closing section includes maps, chronology, people profiles and state facts. Most effective purchasing pattern for this series is acquisition of regionally applicable titles.
SUBJ: Idaho.

979.7 Ph-3 4-6/7 $15.90 L KF092
COCKE, WILLIAM. Historical album of Washington. Millbrook ISBN 1-56294-508-4, 1995. 64p. ill. (some col.), maps. (Historical albums).
Includes chronologies, bibliography, directory and index.
Offers an overview of the history of the state whose flag and seal feature a likeness of George Washington. Back matter supplies addresses for sources of further information and offers a section with timelines, personalities, and fast facts. Recommended for regional purchase.
SUBJ: Washington (State)--History.

979.7 Ph-3 4-6/4 $24.00 L OD KF093
FRADIN, DENNIS B. Washington. By Dennis Brindell Fradin and Judith Bloom Fradin. Childrens Press ISBN 0-516-03847-8; In Canada: Childrens Press, 1994. 64p. col. ill., maps. (From sea to shining sea).
Includes chronology, glossary and index.
Introduces the people, cities, history, and geography of Washington. Closing section provides fast facts, trivia, and an introduction to famous Washingtonians. For regional collections.
SUBJ: Washington (State).

979.7 Ph-3 4-6/6 $17.50 L KF094
POWELL, E. SANDY. Washington. Lerner ISBN 0-8225-2726-X, 1993. 72p. col. ill., maps. (Hello U.S.A.).
Includes glossary and index.
Lively design, colorful photographs, fast facts, and horizontal format add up to an appealing state book. Recommended for regional collections.
SUBJ: Washington (State).

VCR 979.8 Ph-3 A $59.95 OD KF095
FIRST AND LAST FRONTIER (Videocassette). WNET/dist. by PBS Video ISBN 0-7936-0658-6, 1991. 1/2" VHS videocassette color (60min).
(Land of the eagle).
Includes series study guide.
Examines the natural and human histories of Alaska with emphasis on mammals such as walrus, whale, otter, and fur seal. Strong

production values are a feature of the series of which this video is a part. Length requires careful planning for effective use.
SUBJ: Alaska--History./ Indians of North America--Alaska--History.

979.8 Ph-3 4-6/7 $26.60 L KF096
HEINRICHS, ANN. Alaska. Childrens Press ISBN 0-516-00448-4; In Canada: Childrens Press, 1990. 144p. col. ill., maps. (America the beautiful).
Includes chronology and index.
Available from the National Library Service for the Blind and Physically Handicapped on sound recording cassette RC 34649.
Contains reliable, attractive coverage of geography, history, government, cultural and recreational features of the state. Final sections include maps, state facts, chronology, and people profiles. Suggested as a regional purchase.
SUBJ: Alaska.

979.8 Ph-1 3-6/6 $15.95 L KF097
HOYT-GOLDSMITH, DIANE. Arctic hunter. Photos by Lawrence Migdale. Holiday House ISBN 0-8234-0972-4, 1992. 32p. col. ill.
Includes glossary and index.
Selectors' Choice, 19th ed.
Tells of a ten-year-old Inupiat boy living in Alaska north of the Arctic Circle. Appealing color photographs and well-written text impart a strong sense of the mesh of traditional and modern ways present in the everyday life of the children of the Inupiat. Use with other books by the same author in a "how we live today" activity.
SUBJ: Eskimos./ Indians of North America./ Eskimos--Alaska--Social life and customs.

979.8 Ph-1 5-6/7 $13.95 T KF098
JENNESS, AYLETTE. In two worlds: a Yup'ik Eskimo family. By Aylette Jenness and Alice Rivers. Photos by Aylette Jenness. Houghton Mifflin ISBN 0-395-42797-5, 1989. 84p. ill.
Includes bibliography and index.
Describes and documents Yup'ik Eskimo life in a small Alaskan community on the coast of the Bering Sea. A narrative text and captionless black-and-white photographs contrast today's world with that of earlier times; a briefly annotated bibliography and a listing of periodicals about Arctic peoples are added pluses. Despite the incorrect order of the two paragraphs on p.54, this is a strong curriculum item and an interesting awareness expander.
SUBJ: Indians of North America./ Eskimos--Alaska--Social life and customs.

979.8 Ph-3 4-6/7 $17.50 L KF099
JOHNSTON, JOYCE. Alaska. Lerner ISBN 0-8225-2735-9, 1994. 72p. col. ill., maps. (Hello U.S.A.).
Includes glossary and index.
Fast facts, color photographs, lively design, and minor mention of the famous and somewhat prominent add up to an appealing state book. Recommended if regionally appropriate.
SUBJ: Alaska.

979.8 Ph-2 3-6/6 $13.95 L KF100
KENDALL, RUSS. Eskimo boy: life in an Inupiaq Eskimo village. Written and photos. by Russ Kendall. Scholastic ISBN 0-590-43695-3; In Canada: Scholastic, 1992. 40p. col. ill.
Includes glossary.
Depicts a seven-year-old child living on an island off the northwest coast of Alaska. Color photographs show daily routine in a culture which combines old and new. Good social studies support for multicultural units.
SUBJ: Eskimos--Alaska./ Indians of North America--Alaska.

979.8 Ph-2 3-5/8 $15.95 T KF101
MURPHY, CLAIRE RUDOLF. Child's Alaska. Photos by Charles Mason. Alaska Northwest ISBN 0-88240-457-1, 1994. 48p. col. ill., map.
Includes glossary.
Offers intriguing insight into Alaskan life as text and color photographs combine to portray a yearlong cycle of activity in the 49th state. Nature, climate, and recreation receive attention. Use as a cornerstone for study of Alaska.
SUBJ: Alaska.

979.8 Ph-2 4-6/7 $19.90 L KF102
NEWMAN, SHIRLEE PETKIN. Inuits. By Shirlee P. Newman. Watts ISBN 0-531-20073-6, 1993. 64p. col. ill., map. (First book).
Includes glossary, bibliography and index.
"Provides a look at the history, culture, and daily life of the Inuit people who live in the Arctic regions of the world..." (CIP) Final chapter discusses modern Inuit life. Support for social studies and multicultural studies.
SUBJ: Eskimos./ Indians of North America.

980.3   Ph-2 5-6/7 $17.71   L   KF103
NEWMAN, SHIRLEE PETKIN. Incas. Watts ISBN 0-531-20004-3; In Canada: Watts, 1992. 61p. col. ill. (First book).
> Includes glossary, bibliography and index.
> Describes the history and civilization of the Inca empire and discusses the Andean people of today. Writing style is expository; color illustrations bolster the text. Useful for reports and related social studies units.
> SUBJ: Incas./ Indians of South America.

981   Ph-2 3-6/7 $16.95   T   KF104
REYNOLDS, JAN. Amazon Basin: vanishing cultures. Harcourt Brace ISBN 0-15-202831-5; In Canada: Harcourt Brace c/o Canadian Manda, 1993. unp. col. ill., map. (Vanishing cultures).
> Captures the rainforest world of the Yanomama, indigenous people of the Amazon territory of Venezuela. Distinguished color photographs carry the slight storyline. Valuable background builder. For multicultural studies.
> SUBJ: Yanomamo Indians./ Indians of South America./ Amazon River Region--Social life and customs.

981   Ph-2 4-6/7 $15.93   L   KF105
SCHWARTZ, DAVID M. Yanomami: people of the Amazon. Photos by Victor Englebert. Lothrop, Lee & Shepard ISBN 0-688-11158-0, 1995. 48p. col. ill., map. (Vanishing peoples).
> Includes directory.
> Examines the primitive Yanomami living deep in the rain forests in the border region of Venezuela and Brazil. An afterword offers suggestions of ways to help preserve the rain forest and the Yanomami. Useful as supplement material in environmental studies and social studies.
> SUBJ: Yanomamo Indians./ Indians of South America--Amazon River Region.

982   Ph-2 3-6/6 $14.95   T   KF106
BRUSCA, MARIA CRISTINA. On the pampas. Henry Holt ISBN 0-8050-1548-5; In Canada: Fitzhenry & Whiteside, 1991. unp col illus.
> An engaging reminiscence of a summer spent on an estancia on the pampas of Argentina. Endpapers provide definitions and pronunciation of 16 items basic to ranch life. Pleasing to browsers and those interested in comparative activities related to rural life.
> SUBJ: Pampas (Argentina)--Description and travel./ Argentina--Social life and customs./ Gauchos./ Ranch life--Argentina.

982   Ph-3 5-6/8 $14.95   L   KF107
PETERSON, MARGE. Argentina: a wild west heritage. New ed. By Marge and Rob Peterson. Dillon ISBN 0-382-39287-6, 1997. 127p. col. ill. (Discovering our heritage).
> Includes appendix, glossary, bibliography and index.
> Describes geography, history, holidays and educational system of Argentina. Fact pages, a list of consulates in North America, and a glossary are features of this "country book." Useful in units emphasizing South America and for report writers.
> SUBJ: Argentina.

984   Ph-3 4-6/10 $19.95   L   KF108
HERMES, JULES. Children of Bolivia. Carolrhoda ISBN 0-87614-935-2, 1996. 48p. col. ill., map. (World's children).
> Includes index.
> Bolivian children and their families introduce readers to the daily life, celebrations, and cultures of several distinct regions of the country. Vibrant photographs illustrate text and feature appealing scenes of people, places, and activities. Useful for multicultural studies and social studies units on South America.
> SUBJ: Bolivia--Social life and customs./ Family life--Bolivia.

985   Ph-2 A/8 $14.95   L   KF109
MARRIN, ALBERT. Inca and Spaniard: Pizarro and the conquest of Peru. Atheneum ISBN 0-689-31481-7; In Canada: Collier Macmillan, 1989. 211p. ill.
> Includes bibliography and index.
> The Sapa Inca was an absolute ruler of his people and a wealthy one whose treasures enticed Pizarro, de Soto, and an army of conquistadors. This vivid and at times gory description of Incan culture and the tragic events of Pizarro's conquest of the Incan Empire in the early 1500s is enhanced by historic black and white drawings, etchings and maps. The density of the text requires a mature, skilled reader.
> SUBJ: Peru--History--Conquest, 1522-1548./ Incas./ Indians of South America./ Pizarro, Francisco.

985   Ph-2 4-6/6 $14.95   L   KF110
PITKANEN, MATTI A. Grandchildren of the Incas. By Matti A. Pitkanen with Ritva Lehtinen and Kari E. Nurmi. Carolrhoda ISBN 0-87614-397-4, 1991. 40p. col. ill., map. (World's children).
> Includes index.
> Tells of the life of the Quecha Indians of Peru, descendants of the ancient Incas. Color photographs of memorable quality and strong graphic design lift this "country book" well above the average. Useful in curriculum units and as a provider of sense of place.
> SUBJ: Incas./ Quechua Indians./ Indians of South America--Peru.

986.1   Ph-3 4-6/7 $17.95   L OD KF111
MARKHAM, LOIS. Colombia: the gateway to South America. Benchmark Books/Marshall Cavendish ISBN 0-7614-0140-7, 1997. 64p. col. ill., maps. (Exploring cultures of the world).
> Includes glossary, bibliography and index.
> Traces the history and culture of Columbia and discusses modern life in cities and countrysides, family relationships and traditions, holidays, recreation, education, and art. Color photographs illustrate the text. Although there is little emphasis on current politics, this will be useful for regional social studies reports.
> SUBJ: Colombia.

986.6   Ph-3 3-6/9 $19.95   L   KF112
BEIRNE, BARBARA. Children of the Ecuadorean Highlands. Carolrhoda ISBN 1-57505-000-5, 1996. 48p. col. ill., map. (World's children).
> Includes index.
> Life in various parts of Equador is seen through the daily activities of children who live there. Extensively captioned full-color photographs provide additional information. Use for regional studies and multicultural units.
> SUBJ: Ecuador--Social life and customs./ Family life--Ecuador.

986.6   Ph-1 4-A/8 $16.89   L   KF113
MYERS, LYNNE BORN. Galapagos: islands of change. By Lynne Born Myers and Christopher A. Myers. Photos by Nathan Farb. Hyperion ISBN 0-7868-2061-6; In Canada: Little, Brown, 1995. 48p. col. ill., maps.
> Includes glossary.
> Selectors' Choice, 21st ed.
> Wonders of the Galapagos are revealed in text and lush photographs as readers explore the islands' volcanic history from eruptions to recently discovered seamounts. Any Galapagos story must include Darwin and the process of natural selection; this is carefully explained along with adaptive radiation (conditions under which animals evolve into many new species). The documented evolution is amazing, but changes are never complete. Today, the Nazca tectonic plate continues to travel, islands move apart from the volcanic hot spot, and calderas are formed where new life speeds into craggy nooks and crannies. Use with geology, evolution, animal, and environmental studies.
> SUBJ: Natural history--Galapagos Islands./ Galapagos Islands.

VCR 994   Ph-3 4-A $99.00   OD KF114
AUSTRALIA (Videocassette). National Geographic 51444, 1991. 1/2" VHS videocassette color (25min). (Physical geography of the continents).
> Includes Teacher's Guide.
> Examines the range of climate and life forms of the smallest continent and presents rural and urban settings. Production quality is strong. Recommended as budget and need allow.
> SUBJ: Physical geography--Australia./ Australia--Geography.

994   Ph-2 K-4/6 $14.93   L   KF115
BAKER, JEANNIE. Story of rosy dock. Greenwillow ISBN 0-688-11493-8, 1995. unp. col. ill.
> Baker's collages enliven the often barren, searing Australian desert, illustrating the effects of torrential flooding and the invasive spreading of a non-native plant. Use in ecology and habitat studies to illustrate the consequences of haphazard environmental tampering.
> SUBJ: Natural history--Australia./ Plant introduction--Australia./ Man--Influence on nature.

994.06   Ph-3 3-6/7 $14.85   L   KF116
COBB, VICKI. This place is lonely. Illus. by Barbara Lavallee. Walker ISBN 0-8027-6960-8; In Canada: Thomas Allen, 1991. unp. col. ill. (Imagine living here).
> Native plants and animals and the isolation of the outback are portrayed in this colorful presentation. Too narrow in scope to adequately cover Australia, its graphic excellence provides a strong sense of place for portions of the country nonetheless. Use in conjunction with other resources.
> SUBJ: Australia--Description and travel.

994   Ph-2 3-6/6 $16.95   L   KF117
REYNOLDS, JAN. Down under: vanishing cultures. Harcourt Brace ISBN 0-15-224182-5, 1992. unp. col. ill. (Vanishing cultures).
> Includes map on inside covers.

Follows young Amprenula and her family on walkabout on Bathurst Island just off Northern Territory of Australia. Color photographs by the author expand the carefully written text which describes an ancient, rapidly disappearing culture. Valuable in building awareness of varying lifeways.
SUBJ: Tiwi (Australian people)./ Australian aborigines.

994   Ph-2 5-6/3 $14.95   T   KF118
WHEATLEY, NADIA. My place. By Nadia Wheatley and Donna Rawlins. Kane/Miller ISBN 0-916291-42-1, 1992. unp. col. ill., maps.
Includes glossary.
Twenty-one two-paged spreads trace the social history of a single plot of Australian land decade by decade from 1988 back to 1788 using maps and first-person comments from children living there. Works well as a foundation for creative writing activities or for a charting project about changes in students' communities.
SUBJ: Australia--Social life and customs.

994.3   Ph-3 3-6/5 $15.95   L OD KF119
GOUCK, MAURA. Great Barrier Reef. Child's World ISBN 1-56766-008-8, 1993. 32p. col. ill. (Vision book).
Includes index.
Brilliantly colored photographs introduce the unique life forms of the Great Barrier Reef. Half pages of text provide brief factual information about the fascinating creatures. Use for environmental studies when introducing biomes.
SUBJ: Great Barrier Reef (Qld.)./ Coral reef animals--Australia--Great Barrier Reef (Qld.).

994.3   Ph-3 3-6/5 $14.95   L   KF120
MCGOVERN, ANN. Down under, down under: diving adventures on the Great Barrier Reef. Photos by Jim and Martin Scheiner and the author. Macmillan ISBN 0-02-765770-1; In Canada: Collier Macmillan, 1989. 48p. col. ill.
Includes "Getting ready for a dive" and index.
Plunge into the waters surrounding the Great Barrier Reef with a 12-year-old certified diver. Lovely color photos of fantastic creatures yield a stunning arm chair adventure. Use with units on Australia and oceanography. Even reluctant students will enjoy this. Read aloud to lower grades.
SUBJ: Great Barrier Reef (Qld.)./ Coral reef animals--Australia--Great Barrier Reef (Qld.)./ Scuba diving./ Underwater exploration.

996   Ph-1 P-6 $12.95   T   KF121
FEENEY, STEPHANIE. Hawaii is a rainbow. Photos by Jeff Reese. University of Hawaii Press ISBN 0-8248-1007-4, 1985. unp. col. ill. (Kolowalu book).
Selectors' Choice, 16th ed.
Combines rainbow colors with unusually fine photography to introduce preschoolers to colors and to Hawaiian people and life. Arrangement is that of a wordless picture book followed by a note to adults; text on history, plants, animals, and people of the islands; and a section which gives information on items depicted in the portion of the book designed for early childhood use. Can be used creatively in language development or social studies activities at many grade levels.
SUBJ: Hawaii.

996.5   Ph-3 4-6/9 $19.95   L   KF122
HERMES, JULES. Children of Micronesia. Carolrhoda ISBN 0-87614-819-4, 1994. 48p. col. ill., map. (World's children).
Includes glossary and index.
Combines colorful photographs of the children of a variety of Micronesian islands with a text which describes aspects of their daily lives. Provides a strong sense of place while serving as a browser and curriculum-extender. Useful social studies support. For multicultural studies.
SUBJ: Micronesia--Social life and customs./ Family life--Micronesia.

996.9   Ph-3 5-A/6 $39.96   L OD KF123
RAYSON, ANN. Hawai'i: the Pacific State. Rev. and updated edition. By Ann Rayson and Helen Bauer. Bess Press ISBN 1-57306-062-3, 1997. 120p. col. ill., maps.
Revised edition of HAWAI'I: THE ALOHA STATE.
Includes index.
A comprehensive study of Hawaii, covering geology, early history, overthrow of the monarchy by the United States, annexation, and statehood. Photographs of various sites and personalities illustrate the text. Advanced readers looking for in-depth information and current statistics will find this a useful resource for regional studies.
SUBJ: Hawaii./ Physical geography--Hawaii.

VCR 998   Ph-3 4-A $99.00   OD KF124
ANTARCTICA (Videocassette). National Geographic 51443, 1991. 1/2" VHS videocassette color (25min). (Physical geography of the continents).
Includes Teacher's Guide.
Offers a look at the world's "driest, coldest, windiest, and iciest continent" and is designed to increase the viewer's understanding of the climate, landscape, and adaptation of plants and animals to extremes. Production quality is good. Recommended as budget allows.
SUBJ: Physical geography--Antarctica./ Antarctica--Geography.

998   Ph-2 2-6/4 $15.95   T   KF125
EKOOMIAK, NORMEE. Arctic memories. Henry Holt ISBN 0-8050-1254-0; In Canada: NC Press, c1988, 1990. unp. col. ill.
Inuit artist Normee Ekoomiak uses felt applique techniques and acrylic paintings to capture the now vanished life of his Eskimo childhood in arctic Quebec. This pleasing picture book is accompanied by bilingual text in Inuktitut and English.
SUBJ: Eskimos./ Eskimo language materials--Bilingual./ Bilingual materials--Eskimo.

EASY

Ph-2 K-2/2 $13.88   L   KF126
ABOLAFIA, YOSSI. Fox tale. Greenwillow ISBN 0-688-09542-9, 1991.
unp. col. ill.
Fox promises his bushy tail to Bear in exchange for a jar of honey.
When Bear learns from the other animals Fox has cheated, they join
forces to outsmart him. A humorous and satisfying story appropriate
for story time.
SUBJ: Foxes--Fiction./ Animals--Fiction./ Swindlers and swindling--
Fiction.

Ph-3 P-1/2 $14.95   L   KF127
ACCORSI, WILLIAM. Friendship's first Thanksgiving. Holiday House ISBN
0-8234-0963-5, 1992. unp. col. ill.
The story of the Mayflower's arrival and the New Plymouth Colony
including the first Thanksgiving are told by Friendship a small terrier,
who arrived with the Pilgrims. An introduction to the Thanksgiving
story for young children.
SUBJ: Pilgrims (New Plymouth Colony)--Fiction./ Thanksgiving Day--
Fiction./ Dogs--Fiction.

Ph-2 2-4/5 $14.95   T   KF128
ACKERMAN, KAREN. Bingleman's Midway. Illus. by Barry Moser. Boyds
Mills ISBN 1-56397-366-9; In Canada: McClelland & Stewart, 1995.
unp. col. ill.
Captured by the midway magic, young Drew runs away to join
Bingleman's carnival. When Bingleman brings him home in the middle
of the night, his father is not surprised. Masterful watercolor
illustrations, including two wordless doublespreads showing the
carnival's unusual cast of characters, draw the viewer into the story
and the midway's spell.
SUBJ: Carnivals--Fiction./ Fathers and sons--Fiction.

Ph-2 K-2/5 $14.95   L   KF129
ACKERMAN, KAREN. By the dawn's early light. Illus. by Catherine
Stock. Atheneum ISBN 0-689-31788-3; In Canada: Maxwell Macmillan,
1994. unp. col. ill.
Spanish version available AL AMANECER (ISBN 0-689-31917-7,
1994).
Available from the National Library Service for the Blind and
Physically Handicapped on sound recording cassette RC 43023.
While Mom works the graveyard shift at the factory, Nana and the
children have dinner, do homework, and get ready for bed. The
children cherish the early morning hour when Mom returns home and
has time for breakfast and a snuggle. The warm family story includes
references to difficulties, but shows an African-American family that
finds time to be together, nevertheless. For multicultural studies.
SUBJ: Single-parent family--Fiction./ Mothers--Employment--Fiction./
Grandmothers--Fiction./ Afro-Americans--Fiction.

Ph-3 K-2/6 $5.99   P   KF130
ACKERMAN, KAREN. Song and dance man. Illus. by Stephen Gammell.
Knopf ISBN 0-679-81995-9, 1988. unp. col. ill.
Caldecott Medal.
Grandpa is an ex-vaudevillian who treasures the visits of his three
grandchildren as his chance to take them to the attic, don his tap
shoes, his top hat and cane and recreate the often corny routines of
his youth. The shared affection is beautifully depicted as Grandpa
takes center stage before the least critical and most loving of

audiences.
SUBJ: Entertainers--Fiction./ Grandfathers--Fiction.

Ph-2 1-3/4 $15.00   L   KF131
ADA, ALMA FLOR. Gold coin. Translated from the Spanish by Bernice
Randall. Illus. by Neil Waldman. Atheneum ISBN 0-689-31633-X; In
Canada: Collier Macmillan, 1991. unp. col. ill.
Spanish version available from Lectorum LA MONEDA DE ORO
(ISBN 84-241-3338-2, n.d.).
In pursuit of an old woman and her treasure, Juan, a thief, is
transformed by the human generosity he encounters. A quiet story
about the triumph of goodness illustrated with stylized watercolor
illustrations.
SUBJ: Stealing--Fiction./ Conduct of life--Fiction./ Spanish language
materials.

Ph-1 1-2/2 $11.99   T   KF132
ADLER, DAVID A. Young Cam Jansen and the dinosaur game. Illus. by
Susanna Natti. Viking ISBN 0-670-86399-8; In Canada: Penguin, 1996.
32p. col. ill. (Viking easy-to-read).
Cam's uncanny ability to remember small details and her powers of
deduction help her detect deception at a birthday party. Readers
developing independent skills will enjoy unravelling the mystery of this
transitional reader.
SUBJ: Mystery and detective stories./ Parties--Fiction./ Birthdays--
Fiction.

Ph-2 1-2/2 $11.99   T   KF133
ADLER, DAVID A. Young Cam Jansen and the lost tooth. Illus. by
Susanna Natti. Viking ISBN 0-670-87354-3; In Canada: Penguin, 1997.
32p. col. ill. (Viking easy-to-read).
Cam uses her photographic memory and powers of deduction to help
find a classmate's lost tooth. The young Cam Jansen will attract
beginning readers to the popular series and mystery genre.
SUBJ: Teeth--Fiction./ Schools--Fiction./ Mystery and detective stories.

Ph-1 1-2/2 $11.99   T   KF134
ADLER, DAVID A. Young Cam Jansen and the missing cookie. Illus. by
Susanna Natti. Viking ISBN 0-670-86772-1; In Canada: Penguin, 1996.
32p. col. ill. (Viking easy-to-read).
Cam uses her photographic memory and powers of deduction to solve
the mystery of who took Jason's cookie from his lunch box. The mild
suspense in this transitional reader encourages youngsters to read
with comprehension.
SUBJ: Mystery and detective stories./ Cookies--Fiction.

Ph-2 P-2 $15.95   T   KF135
ADLERMAN, DANIEL. Africa calling, nighttime falling. Illus. by Kimberley
M. Adlerman. Whispering Coyote ISBN 1-879085-98-4, 1996. unp. col.
ill.
African animals and landscapes rendered in three-dimensional, mixed-
media collages stand out from framed illustrations. Doublespreads and
poetic rhyming text focus on one animal at a time as nighttime
approaches. Finally, a young child is shown in bed surrounded by toy
animals.
SUBJ: Animals--Fiction./ Africa--Fiction./ Imagination--Fiction./ Stories
in rhyme.

Ph-1 P-3/3 $15.00 T KF136

ADOFF, ARNOLD. Black is brown is tan. Illus. by Emily Arnold McCully. HarperCollins ISBN 0-06-020083-9, 1973. 32p. col. ill.

Poetic text and appealing illustrations picture the daily activities of an interracial family as they work, play, sing, scold and tease. The strong overall feelings are of joy, warmth, harmony, love, affection and respect for individual differences.
SUBJ: Color of man--Fiction./ Marriage, Mixed--Fiction./ Family--Fiction./ Stories in rhyme.

Ph-2 K-2/3 $7.95 T KF137

AGELL, CHARLOTTE. I slide into the white of winter. Tilbury House ISBN 0-88448-115-8, 1994. unp. col. ill. (I love the seasons).

A child describes a day in the snow, noticing colors, the sound of crows, and breath steaming like dragons in the cold air. The free-form illustrations carefully match and enhance the child's perspective offered in the text. The small format of the book will have big appeal for young children.
SUBJ: Snow--Fiction./ Winter--Fiction./ Family life--Fiction.

Ph-2 K-2/2 $7.95 T KF138

AGELL, CHARLOTTE. I wear long green hair in the summer. Tilbury House ISBN 0-88448-113-1, 1994. unp. col. ill. (I love the seasons).

An outing with Papa, so Mama and the baby can rest, turns into frolicking fun at the beach--splashing in waves, shooing seagulls, sculpting sand, and wearing seaweed tresses. Illustrations depict a warm, father-daughter relationship. Small format makes it most suitable for one-on-one sharing.
SUBJ: Beaches--Fiction./ Summer--Fiction./ Fathers and daughters--Fiction.

Ph-2 K-2/2 $7.95 T KF139

AGELL, CHARLOTTE. Mud makes me dance in the spring. Tilbury House ISBN 0-88448-112-3, 1994. unp. col. ill. (I love the seasons).

A young girl spends a spring day outdoors with her family. As she plays in the mud, harvests dandelion, and plants seeds, her baby brother "chirps" with the birds. Illustrations convey the exuberance of the season. Small format will be appreciated by young picture book readers.
SUBJ: Spring--Fiction./ Family life--Fiction./ Imagination--Fiction.

Ph-2 K-2/3 $7.95 T KF140

AGELL, CHARLOTTE. Wind spins me around in the fall. Tilbury House ISBN 0-88448-114-X, 1994. unp. col. ill. (I love the seasons).

Falling leaves, feeding the birds, and choosing a pumpkin for a jack-o-lantern are a few of the characteristic childhood experiences of the season featured in the story and free-form illustrations. The tiny format of the book will fit nicely in small hands, adding to its child appeal.
SUBJ: Autumn--Fiction./ Family life--Fiction.

CE

Ph-2 P-1/3 $3.99 P KF141

AHLBERG, JANET. Each peach pear plum: an "I spy" story. Written and illustrated by Janet and Allan Ahlberg. Penguin ISBN 0-14-050639-X, 1978. unp. col. ill.

Kate Greenaway Medal.
Videocassette available from Weston Woods FOV280V, 1992. 1/2" VHS videocassette color (5min), $39.00.
Brief rhymes and detailed watercolor illustrations create a game of "I spy" in which familiar nursery and storybook characters are hidden within the pictures. Best used on an individual or one to one basis since the hidden characters are almost invisible in some of the pictures.
SUBJ: Stories in rhyme.

Ph-2 P-3/2 $13.93 L KF142

AHLBERG, JANET. Funnybones. Written and illustrated by Janet and Allan Ahlberg. Greenwillow ISBN 0-688-84238-0, c1980, 1981. unp. col. ill.

In a dark, dark cellar of a dark, dark house on a dark, dark street in a dark, dark town live a big skeleton, a little skeleton and a dog skeleton. One night the three skeletons decide to take a walk through the dark, dark, town and frighten somebody. Brightly colored illustrations combine with the rhythmic text to make this perfect for sharing with a group.
SUBJ: Skeleton--Fiction.

Ph-2 K-2/3 $13.95 L KF143

ALBERT, BURTON. Where does the trail lead? Illus. by Brian Pinkney. Simon & Schuster ISBN 0-671-73409-1; In Canada: Simon & Schuster, 1991. 32p. col. ill.

A young African-American boy follows the trail on Summertime Island as it meanders near the edge of the sea and across sandy dunes to a family picnic and campfire at the beach. Scratchboard illustrations provide a suitable accompaniment to the lyrical description of the beach trail. For multicultural studies.
SUBJ: Seashore--Fiction./ Afro-Americans--Fiction.

Ph-2 1-3/6 $13.95 T KF144

ALBERT, RICHARD E. Alejandro's gift. Illus. by Sylvia Long. Chronicle ISBN 0-8118-0436-4; In Canada: Raincoast, 1994. unp. col. ill.

Includes glossary.
Surrounded by the desert and desert wildlife, Alejandro decides to build a water hole for the animals, but he builds the first one too close to his house, and the animals won't come. The second water hole is sheltered and further from his house, and the desert animals enjoy the gift. Lovely illustrations depict the desert habitat and wildlife. Glossary provides a key to the animals pictured in the story. Use to introduce the desert habitat in environmental studies units.
SUBJ: Desert animals--Fiction.

Ph-2 P-1/2 $15.95 T KF145

ALBOROUGH, JEZ. Where's my teddy? Candlewick ISBN 1-56402-048-7; In Canada: Candlewick/dist. by Douglas & McIntyre, 1992. unp. col. ill.

Spanish version available DONDE ESTA MI OSITO from Santillana (ISBN 1-56014-582-X, 1995).
Eddie has lost his teddy in the big, dark woods, but what he finds is a giant teddy bear too large to cuddle and fit in his bed. When a bear stomps through the woods upset because his teddy has shrunk, it becomes apparent that there's a switch. The oversized format, rhyming text, and slight suspense are ideal for story hours.
SUBJ: Teddy bears--Fiction./ Bears--Fiction./ Stories in rhyme./ Spanish language materials.

Ph-1 K-2/2 $18.00 T KF146

ALEXANDER, MARTHA. How my library grew by Dinah. Wilson ISBN 0-8242-0679-7, 1983. unp. col. ill.

A young girl is watching with excitement the progress of construction of a library across the street from her home. On opening day she presents a book she's made tracing the building of the library and finally gets the answers to her questions about real moles and real rainbows. Delightful to use for young children's first visit to a library.
SUBJ: Libraries--Fiction.

Ph-2 K-2/2 $12.95 T KF147

ALEXANDER, MARTHA. You're a genius, Blackboard Bear. Candlewick ISBN 1-56402-238-2; In Canada: Candlewick/dist. by Douglas & McIntyre, 1995. unp. col. ill.

Blackboard Bear and Anthony build a spaceship and make preparations to fly to the moon. As the time of departure nears, Anthony has second thoughts and lets Blackboard Bear travel on his own. Another charming escapade of this warm and friendly bear.
SUBJ: Space flight to the moon--Fiction./ Bears--Fiction.

Ph-2 P-1 $13.89 L KF148

ALIKI. Tabby: a story in pictures. HarperCollins ISBN 0-06-024916-1; In Canada: HarperCollins, 1995. unp. col. ill.

Conveyed entirely in pictures, the story of Tabby, a kitten adopted from an animal shelter, will delight young viewers. The small format and watercolor illustrations encourage the viewer to turn the pages and add details to the wordless story.
SUBJ: Cats--Fiction./ Stories without words.

Ph-2 K-2/4 $14.89 L KF149

ALIKI. Those summers. HarperCollins ISBN 0-06-024938-2; In Canada: HarperCollins, 1996. unp. col. ill.

Reflecting upon childhood summers spent at the beach with extended family, the author captures days of endless fun at the seashore and nights on the boardwalk or listening to the radio. Children and adults will enjoy sharing this fond look at the past and comparing it with contemporary beach vacations.
SUBJ: Summer--Fiction./ Seashore--Fiction./ Beaches--Fiction./ Family--Fiction.

TB

Ph-3 K-2 $11.98 OD KF150

ALL TIME FAVORITE CHILDREN'S STORIES (Talking book). Smarty Pants FTG 4-815 ISBN 1-55886-151-3, 1993. 4 sound cassettes. (Four-to-go).

Features popular children's stories read with expression and music and sound effects as appropriate. The sound quality including use of stereo effects provides an enjoyable listening experience. Although the stories are not read-alongs, they will be useful as listening introductions or follow-ups to the books. The cassettes are packaged in an economical small boxed set that will require different packaging for circulating collections.
Contents: Horton hatches the egg (12min); Tubby the Tuba (14min); The little engine that could! (15min); Little Toot (14min).
SUBJ: Short stories.

CE Ph-1 1-3/3 $13.95 L KF151

ALLARD, HARRY. Miss Nelson is missing. Illus. by James Marshall. Houghton Mifflin ISBN 0-395-25296-2, 1977. 32p. col. ill.
Read-along kit available from Houghton Mifflin ISBN 0-395-45737-8, 1987. 1 paperback book, 1 sound cassette, $7.95.
Available from National Library Service for the Blind and Physically Handicapped in Braille BR06127.
Miss Nelson is the nicest teacher in the school but her class is the worst behaved one in the entire building. One day gentle Miss Nelson is replaced by Viola Swamp who is witchlike in her black dress. She makes the children sit absolutely quiet and still and loads them down with work. Finally the missing teacher returns to a subdued class and only Miss Nelson and the readers know the mystery of her strange disappearance.
The kids in 207 have a fun-filled but non-productive week during their teacher's absence but suddenly shape up when Miss Swamp appears. Thankfully, soon, MISS NELSON IS BACK (ISBN 0-395-32956-6, 1982). In MISS NELSON HAS A FIELD DAY (ISBN 0-395-36690-9, 1985) Viola Swamp takes over coaching the losing Smedley Tornadoes.
SUBJ: Schools--Fiction./ Teachers--Fiction./ Behavior--Fiction./ Humorous stories.

Ph-1 K-2/5 $13.95 L KF152

ALLARD, HARRY. Stupids step out. Illus. by James Marshall. Houghton Mifflin ISBN 0-395-18513-0, 1974. 30p. col. ill.
From a waterless bath to begin the day to bedtime with their feet on the pillows and heads under the cover, the Stupid family and their dog "Kitty" enjoy one slapstick outing after another. The nonsense, humor and ridiculous details of the illustrations account for much of the appeal.
In THE STUPIDS HAVE A BALL (ISBN 0-395-26497-9, 1978) the family celebrates the children's awful report cards. When all the lights go out they all think they're dead in THE STUPIDS DIE (ISBN 0-395-30347-8, 1981). The family flees a visit from a disliked relative in THE STUPIDS TAKE OFF (ISBN 0-395-50068-0, 1989).
SUBJ: Humorous stories./ Family life--Fiction.

CE Ph-2 1-3/2 $14.89 L KF153

ALLEN, LAURA JEAN. Rollo and Tweedy and the ghost at Dougal Castle. HarperCollins ISBN 0-06-020107-X; In Canada: HarperCollins, 1992. 64p. col. ill. (I can read book).
Read-along kit available from HarperChildren's Audio (ISBN 0-69470-053-3, 1996). 1 paperback book, 1 sound cassette (12min), $7.95.
Rollo and Tweedy, two mouse detectives from the United States, are invited to Scotland to solve the case of the ghost that is haunting Dougal Castle. An easy-to-read mystery with the right amount of suspense and false clues.
SUBJ: Castles--Fiction./ Ghosts--Fiction./ Mystery and detective stories.

Ph-2 1-3/4 $14.95 T KF154

ALTMAN, LINDA JACOBS. Amelia's road. Illus. by Enrique O. Sanchez. Lee & Low ISBN 1-880000-04-0, 1993. unp. col. ill.
Available in Spanish EL CAMINO DE AMELIA (ISBN 1-880000-07-5, 1994).
Amelia's family is always on the road from one labor camp to another. As migrant farm workers, they measure time and the seasons by the crops they harvest. Amelia longs for a place to call her own and in her own way finds such a place. For multicultural studies.
SUBJ: Migrant labor--Fiction./ Hispanic Americans--Fiction.

Ph-1 K-3/5 $13.95 L KF155

ANDERSEN, HANS CHRISTIAN. Tinderbox. Newly illustrated ed. Illus. by Warwick Hutton. McElderry ISBN 0-689-50458-6; In Canada: Collier Macmillan, 1988. unp. col. ill.
This version of the classic story of the poor soldier who acquires a tinderbox from a witch that brings him wealth, three saucer-eyed dogs who do his bidding and ultimately save his life so he can marry the king's daughter. The bold and original illustrations with their unusual angles enrich the tale and make this an ideal choice for story hour.
SUBJ: Fairy tales.

Ph-2 2-3/4 $12.95 T KF156

ANDERSON, JOY. Juma and the magic jinn. Illus. by Charles Mikolaycak. Lothrop, Lee & Shepard ISBN 0-688-05443-9, 1986. unp. col. ill.
Sent home from school because he would rather draw pictures and write poems than do his sums, Juma touches the forbidden jar and calls up the magic jinn who grants him all his wishes. The text and handsome, dramatic illustrations reflect the language and Moslem culture of the island of Lamu off the coast of Kenya.
SUBJ: Magic--Fiction./ Lamu (Island)--Fiction.

Ph-2 P-2/1 $13.95 L KF157

ANDERSON, PEGGY PERRY. Time for bed, the babysitter said. Houghton Mifflin ISBN 0-395-41851-8, 1987. 31p. col. ill.
"No" said Joe each time the babysitter says bedtime. The spare and very easy-to-read text paired with exaggerated drawings draws laughter from young listeners and beginning independent readers.
SUBJ: Frogs--Fiction./ Bedtime--Fiction./ Babysitters--Fiction./ Humorous stories.

Ph-2 1-3/3 $13.89 L KF158

ANDREWS, SYLVIA. Rattlebone Rock. Illus. by Jennifer Plecas. HarperCollins ISBN 0-06-023452-0; In Canada: HarperCollins, 1995. unp. col. ill.
When all the spooks and skeletons come out to dance for Halloween in the moonlit graveyard, the townspeople join them. Inspires creative movement to the not-so-scary beat of the rhythmic text. Best for reading aloud.
SUBJ: Halloween--Fiction./ Stories in rhyme.

Ph-3 P-A $5.95 P KF159

ANNO, MITSUMASA. Anno's journey. Putnam ISBN 0-698-11433-7, 1978. unp. col. ill.
Wander through villages, farms and walled cities; view castles and churches; meander through an open-air market and peer in the windows of little shops; visit a circus and a fair; but don't miss the small details in this visual journey around Northern Europe. Meticulous watercolor illustrations, populated with numerous characters and packed with action, invite viewers of all ages to linger over the pages and return to view them again and again. Children may appreciate an adult's guidance in recognizing the scenes from famous art and literature and might be led to learn more about the originals.
Similar detailed illustration and wordless treatment is given to two countries in ANNO'S BRITAIN (ISBN 0-399-20861-5, 1982, OPC) and ANNO'S U.S.A. (ISBN 0-399-20974-3, 1983, OPC Selectors' Choice, 15th ed.).
SUBJ: Europe--Pictorial works./ Stories without words.

Ph-3 P-1/1 $1.95 P KF160

ANTLE, NANCY. Good bad cat. Illus. by John Sandford. School Zone ISBN 0-88743-012-0, 1985. unp. col. ill. (Start to read).
When the cat knocks over chairs, chess games and generally disrupts things it's called "bad cat" but when the cat chases a mouse the refrain becomes "good cat". Children who are just beginning to read will experience success with this simple story accompanied by attractive action-filled illustrations.
SUBJ: Cats--Fiction.

Ph-2 1-3/2 $12.89 L KF161

ANTLE, NANCY. Sam's Wild West Show. Illus. by Simms Taback. Dial ISBN 0-8037-1533-1, 1995. 40p. col. ill. (Dial easy-to-read).
Sam's Wild West Show is quite a performance, but the act turns real when outlaws come to rob the bank and Sam is appointed to serve as marshal. The horseback high jinks and roping techniques of Sam and his cast completely disarm the bandits and save the town. The lively story has illustrations to match, and new readers will handle the beginning reader with success.
SUBJ: Cowboys--Fiction./ Cowgirls--Fiction./ Robbers and outlaws--Fiction./ West (U.S.)--Fiction.

Ph-2 1-3/2 $14.89 L KF162

ANTLE, NANCY. Staying cool. Illus. by E. B. Lewis. Dial ISBN 0-8037-1877-2; In Canada: McClelland & Stewart, 1997. unp. col. ill.
Curtis describes his grandfather's boxing gym and his own ambitions to compete in the Golden Gloves amateur boxing tournament. The values of education, discipline, and self-control are clearly communicated to Curtis by his grandfather. Aspiring young athletes will find inspiration here. For multicultural studies.
SUBJ: Boxing--Fiction./ Grandfathers--Fiction./ Afro-Americans--Fiction.

Ph-2 P-2/5 $15.93 L KF163

APPELT, KATHI. Bayou lullaby. Illus. by Neil Waldman. Morrow ISBN 0-688-12857-2, 1995. unp. col. ill.
Includes glossary.
The bayou has its own nighttime rhythms with bullfrogs, crawdads, and tree frogs as parents put their child to sleep. A pronunciation key provides definitions for the Cajun words interspersed throughout the sleepy rhyming text. Acrylic illustrations transport the reader to the shimmering moonlight on the dark chocolate colored water of the bayou.
SUBJ: Bayous--Fiction./ Cajuns--Fiction./ Bedtime--Fiction./ Sleep--Fiction./ Night--Fiction./ Lullabies./ Stories in rhyme.

Ph-2 K-2/2 $14.95   T   KF164

APPELT, KATHI. Watermelon Day. Illus. by Dale Gottlieb. Henry Holt ISBN 0-8050-2304-6; In Canada: Fitzhenry & Whiteside, 1996. unp. col. ill.

After a long wait for the watermelon to grow big and ripe, and then cool all day in the lake, Jesse and her family enjoy eating the juicy fruit. A summer's anticipation vibrates through the bright pastel illustrations. A seasonal celebration of family and watermelon.
SUBJ: Watermelons--Fiction./ Summer--Fiction.

Ph-2 1-3/4 $16.99   L   KF165

ARMSTRONG, JENNIFER. King Crow. Illus. by Eric Rohmann. Crown ISBN 0-517-59635-0, 1995. unp. col. ill.

Defeated and blinded in battle, Cormac, the king, is imprisoned by his enemy, the warlike Bregant. Cormac uses the news brought to him by a crow to unnerve and eventually defeat Bregant. Making effective use of gold tones and light and shadow, the dark illustrations will appeal to the story's audience. Youngsters who enjoy stories of the Middle Ages and stories of good versus evil will appreciate this one.
SUBJ: Crows--Fiction./ Kings, queens, rulers, etc.--Fiction.

Ph-2 K-2/3 $13.93   L   KF166

ARMSTRONG, JENNIFER. That terrible baby. Illus. by Susan Meddaugh. Tambourine ISBN 0-688-11833-X, 1994. unp. col. ill.

The terrible baby wreaks havoc throughout the house, but older siblings, Eleanor and Mark, get blamed for the damage. When the speedy crawler crawls out the cat door and is poised to fall down the stairs, he is saved by his two siblings. Youngsters with a young crawler at home will howl with delight at the funny story and amusing illustrations.
SUBJ: Babies--Fiction./ Brothers and sisters--Fiction./ Behavior--Fiction.

Ph-2 P-3/5 $14.99   T   KF167

ARNOLD, TEDD. No jumping on the bed! Dial ISBN 0-8037-0038-5; In Canada: Fitzhenry & Whiteside, 1987. unp. col. ill.

Disobeying his father, Walter jumps on his bed just one more time and starts a chaotic descent floor by floor, gathering tenants, food, furniture, etc. from each apartment in the tall building. Finally landing in his own bed, Walter wonders if it's a dream or for real, and then Delbert from the top floor crashes through the ceiling, bed and all. Comical pictures match the hilarity of the story. Very popular with young children.
SUBJ: Apartment houses--Fiction./ Humorous stories.

Ph-2 P-2/2 $15.95   L   KF168

ARNOSKY, JIM. Every autumn comes the bear. Putnam ISBN 0-399-22508-0; In Canada: Putnam, 1993. unp. col. ill.

Breathtaking watercolors illustrate the story of a bear preparing to hibernate. Youngsters are fascinated by the topic, and the illustrations are suitable for group sharing and for discussions about the changing seasons.
SUBJ: Bears--Fiction./ Hibernation--Fiction.

Ph-1 P-2/2 $15.95   T   KF169

ARNOSKY, JIM. Rabbits and raindrops. Putnam ISBN 0-399-22635-4; In Canada: Putnam, 1997. unp. col. ill.

Five baby rabbits scamper out from their nest with their mother only to scurry back when a storm arrives. Attentive to small details and the unique personalities of each rabbit, watercolor illustrations will delight the viewer. An outstanding choice for primary animal units.
SUBJ: Rabbits--Fiction.

Ph-1 P-K/1 $12.88   L   KF170

ARNOSKY, JIM. Watching foxes. Lothrop, Lee & Shepard ISBN 0-688-04260-0, 1985. unp. col. ill.

Selectors' Choice, 15th ed.
When the mother fox leaves the den to go hunting, the four young pups run out to frolic and explore the world around them. Based on notes and sketches the author made while watching a den of red foxes.
SUBJ: Foxes--Fiction.

CDR   Ph-1 1-4 $39.95   OD KF171

ARTHUR'S TEACHER TROUBLE (CD-ROM). Broderbund 48674, 1992. 1 CD-ROM, 1 paperback book. (Living books).

Includes user's guide.
Also available for Macintosh.
Selectors' Choice, 19th ed.
System requirements: Macintosh and Power Macintosh; System 6.0.7 or higher; 16MHz 68020 processor or faster; Power Macintosh; 4MB RAM; 2.5MB free; CD-ROM drive required; Monitor; 12 inch or larger color, 256 colors.
System requirements: Windows 3.1 or Windows 95; 16MHz 386 or faster required; 4MB RAM for Windows 3.1; 8MB RAM for Windows 95; CD-ROM drive or faster required; SVGA monitor/ display card 640x480, 256 colors; Windows compatible sound device.
Product runs on either Macintosh or Windows compatible hardware. Marc Brown's Arthur adventure comes alive in the CD-ROM version which can be used in English or Spanish. Youngsters can have the story read completely or choose to read page by page as they explore what happens when they click on items on the page. For small groups or individual students as part of a whole language classroom.
SUBJ: Schools--Fiction--Software./ Software--Schools--Fiction./ Teachers--Fiction--Software./ Software--Teachers--Fiction./ Animals--Fiction--Software./ Software--Animals--Fiction./ Spanish language materials--Software./ Software--Spanish language materials./ Bilingual materials--Spanish--Software./ Software--Bilingual materials--Spanish./ Interactive media.

Ph-1 P-K/1 $14.93   L   KF172

ARUEGO, JOSE. We hide, you seek. Written and illustrated by Jose Aruego and Ariane Dewey. Greenwillow ISBN 0-688-84201-1, 1979. unp. col. ill.

In their East African habitat a clumsy but good natured rhino plays hide and seek with his many animal friends. This amusing and almost wordless picture book stimulates an awareness of protective coloration occurring in nature.
SUBJ: Hide-and-seek--Fiction./ Camouflage (Biology)--Fiction./ Animals--Habitations--Fiction.

Ph-1 P-2/2 $14.00   L   KF173

ASCH, FRANK. Bear shadow. Prentice-Hall/Simon & Schuster ISBN 0-671-66279-1, 1985. unp. col. ill.

Going fishing, Bear is furious when his shadow frightens the fish away and he then proceeds to try all sorts of activities to get rid of his shadow. Lots of humor but also encourages efforts to understand the sun's relationship to formation of shadows.
SUBJ: Bears--Fiction./ Shadows--Fiction.

CE   Ph-2 P-1/2 $12.95   L   KF174

ASCH, FRANK. Happy birthday, moon. Prentice-Hall ISBN 0-671-66454-9; In Canada: Prentice-Hall, 1982. unp. col. ill.

Available on 1/2" VHS videocassette from Weston Woods HMPV281V (7min). $49.95.
Enamored of the moon, a small bear decides to get a birthday present for his far away friend. How Bear discovers the perfect present, delivers it and gets one himself can create an awareness of echoes, the motion of the moon and the effects of wind in this simple, humorous and warmly-written story that is effective at picture story book time.
Bear and his friend Little Bear are featured in MOONCAKE (ISBN 0-671-06450-6, 1983, OPC); MOONGAME (Simon & Schuster ISBN 0-671-66453-0, 1987, also available in big book from Scholastic ISBN 0-590-65965-0, 1992); and BEAR'S BARGAIN (Simon & Schuster ISBN 0-671-67838-8, 1989, also available in big book from Scholastic ISBN 0-590-72698-6, 1992).
SUBJ: Bears--Fiction./ Moon--Fiction./ Birthdays--Fiction.

Ph-1 P-K/2 $15.00   T   KF175

ASCH, FRANK. Moonbear's pet. Simon & Schuster ISBN 0-689-80794-5; In Canada: Distican, 1997. unp. col. ill.

When their pet fish sprouts limbs, Bear and Little Bird can't agree about whether it will become a bear or a bird. Attentive readers will anticipate their surprise when the "fish" becomes a frog. Uncluttered illustrations are the perfect complement to the straightforward text.
SUBJ: Bears--Fiction./ Birds--Fiction./ Tadpoles--Fiction./ Friendship--Fiction.

CE   Ph-1 K-2/3 $15.95   L   KF176

AUCH, MARY JANE. Eggs mark the spot. Holiday House ISBN 0-8234-1242-3, 1996. unp. col. ill.

Videocassette available from Live Oak Media (ISBN 0-87499-386-5, 1997). 1/2" VHS videocassette color (13min), $37.95. Includes teacher's guide.
Read-along kit available from Live Oak Media (ISBN 0-87499-387-3, 1997). 1 paperback book, 1 sound cassette (13min), $15.95. Includes teacher's guide.
Pauline the hen has a talent for laying eggs with images she has just seen. When she is invited to spend the night at an exhibit of famous paintings, she lays eggs that have her own interpretations of several well-known paintings until she is interrupted by an art thief. Her remarkable skill also helps to capture the thief. The illustrations introduce young viewers to Matisse, Van Gogh, and several other artists. The suspenseful story will capture the attention of young readers while promoting art appreciation. An unusual choice for art classes. Pair with Hurd's ART DOG for an interdisciplinary approach.
SUBJ: Chickens--Fiction./ Painting--Fiction./ Robbers and outlaws--Fiction.

Ph-1 K-2/2 $13.89   L   KF177
AVERILL, ESTHER. Fire cat. HarperCollins ISBN 0-06-020196-7, c1960. 63p. col. ill. (I can read book).
Available from National Library Service for the Blind and Physically Handicapped in Braille BRA06861 and as talking book TB03280. Pickles, a spotted cat, was given a home by Mrs. Goodkind but he ran away. Finally he became a fire cat and lived at the firehouse.
SUBJ: Cats--Fiction./ Fire departments--Fiction.

Ph-2 1-3/3 $13.00   T   KF178
AXELROD, AMY. Pigs in the pantry: fun with math and cooking. Illus. by Sharon McGinley-Nally. Simon & Schuster ISBN 0-689-80665-5; In Canada: Distican, 1997. unp. col. ill.
Includes glossary.
Mrs. Pig is not feeling well, and her family decides to cheer her up by cooking a favorite dish, Firehouse Chili. Well, they do have to call in the fire department! Follow the recipe to understand what Mr. Pig needs to learn about the importance of measurement. Appealing illustrations, cooking, and math provide a recipe for fun.
SUBJ: Cookery--Fiction./ Pigs--Fiction./ Measurement--Fiction.

Ph-1 2-3/2 $13.00   T   KF179
AXELROD, AMY. Pigs on a blanket. Illus. by Sharon McGinley-Nally. Simon & Schuster ISBN 0-689-80505-5; In Canada: Distican, 1996. unp. col. ill.
Join the Pig family for a trip to the beach and calculate how they run out of time for a swim. Basic time concepts are reinforced with humor and brightly colored illustrations. Students will understand the importance of time in planning a family outing. Delightfully funny, will enliven math classes.
SUBJ: Pigs--Fiction./ Beaches--Fiction./ Time--Fiction.

Ph-1 K-2/2 $15.95   T   KF180
AYLESWORTH, JIM. Old black fly. Illus. by Stephen Gammell. Henry Holt ISBN 0-8050-1401-2; In Canada: Fitzhenry & Whiteside, 1992. unp. col. ill.
Big book available (ISBN 0-8050-3925-2, 1995).
The old black fly has had a busy day buzzing through the alphabet and meets an ignoble end. Spattered paint practically drips from every page, following the fly's messy path. Rhyming text is a must for reading aloud. Raucous alternative to most alphabet books.
SUBJ: Flies--Fiction./ Alphabet./ Stories in rhyme.

Ph-2 P-1/3 $13.95   L   KF181
AYLESWORTH, JIM. Two terrible frights. Illus. by Eileen Christelow. Atheneum ISBN 0-689-31327-6, 1987. unp. col. ill.
Going to the kitchen for late night snacks, a little girl child and a little girl mouse meet and each is terrified. In this gently humorous story told in parallel form, both run to their respective mothers eeking and squeaking, are reassured and comforted, and soon are sound asleep dreaming of sharing a bedtime snack with each other.
SUBJ: Bedtime--Fiction./ Mice--Fiction.

Ph-2 P-2/2 $14.89   L   KF182
BABBITT, NATALIE. Bub, or, The very best thing. HarperCollins ISBN 0-06-205045-1; In Canada: HarperCollins, 1994. unp. col. ill.
"Michael di Capua books."
Searching for what is best for their young prince, the king and queen consult books and other people. The young prince knows it's "bub," and the cook's daughter understands he means "love." In the charming illustrations, the dog, wearing a jester's hat, loyally follows the prince and his mother everywhere they go in the castle, demonstrating that he knows the meaning of "bub."
SUBJ: Love--Fiction./ Family--Fiction./ Kings, queens, rulers, etc.--Fiction.

Ph-1 1-3/1 $12.99   T   KF183
BAKER, BARBARA. One Saturday morning. Illus. by Kate Duke. Dutton ISBN 0-525-45262-1, 1994. 48p. col. ill. (Dutton easy reader).
Available from the National Library Service for the Blind and Physically Handicapped on sound recording cassette RC 41965.
One by one, the six members of a bear family wake up, have breakfast, go to the park to play, and come home for lunch. Each of six chapters focuses on one member of the family in an easy-to-read format. Youngsters will relate to the lightly humorous stories and the illustrations depicting typical family life in this appealing beginning reader.
SUBJ: Family life--Fiction./ Bears--Fiction.

Ph-2 1-3/1 $12.99   T   KF184
BAKER, BARBARA. Staying with Grandmother. Illus. by Judith Byron Schachner. Dutton ISBN 0-525-44603-6, 1994. 48p. col. ill. (Dutton easy reader).
Clair misses her parents when they leave her at Grandmother's house where everything seems unfamiliar. As Grandmother introduces her to a new friend, a favorite book, and a beloved stuffed animal that belonged to Clair's mother, Clair feels more comfortable. Youngsters eager to read chapter books will enjoy this easy-to-read intergenerational transitional reader.
SUBJ: Grandmothers--Fiction./ Homesickness--Fiction.

Ph-1 K-2/2 $15.00   L   KF185
BAKER, KAREN LEE. Seneca. Greenwillow ISBN 0-688-14030-0; In Canada: Hearst Book Group, 1997. unp. col. ill.
A young girl describes her daily visit to care for and ride her horse, Seneca. Young horse enthusiasts will especially relate to the realistic story which could also serve as a resource for units on pets. The watercolor artwork is a good match for the gentle text.
SUBJ: Horses--Fiction./ Pets--Fiction.

Ph-1 P-1/2 $12.95   L   KF186
BAKER, KEITH. Hide and snake. Harcourt Brace Jovanovich ISBN 0-15-233986-8; In Canada: Harcourt Brace Jovanovich, 1991. unp. col. ill.
Play hide-and-seek with a rainbow snake as he winds through yarn, cakes, shoes, and other colorful doublespreads. Lots of fun and good for visual discrimination.
SUBJ: Snakes--Fiction./ Picture puzzles./ Stories in rhyme.

Ph-2 P-K/1 $12.95   L   KF187
BAKER, KEITH. Who is the beast? Harcourt Brace Jovanovich ISBN 0-15-296057-0, 1990. unp. col. ill.
Big book available (ISBN 0-15-296059-7, 1991).
The animals in the jungle are frightened by "the beast" (a tiger) until he points out their many similarities. Lush illustrations of jungle vegetation and animals fill double-paged spreads. The simple story will be useful in discussions of the concepts of alike and different.
SUBJ: Tigers--Fiction./ Jungle animals--Fiction./ Stories in rhyme.

Ph-2 1-3/5 $15.95   L   KF188
BAKER, SANNA ANDERSON. Grandpa is a flyer. Illus. by Bill Farnsworth. Whitman ISBN 0-8075-3033-6; In Canada: General, 1995. unp. col. ill.
From the age of nine, when he first sees a plane fly over his yard, Grandpa is fascinated with flying. His dream comes true when his brother helps him save the money to pay for a short flight in a plane and, later as a grown-up, when he buys his own plane. Grandpa imparts his love for flying to his granddaughter as he shares the story with her. Illustrations and story convey the romance of flight in its early days.
SUBJ: Flight--Fiction./ Grandfathers--Fiction.

Ph-2 1-3/2 $14.93   L   KF189
BANG, MOLLY. Dawn. Morrow ISBN 0-688-02404-1, 1983. unp. col. ill.
Freely adapted from the Japanese folktale, "The Crane Wife." A ship builder rescues an injured Canada goose who later returns as a beautiful young sailmaker. He marries her, they have a daughter, Dawn, and he loses her because of his insistence that she make one more perfect sail. Magnificent illustrations, many with unusual borders, make this a compelling book. The text is set in italic calligraphy.
SUBJ: Fairy tales.

Ph-1 P-2/2 $10.95   L   KF190
BANG, MOLLY. Goose. Blue Sky Press/Scholastic ISBN 0-590-89005-0; In Canada: Scholastic, 1996. unp. col. ill.
When a goose egg is blown out of its nest, the gosling hatches and joins a woodchuck family whose best efforts don't entirely convince the goose that she is one of them. A small format and affectionate illustrations offer readers a sense of intimacy. For one-on-one sharing.
SUBJ: Geese--Fiction./ Woodchucks--Fiction./ Identity--Fiction.

CE
Ph-1 K-3/4 $13.93   L   KF191
BANG, MOLLY. Paper crane. Greenwillow ISBN 0-688-04109-4, 1985. unp. col. ill.
Selectors' Choice, 16th ed.
Available from National Library Service for the Blind and Physically Handicapped in Braille BR06126 and as sound recording cassette RC24650.
Unable to pay for his dinner, a poor but gentle man instead gives the restaurant owner an unusual paper crane which comes to life and dances at the clap of hands. Soon word of this unusual bird spreads, the kind restaurateur's dwindling business flourishes, and after success is guaranteed the gentle old man returns, plays his flute and then flies away on the back of the origami crane. Colored photographs bring to life the intricate paper collages and create elegant, three-dimensional pictures with an Oriental flavor.
SUBJ: Cranes (Birds)--Fiction.

Ph-1 P-K $15.93   L   KF192

BANG, MOLLY. Ten, nine, eight. Greenwillow ISBN 0-688-00907-7, 1983. unp. col. ill.
Caldecott Honor book, 1984.
Selectors' Choice, 15th ed.
Big book available from Scholastic (ISBN 0-590-65233-8, 1993).
Board book available from Tupelo Books (ISBN 0-688-14901-4, 1996).
Counting down from ten small toes to one big girl all ready for bed, this title through its bright simple pictures and lilting rhymes emphasizes the love, warmth, and happiness existing between an African-American father and his little girl. A quiet read-aloud. For multicultural studies.
SUBJ: Counting./ Fathers and daughters--Fiction./ Night--Fiction./ Lullabies.

Ph-2 1-3/2 $4.95   P   KF193

BANG, MOLLY. Tye May and the magic brush. Adapted from the Chinese by Molly Garrett Bang. Mulberry/Morrow ISBN 0-688-11504-7, c1981, 1992. 55p. col. ill. (Greenwillow read-alone).
Tye May is a poor orphan who mysteriously is given a magic paint brush. When she paints birds, they sing and fly, and her paintings of fish begin to splash and swim. She uses her magic brush to make things for the poor until the greedy emperor makes her paint for him. When his demands include an ocean, ship, and wind, Tye May's brush enables her to be rid of him forever.
SUBJ: Painting--Fiction./ Magic--Fiction./ Orphans--Fiction.

Ph-2 P-1/2 $14.00   T   KF194

BANKS, KATE. Spider spider. Illus. by Georg Hallensleben. Farrar, Straus and Giroux ISBN 0-374-37151-2; In Canada: HarperCollins, 1996. unp. col. ill.
Originally published as ARAIGNEE, PETITE ARAIGNEE, Editions Gallimard, France, 1996.
"Frances Foster books."
A young boy and his mother talk about what they would do if he were a spider. The son tells the mother that he would come back to her each time she attempts to brush the spider away until she agrees to also become a spider. Imaginative oil paintings and a straightforward text convey the loving and warm story.
SUBJ: Spiders--Fiction./ Imagination--Fiction./ Mothers and sons--Fiction.

Ph-1 K-2/2 $14.95   T   KF195

BANNERMAN, HELEN. Story of Little Babaji. Illus. by Fred Marcellino. HarperCollins ISBN 0-06-205064-8; In Canada: HarperCollins, 1996. unp. col. ill.
"Michael di Capua books."
Feeling grand in his new clothes, Little Babaji goes for a walk in the jungle where he encounters several tigers. They take one article of his clothing at a time, and they end up arguing about who has the grandest attire. The story, originally published as THE STORY OF LITTLE BLACK SAMBO, is now clearly set in India, and the tigers still turn into butter for Babaji's pancakes. The small size and page turns are cleverly designed for optimum humor and suspense. For multicultural studies.
SUBJ: Tigers--Fiction./ India--Fiction./ Humorous stories.

Ph-1 2-A $13.99   L   KF196

BANYAI, ISTVAN. Re-zoom. Viking ISBN 0-670-86392-0; In Canada: Penguin, 1995. unp. col. ill.
Sequential illustrations zoom out and around the world as pictures within pictures surprise the viewer at every turn of the page. The clever visual tour challenges viewers to identify the setting, imagine the stories, and find humor and clues in the details. Entirely without words, the book can be enjoyed on several levels not limited by language. Will have special appeal for reluctant readers and ESL students.
SUBJ: Visual perception--Fiction./ Stories without words.

Ph-1 P-A $13.99   L   KF197

BANYAI, ISTVAN. Zoom. Viking ISBN 0-670-85804-8; In Canada: Penguin, 1995. unp. col. ill.
Selectors' Choice, 20th ed.
In this wordless picture book, illustrations present scenes from increasingly distant perspectives--from a rooster to a child's toy village, to a boy on a cruise ship, to a picture on the side of a city bus, to a television set in a desert that's a stamp on a postcard. A solid black page on the left side offsets the brightly colored illustrations on the facing pages that carry the viewer from close up to far away. Offers a witty insight into the power of the visual to suggest a story or influence our perception. Has applications for visual literacy and creative writing. Will have special appeal for reluctant readers and ESL students.
SUBJ: Visual perception--Fiction./ Stories without words.

Ph-1 K-3/3 $14.95   T   KF198

BARBER, BARBARA E. Saturday at The New You. Illus. by Anna Rich. Lee & Low ISBN 1-880000-06-7, 1994. unp. col. ill.
Shauna spends Saturdays helping her mother at her beauty parlor, The New You. She greets customers, brings them magazines, and does her dolls' hair, but mostly she is an acute observer of the people who come and go and the pride and skill her mother puts in her work. Oil paintings reveal the personalities and hair styles of the people in The New You. The topic will have broad appeal to audiences interested in careers, mother-daughter stories, or hair styles. Excellent book for multicultural studies that depicts a positive mother-daughter relationship, an African-American woman who owns her own business, and a warm neighborhood story.
SUBJ: Afro-Americans--Fiction./ Mothers and daughters--Fiction./ Beauty shops--Fiction.

Ph-1 1-3/5 $14.95   T   KF199

BARKER, MARJORIE. Magical hands. Illus. by Yoshi. Picture Book Studio ISBN 0-88708-103-7, 1989. unp. col. ill.
Available from the National Library Service for the Blind and Physically Handicapped on sound recording cassette RC 36512.
William works magic with his own hands by secretly doing the chores of his three friends for their birthdays. A wonderfully crafted story of friendship and doing for others. A combination of batik and painting on silk create an unusual texture and depth to the illustrations.
SUBJ: Work--Fiction./ Birthdays--Fiction./ Friendship--Fiction.

CE   Ph-1 P-2/2 $14.99   T   KF200

BARRACCA, DEBRA. Adventures of taxi dog. By Debra and Sal Barracca. Illus. by Mark Buehner. Dial ISBN 0-8037-0671-5; In Canada: Fitzhenry & Whiteside, 1990. 31p. col. ill.
Selectors' Choice, 18th ed.
Spanish version LAS ADVENTURAS DE MAXI, EL PERRO TAXISTA available from Penguin Ediciones (ISBN 0-8037-2009-2, 1996).
An exuberant story about Maxi, a stray dog who is adopted by Jim, a cab driver, and becomes his constant companion. The rhyming text is bordered in bright yellow and black and white checks identical to Jim's cab. Large, colorful illustrations attract attention to the dog's happy story.
Taxi dog catches a thief in MAXI, THE HERO (ISBN 0-8037-0939-0, 1991).
SUBJ: Dogs--Fiction./ Taxicabs--Fiction./ New York (N.Y.)--Fiction./ City and town life--Fiction./ Stories in rhyme./ Spanish language materials.

Ph-1 P-2/2 $13.99   T   KF201

BARRACCA, DEBRA. Maxi, the star. By Debra and Sal Barracca. Illus. by Alan Ayers. Dial ISBN 0-8037-1348-7, 1993. unp. col. ill.
Maxi, the taxi dog, is discovered by a producer and goes to Los Angeles to make a commercial for Doggie Bites. Maxi and Jim travel across the country in their bright yellow cab visiting landmarks along the way. A new illustrator maintains the cheery overall brightness of the previous Maxi, the taxi dog, stories, but Maxi and Jim have a different appearance.
SUBJ: Dogs--Fiction./ United States--Description and travel--Fiction./ Television advertising--Fiction./ Stories in rhyme.

Ph-2 P-2/3 $14.99   T   KF202

BARRACCA, DEBRA. Taxi Dog Christmas. By Debra and Sal Barracca. Illus. by Alan Ayers. Dial ISBN 0-8037-1360-6, 1994. unp. col. ill.
Jim and Maxi prepare for the holidays, adopt a stray kitten, and help Santa deliver his presents when his sled breaks down. Rhyming text and bright oil illustrations feature city streets. Fans of the yellow cab driven by Jim and his cheerful companion Maxi, the large brown dog, will enjoy this holiday addition.
SUBJ: Dogs--Fiction./ Christmas--Fiction./ Taxicabs--Fiction./ Stories in rhyme.

Ph-2 P-2/7 $14.95   T   KF203

BARRETT, JUDI. Cloudy with a chance of meatballs. Illus. by Ron Barrett. Atheneum ISBN 0-689-30647-4; In Canada: McClelland & Stewart, 1978. unp. col. ill.
Grandpa tells a tall tale about the town of Chewandswallow where the weather brings food: it rains juice or soup, snows mashed potatoes and blows in frankfurters with mustard clouds. The illustrations add to the slapstick with pancake showers, jello sunsets and drifts of cream cheese and jelly sandwiches. A popular choice for story hour as well as a hilarious departure for units on weather or food.
SUBJ: Weather--Fiction./ Food--Fiction.

BB   Ph-2 P $3.95   T   KF204

BARTON, BYRON. Big machines (Board book). HarperFestival ISBN 0-694-00622-X; In Canada: HarperCollins, 1995. unp. col. ill.
Young children fascinated by large machines will delight in this

colorful board book presentation. Beginning readers will feel successful as they "read" the names of the labeled vehicles.
SUBJ: Machinery./ Vocabulary.

BB   Ph-2   P $3.95   T   KF205
BARTON, BYRON. Dinosaurs (Board book). HarperFestival ISBN 0-694-00621-1; In Canada: HarperCollins, 1995. unp. col. ill.
Colorful dinosaurs fill the pages in this board book for young fans.
SUBJ: Dinosaurs.

Ph-1   P-2/2 $12.89   L   KF206
BARTON, BYRON. I want to be an astronaut. Crowell/HarperCollins ISBN 0-690-04744-4, 1988. unp. col. ill.
The world of the astronaut is presented here in a background of brilliant greens and blues against which the stiff, almost robot like figures of the astronauts go about their tasks. The text is brief but the illustrations are clear and dramatic and invoke the thrill of a journey into space. Good for very young readers interested in space flights.
SUBJ: Astronauts--Fiction./ Astronautics--Fiction./ Space flight--Fiction.

Ph-2   P-K/2 $14.89   L   KF207
BARTON, BYRON. Machines at work. Crowell/HarperCollins ISBN 0-690-04573-5, 1987. unp. col. ill.
Pictures the day in the life of a construction crew as they bulldoze, dig, truck and dump, drill and build a road and a building. Bright, bold, childlike pictures illustrate the bare, simple text.
SUBJ: Building--Fiction./ Construction equipment--Fiction./ Machinery--Fiction.

BB   Ph-2   P $3.95   T   KF208
BARTON, BYRON. Tools (Board book). HarperFestival ISBN 0-694-00623-8; In Canada: HarperCollins, 1995. unp. col. ill.
Men and women use a variety of tools in a bold and colorful board book format. Include in preschool units about community helpers.
SUBJ: Tools./ Vocabulary.

BB   Ph-2   P $3.95   T   KF209
BARTON, BYRON. Zoo animals (Board book). HarperFestival ISBN 0-694-00620-3; In Canada: HarperCollins, 1995. unp. col. ill.
Features zoo animals familiar to the very young in a cheery board book format. Will appeal to preschoolers and beginning readers who are learning sight words.
SUBJ: Zoo animals./ Vocabulary.

Ph-1   1-3/3 $15.93   L   KF210
BARTONE, ELISA. American too. Illus. by Ted Lewin. Lothrop, Lee & Shepard ISBN 0-688-13279-0, 1996. unp. col. ill.
Longing to be American, Rosie is upset about being the queen for the feast of San Gennaro until she plans to dress up as the Statue of Liberty for the parade. Details about the preparations and activities of the Italian celebration provide a counterpoint to Rosie's determination to assimilate. Time and place of New York City's post-World War I Italian community are masterfully communicated through the illustrations. Historical fiction based on an episode in the author's family history.
SUBJ: Italian Americans--Fiction./ Festivals--Fiction./ New York (N.Y.)--Fiction./ Emigration and immigration--Fiction.

Ph-3   1-3/2 $13.93   L   KF211
BARTONE, ELISA. Peppe the lamplighter. Illus. by Ted Lewin. Lothrop, Lee & Shepard ISBN 0-688-10269-7, 1993. unp. col. ill.
Caldecott Honor book, 1994.
Peppe needs a job to support his sick father and their family, but no one in Little Italy is able to hire him except Domenico, the lamplighter, who keeps someone to do his job while he returns to Italy for his wife. Peppe does the job of lighting the street lamps by hand very well, but his father feels the job is beneath him until he realizes how important the light is to the neighborhood. Masterful illustrations depict the turn-of-the-century New York City neighborhood.
SUBJ: Italian Americans--Fiction./ Fathers and sons--Fiction./ Brothers and sisters--Fiction./ New York (N.Y.)--Fiction.

Ph-1   P-A $11.95   T   KF212
BASE, GRAEME. Animalia. Abrams ISBN 0-8109-1939-7, c1986, 1993. unp. col. ill.
"Robert Sessions book."
Armoured armadillos, diabolical dragons, and quivering quails are among the creatures featured in this unique alphabet book. Detailed illustrations invite close inspection as viewers attempt to identify the many words that begin with the featured letter, increasing their vocabularies in the process. A sophisticated alphabet book that can be enjoyed on many levels by all ages. Use to demonstrate alliteration in creative writing classes.
SUBJ: Animals--Fiction./ Alphabet.

Ph-2   1-3/5 $15.95   L   KF213
BATEMAN, TERESA. Ring of Truth: an original Irish tale. Illus. by Omar Rayyan. Holiday House ISBN 0-8234-1255-5, 1997. unp. col. ill.
Patrick, the peddlar, boasts that he can tell the best lies, so the king of the leprechauns decides to teach him a lesson and puts a ring on his finger that will only permit him to tell the truth. When Patrick relates his story of the leprechaun king at the lying contest in Donegal, no one believes him, and he wins the pot of gold. Celtic borders and backgrounds lend flavor to the Irish tale.
SUBJ: Leprechauns--Fiction./ Contests--Fiction./ Honesty--Fiction./ Fairy tales.

Ph-2   P-2/3 $3.95   P   KF214
BECKER, JOHN. Seven little rabbits. Illus. by Barbara Cooney. Scholastic ISBN 0-590-33447-6, 1973. unp. col. ill.
"Seven little rabbits/Walking down the road/To call on old friend Toad." One little rabbit grows tired and takes a nap in Mole's bed and then there are only six little rabbits walking down the road to call on Toad. One by one all seven little rabbits grow tired and end up asleep in Mole's bed. Rhyming, repetitive and charming text supported by humorously detailed, appealing illustrations.
SUBJ: Counting./ Stories in rhyme./ Rabbits--Fiction.

Ph-2   2-5/2 $16.00   T   KF215
BEDARD, MICHAEL. Emily. Illus. by Barbara Cooney. Doubleday ISBN 0-385-30697-0, 1992. unp. col. ill.
A young girl is curious about the reclusive neighbor across the street whom people call the Myth. When her mother is invited to play the piano for the neighbor, the young girl gets to meet the poet, Emily Dickinson. An afterword provides factual information to accompany the story about the famous poet. Rich oil paintings provide interesting details of nineteenth century New England. Useful for studies of Emily Dickinson and her work.
SUBJ: Dickinson, Emily--Fiction./ Neighborliness--Fiction.

Ph-2   K-2/4 $13.95   T   KF216
BEIFUSS, JOHN. Armadillo Ray. Illus. by Peggy Turley. Chronicle ISBN 0-8118-0334-1; In Canada: Raincoast, 1995. unp. col. ill.
Asking other animals about the moon's changing shape, Armadillo Ray gets various answers from each: a serpent, a prairie dog's burrow, or an egg. Bold colors against a dark background are folklike and eye-catching. Facts about the moon follow the story which would be a great introduction to lunar studies.
SUBJ: Armadillos--Fiction./ Desert animals--Fiction./ Moon--Fiction.

Ph-1   1-3/3 $14.95   L   KF217
BELTON, SANDRA. May'naise sandwiches and sunshine tea. Illus. by Gail Gordon Carter. Four Winds ISBN 0-02-709035-3; In Canada: Maxwell Macmillan, 1994. unp. col. ill.
A picnic of mayonnaise sandwiches and sugar water becomes a feast of imagination and dreams for two young African-American girls from different sides of town. Big Mama relates the story to her grandchild about her humble beginnings and the aspirations that led her to be the first one in the family to graduate from college. The sun dances in the delicate watercolor and pencil illustrations as it does in this story about friendship, family, and hope. For multicultural studies.
SUBJ: Grandmothers--Fiction./ Afro-Americans--Fiction./ Family--Fiction.

CE   Ph-1   P-2/4 $15.99   L   KF218
BEMELMANS, LUDWIG. Madeline. Viking ISBN 0-670-44580-0, 1962. unp. col. ill.
Caldecott Honor Book.
Read-along kit available from Live Oak Media (ISBN 0-670-44581-1, 1975). 1 hardback book, 1 sound cassette (8min), $22.95. (Seafarer Reading chest).
Also available in Spanish MADELINE (ISBN 0-670-85154-X, 1993). Spanish read-along kit available from Live Oak Media (ISBN 0-87499-408-X, 1997). 1 paperback book, 1 sound cassette (8min), $15.95. Includes teacher's guide.
Enhanced videocassette available from SRA/McGraw-Hill 87-540348, 1989 (8min), $39.00.
Available from National Library Service for the Blind and Physically Handicapped in Braille BR03644.
Big book available from Puffin (ISBN 0-14-054845-9, 1993), $17.99.
Madeline is the smallest, bravest, and most adventurous of 12 little girls in a Parisian boarding school.
SUBJ: Paris (France)--Fiction./ Schools--Fiction./ Stories in rhyme./ Spanish language materials.

TB   Ph-2   P-2 $11.95   OD   KF219
BEMELMANS, LUDWIG. Madeline and other Bemelmans (Talking book). Told by Carol Channing. HarperAudio/Caedmon; In Canada: dist. by HarperCollins, n.d. 1 sound cassette.
Gay humor and sprightly style combine in these characteristic tales by

a noted author-illustrator.

Contents: Madeline's rescue; Madeline; Madeline and the bad hat; Fifi; Happy place.

SUBJ: Paris (France)--Fiction./ Stories in rhyme.

CE   Ph-1 P-2/2 $14.00   L   KF220

BEMELMANS, LUDWIG. Madeline's rescue. Viking ISBN 0-670-44716-1, c1953. 56p. col. ill.

Caldecott Medal Award.

Sequel to: "Madeline"

Available from National Library Service for the Blind and Physically Handicapped in Braille BRA04718.

Read-along kit available from Live Oak Media 0-670-44718-8, 1978. 1 sound cassette (10min), 8 paperback books (Seafarer Reading chest) $31.95.

Twelve little French girls living at a boarding school adopt a dog who has saved one of them from drowning, only to be told they may not keep her.

SUBJ: Dogs--Fiction./ Paris (France)--Fiction./ Schools--Fiction./ Stories in rhyme.

****   Ph-2 1-3/2 $13.89   L   KF221

BENCHLEY, NATHANIEL. George, the drummer boy. Illus. by Don Bolognese. HarperCollins ISBN 0-06-020501-6, c1977. 61p. col. ill. (I can read history book).

Available from National Library Service for the Blind and Physically Handicapped in Braille BR05088.

George is a British drummer boy who is stationed in Boston at the start of the American Revolution. One night George's company is sent on a secret mission. As they cross the river on barges, wade ashore and make their way to Concord and Lexington, George and his friend Fred are cold and frightened. In this attractively illustrated, easy to read story, these famous skirmishes are seen through the eyes of a young British boy.

SUBJ: Lexington, Battle of, 1775--Fiction./ Concord, Battle of, 1775--Fiction./ United States--History--Revolution, 1775-1783--Campaigns--Fiction.

****   Ph-2 1-3/2 $12.89   L   KF222

BENCHLEY, NATHANIEL. Sam the minuteman. Illus. by Arnold Lobel. HarperCollins ISBN 0-06-020480-X, c1969. 62p. col. ill. (I can read history book).

Available from National Library Service for the Blind and Physically Handicapped as talking book TB03589.

It isn't Sunday, it's the middle of the night when the ringing church bells awaken the farmers of Lexington. Sam is cold and afraid as he takes his gun and goes into the darkness with his father. Neither Sam nor his friend John want to fight and are glad when the outnumbered Minutemen decide to disperse. However after the Red Coats wound John, Sam is angry. The next time the bells warn them, he is anxious to help in the fight for freedom. An attractive, easy to read story that gives information of the way of life and existing conditions at the beginning of the Revolution.

SUBJ: Lexington, Battle of, 1775--Fiction./ United States--History--Revolution, 1775-1783--Fiction.

CDR   Ph-1 K-3 $39.95   OD KF223

BERENSTAIN BEARS GET IN A FIGHT. School ed. (CD-ROM). Random House/Broderbund, 1995. 1 CD-ROM color, 2 paperback books. (Living books).

Includes teacher's guide, user's guide, troubleshooting guide and Judy Blume's THE PAIN AND THE GREAT ONE.

System requirements: Macintosh System 6.0.7 or higher; 256 color monitor; 4MB RAM; CD-ROM drive.

System requirements: IBM or 100% compatible 386SX or higher with 4MB RAM; Windows 3.1; MS-DOS 3.3 or higher; Super VGA (640x480, 256 colors); Sound Blaster or SB Pro and 100% compatible sound card; mouse; CD-ROM drive.

Product runs on either Macintosh or Windows compatible hardware. Based on the text by Stan and Jan Berenstain, this interactive story tells the tale of Brother Bear and Sister Bear getting into a fight. Trademark Broderbund animations and humor make the story very realistic. Options to have the story read in English or Spanish make the tale even more useful. A bonus book about sibling rivalry, THE PAIN AND THE GREAT ONE, accompanies the CD edition.

SUBJ: Behavior--Fiction--Software./ Software--Behavior--Fiction./ Bears--Fiction--Software./ Software--Bears--Fiction./ Friendship--Fiction--Software./ Software--Friendship--Fiction./ Spanish language materials--Software./ Software--Spanish language materials./ Bilingual materials--Spanish--Software./ Software--Bilingual materials--Spanish./ Interactive media.

CDR   Ph-1 K-3 $49.95   OD KF224

BERENSTAIN BEARS IN THE DARK. School ed. (CD-ROM). Random House/Broderbund, 1996. 1 CD-ROM color, 2 paperback books. (Living books).

Includes teacher's guide, user's guide, troubleshooting guide and Charles G. Shaw's IT LOOKED LIKE SPILT MILK.

System requirements: Macintosh System 6.0.7 or higher or Power Macintosh; CD-ROM drive; 256 color monitor; 4MB RAM (8MB RAM for System 7.5 or higher or Power Macintosh).

System requirements: Windows 3.1 or Windows 95; IBM or compatible 386SX or higher with 4MB RAM (486SX or higher with 8MB RAM for Windows 95); Super VGA (640x480, 256 colors); Sound Blaster or SB Pro and 100% compatible sound card; mouse; CD-ROM drive.

Product runs on either Macintosh or Windows compatible hardware. This interactive story based on the book by Stan and Jan Berenstain provides a whimsical look at a young bear with an overactive imagination who is afraid of the dark after hearing a mystery. Options to have the story read to you or to move at your own pace exist. In addition, a concentration game and a picture jumble activity are available. A bonus book, IT LOOKED LIKE SPILT MILK, which corresponds with the theme of imagination is included.

SUBJ: Night--Fiction--Software./ Software--Night--Fiction./ Fear--Fiction--Software./ Software--Fear--Fiction./ Bears--Fiction--Software./ Software--Bears--Fiction./ Interactive media.

CE   Ph-1 K-2/4 $3.25   P   KF225

BERENSTAIN, STAN. Berenstain Bears learn about strangers. By Stan and Jan Berenstain. Random House ISBN 0-394-87334-3; In Canada: Random House, 1985. unp. col. ill.

Because Sister is so outgoing and friendly with anyone and everyone, Brother Bear thinks it is time for her to learn about the possible dangers. Unfortunately, Papa's explanation leaves Sister so frightened that she doesn't even want to go outside, and it isn't until Mama tries another approach and the family works out six important rules that the cubs again feel free to play and be friendly yet sensible.

SUBJ: Strangers--Fiction./ Bears--Fiction./ Safety--Fiction.

****   Ph-2 K-2/4 $3.25   P   KF226

BERENSTAIN, STAN. Berenstain Bears: no girls allowed. By Stan and Jan Berenstain. Random House ISBN 0-394-87331-9, 1986. unp. col. ill. (First time book).

Sister Bear, who used to be a little nuisance when she wanted to tag along, becomes a big nuisance when she runs faster, climbs higher, hits the ball farther and wins more marbles than Brother Bear and his friends so they form a special club with NO GIRLS ALLOWED. Other child-appealing titles in this series are: THE BERENSTAIN BEARS GET STAGE FRIGHT (ISBN 0-394-97337-2, 1986, OPC); "..AND THE WEEK AT GRANDMA'S" (ISBN 0-394-97335-6, 1986); "...AND TOO MUCH BIRTHDAY" (ISBN 0-394-87332-7, 1986); Spanish version LOS OSOS BERENSTAIN Y DEMASIADA FIESTA (ISBN 0-679-84745-6, 1993); "...MOVING DAY" (ISBN 0-394-84838-1, 1981; Spanish version LOS OSOS BERENSTAIN DIA DE MUDANZA (ISBN 0-679-85430-4, 1994) "...GO TO CAMP" (ISBN 0-394-85131-5, 1982); "...AND THE SITTER" (ISBN 0-394-84837-3, 1981; Spanish version LOS OSOS BERENSTAIN Y LA NINERA (ISBN 0-679-84746-4, 1993, OPC); "...GET IN A FIGHT" (ISBN 0-394-85132-3, 1982); "...VISIT THE DENTIST" (ISBN 0-394-94836-5, 1981); "...GO TO THE DOCTOR" (ISBN 0-394-94835-1, 1981 (OPC); "...GET THE GIMMIES" (ISBN 0-394-90566-0, 1988, OPC). Each title is an accurate description of its contents. Even though the series title incorrectly implies ease of reading, this has remained a long enduring popular series.

SUBJ: Bears--Fiction./ Brothers and sisters--Fiction.

****   Ph-2 K-1/1 $7.99   L   KF227

BERENSTAIN, STAN. Inside, outside, upside down. By Stan and Jan Berenstain. Random House ISBN 0-394-91142-3, c1968. unp. col. ill. (Bright and early book).

A bit of nonsense in which a bear-like animal has a brief trip "inside, outside, upside down!" Has great appeal for reluctant primary readers. Useful (on a one-to-one basis) for those who work with children who have perceptual difficulties. In the BERENSTAIN BEARS AND THE SPOOKY OLD TREE (ISBN 0-394-93910-7, 1978) three little bears find themselves up a spooky old tree in the dark and with the shivers after losing their rope, stick and light.

SUBJ: Nonsense verses.

****   Ph-1 K-2/2 $15.99   L   KF228

BEST, CARI. Red light, green light, Mama and me. Illus. by Niki Daly. Orchard ISBN 0-531-08752-2, 1995. unp. col. ill.

"Melanie Kroupa book."

Lizzie finds lots of fun things to do when she spends the day with her mother at work in the Downtown Public Library. The excitement of

spending a day at work with a parent is apparent in the story and watercolor illustrations, especially when the workplace is a library. A first choice for units on career studies or community helpers. For multicultural studies.
SUBJ: Mothers and daughters--Fiction./ Libraries--Fiction./ Work--Fiction./ City and town life--Fiction./ Afro-Americans--Fiction.

CDR Ph-1 K-2 $79.00 OD KF229
BIG ANTHONY'S MIXED-UP MAGIC (CD-ROM). MECC/Learning Company CD-659 ISBN 0-7929-0933-X, 1996. 1 CD-ROM color, 1 paperback book.
Version 1.01.
Includes teacher's guide and companion volume STREGA NONA MEETS HER MATCH by Tomie De Paola.
System requirements: Macintosh 68030 processor or better (LC II or greater); System 7.0 or later Macintosh operating system; 4MB RAM; double-speed or faster CD-ROM drive; 13" color display or larger (256 colors, 640x480).
System requirements: Windows 486 or faster processor; Microsoft Windows 3.1 or Windows for Workgroups 3.11 or Windows 95; 16-color display; 4MB RAM or 8MB RAM for Windows for Workgroups recommended or 8MB RAM for Windows 95; double-speed CD-ROM drive; mouse; Windows-compatible sound card. Product CD-659 (ISBN 0-7929-0933-X) runs on either Macintosh or Windows compatible hardware.
This is an interactive version of the classic STREGA NONA MEETS HER MATCH. Youngsters can either read the story, explore Calabria, or take an adventure with Big Anthony. Excellent sound and consistent operation enable youngsters to use this CD-ROM independently. Works well with small groups or an entire class.
SUBJ: Thought and thinking--Software./ Software--Thought and thinking./ Problem solving--Software./ Software--Problem solving./ Magic tricks--Software./ Software--Magic tricks./ Interactive media.

Ph-2 1-3/3 $15.93 L KF230
BIRCHMAN, DAVID FRANCIS. Jigsaw Jackson. By David F. Birchman. Illus. by Daniel San Souci. Lothrop, Lee & Shepard ISBN 0-688-11633-7, 1996. unp. col. ill.
Jigsaw Jackson, who can piece together a puzzle in record time, becomes a celebrity when he joins Sean McShaker, a puzzle maker. Together they travel from town to town amazing audiences with Jackson's incredible skill. Larger than life, the feats of the jigsaw genius will enthrall both readers and listeners. For reading aloud.
SUBJ: Jigsaw puzzles--Fiction./ Farm life--Fiction./ Domestic animals--Fiction.

Ph-1 K-3/5 $14.95 L KF231
BIRDSEYE, TOM. Air mail to the moon. Illus. by Stephen Gammell. Holiday House ISBN 0-8234-0683-0, 1988. unp. col. ill.
Eagerly awaiting a great gift from the tooth fairy, Ora Mae is furious when she finds nothing under her pillow and accuses each member of her family of stealing her first tooth. She threatens to "open up a can of gotcha and send 'em air mail to the moon". As she vows not to give up until she finds the "lop-eared rascal" who took it, she puts her hands in her pocket and much to her chagrin feels a small, hard, roundish object. Colorful, scratchy illustrations match the humorous hilly-billyish language and setting.
SUBJ: Teeth--Fiction./ Tooth fairy--Fiction.

Ph-2 1-3/5 $13.95 L KF232
BLACKSTONE, STELLA. Grandma went to market: a round-the-world counting rhyme. Illus. by Bernard Lodge. Houghton Mifflin ISBN 0-395-74045-2, 1996. unp. col. ill.
When Grandma goes to market, she goes around the world from Istanbul to Tokyo. On each page, count the items she buys from one to ten until the last page unfolds to show all her purchases. A counting book with extensions to multicultural studies.
SUBJ: Voyages and travels--Fiction./ Geography--Fiction./ Counting./ Stories in rhyme.

CE Ph-2 1-3/3 $8.95 P KF233
BLADES, ANN. Mary of Mile 18. Tundra ISBN 0-88776-059-7; In Canada: Tundra, 1971. unp. col. ill.
Canadian Library Award.
Available from National Library Service for the Blind and Physically Handicapped on sound recording cassette RC15202.
Mary, who lives in a tiny isolated village in northern British Columbia, wishes for something special to alter her winter life of chores and school. Her wish is answered when she finds a pup--part dog and part wolf--but the animal must prove his usefulness before she can keep him. Striking paintings illustrate life in a desolate Mennonite community.
SUBJ: British Columbia (Canada)--Fiction./ Mennonites--Fiction./ Wolves--Fiction.

Ph-1 K-3/6 $4.95 P KF234
BLOOD, CHARLES L. Goat in the rug. By Geraldine, as told to Charles L. Blood and Martin Link. Illus. by Nancy Winslow Parker. Aladdin ISBN 0-689-71418-1, 1990. unp. col. ill.
Geraldine, a goat, describes each process used to make a rug. Glenmae, her Navajo friend, clips, washes, combs, spins and dyes the wool before finally weaving a rug with a design that will never be duplicated.
SUBJ: Navajo Indians--Industries--Fiction./ Rugs--Fiction./ Weaving--Fiction./ Goats--Fiction.

Ph-2 P-2/2 $13.00 T KF235
BLOOM, SUZANNE. Family for Jamie: an adoption story. Potter/Crown ISBN 0-517-57492-6, 1991. unp. col. ill.
Long before they adopt Jamie, his parents lovingly plan to adopt and raise a child. Cheerful illustrations are filled with children and toys in this very child-centered story about the adoption process. Written from the author's experience, this clearly fills a need for materials about the decision, anticipation, and love involved in adoption.
SUBJ: Adoption--Fiction.

Ph-2 2-5/9 $14.93 L KF236
BLOS, JOAN W. Nellie Bly's monkey: his remarkable story in his own words. Illus. by Catherine Stock. Morrow ISBN 0-688-12678-2, 1996. unp. col. ill., map.
Purchased by Nellie Bly in Singapore, McGinty a small monkey relates the story of their journey around the world. The somewhat long text will be most enjoyed by older readers who may use the author's notes to follow up with more research about the life of this remarkable woman. For women's studies.
SUBJ: Bly, Nellie--Fiction./ Monkeys--Fiction./ Journalists--Fiction./ Voyages and travels--Fiction.

CE Ph-2 K-3/2 $15.93 L KF237
BLOS, JOAN W. Old Henry. Illus. by Stephen Gammell. Morrow ISBN 0-688-06400-0, 1987. unp. col. ill.
Available from National Library Service for the Blind and Physically Handicapped on sound recording cassette RC26353.
The neighbors are surprised and alarmed when Henry moves into the dilapidated house and doesn't spruce it up. Their complaints only make him move and then they realize he made a real contribution to the neighborhood. Colorful and lively pencil drawings add tone and texture to this rhyming story that stresses acceptance of individual differences.
SUBJ: Neighborliness--Fiction./ Stories in rhyme.

CE Ph-1 K-3/2 $12.95 L KF238
BLUME, JUDY. One in the middle is the green kangaroo. Illus. by Amy Aitken. Bradbury ISBN 0-02-711055-9, 1981. 39p. col. ill.
Read-along kit available from Listening Library FTR 77 (ISBN 0-8072-0044-1, 1983). 1 paperback book, 1 sound cassette (9min), $14.95. Includes guide.
Being a successful performer in the school play provides a tremendous ego boost for Freddie, the "great big middle nothing" in a family with three children.
SUBJ: Family life--Fiction./ Brothers and sisters--Fiction.

CE Ph-1 K-3/4 $14.95 L KF239
BLUME, JUDY. Pain and the great one. Illus. by Irene Trivas. Bradbury ISBN 0-02-711100-8; In Canada: Collier Macmillan, 1984. unp. col. ill.
Available from National Library Service for the Blind and Physically Handicapped on sound recording cassette RC22718.
Read-along kit available from Listening Library FTR118 (ISBN 0-8072-0122-7, 1988). 1 paperback book, 1 sound cassette (10min), teacher's guide. $14.95. (Follow the reader).
Expounding emphatically as to which has the most faults, and who gets the most attention, love and special favors from their parents, are two monologues; one by the six year old Pain and one from the viewpoint of the eight year old Great One. Although included in 'Free to be...you and me" by Marlo Thomas, it is worthwhile and quite useful as a single title.
SUBJ: Brothers and sisters--Fiction.

Ph-2 1-3/4 $14.95 T KF240
BODKIN, ODDS. Banshee train. Illus. by Ted Rose. Clarion ISBN 0-395-69426-4, 1995. unp. col. ill.
Train Number 1, filled with passengers and headed to Troublesome and Steamboat Springs, is pursued by a mysterious train and forced to stop just short of the Gore Canyon Trestle. Only the train's engineer and the fireman witness the Banshee train as it speeds past their stopped train. Awestruck, they get down from the train and discover the trestle is completely gone. Dark watercolor illustrations join the text in creating the mysterious and ghostly mood perfect for reading aloud.
SUBJ: Railroad accidents--Fiction./ Ghosts--Fiction.

Ph-1 K-2/2 $12.89 L KF241
BOLAND, JANICE. Dog named Sam. Illus. by G. Brian Karas. Dial ISBN 0-8037-1531-5; In Canada: Penguin, 1996. 40p. col. ill. (Dial easy-to-read).
Sam is one of those dogs who fetches everything, jumps in when he's not welcome, and keeps the family awake with his howling. Young readers can't help but love him anyway with his good intentions and endearing expressions. The easy-to-read text and humorous illustrations are accessible to beginning readers.
SUBJ: Dogs--Fiction.

Ph-1 1-2/1 $13.89 L KF242
BONSALL, CROSBY NEWELL. And I mean it, Stanley. HarperCollins ISBN 0-06-020568-7, 1974. 32p. col. ill. (Early I can read book).
As she plays in a fenced, junk filled alley, a little girl talks to invisible Stanley who apparently is on the other side of the fence. Out of the trash and junk she completes a "really neat" tall, scarecrow-like figure just as big, furry, affectionate Stanley finally appears.
SUBJ: Play--Fiction./ Dogs--Fiction.

CE
Ph-2 1-2/2 $12.89 L KF243
BONSALL, CROSBY NEWELL. Case of the hungry stranger. HarperCollins ISBN 0-06-020571-7; In Canada: HarperCollins, c1963. 64p. col. ill. (I can read mystery).
Spanish edition EL CASO DEL FORASTERO HAMBRIENTO available from Harper Arco Iris (ISBN 0-06-444195-4, 1996).
Read-along kit available from Harper Caedmon (ISBN 1-559942-23-1, 1985). 1 paperback book, 1 sound cassette (17min), $7.95.
Wizard, Tubby, Skinny and Snitch are four boys who act as "private eyes" in this easy-to-read mystery series.
Also in this series CASE OF THE CAT'S MEOW (ISBN 0-06-020561-X, 1965); CASE OF THE DUMB BELLS (ISBN 0-06-020624-1, 1966); CASE OF THE SCAREDY CATS (ISBN 0-06-020566-0, 1971), (read-along kit available from Harper Caedmon (ISBN 1-55994-436-6, 1991), 1 paperback book, 1 sound cassette (15min); and CASE OF THE DOUBLE CROSS (ISBN 0-06-020603-9, 1980).
SUBJ: Mystery and detective stories./ Spanish language materials.

Ph-1 1-2/1 $13.89 L KF244
BONSALL, CROSBY NEWELL. Day I had to play with my sister. HarperCollins ISBN 0-06-020576-8, c1972. 32p. col. ill. (Early I can read book).
A little boy tries to teach his toddler sister how to play hide-and-seek, but little sister just doesn't get the idea. Division into chapters, simple easy to read text and humorous illustrations all add to the appeal.
SUBJ: Play--Fiction./ Brothers and sisters--Fiction.

Ph-1 1-2/1 $14.89 L KF245
BONSALL, CROSBY NEWELL. Mine's the best. Newly illustrated ed. HarperCollins ISBN 0-06-027091-8; In Canada: HarperCollins, 1996. 32p. col. ill. (My first I can read book).
Two little boys at the beach have identical balloons, but each insists that his inflated toy is best. The balloons deflate, and each boy blames the other until a smart-alecky little girl goes by. Then the boys join forces and decide "ours was the best."
SUBJ: Balloons--Fiction./ Friendship--Fiction.

Ph-2 P-2/2 $13.89 L KF246
BONSALL, CROSBY NEWELL. Piggle. HarperCollins ISBN 0-06-020580-6, 1973. 64p. col. ill.
Sequel to WHO'S A PEST?
When Homer's sisters, Lolly, Molly, Polly and Dolly won't play with him, he tries to play with Duck, Rabbit and Pig. They won't play either, but finally Homer and Bear have fun playing a good, rhyming word game they call Piggle like wiggle, giggle, sniggle and figgle.
SUBJ: Animals--Fiction./ Word games--Fiction./ Brothers and sisters--Fiction.

Ph-1 K-2/2 $13.89 L KF247
BONSALL, CROSBY NEWELL. Tell me some more. Illus. by Fritz Siebel. HarperCollins ISBN 0-06-020601-2, c1961. 64p. col. ill. (I can read book).
Available from National Library Service for the Blind and Physically Handicapped in Braille BRA06945.
Andrew takes Tim to a place where he can do the most impossible things--carry an elephant, tickle a seal, pet a lion's nose--the public library.
SUBJ: Libraries--Fiction.

Ph-2 P-2/2 $13.89 L KF248
BONSALL, CROSBY NEWELL. Who's a pest? HarperCollins ISBN 0-06-020621-7, c1962. 64p. col. ill. (I can read book).
A little boy does not think that he is a pest even though four sisters, a lizard, a rabbit and a chipmunk believe he is.
SUBJ: Animals--Fiction.

Ph-1 P-1/1 $13.89 L KF249
BONSALL, CROSBY NEWELL. Who's afraid of the dark? HarperCollins ISBN 0-06-020599-7; In Canada: HarperCollins, 1980. 32p. col. ill. (Early I can read book).
A little boy tries to teach his dog, Stella, to be unafraid of the dark and the night noises. But the readers know it's really the boy who's scared and shivery.
SUBJ: Night--Fiction.

Ph-2 K-2/5 $14.88 L KF250
BOOTH, BARBARA D. Mandy. Illus. by Jim LaMarche. Lothrop, Lee & Shepard ISBN 0-688-10339-1, 1991. unp. col. ill.
Mandy, who is deaf, wonders about the sounds of chocolate chip cookie dough dropping onto metal pans, the radio, and tree branches blowing in the wind. When her grandma loses a cherished pin while they are out walking, Mandy bravely searches for it during a thunderstorm. Mandy's point of view, as a deaf child, is unique in a book for young people.
SUBJ: Hearing disorders--Fiction./ Physically handicapped--Fiction./ Grandmothers--Fiction.

Ph-1 3-5/3 $15.00 T KF251
BORDEN, LOUISE. Little ships: the heroic rescue at Dunkirk in World War II. Illus. by Michael Foreman. McElderry ISBN 0-689-80827-5; In Canada: Distican, 1997. 32p. col. ill., map.
The dramatic rescue at Dunkirk aided by small fishing boats and yachts is described through the eyes of a young girl who accompanies her father on his boat, the Lucy. A blend of fact and fiction, the story represents the spirit of the endeavor as the watercolor illustrations convey the wartime scenes. Historical fiction perhaps best appreciated by older readers who have some background and interest in World War II.
SUBJ: Dunkerque (France), Battle of, 1940--Fiction./ World War, 1939-1945--Great Britain--Fiction./ Fathers and daughters--Fiction.

Ph-1 K-2/3 $15.95 L KF252
BORTON, LADY. Junk pile! Illus. by Kimberly Bulcken Root. Philomel ISBN 0-399-22728-8; In Canada: Putnam, 1997. unp. col. ill.
Jamie Kay helps her father around the junkyard salvaging parts and repairing cars. Robert, a neighbor, teases her until one day she helps restart the school bus with a new clutch pin. Jamie Kay earns Robert's friendship by leaving him gifts of spare parts that he uses to build a dog. The power of imagination and the potential beauty of junk are skillfully conveyed in the watercolor illustrations and strong characterization of Jamie Kay.
SUBJ: Junk--Fiction./ Friendship--Fiction./ Appalachian Region--Fiction./ Imagination--Fiction.

VCR
Ph-3 1-4 $14.98 KF253
BOX AND TWO OTHER TITLES FOR FAMILY ENJOYMENT (Videocassette). National Film Board of Canada/Smarty Pants NFV 14009 ISBN 1-55886-159-9; In Canada: National Film Board of Canada, 1992. 1/2" VHS videocassette color.
Originally published in Canada, 1989.
The title story features an artist's paper creation and its adventures in a paper world in a simple fantasy which is technically interesting. "Cinderella" is narrated with young voices and features the illustrations of fifth grade students and may inspire similar productions. "Mary of Mile 18" is presented with very primitive animation but may serve as a complement to the book.
Contents: The box (10min); The story of Cinderella (7min); Mary of Mile 18 (12min).
SUBJ: Fairy tales./ Short stories.

Ph-2 1-3/2 $15.95 L KF254
BOYD, CANDY DAWSON. Daddy, Daddy, be there. Illus. by Floyd Cooper. Philomel ISBN 0-399-22745-8; In Canada: Putnam, 1995. unp. col. ill.
Daddy, be there--listening, sharing, and hugging through happy, scary, sad, and proud moments. This is the plea of children of all races and nationalities expressed in poetic words and evocative pictures. Many children will find themselves reflected in these pages. For multicultural studies.
SUBJ: Father and child--Fiction.

CE
Ph-2 K-2/7 $15.95 T KF255
BOYLE, DOE. Coral reef hideaway: the story of a clown anemonefish. Illustrated by Steven James Petruccio. Soundprints/Smithsonian Institution ISBN 1-56899-182-7; In Canada: Soundprints/dist. by Canadian Manda, 1995. 32p. col. ill. (Smithsonian oceanic collection).
Includes glossary.
Teacher's guide available upon request.
Read-along kit available (ISBN 1-56899-186-X, 1995). 1 hardback book, 1 sound cassette (9min), $19.95.
Percula, a clown anemonefish, evades predators, finds a mate, and

guards her eggs until they hatch in her sea anemone hideaway. Bright illustrations and a text focused on an individual fish convey information and spark interest for young readers.
SUBJ: Clown anemonefish--Fiction./ Fishes--Fiction./ Coral reef animals--Fiction.

Ph-1 1-3/3 $15.99 L KF256
BRADBY, MARIE. More than anything else. Illus. by Chris K. Soentpiet. Orchard ISBN 0-531-08764-6, 1995. unp. col. ill.
"Richard Jackson book."
Young Booker dreams of learning to decipher the black marks on paper while he accompanies his father to the salt mines. His desire and perserverance is so strong that he learns the alphabet and how to spell his name. Allusion is made to Booker T. Washington, but no historical note is provided, leaving the curious to research the connection elsewhere. Watercolor paintings add depth and power to the moving story. For multicultural studies.
SUBJ: Washington, Booker T.--Fiction./ Afro-Americans--Fiction./ Books and reading--Fiction.

Ph-2 P-1/2 $14.00 T KF257
BRANDENBERG, ALEXA. Chop, simmer, season. Harcourt Brace ISBN 0-15-200973-6; In Canada: Harcourt Brace c/o Canadian Manda, 1997. unp. col. ill.
The menu is set on the title page, and the chefs begin at sunrise to prepare the evening meal. Red and white checks border the bright paintings which illustrate one verb on each page. A simple text and appealing illustrations are the recipe for this successful presentation. The behind-the-scenes look at a restaurant kitchen will supplement community helpers units.
SUBJ: Cookery--Fiction./ Restaurants--Fiction.

Ph-1 P-K/1 $12.00 L KF258
BRANDENBERG, ALEXA. I am me! Red Wagon Books/Harcourt Brace ISBN 0-15-200974-4; In Canada: Harcourt Brace c/o Canadian Manda, 1996. unp. col. ill.
Young children describe what they want to be when they grow up and the things they like to do now. Forthright and appealing, framed illustrations and minimal text will appeal to very young listeners and beginning readers. The various careers introduce community helpers.
SUBJ: Occupations--Fiction.

CE   Ph-1 1-3/1 $13.89 L KF259
BRENNER, BARBARA. Wagon wheels. Illus. by Don Bolognese. HarperCollins ISBN 0-06-020669-1; In Canada: HarperCollins, 1978. 64p. col. ill. (I can read history book.)
Available from National Library Service for the Blind and Physically Handicapped in Braille BR05074.
Read along kit available from HarperChildren's Audio (ISBN 0-69470-001-0, 1995). 1 paperback book, 1 sound cassette (15min), $6.95.
Shortly after the war between the states, Johnny, Willie, Little Brother, and Daddy leave Kentucky to homestead and make a new home on the "free dirt" of Kansas. They spend the first hard winter in a dugout in the African-American community of Nicodemus. Spring comes and the children care for themselves until word comes that Mr. Muldie has established a new farm home for them. Depicts relationships between Native Americans and African-Ameican settlers based on true events. For multicultural studies.
SUBJ: Frontier and pioneer life--Fiction./ Afro-Americans--Fiction.

Ph-1 K-3/2 $13.95 L KF260
BRETT, JAN. Annie and the wild animals. Houghton Mifflin ISBN 0-395-37800-1, 1985. unp. col. ill.
When Annie's cat disappears she tries to entice a new pet but each animal attracted by her corn cakes is much too big, wild or fierce to cuddle and pet. Outstanding, detailed water colors containing many folk motifs enhance the simple, predictable story and the pictures in the intricate border design tell stories within the story as they forecast coming events.
SUBJ: Animals--Fiction./ Pets--Fiction./ Cats--Fiction.

Ph-1 K-2/2 $14.95 L KF261
BRETT, JAN. Berlioz the bear. Putnam ISBN 0-399-22248-0; In Canada: Putnam, 1991. unp. col. ill.
Available from the National Library Service for the Blind and Physically Handicapped on sound recording cassette RC 36455.
Concerned about a buzzing noise coming from his double bass, Berlioz the bear joins the other musicians in the bandwagon to go to a ball. When their wagon hits a hole in the road, the mule refuses to pull the wagon further and won't budge despite the efforts of several animals. Finally the source of the buzzing in Berlioz's double bass comes out and stings the mule into action. The story is furthered by another story pictured in the borders of the richly decorated

illustrations.
SUBJ: Bears--Fiction./ Animals--Fiction./ Musicians--Fiction.

Ph-2 P-1/3 $14.95 L KF262
BRETT, JAN. Trouble with trolls. Putnam ISBN 0-399-22336-3; In Canada: Putnam, 1992. unp. col. ill.
One day Treva has trouble with trolls who keep trying to steal her dog as she climbs up Mount Baldy, but each time she manages to trick the trolls. The cutaway view of the trolls' life underground is the most interesting feature of this simple story.
SUBJ: Trolls--Fiction.

Ph-2 K-2/2 $14.95 L KF263
BRETT, JAN. Wild Christmas reindeer. Putnam ISBN 0-399-22192-1; In Canada: Putnam, 1990. unp. col. ill.
Teeka, a young girl who lives in the Arctic near Santa's Winterfarm, is in charge of training the reindeer for Christmas Eve. The story, while pleasant, is secondary to the richly colored and textured illustrations. Useful for a changing display during the holiday season since each page is framed by lavishly decorative borders which picture the elves preparing for Christmas as the calendar moves from the first of December to Christmas Eve.
SUBJ: Reindeer--Fiction./ Christmas--Fiction.

CE   Ph-2 P-2/1 $10.95 L KF264
BRIDWELL, NORMAN. Clifford the big red dog. Scholastic ISBN 0-590-40743-0, c1963, 1985. unp. col. ill.
Also available in Spanish: CLIFFORD EL GRAND PERRO COLORADO. Translated by Frances M. Leos. Scholastic (ISBN 0-590-41380-5, 1988).
Relates funny experiences Emily Elizabeth has with Clifford, her pet dog who is bigger than a two story house. Very easy-to-read and exhibiting humor that appeals to beginning readers. Other popular and very funny titles in the series include: CLIFFORD GETS A JOB (ISBN 0-590-44296-1, 1985); CLIFFORD TAKES A TRIP (ISBN 0-590-44260-0, 1985, Spanish version CLIFFORD VA DE VIAJE ISBN 0-590-40844-5, 1995); CLIFFORD THE SMALL RED PUPPY (ISBN 0-590-43496-9, 1985); CLIFFORD'S GOOD DEEDS (ISBN 0-590-44292-9, 1985, Spanish version LAS BUENAS ACCIONES DE CLIFFORD ISBN 0-590-40179-3, 1978); CLIFFORD AT THE CIRCUS (ISBN 0-590-44293-7, 1985) (read-along kit available from Scholastic ISBN 0-590-63340-6, 1987 $6.95); CLIFFORD'S PALS (ISBN 0-590-33582-0, 1985, OPC); CLIFFORD'S HALLOWEEN (ISBN 0-590-44287-2, 1986); CLIFFORD, WE LOVE YOU (ISBN 0-590-43843-3, 1991); and CLIFFORD'S SPORTS DAY (ISBN 0-590-62971-9, 1996).
SUBJ: Dogs--Fiction./ Humorous stories./ Spanish language materials.

CE   Ph-1 P-1 $16.00 T KF265
BRIGGS, RAYMOND. Snowman. Random House ISBN 0-394-83993-0; In Canada: Random House, 1978. unp. col. ill.
Also available as a 1/2" VHS animated color videocassette (26min) Weston Woods HMPV288V, $49.95.
A little boy invites his snowman into his home and introduces his frozen friend to those common, modern inventions such as TV, electric lights, running water, central heat, freezers, a skate board and even false teeth. An appealing wordless story that even the youngest can "read".
SUBJ: Stories without words./ Dreams--Fiction./ Snow--Fiction.

Ph-2 K-1/2 $15.00 L KF266
BRIMNER, LARRY DANE. Brave Mary. Illus. by Marilyn Mets. Children's Press ISBN 0-516-02056-0; In Canada: Grolier Ltd., 1996. 32p. col. ill. (Rookie reader).
Everyone agrees Brave Mary is brave: she doesn't fear snakes, or heights, or the dark. Limited vocabulary and colorful illustrations convey her courageous character for beginning readers.
SUBJ: Courage--Fiction./ Stories in rhyme.

Ph-2 K-2/3 $14.95 T KF267
BRIMNER, LARRY DANE. Merry Christmas, Old Armadillo. Illus. by Dominic Catalano. Boyds Mills ISBN 1-56397-354-5; In Canada: McClelland & Stewart, 1995. unp. col. ill.
Alone on Christmas Eve in a casita on a mesa in the Southwest, Old Armadillo falls asleep while his friends secretly decorate a tree and the outside of his house. Roadrunner, Rattlesnake, and Peccary are among his native animal friends, and luminarias, red peppers, and a cactus with red blossoms are among the decorations. The story has a repeating refrain that will draw in young listeners while the pastel illustrations celebrate the season.
SUBJ: Friendship--Fiction./ Christmas--Fiction./ Southwest, New--Fiction.

Ph-1 K-3/3 $14.88 L KF268

BRINK, CAROL RYRIE. Goody O'Grumpity. Illus. by Ashley Wolff. North-South Books ISBN 1-55858-328-9; In Canada: North-South Books, 1994. unp. col. ill.

When Goody O'Grumpity bakes a cake, the entire village knows about it. Linoleum block illustrations set the poem in Plymouth Village and depict Goody as a Pilgrim woman. A recipe for spice cake is included. The food and the Pilgrim setting make this an ideal book for Thanksgiving themes.
SUBJ: Baking--Fiction./ Stories in rhyme./ Pilgrims (New Plymouth Colony)--Fiction.

Ph-2 P-1/2 $13.93 L KF269

BROWN, CRAIG. In the spring. Greenwillow ISBN 0-688-10984-5, 1994. unp. col. ill.

Several farm animals and their young are identified individually on doublespread pages with minimal text. Youngsters learning about animals can build their vocabulary with this attractive and simply designed book.
SUBJ: Babies--Fiction./ Birth--Fiction./ Domestic animals--Infancy--Fiction./ Spring--Fiction.

Ph-1 K-1/1 $12.95 L KF270

BROWN, LAURENE KRASNY. Rex and Lilly family time. By Laurie Krasny Brown. Illus. by Marc Brown. Little, Brown ISBN 0-316-11385-9; In Canada: Little, Brown, 1995. 32p. col. ill. (Dino easy reader).

The Dino family prepares a surprise for Mom's birthday, hires a robot housekeeper, and buys fish for pets in three short and easy-to-read stories. The humor in the stories and illustrations will encourage beginning readers to read with pleasure.
SUBJ: Dinosaurs--Fiction./ Brothers and sisters--Fiction./ Family life--Fiction.

CE
Ph-1 K-2/2 $15.95 L KF271

BROWN, MARC TOLON. Arthur goes to camp. Atlantic/Little, Brown ISBN 0-316-11218-6; In Canada: Little, Brown, 1982. unp. col. ill.

Arthur doesn't want to go to summer camp, and after he gets there, everything is just as awful as he thought it would be. Each letter home tells of the "teribul" happenings and ends with "I'm homesick. Please come and get me." Then things reach a climax. It's time for the annual scavenger hunt and Arthur knows that those brutes from Camp Horsewater will win as usual. Since his parents still haven't come for him, Arthur decides to run away. In trying to find his way, he turns on his flashlight and that is all his friends need for Camp Meadowcroak to win the hunt. Arthur is a hero and suddenly camp is great.
In ARTHUR'S FAMILY VACATION (ISBN 0-316-11312-3, 1993; read-along kit available ISBN 0-316-11043-4, 1996) Arthur and his family go to the beach where it rains nearly every day, but Arthur plans several field trips for his family.
In ARTHUR'S NEW PUPPY (ISBN 0-316-11355-7, 1993, also available from the NLSBPH on sound recording cassette RC 41874) the family gets a new pet.
SUBJ: Camping--Fiction./ Aardvark--Fiction.

Ph-1 K-2/2 $15.95 L KF272

BROWN, MARC TOLON. Arthur writes a story. By Marc Brown. Little, Brown ISBN 0-316-10916-9; In Canada: Little, Brown, 1996. unp. col. ill.

Attempting to improve his story about his pet business, Arthur embellishes it with more and more fanciful details until it includes elephants in outer space and a song and dance routine. Finally he realizes that his original story about how he got a pet puppy is the best. The familiar cast of Arthur's friends and family are included in this humorous story about the writing process which is sure to inspire creative writing activities.
SUBJ: Authorship--Fiction./ Animals--Fiction./ Aardvark--Fiction.

Ph-2 P-3/2 $15.95 L KF273

BROWN, MARC TOLON. Arthur's April fool. Atlantic/Little, Brown ISBN 0-316-11196-1; In Canada: Little, Brown, 1983. unp. col. ill.

Read-along kit available (ISBN 0-316-11181-3, 1995). 1 paperback book, 1 sound cassette (10min), $9.95.
Getting pulverized by the school bully worries Arthur so much that he's afraid he won't remember his tricks for the April Fool's magic show. However, Arthur not only puts on an outstanding performance, but changes the brazen, bullying Binky into a pale, screaming coward. Directing the Thanksgiving play is very important to Arthur, but he is also reluctantly forced to be the "turkey" in ARTHUR'S THANKSGIVING (ISBN 0-316-11060-4, 1983).
Holiday books are always in demand and humorous illustrations, realistic school activities and conversations make these and ARTHUR'S CHRISTMAS (ISBN 0-316-11180-5, 1984); ARTHUR'S HALLOWEEN (ISBN 0-316-11116-3, 1982; read-along kit read by the author available ISBN 0-316-11105-8, 1996. 1 paperback book, 1 sound cassette [20min], $9.95; and ARTHUR'S VALENTINE (ISBN 0-316-

11062-0, 1980) popular.
SUBJ: April Fools' Day--Fiction./ Magic tricks--Fiction./ Bullies--Fiction./ Thanksgiving Day--Fiction./ Plays--Fiction./ Schools--Fiction./ Christmas--Fiction./ Halloween--Fiction./ Valentine's Day--Fiction.

Ph-2 K-3/2 $14.95 L KF274

BROWN, MARC TOLON. Arthur's baby. Joy Street/Little, Brown ISBN 0-316-11123-6; In Canada: Little, Brown, 1987. unp. col. ill.

Available from National Library Service for the Blind and Physically Handicapped in Braille BR7488.
Disappointed when his surprise turns out to be a baby instead of a new bicycle, Arthur thinks baby Kate is a real nuisance until the day she stops crying only for Arthur. A familiar childhood problem addressed realistically and with humor.
SUBJ: Babies--Fiction./ Brothers and sisters--Fiction./ Aardvark--Fiction.

Ph-1 K-2/2 $15.95 L KF275

BROWN, MARC TOLON. Arthur's first sleepover. By Marc Brown. Little, Brown ISBN 0-316-11445-6; In Canada: Little, Brown, 1994. unp. col. ill.

When Arthur and his friends spend the night in a backyard tent, they hear strange noises and see unusual lights. Could it be space aliens? When you have a little sister like D.W., anything is possible! Fans of this aardvark and his friends will thoroughly enjoy the amusing story and illustrations.
SUBJ: Sleepovers--Fiction./ Aardvark--Fiction./ Animals--Fiction.

CE
Ph-2 K-2/2 $15.95 L KF276

BROWN, MARC TOLON. Arthur's nose. Atlantic/Little, Brown ISBN 0-316-11193-7; In Canada: Little, Brown, c1976. 32p. col. ill.

Arthur, an aardvark, blames his unhappiness on his unusual nose. He decides to do something about it, but after trying on all kinds of noses he discovers "I'm just not me without my nose." All his friends agree and tell him "It's a nice nose."
In ARTHUR'S PET BUSINESS (ISBN 0-316-11262-3, 1990; read-along kit available ISBN 0-316-11182-1, 1995) Arthur takes care of other people's pets to show his parents that he's ready for the responsibilities of owning a puppy.
In ARTHUR MEETS THE PRESIDENT (ISBN 0-316-11265-8, 1991; read-along kit available ISBN 0-316-11044-2, 1996) Arthur must recite his contest winning essay.
In ARTHUR BABYSITS (Joy Street/Little, Brown ISBN 0-316-11293-3, 1992; read-along kit available ISBN 0-316-11103-1, 1996; videocassette available from SRA/MaGraw-Hill 87-005413, n.d.) Arthur watches the terrible Tibble twins.
In ARTHUR'S EYES (Joy Street/Little, Brown ISBN 0-316-11063-9, 1979; read-along kit available ISBN 0-316-11338-7, 1993; available from the NLSBPH on sound recording cassette RC 41678) Arthur doesn't like his new glasses until he realizes how much better he can see with them on.
In ARTHUR'S CHICKEN POX (ISBN 0-316-11384-0, 1994) Arthur catches chicken pox a week before he is supposed to go to the circus.
SUBJ: Nose--Fiction./ Animals--Fiction./ Humorous stories./ Aardvark--Fiction.

CE
Ph-2 K-3/4 $13.95 L KF277

BROWN, MARC TOLON. Arthur's teacher trouble. Joy Street/Little, Brown ISBN 0-316-11244-5; In Canada: Little, Brown, 1986. unp. col. ill.

Available in Spanish ARTURO Y SUS PROBLEMAS CON EL PROFESOR (ISBN 0-316-11379-4, 1994), $15.95.
Furious because his new teacher assigns homework on the first day of school, Arthur and his friends continue to complain when Mr. Ratburn works them even harder. But all those assignments pay off and Arthur very successfully represents the third grade in the school spellathon. Little sister D.W. is just as pesky as ever but on the last page she gets her comeuppance. Comical, imaginative and busy illustrations extend the humor of another title about Arthur, Francine and their schoolmates.
ARTHUR'S BIRTHDAY (ISBN 0-316-11073-6, 1989) may not turn out to be fun since Muffy is having her party at the same time and has invited the same children.
SUBJ: Schools--Fiction./ Teachers--Fiction./ Animals--Fiction./ Aardvark--Fiction./ Spanish language materials.

CE
Ph-2 1-3/2 $14.95 L KF278

BROWN, MARC TOLON. Arthur's tooth. Joy Street/Little, Brown ISBN 0-316-11245-3; In Canada: Little, Brown, 1985. 30p. col. ill.

Available from National Library Service for the Blind and Physically Handicapped in Braille BR06119.
Depressed and embarrassed because he is the only one in the class who hasn't lost a baby tooth, Arthur is the object of Francine's taunts and class jokes, but loud mouth Francine finally unintentionally solves the problem. Many details in the bright illustrations add humor to the

typical childhood experiences and conversations.
SUBJ: Teeth--Fiction./ Aardvark--Fiction.

Ph-2 K-2/2 $15.95 L KF279
BROWN, MARC TOLON. Arthur's TV trouble. By Marc Brown. Little,
Brown ISBN 0-316-10919-3; In Canada: Little, Brown, 1995. unp. col. ill.
Arthur works hard to earn the money to buy a Treat Timer for his
dog, but he is disappointed when the product doesn't perform as
advertised on TV. This amusing and cautionary tale will be a good
discussion starter for social studies classes examining media influence.
SUBJ: Advertising--Fiction./ Moneymaking projects--Fiction./ Brothers
and sisters--Fiction./ Aardvark--Fiction.

Ph-1 K-3/5 $5.95 P KF280
BROWN, MARC TOLON. Bionic Bunny Show. By Marc Tolon Brown
and Laurene Krany Brown. Joy Street/Little, Brown ISBN 0-316-10992-4;
In Canada: Little, Brown, 1984. 31p. col. ill.
Selectors' Choice, 15th ed.
Transforming an ordinary rabbit into a television super hero is simply
a matter of costume, special effects and careful staging as this
humorous title shows. Very useful as an enjoyable way to raise young
people's consciousness level and initiate a discussion about
perceptions.
SUBJ: Television--Fiction./ Rabbits--Fiction.

Ph-2 P-2/1 $14.95 L KF281
BROWN, MARC TOLON. D.W. flips. Joy Street Books/Little, Brown
ISBN 0-316-11239-9; In Canada: Little, Brown, 1987. unp. col. ill.
Superconfident D.W., Arthur's little sister, joins a gymnastics class
with the expectation of immediately doing superflips, but instead she
is placed in a beginning baby group and discovers she can't even do
a forward roll. Just as determined as she is confident, D.W. learns
that with lots and lots of practice she can perform perfect rolls. Softly
colored pictures capture the lively action and humor of the animal
children performing in class and of plaster falling, chandelier shaking,
and fruit rolling in the grocery store aisles as D.W. practices
everywhere.
In D.W. ALL WET (ISBN 0-316-11077-9, 1988), D.W. insists she
hates the beach and doesn't want to get sunburned or wet, but after
Arthur tricks her and unceremoniously dumps her into the water, she
joyously floats, flips, splashes, and refuses to come out when it's time
to go home. The entertaining pictures are so descriptive that words
are almost unnecessary.
D.W. is a big help at her Aunt Lucy's wedding in D.W. THINKS BIG
(Joy Street/Little, Brown ISBN 0-316-11305-0, 1993).
Arthur's younger sister is also featured in D.W. RIDES AGAIN! (ISBN
0-316-11356-5, 1993).
In D.W. THE PICKY EATER (ISBN 0-316-10957-6, 1995) D.W.
discovers her picky ways are making her miss out on family fun.
Available from the National Library Service for the Blind and
Physically Handicapped on sound recording cassette is D.W. THE
PICKY EATER RC 41641.
SUBJ: Gymnastics--Fiction./ Aardvark--Fiction.

Ph-2 1-2/1 $4.95 P KF282
BROWN, MARC TOLON. True Francine. Joy Street/Little, Brown ISBN
0-316-11243-7; In Canada: Little, Brown, 1987. unp. col. ill.
Francine always seems to be in trouble while Muffy, her best friend,
is teacher's pet and to Mr. Ratburn can do nothing wrong. One day
on a test Muffy copies Francine's answers (right or wrong). When
Muffy says she'd never cheat, Mr. Ratburn punishes Francine, who
says nothing, and keeps her after school for a week. Thus she is
prevented from playing in the big softball game. At the last minute
Muffy confesses and "Slugger" Francine saves the game with a
home run.
SUBJ: Friendship--Fiction./ Honesty--Fiction./ Schools--Fiction.

Ph-2 P-1/3 $14.89 L KF283
BROWN, MARGARET WISE. Big red barn. Illus. by Felicia Bond.
HarperCollins ISBN 0-06-020749-3; In Canada: HarperCollins, c1956,
1989. unp. col. ill.
Spanish edition GRAN GRANERO ROJO available from Harper Arco
Iris (ISBN 0-06-026225-7, 1996).
Cows, cats, horses, sheep, and goats are among the animals happily
living on a farm. Large, clear pictures and the simple rhyming and
rhythmic text follow life from sunrise to sunset. An appealing
predictable book for reading aloud.
SUBJ: Domestic animals--Fiction./ Farm life--Fiction./ Stories in
rhyme./ Spanish language materials.

Ph-2 P/2 $10.95 T KF284
BROWN, MARGARET WISE. Child's good night book. Illus. by Jean
Charlot. HarperCollins ISBN 0-06-021028-1; In Canada: HarperCollins,
c1943, 1992. unp. col. ill.

Caldecott Honor Book.
A bedtime picture story of animals getting ready for bed and finally,
children saying their evening prayers for all "small things that have
no words."
SUBJ: Night--Fiction.

Ph-1 P-K/1 $13.89 L KF285
BROWN, MARGARET WISE. Goodnight moon. Illus. by Clement Hurd.
HarperCollins ISBN 0-06-020706-X, c1947. unp. col. ill.
50th anniversary ed. read-along kit available from HarperChildren's
Audio (ISBN 0-89845-988-5, 1997). 1 paperback book, 1 sound
cassette (4min), $7.95.
Spanish edition BUENAS NOCHES, LUNA available from Harper
Arco Iris (ISBN 0-06-026214-1, 1995).
Spanish edition read-along kit BUENAS NOCHES, LUNA available
from HarperChildren's Audio (ISBN 0-69470-021-5, 1996). 1
paperback book, 1 sound cassette (4min), $10.95.
Read-along kit available from Live Oak Media (ISBN 0-94107-830-2,
1984). 1 hardcover book, 1 sound cassette (4min), $22.95.
Picture available from Peaceable Kingdom Press (15"x24") color
poster, $9.95.
Big book available from Scholastic (ISBN 0-590-73302-8, n.d.),
$19.95.
The illustrations change from bright to soft dark colors as a little
bunny says goodnight to each of the familiar things of his world.
Simple repetitive text sets a cozy bedtime mood in this appealing
predictable book.
SUBJ: Night--Fiction./ Rabbits--Fiction./ Stories in rhyme./ Spanish
language materials.

Ph-2 P-K/2 $13.89 L KF286
BROWN, MARGARET WISE. Little Donkey close your eyes. Illus. by
Ashley Wolff. HarperCollins ISBN 0-06-024483-6; In Canada:
HarperCollins, 1995. unp. col. ill.
A variety of animals in farmyards, forests, and jungles prepare for
sleep. The rhyming text reads like a lullaby while the woodcut
illustrations accentuate nighttime in several environs.
SUBJ: Sleep--Fiction./ Bedtime--Fiction./ Animals--Fiction./ Stories in
rhyme.

Ph-2 P-K/2 $11.89 L KF287
BROWN, MARGARET WISE. Runaway bunny. Illus. by Clement Hurd.
HarperCollins ISBN 0-06-020766-3, c1972. unp. col. ill.
Read-along kit available from Live Oak Media (ISBN 0-941078-78-7,
1985). 1 hardback book, 1 sound cassette (7min), $22.95.
Available from National Library Service for the Blind and Physically
Handicapped in Braille BRA13966.
Picture available from Peaceable Kingdom Press (18"x24") color
poster, $9.95.
Spanish version EL CONEJITO ANDARIN available from Harper Arco
Iris (ISBN 0-06-025434-3, 1995).
Spanish read-along kit available from HarperChildren's Audio (ISBN
0-69470-024-X, 1995). 1 paperback book, 1 sound cassette (7min),
$10.95.
A bunny tries to run away from his mother, but she can always find
him. A new edition of an old favorite with more appealing illustrations
than the earlier one. Omits the music and words of "The song of the
runaway bunny" which appeared on the last page of the old edition.
SUBJ: Rabbits--Fiction./ Spanish language materials.

Ph-1 P-1/1 $10.95 L KF288
BROWN, RUTH. Our puppy's vacation. Dutton ISBN 0-525-44326-6,
1987. unp. col. ill.
Accompanying a large family on their vacation, a young dog romps
on the beach with screeching gulls, joyous children and crashing
waves, chases frogs, digs holes, climbs hills, encounters angry bees
and meets new farm friends. The full-paged illustrations are not only
beautiful but realistic, humorous and sometimes wistful as they picture
the rural scenes and the activities of an appealing puppy.
SUBJ: Vacations--Fiction./ Dogs--Fiction.

Ph-1 K-2/3 $14.99 T KF289
BROWN, RUTH. Toad. Dutton ISBN 0-525-45757-7; In Canada:
McClelland & Stewart, 1997. unp. col. ill.
Originally published in Great Britain, Andersen Press Ltd., 1996.
Toad is slimy, toxic, and covered with warts, but still appealing to the
monster who stalks him until the monster gets a taste and spits Toad
out. Toad eggs fill the endpapers, and the illustrations are
appropriately mucky, concealing the stalker. Fun for reading aloud,
the tale will ignite conversations about animal protection.
SUBJ: Toads--Fiction./ Monsters--Fiction.

Ph-1 P-1/1 $12.89 L KF290
BUCK, NOLA. Oh, cats! Illus. by Nadine Bernard Westcott. HarperCollins
ISBN 0-06-025374-6; In Canada: HarperCollins, 1997. 24p. col. ill. (My
first I can read book).
A young girl tries to make friends with three cats that have their own
ideas about what to play. Cheery illustrations provide clues to the
very limited vocabulary for beginning readers.
SUBJ: Cats--Fiction./ Stories in rhyme.

Ph-1 P-1/1 $14.89 L KF291
BUCK, NOLA. Sid and Sam. Illus. by G. Brian Karas. HarperCollins ISBN
0-06-025372-X, 1996. 29p. col. ill. (My first I can read book).
Sid continues to sing long after Sam is ready to stop. Then she hears
Sam say "so long," and the two friends part. New readers will
enjoy success with the very simple repetitive text.
SUBJ: Singing--Fiction./ Friendship--Fiction.

Ph-2 P-1/1 $12.93 L KF292
BUCKLEY, HELEN E. Grandfather and I. Illus. by Jan Ormerod. Lothrop,
Lee & Shepard ISBN 0-688-12534-4, 1994. unp. col. ill.
Walks with Grandfather are never hurried; there's time to linger and
explore. New illustrations lend a contemporary appearance to the
story first published in 1959. The repetition in the text flows smoothly
when reading aloud. For multicultural studies.
SUBJ: Grandfathers--Fiction./ Afro-Americans--Fiction.

Ph-2 P-1/2 $12.93 L KF293
BUCKLEY, HELEN E. Grandmother and I. Illus. by Jan Ormerod. Lothrop,
Lee & Shepard ISBN 0-688-12532-8, 1994. unp. col. ill.
Grandmother's lap is just right when you have a cold, when there's
lightning outside, or any time you need cuddling. Republished with
contemporary illustrations, the text is repetitive, rhythmic, and
comforting just like Grandmother's rocking chair. For multicultural
studies.
SUBJ: Grandmothers--Fiction./ Afro-Americans--Fiction.

Ph-2 P-2/3 $14.99 L KF294
BUEHNER, CARALYN. Escape of Marvin the ape. By Caralyn and Mark
Buehner. Dial ISBN 0-8037-1124-7, 1992. unp. col. ill.
Spanish version LA ESCAPADA DE MARVIN EL MONO available
from Dial/Peguin Ediciones (ISBN 0-8037-2083-1, 1997).
After escaping from the zoo, Marvin a large ape has several
adventures in the city. He rides on the subway, swings through the
trees in the park, and takes a ferryboat ride all the time eluding two
police officers, who can be spotted in each picture. The illustrations
are a treat and perfect accompaniment to the text.
SUBJ: Apes--Fiction./ City and town life--Fiction./ Spanish language
materials.

Ph-1 1-3/4 $14.89 L KF295
BUEHNER, CARALYN. Fanny's dream. Illus. by Mark Buehner. Dial ISBN
0-8037-1497-1; In Canada: McClelland & Stewart, 1996. unp. col. ill.
Available from the National Library Service for the Blind and
Physically Handicapped on sound recording cassette RC 42614.
Waiting for her fairy godmother to grant her wish to marry a prince,
Fanny passes the time with Heber Jensen eventually agreeing to
marry him. Years later when her fairy godmother finally does appear,
Fanny declines her offer to send her to the ball. Oil paints over
acrylic add depth and shadow to the realistic illustrations. A humorous
variation of the traditional Cinderella story.
SUBJ: Marriage--Fiction./ Farm life--Fiction.

Ph-1 1-2/1 $13.89 L KF296
BULLA, CLYDE ROBERT. Daniel's duck. Illus. by Joan Sandin.
HarperCollins ISBN 0-06-020909-7; In Canada: HarperCollins, 1979.
60p. col. ill. (I can read book).
Daniel and his family spend the long winter evenings in their
Tennessee cabin working on crafts for the Spring Fair. Spring arrives
and they take their moccasins, quilts, carvings, and Daniel's first
project, a carved duck, down the mountain to the village. Hearing the
villagers laugh about his duck, Daniel grabs the carving and runs
away brokenhearted until Mr. Pettigrew, the best carver in Tennessee,
admires it.
SUBJ: Wood-carving--Fiction.

Ph-2 3-5/3 $14.95 L KF297
BUNTING, EVE. Blue and the gray. Illus. by Ned Bittinger. Scholastic
ISBN 0-590-60197-0; In Canada: Scholastic, 1996. unp. col. ill.
Includes bibliography.
Two friends, one African American and one Caucasian, learn about
the history of the field near their homes that once was the scene of a
Civil War battle. Wide doublespread, oil illustrations alternate
peaceful contemporary scenes with scenes of battle. A picture book
for older children interested in the Civil War, local history, or
exploring the causes of conflicts. For multicultural studies.

SUBJ: United States--History--Civil War, 1861-1865--Fiction./
Friendship--Fiction./ Dwellings--Fiction./ Afro-Americans--Fiction./
Stories in rhyme.

Ph-1 1-3/2 $14.95 L KF298
BUNTING, EVE. Day's work. Illus. by Ronald Himler. Clarion ISBN
0-395-67321-6, 1994. 32p. col. ill.
Francisco learns several important lessons when he lies to get
gardening work for his grandfather, who doesn't speak any English.
The haunting story includes several well developed and sympathetic
characters including the man who hires them for the day and forgives
their mistake. Watercolor and gouache illustrations illuminate the
relationships important to the story. For multicultural studies.
SUBJ: Mexican Americans--Fiction./ Grandfathers--Fiction./ Work--
Fiction./ Honesty--Fiction./ Hispanic Americans--Fiction.

Ph-2 P-2/3 $13.95 L KF299
BUNTING, EVE. Flower garden. Illus. by Kathryn Hewitt. Harcourt Brace
ISBN 0-15-228776-0; In Canada: Harcourt Brace c/o Canadian Manda,
1994. unp. col. ill.
A young African-American girl and her father plant a garden in a
window box as a birthday surprise for her mother. Illustrated with
striking oil paintings, the story depicts gardening in an urban setting.
For multicultural studies.
SUBJ: Gardening--Fiction./ Parent and child--Fiction./ Birthdays--
Fiction./ Stories in rhyme.

Ph-1 K-3/2 $14.95 L KF300
BUNTING, EVE. Fly away home. Illus. by Ronald Himler. Clarion ISBN
0-395-55962-6, 1991. 32p. col. ill.
Selectors' Choice, 18th ed.
Available from the National Library Service for the Blind and
Physically Handicapped on sound recording cassette RC35190.
Andrew and his father are homeless and live in an airport where his
father tells him the first rule is not to be noticed. A very moving story
told from Andrew's point of view with honesty and hope for a better
life. A timely topic that deserves notice.
SUBJ: Homeless persons--Fiction./ Airports--Fiction./ Birds--Fiction.

Ph-1 P-2/2 $14.95 L KF301
BUNTING, EVE. Ghost's hour, spook's hour. Illus. by Donald Carrick.
Clarion ISBN 0-89919-484-2, 1987. unp. col. ill.
Available from National Library Service for the Blind and Physically
Handicapped in Braille BR7508.
Awakened by howling winds and strange noises and discovering that
the lamps won't light and his parents' bed is empty, a frightened little
boy carries his equally frightened dog down the stairs, encountering
more harrowing experiences before he and Biff join the parents in a
large sofa bed where they are now comforted and unafraid. Large,
handsome, spooky pictures magnify the mystery and suspense of the
spare text.
SUBJ: Night--Fiction./ Fear--Fiction./ Dogs--Fiction.

Ph-2 1-3/2 $14.89 L KF302
BUNTING, EVE. Going home. Illus. by David Diaz. HarperCollins ISBN
0-06-026297-4; In Canada: HarperCollins, 1996. unp. col. ill.
"Joanna Cotler books."
When a migrant family returns to Mexico for the Christmas holiday,
the children are concerned about leaving their home in the United
States for the home their parents remember in Mexico. The sights
along the way, extended family, and their parents' joy are fresh
discoveries, seen from the point of view of one of the children.
Colorful paintings are framed by photographs of Mexican folk
ornaments, lending the presentation a festive flavor. For multicultural
studies.
SUBJ: Mexicans--United States--Fiction./ Migrant labor--Fiction./
Home--Fiction./ Christmas--Fiction.

Ph-2 1-3/1 $3.95 P KF303
BUNTING, EVE. Jane Martin, dog detective. Illus. by Amy Schwartz.
Harcourt Brace Jovanovich ISBN 0-15-239587-3, 1984. 44p. ill.
Available from National Library Service for the Blind and Physically
Handicapped in Braille BR06572 and on sound recording cassette
RC24512.
Finding missing dogs for twenty-five cents a day keeps Jane very
busy as she successfully solves three mysterious cases. Suspense,
humor and ease of reading make this popular.
SUBJ: Mystery and detective stories./ Dogs--Fiction./ Short stories.

Ph-2 1-3/2 $14.95 L KF304
BUNTING, EVE. Man who could call down owls. Illus. by Charles
Mikolaycak. Macmillan ISBN 0-02-715380-0; In Canada: Collier
Macmillan, 1984. unp. ill.
Available from National Library Service for the Blind and Physically

Handicapped on sound recording cassette RC22429.
When an old man is killed for his power, the owls he has befriended and with whom he communicates take vengeance on the cold, murderous stranger; but his love, knowledge and power are passed on to Con, a thoughtful caring boy of the village. Dramatic black and white drawings bordered in steel blue capture the mood of the haunting tale.
SUBJ: Owls--Fiction.

CE   Ph-2 P-2/2 $14.95   L   KF305
BUNTING, EVE. Mother's Day mice. Illus. by Jan Brett. Clarion/Ticknor & Fields ISBN 0-89919-387-0, 1986. unp. col. ill.
Available from National Library Service for the Blind and Physically Handicapped in Braille BR06148.
Read-along kit available from Houghton Mifflin (ISBN 0-89919-895-3, 1989). 1 paperback book, 1 sound cassette (11min), $7.95.
Searching for Mother's Day presents, three little mice experience some frightening encounters before returning home with three very special gifts: a beautiful, full dandelion puff ball for wishing, a big red strawberry reminding that summer is coming, and Little Mouse's original song telling of love. The gentle affectionate story pictures a generous, sharing feeling between the three siblings and the lushly colored, detailed illustrations add appeal.
SUBJ: Gifts--Fiction./ Mice--Fiction./ Mother's Day--Fiction.

Ph-2 1-3/2 $15.95   L   KF306
BUNTING, EVE. On Call Back Mountain. Illus. by Barry Moser. Blue Sky Press/Scholastic ISBN 0-590-25929-6; In Canada: Scholastic, 1997. unp. col. ill.
Living at the foot of Call Back Mountain, two brothers look forward to the visits of Bosco Burak on his way up the mountain where he watches for fires and signals the family every night. One night Bosco does not signal, and the children learn he has died. The beauty of the wilderness, especially in the moonlight, is imparted by the richness of the watercolor illustrations.
SUBJ: Friendship--Fiction./ Death--Fiction./ Wolves--Fiction./ Fire lookout stations--Fiction.

Ph-2 P-1/2 $13.95   L   KF307
BUNTING, EVE. Our teacher's having a baby. Illus. by Diane De Groat. Clarion ISBN 0-395-60470-2, 1992. 32p. col. ill.
Mrs. Neal is expecting a baby, and her class is very excited but somewhat apprehensive about her being absent. A humorous and childlike approach to the subject of babies is especially useful for classes in a similar situation.
SUBJ: Babies--Fiction./ Schools--Fiction.

Ph-1 P-K/4 $14.45   L   KF308
BUNTING, EVE. Scary, scary Halloween. Illus. by Jan Brett. Clarion ISBN 0-89919-414-1, 1986. unp. col. ill.
Available from National Library Service for the Blind and Physically Handicapped in Braille BR7509.
Electrically hued double-paged spreads portray trick-or-treaters dressed in their frightening best, watched by four pairs of green eyes. Absolutely perfect to share with a group.
SUBJ: Halloween--Fiction./ Cats--Fiction./ Stories in rhyme.

Ph-1 2-5/2 $14.95   L   KF309
BUNTING, EVE. Smoky night. Illus. by David Diaz. Harcourt Brace ISBN 0-15-269954-6; In Canada: Harcourt Brace c/o Canadian Manda, 1994. unp. col. ill.
Caldecott Award, 1995.
There is rioting in the street, and a fire in Daniel's apartment house forces him and his mother to evacuate in the middle of the night. When two missing cats are found, their rescue together bridges the mistrust and fear that existed between two families of different ethnic origins. Collages created from seemingly discarded items form the backgrounds for strong acrylic paintings lending reality and intensity to the story. For multicultural studies.
SUBJ: Riots--California--Los Angeles--Fiction./ Interpersonal relations--Fiction./ Neighborliness--Fiction.

Ph-1 K-2/2 $13.95   L   KF310
BUNTING, EVE. St. Patrick's Day in the morning. Illus. by Jan Brett. Clarion ISBN 0-395-29098-8, 1980. unp. col. ill.
They all say he's too little to walk in the St. Patrick's Day parade but Jamie will show them. Very early in the morning he puts on his mother's raincoat, his dad's black derby hat, Sean's green sash crusted with gold fringe and takes Kevin's flute. With his dog, Nell, he proudly marches through the town and to the very top of Acorn Hill. After greeting the rising sun, Jamie places his Irish flag in the center of the cermonial stage for all to wonder who was first. The large illustrations highlighted by greens and yellows make this a good choice for reading aloud.
SUBJ: St. Patrick's Day--Fiction./ Parades--Fiction.

Ph-2 P-2/2 $15.00   L   KF311
BUNTING, EVE. Sunflower house. Illus. by Kathryn Hewitt. Harcourt Brace ISBN 0-15-200483-1; In Canada: Harcourt Brace c/o Canadian Manda, 1996. unp. col. ill.
A young boy plants sunflower seeds in a circle which grow to create a sunflower house for summer play. When the flowers bend and fall over, the children harvest the seeds to feed the birds and to save for planting next year. The rhyming text and cheerful watercolor and colored pencil illustrations make it suitable for reading aloud as part of gardening units.
SUBJ: Sunflowers--Fiction./ Stories in rhyme.

Ph-2 P-2/2 $13.95   L   KF312
BUNTING, EVE. Turkey for Thanksgiving. Illus. by Diane De Groat. Clarion ISBN 0-89919-793-0, 1991. 32p. col. ill.
Mrs. Moose wants a turkey for Thanksgiving, and Mr. Moose captures one and brings it home for dinner. To the turkey's relief, his presence is desired as a guest at the meal not as part of the meal. A light Thanksgiving story that will amuse young listeners.
SUBJ: Thanksgiving Day--Fiction./ Turkeys--Fiction./ Moose--Fiction.

KIT   Ph-2 2-4 $19.95   KF313
BURNHAM, SARANNE D. Three River Junction: a story of an Alaskan bald eagle preserve (Kit). Illus. by Tom Antonishak. Soundprints/The Native Conservancy ISBN 1-56899-443-5; In Canada: Soundprints/dist. by Canadian Manda, 1997. 1 hardback book, 1 sound cassette (9min).
Teacher's guide available upon request.
Describes the variety of wildlife in the frozen landscape of the Chilkat Bald Eagle Preserve, as an eagle surveys the area for food and rivals. Striking paintings accompany the text which can be paired with a quality sound recording with or without page turning signals. Useful as an appeal to the senses for units on eagles, environmental studies, endangered species, and Alaska.
SUBJ: Bald eagle--Fiction./ Eagles--Fiction./ Alaska--Fiction.

Ph-2 K-2/4 $15.95   L   KF314
BURNINGHAM, JOHN. Cannonball Simp. Candlewick ISBN 1-56402-338-9; In Canada: Candlewick/dist. by Douglas & McIntyre, 1994. unp. col. ill.
Originally published by Bobbs-Merrill, 1967.
Considered unattractive and abandoned by her owner, Simp scavenges for food and looks for a warm place to sleep. She escapes from the dogcatcher and finds a home in the circus where her daring cannonball act earns her a place in the clown's act. The illustrations range from bold close-ups to impressionistic landscapes to detailed pen and ink sketches, always appropriate to the story.
SUBJ: Dogs--Fiction./ Circus--Fiction.

CE   Ph-1 P-2/2 $14.89   L   KF315
BURNINGHAM, JOHN. Come away from the water, Shirley. Crowell/HarperCollins ISBN 0-690-01361-2, c1977. 24p. col. ill.
It's not the kind of day to go swimming at the beach but despite her mother's constant cautions and constraints Shirley, by using her vivid imagination, manages to have a very good time.
In TIME TO GET OUT OF THE BATH, SHIRLEY (ISBN 0-690-01379-5, 1978) her imagination takes her on an exciting adventure down the bathtub drain into a medieval world.
SUBJ: Imagination--Fiction.

Ph-2 K-2/2 $16.95   T   KF316
BURNINGHAM, JOHN. Harvey Slumfenburger's Christmas present. Candlewick ISBN 1-56402-246-3; In Canada: Douglas & McIntyre, 1993. unp. col. ill.
Discovering that he has forgotten to deliver Harvey Slumfenburger's present, Santa walks, rides in an airplane, a jeep, a motorbike, on skis, and finally climbs with a rock climber up Roly Poly Mountain to deliver the gift. The long journey home involves several other modes of transportation until Santa finally climbs into bed. The somewhat oversized book with droll pen and ink and watercolor illustrations is congenial for reading aloud at holiday times.
SUBJ: Santa Claus--Fiction./ Christmas--Fiction./ Transportation--Fiction.

CE   Ph-1 P-2/2 $13.89   L   KF317
BURNINGHAM, JOHN. Mr. Gumpy's motor car. Crowell/HarperCollins ISBN 0-690-00799-X, c1973, 1976. unp. col. ill.
Sequel to MR. GUMPY'S OUTING.
Available from National Library Service for the Blind and Physically Handicapped in Braille BR03270.
Mr. Gumpy and his friends (two children and an assortment of farm animals) pile in an old touring car and go for a ride through the fields. All goes well until a cloudburst lets loose and the big red car gets stuck in the mud.
SUBJ: Automobiles--Fiction./ Animals--Fiction.

CE   Ph-1 P-2/2 $14.95   L   KF318

BURNINGHAM, JOHN. Mr. Gumpy's outing. Henry Holt ISBN 0-8050-0708-3, c1970. unp. col. ill.
> Kate Greenaway Medal.
> Selectors' Choice, 7th ed.
> Available from National Library Service for the Blind and Physically Handicapped as talking book TB04455.
> Big book available from Henry Holt (ISBN 0-8050-3854-X, 1995), $19.95.
> One summer day, Mr. Gumpy, who lives by the river and owns a boat, decides to go for a boat ride. One by one the children, the rabbit, the cat, pig and other farm animals ask to go along. He invites them all, if they promise to behave. All goes along happily until they forget their promises and have the inevitable accident. Mr. Gumpy is an unflappable and forgiving host and gives his friends another chance. An outstanding picture book, easy-to-read and good for reading aloud.
> SUBJ: Boats and boating--Fiction./ Animals--Fiction.

     Ph-1 P-1/4 $14.95   L   KF319

BURTON, VIRGINIA LEE. Katy and the big snow. Houghton Mifflin ISBN 0-395-18155-0, c1943, 1973. 32p. col. ill.
> Available from National Library Service for the Blind and Physically Handicapped in Braille BRA06848.
> A crawler tractor pushes a snow plow in the winter and saves a city when a heavy snow storm comes.
> SUBJ: Tractors--Fiction./ Snow--Fiction.

CE   Ph-2 K-2/2 $13.95   L   KF320

BURTON, VIRGINIA LEE. Little house. Houghton Mifflin ISBN 0-395-18156-9, c1942, 1978. 40p. col. ill.
> Caldecott Medal Award.
> Available from National Library Service for the Blind and Physically Handicapped in Braille BR05903.
> A country house is unhappy when the city with all its houses and traffic grows up around it.
> SUBJ: Houses--Fiction./ Cities and towns--Fiction.

     Ph-2 K-2/3 $15.95   T   KF321

BURTON, VIRGINIA LEE. Maybelle the cable car. Houghton Mifflin ISBN 0-395-82847-3, 1997. 42p. col. ill.
> Recounts efforts of the citizens of San Francisco to save the city's cable cars. The mini-lesson in the democratic process is illustrated with Burton's original artwork. This classic story still has lots of child appeal.
> SUBJ: Cable cars (Streetcars)--Fiction./ San Francisco (Calif.)--Fiction.

CE   Ph-1 P-2/6 $13.95   L   KF322

BURTON, VIRGINIA LEE. Mike Mulligan and his steam shovel. Houghton Mifflin ISBN 0-395-16961-5, c1939. unp. col. ill.
> Videocassette available from Weston Woods HMPV0004V. 1/2" VHS videocassette color, (11min), $49.95.
> Available from National Library Service for the Blind and Physically Handicapped in Braille BRA06817, on sound recording cassette RC25281, and as talking book TB03173.
> Mary Anne, the steam shovel, is old fashioned, but she and her owner prove they can still dig and be of use in the town of Popperville.
> SUBJ: Steam shovels--Fiction./ Spanish language materials./ Italian language materials.

     Ph-2 K-2/2 $15.00   T   KF323

BUSH, TIMOTHY. Grunt!: the primitive cave boy. Crown ISBN 0-517-79967-7, 1995. unp. col. ill.
> Grunt, a cave boy, is a failure as a hunter, but the pictures he draws on cave walls bring plenty of game to feed his tribe. In their greed, the tribesmen kill all the animals and drive several species to extinction. Action-packed, the story and illustrations will appeal to beginning readers. Good discussion starter for environmental studies. For reading aloud.
> SUBJ: Cave dwellers--Fiction./ Cave paintings--Fiction./ Hunting--Fiction.

     Ph-1 K-1/1 $11.99   T   KF324

BYARS, BETSY CROMER. Ant plays Bear. By Betsy Byars. Illus. by Marc Simont. Viking ISBN 0-670-86776-4; In Canada: Penguin, 1997. 32p. col. ill. (Viking easy-to-read).
> Ant plays Bear with his brother, pretends to be a dog, worries about a scratching noise at the window, and discusses what he wants to be when he grows up. Beginning readers will readily identify with the characters. Easy vocabulary and short sentences convey affection and humor. Watercolor illustrations add a light touch.
> SUBJ: Brothers--Fiction.

CE   Ph-1 1-3/1 $15.89   L   KF325

BYARS, BETSY CROMER. Golly sisters go West. Illus. by Sue Truesdell. HarperCollins ISBN 0-06-020884-8; In Canada: HarperCollins, 1986. 64p. col. ill. (I can read book).
> Read-along kit available from HarperChildren's Audio (ISBN 0-69470-027-4, 1995). 1 paperback book, 1 sound cassette (17min), $6.95.
> Available from the National Library Service for the Blind and Physically Handicapped on sound recording cassette RC 40049.
> Six rollicking, slapstick tales about the ever-fussing Golly sisters, May-May and Rose, who learn the hard way how to make their horse stop and go. After this accomplishment and with their covered wagon loaded, they set out for the Western frontier where they put on singing and dancing road shows and even try, unsuccessfully, to get their horse to join in their dances. The humorous watercolors create a real feel of the Old West for beginning readers.
> For more Golly sister adventures, read HOORAY FOR THE GOLLY SISTERS! (ISBN 0-06-020899-6, 1990), and GOLLY SISTERS RIDE AGAIN (ISBN 0-06-021564-X, 1994).
> HOORAY FOR THE GOLLY SISTERS! and THE GOLLY SISTERS RIDE AGAIN are available from the National Library Service for the Blind and Physically Handicapped on sound recording cassette RC 40050 and RC 40051.
> SUBJ: Entertainers--Fiction./ Frontier and pioneer life--Fiction./ West (U.S.)--Fiction.

     Ph-2 2-3/1 $13.95   T   KF326

BYARS, BETSY CROMER. Joy boys. By Betsy Byars. Illus. by Frank Remkiewicz. Delacorte ISBN 0-385-32164-3; In Canada: Bantam Doubleday Dell, 1996. 48p. col. ill. (Yearling first choice chapter book).
> The Joy boys are brothers who narrowly avoid a bull, get in a mud fight, draw a line down the middle of the room they share, and try to catch a wild animal. The short chapters and limited vocabulary create an attractive transitional reader.
> SUBJ: Brothers--Fiction./ Farm life--Fiction./ Dogs--Fiction.

     Ph-1 K-2/1 $11.99   T   KF327

BYARS, BETSY CROMER. My brother, Ant. By Betsy Byars. Illus. by Marc Simont. Viking ISBN 0-670-86664-4; In Canada: Penguin, 1996. 32p. col. ill. (Viking easy-to-read).
> Selectors' Choice, 21st ed.
> Ant's older brother relates four vignettes about Ant in short easy-to-read sentences that convey humor and affection. Typical childhood concerns about monsters under the bed, homework, big bad wolves, and letters to Santa will entertain beginning readers. Small watercolor illustrations perfectly parallel the format and story.
> SUBJ: Brothers--Fiction./ Family life--Fiction.

VCR   Ph-3 P-3 $149.95   OD KF328

CALDECOTT VIDEO LIBRARY. VOL. I (Videocassette). Weston Woods HMPV492V, 1992. 1/2" VHS videocassette color (49min).
> Includes public performance rights.
> Features five Caldecott Award-winning titles on one videocassette. Useful where cost or space would limit ability to have separate videocassettes.
> Contents: WHERE THE WILD THINGS ARE, Maurice Sendak; STONE SOUP, Marcia Brown; AMAZING BONE, William Steig; TIME OF WONDER, Robert McCloskey; GOGGLES!, Ezra Jack Keats.
> SUBJ: Caldecott Medal books.

VCR   Ph-3 P-3 $149.95   OD KF329

CALDECOTT VIDEO LIBRARY. VOL. II (Videocassette). Weston Woods HMPV493V, 1992. 1/2" VHS videocassette color (48min).
> Includes public performance rights.
> Presents five picture book classics which have won the Caldecott Award. Useful for collections where limited budgets or space prohibit purchasing individual videocassettes.
> Contents: OWL MOON, Jane Yolen; MAKE WAY FOR DUCKLINGS, Robert McCloskey; IN THE NIGHT KITCHEN, Maurice Sendak; STREGA NONNA, Tomie de Paola; CROW BOY, Taro Yashima.
> SUBJ: Caldecott Medal books.

VCR   Ph-3 P-3 $149.95   OD KF330

CALDECOTT VIDEO LIBRARY. VOL. III (Videocassette). Weston Woods HMPV494V, 1992. 1/2" VHS videocassette color (50min).
> Includes public performance rights.
> Six popular picture books all of which won the Caldecott Award are presented. Useful for collections where limited budget or space prohibit purchase of individual videocassettes.
> Contents: MADELINE'S RESCUE, Ludwig Bemelmans; SNOWY DAY, Ezra Jack Keats; BLUEBERRIES FOR SAL, Robert McCloskey; DRUMMER HOFF, Barbara Emberley; ANDY AND THE LION, James Daugherty; FROG WENT A-COURTIN', John Langstaff.
> SUBJ: Caldecott Medal books.

Ph-1 K-2/4 $15.93 L KF331
CALHOUN, MARY. Cross-country cat. Illus. by Erick Ingraham. Morrow ISBN 0-688-32186-0, 1979. unp. col. ill.
Henry is an unusual Siamese cat who walks on his hind legs and prances and dances to the music of the stereo. However, he refuses to even try the small skis The Kid makes for him. When he is inadvertently left behind at the family's ski lodge, Henry discovers that he is a superb cross-country skier. He is even fast enough to outrace a hungry coyote.
The remarkable Siamese cat, Henry, stows away in a hot air balloon in HOT-AIR HENRY (ISBN 0-688-00502-0, 1981).
Henry learns to walk a tightrope in HIGH-WIRE HENRY (ISBN 0-688-08984-4, 1991, available from the NLSBPH on sound recording cassette RC34851).
Henry gets his sea legs in HENRY THE SAILOR CAT (ISBN 0-688-10841-5, 1994).
SUBJ: Cats--Fiction./ Cross-country skiing--Fiction.

Ph-1 1-3/2 $15.93 L KF332
CALHOUN, MARY. Flood. Illus. by Erick Ingraham. Morrow ISBN 0-688-13920-5; In Canada: Hearst Book Group, 1997. unp. col. ill.
Determined to remain in their house despite rising waters, a family prepares for a flood and moves to the upstairs. Finally when the levee breaks, the family is forced to evacuate and face the possibility of losing their house. Current events are given a human face and child's perspective through the main character, Sarajean.
SUBJ: Floods--Mississippi River--Fiction./ Family--Fiction./ Natural disasters--Fiction.

Ph-1 1-3/2 $16.99 L KF333
CANNON, ANNIE. Bat in the boot. Orchard ISBN 0-531-08795-6, 1996. unp. col. ill.
"Richard Jackson book."
A family finds a baby bat, feeds it with a dropper, and puts it safely in a shoebox where the baby bat chitters for food almost constantly. After dark, a large bat swoops into the house and carries the baby away. Based on a true story and reviewed by Bat Conservation International, the book will intrigue youngsters and encourage further inquiry into this unusual mammal.
SUBJ: Bats--Fiction./ Wildlife rescue--Fiction.

Ph-1 K-2/3 $16.00 L KF334
CANNON, JANELL. Stellaluna. Harcourt Brace Jovanovich ISBN 0-15-280217-7; In Canada: Harcourt Brace Jovanovich, 1993. unp. col. ill.
Spanish version STELALUNA available from Hispanic Book Distributors (ISBN 84-261-2849-1, 1993).
Separated from her mother, Stellaluna, a young fruit bat, falls into a nest of young birds. Some identity confusion follows as the young birds try to imitate Stellaluna, and she tries to conform to bird behavior. Lots of white space borders the luminous acrylic illustrations and text providing a clean and pleasant design well-suited to group use. Some interesting facts about bats follow the appealing story.
SUBJ: Bats--Fiction./ Birds--Fiction./ Spanish language materials.

TB Ph-2 K-2 $9.98 KF335
CANNON, JANELL. Stellaluna (Talking book). Told by David Holt. Music by Steven Heller. High Windy Audio HW1211C ISBN 0-942303-11-3, 1996. 1 sound cassette.
ALA notable recording, 1997.
Talking book also available as compact disc HW1211D (ISBN 0-942303-12-1, 1996). 1 compact disc (35min), $15.98.
Features a telling of STELLALUNA and two other stories about bats-- one a pourquoi tale about why bats fly at night and the other a story by Don Freeman. Some interesting facts about bats follow.
Contents: Stellaluna (12min); Why the bat flies at night (7min); Hattie, the backstage bat (6min); Amazing bat facts (8min); Stellaluna's theme (1min).
SUBJ: Bats--Fiction./ Birds--Fiction.

Ph-2 K-2/3 $16.00 L KF336
CANNON, JANELL. Verdi. Harcourt Brace ISBN 0-15-201028-9; In Canada: Harcourt Brace c/o Canadian Manda, 1997. unp. col. ill.
Verdi, a bright yellow snake, doesn't want to grow up and turn green. He prefers to jump, climb, and fly through the air until one day he falls back down to earth and is forced to slow down. The antics of Verdi are depicted in luminous color paintings. Includes a doublespread of snake facts.
SUBJ: Pythons--Fiction./ Snakes--Fiction./ Old age--Fiction.

Ph-1 P-2/2 $14.95 L KF337
CAPLE, KATHY. Biggest nose. Houghton Mifflin ISBN 0-395-36894-4, 1985. 32p. col. ill.
Available from National Library Service for the Blind and Physically Handicapped in Braille BR06463 and sound recording cassette RC24669.

Unhappy because Betty, the hippopotamus, and her other classmates tease her about her large nose, Eleanor, a young elephant, unsuccessfully tries to shorten the offending proboscis; but when she realizes that Betty has the biggest mouth, Harold the biggest feet and Lizzard the biggest tail, the teasing of Eleanor ceases. A pleasant and humorous way to teach acceptance of individual differences.
SUBJ: Teasing--Fiction./ Nose--Fiction./ Elephants--Fiction./ Animals--Fiction.

Ph-2 P-1/1 $14.89 L KF338
CAPUCILLI, ALYSSA. Biscuit. By Alyssa Satin Capucilli. Illus. by Pat Schories. HarperCollins ISBN 0-06-026198-6; In Canada: HarperCollins, 1996. 26p. col. ill. (My first I can read book).
Postponing bedtime, Biscuit the puppy wants to play, have a snack, and hear a story before settling down. A very simple and repetitive text will satisfy beginning readers with limited skills.
SUBJ: Dogs--Fiction./ Bedtime--Fiction.

Ph-2 P-1/1 $14.98 L KF339
CAPUCILLI, ALYSSA. Biscuit finds a friend. By Alyssa Satin Capucilli. Illus. by Pat Schories. HarperCollins ISBN 0-06-027413-1; In Canada: HarperCollins, 1997. 24p. col. ill. (My first I can read book).
Eager to play with a duckling, the puppy Biscuit ends up falling in a pond. Beginning readers with limited vocabulary will enjoy success with the simple text.
SUBJ: Dogs--Fiction./ Ducks--Fiction.

Ph-1 P-K/1 $15.00 T KF340
CARLE, ERIC. Do you want to be my friend? Crowell/HarperCollins ISBN 0-690-24276-X, 1971. unp. col. ill. (Very-first-step-to-reading book).
"Do you want to be my friend?" a small mouse asks as a big tail comes into view. On turning the page, the tail becomes a horse too busy eating to be a mouse's friend. The horse is followed by an alligator, then a lion and one by one a procession of animals each preceded by a picture of his tail. Finally there is another little mouse who is eager to be a friend and says "yes". Specially planned as reading readiness material, the story is told almost entirely by pictures and must be "read" from left to right and from front to back thus instilling the idea of linear sequence. Although designed with a purpose, the book is attractive, appealing and fun.
SUBJ: Mice--Fiction./ Friendship--Fiction.

Ph-2 P-K/1 $16.89 L KF341
CARLE, ERIC. From head to toe. HarperCollins ISBN 0-06-023516-0; In Canada: HarperCollins, 1997. unp. col. ill.
Bold, homely paintings on white pages pair animals and children to name different body movements. "I am a buffalo and I raise my shoulders. Can you do it?" "I can do it." The clever scheme effortlessly introduces basic body parts and simple movements. Children will enjoy the vivid animals and strong pictures. The predictable book will work very well for storyhours, prompting lots of discussion and audience participation.
SUBJ: Exercise./ Physical fitness.

Ph-2 P-2/2 $15.89 L KF342
CARLE, ERIC. Grouchy ladybug. New ed. HarperCollins ISBN 0-06-027088-8; In Canada: HarperCollins, 1996. unp. col. ill.
Spanish version LA MARIQUITA MALHUMORADA available from Harper Arco Iris (ISBN 0-06-027089-6, 1996).
In a grouchy mood, a ladybug searches throughout the day for an animal that will fight with her. As the day progresses, the animals she encounters get larger and the narrow pages get wider, the sun rises and sets in the boldly colored illustrations, and a clock insert marks the hour. Useful to explain the concept of time, the story can also be a discussion starter for conflict resolution. The cleverly designed pages will inspire children who are making their own books, but they may limit shelf life.
SUBJ: Ladybugs--Fiction./ Behavior--Fiction./ Spanish language materials.

Ph-2 P-1/1 $14.95 T KF343
CARLE, ERIC. Have you seen my cat? Picture Book Studio ISBN 0-88708-054-5; In Canada: Vanwell, c1973, 1987. unp. col. ill.
Searching for his lost cat, a little boy meets people from many parts of the world, and many members of the cat family--tiger, panther, lion, cheetah, jaguar, etc.--before he finally finds his pet with a litter of new kittens. Vivid collages illustrate the simple, brief story.
SUBJ: Cats--Fiction.

Ph-3 P-2/2 $15.95 T KF344
CARLE, ERIC. House for Hermit Crab. Picture Book Studio ISBN 0-88708-056-1, 1987. unp. col. ill.
Outgrowing his house in January and moving into a big, strong new shell in February Hermit Crab thinks it looks too drab and plain so

month by month he beautifies it with sea anemone, starfish, coral and other marine creatures. By December he has outgrown his lovely home and in January must start the cycle again. Beautifully illustrated in collages of the many bold, brilliant colors found in the oceans. Told as a story but presents information concerning many animals living in the sea.
SUBJ: Hermit crabs--Fiction./ Crabs--Fiction./ Marine animals--Fiction./ Dwellings--Fiction.

Ph-2 P-2/2 $15.95 T KF345

CARLE, ERIC. Rooster's off to see the world. Picture Book Studio ISBN 0-88708-042-1; In Canada: Vanwell, 1972. unp. col. ill.
As Rooster sets off to see the world, he is joined by two cats, three frogs, four turtles and five fish. Young readers are introduced to sets, addition, and subtraction. The simple story is enhanced by bold, colorful collages. Small squares with black and white pictures illustrate the numerical groups and are found in the upper corners of the text pages.
SUBJ: Numbers./ Counting./ Animals--Fiction.

Ph-1 P-2/2 $16.95 L KF346

CARLE, ERIC. Very busy spider. Philomel ISBN 0-399-21166-7, 1985. unp. col. ill.
Selectors' Choice, 15th ed.
Available from National Library Service for the Blind and Physically Handicapped in Braille BR06131.
Invited by many farm animals to participate in their activities, a busy spider ignores them and patiently continues spinning her web. The collage pictures of the farm animals are very handsome and children are intrigued by the three-dimensional effect of the spider, the web and a fly. They are able to both see and feel the web as it develops and finally catches the fly.
SUBJ: Spiders--Fiction./ Spider webs--Fiction./ Domestic animals--Fiction./ Toy and movable books.

Ph-1 P-1/6 $15.95 L KF347

CARLE, ERIC. Very hungry caterpillar. Philomel ISBN 0-399-20853-4, 1981. unp. col. ill.
Available in French LA CHENILLE AFFAMEE (ISBN 0-399-21870-X, 1992).
A small and very hungry caterpillar eats through the days of the week and all sorts of food until he is no longer a small caterpillar. He then builds a cocoon and later emerges as a beautiful butterfly. Large, colorful illustrations are appropriate for use with groups, but individuals also enjoy the die-cut pages.
SUBJ: Caterpillars--Fiction./ Metamorphosis--Fiction.

Ph-2 P-2/2 $19.95 T KF348

CARLE, ERIC. Very lonely firefly. Philomel ISBN 0-399-22774-1; In Canada: Putnam, 1995. unp. col. ill.
A lonely firefly flashes its light looking for another firefly. At first, it finds only other lights, including fireworks, before finally discovering a group of fireflies. Open the last page to see the group of fireflies blinking on and off. A story about belonging for reading aloud to a group, preferably with the lights off. Circulation may be limited by the special flashing lights, although the book includes an opening to replace the battery.
SUBJ: Fireflies--Fiction./ Toy and movable books.

Ph-3 P-K $15.95 L KF349

CARLE, ERIC. 1, 2, 3 to the zoo. Philomel ISBN 0-399-61172-X, c1968. unp. col. ill.
A counting book illustrated with colorful animals traveling in a zoo train. There is no text, but each doublespread page contains a numeral and a corresponding number of animals in a train car. Carle uses a mouse the way Munari used a fly in his ABC.
SUBJ: Counting.

Ph-2 K-2/2 $14.99 L KF350

CARLSON, NANCY. How to lose all your friends. Viking ISBN 0-670-84906-5; In Canada: Penguin, 1994. unp. col. ill.
Never smile, never share, be a bully, be a poor sport, tattle, and whine in order to lose all of your friends. Colorful and funny illustrations demonstrate the obnoxious behaviors that will alienate friends and offer a reverse prescription for friendship.
SUBJ: Behavior--Fiction./ Friendship--Fiction.

Ph-2 P-2/2 $13.50 L KF351

CE
CARLSON, NANCY. Perfect family. Carolrhoda ISBN 0-87614-280-3, 1985. 32p. col. ill.
Read-along kit from Live Oak Media (ISBN 0-87499-037-8, 1987) 1 hardcover book, 1 sound cassette (8min), $22.95.
Envious of her friend George and his large family of twelve, Louanne spends a weekend with them and discovers that her small family is

best for her. There is warmth, love and fun evident in both households, but a picture of the chaos and hilarity in life at the rabbit home is shown in the detailed illustrations.
Other stories about Louanne Pig include MAKING THE TEAM (ISBN 0-87614-281-1, 1985); WITCH LADY (ISBN 0-87614-283-8, 1985); THE TALENT SHOW (ISBN 0-87614-284-6, 1985); MYSTERIOUS VALENTINE (ISBN 0-87614-282-X, 1985) (read-along kit available from Live Oak (ISBN 0-87499-087-4, 1985), 1985) hardcover and cassette (6min), $22.95).
SUBJ: Brothers and sisters--Fiction./ Family life--Fiction.

Ph-2 K-2/2 $13.99 L KF352

CARLSON, NANCY. Sit still! Viking ISBN 0-670-85721-1; In Canada: Penguin, 1996. unp. col. ill.
Patrick knows 101 ways to sit in a chair, but not how to sit still. After taking him to a doctor, his mother provides him with other outlets for his energy. Many youngsters will empathize with Patrick, who enjoys activity and has a hard time sitting still, especially in school.
SUBJ: Behavior--Fiction.

Ph-2 P-2/2 $13.95 L KF353

CARLSON, NANCY. Visit to Grandma's. Viking Penguin ISBN 0-670-83288-X; In Canada: Penguin, 1991. unp col ill.
Tina and her family visit Grandma in her condominium in Florida, expecting a traditional family Thanksgiving, but Grandma meets them at the airport in her convertible, visits with them between aerobics and tap-dancing classes and takes them out to a seafood restaurant for Thanksgiving dinner. Brightly colored illustrations of Tina and her beaver family add to the fun.
SUBJ: Grandmothers--Fiction./ Thanksgiving Day--Fiction.

Ph-1 P-2/3 $14.95 L KF354

CARLSTROM, NANCY WHITE. How does the wind walk? Illus. by Deborah Kogan Ray. Macmillan ISBN 0-02-717275-9; In Canada: Maxwell Macmillan, 1993. unp. col. ill.
The wind walks with a roar of leaves in fall, frosty lips in winter, a bounce in spring, and a small boy's puff in summer. Poetic text introduces the seasons and weather. The striking acrylic doublespreads and language-rich text make it an ideal choice for reading aloud.
SUBJ: Winds--Fiction./ Seasons--Fiction.

Ph-3 P-1/1 $13.95 L KF355

CARLSTROM, NANCY WHITE. I'm not moving, Mama! Illus. by Thor Wickstrom. Macmillan ISBN 0-02-717286-4; In Canada: Collier Macmillan, 1990. unp. col. ill.
A young mouse doesn't want to move and tells his mother she can take everything but he's staying behind. However, his mother continually states why the family needs him and won't leave him behind. A reassuring story reflecting the emotions experienced by young children when a family leaves a familiar home.
SUBJ: Moving, Household--Fiction./ Mother and child--Fiction.

Ph-1 P-K/4 $15.00 L KF356

CARLSTROM, NANCY WHITE. Jesse Bear, what will you wear? Illus. by Bruce Degen. Macmillan ISBN 0-02-717350-X; In Canada: Macmillan, 1986. unp. col. ill.
Available from National Library Service for the Blind and Physically Handicapped in Braille BR7136.
Starting the morning with shirt of red, pulled over his head, Jesse Bear goes through the day and on to bath and bedtime pursuing activities familiar to children and pondering on his sometimes quite unusual attire. Told in lilting rhymes with lots of humor and illustrated with appealing, brightly colored uncluttered watercolors, this presents strong feelings of family love and a happy childhood.
Other stories about Jesse are BETTER NOT GET WET, JESSE BEAR (ISBN 0-02-717280-5, 1988); HOW DO YOU SAY IT, JESSE BEAR? (ISBN 0-02-717276-7, 1990); and HAPPY BIRTHDAY, JESSE BEAR (ISBN 0-02-717277-5, 1994).
SUBJ: Bears--Fiction./ Stories in rhyme.

Ph-1 P-1/2 $15.00 L KF357

CARLSTROM, NANCY WHITE. Let's count it out, Jesse Bear. Illus. by Bruce Degen. Simon & Schuster ISBN 0-689-80478-4; In Canada: Distican, 1996. unp. col. ill.
Jesse Bear is the star of a poem about each number from one through ten. A small inset on each spread features the numeral, the number word, and a picture with objects to count. The numbers 11 through 20 follow with pictures with objects for counting. On target and well designed for the intended audience.
SUBJ: Bears--Fiction./ Counting./ Stories in rhyme.

Ph-2 1-3/4 $14.95 L KF358

CARRICK, CAROL. Foundling. Illus. by Donald Carrick. Clarion ISBN 0-395-28775-8, 1977. unp. col. ill.

After the death of his dog Bodger, Christopher resists getting a new puppy until a homeless stray convinces him to reconsider. Other stories about Christopher and Ben include THE WASHOUT (ISBN 0-89919-850-3, 1978, 1989, OPC) when a storm cuts Christopher and his mother off from civilization; BEN AND THE PORCUPINE (ISBN 0-89919-348-X, 1985) when Christopher must keep his inquisitive dog away from the defensive animal and DARK AND FULL OF SECRETS (ISBN 0-89919-271-3, 1984, OPC) when Christopher begins to explore the bottom of the pond.
SUBJ: Dogs--Fiction.

Ph-1 1-3/2 $13.95   L   KF359
CARRICK, CAROL. Left behind. Illus. by Donald Carrick. Clarion ISBN 0-89919-535-0, 1988. unp. col. ill.
A class trip to the aquarium ends in disaster for Christopher as he becomes separated from his teacher and classmates on the subway ride home. Discovered by the police he is happily reunited with his teacher. The illustrations well convey the impersonal bustle of the subway swirling around the small frightened boy and young readers will take heart from the satisfying conclusion.
SUBJ: Lost children--Fiction.

Ph-1 1-3/2 $14.95   L   KF360
CARRICK, CAROL. Melanie. Illus. by Alisher Dianov. Clarion ISBN 0-395-66555-8, 1996. unp. col. ill.
Searching for her grandfather, Melanie, who is blind, finds her way through a dark forest, helps a trapped elk, and fails to fall under the spell of a horrible troll because she cannot see him. The original story has many characteristics of traditional folktales, and young readers will discern the strength of the young heroine. Illustrations create the once-upon-a-time setting with borders and small details.
SUBJ: Trolls--Fiction./ Grandfathers--Fiction./ Blind--Fiction./ Physically handicapped--Fiction.

CE
Ph-1 K-2/4 $13.95   L   KF361
CARRICK, CAROL. Patrick's dinosaurs. Illus. by Donald Carrick. Clarion ISBN 0-89919-189-4, 1983. unp. col. ill.
Read-along kit available from Houghton Mifflin ISBN 0-395-66496-9, 1987. 1 paperback book, 1 sound cassette (5min) $8.95.
Listening to his older brother Hank show off his knowledge of dinosaurs, young Patrick begins to see the enormous, frightening prehistoric animals just about everywhere. Large realistic pictures are just scary enough and aid the text in presenting accurate information. Patrick's theory about the fate of the dinosaurs follows in WHAT HAPPENED TO PATRICK'S DINOSAURS? (ISBN 0-89919-406-0, 1986) (available from National Library Service for the Blind and Physically Handicapped in Braille BR06150, and on sound recording cassette RC30689), (read-along kit available from Houghton Mifflin ISBN 0-89919-838-4, 1988. 1 paperback book, 1 sound cassette (5min), $8.95).
SUBJ: Dinosaurs--Fiction.

Ph-3 P-2/2 $10.95   T   KF362
CARTER, DAVID A. In a dark, dark wood. Simon & Schuster ISBN 0-671-74134-9; In Canada: Simon & Schuster, 1991. unp. col. ill.
The spooky dark tale begins in a dark, dark wood and culminates with the surprise contents of a dark, dark box. The story ends with a pop-up ghost and is a wonderful choice for Halloween story hours but will not hold up in circulation.
SUBJ: Ghosts--Fiction./ Toy and movable books.

Ph-2 K-2/2 $13.88   L   KF363
CASELEY, JUDITH. Dear Annie. Greenwillow ISBN 0-688-10011-2, 1991. unp. col. ill.
Annie and her grandfather have a correspondence which began when she was born and continues until she is able to read his letters and answer them herself. A pleasant story about the relationship between a young girl and her grandfather which would be a fun introduction to letter writing for children.
SUBJ: Grandfathers--Fiction./ Letters--Fiction.

Ph-2 P-1/2 $12.88   L   KF364
CASELEY, JUDITH. Grandpa's garden lunch. Greenwillow ISBN 0-688-08817-1, 1990. unp. col. ill.
Sarah helps her grandfather plant and tend his garden, and one day she is invited to lunch where everything from the flower arrangement to the zucchini cake comes from the garden. Attractive, cheerful illustrations with borders that extend the garden theme add to the appeal of this quiet story.
SUBJ: Gardening--Fiction./ Vegetables--Fiction./ Grandparents--Fiction.

Ph-1 K-1/2 $13.88   L   KF365
CASELEY, JUDITH. Harry and Willy and Carrothead. Greenwillow ISBN 0-688-09493-7, 1991. unp. col. ill.
Born with no left arm, Harry begins school with a prosthesis which is at first a curiosity to the other children, but is soon accepted as a normal difference like Oscar's red hair. A gentle story of individual differences and friendship with an understated message.
SUBJ: Physically handicapped--Fiction./ Friendship--Fiction.

Ph-2 1-3/4 $13.93   L   KF366
CASELEY, JUDITH. Mama, coming and going. Greenwillow ISBN 0-688-11442-3, 1994. unp. col. ill.
Jenna is a big help to her mother after her baby brother is born and Mama doesn't know whether she's coming or going. Together, they make the best of a series of mishaps. The disruption caused by a new baby will be familiar, and Jenna's good-natured handling of the situation may serve as a model. (Parents' Shelf.)
SUBJ: Babies--Fiction./ Mother and child--Fiction./ Memory--Fiction.

Ph-2 P-1/2 $14.00   T   KF367
CASELEY, JUDITH. Noisemakers. Greenwillow ISBN 0-688-09394-9, 1992. unp. col. ill.
Sam and Laura are two friends who like to make noise together everywhere they go--the library, a restaurant, and a department store. Other people, including their mothers, are not pleased with their noisemaking until they finally find a place where noise is acceptable. The noisy fun of the two friends is joyously apparent in the bright illustrations.
SUBJ: Play--Fiction./ Noise--Fiction.

Ph-2 1-3/2 $14.93   L   KF368
CASELEY, JUDITH. Priscilla twice. Greenwillow ISBN 0-688-13306-1, 1995. unp. col. ill.
Priscilla recognizes the split between her parents before they tell her they plan to divorce, but that doesn't make it any easier for her to accept. Her parents ease the separation by keeping communication open with her and with each other. Bright illustrations including Priscilla's school artwork exhibit her struggle and eventual acceptance of her family's new structure.
SUBJ: Divorce--Fiction./ Parent and child--Fiction.

Ph-2 2-3/2 $14.93   L   KF369
CASELEY, JUDITH. Slumber party! Greenwillow ISBN 0-688-14016-5, 1996. unp. col. ill.
Zoe's slumber party is the best birthday party even though there's an argument about who sleeps next to her and everyone gets frightened by scary stories. Exuberant colorful illustrations portray a favorite childhood activity.
SUBJ: Sleepovers--Fiction./ Birthdays--Fiction.

Ph-2 P-1/4 $13.93   L   KF370
CASELEY, JUDITH. Sophie and Sammy's library sleepover. Greenwillow ISBN 0-688-10616-1, 1993. unp. col. ill.
Dressed in pajamas, Sophie goes with her mother to a library "sleepover" without her younger brother, Sammy, who loves books but doesn't know how to take care of them. The next evening Sophie and Sammy have their own library sleepover at home. This could be a fun introduction to library programming and caring for library materials for new library patrons.
SUBJ: Books and reading--Fiction./ Brothers and sisters--Fiction.

Ph-2 K-2/3 $14.93   L   KF371
CASELEY, JUDITH. Witch Mama. Greenwillow ISBN 0-688-14458-6, 1996. unp. col. ill.
Born on Halloween, Jenna calls her mother "Witch Mama," and they celebrate with trick-or-treating and a party at school. Jenna's small brother, Mickey, is frightened by many of the holiday happenings, and his fears lend a realistic touch to the story. Colorful illustrations capture a traditional Halloween celebration.
SUBJ: Halloween--Fiction./ Mothers and daughters--Fiction./ Brothers and sisters--Fiction.

Ph-2 P-1/2 $6.99   P   KF372
CASEY, PATRICIA. My cat Jack. Candlewick ISBN 1-56402-660-4; In Canada: Candlewick/dist. by Douglas & McIntyre, 1996. unp. col. ill. (Read and wonder.)
Jack is a black and white cat whose yawning, stretching, and playful antics fill the pages in large pen-and-ink illustrations. The simple, bouncy text is a perfect counterpoint to the playful cat poses. Excellent for reading aloud.
SUBJ: Cats--Fiction.

Ph-2 P-K/2 $14.95   L   KF373
CAULEY, LORINDA BRYAN. Clap your hands. Putnam ISBN 0-399-22118-2; In Canada: Putnam, 1992. unp. col. ill.

Clap, shake, wiggle, and hop with a group of exuberant children and clothed animals. The rhyming text is perfect for reading aloud and will spark creative movement.
SUBJ: Play--Fiction./ Stories in rhyme.

Ph-2 P-2/2 $13.99 L KF374
CAZET, DENYS. Fish in his pocket. Orchard ISBN 0-531-08313-6, 1987. unp. col. ill.
Dawdling and playing in Long Meadow Pond on his way to school, Russell accidently drops his arithmetic book into the water. When the teacher opens the soggy book, and a small dead fish falls out, Russell sadly puts the fish in his pocket and worries all day before thinking of a proper and fitting way to dispose of the little orange fish.
Attractive double-paged watercolor paintings of rural and classroom scenes add humor to the sensitive, serious story.
SUBJ: Fishes--Fiction./ Schools--Fiction.

Ph-1 1-3/2 $13.95 L KF375
CHAMPION, JOYCE. Emily and Alice. Illus. by Sucie Stevenson. Harcourt Brace ISBN 0-15-200588-9; In Canada: Harcourt Brace c/o Canadian Manda, 1993. unp. col. ill.
"Gulliver books."
Available from the National Library Service for the Blind and Physically Handicapped on sound recording cassette RC 41390.
Emily goes next door to make friends with the new girl, Alice, and the two like each other immediately. Told in three episodes, the story of their friendship provides an amusing bridge to chapter books. Transitional reader for young readers.
SUBJ: Friendship--Fiction.

Ph-2 1-3/2 $14.00 L KF376
CHAMPION, JOYCE. Emily and Alice again. Illus. by Sucie Stevenson. Gulliver/Harcourt Brace ISBN 0-15-200439-4; In Canada: Harcourt Brace c/o Canadian Manda, 1995. unp. col. ill.
Sequel to EMILY AND ALICE, Harcourt Brace, 1993.
In three episodes best friends Emily and Alice make a trade, wear hats to school, and share a scary story during a sleepover. Fun illustrations are part of the appeal of these short stories which may serve as a transitional reader.
SUBJ: Friendship--Fiction.

Ph-2 K-3/3 $14.89 L KF377
CHAPMAN, CHERYL. Snow on snow on snow. Illus. by Synthia Saint James. Dial ISBN 0-8037-1457-2, 1994. unp. col. ill.
Waking up "under blankets under blankets under blankets" and dressing in "clothes over clothes over clothes" to go out in "snow on snow on snow," a young boy spends a day sledding with friends until his dog, Clancy, is missing. The happy ending is "ever after ever after ever after." The title was taken from a poem by Christina Rossetti, and the simple layered text can be enjoyed by very young children and extended into creative writing activities for older children. Oil and acrylic paintings are striking blocks of bright color against white snow. For multicultural studies.
SUBJ: Snow--Fiction./ Dogs--Fiction./ Sleds--Fiction./ Afro-Americans--Fiction.

Ph-1 P-2/2 $13.95 L KF378
CHARLES, N. N. What am I?: looking through shapes at apples and grapes. Illus. by Leo and Diane Dillon. Blue Sky/Scholastic ISBN 0-590-47891-5; In Canada: Scholastic, 1994. unp. col. ill.
Page through colors, cut-out shapes, and short rhyming clues to guess the different fruits featured in striking doublespread illustrations. Together the colors form a rainbow as the hands of different children on the last spread form "a rainbow of the human race." Use to reinforce the concepts of colors and shapes, to introduce different fruits, or to affirm the diversity of our world in multicultural studies.
SUBJ: Fruit--Fiction./ Color--Fiction./ Shape--Fiction./ Toy and movable books.

Ph-2 P-1/1 $12.95 T KF379
CHARLES, VERONIKA MARTENOVA. Hey! What's that sound? Stoddart ISBN 0-7737-2841-4; In Canada: Stoddart, 1994. unp. col. ill.
Listen to the sounds of Aunt Minnie's visit: singing, barking, and screaming as fun and mayhem ensue. The repetitive text is a spirited storytime selection with bright, active illustrations to match. For reading aloud.
SUBJ: Sound--Fiction./ Humorous stories.

Ph-2 2-3/4 $14.95 L KF380
CHERRY, LYNNE. Great kapok tree: a tale of the Amazon rain forest. Gulliver/Harcourt Brace Jovanovich ISBN 0-15-200520-X, 1990. unp. col. ill.
As a woodcutter sleeps at the base of the great kapok tree in an Amazon rain forest, the animals living in the tree plead with him to spare the source of their food and shelter. He awakes, changes his mind and departs, leaving his ax behind. The full-page color illustrations recreate the richness of forest life, and the endpapers have a map of the world's rain forests with margin illustrations of the animals and insects depicted in the story. An excellent book to include in environmental studies.
SUBJ: Conservation of natural resources--Fiction./ Rain forests--Fiction./ Ecology--Fiction./ Kapok (Tree)--Fiction./ Rain forest ecology--Amazon River Region--Brazil--Fiction.

VCR Ph-2 2-3 $42.00 KF381
CHERRY, LYNNE. Great kapok tree (Videocassette). Based on the book written and illus. by Lynne Cherry. SRA/McGraw-Hill ISBN 0-02-686763-X, 1996. 1/2" VHS videocassette color (10min). (Children's literature series).
Includes teacher's guide.
Includes public performance rights.
A group of animals in the rain forest convinces a woodcutter to spare their source of life--the kapok tree. Visuals highlight the details of Lynne Cherry's intricate illustrations while Brazilian percussion instruments imitate the sounds of the tropics. For environmental studies.
SUBJ: Conservation of natural resources--Fiction./ Rain forests--Fiction./ Ecology--Fiction./ Kapok (Tree)--Fiction./ Rain forest ecology--Amazon River Region--Brazil--Fiction.

CDR Ph-1 P-2 $22.48 OD KF382
CHICKA CHICKA BOOM BOOM (CD-ROM). Narrated by Ray Charles. Davidson/Simon & Schuster 2975 ISBN 0-7849-0965-2, 1996. 1 CD-ROM color.
Includes user's guide.
System requirements: Windows 95 or Windows 3.1 or higher; 256-color Super VGA graphics; 8MB of RAM; 66 MHz 486 or faster; double-speed CD-ROM drive; mouse and hard drive; Windows-compatible sound card required; microphone recommended.
System requirements: Macintosh/Power Macintosh; System 7.1 or higher; Motorola 68040 or Power PC processor; 8MB RAM; minimum 14" 256-color monitor; double-speed CD-ROM drive; microphone recommended.
Product (ISBN 0-7849-0965-2) runs on either Windows or Macintosh compatible hardware.
Narrated by Ray Charles, this CD-ROM includes not only Bill Martin, Jr.'s popular alphabet story but also five additional learning games. Youngsters sing along and play letter line-up and various other activities. Works well with small groups, an entire class, or with individuals. (Parents' Shelf)
SUBJ: Alphabet--Software./ Software--Alphabet./ Reading (Preschool)--Software./ Software--Reading (Preschool)./ Reading games--Software./ Software--Reading games./ Interactive media.

Ph-2 1-3/4 $14.95 T KF383
CHINN, KAREN. Sam and the lucky money. Illus. by Cornelius Van Wright and Ying-Hwa Hu. Lee & Low ISBN 1-880000-13-X, 1995. unp. col. ill.
Unable to decide how to spend the four dollars in "lucky money" he received from his grandparents for Chinese New Year, Sam finally chooses to give it to a barefooted old man sitting in a doorway. The colorful setting in Chinatown is pictured in the watercolor illustrations. Useful for multicultural studies, the story has a universal message about caring for those less fortunate than ourselves.
SUBJ: Chinese New Year--Fiction./ Chinese Americans--Fiction./ Asian Americans--Fiction.

Ph-3 P-K/2 $14.95 L KF384
CHRISTELOW, EILEEN. Five little monkeys sitting in a tree. Clarion ISBN 0-395-54434-3, 1991. 32p. col. ill.
Five little monkeys climb out on a limb and taunt Mr. Crocodile below. One by one, they disappear and worried onlookers fear the crocodile has eaten them, but the truly observant will know differently. A humorous introduction to counting with vibrant illustrations.
The five little monkeys bake a cake for Mama's birthday in DON'T WAKE UP MAMA! (ISBN 0-395-60176-2, 1992 and also available from the National Library Service for the Blind and Physically Handicapped on sound recording cassette RC 38328).
SUBJ: Monkeys--Fiction./ Crocodiles--Fiction./ Counting./ Stories in rhyme.

Ph-1 P-2/2 $14.95 L KF385
CHRISTELOW, EILEEN. Five little monkeys with nothing to do. Clarion ISBN 0-395-75830-0, 1996. 37p. col. ill.
Complaining that they have nothing to do, five little monkeys are assigned various cleanup chores in preparation for Grandma Bessie's visit. Unfortunately, the last assignment to pick berries results in the

undoing of everyone's hard work. The amusing illustrations forecast the ending.
SUBJ: Monkeys--Fiction./ House cleaning--Fiction.

Ph-2 1-3/3 $14.95 L KF386
CHRISTELOW, EILEEN. Five-dog night. Clarion ISBN 0-395-62399-5, 1993. unp. col. ill.
Betty can't understand why her neighbor, Ezra, doesn't need a blanket when the nights get cold. Concerned about Ezra, she visits him one morning and discovers his five dogs keep him warm. Ezra is annoyed about her nosiness, but eventually they both decide there is no substitute for each other's company. A light and humorous story.
SUBJ: Winter--Fiction./ Neighborliness--Fiction./ Dogs--Fiction.

Ph-2 K-2/3 $13.95 T KF387
CHRISTELOW, EILEEN. Gertrude, the bulldog detective. Clarion ISBN 0-395-58701-8, 1992. 32p. col. ill.
Gertrude loves mysteries and decides to become a detective. She annoys her neighbors by spying on them, so they plant some phony clues which lead her to solve a real case. An entertaining mystery for young fans of the genre.
SUBJ: Mystery and detective stories./ Dogs--Fiction.

Ph-2 1-3/2 $14.95 L KF388
CHRISTELOW, EILEEN. Great pig escape. Clarion ISBN 0-395-66973-1, 1994. unp. col. ill.
On the way to market, six piglets escape from the back of a truck and run away to Florida by dressing in clothing they borrow from clotheslines and scarecrows. Several months later the clothes are returned, and Ethel and Bert receive a postcard from the pigs. Much of the humor is in the watercolor and ink illustrations which picture the pigs in their disguises.
SUBJ: Pigs--Fiction.

CE

Ph-2 K-3/4 $13.95 L KF389
CHRISTELOW, EILEEN. Robbery at the Diamond Dog Diner. Clarion ISBN 0-89919-425-7, 1986. unp. col. ill.
Read along kit available from Houghton Mifflin (ISBN 0-89919-894-5, 1989). 1 paperback book, 1 sound cassette (11min), $8.95.
Glenda Feathers has a very clever idea for foiling the diamond robbers, but unfortunately she also has a big mouth and inadvertently alerts the thieves to the hiding place of Lola Dog's diamonds.
Colorful, cartoon-style illustrations add to the suspense and humor of the slapstick tale. Fine for reading aloud.
SUBJ: Robbers and outlaws--Fiction./ Dogs--Fiction./ Animals--Fiction.

Ph-2 1-3/2 $15.00 T KF390
CHRISTIAN, MARY BLOUNT. Toady and Dr. Miracle. Illus. by Christine Jenny. Simon & Schuster ISBN 0-689-80890-9; In Canada: Distican, 1997. 40p. col. ill. (Ready-to-read).
Hired as a toady, Luther puts on such a good performance that he helps Dr. Miracle, a traveling medicine man, cheat the local people. When the fraud becomes evident, Luther outwits the crook and proves he is "right smart." New full-color acrylic illustrations revive the humorous story.
SUBJ: Medicine shows--Fiction./ Conduct of life--Fiction.

Ph-2 2-3/6 $15.99 T KF391
CHRISTIANSEN, CANDACE. Ice horse. Illus. by Thomas Locker. Dial ISBN 0-8037-1400-9, 1993. unp. col. ill.
Jack is proud to be asked by his Uncle Joe to help harvest the ice on the Hudson River where he learns firsthand about the hard work and dangers. Presents an interesting slice of history before refrigerators when the ice harvested from the Hudson River provided the ice for the city of New York. Historical fiction in picture-book format is stunningly illustrated with full-color oil paintings.
SUBJ: Ice industry--Fiction./ Horses--Fiction.

Ph-3 K-2 $4.95 P KF392
CHWAST, SEYMOUR. Alphabet parade. Harcourt Brace Jovanovich ISBN 0-15-200115-8; In Canada: Harcourt Brace c/o Canadian Manda, 1994. unp. col. ill.
"Gulliver books."
The letters of the alphabet parade through the pages of this picture book. Most letters have a page to themselves with people, animals, and objects in the parade or among the spectators that begin with the featured letter. A list of the items to be found follows at the end of the book. Youngsters will enjoy the puzzle as they recognize the letter sounds.
SUBJ: Alphabet./ Stories without words.

Ph-2 K-1 $14.00 L KF393
CLARKE, GUS. E I E I O: the story of Old MacDonald, who had a farm. Illus. by Gus Clarke. Lothrop, Lee & Shepard ISBN 0-688-12215-

9, 1993. unp. col. ill.
A charming version of the classic tale. Cluttered, zany pictures will provoke giggles as Old MacDonald's barnyard overflows with animals.
SUBJ: Folk songs--United States.

Ph-2 P-3/1 $11.88 L KF394
CLEARY, BEVERLY. Growing-up feet. Illus. by DyAnne DiSalvo-Ryan. Morrow ISBN 0-688-06620-8, 1987. unp. col. ill.
Available from the National Library Service for the Blind and Physically Handicapped on sound recording cassette RC35313.
Presents the story of twins Jimmy and Janet who acquire new red boots at the shoe store--rain boots that will grow as their feet grow. The slight story centers on how the four-year-old twins share their excitement and anticipate a good rainy day--until dad provides a hose, some mud, and a most satisfying puddle. Good for oral, primary, and for those just at the beginning-to-read stage.
SUBJ: Shoes--Fiction./ Boots--Fiction./ Twins--Fiction.

Ph-1 2-3/3 $14.93 L KF395
CLEARY, BEVERLY. Petey's bedtime story. Illus. by David Small. Morrow ISBN 0-688-10661-7, 1993. unp. col. ill.
Petey asks for a bedtime story and ends up telling a whopper of his own about his birth. This tall tale features the precocious toddler, Petey, but older students will appreciate the humor while sticking with the lengthy text.
SUBJ: Bedtime--Fiction./ Parent and child--Fiction.

Ph-2 P/2 $11.88 L KF396
CLEARY, BEVERLY. Real hole. Illus. by DyAnne DiSalvo-Ryan. Morrow ISBN 0-688-05851-5, c1960, 1986. unp. col. ill.
Available from National Library Service for the Blind and Physically Handicapped on sound recording cassette RC11666, and in Braille BR7466.
Four-year-old Jimmy surprises his family by digging such a big hole that his father buys a tree to plant in it.
Jimmy and his twin sister Janet are also featured in TWO DOG BISCUITS (ISBN 0-688-05848-5, 1961, 1986) (available from NLSBPH in Braille BR7003) and JANET'S THINGAMAJIGS (ISBN 0-688-06617-8, 1987) (available from NLSBPH in Braille BR7004).
SUBJ: Family life--Fiction.

Ph-1 K-2/5 $15.89 L KF397
CLIMO, SHIRLEY. Cobweb Christmas. Illus. by Joe Lasker. Crowell/ HarperCollins ISBN 0-690-04216-7, 1982. unp. col. ill.
Available from National Library Service for the Blind and Physically Handicapped in Braille BR07031.
Tante and her animals live in a tiny cottage deep in a German forest. In preparation for Christmas, she cleans, polishes, bakes, decorates and sweeps out all the spiders and their cobwebs. On Christmas eve, as she dozes before the fire, Christkindel lets the spiders in to see the wonderful tree. They run up and down the tree and create a magic of their own. And that is why today Christmas trees are decorated with tinsel and strings of gold and silver.
SUBJ: Christmas--Fiction.

Ph-2 1-3/2 $14.95 T KF398
CLIMO, SHIRLEY. Little red ant and the great big crumb: a Mexican fable. Retold by Shirley Climo. Illus. by Francisco X. Mora. Clarion ISBN 0-395-70732-3, 1995. 40p. col. ill.
Includes glossary.
Searching for someone strong to help her carry a cake crumb, a little red ant decides she is the strongest and carries the crumb herself. The many animal characters are named in Spanish (pronunciation guide in the back). This variation of an old Spanish fable set in Mexico will complement studies in Mexican culture and the Spanish language as well as provide an entertaining and colorful story. For multicultural studies.
SUBJ: Ants--Fiction./ Animals--Fiction./ Self-esteem--Fiction.

Ph-1 1-3/2 $13.89 L KF399
COERR, ELEANOR. Buffalo Bill and the Pony Express. Illus. by Don Bolognese. HarperCollins ISBN 0-06-023373-7; In Canada: HarperCollins, 1995. 64p. col. ill. (I can read book).
When young Bill Cody joins the Pony Express and has a series of adventures, his letters home downplay the danger and excitement of his job. Based on the actual life of Buffalo Bill, the action-packed beginning reader will thrill young readers.
SUBJ: Buffalo Bill--Fiction./ Pony express--Fiction.

Ph-2 2-3/2 $13.89 L KF400
COERR, ELEANOR. Chang's paper pony. Illus. by Deborah Kogan Ray. HarperCollins ISBN 0-06-021329-9; In Canada: HarperCollins, 1988. 64p. col. ill. (I can read book).

A young Chinese immigrant in California helps his grandfather run a restaurant in a mining camp and dreams of owning his own horse one day. He even tries, unsuccessfully, to pan for gold, but eventually gets his pony through the help of a friendly miner. Strongly conveys the pride and dignity of the Chinese immigrant in the rough, prejudiced world of the mining camps in an easy to read text.
SUBJ: Chinese--United States--Fiction./ Ponies--Fiction./ Gold mines and mining--Fiction.

CE   Ph-2 1-3/2 $14.89   L   KF401
COERR, ELEANOR. Josefina story quilt. Illus. by Bruce Degen. HarperCollins ISBN 0-06-021349-3; In Canada: HarperCollins, 1986. 64p. col. ill. (I can read book).
  Spanish version JOSEFINA Y LA COLCHA DE RETAZOS available from Harper Arco Iris (ISBN 0-06-025319-3, 1995).
  Available from National Library Service for the Blind and Physically Handicapped in Braille BR7046.
  Read-along kit available from HarperChidren's Audio (ISBN 0-694-70012-6, 1995). 1 paperback book, 1 sound cassette (17min), $7.95.
  During the long, difficult wagon train trip to a new home in California, young Faith creates squares for a quilt that will tell the story of the hazardous journey and will star her beloved pet hen, Josefina. Drama, excitement, sorrow and courage are all elements in appealing, easy-to-read historical fiction.
  SUBJ: Quilting--Fiction./ Chickens--Fiction./ Overland journeys to the Pacific--Fiction./ Spanish language materials.

                              Ph-2 K-2/3 $14.00   L   KF402
COFFELT, NANCY. Dog who cried woof. Gulliver/Harcourt Brace ISBN 0-15-200201-4; In Canada: Harcourt Brace c/o Canadian Manda, 1995. unp. col. ill.
  When Ernie tries to tell his family that the neighbor's cat is stealing his food, no one pays any attention because he barks loudly at every small thing. One day, Ernie loses his voice and as it gradually comes back, he learns to use his voice sparingly with greater effect. Large pastel illustrations make this variant of the "Boy who cried wolf" a delight for reading aloud.
  SUBJ: Dogs--Fiction./ Cats--Fiction./ Noise--Fiction./ Barking--Fiction.

                              Ph-2 P-1/2 $13.95   L   KF403
COFFELT, NANCY. Good night, Sigmund. Harcourt Brace Jovanovich ISBN 0-15-200464-5; In Canada: Harcourt Brace c/o Canadian Manda, 1992. unp. col. ill.
  "Gulliver books."
  Sigmund a grey cat with a sense of humor seems to appear everywhere the young narrator goes until bedtime when he is hiding. The large format includes lots of white space with colorful oil pastels suitable for sharing with a group.
  SUBJ: Cats--Fiction.

CE   Ph-1 K-1/2 $15.00   T   KF404
COHEN, MIRIAM. See you in second grade! Illus. by Lillian Hoban. Greenwillow ISBN 0-688-07138-4, 1989. unp. col. ill.
  Videocassette available from Spoken Arts SAV-9052-4, 1991. 1/2" VHS videocassette color (9min), guide, $44.95.
  The First Grade--so popular over the last 25 years--share a very special year-end outing to the beach because next year they are going to the Second Grade! After a swim and lunch the class enjoys a very special sharing of first grade memories. Readers who love this popular series will like this nostalgic story and appreciate the big step up to the Second Grade.
  In THE REAL-SKIN RUBBER MONSTER MASK (ISBN 0-688-09123-7, 1990), Jim wears a scary mask for Halloween and goes trick-or-treating with his second-grade friends.
  REAL-SKIN RUBBER MONSTER MASK available on videocassette from Spoken Arts SAV-9053-2, 1991. 1/2" VHS videocassette color (11min), guide, $44.95.
  SUBJ: Schools--Fiction./ Picnicking--Fiction.

CE   Ph-1 K-1/2 $13.95   L   KF405
COHEN, MIRIAM. Will I have a friend? Illus. by Lillian Hoban. Macmillan ISBN 0-02-722790-1, c1967. unp. col. ill.
  Jim is very apprehensive about his first day in school and asks his father "Will I have a friend?" The other children are busily playing and all seem to have friends and pay no attention to Jim. However, at rest time Paul notices Jim and afterward they too play together. Traditional concerns and activities of young school-aged children are treated throughout the series: WHEN WILL I READ? (Greenwillow ISBN 0-688-84073-6, 1977); NO GOOD IN ART (Greenwillow ISBN 0-688-84234-8, 1980); SO WHAT? (Greenwillow ISBN 0-688-01203-5, 1982, OPC); JIM'S DOG MUFFINS (Greenwillow ISBN 0-688-02565-X, 1984, OPC); LIAR, LIAR, PANTS ON FIRE! (Greenwillow ISBN 0-688-04245-7, 1985); DON'T EAT TOO MUCH

TURKEY! (Greenwillow ISBN 0-688-07142-2, 1987).
SUBJ: Schools--Fiction./ First day of school--Fiction.

                              Ph-2 2-4/2 $17.00   T   KF406
COLE, BABETTE. Drop dead. Knopf ISBN 0-679-88358-4; In Canada: Random House, 1996. unp. col. ill.
  "Borzoi book."
  Grandma and Grandpa tell their life story from infancy to possible post-death reincarnation to their grandchildren. Slapstick, multicolored illustrations add humorous details and extend the text.
  SUBJ: Grandparents--Fiction./ Death--Fiction./ Reincarnation--Fiction.

                              Ph-2 P-2/2 $15.00   T   KF407
COLE, BROCK. Giant's toe. Farrar, Straus and Giroux ISBN 0-374-32559-6; In Canada: HarperCollins, 1986. unp. col. ill.
  Having hit his foot with a hoe while gardening, a giant is sure that the little figure he picks up is his toe. He soon finds that the toe is an absolute trial and tribulation and tries to rid himself of it only to have the tables constantly turned on him. Hysterically funny and even easy to read, this will be delightful for those children who will not be disconcerted by the unclothed figure.
  SUBJ: Giants--Fiction./ Humorous stories.

                              Ph-2 K-3/2 $15.00   T   KF408
COLE, BROCK. Winter wren. Farrar, Straus & Giroux ISBN 0-374-38454-1; In Canada: HarperCollins, 1984. unp. col. ill.
  Searching for spring, Simon with his little sister on his back encounters ghostly Old Man Winter, who throws ice at them and turns Meg into a bird before the boy finally releases spring and changes the bird back into his little sister. Magnificent water colors enhance the mystical story with the feel of a folktale.
  SUBJ: Spring--Fiction./ Brothers and sisters--Fiction.

                              Ph-1 K-3/3 $15.00   L   KF409
COLE, HENRY. Jack's garden. Greenwillow ISBN 0-688-13501-3, 1995. unp. col. ill.
  Includes directory.
  Seeds nourished by soil and rain turn into plants whose flowers attract insects and birds to Jack's lush garden. As the garden that Jack planted grows so does the cumulative text. Different colored papers form the background for each horizontal doublespread executed in colored pencils. The illustrations extend into the borders which also feature small, labeled details relating to each page. Individuals and classes planning to start a garden shouldn't miss this offering.
  SUBJ: Gardening--Fiction.

                              Ph-2 K-3/2 $12.88   L   KF410
COLE, JOANNA. Doctor Change. Illus. by Donald Carrick. Morrow ISBN 0-688-06136-2, 1986. unp. col. ill.
  Available from National Library Service for the Blind and Physically Handicapped on sound recording cassette RC25418.
  After taking a job with a man he thinks is a doctor, young Tom finds he is a captive of a wicked sorcerer. Very cleverly Tom finally manages to learn the magician's spells, trick Dr. Change, gain his freedom, and put an end to the evil doctor of magic. The fairy tale like fantasy is illustrated with attractive paintings of nineteenth century settings.
  SUBJ: Sorcerers--Fiction.

                              Ph-2 P-2/3 $14.88   L   KF411
COLE, SHEILA. When the tide is low. Illus. by Virginia Wright-Frierson. Lothrop, Lee & Shepard ISBN 0-688-04067-5, 1985. 32p. col. ill.
  Includes glossary.
  Swinging high and low on her swing, a little girl understands more about high and low tide and eagerly awaits low tide when she and her mother will be able to walk the beach and observe and collect clams, crabs, mussels, anemones, and other sea creatures. The pictures of the sea animals are especially clear and very interesting to children who live near the seashore.
  SUBJ: Tides--Fiction./ Beaches--Fiction.

VCR   Ph-1 2-4 $9.95   KF412
CONNELLY, BERNARDINE. Follow the drinking gourd: a story of the Underground Railroad (Videocassette). Told by Morgan Freeman. Music by Taj Mahal. Illus. by Yvonne Buchanan. Rabbit Ears 74041-70736-3 ISBN 1-57099-001-8, 1992. 1/2" VHS videocassette color (30min). (American heroes and legends).
  Mary, her mother, and brother escape from a plantation in Alabama. With the help of Peg Leg Joe and his song about the drinking gourd, they find their way up the Tennessee River to cross the Ohio River and meet their father along the way. Still watercolor pictures are animated with skillful use of video techniques. The music by Taj Mahal perfectly underscores the well-paced narration and the emotions from

fear to hope and joy. For multicultural studies.
SUBJ: Slavery--Fiction./ Underground railroad--Fiction.

Ph-1 2-5/2 $14.89   L   KF413
CONRAD, PAM. Call me Ahnighito. Illus. by Richard Egielski.
HarperCollins ISBN 0-06-023323-0; In Canada: HarperCollins, 1995.
unp. col. ill.
"Laura Geringer book."
Made of star stuff, Ahnighito, a giant meteorite, tells the story of its
arduous journey from the Arctic to the American Museum of Natural
History in New York City. Large illustrations depict the struggle of
numerous people to move the huge rock with chains, boats, and a
horse-drawn cart. Told from an unusual point of view, this story
should not be missed in astronomy and geology studies.
SUBJ: Meteorites--Fiction./ Greenland--Fiction./ Peary, Robert E.
(Robert Edwin)--Fiction.

Ph-1 K-2/3 $15.89   L   KF414
CONRAD, PAM. Rooster's gift. Illus. by Eric Beddows. HarperCollins
ISBN 0-06-023604-3; In Canada: HarperCollins, 1996. unp. col. ill.
"Laura Geringer book."
Thinking he has the gift of waking the sun every morning, Rooster is
disappointed when he learns the sun rises without him, but Smallest
Hen helps him to realize his true gift. Barnyard life and glorious egg-
shaped sunrises are depicted in the illustrations. The warm story is a
fun selection for science units about the sun.
SUBJ: Roosters--Fiction./ Chickens--Fiction./ Pride and vanity--Fiction./
Sun--Fiction.

Ph-1 1-3/4 $14.89   L   KF415
CONRAD, PAM. Tub Grandfather. Illus. by Richard Egielski.
HarperCollins ISBN 0-06-022896-2; In Canada: HarperCollins, 1993.
unp. col. ill.
"Laura Geringer book."
Sequel to TUB PEOPLE, HarperCollins, 1989.
Rescuing a figure from under the radiator, the Tub People recognize
him as the grandfather and slowly revive their lost family member.
SUBJ: Toys--Fiction./ Grandfathers--Fiction.

CE
Ph-1 1-3/4 $14.89   L   KF416
CONRAD, PAM. Tub people. Illus. by Richard Egielski. HarperCollins
ISBN 0-06-021341-8; In Canada: HarperCollins, 1989. unp. col. ill.
Read-along kit available from HarperChildren's Audio (ISBN
0-69470-058-4, 1996). 1 paperback book, 1 sound cassette (12min),
$7.95.
Seven round, stolid wooden toys live on the edge of the tub. They
enjoy lively bathtub games until the Tub Child is tragically sucked
down the drain. He is eventually rescued and the Tub People are
whisked to the safer surroundings of a quilt and windowsill. The
illustrations show the toys in scale dwarfed by cakes of soap and
washcloths and subtly convey their intensely private lives which
guarantee survival in a world they cannot dominate. This will provoke
discussion at storytime.
SUBJ: Toys--Fiction./ Baths--Fiction.

Ph-3 1-3/4 $14.95   T OD KF417
CONWAY, DIANA COHEN. Northern lights: a Hanukkah story. Illus. by
Shelly O. Haas. Kar-Ben Copies ISBN 0-929371-79-8, 1994. unp. col. ill.
A snow squall forces Sara and her father to spend the first night of
Hanukkah in an Eskimo village. When the lights go out in the Yupik
cabin where Sara is staying, she tells the family the story of
Hanukkah, and they light a seal oil lamp in observation of the first
night. Finally the northern lights remind both families of a giant
menorah. Associations drawn between the two cultures emphasize
their commonalities while illuminating unique features of the two
traditions. For multicultural studies.
SUBJ: Hanukkah--Fiction./ Eskimos--Alaska--Fiction./ Indians of North
America--Fiction.

Ph-2 1-3/5 $14.95   L   KF418
COONEY, BARBARA. Hattie and the wild waves. Viking/Penguin ISBN
0-670-83056-9; In Canada: Penguin, 1990. unp. col. ill.
As she grows up, Hattie dreams of becoming an artist until one day
she decides it is time to act on her dreams and she enrolls in Art
School. An engaging portrait of a young girl growing up with
wealthy immigrant parents in Brooklyn and Long Island. Based on the
life of the author's mother, this illustrated story provides readers with
a warm glimpse into another era.
SUBJ: Beaches--Fiction./ Artists--Fiction.

Ph-1 K-3/5 $14.95   L   KF419
COONEY, BARBARA. Miss Rumphius. Viking ISBN 0-670-47958-6; In
Canada: Penguin, 1982. unp. col. ill.
Selectors' Choice, 14th ed.

Available in Spanish, SENORITA EMILIA (Ekare ISBN 980-257-110-
5, n.d.).
Having traveled to many far away places, Great-Aunt Alice has
retired and tries to figure out how to honor her grandfather's request
to make the world more beautiful. Masterful paintings using the blue,
purple, and rose of the lupines that she decides to plant create the
perfect serene background for the simple story.
SUBJ: Aunts--Fiction./ Conduct of life--Fiction./ Spanish language
materials.

KIT
Ph-3 K-3 $7.99   KF420
COONEY, BARBARA. Miss Rumphius (Kit). Puffin StoryTapes ISBN
0-14-095026-5, 1994. 1 paperback book, 1 sound cassette (18min).
The unabridged story of Miss Rumphius, who longed to visit faraway
places and to make the world more beautiful, is presented on side
one of the tape in a read-along version, complete with page turning
signals. Side two extends the story with discussions and songs about
traveling, flowers, and making a more beautiful world. An economical
package.
SUBJ: Aunts--Fiction./ Conduct of life--Fiction.

Ph-2 1-3/3 $15.00   L   KF421
COOPER, ELISHA. Country fair. Greenwillow ISBN 0-688-15531-6; In
Canada: Hearst Book Group, 1997. unp. col. ill.
An agricultural fair complete with farm animals, machinery, rides, and
food fills a large field for several days. The hand-lettered text swoops
and swirls around tiny watercolor and pencil illustrations. The small
scale of the pictures and text add to their charm and appeal, but
probably limit the book to individual enjoyment.
SUBJ: Fairs.

Ph-1 P-1/2 $13.99   T   KF422
COOPER, HELEN. Boy who wouldn't go to bed. Dial ISBN 0-8037-
2253-2, 1997. unp. col. ill.
Published in Great Britain, Transworld, 1996.
Eluding sleep, a small boy drives his car around looking for someone
to play with him, but everyone is sleepy including Mother who finally
carries him to bed. Luminous watercolor paintings evoke a make-
believe world where stuffed animals and toy soldiers are life-sized
and even the moon and stars hang from strings in a mobile. A
charming bedtime composition.
SUBJ: Bedtime--Fiction./ Sleep--Fiction./ Imagination--Fiction.

Ph-2 2-4/2 $14.95   L   KF423
COOPER, SUSAN. Danny and the kings. Illus. by Jos. A. Smith.
McElderry ISBN 0-689-50577-9; In Canada: Maxwell Macmillan, 1993.
unp. col. ill.
Longing for a Christmas tree for his family's trailer, Danny gets a
small one from a friend, but a truck runs over it as he is pulling it
home. The driver and two of his friends are driving east in their three
trucks with Christmas lights around the windshields. When they return
home from the school play, Danny and his family discover a
decorated tree in their trailer and a single bulb in the snow like the
ones that had decorated the trucks of the "three kings." This
heartwarming holiday story evokes the biblical Christmas story which
is the subject of Danny's school play.
SUBJ: Christmas trees--Fiction./ Christmas--Fiction./ Brothers--Fiction.

Ph-2 1-3/3 $13.95   T   KF424
COPELAND, ERIC. Milton, my father's dog. Tundra ISBN 0-88776-339-
1; In Canada: Tundra, 1994. unp. col. ill.
The huge sheep dog his parents bring home is not quite the puppy
Fraser had wanted. In fact, the huge beast smells bad, pulls too hard
on the leash, and wreaks havoc everywhere he goes. Fraser's father
can't see the dog's faults and treats him like one of the children. The
perspective of a child describing a parent's obsession creates
engaging dry humor. Based on a true experience, the story will
appeal to adults and children.
SUBJ: Dogs--Fiction./ Family life--Fiction.

Ph-2 P-1/2 $11.95   L   KF425
COREY, DOROTHY. Will there be a lap for me? Illus. by Nancy Poydar.
Whitman ISBN 0-8075-9109-2; In Canada: General, 1992. unp. col. ill.
Kyle's mother is expecting a baby, and as she gets bigger, her lap
grows smaller, and Kyle misses that special place. After the baby is
born, his mother always seems busy with the new baby. Then one
afternoon while the baby naps, Kyle rediscovers his mother's lap. A
reassuring story about the concerns of older siblings who feel
"crowded out" by a new baby.
SUBJ: Mothers and sons--Fiction./ Babies--Fiction.

Ph-2 K-2/2 $17.27   L   KF426
COSSI, OLGA. Great getaway. Illus. by Ellen Anderson. Gareth Stevens
ISBN 0-8368-0107-5; In Canada: Saunders, 1991. 32p. col. ill.

Elizabeth and Jennifer, two sisters, decide to run away from home where mom and dad are always busy with new twins. They pack their things in a laundry basket strapped to roller skates and set out, but at every corner, something prevents them from crossing the street. They end up going around the block and arrive back home in time to eat. Expressive watercolor illustrations accompany the universal story. For multicultural studies.
SUBJ: Sisters--Fiction./ Runaways--Fiction./ Afro-Americans--Fiction.

Ph-1 K-2/4 $14.95   L   KF427
COTE, NANCY. Palm trees. Four Winds ISBN 0-02-724760-0; In Canada: Maxwell Macmillan, 1993. unp. col. ill.
On a hot, humid day, Millie can't decide what to do with her hair. She puts it in two ponytails on top of her head, but her friend Renee says they look like palm trees. Bright, splashy illustrations accompany the story of hair and friendship. For multicultural studies.
SUBJ: Hair--Fiction./ Self-reliance--Fiction./ Friendship--Fiction./ Afro-Americans--Fiction.

Ph-3 2-4/4 $4.95   P   KF428
COWCHER, HELEN. Rain forest. Farrar, Straus & Giroux ISBN 0-374-46190-2, c1988, 1990. unp. col. ill.
Spanish version available EL BOSQUE TROPICAL (ISBN 0-374-30900-0, 1992).
What appears to be a vividly illustrated picture storybook is really a walloping introduction to rain forest destruction. An attention grabber for elementary units on ecological nightmares.
SUBJ: Rain forests--Fiction./ Spanish language materials.

Ph-2 K-2/2 $14.95   L   KF429
COWEN-FLETCHER, JANE. It takes a village. Scholastic ISBN 0-590-46573-2; In Canada: Scholastic, 1994. unp. col. ill.
After Yemi promises to look after her little brother, Kokou, at the market, she is distressed when she loses him. However, she has no need to worry because all of the people from the village take a part in looking after him. Illustrates the African proverb, "It takes a village to raise a child," with an enjoyable, lightly humorous story and colorful illustrations. A fine adjunct to curriculum units about community. For multicultural studies.
SUBJ: Benin--Fiction./ Brothers and sisters--Fiction.

Ph-1 K-2/1 $15.95   L   KF430
COWLEY, JOY. Gracias, the Thanksgiving turkey. Illus. by Joe Cepeda. Scholastic ISBN 0-590-46976-2; In Canada: Scholastic, 1996. unp. col. ill.
Includes glossary.
Miguel's father, a truck driver, sends him a turkey with instructions to fatten the bird for Thanksgiving. Named Gracias, the bird becomes a pet for Miguel who cannot imagine eating his friend for the holiday. Oil paintings provide the urban setting, and Spanish words are used throughout this unique holiday offering. For multicultural studies.
SUBJ: Turkeys--Fiction./ Thanksgiving Day--Fiction./ Puerto Ricans--New York (N.Y.)--Fiction./ New York (N.Y.)--Fiction.

Ph-2 K-2/2 $15.93   L   KF431
CREWS, DONALD. Bicycle race. Greenwillow ISBN 0-688-05172-3, 1985. unp. col. ill.
Numbering the helmets of twelve bicyclists precedes a race in which the unexpected happens. Although not a counting book for the very young as promoted, it is a brightly colored fun book with the excitement of bicycle road racing.
SUBJ: Bicycle racing--Fiction./ Racing--Fiction.

Ph-2 P-K $13.93   L   KF432
CREWS, DONALD. Carousel. Greenwillow ISBN 0-688-00909-3, 1982. unp. col. ill.
Children climb on their favorite animal and anxiously wait for the carousel to start. The calliope plays, the horses are off, and round and round and faster and faster they go until all is just a blur of color. Soon the music stops, the horses go slower and slower finally stopping. The blur ceases, the ride is over. Full color collages and special photographic techniques are used to create sound and motion.
SUBJ: Merry-go-round--Fiction.

Ph-1 P-K $15.93   L   KF433
CREWS, DONALD. Freight train. Greenwillow ISBN 0-688-84165-1, 1978. unp. col. ill.
Caldecott Honor Book.
Board book available from Tupelo Books (ISBN 0-688-14900-6, 1996).
A black steam engine pulls a freight train with purple, blue, green, yellow, and orange cars and, of course, a red caboose through tunnels, by cities, and across trestles in daylight and into the darkness of night.
SUBJ: Railroads--Trains--Pictorial works./ Color.

Ph-1 P-2/2 $14.93   L   KF434
CREWS, DONALD. Sail away. Greenwillow ISBN 0-688-11054-1, 1995. unp. col. ill.
Few words and full-color, horizontal doublespread illustrations depict a day of sailing through a bright sky, a darkening storm, and the calm of dusk. The minimal text is carefully placed, and the typeface conveys the strong wind, rocky storm, and quiet night. A masterful example of book design and illustration for reading aloud.
SUBJ: Sailing--Fiction./ Boats and boating--Fiction.

Ph-2 P-2/1 $14.93   L   KF435
CREWS, DONALD. School bus. Greenwillow ISBN 0-688-02808-X, 1984. unp. col. ill.
Follows school buses as they transport children to and from school. Large, uncluttered pictures, familiar situations and a very easy to read text make this very popular with beginning readers.
SUBJ: School buses--Fiction./ Buses--Fiction.

Ph-1 K-2/2 $13.93   L   KF436
CREWS, DONALD. Shortcut. Greenwillow ISBN 0-688-06437-X, 1992. unp. col. ill.
A group of children decides to take the shortcut home along the railroad tracks, and a train comes dangerously close to hitting them. Dark, ominous illustrations fill the pages as the train goes klakity-klak down the track. Readers will turn the pages breathlessly to discover the fate of the children. For multicultural studies.
SUBJ: Railroads--Fiction./ Afro-Americans--Fiction.

Ph-2 P-2/2 $14.93   L   KF437
CREWS, DONALD. Ten black dots. Rev. and redesigned ed. Greenwillow ISBN 0-688-06068-4, c1968, 1986. unp. col. ill.
A counting book in which ten black dots as one or in groups of two through ten are used to complete a picture. A brief, rhyming text reinforces the numerical concepts. The bright, bold, uncomplicated pictures are large enough for group story use.
SUBJ: Counting./ Stories in rhyme.

CE   Ph-1 P-K $13.93   L   KF438
CREWS, DONALD. Truck. Greenwillow ISBN 0-688-84244-5, 1980. unp. col. ill.
Caldecott Honor Book.
Big book available from Mulberry (ISBN 0-688-12611-1, 1992), $18.95.
Loaded with tricycles an enormous red truck leaves a loading dock, travels on city streets, through a tunnel, down super highways with appropriate truck stops, and across a bridge to its final destination. Vibrant illustrations with road, highway and traffic signs but no text.
SUBJ: Trucks--Pictorial works./ Stories without words.

Ph-1 K-2/2 $13.89   L   KF439
CROLL, CAROLYN. Too many Babas. HarperCollins ISBN 0-06-021384-1; In Canada: HarperCollins, c1979, 1994. 64p. col. ill. (I can read book).
Too many Babas "spoil the broth" when they each add more salt and spices to soup Baba Edis is making. Crisp illustrations add a Russian flavor to this story. Several pages without text add the perfect touch to this easy-to-read title for beginning readers.
SUBJ: Cookery--Fiction.

Ph-2 1-2/2 $14.89   L   KF440
CUSHMAN, DOUG. Aunt Eater's mystery Christmas. HarperCollins ISBN 0-06-023580-2; In Canada: HarperCollins, 1995. 64p. col. ill. (I can read book).
Aunt Eater solves several yuletide mysteries including what caused the bump and the jingling sound in the middle of the night. Funny, short mysteries in an easy-to-read format will appeal to beginning readers.
SUBJ: Anteaters--Fiction./ Christmas--Fiction./ Mystery and detective stories.

Ph-2 1-3/2 $12.89   L   KF441
CUSHMAN, DOUG. Aunt Eater's mystery vacation. HarperCollins ISBN 0-06-020514-8; In Canada: HarperCollins, 1992. 64p. col. ill. (I can read book).
Aunt Eater is an anteater who loves detective stories, and while on vacation, she solves several mysteries herself. Young fans of the genre will enjoy this appropriately paced and readable selection.
SUBJ: Anteaters--Fiction./ Vacations--Fiction./ Hotels, motels, etc.--Fiction./ Mystery and detective stories.

Ph-2 K-2/3 $14.95   L   KF442
CUTLER, JANE. Mr. Carey's garden. Illus. by G. Brian Karas. Houghton Mifflin ISBN 0-395-68191-X, 1996. unp. col. ill.
The neighbors all have suggestions for how Mr. Carey can rid his garden of snails until one moonlit night, they discover the lovely trails and lacy shadows the snails create. Fosters an appreciation of nature

Ph-2 1-3/7 $14.89 L KF443
CZERNECKI, STEFAN. Hummingbirds' gift. By Stefan Czernecki and Timothy Rhodes. Illustrated by Stefan Czernecki. Straw weavings by Juliana Reyes de Silva and Juan Hilario Silva. Hyperion ISBN 1-56282-605-0, 1994. unp. col. ill.
During an awful drought, a Mexican family makes clay feeders for the hummingbirds and shares their meager supply of water and sugar. To repay their kindness, the small birds show the family how to weave straw figures which the family sells at the Day of the Dead festival. Author's note explains the significance of the straw figures and the celebration of the Mexican holiday to honor ones' ancestors. For multicultural studies.
SUBJ: Hummingbirds--Fiction./ Mexico--Fiction./ All Souls' Day--Mexico--Fiction.

Ph-2 1-3/4 $3.99 P KF444
DAHL, ROALD. Enormous Crocodile. Illus. by Quentin Blake. Puffin ISBN 0-14-036556-7; In Canada: Penguin, c1978, 1993. unp. col. ill.
Spanish version EL COCODRILO ENORME available from Santillana (ISBN 84-2044-7609, n.d.).
Enormous Crocodile brags to all of the forest creatures that he is going to town to eat young children, but one by one the animals foil his dastardly plans. Youngsters will enjoy the humorous story and just ending. Good choice for reading aloud.
SUBJ: Crocodiles--Fiction./ Spanish language materials.

TB
Ph-3 K-3 $11.95 OD KF445
DAHL, ROALD. Enormous crocodile; and, The magic finger (Talking book). HarperCollins/Caedmon CPN1633, 1980. 1 sound cassette.
Read by the author, these two tales reflect Dahl's talent for creating villainous villains and magical magic.
Contents: Side A: Enormous crocodile (17min); Side B: Magic finger (22min).
SUBJ: Fantasy.

Ph-1 P-1/2 $14.95 T KF446
DALE, PENNY. Ten out of bed. Candlewick ISBN 1-56402-322-2; In Canada: Douglas & McIntyre, 1994. unp. col. ill.
A young boy and his stuffed animals count down to sleep as they play games of make-believe. A fun-filled book for counting and bedtime.
SUBJ: Counting./ Bedtime--Fiction./ Sleep--Fiction./ Toys--Fiction./ Animals--Fiction.

Ph-2 1-4/5 $16.00 L KF447
DALY, NIKI. My dad. McElderry ISBN 0-689-50620-1, 1995. unp. col. ill.
Embarrassed by their father's drinking, the children don't tell him about their school concert, but he comes anyway and creates a scene. The realistic portrayal of a father's alcoholism ends hopefully when the father joins Alcoholics Anonymous. Young readers with similar problems will relate to the story while others may better understand the experiences of children with alcoholic parents. The picture book format is suitable for reading aloud in units on substance abuse.
SUBJ: Alcoholism--Fiction./ Fathers--Fiction.

CE
Ph-1 K-3/2 $13.95 T KF448
DALY, NIKI. Not so fast, Songololo. Atheneum ISBN 0-689-50367-9, 1986. unp. col. ill.
Selectors' Choice, 16th ed.
Available from National Library Service for the Blind and Physically Handicapped in Braille BR06145.
Videocassette available from Weston Woods HMPVC351V, 1992. 1/2" VHS iconographic videocassette color (11min) $49.95.
Slow-moving Malusi (affectionately called Songololo by his grandmother) is chosen by his mother to accompany the elderly old lady on her shopping trip to a nearby South African city. Gogo's final and surprising purchase is a new pair of bright red tackies to replace Malusi's old, worn-out hand-me-down sneakers and then Songololo is no longer slow moving. Although not mentioned, the handsome illustrations show (not blatantly) the evidence of apartheid and poverty. Both text and the superb pictures exhibit many strong feelings and emotions; responsibility as Songololo carefully helps his grandmother, strong love and affection existing between the young boy and old lady, sensitivity, patience, gentleness and unselfishness as the grandmother buys new shoes for her grandson when her own shoes are so worn.
SUBJ: Grandmothers--Fiction./ South Africa--Fiction.

Ph-2 1-3/2 $21.95 L KF449
DAVOL, MARGUERITE W. Batwings and the curtain of night. Illus. by Mary GrandPre. Orchard ISBN 0-531-33005-2, 1997. unp. col. ill.
"Melanie Kroupa book."
The Mother of All Things creates light, plants, and animals and weaves a dark curtain for night that the animals try to pull back. Instead bat's claws poke small, starry holes, and the owl tugs a larger moon-shaped opening in the night sky. An original creation and pourquoi story with luminous pastel illustrations that spill over borders.
SUBJ: Creation--Fiction./ Animals--Fiction./ Night--Fiction.

Ph-2 K-2/2 $15.99 L KF450
DAVOL, MARGUERITE W. How Snake got his hiss: an original tale. Illus. by Mercedes McDonald. Orchard ISBN 0-531-08768-9, 1996. unp. col. ill.
"Melanie Kroupa book."
Snake used to have a round shape and make a hup hup sound as he rolled around without a care for anyone else. One day, when he is under the foot of Elephant, he is flattened and stretched out so that only a hissing sound will squeeze out of him. The original pourquoi story includes several other animals whose characteristics are permanently altered by Snake's carelessness. The rhythm of the text and the bright illustrations make it a good choice for reading aloud.
SUBJ: Snakes--Fiction./ Animals--Fiction./ Africa--Fiction.

Ph-2 2-3/2 $14.95 L KF451
DAY, ALEXANDRA. Frank and Ernest on the road. Scholastic ISBN 0-590-45048-4; In Canada: Scholastic, 1994. unp. col. ill.
Includes glossary.
Frank and Ernest learn the language of truckers when they agree to deliver a load of produce. The surefire appeal of CB slang and semis will delight readers. Boldly colored illustrations and a glossary of trucking terms add to the fun.
SUBJ: Citizen band radio--Slang--Fiction./ Truck drivers--Fiction./ Bears--Fiction./ Elephants--Fiction.

Ph-2 2-3/4 $12.95 L KF452
DAY, ALEXANDRA. Frank and Ernest play ball. Scholastic ISBN 0-590-42548-X, 1990. unp. col. ill.
Includes glossary.
"Pepper," "Hot Corner," and "Butterfingers" are among the many new expressions Frank and Ernest, that inimitable animal duo, learn while managing a minor league team. Lively, bright watercolor illustrations add to the enjoyment of this baseball story for fans of the sport and collectors of unusual words. The lyrics and musical arrangement for TAKE ME OUT TO THE BALL GAME are included.
SUBJ: Baseball--Fiction./ English language--Terms and phrases./ Elephants--Fiction./ Bears--Fiction.

Ph-1 P-2/3 $10.99 L KF453
DE BRUNHOFF, JEAN. Story of Babar, the little elephant. Translated from the French by Merle S. Haas. Random House ISBN 0-394-90575-X, c1937, 1960. 47p. col. ill.
Available from National Library Service for the Blind and Physically Handicapped in Braille BR03385 and on sound recording cassette RC11365.
After his mother is shot by hunters a young elephant runs away and lives with a kind old lady in Paris who treats him royally. The cursive text is difficult for youngsters to read independently but this story has been loved for generations.
BABAR AND HIS CHILDREN (ISBN 0-679-80165-0, c1938, 1989) finds all of Celesteville enjoying the childhood scrapes of the three elephant babies.
SUBJ: Elephants--Fiction.

Ph-2 K-2/3 $14.95 T KF454
DE COTEAU ORIE, SANDRA. Did you hear Wind sing your name?: an Oneida song of spring. Illus. by Christopher Canyon. Walker ISBN 0-8027-8350-3; In Canada: Thomas Allen, 1995. unp. col. ill.
Celebrate spring in the white birch standing tall, the new flowers, and the dance of the animals in this representation of the Oneida Indians' thanksgiving for the season. Sparkling doublespread paintings display the breathtaking natural beauty of spring. The author is an Oneida writer, and her notes lend authenticity to the poem for units on Native Americans, the seasons, or multicultural studies.
SUBJ: Spring--Fiction./ Nature--Fiction./ Oneida Indians--Fiction./ Indians of North America--Fiction.

Ph-1 1-3/2 $21.95 L KF455
DEFELICE, CYNTHIA C. Willy's silly grandma. By Cynthia DeFelice. Illus. by Shelley Jackson. Orchard ISBN 0-531-33012-5, 1997. unp. col. ill.
"Richard Jackson book."
Willy thinks his grandmother's superstitions are silly until he encounters the bogeyman in Big Swamp and runs home to Grandma for comfort. While Willy is determined not to be frightened, the ink and crayon

illustrations depict all sorts of spooky creatures and happenings. Perfect for scary storytimes and Halloween.
SUBJ: Grandmothers--Fiction./ Superstition--Fiction.

CE   Ph-1 P-2 $14.89   L   KF456
DEGEN, BRUCE. Jamberry. HarperCollins ISBN 0-06-021417-1; In Canada: HarperCollins, 1983. unp. col. ill.
Read-along kit available from HarperChildren's Audio (ISBN 0-69470-038-X, 1996). 1 paperback book, 1 sound cassette (4min), $7.95.
Using bright, colorful action-filled pictures of a bear and a boy in scenes filled with many kinds of berries, the rhyming text celebrates the wonders of berries and their jams.
SUBJ: Stories in rhyme.

       Ph-2 K-2/2 $14.93   L   KF457
DE GROAT, DIANE. Roses are pink, your feet really stink. Morrow ISBN 0-688-13605-2, 1996. unp. col. ill.
When Gilbert signs someone else's name to the cards and sends mean valentines to two classmates, he regrets the results. Animal characters, acting very much like real children, fill the classroom. A story about getting along with others and forgiveness.
SUBJ: Valentine's Day--Fiction./ Valentines--Fiction.

       Ph-3 1-3/4 $14.95   L   KF458
DELACRE, LULU. Vejigante masquerader. Scholastic ISBN 0-590-45776-4; In Canada: Scholastic, 1993. unp. col. ill.
Includes glossary and bibliography.
Ramon wishes to be a vejigante or masquerader for Carnival during the month of February in Puerto Rico. He secretly sews a costume and saves his money to buy a mask but almost ruins his disguise in an encounter with a goat. Material following the story includes information about other masquerade festivals, instructions for creating a papier mache mask, some vejigante chants, a glossary, and a bibliography. Text is in Spanish and English. Unfortunately the placement of the text frequently detracts from the colorful illustrations.
SUBJ: Puerto Rico--Fiction./ Carnival--Fiction./ Spanish language materials./ Bilingual materials--Spanish.

       Ph-1 K-2/1 $14.98   L   KF459
DELANEY, A. Pearl's first prize plant. HarperCollins ISBN 0-06-027357-7; In Canada: HarperCollins, 1997. unp. col. ill.
When she see the competition at the County Fair Flower Show, Pearl takes the small white flower she has carefully tended back home where it truly is a First Prize Plant. Cheerful illustrations show Pearl caring for her plant while a pink pig cavorts nearby. The sprouting plant and maturing piglet subtly show the growth cycle.
SUBJ: Gardening--Fiction.

       Ph-2 P-K/2 $14.99   T   KF460
DEMUTH, PATRICIA. Busy at day care head to toe. By Patricia Brennan Demuth. Photos by Jack Demuth. Dutton ISBN 0-525-45603-1, 1996. unp. col. ill.
Day care is a busy place where children are actively engaged from head to toe with their surroundings and each other. Rhyming text and full-color photographs attractively arranged against a white background with pastel shapes capture a day in a child-centered environment. For children in full time day care.
SUBJ: Day care centers--Fiction./ Stories in rhyme.

       Ph-1 1-3/2 $15.00   L   KF461
DENSLOW, SHARON PHILLIPS. On the trail with Miss Pace. Illus. by G. Brian Karas. Simon & Schuster ISBN 0-02-728688-6; In Canada: Distican, 1995. unp. col. ill.
When school is over, Miss Pace heads out West to vacation on a ranch where she runs into two of her students Bill and Phil, who are interested in her relationship with Last Bob, a real cowboy. Bits and pieces of rope, wildflowers, bandanas, and an assortment of papers lend reality to the gouache and pencil illustrations. Use this story to introduce the question, "What did you do on your summer vacation?"
SUBJ: Teachers--Fiction./ Twins--Fiction./ West (U.S.)--Fiction./ Cowboys--Fiction.

       Ph-2 1-3/7 $15.00   L   KF462
DENSLOW, SHARON PHILLIPS. Radio boy. Illus. by Alec Gillman. Simon & Schuster ISBN 0-689-80295-1; In Canada: Distican, 1995. unp. col. ill.
On the outskirts of a Kentucky town in the 1870s, a young boy invents "electricals" and fixes a telephone. This fictionalized account of the childhood of Nathan Stubblefield will appeal to young inventors and may encourage research about him and his induction telephone. Historical fiction with uses in social studies and science classes.

SUBJ: Stubblefield, Nathan Beverly--Childhood and youth--Fiction./ Inventors--Fiction.

       Ph-2 P-1/1 $22.79   T   KF463
DENTON, KADY MACDONALD. Would they love a lion? Kingfisher/ dist. by Raintree Steck-Vaughn ISBN 1-85697-546-0, 1995. unp. col. ill.
No one in her family notices Anna. She uses her imagination and a red plaid robe to be a bird, a bear, an elephant, a dinosaur, and a rabbit until finally a lion gets everyone's attention. Large watercolor illustrations delight the viewer as Anna is transformed into the various animals.
SUBJ: Imagination--Fiction./ Animals--Fiction.

CE   Ph-3 K-2/4 $13.95   L   KF464
DE PAOLA, TOMIE. Art lesson. Putnam ISBN 0-399-21688-X, 1989. unp. col. ill.
Read-along kit narrated by the author available from Listening Library PRA 809SP (ISBN 0-8072-6003-7, 1991). 1 paperback book, 1 sound cassette (11min), $15.98, and teacher's guide.
Tommy loves to draw, but art lessons in kindergarten and first grade are very disappointing--the paint literally falls off the paper, and he must use the school crayons. Indignantly he tells his understanding art teacher that real artists just don't copy and is rewarded with free time to improvise. Clearly autobiographical--the last page shows a grown artist at work--this is a pleasant low-keyed story.
SUBJ: Artists--Fiction./ Individuality--Fiction.

       Ph-1 K-2/2 $15.95   L   KF465
DE PAOLA, TOMIE. Baby sister. Putnam ISBN 0-399-22908-6; In Canada: Putnam, 1996. unp. col. ill.
When his mother tells him she's expecting a baby, Tommy hopes it will be a sister with a red ribbon in her hair. Extended family, including his Nana, are included in this story based on the author's life.
SUBJ: Babies--Fiction./ Brothers and sisters--Fiction./ Family--Fiction.

       Ph-1 1-3/5 $14.95   L   KF466
DE PAOLA, TOMIE. Big Anthony and the magic ring. Harcourt Brace Jovanovich ISBN 0-15-207124-5, 1979. unp. col. ill.
Big Anthony has spring fever and decides that a little night life is just what he needs. But when he borrows Strega Nona's magic ring and turns himself into a tall, handsome young man dressed in elegant clothes, his fun and popularity soon turn to disaster. The girls of Calabria won't leave him alone. Amusing illustrations with an Italian village background.
SUBJ: Magic--Fiction.

CE   Ph-1 K-3/6 $13.95   T   KF467
DE PAOLA, TOMIE. Clown of God. Harcourt Brace Jovanovich ISBN 0-15-219175-5, 1978. unp. col. ill.
Selectors' Choice, 12th ed.
Also available on 1/2'' VHS videocassette color (10min) Weston Woods HMPV260V, $49.95.
Giovanni is a very famous juggler but in time he loses his skill and popularity and becomes again a poor, homeless beggar as he had been as a child. On Christmas Eve all in the village bring beautiful gifts for the Christ Child but the old juggler has nothing to give. When the music stops and the monastery church is empty a miracle occurs--old Giovanni has given his only gift.
SUBJ: Jugglers and juggling--Fiction./ Italy--Fiction./ Christmas--Fiction.

       Ph-2 1-3/6 $15.95   T   KF468
DE PAOLA, TOMIE. Days of the blackbird: a tale of northern Italy. Putnam ISBN 0-399-22929-9; In Canada: BeJo Sales, 1997. unp. col. ill.
When the Duke became ill, only the birds' songs could cheer him. One bird La Colomba remained behind through the harsh winter spending the coldest days and nights in the chimney where her white feathers turned permanently black. The Italian architecture featured in the illustrations is echoed by the panels framing text and pictures.
SUBJ: Blackbirds--Fiction./ Fathers and daughters--Fiction./ Italy--Fiction.

       Ph-1 K-3/5 $14.95   L   KF469
DE PAOLA, TOMIE. Early American Christmas. Holiday House ISBN 0-8234-0617-2, 1987. unp. col. ill.
Long ago a German family, moving into a New England village where no one displayed any evidence of Christmas, shared and introduced their family customs to their puritanical neighbors. Gathering bayberries for candle making, saving the reddest apples for the holidays, baking and cooking special foods, carving wooden figures, stringing popcorn and apple rings, all culminate in that final day with the tree, nativity scene, lighted candles in the windows, the Biblical story and the family singing Christmas songs. Attractive,

colorful illustrations picture American homes in the early 1800s, their clothing, and their customs.
SUBJ: Christmas--Fiction.

Ph-2 K-1 $14.95 L KF470
DE PAOLA, TOMIE. Hunter and the animals: a wordless picture book. Holiday House ISBN 0-8234-0397-1, 1981. unp. col. ill.
A young hunter jauntily sets off for the woods but in spite of an abundance of game, there is no kill. Frustrated he naps under the trees while the animals play a trick on him. Awakening confused and frightened, he starts to cry but the animals, feeling sorry for him, return his gun, pouch and hat filled with food. The young hunter breaks his gun and all become friends. Inspired by Hungarian folk art, the handsome stylized pictures are appealing as they present the anti-hunting message.
SUBJ: Hunting--Fiction./ Forest animals--Fiction./ Stories without words.

Ph-1 K-2/5 $14.95 T KF471
DE PAOLA, TOMIE. Knight and the dragon. Putnam ISBN 0-399-20707-4; In Canada: Academic Press, 1980. unp. col. ill.
A young, inexperienced knight gets a book from the library to teach him how to fight a dragon. At the same time an equally young and inexperienced dragon reads literature inherited from his ancestors concerning the fiercest way to battle a knight. The two practice long and arduously and finally engage in the great combat. The outcome is most unexpected. An almost wordless book with vibrant and appealing illustrations.
SUBJ: Knights and knighthood--Fiction./ Dragons--Fiction.

Ph-2 K-2/2 $14.95 L KF472
DE PAOLA, TOMIE. Little Grunt and the big egg: a prehistoric fairy tale. Holiday House ISBN 0-8234-0730-6, 1990. unp. col. ill.
A cave-dwelling prehistoric boy named Little Grunt brings home a large egg which hatches into a baby dinosaur he names George. The Grunts, alarmed by the pet's huge size, send George away but he returns to rescue them when a volcano threatens their cave. The story and the author's droll illustrations will make this a favorite and the low reading level makes it a good choice for beginning reading.
SUBJ: Dinosaurs--Fiction./ Pets--Fiction./ Cave dwellers--Fiction.

Ph-2 K-3/5 $14.95 L KF473
DE PAOLA, TOMIE. Merry Christmas, Strega Nona. Harcourt Brace Jovanovich ISBN 0-15-253183-1, 1986. unp. col. ill.
Preparing for the Christmas Eve festival she always makes for all the villagers, Strega Nona sadly cancels the feast of Natale when bumbling, forgetful Big Anthony forgets to soak the cod and to purchase many items essential for the dinner. After midnight mass, the beloved Witch Grandmother slowly returns home and is surprised by a welcome from all the villagers and a wonderful feast. It is the magic of Christmas.
SUBJ: Witches--Fiction./ Christmas--Fiction.

TB Ph-2 K-3 $9.98 KF474
DE PAOLA, TOMIE. Merry Christmas, Strega Nona (Talking book). Read by Celeste Holm. Carols performed by Tom Glazer. Listening Library FTR 125 ISBN 0-8072-0137-5, 1991. 1 sound cassette (31min).
Preparing for the Christmas Eve festival she always makes for all the villagers, Strega Nona sadly cancels the feast of Natale when bumbling, forgetful Big Anthony forgets to soak the cod and to purchase many items essential for the dinner. After midnight mass, the beloved Witch Grandmother slowly returns home and is surprised by a welcome from all the villagers and a wonderful feast. It is the magic of Christmas. Several traditional Christmas carols sung by Tom Glazer follow the reading of the book.
Contents: Merry Christmas, Strega Nona (11min); What child is this? (4min); Little Bitty Baby (3min); Christmas is coming (2min); Friendly beasts (4min); Twelves days of Christmas (5min); We wish you a merry Christmas (2min); Reprise of Merry Christmas, Strega Nona theme (1min).
SUBJ: Witches--Fiction./ Christmas--Fiction./ Carols.

Ph-1 K-3/6 $4.99 P KF475
DE PAOLA, TOMIE. Nana upstairs and Nana downstairs. Penguin ISBN 0-14-050290-4, c1973, 1978. 32p. col. ill.
Available in Spanish LA ABUELITA DE ARRIBA Y LA ABUELITA DE ABAJO (Norma ISBN 958-04-1495-5, 1991).
Tommy calls his ninety-four year old great-grandmother "Nana Upstairs" because she is always upstairs in bed; and calls his grandmother "Nana Downstairs" for she is usually downstairs cooking and keeping house. Tommy loves them both and looks forward to his weekly visits. But one Sunday, when he runs to see Nana Upstairs her bed is empty and Tommy sadly learns she will never come back except in his memory.
SUBJ: Grandparents--Fiction./ Death--Fiction.

Ph-2 K-3/5 $13.95 L KF476
DE PAOLA, TOMIE. Now one foot, now the other. Putnam ISBN 0-399-20774-0; In Canada: Academic Press, 1981. unp. col. ill.
Available in Spanish PASITO...Y OTRO PASITO (Ekare ISBN 980-257-025-7, 1986).
Bobby's first word was "Bob," his grandfather's name. Bob and Bobby became best friends. The grandfather helped little Bobby learn to walk, played with him, told him stories, and the two had very special times together. When Bobby was five, his grandfather had a stroke and was very ill. He could neither walk nor talk, and his recovery was doubtful. In time, Bobby helped old Bob walk and talk as his grandfather had helped him. The classic intergenerational story depicts the touching relationship between Bobby and his grandfather.
SUBJ: Grandfathers--Fiction./ Physically handicapped--Fiction./ Spanish language materials.

Ph-2 K-2/2 $11.95 L KF477
DE PAOLA, TOMIE. Oliver Button is a sissy. Harcourt Brace Jovanovich ISBN 0-15-257852-8, 1979. 48p. col. ill.
His classmates and even his father think Oliver is a sissy because he prefers to jump rope, read books, draw pictures, sing and dance, and pretend he's a movie star rather than play any kind of ball. But after Oliver takes tap dancing lessons and then performs in a talent show at the local theater some opinions change.
SUBJ: Dancing--Fiction./ Sex role--Fiction.

Ph-2 1-2 $14.95 L KF478
DE PAOLA, TOMIE. Pancakes for breakfast. Harcourt Brace Jovanovich ISBN 0-15-259455-8, 1978. unp. col. ill.
A woman, having decided she'd like to eat some pancakes, gathers the eggs, milks the cow, and churns the butter. When she returns from getting maple syrup she discovers her pet dog and cat have eaten all the other ingredients. She does in the end manage to have "Pancakes for breakfast" in a way that tickles young people's funny bones.
SUBJ: Stories without words./ Food--Fiction.

Ph-2 1-3/2 $14.95 L KF479
DE PAOLA, TOMIE. Strega Nona meets her match. Putnam ISBN 0-399-22421-1; In Canada: Putnam, 1993. unp. col. ill.
Strega Nona is forced out of business by Strega Amelia's more modern cures until Big Anthony goes to work for the competition. Humor abounds in the illustrations and story set in Italy.
SUBJ: Witches--Fiction.

Ph-2 K-2/2 $14.95 L KF480
DE PAOLA, TOMIE. Tom. Putnam ISBN 0-399-22417-3; In Canada: Putnam, 1993. unp. col. ill.
Tommy and his grandfather, who is a butcher, enjoy practical jokes. When his grandfather gives him a pair of chicken feet, Tommy paints the toenails red and takes them to school to scare people. A humorous story based on the author's childhood.
SUBJ: Grandfathers--Fiction./ Humorous stories.

Ph-2 K-2/2 $12.95 L KF481
DE PAOLA, TOMIE. Watch out for the chicken feet in your soup. Prentice-Hall ISBN 0-671-66682-7, 1974. 32p. col. ill.
Joey warns his friend, Eugene, that his old fashioned, Italian grandma talks and acts funny and has strange, old things around. In fact, Joey is a little embarrassed about taking Eugene to see Grandma but the visit is a great success. The boys leave stuffed with soup and spaghetti and carrying special baked goods. "Hey, Joey, I love your grandma." "Me, too," says Joey. A recipe for Bread Dolls is included.
SUBJ: Grandparents--Fiction./ Italians--United States--Fiction.

Ph-2 P-1/2 $14.95 T KF482
DERBY, SALLY. My steps. Illus. by Adjoa J. Burrowes. Lee & Low ISBN 1-880000-40-7, 1996. unp. col. ill.
A young girl describes how she likes to play games of make-believe on her five front steps: circus, stone school, and horseback riding. On really hot days, she splashes in the water from a nearby hydrant. Watercolor illustrations with cut-paper collages focus on the small, imaginary world created on a city stoop throughout the four seasons. For multicultural studies.
SUBJ: Play--Fiction./ Seasons--Fiction./ Afro-Americans--Fiction.

Ph-3 K-1/4 $9.95 L KF483
DE REGNIERS, BEATRICE SCHENK. Little house of your own. Illus. by Irene Haas. Harcourt Brace Jovanovich ISBN 0-15-245787-9, c1954. unp. ill.
The importance of a secret house of one's own as well as suggestions as to where it may be found are explored here in gentle fashion.
SUBJ: Privacy, Right of--Fiction.

Ph-1 1-3/3 $14.93 L KF484

DISALVO-RYAN, DYANNE. City green. Morrow ISBN 0-688-12787-8, 1994. unp. col. ill.

Includes directory.

A neighborhood comes together to turn an empty lot into a flourishing garden. Even the grouchy and cynical Old Man Hammer adds his contribution. Told from the point of view of Marcy, a young girl, the story is a recipe for community action. An end note provides guidance for groups interested in similar projects.

SUBJ: Community gardens--Fiction./ Gardens--Fiction./ City and town life--Fiction.

Ph-1 1-3/2 $16.00 T KF485

DISALVO-RYAN, DYANNE. Uncle Willie and the soup kitchen. Morrow ISBN 0-688-09165-2, 1991. unp. col. ill.

A young boy spends the day working in a soup kitchen with his Uncle Willie and learns about the work involved in preparing the food and the types of people who visit the soup kitchen. The natural curiosity of the boy and his uncle's straightforward replies will answer young readers' questions about this type of community response to hunger. A note about soup kitchens and poverty precedes the compassionate and realistic text.

SUBJ: Hunger--Fiction./ Soup kitchens--Fiction.

Ph-2 P-K/1 $12.95 L KF486

DODDS, DAYLE ANN. Color box. Illus. by Giles Laroche. Little, Brown ISBN 0-316-18820-4; In Canada: Little, Brown, 1992. unp. col. ill.

Alexander the monkey crawls into a black box and then through die-cut holes to successively enter entire double-page spreads of yellow, orange, blue, red, green, purple, and white until he finally finds a door that leads to a full-color scene. Cut paper illustrations add depth and interest to the mono-color spreads which introduce the colors. Printed on heavy stock, however, die-cuts may limit its shelf life.

SUBJ: Color--Fiction./ Monkeys--Fiction./ Toy and movable books.

Ph-3 P-2/1 $2.50 P KF487

DONNELLY, LIZA. Dinosaur day. Scholastic ISBN 0-590-41800-9, 1987. unp. col. ill.

Includes glossary.

Just after a big snow storm, a boy and his dog go off looking for dinosaurs but unearth a car and a bicycle until returning home sadly they are surprised. Minimal text and cartoon-like illustrations will delight the youngest dinosaur fans as will the concluding glossary of nine of the extinct reptiles.

In DINOSAUR BEACH (ISBN 0-590-42175-1, 1989, OPC) the boy and his dog travel on the back of a elasmosaurus to a section of the beach populated by a host of the extinct creatures.

SUBJ: Dinosaurs--Fiction.

Ph-1 P-2/2 $13.95 L KF488

DORROS, ARTHUR. Abuela. Illus. by Elisa Kleven. Dutton ISBN 0-525-44750-4, 1991. unp. col. ill.

Includes glossary.

Spanish edition ABUELA available from Dutton (ISBN 0-525-45438-1, 1995), $15.99.

When Rosalba and her grandmother, Abuela, go for a walk in the park, she imagines them flying over New York City and by the Statue of Liberty. The mixed-media collages sparkle with color and vibrate with different perspectives. Spanish words and phrases are interspersed throughout the text so that their meaning is generally evident from the context. A glossary also follows with definitions and pronunciations. For multicultural studies.

SUBJ: Imagination--Fiction./ Flight--Fiction./ Hispanic Americans--Fiction./ Grandmothers--Fiction./ New York (N.Y.)--Fiction./ Spanish language materials.

VCR Ph-1 P-2 $42.00 KF489

DORROS, ARTHUR. Abuela (Videocassette). Based on the book written by Arthur Dorros; illus. by Eliza Kleven. SRA/McGraw-Hill ISBN 0-02-686245-X, 1994. 1/2" VHS videocassette color (12min). (Children's literature series).

Includes teacher's guide.

Includes public performance rights.

ALA notable video, 1995.

As Rosalba and her grandmother, Abuela, walk in the park, she imagines they are flying over New York City. Latin rhythms bring the city scenes to life while Spanish words and phrases are interspersed throughout the text. For multicultural studies.

SUBJ: Imagination--Fiction./ Flight--Fiction./ Hispanic Americans--Fiction./ Grandmothers--Fiction./ New York (N.Y.)--Fiction.

Ph-2 K-2/2 $15.99 T KF490

DORROS, ARTHUR. Isla. Illus. by Elisa Kleven. Dutton ISBN 0-525-45149-8, 1995. unp. col. ill.

Includes glossary.

Spanish version available, LA ISLA (ISBN 0-525-45422-5), 1995. Abuela's stories take Rosalba flying back to the island, la isla, where her grandmother grew up and raised her children. The collage illustrations sparkle with color and capture the details of tropical villages, the rain forest, and city life on the island. This companion to ABUELA also incorporates Spanish phrases in the text and will enhance multicultural studies.

SUBJ: Caribbean Area--Fiction./ Islands--Fiction./ Grandmothers--Fiction./ Hispanic Americans--Fiction./ Spanish language materials.

Ph-2 2-5/2 $15.89 L KF491

DORROS, ARTHUR. Radio Man: a story in English and Spanish./Don Radio: un cuento en Ingles y Espanol. Spanish translation by Sandra Marulanda Dorros. HarperCollins ISBN 0-06-021548-8; In Canada: HarperCollins, 1993. unp. col. ill.

Includes glossary.

In bilingual text, English and Spanish, readers can follow both the story and colorful pictures that detail the travels of Diego and his migrant farmworker family as they listen to radio stations which broadcast in both languages. The radio programs connect Diego to places on the family's route from field to field, crop to crop, state to state. Illustrations are full of flat, solid colors and tend toward folk art. For multicultural studies.

SUBJ: Migrant labor--Fiction./ Radio--Fiction./ Mexican Americans--Fiction./ Bilingual materials--Spanish.

Ph-1 1-3/4 $13.95 L KF492

DORROS, ARTHUR. Tonight is Carnaval. Arpilleras sewn by members of the Club de Madres Virgen del Carmen, Lima, Peru. Dutton ISBN 0-525-44641-9, 1991. unp. col. ill.

Includes glossary.

Also available in Spanish: POR FIN ES CARNAVAL (ISBN 0-525-44690-7, 1991).

A young boy from the Andes describes the daily activities of his family as they prepare for Carnaval, a village festival. Illustrated with photographs of arpilleras, hand sewn wall hangings, the story is followed by "How arpilleras are made" and a brief glossary. An attractive introduction to Andean culture.

SUBJ: Carnival--South America--Fiction./ South America--Fiction./ Handicraft--South America./ Spanish language materials./ Arpilleras (Handicraft).

CDR Ph-1 P-2 $39.95 OD KF493

DR. SEUSS'S ABC (CD-ROM). Random House/Broderbund ISBN 1-57135-136-1, 1995. 1 CD-ROM color, 1 paperback book. (Living books).

Includes user's guide and trouble shooting guides.

System requirements: Macintosh and Power Macintosh; System 6.0.7 or higher; 16MHz 68020 processor or faster; Power Macintosh; 4MB RAM; 2.5MB free; CD-ROM drive required; monitor: 12 inch or larger color, 256 colors.

System requirements: Windows 3.1 or Windows 95; 16MHz 386 or faster required; 4MB RAM for Windows 3.1; 8MB RAM for Windows 95; CD-ROM drive or faster required; SVGA monitor/display card 640x480, 256 colors; Windows compatible sound device.

Product (ISBN 1-57135-136-1) runs on either Macintosh or Windows compatible hardware.

A wonderfully whimsical work features alliteration and remains true to the Dr. Seuss style. Engaging animations, the traditional ABC song, and opportunities for interaction truly make the literature come alive for the user. Works well as a learning station, with small groups, or with the entire class.

SUBJ: Alphabet--Software./ Software--Alphabet./ English language--Grammar--Software./ Software--English language--Grammar./ Alliteration--Software./ Software--Alliteration./ Interactive media.

Ph-3 K-2/5 $15.95 L KF494

DRAGONWAGON, CRESCENT. Alligator arrived with apples, a potluck alphabet feast. Illustrated by Jose Aruego and Ariane Dewey. Macmillan ISBN 0-02-733090-7; In Canada: Collier Macmillan, 1987. unp. col. ill.

Animals as well as the exciting food each contributes are arranged in alliterative, alphabetical order providing an unusual Thanksgiving feast. Bright illustrations add just the right flavor and humor. Many unfamiliar foods may require adult explanation.

SUBJ: Alphabet./ Animals--Fiction./ Thanksgiving Day--Fiction.

Ph-2 K-2/2 $14.95 L KF495

DRAGONWAGON, CRESCENT. Annie flies the birthday bike. Illus. by Emily Arnold McCully. Macmillan ISBN 0-02-733155-5; In Canada: Maxwell Macmillan, 1993. unp. col. ill.

Annie's dream of getting a real bicycle for her birthday comes true. At first she is unable to ride it, but with practice, persistence, and the help of a boy in the neighborhood, she finally experiences the

freedom of riding on her own. The common childhood experience of learning to ride a bike complete with scrapes and spills, the exhilarating sense of flying, and pride in mastery is portrayed in the illustrations and rhyming text.
SUBJ: Bicycles and bicycling--Fiction./ Birthdays--Fiction.

Ph-2 K-3 $13.95   L   KF496
DRAGONWAGON, CRESCENT. Itch book. Illus. by Joseph Mahler. Macmillan ISBN 0-02-733121-0; In Canada: Collier Macmillan, 1990. unp. col. ill.
Summer heat drenches the pages and makes everyone itch in this story about a blazing hot day in a small Ozark town. As the heat builds everyone sighs and scratches but when dusk comes the whole town heads for the creek and a good cool swim. The illustrations are a wonderful complement to this bouncy itchy summer story, written in blank verse.
SUBJ: Heat--Fiction./ Mountain life--Fiction./ Stories in rhyme.

CE
4   Ph-1 K-2/6 $14.93   L   KF497
DRESCHER, HENRIK. Simon's book. Lothrop, Lee & Shepard ISBN 0-688-02086-0, 1983. unp. col. ill.
Intertwining drawing, dreaming, monsters, snake-like pens and an ink bottle, Simon's book is created. A good scare with humor and a surprise ending. Dramatic, visually exciting illustrations.
SUBJ: Drawing--Fiction./ Monsters--Fiction.

Ph-2 P-2/1 $13.95   L   KF498
DUBANEVICH, ARLENE. Pig William. Bradbury ISBN 0-02-733200-4, 1985. unp. col. ill.
William may be a pig, but he is very much like many children. He's slow to get out of bed and dawdles and misses the bus for the school picnic. However, he wins in the long run: rain cancels the picnic and William's brothers arrive home only to find their brother happily enjoying a picnic with his pets. Cluttered, cartoon-style pictures and text have lots of child appeal.
SUBJ: Pigs--Fiction./ Picnicking--Fiction./ Cartoons and comics.

Ph-2 1-3/2 $13.99   L   KF499
DUBOWSKI, CATHY EAST. Pirate School. By Cathy East Dubowski and Mark Dubowski. Grosset & Dunlap ISBN 0-448-41133-4; In Canada: BeJo Sales, 1996. 48p. col. ill. (All aboard reading).
At the school for pirates, it's important to know how to fight and look for treasure, but as two students discover, cooperation and sharing are also valuable. Tongue-in-cheek, with loads of appeal for beginning readers to practice their new skills.
SUBJ: Pirates--Fiction./ Schools--Fiction./ Treasure hunts--Fiction.

Ph-1 1-3/2 $13.95   T   KF500
DUFFEY, BETSY. Camp Knock Knock. Illus. by Fiona Dunbar. Delacorte ISBN 0-385-32190-2; In Canada: Bantam Doubleday Dell, 1996. 47p. col. ill. (Yearling first choice chapter book).
Challenged to remain the knock-knock king at camp, Willie must think of one more riddle than Crow. Readers bridging to longer books will enjoy the humor and suspense in this easy-to-read chapter book. Length and subject matter will meet the needs of both strong beginning readers and older, reluctant readers.
SUBJ: Jokes--Fiction./ Camps--Fiction./ Contests--Fiction.

Ph-1 1-3/4 $13.93   L   KF501
DUGAN, BARBARA. Loop the loop. Illus. by James Stevenson. Greenwillow ISBN 0-688-09648-4, 1992. unp. col. ill.
Available from the National Library Service for the Blind and Physically Handicapped on sound recording cassette RC 41364.
Annie becomes good friends with Mrs. Simpson, an older woman in Annie's neighborhood who rides by in a wheelchair, does yo-yo tricks, and owns a cat named Bertrand. When Mrs. Simpson breaks her hip and moves into a nursing home, Anne comes to visit her. The somewhat cranky and irreverant personality of Mrs. Simpson, a delightful and memorable character, is captured in story and pictures.
SUBJ: Old age--Fiction./ Friendship--Fiction.

CE
4   Ph-1 K-2/3 $9.99   L   KF502
DUVOISIN, ROGER. Petunia. Knopf ISBN 0-394-90865-1, c1950. unp. col. ill.
Videocassette available from Weston Woods HMPV045, 1985. 1/2" VHS videocassette color (10min), $49.95.
Available from National Library Service for the Blind and Physically Handicapped in Braille BRA05441 and as talking book TB00818.
Even though she cannot read, this silly goose thinks that she will become wise by carrying a book around under her wing.
In PETUNIA BEWARE (ISBN 0-394-90867-8, 1958, OPC) when she goes outside the fence for greener grass Weasel, Fox, Raccoon and Bobcat think she will make a delicious meal, and in PETUNIA, I LOVE YOU (ISBN 0-394-90870-8, 1965, OPC) Raccoon invites her for a

walk intending to feast on her but she wins his love by saving his life. Petunia must find a way to prevent Charles, a neighboring goose, from becoming Christmas dinner in PETUNIA'S CHRISTMAS (ISBN 0-679-80696-2, c1952, 1980).
SUBJ: Geese--Fiction.

Ph-2 2-3/4 $15.95   L   KF503
EASTERLING, BILL. Prize in the snow. Illus. by Mary Beth Owens. Little, Brown ISBN 0-316-22489-8; In Canada: Little, Brown, 1994. unp. col. ill.
Longing to be a hunter like the older boys, a young boy sets a trap in the snow and captures a hungry rabbit which he compassionately releases. The relationship between the boy and the natural world is beautifully conveyed in snowy watercolor illustrations. The many shades of emotion experienced by the boy could serve as a discussion starter about the ethics of hunting.
SUBJ: Hunting--Fiction./ Rabbits--Fiction.

Ph-1 P-1/1 $7.99   L   KF504
EASTMAN, P. D. Are you my mother? Beginner Books/Random House ISBN 0-394-90018-9, c1960. 63p. col. ill. (Beginner books).
Available from National Library Service for the Blind and Physically Handicapped on sound recording cassette RC22795, talking book TB04452, and in Braille BR06107.
Humorous story of a baby bird in search of his mother.
SUBJ: Birds--Fiction.

VCR   Ph-2 P-1 $6.99   KF505
EASTMAN, P. D. Are you my mother? plus two more P.D. Eastman classics (Videocassette). Random House Home Video ISBN 0-679-81358-6, 1991. 1/2" VHS videocasstte color (30min). (Beginner book video).
Closed captioned.
Minimal but effective animation featuring 3 Eastman stories including two of the most popular: ARE YOU MY MOTHER?; and GO, DOG, GO! An inexpensive addition for video collections.
Contents: Are you my mother?; Go, dog, go!; The best nest.
SUBJ: Birds--Fiction./ Dogs--Fiction.

4   Ph-1 P-1/1 $7.99   L   KF506
EASTMAN, P. D. Go, dog, go! Beginner Books/Random House ISBN 0-394-90020-0, c1961. 64p. col. ill. (Beginner books).
Spanish edition available CORRE, PERRO, CORRE! (Lectorum ISBN 1-880507-02-1, 1992), $8.95.
FR   Zany fun about all kinds of dogs and their doings, ending with a party at the top of a tree!
SUBJ: Dogs--Fiction.

Ph-2 P-1/1 $7.99   L   KF507
EASTMAN, P. D. Sam and the firefly. Beginner Books/Random House ISBN 0-394-90006-5, c1958. 62p. col. ill. (Beginner books).
Sam, the owl, meets Gus, the firefly, who does skywriting at night and uses his talents to play tricks.
SUBJ: Fireflies--Fiction./ Owls--Fiction.

SRC   Ph-2 P-3 $10.00   OD KF508
EDGECOMB, DIANE. Pattysaurus and other tales (Sound recording cassette). Music by Tom Megan and Margot Chamberlain. Wilderwalks Productions ISBN 0-9651669-0-2, 1995. 1 sound cassette (48min).
Three tales are told with verve and drama. "Pattysaurus" is an original fable about a girl who is obsessed with dinosaurs; "The old apple tree" asks three children what is the greatest treasure the old tree can give; and "Princess Firefly" is based on a traditional Japanese folktale. The stories can be integrated into units on dinosaurs, insects, and nature and are wonderful for encouraging listening skills. Background sound effects and musical accompaniment enhance listening pleasure. Can be used by individual students or by an entire class.
SUBJ: Short stories./ Folklore.

Ph-2 K-2/2 $13.95   T   KF509
EDWARDS, MICHELLE. Chicken man. Lothrop, Lee & Shepard ISBN 0-688-09708-1, 1991. unp. col. ill.
Chicken Man makes all the jobs on the Kibbutz look fun, but when the hens stop laying eggs because they miss his singing, the work committee assigns him permanently to the chicken coop. Chicken Man is a pleasure to meet and his love of life is joyfully conveyed in the text and colorful illustrations. A note following the story provides more information about life on a Kibbutz in Israel.
SUBJ: Kibbutzim--Fiction./ Occupations--Fiction./ Chickens--Fiction./ Israel--Fiction./ Jews--Israel--Fiction.

Ph-2 1-3/3 $14.89   L   KF510
EDWARDS, PAMELA DUNCAN. Barefoot: escape on the Underground Railroad. Illus. by Henry Cole. HarperCollins ISBN 0-06-027138-8; In

Canada: HarperCollins, 1997. unp. col. ill.
An escaped slave, "the Barefoot," eludes capture from men in heavy boots. Viewed primarily from the ground level point of view of animals, the dark illustrations depict the night setting and skillfully use light and reflection to illuminate the hidden animals whose behavior seems to aid the runaway slave. Serves as an introduction to the Underground Railroad. Historical fiction for younger audiences. For multicultural studies.
SUBJ: Fugitive slaves--Fiction./ Afro-Americans--Fiction./ Animals--Fiction./ Underground railroad--Fiction.

Ph-1 1-3/3 $14.89 L KF511
EDWARDS, PAMELA DUNCAN. Four famished foxes and Fosdyke. Illus. by Henry Cole. HarperCollins ISBN 0-06-024926-9; In Canada: HarperCollins, 1995. 32p. col. ill.
While Fosdyke fixes fabulous feasts, four other foxes attempt to filch fowl from the farmyard and meet with failure. Featuring the letter "F," this funny story is paired with fantastic illustrations for finding objects that start with "F." Follow up with similar creative writing fun!
SUBJ: Foxes--Fiction./ Alliteration.

Ph-2 K-2/2 $14.89 L KF512
EDWARDS, PAMELA DUNCAN. Livingstone Mouse. Illus. by Henry Cole. HarperCollins ISBN 0-06-025870-5; In Canada: HarperCollins, 1996. 32p. col. ill.
In search of a place to live, Livingstone Mouse wants to find China, but every place he finds is occupied or unpleasant until he discovers a broken piece of china which is ideal. Oversized illustrations follow Livingstone's explorations and are ideal for sharing at storytime.
SUBJ: Mice--Fiction./ Dwellings--Fiction.

Ph-1 P-2/3 $14.89 L KF513
EDWARDS, PAMELA DUNCAN. Some smug slug. Illus. by Henry Cole. HarperCollins ISBN 0-06-024792-4; In Canada: HarperCollins, 1996. 32p. col. ill.
Selectors' Choice, 21st ed.
A smug slug slithers and swaggers up a slope ignoring the warnings of other animals until it's too late. The letter "S" is featured in the alliterative text, the illustrations, and the author's and illustrator's notes. Obviously a choice for classes learning about the letter "S," the smart story also suggests similar creative writing activities, and the realistic illustrations support nature study.
SUBJ: Slugs (Mollusks)--Fiction./ Animals--Fiction./ Alliteration.

Ph-1 1-3/2 $14.95 L KF514
EGAN, TIM. Burnt toast on Davenport Street. Houghton Mifflin ISBN 0-395-79618-0, 1997. unp. col. ill.
Sparing the life of a fly, Arthur is granted three wishes which he uses foolishly and skeptically. As a result, he and his wife become stranded on a tropical island, wishing to return home. Watercolor illustrations convincingly move from Davenport Street to the exotic tropical island. The wry story has a satisfying conclusion.
SUBJ: Dogs--Fiction./ Wishes--Fiction./ Humorous stories.

Ph-2 P-K $12.89 L KF515
EHLERT, LOIS. Color farm. Lippincott/HarperCollins ISBN 0-397-32441-3; In Canada: HarperCollins, 1990. unp. col. ill.
Familiar farm animals are formed with brightly colored shapes and cut-out pages. An engaging introduction to shapes.
SUBJ: Domestic animals--Fiction./ Shape--Fiction./ Color--Fiction.

Ph-2 P-1/2 $11.89 L KF516
EHLERT, LOIS. Color zoo. Lippincott ISBN 0-397-32260-7, 1989. unp. col. ill.
Caldecott Honor Book.
Cut-out geometric shapes create different animal faces as the pages are turned in this colorful book. Introduces geometric shapes and colors and may suggest art projects using shapes. The cut-out pages may hold up better if circulation is restricted.
SUBJ: Shape--Fiction./ Color--Fiction.

Ph-1 P-1/2 $13.95 L KF517
EHLERT, LOIS. Feathers for lunch. Harcourt Brace Jovanovich ISBN 0-15-230550-5, 1990. unp. col. ill.
Big book available (ISBN 0-15-230551-3, 1993).
Spanish version available PLUMAS PARA ALMORZAR (ISBN 0-15-201021-1, 1996).
A prowling cat tries to catch 12 common birds for lunch, but only gets a mouthful of feathers. Striking illustrations depict life-size birds and flowering plants, all labelled. The illustrations and story will be enjoyed at storytime and the facts about the birds make this ideal for nature units.
SUBJ: Cats--Fiction./ Birds--Fiction./ Stories in rhyme./ Birds./ Spanish language materials.

Ph-1 P-K/1 $14.95 L KF518
EHLERT, LOIS. Fish eyes: a book you can count on. Harcourt Brace Jovanovich ISBN 0-15-228050-2, 1990. unp. col. ill.
Bright neon fish with cut out eyes swim through the pages of this counting book. A small black fish turns basic counting into addition. The striking paper collage illustrations make this one an attention-grabber.
SUBJ: Fishes--Fiction./ Stories in rhyme./ Counting.

Ph-1 P-2/2 $14.95 L KF519
EHLERT, LOIS. Nuts to you! Harcourt Brace Jovanovich ISBN 0-15-257647-9; In Canada: Harcourt Brace Jovanovich, 1993. unp. col. ill.
Describes the antics of a frisky squirrel who eats bulbs in the flower box, steals birdseed, and gets inside through a hole in the screen. Boldly colored collages feature several plants and birds which are labelled. Section of facts about squirrels follows the rhyming story.
SUBJ: Squirrels--Fiction./ Stories in rhyme.

Ph-1 P-2/2 $15.00 T KF520
EHLERT, LOIS. Snowballs. Harcourt Brace ISBN 0-15-200074-7; In Canada: Harcourt Brace c/o Canadian Manda, 1995. unp. col. ill.
Selectors' Choice, 21st ed.
A collection of seeds, buttons, and other objects are used to decorate snowballs to make a snow family, including pets. Turn the pages vertically to enjoy the snow people created with collage. Information follows about snow and what makes it snow. Wintry fun with applications for science and art activities.
SUBJ: Snow--Fiction./ Winter--Fiction.

Ph-2 K-2/6 $14.99 T KF521
EHRLICH, AMY. Parents in the pigpen, pigs in the tub. Illus. by Steven Kellogg. Dial ISBN 0-8037-0933-1, 1993. unp. col. ill.
Mayhem strikes when the farmyard animals move into the house. The family decides to move out to the barn and sleep in the pigpen instead of putting up with the noisy, sloppy animals. Zany illustrations fit the hilarious story sure to tickle young listeners.
SUBJ: Domestic animals--Fiction./ Farm life--Fiction./ Humorous stories.

Ph-3 P-1/2 $12.95 L KF522
EMBERLEY, ED. Go away, big green monster! Little, Brown ISBN 0-316-23653-5; In Canada: Little, Brown, 1992. unp. col. ill.
Turn the page and die-cuts progressively reveal a big green monster. Turn some more pages and he slowly disappears. The reader has control over the monster in this clever and colorful book suitable for storytime. Format may not circulate well.
SUBJ: Monsters--Fiction./ Fear--Fiction./ Bedtime--Fiction./ Toy and movable books.

Ph-2 1-3/3 $5.95 P KF523
EMBERLEY, MICHAEL. Ruby. Little, Brown ISBN 0-316-23660-8; In Canada: Little, Brown, 1990. unp. col. ill.
Warned by her mother not to talk to strangers, especially cats, Ruby, a young mouse, puts on her red cape and goes through the city to take some pies to her grandmother. A hilarious spoof on the familiar fairy tale, LITTLE RED RIDING HOOD, with comic, detailed illustrations.
SUBJ: Mice--Fiction./ Cats--Fiction.

Ph-2 1-3/3 $14.95 L KF524
EMBERLEY, MICHAEL. Welcome back, Sun. Little, Brown ISBN 0-316-23647-0; In Canada: Little, Brown, 1993. unp. col. ill.
From September through March during "murketiden" or the murky time in Norway, the sun doesn't rise. The family tires of the endless night, and the young daughter longs to climb the Gausta, a high mountain, in search of the sun. When the time is right, the family makes the traditional trek to find the sun. Scandinavian story for multicultural studies.
SUBJ: Sun--Fiction./ Spring--Fiction./ Norway--Fiction.

Ph-1 P-1/3 $15.95 L KF525
EMBERLEY, REBECCA. Three cool kids. Little, Brown ISBN 0-316-23666-7; In Canada: Little, Brown, 1995. unp. col. ill.
Available from the National Library Service for the Blind and Physically Handicapped on sound recording cassette RC 41973.
Three goats lived on a vacant lot in the city. They wanted to move to another lot, but they were fearful of a rat that lived in the sewer under the street. This contemporary retelling of a favorite tale is illustrated by collages which children will admire and perhaps replicate. Inspiration for creative writing activities as well as art activities.
SUBJ: Fairy tales--Parodies, imitations, etc./ Goats--Fiction.

Ph-1 K-2/2 $14.95   T   KF526
ENDERLE, JUDITH ROSS. What would Mama do? By Judith Ross Enderle and Stephanie Gordon Tessler. Illus. by Chris L. Demarest. Boyds Mills ISBN 1-56397-418-5; In Canada: McClelland & Stewart, 1995. unp. col. ill.
  When Little Lily Goose encounters a sly fox on her way into town to do the shopping, she wonders "What would Mama do?" She manages to outsmart and overload the fox with gallons, quarts, pints, bushels, pecks, a catty, a firkin, and various other measures, common and uncommon. The measures are given on the endpapers extending the humorously illustrated story into an introduction to unusual measurements.
  SUBJ: Shopping--Fiction./ Humorous stories./ Weights and measures--Fiction./ Foxes--Fiction./ Geese--Fiction.

Ph-2 1-3/2 $14.95   L   KF527
ENGLISH, KAREN. Neeny coming, Neeny going. Illus. by Synthia Saint James. BridgeWater ISBN 0-8167-3796-7; In Canada: BridgeWater/dist. by Vanwell, 1996. unp. col. ill.
  Coretta Scott King Illustrator Honor book, 1997.
  Returning to visit her cousin Essie on Daufuskie Island off the coast of South Carolina, Neeny doesn't seem to care for island life which she compares to the comforts of life in the city. Essie knows the past is important and gives Neeny her bed quilt as a reminder. Bright patches of color proclaim the beauty and joy of island life and highlight the strong emotions of home and change. For multicultural studies.
  SUBJ: Afro-Americans--Fiction./ Islands--Fiction./ Cousins--Fiction.

CE   Ph-2 1-3/3 $12.93   L   KF528
ERICKSON, RUSSELL E. Toad for Tuesday. Illus. by Lawrence Di Fiori. Lothrop, Lee & Shepard ISBN 0-688-51569-X, 1974. 63p. ill.
  Read-along kit from Listening Library FTR55SP (ISBN 0-8072-0008-5, 1981). 1 sound cassette (61min), 1 paperback book, guide, $15.98.
  Available from National Library Service for the Blind and Physically Handicapped in Braille BR03188 and on sound recording cassette RC12637.
  Warton, a sociable toad, ventures into wintry woods, to visit his Aunt Toolia and is captured by an owl who considers Warton perfect for his birthday dinner. A prisoner for five days, Warton finally escapes with the help of other forest animals, only to discover that the owl is a friend in need.
  SUBJ: Owls--Fiction./ Frogs--Fiction./ Friendship--Fiction.

Ph-2 K-3/4 $14.95   L   KF529
ERNST, LISA CAMPBELL. Ginger jumps. Bradbury/Macmillan ISBN 0-02-733565-8; In Canada: Collier Macmillan, 1990. unp. col. ill.
  A young circus dog longs for a little girl to love. Large cross-hatched outlined illustrations capture the busyness of the circus. An extended read aloud at circus time.
  SUBJ: Circus--Fiction./ Dogs--Fiction.

Ph-1 P-K/2 $14.99   L   KF530
ERNST, LISA CAMPBELL. Letters are lost! Viking ISBN 0-670-86336-X; In Canada: Penguin, 1996. unp. col. ill.
  Scattered around the house, the alphabet blocks are in locations associated with each letter of the alphabet such as L is a pile of leaves. Full-page illustrations are bright and full of child appeal for young initiates to the alphabet.
  SUBJ: Lost and found possessions--Fiction./ Alphabet.

Ph-1 K-2/4 $15.00   L   KF531
ERNST, LISA CAMPBELL. Little Red Riding Hood: a newfangled prairie tale. Simon & Schuster ISBN 0-689-80145-9; In Canada: Distican, 1995. unp. col. ill.
  Retells the familiar story with Red Riding Hood who rides a bike and an independent, feisty grandmother who manages her own farm and turns the wolf into a muffin baking co-worker. The new version set in the Midwest will find an audience seeking originality and humor. The independent and resourceful pair make good role models for girls.
  SUBJ: Fairy tales--Parodies, imitations, etc./ Wolves--Fiction./ Folklore--Parodies, imitations, etc.

Ph-2 1-3/2 $14.95   L   KF532
ERNST, LISA CAMPBELL. Luckiest kid on the planet. Bradbury ISBN 0-02-733566-6; In Canada: Maxwell Macmillan, 1994. unp. col. ill.
  Can you still be the luckiest kid if you discover that Lucky is not your true name, but just a nickname? Herbert (Lucky) Morgenstern doesn't think so until his grandfather's illness makes him aware of how lucky he truly is. The well-told story ably illustrated in pastel, ink, and pencil explores the meaning of luck and how Herbert perceives it and himself.
  SUBJ: Grandfathers--Fiction./ Luck--Fiction./ Self-perception--Fiction.

Ph-2 K-2/5 $15.95   L   KF533
ERNST, LISA CAMPBELL. Squirrel Park. Bradbury ISBN 0-02-733562-3; In Canada: Maxwell Macmillan, 1993. unp. col. ill.
  Stuart likes trees and squirrels, especially his friend Chuck, a squirrel who lives in the town's oldest tree. Stuart likes straight lines as reflected in the tall straight buildings he has designed. Father and son clash while planning a new park on the site of Chuck's tree, but the squirrel helps them find a creative solution. Youngsters will enjoy Stuart's and Chuck's initiative and the large pastel, ink, and pencil illustrations. The story works well with ecology and community units.
  SUBJ: Squirrels--Fiction./ Parks--Fiction./ Conservation of natural resources--Fiction./ Fathers and sons--Fiction.

Ph-1 P-2/3 $14.95   L   KF534
ERNST, LISA CAMPBELL. Walter's tail. Bradbury ISBN 0-02-733564-X; In Canada: Maxwell Macmillan, 1992. unp. col. ill.
  Walter wags his tail all the time. As he grows, so does his tail wagging and wreaking havoc everywhere he goes. To keep him out of trouble, Mrs. Tully takes Walter up a hill away from the town. When her foot gets stuck in a crevice, Walter puts his tail to good use, waves Mrs. Tully's red shawl to alert the townspeople, and saves the day. Endearing illustrations make this an ideal story for sharing with a group.
  SUBJ: Dogs--Fiction./ Tail--Fiction.

Ph-1 P-1/2 $14.00   T   KF535
ERNST, LISA CAMPBELL. Zinnia and Dot. Viking ISBN 0-670-83091-7; In Canada: Penguin, 1992. unp. col. ill.
  Available from the National Library Service for the Blind and Physically Handicapped on sound recording cassette RC 36303.
  Zinnia and Dot are two hens who grudgingly share a chicken coop and rarely speak to each other except to argue. One day a weasel steals all but one of their eggs, and the two hens must share the remaining egg. A humorous story about cooperation with large expressive illustrations.
  SUBJ: Chickens--Fiction./ Eggs--Fiction./ Weasels--Fiction.

CE   Ph-2 P-1/2 $15.99   L   KF536
ETS, MARIE HALL. Gilberto and the wind. Viking ISBN 0-670-34025-1, c1963. 32p. col. ill.
  Spanish version GILBERTO Y EL VIENTO available from Lectorum (ISBN 1-880507-16-1, 1995).
  Spanish version read-along kit GILBERTO Y EL VIENTO available from Live Oak Media (ISBN 0-87499-362-8, 1996). 1 paperback book, 1 sound cassette (10min), $15.95.
  Available from National Library Service for the Blind and Physically Handicapped on sound recording cassette RC11511.
  Read-along kit available from Live Oak Media (ISBN 0-670-34033-2, 1996). 1 paperback book, 1 sound cassette (10min), $15.95.
  A very little boy from Mexico finds that the wind is his playmate. For multicultural studies.
  SUBJ: Winds--Fiction./ Mexico--Fiction./ Spanish language materials.

Ph-2 P-1/2 $3.95   P   KF537
ETS, MARIE HALL. In the forest. Puffin/Penguin ISBN 0-14-050180-0, c1944, 1976. unp. ill.
  Caldecott Honor Book.
  Available from National Library Service for the Blind and Physically Handicapped in Braille BRA01577.
  A small boy wearing a paper hat and blowing a horn walks through the forest. Several animals join him forming a parade.
  SUBJ: Animals--Fiction.

Ph-2 1-3/2 $14.99   L   KF538
ETS, MARIE HALL. Nine days to Christmas. By Marie Hall Ets and Aurora Labastida. Viking Penguin ISBN 0-670-51350-4, c1959. 48p. col. ill.
  Caldecott Medal Award.
  Available from National Library Service for the Blind and Physically Handicapped on sound recording cassette RC22909.
  Available in Spanish NUEVE DIAS PARA NAVIDAD (0-670-84165-X, 1991).
  Ceci, a little Mexican girl, is excited because now she is old enough to buy a pinata for her first Christmas posada, a gay party given before the great holiday.
  SUBJ: Christmas--Fiction./ Mexico--Fiction./ Spanish language materials.

CE   Ph-1 P-1/2 $13.95   L   KF539
ETS, MARIE HALL. Play with me. Viking ISBN 0-670-55977-6, c1955. 31p. col. ill.
  Caldecott Honor Book.
  Available from National Library Service for the Blind and Physically Handicapped in Braille BR04681 and as talking book TB00818.
  A little girl learns that the creatures of the meadow will come to her

Ph-2 K-2/2 $14.95 L KF540
EVERETT, PERCIVAL. One that got away. Illus. by Dirk Zimmer. Clarion ISBN 0-395-56437-9, 1992. 32p. col. ill.
Three cowboys capture a number one and then a herd of ones. When one gets away, they go after it. A humorous word play on "one" with a wild West theme which will interest the interest of youngsters.
SUBJ: Cowboys--Fiction./ One (The number)--Fiction.

Ph-2 K-2/2 $15.99 L KF541
EVERSOLE, ROBYN. Flute player./La Flautista. Illus. by G. Brian Karas. Orchard ISBN 0-531-08769-7, 1995. unp. col. ill.
"Richard Jackson book."
The music of the flute player evokes different sounds for each of the residents of a five story building until one day it won't make a sound. A young girl blows into the flute and releases animals and objects that meet the needs of the apartment dwellers. Full-color impressionistic illustrations create a dream-like background for the story which is written in both English and Spanish.
SUBJ: Flute--Fiction./ Music--Fiction./ Spanish language materials./ Bilingual materials--Spanish.

Ph-2 P-K/1 $14.95 L KF542
FALWELL, CATHRYN. We have a baby. Clarion ISBN 0-395-62038-4, 1993. unp. col. ill.
A older sibling describes the many ways a family shares and cares for a new baby. Pastel illustrations feature Mom and Dad and the older child taking turns with the baby's care. Very young children will relate easily to the simple text.
SUBJ: Babies--Fiction.

Ph-1 K-2 $13.95 T KF543
FANELLI, SARA. My map book. HarperCollins ISBN 0-06-026455-1; In Canada: HarperCollins, 1995. unp. col. ill.
First published by ABC, All Books for Children, England, 1995.
Selectors' Choice, 21st ed.
Childlike maps of my room, my family, my dog, and my heart expand the concept of maps to include much more than streets. The illustrations are big, bold, and appealing with small details that require a second look. Introduces mapping of concepts, objects, and places. Has applications for math and social studies units. Consider removing the book's jacket, which is also a map, before processing.
SUBJ: Maps--Fiction.

Ph-1 K-2/4 $13.95 L KF544
FASSLER, JOAN. Howie helps himself. Illus. by Joe Lasker. Whitman ISBN 0-8075-3422-6, 1974, c1975. 32p. col. ill.
Available from National Library Service for the Blind and Physically Handicapped on sound recording cassette RC11657.
Though he has a happy family life and enjoys his special school, Howie, a child with cerebral palsy wants more than anything to be able to move his wheelchair by himself. Howie, even though handicapped and confined to a wheelchair, is a real little boy with emotions and feelings similar to those felt by most children.
SUBJ: Cerebral palsy--Fiction./ Physically handicapped--Fiction.

Ph-2 1-3/7 $15.99 T KF545
FEELINGS, MURIEL L. Jambo means hello: Swahili alphabet book. Illus. by Tom Feelings. Dial ISBN 0-8037-4346-7, 1974. unp. ill.
Caldecott Honor Book.
For each of the twenty-four letters of the Swahili alphabet an appropriate word has been selected, spelled phonetically, explained in terms of African culture, and beautifully illustrated. Emphasis is on idealistic and positive values, such as respect, family love and pride, beauty, welcome, friendship, and worship. Outstanding illustrations.
SUBJ: Alphabet./ Africa, East--Social life and customs.

Ph-2 K-3 $8.95 T KF546
FEENEY, STEPHANIE. A is for aloha. Photos by Hella Hammid. University of Hawaii Press ISBN 0-8248-0722-7, 1980. unp. ill.
Uses the format of an ABC book and black and white photographs to introduce children to the people, clothes, foods, plants and life in Hawaii. Following the photographic section are two pages of small print text, "About Hawaii," describing the history, geography, customs, holidays, and life style of this fiftieth state. The unfamiliar words found in the alphabetical section are explained and suggestions for sharing the book with children are included.
SUBJ: Alphabet./ Hawaii--Fiction.

Ph-2 1-3/3 $15.00 T KF547
FERGUSON, ALANE. Tumbleweed Christmas. Illus. by Tom Sully. Simon & Schuster ISBN 0-689-80465-2; In Canada: Distican, 1996. unp. col. ill.

Scotty and his mother have car trouble in the middle of the desert on their way to his grandparents' house for Christmas. Rescued by a car mechanic named Jasper who tows them to the Dry Bean Motel, Scotty despairs at the lack of Christmas decorations until he finds a way to decorate a tumbleweed for Jasper. Rust-hued illustrations capture the barren beauty of the desert.
SUBJ: Christmas--Fiction./ Deserts--Fiction.

Ph-1 P-3 $12.95 T KF548
FIELD, RACHEL. General store. Illus. by Nancy Winslow Parker. Greenwillow ISBN 0-688-07353-0, c1926, 1988. unp. col. ill.
A potbellied wood stove, bolts of calico, balls of sting, glass jars filled with candy, tins of tea, an old fashioned cash register, barrels of pickles, and much more are included in a small girl's description of the store she someday hopes to own. Childlike colored pencil drawings accented by watercolor drawings illustrate the appealing poem published in the early twenties. Although there are still a few general stores in existence this title should be a worthwhile addition to material concerning pioneer times and early American history as well as a fun book for enjoyment.
SUBJ: General stores--Fiction./ Stores, Retail--Fiction./ Stories in rhyme.

CE   Ph-1 P-1/2 $12.95 L KF549
FLACK, MARJORIE. Ask Mr. Bear. Macmillan ISBN 0-02-735390-7, c1932. unp. col. ill.
Read-along kit available from Live Oak (ISBN 0-87499-044-0, 1990). 1 hardcover book, 1 sound cassette (8min), $22.95.
Danny does not know what to give his mother for her birthday so he asks many animals for their help.
SUBJ: Animals--Fiction./ Birthdays--Fiction.

CE   Ph-1 P-1/6 $14.00 L KF550
FLACK, MARJORIE. Story about Ping. By Marjorie Flack and Kurt Wiese. Viking Penguin ISBN 0-670-67223-8, c1933. 32p. col. ill.
Spanish version LA HISTORIA DE PING available from Viking Penguin/Ediciones (ISBN 0-670-86958-9, 1996).
Videocassette available from Weston Woods HMPV008V, n.d. 1/2" VHS videocassette color (10min), $49.95.
Read-along kit available from Puffin StoryTapes (ISBN 0-14-095117-2, 1993). 1 paperback book, 1 sound cassette (19min), $6.99.
Available from National Library Service for the Blind and Physically Handicapped in Braille BRA06908 and as talking book TB04445.
Ping, the duck, almost ends in the cook pot when he tries to avoid a spanking.
SUBJ: China--Fiction./ Ducks--Fiction./ Runaways--Fiction./ Spanish language materials./ Italian language materials.

Ph-1 1-3/2 $5.95 P KF551
FLEISCHMAN, PAUL. Time train. Illus. by Claire Ewart. HarperCollins ISBN 0-06-443351-X; In Canada: HarperCollins, 1994. unp. col. ill.
"Charlotte Zolotow book."
A class train trip to study dinosaurs in Utah provides firsthand learning for the students who ride the Rocky Mountain Unlimited back in time to the age of the dinosaurs. The narrator is very matter-of-fact about eating dinosaur eggs, riding on the back of a stegosaurus, and sleeping in giant dinosaur footprints while the expansive illustrations depict the humor and incredulity of the encounters with the huge and extinct creatures.
SUBJ: Dinosaurs--Fiction./ Time travel--Fiction./ School excursions--Fiction.

Ph-1 1-3/5 $13.93 L KF552
FLEISCHMAN, SID. Scarebird. Illus. by Peter Sis. Greenwillow ISBN 0-688-07318-2, 1987. unp. col. ill.
Selectors' Choice, 17th ed.
A lonely old farmer turns to his scarebird (scarecrow) for companionship. He talks to him, dresses him in sensible clothes and watches over him protectively. When a homeless boy asks for work he gradually but gruffly transfers his attentions--and scarebird's clothes--to him. Well written and powerfully illustrated with textured oil paintings this provokes much discussion among children about loneliness and the need for friendship.
SUBJ: Friendship--Fiction./ Scarecrows--Fiction./ Farm life--Fiction.

Ph-1 P-1/3 $15.95 T KF553
FLEMING, DENISE. Barnyard banter. Henry Holt ISBN 0-8050-1957-X; In Canada: Fitzhenry & Whiteside, 1994. unp. col. ill.
The animals on the farm make a lot of noise except for the goose, who is seen in each picture but doesn't make a sound until the last page. Large, doublespread illustrations created with the artist's unique method of papermaking, which incorporates unusual materials such as coffee grounds, oats, and burlap, elevate this farmyard story above the others. Keep the jacket with the book since the artist's technique is

only detailed on the back flap. Predictable text and animal sounds will appeal to preschoolers and beginning readers.
SUBJ: Domestic animals--Fiction./ Animal sounds--Fiction./ Farm life--Fiction./ Stories in rhyme.

Ph-2 P-K $14.95   T   KF554
FLEMING, DENISE. Count! Henry Holt ISBN 0-8050-1595-7; In Canada: Fitzhenry & Whiteside, 1992. unp. col. ill.
Counts the animals one through ten and then by tens to fifty. Doublespread illustrations made of homemade paper in splashy colors provide a vibrant introduction to counting.
SUBJ: Counting--Fiction./ Animals--Fiction.

Ph-1 P-2/1 $15.95   T   KF555
FLEMING, DENISE. In the small, small pond. Henry Holt ISBN 0-8050-2264-3; In Canada: Fitzhenry & Whiteside, 1993. unp. col. ill.
Caldecott Honor book, 1994.
Throughout the seasons, there is activity at the pond as herons plunge, whirligigs twirl, and muskrats stack. Delightful handmade paper illustrations fill doublespreads with brilliant colors while the text tickles the tongue. Great fun for reading aloud.
SUBJ: Pond animals--Fiction./ Stories in rhyme.

Ph-1 P-K/1 $15.95   T   KF556
FLEMING, DENISE. In the tall, tall grass. Henry Holt ISBN 0-8050-1635-X; In Canada: Fitzhenry & Whiteside, 1991. unp. col. ill.
Selectors' Choice, 19th ed.
A caterpillar crawls through the tall grass observing several busy backyard animals. Illustrations were created through an unusual technique involving handmade paper with eye-catching, bright colors. Simple rhyming text accompanies the large illustrations and is a perfect read-aloud to share with a group.
SUBJ: Animals--Fiction./ Stories in rhyme.

Ph-1 P-K/2 $14.95   T   KF557
FLEMING, DENISE. Lunch. Henry Holt ISBN 0-8050-1636-8; In Canada: Fitzhenry & Whiteside, 1992. unp. col. ill.
Having eaten his way through several colorful foods, a frisky mouse returns to his hole for a nap until dinnertime leaving a multicolored trail behind him. Large, brightly hued illustrations created with handmade paper provide visual clues for the next fruit or vegetable. Final page shows the mouse with the different food stains labelled. Delightful group read-aloud to introduce colors and produce.
SUBJ: Mice--Fiction./ Food habits--Fiction./ Color--Fiction.

Ph-1 P-1/2 $15.95   T   KF558
FLEMING, DENISE. Time to sleep. Henry Holt ISBN 0-8050-3762-4; In Canada: Fitzhenry & Whiteside, 1997. unp. col. ill.
Bear tells Snail who passes it along to Skunk that winter is coming until the message cycles back to awaken Bear who has already gone to sleep for the winter. Falling leaves and gold and brown hues herald winter in the handmade paper illustrations. A seasonal choice for storytimes.
SUBJ: Winter--Fiction./ Animals--Fiction./ Hibernation--Fiction.

Ph-2 1-3/4 $14.95   L   KF559
FLORA, JAMES. Fabulous Firework Family. McElderry ISBN 0-689-50596-5; In Canada: Maxwell Macmillan, 1994. unp. col. ill.
A different version (both text and art) of THE FABULOUS FIREWORK FAMILY by James Flora was published by Harcourt Brace and World in 1955.
The Firework Family gathers materials and constructs the fireworks for the town's fiesta, including one very grand castillo in honor of the village patron saint, Santiago. Action-packed, colorful watercolor illustrations capture the festive flavor of the village celebration. A few illustrations are labeled with familiar Spanish words. This lively introduction to Mexican culture is based on a family the author knew when he lived in Mexico. For multicultural studies.
SUBJ: Fireworks--Fiction./ Mexico--Fiction./ Festivals--Mexico--Fiction.

Ph-2 P-1/1 $12.88   L   KF560
FLORIAN, DOUGLAS. Winter day. Greenwillow ISBN 0-688-07352-2, 1987. unp. col. ill.
A brief, rhyming text and bold, child like pictures show how three children and their parents enjoy a snowy, winter day. In similar manner and format a city family packs a picnic lunch and leaves their apartment for a fun day in the country in A SUMMER DAY (ISBN 0-688-07565-7, 1988).
SUBJ: Winter--Fiction./ Summer--Fiction.

Ph-1 K-3/5 $15.99   L   KF561
FLOURNOY, VALERIE. Patchwork quilt. Illus. by Jerry Pinkney. Dial ISBN 0-8037-0097-0, 1985. unp. col. ill.
Selectors' Choice, 16th ed.

Available from National Library Service for the Blind and Physically Handicapped in Braille BR07110.
As she works on her masterpiece, Grandma tells Tanya stories of the family and source of each piece in her quilt. When the old woman becomes very ill, young Tanya continues to work on her grandmother's dream and soon the entire family becomes involved in completing the heirloom quilt with the many memories. Gives a very positive, non-stereotypical picture of a middle class African-American family with an abundance of love throughout the immediate extended family that, with its strong illustrations, is a delight to share with a group. For multicultural studies.
SUBJ: Quilting--Fiction./ Grandmothers--Fiction./ Family life--Fiction./ Afro-Americans--Fiction.

Ph-1 K-3/3 $15.89   L   KF562
FLOURNOY, VALERIE. Tanya's reunion. Illus. by Jerry Pinkney. Dial ISBN 0-8037-1605-2, 1995. unp. col. ill.
Sequel to THE PATCHWORK QUILT, Dial, 1985.
When Tanya accompanies Grandma back to the family farm, the young girl is at first disappointed in what she sees until she begins to view it through Grandma's eyes. Watercolor illustrations focus on the close relationship of the extended family. Celebrates the importance of sharing family memories. An intergenerational story for multicultural studies.
SUBJ: Grandmothers--Fiction./ Farm life--Virginia--Fiction./ Family reunions--Fiction./ Virginia--Fiction./ Afro-Americans--Fiction.

BA   Ph-1 2-4 $22.00   OD KF563
FOLLOW THE DRINKING GOURD. Told by Morgan Freeman. Music by Taj Mahal. Rabbit Ears MMI 740879 ISBN 1-56668-705-5, 1993. 1 hardcover book, 1 compact disc (60min). (American heroes and legends).
Mary, her mother, and brother escape from a plantation in Alabama with the help of Peg Leg Joe and his song about the drinking gourd. They find their way up the Tennessee River to cross the Ohio River and meet their father along the way. The music by Taj Mahal perfectly underscores the emotions from fear to hope and joy of the well-paced narration on the first side. Side two features the music without the narration and would be suitable background music for follow-up activities. For multicultural studies.
SUBJ: Slavery--Fiction./ Underground railroad--Fiction.

Ph-2 1-3/3 $14.95   L   KF564
FOLSOM, MARCIA. Easy as pie: a guessing game of sayings. By Marcia and Michael Folsom . Illus. by Jack Kent. Clarion ISBN 0-89919-303-X, 1985. 64p. col. ill.
Old and familiar sayings are arranged in alphabetical order by the last word, creating a game because of the format. Colorful uncluttered illustrations are imaginative and humorous, adding to the enjoyment of this work by children who already know the alphabet and enjoy word games.
SUBJ: Alphabet.

Ph-2 P-K/1 $13.93   L   KF565
FORD, MIELA. Little elephant. Photos by Tana Hoban. Greenwillow ISBN 0-688-13141-7, 1994. unp. col. ill.
A little elephant likes to play and splash in the water, even falling in then struggling to get out. Of course, mother is nearby, waiting. Photographed at a zoo, the pictures of the baby elephant are endearing, and youngsters will identify with his frolic in the water and return to the comfort of mother.
SUBJ: Elephants--Fiction.

Ph-2 P-1/1 $14.93   L   KF566
FORD, MIELA. Sunflower. Illus. by Sally Noll. Greenwillow ISBN 0-688-13302-9, 1995. unp. col. ill.
Plant a seed and watch it grow into a giant sunflower with seeds for birds and you to eat! A black cat on each page provides contrast, and a child shows the scale of the growing plant in the bright, colorful gouache paintings.
SUBJ: Sunflowers--Fiction./ Flowers--Fiction.

Ph-2 2-3/4 $15.99   T   KF567
FORWARD, TOBY. Ben's Christmas carol. Illus. by Ruth Brown. Dutton ISBN 0-525-45593-0; In Canada: McClelland & Stewart, 1996. unp. col. ill.
Originally published in Great Britain, Andersen Press, Ltd., 1996.
Borrowing liberally from Dickens, Forward depicts Ben, a mouse, when he is shown the meaning of Christmas by a nighttime visitor. The details of a mouse's life in Victorian England are provided in the illustrations which also include allusions to that other CHRISTMAS CAROL. Definitely not a replacement for Dickens, but the story will delight fans familiar wit that story and spur others to read it as well.
SUBJ: Mice--Fiction./ Christmas--Fiction.

Ph-1 K-2/2　$13.93　L　KF568

FOWLER, SUSI GREGG. I'll see you when the moon is full. Illus. by Jim Fowler. Greenwillow ISBN 0-688-10831-8, 1994. unp. col. ill.

Dad is going away for two weeks, and Abe wants to know when he will be home. Dad explains that he'll be back when the moon is full, and he shows Abe how the phases of the moon change. The father's reassurances combine naturally with a small lesson on the phases of the moon. Acrylic illustrations corroborate the warm father and son relationship.
SUBJ: Fathers and sons--Fiction./ Separation anxiety--Fiction./ Moon--Fiction.

Ph-2 P-2/2　$14.95　L　KF569

FOX, MEM. Hattie and the fox. Illus. by Patricia Mullins. Bradbury ISBN 0-02-735470-9; In Canada: Collier Macmillan, 1987. unp. col. ill.

Big book available from Bradbury (ISBN 0-02-735471-7, 1988), $18.95.
Warned by the hen that something is in the bushes, the other farm animals remain undisturbed until they find out it is a fox. The refrain of each animal's comment is quickly chorused by young readers who also delight in the various tissue paper and crayon collage illustrations.
SUBJ: Chickens--Fiction./ Foxes--Fiction./ Domestic animals--Fiction.

TB　　Ph-3 P-2　$9.95　KF570

FOX, MEM. Mem Fox reads (Talking book). Harcourt Brace Jovanovich ISBN 0-15-253173-4, 1992. 1 sound cassette (32min).

Mem Fox reads POSSUM MAGIC and five other stories with sound effects and music.
Contents: GUESS WHAT?; KOALA LOU; NIGHT NOISES; TOUGH BORIS; POSSUM MAGIC; FEATHERS AND FOOLS.
SUBJ: Animals--Fiction.

Ph-2 P-2/4　$13.95　L　KF571

FOX, MEM. Possum magic. Illus. by Julie Vivas. Gulliver/Harcourt Brace Jovanovich ISBN 0-15-200572-2, c1983, 1990. unp. col. ill.

Mastering the magic of making little Hush invisible, Grandma Poss can't find the proper spell to reverse the process, so they leave their home, deep in the Australian bush, and travel all over the continent trying the regional "people" foods until the correct ones solve the problem. Large, bold watercolors against a stark white background mesh perfectly with the story. Not only fun for reading aloud and independent reading, but useful with units on Australia. A simple map and brief glossary of Australian terms are included.
SUBJ: Opossums--Fiction./ Magic--Fiction./ Australia--Fiction.

Ph-2 P-1/2　$15.00　L　KF572

FOX, MEM. Time for bed. Illus. by Jane Dyer. Gulliver/Harcourt Brace ISBN 0-15-288183-2; In Canada: Harcourt Brace c/o Canadian Manda, 1993. unp. col. ill.

Big book available from Harcourt Brace (ISBN 0-15-201014-9, 1996).
Starry endpapers frame this quiet bedtime story as animals tell their young goodnight. Rhyming text and expansive doublespread illustrations will be enjoyed by young listeners.
SUBJ: Bedtime--Fiction./ Animals--Fiction./ Stories in rhyme.

Ph-1 K-2/2　$13.95　L　KF573

FOX, MEM. Tough Boris. Illus. by Kathryn Brown. Harcourt Brace ISBN 0-15-289612-0; In Canada: Harcourt Brace c/o Canadian Manda, 1994. unp. col. ill.

Boris is tough, scruffy, and greedy; all pirates are. Yet when Boris' parrot dies, he cries and cries. A young, violin-playing stowaway, hidden in the watercolor illustrations, is the narrator. The story demonstrates the soft side of even the toughest pirate. Easy-to-read, repetitive text will attract beginning readers.
SUBJ: Pirates--Fiction.

Ph-1 K-3/6　$13.95　T　KF574

FOX, MEM. Wilfrid Gordon McDonald Partridge. Illus. by Julie Vivas. Kane/Miller ISBN 0-916291-04-9, 1985. unp. col. ill.

Also available in Spanish, GUILLERMO JORGES MANUEL JOSE (ISBN 0-916291-04-9, n.d.).
Big book available (ISBN 0-916291-56-1, 1995), $19.95.
Wilfrid Gordon McDonald Partridge has many friends who live in the old people's home next door, but Miss Nancy Alison Delacourt Cooper is his favorite. Unfortunately Miss Nancy has lost her memory so the young boy begins a project to find memories for her and he succeeds. The pastel watercolors, rather straggly but humorously realistic, are appealing and contribute to the warmth of this gentle story that, unfortunately, has a very poor binding.
SUBJ: Memory--Fiction./ Old age--Fiction./ Spanish language materials.

Ph-2 P-1/2　$18.99　L　KF575

FRANKLIN, KRISTINE L. Iguana Beach. Illus. by Lori Lohstoeter. Crown ISBN 0-517-70901-5; In Canada: Random House, 1997. unp. col. ill.

Told to stay out of the waves, Reina is determined to play in the ocean like her older cousins. She runs off with everyone following her until they come to a small, calm lagoon. The beach in the tropics is depicted in the lush illustrations filled with monkeys and iguanas. For multicultural studies.
SUBJ: Swimming--Fiction./ Seashore--Fiction./ Guatemala--Fiction.

Ph-1 1-3/3　$15.93　L　KF576

FRANKLIN, KRISTINE L. Wolfhound. Illus. by Kris Waldherr. Lothrop, Lee & Shepard ISBN 0-688-13675-3, 1996. unp. col. ill.

When he rescues one of the Tsar's wolfhounds from the snow, Pavel is worried that he will be blamed for stealing the dog and tries to return it. Instead he encounters the Tsar in the woods, and the Tsar later sends one of the royal dog's puppies in gratitude. The unusual setting is portrayed in gorgeous, richly hued oil paintings which add another dimension to the solid story of boy and dog.
SUBJ: Dogs--Fiction./ Russia--Fiction.

Ph-2 P-3/5　$13.95　L　KF577

FRASIER, DEBRA. On the day you were born. Harcourt Brace Jovanovich ISBN 0-15-257995-8, 1991. unp. col. ill.

Describes the animals, Earth, Sun, Moon, stars and the people who prepare for and celebrate the birth of a child. Gentle word images of the child in the womb and at birth are accompanied by joyful cut-paper collages showing a welcoming and life-supporting planet. The text is followed by five pages of extensive notes about the world around us.
SUBJ: Earth--Fiction./ Birth--Fiction.

CE　　Ph-1 P-2/2　$12.99　L　KF578

FREEMAN, DON. Corduroy. Viking Penguin ISBN 0-670-24133-4, c1968. 32p. col. ill.

Spanish edition available CORDUROY (Viking ISBN 0-670-82265-5, 1988), $11.95.
Kit from Live Oak Media 0-94107-808-6, 1982. 1 hardcover book, 1 cassette (11min), (Seafarer reading chest), $22.95.
Also available in Spanish as read-along kit from Live Oak (ISBN 0-87499-191-9, 1988). 1 sound cassette (10min), 1 paperback book, $13.95.
1/2" VHS videocassette color (16min) available from Weston Woods HMPV436V, $49.95.
Available from National Library Service for the Blind and Physically Handicapped as talking book TB04797.
Corduroy is a bear who once lived in the toy department of a big store. He was waiting for someone to take him home. One day a little girl decides that he is the very bear she has always wanted but her mother says, "Not today, dear. Besides, he's lost the button to one of his shoulder straps." Corduroy goes in search of his lost button while the little girl searches for a way to take him home--to be her very own bear.
SUBJ: Toys--Fiction./ Spanish language materials.

CE　　Ph-1 K-1/2　$14.00　L　KF579

FREEMAN, DON. Dandelion. Viking Penguin ISBN 0-670-25532-7, c1964. 48p. col. ill.

Kit available from Live Oak Media 0-94107-7811-6 1982. 1 hardcover book, 1 sound cassette (14min), (Seafarer reading chest), $22.95.
Dandelion, the lion, is invited to a party but he primps and preens so much that he is turned away because no one recognizes him!
SUBJ: Lions--Fiction./ Friendship--Fiction.

CE　　Ph-1 K-1/7　$4.99　P　KF580

FREEMAN, DON. Norman the doorman. Penguin ISBN 0-14-050288-2, c1959. 64p. col. ill.

Also available as 1/2" VHS videocassette color (15min) from Weston Woods MPV64, $60.00.
Available from National Library Service for the Blind and Physically Handicapped as talking book TB00522.
Norman is the doorman at the Art Museum and enjoys very much escorting his rodent friends through its treasures. But he can't resist entering a piece of sculpture in an exhibit for himself!
SUBJ: Mice--Fiction./ Museums--Fiction.

CE　　Ph-1 P-2/2　$13.00　L　KF581

FREEMAN, DON. Pocket for Corduroy. Viking Penguin ISBN 0-670-56172-X; In Canada: Penguin, 1978. unp col illus.

Available from National Library Service for the Blind and Physically Handicapped in Braille BR04675.
Spanish version UN BOLSILLO PARA CORDUROY available from Viking Penguin (ISBN 0-670-84483-7, 1992); read-along kit available from Live Oak Media (0-87499-292-X, 1992), 1 hardcover book, 1

sound cassette (13min), $19.95.

Corduroy, Lisa's lovable teddy bear, discovers his pants lack pockets so he starts searching all over the laundromat for suitable pocket material. Instead he almost takes a spin in a clothes dryer and even ends up spending the night in the dark, locked building. Lisa rescues him early the next morning and he soon sports a purple pocket with his name tucked inside.

SUBJ: Toys--Fiction./ Spanish language materials.

Ph-2 1-2/7 $13.95   T   KF582

FREEMAN, LYDIA. Pet of the Met. By Lydia and Don Freeman. Viking Penguin ISBN 0-670-54875-8, c1953. unp. col. ill.

Petrini a music-loving mouse and Mefisto a music-hating cat meet on the stage of the Metropolitan Opera House--and thereby hangs a tale!

SUBJ: Cats--Fiction./ Mice--Fiction./ Opera--Fiction./ Metropolitan Opera House, New York (N.Y.)--Fiction.

Ph-2 K-2/2 $14.95   L   KF583

FRENCH, FIONA. Anancy and Mr. Dry-Bone. Little, Brown ISBN 0-316-29298-2; In Canada: Little, Brown, 1991. unp col illus.

Anancy and Mr. Dry-Bone both want to marry Miss Louise, but she will only marry the man who can make her laugh. Mr. Dry-Bone tries to conjure up something to make her laugh without success. Anancy dresses up in an outrageous outfit borrowed from several animals and wins Miss Louise. An original story based on traditional characters from Caribbean and African folktales illustrated with striking colors with contrasting black and white.

SUBJ: Anansi (Legendary character)--Fiction.

Ph-1 P-2/2 $15.00   L   KF584

FRENCH, VIVIAN. Red Hen and Sly Fox. Illus. by Sally Hobson. Simon & Schuster ISBN 0-689-80010-X; In Canada: Distican, 1995. unp. col. ill.

Originally published in Great Britain, ABC, All Books for Children, 1994.

Red Hen always kept a needle and thread and scissors in her apron pocket. When Sly Fox captured her in a sack, she simply cut a hole, put a rock in the sack, and sewed it shut. Interesting perspectives, shadows, and bright colors fill the viewer's eye in this delightful story perfect for storytime.

SUBJ: Chickens--Fiction./ Foxes--Fiction.

Ph-1 1-3/6 $14.95   L   KF585

FRIEDMAN, AILEEN. Cloak for the dreamer. Illus. by Kim Howard. Scholastic ISBN 0-590-48987-9; In Canada: Scholastic, 1995. unp. col. ill.

"Marilyn Burns brainy day book."

A tailor has three sons and assigns them each the task of creating a cloak for the Archduke. Two sons more than adequately perform the task, creating lovely patchwork capes, but the youngest son, who longs to travel the globe, cuts out and pieces together circles. The father wisely recognizes the calling of the younger son to travel and transforms his circular cape into one of hexagons for his going away present. Watercolor and pencil illustrations portray the old world of fairy tales in this original story with mathematical applications. The pleasant narrative could be followed up with hands-on geometric activities or paired with other stories about patchwork. Includes suggestions for extension activities for parents and teachers. (Parents' Shelf).

SUBJ: Tailors--Fiction./ Individuality--Fiction./ Fathers and sons--Fiction.

Ph-1 1-3/2 $13.95   L   KF586

FRIEDMAN, INA R. How my parents learned to eat. Illus. by Allen Say. Houghton Mifflin ISBN 0-395-35379-3, 1984. 30p. col. ill.

Selectors' Choice, 15th ed.

Available from National Library Service for the Blind and Physically Handicapped on sound recording cassette RC23230.

To explain why "in our house, some days we eat with chopsticks and some days we eat with knives and forks," a young girl tells of the courtship of her American sailor father and her Japanese mother. Told with humor, the tale is entertaining but also informative as the two cultures are portrayed. Clean line drawings with muted watercolors enhance the story.

SUBJ: Japan--Fiction./ Tableware--Fiction./ Manners and customs--Fiction.

Ph-1 P-K $13.88   L   KF587

FRIEDRICH, PRISCILLA. Easter Bunny that overslept. By Priscilla and Otto Friedrich. Illus. by Adrienne Adams. Lothrop, Lee & Shepard ISBN 0-688-01541-7, 1983. unp. col. ill.

Santa Claus gives the bunny a special present so that he will never again sleep past Easter day.

SUBJ: Easter--Fiction./ Rabbits--Fiction.

Ph-3 K-2/3 $15.00   L   KF588

FROEHLICH, MARGARET WALDEN. That Kookoory! Illus. by Marla Frazee. Browndeer/Harcourt Brace ISBN 0-15-277650-8; In Canada: Harcourt Brace c/o Canadian Manda, 1995. unp. col. ill.

Kookoory is a silly rooster who wakes everyone up in the middle of the night to go to the fair and manages to elude a hungry weasel with his foolishness. Young listeners will enjoy the silly story and the colored ink illustrations.

SUBJ: Roosters--Fiction./ Fairs--Fiction.

Ph-2 K-2/2 $14.95   T   KF589

FUCHS, DIANE MARCIAL. Bear for all seasons. Illus. by Kathryn Brown. Henry Holt ISBN 0-8050-2139-6; In Canada: Fitzhenry & Whiteside, 1995. unp. col. ill.

Fox keeps Bear from his winter nap as the two friends discuss the relative merits of the seasons. Finally they decide that friends are best no matter the season. Cozy watercolor and pencil illustrations portray the delights of the seasons.

SUBJ: Bears--Fiction./ Foxes--Fiction./ Seasons--Fiction./ Friendship--Fiction.

Ph-1 K-2/2 $12.95   L   KF590

GACKENBACH, DICK. Mag the magnificent. Clarion ISBN 0-89919-339-0, 1985. unp. col. ill.

When a little boy puts on his Indian suit and draws a monster on his wall, he finds a way to turn the monster into a magnificent, magical creature who plays and entertains him and solves all his problems. When his mother makes him wash his friend from the wall, the little boy devises a clever way to keep Mag safe for another day. Bright, lively, exaggerated pictures add humor to this child-appealing fantasy.

SUBJ: Drawing--Fiction./ Magic--Fiction./ Monsters--Fiction.

Ph-1 P-K $5.95   P   KF591

GAG, WANDA. ABC bunny. Hand lettered by Howard Gag. Coward, McCann/Putnam ISBN 0-698-11438-8, c1933, 1997. unp. ill.

"A B C song" (words and music) on lining-papers.

Newbery Honor Book.

Available from National Library Service for the Blind and Physically Handicapped as talking book TB04814.

The alphabet done in rhyme which describes the activities of a little rabbit.

SUBJ: Alphabet./ Rabbits--Fiction.

CE   Ph-1 P-1/6 $9.95   L   KF592

GAG, WANDA. Millions of cats. Coward, McCann/Putnam ISBN 0-698-20091-8, c1928. unp. ill.

Newbery Honor Book.

Also available on 1/2" VHS videocassette color (10min) from Weston Woods HMPV005V, $49.95.

Available from National Library Service for the Blind and Physically Handicapped in Braille BR01738.

A very old man and a very old woman want one little cat but find themselves with an overwhelming number of them.

SUBJ: Cats--Fiction./ Spanish language materials./ Italian language materials.

Ph-1 1-3/2 $15.95   L   KF593

GAGE, WILSON. My stars, it's Mrs. Gaddy!: the three Mrs. Gaddy stories. Illus. by Marylin Hafner. Greenwillow ISBN 0-688-10514-9, 1991. 96p. col. ill.

Three rollicking adventures of Mrs. Gaddy are compiled into one edition which includes MRS. GADDY AND THE GHOST, THE CROW AND MRS. GADDY, and MRS. GADDY AND THE FAST-GROWING VINE. Episodic chapters appealing to new chapter book readers relate the humorous tales as Mrs. Gaddy encounters a ghost in her kitchen, seeks revenge on a pesky crow, and battles her out-of-control ground cover. Welcome addition to collections where the individual titles (many of which are now out of print) have been popular.

SUBJ: Farm life--Fiction.

CE   Ph-1 P-K/2 $13.95   L   KF594

GALDONE, PAUL. Henny Penny. Retold and illus. by Paul Galdone. Clarion ISBN 0-395-28800-2, c1968. unp. col. ill.

Read-along kit available from Spoken Arts 6520. 1 paperback book, 1 sound cassette $15.90.

Big book available from Scholastic (ISBN 0-590-65121-8, 1992).

The author-artist has added a surprise ending to the familiar tale of Henny Penny who thought the sky was falling.

SUBJ: Animals--Fiction./ Poultry--Fiction.

CE   Ph-2 P-K/2 $13.95   L   KF595

GALDONE, PAUL. Little red hen. Clarion ISBN 0-395-28803-7, c1973. unp. col. ill.

Videocassette available from Weston Woods VC155V, 1991. 1/2"

VHS videocassette color (8min), $60.00.
Available from National Library Service for the Blind and Physically Handicapped in Braille BR02197.
A wise hen shares her home with a dog, cat and mouse. They leave all the chores to the hen until she harvests some wheat and bakes a cake from her grain. When they wish to eat the cake they are refused and realize they must share in the work around the house.
SUBJ: Animals--Fiction./ Chickens--Fiction./ Laziness--Fiction./ Spanish language materials.

Ph-2 P-2/4 $13.95   L   KF596
GALDONE, PAUL. Magic porridge pot. Clarion ISBN 0-8164-3173-6, c1976. 32p. col. ill.
Available from National Library Service for the Blind and Physically Handicapped in Braille BR03881.
After a strange old woman in the forest gives a poor, hungry little girl a magic pot, the little girl and her mother have all the delicious porridge they need. In fact one day there is much too much porridge. The whole village is flooded when the mother forgets the magical words needed to stop the pot from producing bubbling, boiling porridge.
SUBJ: Magic--Fiction./ Mothers and daughters--Fiction.

Ph-1 K-2/3 $13.95   L   KF597
GANTOS, JACK. Rotten Ralph. Illus. by Nicole Rubel. Houghton Mifflin ISBN 0-395-24276-2, 1976. 48p. col. ill.
Ralph is Sarah's cat and she loves him in spite of the fact that he is arrogant, hateful and just plain rotten. One day he goes too far and loses his comfortable home. But Sarah's love wins out and after she rescues him, he learns that being even just a little bit nice can have its rewards.
Rotten Ralph's bad behavior continues in ROTTEN RALPH'S TRICK OR TREAT (ISBN 0-395-38943-7, 1986, OPC). In ROTTEN RALPH'S SHOW AND TELL (ISBN 0-395-44312-1, 1989) he goes to school with Sarah because he's messed up everything else she was thinking of taking to school for show and tell, and his mischief continues as Sarah prepares for his birthday party in HAPPY BIRTHDAY ROTTEN RALPH (ISBN 0-395-53766-5, 1990).
SUBJ: Cats--Fiction./ Behavior--Fiction./ Circus--Fiction.

Ph-2 1-3/2 $14.95   T   KF598
GARAY, LUIS. Pedrito's Day. Orchard ISBN 0-531-09522-3, 1997. unp. col. ill.
First published in Canada, Stoddart Publishing Co. Limited, 1997.
Saving for a bicycle of his own, Pedrito demonstrates his maturity by using his own money to repay his aunt when he loses money she had entrusted to him. Strongly illustrated with cross-hatched, color paintings, the story provides a glimpse at Latin American culture as well as a model of responsibility. For multicultural studies and values education.
SUBJ: Latin Americans--Fiction./ Responsibility--Fiction.

Ph-2 P-K/3 $14.93   L   KF599
GARTEN, JAN. Alphabet tale. New ed., rev. and re-illustrated. Illus. by Muriel Batherman. Greenwillow ISBN 0-688-12703-7, 1994. unp. col. ill.
Wild animal tails and simple rhymes form an alphabet guessing game in this simple picture book. "He's an armor-plated animal/who lives far away from us./This is the tail of a...Xenurus." A bold red letter, the rhyme, and the animal's tail appear on the right hand page. Turning the page reveals a congenial, quickly sketched painting of the animal. This enjoyable scheme is especially suited to very young readers and nursery school classes.
SUBJ: Alphabet./ Animals--Fiction./ Stories in rhyme.

Ph-2 K-2/6 $5.95   P   KF600
GAUCH, PATRICIA LEE. Christina Katerina and the time she quit the family. Illus. by Elise Primavera. Putnam ISBN 0-399-22405-X; In Canada: General, 1987. unp. col. ill.
Blamed for her little brother's misdeeds, Christina decides to change her name, quit the family and partition off part of the house for her own area where she can do what she pleases, and eat what she wants when and where she wants to do it. All is great for awhile but she soon learns that independent living can be very lonely. The pictures are superb in presenting the chaos and activity of a normal household. Adults may think Christina a brat but youngsters admire and love her.
SUBJ: Self-reliance--Fiction./ Family life--Fiction.

Ph-2 K-2/3 $16.95   T   KF601
GEISERT, ARTHUR. After the flood. Houghton Mifflin ISBN 0-395-66611-2, 1994. 32p. col. ill.
After the flood, Noah, his family, and the animals start anew, turning the ark into a home, planting new crops, and multiplying to repopulate the earth. Detailed colored etchings show the hard work

and satisfaction in rebuilding that followed the flood. The story provides a simple celebration of life on earth and a follow-up to the biblical story of Noah's Ark.
SUBJ: Noah (Biblical figure)--Fiction.

Ph-1 2-5/2 $15.95   L   KF602
GEISERT, ARTHUR. Etcher's studio. Houghton Mifflin ISBN 0-395-79754-3, 1997. 32p. col. ill.
"Walter Lorraine books."
Preparing for a studio sale of etchings, a young boy helps his grandfather ready the paper and plates to create proofs for the boy to hand color. Material following the story shows the equipment in the studio and the steps to make an etching.
SUBJ: Etching--Fiction./ Artists--Fiction./ Imagination--Fiction./ Grandfathers--Fiction.

Ph-1 1-3/3 $14.95   T   KF603
GEISERT, ARTHUR. Pigs from A to Z. Houghton Mifflin ISBN 0-395-38509-1, 1986. unp. col. ill.
Seven little pigs build a tree house with each step fitting neatly into an alphabetical arrangement. The illustrations are intricate, full-paged, black and white etchings, one opposite each line or two of text. Each contains pictures of the seven pigs, five forms of the appropriate letter, one form of the preceeding letter and one form of the following letter. Often some of the pigs and some of the letters are hidden in the designs. This is a handsome, challenging and sophisticated alphabet book with the key to the puzzles provided at the end.
SUBJ: Alphabet./ Pigs--Fiction./ Tree houses--Fiction.

Ph-3 1-3/3 $14.95   L   KF604
GEISERT, ARTHUR. Pigs from 1 to 10. Houghton Mifflin ISBN 0-395-58519-8, 1992. 32p. col. ill.
Ten pigs set out on a quest to find a legendary place about which their mother has read to them. The reader is challenged to find the numerals zero through nine cleverly hidden in each doublespread illustration. A key to locating the numerals in the intricately detailed etchings is appended.
SUBJ: Pigs--Fiction./ Picture puzzles./ Counting.

Ph-2 1-3/3 $14.89   L   KF605
GEORGE, JEAN CRAIGHEAD. Dear Rebecca, winter is here. Illus. by Loretta Krupinski. HarperCollins ISBN 0-06-021140-7; In Canada: HarperCollins, 1993. unp. col. ill.
"Winter is here," a grandmother writes to her granddaughter and tells the story of how winter begins its approach on the first day of summer. Beautiful gouache watercolor illustrations depict the changing seasons and wildlife while an author's note describes the tilt of the earth and its effect on the winter and summer solstices. An intergenerational story for the science curriculum.
SUBJ: Winter--Fiction./ Seasons--Fiction./ Nature--Fiction./ Grandmothers--Fiction.

Ph-1 K-2/2 $15.93   L   KF606
GEORGE, LINDSAY BARRETT. Around the pond: who's been here? Greenwillow ISBN 0-688-14377-6, 1996. unp. col. ill.
Exploring around a pond, Cammy and William find tracks and other signs of wildlife. Each clue is followed by an oversized doublespread showing the animal. Brief notes about each animal follow the story. The format is ideal for reading aloud as an introduction to observing wildlife and animal habitats.
SUBJ: Animals--Habits and behavior--Fiction./ Summer--Fiction.

Ph-2 1-3/2 $14.93   L   KF607
GEORGE, LINDSAY BARRETT. In the snow: who's been here? Greenwillow ISBN 0-688-12321-X, 1995. unp. col. ill.
Following a trail through the woods, two children find evidence of several animals who have been there. Gorgeous full-color doublespread illustrations answer the repeated question, "Who's been here?" Includes a short note about each animal. Useful for winter or wildlife units.
SUBJ: Winter--Fiction./ Animal tracks--Fiction.

Ph-2 1-3/3 $15.93   L   KF608
GEORGE, WILLIAM T. Box turtle at Long Pond. Illus. by Lindsay Barrett George. Greenwillow ISBN 0-688-08185-1, 1989. unp. col. ill.
Full-page paintings depict the woodland life of a box turtle. The simple text describes sleeping arrangements, going to the pond for a drink of water, searching for food, hiding from enemies. Not a full life cycle, this is a brief introduction to the habitat and survival strategies of the box turtle set on handsome pages which work well for reading aloud.
SUBJ: Box turtle--Fiction./ Turtles--Fiction.

Ph-1 P-3/2 $14.89   L   KF609
GERINGER, LAURA. Three hat day. Illus. by Arnold Lobel. HarperCollins
ISBN 0-06-021989-0, 1985. 30p. col. ill.
Available from National Library Service for the Blind and Physically
Handicapped on sound recording cassette RC25769.
Collecting hats with a passion, R.R. Pottle the Third finally finds a
wife who shares his unusual love. They live happily in his family
mansion surrounded by canes collected by R.R.'s father, umbrellas
accumulated by his mother and of course hats. Soon little R.R. Pottle
the Fourth is born and she grows up disliking hats, canes and
umbrellas, but she loves shoes. A warm humorous story with clever
illustrations to match. Although the detailed pictures are often small
and better suited to individual viewing, the text is great for reading
aloud.
SUBJ: Hats--Fiction./ Humorous stories.

Ph-1 P-2/2 $14.95   T   KF610
GERSHATOR, DAVID. Bread is for eating. By David and Phillis
Gershator. Illus. by Emma Shaw-Smith. Henry Holt ISBN 0-8050-3173-1;
In Canada: Fitzhenry & Whiteside, 1995. unp. col. ill.
Includes music.
Encouraging her child to eat his bread, Mama sings him a song that
leads into a story about bread from seed to farmer to miller to baker
to bread enjoyed around the world. Lyrics in English and Spanish as
well as the music for the original song follow the story. Full-color ink
illustrations bordered with sketches of bread in its many forms have a
folk art quality suitable to the multicultural theme. The story will have
applications in multicultural studies and nutrition, economics, and plant
units.
SUBJ: Bread--Fiction./ Songs--Fiction./ Hispanic Americans--Fiction.

Ph-1 K-2/2 $15.45   L   KF611
GERSHATOR, PHILLIS. Rata-pata-scata-fata: a Caribbean story. Illus. by
Holly Meade. Little, Brown ISBN 0-316-30470-0; In Canada: Little,
Brown, 1994. unp. col. ill.
Little Junjun wishes his chores would get done by themselves, and
when he says the magic words "rata-pata-scata-fata," they do.
Every child will recognize Junjun's desire and enjoy the chance
fulfillment of each of his wishes. Torn paper illustrations offer large
swatches of color in bright, Caribbean hues.
SUBJ: Caribbean Area--Fiction./ Wishes--Fiction.

Ph-2 1-3/2 $15.00   T   KF612
GERSHATOR, PHILLIS. Sambalena show-off. Illus. by Leonard Jenkins.
Simon & Schuster ISBN 0-689-80314-1; In Canada: Distican, 1995. unp.
col. ill.
Sambalena is a lazy show-off until a pot gets stuck on his head and
he longs to be able to do anything, even work. Set in the Caribbean,
the story was inspired by a Brazilian folk song. One variant of the
song is featured on a Raffi recording: MORE SINGABLE SONGS.
For multicultural studies.
SUBJ: Caribbean Area--Fiction./ Grandmothers--Fiction.

Ph-2 K-2/2 $14.95   L   KF613
GERSHATOR, PHILLIS. Sweet, sweet fig banana. Illus. by Fritz Millevoix.
Whitman ISBN 0-8075-7693-X; In Canada: General, 1996. unp. col. ill.
Soto gives a hand of bananas from his tree to each of three people
who have befriended him on Market day: the hat seller, the fraico
man, and the librarian who has been helping him to read. Bright,
tropical colors accent the Caribbean setting. The inclusion of the
librarian in this simple and appealing multicultural story makes this a
natural for library story times. For multicultural studies.
SUBJ: Banana--Fiction./ Caribbean Area--Fiction./ Gifts--Fiction.

CE
Ph-3 1-2/2 $2.95   P   KF614
GIFF, PATRICIA REILLY. All about Stacy. Illus. by Blanche Sims. Dell
ISBN 0-440-40088-0, 1988. 79p. ill.
Read-along kit available from Listening Library FTR 143 (ISBN
0-8072-0187-1, 1994). 1 paperback book, 1 sound cassette (46min),
$15.98, and teacher's guide.
Stacy's class is constructing "About-Me" boxes, containers that hold
items that are special to the makers. This very easy first chapter book
details Stacy's problems as she decides what should be in her box
and her adventures along the way. Prime transitional reader for newly
established primary readers.
More about the new kids at Polk Street School may be found in B-E-
S-T FRIENDS (ISBN 0-440-40090-2, 1988, read-along kit available
from Listening Library ISBN 0-8072-0178-2, 1994); STACY SAYS
GOOD-BYE (ISBN 0-440-40135-6, 1989, read-along kit available
from Listening Library FTR 141 ISBN 0-8072-0181-2, 1994).
SUBJ: Schools--Fiction./ Self-identity--Fiction.

Ph-3 2-3/2 $2.99   P   KF615
GIFF, PATRICIA REILLY. Powder puff puzzle. Illus. by Blanche Sims. Dell
ISBN 0-440-47180-X, 1987. 75p. ill.

Gives the very young, newly established reader a chance to match
wits with detective Dawn Bosco as she and her cohorts search for
Dawn's escaped cat, Powder Puff, one simmering summer day.
Presented in easy-to-read sentences and short chapters, this book will
reinforce the abilities of the reader who is chasing his/her own first
"chapter mystery book."
More adventure with the polka dot private eye may be found in
GARBAGE JUICE FOR BREAKFAST (ISBN 0-440-40207-7, 1989).
SUBJ: Cats--Fiction./ Mystery and detective stories.

CE
Ph-1 1-2/2 $11.95   L   KF616
GIFF, PATRICIA REILLY. Today was a terrible day. Illus. by Susanna
Natti. Viking ISBN 0-670-71830-0; In Canada: Penguin, 1980. 25p. col.
ill.
Videocassette available from Live Oak Media (ISBN 0-8749-9099-8,
1988). 1/2" VHS videocassette color (8min), $37.95.
Ronald is a second grader who may never get to third grade. He's in
the lowest reading group, signs his own homework, gets into trouble
at the water fountain, loses the ball game and his ice cream money
during recess, and eats the wrong lunch. When his teacher sends a
note home, Ronald makes a big discovery. He can read and he learns
that Miss Tyler is a really understanding person, too.
SUBJ: Reading--Fiction./ Schools--Fiction./ Behavior--Fiction.

KIT
Ph-3 1-2 $6.99   KF617
GIFF, PATRICIA REILLY. Today was a terrible day (Kit). Illus. by
Susanna Natti. Puffin StoryTapes ISBN 0-14-095119-9, 1993. 1
paperback book, 1 sound cassette (16min).
Chronicles the ups and downs of second grader Ronald, who is
learning to read. Side one is a read-along version of the story with
page turning signals. Side two, which features a song, poem, and
discussion about handling terrible days, may extend the use of the
tape for guidance programs.
SUBJ: Reading--Fiction./ Schools--Fiction./ Behavior--Fiction.

Ph-2 P-2/2 $14.95   L   KF618
GILLILAND, JUDITH HEIDE. Not in the house, Newton! Illus. by
Elizabeth Sayles. Clarion ISBN 0-395-61195-4, 1995. 32p. col. ill.
Everything Newton draws with his red crayon-- a ball, a toy car, a
fire engine, and red boots-- becomes real. His mother insists that he
take his new toys outside. Finally, he draws a large red airplane that
takes him out of the house. The illustrations and story provide a
satisfying fantasy that will work well for reading aloud. Combine with
HAROLD AND THE PURPLE CRAYON, the story of another magical
crayon.
SUBJ: Drawing--Fiction./ Crayons--Fiction./ Magic--Fiction.

Ph-2 K-2/3 $15.95   L   KF619
GILMAN, PHOEBE. Gypsy princess. Scholastic ISBN 0-590-86543-9; In
Canada: Northwinds/Scholastic, 1997. unp. col. ill.
Dreaming of life as a princess, Cinnamon is invited to live like a
princess, but she discovers that royal life is not as comfortable or fun
as she imagined and returns to the gypsy camp. Glowing illustrations
touched with gold and small insets add the true enchantment to this
story which lacks depth, but will appeal to fairy tale fans.
SUBJ: Gypsies--Fiction./ Princesses--Fiction.

Ph-2 1-3/5 $9.95   T   KF620
GILMORE, RACHNA. Lights for Gita. Illus. by Alice Priestley.. Tilbury
House ISBN 0-88448-150-6; In Canada: Second Story Press, 1994. unp.
col. ill.
Freezing rain threatens to ruin Gita's first celebration of Divali in her
new home away from India. Divali is a Hindu celebration of lights
observed in October or November with fireworks, parties, and
storytelling. Gita's memories and her family's celebration in their new
country serve as an introduction to the holiday and the difficulties
adjusting to a new home. For multicultural studies.
SUBJ: Fasts and feasts--Hinduism--Fiction./ Emigration and
immigration--Fiction./ East Indian Americans--Fiction./ Divali--Fiction.

Ph-1 P-K/2 $15.88   L   KF621
GINSBURG, MIRRA. Across the stream. Illus. by Nancy Tafuri.
Greenwillow ISBN 0-688-01206-X, 1982. 23p. col. ill.
A duck and her three ducklings ferry a hen and her three chicks
across a deep, wide stream enabling the chickens to escape from a
hungry fox. Simple, rhyming text and large, bright illustrations
combine to create an appealing picture book for very young children.
SUBJ: Chickens--Fiction./ Ducks--Fiction./ Dreams--Fiction./ Stories in
rhyme.

Ph-2 P/1 $13.93   L   KF622
GINSBURG, MIRRA. Asleep, asleep. Inspired by a verse of A.
Vvedensky. Illus. by Nancy Tafuri. Greenwillow ISBN 0-688-09154-7,
1992. unp. col. ill.

A mother soothes a baby, who is awake in the middle of the night, back to sleep just as the animals and other children are "asleep, asleep." Few words in a gentle question-and-answer format along with charming watercolor illustrations of sleeping animals softly lull the listener.
SUBJ: Sleep--Fiction.

Ph-2 P-2/2 $13.95 L KF623
GINSBURG, MIRRA. Mushroom in the rain. Adapted from the Russian of V. Suteyev. Illustrated by Jose Aruego and Ariane Dewey. Macmillan ISBN 0-02-736241-8; In Canada: Collier Macmillan, c1974, 1987. unp. col. ill.
An ant caught in a rainstorm hides under a mushroom and doesn't know what to do when a butterfly and then other creatures try to hide there also. Simply retold from the original Russian and comically illustrated, this is a delight for story hours or for novice readers.
SUBJ: Animals--Fiction./ Mushrooms--Fiction./ Rain and rainfall--Fiction.

Ph-2 P-K/1 $12.93 L KF624
GINSBURG, MIRRA. Sun's asleep behind the hill. Adapted from an Armenian song by Mirra Ginsburg. Illus. by Paul O. Zelinsky. Greenwillow ISBN 0-688-00825-9, 1982. 32p. col. ill.
Growing tired after a long day, the sun, breeze, leaves, a squirrel and a child become still and rest. Only the moon shines in the silence. Striking illustrations are the real power in this quiet mood piece which can be read by a beginning reader.
SUBJ: Bedtime--Fiction./ Night--Fiction./ Stories in rhyme.

Ph-3 K-2/2 $15.00 T KF625
GLASSMAN, PETER. Wizard next door. Illus. by Steven Kellogg. Morrow ISBN 0-688-10645-5, 1993. unp. col. ill.
Though Mr. Myers lives next door, only the young narrator can see the fantastic magic he concocts. Perhaps it's his imagination, but the wizard has the strangest pets, chases robbers with a tornado, and makes a great substitute teacher. Imaginative, extraordinary, and incredibly humorous illustrations complete the enchantment.
SUBJ: Imagination--Fiction./ Magic--Fiction.

Ph-1 K-3/2 $14.95 L KF626
GOBLE, PAUL. Death of the iron horse. Bradbury ISBN 0-02-737830-6; In Canada: Collier Macmillan, 1987. unp. col. ill.
Selectors' Choice, 16th ed.
Wanting to protect their land, homes, women and children and inspired and impressed by the vision of Sweet Medicine, their ancient prophet, a group of young Cheyenne braves set out to destroy the terrifying iron horse. Their success, although short-lived, is a period of triumph, fun and great humor as they investigate the contents of white people's wagons. Stunning illustrations, brightly colored, action-packed, and strong in Indian motifs, add much to the story based on a true incident occurring in 1867 and the only occurrence of a train wreck caused by the Indians.
SUBJ: Cheyenne Indians--History--Fiction./ Indians of North America--History--Fiction./ Railroads--History--Fiction.

Ph-3 K-3/4 $14.95 L KF627
GOBLE, PAUL. Dream wolf. Bradbury ISBN 0-02-736585-9; In Canada: Collier Macmillan, 1990. unp. col. ill.
Revised edition of THE FRIENDLY WOLF (Bradbury, 1974).
Available from the National Library Service for the Blind and Physically Handicapped on sound recording cassette RC 36651.
Tiblo and his little sister Tanksi wander away from berry-picking and when night comes they are lost. They spend the night in a cave that belongs to a wolf who leads them home the next day. The Indians thank and honor the wolf and the story ends with a distinct message about how we have driven the wolves away. Beautiful illustrations depict Native American culture and its reverence for all life including the wolf. Useful for units on Native Americans or endangered species.
SUBJ: Wolves--Fiction./ Indians of North America--Fiction.

CE   Ph-1 K-3/4 $14.95 T KF628
GOBLE, PAUL. Girl who loved wild horses. Bradbury/Macmillan ISBN 0-02-736570-0, 1978. unp. col. ill.
Caldecott Medal Award.
Selectors' Choice, 12th ed.
Videocassette available from SRA/McGraw-Hill 87-510726, 1988. 1/2" enhanced VHS videocassette color (9min), $37.00.
Available from the National Library Service for the Blind and Physically Handicapped on sound recording cassette RC 38551.
Brilliant paintings match the dramatic story of a young Indian girl who has such special love, feeling and understanding for horses that they too understand and follow her. When a violent storm drives the girl and the tribe's horses to faraway hills where the wild horses live, a handsome stallion, leader of the herd, welcomes the newcomers.

Although her family finally finds her, the girl chooses the freedom and happiness found with the wild horses. Legend says she became a beautiful mare--the mate of the mighty stallion.
SUBJ: Indians of North America--Great Plains--Fiction./ Horses--Fiction.

Ph-2 K-3/5 $14.99 L KF629
GOLDIN, BARBARA DIAMOND. Magician's visit: a Passover tale. Adapted from a story by I.L. Peretz. Retold by Barbara Diamond Godin. Illus. by Robert Andrew Parker. Viking ISBN 0-670-84840-9; In Canada: Penguin, 1993. 32p. col. ill.
A penniless couple have nothing for the Passover Seder until a mysterious magician visits them and provides the meal. When the matzah crumbles and the wine pours, they realize the Seder is not a magical illusion but a gift from the Prophet Elijah. Based on a story written in 1904 by I.L. Peretz, the tale portrays dignity and faith. A note follows the story with more information about Passover and the Prophet Elijah.
SUBJ: Passover--Fiction./ Jews--Fiction.

Ph-2 P-K/2 $6.95 T KF630
GOMI, TARO. Who hid it? Millbrook ISBN 1-56294-707-9, 1991. unp. col. ill.
An object is camouflaged as part of an animal in a group and the viewer is asked to identify "Who hid it?" The number of animals in the group ranges from two to twelve successively increasing the difficulty of finding the hidden object.
SUBJ: Visual perception./ Size and shape./ Color.

Ph-1 K-3 $14.95 T KF631
GOODALL, JOHN S. Story of a main street. McElderry ISBN 0-689-50436-5, 1987. unp. col. ill.
Traces the evolution of the market area of a British town from the simplicity of Medieval time to the hustle and bustle of a modern city. Although wordless, the detailed and eloquent watercolors picture activities, inhabitants, interior and exterior views of the buildings and, with the use of many half pages give a feeling of movement.
SUBJ: Cities and towns--Fiction./ Great Britain--Fiction./ Stories without words.

Ph-2 P-2/2 $13.95 L KF632
GOODE, DIANE. Where's our mama? Dutton ISBN 0-525-44770-9, 1991. unp. col. ill.
"Is this your mama?" a gendarme asks two young children about several different women, all of whom fit one description of their mother: beautiful, strong, brave, smart, etc. Finally the children remember that their mother told them to wait at the station where they had been separated and where they are reunited. Set in Paris, the story and illustrations are lightly humorous.
SUBJ: Paris (France)--Fiction./ Mothers--Fiction.

Ph-1 P-2/3 $14.89 L KF633
GRAHAM, MARGARET BLOY. Be nice to spiders. HarperCollins ISBN 0-06-022073-2, c1967. unp. col. ill.
Available from National Library Service for the Blind and Physically Handicapped as talking book TB02342.
Since the new apartment doesn't allow animals, Billy leaves his pet spider, Helen, with the zoo. Because of Helen's special talent for spinning and her appetite for flies, the "zoo becomes a peaceful place where all the animals are happy and contented."
SUBJ: Spiders--Fiction./ Zoos--Fiction.

CE   Ph-1 P-1/4 $16.95 T KF634
GRAMATKY, HARDIE. Little Toot. Putnam ISBN 0-399-22419-X, 1981. unp. col. ill.
Available from National Library Service for the Blind and Physically Handicapped in Braille BRA06872.
Constantly scolded for being playful, Little Toot, the young tugboat, shows the other, larger boats what he can do when there is a disaster at sea. Active watercolor illustrations help tell the story. Young children identify with Little Toot's heroism.
In LITTLE TOOT AND THE LOCH NESS MONSTER (ISBN 0-399-21684-7, 1989, OPC) he travels across the ocean to find out for himself if the famous monster exists.
SUBJ: Tugboats--Fiction.

Ph-2 P-1/2 $13.93 L KF635
GRAVOIS, JEANNE M. Quickly, Quigley. Illus. by Alison Hill. Tambourine ISBN 0-688-13048-8, 1994. unp. col. ill.
Quigley, the penguin, is small and slow and always trying to keep up. One day his younger and smaller brother asks Quigley to slow down so he can keep up. Perky, color illustrations are the key to this story's charm.
SUBJ: Behavior--Fiction./ Penguins--Fiction.

Ph-2 K-2/4　$17.99　L　KF636
GRAY, LIBBA MOORE. Is there room on the feather bed? Illus. by Nadine Bernard Westcott. Orchard ISBN 0-531-33013-3, 1997. unp. col. ill.
"Melanie Kroupa book."
One rainy night the wee fat woman and her wee fat husband allow the animals to join them in their feather bed two at a time. When the skunk crawls into bed, everyone else scurries out into the rain where they soon decide there is room in the feather bed for all. Large, brightly colored illustrations and a repetitive refrain are delightful for sharing at storytime.
SUBJ: Domestic animals--Fiction./ Skunks--Fiction.

Ph-1 P-2/6　$14.99　L　KF637
GRAY, LIBBA MOORE. Small Green Snake. Illus. by Holly Meade. Orchard ISBN 0-531-08694-1, 1994. unp. col. ill.
Just like Mama Snake warned, the sassy Small Green Snake is captured and put into a glass jar. A curious cat inadvertently releases the snake who hurries home to tell his brother and sisters about his adventures. The text hisses and rustles and is great fun for reading aloud. Torn paper used for the collage illustrations was also used for some of the noisier text words adding to the fun and drama. Use with older students to illustrate the concept of onomatopoeia.
SUBJ: Snakes--Fiction.

Ph-2 K-3/1　$13.99　L　KF638
GRAY, NIGEL. Country far away. Illus. by Philippe Dupasquier. Orchard ISBN 0-531-08392-6, 1988. unp. col. ill.
Pictures placed on a split page detail the daily life of two boys; one in an African country and one in a western country. Activities at home, at play, at school and shopping are shown in detailed illustrations accompanied by a simple text which conveys that people of seemingly disparate cultures have more similarities than differences. A good resource for a social studies project.
SUBJ: Boys--Fiction./ Manners and customs--Fiction.

CDR　　　　　Ph-1 K-2　$49.95　　OD KF639
GREEN EGGS AND HAM. School ed. (CD-ROM). Random House/ Broderbund, 1996. 1 CD-ROM color, 1 paperback book, 1 hardback book. (Living books).
Includes teacher's guide, user's guide, troubleshooting guide, activity book and Dr. Seuss' OH SAY CAN YOU SAY?
System requirements: Macintosh System 6.0.7 or higher or Power Macintosh; CD-ROM drive; 256 color monitor; 4MB RAM (8MB RAM for System 7.5 or higher or Power Macintosh).
System requirements: Windows 3.1 or Windows 95; IBM or compatible 386SX or higher with 4MB RAM (486SX or higher with 8MB RAM for Windows 95); Super VGA (640x480, 256 colors); Sound Blaster or SB Pro and 100% compatible sound card; mouse; CD-ROM drive
Product runs on either Macintosh or Windows compatible hardware. The Living Books version of this Dr. Seuss classic presents a delightful animated version for youngsters to use. Sam-I-Am captures the user with his antics, and the variety of animations will keep users' attention. Extension activities in the school edition will make this a true learning experience. A bonus book of Dr. Seuss' tongue twisters OH SAY CAN YOU SAY? is included.
SUBJ: Food--Fiction--Software./ Software--Food--Fiction./ Interactive media.

CE　　　　　Ph-1 K-2/2　$15.98　L　KF640
GREEN, NORMA B. Hole in the dike. Retold by Norma B. Green. Illus. by Eric Carle. Crowell/HarperCollins ISBN 0-690-00676-4, c1974, 1975. 32p. col. ill.
Available from National Library Service for Blind and Physically Handicapped in Braille BR03175.
Retells the familiar story of the young Dutch boy whose resourcefulness, courage and finger save his country from being destroyed by the sea. A simplified adaptation of one chapter in HANS BRINKER OR THE SILVER SKATES by Mary Mapes Dodge. Striking illustrations.
SUBJ: Netherlands--Fiction./ Floods--Fiction.

Ph-2 K-1/2　$14.95　L　KF641
GREENFIELD, ELOISE. Grandpa's face. Illus. by Floyd Cooper. Philomel ISBN 0-399-21525-5; In Canada: Putnam, 1988. unp. col. ill.
Tamika, a young black girl, loves her grandfather's kind face but one day she sees him rehearsing for a play and his loveless expression frightens her. Her grandfather realizes something is bothering her and they go for a "talk walk" where he reaffirms his love for her. Depicts a warm, communicative relationship between grandparent and child.
SUBJ: Grandfathers--Fiction./ Actors and actresses--Fiction.

Ph-2 K-2/3　$14.89　L　KF642
GREENFIELD, ELOISE. Me and Neesie. Illus. by Moneta Barnett. Crowell/HarperCollins ISBN 0-690-00715-9, c1975. 39p. col. ill.
To Janell, her imaginary friend, Neesie, seems very real--especially when the two of them get into mischief.
SUBJ: Imagination--Fiction./ Aunts--Fiction.

Ph-2 K-2/3　$15.00　T　KF643
GREENSTEIN, ELAINE. Mrs. Rose's garden. Simon & Schuster ISBN 0-689-80215-3; In Canada: Distican, 1996. unp. col. ill.
When Mrs. Rose's vegetables exceed her expectations, she secretly transplants several of the gargantuan plants in her competitors' gardens, and everyone wins a blue ribbon at the county fair. The pastel cassein paintings are understated and well matched to Mrs. Rose's generosity which is all the greater because it does not call attention to itself.
SUBJ: Gardening--Fiction./ Vegetables--Fiction./ Contests--Fiction./ Sharing--Fiction./ Fairs--Fiction.

Ph-1 1-3/2　$14.95　L　KF644
GREENWOOD, PAMELA D. What about my goldfish? Illus. by Jennifer Plecas. Clarion ISBN 0-395-64337-6, 1993. 40p. col. ill.
Jamie is worried about moving, transporting his pet dog and goldfish, and especially about making friends in a new school. His goldfish help him to break the ice in his new classroom. Easy-to-read text and short chapters provide an appealing transitional reader.
SUBJ: Moving, Household--Fiction./ Pets--Fiction.

Ph-1 K-2/4　$15.95　L　KF645
GRIFALCONI, ANN. Darkness and the butterfly. Little, Brown ISBN 0-316-32863-4; In Canada: Little, Brown, 1987. unp. col. ill.
Fearless in the daytime, small Osa shivers and cowers in a corner of her African home with the dark of night, but a visit with a wise old woman and an encounter with a yellow butterfly enable the small girl to conquer her fears. Dramatic double-spreads in bold, jewel-like colors picture the African village, homes, lifestyle and jungle.
In OSA'S PRIDE (ISBN 0-316-32865-0, 1990, OPC) her grandmother uses a story cloth to show Osa the foolishness of too much pride.
SUBJ: Fear--Fiction./ Night--Fiction./ Africa--Fiction.

Ph-2 2-4/2　$12.88　L　KF646
GRIFFITH, HELEN V. Emily and the enchanted frog. Illus. by Susan Condie Lamb. Greenwillow ISBN 0-688-08484-2, 1989. 32p. col. ill.
There are three amusing stories in this slender book involving Emily's unusual encounters--one with a frog who does not appreciate becoming a prince, another with a tricky elf who grants her wish to be invisible, and lastly with a sulky crab who thinks it is a mermaid. A good read-aloud with amusing color illustrations.
SUBJ: Wishes--Fiction./ Crabs--Fiction./ Frogs--Fiction.

Ph-1 1-4/1　$13.93　L　KF647
GRIFFITH, HELEN V. Grandaddy's place. Illus. by James Stevenson. Greenwillow ISBN 0-688-06254-7, 1987. unp. col. ill.
Available from the National Library Service for the Blind and Physically Handicapped on sound recording cassette RC 41842. Serves as a prequel to GEORGIA MUSIC and sets the place and emotional background of love and understanding between Janetta, the city child, and her rural grandfather. Quiet and satisfying, using humor and apt descriptions of places, people, and relationships, Griffith's words and Stevenson's watercolors will be good for new chapter book readers and for reading aloud in a story hour. Janetta returns to visit Grandaddy in a companion title GRANDADDY AND JANETTA (ISBN 0-688-11227-7, 1993, available from the NLSBPH on sound recording cassette RC 39079).
SUBJ: Farm life--Fiction./ Grandfathers--Fiction.

Ph-1 1-4/2　$14.93　L　KF648
GRIFFITH, HELEN V. Grandaddy's stars. Illus. by James Stevenson. Greenwillow ISBN 0-688-13655-9, 1995. unp. col. ill.
Available from the National Library Service for the Blind and Physically Handicapped on sound recording cassette RC 41755. Janetta shows Grandaddy the important things in Baltimore: her cat, Star; her room; her school; the playground; and her feather collection. He reaffirms the importance of each with affection and stories of his own. The relationship between Janetta and her grandfather continues in this charming intergenerational story written as a short chapter book. Good transitional reader, particularly for those already familiar with the characters.
SUBJ: Grandfathers--Fiction./ City and town life--Fiction.

Ph-1 P-2/2　$13.93　L　KF649
GRIFFITH, HELEN V. Mine will, said John. New ed. Illus. by Jos. A. Smith. Greenwillow ISBN 0-688-10958-6, 1992. unp. col. ill.
John wants a puppy, but John's parents want to choose a pet for him. When the gerbil cries at night, the chameleon glows in the dark,

and the frogs chew the furniture, they choose a pet that John says won't do any of those things--a puppy. Originally published in 1980, this new edition has bright, humorous illustrations.
SUBJ: Pets--Fiction.

Ph-2 P-K/2 $13.95 L KF650
GROSSMAN, PATRICIA. Night ones. Illus. by Lydia Dabcovich. Harcourt Brace Jovanovich ISBN 0-15-257438-7, 1991. unp. col. ill.
Introduces some of the many people who work at night and the different jobs they do. Simple text and active illustrations show a busy night time city sure to intrigue curious youngsters.
SUBJ: Night work--Fiction./ Occupations--Fiction.

Ph-1 P-1/2 $12.95 L KF651
GUARINO, DEBORAH. Is your mama a llama? Illus. by Steven Kellogg. Scholastic ISBN 0-590-41387-2, 1989. unp. col. ill.
Big book available (ISBN 0-590-65734-8, 1992).
Spanish edition available TU MAMA ES UNA LLAMA? (ISBN 0-590-46275-X, 1993), $4.99.
A young llama goes to a bat, a calf and other animals with the question, "Is your mama a llama?" Indignantly each animal describes their own mother in a riddle and llama solves the riddle on the next page. The rhyming text is simple to follow and the full page illustrations are warm and cheerful. Young readers will enjoy this very much.
SUBJ: Llamas--Fiction./ Animals--Fiction./ Stories in rhyme.

Ph-2 1-3/2 $13.93 L KF652
GUBACK, GEORGIA. Luka's quilt. Greenwillow ISBN 0-688-12155-1, 1994. unp. col. ill.
Upset because the flower quilt her grandmother makes for her only has two colors, Luka won't speak with her until her grandmother proposes a truce, so they can go to the Lei Day celebration together. At the celebration, Luka makes a lei with multicolored flowers that inspires her grandmother to solve the problem with the quilt. The landscapes and traditions of Hawaii are depicted in cut-paper collage illustrations. The grandmother models creative problem-solving. Intergenerational story for multicultural studies.
SUBJ: Grandmothers--Fiction./ Quilts--Fiction./ Hawaii--Fiction.

Ph-2 P-1/3 $11.95 T KF653
GUNDERSHEIMER, KAREN. Happy winter. HarperCollins ISBN 0-06-022172-0, 1982. 33p col ill.
A young girl recites a litany of winter activities. Sledding and making angels in the snow; watching the sleet and ice through lacy, frosted windows; cutting, pasting, and painting presents; and baking a wonderful winter fudge cake help create a happy winter day for the narrator and her younger sister. Small, colorful, detailed pictures create a warm, cozy setting for the rhyming text.
SUBJ: Stories in rhyme./ Winter--Fiction.

Ph-2 2-4/5 $10.95 T KF654
GUTHRIE, DONNA. Rose for Abby. Illus. by Dennis Hockerman. Abingdon Press ISBN 0-687-36586-4, 1988. unp. col. ill.
Abby's father is a minister in an inner city parish. When Abby notices an elderly woman searching through garbage she sets out to help her first by leaving gloves and a hat from the lost and found and then by getting neighbors to set up a soup kitchen. Although simplistic, the story is sure to provoke discussion about the plight of the homeless.
SUBJ: Homeless persons--Fiction./ Churches--Fiction./ City and town life--Fiction.

Ph-1 P-1/1 $15.00 L KF655
GUY, GINGER FOGLESONG. Fiesta! Illus. by Rene King Moreno. Greenwillow ISBN 0-688-14331-8, 1996. unp. col. ill.
Children prepare for a party or fiesta beginning with one basket through ten streamers for the pinata. The bilingual text is a counting book in both English and Spanish. Wide doublespread illustrations are suitable for sharing at storytime. For multicultural studies.
SUBJ: Parties--Fiction./ Counting./ Spanish language materials./ Bilingual materials--Spanish.

Ph-2 K-2/5 $13.95 L KF656
GWYNNE, FRED. Pondlarker. Simon & Schuster ISBN 0-671-70846-5, 1990. unp. col. ill.
Pondlarker, the Frog, sets off to find a princess who will kiss him and turn him into a prince; he finds her but at the last minute decides he'd rather be a frog. A humorous twist on the familiar story which also communicates the value of being happy with who you are.
SUBJ: Fairy tales--Parodies, imitations, etc./ Frogs--Fiction./ Self-acceptance--Fiction.

Ph-2 K-2/2 $15.00 L KF657
HAAS, JESSIE. Sugaring. Illus. by Jos. A. Smith. Greenwillow ISBN 0-688-14200-1, 1996. unp. col. ill.
After accompanying Gramp as he gathers maple sap and cooks it down into syrup, Nora wants to share the sweet treat with the horses who have worked hard. Gram helps her by making maple sugar, a treat for Nora and the horses. The warm intergenerational story offers an introduction to the process of making maple syrup through snowy pictures and vivid text.
SUBJ: Maple syrup--Fiction./ Grandfathers--Fiction./ Horses--Fiction.

Ph-1 K-2/5 $14.95 L KF658
HADER, BERTA. Big snow. By Berta and Elmer Hader. Macmillan ISBN 0-02-737910-8, 1948. unp. col. ill.
Caldecott Medal Award.
Available from National Library Service for the Blind and Physically Handicapped in Braille BR02128.
Realistically descriptive illustrations give feeling to this quiet telling about a heavy snowstorm and of how an old couple feed the animals and birds. Tells the reassuring story of how nature provides for the woodland creatures, how each creature prepares for the coming winter. Thoughtful and informative with considerable text demanding close attention.
SUBJ: Animals--Habits and behavior--Fiction./ Snow--Fiction.

Ph-2 P-2/7 $4.95 P KF659
HADITHI, MWENYE. Crafty chameleon. Illus. by Adrienne Kennaway. Little, Brown ISBN 0-316-33771-4, c1987, 1995. unp. col. ill.
Teased and taunted every morning by Leopard and frightened by Crocodile each evening, Chameleon tires of their treatment and devises a clever plan which causes the two big bullies to leave him alone forever. Pictures of the animals and jungle are handsome and exciting, with many touches of humor.
SUBJ: Chameleons--Fiction.

CE Ph-1 K-3/4 $5.95 P KF660
HADITHI, MWENYE. Hot Hippo. Illus. by Adrienne Kennaway. Little, Brown ISBN 0-316-33718-8; In Canada: Little, Brown, 1986. unp. col. ill.
Available from National Library Service for the Blind and Physically Handicapped in Braille BR7123.
1/2" VHS videocassette color (6min) from Weston Woods HMPV324V, $49.95.
Hippo is so hot living only on land that he strikes a bargain with Ngai, the god of everything and everywhere, and that is why hippopotamuses live on land by night but in cool water by day, and why they frequently open their huge mouths wide saying "Look Ngai! No Fishes!" Large, striking pictures fill the pages with glorious colors that match the heat of the land, cool of the water, the duskiness of the night, and the moods of the story. A good read-aloud.
SUBJ: Hippopotamus--Fiction.

Ph-2 K-3/3 $15.99 T KF661
HALL, DONALD. I am the dog, I am the cat. Illus. by Barry Moser. Dial ISBN 0-8037-1504-8, 1994. unp. col. ill.
Contrasts the distinctive personalities of a dog and cat as they alternately talk about themselves and their likes and dislikes. Fans of these two popular pets will recognize the unique and endearing qualities of each in the humorous text and realistic watercolor illustrations.
SUBJ: Dogs--Fiction./ Cats--Fiction.

Ph-1 1-3/6 $14.95 L KF662
HALL, DONALD. Lucy's Christmas. Illus. by Michael McCurdy. Browndeer/Harcourt Brace ISBN 0-15-276870-X; In Canada: Harcourt Brace c/o Canadian Manda, 1994. unp. col. ill.
In 1909, Lucy begins her preparations for Christmas in August as she makes presents for her family and best friend. Finally, everyone from the town gathers at the church for carols, the children's Christmas pageant, and the opening of gifts. Each gift reflects life in New Hampshire in the early 1900s, including the small replica Lucy receives of her family's new cast-iron range. Old-fashioned scratchboard illustrations suggest times long ago and illustrate the small details of a child's point of view of family life in those days. Historical fiction for the holiday season.
SUBJ: Christmas--Fiction./ Gifts--Fiction./ United States--Social life and customs--1865-1918--Fiction.

CE Ph-1 K-3/7 $15.00 L KF663
HALL, DONALD. Ox-cart man. Illus. by Barbara Cooney. Viking Penguin ISBN 0-670-53328-9; In Canada: Penguin, 1979. unp. col. ill.
Caldecott Medal Award.
Selectors' Choice, 13th ed.
1/2" VHS videocassette available from Live Oak Media 0-87499-079-3 (8min) $37.95.
Read-along kit available from Live Oak Media (ISBN 0-94107-842-6,

1984). 1 hardcover book, 1 sound cassette (6min), $22.95.
Available from National Library Service for the Blind and Physically Handicapped on sound recording cassette RC21584 and in Braille BR05914.
Highly textured illustrations in a primitive style extend the skillfully simplistic text that follows a New England farmer in the mid 1800s who in October loads his ox cart "with everything they made or grew all year long that was left over" (text) and walks his ox and cart to Portsmouth Market. After selling his goods and his cart and ox, and buying a few needed supplies, and a treat for his family he makes the long walk home where he and his family begin again the cycle of making and growing.
SUBJ: New England--Fiction./ Farm life--Fiction.

Ph-2 K-1/1 $14.00   L   KF664
HALL, KIRSTEN. I'm not scared. Illus. by Joan Holub. Childrens Press ISBN 0-516-05366-3; In Canada: Childrens Press, 1994. 31p. col. ill. (My first reader).
Two fearless boys play together and prepare to camp out until the call of an owl frightens them. Emerging readers will appreciate the limited vocabulary and short sentences of this appealing beginning reader.
SUBJ: Courage--Fiction./ Fear--Fiction./ Stories in rhyme.

Ph-2 K-1/1 $14.00   L   KF665
HALL, KIRSTEN. Tooth fairy. Illus. by Nan Brooks. Childrens Press 0-516-05368-X; In Canada: Childrens Press, 1994. 31p. col. ill. (My first reader).
A young boy describes the experience of loosing a tooth and anticipating a visit from the tooth fairy. Emerging readers will appreciate the limited vocabulary and short sentences in this appealing beginning reader.
SUBJ: Tooth fairy--Fiction./ Stories in rhyme./ Teeth--Fiction.

Ph-1 P-2/3 $12.95   L   KF666
HALL, ZOE. It's pumpkin time! Illus. by Shari Halpern. Blue Sky Press/ Scholastic ISBN 0-590-47833-8; In Canada: Scholastic, 1994. unp. col. ill.
Selectors' Choice, 20th ed.
A brother and sister get ready for their favorite holiday, Halloween, in the summer when they prepare the soil and plant the seeds to grow big pumpkins. Collages created with painted paper form striking illustrations that follow the development from seed to pumpkin to jack-o-lantern. Wonderful for story hours.
SUBJ: Pumpkin--Fiction./ Halloween--Fiction./ Jack-o-lanterns--Fiction./ Gardening--Fiction.

Ph-2 P-2/4 $14.93   L   KF667
HAMANAKA, SHEILA. All the colors of the earth. Morrow ISBN 0-688-11132-7, 1994. unp. col. ill.
"Children come in all the colors of the earth" begins this book about the variety of skin and hair colors found among people. A celebration of the many shades of children, families, and the earth in rich oil paintings and brief, poetic text for multicultural studies.
SUBJ: Brotherliness--Fiction./ Stories in rhyme.

Ph-2 1-3/4 $15.93   L   KF668
HAMANAKA, SHEILA. Peace crane. Morrow ISBN 0-688-13816-0, 1995. unp. col. ill.
In poetic text and moving oil paintings, a child's wish for peace is expressed as a memorial to Sadako who folded a thousand paper cranes and as a hope for today's children. The legacy of Sadako continues to fascinate and encourage youth. For multicultural studies.
SUBJ: Peace--Fiction./ Afro-Americans--Fiction.

Ph-3 P-3/2 $11.95   L   KF669
HAMM, DIANE JOHNSTON. Grandma drives a motor bed. Illus. by Charles Robinson. Whitman ISBN 0-8075-3025-5; In Canada: General, 1987. unp. ill.
Available from National Library Service for the Blind and Physically Handicapped on sound recording cassette RC28930.
Helping Grandpa take care of Grandma Josh is intrigued by her motorized hospital bed and very excited when he gets to "test drive" it. Realistically portrays many of the infirmities and unpleasantries of ageing; incontinence and adult disposable diapers, immobility and physical therapy, but also shows family love and caring and a courageous invalid.
SUBJ: Grandmothers--Fiction./ Physically handicapped--Fiction.

Ph-2 P-1/2 $12.95   L   KF670
HAMM, DIANE JOHNSTON. Laney's lost momma. Illus. by Sally G. Ward. Whitman ISBN 0-8075-4340-3; In Canada: General, 1991. unp col illus.
Laney loses her mother in a department store and panics. Then she remembers two things her mother told her: to never leave the store without her and to ask someone behind the counter for help. Soon Laney and her mother are reunited. Young children will recognize the experience and Laney's emotions and may remember her mother's good advice in similar situations. Solid writing and pleasing watercolor illustrations convey the story without being didactic.
SUBJ: Lost children--Fiction./ Department stores--Fiction.

SRC   Ph-3 1-3 $10.00   OD KF671
HARLEY, BILL. Dinosaurs never say please and other stories (Sound recording cassette). Round River RRR 103C, c1987, 1989. 1 sound cassette (40min).
A collection of stories, some original and some folk tales, told in a lively expressive voice with musical accompaniment and tremendous child appeal. In the title story, young Jimmy wakes up one morning a Tyrannosaurus Rex. Fine storytelling useful for improving listening skills and sparking young imaginations.
Similar material is featured on other cassette recordings: COME ON OUT AND PLAY (Round River Records 107C (55min), 1990); and GROWNUPS ARE STRANGE (Round River Records 106C (50min), 1990).
SUBJ: Dinosaurs--Fiction./ Storytelling--Collections.

Ph-2 P-2/2 $15.95   L   KF672
HARLEY, BILL. Sitting down to eat. Illus. by Kitty Harvill. August House LittleFolk ISBN 0-87483-460-0, 1996. unp. col. ill.
Sitting down to eat, a young boy is joined in succession by nine animals--the last a small caterpillar. Combines traditional elements of zipper songs and cumulative stories to create a counting story and bouncy predictable book. Listeners familiar with the author's recordings will especially enjoy the book, despite the fact that the cut-paper illustrations and design don't work as well as a counting book. For reading aloud.
SUBJ: Animals--Fiction./ Counting./ Stories in rhyme.

Ph-2 P-1/2 $14.95   L   KF673
HARPER, ISABELLE. My cats Nick and Nora. Illus. by Barry Moser. Blue Sky Press/Scholastic ISBN 0-590-47620-3; In Canada: Scholastic, 1995. unp. col. ill.
Two cousins play school and dress up a pair of reluctant cats, Nick and Nora. Bright watercolor doublespread illustrations lend enormous appeal to the childlike description of the two cats.
SUBJ: Cats--Fiction.

Ph-2 P-1/1 $13.95   L   KF674
HARPER, ISABELLE. My dog Rosie. Illus. by Barry Moser. Blue Sky Press/Scholastic ISBN 0-590-47619-X; In Canada: Scholastic, 1994. unp. col. ill.
A small girl takes care of her grandfather's large Rottweiler while he works. Large watercolor illustrations and simple text focus attention on the relationship between the young child and the dog. A photograph on the flap shows the illustrator with his granddaughter, Isabelle (the author), and his dog who look exactly like the characters in the book.
SUBJ: Dogs--Fiction.

Ph-1 P-2/1 $14.95   L   KF675
HARPER, ISABELLE. Our new puppy. Illus. by Barry Moser. Blue Sky Press/Scholastic ISBN 0-590-56926-0; In Canada: Scholastic, 1996. unp. col. ill.
Rosie, the pet dog of the family, is not sure about the new rambunctious puppy, Floyd. Large watercolor illustrations are marvelous portraits of the dogs' expressions as well as the family cat's reactions. Though not mentioned in the text, the cat clearly has an opinion of the new puppy as well.
SUBJ: Dogs--Fiction.

Ph-1 P-2/3 $16.99   T   KF676
HARRIS, ROBIE H. Happy birth day! Illus. by Michael Emberley. Candlewick ISBN 1-56402-424-5; In Canada: Candlewick/dist. by Douglas & McIntyre, 1996. unp. col. ill.
A mother describes the first day of life to her baby from birth through the hospital routines, nursing, family welcomes, and doting parents. Realistic illustrations softly done in pastel and pencil provide a sense of warmth and safety. Parents will want to share this lovely book with children who want to hear the story of their own birth days or who are anticipating the birth of a sibling. (Parents' Shelf).
SUBJ: Childbirth--Fiction./ Babies--Fiction.

Ph-1 1-3/5 $12.95   L   KF677
HARVEY, BRETT. Cassie's journey: going West in the 1860s. Illus. by Deborah Kogan Ray. Holiday House ISBN 0-8234-0684-9, 1988. unp. ill.
Available from National Library Service for the Blind and Physically Handicapped on sound recording cassette RC30605.

Seeking a better life, Cassie and her family join other families, form a wagon-train and travel from their midwestern farm to the Sacramento Valley of California. Without being morbid or depressing, the book does picture the hazards, loss of possessions, deaths and other hardships experienced by those courageous Americans on whose diaries the story is based. Soft charcoal drawings match the seriousness of the account.
SUBJ: Overland journeys to the Pacific--Fiction./ Frontier and pioneer life--Fiction./ West (U.S.)--Fiction.

Ph-2 K-3/4 $4.95   P   KF678
HASLER, EVELINE. Winter magic. Illus. by Michele Lemieux. Kids Can Press ISBN 0-92110-371-9, 1989. unp. col. ill.
Peter hates winter until one night after a strange dream he and his cat Sebastian go out into the snow-covered world, investigate under the snow and tree roots, and find food, mice, badger, and many other secrets of winterland. Soft, luminous, evocative illustrations bring magic to the quiet story.
SUBJ: Winter--Fiction./ Cats--Fiction./ Fantasy.

SRC   Ph-2 1-4 $10.00   OD KF679
HAVEN, KENDALL. Fathers and sons (Sound recording cassette). Music by Christopher Hedge. Story Street, USA, 1991. 1 sound cassette (63min).
Presents three stories in the style of radio days, complete with sound effects, of a father trying to relate to his son as his father had related to him. Both humorous and solemn, these stories would be great for promoting listening skills.
Contents: The sawhorse elk (17min); The climbing tree (13min); Baseball magic (30min).
SUBJ: Fathers and sons--Fiction./ Short stories.

Ph-2 K-2/2 $13.95   L   KF680
HAVILL, JUANITA. Jamaica and Brianna. Illus. by Anne Sibley O'Brien. Houghton Mifflin ISBN 0-395-64489-5, 1993. unp. col. ill.
Protecting their own pride, Jamaica and Brianna hurt each other's feelings with unkind comments about each other's boots. Their friendship is repaired when they communicate their true feelings to each other. Demonstrates the type of misunderstanding behind many conflicts among friends and a happy resolution. The illustrations depict Jamaica as an African-American child and Brianna as an Asian-American child, but their friendship and its problems are universal. For multicultural studies.
SUBJ: Jealousy--Fiction./ Boots--Fiction./ Friendship--Fiction./ Afro-Americans--Fiction./ Asian Americans--Fiction.

Ph-2 K-1/2 $13.95   L   KF681
HAVILL, JUANITA. Jamaica's blue marker. Illus. by Anne Sibley O'Brien. Houghton Mifflin ISBN 0-395-72036-2, 1995. unp. col. ill.
When Jamaica learns that Russell is moving, she begins to understand his annoying behavior and how he might feel. A story that may help youngsters empathize with others and look for reasons behind their behavior. For multicultural studies.
SUBJ: Schools--Fiction./ Moving, Household--Fiction./ Afro-Americans--Fiction.

Ph-2 K-2/2 $16.00   L   KF682
HAVILL, JUANITA. Jamaica's find. Illus. by Anne Sibley O'Brien. Houghton Mifflin ISBN 0-395-39376-0, 1986. 32p. col. ill.
Jamaica turns in the red sock hat she finds on the playground, but not the stuffed dog she has also found. Her happiness in finding the new toy soon turns to regret as she thinks about the child who lost it. Finally she decides to return it to the park lost and found. In the process, she finds a new friend. Jamaica's struggle with her conscience is apparent, and young children will identify with her feelings. A good discussion starter for values education. For multicultural studies.
SUBJ: Lost and found possessions--Fiction./ Afro-Americans--Fiction./ Honesty--Fiction.

Ph-2 P-1/2 $13.95   L   KF683
HAVILL, JUANITA. Treasure nap. Illus. by Elivia Savadier. Houghton Mifflin ISBN 0-395-57817-5, 1992. 32p. col. ill.
On a hot afternoon, Alicia convinces Mama to tell the familiar story of how her great-great-grandparents came to the United States from Mexico. The warm story about family history with soft watercolor illustrations is suitable for multicultural studies.
SUBJ: Mexican Americans--Fiction./ Family--Fiction.

Ph-1 2-4/4 $16.99   L   KF684
HAYES, JOE. Spoon for every bite. Illus. by Rebecca Leer. Orchard ISBN 0-531-08799-9, 1996. unp. col. ill.
When a wealthy neighbor brags that he has a spoon for every day of the year, a couple claims to know a friend who has a spoon for

every bite he takes. The neighbor soon goes bankrupt as he discards his spoon with every mouthful. The poor couple lives in comfort on an income from the rich man's discarded silver spoons. The story is based on Hispanic folktales in which the spoon for every bite is a tortilla. For multicultural studies.
SUBJ: Wealth--Fiction./ Pride and vanity--Fiction.

Ph-2 P-2/2 $15.00   T   KF685
HAYES, SARAH. Eat up, Gemma. Illus. by Jan Ormerod. Lothrop, Lee & Shepard ISBN 0-688-08149-5, 1988. unp. col. ill.
Gemma throws her breakfast to the floor, smashes grapes in the supermarket, feeds the party food to the dog, but in church tries to eat artificial fruit on the hat of a woman sitting in front of the family, and that gives her big brother an idea which finally tempts baby Gemma to "Eat up." The warm portrayal of the African-American family is an additional plus. For multicultural studies.
SUBJ: Food habits--Fiction./ Babies--Fiction./ Afro-Americans--Fiction.

Ph-2 P-1/2 $13.95   T   KF686
HAYES, SARAH. Happy Christmas Gemma. Illus. by Jan Ormerod. Lothrop, Lee & Shepard ISBN 0-688-06508-2, 1986. unp. col. ill.
A little boy and his family prepare for Christmas with lots of decorating, package wrapping, and cooking. Baby sister Gemma tries to participate, too, and although she seems to be more destructive than helpful, the family Christmas is a warm loving and happy occasion. Brightly colored pictures placed on a white background are very effective in capturing the happy mood of the story. For multicultural studies.
SUBJ: Afro-Americans--Fiction./ Christmas--Fiction.

Ph-2 P-1/3 $14.00   T   KF687
HAZELAAR, COR. Zoo dreams. Farrar Straus Giroux ISBN 0-374-39730-9; In Canada: HarperCollins, 1997. unp. col. ill.
"Frances Foster books."
The zookeeper checks on the sleepy animals as they settle down for the night. Muted illustrations and a simple text softly evoke nighttime for young readers.
SUBJ: Zoo animals--Fiction./ Zoos--Fiction./ Sleep--Fiction.

Ph-1 P-2/2 $13.95   T   KF688
HAZEN, BARBARA SHOOK. Mommy's office. Illus. by David Soman. Atheneum ISBN 0-689-31601-1; In Canada: Maxwell Macmillan, 1992. unp. col. ill.
Emily accompanies her mother to her office and observes how many of the grown-up things that her mother does at work are similar to the things that she does at school. The parallels drawn between the adult working world and the child's world at school help young children to relate to their parents' jobs.
SUBJ: Mothers and daughters--Fiction./ Work--Fiction.

Ph-1 K-2/1 $4.99   P   KF689
HAZEN, BARBARA SHOOK. Tight times. Illus. by Trina Schart Hyman. Penguin ISBN 0-14-050442-7; In Canada: Penguin, 1983. unp. ill.
Spanish version available TIEMPOS DUROS (ISBN 0-670-84841-7, 1993).
A youngster doesn't understand why something called "tight times" keeps him from getting a dog and causes Mommy to go to work and Daddy to lose his job. But when the child brings home a starved kitten Mommy and Daddy, in spite of all their problems, say the new pet can stay.
SUBJ: Family problems--Fiction.

Ph-2 1-3/5 $15.00   L   KF690
HEARN, DIANE DAWSON. Bad Luck Boswell. Simon & Schuster ISBN 0-689-80303-6; In Canada: Distican, 1995. unp. col. ill.
Boswell, the black cat, brings bad luck to everyone he encounters, including a witch who hopes to use his bad luck powers for her evil spells. When Boswell survives the explosion that kills the witch, the village people decide he has lost at least one of his nine lives: the bad luck one. Pen and ink and acrylic illustrations skillfully use framing to move the story along.
SUBJ: Cats--Fiction./ Luck--Fiction./ Witches--Fiction.

Ph-1 1-3/2 $14.93   L   KF691
HEARNE, BETSY. Seven brave women. Illus. by Bethanne Andersen. Greenwillow ISBN 0-688-14503-5; In Canada: Hearst Book Group, 1997. unp. col. ill.
A young girl briefly describes the accomplishments of her female ancestors, beginning with her great-great-grandmother, a Mennonite who came to this country in a small sailboat from Switzerland. Celebrates the brave women who helped build our country as well as the personal history each of us possesses. A valuable adjunct to units on family history and women's studies.
SUBJ: Genealogy--Fiction./ Courage--Fiction.

Ph-2 P-2/2 $14.95 L KF692
HEATH, AMY. Sofie's role. Illus. by Sheila Hamanaka. Four Winds/Macmillan ISBN 0-02-743505-9; In Canada: Maxwell Macmillan, 1992. unp col illus.

It's Christmas eve and Broadway Pastries is a bustling place as Sofie helps her parents by sweeping, answering the phone, and helping out at the counter. Scrumptious illustrations depict the holiday activity and the appealing confections. For multicultural studies.
SUBJ: Bakers and bakeries--Fiction./ Family life--Fiction./ Christmas--Fiction./ Afro-Americans--Fiction.

Ph-2 1-3/6 $16.00 L KF693
HECKMAN, PHILIP. Waking upside down. Illus. by Dwight Been. Atheneum ISBN 0-689-31930-4; In Canada: Distican, 1996. unp. col. ill.

Waking up on the ceiling, Morton is fascinated by ordinary things like how the water stays in the toilet, the ceiling fan, and his father drinking orange juice straight from the pitcher. Watercolor and pencil illustrations surprise the viewer with a different perspective as Morton explores his house upside down. Introduce a unit on gravity with this upside-down perspective.
SUBJ: Brothers and sisters--Fiction./ Bedrooms--Fiction./ Family life--Fiction./ Bedtime--Fiction./ Gravity--Fiction.

Ph-1 1-3/4 $13.93 L KF694
HEIDE, FLORENCE PARRY. Day of Ahmed's secret. By Florence Parry Heide and Judith Heide Gilliland. Illus. by Ted Lewin. Lothrop, Lee & Shepard ISBN 0-688-08895-3, 1990. unp. col. ill.

As Ahmed rides his donkey cart through the city of Cairo delivering fuel, he describes the sights and sounds of the busy city and thinks about the secret he waits to share with his family. Ahmed's descriptions and the watercolor illustrations provide a glimpse of life in this major Mideast city.
SUBJ: Cairo (Egypt)--Fiction.

Ph-1 2-4/4 $14.95 T KF695
HEIDE, FLORENCE PARRY. Sami and the time of the troubles. By Florence Parry Heide and Judith Heide Gilliland. Illus. by Ted Lewin. Clarion ISBN 0-395-55964-2, 1992. unp. col. ill.

Sami, a ten-year-old boy, describes his family's life during the fighting and bombing in Beirut. They take shelter in an uncle's basement where carpets line the walls reminding them of better days. "Stop the fighting": the children's plea echoes long after this compelling book is closed.
SUBJ: Family life--Fiction./ Lebanon--History--Civil War--Fiction.

Ph-2 K-2/1 $7.99 T KF696
HEILBRONER, JOAN. Robert the rose horse. Illus. by P. D. Eastman. Random House ISBN 0-394-80025-7; In Canada: Random House, 1962. 64p. col. ill. (I can read it all by myself).

Robert is a horse whose allergy to roses is expressed by violent, destructive sneezes. Advised to seek work in the city, his allergy costs him two jobs before finding work as a police horse. When he sniffs a rose to flatten would-be robbers with a sneeze he becomes a hero. Children like the humor of the story which most can read independently.
SUBJ: Horses--Fiction./ Allergy--Fiction.

CE

Ph-2 P-2/6 $14.95 L KF697
HEINE, HELME. Pigs' wedding. McElderry ISBN 0-689-50409-8, c1978, 1986. unp. col. ill.

Smoke signal invitations to the wedding of Porker and Curlytail bring a host of smelly guests who are then bathed and dressed appropriately in painted-on clothes. The double-paged-spread water color illustrations reenforce the humor of the celebration. Fun to share with a group.
SUBJ: Pigs--Fiction./ Weddings--Fiction./ Humorous stories.

Ph-2 2-3/3 $14.95 L KF698
HELLDORFER, MARY CLAIRE. Mapmaker's daughter. Illus. by Jonathan Hunt. Bradbury ISBN 0-02-743515-6; In Canada: Collier Macmillan, 1991. unp. col. ill.

Suchen, the mapmaker's daughter, gives the prince a map to Turnings, an enchanted place from which no one has returned. When her father is arrested, Suchen offers to go after the prince and sets off on a journey fraught with danger. Richly colored watercolors place the original fairy tale in a Mideastern setting, with details that will appeal to fans of this genre.
SUBJ: Fairy tales.

Ph-2 P-1/2 $15.93 L KF699
HELLER, NICHOLAS. This little piggy. Illus. by Sonja Lamut. Greenwillow ISBN 0-688-15175-2; In Canada: Hearst Book Group, 1997. unp. col. ill.

Donald's grandmother elaborates on the story of the five little piggies to include details about what each piggy did and how they were connected. The omission of the lyrics of the original rhyme "This little piggy went to market" unfortunately lessens the utility of the book. The attractive illustrations and slightly comical expressions are a fun extension for the nursery rhyme.
SUBJ: Bedtime--Fiction./ Grandmothers--Fiction./ Pigs--Fiction./ Finger play.

Ph-1 K-2/2 $15.99 T KF700
HENDERSON, KATHY. Year in the city. Illus. by Paul Howard. Candlewick ISBN 1-56402-872-0; In Canada: Candlewick/dist. by Douglas & McIntyre, 1996. unp. col. ill.

January through December in the city there's always something happening. Full-page watercolor and crayon illustrations show the hustle and bustle of urban life through the months and seasons. The pages of text contain thumbnail sketches with more small details, and changing background colors reflect the seasons. A thorough introduction to the months of the year and city life.
SUBJ: City and town life--Fiction./ Seasons--Fiction./ Months--Fiction.

Ph-1 P/2 $14.93 L KF701
HENKES, KEVIN. Biggest boy. Illus. by Nancy Tafuri. Greenwillow ISBN 0-688-12830-0, 1995. unp. col. ill.

Young Billy is getting bigger every day. Soon he'll wear the house like a jacket and the moon as a mustache. Expansive watercolor illustrations and the large format suit the exaggerated growth of Billy. The very young (and small) will relate to Billy's dreams of being giant-sized.
SUBJ: Size--Fiction./ Growth--Fiction.

Ph-1 K-2/5 $13.93 L KF702
HENKES, KEVIN. Chester's way. Greenwillow ISBN 0-688-07608-4, 1988. unp. col. ill.

Available from National Library Service for the Blind and Physically Handicapped on sound recording cassette RC31330.
Alike as two peas in a pod, very conservative best friends Chester and Wilson do everything alike until, bold daring Lilly comes to town. At first resisting her attempts at friendship they do become a threesome and she adopts some of their rigid habits and they some of her high flying ways. And at the end Victor moves into the neighborhood. A fun way to learn the value of accepting individual differences.
SUBJ: Friendship--Fiction./ Individuality--Fiction.

Ph-1 K-2/2 $13.95 T KF703
HENKES, KEVIN. Chrysanthemum. Greenwillow ISBN 0-688-09699-9, 1991. unp. col. ill.

Available from the National Library Service for the Blind and Physically Handicapped on sound recording cassette RC 37639. Chrysanthemum loves her name until she starts school and the other students tease her about it. Chrysanthemum may be a mouse, but children will relate to her dilemma. The watercolor and pen illustrations sparkle with personality.
SUBJ: Names, Personal--Fiction./ Schools--Fiction.

Ph-2 P-2/2 $14.93 L KF704
HENKES, KEVIN. Good-bye, Curtis. Illus. by Marisabina Russo. Greenwillow ISBN 0-688-12828-9, 1995. unp. col. ill.

Retiring after 42 years as a letter carrier, Curtis finds treats and memories along his route and a surprise party at the last address. Boldly colored illustrations against a white background have lots of child appeal. Appropriate for units on community helpers and letter writing.
SUBJ: Postal service--Letter carriers--Fiction./ Occupations--Fiction./ Retirement--Fiction.

Ph-2 P-2/2 $14.88 L KF705
HENKES, KEVIN. Grandpa and Bo. Greenwillow ISBN 0-688-04957-5, 1986. unp. col. ill.

Spending the summer in the country with Grandpa, Bo learns about birds, flowers, grasses, insects, trees, fish, snakes and algae; also how to weave a willow basket and carve soap figures. Though a quiet and sensitive picture of a young boy sharing time with his grandfather, there is also humor. Neatly framed soft pencil drawings enhance the low-keyed affectionate story.
SUBJ: Grandfathers--Fiction.

Ph-2 K-1/2 $11.93 L KF706
HENKES, KEVIN. Jessica. Greenwillow ISBN 0-688-07830-3, 1989. unp. col. ill.

Even though Ruthie's parents keep saying there's no Jessica the little girl ignores them. Brief but active text is paired with exuberant pictures. Youngsters who've had imaginary playmates themselves will enjoy this.
SUBJ: Imaginary playmates--Fiction.

Ph-1 K-3/2 $14.93 L KF707

HENKES, KEVIN. Julius, the baby of the world. Greenwillow ISBN 0-688-08944-5, 1990. unp. col. ill.

Selectors' Choice, 18th ed.

Lilly spends more time than usual in the "uncooperative chair" after the birth of her baby brother, Julius, whom her parents think is "the baby of the world" and Lilly thinks is "disgusting." Lilly and her family are mice but their emotions and behavior are endearingly human and will be recognized by siblings everywhere. The text and illustrations abound with humor and youngsters will take Lilly and her antics to heart.

SUBJ: Babies--Fiction./ Brothers and sisters--Fiction./ Sibling rivalry--Fiction.

Ph-1 K-2/2 $15.93 L KF708

HENKES, KEVIN. Lilly's purple plastic purse. Greenwillow ISBN 0-688-12898-X, 1996. unp. col. ill.

Selectors' Choice, 21st ed.

Lilly loves school and her teacher, Mr. Slinger, until he takes away her musical purple plastic purse, her three shiny quarters, and her movie star sunglasses. She writes him a mean letter which she soon regrets until the next day when the two reach an understanding and all is forgiven. The irrepressible Lilly stars in a story that will wow her young fans with her humor and determination. The illustrations are filled with emotional expression and lead the reader to forget these rodents aren't human.

SUBJ: Schools--Fiction./ Teachers--Fiction.

Ph-1 P-2/2 $15.93 L KF709

HENKES, KEVIN. Owen. Greenwillow ISBN 0-688-11450-4, 1993. unp. col. ill.

Caldecott Honor book, 1994.

Owen loves his fuzzy yellow blanket with all of his heart, and his parents' attempts and a nosey neighbor's suggestions for breaking the attachment are futile until his mother finds the perfect solution. The story is universal in appeal, and the illustrations of the mouse family are touchingly human.

SUBJ: Blankets--Fiction./ Parent and child--Fiction.

VCR Ph-1 P-2 $49.95 OD KF710

HENKES, KEVIN. Owen (Videocassette). Narrated by Sarah Jessica Parker. Music by Ernest Troost. Weston Woods HMPV358V ISBN 0-78820-704-0, 1995. 1/2" VHS videocassette color (13min).

Includes teacher's guide.

Includes public performance rights.

ALA Notable Video, 1996.

Andrew Carnegie Medal, 1996.

Owen's devotion to his blanket and his parents and other people's attempts to break the bond are superbly relayed in this narrated version.

SUBJ: Blankets--Fiction./ Parent and child--Fiction.

Ph-1 P-2/4 $13.93 L KF711

HENKES, KEVIN. Sheila Rae, the brave. Greenwillow ISBN 0-688-07156-2, 1987. unp. col. ill.

Fearless Sheila Rae thinks her little sister is a scaredy-cat until the day Sheila Rae gets lost and it is spunky, little Louise that finds their way home and proves that she's a brave, fearless little mouse too. Humorous, expressive illustrations contribute to the appeal.

SUBJ: Sisters--Fiction./ Courage--Fiction.

Ph-1 P-2/2 $13.88 L KF712

HENKES, KEVIN. Weekend with Wendell. Greenwillow ISBN 0-688-06326-8, 1986. unp. col. ill.

Spending the weekend at Sophie's house, Wendell is a real pest and a rotten guest and Sophie can't wait until he goes home. Before the weekend is over she does get even, but after he goes home Sophie wishes naughty Wendell would come back soon. Soft, attractive watercolors amplify the appealing story.

SUBJ: Play--Fiction.

Ph-1 P-1/3 $13.95 L KF713

HENNESSY, B. G. School days. Illus. by Tracey Campbell Pearson. Viking/Penguin ISBN 0-670-83025-9; In Canada: Penguin, 1990. unp. col. ill.

Youngsters will find much to identify with in the lively illustrations and simple text that outlines a typical school day for early elementary grades. A useful introduction for those starting or anticipating the beginning of school.

SUBJ: Schools--Fiction./ Stories in rhyme.

Ph-2 K-1/2 $3.95 P KF714

HERMAN, R. A. Pal the pony. Illus. by Betina Ogden. Grosset & Dunlap ISBN 0-448-41257-8; In Canada: BeJo Sales, 1996. 32p. col. ill. (All aboard reading).

On the Star Ranch, the animals and cowboys all have important and exciting jobs to do. Pal the pony eventually discovers that he is just right for the young children to ride. Attractive and appropriate for beginning readers.

SUBJ: Ponies--Fiction./ Ranch life--Fiction./ Rodeos--Fiction./ Size--Fiction.

Ph-1 K-3/2 $15.93 L KF715

HEROLD, MAGGIE RUGG. Very important day. Illus. by Catherine Stock. Morrow ISBN 0-688-13066-6, 1995. unp. col. ill.

Includes glossary.

Available from the National Library Service for the Blind and Physically Handicapped on sound recording cassette RC 42567.

As snow falls in New York City, families from around the world travel to the courthouse to take an oath and become citizens of the United States. Watercolor illustrations portray the pride and joy of the naturalized citizens. A note follows which explains the process. Children who are citizens may gain an appreciation of what they have, and new citizens or immigrants may see their own striving reflected in the story. Useful for social studies units on citizenship.

SUBJ: Naturalization--Fiction./ Emigration and immigration--Fiction./ New York (N.Y.)--Fiction.

Ph-1 1-3/3 $13.99 L KF716

HESSE, KAREN. Lester's dog. Illus. by Nancy Carpenter. Crown ISBN 0-517-58358-5, 1993. unp. col. ill.

Available from the National Library Service for the Blind and Physically Handicapped on sound recording cassette RC 38552.

A young narrative voice colorfully describes the sights and sounds of his neighborhood, his friendship with Corey who is deaf, and their adventure rescuing a kitten and getting it past Lester's fierce dog.

SUBJ: Dogs--Fiction./ Fear--Fiction.

Ph-2 P-K/1 $16.99 T KF717

HEST, AMY. Baby Duck and the bad eyeglasses. Illus. by Jill Barton. Candlewick ISBN 1-56402-680-9; In Canada: Candlewick/dist. by Douglas & McIntyre, 1996. unp. col. ill.

Baby Duck isn't happy with her new eyeglasses until Grampa shows her how much she can see and enjoy with them. The large format and cheery illustrations are perfect for sharing with a group. For reading aloud.

SUBJ: Ducks--Fiction./ Eyeglasses--Fiction./ Grandfathers--Fiction.

Ph-2 P-1/2 $16.95 T KF718

HEST, AMY. In the rain with Baby Duck. Illus. by Jill Barton. Candlewick ISBN 1-56402-532-2; In Canada: Candlewick/dist. by Douglas & McIntyre, 1995. unp. col. ill.

Baby Duck doesn't enjoy the wet walk in the rain to Grampa's house for pancakes. When Grampa gives her boots and a matching umbrella, Baby Duck is ready to enjoy the rain. Large, endearing watercolor and pencil illustrations extend the appeal for reading aloud at storytime.

SUBJ: Rain and rainfall--Fiction./ Ducks--Fiction./ Grandfathers--Fiction.

Ph-1 K-2/2 $15.99 T KF719

HEST, AMY. Jamaica Louise James. Illus. by Sheila White Samton. Candlewick ISBN 1-56402-348-6; In Canada: Candlewick/dist. by Douglas & McIntyre, 1996. unp. col. ill.

Jamaica Louise, age eight, brightens the dreary walls of a subway station when she gets the clever idea to hang her paintings there. The text vibrates with the enthusiasm of the young narrator, and the lively gouache and acrylic illustrations provide a positive view of life in the city. For multicultural studies.

SUBJ: Painting--Fiction./ Birthdays--Fiction./ Afro-Americans--Fiction./ Subways--Fiction.

Ph-2 1-3/4 $14.93 L KF720

HEST, AMY. Nana's birthday party. Illus. by Amy Schwartz. Morrow ISBN 0-688-07498-7, 1993. unp. col. ill.

Nana's birthday parties are gala occasions especially for the two cousins Maggie and Brett, who get to sleep over the night before the party. The rule "no presents, except the kind you make yourself" inspires them to collaborate on a gift that showcases their unique talents.

SUBJ: Grandmothers--Fiction./ Cousins--Fiction./ Authors--Fiction./ Artists--Fiction./ Birthdays--Fiction.

Ph-2 K-3/4 $13.95 L KF721

HEST, AMY. Purple coat. Illus. by Amy Schwartz. Four Winds/Macmillan ISBN 0-02-743640-3; In Canada: Collier Macmillan, 1986. unp. col. ill.

Riding the train from the suburbs, changing to a noisy subway, and then going up in a crowded elevator, a little girl and her mother finally reach Grandpa's tailoring shop on the twenty-eighth floor of a

tall building. It's the annual fitting for Gabrielle's new winter coat. As usual Mama insists on classic navy, but Gabby wants purple and it is wise old Grandpa who pleases both. The colorful and detailed pictures express a warm family relationship and give children a realistic view of city life and a tailor shop.
SUBJ: Coats--Fiction./ Grandfathers--Fiction.

Ph-1 P-1/2 $16.99   T   KF722
HEST, AMY. You're the boss, Baby Duck! Illus. by Jill Barton. Candlewick ISBN 1-56402-667-1; In Canada: Candlewick/dist. by Douglas & McIntyre, 1997. unp. col. ill.
Baby Duck may no longer be the baby in the family now that there's Hot Stuff, a new sibling, but she learns that being oldest has some advantages including being the boss. The bright, large format continues to deliver lots of appeal for young readers and listeners.
SUBJ: Ducks--Fiction./ Babies--Fiction./ Grandfathers--Fiction.

Ph-2 P-K/7 $4.95   P   KF723
HEYWARD, DU BOSE. Country bunny and the little gold shoes, as told to Jenifer. Illus. by Marjorie Flack. Houghton Mifflin ISBN 0-395-18557-2, c1939. unp. col. ill.
Available from National Library Service for the Blind and Physically Handicapped in Braille BRA06624.
Cottontail finds a way to become one of the five specially chosen Easter bunnies even though she is the mother of 21 children.
SUBJ: Rabbits--Fiction./ Easter--Fiction.

Ph-2 1-3/6 $15.95   T   KF724
HICKOX, REBECCA. Per and the Dala horse. Illus. by Yvonne Gilbert. Doubleday ISBN 0-385-32075-2; In Canada: Bantam Doubleday Dell, 1995. unp. col. ill.
Per, the youngest of three brothers, and his toy wooden horse succeed where his brothers have failed and retrieve the church's gold communion cup from the trolls. Folklore elements and a Swedish influence are evident in the story and the colored-pencil illustrations.
SUBJ: Fairy tales./ Trolls--Fiction./ Brothers--Fiction./ Sweden--Fiction./ Horses--Fiction.

Ph-2 K-2/4 $11.95   T   KF725
HIDAKA, MASAKO. Girl from the snow country. Translated by Amanda Mayer Stinchecum. Kane/Miller ISBN 0-916291-06-5, 1986. unp. col. ill.
Mi-chan plays in the snow drifts and makes many snow bunnies using camelia leaves for ears but has nothing for eyes. Accompanying her mother to the village market, she finds just the right thing when the flower lady gives her a branch covered with red berries and now her snow bunnies can have red eyes. Large attractive watercolors enhance the oriental setting. May be used as an introduction to Japan and life and customs in small Japanese villages.
SUBJ: Snow--Fiction./ Japan--Fiction.

Ph-1 1-3/2 $13.00   T   KF726
HIGHTOWER, SUSAN. Twelve snails to one lizard: a tale of mischief and measurement. Illus. by Matt Novak. Simon & Schuster ISBN 0-689-80452-0; In Canada: Distican, 1997. unp. col. ill.
Milo, the beaver, needs 36 inches to bridge the hole in his dam and enlists the help of Bubba, the frog, who suggests that he use 36 snails, 3 lizards, or one sinister snake to measure the distance. Comic illustrations add to the fun in this introduction to measurement for math classes.
SUBJ: Measurement--Fiction./ Frogs--Fiction./ Beavers--Fiction.

Ph-1 K-2/2 $13.00   L   KF727
HILL, ELIZABETH STARR. Evan's corner. Illus. by Sandra Speidel. Viking/Penguin ISBN 0-670-82830-0; In Canada: Penguin, c1967, 1991. unp. col. ill.
Evan, who lives with his mother, father, and five brothers and sisters in a two room Harlem flat, longs for privacy and a place of his own. Evan's understanding mother has a fine idea and suggests that each member of the family choose for his very own, one of the eight corners of the flat. Evan works hard to fix up his corner and finds the joy of sharing and helping others when he helps his little brother, Adam, fix up his corner, too. Reissued with new illustrations, this story will appeal to strong independent readers or can be used as a longer read-aloud. For multicultural studies.
SUBJ: Family life--Fiction./ Apartment houses--Fiction./ Afro-Americans--Fiction.

Ph-3 P-2/2 $12.95   T   KF728
HILL, ERIC. Where's Spot? Sign language edition. Putnam ISBN 0-399-21478-X, 1987. unp. col. ill.
Available in Vietnamese language, KI CON DAU ROI NHI, from William Heinemann in London.
The first "lift the flap Spot" story introducing the appealing young puppy is reissued with a Signed English translation accompanying the original text. Should provide satisfaction not only for hearing impaired but for all children.
SUBJ: Hide-and-seek--Fiction./ Sign language--Fiction./ Vietnamese language materials.

Ph-2 1-3/1 $8.98   L   KF729
HIMMELMAN, JOHN. Day-off machine. Silver Press/Silver Burdett ISBN 0-671-69635-1, 1990. 44p. col. ill. (Silver seedling easy reader).
No one will play in the snow with Graham until he convinces his busy beaver family to take two days off. Youngsters will chuckle to themselves as they read this title and THE GREAT LEAF BLAST-OFF (ISBN 0-671-69634-3, 1990); THE SUPER CAMPER CAPER (ISBN 0-671-69636-X, 1991); and THE CLOVER COUNTY CARROT CONTEST (ISBN 0-671-69637-8, 1991).
SUBJ: Beavers--Fiction./ Inventors--Fiction./ Family life--Fiction./ Snow--Fiction.

Ph-2 K-2/3 $14.93   L   KF730
HINES, ANNA GROSSNICKLE. What Joe saw. Greenwillow ISBN 0-688-13124-7, 1994. unp. col. ill.
Joe is the slowest in his class because he lingers behind, and no one sees what he sees: birds, a frog, and a turtle. Until one day, Pete stops to tie his shoe and calls attention to the newly hatched ducks Joe has discovered. Lush watercolor and colored pencil illustrations depict the wildlife that is visible to those who take the time to look.
SUBJ: Nature--Fiction.

CE   Ph-2 K-2/2 $3.50   P   KF731
HOBAN, JULIA. Buzby. Illus. by John Himmelman. HarperCollins ISBN 0-06-444152-0, 1992. 64p. col. ill. (I can read book).
Read-along kit available from HarperChildren's Audio (ISBN 0-69470-044-4, 1996). 1 paperback book, 1 sound cassette (14min), $7.95.
Buzby, a young cat, gets a job at a hotel as a bus boy, and while he doesn't do that job very well, he does make the customers happy and so is given a new job as the hotel cat. An easily read story told with humor and bright illustrations.
SUBJ: Cats--Fiction./ Work--Fiction./ Hotels, motels, etc.--Fiction.

Ph-2 K-2/2 $3.50   P   KF732
HOBAN, JULIA. Buzby to the rescue. Illus. by John Himmelman. HarperCollins ISBN 0-06-444184-9; In Canada: HarperCollins, 1995. 64p. col. ill. (I can read book).
Sequel to BUZBY, 1990.
Buzby helps Serena Lovejoy, the movie star, find her missing ruby.
SUBJ: Cats--Fiction./ Hotels, motels, etc.--Fiction./ Mystery and detective stories.

Ph-1 1-3/2 $14.89   L   KF733
HOBAN, LILLIAN. Arthur's funny money. HarperCollins ISBN 0-06-022344-8; In Canada: HarperCollins, 1981. 64p. col. ill. (I can read book).
Selectors' Choice, 14th ed.
Arthur and Violet team up to raise enough money to buy Arthur a T-shirt and cap. This creative story will be useful to teachers looking for inventive ways to introduce young readers to business concepts.
SUBJ: Moneymaking projects--Fiction./ Chimpanzees--Fiction./ Brothers and sisters--Fiction.

CE   Ph-1 1-3/2 $14.89   L   KF734
HOBAN, LILLIAN. Arthur's honey bear. HarperCollins ISBN 0-06-022370-7, c1964. 62p. col. ill. (I can read book).
Read-along kit available from HarperAudio (ISBN 1-55995-219-3, 1986). 1 paperback book, 1 sound cassette (17min) $7.95.
Available from National Library Service for the Blind and Physically Handicapped in Braille BR02662.
When Arthur cleans out his toy chest, he decides to have a "tag" sale and get rid of all his old treasures. With the help of his little sister, Violet, everything is marked and priced except his old teddy bear. He knows he is too old for it, but he just can't quite part with Honey Bear. His solution is quite ingenious, and Arthur finds great satisfaction in becoming Honey Bear's uncle.
ARTHUR'S CHRISTMAS COOKIES (ISBN 0-06-022368-5, 1972).
ARTHUR'S HALLOWEEN COSTUME (ISBN 0-06-022391-X, 1984; available from the NLSBPH in Braille BR07092).
ARTHUR'S LOOSE TOOTH (ISBN 0-06-022354-5, 1985; available from the NLSBPH in Braille BR06768).
ARTHUR'S GREAT BIG VALENTINE (ISBN 0-06-022407-X, 1989).
ARTHUR'S PRIZE READER (ISBN 0-06-022380-4, 1978; read-along kit available from HarperAudio ISBN 1-55994-220-7, 1985; available from the NLSBPH in Braille BR04679.).
ARTHUR'S CAMP OUT (ISBN 0-06-020526-1, 1993; read-along kit available from HarperChildren's Audio ISBN 0-69470-040-1, 1996).
SUBJ: Brothers and sisters--Fiction./ Toys--Fiction./ Chimpanzees--Fiction.

Ph-1 1-3/2 $14.89   L   KF735

HOBAN, LILLIAN. Arthur's pen pal. HarperCollins ISBN 0-06-022372-3;
In Canada: HarperCollins, c1976. 62p. col. ill.
Selectors' Choice, 11th ed.
Available from the National Library Service for the Blind and
Physically handicapped on Braille BR03332.
Arthur must change his attitude towards his sister when he discovers
that the pen pal he admires is really a girl.
SUBJ: Pen pals--Fiction./ Brothers and sisters--Fiction./ Chimpanzees--
Fiction.

BB   Ph-2 P/1 $5.95   T   KF736

HOBAN, LILLIAN. Big little otter (Board book). HarperFestival ISBN
0-694-00850-8; In Canada: HarperCollins, 1997. unp. col. ill.
Baby Otter wants to swim and splash and fish for supper to show his
mother that he is a big otter. The very short book in a board book
format has a simple text and endearing illustrations.
SUBJ: Otters--Fiction./ Self-confidence--Fiction.

Ph-2 K-2/1 $3.75   P   KF737

HOBAN, LILLIAN. Case of the two masked robbers. HarperCollins ISBN
0-06-444121-0, 1988. 62p. col. ill. (I can read book).
Sneaking out of bed the raccoon twins, Arabella and Albert,
encounter scary, frightening night noises and animals before finding
the culprits who had stolen Mrs. Turtle's eggs from the Meadow
Marsh Bank. Easy reading, just enough suspense, and a surprise
ending make this popular with beginning readers.
SUBJ: Raccoons--Fiction./ Animals--Fiction./ Twins--Fiction./ Mystery
and detective stories.

Ph-2 K-2/2 $13.89   L   KF738

HOBAN, LILLIAN. Silly Tilly's Thanksgiving dinner. HarperCollins ISBN
0-06-022423-1, 1990. 63p. col. ill. (I can read book).
Tilly Mole gets mixed-up when her glasses are smudged and sends
out recipes instead of invitations for Thanksgiving dinner. Her friends
show up anyway and bring the food which Silly Tilly has forgotten to
prepare. Beginning readers will enjoy the antics of Tilly in this and
SILLY TILLY AND THE EASTER BUNNY (ISBN 0-06-022392-8,
1987).
SUBJ: Thanksgiving Day--Fiction./ Moles (Animals)--Fiction./ Animals-
-Fiction.

CE   Ph-1 P-1/2 $14.89   T   KF739

HOBAN, RUSSELL. Bedtime for Frances. Newly ill. ed. Illus. by Garth
Williams. HarperCollins ISBN 0-06-027107-8; In Canada: HarperCollins,
1995. 31p. col. ill.
Spanish edition LA HORA DE ACOSTARSE DE FRANCISCA
available from Harper Arco Iris (ISBN 0-06-025442-4, 1996).
A badger acts like a child as she tries to put off going to bed.
In the other stories about Frances illustrated by Lillian Hoban, BABY
SISTER FOR FRANCES. Newly ill. ed. (ISBN 0-06-022336-7, 1993,
read-along kit available from HarperChildren's Audio ISBN 0-694-
70018-5, 1977. 1 paperback book, 1 sound cassette (16min), $7.95.
Spanish version LA NUEVA HERMANITA DE FRANCISCA available
from Harper Arco Iris ISBN 0-06-443461-3, 1997); BREAD AND
JAM FOR FRANCES. Newly ill. ed. (ISBN 0-06-022360-X, 1993,
Spanish version PAN Y MERMELADA PARA FRANCISCA available
from Harper Arco Iris ISBN 0-06-025328-2, 1995, big book ISBN
0-06-443336-6, 1993); BEST FRIENDS FOR FRANCES. Newly ill. ed.
(ISBN 0-06-022328-6, 1994); and BARGAIN FOR FRANCES. Newly
ill. ed. (ISBN 0-06-022330-8, 1992, Spanish version EL GRAN
NEGOCIO DE FRANCISCA available from Harper Arco Iris ISBN
0-06-444196-2, 1996), the little badger deals with other typical
childhood situations.
Available from NLSBPH are: BREAD AND JAM FOR FRANCES in
Braille BRA05239; BEST FRIENDS FOR FRANCES as talking book
TB02980; BARGAIN FOR FRANCES on sound recording cassette
RC23569 and as talking book TB04011; BABY SISTER FOR
FRANCES on sound recording cassette RC 38623.
SUBJ: Badgers--Fiction./ Bedtime--Fiction./ Fear of the dark--Fiction./
Spanish language materials.

Ph-3 P-1/2 $15.00   T   KF740

HOBAN, RUSSELL. Birthday for Frances. Illus. by Lillian Hoban.
HarperCollins ISBN 0-06-022338-3; In Canada: HarperCollins, c1968,
1995. 32p. col. ill.
Frances, that popular badger child, is so jealous of her younger sister
that she refuses to help with the preparations for Gloria's birthday
party. A wise mother and a supportive father help Frances understand
the struggle within herself, so that she is able to gracefully accept the
fact that Gloria is the birthday girl today.
SUBJ: Birthdays--Fiction./ Badgers--Fiction./ Behavior--Fiction.

Ph-1 P $14.95   L   KF741

HOBAN, TANA. Count and see. Macmillan ISBN 0-02-744800-2, c1972.
unp. col. ill.
Objects, familiar to children, are creatively photographed in this
effective counting book. Full page photographs clearly display the
appropriate number of things: one hydrant, three school busses, five
trashcans, 12 eggs, 20 watermelon seeds still in the slice and 100
peas, ten to a pod.
SUBJ: Counting.

Ph-3 P-1 $18.00   T   KF742

HOBAN, TANA. Is it rough? Is it smooth? Is it shiny? Greenwillow ISBN
0-688-03823-9, 1984. unp. col. ill.
Look at fish, balls of cotton, a whole myriad of things and think
about how they feel. The series of striking photographs should
provoke considerable comment from the very youngest children.
SUBJ: Textures--Pictorial works.

Ph-2 P-1 $13.93   L   KF743

HOBAN, TANA. Look up, look down. Greenwillow ISBN 0-688-10578-
5, 1992. unp col photos.
An engaging collection of color photographs invite the viewer to look
above at skyscrapers and trees and below at ants and bird prints in
the sand. A wonderful introduction to visual perception.
SUBJ: Visual perception.

Ph-2 P-K/1 $14.93   L   KF744

HOBAN, TANA. One little kitten. Greenwillow ISBN 0-688-84222-4,
1979. unp. ill.
Rhyming words and appealing black and white full paged
photographs show a little kitten exploring his surroundings. He tangles
a ball of string, pokes his head into a pair of sneakers, goes under a
big wheel, into a paper sack, behind a broom and finally back to his
mother and his supper.
SUBJ: Cats--Fiction./ Stories in rhyme.

Ph-2 P-K $15.00   L   KF745

HOBAN, TANA. Over, under and through, and other spatial concepts.
Macmillan ISBN 0-02-744820-7, 1973. unp. ill.
Engaging black and white photographs of children and scenes
illustrate the spatial concepts of over, under, through, on, in, around,
across, between, beside, below, against and behind.
SUBJ: Space perception./ Vocabulary./ Concepts.

Ph-2 P-K $13.95   L   KF746

HOBAN, TANA. Push, pull, empty, full: a book of opposites. Macmillan
ISBN 0-02-744820-7, c1972. unp b&w photos.
Clear, large and excellent black and white photographs illustrate a
simple book designed to help young children distinguish the basic
concept of the meaning of opposites.
SUBJ: Concepts./ English language--Synonyms and antonyms.

Ph-1 P-K/1 $13.95   L   KF747

HOBAN, TANA. Where is it? Macmillan ISBN 0-02-744070-2, c1972.
unp. ill.
Over rocks, through grass, flowers and clover, an appealing rabbit
runs and hops searching for something. Where is it? Behind a tree he
finds a special treat, an Easter basket filled with cabbage and carrots.
Outstanding black and white photographs and a brief text tell the
simple story.
SUBJ: Easter--Fiction./ Rabbits--Fiction./ Stories in rhyme.

Ph-1 P-2 $14.93   L   KF748

HOBAN, TANA. 26 letters and 99 cents. Greenwillow ISBN 0-688-
06362-4, 1987. unp. col. ill.
Selectors' Choice, 16th ed.
Combines an alphabet book with one about counting and coins to
produce two handsome books in one. Letters are shown in both upper
and lower case with familiar objects illustrating each. Combinations of
coins are used to count from one to twenty, by fives to fifty, by tens
to ninety and then a combination to make ninety-nine. In many cases
more than one example is given, i.e. seven pennies as well as a nickel
and two pennies are shown to equal seven cents and four nickels as
well as two dimes are shown for twenty cents. Both books are
illustrated with superb, appealing color photographs.
SUBJ: Alphabet./ Counting./ Coins.

Ph-2 P-2/2 $14.00   L   KF749

HOBSON, SALLY. Chicken Little. Simon & Schuster ISBN 0-671-89548-
6; In Canada: Simon & Schuster, 1994. unp. col. ill.
Chicken Little mistakes an acorn for the falling sky and convinces
several birds to follow him to tell the king. They end up in Foxy
Loxy's lair. The repetitive and straightforward text, just right for
reading aloud, is accompanied by striking color illustrations.
Predictable text encourages audience participation.
SUBJ: Animals--Fiction./ Foxes--Fiction./ Poultry--Fiction.

Ph-2 K-2/2 $13.95 L KF750
HOFF, SYD. Arturo's baton. Clarion ISBN 0-395-71020-0, 1995. 32p. col. ill.
 Arturo believes he must have his special baton to conduct beautiful music, but one night when he goes on without it, he discovers he only needs his hands. Conveys a clear message about talent in a satisfying story for youngsters discovering their own gifts.
 SUBJ: Conducting--Fiction.

Ph-2 K-2/1 $15.89 L KF751
HOFF, SYD. Barkley. HarperCollins ISBN 0-06-022448-7, c1975. 32p. col. ill. (Early I can read book).
 Available from National Library Service for the Blind and Physically Handicapped in Braille BR03639.
 When Barkley, an aging circus dog, gets too old to perform, he decides he is useless and runs away. He does tricks for some admiring children who take him back to the circus. Then Barkley discovers that he really is needed to teach tricks to the younger dogs.
 SUBJ: Dogs--Fiction./ Circus--Fiction.

Ph-2 K-2/2 $15.89 L KF752
HOFF, SYD. Captain Cat: story and pictures. HarperCollins ISBN 0-06-020528-8; In Canada: HarperCollins, 1993. 46p. col. ill. (I can read book).
 Captain Cat has more stripes than the soldiers have ever seen. As he joins them in their routines, he becomes a best friend of one soldier named Pete. Appealing, easy-to-read story for beginning readers.
 SUBJ: Cats--Fiction./ United States. Army--Fiction.

CE
Ph-1 K-2/2 $12.89 L KF753
HOFF, SYD. Danny and the dinosaur. HarperCollins ISBN 0-06-022466-5, c1958. 64p. col. ill. (I can read book).
 Available from National Library Service for the Blind and Physically Handicapped in Braille BRA07197.
 Read-along kit available from HarperAudio/Caedmon (ISBN 1-55994-226-6, 1985). 1 sound cassette (11min), 1 paperback book, $7.95.
 Danny goes to a museum, makes friends with a gigantic dinosaur, and shows him around the town.
 SUBJ: Dinosaurs--Fiction./ Spanish language materials.

Ph-2 K-2/2 $14.89 L KF754
HOFF, SYD. Danny and the dinosaur go to camp. HarperCollins ISBN 0-06-026440-3; In Canada: HarperCollins, 1996. 32p. col. ill. (I can read book).
 When the dinosaur accompanies Danny to camp, he joins the children for sports, meals, and hikes; but he can't get comfortable sleeping in the cabins. Fans of this dinosaur will appreciate this easy-to-read story.
 SUBJ: Dinosaurs--Fiction./ Camps--Fiction.

Ph-1 K-2/2 $13.89 L KF755
HOFF, SYD. Grizzwold. HarperCollins ISBN 0-06-022481-9, c1963. 64p. col. ill. (I can read book).
 An enormous, likeable bear searches for a new home after lumbermen destroy his forest haven.
 SUBJ: Bears--Fiction.

Ph-2 K-1/2 $14.89 L KF756
HOFF, SYD. Happy birthday, Danny and the dinosaur! HarperCollins ISBN 0-06-026438-1; In Canada: HarperCollins, 1995. 32p. col. ill. (I can read book).
 Danny invites his friend the dinosaur to his birthday party. The antics of the friendly dinosaur will appeal to beginning readers who can succeed with the easy-to-read text.
 SUBJ: Dinosaurs--Fiction./ Birthdays--Fiction.

Ph-2 K-2/2 $13.89 L KF757
HOFF, SYD. Horse in Harry's room. HarperCollins ISBN 0-06-022483-5, c1970. 32p. col. ill. (Early I can read book).
 Harry insists that he has a horse in his room, but neither his mother nor his father can see it. After a trip to a farm, Harry realizes that "horses should always be free to run and kick and nibble." So, sadly, Harry offers to let his horse go free. Then Harry's horse looks to the left and to the right and just stays right where he is--in Harry's room.
 SUBJ: Imagination--Fiction./ Horses--Fiction.

Ph-1 K-1/1 $13.89 L KF758
HOFF, SYD. Julius. HarperCollins ISBN 0-06-022491-6, c1959. 64p. col. ill. (I can read book).
 Available from National Library Service for the Blind and Physically Handicapped in Braille BRA06637.
 A circus gorilla scares away the people who have come to see him, and when he tries to find them, he gets lost himself.
 SUBJ: Circus--Fiction./ Gorilla--Fiction.

Ph-2 K-2/2 $14.00 L KF759
HOFF, SYD. Mrs. Brice's mice. HarperCollins ISBN 0-06-022452-5; In Canada: HarperCollins, 1988. 32p. col. ill.
 Mrs. Brice has twenty-five mice and twenty-four of them do everything she does, but the very small mouse does most everything differently. Easy-to-read and humorous pictures of child appealing slapstick silliness guarantee popularity.
 SUBJ: Mice--Fiction./ Humorous stories.

Ph-1 K-1/1 $13.89 L KF760
HOFF, SYD. Who will be my friends? HarperCollins ISBN 0-06-022556-4, c1960. 32p. col. ill. (Early I can read book).
 How Freddy moves to a new home and finds new friends.
 SUBJ: Friendship--Fiction.

CE
Ph-1 P-2/4 $14.00 T KF761
HOFFMAN, MARY. Amazing Grace. Illus. by Caroline Binch. Dial ISBN 0-8037-1040-2, 1991. unp. col. ill.
 Selectors' Choice, 19th ed.
 Videocassette available from Weston Woods HMPV354V (ISBN 1-56008-251-8, 1994). 1/2" VHS iconographic videocassette color (10min), $49.95.
 Videocassette available from AIMS Media WW354FE1, 1996. 1/2" VHS videocassette color (10min), $49.95.
 Spanish version available ASOMBROSA GRACIELA (ISBN 0-8037-1938-8, 1996).
 Grace loves stories, especially acting them out, and she longs to be Peter Pan in the class play. When a classmate tells her she can't because she's a girl and African American, Grace heeds her Nana's advice "You can be anything you want, if you put your mind to it," and she gets the part. Exuberant illustrations capture Grace's lively imagination and spirit. The many stories Grace loves and acts out may spur youngsters to read them. For multicultural studies.
 SUBJ: Afro-Americans--Fiction./ Identity--Fiction./ Theater--Fiction./ Spanish language materials.

Ph-1 1-3/5 $14.99 T KF762
HOFFMAN, MARY. Boundless Grace. Illus. by Caroline Binch. Dial ISBN 0-8037-1715-6, 1995. unp. col. ill.
 Sequel to AMAZING GRACE, Dial, 1991.
 Grace and Nana travel to Africa to visit Grace's father and his new wife and family. Grace, a very real and appealing character, struggles with stretching herself between two families as she explores a new country and the definition of family. Authentic, bold watercolor and pencil illustrations were researched during the artist's visits to Gambia. For multicultural studies.
 SUBJ: Stepfamilies--Fiction./ Afro-Americans--Fiction./ Africa--Fiction.

CE
Ph-1 P-2/5 $14.95 T KF763
HOGROGIAN, NONNY. One fine day. Macmillan ISBN 0-02-744000-1, c1971. unp. col. ill.
 Caldecott Medal Award.
 Available from National Library Service for the Blind and Physically Handicapped as talking book TB04463.
 Read-along kit available from Weston Woods PBC153, 1993. 1 paperback book, 1 sound cassette (11min), $12.95. Side one with page turn signal, side two without signal.
 Spanish version UN BUEN DIA available from Aladdin/Libros Colibri (ISBN 0-689-81414-3, 1997).
 A crisp retelling of an old Armenian cumulative tale about a fox who drinks the milk from the pail of an old woman who then cuts off his tail. He begs her to sew it back on, but she won't until he gives back the milk. He appeals to cow, meadow, water, peddler, hen, and others, each of whom ask a favor in return. At last the miller takes pity on the fox and gives him the grain which starts the chain of events required to restore the milk. The predictable book is excellent for reading aloud.
 SUBJ: Foxes--Fiction./ Spanish language materials.

Ph-1 P-2/5 $14.00 L KF764
HOLABIRD, KATHARINE. Angelina and the princess. Illus. by Helen Craig. Potter/dist. by Crown ISBN 0-517-55273-6; In Canada: General, 1984. unp. col. ill.
 After disobeying her mother, Angelina performs poorly in the ballet tryouts but she does rehearse very hard and learns not only her minor part but the leading roles too; and finally her disappointment turns to the pleasure of success. Angelina is introduced in an earlier book, ANGELINA BALLERINA (ISBN 0-517-55083-0, 1983). Delicate illustrations create a rather quaint and old fashioned appearance. More stories about Angelina follow in ANGELINA AT THE FAIR (ISBN 0-517-55744-4, 1985, OPC); ANGELINA'S CHRISTMAS (ISBN 0-517-55823-8, 1985) (Available from National Library Service for the Blind and Physically Handicapped in Braille BR06435 and on sound recording cassette RC23630); ANGELINA ON STAGE (ISBN 0-517-56073-9, 1986); ANGELINA AND ALICE (ISBN 0-517-

56074-7, 1987); ANGELINA'S BIRTHDAY SURPRISE (ISBN 0-517-57325-3, 1989); ANGELINA'S BABY SISTER (ISBN 0-517-58600-2, 1991); and ANGELINA ICE SKATES (ISBN 0-517-59619-9, 1993).
SUBJ: Mice--Fiction./ Ballet dancing--Fiction./ Dancers--Fiction.

TB　　　　　　　　　　　Ph-3 P-2　　$11.00　　　OD KF765
HOLABIRD, KATHARINE. Angelina Ballerina and other stories (Talking book). Performed by Sally Struthers. Music composed by Don Heckman. HarperCollins/Caedmon CP1790, 1986. 1 sound cassette (27min).
Based on the books of the same titles.
Contents: Angelina Ballerina (5min); Angelina and the princess (5min); Angelina at the fair (5min); Angelina's Christmas (6min); Angelina onstage (6min).
SUBJ: Mice--Fiction.

　　　　　　　　　　　Ph-2 1-3/6　　$16.95　　L　KF766
HONG, LILY TOY. Empress and the silkworm. Whitman ISBN 0-8075-2009-8; In Canada: General, 1995. unp. col. ill.
Available from the National Library Service for the Blind and Physically Handicapped on sound recording cassette RC 42943.
One day a cocoon falls from a mulberry tree into the teacup of the Empress Si Ling-Chi, who soon realizes the potential for the silken thread that unwinds from the cocoon. Based on a Chinese legend about the origin of silk, the story is followed by facts about the silk industry and trade. Has applications to units on insects, textiles, and China. For multicultural studies.
SUBJ: Silk--Fiction./ China--Fiction.

　　　　　　　　　　　Ph-2 K-2/2　　$13.95　　L　KF767
HOOKER, RUTH. Matthew the cowboy. Illus. by Cat Bowman Smith. Whitman ISBN 0-8075-4999-1; In Canada: General, 1990. unp. col. ill.
There's trouble at the Rocky 9 ranch and Matthew, a young cowboy, solves the mystery. A Western setting complete with rustlers, cowboys, and a likeable hero insure the book's appeal.
SUBJ: Cowboys--Fiction./ West (U.S.)--Fiction./ Imagination--Fiction.

　　　　　　　　　　　Ph-2 K-2/2　　$24.21　　L　KF768
HOOPER, MEREDITH. Cow, a bee, a cookie, and me. Illus. by Alison Bartlett. Kingfisher/dist. by Raintree Steck-Vaughn ISBN 0-7534-5067-4, 1997. unp. col. ill.
Making honey cookies, Ben and his grandmother talk about the cow, sugarcane, bees, hens, cinnamon bark, and wheat needed for the ingredients. Sunshine bright illustrations burst from the page, and the sweet recipe is included.
SUBJ: Cookies--Fiction./ Baking--Fiction./ Food--Fiction./ Grandmothers--Fiction.

　　　　　　　　　　　Ph-2 K-2/3　　$14.89　　L　KF769
HOOPES, LYN LITTLEFIED. Unbeatable bread. Illus. by Brad Sneed. Dial ISBN 0-8037-1612-5, 1996. unp. col. ill.
Uncle John is baking an unbeatable bread, but who will leave their warm, snowed-in houses to eat it? Uncle John doesn't care, and soon the fabulous aroma awakens children, animals, and bees with the magic promise of winter's end. The rhyming text casts a magic spell for reading aloud, and the aroma of baking bread almost becomes one of the characters in the dreamy illustrations.
SUBJ: Bread--Fiction./ Stories in rhyme.

　　　　　　　　　　　Ph-1 1-3/4　　$15.99　　L　KF770
HOPKINSON, DEBORAH. Sweet Clara and the freedom quilt. Illus. by James Ransome. Knopf ISBN 0-679-92311-X; In Canada: Random House, 1993. unp. col. ill.
Separated from her family, Sweet Clara, a slave, learns to sew from a woman she calls "Aunt Rachel" and gets a job working in the Big House. She stitches a quilt designed as a map to guide runaway slaves to the Underground Railroad. One night Sweet Clara and her friend Jack use the information she has learned while working on the quilt to escape to freedom.
SUBJ: Slavery--Fiction./ Quilts--Fiction.

　　　　　　　　　　　Ph-1 K-3/6　　$15.99　　T　KF771
HOUSTON, GLORIA. Year of the perfect Christmas tree. Illus. by Barbara Cooney. Dial ISBN 0-8037-0299-X; In Canada: Fitzhenry & Whiteside, 1988. unp. col. ill.
In 1918 Ruthie's mother says that they will provide the town's Christmas tree even though Papa hasn't come back from the war to cut it down from it's rocky crag. The tender tone of the story is enhanced by poignant oil paintings that shine with their own light. A superb Christmas story to be enjoyed aloud or silently.
SUBJ: Christmas--Fiction./ Christmas trees--Fiction./ Appalachian Region--Fiction./ World War, 1914-1918--United States--Fiction.

　　　　　　　　　　　Ph-1 1-3/2　　$15.95　　L　KF772
HOWARD, ELIZABETH FITZGERALD. Aunt Flossie's hats (and crab cakes later). Illus. by James Ransome. Clarion ISBN 0-395-54682-6, 1991. unp. col. ill.
Two sisters visit their great-aunt Flossie each Sunday and play with her many hats. Each hat has a story behind it including a big fire in Baltimore, a parade at the end of the War, and a day in the park when Aunt Flossie's hat had to be retrieved from the water by a dog. Colorful oil paintings add to the richness of the stories and sharing between the girls and their beloved great-aunt in the extended black family.
SUBJ: Hats--Fiction./ Great-aunts--Fiction./ Baltimore (Md.)--Fiction.

　　　　　　　　　　　Ph-2 2-4/5　　$14.95　　L　KF773
HOWARD, ELIZABETH FITZGERALD. Chita's Christmas tree. Illus. by Floyd Cooper. Bradbury ISBN 0-02-744621-2; In Canada: Collier Macmillan, 1989. unp. col. ill.
Turn of the century Baltimore is the setting for this Christmas story about Chita, her doctor father, and their annual excursion to pick a Christmas tree in the woods outside the city. The glowing illustrations not only show old fashioned Baltimore, but recreate the rich Christmas tradition of a black professional family.
SUBJ: Christmas--Fiction./ Christmas trees--Fiction./ Baltimore (Md.)--Fiction.

　　　　　　　　　　　Ph-2 K-2/2　　$14.95　　L　KF774
HOWARD, ELIZABETH FITZGERALD. Mac and Marie and the train toss surprise. Illus. by Gail Gordon Carter. Four Winds ISBN 0-02-744640-9; In Canada: Maxwell Macmillan, 1993. unp. col. ill.
Mac and his sister Marie eagerly wait for the Seaboard Florida Limited to pass their house on its way from Florida to New York. Their Uncle Clem works in the train's dining car and has written to them that he will be tossing a package to them as the train goes by their house. Excitement, suspense, and the dreams of a young boy are featured in this well-constructed story. For multicultural studies.
SUBJ: Railroads--Trains--Fiction./ Brothers and sisters--Fiction./ Afro-Americans--Fiction.

　　　　　　　　　　　Ph-2 1-3/2　　$14.00　　L　KF775
HOWARD, ELLEN. Big seed. Illus. by Lillian Hoban. Simon & Schuster ISBN 0-671-73956-5; In Canada: Simon & Schuster, 1993. unp. col. ill.
Bess plants a seed that grows into a huge sunflower plant much to the surprise of her family, who expected a marigold instead. The plant is too big for a marigold but just right for a sunflower, conveying the "just-rightness" of her own small size to Bess.
SUBJ: Size--Fiction./ Self-esteem--Fiction.

　　　　　　　　　　　Ph-2 P-K/8　　$7.99　　T　KF776
HOWARD, JANE R. When I'm sleepy. Illus. by Lynne Cherry. Dutton ISBN 0-525-45561-2; In Canada: Fitzhenry & Whiteside, 1996. unp. col. ill.
Spanish edition available CUANDO TENGO SUENO (ISBN 0-525-45562-0, 1996).
Before falling asleep a little girl imagines herself in the sleep mode of many animals, but decides that her own bed, blanket, and pillow are best. The large, softly colored pictures are not only humorous but also warm and comforting. A gentle bedtime story.
SUBJ: Sleep--Fiction./ Spanish language materials.

　　　　　　　　　　　Ph-1 K-3/2　　$13.88　　L　KF777
HOWE, JAMES. Hot fudge. Illus. by Leslie Morrill. Morrow ISBN 0-688-09701-4, 1990. unp. col. ill.
Includes recipe for "Mr. Monroe's Famous Fudge."
The Monroe's dog, Harold, narrates this story about fudge that mysteriously turns white and then disappears until he and his friends, Chester the cat and Howie the puppy, solve the mystery. A recipe follows for the fudge along with a note reminding readers that chocolate is dangerous for most dogs.
SUBJ: Fudge--Fiction./ Chocolate--Fiction./ Dogs--Fiction./ Cats--Fiction.

　　　　　　　　　　　Ph-2 K-3/2　　$15.95　　L　KF778
HOWE, JAMES. I wish I were a butterfly. Illus. by Ed Young. Gulliver/Harcourt Brace Jovanovich ISBN 0-15-200470-X, 1987. unp. col. ill.
A little cricket believes the frog who's told him he's ugly. Meetings with other insects do not change his mind until he meets a spider. Luminously hued pastel double page spread illustrations help convey the important message of self-esteem.
SUBJ: Friendship--Fiction./ Self-acceptance--Fiction./ Crickets--Fiction.

　　　　　　　　　　　Ph-2 K-3/3　　$14.93　　L　KF779
HOWE, JAMES. Rabbit-Cadabra! Illus. by Alan Daniel. Morrow ISBN 0-688-10403-7, 1993. 48p. col. ill.
At head of title: "Harold & Chester in".
Harold the dog narrates the story about how he, Chester, and Howie

set out to solve the mystery of the Magician Karlovsky, who pulls a rabbit that looks like Bunnicula out of a hat. Chaos and humor ensue in this entertaining picture book featuring the Monroe family pets.
SUBJ: Magicians--Fiction./ Dogs--Fiction./ Cats--Fiction./ Rabbits--Fiction./ Vampires--Fiction.

Ph-1 K-3/3 $16.00 T KF780
HOWE, JAMES. Scared silly: a Halloween treat. Illus. by Leslie Morrill. Morrow ISBN 0-688-07666-1, 1989. unp. col. ill.
As the Monroes prepare for Halloween, Harold, Chester, and Howie look on with interest. It's all make believe, but when the house is dark and an evil witch creeps into the kitchen to brew a potion seemingly meant for Bunnicula the animals are terrified. The witch turns out to be grandma and the potion, cider. Full page color illustrations and a really creepy encounter make this a perfect read aloud.
Harold, Chester and Howie let loose some unusual guests for Howie's birthday in CREEPY-CRAWLY BIRTHDAY (ISBN 0-688-09688-3, 1991).
SUBJ: Halloween--Fiction./ Witches--Fiction./ Dogs--Fiction./ Cats--Fiction.

Ph-2 P-2/2 $13.95 L KF781
HOWE, JAMES. There's a monster under my bed. Illus. by David S. Rose. Atheneum ISBN 0-689-31178-8; In Canada: Collier Macmillan, 1986. unp. col. ill.
Available from National Library Service for the Blind and Physically Handicapped in Braille BR7129.
Lying stiff on his bed and unable to go to sleep in the dark, spooky room, Simon is sure he can hear a monster breathing under his bed. As his imagination grows so does the crowd of strange creatures of varying colors and shapes. Finally brave enough to flash a light at the eyes under the bed, Simon has a real surprise.
SUBJ: Night--Fiction./ Fear--Fiction./ Monsters--Fiction.

Ph-2 P-1/1 $13.95 L KF782
HOWLAND, NAOMI. ABCDrive!: a car trip alphabet. Clarion ISBN 0-395-66414-4, 1994. unp. col. ill.
A young boy with a yellow balloon and his mother travel around the city in this alphabet book which features words related to transportation from "ambulance" to "zoom." The young boy can always be identified in the bright, active illustrations by his balloon. Introduces the alphabet and words about transportation in an appealing format.
SUBJ: Automobiles--Fiction./ Transportation--Fiction./ Alphabet.

Ph-2 K-2/2 $14.89 L KF783
HRU, DAKARI. Magic moonberry jump ropes. Illustrated by E. B. Lewis. Dial ISBN 0-8037-1755-5, 1996. unp. col. ill.
Includes glossary.
April and Erica wish for a third person to help them turn the jump rope. While jumping with the magic moonberry rope that their uncle brought from Tanzania, their wish comes true. Several jump rope rhymes which are included in the text may inspire students to create their own chants. Watercolor illustrations depict an urban African-American neighborhood. For multicultural studies.
SUBJ: Rope skipping--Fiction./ Afro-Americans--Fiction./ Uncles--Fiction.

Ph-1 P-K/2 $4.95 P KF784
HUGHES, SHIRLEY. Alfie gets in first. Lothrop, Lee & Shepard ISBN 0-688-07036-1, 1987. 32p. col. ill.
Available from National Library Service for the Blind and Physically Handicapped in Braille BR05454.
Alfie runs ahead and gets home first. Unfortunately he accidently locks the door and can't get it open for Mommie and baby Annie Rose. Alfie cries, Annie Rose cries, and Mom, the neighbors, the milkman and the window cleaner try to get the door open. Clever double spreads show the frantic outside activity on the left and sad-eyed Alfie on the right.
In ALFIE'S FEET (ISBN 0-688-01660-X, 1982, OPC), Alfie gets new yellow boots and learns about left and right. Hughes' work is particularly noteworthy for the warm loving feelings her characters seem to generate.
SUBJ: Family life--Fiction.

Ph-2 P-3/6 $15.00 T KF785
HUGHES, SHIRLEY. Big Alfie and Annie Rose storybook. Lothrop, Lee & Shepard ISBN 0-688-07672-6, 1988. unp. col. ill.
Breakfast messes, looking at the family album and being part of a wedding are some of the stories about this favorite brother and sister combination. Young children enjoy hearing the tales and older ones will like having a "big book" to read.
The world from Alfie's point of view is deftly captured in THE BIG ALFIE OUT OF DOORS STORYBOOK (ISBN 0-688-11428-8, 1992),

which includes a backyard store, camping, and a pet rock.
SUBJ: Brothers and sisters--Fiction.

Ph-3 P/2 $3.99 P KF786
HUGHES, SHIRLEY. Bouncing. Candlewick ISBN 1-56402-554-3; In Canada: Candlewick/dist. by Douglas & McIntyre, 1995. unp. col. ill.
Bouncing balls, bouncing on beds, and bouncing on each other, a little girl and her baby brother celebrate the popular childhood exercise. The small joys of family life with young children are apparent in the expressive watercolor and pencil illustrations.
SUBJ: Play--Fiction.

Ph-2 P-1/2 $3.99 P KF787
HUGHES, SHIRLEY. Chatting. Candlewick ISBN 1-56402-844-5; In Canada: Candlewick/dist. by Douglas & McIntyre, 1996. unp. col. ill.
A young girl describes the fun of chatting with friends, on the phone, and especially with Dad at bedtime. The simplicity and wonder of a child's world are aptly conveyed in the straightforward text and appealing watercolor and pen illustrations.
SUBJ: Conversation--Fiction.

Ph-1 P-2/3 $14.93 L KF788
HUGHES, SHIRLEY. Dogger. Lothrop, Lee & Shepard ISBN 0-688-07981-4, c1978. 32p. col. ill.
Kate Greenaway Medal.
A young boy is heartsick because his beloved stuffed dog is lost. David finds him for sale at the school fair but doesn't have enough money to buy him back. His sister Bella comes to the rescue. Vibrantly colored and meticulously detailed illustrations combine with the straight forward text to produce this heartwarming story.
SUBJ: Toys--Fiction./ Brothers and sisters--Fiction.

Ph-2 P-K/2 $3.99 P KF789
HUGHES, SHIRLEY. Hiding. Candlewick ISBN 1-56402-845-3; In Canada: Candlewick/dist. by Douglas & McIntyre, 1996. unp. col. ill.
People hiding behind a pillow or a book and the moon hiding behind clouds are among the examples given of a favorite childhood pastime. A young child's warm relationships with family, home, and nature are expressed in the appealing story and illustrations.
SUBJ: Play--Fiction./ Hide-and-seek--Fiction.

Ph-3 P/2 $17.00 L KF790
HUGHES, SHIRLEY. Nursery collection. Lothrop, Lee & Shepard ISBN 0-688-13583-8, c1986, 1994. unp. col. ill.
A collection of five stories introduces the concepts of opposites, counting, colors, shapes and sizes, and sounds. A small girl and her baby brother featured in the warm, appealing illustrations connect the stories in familiar family scenes. Originally published as separate books in Great Britain, the collection is especially suitable for lap sharing.
SUBJ: Stories in rhyme./ Concepts.

Ph-1 K-1/2 $14.89 L KF791
HURD, EDITH THACHER. I dance in my red pajamas. Illus. by Emily Arnold McCully. HarperCollins ISBN 0-06-022700-1; In Canada: Fitzhenry & Whiteside, 1982. unp. col. ill.
Despite her parents' instructions not to be noisy when she spends the day and night with her grandparents, Jenny knows that she'll play "the whirling game" with her grandfather and dance noisily with him after her bath. The illustrations sparkle with vitality, though the back view of Jenny as she stands naked waiting for her bath may provoke some giggles. Useful in conjunction with units on the family and grandparents.
SUBJ: Grandparents--Fiction.

Ph-2 1-3/2 $14.89 L KF792
HURD, THACHER. Art dog. HarperCollins ISBN 0-06-024425-9; In Canada: HarperCollins, 1996. unp. col. ill.
When the moon is full, Arthur Dog becomes Art Dog and paints large murals in the city. Then one night he is arrested when someone steals the Mona Woofa from the museum. Art Dog uses his paint brush and keen sense of smell to apprehend the crooks. Visual references to several well known paintings could serve as an introduction to art appreciation. Pair with Auch's EGGS MARK THE SPOT for an interdisciplinary approach for art classes.
SUBJ: Dogs--Fiction./ Artists--Fiction.

CE
Ph-1 K-3/2 $15.89 L KF793
HURD, THACHER. Mama don't allow. HarperCollins ISBN 0-06-022690-0, 1984. unp. col. ill.
Selectors' Choice, 15th ed.
Videocassette available from SRA/McGraw-Hill 87-509233, 1989. 1/2" iconographic VHS videocassette color (9min), $39.00.
Spanish videocassette edition MAMA NO QUIERE available from

SRA/McGraw-Hill 87-005039, 1989. 1/2" iconographic VHS videocassette color (9min), $39.00.
Talking book available from SRA/McGraw-Hill 87-511618, 1984. 1 sound cassette (9min), $15.00.
Playing on the riverboat for the Alligators' Ball, Miles and the Swamp Band are a loud success but almost end up on the alligators' dinner menu. Vigorous, boldly colored illustrations match the raucous sounds and actions. Older children like it too, and those who play instruments enjoy playing the music for the title song which is included on the last page.
SUBJ: Bands (Music)--Fiction./ Musicians--Fiction./ Alligators--Fiction./ Swamps--Fiction.

Ph-2 K-2/2 $14.93 L KF794
HURWITZ, JOHANNA. New shoes for Silvia. Illus. by Jerry Pinkney. Morrow ISBN 0-688-05287-8, 1993. unp. col. ill.
Silvia receives a pair of shiny red shoes from her Tia Rosita who lives in America. She longs to wear the shoes that are too big for her and regularly tries them on to see if they fit yet. Later she is so busy that she forgets about the shoes, and finally one day she remembers and they fit. Beautiful watercolor illustrations are good for sharing. For multicultural studies.
SUBJ: Shoes--Fiction./ Latin America--Fiction.

CE
Ph-2 P-1 $13.95 L KF795
HUTCHINS, PAT. Changes, changes. Macmillan ISBN 0-02-745870-9, c1971. unp. col. ill.
Sound filmstrip available from Weston Woods SF154C, OPC 1973. 30fr color, 1 sound cassette (6min) $30.00.
1/2" VHS videocassete available from Weston Woods MPV154, OPC (6min) $60.00.
In this wordless picture book, blocks become many things. Two little wooden dolls construct a house with a set of brightly colored building blocks. The house catches on fire and the blocks are rearranged to form a fire engine. But the fire engine pumps so much water that a flood occurs. Then the blocks become a boat and then change into a truck, then a locomotive and finally back into a house again.
SUBJ: Dolls--Fiction./ Stories without words.

CE
Ph-2 P-2/3 $14.93 L KF796
HUTCHINS, PAT. Don't forget the bacon! Greenwillow ISBN 0-688-06788-3, c1976, 1987. unp. col. ill.
Read-along kit available from Live Oak (ISBN 0-87499-253-2, 1992). 1 hardcover book, 1 sound cassette (5min), $19.95.
Big book available from Mulberry (ISBN 0-688-13102-6, 1994), $18.95. Includes study guide.
A little boy tries to remember his mother's simple grocery list but soon his imagination runs riot and six farm eggs become six fat legs, a cake for tea is a cape for me, and a pound of pears becomes a pile of chairs. Potentially destined for failure, his mnemonic attempts provoke laughter and yet demonstrate a potentially useful memory strategy.
SUBJ: Stories in rhyme./ Shopping--Fiction./ Memory--Fiction./ Humorous stories.

CE
Ph-1 P-2/2 $14.93 L KF797
HUTCHINS, PAT. Doorbell rang. Greenwillow ISBN 0-688-05252-5, 1986. unp. col. ill.
Available from National Library Service for the Blind and Physically Handicapped in Braille BR7134.
Big book available from Mulberry (ISBN 0-688-13101-8, 1994), $18.95.
Spanish edition available LLAMAN A LA PUERTA (ISBN 0-688-13807-1, 1994).
Read-along Spanish kit available from Live Oak Media (ISBN 0-87499-370-9, 1996). 1 paperback book, 1 sound cassette (6min), $14.95.
When Ma makes a batch of cookies, there are six for Victoria and six for Sam until the doorbell rings and Tom and Hannah will share, making only three cookies each. Again and again the doorbell rings, and there are more and more people to share only twelve cookies. Then the bell rings once again and it is Grandma who saves the day with an enormous tray of freshly baked cookies. This predictable book with bright doublespreads and brief repetitive text invite participation during mathematics class.
SUBJ: Cookies--Fiction./ Division--Fiction./ Sharing--Fiction.

CE
Ph-1 P-2/3 $13.95 L KF798
HUTCHINS, PAT. Good-night owl. Macmillan ISBN 0-02-745900-4, c1972. unp. col. ill.
Planning to sleep all day, Owl finds the noises made by the bees, the squirrel, the crows and the other inhabitants of the hollow tree disturbing. An appealing and popular story.
SUBJ: Sleep--Fiction./ Owls--Fiction./ Humorous stories.

Ph-1 P-1/2 $13.93 L KF799
HUTCHINS, PAT. Little Pink Pig. Greenwillow ISBN 0-688-12015-6, 1994. unp. col. ill.
While Mother Pig is looking for Little Pink Pig, he is right behind her having a series of funny mishaps as he chases a colorful butterfly. The predictable text incorporates animal sounds and youngsters will find the antics of Little Pink Pig in the illustrations predictable as well. Humor abounds and youngsters will want to hear this story again and again.
SUBJ: Pigs--Fiction./ Domestic animals--Fiction./ Bedtime--Fiction./ Animal sounds--Fiction./ Farm life--Fiction.

Ph-1 P-K $15.93 L KF800
HUTCHINS, PAT. One hunter. Greenwillow ISBN 0-688-00615-9, 1982. 24p. col. ill.
One intense hunter, with shotgun over his shoulder, stalks through the vibrantly colored jungle unaware that he is accumulating quite a following. Finally he turns around and is startled to see that ten parrots, nine snakes, eight monkeys, seven crocodiles, six tigers, five antelopes, four ostriches, three giraffes, and two elephants have been just behind this one stunned hunter. An outstanding counting book with a puzzle element to add to the fun.
SUBJ: Counting./ Animals--Fiction./ Camouflage (Biology)--Fiction.

Ph-2 K-2/4 $4.95 P KF801
HUTCHINS, PAT. One-Eyed Jake. Mulberry ISBN 0-688-13113-1, c1979, 1994. unp. col. ill.
One-Eyed Jake is a mean, terrible pirate who robs every ship in sight. His crew is terrified of him, and although each wishes for another job, they continue to help him steal. Jake's greed finally causes him to plunder one ship too many. Then the cook, the bosun, and Jim the cabin boy all have their wishes fulfilled while terrible One-Eyed Jake and his stolen treasures end up at the bottom of the sea. Brightly colored, detailed illustrations add flavor. A good choice for reading aloud.
SUBJ: Pirates--Fiction.

CE
Ph-1 P-1/1 $16.00 L KF802
HUTCHINS, PAT. Rosie's walk. Macmillan ISBN 0-02-745850-4, c1968. unp. col. ill.
Big book available from Scholastic (ISBN 0-590-64786-5, 1992).
Videocassete available from Weston Woods HMPV125V, 1986. 1/2" VHS videocassete (5min), $49.95.
Read-along kit available from Weston Woods HBC125, 1992. 1 hardcover book, 1 sound cassette (3min), $24.95.
Spanish version EL PASEO DE ROSIE available from Aladdin/Libros Colibri (ISBN 0-689-81317-1, 1997).
The fox is chasing Rosie the hen, but Rosie doesn't know it. She leads him across the yard, around the pond, over the haystack, past the mill, through the fence, and under the beehives-straight into disaster each time! Clear bold figures and bright colors are full of action. Almost wordless, the predictable book is a winning combination of minimal text and expressive illustrations. Excellent either for beginning readers or for storytime.
SUBJ: Poultry--Fiction./ Foxes--Fiction./ Spanish language materials.

Ph-2 P-K/1 $14.93 L KF803
HUTCHINS, PAT. Shrinking mouse. Greenwillow ISBN 0-688-13962-0; In Canada: Hearst Book Group, 1997. unp. col. ill.
Four animal friends notice that a faraway woods looks very small and that each animal appears to shrink as he goes toward it. The full-color illustrations may help viewers understand and discuss perspective and how faraway objects appear smaller.
SUBJ: Size--Fiction./ Animals--Fiction./ Visual perception--Fiction.

CE
Ph-1 1-2/2 $12.88 L KF804
HUTCHINS, PAT. Tale of Thomas Mead. Greenwillow ISBN 0-688-84282-8, 1980. 31p. col. ill. (Greenwillow read-alone).
Thomas Mead refuses to learn to read. Because of his inability to understand signs, a bucket of green paint falls on his head, he pushes the PULL sign and knocks shoppers to the floor, and marches into the ladies restroom causing chaos. Each time when asked "Can't you read?" Thomas replies "Why should I?" But when he jay walks and causes a fender bending traffic jam, a policeman and his parents convince him (the hard way) that it is time he learned to read. Humorous illustrations and a rhyming text.
SUBJ: Reading--Fiction.

Ph-2 P-K/2 $14.93 L KF805
HUTCHINS, PAT. Titch and Daisy. Greenwillow ISBN 0-688-13960-4, 1996. unp. col. ill.
Reluctant to join the fun at a party without each other, Titch and Daisy both hide until they are reunited under a table. Small children may recognize their reluctance and will enjoy the simple text and finding Titch and Daisy who are hidden throughout the colorful

illustrations.
SUBJ: Parties--Fiction./ Friendship--Fiction.

CE　　　　　　　Ph-1 P-2/2　$12.88　L　KF806
HUTCHINS, PAT. Very worst monster. Greenwillow ISBN 0-688-04011-X, 1985. unp. col. ill.
Read-along kit available from Morrow (ISBN 0-688-09038-9, 1989). 1 paperback book, 1 sound cassette (12min). (Mulberry books read-with-me).
Proving that she and not her new brother, Billy, is the very worst monster isn't hard for young Hazel, who has been ignored since the baby's arrival. Bright, imaginative pictures of lots of monsters add to the fun of this tale of sibling dethronement.
The new baby has grown up enough to create chaos all through the house in WHERE'S THE BABY? (ISBN 0-688-05934-1, 1988); and in SILLY BILLY! (ISBN 0-68-10818-0, 1992).
SUBJ: Monsters--Fiction./ Brothers and sisters--Fiction.

　　　　　　　Ph-3 P-1/2　$14.88　L　KF807
HUTCHINS, PAT. Which witch is which? Greenwillow ISBN 0-688-06358-6, 1989. unp. col. ill.
Identical twins attend a costume party dressed as witches. Alert young readers can penetrate their disguise by noticing the difference in their color preferences as the party progresses through games to cake. The illustrations are lively and colorful and the concept will have great appeal to younger readers.
SUBJ: Twins--Fiction./ Parties--Fiction./ Identity--Fiction./ Stories in rhyme.

　　　　　　　Ph-1 P-2/2　$14.93　L　KF808
HUTCHINS, PAT. You'll soon grow into them, Titch. Greenwillow ISBN 0-688-01771-1, 1983. unp. col. ill.
Selectors' Choice, 14th ed.
Titch is growing up but not fast enough to fit his brother's and sister's hand-me-downs. Finally his father takes him shopping for new clothes. Dressed in his new finery he joins Pete and Mary in welcoming Mom and the baby and loses no time offering his old clothes to the new arrival. "They're a bit big for him" shout Pete and Mary, but as he has often been told Titch responds with "He'll soon grow into them." In the first story TITCH (ISBN 0-02-745880-6, 1971, OPC Selectors' Choice, 7th ed.) tired of always being low man on the totem pole finally finds a way to best his older brother and sister. In TIDY TITCH (ISBN 0-688-09964-5, 1991) his older siblings clean out their room and Titch is the happy recipient of their discards.
SUBJ: Brothers and sisters--Fiction./ Clothing and dress--Fiction.

VCR　　　　　　Ph-2 P-1　$72.00　OD KF809
INTRODUCTION TO LETTERS AND NUMERALS (Videocassette). SRA/McGraw-Hill 87-510258, 1985. 1/2" enhanced VHS videocassette color.
Presents two Caldecott honor books, one an alphabet, one a counting book, that have been transferred from filmstrips. While some motion has been added, this form does not need to be purchased if the filmstrips are already owned. Designed to be used separately.
Contents: Lobel, Arnold. On Market Street (12min); Bang, Molly. Ten, Nine, Eight (3min).
SUBJ: Alphabet./ Counting.

　　　　　　　Ph-1 2-5/6　$15.99　L　KF810
ISAACS, ANNE. Swamp Angel. Illus. by Paul O. Zelinsky. Dutton ISBN 0-525-45271-0, 1994. unp. col. ill.
Caldecott Honor book, 1995.
Selectors' Choice, 20th ed.
Angelica Longrider earned the name "Swamp Angel." She was born taller than her mother, built a log cabin by age two, and rescued covered wagons stuck in Dejection Swamp simply by lifting them like twigs. When this legendary giantess meets the giant bear, "Thundering Tarnation," she uses a twister for a lasso, drinks an entire lake, and snores down giant trees, one of which finally finishes off the wily bear. Larger than life, this original tall tale includes the many elements of the traditional American folklore form set in the pioneer days of the American wilderness. Filled with humor and Americana, the oil illustrations painted on wood, the material that was both plentiful and essential to the settlers, are artistic genius. A rollicking book for reading aloud.
SUBJ: Tall tales./ Frontier and pioneer life--Tennessee--Fiction./ Tennessee--Fiction.

　　　　　　　Ph-2 K-2/1　$14.93　L　KF811
ISADORA, RACHEL. At the crossroads. Greenwillow ISBN 0-688-05271-1, 1991. unp. col. ill.
The children of a shanty town in South Africa eagerly prepare for the homecoming of their fathers who have been away for ten months working in the mines. Watercolor illustrations show the stark living conditions of the families but cannot mute the joyous homecoming. Children will recognize the universal emotions and question the adverse circumstance. For multicultural studies.
SUBJ: Fathers--Fiction./ South Africa--Fiction.

VCR　　　　　　Ph-2 K-2　$42.00　　KF812
ISADORA, RACHEL. At the crossroads (Videocassette). Based on the book by Rachel Isadora. SRA/McGraw-Hill ISBN 0-02-686762-1, 1996. 1/2" VHS videocassette color (7min). (Children's literature series).
Includes teacher's guide.
Includes public performance rights.
ALA notable video, 1996.
The sights and sounds of South Africa are vividly brought to life as spirited music and stop-motion video animation portray shanty town children who eagerly await the return of their fathers. Though the focus of the story is the joyous homecoming from the mines, the video also depicts the stark living conditions of the families. For multicultural studies.
SUBJ: Fathers--Fiction./ South Africa--Fiction.

　　　　　　　Ph-1 1-3/3　$13.95　T　KF813
ISADORA, RACHEL. Ben's trumpet. Greenwillow ISBN 0-688-80194-3, c1979. unp. ill.
Caldecott Honor Book.
Selectors' Choice, 13th ed.
Striking black and white illustrations and brief poignant text tell of Ben who each evening sits on the fire escape and plays his trumpet to the music from the Zig Zag Jazz Club. He also plays for his family, on the front stoop and along the street until neighborhood kids tease and taunt him with "Man, you're crazy. You got no trumpet." All along Ben knows it's just a dream. But sometimes dreams come true and so does Ben's. For multicultural studies.
SUBJ: Musicians--Fiction./ Afro-Americans--Fiction.

　　　　　　　Ph-2 P-1　$13.93　L　KF814
ISADORA, RACHEL. City seen from A to Z. Greenwillow ISBN 0-688-01803-3, 1983. unp. ill.
Striking black and white drawings present the alphabet as found in a large multi-ethnic city. No text as such, just the appropriate noun. Good for sharing with a group.
SUBJ: City and town life--Pictorial works./ Alphabet.

　　　　　　　Ph-2 P-2/2　$14.95　L　KF815
ISADORA, RACHEL. Lili at ballet. Putnam ISBN 0-399-22423-8; In Canada: Putnam, 1993. unp. col. ill.
Lili takes dance lessons four days a week and thinks about being the flower fairy in the school performance. Delicate watercolors depict dancers, their attire, and ballet positions and steps.
SUBJ: Ballet dancing--Fiction.

　　　　　　　Ph-2 K-2/3　$15.95　L　KF816
ISADORA, RACHEL. Lili backstage. Putnam ISBN 0-399-23025-4; In Canada: Putnam, 1997. unp. col. ill.
When Lili visits backstage at the dance theater, she enters the exciting world of make-up, costumes, props, and dancers rehearsing. The watercolor illustrations provide a glimpse behind the scenes for young dance devotees.
SUBJ: Ballet companies--Fiction./ Grandfathers--Fiction.

　　　　　　　Ph-2 1-3/2　$13.93　L　KF817
ISADORA, RACHEL. Over the green hills. Greenwillow ISBN 0-688-10510-6, 1992. unp. col. ill.
Zolani a young South African boy and his mother journey on foot across the Transkei, a coastal homeland for Blacks, to visit his grandmother. Expansive watercolor illustrations depict the rural village way of life as well as the colorful countryside.
SUBJ: South Africa--Fiction./ Blacks--South Africa--Fiction.

　　　　　　　Ph-2 P-1/2　$14.89　L　KF818
JACKSON, ELLEN. Brown cow, green grass, yellow mellow sun. Illus. by Victoria Raymond. Hyperion ISBN 0-7868-2006-3; In Canada: Little, Brown, 1995. unp. col. ill.
Yellow butter comes from the yellow sun as this story demonstrates with green grass, a brown cow, and white milk. Introduces colors, a food chain, and recipes for pancakes and butter. The illustrations were modeled with clay and painted with acrylics for an interesting visual effect. The easy text may not be as easy to read because of the use of different typefaces.
SUBJ: Color--Fiction./ Farm life--Fiction./ Dairy products--Fiction.

　　　　　　　Ph-2 K-3/4　$14.95　T　KF819
JACKSON, ELLEN. Impossible riddle. Illus. by Alison Winfield. Whispering Coyote ISBN 1-879085-93-3, 1995. unp. col. ill.
Attempting to prevent the marriage and loss of his daughter, the Tsar

poses a difficult riddle to her suitors. A clever farmer helps the Tsar and his daughter resolve their problem. Lavish borders and illustrations create a fairy tale setting for the folkloric story.
SUBJ: Riddles--Fiction./ Kings, queens, rulers, etc.--Fiction./ Russia--Fiction.

CE   Ph-1 K-2/2 $15.00   L   KF820
JAFFE, NINA. In the month of Kislev: a story for Hanukkah. Illus. by Louise August. Viking ISBN 0-670-82863-7; In Canada: Penguin, 1992. 32p. col. ill.
Available from the National Library Service for the Blind and Physically Handicapped on sound recording cassette RC 38213. Videocassette available from Weston Woods HMPV357V (ISBN 1-56008-295-X, 1993). 1/2" VHS iconographic videocassette color (11min), $49.95.
Mendel, a poor peddler, cannot afford much for his family at Hanukkah, but his children are content simply to smell the latkes cooking at the house of Feivel, a wealthy merchant. On the eighth night of Hanukkah, Feivel catches the girls smelling the latkes and demands Mendel pay a fine. The wise rabbi stipulates a fine, appropriate to the deed. Oil-painted woodcuts accompany the clever holiday story which is followed by a note explaining the Jewish holiday.
SUBJ: Hanukkah--Fiction.

                                          Ph-2 K-2/3 $13.89   L   KF821
JAKOB, DONNA. My bike. Illus. by Nelle Davis. Hyperion ISBN 1-56282-455-4, 1994. unp. col. ill.
Learning to ride a bike has its ups and downs, but once the young narrator has mastered the skill everything goes smoothly. The scratchboard illustrations depict the frustrations and ultimate satisfaction of learning to ride a two-wheeler.
SUBJ: Bicycles and bicycling--Fiction.

                                          Ph-1 P-1/1 $13.89   L   KF822
JAKOB, DONNA. My new sandbox. Illus. by Julia Gorton. Hyperion ISBN 0-7868-2144-2; In Canada: Little, Brown, 1996. unp. col. ill.
A young boy discovers his sandbox is big enough for everyone who wants to be in it waddling, searching, digging, and stomping. The bright, acrylic illustrations, sharp format, and predictable, repetitive text invite young readers. A good book for beginning readers.
SUBJ: Sandboxes--Fiction./ Sharing--Fiction./ Play--Fiction.

                                          Ph-1 K-2/3 $13.99   T   KF823
JAMES, BETSY. Mary Ann. Dutton ISBN 0-525-45077-7, 1994. unp. col. ill.
Amy misses her friend, Mary Ann, who has moved away. She finds a praying mantis which she names "Mary Ann" and keeps it in a terrarium. The praying mantis lays her eggs and soon dies. While Amy and her family go to visit her friend, Mary Ann, the eggs hatch. When they return, praying mantises are all over the house. A page of facts follows the story about friendship, loss, and this fascinating insect.
SUBJ: Praying mantis--Fiction./ Friendship--Fiction.

                                          Ph-2 K-2/2 $15.99   T   KF824
JAMES, SIMON. Leon and Bob. Candlewick ISBN 1-56402-991-3; In Canada: Candlewick/dist. by Douglas & McIntyre, 1997. unp. col. ill.
Lonely in a new town, Leon has an imaginary friend named Bob who keeps him company. Then one day he decides to make friends with the boy next door and discovers Bob is no longer with him. Very straightforward and understated, the story and the line and watercolor illustrations are reassuring. For multicultural studies.
SUBJ: Imaginary playmates--Fiction./ Friendship--Fiction./ Blacks--England--Fiction./ England--Fiction.

                                          Ph-2 P-2/2 $5.99   P   KF825
JAMES, SIMON. Wild woods. Candlewick ISBN 1-56402-637-X; In Canada: Douglas & McIntyre, 1996. unp. col. ill.
Jess leads her grandfather through the wild woods, over fences, across a stream, and over a fallen tree while they converse about keeping a squirrel as a pet. Jess finally agrees the squirrel belongs in the wild, but she convinces her sporting grandfather to return tomorrow. Much of the humor of the intergenerational story is conveyed by the illustrations that show Grandad struggling to keep up with the much younger Jess.
SUBJ: Grandfathers--Fiction./ Squirrels--Fiction.

CE   Ph-2 K-2/5 $15.95   T   KF826
JAY, LORRAINE A. Sea turtle journey: the story of a loggerhead turtle. Illus. by Katie Lee. Soundprints/Smithsonian Institution ISBN 1-56899-189-4; In Canada: Soundprints/dist. by Canadian Manda, 1995. 32p. col. ill. (Smithsonian oceanic collection).
Includes glossary.

Teacher's guide available upon request.
Read-along kit available (ISBN 1-56899-193-2, 1995). 1 hardback book, 1 sound cassette (10min), $19.95.
Follow the life of a female loggerhead turtle from her hatching until she returns to the same location to lay her own eggs. The focus on an individual turtle and attractive doublespread illustrations will capture the interest of young readers.
SUBJ: Loggerhead turtle--Fiction./ Turtles--Fiction.

                                          Ph-2 K-3 $14.95   L   KF827
JENKINS, STEVE. Looking down. Houghton Mifflin ISBN 0-395-72665-4, 1995. unp. col. ill.
Cut-paper collages start with a view of Earth from the moon and gradually move in closer to portray a town on the east coast of the United States and a boy viewing a ladybug through a magnifying glass. Presented entirely without words, the book offers possibilities for studies in art and perspective on mapping and communities.
SUBJ: Visual perception--Fiction./ Stories without words.

                                          Ph-2 K-2/2 $15.95   T   KF828
JENNINGS, SHARON. Jeremiah and Mrs. Ming. Illus. by Mireille Levert. Annick/dist. by Firefly ISBN 1-55037-079-0; In Canada: Annick/dist. by Firefly, 1990. unp. col. ill.
Big book available (ISBN 1-55037-124-X, 1990).
A young boy repeatedly complains that he can't sleep because his books are reading themselves aloud, his toys are singing, and the pictures are jumping off the wall. Each time Mrs. Ming, whose relationship to Jeremiah is unexplained, patiently and creatively resolves the incidents. The text is humorous and sensitive; the watercolor illustrations are delightful; fun for story hours.
SUBJ: Bedtime--Fiction./ Humorous stories./ French language materials.

BB   Ph-3 P/2 $4.95   T   KF829
JOHNSON, ANGELA. Joshua by the sea (Board book). Illus. by Rhonda Mitchell. Orchard ISBN 0-531-06846-3, 1994. unp. col. ill.
A young African-American boy spends the day at the beach with his family. Board book format is suitable for collections serving preschoolers. For multicultural studies.
SUBJ: Seashore--Fiction./ Afro-Americans--Fiction.

BB   Ph-3 P/2 $4.95   T   KF830
JOHNSON, ANGELA. Joshua's night whispers (Board book). Illus. by Rhonda Mitchell. Orchard ISBN 0-531-06847-1, 1994. unp. col. ill.
Awakened by noises in the night, Joshua finds comfort from his father. The board book format is suitable for collections serving preschoolers. The father and son pictured are African American, filling a need for positive images for very young children. For multicultural studies.
SUBJ: Night--Fiction./ Sound--Fiction./ Fathers and sons--Fiction./ Afro-Americans--Fiction.

                                          Ph-1 P-2/2 $14.99   L   KF831
JOHNSON, ANGELA. Julius. Illus. by Dav Pilkey. Orchard ISBN 0-531-08615-1, 1993. unp. col. ill.
Available from the National Library Service for the Blind and Physically Handicapped on sound recording cassette RC 38526.
Julius, the pig, is a present for Maya from her grandfather. Although at first her parents aren't too sure about Julius, Maya and Julius love each other from the beginning and have a raucous time together. Maya and Julius are a magnificent duo, and the illustrations done in acrylic, watercolor, fabric, instant coffee, crayon, and india ink are truly delightful.
SUBJ: Pigs--Fiction.

                                          Ph-2 P-1/2 $15.95   T   KF832
JOHNSON, ANGELA. One of three. Illus. by David Soman. Orchard ISBN 0-531-05955-3, 1991. unp. col. ill.
A young girl describes the many things she does with her two older sisters as "one of three" and the disappointment she feels when left behind. A comforting look at family with warm watercolor illustrations.
SUBJ: Sisters--Fiction./ Family life--Fiction.

BB   Ph-3 P/2 $4.95   T   KF833
JOHNSON, ANGELA. Rain feet (Board book). Illus. by Rhonda Mitchell. Orchard ISBN 0-531-06849-8, 1994. unp. col. ill.
Protected by his yellow slicker, boots, and umbrella, a young African-American boy romps in a rain storm. Board book format is suitable for collections serving preschoolers. For multicultural studies.
SUBJ: Rain and rainfall--Fiction./ Afro-Americans--Fiction.

Ph-1 P-2/6 $14.99   L   KF834
JOHNSON, ANGELA. When I am old with you. Illus. by David Soman.
Orchard ISBN 0-531-08484-1, 1990. unp. col. ill.
Coretta Scott King Honor Book.
A young black child names the many wonderful things they'll do
together "When I am old with you, Grandaddy", while double-
spread watercolor illustrations show them enjoying the activities
together now. A loving tribute to grandfathers.
SUBJ: Grandfathers--Fiction./ Old age--Fiction.

CE   Ph-1 P-2/2 $4.95   P   KF835
JOHNSON, CROCKETT. Harold and the purple crayon. HarperCollins
ISBN 0-06-443347-1; In Canada: HarperCollins, c1955, 1994. unp. col.
ill.
Available on 1/2" VHS videocassette from Weston Woods
HMPV004V (8min), $49.95.
Available from National Library Service for the Blind and Physically
Handicapped as talking book TB00818.
Spanish version HAROLD Y EL LAPIZ COLOR MORADO available
from Harper Arco Iris (ISBN 0-06-025332-0, 1995).
A small boy uses his crayon to draw the things he needs as he goes
for a moonlight walk.
Harold uses his purple crayon again in HAROLD'S TRIP TO THE SKY
(ISBN 0-06-022986-1, 1957); PICTURE FOR HAROLD'S ROOM
(ISBN 0-06-023006-1, 1960), and animated 1/2" VHS videocassette
from Weston Woods HMPV133V, n.d.); HAROLD'S ABC (ISBN
0-06-443023-5, 1963); and HAROLD'S FAIRY TALE: FURTHER
ADVENTURES WITH THE PURPLE CRAYON (ISBN 0-06-443347-1,
1994).
SUBJ: Crayon drawing--Fiction./ Imagination--Fiction./ Spanish
language materials.

Ph-2 K-1/2 $13.95   L   KF836
JOHNSON, DOLORES. What will Mommy do when I'm at school?
Macmillan ISBN 0-02-747845-9; In Canada: Collier Macmillan, 1990.
unp. col. ill.
Anticipating the beginning of school, a young black girl is worried
about how her mother will manage without her company. The
daughter's concern about her mother is a clever twist on the common
childhood anxiety about separation.
SUBJ: Mothers--Fiction./ Schools--Fiction./ Separation anxiety--Fiction.

Ph-2 P-1/2 $16.99   L   KF837
JOHNSON, PAUL BRETT. Farmers' market. Orchard ISBN 0-531-
33014-1, 1997. unp. col. ill.
"Richard Jackson book."
A young girl shares her experiences at the farmer's market where she
helps her family sell vegetables, plays with a friend, and eats ice
cream. A centerfold opens to a large panoramic view of the market
similar to many held around the country. For units on communities and
markets.
SUBJ: Farmers' markets--Fiction.

Ph-1 K-A $14.99   L   KF838
JOHNSON, STEPHEN. Alphabet city. By Stephen T. Johnson. Viking
ISBN 0-670-85631-2; In Canada: Penguin, 1995. unp. col. ill.
Caldecott Honor book, 1996.
Look carefully to find the letters of the alphabet in the realistic
paintings of city scenes. Children will wonder at the artist's technique
which created paintings that look like photographs. A visual treat.
SUBJ: Alphabet.

Ph-1 K-2/5 $14.95   L   KF839
JOHNSTON, TONY. Cowboy and the black-eyed pea. Illus. by Warren
Ludwig. Putnam ISBN 0-399-22330-4; In Canada: Putnam, 1992. unp.
col. ill.
Farethee Well is an independent-minded cowgirl whose father left her
his huge ranch and herd of longhorns with the advice to find a "real
cowboy" known for his sensitivity. She devises a plan to put a pea
under the saddle of each cowboy who courts her and marries the one
who notices the discomfort. THE PRINCESS AND THE PEA is given a
western twist sure to have broad appeal.
SUBJ: Fairy tales--Parodies, imitations, etc./ Cowboys--Fiction./
Texas--Fiction./ West (U.S.)--Fiction.

Ph-2 P-3/2 $14.95   L   KF840
JOHNSTON, TONY. Quilt story. Illus. by Tomie De Paola. Putnam ISBN
0-399-21009-1, 1985. unp. col. ill.
After moving across the country in a covered wagon, young Abigail is
sad and lonely in the new log house in the woods but she does find
comfort in her old patchwork quilt. Generations later another little girl
finds happiness in the ragged old quilt after her family has moved
across the country with their possessions in a big moving van. Stylized
colored drawings in a folk art style match the warmth of the story.
SUBJ: Moving, Household--Fiction.

Ph-2 K-2/2 $12.95   L   KF841
JOHNSTON, TONY. Soup bone. Illus. by Margot Tomes. Harcourt
Brace Jovanovich ISBN 0-15-277255-3, 1990. unp. col. ill.
Looking for a soup bone, a little old lady finds a skeleton. The
skeleton frightens her, then she frightens it until they agree to stop
scaring each other and be friends. A light-hearted Halloween story
with which beginning readers will enjoy success.
SUBJ: Skeleton--Fiction./ Halloween--Fiction./ Friendship--Fiction.

Ph-1 P-2/3 $13.00   L   KF842
JOHNSTON, TONY. Very scary. Illus. by Douglas Florian. Harcourt
Brace ISBN 0-15-293625-4; In Canada: Harcourt Brace c/o Canadian
Manda, 1995. unp. col. ill.
A big, orange pumpkin tries to look scary without success until a girl
carves a face in it and places a candle in the jack-o-lantern. The text
builds well for reading aloud through a not-so-scary "very scary"
ending. The moon shines brightly on pumpkins and Halloween
characters in the watercolor illustrations that are just right for sharing.
SUBJ: Pumpkin--Fiction./ Halloween--Fiction./ Jack-o-lanterns--Fiction.

Ph-2 2-5/2 $15.93   L   KF843
JOHNSTON, TONY. Wagon. Illus. by James E. Ransome. Tambourine
ISBN 0-688-13537-4, 1996. unp. col. ill.
A young boy describes his life growing up as a slave and his eventual
freedom following the Emancipation Proclamation. Rich oil paintings
bring this period of history to vivid life. Historical fiction for
multicultural studies.
SUBJ: Slavery--Fiction./ Afro-Americans--Fiction.

Ph-1 P-1/1 $13.93   L   KF844
JONAS, ANN. Color dance. Greenwillow ISBN 0-688-05991-0, 1989.
unp. col. ill.
Three young girls carrying gossamer veils in red, yellow and blue
dance across the pages of this book mixing colors as they dance. A
boy joins them to introduce white, grey and black. The illustrations
are brilliantly clear and full of swirling motion while the brief, concise
text introduces all the colors of the spectrum. This is wonderful for
classroom use in pre-school and kindergarten and will intrigue older
readers as well.
SUBJ: Color--Fiction./ Dancing--Fiction.

Ph-3 P-K/1 $15.93   L   KF845
JONAS, ANN. Holes and peeks. Greenwillow ISBN 0-688-02538-2,
1984. unp. col. ill.
Frightened by holes, a young child thinks peeks are different and fun.
Both simple text and bold pictures are from a young child's point of
view and all episodes occur in a white tiled bathroom.
SUBJ: Size--Fiction.

Ph-3 K-1/2 $15.93   L   KF846
JONAS, ANN. Quilt. Greenwillow ISBN 0-688-03826-3, 1984. unp. col.
ill.
Remembering with pleasure the sources of the patches on her quilt, a
young black girl falls asleep and has a frightening dream. Handsome,
boldly colored and imaginative pictures are the best part of the book.
SUBJ: Quilts--Fiction./ Bedtime--Fiction.

CE   Ph-1 K-2/2 $15.93   L   KF847
JONAS, ANN. Round trip. Greenwillow ISBN 0-688-01781-9, 1983.
unp. ill.
Read-along kit available from Live Oak (ISBN 0-87499-269-9, 1992)
1 hardcover book, 1 sound cassette (5min), $19.95.
Dazzling black and white pictures and minimal text trace a journey
from the country to the big city and describes the activities. The
return trip is shown by inverting the book and going from back to
front. Viewed with exclamations of delight from young people, it is an
excellent choice for the picture book hour.
SUBJ: Cities and towns--Fiction./ Country life--Fiction.

Ph-1 P-2/1 $14.93   L   KF848
JONAS, ANN. Splash! Greenwillow ISBN 0-688-11052-5, 1995. unp.
col. ill.
Selectors' Choice, 20th ed.
A young girl, a dog, a cat, a turtle, frogs, and fish jump in and out
of a backyard pond, offering the reader a chance to count, add, or
subtract how many are in the pond. One illustration was used as the
background for each scene, but the action, especially the splashes,
changes from scene to scene in bold acrylic paintings. The story can
be read from beginning to end or enjoyed page by page as the
action offers much to discuss. Use in art classes with older students to
demonstrate the technique of using one scene as the background and
adding action separately on clear acetate.
SUBJ: Fishes--Fiction./ Animals--Fiction./ Counting--Fiction.

Ph-1 P-2/4 $14.93 L KF849
JONAS, ANN. Trek. Greenwillow ISBN 0-688-04800-5, 1985. unp. col. ill.
Walking to school becomes an exciting adventure as a young girl sees a jungle and a desert filled with wild animals in the shrubs, hidden in the flowers, trees, etc. Each reviewing of the ingenious water color doublespread paintings are inviting and reveal more subtly hidden surprises. Small pictures with the correct name of the appearing animals are found in a chart at the end of the book.
SUBJ: Jungles--Fiction./ Deserts--Fiction./ Imagination--Fiction.

Ph-3 P-K/2 $14.93 L KF850
JONAS, ANN. When you were a baby. Greenwillow ISBN 0-688-00864-X, 1982. unp. col. ill.
Large, uncluttered, colorful pictures and a very simple text point out to a young child many things he or she could not do as a baby but is able to do now.
SUBJ: Babies--Fiction.

Ph-1 1-2/1 $13.93 L KF851
JONAS, ANN. 13th clue. Greenwillow ISBN 0-688-09743-X, 1992. unp. col. ill.
Selectors' Choice, 19th ed.
Thirteen clues lead the heroine who is disappointed that no one seems to have remembered it's her birthday, and the reader to a birthday party. The clues are hidden, scrambled, or in rebus form, and youngsters will delight in deciphering them.
SUBJ: Birthdays--Fiction./ Parties--Fiction.

Ph-2 P-K/2 $13.95 L KF852
JONES, REBECCA C. Down at the bottom of the deep dark sea. Illus. by Virginia Wright-Frierson. Bradbury ISBN 0-02-747901-3; In Canada: Collier Macmillan, 1991. unp. col. ill.
Andrew doesn't like water, especially the deep dark sea at the beach, until one day when he needs wet sand to build the largest sand city in the world he wades into the ocean. A realistic story about overcoming fears. The illustrator's six-year-old daughter drew the sea monsters that Andrew imagines in the sea, adding to the story's child appeal.
SUBJ: Beaches--Fiction./ Sandplay--Fiction.

Ph-2 1-3/2 $13.99 T KF853
JONES, REBECCA C. Great Aunt Martha. Illus. by Shelley Jackson. Dutton ISBN 0-525-45257-5, 1995. unp. col. ill.
When Great-Aunt Martha comes to visit, the house is clean, the talk is dull, and no one can play because she needs her rest. However, Great-Aunt Martha has other ideas about what to do in a surprising and lively ending. Older relatives can be a lot of fun as this intergenerational story and expressive, colorful illustratons demonstrate.
SUBJ: Great-aunts--Fiction./ Old age--Fiction./ Family life--Fiction.

Ph-1 P-1/2 $14.95 T KF854
JOOSSE, BARBARA M. Mama, do you love me? Illus. by Barbara Lavallee. Chronicle ISBN 0-87701-759-X, 1991. unp. col. ill.
Includes glossary.
Selectors' Choice, 19th ed.
When a young Inuit girl asks her mother how much she loves her, the dialogue between them explores the mother's love with numerous references to the animals and culture of the Arctic. The enduring love between parent and child is universally recognized while the Inuit setting provides an introduction to another culture for young children. Beautiful illustrations and notes following the story extend the listener's horizons. A valuable book for multicultural studies.
SUBJ: Mother and child--Fiction./ Love--Fiction./ Arctic regions--Fiction./ Eskimos--Fiction.

Ph-1 1-3/2 $14.95 L KF855
JOSEPH, LYNN. Island Christmas. Illus. by Catherine Stock. Clarion ISBN 0-395-58761-1, 1992. 31p. col. ill.
Available from the National Library Service for the Blind and Physically Handicapped on sound recording cassette RC 36424.
A young girl describes her family's Christmas on the island of Trinidad including the special foods, music, and traditions. The story is written in dialect and is illustrated with soft watercolors. A note follows the story providing further information about the island customs. Striking for the similarities to American celebrations as well as the differences. For multicultural units.
SUBJ: Trinidad and Tobago--Fiction./ Christmas--Fiction.

Ph-2 1-3/3 $14.93 L KF856
JOSEPH, LYNN. Jasmine's parlour day. Illus. by Ann Grifalconi. Lothrop, Lee & Shepard ISBN 0-688-11488-1, 1994. unp. col. ill.
Jasmine and her mother sell sugar cakes and fresh fish at their parlour on the beach in Trinidad. The reader is introduced to the different fruits, foods, and other products available as Jasmine visits her friends at the beginning of Parlour Day. Brightly colored illustrations expand the Caribbean experience for multicultural studies.
SUBJ: Markets--Trinidad and Tobago--Fiction./ Trinidad and Tobago--Fiction./ Mothers and daughters--Fiction.

Ph-2 1-3/4 $15.00 T KF857
JOYCE, WILLIAM. Bently and egg. HarperCollins ISBN 0-06-020385-4; In Canada: HarperCollins, 1992. unp. col. ill.
"Laura Geringer book."
Available from the National Library Service for the Blind and Physically Handicapped on sound recording cassette RC 36650.
Bently Hopperton is a frog, a songwriter, and an artist. When he is asked to watch the egg of his best friend Kack Kack the duck, he paints the egg with beautiful designs. The egg is mistakenly hidden as an Easter egg, and Bently sets off on a fantastic adventure to retrieve it. Illustrations depict the world from a frog-sized perspective with delightful results.
SUBJ: Frogs--Fiction./ Ducks--Fiction./ Eggs--Fiction.

Ph-2 1-3/4 $14.89 L KF858
JOYCE, WILLIAM. Day with Wilbur Robinson. HarperCollins ISBN 0-06-022968-3, 1990. unp. col. ill.
Wilbur Robinson lives in a most unusual home with most unusual relatives as the astute observer will notice, not so much from the deadpan text but from the outrageous illustrations. Youngsters with a taste for the unusual will appreciate this offbeat visit with Wilbur Robinson's family.
SUBJ: Humorous stories.

Ph-1 K-3/5 $14.89 L KF859
JOYCE, WILLIAM. Dinosaur Bob and his adventures with the family Lazardo. HarperCollins ISBN 0-06-023048-7, 1988. unp. col. ill.
Accompanying the Lazardo family when they return from their annual African safari is a long green dinosaur who they call Bob. Although very friendly and popular with the town's people, he is arrested for disturbing the peace when he chases autos just as the local dogs do, but Bob escapes from jail just in time to swat the winning run for the popular Pimlico Pirates (the worst team in history). Although perhaps ridiculous, both pictures and story are great fun for children and the adults who read to them.
SUBJ: Dinosaurs--Fiction./ Family life--Fiction.

Ph-1 P-2/2 $13.89 L KF860
JOYCE, WILLIAM. George shrinks. HarperCollins ISBN 0-06-023071-1, 1985. unp. col. ill.
Completing the list of chores left by his parents is quite difficult since during his sleep, George has shrunk to the size of a mouse. But with ingenuity, cleverness and lots of fun he follows the orders. The brief text consists largely of the parents' note but the vibrant, action-packed comical illustrations carry the tale.
SUBJ: Size--Fiction.

Ph-1 1-3/3 $15.89 L KF861
JOYCE, WILLIAM. Leaf Men and the brave good bugs. HarperCollins ISBN 0-06-027238-4; In Canada: HarperCollins, 1996. unp. col. ill.
"Laura Geringer book."
Anything can happen on a moonlit night in the garden, and when the doodle bugs brave the Spider Queen to climb the highest tree and call the Leaf Men, unusual and wonderful things do happen. The mysterious and eerie story explores the triumph of good over evil and life over life's destruction.
SUBJ: Old age--Fiction./ Insects--Fiction./ Gardens--Fiction./ Fantasy.

Ph-1 2-4/4 $17.89 L KF862
JOYCE, WILLIAM. Santa calls. HarperCollins ISBN 0-06-021134-2; In Canada: HarperCollins, 1993. unp. col. ill.
"Laura Geringer book."
Art Atchinson Aimesworth, his best friend Spaulding, and his sister Esther receive a package and instructions from S.C.--Santa Claus--to build a "Yuletide Flyer" and fly to the North Pole. There they meet Mr. Claus and battle the Dark Queen and her Dark Elves with a candy bomb and licorice. The unusual illustrations and adventurous story will appeal especially to older listeners who may have thought they had outgrown Santa Claus and picture books. For the POLAR EXPRESS graduate.
SUBJ: Brothers and sisters--Fiction./ Santa Claus--Fiction./ Christmas--Fiction.

CDR Ph-1 P-2 $39.95 OD KF863
JUST GRANDMA AND ME (CD-ROM). Broderbund ISBN 1-55790-714-5, 1992. 1 CD-ROM, 1 paperback book. (Living books).
Version 1.0.
Includes user's guide.

Selectors' Choice, 19th ed.
System requirements: Macintosh and Power Macintosh; System 6.0.7 or higher; 16MHz 68020 processor or faster; Power Macintosh; 4MB RAM, 2.5MB free; CD-ROM drive required; monitor: 12 inch or larger color, 256 colors.
System requirements: Windows 3.1 or Windows 95; 16MHz 386 or faster required; 4MB RAM for Windows 3.1; 8MB RAM for Windows 95; CD-ROM drive or faster required; SVGA monitor/ display card 640x480, 256 colors; Windows compatible sound device.
Product run on either Macintosh or Windows compatible hardware. This picture book comes alive as youngsters can hear the story in English, Japanese, or Spanish, as well as see what is inside Grandma's purse, what happens inside the knothole in the tree, or what shape a cloud at the beach will take. The interactive portion of the program allows the user to click on many of the objects to gather further information or see changes. Helps small groups or individual users become active participants in reading activities.
SUBJ: Beaches--Fiction./ Software--Beaches--Fiction./ Japanese language materials--Software./ Software--Japanese language materials./ Spanish language materials--Software./ Software--Spanish language materials./ Bilingual materials--Spanish--Software./ Software--Bilingual materials--Spanish./ Bilingual materials--Japanese--Software./ Software--Bilingual materials--Japanese./ Interactive media.

CE   Ph-2 P-1/1 $15.00   L   KF864
KALAN, ROBERT. Jump, frog, jump! New ed. Illus. by Byron Barton. Greenwillow ISBN 0-688-13954-X, c1981, 1995. unp. col. ill.
Spanish edition SALTA, RANITA, SALTA! (ISBN 0-688-13805-5, 1994); Spanish edition read-along kit available from Live Oak Media (ISBN 0-87499-367-9, 1996) 1 paperback book, 1 sound cassette (5min), $14.95.
Big book available from Mulberry (ISBN 0-688-14849-2, 1996), $18.95.
Frog jumps to catch a fly and to escape from several types of danger. A repetitive refrain and cumulative story create a predictable text for audience participation. Young readers or listeners will want to join in the fun. Lively and colorful illustrations add to the entertainment.
SUBJ: Frogs--Fiction./ Spanish language materials.

    Ph-1 P-1/1 $14.93   L   KF865
KALAN, ROBERT. Moving day. Illus. by Yossi Abolafia. Greenwillow ISBN 0-688-13949-3, 1996. unp. col. ill.
Introduces the concept of opposites as a hermit crab tries on several shells until he finally finds one that fits just right. The very simple, repetitive text creates an easy-to-read predictable book. Watercolor illustrations offer visual clues and humor, especially in the hermit crab's expressions.
SUBJ: Hermit crabs--Fiction./ Crabs--Fiction./ Shells--Fiction./ Dwellings--Fiction./ Stories in rhyme./ English language--Synonyms and antonyms--Fiction.

    Ph-2 K-2/1 $14.00   T   KF866
KALAN, ROBERT. Stop, thief! Illus. by Yossi Abolafia. Greenwillow ISBN 0-688-11876-3, 1993. unp. col. ill.
A nut exchanges hands several times as one "thief" after another takes it until it is returned to its original owner, a squirrel. A simple repetitive text and humorous illustrations will attract beginning readers.
SUBJ: Animals--Fiction.

    Ph-2 1-3/3 $14.95   L   KF867
KALMAN, MAIRA. Sayonara, Mrs. Kackleman. Viking Kestrel ISBN 0-670-82945-5; In Canada: Penguin, 1989. unp. col. ill.
Alexander and his sister Lulu visit Japan, where their guide, Hiroko, takes them to restaurants, a Godzilla movie and to meet a frog who recites Haiku. An original and quirky introduction to Japanese culture with childlike illustrations and unusual humor.
SUBJ: Japan--Fiction./ Japan--Social life and customs--Fiction.

    Ph-1 K-2/2 $15.00   T   KF868
KARAS, G. BRIAN. Home on the bayou: a cowboy's story. Simon & Schuster ISBN 0-689-80156-4; In Canada: Distican, 1996. unp. col. ill.
During the move from the West to the swamp, Ned's lasso is damaged, and he is forced to use a garden hose instead. Unhappy about the move, Ned has a showdown at school where he puts the garden hose to good use. Humorous and interesting, Ned's story will touch youngsters in similar situations.
SUBJ: Cowboys--Fiction./ Bayous--Fiction./ Swamps--Fiction./ Moving, Household--Fiction.

    Ph-1 P-1/1 $12.89   L   KF869
KARLIN, NURIT. I see, you saw. HarperCollins ISBN 0-06-026678-3; In Canada: HarperCollins, 1997. 24p. col. ill. (My first I can read book).
Two cats create puns with the simplest words such as sea and duck. Limited vocabulary with lots of humor will delight beginning readers.
SUBJ: Cats--Fiction./ Humorous stories.

    Ph-2 P-2/2 $5.95   P   KF870
KASZA, KEIKO. Wolf's chicken stew. Putnam ISBN 0-399-22000-3; In Canada: General, 1987. 32p. col. ill.
Spanish edition available EL ESTOFADO DEL LOBO (Norma ISBN 958-04-1427-0, 1991), $3.95.
A greedy wolf decides to fatten up a hen so that she'll make a better stew. The simple narrative, attractive watercolor pictures and amusing turn-the-tables ending delight young people.
SUBJ: Wolves--Fiction./ Chickens--Fiction./ Humorous stories.

VCR   Ph-1 P-2 $89.95   OD   KF871
KEATS, EZRA JACK. Ezra Jack Keats Library (Videocassette). Weston Woods HMPV496V, 1992. 1/2" VHS videocassette color (45min).
Includes public performance rights.
Six of the author's stories are included on this video. While the individual stories are not as accessible as they would be on separate videos, this collection is a good value and the visit with the author at the end is a special bonus.
Contents: Snowy day; Whistle for Willie; Peter's chair; A letter to Amy; Pet show; The trip; Getting to know Ezra Jack Keats.
SUBJ: Afro-Americans--Fiction./ Pets--Fiction./ Fantasy.

CE   Ph-1 K-2/2 $4.95   P   KF872
KEATS, EZRA JACK. Goggles! Aladdin/Macmillan ISBN 0-689-71157-3, c1969, 1971. unp. col. ill.
Sequel to A LETTER FROM AMY.
Caldecott Honor Book.
Available from National Library Service for the Blind and Physically Handicapped in Braille BRA03646 and as talking book TB03288.
Available on 1/2" VHS videocassette from Weston Woods HMPV152V (6min) $49.95.
Peter of A SNOWY DAY and his friend Archie have great plans for some old goggles which they have just found, but the neighborhood bullies have other ideas for the boys and the goggles. However, Peter and Archie, with the help of Peter's dog, Willie, very cleverly outwit the bullies and reach the safety of Archie's house--goggles, Willie and all.
SUBJ: Eyeglasses--Fiction.

CE   Ph-1 P-2/2 $4.95   P   KF873
KEATS, EZRA JACK. Hi, cat! Aladdin/Macmillan ISBN 0-689-71258-8, c1970, 1988. unp. col. ill.
Read-along kit available from Live Oak (ISBN 0-87499-179-X, 1990). 1 paperback book, 1 sound cassette (5min).
On his way to meet Peter of "A Snowy Day" Archie meets someone new on the block, a stray cat. But that crazy new cat spoils the show Peter and Archie put on for the neighborhood children. Although later Archie complains to his mother about the cat, after awhile he said "You know what, Ma?...I think that cat just kinda liked me."
SUBJ: Cats--Fiction.

CE   Ph-1 P-2/2 $14.89   L   KF874
KEATS, EZRA JACK. Letter to Amy. HarperCollins ISBN 0-06-023109-2, c1968. unp. col. ill.
Available from National Library Service for the Blind and Physically Handicapped in Braille BR01140.
Available on 1/2" VHS videocassette from Weston Woods MPV114 (7min) $60.00.
Peter, the hero of A SNOWY DAY, WHISTLE FOR WILLIE, and PETER'S CHAIR, is growing up. He even wants to invite a girl to his birthday party. As he goes out in a storm to mail the invitation, a burst of wind blows the letter away. Rushing to retrieve the note, he bumps into Amy, knocks her down and makes her cry. Now Peter is sure that she'll never come to his party.
SUBJ: Letter writing--Fiction./ Postal service--Fiction./ Spanish language materials.

    Ph-2 P-2/2 $13.95   L   KF875
KEATS, EZRA JACK. Maggie and the pirate. Four Winds/Macmillan ISBN 0-02-749710-0; In Canada: Collier Macmillan, 1979. unp. col. ill.
Available from National Library Service for the Blind and Physically Handicapped in Braille BR7505.
Maggie's pet cricket is missing and she and her friends search for Niki. Luminous full color watercolor/collage illustrations are stronger than the storyline.
SUBJ: Pets--Fiction./ Friendship--Fiction./ Mystery and detective stories.

CE KEATS, EZRA JACK. Pet show. Aladdin ISBN 0-689-71159-X, 1987. unp. col. ill.   Ph-1 P-2/2 $4.95   P   KF876
Available from National Library Service for the Blind and Physically Handicapped as talking book TB04811.
Videocassette available from Weston Woods HMPV349V, 1992. 1/2" VHS videocassette color (8min), $49.95.
Read-along kit available from Weston Woods HPRA349, 1992. 1 hardcover book, 1 sound cassette (12min), $12.95.
On the day of the pet show, Archie's independent cat (a star in Hi Cat) can't be found anywhere. In a last minute effort to win a ribbon, Archie enters an unusual pet in the show and, believe it or not, his invisible "pet germ" comes through with flying colors.
SUBJ: Pets--Fiction.

CE KEATS, EZRA JACK. Peter's chair. HarperCollins ISBN 0-06-023112-2, c1967. unp. col. ill.   Ph-1 P-2/2 $14.89   L   KF877
Spanish edition LA SILLA DE PEDRO available from Harper Arco Iris (ISBN 0-06-026655-4, 1996).
Videocassette available from Weston Woods HMPV107V, 1969. 1/2" VHS videocassette color (6min), $49.95.
Read-along kit available from HarperChildren's Audio (ISBN 0-694-70009-6, 1995). 1 paperback book, 1 sound cassette (3min), $7.95.
Available from National Library Service for the Blind and Physically Handicapped in Braille BRA13962.
Big book available from HarperCollins (ISBN 0-06-443325-0, 1993).
Peter's cradle, crib, and high chair are taken over by a new baby sister. He even has to give up noisy games because of the new arrival. Before his special little blue chair can be painted that sissyish pink for Susie, he and his dog Willie pack up their prize possessions and run away--but not too far. This is the same Peter of A SNOWY DAY and WHISTLE FOR WILLIE. For multicultural studies.
SUBJ: Children--Growth--Fiction./ Afro-Americans--Fiction./ Spanish language materials.

CE KEATS, EZRA JACK. Snowy day. Viking ISBN 0-670-65400-0; In Canada: Penguin, c1962, 1963. 32p. col. ill.   Ph-1 P-2/2 $13.99   L   KF878
Caldecott Medal Award.
1/2" VHS videocassette available from Weston Woods HMPV061V (6min), $49.95.
Available from National Library Service for the Blind and Physically Handicapped in Braille BR04677.
Read-along kit available from Live Oak (ISBN 0-670-65405-1, 1974). 1 hardcover book, 1 sound cassette (6min), $19.95.
Also available in Spanish, UN DIA DE NIEVE (ISBN 0-670-83747-4, 1991) $12.95. Read-along kit available from Live Oak (ISBN 0-87499-246-X, 1991). 1 hardcover book, 1 sound cassette (6min), $19.95.
A small boy's delight in a new snowfall is vividly told in words and striking pictures. For multicultural studies.
SUBJ: Snow--Fiction./ Afro-Americans--Fiction./ Spanish language materials.

CE KEATS, EZRA JACK. Trip. Greenwillow ISBN 0-688-84123-6, c1978. unp. col. ill.   Ph-1 K-2/2 $14.88   L   KF879
Sequel to LOUIE.
Available on 1/2" VHS videocassette from Westom Woods HMPV245V (6min), $49.95.
Louie's new neighborhood, portrayed in vibrantly colored collage, paint, and pastel, seems lonely and strange. He creates a shoebox diorama and imagines that he flies back through it to see his old friends who are dressed in frightening Halloween costumes. A quick fantasy flight around the city with them and he returns home to join his new neighbors for trick-or-treat.
SUBJ: Halloween--Fiction./ Fantasy.

CE KEATS, EZRA JACK. Whistle for Willie. Penguin ISBN 0-14-050202-5, c1964, 1977. 33p. col. ill.   Ph-1 P-2/3 $4.99   P   KF880
Available on 1/2" VHS videocassette from Weston Woods MPV65 (6min) $60.00.
Available from National Library Service for the Blind and Physically Handicapped as talking book TB03170.
Kit from Live Oak Media 0-670-76239-3, 1975. 1 hardcover book, 1 sound cassette (6min), $22.95 (Seafarer reading chest).
Spanish version: SILBA POR WILLIE (ISBN 0-670-84395-4, 1992). Peter finds that he has a great deal to learn before he can whistle for his dog. For multicultural studies.
SUBJ: Dogs--Fiction./ Afro-Americans--Fiction./ Whistling--Fiction./ Spanish language materials.

KELLER, HOLLY. Geraldine first. Greenwillow ISBN 0-688-14150-1, 1996. unp. col. ill.   Ph-2 K-2/2 $14.93   L   KF881
Geraldine discovers how to take advantage of her younger brother, who always copies everything she does, when she has him help pick up her toys. Charming watercolor illustrations show the pig siblings engaged in behaviors familiar to youngsters with younger brothers or sisters.
SUBJ: Pigs--Fiction./ Brothers and sisters--Fiction./ Family life--Fiction./ Behavior--Fiction.

KELLER, HOLLY. Geraldine's big snow. Greenwillow ISBN 0-688-07514-2, 1988. unp. col. ill.   Ph-2 P-2/4 $12.93   L   KF882
Eagerly awaiting the first big snow, Geraldine places her new sled and boots by the front door, puts on her hat and jacket, goes outside to watch and wait, and discovers her neighbors are also preparing. Mrs. Wilson has lots of food and apples from the market, Mr. Peters lays in a large supply of books from the library, Mr. Harper has a big supply of seeds for the birds and Uncle Albert attaches his snowplow to his truck.
SUBJ: Snow--Fiction.

KELLER, HOLLY. Grandfather's dream. Greenwillow ISBN 0-688-12340-6, 1994. unp. col. ill.   Ph-1 K-2/2 $13.93   L   KF883
The cranes have not returned to the village since the war in Vietnam, but Nam and his grandfather dream of their return while some in the village think the land would be better used to grow rice. One day the magnificent birds do return, and the whole village goes out to see them. As part of a project to save the cranes, the author went to Vietnam to promote wildlife conservation. Her stylized watercolor and pen illustrations are very appealing and capture the landscape and homes of Vietnam. This environmental story is also suitable for multicultural studies.
SUBJ: Vietnam--Fiction./ Cranes (Birds)--Fiction./ Grandfathers--Fiction./ Ecology--Fiction.

KELLER, HOLLY. Harry and Tuck. Greenwillow ISBN 0-688-11463-6, 1993. unp. col. ill.   Ph-2 K-1/2 $13.93   L   KF884
Harrison and Tucker are an appealing pair of twins who do everything together until they start kindergarten in separate classes. They learn to appreciate their differences and time spent apart. Use as an introduction to kindergarten or for a discussion about individual differences.
SUBJ: Twins--Fiction./ Individuality--Fiction./ Kindergarten--Fiction./ Schools--Fiction.

KELLER, HOLLY. Island baby. Greenwillow ISBN 0-688-10580-7, 1992. unp. col. ill.   Ph-2 P-2/3 $13.93   L   KF885
Simon helps Pops, who runs a bird hospital on their Caribbean island, feed and care for the birds. Together they rescue a young flamingo and nurse it back to health. Bold, brightly colored illustrations and borders of tropical birds fill the pages of this satisfying story.
SUBJ: Birds--Fiction./ Wildlife rescue--Fiction./ Islands--Fiction./ Caribbean Area--Fiction.

KELLER, HOLLY. Rosata. Greenwillow ISBN 0-688-05321-1, 1995. unp. col. ill.   Ph-2 K-2/2 $14.93   L   KF886
Camilla names the bird on an old hat she has found, Rosata, and wears her everywhere. When she makes friends with Teresa, she gradually learns to leave Rosata behind. Learning to let go of a favorite article of clothing or toy is part of growing up for many children who will empathize with Camilla's feelings and appreciate Teresa's understanding.
SUBJ: Hats--Fiction./ Friendship--Fiction.

KELLEY, TRUE. I've got chicken pox. Dutton ISBN 0-525-45185-4, 1994. unp. col. ill.   Ph-2 K-3/2 $13.99   T   KF887
Jess thinks the chicken pox are fun until she really starts to itch and the boredom of a long stay at home begins. Jess' story is told in a light, lively style while brief facts about the disease are included on the bottom of each page. Youngsters stricken with the illness will commiserate with Jess and appreciate the facts and helpful hints.
SUBJ: Chicken pox--Fiction./ Sick--Fiction.

KELLOGG, STEVEN. Best friends. Dial ISBN 0-8037-0099-7; In Canada: Fitzhenry & Whiteside, 1986. 32p. col. ill.   Ph-1 K-3/2 $15.99   T   KF888
Available from National Library Service for the Blind and Physically Handicapped on sound recording cassette RC25765.

Lonely when her best friend leaves for a summer vacation in the mountains, and since the two girls have been constant companions to the exclusion of others, Kathy thinks Louise is a traitor when she writes about the new friends she's enjoying. Lively, imaginative and humorous illustrations combine the girl's many fantasies with the realism of life in the suburbs.
SUBJ: Friendship--Fiction.

CE   Ph-1 K-3/5 $14.93   L   KF889
KELLOGG, STEVEN. Chicken Little. Retold and illustrated by Steven Kellogg. Morrow ISBN 0-688-05691-1, 1985. unp. col. ill.
Read-along kit available from Morrow (ISBN 0-688-09041-9, 1989). 1 paperback book, 1 sound cassette (15min) $7.95.
Spanish edition available POLLITA PEQUENITA (Everest ISBN 84-241-3331-5, 1991), $11.95.
Adds a crashing helicopter and other modern touches to the old story of Chicken Little who thinks the sky is falling and his encounter with sly, scheming Foxy Loxy. Lively text, humorous, vital illustrations and plays on words (poulice, hippoliceman) continue the popularity of this timeless, cumulative tale.
SUBJ: Foxes--Fiction./ Animals--Fiction.

CE   Ph-2 K-3/5 $15.99   T   KF890
KELLOGG, STEVEN. Island of the skog. Dial ISBN 0-8037-3842-0, c1973. unp. col. ill.
Also available as 1/2" VHS videocassette (11min) from Weston Woods HMPV174V, $49.95.
A group of mice sail away in hopes of finding a place free of cats, dogs, and other city hazards. After a rough and frightening voyage, they finally land on an island inhabited by one Skog. Not knowing what a Skog is but finding enormous footprints, the mice set a trap and are pleasantly surprised when their efforts succeed.
SUBJ: Mice--Fiction./ Islands--Fiction./ Ecology--Fiction./ Spanish language materials.

                             Ph-1 K-2/2 $12.95   T   KF891
KELLOGG, STEVEN. Much bigger than Martin. Dial ISBN 0-8037-5809-X, c1976. 32p. col. ill.
Henry hates being Martin's little brother. It's no fun being last in line, getting the smallest piece of cake, and being the butt of all jokes when the big boys are around. Trying to become taller, Henry stretches himself, waters himself and eats lots of apples before he finally finds an ingenious solution that really does put him head and shoulders above Martin.
SUBJ: Brothers--Fiction./ Size--Fiction.

                             Ph-1 P-2/2 $3.50   P   KF892
KELLOGG, STEVEN. Mystery of the missing red mitten. Dial ISBN 0-8037-5749-2, 1974. unp. col. ill.
When she loses her fifth mitten, Annie and her dog Oscar search everywhere but only find Ralph's boots, mice, or a hat for a baby hawk, or even as a seed for a mitten tree. The mitten's appearance as the heart of a snowman is a real surprise.
SUBJ: Gloves--Fiction.

                             Ph-3 P-1/2 $3.95   P   KF893
KELLOGG, STEVEN. Mystery of the stolen blue paint. Dial ISBN 0-8037-0285-X, 1982. unp. col. ill.
Belinda plans to paint a special blue picture but is interrupted first by her pesky little cousin Jason, then by Jason and his friends and Lou Anne, and finally by a sudden windstorm. She gives up and packs up her painting supplies but discovers her blue paint is missing. Belinda blames the little kids, but each one denies any involvement. There is no evidence under their fingernails but when Belinda's dog Homer starts kissing everyone the mystery is solved.
SUBJ: Mystery and detective stories.

CE   Ph-1 P-2/2 $16.99   T   KF894
KELLOGG, STEVEN. Pinkerton, behave. Dial ISBN 0-8037-6573-8, 1979. unp. col. ill.
Selectors' Choice, 13th ed.
Pinkerton, a huge loveable dog, can't learn the proper responses to commands so he is enrolled in an obedience school. There he gets "F's" in all phases and even worse disrupts the entire class. Though sent home in disgrace, that night he proves his worth. Truly hilarious text and large watercolor illustrations make this a perfect candidate for picture story time.
In ROSE FOR PINKERTON (ISBN 0-8037-0060-1, 1984) the family acquires a kitten named Rose for him and the two disrupt the International Pet Show and in TALLYHO, PINKERTON (ISBN 0-8037-8731-6, 1982) the two inadvertently become involved with Dr. Aleasha Kibble's snobbish Hunting Academy.
SUBJ: Dogs--Fiction./ Humorous stories./ Dogs--Training--Fiction.

                             Ph-1 P-3/5 $12.89   L   KF895
KELLOGG, STEVEN. Prehistoric Pinkerton. Dial ISBN 0-8037-0323-6; In Canada: Fitzhenry & Whiteside, 1987. unp. col. ill.
Disguised in a stegosaurus costume, Pinkerton accompanies his young mistress and her class on a special Dinosaur Day trip to the museum of natural history. Unfortunately the lovable, affectionate but unpredictable Great Dane is "teething" and the special, prized exhibit is soon in jeopardy and chaos. Both text and pictures present the slapstick humor popular and appealing to children.
SUBJ: Dogs--Fiction./ Museums--Fiction./ Fossils--Fiction.

CE   Ph-2 K-2/4 $14.00   L   KF896
KENT, JACK. Caterpillar and the polliwog. Prentice-Hall ISBN 0-671-66280-5; In Canada: Prentice-Hall, 1982. unp. col. ill.
Animated 1/2" VHS videocassette color (7min) available from Weston Woods HMPV312V, $49.95.
Boasting that when she grows up she'll turn into a butterfly, a caterpillar catches the attention of a polliwog who also desires to turn into a butterfly but is so busy watching the caterpillar change that he doesn't notice his own transformation into a frog. A lively tale with large, bold illustrations ideal for storytelling and to use in conjunction with units on metamorphosis.
SUBJ: Caterpillars--Fiction./ Tadpoles--Fiction./ Metamorphosis--Fiction.

                             Ph-2 1-2/1 $13.89   L   KF897
KESSLER, ETHEL. Stan the hot dog man. By Ethel and Leonard Kessler. HarperCollins ISBN 0-06-023280-3, 1990. 64p. col. ill. (I can read book).
Since Stan retired from the bakery he's been selling hot dogs from a truck and on a snowy winter day is able to help the driver and passengers of a stranded school bus. The unusual subject and slight plot tension appeals to beginning independent readers.
SUBJ: Frankfurters--Fiction./ Occupations--Fiction./ Snow--Fiction.

CE   Ph-2 1-2/2 $11.89   L   KF898
KESSLER, LEONARD. Here comes the strikeout. HarperCollins ISBN 0-06-023156-4, c1965. 64p. col. ill. (Sports I can read book).
Also available in Spanish from the National Library Service for the Blind and Physically Handicapped in Braille BRF00122.
Spanish version AQUI VIENE EL QUE SE PONCHA! available from Harper Arco Iris (ISBN 0-06-025437-8, 1995).
Available from National Library Service for the Blind and Physically Handicapped in Braille BRA13176.
Read-along kit from HarperAudio (ISBN 0-55994-231-2). 1 paperback book, 1 sound cassette (16min), $7.95.
After Bobby strikes out 21 times, he asks Willie to coach him and learns that only hard work will help him hit the ball.
SUBJ: Baseball--Fiction./ Spanish language materials.

                             Ph-2 1-2/2 $13.89   L   KF899
KESSLER, LEONARD. Kick, pass, and run. HarperCollins ISBN 0-06-023160-2, c1966. 64p. col. ill. (Sports I can read book).
Includes glossary.
Available from National Library Service for the Blind and Physically Handicapped in Braille BR03640.
An assorted group of animals are quite puzzled over a large brown "egg." The mystery is solved when some boys recover it and continue their football game. Intrigued with this new sport, the animals too play a game. In spite of makeshift balls and unexpected difficulties, the game goes to an exciting finish. Lists famous football players, gives some cheers, and provides pictorial explanations of football terms in an easy to read vocabulary.
SUBJ: Football--Fiction./ Animals--Fiction.

                             Ph-2 1-2/1 $13.89   L   KF900
KESSLER, LEONARD. Last one in is a rotten egg. HarperCollins ISBN 0-06-023158-0, c1969. 64p. col. ill. (Sports I can read book).
Available from National Library Service for the Blind and Physically Handicapped as talking book TB03224.
Spanish version EL ULTIMO EN TIRARSE ES UN MIEDOSO available from Harper Arco Iris (ISBN 0-06-444194-6, 1995).
Freddy can't swim well enough to go in the deep water, so he doesn't have as much fun at the city pool as his friends, Bobby and Willie. When some bullies push Freddy into the deep water, he almost drowns. After that frightening experience, he doesn't want to go swimming. Finally, he gets enough courage to return to the pool, and this time he is determined to learn to swim. Gives water safety rules and some simple instructions for learning to swim.
SUBJ: Swimming--Fiction./ Spanish language materials.

                             Ph-1 K-3/2 $13.93   L   KF901
KESSLER, LEONARD. Old Turtle's soccer team. Greenwillow ISBN 0-688-07158-9, 1988. 47p. col. ill. (Greenwillow read-alone).
Cat, Dog, Rabbit and the other friends agree to a game of soccer

against the Rockets but unfortunately they don't know how to play until Old Turtle offers to coach them. Soccer rules and skills are presented in a simple, easily understood manner. Many positive features: both boy and girl animals are on the teams, arranged in chapters, humorous text and pictures and easy to read.
More tall tales can be found in OLD TURTLE'S BASEBALL STORIES (ISBN 0-688-00723-6, 1982, OPC) and THE BIG MILE RACE (ISBN 0-688-01420-8, 1983).
SUBJ: Soccer--Fiction./ Sportsmanship--Fiction./ Animals--Fiction.

Ph-2 P-2/5 $13.95   L   KF902
KHALSA, DAYAL KAUR. I want a dog. Potter/Crown ISBN 0-517-56532-3, 1987. unp. col. ill.
Trying every trick imaginable, even leashing, walking and caring for a roller skate, May, after a couple of years, convinces her parents that she can care for a real dog. Vivid, detailed pictures add to the humor.
SUBJ: Dogs--Fiction./ Imagination--Fiction.

Ph-1 2-4/3 $15.95   L   KF903
KIMMEL, ERIC A. Bernal and Florinda: a Spanish tale. Illus. by Robert Rayevsky. Holiday House ISBN 0-8234-1089-7, 1994. unp. col. ill.
Bernal wishes to marry Florinda, but her greedy father won't let a man who only owns a field of grasshoppers marry his daughter. Bernal swears he will make his fortune on the grasshoppers, and he does, winning the hand of Florinda in the process. Written in the tradition of the Spanish picaresque tale with theatrical illustrations, this is a broadly humorous and delightful story for sharing or individual enjoyment.
SUBJ: Fairy tales./ Spain--Fiction.

Ph-1 K-3/2 $15.95   L   KF904
KIMMEL, ERIC A. Magic dreidels: a Hanukkah story. Illus. by Katya Krenina. Holiday House ISBN 0-8234-1256-3, 1996. unp. col. ill.
Jacob loses two magic dreidels he has acquired from a goblin when the neighborhood busybody exchanges them for ordinary dreidels. The goblin helps him to get the magic dreidels back, and he shares the latkes and gelt they spin out with his neighbors. Striking illustrations illuminate the clever Hanukkah story that uses elements from traditional folktales.
SUBJ: Fairy tales./ Swindlers and swindling--Fiction./ Dreidel (Game)--Fiction./ Hanukkah--Fiction./ Jews--United States--Fiction.

Ph-1 2-3/2 $13.99   L   KF905
KINSEY-WARNOCK, NATALIE. Bear that heard crying. By Natalie Kinsey-Warnock and Helen Kinsey. Illus. by Ted Rand. Cobblehill/Dutton ISBN 0-525-65103-9, 1993. unp. col. ill.
Encountering a black bear in the woods, three-year-old Sarah thinks it's a big dog and cuddles up with it. After four days, a search party led by a stranger's dream finds her beneath a tree surrounded by bear tracks. Youngsters will enjoy the suspenseful story especially because it is based on a true story about the author's great-great-great-great-great aunt. Illustrations are the perfect accompaniment for reading aloud, including several dramatic doublespreads.
SUBJ: Lost children--Fiction./ Survival--Fiction./ Bears--Fiction.

Ph-2 P-2/3 $14.99   L   KF906
KINSEY-WARNOCK, NATALIE. When spring comes. Illus. by Stacey Schuett. Dutton ISBN 0-525-45008-4, 1993. unp. col. ill.
In the midst of winter, a young girl dreams about spring, making syrup, fishing, and planting the garden until the jingle of bells brings her back to the present and a sleigh ride through the snow. The story and luminous illustrations provide a glimpse into the early 1900's and portray the pleasures of the seasons.
SUBJ: Farm life--Fiction./ Spring--Fiction./ Family life--Fiction.

Ph-1 K-2/4 $14.89   L   KF907
KIRK, DANIEL. Lucky's 24-hour garage. Hyperion ISBN 0-7868-2168-X; In Canada: Little, Brown, 1996. unp. col. ill.
All sorts of late night travelers stop by Lucky's 24-hour Garage during Angelo's all night shift. Set in 1939 in New York and illustrated with oil paintings that reflect the era, the story has a timeless appeal for fans of automobiles and their service stations. Historical fiction from an unusual perspective.
SUBJ: Service stations--Fiction./ United States--History--1933-1945--Fiction.

Ph-1 K-2/3 $15.95   L   KF908
KIRK, DANIEL. Trash trucks. Putnam ISBN 0-399-22927-2; In Canada: Putnam, 1997. unp. col. ill.
Selectors' Choice, 21st ed.
Trash trucks rumble through the street, grind up the trash, and haul it away in this celebraton of the service they provide. Trash overflows, forms letters of the text, and ultimately ends up in the jaws of the ravenous trucks. Obviously a choice for units on community helpers, this will delight youngsters anytime.
SUBJ: Refuse and refuse disposal--Fiction./ Trucks--Fiction./ Stories in rhyme.

Ph-1 K-2/2 $14.00   T   KF909
KITAMURA, SATOSHI. UFO diary. Farrar, Straus & Giroux ISBN 0-374-38026-0, 1989. unp. col. ill.
A UFO floating through the universe is attracted by the luminous globe of earth. Landing in a meadow, the alien--never glimpsed--meets his first human, a boy, and after sharing his day takes him on a brief ride through space returning him to his own home. The pictures give a marvelous view of space and earth as seen by the invisible narrator. A must for young UFO fans.
SUBJ: Unidentified flying objects--Fiction.

Ph-2 K-2/2 $15.99   T   KF910
KLEVEN, ELISA. Hooray! A pinata! Dutton ISBN 0-525-45605-8; In Canada: McClelland & Stewart, 1996. unp. col. ill.
Spanish version VIVA! UNA PINATA! available (ISBN 0-525-45606-6, 1996).
When Clara becomes attached to the dog pinata she has chosen for her birthday party, she doesn't want to fill it with candy and have it broken open. Her friend Samson knows what to get her as a present: another pinata that is larger and scary looking. Confirming Clara's affection for the dog pinata, the illustrations, a magical mixture of collage and paint, exhibit her growing attachment. For multicultural studies.
SUBJ: Pinatas--Fiction./ Dogs--Fiction./ Parties--Fiction./ Hispanic Americans--Fiction./ Birthdays--Fiction./ Spanish language materials.

Ph-1 P-2/2 $15.95   T   KF911
KLINTING, LARS. Bruno the baker. Henry Holt ISBN 0-8050-5506-1, 1997. unp. col. ill.
Bruno bakes a cake for his birthday with the help of Felix, another beaver. Similar in format and style to the other Bruno books, the story and watercolor and colored pencil illustrations present the utensils, steps, and recipe for baking a cake.
SUBJ: Baking--Fiction./ Birthday cakes--Fiction./ Cake--Fiction./ Beavers--Fiction.

Ph-1 K-2/2 $14.95   T   KF912
KLINTING, LARS. Bruno the carpenter. Henry Holt ISBN 0-8050-4501-5, 1996. unp. col. ill.
Follow the steps as Bruno the beaver builds a toolbox. At each step, the tool he uses is shown in clear illustrations. The final doublespread includes plans for building a toolbox. Youngsters with a fascination for tools will love the clarity of this book. A fun adjunct to units on simple machines.
SUBJ: Carpenters--Fiction./ Beavers--Fiction./ Tools--Fiction.

Ph-1 K-2/2 $14.95   T   KF913
KLINTING, LARS. Bruno the tailor. Henry Holt ISBN 0-8050-4500-7, 1996. unp. col. ill.
Bruno the beaver decides to sew a new apron. When the first results are less than perfect, he solves the problem. The sewing steps are clearly outlined in the story and distinct watercolor and colored pencil illustrations. A pattern and sewing tips follow the text.
SUBJ: Tailors--Fiction./ Beavers--Fiction./ Sewing--Fiction.

Ph-2 P-2/3 $14.95   L   KF914
KNUTSON, KIMBERLEY. Ska-tat! Macmillan ISBN 0-02-750846-3; In Canada: Maxwell Macmillan, 1993. unp. col. ill.
Three children frolic in the autumn leaves: crunching them underfoot, raking them into mountains, and grinding them into magic dust. The joyous celebration of autumn is conveyed in the handmade paper collage illustrations and the noisy text.
SUBJ: Leaves--Fiction./ Autumn--Fiction.

Ph-2 K-2/2 $13.95   L   KF915
KOSCIELNIAK, BRUCE. Geoffrey Groundhog predicts the weather. Houghton Mifflin ISBN 0-395-70933-4, 1995. unp. col. ill.
Geoffrey Groundhog becomes a celebrity when his prediction for spring weather proves to be true. The next winter he oversleeps and can't see his shadow because of all the television cameras. Eventually he makes the proper prediction with the help of his mother who always looks for her shadow. A title to share on Groundhog Day.
SUBJ: Groundhog Day--Fiction./ Woodchucks--Fiction.

Ph-2 2-3/2 $17.99   L   KF916
KOTZWINKLE, WILLIAM. Million-Dollar Bear. Illus. by David Catrow. Knopf ISBN 0-679-95295-0; In Canada: Random House, 1995. unp. col. ill.
"Borzoi book."

The Million-Dollar Bear is kept in a vault first by Argyle Oldhouse and then by J.P. Plumpgarden. He is accidentally removed by a cleaning company and falls out of the truck and into the lives of an ordinary family who doesn't think he's worth anything but their affection. The long story is filled with humor and adventure for true bear fans.
SUBJ: Teddy bears--Fiction./ Greed--Fiction.

Ph-2 K-2/2 $13.88 L KF917
KOVALSKI, MARYANN. Pizza for breakfast. Morrow ISBN 0-688-10410-X, 1991. unp. col. ill.
Originally published in Canada: FRANK AND ZELDA, Kids Can Press, 1990.
Frank and Zelda wish in turn for business in their restaurant to be better, for more help, and for a bigger building. When things get out of hand, they receive their final wish for a return to life before the wishes and make a plan that proves smaller is sometimes better. Watercolor illustrations reveal the extent of their predicament, and its satisfactory solution.
SUBJ: Restaurants--Fiction./ Wishes--Fiction.

CE Ph-1 P-2/2 $14.89 L KF918
KRAUS, ROBERT. Leo the late bloomer. Illus. by Jose Aruego. Crowell/HarperCollins ISBN 0-87807-043-5, 1971. 32p. col. ill. (Windmill book).
Selectors' Choice, 7th ed.
Distressed by his inability to read, write, draw, eat neatly, or talk young Leo feels even worse when his father expresses concern about his backwardness. His mother's reassuring and accurate statement, "Leo is just a late bloomer" has proved to be especially comforting to many children who identify with the young tiger.
SUBJ: Tigers--Fiction./ Self-acceptance--Fiction.

CE Ph-1 P-1/1 $13.95 L KF919
KRAUS, ROBERT. Whose mouse are you? Illus. by Jose Aruego. Macmillan ISBN 0-02-751190-1; In Canada: Collier Macmillan, c1970. unp. col. ill.
A little mouse is lonely because he thinks he is nobody's mouse. He says his mother is in the cat, his father in a trap, his sister far, far away and he has no brother. Soon, however, all is well--the young mouse rescues his mother, father and sister and even gets a brand new brother. Brief, rhyming text in question and answer form. Bright, enchanting illustrations.
Bold illustrations and simple humorous text are also the keystones of WHERE ARE YOU GOING LITTLE MOUSE? (ISBN 0-688-04295-3, 1986) and COME OUT AND PLAY, LITTLE MOUSE (ISBN 0-688-05838-8, 1986).
SUBJ: Mice--Fiction./ Stories in rhyme.

CE Ph-1 P-2/2 $13.95 T KF920
KRAUSS, RUTH. Carrot seed. Illus. by Crockett Johnson. HarperCollins ISBN 0-06-023350-8; In Canada: HarperCollins, c1945. unp. col. ill.
Read-along kit available from Live Oak (ISBN 0-87499-177-3, 1990). 1 hardcover book, 1 sound cassette (3min), $22.95.
Big book available from Scholastic (ISBN 0-590-73301-X, 1978).
Even when his family tease him, a little boy persists in his belief that a plant will grow from the seed he planted.
SUBJ: Seeds--Fiction./ Gardening--Fiction.

Ph-1 P-2/2 $14.89 L KF921
KRAUSS, RUTH. Happy day. Illus. by Marc Simont. HarperCollins ISBN 0-06-023396-6, c1945, 1949. unp. col. ill.
Caldecott Honor Book.
Spanish version UN DIA FELIZ available from Harper Arco Iris (ISBN 0-06-443414-1, 1995).
Slight text, beautifully illustrated, describes the animals' joy as winter comes to an end.
SUBJ: Animals--Fiction./ Spring--Fiction./ Spanish language materials.

CE Ph-3 P-2/2 $14.95 T KF922
KRAUSS, RUTH. Hole is to dig: a first book of first definitions. Illus. by Maurice Sendak. HarperCollins ISBN 0-06-023405-9; In Canada: HarperCollins, c1952. unp. ill.
Available from National Library Service for the Blind and Physically Handicapped in Braille BR03175.
Read-along kit available from Live Oak (ISBN 0-87499-174-9, 1990). 1 hardbound book, 1 sound cassette (8min), $22.95.
Whimsical illustrations enhance completely childlike explanations such as "A hat is to wear on a train"--"The world is so you have something to stand on."
SUBJ: Humorous stories.

Ph-2 P-1/1 $13.89 L KF923
KRAUSS, RUTH. Very special house. Illus. by Maurice Sendak. HarperCollins ISBN 0-06-023456-3, c1953. unp. col. ill.

Caldecott Honor Book.
Anything is possible and lots of silly things happen in "a very special house" that exists in a young boy's imagination. The expressive text does well when read aloud.
SUBJ: Imagination--Fiction.

Ph-1 K-2/2 $3.50 P KF924
KRENSKY, STEPHEN. Lionel at large. Illus. by Susanna Natti. Dial ISBN 0-8037-0556-5; In Canada: Fitzhenry & Whiteside, 1986. 56p. col. ill. (Dial easy-to-read).
Available from National Library Service for the Blind and Physically Handicapped in Braille BR06956.
Tells five easy-to-read stories about a little boy who eats unpleasant green beans, so he can have dessert; doesn't mind going to the doctor's for a checkup, but dreads the shots; hates snakes and has a horrible time when his big sister, Louise, loses her pet snake in his room; learns that babies can be lots of trouble when he and his friend build a sandbox for Jeffrey's expected new baby brother or sister; and finally sleeps over at Jeffrey's house--Lionel's first night away from home without his mother. The colorful pictures add warmth and quiet humor, and reinforce the feeling that most little boys react in a manner very similar to Lionel's.
Other easy-to-read titles featuring Lionel include: LIONEL IN THE FALL (ISBN 0-8037-0683-9, 1989, OPC); LIONEL IN THE SPRING (ISBN 0-8037-0631-6, 1990, OPC); LIONEL AND LOUISE (ISBN 0-14-038617-3, 1997); and LIONEL IN THE WINTER (ISBN 0-14-038322-0, 1996).
SUBJ: Family life--Fiction.

Ph-1 1-3/2 $13.95 T KF925
KRENSKY, STEPHEN. Three blind mice mystery. Illus. by Lynn Munsinger. Delacorte ISBN 0-385-32131-7; In Canada: Bantam Doubleday Dell, 1995. 48p. col. ill. (Yearling first choice chapter book).
Several nursery rhyme characters provide the clues for Simple Simon, the detective, to locate one of the three blind mice who is missing. An easy-to-read format, short chapters, and amusing illustrations combine in this transitional reader with mystery, humor, and familiar characters for a fun read sure to appeal to new and reluctant readers.
SUBJ: Mystery and detective stories./ Mice--Fiction.

Ph-1 1-3/2 $16.95 T KF926
KROEGER, MARY KAY. Paperboy. By Mary Kay Kroeger and Louise Borden. Illus. by Ted Lewin. Clarion ISBN 0-395-64482-8, 1996. 31p. col. ill.
Proud of his job as paperboy at the corner of Hunt and Main, Willie signs up to sell the extra edition after the Dempsey-Tunney boxing match. The appealing historical fiction for young readers captures the pride of a boy working to help his family and the year 1927 when the family gathers around the radio to listen to the boxing match. Richly expressive watercolor illustrations effectively use black and white insets to depict the fight action the family hears on the radio.
SUBJ: Newspaper carriers--Fiction./ Boxing--Fiction./ Loyalty--Fiction.

Ph-2 K-1/6 $13.95 L KF927
KROLL, STEVEN. Candy witch. Illus. by Marylin Hafner. Holiday House ISBN 0-8234-0359-9, 1979. unp. col. ill.
Mama Witch, Papa Warlock and Brother John seem to ignore all the kind deeds young Maggie Witch performs. In order to gain attention from her family Maggie decides to reverse her behavior. So she goes all over the town and school casting bad spells and tricks. She manages to create a Halloween to remember.
SUBJ: Confectionery--Fiction./ Witches--Fiction./ Halloween--Fiction.

Ph-2 K-2/2 $14.95 L KF928
KROLL, STEVEN. Happy Father's Day. Illus. by Marylin Hafner. Holiday House ISBN 0-8234-0671-7, 1988. unp. col. ill.
Mom and six children surprise Dad on Father's Day.
SUBJ: Father's Day--Fiction.

Ph-2 K-2/4 $14.95 L KF929
KROLL, STEVEN. It's groundhog day! Illus. by Jeni Bassett. Holiday House ISBN 0-8234-0643-1, 1987. unp. col. ill.
When Godfrey Groundhog has a hunch that he won't see his shadow on February second and spring will be early, all his friends and Roland Raccoon are delighted. Roland is afraid his ski resort business will be devastated so he plans a trick to keep Godfrey inside on the telltale day. The story and pictures are fun but the many scenes of life underground offer an added attraction and source of information.
SUBJ: Groundhog Day--Fiction./ Woodchucks--Fiction./ Animals--Fiction.

Ph-2 K-2/2 $13.95 L KF930
KROLL, STEVEN. One tough turkey: a Thanksgiving story. Illustrated by John Wallner. Holiday House ISBN 0-8234-0457-9, 1982. unp. col. ill.

After a hard year in the New World, the Pilgrims plan the first Thanksgiving. Since everyone wants turkey, the men and boys under the leadership of Captain Bill Fitz, set off for the woods with loaded muskets. However, they hadn't counted on Solomon, one wise and tough turkey, who doesn't want his family or friends to be anyone's dinner. He leads the Pilgrims on such a wild, slapstick chase, that instead of turkey, squash is the main course for the first Thanksgiving. A tongue in cheek tale with lots of nonsensical humor of the type that appeals to children.
SUBJ: Thanksgiving Day--Fiction./ Turkeys--Fiction.

CE

Ph-1 K-2/6 $13.95   L   KF931
KROLL, STEVEN. Tyrannosaurus game. Illus. by Tomie De Paola. Holiday House ISBN 0-8234-0275-4, c1976. 39p. col. ill.
Read-along kit available from Live Oak (ISBN 0-87499-096-3, 1986). 1 hardcover book, 1 sound cassette (9min), $19.95.
On a dull, rainy day when school seems blah and boring, the class livens things up with an old game now given a new name--the tyrannosaurus game.
SUBJ: Dinosaurs--Fiction./ Games--Fiction.

Ph-2 K-2/5 $15.00   T   KF932
KROLL, VIRGINIA L. Can you dance, Dalila? By Virginia Kroll. Illus. by Nancy Carpenter. Simon & Schuster ISBN 0-689-80551-9; In Canada: Distican, 1996. unp. col. ill.
In search of her own style, Dalila tries the fox trot, jigs, ballet, and tap. It isn't until a troupe of West African dancers invites others to join the akpasa and dance the way the music makes them feel that Dalila shines. Dalila's exploration of dances from different cultures relates well to multicultural studies.
SUBJ: Afro-Americans--Fiction./ Dancing--Fiction.

Ph-2 1-3/5 $15.00   L   KF933
KROLL, VIRGINIA L. Fireflies, peach pies and lullabies. Illus. by Nancy Cote. Simon & Schuster ISBN 0-689-80291-9; In Canada: Distican, 1995. unp. col. ill.
Following the death of her Great-Granny Annabel, Francie collects written memories from family and friends who remember the times before Annabel became sick and confused. Children dealing with a death in the family will relate to Francie's feelings and actions as she creates a powerful memorial. (Parents' Shelf).
SUBJ: Death--Fiction./ Memory--Fiction./ Alzheimer's disease--Fiction.

Ph-2 K-2/4 $13.95   L   KF934
KROLL, VIRGINIA L. Masai and I. Illus. by Nancy Carpenter. Four Winds/Macmillan ISBN 0-02-751165-0; In Canada: Maxwell Macmillan, 1992. unp col illus.
A young African-American girl compares her daily activities with what they would be if she were an East African Masai. Facing pages depict the two cultures side by side. For multicultural studies.
SUBJ: Masai (African people)--Fiction./ Afro-Americans--Fiction.

Ph-2 K-3/5 $14.95   L   KF935
KROLL, VIRGINIA L. Seasons and Someone. Illus. by Tatsuro Kiuchi. Harcourt Brace ISBN 0-15-271233-X; In Canada: Harcourt Brace c/o Canadian Manda, 1994. unp. col. ill.
Someone will enjoy the last berries of the season and save the seeds throughout the changing seasons in the cold North until it is time to pick berries again and plant the seeds. A young eskimo girl is refered to as "Someone" because of the Eskimo belief that it is bad luck to say one's own name aloud. Her story includes rich references to the Eskimo way of life, accompanied by beautiful oil paintings of the wildlife and landscape of Alaska. For multicultural studies.
SUBJ: Eskimos--Fiction./ Indians of North America--Fiction./ Seasons--Fiction.

Ph-2 2-4/4 $15.95   L   KF936
KRULL, KATHLEEN. Maria Molina and the Days of the Dead. Illus. by Enrique O. Sanchez. Macmillan ISBN 0-02-750999-0; In Canada: Maxwell Macmillan, 1994. unp. col. ill.
Includes bibliography.
Maria's family honors their ancestors with offerings and memories during a celebration of the Days of the Dead. She contrasts it with the American holiday of Halloween, especially when her family relocates to the United States. The warm family story and acrylic gouache illustrations convey the spirit and specific customs of the three-day Mexican celebration. A note follows with more specific details and a list of sources for further information. A recipe for "Bread of the Dead" is also included. For multicultural studies.
SUBJ: All Souls' Day--Mexico--Fiction./ Mexico--Fiction.

Ph-1 1-3/6 $15.00   L   KF937
KURTZ, JANE. Pulling the lion's tail. Illus. by Floyd Cooper. Simon & Schuster ISBN 0-689-80324-9; In Canada: Distican, 1995. unp. col. ill.

Approaching a lion with courage and patience, young Almaz pulls a hair from its tail and in the process learns how to forge a relationship with her father's new wife. Although set in Ethiopia, the story of a young girl's struggle to relate to a new stepmother will be familiar to readers who will identify with Almaz. For multicultural studies.
SUBJ: Ethiopia--Fiction./ Stepmothers--Fiction./ Patience--Fiction./ Grandfathers--Fiction.

Ph-2 K-2/5 $15.00   L   KF938
KUSKIN, KARLA. James and the rain. Illus. by Reg Cartwright. Simon & Schuster ISBN 0-671-88808-0; In Canada: Distican, 1995. unp. col. ill.
James goes for a walk in the rain and meets one cow, two ducks, three toads, and more who join him until they meet ten cats, who suggest they all go inside to sit by the fire. The repetitive text is fun for reading aloud as each set of animals has another idea for a rainy day game. The stylized illustrations have a folk art quality and will intrigue young viewers.
SUBJ: Rain and rainfall--Fiction./ Counting--Fiction./ Stories in rhyme./ Animals--Fiction.

Ph-1 K-3/5 $14.95   T   KF939
KUSKIN, KARLA. Philharmonic gets dressed. Illus. by Marc Simont. HarperCollins ISBN 0-06-023622-1; In Canada: HarperCollins, 1982. unp. col. ill.
Selectors' Choice, 14th ed.
One hundred and five musicians prepare for their concert. Some take showers, some bubble baths and one man reads in the tub while his cat watches. After bathing each gets dressed. Some start with briefs, some shorts, some panty hose, some girdles and one wears long johns. Finally all are dressed in evening apparel and leave for the concert hall. They travel by cab, car, subway or bus. Only one, the conductor, dresses more elegantly and rides in a limousine. Clean cut though often subtle pictures add humor to the matter of fact text.
SUBJ: Clothing and dress--Fiction./ Orchestra--Fiction.

Ph-2 P-1 $13.89   L   KF940
KUSKIN, KARLA. Roar and more. HarperCollins ISBN 0-06-023619-1, c1956, 1990. unp. col. ill.
Rhymed stanzas describe animal sounds. The simple illustrations and the double page spread of the sounds make this perfect to share with a group.
SUBJ: Animal sounds--Fiction./ Animals--Fiction./ Stories in rhyme.

Ph-2 1-3/2 $12.89   L   KF941
KWITZ, MARY DEBALL. Little Vampire and the Midnight Bear. Illus. by S. D. Schindler. Dial ISBN 0-8037-1529-3, 1995. 48p. col. ill. (Dial easy-to-read).
Wishing for a puppy for his birthday, Little Vampire gets a cape to wear when he learns to fly instead. When the Midnight Bear threatens Baby Vampira, Little Vampire forgets that he can't fly and saves his younger sibling. In an easy-to-read format, the subject matter will appeal to beginning and reluctant readers.
SUBJ: Vampires--Fiction./ Bears--Fiction./ Flight--Fiction./ Family life--Fiction.

Ph-1 1-3/2 $14.95   L   KF942
LAKIN, PATRICIA. Dad and me in the morning. Illus. by Robert G. Steele. Whitman ISBN 0-8075-1419-5; In Canada: General, 1994. unp. col. ill.
A young boy wakes his father early one morning, so they can watch the sun rise over the ocean. In this warm family story, it hardly seems to matter that the boy has a hearing impairment. Small allusions to hearing aids, a special alarm clock, lip reading, and sign language seem incidental to the universal story of togetherness and enjoying nature's beauty. Prime choice for units on persons with disabilities.
SUBJ: Fathers and sons--Fiction./ Deaf--Fiction./ Physically handicapped--Fiction./ Morning--Fiction./ Seashore--Fiction.

Ph-2 1-3/3 $13.93   L   KF943
LAKIN, PATRICIA. Palace of stars. Illus. by Kimberly Bulcken Root. Tambourine ISBN 0-688-11177-7, 1993. unp. col. ill.
Amanda turns the tables on her great-uncle and takes him for a Saturday outing at the movies. Set in the days when movie theaters were ornate palaces, the story and illustrations have an old-fashioned charm that appeals to many young readers. A warm intergenerational story.
SUBJ: Great-uncles--Fiction./ Family life--Fiction./ Motion pictures--Fiction.

Ph-3 P-2/2 $12.95   T OD KF944
LANTON, SANDY. Daddy's chair. Illus. by Shelly O. Haas. Kar-Ben Copies ISBN 0-929371-51-8, 1991. unp. ill.
Michael slowly begins to come to terms with his father's death during the week when his family sits Shiva, observing the Jewish week of

mourning. Sepia-toned illustrations set the serious mood for the story. Conveys respect for the feelings of children and some information about the Jewish observance of Shiva.
SUBJ: Death--Fiction./ Jews--Fiction.

Ph-2 1-3/1 $15.00   T   KF945
LAPOINTE, CLAUDE. Out of sight! Out of mind! Creative Editions/ Harcourt Brace ISBN 0-15-200956-6; In Canada: Harcourt Brace c/o Canadian Manda, 1995. unp. col. ill.
Three children decide nothing ever happens outside, but as they play a video game inside, the doublespread illustrations show a flurry of activity outside. The illustrations in the almost wordless picture book invite viewers to spend time poring over the details and talking about their observations.
SUBJ: Nature--Fiction./ Animals--Fiction.

Ph-1 K-2/2 $14.95   L   KF946
LASKY, KATHRYN. Lunch bunnies. Illus. by Marylin Hafner. Little, Brown ISBN 0-316-51525-6; In Canada: Little, Brown, 1996. unp. col. ill.
Worried about carrying a tray and the mean lunch ladies in the cafeteria, Clyde is anxious about starting school. He discovers the staff is friendly and protective of the younger students, and he makes a friend with another rabbit, Rosemary. Reassuring for new students, the story will also appeal to veterans who remember those first day jitters. A clear choice for the first day of school.
SUBJ: First day of school--Fiction./ Schools--Fiction./ Rabbits--Fiction.

Ph-2 1-3/2 $14.95   L   KF947
LATIMER, JIM. Moose and friends. Illus. by Carolyn Ewing. Scribner's ISBN 0-684-19335-3; In Canada: Maxwell Macmillan, 1993. unp. col. ill.
Moose and his animal friends are featured in a collection of episodic stories about cooking, whistling, Halloween, and Moose's birthday. Useful as a transitional reader or for reading aloud.
SUBJ: Moose--Fiction./ Animals--Fiction.

Ph-3 2-3/2 $13.89   L   KF948
LATTIMORE, DEBORAH NOURSE. Flame of peace, a tale of the Aztecs. HarperCollins ISBN 0-06-023709-0, 1987. 40p. col. ill.
Learning that his father has been killed by Tezozomois' warriors, an Aztec boy, Two Flint, takes up his search for peace by leaving to find Lord Morning Star. Using his wits, not his sword, he overcomes the nine evil ones to gain the New fire for his people. While focusing on a message of peace, the stylized illustrations and detailed endpapers provide information helpful in studies of the Aztec culture.
SUBJ: Aztecs--Fiction./ Indians of Mexico--Fiction.

Ph-2 1-3/2 $14.95   L   KF949
LATTIMORE, DEBORAH NOURSE. Frida Maria: a story of the old Southwest. Browndeer/Harcourt Brace ISBN 0-15-276636-7; In Canada: Harcourt Brace c/o Canadian Manda, 1994. unp. col. ill.
Includes glossary.
Frida Maria's independent spirit is sometimes less than ladylike, but she tries to please her mother for the Fiesta. However, when it looks as if the race will be lost to Don Ramon's horse, Frida Maria leaps into action and rides Diablo to victory. Illustrations are styled to look like frescos and reflect the art and architecture of the Southwest missions. Spanish words are included throughout the text, and a glossary provides pronuniciation and definitions. For multicultural studies.
SUBJ: Sex role--Fiction./ Southwest, New--Fiction.

Ph-2 3-5/4 $14.95   L   KF950
LATTIMORE, DEBORAH NOURSE. Punga, the goddess of ugly. Harcourt Brace ISBN 0-15-292862-6; In Canada: Harcourt Brace c/o Canadian Manda, 1993. unp. col. ill., map.
Includes glossary.
When twin sisters are told the legend of Punga, the ugly, by their grandmother, Maraweia continues to make ugly faces and finds herself in the hands of the goddess. To rescue her, Kiri teaches her, Lizard, and Mudfish to make beautiful motions and stick out their tongues in a comely fashion. The illustrations incorporate traditional Maori designs, giving the original tale an authentic flavor. For multicultural studies and units on New Zealand.
SUBJ: Maori (New Zealand people)--Fiction./ Twins--Fiction./ Sisters--Fiction./ New Zealand--Fiction.

Ph-1 1-3/4 $16.00   T   KF951
LAUTURE, DENIZE. Running the road to ABC. Illus. by Reynold Ruffins. Simon & Schuster ISBN 0-689-80507-1; In Canada: Distican, 1996. unp. col. ill.
Coretta Scott King Illustrator Honor book, 1997.
A group of children in Haiti awake before the roosters to run the distance to their school where they learn to read and write. Poetic text and crisp, colorful acrylic paintings of the tropical landscape

celebrate the road to learning based on the author's childhood. Offers a multicultural flavor for back-to-school storytimes. For multicultural studies.
SUBJ: Blacks--Haiti--Fiction./ Haiti--Fiction./ Schools--Fiction.

Ph-2 K-3/5 $14.93   L   KF952
LEAF, MARGARET. Eyes of the dragon. Illus. by Ed Young. Lothrop, Lee & Shepard ISBN 0-688-06156-7, 1987. unp. col. ill.
Proud of a wall he's had built around the village, a magistrate decides to complete it by having a dragon painted on it. The richly hued expansive illustrations are lush but, at times, make the text unreadable. The presentation of what happens when a historic law is broken is a striking readaloud.
SUBJ: Dragons--Fiction./ Artists--Fiction./ China--Fiction.

CE
Ph-1 P-1/3 $13.00   L   KF953
LEAF, MUNRO. Story of Ferdinand. Illus. by Robert Lawson. Viking Penguin ISBN 0-670-67424-9; In Canada: Penguin, c1936. unp. ill.
Read-along kit available from Live Oak Media (ISBN 0-670-67427-3, 1978). 1 hardback book, 1 sound cassette (10min), $22.95.
Spanish version read-along kit, EL CUENTO DE FERDINANDO available from Live Oak (ISBN 0-87499-189-7, 1990). 1 hardbound book, 1 sound cassette (11min), $19.95.
Available from National Library Service for the Blind and Physically Handicapped in Braille BRA06862, on sound recording cassette RC25500, and as talking book TB03858.
A young bull in Spain refuses to fight. Instead, he sits and smells the flowers--until he sits on a bee!
SUBJ: Bulls--Fiction./ Bullfights--Fiction./ Spanish language materials.

Ph-2 K-3 $13.95   T   KF954
LECOURT, NANCY. Abracadabra to zigzag: an alphabet book. Illus. by Barbara Lehman. Lothrop, Lee & Shepard ISBN 0-688-09481-3, 1991. unp. col. ill.
Includes glossary.
A vocabulary-stretching alphabet book which features unusual words like bigwig, dilly-dally, pitter-patter and wigwam. A glossary follows which gives the history and meaning of the words. Features words and illustrations that children will chuckle over and enjoy learning.
SUBJ: Alphabet.

Ph-2 1-3/2 $15.95   T   KF955
LEE, HUY VOUN. In the snow. Henry Holt ISBN 0-8050-3172-3; In Canada: Fitzhenry & Whiteside, 1995. unp. col. ill.
Xiao Ming practices drawing Chinese characters in the snow with his mother who helps him picture what they mean. A fine introduction to Chinese characters against the background of snowy collages. A fun glimpse at Chinese writing appropriate for midwinter Chinese New Year's celebrations. For multicultural studies.
SUBJ: Snow--Fiction./ Mothers and sons--Fiction./ Chinese Americans--Fiction./ Chinese language--Vocabulary./ Asian Americans--Fiction.

Ph-2 P-2/4 $14.95   T   KF956
LEE, JEANNE M. Silent Lotus. Farrar, Straus & Giroux ISBN 0-374-36911-9; In Canada: HarperCollins, 1991. unp. col. ill.
Lotus, a young girl who cannot speak or hear, leads a lonely life until her parents take her to the temple in the city. When she feels the vibrations of the music and watches the dancers, she learns to dance. Graceful illustrations depict the people and countryside of Cambodia. An original story based on the decorations on the temple at Angkor Wat.
SUBJ: Dancing--Fiction./ Mutism--Fiction./ Deaf--Fiction./ Physically handicapped--Fiction./ Cambodia--Fiction.

Ph-2 1-3/2 $14.95   L   KF957
LEEDY, LOREEN. Monster money book. Holiday House ISBN 0-8234-0922-8, 1992. unp col illus.
Includes glossary.
The members of the Monster Club meet to decide what to do with the money they have raised from dues and club projects. Slim storyline, however, young readers are introduced to basic economics including interest, budgets and checking accounts. Useful and fun for the economics curriculum.
SUBJ: Money--Fiction./ Clubs--Fiction./ Monsters--Fiction.

Ph-1 1-2/1 $7.99   T   KF958
LESIEG, THEO. Eye book. Illus. by Roy McKie. Random House ISBN 0-394-81094-5, c1968. unp. col. ill. (Bright and early book).
Humorous drawings, brief sentences and rhyming, familiar words enable beginning readers and primary children with reading difficulties gain a feeling of success. They can read, with little help, of many things to be seen with our eyes. Useful for work with children who have perceptual difficulties.
SUBJ: Eye--Fiction./ Stories in rhyme.

Ph-1 1-2/1 $7.99 L KF959

LESIEG, THEO. Ten apples up on top! Illus. by Roy McKie. Beginner Books/Random House ISBN 0-394-90019-7, c1961. 59p. col. ill. (Beginner books).

A lion, a dog, and a tiger pile apples on their heads, are chased by an unfriendly bear, and everyone ends up with ten apples on his head.

SUBJ: Apples--Fiction./ Animals--Fiction./ Counting./ Stories in rhyme.

Ph-3 K-2/2 $7.99 L KF960

LESIEG, THEO. Tooth book. Illus. by Roy McKie. Beginner Books/ Random House ISBN 0-394-94825-4; In Canada: Random House, 1981. unp. col. ill. (Bright and early book).

Rhymes and cartoonish drawings tell who has teeth and what they're used for and who doesn't have teeth and what they cannot do. Also gives lots of "don'ts" and "do's" for taking care of one's teeth.

SUBJ: Teeth--Fiction./ Stories in rhyme.

Ph-2 1-2/1 $7.99 L KF961

LESIEG, THEO. Wacky Wednesday. Illus. by George Booth. Beginner Books/Random House ISBN 0-394-92912-8, c1974. unp. col. ill.

A boy, just getting out of bed, soon decides that it must be wacky Wednesday. It all begins with a shoe on the wall, and then he sees more and more things that are strange, or wacky, or out of place. Young readers have fun searching each page for all the silly things that are wrong.

SUBJ: Counting./ Stories in rhyme./ Humorous stories.

Ph-2 1-3 $14.93 L KF962

LESSAC, FRANE. Caribbean alphabet. Tambourine ISBN 0-688-12953-6, 1994. unp. col. ill.

Includes glossary.

Agouti, dasheen, Junkanoo, reggae and other rhythmical words from the West Indies are featured in this alphabet book. Brilliant colors of the tropics intensify the primitive-style illustrations. A glossary gives brief definitions of the unusual words. The brevity of the information only offers an introduction; the curious will want to look elsewhere for more information. For multicultural studies.

SUBJ: Caribbean Area./ Alphabet.

Ph-2 K-2/3 $17.99 L KF963

LESSER, CAROLYN. What a wonderful day to be a cow. Illus. by Melissa Bay Mathis. Knopf ISBN 0-679-92430-2; In Canada: Random House, 1995. unp. col. ill.

"Borzoi book."

On and around the farm, each month has its own special qualities which are ideal for the various animals. A different animal enjoys the weather for each of the months of the year in descriptive text and richly colored illustrations suitable for sharing. For reading aloud.

SUBJ: Domestic animals--Fiction./ Months--Fiction./ Seasons--Fiction.

Ph-2 K-2/2 $14.95 L KF964

LESTER, HELEN. Listen Buddy. Illus. by Lynn Munsinger. Houghton Mifflin ISBN 0-395-72361-2, 1995. 32p. col. ill.

"Walter Lorraine books."

Buddy, a rabbit, has beautiful big ears, but he doesn't listen well which lands him in a lot of trouble with Scruffy Varmint. Buddy's poor listening skills have humorous consequences which are captured in the amusing illustrations. Makes a point about listening and following directions with lighthearted technique.

SUBJ: Rabbits--Fiction./ Listening--Fiction.

Ph-2 K-2/2 $14.95 L KF965

LESTER, HELEN. Princess Penelope's parrot. Illus. by Lynn Munsinger. Houghton Mifflin ISBN 0-395-78320-8, 1996. 32p. col. ill.

"Walter Lorraine books."

When she tries to persuade her new parrot to talk, Princess Penelope is extremely rude. The parrot chooses not to talk until the prince comes to visit and is frightened away by Penelope's rudeness. Comical illustrations depict a spoiled Penelope and a prince who arrives on a toy horse, confirming the intent of the story to be pure fun.

SUBJ: Princesses--Fiction./ Parrots--Fiction./ Behavior--Fiction.

Ph-1 K-3/2 $15.89 L KF966

LESTER, JULIUS. Sam and the tigers: a new telling of LITTLE BLACK SAMBO. Illus. by Jerry Pinkney. Dial ISBN 0-8037-2029-7, 1996. unp. col. ill.

Sporting a new colorful outfit, Sam meets several tigers on his way to school and offers each an article of clothing to keep from being eaten. The tigers argue over which is the most handsome and turn to butter as they chase each other. Sam gets his clothes back and pancakes for supper. Catchy dialog and a lively text extend the story with details about the market in Sam-sam-samara. Plants have faces and animals wear clothes in the large watercolor illustrations

appropriate for sharing. For multicultural studies.

SUBJ: Tigers--Fiction./ Humorous stories.

Ph-1 1-3/1 $13.89 L KF967

LEVINSON, NANCY SMILER. Clara and the bookwagon. Illus. by Carolyn Croll. HarperCollins ISBN 0-06-023838-0, 1988. 64p. col. ill. (I can read book).

Clara, a young Maryland farm girl, helps her mother with the younger children and the household chores and her father with the farm work. It is a happy, hard-working life but Clara longs to know about the world and read books but since there are no schools for farm children she has no chance to learn to read until the wonderful day when a big, black wagon filled with books and driven by a persistent, caring librarian, Mary Titcomb, comes up the road and Clara borrows her first library book. Based on a true 1905 incident.

SUBJ: Libraries, Traveling--Fiction./ Books and reading--Fiction./ Farm life--Fiction.

Ph-1 P-2/4 $14.95 L KF968

LEVINSON, RIKI. Emperor's new clothes. Hans Christian Andersen; retold by Riki Levinson. Illus. by Robert Byrd. Dutton ISBN 0-525-44611-7, 1991. unp. col. ill.

The beloved and classic tale about the vain and foolish emperor and the crooked tailors who deceive him is competently retold. Elaborate illustrations depict the royal palace and the animal characters.

SUBJ: Fairy tales.

Ph-1 K-2/2 $5.99 P KF969

LEVINSON, RIKI. Watch the stars come out. Illus. by Diane Goode. Penguin ISBN 0-14-055506-4, c1985, 1995. unp. col. ill.

Available in Spanish: MIRA COMO SALEN LAS ESTRELLAS (ISBN 0-525-44958-2, 1992).

Journeying across the ocean in a large ship to join their parents in a new country a young girl, the narrator's great-grandmother, and her brother are nervous and excited about their new life. Superb illustrations reenforce the tender tone of continuity and the title can be shared with a group or read with pleasure by young independent readers.

SUBJ: United States--Emigration and immigration--Fiction./ Grandmothers--Fiction./ Spanish language materials.

Ph-2 K-2/3 $14.95 T KF970

LEVITIN, SONIA. Man who kept his heart in a bucket. Illus. by Jerry Pinkney. Dial ISBN 0-8037-1029-1, 1991. unp. col. ill.

Jack keeps his heart safe in a bucket where it can't be broken, but it is stolen by a beautiful maiden who challenges him to solve her riddle in order to get his heart back. He solves the riddle and learns to keep his heart in the right place. Pinkney's pencil and watercolor illustrations add a magical quality to the folklorish tale.

SUBJ: Love--Fiction.

Ph-2 K-2/2 $10.89 L KF971

LEVITT, SIDNEY. Mighty Movers. Hyperion ISBN 1-56282-422-8, 1994. unp. col. ill.

Fred and Ted can move anything, at least they think so until they meet Hamilton, the ghost who won't move to the Quimbys' new house. Simple illustrations and easy-to-read text have child appeal.

SUBJ: Ghosts--Fiction.

CE Ph-2 1-3/3 $2.99 P KF972

LEVY, ELIZABETH. Something queer is going on (a mystery). Illus. by Mordicai Gerstein. Dell ISBN 0-440-47974-6, C1973. 48p. ill.

Read-along kit available from Listening Library FTR 78 SP (ISBN 0-8072-0070-0, 1983). 1 paperback book, 1 sound cassette (19min), $14.95. Includes guide. (Follow the reader).

The mysterious dognapping of Jill's friendly but inert basset hound leads Jill and her friend Gwen on a frantic search that ends up in front of a TV camera shooting a dog food commercial. Gwen and Jill solve further mysteries in SOMETHING QUEER AT THE BALL PARK (Delacorte ISBN 0-385-28975-8, 1975); SOMETHING QUEER AT THE HAUNTED SCHOOL (ISBN 0-440-48461-8, 1982) (kit from Listening Library FTR90SP (19min) $14.95); SOMETHING QUEER AT THE LEMONADE STAND (ISBN 0-440-48495-2, 1982); SOMETHING QUEER IN ROCK 'N ROLL (Delacorte ISBN 0-385-29547-2, 1987); SOMETHING QUEER AT THE BIRTHDAY PARTY (Delacorte ISBN 0-385-29973-7, 1990, OPC); and SOMETHING QUEER IN OUTER SPACE (Hyperion, ISBN 1-56282-566-6, 1993).

SUBJ: Dogs--Fiction./ Mystery and detective stories.

Ph-2 K-2/2 $14.95 T KF973

LEWIN, BETSY. Booby hatch. Clarion ISBN 0-395-68703-9, 1995. 32p. col. ill., map.

A blue-footed booby hatches on the Galapagos Islands, avoids

predators, and grows to adulthood. The simple text successfully conveys the life cycle of a booby without attributing human emotions and actions to it. The writer visited the islands to research the text and the watercolor illustrations.
SUBJ: Blue-footed booby--Fiction./ Galapagos Islands--Fiction./ Birds--Fiction.

Ph-2 K-2/5 $14.95 L KF974
LEWIN, TED. Amazon boy. Macmillan ISBN 0-02-757383-4; In Canada: Maxwell Macmillan, 1993. unp. col. ill.
For his birthday, Paulo and his father journey from their home in the jungle down the Amazon to the city of Belem. They visit the old part of the city, the harbor, and the market where the fishermen bring the many kinds of fish they catch in the river and the ocean. Paulo's father cautions him that these gifts from the river may disappear if people are not careful. Vivid illustrations depict the Amazon River Valley and the market brimming with life. Useful for units on Latin America and multicultural studies as well as environmental units.
SUBJ: Brazil--Fiction./ Amazon River Region--Fiction./ Environmental protection--Fiction.

Ph-1 1-3/4 $15.99 T KF975
LEWIS, J. PATRICK. Christmas of the reddle moon. Illus. by Gary Kelley. Dial ISBN 0-8037-1566-8, 1994. unp. col. ill.
Lost on the heath in a snowstorm on Christmas eve, two children are rescued by the reddlewoman, Wee Mary Fever whose mysterious powers include summoning Santa to their rescue while the children sleep. Dark, reddish pastel illustrations, including several wordless doublespreads, are the perfect accompaniment to the haunting story. An author's note describes the heath and explains that reddle was a red clay used to mark sheep. Unique among Christmas stories.
SUBJ: Christmas--Fiction./ Magic--Fiction./ Santa Claus--Fiction./ England--Fiction.

Ph-2 P-1/2 $15.95 T KF976
LEWIS, KIM. My friend Harry. Candlewick ISBN 1-56402-617-5; In Canada: Douglas & McIntyre, 1995. unp. col. ill.
James and Harry, his stuffed elephant, are inseparable playing, bathing, and sleeping together until James starts school without him. In the story and the realistic colored pencil illustrations, Harry has a definite personality without violating the bounds of reality. Youngsters with a beloved stuffed companion will relate to the warm, believable story.
SUBJ: Toys--Fiction./ Elephants--Fiction.

Ph-2 1-3/3 $9.95 P KF977
LEWIS, PAUL OWEN. Davy's dream. Beyond Words ISBN 0-941831-28-0; In Canada: Publishers Group West, 1988. unp. col. ill.
Dreaming of sailing with wild Orca whales, Davy paints the bottom of his boat whale colors, and his dreams are realized. Doublespread illustrations framed in blue convey the sequence of the story which will appeal to young whale enthusiasts.
SUBJ: Whales--Fiction./ Dreams--Fiction.

Ph-2 K-1/3 $8.95 P KF978
LEWIS, PAUL OWEN. P. Bear's New Year's party!: a counting book. Beyond Words ISBN 0-941831-29-9; In Canada: Beyond Words/dist. by Publishers Group West, 1989. unp. ill.
Countdown to midnight and the new year as guests arrive on each hour from one to twelve. Black and white illustrations are highlighted with small red details. A clock shows each hour and the animals come in numbers to match the hour providing practice in counting and telling time.
SUBJ: Bears--Fiction./ Counting./ New Year--Fiction./ Time--Fiction.

Ph-2 1-2/1 $13.89 L KF979
LEXAU, JOAN M. Rooftop mystery. Illus. by Syd Hoff. HarperCollins ISBN 0-06-023865-8, c1968. 64p. col. ill. (I can read mystery).
Available from National Library Service for the Blind and Physically Handicapped in Braille BR00958.
On his family's moving day, Sam and his friend Albert are very helpful. But while trying to move Iris' big doll without being seen by their friends, they run into a few problems and the doll disappears. It takes some clever detective work to solve the mystery and return the doll to Iris.
SUBJ: Dolls--Fiction./ Mystery and detective stories.

Ph-1 K-3/2 $16.00 T KF980
LIED, KATE. Potato: a tale from the Great Depression. Illus. by Lisa Campbell Ernst. National Geographic/dist. by Publishers Group West ISBN 0-7922-3521-5, 1997. unp. col. ill.
During the Great Depression, a young couple who cannot find work go to Idaho with their young daughter to pick potatoes. Written by an eight-year-old who heard it from an aunt, the family story is simply

told and ably illustrated. Illuminates a period of United States history, models writing for creative writing classes, and affirms the value of family stories.
SUBJ: Depressions--1929--Fiction./ Potatoes--Fiction./ Children's writings.

Ph-2 P-K/1 $13.93 L KF981
LILLIE, PATRICIA. Everything has a place. Illus. by Nancy Tafuri. Greenwillow ISBN 0-688-10083-X, 1993. unp. col. ill.
A young child observes many things in their place: a cow in a barn, a flower in a garden, and a family in a house. Bold shapes and bright colors distinguish the warm illustrations which accompany the easy-to-read text. A good point-and-say book for preschoolers and a first reader for emerging readers.
SUBJ: Perception--Fiction.

Ph-2 P-1/2 $15.00 L KF982
LILLIE, PATRICIA. Floppy teddy bear. Illus. by Karen Lee Baker. Greenwillow ISBN 0-688-12570-0, 1995. unp. col. ill.
Big sister can't keep her teddy bear away from little sister. Then big sister and Mama solve the problem by getting little sister her own teddy bear. Watercolor illustrations picture the sibling conflict and the travails of teddy. Told in a rhyming pattern with repetition and rhythm, the story is a good choice for reading aloud.
SUBJ: Teddy bears--Fiction./ Sisters--Fiction.

Ph-2 1-3/2 $15.99 T KF983
LINDBERGH, REEVE. Nobody owns the sky: the story of "Brave Bessie" Coleman. Illus. by Pamela Paparone. Candlewick ISBN 1-56402-533-0; In Canada: Candlewick/dist. by Douglas & McIntyre, 1996. unp. col. ill.
Celebrates the life and courage of Bessie Coleman, the first African-American woman licensed to fly in the world. Told in verse accompanied by attractive acrylic illustrations, Bessie Coleman's life may inspire others to reach for their dreams. Students may also be motivated to look elsewhere for more detail and facts about her life. For multicultural studies and women's studies.
SUBJ: Coleman, Bessie--Fiction./ Air pilots--Fiction./ Afro-Americans--Fiction./ Women air pilots--Fiction./ Stories in rhyme.

Ph-1 P-1/2 $4.99 P KF984
LINDEN, ANN MARIE. One smiling grandma: a Caribbean counting book. Illus. by Lynne Russell. Penguin ISBN 0-14-055341-X; In Canada: Penguin, 1995. unp. col. ill.
Count from "one smiling grandma" to "ten sleepy mongooses" in this Caribbean counting book. Sunny illustrations convey the flavor of the tropics in generous doublespreads.
SUBJ: Caribbean Area--Fiction./ Counting./ Stories in rhyme.

Ph-2 1-2/2 $13.95 T KF985
LINDGREN, ASTRID. Lotta's Christmas surprise. Illus. by Ilon Wikland. R&S/dist. by Farrar, Straus & Giroux ISBN 91-29-59782-X, c1977, 1990. unp. col. ill.
Lotta thinks she can do anything and she does manage to rescue Teddy from the garbage man and find a Christmas tree for her family when there are none to be found. Illustrations show the snow-covered town and the family's preparations for Christmas. A longer story for sharing or for good independent readers.
SUBJ: Christmas--Fiction.

CE Ph-3 K-2/3 $5.95 P KF986
LINDGREN, ASTRID. Tomten. Adapted by Astrid Lindgren from a poem by Viktor Rydberg. Illus. by Harald Wiberg. Coward-McCann/Putnam ISBN 0-698-11591-0, c1965, 1997. unp. col. ill.
Available on 1/2" VHS videocassette (8min) from Weston Woods VC66, 1982, $60.00.
A troll moves quietly about the Swedish countryside at night talking with the animals.
In THE TOMTEN AND THE FOX (Sandcastle ISBN 0-698-20644-4, c1966, 1989) the hungry fox comes to the farmyard, which is protected by the Tomten, looking for something to eat.
SUBJ: Fairy tales./ Winter--Fiction./ Sweden--Fiction.

Ph-2 K-2/2 $3.50 P KF987
LING, BETTINA. Fattest, tallest, biggest snowman ever. Illus. by Michael Rex. Math activities by Marilyn Burns. Scholastic ISBN 0-590-97284-7; In Canada: Scholastic, 1997. unp. col. ill. (Hello math reader).
"Cartwheel books."
Wanting to be the best at something, Jeff builds what he hopes is the biggest snowman. Maria's snowman seems to be as big, so the two attempt to measure their snowmen. Several activities follow the simple introduction to measurement and problem-solving.
SUBJ: Measurement--Fiction./ Snow--Fiction.

Ph-1 P-1/4 $5.99   P   KF988

LIONNI, LEO. Alexander and the wind-up mouse. Knopf ISBN 0-394-82911-5, 1987. unp. col. ill.

Caldecott Honor Book.

Available from National Library Service for the Blind and Physically Handicapped on talking book TB03289 and in Braille BRA02850 and BRA04099.

Poor Alexander--he just wants to be friendly and get a few crumbs to eat. But every time he appears in Annie's house, shrieks and commotion accompany his visit. Oh, how he wishes he could be as welcome and loved as is his friend Willie, a wind-up toy mouse. At last, with the help of the Magic Lizard, he is able to have one wish come true.

SUBJ: Mice--Fiction.

Ph-1 1-2/3 $4.99   P   KF989

LIONNI, LEO. Alphabet tree. Knopf ISBN 0-679-80835-3; In Canada: Random House, c1968, 1990. unp. col. ill.

Have you ever heard of an alphabet tree where a funny red, black and yellow word bug teaches the letters to "get together in threes and fours" and make words that even the strongest wind can't blow away? If you read about the alphabet tree you will also know about a fuzzy purple caterpillar who teaches the words how to get together to make a special message for the President.

SUBJ: Alphabet.

Ph-3 K-2/5 $6.99   P   KF990

LIONNI, LEO. Color of his own. Random House ISBN 0-679-88785-7, c1975, 1997. 32p. col. ill.

A sad chameleon has a problem. Unlike other animals, he has no color of his own but changes color to match his surroundings. He gains happiness when he meets another chameleon and they decide to stay together, and though they still change color, the two friends are always alike.

SUBJ: Chameleons--Fiction./ Friendship--Fiction.

Ph-1 1-3/2 $15.99   L   KF991

LIONNI, LEO. Extraordinary egg. Knopf ISBN 0-679-95840-1; In Canada: Random House, 1994. unp. col. ill.

"Borzoi book."

Jessica the frog discovers a wondrous pebble that is really an egg. When it hatches into an alligator, the silly frogs think it is a chicken. The funny story and doublespread illustrations make it a good choice for reading aloud.

SUBJ: Frogs--Fiction./ Alligators--Fiction./ Friendship--Fiction./ Identity--Fiction.

Ph-1 P-2/2 $15.99   L   KF992

LIONNI, LEO. Frederick. Knopf ISBN 0-394-91040-0, c1967. unp. col. ill.

Caldecott Honor Book.

Available from National Library Service for the Blind and Physically Handicapped in Braille BR00760.

Available in French: FREDERIC (L'ecole des loisirs $7.95).

While all other field mice store food for the coming winter, Frederick gathers the sun's rays and lazily dreams away the summer. But when all the food is gone and winter seems so cold and gray, Frederick brings out his magic treasures--the warmth of the sun, the colors of the flowers and the poetry of words.

SUBJ: Mice--Fiction./ French language materials.

Ph-3 P-2/4 $29.99   L   KF993

LIONNI, LEO. Frederick's fables: a Leo Lionni treasury of favorite stories. Rev. ed. With an introduction by Bruno Bettelheim. Random House ISBN 0-679-98826-2; In Canada: Random House, 1997. 132p. col. ill.

Available from National Library Service for the Blind and Physically Handicapped on sound recording cassette RC24444.

An anthology of thirteen most popular of Lionni's picture books. The stories are complete but some of the pictures have been deleted. This collection may be useful but the individual titles are more effective and have greater appeal for young children.

SUBJ: Animals--Fiction.

VCR   Ph-3 P-2 $71.00   OD   KF994

LIONNI, LEO. Leo Lionni's Caldecotts (Videocassette). SRA/McGraw-Hill 87-510158, 1985. 1/2" VHS videocassette color.

Features three well loved stories by the award winning illustrator. Transferred directly from the filmstrips, the videos contain minimum action. The cassette is recommended for purchase if the original filmstrips are not owned.

Contents: Swimmy (3min); Frederick (4min); Alexander and the wind-up Mouse (7min).

SUBJ: Animals--Fiction.

Ph-1 K-2/6 $18.99   L   KF995

LIONNI, LEO. Swimmy. Pantheon ISBN 0-394-91713-8; In Canada: Random House, c1968. unp. col. ill.

Caldecott Honor Book, 1964.

A little fish is able to protect many fish in an ingenious manner. Outstanding illustrations create a realistic underwater world.

SUBJ: Fishes--Fiction.

Ph-2 1-3/2 $14.00   L   KF996

LITTLE, JEAN. Revenge of the small Small. Illus. by Janet Wilson. Viking ISBN 0-670-84471-3; In Canada: Penguin, 1992. unp. col. ill.

Patsy, the youngest Small, has the chicken pox, and her three older siblings don't have the time to play with her. When she builds a model village and puts them in the cemetery, they realize how mean they have been to her. Portrays sibling relationships with humor and realism.

SUBJ: Family life--Fiction./ Brothers and sisters--Fiction.

Ph-2 3-5/2 $16.00   T   KF997

LITTLE, MIMI OTEY. Yoshiko and the foreigner. Farrar, Straus and Giroux ISBN 0-374-32448-4; In Canada: HarperCollins, 1996. unp. col. ill.

"Frances Foster books."

Based on her own life, the author recounts how she met and eventually married a United States Air Force officer. Because custom dictated that a proper Japanese female not talk to a foreigner, her daring to respond to him was a breach of Japanese etiquette. Little's bright illustrations recreate that long-ago experience. As in Say's HOW MY PARENTS LEARNED TO EAT, the meeting of two very different cultures is explained as the couple learns the manners, customs, and personalities of each other. An interesting visual and cultural experience for multicultural studies.

SUBJ: Prejudices--Fiction./ Japan--Fiction./ Interracial marriage--Fiction.

Ph-2 2-5/1 $15.95   L   KF998

LITTLEFIELD, HOLLY. Fire at the Triangle Factory. Illus. by Mary O'Keefe Young. Carolrhoda ISBN 0-87614-868-2, 1996. 48p. col. ill. (Carolrhoda on my own book).

Transcending their ethnic and religious differences, Tessa and Minnie, fourteen-year-old girls, work together at the Triangle Factory in New York City and save each other's lives when fire breaks out. Easy-to-read, but mature in subject matter, the story may interest reluctant readers. Author's note provides background for the historical fiction account.

SUBJ: Triangle Shirtwaist Company--Fire, 1911--Fiction./ Jews--Fiction./ Italian Americans--Fiction./ Friendship--Fiction.

Ph-2 P-2/2 $14.93   L   KF999

LOBEL, ANITA. Alison's zinnia. Greenwillow ISBN 0-688-08866-X, 1990. unp. col. ill.

From Alison to Zena and from Amaryllis to Zinnia, a girl's name, a verb and a flower are featured for each letter of the alphabet. Lush illustrations of the flowers fill over half of each page while a small insert pictures the action described. The alphabetic formula restricts the text but the beauty of the flowers fills the pages.

SUBJ: Flowers--Fiction./ Alphabet.

VCR   Ph-3 1-3 $135.00   OD   KG000

LOBEL, ARNOLD. Arnold Lobel video showcase (Videocassette). SRA/McGraw-Hill 87-510174, 1985. 16 stories on 1 1/2" VHS videocassette.

Combines selections from four books by the well known author-illustrator and an interview with him. Transferred from the filmstrips, this format has a modicum of action. The sections should be used separately and the videocassette purchased only if the filmstrips are not already owned.

Contents: Selections from Frog and Toad Together (7min); Selections from Frog and Toad are Friends (9min); Selections from Fables (16min); Selections from Mouse Soup (11min); Meet the Author: Arnold Lobel (9min).

SUBJ: Animals--Fiction./ Lobel, Arnold.

Ph-1 K-2/1 $13.89   L   KG001

LOBEL, ARNOLD. Days with Frog and Toad. HarperCollins ISBN 0-06-023964-6; In Canada: Fitzhenry & Whiteside, 1979. 64p. col. ill. (I can read book).

Spanish version DIAS CON SAPO Y SEPO available from Santillana (ISBN 84-204-37433, 1995).

Those two good friends, Frog and Toad, clean house, fly a kite, tell ghost stories, have a problem with a birthday hat that is too big, and spend most of their time together. But when Frog goes off by himself, Toad fears he has lost a friend until Frog explains that solitude is important even with best friends.

SUBJ: Frogs--Fiction./ Toads--Fiction./ Friendship--Fiction./ Spanish language materials.

CE   Ph-1 K-2/1 $13.89   L   KG002
LOBEL, ARNOLD. Frog and Toad all year. HarperCollins ISBN 0-06-023951-4, c1976. 64p. col. ill. (I can read book).
    Selectors' Choice, 11th ed.
    Read-along kit available from HarperAudio (ISBN 1-55994-228-2, 1985). 1 paperback book, 1 sound cassette (21min), $7.95.
    Available from National Library Service for the Blind and Physically Handicapped in Braille BR03334.
    Spanish version SAPO Y SEPO UN ANO ENTERO available from Santillana (ISBN 84-204-30528, n.d.).
    Five more humorous, gentle and easy-to-read stories follow this endearing pair of friends through all the seasons. There's a wild sled ride on winter's snow, they look for spring that is just around the corner, chocolate ice cream melting in the summer sun turns Toad into a brown, horned monster, autumn leaves are raked, and finally the good friends share a happy Christmas in spite of all the terrible things Toad imagines happening to his dear friend Frog.
    SUBJ: Frogs--Fiction./ Friendship--Fiction./ Toads--Fiction./ Spanish language materials.

CE   Ph-1 K-2/2 $13.89   L   KG003
LOBEL, ARNOLD. Frog and Toad are friends. HarperCollins ISBN 0-06-023958-1, c1972. 64p. col. ill. (I can read book).
    Caldecott Honor Book.
    Read-along kit from HarperAudio (ISBN 0-694-00027-2, 1985). 1 paperback book, 1 sound cassette (25min), $7.95.
    Spanish version SAPO Y SEPO SON AMIGOS available from Santillana (ISBN 84-204-30439, n.d.).
    Toad wants to sleep in his dark house instead of play in the melting snow with his best friend, Frog. He says he'll get up when it is May. Frog solves the problem by tearing the pages for November, December, January, February, March, and even April from the calendar. There are five chapters, each telling, with humor and affection, the adventures of these two best friends.
    SUBJ: Frogs--Fiction./ Friendship--Fiction./ Toads--Fiction./ Spanish language materials.

CE   Ph-1 K-2/2 $13.89   L   KG004
LOBEL, ARNOLD. Frog and Toad together. HarperCollins ISBN 0-06-023960-3, c1972. 64p. col. ill. (I can read book).
    Newbery Honor Book.
    Selectors' Choice, 8th ed.
    Read-along kit available from HarperAudio (ISBN 1-55994-230-4, 1985). 1 paperback book, 1 sound cassette read by the author (24min), $7.95.
    Available from National Library Service for the Blind and Physically Handicapped as talking book TB04809.
    Spanish version SAPO Y SEPO INSEPARABLES available from Santillana (ISBN 84-204-30471, n.d.).
    Five additional episodes in the daily life of those two best friends, Frog and Toad, are told with the same warmth and humor as in FROG AND TOAD ARE FRIENDS. When Toad loses his list of things to do for the day, he can't do anything until Frog comes up with a clever solution. Another day Frog gives Toad some seeds, but when the seeds don't sprout immediately Toad gets impatient and then worried and ends up reading stories by candlelight to his frightened seeds. In another episode Frog and Toad try to resist eating Toad's freshly baked cookies and thus develop will power.
    SUBJ: Frogs--Fiction./ Friendship--Fiction./ Toads--Fiction./ Spanish language materials.

CE   Ph-1 K-2/2 $12.89   L   KG005
LOBEL, ARNOLD. Grasshopper on the road. HarperCollins ISBN 0-06-023962-X; In Canada: Fitzhenry & Whiteside, 1978. 62p. col. ill. (I can read book).
    Available from National Library Service for the Blind and Physically Handicapped in Braille BR05082.
    Read-along kit available from Harper Caedmon (ISBN 1-55994-436-6, 1991); 1 paperback book, 1 sound cassette (15min), $6.95.
    Lighthearted Grasshopper is a real non-conformist who decides to find a road and follow it wherever it goes. As he goes along his journey, he meets a club of beetles, a worm, a housefly, a mosquito, three butterflies, and a pair of dragonflies. All have compulsive habits that allow no time for change, appreciation of nature, or adventure.
    SUBJ: Animals--Fiction.

CE   Ph-1 K-2/1 $14.93   L   KG006
LOBEL, ARNOLD. Ming Lo moves the mountain. Greenwillow ISBN 0-688-00611-6, 1982. 32p. col. ill.
    Available from National Library Service for the Blind and Physically Handicapped in Braille BR7143.
    Videocassette available from Reading Adventures 1002 (ISBN 1-882869-51-6, 1993). 1/2" VHS videocassette color (10min), $42.50.

Full page, bordered, watercolor illustrations help tell the folklore-like story of Ming Lo and his wife who attempt to move the mountain which towered over their home. Following the advice of the wise man they try to push it, frighten it away with loud noises, and bribe it. Finally, however, their home is no longer overshadowed by the mountain in a very funny resolution. Perfect to read aloud.
    SUBJ: Mountains--Fiction./ Dwellings--Fiction.

CE   Ph-1 K-2/1 $13.89   L   KG007
LOBEL, ARNOLD. Mouse soup. HarperCollins ISBN 0-06-023968-9, c1977. 63p. col. ill. (I can read book).
    Read-along kit from Harper Audio 1-55994-237-1, 1986. 1 sound cassette read by the author (16min), 1 paperback book, $6.95.
    Available from National Library Service for the Blind and Physically Handicapped in Braille BR04672 and on sound recording cassette RC12227.
    Mouse, about to become the main ingredient in Weasel's soup, convinces his captor that the soup will be much tastier with the addition of some stories. So Mouse proceeds to tell tales about a nest of bees, two large stones, some noisy crickets and finally the story of an old lady and a thorn bush growing in her chair. Then while the gullible weasel collects the bees, stones, crickets, and thorn bush, Mouse hurries home to safety.
    SUBJ: Mice--Fiction./ Weasels--Fiction.

CE   Ph-1 K-2/2 $13.89   L   KG008
LOBEL, ARNOLD. Mouse tales. HarperCollins ISBN 0-06-023942-5, c1972. 61p. col. ill. (I can read book).
    Read-along kit from HarperAudio 1-55994-239-8, 1985. 1 sound cassette read by the author (18min), 1 paperback book, $6.95.
    Father Mouse has seven lively sons. Each night he tells them bed time stories. The seven nonsensical tales, one for each son, have soft, imaginative illustrations.
    Contents: The wishing well; Clouds; Very tall mouse and very short mouse; The mouse and the winds; The journey; The old mouse; The bath.
    SUBJ: Mice--Fiction./ Short stories.

     Ph-1 P-1/6 $13.93   L   KG009
LOBEL, ARNOLD. On Market Street. Illus. by Anita Lobel. Greenwillow ISBN 0-688-84309-3, 1981. unp. col. ill.
    Caldecott Honor Book.
    Selectors' Choice, 13th ed.
    Big book available from Scholastic (ISBN 0-590-71697-2, 1986).
    Market Street has old fashioned shops filled with wonderful things for a young boy to buy. These items are arranged in ABC order and illustrated by figures of persons constructed of appropriate objects. A is a woman made of apples and M is man composed of horns, drums, violins and other musical instruments. Handsome, detailed illustrations inspired by seventeenth-century French trade engravings.
    SUBJ: Shopping--Fiction./ Alphabet./ Stories in rhyme.

     Ph-1 K-2/1 $13.89   L   KG010
LOBEL, ARNOLD. Owl at home. HarperCollins ISBN 0-06-023949-2, c1975. 64p. col. ill. (I can read book).
    Selectors' Choice, 10th ed.
    Available from National Library Service for the Blind and Physically Handicapped on sound recording cassette RC13456.
    Five episodes about lovable Owl and life in and around his cozy house. One cold night Winter comes to visit and blows out Owl's fire. Another night Owl is terrified when he discovers two strange bumps at the foot of his bed. But each time he looks under the covers for the bumps, all he sees are his own two feet. On another occasion Owl races up and down the stairsteps trying to be both upstairs and downstairs.
    SUBJ: Owls--Fiction./ Night--Fiction.

     Ph-1 K-3 $15.93   L   KG011
LOBEL, ARNOLD. Rose in my garden. Illus. by Anita Lobel. Greenwillow ISBN 0-688-02587-0, 1984. unp. col. ill.
    Selectors' Choice, 15th ed.
    Available from National Library Service for the Blind and Physically Handicapped on sound recording cassette RC22445.
    Introduces flowers of a garden, one by one and page by page. The addition of a bee, fieldmouse and cat, and other fauna pictured but not mentioned in the text, creates humor in this cumulative rhyming tale. A book of appeal and strength for children and adults.
    SUBJ: Schools--Fiction./ Bees--Fiction./ Stories in rhyme.

     Ph-1 K-2/2 $13.89   L   KG012
LOBEL, ARNOLD. Small pig. HarperCollins ISBN 0-06-023932-8, c1969. 63p. col. ill. (I can read book).
    Available from National Library Service for the Blind and Physically Handicapped in Braille BR01142.

When the farmer's wife goes on a cleaning spree and scrubs everything in sight including Small Pig, he runs away. At last he finds some lovely, soft stuff, almost like his favorite mud, and he sits and sinks in it to his heart's content. But what a shock when he discovers that he is trapped in this nice new sidewalk!
SUBJ: Pigs--Fiction.

Ph-1 P-2/4 $13.93 L KG013
LOBEL, ARNOLD. Treeful of pigs. Illus. by Anita Lobel. Greenwillow ISBN 0-688-84177-5, 1979. unp. col. ill.
When it's time to do the work involved with raising baby pigs, a lazy farmer assures his wife he will help when "pigs bloom in the garden like flowers", or "grow in trees like apples" or "fall out of the sky like rain". But each time these strange events occur the farmer goes back on his word. Finally his exasperated wife uses drastic means to get him to change his lazy ways.
SUBJ: Laziness--Fiction.

Ph-2 K-1/1 $13.89 L KG014
LOBEL, ARNOLD. Uncle Elephant. HarperCollins ISBN 0-06-023980-8; In Canada: HarperCollins, 1981. 62p. col. ill. (I can read book).
A young elephant is left alone when his parents are missing at sea. But soon his wrinkled old Uncle Elephant appears and takes the youngster on a train ride to his home. There the old uncle shows his nephew the garden, tells him stories, writes songs for him and comforts him when he mourns for his parents. Joyfully they celebrate the return of the young elephant's Mother and Father but vow to see each other often. An easy to read story that is good enough to read aloud.
SUBJ: Elephants--Fiction./ Uncles--Fiction.

Ph-2 P-1/5 $12.89 L KG015
LOBEL, ARNOLD. Zoo for Mister Muster. HarperCollins ISBN 0-06-023991-3, c1962. unp. col. ill.
The animals help to make it possible for their friend to become their keeper.
SUBJ: Animals--Fiction./ Zoos--Fiction.

Ph-1 K-3/5 $16.95 T KG016
LOCKER, THOMAS. Where the river begins. Dial/Dutton ISBN 0-8037-0089-X; In Canada: Fitzhenry & Whiteside, 1984. unp. col. ill.
Seeking the source of the river that flows past their home, Josh, Aaron, their grandfather and their dog hike through the forest, up the mountain, camp by the narrowing stream and finally reach a small, peaceful place where their search is ended at a still pond. The text is minimal and somewhat stilted though the full page landscape oil paintings give this book dramatic impact. While it can be used with a group, more of the details in the paintings can be seen if individuals or small groups have the opportunity to pore over them.
SUBJ: Grandfathers--Fiction./ Camping--Fiction./ Rivers--Fiction.

Ph-1 P-2/2 $13.99 L KG017
LOH, MORAG. Tucking mommy in. Illus. by Donna Rawlins. Orchard ISBN 0-531-08340-3, 1987. unp. col. ill.
Selectors's Choice, 17th ed.
When Sue says she'll tell the bedtime story because Mommy is so tired neither she nor Jenny expect her to fall asleep. The young sisters gently guide Mommy to her own bed, undress her and tell her a bedtime story which puts her right back to sleep. The large water colors contribute much to the success of this gentle, loving story of a family with members taking care of each other.
SUBJ: Sisters--Fiction./ Mothers and daughters--Fiction./ Bedtime--Fiction.

Ph-1 K-3/3 $14.99 T KG018
LOMONACO, PALMYRA. Night letters. Illus. by Normand Chartier. Dutton ISBN 0-525-45387-3; In Canada: McClelland & Stewart, 1996. unp. col. ill.
At the end of the day, Lily gathers messages from the ants, a rock, fireflies, and a tree and records these "letters" in her notebook. The rosy color of dusk is depicted in watercolor illustrations. Recording her observations of the natural world, Lily models an important component of the scientific process. Use in interdisciplinary units which combine nature study with creative writing activities.
SUBJ: Nature--Fiction./ Night--Fiction./ Diaries--Fiction.

Ph-1 K-3/3 $15.93 L KG019
LONDON, JONATHAN. Ali, child of the desert. Illus. by Ted Lewin. Lothrop, Lee & Shepard ISBN 0-688-12561-1; In Canada: Hearst Book Group, 1997. unp. col. ill.
Includes glossary.
Separated from his father in a sandstorm, Ali spends the night with a goatherd and the day alone in the Sahara desert until his father hears his gunshot and finds him. Dramatic watercolor illustrations underscore the survival theme and the Mideast desert setting. For multicultural studies.
SUBJ: Sahara--Fiction./ Deserts--Fiction./ Lost children--Fiction.

Ph-1 P-2/2 $14.99 L KG020
LONDON, JONATHAN. Fireflies, fireflies, light my way. Illus. by Linda Messier. Viking ISBN 0-670-85442-5; In Canada: Penguin, 1996. unp. col. ill.
Fireflies light the way as a young boy discovers the wildlife connected by the river. Richly colored illustrations overflow with lush vegetation and hidden animals. The predictable book with lyrical repetitive text is good for reading aloud for nature study or pure pleasure.
SUBJ: Animals--Fiction./ Nature--Fiction./ Fireflies--Fiction./ Stories in rhyme.

Ph-2 P-K/2 $13.99 L KG021
LONDON, JONATHAN. Froggy gets dressed. Illus. by Frank Remkiewicz. Viking Penguin ISBN 0-670-84249-4; In Canada: Penguin, 1992. unp. col. ill.
Spanish version available from Penguin Ediciones FROGGY SE VISTE (ISBN 0-670-87414-0, 1997).
Big book available from Puffin (ISBN 0-14-055378-9, 1995).
Frogs are supposed to sleep in the winter, but Froggy jumps out of bed to play in the snow. When he has to come back inside several times to finish getting dressed, he becomes exhausted. A fun introduction to clothing and snowy weather with crisp illustrations.
SUBJ: Frogs--Fiction./ Clothing and dress--Fiction./ Snow--Fiction./ Spanish language materials.

Ph-2 P-1/2 $13.99 L KG022
LONDON, JONATHAN. Froggy goes to school. Illus. by Frank Remkiewicz. Viking ISBN 0-670-86726-8; In Canada: Penguin, 1996. unp. col. ill.
Froggy's first day of school begins with a dream about going to school undressed and ends with a happy, but forgetful Froggy hopping off the bus to greet his parents. The appealing character of Froggy continues to amuse beginning readers.
SUBJ: First day of school--Fiction./ Schools--Fiction./ Frogs--Fiction.

Ph-2 K-2/5 $4.99 P KG023
LONDON, JONATHAN. Gray Fox. Illus. by Robert Sauber. Penguin ISBN 0-14-055482-3; In Canada: Penguin, c1993, 1995. unp. col. ill.
Gray Fox runs wild through fields and forests until one night he chases a rabbit into the road and is killed by a truck. A young boy finds the dead animal and carries him to a secluded spot by the river. The boy's reverent treatment of the fox and his wish for Gray Fox's spirit to be free are a moving tribute to wildlife.
SUBJ: Foxes--Fiction./ Nature--Fiction.

Ph-2 P-K/2 $12.99 L KG024
LONDON, JONATHAN. Let's go, Froggy! Illus. by Frank Remkiewicz. Viking ISBN 0-670-85055-1; In Canada: Penguin, 1994. unp. col. ill.
Getting ready for a bike trip with his father, Froggy has to search everywhere for each item he needs until finally he is ready, and his father can't find his backpack. Sound effects in the humorous text and the illustrations of the silly frog make this a great choice for reading aloud.
SUBJ: Frogs--Fiction./ Fathers and sons--Fiction./ Lost and found possessions--Fiction.

Ph-1 P-2/2 $13.95 L KG025
LONDON, JONATHAN. Lion who had asthma. Illus. by Nadine Bernard Westcott. Whitman ISBN 0-8075-4559-7; In Canada: General, 1992. unp. col. ill.
Sean likes to imagine that he is a lion, a hippo, or a giant, but when he has an asthma attack and requires treatment with a nebulizer, he no longer feels like pretending. His parents help him to imagine being a pilot connected to the machine, and he soars through the treatment. A realistic and comforting book about the most common chronic childhood illness.
SUBJ: Asthma--Fiction./ Imagination--Fiction.

Ph-2 P-2/3 $13.99 L KG026
LONDON, JONATHAN. Owl who became the moon. Illus. by Ted Rand. Dutton ISBN 0-525-45054-8, 1993. unp. col. ill.
A train whistles through a snowy woods on a moonlit night providing the only sound except for the call of an owl. The poetic images in this nighttime journey are given dramatic shape by the Japanese sumi brush strokes used in the illustrations.
SUBJ: Night--Fiction./ Railroads--Trains--Fiction./ Animals--Fiction.

Ph-1 P-1/3 $14.99 L KG027
LONDON, JONATHAN. Puddles. Illus. by G. Brian Karas. Viking ISBN 0-670-87218-0; In Canada: Penguin, 1997. unp. col. ill.

Grass glistens and puddles beckon two young children after a night of rain. Childlike illustrations and a crisp text celebrate the pleasures of mud, water, and nature.
SUBJ: Rain and rainfall--Fiction.

Ph-2 K-3/4 $15.99 T KG028
LONDON, JONATHAN. Red wolf country. Illus. by Daniel San Souci. Dutton ISBN 0-525-45191-9; In Canada: McClelland & Stewart, 1996. unp. col. ill.
A pair of red wolves travel around coastal wetlands, through snow, past skunks, people, and alligators to find food and a place to den. Once extinct in the wild, red wolves have been reintroduced in the Southeast. Their experiences have been similar to those of the pair in the story. Beautiful paintings fill doublespreads with the majesty of this species. A map on the back jacket cover shows their former range and current release sites. For environmental studies.
SUBJ: Red wolf--Fiction./ Wolves--Fiction.

Ph-2 2-3/6 $14.99 T KG029
LONDON, JONATHAN. Village basket weaver. Illus. by George Crespo. Dutton ISBN 0-525-45314-8; In Canada: McClelland & Stewart, 1996. unp. col. ill.
Tavio learns to weave baskets from his grandfather who is the village basket weaver. When his grandfather is too old and weak to complete the cassava basket needed to make the cassava bread for the whole village, Tavio asks to finish it. Bordered with weaving patterns, the illustrations depict the people and culture of a fishing village in Belize. Well researched text and illustrations depict customs and traditional crafts of the Caribbean nation. For multicultural studies.
SUBJ: Black Carib Indians--Fiction./ Indians of Central America--Fiction./ Grandfathers--Fiction./ Belize--Fiction.

Ph-1 P-1/1 $13.95 L KG030
LONG, EARLENE. Gone fishing. Illus. by Richard Brown. Houghton Mifflin ISBN 0-395-35570-2, 1984. 32p. col. ill.
Selectors' Choice, 15th ed.
Starting with "A big breakfast for my daddy. A little breakfast for me," a small boy shares a wonderful day with his father; a day that ends with "Going home to my mommy" with fish for her to see, "A big fish and a little fish for my daddy" and "A little fish and a big fish for me." Large bold pictures and a single line of text on each page convey love, warmth and fun as well as the concept of big and little.
SUBJ: Fathers and sons--Fiction./ Fishing--Fiction.

Ph-2 P-2/2 $14.95 L KG031
LOOMIS, CHRISTINE. In the diner. Illus. by Nancy Poydar. Scholastic ISBN 0-590-46716-6; In Canada: Scholastic, 1994. unp. col. ill.
Sizzling bacon and twirling stools are among the happenings at Joe's Diner depicted in simple, rhyming two word sentences with inviting illustrations. The vocabulary is not simple, but the rhyme and sentence length make this accessible for beginning readers.
SUBJ: Restaurants--Fiction./ Stories in rhyme.

Ph-1 K-2/2 $15.95 T KG032
LOPEZ, LORETTA. Birthday swap. Lee & Low ISBN 1-880000-47-4, 1997. unp. col. ill.
Includes glossary.
Expecting a celebration for her older sister's birthday, Lori is surprised when the summer party is for her birthday which isn't until December. Borders around the text and brightly colored illustrations highlight Lori's search for the perfect present for her sister and her own perfect party. Features an extended family with relatives on both sides of the border between the United States and Mexico. For multicultural studies.
SUBJ: Birthdays--Fiction./ Mexican Americans--Fiction./ Sisters--Fiction.

Ph-3 K-1/1 $7.99 L KG033
LOPSHIRE, ROBERT. Put me in the zoo. Beginner Books/Random House ISBN 0-394-90017-0, c1960. 58p. col. ill. (Beginner books).
Available from National Library Service for the Blind and Physically Handicapped in Braille BR06105 and on sound recording cassette RC22797.
A huge dotted dog learns that he really belongs in a circus, not a zoo.
SUBJ: Animals--Fiction./ Stories in rhyme.

Ph-1 K-2/3 $15.95 L KG034
LOREDO, ELIZABETH. Boogie Bones. Illus. by Kevin Hawkes. Putnam ISBN 0-399-22763-6; In Canada: Putnam, 1997. unp. col. ill.
Boogie Bones, a dancing skeleton, dresses up to leave the graveyard for a dance contest in town. He gets so carried away at the contest that his disguise falls off, scaring everyone except Maggie who joins

him on the dance floor to win the trophy. A humorous addition to skeleton storytimes.
SUBJ: Dancing--Fiction./ Skeleton--Fiction./ Contests--Fiction.

Ph-2 P-2/2 $2.95 P KG035
LOW, ALICE. Popcorn shop. Illus. by Patti Hammel. Scholastic ISBN 0-590-47121-X, 1993. unp. col. ill. (Hello reader!).
"Cartwheel books."
Popcorn Nell's popcorn is so popular she buys a big machine to pop it, and one day it won't stop popping. Soon the townspeople are wading through popcorn and begging Nell to stop. The rhyming text is a popping pleasure for reading aloud or independent reading.
SUBJ: Popcorn--Fiction./ Stories in rhyme.

Ph-1 P-2/2 $4.95 P KG036
LOW, JOSEPH. Mice twice. Atheneum ISBN 0-689-71060-7; In Canada: Collier Macmillan, 1980. unp. col. ill.
Caldecott Honor Book.
With ulterior motives hungry Cat invites Mouse to dinner. He is especially pleased when she accepts and even asks to bring a friend. Much to Cat's surprise and anger Mouse's friend turns out to be Dog. Thus Cat's plans are changed and there are no juicy mice for dinner. Returning the invitation Dog is prepared when Cat brings Wolf along. He has Crocodile in attendance. And so continues a round of invitations with larger and fiercer guests until Mouse ends it with a small but very effective friend. Bright colorful illustrations add to the humor and appeal.
SUBJ: Animals--Fiction.

Ph-1 K-2/3 $15.95 T KG037
LOW, WILLIAM. Chinatown. Henry Holt ISBN 0-8050-4214-8; In Canada: Fitzhenry & Whiteside, 1997. unp. col. ill.
A young boy describes his neighborhood as he and his grandmother go for a morning walk, and he remembers his favorite time: Chinese New Year. Oil paintings immerse the viewer in the activities and culture of Chinatown. For multicultural studies.
SUBJ: Chinatown (New York, N.Y.)--Fiction./ Chinese Americans--Fiction./ Chinese New Year--Fiction./ Grandmothers--Fiction.

Ph-1 1-3/3 14.95 T KG038
LOWELL, SUSAN. Little Red Cowboy Hat. Illus. by Randy Cecil. Henry Holt ISBN 0-8050-3508-7; In Canada: Fitzhenry & Whiteside, 1997. unp. col. ill.
Little Red Riding Hood has a decidedly western and spicy flavor in this variation set among canyons and cacti. Red is a cowgirl and her granny is no meek morsel for a wolf, but an ax-wielding, horseback riding force to be reckoned with. Add this to the growing body of folktale parodies popular with young audiences.
SUBJ: Fairy tales--Parodies, imitations, etc./ Folklore--Parodies, imitations, etc./ Grandmothers--Fiction./ Wolves--Fiction./ Southwest, New--Fiction.

Ph-1 K-2/4 $14.95 T KG039
LOWELL, SUSAN. Three little javelinas. Illus. by Jim Harris. Northland ISBN 0-87358-542-9, 1992. unp. col. ill.
Selectors' Choice, 19th ed.
Bilingual Spanish edition available LOS TRES PEQUENOS JABALIES/THE THREE LITTLE JAVELINAS (ISBN 0-87358-661-1, 1996), $14.95.
Three javelinas, wild and hairy southwestern cousins of pigs, outsmart a coyote in this delightful version of the traditional story of THE THREE LITTLE PIGS. Humorous illustrations are filled with regional details.
SUBJ: Pigs--Fiction./ Coyotes--Fiction./ Southwest, New--Fiction./ Bilingual materials--Spanish./ Spanish language materials.

Ph-2 K-2/3 $14.95 T KG040
LOWELL, SUSAN. Tortoise and the jackrabbit. Illus. by Jim Harris. Northland ISBN 0-87358-586-0, 1994. unp. col. ill.
The well-worn story of the tortoise and the hare is given a southwestern flavor in this version featuring a desert tortoise and a jackrabbit. Rattlesnakes, saguaro cactus, tarantulas, and other desert plants and animals depicted in watercolor and acrylic illustrations lend local color to the familiar race. Fans of THE THREE JAVELINAS will enjoy finding those characters in this story.
SUBJ: Turtles--Fiction./ Rabbits--Fiction./ Southwest, New--Fiction./ Deserts--Fiction.

CE
Ph-2 K-2/2 $13.95 L KG041
LUENN, NANCY. Nessa's fish. Illus. by Neil Waldman. Atheneum ISBN 0-689-31477-9; In Canada: Collier Macmillan, 1990. unp. col. ill.
Also available in Spanish LA PESCA DE NESSA (ISBN 0-689-31977-0, 1994).
Available from the National Library Service for the Blind and

Physically Handicapped on sound recording cassette RC35303. Videocassette available from Reading Adventures 1007 (ISBN 1-88286-956-7, 1993), 1/2" VHS videocassette color (6min), $42.50.

When her grandmother becomes ill and they cannot return to camp with all the fish they've caught, young Nessa manages to ward off the animals that come after the fish. Luminous, highly stylized watercolor wash illustrations enhance the simply told text. A useful adjunct to units on family or cultural differences. For multicultural studies.

SUBJ: Eskimos--Fiction./ Indians of North America--Fiction./ Arctic tundra--Fiction./ Grandmothers--Fiction.

Ph-1 K-3/2 $14.99   L   KG042
LYON, GEORGE ELLA. Cecil's story. Illus. by Peter Catalanotto. Orchard ISBN 0-531-08512-0, 1991. unp. col. ill.

Left with neighbors while his mother goes to fetch his father, who has been wounded in the Civil War, Cecil ponders the possible outcomes. A brief text and impressionistic illustrations powerfully convey the impact of war on a child's world. Although the setting is historical, the story can ring true whenever war threatens.

SUBJ: War--Fiction./ United States--History--Civil War, 1861-1865--Fiction.

Ph-1 K-3/2 $14.99   L   KG043
LYON, GEORGE ELLA. Come a tide. Illus. by Stephen Gammell. Orchard ISBN 0-531-08454-X, 1990. unp. col. ill.

In the Kentucky hills rain is pouring down and the swelling creeks make Grandma predict "It'll come a tide." It does as floods come rushing down and everyone flees to higher ground. As the sun comes out and they assess the damage, Grandma says "make friends with a shovel." The light-hearted illustrations mesh with the text to show the commonsense and courage of the mountain folk.

SUBJ: Floods--Fiction./ Country life--Fiction.

Ph-1 2-3/3 $15.95   L   KG044
LYON, GEORGE ELLA. Mama is a miner. Illus. by Peter Catalanotto. Orchard ISBN 0-531-08703-4, 1994. unp. col. ill.

"Richard Jackson book."

In a warm, bright kitchen with the family gathered together, a young child reflects on her mother's day spent working deep in the mines. Watercolor illustrations bounce and fade from the dark mines to the well lit kitchen, from Mama's dangerous job to the safety of home, and from hard work to family togetherness. Sometimes wishing her mother had a safer job, the young narrator is clearly proud of her mother's hard work.

SUBJ: Mothers--Fiction./ Miners--Fiction./ Work--Fiction./ Stories in rhyme.

Ph-1 P-1/1 $6.95   L   KG045
MACCARONE, GRACE. Cars! cars! cars! Illus. by David A. Carter. Scholastic ISBN 0-590-47572-X; In Canada: Scholastic, 1995. unp. col. ill. (Story corner).

"Cartwheel books."

Presents dogs in all kinds of cars in a simple and repetitive text. Uncluttered, attractive illustrations and plenty of white space complement the easy, predictable story. Emergent readers, especially the many infatuated with cars, dogs, or both will particularly enjoy this book. Reminiscent of GO, DOG, GO!, many of the rhyming pairs introduce the concept of opposites.

SUBJ: Automobiles--Fiction./ Stories in rhyme./ English language--Synonyms and antonyms--Fiction.

Ph-2 K-1/2 $2.95   P   KG046
MACCARONE, GRACE. Classroom pet. Illus. by Betsy Lewin. Scholastic ISBN 0-590-26264-5; In Canada: Scholastic, 1995. unp. col. ill. (Hello reader!).

"Cartwheel books."

When Sam loses the class hermit crab during Christmas vacation, he finds it in a surprising place. The easy-to-read text is accompanied by lively illustrations which offer visual clues. Part of the "First-Grade Friends series," the story will appeal to beginning readers who enjoy reading different books about the same characters.

SUBJ: Hermit crabs--Fiction./ Crabs--Fiction./ Schools--Fiction./ Stories in rhyme.

Ph-2 P-1/1 $2.95   P   KG047
MACCARONE, GRACE. Pizza party! Illus. by Emily Arnold McCully. Scholastic ISBN 0-590-47563-0; In Canada: Scholastic, 1994. unp. col. ill. (Hello reader!).

"Cartwheel books."

Four children scoop, fill, spill, clean, roll, and eat a pizza together. Very short sentences create an easy-to-read story and the cast has something for everyone. For multicultural studies.

SUBJ: Pizza--Fiction./ Stories in rhyme.

Ph-2 K-2/2 $14.95   L   KG048
MACDONALD, AMY. Cousin Ruth's tooth. Illus. by Marjorie Priceman. Houghton Mifflin ISBN 0-395-71253-X, 1996. 32p. col. ill.

Everyone gets involved in the search for Cousin Ruth's lost tooth, until they finally look in her mouth and see that a new one has taken its place. Absurd rhymes and funny illustrations delight clever audiences who know exactly what happens when you lose a tooth.

SUBJ: Teeth--Fiction./ Stories in rhyme.

Ph-2 P-K/1 $14.95   T   KG049
MACDONALD, AMY. Little Beaver and The Echo. Illus. by Sarah Fox-Davies. Putnam ISBN 0-399-22203-0, 1990. unp. col. ill.

In search of the voice across the pond, Little Beaver makes friends with a duck, an otter, and a turtle. He meets a wise old beaver who tells him the voice across the pond is the Echo. Youngsters may require further explanations about echoes since little information is offered here.

SUBJ: Friendship--Fiction./ Beavers--Fiction./ Animals--Fiction./ Echoes--Fiction.

Ph-2 K-2/2 $13.95   L   KG050
MACDONALD, AMY. Rachel Fister's blister. Illus. by Marjorie Priceman. Houghton Mifflin ISBN 0-395-52152-1, 1990. 32p. col. ill.

Rachel Fister finds a blister on her toe and everyone in town offers their suggestions, until Queen Alice suggests the perfect cure. A lot of fuss and silly rhymes, perfect for reading aloud.

SUBJ: Wounds and injuries--Fiction./ Stories in rhyme.

Ph-1 P-2 $15.95   T   KG051
MACDONALD, SUSE. Alphabatics. Bradbury ISBN 0-02-761520-0; In Canada: Collier Macmillan, 1986. unp col illus.

Caldecott Honor book.

Available from National Library Service for the Blind and Physically Handicapped in Braille BR7141.

An unusual alphabet book in which each letter of the alphabet gradually changes into an object illustrating that letter. A capital A frame by frame turns until it is upside down on a sea of blue and has become an ark. Some of the transformations are more complicated but the end result of each is a large, uncluttered and visually stimulating picture of the appropriate object.

SUBJ: Alphabet.

Ph-1 P-1/1 $11.95   L   KG052
MACK, STANLEY. 10 bears in my bed: a goodnight countdown. Pantheon ISBN 0-394-92902-0, 1974. 28p. col. ill.

When the "little one" says "Roll over, Roll over", one by one ten bears leave a little boy's bed until there are none, and then the "little one" says "Goodnight". Based on an old counting song, this simple book has strong child appeal.

SUBJ: Counting./ Nursery rhymes./ Bears--Fiction.

Ph-1 1-4/5 $14.89   L   KG053
MACLACHLAN, PATRICIA. All the places to love. Illus. by Mike Wimmer. HarperCollins ISBN 0-06-021099-0, 1994. unp. col. ill.

Selector's Choice, 20th ed.

When Eli is born, his grandfather carves his name on the rafter in the barn. As he grows up, he learns about the many places to love on the farm and surrounding countryside. When Eli's baby sister is born, he helps his grandfather add her name to the rafter and plans to show her the places to love. Rich language and striking oil paintings convey a strong sense of family and of place.

SUBJ: Farms--Fiction./ Country life--Fiction.

Ph-2 2-3/1 $14.89   L   KG054
MACLACHLAN, PATRICIA. Mama One, Mama Two. Illus. by Ruth Lercher Bornstein. HarperCollins ISBN 0-06-024082-2; In Canada: HarperCollins, 1982. unp. col. ill.

Selectors' Choice, 14th ed.

Maudie and her Mama (Mama One) are separated when the mother, in a state of deep depression, must be institutionalized. Fortunately for Maudie her foster mother, Mama Two, is loving, careing and understanding. Richly hued, softly textured illustrations complement the mood of the story.

SUBJ: Foster home care--Fiction./ Mothers and daughters--Fiction./ Mentally ill--Fiction.

Ph-2 2-3/5 $14.89   L   KG055
MACLACHLAN, PATRICIA. Three Names. Illus. by Alexander Pertzoff. HarperCollins ISBN 0-06-024036-9; In Canada: HarperCollins, 1991. 31p. col. ill.

"Charlotte Zolotow book."

Available from the National Library Service for the Blind and Physically Handicapped on sound recording cassette RC 36329.

Great grandfather had a dog named "Three Names" who accompanied him to a one-room schoolhouse on the prairie where

they lived. Warm story of a boy and his dog depicts an earlier time in slow-paced text and impressionistic illustrations.
SUBJ: Grandfathers--Fiction./ Schools--Fiction./ Dogs--Fiction./ West (U.S.)--Fiction.

CE   Ph-1 K-4/5 $13.99   T   KG056
MAHY, MARGARET. Great white man-eating shark: a cautionary tale. Illus. by Jonathan Allen. Dial ISBN 0-8037-0749-5, 1989. unp. col. ill.
Animated videocassette available from Weston Woods HMPV348V, 1991. 1/2" VHS videocassette color (10min), $49.95.
Read-along kit available from Weston Woods HRA348, 1992. 1 hardback book, 1 sound cassette (19min), $12.95.
Young Norville is a great actor, but his sharklike face limits his parts. A great swimmer, he turns his theatrical talents to impersonating a shark (aided by a fake dorsal fin) and driving the swimmers from his favorite cove. But an approach from an amorous female shark catapults him to shore. Very amusing watercolor illustrations complement his hilarious story. Good for reading aloud.
SUBJ: Sharks--Fiction./ Greed--Fiction.

       Ph-2 K-2/5 $14.99   T   KG057
MAHY, MARGARET. Rattlebang picnic. Illus. by Steven Kellogg. Dial ISBN 0-8037-1318-5, 1994. unp. col. ill.
Available from the National Library Service for the Blind and Physically Handicapped on sound recording cassette RC 41713.
Mr. and Mrs. McTavish decide to have seven children and make do with an old rattlebang car instead of a speedy new car. The car serves them well on a family picnic and safely delivers them from atop Mount Fogg when the volcano erupts. Raucous humor also erupts from every page with an unforgettable cast of characters and energetic illustrations.
SUBJ: Picnicking--Fiction./ Automobiles--Fiction.

       Ph-2 1-3/2 $18.60   L   KG058
MANN, PAMELA. Frog Princess? Illus. by Jill Newton. Gareth Stevens ISBN 0-8368-1352-9, 1995. unp. col. ill.
First published in Great Britain, ABC, All Books for Children, 1995.
When a horse named Beauty and other story characters claim to have had a book written about them, an ugly frog answers, "Reddit." Finally a well-read prince who believes the frog kisses it, and he transforms the frog into a beautiful and well-read princess. An entertaining variant of the popular Frog Prince story with references to other well-known fairy tales.
SUBJ: Frogs--Fiction./ Princes--Fiction./ Librarians--Fiction./ Fairy tales--Parodies, imitations, etc.

       Ph-2 1-3/2 $14.95   L   KG059
MANUSHKIN, FRAN. Matzah that Papa brought home. Illus. by Ned Bittinger. Scholastic ISBN 0-590-47146-5; In Canada: Scholastic, 1995. unp. col. ill.
A family's celebration of the Passover Seder is told in a cumulative verse. Rich oil paintings depict the extended family eating the symbolic foods and enjoying the rituals of the holiday. "The Story of Passover" follows the text, providing historical background and outlining several of the foods and rituals including the four questions.
SUBJ: Seder--Fiction./ Passover--Fiction./ Stories in rhyme.

       Ph-1 P-2/2 $14.95   L   KG060
MANUSHKIN, FRAN. Peeping and sleeping. Illus. by Jennifer Plecas. Clarion ISBN 0-395-64339-2, 1994. 32p. col. ill.
Peeping noises frighten Barry as he prepares for sleep. His father takes him outside with a flashlight to see the small frogs called spring peepers who are making all of the noise. Returning to bed, Barry hears one of the peepers inside and discovers it in his slipper. A gentle nighttime story illustrated with soothing pastels and colored pencils.
SUBJ: Frogs--Fiction./ Night--Fiction./ Sound--Fiction./ Fathers and sons--Fiction.

       Ph-2 1-3/2 $15.00   L   KG061
MANUSHKIN, FRAN. Starlight and candles: the joys of the Sabbath. Illus. by Jacqueline Chwast. Simon & Schuster ISBN 0-689-80274-9; In Canada: Distican, 1995. unp. col. ill.
Includes glossary.
An extended family's observance of the Jewish Sabbath highlights the traditions and history of the weekly celebration. Stylized cut-paper and watercolor illustrations are an elegant addition to the story.
SUBJ: Sabbath--Fiction./ Jews--Fiction.

CDR   Ph-1 K-4 $39.95   OD   KG062
MARC BROWN'S ARTHUR'S BIRTHDAY. School ed. (CD-ROM). Random House/Broderbund, 1994. 1 CD-ROM color, 1 paperback book, 1 sound cassette. (Living books).
Includes teacher's guide, user's guide and Sharon, Lois and Bram's

HAPPY BIRTHDAY sound recording cassette.
System requirements: Macintosh: System 6.0.7 or later; 4MB RAM; 256 color monitor LC series or higher; CD-ROM drive.
System requirements: IBM and 100% compatibles: MPC compatible CD-ROM drive; Windows 3.0 with multimedia extensions or Windows 3.1; 16 MHz 386 or faster; SVGA; mouse and sound card.
Product runs on either Macintosh or Windows compatible hardware.
Yet another story about Arthur, this one tells of Arthur's dilemma when a fellow student schedules another party on the same date as Arthur's birthday party. An ingenious solution makes for a happy ending. The excellent animations, standard for this series, options to have the story read in English or Spanish, and superb sound captivate young readers. A sound recording of birthday songs and music recorded by Sharon, Lois and Bram is included.
SUBJ: Parties--Fiction--Software./ Software--Parties--Fiction./ Birthdays--Fiction--Software./ Software--Birthdays--Fiction./ Friendship--Fiction--Software./ Software--Friendship--Fiction./ Spanish language materials--Software./ Software--Spanish language materials./ Bilingual materials--Spanish--Software./ Software--Bilingual materials--Spanish./ Interactive media.

CDR   Ph-1 K-3 $39.95   OD   KG063
MARK SCHLICHTING'S HARRY AND THE HAUNTED HOUSE. School ed. (CD-ROM). Random House/Broderbund, 1994. 1 CD-ROM color, 2 paperback books. (Living books).
Includes teacher's guide, user's guide, troubleshooting guide and Harry Allard's MISS NELSON IS MISSING.
System requirements: Macintosh System 6.0.7 or higher; CD-ROM drive; 256 color monitor; 4MB RAM.
System requirements: IBM/Tandy or 100% compatible; 386SX or higher with 4MB RAM; Windows 3.1; MS-DOS 3.3 or higher; Super VGA (640x480, 256 colors); Sound Blaster or SB Pro and 100% compatible sound card; mouse; CD-ROM drive.
Product runs on either Macintosh or Windows compatible hardware.
Follows the book HARRY AND THE HAUNTED HOUSE by Mark Schlichting in which a baseball hit into the haunted house begins Harry's adventure with his friends. Trademark animations and humor as well as excellent graphics and sound make the tale also a hit with youngsters. The story can be read in English or Spanish. A bonus book, MISS NELSON IS MISSING, about another mysterious occurrence is included.
SUBJ: Haunted houses--Fiction--Software./ Software--Haunted houses--Fiction./ Animals--Fiction--Software./ Software--Animals--Fiction./ Spanish language materials--Software./ Software--Spanish language materials./ Bilingual materials--Spanish--Software./ Software--Bilingual materials--Spanish./ Interactive media.

CE   Ph-1 K-2/1 $3.50   P   KG064
MARSHALL, EDWARD. Fox and his friends. Illus. by James Marshall. Penguin ISBN 0-14-037007-2, 1994. 56p. col. ill. (Dial easy-to-read).
Read-along kit from Listening Library FTR92, 1985. 1 sound cassette (15min), 1 paperback book, guide $15.98.
Spanish version available from Penguin Ediciones ZORRO Y SUS AMIGOS (ISBN 0-14-038020-5, 1996).
It's Saturday and Fox plans a great time with his friends, but instead he must babysit his little sister, Louise. Another time he has swimming plans with friends, Dexter, Carmen, and Junior, but again he has to let Louise tag along. Sometimes watching Louise is a bore, but more often than not, she causes real excitement.
Humorous, easy-to-read, and familiar childhood experiences also follow in FOX IN LOVE (ISBN 0-14-036843-4, 1994) (kit from Listening Library FTR94); FOX AT SCHOOL (ISBN 0-8037-2674-0, 1983, OPC) (kit from Listening Library FTR91); FOX ON WHEELS (ISBN 0-8037-0002-4, 1983, OPC) (kit from Listening Library FTR95); FOX ON STAGE (ISBN 0-8037-1357-6, 1993), and FOX ALL WEEK (ISBN 0-14-037708-5, c1984, 1992).
SUBJ: Foxes--Fiction./ Humorous stories./ Brothers and sisters--Fiction./ Spanish language materials.

       Ph-1 P-2/4 $14.99   T   KG065
MARSHALL, EDWARD. Space case. Illus. by James Marshall. Dial ISBN 0-8037-8005-2, 1980. unp. col. ill.
Selectors' Choice, 13th ed.
A round, yellow, robot-like creature from outer space lands on earth to have a look around. He soon joins a group of "trick-or-treaters" who think he is the new kid down the block with a great costume. After an evening of Halloween fun, the "Thing" spends the night with Buddy McGee and even goes to school with him next day. When Buddy is unprepared with his space project, his new friend saves the day and helps Buddy gets an A minus. Humorous, strongly colored illustrations make this a good candidate for sharing.
SUBJ: Science fiction./ Halloween--Fiction.

CE Ph-2 K-3/1 $3.50 P KG066
MARSHALL, EDWARD. Three by the sea. Illus. by James Marshall. Dial ISBN 0-8037-8671-9, 1981. 48p. col. ill.
> Read-along kit from Listening Library FTR82 (ISBN 0-8072-0054-9, 1984). 1 sound cassette (12min), 1 paperback book, guide, $15.98. Available from National Library Service for the Blind and Physically Handicapped in Braille BR06307 and on sound recording cassette RC23153.
> After a big picnic on the beach, Lolly, Sam and Spider are too full to swim so decide to tell stories. Lolly reads one first. Her friends say it is too dull. Then Sam tells a story about a rat who buys a cat for a pet. Spider thinks it has a dumb ending so he tells a scary one about a fierce looking sea monster with sharp green teeth and long black claws and who likes to eat kids on toast.
> Sam, Spider and Lolly spin more yarns in FOUR ON THE SHORE (ISBN 0-8037-0155-1, 1985, Spanish version LA PANDILLA EN LA ORILLA available from Santillana ISBN 84-204-46785, n.d.)); and THREE UP A TREE (ISBN 0-8037-0329-5, 1986, Spanish version TRES EN UN ARBOL available from Santillana ISBN 84-240-46378, n.d.).
> SUBJ: Storytelling--Fiction./ Spanish language materials.

Ph-1 K-3/2 $4.99 P KG067
MARSHALL, JAMES. Fox on the job. Penguin ISBN 0-14-036191-X, c1988, 1990. 48p. col. ill. (Dial easy-to-read).
> Showing off for the girls, Fox wrecks his bike and when no one in the family will give him the needed money he must get a job to buy a new one. His lack of success in several jobs before finding the position that just suits him provides much humor in this easy to read and appealing story.
> More stories of Fox showing off are found in FOX BE NIMBLE (ISBN 0-8037-0760-6, 1990); and FOX OUTFOXED (ISBN 0-8037-1037-2, 1992).
> SUBJ: Foxes--Fiction./ Humorous stories.

CE Ph-2 P-2/3 $13.95 L KG068
MARSHALL, JAMES. George and Martha. Houghton Mifflin ISBN 0-395-16619-5, c1972. 46p. col. ill.
> Read-along kit available from Houghton Mifflin 0-395-45739-4, 1987. 1 sound cassette, 1 paperback book, $7.95.
> Five brief stories about two hippopotamuses portray the joys and delights of having a friend to cheer you, care, and spare your feelings. Upon discovering that George has eaten ten bowls of her special pea soup before pouring the eleventh in his loafers rather than hurt her feelings by admitting that he hates pea soup, Martha says "Friends should always tell each other the truth", and besides "I don't like pea soup myself", GEORGE AND MARTHA 'ROUND AND 'ROUND (ISBN 0-395-46763-2, 1988) adds five more easy to read stories about these popular friends.
> More stories about these two good friends follow in GEORGE AND MARTHA ENCORE (ISBN 0-395-17512-7, 1973); GEORGE AND MARTHA ONE FINE DAY (ISBN 0-395-27154-1, 1978); GEORGE AND MARTHA RISE AND SHINE (ISBN 0-395-24738-1, 1976); and GEORGE AND MARTHA BACK IN TOWN (ISBN 0-395-35386-6, 1984).
> SUBJ: Hippopotamus--Fiction./ Friendship--Fiction.

Ph-2 K-2/1 $15.95 L KG069
MARTIN, ANN M. Rachel Parker, kindergarten show-off. Illus. by Nancy Poydar. Holiday House ISBN 0-8234-0935-X, 1992. unp. col. ill.
> Rachel Parker moves in next door to Olivia and is in her kindergarten class. The two girls frequently find themselves in competition with each other but eventually become good friends. The subject and reading level are on target for the concerns of this age group when first friendships are developing.
> SUBJ: Friendship--Fiction./ Kindergarten--Fiction./ Schools--Fiction.

Ph-2 P-2/4 $13.95 L KG070
MARTIN, ANTOINETTE TRUGLIO. Famous seaweed soup. Illus. by Nadine Bernard Westcott. Whitman ISBN 0-8075-2263-5; In Canada: General, 1993. unp. col. ill.
> Sara gathers seaweed, snails, and other ingredients from the beach all by herself to make her famous seaweed soup. Since no one helped to make it, she tells her family they will all have to help eat it. A bright selection for units on the beach and for comparison with the traditional LITTLE RED HEN.
> SUBJ: Seashore--Fiction./ Soups--Fiction.

Ph-2 P-3/3 $13.95 T KG071
MARTIN, JR., BILL. Barn dance! By Bill Martin, Jr. and John Archambault. Illus. by Ted Rand. Henry Holt ISBN 0-8050-0089-5; In Canada: Fitzhenry & Whiteside, 1986. unp. col. ill.
> Everyone else is asleep but a very curious young farm boy investigates the sounds of a fiddle coming from the cornfield and soon from a hoe-down in the barn. The rhyming text has the rhythm and often the words of square dance calls and the skinny young boy goes through the dance steps with the animals. The effective and often humorous illustrations capture the feel of full moonlight on a farm and all the animals who participate in the get-together.
> SUBJ: Stories in rhyme./ Dancing--Fiction./ Country life--Fiction.

Ph-1 P-K/1 $14.95 T KG072
MARTIN, JR., BILL. Brown bear, brown bear, what do you see? Illus. by Eric Carle. Henry Holt ISBN 0-8050-1744-5; In Canada: Fitzhenry & Whiteside, 1992. unp. col. ill.
> Questioning "What do you see?" begins a chain of responses which in turn leads to further queries all incorporating animals and colors. Highly popular with young children, this new edition of a perennial favorite uses new and brighter collages. A favorite choice for emerging readers. A similar question and response format with colorful animal illustrations follows in POLAR BEAR, POLAR BEAR, WHAT DO YOU HEAR? (ISBN 0-8050-1759-3, 1991) Big book available for POLAR BEAR, POLAR BEAR, WHAT DO YOU HEAR? (ISBN 0-8050-2346-1, 1992)
> SUBJ: Color--Fiction./ Animals--Fiction./ Stories in rhyme.

Ph-1 P-1/2 $13.95 L KG073
MARTIN, JR., BILL. Chicka chicka boom boom. By Bill Martin, Jr. and John Archambault. Illus. by Lois Ehlert. Simon & Schuster ISBN 0-671-67949-X, 1989. unp. col. ill.
> Selectors' Choice, 18th ed.
> An amusing alphabet book about letters who dare each other to climb a coconut tree. As they climb, the tree bends under their weight and they all "chicka chicka... boom boom" come crashing down. The vividly colored illustrations convey the manic energy of the competitive alphabet letters.
> SUBJ: Alphabet./ Stories in rhyme.

KIT Ph-1 P-1 $19.95 KG074
MARTIN, JR., BILL. Chicka chicka boom boom (Kit). By Bill Martin, Jr. and John Archambault. Illus. by Lois Ehlert. Simon & Schuster ISBN 0-671-74894-7, 1991. 1 hardcover book, 1 sound cassette (20min).
> Selectors' Choice, 19th ed.
> Contains five versions of the lively alphabet book. Ray Charles reads two, one of which has a drum beat to indicate page-turning for reading along. The third version on side A is done by children, and youngsters are invited to join in. Side B includes two musical versions with similar jump rope rhymes, and John Archambault discussing the origin of the idea for the text. The musical text and jump rope rhymes can be extended as an introduction to rhythm for music or physical education classes.
> SUBJ: Alphabet./ Stories in rhyme.

Ph-1 K-3/2 $13.45 L KG075
MARTIN, JR., BILL. Ghost-eye tree. By Bill Martin, Jr. and John Archambault. Illus. by Ted Rand. Henry Holt ISBN 0-8050-0208-1; In Canada: Fitzhenry & Whiteside, 1985. unp. col. ill.
> On a dark and windy autumn night a brother and sister are sent to the far end of town for a bucket of milk. They safely pass the fearful ghost-eye tree while accusing each other of being a "fraidy-cat." But on the way home they are not so fortunate; a sound going eeeooowowowooowowo pierces the air, the ghost-eye tree reaches out to grab them and when they reach safety both admit they had been very scared. Dramatic, dark, shadowy pictures with highlights on the children's expressive faces superbly create just the right spooky atmosphere. Excellent for reading aloud, especially at Halloween.
> SUBJ: Ghosts--Fiction./ Fear--Fiction./ Brothers and sisters--Fiction.

Ph-2 P-1/2 $14.95 L KG076
MARTIN, JR., BILL. Here are my hands. By Bill Martin, Jr. and John Archambault. Illus. by Ted Rand. Henry Holt ISBN 0-8050-0328-2, 1987. unp. col. ill.
> Hands, feet, head, nose, eyes, ears, neck, cheeks, teeth, are among the body parts for which uses are listed in simple rhyming text. Could easily be set to a melody and/or become a game.
> SUBJ: Body, Human--Fiction./ Stories in rhyme.

Ph-2 P-2 $14.95 L KG077
MARTIN, JR., BILL. Listen to the rain. By Bill Martin, Jr. and John Archambault. Illus. by James Endicott. Henry Holt ISBN 0-8050-0682-6; In Canada: Fitzhenry & Whiteside, 1988. unp. col. ill.
> Whispering, splish and splash and splatter, hurly-burly, lashing, are among the words used to describe the nature of rain in this poetic, sound evolving text. Set against stylized and textured double paged spread water color illustrations this sparks young children's own creativity.
> SUBJ: Rain and rainfall--Fiction./ Sound--Fiction./ Stories in rhyme.

Ph-1 K-3/2 $5.95 P KG078
MARTIN, JR., BILL. White Dynamite and Curly Kidd. By Bill Martin, Jr. and John Archambault. Illus. by Ted Rand. Henry Holt ISBN 0-8050-1018-1; In Canada: Fitzhenry & Whiteside, c1986, 1989. unp. col. ill.
Curly Kidd, the toughest bull rider around, rides White Dynamite, the meanest bull in the whole United States, while Curly's child Lucky proudly but nervously cheers him on. Superb doublespreads capture the excitement of a rodeo and the actions of the bull and rider. The text consists of dialog and chants that children enjoy repeating. The final illustration shows a surprising picture of young Lucky.
SUBJ: Rodeos--Fiction./ Fathers and daughters--Fiction.

Ph-1 1-4/3 $14.95 T KG079
MARTIN, JACQUELINE BRIGGS. Grandmother Bryant's pocket. Illus. by Petra Mathers. Houghton Mifflin ISBN 0-395-68984-8, 1996. 48p. col. ill.
Includes glossary.
Selectors' Choice, 21st ed.
Mourning the loss of her dog, Patches, in a barn fire, eight-year-old Sarah goes to stay with her Grandmother Bryant whose healing skills and pocket embroidered with "Fear Not" help the young girl recover. The pocket is actually a cloth pouch worn inside clothing. The story's setting in 1787 is evoked by the many details in the short chapters and minimal illustrations. A small treasure of historical fiction which will itself fit in a pocket.
SUBJ: Fear--Fiction./ Nightmares--Fiction./ Grandparents--Fiction./ Maine--Fiction.

CE Ph-1 1-3/2 $15.95 L KG080
MARTIN, RAFE. Will's mammoth. Illus. by Stephen Gammell. Putnam ISBN 0-399-21627-8; In Canada: Putnam, 1989. unp. col. ill.
Selectors' Choice, 18th ed.
Videocassette available from SRA/McGraw-Hill 87-909894 (ISBN 0-07-909894-0, 1991). 1/2" VHS videocassette color (8min), guide, $39.00. (Children's literature series).
Young Will is fascinated by woolly mammoths. One day he trudges up a snowy hill and finds a genial mammoth who carries him through a winter landscape of prehistoric people and beasts. The brief text, hand lettered in rainbow-like colors, sets the scene for Will's secret adventure while the exuberant color illustrations are packed with action and humorous detail. Readers of prehistoric animal books will find their imagination stretched by this fanciful journey.
SUBJ: Mammoths--Fiction.

Ph-2 K-2/1 $3.50 P KG081
MARZOLLO, JEAN. I'm a seed. Illus. by Judith Moffatt. Scholastic ISBN 0-590-26586-5; In Canada: Scholastic, 1996. unp. col. ill. (Hello science reader!).
"Cartwheel books."
Two seeds grow into very different plants: a marigold and a pumpkin. A very easy-to-read text illustrated with bold collages introduces elementary botany concepts. An excellent presentation for beginning readers.
SUBJ: Seeds--Fiction./ Pumpkin--Fiction./ Flowers--Fiction.

Ph-2 P-1 $14.99 T KG082
MARZOLLO, JEAN. Pretend you're a cat. Illus. by Jerry Pinkney. Dial ISBN 0-8037-0773-8, 1990. unp. col. ill.
Rhyming text invites listeners to imagine they are 12 different animals including a cat, a fish, a pig, a seal and a bear. The animal is depicted along with pictures of children pretending to be the animal. A wonderful springboard for imaginative play or creative movement, each verse ends with an open-ended question "What else can you do like a ...?"
SUBJ: Animals--Fiction./ Stories in rhyme.

Ph-1 P-1/2 $15.88 L KG083
MASUREL, CLAIRE. No, no, Titus! Illus. by Shari Halpern. North-South Books ISBN 1-55858-726-8; In Canada: North-South Books/dist. by Vanwell, 1997. unp. col. ill.
Titus, the new dog, wants to be useful on the farm like everyone else. Then he chases a fox away from the hen house. Cut-paper and fabric collage illustrations are a bold and simple match to the easy-to-read text for beginning readers.
SUBJ: Dogs--Fiction./ Farm life--Fiction.

CE Ph-3 P-1 $3.99 P KG084
MAYER, MERCER. Boy, a dog and a frog. Dial ISBN 0-8037-0769-X, c1967. unp. ill.
Videocassette (dramatization) from Phoenix Films & Video, 1981. 1/2" VHS videocassette color (9min) $89.59.
A little boy and his dog are unsuccessful in their attempt to catch a frog, but they do gain an unusual bath time playmate in this small, picture "story-without-words."
More funny wordless stories follow in FROG WHERE ARE YOU?

(ISBN 0-8037-2729-1, 1969); FROG ON HIS OWN (ISBN 0-8037-2716-X, 1973); FROG GOES TO DINNER (ISBN 0-8037-2733-X, 1974); and ONE FROG TOO MANY (ISBN 0-8037-4858-2, 1975).
SUBJ: Dogs--Fiction./ Frogs--Fiction./ Stories without words.

Ph-2 P-2/2 $14.99 T KG085
MAYER, MERCER. There's an alligator under my bed. Dial ISBN 0-8037-0374-0, 1987. unp. col. ill.
Tired of walking a plank to his bed each night a boy lays a trail of goodies to lure the alligator into the garage. Silly enough to provoke guffaws of laughter at storytime this has the advantage of being easy to read.
SUBJ: Alligators--Fiction./ Bedtime--Fiction./ Humorous stories.

Ph-2 K-2/1 $7.99 T KG086
MCCLINTOCK, MIKE. Stop that ball. Illustrated by Fritz Siebel. Beginner Books/Random House ISBN 0-394-80010-9; In Canada: Random House, c1959, 1987. unp. col. ill. (I can read it all by myself).
Laugh-provoking things happen as a boy tries to retrieve his ball.
SUBJ: Humorous stories.

CE Ph-1 P-2/7 $15.00 L KG087
MCCLOSKEY, ROBERT. Blueberries for Sal. Viking ISBN 0-670-17591-9, c1948. 54p. col. ill.
Caldecott Honor Book.
Videocassette available from Weston Woods HMPV41V, n.d. 1/2" VHS videocassette color (9min), $49.95.
Available from National Library Service for the Blind and Physically Handicapped in Braille BRA06793 and on sound recording cassette RC10774.
Read-along kit available from Puffin StoryTapes (ISBN 0-14-095110-5, 1993). 1 paperback book, 1 sound cassette (20min), $6.99.
Adventures of a little girl and her mother as they go blueberrying in Maine and meet a Mother Bear and her cub.
SUBJ: Maine--Fiction./ Bears--Fiction.

CE Ph-1 1-3/6 $3.95 P KG088
MCCLOSKEY, ROBERT. Lentil. Puffin/Penguin ISBN 0-14-050287-4, c1940. unp. ill.
Videocassette available from Weston Woods HMPV014V. 1/2" VHS videocassette color (9min) $49.95.
Available from National Library Service for the Blind and Physically Handicapped in Braille BRA04987 and as talking book TB04460.
A boy practices playing the harmonica in many places, including the bathtub, and becomes so adept he saves the day when the town band cannot operate.
SUBJ: Ohio--Fiction./ Mouth-organ--Fiction./ Spanish language materials.

CE Ph-1 P-1/4 $15.99 L KG089
MCCLOSKEY, ROBERT. Make way for ducklings. Viking ISBN 0-670-45149-5, c1941, 1963. unp. ill.
Caldecott Medal Award.
Spanish version available from Penguin Ediciones ABRAN PASO A LOS PATITOS (ISBN 0-670-86830-2, 1996).
1/2" VHS videocassette color available from Weston Woods HMPV003V, 1985. $49.95.
Read-along kit available from Live Oak Media (ISBN 0-670-45157-6, 1975). 1 paperback book, 1 sound cassette (11min), $15.95.
Available from National Library Service for the Blind and Physically Handicapped in Braille BR01739, talking book TB02166, and sound recording cassette RC 42913.
Boston is the setting for this modern classic of a mallard family's search for a home.
SUBJ: Boston (Mass.)--Fiction./ Ducks--Fiction./ Spanish language materials.

Ph-1 1-3/6 $14.00 L KG090
MCCLOSKEY, ROBERT. One morning in Maine. Viking ISBN 0-670-52627-4, c1952, 1962. 64p. ill.
Caldecott Honor Book.
Available from National Library Service for the Blind and Physically Handicapped in Braille BR04300.
Many things happen on the day Sally loses her first tooth.
SUBJ: Maine--Fiction./ Family life--Fiction.

CE Ph-1 P-A/6 $16.00 L KG091
MCCLOSKEY, ROBERT. Time of wonder. Viking ISBN 0-670-71512-3, c1957, 1962. 63p. col. ill.
Caldecott Medal Award.
1/2" VHS videocassette available from Weston Woods HMPV031V (13min), $49.95.
Available from National Library Service for the Blind and Physically Handicapped in Braille BR05624.

A soft, quietly poetic text and beautiful illustrations describe a family on an island in Maine as they experience a summer hurricane.
SUBJ: Maine--Fiction./ Hurricanes--Fiction.

Ph-1 2-4/4 $14.89   L   KG092
MCCULLY, EMILY ARNOLD. Little Kit or, The Industrious Flea Circus girl. Dial ISBN 0-8037-1674-5, 1995. unp. col. ill.
Mistaken for a boy, Little Kit goes to work for the cruel Professor Malefetta, helping with his remarkable flea circus. Her adventures traveling through Victorian London and trying to keep the Professor from learning she is a girl are captivating and suspenseful. Kit is a memorable and resourceful character, and her story provides a fascinating glimpse into an unusual entertainment and the historical period. The watercolor illustrations make striking use of light, dark, and shadow to convey poor conditions, relatively scary scenes, and Kit's emotions.
SUBJ: Orphans--Fiction./ England--Fiction./ Fleas--Fiction.

Ph-1 1-3/2 $14.95   L   KG093
MCCULLY, EMILY ARNOLD. Mirette on the high wire. Putnam ISBN 0-399-22130-1; In Canada: Putnam, 1992. unp col illus.
Caldecott Award.
Available from the National Library Service for the Blind and Physically Handicapped on sound recording cassette RC 36482.
Mirette's mother runs a boardinghouse in Paris where Bellini, a retired high-wire walker, comes to stay. Mirette discovers he is the Great Bellini who used to perform many high-wire feats until he lost his nerve. The young Mirette becomes his protege and helps him regain his courage. A heartwarming story with watercolor illustrations of nineteenth century Paris.
SUBJ: Tightrope walking--Fiction./ Paris (France)--Fiction.

CE   Ph-1 P-2 $12.95   T   KG094
MCCULLY, EMILY ARNOLD. Picnic. HarperCollins ISBN 0-06-024100-4, 1984. unp. col. ill.
Available on 1/2" VHS videocassette color (10min) from Weston Woods VC306V, 1991, $120.00.
Piling into their old red pickup truck, a very large family of mice heads for the country and a day of fun and picnicking. Along the way one small mouse bounces out of the truck unnoticed, but all does end well. Appealing, colorful and well designed pictures tell this wordless story.
SUBJ: Stories without words./ Mice--Fiction./ Picnicking--Fiction.

Ph-2 P-K $13.89   L   KG095
MCCULLY, EMILY ARNOLD. School. HarperCollins ISBN 0-06-024133-0, 1987. unp. col. ill.
After watching her brothers and sisters hustle and bustle and finally leave for school, the baby of the family finds home too quiet and lonely so she decides to sneak off for the school and discover what really happens there. A wordless story about the mouse family of PICNIC and FIRST SHOW.
SUBJ: Schools--Fiction./ Mice--Fiction./ Stories without words.

Ph-1 P-2/5 $16.95   L   KG096
MCDERMOTT, GERALD. Papagayo the mischief maker. Harcourt Brace Jovanovich ISBN 0-15-259465-5; In Canada: Harcourt Brace Jovanovich, 1992. unp. col. ill.
The animals of the rain forest are worried because every night the moon-dog takes another bite of the moon. Papayago, the lively and noisy parrot, tells them to make a lot of noise to frighten the moon-dog away. When their plan succeeds, Papagayo warns then that moon-dog will return and reminds them to remember what to do. Bright colors predominate in the gouache and colored pencil illustrations. Use in discussions about phases of the moon.
SUBJ: Parrots--Fiction./ Rain forests--Fiction./ Moon--Fiction.

Ph-1 1-3/2 $14.99   L   KG097
MCDONALD, MEGAN. Insects are my life. Illus. by Paul Brett Johnson. Orchard ISBN 0-531-08724-7, 1995. unp. col. ill.
"Richard Jackson book."
Amanda loves bugs. She collects insects and mosquito bites, opens her window at night to let the bugs inside, and wears a shirt that says "Amanda Frankenstein: Friend of Bugs." Watercolor, colored pencil, and pastel illustrations convey Amanda's distinct personality and passion for insects. This title is an obvious choice for units on insects, but is also appropriate for classroom discussions about individual differences.
SUBJ: Insects--Fiction./ Schools--Fiction./ Family life--Fiction./ Individuality--Fiction.

Ph-1 K-3/5 $14.99   L   KG098
MCDONALD, MEGAN. Potato man. Illus. by Ted Lewin. Orchard ISBN 0-531-08514-7, 1991. unp. col. ill.

Grampa tells his grandchildren about his boyhood encounters with the Potato Man, who sold fruits and vegetables from a horse-drawn wagon. The Potato Man had lost an eye in the war and his lumpy face was the object of fear and ridicule until the day when he and Grampa met face to face. The story and watercolor illustrations capture an earlier time when peddlers were common.
In THE GREAT PUMPKIN SWITCH (ISBN 0-531-08600-3, 1992) Grandpa tells the story about the time his friend Otto and he have to replace his sister's prized pumpkin.
SUBJ: Peddlers and peddling--Fiction.

Ph-1 P-K/3 $16.99   T   KG099
MCDONNELL, FLORA. Flora McDonnell's ABC. Candlewick ISBN 0-7636-0118-7; In Canada: Candlewick/dist. by Douglas & McIntyre, 1997. unp. col. ill.
In an oversized format, upper and lower case letters from A to Z are each depicted with at least a full-page illustration with two objects. A simple alphabet book appropriate for very young children who are learning their letters.
SUBJ: Alphabet.

Ph-1 P-1/2 $14.95   T   KG100
MCDONNELL, FLORA. I love animals. Candlewick ISBN 1-56402-387-7; In Canada: Candlewick/dist. by Douglas & McIntyre, 1994. unp. col. ill.
Big book available (ISBN 1-56402-662-0, 1996), $19.99.
A series of oversized doublespreads depict the animals a young girl loves. The simple text and large typeface are ideal for beginning readers. The large acrylic and gouache illustrations can be seen across the room, enhancing their immense appeal for young children. For reading aloud.
SUBJ: Domestic animals--Fiction./ Farm life--Fiction.

Ph-1 P-1/3 $15.95   T   KG101
MCDONNELL, FLORA. I love boats. Candlewick ISBN 1-56402-539-X; In Canada: Candlewick/dist. by Douglas & McIntyre, 1995. unp. col. ill.
Selectors' Choice, 20th ed.
As she describes different boats, a young girl says she loves each one. Oversized, doublespread acrylic and gouache illustrations show each boat as it would look at sea with all the people on it. The last page reveals the narrator in the bathtub with all of the boats. Careful use of white space and a large typeface add to the readability of this slightly predictable book.
SUBJ: Baths--Fiction./ Boats and boating--Fiction.

Ph-2 K-2/2 $12.95   T   KG102
MCGEORGE, CONSTANCE W. Boomer's big day. Illus. by Mary Whyte. Chronicle ISBN 0-8118-0526-3; In Canada: Raincoast, 1994. unp. col. ill.
Moving day is described from the point of view of Boomer the family dog, who really doesn't understand what is happening. The color illustrations express Boomer's good-natured perplexity.
SUBJ: Dogs--Fiction./ Moving, Household--Fiction.

Ph-1 1-3/2 $14.95   T   KG103
MCGOVERN, ANN. Lady in the box. Illus. by Marni Backer. Turtle Books/dist. by Publishers Group West ISBN 1-890515-01-9, 1997. unp. col. ill.
A brother and sister befriend a homeless woman who lives in a box and sneak food and a warm scarf to her until their mother discovers the missing items. Oil painting illustrations are especially effective in the snow-flecked and impressionistic city scenes. The warm and realistic story is dignified and compassionate in its treatment of the homeless.
SUBJ: Homeless persons--Fiction./ Helpfulness--Fiction./ Neighborhood--Fiction.

Ph-2 1-3/1 $13.99   L   KG104
MCGUIRE, RICHARD. Night becomes day. Viking ISBN 0-670-85547-2; In Canada: Penguin, 1994. unp. col. ill.
Travel through the day and from the country into the city through a series of transformations: some everyday and predictable like "Stream becomes river And river becomes ocean" and some surprisingly logical like "City becomes building And building becomes cloud." The retro-style illustrations use unusual blocks of color to depict the story transformations. Fun language pattern to use for creative writing activities.
SUBJ: Time--Fiction./ Day--Fiction.

CE   Ph-1 K-3/2 $14.99   T   KG105
MCKISSACK, PAT. Flossie and the fox. By Patricia C. McKissack. Illus. by Rachel Isadora. Dial ISBN 0-8037-0250-7; In Canada: Fitzhenry & Whiteside, 1986. unp. col. ill.
Selectors' Choice, 16th ed.
Videocassette available from Weston Woods HMPV327V, 1992.

1/2″ VHS videocassette color (14min) $49.95.
Delivering a basket of fresh eggs to Miz Viola who lives on the other side of the woods, young Flossie encounters a fox who has designs on the eggs, but the spunky little African-American girl out-maneuvers and frustrates the scheming fox by continually questioning his identity. Based on a story told by the author's grandfather and retold in the same colorful dialect of the rural South. The dramatic tale, enhanced by vibrant full-page color pictures, is excellent for reading aloud. For multicultural studies.
SUBJ: Foxes--Fiction./ Tricks--Fiction./ Afro-Americans--Fiction.

Ph-1 1-3/4 $6.99   P   KG106
MCKISSACK, PAT. Million fish...more or less. By Patricia C. McKissack. Illus. by Dena Schutzer. Knopf ISBN 0-679-88086-0; In Canada: Random House, c1992, 1996. unp. col. ill.
Fishing in the Bayou Clapateaux, Hugh Thomas invents a tall tale about catching a million fish--more or less. Gators, raccoon pirates, and 20 foot snakes are among the animals Hugh Thomas encounters in places with names like Napoleon's Elbow and Mossland Mansion in this rollicking read-aloud accompanied by lively oil paintings.
SUBJ: Fishing--Fiction./ Afro-Americans--Fiction./ Tall tales.

CE   Ph-1 1-3/6 $15.99   L   KG107
MCKISSACK, PAT. Mirandy and Brother Wind. By Patricia C. McKissack. Illus. by Jerry Pinkney. Knopf ISBN 0-394-98765-9; In Canada: Random House, 1988. unp. col. ill.
Caldecott Honor book.
Coretta Scott King Award.
Selectors' Choice, 17th ed.
After several futile attempts, Mirandy finally catches the wind and on the night of her first dance contest she and clumsy Ezel with the help of Brother Wind and the scarves of Miss Poinsettia (a conjure woman) strut, swirl, prance, and reel with such animation, style and grace that they win the junior cakewalk. The text is paired with large, brightly colored and detailed pencil and watercolor wash pictures which bring life, action, and sparkle to the story based on the culture, activities and surroundings of an early twentieth century rural African-American community. Author's note provides background information about the cakewalk. For multicultural studies.
SUBJ: Dancing--Fiction./ Winds--Fiction./ Afro-Americans--Fiction.

Ph-2 1-3/4 $15.00   T   KG108
MCKISSACK, PAT. Nettie Jo's friends. By Patricia C. McKissack. Illus. by Scott Cook. Knopf ISBN 0-394-89158-9; In Canada: Random House, 1989. unp. col. ill.
While trying to find a needle to sew a new dress for her beloved doll, Nettie Jo helps three animals who finally return the favor. The large impressionistic paintings that illustrate this folklore-like tale are best seen at a distance making this a prime choice to read aloud to a group.
SUBJ: Animals--Fiction./ Dolls--Fiction.

CE   Ph-3 P-2/2 $5.95   P   KG109
MCLEOD, EMILIE WARREN. Bear's bicycle. Illus. by David McPhail. Atlantic/Little, Brown ISBN 0-316-56206-8, c1975, 1986. 31p. col. ill.
Read-along kit available from Live Oak Media (ISBN 0-87499-023-8) 1 paperback book, 1 sound cassette (5min), $15,95.
A little boy and his bear have an exciting bicycle ride. The boy explains and practices all the rules of safety, but his teddy bear, suddenly grown to grizzly bear proportions, falls into many of the pitfalls and horrors of careless bicycle riding.
SUBJ: Bears--Fiction./ Bicycles and bicycling--Safety measures--Fiction.

CE   Ph-1 K-3/2 $14.88   L   KG110
MCLERRAN, ALICE. Roxaboxen. Illus. by Barbara Cooney. Lothrop, Lee & Shepard ISBN 0-688-07593-2, 1991. unp. col. ill.
Selectors' Choice, 18th ed.
Videocassette available from Spoken Arts 9076, 1991. 1/2″ VHS videocassette color (9min), guide, $44.95.
In Roxaboxen, rocks, sand, old boxes and cactus are transformed by neighborhood children into a town complete with houses, a bakery, a jail and a cemetery. Based on the experiences of the author's mother, Roxaboxen will be recognized by the many children who understand how a few materials, a lot of imagination and a group of friends can create something wondrous out of practically nothing. Desert-hued illustrations recreate the simple world of Roxaboxen and evoke the viewer's imagination of its possibilities.
SUBJ: Play--Fiction./ Imagination--Fiction.

Ph-1 K-3/1 $15.95   L   KG111
MCMILLAN, BRUCE. Mouse views: what the class pet saw. Written and photo-illustrated by Bruce McMillan. Holiday House ISBN 0-8234-1008-0, 1993. 32p. col. ill.
Selectors' Choice, 20th ed.

The class pet is loose. Close-up photographs capture the mouse's view of rulers, pencils, and computer keys. A map with a key shows the route the mouse takes through the school. Useful for discussions about point of view as well as map skills. Children will enjoy the guessing game aspect of the story.
SUBJ: Mice--Fiction./ Schools--Fiction./ Visual perception.

Ph-1 P-K/3 $6.95   T   KG112
MCMULLAN, KATE. If you were my bunny. Illus. by David McPhail. Scholastic ISBN 0-590-52749-5; In Canada: Scholastic, 1996. unp. col. ill. (Story corner).
"Cartwheel books."
A mother tells her young child the songs she would sing if he was her bunny, her bear cub, her kitten, her duckling, or her puppy. The original lyrics can be sung to the tunes of traditional lullabies which are named in a note to parents in the back of the book. Cozy illustrations enhance the gentle mood of the lullabies. For reading aloud or singing with individuals or small groups. (Parents' Shelf).
SUBJ: Babies--Fiction./ Mother and child--Fiction./ Bedtime--Fiction./ Animals--Infancy--Fiction./ Lullabies.

Ph-2 1-3/3 $16.95   T   KG113
MCNAUGHTON, COLIN. Captain Abdul's pirate school. Candlewick ISBN 1-56402-429-6; In Canada: Candlewick/dist. by Douglas & McIntyre, 1994. unp. col. ill.
A young girl and several other students attend a pirate school where bad behavior is encouraged and the curriculum includes pirate poetry, geography, and sail-making. When the students realize the pirates intend to kidnap them, they plan a mutiny and take over the ship. Amusing and fun, the story and illustrations will appeal to fans of pirate stories.
SUBJ: Pirates--Fiction./ Schools--Fiction.

Ph-3 1-3/2 $4.95   P   KG114
MCNULTY, FAITH. Lady and the spider. Illus. by Bob Marstall. HarperCollins ISBN 0-06-443152-5; In Canada: HarperCollins, 1986. unp. col. ill.
Having made its home in a garden, a spider is carried into a lady's home when the head of lettuce in which it is living is harvested. Small in size but not in meaning, this celebrates respect for life no matter the form it takes. Ideal to read aloud.
SUBJ: Spiders--Fiction.

Ph-1 1-3/2 $14.95   L   KG115
MCNULTY, FAITH. Snake in the house. Illus. by Ted Rand. Scholastic ISBN 0-590-44758-0; In Canada: Scholastic, 1994. unp. col. ill.
Escaping from a jar, a small snake is loose in the house and tries to find its way back outdoors. The young boy who captured it in the first place, inadvertently takes the snake back to the pond in a basket. After discovering the snake, he returns the reptile to the pond shore. The snake's adventures among the pots and pans, avoiding the cat and the vacuum cleaner, and coiled in a sewing box are delightfully portrayed in the illustrations. Youngsters with an interest in snakes will especially enjoy this story.
SUBJ: Snakes--Fiction.

CE   Ph-1 K-2/2 $14.95   L   KG116
MCPHAIL, DAVID. Bear's toothache. Joy Street/Little, Brown ISBN 0-316-56312-9, c1972. 31p. col. ill.
Kit available from Live Oak Media (ISBN 0-8749-9081-5, 1980). 1 hardcover book, 1 sound cassette (5min) $22.95.
Available from National Library Service for the Blind and Physically Handicapped in Braille BR02473.
A small boy's sleep is disturbed by the howling of a big bear with a toothache. After inviting the bear in, the boy tries to cure the ache by pulling the tooth. Tugging on the tooth fails, eating steak and all else in the refrigerator doesn't work, but eventually the tooth does come out. The happy bear goes on his way and the little boy sleeps with an enormous tooth under his pillow.
SUBJ: Bears--Fiction./ Teeth--Fiction.

Ph-1 K-2/3 $15.95   L   KG117
MCPHAIL, DAVID. Edward and the pirates. Little, Brown ISBN 0-316-56344-7; In Canada: Little, Brown, 1997. unp. col. ill.
Sequel to: SANTA'S BOOK OF NAMES, Little, Brown, 1993.
Edward is a voracious reader; sometimes the characters in his books seem to come to life, including a group of pirates who think the book he's reading will lead them to their lost treasure. Large acrylic paintings transport readers into Edward's adventures. The scary pirates, as it turns out, can't read and need Edward to read to them. An imaginative story which reinforces the importance of reading.
SUBJ: Books and reading--Fiction./ Imagination--Fiction./ Pirates--Fiction.

Ph-2 P-1/2 $3.95 L KG118
MCPHAIL, DAVID. Farm morning. Harcourt Brace Jovanovich ISBN 0-15-227300-X, c1985, 1991. unp. col. ill.
Getting up even before the cock crows, a little girl and her father feed the animals on their old-fashioned farm. The full-paged subdued water color paintings and the very brief text picture the various noisy barnyard animals, a warm, loving father-daughter relationship, and lots of subtle humor. The large pictures make this suitable for group story hours and useful in study units on farms and animals.
SUBJ: Fathers and daughters--Fiction./ Farm life--Fiction./ Domestic animals--Fiction.

Ph-2 P-1/2 $14.95 L KG119
MCPHAIL, DAVID. Lost! Joy Street/Little, Brown ISBN 0-316-56329-3; In Canada: Little, Brown, 1990. unp. col. ill.
Leading a lost bear from the big city back to the forest, a young boy finds he is the one who is lost. Humorous illustrations depict the small boy and his large furry friend in a elevator, on a playground and in numerous other places around the city. Children relate easily to the theme and the warm friendship of the unusual pair.
SUBJ: Lost children--Fiction./ Bears--Fiction.

Ph-2 1-3/4 $12.95 T KG120
MCPHAIL, DAVID. Moony B. Finch, the fastest draw in the West. Western Publishing ISBN 0-307-17554-5; In Canada: Western Publishing, 1994. unp. col. ill.
"Artists and Writers Guild book."
Moony B. Finch's drawings sometimes become real. When he draws an old passenger train and boards it, the train is held up by a cowboy. Moony B. Finch takes out his eraser and reduces the robber to ridicule. A satisfactory fantasy with humorous illustrations.
SUBJ: Drawing--Fiction./ Magic--Fiction./ Railroads--Trains--Fiction./ Robbers and outlaws--Fiction.

Ph-2 P-2/3 $14.99 T KG121
MCPHAIL, DAVID. Pigs ahoy! Dutton ISBN 0-525-45334-2, 1995. unp. col. ill.
Pigs on board a cruise ship create havoc with their piggy manners until the crew sends them ashore in a small boat. The funny rhyming text and illustrations will provoke giggles.
SUBJ: Cruise ships--Fiction./ Pigs--Fiction./ Voyages and travels--Fiction./ Stories in rhyme.

Ph-1 P-2/2 $13.99 L KG122
MCPHAIL, DAVID. Pigs aplenty, pigs galore! Dutton ISBN 0-525-45079-3, 1993. unp. col. ill.
Available from the National Library Service for the Blind and Physically Handicapped on sound recording cassette RC 38579. Spanish version CERDOS A MONTONES, CERDOS A GRANEL! available (ISBN 0-525-45590-6, 1996).
Late at night, a man discovers pigs of every type eating in his kitchen. The silly, rhyming text and the outrageously funny illustrations provide marvelous humor for reading aloud.
SUBJ: Pigs--Fiction./ Stories in rhyme./ Spanish language materials.

Ph-1 K-3/2 $14.95 L KG123
MEDDAUGH, SUSAN. Hog-eye. Houghton Mifflin ISBN 0-395-74276-5, 1995. 32p. col. ill.
"Walter Lorraine books."
Captured by a wolf who intends to put her in soup, a clever pig tricks the wolf, who can't read the cookbook, into going after several unusual ingredients including a three-leafed plant that causes him to itch. Watercolor illustrations with speech balloons interject humor into the story. A good introduction to the importance of reading, the story will be entertaining for reading aloud as well as an appealing lesson on the dangers of poison ivy.
SUBJ: Pigs--Fiction./ Wolves--Fiction./ Reading--Fiction./ Poison ivy--Fiction.

Ph-1 K-2/2 $14.95 L KG124
MEDDAUGH, SUSAN. Martha blah blah. Houghton Mifflin ISBN 0-395-79755-1, 1996. 32p. col. ill.
"Walter Lorraine books."
In a cost-cutting move, the soup company leaves some of the letters out of the alphabet soup which Martha depends on for speech. Suddenly she doesn't make any sense until she finds one leftover can with every letter and frightens Granny Flo into putting all letters back into the soup. Lots of fun with possibilities for creative writing activities.
SUBJ: Dogs--Fiction./ Soups--Fiction.

Ph-2 1-3/2 $13.95 L KG125
MEDDAUGH, SUSAN. Witches' supermarket. Houghton Mifflin ISBN 0-395-57034-4, 1991. 32p. col. ill.
It's Halloween night and Helen, dressed like a witch, follows an old

lady into an unusual supermarket which sells poisoned apples, lizard gizzards, and lots of brooms. Color illustrations display the extraordinary selection on the market shelves. A humorous holiday selection with details to thrill young readers.
SUBJ: Witches--Fiction./ Dogs--Fiction./ Halloween--Fiction.

Ph-2 K-1/2 $3.50 P KG126
MEDEARIS, ANGELA SHELF. Here comes the snow. Illus. by Maxie Chambliss. Scholastic ISBN 0-590-26266-1; In Canada: Scholastic, 1996. unp. col. ill. (Hello reader!).
"Cartwheel books."
Anticipating the snow, children are excited when it finally arrives and they can sled, throw snowballs, and make a snowman. A very simple text and expressive illustrations convey the excitement for beginning readers.
SUBJ: Snow--Fiction./ Stories in rhyme./ Winter--Fiction./ Afro-Americans--Fiction.

Ph-1 2-3/5 $14.93 L KG127
MELMED, LAURA KRAUSS. Rainbabies. Illus. by Jim LaMarche. Lothrop, Lee & Shepard ISBN 0-688-10756-7, 1992. unp. col. ill.
An old woman and her husband have everything they need, but not the one thing they want the most: a child. One night they awaken to a full moon and a rainshower and find a dozen babies, each no bigger than a big toe. They tenderly care for and fiercely protect the small babies until Mother Moonshower comes to claim them leaving behind a gift. A magical story with captivating illustrations written in classic folktale tradition.
SUBJ: Fairy tales.

Ph-1 1-3/7 $14.95 T KG128
MENDELSON, S. T. Emperor's new clothes. H. C. Andersen; retold and illus. by S. T. Mendelson. Stewart, Tabori & Chang ISBN 1-55670-232-9; In Canada: Stewart, Tabori & Chang/dist. by General, 1992. unp. col. ill.
Humor abounds in this retelling of the story of the vain emperor whose foolishness and nakedness is revealed by a child. The opulent illustrations portray the personalities of the characters in animal form in a showy Byzantine setting. Casting the emperor as an ape seems especially apt, although his bare bottom will still provoke giggles.
SUBJ: Fairy tales.

Ph-2 K-2/4 $13.00 L KG129
MENNEN, INGRID. Somewhere in Africa. By Ingrid Mennen and Niki Daly. Illus. by Nicolaas Maritz. Dutton ISBN 0-525-44848-9, 1992. unp col illus.
Somewhere in Africa there are lions, crocodiles, and zebras but not in the large city at the tip of the African continent where Ashraf lives. Mennen captures the flavor of life in a large city and contrasts it with the wild and untamed parts of Africa that Ashraf reads about in his favorite library book.
SUBJ: Africa--Fiction./ City and town life--Fiction./ Imagination--Fiction.

CDR Ph-1 K-3 $39.95 OD KG130
MERCER MAYER'S LITTLE MONSTER AT SCHOOL. School ed. (CD-ROM). Random House/Broderbund, 1994. 1 CD-ROM color, 2 paperback books. (Living books).
Includes teacher's guide, troubleshooting guide and Byrd Baylor's EVERYBODY NEEDS A ROCK.
System requirements: Macintosh System 6.0.7 or higher; CD-ROM drive; 256 color monitor; 4MB RAM.
System requirements: IBM/Tandy or 100% compatible; 386SX or higher with 4MB RAM; Windows 3.1; MS-DOS 3.3 or higher; Super VGA (640x480, 256 colors); Sound Blaster or SB Pro and 100% compatible sound card; mouse; CD-ROM drive.
Product runs on either Macintosh or Windows compatible hardware. Youngsters will be delighted with the interactive version of this Mercer Mayer story. Available in English or Spanish, the story can be read to youngsters, or they can move along at their own pace. Excellent graphics, animations, and sound truly do make this a Living Book. A bonus book, EVERYBODY NEEDS A ROCK, which coordinates with the extension activities is included.
SUBJ: Schools--Fiction--Software./ Software--Schools--Fiction./ Monsters--Fiction--Software./ Software--Monsters--Fiction./ Spanish language materials--Software./ Software--Spanish language materials./ Bilingual materials--Spanish--Software./ Software--Bilingual materials--Spanish./ Interactive media.

Ph-2 P-1/2 $16.00 L KG131
MERRIAM, EVE. Hole story. Designed and illus. by Ivan Chermayeff. Simon & Schuster ISBN 0-671-88353-4; In Canada: Distican, 1995. unp. col. ill.
All types of holes from buttonholes to holes in drinking straws to the

holes in the soles of sandals are featured in large visually impressive illustrations created from sharp photographs, collage, and a combination of the two mediums. The rhyming text is quite easy to read, except that the clever use of holes in place of the letter "O" may slow inexperienced readers.
SUBJ: Holes--Fiction./ Stories in rhyme.

Ph-2 2-4/5 $14.95 L KG132
MERRILL, JEAN. Girl who loved caterpillars: a twelfth-century tale from Japan. Adapted by Jean Merrill. Illus. by Floyd Cooper. Philomel ISBN 0-399-21871-8; In Canada: Putnam, 1992. unp. col. ill.
Izumi's love of caterpillars and other crawling creatures embarrasses her parents and alienates her ladies-in-waiting, but still she pursues her interests. The story from twelfth-century Japan has a strong contemporary message about independent choice and societal expectations.
SUBJ: Japan--Fiction./ Conduct of life--Fiction.

Ph-2 1-3/4 $12.95 T KG133
MICHL, REINHARD. Day on the river. Barron's ISBN 0-8120-5715-5; In Canada: Barron's, 1986. unp. col. ill.
Playing hooky, three good friends spend the day navigating down the river on their big inner tube, under overhanging tree limbs, past huge submerged roots with maybe a sea monster, a stop at Puma Island, on through the jungle and an inspection of the Iron Monster. This nostalgic remembrance of the author's boyhood adventures presents a plea for conservation and preservation of our natural heritage, "not only for the mallard, kingfisher and the heron, but for ourselves," and is enhanced by beautiful doublespread watercolors, end papers showing a map of the river trip, and pictures of the wildlife with identifications indicated.
SUBJ: Rivers--Fiction.

Ph-1 1-3/4 $4.95 P KG134
MILHOUS, KATHERINE. Egg tree. Aladdin/Macmillan ISBN 0-689-71568-4; In Canada: Maxwell Macmillan, c1950, 1992. unp col illus. Caldecott Medal Award.
Hunting for Easter eggs, Katy discovers six beautiful eggs packed away in the attic. Grandmom recognizes eggs she had decorated as a young girl. When she makes an egg tree to hang them, she starts a new spring tradition. The illustrations and decorated eggs show the folk art of the Pennsylvania Dutch. Includes instructions for making an egg tree.
SUBJ: Easter eggs--Fiction./ Easter--Fiction./ Pennsylvania Dutch--Fiction.

Ph-2 P/2 $14.93 L KG135
MILLER, MARGARET. Now I'm big. Greenwillow ISBN 0-688-14078-5, 1996. unp. col. ill.
Now that they are "big," six preschool children compare themselves to when they were smaller and less independent. Photographs depict their progression of skills. A celebration of growing up for preschool programs, it will also be useful for children who have new siblings. (Parents' Shelf).
SUBJ: Babies--Fiction./ Growth--Fiction./ Size--Fiction.

Ph-2 P-K/1 $13.93 L KG136
MILLER, MARGARET. Where does it go? Greenwillow ISBN 0-688-10929-2, 1992. unp. col. ill.
Simple lessons in logic feature a guessing game with appealing photographs of children with toys, clothes, food, and other familiar objects. "Where does Jaclyn put her bicycle?" Four choices are offered in small photographs facing the initial, larger illustration; the answer on the succeeding doublespread pages completes the set. A nice choice for read-aloud and discussion with nursery school and day-care groups.
SUBJ: Clothing and dress--Fiction./ Toys--Fiction.

Ph-2 K-2/2 $13.95 T KG137
MILLER, SARA SWAN. Three stories you can read to your cat. Illus. by True Kelley. Houghton Mifflin ISBN 0-395-78831-5, 1997. unp. col. ill.
Read these three cat stories about rainy days, bad tasting bugs, and good things to do alone in the house for a cat, of course! Amusing illustrations and episodic stories will appeal to cat owners.
SUBJ: Cats--Fiction.

Ph-2 K-2/2 $14.95 L KG138
MILLS, CLAUDIA. Phoebe's parade. Illus. by Carolyn Ewing. Macmillan ISBN 0-02-767012-0; In Canada: Maxwell Macmillan, 1994. unp. col. ill.
Phoebe's brothers aren't sufficiently impressed that she gets to march in the Fourth of July parade. When she throws her baton into the crowd and loses her place in the parade, her brothers retrieve it, and they all get to ride on the fire engine. Phoebe's enthusiasm and her sibling relationships are typical.

SUBJ: Parades--Fiction./ Drum majorettes--Fiction./ Brothers and sisters--Fiction.

Ph-1 2-3/4 $14.95 L KG139
MILLS, LAUREN A. Rag coat. Little, Brown ISBN 0-316-57407-4; In Canada: Little, Brown, 1991. unp col illus.
Available from the National Library Service for the Blind and Physically Handicapped on sound recording cassette RC 36292.
Minna wants to go to school but she doesn't have a coat to wear because her father has recently died and her family can't afford to buy her one. Her mother and several other mothers who quilt together make her a very special coat quilted from rags with stories of their own. A very heartwarming Appalachian story.
SUBJ: Coats--Fiction./ Appalachian region--Fiction.

Ph-2 P-K/2 $13.93 L KG140
MINARIK, ELSE HOLMELUND. Am I beautiful? Illus. by Yossi Abolafia. Greenwillow ISBN 0-688-09912-2, 1992. unp. col. ill.
Young Hippo goes for a walk and observes several animal mothers telling their children how beautiful they are. "Am I beautiful?" he asks, but no one gives him the right answer until he returns home and asks his mother. A loving story extended by the warm, expressive illustrations.
SUBJ: Hippopotamus--Fiction./ Animals--Fiction.

CE Ph-1 P-1/2 $14.89 L KG141
MINARIK, ELSE HOLMELUND. Little Bear. Illus. by Maurice Sendak. HarperCollins ISBN 0-06-024241-8, c1961. 63p. col. ill. (I can read book).
Read-along kit available from Harper Caedmon (ISBN 1-55994-234-7, 1986), 1 paperback book, 1 sound cassette (21min), $7.95. Spanish version, OSITO, available from Santillana (ISBN 84-204-30447), $9.95.
Available from National Library Service for the Blind and Physically Handicapped in braille BR00267 and as talking book TB03844.
Four stories center around Mother Bear and Little Bear, who not only takes a trip to the moon but also has a birthday party.
Other appealing stories in this popular series are: FATHER BEAR COMES HOME (ISBN 0-06-024231-0, 1959); read-along kit available from HarperChildren's Audio (ISBN 0-69470-010-X, 1995), 1 paperback book, 1 sound cassette (17min), $7.95; Spanish version, PAPA OSO VUELVE A CASA, available from Santillana (ISBN 84-204-3048X): available from National Library Service for the Blind and Physically Handicapped as talking book TB01121.
LITTLE BEAR'S FRIEND (ISBN 0-06-024256-6, 1960); read-along kit available from Harper Caedmon (ISBN 1-55994-235-5, 1990), $7.95; Spanish version, AMIGOS DE OSITO, available from Santillana (ISBN 84-204-30498); available from National Library Service for the Blind and Physically Handicapped in braille BRA06818.
KISS FOR LITTLE BEAR (ISBN 0-06-024299-X, 1968); read-along kit available from Harper Caedmon (ISBN 1-55994-263-0, 1991), $7.95; Spanish version, BESO PARA OSITO(Santillana (ISBN 84-204-30501, OPC).
LITTLE BEAR'S VISIT (ISBN 0-06-024266-3, 1961); read-along kit available from Harper Caedmon (ISBN 1-55994-236-3, 1961), $7.95; Spanish version, VISITA DE OSITO, available from Santillana (ISBN 84-204-3051X, 1994); available from National Library Service for the Blind and Physically Handicapped in braille BRA06820.
SUBJ: Bears--Fiction./ Mothers--Fiction./ Spanish language materials.

Ph-1 2-3/3 $14.99 L KG142
MINTERS, FRANCES. Sleepless Beauty. Illus. by G. Brian Karas. Viking ISBN 0-670-87033-1; In Canada: Penguin, 1996. unp. col. ill.
SLEEPING BEAUTY is given a contemporary twist: Beauty lives in an urban apartment, pricks her finger on a phonograph needle, and is awakened by rock and roll music blaring from her alarm clock. The rhyming text, small asides, and a musician are complemented by quirky illustrations and varying page designs. Older students familiar with the traditional story will enjoy the humor and twist.
SUBJ: Fairy tales--Parodies, imitations, etc./ Folklore--Parodies, imitations, etc./ Stories in rhyme.

Ph-1 P-A/4 $14.95 T KG143
MITCHELL, ADRIAN. Ugly Duckling. By Hans Christian Andersen. Retold by Adrian Mitchell. Woodcuts by Jonathan Heale. DK Publishing ISBN 1-56458-557-3, 1994. 32p. col. ill.
Perhaps one of the most well-known and beloved of Andersen's stories is retold with language faithful to the original. Accompanied by woodcut illustrations which give the story an old-fashioned and classic quality. An elegant retelling with broad appeal.
SUBJ: Fairy tales./ Swans--Fiction.

Ph-1 1-3/2 $14.93 L KG144
MITCHELL, BARBARA. Down Buttermilk Lane. Illus. by John Sandford. Lothrop, Lee & Shepard ISBN 0-688-10115-1, 1993. unp. col. ill.
An Amish family rides in their horse and buggy into town to the general store and the Farmer's Market then to Dawdi's for a big meal before heading back home to do the milking. The gold and bronze hues of autumn predominate the doublespread illustrations which depict the farming countryside, the people, and homes of the Amish.
SUBJ: Amish--Fiction.

Ph-2 1-3/4 $15.93 L KG145
MITCHELL, BARBARA. Red Bird. Illus. by Todd L. W. Doney. Lothrop, Lee & Shepard ISBN 0-688-10860-1, 1996. unp. col. ill.
Red Bird and her family go to a Nanticoke powwow where they participate in dancing, feasting, and storytelling with extended family members and Native Americans representing tribes from Canada and the United States. Striking oil paintings focus attention on a contemporary celebration of Native American culture. Useful for multicultural studies and family history units.
SUBJ: Nanticoke Indians--Fiction./ Indians of North America--Fiction./ Powwows--Fiction./ Indians of North America--Rites and ceremonies--Fiction.

Ph-1 1-3/2 $14.95 L KG146
MITCHELL, MARGAREE KING. Granddaddy's gift. Illus. by Larry Johnson. BridgeWater ISBN 0-8167-4010-0; In Canada: BridgeWater/ dist. by Vanwell, 1997. unp. col. ill.
An African-American girl relates the story of her grandfather who had the courage to register to vote in spite of racial barriers, community attitudes, and a test on the Mississippi Constitution which he was required to take. The history of voting rights becomes immediate through the story and illustrations. For multicultural studies.
SUBJ: Afro-Americans--Mississippi--Fiction./ Mississippi--Fiction./ Grandfathers--Fiction./ Voting--Fiction.

Ph-1 1-3/4 $15.00 L KG147
MITCHELL, MARGAREE KING. Uncle Jed's barbershop. Illus. by James Ransome. Simon & Schuster ISBN 0-671-76969-3; In Canada: Simon & Schuster, 1993. unp. col. ill.
Coretta Scott King Honor book, 1994.
Uncle Jed dreams about owning his own barbershop, but when his niece, Sarah Jean, needs an operation, he spends some of his barbershop savings to save her life. Bank failure and the Great Depression further delay his plans until finally on his seventy-ninth birthday, he opens his own barbershop. Told from the point of view of Sarah Jean, this poignant story shows the segregated South in the 1920s, close family relationships, and dreams fulfilled. Oil paintings and a rich design add depth and beauty to the story. Historical fiction for multicultural studies.
SUBJ: Uncles--Fiction./ Barbers--Fiction./ Afro-Americans--Fiction./ United States--History--1919-1933--Fiction.

Ph-3 K-2/2 $15.00 T KG148
MODELL, FRANK. Look out, it's April Fools' Day. Greenwillow ISBN 0-688-04016-0, 1985. 24p. col. ill.
Playing jokes on Milton isn't much fun for Marvin even on April Fools' Day since Milton just won't be fooled. Silly but children think it funny.
SUBJ: April Fools' Day--Fiction./ Jokes--Fiction.

Ph-2 P-1/1 $3.95 P KG149
MOFFATT, JUDITH. Who stole the cookies? Grosset & Dunlap ISBN 0-448-41127-X; In Canada: BeJo Sales, 1996. 32p. col. ill. (All aboard reading).
Did Cat, Puppy, Mouse, Squirrel, or Turtle take the cookies from the cookie jar? No, but when they find out who did, everyone shares a new batch of cookies. Beginning readers familiar with the similar song will enjoy this easy-to-read predictable book complete with cut-paper illustrations.
SUBJ: Cookies--Fiction./ Animals--Fiction./ Stories in rhyme.

Ph-2 K-2/3 $14.95 T KG150
MOLLEL, TOLOLWA M. Big boy. Illustrated by E. B. Lewis. Clarion ISBN 0-395-67403-4, 1995. unp. col. ill.
Wishing he were big like his brother who can go bird hunting, Oli dreams he is a giant who can cross the woods in a step, start a stampede with a sneeze, and begin a mountain slide with a jump. Using a motif from African folklore, the author has crafted a story with appeal for every child who longs to be bigger. Watercolor illustrations place the story in a contemporary African setting. For multicultural studies.
SUBJ: Size--Fiction./ Growth--Fiction./ Africa--Fiction.

Ph-1 1-3/2 $14.89 L KG151
MONJO, F. N. Drinking gourd. Newly illustrated ed. Illus. by Fred Brenner. HarperCollins ISBN 0-06-024330-9; In Canada: HarperCollins, 1993. 62p. col. ill. (I can read book).
Selectors' Choice, 6th ed.
Available from National Library Service for the Blind and Physically Handicapped in Braille BR01553.
Spanish version available from Harper Arco Iris OSA MENOR: UNA HISTORIA DEL FERROCARRIL SUBTERRANEO (ISBN 0-06-444217-9, 1997).
Helping his father Deacon Fuller escort an African-American family on the way to freedom in Canada, rapscallion Tommy finds himself deliberately misleading the marshall and his posse. Simply written, this tale of the functioning of the Underground Railroad has proven to be appealing to beginning readers. For multicultural studies
SUBJ: Slavery--Fiction./ Underground railroad--Fiction./ New England--Fiction./ Spanish language materials.

Ph-2 K-2/2 $14.89 L KG152
MONSON, A. M. Wanted: best friend. Illus. by Lynn Munsinger. Dial ISBN 0-8037-1485-8; In Canada: McClelland & Stewart, 1997. unp. col. ill.
Following a disagreement with Mouse, Cat advertises for a new friend, but discovers that old friends like Mouse are the best. Expressive illustrations place this book ahead of the pack of friendship stories.
SUBJ: Cats--Fiction./ Mice--Fiction./ Friendship--Fiction.

Ph-2 P-1/2 $14.99 T KG153
MOON, NICOLA. Lucy's picture. Illus. by Alex Ayliffe. Dial ISBN 0-8037-1833-0, 1995. unp. col. ill.
Lucy makes a special picture for Grandpa at school. A painting won't do, so she cuts out paper and collects objects including a snippet of her own hair to create a collage that Grandpa, who is blind, can "see" with his hands. The collage illustrations are exuberant and childlike as is Lucy's thoughtfulness. A charming story which depicts warm family relationships and sensitivity to persons with disabilities.
SUBJ: Grandfathers--Fiction./ Blind--Fiction./ Physically handicapped--Fiction./ Art--Fiction.

Ph-2 K-2/4 $16.00 T KG154
MOORE, ELAINE. Grandma's house. Illus. by Elise Primavera. Lothrop, Lee & Shepard ISBN 0-688-04115-9, 1985. unp. col. ill.
Spending the summers in the country with Grandma is a very special time for Kim as they pick strawberries, peaches, and almost plums, and celebrate half-birthdays at the village ice-cream parlor. Pictures an active, loving grandmother and a deep, tender relationship existing between the pair. Pleasant pastel drawings match the mood of the gentle story.
Kim makes her first winter visit to grandma's and the two of them experience a snowstorm and the ensuing power failure in GRANDMA'S PROMISE (ISBN 0-688-06741-7, 1988).
SUBJ: Grandmothers--Fiction./ Country life--Fiction.

Ph-2 P-1/3 $14.95 T KG155
MORA, PAT. Uno, dos, tres: one, two, three. Illus. by Barbara Lavallee. Clarion ISBN 0-395-67294-5, 1996. 45p. col. ill.
Count to ten in Spanish and English while accompanying two girls as they visit the market to buy Mama a birthday present. The predictable book with rhyming text will reinforce reading skills and counting in both languages. For multicultural studies.
SUBJ: Birthdays--Fiction./ Counting./ Stories in rhyme./ Spanish language materials./ Bilingual materials--Spanish.

Ph-2 1-2/3 $6.95 P KG156
MORGAN, ALLEN. Matthew and the midnight pilot. Illus. by Michael Martchenko. Stoddart Kids ISBN 0-7737-5852-6; In Canada: Stoddart Kids, 1997. unp. col. ill.
Matthew's model glider is stuck in a tree, and his mother is expecting a package. In the middle of the night, he helps a pilot free his plane from the tree, and the two join an air show, pick up the package, and release Matthew's glider from the tree. A lively fantasy with active illustrations.
SUBJ: Airplanes--Fiction./ Fantasy.

Ph-1 K-3/3 $15.00 L KG157
MOSS, LLOYD. Zin! zin! zin! a violin. Illus. by Marjorie Priceman. Simon & Schuster ISBN 0-671-88239-2; In Canada: Distican, 1995. unp. col. ill.
Caldecott Honor book, 1996.
The trombone plays a solo then one by one other instruments join in for a duo, trio, quartet, and so on up to a chamber group of ten and then finally: the orchestra. A lively, rhyming introduction to the instruments in the orchestra and to the vocabulary that describes the number of musicians in a musical group as well as a counting book. The antics of a pair of cats, a dog, and a mouse add to the

playfulness of the gouache illustrations.
SUBJ: Musical instruments--Fiction./ Music--Fiction./ Counting./ Stories in rhyme.

Ph-2 K-2/2 $13.95   L   KG158
MOSS, MARISSA. Mel's Diner. BridgeWater ISBN 0-8167-3460-7; In Canada: BridgeWater/dist. by Vanwell., 1994. unp. col. ill.
Mabel describes the customers, food, and fun she has at her family's diner. Watercolor illustrations depict a lively neighborhood establishment with a diverse clientele. For multicultural studies.
SUBJ: Diners (Restaurants)--Fiction./ Afro-Americans--Fiction.

Ph-1 1-4/3 $15.99   T   KG159
MOSS, THYLIAS. I want to be. Illus. by Jerry Pinkney. Dial ISBN 0-8037-1286-3, 1993. unp. col. ill.
Dreaming about what she wants to be, a young African-American girl describes all of the qualities she would like to have concluding, "I want to be life doing, doing everything." Dreamlike colored pencil and watercolor illustrations sparkle beside the poetic text. A great springboard for creative writing. For multicultural studies.
SUBJ: Growth--Fiction./ Self-realization--Fiction./ Afro-Americans--Fiction.

Ph-1 1-3/2 $14.95   T   KG160
MOST, BERNARD. Hippopotamus hunt. Harcourt Brace ISBN 0-15-234520-5; In Canada: Harcourt Brace c/o Canadian Manda, 1994. unp. col. ill.
Join a group of youngsters as they hunt for the words you can make from the letters in the word "hippopotamus." The words they find appear in the colorful illustrations and in the text of the story about the hunt. In the end the "most" words are found in the library. Use for storytime and follow with a word hunt activity, perhaps, extended with a creative writing activity.
SUBJ: English language--Spelling--Fiction./ Hippopotamus--Fiction./ Word games--Fiction.

VCR   Ph-3 K-2 $44.95   OD KG161
MOUSE SOUP (Videocassette). SVE/Churchill Media C80420-HAVT ISBN 0-7932-2680-5, 1992. 1/2" VHS videocassette color (25min).
A faithful adaptation of the popular book which uses three-dimensional animation and lively music. The expense makes this an appropriate selection for larger collections.
SUBJ: Mice--Fiction./ Weasels--Fiction.

Ph-3 P-1/1 $11.95   L   KG162
MUELLER, VIRGINIA. Halloween mask for Monster. Illus. by Lynn Munsinger. Whitman ISBN 0-8075-3134-0; In Canada: General, 1986. unp. col. ill.
A young monster tries to find just the perfect mask for Halloween. Simple and appealing to toddlers but also useful for very beginning readers who want a Halloween story.
SUBJ: Halloween--Fiction./ Monsters--Fiction.

Ph-1 P-1/1 $14.89   L   KG163
MURPHY, STUART J. Best bug parade. Illus. by Holly Keller. HarperCollins ISBN 0-06-025872-1; In Canada: HarperCollins, 1996. 33p. col. ill. (MathStart).
Includes bibliography.
Compare bugs--big, small, long, and short--in the best bug parade. A colorful introduction to the concepts of size and comparisons which are important language and math skills. The predictable book will be welcome in math classes.
SUBJ: Insects--Fiction./ Size--Fiction./ Parades--Fiction./ Stories in rhyme.

Ph-1 K-2/2 $14.89   L   KG164
MURPHY, STUART J. Best vacation ever. Illus. by Nadine Bernard Westcott. HarperCollins ISBN 0-06-026767-4; In Canada: HarperCollins, 1997. 33p. col. ill. (MathStart).
Includes bibliography.
A young girl helps her family decide where to go for vacation by collecting data about everyone's preferences and creating charts to show the results. Simple and appealing text and illustrations model a decision-making process.
SUBJ: Vacations--Fiction./ Problem solving--Fiction./ Stories in rhyme.

Ph-2 1-3/3 $14.89   L   KG165
MYERS, WALTER DEAN. Story of the three kingdoms. Illus. by Ashley Bryan. HarperCollins ISBN 0-06-024287-6; In Canada: HarperCollins, 1995. unp. col. ill.
Available from the National Library Service for the Blind and Physically Handicapped on sound recording cassette RC 42064.
Elephant, Shark, and Hawk are each the master of his own kingdom until the People learn to master each kingdom by sharing wisdom

through stories. In turn, they decide to share rather than rule. Watercolor illustrations rich in pattern frame the almost mythic tale about the power of story.
SUBJ: Animals--Fiction./ Human-animal relationships--Fiction./ Storytelling--Fiction.

CE   Ph-2 P-2/2 $13.95   L   KG166
NARAHASHI, KEIKO. I have a friend. McElderry ISBN 0-689-50432-2; In Canada: Collier Macmillan, 1987. unp. col. ill.
A small boy tells about his friend, a blue shadow, who is with him wherever he goes until the sun goes down. The subtle, deceptively simple story is accompanied by visually stimulating full page and double spread water color paintings.
SUBJ: Shadows--Fiction.

Ph-2 K-3/2 $13.95   L   KG167
NAYLOR, PHYLLIS REYNOLDS. King of the playground. Illus. by Nola Langner Malone. Atheneum ISBN 0-689-31558-9; In Canada: Collier Macmillan, 1991. unp. col. ill.
Kevin is bothered on the playground by Sammy, a bully, but his father helps him see the weaknesses in Sammy's threats. When Kevin finds the courage to stand up to Sammy, the two become friends. A useful story about cooperation and friendship.
SUBJ: Bullies--Fiction./ Courage--Fiction./ Playgrounds--Fiction./ Friendship--Fiction.

Ph-2 P-2/2 $13.93   L   KG168
NEITZEL, SHIRLEY. Jacket I wear in the snow. Illus. by Nancy Winslow Parker. Greenwillow ISBN 0-688-08030-8, 1989. unp. col. ill.
Big book available from Mulberry Books (ISBN 0-688-12771-1, 1997), $18.95.
A list of the clothing a young girl wears to play in the snow is set to the rhythm and cumulative pattern of THE HOUSE THAT JACK BUILT. The name of each clothing item is matched to an illustration which then becomes part of the rebus text. The dressing and undressing of the little girl is thoroughly satisfying during story hours.
A similar format follows in THE DRESS I'LL WEAR TO THE PARTY (ISBN 0-688-09960-2, 1992).
SUBJ: Clothing and dress--Fiction./ Snow--Fiction./ Stories in rhyme./ Rebuses.

Ph-2 P-1/2 $14.93   L   KG169
NEITZEL, SHIRLEY. We're making breakfast for Mother. Illus. by Nancy Winslow Parker. Greenwillow ISBN 0-688-14576-0; In Canada: Hearst Book Group, 1997. unp. col. ill.
Preparing breakfast for Mother seems to be going smoothly. Then everything spills or drops on the way to the bedroom, and the family goes out for breakfast. The cumulative story rhymes and includes small rebus pictures in a format with lots of appeal for young children. An attractive choice for Mother's Day units.
SUBJ: Breakfasts--Fiction./ Stories in rhyme./ Rebuses.

Ph-1 K-2/2 $15.00   T   KG170
NETHERY, MARY. Hannah and Jack. Illus. by Mary Morgan. Atheneum ISBN 0-689-80533-0; In Canada: Distican, 1996. unp. col. ill.
While visiting her grandparents, Hannah misses her cat, Jack, and sends him numerous postcards. Attractive watercolor and gouache illustrations pair with the affectionate text in a satisfying story about a family pet. Use to introduce an activity designing and writing postcards after reading the story aloud. For multicultural studies.
SUBJ: Cats--Fiction./ Vacations--Fiction./ Grandmothers--Fiction./ Afro-Americans--Fiction.

Ph-2 1-3 $13.93   L   KG171
NEUMEIER, MARTY. Action alphabet. By Marty Neumeier and Byron Glaser. Greenwillow ISBN 0-688-05704-7, 1985. unp. ill.
Stunning black and white graphics give meaning to twenty-six alphabetically arranged words. Not a teaching tool for the very young but a stimulant of imagination and a visual delight for all ages.
SUBJ: Alphabet.

Ph-2 1-3/6 $14.95   T   KG172
NEWMAN, LESLEA. Too far away to touch. Illus. by Catherine Stock. Clarion ISBN 0-395-68968-6, 1995. 32p. col. ill.
Zoe worries about her uncle who has AIDS. When she visits the beach with Uncle Leonard and his companion, Nathan, she wonders if he will die and where he will go when he dies. As they look at the stars together, he answers "Too far away to touch, but close enough to see." Watercolor illustrations depict the warm relationship and the uncle's deteriorating health with hope and affirmation of life's beauty. A timely and dignified portrayal of a child's approach to a potential loss.
SUBJ: AIDS (Disease)--Fiction./ Uncles--Fiction./ Death--Fiction./ Stars--Fiction.

Ph-2 P-K/2 $15.95 T KG173

NIKOLA-LISA, W. One hole in the road. Illus. by Dan Yaccarino. Henry Holt ISBN 0-8050-4285-7; In Canada: Fitzhenry & Whiteside, 1996. unp. col. ill.

"Bill Martin book."

Tally one hole in the road through ten workers in a flurry in this counting book featuring roadwork. Bold, stylized shapes form easy objects for counting in a format designed to appeal to young children.

SUBJ: Roads--Maintenance and repair--Fiction./ Counting.

Ph-2 P-1/2 $14.95 L KG174

NIKOLA-LISA, W. Storm. Illus. by Michael Hays. Atheneum ISBN 0-689-31704-2; In Canada: Maxwell Macmillan, 1993. unp. col. ill.

As a storm approaches, two children run inside to watch through the window until it passes, and they can go outside again. Short descriptive sentences and sweeping doublespread illustrations capture a child's view of a summer storm.

SUBJ: Thunderstorms--Fiction.

Ph-1 K-3/6 $14.99 T KG175

NOBLE, TRINKA HAKES. Apple tree Christmas. Dial/Dutton ISBN 0-8037-0102-0; In Canada: Fitzhenry & Whiteside, 1984. unp. col. ill.

Saddened by the loss of her favorite apple tree during a fierce blizzard on their midwestern farm, Katrina feels that Christmas is hardly worth celebrating until her parents show their understanding by the gifts she and her sister Josie get. Set in the late 1800s and attractively illustrated with much detail, the title contributes information about pioneer life.

SUBJ: Farm life--Fiction./ Blizzards--Fiction./ Christmas--Fiction./ Trees--Fiction.

CE
Ph-1 K-2/2 $15.99 T KG176

NOBLE, TRINKA HAKES. Day Jimmy's boa ate the wash. Illus. by Steven Kellogg. Dial ISBN 0-8037-1723-7, 1980. unp. col. ill.

Spanish version DIA QUE LA BOA DE JIMMY SE COMIO LA ROPA available from Dial/Penguin Ediciones (ISBN 0-8037-2035-1, 1997). Videocassette available from Weston Woods HMPV303V, 1992. 1/2" VHS videocassette color (8min), $49.95.

Available from National Library Service for the Blind and Physically Handicapped in Braille BR7131.

A hilarious juxtaposition of tone. The matter-of-fact quality of a girl's explanation to her mother of the events occurring on her class' trip to a farm is contradicted by the vibrant watercolor wash illustrations and nature of the incidents. A cow cried, a haystack fell over, pigs were on the school bus, an egg fight broke out--all because Jimmy brought his pet snake along.

In JIMMY'S BOA BOUNCES BACK (ISBN 0-8037-0228-0, 1984) a funny series of events occur at the garden club meeting when Jimmy's pet snake wakes up and eats the rare yellow-spotted Bongo plant; and everyone ends up in the big tank in JIMMY'S BOA AND THE BIG SPLASH BIRTHDAY BASH (ISBN 0-8037-0539-5, 1989).

Available from NLSBPH is JIMMY'S BOA BOUNCES BACK in Braille BR7132.

SUBJ: Boa constrictors--Fiction./ Snakes--Fiction./ Farms--Fiction./ Schools--Fiction./ Spanish language materials.

Ph-1 P-1/1 $13.89 L KG177

NODSET, JOAN L. Go away, dog. Illus. by Crosby Newell Bonsall. HarperCollins ISBN 0-06-024556-5; In Canada: HarperCollins, c1963, 1993. unp. col. ill.

Since Jimmy doesn't like dogs, he is not a bit happy with the new puppy Uncle George sends him for his birthday. In fact, over and over again he tells the little dog to "go away" even though the persistent pup does trick after trick to win Jimmy's approval. Brief, repetitive, easy to read text and engaging illustrations appeal to young children.

SUBJ: Dogs--Fiction.

Ph-1 2-3/5 $14.95 L KG178

NOLAN, DENNIS. Dinosaur dream. Macmillan ISBN 0-02-768145-9; In Canada: Collier Macmillan, 1990. unp. col. ill.

Drifting off to sleep, Wilbur hears a tapping at the window and discovers a small dinosaur. Together they travel back through the Ice Age, the Age of Mammals, and the Cretaceous period to the Jurassic period where Gideon, the young dinosaur, belongs. A thrilling blend of fact and fantasy essential for dinosaur units.

SUBJ: Dinosaurs--Fiction./ Time travel--Fiction./ Dreams--Fiction.

Ph-2 P-K/2 $14.93 L KG179

NOLL, SALLY. Surprise! Greenwillow ISBN 0-688-15171-X; In Canada: Hearst Book Group, 1997. unp. col. ill.

Count the objects from one to ten as a young girl opens a present to discover a birthday surprise. Large boldly colored, gouache illustrations fill the pages.

SUBJ: Cats--Fiction./ Birthdays--Fiction./ Counting./ Stories in rhyme.

Ph-2 K-2/3 $14.99 L KG180

NOVAK, MATT. Mouse TV. Orchard ISBN 0-531-08706-9, 1994. unp. col. ill.

"Richard Jackson book."

The mouse family all enjoy watching television; the problem is they can't agree on which channel because everyone has a different favorite. One night the TV set doesn't work and they have a great time playing together and sharing a bedtime story; all without commercials. The illustrations abound with humor including a major clue about what is wrong with the TV set.

SUBJ: Television--Fiction./ Family life--Fiction./ Mice--Fiction.

Ph-2 1-3/2 $14.89 L KG181

NOVAK, MATT. Newt. HarperCollins ISBN 0-06-024502-6; In Canada: HarperCollins, 1996. 48p. col. ill. (I can read book).

In three short chapters, Newt, a small salamander, makes a friend, finds a special bug, and coaxes the moon out from behind the trees. An additional title for easy-to-read collections for beginning readers.

SUBJ: Newts--Fiction./ Salamanders--Fiction./ Friendship--Fiction.

Ph-2 K-2/2 $14.00 T KG182

NUMEROFF, LAURA JOFFE. Why a disguise? By Laura Numeroff. Illus. by David McPhail. Simon & Schuster ISBN 0-689-80513-6; In Canada: Distican, 1996. unp. col. ill.

A disguise is handy when you visit the dentist, want to avoid the school bully, and play hide-and-seek. The comical illustrations and story's premise are fun for sharing. For reading aloud.

SUBJ: Disguise--Fiction./ Identity--Fiction.

Ph-2 2-3/3 $14.95 L KG183

NUNES, SUSAN. Last dragon. By Susan Miho Nunes. Illus. by Chris K. Soentpiet. Clarion ISBN 0-395-67020-0, 1995. unp. col. ill.

Peter Chung is unhappy about spending the summer in Chinatown with Great Aunt until he discovers an old dragon in disrepair. With Peter's determination and the help of many different people, the great dragon is revived. Many different shops and streets in Chinatown are depicted in the text and watercolor illustrations which convey the story of a young boy restoring a piece of his cultural heritage. For multicultural studies.

SUBJ: Chinese Americans--Fiction./ Dragons--Fiction./ Great-aunts--Fiction./ Asian Americans--Fiction.

Ph-1 2-4/2 $14.95 T KG184

OBERMAN, SHELDON. Always Prayer Shawl. Illus. by Ted Lewin. Boyds Mills ISBN 1-878093-22-3; In Canada: McClelland & Stewart, 1994. unp. col. ill.

"Some things change. And some things don't." These are the words along with the prayer shawl that are passed from grandfather to grandson in this story which spans the generations as Adam grows from boyhood in Russia to manhood, parenthood, and grandparenthood in the United States. Black and white illustrations change to full color as the boy becomes a man. A powerful intergenerational story about tradition and change.

SUBJ: Jews--Social life and customs--Fiction./ Family--Religious life--Fiction./ Grandfathers--Fiction.

Ph-2 K-2/2 $14.00 L KG185

OBLIGADO, LILIAN. Chocolate cow. Simon & Schuster ISBN 0-671-73852-6; In Canada: Simon & Schuster, 1993. unp. col. ill.

Pierre's father is planning to sell their cow Melody because she no longer gives much milk. Pierre joins his father for the "poya" the traditional climb with the cows up the mountains in Switzerland for better grazing and cheese-making. High in the mountains, Melody shows her worth and is chosen as the queen to lead the procession back down the mountain. The heartwarming story is a good introduction to Switzerland and Swiss customs and traditions.

SUBJ: Cows--Fiction./ Switzerland--Fiction.

Ph-2 P-2/3 $10.95 T KG186

O'BRIEN, CLAIRE. Sam's sneaker search. Illus. by Charles Fuge. Simon & Schuster ISBN 0-689-80169-6; In Canada: Distican, 1997. unp. col. ill.

Sam encounters several wild animals in unlikely places as she searches for her sneaker. When the elephant outside finds it, the billy goat has chewed it, and the search begins again for her sandals. The colorful watercolor illustrations of realistic animals in unrealistic places are the most fun. Pure foolishness!

SUBJ: Sneakers--Fiction./ Lost and found possessions--Fiction./ Shoes--Fiction.

Ph-2 P-2/4 $18.95 L KG187

OCHS, CAROL PARTRIDGE. When I'm alone. Illus. by Vicki Jo Redenbaugh. Carolrhoda ISBN 0-87614-752-X, 1993. unp col illus.

A young girl claims she didn't make a mess of her room by herself but with the help of ten aardvarks, nine lions, eight turtles, and so on down to one kitten. A clever rhyming text and the familiar story of

imaginary creatures making a mess combine to create a counting story which is a zippy read-aloud.
SUBJ: Cleanliness--Fiction./ Imagination--Fiction./ Animals--Fiction./ Counting./ Stories in rhyme.

Ph-1 K-3/2 $14.89   L   KG188
O'CONNOR, JANE. Lulu and the witch baby. Illus. by Emily Arnold McCully. HarperCollins ISBN 0-06-024627-8; In Canada: HarperCollins, 1986. 64p. col. ill. (I can read book).
Jealous of her baby sister and frustrated by the baby's destructive habits, Lulu makes a disappearing potion, sprinkles it on the baby and when she can't be found, Lulu is sorry for her actions and frantically tries to concoct a new spell to bring the witch baby back. The illustrations showing spooky clutter in the witches' home, the monster yummies for the pets, and ghoulish items such as bottles of bat blood in the magic room all add to the fun.
SUBJ: Witches--Fiction./ Sisters--Fiction./ Jealousy--Fiction.

Ph-2 P-1/1 $7.99   L   KG189
O'CONNOR, JANE. Nina, Nina ballerina. Illus. by DyAnne DiSalvo-Ryan. Grosset & Dunlap ISBN 0-448-40512-1; In Canada: Putnam, 1993. 32p. col. ill. (All aboard reading).
Nina has a small part as one of several butterflies in the ballet, and she is worried that her mother won't know which one she is. When she breaks her arm and has to wear a cast, there is no doubt about which butterfly is Nina.
SUBJ: Ballet dancing--Fiction.

Ph-1 P-2/2 $14.93   L   KG190
OGBURN, JACQUELINE K. Noise lullaby. Illus. by John Sandford. Lothrop, Lee & Shepard ISBN 0-688-10453-3, 1995. unp. col. ill.
There are many outdoor and indoor noises at bedtime, but finally the ticking of the clock lulls the young narrator to sleep. The text is primarily composed of the sounds of the night: cars outside, crickets, a rocking chair, and footsteps. The pastel illustrations help the reader decipher the familiar sounds.
SUBJ: Bedtime--Fiction./ Sound--Fiction.

Ph-2 1-3/2 $15.00   T   KG191
O'MALLEY, KEVIN. Who killed Cock Robin? Lothrop, Lee & Shepard ISBN 0-688-12430-5, 1993. unp. col. ill.
The feathered nursery rhyme that asks who killed, buried, and mourned Cock Robin is the framework for a mystery. The older picture book audience will enjoy looking for clues in the almost sinister illustrations. A fun introduction to the mystery genre or for a unit on nursery rhymes.
SUBJ: Mystery and detective stories./ Nursery rhymes./ Birds--Fiction.

VCR   Ph-1 P-A $19.95   OD KG192
ON THE DAY YOU WERE BORN (Videocassette). Read by Debra Frasier. Featuring the Minnesota Orchestra. Music by Steve Heitzeg. What a Gal Productions/dist. by Minnesota Orchestra Visual Entertainment ISBN 0-9653818-0-3, 1996. 1/2" VHS videocassette color (30min). (Notes Alive! StoryConcert series).
Andrew Carnegie Medal, 1997.
ALA notable video, 1997.
Several dimensions are added to the book with music performed by the Minnesota Orchestra, animation of the illustrations, and narration by the author. Close-ups of the musicians performing, author reading, and conductor leading the orchestra provide a concert experience. Interviews with the author and composer offer insight into the creative process. Can be used as an author study and enjoyed on several levels with applications to music, art, literature, and nature study.
SUBJ: Earth--Fiction./ Birth--Fiction./ Music appreciation.

Ph-2 P-1 $12.95   L   KG193
OPPENHEIM, JOANNE. You can't catch me! By Joanne F. Oppenheim. Illus. by Andrew Shachat. Houghton Mifflin ISBN 0-395-41452-0, 1986. unp. col. ill.
Available from National Library Service for the Blind and Physically Handicapped on sound recording cassette RC26262.
A bothersome black fly pesters many animals while boasting "No matter how hard you try, try, try you can't catch me"; and he does get away from a cow, goat, horse, fox, bear, pig, sheep, lamb, and a ram but he meets his comeuppance when he encounters a sleeping turtle. Jaunty, lilting verses and droll colorful paintings work well together in this variant of the Gingerbread boy.
SUBJ: Fly (Insect)--Fiction./ Animals--Fiction./ Stories in rhyme.

Ph-3 2-3/2 $7.95   P   KG194
OPPENHEIM, SHULAMITH LEVEY. Hundredth name. Illus. by Michael Hays. Boyds Mills ISBN 1-56397-694-3; In Canada: McClelland & Stewart, c1995, 1997. unp. col. ill.
Salah worries about his camel, Quadiim who is unhappy. One night

Salah performs the prayer ritual he has watched his father use to pray to Allah. "He prays that the camel will learn Allah's hundredth name, which is unknown to man." (CIP) In the morning, Quadiim has a look of happiness and wisdom which Salah attributes to Allah's revealing to the camel His hundredth name. The acrylic paintings have the texture of the linen on which they were painted and the sandy color of the desert. An attractive introduction to Muslim Egypt. For multicultural studies.
SUBJ: Egypt--Fiction./ Camels--Fiction.

Ph-2 P-1 $15.00   T   KG195
ORMEROD, JAN. Moonlight. Lothrop, Lee & Shepard ISBN 0-688-00846-1, 1982. unp. col. ill.
Supper, doing the dishes, an evening bath and picking up the toys are followed by Daddy's bedtime story. Then the usual stalls--a drink, a fright, Daddy sitting by her bed until (instead of the child) he goes to sleep. The little girl gets up and reads with Mommie until the mother goes to sleep. Finally the whole family sleeps. Warmth, humor and a close family relationship are pictured in this wordless story of a young family.
SUBJ: Bedtime--Fiction./ Stories without words.

Ph-2 P-1 $3.95   P   KG196
ORMEROD, JAN. Sunshine. Lothrop, Lee & Shepard ISBN 0-688-09353-1, 1981. unp. col. ill.
When the sun shines in her eyes a little girl awakens, plays with her doll, reads her book and then wakes her Daddy. The two of them get breakfast and then take a tray to still sleeping Mommie. After a slow, sleepy beginning, suddenly there is a rush of activity and soon all leave home for the day's activity. Wordless, simple but very effective.
SUBJ: Family life--Fiction./ Stories without words.

Ph-3 P-K $15.93   L   KG197
ORMEROD, JAN. 101 things to do with a baby. Lothrop, Lee & Shepard ISBN 0-688-03802-6, 1984. unp. col. ill.
Lists and pictures with humorous illustrations one hundred and one things a young contemporary family, consisting of a mother, father and big sister, can do with the family baby.
SUBJ: Babies--Fiction./ Brothers and sisters--Fiction.

Ph-2 K-2/2 $18.95   L   KG198
ORR, KATHERINE. My grandpa and the sea. Carolrhoda ISBN 0-87614-409-1, 1990. unp. col. ill.
Lila's grandfather is a fisherman on a Caribbean island who shares his reverence for the sea and for life with his granddaughter. When he can no longer make a living fishing, he devises a plan to raise sea moss, telling Lila "If we give back something for everything we take, we will always meet with abundance." An ecological story with illustrations that depict the natural beauty of the tropical island.
SUBJ: Fishers--Fiction./ Wildlife conservation--Fiction./ Marine ecology--Fiction./ Grandfathers--Fiction.

Ph-2 1-3/6 $18.95   L   KG199
ORR, KATHERINE. Story of a dolphin. Carolrhoda ISBN 0-87614-777-5, 1993. unp. col. ill.
When a friendly dolphin plays with the people on a Caribbean Island, there are some problems because the animal and the people don't understand each other. A dolphin expert is consulted to help resolve the misunderstandings. Tropical colors and ocean hues predominate in the illustrations. Based on a true event, the enjoyable story is suitable for studies about dolphins and about relationships between humans and animals.
SUBJ: Caribbean Area--Fiction./ Dolphins--Fiction.

Ph-1 K-2/5 $14.99   L   KG200
OSOFSKY, AUDREY. Dreamcatcher. Illus. by Ed Young. Orchard ISBN 0-531-08588-0, 1992. unp. col. ill.
The dreamcatcher is a woven net hung over the baby's cradle which catches the bad dreams while letting the good ones pass through. Poetic text and impressionistic pastel illustrations with flowery borders softly reveal numerous aspects of Ojibway life and culture.
SUBJ: Ojibwa Indians--Fiction./ Indians of North America--Fiction./ Babies--Fiction./ Dreams--Fiction./ Family life--Fiction.

Ph-1 K-2/2 $14.95   T   KG201
OSOFSKY, AUDREY. My Buddy. Illus. by Ted Rand. Henry Holt ISBN 0-8050-1747-X; In Canada: Fitzhenry & Whiteside, 1992. unp. col. ill.
A young boy with muscular dystrophy tells about the dog that is his constant companion and is trained to help him. Information is provided about the training they each receive in order to work together, and several examples are given of the many tasks from turning on light switches to answering the phone that the dog is trained to do. A heartwarming story with emphasis on the independence provided to the boy and the friendship between the

boy and his dog.
SUBJ: Muscular dystrophy--Fiction./ Service dogs--Fiction./ Dogs--Fiction.

CE   Ph-2 K-2/3 $15.95   T   KG202
OTTO, CAROLYN. Raccoon at Clear Creek Road. By Carolyn B. Otto.
Illus. by Cathy Trachok. Soundprints/Smithsonian Institution ISBN
1-56899-175-4; In Canada: Soundprints/dist. by Canadian Manda,
1995. 32p. col. ill. (Smithsonian's backyard).
Includes glossary.
Teacher's guide available upon request.
Read-along kit available (ISBN 1-56899-179-7, 1995). 1 hardback
book, 1 sound cassette (9min), $19.95.
Raccoon leaves her babies to search for food, avoiding dangers such
as humans, swift creek currents, and a hungry owl. The focus on an
individual animal gives the facts immediacy. Strong doublespread
illustrations provide drama and encourage interest in this common
nocturnal animal.
SUBJ: Raccoons--Fiction.

                                                 Ph-2 P-K/2 $3.99   P   KG203
OXENBURY, HELEN. Grandma and grandpa. Puffin ISBN 0-14-054978-
1; In Canada: Penguin, c1984, 1993. unp. col. ill.
"Puffin Pied Piper."
Visiting Grandma and Grandpa every weekend is great fun for a little
girl, and her grandparents enjoy the activities too, but finish the
weekend in a state of exhaustion. The appealing illustrations and the
simple story present an excellent picture of an ideal grandparent-
grandchild relationship.
SUBJ: Grandparents--Fiction.

                                                 Ph-2 K-1/1 $14.00   L   KG204
PACKARD, MARY. Christmas kitten. Illus. by Jenny Williams. Childrens
Press ISBN 0-516-05364-7; In Canada: Childrens Press, 1994. 31p. col.
ill.
The stray kitten Santa finds is always in the way, but Santa knows
how to find a home for the Christmas kitten. Emerging readers will
appreciate the limited vocabulary and short sentences in this beginning
reader.
SUBJ: Christmas--Fiction./ Cats--Fiction./ Santa Claus--Fiction./ Stories
in rhyme.

                                                 Ph-2 K-1/1 $14.00   L   KG205
PACKARD, MARY. I am king! Illus. by Leonid Gore. Childrens Press
ISBN 0-516-05365-5; In Canada: Childrens Press, 1994. 31p. col. ill.
(My first reader).
A young boy pretends he is king and directs an army of toy soldiers.
Emerging readers will appreciate the limited vocabulary and short
sentences in this appealing beginning reader.
SUBJ: Kings, queens, rulers, etc.--Fiction./ Imagination--Fiction./
Stories in rhyme.

                                                 Ph-2 1-3/2 $14.95   L   KG206
PALACIOS, ARGENTINA. Christmas surprise for Chabelita. Illus. by Lori
Lohsteeter. BridgeWater ISBN 0-8167-3131-4; In Canada:
BridgeWater/dist. by Vanwell, 1993. unp. col. ill.
Also available in Spanish, SORPRESA DE NAVIDAD PARA
CHABELITA (ISBN 0-8167-3545-X, 1994).
Chabelita lives with her grandparents while her mother works in
another city. One day she receives a package from her mother with a
red dress and shiny black shoes. She wears them for special occasions
including the first day of school and the holiday program in which she
recites "Caperucita Roja" a Spanish poem about Little Red Riding
Hood. Based on the author's childhood in Panama and illustrated in
full color, the warm family story offers insights into growing up in
Central America. For multicultural studies.
SUBJ: Mothers and daughters--Fiction./ Grandparents--Fiction./
Panama--Fiction./ Christmas--Fiction./ Spanish language materials.

                                                 Ph-1 1-5/2 $13.95   L   KG207
PALATINI, MARGIE. Piggie Pie! Illus. by Howard Fine. Clarion ISBN
0-395-71691-8, 1995. unp. col. ill.
Searching for the main ingredient for her Piggie Pie, Gritch the Witch
is fooled by pigs dressed as ducks, cows, chickens, and a farmer. The
ending finds her commiserating with a battered wolf who has had a
recent run-in with three little pigs. The hilarious story includes allusions
to Old MacDonald and the Wizard of Oz for the astute audience.
Should find broad appeal with a range of age groups.
SUBJ: Witches--Fiction./ Domestic animals--Fiction./ Humorous stories.

                                                 Ph-2 K-1/1 $12.50   L   KG208
PALAZZO-CRAIG, JANET. Max and Maggie in spring. By Janet Craig.
Illus. by Paul Meisel. WhistleStop/Troll ISBN 0-8167-3350-3, 1995. 32p.
col. ill. (Nice mice).

Max and Maggie, two mouse friends, share spring cleaning and the
meaning of "April showers bring May flowers." Charming watercolor
and pen illustrations depict the season and the friendship of the mice.
Max and Maggie are featured in brief stories for each of the other
seasons in MAX AND MAGGIE IN SUMMER (ISBN 0-8167-3352-X,
1994), MAX AND MAGGIE IN AUTUMN (ISBN 0-8167-3348-1,
1994), and MAX AND MAGGIE IN WINTER (ISBN 0-8167-3354-6,
1995).
SUBJ: Mice--Fiction./ Friendship--Fiction./ Seasons--Fiction.

                                                 Ph-1 K-2/2 $7.99   L   KG209
PALMER, HELEN. Fish out of water. Illus. by P. D. Eastman. Beginner
Books/Random House ISBN 0-394-90023-5, c1961. 64p. col. ill.
(Beginner books).
Available from National Library Service for the Blind and Physically
Handicapped on sound recording cassette RC12096.
A youngster feeds his fish too much and it quickly grows into a
monstrous size!
SUBJ: Fishes--Fiction.

                                                 Ph-2 1-2/2 $11.88   L   KG210
PARISH, HERMAN. Bravo, Amelia Bedelia! Illus. by Lynn Sweat.
Greenwillow ISBN 0-688-15155-8; In Canada; Hearst Book Group,
1997. 40p. col. ill.
Amelia Bedelia takes everything literally at the school concert,
including playing by ear, using a bow, and making a drum roll. The
conductor is relieved when she decides to confine her fiddling around
to home. The slapstick wordplay will thrill young fans.
SUBJ: Concerts--Fiction./ Humorous stories.

                                                 Ph-2 K-3/4 $13.88   L   KG211
PARISH, PEGGY. Amelia Bedelia's family album. Illus. by Lynn Sweat.
Greenwillow ISBN 0-688-07677-7, 1988. 48p. col. ill.
In celebration of the many many years Amelia has been their maid,
Mr. and Mrs. Rogers plan a party in her honor and invite all her
relatives. In typical Amelia Bedelia style the literal maid describes her
many relatives--her mother is a loafer (she makes loaves of bread),
Cousin Calvin the boxer packs things in boxes, Cousin Clara is a
bookkeeper (she never returns borrowed library books) and on and
on. Bright illustrations extend and clarify the many jokes.
SUBJ: Family--Fiction./ Humorous stories.

                                                 Ph-2 1-2/1 $14.00   T   KG212
PARISH, PEGGY. Be ready at eight. Illus. by Cynthia Fisher. Simon &
Schuster ISBN 0-689-80792-9; In Canada: Distican, 1996. 64p. col. ill.
(Ready-to-read).
Miss Molly can't remember what's so special about the day until her
friends come to wish her a happy birthday. Beginning readers
progressing to longer books can manage this story with success and
enjoyment.
SUBJ: Memory--Fiction./ Birthdays--Fiction.

                                                 Ph-1 K-2/2 $14.89   L   KG213
PARISH, PEGGY. Come back, Amelia Bedelia. Newly illustrated ed. Illus.
by Wallace Tripp. HarperCollins ISBN 0-06-026691-0; In Canada:
HarperCollins, 1995. 64p. col. ill. (I can read book).
When Mrs. Rogers fires her, Amelia Bedelia looks for work
elsewhere, but her literal style continues to get her into trouble until
Mrs. Rogers asks her to come back. The ever popular character of
Amelia Bedelia will continue to delight beginning readers. Includes
updated illustrations by the original artist.
SUBJ: Work--Fiction./ Humorous stories.

CE   Ph-1 1-3/2 $14.00   L   KG214
PARISH, PEGGY. Good work, Amelia Bedelia. Illus. by Lynn Sweat.
Greenwillow ISBN 0-688-84022-1, c1976. 56p. col. ill. (Greenwillow
read-alone).
Amelia Bedelia does the household chores and gets dinner in her
usual literal minded manner. To Amelia a sponge cake is one made
from sponges and a chicken dinner is one of cracked corn as a
chicken would like to eat.
Amelia Bedelia continues to take everything literally in TEACH US,
AMELIA BEDELIA (ISBN 0-688-80069-6, 1977); AMELIA BEDELIA
GOES CAMPING (ISBN 0-688-04058-6, 1985); and MERRY
CHRISTMAS, AMELIA BEDELIA (ISBN 0-688-06102-8, 1986) (read-
along kit available from Listening Library FTR130, 1987, 1 paperback
book, 1 sound cassette (36min) $15.98).
SUBJ: Humorous stories./ Cookery--Fiction.

                                                 Ph-3 K-1/1 $13.89   L   KG215
PARISH, PEGGY. No more monsters for me! Illus. by Marc Simont.
HarperCollins ISBN 0-06-024658-8; In Canada: HarperCollins, 1981.
64p. col. ill. (I can read book).
"No pets" yells Mom, so Minneapolis Simpkins storms out of the

house. When she finds a baby monster crying in the bushes Minn decides to take it home since monsters aren't really pets. Still not sure her mother will allow her to keep it she hides the creature in the basement. But keeping this monster hidden is a real problem. He eats everything in sight and grows bigger and bigger and bigger.
SUBJ: Monsters--Fiction./ Pets--Fiction.

Ph-1 1-3/2 $14.89 L KG216
PARISH, PEGGY. Play ball, Amelia Bedelia. Illus. by Wallace Tripp. HarperCollins ISBN 0-06-026701-1; In Canada: HarperCollins, 1996. 64p. col. ill. (I can read book).
Joining the Grizzlies for a game of baseball, Amelia Bedelia takes everything literally, including tagging, stealing bases, and running home. Her well-known talent for misinterpretation has gained her a wide following among primary students and teachers. New illustrations give this timeless story for beginning readers a more up-to-date appearance.
SUBJ: Baseball--Fiction./ Humorous stories.

Ph-2 K-3/1 $12.89 L KG217
PARISH, PEGGY. Scruffy. Illus. by Kelly Oechsli. HarperCollins ISBN 0-06-024660-X, 1988. 64p. col. ill. (I can read book).
For his birthday Todd is allowed to choose a much desired kitten from the animal shelter. The decision is difficult with so many cute baby kittens and other animals too, but finally Todd decides on an older kitten with a crooked tail and he appropriately names him Scruffy. An appealing, well written, easy to read story providing information on pet care and the importance of animal shelters and pet neutering.
SUBJ: Cats--Fiction./ Birthdays--Fiction.

CE
Ph-1 1-3/2 $13.89 L KG218
PARISH, PEGGY. Thank you, Amelia Bedelia. Rev. ed. Illus. by Barbara Siebel Thomas. Based on the original drawings by Fritz Siebel. HarperCollins ISBN 0-06-022980-2; In Canada: HarperCollins, 1993. 64p. col. ill. (I can read book).
Read along kit available from HarperChildren's Audio (ISBN 0-69-470002-9, 1995). 1 paperback book, 1 sound cassette (8min), $6.95.
Literal-minded Amelia Bedelia strips the sheets, checks the shirts, and makes a jelly roll in preparation for a visit from Great-Aunt Myra. Reissued with full-color illustrations, this adventure will remain a perennial favorite.
SUBJ: Household employees--Fiction./ Humorous stories.

Ph-2 P-2/1 $14.95 L KG219
PARNALL, PETER. Feet! Macmillan ISBN 0-02-770110-7; In Canada: Collier Macmillan, 1988. unp. col. ill.
Bold pictures and brief descriptions of many animal feet. Almost hidden in each doublespread showing the feet is a small, often faintly shown picture of the entire animal. An after note lists each of the animals in order seen.
SUBJ: Foot--Fiction./ Animals--Fiction.

Ph-3 P-1/2 $13.93 L KG220
PATRICK, DENISE LEWIS. Red dancing shoes. Illustrated by James E. Ransome. Tambourine ISBN 0-688-10393-6, 1993. unp. col. ill.
A young girl receives shiny red dancing shoes from her grandmother and goes out to show them off. She slips and the red shoes get muddy, but her Great-aunt Nen polishes them to look like new. Colorful oil paintings provide a rich accompaniment to the story. For multicultural studies.
SUBJ: Shoes--Fiction./ Dancing--Fiction./ Afro-Americans--Fiction.

Ph-2 1-3/4 $15.95 T KG221
PAULSEN, GARY. Dogteam. Illus. by Ruth Wright Paulsen. Delacorte ISBN 0-385-30550-8; In Canada: Bantam Doubleday Dell, 1993. unp. col. ill.
A dog team pulls a sled through the woods at night past wolves and the aurora borealis. Poetic text and wide doublespread watercolors convey the thrill of a wintry nighttime run. A worthy text for reading aloud that also provides an adjunct to longer books about dogsled racing.
SUBJ: Dogsledding--Fiction./ Sled dogs--Fiction./ Sled dog racing--Fiction.

Ph-1 K-2/2 $15.00 L KG222
PAULSEN, GARY. Worksong. Illus. by Ruth Wright Paulsen. Harcourt Brace ISBN 0-15-200980-9; In Canada: Harcourt Brace c/o Canadian Manda, 1997. unp. col. ill.
The importance of work receives dignified treatment in a lyrical text and rich oil paintings. This tribute to the variety of jobs needed to provide the products and services essential to our society and to the people who do them is a clear choice for community helper units and career studies.
SUBJ: Occupations--Fiction./ Work--Fiction./ Stories in rhyme.

Ph-2 K-3/5 $13.95 L KG223
PEET, BILL. Ant and the elephant. Houghton Mifflin ISBN 0-395-16963-1, c1972. 46p. col. ill.
When an ant finds himself stranded on a twig in the jungle river, he asks the turtle to rescue him, but is refused. Later when the selfish turtle finds himself in a predicament and asks the hornbill for help he is refused in turn. One by one, a series of animals who have declined to offer a helping hand, are themselves entrapped. Finally, the elephant rescues each animal from his plight. Later when the elephant falls into a ravine, it is the grateful ant who returns the good turn.
SUBJ: Animals--Fiction./ Kindness--Fiction.

Ph-1 K-3/3 $13.95 L KG224
PEET, BILL. Big bad Bruce. Houghton Mifflin ISBN 0-395-25150-8, 1977. 38p. col. ill.
Big Bruce thinks it great fun to roll boulders down the hill frightening rabbits, quail and other small creatures who live in Forevergreen Forest. But one day this bully bear makes a big mistake when he almost hits Roxy, a spunky, foxy, little witch.
SUBJ: Bears--Fiction./ Witches--Fiction.

Ph-1 K-2/6 $13.95 L KG225
PEET, BILL. Cowardly Clyde. Houghton Mifflin ISBN 0-395-27802-3, 1979. 38p. col. ill.
Clyde is a huge war-horse who pretends to be very brave but in reality is a hopeless coward. However, in spite of his terrible, shivering fear, he manages to heroically rescue his brave master, Sir Galavant, and rid the country of a fierce and horrible monster.
SUBJ: Courage--Fiction./ Horses--Fiction.

Ph-2 K-2/7 $13.95 L KG226
PEET, BILL. Encore for Eleanor. Houghton Mifflin ISBN 0-395-29860-1, 1981. 38p. col. ill.
Eleanor has been a circus star for forty years before her legs give out and she is retired to the city zoo. The old elephant misses all the excitement and glamour of circus life and is moody and miserable until she discovers a hidden talent and embarks on a new career filled with applause.
SUBJ: Elephants--Fiction./ Artists--Fiction.

Ph-1 K-2 $13.95 L KG227
PEET, BILL. Farewell to Shady Glade. Houghton Mifflin ISBN 0-395-18975-6, c1966. 38p. col. ill.
When bulldozers come to clear the land where sixteen animals have been living happily, they are forced to try to find a new home. The old raccoon takes them on their first train ride, and a merry train it is, packed with frogs, rabbits, possums, skunks and other dispossessed animals.
SUBJ: Animals--Fiction./ Wildlife conservation--Fiction.

Ph-1 K-2/7 $13.95 L KG228
PEET, BILL. Jennifer and Josephine. Houghton Mifflin ISBN 0-395-18225-5, c1967. 46p. col. ill.
Jennifer is an ancient touring car languishing in an auto junk yard with only the cat Josephine as a friend. They embark on a hair-raising series of adventures when Jennifer is bought by a "large, long-legged fellow with two suitcases and puffing a cigar." Their reckless ride does end in disaster but not total disaster! The reckless foolhardy driver breaks all the laws of safety but Jennifer and Josephine both eventually reach safe harbor.
SUBJ: Automobiles--Fiction./ Cats--Fiction.

Ph-2 1-3/4 $13.95 L KG229
PEET, BILL. Jethro and Joel were a troll. Houghton Mifflin ISBN 0-395-43081-X, 1987. 32p. col. ill.
"Once upon a time there was a gigantic two-headed turnip-eating troll named Jethro and Joel..." Jethro was peaceful but Joel complained that as a troll they should be on a rampage. Joel's plans are doomed to failure in this account of outlandish high jinks.
SUBJ: Trolls--Fiction./ Humorous stories.

Ph-1 1-3/7 $14.95 L KG230
PEET, BILL. Wump World. Houghton Mifflin ISBN 0-395-19841-0, c1970. 44p. ill.
The fuzzy, furry, little Wumps spend most of their happy days eating the tall tender grass that grows in their meadows, and cooling themselves in their crystal-clear rivers and lakes. Suddenly, one day, their happiness ends and they are forced to hide in a cave. Their lovely world is overrun by Pollutians from the despoiled planet Pollutus. In time the Pollutians ruin the Wump World and again set off in their spaceships in search of a new and better world. The

message, though obvious, is very timely.
SUBJ: Pollution--Fiction.

Ph-2 K-3/4 $12.95 L KG231
PEET, BILL. Zella, Zack and Zodiac. Houghton Mifflin ISBN 0-395-41069-X, 1986. 32p. col. ill.
Available from National Library Service for the Blind and Physically Handicapped on sound recording cassette RC25694.
Rhymed text tells of the adventures of the ostrich chick Zack who is rescued by a zebra named Zella and how he in turn guards her large-footed colt Zodiac. Popular reading aloud fare.
SUBJ: Ostriches--Fiction./ Zebras--Fiction./ Friendship--Fiction./ Stories in rhyme.

Ph-1 P-1/2 $14.95 L KG232
PELLEGRINI, NINA. Families are different. Holiday House ISBN 0-8234-0887-6, 1991. unp. col. ill.
Nico describes many different families including several blended through adoption, divorce, or remarriage like her own which includes her sister and herself, both of Korean descent and adopted. All of these families, her mother points out, are bonded by the strong glue of love for each other. The story and warm family portraits are a strong affirmation of families no matter how they're configured.
SUBJ: Family--Fiction./ Adoption--Fiction./ Korean Americans--Fiction.

Ph-1 K-2/5 $14.93 L KG233
PERKINS, LYNNE RAE. Home lovely. Greenwillow ISBN 0-688-13688-5, 1995. unp. col. ill.
When Tiffany transplants some seedlings she finds near the garbage can outside their trailer, she hopes they will grow into flowers or trees. She is upset when the friendly mail carrier, Bob, tells her they are vegetables. As the plants grow, so does her friendship with Bob and pride in her vegetable plants. Bright illustrations trace the transformation of small sprouts into large, bushy plants. A warm story about creating a home and friendship.
SUBJ: Gardening--Fiction./ Friendship--Fiction./ Single-parent family--Fiction./ Mothers and daughters--Fiction.

Ph-2 K-2/2 $14.95 L KG234
PETERSEN, P. J. Some days, other days. Illus. by Diane De Groat. Scribner's ISBN 0-684-19595-X; In Canada: Maxwell Macmillan, 1994. unp. col. ill.
Jimmy doesn't want to get out of bed because he isn't sure if today is going to be a good day or one of those other days in which nothing seems to go right. His understanding mother suggests they get off to a good start with a hug and make it a great day. The watercolor illustrations depict the good days as the primary picture with an illustration of the other days in a boxed insert. Familiar experiences at home and school provide examples for the two kinds of days. Pair with Viorst's classic ALEXANDER AND THE TERRIBLE, HORRIBLE, NO GOOD, VERY BAD DAY.
SUBJ: Family life--Fiction./ Schools--Fiction.

CE
Ph-1 P-2/3 $13.95 L KG235
PETERSHAM, MAUD. Circus baby. A picture book by Maud and Miska Petersham. Macmillan ISBN 0-02-771670-8, c1950. unp. col. ill.
Videocassette available from Weston Woods MPV13, 1965. 1/2" VHS videocassette color (5min), $60.00.
A mother elephant tries to teach her baby to eat the way the baby clown does, with disastrous results.
SUBJ: Circus--Fiction./ Elephants--Fiction./ Spanish language materials.

Ph-2 2-3/3 $12.95 L KG236
PILKEY, DAV. Dog breath: the horrible trouble with Hally Tosis. Blue Sky/Scholastic ISBN 0-590-47466-9; In Canada: Scholastic, 1994. unp. col. ill.
Hally Tosis is a dog with such bad breath that it offends everything: a picture on the wall, the sun, and everyone behind her on a roller coaster ride. When her horrendous breath knocks out a pair of notorious robbers, Hally becomes a hero. The text and illustrations reek with puns and will tickle many funny bones.
SUBJ: Dogs--Fiction./ Bad breath--Fiction./ Humorous stories.

Ph-2 K-2/2 $12.95 L KG237
PILKEY, DAV. Hallo-wiener. Blue Sky Press/Scholastic ISBN 0-590-41703-7; In Canada: Scholastic, 1995. unp. col. ill.
Available from the National Library Service for the Blind and Physically Handicapped on sound recording cassette RC 42615.
Oscar, a dachshund, is teased for his funny shape, and the teasing is only compounded when his mother makes him a Halloween costume that's a hot dog bun complete with mustard. Replete with puns and bright illustrations, the funny story will be a hit for holiday storytimes. For reading aloud.
SUBJ: Dachshunds--Fiction./ Dogs--Fiction./ Halloween--Fiction.

Ph-1 K-2/2 $15.99 L KG238
PILKEY, DAV. Paperboy. Orchard ISBN 0-531-08856-1, 1996. unp. col. ill.
"Richard Jackson book."
Caldecott Honor book, 1997.
Selectors' Choice, 21st ed.
Rising before the sun is up, the paperboy and his dog deliver newspapers as the town awakens. Acrylic and ink illustrations start the story before the text as a van delivers the newspapers to the boy's house and continue as night turns to day and the boy completes his route. Text and illustrations capture the gentleness of early morning, the ease of routine, and the young boy's dedication to his job. For multicultural studies.
SUBJ: Newspaper carriers--Fiction./ Morning--Fiction./ Afro-Americans--Fiction.

VCR
Ph-2 P-2 $14.98 KG239
PINDAL, KAJ. Peep and the big wide world (Videocassette). Narrated by Peter Ustinov. National Film Board of Canada/Smarty Pants NFV 14005 ISBN 1-55886-129-7, 1991. 1/2" VHS videocassette color (30min).
Peep, a newly hatched chick, and her friends Quack, a duck, and Chirp, a robin, discover the world in three episodes. The naivete of the three birds is delightful and will strike the funny bones of the youngest viewers who already know much more about the "big wide world." Ustinov's narration creates distinct voices for each of the characters. Animation is bold and effective, while very simple. Episodes are brief enough to show separately and would be a fun complement to units on how types of birds differ from each other and from other animals.
SUBJ: Birds--Fiction.

Ph-2 1-3/4 $15.99 T KG240
PINKNEY, GLORIA JEAN. Back home. Illus. by Jerry Pinkney. Dial ISBN 0-8037-1168-9, 1992. unp. col. ill.
Young Ernestine arrives on a train from a city in the North to visit her great-uncle and other relatives in North Carolina. She rides in the same pickup truck in which her mother rode to school, makes friends with her cousin Jack, and visits the house where she was born. Watercolor and color pencil illustrations evoke the gentle pace of summer in the country.
SUBJ: Farm life--Fiction./ North Carolina--Fiction./ Afro-Americans--Fiction.

Ph-1 1-3/2 $14.99 T KG241
PINKNEY, GLORIA JEAN. Sunday outing. Illus. by Jerry Pinkney. Dial ISBN 0-8037-1198-0, 1994. unp. col. ill.
Ernestine dreams about riding the train from Philadelphia to Lumberton, North Carolina, where she was born. She and her parents manage to save the money for the trip, and at last she is ready to ride the Silver Star. This prequel presents the events leading up to Ernestine's visit in BACK HOME. For multicultural studies.
SUBJ: Railroads--Fiction./ Afro-Americans--Fiction.

Ph-1 K-2/3 $16.00 T KG242
PINKNEY, J. BRIAN. Adventures of Sparrowboy. By Brian Pinkney. Simon & Schuster ISBN 0-689-81071-7; In Canada: Distican, 1997. unp. col. ill.
Selectors' Choice, 21st ed.
Inspired by a comic book hero, Henry has a collision with a sparrow that leaves him with superhuman powers to rescue the neighborhood from the bully, Bruno, and his ferocious dog. Scratchboard and gouache illustrations soar in a comic book format filled with action and power.
SUBJ: Flight--Fiction./ Cartoons and comics--Fiction./ Newspaper carriers--Fiction.

Ph-1 K-3/2 $15.00 L KG243
PINKNEY, J. BRIAN. JoJo's flying side kick. By Brian Pinkney. Simon & Schuster ISBN 0-689-80283-8; In Canada: Distican, 1995. unp. col. ill.
Available from the National Library Service for the Blind and Physically Handicapped on sound recording cassette RC 42920.
JoJo finds the right combination of advice from others and self-confidence to earn her yellow belt in Tae Kwan Do and overcome her fear of the creepy bandit tree. Illustrations done in oil and scratchboard effectively convey JoJo's emotions and eventual triumph. Always a popular topic, the martial arts will find broad appeal in the courage and character of the strong female protagonist--JoJo. For multicultural studies.
SUBJ: Martial arts--Fiction./ Courage--Fiction./ Afro-Americans--Fiction.

Ph-2 P-2/2 $3.95 P KG244
PINKWATER, DANIEL MANUS. Aunt Lulu. By Daniel Pinkwater. Simon & Schuster ISBN 0-689-71413-0; In Canada: Distican, 1991. unp. col. ill.

After years of taking books to the gold miners in the wilds of Alaska by means of a "book sled," librarian Aunt Lulu retires to New Jersey accompanied by her fourteen huskies, the dog sled and her parka. In winter the sled works just fine but in the New Jersey summer she adds wheels and sun glasses for all the dogs and herself.
SUBJ: Aunts--Fiction./ Librarians--Fiction./ Alaska--Fiction./ Humorous stories./ Sled dogs--Fiction.

Ph-2 1-3/2 $12.95 L KG245
PINKWATER, DANIEL MANUS. Doodle flute. By Daniel Pinkwater. Macmillan ISBN 0-02-774635-6; In Canada: Collier Macmillan, 1991. unp. col. ill.
Kevin Spoon has almost everything a kid could want, but he doesn't have a doodle flute. There's only one doodle flute and the owner won't trade or sell it. He gives it to Kevin when he asks for it, but then Kevin doesn't know how to play it. The two finally work out a satisfying solution in this lightly humorous story which is easily read by independent readers.
SUBJ: Flute--Fiction./ Friendship--Fiction.

CE Ph-1 P-K/4 $5.95 T KG246
PIPER, WATTY. Little engine that could. The complete, original edition; retold by Watty Piper. Illustrated by George and Doris Hauman. Platt & Munk/Grossett & Dunlap ISBN 0-448-40520-2, c1961. unp. col. ill.
Spanish version: LA PEQUENA LOCOMOTORA QUE SI PUDO (ISBN 0-448-41096-6, 1992).
Read-along kit available from Listening Library FTR 113 SP (ISBN 0-8072-0112-X, 1985). 1 hardcover book, 1 sound cassette (13min), Teacher's Guide, $15.98.
Available from National Library Service for the Blind and Physically Handicapped in Braille BR02259, and as talking book TB02625.
Everyone wonders what can be done when the train that carries good things for children breaks down and cannot go over the mountain.
SUBJ: Locomotives--Fiction./ Perseverance (Ethics)--Fiction./ Spanish language materials.

Ph-1 K-2/2 $15.95 T KG247
PLOURDE, LYNN. Pigs in the mud in the middle of the rud. Illus. by John Schoenherr. Blue Sky Press/Scholastic ISBN 0-590-56863-9; In Canada: Scholastic, 1997. unp. col. ill.
The Model T Ford can't pass in the muddy road because there are pigs, hens, sheep, and bulls in the road. One by one the family members try to shoo the animals out of the way until granny gets out and yells, "time for sup." The exuberant text rolls off the tongue with rhyme, repetition, and exclamations. A predictable book that will be fun for reading aloud.
SUBJ: Automobile driving--Fiction./ Domestic animals--Fiction./ Grandmothers--Fiction./ Stories in rhyme.

Ph-1 2-4/2 $15.95 L KG248
POLACCO, PATRICIA. Aunt Chip and the great Triple Creek Dam affair. Philomel ISBN 0-399-22943-4; In Canada: Putnam, 1996. unp. col. ill.
Television reigns and books are being used for everything but reading in the town of Triple Creek until Aunt Chip finds out what has happened and teaches the children to read. When the dam (made of books) breaks and the TV tower tumbles, the townsfolk rediscover reading, and their quality of life improves. Empowered by books, children are the heroes which delights young audiences. An enjoyable rally for reading. For reading aloud.
SUBJ: Literacy--Fiction./ Books and reading--Fiction./ Television--Fiction.

Ph-2 1-3/5 $15.95 L KG249
POLACCO, PATRICIA. Babushka Baba Yaga. Philomel ISBN 0-399-22531-5; In Canada: Putnam, 1993. unp. col. ill.
Baba Yaga, the witch-like character from Russian folklore, dresses up like a grandmother and becomes the babushka to a young child in the village. Fearful that her identity will be revealed, she disappears but returns in her true form when the child is in danger. Colorful and expressive illustrations provide warmth and charm to the folkloric story.
SUBJ: Baba Yaga (Legendary character)--Fiction./ Grandmothers--Fiction./ Russia--Fiction.

Ph-2 K-2/3 $14.95 L KG250
POLACCO, PATRICIA. Bee tree. Philomel ISBN 0-399-21965-X; In Canada: Putnam, 1993. unp. col. ill.
Grampa demonstrates to Mary Ellen how some of the sweetest things like honey and reading are worth pursuing as he leads her on a bee chase to find the honey tree. A crowd of people join the exuberant chase in this rollicking tale.
SUBJ: Books and reading--Fiction./ Bees--Fiction.

Ph-2 1-3/2 $14.95 T KG251
POLACCO, PATRICIA. Chicken Sunday. Philomel ISBN 0-399-22133-6; In Canada: Putnam, 1992. unp col illus.
A young girl narrates the story about her two friends, Stewart and Winston and their Grandmother, Eula, who sings in the church choir and prepares chicken dinners for them on Sundays. The three friends hope to earn the money to buy her the Easter bonnet in Mr. Kodinski's shop window. When they learn how to make Pysanky eggs, they find a way. A richly woven story about friendship that spans cultures and generations with expressive illustrations.
SUBJ: Egg decoration--Fiction./ Easter--Fiction./ Friendship--Fiction.

CE Ph-1 K-3/6 $14.95 L KG252
POLACCO, PATRICIA. Keeping quilt. Simon & Schuster ISBN 0-671-64963-9, 1988. unp. col. ill.
Videocassette available from Reading Adventures 1008 (ISBN 1-882869-57-5, 1993). 1/2" VHS videocassette color (11min), $42.50..
A quilt made from pieces of clothing brought by an immigrant Jewish family from "backhome Russia" is passed through four generations where it is used many times; as a table cloth for special occasions, a wedding canopy, a wrapper for new babies and for warmth and comfort for the elderly and dying. It is always a link to the past and a reminder of the love and faith of the family. Tells of Jewish customs and their changes through the years. The text is rather brief but the pencil pictures highlighted by the colorful quilt are large and reflect the moods of the story.
SUBJ: Quilts--Fiction./ Jews--Fiction./ Emigration and immigration--Fiction.

Ph-2 1-3/2 $5.99 P KG253
POLACCO, PATRICIA. Mrs. Katz and Tush. Delacorte ISBN 0-440-40936-5; In Canada: Bantam, 1992. unp. col. ill.
Available from the National Library Service for the Blind and Physically Handicapped on sound recording cassette RC 36799.
Mrs. Katz agrees to take a kitten from Larnel with the condition that he will visit her daily to help care for it. A strong friendship develops between the two as Mrs. Katz introduces him to her Jewish heritage, drawing parallels between it and Larnel's African-American heritage. For multicultural studies.
SUBJ: Friendship--Fiction./ Jews--Fiction./ Afro-Americans--Fiction./ Cats--Fiction.

Ph-2 1-3/3 $15.95 L KG254
POLACCO, PATRICIA. My ol' man. Philomel ISBN 0-399-22822-5; In Canada: Putnam, 1995. unp. col. ill.
When their father loses his job as a traveling salesman, Patricia and Richard know the rock and stories their father has told them will work magic, and they do. Based on the author's childhood, the story has the warmth of a family's faith in themselves despite hard times.
SUBJ: Fathers--Fiction./ Magic--Fiction./ Rocks--Fiction./ Storytelling--Fiction.

Ph-1 1-3/3 $15.00 L KG255
POLACCO, PATRICIA. My rotten redheaded older brother. Simon & Schuster ISBN 0-671-72751-6; In Canada: Simon & Schuster, 1994. unp. col. ill.
Available from the National Library Service for the Blind and Physically Handicapped on sound recording cassette RC 39831.
In the sibling competition between Patricia and her brother, Richard, he always outdoes her no matter how outrageous the contest: burping, spitting, or even eating rhubarb. When she falls off the merry-go-round and requires stitches, he finally concedes that she has outdone him. Based on the author's relationship with her redheaded brother, Richard, the story includes authentic black and white photographs of the author and her brother on the endpapers and in some of the painted illustrations. Use in units on family history, on this prolific author, or for fun storytelling.
SUBJ: Brothers--Fiction./ Sibling rivalry--Fiction.

CE Ph-2 1-3/5 $14.95 L KG256
POLACCO, PATRICIA. Rechenka's eggs. Philomel ISBN 0-399-21501-8, 1988. unp. col. ill.
Videocassette narrated by the author available from Spoken Arts SAV 9051, 1991. 1/2" VHS videocassette color (11min), $44.95.
An old peasant woman carefully paints eggs in the Ukranian style for the Easter festival. The wounded goose she has taken in breaks them accidentally but manages to replace them. The pencil and paint illustrations and the warmth of the text make this a delight to share.
SUBJ: Geese--Fiction./ Easter eggs--Fiction./ Eggs--Fiction./ Soviet Union--Fiction.

Ph-2 K-2/4 $14.95 L KG257
POLACCO, PATRICIA. Some birthday! Simon & Schuster ISBN 0-671-72750-8, 1991. unp col illus.

Patricia worries that her father has forgotten her birthday especially when he suggests they try to photograph the Monster at Clay Pit Bottoms. They do enjoy a family outing and a good scare but return home for cake and presents. The color illustrations convey humor and personality and the slight suspense.
SUBJ: Birthdays--Fiction./ Fathers--Fiction.

CE   Ph-1 1-3/4 $14.95   L   KG258
POLACCO, PATRICIA. Thunder cake. Philomel ISBN 0-399-22231-6; In Canada: Putnam, 1990. unp. col. ill.
Videocassette read by author available from Spoken Arts 9024, 1990. 1/2" VHS videocassette color (14min), guide, $39.95.
A young girl is terrified when thunderstorms approach her grandmother's Michigan farm. The wise Russian grandmother tells her to gather the ingredients for a Thunder Cake. They collect eggs, milk the cow and mix the ingredients as the storm approaches. When it bursts above them they are happily eating cake. A reassuring story richly illustrated in vivid folk art style. The Thunder Cake recipe is appended.
SUBJ: Thunderstorms--Fiction./ Fear--Fiction./ Grandmothers--Fiction.

                        Ph-2 1-3/2 $15.95   T   KG259
POLACCO, PATRICIA. Tikvah means hope. Doubleday ISBN 0-385-32059-0; In Canada: Bantam Doubleday Dell, 1994. unp. col. ill.
After a fire destroys much of their neighborhood in Oakland, families return to find a neighbor's Sukkah and a cat have miraculously been spared. Illustrations depict a multicultural community drawn together to rebuild following a disaster.
SUBJ: Fires--California--Oakland--Fiction./ Judaism--Customs and practices--Fiction./ Sukkot--Fiction./ Cats--Fiction.

                        Ph-1 1-3/3 $16.00   T   KG260
POLACCO, PATRICIA. Trees of the dancing goats. Simon & Schuster ISBN 0-689-80862-3; In Canada: Distican, 1996. unp. col. ill.
When their neighbors are too sick to prepare for their Christmas celebration, Trish and her family who are Jewish prepare food and decorate trees to surprise them. Illustrations bustle with family and color, including grandfather's carved wooden animals. The warm story about sharing traditions is especially relevant in schools attempting to recognize diversity during the winter holidays.
SUBJ: Hanukkah--Fiction./ Christmas--Fiction./ Jews--Fiction./ Grandparents--Fiction./ Russian Americans--Fiction.

                        Ph-3 1-3/6 $14.95   L   KG261
POLACCO, PATRICIA. Uncle Vova's tree. Philomel ISBN 0-399-21617-0; In Canada: Putnam, 1989. unp. col. ill.
An immigrant Russian family gathers at an uncle's farm to celebrate Christmas with beloved traditions like psanky eggs and decorating an outside fir tree with food for birds and animals. The next year they gather saddened by their uncle's death, but to their delight the animals have decorated the tree in his memory. The vividly colored illustrations are full of the rich details of the Russian tradition.
SUBJ: Christmas--Fiction./ Russian Americans--Fiction.

CE   Ph-2 K-3/6 $13.95   L   KG262
POLITI, LEO. Song of the swallows. Scribner's ISBN 0-684-18831-7, c1949, 1987. unp. col. ill.
Caldecott Medal.
Available from National Library Service for the Blind and Physically Handicapped in Braille BR06101.
A story from California telling about the birds who return to the mission on the same day every springtime.
SUBJ: Missions--Fiction./ Swallows--Fiction./ California--Fiction.

                        Ph-3 1-3/2 $4.95   P   KG263
POMERANTZ, CHARLOTTE. Chalk doll. Illus. by Frane Lessac. HarperCollins ISBN 0-06-443333-1, c1989, 1993. 30p. col. ill.
Selectors' Choice, 17th ed.
Rose is in bed with a cold and her mother tells her stories of her own childhood on the island of Jamaica. Brightly colored, full page primitive style paintings capture the images projected by the gentle, descriptive text. Set in chapter-like episodes this is a fine independent reading choice for secure independent readers.
SUBJ: Dolls--Fiction./ Mothers and daughters--Fiction./ Short stories.

                        Ph-2 1-3/3 $15.93   L   KG264
POMERANTZ, CHARLOTTE. Mangaboom. Illus. by Anita Lobel. Greenwillow ISBN 0-688-12957-9; In Canada: Hearst Book Group, 1997. unp. col. ill.
Daniel befriends a giant lady, Mangaboom, who speaks both English and Spanish and is courted by a mysterious admirer whose address has been eaten by a goat. All ends well in this oversized romance. Bright illustrations depict Mangaboom from many perspectives though the giant protagonist never quite fits on the large pages.
SUBJ: Giants--Fiction.

                        Ph-1 P-1/1 $13.93   L   KG265
POMERANTZ, CHARLOTTE. One duck, another duck. Illustrated by Jose Aruego and Ariane Dewey. Greenwillow ISBN 0-688-03745-3, 1984. unp. col. ill.
Learning to count, Danny, a young owl, has the help of his grandmother as they watch ducks on a nearby pond. Bright illustrations, lots of humor and an easy to read text make counting to ten fun.
SUBJ: Counting--Fiction./ Birds--Fiction.

CE   Ph-1 P-2/2 $13.89   L   KG266
POMERANTZ, CHARLOTTE. Outside dog. Illus. by Jennifer Plecas. HarperCollins ISBN 0-06-024783-5; In Canada: HarperCollins, 1993. 64p. col. ill. (I can read book).
Includes glossary.
Available from the National Library Service for the Blind and Physically Handicapped on sound recording cassette RC 39556.
Read-along kit available from HarperChildren's Audio (ISBN 0-69470-050-9, 1996). 1 paperback book, 1 sound cassette (21min), $7.95.
Marisol's grandfather tells her not to feed the stray dog, or he will think they own him. Gradually Marisol names the dog, "Pancho," and he does become their "outside dog." The caring relationship between the young girl and her grandfather is clearly apparent as they accept the dog into their lives. Set in Puerto Rico, this easy-to-read title includes several Spanish words. Intergenerational story for multicultural studies.
SUBJ: Dogs--Fiction./ Grandfathers--Fiction./ Puerto Rico--Fiction.

                        Ph-1 1-3/2 $15.93   L   KG267
PORTE, BARBARA ANN. Harry's dog. Illus. by Yossi Abolafia. Greenwillow ISBN 0-688-02556-0, 1984. 47p. col. ill. (Greenwillow read-alone).
Solving the problem created by his father's allergies and Harry's strong desire for a dog isn't easy, but Aunt Rose comes up with the best answer. Breakfast and lunch are awful, the morning is slow moving and boring, but afternoon brings a pleasant surprise in HARRY'S VISIT, Dell (ISBN 0-440-40331-4, c1983, 1990, OPC). Though easy-to-read, these titles are well-written and are very appealing to youngsters. Pen and wash line drawings are excellent in capturing the mood of the stories. Small flip pictures in the lower corners of the right-hand pages add interest. HARRY IN TROUBLE (ISBN 0-688-07722-6, 1989) finds him concerned about losing his library card.
Aunt Rose is getting married and Harry is the ring boy in HARRY GETS AN UNCLE (ISBN 0-688-09389-2, 1991). In HARRY'S BIRTHDAY (ISBN 0-688-12143-8, 1994) his wish for a cowboy hat is fulfilled.
In HARRY'S PONY (ISBN 0-688-14826-3, 1997) he contributes a pony he won to a farm where children with disabilities can ride it.
SUBJ: Dogs--Fiction./ Allergy--Fiction.

                        Ph-2 P-2/2 $8.95   T   KG268
POTTER, BEATRIX. Hill top tales. Warne ISBN 0-7232-3548-1; In Canada: Penguin, c1907, 1987. 128p. col. ill.
Four tales set in and around Hill Top Farm, Beatrix Potter's home in England's Lake District. The tales included in this volume are "The Tale of Tom Kitten," "The Tale of Jemima Puddle-Duck," "The Tale of Samuel Whiskers or The Roly-Poly Pudding" and "The Tale of Ginger and Pickles." They are the original, authorized editions with new color reproductions.
SUBJ: Animals--Fiction.

                        Ph-2 K-2/4 $5.95   L   KG269
POTTER, BEATRIX. Story of Miss Moppet. Warne ISBN 0-7232-3480-9, 1987. 34p. col. ill.
Available from National Library Service for the Blind and Physically Handicapped on sound recording cassette RC13917.
A pussycat is fooled by a mouse.
SUBJ: Cats--Fiction.

                        Ph-1 P-3/7 $5.95   L   KG270
POTTER, BEATRIX. Tailor of Gloucester. Warne ISBN 0-7232-3462-0, c1931, 1987. 58p. col. ill.
Available from National Library Service for the Blind and Physically Handicapped on sound recording cassette RC13917.
A Christmas story about the mice who help a tailor finish his sewing on time.
SUBJ: Christmas--Fiction./ Tailors--Fiction./ Mice--Fiction./ French language materials.

VCR   Ph-3 1-3 $9.95   KG271
POTTER, BEATRIX. Tailor of Gloucester (Videocassette). Read by Meryl Streep. Music by The Chieftains. Illus. by David Jorgensen. Rabbit Ears, 1988. 1/2" VHS videocassette color (30min). (Holiday classics).

Talking book available from Rabbit Ears as sound cassette (ISBN 1-56668-818-3, 1988), 1 sound cassette (35min), $10.95.
The mice in Gloucester help a poor tailor who has taken ill to finish a cloak and waistcoat in time for the Mayor's wedding on Christmas day. The music of the Chieftains, including harpsichord, fiddles, and tin whistle offers an authentic setting and an outstanding listening experience. Narration of Meryl Streep complements the story, but the muted illustrations and minimal animation move a bit slowly. While the author's original illustrations are preferred, this selection may be useful where a video production of the story is needed.
SUBJ: Christmas--Fiction./ Tailors--Fiction./ Mice--Fiction.

Ph-1 P-2/8 $5.95 L KG272
POTTER, BEATRIX. Tale of Benjamin Bunny. Warne ISBN 0-7232-3463-9, c1932, 1987. 58p. col. ill.
Available in Spanish EL CUENTO DEL CONEJITO BENJAMIN (ISBN 0-7232-3558-9, 1988).
When Benjamin Bunny and his cousin, Peter Rabbit, go into Mr. McGregor's garden, they see a big cat and run and hide from her for five long hours!
SUBJ: Rabbits--Fiction.

Ph-1 P-2/6 $5.95 L KG273
POTTER, BEATRIX. Tale of Jemima Puddle-Duck. Warne ISBN 0-7232-3468-X, c1936, 1987. 58p. col. ill.
Available from National Library Service for the Blind and Physically Handicapped on sound recording cassette RC25766 and in Braille BRA06024.
Available in Spanish EL CUENTO DE LA OCA CARLOTA (ISBN 0-7232-3557-0, 1988).
Large type available (ISBN 0-7232-7231-3, 1996).
A silly duck makes a nest in a fox's wood shed.
SUBJ: Ducks--Fiction.

Ph-2 P-2/8 $5.95 L KG274
POTTER, BEATRIX. Tale of Johnny Town-Mouse. Warne ISBN 0-7232-3472-8, c1946, 1987. 58p. col. ill.
Available in Spanish EL CUENTO DE JUANITO RATON DE LA CIUDAD (ISBN 0-7232-3560-0, 1988).
Timmy Willie, a country mouse, and Johnny Town-Mouse, find that each likes his own home best.
SUBJ: Mice--Fiction.

Ph-2 K-2/7 $14.95 T KG275
POTTER, BEATRIX. Tale of Mr. Jeremy Fisher. Illus. by David Jorgensen. Rabbit Ears ISBN 0-88708-094-4, 1989. unp. col. ill.
Presents the familiar text of Beatrix Potter's story in a larger format with pastel illustrations suitable for sharing with a group. Does not take the place of the edition with Potter's original illustrations, but provides another vehicle for introducing the story.
SUBJ: Frogs--Fiction.

Ph-2 P-2/7 $5.95 L KG276
POTTER, BEATRIX. Tale of Mrs. Tiggy-Winkle. Warne ISBN 0-7232-3465-5, c1905, 1987. 58p. col. ill.
When Lucie loses her handkerchiefs, she finds them at the home of a little hedgehog who is busy ironing animals' clothes.
SUBJ: Hedgehogs--Fiction.

Ph-2 P-2/7 $5.95 L KG277
POTTER, BEATRIX. Tale of Mrs. Tittlemouse. Warne ISBN 0-7232-3470-1, c1938, 1987. 59p. col. ill.
Available from National Library Service for the Blind and Physically Handicapped on sound recording cassette RC13917.
About a wood-mouse who has so many visitors that she works all the time keeping her house tidy.
SUBJ: Mice--Fiction.

Ph-1 P-2/6 $5.95 L KG278
POTTER, BEATRIX. Tale of Peter Rabbit. Warne ISBN 0-7232-3460-4, n.d., 1987. 58p. col. ill.
Available in French L'HISTOIRE DE PIERRE LAPIN (Dover ISBN 0-486-25313-9), $2.50.
Available in Spanish EL CUENTO DE PEDRO, EL CONEJO (Dover ISBN 0-486-25314-7), $2.50.
Available from National Library Service for the Blind and Physically Handicapped in Braille BR05087, sound recording cassette RC13917, talking book TB00818.
Big book available from Warne (ISBN 0-7232-4029-9, c1902, 1993).
The disobedient rabbit goes into Mr. McGregor's garden, contrary to his mother's wish.
SUBJ: Rabbits--Fiction./ Spanish language materials./ French language materials.

TB Ph-1 P-2 $9.95 OD KG279
POTTER, BEATRIX. Tale of Peter Rabbit, and four other stories (Talking book). Read by Clarie Bloom. HarperAudio/Caedmon ISBN 0-89845-575-8; In Canada: dist. by HarperCollins, 1984. 1 sound cassette.
Claire Bloom reads THE TALE OF PETER RABBIT, THE TALE OF BENJAMIN BUNNY, THE TALE OF TWO BAD MICE, THE TALE OF MRS. TIGGY-WINKLE, THE TALE OF MR. JEREMY FISHER. Clear enunciation and excellent technical production make this an outstanding recording.
SUBJ: Animals--Fiction.

Ph-1 P-2/7 $5.95 L KG280
POTTER, BEATRIX. Tale of Squirrel Nutkin. Warne ISBN 0-7232-3461-2, c1931, 1987. 58p. col. ill.
Available from National Library Service for the Blind and Physically Handicapped on sound recording cassette RC13917.
When the other squirrels are busy gathering nuts, bad little Nutkin asks Old Mr. Brown Owl so many riddles that at last he becomes angry.
SUBJ: Squirrels--Fiction.

Ph-2 P-2/7 $5.95 L KG281
POTTER, BEATRIX. Tale of the Flopsy Bunnies. Warne ISBN 0-7232-3469-8, c1937, 1987. 59p. col. ill.
Available from National Library Service for the Blind and Physically Handicapped on sound recording cassette RC13917.
When Farmer McGregor puts the six little rabbits into a sack, a mouse tries to save them.
SUBJ: Rabbits--Fiction.

Ph-2 K-2/5 $5.95 L KG282
POTTER, BEATRIX. Tale of the pie and the patty-pan. Warne ISBN 0-7232-3476-0, c1933, 1987. 74p. col. ill.
A cat, Ribby, and a little dog, Duchess, have tea together.
SUBJ: Cats--Fiction./ Dogs--Fiction.

Ph-2 P-2/7 $5.95 L KG283
POTTER, BEATRIX. Tale of Tom Kitten. Warne ISBN 0-7232-3467-1, c1935. 59p. col. ill.
Available in Spanish EL CUENTO DEL GATO TOMAS (ISBN 0-7232-3565-1, 1988).
Even though they are wearing their best clothes for company, Tom Kitten and his sisters, Mittens and Moppet, get into trouble.
SUBJ: Cats--Fiction.

Ph-1 P-2/6 $5.95 L KG284
POTTER, BEATRIX. Tale of two bad mice. Warne ISBN 0-7232-3464-7, c1932, 1987. 58p. col. ill.
Available in Spanish EL CUENTO DE LOS DOS MALVADOS RATONES (ISBN 0-7232-3559-7, 1988).
Tom Thumb, a mouse, and his wife, Hunca Munca, go into the doll's house and upset it.
SUBJ: Mice--Fiction.

Ph-2 P-1/2 $14.95 L KG285
POYDAR, NANCY. Busy Bea. McElderry ISBN 0-689-50592-2; In Canada: Maxwell Macmillan, 1994. unp. col. ill.
Bea is so busy she loses everything, but she is also good at finding things. At school when she searches for the yellow sweater her grandmother knit her, she finds not only her sweater but also many of her other missing items in the lost and found. Cheerful watercolor illustrations depict a carefree Bea and a typical childhood problem. For multicultural studies.
SUBJ: Lost and found possessions--Fiction./ Grandmothers--Fiction./ Afro-Americans--Fiction.

Ph-2 1-3/2 $9.99 L KG286
PRAGER, ANNABELLE. Baseball birthday party. Illus. by Marilyn Mets. Random House ISBN 0-679-94171-1; In Canada: Random House, 1995. 48p. col. ill. (Step into reading).
Billy is new in the neighborhood and decides to have a baseball birthday party to show the other kids how well he can play, but no one responds to his invitation. His young friend, Dan put the invitations in a box marked "litter" which he mistakenly thought said "letter." Emerging readers will relate to Dan's mistake and cheer for the happy resolution in this delightful beginning reader.
SUBJ: Baseball--Fiction./ Parties--Fiction./ Birthdays--Fiction.

Ph-1 1-3/2 $7.99 L KG287
PRAGER, ANNABELLE. Spooky Halloween party. Illus. by Tomie De Paola. Pantheon ISBN 0-394-94961-7; In Canada: Random House, 1981. 45p. ill. (I am reading book).
Albert thinks he's too big to be scared and is sure that he'll know all the gang at Nicky's Halloween party in spite of their costumes. But

Albert is in for a real surprise. He gets increasingly worried when he can't recognize any of the other guests even after they remove their masks.
SUBJ: Halloween--Fiction./ Parties--Fiction./ Apartment houses--Fiction.

Ph-1 K-2/3 $15.99   L   KG288
PRICEMAN, MARJORIE. How to make an apple pie and see the world. Knopf ISBN 0-679-93705-6; In Canada: Random House, 1994. unp. col. ill., map.
"Borzoi book."
You want to make an apple pie, but the market is closed. Get on a boat and go around the world for the ingredients: wheat from Italy, cinnamon from Sri Lanka, and sugar from Jamaica. A young girl takes you on the tour, and a recipe for the pie follows the story. A map of the world in front and back of the book provides the geographical references for the story that has numerous applications across the curriculum. It's delicious fun as well!
SUBJ: Pies--Fiction./ Food--Fiction./ Voyages and travels--Fiction./ Humorous stories.

Ph-3 K-2/5 $16.95   L   KG289
PROVENSEN, ALICE. Owl and three pussycats. By Alice and Martin Provensen. Browndeer/Harcourt Brace ISBN 0-15-200183-2, 1994. unp. col. ill.
Originally published by Atheneum, 1981.
When a spring storm dislodges a very small owl from his home in an old, old tree, the baby orphan is rescued by the farm family of Maple Hill. They feed him, care for him, and play with him until he is old enough and wise enough to be free and independent. In the second story three kittens--Fat Boy, Crook, and Webster--each with very different personalities join the family. They live in the house until their wild though humorous antics cause banishment to the barn. The oversized book with the Provensens' usual high quality illustrations will be enjoyed by young listeners on a one-to-one basis.
SUBJ: Owls--Fiction./ Cats--Fiction./ Farm life--Fiction.

Ph-1 K-2/4 $3.95   P   KG290
PROVENSEN, ALICE. Year at Maple Hill Farm. By Alice and Martin Provensen. Atheneum ISBN 0-689-71270-7, 1978. unp. col. ill.
Describes and pictures for each month of the year the seasonal habits, activities and changes that take place with farm animals and the people who live at Maple Hill Farm.
OUR ANIMAL FRIENDS AT MAPLE HILL FARM (Random House ISBN 0-394-92123-2, 1974) introduces the many animals who live on or near Maple Hill Farm in a matter of fact but humorous manner with many colorful, detailed illustrations.
SUBJ: Farm life--Fiction./ Seasons--Fiction./ Spanish language materials.

Ph-2 2-3/5 $14.93   L   KG291
PRYOR, BONNIE. Dream jar. Illus. by Mark Graham. Morrow ISBN 0-688-13062-3, 1996. unp. col. ill.
Valentina wants to help earn money towards her father's dream of owning a store. When neighbors pay her to teach them to read, she is able to make contributions to the dream jar. Finally her father finds a small store for his family. One of numerous stories about immigrant families, this one places a value on reading and one girl's contribution as a teacher.
SUBJ: Emigration and immigration--Fiction./ Family life--Fiction./ Russian Americans--Fiction.

Ph-2 K-3/4 $14.88   L   KG292
PRYOR, BONNIE. House on Maple Street. Illus. by Beth Peck. Morrow ISBN 0-688-06381-0, 1987. unp. col. ill.
Starting and concluding with two contemporary sisters, this capsule history of 300 years in America's Midwest traces the evolution of woods and streams to a busy subdivision. Personalized by a lost arrowhead and a lost china cup and interpreted in beautiful earthtone paintings which capture the people and surroundings of the passing eras this will be useful in the social studies curriculum.
SUBJ: Time--Fiction./ Change--Fiction.

Ph-2 K-2/2 $13.89   L   KG293
PULVER, ROBIN. Nobody's mother is in second grade. Illus. by G. Brian Karas. Dial ISBN 0-8037-1211-1, 1992. unp. col. ill.
None of the other mothers ever came to second grade so Cassandra's mother disguises herself as a plant to accompany her to school. A lightly humorous and affectionate school story.
SUBJ: Plants--Fiction./ Mothers and daughters--Fiction./ Schools--Fiction.

Ph-2 2-4/6 $15.95   L   KG294
PYLE, HOWARD. Swan Maiden. Afterword by Ellin Greene. Illus. by Robert Sauber. Holiday House ISBN 0-8234-1088-9, 1994. unp. col. ill.

In order to marry the Swan Maiden, a young prince must perform three seemingly impossible tasks for the witch with three eyes. With the magic help of the Swan Maiden, he performs the tasks and outsmarts the witch, returning to his home with the maiden and three magic eggs. Richly colored and boldly framed illustrations add to the story's enchantment.
SUBJ: Fairy tales./ Princes--Fiction.

Ph-2 1-3/2 $14.95   T   KG295
QUINLAN, PATRICIA. My dad takes care of me. Illus. by Vlasta Van Kampen. Annick/dist. by Firefly ISBN 0-920303-79-X; In Canada: Annick/dist. by Firefly, 1987. unp. col. ill.
Luke's father is home all the time now since the factory in which he worked closed. Luke's confusion about the changes soon gives way to the pleasure that he doesn't have to go to a sitter and that he and his dad have time to talk, work and play together. A quietly reassuring book for children in similar circumstances.
SUBJ: Unemployed--Fiction./ Family problems--Fiction./ Fathers and sons--Fiction.

Ph-2 P-2/2 $13.95   L   KG296
RABE, BERNIECE. Where's Chimpy? Photos by Diane Schmidt. Whitman ISBN 0-8075-8928-4; In Canada: General, 1988. unp. col. ill.
Daddy is ready to read Misty a bedtime story but Misty can't settle down for sleep because Chimpy is missing. The two reenact the day's activities as they search through the house and yard before finally finding the beloved stuffed monkey. Appealing, perceptive full color photographs enrich the simple loving story of a true family whose Down's syndrome child is the star. Introductory material concerning Down's syndrome is included.
SUBJ: Down's syndrome--Fiction./ Mentally handicapped--Fiction./ Lost and found possessions--Fiction.

Ph-2 2-4/4 $14.95   L   KG297
RABIN, STATON. Casey over there. Illus. by Greg Shed. Harcourt Brace ISBN 0-15-253186-6; In Canada: Harcourt Brace c/o Canadian Manda, 1994. unp. col. ill.
Worried about his older brother, Casey, a soldier in France during the "Great War," Aubrey writes a letter to Uncle Sam asking when his brother will be back. He receives an answer from President Wilson. Sepia-toned illustrations show contrasting scenes of Aubrey playing at home and his older brother in the trenches. Historical fiction for the primary grades.
SUBJ: World War, 1914-1918--Fiction./ Brothers--Fiction.

Ph-2 1-3/4 $14.95   T   KG298
RAHAMAN, VASHANTI. O Christmas tree. Illus. by Frane Lessac. Boyds Mills ISBN 1-56397-237-9; In Canada: McClelland & Stewart, 1996. unp. col. ill.
Disappointed when a shipment of Christmas trees arrives on his Caribbean Island dry and needleless, Anslem tries to use paint and pine cleaner to transform two bare trees into a Christmas tree. The familiar and foreign blend in the dialog that slips into West Indian dialect and in the adoption of familiar traditions in an unfamiliar setting. A holiday book for multicultural studies.
SUBJ: Christmas trees--Fiction./ Christmas--Fiction./ West Indies--Fiction./ Caribbean Area--Fiction.

Ph-1 1-3/3 $15.95   T   KG299
RAND, GLORIA. Aloha, Salty! Illus. by Ted Rand. Henry Holt ISBN 0-8050-3429-3; In Canada: Fitzhenry & Whiteside, 1996. unp. col. ill.
Near the end of their sailing trip to Hawaii, Zack and Salty are washed overboard in a rough storm. The adventure is realistic and suspenseful, and the wide watercolor illustrations are action-packed. A great story about water safety with strong appeal for adventure fans.
SUBJ: Sailing--Fiction./ Storms--Fiction./ Dogs--Fiction./ Hawaii--Fiction.

Ph-2 2-3/4 $14.95   T   KG300
RAND, GLORIA. Prince William. Illus. by Ted Rand. Henry Holt ISBN 0-8050-1841-7; In Canada: Fitzhenry & Whiteside, 1992. unp. col. ill.
Following a large oil spill in Prince William Sound, Denny finds a baby seal covered in oil and names him Prince William. She takes the seal pup to a rescue center where he is cleaned up and then taken to an animal hospital to recuperate. Details are provided about the devastating effects of an oil spill and about animal rescue, specifically the rehabilitation and release of a seal pup. Useful for environmental units.
SUBJ: Seals (Animals)--Fiction./ Wildlife rescue--Fiction./ Oil spills--Fiction./ Pollution--Fiction./ Alaska--Fiction.

Ph-2 2-3/5 $4.95   P   KG301
RAND, GLORIA. Salty dog. Illus. by Ted Rand. Henry Holt ISBN 0-8050-1847-6; In Canada: Fitzhenry & Whiteside, 1991. unp. col. ill.

Accustomed to riding the ferry with his master and staying at the boatyard while he builds his sailboat, Salty is upset when he's left behind because he's too big to stay in a box. Based on facts this combines a dog story with an overview of boat building. The colorful illustrations and matter-of-fact text appeal at storytime.
The intrepid dog and Zack set sail to Alaska - a voyage that proves to have many adventures in SALTY SAILS NORTH (ISBN 0-8050-2118-4, 1992, OPC) and in SALTY TAKES OFF (ISBN 0-8050-1159-5, 1991, OPC) Salty falls from an airplane but is reunited with Zack.
SUBJ: Dogs--Fiction./ Boats and boating--Fiction./ Sailboats--Fiction.

Ph-2 K-2/3 $15.00 L KG302
RAND, GLORIA. Willie takes a hike. Illus. by Ted Rand. Harcourt Brace ISBN 0-15-200272-3; In Canada: Harcourt Brace c/o Canadian Manda, 1996. unp. col. ill.
Despite a warning not to hike alone, Willie, a mouse, explores the junkyard and becomes truly lost. A search and rescue team finds him the next morning, and now Willie always remembers to follow hiking safety rules. A cautionary tale for young listeners who will enjoy the suspense and adventure and may remember some of the safety rules.
SUBJ: Mice--Fiction./ Hiking--Fiction./ Safety--Fiction./ Lost children--Fiction.

Ph-2 P-1/2 $14.89 L KG303
RANSOM, CANDICE F. Big green pocketbook. Illus. by Felicia Bond. HarperCollins ISBN 0-06-020849-X; In Canada: HarperCollins, 1993. unp. col. ill.
"Laura Geringer book."
A litte girl fills her big green pocketbook with small mementos from a trip into town with her mother. The child's joy in the day's activities and her own possessions is clear from the illustrations which depict a pocketbook about half her size. When the pocketbook is left behind on the bus, readers will feel the loss and the joy when it is returned.
SUBJ: City and town life--Fiction./ Mothers and daughters--Fiction./ Handbags--Fiction.

Ph-2 K-2/2 $14.95 T KG304
RANSOM, CANDICE F. Shooting star summer. Illus. by Karen Milone. Caroline House/Boyds Mills ISBN 1-56397-005-8, 1992. unp. col. ill.
Two cousins are very different. When one comes for a summer visit, they are uncertain about each other but soon become good friends. The illustrations include some that look like photographs and reinforce the mood of summer vacations remembered.
SUBJ: Friendship--Fiction.

Ph-1 1-3/2 $15.93 L KG305
RANSOM, CANDICE F. When the whippoorwill calls. Illus. by Kimberly Bulcken Root. Tambourine ISBN 0-688-12730-4, 1995. unp. col. ill.
Displaced by the Shenandoah National Park, Polly and her family leave their home in the Blue Ridge Mountains of Virginia, but return for a visit. Details about their lives in the mountains and the flatlands fill the text and illustrations. The family story about moving also offers an understanding of the loss often caused by progress. Historical fiction could be used as a discussion starter in Virginia history units.
SUBJ: Mountain life--Virginia--Fiction./ Blue Ridge Mountains--Fiction./ Virginia--Fiction./ Moving, Household--Fiction.

Ph-1 K-3/2 $12.89 L KG306
RAPPAPORT, DOREEN. Boston coffee party. Illus. by Emily Arnold McCully. HarperCollins ISBN 0-06-024825-4, 1988. 63p. col. ill. (I can read book).
During the difficult times of the Revolutionary War and remembering the Boston Tea Party, the patriotic women and children of Boston decide to hold a coffee party and teach greedy, profiteering merchant Thomas a lesson he won't forget. Based on a true incident described in a letter from Abigail Adams to her husband John, the account and illustrations provide just enough suspense, humor and historical information for young primaries.
SUBJ: United States--History--Revolution, 1775-1783--Fiction./ Boston (Mass.)--Fiction.

Ph-1 P-3/1 $14.99 L KG307
RASCHKA, CHRIS. Yo! Yes?. Orchard ISBN 0-531-08619-4, 1993. unp. col. ill.
Caldecott Honor book, 1994.
Selectors' Choice, 19th ed.
A friendship is formed with much expression and few words between two strangers. Although easy-to-read, this story is not at all babyish and has a lot of street spunk in the illustrations and minimal text. For multicultural studies.
SUBJ: Friendship--Fiction./ Race relations--Fiction./ Afro-Americans--Fiction.

Ph-1 K-2/2 $3.95 P KG308
RASKIN, ELLEN. Nothing ever happens on my block. Atheneum ISBN 0-689-71335-5, c1966. unp. col. ill.
Chester, a dull boy, sits on a curb complaining of boredom while behind him, children play, a house burns, cops and robbers appear and a parachutist lands.
SUBJ: Cities and towns--Fiction.

Ph-1 K-2/1 $13.95 L KG309
RATHMANN, PEGGY. Good night, Gorilla. Putnam ISBN 0-399-22445-9; In Canada: Putnam, 1994. unp. col. ill.
As the zookeeper makes his rounds telling all of the animals, "goodnight," Gorilla, who has stolen the zookeeper's keys, lets them out. In single file, the animals follow the zookeeper home and to bed. Delightfully humorous, the almost wordless story is conveyed in the expressive, colorful illustrations which include the antics of a small mouse dragging a banana.
SUBJ: Zoo animals--Fiction./ Zoos--Fiction./ Gorilla--Fiction.

Ph-1 K-2/3 $15.95 L KG310
RATHMANN, PEGGY. Officer Buckle and Gloria. Putnam ISBN 0-399-22616-8; In Canada: Putnam, 1995. unp. col. ill.
Caldecott Medal Award, 1996.
Officer Buckle and his canine partner, Gloria, are a team as they go from school to school giving safety speeches. Officer Buckle's discovery of how Gloria has been dramatizing the safety tips behind his back almost threatens their partnership. Expressive cartoon-like illustrations highlight their friendship and provide the hilarity. Although the applications to discussions about community helpers and health and safety units are clear, the delightful delivery is the reason to share this story again and again.
SUBJ: Safety--Fiction./ Police--Fiction./ Police dogs--Fiction./ Schools--Fiction.

Ph-1 K-2/2 $12.95 L KG311
RATHMANN, PEGGY. Ruby the copycat. Scholastic ISBN 0-590-43747-X; In Canada: Scholastic, 1991. unp. col. ill.
Ruby copies everything Angela does from the red bow she wears in her hair to the poem she recites in class. Angela is a good sport at first, but it soon becomes too much for her until Ruby finally demonstrates her individuality. Ruby's copycat style as portrayed in story and pictures is truly original and delightful.
SUBJ: Behavior--Fiction./ Teacher-student relationships--Fiction./ Schools--Fiction.

Ph-2 1-3/2 $15.95 L KG312
RATTIGAN, JAMA KIM. Dumpling soup. Illus. by Lillian Hsu-Flanders. Little, Brown ISBN 0-316-73445-4; In Canada: Little, Brown, 1993. unp. col. ill.
Includes glossary.
A young Hawaiian girl whose family traditions come from Korea, Japan, and China as well as Hawaii describes her family's preparations for the New Year celebrations, including her introduction to cooking the traditional dumplings. Glossary provides pronunciations and definitions for the many words originating in the various languages. For multicultural studies.
SUBJ: Family life--Fiction./ Cookery--Fiction./ Hawaii--Fiction.

Ph-1 K-1/2 $15.00 L KG313
RAU, DANA MEACHEN. Box can be many things. Illus. by Paige Billin-Frye. Children's Press ISBN 0-516-20317-7; In Canada: Grolier Ltd., 1997. 32p. col. ill. (Rookie reader).
Retrieving a large cardboard box from the trash, two children fantasize that it's a cave and a car. When the box falls apart, the torn pieces become costumes for more creative play. Watercolor illustrations offer clues to the simple text for beginning readers.
SUBJ: Boxes--Fiction./ Imagination--Fiction./ Play--Fiction.

CE Ph-2 K-2/3 $15.95 T KG314
RAU, DANA MEACHEN. Robin at Hickory Street. Illus. by Joel Snyder. Soundprints/Smithsonian Institution ISBN 1-56899-168-1; In Canada: Soundprints/dist. by Canadian Manda, 1995. 32p. col. ill. (Smithsonian's backyard).
Includes glossary.
Teacher's guide available upon request.
Read-along kit available (ISBN 1-56899-172-X, 1995) 1 hardback book, 1 sound cassette (9min), $19.95.
Young Robin finds a home, uninhabited by other robins, which he guards welcoming a female mate to build a nest. Cheery doublespread illustrations will catch the interest of young readers, and the focus on an individual bird provides facts about this common backyard sign of spring.
SUBJ: Robins--Fiction./ Birds--Fiction./ Spring--Fiction.

Ph-2 2-3/2 $15.95   L   KG315

RAVEN, MARGOT. Angels in the dust. By Margot Theis Raven. Illus. by Roger Essley. BridgeWater ISBN 0-8167-3806-8; In Canada: BridgeWater/dist. by Vanwell, 1997. unp. col. ill.

Annie relates the story of her youth during the Dust Bowl in Oklahoma to her great grandchildren. The hardships of losing a parent, trying to maintain a garden, and a house fire are lightened by family and community and undying hope. Pastel illustrations are suitably dark and gritty. Historical fiction for beginning readers.
SUBJ: Dust storms--Great Plains--Fiction./ Droughts--Great Plains--Fiction./ Farm life--Oklahoma--Fiction./ Family life--Fiction.

Ph-2 P-2/2 $15.00   L   KG316

RAY, MARY LYN. Mud. Illus. by Lauren Stringer. Harcourt Brace ISBN 0-15-256263-X; In Canada: Harcourt Brace c/o Canadian Manda, 1996. unp. col. ill.

Spring thaw turns the frozen earth into a wonderful substance for play: mud! Large doublespread acrylic illustrations focus on bare feet and squishy mud. An outstanding choice for reading aloud when the seasons turn from winter to spring.
SUBJ: Spring--Fiction./ Mud--Fiction.

Ph-1 K-2/4 $14.95   L   KG317

RAYNER, MARY. Mr. and Mrs. Pig's evening out. Atheneum ISBN 0-689-30530-3, c1976. 32p. col. ill.

Available from National Library Service for the Blind and Physically Handicapped in Braille BR03638.
The agency sitter engaged by Mrs. Pig seems very nice and quite competent but during the long evening her true nature becomes evident. She attempts to convert rosy, plump, pink Garth Pig into a juicy snack. However, she doesn't count on the cleverness of the other nine young piglets who save their brother and Mrs. Wolfe ends up in the river. The Pig family returns in a collection of adventures: GARTH PIG AND THE ICE CREAM LADY (Atheneum ISBN 0-689-30598-2, 1977); MRS. PIG'S BULK BUY (Atheneum ISBN 0-689-30831-0, 1981); MRS. PIG GETS CROSS AND OTHER STORIES (ISBN 0-525-44280-4, 1987); GARTH PIG STEALS THE SHOW (ISBN 0-525-45023-8, 1993, OPC).
In GARTH PIG AND THE ICE CREAM LADY (ISBN 0-689-30598-2, 1977) Garth Pig sets out to buy whooshes for his brothers and sisters only to find that the ice cream lady, Madame Lupino is not what she appears to be, and in MRS. PIG'S BULK BUY (ISBN 0-689-30831-0, 1981) Mrs. Pig serves ketchup for every meal and snack until the piglets finally lose their appetite for it. The pig family returns in a collection of stories MRS. PIG GETS CROSS AND OTHER STORIES (Dutton ISBN 0-525-44280-4, 1987, OPC) and in GARTH PIG STEALS THE SHOW (Dutton ISBN 0-525-45023-8, 1993).
Also available from NLSBPH is GARTH PIG AND THE ICE CREAM LADY in Braille BR04669 and on sound recording cassette RC16120.
SUBJ: Pigs--Fiction./ Babysitters--Fiction./ Problem solving--Fiction.

Ph-1 P-3/2 $14.93   L   KG318

REISER, LYNN. Beach feet. Greenwillow ISBN 0-688-14401-2, 1996. unp. col. ill.

Lots of different feet can be found at the beach including those of birds, dogs, and sea creatures. A repetitive text and splendid illustrations form the footing for the book while numerous footnotes offer thumbnail descriptions of various beach creatures and their feet. The interdisciplinary approach may be enjoyed on various levels--as an easy-to-read story, for units on the seashore, or even as an introduction to footnotes.
SUBJ: Foot--Fiction./ Beaches--Fiction./ Animals--Fiction.

Ph-1 P-2/2 $13.93   L   KG319

REISER, LYNN. Surprise family. Greenwillow ISBN 0-688-11672-8, 1994. unp. col. ill.

A young boy hatches and raises a chick until she grows up and wants a family of her own. He finds a nest of eggs for her, and when baby ducklings hatch, she raises them as her own until one day they decide to go swimming without her. The quilt pattern on the endpapers offers a homelike frame for the loving story about families and attachment.
SUBJ: Chickens--Fiction./ Ducks--Fiction./ Family--Fiction.

Ph-2 P-2/3 $14.93   L   KG320

REISER, LYNN. Two mice in three fables. Greenwillow ISBN 0-688-13390-8, 1995. 32p. col. ill.

Three original fables are connected by two mice: an indoor and an outdoor one. They scurry together outdoors and foil a snake, a raccoon, and an owl attempting to eat the two. The illustrations include small details that connect the three stories, such as a family reading together at the beginning of each story and the many animal characters peering through a window on the last page.
SUBJ: Fables./ Animals--Fiction./ Mice--Fiction.

Ph-2 P-1 $13.95   L   KG321

REISS, JOHN J. Numbers. Bradbury ISBN 0-02-776150-9, c1971. unp. col. ill.

Bold numbers, bright colors and recognizable objects make this an exceptionally good counting book. After twenty the counting is by tens to one hundred. Objects are grouped so that children can discover many number facts for themselves, i. e. four fours are sixteen, six fives are thirty, etc.
SUBJ: Counting.

Ph-1 P-2/2 $12.95   L   KG322

REY, H. A. Curious George. Houghton Mifflin ISBN 0-395-15993-8, c1941. 56p. col. ill.

Available from National Library Service for the Blind and Physically Handicapped BRA06644, talking book TB03845, and sound recording cassette RC28932.
Available in Spanish JORGE EL CURIOSO (ISBN 0-395-17075-3).
Available in big book (ISBN 0-395-69803-0, 1994).
A mischievous monkey who has just come to a city from the jungle, leads his owner, the man with the yellow hat, on a merry chase.
SUBJ: Monkeys--Fiction./ Spanish language materials.

TB   Ph-1 P-2 $5.99   OD   KG323

REY, H. A. Curious George and other stories about Curious George (Talking book). Read by Julie Harris. HarperAudio/Caedmon CDL51420 ISBN 1-55994-915-5; In Canada: dist. by HarperCollins, 1973. 1 sound cassette.

Straight narrative reading by actress Julie Harris of Curious George takes a job; Curious George rides a bike and Curious George gets a medal; Can have a fairly wide span of appeal from pre-school through primary grades.
SUBJ: Monkeys--Fiction.

Ph-3 P-2/2 $13.95   L   KG324

REY, H. A. Curious George gets a medal. Houghton Mifflin ISBN 0-395-16973-9, 1957. 47p. col. ill.

Available from National Library Service for the Blind and Physically Handicapped in Braille BRA02484.
This little monkey has a very exciting day filled with soap bubbles, pigs, a museum and finally a ride into space.
SUBJ: Monkeys--Fiction.

Ph-3 P-2/2 $13.95   L   KG325

REY, H. A. Curious George learns the alphabet. Houghton Mifflin ISBN 0-395-16031-6, c1963. 72p. col. ill.

Available from National Library Service for the Blind and Physically Handicapped on sound recording cassette RC23186.
How his friend, the man in the yellow hat, teaches a monkey to read.
SUBJ: Alphabet./ Monkeys--Fiction.

CE   Ph-1 P-2/1 $13.45   L   KG326

REY, H. A. Curious George rides a bike. Houghton Mifflin ISBN 0-395-16964-X, c1952. 45p. col. ill.

Videocassette available from Weston Woods HMPV017V, 1985.
1/2" VHS videocassette color (10min), $49.95.
Read-along kit available from Weston Woods PBC17, 1993. 1 paperback book, 1 sound cassette (24min), $14.80. Side one with page turn signal, side two without signal.
After many humorous episodes, a friendly monkey gets a job in a show.
SUBJ: Monkeys--Fiction./ Bicycles and bicycling--Fiction.

Ph-3 P-2/3 $13.95   L   KG327

REY, H. A. Curious George takes a job. Houghton Mifflin ISBN 0-395-15086-8, c1947. 47p. col. ill.

Available from National Library Service for the Blind and Physically Handicapped in Braille BR04662.
A lively monkey escapes from a zoo and gets into spaghetti, paint, breaks a leg and in general leads a merry life.
SUBJ: Monkeys--Fiction.

Ph-3 P-2/1 $13.95   L   KG328

REY, MARGRET. Curious George flies a kite. Illus. by H.A. Rey. Houghton Mifflin ISBN 0-395-16965-8, c1958. 80p. col. ill.

Available from National Library Service for the Blind and Physically Handicapped in Braille BR01741.
The antics of a lovable monkey end with his rescue by helicopter.
SUBJ: Monkeys--Fiction.

Ph-1 P-2/2 $12.95   L   KG329

REY, MARGRET. Curious George goes to the hospital. By Margret and H.A. Rey in collaboration with the Children's Hospital, Boston. Houghton Mifflin ISBN 0-395-18158-5, c1966. 48p. col. ill.

Available from National Library Service for the Blind and Physically Handicapped in Braille BR05079.

The lively monkey swallows a piece of a jigsaw puzzle and goes to the hospital for an operation and soon becomes the favorite of the children's ward. Written in collaboration with the Children's Medical Center of Boston, this is a fine way of preparing a child for his trip to a hospital.
SUBJ: Monkeys--Fiction./ Hospitals--Fiction.

Ph-1 P-2/2 $13.93   L   KG330
RICE, EVE. Benny bakes a cake. Greenwillow ISBN 0-688-11580-2, c1981, 1993. unp. col. ill.
It's Benny's birthday and he and his mother bake a beautiful cake while his big dog, Ralph, watches. Everything is ready and there is still time for a walk. But where is Ralph? He's in the kitchen eating Benny's cake. Although his mother tries to comfort him, Benny cries and cries until there is a knock at the door, Papa appears and there is a birthday party after all.
SUBJ: Birthdays--Fiction./ Cake--Fiction.

Ph-1 2-3/2 $15.95   T   KG331
RIGGIO, ANITA. Secret signs: along the Underground Railroad. Boyds Mills ISBN 1-56397-555-6; In Canada: McClelland & Stewart, 1997. unp. col. ill.
A young deaf boy bravely conveys the signal of a change in a stop along the Underground Railroad through his skill as an artist. Watercolor illustrations portray the danger to the boy from a slave catcher. Sign language plays an important role in the dramatic historical fiction account for beginning readers.
SUBJ: Underground railroad--Fiction./ Deaf--Fiction.

Ph-1 2-4/5 $14.89   L   KG332
RINGGOLD, FAITH. Dinner at Aunt Connie's house. Hyperion ISBN 1-56282-426-0, 1993. unp. col. ill.
Aunt Connie's paintings of famous African-American women tell their stories to Melody and her cousin, Lonnie, when they discover them during a family gathering. This longer picture book illustrated with portraits may serve as an introduction to a study of African-American history or as an enjoyable summation for multicultural studies. For reading aloud.
SUBJ: Afro-Americans--Fiction./ Dinners and dining--Fiction.

Ph-1 2-3/4 $16.99   L   KG333
RINGGOLD, FAITH. Tar beach. Crown ISBN 0-517-58031-4, 1991. unp. col. ill.
Caldecott Honor Book.
Coretta Scott King Award (Illustrator).
Selectors' Choice, 18th ed.
From a rooftop in Harlem, 8-year-old Cassie dreams of flying over the city and the George Washington Bridge and of a better life for her family. The African-American folk motif of flying represents freedom, and is richly depicted in the author's quilt paintings. A beautifully optimistic story of rising above difficult circumstances. For multicultural studies.
SUBJ: Afro-Americans--Fiction./ Harlem (New York, N.Y.)--Fiction./ Flight--Fiction./ Dreams--Fiction.

Ph-3 P-1/1 $4.95   P   KG334
ROBART, ROSE. Cake that Mack ate. Illus. by Maryann Kovalski. Joy Street/Little, Brown ISBN 0-316-74891-9; In Canada: Kids Can Press, 1986. unp. col. ill.
The farmer's wife lit the candles, the farmer planted the seed, the hen laid an egg and all of that contributed to "the cake that Mack ate." Told in cumulative text similar in rhythm to "The House that Jack built" this is fun to share with a group or for beginning readers to handle on their own.
SUBJ: Cake--Fiction.

Ph-2 P-1/3 $15.93   L   KG335
ROBERTS, BETHANY. Camel caravan. By Bethany Roberts and Patricia Hubbell. Illus. by Cheryl Munro Taylor. Tambourine ISBN 0-688-13940-X, 1996. unp. col. ill.
Escaping from a caravan, camels clump, jump, pump, and stump across the desert using a variety of transportation. Silly, but fun, predictable book which children will enjoy for the sound of the rhyming words and the wide doublespread cut-paper collage illustrations.
SUBJ: Camels--Fiction./ Vehicles--Fiction./ Deserts--Fiction./ Stories in rhyme.

Ph-2 P-1/3 $12.95   L   KG336
ROBERTS, BETHANY. Halloween mice! Illus. by Doug Cushman. Clarion ISBN 0-395-67064-0, 1995. 32p. col. ill.
Mice in costumes cavort in a pumpkin patch on Halloween night and scare the cat with a spooky shadow. The simple rhyming text and playful illustrations will appeal to the youngest Halloween fans. For

storytime and independent reading.
SUBJ: Mice--Fiction./ Cats--Fiction./ Halloween--Fiction.

CE   Ph-2 K-1/4 $14.95   L   KG337
ROBERTUS, POLLY M. Dog who had kittens. Illus. by Janet Stevens. Holiday House ISBN 0-8234-0860-4, 1991. unp. col. ill.
Read-along kit available from Live Oak Media (ISBN 0-87499-285-0, 1992). 1 hardcover book, 1 sound cassette (14min), $19.95.
Videocassette available from Live Oak Media (ISBN 0-87499-283-4, 1992). 1/2" VHS videocassette color (14min), $36.95.
Baxter, a basset hound, befriends a litter of kittens despite his shaky relationship with their mother, Eloise, the family cat. Baxter is heartbroken when the kittens are given away but finds he and Eloise have a new understanding. The characters of Baxter and Eloise are great fun in the story along with the large humorous illustrations.
SUBJ: Dogs--Fiction./ Cats--Fiction.

Ph-2 K-2/1 $13.89   L   KG338
ROBINS, JOAN. Addie meets Max. Illus. by Sue Truesdell. HarperCollins ISBN 0-06-025064-X; In Canada: HarperCollins, 1985. 32p. col. ill. (Early I can read book).
Getting acquainted with the new boy next door isn't easy and starts out with a bike collision, skinned knees and a lost tooth, but Addie and Max do soon become good friends and Addie discovers that the new dog, Ginger, isn't fierce after all. Brief, easy to read and children like it.
SUBJ: Friendship--Fiction.

Ph-2 K-1/2 $13.89   L   KG339
ROBINS, JOAN. Addie's bad day. Illus. by Sue Truesdell. HarperCollins ISBN 0-06-021298-5; In Canada: HarperCollins, 1993. 32p. col. ill. (I can read book).
Addie wants to attend Max's birthday party, but she is embarrassed by her new haircut. How she and Max cleverly solve her dilemma is humorously depicted.
SUBJ: Haircutting--Fiction./ Beauty, Personal--Fiction./ Friendship--Fiction.

Ph-2 P-3/3 $13.95   L   KG340
ROCKWELL, ANNE F. At the beach. By Anne and Harlow Rockwell. Macmillan ISBN 0-02-777940-8; In Canada:: Collier Macmillan, 1987. unp. col. ill.
Evokes, with perceptive text and fresh illustrations, the feeling of being at the beach on a mid-July day. Certainly pleasurable reading but also can be used to support safety and beginning science units; also has potential for English as a second language use.
SUBJ: Seashore--Fiction./ Beaches--Fiction.

Ph-1 K-2/3 $14.95   L   KG341
ROCKWELL, ANNE F. Ducklings and pollywogs. By Anne Rockwell. Illus. by Lizzy Rockwell. Macmillan ISBN 0-02-777452-X; In Canada: Maxwell Macmillan, 1994. unp. col. ill.
Throughout a year, a young girl and her father visit a pond and chronicle the changes they notice in the wildlife including ducks hatching and growing up to fly away when the weather gets cold. A simple text and bold watercolor illustrations highlight the plants and animals found in and around the pond. This worthwhile effort introduces facts about a pond habitat in a straightforward narrative easy for young listeners to follow. For environmental studies.
SUBJ: Ponds--Fiction./ Seasons--Fiction./ Fathers and daughters--Fiction./ Ducks--Fiction.

Ph-2 P-1/2 $13.95   L   KG342
ROCKWELL, ANNE F. First snowfall. By Anne and Harlow Rockwell. Macmillan ISBN 0-02-777770-7; In Canada: Collier Macmillan, 1987. unp. col. ill.
A young child enjoys the first snowfall as she and her father go sledding in the park, watch her mother ski and then enjoys hot cocoa before going out to play in the snow again. The brief, simple text is enhanced by the bright, uncluttered pictures.
SUBJ: Snow--Fiction.

Ph-1 P-1/2 $17.99   L   KG343
ROCKWELL, ANNE F. I fly. Illus. by Annette Cable. Crown ISBN 0-517-59684-9; In Canada: Random House, 1997. unp. col. ill.
A young boy traveling with his family to visit cousins describes the airplane flight. The realistic description will answer questions about the experience of flying. Slightly stylized illustrations offer aerial views. For transportation units or youngsters curious about what it's like to fly in an airplane.
SUBJ: Flight--Fiction./ Airplanes--Fiction./ Travel--Fiction.

Ph-2 P-K/2 $14.93 L KG344
ROCKWELL, ANNE F. Once upon a time this morning. By Anne
Rockwell. Illus. by Sucie Stevenson. Greenwillow ISBN 0-688-14707-0; In
Canada: Hearst Book Group, 1997. 23p. col. ill.
Everyday happenings like waking up early, buying new shoes, and
resisting bathtime can make great stories, especially if they start
"once upon a time." The very young will relate to the simple stories
and appealing illustrations.
SUBJ: Behavior--Fiction./ Short stories.

Ph-2 P-K/2 $14.89 L KG345
ROCKWELL, ANNE F. Show and tell day. By Anne Rockwell. Illus. by
Lizzy Rockwell. HarperCollins ISBN 0-06-027301-1; In Canada:
HarperCollins, 1997. unp. col. ill.
Describing everyone else's show and tell object, a young boy saves
his contribution, a scary mask, for last. Bright illustrations convey the
diversity of the children and their choices for sharing. Introduces a
favorite school activity for young children. For multicultural studies.
SUBJ: Show-and-tell presentations--Fiction./ Schools--Fiction.

Ph-2 P-2/2 $12.95 L KG346
ROE, EILEEN. With my brother/Con mi hermano. Illus. by Robert Casilla.
Bradbury ISBN 0-02-777373-6; In Canada: Collier Macmillan, 1991.
unp. col. ill.
A young boy describes the things he and his older brother do
together as well as the things his brother does that he will be able to
do when he gets bigger. Strongly-colored double-spread watercolor
illustrations are ideal for sharing with a group. The text is written in
both English and Spanish and the brothers shown are Hispanic,
widening the usefulness of the book to include Spanish language
classes or groups whose primary language is Spanish.
SUBJ: Brothers--Fiction./ Spanish language materials./ Bilingual
materials--Spanish.

Ph-2 K-3/5 $12.93 L KG347
ROGERS, JEAN. King Island Christmas. Illus. by Rie Munoz.
Greenwillow ISBN 0-688-04237-6, 1985. unp. col. ill.
High seas and the approaching ice floe may prevent the new priest
from leaving the big freighter and reaching the tiny Alaskan island in
the Bering Sea. But determined villagers carry their oomiak up the
cliffs and over to the lee of the island where the sea is calmer. Father
Carroll is brought ashore, the happy Eskimos return to their village,
and later there are festive celebrations and an extra special Christmas
Mass. Spare, restrained text printed in boxes and the almost abstract,
colorful pictures capture the lifestyle, customs and habitat of these
islanders.
SUBJ: Christmas--Fiction./ Eskimos--Fiction.

Ph-1 P-2/4 $14.93 L KG348
ROGERS, JEAN. Runaway mittens. Illus. by Rie Munoz. Greenwillow
ISBN 0-688-07054-X, 1988. unp. col. ill.
Pica, a young Eskimo boy, is very proud of his bright red mittens knit
for him by his Grandmother, but unfortunately he keeps losing them.
They are found on the family drying shelf, behind the stove, in his
pockets and other likely places but finally Pica lets his red mittens
remain in the last surprising location. Both the simple story and the
bold somewhat primitive illustrations contain considerable information
about Eskimo life.
SUBJ: Eskimos--Fiction./ Indians of North America--Fiction./ Mittens--
Fiction.

Ph-2 1-3 $15.99 L KG349
ROHMANN, ERIC. Time flies. Crown ISBN 0-517-59599-0, 1994. unp.
col. ill.
Caldecott Honor book, 1995.
A small bird flies into a museum hall filled with giant dinosaur
skeletons. The prehistoric giants take on flesh, and one swallows the
bird who flies through the skeleton to freedom. Entirely wordless, the
story conveyed by the striking doublespread oil paintings is
ambiguous. Students may be inspired to flesh out the fantasy in
creative writing classes.
SUBJ: Stories without words./ Birds--Fiction./ Dinosaurs--Fiction./
Museums--Fiction.

Ph-2 K-3/6 $16.99 T KG350
ROOT, PHYLLIS. Aunt Nancy and Old Man Trouble. Illus. by David
Parkins. Candlewick ISBN 1-56402-347-8; In Canada: Candlewick/dist.
by Douglas & McIntyre, 1996. unp. col. ill.
Aunt Nancy knows Old Man Trouble is coming when the spring dries
up, but she foils his attempts to bother her by acting like his trouble is
good fortune instead. Black and white silhouettes and the expressions
of Old Man Trouble and sly Aunt Nancy fit perfectly with this battle
of wits. Enjoyable for reading aloud.
SUBJ: Tricks--Fiction.

Ph-2 P-2/2 $13.93 L KG351
ROOT, PHYLLIS. Coyote and the magic words. Illus. by Sandra Speidel.
Lothrop, Lee & Shepard ISBN 0-688-10309-X, 1993. unp. col. ill.
In this original creation story, words are the only magic needed for
eating, drinking, and sleeping. Coyote is bored with the simplicity and
causes trouble. The Maker-of-all-things takes away the magic of
words except for storytelling. The clever introduction to storytelling
can be used to initiate the activity. Pastel illustrations add zest to the
fun story.
SUBJ: Coyote (Legendary character)--Fiction./ Creation--Fiction.

Ph-1 2-3/6 $15.00 L KG352
ROSEN, MICHAEL J. Bonesy and Isabel. Illus. by James Ransome.
Harcourt Brace ISBN 0-15-209813-5; In Canada: Harcourt Brace c/o
Canadian Manda, 1995. unp. col. ill.
Isabel, a young girl from El Salvador, struggles to learn the language
of her adoptive American family, Vera and Ivan. The couple's dogs
and cats, many rescued strays, demonstrate a language without
words as they return the couple's clear affection. Isabel is especially
fond of Bonesy, an older dog allowed in the house, and his death
draws the family together in an experience that transcends words. Oil
paintings, predominately in sunny greens and yellows, illustrate the
story, affirming life's continuation. The heartwarming story will find a
place in multicultural studies.
SUBJ: Salvadoran Americans--Fiction./ Adoption--Fiction./ Dogs--
Fiction./ Death--Fiction.

Ph-2 K-2/2 $16.99 L KG353
ROSENBERG, LIZ. Big and little alphabet. Illus. by Vera Rosenberry.
Orchard ISBN 0-531-33050-8, 1997. unp. col. ill.
"Richard Jackson book."
Features the upper and lower case letters of the alphabet illustrated
with a cast of animals acting out verbs which begin with each letter.
The pen-and-ink and gouache illustrations are silly, and a key at the
end lists the items that begin with each letter.
SUBJ: Animals--Fiction./ Alphabet.

Ph-2 K-2/4 $14.95 L KG354
ROSENBERG, LIZ. Monster mama. Illus. by Stephen Gammell. Philomel
ISBN 0-399-21989-7; In Canada: Putnam, 1993. unp. col. ill.
Patrick Edward's mother is a true monster. Usually she stays out of
the sight of Patrick Edward's friends, but when he is troubled by
three bullies on his way home from the market, she makes an
appearance and fiercely defends him. Grotesque illustrations will
appeal especially to boys as will the surprising tenderness of Patrick
Edward's "Monster Mama."
SUBJ: Mothers and sons--Fiction./ Bullies--Fiction.

VCR Ph-2 K-2 $42.00 KG355
ROSENBERG, LIZ. Monster mama (Videocassette). Based on the book
written by Liz Rosenberg; illus. by Stephen Gammell. SRA/McGraw-Hill
ISBN 0-02-686761-3, 1996. 1/2" VHS videocassette color (10min).
(Children's literature series).
Includes teacher's guide.
Includes public performance rights.
Computer animated graphics create a "Monster Mama" who is at
once fierce and endearing. Children will identify with Patrick Edward
who needs his mother's protection, but wants his independence. An
unusual selection for Mother's Day to inspire creative writing and art
activities.
SUBJ: Mothers and sons--Fiction./ Bullies--Fiction.

Ph-2 P-1/2 $12.89 L KG356
ROTH, SUSAN L. My love for you. Dial ISBN 0-8037-2032-7; In
Canada: McClelland & Stewart, 1997. unp. col. ill.
A mouse measures his love as greater than a series of animals from
one to ten. Tender, tissue paper collages accompany the affectionate
text and provide an opportunity to count from one to ten.
SUBJ: Love--Fiction./ Mice--Fiction./ Counting.

Ph-2 P-2/3 $14.95 L KG357
ROTNER, SHELLEY. Ocean day. Written by Shelley Rotner and Ken
Kreisler. Photos. by Shelley Rotner. Macmillan ISBN 0-02-777886-X; In
Canada: Maxwell Macmillan, 1993. unp. col. ill.
Describes the many things a young girl sees at the beach. Striking
color photographs of the surf and sand as well as close-ups of sea
creatures and shells are the outstanding features of this beach visit.
SUBJ: Seashore--Fiction.

Ph-2 K-2/3 $15.95 L KG358
ROUNDS, GLEN. Once we had a horse. Holiday House ISBN 0-8234-
1241-5, 1996. unp. col. ill.
Despite the horse's gentle patience, two children struggle most of the
summer with various attempts to mount, stay on, and ride an old
horse. The straightforward text is humorously honest and

accompanied by expressive drawings.
SUBJ: Horses--Fiction./ Ranch life--Fiction.

Ph-1 P-1/1 $13.95 L KG359
RUBINSTEIN, GILLIAN. Dog in, cat out. Illus. by Ann James. Ticknor & Fields ISBN 0-395-66596-5, 1993. unp. col. ill.
A charming cuckoo clock shows the hours of the day. As the family dog and cat go in and out, a small cat and dog go in and out on the clock. The four words in the title in different combinations--one in and one out, both out, or both in--comprise the entire text. Humorous illustrations show the family's activities including the pets. A great story with repetition and visual clues for beginning readers.
SUBJ: Dogs--Fiction./ Cats--Fiction./ English language--Synonyms and antonyms--Fiction.

Ph-2 K-2/2 $14.93 L KG360
RUSSO, MARISABINA. Grandpa Abe. Greenwillow ISBN 0-688-14098-X, 1996. unp. col. ill.
When Sarah is a year old, her grandmother marries Abe. As the years pass, Sarah forms an attachment to Abe as her grandfather, and she has difficulty accepting his death. Gouache paintings highlight the warm family relationship and shared emotions. The intergenerational story is especially valuable for children dealing with the loss of a grandparent.
SUBJ: Grandfathers--Fiction./ Death--Fiction.

Ph-2 1-3/2 $14.93 L KG361
RUSSO, MARISABINA. I don't want to go back to school. Greenwillow ISBN 0-688-04602-9, 1994. unp. col. ill.
Ben is anxious about returning to school for second grade. His big sister Hannah doesn't help as she teases: what if his teacher is mean?, his friends don't remember him?, or the bus misses his stop? School begins, and everything turns out great. The familiar childhood concerns are illustrated with bold gouache paintings.
SUBJ: Schools--Fiction./ Brothers and sisters--Fiction.

Ph-2 P-1/1 $12.95 T KG362
RUSSO, MARISABINA. Line up book. Greenwillow ISBN 0-688-06204-0, 1986. unp. col. ill.
Sam lines up his blocks while his mother calls him for lunch. Sam lines up his books and his mother still calls "Come on Sam"; he continues to line up various objects and she continues to call, and finally Sam's line reaches the kitchen and they both reach a compromise.
SUBJ: Play--Fiction.

Ph-2 P-K/2 $14.93 L KG363
RUSSO, MARISABINA. Under the table. Greenwillow ISBN 0-688-14603-1; In Canada: Hearst Book Group, 1997. unp. col. ill.
Under the table is a good place for playing, hiding, and imagining, but not for drawing on the underside of the table as the young narrator discovers. Respectful of the child's point of view, the story conveys innocence, understanding, and forgiveness.
SUBJ: Tables--Fiction./ Drawing--Fiction./ Parent and child--Fiction.

Ph-2 P-2/2 $13.95 T KG364
RUURS, MARGRIET. Emma's eggs. Illus. by Barbara Spurll. Stoddart ISBN 0-7737-2972-0; In Canada: Stoddart, 1996. unp. col. ill.
Emma, the hen, is not quite sure what to do with her eggs; she tries scrambling them, putting them in a pot of water, painting them, and hiding them until finally she hatches one! The humor is apparent in the bright, almost comic illustrations. A good choice for storytimes which has possibilities for the Easter holiday.
SUBJ: Chickens--Fiction./ Eggs--Fiction.

Ph-1 K-3/6 $13.95 L KG365
RYAN, CHELI DURAN. Hildilid's night. Illus. by Arnold Lobel. Macmillan ISBN 0-02-777260-8; In Canada: Collier Macmillan, c1971, 1986. unp. ill.
Caldecott Honor book.
Available from National Library Service for the Blind and Physically Handicapped as talking book TB04444.
Attempting to drive away the night Hildilid sweeps, scrubs, scours, boils, pushes, burns, shears, sings, stamps, spanks, spits and even digs a grave for it until by sunrise she is so exhausted she sleeps all day. Humorous and clever with great illustrations.
SUBJ: Night--Fiction.

Ph-2 K-2 $14.93 L KG366
RYDER, JOANNE. My father's hands. Illus. by Mark Graham. Morrow ISBN 0-688-09190-3, 1994. unp. col. ill.
In her father's hands, a young girl discovers small creatures from the backyard, including a praying mantis. A warm and secure father and daughter relationship is conveyed in the story and delicate oil paintings.
SUBJ: Fathers and daughters--Fiction./ Gardening--Fiction./ Insects--Fiction.

Ph-1 P-2/2 $13.95 L KG367
RYDER, JOANNE. Night gliders. Illus. by Melissa Bay Mathis. BridgeWater ISBN 0-8167-3820-3; In Canada: BridgeWater/dist. by Vanwell, 1996. unp. col. ill.
Four flying squirrels glide through a moonlit night. Gentle verse lulls the listener and, paired with the illustrations, creates a sense of enchantment. An author's note provides further facts about flying squirrels to round out this introduction to these unique creatures.
SUBJ: Flying squirrels--Fiction./ Squirrels--Fiction.

Ph-2 P-1/2 $5.95 P KG368
RYLANT, CYNTHIA. Birthday presents. Illus. by Sucie Stevenson. Orchard ISBN 0-531-07026-3, 1991. unp. col. ill.
Emphasizing family love, a young girl of five and her parents remember six past birthday celebrations starting and closing with her real birthday, the day she was born. The joyous, cheerful pictures perfectly compliment the loving story.
SUBJ: Birthdays--Fiction./ Parent and child--Fiction.

Ph-2 K-2/2 $14.95 L KG369
RYLANT, CYNTHIA. Bookshop dog. Blue Sky Press/Scholastic ISBN 0-590-54331-8; In Canada: Scholastic, 1996. unp. col. ill.
Martha Jane goes everywhere with the woman who owns her, especially to work at the bookstore named for her, but when the woman needs to go to the hospital, Martha Jane can't go with her. The man in the green coat who loves Martha Jane takes care of her and eventually marries her owner. Appealing bright colors highlight the primitive illustrations.
SUBJ: Dogs--Fiction./ Neighborliness--Fiction.

BB Ph-3 P-K/2 $4.95 T KG370
RYLANT, CYNTHIA. Everyday children (Board book). Bradbury ISBN 0-02-778022-8; In Canada: Maxwell Macmillan, 1993. unp. col. ill. (Everyday book).
Cut-paper illustrations and a simple rhyming text depict children playing in the rain, hiding in trees, and sleeping with bears. Primary colors and simple shapes create an appealing board book for young listeners and beginning readers.
SUBJ: Play--Fiction./ Children--Fiction./ Stories in rhyme.

BB Ph-3 P-K/2 $4.95 T KG371
RYLANT, CYNTHIA. Everyday garden (Board book). Bradbury ISBN 0-02-778023-6; In Canada: Maxwell Macmillan, 1993. unp. col. ill. (Everyday book).
A bountiful garden complete with rabbits, birds, and insects comes to life in cut-paper designs. The board book with easy-to-read, rhyming text and bright colors will appeal to preschoolers as well as beginning readers. Useful for art teachers to demonstrate collage techniques.
SUBJ: Gardens--Fiction./ Stories in rhyme.

BB Ph-3 P-K/2 $4.95 T KG372
RYLANT, CYNTHIA. Everyday house (Board book). Bradbury ISBN 0-02-778024-4; In Canada: Maxwell Macmillan, 1993. unp. col. ill. (Everyday book).
Brightly colored, cut-paper illustrations depict the inside and outside of a house. Simple sentences and rhyming text will appeal to young prereaders as well as beginning readers. A board book with multiple uses.
SUBJ: Dwellings--Fiction./ Stories in rhyme.

BB Ph-3 P-K/2 $4.95 T KG373
RYLANT, CYNTHIA. Everyday pets (Board book). Bradbury ISBN 0-02-778025-2; In Canada: Maxwell Macmillan, 1993. unp. col. ill. (Everyday book).
Colorful cut-paper designs combine with simple rhyming text to present a parade of pets. Young listeners will delight at naming the animals while beginning readers will enjoy reading the board book all by themselves.
SUBJ: Pets--Fiction./ Animals--Fiction./ Stories in rhyme.

BB Ph-3 P-K/2 $4.95 T KG374
RYLANT, CYNTHIA. Everyday town (Board book). Bradbury ISBN 0-02-778026-0; In Canada: Maxwell Macmillan, 1993. unp. col. ill. (Everyday book).
Cut-paper collages illustrate both daytime and nighttime activities in a town. Primary colors and simple rhyming text have strong child appeal. Try this board book with both nonreaders and beginning readers.
SUBJ: City and town life--Fiction./ Stories in rhyme.

CE
Ph-1 K-3/2 $14.00   L   KG375
RYLANT, CYNTHIA. Henry and Mudge: the first book. Illus. by Sucie Stevenson. Simon & Schuster ISBN 0-689-81004-0; In Canada: Distican, 1987. 39p. col. ill.
Available from National Library Service for the Blind and Physically Handicapped in Braille BR7040.
Spanish version HENRY Y MUDGE: EL PRIMER LIBRO DE SUS AVENTURAS available from Aladdin (ISBN 0-689-80684-1, 1996). Henry has no brothers or sisters and no children in his neighborhood and is a lonely little boy until he gets a dog named Mudge. They play together, get in trouble together, and they love each other completely.
Other beginning reader adventures of Henry and Mudge which are simple and very appealing to primary aged children are: HENRY AND MUDGE IN PUDDLE TROUBLE (ISBN 0-689-71400-9, 1990) (animated 1/2" VHS videocassette color (10min) from SRA/McGraw-Hill 87-509213, 1987, (11min) $39.00, Spanish version HENRY Y MUDGE CON BARRO HASTA EL RABO ISBN 0-689-80687-6, 1996); HENRY AND MUDGE IN THE GREEN TIME (ISBN 0-689-81000-8, 1987); HENRY AND MUDGE UNDER THE YELLOW MOON (ISBN 0-689-81020-2, 1997) (Animated videocassette available from SRA/McGraw-Hill 87-509221, 1989. 1/2" VHS videocassette color (11min), $39.00); HENRY AND MUDGE AND THE FOREVER SEA (ISBN 0-689-81016-4, 1989); HENRY AND MUDGE IN THE SPARKLE DAYS (ISBN 0-689-81018-0, 1988) (Animated videocassette available from SRA/McGraw-Hill 87-540347, 1989. 1/2" VHS videocassette color (11min), $39.00); HENRY AND MUDGE AND THE BEDTIME THUMPS (ISBN 0-689-81011-3, 1991); HENRY AND MUDGE GET THE COLD SHIVERS (ISBN 0-689-81014-8, 1989); HENRY AND MUDGE AND THE HAPPY CAT (ISBN 0-689-81012-1, 1990); HENRY AND MUDGE TAKE THE BIG TEST (ISBN 0-689-81010-5, 1991); HENRY AND MUDGE AND THE LONG WEEKEND (ISBN 0-689-81009-1, 1992); HENRY AND MUDGE AND THE WILD WIND (ISBN 0-02-778014-7, 1993); HENRY AND MUDGE AND THE CAREFUL COUSIN (0-689-81007-5, 1994); and HENRY AND MUDGE AND THE BEST DAY OF ALL (ISBN 0-689-81006-7, 1995, Spanish version HENRY Y MUDGE Y EL MEJOR DIA DEL ANO available from Listos-para-leer/Libros Colibri Aladdin (ISBN 0-689-81469-0, 1997).
Available from National Library Service for the Blind and Physically Handicapped on sound recording cassette RC30725, and in Braille BR7257 is HENRY AND MUDGE UNDER THE YELLOW MOON; in Braille BR7256 is HENRY AND MUDGE IN THE GREEN TIME; in Braille BR7210 is HENRY AND MUDGE IN PUDDLE TROUBLE; and on sound recording cassette RC 41395 HENRY AND MUDGE AND THE CAREFUL COUSIN.
SUBJ: Dogs--Fiction./ Spanish language materials.

Ph-2 P-2/6 $5.95   P   KG376
RYLANT, CYNTHIA. Mr. Griggs' work. Illus. by Julie Downing. Orchard ISBN 0-531-07037-9, c1989, 1993. unp. col. ill.
The postmaster in a small town truly loves his work and is upset when he becomes ill and must stay at home. Softly hued and textured color pencil drawings complement the gentle story. A fine title to share when talking about community helpers.
SUBJ: Postal service--Fiction./ Occupations--Fiction.

Ph-1 1-3/2 $10.95   T   KG377
RYLANT, CYNTHIA. Mr. Putter and Tabby bake the cake. Illus. by Arthur Howard. Harcourt Brace ISBN 0-15-200205-7; In Canada: Harcourt Brace c/o Canadian Manda, 1994. unp. col. ill.
Available from the National Library Service for the Blind and Physically Handicapped on sound recording cassette RC 43114.
Mr. Putter wants to bake the perfect cake to give his neighbor, Mrs. Teaberry, for Christmas.
SUBJ: Christmas--Fiction./ Cake--Fiction./ Gifts--Fiction.

Ph-1 K-2/2 $11.00   T   KG378
RYLANT, CYNTHIA. Mr. Putter and Tabby fly the plane. Illus. by Arthur Howard. Harcourt Brace ISBN 0-15-256253-2; In Canada: Harcourt Brace c/o Canadian Manda, 1997. unp. col. ill.
Mr. Putter buys a radio-controlled toy airplane, but Tabby, his cat, is not too sure about the contraption. The two characters fill the easy-to-read text and illustrations with personality and humor. For beginning readers.
SUBJ: Toys--Fiction./ Cats--Fiction./ Old age--Fiction.

Ph-1 1-3/2 $11.00   T   KG379
RYLANT, CYNTHIA. Mr. Putter and Tabby pick the pears. Illus. by Arthur Howard. Harcourt Brace ISBN 0-15-200245-6; In Canada: Harcourt Brace c/o Canadian Manda, 1995. unp. col. ill.
Mr. Putter's cranky legs won't allow him to climb the ladder to pick the pears he needs to make pear jelly, and he gets carried away zinging apples with his homemade slingshot. Everything turns out okay

for Mr. Putter and his companion Tabby in the delightful ending. Short chapters and expressive illustrations will continue to attract beginning readers to this series.
SUBJ: Fruit--Fiction./ Old age--Fiction./ Cats--Fiction.

Ph-1 1-3/2 $10.95   T   KG380
RYLANT, CYNTHIA. Mr. Putter and Tabby pour the tea. Illus. by Arthur Howard. Harcourt Brace ISBN 0-15-256255-9; In Canada: Harcourt Brace c/o of Canadian Manda, 1994. unp. col. ill.
Mr. Putter longs for someone to share teatime and stories. He chooses an older cat, Tabby, from the animal shelter, and they become perfect company for each other. Short chapters with numerous illustrations are ideal for beginning readers.
SUBJ: Cats--Fiction./ Old age--Fiction.

Ph-1 K-2/2 $11.00   T   KG381
RYLANT, CYNTHIA. Mr. Putter and Tabby row the boat. Illus. by Arthur Howard. Harcourt Brace ISBN 0-15-256257-5; In Canada: Harcourt Brace c/o Canadian Manda, 1997. unp. col. ill.
Retreating from the sweaty heat, Mr. Putter, Tabby, and their neighbors Mrs. Teaberry and Zeke spend the day at the big pond. Light touches of humor in the dry, easy-to-read text and watercolor illustrations will entice beginning readers.
SUBJ: Heat--Fiction./ Pets--Fiction./ Picnicking--Fiction./ Summer--Fiction.

Ph-1 1-3/2 $10.95   T   KG382
RYLANT, CYNTHIA. Mr. Putter and Tabby walk the dog. Illus. by Arthur Howard. Harcourt Brace ISBN 0-15-256259-1; In Canada: Harcourt Brace c/o Canadian Manda, 1994. unp. col. ill.
Mr. Putter and Tabby offer to walk their neighbor's dog whose behavior is nightmarish.
SUBJ: Dogs--Fiction./ Cats--Fiction./ Neighborliness--Fiction.

Ph-1 1-3/2 $15.00   L   KG383
RYLANT, CYNTHIA. Old woman who named things. Illus. by Kathryn Brown. Harcourt Brace ISBN 0-15-257809-9; In Canada: Harcourt Brace c/o Canadian Manda, 1996. unp. col. ill.
Having outlived all of her friends, the old woman only names things that she will never outlive such as her car, her chair, and her bed. She refuses to name the young dog who becomes a part of her life until he is lost. Outstanding watercolor illustrations give personalities to the inanimate objects she has named. A touching story for reading aloud.
SUBJ: Old age--Fiction./ Dogs--Fiction.

Ph-1 K-2/2 $13.95   T   KG384
RYLANT, CYNTHIA. Poppleton. Illus. by Mark Teague. Blue Sky Press/Scholastic ISBN 0-590-84782-1; In Canada: Scholastic, 1997. 48p. col. ill.
"Book one."
Poppleton the pig fixes a misunderstanding with his new neighbor, Cherry Sue; visits the library; and helps a sick friend. Three short, episodic chapters comprise the easy-to-read text accompanied by perky color illustrations. For beginning readers.
SUBJ: Pigs--Fiction./ Friendship--Fiction./ Books and reading--Fiction.

Ph-1 K-3/8 $14.95   L   KG385
RYLANT, CYNTHIA. Relatives came. Illus. by Stephen Gammell. Bradbury ISBN 0-02-777220-9; In Canada: Collier Macmillan, 1985. unp. col. ill.
Caldecott Honor book.
Selectors' Choice, 16th ed.
Available from National Library Service for the Blind and Physically Handicapped in Braille BR06124.
Very early in the morning an old station wagon bursting with people, lunches, soda pop and luggage leaves the hills of rural Virginia, travels over the mountains and late at night finally arrives at another dilapidated mountain home. The relatives have come! There is much hugging, loving, eating, repairing, music making, and sleeping on pallets on the floor during the happy days and nights of the extended visit. This unsophisticated homespun group, perhaps below the poverty level according to their bank accounts, is very rich in family love. The plot, although simple and uncomplicated, gives a strong feeling of fun and family love and support. The animated, colorful pencil drawings work perfectly as they extend the humor and love in the text. Excellent for picturebook story time.
SUBJ: Family life--Fiction.

Ph-2 1-3/2 $16.99   L   KG386
RYLANT, CYNTHIA. Silver packages: an Appalachian Christmas story. Illus. by Chris K. Soentpiet. Orchard ISBN 0-531-33051-6, 1997. unp. col. ill.
"Richard Jackson book."
Remembering the Christmas train and the man who threw out silver

packages to the children, a young doctor returns to the rural community to share his gifts. Originally published in a collection of short stories, the heartwarming story is brought to life in warm watercolor paintings.
SUBJ: Appalachian Region--Fiction./ Christmas--Fiction./ Railroads--Trains--Fiction.

CE   Ph-1 K-3/6 $14.00   L   KG387
RYLANT, CYNTHIA. When I was young in the mountains. Illus. by Diane Goode. Dutton ISBN 0-525-42525-X; In Canada: Fitzhenry & Whiteside, 1982. 32p. col. ill.
Caldecott Honor book.
Talking book available from SRA/McGraw-Hill 87-511310, 1983. 1 sound cassette (6min), $14.00.
A young girl recalls her childhood days living with her younger brother and her loving grandparents in rural southern mountains. Lyric text describes cornbread, beans, fried okra and hot cocoa, toilet facilities located in an outdoor "johnny-house", water pumped from a deep well, church held in the school house and baptisms in the swimming hole. The detailed illustrations in blues, greens, and browns help tell of a life style unfamiliar to many children. Best used to share at picture storybook hours.
SUBJ: Mountain life--Fiction./ United States--Social life and customs--20th century, 1900-1999--Fiction./ Appalachian Mountains--Fiction.

                    Ph-2 K-2/2 $14.89   L   KG388
SALTZBERG, BARNEY. Show-and-tell. Hyperion ISBN 0-7868-2016-0; In Canada: Little, Brown, 1994. unp. col. ill.
Phoebe wants to bring a star-shaped leaf or a chicken bone that looks like a dinosaur bone for show-and-tell, but her well meaning parents overdo it with a real palm tree and a tyrannosaurus rex skeleton. Youngsters will relate to the humorous story about a common school day activity and the exaggerated interference of Phoebe's parents.
SUBJ: Schools--Fiction./ Parent and child--Fiction.

                    Ph-3 P-K/2 $14.95   T   KG389
SAMTON, SHEILA WHITE. World from my window. Caroline House ISBN 1-878093-15-0, c1985, 1991. unp. col. ill.
The reader counts the objects seen through a window from one moon to ten stars. A quiet rhyming text and uncluttered illustrations introduce counting and numerals. In the final doublespread illustration, all the items are combined to be counted again.
SUBJ: Night--Fiction./ Stories in rhyme./ Counting.

                    Ph-1 1-3/3 $16.00   T   KG390
SANDERS, SCOTT R. Place called Freedom. By Scott Russell Sanders. Illus. by Thomas B. Allen. Atheneum ISBN 0-689-80470-9; In Canada: Distican, 1997. unp. col. ill.
A young boy describes the settlement of Freedom, begun by his family who were freed slaves, and how it grew to become a town of farmers, teachers, carpenters, and many others. Gentle pastel illustrations focus on the people and their hard work. Historical fiction that moves beyond the many stories of slavery and the Underground Railroad to show the establishment of a successful community. Based on the settlement of Lyes Station, Indiana. For multicultural studies.
SUBJ: Afro-Americans--History--1815-1861--Fiction./ Frontier and pioneer life--Indiana--Fiction./ Family life--Fiction./ Indiana--Fiction.

                    Ph-1 1-3/2 $14.89   L   KG391
SANDIN, JOAN. Long way to a new land. HarperCollins ISBN 0-06-025194-8; In Canada: HarperCollins, 1981. 63p. col. ill. (I can read history book).
Includes author's note.
Selectors' Choice, 14th ed.
After drought, hard times and famine a Swedish family decides to go to America where Uncle Axel writes they will all have a better future. Young Carl Erik tells of the preparations, disposal of possessions, family farewells and the journey by cart, train and steamship. After days of stormy weather and sea sickness the emigrants finally reach New York, America and new hope.
In the LONG WAY WESTWARD (ISBN 0-06-025207-3, 1989) the family has disembarked in New York and makes the long journey westward to Minnesota by train and boat to join their relatives. An excellent introduction to immigration for young readers.
SUBJ: United States--Emigration and immigration--Fiction./ Sweden--Emigration and immigration--Fiction.

                    Ph-2 2-3/6 $14.00   L   KG392
SAN SOUCI, ROBERT D. Boy and the ghost. Illus. by J. Brian Pinkney. Simon & Schuster ISBN 0-671-67176-6, 1989. unp. col. ill.
Thomas is a poor black boy who leaves his family's farm to earn money. Sharing his lunch with an old man, he hears about a nearby haunted house where legend has it that buried treasure will go to the

one who spends the night. Thomas bravely enters the house, withstands the spooky apparition and gains the treasure. An old tale retold, this is distinctive for its rural black setting.
SUBJ: Ghosts--Fiction./ Haunted houses--Fiction.

                    Ph-2 3-5/6 $15.89   L   KG393
SAN SOUCI, ROBERT D. Red heels. Illus. by Gary Kelley. Dial ISBN 0-8037-1134-4, 1996. unp. col. ill.
After making her a new pair of shoes, Jonathan becomes infatuated by Rebecca, the mysterious young woman with the red heels. He follows her one night up the chimney to dance among the trees. Early American in speech and dress, the romantic and mysterious tale will enchant readers and listeners.
SUBJ: Shoes--Fiction./ Witches--Fiction./ United States--History--Colonial period, ca. 1600-1775--Fiction.

                    Ph-2 P-1/2 $12.00   L   KG394
SATHRE, VIVIAN. Mouse chase. Illus. by Ward Schumaker. Harcourt Brace ISBN 0-15-200105-0; In Canada: Harcourt Brace c/o Canadian Manda, 1995. unp. col. ill.
Mouse gets away from Cat by hitching a ride on a swirling leaf. Expressive color and ink illustrations and two word sentences convey the action. The simple story will satisfy beginning readers.
SUBJ: Mice--Fiction./ Cats--Fiction./ Winds--Fiction.

                    Ph-1 K-3/4 $14.95   L   KG395
SAY, ALLEN. Bicycle man. Houghton Mifflin ISBN 0-395-32254-5, 1982. unp. col. ill.
Selectors' Choice, 14th ed.
It's the first sportsday after the end of World War II and the Japanese children, teachers and parents of a small mountain school enjoy a day of games, contests and picnics. Suddenly two American occupation soldiers appear. At first fearful of the tall strangers, the children are soon laughing and cheering as the soldier with the "face as black as earth" performs a dazzling exhibition of bicycle stunts while the white faced one with the red hair assists and waves him on. The quiet, understated story with full page delicately hued pen and ink illustrations fosters an understanding of different cultures and will be useful for study units on Japan.
SUBJ: Bicycles and bicycling--Fiction./ Japan--Fiction./ Schools--Fiction.

                    Ph-2 1-3/3 $16.95   L   KG396
SAY, ALLEN. Emma's rug. Houghton Mifflin ISBN 0-395-74294-3, 1996. 32p. col. ill.
"Walter Lorraine book."
Emma, a very talented young artist, gets her ideas from a small shaggy carpet in her room. One day her mother washes the carpet, and it no longer looks the same. Emma refuses to paint and throws away all her artwork and the rug, but she can still see the images she once saw in it. Raises deep questions about the origin of creativity which may touch sensitive children. The illustrations are small masterpieces themselves.
SUBJ: Creativity--Fiction./ Rugs--Fiction./ Drawing--Fiction.

                    Ph-1 2-4/5 $16.95   L   KG397
SAY, ALLEN. Grandfather's journey. Houghton Mifflin ISBN 0-395-57035-2, 1993. 32p. col. ill.
Caldecott Award, 1994.
Moving from Japan to the United States, a grandson understands the pull his grandfather felt between two worlds: the village in Japan where he was born and the vast United States he also grew to love. He expresses the feelings of many attempting to bridge two cultures when he says no matter which country he is in, he is homesick for the other. Expressive of love and longing, watercolor paintings draw the viewer in to close-up portraits and breathtaking landscapes. For multicultural studies.
SUBJ: Grandfathers--Fiction./ Voyages and travels--Fiction./ Homesickness--Fiction./ Japan--Fiction./ United States--Description and travel--Fiction./ Japanese Americans--Fiction./ Emigration and immigration--Fiction.

                    Ph-2 1-3/2 $14.95   L   KG398
SAY, ALLEN. Lost lake. Houghton Mifflin ISBN 0-395-50933-5, 1989. 32p. col. ill.
A boy living with his father for the first time is lonely and bored until his father takes him on a backpacking trip to find his favorite lake. It is crowded with people so they strike off cross country and find a new "lost lake." The glowing watercolor illustrations not only convey the beauty of the back country but the growing closeness between father and son.
SUBJ: Fathers and sons--Fiction./ Camping--Fiction.

Ph-2 K-3/4 $14.95   L   KG399
SAY, ALLEN. River dream. Houghton Mifflin ISBN 0-395-48294-1, 1988. 30p. col. ill.
Mark and his uncle are fishing buddies, so when the young boy is very sick with a high fever, Uncle Scott sends him a special box of flies. The sight of the flies sends Mark into a realistic dream sequence in which he and Uncle Scott enjoy the fun of catching enormous rainbow trout and then releasing them so that they may leave the river just the way they found it. Quiet, uncluttered full paged pictures match the dream like mood of the story.
SUBJ: Fishing--Fiction./ Sick--Fiction./ Uncles--Fiction.

Ph-1 1-3/4 $16.95   T   KG400
SAY, ALLEN. Tree of cranes. Houghton Mifflin ISBN 0-395-52024-X, 1991. 32p. col. ill.
Selectors' Choice, 19th ed.
A young Japanese boy wonders why his mother is behaving strangely until she explains that it is Christmas where she used to live in California. Together they decorate a tree with paper cranes and candles. A traditional Japanese house is depicted in the elegantly simple illustrations. A young boy's introduction to American holiday traditions provides a glimpse of Japanese culture for readers.
SUBJ: Christmas--Fiction./ Mothers--Fiction./ Japan--Fiction.

Ph-2 1-3/5 $14.99   T   KG401
SCHACHNER, JUDITH BYRON. Willy and May. Dutton ISBN 0-525-45347-4, 1995. unp. col. ill.
A young girl narrates the story of her special visits with her Great-Aunt May and her small yellow bird, Willy. Family illness and a winter snowstorm almost prevent a Christmas visit, but May and Willy arrive with the sound of bells and a jolly man's laughter. Warm watercolor illustrations depict the antics of Willy, the special friendship, and the magic of the Christmas season.
SUBJ: Great-aunts--Fiction./ Canaries--Fiction./ Christmas--Fiction.

Ph-1 P-2/3 $18.99   L   KG402
SCHAEFER, CAROLE LEXA. Squiggle. Illus. by Pierr Morgan. Crown ISBN 0-517-70048-4; In Canada: Random House, 1996. unp. col. ill.
A piece of string is only a squiggle, but in a young girl's imagination the line becomes a dragon, part of the Great Wall, and a ripple in a pool. The illustrations have an Asian flair and are a graceful complement to the playful story. Use with art classes, creative movement activities, and multicultural studies.
SUBJ: Imagination--Fiction./ String--Fiction.

Ph-1 P-A/2 $14.95   T   KG403
SCHEER, JULIAN. Rain makes applesauce. By Julian Scheer and Marvin Bileck. Holiday House ISBN 0-8234-0091-3, c1964. unp. col. ill.
Caldecott Honor Book.
"Oh you're just talking silly silly talk/I know I'm talking silly talk/But-/Rain makes apple sauce"; a series of silly statements illustrated by double-page pictures full of "tiny, fey graphic details, of captivating scenes and lyrical phrases that stretch the imagination."
SUBJ: Nonsense verses.

Ph-2 K-2/4 $14.93   L   KG404
SCHERTLE, ALICE. Jeremy Bean's St. Patrick's Day. Illus. by Linda Shute. Lothrop, Lee & Shepard ISBN 0-688-04814-5, 1987. unp. col. ill.
Having forgotten to wear his green sweater to school Jeremy tries to hide in the closet to avoid being teased by his classmates and even worse, being scolded by the principal. The watercolor illustrations successfully interpret the text and many children will identify with Jeremy's first reaction and cheer the resolution.
SUBJ: St. Patrick's Day--Fiction./ Schools--Fiction.

Ph-1 1-3/4 $15.93   L   KG405
SCHERTLE, ALICE. Maisie. Illus. by Lydia Dabcovich. Lothrop, Lee & Shepard ISBN 0-688-09311-6, 1995. unp. col. ill.
Maisie is a remarkable woman whose life began in a small red house with a dresser drawer as her first bed. She grows up, marries, and has children, grandchildren, and great grandchildren who all gather around her for her ninetieth birthday. As Maisie's life spans ninety years so do the colorful, active illustrations that depict changing times and the constancy of family. Young readers may be inspired to investigate their own family history.
SUBJ: Family life--Fiction./ Farm life--Fiction.

Ph-2 K-2/2 $12.95   L   KG406
SCHINDEL, JOHN. Dear Daddy. Illus. by Dorothy Donohue. Whitman ISBN 0-8075-1531-0; In Canada: General, 1995. unp. col. ill.
Sad because his father lives very far away, Jesse writes letters and anxiously awaits his father's reply. Finally an answer arrives on a long roll of paper. Children coping with divorce and geographical separation from parents will relate to this story and to the father's words that "letters give you something to hold on to."
SUBJ: Fathers and sons--Fiction./ Letters--Fiction./ Divorce--Fiction.

Ph-2 P-1/2 $14.93   L   KG407
SCHINDEL, JOHN. What's for lunch? Illus. by Kevin O'Malley. Lothrop, Lee & Shepard ISBN 0-688-13599-4, 1994. unp. col. ill.
Sidney, a mouse, escapes becoming a cat's lunch through a series of actions by different animals which culminate when a loud "Boo" from another mouse frightens everyone away. Young listeners will join in with the repetitive and predictable text and delight in the boisterous ending.
SUBJ: Food--Fiction./ Animals--Fiction./ Mice--Fiction.

Ph-2 2-4/7 $14.95   T   KG408
SCHMID, ELEONORE. Water's journey. North-South Books/dist. by Picture Book Studios ISBN 1-55858-013-1, 1989. unp. col. ill.
This is a fictional account of the water cycle from the snowfall of the mountains, through brooks, streams and river, and ultimately to the ocean where it will return to earth as snow or rain. The text is concise (long sentences account for high Fry level) and covers such necessary information as irrigation, reservoirs and pollution in full page color illustrations that are a story in themselves. A useful introduction to the water cycle.
SUBJ: Water--Fiction.

Ph-2 2-3/4 $15.93   L   KG409
SCHNUR, STEVEN. Tie man's miracle: a Chanukah tale. Illus. by Stephen T. Johnson. Morrow ISBN 0-688-13464-5, 1995. unp. col. ill.
Includes glossary.
On the last night of Chanukah, Mr. Hoffman, a peddler selling ties, is invited to join the family for the lighting of the menorah. He reveals that his family was lost in the Holocaust and shares rememberances from his childhood. The old man's stories transform the way Seth and his sister, Hannah, view the miracle of Chanukah. The quietly moving story for the holiday can also serve as an introduction to the Holocaust.
SUBJ: Hanukkah--Fiction./ Jews--Fiction.

Ph-1 K-2/2 $15.95   L   KG410
SCHOTTER, RONI. Passover magic. Illus. by Marylin Hafner. Little, Brown ISBN 0-316-77468-5; In Canada: Little, Brown, 1995. unp. col. ill.
Passover is a special time for family that seems more magical with Uncle Harry's magic tricks. The traditional seder, Four Questions, and hiding the afikomen are featured in the warm story of extended family as seen through the eyes of a young girl. The story of Passover follows the text.
SUBJ: Passover--Fiction./ Jews--Fiction.

Ph-2 1-5/3 $14.89   L   KG411
SCHROEDER, ALAN. Carolina shout! Illus. by Bernie Fuchs. Dial ISBN 0-8037-1678-8, 1995. unp. col. ill.
Young Delia hears the music in Charlestown around every corner as the vendors shout, children chant, and workers sing. An author's note offers historical and cultural information about the vendor's shouts, a few of which have been preserved in sources cited by the author. Historical fiction which provides an interesting complement to units on folk rhymes as well as offering a glimpse of South Carolina history.
SUBJ: Charleston (S.C.)--Social life and customs--Fiction./ Afro-Americans--Fiction./ City sounds--Fiction./ Peddlers and peddling--Fiction.

Ph-2 1-3/4 $15.89   L   KG412
SCHUR, MAXINE ROSE. Day of delight: a Jewish Sabbath in Ethiopia. Illus. by Brian Pinkney. Dial ISBN 0-8037-1414-9, 1994. unp. col. ill.
Includes glossary.
Preparing for the Jewish Sabbath, Menelik, the son of a blacksmith in Ethiopia, details the traditional daily life in the village where he lives. The story and scratchboard illustrations reveal a unique and vanishing culture encompassing the diversity of geography and religious traditions. An author's note provides some background about black Jews called "Falashas" or strangers by the Ethiopians and offers a pronunciation guide and glossary. For multicultural studies.
SUBJ: Jews--Ethiopia--Fiction./ Sabbath--Fiction./ Ethiopia--Social life and customs--Fiction.

CE   Ph-1 P-2/1 $5.95   P   KG413
SCHWARTZ, AMY. Annabelle Swift, Kindergartner. Orchard ISBN 0-531-07027-1, 1988. unp. col. ill.
Read-along kit available from Live Oak Media (ISBN 0-87499-355-5, 1996). 1 paperback book, 1 sound cassette (12min), $14.95.
Thoroughly coached by her third grade sister, Annabelle enters kindergarten with great confidence, but unfortunately some of the advice backfires, and the new kindergartner is the object of several class laughs. However, Lucy's counting lessons do pay off, and Annabelle is the only member of the class qualified to be the Milk Monitor. Attractive watercolors picturing familiar school activities and environment along with the humorous text create an appealing book for the intended audience.
SUBJ: Kindergarten--Fiction./ Schools--Fiction./ Sisters--Fiction.

Ph-2 K-3/2 $14.95 L KG414
SCHWARTZ, AMY. Oma and Bobo. Bradbury ISBN 0-02-781500-5; In Canada: Collier Macmillan, 1987. unp. col. ill.
Alice's new dog Bobo is more interested in Oma's potholder than in following commands, and Alice is afraid he'll fail obedience school. Oma's secret plan to help her beloved granddaughter and the dog she's come to care for is touching. The watercolor washed pen and ink drawings add to the book's appeal at storytime.
SUBJ: Dogs--Fiction./ Grandmothers--Fiction.

Ph-1 P-2/2 $15.99 L KG415
SCHWARTZ, AMY. Teeny tiny baby. Orchard ISBN 0-531-08668-2, 1994. unp. col. ill.
"Richard Jackson book."
The baby may be tiny, but he knows how to get what he wants-- going places, eating on demand, and sleeping wherever he pleases. The baby narrates this funny story that will be enjoyed by older children looking back at their own infancy or thinking of an infant in the family. The adorable gouache illustrations show the baby in all sorts of places and poses and with every type of expression. Reinforces the big needs of small babies.
SUBJ: Babies--Fiction./ City and town life--Fiction.

Ph-1 K-3/5 $13.88 L KG416
SCHWARTZ, DAVID M. Supergrandpa. Illus. by Bert Dodson. Lothrop, Lee & Shepard ISBN 0-688-09899-1, 1991. unp. col. ill.
Selectors' Choice, 18th ed.
At 66, Gustaf is told he is too old to enter the Tour of Sweden bicycle race, but by riding while the other racers are resting, he wins the race. Gustaf becomes a folk hero and is given the nickname "Supergrandpa." An unusual story about perseverance and overcoming stereotypes, based on a real person.
SUBJ: Grandfathers--Fiction./ Bicycle racing--Fiction./ Sweden--Fiction.

Ph-2 1-3/2 $16.99 L KG417
SCHWARTZ, HARRIET BERG. When Artie was little. Illus. by Thomas B. Allen. Knopf ISBN 0-679-93236-4; In Canada: Random House, 1996. unp. col. ill.
"Borzoi book."
Artie remembers the highlights from his childhood, especially the time he rode in a plane with a barnstormer. Provides a look at times past and the shaping of memories. Sepia-toned photographs on the endpapers show the actual Artie.
SUBJ: Old age--Fiction./ Family life--Fiction./ Flight--Fiction.

Ph-2 P-2/2 $5.95 P KG418
SCHWARTZ, HENRY. How I captured a dinosaur. Illus. by Amy Schwartz. Orchard ISBN 0-531-07028-8, c1989, 1993. unp. col. ill.
Camping in Baja gives Liz the chance to see if she can capture a dinosaur. The matter-of-factness of the text is funny and the oversized water color illustrations contain delightful details. Read aloud and compare with "Dinosaur Bob."
Liz and her dinosaur, Albert are back home in Los Angeles where Albert gets a job in the movies in ALBERT GOES HOLLYWOOD (ISBN 0-531-08580-5, 1992, OPC).
SUBJ: Dinosaurs--Fiction.

Ph-1 1-3/4 $14.95 L KG419
SCIESZKA, JON. Frog Prince, continued. Illus. by Steve Johnson. Viking/Penguin ISBN 0-670-83421-1; In Canada: Penguin, 1991. unp. col. ill.
Available from the National Library Service for the Blind and Physically Handicapped on sound recording cassette RC34881.
Unable to adjust to life and marriage as a human, the frog prince runs off to find a witch to turn him back into a frog. Instead he experiences some close calls with the menacing witches from Sleeping Beauty, Snow White, and Hansel and Gretel, and finally Cinderella's fairy godmother. Fractures several familiar fairy tales and provides a surprise twist for the ending of the FROG PRINCE. A wacky alternative to the usual fairy tales, especially for children well acquainted with the originals.
SUBJ: Fairy tales--Parodies, imitations, etc./ Princes--Fiction./ Frogs-- Fiction.

Ph-1 2-5/3 $16.99 L KG420
SCIESZKA, JON. Math curse. Illus. by Lane Smith. Viking ISBN 0-670-86194-4; In Canada: Penguin, 1995. unp. col. ill.
Selectors' Choice, 21st ed.
Available from the National Library Service for the Blind and Physically Handicapped on sound recording cassette RC 42748.
What if everything suddenly seemed like a math problem? When Mrs. Fibonacci suggests that possibility, the whole day becomes a series of outrageous computational problems from breakfast through dinner, including social studies, English, and phys. ed. classes, and, of course, the division of 24 cupcakes among 25 people for snack. The math

theme is carried throughout the design and illustration of the book including the price, dedication, and author information. The back cover contains all the answers, but be careful, there may be an error!
SUBJ: Math anxiety--Fiction./ Mathematics--Fiction./ Schools--Fiction.

CE Ph-1 K-3/2 $15.99 L KG421
SCIESZKA, JON. True story of the 3 little pigs. By A. Wolf, as told to Jon Scieszka. Illus. by Lane Smith. Viking ISBN 0-670-82759-2; In Canada: Penguin, 1989. unp. col. ill.
Available in Spanish, LA VERDADERA HISTORIA DE LOS TRES CERDITOS! (ISBN 0-670-84162-5, 1991).
Spanish read-along kit VERDADERA HISTORIA DE LOS TRES CERDITOS available from Live Oak Media (ISBN 0-87499-417-0, 1997). 1 paperback book, 1 sound cassette (13min), $15.95.
The familiar story of the three pigs is told from the unfamiliar point of view of the wolf, who says he only went out to borrow a cup of sugar and just happened to sneeze, blowing down the homes of the first two pigs. Offbeat illustrations include many humorous details and are fun for individual readers to pore over. This is also a hilarious choice for seasoned storyhour listeners who are familiar with the original tale.
SUBJ: Fairy tales--Parodies, imitations, etc./ Pigs--Fiction./ Wolves-- Fiction./ Spanish language materials.

Ph-2 P-K/2 $14.95 L KG422
SCOTT, ANN HERBERT. Hi. Illus. by Glo Coalson. Philomel ISBN 0-399-21964-1; In Canada: Putnam, 1994. unp. col. ill.
"Hi," Margarita says to everyone she meets with her mother in the post office, but the people are too busy to notice her. Finally, she gets to the counter, and the lady says "hi" back. Illustrations and text capture the young child's friendliness and enthusiasm.
SUBJ: Postal service--Fiction./ Interpersonal relations--Fiction.

Ph-2 P-K/2 $14.95 L KG423
SCOTT, ANN HERBERT. On mother's lap. Illus. by Glo Coalson. Clarion ISBN 0-395-58920-7, c1972, 1992. 32p col illus.
Available from National Library Service for the Blind and Physically Handicapped in Braille BR02474.
Michael, a little Eskimo boy, is especially happy when he cuddles under his reindeer blanket on Mother's lap with his puppy and his toys and rocks back and forth. He thinks there's not room enough for his baby sister, but to his surprise, Michael learns that Mother's lap is very special--there is always room for everyone.
SUBJ: Eskimos--Fiction./ Mothers and sons--Fiction./ Family life-- Fiction./ Indians of North America--Fiction.

Ph-2 K-2/2 $12.88 L KG424
SCOTT, ANN HERBERT. One good horse: a cowpuncher's counting book. Illus. by Lynn Sweat. Greenwillow ISBN 0-688-09147-4, 1990. unp. col. ill.
Riding out with his father, a young boy counts a variety of things from the horse they're riding through clumps of sagebrush, fence posts, and a herd of cattle. The transparent oil and colored pencil illustrations are attractively textured and hued. A counting book appealing to boys particularly.
SUBJ: Counting./ West (U.S.)--Fiction./ Cowboys--Fiction./ Ranch life--Fiction.

Ph-2 1-3/2 $15.99 L KG425
SEABROOK, ELIZABETH. Cabbage and kings. Illus. by Jamie Wyeth. Viking ISBN 0-670-87462-0; In Canada: Penguin, 1997. unp. col. ill.
Albert an asparagus stalk befriends Herman a cabbage in the garden, offering advice about avoiding rabbits (look tough) and winning a prize at the fair. Careful viewers will notice faces and their expressions in the rich paintings. Unusual characters provide humor and suspense in the somewhat long story.
SUBJ: Asparagus--Fiction./ Cabbage--Fiction./ Gardens--Fiction.

Ph-1 K-3/6 $17.00 T KG426
SEGAL, LORE. Tell me a Mitzi. Illus. by Harriet Pincus. Farrar, Straus & Giroux ISBN 0-374-37392-2, c1970. unp. col. ill.
Available from National Library Service for the Blind and Physically Handicapped in Braille BR01432.
"Tell me a Mitzi" begs Martha. And here we have three humorous, warm, homey, "once upon a time there was a Mitzi" fantasies. In the first Mitzi diapers, feeds and dresses baby Jacob and while their parents still sleep starts for Grandma and Grandpa's house. Unfortunately when the taxi driver asks for the address, Mitzi doesn't know. In the second tale the whole family suffers the miseries of the common cold. And in the third episode a presidential parade is reversed to satisfy baby Jacob's wishes.
SUBJ: Family life--Fiction./ Humorous stories./ Short stories.

Ph-1 K-3/4 $17.00 T KG427

SEGAL, LORE. Tell me a Trudy. Illus. by Rosemary Wells. Farrar, Straus & Giroux ISBN 0-374-37392-2, c1977, 1981. unp. col. ill.
Sequel to TELL ME A MITZI.
Hilarity abounds in these three further episodes of Trudy, Jacob and their parents. In "Trudy and the copycats" everyone (father included) mimics everything Mother says but still won't get ready for bed until Grandma comes to the rescue. In "Trudy and the dump truck" sharing by the children leads to arguments between adults, and in "Trudy and Superman" a letter to Superman about the robbers or Martians lurking in the bathroom brings a quick and dramatic response. Rosemary Wells' illustrations make this a prime candidate for picture story time.
SUBJ: Family life--Fiction./ Humorous stories./ Short stories.

BB Ph-3 P $3.95 T KG428

SEIDEN, ART. Trucks (Board book). Platt & Munk/Grossett & Dunlap ISBN 0-448-40873-2, 1983. unp col illus. (Teddy board books).
Printed on sturdy boards are colorful pictures of eleven large vehicles such as a fire truck, steam shovel, concrete mixer, dump truck, and tow truck. Wordless except for the names of each machine, this type of book is very popular with the preschool set.
SUBJ: Trucks.

CE Ph-2 P-1 $12.89 L KG429

SENDAK, MAURICE. Alligators all around: an alphabet. HarperCollins ISBN 0-06-025530-7, c1962. unp. col. ill.
This edition size: 5 1/4 x 7 1/8 inches.
1/2" VHS videocassette available from Weston Woods HMPV222V (2min), $49.95.
From "A Alligators all around" all the way to "Z Zippity Zound! Alligators ALL around."
SUBJ: Alphabet.

CE Ph-1 P-1 $12.89 L KG430

SENDAK, MAURICE. Chicken soup with rice: a book of months. HarperCollins ISBN 0-06-025535-8, c1962. 48p. col. ill.
This edition size: 5 1/4 x 7 1/8 inches.
Big book available from Scholastic (ISBN 0-590-71789-8, 1992).
1/2" VHS videocassette available from Weston Woods HMPV223V (5min), $49.95.
Read-along kit, sung by Carly Simon, available from Weston Woods HPRA223. 1 paperback book, 1 sound cassette (5min), $12.95.
"I told you once/ I told you twice/ All seasons of the year are nice/ For eating chicken soup with rice!"
SUBJ: Seasons--Fiction./ Stories in rhyme.

Ph-3 1-3/6 $14.89 L KG431

SENDAK, MAURICE. Higglety pigglety pop, or, There must be more to life. HarperCollins ISBN 0-06-025488-2, c1967. 69p. ill.
Available from National Library Service for the Blind and Physically Handicapped in Braille BR00796.
Jennie is a little dog whose master loves her and she has everything. But one night she decides that "There must be more to life than having everything." So she packs up and runs away. She finds she can't get a job because she lacks experience, so she takes a job as nurse to Baby. She wants above all to secure the job of leading lady in the World Mother Goose Theatre. She has many fantastic adventures and conversations--before she gets her wish. Pages 52-68 show the Theatre performance. Excellent for reading aloud.
SUBJ: Fantasy./ Animals--Fiction./ Dogs--Fiction.

CE Ph-2 K-3/3 $15.95 T KG432

SENDAK, MAURICE. In the night kitchen. HarperCollins ISBN 0-06-066668-6, c1970. unp. col. ill.
Caldecott Honor Book.
Videocassette available from Weston Woods HMPV302V. 1/2" VHS videocassette color (6min), $49.95.
Videocassette available from Weston Woods in Spanish, HVC302VSP. 1/2" VHS videocassette color (6min), $49.95.
Picture from Peaceable Kingdom Press 18" x 24" color poster, $9.95.
Spanish version LA COCINA DE NOCHE available from Santillana (ISBN 84-204-45703, 1997).
Available from National Library Service for the Blind and Physically Handicapped as talking book TB04079.
Mickey is suddenly awakened by a thumpy, dumpy, clumpy racket in the night. After shouting "Quiet down there," he falls through the dark, out of his clothes, past the moon, and into the cake batter of the night kitchen. Mickey kneads and punches and pounds and pulls the dough into an airplane. He then flies off to the Milky Way where he gets all the milk the three bakers need. "And that's why, thanks to Mickey, we have cake every morning."
SUBJ: Fantasy./ Spanish language materials.

VCR Ph-2 P-2 $89.00 OD KG433

SENDAK, MAURICE. Maurice Sendak Library (Videocassette). Weston Woods HMPV491V, 1992. 1/2" VHS videocassette color (35min).
Includes public performance rights.
Several popular titles by this author are presented followed by the author talking briefly about his work. The four titles from the Nutshell library are performed musically by Carole King.
Contents: Nutshell Kids: Alligators all around, Pierre, One was Johnny, Chicken soup with rice; Where the wild things are; In the night kitchen; Getting to know Maurice Sendak.
SUBJ: Stories in rhyme./ Fantasy.

VCR Ph-2 P-2 $30.00 OD KG434

SENDAK, MAURICE. Nutshell library (Videocassette). Weston Woods PBV003, 1987. 1/2" VHS videocassette color (16min). (Picture book parade).
Excerpted from the film "Really Rosie" these fully animated interpretations of Sendak's beloved tiny books can help young children learn or reinforce the alphabet, numbers, months, or a moral about caring.
Contents: Alligators all around (2min); One was Johnny (3min); Pierre (6min); Chicken soup with rice (5min).
SUBJ: Stories in rhyme.

CE Ph-2 P-1 $12.89 L KG435

SENDAK, MAURICE. One was Johnny: a counting book. HarperCollins ISBN 0-06-025540-4, c1962. unp. col. ill.
This edition size: 5 1/4 x 7 1/8 inches.
1/2" VHS videocassette available from Weston Woods HMPV221V (3min) $30.00.
A book to help you count from one to ten by telling you about the queer creatures who infested Johnny's house and how he got rid of them!
SUBJ: Arithmetic--Fiction./ Counting.

CE Ph-2 P-1 $12.89 L KG436

SENDAK, MAURICE. Pierre: a cautionary tale in five chapters and a prologue. HarperCollins ISBN 0-06-025965-5, c1962. unp. col. ill.
This edition size: 5 1/4 x 7 1/8 inches.
1/2" VHS videocassette available from Weston Woods MPV220 (6min) $60.00.
"There once was a boy named Pierre/ Who only would say, 'I don't care!'/ Read his story, my friend/ For you'll find at the end/ That a suitable moral lies there."
SUBJ: Nonsense verses./ Behavior--Fiction.

TB Ph-1 P-2 $11.95 OD KG437

SENDAK, MAURICE. Where the wild things are and other stories (Talking book). Read by Tammy Grimes. HarperAudio/Caedmon ISBN 0-89845-792-0; In Canada: dist. by HarperCollins, 1977. 1 sound cassette (42min).
Tammy Grimes reads eight popular stories written by Maurice Sendak. Selections from works of Mozart are very effectively used as background music.
Contents: Side A: "Alligators all around"; "One was Johnny;" "Pierre"; "Chicken soup with rice"; "Very far away"; and "Where the wild things are". Side B: "The sign on Rosie's door", and "In the night kitchen".
SUBJ: Animals--Fiction./ Fantasy.

CE Ph-1 P-3/2 $14.89 L KG438

SENDAK, MAURICE. Where the wild things are. 25th anniv. ed. HarperCollins ISBN 0-06-025493-9, c1963, 1988. unp. col. ill.
Caldecott Medal Award.
Videocassette available from Weston Woods HMPV906V. 1/2" VHS videocassette color (8min), $49.95.
Spanish version DONDE VIVEN LOS MONSTRUOS available from HarperTrophy (ISBN 0-06-443422-2, 1996), $5.95; videocassette in Spanish available from Weston Woods HVC084VSP n.d. 1/2" VHS videocassette color (7min), $49.95.
Picture available from Peaceable Kingdom Press (18"x24") color poster, $9.95.
Available from National Library Service for the Blind and Physically Handicapped in Braille BR05919, on sound recording cassette RC22906, and talking book TB03167.
Max dreams of a voyage to the island where the wild things are after he is sent to bed without supper for behaving like a wild thing.
SUBJ: Fantasy./ Spanish language materials.

Ph-2 P-K/2 $14.95 L KG439

SERFOZO, MARY. Benjamin Bigfoot. Illus. by Jos. A. Smith. McElderry ISBN 0-689-50570-1; In Canada: Maxwell Macmillan, 1993. unp. col. ill.
Benjamin loves to splash, crunch, and scuffle in the big shoes that used to belong to his father. He wants to wear oversized shoes to

kindergarten until he visits the school, meets his new teacher, and realizes what a great place it will be. Humorous and reassuring, this is on target for youngsters starting school.
SUBJ: Kindergarten--Fiction./ Schools--Fiction./ Shoes--Fiction.

Ph-2 P-K/1 $15.95   L   KG440
SERFOZO, MARY. Joe Joe. Illus. by Nina S. Montezinos. McElderry ISBN 0-689-50578-7; In Canada: Maxwell Macmillan, 1993. unp. col. ill.
Joe Joe runs up and down the street banging a fence with a stick, clanging a toy fire engine, and splashing in puddles. In each pastel and colored pencil doublespread, a single word of text imparts what Joe Joe is doing. The word appears a second time as part of the illustration providing a visual clue to the word's meaning. The illustrations sparkle, the activities are very childlike, and the text invites very beginning readers to use their skills.
SUBJ: Sound--Fiction.

Ph-1 P-1/4 $13.95   L   KG441
SERFOZO, MARY. Rain talk. Illus. by Keiko Narahashi. McElderry ISBN 0-689-50496-9; In Canada: Collier Macmillan, 1990. unp. col. ill.
The delight of a summer rain is evident in a young black girl's description of the sights and especially the sounds the rain makes. The many different sounds of rain are aptly mimicked by the text while watercolor illustrations perfectly match the rainy story. A pleasing choice for rainy days or fun with onomatopoeia.
SUBJ: Rain and rainfall--Fiction.

Ph-2 P-1/1 $6.95   T   KG442
SERFOZO, MARY. There's a square: a book about shapes. Illus. by David A. Carter. Scholastic ISBN 0-590-54426-8; In Canada: Scholastic, 1996. unp. col. ill. (Story corner).
"Cartwheel books."
Launches youngsters into the world of geometric shapes with simple rhyming text and illustrations created from various shapes. Fun combination for math and art units.
SUBJ: Shape--Fiction./ Stories in rhyme.

Ph-1 P-1/2 $15.00   T   KG443
SERFOZO, MARY. What's what?: a guessing game. Illus. by Keiko Narahashi. McElderry ISBN 0-689-80653-1; In Canada: Distican, 1996. unp. col. ill.
Designed as a guessing game, the book answers a series of questions with each turn of a page about what's soft, hard, warm, cold, wet, dry, long, short, light, and dark with a surprise ending about something which has all of those qualities. Bright watercolor illustrations and rhyming text provide delightful answers to each question. Predictable book about opposites that's perfect for sharing at storytime. For multicultural studies.
SUBJ: English language--Synonyms and antonyms--Fiction./ Dogs--Fiction./ Afro-Americans--Fiction.

Ph-1 P-K/2 $15.00   L   KG444
SERFOZO, MARY. Who said red? Illus. by Keiko Narahashi. McElderry ISBN 0-689-50455-1; In Canada: /Distican, 1988. unp. col. ill.
As a small boy searches for his kite, his older sister accompanies him and continually asks questions involving red and other colors but the small boy insists "I said RED." An addition to the many concept books introducing colors, it has very appealing pictures and a text consisting of brief, bouncy verses.
SUBJ: Color--Fiction.

Ph-1 K-2/2 $15.99   L   KG445
SEUSS, DR. And to think that I saw it on Mulberry Street. Random House ISBN 0-394-94494-1, c1937, 1964. unp. col. ill.
"Vanguard Press book."
Available from the National Library Service for the Blind and Physically Handicapped in talking book TB00636.
Walking to school and back, young Marco only sees a horse and wagon on Mulberry Street, but he imagines all sorts of fantastic sights that he could report. The snappy text and increasingly elaborate illustrations never cease to delight young and old.
SUBJ: Imagination--Fiction./ Nonsense verses./ Stories in rhyme.

Ph-1 P-3/6 $12.99   L   KG446
SEUSS, DR. Bartholomew and the oobleck. Random House ISBN 0-394-90075-8, c1949. unp. col. ill.
Sequel to 500 HATS OF BARTHOLOMEW CUBBINS.
Caldecott Honor Book.
A king who is tired of having the snow, fog, sunshine and rain fall on his kingdom has real trouble when green, sticky oobleck falls instead, but his page boy saves the day.
SUBJ: Fantasy.

Ph-2 K-3/5 $12.99   L   KG447
SEUSS, DR. Butter battle book. Random House ISBN 0-394-96580-9; In Canada: Random House, 1984. unp. col. ill.
Available from National Library Service for the Blind and Physically Handicapped in Braille BR05904, and sound recording cassette RC20248.
Warning of the danger of an arms race and the fallacy of trying to match and outdistance the enemy is the message in this story of the Zooks who eat their bread with the buttered side down and the Yooks who prefer their bread with the buttered side up. Initial Seuss appeal soon dissipates and children may be confused by the unresolved ending.
SUBJ: War--Fiction./ Stories in rhyme.

CE   Ph-1 P-2/1 $7.99   L   KG448
SEUSS, DR. Cat in the hat. Beginner Books/Random House ISBN 0-394-90001-4, c1957. 61p. col. ill. (Beginner books).
Read-along kit also available in Spanish EL GATO ENSOMBRERADO (ISBN 0-679-84329-9, 1993). 1 paperback book, 1 sound cassette, $6.95.
A fantastic cat entertains two children in a most unusual way.
In THE CAT IN THE HAT COMES BACK (ISBN 0-394-90002-2, 1958) the cat returns to create more unusual entertainment.
SUBJ: Cats--Fiction./ Nonsense verses./ Stories in rhyme.

VCR   Ph-3 K-2 $9.95   KG449
SEUSS, DR. Cat in the Hat gets grinched (Videocassette). Random House ISBN 0-679-83076-6, 1982. 1/2" VHS videocassette color (30min).
Formerly released as THE GRINCH GRINCHES THE CAT IN THE HAT.
Closed-captioned.
The Cat in the Hat meets the Grinch who tries his best to mess up the cat's day until the Cat in the Hat ungrinches the Grinch. Lively and fun, the video features two favorite Seuss characters and the inevitable conflict that ensues when the two personalities meet.
SUBJ: Cats--Fiction./ Nonsense verses./ Songs.

VCR   Ph-3 1-3 $137.00   OD KG450
SEUSS, DR. Dr. Seuss' Caldecotts (Videocassette). SRA/McGraw-Hill 87-510142, 1985. 3 stories on 1 1/2" VHS videocassette color.
Videocassettes avaiable separately, $39.00.
Originally Caldecott Honor Books, these Dr. Seuss titles have been transferred from the filmstrip versions to videocassette with a minimum of motion. Each story should be shown separately and the videocassette should be purchased only if the filmstrips are not owned.
Contents: McElligot's Pool (9min); If I Ran the Zoo (17min); Bartholomew and the Oobleck (26min).
SUBJ: Humorous stories.

CE   Ph-2 P-2/2 $7.99   L   KG451
SEUSS, DR. Dr. Seuss's ABC. Beginner Books/Random House ISBN 0-394-90030-8, c1963. 63p. col. ill. (I can read it all by myself).
Talking book available from SRA/McGraw-Hill 87-508370, n.d. 1 sound cassette (7min), $15.00.
A lively alphabet book filled with funny, imaginary creatures.
SUBJ: Alphabet./ Nonsense verses.

Ph-1 P-1/1 $7.99   L   KG452
SEUSS, DR. Foot book. Random House ISBN 0-394-90937-2, c1968. unp. col. ill. (Bright and early book).
Familiar Dr. Seuss characters leap and parade across the pages as easy words describe for beginning readers many different kinds of feet such as "Slow feet- Quick feet- Trick feet- Sick feet." Useful for work with children who have perceptual difficulties.
SUBJ: Foot--Fiction./ Stories in rhyme.

Ph-2 P-2/2 $7.99   L   KG453
SEUSS, DR. Fox in socks. Beginner Books/Random House ISBN 0-394-90038-3, c1965. 61p col illus. (Beginner books).
Filled with tongue twisters beginning with easy ones and progressing into those more difficult.
SUBJ: Nonsense verses.

CE   Ph-1 P-2/1 $7.99   L   KG454
SEUSS, DR. Green eggs and ham. Beginner Books/Random House ISBN 0-394-90016-2; In Canada: Random House, 1960. 62p. col. ill. (Beginner books).
Videocassette available from BFA/Phoenix 71542, n.d. 1/2" VHS videocassette color (9min), $89.95.
Spanish edition available HUEVOS VERDES CON JAMON (Lectorum ISBN 1-880507-01-3, 1992), $8.95.
"I do not like them Sam-I-am. I do not like green eggs and ham."
But Sam-I-am persists in offering them here, there, with a mouse, in a

house, with a fox, in a box, in a tree, on a train, in the rain, with a goat, and on a boat.
SUBJ: Stories in rhyme./ Food--Fiction.

Ph-2 P-1/1 $7.99   L   KG455
SEUSS, DR. Hop on pop. Beginner Books/Random House ISBN 0-394-90029-4, c1963. 64p. col. ill. (Beginner books).
Available from National Library Service for the Blind and Physically Handicapped in Braille BR02258.
A fun book for boys and girls who want a "book to begin on."
SUBJ: Nonsense verses.

CE   Ph-1 P-3/3 $13.99   L   KG456
SEUSS, DR. Horton hatches the egg. Random House ISBN 0-394-90077-4, c1940. unp. col. ill.
Available from National Library Service for the Blind and Physically Handicapped in Braille BRA04740.
A kindly, good natured elephant helps an ungrateful bird by caring for her nest as she flies off on vacation.
In HORTON HEARS A WHO (ISBN 0-394-90078-2, 1954) (available from NLSBPH in Braille BR03886) he hears a tiny cry coming from a small speck of dust and discovers an almost microscopic group of creatures with a complete civilization. (Kit narrated by Dustin Hoffman available from Random House ISBN 0-679-80003-4, 1990. 1 sound cassette (17min), 1 paperback book, $10.95.)
SUBJ: Elephants--Fiction./ Nonsense verses./ Stories in rhyme.

VCR   Ph-3 P-3 $6.99   KG457
SEUSS, DR. Horton hatches the egg./If I ran the circus (Videocassette). Narrated by Billy Crystal. Random House ISBN 0-679-82819-2, 1992. 1/2" VHS videocassette color (30min). (Dr. Seuss video classics).
Closed captioned.
Two popular Seuss stories are offered on one economical videocassette. Billy Crystal reads HORTON HATCHES THE EGG, and a child's voice reads IF I RAN THE CIRCUS. Both feature minimal animation of the books' illustrations.
SUBJ: Elephants--Fiction./ Circus--Fiction./ Nonsense verses./ Stories in rhyme.

VCR   Ph-2 P-3 $9.95   KG458
SEUSS, DR. Horton hears a Who!/Thidwick the big-hearted moose (Videocassette). Narrated by Dustin Hoffman. Random House ISBN 0-679-82817-6, 1992. 1/2" VHS videocassette color (30min). (Dr. Seuss video classics).
Closed captioned.
Two stories by Seuss are faithfully presented with minimal animation. Well paced and enjoyable.
SUBJ: Elephants--Fiction./ Moose--Fiction./ Nonsense verses./ Stories in rhyme.

Ph-1 P-3 $15.99   L   KG459
SEUSS, DR. How the Grinch stole Christmas. Random House ISBN 0-394-90079-0, c1957. unp. col. ill.
Available from National Library Service for the Blind and Physically Handicapped in Braille BR04656 and sound recording cassette RC12236.
A mean old creature tries to find a way to do away with Christmas but he learns his lesson.
SUBJ: Christmas--Fiction./ Nonsense verses./ Stories in rhyme.

Ph-3 K-3/2 $10.99   L   KG460
SEUSS, DR. Hunches in bunches. Random House ISBN 0-394-95502-1; In Canada: Random House, 1982. unp. col. ill.
Making decisions is difficult, especially when the hero is pulled in all directions by bunches of good and bad hunches. The jingling rhymes, nonsensical humor, and bright illustrations are typical Seuss.
SUBJ: Stories in rhyme./ Decision making--Fiction.

Ph-1 1-3/2 $7.99   L   KG461
SEUSS, DR. I am not going to get up today! Illus. by James Stevenson. Beginner Books/Random House ISBN 0-394-99217-2; In Canada: Random House, 1987. unp. col. ill. (Beginner books).
Available from National Library Service for the Blind and Physically Handicapped in Braille BR7339.
A sleepy young boy vows that nothing, not even a strawberry flip, a marshmallow dip, a pineapple butterscotch ding dang doo, a big brass band, or a multitude of other intriguing fantasies will tempt him to get out of bed. Seuss's rhyming words and Stevenson's humorous pictures work perfectly in creating a title very appealing to young primaries.
SUBJ: Sleep--Fiction./ Beds--Fiction./ Humorous stories./ Stories in rhyme.

VCR   Ph-2 1-3 $6.99   KG462
SEUSS, DR. I am not going to get up today! plus three more Dr. Seuss classics (Videocassette). Random House Home Video ISBN 0-679-81031-5, 1991. 1/2" VHS videocassette color (25min). (Beginner book video).
Closed captioned.
Minimal but effective animation is featured with the title Seuss story and 3 lesser known stories. If purchased only for the first title, this is still an inexpensive addition for video collections.
Contents: I am not going to get up today; The Shape of me and other stuff; Great day for up; In a people house.
SUBJ: Sleep--Fiction./ Beds--Fiction./ Humorous stories./ Stories in rhyme.

Ph-1 P-2/2 $7.99   L   KG463
SEUSS, DR. I can read with my eyes shut. Beginner Books/Random House ISBN 0-394-93912-3; In Canada: Random House, 1978. unp. col. ill. (Beginner books).
That old, familiar favorite, the Cat in the Hat is back again. This time he takes Young Cat all around and shows him how much fun it is to read, how much he can learn, and how far he can go especially if he keeps his eyes open while he reads.
SUBJ: Stories in rhyme./ Reading--Fiction.

Ph-2 P-3/4 $13.99   L   KG464
SEUSS, DR. If I ran the circus. Random House ISBN 0-394-90080-4, c1956. unp. col. ill.
Available from National Library Service for the Blind and Physically Handicapped in Braille BR02368.
A boy, Morris McGurk, imagines what could happen if he should have his own circus.
SUBJ: Circus--Fiction./ Nonsense verses./ Stories in rhyme.

Ph-2 P-3/5 $13.99   L   KG465
SEUSS, DR. If I ran the zoo. Random House ISBN 0-394-90081-2; In Canada: Random House, 1950. 56p. col. ill.
Caldecott Medal Award.
Available from National Library Service for the Blind and Physically Handicapped in Braille BR04661, as talking book TB00636, and on sound recording cassette RC34725.
Young Gerald McGrew imagines a new kind of zoo filled with astounding and unusual animals.
SUBJ: Nonsense verses./ Zoos--Fiction./ Animals--Fiction./ Stories in rhyme.

CE   Ph-3 P-3/3 $12.00   T   KG466
SEUSS, DR. Lorax. Random House ISBN 0-394-82337-0, c1971. unp. col. ill.
Available from National Library Service for the Blind and Physically Handicapped on sound recording cassette RC31231.
Read-along kit, narrated by Ted Danson, available from Random House (ISBN 0-679-82273-9, 1992). 1 paperback book, 1 sound cassette (8min), $13.00.
Spanish edition available EL LORAX (Lectorum ISBN 1-880507-04-8, 1993), $13.95.
The Once-ler tells a little boy how his family's greed has destroyed a glorious place. They cut down the trees to manufacture goods. Their factories polluted the soil, the air and the water until all the animals who had not died left. When the last tree was cut down, the Lorax who had tried to stop the destruction of the Once-lers departed with the warning that unless someone, like the little boy, comes along who cares about his environment nothing will get better.
SUBJ: Stories in rhyme./ Pollution--Fiction./ Ecology--Fiction./ Spanish language materials.

Ph-1 P-3 $11.99   L   KG467
SEUSS, DR. McElligot's pool. Random House ISBN 0-394-90083-9, c1947. unp. col. ill.
Caldecott Honor Book.
Available from National Library Service for the Blind and Physically Handicapped in Braille BR02367.
As a boy tries to catch a fish, he begins to imagine extraordinary fish that might come his way.
SUBJ: Fishes--Fiction./ Nonsense verses./ Stories in rhyme.

Ph-2 K-2/2 $17.99   L   KG468
SEUSS, DR. My many colored days. Illus. by Steve Johnson and Lou Fancher. Knopf ISBN 0-679-97597-7; In Canada: Random House, 1996. unp. col. ill.
"Borzoi book."
Different moods are like different colored days: yellow feels busy and purple is sad. Oil paintings carefully match the mood and content of the text. Can be used on several levels as a book about colors or about emotions.

SUBJ: Color--Fiction./ Day--Fiction./ Emotions--Fiction./ Stories in rhyme.

Ph-1 1-3/2 $13.99 L KG469
SEUSS, DR. Oh, the places you'll go! Random House ISBN 0-679-90527-8; In Canada: Random House, 1990. unp. col. ill.
Available from National Library Service for the Blind and Physically Handicapped on sound recording cassette, RC30795.
Spanish edition available OH, CUAN LEJOS LLEGARAS! (Lectorum ISBN 1-880507-05-6, 1993), $13.95.
"You have brains in your head. You have feet in your shoes. You can steer yourself any direction you choose." Rhyming text and humorous, colorful illustrations urge the hero (and young reader) forward despite the difficulties that will be encountered. This very up-beat but realistic presentation encourages independence.
SUBJ: Success--Fiction./ Stories in rhyme.

Ph-1 P-3/6 $13.99 L KG470
SEUSS, DR. On beyond zebra. Random House ISBN 0-394-90084-7; In Canada: Random House, 1955. unp. col. ill.
Young Conrad Cornelius o'Donald o'Dell learns, in scintillating language, that the alphabet can go beyond the original 26 letters particularly for describing some most unusual creatures. For creative writing, for appreciating the expressive quality of language, or just for laughs.
SUBJ: Alphabet./ Creative ability--Fiction./ Stories in rhyme.

Ph-1 P-1/1 $7.99 L KG471
SEUSS, DR. One fish, two fish, red fish, blue fish. Beginner Books/ Random House ISBN 0-394-90013-8, c1960. 62p. col. ill. (Beginner books).
Available from National Library Service for the Blind and Physically Handicapped in Braille BR06106 and on sound recording cassette RC22796.
From here to there, funny things like a Zans, a Gox, a Yink, and Ying, are everywhere.
SUBJ: Nonsense verses.

CE Ph-3 P-3/3 $13.99 L KG472
SEUSS, DR. Yertle the turtle, and other stories. Random House ISBN 0-394-90087-1, c1958. unp. col. ill.
Available from National Library Service for the Blind and Physically Handicapped on sound recording cassette RC34061.
Closed-captioned video, narrated by John Lithgow from the Dr. Seuss video classics series, is available from Random House (ISBN 0-679-82820-6, 1992) 1/2" VHS videocassette color (30min), $6.99.
Yertle, ambitious king of the turtles, wants to see and rule the entire world from his high position on top of many, many other turtles, but a lowly burp precipitates his downfall to king of the mud. The other zany tales in this collection are about Gertrude, a bird who wants more tail feathers than her friend, and Rabbit and Bear who wage a ridiculous bragging contest.
SUBJ: Stories in rhyme./ Animals--Fiction./ Short stories.

Ph-2 P-A/6 $15.99 L KG473
SEUSS, DR. 500 hats of Bartholomew Cubbins. Random House ISBN 0-394-94484-4, c1938, 1989. unp. col. ill.
Available from National Library Service for the Blind and Physically Handicapped in Braille BRA06574 and as talking book TB00636.
Every time the boy tries to take his hat off before the king, a new one appears making the king very angry.
SUBJ: Hats--Fiction./ Humorous stories.

Ph-2 1-3/2 $15.99 L KG474
SEYMOUR, TRES. Hunting the white cow. Illus. by Wendy Anderson Halperin. Orchard ISBN 0-531-08646-1, 1993. unp. col. ill.
"Richard Jackson book."
The white cow eludes all attempts to catch her, but only temporarily. Soft watercolor illustrations match the understated mood of the story while adding details and humor.
SUBJ: Cows--Fiction.

Ph-2 2-5/6 $15.95 L KG475
SHANNON, DAVID. Amazing Christmas extravaganza. Blue Sky Press/ Scholastic ISBN 0-590-48090-1; In Canada: Scholastic, 1995. unp. col. ill.
Mr. Merriweather gets carried away with decorating the house for Christmas until his house becomes a spectacle of colored lights and giant plastic figures that cause his neighbors to revolt. The acrylic illustrations build to a vertical doublespread as Mr. Merriweather piles on the decorations.
SUBJ: Christmas decorations--Fiction./ Christmas--Fiction.

Ph-1 2-5/6 $14.95 L KG476
SHANNON, DAVID. How Georgie Radbourn saved baseball. Blue Sky Press/Scholastic ISBN 0-590-47410-3; In Canada: Scholastic, 1994. unp. col. ill.
Baseball and any mention of baseball have been outlawed by Boss Swaggert. Georgie Radbourn can hardly open his mouth without uttering a baseball phrase which results in his arrest and trial. Georgie proposes a contest of skills in a baseball game. When he strikes out the Boss, baseball returns to America. An ominous story with dark illustrations in which a youngster is the hero. Layered meanings can be explored by many different ages.
SUBJ: Baseball--Fiction.

Ph-2 P-1/2 $14.93 L KG477
SHANNON, GEORGE. April showers. Illus. by Jose Aruego and Ariane Dewey. Greenwillow ISBN 0-688-13122-0, 1995. unp. col. ill.
A group of frogs dance in the rain with snake who may not be quite what he appears. The text bounces and the brilliant watercolor illustrations convey the humor and action in the story. A celebration for rainy days especially in April.
SUBJ: Frogs--Fiction./ Snakes--Fiction./ Dancing--Fiction./ Rain and rainfall--Fiction.

Ph-2 K-2/2 $13.95 L KG478
SHANNON, GEORGE. Seeds. Illus. by Steve Bjorkman. Houghton Mifflin ISBN 0-395-66990-1, 1994. unp. col. ill.
Missing his neighbor Bill and his garden, Warren, who has moved far away, writes and asks for seeds to start his own garden. Bill, who is an artist, sends him seeds and a picture of a squirrel. His letter explains that Warren's request gave him the idea for a story about two squirrels, separated by a move, who share seeds. Watercolor illustrations depict the interracial and intergenerational friendship. For multicultural studies.
SUBJ: Friendship--Fiction./ Gardens--Fiction./ Moving, Household--Fiction.

Ph-1 K-2/2 $15.93 L KG479
SHANNON, GEORGE. Tomorrow's alphabet. Illus. by Donald Crews. Greenwillow ISBN 0-688-13505-6, 1996. unp. col. ill.
"A is for seed," when the seed will be an apple tomorrow. A clever alphabet book leads youngsters through the letters A to Z with this surprising twist. For reading aloud as a challenging guessing game and for creative writing.
SUBJ: Alphabet.

Ph-1 K-2/2 $14.95 L KG480
SHARMAT, MARJORIE WEINMAN. Gila monsters meet you at the airport. Illus. by Byron Barton. Macmillan ISBN 0-02-782450-0; In Canada: Maxwell Macmillan, 1980. unp. col. ill.
A young Manhattan boy doesn't want to move West. He thinks there is cactus everywhere, that he'll have to ride a horse to school and won't have time for baseball since everyone will be busy chasing buffaloes. What a surprise when the plane lands and there is no gila monster waiting only a western boy who is very apprehensive about moving East. The young westerner is expecting gangsters, snow all the time, planes zooming through the apartment and alligators escaping from the sewers.
SUBJ: West (U.S.)--Fiction./ Perception--Fiction.

Ph-2 P-1/3 $13.95 L KG481
SHARMAT, MARJORIE WEINMAN. I'm terrific. Illus. by Kay Chorao. Holiday House ISBN 0-8234-0282-7, 1977. 28p. col. ill.
Jason Everett Bear thinks he's so terrific that he awards himself gold stars for his outstanding performances. Unfortunately he's almost friendless since the other young animals think Jason is a boring mama's boy and a conceited show-off.
SUBJ: Pride and vanity--Fiction./ Animals--Fiction.

Ph-2 K-2/1 $14.95 L KG482
SHARMAT, MARJORIE WEINMAN. I'm the best! Illus. by Will Hillenbrand. Holiday House ISBN 0-8234-0859-0, 1991. unp. col. ill.
Dudley has had many names and many owners until a family adopts him from the animal shelter. Expressive illustrations and a heart warming story chronicle the growing trust between Dudley and his new family.
SUBJ: Dogs--Fiction.

Ph-2 K-3/1 $14.00 T KG483
SHARMAT, MARJORIE WEINMAN. Mitchell is moving. Illus. by Jose Aruego and Ariane Dewey. Simon & Schuster ISBN 0-689-80875-5; In Canada: Distican, 1978. 47p. col. ill. (Ready-to-read).
Margo tries to keep her best friend and longtime neighbor from moving, but Mitchell is determined. After moving, the dinosaur is excited and pleased with his new bed and new kitchen. In fact, he is happy with his whole new house, but something very important is

missing.
SUBJ: Moving, Household--Fiction./ Friendship--Fiction./ Dinosaurs--Fiction.

CE   Ph-2 1-3/2 $14.95   T   KG484
SHARMAT, MARJORIE WEINMAN. Nate the Great. Illus. by Marc Simont. Coward-McCann/Putnam ISBN 0-698-20627-4; In Canada: Putnam, c1972. 60p. col. ill.
Available from National Library Service for the Blind and Physically Handicapped in Braille BR02470.
Nate the Great, boy detective, puts on his Sherlock Holmes outfit and sets out to solve the mystery of the missing painting. He describes his exploits in a clipped, deadpan style. "I hate to eat on the job. But I must keep up my strength", Nate says, when he devours a stack of pancakes. His observations of people are keen: Rosamond has "black hair, green eyes, and cat hair all over".
Nate the Great investigates further in NATE THE GREAT GOES UNDERCOVER (Delacorte ISBN 0-440-46302-5, c1974, 1978) (available from NLSBPH in Braille BR03086, read-along kit available from Listening Library FTR 172 ISBN 0-8072-0304-1, 1995); ...AND THE LOST LIST (ISBN 0-440-46282-7, 1981) (available from NLSBPH in Braille BR7612); ...AND THE PHONY CLUE (Dell ISBN 0-440-46300-9, 1981); ...AND THE STICKY CASE (ISBN 0-698-20629-0, 1978, OPC); ...AND THE MISSING KEY (ISBN 0-698-20630-4, 1981, OPC) (read-along kit from Listening Library FTR75 ISBN 0-8072-0040-9, 1989); ...AND THE SNOWY TRAIL (ISBN 0-698-20628-2, 1982, OPC) (available from NLSBPH in Braille BR7559); ...AND THE FISHY PRIZE (ISBN 0-698-20639-8, 1985, OPC) (available from NLSBPH in Braille BR7560); ...STALKS STUPIDWEED (Dell ISBN 0-440-40150-X, 1989); ...GOES DOWN IN THE DUMPS (ISBN 0-698-20636-3, 1989, OPC); ...AND THE HALLOWEEN HUNT (Dell ISBN 0-440-40341-3, 1990); and ...AND THE STOLEN BASE (ISBN 0-698-20708-4, 1992).
SUBJ: Mystery and detective stories./ Detectives--Fiction.

Ph-1 2-4/2 $13.95   T   KG485
SHARMAT, MARJORIE WEINMAN. Nate the Great and the crunchy Christmas. By Marjorie Weinman Sharmat and Craig Sharmat. Illus. by Marc Simont. Delacorte ISBN 0-385-32117-1; In Canada: Bantam Doubleday Dell, 1996. 42p. col. ill.
With deduction and determination, Nate the detective solves the holiday mystery of what happened to Fang's annual Christmas card from his mother. A worthwhile addition to the popular mystery series for beginning readers.
SUBJ: Mystery and detective stories./ Dogs--Fiction./ Christmas--Fiction.

Ph-1 1-3/1 $12.95   T   KG486
SHARMAT, MARJORIE WEINMAN. Nate the Great and the pillowcase. By Marjorie Weinman Sharmat and Rosalind Weinman. Illus. by Marc Simont. Delacorte ISBN 0-385-31051-X; In Canada: Bantam Doubleday Dell, 1993. 48p. col. ill.
Awakened in the middle of the night, Nate the Great helps Rosamond locate her cat's missing pillowcase. A worthwhile addition to the mystery series for beginning readers.
SUBJ: Mystery and detective stories.

Ph-1 1-3/2 $13.95   T   KG487
SHARMAT, MARJORIE WEINMAN. Nate the Great and the tardy tortoise. By Marjorie Weinman Sharmat and Craig Sharmat. Illus. by Marc Simont. Delacorte ISBN 0-385-32111-2; In Canada: Bantam Doubleday Dell, 1995. 42p. col. ill.
Nate and his dog, Sludge, pursue the trail of a slowly moving tortoise in search of its home. A worthy addition to the easy-to-read mystery series for beginning readers.
SUBJ: Turtles--Fiction./ Mystery and detective stories.

Ph-2 K-2/4 $14.95   L   KG488
SHARMAT, MITCHELL. Gregory, the terrible eater. Illus. by Jose Aruego and Ariane Dewey. Four Winds/Macmillan ISBN 0-02-782250-8, 1980. unp. col. ill.
Gregory's parents are very worried because their young son is such a finicky eater. He prefers junk foods such as fruits, vegetables, eggs and milk to the normal diet of tin cans, bottle caps, shirts and buttons. However, a visit to Dr. Ram provides the perfect prescription to solve Gregory's eating problems.
SUBJ: Goats--Fiction./ Diet--Fiction.

Ph-1 K-3/2 $13.45   L   KG489
SHAW, NANCY. Sheep in a jeep. Illus. by Margot Apple. Houghton Mifflin ISBN 0-395-41105-X, 1986. 32p. col. ill.
Piling into a red jeep, a frisky flock of sheep experience a wild, muddy ride with sheep and jeep ending in a heep. Large, softly colored doublespreads capture the many expressions of the sheep

and the actions of this silly but very humorous, very brief tale. Adventures of the sheep are continued in SHEEP ON A SHIP (ISBN 0-395-48160-0, 1989) SHEEP IN A SHOP (ISBN 0-395-53681-2, 1991, available from the NLSBPH on sound recording cassette RC 36515), and SHEEP OUT TO EAT (ISBN 0-395-61128-8, 1992, available from the NLSBPH on sound recording cassette RC 36514).
SUBJ: Stories in rhyme./ Sheep--Fiction.

Ph-2 P-2/2 $14.95   T   KG490
SHEA, PEGI DEITZ. New moon. Illus. by Cathryn Falwell. Boyds Mills ISBN 1-56397-410-X; In Canada: McClelland & Stewart, 1996. unp. col. ill.
Fascinated when her big brother shows her the moon, Vinnie looks for it every night until one day her brother hurries home to show her the moon during the day. Cut-paper illustrations spotlight the warm sibling relationship and the attraction of the moon. The cozy family story could be used to introduce a discussion of the phases of the moon. For multicultural studies.
SUBJ: Moon--Fiction./ Winter--Fiction./ Brothers and sisters--Fiction.

Ph-2 1-3/5 $13.95   T   KG491
SHEEHAN, PATTY. Gwendolyn's gifts. Illus. by Claudia Bumgarner-Kirby. Pelican ISBN 0-88289-845-0, 1991. unp. col. ill.
Queen Gwendolyn is bored with her royal life and having others do everything for her, so she takes a vacation and works sewing, making jewelry, and doing carpentry. Gwendolyn is a modern and likeable heroine who may inspire youngsters to learn to do things for themselves.
SUBJ: Kings, queens, rulers, etc.--Fiction./ Artists--Fiction.

Ph-2 1-3/2 $14.95   L   KG492
SHEFELMAN, JANICE. Peddler's dream. Illus. by Tom Shefelman. Houghton Mifflin ISBN 0-395-60904-6, 1992. 32p. col. ill.
Arriving in America from Lebanon, Solomon works as a peddler. Then through a series of misfortunes and fortunes, he eventually marries his beloved, and together they raise a family and build the store of his dreams. A classic story of the American dream.
SUBJ: Lebanese Americans--Fiction./ Success--Fiction.

Ph-1 1-3/3 $15.99   L   KG493
SHELBY, ANNE. Homeplace. Illus. by Wendy Anderson Halperin. Orchard ISBN 0-531-08732-8, 1995. unp. col. ill.
"Richard Jackson book."
Starting as a log cabin, a house and its accompanying land go through several transformations and generations beginning with the great-great-great-great-grandpa of the young child hearing the story from her grandmother. Decorative and numerous watercolor illustrations detail changing times and family connected through the years by the place they call "home." The cozy design invites readers to linger over the illustrations, looking for small clues about the past.
SUBJ: Genealogy--Fiction./ Family life--Fiction.

Ph-2 1-3/3 $13.99   L   KG494
SHIELDS, CAROL DIGGORY. I am really a princess. Illus. by Paul Meisel. Dutton ISBN 0-525-45138-2, 1993. unp. col. ill.
A true princess would not be expected to do chores, eat lima beans, or go to bed when she is told. A young girl fantasizes about how things will be different when her family realizes she is a real princess. Her fantasy is played out in the humorous illustrations. Youngsters will enjoy this comical retreat from reality.
SUBJ: Princesses--Fiction./ Parent and child--Fiction.

Ph-2 P-1/1 $13.89   L   KG495
SHOWERS, PAUL. Listening walk. Illus. by Aliki. HarperCollins ISBN 0-06-021638-7; In Canada: HarperCollins, c1961, 1991. unp. col. ill.
Spanish edition LOS SONIDOS A MI ALREDEDOR available from Harper Arco Iris (ISBN 0-06-026228-1, 1996).
When a young girl, accompanied by her father, walks her dog, she notices the many sounds that can be heard if you take your time and listen. New cheerful illustrations and the many sounds included in the text will encourage youngsters to pay attention to the sounds around them.
SUBJ: Sound--Fiction./ Fathers and daughters--Fiction./ Spanish language materials.

Ph-1 K-2/2 $14.00   L   KG496
SHUB, ELIZABETH. Seeing is believing. Illus. by Rachel Isadora. Greenwillow ISBN 0-688-13647-8, 1979. 63p. ill. (Greenwillow read-alone).
Tom is a farm boy who lives in County Cork where everyone talks about fairies and elves but no one has ever seen one. Tom does meet up with one of the wee folk and thinks he will get the hidden gold but the clever leprechaun outwits the young boy. When Tom grows older he moves to Cornwall and there one night he has a run-in with

some piskies, those tiny elves who ride through the moors at night.
SUBJ: Leprechauns--Fiction.

Ph-2 1-3/2 $15.93 L KG497
SHUB, ELIZABETH. White stallion. Illus. by Rachel Isadora. Greenwillow ISBN 0-688-01211-6, 1982. unp. ill.
Selectors' Choice, 14th ed.
Available from National Library Service for the Blind and Physically Handicapped in Braille BR05520, and on sound recording cassette RC20193.
In 1845 Gretchen and her family travel West in a Conestoga wagon with a group of friends. Somewhere in Texas, the little girl and Anna, the family mare, are separated from the wagon train. Hopelessly lost they are rescued from a band of wild horses by a magnificent white stallion. Retold from James Frank Dobie's "Tales of the Mustang". Spare text and dramatic illustrations create a suspenseful story with historical background.
SUBJ: Horses--Fiction./ West (U.S.)--Fiction.

Ph-1 K-2/2 $16.00 T KG498
SHULEVITZ, URI. Dawn. Farrar, Straus & Giroux ISBN 0-374-31707-0, 1974. 32p. col. ill.
Under a tree by the lake an old man and his grandson are curled up in their blankets. Slowly the darkness of night lightens and the two awaken, break camp and push off into the water. As their old boat reaches the middle of the lake, day breaks with a spectacular sunrise. Inspired by an old Chinese poem, the spare text is superbly illustrated.
SUBJ: Grandparents--Fiction./ Nature--Fiction.

Ph-2 P-2/2 $3.95 P KG499
SHULEVITZ, URI. Rain, rain rivers. Farrar, Straus & Giroux ISBN 0-374-46195-3, c1969, 1998. unp. col. ill.
From the warmth and safety of her city home a little girl watches the rain and thinks of all the fields, hills, ponds and streams from which the rain rushes on to make rivers, seas and oceans. But the rain will stop and there will be sunshine, puddles to jump and warm mud in which the children can stamp their bare feet. Brief text with beautiful illustrations.
SUBJ: Rain and rainfall--Fiction.

Ph-1 P-1/1 $12.95 L KG500
SIDDALS, MARY MCKENNA. Tell me a season. Illus. by Petra Mathers. Clarion ISBN 0-395-71021-9, 1997. 26p. col. ill.
Colors change with the seasons in the yard of a small house inhabited by two children. The small format, spare text, and watercolor illustrations are just right for beginning readers.
SUBJ: Seasons--Fiction./ Color--Fiction./ Bedtime--Fiction.

Ph-1 P-3 $15.89 L KG501
SIEBERT, DIANE. Train song. Illus. by Mike Wimmer. Crowell/HarperCollins ISBN 0-690-04728-2, 1990. unp. col. ill.
Captures the many sights and sounds of trains as they go clickety-clacking across the country. Richly-hued doublespread paintings draw in the viewer while the rolling, rhyming text preserves the motion and sounds of train travel.
SUBJ: Railroads--Trains--Fiction./ Stories in rhyme.

CE
Ph-2 P-1 $15.89 L KG502
SIEBERT, DIANE. Truck song. Illus. by Byron Barton. Crowell/HarperCollins ISBN 0-690-04411-9, 1984. unp. col. ill.
Read-along kit available from Live Oak (ISBN 0-87499-093-9). 1 hardcover book, 1 sound cassette (6min), $19.95.
Available from National Library Service for the Blind and Physically Handicapped in Braille BR06123.
Live action videocassette available from Pied Piper/AIMS Multimedia Q9991, 1992. 1/2" VHS videocassette color (17min), study guide, $49.95.
Crossing the entire continent is a big yellow truck and its driver. The hills, mountains, farm lands, truck stops, cities and many, many other trucks are pictured in colorful goaches. The text, for which a readability estimate cannot be determined, presents the rhythmic sounds of the trucks, the CB lingo, and the feel of country music.
SUBJ: Stories in rhyme./ Trucks--Fiction.

Ph-2 1-3/3 $14.00 L KG503
SIERRA, JUDY. House that Drac built. Illus. by Will Hillenbrand. Gulliver/Harcourt Brace ISBN 0-15-200015-1; In Canada: Harcourt Brace c/o Canadian Manda, 1995. unp. col. ill.
Manticores, zombies, and fiends haunt the house that Drac built until a group of children dressed for Halloween tame the dreadful monsters. Following the cumulative format of the familiar nursery rhyme, the story and pictures are just creepy enough to delight young listeners. The predictable book will be popular throughout the year.

SUBJ: Haunted houses--Fiction./ Halloween--Fiction./ Nursery rhymes--Adaptations./ Stories in rhyme.

Ph-1 P-2/2 $14.95 L KG504
SILVERMAN, ERICA. Big pumpkin. Illus. by S. D. Schindler. Macmillan ISBN 0-02-782683-X; In Canada: Maxwell Macmillan, 1992. unp. col. ill.
Available from the National Library Service for the Blind and Physically Handicapped on sound recording cassette RC 38028.
A witch grows a huge pumpkin for a pie, but when it's time to pick it, she can't get it to budge. One by one a ghost, a vampire, and a mummy each try without success. A small bat suggests they all pull together, and it works. While not an original story, the seasonal twist and illustrations give it new life. Suitable choice for holiday read-aloud.
SUBJ: Witches--Fiction./ Monsters--Fiction./ Pumpkin--Fiction./ Halloween--Fiction./ Cooperativeness--Fiction.

Ph-2 P-2/2 $15.00 L KG505
SILVERMAN, ERICA. Don't fidget a feather! Illus. by S. D. Schindler. Macmillan ISBN 0-02-782685-6; In Canada: Maxwell Macmillan, 1994. unp. col. ill.
Available from the National Library Service for the Blind and Physically Handicapped on sound recording cassette RC 41969.
Duck and Gander have a series of contests to see who is the champion, but the final contest to see who can hold still the longest almost lands them both in Fox's soup pot. Friendship wins over the pair's pride and rivalry in a humorous story illustrated with pastels.
SUBJ: Competition (Psychology)--Fiction./ Ducks--Fiction./ Geese--Fiction.

Ph-2 K-2/2 $14.95 L KG506
SILVERMAN, ERICA. Gittel's hands. Illus. by Deborah Nourse Lattimore. BridgeWater ISBN 0-8167-3798-3; In Canada: BridgeWater/dist. by Vanwell, 1996. unp. col. ill.
Includes glossary.
Because of Yakov's exaggerated boasting about the skills of his daughter, Gittel, she is assigned impossible tasks by the hay merchant. Gittel's warm heart and generosity capture the attention of the prophet Elijah who appears to assist her. In this RUMPELSTILTSKIN variant, the folkloric story and Chagall-style illustrations highlight Passover traditions. Combine with other RUMPELSTILTSKIN variants, Zemach's DUFFY AND THE DEVIL and Moser's TUCKER PFEFFERCORN.
SUBJ: Elijah (Biblical prophet)--Fiction./ Jews--Europe--Fiction./ Fathers and daughters--Fiction./ Passover--Fiction.

Ph-1 K-1/2 $15.00 L KG507
SIMON, CHARNAN. One happy classroom. Illus. by Rebecca McKillip Thornburgh. Children's Press ISBN 0-516-20318-5; In Canada: Grolier Ltd., 1997. 32p. col. ill. (Rookie reader)
From one happy classroom to ten crunchy apples and back again, readers can count as they follow a busy school day. School is a happy and active place in the watercolor illustrations and easy-to-read text for beginning readers.
SUBJ: Kindergarten--Fiction./ Schools--Fiction./ Counting.

Ph-2 P-1/3 $12.95 T KG508
SIMON, NORMA. Wet world. Illus. by Alexi Natchev. Candlewick ISBN 1-56402-190-4; In Canada: Candlewick/dist. by Douglas & McIntyre, 1995. unp. col. ill.
Outside is wet, but inside is warm in a young girl's description of her rainy day. "Wet" and "warm" cycle through the repetitive, alliterative text for beginning readers to enjoy. The watercolor illustrations appear dripping with water, enhancing the day's description. The ideal book for reading aloud in primary classes on "W" day.
SUBJ: Rain and rainfall--Fiction.

Ph-2 2-3/5 $15.00 L KG509
SINGER, MARILYN. In the palace of the Ocean King. Illus. by Ted Rand. Atheneum ISBN 0-689-31755-7; In Canada: Distican, 1995. unp. col. ill.
Spanish version EN EL PALACIO DEL REY DEL OCEANO available (ISBN 0-689-31983-5, 1995).
Mariana has never been in love and fears nothing but the deep sea until she accompanies her father to the seaside castle of a duke and meets his son, Sylvain. When Sylvain is reported drowned at sea, she realizes her love for him and overcomes her fear to rescue him from the merciless Ocean King. Acrylic illustrations and the clever placement of text on white banners reinforce the romantic quality of this original tale of enchantment.
SUBJ: Fairy tales./ Sea stories./ Spanish language materials.

Ph-2 K-1/1 $11.89 L KG510

SIRACUSA, CATHERINE. Bingo, the best dog in the world. Illus. by Sidney Levitt. HarperCollins ISBN 0-06-025813-6; In Canada: HarperCollins, 1991. 64p. col. ill. (I can read book).

Sam and Stuart trick Bingo into a bath and then get a ride in a police car before entering the dog show. Simply told and illustrated, this story is a winner for new readers.
SUBJ: Dogs--Fiction./ Brothers and sisters--Fiction./ Dog shows--Fiction.

Ph-2 P-2 $15.00 T KG511

SIS, PETER. Going up! A color counting book. Greenwillow ISBN 0-688-08125-8, 1989. unp. col. ill.

Mary gets on the elevator in her apartment house with a bouquet of flowers and on each of the succeeding ten stops another person dressed in a differently colored costume joins her. The watercolor and pen and ink drawings are lively and attractive. An enjoyable introduction to colors and counting.
SUBJ: Elevators--Fiction./ Apartment houses--Fiction./ Counting./ Birthdays--Fiction.

Ph-2 P-2 $12.88 L KG512

SIS, PETER. Waving: a counting book. Greenwillow ISBN 0-688-07160-0, 1988. unp. col. ill.

Standing on a curb, Mary's mother waves for one taxi as two bicyclists wave back. The waving and counting continue along the city street as five mailmen, six police officers, nine girl scouts, thirteen little leaguers are all waving and finally "fifteen taxi drivers waved at everybody waving at them." A friendly counting book.
SUBJ: Counting./ Walking--Fiction.

Ph-1 1-3/2 $14.95 L KG513

SISULU, ELINOR. Day Gogo went to vote: South Africa, April 1994. By Elinor Batezat Sisulu. Illustrated by Sharon Wilson. Little, Brown ISBN 0-316-70267-6; In Canada: Little, Brown, 1996. unp. col. ill.

Includes glossary.
Thembi's great-grandmother, Gogo, insists that she will vote in the first election in which black South Africans can participate. Thembi conveys the historic moment with a child's straightforward wonder. A compelling addition to multicultural studies and discussions of voting rights.
SUBJ: Blacks--South Africa--Fiction./ Voting--Fiction./ South Africa--Fiction./ Great-grandmothers--Fiction.

Ph-2 1-3/2 $14.89 L KG514

SKOFIELD, JAMES. Detective Dinosaur. Illus. by R. W. Alley. HarperCollins ISBN 0-06-024908-0; In Canada: HarperCollins, 1996. 48p. col. ill. (I can read book).

Detective Dinosaur and Officer Pterodactyl solve the mysteries of a missing hat, a squeaking shoe, and the strange noises in a dark alley. Pronunciations are given for the dinosaur names for beginning readers who will enjoy the easy-to-read format, colorful illustrations, and humorous story.
SUBJ: Dinosaurs--Fiction./ Mystery and detective stories.

Ph-1 P-K/2 $14.99 T KG515

SLATE, JOSEPH. Miss Bindergarten gets ready for kindergarten. Illus. by Ashley Wolff. Dutton ISBN 0-525-45446-2; In Canada: McClelland & Stewart, 1996. unp. col. ill.

Run through the alphabet as students prepare for kindergarten and on alternating doublespreads Miss Bindergarten, their teacher, prepares the classroom. Humor and delight fill the pages with animal characters and small playful touches like the price tag still on Miss Bindergarten's new jumper. A first choice for the first day of kindergarten.
SUBJ: Alphabet./ Animals--Fiction./ Kindergarten--Fiction./ First day of school--Fiction./ Schools--Fiction./ Stories in rhyme.

Ph-2 K-2/2 $3.50 P KG516

SLATER, TEDDY. Stay in line. Illus. by Gioia Fiammenghi. Scholastic ISBN 0-590-22713-0; In Canada: Scholastic, 1996. unp. col. ill. (Hello math reader).

"Cartwheel books."
While on a field trip to the zoo, twelve classmates group together in a variety of ways. Sprightly illustrations and the easy-to-read text are the appeal of this introduction to the mathematics of a dozen. Hands-on math activities follow the short story. For interdisciplinary curriculum. (Parents' Shelf).
SUBJ: Zoos--Fiction./ School field trips--Fiction./ Arithmetic--Fiction./ Stories in rhyme.

Ph-2 K-2/2 $15.95 L KG517

SLEPIAN, JAN. Lost moose. Illus. by Ted Lewin. Philomel ISBN 0-399-22749-0; In Canada: Putnam, 1995. unp. col. ill.

When a young moose is separated from its mother and wanders close

to a camp, a young boy mistakes it for one of Santa's reindeer. Opulent watercolor paintings display the beauty of the woods in landscape scenes and the emotion of the encounter in closeups. The references to Santa's reindeer make this a unique selection for the Christmas season which youngsters will enjoy.
SUBJ: Moose--Fiction.

VCR Ph-3 P-2 $30.00 OD KG518

SLIGHTLY SCARY STORIES (Videocassette). Weston Woods PBV004, 1987. 1/2" VHS videocassette color (15min). (Picture book parade).

Eerie sounds and music accent the reading of these slightly scary books which use animation occasionally to visualize action in the story. Good use of zoom and panning of illustrations.
Contents: Keats, Ezra Jack. The trip (5min); Bright, Robert. Georgie (6min); Brown, Ruth. A dark dark tale (4min).
SUBJ: Ghosts--Fiction.

CE Ph-1 P-2/1 $12.89 L KG519

SLOBODKINA, ESPHYR. Caps for sale: a tale of a peddler, some monkeys and their monkey business. HarperCollins ISBN 0-06-025778-4, c1947. unp. col. ill.

Read-along kit available from Live Oak Media (ISBN 0-87499-059-9, 1987). 1 hardback book, 1 sound cassette (9min), guide, $19.95.
Read-along kit available from HarperChildren's Audio (ISBN 0-694-70004-5, 1995). 1 paperback book, 1 sound cassette (7min), $7.95.
Videocassette available from Weston Woods HMPV012V, n.d. 1/2" VHS videocassette color (5min), $49.95
Big book available from HarperTrophy (ISBN 0-06-443313-7, 1996), $19.95.
Spanish version SE VENDEN GORRAS: LA HISTORIA DE UN VENDEDOR AMBULANTE, UNOS MONOS Y SUS TRAVESURAS available from Harper Arco Iris (ISBN 0-06-025330-4, 1995). Read-along kit available from HarperChildren's Audio (ISBN 0-69470-025-8, 1995); 1 paperback book, 1 sound cassette (7min), $10.95.
The monkeys steal the peddler's caps while he is asleep. If the monkeys had not imitated him, they would still be wearing his caps!
SUBJ: Monkeys--Fiction./ Peddlers and peddling--Fiction./ Hats--Fiction./ Spanish language materials.

Ph-2 K-2/2 $15.00 T KG520

SMALL, DAVID. Fenwick's suit. Farrar Straus Giroux ISBN 0-374-32298-8; In Canada: HarperCollins, 1996. unp. col. ill.

Fenwick hopes a new suit will attract attention and friends at the office, but the suit doesn't need Fenwick, and it goes to the office without him. A slapstick chase follows until Fenwick ends up being worn in the pocket of the suit, and the story unravels from there. The flamboyant yellow suit depicted in the illustrations carries the silly story.
SUBJ: Clothing and dress--Fiction.

Ph-2 1-3/5 $16.00 T KG521

SMALL, DAVID. Hoover's bride. Crown ISBN 0-517-59707-1, 1995. unp. col. ill.

Rescued from a mountain of dust by a vacuum machine named Elektra, Hoover marries the machine in gratitude. On their honeymoon, Elektra runs off with a lawn mower, and Hoover falls in love with the woman who was married to the lawn mower. The wacky story is conveyed in rhyme and cartoon-like illustrations to tickle the funnybones of those with a taste for the unusual.
SUBJ: Vacuum cleaners--Fiction./ Marriage--Fiction./ Stories in rhyme./ Humorous stories.

CE Ph-1 P-2/6 $12.95 L KG522

SMALL, DAVID. Imogene's antlers. Crown ISBN 0-517-55564-6, 1985. 32p. col. ill.

Read-along kit available from Live Oak Media (0-874-99323-7, 1994). 1 paperback book, 1 sound cassette (5min), $22.95.
Surprised but nonchalant, Imogene awakens to find a large set of antlers growing from her head. They create some difficulty in dressing and going through doors. Her pompous mother repeatedly faints away, but the cook and maid find them quite useful. Imogene is almost disappointed next morning to find the antlers gone, but she does have another surprise. Both story and pictures are hilarious, but there is a plug for accepting individual differences.
SUBJ: Humorous stories.

Ph-1 1-3/4 $12.00 T KG523

SMALL, DAVID. Ruby Mae has something to say. Crown ISBN 0-517-58248-1, 1992. unp. col. ill.

Nada, Texas is a small town, but the World Headquarters for Universal Peace and Understanding is located there in the home of Ruby Mae Foote. Ruby Mae dreams of bringing her message to the United States, but she can't speak without mixing up words. Her nephew, Billy Bob, creates an amazing hat that allows Ruby Mae to

rise to fame, but on the day she is scheduled to speak at the United Nations, disaster strikes. A truly funny and creative story with an important message.
SUBJ: Speech disorders--Fiction./ Inventions--Fiction./ United Nations--Fiction.

Ph-2 2-3/3 $14.00   L   KG524
SMITH, LANE. Glasses: who needs 'em?. Viking ISBN 0-670-84160-9; In Canada: Penguin, 1991. unp. col. ill.
When a young fellow doesn't want to wear glasses, his wacky doctor describes the many people, animals, and vegetables who (he claims) wear spectacles. In an irreverant look at eyewear, the endpapers are antique optical advertisements, and even the barcode on the back cover becomes part of the statement. Youngsters who need glasses will enjoy viewing them through the offbeat lens of this book.
SUBJ: Eyeglasses--Fiction.

Ph-1 K-3/6 $16.95   T   KG525
SNYDER, DIANNE. Boy of the three-year nap. Illus. by Allen Say. Houghton Mifflin ISBN 0-395-44090-4, 1988. 32p. col. ill.
Caldecott Honor Book, 1989.
Spanish version SIESTA DE TRES ANOS available from Santillana (ISBN 1-56014-182-4, 1995).
Taro, the lazy son of a hard working seamstress, tricks a rich rice merchant and marries his young daughter. The trick backfires and lazy Taro now must work very hard for his riches, but to his surprise, he is also happy. Traditional Japanese, black-bordered paintings contribute a strong Asian flavor to the well-written story based on a Japanese folk tale. For multicultural studies.
SUBJ: Laziness--Fiction./ Japan--Fiction./ Spanish language materials.

Ph-2 1-4/4 $14.93   L   KG526
SORENSEN, HENRI. New Hope. Lothrop, Lee & Shepard ISBN 0-688-13926-4, 1995. unp. col. ill.
When Jimmy asks his grandfather about the statue in the town of New Hope, his grandfather tells him the story of Lars Jensen. After bringing his family to America from Denmark, Lars Jensen started the town of New Hope when a broken axle forced him to stop his trek across the Great Plains. The story within a story relates a slice of American history, and the acrylic illustrations show the changing landscape.
SUBJ: Frontier and pioneer life--Fiction./ Family life--Fiction./ United States--Emigration and immigration--Fiction.

Ph-1 1-3/5 $6.95   P   KG527
SOTO, GARY. Chato's kitchen. Illus. by Susan Guevara. Putnam ISBN 0-698-11600-3; In Canada: Putnam, c1995, 1997. unp. col. ill.
Includes glossary.
Available from the National Library Service for the Blind and Physically Handicapped on sound recording cassette RC 41971. Spanish version CHATO Y SU CENA available (ISBN 0-689-11601-1).
Expecting to enjoy the mouse family as part of the Latin American feast he has prepared, Chato, a cool cat, is surprised when one of the guests is a dog. The dialog and menu are spiced with Spanish words often understood from the context though a glossary is included. The personalities of the characters emanate from the expressive illustrations rich in color and detail. For multicultural studies.
SUBJ: Cats--Fiction./ Mice--Fiction./ Los Angeles (Calif.)--Fiction./ Spanish language materials.

Ph-2 K-2/2 $15.95   L   KG528
SOTO, GARY. Old man and his door. Illus. by Joe Cepeda. Putnam ISBN 0-399-22700-8; In Canada: BeJo Sales, 1996. unp. col. ill.
Includes glossary.
El viejo, an old man, hears his wife wrong and brings a door, la puerta, instead of a pig, el puerco, to a barbecue. Along the way, the door serves several purposes as a shield, a raft, and a ramp; and the old man arrives at the barbecue with honey, a fish, and watermelons. Spanish world are sprinkled throughout the text. Youngsters learning a new language will appreciate the confusion. For multicultural studies.
SUBJ: Doors--Fiction./ Parties--Fiction.

Ph-1 K-2/2 $15.95   L   KG529
SOTO, GARY. Snapshots from the wedding. Illus. by Stephanie Garcia. Putnam ISBN 0-399-22808-X; In Canada: Putnam, 1997. unp. col. ill.
Includes glossary.
Maya, the flower girl, describes the wedding of Isabel and Rafael with a cast that includes the wedding party, a mariachi band, and extended family. Stunning three dimensional dioramas featuring sculpy clay figures, lots of lace, flowers, and other found objects form a remarkable wedding album. Young children attending or participating in a wedding will especially enjoy this selection which is appropriate

for units on the family. May inspire three-dimensional art activities. For multicultural studies.
SUBJ: Weddings--Fiction./ Mexican Americans--Fiction.

Ph-1 K-3/3 $15.95   L   KG530
SOTO, GARY. Too many tamales. Illus. by Ed Martinez. Putnam ISBN 0-399-22146-8; In Canada: Putnam, 1993. unp. col. ill.
When she finds her mother's diamond ring on the counter, Maria can't resist putting it on her finger. Helping to prepare tamales for the family's Christmas celebration, she loses the ring in the batter and convinces her cousins to help her eat all of the tamales in search of the missing ring. A Mexican-American family's celebration of the holiday is depicted in this amusing story for multicultural studies.
SUBJ: Christmas--Fiction./ Mexican Americans--Fiction./ Rings--Fiction.

Ph-1 P-2 $12.99   L   KG531
SPIER, PETER. Dreams. Doubleday ISBN 0-385-19337-8, 1986. unp col illus.
After romping with their dogs, two children relax on a grassy slope and imagine many exciting things in the moving clouds. Almost wordless.
SUBJ: Imagination--Fiction./ Clouds--Fiction.

Ph-1 P-2/4 $16.00   T   KG532
SPIER, PETER. Peter Spier's circus! Doubleday ISBN 0-385-41969-4; In Canada: Bantam, 1992. unp. col. ill.
Detailed illustrations and a brief, descriptive text show the many activities behind-the-scenes and during the performance of a circus. Youngsters will be fascinated with the many goings-on especially when the circus is in town.
SUBJ: Circus--Fiction.

Ph-2 1-2/1 $14.98   L   KG533
SPIRN, MICHELE. Know-Nothing birthday. By Michele Sobel Spirn. Illus. by R. W. Alley. HarperCollins ISBN 0-06-027274-0; In Canada: HarperCollins, 1997. 48p. col. ill. (I can read book).
Boris thinks his friends have forgotten his birthday, but the Know-Nothings are preparing in their own foolish ways. Slapstick silliness in story and illustrations will appeal to beginning readers.
SUBJ: Birthdays--Fiction./ Friendship--Fiction./ Humorous stories.

Ph-2 K-2/1 $11.99   T   KG534
SPOHN, KATE. Dog and Cat shake a leg. Viking ISBN 0-670-86758-6; In Canada: Penguin, 1996. 31p. col. ill. (Viking easy-to-read).
Dog and Cat are best friends who enjoy doing things together--dancing, buying hats, reading, and rollerblading. Small watercolor illustrations spotlight the simple stories. Suggested where additional titles are needed to meet the needs of beginning readers.
SUBJ: Dogs--Fiction./ Cats--Fiction./ Friendship--Fiction.

Ph-1 K-2/3 $18.99   L   KG535
STANDIFORD, NATALIE. Astronauts are sleeping. Illus. by Allen Garns. Knopf ISBN 0-679-96999-3; In Canada: Random House, 1996. unp. col. ill.
"Borzoi book."
Drifting in space, astronauts are dreaming not of faraway planets but of Earth's beaches, forests, homes, and families. Lush pastel illustrations and rhyming questions depict astronauts floating in space past the planets and then through scenes of home. A celebration of the planets especially our Earth.
SUBJ: Astronauts--Fiction./ Dreams--Fiction./ Stories in rhyme.

Ph-1 2-3/2 $11.95   L   KG536
STANEK, MURIEL. All alone after school. Illus. by Ruth Rosner. Whitman ISBN 0-8075-0278-2; In Canada: General, 1985. unp. col. ill. (Concept book).
Selectors' Choice, 15th ed.
Fortified by a practice run and armed with a lucky white stone, a list of rules and some important phone numbers, Josh meets the challenge of staying alone until his mother gets home from work each day. A pleasant story providing important information for the many, many latchkey children.
SUBJ: Self-reliance--Fiction./ Mothers--Employment--Fiction.

Ph-1 2-5/3 $14.93   L   KG537
STANLEY, DIANE. Rumpelstiltskin's daughter. Morrow ISBN 0-688-14328-8; In Canada: Hearst Book Group, 1997. unp. col. ill.
The Miller's daughter marries Rumpelstiltskin which is only the first twist in this take-off from the familiar fairy tale. Their daughter grows up and returns to the king's castle to correct the social wrongs of the king who has squandered all the kingdom's resources on himself. Full-color illustrations spoof more than the story as the king's face appears in reproductions of famous paintings throughout the castle, his dog wears a matching, color-coordinated ribbon, and his guard

clones gnash teeth and wield swords. Older readers will most appreciate the humorous and political nuances.
SUBJ: Fairy tales--Parodies, imitations, etc./ Greed--Fiction.

Ph-1 1-3/4 $15.95 L KG538
STANLEY, DIANE. Saving Sweetness. Illus. by G. Brian Karas. Putnam ISBN 0-399-22645-1; In Canada: Putnam, 1996. unp. col. ill.
Rescuing the runaway orphan Sweetness from the dangers of the desert, a kindly sheriff finally gets the message and adopts the darling as well as the other seven orphans. Rollicking and fun for reading aloud, the text is accompanied by desert-toned illustrations that blend photographs with gouache, acrylic, and pencil.
SUBJ: Orphans--Fiction./ West (U.S.)--Fiction./ Humorous stories.

CE Ph-1 1-3/5 $17.00 T KG539
STEIG, WILLIAM. Amazing bone. Farrar, Straus & Giroux ISBN 0-374-30248-0, 1976. 32p. col. ill.
Caldecott Honor Book.
Read-along kit available from Weston Woods PBC301, c1986, 1993. 1 paperback book, 1 sound cassette (28min), $12.95. Side one with page turn signal, side two without signal.
Available from National Library Service for the Blind and Physically Handicapped on sound recording cassette RC11455.
Videocassette available from Weston Woods HMPV301V, 1986. 1/2" VHS videocassette color (11min), $49.95.
Available in Spanish EL HUESO PRODIGIOSO (Mirasol ISBN 0-374-33504-4, 1993). $17.00.
On a beautiful spring day Pearl, the pig, is dallying in the forest when she finds a bone that talks to her. She picks it up and starts home thinking how surprised her parents will be. But she meets highway robbers and a fox; the amazing bone deals with these threats in an amazing way.
SUBJ: Supernatural--Fiction./ Pigs--Fiction./ Spring--Fiction.

CE Ph-1 1-3/7 $17.00 T KG540
STEIG, WILLIAM. Amos and Boris. Farrar, Straus & Giroux ISBN 0-374-30278-2; In Canada: HarperCollins, c1971. unp. col. ill.
Selectors' Choice, 7th ed.
Spanish version available AMOS Y BORIS (ISBN 0-374-30279-0, 1992).
Amos, a young mouse, falls off his boat while adventuring on the high seas. Just as his strength is giving out, a huge head bursts through the surface of the water and Amos is saved by Boris, a whale. The two mammals develop a deep admiration for one another and become fast friends. As they part, Amos promises to give help to Boris if the whale ever needs it. Strangely enough the time does come when the small mouse saves the huge whale.
SUBJ: Mice--Fiction./ Whales--Fiction./ Friendship--Fiction./ Spanish language materials.

CE Ph-1 K-3/3 $17.00 T KG541
STEIG, WILLIAM. Brave Irene. Farrar, Straus & Giroux ISBN 0-374-30947-7; In Canada: HarperCollins, 1986. unp. col. ill.
Animated videocassette available from Weston Woods HMPV331V, 1990. 1/2" VHS videocassette color (12min), $49.95.
Available from National Library Service for the Blind and Physically Handicapped on sound recording cassette RC25669.
Available in Spanish: IRENE, LA VALIENTE (ISBN 0-374-30948-5, 1991).
Since her seamstress mother is too sick to go out, Irene struggles through darkness, a raging blizzard, bitter cold and deep snow and delivers the duchess' beautiful new gown in time for the grand ball. For her bravery and determination she receives exciting rewards as well as medical help for her mother. The illustrations (almost full-paged) are very effective in picturing the fierceness of the storm and the persistence of sturdy little Irene.
SUBJ: Courage--Fiction./ Mothers and daughters--Fiction./ Spanish language materials.

CE Ph-1 P-3/4 $16.00 T KG542
STEIG, WILLIAM. Doctor De Soto. Farrar, Straus & Giroux ISBN 0-374-31803-4; In Canada: McGraw-Hill Ryerson, 1982. unp. col. ill.
Newbery Honor book.
Talking book read by Ian Thompson from Weston Woods, LTR284C. 1 sound cassette (9min) $8.95.
Read-along kit available from Weston Woods HPRA284. 1 hardcover book, 1 sound cassette (9min), $12.95.
Available on 1/2" VHS videocassette color (10min) from Weston Woods HMPV284V, $49.95.
Available in Spanish on videocassette, Weston Woods V284SP. 1/2" VHS videocassette color (10min), $60.00.
Available from National Library Service for the Blind and Physically Handicapped in Braille BR 05462.
Available in Spanish DOCTOR DE SOTO (Santillana ISBN 84-372-

6616-5, 1991).
Doctor and Mrs. De Soto, a pair of mice, are very successful dentists in spite of their small size. Treating large animals creates quite a challenge and requires unusual equipment. Cats and other dangerous animals are refused treatment until in a moment of compassion they agree to relieve the excruciating pain caused by Mr. Fox's decaying bicuspid. This sympathetic action proves almost fatal, but the clever De Sotos manage to carry out their professional duties and outwit the scheming animal as well.
And in DOCTOR DE SOTO GOES TO AFRICA (ISBN 0-06-205003-6, 1992); also available from HarperChildren's Audio on sound cassette (ISBN 0-69470-003-7, 1995); and also available from the National Library Service for the Blind and Physically Handicapped on sound recording cassette RC 38143, the De Sotos are called to Africa to help an ailing elephant with a toothache.
SUBJ: Dentists--Fiction./ Mice--Fiction.

Ph-2 K-3/6 $4.95 P KG543
STEIG, WILLIAM. Farmer Palmer's wagon ride. Farrar, Straus & Giroux ISBN 0-374-42268-0; In Canada: HarperCollins, c1974, 1992. unp. col. ill.
"Sunburst book."
Farmer Palmer (a pig) and Ebenezer, his hired hand (strongly resembling Sylvester the donkey) uneventfully take a load of vegetables to market. The trip home, however, is filled with calamities, and only by persistence and determination does Farmer Palmer arrive home along with Ebenezer, a tool chest, a harmonica, a camera, and a tripod, all on one bicycle.
SUBJ: Humorous stories./ Pigs--Fiction./ Donkeys--Fiction.

CE Ph-1 K-2/6 $14.00 L KG544
STEIG, WILLIAM. Sylvester and the magic pebble. Simon & Schuster ISBN 0-671-66154-X, c1969, 1988. unp. col. ill.
Caldecott Medal Award.
Also available in Spanish, SILVESTRE Y LA PIEDRECITA MAGICA, Lectorum (ISBN 0-9625162-0-1), 1990.
Spanish version read-along kit SILVESTRE Y LA PIEDRECITA MAGICA available from Live Oak Media (ISBN 0-87499-272-9, 1992) 1 hardback book, 1 sound cassette, (21min), $19.95.
Sylvester Duncan, a young donkey, finds a red, shiny pebble with extraordinary powers. When he touches the magic pebble, his wishes come true. Hurrying home to share his good fortune with his family, Sylvester meets a vicious lion. In a panic he wishes he were a rock; the magic works. Unfortunately, Sylvester is separated from the wonderful, red pebble and seems destined to remain a large boulder on Strawberry Hill.
SUBJ: Donkeys--Fiction./ Magic--Fiction./ Spanish language materials.

VCR Ph-1 K-2 $60.00 OD KG545
STEIG, WILLIAM. Sylvester and the magic pebble (Videocassette).
Weston Woods VC352V, 1992. 1/2" VHS videocassette color (10min).
ALA notable video, 1994.
Sylvester Duncan, a young donkey, finds a red, shiny pebble with extraordinary powers. When he touches the magic pebble, his wishes come true. Hurrying home to share his good fortune with his family, Sylvester meets a vicious lion. In a panic he wishes he were a rock; the magic works. Unfortunately, Sylvester is separated from the wonderful, red pebble and seems destined to remain a large boulder on Strawberry Hill. Steig's classic is enhanced by expert animation and an original musical score in this video version.
SUBJ: Donkeys--Fiction./ Magic--Fiction.

Ph-2 P-1/2 $13.95 T KG546
STEIG, WILLIAM. Toby, where are you? Illus. by Teryl Euvremer. HarperCollins ISBN 0-06-205082-6; In Canada: HarperCollins, 1997. unp. col. ill.
"Michael di Capua books."
As Toby's parents search everywhere for him, he is successfully hidden, but visible to careful viewers. Beginning readers will delight in their success with the text and search for Toby.
SUBJ: Hide-and-seek--Fiction./ Animals--Fiction.

Ph-1 2-5/6 $14.89 L KG547
STEIG, WILLIAM. Toy brother. HarperCollins ISBN 0-06-205079-6; In Canada: HarperCollins, 1996. unp. col. ill.
"Michael di Capua books."
Yorick has a typical older sibling's disdain for his younger brother, Charles. Then Yorick creates a potion in their alchemist father's lab that shrinks Yorick to peanut size. Charles must protect his brother while they try to concoct an antidote. Familiar sibling rivalries, humor, and alchemy abound in the clever story and wry illustrations.
SUBJ: Brothers--Fiction./ Sibling rivalry--Fiction./ Magic--Fiction.

VCR Ph-1 1-3 $90.00 OD KG548
STEIG, WILLIAM. William Steig library (Videocassette). Weston Woods HMPV499V ISBN 0-78820-703-2, 1995. 1/2" VHS videocassette color.
Includes teacher's guide.
Includes public performance rights.
Features four of the author's popular stories with outstanding narration, including John Lithgow reading two of the stories, and lively music. The short visit with the author at the end extends the usefulness of the collection for author and illustrator units.
Contents: Sylvester and the magic pebble (11min); The amazing bone (11min); Doctor De Soto (10min); Brave Irene (12min); Getting to know William Steig (8min).
SUBJ: Humorous stories./ Steig, William.

Ph-1 1-3/6 $15.00 T KG549
STEIG, WILLIAM. Zeke Pippin. HarperCollins ISBN 0-06-205076-1; In Canada: HarperCollins, 1994. unp. col. ill.
"Michael di Capua books."
Zeke, a pig, finds a harmonica. Everytime he plays it for his family, they fall asleep, so he runs away from home. The harmonica has an unusual magic that gets Zeke both in and out of a lot of trouble until he finally makes it back home. The animals are always in character whether as villainous dogs or a grieving family of pigs in the watercolor and pen illustratons. Many elements common to the author's work are incorporated, including his hallmark humor and choice language.
SUBJ: Pigs--Fiction./ Harmonica--Fiction./ Runaways--Fiction.

CDR Ph-1 K-3 $49.95 OD KG550
STELLALUNA (CD-ROM). Random House/Broderbund ISBN 1-57135-185-X, 1996. 1 CD-ROM color, 1 paperback book. (Living books).
Includes user's guide and troubleshooting guide.
System requirements: Windows 3.1+ or Windows 95; IBM or compatible 486SX or higher; 8MB RAM for Windows 3.1+ and Windows 95; double-speed CD-ROM drive; Super VGA (640x480, 256 colors); Sound Blaster or SB Pro and 100% compatible sound cards; mouse.
System requirements: Macintosh System 7.0 or higher; IIci, LCIII, Performa 400, or higher; 8MB RAM for Macintosh and PowerMac; double-speed CD-ROM drive; 256 color monitor.
Product (ISBN 1-57135-185-X) runs on either Windows or Macintosh compatible hardware.
Another Living Books creation, this story of a young bat separated from her mother, raised by birds, and finally reunited with her mother will have wide appeal. The excellent animations and African landscapes add yet another dimension to the story. A bat quiz, which provides an additional science lesson, is also included.
SUBJ: Bats--Fiction--Software./ Software--Bats--Fiction./ Birds--Fiction-Software./ Software--Birds--Fiction./ Interactive media.

Ph-2 P-K $13.93 L KG551
STEPTOE, JOHN. Baby says. Lothrop, Lee & Shepard ISBN 0-688-07424-3, 1988. unp. col. ill.
Although frequently annoyed by the baby's actions, an older brother shows patience, warmth and love as he plays with the busy, younger child. Appealing, softly shaded, full paged pictures of the two young black children extend an almost wordless text. For multicultural studies.
SUBJ: Brothers--Fiction./ Babies--Fiction./ Afro-Americans--Fiction.

CE Ph-1 K-3/5 $15.93 L KG552
STEPTOE, JOHN. Mufaro's beautiful daughters: an African tale. Lothrop, Lee & Shepard ISBN 0-688-04046-2, 1987. unp. col. ill.
Caldecott Honor Book.
Coretta Scott King Award.
Selectors' Choice, 16th ed.
Unanimated 1/2" VHS iconographic videocassette color (15min) available from Weston Woods HMPV334V, 1988, $49.95.
Mufaro, who lives in a small African village, has two beautiful daughters. Manyara is clever, strong and beautiful, but also aggresive, bad tempered, and greedy while Nyasha is gentle, kind and retiring. The Great King from the city wants to choose a bride from the most worthy and beautiful daughters in the land. Whom will he choose; will it be Manyara, who gets there first, or will it be Nyasha, who befriends a small snake in her garden and stops on the way to the city to share her food with a hungry child and an old woman? Dramatic paintings with minute details of stone work, brick work, pottery, baskets, cloth, fauna and flora, and facial features of the human characters illustrate this tale inspired by an African folktale.
SUBJ: Africa--Fiction./ Pride and vanity--Fiction.

Ph-1 K-3/3 $12.89 L KG553
STEPTOE, JOHN. Stevie. HarperCollins ISBN 0-06-025764-4, c1969. unp. col. ill.

Spanish version STEVIE available from Harper Arco Iris (ISBN 0-06-027038-1, 1996).
Available from National Library Service for the Blind and Physically Handicapped as talking book TB03225.
That old crybaby Stevie is a real pest when he moves in with Robert's family, because his own Mother works. He spoils everything for Robert. He tags after Robert and his friends, breaks Robert's toys, and worst of all, Robert's "Momma never says nothin to him." What a relief when Stevie's parents say they are moving and take Stevie away for good. But much to his surprise, Robert is lonesome and decides that maybe Stevie wasn't so bad after all. In fact "He was a nice little guy. He was kinda like a little brother. Little Stevie." For multicultural studies.
SUBJ: Friendship--Fiction./ Afro-Americans--Fiction./ Spanish language materials.

CE Ph-2 1-3/3 $14.95 T KG554
STEVENS, JAN ROMERO. Carlos and the skunk./Carlos y el zorrillo. Illus. by Jeanne Arnold. Rising Moon ISBN 0-87358-591-7, 1997. unp. col. ill.
When Carlos is sprayed by a skunk, he tries to rid himself of the odor, but he forgets about his shoes. Then everyone must evacuate the church because of the smell. Based on a true incident, the humorous story has a strong sense of place conveyed in a bilingual text and desert illustrations. For multicultural studies.
SUBJ: Skunks--Fiction./ Farm life--New Mexico--Fiction./ New Mexico--Fiction./ Spanish language materials./ Bilingual materials--Spanish.

CE Ph-2 K-2/2 $15.95 L KG555
STEVENS, JANET. Princess and the pea. Holiday House ISBN 0-8234-0442-0, 1982. unp. col. ill.
Read-along kit available from Live Oak Media (ISBN 0-87499-352-0, 1996). 1 paperback book, 1 sound cassette (8min), $14.95.
An adaptation of Hans Christian Andersen's classic tale with a new twist. Preposterous perhaps but hilarious too, due to the very amusing illustrations of the many animals who are the main characters.
SUBJ: Fairy tales--Parodies, imitations, etc./ Princesses--Fiction.

Ph-2 P-1/2 $14.89 L KG556
STEVENSON, HARVEY. Grandpa's house. Hyperion ISBN 1-56282-589-5, 1994. unp. col. ill.
Woody and Grandpa are inseparable friends during vacation as they canoe, pick raspberries, and enjoy each other's company. The friendship shared across the generations is depicted in the lighthearted text and joyful illustrations. A warm, intergenerational story suitable for beginning readers.
SUBJ: Grandfathers--Fiction.

Ph-2 1-3/2 $14.93 L KG557
STEVENSON, JAMES. All aboard! Greenwillow ISBN 0-688-12439-9, 1995. unp. col. ill.
On the way to New York for the 1939 World's Fair, Hubie boards the wrong train and begins a series of adventures finally parachuting into the fair from a plane flown by the famous aviatrix, Miss Betty Beagle. Cartoon illustrations complete with speech bubbles invite the reader to follow Hubie on his escapades.
SUBJ: Mice--Fiction./ Railroads--Fiction./ Adventure and adventurers-Fiction.

CE Ph-1 K-3/4 $3.95 P KG558
STEVENSON, JAMES. Could be worse. Greenwillow ISBN 0-688-07035-3, c1977, 1987. 32p. col. ill.
Mary Ann and Louie think Grandpa's life dull and uneventful and his usual comment "could be worse" just plain boring. One morning, however, Grandpa surprises the pair with a tall, tall tale of adventure to which Mary Ann and Louie surprisingly respond "Could be worse".
Grandpa amazes Mary Ann and Louie with more tall tales in THAT TERRIBLE HALLOWEEN NIGHT (ISBN 0-688-80281-8, 1980); WE CAN'T SLEEP (ISBN 0-688-01214-0, 1982, OPC); GREAT BIG ESPECIALLY BEAUTIFUL EASTER EGG (ISBN 0-688-01791-6, 1983, OPC); and WHAT'S UNDER MY BED (ISBN 0-688-02327-4, 1983) (1/2" VHS videocassette from Weston Woods VCV299 (8min), $60.00). In GRANDPA'S TOO-GOOD GARDEN (ISBN 0-688-08486-9, 1989, OPC) he describes the problems he and Uncle Wainey had after they grew huge vegetables.
SUBJ: Dreams--Fiction./ Grandfathers--Fiction./ Humorous stories.

Ph-2 1-3/3 $14.00 T KG559
STEVENSON, JAMES. Flying Acorns. Greenwillow ISBN 0-688-11418-0, 1993. unp. col. ill.
The Flying Acorns are three squirrels who can't quite get their acrobatic act together for the circus, but they all end up in the circus

in some unanticipated acts. Humor abounds in this cartoon format.
SUBJ: Acrobats--Fiction./ Squirrels--Fiction.

Ph-2 P-2/2 $13.93   L   KG560
STEVENSON, JAMES. Fried feathers for Thanksgiving. Greenwillow ISBN 0-688-06676-3, 1986. unp. col. ill.
Plotting how to have Thanksgiving dinner without all the work Lavina and Dolores, two witches, try to trick young witch Emma and her animal friends. The tables are turned in this fun-filled story in Stevenson's usual cartoon style.
SUBJ: Thanksgiving Day--Fiction./ Witches--Fiction.

Ph-1 1-3/2 $14.93   L   KG561
STEVENSON, JAMES. Mud Flat mystery. Greenwillow ISBN 0-688-14966-9; In Canada: Hearst Book Group, 1997. 56p. col. ill.
A box is delivered to Duncan's house while he is away on vacation, and the residents of Mud Flat want to solve the mystery. The short chapters are filled with comedy and droll watercolor illustrations.
SUBJ: Boxes--Fiction./ Curiosity--Fiction.

Ph-2 1-3/2 $14.63   L   KG562
STEVENSON, JAMES. Mud Flat Olympics. Greenwillow ISBN 0-688-12924-2, 1994. 56p. col. ill.
Available from the National Library Service for the Blind and Physically Handicapped on sound recording cassette RC 42055. The contestants in the Mud Flat Olympics are all animals, and the events include the All-Snail High Hurdles, Smelliest Skunk, and The River-cross Freestyle. The events are unusual, the judging unconventional, and the humor abundant in the short vignettes of this transitional reader. Fun to read at any time, but especially during Olympics seasons.
SUBJ: Animals--Fiction./ Games--Fiction.

Ph-2 K-2/1 $12.88   L   KG563
STEVENSON, JAMES. National worm day. Greenwillow ISBN 0-688-08772-8, 1990. 40p. col. ill.
Three hilarious short stories interrelate the adventures of Herbie the worm, Amelia the snail, and Rupert the rhinoceros. The fey watercolor and pen and ink illustrations capture the silliness and sheer fun of the stories.
SUBJ: Animals--Fiction./ Humorous stories.

CE   Ph-1 K-2/2 $13.88   L   KG564
STEVENSON, JAMES. Night after Christmas. Greenwillow ISBN 0-688-00548-9, 1981. unp. col. ill.
Annie, a doll, and Teddy, a toy bear, are thrown out with the garbage when the kids that own them get new, more sophisticated Christmas toys. But soon these old toys are rescued by Chauncey, a street-wise stray dog, who uses an ingenious plan for getting new homes and owners for Annie and Teddy. Simple, well told and appealingly illustrated.
SUBJ: Teddy bears--Fiction./ Dolls--Fiction./ Toys--Fiction./ Spanish language materials.

Ph-2 P-2/2 $14.93   L   KG565
STEVENSON, JAMES. Oldest elf. Greenwillow ISBN 0-688-13756-3, 1996. unp. col. ill.
Elwyn, the oldest elf, almost misses Christmas because he doesn't finish before Santa has left. Blitzen, a retired reindeer, decides he has one flight left in him, and the two take off to deliver presents. The pleasant story with a large format is suitable for reading aloud during holiday storytimes.
SUBJ: Christmas--Fiction./ Santa Claus--Fiction./ Elves--Fiction.

Ph-2 P-K/2 $13.93   L   KG566
STEVENSON, JAMES. Rolling Rose. Greenwillow ISBN 0-688-10675-7, 1992. unp. col. ill.
Available from the National Library Service for the Blind and Physically Handicapped on sound recording cassette RC 39336. Baby Rose rolls in her walker right out the door and down the street where a parade of babies in walkers join her as they roll out of town. Youngsters with small siblings will enjoy the adventures of Rose in her walker in this tall tale.
SUBJ: Babies--Fiction.

Ph-1 K-3/3 $14.93   L   KG567
STEVENSON, JAMES. Sea View Hotel. Greenwillow ISBN 0-688-13470-X, c1978, 1994. unp. col. ill.
Alf, a fascinating handyman with lots of interesting hobbies, saves Hubert from an absolutely boring two weeks at a quiet, all adult, victorian, seaside, resort hotel.
SUBJ: Summer resorts--Fiction./ Vacations--Fiction./ Animals--Fiction./ Cartoons and comics.

Ph-2 1-3/2 $14.93   L   KG568
STEVENSON, JAMES. Village full of valentines. Greenwillow ISBN 0-688-13603-6, 1995. 40p. col. ill.
The animals who live in the village each have their particular problems and solutions for making and giving valentines to their friends. Short chapters are loosely connected and illustrated with small watercolor and pen art. Use the amusing vignettes for reading aloud for the holiday.
SUBJ: Valentines--Fiction./ Valentine's Day--Fiction.

Ph-1 P-3/2 $12.88   L   KG569
STEVENSON, JAMES. We hate rain! Greenwillow ISBN 0-688-07787-0, 1988. unp. col. ill.
Complaining because two days of continuous rain have spoiled their play, Mary Ann and Louie have a change of viewpoint when Grandpa tells of the great month long rain he and little brother Wainey endured as water filled their house including the attic. Another hilarious tall tale about this familiar trio.
SUBJ: Rain and rainfall--Fiction./ Grandfathers--Fiction.

Ph-2 K-3/4 $13.93   L   KG570
STEVENSON, JAMES. Worst person in the world. Greenwillow ISBN 0-688-84127-9, c1978. unp. col. ill.
The worst person in the world lived all alone in a messy uncomfortable house surrounded by weeds, poison ivy, and signs saying "GO AWAY" and "KEEP OUT." One day Mr. Worst met the ugliest thing in the world. This strange creature though called "Mr. Ugly" had a friendly, outgoing personality, and soon even Mr. Worst had an enormous change in his life-style.
In THE WORST PERSON'S CHRISTMAS (ISBN 0-688-10211-5, 1992, OPC) the worst person in the world is back, and he even makes Scrooge look like a nice fellow.
What could be worse for the worst person in the world than having his great-nephew come for a visit in WORSE THAN THE WORST (ISBN 0-688-12250-7, 1994).
In THE WORST GOES SOUTH (ISBN 0-688-13060-7, 1995) a trip to Florida to escape his town's harvest festival includes an unexpected surprise for the worst.
SUBJ: Friendship--Fiction.

Ph-1 K-3/2 $15.00   T   KG571
STEWART, SARAH. Gardener. Illus. by David Small. Farrar Straus Giroux ISBN 0-374-32517-0; In Canada: HarperCollins, 1997. unp. col. ill.
Selectors' Choice, 21st ed.
When Lydia must go to the city to live with her cantankerous Uncle Jim, she is determined to make him smile as she cultivates a garden on the rooftop. The text consists entirely of Lydia's letters, but the flourishing Lydia and her flowers blossom in the illustrations.
SUBJ: Gardening--Fiction./ Letters--Fiction.

CE   Ph-1 K-3/3 $15.00   T   KG572
STEWART, SARAH. Library. Illus. by David Small. Farrar Straus Giroux ISBN 0-374-34388-8; In Canada: HarperCollins, 1995. unp. col. ill.
Videocassette available from Live Oak Media (ISBN 0-87499-358-X, 1996). 1/2" VHS videocassette color (5min), $37.95. Includes teacher's guide.
Read-along kit available from Live Oak Media (ISBN 0-87499-359-8, 1996). 1 hardback book, 1 sound cassette (9min), $22.95.
From an early age, books are Elizabeth Brown's life until as an adult her home is overflowing with books. When they block the front door, she realizes something must be done and donates her house and books to the town which turns it into a free library. The rhyming story reads swiftly, celebrating books and the people who love them. For reading aloud.
SUBJ: Books and reading--Fiction./ Stories in rhyme.

Ph-2 1-3/3 $14.95   T   KG573
STILZ, CAROL CURTIS. Grandma Buffalo, May, and me. Illus. by Constance R. Bergum. Sasquatch Books ISBN 1-57061-015-0; In Canada: Raincoast, 1995. unp. col. ill.
Journeying to visit her grandmother in Montana, a young girl and her mother camp and fish along the way. They share stories of her great-grandmother May who planted apple trees and fed buffaloes. Attractively illustrated with watercolor paintings, the story is a unique addition to family history stories.
SUBJ: Great-grandmothers--Fiction./ Family--Fiction./ Bison--Fiction.

Ph-2 P-K/2 $11.95   L   KG574
STOCK, CATHERINE. Halloween monster. Bradbury ISBN 0-02-788404-X; In Canada: Maxwell Macmillan, 1990. unp. col. ill.
A young boy and his family prepare for Halloween but the holiday frightens him until his mother explains that there are no monsters, ghosts or witches but children dressed up like them. Warm watercolor illustrations and sensitive text feature the experiences of young

children at the holidays and special occasions in this story and the companions THANKSGIVING TREAT (ISBN 0-02-788402-3, 1990); CHRISTMAS TIME (ISBN 0-02-788403-1, 1990); EASTER SURPRISE (ISBN 0-02-788371-X, 1991); SECRET VALENTINE (ISBN 0-02-788372-8, 1991, OPC); and BIRTHDAY PRESENT (ISBN 0-02-788401-5, 1991).
SUBJ: Halloween--Fiction./ Holidays--Fiction.

Ph-1 K-3/3 $14.93   L   KG575
STOCK, CATHERINE. Where are you going Manyoni? Morrow ISBN 0-688-10353-7, 1993. unp. col. ill.
Includes glossary.
Manyoni walks to school past the baobab tree, fig trees, and malala palms across the countryside in Zimbabwe. From the endpapers copied from cave paintings to the detailed watercolors with hidden wildlife, the illustrations reflect careful research and observation. Youngsters will relate to the universal experiences of traveling to school as they enjoy the challenge of finding the animals identified at the end of the book. For multicultural studies.
SUBJ: Animals--Fiction./ Zimbabwe--Fiction.

Ph-1 P-K/2 $12.99   T   KG576
STOEKE, JANET MORGAN. Hat for Minerva Louise. Dutton ISBN 0-525-45328-8, 1994. unp. col. ill.
Minerva Louise is a chicken who loves the snow, but she needs a hat or a scarf to keep warm. After mistaking a garden hose for a scarf, gloves for shoes, and a flower pot for a hat, Minerva finally finds the ideal hat: a pair of mittens--one for her head and one for her tail. Crisp illustrations framed in white offer much of the humor to be enjoyed by young listeners at story hour.
SUBJ: Chickens--Fiction./ Hats--Fiction./ Winter--Fiction.

Ph-1 P-1/2 $13.99   T   KG577
STOEKE, JANET MORGAN. Minerva Louise at school. Dutton ISBN 0-525-45494-2; In Canada: McClelland & Stewart, 1996. unp. col. ill.
Minerva Louise visits a school and in her hen-like way interprets everything she sees as something from the farm: classrooms are stalls and cubby holes are nesting boxes. The bold colors and light humor are a hit with young listeners. Try as a first day of school icebreaker.
SUBJ: Schools--Fiction./ Chickens--Fiction./ First day of school--Fiction.

Ph-1 K-3/4 $14.89   L   KG578
STOLZ, MARY. Storm in the night. Illus. by Pat Cummings. HarperCollins ISBN 0-06-025913-2, 1988. unp. col. ill.
Coretta Scott King Award.
Frightened by the fierce, night time storm, but not admitting it, Thomas is comforted by his grandfather who tells the young black boy about his own fear of storms when he was young. The striking, full paged illustrations are somber but effective in matching the mood of the sensitive, loving and poetic text.
SUBJ: Thunderstorms--Fiction./ Grandfathers--Fiction./ Fear--Fiction.

Ph-2 K-2/2 $14.93   L   KG579
STRETE, CRAIG KEE. They thought they saw him. Illus. by Jose Aruego and Ariane Dewey. Greenwillow ISBN 0-688-14195-1, 1996. unp. col. ill.
Several predators think they see chameleon, but when they look again, he is gone. Sharp eyes will spot the chameleon who has changed to the color of his surroundings. Young listeners will cheer for the chameleon as he eludes capture and will enjoy the puzzle of finding him. Use as a discussion starter about protective coloring in nature. For reading aloud.
SUBJ: Chameleons--Fiction./ Camouflage (Biology)--Fiction.

Ph-2 2-3/4 $15.99   T   KG580
STROUD, VIRGINIA A. Doesn't Fall Off His Horse. Dial ISBN 0-8037-1634-6, 1994. unp. col. ill.
Includes glossary.
As a young Kiowa brave, grandfather earned his name "Doesn't Fall Off His Horse" when he was wounded in a daring raid to steal horses from a Comanche camp. Based on a story the author heard from her adoptive Kiowa grandfather, the adventure is fraught with danger and suspense that will hold the attention of young readers. Colorful acrylic illustrations transport the viewer to a Kiowa camp. For multicultural studies.
SUBJ: Kiowa Indians--Fiction./ Indians of North America--Fiction./ Grandfathers--Fiction.

Ph-1 K-2/2 $14.88   L   KG581
STURGES, PHILEMON. Ten flashing fireflies. Illus. by Anna Vojtech. North-South ISBN 1-55858-421-8; In Canada: North-South/dist. by Vanwell, 1995. unp. col. ill.
On a summer night, children catch ten fireflies one by one and put them in a jar. Count how many are in the jar and how many are left twinkling in the summer night. Fireflies glow on the dark, shadowy pages as a favorite children's summertime activity becomes a counting, addition, and subtraction exercise.
SUBJ: Fireflies--Fiction./ Night--Fiction./ Counting./ Mathematics--Fiction./ Stories in rhyme.

Ph-2 1-3/3 $15.93   L   KG582
STUTSON, CAROLINE. By the light of the Halloween moon. Illus. by Kevin Hawkes. Lothrop, Lee & Shepard ISBN 0-688-12046-6, 1993. unp. col. ill.
A cat, a witch, a bat, a ghoul, a ghost, and a sprite are each thwarted in their attempts to grab the tapping toe of a young girl as she sits on a bridge playing the fiddle on Halloween night. Cumulative story for reading aloud.
SUBJ: Halloween--Fiction.

Ph-2 1-3/3 $15.99   T   KG583
STUTSON, CAROLINE. Prairie primer A to Z. Illus. by Susan Condie Lamb. Dutton ISBN 0-525-45163-3; In Canada: McClelland & Stewart, 1996. unp. col. ill.
A rhyming text and expansive illustrations move through the alphabet highlighting features of family life on the prairie at the turn of the century. Young readers will appreciate this additional title for social studies and literature units focusing on prairie life.
SUBJ: Frontier and pioneer life--Fiction./ Stories in rhyme./ Alphabet.

Ph-2 1-3/2 $3.95   P   KG584
SURAT, MICHELE MARIA. Angel child, dragon child. Illus. by Dinh Mai Vo. Scholastic ISBN 0-590-42271-5, c1983, 1989. 35p. col. ill.
Available from the National Library Service for the Blind and Physically Handicapped on sound recording cassette RC 37510.
Missing her mother who is still in Vietnam, being teased by other children, and the strange new ways make adjusting to her American school very difficult for Nguyen Hoa. The soft, colored pencil drawings are well done and appealing. Though the story is purposeful, it is thought provoking for children. An afterword tells of legend and customs of Vietnam.
SUBJ: Vietnamese--United States--Fiction./ Schools--Fiction.

Ph-1 P-1/1 $14.95   L   KG585
SUTEEV, V. Chick and the duckling. Translated from the Russian of V. Suteyev by Mirra Ginsburg. Illus. by Jose Aruego and Ariane Dewey. Macmillan ISBN 0-02-735940-9; In Canada: Collier Macmillan, 1972. unp. col. ill.
Selectors' Choice, 8th ed.
A duckling and a chick hatch at the same time and become constant companions. It's a game of follow the leader with everything the duckling does followed by the chick saying "me too". When the duckling decides to go swimming, the chick's "me too" almost ends in disaster; but when duckling decides to go for another swim, chick says "not me". The bright, humorous illustrations and the simple, easy to read text are appealing to young children.
SUBJ: Poultry--Fiction.

Ph-2 P-1/2 $14.00   T   KG586
SYKES, JULIE. This and that. Illus. by Tanya Linch. Farrar, Straus and Giroux ISBN 0-374-37492-9, 1996. unp. col. ill.
Cat collects various items from the animals on the farm. When they ask what she will do with each, she answers, "This and that." The ending reveals two kittens, whom the animals name "This and That." Careful listeners will begin to chime in with the predictable text and guess the names for the kittens.
SUBJ: Cats--Fiction./ Domestic animals--Fiction./ Farms--Fiction.

Ph-2 P-2 $12.95   T   KG587
TAFURI, NANCY. Do not disturb. Greenwillow ISBN 0-688-06541-4, 1987. unp. col. ill.
Camping, splashing, fishing, playing ball, flying a kite and cooking out, a family enjoys the first day of summer without noticing the wildlife they disturb. But after the family is asleep in their tent, the animal chorus begins and turns the tables. Told almost exclusively through pictures this can be enjoyed by even the youngest "readers."
SUBJ: Camping--Fiction./ Animals--Fiction./ Stories without words.

Ph-2 P $14.93   L   KG588
TAFURI, NANCY. Early morning in the barn. Greenwillow ISBN 0-688-02329-0, 1983. unp. col. ill.
Announcing the arrival of a new day on the farm are the rising sun, crowing rooster, cheeping chicks, quacking ducks, mooing cows, and other barnyard animals. The page-filling pictures are bright, cheerful and though simple manage to semi-hide some humorous incidents. Appeal is largely to preschoolers, but could be used in primary farm and animal units.
SUBJ: Stories without words./ Domestic animals--Pictorial works.

Ph-1 P-2 $13.88   L   KG589
TAFURI, NANCY. Follow me! Greenwillow ISBN 0-688-08774-4, 1990. unp. col. ill.
A young sea lion resting under its mother's flipper is interested in the bright red crab scuttling along. Told entirely by the wonderful watercolor ink and pen illustrations, this is a joy for children who will tell their own stories.
SUBJ: Sea lions--Fiction./ Crabs--Fiction./ Stories without words.

Ph-1 P-K/1 $15.88   L   KG590
TAFURI, NANCY. Have you seen my duckling? Greenwillow ISBN 0-688-02798-9, 1984. unp. col. ill.
Board book available from Tupelo Books (ISBN 0-688-14899-9, 1996).
Asking over and over just one question, "Have you seen my duckling?" a worried mother duck leads the rest of her brood all over the pond as she searches for the missing adventurer. Large colorful pictures give children an opportunity to count the baby ducks, learn about other pond residents and be reassured of the mother's concern.
SUBJ: Lost children--Fiction./ Ducks--Fiction./ Ponds--Fiction.

Ph-1 P-1/1 $13.93   L   KG591
TAFURI, NANCY. This is the farmer. Greenwillow ISBN 0-688-09469-4, 1994. unp. col. ill.
A farmer kisses his wife and begins a sequence of events that eventually opens the gate for him to walk through to milk the cow. Large bold text accompanies doublespread, color illustrations of the farmyard. Beginning readers will enjoy the simple text and visual clues in the pictures.
SUBJ: Farm life--Fiction.

Ph-1 P-K $16.00   T   KG592
TAFURI, NANCY. Who's counting? Greenwillow ISBN 0-688-06130-3, 1986. unp. col. ill.
Follow the puppy as he counts one squirrel, two birds, three moles and on to a surprise at ten. Bold, striking double-page spreads are the real attraction of this excellently designed counting book for young children.
SUBJ: Counting.

Ph-2 1-3/2 $15.00   L   KG593
TAMAR, ERIKA. Garden of happiness. Illus. by Barbara Lambase. Harcourt Brace ISBN 0-15-230582-3; In Canada: Harcourt Brace c/o Canadian Manda, 1996. unp. col. ill.
When Marisol's neighbors turn a vacant garbage-filled lot into a garden, Marisol plants a seed at the edge of the fence that grows into a huge sunflower. Expressive oil paintings burst from the pages with the exuberance of a community garden. Features a multiethnic neighborhood committed to working together to create a growing space in the city. For multicultural studies.
SUBJ: Community gardens--Fiction./ Gardens--Fiction./ City and town life--Fiction.

Ph-1 K-2/2 $13.95   L   KG594
TEAGUE, MARK. Field beyond the outfield. Scholastic ISBN 0-590-45173-1; In Canada: Scholastic, 1992. unp. col. ill.
Ludlow has an active imagination, so his parents decide to sign him up for baseball. In his first game, he is put so far out in the field that he finds himself part of another game with six-legged creatures and monsters cheering in the stands. A delightful twist on America's favorite pastime sure to delight young daydreamers and other fans.
SUBJ: Fear--Fiction./ Baseball--Fiction.

Ph-2 K-2/2 $13.95   L   KG595
TEAGUE, MARK. Pigsty. Scholastic ISBN 0-590-45915-5; In Canada: Scholastic, 1994. unp. col. ill.
At first Wendell Fultz likes living with pigs in a room that's a pigsty, but eventually he tires of their mess and enlists their help to clean his room. Rotund pigs lounge around reading comic books and snacking on potato chips in the humorous acrylic illustrations.
SUBJ: Pigs--Fiction./ Cleanliness--Fiction./ Orderliness--Fiction.

Ph-2 1-3/2 $14.95   L   KG596
TEAGUE, MARK. Secret shortcut. Scholastic ISBN 0-590-67714-4; In Canada: Scholastic, 1996. unp. col. ill.
Wendell and Floyd are always late for school because they are waylaid by aliens, pirates, and frogs. One day they decide to take a shortcut which leads through the jungle where they encounter crocodiles, but they make it to school on time! A tall tale with lots of adventure and imaginative acrylic illustrations.
SUBJ: Promptness--Fiction./ Schools--Fiction./ Adventure and adventurers--Fiction./ Imagination--Fiction.

Ph-1 P-2/4 $14.95   T   KG597
TEJIMA, KEIZABURO. Fox's dream. Philomel ISBN 0-399-21455-0; In Canada: General, 1987. unp col illus.
Available in Spanish EL SUENO DEL ZORRO (Juventud ISBN 84-261-2450-X, 1989).
Dramatic woodcuts and a brief, poetic text picture a solitary fox wandering through the silent, snow covered, and almost deserted woods. He is very lonely until he encounters a vixen and the two foxes become mates.
SUBJ: Foxes--Fiction.

Ph-2 K-2/2 $3.99   P   KG598
TELLO, JERRY. Abuelo y los tres osos./Abuelo and the three bears. Illus. by Ana Lopez Escriva. Scholastic ISBN 0-590-04320-X; In Canada: Scholastic, 1997. 16p. col. ill.
"Mariposa Scholastic in Espanol."
Includes glossary.
The story of the three bears is given a Latin American twist as the bears are preparing frijoles instead of oatmeal, Goldilocks is named Trencitas, and a few Spanish words are sprinkled throughout the text. Turn the book over and the familiar story is in Spanish. Useful in schools where Spanish is the first or second language of students.
SUBJ: Bears--Fiction./ Fairy tales--Parodies, imitations, etc./ Spanish language materials.

Ph-1 K-3/2 $14.95   L   KG599
TEMPLE, CHARLES. Train. Illus. by Larry Johnson. Houghton Mifflin ISBN 0-395-69826-X, 1996. unp. col. ill.
A family rides a C & O train out of town, past fields and cows, through the day, and into the night. The rhythm of the train as it sways and clacks and rumbles over the tracks is conveyed in the musical text. Rich oil paintings are the perfect accompaniment and portray a contemporary African-American family enjoying the journey. Worth reading aloud for the poetry. For multicultural studies and transportation units.
SUBJ: Railroads--Trains--Fiction./ Stories in rhyme./ Afro-Americans--Fiction.

VCR   Ph-3 1-3 $14.98   KG600
TENDER TALE OF CINDERELLA PENGUIN (Videocassette). National Film Board of Canada/Smarty Pants NFV 14001 ISBN 1-55886-124-6; In Canada: National Film Board of Canada, 1990. 1/2" VHS videocassette color.
Originally published in Canada, 1981.
Five brief, unrelated film vignettes comprise this video. The title story is the most outstanding. Penguin characters recreate Cinderella in wordless and amusing animation. The traditional "Frog went a-courting" is simply animated, and the "Owl and the raven" uses puppets and Eskimo language overlaid with English narration to dramatize an Eskimo legend. The remaining two films are exercises in animation that will have limited appeal.
Contents: The tender tale of Cinderella Penguin (10min); Metamorphoses (3min); Mr. Frog went a-courting (5min); The sky is blue (5min); The owl and the raven (7min).
SUBJ: Fairy tales./ Short stories.

Ph-2 1-3/2 $13.95   L   KG601
TESTA, MARIA. Thumbs up, Rico! Illus. by Diane Paterson. Whitman ISBN 0-8075-7906-8; In Canada: General, 1994. unp. col. ill.
Rico is a good basketball player, friend, and brother, but he struggles with drawing. Rico, who has Down's syndrome, narrates the three short chapters which depict his winning ways and positive attitude. The transitional reader effectively portrays persons with disabilities.
SUBJ: Down's syndrome--Fiction./ Mentally handicapped--Fiction./ Brothers and sisters--Fiction.

Ph-2 1-3/5 $14.95   L   KG602
TEWS, SUSAN. Gingerbread doll. Illus. by Megan Lloyd. Clarion ISBN 0-395-56438-7, 1993. 32p. col. ill.
Great-Grandma tells a story about the gingerbread doll her mother made her one Christmas when she longed for a doll though the family was very poor. The dough doll doesn't last, but the rag dress and love remain for generations.
SUBJ: Dolls--Fiction./ Christmas--Fiction.

Ph-3 1-3/2 $13.93   L   KG603
THAYER, JANE. Puppy who wanted a boy. Illus. by Lisa McCue. Morrow ISBN 0-688-05945-7, c1958, 1986. unp. col. ill.
Available from National Library Service for the Blind and Physically Handicapped on sound recording cassette RC25615.
A lonely puppy finds a boy just in time for Christmas.
SUBJ: Christmas--Fiction./ Dogs--Fiction.

Ph-2 1-3/3 $14.89 L KG604
THOMAS, JANE RESH. Celebration! Illus. by Raul Colon. Hyperion ISBN 0-7868-2160-4; In Canada: Little, Brown, 1997. unp. col. ill.
Maggie's grandmother, aunts and uncles, and lots of cousins bring food to the family picnic for the Fourth of July. Truly a celebration of family, the illustrations and story overflow with children, games, food, and fun. For multicultural studies.
SUBJ: Family life--Fiction./ Picnicking--Fiction./ Fourth of July--Fiction./ Afro-Americans--Fiction.

Ph-2 K-3/2 $15.93 L KG605
THOMAS, PATRICIA. Stand back, said the elephant, I'm going to sneeze! Illus. by Wallace Tripp. Lothrop, Lee & Shepard ISBN 0-688-09339-6, c1971, 1990. unp. col. ill.
Elephant's warning triggers responses from all the animals who want him to stifle the forthcoming sneeze so they won't be sent "tumbling and bumbling", and lose their feathers, stings and wings, fur, scales, stripes, and spots. Wildly funny in both text and illustrations, this is a sure fire hit when read aloud.
SUBJ: Animals--Fiction./ Stories in rhyme.

Ph-2 P-2/2 $13.95 L KG606
THOMAS, SHELLEY MOORE. Putting the world to sleep. Illus. by Bonnie Christensen. Houghton Mifflin ISBN 0-395-71283-1, 1995. unp. col. ill.
A soothing cumulative text describes the world's preparations for sleep as a mother puts her children to bed. Wood engravings edged in black draw in the listener with the charm of night. The easy-to-read, predictable text will ensure success for beginning readers.
SUBJ: Night--Fiction./ Bedtime--Fiction.

Ph-2 P-1/4 $14.00 T KG607
THREADGALL, COLIN. Proud rooster and the fox. Tambourine/Morrow ISBN 0-688-11123-8, 1992. unp. col. ill.
Everytime the fox tries to sneak into the barnyard, the rooster crows signaling the farmer to come out with his gun. One day the wily fox tricks the rooster into playing a game that causes him to lose his voice, and the fox gets away with the hens. Bright colors and a humorous ending combine for a lively read-aloud.
SUBJ: Pride and vanity--Fiction./ Roosters--Fiction./ Foxes--Fiction.

Ph-2 P-2/2 $12.93 L KG608
TITHERINGTON, JEANNE. Place for Ben. Greenwillow ISBN 0-688-06494-9, 1987. unp. col. ill.
Ezra is everywhere and Ben longs to have some privacy until he discovers that being by himself isn't as much fun as he thought it would be. Muted pastel pencil drawings make this a story that will best be enjoyed in a small group or on an individual basis.
SUBJ: Babies--Fiction./ Brothers--Fiction.

Ph-2 P-2/1 $13.93 L KG609
TITHERINGTON, JEANNE. Pumpkin pumpkin. Greenwillow ISBN 0-688-05696-2, 1986. 24p. col. ill.
Big book available from Scholastic (ISBN 0-590-72452-5, 1990).
Jamie plants a seed and it sprouts, grows into a plant, flowers and produces a pumpkin that grows and grows until Jamie picks it and carves it into a jack-o'-lantern, but he does save six seeds for planting the next spring. Full-paged, pastel-hued colored pencil drawings could tell the story without use of the simple words. A fine introduction to the botanical phase of beginning science and also useful during the Halloween season.
SUBJ: Pumpkin--Fiction./ Gardening--Fiction.

Ph-2 P-K/3 $12.88 L KG610
TITHERINGTON, JEANNE. Where are you going, Emma? Greenwillow ISBN 0-688-07082-5, 1988. unp. col. ill.
Accompanying Grandpa to the apple orchard, Emma decides to climb the stone wall and investigate the outside world. Softly colored, full paged pictures have the appearance of photographs.
SUBJ: Grandfathers--Fiction.

Ph-2 P-K/1 $12.95 T KG611
TITUS, EVE. Kitten who couldn't purr. Illus. by Amrei Fechner. Morrow ISBN 0-688-09363-9, 1991. unp. col. ill.
Jonathan, a kitten who can't purr, asks a hen, a duck, a pig, a cow, and a donkey each in turn to help him but they can only cluck, quack, oink, moo and hee-haw. Finally Toto, a puppy, helps Jonathan find another way to express himself. Young listeners will enjoy the repetition and animal sounds and the satisfying resolution. Recommeneed for story time.
SUBJ: Cats--Fiction./ Animal sounds--Fiction.

Ph-2 K-3/5 $16.00 L KG612
TOMPERT, ANN. Carol for Christmas. Illus. by Laura Kelly. Macmillan ISBN 0-02-789402-9; In Canada: Maxwell Macmillan, 1994. unp. col. ill.
A young mouse narrates the tale about how the carol "Silent Night" originated in the village of Oberndorf, Austria. When the mice family have eaten the leather connections for the church organ keys, the pastor is forced to compose Christmas music for the guitar. Based on a legend, the story has been brought to life by the author and illustrator.
SUBJ: Carols--Fiction./ Mice--Fiction./ Christmas--Fiction.

Ph-2 2-3/4 $15.99 L KG613
TOMPERT, ANN. Grandfather Tang's story. Illus. by Robert Andrew Parker. Crown ISBN 0-517-57272-9, 1990. unp. col. ill.
Seven tangram pieces are moved as Grandfather Tang tells Little Soo a story about two fox fairies who try to out do each other by changing shapes. Watercolor wash and pen illustrations extend the text and tangram pictures. After story hour, youngsters can replicate the tangrams themselves.
SUBJ: Storytelling--Fiction./ Foxes--Fiction./ Fairies--Fiction./ Tangrams--Fiction.

Ph-2 K-2/5 $15.00 L KG614
TORRES, LEYLA. Saturday sancocho. Farrar Straus Giroux ISBN 0-374-36418-4; In Canada: HarperCollins, 1995. unp. col. ill.
Spanish version EL SANCOCHO DEL SABADO available from Mirasol/Farrar Straus Giroux (ISBN 0-374-31997-9, 1995), $15.00.
Maria Lili accompanies her grandmother to the market where she trades a dozen eggs for the ingredients to make chicken sancocho. A South American market features prominently in the airy, watercolor illustrations as Maria Lili and her grandmother gather the ingredients. A recipe for the sancocho follows the story. For multicultural studies.
SUBJ: Cookery--Fiction./ Barter--Fiction./ Grandmothers--Fiction./ South America--Fiction./ Spanish language materials.

Ph-1 K-2 $15.93 L KG615
TRESSELT, ALVIN. Hide and seek fog. Illus. by Roger Duvoisin. Lothrop, Lee & Shepard ISBN 0-688-51169-4, c1965. unp. col. ill.
Caldecott Honor Book.
When a fog comes and stays for three days at a little seaside village, children find ways of enjoying the time.
SUBJ: Fog--Fiction./ Cape Cod (Mass.)--Fiction.

Ph-2 1-3/5 $14.95 T KG616
TRESSELT, ALVIN. Wake up, city! Illustrated by Carolyn Ewing. Morrow ISBN 0-688-08654-3, c1957, 1990. unp. col. ill.
Available from the National Library Service for the Blind and Physically Handicapped on sound recording cassette RC34733.
A medium-sized city awakens at dawn when city workers report to work. The harbor stirs, the markets bustle and the city dwellers prepare to start their day. Realistic color illustrations enhance this updated re-issue of a book originally published in 1957. Useful for lower primary grades as an adjunct to a unit studying cities and towns.
SUBJ: Day--Fiction./ City and town life--Fiction.

Ph-2 P-2/4 $12.95 T KG617
TRINCA, ROD. One woolly wombat. By Rod Trinca and Kerry Argent. Kane/Miller ISBN 0-916291-00-6, 1985. unp. col. ill.
Introduces fourteen Australian animals by means of rhyming text and counting book format. Many touches of humor are included in the handsome, vivid illustrations.
SUBJ: Zoology--Australia--Fiction./ Australia--Fiction./ Counting./ Stories in rhyme.

Ph-2 P-3/6 $14.99 L KG618
TRIVAS, IRENE. Emma's Christmas: an old song. Re-sung and pictured by Irene Trivas. Orchard ISBN 0-531-08380-2, 1988. unp. col. ill.
This variant of the traditional Christmas carol, "The Twelve Days of Christmas" adds up to lots of fun, confusion, birds, fruit, milkmaids, cows, dancers, pipers, and golden rings when a prince wooing a farm girl sends her all the three hundred and sixty-four gifts (not including the forty cows) mentioned in the song. Wonderfully drawn colored sketches, detailed but not cluttered, emphasize the humor and frenzy of the tale.
SUBJ: Christmas--Fiction./ Humorous stories./ Twelve days of Christmas (English folk song)--Adaptations.

Ph-1 P-3/4 $16.00 L KG619
TRIVIZAS, EUGENE. Three little wolves and the big bad pig. Illus. by Helen Oxenbury. McElderry ISBN 0-689-50569-8; In Canada: Maxwell Macmillan, 1993. unp. col. ill.
Spanish version TRES LOBITOS Y EL COCHINO FEROZ available from Ediciones Ekare/dist. by Kane/Miller (ISBN 980-257-177-6, 1995).
Turn about is fair play in this altered retelling which pits three innocent wolves against a determined and destructive pig. Witty, watercolor illustrations match the humor inherent in the text.

SUBJ: Fairy tales--Parodies, imitations, etc./ Pigs--Fiction./ Wolves--Fiction./ Spanish language materials.

Ph-1 P-1 $16.00 L KG620

TRYON, LESLIE. Albert's alphabet. Atheneum ISBN 0-689-31642-9; In Canada: Maxwell Macmillan, 1991. unp. col. ill.
Albert is a very resourceful duck and school carpenter who constructs the twenty-six letters of the alphabet using wood scraps and other found materials. An inventive twist on the usual alphabet books.
In ALBERT'S PLAY (ISBN 0-689-31525-2, 1992) the inventive duck directs a school production of "The Owl and the Pussycat."
Albert takes a class to visit an apple farm in ALBERT'S FIELD TRIP (ISBN 0-689-31821-9, 1993).
Join the residents of Pleasant Valley for a game in ALBERT'S BALLGAME (ISBN 0-689-80187-4, 1996).
SUBJ: Alphabet./ Building--Fiction./ Ducks--Fiction.

Ph-1 K-2/2 $14.95 L KG621

TRYON, LESLIE. Albert's Thanksgiving. Atheneum ISBN 0-689-31865-0; In Canada: Maxwell Macmillan, 1994. unp. col. ill.
Knowing what a hard worker Albert is, the PTA president asks him to do a multitude of tasks to prepare for the Thanksgiving feast, including making the table, assembling the turkeys, and preparing the pumpkin pie pizzas. The requests come in the form of letters which make up most of the text. The story about a school celebrating Thanksgiving will be welcomed, especially with the familiar character of Albert, the industrious duck. A recipe for pumpkin pie pizza is provided. Use to initiate letter writing activities or cooking in the classroom.
SUBJ: Ducks--Fiction./ Thanksgiving Day--Fiction./ Animals--Fiction./ Letters--Fiction.

Ph-1 K-2/2 $13.95 L KG622

TURKLE, BRINTON. Do not open. Dutton ISBN 0-525-28785-X; In Canada: Fitzhenry & Whiteside, 1981. unp. col. ill.
Selectors' Choice, 14th ed.
Available from National Library Service for the Blind and Physically Handicapped in Braille BR05505.
After a violent September storm Miss Moody and her cat, Captain Kidd, search the beach for washed up treasures. They find an unusual deep purple bottle with "DO NOT OPEN" scratched on it. Tricked by a strange voice, Miss Moody opens the bottle and out pops the biggest, ugliest creature she has ever seen. Unafraid of the snarling monster, Miss Moody cleverly gets rid of him and she and Captain Kidd return to their cozy seaside cottage with their new-found possessions. The illustrations are splendid and vibrant.
SUBJ: Seashore--Fiction./ Cats--Fiction./ Magic--Fiction./ Monsters--Fiction.

Ph-1 K-3/5 $4.99 P KG623

TURKLE, BRINTON. Thy friend, Obadiah. Penguin ISBN 0-14-050393-5, c1969. unp. col. ill.
Caldecott Honor Book.
Available from National Library Service for the Blind and Physically Handicapped in Braille BR01433.
A little Quaker boy is annoyingly followed by a persistant sea gull. However, when the bird disappears on a bitter November evening Obadiah gets worried. Glowing pictures of Nantucket make this an outstanding picture storybook.
In RACHEL AND OBADIAH (Dutton ISBN 0-525-38020-5, 1978, Selectors' Choice, 12th ed., available from the NLSBPH in Braille BR05085), Rachel beats her older brother Obadiah in a foot race (reminiscent of the tortoise and the hare).
SUBJ: Gulls--Fiction./ Nantucket (Mass.)--Fiction./ Quakers--Fiction./ United States--History--Colonial period, ca. 1600-1775--Fiction.

Ph-1 1-3/6 $13.95 L KG624

TURNER, ANN. Dakota dugout. Illus. by Ronald Himler. Macmillan ISBN 0-02-789700-1; In Canada: Collier Macmillan, 1985. unp. col. ill.
Traveling to the West to join her young pioneer husband, the narrator cries when she sees their primitive sod house home. Loneliness, severe weather, and crop failure finally are followed by success and a fine new house, but she remembers fondly life in their first simple home. Striking black and white drawings expand the spare text.
SUBJ: Frontier and pioneer life--Fiction./ Great Plains--Fiction.

Ph-2 2-5/2 $14.89 L KG625

TURNER, ANN. Dust for dinner. Illus. by Robert Barrett. HarperCollins ISBN 0-06-023377-X; In Canada: HarperCollins, 1995. 64p. col. ill. (I can read book).
Forced from their farm by dust storms, Jake and Maggy and their parents head for California looking for work along the way. The easy-to-read historical fiction introduces the trials of the Dust Bowl and the Great Depression to beginning readers.

SUBJ: Depressions--1929--Fiction./ Family life--Fiction./ Farm life--Fiction.

Ph-2 1-3/3 $14.89 L KG626

TURNER, ANN. Heron Street. Illus. by Lisa Desimini. HarperCollins ISBN 0-06-026185-4, 1989. unp. col. ill.
At first a marsh houses wildlife but then people come. Jeweltoned paintings and spare text show how, over many years, the land changes. A good introduction to ecology and urbanization studies.
SUBJ: Man--Influence on nature--Fiction.

Ph-2 3-5/3 $13.95 L KG627

TURNER, ANN. Katie's trunk. Illus. by Ronald Himler. Macmillan ISBN 0-02-789512-2; In Canada: Maxwell Maxmillan, 1992. unp. col. ill.
Katie is the middle child in a Tory family during the Revolutionary War. When the rebels come, her family hides in the woods, but Katie sneaks back home. As the rebels ransack her house, she climbs in a trunk. One of the men discovers her but calls his friends away to protect her. Suspenseful historical fiction for reading aloud.
SUBJ: United States--History--Revolution, 1775-1783--Fiction.

Ph-2 1-3/6 $14.95 L KG628

TURNER, ANN. Sewing quilts. Illus. by Thomas B. Allen. Macmillan ISBN 0-02-789285-9; In Canada: Maxwell Macmillan, 1994. unp. col. ill.
A young girl describes the quilts she, her mother, and her sister are making: School House, Bear Claw, and a red, white, and blue doll's quilt. Pieces of the quilts are connected with the pieces of their lives in rich prose and muted pastel illustrations. A quiet story for reading aloud especially as part of units on pioneer life or quilting.
SUBJ: Quilts--Fiction./ Quilting--Fiction./ Frontier and pioneer life--Fiction.

CE Ph-1 P-2/1 $13.89 L KG629

TURNER, ANN. Through moon and stars and night skies. Illus. by James Graham Hale. HarperCollins ISBN 0-06-026190-0; In Canada: HarperCollins, 1990. unp. col. ill.
Read-along kit available from HarperChildren's Audio (ISBN 0-69470-013-4, 1995). 1 paperback book, 1 sound cassette (5min), $7.95.
A little boy carefully carries a photograph of the man and woman who will become his parents all through the long frightening plane ride through the long frightening night. This wonderfully gentle and loving story is enhanced by quietly appealing watercolor illustrations. Use in discussions of families. (Parents' Shelf).
SUBJ: Adoption--Fiction./ Parent and child--Fiction.

Ph-2 1-3/3 $15.00 T KG630

TURNER, PRISCILLA. War between the Vowels and the Consonants. Illus. by Whitney Turner. Farrar Straus Giroux ISBN 0-374-38236-0; In Canada: HarperCollins, 1996. unp. col. ill.
Vowels and Consonants didn't trust each other, and eventually their differences turn into war. When a sprawling, scribbled line appears, the letters cooperate to form words and chase the scrawl out of town. Humorous illustrations show letters dressed and acting like people. Teachers and students will have fun with this bit of nonsense and the possibilities when vowels and consonants join to form words. Useful in creative writing activities as well as units on conflict resolution.
SUBJ: War--Fiction./ English language--Vowels--Fiction./ English language--Consonants--Fiction./ Alphabet.

Ph-1 2-5/3 $14.95 L KG631

UCHIDA, YOSHIKO. Bracelet. Illus. by Joanna Yardley. Philomel ISBN 0-399-22503-X; In Canada: Putnam, 1993. unp. col. ill.
Emi and her family are Japanese Americans who are sent to an internment camp during World War II. Arriving at the camp, Emi realizes she has lost the bracelet her best friend, Laurie, had given her before she left. The emotional pain experienced by Emi and her family is clearly expressed as is their ability to rise above their circumstances and hold onto the people and places in their hearts. Subdued watercolor illustrations illuminate this dark chapter in American history, and an afterword provides historical context. Historical fiction for multicultural studies.
SUBJ: Japanese Americans--Evacuation and relocation, 1942-1945--Fiction./ World War, 1939-1945--United States--Fiction./ Friendship--Fiction.

Ph-3 P-1/2 $12.89 L KG632

UDRY, JANICE MAY. Let's be enemies. Illus. by Maurice Sendak. HarperCollins ISBN 0-06-026131-5, c1961. unp. col. ill.
John is unhappy because his friend is too bossy. When he tells him this, the two boys say they will stop being friends.
SUBJ: Friendship--Fiction.

Ph-1 K-2/2 $14.89   L   KG633
UDRY, JANICE MAY. Tree is nice. Illus. by Marc Simont. HarperCollins
ISBN 0-06-026156-0, c1956. unp. col. ill.
Caldecott Medal Award.
Available from National Library Service for the Blind and Physically
Handicapped in Braille BR06122.
Spanish version UN ARBOL ES HERMOSO available from Harper
Arco Iris (ISBN 0-06-025317-7, 1995).
A child's book about the wonder of trees, why they are so important,
and the many kinds of fun they afford children. For environmental
studies.
SUBJ: Trees--Fiction./ Spanish language materials.

Ph-2 K-2 $12.89   L   KG634
UNGERER, TOMI. Crictor. HarperCollins ISBN 0-06-026181-1, c1958.
32p. col. ill.
A big snake comes to live in a town in France where he makes
friends with the children who even use him for a jump-rope.
SUBJ: Snakes--Fiction./ France--Fiction.

VCR   Ph-3 K-2 $90.00   OD KG635
UNGERER, TOMI. Tomi Ungerer Library (Videocassette). Weston Woods
MPV 497V, 1993. 1/2" VHS videocassette color (35min).
Includes teacher's guide.
Includes public performance rights.
A selection of four of the author's books is followed by a short visit
with the author. Useful where cost or space constraints allow for only
one videocassette instead of four separate ones.
Contents: The three robbers; Moon Man; The hat; The beast of
Monsieur Racine; Getting to know Tomi Ungerer.
SUBJ: Robbers and outlaws--Fiction./ Moon--Fiction./ Hats--Fiction./
Monsters--Fiction.

Ph-2 K-2/2 $13.95   L   KG636
USHINSKY, KONSTANTIN. How a shirt grew in the field. Adapted from
the Russian by Marguerita Rudolph. Illus. by Erika Weihs. Clarion ISBN
0-395-59761-7, 1992. 31p. col. ill.
A young Ukranian boy describes the steps involved in making his shirt
from planting the flax seeds in the field through harvesting the flax,
spinning, weaving, and sewing the shirt. A note following the story
further explains the process.
SUBJ: Soviet Union--Fiction./ Clothing and dress--Fiction.

Ph-2 1-3/3 $17.95   L   KG637
VAN ALLSBURG, CHRIS. Bad day at Riverbend. Houghton Mifflin ISBN
0-395-67347-X, 1995. unp. col. ill.
Sheriff Ned Hardy is determined to find and stop the evil that is
covering animals, people, and their surroundings in greasy streaks.
What the sheriff doesn't know is that he and Riverbend exist in a
child's coloring book, and the greasy streaks are crayon markings.
Black and white illustrations mysteriously scribbled with crayons
provide clues for the surprising ending.
SUBJ: Cowboys--Fiction./ Coloring books--Fiction./ Crayons--Fiction.

CE   Ph-1 1-3/5 $15.95   L   KG638
VAN ALLSBURG, CHRIS. Garden of Abdul Gasazi. Houghton Mifflin
ISBN 0-395-27804-X, 1979. unp. ill.
Caldecott Honor Book.
Talking book available from SRA/McGraw-Hill 87-511226, 1983. 1
sound cassette, $15.00.
Available from the National Library Service for the Blind and
Physically Handicapped on sound recording cassette RC34174.
While trying to retrieve Miss Hester's bad-mannered dog Fritz, Alan
Mitz has a terrifying trip through Abdul Gasazi's forbidden garden.
Sadly he returns to tell Miss Hester how the retired magician has
turned Fritz into a duck who then has flown away with Alan's cap.
Miss Hester assures the tearful boy that no one can turn a dog into
a duck and as Fritz bounds out of the kitchen Alan is convinced. But
how did Alan's cap get back into the front yard?
SUBJ: Magicians--Fiction./ Dogs--Fiction.

Ph-1 1-3/4 $16.95   L   KG639
VAN ALLSBURG, CHRIS. Two bad ants. Houghton Mifflin ISBN 0-395-
48668-8, 1988. 31p. col. ill.
Suspenseful drama, and magnificent, somber colored illustrations as
seen from an insect's point of view are incorporated in the story of
two bold ants who decide to remain behind when the clan returns
from a sweet crystal transporting mission. Stuffed with sugar they fall
asleep only to awaken and find themselves almost drowned in hot,
brown liquid, roasted when they hide on an English muffin, battered
and bruised as they escape a grinding disposal and shocked across
the room when they hide in a strange dark tunnel. When night comes
and the workers return for more food the now not so bold pair
eagerly accompany them back to the queen.
SUBJ: Ants--Fiction.

Ph-2 2-A $16.95   T   KG640
VAN ALLSBURG, CHRIS. Z was zapped. Houghton Mifflin ISBN 0-395-
44612-0, 1987. unp. ill.
Using the format of a play with twenty-six acts, each letter of the
alphabet encounters a mishap. Dramatic, full-paged, sculptured, black
and white pictures portray the event while a brief text on the reverse
page describes each disasterous accident. The episodes such as "The
A was in an Avalanche", "The E was slowly Evaporating", "The N
was Nailed and Nailed again" and "The Q was neatly Quartered"
are rather violent but also provide a vocabulary stretching, puzzle
like, game element.
SUBJ: Alphabet.

Ph-2 1-3/2 $15.95   L   KG641
VAN LAAN, NANCY. Boda: a Mexican wedding celebration. Illus. by
Andrea Arroyo. Little, Brown ISBN 0-316-89626-8; In Canada: Little,
Brown, 1996. unp. col. ill.
Includes glossary.
In a Mexican town, a young girl and her grandmother observe a
traditional Zapotec Indian wedding from the preparations through the
ceremony and celebrations. Spanish words throughout the text are
translated within the context of the story. Language and culture
depicted in the text and watercolor illustrations will be useful for
multicultural studies.
SUBJ: Zapotec Indians--Social life and customs--Fiction./ Indians of
Mexico--Social life and customs--Fiction./ Weddings--Fiction.

Ph-2 K-2/2 $14.99   L   KG642
VAN LAAN, NANCY. Possum come a-knockin'. Illus. by George Booth.
Knopf ISBN 0-394-92206-9; In Canada: Random House, 1990. unp. col.
ill.
A rural family hears a-knockin' on the door as they are knittin', fixin',
cookin' and a'whittlin'. It's possum all right, but by the time they stop
what they're doing and go to the door, he's back up the tree
laughing at his trick. The color illustrations showing the family through
the window with the teasing possum at the door are very funny. The
rhythms make this good for reading aloud.
SUBJ: Family life--Fiction./ Opossums--Fiction./ Stories in rhyme.

Ph-2 P-2/3 $13.89   L   KG643
VAN LAAN, NANCY. Round and round again. Illus. by Nadine Bernard
Westcott. Hyperion ISBN 0-7868-2005-5; In Canada; Little, Brown,
1994. unp. col. ill.
Environmentalists can rejoice in this story about a mother who recycles
everything. Rollicking, repetitive rhymes and zany, colorful illustrations
create an inventive tall tale about discovering the usefulness in all
things. Fun for reading aloud, it will be useful for environmental
studies units.
SUBJ: Recycling (Waste)--Fiction./ Stories in rhyme.

Ph-2 P-2/3 $15.95   L   KG644
VAN LAAN, NANCY. Sleep, sleep, sleep: a lullaby for little ones around
the world. Illus. by Holly Meade. Little, Brown ISBN 0-316-89732-9; In
Canada: Little, Brown, 1995. unp. col. ill.
Different people and animals around the world sing their babies to
sleep. Torn paper collages lead the viewer around the globe,
alternating full doublespreads with frames split vertically or
horizontally for the visual tour. Refrains lull the listener with foreign
words spelled phonetically. For multicultural studies.
SUBJ: Lullabies./ Mother and child--Fiction./ Animals--Fiction.

Ph-2 2-4/4 $15.99   T   KG645
VAN LEEUWEN, JEAN. Across the wide dark sea: the Mayflower
journey. Illus. by Thomas B. Allen. Dial ISBN 0-8037-1166-2, 1995. unp.
col. ill.
A small boy describes a long ocean voyage in a crowded, leaky ship
with little to eat and much illness and the first difficult months in the
new land. Based on the Mayflower journey, the story, told from the
point of view of a young boy, offers immediacy to young readers
while an author's note provides historical sources. Charcoal, pastel,
and colored pencil illustrations are somewhat hazy, but they do not
detract from the compelling historical fiction which will be in demand
for Thanksgiving units.
SUBJ: Pilgrims (New Plymouth Colony)--Fiction./ Massachusetts--
History--New Plymouth, 1620-1691--Fiction./ Mayflower (Ship)--
Fiction.

Ph-2 K-2/2 $13.89   L   KG646
VAN LEEUWEN, JEAN. Emma Bean. Illus. by Juan Wijngaard. Dial
ISBN 0-8037-1393-2, 1993. 40p. col. ill.
Emma Bean is a rabbit who has had a girl named Molly since Molly
was a baby. As Molly grows up, Emma Bean endures feedings,
dressing up, and rough play as well as songs, whispered secrets, and
endless companionship. A gentle and endearing story.
SUBJ: Toys--Fiction./ Rabbits--Fiction./ Growth--Fiction.

Ph-1 2-5/2 $14.89   L   KG647
VAN LEEUWEN, JEAN. Fourth of July on the plains. Illus. by Henri Sorensen. Dial ISBN 0-8037-1772-5; In Canada: McClelland & Stewart, 1997. unp. col. ill.
Celebrating the Fourth of July in 1852 along the Oregon Trail, everyone on the wagon train contributes--food, speeches, a flag sewn from fabric scraps, and even a parade led by the young narrator beating a washtub drum. Based on a diary account, the focus on the American holiday rings authentic. Historical fiction for beginning readers.
SUBJ: Frontier and pioneer life--Fiction./ Overland journeys to the Pacific--Fiction./ Fourth of July--Fiction.

CE   Ph-1 K-2/1 $3.50   P   KG648
VAN LEEUWEN, JEAN. Oliver Pig at school. Illus. by Ann Schweninger. Puffin ISBN 0-14-037145-1, 1994. 48p. col. ill.
Four easy-to-read stories about Oliver's first day at school. These stories and others about Oliver and Amanda Pig are great for beginning chapter book readers.
Other titles in this series include AMANDA PIG AND HER BIG BROTHER, OLIVER available from Puffin (ISBN 0-14-037008-0, 1994) (read-along kit from Listening Library FTR81 (ISBN 0-8072-0052-2, 1984), 1 paperback book, 1 sound cassette (24min), $15.98); TALES OF AMANDA PIG available from Puffin (ISBN 0-14-036840-X, 1994); MORE TALES OF AMANDA PIG (ISBN 0-14-036205-3, c1985, 1988); OLIVER, AMANDA, AND GRANDMOTHER PIG (ISBN 0-8037-0745-2, c1987, 1990); AMANDA PIG ON HER OWN (ISBN 0-8037-0893-9, 1991); OLIVER AND AMANDA'S HALLOWEEN (ISBN 0-8037-1237-5, 1992); OLIVER AND AMANDA'S CHRISTMAS (ISBN 0-8037-0636-7, 1989); OLIVER AND AMANDA AND THE BIG SNOW (ISBN 0-8037-1763-6, 1995); and AMANDA PIG, SCHOOLGIRL (ISBN 0-8037-1981-7, 1997).
Available from National Library Service for the Blind and Physically Handicapped, TALES OF AMANDA PIG in Braille BR5608.
SUBJ: Pigs--Fiction./ Schools--Fiction./ First day of school--Fiction.

CE   Ph-1 K-2/1 $3.50   P   KG649
VAN LEEUWEN, JEAN. Tales of Oliver Pig. Illus. by Arnold Lobel. Dial ISBN 0-8037-8737-5, 1979. 64p. col. ill. (Dial easy-to-read).
Read-along kit available from Listening Library FTR74 (ISBN 0-8072-0038-7, 1983). 1 paperback book, 1 sound cassette (24min), $15.98. Includes guide.
Spanish version available from Penguin Ediciones CUENTOS DEL CERDITO OLIVER (ISBN 0-14-038111-2, 1996).
Oliver is a member of the pig family, but in the five easy-to-read chapters, he behaves much like many little boys. He bakes cookies with his mother; plays with his toys; and squabbles with his little sister, Amanda; shares a visit with his grandmother; comforts his exasperated mother; is tucked into bed by his father; and all in all enjoys a warm, happy family life.
SUBJ: Pigs--Fiction./ Family life--Fiction./ Spanish language materials.

Ph-2 1-3/7 $13.93   L   KG650
VARLEY, SUSAN. Badger's parting gifts. Lothrop, Lee & Shepard ISBN 0-688-02703-2, 1984. unp. col. ill.
Remembering happy times and special things Badger had taught them helps his many animal friends finally overcome their grief, and keeps him as a part of their lives after the death of their old friend. Thoughtful, gentle and tender without being too sentimental. Warm, appealing pictures match the mood of the story.
SUBJ: Death--Fiction./ Badgers--Fiction./ Animals--Fiction.

Ph-2 K-2/2 $14.95   L   KG651
VAUGHAN, MARCIA K. Snap! By Marcia Vaughan. Illus. by Sascha Hutchinson. Scholastic ISBN 0-590-60377-9; In Canada: Scholastic, 1996. unp. col. ill.
Includes glossary.
Joey, the baby kangaroo, wants to play games with the mouse, snake, platypus, and echidna, but when they ask Sly-tooth, the crocodile, to join, the game turns dangerous. The repetition and rhyme are ideal for reading aloud, and the happy ending will please a storytime audience. Cut-paper illustrations and an animal glossary introduce the animals native to Australia.
SUBJ: Kangaroos--Fiction./ Animals--Fiction./ Zoology--Australia--Fiction./ Australia--Fiction./ Games--Fiction.

Ph-2 P-2/4 $8.95   T   KG652
VAUGHAN, MARCIA K. Wombat stew. Illus. by Pamela Lofts. Silver Burdett ISBN 0-382-09211-2, c1984. unp. col. ill.
Catching a wombat, a very clever dingo decides to make wombat stew. However, Wombat's friends Platypus, Emu, Old Blue Tongue the Lizard, Echidna, and Koala are even more clever and contribute an assortment of items to the stew so that when the clever dingo samples the concoction (just before adding Wombat), he thinks he's poisoned, screams, howls, and runs away"...deep in the bush, never again to sing...Wombat stew, Wombat stew, Goo-ey, brew-y, Yummy chew-y, Wombat stew!" Animated, humorous full-page colored pictures extend the rollicking text. Music for the recurring refrain is included.
SUBJ: Australia--Fiction./ Animals--Fiction./ Humorous stories.

Ph-2 P-3/2 $13.95   L   KG653
VIGNA, JUDITH. I wish Daddy didn't drink so much. Whitman ISBN 0-8075-3523-0; In Canada: General, 1988. unp. col. ill.
Daddy can be loving and kind but most of the time he is mad and abusive and worst of all he spoils Christmas. Her mother says he is sick but Lisa says "No, he's drunk". They do salvage some Christmas joy when Lisa and her mother put the big turkey with all the stuffing on her new sled and take it to the home of Mrs. Field, a new friend Lisa's mother met at Al-Anon. A realistic, sensitive and sympathetic approach but with no easy or false solution to a problem faced by many children. A note to adults provides insight into the conflicting feelings experienced by the children and gives addresses and phone numbers of organizations that can provide resources and help for troubled families.
SUBJ: Alcoholism--Fiction./ Fathers--Fiction.

Ph-2 1-3/3 $13.95   L   KG654
VIGNA, JUDITH. When Eric's mom fought cancer. Whitman ISBN 0-8075-8883-0, 1993. unp. col. ill.
Attempting to deal with his mother's recovery from surgery and treatments for breast cancer, a young boy experiences a range of emotions including sadness, anger, and fear. Gentle watercolor illustrations set the tone for this realistic, but reassuring story. Deals with the emotional rather than the medical aspects of the disease and may help youngsters understand when a friend or classmate has a similar experience.
SUBJ: Cancer--Fiction./ Parent and child--Fiction./ Sick--Family relationships--Fiction.

Ph-1 P-2/2 $11.9388   L   KG655
VINCENT, GABRIELLE. Ernest and Celestine at the circus. Greenwillow ISBN 0-688-08685-3, 1988. unp. col. ill.
The two friends dress up as clowns and head off to visit the circus. Just as gentle as the other stories this will be enjoyed by very young children and beginning independent readers.
SUBJ: Circus--Fiction./ Clowns--Fiction./ Friendship--Fiction./ Bears--Fiction./ Mice--Fiction.

Ph-1 P-2/1 $15.93   L   KG656
VINCENT, GABRIELLE. Ernest and Celestine's picnic. Greenwillow ISBN 0-688-01252-3, 1982. unp. col. ill.
Child-like mouse Celestine is terribly disappointed when it appears that the picnic must be cancelled because of the rain. Father-like bear Ernest has a great idea. With tarpaulin, boots, umbrellas, and raincoats they have a marvellous outing--even meeting a new friend--in spite of the downpour. Superbly drawn illustrations augment the brief but effective plot. An affection filled story that can be read aloud or will be enjoyed by just beginning readers who can manage it on their own.
Other titles in the series are ERNEST AND CELESTINE (ISBN 0-688-06525-2, 1982); BRAVO ERNEST AND CELESTINE! (ISBN 0-688-00858-5, 1982, OPC); SMILE, ERNEST AND CELESTINE (ISBN 0-688-01249-3, 1982, OPC); and WHERE ARE YOU, ERNEST AND CELESTINE? (ISBN 0-688-06235-0, 1986).
SUBJ: Bears--Fiction./ Mice--Fiction./ Friendship--Fiction.

CE   Ph-1 P-3/7 $13.95   L   KG657
VIORST, JUDITH. Alexander and the terrible, horrible, no good, very bad day. Illus. by Ray Cruz. Atheneum ISBN 0-689-30072-7; In Canada: Collier Macmillan, c1972. unp. ill.
Available from National Library Service for the Blind and Physically Handicapped on talking book TB04810, and on sound recording cassette RC30872.
Spanish version, ALEXANDER Y EL DIA TERRIBLE, HORRIBLE, ESPANTOSO, HORROROSO, (Atheneum ISBN 0-689-31591-0, 1989); (available as a read-along kit from Live Oak (ISBN 0-87499-220-6, 1991). 1 hardbound book, 1 sound cassette (9min), $19.95). Starting with gum in his hair and no prize in his cereal, all day long, everything goes wrong for Alexander--at home, in his car pool, at school, at the dentist's, and at Daddy's office. He decides he'll run away to Australia, but his mother convinces him that some days are bad, even in Australia.
SUBJ: Family life--Fiction./ Behavior--Fiction./ Spanish language materials.

TB Ph-1 P-3 $11.00 OD KG658
VIORST, JUDITH. Alexander and the terrible, horrible, no good, very bad day and other stories and poems (Talking book). Read by Blythe Danner. Music composed and conducted by Don Heckman. HarperCollins/Caedmon CP722, 1984. 1 sound cassette.
Read expressively, this recording of five favorite picture story books and a sampling of Viorst's verse proved to be an appealing independent listening experience.
Contents: Alexander who used to be rich last Sunday (6min); Alexander and the terrible, horrible, no good very bad day (5min); Rosie and Michael (6min); My mama says there aren't any zombies, ghosts, vampires, creatures, demons, monsters, fiends, goblins or things (5min); The tenth good thing about Barney (6min); If I were in charge of the world (24min).
SUBJ: Family life--Fiction./ Humorous stories./ Stories in rhyme.

CE Ph-2 P-3/5 $13.95 L KG659
VIORST, JUDITH. Alexander, who used to be rich last Sunday. Illus. by Ray Cruz. Atheneum ISBN 0-689-30602-4; In Canada: Collier Macmillan, c1978. 28p. ill.
Spanish version ALEXANDER, QUE ERA RICO EL DOMINGO PASADO, (Atheneum ISBN 0-689-31590-2, 1989); read-along kit available for Live Oak (ISBN 0-87499-223-0, 1991). 1 hardbound book, 1 sound cassette (12min), $22.95.
Despondent over his impoverished finances and jealous of his brothers, Anthony and Nick, who seem to have no trouble accumulating money, Alexander sadly ponders the rapid disappearance of the dollar his grandparents had given him last Sunday. Alexander is just a foolish spendthrift.
SUBJ: Finance, Personal--Fiction./ Saving and investment--Fiction./ Spanish language materials.

Ph-1 1-3/2 $14.00 L KG660
VIORST, JUDITH. Alexander, who's not (Do you hear me? I mean it!) going to move. Illus. by Robin Preiss Glasser. Atheneum ISBN 0-689-31958-4; In Canada: Distican, 1995. unp. ill.
Spanish version ALEXANDER, QUE DE NINGUNA MANERA (LE OYEN? LO DICE EN SERIO!) SE VA A MUDAR available from Colibri/Simon & Schuster (ISBN 0-689-31984-3, 1995).
Alexander says he will not move. He ponders the alternatives, thinks about the things he will miss, says goodbye, considers what there might be at his new home, and reluctantly begins to accept the move and pack. Alexander's feelings about moving are conveyed with humor and realism that will appeal to youngsters in a similar situation. Amusing black and white illustrations in the style of Ray Cruz extend the story.
SUBJ: Moving, Household--Fiction./ Spanish language materials.

Ph-2 1-3/2 $13.95 L KG661
VIORST, JUDITH. Earrings! Illus. by Nola Langner Malone. Atheneum ISBN 0-689-31615-1; In Canada: Collier Macmillan, 1990. unp. col. ill.
No matter how often she asks, begs or argues, the young narrator can't convince her parents to let her get pierced ears. Youngsters in similar predicaments will relate to the young girl's desperate and often humorous pleas.
SUBJ: Earrings--Fiction.

Ph-1 P-2/2 $13.95 L KG662
VIORST, JUDITH. Good-bye book. Illus. by Kay Chorao. Atheneum ISBN 0-689-31308-X, 1988. unp. col. ill.
Selectors' Choice, 17th ed.
In a familiar family situation a determined young boy puts on all sorts of acts in an attempt to keep his parents from going out to a French restaurant and abandoning him to a baby sitter. Imaginative, expressive colored pencil pictures show lots of humor along with the frustrations of both child and parents. A real winner.
SUBJ: Separation anxiety--Fiction./ Parent and child--Fiction.

Ph-1 P-3/4 $13.95 L KG663
VIORST, JUDITH. My mama says there aren't any zombies, ghosts, vampires, creatures, demons, monsters, fiends, goblins, or things. Illus. by Kay Chorao. Atheneum ISBN 0-689-30102-2, 1973. 44p. ill.
Each time Nick is troubled about imaginary monsters his mama assures him they don't exist. But the little boy isn't really sure he can believe her since his mama often makes mistakes such as the time "she said my wriggly tooth would fall out Thursday and then it stayed in till Sunday after lunch." Lots of horrible monsters and many humorous, family incidents that appeal to children.
SUBJ: Mothers--Fiction./ Monsters--Fiction.

Ph-1 K-3/2 $3.95 P KG664
VIORST, JUDITH. Tenth good thing about Barney. Illus. by Erik Blegvad. Atheneum ISBN 0-689-71203-0, c1971. 25p. ill.
Selectors' Choice, 8th ed.

A little boy is very sad when his cat dies. He doesn't want to watch TV, he can't eat chocolate pudding, he just goes to bed and cries. His mother tries to console him and suggests that he think of ten good things about Barney and say them at a funeral for his pet. He can think of only nine good things, but later when he and his Father are gardening he thinks of the tenth. "Barney is in the ground and he's helping grow flowers."
SUBJ: Cats--Fiction./ Death--Fiction.

Ph-2 2-3/2 $5.99 P KG665
VOZAR, DAVID. M.C. Turtle and the Hip Hop Hare: a nursery rap. Illus. by Betsy Lewin. Delacorte ISBN 0-440-41394-X; In Canada: Bantam Doubleday Dell, 1997. unp. col. ill.
Retells the familiar story of the race between the Tortoise and the Hare with a contemporary rap beat and cartoonish illustrations. Great fun for those who already know the original story. May inspire writing rap versions of other familiar stories as creative writing activities.
SUBJ: Turtles--Fiction./ Hares--Fiction./ Stories in rhyme./ Fables--Parodies, imitations, etc.

Ph-2 1-3/2 $14.95 L KG666
WABER, BERNARD. Gina. Houghton Mifflin ISBN 0-395-74279-X, 1995. unp. col. ill.
"Walter Lorraine books."
Gina, the only girl in her new neighborhood, is lonely until the boys learn she can throw a ball and enjoys many of the same activities as they do. The light, humorous story about accepting others and oneself is augmented by numerous color illustrations.
SUBJ: Friendship--Fiction./ Moving, Household--Fiction./ Stories in rhyme.

Ph-1 P-2/3 $14.95 L KG667
WABER, BERNARD. House on East 88th Street. Houghton Mifflin ISBN 0-395-18157-7, c1962. 48p. col. ill.
The Primm family finds Lyle, a performing crocodile, in the bathtub in their new apartment. To everyone's surprise all become great friends. In FUNNY, FUNNY LYLE (ISBN 0-395-43619-2, 1987) Lyle's mother returns, acquires the name "Felicity" and after a brush with the law becomes a permanent resident, an excellent nurse and helps care for the Primm's new baby.
SUBJ: Crocodiles--Fiction.

CE Ph-1 K-2/2 $13.95 L KG668
WABER, BERNARD. Ira sleeps over. Houghton Mifflin ISBN 0-395-13893-0, c1972. 48p. col. ill.
Read-along kit available from Live Oak Media (ISBN 0-941078-34-5, 1984), 1 hardback book, 1 sound cassette (14min), $37.95.
Available in Spanish QUIQUE DUERME FUERA DE CASA (Sitesa ISBN 968-6570-15-X, 1991).
Videocassette available from Live Oak Media (ISBN 0-87499-057-2). 1/2" VHS videocassette color (14min), $36.95.
Ira is happy and excited at the prospect of spending the night at Reggie's house until his sister brings up the problem that his teddy bear will create. Ira's never slept without his teddy bear, but if he takes the toy, Reggie may laugh. He decides to be brave and go without his teddy bear. The boys have an evening of fun, wrestling, pillow fights, ghost stories and finally bed. Best of all is Ira's discovery that Reggie too has a comforting bedtime teddy bear. As is often inevitable two best friends must spearate and that happens when Reggie moves away and IRA SAYS GOODBYE (ISBN 0-385-48315-8, 1988), as an unanimated but well paced 1/2" VHS videocassette color (18min) from Live Oak Media, 1989 (ISBN 0-87499-137-4) $34.95; and as read-along kit, Live Oak Media (ISBN 0-87499-240-0, 1991). 1 hardback book, 1 sound cassette (18min), $37.95.
SUBJ: Friendship--Fiction./ Toys--Fiction./ Family life--Fiction.

Ph-2 P-2/3 $14.95 L KG669
WABER, BERNARD. Lyle and the birthday party. Houghton Mifflin ISBN 0-395-15080-9, c1966. 48p. col. ill.
Sequel to LYLE, LYLE, CROCODILE.
Lyle, that lovable crocodile, is helping the Primms prepare for Joshua's birthday party. Suddenly he becomes "green jealous" and sulks and loses his appetite. Mrs. Primm knows he must be sick and calls a doctor. By mistake Lyle lands in a hospital for people, where he soon recovers his normal good nature and trots about (in a hospital gown) entertaining the other patients.
SUBJ: Crocodiles--Fiction./ Birthdays--Fiction./ Hospitals--Fiction.

Ph-2 K-2/3 $14.95 L KG670
WABER, BERNARD. Lyle at the office. Houghton Mifflin ISBN 0-395-70563-0, 1994. unp. col. ill.
Available from the National Library Service for the Blind and

Physically Handicapped on sound recording cassette RC 41711. Everyone in the Primm family including Lyle finds a job after Mr. Primm is dismissed because he won't allow the jovial Lyle to advertise Krispie Krunchie Krackles cereal. A humorous addition to the well-loved stories featuring the friendly crocodile.
SUBJ: Crocodiles--Fiction./ Work--Fiction.

Ph-2 P-2/3 $13.95 L KG671
WABER, BERNARD. Lyle finds his mother. Houghton Mifflin ISBN 0-395-19489-X, 1974. 47p. col. ill.
Lyle, that lovable crocodile, is very happy in the house on East 88th Street with the Primms for a family until Hector P. Valenti entices him back to their stage career with the notion that they should find Lyle's mother.
SUBJ: Crocodiles--Fiction./ Mothers--Fiction./ Theater--Fiction.

CE
Ph-1 P-2/3 $13.95 L KG672
WABER, BERNARD. Lyle, Lyle, crocodile. Houghton Mifflin ISBN 0-395-16995-X, c1965. 48p col illus.
Read-along kit available from Houghton Mifflin (ISBN 0-395-66502-7, 1987), 1 paperback book, 1 sound cassette (15min) $7.95.
A contented crocodile living happily with a family is put in a zoo by a cross neighbor but manages to escape and becomes a hero in a fire.
More fun with LOVABLE LYLE (ISBN 0-395-19858-5, 1977) which is also available from the National Library Service for the Blind and Physically Handicapped in Braille BR01148.
SUBJ: Crocodiles--Fiction./ New York (N.Y.)--Fiction.

Ph-2 1-2/2 $15.95 L KG673
WABER, BERNARD. You look ridiculous said the rhinoceros to the hippopotamus. Houghton Mifflin ISBN 0-395-07156-9, c1966. 32p. col. ill.
A fable wherein a hippopotamus dreams that she has acquired the features of a variety of animals each of whom has suggested that his fine point was lacking in her.
SUBJ: Hippopotamus--Fiction./ Animals--Fiction.

Ph-2 P-K/3 $14.95 T KG674
WADDELL, MARTIN. Can't you sleep, Little Bear? 2nd ed. Illus. by Barbara Firth. Candlewick ISBN 1-56402-007-X; In Canada: Candlewick, c1988, 1992. unp. col. ill.
Little Bear can't sleep because of the dark despite the bigger and bigger lanterns that Big Bear brings to his room in their cave. There's still the big dark "out there"--outside the cave, so Big Bear gently carries Little Bear out to see the moon and the stars. Cozy illustrations of the cave's interior and the charming bears along with the gentle cadence of the text lull the listener.
SUBJ: Bears--Fiction./ Fear of the dark--Fiction./ Bedtime--Fiction.

Ph-2 P-1/2 $15.95 T KG675
WADDELL, MARTIN. Farmer duck. Illus. by Helen Oxenbury. Candlewick ISBN 1-56402-009-6; In Canada: Candlewick, 1992. unp. col. ill.
Big book available (ISBN 1-56402-964-6, 1996), $19.99.
"How goes the work?" asks the lazy farmer, and the overworked duck answers, "Quack" as he brings in the animals, saws logs, hoes the garden, and does all the other chores around the farm. One night the animals make a plan and chase the no-good farmer away. Youngsters will sympathize with the overworked duck, delightfully depicted in the droll illustrations, and cheer for the happy ending.
SUBJ: Domestic animals--Fiction./ Farm life--Fiction.

Ph-2 P-K/3 $14.95 T KG676
WADDELL, MARTIN. Let's go home, Little Bear. Illus. by Barbara Firth. Candlewick ISBN 1-56402-131-9; In Canada: Candlewick/dist. by Douglas & McIntyre, 1993. 32p. col. ill.
When Big Bear and Little Bear go walking in the snow, Little Bear is frightened by the sounds he hears in the woods. Big Bear comforts him and explains the strange noises as he carries him home. Soft, expressive watercolor illustrations extend the text.
SUBJ: Bears--Fiction./ Fear--Fiction./ Noise--Fiction.

Ph-2 P-K/1 $15.99 T KG677
WADDELL, MARTIN. You and me, Little Bear. Illus. by Barbara Firth. Candlewick ISBN 1-56402-879-8; In Canada: Candlewick/dist. by Douglas & McIntyre, 1996. unp. col. ill.
Little Bear wants to play, but Big Bear has work to do. Finally the two enjoy a game of hide-and-seek together. An additional title for fans of the appealing bear pair who have a parent and child relationship.
SUBJ: Bears--Fiction./ Play--Fiction./ Helpfulness--Fiction.

Ph-2 1-3/2 $15.95 L KG678
WALLNER, ALEXANDRA. Alcott family Christmas. Holiday House ISBN 0-8234-1265-2, 1996. unp. col. ill.
The Alcott family gives their Christmas dinner to a less fortunate family and celebrates the holiday with other forms of sharing. The fictionalized story, based on the life and writings of Louisa May Alcott, conveys the spirit of Christmas and the generosity of the Alcott family. Readers may be led to other books about the author.
SUBJ: Alcott, Louisa May--Fiction./ Christmas--Fiction./ Family life--Fiction./ Sharing--Fiction.

Ph-2 P-K/2 $13.95 L KG679
WALSH, ELLEN STOLL. Hop jump. Harcourt Brace ISBN 0-15-292871-5; In Canada: Harcourt Brace c/o Canadian Manda, 1993. unp. col. ill.
All of the frogs hop and jump until one blue frog, Betsy, introduces them to dancing. Daring to be different, Betsy also allows room for others to move in their own way. Cut-paper collage illustrations displayed with plenty of white space and easy-to-read text will appeal to the very young. Use as a springboard for creative movement activities.
SUBJ: Frogs--Fiction./ Dancing--Fiction.

Ph-2 P-1/2 $12.00 L KG680
WALSH, ELLEN STOLL. Mouse paint. Harcourt Brace ISBN 0-15-256025-4; In Canada: Harcourt Brace c/o Canadian Manda, 1989. unp. col. ill.
A trio of white mice frolic in red, blue, and yellow paint while the cat sleeps. As the mice play, they mix colors to create green, orange, and purple, washing themselves in the cat's water dish. Cut-paper collages surrounded by plenty of white space introduce color to young viewers. For art classes.
SUBJ: Color--Fiction./ Mice--Fiction.

Ph-2 K-2/2 $14.00 L KG681
WALSH, ELLEN STOLL. Samantha. Harcourt Brace ISBN 0-15-252264-6; In Canada: Harcourt Brace c/o Canadian Manda, 1996. unp. col. ill.
Samantha, a young mouse, seeks protection from her rough brothers and sisters and finds it with her fairy godmother. Eventually Samantha decides she's too safe. Cut-paper illustrations are whimsical and light.
SUBJ: Brothers and sisters--Fiction./ Fairies--Fiction./ Mice--Fiction.

Ph-2 P-K/2 $13.95 L KG682
WALSH, ELLEN STOLL. You silly goose. Harcourt Brace Jovanovich ISBN 0-15-299865-9; In Canada: Harcourt Brace Jovanovich c/o Canadian Manda, 1992. unp. col. ill.
George, a brown mouse, brings news to his geese friends that he has seen the fox. When he starts to describe the fox, Lulu, a foolish goose, thinks George is the fox. A real fox comes along and almost gets the goose, but clever George saves his friend. Accompanied by attractive cut-paper collage illustrations.
SUBJ: Geese--Fiction./ Foxes--Fiction.

Ph-2 2-3/6 $15.00 L KG683
WALSH, JILL PATON. Pepi and the secret names. Illus. by Fiona French. Lothrop, Lee & Shepard ISBN 0-688-13428-9, 1995. unp. col. ill.
Available from the National Library Service for the Blind and Physically Handicapped on sound recording cassette RC 41520.
Knowing the secret names of the lion, the cobra, the hawk, and the crocodile, Pepi convinces them to pose for his father who is decorating the tomb of Prince Dhutmose. Set in ancient Egypt, the long story is elaborately illustrated in brilliant colors and Egyptian motifs. The secret names of the fierce animals are given in hieroglyphics with a key following the story.
SUBJ: Egypt--Fiction./ Animals--Fiction./ Cats--Fiction.

Ph-1 1-3/2 $14.93 L KG684
WALTER, MILDRED PITTS. Brother to the wind. Illustrated by Diane and Leo Dillon. Lothrop, Lee & Shepard ISBN 0-688-03812-3, 1985. 32p. col. ill.
Believing that Good Snake can make his wish come true, Emeke, a young African boy, with help from Hyena, Elephant and Rhinoceros, follows the reptile's instructions, builds an enormous kite and achieves his dream. He flies from the mountain top down to his village much to the chagrin of the villagers who have ridiculed him. Handsome, often subdued, paintings combine realism and mysticism to illustrate an imaginative, compelling folk-like story.
SUBJ: Africa--Fiction./ Flying--Fiction./ Wishes--Fiction.

Ph-2 P-2/1 $14.93 L KG685
WALTER, MILDRED PITTS. My mama needs me. Illus. by Pat Cummings. Lothrop, Lee & Shepard ISBN 0-688-01671-5, 1983. unp. col. ill.
Coretta Scott King Award.
Anxious to care for his new baby sister, Jason is unwilling to play with his friends, visit a neighbor, or go to the pond and feed the ducks in case his mother needs him. The striking illustrations combine

with the simple text to portray the mixed feelings of many children when they gain a younger sibling. Share with a group.
SUBJ: Babies--Fiction.

Ph-2 1-3/2 $14.95 L KG686
WALTER, MILDRED PITTS. Ty's one-man band. Illus. by Margot Tomes. Four Winds/Macmillan ISBN 0-02-792300-2; In Canada: Collier Macmillan, c1980, 1987. unp. col. ill.
Ty's friends ridicule him when he says his new, peg-legged friend is coming to town and will dance and make music with a washboard, wooden spoons, comb and tin pail. Soon, however, the hot, night air explodes with music and all the town's folks fill the street with dancing. Colorful, realistic pictures portray an African-American community of an old southern town. For multicultural studies.
SUBJ: Music--Fiction./ Afro-Americans--Fiction.

Ph-2 K-2/3 $14.93 L KG687
WALTON, RICK. Noah's square dance. Illus. by Thor Wickstrom. Lothrop, Lee & Shepard ISBN 0-688-11187-4, 1995. unp. col. ill.
The animals grab their partners, and Noah does the calling for a great square dance to the beat of the rain on the ark. Richly illustrated with doublespread paintings, the toe-tapping, rhyming text is ideal for reading aloud. This NOAH'S ARK variation is appropriate for general audiences.
SUBJ: Noah's ark--Fiction./ Square dancing--Fiction./ Animals--Fiction./ Stories in rhyme.

CE
Ph-1 1-3/3 $14.95 L KG688
WARD, LYND. Biggest bear. Houghton Mifflin ISBN 0-395-14806-5, c1952. 84p. ill.
Caldecott Medal Award.
Available from National Library Service for the Blind and Physically Handicapped on talking book TB02166 and in Braille BR05917 and BRA02347.
Read-along kit available from Weston Woods PBC10, 1993. 1 paperback book, 1 sound cassette (18min), $15.70. Side one with page turn signal, side two without signal.
Johnny wants a bearskin for his barn, but instead gets a live bear.
SUBJ: Bears--Fiction.

Ph-2 P-1 $15.00 T KG689
WATSON, CLYDE. AppleBet; an ABC. Illus. by Wendy Watson. Farrar, Straus & Giroux ISBN 0-374-30384-3; In Canada: McGraw-Hill Ryerson, 1982. unp. col. ill.
An alphabet book that uses brightly colored homey pictures and rhyming couplets to tell the story of Bets and her mother and their trip to the country fair with their cart filled with apples to sell. Introduces not only the letters usually found in ABC books but also ch, sh, th, wh, and the soft sounds of c and g.
SUBJ: Alphabet.

Ph-1 1-3/5 $14.95 T KG690
WEATHERFORD, CAROLE BOSTON. Juneteenth jamboree. Illus. by Yvonne Buchanan. Lee & Low ISBN 1-880000-18-0, 1995. unp. col. ill.
Cassandra and her family celebrate "Juneteenth," a commemoration of June 19, 1865 when the slaves in Texas finally learned of the Emancipation Proclamation. A brief author's note provides historical background for readers unfamiliar with this Texas holiday. Watercolor illustrations and the family story in this historical fiction piece will have broad appeal. For multicultural studies.
SUBJ: Afro-Americans--Fiction./ Texas--Fiction./ Family life--Fiction.

Ph-2 K-2/2 $14.89 L KG691
WEEKS, SARAH. Hurricane City. Illus. by James Warhola. HarperCollins ISBN 0-06-021573-9; In Canada: HarperCollins, 1993. unp. col. ill.
"Laura Geringer book."
Hurricanes big and small from A to Z come to "Hurricane City." Zany illustrations accompany each letter of the alphabet with a name and personality for each hurricane as it blows through town. This romp through the alphabet would be a fun accompaniment to primary units on weather.
SUBJ: Alphabet./ Hurricanes--Fiction./ Stories in rhyme.

Ph-2 P-2/2 $16.00 L KG692
WEISS, GEORGE DAVID. What a wonderful world. By George David Weiss and Bob Thiele. Illus. by Ashley Bryan. Atheneum ISBN 0-689-80087-8; In Canada: Distican, 1995. unp. col. ill.
"Jean Karl book."
Vivid illustrations bring the lyrics of this exuberant song to life. Children of varied cultures are depicted in a puppet show which includes Louis Armstrong, the musician who made the song famous. An optimistic, joyful view of the world. Good for multicultural studies.
SUBJ: Songs./ Jazz.

Ph-2 K-2/2 $13.93 L KG693
WEISS, NICKI. Stone men. Greenwillow ISBN 0-688-11016-9, 1993. unp. col. ill.
Grandma tells Arnie a story about the peddler, Isaac, who traveled from town to town building people from stones to keep him company. One night near Passover, he hears the czar's soldiers planning to attack the village he has just visited. Isaac builds a row of stone men outside the village, and in the early morning darkness, the soldiers turn away when they think they see an army.
SUBJ: Peddlers and peddling--Fiction./ Jews--Fiction./ Grandmothers--Fiction.

Ph-2 K-2/3 $13.95 L KG694
WELCH, WILLY. Playing right field. Illus. by Marc Simont. Scholastic ISBN 0-590-48298-X; In Canada: Scholastic, 1995. unp. col. ill.
Out in right field, there's not much to do except study the dandelions and dream of great baseball players until a ball comes your way and lands in your glove. The range of emotions experienced by a young boy picked last for the team and placed in right field are perfectly portrayed in the watercolor and charcoal illustrations. The rhyming text is also a song recorded by Peter, Paul and Mary.
SUBJ: Baseball--Fiction./ Stories in rhyme.

Ph-2 1-3/4 $14.95 L KG695
WELLER, FRANCES WARD. Riptide. Illus. by Robert J. Blake. Philomel ISBN 0-399-21675-8; In Canada: Putnam, 1990. unp. col. ill.
A young boy growing up on Cape Cod has a golden haired dog named Riptide - who loves to run the beach and plunge into the sea. When a real riptide menaces the swimmers, he swims out to save a girl and is nearly swept away himself. The superb oil paintings combine with well written text to provide a classic animal story and a first rate read-aloud.
SUBJ: Dogs--Fiction./ Cape Cod (Mass.)--Fiction.

Ph-1 P-1/2 $13.89 L KG696
WELLS, ROSEMARY. Bunny cakes. Dial ISBN 0-8037-2144-7; In Canada: McClelland & Stewart, 1997. unp. col. ill.
Selectors' Choice, 21st ed.
Wanting to help Ruby make a surprise cake for Grandma, Max tries to add Red Hot Marshmallow Squirters to each shopping list she gives him, but the grocer can't read his scribbles. Finally Max gets the bright idea to draw the candies which he finally gets to decorate his earthworm cake. The characters of Max and Ruby are perfectly conveyed in the expressive ink and watercolor illustrations and story which are on target for young audiences.
SUBJ: Rabbits--Fiction./ Brothers and sisters--Fiction./ Baking--Fiction./ Cake--Fiction.

Ph-2 P-K/2 $7.99 T KG697
WELLS, ROSEMARY. Edward in deep water. Dial ISBN 0-8037-1882-9, 1995. unp. col. ill. (Edward the unready).
Spanish version EDUARDO CUMPLEANOS EN LA PISCINA available from Santillana (ISBN 1-56014-664-8, 1996).
Invited to a swim party, Edward insists on wearing his water wings, but still needs to leave the party early. The adults accept that Edward is not quite ready and treat his feelings with respect. The small format and endearing illustrations are comfortable in the hands of youngsters who may identify with Edward.
SUBJ: Bears--Fiction./ Fear--Fiction./ Birthdays--Fiction./ Swimming--Fiction./ Spanish language materials.

Ph-2 P-K/2 $7.99 T KG698
WELLS, ROSEMARY. Edward unready for school. Dial ISBN 0-8037-1884-5, 1995. unp. col. ill. (Edward the unready).
Spanish version EDUARDO: EL PRIMER DIA DE COLEGIO available from Santillana (ISBN 1-56014-620-6, 1997).
School is a happy and busy place, but not for Edward who wants to go home. His teacher and parents agree that not everyone is ready for school at the same time. The lack of pressure to achieve is unique and reassuring for youngsters in similar circumstances.
SUBJ: Bears--Fiction./ Play schools--Fiction./ Schools--Fiction.

Ph-2 P-1/2 $7.99 T KG699
WELLS, ROSEMARY. Edward's overwhelming overnight. Dial ISBN 0-8037-1883-7, 1995. unp. col. ill. (Edward the unready).
When snow forces Edward to stay the night at a friend's house, he's overwhelmed and unhappy with the experience. Edward's sympathetic hosts shovel snow and put chains on the car in order to take him home. Many young children will relate to Edward's feelings and find reassurance in his family's understanding.
SUBJ: Bears--Fiction./ Sleepovers--Fiction./ Snow--Fiction./ Growth--Fiction.

Ph-1 P-1/3 $11.99   T   KG700

WELLS, ROSEMARY. Max and Ruby's first Greek myth: Pandora's box. Dial ISBN 0-8037-1524-2, 1993. unp. col. ill.
> The Greek myth "Pandora's box" gets an original twist when Ruby reads the story about "sneaking and peeking" to Max. In Ruby's version, Pandora opens her mother's jewelry box to release a horde of insects with one hope: a little green spider who spins a web to capture the insects. A new and younger audience will delight in this humorous introduction to the traditional myth through the familiar and beloved characters of Max and Ruby.
> SUBJ: Brothers and sisters--Fiction./ Curiosity--Fiction./ Rabbits--Fiction./ Mythology, Greek--Fiction.

Ph-1 P-1/3 $12.99   T   KG701

WELLS, ROSEMARY. Max and Ruby's Midas: another Greek myth. Dial ISBN 0-8037-1782-2, 1995. unp. col. ill.
> Max's overwhelming greed for cupcakes and sweets prompts Ruby to relate the story of Midas who turned vegetables, and inadvertently his family, into ice cream and other confections. Humorous illustrations and a clever design including Greek statues on the endpapers provide a delightful vehicle for this modern twist on ancient mythology.
> SUBJ: Food habits--Fiction./ Brothers and sisters--Fiction./ Rabbits--Fiction./ Mythology, Greek--Fiction.

CE   Ph-1 P-2/2 $9.95   T   KG702

WELLS, ROSEMARY. Max's chocolate chicken. Dial ISBN 0-8037-0585-9; In Canada: Fitzhenry & Whiteside, 1989. unp. col. ill.
> Animated videocassette available from Weston Woods HMPV344V, 1991. 1/2" VHS videocassette color (4min) $49.95.
> Even though he wants to eat the chocolate chicken he found in the birdbath Max is not willing to hunt for eggs to win it. Ruby's scoldings come to no avail but Max, as always, gains his heart's desire. Certain to provoke giggles.
> SUBJ: Easter eggs--Fiction./ Easter--Fiction./ Rabbits--Fiction.

CE   Ph-1 P-1/2 $9.89   L   KG703

WELLS, ROSEMARY. Max's Christmas. Dial ISBN 0-8037-0290-6; In Canada: Fitzhenry & Whiteside, 1986. unp. col. ill.
> Animated 1/2" VHS videocassette color (5min) available from Weston Woods HMPV322V, $49.95.
> Answering all his questions with an abrupt "Because," big sister Ruby leaves young Max uncertain concerning the mysteries of Santa Claus, so the curious little rabbit sneaks downstairs and has a surprising encounter with the jolly old gent.
> SUBJ: Christmas--Fiction./ Santa Claus--Fiction./ Rabbits--Fiction.

BB   Ph-3 P/1 $4.50   T   KG704

WELLS, ROSEMARY. Max's first word (Board book). Dial ISBN 0-8037-6066-3, 1979. unp. col. ill.
> Ruby patiently tries to teach her baby brother, Max, the correct words for various objects, but Max has his own ideas and calls everything Bang until Ruby shows him an apple. A small, brief, bright book with heavy board pages.
> In MAX'S NEW SUIT (ISBN 0-8037-6065-5, 1979) Ruby tries to help Max dress for a party but he does it himself with decidedly unconventional results, and in MAX'S RIDE (ISBN 0-8037-6069-8, 1979) Max takes a wild carriage ride.
> SUBJ: Brothers and sisters--Fiction./ Rabbits--Fiction./ Humorous stories.

Ph-2 K-2/2 $12.89   L   KG705

WELLS, ROSEMARY. McDuff comes home. Illus. by Susan Jeffers. Hyperion ISBN 0-7868-2259-7; In Canada: Little, Brown, 1997. unp. col. ill.
> Chasing a rabbit, McDuff gets lost in the garden of Mrs. Higgins who helps him return home. Brightly colored illustrations are the attraction in the simple story about the adorable McDuff.
> SUBJ: Dogs--Fiction.

Ph-2 K-2/2 $12.89   L   KG706

WELLS, ROSEMARY. McDuff moves in. Illus. by Susan Jeffers. Hyperion ISBN 0-7868-2257-0; In Canada: Little, Brown, 1997. unp. col. ill.
> Falling out of the dogcatcher's truck, a small white terrier looks for a home. Following the smell of vanilla rice pudding and sausages, he comes to the home of Lucy and Fred who adopt him and name him, McDuff. Richly colored illustrations focus on the fluffy white dog who wins the hearts of readers.
> SUBJ: Dogs--Fiction.

CE   Ph-1 K-1/4 $14.89   L   KG707

WELLS, ROSEMARY. Noisy Nora. With all new illustrations by Rosemary Wells. Dial ISBN 0-8037-1836-5; In Canada: McClelland & Stewart, 1997. unp. col. ill.
> Spanish version NORA LA REVOLTOSA available from Dial/Penguin Ediciones (ISBN 0-8037-2065-3, 1997).

Big book available from Scholastic (ISBN 0-590-64658-3, 1979). Read-along kit available from Weston Woods HRA175, 1993. 1 hardback book, 1 sound cassette (6min), $14.00.
> Kate gets special attention because she's older and baby Jack because he's younger. So Nora, the middle child in the mouse family, must resort to noise and naughtiness in hopes of gaining parental attention. Even then all she hears is "hush" or "quiet" from her parents or "Why are you so dumb?" from Kate. Finally Nora discovers a special silence and quietness that brings worried responses from Mother, Father, and even sister Kate. Newly illustrated in bright colors with a large format.
> SUBJ: Behavior--Fiction./ Family life--Fiction./ Mice--Fiction./ Stories in rhyme./ Spanish language materials.

VCR   Ph-1 K-1 $60.00   OD   KG708

WELLS, ROSEMARY. Noisy Nora (Videocassette). Weston Woods C175 ISBN 0-89719-339-3, 1993. 1/2" VHS videocassette color (6min).
> Includes teacher's guide.
> ALA notable video, 1995.
> Kate gets special attention because she's older and baby Jack because he's younger. So Nora, the middle child in the mouse family, must resort to noise and naughtiness in hopes of gaining parental attention. In this delightful production with just the right amount of drama and humor, Nora finally discovers a special silence and quietness that brings worried responses from Mother, Father, and even sister Kate.
> SUBJ: Behavior--Fiction./ Family life--Fiction./ Mice--Fiction./ Stories in rhyme.

Ph-2 K-2/2 $9.99   L   KG709

WHEELER, CINDY. Bookstore cat. Random House ISBN 0-394-94109-8; In Canada: Random House, 1994. 32p. col. ill. (Step into reading).
> Mulligan, the cat, works in the bookstore and disrupts story hour one morning when a pigeon strays into the shop. The action-packed and colorful illustrations will attract beginning readers who will be rewarded with a simple, easy-to-read text.
> SUBJ: Cats--Fiction./ Bookstores--Fiction.

Ph-2 K-2/5 $11.95   T   KG710

WHELAN, GLORIA. Week of raccoons. Illus. by Lynn Munsinger. Knopf ISBN 0-394-98396-3; In Canada: Random House, 1988. unp col illus.
> Raccoons have made pests of themselves at Mr. and Mrs. Twerkle's house so he traps them and moves them to the woods but they spend their time trying to figure out how to get back. Pastel illustrations and humorous text make this one fun to read aloud.
> SUBJ: Raccoons--Fiction.

Ph-2 P-2/2 $14.95   L   KG711

WIDMAN, CHRISTINE. Lemon drop jar. Illus. by Christa Kieffer. Macmillan ISBN 0-02-792759-8; In Canada: Maxwell Macmillan, 1992. unp. col. ill.
> A young girl visits her great-aunt Emma and learns the story of the large glass jar in which she keeps lemon drops. The yellow of the lemon drops is carried throughout in the warm illustrations and in references in the text to yellow leaves, a yellow cat, and the yellow glow of a lamp. A well-crafted story that appeals to each of the senses.
> SUBJ: Great-aunts--Fiction.

Ph-1 K-2/2 $15.95   L   KG712

WIESNER, DAVID. Hurricane. Clarion ISBN 0-395-54382-7, 1990. unp. col. ill.
> Two brothers experience the excitement of a passing hurricane, and the following day a fallen tree fuels their imaginations. Masterful illustrations depict the preparations for the storm and the fantasy the boys create with the tree.
> SUBJ: Hurricanes--Fiction./ Brothers--Fiction./ Imagination--Fiction.

Ph-1 1-5/4 $15.95   L   KG713

WIESNER, DAVID. June 29, 1999. Clarion ISBN 0-395-59762-5, 1992. unp. col. ill.
> A young girl suspects her science project is the cause of giant vegetables falling from the sky until vegetables that weren't part of her experiment float down to earth. Bizarre illustrations of giant backyard broccoli and monstrous peas floating down the Mississippi have a surreal and humorous quality. A marvelous story on its own with numerous possiblities for the curriculum including science projects, geography, and creative writing.
> SUBJ: Science--Experiments--Fiction./ Vegetables--Fiction.

Ph-1 P-3 $15.95   L   KG714

WIESNER, DAVID. Tuesday. Clarion ISBN 0-395-55113-7, 1991. unp. col. ill.
> Caldecott Medal.

Selectors' Choice, 18th ed.
One sleepy Tuesday night frogs set sail on their "magic carpet" lily pads and fly through town, getting tangled in a clothesline, watching television and chasing a startled dog. The police are bewildered by lily pad strewn streets the next morning. There is very little text, allowing viewers of all ages to laugh aloud at the fantastic illustrations of frogs flying, winking and waving. Tuesdays will never again be mundane.
SUBJ: Frogs--Fiction.

Ph-2 P-K/1 $15.99 L KG715
WIKLER, LINDA. Alfonse, where are you? Crown ISBN 0-517-70046-8, 1996. unp. col. ill.
When Little Bird can't find Alphonse, she hides from him. A goose chase ensues as all the geese join in the search for Little Bird. The simple story will delight young readers who will enjoy finding Little Bird hidden in the doublespread watercolor illustrations. Repetitive phrases in the predictable book make it a good choice for beginning readers.
SUBJ: Hide-and-seek--Fiction./ Geese--Fiction./ Birds--Fiction.

Ph-2 1-3/3 $14.95 L KG716
WILD, MARGARET. Going home. Illus. by Wayne Harris. Scholastic ISBN 0-590-47958-X; In Canada: Scholastic, 1993. unp. col. ill.
Wishing for home, Hugo looks out of his hospital window to the zoo next door and dreams about going home with the animals to African grasslands, the Amazon jungle, and the Himalayas. In contrast to the white space on the pages that depict the hospital, Hugo's imaginative journeys are depicted in full-color doublespreads. Youngsters who have been away from home, especially for a hospital visit, will understand the young boy's yearning in this well-designed, appealing, and hopeful fantasy.
SUBJ: Hospitals--Fiction./ Dreams--Fiction./ Voyages and travels--Fiction./ Zoo animals--Fiction.

Ph-1 P-2 $13.95 T KG717
WILD, MARGARET. Our granny. Illus. by Julie Vivas. Ticknor & Fields ISBN 0-395-67023-3, 1994. unp. col. ill.
Grannies come in all shapes and sizes, live in different places, and enjoy different activities. The two children who narrate this book know their granny is special, and they love her. Poetic text and watercolor illustrations joyously depict the variety of grannies.
SUBJ: Grandmothers--Fiction.

Ph-2 1-3/3 $13.95 T KG718
WILD, MARGARET. Toby. Illus. by Noela Young. Ticknor & Fields ISBN 0-395-67024-1, 1994. unp. col. ill.
Toby has been the family dog since Sara, the big sister was a baby. A younger brother describes the family's reaction to Toby's aging and approaching death, including Sara's apparent meanness and inability to accept the loss. The story and illustrations realistically portray the varied means of dealing with grief among the family members.
SUBJ: Death--Fiction./ Dogs--Fiction.

Ph-2 K-3/4 $11.89 L KG719
WILDER, LAURA INGALLS. Dance at Grandpa's. Adapted from the Little House books by Laura Ingalls Wilder. Illus. by Renee Graef. HarperCollins ISBN 0-06-023879-8; In Canada: HarperCollins, 1994. unp. col. ill. (My first Little House books).
Laura and her family travel to Grandpa's for a party in this episodic story adapted from LITTLE HOUSE IN THE BIG WOODS. Designed to introduce the "Little House" books to younger readers, the adaptation maintains the warmth and appeal of the original. Full-color illustrations imitate the style of Garth Williams.
SUBJ: Frontier and pioneer life--Fiction./ Family life--Fiction./ Wisconsin--Fiction./ Parties--Fiction.

Ph-2 K-3/4 $11.89 L KG720
WILDER, LAURA INGALLS. Winter days in the Big Woods. Adapted from the Little House books by Laura Ingalls Wilder. Illus. by Renee Graef. HarperCollins ISBN 0-06-023022-3; In Canada: HarperCollins, 1994. unp. col. ill. (My first Little House books).
Introduces Laura, the Wilder family, and their daily and seasonal routines while living in the little house in the Big Woods in Wisconsin. Doublespread, full-color illustrations and brief text offer a visual introduction to the Little House series or serve as an accompaniment to the longer books for young children who would like to see an artist's interpretation of pioneer life. The illustrations where inspired by the work of Garth Williams with his permission and like the text are true to the original work. Not a substitute for the original books, but a worthy extension of the popular series.
SUBJ: Frontier and pioneer life--Fiction./ Family life--Fiction./ Wisconsin--Fiction.

Ph-1 P-1 $6.95 P KG721
WILDSMITH, BRIAN. Brian Wildsmith's ABC. Millbrook ISBN 1-56294-906-3, 1995. unp. col. ill.
Originally published in England, Oxford University Press, 1962. Features the letters of the alphabet in upper and lower case with an accompanying animal or object. Bold colors and crisp graphic design create eye-catching illustrations. The simple design makes it a good alphabet book for teaching letter recognition.
SUBJ: Alphabet.

Ph-1 K-2/5 $14.95 T KG722
WILDSMITH, BRIAN. Professor Noah's spaceship. Oxford ISBN 0-19-279741-7, 1980. unp col illus.
A modern Noah builds a spaceship and takes off for a journey of 40 days and nights to a distant planet. With him he takes all Earth's animals to save them from the terrible pollution that is destroying their lives. Repair to the time guidance fin results in an accidental adjustment backwards. When the ship finally lands it is back on Earth, no longer a polluted planet, but as it was hundreds of years ago when it was beautiful and clean. Striking, handsome pictures illustrate a message worth telling.
SUBJ: Space flight--Fiction./ Pollution--Fiction./ Ecology--Fiction.

Ph-2 K-2/2 $15.95 T KG723
WILHELM, HANS. Royal raven. Scholastic ISBN 0-590-54337-7; In Canada: Scholastic, 1996. unp. col. ill.
"Cartwheel books."
Not satisfied to be an ordinary black raven, Crawford asks a witch to turn him into a flashy colored bird. When he is caged by a princess for his remarkable feathers, he eventually decides his freedom is more important and plucks the feathers out. Glitter-enhanced illustrations attract youngsters to the story and personality of Crawford. The amusing story includes a lesson about self-esteem.
SUBJ: Birds--Fiction./ Self-acceptance--Fiction./ Princesses--Fiction.

Ph-1 K-3/6 $4.95 P KG724
WILLARD, NANCY. Simple pictures are best. Illus. by Tomie De Paola. Harcourt Brace Jovanovich ISBN 0-15-682625-9, c1977. 32p. col. ill.
The shoemaker and his wife Ellen are having their picture taken for their anniversary. The debates over what they will wear and what will be included in the photograph are resolved by the photographer's assistant James who manages to add things despite the photographer's warning that simple pictures are best. The purposefully dead-pan illustrations juxtapositioned with the detailed descriptions of the couple will prove hilariously funny at picture-story time.
SUBJ: Photography--Fiction./ Humorous stories.

Ph-1 K-2/3 $15.95 L KG725
WILLARD, NANCY. Starlit somersault downhill. Illus. by Jerry Pinkney. Little, Brown ISBN 0-316-94113-1; In Canada: Little, Brown, 1993. unp. col. ill.
A bear invites a rabbit to join him for a winter's nap, but the rabbit soon discovers it's not in his nature to sleep through the season. The rabbit's infectious joy in the first snowfall is shown through the poetic text and the watercolor illustrations. A foldout page offers surprise action at the end of the story about hibernation.
SUBJ: Bears--Fiction./ Rabbits--Fiction./ Winter--Fiction./ Hibernation--Fiction./ Stories in rhyme.

Ph-2 2-4/4 $16.00 T KG726
WILLIAMS, DAVID. Grandma Essie's covered wagon. Illus. by Wiktor Sadowski. Knopf ISBN 0-679-80253-3; In Canada: Random House, 1993. unp. col. ill.
"Borzoi book."
Born in a log cabin in Missouri around the turn of the century, Essie tells about the many moves her family made in a covered wagon to Kansas, Oklahoma, and back to Missouri in search of a more prosperous life. Based on the stories of the author's grandmother and told in her voice, the words and illustrations offer a glimpse into the history of the Midwest.
SUBJ: Frontier and pioneer life--Fiction./ Middle West--Fiction.

CE
Ph-1 1-2/2 $13.88 L KG727
WILLIAMS, KAREN LYNN. Galimoto. Illus. by Catherine Stock. Lothrop, Lee & Shepard ISBN 0-688-08790-6, 1990. unp. col. ill.
Videocassette available from Reading Adventures 1003, 1993. 1/2" VHS videocassette color (9min), $42.50.
Read-along kit available from Reading Adventures 1390, 1993. 1 hardback book, 1 sound cassette (18min), $24.95
A 7-year-old boy, Kondi, scours his African village for enough wire to build a "galimoto", a push toy made in the shape of a car. A satisfying story of a young boy's perseverance and ingenuity which might also serve as an introduction to African village life.
SUBJ: Toy making--Fiction./ Africa--Fiction.

CE   Ph-2 K-2/2 $14.95   L   KG728
WILLIAMS, KAREN LYNN. Tap-tap. Illus. by Catherine Stock. Clarion
ISBN 0-395-65617-6, 1994. 34p. col. ill.
Read-along kit available from Clarion (ISBN 0-395-72087-7, 1996). 1
paperback book, 1 sound cassette (23min), $8.95.
After a busy day at the market, Sasifi uses the coins she has earned
to purchase a ride home in the "tap-tap," a brightly decorated
truck. The colorful Haitian countryside, market, and produce fill the
watercolor illustrations. For multicultural studies.
SUBJ: Haiti--Fiction./ Trucks--Fiction./ Markets--Fiction./ Mothers and
daughters--Fiction.

                      Ph-2 K-3/2 $15.95   T   KG729
WILLIAMS, KAREN LYNN. When Africa was home. Illus. by Floyd
Cooper. Orchard ISBN 0-531-05925-1, 1991. unp. col. ill.
Peter, a small golden-haired boy, considers Africa his home and
misses it when his family returns to America. A superb introduction to
another culture through the experiences of a boy whose American
parents live and work in Africa.
SUBJ: Africa--Fiction.

CE   Ph-1 P-2/4 $14.89   L   KG730
WILLIAMS, LINDA. Little old lady who was not afraid of anything. Illus.
by Megan Lloyd. HarperCollins/Crowell ISBN 0-690-04586-7; In
Canada: HarperCollins, 1986. unp. col. ill.
Read-along kit available from HarperChildren's Audio (ISBN 0-694-
70015-0, 1995). 1 paperback book, 1 sound cassette (6min), $7.95.
Spanish version, LA VIEJECITA QUE NO LE TENIA MIEDO A
NADA, available from Harper Arco Iris (ISBN 0-06-026238-9, 1996),
$15.95.
Coming home through the woods late at night, a little old lady sees
two big shoes in her path and tells them to get out of her way, but
they follow her going CLOMP, CLOMP. In like manner she adds to
her following a pair of pants going WIGGLE, WIGGLE; a shirt going
SHAKE, SHAKE; gloves going CLAP, CLAP; and a hat going NOD,
NOD; but when a big, scary orange pumpkin head goes BOO, BOO
and joins the group, the little old lady races home without looking
back. Full-paged, detailed, folk art-style pictures echo the repetition
and cumulative chant of the tale. Fine for reading aloud anytime and
a good addition to the Halloween collection.
SUBJ: Fear--Fiction./ Spanish language materials.

                      Ph-1 1-3/2 $14.95   L   KG731
WILLIAMS, SHERLEY ANNE. Working cotton. Illus. by Carole Byard.
Harcourt Brace Jovanovich ISBN 0-15-299624-9; In Canada: Harcourt
Brace Jovanovich, 1992. unp. col. ill.
Caldecott Honor book, 1993.
Coretta Scott King Award, 1993.
A young girl describes a day with her family picking cotton from
sunup to sundown. The family's pride and happiness together is
apparent although the hardships of their poverty and difficult working
conditions leave a strong impression on the reader. Sweeping
doublespread illustrations dramatically portray the migrant experience.
Use of dialect provides an opportunity to introduce language patterns
and point of view to young listeners. For multicultural studies.
SUBJ: Migrant labor--Fiction./ Cotton picking--Fiction./ Family life--
Fiction./ Afro-Americans--Fiction.

CE   Ph-1 P-1/1 $14.95   L   KG732
WILLIAMS, SUE. I went walking. Illus. by Julie Vivas. Gulliver/Harcourt
Brace Jovanovich ISBN 0-15-200471-8, 1990. unp. col. ill.
Selectors' Choice, 18th ed.
Big book available from Harcourt Brace (ISBN 0-15-238010-8,
1991).
Spanish version SALI DE PASEO available from Libros Viajeros/
Harcourt Brace (ISBN 0-15-200288-X, 1995); Spanish version read-
along kit available from Live Oak Media (ISBN 0-87499-365-2,
1996) 1 paperback book, 1 sound cassette (6min), $14.95.
As a young boy goes walking, he sees farmyard animals of different
colors who end up following him. Large doublespread illustrations and
a simple, repetitive question and answer text make this predictable
book a pure delight for sharing in a group and for beginning readers
to use independently.
SUBJ: Walking--Fiction./ Color--Fiction./ Animals--Fiction./ Stories in
rhyme./ Spanish language materials.

                      Ph-1 1-3/2 $13.95   T   KG733
WILLIAMS, SUZANNE. Edwin and Emily. Illus. by Abby Carter.
Hyperion ISBN 0-7868-0129-8; In Canada: Little, Brown, 1995. 48p. ill.
(Hyperion chapters).
Emily manages to get the best of her big brother, Edwin, whether it's
his hat and mittens, his favorite car, or his candy bar. Amusing short
chapters and well-placed black and white illustrations portray a
typical sibling relationship in an appealing transitional reader format.
SUBJ: Brothers and sisters--Fiction.

                      Ph-1 P-3/3 $14.93   L   KG734
WILLIAMS, VERA B. Chair for my mother. Greenwillow ISBN 0-688-
00915-8, 1982. unp. col. ill.
Caldecott Honor book.
Spanish available SILLON PARA MI MAMA (ISBN 0-688-13616-8,
1994).
Spanish read-along kit available from Live Oak Media (ISBN
0-87499-335-0, 1994). 1 paperback book, 1 sound cassette (12min),
$15.95, and teacher's guide.
Big book available from Mulberry (ISBN 0-688-12612-X, 1992),
$18.95.
A young girl describes her life with Mama, a waitress, and Grandma,
who seems always to stay at home. A fire destroys their home and all
of their belongings, but friends, neighbors and relatives come to their
aid and contribute the essentials needed to set up a new home.
Unfortunately there is not a comfortable chair, only three useful but
hard, straight kitchen chairs. So they start putting all their coins in a
large jar until the day they have enough money to buy a big,
flowered, overstuffed chair so that Grandma can sit by the window
and talk to passersby, Mama can rest after work and the little girl
can curl up with Mama until she falls asleep. Brightly colored primitive
style illustrations add drama to this title at picture storybook time.
SUBJ: Family life--Fiction./ Saving and investment--Fiction./ Chairs--
Fiction.

                      Ph-1 K-3/2 $13.93   L   KG735
WILLIAMS, VERA B. Cherries and cherry pits. Greenwillow ISBN 0-688-
05146-4, c1965, 1984. unp. col. ill.
As she draws her beautiful pictures, Bidemmi, a young Black girl, tells
stories of a loving father, a giving grandmother and a thoughtful,
agile big brother. Incorporated in each story is a bag of cherries
requiring someone to spit out the pits, which in the final story leads to
a dream of an orchard with cherries for the entire neighborhood.
SUBJ: Drawing--Fiction./ Imagination--Fiction.

                      Ph-1 P-K/2 $12.93   L   KG736
WILLIAMS, VERA B. More more more, said the baby. Greenwillow ISBN
0-688-09174-1, 1990. unp. col. ill.
Caldecott Honor Book.
Three brief stories about three babies and a parent or grandparent
who exuberantly chases, swings, nuzzles and clearly loves each one.
Each story features a child of a different race in boldly colored
gouache paintings with colorful borders and even colorful lettering for
the text. Young listeners are caught up in the joyful expression of
family love.
SUBJ: Babies--Fiction./ Parent and child--Fiction.

                      Ph-1 P-3/4 $14.93   L   KG737
WILLIAMS, VERA B. Music, music for everyone. Greenwillow ISBN
0-688-02604-4, 1984. unp. col. ill.
Sequel to A CHAIR FOR MY MOTHER, 1982 and SOMETHING
SPECIAL FOR ME, 1983.
Spanish edition MUSICA PARA TODO EL MUNDO! available from
Mulberry Books (ISBN 0-688-14035-1, 1995).
Available from National Library Service for the Blind and Physically
Handicapped on sound recording cassette RC22428.
Organizing the Oak Street Band, Rosa and her friends play for
neighborhood parties and soon are able to start filling the big glass
money jar which has been emptied because Grandma is sick and
needs expensive care. Shows the same love, warmth, and caring
within both the family and the community as was found in the earlier
books. For multicultural studies.
SUBJ: Family life--Fiction./ Bands (Music)--Fiction./ Grandmothers--
Fiction./ Spanish language materials.

                      Ph-1 P-3/2 $15.93   L   KG738
WILLIAMS, VERA B. Something special for me. Greenwillow ISBN
0-688-01807-6, 1983. unp. col. ill.
Sequel to A CHAIR FOR MY MOTHER (1982).
Available in Spanish ALGO ESPECIAL PARA MI (ISBN 0-688-
13803-9, 1994).
Emptying the coin jar again in order to buy Rosa a very special
birthday present, she and her mother go from store to store until the
absolutely perfect birthday present is finally found. Full-paged,
vibrantly colored and bordered pictures reinforce the warmth,
sensitivity, and loving relationships shown in the text. Excellent for
story hours.
SUBJ: Family life--Fiction./ Gifts--Fiction.

                      Ph-2 K-A/2 $13.93   L   KG739
WILLIAMS, VERA B. Stringbean's trip to the shining sea. By Vera B. and
Jennifer Williams. Greenwillow ISBN 0-688-07162-7, 1988. unp. col. ill.
Selectors' Choice, 17th ed.
Post cards and photographs sent to the family back home and
arranged in an album format tell of the wonderful adventures

Stringbean Coe experiences when he and his big brother drive Fred's truck, modified as a camper, from Jeloway, Kansas, to the Pacific Ocean. The childlike messages, the varying addresses, and especially the stamps provide readers and viewers with additional intriguing details and jokes with each rereading. Text and pictures are superbly designed and work perfectly together.
SUBJ: Postcards--Fiction./ Travel--Fiction./ West (U.S.)--Fiction.

Ph-1 K-3/5 $14.93   L   KG740
WILLIAMS, VERA B. Three days on a river in a red canoe. Greenwillow ISBN 0-688-84307-7, 1981. unp. col. ill.
Two cousins and their mothers put their money together and buy a red canoe. They all set out for a weekend trip on the river. It's an exciting time: setting up the tent, building a campfire and cooking over it (recipes included), paddling through a fog, lowering the canoe over a waterfall, stargazing, watching wild animals, and coping with the wild winds of a sudden storm. Attractive, crayon-colored illustrations are informative and intriguing.
SUBJ: Canoes and canoeing--Fiction./ Camping--Fiction.

Ph-2 1-3/2 $13.95   L   KG741
WILLNER-PARDO, GINA. Natalie Spitzer's turtles. Illus. by Molly Delaney. Whitman ISBN 0-8075-5515-0; In Canada: General, 1992. 32p. col. ill.
Jess starts second grade looking forward to spending time with her old friend Molly but there are two new girls at school: Abigail who is immediately popular but very bossy and Natalie who is quiet and keeps to herself. Five short chapters and the reading level fill the need for bridge books for this age.
SUBJ: Friendship--Fiction./ Schools--Fiction./ Turtles--Fiction.

Ph-2 1-3/2 $15.00   T   KG742
WING, NATASHA. Jalapeno bagels. Illus. by Robert Casilla. Atheneum ISBN 0-689-80530-6; In Canada: Distican, 1996. unp. col. ill. Includes glossary.
As he attempts to select something from his family's bakery to take to school for International Day, Pablo has an interesting choice to make between his mother's Mexican and his father's Jewish heritages. Finally, he settles on jalapeno bagels, a mixture of both. Recipes from a real Mexican-Jewish-American bakery follow the story along with a glossary of Spanish and Yiddish terms. Clearly a choice for multicultural studies, the cheerful illustrations and story are great for reading aloud.
SUBJ: Bakers and bakeries--Fiction./ Bagels--Fiction./ Cookery, Jewish--Fiction./ Cookery, Mexican American--Fiction.

Ph-2 1-3/6 $15.00   L   KG743
WINTER, JEANETTE. Josefina. Harcourt Brace ISBN 0-15-201091-2; In Canada: Harcourt Brace c/o Canadian Manda, 1996. unp. col. ill.
Josefina is an artist who shapes a world out of clay. Inspired by a Mexican folk artist, the book is a tribute to the artist, a counting book, and a study in Mexican culture. For multicultural studies.
SUBJ: Artists--Fiction./ Mexico--Fiction./ Counting.

Ph-1 P-1/1 $14.95   L   KG744
WINTHROP, ELIZABETH. Bear and Mrs. Duck. Illus. by Patience Brewster. Holiday House ISBN 0-8234-0687-3, 1988. unp. col. ill.
Bear doesn't want a babysitter and thinks of all sorts of reasons to dislike Mrs. Duck. But with her big feet and large, floppy, flowered hat, but to his surprise he soon begins to like her, admires her flying and swimming abilities, has lots of fun and is eager for her return. The superb illustrations add both humor and warmth to a story that addresses a very common childhood problem: babysitter apprehension.
In BEAR'S CHRISTMAS SURPRISE (ISBN 0-8234-0888-4, 1991) Bear wants a train for Christmas but when he accidentally finds some presents and takes a peek he is disappointed.
SUBJ: Babysitters--Fiction./ Bears--Fiction./ Ducks--Fiction.

CE   Ph-2 P-K/4 $14.89   L   KG745
WINTHROP, ELIZABETH. Shoes. Illus. by William Joyce. HarperCollins ISBN 0-06-026592-2, 1986. 19p. col. ill.
Read-along kit available from HarperChildren's Audio (ISBN 0-69470-037-1, 1996). 1 paperback book, 1 sound cassette (3min), $7.95.
Available from National Library Service for the Blind and Physically Handicapped on sound recording cassette RC25654.
Big book available (ISBN 0-06-443320-X, 1993), $19.95.
Jaunty rhymes and animated pictures shown from a small child's angle of perception describe many kinds of shoes and the activities appropriate for each type. A closing riddle furnishes a funny and surprising ending.
SUBJ: Shoes--Fiction./ Foot--Fiction./ Stories in rhyme.

Ph-2 P-K/2 $12.89   L   KG746
WINTHROP, ELIZABETH. Sledding. Illus. by Sarah Wilson. HarperCollins ISBN 0-06-026566-3, 1989. 30p. col. ill.
Bundled up, two young children go sledding down a long snow-covered hill and end up covered in snow. A rambunctious description of winter sledding and expressive illustrations capture the children's excitement and joy. The rhyming text is easy to read.
SUBJ: Sleds--Fiction./ Stories in rhyme.

Ph-2 K-2/2 $14.95   L   KG747
WINTHROP, ELIZABETH. Very noisy girl. Illus. by Ellen Weiss. Holiday House ISBN 0-8234-0858-2, 1991. unp. col. ill.
Elizabeth, a very noisy girl, pretends to be a quiet dog and her mother decides the noisy girl is much more fun. Children as well as adults will enjoy the antics of Elizabeth, the noisy girl, and Elizabeth, the quiet dog.
SUBJ: Noise--Fiction./ Mothers and daughters--Fiction./ Imagination--Fiction.

Ph-2 K-2/1 $15.95   L   KG748
WISEMAN, BERNARD. Morris and Boris. Putnam ISBN 0-399-21905-6, c1974, 1991. 64p. col. ill.
Available from National Library Service for the Blind and Physically Handicapped in Braille BR03031.
Know-it-all Boris the Bear is frustrated and exasperated when he tries to teach fun loving Morris the Moose how to ask riddles, repeat tongue-twisters, and play hide-and-seek. Silly, slapstick humor that children find hilarious.
Ease of reading and silly misinterpretations of many words contribute to the popularity of this and the other titles: HALLOWEEN WITH MORRIS AND BORIS (Scholastic ISBN 0-590-41498-4, c1975, 1986, OPC); MORRIS HAS A COLD (Putnam ISBN 0-399-21906-4, c1978, 1997); and CHRISTMAS WITH MORRIS AND BORIS (Little, Brown ISBN 0-316-94855-1, 1983, OPC); MORRIS AND BORIS AT THE CIRCUS (HarperCollins ISBN 0-06-026478-0, 1988).
SUBJ: Moose--Fiction./ Bears--Fiction./ Humorous stories.

Ph-1 K-2/2 $13.89   L   KG749
WISEMAN, BERNARD. Morris goes to school. HarperCollins ISBN 0-06-026548-5, 1970. 64p. col. ill. (I can read book).
Because he can't read, Morris the moose goes to the fish store to buy candy, and because he can't count he has a problem when he tries to pay for his gumdrops. The candy man tells him about a place called school. Morris decides to go there and learn to read and count. A moose in school--the children can't believe it. But Morris and the boys and girls have great fun and Morris does learn many things, even that some "B's" are not the stinging kind.
SUBJ: Moose--Fiction./ Schools--Fiction.

CE   Ph-2 K-2/2 $15.89   L   KG750
WISEMAN, BERNARD. Morris the Moose. HarperCollins ISBN 0-06-026476-4, 1989. 32p. col. ill. (Early I can read book).
Read-along kit available from HarperChildren's Audio (ISBN 0-69470-005-3, 1996). 1 paperback book, 1 sound cassette (6min), $7.95.
Sure that every four legged animal with horns and a tail is a moose like himself, Morris makes a pest of himself when they disagree. For established beginning readers.
SUBJ: Moose--Fiction./ Animals--Fiction./ Humorous stories.

CE   Ph-1 2-3/4 $16.95   L   KG751
WISNIEWSKI, DAVID. Rain player. Clarion ISBN 0-395-55112-9, 1991. unp. col. ill.
Read-along kit available from Clarion (ISBN 0-395-72084-2, 1996). 1 paperback book, 1 sound cassette (10min), $8.95.
In order to bring rain to his people, Pik challenges Chac, the rain god, to a game of pok-a-tok, and with the help of Jaguar, Quetzal, and the Cenote, an underground river, he succeeds. Intricate cut-paper illustrations amaze the viewer. Author's note provides background about the Mayan culture which is the setting for the exciting story. For multicultural studies.
SUBJ: Mayas--Fiction./ Indians of Central America--Fiction./ Games--Fiction.

Ph-2 1-3/5 $14.93   L   KG752
WISNIEWSKI, DAVID. Warrior and the wise man. Lothrop, Lee & Shepard ISBN 0-688-07890-7, 1989. unp. col. ill.
Guarded by demons, the five essential elements are sought by twin brothers who each hope to become the next Emperor of Japan. Stunningly dramatic papercut illustrations enhance the folkloric nature of the story. While the pictures can be seen at a distance their detail and texture are best appreciated on an individual basis.
SUBJ: Japan--Fiction./ Twins--Fiction.

Ph-2 1-3/6 $16.95 L KG753
WISNIEWSKI, DAVID. Wave of the Sea-Wolf. Clarion ISBN 0-395-66478-0, 1994. unp. col. ill.
Kchokeen, a Tlingit princess, is revered by her people because she can predict the giant waves created by Gonakadet, the Sea-Wolf. When Europeans attempt to force th Tlingits to trap and trade more furs, Kchokeen asks the Sea-Wolf for help, and in a war canoe, she leads the Europeans to their destruction by giant waves. Intricate cut-paper illustrations remarkably capture the dense woodlands and the angry sea. The original story is followed by a note about the Tlingit people and the earthquakes that caused the giant waves. For multicultural studies.
SUBJ: Fairy tales./ Tlingit Indians--Fiction./ Indians of North America--Northwest, Pacific--Fiction.

Ph-1 P-3/4 $5.95 P KG754
WITTMAN, SALLY. Special trade. Illus. by Karen Gundersheimer. HarperCollins ISBN 0-06-443071-5, 1978. unp. col. ill.
Selectors' Choice, 12th ed.
Old Bartholomew and young Nelly are neighbors and good friends. Over the years their very real understanding of each other helps their friendship grow and change according to need. Charming and detailed pen and ink drawings follow and expand the text.
SUBJ: Friendship--Fiction./ Old age--Fiction.

Ph-2 K-2/2 $14.93 L KG755
WOLF, JAKE. Daddy, could I have an elephant? Illus. by Marylin Hafner. Greenwillow ISBN 0-688-13295-2, 1996. unp. col. ill.
A young boy who lives in an apartment asks his father for a series of outrageous pets: an elephant, a pony, a twenty-foot python, sheep, gorillas, a parrot, and a dolphin. In each case, imaginative illustrations show the animals hanging out the windows, sprawling over the furniture, or swimming in the apartment. Finally he asks for a puppy which Dad concedes is a possibility.
SUBJ: Animals--Fiction./ Pets--Fiction.

Ph-1 P-1/3 $12.99 T KG756
WOLFF, ASHLEY. Stella and Roy. Dutton ISBN 0-525-45081-5, 1993. unp. col. ill.
Selectors' Choice, 20th ed.
As she races her younger brother around the lake, Stella has a much faster bike than Roy, but she is distracted several times along the way. Roy keeps a steady pace and wins the race in this variant of THE TORTOISE AND THE HARE. The linoleum block illustrations hand-tinted with watercolor are appealing, and many include a rabbit and a turtle for the observant viewer.
SUBJ: Parks--Fiction./ Bicycles and bicycling--Fiction./ Racing--Fiction./ Nature--Fiction.

Ph-1 P-K/1 $11.95 L KG757
WOLFF, ASHLEY. Year of beasts. Dutton ISBN 0-525-44240-5; In Canada: Fitzhenry & Whiteside, 1986. unp. col. ill.
Records seasonal changes as they affect the activities of Ellie, Peter and many animals seen around the family's farm. For each month of the year there is a handsome doublespread block print showing an appropriate scene and activity. Simple yet dramatic.
SUBJ: Animals--Fiction./ Seasons--Fiction./ Country life--Fiction.

Ph-1 1-3/2 $13.93 L KG758
WOLFF, FERIDA. Seven loaves of bread. Illus. by Katie Keller. Tambourine ISBN 0-688-11112-2, 1993. unp. col. ill.
Every day Milly makes seven loaves of bread to feed the various animals and people around the farm. While Milly is sick, Rose, who doesn't believe in hard work, bakes fewer and fewer loaves of bread until the farm begins to fall apart around her. Rose decides that it is easier to bake seven loaves.
SUBJ: Farm life--Fiction./ Baking--Fiction./ Bread--Fiction.

Ph-1 1-3/2 $13.00 L KG759
WOLFF, PATRICIA RAE. Toll-bridge troll. Illus. by Kimberly Bulcken Root. Browndeer/Harcourt Brace ISBN 0-15-277665-6; In Canada: Harcourt Brace c/o Canadian Manda, 1995. unp. col. ill.
Crossing a bridge each morning on his way to school, Trigg is confronted by a troll who demands a toll. Each day Trigg manages to trick the troll with a riddle. The familiar folklore motif is given a contemporary twist with a clever ending. The humorous dialog between Trigg and the troll is suitable for reading aloud and will be enjoyed at story hour. Compare and contrast with other troll under the bridge stories.
SUBJ: Trolls--Fiction./ Schools--Fiction./ Riddles--Fiction.

Ph-1 1-5/6 $15.95 L KG760
WOOD, AUDREY. Bunyans. Illus. by David Shannon. Blue Sky Press/Scholastic ISBN 0-590-48089-8; In Canada: Scholastic, 1996. unp. col. ill.
When Paul Bunyan marries giant Carrie McIntie, their family activities result in Niagara Falls, Bryce Canyon, and the Great Sand Dunes of Colorado along with other American landmarks. Larger than life, the original tall tale and rich oil illustrations will delight listeners of all ages and extend social studies units on United States geography.
SUBJ: Bunyan, Paul (Legendary character)--Fiction./ Tall tales./ Natural monuments--Fiction./ National parks and reserves--Fiction.

Ph-2 2-4/3 $14.95 T KG761
WOOD, AUDREY. Flying Dragon Room. Illus. by Mark Teague. Blue Sky Press/Scholastic ISBN 0-590-48193-2; In Canada: Scholastic, 1996. unp. col. ill.
Elderly Mrs. Jenkins, handyperson, carpenter, and painter also makes magic. With the help of her tools, Patrick creates a magical place with dragons, sailing ships, dinosaurs, a bubble room, and a rather horrid enormous snake. The full-color, full-page acrylics wittingly or unwittingly serve as a tribute to William Joyce's style and imagination in this "oh-that-it-might-be" fantasy.
SUBJ: Magic--Fiction./ Imagination--Fiction.

Ph-2 K-3/3 $14.95 L KG762
WOOD, AUDREY. Heckedy peg. Illus. by Don Wood. Harcourt Brace Jovanovich ISBN 0-15-233678-8, 1987. unp. col. ill.
Tricked and transformed into seven different foods by a wicked witch, seven children (named after the seven days of the week) are returned to their normal form after their clever mother confronts the witch and solves a difficult riddle. Stunning, luminous paintings, many full-paged and double spreads, enhance the original folk-like tale.
SUBJ: Witches--Fiction.

CE
Ph-1 P-2/1 $15.00 L KG763
WOOD, AUDREY. King Bidgood's in the bathtub. Illus. by Don Wood. Harcourt Brace ISBN 0-15-242730-9, 1985. unp. col. ill.
Caldecott Honor book.
Big book available (ISBN 0-15-242732-5, 1993).
Sound filmstrip available from SRA/McGraw-Hill 87-511682. 79fr color, 1 sound cassette (8min), guide. $39.00.
Videocassette available from SRA/McGraw-Hill 87-510714, 1988. 1/2" VHS videocassette color (8min), guide. $39.00.
Available from National Library Service for the Blind and Physically Handicapped on sound recording cassette RC24651.
Refusing to get out of his bath, King Bidgood causes turmoil in the palace. Neither the knight nor the queen, neither the duke nor the court can persuade the king to dry off and get on with the business of the kingdom and all end up with him in the sudsy water while dressed in their elegant finery. Finally the young page, with common sense, solves the problem and soon the tub is empty of both water and royalty. Parallel in theme to Thurber's "Many Moons" which has its humor in the text, this succeeds with young people because of the easy-to-read text and the fine doublespread paintings which show many details of Renaissance court life and portray much humor in the bathtub scenes.
SUBJ: Kings, queens, rulers, etc.--Fiction./ Baths--Fiction.

CE
Ph-1 P-2/7 $13.95 L KG764
WOOD, AUDREY. Napping house. Illus. by Don Wood. Harcourt Brace Jovanovich ISBN 0-15-256708-9, 1984. unp. col. ill.
Available on 1/2" VHS videocassette color (5min) from Weston Woods HMPV307V, $49.95.
Available from National Library Service for the Blind and Physically Handicapped in Braille BR06117.
Big book available (ISBN 0-15-256711-9, 1991).
Piling on top of sleeping, snoring Granny, a young child is soon dreaming and followed by a dozing dog, a snoozing cat, a slumbering mouse, and finally a flea who does not sleep but bites the mouse and starts a chain of chaotic events that waken all the napping inhabitants of the house. The full paged pictures gradually change from the subdued blues and grays of a sleepy, rainy day to the brightness of a clearing, sunny, wide awake one. The appealing cumulative text and superb illustrations combine to make a fine choice for story hours.
SUBJ: Sleep--Fiction./ Fleas--Fiction.

TB
Ph-2 P-3 $11.95 OD KG765
WOOD, AUDREY. Napping house and other stories (Talking book). Performed by Lynn Redgrave. HarperAudio/Caedmon ISBN 0-89845-747-5, 1987. 1 sound cassette.
Expressive readings of favorite stories alternate with lively musical interpretations of others. For independent listening.
Contents: Moonflute (16min); King Bidgood's in the bathtub (3min); The napping house (4min); Heckedy Peg (8min); Elbert's bad word (4min).
SUBJ: Humorous stories.

Ph-2 P-K/2 $13.95 L KG766
WOOD, AUDREY. Silly Sally. Harcourt Brace Jovanovich ISBN 0-15-274428-2; In Canada: Harcourt Brace Jovanovich, 1992. unp. col. ill.
"Silly Sally went to town, walking backwards, upside down," and along the way she meets several equally silly animals. A nonsensical, repetitive, and rhyming verse accompanied by splashy, bright illustrations sure to capture the attention of young listeners or beginning readers.
SUBJ: Humorous stories./ Stories in rhyme.

Ph-2 K-2/4 $11.89 L KG767
WOOD, AUDREY. Weird parents. Dial ISBN 0-8037-0649-9; In Canada: Fitzhenry & Whiteside, 1990. unp col illus.
A conventional boy has weird parents who always embarass him in public. He wishes they were like other parents or that other parents were like them, but he realizes that's not possible and that they're okay after all because they're his parents. Gaudy illustrations show some truly unusual but lovable parents to young listeners who will enjoy the humor.
SUBJ: Parent and child--Fiction.

Ph-1 P-K/1 $13.95 L KG768
WOOD, DON. Piggies. By Don and Audrey Wood. Illustrated by Don Wood. Harcourt Brace Jovanovich ISBN 0-15-256341-5, 1991. unp. col. ill.
Ten little piggies cavort on the fingers of a child's hands in sun, snow, soap bubbles and mud until bedtime. The outlandish illustrations of pigs reading, dancing, sunbathing, skiing, fishing and engaged in numerous other silly activities invite returning again and again to this extended finger play.
SUBJ: Bedtime--Fiction./ Finger play./ Pigs--Fiction.

Ph-2 P-K/1 $12.00 L KG769
WOOD, JAKKI. Dads are such fun. Illus. by Rog Bonner. Simon & Schuster ISBN 0-671-75342-8; In Canada: Simon & Schuster, 1992. unp. col. ill.
Animal fathers are shown swinging, playing peekaboo, and nuzzling and kissing their young. Concludes with a human family. Endearing watercolor illustrations depict pairs of fathers and youngsters.
SUBJ: Father and child--Fiction./ Animals--Fiction.

Ph-1 P-2/3 $19.95 T KG770
WORMELL, CHRISTOPHER. Number of animals. Text by Kate Green. Creative Education ISBN 0-88682-625-X, 1993. unp. col. ill.
A small chick searches the barnyard for its mother. Woodcut illustrations and an expansive design invite the reader to count the animals from one through ten as the small chick wanders among the farm animals.
SUBJ: Counting--Fiction./ Domestic animals--Fiction.

Ph-2 K-3/5 $15.95 L KG771
WRIGHT, COURTNI C. Jumping the broom. Illus. by Gershom Griffith. Holiday House ISBN 0-8234-1042-0, 1994. unp. col. ill.
The slaves on the plantation prepare for a wedding or "jumping the broom" by quilting, cooking, and making wooden tools for the new couple. Lettie, an eight-year-old girl, tells the story about her sister's wedding which includes several details about life on a plantation. Historical fiction for multicultural studies.
SUBJ: Weddings--Fiction./ Slavery--Fiction./ Afro-Americans--Fiction.

CE
Ph-1 1-3/3 $14.99 L KG772
YASHIMA, TARO. Crow Boy. Viking ISBN 0-670-24931-9, 1955. 37p. col. ill.
Caldecott Honor Book.
Available from National Library Service for the Blind and Physically Handicapped on talking book TB00818 and in Braille BRA01599.
Read-along kit from Live Oak Media 0-670-24939-4, 1985. 1 sound cassette (10min), 1 paperback book, $15.95.
A Japanese story in which a very shy boy, under the influence of an understanding teacher, surprises everyone with his talent.
SUBJ: Japan--Fiction./ Schools--Fiction./ Individuality--Fiction.

CE
Ph-1 P-K/2 $13.95 L KG773
YASHIMA, TARO. Umbrella. Viking ISBN 0-670-73858-1, c1958. 30p. col. ill.
Caldecott Honor Book.
Available from National Library Service for the Blind and Physically Handicapped on talking book TB04451.
Read-along kit from Live Oak Media 0-670-73864-6, 1985. 1 sound cassette (9min), 1 hardback book $22.95.
Tells about three-year-old Momo who has new red boots and umbrella and impatiently awaits the arrival of rain so that she may put them to use.
SUBJ: Umbrellas and parasols--Fiction.

Ph-2 K-3/4 $6.95 T KG774
YEOMAN, JOHN. Old Mother Hubbard's dog dresses up. By John Yeoman and Quentin Blake. Houghton Mifflin ISBN 0-395-53358-9, c1989, 1990. unp. col. ill.
Old Mother Hubbard and her unpredictable dog are back and every time she turns around he's dressed up as an artist, a sailor, a clown, a burglar, a baby, or a knight in armor with antics to match. Children familiar with the original nursery rhyme especially enjoy the humorous text and illustrations.
More silly stories about Old Mother Hubbard and her dog can be found in ....LEARNS TO PLAY (ISBN 0-395-53360-0, 1990);
....NEEDS A DOCTOR (ISBN 0-395-53359-7, 1990); and ....TAKES UP SPORT (ISBN 0-395-53361-9, 1990).
SUBJ: Dogs--Fiction./ Stories in rhyme.

Ph-2 1-3/5 $14.95 L KG775
YEP, LAURENCE. City of dragons. Illus. by Jean and Mou-sien Tseng. Scholastic ISBN 0-590-47865-6; In Canada: Scholastic, 1995. unp. col. ill.
Possessed with the saddest face, a young boy leaves his family and joins a caravan of giants who believe he will bring good luck. In the city of dragons, his face causes tears of pearls to flow once again, bringing wealth and luck to the boy and the giants. The Asian setting is depicted in watercolor illustrations that accompany the folkloric story about appearances. For multicultural studies.
SUBJ: Prejudices--Fiction./ Giants--Fiction./ Dragons--Fiction./ China--Fiction.

Ph-2 K-1/3 $14.95 T KG776
YOLEN, JANE. All in the woodland early: an ABC book. Illus. by Jane Breskin Zalben. Caroline House/Boyd Mills ISBN 1-878093-62-2, c1979, 1991. unp col illus.
Includes musical score and lyrics.
Exquisite, full-color illustrations meticulously executed and rhyming verses with frequently repeated refrains portray woodland creatures representing each letter of the alphabet. Some of the animals such as an ANT running, a swift EAGLE, and a YELLOW JACKET a-buzzing are familiar, but others such as an URBANUS, a velvety VOLE, XYLEBORUS, and a ZEMMI are not often encountered.
SUBJ: Alphabet./ Animals--Fiction.

Ph-1 1-3/5 $15.95 L KG777
YOLEN, JANE. Letting Swift River go. Illus. by Barbara Cooney. Little, Brown ISBN 0-316-96899-4; In Canada: Little, Brown, 1992. unp. col. ill.
Selectors' Choice, 19th ed.
Available from the National Library Service for the Blind and Physically Handicapped on sound recording cassette RC 36180.
The city of Boston needs water, and the decision is made to "drown" the towns along the Swift River by flooding them to form a reservoir. A young girl remembers the town before it was flooded and describes the experience of moving it: moving graves and cutting down trees, moving some houses and bulldozing others. The lyrical story and soft illustrations recreate the human history of a reservoir and will provoke thoughtful discussions in units on communities and water.
SUBJ: Swift River (Mass.)--Fiction./ Massachusetts--Fiction./ Country life--Fiction./ Change--Fiction.

CE
Ph-1 P-3/2 $15.95 L KG778
YOLEN, JANE. Owl moon. Illus. by John Schoenherr. Philomel ISBN 0-399-21457-7; In Canada: General, 1987. unp. col. ill.
Caldecott Medal.
Unanimated 1/2" VHS videocassette color (9min) available from Weston Woods HMPV333V, 1989, $49.95.
Trudging through a moonlit, snow covered field and into a dark woods, a little girl and her father go owling. Although quiet and low-keyed, this expressive, poetic, mood piece is illustrated by dramatic pictures of shadows in the moonlight, foreboding darkness of the woods, culminating in the magnificent doublespread of the large owl staring back at father and child. Works best in an individual basis or in a one to one or small group sharing.
SUBJ: Owls--Fiction./ Fathers and daughters--Fiction.

Ph-1 K-3/4 $14.95 L KG779
YOLEN, JANE. Piggins. Illus. by Jane Dyer. Harcourt Brace Jovanovich ISBN 0-15-261685-3, 1987. unp. col. ill.
Piggins, a very proper English butler, combines his household duties with detective work, and on the night of his employer's elegant dinner party solves the mystery of the disappearing diamond necklace. When the butler takes the Reynard children on an outing in PICNIC WITH PIGGINS (ISBN 0-15-261535-0, c1988, 1993) young Rexy disappears and when Piggins solves the mystery of his disappearance gets a real surprise. In PIGGINS AND THE ROYAL WEDDING (ISBN 0-15-261687-X, 1988) Rexy, serving as ringbearer in the royal wedding, is accused of stealing the wedding ring until Piggins again

comes to the rescue. Ornate, meticulously detailed colored pencil and watercolor illustrations picture a lifestyle of the Edwardian era. The "spoof" tone of the stories adds to the fun.
SUBJ: Mystery and detective stories./ Humorous stories./ Pigs--Fiction.

Ph-2 2-3/6 $15.95 L KG780
YOLEN, JANE. Sky dogs. Illus. by Barry Moser. Harcourt Brace Jovanovich ISBN 0-15-275480-6, 1990. unp. col. ill.
Available from the National Library Service for the Blind and Physically Handicapped on sound recording cassette RC34865.
He-Who-Loves-Horses, an elderly member of the Piegan band of the Blackfeet, tells how he got his name when his people first saw horses which they called "Sky dogs". An author's note follows with information about the many legends surrounding the coming of the horse and about the Blackfeet tribe. Amber-toned watercolor illustrations lend a quiet dignity to the poetic story.
SUBJ: Siksika Indians--Fiction./ Indians of North America--Fiction./ Horses--Fiction.

Ph-1 1-3/3 $15.95 T KG781
YORINKS, ARTHUR. Hey, Al. Illus. by Richard Egielski. Farrar, Straus & Giroux ISBN 0-374-33060-3; In Canada: HarperCollins, 1986. unp. col. ill.
Caldecott Medal Award.
Available from National Library Service for the Blind and Physically Handicapped in Braille BR07117.
Bemoaning their drab existence in a one-room tenement flat, Al, a janitor, and his dog Eddie accept the invitation of a large, strangely-colored bird and fly away to a lush, bird-inhabited island in the sky. It is ecstasy until one morning Al discovers that he and Eddie are turning into birds too, and in panic they make a hazardous return trip home. Outstanding pictures blend perfectly with the story.
SUBJ: Fantasy.

Ph-2 K-3/4 $13.95 T KG782
YORINKS, ARTHUR. Louis the fish. Illus. by Richard Egielski. Farrar, Straus & Giroux ISBN 0-374-34658-5, 1980. unp. col. ill.
Because his grandfather and father were butchers, Louis is expected to be one too. But Louis loathes meat and would rather clean fish tanks than work in the market. After the death of his parents he dutifully takes over the business. He is miserable most of the time only finding happiness when he sits in the large refrigerator drawing pictures of fish. Finally permanent joy comes when Louis turns into a big, handsome salmon. Intriguing illustrations and the unusual fantasy work perfectly together.
SUBJ: Fantasy.

Ph-2 1-4/5 $15.95 T KG783
YORINKS, ARTHUR. Oh, brother. Illus. by Richard Egielski. Farrar, Straus & Giroux ISBN 0-374-35599-1, 1989. unp. col. ill.
Orphaned in a spectacular shipwreck, twin brothers land in New York. Arguing loudly, they fail at a circus job, selling apples and even street singing. Finally a kindly tailor takes them in, endures their arguments, and teaches them to tailor, a skill which reunites them with their long-lost parents.
SUBJ: Twins--Fiction./ Orphans--Fiction.

Ph-2 K-3/2 $15.95 T KG784
YOSHI. Who's hiding here? Picture Book Studio ISBN 0-88708-041-3, 1987. unp. col. ill.
Striking batik on silk paintings, die cut pages and rhyming, riddle like text introduce young readers to camouflage and mimicry as found in nature. Not only useful in science and nature study discussions but also in teaching various art forms.
SUBJ: Camouflage (Biology)--Fiction./ Animals--Fiction./ Stories in rhyme./ Toy and movable books.

Ph-3 P/4 $12.95 L KG785
ZALBEN, JANE BRESKIN. Beni's first Chanukah. Henry Holt ISBN 0-8050-0479-3; In Canada: Fitzhenry & Whiteside, 1988. unp. col. ill.
According to Beni, the first Chanukah he is old enough to remember is the very best ever. In the morning Beni and Sara help Mama and Papa prepare the latkes and applesauce and fry jelly doughnuts and that evening join the entire extended family in the prayer, lighting the menorah, singing, opening presents, and hearing Grandpa tell the story of Chanukah. Although Beni and his family are bears, young children will readily relate to the warm family story with cozy, detailed pictures. A recipe for Mama's Latkes is provided at the close of the story.
In LEO AND BLOSSOM'S SUKKAH (ISBN 0-8050-1226-5, 1990), a family of bears celebrates the Jewish harvest festival of Sukkot and makes comparisons to the American Thanksgiving holiday.
SUBJ: Hanukkah--Fiction./ Bears--Fiction.

Ph-1 P-2/1 $15.95 L KG786
ZAMORANO, ANA. Let's eat! Illus. by Julie Vivas. Scholastic ISBN 0-590-13444-2; In Canada: Scholastic, 1997. unp. col. ill.
Originally published by Omnibus Books, 1996.
Includes glossary.
Everyday at two, Antonio's family gathers to eat the large meal that Mama has prepared. One week there is a different person missing from the table each day, including Mama who has gone to the hospital to have a baby. Watercolor illustrations overflow with family and affection, especially as they depict the family gathered around the big table. Spanish words are interspersed throughout with a glossary provided at the end. For multicultural studies.
SUBJ: Dinners and dining--Fiction./ Family life--Fiction./ Spaniards--Fiction.

CE
Ph-1 P-3/2 $17.00 T KG787
ZEMACH, HARVE. Judge, an untrue tale. Illus. by Margot Zemach. Farrar, Straus & Giroux ISBN 0-374-33960-0, c1969. unp. col. ill.
Caldecott Honor Book.
Available from National Library Service for the Blind and Physically Handicapped in Braille BR01434.
One after the other five prisoners warn the Judge that "A horrible thing is coming this way, Creeping closer day by day. Its eyes are scary. Its tail is hairy." Unfortunately the old Judge ignores the warnings and sends each prisoner back to jail. But in the end justice is done and the arrogant judge pays for his disbelief. A rhyming, cumulative tale with exciting, humorous illustrations.
SUBJ: Judges--Fiction./ Stories in rhyme.

Ph-2 P-1/1 $4.95 P KG788
ZEMACH, HARVE. Mommy, buy me a china doll. Illus. by Margot Zemach. Farrar, Straus & Giroux ISBN 0-374-45286-5; In Canada: HarperCollins, 1966. unp. col. ill.
Small Eliza Lou, who lives in the Ozarks, wants a doll. When her mother asks how they can buy one, Eliza Lou suggests that they trade her daddy's featherbed. He can sleep in the stable; the horse in her sister's bed; and on and on until they come around to Eliza Lou again! From an old mountain song, it is fun to read aloud.
SUBJ: Folk songs--Southern States.

Ph-2 K-2/2 $4.95 P KG789
ZEMACH, HARVE. Penny a look. Illus. by Margot Zemach. Farrar, Straus & Giroux ISBN 0-374-45758-1; In Canada: HarperCollins, c1971. unp. col. ill.
A retelling of an old tale about a red-headed rascal who convinces his lazy, good-for-nothing brother to help him capture a one-eyed man so that he can display the freak in the market place and make millions by charging a "penny a look". The scheme back-fires, and the conniving rascal gets his due.
SUBJ: Humorous stories./ Brothers--Fiction./ Fairy tales.

Ph-1 P-K/2 $14.00 T KG790
ZEMACH, MARGOT. Little red hen, an old story. Farrar, Straus & Giroux ISBN 0-374-34621-6; In Canada: HarperCollins, 1983. unp. col. ill.
Spanish version: LA GALLINITA ROJA, UN VIEJO CUENTO (ISBN 0-374-34285-7, 1992).
Retells the old story of the industrious red hen and her lazy friends. In this case the friends are a goose, cat and pig instead of the dog, cat and mouse in other versions. The crisp text and colorful, whimsical pictures create a mood of no-nonsense yet one with humor and the feel of folklore.
SUBJ: Chickens--Fiction./ Laziness--Fiction./ Animals--Fiction./ Spanish language materials.

Ph-3 P-1/1 $9.00 T KG791
ZIEFERT, HARRIET. Clown games. Illus. by Larry Stevens. Viking Penguin ISBN 0-670-84652-X; In Canada: Penguin, 1993. unp. col. ill. (Hello reading!).
Brightly colored clowns frolic along side a simple repetitive text appealing to emerging readers.
SUBJ: Clowns--Fiction.

Ph-3 K-2/1 $3.25 P KG792
ZIEFERT, HARRIET. Jason's bus ride. Illus. by Simms Taback. Penguin ISBN 0-14-036536-2; In Canada: Penguin, c1987, 1993. unp. col. ill. (Hello reading!).
Jason's bus ride is interrupted by a big spotted dog who sits in front of the bus and refuses to move. Many people try in many different ways to move him but only Jason knows the trick to get the dog out of the way. A simple story with bright, cartoonish pictures attractive to beginning readers.
SUBJ: Dogs--Fiction.

Ph-2 K-1/2 $11.99 T KG793
ZIEFERT, HARRIET. Little red hen. Retold by Harriet Ziefert. Illus. by Emily Bolam ISBN 0-670-86050-6; In Canada: Penguin, 1995. unp. col. ill. (Viking easy-to-read classic).
A red hen seeks help from her friends dog, goose, and cat to plant, harvest, and use wheat to make bread. They refuse to help her, so, in the end, she eats all the bread. Cartoon-like illustrations. Predictable story for beginning readers.
SUBJ: Chickens--Fiction./ Animals--Fiction./ Laziness--Fiction.

Ph-3 K-2/1 $3.50 P KG794
ZIEFERT, HARRIET. Mike and Tony: best friends. Illus. by Catherine Siracusa. Penguin ISBN 0-14-036853-1; In Canada: Penguin, 1987. unp. col. ill. (Hello reading!).
Mike and Tony share almost everything, constantly play together, and on weekends "sleep over," but like many best friends they sometimes disagree and get into fights. Bright pictures, familiar activities, and easy reading make this a good choice for beginning readers.
SUBJ: Friendship--Fiction.

Ph-2 P-1/1 $3.25 P KG795
ZIEFERT, HARRIET. Nicky upstairs and down. Illus. by Richard Brown. Puffin Books ISBN 0-14-036852-3; In Canada: Penguin, c1987, 1994. unp. col. ill. (Puffin easy-to-read).
A small cat's antics illustrate the meaning of up and down. Appealing illustrations and a pleasant story provide a fun way for young children to learn these concepts.
SUBJ: English language--Synonyms and antonyms--Fiction./ Space perception--Fiction.

Ph-2 K-2/1 $11.99 L KG796
ZIEFERT, HARRIET. Princess and the pea. Retold by Harriet Ziefert. Illus. by Emily Bolam. Viking ISBN 0-670-86054-9; In Canada: Penguin, 1996. unp. col. ill. (Viking easy-to-read classic).
The traditional story of the true princess who couldn't sleep with a pea under a stack of mattresses is told in very simple language. The easy-to-read format loses the suspense and detail of the original story, but beginning readers who have heard that story will enjoy reading this independently. The simple and colorful illustrations match the straightforward text.
SUBJ: Fairy tales.

Ph-2 P-1/1 $3.50 P KG797
ZIEFERT, HARRIET. Three wishes. Illus. by David Jacobson. Penguin ISBN 0-14-038323-9; In Canada: Penguin, c1993, 1996. unp. col. ill. (Hello reading!).
Three very short chapters detail a boy's three wishes: to catch two hundred and twenty-two fishes, to be in charge of the kitchen, and to climb a tree and get a piece of the moon. Childlike and easy-to-read with colorful pictures that provide clues to the text.
SUBJ: Wishes--Fiction.

Ph-3 P-1/2 $12.99 L KG798
ZIEFERT, HARRIET. What rhymes with eel?: a word-and-picture flap book. Illus. by Rick Brown. Viking ISBN 0-670-86670-9; In Canada: Penguin, 1996. unp. col. ill.
Lift the flaps to change initial consonants and reveal a picture of the new word. Numerous combinations are possible to allow for spelling games or reading the rhyming words. Fun wordplay will encourage students to make their own rhyming books in reading or art classes.
SUBJ: Vocabulary--Fiction./ English language--Spelling--Fiction./ Toy and movable books.

Ph-1 P-1/2 $5.95 P KG799
ZIEFERT, HARRIET. Who said moo? Illus. by Simms Taback. HarperFestival ISBN 0-694-00854-0; In Canada: HarperCollins, 1996. unp. col. ill.
Determined to find out who answered his "cock-a-doodle do" with a "moo," Red Rooster asks all the farm animals until he finds the cow. Bright illustrations and heavy split pages provide action and set this animal sounds book above the rest for individual and group fun. Easy-to-read, predictable text will enable beginning readers to be successful.
SUBJ: Domestic animals--Fiction./ Animal sounds--Fiction./ Toy and movable books.

CE Ph-1 P-2/2 $14.89 L KG800
ZION, GENE. Harry the dirty dog. Illus. by Margaret Bloy Graham. HarperCollins ISBN 0-06-026866-2; In Canada: HarperCollins, c1956. unp. col. ill.
Spanish edition HARRY EL PERRITO SUCIO available from Harper Arco Iris (ISBN 0-06-443443-5, 1996).
Available from National Library Service for the Blind and Physically Handicapped in Braille BR03390.

A white dog with black spots hates baths and runs away. He returns in such a sad condition that even the family does not recognize him. HARRY AND THE LADY NEXT DOOR (ISBN 0-06-026852-2, 1960; read-along kit available from HarperChildren's Audio ISBN 0-69470-035-5, 1996. 1 paperback book, 1 sound cassette (16min), $7.95. NO ROSES FOR HARRY (ISBN 0-06-026890-5, 1958). Spanish version HARRY NO QUIERE ROSAS available from Harper Arco Iris (ISBN 0-06-443457-5, 1997).
HARRY BY THE SEA (ISBN 0-06-026856-5, 1965).
SUBJ: Dogs--Fiction./ Spanish language materials.

Ph-2 K-2/2 $4.95 P KG801
ZOLOTOW, CHARLOTTE. Hating book. Illus. by Ben Shecter. HarperCollins ISBN 0-06-443197-5; In Canada: HarperCollins, c1969, 1989. 32p. col. ill.
Even though her mother keeps telling her to ask why her friend is angry a little girl can't. Instead she lists all the things her former friend has done that are wrong. The common childhood situation is handled in a supportive manner and can spark a discussion about misunderstandings.
SUBJ: Friendship--Fiction.

Ph-1 K-2/6 $15.93 L KG802
ZOLOTOW, CHARLOTTE. I know a lady. Illus. by James Stevenson. Greenwillow ISBN 0-688-03838-7, 1984. unp. col. ill.
Available from National Library Service for the Blind and Physically Handicapped on sound recording cassette RC22248.
An old lady who knows your name and the names of all your pets and shares her spring and summer garden and her Christmas tree and gives you Halloween treats is a neighbor worth knowing and loving. The illustrations are very attractive and the pictures of the various flowers are exceptionally fine.
SUBJ: Old age--Fiction.

Ph-2 K-2/5 $14.93 L KG803
ZOLOTOW, CHARLOTTE. Moon was the best. Photographs by Tana Hoban. Greenwillow ISBN 0-688-09941-6, 1993. unp. col. ill.
After a recent visit, a mother remembers the ordinary sights of Paris and shares them with her daughter. Striking color photographs capture the beauty of this famous city and provide a memorable introduction to everyday Parisian life.
SUBJ: Paris (France)--Fiction./ Mothers and daughters--Fiction.

CE Ph-1 P-2/2 $14.95 T KG804
ZOLOTOW, CHARLOTTE. Mr. Rabbit and the lovely present. Illus. by Maurice Sendak. HarperCollins ISBN 0-06-026945-6, c1962. unp. col. ill. Caldecott Honor Book.
Read-along kit from Live Oak Media 0-87499-046-7, 1987. 1 sound cassette (10min), 1 paperback book, $15.95.
Available from National Library Service for the Blind and Physically Handicapped in Braille BR03387.
Spanish version EL SENOR CONEJO Y EL HERMOSO REGALO available from Harper Arco Iris (ISBN 0-06-025326-6, 1995).
A little girl asks the rabbit to help find a birthday present for her mother who likes things that are red, yellow, green and blue.
SUBJ: Rabbits--Fiction./ Color--Fiction./ Birthdays--Fiction./ Spanish language materials.

Ph-1 K-2/2 $13.89 L KG805
ZOLOTOW, CHARLOTTE. My grandson Lew. Illus. by William Pene Du Bois. HarperCollins ISBN 0-06-026962-6, c1974. 30p. col. ill.
Six year old Lewis awakens in the night. When his mother comes to comfort him, they share happy, loving memories of Lew's Grandpa. The mother is very surprised because Grandpa died when Lew was two and until this night Lew had never mentioned his grandfather. "But now we will remember him together and neither of us will be lonely as we would if we had to remember him alone."
SUBJ: Grandfathers--Fiction./ Family life--Fiction./ Death--Fiction.

Ph-1 K-2/2 $14.89 L KG806
ZOLOTOW, CHARLOTTE. Old dog. Rev. and newly illustrated ed. Illus. by James Ransome. HarperCollins ISBN 0-06-024412-7; In Canada: HarperCollins, 1995. unp. col. ill.
One morning, Ben's old dog won't move, and his father says she is dead. A child's understanding of death is conveyed in a gentle text and burnished oil paintings. New illustrations by James Ransome feature a loving African-American family. For multicultural studies.
SUBJ: Dogs--Fiction./ Pets--Fiction./ Death--Fiction./ Grief--Fiction./ Afro-Americans--Fiction.

Ph-2 P-2/2 $14.89 L KG807
ZOLOTOW, CHARLOTTE. Over and over. Illus. by Garth Williams. HarperCollins ISBN 0-06-026956-1, c1957. unp. col. ill.
A tiny girl not yet understanding about seasons and holidays, enjoys

the special days and on her birthday wishes that all the good times
would happen again.
SUBJ: Holidays--Fiction.

Ph-1 K-2/4 $12.88   L   KG808

ZOLOTOW, CHARLOTTE. Tiger called Thomas. Illus. by Catherine Stock.
Lothrop, Lee, & Shepard ISBN 0-688-06697-6, c1963, 1988. unp. col.
ill.
Available from National Library Service for the Blind and Physically
Handicapped on sound recording cassette RC15285 and in Braille
BR050667.
Staying on the front porch of his new home because he's got the
feeling he won't be liked by the neighbors young Thomas is
emboldened by his tiger suit to go trick or treating on Halloween. The
new softly hued watercolor and colored pencil illustrations capture the
gentle tone of the story.
SUBJ: Moving, Household--Fiction./ Friendship--Fiction.

Ph-2 K-2/4 $14.89   T   KG809

ZOLOTOW, CHARLOTTE. When the wind stops. Rev. and newly
illustrated ed. Illus. by Stefano Vitale. HarperCollins ISBN 0-06-026972-
3; In Canada: HarperCollins, 1995. unp. col. ill.
As the day ends, a young boy talks with his mother about the
continuous cycles in nature where nothing ends without another
beginning. Illustrations painted on wood reveal the texture and
strength of their backgrounds. Challenges listeners to think about
other beginnings and endings in nature as part of science or creative
writing activities. For reading aloud.
SUBJ: Nature--Fiction.

Ph-1 P-2/4 $13.89   L   KG810

ZOLOTOW, CHARLOTTE. William's doll. Illus. by William Pene Du Bois.
HarperCollins ISBN 0-06-027048-9, c1972. 30p. col. ill.
Available from National Library Service for the Blind and Physically
Handicapped in Braille BR02214.
William's desire for a doll is finally satisfied by his grandmother,
despite his father's and brother's insistence that "dolls are sissy".
William, however, is not a sissy. He's very good at shooting baskets
and maneuvering electric trains, but he still wants a doll. The
grandmother's understanding and explanation of this desire should
make sense to young children and to the adults who read this story
to them.
SUBJ: Dolls--Fiction./ Behavior--Fiction.

FICTION

Ph-2 4-6/5 $13.95   T   KG811
AAMUNDSEN, NINA RING. Two short and one long. Translated from Norwegian by the author. Houghton Mifflin ISBN 0-395-52434-2, 1990. 103p.

"Jonas and Einar, two Norwegian boys, must come to terms with each other and their prejudices when a large Afghanistan family moves into the neighborhood." (CIP) On the surface, this is a humorous story of friendship and the adventures of two young boys (e.g., the short and long of the title are burps the boys use as a signal), but it carries with it several distinctly unfunny situations: Einar's unhappy past, race prejudice toward the Afghani family, and a girl who lives on the streets. Yet, the basic decency of most of the characters and the excellent diction make this a story that creates empathy and sympathy. It would be useful to start discussions about prejudice and can show the universality of both the negative and positive sides of society without being in any way didactic.
SUBJ: Friendship--Fiction./ Norway--Fiction./ Prejudices--Fiction.

Ph-2 3-4/8 $14.00   T   KG812
ACKERMAN, KAREN. Night crossing. Illus. by Elizabeth Sayles. Knopf ISBN 0-679-83169-X; In Canada: Random House, 1994. 56p. ill.
"Borzoi book."
On the eve of World War II, Clara and her family, who are Austrian Jews, must flee over the mountains into Switzerland to escape persecution. The arduous journey is accomplished with danger every step of the way in a first look at the Holocaust for younger readers. Historical fiction for the social studies curriculum.
SUBJ: Holocaust, Jewish (1939-1945)--Fiction./ Jews--Austria--Fiction./ Austria--Fiction.

Ph-1 6-A/5 $40.00   T   KG813
ADAMS, RICHARD. Watership Down. Macmillan ISBN 0-02-700030-3, c1972, 1974. 429p. maps.
Carnegie Medal.
Available from National Library Service for the Blind and Physically Handicapped in Braille BR02514.
Adventures develop for a group of rabbits in search of a safe location for a new warren. Fiver, the visionary with ESP; Hazel, his brother who is the modest, unassuming leader; the impetuous fighter Bigwig; and the others finally find a safe haven on Watership Down. The shadowy half god-like figure of El-ahrairah, the rabbit folk hero, adds to the enigma of this fascinating and much-praised story. Especially recommended for reading aloud by an adult.
SUBJ: Rabbits--Fiction./ Fantasy.

Ph-2 4-6/5 $13.95   T   KG814
ADLER, C. S. That horse Whiskey! Clarion ISBN 0-395-68185-5, 1994. 152p.
Horse lovers will welcome Lainey, a mature thirteen-year-old, who trains Whiskey, a marvelous steed that has a mind of its own and can be dangerous to riders. She also helps Ryan, the visiting son of a local developer, accept his father as she makes Whiskey into a tractable, but spirited horse. Characters, including four-footed ones, are reasonable, and readers will empathize with Lainey as she works with Whiskey and as her family undergoes financial problems.
SUBJ: Horses--Fiction.

Ph-2 2-4/2 $12.99   L   KG815
ADLER, DAVID A. Cam Jansen and the ghostly mystery. Illus. by Susanna Natti. Viking ISBN 0-670-86872-8; In Canada: Penguin, 1996. 58p. ill.
Fifth grader Cam Jansen, girl detective, apprehends robbers who are disguised as ghosts. As usual, Cam's quick wit and photographic memory save the day in this transitional reader which is one in a voluminous series.
SUBJ: Robbers and outlaws--Fiction./ Ghosts--Fiction./ Mystery and detective stories.

CE
Ph-2 2-4/4 $12.99   L   KG816
ADLER, DAVID A. Cam Jansen and the mystery of the dinosaur bones. Illus. by Susanna Natti. Viking Penguin ISBN 0-670-20040-9, 1981. 64p. ill.
Available from National Library Service for the Blind and Physically Handicapped in Braille BR6995.
Read-along kit from Listening Library (ISBN 0-8072-0056-5, 1989). 1 sound cassette (45min), 1 paperback book, guide, $15.98.
Using her photographic memory, Cam discovers bones are missing from a dinosaur skeleton at the museum, and she and her friend Eric track them down. Entertaining and a good bridge book.
SUBJ: Mystery and detective stories.

Ph-2 2-4/3 $12.99   L   KG817
ADLER, DAVID A. Cam Jansen and the mystery of the stolen diamonds. Illus. by Susanna Natti. Viking ISBN 0-670-20039-5, 1980. 58p. ill.
Available from National Library Service for the Blind and Physically Handicapped in Braille BR6988.
Cam has a photographic memory so while she's sitting with her friend Eric and his baby sister she watches and records the strange goings-on when there is a hold-up in the jewelry store. Eventually, because of her keen observation, she and Eric are able to help the police correctly identify the real thieves.
Quick and easy reading in this story and its sequels: CAM JANSEN AND THE MYSTERY OF THE UFO (ISBN 0-670-20041-7, 1980); "...OF THE TELEVISION DOG" (ISBN 0-670-20042-5, 1981); "...OF THE GOLD COINS" (ISBN 0-670-20038-7, 1982); "...OF THE BABE RUTH BASEBALL" (ISBN 0-670-20037-9, 1982); "...OF THE CIRCUS CLOWN" (ISBN 0-670-20036-0, 1983); "...OF THE MONSTER MOVIE" (ISBN 0-670-20035-2, 1984); "...OF THE CARNIVAL PRIZE" (ISBN 0-14-036022-0, c1984, 1992); "...AT THE MONKEY HOUSE" (ISBN 0-670-80782-6, 1985); "...OF FLIGHT 54" (ISBN 0-670-81841-0, 1989); and "...AT THE HAUNTED HOUSE" (ISBN 0-670-83419-X, 1992).
Available in Braille from the NLSBPH are: CAM JANSEN AND THE MYSTERY OF THE BABE RUTH BASEBALL BR6992; CAM JANSEN AND THE MYSTERY OF THE CARNIVAL PRIZE BR6994; CAM JANSEN AND THE MYSTERY OF THE GOLD COINS BR6991; CAM JANSEN AND THE MYSTERY OF THE MONSTER MOVIE BR6993; CAM JANSEN AND THE MYSTERY OF THE TELEVISION DOG BR6990; and CAM JANSEN AND THE MYSTERY OF THE UFO BR6989.
SUBJ: Mystery and detective stories.

Ph-2 3-5/4 $16.00   T   KG818
ADLER, DAVID A. One yellow daffodil: a Hanukkah story. Illus. by Lloyd Bloom. Gulliver/Harcourt Brace ISBN 0-15-200537-4; In Canada:

Harcourt Brace c/o Canadian Manda, 1995. unp. col. ill.

A special Hanukkah story is told in simple text and sometimes moody acrylics. Two children befriend the local florist, Morris Kaplan, a Holocaust survivor. By offering friendship and the necessary companionship of the holiday, they bring the old man back to his religion--and life with people, not only flowers. The daffodil is symbolic of his survival in a tale that would be good for reading aloud, not only at Hanukkah.

SUBJ: Hanukkah--Fiction./ Holocaust survivors--Fiction./ Florists--Fiction./ Jews--United States--Fiction.

Ph-2 2-3/2 $11.99 L KG819
ADLER, DAVID A. Onion sundaes. Illus. by Heather Harms Maione. Random House ISBN 0-679-94697-7; In Canada: Random House, 1994. 72p. ill. (Houdini Club magic mystery).

"First Stepping Stone book."

Customers are losing their money in the supermarket, and nine-year-old Herman "Houdini" Foster and his cousin, Janet, solve the crime. New chapter book readers will find this mystery with short chapters and occasional illustrations attractive. Instructions for a magic trick following the story will add to the appeal of this satisfying transitional reader.

SUBJ: Stealing--Fiction./ Magic tricks--Fiction./ Supermarkets--Fiction./ Mystery and detective stories.

Ph-2 3-5/7 $13.99 T KG820
AHLBERG, ALLAN. Giant baby. Illus. by Fritz Wegner. Viking ISBN 0-670-84864-6; In Canada: Penguin, 1994. 156p. ill.

Utilizes the wildest imagination and a set of characters which could appear in a fast slapstick film. The story of the Hicks family, especially older sister Alice and her new baby brother, an infant of enormous proportions, leads to baby-naping by an evil scientist. A circus crew, neighborhood children, police constables, and a host of others are all involved in one way or the other with the remarkable baby boy. The hilarious romp is fine for reading aloud and will bring forth chortles from those who read it to themselves.

SUBJ: Babies--Fiction./ Kidnapping--Fiction./ Humorous stories.

Ph-2 3-6/6 $3.99 P KG821
AHLBERG, JANET. Bear nobody wanted. By Janet and Allan Ahlberg. Penguin ISBN 0-14-034809-3; In Canada: Penguin, c1992, 1995. 142p. ill.

Details the life of a stuffed bear who, through accident and unfortuitous events, learns what it is like to be a special bear to one person. Charmingly old-fashioned, it will be good for reading aloud especially if the many Briticisms are explained. Children who like to read about dolls and toys will enjoy the book and the added dimension of charming black and white illustrations. Unlike THE VELVETEEN RABBIT, this toy is not a sentimentalist, and the humor may be appreciated by the more sophisticated reader.

SUBJ: Teddy bears--Fiction./ Family life--Fiction.

Ph-1 3-5/6 $14.99 T KG822
AHLBERG, JANET. It was a dark and stormy night. By Janet and Allan Ahlberg. Viking ISBN 0-670-84620-1; In Canada: Penguin, 1993. unp. col. ill.

Nonsensical text full of delightful wordplay recounts the story of young Antonio kidnapped by cowardly and bumbling brigands who want the boy to tell them stories--but not scary ones. Colorful, active illustrations are dynamic and serve as a fine counterpoint to the somewhat lengthy text. This ridiculous silliness is perfect for reading aloud.

SUBJ: Storytelling--Fiction./ Robbers and outlaws--Fiction./ Pirates--Fiction.

Ph-1 5-A/5 $15.95 T KG823
AIKEN, JOAN. Cold Shoulder Road. Delacorte ISBN 0-385-32182-1; In Canada: Bantam Doubleday Dell, 1995. 283p.

Available from the National Library Service for the Blind and Physically Handicapped on sound recording cassette RC 42999.

In a complex, tense adventure, Is Twite and her cousin Arun search for her missing aunt, and they find themselves in danger from the evil Dominic de la Twite, leader of the Silent Sect.

SUBJ: Sects--Fiction./ Adventure and adventurers--Fiction./ Extrasensory perception--Fiction./ England--Fiction.

Ph-1 5-A/7 $15.00 T KG824
AIKEN, JOAN. Is underground. Delacorte ISBN 0-385-30898-1; In Canada: Bantam Doubleday Dell, 1993. 242p.

Originally published IS, Britain, 1992.

Available from the National Library Service for the Blind and Physically Handicapped on sound recording cassette RC 39525.

The Twite family returns as Is, Dido's brave and resourceful younger sister, outwits a frighteningly cruel uncle who spirits children from London to work under inhuman conditions in his mines and factories. Thanks to a few courageous and well characterized souls, he is overthrown in this suspenseful adventure filled with Aiken's original language and settings and characters reminiscent of Charles Dickens. Good for reading aloud and private shivers.

SUBJ: Adventure and adventurers--Fiction./ Coal mines and mining--Fiction./ England--Fiction./ Mystery and detective stories.

Ph-2 4-6/6 $12.95 T KG825
AIKEN, JOAN. Up the chimney down and other stories. HarperCollins ISBN 0-06-020036-7, 1987. 248p.

Available from National Library Service for the Blind and Physically Handicapped in Braille BR06520.

Infuriated when Mrs. Armitage outbids her for a mirror, Miss Hooting leaves her two ancient robots whose behavior is indeed strange. The eleven short stories in this collection are peopled with memorable characters and macabre circumstances.

SUBJ: Short stories./ Ghosts--Fiction.

CE Ph-1 5-A/7 $4.50 P KG826
AIKEN, JOAN. Wolves of Willoughby Chase. Dell ISBN 0-440-49603-9; In Canada: Bantam Doubleday Dell, c1962, 1987. 168p.

Available from National Library Service for the Blind and Physically Handicapped in Braille BRA07122, and on sound recording cassette RC30653.

Sound recording cassette available from Caedmon CDL51540; In Canada: dist. by HarperCollins, 1978. 1 sound cassette. $8.98 (OPC).

Surrounded by villains of the first order, brave Bonnie and her gentle cousin, Sylvia, conquer all obstacles in this Victorian melodrama. Followed by BLACK HEARTS IN BATTERSEA (ISBN 0-440-40904-7, c1964, OPC), (available from National Library Service for the Blind and Physically Handicapped in Braille BRA08984); NIGHTBIRDS ON NANTUCKET (ISBN 0-440-46370-X, c1969, OPC), (available from NLSBPH in Braille BRA05013 and as talking book TB01930); DIDO AND PA (ISBN 0-440-40052-X, 1986, OPC); and THE STOLEN LAKE (ISBN 0-440-40037-6, 1988, OPC).

SUBJ: England--Fiction./ Mystery and detective stories.

Ph-2 5-6/6 $6.95 P KG827
ALCOCK, VIVIEN. Haunting of Cassie Palmer. Houghton Mifflin ISBN 0-395-81653-X, 1990. 149p.

Tradition has it that the seventh child of a seventh child will have psychic powers. Cassie Palmer is not interested. When her mother, who earns money as a medium, is caught cheating, Cassie must put her potential powers to the test and save the family fortunes. Deverill, a ghost from the 18th century, appears and brings terror as well as eventual good fortune to the family in an unusual ghost story with interesting characters and an exciting plot.

SUBJ: Ghosts--Fiction./ Clairvoyance--Fiction.

Ph-1 5-A/4 $15.95 T KG828
ALCOCK, VIVIEN. Red-eared ghosts. Houghton Mifflin ISBN 0-395-81660-2, 1997. 264p.

Selectors' Choice, 21st ed.

Mary Frewin, daughter of an English working-class family, has seen "red-eared ghosts" since she was in her pram. Apparently her "condition," about which her parents are aware, can be traced to a great-great grandmother, a servant who disappeared in a flash of light generations ago. Searching for the cause of her apparitions and her ancestor, Mary somehow crosses to "the other side," where a society in the future lives among the wreckage of the past. Mary matures in the alternative time-space world, becomes spunkier, thinks more, and, with some help from an unexpected source, returns to her own world. Those who have wondered about tesseracts (WRINKLE IN TIME) will welcome this complex, strongly written novel which contains superbly developed characters and tense situations.

SUBJ: Space and time--Fiction.

Ph-1 5-A/7 $16.95 T KG829
ALCOTT, LOUISA MAY. Little men: life at Plumfield with Jo's boys. Illus. by Douglas W. Gorsline. Grosset & Dunlap ISBN 0-448-06018-3; In Canada: Grosset & Dunlap, c1947, 1982. 372p. ill. (some col.). (Illustrated junior library).

Sequel to LITTLE WOMEN.

Available from National Library Service for the Blind and Physically Handicapped in Braille BR01037, on sound recording cassette RC00523, and as talking book TB04055.

Aunt March's house has been turned into a school by Jo and her husband. Dr. Bhaer's nephews, Meg's and John's twins, the orphaned Nat Blake, the irrepressible Tommy Bangs, and a group of other interesting characters keep Plumfield an exciting place. A sentimental tale that still has ardent fans.

Followed by JO'S BOYS available from Penguin (ISBN 0-14-

035015-2, 1984).
SUBJ: Boys--Fiction./ Schools--Fiction.

TB Ph-2 5-A $11.00 OD KG830
ALCOTT, LOUISA MAY. Little women (Talking book). Three excerpts
read by Julie Harris. HarperAudio/Caedmon ISBN 1-55994-371-8; In
Canada: dist. by Heath, 1975. 1 sound cassette (60min).
   Based on book of the same title, Julie Harris reads three outstanding
selections from this tale, still beloved by children and adults. Excellent
for introduction and motivation for further reading.
   Contents: Side A: A Merry Christmas; Gossip, Part 1. Side B: Gossip,
Part 2; The First wedding.
   SUBJ: Family life--Fiction./ New England--Fiction./ United States--
History--Civil War, 1861-1865--Fiction./ Girls--Fiction.

Ph-1 5-6/7 $17.95 T KG831
ALCOTT, LOUISA MAY. Rose in bloom: a sequel to Eight cousins.
Uniform ed. Little, Brown ISBN 0-316-03782-6; In Canada: Little, Brown,
c1876, 1995. 302p.
   Available from National Library Service for the Blind and Physically
Handicapped in Braille BRA06928.
   When Rose returns from her travels, her six male cousins are surprised
to see that the tomboyish playmate they remember has "bloomed"
into a proper young lady.
   SUBJ: Cousins--Fiction./ Self-reliance--Fiction.

Ph-1 5-A/5 $16.99 T KG832
ALEXANDER, LLOYD. Arkadians. Dutton ISBN 0-525-45415-2, 1995.
272p.
   Selectors' Choice, 20th ed.
   Available from the National Library Service for the Blind and
Physically Handicapped on sound recording cassette RC 42693.
   Traveling through mythological realms mapped out by Homer and
Virgil, Lucian, a royal "bean counter" on the run; Joy-in-the-Dance,
an oracle; Fronto, a poet turned into a jackass; and a large cast of
characters, each resembling someone in Greek myths, find love,
adventure, and exist on the edge of danger. Suspense,
characterization, and language are all strongly developed in an
enchanting book that can also be the beginning of a mythology unit
in which readers trace the origins of the characters--starting with the
title. Once again, Alexander has taken elements and reworked them
into a humorous book just right for reading aloud because of its
storytelling qualities.
   SUBJ: Fantasy./ Mythology--Fiction.

Ph-1 6-A/6 $16.95 L KG833
ALEXANDER, LLOYD. Book of three. Henry Holt ISBN 0-8050-0874-8;
In Canada: Fitzhenry & Whiteside, 1964. 217p. ill.
   Available from National Library Service for the Blind and Physically
Handicapped in Braille BRA09471, on sound recording cassette
RC25013, and talking book TB00881.
   A series of five tales all based on Welsh and Celtic mythological
characters and events in which Taran, the assistant pig keeper
becomes the leader of the forces of good fighting against those of
evil. Rich in language and characterization, these titles are a
challenging but rewarding reading experience.
   Others in this series are: THE BLACK CAULDRON (ISBN 0-8050-
0992-2, 1965); THE CASTLE OF LLYR (ISBN 0-8050-1115-3, 1989);
THE TARAN WANDERER (Dell ISBN 0-440-48483-9, 1967); and the
Newbery Award title THE HIGH KING (ISBN 0-8050-1114-5, 1968)
Also available from NLSBPH are: THE BLACK CAULDRON in Braille
BRA00513, on sound recording cassette RC25014, and talking book
TB01179; THE TARAN WANDERER in Braille BRA15235 and talking
book TB01973; THE CASTLE OF LLYR on sound recording cassette
RC34708.
   SUBJ: Fantasy.

Ph-1 2-5/5 $15.00 L KG834
ALEXANDER, LLOYD. Fortune-tellers. Illus. by Trina Schart Hyman.
Dutton ISBN 0-525-44849-7, 1992. unp. col. ill.
   Selectors' Choice, 19th ed.
   A young carpenter, discontented with his job, consults a fortune-teller.
When the fortune-teller disappears, the young man is mistaken for the
new fortune-teller, a role he ably fills. Humor abounds as he foresees
the future with predictions such as you will be "enormously rich as
soon as you gain a lot of money." Detailed illustrations depict the
rich beauty of the people and the country of Cameroon.
   SUBJ: Fortune telling--Fiction./ Humorous stories./ Blacks--Fiction.

Ph-2 4-A/5 $3.50 P KG835
ALEXANDER, LLOYD. Foundling and other tales of Prydain. Dell ISBN
0-440-42536-0, c1973, 1982. 122p.
   Selectors' Choice, 9th ed.
   The charm and wit of Princess Angharad, the grim tale of the sword

Dyrnwn, and the childhood of Dalben are among the six tales
recounted in this collection from the realm of Prydain. "Author's
note" informs readers that the tales deal with happenings before the
birth of Taran and therefore precede the chronicles of Prydain.
Dedication is "for friends of Prydain who promised to read more if I
promised to write more." A real treat is in store for such friends.
   SUBJ: Fantasy./ Short stories.

Ph-1 3-5/4 $15.99 T KG836
ALEXANDER, LLOYD. House Gobbaleen. Illus. by Diane Goode. Dutton
ISBN 0-525-45289-3, 1995. unp. col. ill.
   When Tooley, who is always bemoaning his bad luck, doesn't listen to
his cat Gladsake's advice about not inviting Hooks into his house, he
soon rues his invitation as the decidedly UNfriendly gobbaleen eats
him out of house and home and totally takes over. Thanks to a ruse
suggested by the cat, the little goblin eventually leaves. In a
humorous, original "fakelore" story just right for the storyteller's
collection, Goode's multicolored art reflects the humor and characters
well. Fun.
   SUBJ: Luck--Fiction./ Cats--Fiction.

Ph-1 5-A/5 $3.99 P KG837
ALEXANDER, LLOYD. Illyrian adventure. Dell ISBN 0-440-40297-2; In
Canada: Fitzhenry & Whiteside, 1986. 132p.
   Available from National Library Service for the Blind and Physically
Handicapped on sound recording cassette RC25144.
   Determined to restore her late father's reputation as a scholar, Vesper
travels with her bumbling but kind guardian, Brinnie, to the Middle
European kingdom of Illyria where they search for an archeological
treasure that has meaning for the present. Packed with tongue-in-
cheek humor, the rapid pace and well-developed characters can give
the average and better than average reader a resounding vicarious
adventure. In THE EL DORADO ADVENTURE (ISBN 0-525-44313-4,
1987, Selectors' Choice, 16th ed.), Vesper and her guardian travel to
Central America where they help defeat the devious Helvetius. In THE
DRACKENBERG ADVENTURE (ISBN 0-525-44389-4, 1988), Vesper
and Brinnie and his wife, Mary, visit the diamond jubilee celebration
which brings another encounter with Helvetius. In THE PHILADELPHIA
ADVENTURE (ISBN 0-440-40605-6, 1992), Vesper and friends save
the Philadelphia Centennial Exposition from Dr. Helvitius's dastardly
plans and the reader meets some new characters. A knowledge of
scoundrels in U.S. History will help the reader.
   SUBJ: Adventure and adventurers--Fiction./ Fantasy./ Central
America--Fiction.

Ph-1 6-A/6 $16.99 T KG838
ALEXANDER, LLOYD. Iron ring. Dutton ISBN 0-525-45597-3; In Canada:
McClelland & Stewart, 1997. 283p., map.
   Includes glossary.
   Selectors' Choice, 21st ed.
   Set in an imaginary ancient India, the story is replete with heroes,
cowards, people of honor, people of dishonor, humorous
philosophers, and the protagonist, young King Tamar of a smallish
kingdom. The reader adventures with him on his quest to follow his
"dharma" or honor--and meets many unusual and well developed
characters. Tamar's sense of honor tends to the heroic, but he often
uses his sword before he thinks. Fortunately, some of his companions,
especially the cow-tender Mirri, a young woman of uncommon
common sense, change him into a more thoughtful person. Full of
tense events, the adventure/fantasy shows Alexander to be a wise
observer of humankind and an imaginative inventor of many strange
beings. A strong, fine book which is great for reading aloud despite
its length.
   SUBJ: Fantasy.

Ph-1 5-A/7 $3.99 P KG839
ALEXANDER, LLOYD. Jedera adventure. Delacorte ISBN 0-440-40295-6,
1990. 152p.
   Available from National Library Service for the Blind and Physically
Handicapped on sound recording cassette RC30583.
   Continues the humorous, and sometimes cliff-hanging adventures of
Vesper Holly as she and Brinnie travel to a far desert country to
return a valuable book to an ancient library. In that well described
land, Holly and various allies manage to free the enslaved inhabitants
from the ubiquitous Dr. Helvitius (again). Concise in its construction
and characterization, this is a fun-filled book for reading aloud or for
private reading.
   SUBJ: Adventure and adventurers--Fiction./ Middle East--Fiction.

Ph-1 6-A/6 $15.99 T KG840
ALEXANDER, LLOYD. Remarkable journey of Prince Jen. Dutton ISBN
0-525-44826-8, 1991. 273p.
   Alexander's complex interweaving of several plot lines creates an
adventure filled with delightful characters and his trademark humor

which supports philosophical and moral precepts without didacticism. Prince Jen must find a mysterious city known for its perfection, but his journey is filled with snags. The reader will meet characters who rationalize "wrong deeds" to make them right, strong women (a historic feature of Alexander's fiction), and aphorisms which are worth quoting. The adventures are fraught with suspense in this well crafted fantasy that speaks to the modern condition of people in search of a greater, as yet unrealized good. Prime for oral presentation, and a special treat for the better reader.
SUBJ: Adventure and adventurers--Fiction./ Princes--Fiction./ Fantasy.

Ph-1 5-6/6 $4.50   P   KG841
ALEXANDER, LLOYD. Westmark. Dutton ISBN 0-440-99731-3; In Canada: Fitzhenry & Whiteside, 1982. 184p.
Available from National Library Service for the Blind and Physically Handicapped in Braille BRA17496 and on sound recording cassette RC18341.
Theo, a printer's devil, falls into serious trouble when Cabbarus the power-mad minister has him and his master Anton arrested for printing "seditious" pamphlets. The King's daughter's death leaves the king too depressed to rule. A charlatan, Mickle (a deserted street waif), and a group of revolutionaries are among the small army of rebels who join with Theo in this story of medieval times with many contemporary overtones. An excellent tale in every way.
In THE KESTREL (ISBN 0-525-45110-2, 1982, OPC) Mickle has become Queen and Theo develops into a military leader when courtiers plot to take over the monarchy. In THE BEGGAR QUEEN (Dell ISBN 0-440-90548-6, 1984) internal strife threatens the kingdom.
Also available from NLSBPH is THE KESTREL on sound recording cassette RC21047; THE BEGGAR QUEEN on sound recording cassette RC21569.
SUBJ: Revolutions--Fiction./ Adventure and adventurers--Fiction.

Ph-3   A/6 $4.99   P   KG842
ALFRED HITCHCOCK'S SUPERNATURAL TALES OF TERROR AND SUSPENSE. Random House ISBN 0-394-85622-8; In Canada: Random House, c1973, 1983. 213p.
Likely to satisfy even the most avid fan of this genre, these eleven short stories by such authorities as Muriel Spark, Alexis Tolstoy and Raymond Chandler contain plenty of suspense and horror.
SUBJ: Supernatural--Fiction./ Short stories./ Horror stories.

Ph-2 4-6/7 $22.89   L   KG843
AMERICAN FAIRY TALES: FROM RIP VAN WINKLE TO THE ROOTABAGA STORIES. Compiled by Neil Philip. Illus. by Michael McCurdy. Preface by Alison Lurie. Hyperion ISBN 0-7868-2171-X; In Canada: Little, Brown, 1996. 160p. ill.
Includes bibliography.
Gathers 12 fairy tales written by Americans from Washington Irving's day to the twentieth century, including selections by such familiar favorites as Hawthorne, Pyle, Baum, and Sandburg. Scratchboard drawings add atmosphere. Good for reading aloud.
SUBJ: Fairy tales./ Short stories.

Ph-3 3-5/4 $17.00   T   KG844
AMMON, RICHARD. Amish Christmas. Illus. by Pamela Patrick. Atheneum ISBN 0-689-80377-X; In Canada: Distican, 1996. unp. col. ill.
Presents in text and colorful illustrations rendered in pastels the Christmas celebration at home and school of an Amish family and community. It is a simple celebration with fun, especially for the children, and a time for gathering of extended families. Some Amish customs are explained, and the paintings depict clothing, activities, and setting well. Useful for units on religion and religious groups in the United States.
SUBJ: Amish--Fiction./ Christmas--Fiction.

Ph-2 3-6/2 $14.89   L   KG845
ANAYA, RUDOLFO. Farolitos of Christmas. Illus. by Edward Gonzales. Hyperion ISBN 0-7868-2047-0; In Canada: Little, Brown, 1995. unp. col. ill.
Includes glossary.
Historical fiction set in New Mexico during World War II a few days before Christmas depicts holiday traditions in the Hispanic culture. Young Luz creates farolitos, little lanterns, when her grandfather is unable to chop the wood for the traditional luminarias, lights to guide those who reenact the shepherds' journey to Bethlehem. Filled with family warmth and the warmth of the season, the full color art reflects a text just right to use for reading aloud. The tone of the book is enhanced by the use of several Spanish words, which are explained (but not pronounced) in the glossary. Good for multicultural studies.
SUBJ: Christmas--Fiction./ Mexican Americans--Fiction./ Grandfathers--Fiction./ New Mexico--Fiction./ Hispanic Americans--Fiction.

SRC   Ph-1 4-6 $8.95   OD KG846
ANDERSEN, HANS CHRISTIAN. Hans Christian Andersen in Central Park (Sound recording cassette). Stories told by Diane Wolkstein. Weston Woods WW713, 1981. 1 sound cassette (54min).
Notes on sleeve.
The well-known story teller, "New York City's Official Storyteller," tells six stories with background and transition music provided by a kazoo, guitar, recorder, gong, and other traditional instruments. Slightly abridged, the recording includes several stories not found in most anthologies.
Contents: Side 1: Hans Clodhopper (10min); The goblin and the grocer (8min); The ugly duckling (9min); Side 2: The emperor's new clothes (9min); The nightingale (15min); Dance, dance dolly mine (4min).
SUBJ: Fairy tales./ Short stories.

Ph-2 2-5/5 $14.95   T   KG847
ANDERSEN, HANS CHRISTIAN. Swineherd. Translated by Anthea Bell. Illus. by Lisbeth Zwerger. North-South Books ISBN 1-55858-428-5; In Canada: North-South Books/dist. by Vanwell, 1995. unp. col. ill.
"Michael Neugebauer book."
Intending to marry the emperor's daughter, a poor prince disguises himself as a swineherd to work for the emperor. The princess foolishly gives away kisses for a toy, and the prince is glad that she would not agree to marry him. The delightful translation is illustrated with expressive watercolor illustrations.
SUBJ: Fairy tales./ Princes--Fiction./ Princesses--Fiction.

Ph-1 3-6/5 $19.95   L   KG848
ANDERSEN, HANS CHRISTIAN. Twelve tales. Selected, translated, and illus. by Erik Blegvad. McElderry ISBN 0-689-50584-1; In Canada: Maxwell Macmillan, 1994. 92p. col. ill.
Blegvad, himself of Danish birth, gathers, translates, and illustrates in color twelve of the more accessible tales of Andersen. The illustrations are nineteenth century in appearance and enliven these shorter tales including "The Princess and the pea," "The Emperor's new clothes," "The fir tree," and others which are less well known. The book is a generous package and should be considered as more than a relacement copy.
SUBJ: Fairy tales./ Short stories.

VCR   Ph-2 2-5 $49.95   OD KG849
ANDERSEN, HANS CHRISTIAN. Ugly duckling (Videocassette). Illus. by Svend Otto S. Weston Woods HMPV187V, 1977. 1/2" VHS videocassette color (17min).
Includes picture-cued text booklet.
The ugly duckling who becomes a graceful swan is dramatized and adapted with care. An excellent listening/viewing experience as well as motivation for reading more Andersen by older students.
SUBJ: Fairy tales./ Swans--Fiction.

Ph-1 6-A/6 $5.95   P   KG850
ANDERSON, RACHEL. Bus people. Henry Holt ISBN 0-8050-4250-4; In Canada: Fitzhenry & Whiteside, 1995. 102p.
"The lives of the passengers on Bertram's 'fruit-cake bus' are shaped by the experiences and problems each has faced because of different disabilities." (CIP) Sharply realistic and clearly described interior monologues of the protagonists and of an omniscient narrator portray episodes about mentally and physically disabled young people. May help further understanding of those who are not quite like the average child. Will need a mature reader, but might be read aloud to help sensitize children to the hopes, dreams, and frustrations of the differently-abled.
SUBJ: Handicapped--Fiction./ School buses--Fiction./ England--Fiction.

CE   Ph-1 4-A/4 $14.89   L   KG851
ARMSTRONG, WILLIAM H. Sounder. Illus. by James Barkley. HarperCollins ISBN 0-06-020144-4, c1969. 116p. ill.
Newbery Medal Award.
Available from National Library Service for the Blind and Physically Handicapped in Braille BR06227, on sound recording cassette RC22898, and talking book TB03219.
Talking book available from Caedmon/Harper Audio DNC 2322 (ISBN 1-55994-671-7, 1992). 2 sound cassettes (180min), $16.95. Spanish version available from Everest TRUENO (ISBN 84-241-3187-8, 1996).
The sharecropper wasn't weak or wicked, but crops were poor and his children were hungry. He stole a ham and some sausage and was arrested. The sheriff nearly kills the hunting dog in a profoundly moving tale of the great courage of a boy, his father, his mother, and the dog, Sounder. For multicultural studies.
SUBJ: Afro-Americans--Fiction./ Dogs--Fiction./ Poverty--Fiction./ United States--History--1933-1945--Fiction./ Spanish language materials.

Ph-2 5-A/6 $12.95   T   KG852
ARNOSKY, JIM. Long Spikes: a story. Clarion ISBN 0-395-58830-8, 1992. 90p. ill.
Details the life of a buck white-tailed deer from birth to his sexual maturity. Violence in nature is part of his story as are changing seasons, territories, birth, and death. As in Chaffee's books and those of Jean George, animals are portrayed in a realistic fashion, at once interesting and educational.
SUBJ: Deer--Fiction.

Ph-2 3-5/3 $14.95   T   KG853
ATKINS, JEANNINE. Aani and the tree huggers. Illus. by Venantius J. Pinto. Lee & Low ISBN 1-880000-24-5, 1995. unp. col. ill.
"Based on true events in India in the 1970s, young Aani and the other women in her village defend their forest from developers by wrapping their arms around the trees, making it impossible to cut them down." (CIP) Pinto's colorful East Indian style gouaches, many full page, present not only a small slice of history, but also a setting in rural India and inspiration for what a few determined people can do to help control their own lives. Historical fiction useful for units on environmental studies, multicultural studies, and women's studies, the book will also find a place in units on conflict resolution. For reading aloud.
SUBJ: Trees--Fiction./ Conservation of natural resources--Fiction./ India--Fiction.

CE   Ph-1 3-5/4 $16.95   T   KG854
ATWATER, RICHARD. Mr. Popper's penguins. By Richard and Florence Atwater. Illus. by Robert Lawson. Little, Brown ISBN 0-316-05842-4, c1938. 138p. ill.
Newbery Honor Book.
Talking book available from SRA/McGraw-Hill 87-508017, 1975. 1 sound cassettes $16.00.
Available from National Library Service for the Blind and Physically Handicapped on sound recording cassette RC23301 and talking book TB04525.
Mr. Popper changes his occupation from house painter to trainer of a penguin vaudeville troupe.
SUBJ: Penguins--Fiction./ Humorous stories.

Ph-2 3-5/4 $14.95   L   KG855
AUCH, MARY JANE. Latchkey dog. Illus. by Cat Bowman Smith. Little, Brown ISBN 0-316-05916-1; In Canada: Little, Brown, 1994. 120p. ill.
Sam is faced with the possibility of giving up his beloved golden retriever when his mother begins working outside the home. He searches for solutions that will allow him to keep the dog, take care of his younger sister after school, and not find himself in the care of a disliked baby-sitter. His solution of taking the dog to visit at a nursing home is a good one in a very human book with very real characters.
SUBJ: Dogs--Fiction./ Latchkey children--Fiction./ Single-parent family--Fiction.

Ph-1 5-A/3 $15.99   L   KG856
AVI. Barn. Orchard ISBN 0-531-08711-5, 1994. 106p.
"Richard Jackson book."
Selectors' Choice, 20th ed.
Available from the National Library Service for the Blind and Physically Handicapped on sound recording cassette RC 41373.
"In an effort to fulfill their dying father's last request, nine-year-old Ben and his brother and sister construct a barn on their land in the Oregon Territory." (CIP) Set in the Willamette Valley in 1855, this short, concise, and tightly packed realistic novel is absolutely gripping as readers learn about all the characters, even the dead mother. Ben, the brightest, is convinced that if he, his older brother, and sister can build a barn for their hardworking but feckless father who has been struck down by "a fit of palsy," he will recover. It is built, he does not recover, but there is so much suspense that few readers will be able to put this story down. First choice to use for reading aloud and units on family life, homesteading, and interpersonal relationships. Discussing the characters, situation, solution, and all the details should prove fruitful, too. Recommended for reluctant readers.
SUBJ: Father and child--Fiction./ Sick--Fiction./ Building--Fiction./ Farm life--Fiction.

Ph-1 6-A/5 $19.99   L   KG857
AVI. Beyond the western sea: book one: the escape from home. Orchard ISBN 0-531-08863-4, 1996. 295p.
"Richard Jackson book."
Selectors' Choice, 21st ed.
Avi has written an engrossing tale in the style of the Victorian magazine serials. Cliffhanger chapters present the Dickensian characters Maura and Patrick O'Connell, who are fleeing the Irish potato famine, and Sir Laurence Kirkle, the son of a rich, greedy English lord. All depart from Liverpool in the hopes of starting a better life in the New World. Blends historical fiction with suspense-filled adventure to create a captivating story. For reading aloud.
SUBJ: Emigration and immigration--Fiction./ Runaways--Fiction./ England--Fiction./ Adventure and adventurers--Fiction.

Ph-1 6-A/5 $19.99   L   KG858
AVI. Beyond the western sea: book two: Lord Kirkle's money. Orchard ISBN 0-531-08870-7, 1996. 380p.
"Richard Jackson book."
Selectors' Choice, 21st ed.
The saga begun in book one continues throughout the dangerous ocean voyage across the Atlantic, ending in the sewing factories of Lowell, Massachusetts. The interactions and destinies of all the characters culminate in an explosive conclusion during the midst of the anti-immigration sentiment of mid-nineteenth century America. Compelling historical fiction for reading aloud.
SUBJ: Emigration and immigration--Fiction./ Runaways--Fiction./ United States--History--19th century--Fiction./ Adventure and adventurers--Fiction.

Ph-1 5-A/7 $4.95   P   KG859
AVI. History of Helpless Harry: to which is added a variety of amusing and entertaining adventures. Illus. by Paul O. Zelinsky. Morrow ISBN 0-688-05303-3, c1980, 1995. 179p. ill.
Originally published by Pantheon, 1980.
Helpless Harry's parents thought he was a helpless frail thing. When left alone with a seventeen-year-old guardian, he finds all manner of trouble. Historical fiction set in 1845, similiar in style to the author's EMILY UPHAM'S REVENGE and Joan Aiken's stories such as WOLVES OF WILLOUGHBY CHASE. For stronger readers, tongue-in-cheek pen and ink illustrations add flavor.
SUBJ: Robbers and outlaws--Fiction./ Humorous stories.

Ph-1 5-A/6 $15.00   L   KG860
AVI. Night journeys. Morrow ISBN 0-688-05298-3, c1979, 1994. 143p.
Taken into the home of Everett Shinn, a Quaker, in pre-Revolutionary Pennsylvania, orphaned Peter York joins a search party for two escaped indentured servants. Historical fiction with excellent characterization and plot that makes positive contributions to the social studies curriculum.
The sequel, ENCOUNTER AT EASTON (ISBN 0-688-05295-9, c1980, 1994), continues the desperate efforts of Elizabeth Mawes and Robert Linnly to escape their cruel master.
SUBJ: Indentured servants--Fiction./ Quakers--Fiction./ Pennsylvania--Fiction./ Runaways--Fiction.

Ph-1 6-A/5 $17.99   L   KG861
AVI. Nothing but the truth: a documentary novel. Orchard ISBN 0-531-08559-7, 1991. 177p.
Newbery Honor Book.
Available from the National Library Service for the Blind and Physically Handicapped on sound recording cassette RC35549.
Smart-mouthed ninth grader Philip Malloy is resentful that he cannot join the track team because of his grade in English class. His actions open a can of worms which eventually eat through the life of a fine English teacher and Philip, himself. A frightening book, the story develops through a series of short documents: letters, newspaper articles and diary entries which present the differing perspectives of Philip, his parents, his English teacher, school administrators, a candidate for the school board and a host of others.
SUBJ: High schools--Fiction./ Schools--Fiction.

Ph-1 3-5/6 $16.99   L   KG862
AVI. Poppy. Illus. by Brian Floca. Orchard ISBN 0-531-08783-2, 1995. 147p. ill., map.
"Richard Jackson book."
With the help of the once-feared porcupine, Poppy, the young, resourceful, and brave deer mouse, saves her large--and growing larger--family from the depredations of the bullying Mr. Ocax, a great horned owl, dictator of the territory. Her tense and well-described adventures bring the charming animal fable to a happy conclusion. Black and white illustrations add to the liveliness of the story. An excellent choice to use for reading aloud.
SUBJ: Mice--Fiction./ Owls--Fiction./ Survival--Fiction.

Ph-1 5-A/6 $14.95   L   KG863
AVI. Punch with Judy. Illus. by Emily Lisker. Bradbury ISBN 0-02-707755-1; In Canada: Maxwell Macmillan, 1993. 167p. ill.
"An outcast eight-year-old boy, orphaned by the Civil War, is taken in by the owner of a traveling medicine show and, despite the doubts of others, years later he confirms the man's faith in him." (CIP) Punch, the boy, and Judy, daughter of the boss of the failing show, and a cast of circus performers are constantly on the run from a low-down sheriff determined to close the show. The high jinks accompany

FICTION

fast paced events, sharp characterizations, and a suspenseful, cinematic, comical story that will engage readers and listeners. Black and white illustrations add to the fun.
SUBJ: Medicine shows--Fiction./ Orphans--Fiction./ Self-confidence--Fiction.

Ph-1 4-6/5 $16.00 L KG864
AVI. Smugglers' Island. Morrow ISBN 0-688-12796-7, 1994. 178p.
Originally published as SHADRACH'S CROSSING, Pantheon, 1983.
Warned not to try to find out anything about the mysterious smuggling that is dominating the tiny community on the economically depressed island, Shadrach is determined to rid the island of its pernicious influence. Suspenseful and believable with well-developed characters, this title should prove popular with the most reluctant of readers.
SUBJ: Smuggling--Fiction./ Islands--Fiction.

Ph-2 5-A/6 $15.00 T KG865
AVI. S.O.R. losers. Bradbury ISBN 0-02-793410-1, 1984. 112p.
Available from National Library Service for the Blind and Physically Handicapped in Braille BR06317 and on sound recording cassette RC23326.
Having avoided team sports up to now, eleven seventh grade students at South Orange River Middle School find themselves placed together on a soccer team. By stating a case for those disinterested and/or unskilled in sports and the entire "must win" sentiment, the title addresses sports participation from a different perspective. An unusual read aloud that can lead to very fruitful discussions.
SUBJ: Soccer--Fiction./ Schools--Fiction./ Individuality.

Ph-2 3-6/4 $15.00 L KG866
AVI. Tom, Babette, and Simon: three tales of transformation. Illus. by Alexi Natchev. Macmillan ISBN 0-02-707765-9; In Canada: Distican, 1995. 100p. ill.
"Three original stories in which a boy and a cat change places, a young man learns the price of selfishness, and an invisible princess learns to see herself." (CIP) Each of these fairy tales is so sharply characterized and active that persons and places come alive. The stories can be read by reluctant readers, younger strong readers, and are good choices for reading aloud.
SUBJ: Fairy tales./ Short stories.

Ph-1 5-A/6 $16.95 T KG867
AVI. True confessions of Charlotte Doyle. Decorations by Ruth E. Murray. Orchard ISBN 0-531-05893-X, 1990. 215p.
Newbery Honor Book.
Selectors' Choice, 19th ed.
Talking book available from Recorded Books (ISBN 1-55690-593-9, 1992). 5 sound cassettes (420min), $42.00.
From the first sentence, "Not every thirteen-year-old girl is accused of murder, brought to trial and found guilty," to its last, the suspense is palpable and constant. Set on a transatlantic sailing ship in 1832 with a murderous captain and a crew constantly on the edge of mutiny, the plot centers on Charlotte who both acts and is acted upon in tightly written historical fiction that is prime for reading aloud and private reading--guaranteed to keep the reader at the edge of a chair. Good for units on U.S. history, and slavery, it also provides background for ocean travel by sailing ship.
SUBJ: Sea stories.

Ph-1 5-6/8 $13.00 T KG868
BABBITT, NATALIE. Devil's other storybook. Farrar, Straus & Giroux ISBN 0-374-31767-4; In Canada: HarperCollins, 1987. 82p. ill.
Selectors' Choice, 16th ed.
Rousted by a parrot formerly owned by a clergyman, the debonair Devil is forced back to Hell. The other nine tales in this collection also describe his attempts at mischief that do not always succeed and require reading between the lines for fullest effect. The stories will be most enjoyed by skilled readers or when read aloud.
SUBJ: Short stories./ Devil--Fiction.

CE Ph-1 3-5/4 $10.95 T KG869
BABBITT, NATALIE. Devil's storybook. Mirasol/Farrar, Straus & Giroux ISBN 0-374-31770-4, 1974. 101p. ill.
Spanish version CUENTOS DEL POBRE DIABLO available (ISBN 0-374-31769-0, 1994).
Ten original stories about the exploits and adventures of the devil which paint him as a humorous, almost likeable character, who loses as often as he wins. In spite of the easy reading level, the story will appeal primarily to special or gifted readers; recommended also for reading aloud.
SUBJ: Short stories./ Devil--Fiction.

Ph-2 5-6/6 $14.95 T KG870
BABBITT, NATALIE. Goody Hall. Farrar, Straus & Giroux ISBN 0-374-32745-9; In Canada: Maxwell Macmillan, c1971, 1992. 176p illus.
Available from National Library Service for the Blind and Physically Handicapped as talking book TB04431.
The blacksmith said something was going to happen and it did. Hercules Feltwright, a one-time actor, tutors Willet Goody, has a seance with the gypsy girl and decides to help Willett find his father. He finds that nobody is in the family tomb. A Gothic mystery of robbers and diamonds and false identities, much in the style of Joan Aiken's tales.
SUBJ: Mystery and detective stories./ Robbers and outlaws--Fiction.

CE Ph-1 4-6/6 $15.00 T KG871
BABBITT, NATALIE. Knee-Knock Rise. Farrar, Straus & Giroux ISBN 0-374-34257-1, c1970. 117p. ill.
Newbery Honor book.
Selectors' Choice, 6th ed.
Available from National Library Service for the Blind and Physically Handicapped as talking book TB03787.
Talking book available from Listening Library YA 902 (ISBN 0-8072-7617-0, 1996). 2 sound cassettes (104min), $16.98.
The Megrimum, a mysterious creature purported to live at the top of Knee-Knock Rise, is of interest to the entire countryside, which is one reason the yearly fair is so successful. Visitors come hoping to hear the Megrimum put on a noisy show. Young Egan visits relatives in Instep and climbs the mountains to see the Megrimum, but it is said the Megrimum eats people.
SUBJ: Mountains--Fiction./ Mystery and detective stories.

CE Ph-1 4-6/5 $16.00 T KG872
BABBITT, NATALIE. Search for delicious. Farrar, Straus & Giroux ISBN 0-374-36534-2; In Canada: McGraw-Hill Ryerson, c1969. 167p. ill.
Available from National Library Service for the Blind and Physically Handicapped as talking book TB03069.
Talking book available from Listening Library YA 889 (ISBN 0-8072-7596-4, 1995). 2 sound cassettes (161min), $16.98.
The Prime Minister needed a definition for delicious, but everyone disagreed and fought. Gaylen, the Prime Minister's son, was sent as the King's messenger to find out the people's choice, but he finds the kingdom in a turmoil. This "quest story," which incorporates the tale of an ancient spring, a mermaid, and a lost key, ends in Gaylen's saving the kingdom from havoc. A folktale-like story of much appeal.
SUBJ: Fantasy./ Fairy tales.

CE Ph-1 4-6/4 $15.00 T KG873
BABBITT, NATALIE. Tuck everlasting. Farrar, Straus & Giroux ISBN 0-374-37848-7, c1975. 139p.
Available in Spanish, TUCK PARA SIEMPRE (ISBN 0-374-37849-5, 1991, and from the NLSBPH on sound recording cassette RC33900).
Read-along kit available from Listening Library LB 4 SP (ISBN 0-8072-8511-0, 1988). 1 paperback book, 1 sound cassette (210min), $20.98.
Available from National Library Service for the Blind and Physically Handicapped on sound recording cassette RC10358.
The story of Winnie Foster and her adventures with the Tuck family involves a kidnapping, a murder, a jailbreak, and the possibility of eternal youth. It is far more than that however, because the Tuck family, which lived near the village of Treegap in the 1880s had years before found and drunk from a spring which gave them life everlasting. A most unusual story for readers, and excellent as a read-aloud.
SUBJ: Fantasy./ Life--Fiction./ Kidnapping--Fiction./ Murder--Fiction./ Prisons--Fiction./ Spanish language materials.

Ph-1 4-A/5 $18.00 L KG874
BAGNOLD, ENID. National Velvet. Illus. by Ted Lewin. Morrow ISBN 0-688-05788-8, c1935, 1985. 258p. col. ill.
Available from National Library Service for the Blind and Physically Handicapped in Braille BRA01731, on sound recording cassette RC12453, and talking book TB00589.
Fourteen-year-old Velvet Brown wins "The Pie," a spirited, difficult horse, in a village lottery, trains him and rides him in Great Britain's Grand National Steeplechase. A classic story for horse lovers.
SUBJ: Horses--Fiction.

CE Ph-3 4-6/4 $15.99 L KG875
BAILEY, CAROLYN SHERWIN. Miss Hickory. Illus. with lithographs by Ruth Gannett. Viking ISBN 0-670-47940-3, c1946. 120p. ill.
Newbery Medal Award.
Talking book available from Live Oak Media ISBN 0-670-47943-8, 1972. 1 sound cassette $9.95.
Available from National Library Service for the Blind and Physically Handicapped on sound recording cassette RC22824.
Miss Hickory, the doll with a hickory nut head and apple wood body,

was left behind when the family decided to winter in Boston. Her winter adventures with animal life of field and forest are enchanting.
SUBJ: Dolls--Fiction./ New Hampshire--Fiction.

Ph-2 1-3/2 $13.00   T   KG876
BALL, DUNCAN. Emily Eyefinger. Illus. by George Ulrich. Simon & Schuster ISBN 0-671-74618-9; In Canada: Simon & Schuster, 1992. 82p. ill.
Though Emily was born with an extra eye (on the end of her finger), she doesn't mind being different from the other children. In fact, she finds it useful. The humorous text combines with tongue-in-check, black and white illustrations to create a first-rate transitional reader.
SUBJ: Eye--Fiction./ Humorous stories./ Self-acceptance--Fiction.

Ph-2 5-A/6 $14.95   T   KG877
BALL, ZACHARY. Bristle Face. Holiday House ISBN 0-8234-0915-5, 1990. 206p.
In this story set in the Southern Mountains, an orphan boy first finds an odd looking dog and then a home for himself as the dog proves to be a rare tracker.
SUBJ: Mississippi--Fiction./ Fox hunting--Fiction./ Dogs--Fiction.

Ph-2 4-6/6 $7.99   P   KG878
BARBER, ANTONIA. Catkin. Illus. by P. J. Lynch. Candlewick ISBN 1-56402-976-X; In Canada: Candlewick/dist. by Douglas & McIntyre, 1996. unp. col. ill.
"When a tiny, magical cat carelessly allows a young girl to be captured by the Little People, he must confront her captors and solve three cunning riddles in order to rescue her." (CIP) The original story based on several older sources includes elements from the Greek myth about Persephone and Demeter. Multicolored and finely detailed illustrations help make this a dramatic and handsome book, good for the telling or for the perusal of the art. Use in multicultural studies when discussing and comparing cultures and folktale motifs.
SUBJ: Fairy tales./ Cats--Fiction.

Ph-1 4-6/6 $14.95   L   KG879
BARBER, ANTONIA. Mousehole cat. Illus. by Nicola Bayley. Macmillan ISBN 0-02-708331-4, 1990. unp. col. ill.
Based on the old Cornish legend of Tom Bawcock, the tale about a fisherman and his cat and how they save their town from starvation on Christmas Eve is retold in glowing language and glowing art. Perfect for oral presentation for younger and older listeners who will also be enchanted by the stunning art work. Artist, author, and publisher have presented a book that shows the unity of author's words and artist's paintings.
SUBJ: Cats--Fiction./ Cornwall (England)--Folklore./ Folklore--Cornwall (England).

Ph-2 6-A/4 $15.95   T   KG880
BAUER, JOAN. Sticks. Delacorte ISBN 0-385-32165-1; In Canada: Bantam Doubleday Dell, 1996. 182p. ill.
In the first person, ten-year-old Mickey details how he prepares for a pool championship with the help of various people, including his best friend, a math genius who explains the physics of pocket billiards. Full of action, albeit wordy, the novel is above all a character study of Mickey coming to terms with himself and the past--especially his father who abandoned him. Illustrations of various angle shots should help the neophyte.
SUBJ: Pool (Game)--Fiction./ Mothers and sons--Fiction./ Fathers and sons--Fiction./ Grandmothers--Fiction./ Friendship--Fiction./ Mathematics--Fiction.

Ph-2 4-6/6 $13.95   L   KG881
BAUER, MARION DANE. Ghost eye. Illus. by Trina Schart Hyman. Scholastic ISBN 0-590-45298-3; In Canada: Scholastic, 1992. 82p. ill.
Once a prizewinning cat, Purrloom Popcorn adopts Lydia, a lonely little girl who loves him. His ability to summon ghost cats creates problems in this different, active, and well-characterized short novel.
SUBJ: Cats--Fiction./ Animal ghosts--Fiction./ Ghosts--Fiction.

CE   Ph-1 5-6/7 $15.00   T   KG882
BAUER, MARION DANE. On my honor. Clarion ISBN 0-89919-439-7, 1986. 90p.
Newbery Honor Book.
Selectors' Choice, 16th ed.
Available from National Library Service for the Blind and Physically Handicapped in Braille BR06959.
Talking book available from Listening Library YA 839 CX (ISBN 0-8072-7369-4, 1992). 2 sound cassettes (120min), $16.98.
Raised by his parents to keep his word, twelve-year-old Joel is terrified to tell the adults in his life that his friend, Tony, has drowned in a place where Joel had promised he would not go. But Tony was a headstrong show-off, a person who heeded no one's warnings and

especially not Joel's. The mental tension in this short novel is almost physical and while better readers will understand this easily, it could be an intense oral reading experience.
SUBJ: Promises--Fiction./ Obedience--Fiction./ Accidents--Fiction.

Ph-1 5-A/6 $14.95   L   KG883
BAUER, MARION DANE. Question of trust. Scholastic ISBN 0-590-47915-6; In Canada: Scholastic, 1994. 130p.
Each character is carefully and understandably delineated in a fast-paced story about two children torn by the separation of their parents. Brad, about 11, is determined to force his mother to return by refusing to speak with her or see her and swears his younger brother Charlie to the same action. They adopt a homeless cat that gives birth to two kittens, one of which dies. As Brad takes care of the remaining kitten, he learns that the mother cat did not kill her kitten nor desert them. The cat is, of course, symbolic of his own mother in this sensitive character study of a very unhappy boy in a tramatic situation in which maturing and learning develop--but at a high cost to everyone.
SUBJ: Mothers and sons--Fiction./ Cats--Fiction.

Ph-1 4-6/7 $16.95   L   KG884
BAUM, L. FRANK. Road to Oz. Illus. by John R. Neill. Books of Wonder/Morrow ISBN 0-688-09997-1, 1991. 267p. ill.
Available from the National Library Service for the Blind and Physically Handicapped on sound recording cassette RC34766.
In the fifth Oz adventure, Dorothy and Toto encounter Scoodlers and Johnny Dooit in addition to their old friends, the Scarecrow and the Wizard. This is the edition of choice where a replacement copy is needed. Facsimile of first edition with original Neill illustrations and multicolored paper stocks.
More enjoyment can be found in the sixth Oz book THE EMERALD CITY OF OZ (ISBN 0-688-11558-6, 1993) with several new kingdoms and a plot against Oz revealed.
OZMA OF OZ (Reilly & Britton/Morrow ISBN 0-688-06632-1, 1989) finds Dorothy, the Scarecrow, the Tin Woodman, and Cowardly Lion trying to release the Queen of Ev and her children from the power of the Nome King.
Baum introduces a new set of characters in THE PATCHWORK GIRL OF OZ (Books of Wonder/Morrow ISBN 0-688-13354-1, 1995) who discover the wonders of Oz, including a living girl made from patchwork quilts and cotton stuffing. Facsimile of the 1913 edition.
In TIK-TOK OF OZ (Books of Wonders/Morrow ISBN 0-688-13355-X, 1996), a facsimile edition of the 1914 Oz book, Queen Anne, ruler of a small kingdom, has warlike aspirations to conquer Oz.
SUBJ: Fantasy.

Ph-1 4-6/7 $22.00   L   KG885
BAUM, L. FRANK. Scarecrow of Oz. Illus. by John R. Neill. Afterword by Peter Glassman. Books of Wonder/Morrow ISBN 0-688-14719-4, 1997. 291p. ill. (some col.).
The Scarecrow uses his new brains to rescue Trot, Cap'n Bill, Button-Bright, and Ork from the evil clutches of King Krewl. Facsimile of the 1915 first edition.
SUBJ: Fantasy.

CE   Ph-1 4-6/6 $22.00   L   KG886
BAUM, L. FRANK. Wonderful Wizard of Oz. Illus. by W. W. Denslow. Morrow ISBN 0-688-06944-4, 1987. 267p. col. ill. (Books of wonder).
Available from National Library Service for the Blind and Physically Handicapped as talking book TB03579 and in Braille BRA06321.
Available as talking book MARVELOUS LAND OF OZ, from Audio Book Contractors (ISBN 1-55685-290-8, 1993). 3 sound cassettes (270min.), $24.95.
Spanish version EL MAGO DE OZ available from Santillana (ISBN 84-204-35090, 1987).
Presents a facsimile edition of the 1900 edition, with clear type, Denslow illustrations, and the feel of an old story forever new. Dorothy and her friends have adventures in Oz among many strange, and sometimes fearsome, characters as they each seek their heart's desire. Collections needing a new edition of Oz, one of the most American of American books, will not go wrong with this.
SUBJ: Fantasy./ Spanish language materials.

Ph-2 4-6/4 $14.89   L   KG887
BAWDEN, NINA. Carrie's war. HarperCollins ISBN 0-397-31450-7, c1973. 159p.
Carrie, now grown up with children of her own, takes the children back to see the house she loved and visited when she and her little brother were evacuated from war-torn London. They lived with a penny-pinching shop-keeper and his mouse of a sister, but found love and warmth in Druid's Bottom, whose mystery is slowly revealed as Carrie remembers her days there. An exciting and different kind of mystery by a masterly writer.
SUBJ: Family life--Fiction./ Wales--Fiction.

FICTION

Ph-1 5-A/4 $14.95 T KG888
BAWDEN, NINA. Granny the Pag. Clarion ISBN 0-395-77604-X, 1996. 184p.
"Originally abandoned by her actor parents who later attempt to gain custody, Cat wagers a spirited campaign to decide her own fate and remain with her grandmother." (CIP) In another example of sharp and brilliant writing, Bawden once again demonstrates how to create vital characters in interesting, odd situations. Cat's perceptions of her psychoanalyst, free-spirited grandmother, the Pag, her selfish, always-on-stage mother, her friends, and her enemies (particularly the school bully) are realized in a true-to-life, intergenerational story with very human and, alas, real people. More mature readers will appreciate the skill of the writer--and the characters in the book.
SUBJ: Grandmothers--Fiction./ Parent and child--Fiction./ Schools--Fiction.

Ph-1 5-A/5 $13.95 T KG889
BAWDEN, NINA. Handful of thieves. Clarion ISBN 0-395-58634-8, c1967, 1991. 177p.
Available from the National Library Service for the Blind and Physically Handicapped on sound recording cassette RC 37879.
A small English community is nearly turned upside down when Fred McAlpine and his friends decide to retrieve the picture and the money stolen from his grandmother by a "con man." Gran doesn't want to report the theft to the police. Finally Fred's gang finds that the only way they can retrieve the money is to become thieves themselve.
SUBJ: Mystery and detective stories.

Ph-1 5-A/7 $13.95 T KG890
BAWDEN, NINA. House of secrets. Clarion ISBN 0-395-58670-4, c1963, 1992. 187p.
Published in England as THE SECRET PASSAGE, c1963.
When the three Mallory children go to live with a hitherto unknown aunt in England, leaving their warm and happy home in Kenya, they have many adjustments to make. The discovery of a mysterious deserted house--which they decide to call the House of Secrets--next door to their aunt's boarding house, captures their interest. A strange disagreeable girl, Aunt Mabel's two boarders, rich old Mr. Reynolds and the small jade horse which Miss Pin gave Ben add up to an enthralling story.
SUBJ: Mystery and detective stories./ England--Fiction.

Ph-1 5-A/5 $13.95 T KG891
BAWDEN, NINA. Humbug. Clarion ISBN 0-395-62149-6, 1992. 133p.
Bawden has created such strong characters and such unpleasant situations that readers' empathies will be immediately aroused as they follow the torture which Angelica, a seemingly psychopathic girl, inflicts upon Cora. Cora is staying with Angel's family, and she is victimized until Angel's grandmother and her own excellent intelligence lead to a rescue. As usual with Bawden, story construction, plot details, and character are strong, and her prose is concise and active. Fine choice for reading aloud or quiet reading.
SUBJ: Honesty--Fiction./ Old age--Fiction./ Parent and child--Fiction./ Self-reliance--Fiction.

Ph-1 6-A/6 $13.95 T KG892
BAWDEN, NINA. Real Plato Jones. Clarion ISBN 0-395-66972-3, 1993. 166p.
Available from the National Library Service for the Blind and Physically Handicapped on sound recording cassette RC 38145.
"Thirteen-year-old Plato Jones tries to come to terms with his mixed heritage while visiting Greece, as he finds out more about his Welsh grandfather, a World War II hero, and his Greek grandfather, a supposed traitor." (CIP) As Bawden uncovers the layers of story, the reader will realize that situations are complex, that on the surface what appears to be simple is not, and that stories have hidden parts which historic fact dredged from memory can bring to light. Once again the author has created a gripping story with strong characters and a well-described setting. Essentially a fascinating character study, the novel probably needs a strong reader because of the complex situations and the somewhat daunting typeface.
SUBJ: Greece--Fiction./ Grandfathers--Fiction./ World War, 1939-1945--Greece--Fiction./ Identity--Fiction.

Ph-2 5-A/6 $13.95 T KG893
BAWDEN, NINA. Witch's daughter. Clarion ISBN 0-395-58635-6, c1966, 1991. 184p.
Perdita, a lonely child living on the Scottish island of Skua, has no friends until two English children, blind Janey and her brother Tim, come to the island for a holiday. The children are involved in a real cops-and-robbers chase and it is Janey who saves them when they are trapped in a cave. The island children are forced to recognize their unfairness in labeling Perdita a witch.
SUBJ: Blind--Fiction./ Mystery and detective stories./ Friendship--Fiction./ Scotland--Fiction.

Ph-2 5-A/7 $4.95 P KG894
BELL, FREDERIC. Jenny's corner. Illus. by Zenowij Onyshkewych. Farrar, Straus and Giroux ISBN 0-374-43744-0; In Canada: HarperCollins, 1995. 58p. ill.
"Sunburst book."
Originally published by Random House, 1974.
In a novella, largely descriptive in style, the Pennsylvania wilderness of the mid-nineteenth century serves as the setting for the story of Jenny, nine, and how her love for the deer forever makes the area a place where no hunting will take place. Although a neighboring family depends on deer for food and clothing, they no longer hunt "Jenny's Corner" and prevent others from killing, too, because of the near death of Jenny. Sentimental and often gripping historical fiction for reading aloud.
SUBJ: Hunting--Fiction./ Pennsylvania--History--Fiction.

Ph-3 6-A/6 $3.99 P KG895
BELLAIRS, JOHN. Dark secret of Weatherend. Peguin ISBN 0-14-038006-X, c1984. 182p.
Available from National Library Serivce for the Blind and Physically Handicapped in Braille BRA17851 and on sound recording cassette RC22738.
Surreptitiously exploring the decrepit Weatherend mansion fourteen-year-old Anthony Monday and sprightly, nonconformist, sixty-eight-year old librarian, Miss Eells discover a diary which urges the cleansing of the world by turbulent weather and which leads them to wonder about the recent increase in atypical storms. While exciting and dramatic the language is more vernacular and the title's appeal is to the more mature reader.
In THE TREASURE OF ALPHEUS WINTERBORN (ISBN 0-14-038009-4, 1997) Anthony and Miss Eells try to find the treasure hidden by old Mr. Winterborn and in THE LAMP FROM THE WARLOCK'S TOMB (ISBN 0-8037-0535-2, 1988, OPC), Anthony and Miss Eells unleash monstrous forces when they light an old oil lamp; Anthony, Miss Eells and Emerson Eells travel to another dimension and destroy the Autarchs who plan to take over the earth in THE MANSION IN THE MIST (ISBN 0-14-034933-2, 1993). THE TREASURE OF ALPHEUS WINTERBORN is available from NLSBPH in Braille BRA15470 and on sound recording cassette RC12810.
SUBJ: Magic--Fiction./ Weather--Fiction./ Minnesota--Fiction./ Librarians--Fiction./ Mystery and detective stories.

Ph-2 4-6/6 $14.89 L KG896
BELLAIRS, JOHN. Doom of the haunted opera. By John Bellairs; completed by Brad Strickland. Frontispiece by Edward Gorey. Dial ISBN 0-8037-1465-3, 1995. 153p.
Lewis and Rose Rita discover an old opera score and unleash a sorcerer who wants to rule the world--by reviving the dead.
SUBJ: Wizards--Fiction./ Magic--Fiction./ Supernatural--Fiction.

Ph-2 4-6/5 $3.99 P KG897
BELLAIRS, JOHN. House with a clock in its walls. Illus. by Edward Gorey. Penguin ISBN 0-14-036336-X, c1973. 179p. ill.
Lewis discovers that his Uncle Jonathan, who adopts him when his parents are accidentally killed, is a wizard. And so is their next-door neighbor Mrs. Zimmermann. Worse still, he discovers that there is a magic clock ticking away the hours to Doomsday, hidden in the walls of the house. The ingredients of this story of both black and white witchcraft include cozy fireplaces, chocolate-chip cookies, raisings from the dead, and many other wacky and hair-raising events--before the clock is found and destroyed.
Further adventures of Lewis the timid hero are found in THE FIGURE IN THE SHADOWS (ISBN 0-140-36337-8, 1993); THE LETTER, THE WITCH, AND THE RING (Viking ISBN 0-14-036338-6, c1976, 1993); THE GHOST IN THE MIRROR (Dial ISBN 0-8037-1370-3, 1993).
SUBJ: Witchcraft--Fiction.

Ph-2 3-5/5 $13.95 T KG898
BERENZY, ALIX. Frog prince. Henry Holt ISBN 0-8050-0426-2; In Canada: Fitzhenry & Whiteside, 1989. unp. col. ill.
Presents a "Once upon a time" story of a frog prince who really is a frog and who journeys through several kingdoms to find a true princess--a lovely and loving frog. In a humorous twist of the well known folk tale, colorfully illustrated in true fairy tale style, the young reader or listener can gain a new perspective on an old favorite.
SUBJ: Frogs--Fiction./ Fairy tales.

Ph-1 6-A/7 $13.89 L KG899
BERRY, JAMES. Ajeemah and his son. HarperCollins ISBN 0-06-021044-3, 1992. 83p.
"Willa Perlman books."
Selectors' Choice, 19th ed.
Available from the National Library Service for the Blind and

Physically Handicapped on sound recording cassette RC 36259.
Presents the fate of Ajeemah and his son, Atu, as they are captured in Africa by African slave dealers and sold to neighboring British sugar planters in Jamaica. The moving story, told in easy enough language for reader comprehension, will raise strong emotions about the injustices of slavery and its aftermath. Highly recommended.
SUBJ: Slavery--Jamaica--Fiction./ Fathers and sons--Fiction./ Jamaica--Fiction.

Ph-1 5-A/6 $15.00   L   KG900
BIRTHDAY SURPRISES: TEN GREAT STORIES TO UNWRAP. Edited by Johanna Hurwitz. Morrow ISBN 0-688-13194-8, 1995. 119p.
Includes bibliography.
Gathers nine original stories and one story poem (Kuskin's), all out of the ordinary about birthdays and birthday presents by such authors as Richard Peck, Ellen Conford, Barbara Ann Porte and others whose names readers will recognize. The variety is excellent and includes good choices for reading aloud.
SUBJ: Birthdays--Fiction./ Short stories.

Ph-1 3-5/5 $14.95   T   KG901
BLANC, ESTHER SILVERSTEIN. Berchick. Illus. by Tennessee Dixon. Volcano Press ISBN 0-912078-81-2, 1989. unp. col. ill.
Includes glossary.
Selectors' Choice, 18th ed.
An orphaned colt becomes the pet of a Jewish family homesteading in Wyoming in the early 1900s. Enhanced by glowing and realistic watercolor wash illustrations this tender and loving story shows the sometimes-hard life of pioneer farmers. Adds a valued perspective to units on settling of the West whether read aloud or independently.
SUBJ: West (U.S.)--Fiction./ Jews--United States--Fiction./ Family life--Fiction./ Frontier and pioneer life--Fiction./ Horses--Fiction./ Wyoming--Fiction.

Ph-3 2-4/6 $14.95   L   KG902
BLANCO, ALBERTO. Angel's kite/La estrella de Angel. English translation by Dan Bellm. Illus. by Rodolfo Morales. Children's Book Press ISBN 0-89239-121-9, 1994. 32p. col. ill.
"A young boy makes a kite that mysteriously restores a long-missing bell to the town church." (CIP) Bright, folklorish, collage illustrations help tell the simple quest story and will add to the understanding of a reader. The engaging story is told in English and Spanish. The English translation lacks variety in word choice, overusing forms of "to get" and the term "beautiful" when other verbs and adjectives could have added greatly to the language, especially for a reader who is learning English.
SUBJ: Kites--Fiction./ Bells--Fiction./ Spanish language materials./ Bilingual materials--Spanish.

Ph-2 3-6/2 $13.95   T   KG903
BLEDSOE, LUCY JANE. Big bike race. Illus. by Sterling Brown. Holiday House ISBN 0-8234-1206-7, 1995. 90p. ill.
"Ernest Peterson's hopes of winning the Washington, D.C., Citywide Cup bicycle race are shattered when his grandmother gives him a huge, clunky, yellow bike for his tenth birthday." (CIP) When he meets Sonny whose hobby is bicycle racing, he learns exercises and techniques to build himself into a first-class racer--even one without a proper bike because of family economics. The internal tension will keep readers' attention, and large type, wide leading, and low reading level will appeal to reluctant readers.
SUBJ: Bicycles and bicycling--Fiction./ Bicycle racing--Fiction./ Winning and losing--Fiction./ Grandmothers--Fiction./ Afro-Americans--Fiction.

Ph-1 4-6/6 $15.00   L   KG904
BLOS, JOAN W. Brooklyn doesn't rhyme. Illus. by Paul Birling. Scribner's ISBN 0-684-19694-8; In Canada: Maxwell Macmillan, 1994. 86p. ill.
Includes chronology.
Edwina Rose Sachs (Rosey) records events in the lives of her Polish immigrant family in Brooklyn in the early 1900s. The diction adds to the atmosphere of the novel since it seems to be in the locutions of Yiddish based English, and the small details the author and illustrator provide add to a feeling for the times and people. Blos presents a slice of life peopled by very human characters. Solid historical fiction.
SUBJ: Polish Americans--Fiction./ Jews--United States--Fiction./ Family life--Brooklyn (New York, N.Y.)--Fiction./ Brooklyn (New York, N.Y.)--Fiction.

CE   Ph-1 4-6/5 $16.00   T   KG905
BLUME, JUDY. Are you there God? It's me, Margaret. Bradbury/Macmillan ISBN 0-02-710991-7, c1970, 1982. 149p.
Also available in Spanish, ESTAS AHI DIOS? SOY YO, MARGARET (ISBN 0-02-710950-X, 1985).
Available from National Library Service for the Blind and Physically

Handicapped in Braille BR7171.
Read-along kit available from Listening Library SWR52 (ISBN 0-8072-7869-6, 1985). 1 paperback book, 1 sound cassette (83min) $20.98.
Eleven-year-old Margaret, newly moved from New York City to a New Jersey suburb, is the daughter of a Jewish father and a Catholic mother. Getting acquainted in the new school, working on her chosen project (what church does she want to belong to, if any) are subordinate to the agony of waiting for the hoped-for signs of physical maturation. Her daily prayers to God form a thread on which this pre-teen story runs.
SUBJ: Adolescence--Fiction./ Religions--Fiction./ New Jersey--Fiction./ Suburban life--Fiction./ Spanish language materials.

Ph-1 4-6/3 $16.00   T   KG906
BLUME, JUDY. Blubber. Bradbury/Macmillan ISBN 0-02-711010-9, 1974. 153p.
Also available in Spanish, LA BALLENA (ISBN 0-02-710940-2, 1983), translated by Alma Flor Ada.
Available from National Library Service for the Blind and Physically Handicapped in Braille BR04527 and on sound recording cassette RC15962.
Jill is a not-too-bright and often nasty eleven-year-old. She falls right in with one of her friends who sets out to torment an obese classmate they nickname "Blubber". Forcing her to eat "chocolate ants", being stripped in the girls' locker room, and other sadistic experiences are a few of the trials to which they subject her. When Jill turns against the leader and sticks up for Blubber, she then becomes the next victim. True-to-life, entertaining, a favorite of pre-teen girls.
SUBJ: Schools--Fiction./ Prejudices--Fiction./ Weight control--Fiction./ Spanish language materials.

Ph-2 6/4 $14.95   T   KG907
BLUME, JUDY. Deenie. Bradbury ISBN 0-02-711020-6, 1973. 159p.
Available from National Library Service for the Blind and Physically Handicapped in Braille BR7354 and on sound recording cassette RC34307.
Thirteen-year-old Deenie is a beautiful girl and her mother's one ambition is for her to be a fashion model. Deenie, however, has scoliosis, a deformity of her spine that requires her to wear a brace for four years. Deenie's physical maturation, her adjustment to the difficulties of wearing the brace, and friends' adjustment to her appearance and other difficulties are described in a compelling style with which middle-class children will identify. Includes a teacher's deft handling of questions about masturbation.
SUBJ: Physically handicapped--Fiction./ Adolescence--Fiction./ Scoliosis--Fiction.

CE   Ph-2 2-4/3 $15.00   L   KG908
BLUME, JUDY. Freckle juice. Illus. by Sonia O. Lisker. Four Winds/Macmillan ISBN 0-02-711690-5, 1971. 40p. ill.
Read-along kit available from Listening Library FTR64 (ISBN 0-8072-0018-2, 1982). 1 paperback book, 1 sound cassette (15min), $15.98, guide.
Available from National Library Service for the Blind and Physically Handicapped in Braille BR02350 and on sound recording cassette RC16625.
Spanish version JUGO DE PECAS available from Santillana (ISBN 84-372-19299, n.d.).
Most children don't want freckles, but Andrew's greatest ambition is to have them. His friend Nicky has 86. Teasing Sharon overhears him asking Nicky how he, too, can have freckles. She gives Andrew a recipe for freckle juice. Unexpected problems result in this warm and hilarious story.
SUBJ: Schools--Fiction./ Spanish language materials.

CE   Ph-1 4-6/3 $13.99   L   KG909
BLUME, JUDY. Fudge-a-mania. Dutton ISBN 0-525-44672-9, 1990. 147p.
Talking book available from Listening Library YA 841 CX (ISBN 0-8072-7377-5, 1992). 2 sound recording cassettes (180min), $16.98.
Pete and Fudge return--and will be welcomed by the legions of SUPERFUDGE fans as their family joins with the much disliked Sheila Tubman and her family to share a vacation house in Maine. Packed with Blume's usual perceptive situations, humor, and sharp character development, a new generation of Blume readers will snatch this up with the same pleasure others have in the past.
SUBJ: Vacations--Fiction./ Brothers--Fiction./ Family life--Fiction./ Humorous stories.

Ph-1 6-A/6 $15.95   T   KG910
BLUME, JUDY. Here's to you, Rachel Robinson. Orchard ISBN 0-531-106801-3, 1993. 196p.

527

FICTION

"Richard Jackson book."
Sequel to JUST AS LONG AS WE'RE TOGETHER, 1987.
Returning to the characters who appear in JUST AS LONG AS WE'RE TOGETHER, Blume concentrates, this time, on the gifted and shy Rachel, now in seventh grade. Matters hinted at in the previous book are now fully explicated, including brother Charles who can be "rude and obnoxious," but whose motivations and other side are now revealed. Rachel, who has always said "yes" to any request for work or to be in special classes, learns that "no" is, at times, a healthier answer. Blume brings characters and action to life through her superb diction and her understanding of adolescents and the way they sound. She is unparalleled in her depiction of teenagers.
SUBJ: Brothers and sisters--Fiction./ Family problems--Fiction./ Gifted children--Fiction./ Friendship--Fiction.

Ph-1 4-6/4 $15.00   T   KG911
BLUME, JUDY. It's not the end of the world. Bradbury ISBN 0-02-711050-8, c1972. 169p.
Available from National Library Service for the Blind and Physically Handicapped in Braille BR02191 and on sound recording cassette RC16560.
It is the middle of the night and Amy, six, is still awake, afraid to go to sleep because all of the family may be gone when she awakens. She doesn't understand divorce, and her older sister and brother, Karen, twelve, and Jeff, fourteen, can't help her either. The pain of a family breakup is tastefully and realistically conveyed.
SUBJ: Divorce--Fiction.

Ph-3 4-6/4 $11.95   L   KG912
BLUME, JUDY. Otherwise known as Sheila the Great. Dutton ISBN 0-525-36455-2, 1972. 118p.
Spanish version SHEILA LA MAGNIFICA available from Santillana (ISBN 84-204-45770, 1991).
Sheila Tubman feels inferior to other folks and at the same time thinks she is really Sheila the Great. When her family moves to the suburbs for the summer holiday, she makes friends with Mouse Ellis, holds up the props in the day camp production of Peter Pan, and even survives a slumber party in which she's revealed as a sham. A funny and perceptive tale of pre-teen problems.
SUBJ: Adolescence--Fiction./ Friendship--Fiction./ Suburban life--Fiction./ Humorous stories./ Spanish language materials.

CE   Ph-1 2-4/2 $13.99   L   KG913
BLUME, JUDY. Superfudge. Dutton ISBN 0-525-40522-4; In Canada: Fitzhenry & Whiteside, 1980. 166p.
Sequel to: TALES OF A FOURTH GRADE NOTHING (1972).
Available from National Library Service for the Blind and Physically Handicapped in Braille BR7172.
Read-along kit available from Listening Library (ISBN 0-8072-7407-0, 1994). 1 paperback book, 2 sound cassettes (3hrs), $20.98.
Spanish version SUPERFUDGE available from Santillana (ISBN 1-56014-665-6, 1996).
Four-year-old Fudgie is being a big pain and his parents tell him there's going to be a new baby. When Tootsie is born, there are even more problems and then his parents decide, without consulting him, to live in Princeton, New Jersey, for a year. Coping with Fudgie, who says and does whatever comes to his mind (even in school), the demands a baby makes, and moving, upset Peter who feels left out. Bright and humorous dialogue should make this highly popular with middle grade readers.
SUBJ: Brothers and sisters--Fiction./ Family life--Fiction./ Humorous stories.

CE   Ph-1 2-4/3 $13.99   L   KG914
BLUME, JUDY. Tales of a fourth grade nothing. Illus. by Roy Doty. Dutton ISBN 0-525-40720-0, 1972. 120p. ill.
Available from the National Library Service for the Blind and Physically Handicapped on sound recording cassette RC 39643 and in Braille BR7203.
Talking book available from Listening Library YA 911 CX (ISBN 0-8072-7759-2, 1996). 2 sound cassettes (153min), $16.98.
Two things are of great importance to Peter: his pet turtle Dribble which he was given at a birthday party and his younger brother Fudge, aged two-and-a-half. Fudge, usually the center of attention in his family, behaves dreadfully and causes a series of disasters to befall Peter who considers himself "a fourth grade nothing."
SUBJ: Brothers--Fiction./ Humorous stories./ Turtles--Fiction.

Ph-2 6-A/5 $16.00   T   KG915
BLUME, JUDY. Then again, maybe I won't. Bradbury ISBN 0-02-711090-7, 1971. 164p.
Available from National Library Service for the Blind and Physically Handicapped in Braille BRA13030.
Spanish version QUIZA NO LO HAGA available from Santillana

(ISBN 84-204-46262, 1995).
Thirteen-year-old Tony Miglione is adjusting to a new suburban home, attempting to figure out what to do about a friend who shoplifts, and, most urgently, learning how to deal with his new physical maturation. Perhaps overly loaded with problems, this title offers a measure of support to boys starting to wonder about adolescence.
SUBJ: Adolescence--Fiction./ Puberty--Fiction./ Moving, Household--Fiction./ Spanish language materials.

Ph-1 2-4/5 $14.95   T   KG916
BOND, MICHAEL. Bear called Paddington. Illus. by Peggy Fortnum. Houghton Mifflin ISBN 0-395-06636-0, c1958. 128p. ill.
Available from National Library Service for the Blind and Physically Handicapped in Braille BRA03802, and as talking book TB03354. Availbe in large print from Windrush/dist. by Cornerstone (ISBN 1-85089-938-X, $13.95).
A small bear from Peru is found in Paddington Station in London. When Mr. and Mrs. Brown take him into their home, life is never again the same. The ensuing humorous adventures of this resilient and resourceful bear are told in a number of other books. Some of them are PADDINGTON ON TOP (ISBN 0-395-21897-7, 1980, OPC), PADDINGTON TAKES THE TEST (ISBN 0-395-29519-X, 1980), and PADDINGTON ON SCREEN (ISBN 0-395-32950-7, 1982).
SUBJ: Bears--Fiction.

TB   Ph-3 2-4 $25.00   OD KG917
BOND, MICHAEL. Paddington audio collection (Talking book). Read by Michael Bond. Music composed and conducted by Don Heckman. HarperAudio/Caedmon ISBN 1-55994-502-8; In Canada: dist. by HarperCollins, 1978. 4 sound cassettes.
Includes teacher's guide.
Adapted from the books in the series by Michael Bond. This set makes available to listeners the full panoply of Paddington stories, with the author reading selections from the books in a clear, clipped British voice against bridges of background music. Highly recommended as excellent listening experiences for upper primary and lower middle listeners.
Contents: Bear Called Paddington, (57min); Paddington: a disappearing trick and other stories, (53min); Paddington for Christmas, (61min); Paddington turns detective, (53min).
SUBJ: Bears--Fiction./ Christmas--Fiction./ Mystery and detective stories.

Ph-2 3-6/5 $21.95   L   KG918
BOND, MICHAEL. Paddington's storybook. Illus. by Peggy Fortnum. Houghton Mifflin ISBN 0-395-36667-4, 1984. 159p. ill.
Available from National Library Service for the Blind and Physically Handicapped in Braille BR06261.
Celebrating Paddington's 25th birthday, Michael Bond has chosen ten of his favorite Paddington stories to include in this collection. Full colored illustrations accompany stories such as "A Spot of Decorating," "Paddington Cleans up," "Paddington Dines Out," "A Day by the Sea," "Something Nasty in the Kitchen," and others.
SUBJ: Bears--Fiction.

Ph-1 4-A/6 $6.00   P   KG919
BOSTON, LUCY M. Children of Green Knowe. Illus. by Peter Boston. Harcourt Brace ISBN 0-15-217151-7, c1955, 1983. 157p. ill.
Available from National Library Service for the Blind and Physically Handicapped in Braille BRA06061 and on sound recording cassette RC10608.
Large type available from Lythway (ISBN 0-745-10626-9, 1987).
The first of a series of five superbly written titles centered on Tolly and his great grandmother. All of the tales take place at Green Knowe, Mrs. Oldknowe's ancient house, now Tolly's home. In this tale Mrs. Oldknowe tells Tolly of Alexander, Toby and Lennett who lived in the house during the 17th century. TREASURE OF GREEN KNOWE (Harcourt Brace Jovanovich ISBN 0-15-289982-0, 1989) tells how Tolly discovers a treasure lost since Norman times. In RIVER AT GREEN KNOWE (ISBN 0-15-267450-0, 1989) Ping, a refugee child, and two old ladies explore the river. STRANGER AT GREEN KNOWE, a Carnegie Medal Winner, (Harcourt Brace Jovanovich ISBN 0-15-281755-7, c1961, 1989) relates Tolly's adventures with Hanno, an escaped gorilla from the London zoo. The final title, ENEMY AT GREEN KNOWE (ISBN 0-15-225973-2, 1964), brings Tolly, Ping and Mrs. Oldknowe into contact with a modern witch who seeks an old book of magic.
Also available from NLSBPH are: TREASURE OF GREEN KNOWE in Braille BRA06059 and on sound recording cassette RC10597; STRANGER AT GREEN KNOWE on sound recording cassette RC10670; ENEMY AT GREEN KNOWE on sound recording cassette RC10508.
SUBJ: Fairy tales./ Great Britain--Fiction./ Time--Fiction.

Ph-1 5-A/7 $19.95 T KG920
BRADBURY, RAY. Halloween tree. Illus. by Joseph Mugnaini. Knopf ISBN 0-394-82409-1; In Canada: Random House, c1982. 145p. ill. "Borzoi book."
Eight trick-or-treaters set out on Halloween, but where is Pipkin, the leader of their band? Carapace Clavicle Moundshroud, climbing out of a pile of leaves under the Halloween tree, offers to explain the origins of Halloween to them. He leads them on a leaf-tossed, kite-flying, broomstick-riding trip, with an absolutely stunning--and satisfying--end. "Well", he asked at journey's end "which was it-- trick or treat?" And all will agree--"Both."
SUBJ: Fantasy./ Halloween--Fiction./ Relativity (Physics)--Fiction.

Ph-2 6-A/5 $16.95 T OD KG921
BRADFORD, KARLEEN. There will be wolves. HarperCollins Publishers Ltd. ISBN 0-00-223892-6; In Canada: HarperCollins, 1992. 210p.
Recounts many historical facts in a fictional form of the First Crusade under Peter the Hermit. The story centers on an almost too perfect young woman healer, Ursula of Cologne. The horrors of the times and the aims of the Crusaders come to life in swift prose. This almost-intimate view of the era, although at times anachronistic as to attitudes, is a recapitulation of the First Crusade and is an excellent historical fiction choice for units on medieval history and life.
SUBJ: Crusades--Fiction.

CE
Ph-1 4-6/6 $16.00 L KG922
BRINK, CAROL RYRIE. Caddie Woodlawn. New ed. Illus. by Trina Schart Hyman. Macmillan ISBN 0-02-713670-1, 1973. 275p. ill.
Includes "Author's note".
Newbery Medal Award.
Talking book available from SRA/McGraw-Hill 87-507897. 1 sound cassette $16.00.
The adventures of this pioneer tomboy add to our understanding of the life of the time, in spite of the perpetuation of a few stereotypes. More fun and adventure with Caddie continue in MAGICAL MELONS (Aladdin ISBN 0-689-71416-5, 1939), also available from the National Library Service for the Blind and Physically Handicapped as talking book TB03356.
SUBJ: Frontier and pioneer life--Fiction./ Wisconsin--Fiction./ Girls--Fiction.

Ph-2 3-6/5 $14.89 L KG923
BRITTAIN, BILL. Dr. Dredd's wagon of wonders. Illus. by Andrew Glass. HarperCollins ISBN 0-06-020714-0, 1987. 168p. ill.
Stalking the quiet New England town of Coven Tree are happenings that only the strong-hearted can enjoy. Now, in this place beset by drought, arrives the fascinating Dr. Dredd with his magic wagon of things ancient, mysterious, and of the darkest intent. Fortunately, New England teen-age girls know a thing or two and gain the upper hand and reduce the dreadful Dr. Dredd to a mere candlewick of his former self. Excellent diction and internal suspense makes this little witchy tale a good choice for the oral telling.
SUBJ: Devil--Fiction./ Magic--Fiction./ Witches--Fiction.

Ph-2 2-4/4 $12.89 L KG924
BRITTAIN, BILL. Mystery of the several sevens. Illus. by James Warhola. HarperCollins ISBN 0-06-024462-3; In Canada: HarperCollins, 1994. 79p. ill.
Simon and Becky enter fairyland with Mr. Merlin, the magical substitute teacher. By answering riddles and using math, they solve the mystery of who stole the seven dwarfs' diamonds.
SUBJ: Magic--Fiction./ Characters and characteristics in literature--Fiction./ Riddles--Fiction.

Ph-1 3-6/7 $14.89 L KG925
BRITTAIN, BILL. Wish giver. Illus. by Andrew Glass. HarperCollins ISBN 0-06-020687-X; In Canada: HarperCollins, 1983. 181p. ill.
Newbery Honor Book.
Selectors' Choice, 14th ed.
Available from National Library Service for the Blind and Physically Handicapped on sound recording cassette RC21758.
Thaddeus Blinn guarantees that the white card with the red spot will make a wish come true. And so it does, but not the way Polly Kemp, Rowena Jervis, and Adam Fiske had intended. Polly had wanted attention but not because she croaked like a frog. Rowena had wanted a traveling salesman to put down roots but not turn into a tree. And Adam Fiske had wanted water on the farm but not gushers everywhere. Humor and suspense are mixed together in this excellent title for reading aloud.
SUBJ: Wishes--Fiction./ Magic--Fiction.

Ph-2 2-4/4 $11.89 L KG926
BRITTAIN, BILL. Wizards and the monster. Illus. by James Warhola. HarperCollins ISBN 0-06-024456-9; In Canada: HarperCollins, 1994. 79p. ill.

Becky and Simon are transported to an ancient castle by Mr. Merlin, their extraordinary substitute teacher. Their exciting adventures with magic and monsters will keep readers spellbound.
SUBJ: Magic--Fiction./ Middle Ages--Fiction./ Time travel--Fiction.

Ph-1 5-A/5 $15.00 T KG927
BROOKE, WILLIAM J. Teller of tales. HarperCollins ISBN 0-06-023399-0; In Canada: HarperCollins, 1994. 170p.
Selectors' Choice, 20th ed.
The stories within this gathering indicate its twists: "The Emperor's clothes are news," "Rumplestiltskin by any other name," "Gold in Locks," "Little Well-Read Riding Hood," and two more less indicatively titled tales which unify the book. These are "old stories told new" (p. 79) in a thoughtful, original manner in which the author begins with a small idea and builds into a whole imaginative alternative to the old and familiar. A perfect choice for reading aloud to middle and upper graders, the tales are good discussion starters. Another welcome addition from Brooke and his different universe to compare and contrast with traditional versions.
SUBJ: Fairy tales./ Short stories.

Ph-1 5-A/7 $15.00 T KG928
BROOKE, WILLIAM J. Telling of the tales: five stories. Illus. by Richard Egielski. HarperCollins ISBN 0-06-022399-0, 1994. 132p.
New and humorous versions of five classic tales: Sleeping Beauty; Paul Bunyan; Cinderella; John Henry; and Jack and the Beanstalk. Each tale, meant for the telling, not only contains humor but also seeds of a serious philosophical statement, e.g., Johnny Appleseed teaches Paul Bunyan that it's easy to cut down a forest but hard to grow a tree. Will be ideal for lessons comparing different versions of stories.
SUBJ: Short stories./ Fairy tales.

Ph-1 6-A/7 $14.89 L KG929
BROOKE, WILLIAM J. Untold tales. HarperCollins ISBN 0-06-020272-6; In Canada: HarperCollins, 1992. 165p.
Entirely original, sophisticated and challenging, the contemporary reworkings of several classic fairy tales about frogs, beauties, princes, and queens will provide a mental workout for readers who won't be quite sure that "they lived happily ever after." A knowledge of the original tales, computers, sit-coms, advertising, and the creative writing process will greatly enhance the reading of this intricately constructed book.
SUBJ: Fairy tales./ Short stories.

VCR
Ph-2 6-A $29.95 KG930
BROTHER FUTURE (Videocassette). WonderWorks/dist. by Bonneville Worldwide ISBN 0-7800-0695-X, c1991, 1997. 1/2" VHS videocassette color (116min). (WonderWorks).
Includes teacher's guide.
Includes public performance rights.
Closed-captioned.
Teachers strive to make history come alive, but they can't arrange time travel. That's probably fortunate if T.J.'s time travel adventure is any indication of what students could expect. He experiences the grim realities of slavery in 1822. Use for United States and African-American history units or to stimulate discussion of the past's influence on the future.
SUBJ: Time travel--Fiction./ Charleston (S.C.)--Fiction./ Slavery--Fiction.

Ph-1 2-4/5 $15.89 L KG931
BROWN, JEFF. Flat Stanley. Illus. by Tomi Ungerer. HarperCollins ISBN 0-06-020681-0, c1964, 1989. unp. col. ill.
Stanley is flattened when his bulletin board falls on him. He's only an inch deep but he rather enjoys sliding under doors, being mailed in an envelope to visit a friend and catching an art thief by hanging on the wall of a museum. When his brother reinflates him with a bicycle pump he is glad to be round Stanley. A welcome reissue, this very funny story is a super read aloud.
SUBJ: Humorous stories.

Ph-2 2-4/3 $3.95 P KG932
BROWN, JEFF. Stanley and the magic lamp. Illus. by Steve Bjorkman. HarperTrophy ISBN 0-06-442028-0; In Canada: HarperCollins, 1996. 87p. ill. (Trophy chapter book).
Originally published as A LAMP FOR THE LAMBCHOPS, Harper & Row, 1983.
Sequel to: FLAT STANLEY, HarperCollins, 1989.
This sequel to the stronger book, FLAT STANLEY, relates the story of the Lambchop family when a genie enables them to fly and grants their wishes for fame and power. Each reacts differently and not everything works out quite as the Lambchops wish. A funny transitional reader which first chapter book readers will enjoy.
SUBJ: Wishes--Fiction./ Magic--Fiction.

Ph-2 6-A/6 $19.95   T   KG933
BROWN, ROBERTA SIMPSON. Queen of the cold-blooded tales.
August House ISBN 0-87483-332-9, 1993. 175p.
Gathers several original tales largely macabre in nature. Best for
reading aloud.
SUBJ: Horror stories.

Ph-2 4-6/5 $14.95   T   KG934
BRUCHAC, JOSEPH. Dog people: native dog stories. Illus. by Murv
Jacob. Fulcrum Kids ISBN 1-55591-228-1, 1995. 64p. ill. (World
stories).
Includes glossary.
In a series of stories set among the Abenaki Indians of Northern New
England, the Abenaki author Bruchac depicts the ancient relationship
between his native group and animals, especially dogs. Considered
"Dog People," each of the dogs is well personalized and gives the
feeling of the people, their land, and the animals. The tales are meant
for storytelling and will amuse and instruct. (Glossary--but no
pronunciation key.). For multicultural studies.
SUBJ: Abenaki Indians--Fiction./ Indians of North America--Fiction./
Dogs--Fiction./ Short stories.

Ph-2 4-A/5 $3.99   P   KG935
BUDBILL, DAVID. Bones on Black Spruce Mountain. Puffin ISBN 0-14-
036854-X; In Canada: Penguin, c1978, 1994. 126p. map.
Seth and Daniel finally realize their dream to hike up to the very top
of Black Spruce Mountain. They are experienced backpackers,
intrigued by the legend of a boy lost on the mountain years ago--a
tale especially meaningful to Daniel, who is an orphan like the lost
boy. The relationship of the two boys and Daniel's recognition that he
does belong make this an especially fine tale and a tense adventure.
SUBJ: Orphans--Fiction./ Backpacking--Fiction.

Ph-1 2-4/2 $11.99   L   KG936
BULLA, CLYDE ROBERT. Chalk box kid. Illus. by Thomas B. Allen.
Random House ISBN 0-394-99102-8, 1987. 59p. ill. (Stepping stone
book).
Selectors' Choice, 17th ed.
Available from the National Library Service for the Blind and
Physically Handicapped on sound recording cassette RC35202.
Gregory is a child in a new school, house, and neighborhood, and
the reader sees this new world through his young eyes. He creates a
garden on a blank wall and from his chalked drawings grow the
beginnings of friendship and respect for his talent. This understated
short novel will be ideal as a read along to primary children and a
good first reading experience for the early independent reader.
SUBJ: Artists--Fiction./ Imagination--Fiction./ Gardens--Fiction.

Ph-2 2-4/2 $4.50   P   KG937
BULLA, CLYDE ROBERT. Pirate's promise. Illus. by Peter Burchard.
HarperTrophy ISBN 0-06-440457-9; In Canada: HarperCollins, c1986,
1994. 87p. ill. (Trophy chapter book).
Tom Pippin, twelve, is sold by his uncle as a deckhand on a ship
sailing from London to the New World in 1716. When pirates attack,
Captain Land, the pirate chief, saves Tom. His treatment by the
pirates is preferable to that which he received from his uncle and as a
bonded boy aboard ship. All ends well in this historical fiction for the
first chapter book reader who will follow Tom's adventures and hopes
with empathy and sympathy in an exciting transitional reader.
SUBJ: Pirates--Fiction.

Ph-1 3-5/2 $14.89   L   KG938
BULLA, CLYDE ROBERT. Shoeshine girl. Illus. by Leigh Grant. Crowell/
HarperCollins ISBN 0-690-04830-0, 1975. 84p. ill.
Available from National Library Service for the Blind and Physically
Handicapped in Braille BR03268.
Sarah is an angry, obnoxious but tough ten-year-old. Her family has
sent her to spend the summer with Aunt Claudia. She wants money in
her pockets but doesn't really understand its value. She becomes a
shoeshine girl and learns about friendship--and earning money.
SUBJ: Friendship--Fiction./ Work--Fiction.

Ph-1 3-5/2 $14.89   L   KG939
BULLA, CLYDE ROBERT. Sword in the tree. Illus. by Paul Galdone.
Crowell/HarperCollins ISBN 0-690-79909-8, c1956. 113p. ill.
Available from National Library Service for the Blind and Physically
Handicapped in Braille BRA01900.
The victory of justice in the times of King Arthur.
SUBJ: Arthur, King--Fiction./ Knights and knighthood--Fiction.

Ph-1 1-6/2 $6.99   L   KG940
BULLA, CLYDE ROBERT. White bird. Illus. by Donald Cook. Random
House ISBN 0-679-80662-8; In Canada: Random House, c1966, 1990.
63p. ill. (Stepping stone book).
John Thomas, who lives in the Tennessee backwoods in the 1880s

with his strict and uncommunicative guardian, finds and cares for a
white crow, the first living thing he has to love. When the bird
disappears, John Thomas runs away to find him and sees the larger
world for the first time in a book that is suspenseful, well
characterized, and sympathetic. Would be good for oral presentation
and is simple enough for newly independent readers--and older
reluctant ones. A newly illustrated edition.
SUBJ: Hermits--Fiction./ Mountain life--Fiction./ Orphans--Fiction.

Ph-1 3-5/2 $14.95   L   KG941
BUNTING, EVE. Cheyenne again. Illus. by Irving Toddy. Clarion ISBN
0-395-70364-6, 1995. unp. col. ill.
"In the late 1880's, a Cheyenne boy named Young Bull is taken to a
boarding school to learn the white man's ways." (CIP) Historical
fiction is based on the unfortunately true experiences of Native
American children who were forcibly enrolled in Bureau of Indian
Affairs schools to try and suppress their culture. Young Bull finally
realized he must retain his memories to keep his values and tribal
customs alive. Illustrations in colored acrylics and oil convey settings
well, but people are less well done. First choice for units on Native
Americans and the clash with official United States government
policies. For multicultural studies. Pair with LEDGERBOOK OF
THOMAS BLUE EAGLE.
SUBJ: Cheyenne Indians--Ethnic identity--Fiction./ Boarding schools--
Fiction./ Schools--Fiction./ Indians of North America--Ethnic identity--
Fiction.

Ph-2 3-5/2 $15.00   L   KG942
BUNTING, EVE. Dandelions. Illus. by Greg Shed. Harcourt Brace ISBN
0-15-200050-X; In Canada: Harcourt Brace c/o Canadian Manda, 1995.
unp. col. ill.
Zoe and her family travel by covered wagon from Illinois to the
unknown territory of Nebraska and establish a home. This tale of
pioneer life on the high plains, strongly illustrated in textured
gouache, has its heart in Zoe gathering and planting dandelions on
the roof of their soddy as a birthday gift for her mother. The journey
was a long, hard dirty trip, but the art does not reflect that nor the
constant dirt in the soddies. Text and art tend to soften the
experience in an otherwise acceptable, perhaps romanticized, book.
SUBJ: Frontier and pioneer life--Nebraska--Fiction./ Family life--
Nebraska--Fiction./ Nebraska--Fiction.

Ph-1 4-6/4 $13.89   L   KG943
BUNTING, EVE. In-between days. Illus. by Alexander Pertzoff.
HarperCollins ISBN 0-06-023612-4; In Canada: HarperCollins, 1994.
119p. ill.
Available from the National Library Service for the Blind and
Physically Handicapped on sound recording cassette RC 40053.
Living on Dove Island, a community of 43 families who sometimes are
unable to reach the mainland because boats cannot ply the frozen
waters, George, eleven, becomes increasingly disturbed when it
appears that his widowed father will marry Caroline, a mainlander.
George works himself into a jealous rage and destroys the
relationship so desired by his younger brother and his father. His
actions are despicable, and tension mounts as a reader becomes
concerned in the reestablishment of the adults' relationship. The
tension is similar to that developed in Maclachlan's SARAH, PLAIN
AND TALL. Black and white, full-page portraits do not interfere with
a reader's conception of character and setting.
SUBJ: Single-parent family--Fiction./ Islands--Fiction.

Ph-1 6-A/6 $14.95   T   KG944
BUNTING, EVE. Spying on Miss Muller. Clarion ISBN 0-395-69172-9,
1995. 179p.
Drawing on her own experiences in a boarding school in Belfast,
Northern Ireland during World War II, the author recreates the lives
of several of the girls and their growing suspicion that the German
teacher, Miss Muller, is a Nazi spy who is guiding planes over Belfast
during bombing raids. The narrator, thirteen-year-old Jessie, is very
fond of the sympathetic teacher and is also concerned about her own
father's alcoholism. Nonetheless, she joins with the other girls,
including a Jewish refugee who has lost her family, to spy on Miss
Muller and finally taunt the teacher into a self-destructive act. Active
and strongly characterized historical fiction, the novel presents a
different perception of war--and the love for a parent with whom the
daughter is unhappy, whether Miss Muller's or Jessie's.
SUBJ: World War, 1939-1945--Northern Ireland--Belfast--Fiction./
Boarding schools--Fiction./ Schools--Fiction./ Fathers and daughters--
Fiction./ Ireland--Fiction.

Ph-2 3-5/4 $15.00   T   KG945
BUNTING, EVE. Train to Somewhere. Illus. by Ronald Himler. Clarion
ISBN 0-395-71325-0, 1996. 32p. col. ill.
Available from the National Library Service for the Blind and

Physically Handicapped on sound recording cassette RC 42580. Fourteen children travel with a matron by rail from New York to the West on an Orphan Train in the late nineteenth century. Illustrated in instructive and personalized watercolors and gouaches, both the communities through which they pass, and the major child figure, Marianne (about 10), are clearly pictured and add interest to a story based on history. Readers will empathize and sympathize when little Nora must leave Marianne to be "adopted" and when the latter seems not to find a family. Historical fiction good for units on the settling of the West.
SUBJ: Orphans--Fiction./ Orphan trains--Fiction.

Ph-2 5-A/4 $14.95 T KG946
BURANDT, HARRIET. Tales from the homeplace: adventures of a Texas farm girl. By Harriet Burandt and Shelley Dale. Henry Holt ISBN 0-8050-5075-2; In Canada: Fitzhenry & Whiteside, 1997. 154p.
"Nine stories capture the life of twelve-year-old Irene Hutto growing up on a cotton farm in Texas in the 1930s, based on the life of Harriet Burandt's mother." (CIP) Scenes and people show the tough life--but with family warmth and support and fun, too--and the chores and interactions of an active family of several children. Relates encounters with a rattler, a hurricane, being tossed from a horse, and other events in Irene's young womanhood. Historical fiction told in an appealing and understandable manner which summons both people and place.
SUBJ: Family life--Texas--Fiction./ Farm life--Texas--Fiction./ Texas--Fiction.

Ph-2 6-A/6 $14.95 T KG947
BURGESS, BARBARA HOOD. Fred Field. Delacorte ISBN 0-385-31070-6; In Canada: Bantam Doubleday Dell, 1994. 180p.
Sequel to OREN BELL, Delacorte, 1991.
"The summer after he finished seventh grade, Oren is occupied with turning an empty lot into a memorial ball field honoring his best friend, who was murdered there, and with finding the killer and making him confess." (CIP) Featuring the same characters who appeared in OREN BELL, the sequel carries the family and friends into other happenings. The Bells and their friends are redeeming without being either didactic or smarmy in this sophisticated continuation. It is, however, necessary to read the first book to know the cast and the inner city Detroit setting. For multicultural studies.
SUBJ: Afro-Americans--Fiction./ Detroit (Mich.)--Fiction./ Mystery and detective stories.

Ph-1 5-A/7 $4.95 P KG948
BURGESS, MELVIN. Cry of the wolf. Morrow ISBN 0-688-13625-7, 1994. 128p.
The hunter, a maniacal, menacing presence, kills all but one of the last wolves in England. His life and the lives of the wolves, especially the last one, Graycub, cross and recross over the years until the hunter becomes the prey. In this well-developed, astoundingly tense book, readers will long for the destruction of the human. First choice for reading aloud.
SUBJ: Wolves--Fiction.

Ph-2 5-A/8 $16.00 T KG949
BURNETT, FRANCES HODGSON. Little princess. Illus. by Tasha Tudor. HarperCollins ISBN 0-397-30693-8, c1963. 240p. ill.
At first a rich, privileged student as Miss Minchin's school, Sara Crewe is suddenly a poor outcast reduced to the meanest work. Sara is rescued but the sympathetic reader will cry when she is cold and hungry, and delight in the change in her fortunes. This older book still has appeal for better readers who have been held by THE SECRET GARDEN.
SUBJ: Boarding schools--Fiction./ England--Fiction./ Orphans--Fiction.

Ph-2 4-6/7 $3.50 P KG950
BURNETT, FRANCES HODGSON. Sara Crewe. Illus. by Brian Wildsmith. Scholastic ISBN 0-590-42323-1; In Canada: Scholastic, 1986. 96p. ill.
Raised in India, young Sara is placed in a boarding school in England by her father, whose death drastically affects the way in which she is treated. The melodramatic story has been enduringly popular in this, its original form and in the expanded version of the story, A LITTLE PRINCESS (Bantam, 1987).
SUBJ: Boarding schools--Fiction./ England--Fiction./ Orphans--Fiction.

CE Ph-1 3-6/5 $4.95 P KG951
BURNETT, FRANCES HODGSON. Secret garden. Illus. by Tasha Tudor. HarperCollins ISBN 0-06-440188-X, c1987. 311p. ill. (some col.).
Talking book available from Audio Partners 61040 (ISBN 1-57270-040-8, 1997). 6 sound cassettes (465min), $24.95.
Coming to live in a grand but gloomy house on the Yorkshire moor after her parents have died in India, Mary Lenox finds her life similar in some ways but vastly different in others as she and her companions

bring life to a mysterious locked garden, and to the house and its human inhabitants. The long standing favorite includes classic illustrations in the well-known style of Tasha Tudor. The romantic sense of the story is fulfilled in this attractive edition.
SUBJ: Orphans--Fiction./ Gardens--Fiction./ Physically handicapped--Fiction./ Yorkshire (England)--Fiction.

Ph-2 4-6/5 $14.93 L KG952
BUSHNELL, JACK. Circus of the wolves. Illus. by Robert Andrew Parker. Lothrop, Lee & Shepard ISBN 0-688-12555-7, 1994. unp. col. ill.
Kael, a timber wolf, is captured and trained as a performing circus animal by a gentle man, but the wolf always longs for his life in the wild. When opportunity presents itself, he flees and returns to his life of freedom in a story meant for reading aloud. Parker's color washes carry the story well and unite with the somewhat long text nicely. An addendum provides information about captive wolves.
SUBJ: Wolves--Fiction./ Circus--Fiction.

Ph-2 2-3/2 $13.88 L KG953
BUSSER, MARIANNE. King Bobble. By Marianne Busser and Ron Schroder. Illus. by Hans de Beer. Translated by J. Alison James. North-South Books ISBN 1-55858-592-3; In Canada: North-South Books/dist. by Vanwell, 1996. 63p. col. ill.
Helping a child develop a healthy sense of humor and nonsense is surely "a good thing." King Bobble and his wife are the Royal Stupids (James Marshall) in a book for beginning readers. The Bobbles are an exemplary family--although silly to the nth degree. The birth of Baby Bobble adds to the fun--and family. Lively color illustrations exaggerate the humor in this transitional reader which is sure to tickle young funny bones.
SUBJ: Kings, queens, rulers, etc.--Fiction./ Humorous stories.

Ph-2 3-4/2 $5.95 P KG954
BUSSER, MARIANNE. On the road with Poppa Whopper. By Marianne Busser and Ron Schroder. Illus. by Hans de Beer. Translated by J. Alison James. North-South Books ISBN 1-55858-776-4; In Canada: North-South Books, 1997. 63p. col. ill.
Presents a series of silly events about the Whopper family, father and daughter, as they travel around in their van doing various jobs--all silly. Colorful, full-page illustrations add to the fun of a family somewhat brighter than Marshall's "Stupids." For a transitional reader with fun, try a Whopper.
SUBJ: Fathers and daughters--Fiction./ Occupations--Fiction.

Ph-1 3-5/4 $16.95 L KG955
BUTTERWORTH, OLIVER. Enormous egg. Little, Brown ISBN 0-316-11904-0, c1956. 188p. ill.
Twelve-year-old Nate Twitchell is surprised when one of the hens lays a 3-1/4 lb. egg--and is astonished when it hatches into a Triceratops. The ludicrous nature of the response to the creature has kept young people chuckling for over thirty years.
SUBJ: Fantasy./ Dinosaurs--Fiction./ Humorous stories.

Ph-3 3-5/5 $13.95 L KG956
BUTTERWORTH, OLIVER. Visit to the big house. Illus. by Susan Avishai. Houghton Mifflin ISBN 0-395-52805-4, 1993. 47p. ill.
Originally published as UNA VISITA A LA CASA GRANDE/A VISIT TO THE BIG HOUSE, 1987.
Willy, Rose, and their mother visit their father/husband in prison for the first time. Illustrated with black and white drawings, the story of a difficult visit honestly portrays the feelings of the children as they adjust to their family's situation. A very human and useful book.
SUBJ: Prisons--Fiction./ Prisoners--Fiction./ Fathers--Fiction.

Ph-1 5-A/5 $12.95 T KG957
BYARS, BETSY CROMER. Bingo Brown and the language of love. Viking Penguin ISBN 0-670-82791-6, 1989. 160p.
Bingo faces life, the possibility of shaving, growing up, further questions about "mixed-sex conversations" and falling in and out of love. He also learns his mother (at 38) is pregnant and comes to terms with the idea of "big brotherhood" in a delightful, fast paced novel marked by humor, serious undertones, lively diction, and deft writing. Excellent for oral or individual reading.
In BINGO BROWN'S GUIDE TO ROMANCE (ISBN 0-670-84491-8, 1992, Large type available from Curley Publishing ISBN 0-74512-037-7, 1994, OPC) Melissa returns, Bingo has "the best mixed-sex conversation in the history of the world", and begins to understand romance.
SUBJ: Adolescence--Fiction./ Humorous stories.

Ph-1 5-A/5 $3.99 P KG958
BYARS, BETSY CROMER. Burning questions of Bingo Brown. Penguin ISBN 0-14-032479-8, 1990. 166p. ill.
Selectors' Choice, 17th ed.

Interwoven with the joys and problems of the average twelve-year-old boy: girls, school assignments, hair styles, is the suicidal tendency and talk of Bingo's favorite teacher. The novel, seemingly light and humorous, builds to the attempted suicide and the value Bingo finds in himself and life--a value he helps Mr. M., his teacher, understand. A fine mixture of light and dark.
SUBJ: Schools--Fiction./ Adolescence--Fiction.

Ph-1 4-6/3 $13.95 L KG959
BYARS, BETSY CROMER. Cartoonist. Illus. by Richard Cuffari. Viking ISBN 0-670-20556-7, 1978. 119p. ill.
Alfie treasures his private room, the attic, which can be reached only by a ladder and a trap door. It not only gives him privacy from his mother's nagging and his grandfather's endlessly repeated stories, but he can draw his cartoons of "Super Caterpillar" and his own pigeon footed walk. But when Bubba loses his job and his mother offers his family a home, Alfie's privacy is threatened. A poignant story of a boy's determination to protect his own "turf".
SUBJ: Family life--Fiction./ Privacy, Right of--Fiction.

CE   Ph-1 4-6/5 $13.99 T KG960
BYARS, BETSY CROMER. Dark stairs. Viking ISBN 0-670-85487-5; In Canada: Penguin, 1994. 130p. (Herculeah Jones mystery).
Talking book available from Listening Library YA 883 (ISBN 0-8072-7571-9, 1995). 2 sound cassettes (148min), $16.98.
Available from the National Library Service for the Blind and Physically Handicapped on sound recording cassette RC 41485.
Presents Herculeah Jones, girl detective, as she helps her mother, a private detective who specifically has forbidden her daughter to snoop, to solve the mystery of a long lost person--dead or alive. The dangers Herculeah faces as she is locked into a dark cellar and hears the approaching footsteps of the fearful Moloch, alias William Crewell, will hold a reader. Mystery fans should enjoy this well-developed and fast-paced series.
Other episodes include DEAD LETTER (ISBN 0-670-86860-4, 1996) in which Herculeah and Meat seek the writer of a mysterious note; DEATH'S DOOR (ISBN 0-670-87423-X, 1997) in which Herculeah experiences dangerous adventures as she investigates an attempted murder; and in TAROT SAYS BEWARE (ISBN 0-670-85575-8, 1995; Talking book available from Listening Library YA 913 CX, ISBN 0-8072-7753-3, 1996, 2 sound cassettes [165min], $16.98) Herculeah falls into tense situations as she searches for the murderer of Madame Rosa.
SUBJ: Mystery and detective stories.

Ph-1 5-A/5 $13.99 T KG961
BYARS, BETSY CROMER. McMummy. Viking ISBN 0-670-84995-2; In Canada: Penguin, 1993. 150p.
Mozie takes care of the absent professor's greenhouse and becomes involved with the pod that grows there--an animate plant with a heart--that can walk. Characters are quirky. Story is at once funny, scary, poignant, mysterious, and very human.
SUBJ: Moneymaking projects--Fiction./ Supernatural--Fiction./ Single-parent family--Fiction.

CE   Ph-1 4-A/4 $3.99 P KG962
BYARS, BETSY CROMER. Not-just-anybody family. Illus. by Jacqueline Rogers. Dell ISBN 0-440-45951-6, 1986. 149p. ill.
When Pap (Grandpa) is jailed for disturbing the peace and Junior falls off the barn and breaks both legs, Maggie and Vern Blossom struggle to untangle the family's affairs. This humorous, quickly paced story features three concentric plots and vibrant oddball characters in an oddball situation in which loyalty and affection are major strengths.
In BLOSSOMS MEET THE VULTURE LADY (ISBN 0-440-40672-3, 1986) Junior is kidnapped by Mad Mary the hermit. In BLOSSOMS AND THE GREEN PHANTOM (ISBN 0-440-40069-4, c1987, 1988) Junior discovers an exciting new invention. The adventures of this irrepressible family continue in A BLOSSOM PROMISE (ISBN 0-440-40137-2, 1990); and Mud is put on trial for a crime he did not commit in WANTED...MUD BLOSSOM (ISBN 0-385-30428-5, 1991, available from NLSBPH on sound recording cassette RC 37382, talking book available from Listening Library YA 871, ISBN 0-8072-7521-2, 1995).
SUBJ: Brothers and sisters--Fiction./ Family problems--Fiction.

CE   Ph-1 5-6/3 $14.89 L KG963
BYARS, BETSY CROMER. Pinballs. HarperCollins ISBN 0-06-020918-6, c1977. 136p.
Read-along kit available from Listening Library LB 2 SP (ISBN 0-8072-8536-6, 1988), 1 hardcover book, 2 sound cassettes (168min), $20.98.
Available from National Library Service for the Blind and Physically Handicapped on sound recording cassette RC11982.

Three lonely and alienated children are thrown together in a foster home. Harvey, whose own father ran over him with a car and broke both his legs in a fit of anger, Carlie and Thomas J. figure that they are all pinballs--they don't settle where they want. With the help of the foster parents--and Carlie in particular--they eventually work out their problems in a funny and poignant story. Good for readers of Paterson's GREAT GILLY HOPKINS.
SUBJ: Foster home care--Fiction./ Friendship--Fiction.

CE   Ph-1 5-6/6 $15.99 L KG964
BYARS, BETSY CROMER. Summer of the swans. Illus. by Ted CoConis. Viking ISBN 0-670-68190-3, c1970. 142p. ill.
Newbery Medal Award.
Talking book available from Live Oak Media ISBN 0-670-68193-8, 1972, $9.95.
Available from National Library Service for the Blind and Physically Handicapped on sound recording cassette RC23118.
Sarah, a moody eighth grader, forgets her small miseries when Charlie, her mentally retarded younger brother, disappears. Together with her most despised enemy, Joe Malley, she finds Charlie and the longest day of the summer brings a great change in Sarah. A well-written book and full of meaning especially for upper elementary graders.
SUBJ: Adolescence--Fiction./ Mentally handicapped--Fiction.

Ph-2 2-5/3 $13.89 L KG965
BYARS, BETSY CROMER. Tornado. By Betsy Byars. Illus. by Doron Ben-Ami. HarperCollins ISBN 0-06-026452-7; In Canada: HarperCollins, 1996. 49p. ill.
"As they wait out a tornado in their storm cellar, a family listens to their farmhand tell stories about the dog that was blown into his life by another tornado when he was a boy." (CIP) Told in simple, but effective, language and produced in large type with wide leading, the gentle and sometimes humorous stories are holding. Ben-Ami's full-page illustrations show people and setting well in a soft, but realistic, fashion. The transitional reader will appeal to first chapter book readers and older reluctant ones. The stories are very oral in nature and will work well for reading aloud.
SUBJ: Dogs--Fiction./ Tornadoes--Fiction.

Ph-2 4-6/4 $13.89 L KG966
CALHOUN, MARY. Katie John. Illus. by Paul Frame. HarperCollins ISBN 0-06-020951-8, c1960. 134p. ill.
Katie John and her family move into an inherited home in order to sell it--but grow to love it and decide to stay. Her friend Sue claims the house is haunted and together they find the explanation.
Followed by DEPEND ON KATIE JOHN (ISBN 0-06-440299-1, c1961, 1990, OPC) and HONESTLY, KATIE JOHN (ISBN 0-06-020936-4, 1963, OPC).
SUBJ: Dwellings--Fiction./ Family life--Fiction./ Girls--Fiction.

Ph-1 2-4/2 $3.99 P KG967
CAMERON, ANN. Julian's glorious summer. Illus. by Dora Leder. Random House ISBN 0-394-89117-1, 1987. 62p. ill. (Stepping stone book).
Available from National Library Service for the Blind and Physically Handicapped in Braille BR7447.
Julian, his friends, and his warm and loving family return in a single story about the summer when Julian, in order to avoid learning to ride Gloria's new bike because of his fear of falling, insists he must work in the house and garden so that he will not have even a moment for bikes. A sympathetic portrait of a child and his world with a satisfying ending. Good for newly established readers and excellent for oral presentation.
SUBJ: Fear--Fiction./ Bicycles and bicycling--Fiction.

Ph-2 2-4/2 $13.00 T KG968
CAMERON, ANN. More stories Huey tells. Illus. by Lis Toft. Farrar, Straus and Giroux ISBN 0-374-35065-5; In Canada: HarperCollins, 1997. 118p. ill.
"Frances Foster books."
Presents five more stories about Huey and his family, especially older brother Julian, in which they plant a garden, play basketball (but Julian won't let Huey share), try to convince their father to give up smoking, and other tales. The new illustrator seems to make Huey and Julian much younger than they have been in previous books. The family situations are still holding. For multicultural studies.
SUBJ: Brothers--Fiction./ Family life--Fiction./ Afro-Americans--Fiction.

Ph-1 2-4/2 $16.99 L KG969
CAMERON, ANN. Stories Huey tells. Illus. by Roberta Smith. Knopf ISBN 0-679-96732-X; In Canada: Random House, 1995. 102p. ill.
"Borzoi book."
Huey, Julian's younger brother, now steps on stage in five episodes

centering on the warmth of his family and Huey's part in it. The problems of eating a fish when its eye is staring at you, cooking a meal, and other gentle adventures should be welcomed by newly established readers--even in late first grade. It's nice to have this good family back. Black and white illustrations add to its easy readability. This transitional reader could also be good for reading aloud. For multicultural studies.
SUBJ: Brothers--Fiction./ Family life--Fiction./ Afro-Americans--Fiction.

Ph-1 3-4/4 $15.99 L KG970
CAMERON, ANN. Stories Julian tells. Illus. by Ann Strugnell. Pantheon ISBN 0-394-94301-5; In Canada: Random House, 1981. 71p. ill.
Available from National Library Service for the Blind and Physically Handicapped on sound recording cassette RC26051 and in Braille BR06945.
Julian invariably manages to trick his gullible younger brother Huey in these five episodes in the life of a middle class African-American family. For multicultural studies.
Julian relates five charming stories about frogs wearing shoes, moving the sun, and other whimsical tales firmly set in real children in a warm, real family in MORE STORIES JULIAN TELLS (ISBN 0-394-82454-7, 1989, Selectors' Choice, 16th ed.), and Julian and Huey try to find the perfect birthday gift for Dad in JULIAN, DREAM DOCTOR (Random House ISBN 0-679-90524-3, 1990).
Available from NLSBPH in Braille BR6945 is MORE STORIES JULIAN TELLS.
SUBJ: Afro-Americans--Fiction./ Brothers--Fiction./ Short stories.

CE

Ph-1 4-A/6 $19.00 T KG971
CAPOTE, TRUMAN. Christmas memory. Illus. by Beth Peck. Knopf ISBN 0-679-80040-9; In Canada: Random House, c1956. unp. col. ill.
Also available as a kit, narrated by Celeste Holm (ISBN 0-394-82500-4, 1985) 1 hardcover book, 1 sound cassette (29min) $19.95. (Knopf book and cassette classic).
The call for the faded straw hat and the rickety old baby buggy are the sign that preparations for Christmas are about to begin. This tender autobiographical story about the author as a young boy and his aged companion aunt is presented in a newly illustrated edition that suits the tone and time of the tale well. Perfect for oral, the loving and warm story will also be enjoyed by the able middle-grade reader as well as adults.
SUBJ: Christmas--Fiction./ Aunts--Fiction./ Friendship--Fiction.

Ph-1 5-A/8 $19.00 T KG972
CAPOTE, TRUMAN. Thanksgiving visitor. Illus. by Beth Peck. Knopf ISBN 0-679-83898-8; In Canada: Random House, 1996. unp. col. ill.
"Borzoi book."
Episodic historical fiction recreates the time in 1932 when a bullying schoolmate, Odd Henderson, torments Buddy's life away from home and the love and security of his aged relative, Miss Sook. Through a simple gesture of kindness, she changes Odd's attitude toward the fearful Buddy and teaches Buddy a gentle lesson in acceptance and understanding. Peck's full-page color illustrations give the story a new, and welcome, life and add to Capote's atmospheric words. Good selection for reading aloud, but also encourage its use for quiet individual reading. Companion piece to Capote's novella A CHRISTMAS MEMORY.
SUBJ: Alabama--Fiction./ Bullies--Fiction./ Thanksgiving Day--Fiction./ Friendship--Fiction.

Ph-1 3-6/5 $14.95 T KG973
CAREY, PETER. Big Bazoohley. Illus. by Abira Ali. Henry Holt ISBN 0-8050-3855-8, 1995. 135p.
"John Macrae book."
The son of a charming gambler father and a talented artist mother, Sam Kellow and his family once again find themselves in a not-unfamiliar situation: being in an expensive hotel with only $53.20 to their names. Sam's father is always waiting for "The Big Bazoohley," a big payoff, but this time it is Sam who rescues the family when unusual strangers force him to enter a contest to be selected "A Perfecto Kid" for a cosmetics firm. In this comical novel peopled with memorable characters, Sam does win "The Big Bazoohley" through fortuitous happenstance. Well characterized and fast paced, it will be good for reading aloud or for recreational reading for youngsters who do not fully accept the lure of advertising.
SUBJ: Parent and child--Fiction./ Luck--Fiction./ Contests--Fiction./ Toronto (Ont.)--Fiction.

Ph-3 3-5/4 $14.89 L KG974
CARLSON, NATALIE SAVAGE. Family under the bridge. Illus. by Garth Williams. HarperCollins ISBN 0-06-020991-7, c1958. 99p. ill.
Newbery Honor Book.
Available from National Library Service for the Blind and Physically Handicapped on sound recording cassette RC18427 and in Braille BRA09321.
When the old French hobo, Armand, finds his winter quarters occupied, he plans to move on. However, the three children in the tunnel under the bridge change his plans and also end his hobo days.
SUBJ: Gypsies--Fiction./ Paris (France)--Fiction./ Family life--Fiction./ Christmas--Fiction.

Ph-1 4-6/3 $15.99 T KG975
CARRIER, ROCH. Basketball player. Translated by Sheila Fischman. Illus. by Sheldon Cohen. Tundra ISBN 088776-367-7; In Canada: Tundra, 1996. unp. col. ill.
French edition LE JOUEUR DE BASKET-BALL (ISBN 0-88776-368-5, 1996) available.
Carrier and Cohen seem to be the chroniclers of a French-Canadian boy's life of several decades ago. Now, in his quirky, colorful, and active art, the illustrator joins with the author to relate Roch's first unhappy days at a Catholic boarding school where he is forced to play basketball, a game previously unknown to him. Everything away from home is different, and his adjustment to "everything" is at once humorous and frustrating. The book provides a picture of one boy and a particular life style in that time and place.
SUBJ: Basketball--Fiction./ Boarding schools--Fiction./ Schools--Fiction./ French language materials.

Ph-3 4-6/2 $15.95 T KG976
CARRIER, ROCH. Boxing champion. Translated from the original French by Sheila Fischman. Illus. by Sheldon Cohen. Tundra ISBN 0-88776-249-2; In Canada: Tundra, 1991. unp. col. ill.
Also available in the original French edition, UN CHAMPION (ISBN 0-88776-250-6).
Tells the dreams-of-glory of a young French Canadian to exercise, become strong, and defeat the neighborhood boxing champion. Set in the era when Joe Louis was world champ, and Maurice Richard was the ice hockey hero, the would-be champion boxer never quite succeeds--but finds the sympathetic smile of the prettiest girl in the class a shy reward for being knocked out. The art is splendid, active, original, amusing, and is worth the price of admission to the chalk drawn ring.
SUBJ: Boxing--Fiction./ French language materials./ Quebec (Province)--Fiction.

Ph-2 2-4/4 $15.95 T KG977
CARRIER, ROCH. Longest home run. Translated and adapted from the original French by Sheila Fischman. Illus. by Sheldon Cohen. Tundra ISBN 0-88776-300-6; In Canada: Tundra, 1993. unp. col. ill.
Available in French LE PLUS LONG CIRCUIT (ISBN 0-88776-301-4, 1993).
Available in Spanish EL JONRON MAS LARGO (ISBN 0-8876-304-9, 1993).
"The longest home run in the history of baseball was hit by a girl." Thus begins a colorful, active text and illustrations about life in a small Quebec village when a magician and his daughter come to town.
SUBJ: Baseball--Fiction./ Quebec (Province)--Fiction.

Ph-1 4-6/5 $14.95 L KG978
CARRIS, JOAN DAVENPORT. Aunt Morbelia and the screaming skulls. By Joan Carris. Illustrated by Doug Cushman. Little, Brown ISBN 0-316-12945-3; In Canada: Little, Brown, 1990. 134p. ill.
Aunt Morbelia has a fascination with superstition and the supernatural. When she moves in with Todd's family, he expects the worst, but her talents as a teacher and superb organizer help Todd remediate his dyslexia and add to the life of the school and community. At times humorous, Carris' character study presents interesting characters and a good portrait of an energetic older person.
SUBJ: Dyslexia--Fiction./ Aged--Fiction.

Ph-2 5-A/5 $14.95 T KG979
CARRIS, JOAN DAVENPORT. Beware the ravens, Aunt Morbelia. By Joan Carris. Little, Brown ISBN 0-316-12961-5; In Canada: Little, Brown, 1995. 141p.
Sequel to: AUNT MORBELIA AND THE SCREAMING SKULLS, Little, Brown, 1990.
Aunt Morbelia and Todd Fearing have an adventure filled with mystery, rumor, and danger in their ancestral British mansion, Harrowwood. Shadowed everywhere by strangely disguised characters, Todd and his friend Jeff unravel the puzzle when a clever ruse puts an end to the mystery and lays the ghosts of Harrowwood to rest. Readers of the genre will relish the sometimes-tense adventures.
SUBJ: Aunts--Fiction./ London (England)--Fiction./ Mystery and detective stories.

Ph-1 5-A/7 $16.00   L   KG980
CARROLL, LEWIS. Alice's adventures in Wonderland. Illus. by John Tenniel. Morrow ISBN 0-688-11087-8, c1865, 1992. 196p. ill. (Books of wonder).

When Alice falls down a rabbit hole, she enters a bizarre fantasy world filled with nonsensical creatures such as the Mad Hatter, the Cheshire Cat, and the White Rabbit. This reissue of the classic fantasy story includes 42 reproductions of the original, subtly detailed engravings of John Tenniel. Her humorous adventures are suitable for reading aloud.
SUBJ: Fantasy.

Ph-1 5-A/7 $16.00   T   KG981
CARROLL, LEWIS. Through the looking-glass and what Alice found there. Illus. by John Tenniel. Morrow ISBN 0-688-12049-0, c1872, 1993. 228p. ill. (Books of wonder).

Alice's curiosity takes her through a mirror into a strange land where she meets Tweedledum and Tweedledee, the Jabberwock, and Humpty Dumpty. This edition of the classic fantasy tale, the sequel to ALICE'S ADVENTURES IN WONDERLAND, includes detailed reproductions of 50 of the original engravings by John Tenniel.
SUBJ: Fantasy.

Ph-1 4-6/4 $13.95   T   KG982
CARUSONE, AL. Don't open the door after the sun goes down: tales of the real and unreal. Illus. by Andrew Glass. Clarion ISBN 0-395-65225-1, 1994. 83p. ill.

Gathers nine original, very scary stories just right for reading or telling aloud. Glass' black and white drawings help convey the suspense of the text.
SUBJ: Horror stories./ Short stories.

Ph-1 3-5/4 $15.00   L   KG983
CASELEY, JUDITH. Dorothy's darkest days. Greenwillow ISBN 0-688-13422-X; In Canada: Hearst Book Group, 1997. 117p. ill.

In the fourth grade, Dorothy must face many new challenges, including the sudden death of a classmate. At times both humorous and touching, the story is related through classroom scenes and family interactions that are true-to-life.
SUBJ: Brothers and sisters--Fiction./ Family life--Fiction./ Death--Fiction.

Ph-1 3-5/6 $14.00   L   KG984
CASELEY, JUDITH. Harry and Arney. Greenwillow ISBN 0-688-12140-3, 1994. 138p.

A new baby brother arrives and Harry discovers much about science, history, other people, and himself in this gentle, humorous book.
SUBJ: Babies--Fiction./ Brothers and sisters--Fiction./ Family life--Fiction.

Ph-1 3-5/4 $13.95   L   KG985
CASELEY, JUDITH. Hurricane Harry. Greenwillow ISBN 0-688-10027-9, 1991. 106p. ill.

When he is five, Harry and his family move from a city apartment to a house in the country. This episodic story centers on the largely humorous events in Harry's life: entering kindergarten where he is placed in a room of second-graders by mistake, the acquisition and death of his pet turtle, and a trip to the hospital to see his sick grandmother. Throughout, Harry and his family seem like real people with very human and warm qualities. Character is nicely realized in this gentle book with a heart.
In CHLOE IN THE KNOW (ISBN 0-688-11055-X, 1993) Chloe, oldest of the Kane children, shows how to be a fine oldest sister in another story featuring the loving, very human family.
SUBJ: Moving, Household--Fiction./ Family life--Fiction.

Ph-1 6-A/5 $14.89   L   KG986
CASSEDY, SYLVIA. Behind the attic wall. Crowell/HarperCollins ISBN 0-690-04337-6; In Canada: HarperCollins, 1983. 315p.
Selectors' Choice, 15th ed.

Following the sound of the mysterious voices in the old mansion where she's now living with her intimidating great aunts, Maggie, who has been ejected from a lengthy series of boarding schools and foster homes, discovers a latched door leading to a hidden room off the attic populated by Miss Christabel, Timothy John, and Juniper the dog--dolls, or are they? A low keyed, sensitive story by an author who demonstrates the ability to use even the nuances of words successfully. Recommended for the particularly perceptive reader.
SUBJ: Orphans--Fiction./ Ghosts--Fiction./ Fantasy.

Ph-1 6-A/7 $4.50   P   KG987
CASSEDY, SYLVIA. Lucie Babbidge's house. Avon ISBN 0-380-71812-X, 1993. 243p.

Living as a misunderstood and unhappy scapegoat at Norwood Hall, an orphanage, Lucie Babbidge finds a dollhouse and creates a magical world in which she is part of a loving family and is herself loved. Her powers of imagination change Lucie and will change the better reader of this powerful book for those who have lived in THE SECRET GARDEN (Burnett) and the BEAR'S HOUSE (Sachs). Good for oral presentation.
SUBJ: Orphans--Fiction./ Dolls--Fiction./ Emotional problems--Fiction.

Ph-2 3-4/5 $15.95   L   KG988
CHILDRESS, MARK. Joshua and the big bad blue crabs. Illus. by Mary Barrett Brown. Little, Brown ISBN 0-316-14118-6; In Canada: Little, Brown, 1996. unp. col. ill.

On the Magnolia River, perhaps in a bayou, Joshua paddles his boat to visit Granny and deliver one of his mother's superior huckleberry pies. The blue crabs that inhabit the river are tired of being someone's dinner and kidnap the boat and the pie until people and crustaceans come to a fair accommodation. A tall tale meant for telling and reading aloud. Compare and contrast with "Little Red Riding Hood." Characters and settings are portrayed in a humorous and lively fashion.
SUBJ: Crabs--Fiction.

Ph-2 2-3/2 $15.00   T   KG989
CHRISTIANSEN, C. B. Snowman on Sycamore Street. Illus. by Melissa Sweet. Atheneum ISBN 0-689-31927-4; In Canada: Distican, 1996. 40p. col. ill.

Throughout the year, Angel, Chloe, and Rupert share a friendship that helps them through life's ups and downs. Lively watercolor illustrations portray their wintertime activities, and realistic episodes in the short chapters will endear the trio to readers. A solid choice for students looking for transitional readers.
SUBJ: Snowman--Fiction./ Winter--Fiction./ Friendship--Fiction.

Ph-2 5-A/4 $14.95   L   KG990
CHRISTOPHER, JOHN. Dusk of Demons. Simon & Schuster ISBN 0-02-718425-0; In Canada: Distican, 1994. 175p.

Christopher peoples the future world of Old Isle with a society that is more like the nontechnological past than the present. Young Ben and his allies must fight the destructive Demons, who wish to overthrow the rule of "the Master," an autocratic, but beneficent ruler. In the suspenseful battle between truth and supersitition, a thorough study of the past, contained in books, is the only way to wage and win the war with the Demons. Settings are very clear, and readers will know the geography of the place as well as the inhabitants.
SUBJ: Science fiction.

Ph-1 4-6/6 $16.00   L   KG991
CHRISTOPHER, JOHN. White Mountains. Macmillan ISBN 0-02-718360-2; In Canada: Collier Macmillan, 1967. 184p.
Available from National Library Service for the Blind and Physically Handicapped on sound recording cassette RC26091, as talking book TB01440, in Braille BR05009.

Will lives in a future time when all the cities have been destroyed and technology has reverted to a primitive state. The world has been taken over by Tripods, metal structures inhabited by beings from outer space. They take young people at 13 and "cap them", insert a metal plate which controls their behavior and makes them subservient. Will and Henry, joined by Beanpole, run away to the White Mountains, pursued by Tripods, to escape to freedom. In CITY OF GOLD AND LEAD (Aladdin ISBN 0-02-042701-8, 1989) the three boys continue their guerilla warfare against the Tripods who plan to kill the earth by changing the atmosphere. In THE POOL OF FIRE (ISBN 0-02-718350-5, 1968) this exciting trilogy is brought to a triumphant conclusion.
Also available from NLSBPH is: CITY OF GOLD AND LEAD in talking book TB01940; POOL OF FIRE in Braille BRA04270 and talking book TB02610.
SUBJ: Science fiction./ Future--Fiction.

Ph-1 2-5/3 $15.93   L   KG992
CLEARY, BEVERLY. Beezus and Ramona. Illus. by Louis Darling. Morrow ISBN 0-688-31076-1, 1955. 192p. ill.
Sequel to RAMONA THE PEST. (1968)
Available from National Library Service for the Blind and Physically Handicapped in Braille BRA13483.

Four-year-old Ramona spreads distraction and destruction when she goes to school in her "rabbit ears". Big and well-behaved sister Beezus saves the day, however.
SUBJ: Sisters--Fiction./ Schools--Fiction.

Ph-1 4-A/4 $15.93   L   KG993
CLEARY, BEVERLY. Dear Mr. Henshaw. Illus. by Paul O. Zelinsky. Morrow ISBN 0-688-02406-8, 1983. 133p. ill.
Newbery Medal Award.
Selectors' Choice, 15th ed.

Available from National Library Service for the Blind and Physically Handicapped in Braille BR05629 and on sound recording cassette RC21309.
Spanish edition available QUERIDO SENOR HENSHAW (Austral, 1986), $15.95.
Writing to his favorite author initially in a series of letters and then in an unsent journal, Leigh Botts, age ten, pours out his frustrations about his parents' divorce and his move to a new school. Humor is used as a major adjunct in the realistic portrayal of a child's adjustment to a recent divorce.
SUBJ: Divorce--Fiction./ Parent and child--Fiction./ Schools--Fiction.

Ph-1 2-4/3 $15.93   L   KG994
CLEARY, BEVERLY. Ellen Tebbits. Illus. by Louis Darling. Morrow ISBN 0-688-31264-0, 1951. 160p. ill.
Available from National Library Service for the Blind and Physically Handicapped in Braille BR7180.
Ellen takes dancing lessons, wears woolen underwear, has braces on her teeth and is in third grade. Her life is without problems except when classmate Otis Spofford teases or there are quarrels with her girl friend, Austine.
SUBJ: Schools--Fiction.

CE   Ph-1 2-5/3 $15.93   L   KG995
CLEARY, BEVERLY. Henry and Beezus. Illus. by Louis Darling. Morrow ISBN 0-688-31383-3, c1952. 192p. ill.
Sequel to: HENRY HUGGINS (1950).
Available from National Library Service for the Blind and Physically Handicapped as talking book TB01014 and in Braille BRA02405.
Talking book available from Listening Library YA 897 (ISBN 0-8072-7606-5, 1997). 2 sound cassettes (151min), $16.98.
Henry Huggins, his dog Ribsy, and his friend Beezus busy themselves with trying to earn enough money for Henry to buy a bicycle.
Followed by RIBSY (ISBN 0-688-31662-X, 1964).
Available also from NLSBPH is RIBSY in Braille BRA01721, as talking book TB03583.
SUBJ: Friendship--Fiction./ Dogs--Fiction.

Ph-1 3-5/4 $15.93   L   KG996
CLEARY, BEVERLY. Henry Huggins. Illus. by Louis Darling. Morrow ISBN 0-688-31385-X, 1950. 155p. ill.
Available from National Library Service for the Blind and Physically Handicapped in Braille BR07178, and on sound recording cassette RC35642.
Spanish version available (Beech Tree ISBN 0-688-14887-5, 1996).
Henry Huggins picks up a stray dog, names him Ribsy and sets out on numerous adventures with him, including breeding hundreds of fish and collecting over a thousand worms.
Readers who enjoy this story will no doubt demand HENRY AND THE PAPER ROUTE (ISBN 0-688-31380-9, 1954) and HENRY AND RIBSY (ISBN 0-688-31382-5, 1957) and the other highly popular titles.
Available also from NLSBPH are: HENRY AND THE PAPER ROUTE in Braille BRA07794; HENRY AND RIBSY as talking book TB01014, and in Braille BR7214.
SUBJ: Dogs--Fiction./ Spanish language materials.

CE   Ph-1 3-5/5 $15.93   L   KG997
CLEARY, BEVERLY. Mouse and the motorcycle. Illus. by Louis Darling. Morrow ISBN 0-688-31698-0, 1965. 160p. ill.
Available from National Library Service for the Blind and Physically Handicapped on sound recording casssette RC24692, in Braille BR06649, BRA00951, and as talking book TB01326, TB03358.
Talking book available from Listening Library YA 878 (ISBN 0-8072-7543-3, 1995). 2 sound cassettes (145min), $16.98.
The old and somewhat dilapidated Mountain View Inn is the home of Ralph, an extraordinary mouse whose adventures are chronicled in three delightful stories. In the first he makes friends with a young visitor who provides him with a toy motorcycle with which he has many adventures. In RUNAWAY RALPH (ISBN 0-688-31701-4, 1977; also available as talking book from Listening Library YA 880 (ISBN 0-8072-7537-9, 1995, $16.98) he puts on his half ping pong ball helmet, climbs on his motorcycle, and rides down to Happy Acres Camp where he finds more adventure than he desired.
In RALPH S. MOUSE (ISBN 0-688-01455-0, 1982; also available as talking book from SRA/McGraw-Hill 87-511300, $17.15, or from Listening Library YA 879 (ISBN 0-8072-7546-8, 1995, $16.98) he goes to school with the housekeeper's son and gains unwelcomed notoriety. Particularly appealing to middle grade boys.
Available also from NLSBPH are: RALPH S. MOUSE in Braille BR06619, on sound recording cassette RC24694; RUNAWAY RALPH as talking book TB03358, on sound recording cassette RC24693, in Braille BR06631.
SUBJ: Mice--Fiction./ Fantasy.

Ph-3 3-5/5 $15.93   L   KG998
CLEARY, BEVERLY. Muggie Maggie. Illus. by Kay Life. Morrow ISBN 0-688-08554-7, 1990. 70p. ill.
Any child who has ever struggled to learn cursive writing and fought with teachers' attitudes towards it, will sympathize with third grader Maggie as she is forced to switch from clear printing--and her knowledge of a computer and its printout--in this small slice of life story that quietly presents an interesting child, a kind family, realistic school situations, and Maggie's final triumph. Cleary fans will demand the book but they should not expect another Ramona. They will, however, meet Maggie.
SUBJ: Penmanship--Fiction./ Schools--Fiction.

Ph-1 3-5/6 $14.93   L   KG999
CLEARY, BEVERLY. Otis Spofford. Illus. by Louis Darling. Morrow ISBN 0-688-31720-0, 1953. 191p. ill.
Available from National Library Service for the Blind and Physically Handicapped in Braille BR06056.
Otis Spofford is uncontrollable and creates excitement wherever he goes. When he cuts Ellen Tebbits' hair for fun she proves to be his match.
SUBJ: Schools--Fiction.

VCR   Ph-1 3-5 $44.95   OD   KH000
CLEARY, BEVERLY. Ralph S. Mouse (Videocassette). SVE/Churchill Media C80408-HAVT, 1990. 1/2" VHS videocassette color (40min).
Carnegie Medal.
Ralph goes to school with the housekeeper's son and gains unwelcomed notoriety. Based on the children's classic, the video features John Matthews' handcrafted dimensional animation. Particularly appealing to middle grade boys.
SUBJ: Mice--Fiction./ Fantasy.

Ph-1 3-5/7 $15.93   L   KH001
CLEARY, BEVERLY. Ramona and her father. Illus. by Alan Tiegreen. Morrow ISBN 0-688-32114-3, 1977. 186p. ill.
Sequel to RAMONA THE BRAVE (1968).
Newbery Honor Book.
Available from National Library Service for the Blind and Physically Handicapped in Braille BR03913 and on sound recording cassette RC12425.
Spanish edition available RAMONA Y SU PADRE (Austral, 1987), $15.95.
Ramona is now in second grade, Beezus in seventh. When her father loses his job, the whole family is affected, Ramona more than the others. She practices TV commercials (to find a job on TV), she succeeds in insulting her teacher, and she works on her father to make him quit smoking. The Quimby family copes with all the crises, however, and everything ends well. Cleary's wise and funny books remain up-to-date and appeal to children.
SUBJ: Fathers and daughters--Fiction./ Family life--Fiction./ Domestic relations--Fiction./ Spanish language materials.

CE   Ph-1 3-5/6 $16.93   L   KH002
CLEARY, BEVERLY. Ramona and her mother. Illus. by Alan Tiegreen. Morrow ISBN 0-688-32195-X, 1979. 207p. ill.
Sequel to: RAMONA AND HER FATHER.
Available from National Library Service for the Blind and Physically Handicapped on sound recording cassette RC24836.
Spanish edition available RAMONA Y SU MADRE (Austral, 1989), $15.95.
The fifth in the Ramona series in which we see the highs and the lows in Mrs. Quimby's life from the point of view of 7-1/2-year-old Ramona. Domestic quarrels, hairdo problems, and Ramona's habit of twitching her nose add up to Ramona's realization that, despite the fact that her mother is often tired and harassed from working, she loves her.
SUBJ: Family life--Fiction./ Mothers and daughters--Fiction./ Spanish language materials.

Ph-1 3-5/6 $15.93   L   KH003
CLEARY, BEVERLY. Ramona forever. Illus. by Alan Tiegreen. Morrow ISBN 0-688-03786-0, 1984. 182p. ill.
Available from National Library Service for the Blind and Physically Handicapped on sound recording cassette RC23106 and in Braille BR06284.
Growing up just seems to mean more problems for third grader Ramona who dislikes the long-standing after school arrangements, is worried about her father's ability to find a teaching job so they won't have to move, and isn't quite sure how she feels about the coming baby. Striking a balance between the humor of earlier books and the character's own maturation shows normal growth and Ramona's fans will want to read the book.
SUBJ: Family life--Fiction.

CE   Ph-1 3-5/5 $15.93   L   KH004
CLEARY, BEVERLY. Ramona Quimby, age 8. Illus. by Alan Tiegreen.
Morrow ISBN 0-688-00478-4, 1981. 190p. ill.
Newbery Honor Book.
Talking book available from SRA/McGraw-Hill 87-508707, 1981.
$17.15, (26min).
Available from National Library Service for the Blind and Physically
Handicapped in Braille BR05155.
Spanish edition available RAMONA EMPIEZA EL CURSO (Austral,
1989), $15.95
In this addition to the series, Ramona is rejoicing that she is entering
the third grade and can ride on the bus alone. Father Quimby is
going to school and Mother is working as a doctor's receptionist, so
there are many stresses at home and at school. She "hangs in
there" and proves herself to be "big enough for the family to
depend on."
SUBJ: Family life--Fiction./ Spanish language materials.

                          Ph-1 3-5/6 $15.95   L   KH005
CLEARY, BEVERLY. Ramona the brave. Illus. by Alan Tiegreen. Morrow
ISBN 0-688-32015-5, 1975. 189p. ill.
Sequel to RAMONA THE PEST.
Available from National Library Service for the Blind and Physically
Handicapped in Braille BRA15281.
Ramona is in first grade feeling brave and grown-up. But she quickly
finds that her teacher doesn't like children who are different or who
have imagination. Finally, after a number of funny and sad
experiences because she has spunk, she makes truce with the teacher.
Followed by RAMONA AND HER FATHER.
SUBJ: Schools--Fiction./ Teachers--Fiction.

                          Ph-1 3-5/5 $13.88   L   KH006
CLEARY, BEVERLY. Ramona the pest. Illus. by Louis Darling. Morrow
ISBN 0-688-31721-9, c1968. 192p illus.
Sequel to BEEZUS AND RAMONA.
Available from National Library Service for the Blind and Physically
Handicapped on sound recording cassette RC24837 and as talking
book TB02781, and in Braille BR7197.
Spanish version RAMONA LA CHINCHE available from Morrow,
1984.
Ramona, who has only been met before as Beezus' exasperating little
sister and as Henry Huggins' constant tormentor, has started
kindergarten. Her good intentions and uncontrollable curiosity lead her
to become a "Kindergarten Dropout."
Followed by RAMONA THE BRAVE.
SUBJ: Kindergarten--Fiction./ Schools--Fiction./ Spanish language
materials.

                          Ph-3 3-4/6 $15.93   L   KH007
CLEARY, BEVERLY. Socks. Illus. by Beatrice Darwin. Morrow ISBN
0-688-30067-7, c1973. 156p. ill.
Read-along kit available from Listening Library SWR 50SP, 1985,
OPC. 1 sound cassette (60min), 1 paperback book, teacher's guide.
$14.95.
Available from National Library Service for the Blind and Physically
Handicapped on sound recording cassette RC10399.
Socks, a determined and arrogant cat, finds that he has ceased to
become the center of attraction when a new-born baby enters his
household. Socks craves attention and food, but his only consolation
is left-over baby formula. Socks overcomes obesity, neglect, and
laziness, as he and the baby become friends and partners in mischief.
SUBJ: Cats--Fiction./ Jealousy--Fiction.

                          Ph-1 5-A/4 $15.93   L   KH008
CLEARY, BEVERLY. Strider. Illus. by Paul O. Zelinsky. Morrow ISBN
0-688-09901-7, 1991. 179p. ill.
Available from the National Library Service for the Blind and
Physically Handicapped on sound recording cassette RC34585.
Leigh Botts, now 14, presents another diary in which he details his life
in a beautifully observed novel brimming with real voices and well
defined characters. His contemplations about his father, about an
abandoned dog, Strider, and a track team friend, Geneva, carry the
genuine voice of Leigh--one that readers will enjoy and understand.
Leigh has matured and it is a pleasure to spend time with him once
more.
SUBJ: Dogs--Fiction./ Divorce--Fiction./ High schools--Fiction./
Schools--Fiction./ Diaries--Fiction.

                          Ph-1 5-6/6 $15.00   T   KH009
CLEAVER, VERA. Where the lilies bloom. By Vera and Bill Cleaver. Illus.
by Jim Spanfeller. Lippincott/HarperCollins ISBN 0-397-31111-7, c1969.
174p. ill.
Available from National Library Service for the Blind and Physically
Handicapped on sound recording cassette RC24749.

Mary Call is charged by her tenant-farmer father, when his death
approaches, to take care of the children and to see that they are not
sent to the county charity home. How she conceals his death from the
neighbors and solves their problems makes this tale of the wildcrafters
of the Appalachian Mountains a moving experience.
SUBJ: Orphans--Fiction./ Appalachian Mountains--Fiction./ Family--
Fiction.

CE   Ph-3 A/6 $16.00   L   KH010
COATSWORTH, ELIZABETH. Cat who went to heaven. New ed. Illus. by
Lynd Ward. Macmillan ISBN 0-02-719710-7, c1958. 62p. col. ill.
Newbery Medal Award.
Talking book available from SRA/McGraw-Hill 87-507901, $17.15.
The cat "Good Fortune" watches the Japanese artist as he paints
the animals they go one by one to pay homage to the Buddha. At
long last, a miracle brings the cat into the picture.
SUBJ: Cats--Fiction./ Fairy tales./ Japan--Fiction.

                          Ph-3 4-6/6 $14.95   T   KH011
COCHRANE, PATRICIA A. Purely Rosie Pearl. Delacorte ISBN 0-385-
32193-7; In Canada: Bantam Doubleday Dell, 1996. 135p.
"In 1936 twelve-year-old Rosie Pearl Bush and her family of migrants
endure the hardships of the Great Depression as they find work
picking fruit in the California Valley." (CIP) She and her family had
been living in the Dust Bowl and were blown off their land by the
conditions there. Although migrant work is described well, as are
many of the characters, the book is ultimately weakened by the
characterization of the foreman as all bad and most others as all
good. The contrivance of finding a lost brooch which leads to the
betterment of the Bush family is heavy-handed. California libraries will
want historical fiction set in that state, and in other states, the book
will also speak to readers.
SUBJ: Depressions--1929--Fiction./ Migrant labor--Fiction./ California-
-Fiction.

CE   Ph-1 1-3/4 $15.93   L   KH012
COHEN, BARBARA. Molly's pilgrim. Illus. by Michael J. Deraney.
Lothrop, Lee & Shepard ISBN 0-688-02104-2, 1983. unp. ill.
Selectors' Choice, 15th ed.
Available from National Library Service for the Blind and Physically
Handicapped in Braille BR05741 and on sound recording cassette
RC21685.
Videocassette available from Phoenix/BFA 21285, 1985. 1/2" VHS
videocassette color (23min), $50.00.
Spanish version MOLLY Y LOS PEREGRINOS available from
Lectorum (ISBN 1-880507-17-X, 1995).
Embarrassed by her clothes, uncertain about her grasp of English, and
teased by her third grade classmates, Molly doesn't want to live in
small town America--until her mother makes a unique pilgrim doll for
Thanksgiving. Historical fiction set in the 1930s, this short story,
though a bit didactic, reconfirms the U.S. as a magnet to modern
pilgrims seeking religious freedom. Detailed charcoal drawings add a
nice touch to this alternative to the usual turkey and pumpkin pie
stories. For reading aloud.
SUBJ: Jews--United States--Fiction./ Schools--Fiction./ Thanksgiving
Day--Fiction./ Emigration and immigration--Fiction./ Russians--United
States--Fiction./ Spanish language materials.

                          Ph-1 4-A/4 $4.95   P   KH013
COHEN, BARBARA. Thank you, Jackie Robinson Illus. by Richard
Cuffari. Beech Tree ISBN 0-688-15293-7, 1997. 125p. ill.
Originally published by Lothrop, Lee & Shepard, 1974.
Life, death, love, and baseball combine in the story of young Sam
and Davy, the African-American cook at Sam's mother's inn. Man
and boy are enthusiastic about the Brooklyn Dodgers and share
baseball talk, games, and matters important to a growing boy.
Friendship and love are at the heart of this warm, tender, and
sometimes humorous historical fiction. A memorable reading
experience; good for reading aloud, middle grades and up. For
multicultural studies.
SUBJ: Brooklyn Dodgers (Baseball team)--Fiction./ Robinson, Jackie--
Fiction./ Baseball--Fiction./ Friendship--Fiction.

                          Ph-2 3-4/4 $15.95   L   KH014
COLEMAN, EVELYN. White socks only. Illus. by Tyrone Geter. Whitman
ISBN 0-8075-8955-1; In Canada: General, 1996. unp. col. ill.
"Grandma tells the story about her first trip alone into town during
the days when segregation still existed in Mississippi." (CIP) When
the young African-American girl drank from the "Whites Only"
fountain, one of the white adult town bullies menacingly approached
her. He is only stopped when other black people in the town band
together and when the Chicken Man--someone who is believed to be
able to cast spells--joins them. Illustrated in colorful, full-page oils, the
times and people are clear, and the story is a holding but simple

one--just right to use for reading aloud as a discussion starter. Historical fiction for multicultural studies.
SUBJ: Afro-Americans--Fiction./ Race relations--Fiction./ Mississippi--Fiction.

Ph-2 5-6/5 $4.50 P KH015
COLLIER, JAMES LINCOLN. Jump ship to freedom. By James Lincoln Collier and Christopher Collier. Dell ISBN 0-440-44323-7, 1981. 198p.
14-year-old Daniel Arabus is determined to have his owner, Captain Ivers, return the Continental notes his father, now dead, had earned fighting during the Revolutionary War. He sets a mock fire and takes the script. When the captain realizes the notes are gone, he sends Daniel to sea so that he won't be able to buy his and his mother's freedom. Heavy storms, an escape to Bedloe's Island, involvement with the old Quaker who has an important message for the Continental Congress, all make an exciting adventure. For multicultural studies.
"How much of this story is true?" p191-198.
SUBJ: Slavery--Fiction./ Afro-Americans--Fiction./ United States. Constitutional Convention (1787)--Fiction.

Ph-1 5-6/5 $17.00 T KH016
COLLIER, JAMES LINCOLN. My brother Sam is dead. By James Lincoln Collier and Christopher Collier. Four Winds/Macmillan ISBN 0-02-722980-7, 1974. 216p.
Newbery Honor Book.
Impetuous, idealistic Sam Meeker, 16-year-old Yale student in 1775, defies his Tory sympathizing father, an innkeeper at Redding, Connecticut, to join the Continentals. Younger brother Tim is left to help at the tavern where the reader sees through Tim's eyes the hardships, bitterness, and conflicting beliefs that affect the lives of ordinary people during the Revolution.
SUBJ: United States--History--Revolution, 1775-1783--Fiction./ Brothers--Fiction.

Ph-2 5-6/6 $4.99 P KH017
COLLIER, JAMES LINCOLN. War comes to Willy Freeman. By James Lincoln Collier and Christopher Collier. Dell ISBN 0-440-49504-0, 1983. 178p.
Wilhamina (usually disguised as the boy Willy), witnesses her father's death fighting the Redcoats and finds her mother has been captured and taken to the prison ship in New York harbor. Willy's courage and perseverance take her to New York, where she works for the owner of Fraunces' Tavern and is eventually involved in a court case in which her Uncle Arabus wins his freedom. This exciting tale of African-American freedom fighters is a companion title to JUMP SHIP TO FREEDOM. For multicultural studies.
"How much of this book is true?" p.175-178.
SUBJ: United States--History--Revolution, 1775-1783--Fiction./ Afro-Americans--Fiction./ Slavery--Fiction.

Ph-1 5-A/6 $13.95 T KH018
COMAN, CAROLYN. What Jamie saw. Front Street ISBN 1-886910-02-2; In Canada: Publishers Group West, 1995. 126p.
Newbery Honor book, 1996.
Selectors' Choice, 21st ed.
Although the subject is "Child abuse--Fiction," this book only commences with an act of abuse. It is, rather, an example of stunning, concise writing with nary an extra word. The reader will observe and feel everything through third grader Jamie's eyes and viscera after he, his mother, and his baby sister escape from Van, his mother's boyfriend. Jamie's fears and wishes are so palpable as to be a reader's, especially a sophisticated one. Each character seems real--is real--and this strong novel is a sure discussion starter. Use for reading aloud to reach a wider audience.
SUBJ: Child abuse--Fiction./ Family problems--Fiction.

Ph-2 4-A/3 $15.95 T KH019
CONFORD, ELLEN. Frog Princess of Pelham. Little, Brown ISBN 0-316-15246-3; In Canada: Little, Brown, 1997. 106p.
"When a kiss from (classmate) Danny turns Chandler, a wealthy but lonely orphan, into a frog, Danny's humorous attempts to change her back into a human land the pair on a television talk show." (CIP) and into a host of other funny and entirely improbable situations. Some sharp commentary on talk shows, tabloid magazines, and gossip sheets add to the general and speedy nonsense. Great dialogue.
SUBJ: Orphans--Fiction./ Frogs--Fiction./ Humorous stories.

Ph-2 5-6/6 $14.89 L KH020
CONLY, JANE LESLIE. Racso and the rats of NIMH. Illus. by Leonard Lubin. HarperCollins ISBN 0-06-021362-0, 1986. 278p. ill.
Sequel to MRS. FRISBY AND THE RATS OF NIMH by Robert C. O'Brien.

Available from National Library Service for the Blind and Physically Handicapped in Braille BR06978 and on sound recording cassette RC26785.
The surviving original rats of NIMH and their descendants try to thwart the destruction of their home in Thorne Valley by a politician whose sole purpose is profit. More didactic than its predecessor and perhaps too wordy in places, the story is fast-paced and contains a good deal of cliffhanger suspense. Fans of the earlier title read it with relish.
SUBJ: Mice--Fiction./ Rats--Fiction./ NIMH--Fiction.

Ph-2 6-A/5 $15.95 T KH021
CONLY, JANE LESLIE. Trout summer. Henry Holt ISBN 0-8050-3933-3; In Canada: Fitzhenry & Whiteside, 1995. 234p.
Available from the National Library Service for the Blind and Physically Handicapped on sound recording cassette RC 42758.
Told in the first person by Shana, thirteen, the story takes place the summer when she and her moody twelve-year-old brother live in the woods and meet a crusty, sometimes unpleasant, old man who is trying to save a Pennsylvania stream, Native American artifacts, and wilderness. It should interest young people who enjoyed George's MY SIDE OF THE MOUNTAIN and other books dealing with wilderness preservation. Both children grow and begin to accept their parents' failed marriage and their feckless father. The depiction of character and setting is strong. Probably, because of its length, it needs a strong reader--but it is worth reading. For environmental studies.
SUBJ: Brothers and sisters--Fiction./ Old age--Fiction./ Rivers--Fiction./ Canoes and canoeing--Fiction./ Summer--Fiction.

Ph-2 4-6/7 $14.95 L KH022
CONRAD, PAM. Our house: the stories of Levittown. Illus. by Brian Selznick. Scholastic ISBN 0-590-46523-6; In Canada: Scholastic, 1995. 65p. ill.
After World War II, a community of small wood-frame houses was built on Long Island, New York. Veterans quickly acquired them, and Levittown, named after the builders, became an example of the planned housing community, now common throughout the United States. Conrad takes a reader through the decades from 1947 to the 1990s and relates six stories, each centering on a young person, to provide the flavor of the place and the times in an interesting and unusual slice-of-life presentation.
SUBJ: Levittown (N.Y.)--Fiction./ Short stories.

Ph-1 5-A/7 $14.89 L KH023
CONRAD, PAM. Prairie songs. Illus. by Darryl S. Zudeck. HarperCollins ISBN 0-06-021337-X; In Canada: HarperCollins, 1985. 167p. ill.
Predestined not to survive a life on the prairie, the new doctor's wife captivates Louisa and her young brother with her beauty and weakness, like a "hot house flower", in this memorable portrayal of settler life on the Nebraska prairie.
SUBJ: Frontier and pioneer life--Fiction./ Nebraska--Fiction./ Family life--Fiction.

Ph-2 5-A/4 $4.95 P KH024
COOPER, AMY JO. Dream quest. Annick/Firefly ISBN 0-92030384-62; In Canada: Annick/Firefly, 1987. 155p. ill. (Spirit Bay)
Presents two stories (based on films of the same titles) showing the clash of two cultures: the modern non-practicing Ojibway Indians of the Spirit Bay Reserve in Northern Ontario, Canada, and those who follow ancient tribal rites. In "Big Save", a young girl with tribal knowledge saves a bus load of others from the harsh winter; in "Hack's Choice," a boy realizes that he must follow the ways of his ancestors and not the plastic glamour of non-tribal ways. Many subtle clues in the writing may mean that the less mature readers need some guidance. Would be good for oral reading when discussing Native American culture.
SUBJ: Ojibwa Indians--Fiction./ Indians of North America--Canada--Fiction./ Short stories.

Ph-2 5-A/4 $13.89 L KH025
COOPER, ILENE. Buddy Love: now on video. HarperCollins ISBN 0-06-024664-2; In Canada: HarperCollins, 1995. 183p.
At thirteen and a half, Buddy, an average boy in an average family, discovers himself and his family to be not so average when he videotapes them for a school project. In finding himself, he finally stands up to the boy he has considered to be his best friend for years, someone who had continually humiliated him. Characters and situations reflect eighth grade well in this humorous coming-of-age story.
SUBJ: Self-acceptance--Fiction./ Family life--Fiction./ Interpersonal relations--Fiction.

CE   Ph-1 6-A/7 $15.00   T   KH026
COOPER, SUSAN. Boggart. McElderry ISBN 0-689-50576-0; In
Canada: Maxwell Macmillan, 1993. 196p.
    Available from the National Library Service for the Blind and
    Physically Handicapped on sound recording cassette RC 36547.
    Talking book available from Listening Library YA 863 (ISBN 0-8072-
    7431-3, 1994). 4 sound cassettes (287min), $29.98.
    "So the Boggart looked ahead in happy anticipation, [to new owners
    of Castle Keep, Canadians of Scottish ancestry] not knowing that he
    was living now in a world which no longer believed in boggarts, a
    world which had driven out the Old Things and buried the Wild
    Magic deep under layers of reason and time." (p.67) Yet the
    Canadian children and a computer restore the mischievous being to
    his ancient castle in Scotland after several unpleasant events. Prime
    for fantasy/supernatural readers and computer buffs.
    SUBJ: Supernatural--Fiction./ Scotland--Fiction./ Canada--Fiction.

                                Ph-1 5-A/6 $16.00   T   KH027
COOPER, SUSAN. Boggart and the monster. McElderry ISBN 0-689-
81330-9; In Canada: Distican, 1997. 185p.
    Companion to: THE BOGGART, McElderry, 1993.
    Selectors' Choice, 21st ed.
    The Boggart, who went to Canada and was returned to the lochs of
    Scotland via a computer program, now reappears in all his mischief
    and personality. Boggart who is a shape-shifter awakens Nessie of
    Loch Ness from his long and deep sleep and, in a series of taut
    adventures, returns the lonely Nessie to his true boggart shape,
    personality, and character. The visiting children, Jessup and Emily,
    Tommy Cameron, and others assist a group of scientists who pursue
    the "monster" with all the advantages that modern exploration
    provides. For reading aloud.
    SUBJ: Supernatural--Fiction./ Loch Ness monster--Fiction./ Scotland--
    Fiction.

                                Ph-1 A/5 $16.00   T   KH028
COOPER, SUSAN. Over sea, under stone. Harcourt Brace Jovanovich
ISBN 0-15-259034-X, 1966. 252p. ill.
    Available from National Library Service for the Blind and Physically
    Handicapped on sound recording cassette RC08832.
    Available in large-type from Windrush/dist. by Cornerstone (ISBN
    1-85089-932-0, 1988).
    The three Drews, their Great-Uncle Merry, and the mysterious Will
    Stanton battle the forces of evil while searching for the treasures that
    will vanquish the dark.
    The exciting saga is continues: GREENWITCH (ISBN 0-689-30426-9,
    1974, Large type available from Windrush/Cornerstone ISBN
    1-85089-934-7, 1988, available from NLSBPH in Braille BRA16519
    and on sound recording cassette RC08041); SILVER ON THE TREE
    (ISBN 0-689-50088-2, 1977. available from NLSBPH on sound
    recording cassette RC16112.
    Available in large print from Windrush/dist. by Cornerstone: OVER
    SEA, UNDER STONE (ISBN 1-85089-932-0); GREENWITCH (ISBN
    1-85089-934-7); and SILVER ON THE TREE (ISBN 1-85089-936-3).
    SUBJ: Fantasy./ Great Britain--Fiction./ Good and evil--Fiction.

                                Ph-3 2-4/5 $12.95   T OD KH029
CORBALIS, JUDY. Porcellus, the flying pig. Illus. by Helen Craig. Dial
ISBN 0-8037-0486-0, 1988. unp. col. ill.
    Porcellus is in a litter of 14 lively piglets but is born with odd bumps
    on his back which puzzle and shame him. Their purpose is made clear
    when moonlighting as a bank guard his bank is robbed by the
    dastardly Al Porcone--an underworld pig. Porcellus suddenly sprouts
    huge multi-colored wings and foils the robbers. Despite the picture
    book format this has a substantial text making this humorous
    adventure appeal to slightly older readers.
    SUBJ: Pigs--Fiction./ Robbers and outlaws--Fiction./ Humorous stories.

                                Ph-3 4-5/4 $3.99   P   KH030
CORBETT, SCOTT. Lemonade trick. Illus. by Paul Galdone. Scholastic
ISBN 0-590-32197-8, 1960. 103p. ill.
    Given a mysterious chemistry set by a mysterious woman (a witch?)
    he meets in the park, Kerby Maxwell experiments and becomes a
    too-model child, vanquishes the local bully, and worries considerably
    about what will occur if the potion he put in the lemonade wears off-
    -or doesn't wear off. Just right for middle-grade boys, this humorous
    adventure has been a very popular book since its first appearance in
    1960.
    Another title in the author's long line of books in the "Tricks" series
    include HOCKEY TRICK (Little, Brown ISBN 0-316-15716-3, 1974).
    SUBJ: Magic--Fiction./ Humorous stories.

                                Ph-1 6-A/5 $3.50   P   KH031
COTTONWOOD, JOE. Adventures of Boone Barnaby. Scholastic ISBN
0-590-43547-7, 1992. 227p.

"Boone Barnaby and his two best friends learn about the adult
version of truth and justice through their adventures in a small
California town." (CIP) At times humorous, at times realistically
unpleasant, this first person narration moves along at a good pace
and offers much in the way of events, leaving a reader with many
questions to ponder. Ideal reading for 6th grade--both oral and silent.
SUBJ: Friendship--Fiction./ California--Fiction.

                                Ph-2 6-A/3 $15.95   T   KH032
COTTONWOOD, JOE. Babcock. Scholastic ISBN 0-590-22221-X; In
Canada: Scholastic, 1996. 316p.
    Companion book to ADVENTURES OF BOONE BARNABY, 1992
    and DANNY AIN'T, 1992.
    The third book set in the small town of San Puerco, California, now
    features Babcock, a seventh grade African-American boy who "likes
    dragonflies, poetry, and music, (and who) falls in love with Kirsten, a
    blonde," (CIP) but her mother rejects him because of his color. His
    sometimes abusive uncle moves in with the family, but he proves to be
    a better person than first appearances suggest. Babcock is an
    interesting person in this active character study, especially for those
    who have journeyed--in reading--to the town. For multicultural studies.
    SUBJ: Love--Fiction./ Friendship--Fiction./ Uncles--Fiction./ Afro-
    Americans--Fiction.

                                Ph-1 6-A/6 $13.95   L   KH033
COTTONWOOD, JOE. Danny ain't. Scholastic ISBN 0-590-45067-0; In
Canada: Scholastic, 1992. 288p.
    Companion book to ADVENTURES OF BOONE BARNABY, 1990.
    Selectors' Choice, 19th ed.
    People in the small town of San Puerco, California try to help Danny
    whose father is in the nearby veteran's hospital suffering another
    serious flashback to his service in Vietnam. Danny, trying to survive on
    his own, finds unexpected help from a new neighbor, a rich and
    overprotected boy. However, he finds strength in himself. The many
    elements of the novel, some humorous, some deadly serious, blend
    together in a strongly characterized and fascinating book just right for
    the better, more mature reader.
    SUBJ: Fathers and sons--Fiction./ Family problems--Fiction./ Self-
    perception--Fiction.

                                Ph-2 5-A/5 $13.95   L   KH034
COTTONWOOD, JOE. Quake!: a novel. Scholastic ISBN 0-590-22232-
5; In Canada: Scholastic, 1995. 146p.
    Set near Santa Cruz, CA, on October 17, 1989 the day of the
    "World Series" earthquake and the few days following, the novel
    describes the shaker, the damage to people and property, and the
    gradual beginnings of a cleanup. Centering on Franny, fourteen, her
    younger brother, and a visiting friend, the novel develops empathy
    and will provide a feeling of quakes to those who have not lived
    through them. Aside from a few politically correct elements about a
    migratory farm worker couple, the book is fast and holding--as tense
    as a quake is to those who have experienced one.
    SUBJ: Earthquakes--California--Fiction./ Brothers and sisters--Fiction./
    Family life--California--Fiction./ California--Fiction.

                                Ph-2 4-6/5 $14.00   T   KH035
COVILLE, BRUCE. Aliens ate my homework. Illus. by Katherine Coville.
Pocket ISBN 0-671-87249-4; In Canada: Simon & Schuster, 1993. 179p.
ill.
    "Minstrel book."
    Presents a fluffy science-funtasy [sic] about sixth-grader Rod Allbright
    and his mishaps and adventures when a miniature spaceship, complete
    with several small beings, lands. The aliens need his assistance to
    capture a space criminal and repair their spacecraft, so they can
    return to their galaxy. Despite some interesting, pointed comments on
    how young people are treated in our society (or perhaps because of
    them), the fast-paced novel will be fun to read.
    SUBJ: Extraterrestrial beings--Fiction./ Science fiction.

CE   Ph-1 4-A/4 $16.95   T   KH036
COVILLE, BRUCE. Jeremy Thatcher, dragon hatcher: a magic shop book.
Illus. by Gary A. Lippincott. Harcourt Brace ISBN 0-15-200748-2; In
Canada: Harcourt Brace c/o Canadian Manda, 1991. 148p. ill.
    "Jane Yolen book."
    Talking book available from Listening Library YA 873 (ISBN 0-8072-
    7531-1, 1995). 2 sound cassettes (160min), $16.98.
    Jeremy Thatcher hatches a dragon's egg which he has acquired
    through a series of untoward events. Both boy and dragon are
    attractive characters and the emotional level of the charmingly written
    book is holding. Readers will also glimpse a teacher who is more than
    he appears to be. Adventures just right for reading aloud.
    SUBJ: Dragons--Fiction./ Friendship--Fiction./ Pets--Fiction./ Drawing--
    Fiction./ Size--Fiction.

Ph-1 5-A/5 $15.89   L   KH037
CREECH, SHARON. Walk two moons. HarperCollins ISBN 0-06-023337-0; In Canada: HarperCollins, 1994. 280p.
Newbery Award, 1995.
Selectors' Choice, 20th ed.
Seemingly intricate in construction with many themes, this novel pulls together into a perfect unity thanks to the gripping diction, situations, and characters. After her mother leaves home, Sal(amanca) Tree Hiddle, thirteen, leaves her Kentucky farm home for Ohio with her father and then travels to Idaho with her paternal grandparents to trace her mother's journey. Phoebe, a neighbor and classmate in Ohio who possesses a hyperbolic imagination, also has a mother who has deserted her. It is Phoebe's story, intertwined with her own, that Sal narrates to her marvelously eccentric grandparents on the trip west. The book is memorable and intriguing from beginning to end.
SUBJ: Death--Fiction./ Grandparents--Fiction./ Family life--Fiction./ Friendship--Fiction.

Ph-1 3-5/5 $13.95   L   KH038
CRESSWELL, HELEN. Meet Posy Bates. Illus. by Kate Aldous. Macmillan ISBN 0-02-725375-9; In Canada: Maxwell Macmillan, 1992. 95p. ill.
Posy Bates, a spunky, active girl who is always on the go, sometimes thinks after the action, not before. Like Cleary's Ramona, Posy is fully involved with what she does whether she is concerned about the local bag lady or interested in insects with whom she shares her secrets. Her adventures are funny--albeit set in reality. Posy will be a welcome addition to the field of "girls who do."
SUBJ: Pets--Fiction./ Insects as pets--Fiction.

Ph-1 3-5/3 $13.95   L   KH039
CRESSWELL, HELEN. Posy Bates, again! Illus. by Kate Aldous. Macmillan ISBN 0-02-725372-4; In Canada: Maxwell Macmillan, 1994. 112p. ill.
Posy continues to be Posy, insatiably curious and constantly into mischief. She now has the dog of her dreams and the same basic instincts to do good to almost everyone.
SUBJ: Family life--Fiction./ Dogs--Fiction.

Ph-1 5-A/3 $15.95   L   KH040
CRESSWELL, HELEN. Watchers: a mystery at Alton Towers. Macmillan ISBN 0-02-725371-6; In Canada: Maxwell Macmillan, 1994. 206p.
"Two runaway children hide out in a theme park and become enmeshed in an unearthly battle between the forces of good and evil." (CIP) Besides the interesting details about how Katy and Josh survive (readers of Konigsburg's THE MIXED-UP FILES OF MRS. BASIL E. FRANKWEILER and Fox's HOW MANY MILES TO BABYLON will appreciate Cressell's version of runaways), the palpable evil of someone who represents pure evil and calls himself the "King" set against the happy fun of the amusement park is intriguing and suspenseful. When readers discover that the "King" is a human teenager, the danger becomes even more real in this compelling mystery.
SUBJ: Runaways--Fiction./ Amusement parks--Fiction./ Friendship--Fiction./ Space and time--Fiction./ Magic--Fiction.

Ph-1 4-A/5 $14.00   T   KH041
CREW, LINDA. Nekomah Creek. Illus. by Charles Robinson. Delacorte ISBN 0-385-30442-0; In Canada: Bantam Doubleday Dell, 1991. 191p. ill.
Living in a noisy, loving, unconventional family, Robby, nine, who merely wants to be left alone at school, reads during recess and enjoys the quiet. His rather unsympathetic teacher worries about his escape from group sports, and the school counselor's questions make Robby feel that he might be removed from his family. Although a serious story, it is presented in a humorous way. Robby's problems with school employees, a class bully, and his harum-scarum home are sympathetic and humorous situations which will be understandable to many. Try reading aloud.
SUBJ: Family life--Fiction./ Schools--Fiction.

Ph-2 4-6/4 $14.95   T   KH042
CREW, LINDA. Nekomah Creek Christmas. Illus. by Charles Robinson. Delacorte ISBN 0-385-32047-7; In Canada: Bantam Doubleday Dell, 1994. 147p. ill.
Companion to: NEKOMAH CREEK, Delacorte, 1991.
The story is narrated in the first person by major protagonist Robby, ten, who tells of the happenings at home and school during one Christmas season. His somewhat eccentric, but always thoughtful and loving, family supports him when he asks probing questions and understands his reluctance to be in a school play. His questions about different religions and the "true spirit of Christmas" add depth to the novel. For reading aloud.
SUBJ: Christmas--Fiction./ Plays--Fiction./ Schools--Fiction./ Family life--Fiction./ Oregon--Fiction.

Ph-1 6-A/6 $15.95   T   KH043
CROSS, GILLIAN. Great American elephant chase. Holiday House ISBN 0-8234-1016-1, 1993. 193p.
Set in the 1880s, this melodramatic, exciting book relates the lives of Tad, a runaway from his cruel aunt's home, and Cissie, the imperious daughter of the owner of a medicine show. After the death of Cissie's father and sister, the children and Khush, an elephant, who is the show's star attraction, travel by various means from Pennsylvania to Nebraska to find the one person Cissie loves. Their travels are full of difficulty because they are chased by two scheming people determined to have Khush as their own. The engrossing story is well characterized (including Khush) and will hold a reader fully. Try this as a read-aloud, too.
SUBJ: Elephants--Fiction./ Nebraska--Fiction.

Ph-1 6-A/5 $15.95   T   KH044
CROSS, GILLIAN. New world. Holiday House ISBN 0-8234-1166-4, 1995. 171p.
Players of computer games involving virtual reality will appreciate this sophisticated book in which two teenagers, a girl and a boy, test a new game based on their most secret fears. As the game proceeds, it begins to affect their real lives, and they can be freed from its dangerous malevolence only when they unmask the game's creator. The suspenseful writing and situations in this psychological thriller will hold better readers.
SUBJ: Computer games--Fiction./ Virtual reality--Fiction./ Nightmares--Fiction./ Fear--Fiction.

Ph-1 A/6 $13.95   T   KH045
CROSS, GILLIAN. Wolf. Holiday House ISBN 0-8234-0870-1, 1991. 140p.
Suspenseful, fast paced, and holding from first word to last, Cross' complex and sometimes difficult interweaving of the threat of a terrorist father and the threat of extinction to the wolves, will grip the better reader. Cassy's unweaving of the mystery of her father and her realization of the life and death situation is a well developed "tour de force" in which every word is important. A mature reader will be rewarded--and breathless--at the end of the novel. Some Briticisms, but the better reader will understand them.
SUBJ: Communal living--Fiction./ Terrorism--Fiction./ Wolves--Fiction.

Ph-1 5-A/7 $8.95   P   KH046
CUMMING, PETER. Mogul and me. Illus. by P. John Burden. Ragweed Press/dist. by Inland Book Company ISBN 0-920304-82-6; In Canada: Ragweed Press, 1989. 164p. ill.
Set in New Brunswick, Canada and on a ship traveling from Saint John to Portland, Maine in 1836, the adventure novel is based loosely on a factual incident about a burning ship carrying a traveling circus. Details the friendship of a farm boy and Mogul the circus elephant. Black and white silhouette illustrations add to the mood, weakened only by the last sentences which tend toward a sentimental moral. Gripping throughout, it is a strong choice for reading aloud.
SUBJ: Elephants--Fiction./ Friendship--Fiction.

Ph-1 5-A/6 $16.00   L   KH047
CURRY, JANE LOUISE. Big Smith snatch. McElderry ISBN 0-689-50478-0; In Canada: Maxwell Macmillan, 1989. 220p.
Foster parents, willing to take all four children when their mother is hospitalized just as they are about to move to join their father in another state, prove to be masterminds of a burglary ring. And older sister, Belinda, with the help of a homeless woman, manage to knit together enough clues to help the four lost ones. Character development is realistic and suspense is palpable in this fine choice for oral presentation that will leave the listener--or reader--literally on the edge of a chair.
Now in Pittsburgh, Pennsylvania, the several Smith children find the forgers of property deeds and restore stolen houses to elderly neighbors in THE GREAT SMITH HOUSE HUSTLE (ISBN 0-689-50580-9, 1993).
SUBJ: Kidnapping--Fiction./ Brothers and sisters--Fiction./ Stealing--Fiction.

CE
Ph-1 6-A/7 $14.95   T   KH048
CURTIS, CHRISTOPHER PAUL. Watsons go to Birmingham--1963: a novel. Delacorte ISBN 0-385-32175-9; In Canada: Bantam Doubleday Dell, 1995. 210p.
Newbery Honor book, 1996.
Coretta Scott King Author Honor book, 1996.
Talking book available from Bantam Doubleday Dell BDDAP 679 (ISBN 0-553-47786-2, 1996). 4 sound cassettes (300min), $18.99.
Available from the National Library Service for the Blind and Physically Handicapped on sound recording cassette RC 41921.
"The ordinary interactions and everyday routines of the Watsons, an African American family living in Flint, Michigan, are drastically changed after they go to visit Grandma in Alabama in the summer of

1963." (CIP) On the surface, two stories, one explains why older brother Bryon is out of control and his father thinks that spending time "down South will open his eyes." (p. 123) The second, at the heart of the novel, tells of the Sunday when four little girls lost their lives to a bomb while attending church and how the tragedy affects everyone, especially younger brother Kenny. Interwoven, too, is the story of the migration of African-American southerners to the industrial north and their sometimes hard lives. Gripping historical fiction, the book needs a strong, mature reader, but might be good for reading aloud, especially for units about the civil rights movement and multicultural studies.
SUBJ: Afro-Americans--Fiction./ Family life--Fiction./ Prejudices--Fiction./ Brothers and sisters--Fiction./ Flint (Mich.)--Fiction.

CE   Ph-1 5-A/7 $15.00   T   KH049
CUSHMAN, KAREN. Ballad of Lucy Whipple. Clarion ISBN 0-395-72806-1, 1996. 195p.
Includes bibliography.
Selectors' Choice, 21st ed.
Talking book available from Recorded Books 95030 (ISBN 0-7887-0892-9, 1997). 4 sound cassettes (285min), $34.00.
In 1849, California Morning Whipple, age twelve, moves with her adventuresome widowed mother and her younger siblings to a mining camp in California. Lucy, as she prefers to be known, dreams of their house in Massachusetts and longs for the civilization of home. She loses herself in books, even as she takes on the work of helping her mother run a boarding house, and meets various characters, some good and high-minded, some as scruffy as the Lucky Diggins, the camp. Cushman presents believable people in realistic settings and situations. The rise and fall of one mining camp is clearly conveyed through Lucy's eyes in a prime example of historical fiction that will be excellent for individual reading, for reading aloud, and for units in United States history, the history of California, the westward movement, and pioneering. The author's note (and bibliography) provide good historical background.
SUBJ: Frontier and pioneer life--California--Fiction./ Family life--California--Fiction./ California--Gold discoveries--Fiction.

CE   Ph-1 6-A/6 $14.95   T   KH050
CUSHMAN, KAREN. Catherine, called Birdy. Clarion ISBN 0-395-68186-3, 1994. 169p.
Newbery Honor book, 1995.
Available from the National Library Service for the Blind and Physically Handicapped on sound recording cassette RC 39832.
Abridged talking book available from Bantam Doubleday Dell Audio BDDAP 607 (ISBN 0-553-47669-6, 1996). 2 sound cassettes (180min), $16.99. This abridgement has been approved by the author.
Historical fiction is set in the year 1290 through the lively diary of fourteen-year-old Catherine (Birdy) as she observes and revolts against her station as a female in a smallish manor in late medieval England. Birdy's day-to-day account of life, customs, people, and contemporary history are informative and interesting. Birdy is independent, sometimes full of mischief, sometimes serious as she contemplates her future and other matters. Prime source for units on women's studies and European history.
SUBJ: Middle Ages--Fiction./ England--Fiction./ Diaries--Fiction.

CE   Ph-1 6-A/5 $10.95   T   KH051
CUSHMAN, KAREN. Midwife's apprentice. Clarion ISBN 0-395-69229-6, 1995. 122p.
Newbery Award, 1996.
Abridged talking book available from Bantam Doubleday Dell Audio BDDAP 697 (ISBN 0-553-47798-6, 1996). 2 sound cassettes (150min), $16.99. This abridgment approved by the author.
Continuing to throw light on medieval life in England, Cushman now concentrates on a homeless, nameless girl who learns midwifery from an unpleasant practitioner. However, Brat, whose home had too often been a dung heap, knows more about human nature and kindness than her preceptor and becomes more successful and sought after as she finds her place in the world. Well-characterized and strongly set historical fiction is a solid selection for women's studies and medieval history.
SUBJ: Middle Ages--Fiction./ Midwives--Fiction.

     Ph-2 5-A/4 $15.00   T   KH052
CUTLER, JANE. My wartime summers. Farrar Straus Giroux ISBN 0-374-35111-2; In Canada: HarperCollins, 1994. 153p.
Set during World War II on the home front, the story brings the years 1942-1945 to life through the thoughts and adventures of eleven-year-old Ellen. Her suspicion that a refugee girl from Germany is a spy is a very real and disturbing scene when the war games the children play stop being fun. Other scenes, as Ellen grows and begins to learn the seriousness of war, are well developed. For units on

World War II and modern United States history this historical fiction will serve nicely.
SUBJ: World War, 1939-1945--United States--Fiction./ Family life--Fiction.

     Ph-2 4-A/2 $14.99   T   KH053
CUTLER, JANE. Spaceman. Dutton ISBN 0-525-45636-8; In Canada: McClelland & Stewart, 1997. 138p.
Gary is learning disabled as well as dyslexic, a basically nice fifth grader who is bullied by other boys and is suffering with a first year male teacher who has all the sensitivity of sandpaper. He is eventually placed in a special county class to help him with his social problems and to develop an individual learning style. His new teacher, Mrs. Block, appears disorganized, is strict and no-nonsense, and cares very much for Gary and his colleagues in the special class, each of whom have various severe social and educational problems. Readers will begin to understand what Gary and the others have suffered in life and in school. A fine choice as a discussion starter about persons with disabilities, individuality, and bullying. The low reading level makes it appropriately accessible to reluctant readers who may have learning disabilities themselves.
SUBJ: Learning disabilities--Fiction./ Special education--Fiction./ Emotional problems--Fiction./ Schools--Fiction.

     Ph-1 4-6/6 $4.99   P   KH054
DAHL, ROALD. Danny, the champion of the world. Illus. by Jill Bennett. Penguin ISBN 0-14-032873-4, c1975, 1988. 196p. ill.
Selectors' Choice, 10th ed.
Danny and his father live together and share a beautiful life, in a small caravan with the father's workshop and filling station nearby. Danny's father tells him, "You must easily be the best five-year-old mechanic in the world". When Danny finds that his father leaves him at night, he discovers that he is poaching and outwitting the rich bully who owns the forest. Danny himself invents the best trick for poaching but it backfires in a way that makes this a hilarious and also lovely father-and-son tale. Based on an earlier short story for adults.
SUBJ: Fathers and sons--Fiction./ Poaching--Fiction.

     Ph-1 3-5/3 $14.99   T   KH055
DAHL, ROALD. Magic finger. Illus. by Quentin Blake. Viking ISBN 0-670-85252-X; In Canada: Penguin, 1995. 64p. ill.
Dahl's cautionary tale about a girl who turns heartless animal hunters into hunted animals with the powers of her magic finger is newly illustrated in Blake's typical active line sketches. The thought-provoking fantasy will make a good discussion starter. Try reading aloud.
SUBJ: Hunting--Fiction./ Magic--Fiction.

     Ph-1 5-A/7 $15.99   T   KH056
DAHL, ROALD. Matilda. Illus. by Quentin Blake. Viking Penguin ISBN 0-670-82439-9; In Canada: Penguin, 1988. 240p. ill.
Available from National Library Service for the Blind and Physically Handicapped on sound recording cassette RC31793.
Spanish version MATILDA available from Santillana (ISBN 84-204-46386, 1995).
The very young Matilda is the precocious genius child of selfish, uncaring parents, and the primary school she attends is run by an ogress of a head-mistress. Matilda and her uncanny abilities, intellectual and psychic, manage to put the bad in their place and restore goodness, honesty, and just-plain-decency to the good. A cautionary tale that is sure to offend some adults, the modern fairy tale is also sure to delight the sense of justice and humor in children who often perceive their teachers and parents as monstrous and overly powerful individuals. A great choice for reading aloud.
SUBJ: Schools--Fiction./ Humorous stories./ Magic--Fiction./ Spanish language materials.

     Ph-2 1-4/4 $15.00   L   KH057
DALGLIESH, ALICE. Bears on Hemlock Mountain. Illus. by Helen Sewell. Scribner's ISBN 0-684-19169-5; In Canada: Collier Macmillan, c1952, 1990. unp. col. ill.
Newbery Honor book.
When young Jonathan must carry his aunt's large cooking pot over Hemlock Mountain after dark, he hears many scary sounds and thinks about the bears he has been told once lived in the region. He keeps up his courage and hides under the pot until he is rescued and learns that indeed there are bears in this appealing folktale-like book, excellent for oral telling and quiet reading.
SUBJ: Bears--Fiction.

CE   Ph-1 3-5/3 $15.00   L   KH058
DALGLIESH, ALICE. Courage of Sarah Noble. Illus. by Leonard Weisgard. Simon & Schuster ISBN 0-684-18830-9, c1954, 1987. 52p. ill.
Newbery Honor Book.

Talking book available from SRA/McGraw-Hill 507863-5, 1978, narrated by Marian Seldes (49min), $14.00.
Available from National Library Service for the Blind and Physically Handicapped in Braille BRA08354 and on sound recording cassette RC20012.
Spanish version available from Lectorum EL CORAJE DE SARAH NOBLE (ISBN 84-279-3462-9, n.d.).
Sarah finds courage to accompany her father into the wilderness while he prepares a home for the family.
SUBJ: Indians of North America--Fiction./ Frontier and pioneer life--Connecticut--Fiction./ Spanish language materials.

Ph-2 2-4/4 $13.95 L KH059
DANZIGER, PAULA. Amber Brown goes fourth. Illus. by Tony Ross. Putnam ISBN 0-399-22849-7; In Canada: Putnam, 1995. 101p. ill.
Spanish version available AMBAR EN CUARTO Y SIN SU AMIGO from Santillana (ISBN 84-204-4412-X, 1995).
Available from the National Library Service for the Blind and Physically Handicapped on sound recording cassette RC 42372.
In fourth grade, Amber is in the midst of finding a new friend, adjusting to a new teacher, and puzzled and unhappy about her parents and their divorce. Brandi, who appeared in the first book, AMBER BROWN IS NOT A CRAYON, and Amber form a friendship based on testing themselves and each other and gradually come to a happy accommodation. The bright, lively plot shows the personal problems of some children. Readers of Cleary's Ramona books will be happy to meet Amber and her friends.
SUBJ: Friendship--Fiction./ Divorce--Fiction./ Schools--Fiction./ Spanish language materials.

Ph-2 2-4/6 $13.95 T KH060
DANZIGER, PAULA. Amber Brown is not a crayon. Illus. by Tony Ross. Putnam ISBN 0-399-22509-9; In Canada: Putnam, 1994. 80p. ill.
Available in Spanish, SEQUIREMOS SIENDO AMIGOS (Dist. by Santillana ISBN 84-204-4857-5, 1994).
Finally, Danziger has written books for younger readers showing the same humor, strong characterization, and human problems that the author demonstrated in her books for older readers. Readers will meet third grader Amber and her special friend, Justin. When Justin and his family move to Alabama, Amber is faced with a world without her best friend. Snappy dialogue and a depiction of life in third grade are vibrantly real. Amber is bound to be popular.
SUBJ: Friendship--Fiction./ Moving, Household--Fiction./ Schools--Fiction./ Spanish language materials.

Ph-2 2-4/4 $13.95 L KH061
DANZIGER, PAULA. Amber Brown wants extra credit. Illus. by Tony Ross. Putnam ISBN 0-399-22900-0; In Canada: Putnam, 1996. 120p. ill.
Sequel to: AMBER BROWN GOES FOURTH, Putnam, 1995.
When her parents divorce, Amber goes through changes as she deals with her anger. The spunky heroine provides a lighthearted look at a serious situation which many children face.
SUBJ: Divorce--Fiction./ Schools--Fiction.

Ph-2 2-4/4 $13.95 T KH062
DANZIGER, PAULA. Forever Amber Brown. Illus. by Tony Ross. Putnam ISBN 0-399-22932-9; In Canada: Putnam, 1996. 101p. ill.
When her mother contemplates marrying Max, a thoroughly decent man, Amber's life is thrown into a turmoil. Now more than ever, she needs to talk to her best friend Justin, who has moved to another state. A humorous, realistic portrayal of a young girl's reaction to her mother's romance.
SUBJ: Family life--Fiction./ Remarriage--Fiction./ Friendship--Fiction./ Schools--Fiction.

Ph-1 4-A/8 $4.98 T KH063
DAY, DAVID. Emperor's panda. Illus. by Eric Beddows. McClelland and Stewart ISBN 0-7710-2573-4; In Canada: McClelland and Stewart, c1986, 1987. 111p. ill.
"In the time of China's ancient Celestial Empire, the world was filled with a multitude of mythic and mythic creatures." (front flap)
Among them was Lord Beishung, Master Panda, the first Panda in the world, magical, wise, and omniscient. The shepherd boy Kung the Fluteplayer is sent on a dangerous quest to banish evil forces with the advice and magic of Lord Beishung. In a series of thrilling adventures, Kung helps restore goodness although his journey is fraught with danger. Descriptions resemble old Chinese scroll paintings, as do many of Beddows black and white illustrations. Those who have quested with Lloyd Alexander will find similar adventures and characters here. For reading aloud.
SUBJ: Pandas--Fiction./ Magic--Fiction./ China--Fiction.

Ph-1 4-6/6 $16.95 T KH064
DE ANGELI, MARGUERITE. Door in the wall. Doubleday ISBN 0-385-07283-X, c1949, 1989. 121p. ill.
Newbery Medal.
Just before ten-year-old Robin takes up his duties as a page, he is stricken with an illness that leaves him unable to walk. With both parents away he is alone because of the plague that has devastated London until Brother Luke takes him to St. Mark's hospice. Robin cannot adjust to the rapid changes in the direction of his life until the monks show him new skills. This enthralling account of life in medieval England is a fine introduction to historical fiction.
SUBJ: Great Britain--History--Edward III, 1327-1377--Fiction./ Middle Ages--Fiction./ Physically handicapped--Fiction.

Ph-2 4-6/4 $13.99 T KH065
DECLEMENTS, BARTHE. Pickle song. Viking ISBN 0-670-85101-9; In Canada: Penguin, 1993. 151p.
Sheltering the new girl, Sukey, Paula becomes involved in the life of a family forced to live in their car because of bad luck. With the help of Paula's strong, straightforward, and quirky grandmother, Sukey and her mother begin to find themselves and Paula learns about herself and tough love in a story as current as today's front page. Good for units on current events.
SUBJ: Friendship--Fiction./ Interpersonal relations--Fiction.

CE
Ph-1 5-A/6 $4.50 P KH066
DEFELICE, CYNTHIA C. Apprenticeship of Lucas Whitaker. By Cynthia DeFelice. Avon ISBN 0-380-72720-2; In Canada: HarperCollins, 1998. 151p.
Talking book available from Recorded Books 95023 (ISBN 0-7887-0885-6, 1997). 3 sound cassettes (252min), $26.00.
DeFelice re-creates time, place, and character of nineteenth century New England when it was believed that digging up the first person in a family who died of consumption and burning the heart of the corpse would cure other consumptives. Lucas, twelve, an orphan whose entire family succumbed to the white plague, runs from his home and apprentices with a doctor. Doc is kindly, follows scientific methods, eschews superstitions, and teaches Lucas to be rational and honest. A fine piece of well characterized historical fiction, it reads smoothly and will be good for units on the history of disease, superstition, history of science, and United States history.
SUBJ: Apprentices--Fiction./ Orphans--Fiction./ Physicians--Fiction./ Medicine--History--Fiction./ Tuberculosis--Fiction.

Ph-2 4-A/6 $15.00 L KH067
DEFELICE, CYNTHIA C. Lostman's River. Macmillan ISBN 0-02-726466-1, 1994. 160p.
"In the early 1900s, thirteen-year-old Tyler encounters vicious hunters whose actions threaten to destroy the Everglades ecosystem, and as a result joins the battle to protect that fragile environment." (CIP) Although the reason Tyler's family is living in the Everglades is contrived, the taut story of destroyers of animal life and Governor Broward's allowing dredging to occur set a good historical background for the current conditions in that region of Florida. Character is secondary, but setting is very clear as are the results of destruction of natural resources--very much affecting the area almost a century later. The story of the first game warden hired by the Audubon Society is also related in a book of historical fiction that would be of great use for environmental studies.
SUBJ: Everglades (Fla.)--Fiction./ Environmental protection--Fiction./ Conduct of life--Fiction./ Man--Influence on nature.

Ph-1 5-A/7 $26.00 L KH068
DEFOE, DANIEL. Robinson Crusoe. Illus. by N. C. Wyeth. Scribner's ISBN 0-684-17946-6, 1983. 368p. col. ill.
Surviving a shipwreck, Crusoe lives alone on an island for many years before he is rescued in this classic tale of survival that is referred to in many literary works. The difficulty of the archaic vocabulary puts this out of reach of all but the most accomplished and motivated readers. Good for oral presentation.
SUBJ: Shipwrecks--Fiction./ Survival--Fiction.

Ph-2 2-3/5 $4.50 P KH069
DEJONG, MEINDERT. Shadrach. Illus. by Maurice Sendak. HarperCollins ISBN 0-06-440115-4, c1953. 182p. ill.
Available from National Library Service for the Blind and Physically Handicapped as talking book TB01131.
Davie had been ill and as a result spends the afternoons with his grandparents on their farm. He has been promised a little black rabbit and he gloats in anticipation for a whole week, falling into trouble when he gathers three bags of the wrong kind of clover for the rabbit to eat when it arrives. The little boy's emotions and deep devotion for his pet will provide identification for any child who has had a beloved pet. Recommend for reading aloud to primary grades.
SUBJ: Rabbits--Fiction./ Pets--Fiction.

Ph-1 4-6/3 $14.89   L   KH070
DEJONG, MEINDERT. Wheel on the school. Illus. by Maurice Sendak. HarperCollins ISBN 0-06-021586-0, c1954. 298p. ill.
Newbery Medal Award.
Available from National Library Service for the Blind and Physically Handicapped in Braille BRA06215 and on sound recording cassette RC23202.
Children of Shora, a Netherlands village, are determined to bring storks back to their town.
SUBJ: Netherlands--Fiction./ Storks--Fiction.

Ph-2 3-5/4 $11.95   T   KH071
DERBY, SALLY. Jacob and the stranger. Illus. by Leonid Gore. Ticknor & Fields ISBN 0-395-66897-2, 1994. 32p. ill.
Happy-go-lucky Jacob plant-sits a magical plant which grows a large variety of felines. The owner of the plant, a man as mean as the devil, and indeed, perhaps the devil himself, is tricked into allowing Jacob to keep a very small panther and giving him the money which had been promised. The story, folklike in its telling, will be a good addition to the storyteller's pack and is just right for reading aloud. Gore's dark illustrations fit the story well.
SUBJ: Cats--Fiction./ Plants--Fiction./ Magic--Fiction.

Ph-2 4-6/6 $4.95   P   KH072
DEXTER, CATHERINE. Doll who knew the future. Beech Tree ISBN 0-688-13117-4, 1994. 195p.
Originally published as ORACLE DOLL, Four Winds/Macmillan, 1985. This mystery adventure features a doll that foretells the future. Asking questions can be tricky because the doll contains the spirit and voice of the Oracle of Delphi, know in ancient lore as one who responded in riddles. The children's adventures are sometimes dangerous, and the antagonists are not ancient spirits, but modern neighborhood children who are overindulged and truly nasty. Readers will stick with this to learn how Rose, Lucy, and James solve a dangerous situation.
SUBJ: Prophecies--Fiction./ Oracles--Fiction./ Mythology, Greek--Fiction./ Dolls--Fiction.

Ph-2 3-5/4 $4.95   P   KH073
DEXTER, CATHERINE. Gertie's green thumb. Illus. by Ellen Eagle. Beech Tree/Morrow ISBN 0-688-13090-9, 1995. 119p. ill.
Originally published by Macmillan, 1983.
Finding a wishbone in the park brings Gertie far more than she expected when her house becomes totally overrun by plants, creating a national tourist attraction. A slapstick comedy likely to attract reluctant readers.
SUBJ: Wishes--Fiction./ Nature--Fiction./ Humorous stories.

CE   Ph-1 4-6/5 $18.95   T   KH074
DICKENS, CHARLES. Christmas Carol in prose, being a ghost story of Christmas. Illus. by Trina Schart Hyman. Holiday House ISBN 0-8234-0486-2, 1983. 118p. col. ill.
Sound recording disc performed by Sir Ralph Richardson and others from Caedmon TC 1135, 2s 12in 33rpm, $8.98 (OPC).
Available from National Library Service for the Blind and Physically Handicapped in Braille BRA01907.
Meeting the Ghosts of Christmas Past, Present and Future in a series of dreams, the miser Scrooge changes his way of celebrating Christmas and his general outlook on life. The large, attractive typeface and the robustly colored illustrations, unfortunately often poorly placed, make this edition attractive.
SUBJ: Christmas--Fiction./ Misers--Fiction./ Ghosts--Fiction./ England--Fiction.

Ph-1 6-A/7 $16.00   T   KH075
DICKINSON, PETER. Bone from a dry sea. Delacorte ISBN 0-385-30821-3, 1993. 199p.
"In two parallel stories, an intelligent female member of a prehistoric tribe becomes instrumental in advancing the lot of her people, and the daughter of a paleontologist is visiting him on a dig in Africa when important fossil remains are discovered." (CIP) As the two stories, one of apelike prehominids and the other of contemporaries, merge from the strata being dug, personalities of present and past emerge. Filled with interesting characterizations, the novel will give the better, more mature reader a window into two levels of civilization and the players therein. Gripping adjunct to units on prehistory and archaeology.
SUBJ: Prehistoric peobles--Fiction./ Paleontology--Fiction./ Fossils--Fiction.

Ph-2 4-6/7 $14.95   T   KH076
DICKINSON, PETER. Chuck and Danielle. Illus. by Kees de Kiefte. Delacorte ISBN 0-385-32188-0; In Canada: Bantam Doubleday Dell, 1996. 115p. ill.
Chuck is the world's most terrified, cowardly whippet, a stylish dog and loving one to his owner, Danielle. Dickinson enters the dog's mind perfectly, and readers will share a Chuck's eye view of his universe. Although very British, dog lovers will jump hurdles to stick with the humorous, episodic adventures of a very nervous canine. Black and white sketches add to the humor.
SUBJ: Dogs--Fiction./ England--Fiction./ Fear--Fiction./ Humorous stories.

Ph-1 3-A/8 $16.95   T   KH077
DICKINSON, PETER. Time and the clockmice etcetera. Illus. by Emma Chichester-Clark. Delacorte ISBN 0-385-32038-8; In Canada: Bantam, 1994. 128p. col. ill.
Selectors' Choice, 20th ed.
In a delightful collaboration between illustrator and writer, the adventures of the human beings and clockmice involved with the Branton Town Hall Clock come alive in a detailed, funny, and fast-paced book. The interior essays on clocks, mice, science, time, and other topics are essential to the progress of the novel but are all understandable. The very special mice will charm listeners and readers. Illustrations in color and black and white fit the text and add to it. This seemingly detached study shouldn't work because of its many subjects--but does, and it will be good for reading aloud to younger children.
SUBJ: Mice--Fiction./ Clocks and watches--Fiction.

Ph-2 5-A/6 $16.99   L   KH078
DOHERTY, BERLIE. Street child. Orchard ISBN 0-531-08714-X, 1994. 154p.
Recreates the very mean streets of nineteenth century London and the endless cruelty of the poor to the poor, the "guardians" of the workhouse to the inmates, and the unthinking rich to everyone. As a young boy, Jim loses his sisters and then his mother and must devise various wretched ways to earn something to provide for himself. The conditions described are those which Dickens lived as a boy and later recreated in novels. Loosely based on "the true story of Jim Jarvis, an orphan boy whose plight led [Dr. Bernardo] to set up Britain's first children's refuge." (flap copy) Excellent historical fiction for units on the history of childhood, child labor, and social conditions.
SUBJ: Orphans--Fiction./ Homeless persons--Fiction./ London (England)--Fiction./ Children--Employment--Fiction.

Ph-2 5-A/7 $13.89   L   KH079
DORRIS, MICHAEL. Guests. Hyperion ISBN 0-7868-2036-5; In Canada: Little, Brown, 1994. 119p.
Moss, a Native American boy on the edge of the manhood rite, resents it when his father invites strangers from a vastly different culture to the major, yearly harvest feast. Although it is never stated, readers will know (with a little adult help) that the guests are the Pilgrims in New England during their first year in the New World. With the help of Trouble, a runaway girl, he begins to find answers and his role in the community. The foreshadowing of what will happen to Moss' group, and Native Americans throughout the New World, is never overtly stated, but wiser readers will comprehend it in the cleanly written, creative historical fiction. For multicultural studies.
SUBJ: Algonquin Indians--Fiction./ Indians of North America--Fiction./ America--Discovery and exploration--English--Fiction.

Ph-2 6-A/7 $12.95   T   KH080
DORRIS, MICHAEL. Morning Girl. Hyperion ISBN 1-56282-284-5; In Canada: Hyperion, 1992. 74p.
Spanish version TAINOS available from Santillana (ISBN 84-204-4757-9, 1995).
Available from the National Library Service for the Blind and Physically Handicapped on sound recording cassette RC 37957.
"Morning Girl, who loves the day, and her younger brother Star Boy, who loves the night, take turns describing their life on an island in pre-Columbian America; in Morning Girl's last narrative, she witnesses the arrival of the first Europeans to her world." (CIP) Portrays an idealized life on a Caribbean island before Columbus' first expedition. The drama is in the last lines when the reader realizes whose boats are landing on the shores. Audience for this is uncertain, however, reading it aloud might lead to interesting discussions.
SUBJ: Arawak Indians--Fiction./ Indians of the West Indies--Fiction./ Brothers and sisters--Fiction./ America--Discovery and exploration--Spanish--Fiction./ Spanish language materials.

Ph-1 5-A/4 $14.89   L   KH081
DORRIS, MICHAEL. Sees Behind Trees. Hyperion ISBN 0-7868-2215-5; In Canada: Little, Brown, 1996. 104p.
"A Native American boy with a special gift to 'see' beyond his poor eyesight journeys with an old warrior to a land of mystery and beauty." (CIP) Walnut, whose manhood name is Sees Behind Trees because of his ability to hear with his ears and his mind, narrates his own quest story. The mystical journey leads to the old man's past and to his own realization that "What will happen...will be up to

him,...As it is, finally, for each of us." (p.48) A lyrical coming-of-age story for multicultural studies. For reading aloud.
SUBJ: Indians of North America--Fiction./ Blind--Fiction./ Physically handicapped--Fiction.

Ph-1 6-A/7 $20.00   L   KH082
DOYLE, ARTHUR CONAN. Adventures of Sherlock Holmes. Illus. by Barry Moser. Morrow ISBN 0-688-10782-6, 1992. 342p. col. ill. (Books of wonder).
Twelve Holmes' adventures are presented in a deluxe edition.
Complete text of the original collection of Doyle's short stories will captivate the good reader.
SUBJ: Mystery and detective stories./ Short stories.

Ph-2 5-A/5 $16.95   T   KH083
DOYLE, BRIAN. Uncle Ronald. Groundwood/dist. by Publishers Group West ISBN 0-88899-266-1; In Canada: Groundwood/Douglas & McIntyre, 1997. 138p.
At the age of 112, Old Mickey remembers when he was a boy of 12 and was sent from his shack of a home in Ottawa (Canada) to the small town where his mother's relatives lived. Abused by his drunkard of a father, he is spirited away by his mother, so that he will find love and protection. In his new home with eccentric, but kind and loving relatives, he lives a "normal" life, stops wetting his bed, and begins to be happy. His kind giant of an uncle, Ronald, particularly, leaves a positive impression on the boy.
SUBJ: Uncles--Fiction./ Aunts--Fiction./ Canada--Fiction.

Ph-1 4-A $14.89   L   KH084
DRAANEN, WENDELIN VAN. How I survived being a girl. HarperCollins ISBN 0-06-026672-4; In Canada: HarperCollins, 1997. 163p.
Sixth-grader Carolyn's story about her passage from the asexual, "tom-boyish" stage of a girl's life into the realization that there is a difference between boys and girls is so immediate that a reader might well wonder if the story is autobiographical. At the end of the story, when her new sister is born, Carolyn begins to see things in a different, more female way. All the rules which society applies to girls--and not boys--that she relates in the first person narrative may very well strike a chord in young readers of both sexes--but especially girls. Carolyn is remarkable and admirable, and many girls (and ex-girls) will agree with her. Fine descriptive writing and strong character development.
SUBJ: Self-acceptance--Fiction./ Brothers and sisters--Fiction./ Family life--Fiction.

Ph-2 6-A/6 $19.95   L   KH085
DUBOIS, MURIEL L. Abenaki Captive. Carolrhoda ISBN 0-87614-753-8, 1994. 180p. map.
"Adventures in time books."
Includes glossary and bibliography.
In 1752, eighteen-year-old Abenaki warrior Ogistin is present when two colonial Americans are captured and taken to Canada. His original hatred of the English trappers gradually changes to brotherhood as he develops a bond with John Stark. Much about Abenaki customs and character is supplied in an often suspenseful book which gives details about the colonists' depredation of the native populations. Though historical fiction, this is a strong contribution to units on colonial American life and indigenous populations.
SUBJ: Stark, John--Fiction./ Abenaki Indians--Captivities--Fiction./ Canada--Fiction.

Ph-2 3-5/4 $13.00   T   KH086
DUFFEY, BETSY. Lucky Christmas. Illus. by Leslie Morrill. Simon & Schuster ISBN 0-671-86425-4; In Canada: Simon & Schuster, 1994. 74p. ill.
When Great-Aunt Octavia visits, George's worst fears come true as Lucky is banished from the household on his first Christmas. The comical story contains some superb dog's-eye views of human habits and expectations.
SUBJ: Dogs--Fiction./ Great-aunts--Fiction./ Christmas--Fiction.

Ph-2 4-6/5 $13.99   L   KH087
DUFFEY, BETSY. Utterly yours, Booker Jones. Viking ISBN 0-670-86007-2; In Canada: Penguin, 1995. 116p.
Sixth-grader Booker Jones of Pickle Springs, Arkansas, is determined to be a published author, but he encounters troubles when his grandfather moves into his room, causing problems at home and school. Booker's novels and the letters he sends to publishers are very funny, but the negatives in his life are clearly developed to show how frustrating the situations are. Booker is a different and likeable character. When some of his words are published in a newspaper and he becomes a school hero, it is all very satisfying for the reader.
SUBJ: Authorship--Fiction./ Grandfathers--Fiction./ Middle schools--Fiction./ Schools--Fiction./ Family life--Fiction.

Ph-2 1-4/2 $13.99   L   KH088
DUFFEY, BETSY. Virtual Cody. Illus. by Ellen Thompson. Viking ISBN 0-670-87470-1; In Canada: Penguin, 1997. 85p. ill.
Cody and his third grade classmates have been assigned to report about their names. Cody, who has a great fantasy life, imagines he was named for Wild Bill Cody--Buffalo Bill. Reality smacks against his fantasy when he learns the true origins of his name. The humor the kids show seems very real, especially in the eternal battle between third grade girls and boys. The light transitional reader, good for first-chapter book readers, should amuse since names are important to them and they can be very cruel about them.
SUBJ: Names, Personal--Fiction./ Schools--Fiction./ Humorous stories.

Ph-3 A/5 $3.99   P   KH089
DUNCAN, LOIS. Third eye. Dell ISBN 0-440-98720-2, 1984. 220p.
Available from National Library Service for the Blind and Physically Handicapped on sound recording cassette RC22591.
Worried by her psychic powers, Karen overcomes her fears and helps the police locate missing children. Definitely for advanced, mature readers who like romances, mysteries and are interested in psychic abilities.
Other stories involving the supernatural include DOWN A DARK HALL (ISBN 0-316-19547-2, 1975) and STRANGER WITH MY FACE (ISBN 0-316-19551-0, 1981).
Also available from NLSBPH are: DOWN A DARK HALL on sound recording cassette RC22689; STRANGER WITH MY FACE on sound recording cassette RC18949.
SUBJ: Extrasensory perception--Fiction./ Kidnapping--Fiction./ Mystery and detective stories.

Ph-2 6-A/7 $14.00   L   KH090
DYGARD, THOMAS J. Backfield package. Morrow ISBN 0-688-11471-7, 1992. 202p.
The star of Hillcrest High's championship team, Joe Mitchell, wants to attend the same college as his three friends whom he feels make him effective as a quarterback. Clearly shows the psychological effects of being courted by colleges and presents some fine action packed games in a eminently readable book. Appealing to fans who can appreciate the many facets of sports.
SUBJ: Football--Fiction./ Friendship--Fiction./ High schools--Fiction./ Schools--Fiction.

Ph-2 5-A/6 $11.95   L   KH091
DYGARD, THOMAS J. Forward pass. Morrow ISBN 0-688-07961-X, 1989. 186p.
Selecting a young woman who has fine athletic abilities as a wide receiver on the football team opens several cans of worms, all of which manage to eat at the vitals of other high school coaches and others who have a stereotyped view of the role of females. Combining some swift play action with good characters makes this a good choice for football fans and those for whom Zan Hagan (Knudsen) is a role model. Correct the typo on the last line of p128.
SUBJ: Schools--Fiction./ High schools--Fiction./ Football--Fiction./ Sex role--Fiction.

Ph-2 5-A/8 $14.00   T   KH092
DYGARD, THOMAS J. Game plan. Morrow ISBN 0-688-12007-5, 1993. 220p.
Brainy but nonathletic, football team manager Beano Hatton is forced to take over coaching the high school team when the coach is hospitalized. How Beano manages the self-centered quarterback and achieves a victory creates an active story with a different slant on a football hero. The situation and the well-developed characters will be sure to hold readers of sports books.
SUBJ: Football--Fiction./ High schools--Fiction./ Schools--Fiction.

Ph-2 5-A/7 $16.00   L   KH093
DYGARD, THOMAS J. Infield hit. Morrow ISBN 0-688-14037-8, 1995. 149p.
"After transferring to a new high school during his junior year, Hal tries to make friends, gain a starting position on the baseball team, and hide the fact that his father is a famous ex-major leaguer." (CIP) Following Dygard's tried-and-true formula of a protagonist with a problem, a teammate who is less than perfect, descriptive game play, and a solution to the antagonism, this title will appeal to baseball fans and readers of better than average sports books.
SUBJ: Baseball--Fiction./ Moving, Household--Fiction./ Friendship--Fiction.

Ph-2 4-6/6 $3.95   P   KH094
EAGER, EDWARD. Magic or not? Illus. by N. M. Bodecker. Harcourt Brace Jovanovich ISBN 0-15-251160-1, c1959, 1985. 190p. ill.
Available from National Library Service for the Blind and Physically Handicapped on sound recording cassette RC09809.
Despite what the girl on the train said, James and Laura aren't really

sure that the well by their new house is really magical, because even though the wishes come true, perhaps it is their actions that bring about the desired results. Quickly paced and with humor, this and THE WELL WISHERS (ISBN 0-15-294992-5, 1960, OPC), THE TIME GARDEN (ISBN 0-15-288190-5, c1958), KNIGHT'S CASTLE (ISBN 0-15-647350-X, c1956, 1984) and HALF MAGIC (ISBN 0-15-233078-X, c1954, 1982) are still popular reading fare.
Available also from NLSBPH are: THE WELL WISHERS on sound recording cassette RC09812; KNIGHT'S CASTLE on sound recording cassette RC10134.
SUBJ: Magic--Fiction.

Ph-2 4-6/6 $6.00   P   KH095
EAGER, EDWARD. Seven-day magic. Illus. by N. M. Bodecker. Harcourt Brace Jovanovich ISBN 0-15-272916-X, c1962. 156p. ill.
Sequel to: HALF MAGIC (1954).
Available from National Library Service for the Blind and Physically Handicapped in Braille BRA12283 and on sound recording cassette RC10136.
Abbie picked up the book and checked it out at the end of their visit to the library. When she began to read it, however, she found that it was really a magic book--and about them--just as she had wished. The two families of children--Barnaby, John, Susan, Abbie and Fredericka--have many exciting adventures with the book, but at the end of the seven-day loan period must return it to the library.
SUBJ: Magic--Fiction.

Ph-2 3-5/7 $15.89   L   KH096
EAGLE WALKING TURTLE. Full moon stories: thirteen Native American legends. Hyperion ISBN 0-7868-2175-2; In Canada: Little, Brown, 1997. 47p. col. ill.
"Grandpa Iron tells thirteen stories, one for each full moon of the year, that convey some of the traditions and beliefs of Native Americans, particularly his Arapaho people." (CIP) The stories, told by the author's grandpa, are about Mother Earth and her creatures. Use as an example of the beliefs of one group; they are also good to use for reading aloud, especially when studying Native American culture. Illustrations resemble colorful petroglyphs. For multicultural studies.
SUBJ: Arapaho Indians--Fiction./ Indians of North America--Great Plains--Fiction.

Ph-1 6-A/7 $5.95   P   KH097
ECKERT, ALLAN W. Incident at Hawk's Hill. Illus. by John Schoenherr. Little, Brown ISBN 0-316-20948-1, 1971. 173p. ill.
Newbery Honor Book.
Available from the National Library Service for the Blind and Physically Handicapped in Braille BR 01771 and on sound recording cassette RC 38913.
On a June day in 1870, Ben MacDonald vanishes in the prairie grass which stretches around his home. Ben is given up as dead after several days. How could a six-year-old, the size of a three-year-old, shy and peculiar, survive in the treacherous wilderness? He is a keen observer and a lover of wildlife, and mimicks animals with great accuracy. He is adopted by a badger and lives in her den. Within two months he is a wild boy with faint memories of home and family.
SUBJ: Wilderness areas--Fiction./ Survival--Fiction./ Badgers--Fiction.

Ph-2 2-4/2 $3.95   P   KH098
ELSTE, JOAN. True Blue. Illus. by DyAnne DiSalvo-Ryan. Grosset & Dunlap ISBN 0-448-41264-0; In Canada: BeJo Sales, 1996. 48p. col. ill. (All aboard reading).
"When Blue goes missing, young J.D. goes off to find the dog." (CIP) J.D. bravely trails the dog until she finds it as well as a dog that has been hurt by poachers. Both dog and young girl are heroes in this easy-to-read, but interesting transitional reader for first chapter book readers.
SUBJ: Dogs--Fiction./ Hunting--Fiction./ Friendship--Fiction.

Ph-2 4-6/5 $12.95   T   KH099
ENRIGHT, ELIZABETH. Saturdays. Dell ISBN 0-8050-0291-X, c1941, 1988. 175p. ill.
Available from National Library Service for the Blind and Physically Handicapped in Braille BRA06165.
Four motherless children and their father devise a scheme for taking turns on Saturdays, for spending their allowance on the pleasures and adventures to be found in their home town of New York City. Old fashioned but of enduring popularity.
Other stories about the Melendy family follow in THE FOUR-STORY MISTAKE (ISBN 0-440-42514-X, 1987, OPC); and SPIDERWEB FOR TWO (ISBN 0-440-48203-8, 1987, OPC).
SUBJ: Family life--Fiction./ New York (N.Y.)--Fiction.

CE   Ph-3 4-6/6 $16.95   L   KH100
ENRIGHT, ELIZABETH. Thimble summer. Henry Holt ISBN 0-8050-0306-1, 1966. 124p. col. ill.
Newbery Medal Award.
Talking book available from SRA/McGraw-Hill 87-508065, $16.00.
Available from National Library Service for the Blind and Physically Handicapped on sound recording cassette RC23207 and talking book TB01897.
Garnet believes that most of the happiness and good luck of the summer she spends on a Wisconsin farm comes from her finding of the thimble in the dry creek bed.
SUBJ: Wisconsin--Fiction./ Farm life--Fiction.

Ph-3 3-5/3 $16.00   L   KH101
ESTERL, ARNICA. Okino and the whales. Illus. by Marek Zawadzki. Harcourt Brace ISBN 0-15-200377-0; In Canada: Harcourt Brace c/o Canadian Manda, 1995. unp. col. ill.
Translated from the German and set in Japan, the story within a story features a mother and child waiting for the return of the whales. The mother tells, in folkloric language, the tale of a girl who visited the enchanted palace of Iwa, the Great Mother of the Ocean in olden times. Although the art is dark as befits life undersea, it and the text are clear, and the book is a good choice for reading aloud. The art is striking and shows the magical elements of the text.
SUBJ: Whales--Fiction./ Mother and child--Fiction./ Japan--Fiction.

Ph-1 2-4/6 $16.00   T   KH102
ESTES, ELEANOR. Hundred dresses. Illus. by Louis Slobodkin. Harcourt Brace Jovanovich ISBN 0-15-237374-8, c1944. 80p. col. ill.
Newbery Honor Book.
Available from National Library Service for the Blind and Physically Handicapped in Braille BR01416 and on sound recording cassette RC 42016.
Maddie and Peggy make Wanda, a recent Polish immigrant, the brunt of heartless teasing.
SUBJ: Poles--United States--Fiction./ Poverty--Fiction.

Ph-2 3-5/3 $16.00   T   KH103
ESTES, ELEANOR. Moffats. Illus. by Louis Slobodkin. Harcourt Brace Jovanovich ISBN 0-15-255095-X, c1941. 290p. ill.
Available from National Library Service for the Blind and Physically Handicapped in Braille BR05890, on sound recording cassette RC22178, as talking book TB01022.
Nine-year-old Janey, her family of brothers and sisters and Mama, are not poverty-stricken but just poor; their life, however, is never commonplace.
Followed by THE MOFFAT MUSEUM (ISBN 0-15-255086-0, 1983). Also available from NLSBPH is: THE MOFFAT MUSEUM in Braille BR05934 and on sound recording cassette RC22556.
SUBJ: Family life--Fiction.

Ph-2 3-5/4 $14.95   T   KH104
EVANS, DOUGLAS. Classroom at the end of the hall. Illus. by Larry Di Fiori. Front Street ISBN 1-886910-07-3, 1996. 132p. ill.
"Strange things are happening in the classroom at the end of the hall, like a chalk dust genie that appears while the erasers are being cleaned, and the new art teacher who resembles a stick figure." (CIP) The gentle, humorous tales of the supernatural, illustrated in amusing black and white sketches, will best be read as individual chapters, both for reading aloud or for private entertainment. Unlike some school stories about out-of-the-ordinary schools, there is no meanness in this--refreshing.
SUBJ: Schools--Fiction./ Supernatural--Fiction./ Behavior--Fiction.

Ph-1 4-6/5 $4.99   P   KH105
FARLEY, WALTER. Black Stallion. Illus. by Keith Ward. Random House ISBN 0-679-81347-0, c1941, 1994. 213p. ill.
Available from National Library Service for the Blind and Physically Handicapped in Braille BRA07167.
A tale of the devotion between a boy and a spirited horse. This popular author has written numerous sequels about the great black stallion: e.g. THE BLACK STALLION AND THE GIRL (Knopf ISBN 0-679-82021-3, c1971, 1992, OPC); YOUNG BLACK STALLION (ISBN 0-679-81348-9, 1991); THE BLACK STALLION MYSTERY (Knopf ISBN 0-679-82700-5, c1957, 1992, OPC); THE BLACK STALLION'S COURAGE (Knopf ISBN 0-679-83231-9, c1956, 1992); BLACK STALLION AND FLAME (ISBN 0-679-82020-5,/c1960, 1991); BLACK STALLION'S GHOST (ISBN 0-679-86950-6, c1969, 1995).
SUBJ: Horses--Fiction./ Horse racing--Fiction.

Ph-3 5-6/6 $4.99   P   KH106
FARLEY, WALTER. Man O'War. Random House ISBN 0-394-86015-2; In Canada: Random House, c1962. 339p.

Going to the New Aqueduct Race Track for Man O'War Day brings back the memories of the champion horse's illustrious career to Danny Ryan, his former groom. This detailed fictionalized biography of "the mightiest thoroughbred the American turf has ever known" is, because of its length, for the devoted horse fancier.
SUBJ: Man O'War (Racehorse)./ Horse racing--Fiction.

Ph-1 4-A/5 $16.99 L KH107
FARMER, NANCY. Do you know me. Illus. by Shelley Jackson. Orchard ISBN 0-531-08624-0, 1993. 105p. ill.
"Richard Jackson book."
Includes glossary.
Set in Harare, Zimbabwe, the ten episodes feature Uncle Zeka, fresh from Mozambique, and his niece Tapiwa. Uncle knows a great deal about everything classically African: plants, animals, natural medicines, and crafts but nothing about the modern world of cars, hospitals, etc. When the two worlds clash, Zeka causes endless trouble in his innocence. A fascinating view of different cultures comes alive in these events. For multicultural units.
SUBJ: Zimbabwe--Fiction./ Uncles--Fiction./ Family life--Fiction.

Ph-1 6 A/4 $19.99 L KH108
FARMER, NANCY. Ear, the Eye and the Arm: a novel. Orchard ISBN 0-531-08679-8, 1994. 311p. ill.
"Richard Jackson book."
Newbery Honor book, 1995.
Set in Zimbabwe in the year 2194, the realistic, science fiction novel suspensefully relates the story of the three children of the nation's leader when they are kidnapped. Three mutant detectives (the title characters), each with a special ability, folkloric in nature, help search for the children. The length of the book, which is fraught with tension, should not bother strong readers or listeners. Excellent characterization and a strongly imagined setting distinguish this original creation inspired by Shona mythology. For reading aloud.
SUBJ: Science fiction./ Zimbabwe--Fiction./ Blacks--Zimbabwe--Fiction.

Ph-1 6-A/5 $20.99 L KH109
FARMER, NANCY. Girl named Disaster. Orchard ISBN 0-531-08889-8, 1996. 309p., maps.
"Richard Jackson book."
Includes glossary and bibliography.
Newbery Honor book, 1997.
"While journeying to Zimbabwe, eleven-year-old Nhamo struggles to escape drowning and starvation and in so doing comes close to the luminous world of the African spirits." (CIP) Nhamo, an orphan, flees her village because she has been promised in marriage as a junior wife to a cruel and very sick older man. Her adventures are full of details of customs, culture, beliefs, religions, and history. Although long, the suspenseful survival story, akin to JULIE OF THE WOLVES (George), and Nhamo's character will hold stronger readers and pull them into the situations and settings. Excellent for units on modern and tribal African history, especially that of the Shona. For multicultural studies.
SUBJ: Zimbabwe--Fiction./ Supernatural--Fiction./ Survival--Fiction./ Adventure and adventurers--Fiction.

Ph-1 4-A/3 $16.99 L KH110
FARMER, NANCY. Warm Place. Orchard ISBN 0-531-08738-7, 1995. 152p.
"Richard Jackson book."
Selectors' Choice, 20th ed.
Starring animal, vegetable, and human characters including a gang of evil, selfish baddies, the adventures of our heroes come close to the captured giraffe in a zoo. Readers follow the suspenseful adventures of the brave band and one fine human boy, as Ruva escapes and returns to "the Warm Place"--home. The Kiplingesque prose, strong choice of verbs, delightful character development, and smooth, humorous narration make it perfect for reading aloud. Farmer's fantasy is a gift to listeners and readers.
SUBJ: Giraffes--Fiction./ Home--Fiction./ Animals--Fiction./ Poaching--Fiction./ Zoos--Fiction.

Ph-2 5-A/4 $14.00 T KH111
FARRELL, MAME. Marrying Malcolm Murgatroyd. Farrar Straus Giroux ISBN 0-374-34838-3; In Canada: HarperCollins, 1995. 122p.
Because her parents and Malcolm's parents continually joke about Hannah marrying Malcolm, she has taken upon herself to be his protector. Malcolm seems truly quirky in appearance and actions until he provides comfort and humor to Hannah's younger brother who is confined to a wheelchair because of muscular dystrophy. The interesting and very human interweaving of family life and life in the sixth grade make this an attractive and sometimes thoughtful first novel. Use in units on persons with disabilities.
SUBJ: Interpersonal relations--Fiction./ Popularity--Fiction./ Muscular dystrophy--Fiction./ Physically handicapped--Fiction.

Ph-2 5-A/7 $15.00 T KH112
FEIFFER, JULES. Man in the ceiling. HarperCollins ISBN 0-06-205035-4; In Canada: HarperCollins, 1993. 185p. ill.
"Michael di Capua books."
Jimmy is not interested in sports or school. His only ambition is to be a cartoon artist. The story of his successes and failures as he and his typically middle class family learn about doing what is important is told in prose with comic strip illustrations.
SUBJ: Family life--Fiction./ Uncles--Fiction./ Cartooning--Fiction.

Ph-2 5-6/7 $13.95 T KH113
FIENBERG, ANNA. Wiggy and Boa. Illus. by Ann James. Houghton Mifflin ISBN 0-395-53704-5, c1988, 1990. 99p. ill.
Spanish edition available VICO Y BOA (Fondo de Cultura ISBN 968-16-3747-X, 1992).
Wiggy (Ludwig) and Boa (Boadicea) manage to summon and then housebreak both Boa's grandfather and four fearsome pirates in a tale replete with nonsense, high jinks, and silly characters. Younger children may enjoy hearing this funny story and realize that good does triumph over all types of bad people, whether on the playground or Australian pirates longing for revenge.
SUBJ: Magic--Fiction./ Pirates--Fiction./ Friendship--Fiction./ Australia--Fiction./ Humorous stories./ Spanish language materials.

Ph-1 3-5/4 $15.89 L KH114
FITZHUGH, LOUISE. Harriet the spy. HarperCollins ISBN 0-06-021911-4, c1964. 298p. ill.
Available from National Library Service for the Blind and Physically Handicapped in Braille BRA04264, on sound recording cassette RC24815, and as talking book TB03360.
Eleven-year-old Harriet who goes to a private school in New York, jots down her thoughts about people, places, and things, in preparation for a writing career. When her classmates obtain the notebook and read about themselves they make life miserable for Harriet--until Harriet learns something she never suspected. Further adventures of this lively girl appear in THE LONG SECRET (ISBN 0-06-440332-7, c1965, 1990) (available from National Library Service for the Blind and Physically Handicapped as talking book TB04531).
SUBJ: Schools--Fiction./ Authors--Fiction.

Ph-1 6-A/5 $14.95 T KH115
FLEISCHMAN, PAUL. Borning room. HarperCollins ISBN 0-06-023762-7; In Canada: HarperCollins, 1991. 101p.
Available from the National Library Service for the Blind and Physically Handicapped on sound recording cassette RC 36553.
Can a segment of frontier and human history be told through an inanimate room? Yes--if a reader can understand and "cooperate" with a writer; no, if a reader is a mere peruser. The borning room was also the dying room, the place where the two most intimate acts of life took place: birth and death. In this room in a house on the Ohio frontier, Georgina remembers the moments of her life, the deaths of others and the births of her children. Not for oral presentation, but for quiet moments and mature younger readers.
SUBJ: Frontier and pioneer life--Fiction./ Ohio--Fiction.

Ph-1 5-A/5 $14.89 L KH116
FLEISCHMAN, PAUL. Bull Run. Woodcuts by David Frampton. HarperCollins ISBN 0-06-021447-3; In Canada: HarperCollins, 1993. 104p. ill.
"Laura Geringer book."
Available from the National Library Service for the Blind and Physically Handicapped on sound recording cassette RC 37371.
In an impressive, clear presentation, several first person vignettes describe people, actions, and settings before, during, and after First Manassas (Battle of Bull Run during the Civil War). People from all walks of life give their views of events and show the change from ideas about the glory of war to its ultimate gory, painful, and dirty death. Small woodcuts help identify speakers and add to this handsome, gripping, and understandable work of historical fiction. Use for individual dramatic readings in United States history classes.
SUBJ: Bull Run, 1st Battle of, Va., 1861--Fiction./ United States--History--Civil War, 1861-1865--Campaigns--Fiction.

Ph-2 6/7 $4.50 P KH117
FLEISCHMAN, PAUL. Half-a-Moon Inn. Illus. by Kathy Jacobi. HarperCollins ISBN 0-06-440364-5; In Canada: HarperCollins, c1980, 1991. 88p. ill.
Available from National Library Service for the Blind and Physically Handicapped in Braille BR05264.
When Aaron's mother leaves him alone for the first time in his life, he must face the problem of what to do when she fails to return from the trip to the village. He had been born mute and communicates by writing. He goes out to find her, in a blizzard, and falls into a trap at Half-a-Moon Inn where the evil Miss Grackle manages a world of

deception and thievery. An enticing story, best used for reading aloud.
SUBJ: Kidnapping--Fiction./ Mutism--Fiction./ Physically handicapped--Fiction./ Hotels, motels, etc.--Fiction.

Ph-1 5-A/5 $13.89 L KH118
FLEISCHMAN, PAUL. Seedfolks. Illus. by Judy Pedersen. HarperCollins ISBN 0-06-027472-7; In Canada: HarperCollins, 1997. 69p. ill.
"Joanna Cotler books."
"One by one, a number of people of varying ages and backgrounds transform a trash-filled inner-city lot into a productive and beautiful garden, and in doing so, are themselves transformed." (CIP) The story is told in the first person by each of the workers in the garden in Cleveland (Ohio). The change and growth of the empty lot and in the sometimes empty lives of the people reflect different people from different cultures as they all flower. Try this with reluctant older readers. For multicultural studies.
SUBJ: Gardens--Fiction./ City and town life--Fiction./ Neighborhood--Fiction.

Ph-1 4-6/4 $16.95 L KH119
FLEISCHMAN, SID. By the Great Horn Spoon! Illus. by Eric Von Schmidt. Atlantic/Little, Brown ISBN 0-316-28577-3, c1963. 193p. ill.
Available from National Library Service for the Blind and Physically Handicapped on sound recording cassette RC23517.
Jack Flagg, an orphan, runs away from home accompanied by the butler, Praiseworthy, and is involved in the California Gold Rush of 1849. The pompous and ubiquitous butler involves them in many tall tale adventures.
SUBJ: California--Gold discoveries--Fiction./ Orphans--Fiction./ Humorous stories.

Ph-2 4-6/5 $15.00 L KH120
FLEISCHMAN, SID. Chancy and the Grand Rascal. Illus. by Eric Von Schmidt. Greenwillow ISBN 0-688-14923-5, c1966, 1997. 182p. ill.
Available from National Library Service for the Blind and Physically Handicapped on sound recording cassette RC10281.
Chancy sets out from the Ohio farm where he'd lived for four years with the Starbuck family, determined to find his sisters Indiana and Mirandy and his little brother, Jamie. "Kin belonged together, didn't they?" His Uncle Will finds Chancy and is revealed as the grandest rascal of all, a man who "could out-talk, out-laugh, and out-fox any man" on the Ohio or Mississippi rivers.
SUBJ: Adventure and adventurers--Fiction./ Humorous stories./ Frontier and pioneer life--Kansas--Fiction.

Ph-1 5-A/7 $16.00 L KH121
FLEISCHMAN, SID. Ghost in the noonday sun. Illus. by Peter Sis. Greenwillow ISBN 0-688-08410-9, 1965. 131p. ill.
Shanghaied by a pirate band, Oliver Finch adventures on a sailing ship and manages to outwit the pirates and Captain Scratch, possibly the most superstitious and well characterized sea rover in humorous storydom. A "grandacious" reading experience in a new edition, perfect for oral, perfect for imaginative, adventuring readers.
SUBJ: Pirates--Fiction./ Buried treasure--Fiction.

Ph-1 3-5/4 $15.00 L KH122
FLEISCHMAN, SID. Ghost on Saturday night. Illus. by Laura Cornell. Greenwillow ISBN 0-688-14919-7, 1997. 53p. ill.
Available from National Library Service for the Blind and Physically Handicapped on sound recording cassette RC08743.
Opie is the only boy in town who can earn money by guiding people home in a tule fog. When he leads the mean-looking stranger to his hotel, his pay is two tickets to a ghost-raising show. He doesn't realize they are tickets for front row seats at a bank robbery.
SUBJ: Ghosts--Fiction./ Robbers and outlaws--Fiction./ Fog--Fiction./ West (U.S.)--Fiction.

Ph-1 4-A/6 $16.00 L KH123
FLEISCHMAN, SID. Jim Ugly. Illus. by Jos. A. Smith. Greenwillow ISBN 0-688-10886-5, 1992. 130p. ill.
Available from the National Library Service for the Blind and Physically Handicapped on sound recording cassette RC 37504.
Assumed dead, gone, missing: Jake's actor father was supposedly buried, but the evidence is not definitive. Jim Ugly, his father's dog, trails the scent of the actor from small towns and farms in the Sierra Nevada to San Francisco. Jake becomes an actor, is often in danger, and with Jim Ugly, solves the mystery in a humorous fast paced book which gives a good picture of the Old West of the nineteenth century. High jinks and well defined characters fill a most enjoyable novel. Try reading aloud.
SUBJ: Dogs--Fiction./ West (U.S.)--Fiction./ Mystery and detective stories.

Ph-1 3-6/4 $14.00 L KH124
FLEISCHMAN, SID. McBroom's wonderful one-acre farm: three tall tales. Illus. by Quentin Blake. Greenwillow ISBN 0-688-11159-9, 1992. 63p. ill.
Sid Fleischman, modern master of the tallest of tall tales starring the infamous Josh McBroom, is the model of hyperbole and the ridiculous in newly reissued exaggerations told tongue in cheek and illustrated with lively lines by Quentin Blake. Previously published as individual titles (MCBROOM TELLS THE TRUTH, MCBROOM AND THE BIG WIND, MCBROOM'S EAR, MCBROOM THE RAINMAKER, MCBROOM'S GHOST, and MCBROOM'S ZOO) the stories are perfect for reading aloud and will cause belly laughs for individual readers. McBroom is becoming a classic of the genre.
HERE COMES MCBROOM!: THREE MORE TALL TALES (ISBN 0-688-11160-2, 1992) keeps the tales coming.
SUBJ: Farms--Fiction./ Humorous stories./ Tall tales.

Ph-1 5-A/4 $16.00 L KH125
FLEISCHMAN, SID. Midnight horse. Illus. by Peter Sis. Greenwillow ISBN 0-688-09441-4, 1990. 84p. ill.
Selectors' Choice, 19th ed.
"Touch enlists the help of The Great Chuffalo, a ghostly magician, to thwart his great-uncle's plans to put Touch into the orphan house and swindle The Red Raven Inn away from Miss Sally." (CIP) Replete with humor, brilliantly named characters, and told at a swift pace, this imaginative and gripping tale is just right for oral presentation and for a fun-filled private reading experience. Sis's black and white illustrations add an extra dimension.
SUBJ: Adventure and adventurers--Fiction./ Magicians--Fiction./ Ghosts--Fiction./ Orphans--Fiction.

Ph-2 3-6/6 $15.00 L KH126
FLEISCHMAN, SID. Mr. Mysterious and Company. Illus. by Eric Von Schmidt. Greenwillow ISBN 0-688-14921-9, c1962, 1997. 154p. ill.
A family of traveling magicians do one-night stands in frontier towns during the 1870s in a comedic, adventurous story.
SUBJ: Magic--Fiction./ Overland journeys to the Pacific--Fiction./ Humorous stories.

CE
Ph-1 5-A/6 $15.00 L KH127
FLEISCHMAN, SID. 13th floor: a ghost story. Illus. by Peter Sis. Greenwillow ISBN 0-688-14216-8, 1995. 134p. ill.
Talking book available from Listening Library YA 900 (ISBN 0-8072-7614-6, 1995). 2 sound cassettes (181min), $16.98.
"When his older sister disappears, twelve-year-old Buddy Stebbins follows her back in time and finds himself aboard a seventeenth-century pirate ship captained by a distant relative." (CIP) When the ship founders, he is washed up in New England where he finds a distant ancestor, Abigail, ten, about to be hanged for witchcraft. Through skill, stealth, bravery, and the help of a few friends from the past, she is saved, and he finds his sister and returns to the present in a typically fast paced, humorous, and always exciting Fleischman adventure. Use this for reading aloud and be delighted as the audience shares the suspense, humor, and plot detail fireworks--and even learns about the past.
SUBJ: Time travel--Fiction./ Pirates--Fiction./ Brothers and sisters--Fiction.

Ph-1 5-6/7 $3.99 P KH128
FLEMING, IAN. Chitty Chitty Bang Bang: the magical car. Illus. by John Burningham. Knopf ISBN 0-394-81948-9, c1964, 1989. 114p. ill.
Although rackety when starting (witness her name) the old touring car, restored to her original grandeur by Commander Potts, proves to be magical and takes the family on a series of rousing adventures. Fast-paced and told with humor accented by the use of words printed in full caps, this is popular reading fare.
SUBJ: Automobiles--Fiction./ Magic--Fiction./ Humorous stories.

Ph-1 5-A/4 $15.00 T KH129
FLETCHER, RALPH. Fig pudding. Clarion ISBN 0-395-71125-8, 1995. 136p.
Nine episodes in the lives of the Abernathy family are told in the first person by the oldest of the six children, Cliff who is eleven. Each child is an individual as are the parents and all the relatives to whom the reader is introduced in this sometimes humorous, sometimes sad book. It summons the activity, closeness, and problems of life and death in a large, loving family. Those wanting a family story for reading aloud will do well to choose this.
SUBJ: Family life--Fiction./ Death--Fiction.

Ph-1 2-4/6 $14.93 L KH130
FLOURNOY, VANESSA. Celie and the harvest fiddler. By Vanessa and Valerie Flournoy. Illustrated by James E. Ransome. Tambourine ISBN 0-688-11458-X, 1995. unp. col. ill.
On All Hallows' Eve a mysterious Fiddler has Celie, a young African-

American girl, try on a magical African mask. Those who touch the mask become what they wish to be. Through a series of fast-paced and scary events, Celie has an altogether different All Hallows' Eve. Strongly illustrated in Ransome's active and expressive paintings. Try reading aloud, but be sure to share the art.
SUBJ: Halloween--Fiction./ Masks--Fiction./ Afro-Americans--Fiction.

CE
Ph-1 4-6/6 $15.00 T KH131
FORBES, ESTHER. Johnny Tremain: a novel for old and young. Illus. by Lynd Ward. Houghton Mifflin ISBN 0-395-06766-9, c1943, 1971. 256p. col. ill., map.
Newbery Medal Award.
Talking book (Dramatization) available from SRA/McGraw-Hill 87-507977, 1970, $16.00.
Available from National Library Service for the Blind and Physically Handicapped in Braille BRA08887, on sound recording cassette RC22808, as talking book TB02758.
On the eve of the American Revolution, a young boy, apprentice to a silversmith, has an accident which terminates his planned career and results in his involvement in the politics of the times. Characters are one-dimensional but the picture of Boston in the 1770s provides good historical atmosphere.
SUBJ: Boston (Mass.)--Fiction./ United States--History--Revolution, 1775-1783--Fiction.

Ph-2 6-A/4 $14.99 T KH132
FORD, BARBARA. Most wonderful movie in the world. Dutton ISBN 0-525-45455-1; In Canada: Penguin, 1996. 156p.
Moira, a seventh grader, attends Catholic parochial school, and the film of her favorite book GONE WITH THE WIND will be showing in her town. However, it has been condemned as unfit for viewing by the Legion of Decency, and her dilemma, a serious one, is whether to sneak off and see the film or resist. Embroidered around this central theme are her daily activities in late 1941 when the United States is on the verge of entering World War II. Modern historical fiction which examines times and attitudes.
SUBJ: Gone with the wind (Motion picture)--Fiction./ Catholics--Fiction./ Conscience--Fiction./ Schools--Fiction.

Ph-2 5-A/6 $15.99 T KH133
FORRESTER, SANDRA. Sound the jubilee. Lodestar/Dutton ISBN 0-525-67486-1; In Canada: McClelland & Stewart, 1995. 183p.
Available from the National Library Service for the Blind and Physically Handicapped on sound recording cassette RC 42885.
Maddie and her family, plantation slaves, escape to Roanoke Island, North Carolina when Union forces capture it during the Civil War. Eventually a colony of ex-slaves is established despite great hardship, death, and destructive acts of some Union soldiers. The terrors of slavery are well delineated as are the strengths of individuals for whom freedom is worth the cost of great difficulties. Although the characters are not fully dimensional, this historical fiction paints the times well in a situation based on a little known event in United States history. For multicultural studies.
SUBJ: Slavery--Fiction./ Roanoke Island (N.C.)--History--Fiction./ United States--History--Civil War, 1861-1865--Fiction.

Ph-1 4-6/4 $15.00 L KH134
FORWARD, TOBY. Traveling backward. Illus. by Laura Cornell. Tambourine ISBN 0-688-13076-3, 1994. 123p. ill.
Fanny's beloved Grandpa is dying, but with the help of a magic potion, he becomes younger and younger leading to various humorous problems. There is also a serious tone as Grandpa remembers the fire bombings and deaths during World War II and eventually realizes that he cannot live forever and welcomes death. Both major protagonists are realistically portrayed, but some minor ones are overdrawn for the sake of humor. Older readers who know Babbitt's TUCK EVERLASTING might find some similarities in a book that is smoothly developed and contains more than meets the eye. Thought-provoking, intergenerational story for reading aloud.
SUBJ: Grandfathers--Fiction./ Death--Fiction./ Magic--Fiction.

Ph-1 4-6/4 $15.00 L KH135
FOX, PAULA. Likely place. Illus. by Edward Ardizzone. Macmillan ISBN 0-02-735761-9; In Canada: Collier Macmillan, c1967, 1986. 57p. ill.
Lewis, 9, is that child who cannot win for losing. His over-demanding and over-protective parents will not let him be himself and tend to see him as an eternal problem, not an imaginative, growing little boy. A week with a most unusual babysitter allows him to follow his fantasies and finally meet an old man, a retired Spanish shoemaker whose family treats the dignified old man in much the same way as Lewis is treated. A very real situation is developed with very real characters. Good for oral presentation for middle grades and a sure-fire discussion starter.
SUBJ: Babysitters--Fiction./ Self-reliance--Fiction.

Ph-1 3-6/4 $16.99 T KH136
FOX, PAULA. Little swineherd and other tales. Illus. by Robert Byrd. Dutton ISBN 0-525-45398-9, 1996. 135p. ill.
Fox's 1978 series of tongue-in-cheek short stories, understated in their humor, is now reissued with imaginative black and white illustrations. The goose tells the six quasi-fable-like tales to the duck, a would-be powerful theatrical impresario. Each, except for the title story, features an animal or animals including a conceited rooster, an alligator, a raccoon, and a parade of various animals in a cumulative telling. Just right for reading aloud, the stories might also convert nicely to one act plays.
SUBJ: Animals--Fiction./ Short stories./ Fables.

Ph-1 6-A/6 $16.99 L KH137
FOX, PAULA. Monkey island. Orchard ISBN 0-531-08562-7, 1991. 151p.
Available from the National Library Service for the Blind and Physically Handicapped on sound recording cassette RC35595.
Fox details the life of Clay, an eleven-year-old forced by circumstances of his mother's illness to exist on the streets and in parks because of his homeless condition. Once, he and his parents lived in a comfortable middle-class style, but unemployment and economic conditions worked against reconstruction of that life. Clay and the people he meets are real in this gripping survival story that reflects a segment of contemporary life in the U.S. The better, more mature reader will appreciate Fox's superb writing.
SUBJ: Homeless persons--Fiction./ New York (N.Y.)--Fiction.

Ph-2 A/7 $14.95 T KH138
FOX, PAULA. One-eyed cat. Bradbury ISBN 0-02-735540-3, 1984. 216p.
Newbery Honor.
Available from National Library Service for the Blind and Physically Handicapped on sound recording cassette RC22756.
Feeling guilty because he disobeyed his minister father by firing his birthday present, an air rifle, Ned is even more distressed when he believes that the single shot wounded a stray cat. Trying to care for the cat without letting anyone know his secret adds dramatic tension to this essentially introspective tale that will be enjoyed by the mature reader.
SUBJ: Firearms--Fiction./ Cats--Fiction.

CE
Ph-1 5-6/6 $16.00 T KH139
FOX, PAULA. Slave dancer: a novel. Illus. by Eros Keith. Bradbury ISBN 0-02-735560-8, c1973. 176p. ill.
Newbery Medal Award.
Available from National Library Service for the Blind and Physically Handicapped in Braille BR02653 and on sound recording cassette RC08551.
Talking book available from Bantam Doubleday Dell BDDAP 654A (ISBN 0-553-47696-3, 1996). 4 sound cassettes (240min), $18.99.
Thirteen-year-old Jessie Bollier was kidnapped from his New Orleans home in 1840 to play his fife on the slave ship "Moonlight." His hateful duty began after the slaves had been brought on board at the Bight of Benin. They were forced to "dance" to keep them strong and profitable. Details of the slave trade, its brutalizing effect on the sailors, and the terrible hardships of the black people are graphically portrayed in an important book. Historical fiction for reading aloud and for units on United States history and multicultural studies.
SUBJ: Slave trade--Fiction./ Kidnapping--Fiction.

Ph-1 4-6/3 $3.95 P KH140
FOX, PAULA. Stone-faced boy. Illus. by Donald A. Mackay. Aladdin ISBN 0-689-71127-1, 1987. 106p. ill.
Available from National Library Service for the Blind and Physically Handicapped in Braille BR00974.
Gus is the third child in a family of five and he appears to be the butt of the jokes of family and schoolmates. He learned to protect himself by neither smiling nor frowning, until he thinks his face has turned to stone. A visit from an unusual aunt and his own search for a lost dog at night in the middle of a snow storm climax the nightmare life has become for him. He does return home safe, however, and even learns to smile.
SUBJ: New England--Fiction.

Ph-1 5-A/5 $17.99 L KH141
FOX, PAULA. Western wind: a novel. Orchard ISBN 0-531-08652-6, 1993. 201p.
"Richard Jackson book."
Available from the National Library Service for the Blind and Physically Handicapped on sound recording cassette RC 39006.
Elizabeth, twelve, is sent to stay with her artist grandmother on a small, isolated Maine island after the birth of a new brother. There she conquers her resentment and begins to appreciate the island and its inhabitants, especially after a neighbor girl introduces her to places

on the island and what may have been a mysterious death. Every word is carefully chosen and creates strong characters and understandable situations. Good choice for reading aloud, it will certainly be appreciated by stronger readers.
SUBJ: Grandmothers--Fiction./ Brothers and sisters--Fiction./ Islands--Fiction.

Ph-1 5-A/5 $15.00   L   KH142
FREEMAN, SUZANNE. Cuckoo's child. Greenwillow ISBN 0-688-14290-7, 1996. 249p.
Selectors' Choice, 21st ed.
In a novel at once humorous, active, and sad, a reader will meet Mia as she and her older sisters move from Beirut, Lebanon, to a small town in Tennessee in 1962 because their parents are lost at sea. In Beirut, she had longed for life as an American girl, something about which she knows little from first-hand experience. The story centers on character development, especially Mia's, who grows to learn that in life and geography, "I can't go back. I tried it, and now I know. Sinclair, [her wonderfully wacky friend in Tennessee], I can't be just regular." (p.247) Her activities and revolt against what is--the nest into which she has been put--leave everyone different, especially herself. A very strong and appealing first novel that is a gradual, sometimes painful revelation to reader and characters.
SUBJ: Separation anxiety--Fiction./ Parent and child--Fiction./ Family life--Fiction.

Ph-2 4-6/6 $14.95   T   KH143
FRITZ, JEAN. Cabin faced west. Illus. by Feodor Rojankovsky. Coward-McCann/Putnam ISBN 0-698-20016-0, c1958. 124p. ill.
Booktalk videocassette available from WETA Television, 1987, OPC. 1/2" VHS videocassette color (15min) $49.95. (Books from cover to cover) Teacher's guide available for $2.50.
Ann finds the western Pennsylvania frontier of 1784 very lonely until she makes new friends, General Washington comes for a visit, and her mother helps her have a tea party.
SUBJ: Frontier and pioneer life--Fiction./ Pennsylvania--Fiction./ Scott, Ann (Hamilton)--Fiction.

Ph-1 5-A/6 $4.99   P   KH144
FRITZ, JEAN. Early thunder. Illus. by Lynd Ward. Putnam ISBN 0-14-032259-0, c1967, 1987. 255p. ill., map.
Available from National Library Service for the Blind and Physically Handicapped as talking book TB02105.
In 1775 when the early thunder of the Revolution rolled over Massachusetts, the town of Salem was a tinder box of contradictory factions--Whig and Tory. Daniel West was especially torn by loyalty to his Tory father and his friend Beckett Foote on one hand, and by his own growing independence of judgment and recognition of injustices to the "Yankees" on the other. The climax of the story occurs when the Red Coats are confronted by the men of Salem at the drawbridge and Daniel shows his true colors.
SUBJ: United States--History--Colonial period, ca. 1600-1775--Fiction./ Salem (Mass.)--Fiction.

Ph-1 4-A/4 $15.95   T   KH145
FRITZ, JEAN. Homesick: my own story. Illus. by Margot Tomes. Putnam ISBN 0-399-20933-6; In Canada: General, 1982. 163p. ill.
"Background of Chinese history 1913-1927" p161-163.
Newbery Honor book.
Selectors' Choice, 14th ed.
Available from National Library Service for the Blind and Physically Handicapped on sound recording cassette RC19266.
The noted author of historical fiction and biographies recounts her childhood experiences living in Hankow, China, during the 1920s. Jean was subjected to various trials: at school where she struggled to establish herself as an American; being called a "foreign devil" by a small Chinese boy; and the looming threat of Chinese Communists. Then the family must be evacuated and Jean goes home to Washington, Pa., where she begins the adjustment to the life she had been longing for with bittersweet memories. An excellent story of a period and place not treated in other books for young people and because of its readable style and humor, very popular.
SUBJ: Fritz, Jean--Fiction./ China--Fiction.

Ph-2 5-A/7 $14.95   L   KH146
FROMENTAL, JEAN-LUC. Broadway chicken. Translated by Suzi Baker. Illus. by Miles Hyman. Hyperion ISBN 0-7868-2048-9; In Canada: Little, Brown, 1995. unp. col. ill.
Originally published in France, LE POULET DE BROADWAY, 1993.
In a tongue-in-beak telling, replete with sophisticated wordplay, the story of Charlie, the talented chicken, and his rise from a small Canal Street (N.Y.C.) arcade to the heights of Broadway and Hollywood--and his fall--is detailed in hilarious text and bright, dry pastel art. Charlie danced, sang, acted until impulses fueled by his own vanity

ended his stardom as did a greedy agent. The art which is reminiscent of that of William Joyce and the humor, similar to Maira Kalman's writing, delight children who can play word games and understand the mock heroic tones of biography. Alas, the typeface is an impossible sans serif which will require a strong reader, but the book is fun.
SUBJ: Chickens--Fiction./ Entertainers--Fiction.

Ph-1 5-A/5 $16.00   L   KH147
GAEDDERT, LOUANN. Breaking free. Atheneum ISBN 0-689-31883-9; In Canada: Maxwell Macmillan, 1994. 136p.
"Jean Karl book."
Available from the National Library Service for the Blind and Physically Handicapped on sound recording cassette RC 40067.
Richard, almost twelve, is bound out to his rough uncle who lives on a farm in New York State in 1800. The boy is educated, reads, and has a passion for music, attributes which are considered useless by his uncle and one of his cousins. He secretly teaches Gee Gee, a young slave, to read and helps her and Boy, an adult slave, to escape. This picture of Northern slavery, farm life, and an unusual character is often engaging and will be of special use in units on United States history and the history of slavery. Historical fiction for multicultural studies.
SUBJ: Slavery--Fiction./ Farm life--Fiction./ Literacy--Fiction.

Ph-1 5-A/6 $14.00   L   KH148
GAEDDERT, LOUANN. Hope. Atheneum ISBN 0-689-80128-9; In Canada: Distican, 1995. 165p.
"Jean Karl book."
Placed in the care of a Shaker community in 1851 by their unfeeling and selfish uncle, Hope and her younger brother John find a way of life that is strange although comfortable and secure. The Shakers' history and practices are presented in a nondidactic way. Readers will understand why John takes to these gentle people and why Hope wishes to join her supposedly lost father in California when he is found. While meeting an appealing cast of characters, readers will learn much about the Shakers. Historical fiction for units on religion and United States history.
SUBJ: Shakers--Fiction./ Orphans--Fiction.

Ph-1 3-5/6 $14.95   T   KH149
GANNETT, RUTH STILES. My father's dragon. Illus. by Ruth Chrisman Gannett. Random House ISBN 0-394-88460-4, c1948, 1986. 86p. col. ill., map.
Newbery Honor Book.
Available from National Library Service for the Blind and Physically Handicapped in Braille BRA07124, on sound recording cassette RC25589, and as talking book TB01905.
Elmer goes to the South Seas and rescues an over-worked dragon with the help of chewing gum, toothpaste, and lollipops. A real "noodlehead story" with "noodlehead" sequels; ELMER AND THE DRAGON (ISBN 0-394-89049-3, c1950, 1987) and DRAGONS OF BLUELAND (ISBN 0-394-91092-3, 1963).
Also available from NLSBPH is ELMER AND THE DRAGON in Braille BRA07120 and as talking book TB01905.
SUBJ: Dragons--Fiction./ Animals--Fiction./ Fairy tales./ Humorous stories.

Ph-1 5-A/4 $16.00   T   KH150
GANTOS, JACK. Heads or tails: stories from the sixth grade. Farrar Straus Giroux ISBN 0-374-32909-5; In Canada: HarperCollins, 1994. 151p.
Detailing the activities of Jack and his family when they are living in Fort Lauderdale, Florida, this is no doubt based on the author's life. His family seems to be continually either in or out of fortune, but they are always somewhat crazy. His actions and situations are hilarious and, although he tries, he is not always a model boy. It's easy to see that the "Rotten Ralph" books were probably based on rotten Jack. A welcome addition to an all too small selection of books about "average" boys.
SUBJ: Family life--Fiction./ Schools--Fiction./ Humorous stories.

Ph-1 5-A/4 $16.00   T   KH151
GANTOS, JACK. Jack's new power: stories from a Caribbean year. Farrar, Straus & Giroux ISBN 0-374-33657-1; In Canada: HarperCollins, 1995. 214p.
Sequel to HEADS OR TAILS: STORIES FROM THE SIXTH GRADE, Farrar Straus Giroux, 1994.
Now living in Barbados, Jack continues his diary the summer after sixth grade. His crazy (in a nice way, most of the time) family and his own misadventures add up to another series of events, many humorous. But Jack's father seems almost sadistic at times, although often he shows warmth, guidance, and affection. As a guide to "growing up" and family life, it is hardly a model, but it's real--bad

times, good times, and all.
SUBJ: Family life--Fiction./ Americans--Barbados--Fiction./ Barbados--Fiction./ Islands--Fiction.

Ph-3 4-6/6 $3.99   P   KH152
GARDINER, JOHN REYNOLDS. General Butterfingers. Illus. by Cat Bowman Smith. Puffin ISBN 0-14-036355-6; In Canada: Penguin, c1986, 1993. 84p. ill.
Marches three retired World War II elite commandos into a book brimming with nonstop zany action. The three vets are roused to action by young Walter, the housekeeper's son, when the heroes are to be evicted from their retirement home. Fun read-aloud.
SUBJ: Old age--Fiction.

Ph-2 3-5/7 $13.95   T   KH153
GAUCH, PATRICIA LEE. This time, Tempe Wick? Illus. by Margot Tomes. Putnam ISBN 0-399-21880-7; In Canada: Putnam, c1974, 1992. 43p. ill. (some col.).
Available from National Library Service for the Blind and Physically Handicapped on sound recording cassette RC09497.
Tempe (Temperance) Wick who lived near Morristown, New Jersey, in 1780 was a daring girl. She could wrestle and race her horse Bonny and she seemed to keep on growing. When ten thousand soldiers camped on her farm she pitched in to help. But when the soldiers mutinied it was too much. What happened when Tempe became angry makes a humorous tale and one that throws a new light on the people who lived through the Revolution.
SUBJ: United States--History--Revolution, 1775-1783--Fiction./ New Jersey--History--Revolution, 1775-1783--Fiction./ Mutiny--Fiction.

Ph-2 4-6/5 $14.95   L   KH154
GAUTHIER, GAIL. My life among the aliens. Putnam ISBN 0-399-22945-0; In Canada: Putnam, 1996. 104p. ill.
"Two brothers begin to wonder if it is their mother's unusual cooking that is attracting the aliens that keep showing up at their house." (CIP) Told in a light tone by nine-year-old Will, the story portrays the various and diverse aliens who cause major and minor problems for the brothers in a humorous book that would have been stronger had there been less of it. But for simple fun, the book is a good choice.
SUBJ: Extraterrestrial beings--Fiction./ Brothers--Fiction./ Mothers and sons--Fiction./ Humorous stories.

Ph-1 6-A/6 $14.95   T   KH155
GEE, MAURICE. Fire-raiser. Houghton Mifflin ISBN 0-395-62428-2, 1992. 172p.
Set in a small New Zealand town in 1915, Gee's tightly woven and logically developed story about an arsonist is gripping from first to last. The phsyclogical reasons for the pyromaniac's actions are revealed as is the character of all the people in the book. Attitudes towards Germans during World War I are clear, and the danger throughout is maintained. A few children manage to discover who the arsonist is and are put on the edge of serious harm. Adult women come off as second best, but this is consistent with the time and place of the novel. Prime choice to read aloud or to hold an individual reader in suspense.
SUBJ: Arson--Fiction./ New Zealand--Fiction./ Mystery and detective stories.

Ph-2 5-A/3 $14.89   L   KH156
GEORGE, JEAN CRAIGHEAD. Julie. Illus. by Wendell Minor. HarperCollins ISBN 0-06-023529-2; In Canada: HarperCollins, 1994. 227p., ill.
Sequel to: JULIE OF THE WOLVES, 1972.
Available from the National Library Service for the Blind and Physically Handicapped on sound recording cassette RC 40306.
Julie returns to live with her father and his new wife (not an Eskimo) and finds him willing to destroy anything, including wolves, that stands in the way of the economic development of his group. Once again, Julie goes on a trek into the wilds and shows enormous talent for reading the signs of the tundra and its animal inhabitants. Readers will follow her every step of the way as she searches for the wolf pack that had become her family in JULIE OF THE WOLVES. The wolves are the most memorable characters even as Julie meets a young man, a Siberian Eskimo. For multicultural studies.
SUBJ: Eskimos--Fiction./ Indians of North America--Alaska--Fiction./ Wolves--Fiction.

CE   Ph-1 6-A/6 $14.89   L   KH157
GEORGE, JEAN CRAIGHEAD. Julie of the wolves. Illus. by John Schoenherr. HarperCollins ISBN 0-06-021944-0, c1972. 170p. ill.
Newbery Medal Award.
Selectors' Choice, 8th ed.
Talking book read by Irene Worth available from HarperAudio/Caedmon (ISBN 1-55994-047-6, 1977). 1 sound cassette (60min),

$11.95.
Available from National Library Service for the Blind and Physically Handicapped in Braille BRA13071.
Miyax, a thirteen-year-old Inuit girl, runs away from her husband. She thinks she will go to her pen pal in San Francisco, but becomes lost on the Arctic tundra. Alone except for a pack of wolves, she rethinks her Eskimo past, is slowly accepted as a member of the wolf pack, and learns that her future will never be easy. A fine story of courage and the will to survive. For multicultural studies.
SUBJ: Eskimos--Fiction./ Wilderness survival--Fiction./ Courage--Fiction./ Wolves--Fiction.

TB   Ph-1 6-A $26.00   OD   KH158
GEORGE, JEAN CRAIGHEAD. Julie of the wolves (Talking book). Read by Christina Moore. Recorded Books 93138 ISBN 1-55690-777-X, 1993. 3 sound cassettes (270min).
ALA notable recording, 1994.
The narrator transports listeners to the frozen tundra as Miyax, a thirteen-year-old Inuit girl, runs away from her husband. She thinks she will go to her pen pal in San Francisco, but becomes lost in the Arctic. Alone except for a pack of wolves, she rethinks her Eskimo past, is slowly accepted as a member of the wolf pack, and learns that her future will never be easy. A fine story of courage and the will to survive. For multicultural studies.
SUBJ: Eskimos--Fiction./ Wilderness survival--Fiction./ Courage--Fiction./ Wolves--Fiction.

Ph-1 5-6/6 $15.00   L   KH159
GEORGE, JEAN CRAIGHEAD. My side of the mountain. Dutton ISBN 0-525-44392-4, c1959. 178p. ill.
Newbery Honor Book.
Available from National Library Service for the Blind and Physically Handicapped in Braille BRA05078 and on sound recording cassette RC09825.
Sam Gribley does what many boys dream of doing--spends a winter alone on the mountain in the Catskills.
SUBJ: Nature study--Fiction./ Outdoor life--Fiction./ Catskill Mountains Region (N.Y.)--Fiction.

Ph-1 5-A/5 $4.99   P   KH160
GEORGE, JEAN CRAIGHEAD. Vulpes, the red fox. By Jean Craighead George and John George. Illus. by Jean Craighead George. Peguin ISBN 0-14-037623-2; In Canada: McClelland & Stewart, c1948, 1996. 226p. ill.
Now reissued, almost a half of a century after its first publication, the parallel stories of the life, world, and habits of a red fox, Vulpes, and that of Buck Queen, a determined hunter, will be welcomed by those who wish to read a holding nature story--well told and well illustrated. Although animals are somewhat anthropomorphized, their characterizations and actions will help readers identify. The black and white art, Chinese inks and brush, are expressive and minimalistic.
SUBJ: Red fox--Fiction./ Foxes--Fiction.

Ph-1 5-A/7 $14.89   L   KH161
GEORGE, JEAN CRAIGHEAD. Who really killed Cock Robin?: an ecological mystery. HarperCollins ISBN 0-06-021981-5; In Canada: HarperCollins, c1971, 1991. 160p.
Selectors' Choice, 7th ed.
As timely today as it was prescient in 1971, the ecological mystery about what is killing the town's best known robin is solved. With scientific method and doggedness, eighth grader Tony describes and traces the ecological imbalances caused by chemical dumping in the town's river. In fact, this work is more important and timely today than it was 20 years ago--the perfect book for ecology and social studies units.
SUBJ: Ecology--Fiction./ Environmental protection--Fiction.

Ph-1 2-4/3 $13.95   T   KH162
GERSTEIN, MORDICAI. Behind the couch. Hyperion ISBN 0-7868-0116-6; In Canada: Little, Brown, 1996. 57p. ill. (Hyperion chapters).
The author/illustrator has brought so much imagination, strong character development, and action to this book that it will hold newly established readers on their way to other books of fantasy. "When Zachary loses his oldest toy and first friend, he searches for it behind the couch where he discovers a wonderful, imaginary world." (CIP) But the world is not imaginary: it seems very real and is peopled with dynamic characters. Black and white illustrations will aid the reader of this transitional reader which is a first-rate adventure.
SUBJ: Lost and found possessions--Fiction./ Imagination--Fiction.

Ph-1 5-A/7 $13.95   T   KH163
GIFALDI, DAVID. Gregory, Maw, and the Mean One. Decorations by Andrew Glass. Clarion ISBN 0-395-60821-X, 1992. 136p.

"In 1906, when the foul-tempered Mean One threatens a small Western town, a young boy and the crow that raised him take the varmint back in time to uncover the cause of his rotten disposition." (CIP) The delightful and entirely farfetched tall tale filled with hyperbolic improbability is eminently readable and should please readers of Sid Fleischman's stories. Good selection for reading aloud.
SUBJ: Humorous stories./ Behavior--Fiction./ West (U.S.)--Fiction./ Time travel--Fiction.

Ph-2 4-6/6 $3.25 P KH164
GIFF, PATRICIA REILLY. Fourth-grade celebrity. Illus. by Leslie Morrill. Dell ISBN 0-440-42676-6, 1981. 117p. ill.
Casey Valentine manages to be selected as fourth grade class president, then decides she must make herself a celebrity to outshine her older sister. In the companion story THE GIRL WHO KNEW IT ALL (Dell ISBN 0-440-42855-6, 1984) her pen pal, Tracy Matson, lives in a very small country town, is delighted to meet Casey on a vacation trip, but she too has problems similar to Casey's, and the addition of great difficulty in learning to read.
THE WINTER WORM BUSINESS (ISBN 0-440-49259-9, 1981) finds Casey's friend, Leroy, trying to sell worms to ice fishermen. In LEFT-HANDED SHORTSTOP (ISBN 0-440-44672-4, 1980) Casey tries to help her clumsy friend, Walter, be a successful baseball player.
SUBJ: Schools--Fiction.

Ph-2 5-A/5 $14.95 T KH165
GIFF, PATRICIA REILLY. Lily's crossing. Delacorte ISBN 0-385-32142-2; In Canada: Bantam Doubleday Dell, 1997. 180p.
Lily Mollahan is a born exaggerator, lively, overimaginative, and nosy with a mind overstimulated by war films. During World War II in 1944, she spends the summer with her grandparents in Rockaway Beach on New York's Long Island and meets a younger boy, a Hungarian refugee living with a neighboring family. She worries about her father on his way to fight in Europe, and Albert worries about his family caught in Europe. Her lies lead her to assure Albert that they can row out to a troop ship, board it, and sail to Europe. This notion almost causes Albert's drowning, but pulls Lily back into reality and changes her. The picture of life during the war rings true, and character is the strongest element in a book that recreates the time well without resorting to nostalgia. Historical fiction for recreational reading.
SUBJ: World War, 1939-1945--United States--Fiction./ Friendship--Fiction./ Refugees--Fiction./ Beaches--Fiction.

Ph-2 3-5/3 $3.25 P KH166
GIFF, PATRICIA REILLY. Rat teeth. Illus. by Leslie Morrill. Dell ISBN 0-440-47457-4, c1984. 130p. ill.
Acting tough is the only way ten-year-old Cliffie can keep from crying over his parents' divorce. Lonely in a new school, unhappy about dragging himself and his suitcase between two homes twice a week, Cliff considers running away as the ultimate answer to all of his problems. Part of a series of books about Casey Valentine and her friends.
SUBJ: Divorce--Fiction./ Teeth--Fiction.

Ph-2 4-6/4 $14.95 T KH167
GILBERT, SUZIE. Hawk Hill. Illus. by Sylvia Long. Chronicle ISBN 0-8118-0839-4; In Canada: Chronicle/dist. by Raincoast, 1996. unp. col. ill.
Alone and lonely when he moves to a new town, Pete finds a friend in a seemingly taciturn old woman who works in a rehabilitation center for birds of prey. As he comes out of himself, Mary begins to speak more although she husbands her words carefully. He learns a great deal about raptors, their care, their rehabilitation, and the need to allow them to fly free. Full-page pen, ink, and watercolor illustrations are especially strong showing birds, but are clumsy depicting humans. Good for units on wildlife conservation, environmental studies, and avian life.
SUBJ: Hawks--Fiction./ Friendship--Fiction./ Moving, Household--Fiction.

Ph-2 3-5/6 $13.00 L KH168
GILSON, JAMIE. Hobie Hanson, you're weird. Illustrated by Elise Primavera. Lothrop, Lee & Shepard ISBN 0-688-06700-X, 1987. 169p. ill.
Ten-year-old Hobie's sure that the summer will be boring with his best friend away and everyone else busy. Full of dialog and humor, this should prove to be popular reading fare.
HOBIE HANSON, GREATEST HERO OF THE MALL (ISBN 0-688-08968-2, 1989) finds the children attending school in a vacant department store after a major flood hits the town.
In STICKS AND STONES AND SKELETON BONES, illustrated by Dee DeRosa (ISBN 0-688-10098-8, 1991) Hobie and Nick fight but learn how to solve their problems through mediation.
SUBJ: Vacations--Fiction./ Humorous stories.

Ph-2 3-5/5 $12.00 L KH169
GILSON, JAMIE. Soccer circus. Illus. by Dee deRosa. Lothrop, Lee & Shepard ISBN 0-688-12021-0, 1993. 177p. ill.
Available from the National Library Service for the Blind and Physically Handicapped on sound recording cassette RC 39438.
When Hobie and his teammates play in an out-of-town soccer tournament, they attend a wedding with clowns and get mixed up in a mystery club murder staged at their hotel.
SUBJ: Hotels, motels, etc.--Fiction./ Mystery and detective stories./ Soccer--Fiction.

CE   Ph-1 A/7 $21.00 T KH170
GIPSON, FRED. Old Yeller. Illus. by Carl Burger. HarperCollins ISBN 0-06-011545-9, c1956. 158p. ill.
Newbery Honor Book.
Talking book adapted by Elise Bell; narrated by Bob Kaliban; available from SRA/McGraw-Hill 87-508069, 1973. $16.00, (40min).
Available from National Library Service for the Blind and Physically Handicapped in Braille BRA01734, on sound recording cassette RC15325, as talking book TB01218.
Travis and his dog, Old Yeller, live through a hard summer while his father drives the herd from Texas to the Kansas market. The dog is more than a match for thieving raccoons, fighting bulls, grizzly bears, and even wolves.
SUBJ: Dogs--Fiction./ Frontier and pioneer life--Fiction./ Texas--Fiction.

Ph-2 1-3/2 $13.95 T KH171
GLASER, LINDA. Rosie's birthday rat. Illus. by Nancy Poydar. Delacorte ISBN 0-385-32172-4; In Canada: Bantam Doubleday Dell, 1996. 47p. col. ill. (Yearling first choice chapter book).
Adventures with a pet rat which, of course, escapes in a house with a cat. Rat behavior is accurately described in this appealing transitional reader.
SUBJ: Rats as pets--Fiction./ Pets--Fiction./ Mothers and daughters--Fiction.

Ph-2 3-5/6 $15.95 T KH172
GLASS, ANDREW. Folks call me Appleseed John. Doubleday ISBN 0-385-32045-0; In Canada: Bantam Doubleday Dell, 1995. unp. col. ill. Includes bibliography.
Available from the National Library Service for the Blind and Physically Handicapped on sound recording cassette RC 42557.
Presents in lively, colorful oils and text an episode in the life of John Chapman, Johnny Appleseed. Chapman's half brother Nathaniel joins the great planter in Western Pennsylvania, but he can't quite cope with the harshness of frontier life until some local Senecas rescue him. Glass's notes on what facts are known about Chapman and his sources make this active and humorous tall tale an excellent supplement to other works on Johnny Appleseed. Too bad that the map of his travels is on the endpapers. Otherwise, a good choice-- and fine for reading aloud.
SUBJ: Appleseed, Johnny--Fiction./ Frontier and pioneer life--Fiction.

Ph-1 3-5/4 $11.00 T KH173
GLEITZMAN, MORRIS. Blabber mouth. Harcourt Brace ISBN 0-15-200369-X; In Canada; Harcourt Brace c/o Canadian Manda, 1995. 137p.
Available from the National Library Service for the Blind and Physically Handicapped on sound recording cassette RC 41704.
Mute since birth, Rowena has learned to communicate through sign language, but how can she tell her father she is embarrassed by his behavior and his outlandish clothing? Genuinely funny depiction of a unique father-daughter relationship. Use in units on persons with disabilities.
SUBJ: Fathers and daughters--Fiction./ Mutism--Fiction./ Physically handicapped--Fiction./ Australia--Fiction.

Ph-1 5-A/7 $12.95 T KH174
GLEITZMAN, MORRIS. Misery guts. Harcourt Brace Jovanovich ISBN 0-15-254768-1; In Canada: Harcourt Brace Jovanovich c/o Canadian Manda, 1993. 122p.
Trying to make his "misery guts" (gloomy) parents happy, Keith devises schemes which never are 100% successful. In fact, his humorous efforts cause disasters. Emigration to Australia solves some problems and causes others in a book about an incurably sweet optimist. First published in Australia in 1991; occasional Briticisms are clear in context.
Now in Australia, Keith, mom, and dad are all worry warts. Keith sets off to the opal fields in further adventures in WORRY WARTS (ISBN 0-15-299666-4, 1993).
SUBJ: Cheerfulness--Fiction./ Behavior--Fiction./ Parent and child--Fiction./ England--Fiction./ Australia--Fiction./ Humorous stories.

Ph-1 5-A/5 $12.00 T KH175
GLEITZMAN, MORRIS. Puppy fat. Harcourt Brace ISBN 0-15-200047-X;
In Canada: Harcourt Brace c/o Canadian Manda, 1995. 182p.
    Companion to: MISERY GUTS, 1993 and WORRY WARTS, 1993.
Keith is a perpetual "worry wart." When his parents divorce, he
worries that they will not find new partners. He tries to remake his
very real and loving parents and learns he cannot change them into
different people.
    SUBJ: Divorce--Fiction./ Worry--Fiction./ Beauty, Personal--Fiction./
London (England)--Fiction.

Ph-1 3-5/4 $11.00 T KH176
GLEITZMAN, MORRIS. Sticky Beak. Harcourt Brace ISBN 0-15-
200366-5; In Canada: Harcourt Brace c/o Canadian Manda, 1995.
140p.
    Sequel to BLABBER MOUTH, Harcourt Brace, 1995.
    Available from the National Library Service for the Blind and
Physically Handicapped on sound recording cassette RC 41705.
It was awkward when Rowena's father married her teacher, Ms.
Dunning. Now that they are expecting a baby, it's downright
embarrassing. Secretly, she worries that the baby may be born mute
like her. As she copes with her concerns, Rowena handles the ups and
downs of daily life with humor and aplomb. Use in units on persons
with disabilities.
    SUBJ: Stepmothers--Fiction./ Fathers and daughters--Fiction./ Mutism-
-Fiction./ Physically handicapped--Fiction./ Schools--Fiction./
Australia--Fiction.

Ph-3 2-4/4 $14.95 L KH177
GOBLE, PAUL. Beyond the ridge. Bradbury ISBN 0-02-736581-6; In
Canada: Collier Macmillan, 1989. unp. col. ill.
    Available from the National Library Service for the Blind and
Physically Handicapped on sound recording cassette RC34765.
An old Plains Indian woman dies. As her family mourns and prepares
her body for the spirit world--her spirit moves towards the afterlife
her people have envisioned--a beautiful earthly paradise. The author's
stylized illustrations are attractive and authentic and the book would
be useful in a unit on the Plains Indians. ANNIE AND THE OLD
ONE, by Miles is a different exploration of death and afterlife.
    SUBJ: Indians of North America--Great Plains--Fiction./ Death--Fiction.

Ph-2 5-A/6 $3.99 P KH178
GODDEN, RUMER. Listen to the nightingale. Penguin ISBN 0-14-
036091-3; In Canada: Penguin, c1992, 1994. 198p.
    Available from the National Library Service for the Blind and
Physically Handicapped on sound recording cassette RC 38271.
The story of orphaned Lottie and her beloved puppy involves the
usual cast of characters in a ballet story: the rich snobs, the trouble-
making genius, a loving and superior cast of ballet instructors,
problems, and the final triumph of the orphan and her dog. Although
the story is formulaic, balletomanes will want to read this rapidly
paced book.
    SUBJ: Ballet dancing--Fiction./ Orphans--Fiction./ Dogs--Fiction./
England--Fiction.

Ph-2 3-5/4 $15.00 T KH179
GODDEN, RUMER. Story of Holly and Ivy. Illus. by Barbara Cooney.
Viking Penguin ISBN 0-670-80622-6; In Canada: Penguin, 1985. 31p.
col. ill.
    Available from National Library Service for the Blind and Physically
Handicapped in Braille BR06458 and on sound recording cassette
RC24615.
An orphan named Ivy, a Christmas doll unsold on Christmas eve and
a childless couple are joyfully united on Christmas day. Text and
illustrations blend perfectly in this sentimental, but enchanting, holiday
classic.
    SUBJ: Dolls--Fiction./ Christmas--Fiction.

Ph-1 3-6/6 $3.45 P KH180
GOFFSTEIN, M. B. Goldie, the dollmaker. Farrar, Straus & Giroux ISBN
0-374-42740-2, 1969. 55p. ill.
    Goldie is independent and lives alone. She gives loving attention to
the dolls she carves and the world of love and warmth she makes.
Illustrations by the author add further to the impression of simplicity,
but the story is many layered.
    SUBJ: Dolls--Fiction./ Handicraft--Fiction.

Ph-3 2-3/2 $13.95 L KH181
GOLDIN, BARBARA DIAMOND. World's birthday: a Rosh Hashanah
story. Illus. by Jeanette Winter. Harcourt Brace Jovanovich ISBN 0-15-
299648-6, 1990. unp. col. ill.
    Daniel arranges a birthday party for the world on Rosh Hashanah,
the Jewish holy day that marks the birthday of the world. Nicely
illustrated in autumnal colors and peopled with distinct portraits of
Daniel's neighbors and family, this tale about the Jewish New Year is

good for oral presentation and will be a welcome addition to
collections which generally do not have a sufficient quantity of
instructive, amusing stories about Jewish festivals.
    SUBJ: Rosh Hashanah--Fiction.

Ph-2 5-A/3 $4.50 P KH182
GORMAN, CAROL. Miraculous makeover of Lizard Flanagan.
HarperCollins ISBN 0-06-440570-2; In Canada: HarperCollins, c1994,
1996. 185p.
    Lizard, a.k.a. Elizabeth, is athletic and best friends with a boy. As she
enters sixth grade, she has no interest in makeup, frilly clothing--even
skirts--and certainly not dances. With the help of her friend Mary
Ann, she begins to come to terms with the changes an eleven-year-old
must meet as she enters adolescence in this fast paced and humorous
book.
    SUBJ: Sex role--Fiction./ Schools--Fiction./ Friendship--Fiction.

Ph-2 4-6/4 $13.89 L KH183
GOROG, JUDITH. In a creepy, creepy place and other scary stories.
Illus. by Kimberly Bulcken Root. HarperCollins ISBN 0-06-025132-8; In
Canada: HarperCollins, 1996. 51p. ill.
    Gorog's five short stories feature the strange and the humorous:
extended events about those who fear the unknown that makes itself
known. Why is the large doll, the creature known as Frankenflopper,
created by a child who is not allowed to play with her older siblings,
so fearsome? What IS on that corner by the mailbox? A creature or
rumors of a creature? As usual, just right for the telling and good for
reading aloud. The illustrations add very little since Gorog's specialty
is words that make pictures and situations in the mind's eye.
    SUBJ: Horror stories./ Short stories.

Ph-2 4-6/6 $14.95 T KH184
GOROG, JUDITH. In a messy, messy room. Illus. by Kimberly Bulcken
Root. Philomel ISBN 0-399-22218-9; In Canada: Putnam, 1990. 48p. ill.
    Gathers five original short stories that are humorously grotesque and
short enough for fast reading. Each has a surprise ending and each is
just on the edge of horror. Good for the story teller and the younger
reader who might someday indulge in Saki's (H.H. Munro) works.
    SUBJ: Horror stories./ Short stories.

Ph-2 6-A/7 $3.50 P KH185
GOROG, JUDITH. Please do not touch: a collection of stories. Scholastic
ISBN 0-590-46683-6; In Canada: Scholastic, c1993, 1995. 131p.
    Presents "A collection of ten spooky stories based on exhibits at a
strange art gallery, including a house that records all sounds, a
coffeepot that won't take 'I don't want to' for an answer, and a
haunted car." (CIP) All original, the stories create a haunting
atmosphere reminiscent of Ray Bradbury's work. They feature
inanimate objects which become animated and characters who are not
quite what they seem when only their surface is examined. For
reading aloud.
    SUBJ: Horror stories./ Short stories.

Ph-2 5-A/5 $16.00 T KH186
GRAHAM, HARRIET. Boy and his bear. McElderry ISBN 0-689-80943-3;
In Canada: Distican, 1996. 196p.
    First published in London, England, Scholastic Children's Books,
1994.
Set in Elizabethan England, the story of Dickon, an unhappy
apprentice to a tanner, his rescue of a bear cub from the London
Bear Garden, and his escape from London to France is fraught with
suspense that should hold the better reader and more patient listener.
The atmosphere of Shakespeare's London and the world of the early
seventeenth century in England is nicely developed.
    SUBJ: Bears--Fiction./ Friendship--Fiction./ England--Fiction.

CE   Ph-2 3-6/7 $8.95 L KH187
GRAHAME, KENNETH. Reluctant dragon. Illus. by Ernest H. Shepard.
Holiday House ISBN 0-8234-0093-X, c1938. unp. ill.
    Selectors' Choice, 15th ed.
    Available from National Library Service for the Blind and Physically
Handicapped in Braille BRA01597 and on sound recording cassette
RC17014.
    Available on 1/2" VHS videocassette color (12min) from Churchill
Films #70, 1981. $79.00. Includes study guide.
The boy discovers a dragon who has slept in a cave on the downs
long after all others of his kind are gone. He makes him his friend
and arranges for St. George and the dragon to have a battle.
    SUBJ: Dragons--Fiction./ Fantasy./ Humorous stories.

CE   Ph-1 3-6/6 $14.95 T KH188
GRAHAME, KENNETH. Reluctant dragon. Illus. by Michael Hague.
Henry Holt ISBN 0-8050-1112-9; In Canada: Fitzhenry & Whiteside,
1983. 41p col illus.
    Sound recording cassette read by Boris Karloff available from

Caedmon CDL5-1074, $8.98 (OPC).
Realizing that he prefers to loll about, eat regularly, and compose poetry, the dragon that has suddenly appeared on the Downs and the boy who has befriended him plot how to evade St. George's challenge. The tongue-in-cheek humor and illustrations with the luminous hues of a medieval manuscript combine to create a special read-aloud experience.
SUBJ: Dragons--Fiction./ Humorous stories./ Fantasy.

Ph-1 5-6/8 $19.95 T KH189
GRAHAME, KENNETH. Wind in the willows. Illus. by Michael Hague. Henry Holt ISBN 0-8050-0213-8, 1980. 205p. col. ill., map.
Includes "Illustrator's note."
The now classic story of the animals of the river bank and woods as they fight to regain for Toad his ancestral home of Toad Hall, illustrated anew and in an attractive larger-size format. Unusually legible print, five in full color openings, as well as numerous page-size and end-piece illustrations, and handsome end-papers of "A map of Toad Hall and the surrounding countryside" make this book worth the expense for a second copy.
SUBJ: Animals--Fiction./ Friendship--Fiction./ Fantasy.

Ph-1 5-6/8 $19.00 T KH190
GRAHAME, KENNETH. Wind in the willows. 75th anniversary edition. Illus. by Ernest H. Shepard. Scribner's ISBN 0-684-17957-1, 1983. 259p. ill.
Available from National Library Service for the Blind and Physically Handicapped in Braille BR02183, on sound recording cassette RC24592, and as talking book TB00625.
The adventures of Toad, Rat, Mole and Badger who fight the weasels, ferrets and stoats and regain the ancestral home, Toad Hall.
SUBJ: Animals--Fiction./ Fantasy./ Friendship--Fiction.

Ph-2 1-3/2 $13.89 L KH191
GRAVES, BONNIE B. Mystery of the Tooth Gremlin. By Bonnie Graves. Illus. by Paige Billin-Frye. Hyperion ISBN 0-7868-2238-4, 1997. 54p. ill. (Hyperion chapters).
When his lost tooth is stolen, Jesse enlists the aid of classmate, Monica, to solve the mystery. She recommends he read several mysteries which help him solve the case and meet the class goal for book reports. Beginning readers ready for chapter books will enjoy the suspense and story's resolution in this transitional reader.
SUBJ: Teeth--Fiction./ Reading--Fiction./ Schools--Fiction./ Mystery and detective stories.

Ph-1 3-6/4 $13.95 T KH192
GRAVES, ROBERT. Big green book. Illus. by Maurice Sendak. Macmillan ISBN 0-02-736810-6; In Canada: Collier Macmillan, c1962, 1990. unp. ill.
Turn about is better than fair play when little Jack finds a big green book full of magic spells, turns himself into a little old man with a very long beard, causes rabbits to chase dogs, and wins every game he plays with his unsympathetic uncle and aunt. Magical and merry, this reissue is the stuff of the "dreams of glory"--and magic of many young people. Great for oral presentation and private chuckles. Enhanced by some of Sendak's most humorous illustrations.
SUBJ: Fantasy./ Humorous stories.

SRC   Ph-1 3-6 $11.95 OD KH193
GRAVEYARD TALES (Sound recording cassette). National Storytellers Association 107C ISBN 1-879991-02-0, 1984. 1 sound cassette (43min).
Spine-tingling, ghostly stories from various world cultures are told by master storytellers. A superb listening experience.
Contents: The skeleton woman, told by Gayle Ross (6min); The ghoul, told by Barbara Freeman and Connie Reagan-Blake (1min); The hole that would not stay filled, told by Kathryn Windham (8min); Dead Aaron, told by Mary Carter Smith (6min); The woodcutter, told by Laura Simms with Steve Gorn (13min); The monkey's paw, told by Jackie Torrence (10min).
Stories told by the settlers moving westward are found in HOMESPUN TALES (Sound recording cassette), 105C (ISBN 1-879991-03-9, 1986). 1 sound cassette (48min) $11.95.
SUBJ: Horror stories./ Short stories./ Storytelling.

CE   Ph-2 5-6/6 $15.95 L KH194
GRAY, ELIZABETH JANET. Adam of the road. Illus. by Robert Lawson. Viking ISBN 0-670-10435-3; In Canada: Penguin, c1942, 1970. 317p. ill., map.
Newbery Medal Award.
Talking book available from Live Oak ISBN 0-670-10438-5, 1980. 1 sound cassette (61min) $9.95.
Available from National Library Service for the Blind and Physically Handicapped in Braille BRA07490, on sound recording cassette RC23486, and as talking book TB02762.

Adam has been in school while his father, a famous minstrel, is in France learning new songs. He withstands loneliness through his friendship with Perkin and the companionship of Nick, his red spaniel. When Roger returns, Adam and his dog join him on the road. His multiple adventures are exciting and provide insights into the late middle ages in England.
SUBJ: Great Britain--History-- Plantagenets, 1154-1399--Fiction./ Middle Ages--Fiction./ Minstrels--Fiction./ Dogs--Fiction.

Ph-1 5-A/6 $13.95 T KH195
GRAY, LULI. Falcon's egg. Houghton Mifflin ISBN 0-395-71128-2, 1995. 133p.
"Taking care of her younger brother and a loving but flighty [illustrator] mother has made Falcon [a] very responsible eleven-year-old, but she needs the help of her great-great aunt, a friendly neighbor, and an ornithologist when she finds an unusual egg in Central Park." (CIP) The presentation of character, each a clear-cut individual, and the situation of allowing the dragon to grow too large to be confined make this book memorable and holding. When Falcon realizes she must free Egg, the dragon, her growth is demonstrated as is the fact that allowing something one loves freedom is true growth. It will be an unimaginative reader who does not follow every turn of this book with suspense and the need to know more. A fine choice for reading aloud.
SUBJ: Dragons--Fiction./ Mothers and daughters--Fiction./ New York (N.Y.)--Fiction.

Ph-2 6-A/5 $13.95 L KH196
GREEN, CONNIE JORDAN. Emmy. McElderry ISBN 0-689-50556-6; In Canada: Maxwell Macmillan, 1992. 152p.
When Mr. Mourfield is injured in a coal mining accident, Emmy, eleven-and-a-half, and her family must all pitch in to maintain their home. To keep the family from being evicted from their company house, Emmy's fourteen-year-old brother must work in the mines. The portraits of this decent family struck by hard luck despite endless hard work are full, and Green's writing will raise empathy and sympathy in the better reader. Historical fiction with a strong sense of setting and situation.
SUBJ: Coal mines and mining--Fiction./ Family life--Fiction./ Country life--Fiction.

Ph-1 A/8 $4.99 P KH197
GREENE, BETTE. Summer of my German soldier. Delacorte ISBN 0-440-21892-6, c1973, 1993. 230p.
Twelve-year-old Patty Bergen, who is Jewish, is fascinated when a truckload of German POWs arrive to be interned in her small Arkansas town and strikes up an acquaintance with one of them, Anton, an anti-Nazi. The repercussions after he escapes and she hides him over the garage make this a very powerful story for mature readers.
SUBJ: World War, 1939-1945--United States--Fiction./ Prisoners of war--Fiction.

Ph-2 5-6/4 $3.99 P KH198
GREENE, CONSTANCE C. Beat the turtle drum. Illus. by Donna Diamond. Puffin ISBN 0-14-036850-7; In Canada: Penguin, c1976, 1994. 119p. ill.
Selectors' Choice, 11th ed.
Available from National Library Service for the Blind and Physically Handicapped on sound recording cassette RC10889.
Kate is thirteen and her beloved sister, Joss, eleven. Joss is a much loved special person whose aim is to rent a horse for a week. When she finally achieves this, she and all her friends have a magical week. And then, "in a few irrevocable seconds, Kate's world is changed forever."... "Beat the turtle drum,/ That youth may last forever/ And sorrow never come" as Joss dies in an accident.
SUBJ: Brothers and sisters--Fiction./ Death--Fiction./ Horses--Fiction.

Ph-2 4-6/6 $2.95 P KH199
GREENFIELD, ELOISE. Koya DeLaney and the good girl blues. Scholastic ISBN 0-590-43299-0; In Canada: Scholastic, c1992, 1995. 124p.
Because she has always defused confrontations with jokes and humor, Koya, an eleven-year-old African-American girl, must learn to vent her honest anger at a friend who has deeply hurt her sister's feelings. The novel is reasonably developed and might stir discussion about anger, jealousy, and other psychological motivations. For multicultural studies.
SUBJ: Afro-Americans--Fiction./ Anger--Fiction.

Ph-2 3-5/4 $15.99 L KH200
GREENWALD, SHEILA. Rosy Cole: she grows and graduates. Orchard ISBN 0-531-33022-2, 1997. 92p. ill.
Rosy and her friends, now in the eighth grade, worry about being admitted into high school. Readers who are just discovering Rosy as well as fans of her earlier books will enjoy the humorous, but honest,

look at school pressures.
SUBJ: Self-acceptance--Fiction./ Friendship--Fiction./ Schools--Fiction.

Ph-2 3-6/3 $14.95   L   KH201
GREENWALD, SHEILA. Rosy Cole: she walks in beauty. Little, Brown
ISBN 0-316-32743-3; In Canada: Little, Brown, 1994. 83p. ill.
Rosy learns that beauty is deeper than skin as Donald helps her see
beyond surfaces. As Rosy finds her own image, she has many
humorous encounters. A realistic look at the preadolescent struggle to
find oneself while fitting in with one's peers.
SUBJ: Beauty, Personal--Fiction.

Ph-3 5-A/6 $15.95   T   KH202
GREGORY, KRISTIANA. Earthquake at dawn. Harcourt Brace
Jovanovich ISBN 0-15-200446-7; In Canada: Harcourt Brace c/o
Canadian Manda, 1992. 192p. ill. (Great episodes).
"Gulliver books."
Includes bibliography.
Based on a letter by photographer Edith Irvine, (of the Irvine Ranch
family) who was 22 at the time of San Francisco's earthquake and
fire of 1906, the fictional retelling has all the frightening details of
the quake, fire, and the lives of people during and immediately following
the phenomenal events. Although it is a straightforward telling, the
introduction of Barrymore, Caruso, and Jack London, whether or not
Edith actually saw them all, is a bit much. Of particular importance
for California regional collections.
SUBJ: Irvine, Edith--Fiction./ Earthquakes--California--San Francisco--
Fiction./ San Francisco (Calif.)--Fiction./ Photography--Fiction.

Ph-2 5-6/5 $7.95   P   KH203
GRIESE, ARNOLD A. Way of our people. Boyds Mills ISBN 1-56397-
648-X, 1997. 86p., map.
Originally published by Thomas Y. Crowell, 1977.
Kano, an Athabaskan Indian, lived in the Alaskan village of Anvik in
the 1830s. When he celebrates his coming of age, he kills a moose
and the men feast. But it brings him no joy because he fears hunting
alone. The story of how he learns to conquer his fear and to serve
the people of his village is historical fiction with a universal theme and
portrays Eskimo life of many generations ago. For multicultural
studies.
SUBJ: Alaska--Fiction./ Eskimos--Fiction./ Fear--Fiction./ Indians of
North America--Fiction.

Ph-2 4-6/4 $12.95   L   KH204
GRIFFITH, HELEN V. Caitlin's Holiday. Illus. by Susan Condie Lamb.
Greenwillow ISBN 0-688-09470-8, 1990. 96p. ill.
Caitlin surreptitiously leaves her favorite doll, Jodi, at a next-to-new
shop and exchanges it for Holiday, a teen-age doll complete with a
massive wardrobe. Holiday is a living, self-centered, unpleasant doll
and she dictates Caitlin's life until an exchange is made which restores
Jodi to her rightful place and frees Caitlin's conscience in a
sometimes-suspenseful story with crackling characterization and a very
different doll.
Caitlin's adventures with Holiday continue as her old and once loved
doll, Jodi, comes to life in DOLL TROUBLE (ISBN 0-688-12421-6,
1993, OPC).
SUBJ: Dolls--Fiction.

Ph-1 4-6/3 $19.95   L   KH205
GUCCIONE, LESLIE D. Come morning. By Leslie Davis Guccione.
Carolrhoda ISBN 0-87614-892-5, 1995. 120p.
"Adventures in time books."
"Twelve-year-old Freedom (Newcastle), the son of a freed slave
living in Delaware in the early 1850s, takes over his father's work in
the Underground Railroad when his father disappears." (CIP) The
lives of the Newcastles and their Quaker neighbors are shown as they
contend with the ever-present danger of patrollers who gather human
cargo, whether free or slave, after the Fugitive Slave Law of 1850.
Details the enormous dangers and the unlimited power given
patrollers--legal and illegal. It does seem strange, however, that all
characters in the book speak fine English except for the bounty
hunters. Historical fiction good for units in United States history,
multicultural studies, and the history of slavery. Try reading aloud
because the suspense will hold listeners--and readers.
SUBJ: Underground railroad--Fiction./ Slavery--Fiction./ Afro-
Americans--Fiction.

Ph-2 3-5/4 $13.95   L   KH206
HAARHOFF, DORIAN. Desert December. Illus. by Leon Vermeulen.
Clarion ISBN 0-395-61300-0, 1992. unp. ill.
"A South African boy makes a long journey through the desert to
join his parents in a mining village, reaching them on Christmas Day
and seeing his new baby sister." (CIP) On his way, he is helped by
several, possibly magic, beings--animal and human--who give him

advice to make a safe journey. Illustrations in brown washes show
character and setting clearly in a different "flight into Egypt." For
reading aloud and silent reading throughout the year.
SUBJ: South Africa--Fiction./ Blacks--Fiction./ Deserts--Fiction./
Babies--Fiction./ Christmas--Fiction./ Brothers and sisters--Fiction.

Ph-2 4-6/5 $3.50   P   KH207
HAAS, DOROTHY. Burton's zoom zoom va-rooom machine. Pocket Book
ISBN 0-671-74702-9, 1996. 138p. ill.
An evil though silly antagonist tries to steal the jet propelled
skateboard developed by a young inventor. Humorous and peopled
with inventively created characters, ridiculous food combinations, and
a brave dachshund, this is the stuff for those for whom stories just
this side of silly are first choices, as was Haas's DILLY MCBEAN.
Good for oral presentation and easy enough for better young
readers.
In BURTON AND THE GIGGLE MACHINE (ISBN 0-02-738203-6,
1992) there are more inventions, one in particular to make people
happy--and maybe reform the evil Professor Savvy.
SUBJ: Inventors--Fiction.

Ph-2 3-5/2 $14.00   L   KH208
HAAS, JESSIE. Be well, Beware. Illus. by Jos. A. Smith. Greenwillow
ISBN 0-688-14545-0, 1996. 66p. ill.
Sequel to BEWARE THE MARE, Greenwillow, 1993.
Available from the National Library Service for the Blind and
Physically Handicapped on sound recording cassette RC 42785.
Beware is very ill, but Lily, her family, and a vet nurse the mare back
to health. A sensitive horse story that contains a good deal of
information about horse care.
SUBJ: Horses--Fiction.

Ph-2 3-5/4 $13.00   L   KH209
HAAS, JESSIE. Beware the mare. Illus. by Martha Hass. Greenwillow
ISBN 0-688-11762-7, 1993. 64p. ill.
Available from the National Library Service for the Blind and
Physically Handicapped on sound recording cassette RC 42550.
Lily and her grandfather try to learn why a mare was named
"Beware" by her previous owners and if she is dangerous. Despite
the annoying use of present tense, "horse book" readers will trot
right through the book.
SUBJ: Horses--Fiction./ Grandfathers--Fiction.

Ph-2 4-6/4 $14.00   L   KH210
HAAS, JESSIE. Uncle Daney's way. Greenwillow ISBN 0-688-12794-0,
1994. 117p.
"When his great-uncle Daney comes to live with Cole's family after
being crippled in a logging accident, the two work together all
summer to find a way to make enough money to buy feed so they
can keep Daney's old horse." (CIP) Daney has taught his skidding
horse to obey oral commands, and he teaches Cole to work with Nip
to enter a pulling contest. Readers will pull with Cole in the contest
and admire Daney's ability to be independent with the assistance of
Nip, despite the fact that he uses a wheelchair. Character
development is gentle and different, and the plot which portrays the
coping skills of persons with disabilities will also appeal to horse
lovers.
SUBJ: Great-uncles--Fiction./ Horses--Fiction./ Country life--Fiction./
Handicapped--Fiction.

Ph-1 5-A/5 $15.00   L   KH211
HADDIX, MARGARET PETERSON. Running out of time. Simon &
Schuster ISBN 0-689-80084-3; In Canada: Distican, 1995. 184p.
"When a diphtheria epidemic hits her 1840 village, thirteen-year-old
Jessie discovers it is actually a 1996 tourist site under unseen
observation by heartless scientists, and it's up to Jessie to escape the
village and save the lives of the dying children." (CIP) The
suspenseful, dangerous flight from 1840 to the world of 1996 is
interesting and complex, but reasonable. Not exactly a mystery, and
not exactly historical fiction, the imaginative work is essentially a
well-developed adventure which should also attract science fiction
readers.
SUBJ: Mystery and detective stories./ Indiana--Fiction./ Diphtheria--
Fiction.

Ph-2 4-6/6 $16.00   T   KH212
HALL, DONALD. When Willard met Babe Ruth. Illus. by Barry Moser.
Browndeer/Harcourt Brace ISBN 0-15-200273-1; In Canada: Harcourt
Brace c/o Canadian Manda, 1996. 42p. col. ill.
At twelve, New Hampshire farm boy Willard Babson met Babe Ruth
when the Babe's car went into a ditch. After that, he follows the
Babe's life and extraordinary feats. The story, illustrated in full-page
watercolor portraits, also details Willard's life as he grows from boy
to man to father to grandfather in a gentle fictionalized biography of

people and their times. Appealing historical fiction that quietly reflects a bygone era.
SUBJ: Ruth, Babe--Fiction./ Baseball--Fiction.

Ph-2 6-A/5 $14.95 L KH213
HAMILTON, VIRGINIA. Cousins. Philomel ISBN 0-399-22164-6; In Canada: Putnam, 1990. 110p.
Spanish version PRIMOS available from Santillana (ISBN 84-204-47471, 1995).
Develops the relationship between cousins and the tragedy which occurs when Patty Ann, the "perfect" child, drowns while rescuing another girl. Largely a character study written in Hamilton's sure style. Love, humor, and, above all, character, emerge in a quiet story for the more sensitive and mature reader for whom Bauer's ON MY HONOR was a gripping reading experience.
SUBJ: Death--Fiction./ Cousins--Fiction./ Grandmothers--Fiction./ Spanish language materials.

Ph-1 4-6/4 $18.95 L KH214
HAMILTON, VIRGINIA. Drylongso. Illus. by Jerry Pinkney. Harcourt Brace Jovanovich ISBN 0-15-224241-4; In Canada: Harcourt Brace Jovanovich, 1992. 54p col illus.
Drylongso blows into Lindy's family's farm during a dust storm and dowses for the water that sets the family on the way to a better life. Pinkney's illustrations capture the mood, setting, and characters well, working perfectly with the text. The description of conditions in a dust bowl and the miracle of Drylongso are holding. Excellent choice for oral presentation and to accompany ecology units and history units about drought or the Dust Bowl period. For multicultural studies.
SUBJ: Droughts--Fiction./ Dust storms--Fiction./ Farm life--Fiction./ Afro-Americans--Fiction.

CE Ph-1 4-6/5 $15.95 L KH215
HAMILTON, VIRGINIA. House of Dies Drear. Illus. by Eros Keith. Macmillan ISBN 0-02-742500-2, c1968. 246p. ill.
Available from National Library Service for the Blind and Physically Handicapped in Braille BRA15778 and talking book TB02546.
Videocassette available from Bonneville Worldwide (ISBN 0-7800-0232-6, c1984, 1997). 1/2" VHS videocassette color (116min), $29.95.
This story, through the eyes of Thomas the older of three children, unravels the mystery of an enormous old house in a southern Ohio college town. His father, a new faculty member, rents it because it had been a station on the Underground Railway. The house holds many secrets, and also danger, for Thomas' family. His share in the unravelling of the mystery makes this a tremendously exciting, and timely, but demanding book. For multicultural studies.
In THE MYSTERY OF DREAR HOUSE (Greenwillow ISBN 0-688-04026-8, 1987) the treasure is protected until a new home for it can be found.
SUBJ: Mystery and detective stories./ Ghosts--Fiction./ Afro-Americans--Fiction.

Ph-2 A/4 $15.95 T KH216
HAMILTON, VIRGINIA. M.C. Higgins, the great. Macmillan ISBN 0-02-742480-4, 1974. 278p.
Perfectly written, but difficult to understand. For very mature reader
Newbery Medal Award.
National Book Award.
Available from National Library Service for the Blind and Physically Handicapped in Braille BR02749.
M.C. Higgins the Great sits on top of a gleaming forty-foot pole at his home on Sarah's Mountain and dreams of escape for himself and his family. Two strangers enter his world--a "dude" who thinks M.C.'s mother can become a great singing star and Lurhetta, a young wanderer. His friend, Ben Killburn, and the strangers force him to realize that safety does not lie in leaving home. Complex writing. For multicultural studies.
SUBJ: Family life--Fiction./ Home--Fiction./ Ohio--Fiction./ Afro-Americans--Fiction.

Ph-1 6-A/5 $13.95 L KH217
HAMILTON, VIRGINIA. Plain City. Blue Sky/Scholastic ISBN 0-590-47364-6; In Canada: Scholastic, 1993. 194p.
Available from the National Library Service for the Blind and Physically Handicapped on sound recording cassette RC 37904.
"Twelve-year-old Buhlaire, a 'mixed' child who feels out of place in her community, struggles to unearth her past and her family history as she gradually discovers more and more about her long-missing father." (CIP) Character and setting are strongly developed while action is caused by the interplay and revelations of people who are drawn with memorable strength in this understandable book. Mature readers will appreciate Hamilton's finely tuned and remarkable writing. For multicultural studies.

SUBJ: Fathers and daughters--Fiction./ Afro-Americans--Fiction./ Racially mixed people--Fiction./ Identity--Fiction.

CE Ph-1 A/6 $14.95 T KH218
HAMILTON, VIRGINIA. Planet of Junior Brown. Macmillan ISBN 0-02-742510-X, c1971. 210p.
Newbery Honor Book.
Selectors' Choice, 7th ed.
Talking book available from SRA/McGraw-Hill 87-508029, 1975, $16.00.
The three main characters in this story--Junior Brown, Buddy Clark, and Mr. Pool--are among the most unusual you may meet in a lifetime of reading. Junior is a 300-pound musical prodigy, Buddy a "loner" who is the leader, the "Tomorrow, Billy" for a group of smaller boys living in an abandoned tenement, and Mr. Pool a former school teacher now working as a janitor with whom the two spend their days playing hooky. When they are caught, their world begins to come apart, and society closes in on them, even destroying the planetary system built by Mr. Pool. A most unusual and complex story of courage and strength. For multicultural studies.
SUBJ: Schools--Fiction./ Afro-Americans--Fiction.

Ph-2 5-6/3 $14.00 L KH219
HAMILTON, VIRGINIA. Willie Bea and the time the Martians landed. Greenwillow ISBN 0-688-02390-8, 1983. 208p.
Available from National Library Service for the Blind and Physically Handicapped on sound recording cassette RC23390.
Anticipating the usual fun-filled spooky Halloween evening in rural Ohio, twelve-year-old Willie Bea strides out on her stilts to confront the unexpected monsters unleashed by Orson Welles' famous 1938 radio broadcast. Although slow starting, the title presents the complex relationships among the individualistic characters in this loving, extended African-American family. For multicultural studies.
SUBJ: Afro-Americans--Fiction./ Halloween--Fiction./ Extraterrestrial beings--Fiction./ Radio broadcasting--Fiction./ Farm life--Fiction.

Ph-2 4-A/4 $14.50 L KH220
HAMILTON, VIRGINIA. Zeely. Illus. by Symeon Shimin. Macmillan ISBN 0-02-742470-7, c1967. 122p. ill.
Available from National Library Service for the Blind and Physically Handicapped in Braille BRA04095, as talking book TB02310.
"Zeely was more than six and a half feet tall, thin and deeply dark as a pole of Ceylon ebony. Geeder couldn't say what expression she saw in Zeely's face...it...was the most beautiful she had ever seen." A few days later, eleven-year-old Geeder finds a picture in a magazine which convinces her Zeely is really a queen. In the end, Geeder still thinks Zeely is a queen, but a different kind and her understanding of who and what Geeder is, increases. For multicultural studies.
SUBJ: Farm life--Fiction./ Friendship--Fiction./ Afro-Americans--Fiction.

Ph-3 3-5/5 $12.95 L KH221
HARVEY, BRETT. Immigrant girl: Becky of Eldridge Street. Illus. by Deborah Kogan Ray. Holiday House ISBN 0-8234-0638-5, 1987. unp. ill. Includes glossary.
Living on New York's East Side in 1910 is crowded but for 10-year-old Becky it is far better than living in Russia and facing persecution. The details of daily life many immigrants faced are presented in text and soft pencil illustrations. This will be a useful resource for units on immigration.
SUBJ: Emigration and immigration--Fiction./ Jews--New York (N.Y.)--Fiction./ Russians--United States--Fiction./ New York (N.Y.)--Fiction.

Ph-2 2-4/4 $14.95 L KH222
HARVEY, BRETT. My prairie Christmas. Illus. by Deborah Kogan Ray. Holiday House ISBN 0-8234-0827-2, 1990. unp. col. ill.
Christmas in their new home on the prairie is different from celebrations in their old home in Maine. Eleanor, who seems younger in Ray's atmospheric illustrations than in the text, her mother and family try to recreate as much of the holiday as they can when a snowstorm keeps their father away. A warm family story, it should be enjoyed both orally and as a reading experience--not only at Christmas.
SUBJ: Christmas--Fiction./ Frontier and pioneer life--Fiction./ West (U.S.)--Fiction.

Ph-1 4-A/6 $13.95 T KH223
HARVEY, DEAN. Secret elephant of Harlan Kooter. Illus. by Mark Richardson. Houghton Mifflin ISBN 0-395-62523-8, 1992. 130p. ill.
Available from the National Library Service for the Blind and Physically Handicapped on sound recording cassette RC 39080.
Escaping from a circus, the young, but large, African elephant Hannibal takes refuge in Harlan Kooter's garage. Harlan hides the bright, appealing creature from elephant hunters from the circus who, understandably, want him back. Through a series of fast paced and

suspenseful events, large Hannibal and Harlan, the smallest boy in the school, manage to save the townspeople from a flooding hurricane. Just right for reading aloud, but be sure that listeners see the lively and charming black and white sketches.
SUBJ: Elephants--Fiction./ Friendship--Fiction./ Florida--Fiction.

Ph-2 4-6/5 $12.95   T   KH224
HASELEY, DENNIS. Shadows. Illus. by Leslie W. Bowman. Farrar, Straus & Giroux ISBN 0-374-36761-2; In Canada: HarperCollins, 1991. 74p. ill.
Sent to live with cold relatives while his widowed mother seeks a teaching position, Jamie, a self-contained boy, meets his imaginative grandfather who teaches him to make shadows on the wall and create stories about them. When his grandfather is threatened by an accident, the shadows lead Jamie to save him. Somewhat mystical and quiet in tone, the fantasy of the shadows is in nice contrast to the reality of Jamie's family history and his situation. Good choice for oral presentation.
SUBJ: Family--Fiction./ Grandfathers--Fiction.

Ph-2 6-A/3 $15.99   L   KH225
HATRICK, GLORIA. Masks. Orchard ISBN 0-531-08864-2, 1996. 120p. "Melanie Kroupa book."
"Desperate to help his older brother Will who has become paralyzed by a rare disease, Pete uses tribal animal masks to communicate with Will, allowing him to escape his useless body and embark on a series of strange and powerful dream journeys." (CIP) Because the boys' father is an anthropologist, it is logical for masks to be available for the transformations and mind transfers that Pete provides for Will, who is ill with Guillain-Barre syndrome. Throughout, the author provides interesting perceptions about medical personnel who do not speak to patients, but about them. The book is subtle and will probably require a strong reader.
SUBJ: Guillain-Barre syndrome--Fiction./ Brothers--Fiction./ Physically handicapped--Fiction./ Dreams--Fiction.

CE   Ph-1 6-A/6 $14.95   T   KH226
HAUGAARD, ERIK CHRISTIAN. Boy and the Samurai. Houghton Mifflin ISBN 0-395-56398-4, 1991. 221p.
Talking book available from Recorded Books 93135, 1993 (ISBN 1-55690-780-X). 5 sound cassettes (420min), $42.00.
Orphaned very young and living on the teeming, war-torn city streets of sixteenth century Japan, Saru (monkey) learns to fend for himself. The reader will observe the social hierarchy and the philosophical contemplations of the boy as he grows and survives the strife-filled times. The better reader will care about Saru and learn much about the civil wars in the time of the Samurai and the choices people must make. Excellent historical fiction for units on Japanese history.
SUBJ: Japan--History--Period of civil wars, 1480-1603--Fiction.

Ph-1 A/6 $17.50   T   KH227
HAUGAARD, ERIK CHRISTIAN. Little fishes. Illus. by Milton Johnson. Peter Smith ISBN 0-8446-6245-3, c1967, 1987. 223p. ill.
Jane Addams Book Award.
Available from National Library Service for the Blind and Physically Handicapped in Braille BRA11064 and on talking book TB02141.
Twelve-year-old orphan beggar Guido, his friend Anna and her four-year-old brother are in Naples during the wartime siege and later adrift on Italian roads toward Monte Cassino where they are caught in the long siege. This story of many things: of the people, the smells, the feels of war--its devastation, poverty, horror and bravery, is especially about the "little fishes"--the small people caught in the tide of war, only some of whom will escape. The unattractive, tight binding will require the book be introduced.
SUBJ: World War, 1939-1945--Children--Fiction./ Italy--History--1914-1946--Fiction.

Ph-3 6-A/5 $14.95   T   KH228
HAUGAARD, ERIK CHRISTIAN. Samurai's tale. Houghton Mifflin ISBN 0-395-34559-6, 1984. 234p.
Available from National Library Service for the Blind and Physically Handicapped on sound recording cassette RC24357.
Taro's world changed totally: knight's son to a servant, eventually he became a samurai in the tumultuous 1500s in Japan. Based on the author's extensive research into the period, this stirring tale for skilled readers will also be a useful adjunct in the social studies curriculum.
SUBJ: Japan--History--Period of civil wars, 1480-1603--Fiction./ Samurai--Fiction.

Ph-2 5-A/4 $13.95   T   KH229
HAWKINS, LAURA. Figment, your dog, speaking. Houghton Mifflin ISBN 0-395-57032-8, 1991. 155p.
Available from the National Library Service for the Blind and Physically Handicapped on sound recording cassette RC 38187.
Not given enough attention by her loving, but overly busy parents,

fourth-grader Marcella resorts to lies to gain recognition. A talking dog, Figment, appears and changes her life. The detailing of Marcella's continuing concern for many different, believable characters is an active character study of a child who finds herself. The imaginative novel is set in a lonely childhood and is an interesting working out of a common situation among too many contemporary children.
SUBJ: Dogs--Fiction./ Honesty--Fiction.

Ph-2 2-3/3 $12.95   T   KH230
HAYWOOD, CAROLYN. "B" is for Betsy. Harcourt Brace Jovanovich ISBN 0-15-204975-4, c1939. 159p. ill.
Available from National Library Service for the Blind and Physically Handicapped on sound recording cassette RC10306 and in Braille BRA09329.
This first story about Betsy tells of her first year in school, and her vacation on a farm. It is followed by many tales about her, including BETSY AND BILLY (ISBN 0-15-206765-5, c1941, 1988); BETSY AND THE BOYS (ISBN 0-15-206947-X, c1945) her 4th year at school; SNOWBOUND WITH BETSY (Dell ISBN 0-440-40246-8, c1962, OPC) and MERRY CHRISTMAS FROM BETSY (Dell ISBN 0-440-40187-9, 1970, OPC) are among other popular titles in the series. Also available from NLSBPH are: BETSY AND THE BOYS in Braille BRA05157 and on sound recording cassette RC10294; BETSY AND BILLY in Braille BR00563.
SUBJ: Schools--Fiction./ Girls--Fiction.

VCR   Ph-3 4-6 $29.95   KH231
HECTOR'S BUNYIP (Videocassette). WonderWorks/dist. by Bonneville Worldwide ISBN 0-7800-0114-1, c1986, 1997. 1/2" VHS videocassette color (58min). (WonderWorks).
Includes teacher's guide.
Includes public performance rights.
Closed-captioned.
Sometimes imaginary creatures can come in handy--Hector's bunyip certainly does. This funny yet sentimental story contrasts the bureaucracy and greed of society with the nuturing and imagination of Hector's loving foster family. The Australian setting and Hector's physical disability provide additional dimensions to this engaging tale.
SUBJ: Foster home care--Fiction./ Imagination--Fiction./ Orphans--Fiction./ Australia--Fiction.

CE   Ph-1 3-A/6 $12.95   L   KH232
HEIDE, FLORENCE PARRY. Shrinking of Treehorn. Illus. by Edward Gorey. Holiday House ISBN 0-8234-0189-8, c1971. unp. ill.
Read-along kit available from Listening Library FTR 53 SP (ISBN 0-8072-0215-0, 1983).1 paperback book, 1 sound cassette (22min), $15.98. Includes guide. (Follow the reader).
Available from National Library Service for the Blind and Physically Handicapped on sound recording cassette RC 42734.
Treehorn is shrinking--literally becoming so small he can no longer reach things and even trips over his now too long pant legs. "I must be shrinking or something", he tells his parents and teachers. But none of the adults takes him seriously. No one sees Treehorn--a child. TREEHORN'S TREASURE (ISBN 0-8234-0425-0, 1981, OPC). TREEHORN'S WISH (ISBN 0-8234-0493-5, 1984, OPC).
SUBJ: Size--Fiction.

Ph-2 2-5/2 $15.00   T   KH233
HEIDE, FLORENCE PARRY. Tales for the perfect child. Illus. by Victoria Chess. Lothrop, Lee & Shepard ISBN 0-688-03892-1, 1985. 79p. col. ill.
Available from National Library Service for the Blind and Physically Handicapped in Braille BR06633.
Tells seven brief tales about some clever and some totally obnoxious children who manipulate and outsmart their parents and other adults. The tongue-in-cheek humor of the text is matched by pictures with deadpan expressions on the monsterish animals. Children really enjoy the fun in reading about adults being bested. The appearance of a "real" book (not a picture book), arrangement in chapters and the low reading level make it useful with fourth and fifth graders who read below grade level and have a well developed sense of humor.
SUBJ: Conduct of life--Fiction./ Short stories.

Ph-1 3-5/6 $14.93   L   KH234
HEINS, ETHEL. Cat and the cook and other fables of Krylov. Retold by Ethel Heins. Illus. by Anita Lobel. Greenwillow ISBN 0-688-12311-2, 1995. 32p. col. ill.
The clever wit of the Russian fabulist, Krylov, is accessible in this collection of fables ably translated from Russian verse to English prose and illustrated in lush watercolor and gouache panels. An author's note provides biographical information about the popular Russian author and sources are also included. A useful resource for units on fables and comparison with Aesop and LaFontaine.
SUBJ: Fables./ Short stories.

Ph-3 4-A/3 $14.95 T KH235
HEINZ, BRIAN J. Kayuktuk: an Arctic quest. By Brian Heinz. Illus. by Jon Van Zyle. Chronicle ISBN 0-8118-0411-9; In Canada: Raincoast, 1996. unp. col. ill.
Includes glossary.
The tale about young Aknik and his trials as he tries to have a successful hunt to prove he is worthy of being considered a man shows life, habits, and customs of the Inupiat (Eskimos) in the North American Arctic region. After several unsuccessful hunts, he finally has a fox as his prey, but he does not kill it because it is a vixen with six kits. An elder of the tribe approves his action, and, at last, he is accepted as a man. The use of Inupiat language is explained in context and a glossary. Illustrations in acrylics extend the text and show setting, character, and the vastness of the tundra. The story will be useful in units on Native North Americans, environmental studies, and life in the Arctic regions. For multicultural studies.
SUBJ: Arctic regions--Fiction./ Eskimos--Fiction./ Indians of North America--Alaska--Fiction.

Ph-2 5-A/6 $11.95 L KH236
HELFMAN, ELIZABETH. On being Sarah. Illustrated by Lino Saffioti. Whitman ISBN 0-8075-6068-5; In Canada: General Publishing, 1993. 172p. front.
Reveals the thoughts of twelve-year-old Sarah, who has spastic cerebral palsy which has left her unable to speak, walk, or control her limbs. She communicates with a Blissymbol board and is obviously bright and sensitive. Like Wolff's PROBABLY STILL NICK SWANSEN, and Anderson's THE BUS PEOPLE, this explains the interior of a disabled person with a reality that will help others understand. Characterization is generally good although Sarah's father's actions are enigmatic and sometimes inexplicable. Good for reading aloud.
SUBJ: Cerebral palsy--Fiction./ Physically handicapped--Fiction./ Family life--Fiction./ Friendship--Fiction.

Ph-1 6-A/5 $16.00 T KH237
HENEGHAN, JAMES. Wish me luck. Farrar Straus Giroux ISBN 0-374-38453-3; In Canada: HarperCollins, 1997. 198p.
"Frances Foster books."
During World War II, children from England in danger during Nazi bombing raids were separated from their homes and shipped to Canada. Based on an actual incident, the U-boat sinking of the "Benares," the novel centers on narrator twelve-year-old Jamie Monaghan from the deepest slums of Liverpool. Realistic details and language, not all pleasant but not at all gratuitous, tell of life before the voyage, his neighbors, his friends, the mischief of the boys, family attitudes, night bombing raids, and the trip in the unimagined luxury aboard the ship. Its sinking and the days Jamie and a few others survive at sea are gripping and horrifying and will hold readers. Character and suspense are very well developed. Good as adventure reading and as historical fiction--a small slice of life during the war told from the viewpoint of an ordinary boy. (Author's note gives the history of the sinking of the "Benares.")
SUBJ: City of Benares (Ship)--Fiction./ World War, 1939-1945--Great Britain--Fiction./ Survival--Fiction./ Voyages and travels--Fiction.

Ph-1 5-A/6 $15.00 L KH238
HENKES, KEVIN. Protecting Marie. Greenwillow ISBN 0-688-13958-2, 1995. 195p.
"Secondhand pain is the hardest to deal with," (p. 63) Fanny's mother tells her. Her father, an artist, does inexplicable and sometimes cruel things to his family, including giving away his twelve-year-old daughter's beloved dog. The center of the novel is the relationship, at times loving and indulgent, between father and daughter. Mood, scenes, characters, and actions are set forth in small, telling details to form a fine, occasionally humorous novel. Advanced readers should find the novel a fascinating character study.
SUBJ: Fathers and daughters--Fiction./ Dogs--Fiction.

Ph-1 5-A/6 $15.00 L KH239
HENKES, KEVIN. Sun and spoon. Greenwillow ISBN 0-688-15232-5; In Canada: Hearst Book Group, 1997. 135p.
Spoon Gilmore, ten, is another of Henkes sensitive and very human characters painted in words as strongly as the artist illustrates in paints. The story details the boy's search for something meaningful, something very special, to remember his beloved grandmother who has recently died. Family relationships--with his grandfather, his younger sister, and his parents--are very real as are the lively dialogue and description of interior and exterior mood. How Spoon comes to grips with his loss is also how he comes to grips with life in an affecting and strongly written novel.
SUBJ: Grandmothers--Fiction./ Grandfathers--Fiction./ Death--Fiction./ Grief--Fiction.

Ph-1 5-A/6 $14.00 L KH240
HENKES, KEVIN. Words of stone. Greenwillow ISBN 0-688-11356-7, 1992. 152p.
"Busy trying to deal with his many fears and his troubled feelings for his dead mother, ten-year-old Blaze has his life changed when he meets the boisterous and irresistible Joselle." (CIP) At first, she seems cruel when she leaves messages written in stones for him to find. As they begin to know each other better, she helps pull him from his habitual timidity and superstition. Each has a story that intertwines in the book. Sensitive readers will comprehend the different, sometimes lost persons who affirm each other and give rise to self-affirmation.
SUBJ: Friendship--Fiction./ Mother and child--Fiction./ Fear--Fiction.

Ph-2 5-A/5 $3.95 P KH241
HENRY, MARGUERITE. Born to trot. Illus. by Wesley Dennis. Aladdin/Macmillan ISBN 0-689-71692-3; In Canada: Maxwell Macmillan, c1950, 1993. 223p. ill.
In a story within a story, the history of the Hambletonian, the largest harness racing meet in the world, is traced as are the hopes of Gibson White who wants to be a driver. Too many exclamation points mar the internal excitement of a book which will interest fans of horse stories and also those who want a fast reading experience.
SUBJ: Hambletonian 10 (Horse)--Fiction./ Harness racing--Fiction./ Horse racing--Fiction./ Horses--Fiction.

CE Ph-2 4-5/5 $3.95 P KH242
HENRY, MARGUERITE. Brighty of the Grand Canyon. Illus. by Wesley Dennis. Aladdin ISBN 0-689-71485-8, c1953, 1991. 222p. col. ill., map.
Available from National Library Service for the Blind and Physically Handicapped in Braille BRA05964, and as talking book TB00754.
A shaggy gray burro witnesses the destruction of his friend, the old man. Years later he vindicates his friend's death by helping capture the murderer.
SUBJ: Donkeys--Fiction./ Grand Canyon National Park (Ariz.)--Fiction.

CE Ph-1 4-6/5 $13.95 L KH243
HENRY, MARGUERITE. King of the wind. Illus. by Wesley Dennis. Macmillan ISBN 0-02-743629-2, c1948, 1990. 172p. col. ill.
Newbery Medal Award.
Talking book available from SRA/McGraw-Hill 87-507987, 1971, $16.00.
Available from National Library Service for the Blind and Physically Handicapped in Braille BRA05965 and on sound recording cassette RC16570.
The ancestor of Man O' War, the Godolphin Arabian, has many sad and exciting adventures on his journey from his homeland to safe harbor in England, faithfully cared for by the mute stableboy.
SUBJ: Horses--Fiction./ Arabian horse--Fiction./ Mutism--Fiction.

CE Ph-1 3-5/4 $13.95 L KH244
HENRY, MARGUERITE. Misty of Chincoteague. Illus. by Wesley Dennis. Macmillan ISBN 0-02-743622-5, c1947. 173p. col. ill., maps.
Newbery Honor Book.
1/2" VHS videocassette color (27min) available from SRA/McGraw-Hill 87-510582, 1988, $72.00. (Newbery video collection).
Available from National Library Service for the Blind and Physically Handicapped in Braille BRA14544 and on sound recording cassette RC25353.
A story of the wild horses which live on an island off the Eastern shore of Virginia, and of one particular freedom-loving horse.
Followed by STORMY, MISTY'S FOAL (ISBN 0-02-688762-2, 1963) and SEA-STAR: ORPHAN OF CHINCOTEAGUE (ISBN 0-02-743627-6, 1970).
STORMY, MISTY'S FOAL is available from NLSBPH in Braille BRA00478, on sound recording cassette RC15203, and as talking book TB00754.
SUBJ: Ponies--Fiction./ Assateague Island (Md. and Va.)--Fiction./ Chincoteague Island (Va.)--Fiction.

Ph-2 5-6/5 $3.95 P KH245
HENRY, MARGUERITE. Mustang, wild spirit of the West. Illus. by Robert Lougheed. Aladdin/Macmillan ISBN 0-689-71601-X, c1966, 1992. 224 b&w illus.
Available from National Library Service for the Blind and Physically Handicapped in Braille BRO03316 and on sound recording cassette RC17029.
Expert rider Annie Bronn wins a battle with polio and grows up to become "Wild Horse Annie" because of her crusade for the wild mustangs who are being ruthlessly slaughtered by pet food companies. She wins this battle, too, when Congress passes a bill outlawing roundups by planes or trucks. An inspiring fictional retelling of a true story about what can be done by one dedicated and determined person.
SUBJ: Johnston, Annie Bronn--Fiction./ Horses--Fiction./ Mustang--Fiction./ Wildlife conservation--Fiction.

Ph-2 4-6/6 $14.95 L KH246
HENRY, MARGUERITE. White stallion of Lipizza. Illus. by Wesley Dennis. Macmillan ISBN 0-02-743628-4; In Canada: Maxwell Macmillan, c1964, 1994. 112p. ill.
Hans the baker boy's dearest ambition is to become a part of the world of the Lipizzaner--the famous white dancing stallions of Vienna. How he realizes that ambition is an absorbing story. Readers learn much about the marvelous steeds, their riders, and the training of both.
SUBJ: Lipizzaner horse--Fiction./ Vienna. Spanish Riding School--Fiction./ Horsemanship--Fiction.

Ph-2 3-4/7 $13.99 T KH247
HERMAN, CHARLOTTE. Millie Cooper and friends. Illus. by Helen Cogancherry. Viking ISBN 0-670-86043-3; In Canada: Penguin, 1995. 84p. ill.
Millie Cooper, protagonist of MILLIE COOPER, 3B and MILLIE COOPER, TAKE A CHANCE, is now in fourth grade. She and her best friend Sandy expect it to be the best year ever until they are shocked to learn that the feared Miss Brennan will once again be their teacher. To top off that unpleasantness, it appears that Sandy has become best friends with a new girl, leaving Millie out in the cold, at times. Scenes, styles, and habits of 1947 come to life in this historical fiction aided greatly by black and white illustrations.
SUBJ: Friendship--Fiction./ Schools--Fiction.

Ph-2 5-6/3 $3.99 P KH248
HERMES, PATRICIA. Kevin Corbett eats flies. Illus. by Carol Newsom. Pocket Book ISBN 0-671-69183-X, 1989. 160p. ill.
For the first time since his mother's death fifth-grader Kevin Corbett is living in a town where he feels happy. When his wanderlust-stricken father shows signs of wanting to move on, Kevin plots with his friend Bailey to introduce him to Miss Holt, the attractive young teacher, in hopes romance will strike. The dialog is snappy and humorous while the characters: students, parents, and teachers, seem quite real. A good choice for reluctant readers. In the sequel, HEADS, I WIN (ISBN 0-671-67408-0, 1989) shunted and shuttled from foster home to foster home, fifth-grader Bailey, unpopular in school with the other girls, believes she must become class president to show up the class snob and remain with her current foster mother. Bailey and her friend, Kevin Corbett, are at once tough and sympathetic characters and everyone seems true-to-life in a novel that would be good for oral presentation or silent reading for the better middle-grade reader.
SUBJ: Friendship--Fiction./ Moving, Household--Fiction./ Fathers and sons--Fiction.

Ph-2 4-6/6 $3.50 P KH249
HERMES, PATRICIA. Nothing but trouble, trouble, trouble. Scholastic ISBN 0-590-48747-7; In Canada: Scholastic, 1995. 182p.
Available from the National Library Service for the Blind and Physically Handicapped on sound recording cassette RC 39915.
In a frenetically paced book, Alex tries to prove that she is responsible by staying clear of trouble for two weeks. Because she doesn't think through possible consequences of her actions, she continually causes trouble for herself and her friend. The series of cinematic situations will amuse readers, but they will all feel better when Alex finally does something that shows responsibility.
SUBJ: Behavior--Fiction./ Growth--Fiction.

Ph-2 6-A/7 $14.95 T KH250
HERMES, PATRICIA. Someone to count on: a novel. Little, Brown ISBN 0-316-35925-4; In Canada: Little, Brown, 1993. 184p.
Available from the National Library Service for the Blind and Physically Handicapped on sound recording cassette RC 40026.
Samantha, "Sam," eleven, is the responsible child of a mercurial, but loving mother. When her mother decides to pursue yet another of her occupational dreams, Sam is left with her aged grandfather on his large ranch in a desolate area of Colorado. She learns a great deal about him, nature, and herself and finally gains a feeling of permanence in an established home. Eventually, she must choose between the safety of a home and being with her mother during another period of vagabondage.
SUBJ: Mothers and daughters--Fiction./ Grandfathers--Fiction./ Ranch life--Fiction.

Ph-1 2-3/2 $4.95 P KH251
HESSE, KAREN. Lavender. Illus. by Andrew Glass. Henry Holt ISBN 0-8050-4257-1; In Canada: Fitzhenry & Whiteside, 1995. 40p. ill. (Redfeather book).
Anxious about her Aunt Alix, who has gone to the hospital to have her baby, Codie finishes the quilt she has secretly been making for her new cousin. Short chapters and simple language convey the emotional ties that bind this extended family. This transitional reader is a small treasure.
SUBJ: Babies--Fiction./ Cousins--Fiction./ Aunts--Fiction.

Ph-1 5-A/3 $14.95 T KH252
HESSE, KAREN. Music of dolphins. Scholastic ISBN 0-590-89797-7; In Canada: Scholastic, 1996. 181p.
Told in the first person through the perceptions and language of a "wild human child," this thought-provoking story depicts a girl who has been raised by dolphins, but is captured by a research institute and becomes an object of scientific study. Mila (Spanish for miracle) does learn human language and ways, but she always longs for the sea and her dolphin family. Although the book will need a better reader to understand the narrative in the beginning, it becomes clear as the story unfolds and reader sympathy and empathy develop. An unusual novel, it should be a good discussion starter about ethics and language acquisition.
SUBJ: Feral children--Fiction./ Diaries--Fiction./ Dolphins--Fiction.

Ph-2 3-5/4 $14.95 T KH253
HESSE, KAREN. Sable. Illus. by Marcia Sewall. Henry Holt ISBN 0-8050-2416-6; In Canada: Fitzhenry & Whiteside, 1994. 81p. ill. (Redfeather book).
"Tate Marshall is delighted when a stray dog turns up in the yard one day, but Sable, named for her dark, silky fur, causes trouble with the neighbors and has to go." (CIP) She unsuccessfully tries to train Sable, and the dog is given to someone miles away but escapes to return to Tate and her family. This nicely personalized book features well-drawn, good people. Aided by active black and white illustrations, it is within the reading abilities of first chapter book readers.
SUBJ: Dogs--Fiction./ Fathers and daughters--Fiction./ Carpentry--Fiction.

Ph-2 A/7 $7.95 P KH254
HEWITT, MARSHA. One proud summer. By Marsha Hewitt and Claire Mackay. Women's Educational Press ISBN 0-88961-048-7; In Canada: Women's Educational Press, 1981. 159p. ill.
Includes "Author's note", "Historical note", and bibliography.
13-year-old Lucie Laplante goes to work in the textile mills in a small Quebec town after the accidental death of her father in 1946. Both she and her mother work under inhuman conditions enforced by the mill owners. The strike by the workers brings recognition of the union and the beginning of improved working conditions. An interesting look at the rise of trade unions.
SUBJ: Dominion Textile Company Strike, 1946--Fiction./ Strikes and lockouts--Textile industry--Fiction./ Quebec (Province)--Valleyfield--Fiction.

Ph-2 2-4/4 $12.95 L KH255
HEYMSFELD, CARLA. Coaching Ms. Parker. Illus. by Jane O'Conor. Bradbury ISBN 0-02-743715-9; In Canada: Maxwell Macmillan, 1992. 85p. ill.
The teacher-student softball game is set, but Mike's teacher, Ms. Parker, hasn't a chance. Mike and his friends in the fourth grade coach her, and she becomes a passable player, even as she coaches him to become a better reader. The tale is friendly and the training and game are quite realistic.
SUBJ: Baseball--Fiction./ Schools--Fiction./ Teacher-student relationships--Fiction.

Ph-1 6-A/7 $14.00 L KH256
HICKMAN, JANET. Jericho: a novel. Greenwillow ISBN 0-688-13398-3, 1994. 135p.
Interweaves the life of her great-grandmother, now on her deathbed, with an account of twelve-year-old Angela's visit to Gatesville, once called Jericho. Past and present meet as GrandMin, who cannot remember today--or Angela and her family, recalls her past and the details of a life sometimes happy, sometimes cruelly unhappy, but always hard. In this concise novel, Angela's day-to-day life in the present serves as a counterpoint to the life of the elderly woman. Like Fleischman's THE BORNING ROOM, this is an intimate and understandable portrait, at once tender and realistic.
SUBJ: Great-grandmothers--Fiction./ Family life--Fiction.

Ph-2 6-A/6 $17.00 T KH257
HICYILMAZ, GAYE. Frozen waterfall. Farrar Straus Giroux ISBN 0-374-32482-4, 1994. 325p.
In a somewhat daunting book because of its length, the situation of "guest workers," Turkish citizens in Switzerland, is shown through the eyes and actions of Selda, twelve. The attitudes of Turks toward other ethnic groups and the plight of illegal, i.e., undocumented, workers is particularly sharp and shocking. At a time when similar events are taking place in the United States, the book is especially relevant and presents well developed characters and situations. Especially useful in units about immigration, national attitudes, contemporary history, and discussions about why people leave their native soil. For multicultural studies.
SUBJ: Immigrants--Fiction./ Turks--Switzerland--Fiction./ Switzerland--Fiction.

FICTION

Ph-2 3-6/5 $13.95 L KH258
HILDICK, E. W. Case of the weeping witch. Macmillan ISBN 0-02-743785-X; In Canada: Maxwell Macmillan, 1992. 158p.
Available from the National Library Service for the Blind and Physically Handicapped on sound recording cassette RC 41620. With the aid of their walkie talkies, McGurk and his detective club members travel back to the year 1692. When they try to keep Hester Bidgood from being hung as a witch, they find themselves accused of witchcraft. Fans of McGurk mysteries will enjoy this time travel fantasy.
SUBJ: Time travel--Fiction./ Witchcraft--Fiction.

Ph-1 4-A/7 $12.95 T KH259
HILL, ANTHONY. Burnt stick. Illus. by Mark Sofilas. Houghton Mifflin ISBN 0-395-73974-8, 1995. 53p. ill.
"It was the practice of the authorities in many parts of Australia, until as late as the 1960s, to take aboriginal children of mixed parentage away from their mothers, and to have them brought up either in institutions or with foster parents." (author's note, p.v) Like the practices of the Bureau of Indian Affairs in the United States, official policy was to remove children from their culture and change them to the customs of the dominant population. Thus, John Jagamarra is taken at an early age (5) from his band although his mother more than once covers him with ashes to disguise his skin color. Once removed, he never again sees his mother or his group. Told in almost clinical "just the facts" style, incorporating a few aboriginal stories, and illustrated with handsome black and white sketches, the book is holding and thoughtful. Good historical fiction for units on Native Americans and United States government policies to compare the experiences of aboriginal populations. For multicultural studies.
SUBJ: Australian aborigines--Fiction./ Australia--Fiction./ Mothers and sons--Fiction./ Missions--Australia--Fiction.

Ph-2 6-A/4 $14.99 T KH260
HILL, DAVID. Take it easy. Dutton ISBN 0-525-45763-1; In Canada: McClelland & Stewart, 1997. 163p.
Originally published in New Zealand, Mallinson Rendel Publishers, 1995.
Six teenagers, three male and three female, become lost in a remote and dangerous New Zealand wilderness after their guide suffers a fatal heart attack. Rob, the most experienced of the group, ignores the rules that he knows about survival when Carl panics and causes the rest to follow him ill-prepared and without a plan. They encounter life-threatening danger in a fast paced adventure which sketches rather than fully develops characterization. The tension and surface psychological examination of the characters is reasonable and will hold readers.
SUBJ: Survival--Fiction./ Hiking--Fiction./ Fathers and sons--Fiction./ New Zealand--Fiction.

Ph-2 4-6/6 $12.95 L KH261
HILL, KIRKPATRICK. Toughboy and sister. McElderry ISBN 0-689-50506-X; In Canada: Collier Macmillan, 1990. 121p.
Set in an isolated Athabascan Indian family fish camp on the Yukon River, this survival tale relates the tense events when Toughboy, eleven, and Little Sister, eight, are left alone after their father dies in a drunken state. The children learn that people "Don't need to be big to be grown-up." (p. 120) and manage to survive, albeit just on the edge of winter with its freezing weather and their lack of food. Characters speak as children do and diction seems real in this suspenseful telling, which may lead to discussions relating to the problems (alcoholism) experienced by some native peoples after the arrival of the settlers. For multicultural studies.
SUBJ: Yukon Territory--Fiction./ Survival--Fiction./ Brothers and sisters--Fiction.

Ph-2 5-A/6 $14.95 L KH262
HILL, KIRKPATRICK. Winter camp. McElderry ISBN 0-689-50588-4; In Canada: Maxwell Macmillan, 1993. 185p.
Sequel to TOUGHBOY AND SISTER.
Available from the National Library Service for the Blind and Physically Handicapped on sound recording cassette RC 38850. After their parents die, John (Toughboy) and Annie Laurie (Sister) live with Natasha, the old Athabascan woman, who takes them to her winter trapping camp and tries to teach them the old ways. The children are caught in emergency situations and must try to survive the bitter winter and save an old trapper. They learn that neither old nor new ways are best, but that a combination of the two may be. Tense and filled with details of Athabascan culture, the survival story can be used for multicultural studies.
SUBJ: Survival--Fiction./ Athabascan Indians--Fiction./ Eskimos--Fiction./ Indians of North America--Fiction./ Alaska--Fiction.

Ph-2 3-5/4 $14.95 T KH263
HINTON, S. E. Puppy sister. Illus. by Jacqueline Rogers. Delacorte ISBN 0-385-32060-4; In Canada: Bantam Doubleday Dell, 1995. 122p. ill.
Why and how the puppy Aleasha transforms from a canine to a human female child is a matter of faith, but the description of the puppy's view of the world and her eventual-brother Nick's sometimes embarrassment provide comical situations. Rogers' black and white illustrations add humor, and the large type and wide leading make the book a very approachable transitional reader.
SUBJ: Dogs--Fiction./ Brothers and sisters--Fiction./ Family life--Fiction./ Humorous stories.

VCR Ph-3 5-A $29.95 KH264
HIROSHIMA MAIDEN (Videocassette). WonderWorks/dist. by Bonneville Worldwide ISBN 0-7800-0003-X, c1988, 1997. 1/2" VHS videocassette color (58min). (WonderWorks).
Includes teacher's guide.
Includes public performance rights.
Twenty-five young Japanese survivors of the atomic bomb come to the United States for plastic surgery. This fictional story based on the historical event illustrates not only the aftereffects of war but also the scars that can be caused by ignorance and prejudice. Useful for global education and units on World War II.
SUBJ: Japanese--United States--Fiction./ Family life--Fiction./ Physically handicapped--Fiction./ Prejudices--Fiction.

Ph-2 5-A/7 $15.95 T KH265
HITE, SID. Dither Farm: a novel. Henry Holt ISBN 0-8050-1871-9; In Canada: Fitzhenry & Whiteside, 1992. 215p.
Available from the National Library Service for the Blind and Physically Handicapped on sound recording cassette RC 40236. Combines fantasy, humor (in the nature of a l-o-n-g joke), and character ("What a character!") development, with a series of adventures all of which tie up in a well-knit story of the Dither family and the suspenseful and magical adventures which befall them. Although the first chapter is necessary to lay the groundwork, it may discourage some readers who do not take to description. However, introduced orally, readers who quest after Dan Elish, Lloyd Alexander, and D. Manus Pinkwater will stick with the magic carpets, the remarkable Dither family, and their neighbors. Good read-aloud for someone looking for a longer, somewhat picaresque novel.
SUBJ: Family life--Fiction./ Country life--Fiction./ Supernatural--Fiction./ Virginia--Fiction.

Ph-1 5-A/6 $14.95 T KH266
HITE, SID. Even break. Henry Holt ISBN 0-8050-3837-X; In Canada: Fitzhenry & Whiteside, 1995. 92p.
Frank, twelve, is envied by every boy in his small southern town when he is hired for a summer job to manage the local pool hall. He does his work well, becomes a champion pool player, and finds himself in the finals of a pool tournament against a girl his own age. The tension of the tournament is strongly developed, as are action and character. A fast paced sports story peopled with real people.
SUBJ: City and town life--Fiction./ Pool (Game)--Fiction.

Ph-2 5-A/6 $15.00 L KH267
HOBBS, WILL. Ghost canoe. Morrow ISBN 0-688-14193-5; In Canada: Hearst Books, 1997. 195p., map.
"Fourteen-year-old Nathan, fishing with the Makah in the Pacific Northwest, finds himself holding a vital clue when a mysterious stranger comes to town looking for Spanish treasure." (CIP) Set in the Washington Territory in 1874, this old-fashioned adventure story centers around the son of a lighthouse keeper, Nathan who is self-reliant, almost too good. Characterization is nil, writing style is wordy, although a few details of Makah culture come through. Despite these faults, adventure seekers will want to read the suspense-filled book.
SUBJ: Buried treasure--Fiction./ Northwest, Pacific--Fiction./ Makah Indians--Fiction./ Indians of North America--Northwest, Pacific--Fiction./ Adventure and adventurers--Fiction.

Ph-2 3-5/5 $16.85 L KH268
HOESTLANDT, JO. Star of fear, star of hope. Illus. by Johanna Kang. Translated from the French by Mark Polizzotti. Walker ISBN 0-8027-8374-0; In Canada: Thomas Allen, 1995. unp. col. ill.
Originally published in France, LA GRANDE PEUR SOUS LES ETOILES, 1993.
During the German occupation of Paris during World War II, Helen, nine, is confused at the disappearance of her best friend, the Jewish child Lydia. Full-page illustrations in sepia-toned pencils and chalks reflect the mood of the work of historical fiction, showing day-to-day life and the roundup of the Jewish inhabitants of Paris. The story of this Batchelder Honor book is moving and simple enough to be understood. Why, on the back of the dust jacket, the illustrator had the star badge read "Jude" is questionable since the badge in France read "Juif."

SUBJ: Holocaust, Jewish (1939-1945)--France--Paris--Fiction./ Jews--France--Paris--Fiction./ Paris (France)--History--1940-1944--Fiction./ Friendship--Fiction.

Ph-2 2-4/6 $3.99   P   KH269
HOFFMAN, MARY. Four-legged ghosts. Illus. by Laura L. Seeley. Penguin ISBN 0-14-037601-1, 1995. 90p. ill.
Previously published as: THE GHOST MENAGERIE, Orchard, 1992. Gifted with the unusual power to bring back ghosts of animals who have lived in the old house, Cedric the tiny white mouse, pet of the Brodie children, leads them on a merry chase as more and more and larger and larger ghost animals begin to inhabit the house and endanger the children. With the fortuitous arrival of a boarder who is a magician, all is solved in this light fantasy filled with funny situations. Black and white art adds to the book which is easily read because of type size and wide leading between the lines.
SUBJ: Animal ghosts--Fiction./ Ghosts--Fiction./ Magic--Fiction./ Mice--Fiction./ Pets--Fiction./ Asthma--Fiction.

Ph-3 6-A/6 $2.95   P   KH270
HOLLAND, ISABELLE. Journey home. Scholastic ISBN 0-590-43111-0, 1993. 212p.
Available from the National Library Service for the Blind and Physically Handicapped on sound recording cassette RC34842.
Two Irish Catholic orphans go from the slums of New York to Kansas on an orphan train in the late-middle nineteenth century. Maggie, 12, and little sister Annie are taken in by a Kansas farming family and adjust to life on the high plains and meet some of the anti-Irish, anti-Catholic attitudes, then prevalent. People stereotyped as "good", defend them; others, stereotyped as "bad", attack them. Holland presents an orphan train story with insight into attitudes and conditions. Might be used in units on U.S. History and prejudice.
SUBJ: Orphans--Fiction./ Sisters--Fiction./ West (U.S.)--Fiction.

Ph-1 4-6/5 $16.95   L   KH271
HOLLING, HOLLING CLANCY. Paddle-to-the-sea. Houghton Mifflin ISBN 0-395-15082-5, c1941. unp. col. ill., map.
Caldecott Honor Book.
A toy canoe with an Indian figure is launched in Lake Nipigon and finally travels through the Great Lakes, to the St. Lawrence River, and the Atlantic Ocean in an instructive and colorfully illustrated book.
SUBJ: Great Lakes--Fiction.

Ph-2 5-6/5 $16.95   L   KH272
HOLLING, HOLLING CLANCY. Seabird. Houghton Mifflin ISBN 0-395-18230-1, c1948. 58p. col. ill.
Newbery Honor Book.
Available from National Library Service for the Blind and Physically Handicapped in Braille BRA06007 and on sound recording cassette RC10317.
An ivory gull carved by Ezra Brown in 1832 when he was a boy on a whaling ship brings luck to him and his descendants as they journey the seven seas.
SUBJ: Sea stories./ Whaling--Fiction.

Ph-2 5-6/5 $16.95   L   KH273
HOLLING, HOLLING CLANCY. Tree in the trail. Houghton Mifflin ISBN 0-395-18228-X, c1942. unp. col. ill., maps.
Available from National Library Service for the Blind and Physically Handicapped in Braille BRA06221 and on sound recording cassette RC22800.
Many things happen to the cottonwood sapling as the years pass: A landmark to travelers, a peace-medicine tree to the Indians, carved into a yoke for oxen who plod the Santa Fe Trail.
SUBJ: Santa Fe Trail--Fiction./ Trees--Fiction.

CE
Ph-1 6-A/7 $13.95   L   KH274
HOLMAN, FELICE. Slake's limbo. Scribner's ISBN 0-684-13926-X, 1974. 117p.
Videocassette RUNAWAY available from Bonneville. 1/2" VHS videocassette color (58min), $29.95. (WonderWorks.)
Beset by the gangs in his neighborhood, thirteen-year-old Aremis Slake is harassed by fear and misfortune. Desperate, he goes underground--into the subway--where he lives for 121 days. A powerful story of "the dispossessed and the unwanted in our society," saved at the end by the unexpected working together of two lives, which do occasionally touch. This strongly characterized novel, more contemporary now than in the year of its original publication, is bound to be a classic.
SUBJ: Subways--Fiction./ New York (N.Y.)--Fiction./ Fear--Fiction.

VCR
Ph-1 2-6 $15.98   KH275
HOLT, DAVID. Hogaphone and other stories (Videocassette). High Windy Audio ISBN 0-942303-40-7, 1991. 1/2" VHS videocassette color (30min).
Selector's Choice, 19th ed.
Five stories from the repertoire of David Holt are told with music and sound effects. "The Hambone Fan" will prompt students to want to create music on their own--adults will want to join in the fun too.
Contents: The first motorcycle in Black Mountain, North Carolina; The hambone fan; The hogaphone; Barney McCabe; The water tower.
SUBJ: Storytelling./ Humorous stories.

VCR   Ph-3 5-A $29.95   KH276
HOME AT LAST (Videocassette). WonderWorks/dist. by Bonneville Worldwide ISBN 0-7800-0699-2, c1988, 1997. 1/2" VHS videocassette color (58min). (WonderWorks).
Includes teacher's guide.
Includes public performance rights.
Closed-captioned.
For seventy years, orphans from New York City were sent on Orphan Trains to new homes in the Midwest. This is the story of one such boy and his adjustment to farm life in Nebraska. An interesting but rather sentimental look at a little-known part of American history.
SUBJ: Orphans--Fiction./ Adoption--Fiction./ Family life--Fiction./ Farm life--Nebraska--Fiction.

Ph-2 3-5/4 $3.50   P   KH277
HONEYCUTT, NATALIE. All new Jonah Twist. Avon ISBN 0-380-70317-3, 1987. 110p.
Willing to change and become the person his teachers, parents, and world want him to be, Jonah's third grade school year is one of challenge, mainly to himself. Yet, at the heart of this comical small novel, there is a sad recognition: no matter what our society says about nonconformity, it is the purpose of the schools to discourage it and to protect the status quo. Middle-graders who are over-burdened with older, "talented" siblings, fear of other children, and a sensitivity to their own failings, real and imagined, may identify strongly with Jonah.
More adventures of Jonah Twist may be found in THE BEST-LAID PLANS OF JONAH TWIST (ISBN 0-02-744850-9, 1988); and in JULIET FISHER AND THE FOOLPROOF PLAN (ISBN 0-02-744845-2, 1992). Juliet's best efforts to reform priggish Lydia Jane are failing until Jonah and his friend Granville Jones become involved.
SUBJ: Schools--Fiction./ Friendship--Fiction.

Ph-2 6-A/6 $17.99   L   KH278
HONEYCUTT, NATALIE. Twilight in Grace Falls. Orchard ISBN 0-531-33007-9, 1997. 181p.
"Richard Jackson book."
Centering on eleven-year-old Dasie Jenson's family and neighbors, all of whom are in some way connected with the woods or the lumber mill, the novel portrays the family in the good times and in the days when the mill closes. Characters seem very real: some, like Dasie's older brother, escape to the armed services because they know there is no future in the woods; some, like cousin Warren, want only to fell timber. Tragedy eventually ensues--possibly Warren as a suicide--but the Jensons do change and move after a lifetime in Grace Falls. Although Dasie seems too philosophical and wise for her years, the story of a lumber town rings true. Like Vicki Grove's GOOD-BYE, MY WISHING STAR, which tells of a family forced to leave its farm, Honeycutt's novel is as modern as today--and is sadly holding.
SUBJ: Lumbermen--Fiction./ Lumber and lumbering--Fiction./ Family life--Fiction./ Death--Fiction./ Grief--Fiction./ Logging--Fiction.

Ph-1 4-6/3 $17.99   L   KH279
HOOKS, WILLIAM H. Freedom's fruit. Illus. by James Ransome. Knopf ISBN 0-679-92438-8; In Canada: Random House, 1996. unp. col. ill.
"Borzoi book."
Based on a "conjure tale" the author heard as a child, the story tells how the slave woman, Mama Marina, casts a spell on the master's grapes to win freedom for her daughter and the man Sheba loves. Ransome's full-page and doublespread illustrations show setting and personality and add to the book that can be used in units on the history of slavery and for multicultural studies. Fine addition for storytelling or reading aloud.
SUBJ: Slavery--Fiction./ Afro-Americans--Fiction./ Magic--Fiction.

Ph-2 5-A/5 $13.00   T   KH280
HOOVER, H. M. Only child. Dutton ISBN 0-525-44865-9, 1992. 122p.
Conceived and born on a space craft, Cody is the sole child in a new world operated by a megacorporation. When he discovers large intelligent insectlike beings who are being exterminated illegally by the settlers, he promises to help them. A fine portrayal of colonialism and commercial imperialism in a future world in which might still makes right. Useful for units on the future or as an analogy to past colonialism.
SUBJ: Science fiction./ Future--Fiction./ Extraterrestrial beings--Fiction.

FICTION

Ph-2 6-A/4 $14.99 T KH281
HOOVER, H. M. Winds of Mars. Dutton ISBN 0-525-45359-8, 1995.
181p.
"When rebel forces strike against her father, the all-powerful
president of Mars, teenager (17) Annalyn finds her comfortable
existence turned upside down and her life threatened from unexpected
sources." (CIP) The fast-paced, if sometimes wordy, action and
almost constant tension created by android and human enemies
should hold science fiction readers. The vision of future society is
chilling but is redeemed by the conduct of Annalyn and others.
SUBJ: Science fiction.

Ph-2 3-5/3 $15.00 T KH282
HOPKINSON, DEBORAH. Birdie's lighthouse. Illus. by Kimberly Bulcken
Root. Atheneum ISBN 0-689-81052-0; In Canada: Distican, 1997. unp.
col. ill.
"Anne Schwartz book."
Told as a series of diary entries of a ten-year-old girl, Birdie, who
lives and works in a lighthouse off the coast of Maine in the 1850s,
the story and art reveal much about the dangers and labors of those
who maintained the often-lonely coastal watches to help guide sailors.
The tall format of the book and Root's pen-and-ink and watercolor
illustrations add dimension to an interesting work. An author's note
adds facts about some women lighthouse keepers. For women's
studies.
SUBJ: Lighthouses--Fiction./ Maine--Fiction./ Diaries--Fiction.

Ph-1 4-6/6 $15.00 T KH283
HORVATH, POLLY. Happy yellow car. Farrar Straus Giroux ISBN
0-374-32845-5; In Canada: HarperCollins, 1994. 151p.
Filled with complex incidents and characters' names that are funny
enough to cause giggles, the novel is humorous--but sad, too. Sixth
grader Betty Grunt, whose family is poverty-stricken during a financial
depression, has been elected the Pork-Fry Queen but doubts that she
can raise the dollar her teacher insists will be needed for flowers.
Meanwhile Gunther Grunt, a loving but feckless father, purchases an
old yellow car with money the hardworking mother has saved for
Betty's college education. The plot consists of Betty's machinations as
she attempts to raise the flower money. Presents a large group of
well-developed characters--all of whom are different--and well-detailed
incidents. For reading aloud.
SUBJ: Family life--Missouri--Fiction./ Depressions--1929--Fiction./
Missouri--Fiction.

Ph-2 5-6/8 $13.95 T KH284
HORVATH, POLLY. Occasional cow. Illus. by Gioia Fiammenghi. Farrar,
Straus & Giroux ISBN 0-374-35559-2; In Canada: HarperCollins, 1989.
132p. ill.
Forced to spend a summer with relatives on an Iowa farm,
sophisticated New Yorker, Imogene, finds that the Mid-west offers
fun, adventures, and a chance at friendship and affection for her
cousins. Although the author's hand is evident in dialogue and
narration, good fun abounds in this wacky novel. The pig talent show
is a sure winner--even if the judging isn't fair.
SUBJ: Iowa--Fiction./ Cousins--Fiction./ Vacations--Fiction.

Ph-1 3-6/5 $13.95 L KH285
HOWE, DEBORAH. Bunnicula: a rabbit-tale mystery. By Deborah and
James Howe. Illus. by Alan Daniel. Atheneum ISBN 0-689-30700-4; In
Canada: Collier Macmillan, 1979. 98p. ill.
Available from National Library Service for the Blind and Physically
Handicapped in Braille BR04392 and on sound recording cassette
RC16703.
Spanish edition available BONICULA (Fondo de Cultura ISBN 968-
16-3770-4, 1992).
A story written by Harold the dog who lives with the Monroe family,
and Chester the cat and the bunny, a newcomer whom the family
names Bunnicula. The discovery by Chester that the bunny is really a
vampire results in a number of funny but unsuccessful efforts by the
animals to communicate this finding to the human beings. A tale with
much of the humor and similar theme to Selden's CRICKET IN TIMES
SQUARE.
James Howe continues the adventures of Harold and Chester in
HOWLIDAY INN (ISBN 0-689-30846-9, 1982, available from
NLSBPH in Braille BR02119); THE CELERY STALKS AT MIDNIGHT
(ISBN 0-689-30987-2, 1983, available from NLSBPH Braille BR05874
and on sound recording cassette RC2119); and RETURN TO
HOWLIDAY INN (ISBN 0-689-31661-5, 1992).
SUBJ: Rabbits--Fiction./ Vampires--Fiction./ Mystery and detective
stories./ Spanish language materials.

Ph-3 6-A/5 $13.95 T KH286
HUDSON, JAN. Sweetgrass. Philomel ISBN 0-399-21721-5; In Canada:
Tree Frog Press, 1989. 159p.
Includes bibliography.
Canadian Library Association Award.
"Living on the western Canadian prairie in the nineteenth century,
Sweetgrass, a fifteen-year-old Blackfoot Indian girl, saves her family
from a smallpox epidemic and proves her maturity to her father."
(CIP). Based on written records of the Blackfoot, the story centers on
Sweetgrass and describes many of the customs and attitudes, and
shows the lives, happy and tragic, of a native Canadian group. It will
be of particular use for study of one tribe and can be enjoyed by a
mature reader.
SUBJ: Siksika Indians--Fiction./ Indians of North America--Canada--
Fiction./ Smallpox--Fiction.

Ph-2 5-A/6 $15.00 T KH287
HUGHES, MONICA. Golden Aquarians. Simon & Schuster ISBN 0-671-
50543-2; In Canada: Distican, 1995. 182p.
Hughes worries, quite rightly, that the territorial acquisition of planets,
asteroids, etc. will lead to the same depredation and degradation that
occurred on earth. Set in 2092, this science fiction novel details the
battle against naked power which threatens to destroy an intellignet
native species. Two young people, one the son of planet Aqua's
chief, fight against the destroying invaders from earth. Technology
versus ethics is at the center of this suspenseful and well described
story. Might spark discussions about the ends of technology as well
as preservation of endangered life forms. For environmental studies.
SUBJ: Fathers and sons--Fiction./ Environmental protection--Fiction./
Extraterrestrial beings--Fiction./ Science fiction.

Ph-1 6-A/6 $3.95 P KH288
HUGHES, MONICA. Invitation to the game. Aladdin ISBN 0-671-
86692-3, 1993. 183p.
Available from the National Library Service for the Blind and
Physically Handicapped on sound recording cassette RC 38939.
In a robotized future, society needs no workers so Lisse and other
graduates of high school are invited to participate in "The Game," a
test of survival in a bleak, deserted wilderness. That experience calls
on the skills of each gamer in an adventure which should hold readers
and cause thought about the future in a mechanized, over-populated
world. It is well characterized and the setting is memorably created.
Paperback jacket art is holding; trade edition is off-putting.
SUBJ: Science fiction.

Ph-1 3-6/3 $4.95 P KH289
HUGHES, TED. Iron giant: a story in five nights. Illus. by Dirk Zimmer.
HarperCollins ISBN 0-06-440214-2, 1988. 58p. ill.
Available from National Library Service for the Blind and Physically
Handicapped on sound recording cassette RC30579.
Creates a new fairy tale fantasy about an enormous iron giant who
first destroys the countryside and then saves earth from a world-
eating dragon in a fight to the finish. Poetically told, there is much
suspense in this fantasy. Great for storytelling.
SUBJ: Fantasy.

Ph-1 4-A/5 $13.95 L KH290
HUGHES, TED. Tales of the early world. Illustrated by Andrew
Davidson. Farrar, Straus & Giroux ISBN 0-374-37377-9, 1991. 122p. ill.
Selectors' Choice, 19th ed.
Available from the National Library Service for the Blind and
Physically Handicapped on sound recording cassette RC 36263.
England's Poet Laureate provides another explanation for God's
creation when it was newly underway. Ten original tales tell why and
how creatures are as they are. In these versions, God was sometimes
surprised by the results of His (yes, It is a male) work. A delightfully
original and humorous book, it may offend literal interpreters of
testament. Perfect for oral and, where needed, for comparative
versions of creation stories.
SUBJ: Creation--Fiction./ Animals--Fiction.

CE Ph-1 5-A/5 $3.50 P KH291
HUNT, IRENE. Across five Aprils. Berkeley ISBN 0-425-10241-6, 1984.
192p.
Newbery Honor book.
Talking book available from SRA/McGraw-Hill 87-507877, 1973,
$16.00.
Available from National Library Service for the Blind and Physically
Handicapped in Braille BRA14637, on sound cassette RC26336, and
as talking book TB00691.
Jethro, who is nine years old when the first April blooms, must run
the southern Illinois farm almost alone during the Civil War. Dangers
on the home front prove as exciting as those in battle. Although
interest level is high, the story is fairly easy reading for upper grades
and adds personal insight to the social studies curriculum.
SUBJ: Illinois--Fiction./ United States--History--Civil War, 1861-1865--
Fiction.

Ph-3 A/7 $10.95 T KH292
HUNT, IRENE. Up a road slowly. Silver Burdett ISBN 0-382-24366-8, 1993. 192p.
Newbery Medal Award.
Available from National Library Service for the Blind and Physically Handicapped in Braille BRA14015, on sound recording cassette RC22915, as talking book TB01620.
After her mother's death, Julie goes to live with her Aunt Cordelia in the country. School teacher Aunt Cordelia is exact about everything. She insists upon calling Julie "Julia." She never permits her to leave dishes unwashed and very rarely does she allow eating in the living room. Yet later when her father's remarriage permits a return home, Julie elects to remain with Aunt Cordelia.
SUBJ: Adolescence--Fiction./ Aunts--Fiction.

Ph-2 A/7 $4.50 P KH293
HUNTER, MOLLIE. Stranger came ashore. HarperCollins ISBN 0-06-440082-4; In Canada: HarperCollins, c1975. 163p.
On the night of a wild storm in the Shetland Islands, a stranger comes to the Henderson's, close to Black Ness. Slowly, Robbie, the youngest, realizes the stranger is not a shipwrecked sailor but the Great Selbie, Master of the Seal Folk. With the help of Garl Corbie, the school teacher and a wizard, he musters all the ancient magic taught him by his grandfather to counteract the evil designs against his sister Janet and send him back to his kingdom under the sea.
SUBJ: Fantasy./ Good and evil--Fiction.

Ph-2 A/7 $3.99 P KH294
HUNTER, MOLLIE. Third eye. Dell ISBN 0-440-98720-2, 1991. 276p.
Available from National Library Service for the Blind and Physically Handicapped on sound recording cassette RC16188.
An engrossing story, told primarily in flashback, of the experiences of Jinty who possessed the "third eye" (extrasensory perception). The secrets behind the village rumors about the "Ballinford Doom" are slowly unravelled by Jinty and by the Earl of Ballinford. The Scottish setting is effectively pictured along with the mounting tension of Jinty's story. Primarily for the special reader.
SUBJ: Scotland--Fiction./ Extrasensory perception--Fiction.

Ph-2 6-A/8 $5.00 P KH295
HUNTER, MOLLIE. Walking stones. Magic Carpet/Harcourt Brace ISBN 0-15-200995-7, 1996. 168p.
Originally published by Harper & Row, 1970.
Three men come into the green Highland Glen to build a great hydroelectric dam. But the Bodach had foretold their coming, and he and young Donald combine their great powers to assure that the dam will not operate until the time is right--when the great stones walk.
SUBJ: Supernatural--Fiction./ Friendship--Fiction./ Scotland--Fiction.

Ph-1 4-6/6 $14.93 L KH296
HURWITZ, JOHANNA. Aldo Applesauce. Illustrated by John Wallner. Morrow ISBN 0-688-32199-2, 1979. 128p. ill.
Available from National Library Service for the Blind and Physically Handicapped on sound recording cassette RC20086.
A tender and humorous story in which Aldo's only friend is a girl who wears a false mustache.
MUCH ADO ABOUT ALDO (Puffin ISBN 0-14-034082-3; In Canada: Penguin, c1978, 1989) finds the 8 year old giving up meat. In ALDO PEANUT BUTTER, illustrated by Diane de Groat, (ISBN 0-688-09751-0, 1990) when the parents are away the Sossi children cope with too many dogs, a nasty neighbor, and other family problems with humor and some success.
Another of the pleasant stories is ALDO ICE CREAM (ISBN 0-688-00374-5, 1981) (also available from the NLSBPH on sound recording cassette RC19704 and Braille BR05175) in which Aldo helps his mother deliver Meals on Wheels, learns about fish, and wins a contest for the dirtiest sneakers.
SUBJ: Vegetarianism--Fiction./ Humorous stories.

Ph-2 4-6/6 $12.93 L KH297
HURWITZ, JOHANNA. Baseball fever. Illus. by Ray Cruz. Morrow ISBN 0-688-00711-2, 1981. 128p. ill.
Available from National Library Service for the Blind and Physically Handicapped on sound recording cassette RC20427.
Nine-year-old Ezra is an ardent baseball fan and can quote statistics and other data at the drop of a hat. His radiologist mother is calm about his single-mindedness but his European born, PhD father cannot comprehend Ezra's fascination with what he perceives as a waste of time. A weekend visit with his older brother at Princeton and a chance encounter with one of his father's colleagues lead Ezra and his father to an effective compromise.
SUBJ: Fathers and sons--Fiction./ Baseball--Fiction.

Ph-1 2-4/4 $13.00 L KH298
HURWITZ, JOHANNA. Class clown. Illus. by Sheila Hamanaka. Morrow ISBN 0-688-06723-9, 1987. 98p. ill.
Selectors' Choice, 17th ed.
Presents the very real story of third-grader Lucas Cott who is extremely smart and also the "class clown" and his attempts to become the "perfect" student. Humorous, human, and amazingly true-to-life, this amusing chapter book will elicit the sympathy and empathy of middle graders. All characters are well developed. An excellent choice for reading aloud.
In CLASS PRESIDENT (ISBN 0-688-09114-8, 1990, also available from NLSBPH on sound recording cassette RC 36364) Lucas and Cricket are vying for the office when a surprise nomination changes the results.
Lucas Cott spends a summer helping the French au pair with his twin brothers, falls into mischief, and is revealed as a pretty nice person in SCHOOL'S OUT (ISBN 0-688-09938-6, 1991); and in SCHOOL SPIRIT (ISBN 0-688-12825-4, 1994), Julio, along with other students, rally the public to prevent the closure of Edison-Armstrong School.
SUBJ: Schools--Fiction./ Behavior--Fiction.

Ph-1 2-4/6 $12.88 L KH299
HURWITZ, JOHANNA. New neighbors for Nora. Illus. by Lillian Hoban. Morrow ISBN 0-688-09948-3, c1979, 1991. 78p. ill.
Six brief stories about irrepressible seven-year-old Nora which recount her experiences with various friends and neighbors in the big city apartment house. Her contacts with the stuck-up Eugene Spencer, two attacks of chicken-pox--a fake and a real one--and learning to blow bubble-gum are some of the episodes in these tales. Similar theme and appeal as stories by Cleary.
SUBJ: Apartment houses--Fiction./ Cities and towns--Fiction./ Brothers and sisters--Fiction./ Friendship--Fiction.

Ph-1 2-4/4 $12.95 T KH300
HURWITZ, JOHANNA. Nora and Mrs. Mind-your-own business. Illus. by Lillian Hoban. Morrow ISBN 0-688-09945-9, c1977, 1991. 79p. ill.
A series of episodes in the life of first grader Nora and little brother Teddy. Teddy gets lost, Mrs. Mind-your-own business comes to baby sit for them, and they transform her into a friend.
SUBJ: Apartment houses--Fiction./ Brothers and sisters--Fiction./ Cities and towns--Fiction./ Friendship--Fiction.

Ph-1 3-5/4 $15.00 L KH301
HURWITZ, JOHANNA. Ozzie on his own. Illus. by Eileen McKeating. Morrow ISBN 0-688-13742-3, 1995. 115p. ill.
Available from the National Library Service for the Blind and Physically Handicapped on sound recording cassette RC 41428.
When his best friend and niece Roz vacations in England, Ozzie must make his own fun and face the serious problem of his father's sudden heart attack. Ozzie makes friends, realistically worries about his father, and finally decides to let his relatives in England know about the heart attack. As usual, Hurwitz's characters are recognizable people which helps readers identify with them and their situations-- gentle realistic fiction for middle graders.
SUBJ: Death--Fiction./ Fathers and sons--Fiction./ Family life--Fiction.

Ph-2 3-5/5 $13.00 L KH302
HURWITZ, JOHANNA. Roz and Ozzie. Illus. by Eileen McKeating. Morrow ISBN 0-688-10945-4, 1992. 114p. ill.
Available from the National Library Service for the Blind and Physically Handicapped on sound recording cassette RC 38152.
Uncle Ozzie, six, is a pest to his eight-year-old niece Roz as she tries to adjust to a new school where he follows her everywhere and continually annoys her. Eventually, after some mishaps, he learns to be more careful, and he and Roz become friends. A light, easy-to-read, and nicely characterized book which will be enjoyed by established early readers.
SUBJ: Uncles--Fiction./ Family life--Fiction.

Ph-1 2-4/4 $16.00 T KH303
HURWITZ, JOHANNA. Russell Sprouts. Illus. by Lillian Hoban. Morrow ISBN 0-688-07165-1, 1987. 68p. ill.
Russell is now six and determined to be a successful first-grader. Although there are some rough spots on the road, Russell does have his triumphs as he grows a plant, receives a report card, and learns the small fine distinctions of growing up in a usual school situation and a warm and loving family. Excellent choice for reading aloud to second and third graders and a pleasurable reading experience for those just entering chapter books.
RUSSELL AND ELISA (ISBN 0-688-08792-2, 1989) features six more typical family happenstances, this time adding in three-year-old Elisa as an important character. In E IS FOR ELISA (ISBN 0-688-10440-1, 1991, available from the NLSBPH on sound recording cassette RC 36486) Russell's small sister now becomes a growing, learning major character. In MAKE ROOM FOR ELISA (ISBN 0-688-0-688-12404-6)

Elisa, at five, takes center stage in a series of episodes.
When new baby Marshall changes five-year-old Elisa's position in the family, she adjusts in several warm, humorous episodes in ELISA IN THE MIDDLE (ISBN 0-688-14050-5, 1995).
SUBJ: Growth--Fiction./ Schools--Fiction.

Ph-1 2-4/4 $12.95 T KH304
HURWITZ, JOHANNA. Superduper Teddy. Illus. by Lillian Hoban. Morrow ISBN 0-688-09094-X, c1980, 1990. 80p. ill.
Five-year-old, very real, Teddy is not like his big 7-year-old sister Nora. She is outgoing and he is shy. His superman cape helps him feel "bigger and stronger and smarter than Nora" (p.13), but after he attends his first birthday party, cat sits for his neighbor, and finds an acceptable family pet, he has the courage to invite his class to his apartment and contributes his beloved cape to the class costume box.
SUBJ: Brothers and sisters--Fiction./ City and town life--Fiction./ Apartment houses--Fiction.

Ph-3 3-5/4 $13.00 L KH305
HURWITZ, JOHANNA. Teacher's pet. Illus. by Sheila Hamanaka. Morrow ISBN 0-688-07506-1, 1988. 116p. ill.
Tells the story of Cricket Kaufman, now in fourth grade, and her self-centered expectation of being "teacher's pet" as she has been throughout her school career. Humorous, with well developed characterizations, Cricket learns there is more to life than thinking she is best, particularly when friendship becomes an important element. A prime middle-grade novel with a finely characterized teacher.
SUBJ: Schools--Fiction./ Teachers--Fiction./ Friendship--Fiction.

Ph-2 4-6/6 $4.95 P KH306
HUTCHINS, H. J. Anastasia Morningstar and the crystal butterfly. Rev. ed. Illus. by Barry Trower. Annick/Firefly ISBN 0-920236-95-2; In Canada: Annick/Firefly, 1984. 92p. ill. (Annick young novels).
Sarah and Ben observe the clerk at the corner grocery store turn a not-so-nice boy into a frog. They become friendly with Anastasia, the woman who appears ordinary, but possesses magic. Following their gentle adventures should please readers of fantasy.
SUBJ: Magic--Fiction./ Science projects--Fiction./ Fantasy.

Ph-2 3-5/6 $6.95 P OD KH307
HUTCHINS, H. J. Cat of Artimus Pride. By Hazel Hutchins. Illus. by Ruth Ohi. Annick/dist. by Firefly ISBN 1-55037-199-1; In Canada: Annick/dist. by Firefly, 1991. 95p. ill. (Annick young novels).
Cortez is a 100 year-old-cat who talks to Claire, eleven, and leads her and her friends to find the 100 plus year-old diary of one of the cat's masters. The diary clears the name of diarist Artimus Pride and reveals the origins of the small Canadian town. Character and action meld well into a pleasant bit of historical mystery in a contemporary setting.
SUBJ: Cats--Fiction./ Frontier and pioneer life--Canada--Fiction.

Ph-1 4-6/5 $14.95 L KH308
HUTCHINS, H. J. Prince of Tarn. By Hazel Hutchins. Illus. by Ruth Ohi. Annick Press/dist. by Firefly ISBN 1-55037-439-7; In Canada: Annick Press/dist. by Firefly, 1997. 144p. ill., map. (Annick young novels).
The entirely obnoxious Prince of Tarn, a character in an unpublished book written by Fred's deceased mother, is banished from his kingdom by a wizard and takes up life with Fred, his father, and his friend. The Prince is accustomed to having his every order obeyed, and Fred and Rebecca try to cope with his ways. Sometimes results are humorous; sometimes, not. The fantasy is solved in a magical and dangerous way, and the way the children deal with the Prince should amuse and hold readers. Try reading aloud to fantasy buffs. Black and white art is stiff.
SUBJ: Fantasy./ Princes--Fiction.

Ph-2 3-5/4 $16.95 L KH309
HUTCHINS, H. J. Tess. Illus. by Ruth Ohi. Annick/dist. by Firefly ISBN 1-55037-395-1; In Canada: Annick/dist. by Firefly, 1995. unp. col. ill.
In the Canadian West in the 1930s, young Tess and her brother, children of immigrants, must collect cow patties to heat their house during the bitter winter. Ashamed to be seen gathering the fuel, they avoid a neighbor who seems unfriendly until Tess saves his dog from coyotes which leads to understanding between the man and the child. Readers of Wilder's "Little House" series and Maclachlan's SARAH, PLAIN AND TALL will recognize situations similar to pioneer life on the Great Plains of the United States, adding a new dimension to their knowledge of the hardships of life in hard times. Illustrations, often full page, are rendered in pale watercolors. Historical fiction good for units on pioneer life and for units which compare Canadian and United States development.
SUBJ: Frontier and pioneer life--Canada--Fiction.

Ph-2 4-6/6 $4.95 P KH310
HUTCHINS, H. J. Three and many wishes of Jason Reid. Illus. by John Richmond. Annick/dist. by Firefly ISBN 0-920236-61-8; In Canada: Annick/dist. by Firefly, 1988. 79p. ill.
Available from the National Library Service for the Blind and Physically Handicapped on sound recording cassette RC 35441.
Who has not wished that the third wish would grant more wishes? Jason manages to come to such an arrangement with Quicksilver, the elf he has encountered. He learns the rules of wishing in this book that has humorous undertones, but which treats the theme of wishes quite seriously. Good for reading aloud to middle graders.
SUBJ: Wishes--Fiction./ Humorous stories.

Ph-2 5-A/4 $14.95 L KH311
HUTCHINS, H. J. Within a painted past. Illus. by Ruth Ohi. Annick Press/dist. by Firefly ISBN 1-55037-369-2; In Canada: Annick Press/dist. by Firefly, 1994. 160p. ill. (Annick young novels).
While visiting with her aunt and uncle near Banff in the Canadian Rockies, Allison, twelve, steps through a painting in her room and is magically transported to the cabin of a miner in 1898. There she meets Lily, also twelve. During several journeys through different seasonal paintings, she helps Lily and begins to learn about her and her life. This time fantasy is set in the interesting historical reality of frontier Canada. The explanation of her uncle as possibly having two lives is somewhat confusing, but the fast-paced story will hold a better reader. For a book in which art is so important, it is too bad the illustrations seem so off-putting.
SUBJ: Fantasy./ Canada--Fiction.

Ph-1 4-6/5 $19.95 L KH312
HYATT, PATRICIA RUSCH. Coast to coast with Alice. Carolrhoda ISBN 0-87614-789-9, 1995. 72p. ill., map.
Includes bibliography.
The story, based on a true cross-country (United States) automobile trip in 1909, should put an end to the shibboleth, "Women drivers, hmmph,....." Illustrated with period photos and anonymous cartoon drawings, the adventures of four women, with driver Alice Ramsey at the helm of the Maxwell, are taken from the diary of passenger sixteen-year-old Minna Jahns. Beset by broken axles, punctured tires, mud, dust, rain, storms, a murder, washed out bridges, bedbugs, and much more, the 59 day transcontinental trip between New York City and San Francisco gives a lively idea of the nation as it was then at the beginning of "automobiling." Historical fiction with first class writing depicts strong female protagonists and is suitable for women's studies. Includes a bibliography and an afterword about the participants post 1909.
SUBJ: Jahns, Hermine--Fiction./ Ramsey, Alice--Fiction./ Automobile travel--Fiction./ Sex role--Fiction./ Diaries--Fiction.

Ph-2 4-6/6 $13.95 T KH313
HYPPOLITE, JOANNE. Seth and Samona. Illus. by Colin Bootman. Delacorte ISBN 0-385-32093-0; In Canada: Bantam Doubleday Dell, 1995. 121p. ill.
"A Haitian American boy and an African American girl deal with the fun and problems of friendship and family life." (CIP) Samona is entirely her own person--lively, bright, concerned. Seth tends towards caution and is embarrassed at Samona's dress and daring actions. The warmth of family and community life is everywhere apparent in this sometimes humorous, always human, and loving story. Fine choice for reading aloud. Highly recommended. For multicultural studies.
SUBJ: Haitian Americans--Fiction./ Friendship--Fiction./ Family life--Fiction./ Afro-Americans--Fiction.

Ph-1 6-A/9 $16.95 L KH314
IRVING, WASHINGTON. Legend of Sleepy Hollow. Illus. by Arthur Rackham. Morrow ISBN 0-688-05276-2, c1928, 1990. 105. col. ill.
Classic Rackham illustrations in a facsimile of the 1928 edition of Irving's early U.S. folkloric tale.
SUBJ: New York (State)--Fiction./ Folklore--United States./ United States--Folklore.

Ph-1 4-A/9 $15.00 L KH315
IRVING, WASHINGTON. Rip Van Winkle. Illus. by N. C. Wyeth. Morrow ISBN 0-688-07459-6, 1987. 94p. col. ill. (Books of wonder).
Available from National Library Service for the Blind and Physically Handicapped in Braille BRA09660 and sound recording cassette RC16731.
Presents a facsimile of the 1921 edition of the N.C. Wyeth illustrations and clear typeface and wide leading. Where new copies are needed, this would be the edition of choice. The story, itself, is best read aloud to groups since Irving's style is not meant for children.
SUBJ: Folklore--United States./ United States--Folklore./ New York (State)--Fiction.

TB Ph-2 5-6 $20.95   OD KH316
IRVING, WASHINGTON. Rip Van Winkle; and, The Legend of Sleepy Hollow (Talking book). Narrated by John McDonald. Audio Book Contractors, 1986. 1 sound cassette.
"Rip Van Winkle" is the story of a man, who, in order to escape work and the sharp tongue of his wife, strolled into the Catskill Mountains, where he joined some wee fellows in drink, fell asleep, and slept for twenty years; paired with THE LEGEND OF SLEEPY HOLLOW, the legendary tale of the schoolmaster, Ichabod Crane and his encounter with the headless horseman.
Contents: Rip Van Winkle (90min); Legend of Sleepy Hollow (60min).
SUBJ: New York (State)--Fiction./ Short stories./ Folklore--United States./ United States--Folklore.

Ph-2 4-6/5 $13.99   T   KH317
JACKSON, ALISON. Blowing bubbles with the enemy. Dutton ISBN 0-525-45056-4, 1993. 165p.
Super basketball player, Bobby, a sixth-grade female, tries out for the boys' basketball team, but she is cheated out of a spot by the egregiously sexist male coach. When she joins the girls' team, they prove to be a strong team after hard practice and challenge the boys. The description of the game is fast, and Bobby's problems about the boys not defending her during the tryout and her worries about a boy she likes all are a part of an enjoyable story. Some of the repetitive references to bubble gum could have been edited.
SUBJ: Basketball--Fiction./ Sex role--Fiction./ Schools--Fiction.

Ph-1 3-5/4 $14.99   L   KH318
JACKSON, ISAAC. Somebody's new pajamas. Illus. by David Soman. Dial ISBN 0-8037-1570-6, 1996. unp. col. ill.
Available from the National Library Service for the Blind and Physically Handicapped on sound recording cassette RC 43110.
Jerome's family does not live in the luxury that Robert's does, although both families are loving and supportive. What makes the story unusual is the interaction of the two boys from different economic backgrounds when they stay at each others' homes for a sleep-over. When Robert wears pajamas to bed, Jerome wants a pair and finally receives them as a gift--but he continues to sleep in clean underwear, most of the time. A pair of pj's showing the economic status of the two families is a simple, but telling, reality in this warm book suitable for reading aloud. For multicultural studies.
SUBJ: Pajamas--Fiction./ Sleepovers--Fiction./ Family life--Fiction./ Friendship--Fiction./ Afro-Americans--Fiction.

Ph-2 5-A/6 $15.95   T   KH319
JACOBS, PAUL SAMUEL. James Printer: a novel of rebellion. Scholastic ISBN 0-590-16381-7; In Canada: Scholastic, 1997. 220p.
Set in colonial Massachusetts during the time of King Philip's War, the story tells of James Printer, a Nipmuck Indian who adopted English ways and became an apprentice printer. The attitude of many New Englanders to the original inhabitants is clearly shown as James is attacked and finally flees into Metacom's (King Philip's) camp to help avenge the deaths of other Native Americans and protect himself from the constant threat of being murdered by Indian-hating colonists. Although the pace is sometimes slow, the historical fiction summons attitudes, actions, and settings well. Good for units on Colonial American history or multicultural studies.
SUBJ: King Philip's War, 1675-1676--Fiction./ Printer, James--Fiction./ Indians of North America--Massachusetts--Fiction./ Massachusetts--History--Colonial period, ca. 1600-1775--Fiction./ Printers--Fiction.

Ph-1 5-A/6 $16.95   T   KH320
JACQUES, BRIAN. Redwall. Illus. by Gary Chalk. Philomel ISBN 0-399-21424-0, 1986. 351p. ill.
The animals of Redwall Abbey forced to do battle with the evil rat Cluny and his band of thugs, find a most unexpected hero in young Matthias. Exact language use yields strong, active images and individual characterizations. The smoothly flowing story is tension filled and will be superb for oral reading.
SUBJ: Fantasy./ Good and evil--Fiction./ Mice--Fiction.

Ph-2 2-3/2 $14.95   T   KH321
JAM, TEDDY. Charlotte stories. Illus. by Harvey Chan. Groundwood/dist. by Publisher's Group West ISBN 0-88899-210-6; In Canada: Groundwood/Douglas & McIntype, 1994. 48p. col. ill.
In a humorous transitional reader, seven-year-old Charlotte and her friends, including a new boy who is at first regarded suspiciously, are featured in three stories that illuminate the thinking processes and conduct of young children: pleasant, unpleasant, selfish, generous. The plots are somewhat akin to Nabb's Josie Smith stories and the art in colored pencil and watercolors is well characterized and lively.
SUBJ: Friendship--Fiction./ Humorous stories.

Ph-2 6-A/6 $13.95   L   KH322
JAMES, MARY. Frankenlouse. Scholastic ISBN 0-590-46528-7; In Canada: Scholastic, 1994. 184p.
Nick, fourteen, is forced to live with his father, the strict head of a military academy. He and several other cadets revolt against the militaristic regimen. Nick wants to become a cartoonist and invents a monster cartoon character, "Frankenlouse" who resembles his father. The stories of the other cadets and their not-very-happy home lives are interwoven as Nick begins to assert himself more and be his own person, not his father's. Interestingly developed characters and situations will hold readers especially those who are questioning the status quo.
SUBJ: Schools--Fiction./ Cartoons and comics--Fiction./ Fathers and sons--Fiction.

Ph-1 6-A/6 $3.50   P   KH323
JAMES, MARY. Shoebag. Scholastic ISBN 0-590-43030-0, 1992. 134p.
A cockroach is horrified to find himself transformed (a la Kafka's METAMORPHOSIS with a twist) into a boy. Told very tongue-in-cheek with each character stereotyped larger than life. A prime choice for reading aloud so the reader can explain some of the in-jokes, e.g., the school hero is named Gregor Samsa and others have less literary character names.
SUBJ: Cockroaches--Fiction./ Fantasy./ Humorous stories.

Ph-1 6-A/6 $15.95   T   KH324
JAMES, MARY. Shoebag returns. Scholastic ISBN 0-590-48711-6; In Canada: Scholastic, 1996. 144p.
Sequel to SHOEBAG, Scholastic, 1990.
Shoebag returns as a human boy--Stuart Bagg at the wretched Miss Rattray's School fo Girls, but he's a boy. He destroys the snobs and escapes to Tennessee (as a roach), but readers will see his likes again. Humorous and pointed.
SUBJ: Cockroaches--Fiction./ Schools--Fiction.

Ph-1 3-6/7 $4.95   P   KH325
JANSSON, TOVE. Finn Family Moomintroll. Farrar, Straus & Giroux ISBN 0-374-42307-5; In Canada:: HarperCollins, c1948, 1990. 170p. ill.
Published earlier as: THE HAPPY MOOMINS, 1952.
Large type available from Windrush (ISBN 1-850-89976-2, 1989).
The Hobgoblin's hat, found by Moomintroll and his friends Snufkin and Sniff, "casts a spell on the Valley of the Moomin, and...before long they...all see strange things." (p.20) The delightful fantasy adventures of the Finnish Moomins are infused with a magic just right for reading aloud in grades 2-3 as well as pleasurable reading by older youngsters.
Additional stories include COMET IN MOOMINLAND (ISBN 0-374-31526-4, c1946, 1990); MOOMINSUMMER MADNESS (ISBN 0-374-35039-6, c1954, 1991); MOOMINLAND MIDWINTER (ISBN 0-374-35041-8, c1958, 1992); MOOMINPAPPA AT SEA (ISBN 0-374-35044-2, 1993); MOOMINPAPPA'S MEMOIRS (ISBN 0-374-35045-0, 1994); and TALES FROM MOOMINVALLEY (ISBN 0-374-37379-5, c1964, 1995).
Available from the National Library Service for the Blind and Physically Handicapped is MOOMINLAND MIDWINTER on sound recording cassette RC 41421, MOOMINPAPPA'S MEMOIRS on sound recording cassette RC 41676, MOOMINPAPPA AT SEA on sound recording cassette RC 41674, and COMET IN MOOMINLAND on sound recording cassette RC 41675.
SUBJ: Fantasy.

Ph-1 5-A/6 $14.89   L   KH326
JARRELL, RANDALL. Animal family. Decorations by Maurice Sendak. HarperCollins ISBN 0-06-205089-3; In Canada: HarperCollins, 1995. 179p. ill.
Newbery Honor book.
Available from National Library Service for the Blind and Physically Handicapped in Braille BR01670, on sound recording cassette RC25834 and talking book TB01559.
"Say what you like, but such things do happen--" a family with a hunter, a mermaid, a bear, a lynx and a boy live in a log house near the sea. Lyrical yet restrained in style, the fantasy projects an aura of mystery that will appeal most to the sensitive reader.
SUBJ: Fantasy.

Ph-1 4-A/6 $11.89   L   KH327
JARRELL, RANDALL. Bat-poet. Illus. by Maurice Sendak. HarperCollins ISBN 0-06-205085-0; In Canada: HarperCollins, 1996. 43p. ill.
Originally published by Macmillan, 1964.
"Michael di Capua books."
A young bat who becomes aware of the beauty of sunshine and daytime life is inspired to create poetry about his new experiences. Unappreciated by his fellow-bats and a condescending mockingbird, the timid poet finds encouragement from a friendly chipmunk until the time comes for both animals to hibernate. This deceptively simple tale

of the loneliness and struggle of creativity and the haunting need for communication will be appreciated as an appropriate introduction to poetry and creative writing activities. For reading aloud.
SUBJ: Bats--Fiction./ Creative writing--Fiction./ Poets--Fiction./ Animals--Fiction.

Ph-1 3-5/6 $14.89 L KH328
JOHNSTON, TONY. Ghost of Nicholas Greebe. Illus. by S. D. Schindler. Dial ISBN 0-8037-1649-4; In Canada: McClelland & Stewart, 1996. unp. col. ill.
After Nicholas Greebe is buried in a shallow grave because he died during a high winter in colonial Massachusetts, a dog digs up one of his bones. By happenstance it travels the globe, but eventually returns as a scrimshaw and is reinterred by the dog. This tall tale is magnificently and humorously illustrated in suitable darkly colored inks and theatrically illuminates people, the dog, and settings on land and sea. The ghost is sufficiently scary, albeit humorous, in a rollicking, fast moving tale meant for the telling or reading aloud. Ghostly fun.
SUBJ: Ghosts--Fiction./ Bones--Fiction./ Dogs--Fiction.

Ph-2 A/6 $12.00 T KH329
JONES, DIANA WYNNE. Archer's goon. Greenwillow ISBN 0-688-02582-X, 1984. 241p.
Opening the door to a "goon" who moves into their house starts thirteen-year-old Howard Sykes on the road to discovering some amazing facts about his father and the seven wizards who run the town. Although the premise of this book would suffer in the hands of a lesser storyteller, this is a believable, suspenseful, fun mystery which should satisfy fantasy readers.
SUBJ: Magicians--Fiction./ Fantasy.

Ph-1 6-A/6 $13.95 L KH330
JONES, DIANA WYNNE. Aunt Maria. Greenwillow ISBN 0-688-10611-0, 1991. 214p.
Great-aunt Maria is another of Diana Wynne Jones' impossibly fascinating characters. She oozes power and the terror that accompanies it in a novel in which the entire male population of Cranbury appears to be zombies. Visiting Mig and Chris go through humorous and harrowing adventures to conquer the ancient evil woman and her vicious magic in a complex story which will hold the better reader.
SUBJ: Great-aunts--Fiction./ Magic--Fiction.

Ph-2 6-A/6 $15.00 T KH331
JONES, DIANA WYNNE. Cart and cwidder. Greenwillow ISBN 0-688-13360-6, c1977, 1995. 214p., map. (Dalemark quartet).
Two kingdoms exist isolated yet hostile to each other: the North believes in freedom; the South in tyranny. A gaudy horse-drawn cart driven by Moril's father moves from one kingdom to another, and the family gives performances, covering up a spy operation. In the end, the lute-like cwidder proves to have magical powers and helps Moril save the day. For more advanced readers of fantasy.
The saga of the mythical kingdom of Dalemark continues in DROWNED AMMET (ISBN 0-688-13361-4, c1978, 1995); SPELLCOATS (ISBN 0-688-13362-2, c1979, 1995); and CROWN OF DALEMARK (ISBN 0-688-13363-0, 1995).
SUBJ: Fantasy.

Ph-1 6-A/7 $12.95 L KH332
JONES, DIANA WYNNE. Castle in the air. Greenwillow ISBN 0-688-09686-7, 1991. 199p.
Selectors' Choice, 19th ed.
Howl is back and all the trouble and magic gone awry that Howl can create reside in the high humor from the magnificent imagination of Diana Wynne Jones. Abdullah, the protagonist, is a poor young carpet merchant who becomes involved with a flying carpet and the stuff dreams--and nightmares--are made of, in this series of adventures peopled with memorable genies, meanies, dogs, cats, princesses, djinns, confusion, and witty fantasy. Uses contemporay idioms perfectly to create Lloyd Alexander-like humor and diction in a complex, fast moving fantasy full of wonder and strong writing.
SUBJ: Fantasy.

Ph-1 A/7 $13.00 L KH333
JONES, DIANA WYNNE. Howl's moving castle. Greenwillow ISBN 0-688-06233-4, 1986. 212p.
Cast under a spell by the Witch of Waste and transformed into an ugly old woman, Sophie, the exploited eldest daughter, sets off to seek her fortune and becomes the housekeeper for the Wizard of Howl in his lopsided whirling castle while she tries to break out of the spell. Complex but lucid and developed with great humor, this upbeat fantasy replete with word play should challenge advanced readers of the genre.
SUBJ: Fantasy.

Ph-1 5-A/6 $14.00 L KH334
JONES, DIANA WYNNE. Stopping for a spell: three fantasies. Illus by Jos. A. Smith. Greenwillow ISBN 0-688-11367-2, 1993. 148p. ill.
Originally published as individual titles, three distinct stories, all fantastical, present characters who combine humor and horror. "Chair Person" portrays a chair that becomes alive and takes over everything. "Four Grannies" depicts four grannies who take care of the children while Erg solves the problem with his Invention. "Who Got Rid of Angus Flint?" describes the man who comes to visit and stays and stays and stays until the children rid themselves of the pesty guest. Prime for a read-aloud, it is written with Jones' usual wit and skill.
SUBJ: Humorous stories./ Short stories./ Magic--Fiction.

Ph-1 6-A/6 $14.00 L KH335
JONES, DIANA WYNNE. Witch week. New ed. Greenwillow ISBN 0-688-01534-4, c1982, 1993. 213p.
Sequel to: CHARMED LIFE, LIVES OF CHRISTOPHER CHANT, and THE MAGICIANS OF CAPRONA.
An anonymous note is sent to the teacher of class 6B saying "Someone in this class is a witch." The school is torn with all sorts of magic tricks and disasters. Only when the Chrestomanci, the enchanter, save them are the school children calmed down with the recognition that they won't be burned at the stake.
SUBJ: Witchcraft--Fiction./ Boarding schools--Fiction./ Schools--Fiction./ England--Fiction.

Ph-1 3-5/4 $13.95 L KH336
JORDAN, MARYKATE. Losing Uncle Tim. Illus. by Judith Friedman. Whitman ISBN 0-8075-4756-5; In Canada: General, 1989. unp. col. ill.
Sensitively tells of the warm relationship between young Daniel and Tim, his uncle who has AIDS. Daniel is unsure about the disease and death, but his family and Tim help him come to terms with his loss and the fact that AIDS cannot be transmitted when he visits his uncle. A warmly illustrated book, it is a good choice for oral presentation in the lower grades and within the reach of middle grade independent readers.
SUBJ: AIDS (Disease)--Fiction./ Death--Fiction./ Uncles--Fiction.

Ph-1 5-A/5 $14.95 T KH337
JOYCE, WILLIAM. Buddy: based on the true story of Gertrude Lintz. HarperCollins ISBN 0-06-027660-6; In Canada: HarperCollins, 1997. 48p. ill.
"Laura Geringer book."
Few author-illustrators succeed in the development of ridiculous nonsense better than Joyce. His almost-realistic art, in sepias, presents amusing characters, e.g., an eyeglass wearing dachshund and a formally dressed gorilla, Buddy. The adventures of the remarkable Gertrude Lintz, who believes animals should not be caged, and her extraordinary household, animal and human, can almost be considered a fantasy. Set in the 1930s, time, character, setting, and nonsense are presented to readers who would do well to suspend disbelief and enjoy the fun--whether it is, indeed, a true story or a figment of Joyce's delightful imagination and art.
SUBJ: Lintz, Gertrude--Fiction./ Gorilla--Fiction./ Animals--Treatment--Fiction.

Ph-1 5-6/7 $7.99 P KH338
JUKES, MAVIS. Like Jake and me. Illus. by Lloyd Bloom. Knopf ISBN 0-394-89263-1, 1984. unp. col. ill.
Newbery Honor.
Read-along kit available from American School Publishers 511546-8, 1986. 1 sound cassette (15min), 1 hardcover book, $25.00.
Available from National Library Service for the Blind and Physically Handicapped on sound recording cassette RC23104.
Exhibiting his fright at having a wolf spider in his clothing to his insecure stepson Alex, Jake, a cowboy, finds that the gap between stepfather and stepson begins to close. Although the reading is more difficult than the readability estimate indicates because of cross-purposes dialogue, the story lends itself well to read-aloud situations.
SUBJ: Stepfathers--Fiction./ Spiders--Fiction.

CE
Ph-1 4-6/6 $19.95 T KH339
JUSTER, NORTON. Phantom tollbooth. Special 35th anniversary ed. Illustrated by Jules Feiffer. With an appreciation by Maurice Sendak. Random House ISBN 0-394-81500-9; In Canada: Random House, 1996. 256p. ill.
Originally published by Epstein & Carroll Associates, Inc., 1961 and subsequently published by Random House, Inc., 1964.
Available from National Library Service for the Blind and Physically Handicapped in Braille BR03041, on sound recording cassette RC23208, and as talking book TB00476.
Milo is both bored and lazy until he receives a tollbooth as a gift that admits him to a land where many adventures take place--words are sold in the market place and a spelling bee buzzes around the

castle in the air. This favorite fantasy, filled with wordplay, is fun for reading aloud, especially in language arts classes.
SUBJ: Fantasy.

Ph-1 4-A/3 $15.00 L KH340

KALMAN, MAIRA. Ooh-la-la (Max in love). Viking Penguin ISBN 0-670-84163-3; In Canada: Penguin, 1991. unp col illus.

A Dadaist encounter awaits the participant in Kalman's extraordinary art and continuous humor--every single stroke and word of which deserves constant reader attention, time after time, to experience every single delightful nuance in the Parisian travels of Max, "the millionaire poet dog." Although presented as a picture book, it will take a mature reader to see beyond the complex openings, artistic jokes, and constant word play. The person with a sense of humor and a sense of the ridiculous will relish Kalman's work--and one hopes that French language and fine art classes will also be exposed to this grand tour.
SUBJ: Dogs--Fiction./ Paris (France)--Fiction.

Ph-1 5-A/4 $16.00 T KH341

KARR, KATHLEEN. Cave. Farrar Straus Giroux ISBN 0-374-31230-3; In Canada: HarperCollins, 1994. 165p.

Set in South Dakota during a three-year drought in the Great Depression of the 1930s, the story of Christine and her farming family during the hard times is totally realistic. When she finds a cave with an underground river, she must decide if she will keep it as a private place or use the river to irrigate the land her family farms. Historical fiction that presents a well drawn portrait of a family on the edge in a painful period of United States history.
SUBJ: Caves--Fiction./ Droughts--Fiction./ Farm life--South Dakota--Fiction./ South Dakota--Fiction./ Depressions--1929--Fiction.

Ph-1 5-A/Y $16.00 T KH342

KARR, KATHLEEN. Oh, those Harper girls!; or Young and dangerous. Farrar, Straus & Giroux ISBN 0-374-35609-2; In Canada: HarperCollins, 1992. 182p.

Set in West Texas at the turn of the century (1902) and narrated by Lily, youngest of the six Harper girls, this comic novel, cinematic in its action, is a nonstop hoot. The girls resort to lawless acts to save their feckless father's run-down ranch. The girls' holdup of a stagecoach attracts attention from the newspapers and throws the Harpers into a show business tour. Although the book is long, it's a madcap ride all the way and should keep the attention of better readers.
SUBJ: Texas--Fiction./ Frontier and pioneer life--Texas--Fiction./ Girls--Fiction.

Ph-2 /7 $14.95 L KH343

KELLY, ERIC P. Trumpeter of Krakow. New ed. Forward by Louise Seaman Bechtel. Illus. by Janina Domanska. Macmillan ISBN 0-02-750140-X, c1966, 1973. 224p. ill.

Newbery Medal Award.

Available from National Library Service for the Blind and Physically Handicapped on sound recording cassette RC22916 and talking book TB02675.

Exciting mystery story centers on an attack on Krakow in Medieval Poland. Even today the trumpeter sounds a warning, with incomplete tune, to commemorate the boy whose warning was cut short by an arrow.
SUBJ: Poland--Social life and customs--Fiction./ Poland--History--Fiction./ Middle Ages--Fiction.

Ph-1 5-6/7 $3.95 P KH344

KENDALL, CAROL. Gammage Cup. Illus. by Erik Blegvad. Harcourt Brace Jovanovich ISBN 0-15-230575-0, c1959. 221p. ill.

Newbery Honor Book.

Available from National Library Service for the Blind and Physically Handicapped in Braille BRA01613 and on talking book TB01387.

The Minnipins live in isolation and conformity. When their enemies, The Hairless Ones threaten them, they are saved by a few village 'characters' who show initiative and daring.
SUBJ: Fantasy.

Ph-1 3-5/6 $5.99 P KH345

KHALSA, DAYAL KAUR. Tales of a gambling grandma. Clarkson Potter ISBN 0-517-88262-0, 1986. 32p. col. ill.

"Dragonfly book."

Recalling her grandmother's words of advice, her addiction to poker, and her eccentric habits, the narrator recollects the strong influence she had on her life. No stereotypes of senior citizens here--Grandmother is presented as a warm, independent, and original character. Strong and attractive illustrations expand the appeal of this intergenerational story.
SUBJ: Grandmothers--Fiction./ Family life--Fiction.

CE Ph-1 2-5/5 $11.95 L KH346

KING-SMITH, DICK. Babe: the gallant pig. Illus. by Mary Rayner. Harcourt Brace ISBN 0-15-302228-0, 1994. 118p. ill.

Originally published in Great Britain as the SHEEP-PIG.

Selectors' Choice, 18th ed.

Talking book available from HighBridge/dist. by Listening Library W 6264 CX (ISBN 1-56511-174-5, c1986, 1996). 2 sound cassettes (110min), $13.95.

Winning Babe, a piglet, in a weight-guessing contest has unexpected consequences for Farmer and Mrs. Hogget when Babe is adopted by their sheepdog Fly and learns how to be a "sheep-pig." This funny, warm book is filled with easy-to-read dialog and Rayner's sketches complement the text nicely. Delightful for reading aloud or for independent reading.

Babe, the gallant pig's great-great grandson makes a name for himself and becomes a national TV star in ACE, THE VERY IMPORTANT PIG, illustrated by Lynette Hemmant (ISBN 0-679-81931-2, c1990, 1992).
SUBJ: Pigs--Fiction./ Domestic animals--Fiction.

Ph-2 4-6/6 $13.89 L KH347

KING-SMITH, DICK. Cuckoo child. Illus. by Leslie W. Bowman. Hyperion ISBN 1-56282-351-5, 1993. 127p. ill.

Available from the National Library Service for the Blind and Physically Handicapped on sound recording cassette RC 38265.

The day Jack, who loves birds more than anything, saw an ostrich for the first time at Wildlife Park, he knew he had to have one. When the ranger let his class handle some ostrich eggs, Jack kept one. How Jack manages to hatch and raise an ostrich with the help of his geese makes a delightful story for reading aloud which is sure to please animal lovers.
SUBJ: Ostriches--Fiction./ Geese--Fiction./ Farm life--Fiction.

Ph-1 5-A/7 $4.99 P KH348

KING-SMITH, DICK. Harry's Mad. Illus. by Jill Bennet. Knopf ISBN 0-679-88688-5, c1984, 1997. 123p. ill.

Originally published in Great Britain, Victor Gollancz Ltd., 1984.

Published by Crown, 1987.

Large type available from Lythway (ISBN 0-745-11101-7, 1990).

Receiving his inheritance--an African gray parrot--from his Great Uncle George is the beginning of a strange and wonderful friendship for ten-year-old Harry. Mad (short for Madison) is articulate and intelligent, and when he is captured by a burglar, his loss and recovery turn this lively tale into an unexpected adventure. Dialog and a healthy dose of humor make this prime for reading aloud as well as pleasurable for independent reading.
SUBJ: Parrots--Fiction./ Inheritance and succession--Fiction.

Ph-2 2-4/5 $13.95 T KH349

KING-SMITH, DICK. Jenius: the amazing guinea pig. Illus. by Brian Floca. Hyperion ISBN 0-7868-0243-X; In Canada: Little, Brown, 1996. 52p. ill.

Judy, eight, trains her guinea pig to do tricks: sit, play dead, stay, etc. Thus, in Judy's eyes and his, the pet earns the name Jenius, in the child's inimitable spelling, and both preen, perhaps over much, because pride does goeth before the fall. When Judy takes Jenius to school for show-and-tell, he does not perform. The transitional reader is amusing, and first chapter book readers will enjoy the training and adventures of child and beast as seen through the eyes of both. Floca's black and white sketches are suitably charming.
SUBJ: Guinea pigs--Fiction./ Schools--Fiction.

TB Ph-2 4-6 $16.98 KH350

KING-SMITH, DICK. Lady Daisy (Talking book). Read by Nigel Lambert. Listening Library YA 872 ISBN 0-8072-7550-6, 1995. 2 sound cassettes (174min).

ALA notable recording, 1996.

While exploring his grandmother's attic, Ned finds a doll from 1901 who speaks only to him. A multigenerational tale with British history, customs, politics, games, television, and a mystery within the story is bound to hold doll-story readers, as performed by Nigel Lambert.
SUBJ: Dolls--Fiction./ Sex role--Fiction./ England--Fiction.

Ph-2 3-5/3 $17.99 L KH351

KING-SMITH, DICK. Mouse called Wolf. Illus. by Jon Goodell. Crown ISBN 0-517-70974-0, 1997. 98p. ill.

Readers of the imaginative King-Smith will find new pleasures in his readable story about the smallest mouse in Mrs. Mouse's litter, Wolfgang Amadeus Mouse, "Wolf" for short. His family, no doubt related to the Trins of athletic fame, produces a mouse who can sing--and sing beautifully--and who also composes music. He becomes enchanted by the piano playing and singing of the owner of the house, Mrs. Honeybee, and imitates her. Their friendship and her training of small Wolf provide a scherzo romp and a humorous

situation. Black and white illustrations are suitably lively. For reading aloud.
SUBJ: Mice--Fiction./ Music--Fiction.

Ph-2 3-5/2 $13.89 L KH352
KING-SMITH, DICK. Mr. Potter's pet. Illus. by Mark Teague. Hyperion ISBN 0-7868-2146-9; In Canada: Little, Brown, 1996. 63p. ill.
Mr. Potter, a bachelor of regulated habits, changes his life and ways after purchasing an extremely intelligent mynah bird, Everest. The avian friend engages him in full conversations, and all eventually leads to Mr. Potter's marriage. Fun, typical King-Smith who takes animals into another dimension. Black and white illustrations are suitably humorous and characterize all participants well. Try reading aloud, although it is a transitional reader well within the range of first-chapter-book readers.
SUBJ: Pets--Fiction./ Mynahs--Fiction./ Friendship--Fiction.

Ph-2 3-5/7 $13.89 L KH353
KING-SMITH, DICK. School mouse. Illus. by Cynthia Fisher. Hyperion ISBN 0-7868-2029-2, 1995. 124p. ill.
Flora, a member of a mouse family that lives in a school, learns to read; becomes something of a literary critic; and saves her family when bait is set by an exterminator. All the mice, including the escaped white mouse who becomes the remarkable Flora's husband, are nicely developed as characters. Humor and suspense make the book prime as a transitional reader and for reading aloud. Black and white illustrations add to another of King-Smith's well constructed and most enjoyable books.
SUBJ: Mice--Fiction./ Reading--Fiction./ Schools--Fiction./ Family life--Fiction.

Ph-2 2-4/6 $14.95 T KH354
KING-SMITH, DICK. Sophie hits six. Illus. by David Parkins. Candlewick ISBN 1-56402-216-1; In Canada: Douglas & McIntyre, 1993. 128p. ill.
Sophie, almost six, wants to be a farmer when she is older. She hopes to add a dog to her menagerie of cats and a pet rabbit, but her parents don't think "almost six" demonstrates sufficient responsibility. The irrepressible Sophie shows them otherwise in an active character study of a most interesting child, similar to Nabb's JOSIE SMITH.
SUBJ: Pets--Fiction.

Ph-2 3-5/6 $3.99 P KH355
KING-SMITH, DICK. Sophie in the saddle. Illus. by David Parkins. Candlewick ISBN 1-56402-607-8; In Canada: Candlewick c/o Douglas & McIntyre, 1996. 93p. ill.
Now six, Sophie acquires a puppy for her menagerie, meets a Vietnamese pot-bellied pig, and learns to ride a pony. Her slaughter of polysyllabic words continues to amuse--as does she.
SUBJ: Pets--Fiction.

Ph-2 3-4/8 $14.99 T KH356
KING-SMITH, DICK. Sophie's Lucky. Illus. by David Parkins. Candlewick ISBN 1-56402-869-0; In Canada: Candlewick/dist. by Douglas & McIntyre, 1996. 111p. ill.
Sophie, eight, visits her Great-Great-Aunt Al in Scotland and learns more about farms, especially ponies.
SUBJ: Great-aunts--Fiction./ Scotland--Fiction./ Ponies--Fiction.

Ph-2 3-5/5 $3.99 P KH357
KING-SMITH, DICK. Sophie's Tom. Illus. by David Parkins. Candlewick ISBN 1-56402-373-7; In Canada: Candlewick/dist. by Douglas & McIntyre, c1991, 1994. 111p. ill.
Sequel to SOPHIE'S SNAIL, Delacorte, 1988 (OPC).
Five-year-old Sophie, who had decided she would be a "lady farmer" when she grows up, adopts a black cat, names it Tom, and fights to keep it. Of course, it is misnamed and produces kittens--more animals for her to nurture and love. She and her family are very real people--especially when adults seem to raise eyebrows at her speech and actions. King-Smith is never condescending and presents the child as seriously as the child regards herself. She is a delight and should amuse newly established readers. For reading aloud.
SUBJ: Cats--Fiction./ England--Fiction.

CE Ph-1 3-5/6 $15.99 L KH358
KING-SMITH, DICK. Three terrible trins. Illus. by Mark Teague. Crown ISBN 0-517-59829-9, 1994. 105p. ill.
Talking book available from Listening Library YA 890 (ISBN 0-8072-7600-6, 1996). 2 sound cassettes (102min), $16.98. ALA notable recording, 1997.
"Three mice brothers, ignoring the class system separating the four clans of rodents in their farmhouse, befriend a lower class mouse and form a team to fight cats." (CIP) In this upstairs-downstairs tale of the heroic and hilarious doings of the mice, who are magnificently

trained to outwit felines by their oft-widowed mother, the inventive, imaginative, and creative characters (both human and animal), their games, their diction, and their actions will hold and delight readers and listeners. The first-rate story is a prime choice for reading aloud.
SUBJ: Mice--Fiction./ Cats--Fiction.

Ph-2 3-5/8 $15.88 L KH359
KIPLING, RUDYARD. Beginning of the armadillos. Illus. by John A. Rowe. North-South Books ISBN 1-55858-483-8; In Canada: North-South Books/dist. by Vanwell, 1995. unp. col. ill.
"Michael Neugebauer book."
Presents, in a newly illustrated edition, one of the rarely reprinted "Just So" stories, the funny fable of how the tortoise and the hedgehog became the armadillo, replete with Kiplingesque wordplay. Rowe's paintings, in color, tend toward the semiabstract, but all the major players are recognizable. For reading aloud.
SUBJ: Armadillos--Fiction./ Animals--Fiction./ Jungles--Fiction.

Ph-2 3-5/7 $19.99 T KH360
KIPLING, RUDYARD. Complete Just so stories. Illus. by Isabelle Brent. Viking ISBN 0-670-85196-5; In Canada: Penguin, 1993. 157p. col. ill.
"Albion book."
The original 12 JUST SO STORIES and two additional Kipling tales are illustrated with luminous, patterned paintings. For reading aloud.
SUBJ: Animals--Fiction./ Short stories.

VCR Ph-2 2-5 $9.95 KH361
KIPLING, RUDYARD. How the rhinoceros got his skin; and, How the camel got his hump (Videocassette). Read by Jack Nicholson. Music by Bobby McFerrin. Illus. by Tim Raglin. Rabbit Ears H0627 ISBN 0-7192-0011-6, 1987. 1/2" VHS videocassette color (30min). (Storybook classics).
Combines minimal animation, musical sound effects, and slowly paced narration in an effective visual and auditory presentation of two of Kipling's "Just so Stories." Kipling's stories may be best as intended, read aloud, but some youngsters may be enticed by a video introduction. More sophisticated students could compare this medium to print or sound recordings of the stories; or could launch into their own writing of pourquoi stories for language arts or animal studies.
SUBJ: Rhinoceroses--Fiction./ Camels--Fiction./ Animals--Fiction.

KIT Ph-3 3-5 $19.95 KH362
KIPLING, RUDYARD. How the rhinoceros got his skin (Kit). Illus. by Tim Raglin. Read by Jack Nicholson. Music by Bobby McFerrin. Rabbit Ears ISBN 0-88708-083-9; In Canada: Vanwell, 1988. 1 hardback book, 1 sound cassette (10min).
Kipling's classic pourquoi story explains how the rhinoceros developed a bad temper and baggy, wrinkly skin. Musical score augments the text. Story repeats on both sides of the cassette, so children can listen again by flipping the tape.
SUBJ: Rhinoceroses--Fiction.

Ph-2 6-A/7 $20.00 L KH363
KIPLING, RUDYARD. Jungle book: the Mowgli stories. Afterword by Peter Glassman. Illus. by Jerry Pinkney. Books of Wonder/Morrow ISBN 0-688-09979-3, 1995. 258p. col. ill.
Illustrated with 17 of Pinkney's lush, full-color watercolors, the centenary edition of the Mowgli stories drawn from the two JUNGLE BOOKS (and "Rikki-Tikki-Tavi") makes a good replacement edition. Mowgli, the boy raised by wolves in the jungles of India, is often best used for reading aloud.
SUBJ: Jungles--Fiction./ Animals--Fiction./ India--Fiction./ Short stories.

TB Ph-1 4-6 $11.00 OD KH364
KIPLING, RUDYARD. Rikki-Tikki-Tavi and Wee Willie Winkie (Talking book). HarperAudio ISBN 0-694-50680-X, n.d. 1 sound cassette.
Two favorite stories from the JUNGLE BOOKS are read expressively by Anthony Quayle.
SUBJ: Animals--Fiction./ India--Fiction.

Ph-1 6-A/7 $15.95 T KH365
KJELGAARD, JIM. Big Red: the story of a champion Irish setter and a trapper's son who grew up together, roaming the wilderness. New ed. Illus. by Bob Kuhn. Holiday House ISBN 0-8234-0007-7, c1945, 1956. 254p. ill.
Available from National Library Service for the Blind and Physically Handicapped in Braille BRA05960 and on sound recording cassette RC10856.
Danny and his Irish setter roam the Wintapi Wilderness and eventually track down a great outlaw bear.
SUBJ: Dogs--Fiction./ Outdoor life--Fiction.

Ph-2 3-4/3 $3.99 P KH366
KLINE, SUZY. Herbie Jones and the birthday showdown. Illus. by Carl Cassler. Penguin ISBN 0-14-037500-7; In Canada: Penguin, 1995. 94p. ill.
A birthday "showdown" between Herbie's best friend Ray and rich John turns out to be fun for all.
SUBJ: Birthdays--Fiction./ Parties--Fiction./ Schools--Fiction./ Friendship--Fiction.

Ph-2 3-4/2 $3.99 P KH367
KLINE, SUZY. Herbie Jones and the class gift. Illus. by Richard Williams. Penguin ISBN 0-14-032723-1; In Canada: Penguin, 1989. 94p. ill.
Wanting to participate in the end of year gift giving for their teacher, third grader Herbie Jones and his best friend Raymond must devise a way to earn two dollars. An unforeseen accident causes them to break the beautiful ceramic owl and come up with an alternative. Short chapters, large print and the development of a third grade "Henry Higgins" or "Soup" make this an excellent choice for middle grade independent reading or class read-aloud.
In HERBIE JONES AND HAMBURGER HEAD (ISBN 0-399-21748-7, 1989) Herbie acquires a dog and foils a bank robber.
SUBJ: Schools--Fiction./ Gifts--Fiction./ Humorous stories.

Ph-2 2-4/2 $10.95 L KH368
KLINE, SUZY. Horrible Harry and the green slime. Illus. by Frank Remkiewicz. Viking Penguin ISBN 0-670-82468-2; In Canada: Penguin, 1989. 58p. ill.
Available from the National Library Service for the Blind and Physically Handicapped on sound recording cassette RC 38612.
Recounts the happenings in Harry's second grade class with Harry, who is not at all horrible, in five episodes just right for the newly established reader. Laughter and serious concerns unite in a good first chapter book--even for an advanced first grade reader.
In HORRIBLE HARRY'S SECRET (ISBN 0-670-82470-4, 1990), Harry stops fighting because of Song Lee and loses two front "pearly whites." Every child should be lucky enough to have a teacher like Miss Mackle.
SUBJ: Schools--Fiction./ Friendship--Fiction.

Ph-2 1-3/4 $13.95 T KH369
KLINE, SUZY. Mary Marony hides out. Illus. by Blanche Sims. Putnam ISBN 0-399-22433-5; In Canada: Putnam, 1993. 80p. ill.
Mary Marony, who stutters, is embarrassed when she stammers at a school assembly for her favorite author. Encouraged by her speech therapist and other second graders, Mary becomes confident enough to attend a luncheon with the author.
SUBJ: Stuttering--Fiction./ Authors--Fiction./ Schools--Fiction.

Ph-1 4-6/5 $16.95 T KH370
KNIGHT, ERIC. Lassie come-home. Illus. by Marguerite Kirmse. Henry Holt ISBN 0-8050-0721-0; In Canada: Fitzhenry & Whiteside, 1978. 248p. ill., map.
Available from National Library Service for the Blind and Physically Handicapped on sound recording cassette RC22763, as talking book TB00661.
A reissue of the original edition. Lassie, a collie, sold to a new owner in Scotland, makes a gruelling four hundred mile journey back to the Yorkshire miner's son who was her original owner and who still loved her. A story of animal endurance and love similar to Burnford's THE INCREDIBLE JOURNEY.
SUBJ: Dogs--Fiction./ Courage--Fiction.

Ph-1 A/5 $3.99 P KH371
KOERTGE, RON. Harmony Arms. Little, Brown ISBN 0-380-72188-0; In Canada: Little, Brown, 1994. 177p.
Fourteen-year-old Gabriel spends the summer in a most unusually peopled Los Angeles apartment house. A typical teen embarrassed by his father, he begins to change with the help of the other occupants especially Tess, a creative, imaginative teenager. The sophisticated novel, as eccentric as the people in the Harmony Arms, is at once philosophical (but not too heavily), marvelously characterized, and a very funny reading experience.
SUBJ: Fathers and sons--Fiction./ Los Angeles (Calif.)--Fiction.

Ph-2 A/6 $13.95 L KH372
KONIGSBURG, E. L. Altogether, one at a time. Illustrated by Gail E. Haley, et al. Atheneum ISBN 0-689-20638-0, c1971. 79p. ill.
Four young people find their perceptions about others and themselves change dramatically in these short stories. Hallmarked by strong characters, subtlety, and skilled writing, these are for advanced mature readers.
Contents: Inviting Jason; The Night of the Leonids; Camp Fat; Momma at the Pearly Gates.
SUBJ: Short stories.

CE Ph-1 4-6/7 $13.95 L KH373
KONIGSBURG, E. L. From the mixed-up files of Mrs. Basil E. Frankweiler. Atheneum ISBN 0-689-20586-4, c1967. 162p. ill.
Newbery Medal Award.
Read-along kit available from Listening Library LB 5 SP (ISBN 0-8072-8538-2, 1988), 1 hardcover book, 3 sound cassettes (225min), $20.98.
Available from National Library Service for the Blind and Physically Handicapped in Braille BRA04504, on sound recording cassette RC22914, and as talking book TB02048.
Eleven-year-old Claudia Kincaid wants to run away from home, but insists on doing it in style. She goes with her younger brother, Jamie, to set up residence in New York City at the Metropolitan Museum of Art. A funny, mysterious and exciting story.
SUBJ: New York (N.Y.) Metropolitan Museum of Art--Fiction./ Runaways--Fiction./ Museums--Fiction.

CE Ph-2 3-6/4 $13.95 L KH374
KONIGSBURG, E. L. Jennifer, Hecate, Macbeth, William McKinley, and me, Elizabeth. Atheneum ISBN 0-689-30007-7, c1967. 117p. ill.
Newbery Honor Book.
Available from National Library Service for the Blind and Physically Handicapped as talking book TB02048.
Take two lonely, sensitive children. Make one a witch and the other her apprentice. Stir in a mean little girl, a pair of great relatives, and a toad named Hilary Ezra and the reader has a brew that makes a beautiful tale of friendship.
SUBJ: Witchcraft--Fiction./ New York (N.Y.)--Fiction./ Friendship--Fiction./ Girls--Fiction.

Ph-1 6-A/7 $13.95 T KH375
KONIGSBURG, E. L. T-backs, T-shirts, COAT, and suit. Atheneum ISBN 0-689-31855-3; In Canada: Maxwell Macmillan, 1993. 165p.
"Jean Karl book."
Available from the National Library Service for the Blind and Physically Handicapped on sound recording cassette RC 38298.
Visiting with her Aunt Bernadette in Florida, Chloe, twelve, controlled, tight, and bright, becomes involved in a controversy about the clothing (or lack thereof) people wear to call attention to their "meals-on-wheels" vans. Her aunt will not wear T-back swimsuits, but other drivers do, and a religious group objects so strongly that bonfires and incredible media coverage follows. Characterization is strong, and the past helps explain the present as Chloe learns much about her admirable aunt and about herself. The book is as current as today's date, but the humans are people from any time. Fascinating book and good discussion starter about rights and responsibilities.
SUBJ: Aunts--Fiction./ Protest movements--Fiction./ Florida--Fiction./ Prejudices--Fiction.

Ph-2 5-6/6 $3.95 P KH376
KONIGSBURG, E. L. Throwing shadows. Macmillan ISBN 0-02-044140-1; In Canada: Collier Macmillan, 1979. 151p.
Available from National Library Service for the Blind and Physically Handicapped in Braille BR05002 and on sound recording cassette RC18645.
Five crystalline stories of different young people: Phillip--recording the life story of an ugly old woman; Antonio--selling weavings to tourists in Ecuador; Avery--finding himself in constant trouble; William--helping his mother develop a new career; and Ned--hunting for sharks teeth. In each perceptive story the central character realizes and verbalizes what and who he is.
SUBJ: Self--Fiction./ Short stories.

Ph-1 5-A/7 $16.00 T KH377
KONIGSBURG, E. L. View from Saturday. Atheneum ISBN 0-689-80993-X; In Canada: Distican, 1996. 163p.
"Jean Karl book."
Newbery Award, 1997.
Selectors' Choice, 21st ed.
In a fascinatingly constructed, suspenseful novel, several characters are first presented as individuals and then as a team. Told in the first person in alternate chapters by the protagonists, unusual sixth graders, and in the third person to propel actions and relationships, the story explains how the unlikely group becomes an Academic Bowl team--and wins a championship. Filled with superb characterizations, some hilarious scenes, and tension about the outcome of the contests, the enjoyable novel will have readers rooting for the team and its teacher, a paraplegic who is confined to a wheelchair. Academically minded children may very well find themselves in the cast. A book about individual differences which can be used in units on persons with disabilities. For reading aloud.
SUBJ: Teacher-student relationships--Fiction./ Friendship--Fiction./ Schools--Fiction./ Contests--Fiction./ Physically handicapped--Fiction.

Ph-1 5-A/7 $3.99   P   KH378
KORMAN, GORDON. Zucchini warriors. Scholastic ISBN 0-590-44174-4, 1991. 198p.

Hilarity abounds when the students at Macdonald Hall school find themselves with a football stadium and a gung ho fried zucchini stick sponsor. Fast paced recreational reading.

Other adventures with the students at Macdonald Hall are found in THIS CAN'T BE HAPPENING AT MACDONALD HALL! (ISBN 0-590-44213-9, 1978); GO JUMP IN THE POOL! (ISBN 0-590-44209-0, 1979); THE WAR WITH MR. WIZZLE (ISBN 0-590-44206-6, 1982, OPC); and MACDONALD HALL GOES HOLLYWOOD (ISBN 0-590-43940-5, 1991, OPC).

In SOMETHING FISHY AT MACDONALD HALL (ISBN 0-590-25521-5, 1995) Bruno and Boots are outwitted by a master practical joker.

SUBJ: Football--Fiction./ Schools--Fiction./ Humorous stories./ Boarding schools--Fiction.

Ph-2 3-5/3 $13.95   T   KH379
KRAAN, HANNA. Tales of the wicked witch. Translated by Elisabeth Koolschijn. Illus. by Annemarie van Haeringen. Front Street/Lemniscaat ISBN 1-886910-04-9; In Canada: Publishers Group West, 1995. 107p. ill.

Presents 14 episodes in the lives of gentle forest creatures and a not so wicked witch. Her attempts at mischief go awry and turn into pleasant experiences until the forest creatures convince her she is welcome in the forest. The line sketches add to the charm and humor in this book translated from the Dutch. Excellent for reading aloud. WICKED WITCH IS AT IT AGAIN (ISBN 1-886910-18-9, 1997) contains more stories about the forest creatures--sometimes very charming, and the wicked witch--whose charms are sometimes alarming.

SUBJ: Witches--Fiction./ Forest animals--Fiction.

Ph-2 3-6/4 $17.95   T   KH380
KRAMER, STEPHEN P. Theodoric's rainbow. By Stephen Kramer. Illustrated by Daniel Mark Duffy. W. H. Freeman ISBN 0-7167-6603-5, 1995. unp. col. ill.

"Scientific American books for young readers."

A fictionalized telling of the life of Theodoric of Freiberg, a Dominican monk living in the 14th century, explains how he may have developed his theory that rainbows are produced by the combination of sunlight and drops of water. The multicolored art is static, but provides a feeling for the times and an imagined portrait of Theodoric. A brief end note gives factual information about him and his uniqueness as a scientist who used observation rather than theory to explain natural phenomena. Use in science classes when discussing scientific inquiry.

SUBJ: Theodoric of Freiberg--Fiction./ Rainbow--Fiction./ Friars--Fiction.

Ph-3 3-5/2 $3.99   P   KH381
KRENSKY, STEPHEN. Iron dragon never sleeps. Illus. by John Fulweiler. Delacorte ISBN 0-440-41136-X; In Canada: Bantam Doubleday Dell, 1995. 90p. ill., map.

"In 1867, while staying with her father in a small California mining town, ten-year-old Winnie meets a Chinese boy close to her age and discovers the role of his people in completing the transcontinental railroad." (CIP) The wretched treatment of the Chinese railroad workers is clearly depicted, as is their skill in blasting through the Sierra Nevada. Black and white, full-page illustrations add little, and some of the author's generalized statements need more careful word choice, e.g., not everyone called the Chinese "Celestials" and not all wore the blue jacket. While there is nothing outstanding about the book, it will serve nicely as historical fiction for California history, United States history, and multicultural studies.

SUBJ: Railroads--Fiction./ Frontier and pioneer life--California--Fiction./ California--Fiction./ Chinese Americans--Fiction./ Strikes and lockouts--Fiction.

CE   Ph-3 6-A/5 $16.00   T   KH382
KRUMGOLD, JOSEPH. And now Miguel. Illus. by Jean Charlot. Crowell/HarperCollins ISBN 0-690-09118-4; In Canada: HarperCollins, 1953. 245p. ill.

Newbery Medal.

Available from National Library Service for the Blind and Physically Handicapped on sound recording cassette RC23489, talking book TB01473, and in Braille BRA06089.

Wanting to be considered a man and go into the Sangre de Cristo Mountains with the herds of sheep, 12-year-old Miguel is distressed when his wish is granted through a twist of fate. Slowly paced, this rite of passage title is not for everyone but will be appreciated by the more thoughtful, mature reader. Try oral presentation.

SUBJ: Sheep--Fiction./ Brothers--Fiction./ Maturity--Fiction./ New Mexico--Fiction./ Mexican Americans--Fiction.

Ph-3 3-4/5 $7.95   P   KH383
KURUSA. Streets are free. Rev. ed. Illus. by Monika Doppert. Translated by Karen Englander. Annick/dist. by Firefly ISBN 1-55037-370-6; In Canada: Annick/dist. by Firefly, 1995. unp. col. ill.

Originally published in Venezuela, LA CALLE ES LIBRE, 1981. The children of crowded barrios on the outskirts of Caracas, Venezuela need a place to play. The librarian helps them with plans, posters, and a request to the mayor; politicians promise but do nothing. After a long, disappointing wait, the children and their parents cooperate and build a place to play. The illustrations are successful in capturing the varying moods of the story and its characters and of the physical changes of the area from forests and streams to uncontrolled urban sprawl. Despite the picture-book format, the audience for this story is older. Those who remember A BIG PILE OF DIRT will see that the same situation occurs in the United States.

SUBJ: Venezuela--Fiction./ City and town life--Fiction.

Ph-3 4-6/4 $15.95   L   KH384
KUSUGAK, MICHAEL. Baseball bats for Christmas. By Michael Arvaarluk Kusugak. Illus. by Vladyana Krykorka. Annick/dist. by Firefly ISBN 1-55037-145-2; In Canada: Annick/Firefly, 1990. unp. col. ill.

Set north of the Arctic Circle in Repulse Bay, Canada, this colorfully illustrated story tells about the Christmas when the supply airplane brought strange green things with "spindly branches all over"--Christmas trees, previously unknown to the inhabitants. The trees were eventually made into baseball bats and the game was played throughout the year. From front end papers to back, story and illustrations provide a view of a way of life in a different culture and place.

SUBJ: Baseball--Fiction./ Christmas trees--Fiction./ Arctic regions--Fiction./ Eskimos--Fiction.

Ph-2 4-6/5 $3.95   P   KH385
LANGTON, JANE. Diamond in the window. Illus. by Erik Blegvad. HarperTrophy ISBN 0-06-440042-5; In Canada: HarperCollins, c1962, 1973. 242p. ill.

Originally published by Harper & Row, 1962.

Available from National Library Service for the Blind and Physically Handicapped in Braille BRA12563.

Eleanor and Edward live in a funny Victorian house in Concord, MA with their Aunt Eleanor and crazy Uncle Freddy, who are harassed by the local banker because their taxes are in arrears. Through a series of fantastic experiences, they search for a treasure supposed to have been left by an Indian prince, hoping to solve their financial problems. An "oldie" which still has high appeal for its combination of mystery and fantasy.

SUBJ: Mystery and detective stories./ Fantasy.

Ph-3 3-5/5 $14.89   L   KH386
LASKY, KATHRYN. She's wearing a dead bird on her head! Illus. by David Catrow. Hyperion ISBN 0-7868-2052-7; In Canada: Little, Brown, 1995. unp. col. ill.

Gives "a fictionalized account of the activities of Harriet Hemenway and Minna Hall, founders of the Massachusetts Audubon Society..." (CIP) At a time when women's hats were decorated and over decorated with the feathers of birds, some soon to become extinct thanks to stylish fads, the two women raised public consciousness and changed fashion. Catrow's watercolor and ink illustrations make human beings, especially women, funny looking and distract from the story. They are, in fact, insulting caricatures perhaps to create humor. Nonetheless, the story, although fictionalized, will be useful in environmental studies.

SUBJ: Hemenway, Harriet--Fiction./ Hall, Minna--Fiction./ Massachusetts Audubon Society--Fiction./ Birds--Protection--Fiction.

Ph-2 5-A/6 $13.95   T   KH387
LAWSON, JOHN. If pigs could fly. Houghton Mifflin ISBN 0-395-50928-9, 1989. 136p.

Told in the tradition of the very tall tale, this relates the humorous adventures of Morgan James as he wanders on the U.S. frontier, meets danger, romance, rascals, and magic at the time of the War of 1812. Akin to Sandburg's ROOTABAGA STORIES in tone and even some incidents in Twains's HUCKLEBERRY FINN, these humorous and fast paced episodes should delight the better reader who knows nonsense when it appears. It will also be a good choice for reading aloud.

SUBJ: Tall tales./ United States--History--War of 1812--Fiction./ Humorous stories.

Ph-2 3-5/5 $14.95   T   KH388
LAWSON, ROBERT. Ben and me: a new and astonishing life of Benjamin Franklin, as written by his good mouse Amos; lately discovered. Little, Brown ISBN 0-316-51732-1, c1939. 113p. ill.

Available from National Library Service for the Blind and Physically

Handicapped on talking book TB01431 and in Braille BRA06093.
Amos Mouse moves into Ben Franklin's hat and serves so successfully
as his advisor that Franklin becomes renowned.
SUBJ: Franklin, Benjamin--Fiction./ Mice--Fiction.

Ph-3 5-6/7 $5.95 P KH389
LAWSON, ROBERT. Mr. Revere and I: being an account of certain
episodes in the career of Paul Revere, Esq., as recently revealed by his
horse, Scheherazada, late pride of His Royal Majesty's 14th Regiment of
Foot. Set down and embellished with numerous drawings by Robert
Lawson. Little, Brown ISBN 0-316-51729-1, c1953. 152p. ill.
Available from National Library Service for the Blind and Physically
Handicapped in Braille BRA08388 and as talking book TB01031.
Paul Revere's horse, Scheherazade, tells the story of how he advised
and led the hero of the American Revolution to fame.
SUBJ: Horses--Fiction./ Revere, Paul--Fiction./ United States--History--
Revolution, 1775-1783--Fiction.

CE   Ph-2 4-6/7 $14.00 L KH390
LAWSON, ROBERT. Rabbit Hill. Viking ISBN 0-670-58675-7, c1944,
1962. 127p. ill.
Newbery Medal Award.
Read- along kit available from Live Oak Media (ISBN 0-670-58680--
3, 1972). 1 paperback book, 1 sound cassette (50min), $15.95.
Available from National Library Service for Blind and Physically
Handicapped in Braille BRA13266, on sound recording cassette
RC23114, and as talking book TB03104.
All the animals are excited because new folks are coming to live in
the house on the hill. The question for Little Georgie, Mother and
Father Rabbit, and the other animals is "Will the new folks be good
providers?"
SUBJ: Animals--Fiction.

Ph-1 2-4/5 $16.00 T KH391
LEE, MILLY. Nim and the war effort. Illus. by Yangsook Choi. Farrar,
Straus and Giroux ISBN 0-374-35523-1; In Canada: HarperCollins,
1997. unp. col. ill.
"Frances Foster books."
Nim is anxious to bring honor to her Chinese-American family by
winning the paper drive at her school in 1943. Her persistance almost
leads to trouble when she is seen riding in a police car. The
dimensions of Chinese family life, cultural tensions during World War
II, and community war efforts are tightly woven into compelling
historical fiction. Rich illustrations further the impact of the story. For
multicultural studies.
SUBJ: World War, 1939-1945--United States--Fiction./ Chinese
Americans--Fiction./ Competition (Psychology)--Fiction./
Grandfathers--Fiction.

Ph-1 6-A/7 $16.95 L KH392
LE GUIN, URSULA K. Wizard of Earthsea. Atheneum ISBN 0-689-
31720-4, c1968, 1991. 208p., maps.
Available from National Library Service for the Blind and Physically
Handicapped as talking book TB04709.
The boy Sparrowhawk slowly and painfully achieves his ambition to
become a wizard. His preparation by the Master wizard, rigorous
training at the School for Wizards, and encounters with evil shadows
make an enthralling fantasy.
In THE FARTHEST SHORE (Bantam Doubleday Dell ISBN 0-553-
26847-3, 1987) Ged has become the Archmage of Earthsea and
helps the Wizards of the South regain their magic.
In TEHANU: THE LAST BOOK OF EARTHSEA (ISBN 0-689-31595-3,
1990), the final book in the series, Ged has lost his powers and
comes to live with Tenar, a widow, and Therru, a badly burned girl
with a mysterious background.
Available from NLSBPH is THE FARTHEST SHORE on sound
recording disc RD06778.
SUBJ: Fantasy.

Ph-2 5-6/7 $15.95 T KH393
L'ENGLE, MADELEINE. Wind in the door. Farrar, Straus & Giroux ISBN
0-374-38443-6, c1973. 211p.
Sequel to: A WRINKLE IN TIME.
Selectors' Choice, 9th ed.
Available' from the National Library Service for the Blind and
Physically Handicapped on sound recording cassette RC 41596.
Meg becomes concerned about Charles Wallace's problems in
adapting to school life. The precocious little boy is not only disliked
and bullied by his playmates but his health deteriorates. When he
insists that there are "dragons in the twins' garden", she investigates
and finds the dragons are indeed there and other alien creatures, as
well. They lead her and Charles into a fantastic and terrifying series
of adventures, and the ultimate conflict of good and evil.
SUBJ: Science fiction./ Fantasy.

CE   Ph-1 4-6/6 $15.95 T KH394
L'ENGLE, MADELEINE. Wrinkle in time. Farrar, Straus & Giroux ISBN
0-374-38613-7, c1962. 211p.
Followed by: WIND IN THE DOOR (1973).
Newbery Medal Award.
Available from National Library Service for the Blind and Physically
Handicapped on sound recording cassette RC09768 and in Braille
BRO1546.
Meg and her friends are spirited to another world by three
extraterrestrial beings--Mrs. Whatsit, Mrs. Who, and Mrs. Which--
where they find her father and undergo many adventures and terrors
before they can free him from captivity.
SUBJ: Science fiction.

Ph-1 6-A/6 $13.99 T KH395
LESTER, JULIUS. Long journey home: stories from Black history. Dial
ISBN 0-8037-4953-8, c1972, 1993. 147p.
Six very simple and well-told stories, based on the lives of African
Americans, tell of the farmers, a guitar player, and a land owner
called Satan; Louis, a slave about to be sold; Ben a slave on a
Kentucky plantation who could read and write and who ran the
plantation; an ex-slave who for a short while lived with a herd of wild
mustangs; and the last "Long journey home" in which a group of
slaves walked into the ocean on their way to Africa (their eternal
home). Sources documented by the author in Introduction and Notes;
they are the kind of stories told to the first free-born generation. For
multicultural studies.
SUBJ: Afro-Americans--Fiction./ Short stories.

Ph-1 5-A/4 $15.00 L KH396
LEVIN, BETTY. Fire in the wind. Greenwillow ISBN 0-688-14299-0,
1995. 138p.
"In 1947 in Maine, a raging fire that threatens their farm and the
nearby town makes the members of Meg's extended family see their
strained relationships in a new light." (CIP) Short, snappy self-
contained chapters present the story of the fire and Meg's complex
relationships as she takes care of her younger brother and tries to
protect her older, mentally slow cousin from charges of arson.
Readers will discover both the terrible suspense of the fire as it
surrounds everyone and the unraveling of character in an active novel
which combines with a character study. Meg's thinking is clear,
despite the complexity of the situations.
SUBJ: Family life--Maine--Fiction./ Brothers and sisters--Fiction./
Cousins--Fiction./ Fires--Fiction./ Maine--Fiction.

Ph-1 5-A/5 $14.98 L KH397
LEVINE, GAIL CARSON. Ella enchanted. HarperCollins ISBN 0-06-
027511-1; In Canada: HarperCollins, 1997. 232p.
In a fantasy-novel based on the Cinderella story, Ella is forced to
always follow requests because of a curse placed on her by a silly
and dangerous witch. She is brave, spirited, and daring and has the
capacity for understanding others and making friends. Her greedy
father's new wife and her two mean spirited, greedy, and unintelligent
daughters manage to make life impossible for Ella whose escape
leads her into magical situations, dangerous escapades, and a
reacquaintance with a delightful, but down-to-earth, prince. The
adventure and romance combined with strong characterizations and
humor are bound to attract readers of Robin McKinley's BEAUTY and
other reworkings of old tales.
SUBJ: Fantasy.

Ph-1 5-A/5 $15.00 L KH398
LEVITIN, SONIA. Journey to America. Illus. by Charles Robinson.
Atheneum ISBN 0-689-31829-4; In Canada: Maxwell Macmillan, c1970,
1993. 150p. ill.
Available from National Library Service for the Blind and Physically
Handicapped on talking book TB04099.
As more and more hostilities towards Jews occur in Berlin under the
Nazi regime, the Platt family separates; the father to the U.S. and
mother and daughters seeking refuge in Switzerland until Mr. Platt
can send for them. The difficulties they encounter and the tensions
under which they live involve the reader.
The Platt family reunites, moves from New York City to Los Angeles,
and tries to keep some of their traditions while adjusting to their new
country in SILVER DAYS (ISBN 0-689-71570-6, 1992).
Annie, about to turn 13, gains new insights into her family, the world
situation, and other people in a biographical novel in which character
is particularly well developed in ANNIE'S PROMISE (ISBN 0-689-
31752-2, 1993)
SUBJ: Jews--Germany--1933-1945--Fiction./ World War, 1939-1945-
-Refugees--Fiction.

SRC   Ph-1 4-6 $9.95   KH399
LEVITT, MARC JOEL. Tales of an October moon: haunting stories from New England (Sound recording cassette). August House Audio ISBN 0-87483-209-8, 1992. 1 sound cassette (60min).

     Four ghostly stories of towns, a reservoir, stonewalls, and devil worship are retold by a master storyteller. A surefire pleaser at Halloween, this tape will inspire listeners to track down and record local tales.
     SUBJ: Ghosts--Fiction./ New England--Fiction./ Halloween--Fiction./ Short stories.

                Ph-2 4-6/7 $3.95   P   KH400
LEVOY, MYRON. Witch of Fourth Street, and other stories. Illus. by Gabriel Lisowski. HarperCollins ISBN 0-06-440059-X, c1972. 110p illus.

     This series of short stories capture the essence of what it was like to live on the lower East Side of New York City in the early twentieth century. "Andreas and the magic bells", "Keplik, the match man", and "The Hanukkah Santa Claus" are among the most unusual of the stories.
     SUBJ: United States--Foreign population--Fiction./ New York (N.Y.)--Fiction./ Short stories./ United States--History--1919-1933--Fiction.

KIT   Ph-2 4-6 $14.95   OD KH401
LEVOY, MYRON. Witch of Fourth Street and other stories (Kit). Listening Library SWR 13, 1978. 1 sound cassette (27min), 1 paperback book. (Soundways to reading).

     Includes teacher's guide.
     Adapted from book of the same title. A warm female voice introduces the stories in this book, then reads aloud the text of the first and title story. A "book-talk type" introduction to the other stories then follows as well as an invitation to read about the other characters in Manhattan at the early 20th century. An excellent format for reading motivation.
     SUBJ: United States--Foreign population--Fiction./ New York (N.Y.)--Fiction./ Short stories./ United States--History--1919-1933--Fiction.

                Ph-2 3-5/5 $12.89   L   KH402
LEVY, ELIZABETH. Keep Ms. Sugarman in the fourth grade. Illus. by Dave Henderson. HarperCollins ISBN 0-06-020427-3; In Canada: HarperCollins, 1992. 85p. ill.

     Available from the National Library Service for the Blind and Physically Handicapped on sound recording cassette RC 38367.
     Now in fourth grade, Jackie, who has always been in trouble in school, discovers, with the help of a challenging teacher, that she likes school and can do well. When Ms. Sugarman is made the principal, Jackie begins a revolt to keep her as her teacher. Fortunately, Sugarman understands children, especially Jackie, and the story is resolved in a realistic fashion.
     SUBJ: Schools--Fiction./ Teacher-student relationships--Fiction./ Self-confidence--Fiction.

                Ph-2 3-5/3 $14.95   T   KH403
LEVY, ELIZABETH. Something queer at the scary movie. Illus. by Mordicai Gerstein. Hyperion ISBN 0-7868-0150-6; In Canada: Little, Brown, 1995. unp. col. ill.

     "Gwen must try to figure out who wants to prevent her from completing the scary movie she and Jill are making during summer vacation." (CIP) For a slightly older readership than other books in the series, the story is given an added dimension by supplying information about movie-making techniques and jargon. The illustrations in color gouaches add liveliness and actually help demonstrate production techniques. Although the author's verb choice is scant, the book will hold first mystery readers.
     SUBJ: Motion pictures--Production and direction--Fiction./ Mystery and detective stories.

                Ph-2 1-3/5 $14.95   L   KH404
LEVY, JANICE. Spirit of Tio Fernando: a Day of the Dead story./El espiritu de tio Fernando: una historia del Dia de los Muertos. Illus. by Morella Fuenmayor. Translated by Teresa Mlawer. Whitman ISBN 0-8075-7585-2; In Canada: General, 1995. unp. col. ill.

     Nando's numerous preparations to honor the spirit of his Uncle Fernando on the Day of the Dead provide information on the observance of this holiday celebrated throughout Mexico and Central America. Lively full-color illustrations accompany the bilingual text. Use for holidays and multicultural studies.
     SUBJ: All Souls' Day--Mexico--Fiction./ Uncles--Fiction./ Mexico--Fiction./ Spanish language materials./ Bilingual materials--Spanish.

CE   Ph-1 5-A/6 $14.89   L   KH405
LEWIS, C. S. Lion, the witch and the wardrobe. Illus. by Pauline Baynes. HarperCollins ISBN 0-06-023482-2; In Canada: HarperCollins, 1994. 189p. ill.

     Talking book available CHRONICLES OF NARNIA SUPER-SOUND BOOK from HarperAudio (ISBN 1-55994-856-6, 1993). 7 sound cassettes, $50.00.
     Available from National Library Service for the Blind and Physically Handicapped on sound recording cassette RC16982, in Braille BRA02301, and talking book TB01476.
     Videocassette available from Bonneville Worldwide Entertainment (ISBN 1-57742-038-1, 1988). 2 1/2" VHS videocassettes color (169min), $24.95. (WonderWorks).
     Spanish version LEON, LA BRUJA, Y EL ARMARIO available from Santillana (ISBN 84-204-45649, n.d.).
     Seven stories of fantasy on the theme of the battle between good and evil, which started when the land of Narnia was new and animals talked. The children, Peter, Susan, Edmund and Lucy meet the witch, the mighty lion Aslan, and other characters who live in Narnia. In order of happening the stories are: LION, THE WITCH AND THE WARDROBE; PRINCE CASPIAN: THE RETURN TO NARNIA (ISBN 0-06-023484-9, 1994, Spanish version PRINCIPE CASPIO available from Santillana ISBN 84-204-46300, 1995); VOYAGE OF THE DAWN TREADER (ISBN 0-06-023487-3, 1994, Spanish version VIAJE DEL AMANECER available from Santillana 84-204-4670X, n.d.); SILVER CHAIR (ISBN 0-06-023496-2, 1994, Spanish version SILLON DE PLATA available from Santillana ISBN 84-204-46998, n.d.); HORSE AND HIS BOY (ISBN 0-06-021430-0, 1994, Spanish version CABALLO Y SU JINETE available from Santillana 84-204-46092, 1995); MAGICIAN'S NEPHEW (ISBN 0-06-023497-0, 1994); and the LAST BATTLE, a Carnegie Medal winner, (ISBN 0-06-023494-6, 1994, Spanish version ULTIMA BATALLA available from Santillana 84-204-4698x, n.d.). All children should have the opportunity to read or hear this fine series.
     Also available on videocassette from Bonneville Worldwide Entertainment: SILVER CHAIR (ISBN 1-57742-040-3, 1990) and PRINCE CASPIAN AND THE VOYAGE OF THE DAWN TREADER (ISBN 1-57742-039-X, 1989). (WonderWorks).
     Also available from NLSBPH are: PRINCE CASPIAN in Braille BRA01375, on sound recording cassette RC16984, as talking book TB01476; VOYAGE OF THE DAWN TREADER in Braille BRA00382, on sound recording cassette RC16985, as talking book TB01479; SILVER CHAIR in Braille BRA00731, on sound recording cassette RC16986, as talking book TB01478; HORSE AND HIS BOY in Braille BRA02008, on sound recording cassette RC17438, as talking book TB01475; MAGICIAN'S NEPHEW in Braille BRA06382, on sound recording cassette RC16987, as talking book TB01477; LAST BATTLE in Braille BRA01381, on sound recording cassette RC16988, as talking book TB01474.
     SUBJ: Fantasy./ Good and evil--Fiction./ Spanish language materials.

                Ph-3 4-6/5 $11.00   T   KH406
LIGHTFOOT, D. J. Trail fever: the life of a Texas cowboy. Illus. by John Bobbish. Lothrop, Lee & Shepard ISBN 0-688-11537-3, 1992. 76p. ill.

     Includes bibliography.
     Available from the National Library Service for the Blind and Physically Handicapped on sound recording cassette RC 37902.
     Presents a fictionalized biography of George Saunders from his early childhood to his life as a cowboy before, during, and after the Civil War. Depicts cattle drives, skirmishes with Native Americans, stampedes, and life on the Texas frontier over a period of several years. Historical fiction useful for units on cowboys, frontier and pioneer life, and United States and Texas history.
     SUBJ: Saunders, George W. (George Washington)--Fiction./ Cowboys--Fiction./ Texas--Fiction./ Frontier and pioneer life--Texas--Fiction./ West (U.S.)--Fiction.

CE   Ph-1 3-5/4 $3.99   P   KH407
LINDGREN, ASTRID. Pippi Longstocking. Translated from the Swedish by Florence Lamborn. Illus. by Louis S. Glanzman. Penguin ISBN 0-14-030957-8; In Canada: Penguin, c1950, 1978. 158p. ill.

     Talking book performed by the High Tor Repertory Players, Live Oak Media, (ISBN 0-670-55748-X, 1973), $9.95.
     Available from National Library Service for the Blind and Physically Handicapped on sound recording cassette RC24423, in Braille BRA02436, as talking book TB04172.
     Large type available from Windrush (ISBN 1-85089-906-1, 1987).
     Pippi lives alone although she is only nine. She does many other curious magical things, such as tying brushes to her feet and skating in suds to scrub a floor.
     Followed by PIPPI GOES ON BOARD (ISBN 0-670-55677-7, 1957) and PIPPI IN THE SOUTH SEAS (ISBN 0-670-55711-0, 1959).
     Also available from NLSBPH are: PIPPI GOES ON BOARD in Braille BRA00182 and as talking book TB01023; and PIPPI IN THE SOUTH SEAS as talking book TB04172.
     SUBJ: Sweden--Fiction./ Humorous stories.

Ph-1 6-A/6 $13.99   L   KH408
LISLE, JANET TAYLOR. Afternoon of the elves. Orchard ISBN 0-531-08437-X, 1989. 122p.
Newbery Honor Book, 1990.
Develops a gripping story with solid characterization about imagination and its allure to "nice" middle-class Hillary as "dangerous", poverty-stricken Sara-Kate creates a world of elves in her unkempt yard. Hillary is totally fascinated and begins to help Sara-Kate and her mentally ill mother survive. The depiction of the necessary cruelty that calls itself kindness is startling and totally believable. A superb reading experience for the more mature reader who understood Sachs' BEARS' HOUSE books.
SUBJ: Friendship--Fiction./ Mentally ill--Fiction./ Imagination--Fiction./ Poverty--Fiction.

Ph-1 5-A/7 $15.99   L   KH409
LISLE, JANET TAYLOR. Forest. Orchard ISBN 0-531-08653-4, 1993. 150p.
"Richard Jackson book."
Available from the National Library Service for the Blind and Physically Handicapped on sound recording cassette RC 38555. Amber, a twelve-year-old girl, and Woodbine, an imaginative and unconventional squirrel, work with (or against) their own species to save a large band of squirrels from destruction by humans and the humans from attacks by the squirrels. Tense and suspenseful, the dynamic novel develops the protagonists and antagonists well in a fantasy with a few nondidactic lessons about ecology. Dust jacket art is so off-putting that the book may need enthusiastic book talking. For reading aloud and environmental studies.
SUBJ: Squirrels--Fiction./ Fantasy.

Ph-1 4-6/7 $14.99   L   KH410
LISLE, JANET TAYLOR. Gold dust letters. Orchard ISBN 0-531-08680-1, 1994. 116p. (Investigators of the unknown).
"Richard Jackson book."
Available from the National Library Service for the Blind and Physically Handicapped on sound recording cassette RC 38848.
"When nine-year-old Angela and her friends begin investigating the letters she has received from her fairy godmother, it helps take Angela's mind off her strained relationship with her father." (CIP) The letters seem magical to Angela and her two friends. Although the readers discover who sent them, a question remains at the end. Was there an element of magic in the letters, or was it all hocus-pocus for a good cause? As in most Lisle books, plot development, diction, character, and situation are strongly logical, but with one foot in the real world and one in a world beyond. For readers of the supernatural and fantasy.
SUBJ: Fathers and daughters--Fiction./ Divorce--Fiction./ Friendship--Fiction./ Supernatural--Fiction.

Ph-1 5-6/6 $11.99   L   KH411
LISLE, JANET TAYLOR. Great dimpole oak. Illus. by Stephen Gammell. Orchard ISBN 0-531-08316-0, 1987. 134p. ill.
Growing in a field just outside the town, the mighty Dimpole oak signifies mystery and mayhem to the old farmer, history and romance to the teacher and postal clerk, adventure and treasure to two young boys, and holiness to a swami in far off India. Well drawn characters, humor, and an aura of the supernatural converge beneath the tree's great branches to the delight of readers who have also enjoyed Brittain's stories of Coven Tree.
SUBJ: Trees--Fiction.

Ph-2 4-6/6 $14.99   L   KH412
LISLE, JANET TAYLOR. Looking for Juliette. Orchard ISBN 0-531-08720-4, 1994. 120p. (Investigators of the unknown).
"Richard Jackson book."
Available from the National Library Service for the Blind and Physically Handicapped on sound recording cassette RC 38849.
In THE GOLD DUST LETTERS, three girls Poco, Georgina, and Angela become involved in a magical fantasy. Now, Angela has left, for a time, and the others are charged with caring for Angela's cat Juliette, that inexplicably disappears. With the help of a rather strange boy and a Ouija board, they search for the cat that eventually, also inexplicably, returns. What the "unknown" is, remains a mystery, and the book has fewer seemingly supernatural events than the first. It is, nonetheless, a satisfying reading experience, although not as dramatic as the first title.
SUBJ: Supernatural--Fiction./ Cats--Fiction./ Old age--Fiction./ Friendship--Fiction.

Ph-3 4-6/5 $13.95   L   KH413
LITCHFIELD, ADA BASSETT. Words in our hands. Illus. by Helen Cogancherry. Whitman ISBN 0-8075-9212-9; In Canada: General, 1980. unp. col. ill. (Concept book).
Michael tells the story of his family, and especially of his parents, both of whom are deaf. He describes the various ways in which they communicate--by sign spelling, by sign language, by body language and by writing--as well as speaking. He is upset when they move to a new town and some boys make fun of his parents. A performance by the National Theatre of the Deaf helps explain to the students in his school about "signing."
SUBJ: Deaf--Fiction./ Physically handicapped--Fiction.

Ph-2 5-A/5 $13.99   T   KH414
LITTLE, JEAN. Mine for keeps. Viking ISBN 0-670-85967-2; In Canada: Penguin, c1962, 1994. 213p.
Originally published by Little, Brown, 1962.
Sarah Jane Copeland expects special treatment when she returns to her home after spending five years at a Cerebral Palsy center. Her family treats her as an able member, with no special privileges. Her schoolmates do, too, so Sarah must change her thinking.
SUBJ: Cerebral palsy--Fiction./ Dogs--Fiction./ Physically handicapped--Fiction.

Ph-2 4-6/7 $19.95   L   KH415
LIVELY, PENELOPE. Ghost of Thomas Kempe. Illus. by Antony Maitland. Dutton ISBN 0-525-30495-9, c1973. 186p. ill.
Carnegie Medal.
When James Harrison and his family move to East End Cottage, odd events began to take place, the kind a mischievous boy could perpetrate. But James is not the culprit. He decides it is a ghost of Thomas Kempe who lived in the cottage several hundred years earlier. Thomas is a stubborn ghost, but James finally manages to "lay him" with the help of several friends and the community.
SUBJ: Ghosts--Fiction.

Ph-1 3-A/5 $14.89   L   KH416
LOBEL, ARNOLD. Fables. HarperCollins ISBN 0-06-023974-3, 1980. 40p. col. ill.
Caldecott Medal Award.
Spanish version FABULAS available from Santillana (ISBN 84-204-45525, 1980).
Twenty fables about animals which Aesop never thought of--"The crocodile in the bedroom," "The frogs at the rainbow's end," "The pig at the candy store," and many others. Lobel's inimitable illustrations adroitly match the zany situations in which the animals are involved, and the wry morals at the end of each tale provide their own perspective on the world today.
SUBJ: Animals--Fiction./ Fables./ Spanish language materials.

Ph-3 6-A/6 $3.99   P   KH417
LONDON, JACK. White Fang. Puffin/Penguin ISBN 0-14-035045-4; In Canada: Penguin, c1905, 1985. 272p.
Available from National Library Service for the Blind and Physically Handicapped on sound recording cassette RC10123, in Braille BR02591, and as talking book TB02856.
"Born in the primitive, frozen wilds of north-west Canada, White Fang is destined for a life of hardship, where only the strong survive. Through his eyes we experience every one of his adventures; his triumphant first kill, his discovery of mankind, his harsh time as a sledge dog, his rescue from cruel slavery..." (Blurb). This is an excellent choice as a read-aloud.
SUBJ: Sled dogs--Fiction./ Canada--Fiction./ Wolves--Fiction.

Ph-1 4-A/5 $13.95   L   KH418
LOTTRIDGE, CELIA BARKER. Ticket to Canada. Illus. by Wendy Wolsak-Frith. Silver Burdett ISBN 0-382-39145-4, 1996. 144p. ill.
Originally published in Canada as TICKET TO CURLEW, Groundwood/Douglas & McIntyre, 1992.
Wilder's "Little House" books depict westering and pioneering experiences in the United States. Lottridge's books do the same for the Canadian settlers' experiences in 1915 in the town of Curlew in western Alberta. The two experiences are more similar than dissimilar. Sam Farrier who is about twelve and his father go to Canada from Iowa to build a house so that the rest of the family can join them. Through Sam's eyes, although told in the third person, the reader meets other settlers, neighbors, and townspeople including a Ukrainian family so poor that they have neither paper nor a writing implement. Sam's experiences as the house is built and the farm started and his thoughts about the many buffalo that once lived on the flat treeless land are made clear in understated writing that summons character and atmosphere well. Historical fiction which is excellent for units on westering both in Canada and the United States, the book is highly recommended.
SUBJ: Farm life--Canada--Fiction./ Canada--Fiction./ Frontier and pioneer life--Canada--Fiction.

Ph-1 5-A/5 $15.95   T   KH419
LOTTRIDGE, CELIA BARKER. Wings to fly. Illus. by Mary Jane Gerber. Groundwood/dist. by Publishers Group West ISBN 0-88899-293-9; In Canada: Groundwood/Douglas & McIntyre, 1997. 209p. ill.
Sequel to TICKET TO CANADA, Silver Burdett, 1996.
Set three years after the whole family arrives on their farm outside the small, but growing, town of Curlew, the story features Josie, eleven, as the central character, and readers follow her--and care about her and all the characters--as they grow and change. Set after World War I and at the beginning of the women's rights movement in Canada, it depicts the changes that war and time cause including education and careers. Readers will also be able to follow Sam, the neighbors, and the growth of the region. Historical fiction which is excellent for both the westering experience and studies about women's rights.
SUBJ: Farm life--Canada--Fiction./ Canada--Fiction./ Friendship--Fiction.

Ph-1 3-6/4 $14.21   L   KH420
LOWERY, LINDA. Laurie tells. Illus. by John Eric Karpinski. Carolrhoda ISBN 0-87614-790-2, 1994. unp. col. ill.
"When her mother doesn't believe her, eleven-year-old Laurie tells a supportive aunt that she is being sexually abused by her father." (CIP) Told in the first person, the story of Laurie's trauma and untenable situation is accessible to the reader, as is her dilemma of whom to tell and how to escape the situation about which she is deeply ashamed and unhappy. The art is in dreamy washes and increases in size from page to page until it fills the doublespreads as she finds relief, comfort, and solution with her aunt's help. Those who are victims of incest may begin to find help in this book. (Parents' Shelf)
SUBJ: Child sexual abuse--Fiction./ Incest--Fiction./ Fathers and daughters--Fiction.

Ph-1 3-5/4 $13.95   T   KH421
LOWRY, LOIS. All about Sam. Illus. by Diane De Groat. Houghton Mifflin ISBN 0-395-48662-9, 1988. 135p. ill.
Selectors' Choice, 17th ed.
Available from National Library Service for the Blind and Physically Handicapped on sound recording cassette RC30858.
Unraveling the mysteries of the world is a task Sam Krupnik, Anastasia's little brother, takes on with gusto from the day he leaves the hospital as a newborn to his days in nursery school. While the voice may seem more sophisticated than Sam, this is a very funny book which will appeal to fans already acquainted with the Krupnik family, but will work with all ages.
ATTABOY, SAM! (ISBN 0-395-61588-7, 1992; availabe from the NLSBPH on sound recording cassette RC35603) is another well developed, humorous romp with the Krupniks as each tries to create a gift for mom's birthday.
SUBJ: Family life--Fiction.

Ph-1 4-A/6 $13.95   L   KH422
LOWRY, LOIS. Anastasia, absolutely. Houghton Mifflin ISBN 0-395-74521-7, 1995. 119p.
When Anastasia, now thirteen, accidentally puts wrapped dog feces in the mailbox instead of her mother's letter, she is faced with the dire possibility of having committed a federal crime. She also faces a values class in school, which intertwines perfectly with her mailbox dilemma and shows how she thinks. Lowry's observations of dog conduct are right on target, as are her observations of humans. The author's presentation of Anastasia and her friends shows that ever-so-real combination of sophistication and misinformation. The delightful book with artful, unpretentious writing is a pleasure to read.
SUBJ: Values--Fiction./ Schools--Fiction./ Friendship--Fiction./ Dogs--Fiction./ Humorous stories.

Ph-1 4-6/7 $13.95   T   KH423
LOWRY, LOIS. Anastasia has the answers. Houghton Mifflin ISBN 0-395-41795-3, 1986. 123p.
Available from National Library Service for the Blind and Physically Handicapped on sound recording cassette RC25090.
Being thirteen can be dangerous as Anastasia discovers as she attempts to conquer rope climbing in gym, deal with a crush on her gym teacher, and arrange a date for her widowed Uncle George. Although her motives are pure, her maneuvers are suspect, all of which leads to a very satisfying story for Krupnik addicts.
SUBJ: Family life--Fiction./ Humorous stories.

Ph-1 4-6/7 $13.95   T   KH424
LOWRY, LOIS. Anastasia Krupnik. Houghton Mifflin ISBN 0-395-28629-8, 1979. 113p.
Available from National Library Service for the Blind and Physically Handicapped on sound recording cassette RC16624 and in Braille BR04791.

Spanish edition available ANASTASIA KRUPNIK (Espasa Calpe, 1987), $14.50
Ten-year-old Anastasia was keept lists of the things she loved and the things she hated. On the former were: making lists, her wart, her goldfish, and Washburn Cummings. On the latter: her teacher, the forthcoming baby, and her name which was too long to fit on a T-shirt. Well-developed portrait of a spirited girl and her understanding family.
Further adventures of this realistic family are told in ANASTASIA AGAIN (ISBN 0-395-31147-0, 1981) when the family moves from the city to suburbia and ANASTASIA AT YOUR SERVICE (ISBN 0-395-32865-9, 1982) when Anastasia decides she must earn a living. In ANASTASIA ASK YOUR ANALYST (ISBN 0-395-36011-0, 1984) a bust of Sigmund Freud purchased at a garage sale becomes the recipient of Anastasia's list of woes about school projects and the pains of growing up.
Also available from NLSBPH are: ANASTASIA AGAIN in Braille BR05253 and on sound recording cassette RC18817; ANASTASIA AT YOUR SERVICE in Braille BR05425 and on sound recording cassette RC19179; and ANASTASIA ASK YOUR ANALYST in Braille BR06060 and on sound recording cassette RC22029.
SUBJ: Family life--Fiction.

Ph-1 4-6/6 $13.95   T   KH425
LOWRY, LOIS. Anastasia on her own. Houghton Mifflin ISBN 0-395-38133-9, 1985. 131p.
Available from National Library Service for the Blind and Physically Handicapped in Braille BR06736 and on sound cassette RC24986.
Coping with the house and Sam's case of chicken pox while their mother is out of town, thirteen-year-old Anastasia also attempts a gourmet dinner for her first date and entertains her father's first girlfriend. Fast paced, and eventually turning into a mammoth comedy of errors, this will be read avidly by Anastasia's fans.
Anastasia takes a modeling class in ANASTASIA'S CHOSEN CAREER (ISBN 0-395-42506-9, 1987), and in ANASTASIA AT THIS ADDRESS (ISBN 0-395-56263-5, 1991) Anastasia begins a correspondence with a "SWM, 28" whose name she has gleaned in a magazine.
SUBJ: Family life--Fiction.

Ph-1 5-A/6 $13.95   T   KH426
LOWRY, LOIS. Giver. Houghton Mifflin ISBN 0-395-64566-2, 1993. 180p.
Newbery Award, 1994.
Available from the National Library Service for the Blind and Physically Handicapped on sound recording cassette RC 37689.
This extended allegory, which can be read as science fiction, slowly reveals a future, totally controlled society and what the civilization gave up to achieve its colorless perfection without the choices which allow error. Jonas, the protagonist, becomes the "Receiver of Memories" and begins to experience emotions of love, hate, and destruction, to see colors, and to learn memories of past history. He escapes the total control of his birthright so that he might truly be human--with all its faults, joys, and tragedies. This impressive novel will be thought provoking for the more mature reader and is a fine choice as a read-aloud.
SUBJ: Science fiction.

Ph-2 5-6/5 $13.45   T   KH427
LOWRY, LOIS. Number the stars. Houghton Mifflin ISBN 0-395-51060-0, 1989. 137p.
Newbery Medal Book.
Ten-year-old Annemarie finds the Nazi occupation of Denmark is beginning to encroach on her daily life and, more dangerously, that of her Jewish friend, Ellen Rosen and her family. Unfortunately overly simplistic in its development, this still provides insight into a less well known aspect of World War II.
SUBJ: World War, 1939-1945--Denmark--Fiction./ World War, 1939-1945--Jews--Rescue--Fiction./ Friendship--Fiction./ Denmark--Fiction.

Ph-1 3-6/6 $14.95   L   KH428
LOWRY, LOIS. See you around, Sam! Illus. by Diane de Groat. Houghton Mifflin ISBN 0-395-81664-5, 1996. 113p., ill.
"Walter Lorraine books."
When preschooler Sam, Anastasia Krupnik's little brother, wants to wear a pair of fangs, his mother absolutely forbids it, so he runs away from home--to Alaska. All the neighbors, some readers have previously met, and even the mail carrier are involved in Sam's escape in a way that convinces the four-year-old to return to the loving bosom of his family and remain in the supportive and caring neighborhood. Black and white illustrations become progressively more detailed and humorous to reflect Sam's situation. Funny, yet touching in the many frustrations of childhood, Sam's escapade is perfect for

reading aloud.
SUBJ: Runaways--Fiction./ Neighborhood--Fiction./ Humorous stories.

Ph-2 6-A/7 $13.95   T   KH429
LUTZEIER, ELIZABETH. Coldest winter. Holiday House ISBN 0-8234-0899-X, 1991. 153p.
During "the great hunger," the Irish potato blight of 1846-48, Eamonn, eleven, and his family see British soldiers tearing down their small house and flee. The author reflects the desperate conditions throughout Ireland well: starvation, death, disease, and the eventual hope of sailing to the New World. Although the novel contains some improbabilities, it will serve well to portray the terrible years in nineteenth century Ireland. Historical fiction for better readers.
SUBJ: Victims of famine--Fiction./ Ireland--Fiction.

Ph-1 4-6/4 $13.95   L   KH430
LYONS, MARY E. Letters from a slave girl: the story of Harriet Jacobs. Scribner's ISBN 0-684-19446-5; In Canada: Maxwell Macmillan, 1992. 146p.
Includes glossary and bibliography.
Harriet Jacobs was subjected to every kind of insult to body and emotions that a young slave could endure, and she still survived because of her belief that one day she would be free. Her letters depict with vivid detail the day-to-day life of slavery in this unforgettable account. Basic reading for African-American history units. For multicultural studies.
SUBJ: Jacobs, Harriet A. (Harriet Ann)--Fiction./ Slavery--Fiction./ Afro-Americans--Fiction./ Letters--Fiction.

Ph-2 5-A/7 $13.95   T   KH431
MACAULAY, DAVID. Baaa. Houghton Mifflin ISBN 0-395-38948-8, 1985. 61p. ill.
Satirizing the excessive consumption of modern civilization, the author suggests that after the last person has left the earth, the sheep take over, make the same mistakes and ultimately become extinct. Done as an illustrated allegory, this short novel would be useful for discussions of modern civilization and future trends.
SUBJ: Sheep--Fiction./ Civilization--Fiction./ Allegories.

Ph-1 3-A/5 $14.95   T   KH432
MACAULAY, DAVID. Black and white. Houghton Mifflin ISBN 0-395-52151-3, 1990. unp. col. ill.
Caldecott Award.
A jig-saw puzzle of a book with four stories in words and pictures...or is it one story? The many interesting interlocking, or non-interlocking, pieces are united by black-and-white patterns throughout. Imaginative readers and picture viewers can put the stories together as they wish in this artistic joke of artist, author, designer, and printer. A book to refer to over and over.
SUBJ: Literary recreations./ Puzzles--Fiction.

Ph-2 5-6/8 $19.95   T   KH433
MACAULAY, DAVID. Ship. Houghton Mifflin ISBN 0-395-52439-3, 1993. 96p. col. ill., maps.
Follows the search in the Caribbean for a long-lost caravel. Illustrations of underwater archeology and shipbuilding of the past combine with the text to provide a fictionalized account based on modern research. Imagination-trigger and knowledge-expander provides a wealth of historical and technical information that is at once fascinating and mysterious.
SUBJ: Caravels--Fiction./ Ships--Fiction./ Underwater archaeology--Fiction./ Shipwrecks--Fiction./ Caribbean Sea--Antiquities--Fiction./ Diaries--Fiction.

Ph-1 3-A/3 $15.95   T   KH434
MACAULAY, DAVID. Shortcut. Houghton Mifflin ISBN 0-395-52436-9, 1995. unp. col. ill.
"Walter Lorraine books."
Nine short chapters and an epilogue, all generously illustrated in active, colorful, and humorous paintings, present the cinematic story of several characters, animal and human, and the results of a shortcut to market that raises hob and confusion with each of them. Readers will want to study each painting more than once to find further clues about the hilarious events. The text is minimal, but the story is full thanks to the art. It's a hoot.
SUBJ: Literary recreations./ Picture puzzles.

Ph-2 4-A/7 $13.95   L   KH435
MACAULAY, DAVID. Why the chicken crossed the road. Houghton Mifflin ISBN 0-395-44241-9, 1987. 32p. col. ill.
By merely crossing a road, a chicken starts a circular chain of uproarious events that seems destined to continue forever. Told in long sentences, with characters having punnish names and paired with wild, brilliantly colored, detailed, comical pictures, this read aloud has

appeal for all ages.
SUBJ: Humorous stories.

Ph-1 4-6/6 $15.89   L   KH436
MACBRIDE, ROGER LEA. Little house on Rocky Ridge. Illus. by David Gilleece. HarperCollins ISBN 0-06-020843-0; In Canada: HarperCollins, 1993. 353p. ill. (Little House: the Rocky Ridge years).
Continuing the saga of Laura Ingalls Wilder, these episodes concentrate on the 1894 journey from North Dakota to Missouri that she made with her husband and daughter, Rose. Told largely through Rose's eyes, the story of their travels and the settling of their new home will be welcome by "Little House" fans.
The Wilder family works together to produce crops and to make a new home of their Missouri farm in LITTLE FARM IN THE OZARKS (ISBN 0-06-024246-9, 1994).
IN THE LAND OF THE BIG RED APPLE (ISBN 0-06-024964-1, 1995, available from the NLSBPH on sound recording cassette RC 42000) depicts the farm life of nine-year-old Rose Wilder and her family in 1896 in Missouri.
The routine cycle of farm life--cider pressing, butchering, and corn shucking--is described along with its hazards and blessings in ON THE OTHER SIDE OF THE HILL (ISBN 0-06-024968-4, 1995).
Fire and drought force Rose and her family to move to town in LITTLE TOWN IN THE OZARKS (ISBN 0-06-024970-6, 1996).
SUBJ: Wilder, Laura Ingalls--Fiction./ Frontier and pioneer life--Missouri--Fiction./ Missouri--Fiction./ Farm life--Missouri--Fiction.

Ph-1 4-6/6 $15.99   L   KH437
MACDONALD, AMY. No more nice. Illus. by Cat Bowman Smith. Orchard ISBN 0-531-08892-8, 1996. 123p. ill.
"Melanie Kroupa book."
What a good turnabout when an overly well-mannered boy, Simon, visits his unconventional great-aunt and her companion and learns to be as unconventional as they are. He begins to think for himself, tells the truth as he sees it, burps aloud, uses "real" language instead of euphemisms, and, in short, becomes a kid who has fun. And...the book is FUN. Full of humor and laugh-out-loud situations that any child who has been constrained will enjoy. For reading aloud.
SUBJ: Behavior--Fiction./ Great-aunts--Fiction./ Individuality--Fiction./ Humorous stories.

Ph-2 3-5/6 $15.99   L   KH438
MACDONALD, AMY. No more nice. Illus. by Cat Bowman Smith. Orchard ISBN 0-531-08892-8, 1996. 123p. ill.
"Melanie Kroupa book."
Fifth grader Simon's parents and unpleasant aunt and uncle have drilled manners into him until his life is circumscribed on all sides by sometimes unpleasant conventions. When he visits his aged, but very lively and unconventional great aunt and uncle, he learns a freer, different way of living which releases him from the far-too-many inhibitions which have made him a rigid boy. The fun in the book is what he learns and how it makes him a more courageous, pleasant individual. Overly inhibited children should appreciate the unfreezing of Simon.
SUBJ: Behavior--Fiction./ Great-aunts--Fiction./ Individuality--Fiction.

Ph-2 4-5/5 $15.00   T   KH439
MACDONALD, GEORGE. Light princess. Illus. by Maurice Sendak. Farrar, Straus & Giroux ISBN 0-374-34455-8, 1977. 120p.
Available from National Library Service for the Blind and Physically Handicapped on sound recording cassette RC23584, in Braille BR06725, and as talking book TB02624.
Weighing nothing and spending most of her life floating, the little princess really enjoys swimming, where her lack of gravity is no handicap. The modern fairy tale--perhaps somewhat old fashioned--is still enjoyed by today's readers.
SUBJ: Fantasy./ Fairy tales.

Ph-1 2-3/2 $13.95   T   KH440
MACDONALD, MARYANN. No room for Francie. Illus. by Eileen Christelow. Hyperion ISBN 0-7868-0032-1; In Canada: Little, Brown, 1995. 62p. ill. (Hyperion chapters).
The only space Francie doesn't have to share is an old toolshed that no one in her large family has time to help her fix. When her friends from parochial school visit, they are more interested in playing with her siblings than in her clubhouse. Short chapters and few illustrations denote this appealing story as a transitional reader.
SUBJ: Family life--Fiction./ Brothers and sisters--Fiction./ Clubs--Fiction.

Ph-2 4-A/5 $3.95   P   KH441
MACDONALD, REBY EDMOND. Ghosts of Austwick Manor. Aladdin/ Macmillan ISBN 0-689-71533-1; In Canada: Maxwell Macmillan, c1983, 1991. 144p.

This well written fantasy moves between Canada and England. In Canada, young Donald MacDonald inherits a portrait, some old account books, and a magnificent model of the old family house, Austwick Manor, complete with dolls representing the family. His younger sisters are drawn to the model and go back in time where they learn the MacDonald history and halt a family curse which could claim Donald's life.
SUBJ: Mystery and detective stories./ Time travel--Fiction.

Ph-1 5-A/3 $14.00 L KH442
MACKEN, WALTER. Flight of the doves. Simon & Schuster ISBN 0-671-73801-1; In Canada: Simon & Schuster, 1992. 216p.
Selectors' Choice, 19th ed.
The Dove children, Finn, twelve, and his younger sister, Derval, escape from their abusive stepfather, "Uncle" Toby, in England and try to reach a distantly remembered grandmother somewhere in Ireland. Despite the publicity of their flight and having the police on their trail, the children do succeed in their quest in a suspenseful, breathless chase that will rush better readers from word to word and enthral listeners.
SUBJ: Runaways--Fiction./ Brothers and sisters--Fiction./ Orphans--Fiction./ Ireland--Fiction.

Ph-2 4-6/7 $13.89 L KH443
MACLACHLAN, PATRICIA. Arthur, for the very first time. Illus. by Lloyd Bloom. HarperCollins ISBN 0-06-024047-4; In Canada: HarperCollins, 1980. 117p. col. ill.
Available from National Library Service for the Blind and Physically Handicapped on sound recording cassette RC21620.
Arthur is a rather stuffy ten-year-old whose pregnant mother and abstracted father send him to spend the summer with his eccentric great-aunt and great-uncle. It is a summer of surprises--talking French to a pet hen, becoming oddly protective of a pregnant sow, and becoming friends with the zany granddaughter of the local vet. Fine writing and a flair for characterization makes Arthur's growth, as reflected in his journal, a natural outcome of an unusual summer.
SUBJ: Vacations--Fiction./ Humorous stories.

CE
Ph-1 3-5/4 $12.89 L KH444
MACLACHLAN, PATRICIA. Sarah, plain and tall. Illus. by Marcia Sewall. HarperCollins ISBN 0-06-024102-0, 1985. 64p. ill.
Newbery Medal.
Selectors' Choice, 15th ed.
Talking book performed by Glen Close from Caedmon/Harper Audio TC1793, 1986. 1 sound cassette (61min) $11.95.
Available from National Library Service for the Blind and Physically Handicapped on sound recording cassette RC23524.
Spanish version available from Lectorum SARAH, SENCILLA Y ALTA (ISBN 84-279-3421-1, n.d.).
Yearning for the mother who died at his birth, Caleb and his sister are surprised and excited to find their father has advertised for a bride and that Sarah Wheaton from Maine will come to their home. Sarah--plain, tall and independent--misses the sea and the family worries she will leave, but she announces she would miss them more and will marry their father. A treasure of a book. Good reading aloud.
SUBJ: Family life--Fiction./ Individuality--Fiction./ Frontier and pioneer life--Fiction./ Spanish language materials.

Ph-1 3-5/3 $11.89 L KH445
MACLACHLAN, PATRICIA. Skylark. HarperCollins ISBN 0-06-023333-8; In Canada: HarperCollins, 1994. 87p.
Sequel to: SARAH, PLAIN AND TALL, HarperCollins, 1985.
Good times, then drought on the prairie cause Sarah, Ann, and Caleb to return to Maine for a time.
SUBJ: Stepmothers--Fiction./ Droughts--Fiction./ Frontier and pioneer life--Fiction./ Prairies--Fiction.

Ph-1 4-6/7 $14.99 T KH446
MAHY, MARGARET. Five sisters. Illus. by Patricia MacCarthy. Viking ISBN 0-670-87042-0; In Canada: Penguin, 1997. 80p. ill.
First published in Great Britain, Hamish Hamilton Ltd., 1996.
The five sisters are joined paper dolls who like Andersen's "The Tin Soldier" travel widely by means of accidental winds, water, and the like. Each develops character and personality as various people they meet add features and other details to the blank forms. Thus, inanimate objects become animated. They talk, think, and meet new experiences until they are returned--by happenstance--to the place where, years and many adventures before, they were cut by Sally's Nana. Mystical, magical, and full of witty wordplay, poetry, musings, and even puns, the book is holding and seems meant for reading aloud. Black and white art follows the adventures and expands on them as the dolls change.
SUBJ: Paper dolls--Fiction./ Fantasy.

Ph-2 3-5/4 $3.50 P KH447
MAHY, MARGARET. Fortune branches out. Illus. by Marian Young. Dell ISBN 0-440-41102-5; In Canada: Bantam Doubleday Dell, c1994, 1995. 83p. ill.
"Vanessa Hamilton book."
Tessa is determined to raise $100 for the New Zealand National Telethon. With the help of her cousins and her unique moneymaking schemes, she is sure to reach her goal. Her humorous solutions to fund-raising will amuse readers.
SUBJ: Fund raising--Fiction./ Moneymaking projects--Fiction./ Cousins--Fiction./ New Zealand--Fiction.

Ph-2 3-5/7 $13.95 T KH448
MAHY, MARGARET. Good Fortunes gang. Illus. by Marian Young. Delacorte ISBN 0-385-31015-3; In Canada: Bantam Doubleday Dell, 1993. 100p. ill.
"Vanessa Hamilton book."
Available from the National Library Service for the Blind and Physically Handicapped on sound recording cassette RC 38377.
When Pete Fortune finally settles in his father's New Zealand home instead of constantly traveling about Australia, he meets his extended family. Before his Anzac cousins will accept him, he must undergo several, sometimes unkind, challenges. Readers will empathize with Pete's fears and his gumption in taking on the cousins, especially Tracey, a girl with an undeniable mean streak. Lightly humorous book full of "different" characters. Black and white illustrations add little.
SUBJ: Moving, Household--Fiction./ Cousins--Fiction./ New Zealand--Fiction.

Ph-2 5-A/7 $11.95 T KH449
MAHY, MARGARET. Great piratical rumbustification and The librarian and the robbers. Illus. by Quentin Blake. Godine ISBN 0-87923-629-9, c1978, 1986. 62p. ill.
Available from National Library Service for the Blind and Physically Handicapped on sound recording cassette RC26265.
Entertaining and outrageous, these two wacky and wild stories present pirates, robbers and librarians in a new light. Readers will enjoy the great piratical rumbustification organized by Orpheus Clink, the babysitter for the Terrapin family, who is actually an unreformed pirate. In the second story, bookish, but beautiful, Serena Laburnum, the lovely librarian, outwits the robbers, marries their leader and converts the rest of the band to librarians! Great fun--not to be taken seriously.
More riotous fun may be found in THE BIRTHDAY BURGLAR, AND A VERY WICKED HEADMISTRESS (ISBN 0-87923-720-1, 1984, OPC).
SUBJ: Humorous stories./ Librarians--Fiction./ Pirates--Fiction.

CE
Ph-1 4-A/7 $13.99 T KH450
MAHY, MARGARET. Greatest show off earth. Illus. by Wendy Smith. Viking ISBN 0-670-85736-X; In Canada: Penguin, 1994. 186p. ill.
"Vanessa Hamilton book."
Talking book available from Listening Library YA 870 (ISBN 0-8072-7518-2, 1995). 3 sound cassettes (178min), $23.98.
Available from the National Library Service for the Blind and Physically Handicapped on sound recording cassette RC 42096.
Hyperspace, a circus lost there, dark forces whose aim is to destroy anything that resembles fun, and a super meanie in the person of ten-year-old Delphinium's ex-nanny, Molly alias La Mollerina, combine to give readers yet another book of fast-paced fun from the master of the ridiculous, Margaret Mahy. The nonsense is nonstop and logically developed as Delphinium is joined by Jason to defeat the evildoers in a book that is a complete delight. Just right for reading aloud.
SUBJ: Circus--Fiction./ Science fiction.

CE
Ph-1 5-A/6 $13.95 T KH451
MAHY, MARGARET. Haunting. Atheneum ISBN 0-689-50243-5, 1982. 135p.
Carnegie Medal.
Available from National Library Service for the Blind and Physically Handicapped on sound recording cassette RC21801 and in Braille BR05514.
Videocassette HAUNTING OF BARNEY PALMER available from WonderWorks/dist. by Bonneville Worldwide (ISBN 0-7800-0703-4, 1986). 1/2" VHS videocassette color (58min), $29.95.
The placid life of a New Zealand family conceals seething tension as young Barney copes with constant ghostly whispers and visions. It is the dangerous great uncle Cole with his magic gifts and he is confronted and defeated by the family who have learned through a series of conversations with their multi-generational family that in each generation there is the gift of ESP and magic. This well written family story is interesting because of the gradual acceptance of occult gifts.
SUBJ: Extrasensory perception--Fiction./ Supernatural--Fiction.

TB   Ph-2 3-A $26.95   KH452
MAHY, MARGARET. Horrible story and others (Talking book). Read by Richard Mitchley. Chivers Press/dist. by G.K. Hall ISBN 0-8161-7557-8, 1992. 3 sound cassettes (180min).
Characteristic droll wit of Margaret Mahy is found in 21 complete and unabridged stories ranging from the humorous to the horrible. Clear diction will help listeners understand the few Briticisms which will be easy to comprehend from context.
SUBJ: Humorous stories./ Horror stories./ Short stories.

                                Ph-1 4-6/4 $15.95   L   KH453
MAHY, MARGARET. Tall story and other tales. Illus. by Jan Nesbitt. McElderry ISBN 0-689-50547-7, 1992. 88p b&w and col illus.
Eleven stories demonstrating typical Mahy characteristics of quirky characters and odd happenings are gathered from the First, Second, and Third Mahy story books and illustrated in lively and colorful fashion. The various themes, at once humorous, fantastical, and whimsical, are prime for oral presentation to third-graders and will be enjoyed by better readers who still want fairy tales, but who need new and different ones.
SUBJ: Fairy tales./ Short stories.

                                Ph-1 3-6/5 $13.99   T   KH454
MAHY, MARGARET. Tingleberries, tuckertubs and telephones: a tale of love and ice-cream. Illus. by Robert Staermose. Viking ISBN 0-670-86331-9; In Canada: Penguin, 1996. 96p. ill.
First published in Great Britain, Hamish Hamilton Ltd., 1995.
"Vanessa Hamilton book."
Nonsense--sheer, silly, wonderful nonsense--based on nonsensical characters, silly adventures, and high imagination. Once again, Mahy returns to pirates--modern executive pirates with phones (cell phones, natch). The pirates are seemingly dangerous, but fools at heart, as shy orphan Saracen Hobday defeats them, becomes the world's entrepreneur of tingleberries, and falls in love. No sense in looking for a plot, just enjoy the nonsense--and use for reading aloud, too.
SUBJ: Pirates--Fiction./ Humorous stories.

                                Ph-1 6-A/6 $14.00   T   KH455
MAHY, MARGARET. Underrunners. Viking ISBN 0-670-84179-X; In Canada: Penguin, 1992. 169p.
"Tris and Winola find the underrunners, a vast network of tunnels, the ideal place to escape their unhappy lives and act out their fantasies, but the tunnels become a dangerous place when invaded by an unseen stranger." (CIP) Suspenseful and tense throughout with well-developed, interesting, and imaginative characters, the world that is created is easily visualized by the reader as are all the characters. The imaginary worlds the children invent are fantastic, but the real world in which Winola's father kidnaps her and Tris is frighteningly real. The better reader will empathize with the children and it might be a holding experience for a listener if read aloud.
SUBJ: Mystery and detective stories.

                                Ph-1 6-A/6 $3.50   P   KH456
MARINO, JAN. Day that Elvis came to town. Avon ISBN 0-380-71672-0, 1993. 204p.
When Mercedes, a glamorous night club singer, becomes a boarder, Wanda, at first resentful, comes to admire and respect the "sparkling" woman who helps her to understand her parents and their problems. Wanda convinces herself that Mercedes knows Elvis Presley and constructs a fantasy about Mercedes, Elvis, and herself. Set in Georgia in the early 1960s, the novel also involves bigotry against Mercedes, who is half Caucasian, half African-American. Well characterized, the book reveals many layers of human conduct, both decent and indecent, and presents realistic characters against a clear background of time and place. For multicultural studies.
SUBJ: Southern States--Fiction./ Afro-Americans--Fiction./ Prejudices--Fiction./ Alcoholism--Fiction.

                                Ph-2 2-4/3 $12.95   L   KH457
MARKHAM, MARION M. St. Patrick's Day shamrock mystery. Illus. by Karen A. Jerome. Houghton Mifflin ISBN 0-395-72137-7, 1995. 47p. ill.
Set in an easy-reader format, this small mystery, peopled with "nice" folk, is accessible to first readers and older ones who are becoming independent. The transitional reader doesn't deal with St. Patrick's Day traditions, but it will introduce the reader to twins, a gifted younger child, and a slight mystery.
SUBJ: Twins--Fiction./ St. Patrick's Day--Fiction./ Mystery and detective stories.

                                Ph-1 1-4/2 $12.99   T   KH458
MARSHALL, JAMES. Rats on the range and other stories. Dial ISBN 0-8037-1384-3, 1993. 80p.
Sequel to: RATS ON THE ROOF.
Rats on a dude ranch? A mouse housekeeper for a cat with a specific

appetite? Pigs in school and on the job market? Eight more wacky tales (tails?) to delight those who relish laughter. Alas, not illustrated since it was published after Marshall's death.
SUBJ: Animals--Fiction./ Short stories.

                                Ph-1 1-4/2 $12.89   L   KH459
MARSHALL, JAMES. Rats on the roof and other stories. Dial ISBN 0-8037-0835-1, 1991. 79p. ill.
Selectors' Choice, 19th ed.
Available from the National Library Service for the Blind and Physically Handicapped on sound recording cassette RC35447.
Tumbling from the fertile and somewhat satiric brain of Marshall come seven delightful stories dealing with fanciful creatures who start out on the wrong foot and somehow end up on the right one. Cats, rats, wolves, sheep, cows, and other humorously illustrated characters inhabit a choice, easy-to-read short story collection just right for new readers and for chuckle-filled oral presentation.
SUBJ: Animals--Fiction./ Short stories.

                                Ph-2 3-5/6 $14.95   T   KH460
MASTERS, SUSAN ROWAN. Libby Bloom. Illus. by Beata Szpura. Henry Holt ISBN 0-8050-3374-2; In Canada: Fitzhenry & Whiteside, 1995. 86p. ill. (Redfeather book).
Frequently in trouble caused by accident not through purposeful actions, klutzy fourth grader Libby is removed from the school chorus and put in band. There, she begins to master the tuba--and herself--helped by a delightful and perceptive band teacher. Readers, male and female, who suffer from embarrassment from their own untoward actions will empathize with Libby and root for her--and perhaps hope to triumph as she does.
SUBJ: Self-confidence--Fiction./ Schools--Fiction./ Tuba--Fiction./ Sisters--Fiction.

CE   Ph-1 4-6/4 $15.00   L   KH461
MATHIS, SHARON BELL. Hundred penny box. Viking ISBN 0-670-38787-8, 1975. 47p. ill.
Newbery Honor Book.
Available from National Library Service for the Blind and Physically Handicapped on sound recording cassette RC10920.
Videocassette available from SVE/Churchill Media C80286-HAKT, 1979. 1/2" VHS videocassette color (18min), $99.95.
Talking book available from SRA/McGraw-Hill 87-507865, 1977. 1 sound cassette, $15.00.
When Michael's one-hundred-year-old, Great-Great-Aunt Dew comes to live with them, she brings an old beat-up box, which contains as many pennies as her age. He loves to hear the tales she tells about the year she received each penny. A warm story of the love between old age and youth.
SUBJ: Family life--Fiction./ Human relations--Fiction./ Aunts--Fiction./ Coins--Fiction.

                                Ph-3 4-6/4 $15.95   L   KH462
MATTHEWS, MARY. Magid fasts for Ramadan. Illustrated by E. B. Lewis. Clarion ISBN 0-395-66589-2, 1996. 48p. col. ill.
Includes glossary.
Magid, eight, and his family are practicing Muslims who live in Egypt. When the family is celebrating Ramadan, he is determined to fast like the adults although he is far too young. The explanation of the holiday and the view of a warm Muslim family will add greatly to multicultural studies or world religion classes.
SUBJ: Ramadan--Fiction./ Fasts and feasts--Islam--Fiction./ Cairo (Egypt)--Fiction.

                                Ph-2 3-5/4 $13.89   L   KH463
MAZER, ANNE. Accidental witch. Hyperion ISBN 0-7868-2073-X; In Canada: Little, Brown, 1995. 123p. ill.
Sorcery goes awry when klutzy Bee (Phoebe), ten, falls from a tree into a coven of witches and must learn witchy magic more or less on her own. Humorous and fast paced, the accidental witch's adventures should hold readers, provided they accept the premise that in Bee's town witches are to be expected and accepted although their magic is never bad.
SUBJ: Witches--Fiction./ Magic--Fiction.

                                Ph-2 A/6 $3.25   P   KH464
MAZER, HARRY. Island keeper. Dell ISBN 0-440-94774-X, 1981. 165p.
Overwhelmed by the grief of her sister's death and feeling unloved by her family, Cleo runs away to live alone on an island in Canada owned by her father. Arriving with no skills, she sets to work to organize her life, finding food and shelter and taking charge of her environment in a way that helps her evolve as an independent, self-confident young woman. Useful for survival units since it provides a female alternative to HATCHET and THE ISLAND.
SUBJ: Runaways--Fiction./ Survival--Fiction./ Islands--Fiction./ Family life--Fiction.

Ph-1 6-A/4 $3.50   P   KH465
MAZER, HARRY. Last mission. Dell ISBN 0-440-94797-9, c1979, 1986.
182p.
World War II buffs will accept this action filled story of a fifteen-
year-old Jewish New Yorker who longs to avenge the Holocaust.
Aided by a 4-F older brother's birth certificate and a mature
appearance, he lies his way into the U. S. Air Force. After 24
bombing missions he's shot down over Czechoslovakia, the crew's
sole survivor, and taken POW but fortunately escapes in the collapse
of the German front. Some salty language but based on the author's
wartime experiences.
SUBJ: World War, 1939-1945--Aerial operations--Fiction./ Prisoners
of war--Fiction./ Jews--United States--Fiction.

Ph-1 6-A/6 $5.99   P   KH466
MCCAFFREY, ANNE. Dragonsong. Bantam ISBN 0-553-25852-4; In
Canada: Bantam Doubleday Dell, c1976, 1986. 202p., map.
Menolly lives on the planet Pern where huge flying dragons guard
against burning spores called Threadfall. A gifted musician, she is
barred by her sex from entry to Harperhall. But goaded by her
father, she runs away during Threadfall and makes friends with a
group of tiny enchanting fire lizards she trains to sing, an action so
unusual that she is accepted at Harperhall. In DRAGONSINGER
(Atheneum ISBN 0-689-30570-2, 1977) Menolly feels she is a failure
at Harperhall, and that Masterharper Robinton finds her music inferior
and her fire lizards a nuisance. She is unaware of the growing
respect for her courage and intelligence. In DRAGONDRUMS (ISBN
0-553-25855-9, 1980) the quickwitted boy Piemur, met in
DRAGONSINGER, finds his days at Harperhall numbered when his
voice changes but then is plunged into exciting political intrigue by the
Masterharper, Menolly and her fiancee, Sebell. Sometimes slow
moving and episodic, this trilogy has a large following.
Also available from NLSBPH are: DRAGONDRUMS in Braille
BRA17918 and on sound recording cassette RC15984;
DRAGONSINGER in Braille BRA17767 and on sound recording
cassette RC15983.
SUBJ: Fantasy./ Dragons--Fiction./ Musicians--Fiction.

Ph-2 3-5/4 $15.95   L   KH467
MCCLINTOCK, BARBARA. Fantastic drawings of Danielle. Houghton
Mifflin ISBN 0-395-73980-2, 1996. unp. col. ill.
Danielle, a young and very imaginative artist living in Paris, France, a
century ago, paints the world as she sees it in her mind's eye. Her
paintings are disconcerting to her photographer father who sees the
world as the camera sees it. When she meets another artist, Mme.
Beton, whose art is as imaginative and creative as her own, Danielle
knows that despite her father's lack of understanding of her work, she
is doing the right thing--for her. The artistically produced and
designed book features mixed media paintings in color which tell the
story and extend character, setting, and the artistic world of the child.
The use of sepia adds atmospheric tones of the photography at the
turn of the century. Like Allen Say's EMMA'S RUG and M.B.
Goffstein's GOLDIE THE DOLLMAKER, this shows the artist and the
personal artistic vision that creates a world beyond the obvious.
SUBJ: Artists--Fiction./ Fathers and daughters--Fiction.

CE   Ph-1 P-A/6 $15.95   L   KH468
MCCLOSKEY, ROBERT. Burt Dow, deep-water man: a tale of the sea in
the classic tradition. Viking ISBN 0-670-19748-5, c1963. 61p. col. ill.
Videocassette available from Weston Woods HMPV2672V. 1/2"
VHS videocassette color (10min), $49.95.
Read-along kit available from Weston Woods HPRA 262, 1990. 1
hardcover book, 1 sound cassette (13min), $12.95.
Tall tale of an old fisherman who catches a whale by the tail and
uses a candy-striped band aid to cover the hole.
SUBJ: Whales--Fiction./ Humorous stories.

VCR   Ph-2 2-6 $49.95   OD KH469
MCCLOSKEY, ROBERT. Doughnuts (Videocassette). Weston Woods
HMPV400V, 1984. 1/2" VHS videocassette color (26min).
From HOMER PRICE.
Left in charge of the new doughnut machine while Uncle Ulysses is
visiting with his friends in back of the barbershop, young Homer, the
sandwich board man, and the visiting rich lady soon find there's a
superabundance of doughnuts. Set in the 1940s, this farcical episode
is perhaps not quite as funny to today's technologically oriented
audience, but still serves well as program material.
SUBJ: Humorous stories.

CE   Ph-1 3-6/5 $14.00   L   KH470
MCCLOSKEY, ROBERT. Homer Price. Viking Penguin ISBN 0-670-
37729-5, c1943. 149p. ill.
Read-along kit available from Live Oak Media (ISBN 0-670-37734-1,
1973). 1 paperback book, 1 sound cassette (50min), $15.95.
Available from National Library Service for the Blind and Physically

Handicapped on sound recording cassette RC24724 and as talking
book TB02977.
Hilarious complications result when Homer becomes involved with
bank robbers, a doughnut machine, and Super Duper, a comic strip
hero.
In CENTERBURG TALES (ISBN 0-670-20977-5, 1951) Homer,
Grampa, and others keep preposterous things happening.
Also available from NLSBPH is CENTERBURG TALES in Braille
BRA05899.
SUBJ: Humorous stories./ Short stories.

TB   Ph-1 3-6 $8.95   OD KH471
MCCLOSKEY, ROBERT. Homer Price stories (Talking book). Read by
Robert McCloskey. Weston Woods WW400C, n.d. 1 sound cassette
(60min).
Based on book of the same title. McCloskey's Maine drawl and
effective story-telling style make these selections an excellent listening
experience.
Contents: The doughnuts; The cosmic comic; Nothing new under the
sun (The musical mousetrap).
SUBJ: Humorous stories.

Ph-2 6-A/7 $4.95   P   KH472
MCCLUNG, ROBERT M. Hugh Glass, mountain man. Morrow ISBN
0-688-04595-2, 1993. 166p. ill.
Includes bibliography.
Available from the National Library Service for the Blind and
Physically Handicapped on sound recording cassette RC 35571.
Presents a factual fictionalized biography of one year in the life of
hunter-trapper Hugh Glass in the U.S. wilderness in 1823. Glass, left
for dead by his companions after being almost fatally mauled by a
grizzly bear, recovered and crawled two hundred miles to the nearest
settlement. Native groups and Anglos are neither all good nor all bad
in a book that recreates the frontier with much suspense, a
bibliographical essay, reproduction of period prints, and a map. Top
flight historical factual-fiction for recreational reading and units on
frontier exploration.
SUBJ: Glass, Hugh--Fiction./ Survival--Fiction./ Frontier and pioneer
life--Fiction./ West (U.S.)--Fiction.

Ph-2 1-3/2 $18.99   L   KH473
MCCULLY, EMILY ARNOLD. Ballot box battle. Knopf ISBN 0-679-
97938-7; In Canada: Random House, 1996. unp. col. ill.
"Borzoi book."
A fictionalized account of the attempts of Elizabeth Cady Stanton to
cast a vote in the 1880 election is told through the eyes of her young
neighbor Cordelia, who accompanies her to the poll, observes events,
and proves her own courage in the face of taunts from her brother
and his friends. Full-color illustrations are softly focused. Will serve as
a good discussion starter about women's issues and voting rights for
early grades. For reading aloud.
SUBJ: Stanton, Elizabeth Cady--Fiction./ Feminists--Fiction./
Suffragists--Fiction./ Women--Suffrage--Fiction.

Ph-1 4-6/6 $14.00   T   KH474
MCEWAN, IAN. Daydreamer. Illus. by Anthony Browne. HarperCollins
ISBN 0-06-024426-7; In Canada: HarperCollins, 1994. 192p. ill.
Peter Fortune, ten, seems controlled by his active, imaginative
daydreams which are recounted in several lively adventures. He enters
the body of a cat, catches a most unexpected neighborhood thief,
meets an unpleasant doll that comes to life, encounters the school
bully, and experiences other incidents. Browne's portraits add to the
strong text. Children who are too often told, "Stop daydreaming,"
will appreciate the extraordinary fantasies, as will the less imaginative.
Large type, a clean page, and wide leading create an aesthetically
pleasing book. Episodes make good excerpts for reading aloud in
third grade and above.
SUBJ: Imagination--Fiction./ Family life--Fiction.

Ph-2 5-A/6 $16.00   T   KH475
MCGRAW, ELOISE JARVIS. Moorchild. By Eloise McGraw. McElderry
ISBN 0-689-80654-X; In Canada: Distican, 1996. 241p.
Newbery Honor book, 1997.
"Feeling that she is neither fully human nor 'Folk,' a changeling learns
her true identity and attempts to find the human child whose place
she has been given." (CIP) Saaski, known as Moql among the fairy
folk, is the half-human, half-folk daughter of the fairies who suffers in
the world of humans. Only hard won magic unknots the history of her
birth and provides a means of escape. Her adventures are tense,
characterization is strong, plot movement is fast, and settings are well
defined. It is too bad that Romany, who are only tangential to the
story, are unnecessarily stereotyped. Stonger readers, particularly
readers of fantasy, should appreciate this book.
SUBJ: Fantasy./ Fairies--Fiction./ Identity--Fiction.

Ph-1 5-8/6 $15.00 T KH476
MCKAY, HILARY. Amber cat. McElderry ISBN 0-689-81360-0, 1997. 134p.
Readers who enjoyed McKay's DOG FRIDAY will meet many of the same characters again in a story which can be read independently of the first book. Now Robin, Dan, and Sun Dance stay together at Porridge Hall when they have chicken pox. To entertain them, Mrs. Brogan relates an incident from 27 years before in which three children meet a strange girl, Harriet, on the beach and spend time playing and adventuring with her. The story in the present is humorous, largely sparked by fast, brittle dialogue which appears absolutely realistic, but the story in the past carries with it an edge of sadness as we learn who the children were and realize that Harriet, even decades before, was a ghost. It is a well constructed, rapid book, with well-developed characters and mixes humorous incidents with serious ones. For reading aloud.
SUBJ: Friendship--Fiction./ Seashore--Fiction./ Ghosts--Fiction./ England--Fiction.

Ph-1 4-A/7 $15.00 L KH477
MCKAY, HILARY. Dog Friday. McElderry ISBN 0-689-80383-4; In Canada: Distican, 1995. 135p.
First published in Great Britain, Victor Gollancz Ltd., 1994.
Robin Brogan, ten, has a fear of dogs until new neighbors move in next door. The Robinson children have a "total ruthlessness" (p.51) and fearlessness that help liberate Robin even as he looks on their deeds and doings with amazement. He eventually rescues a dog at the beach. The novel, typical of McKay (THE EXILES), presents outrageous, believable characters in fast-paced, humorous situations. Too many !'s spoil the style, but otherwise it is a serious and hilarious romp.
SUBJ: Dogs--Fiction./ Police--Fiction./ England--Fiction.

Ph-1 6-A/7 $14.95 L KH478
MCKAY, HILARY. Exiles. McElderry ISBN 0-689-50555-8; In Canada: Maxwell Macmillan, 1992. 217p.
Available from the National Library Service for the Blind and Physically Handicapped on sound recording cassette RC 38569.
The four Conroy sisters, ages thirteen, eleven, eight, and six, are forced to spend a summer at the seaside country home of their eccentric grandma. All are voracious readers, but Big Grandma gives them assorted tasks to show them that life also exists outside books. In a fast-paced, well-characterized series of episodes, readers will meet adventures, anger, changes of mind, and a host of eccentric people. Fun.
SUBJ: Sisters--Fiction./ Grandmothers--Fiction./ Humorous stories.

Ph-1 5-A/7 $15.95 L KH479
MCKAY, HILARY. Exiles at home. McElderry ISBN 0-689-50610-4; In Canada: Maxwell Macmillan, 1994. 200p.
Sequel to THE EXILES, McElderry, 1992.
Without the permission of their parents, the Conroys, four sisters, raise money to sponsor a ten-year-old student in a school in Africa. Their efforts to earn the monthly fees and their letters--and those of the boy in Africa--give rise to several difficult, but humorous, situations. Well characterized throughout, the book is meant for better readers--those who read and enjoyed Alcott's LITTLE WOMEN.
SUBJ: Sisters--Fiction./ Family life--Fiction./ Moneymaking projects--Fiction./ Grandmothers--Fiction./ England--Fiction./ Humorous stories.

Ph-2 3-5/6 $14.95 T KH480
MCKAY, JR., LAWRENCE. Caravan. Illus. by Darryl Ligasan. Lee & Low ISBN 1-880000-23-7, 1995. unp. col. ill., map.
Based on the caravan journeys of the Kirghiz of Afghanistan, the brightly illustrated book (in acrylics) presents the ten-day, 125 mile journey of a camel caravan from the mountains to the regional capital where the markets are. A map (alas, lacking a compass rose and scale) shows the rough terrain over which they travel as do the pictures. Good for units on trade and for multicultural studies, the book, while not inspiring, is instructive, especially about a different and exotic subject.
SUBJ: Caravans--Fiction./ Barter--Fiction./ Fathers and sons--Fiction./ Afghanistan--Fiction.

Ph-2 3-4/4 $13.95 L KH481
MCKENNA, COLLEEN OSHAUGHNESSY. Good grief, third grade. Illus. by Richard Williams. Scholastic ISBN 0-590-45123-5; In Canada: Scholastic, 1993. 152p. ill.
"Marsha Cessano, Collette Murphy's neighbor, is determined to be good in third grade--no messy desk, no temper, no tricks--but Roger Friday is making it difficult." (CIP) When the new student teacher assigns the class partners to work on a project, Marsha begins to appreciate Roger and inspect some of her previous notions about him--based on assumption not fact. Amusing story with believable protagonists whom one might meet in almost any school in a middle-class neighborhood.
SUBJ: Schools--Fiction./ Interpersonal relations--Fiction.

Ph-2 3-5/4 $3.50 P KH482
MCKENNA, COLLEEN OSHAUGHNESSY. Valentine's Day can be murder. Scholastic ISBN 0-590-67985-6; In Canada: Scholastic, 1996. 115p.
"Apple paperback."
In a comedy of confusion, Roger is enmeshed in trouble over "mushy" Valentine's poems which go astray. Though the insults between Roger and Marsha--who can be a pain--reflect typical fifth grade behavior, they can become tedious.
SUBJ: Valentine's Day--Fiction./ Valentines--Fiction./ Schools--Fiction./ Friendship--Fiction.

Ph-1 3-5/4 $4.95 P KH483
MCKENZIE, ELLEN KINDT. King, the princess, and the tinker. Illus. by William Low. Henry Holt ISBN 0-8050-9251-6; In Canada: Fitzhenry & Whiteside, 1992. 69p. ill. (Redfeather book).
The king, father of the youngest princess and several other children, shuts himself away from all company, even his children, to gloat over his wealth. Through a series of mishaps, all of which will delight readers, a simple, loving tinker becomes king and reunites the lonely Princess Sweet Rosilla with her father. Readers will enjoy this old-fashioned tale of good rewarded, folly remedied, and the innocence of children. Illustrations add to the whole of this Thurber-like story. Try reading aloud.
SUBJ: Kings, queens, rulers, etc.--Fiction./ Father and child--Fiction.

Ph-1 3-5/5 $13.95 T KH484
MCKENZIE, ELLEN KINDT. Stargone John. Illustrated by William Low. Henry Holt ISBN 0-8050-1451-9; In Canada: Fitzhenry & Whiteside, 1990. 67p. ill. (Redfeather book).
Selectors' Choice, 18th ed.
Clearly depicts John Bain's fearful shyness and silent withdrawal through the eyes of his older sister, Lisa, 9, as a teacher tries to make him conform to unyielding methods, punishments, and ridicule in the first grade of a rural one-room school. Called "Stargone," (i.e., dreamy), John has special talents recognized by the old blind, retired teacher who has secretly taught him to read and write. Because of this secret friendship with her and the ability to communicate that she has developed in him, he helps save her life. Low's black and white illustrations add an extra dimension to this gripping book that shows both the tender and cruel sides of life. Good choice for oral presentation and a pleasurable independent reading experience.
SUBJ: Emotional problems--Fiction./ Schools--Fiction./ Teachers--Fiction./ Blind--Fiction./ Physically handicapped--Fiction.

Ph-1 6-A/6 $15.89 L KH485
MCKINLEY, ROBIN. Beauty: a retelling of the story of Beauty and the Beast. HarperCollins ISBN 0-06-024150-0; In Canada: HarperCollins, 1978. 247p.
Selectors' Choice, 12th ed.
Available from National Library Service for the Blind and Physically Handicapped in Braille BR06800 and on sound recording cassette RC14411.
Beauty, who thinks she is ugly, takes responsibility for her father's promise to the Beast and goes to live in the enchanted castle. Slowly she comes to love the Beast and releases him from the enchantment. Magnificent telling of the classic fairy tale, embellished and enlarged for gifted readers.
SUBJ: Fairy tales./ Love--Fiction.

Ph-1 A/7 $15.00 T KH486
MCKINLEY, ROBIN. Blue sword. Greenwillow ISBN 0-688-00938-7, 1982. 272p.
Newbery Honor book.
Available from National Library Service for the Blind and Physically Handicapped on sound recording cassette RC23523.
Harry Crewe is a restless, independent girl drawn to the mountain home of the Hillfolk rising across the desert from the strict, regimented Homelander outpost where she lives with her brother. Kidnapped by Corlath, King of the Hillfolk, who sees in Harry a part of his people's destiny, she grows to love her life, rises to be guardian of the Blue Sword and helps win an epic battle against the Northerners, winning Corlath's love and admiration. This intricate, well written fantasy which concludes with their marriage is the first of a series.
SUBJ: Fantasy.

Ph-1 4-6/6 $12.95 T KH487
MCKINLEY, ROBIN. Door in the hedge. Greenwillow ISBN 0-688-00312-5, 1981. 216p.
Selectors' Choice, 13th ed.

Rich retellings and skillful creation of two new folklore-like tales mark this volume. Excellent for reading aloud, it may also be a source of inspiration for creative writing.
Contents: "Door in the hedge." "Princess and the frog." "Golden Hind." "Twelve Dancing Princesses."
SUBJ: Fairy tales.

Ph-1 5-A/7 $15.00 T KH488
MCKINLEY, ROBIN. Hero and the crown. Greenwillow ISBN 0-688-02593-5, 1984. 246p.
Newbery Medal.
Selectors' Choice, 15th ed.
Available from National Library Service for the Blind and Physically Handicapped on sound recording cassette RC25926.
Having established herself as a dragon slayer to gain esteem in the eyes of the people of her father's kingdom, Princess Aerin finds herself in battle with the huge dragon, Maur. The fate of the country of Damar hangs in the balance. Set several hundred years before THE BLUE SWORD, the dramatically romantic fantasy is hallmarked by splendid characterization and prose that is simultaneously richly descriptive and restrained. A superb suspenseful read-aloud as well as a joyful experience for fans of the genre.
SUBJ: Fantasy.

Ph-1 6-A/7 $14.00 L KH489
MCKINLEY, ROBIN. Knot in the grain and other stories. Greenwillow ISBN 0-688-09201-2, 1994. 195p.
Gathers five longish short stories, all featuring careful, thoughtful, and smooth development and style. Four are fantasies set in Damar, and one, the title story, is very contemporary and shows unexplained magic. Readers of fantasy and fans of McKinley will welcome these complex, holding creations.
SUBJ: Short stories./ Supernatural--Fiction.

Ph-1 A/8 $13.00 T KH490
MCKINLEY, ROBIN. Outlaws of Sherwood. Greenwillow ISBN 0-688-07178-3, 1988. 282p.
By killing a man, Robin determines his own fate and must thereafter dwell in a vast forest with his trustworthy band. Marian's love for him brings about a confrontation with the Sheriff and finally understanding from the king. Skilled readers relish this romance and may enjoy comparing it with traditional versions. Try oral presentation.
SUBJ: Robin Hood (Legendary character)--Fiction.

Ph-1 5-A/6 $16.00 T KH491
MCKISSACK, PAT. Dark-thirty: Southern tales of the supernatural. By Patricia C. McKissack. Illus. by Brian Pinkney. Knopf ISBN 0-679-8186349; In Canada: Distican, 1992. 122p. ill.
Newbery Honor Book, 1993.
Coretta Scott King Award, 1993.
Selectors' Choice, 19th ed.
Available from the National Library Service for the Blind and Physically Handicapped on sound recording cassette RC 36183.
The "dark-thirty," the half hour before sunset (CIP), presents "a collection of original stories rooted in African-American history and the oral storytelling tradition." (Author's note, p. iv) The ten stories, suitably illustrated with b&w scratchboard, deal with sleeping car porters, a Klan lynching and ghostly revenge, an evil African talisman, the ghost of a mother and young child whom a racist bus driver would not pick up on a snowy night, and other tales with elements of the supernatural and horror. All will tell well and add an extra dimension to the study of African-American history and life. For multicultural studies.
SUBJ: Ghosts--Fiction./ Horror stories./ Afro-Americans--Fiction./ Short stories.

Ph-1 3-5/4 $16.00 T KH492
MCKISSACK, PAT. Ma Dear's aprons. By Patricia C. McKissack. Illus. by Floyd Cooper. Atheneum ISBN 0-689-81051-2; In Canada: Distican, 1997. unp. col. ill.
"Anne Schwartz book."
Cooper's oil washes and the text based on a memory of the author's great-grandmother, Ma Dear, glow with affection as the story of the aprons, one for each day and each day's activity (ironing, doing the laundry for others, etc.), is revealed. Only on Sunday does she not wear an apron. The honesty and dignity of the woman and her labor and the love between mother and child are tender and very real. For multicultural studies.
SUBJ: Aprons--Fiction./ Mothers and sons--Fiction.

Ph-1 5-A/5 $14.00 T KH493
MEAD, ALICE. Junebug. Farrar Straus Giroux ISBN 0-374-33964-3; In Canada: HarperCollins, 1995. 102p.
Mean streets, housing projects, a single parent family, and a tenth

birthday come together in a graphic picture of the life of Reeve McLain, Jr., Junebug, who does not want to become that's when boys are expected to join a gang. The picture of the world he faces and the move from the projects give hope in the concisely written novel which is, above all, a portrait of a child who is totally realistic about his world. All characters are well-developed, and reader sympathy and empathy should be developed thanks to Mead's writing. For multicultural studies.
SUBJ: Single-parent family--Fiction./ Brothers and sisters--Fiction./ Inner cities--Fiction./ Afro-Americans--Fiction.

Ph-2 2-3/2 $15.95 L KH494
MEDEARIS, ANGELA SHELF. Adventures of Sugar and Junior. Illus. by Nancy Poydar. Holiday House ISBN 0-8234-1182-6, 1995. 32p. col. ill.
"Santiago Antonio Ramirez, also known as Junior, enjoys playing games, making cookies, and going to the movies with Sugar, the new girl next door." (CIP) Illustrated in bright colors, with many lively pictures covering full pages, the simple stories in this transitional reader feature political correctness and multiethnic characters, but are not at all didactic. The four easy-to-read stories of friendship appear to be within reach of beginning readers--and they may enjoy them. For multicultural studies.
SUBJ: Friendship--Fiction./ Hispanic Americans--Fiction./ Afro-Americans--Fiction.

Ph-3 4-6/4 $15.95 L KH495
MEDEARIS, ANGELA SHELF. Haunts: five hair-raising tales. Illus. by Trina Schart Hyman. Holiday House ISBN 0-8234-1280-6, 1996. 37p. ill.
"A collection of stories mainly set in Texas and based on tales of local ghosts." (CIP) Although most useful to readers in Texas, the stories will be good for storytelling, and readers in other sections of the nation may recognize variants of the ghost stories as tales from their own regions. Black and white illustrations are suitably atmospheric.
Contents: The fiddler man -- Scared silly -- Last dance at the Dew Drop Inn -- The rainmaker -- Waiting for Mr. Chester.
SUBJ: Ghosts--Fiction./ Texas--Fiction./ Short stories.

Ph-1 4-6/4 $14.95 L KH496
MILES, MISKA. Annie and the old one. Illus. by Peter Parnall. Atlantic/Little, Brown ISBN 0-316-57117-2, c1971. unp. col. ill.
Newbery Honor Book.
Available from National Library Service for the Blind and Physically Handicapped in Braille BR02228.
Available in Spanish ANI Y LA ANCIANA (Fondo de Cultura Economica ISBN 968-16-3748-8, 1992).
The Old One who is about to die says she will return to earth when Annie's mother finishes the new rug on the loom. Unable to accept her grandmother's death, Annie tries to check work on the rug by pulling out the strands woven each day. This gives grandmother the chance to teach Annie a final lesson of wonder and beauty--that she is part of earth, always has been, and always will be. Set in Southwestern United States, this tale teaches attitudes toward life and death from the point of view of another culture.
SUBJ: Indians of North America--Fiction./ Grandmothers--Fiction./ Death--Fiction./ Spanish language materials.

Ph-1 K-6/3 $9.95 L KH497
MILNE, A. A. House at Pooh Corner. With decorations by Ernest H. Shepard. Dutton ISBN 0-525-44444-0, c1956. 180p. ill.
Sequel to WINNIE-THE-POOH.
Available from National Library Service for the Blind and Physically Handicapped in Braille BR06318, on sound recording cassette RC13967, talking book TB01359.
Christopher Robin and his good friends populate this book: Eeyore, the melancholy donkey, Piglet, Tigger, and of course Pooh Bear, and many others in episodes serious at heart but light on the exterior.
SUBJ: Toys--Fiction./ Stuffed animals--Fiction.

Ph-1 K-6/3 $10.99 T KH498
MILNE, A. A. Winnie-the-Pooh. Illus. by Hilda Scott. With decorations by Ernest H. Shepard. Dutton ISBN 0-525-44443-2, 1974. 161p. col. ill.
Available from National Library Service for the Blind and Physically Handicapped in Braille BR02182, on sound recording cassette RC13967, talking book TB01359.
Pooh (bear) and Christopher Robin are the main characters in this story, full of the 'hums of Pooh' and adventures with Kanga and Roo, Piglet, and of course Eeyore.
Followed by THE HOUSE AT POOH CORNER.
SUBJ: Toys--Fiction./ Stuffed animals--Fiction.

Ph-3 K-6/3 $17.50 L KH499
MILNE, A. A. World of Pooh: the complete "Winnie-the-Pooh" and "The House at Pooh Corner." With decorations and new illustrations in

full color by Ernest H. Shepard. Dutton ISBN 0-525-44447-5, c1957. 314p. col. ill.
Available from National Library Service for the Blind and Physically Handicapped on sound recording cassette RC13967, and talking book TB01359.
The complete WINNIE-THE-POOH and THE HOUSE AT POOH CORNER, in larger format, and with some new illustrations.
SUBJ: Toys--Fiction./ Stuffed animals--Fiction.

Ph-1 4-A/6 $14.95 L KH500
MOCHIZUKI, KEN. Baseball saved us. Illus. by Dom Lee. Lee & Low ISBN 1-880000-01-6, 1993. unp. col. ill.
Available in Spanish, BEISBOL NOS SALVO (ISBN 1-880000-21-0, 1995).
Interned in a concentration camp for Japanese Americans during World War II, the first person narrator recounts how the internees built a baseball field, sewed uniforms, and played baseball to try to establish some positive activity in their guarded camp. When the war ended, the boy, now freed, is still bedeviled by others for his ancestry, but he proves that he can play baseball well. The dark illustrations, some of which are based on Ansel Adams' photographs of Manzanar, fit the somber text well and will add to a reader's knowledge of a shameful period in United States history. Try reading this aloud. For multicultural studies.
SUBJ: Japanese Americans--Evacuation and relocation, 1942-1945--Fiction./ World War, 1939-1945--Fiction./ Baseball--Fiction./ Prejudices--Fiction./ Spanish language materials.

Ph-1 3-5/4 $14.95 T KH501
MOCHIZUKI, KEN. Heroes. Illus. by Dom Lee. Lee & Low ISBN 1-880000-16-4, 1995. unp. col. ill.
When young Japanese-American Donnie becomes tired of always being the enemy bad guy in the war games he and the other children play, he enlists his uncle and father to show that they, too, were "good guys" and heroes when they served in the United States Army during World War II and the Korean War. The obvious prejudice of Donnie's companions may be unthinking, but it is hurtful. The moving text and evocative, full-page illustrations will be excellent for units on multicultural studies, prejudice, and modern United States history and should stir discussion.
SUBJ: Japanese Americans--Fiction./ Prejudices--Fiction.

Ph-2 1-3/2 $13.99 T KH502
MONFRIED, LUCIA. No more animals! Illus. by Betsy James. Dutton ISBN 0-525-45390-3, 1995. 64p. ill. (Speedsters).
Just right for a first reader, this highly illustrated book (black and white sketches) recounts Charlie's problems with his unusual pets, especially their escape and capture. A new pet, a skink, is the last straw for mother, but she eventually concedes the lizard is likable. A funny and fast transitional reader in which the illustrations also provide comic sound effects. Fun.
SUBJ: Pets--Fiction./ Skinks--Fiction.

Ph-1 4-A/6 $3.50 P KH503
MONTGOMERY, LUCY M. Anne of Green Gables. Illus. by Jody Lee. Bantam Doubleday Dell ISBN 0-553-15327-7, c1908, 1983. 382p. ill.
Available from National Library Service for the Blind and Physically Handicapped in Braille BR06394.
Anne is an orphan who is delivered to a lonely middle-aged brother and sister on a farm on Prince Edward Island in Maritime Canada of the late 19th century. They decide to keep her because her pixie face, wild imagination, and her ability to find mischief appeals to them and lightens their lives. The story tells of her school experiences, her battle with Gilbert Blythe and their eventual reconciliation. Sentimental but still highly appealing. Other titles in the series: ANNE OF AVONLEA (Bantam ISBN 0-553-21314-8, 1976); ANNE OF THE ISLAND (Bantam ISBN 0-553-21317-2, 1976); ANNE OF WINDY POPLARS (Bantam ISBN 0-553-21316-4, 1981); ANNE'S HOUSE OF DREAMS (Bantam ISBN 0-553-21318-0, 1981); ANNE OF THE ISLAND: AN ANNE OF GREEN GABLES STORY (Grosset & Dunlap ISBN 0-448-40311-0, 1992); ANNE OF INGLESIDE (Bantam ISBN 0-553-21315-6, 1981) trace Anne's development to grown womanhood.
In RAINBOW VALLEY (Bantam ISBN 0-553-26921-6, 1985) and RILLA OF INGLESIDE (Bantam ISBN 0-553-26922-4, 1985) Anne and Gilbert's children are growing up and finding themselves as individuals. Further mishaps develop in ANNE OF AVONLEA (ISBN 0-553-15114-2, 1976); and ANNE OF THE ISLAND (ISBN 0-553-48066-9, 1976).
Also available from NLSBPH are: ANNE OF AVONLEA on sound recording cassette RC14907 and in Braille BR7431; ANNE OF THE ISLAND on sound recording cassette RC14226 and in Braille BR7482; ANNE OF WINDY POPLARS on sound recording cassette RC23806 and in Braille BR7430; ANNE'S HOUSE OF DREAMS on sound recording cassette RC23805 and in Braille BR7429; ANNE OF

INGLESIDE on sound recording cassette RC23851; RILLA OF INGLESIDE on sound recording cassette RC34118.
SUBJ: Prince Edward Island (Canada)--Fiction./ Friendship--Fiction./ Girls--Fiction./ Canada--Fiction.

Ph-1 2-4/4 $12.95 L KH504
MOORE, LILIAN. Don't be afraid, Amanda. Illus. by Kathleen Garry McCord. Atheneum ISBN 0-689-31725-5; In Canada: Maxwell Macmillan, 1992. 57p. ill.
"Jean Karl book."
Available from the National Library Service for the Blind and Physically Handicapped on sound recording cassette RC 36340.
In this sequel to I'LL MEET YOU AT THE CUCUMBERS, city mouse Amanda visits her country pen pal, Adam. Discovering the dangers and pleasures of country life, Amanda has a close call with a hawk, is frightened by a scarecrow, and beholds fireflies. Her adventures inspire Adam's poetry which is included in the text. For reading aloud and for creative writing units.
SUBJ: Mice--Fiction./ Country life--Fiction./ Friendship--Fiction.

Ph-1 2-4/5 $12.95 L KH505
MOORE, LILIAN. I'll meet you at the cucumbers. Illus. by Sharon Wooding. Atheneum ISBN 0-689-31243-1, 1988. 63p. ill.
Accompanying his friend, Junius Mouse to the big city to visit his pen friend, Amanda, is a major accomplishment for country loving, Adam Mouse. Absorbing all the new sights, sounds, and experiences, Adam has his eyes opened to a whole new world, and also learns that he is a poet. The themes of friendship, poetry, learning about oneself, and the contrast of city and country life are intertwined in this story for middle graders.
SUBJ: Mice--Fiction./ Friendship--Fiction.

Ph-1 6-A/5 $14.95 T KH506
MOORE, MARTHA. Under the mermaid angel. Delacorte ISBN 0-385-32160-0; In Canada: Bantam Doubleday Dell, 1995. 168p.
Although classified as a young adult novel, stronger readers should take to this story about Jesse Cowan, thirteen, a child living in a small Texas town and the people she meets, especially her next door neighbor, the fascinating Roxanne, a woman of faith in imagination. Through her contact with the thirty-year-old Roxanne, Jesse learns that appearances are only appearances and what a person is can be found within. The author's use of strong, short descriptions and metaphors of persons and places brings this remarkable novel, peopled with very southern eccentrics, to life in narrative and dialogue.
SUBJ: Friendship--Fiction./ Schools--Fiction./ Texas--Fiction./ Brothers and sisters--Fiction.

Ph-2 3-5/4 $14.95 T KH507
MORA, PAT. Gift of the poinsettia./El regalo de la flor de nochebuena. By Pat Mora and Charles Ramirez Berg. Illus. by Daniel Lechon. Pinata Books ISBN 1-55885-137-2, 1995. unp. col. ill.
Includes music.
"As he participates in the festivities of Las Posadas, preparing for the birth of Christ, a young Mexican boy worries about what gift he will have for baby Jesus." (CIP) Presented in English and Spanish, the customs of the season are explained and are illustrated in bright colors. The book includes the music and lyrics for three Posada songs. Will be useful for multicultural studies and for students of Spanish-- and English.
SUBJ: Christmas--Fiction./ Posadas (Social custom)--Fiction./ Mexico--Fiction./ Spanish language materials./ Bilingual materials--Spanish.

Ph-2 5-A/6 $15.99 L KH508
MOREY, WALT. Gentle Ben. Reissued. Illus. by John Schoenherr. Dutton ISBN 0-525-30429-0; In Canada: McClelland & Stewart, c1965, 1997. 191p. ill.
Available from National Library Service for the Blind and Physically Handicapped in Braille BR00448 and on sound recording cassette RC15318.
Gentle Ben is a huge Alaskan brown bear raised by a heartless man and befriended by eleven-year-old Mark Andersen. Mark eventually cares for Ben, and all is well until the bear almost kills his former owner. Thereafter, Mark struggles to save Ben's life.
SUBJ: Bears--Fiction./ Alaska--Fiction.

Ph-2 5-A/5 $6.95 P KH509
MOREY, WALT. Home is the North. Blue Heron Publishing ISBN 0-936085-11-8, c1967, 1990. 162p. (Walt Morey adventure library).
Originally published by E.P. Dutton (1967).
Brad, fifteen, loves his home in the Alaska wilderness, its climate, openness, the freedom he has, its people (with the notable exception of one super meany), and his dog, Mickie. On the death of his grandmother, the court determines he must live in Seattle with his only

living kin. How he and Mickie manage to escape city life is at the
heart of this adventure which narrates his long trek. Popular
adventure reading.
SUBJ: Alaska--Fiction./ Dogs--Fiction.

Ph-2 4-6/6 $14.95   L   KH510
MOREY, WALT. Kavik, the wolf dog. Illus. by Peter Parnall. Dutton ISBN
0-525-33093-3, c1968. 192p. ill.
The story of Kavik (one-quarter wolf), how he won the North
American Sled Dog Derby, only to meet incredible disaster and
hardship. Through everything, even the loss of his mate, he was
determined to find the only master, Andy Evans, who had returned his
love and devotion. Another story of an "Incredible Journey" by a
great dog.
SUBJ: Dogs--Fiction./ Alaska--Fiction./ Sled dogs--Fiction.

Ph-2 5-A/6 $6.95   P   KH511
MOREY, WALT. Scrub dog of Alaska. Blue Heron Publishing ISBN
0-936085-13-4, c1971, 1989. 152p. (Walt Morey adventure library).
Originally published by E.P. Dutton, 1971.
Scrub the Alaska sled dog was the scrub of the litter and ejected
from his home. Yet he grew into a fine dog, one of the best in
Alaska, due to the love and care given to him by the boy, Dave
Martin. Scrub repays Dave by saving his inheritance from a thief.
Readers of CALL OF THE WILD will enjoy this similar story.
SUBJ: Dogs--Fiction./ Alaska--Fiction./ Sled dogs--Fiction.

Ph-1 5-A/5 $14.99   T   KH512
MORPURGO, MICHAEL. Butterfly lion. Viking ISBN 0-670-87461-2; In
Canada: Penguin, 1997. 90p.
First published in Great Britain, Collins Children's Books, 1996.
A lonely boy, attempting to escape from a boarding school in
England, meets an old woman who tells him the story of another boy.
Many years ago before World War I, he also ran away and
dreamed of reuniting with a white lion he had rescued as a cub in
South Africa. The story tells smoothly, although somewhat sentimently,
moves at a rapid pace, and develops characters, situations, and the
times well. Readers will wonder if the modern boy really meets the
old woman or her ghost, part of the intrigue of the tale. For reading
aloud.
SUBJ: Lions--Fiction./ England--Fiction.

Ph-1 4-6/5 $13.95   T   KH513
MORPURGO, MICHAEL. Dancing bear. Illus. by Christian Birmingham.
Houghton Mifflin ISBN 0-395-77980-4, 1996. 53p. ill.
"Walter Lorraine books."
Originally published in Great Britain, Youngs Lions, 1994.
Young Roxanne, a lonely girl living in a remote community, brings
fame, money, and the outside world to the distant town when she
adopts a bear cub. A film company arrives to shoot a video with a
teen idol and the bear and Roxanne are faced with separation. A
tender story that moves at a good clip, it will be good for reading
aloud and encouraging discussion of friendship, greed, and basic
values. Black and white illustrations add to the mood.
SUBJ: Bears--Fiction./ Mountain life--Fiction./ Friendship--Fiction.

Ph-2 5-A/6 $22.00   T   KH514
MORPURGO, MICHAEL. Robin of Sherwood. Illus. by Michael Foreman.
Harcourt Brace ISBN 0-15-201315-6; In Canada: Harcourt Brace c/o
Canadian Manda, 1996. 113p. col. ill.
First published in Great Britain, Pavilion Books.
A retelling of the Robin Hood legend includes the familiar characters,
but with different physical characteristics and character traits. Robin
marries and his son is kidnapped by the Sheriff of Nottingham.
Robin's loyalty to King Richard takes him to the court where he falls
under the sway of riches. Too late, he attempts to return to the forest
and family he loves. A rousing good adventure story.
SUBJ: Robin Hood (Legendary character)--Fiction./ Great Britain--
History--Richard I, 1189-1199--Fiction.

Ph-1 5-A/7 $13.00   T   KH515
MORPURGO, MICHAEL. Waiting for Anya. Viking/Penguin ISBN
0-670-83735-0; In Canada: Penguin, 1991. 172p.
Set in a small town in Nazi occupied France during W.W. II, the
story centers on Jo, son of a German prisoner of war, who becomes
involved with a group of fleeing Jewish children. Through a ruse and
the connivance of the other villagers and even a German soldier, a
rescue is effected, although not without loss. Setting and character
are nicely delineated and the better reader will be caught in the
tension of the situation.
SUBJ: World War, 1939-1945--France--Fiction.

Ph-1 4-6/3 $14.99   L   KH516
MORPURGO, MICHAEL. Wreck of the Zanzibar. Illus. by Francois Place.
Viking ISBN 0-670-86360-2; In Canada: Penguin, 1995. 69p. col. ill.
Originally published in France by Gallimard Jeunesse, 1994.
A blending of stylized watercolor illustrations and a diary text depicts
the life of Laura, fourteen, and her family on the oft storm-tossed Isles
of Scilly in 1907. It is gripping in its everyday details and in the
depiction of destructive storms, character, and the girl's quiet
determination. Nature at its most violent and its effect on people,
especially Laura's family, is as modern as the latest hurricane yet set
in its time by art and text. The short historical fiction is fascinating
and a good choice for reading aloud.
SUBJ: Shipwrecks--Fiction./ Scilly, Isles of (England)--Fiction./ Islands-
-Fiction./ Diaries.

Ph-2 5-6/4 $16.00   T   KH517
MORROW, HONORE. On to Oregon. Illus. by Edward Shenton.
Morrow ISBN 0-688-21639-0, c1954. 239p. ill.
Available from National Library Service for the Blind and Physically
Handicapped as talking book TB04385.
The story of John Sager and his brothers and sisters has been called
"an American classic...beside Huckleberry Finn." When his father and
mother died on the two-thousand mile journey from their home in
Missouri to a new home in Oregon, John, only thirteen, continued as
the leader of the family and despite tremendous hardships successfully
completed the trek. Shenton's elegant drawings add greatly to the
appeal of the story.
SUBJ: Overland journeys to the Pacific--Fiction./ Frontier and pioneer
life--Fiction./ Oregon Trail--Fiction./ Brothers and sisters--Fiction.

Ph-2 5-6/6 $15.95   T   KH518
MOWAT, FARLEY. Lost in the barrens. Illus. by Charles L. Geere. Little,
Brown ISBN 0-316-58638-2; In Canada: McClelland & Stewart, 1962.
244p. ill., maps.
Canadian Library Award.
Available from the National Library Service for the Blind and
Physically Handicapped in Braille BRA08322.
Jamie, new to northern Canada and its wilds, and Awasin Meewasin
seem like an odd pair. Awasin, the son of a Cree Indian headman,
appoints himself to be Jamie's teacher. They leap at the chance to
explore the wasteland to the far north where the "Eaters of the
Deer" live. Their adventures, including the discovery of a Viking
treasure trove, test all their skill and courage to survive.
SUBJ: Northwest, Canadian--Fiction./ Indians of North America--
Fiction./ Buried treasure--Fiction.

Ph-3 3-5/2 $14.95   L   KH519
MUNSCH, ROBERT. Promise is a promise. By Robert Munsch and
Michael Kusugak. Illus. by Vladyana Krykorka. Annick Press/dist. by
Firefly ISBN 1-55037-009-X; In Canada: Annick Press/dist. by Firefly,
1988. unp. col. ill.
Based on the imaginary Inuit creature the Qallupilluq, a figure used to
caution children to avoid cracks in the ice, this original tale tells
about a little girl who has promised not to go near the cracks--and does.
The Qallupilluq grabs her, but a clever ruse frees the child--who has
learned to keep her promises--as does the creature. Use for units on
Inuits, multicultural studies, and "creative" folkore.
SUBJ: Promises--Fiction./ Eskimos--Fiction.

Ph-1 4-5/7 $4.50   P   KH520
MURPHY, JILL. Jeffrey Strangeways. Candlewick ISBN 1-56402-283-8;
In Canada: Douglas & McIntyre, 1994. 144p. ill.
Fast paced, nonsensical, improbable happenings will keep readers
following the mishaps of Jeffrey, a very poor boy, who manages to
fulfill his heart's desire and become a knight. He meets Sir Walter, an
employee of Free Lance Rescue Services, and a series of accidents
helps Jeffrey aid the knight. Good reading experience for those who
enjoy puns and wordplay and a good read-aloud. Black and white
illustrations add to the mood.
SUBJ: Knights and knighthood--Fiction.

Ph-1 4-A/4 $14.95   T   KH521
MYERS, ANNA. Rosie's tiger. Walker ISBN 0-8027-8305-8; In Canada:
Thomas Allen, 1994. 121p.
"In 1952 in Oklahoma, sixth grader Rosie enlists the aid of her new
best friend, the flamboyant Cassandra, in trying to get rid of the
Korean wife and stepson her older brother has brought back from the
war." (CIP) Ronny has always been a supportive, loving brother
especially since their mother died. Their father, too, is supportive, but
Rosie fears that the new wife and child will alienate her brother's
affections. Through a dramatic accident, Rosie learns that love can
stretch a great deal--including her own. Told in the first person, the
historical fiction convincingly conveys life in a small town in the 1950s.
Characterization is strong in this different family story for multicultural
studies.

SUBJ: Korean Americans--Fiction./ Asian Americans--Fiction./ Brothers and sisters--Fiction./ Friendship--Fiction./ Oklahoma--Fiction.

Ph-1 6-A/6 $14.95   L   KH522

MYERS, WALTER DEAN. Glory Field. Scholastic ISBN 0-590-45897-3; In Canada: Scholastic, 1994. 375p.

Available from the National Library Service for the Blind and Physically Handicapped on sound recording cassette RC 40028. The Glory Field is the plot of land in South Carolina that members of the Lewis family have farmed, first as slaves, then as free people, from the 1750s to the present day. Starting with the captured African boy who is forced into slavery, the family's history and changes are detailed in several chapters concentrating on several generations of the Lewis family through good times and bad. Sharply delineated characters are memorable. A ROOTS for younger readers, the historical fiction will need a strong reader. Once engaged, readers will avidly follow the story from beginning to end. For multicultural studies.
SUBJ: Afro-Americans--Fiction./ Family--Fiction.

Ph-1 5-A/7 $4.50   P   KH523

MYERS, WALTER DEAN. Righteous revenge of Artemis Bonner. HarperCollins ISBN 0-06-440462-5; In Canada: HarperCollins, 1994. 140p.

In a very tall tale, first person narrative, Artemis Bonner tells of his adventures throughout the wild West in the 1880s. A fifteen-year-old African American, he has as his purpose, in these edge-of-the-chair events, vengeance on the head of Catfish Grimes who killed his uncle. High jinks and hyperbole, none of which is meant to be believed, are great fun in a book reminiscent of Sid Fleischman's work. Once again Myers displays a great sense of humor that will appeal to less literal youth. Good for reading aloud in fourth to sixth grades. For multicultural studies.
SUBJ: Revenge--Fiction./ Buried treasure--Fiction./ West (U.S.)--Fiction./ Afro-Americans--Fiction.

Ph-1 5-6/6 $4.99   P   KH524

MYERS, WALTER DEAN. Young landlords. Puffin/Penguin ISBN 0-14-034244-3; In Canada: Penguin, c1979. 197p.

Coretta Scott King Award.
Available from National Library Service for the Blind and Physically Handicapped on sound recording cassette RC23501.
Fifteen-year-old Paul and his friends form an Action Group. Innocently acquiring a run-down Harlem tenement for a dollar, they find themselves with an eccentric group of tenants and a profit margin of zero. Since they are also involved in helping a friend falsely accused of theft, the group finds more "action" than they expected. Fast moving and funny.
SUBJ: Harlem (New York, N.Y.)--Fiction./ Landlord and tenant--Fiction./ Friendship--Fiction.

Ph-2 4-6/7 $15.95   T   KH525

NABB, MAGDALEN. Enchanted horse. Illus. by Julek Heller. Orchard ISBN 0-531-06805-6, 1993. 90p. ill.

"A lonely young girl living on a remote farm with her work-obsessed parents cares for an old and battered wooden horse with such devotion that it comes to life." (CIP) Nabb's lovingly created development of Irina should help readers identify with the peasant child whose wooden horse becomes real at night and eventually runs away with wild horses. Active black and white sketches add to the magic and reality of a book that will appeal to horse lovers and fantasy readers alike.
SUBJ: Horses--Fiction./ Magic--Fiction./ Farm life--Fiction.

Ph-1 6-A/6 $14.89   L   KH526

NAIDOO, BEVERLEY. No turning back: a novel of South Africa. HarperCollins ISBN 0-06-027506-5; In Canada: HarperCollins, 1997. 189p.

Includes glossary.
When his stepfather continues to abuse him in their slum home, Sipho, twelve, escapes to post-apartheid Johannesburg where other children teach him to survive--but then just barely--on the streets of the city where some people still treat him as an inferior because of his color. Using many words and phrases from the Zulu language, the story depicts in a natural way the dangerous conditions Sipho encounters and some of the better ones, too. The picture of one boy and those he meets is not a pretty one, but it provides an absorbing view of a desperate boy, who is a sympathetic character in an unbearable situation. The novel's ending is upbeat and is not forced. Better readers will identify with Sipho, and the book is a strong choice for multicultural studies and modern African history.
SUBJ: Street children--Fiction./ South Africa--Fiction./ Blacks--South Africa--Fiction.

Ph-2 3-6/5 $15.95   L   KH527

NAMIOKA, LENSEY. Yang the third and her impossible family. Illus. by Kees de Kiefte. Little, Brown ISBN 0-316-59726-0; In Canada: Little, Brown, 1995. 144p. ill.

Sequel to: YANG THE YOUNGEST AND HIS TERRIBLE EAR, Joy Street/Little, Brown, 1992.
Once again a window opens on the lives of the musical Yang family, this time concentrating on the next to youngest, Yingmei, known as Mary in the United States. When she adopts a kitten to try and impress a classmate and fellow school orchestra player, she must take care of it while keeping it hidden from everyone in the family except her younger brother. Her sometimes ill ease with her family's retention of many Chinese customs in a new and different land is at the heart of the story. Although less funny than the first Yang book, its presentation of people and customs is interesting and portrays adjusting to differences while accepting one's own culture and family as worthwhile and valuable. For multicultural studies.
SUBJ: Chinese Americans--Fiction./ Family life--Fiction./ Friendship--Fiction./ Cats--Fiction./ Asian Americans--Fiction.

Ph-1 5-A/5 $3.99   P   KH528

NAMIOKA, LENSEY. Yang the youngest and his terrible ear. Illus. by Kees de Kiefte. Dell ISBN 0-440-40917-9, 1994. 134p. ill.

Recent immigrants to the United States from China, Yingtao and his family seek to establish a life in a new land. His parents and siblings are talented musicians, but Yingtao, the youngest, has a tin ear and knows that his screechy second violin destroys all harmony. Learning to play baseball, he becomes more Americanized and discovers a talent for sports. Descriptions of being a stranger, unaware of custom and language, are telling in a story that is entirely reasonable and possible. Excellent choice for reading aloud and for multicultural units.
SUBJ: Chinese Americans--Fiction./ Moving, Household--Fiction./ Violin--Fiction./ Identity--Fiction.

Ph-1 3-5/6 $14.99   T   KH529

NAPOLI, DONNA JO. Bravest thing. Dutton ISBN 0-525-45397-0; In Canada: McClelland & Stewart, 1995. 135p.

Laurel, ten, has had many pets and truly loves them, but they all seem to die for reasons not of her making. When her pet rabbit refuses to nurse its litter and the newborns die, Laurel, with the help of others, realizes that all living things must die even if they are loved. More than a girl-and-pet story, it is a picture of real people in real situations, and the seemingly simple writing brings out the depth of characters and situations. For reading aloud.
SUBJ: Rabbits as pets--Fiction./ Pets--Fiction./ Death--Fiction./ Scoliosis--Fiction.

Ph-1 3-A/3 $14.99   T   KH530

NAPOLI, DONNA JO. Jimmy, the pickpocket of the palace. Illus. by Judith Byron Schachner. Dutton ISBN 0-525-45357-1, 1995. 166p. ill.

Sequel to PRINCE OF THE POND: OTHERWISE KNOWN AS DE FAWG PIN, Dutton, 1992.
The prince's son, Jimmy, unhappily transformed into a human by an old hag, turns up at the palace. Once again the problems and the humor inherent to his transformation create delightful situations as he races against time to save the pond and a special female frog. Black and white illustrations add to the whole in a book to read for fun or for reading aloud.
SUBJ: Frogs--Fiction./ Fantasy.

Ph-1 3-A/3 $13.00   L   KH531

NAPOLI, DONNA JO. Prince of the pond: otherwise known as De Fawg Pin. Illus. by Judith Byron Schachner. Dutton ISBN 0-525-44976-0, 1992. 151p. ill.

Selectors' Choice, 19th ed.
Converted into a frog by the wicked hag of the pond, the prince must learn frog habits, defenses, language, and mating customs. With the help of the narrator, a small female frog he names Jade, he becomes leader and defender of the pond and the happy father of many tadpoles. His language lacks certain sounds so his locutions are hilarious but understandable thanks to Jade's explanations and the reader's ability to interpret after a short while. Fun, fast, with excellent art and design, Napoli's book is a winner.
SUBJ: Frogs--Fiction.

Ph-1 5-6/6 $13.95   T   KH532

NAYLOR, PHYLLIS REYNOLDS. Agony of Alice. Atheneum ISBN 0-689-31143-5; In Canada: Collier Macmillan, 1985. 119p.

Available from National Library Service for the Blind and Physically Handicapped on sound recording cassette RC25250.
Booktalk videocassette available from WETA Television, 1987. 1/2" VHS videocassette color (15min) $49.95. (Books from cover to cover) Teacher's guide available for $2.50.
Making one embarrassing mistake after another at home and at school, Alice is sure she'll never survive sixth grade and become a

sophisticated teenager if she can't silently adopt a mother to help her. When to her horror pear-shaped Mrs. Plotkin is her teacher rather than Ms. Cole, she's sure that she'll never be straightened out. The fast pace, the use of humor and lively dialog combine to portray an eleven-year-old whom other girls her age will appreciate readily.
SUBJ: Teacher-student relationships--Fiction./ Self-perception--Fiction.

Ph-1 6-A/6 $15.00   L   KH533
NAYLOR, PHYLLIS REYNOLDS. Alice in rapture, sort of. Atheneum ISBN 0-689-31466-3; In Canada: Maxwell Macmillan, 1989. 166p.
Warned that she'll be a nobody if she starts junior high school without a boyfriend, Alice finds herself in one predicament after another. Lighthearted and fun, this appeals to pre-adolescent and young adolescent girls.
In RELUCTANTLY ALICE (ISBN 0-689-31681-X, 1991, also available from the NLSBPH on sound recording cassette RC35493) Alice is in seventh grade and tries to encourage romances involving her (much) older brother. She would also like her father, a widower, to remarry. Still in the seventh grade, Alice worries about her course "Changing Bodies," about love, and learns a great deal about girl-boy relationships in ALL BUT ALICE (ISBN 0-689-31773-5, 1992, also available from the National Library Service for the Blind and Physically Handicapped on sound recording cassette RC35260). Alice, now twelve, is changing, maturing, confronting the facts of life and death, and throwing a birthday party that is not a great success in ALICE IN APRIL (ISBN 0-689-31805-7, 1993). In the summer before eighth grade, Alice and her friends face problems, and solve them in ALICE THE BRAVE (ISBN 0-689-80095-9, 1995).
SUBJ: Single-parent family--Fiction./ Adolescence--Fiction./ Humorous stories.

Ph-2 5-6/6 $13.95   L   KH534
NAYLOR, PHYLLIS REYNOLDS. Beetles, lightly toasted. Atheneum ISBN 0-689-31355-1, 1987. 134p.
Wanting more than anything to win the fifty dollar prize for the Roger B. Sudermann essay contest and have his picture in the local newspaper, fifth grader Andy Moller takes an unusually creative approach to conservation - designing and testing recipes using insects as a main ingredient. This rollicking tale will be enjoyed by fans of HOW TO EAT FRIED WORMS who have already proved they have strong stomachs.
SUBJ: Insects as food--Fiction./ Cousins--Fiction./ Contests--Fiction.

Ph-2 4-6/5 $2.99   P   KH535
NAYLOR, PHYLLIS REYNOLDS. Bodies in the Bessledorf Hotel. Avon ISBN 0-380-70485-4, 1988. 132p.
Disappearing bodies are among the strange happenings at the Bessledorf Hotel in Indiana, managed by Bernie Magruder's father. Bernie eventually becomes the hero, but this story actually contains more humor than mystery. The fast-moving plot will appeal to upper elementary readers.
In BERNIE AND THE BESSLEDORF GHOST (ISBN 0-689-31499-X, 1990) panic sets in "when a ghost begins to make a regular appearance in the hotel." (Blurb); and in FACE IN THE BESSLEDORF FUNERAL PARLOR (ISBN 0-689-31802-2, 1993) the Magruders, especially Bernie, try to uncover a thief at the funeral parlor next door to the hotel.
SUBJ: Mystery and detective stories./ Humorous stories.

Ph-1 3-6/7 $13.95   L   KH536
NAYLOR, PHYLLIS REYNOLDS. Grand escape. Illus. by Alan Daniel. Atheneum ISBN 0-689-31722-0; In Canada: Maxwell Macmillan, 1993. 148p. ill.
Marco and Polo, two house cats, escape to the outdoors and embark on a series of adventures with a group of cats known as the Club of Mysteries. Humorously developed, with excellent descriptions of the kinesthetic antics of cats, the adventures and personalities of the characters will be just right for feline fantasy fans. For reading aloud.
SUBJ: Cats--Fiction./ Adventure and adventurers--Fiction.

Ph-2 4-A/4 $15.00   T   KH537
NAYLOR, PHYLLIS REYNOLDS. Saving Shiloh. Atheneum ISBN 0-689-81460-7; In Canada: Distican, 1997. 137p.
Sequel to: SHILOH SEASON, Atheneum, 1996.
"Marty and his family try to help their rough neighbor, Judd Travers, change his mean ways, even though their West Virginia community continues to expect the worst of him." (CIP) Marty's parents want him to know that everyone--even (or especially) Judd--deserves a second chance and to judge on evidence, not prejudice, especially when it may be a case of murder. Once again, most people are decent, especially Marty's family, and Judd does change to the point that even Shiloh will approach him. SHILOH readers will welcome more news of the family.
SUBJ: Dogs--Fiction./ Family life--West Virginia--Fiction./ West Virginia--Fiction./ Prejudices--Fiction.

CE   Ph-1 4-6/6 $15.00   T   KH538
NAYLOR, PHYLLIS REYNOLDS. Shiloh. Atheneum ISBN 0-689-31614-3; In Canada: Distican, 1991. 144p.
Newbery Medal Book.
Talking book performed by Peter MacNicol, available from Bantam Audio (ISBN 0-553-47116-3, 1992). 2 sound cassettes (183min), $15.99.
Available from the National Library Service for the Blind and Physically Handicapped on sound recording cassette RC35064.
In a folksy idiom, eleven-year-old Marty tells his story of a runaway beagle pup, the property of a cruel, gun-toting neighbor in the hills of rural West Virginia. Marty puts himself on the line to save the pup, Shiloh, from Judd, who treats man and beast as cruelly as he had been treated as a child. Unlike books where prayers are always answered, e.g. WHERE THE RED FERN GROWS, this holding novel speaks in tones of reality, where human effort, not divine intervention, helps the boy earn his pup. A good choice for reading aloud and prime for animal lovers.
SUBJ: Dogs--Fiction./ Animals--Treatment--Fiction./ West Virginia--Fiction.

Ph-2 4-A/4 $15.00   T   KH539
NAYLOR, PHYLLIS REYNOLDS. Shiloh season. Atheneum ISBN 0-689-80647-7; In Canada: Distican, 1996. 120p.
Sequel to: SHILOH, Atheneum, 1991.
Marty and his family are concerned because Judd, the man from whom Marty earned his dog, Shiloh, is constantly drunk--a danger to everyone and himself. Marty continues to worry that Judd will somehow kill Shiloh. Then Judd is nearly killed in a truck accident, and Marty learns to extend kindness even to someone he fears.
SUBJ: Dogs--Fiction./ Kindness--Fiction./ West Virginia--Fiction.

Ph-1 6-A/6 $15.99   L   KH540
NELSON, THERESA. Earthshine: a novel. Orchard ISBN 0-531-08717-4, 1994. 182p.
"Richard Jackson book."
Slim (Margery Grace, age twelve) watches her charming and supportive father die from AIDS in a heartfelt and very California novel. Everything leads to a pilgrimage by Slim's PWA (People with AIDS) group to a supposed miracle healer in the nearby mountains, but the miracle isn't her father's cure. It is, instead, a self-awareness and the knowledge that death and life are themselves miracles. A sympathetic, very realistic, contemporary book.
SUBJ: AIDS (Disease)--Fiction./ Fathers and daughters--Fiction.

Ph-2 5-6/7 $2.99   P   KH541
NESBIT, E. Enchanted castle. Illus. by H. R. Millar. Puffin/Penguin ISBN 0-14-035057-8, c1907, 1985. 252p. ill.
Available from National Library Service for the Blind and Physically Handicapped on sound recording cassette RC11778 and in Braille BRJ01535.
Gerald, Jimmy, and Cathy spend a summer investigating an enchanted castle. With the help of a magic ring they discover that the statues in the garden come alive and that the Ugli-Wuglis have a strange power.
SUBJ: Great Britain--Fiction./ Fantasy.

Ph-1 5-A/6 $20.00   T   KH542
NESBIT, E. Enchanted castle. Illus. by Paul O. Zelinsky. Morrow ISBN 0-688-05435-8, 1992. 292p. col. ill. (Books of wonder).
Nesbit's classic tells of four children and their discovery of an enchanted castle and a magic ring. Things are never quite as they seem in this sometimes captivating, sometimes frightening magic place where the children meet fairy tale characters and much adventure. Zelinsky's watercolors fit the mood of the story well. Modern readers should enjoy meeting the Ugly-Wuglies and the magic of the castle.
SUBJ: Fantasy./ England--Fiction.

Ph-2 4-5/7 $3.99   P   KH543
NESBIT, E. Railway children. Illus. by C. E. Brock. Puffin/Penguin ISBN 0-14-036671-7; In Canada: Penguin, 1994. 240p. ill.
Available in large print from Windrush/dist. by Cornerstone (ISBN 0-85089-940-1, $14.95).
The railroad is the high point of Roberta's, Peter's, and Phyllis's new surroundings when they move to the country after father goes away suddenly and they and mother move from London to a tiny cottage in the country. Old fashioned, this still charms middle grade readers who like gentle stories.
SUBJ: Railroads--Trains--Fiction./ Brothers and sisters--Fiction./ Single-parent family--Fiction.

Ph-2 5-6/7 $2.99   P   KH544
NESBIT, E. Story of the treasure seekers. Illus. by Cecil Leslie. Puffin/Penguin ISBN 0-14-036706-3; In Canada: Penguin, 1986. 208p. ill.

The five Bastable children try to recoup the family fortunes with little success but much fun and adventure. In THE WOULDBEGOODS (ISBN 0-14-035059-4, 1985), they and their dog are sent to the country after behaving disasterously at their uncle's home. These lively adventures have long been popular with children.
SUBJ: Great Britain--Fiction./ Brothers and sisters--Fiction./ Behavior--Fiction.

Ph-2 4-A/5 $20.95 T KH545
NEUFELD, JOHN. Edgar Allan: a novel. Phillips ISBN 0-87599-149-1, c1968. 95p.
Available from National Library Service for the Blind and Physically Handicapped in Braille BR00965.
Michael Ficket, twelve-years-old, tells the story of the events, and the motivations behind them, which occurred in his family when his parents adopted a little African-American boy, Edgar Allan. Edgar Allan's arrival means a testing of everything in which Michael believes, including his father's actions and motives. Divided loyalties finally make the family realize that good intentions are not enough. For multicultural studies.
SUBJ: Adoption--Fiction./ Afro-Americans--Fiction./ Family life--Fiction.

Ph-1 6-A/7 $16.00 T KH546
NEUFELD, JOHN. Gaps in stone walls. Atheneum ISBN 0-689-80102-5; In Canada: Distican, 1996. 186p.
Includes bibliography.
"Twelve-year-old Merry Skiffe, who lives on Martha's Vineyard in the 1880s, runs away from home because she is suspected of having committed a murder." (CIP) According to historical records, many of the residents of the island at that time were genetically deaf, as are many of Neufeld's characters. Neufeld distinguishes the speech of those who used spoken word from those who used sign language with punctuation. Merry's island life, family, friends, and other characters are fully developed, and the straightforward plot, often causing reader empathy, moves at a good pace in a well developed and different murder mystery. Interesting historical fiction which can also be used as an adjunct to units on persons with disabilities.
SUBJ: Murder--Fiction./ Runaways--Fiction./ Deaf--Fiction./ Physically handicapped--Fiction.

CE
Ph-2 5-6/6 $14.89 L KH547
NEVILLE, EMILY CHENEY. It's like this, Cat. Illus. by Emil Weiss. HarperCollins ISBN 0-06-024391-0, c1963. 180p. ill.
Newbery Medal Award.
Talking book available from SRA/McGraw-Hill 87-507973, 1970, $16.00.
Available from National Library Service for the Blind and Physically Handicapped in Braille BRA09431, on sound recording cassette RC22850, and as talking book TB03586.
Fourteen-year-old Dave Mitchell, growing up in New York City, tells of his affection for a tomcat and his first friendship with a girl.
SUBJ: Cats--Fiction./ New York (N.Y.)--Fiction.

Ph-2 5-6/5 $16.95 T KH548
NEWBERY HALLOWEEN: A DOZEN SCARY STORIES BY NEWBERY AWARD-WINNING AUTHORS. Selected by Martin H. Greenberg and Charles G. Waugh. Delacorte ISBN 0-385-31028-5; In Canada: Bantam Doubleday Dell, 1993. 189p.
Gathers twelve Halloween-type stories by Newbery authors such as Paul Fleischman, Beverly Cleary, and Charles J. Finger. Some selections stand alone; some are excerpted from longer works. For reading aloud.
SUBJ: Halloween--Fiction./ Short stories.

Ph-2 4-6/4 $15.95 T KH549
NICHOL, BARBARA. Beethoven lives upstairs. Illus. by Scott Cameron. Orchard ISBN 0-531-06828-5, 1994. unp. col. ill.
Spanish version BEETHOVEN VIVE ARRIBA available from Santillana (ISBN 1-56014-619-2, 1996).
Based on incidents in Beethoven's life after he lost his hearing, the story is told through letters between Christoph and his almost-unknown musician Uncle Karl. At first infuriated by the eccentricities of the composer, the boy eventually begins to see Beethoven as an extraordinary musician. Full-page oil illustrations show the people and the setting of Vienna in 1822-1824 well. Prime historical fiction for music appreciation classes based on the author's cassette/CD.
SUBJ: Beethoven, Ludwig van--Fiction./ Uncles--Fiction./ Letters--Fiction./ Spanish language materials.

VCR Ph-2 4-6 $14.98 KH550
NICHOL, BARBARA. Beethoven lives upstairs (Videocassette). Children's Group/dist. by Silo CG83000, 1992. 1/2" VHS videocassette color (52min).
Talking book available from Children's Group/dist. by Silo as sound

cassette (ISBN 1-895404-00-2, 1991), 1 sound cassette (45min), $9.98; or compact disc (CG 4236J, 1991), 1 compact disc (45min), $11.49.
Based on incidents in Beethoven's life after he lost his hearing, the story is told through letters between Christoph and his almost-unknown musician Uncle Karl. At first infuriated by the eccentricities of the composer, the boy eventually begins to see Beethoven as an extraordinary musician. Incorporates over two dozen excerpts from Beethoven's best loved works including Symphonies #5 through #9, "Moonlight Sonata," "Minuet in G major," and "Fur Elise." Prime historical fiction for music appreciation classes.
SUBJ: Beethoven, Ludwig van--Fiction./ Uncles--Fiction./ Letters--Fiction./ Music appreciation.

Ph-1 6-A/5 $17.99 L KH551
NIMMO, JENNY. Griffin's castle. Orchard ISBN 0-531-33006-0, 1997. 198p.
First published in Great Britain, Methuen Children's Books, 1994.
Dinah, eleven, is a very bright, imaginative person--an extraordinary child, more mature than her mother. Her childhood is really quite wretched, but she improves on it with her abilities and her imaginative creativity. "After years of having moved around...Dinah determines to make a huge, dilapidated old mansion into a home for her mother and herself, but the wild beasts she summons from a stone wall to protect her may also imprison her." (CIP) A realistic fantasy in which creation of character, setting, and pace are brilliantly accomplished. Stronger readers should be sympathetic and empathetic to Dinah. For reading aloud.
SUBJ: Mothers and daughters--Fiction./ Supernatural--Fiction./ Wales--Fiction.

Ph-2 4-A/5 $7.00 P KH552
NORTON, MARY. Are all the giants dead? Illus. by Brian Froud. Magic Carpet Books/Harcourt Brace ISBN 0-15-201523-X; In Canada: Harcourt Brace c/o Canadian Manda, c1975, 1997. 123p. ill.
Originally published in Great Britain, J.M. Dent & Sons Ltd., 1975.
Available from National Library Service for the Blind and Physically Handicapped in Braille BR04285.
James and his bridge to adventure, Mildred, go to the land where the fairy-tale characters still live. He meets Jack-and-the-Beanstalk and Jack-the-Giant-Killer, now old men, and Dulcibel who has lost her golden apple and must marry the frog, as well as Beauty and her Beast, now "in the prime of life". An enchanting story, perfectly illustrated with horrendous giants, provides an interesting follow-up of favorite story-book characters.
SUBJ: Fairy tales./ Fantasy./ Frogs--Fiction./ Giants--Fiction.

Ph-1 4-6/5 $3.95 P KH553
NORTON, MARY. Bed-knob and broomstick. Illus. by Erik Blegvad. Harcourt Brace Jovanovich ISBN 0-15-206231-9, c1957. 189p. ill.
Available from National Library Service for the Blind and Physically Handicapped in Braille BR01018.
Charles, Carey, and Paul Wilson meet a spinster who is studying to become a witch. She gives the children magic powers and they go on a number of exciting and gruesome trips. Two books in one: The MAGIC BED-KNOB and BONFIRES AND BROOMSTICKS.
SUBJ: Fairy tales./ Witchcraft--Fiction.

CE Ph-1 4-6/6 $4.95 P KH554
NORTON, MARY. Borrowers. Illus. by Beth and Joe Krush. Harcourt Brace Jovanovich ISBN 0-15-209990-5, c1953, 1989. 180p. ill.
Carnegie Medal.
Available from National Library Service for the Blind and Physically Handicapped in Braille BR01017.
A charming story of the tiny people no taller than a pencil who live in a quiet old country house and "borrow" the things they need, objects human beings have let fall through the cracks of the floor. Their further adventures may be followed in THE BORROWERS AFIELD (ISBN 0-15-210166-7, 1970), THE BORROWERS AFLOAT (ISBN 0-15-210345-7, 1955), THE BORROWERS ALOFT (ISBN 0-15-210524-7, 1961), and THE BORROWERS AVENGED (ISBN 0-15-210530-1, 1986, Selectors' Choice, 14th ed.).
Also available from NLSBPH are: BORROWERS AFIELD in Braille BR07026; BORROWERS AFLOAT on sound recording cassette RC 42267; BORROWERS ALOFT in Braille BRA05108, on sound recording cassette RC 42268; BORROWERS AVENGED in Braille BR07033 and on sound recording cassette RC19618.
SUBJ: Fantasy.

Ph-1 4-6/2 $16.95 T KH555
OBERMAN, SHELDON. White stone in the castle wall. Illus. by Les Tait. Tundra ISBN 0-88776-333-2; In Canada: Tundra, 1995. unp. col. ill.
In a book truly expanded by its realistic, active, and colorful paintings, the story provides a possible explanation for the single

large white stone in the otherwise dull wall surrounding Sir Henry Pellatt's palatial mansion Casa Loma in Toronto in 1914. The historical fiction describes the activities of one poor boy, John Tommy Fiddich. The tale of Casa Loma is true, and the creation of John Tommy imaginatively portrays a very human person trying to earn money any honest way he can. The art shows time and place settings and characters well. A note provides information about Sir Henry Pellatt. Of special interest to Canadians, the story and illustrations should also hold readers in the United States.
SUBJ: Casa Loma (Toronto, Ont.)--Fiction./ Pellatt, Henry Mill, Sir--Fiction./ Canada--History--Fiction.

Ph-1 4-A/6 $14.95   L   KH556
O'BRIEN, ROBERT C. Mrs. Frisby and the rats of NIMH. Illus. by Zena Bernstein. Atheneum ISBN 0-689-20651-8, c1971. 233p. ill.
Newbery Medal Award.
Selectors' Choice, 7th ed.
Available from National Library Service for the Blind and Physically Handicapped in Braille BRA12967, on sound recording cassette RC23562, and talking book TB04336.
Spanish edition available LA SENORA FRISBY Y LAS RATAS DE NIMH (Ediciones SM ISBN 84-348-1601-6, 1985), $9.95.
Super-rats, subjects of experiments at a laboratory (NIMH--National Institute of Mental Health) learn to read, write, and in fact do many things that men do. Science fiction, but also a telling commentary on our own way of life in an adventure in which the animals need all their wits and super-intelligence to survive.
SUBJ: Mice--Fiction./ Rats--Fiction./ Courage--Fiction./ Spanish language materials.

CE   Ph-1 5-6/5 $14.95   T   KH557
O'DELL, SCOTT. Black pearl. Illus. by Milton Johnson. Houghton Mifflin ISBN 0-395-06961-0, c1967. 140p. ill.
Newbery Honor Book.
Talking book available from SRA/McGraw-Hill 87-507893, $16.00.
Available from National Library Service for the Blind and Physically Handicapped in Braille BR00764.
Spanish version available from Lectorum LA NEGRA PERLA (ISBN 84-279-3112-3, n.d.).
Legends of Baja, California, say Manta Diablo, a monstrous manta ray, "owns" a great black pearl. To sixteen-year-old Ramon Salazar, the finding of that pearl is the proof of his manhood and he will risk the sea devil's wrath to claim it for his own.
SUBJ: Baja California--Fiction./ Pearl fisheries--Fiction./ Spanish language materials.

Ph-2 6-A/6 $14.95   T   KH558
O'DELL, SCOTT. Captive. Houghton Mifflin ISBN 0-395-27811-2, 1979. 210p.
Shipwrecked on a desert island Julian, a sixteen-year-old Spanish seminarian, finds himself forced to impersonate a lost fair-haired Mayan god and is caught in the violence and intrigue of the Spanish invasion of Mexico. This excellent first volume of a trilogy is followed by THE FEATHERED SERPENT (ISBN 0-395-30851-8, 1981, OPC). Exploiting his power as a so-called god, Julian is deeply shaken when he visits the mighty Aztecs and sees Cortes destroy Montezuma. Unfortunately the third volume, THE AMETHYST RING (ISBN 0-395-33886-7, 1983, OPC), is overcrowded with disparate events. Julian ventures to ask a haughty bishop for ordination to work among the Mayas, is refused and executes him Maya fashion. He then joins Pizarro for the onslaught on the Incas, makes his way to Machu Picchu and then abruptly returns to Spain to enter a monastary. Although weakened by the third volume, the trilogy fills a void for there is a lack of historical fiction set in this period and place.
SUBJ: Mexico--History--Conquest, 1519-1540--Fiction./ Mayas--Fiction./ Indians of Mexico--Fiction.

Ph-1 5-6/6 $13.95   T   KH559
O'DELL, SCOTT. Island of the Blue Dolphins. Houghton Mifflin ISBN 0-395-06962-9, c1960. 184p.
Newbery Medal Award.
Available from National Library Service for the Blind and Physically Handicapped in Braille BR06230, on sound recording cassette RC22397, as talking book TB01814.
This classic story tells of Karana, a young Indian girl, marooned on an island off the coast of California for 18 years. Based on fact, the book's enduring popularity is rooted in Karana's courage and serenity in the face of devastating loneliness and physical danger.
Followed by ZIA.
SUBJ: San Nicolas Island (Calif.)--Fiction./ Survival--Fiction./ Indians of North America--Fiction./ Islands--Fiction.

Ph-1 5-6/6 $18.95   T   KH560
O'DELL, SCOTT. Island of the Blue Dolphins. Illus. by Ted Lewin. Houghton Mifflin ISBN 0-395-53680-4, c1960, 1990. 181p. col. ill.
Includes "Author's Note".
Newbery Medal.
Followed by ZIA.
The ever popular and gripping novel about the survival of a young Native American girl off the California coast is reissued in a generous format with 12 color illustrations that show settings and characters. Karana's story, based on an actual event, is a favorite of California children and remains as vibrant today as it was in 1960 when it deservedly received the John Newbery Medal. A must for every collection.
SUBJ: Indians of North America--Fiction./ Survival--Fiction./ Islands--Fiction./ San Nicolas Island (Calif.)--Fiction.

Ph-1 5-6/5 $14.95   T   KH561
O'DELL, SCOTT. Sarah Bishop. Houghton Mifflin ISBN 0-395-29185-2, 1980. 184p.
Includes "Author's foreword."
Selectors' Choice, 13th ed.
Available from National Library Service for the Blind and Physically Handicapped in Braille BR05156 and on sound recording cassette RC18158.
Sarah is fifteen when the Revolutionary War breaks out. Her father dies because he is a Tory and has been tarred and feathered for his belief. Her brother joins the patriot army and dies aboard a British prison ship. Sickened by such brutality, she flees Long Island for northern Westchester where she lives off the land as a recluse helped only by an Indian couple and a young Quaker who defends her from witchcraft charges because he senses the strong principles that underlie her unconventional behavior. A book which will invite discussion in both library and classroom.
SUBJ: United States--History--Revolution, 1775-1783--Fiction./ American loyalists--Fiction.

CE   Ph-1 5-6/3 $14.95   T   KH562
O'DELL, SCOTT. Sing down the moon. Houghton Mifflin ISBN 0-395-10919-1, c1970. 137p.
Newbery Honor Book.
Selectors' Choice, 6th ed.
Talking book available from SRA/McGraw-Hill 87-508061, 1973) $16.00.
Available from National Library Service for the Blind and Physically Handicapped on sound recording cassette RC25275 and talking book TB03811.
Enhanced videocassette available from SRA/McGraw-Hill 87-510594 (ISBN 0-07-510594-2, 1986). 1/2" VHS videocassette color (36min), $72.00. (Newbery Award series).
In the spring of 1864, life in the Canyon de Chelly was abundant and beautiful. Bright Morning, a young Navaho girl, watched the sheep which would soon be her own and chatted with her friends about Tall Boy whom she expects to marry. All this is shattered when the Long Knives, the U.S. soldiers, come and burn their village and drive them on the Long March. Based on historical fact.
SUBJ: Navajo Indians--Fiction.

Ph-2 5-A/5 $14.95   T   KH563
O'DELL, SCOTT. Thunder rolling in the mountains. By Scott O'Dell and Elizabeth Hall. Houghton Mifflin ISBN 0-395-59966-0, 1992. 128p.
Available from the National Library Service for the Blind and Physically Handicapped on sound recording cassette RC 38901.
Narrates the tragic defeat of the Nez Perce in 1877 through the eyes of Sound of Running Feet, the daughter of Chief Joseph. The forewarning when white men are seen panning for gold, the attempts at unity among the Native Americans, and the tragic flight of Chief Joseph's band are detailed in this fast-paced book which presents the betrayal of Nez Perce by the U.S. government and its agents. Includes a map (lacking a compass rose and scale marker) and summary afterword.
SUBJ: Nez Perce Indians--Fiction./ Indians of North America--Fiction.

CE   Ph-2 6-A/7 $14.95   T   KH564
O'DELL, SCOTT. Zia. Houghton Mifflin ISBN 0-395-24393-9, 1976. 179p.
Sequel to ISLAND OF THE BLUE DOLPHINS.
Talking book available from Recorded Books 93311 (ISBN 1-55690-869-5, 1993). 3 sound cassettes (240min), $26.00.
The young Indian girl Zia is caught between two worlds: that of her people and their chief who had lived far away on the ocean shore near the mountains and her present life under the padres at Santa Barbara mission. On the Island of the Blue Dolphins, her aunt Karana is the remaining link between Zia and her past. How Zia determines her life through her search and knowledge of herself makes an absorbing story.

SUBJ: Indians of North America--Missions--Fiction./ Indians of North America--California--Fiction.

Ph-2 3-5/2 $13.89   L   KH565
ORGEL, DORIS. Don't call me Slob-o. Illus. by Bob Dorsey. Hyperion ISBN 0-7868-2086-1, 1996. 71p. ill. (West Side kids).
"Bank Street."
Filomeno Pazzalini, a.k.a. Shrimp because he is the smallest boy in his class, must decide whether to join others who tease a new, older boy, Slobodan Vladic, who has recently arrived from Split (in the former Yugoslavia). Shrimp, too, has been teased for his size, and his father had been similarly tormented when he was newly arrived in the United States years earlier. The story line provides lessons about differences and the cruelty of others about those differences and, perhaps, a lesson in acceptance.
SUBJ: Croatian Americans--Fiction./ Popularity--Fiction./ Friendship--Fiction./ City and town life--Fiction.

Ph-1 5-A/6 $13.95   L   KH566
ORLEV, URI. Island on Bird Street. Translated from the Hebrew by Hillel Halkin. Houghton Mifflin ISBN 0-395-33887-5, 1983. 162p.
Batchelder Award, 1985.
Selectors' Choice, 15th ed.
Available from National Library Service for the Blind and Physically Handicapped on sound recording cassette RC23594.
Escaping the last roundup in the Warsaw Ghetto, eleven-year-old Alex lives in a clever hideout in the almost deserted ghetto. His mother is dead, his father with partisans; but Alex is lucky and resourceful, daring even to cross the ghetto. Every day of this long year he fears he will be found, but his incredible inner strength and optimism is given new meaning when his father returns for him. A survivor of the ghetto, the author has written a classic Holocaust story for younger readers.
SUBJ: Holocaust, Jewish (1939-1945)--Fiction./ Jews--Poland--Fiction./ World War, 1939-1945--Poland--Fiction./ Warsaw (Poland)--Fiction./ Poland--History--Occupation, 1939-1945--Fiction.

Ph-1 5-A/6 $13.95   T   KH567
ORLEV, URI. Man from the other side. Translated from the Hebrew by Hillel Halkin. Houghton Mifflin ISBN 0-395-53808-4, 1991. 186p.
Batchelder Award, 1992.
Available from the National Library Service for the Blind and Physically Handicapped on sound recording cassette RC 36966.
The "other side" is the "free" side of the wall surrounding the Warsaw Ghetto during World War II. Marek, 14, a Polish non-Jew, becomes involved in trying to rescue some of the people in the ghetto by bringing them food and weapons and by leading them out through the noxious and dangerous sewers. Tense, atmospheric, and realistic, this well characterized novel depicts "righteous Gentiles" and cruel profiteers and is excellent for oral presentation and for units on World War II, bigotry, and the difference individuals can make against unabashed, arrogant power.
SUBJ: World War, 1939-1945--Poland--Fiction./ Holocaust, Jewish (1939-1945)--Poland--Fiction./ Jews--Poland--Fiction./ Poland--History--Occupation, 1939-1945--Fiction.

Ph-1 3-5/6 $4.95   P   KH568
O'ROURKE, FRANK. Burton and Stanley. Illus. by Jonathan Allen. Farrar, Straus and Giroux ISBN 0-374-40989-7; In Canada: HarperCollins, 1996. 55p. ill.
"Sunburst book."
Originally published by Godine, 1993.
Two marabou storks, the title characters, are blown from Africa to the United States Midwest where a station master who knows Morse code manages to communicate with the beak-tapping avians. The railroad agent, the children, and a congress of birds save the storks and lead them to a ship which returns them to their native nests. Humorously illustrated in black and white sketches. For reading aloud.
SUBJ: Storks--Fiction./ Human-animal communications--Fiction.

Ph-3 6-A/7 $19.00   T   KH569
OXFORD BOOK OF SCARYTALES. Edited by Dennis Pepper. Oxford ISBN 0-19-278131-6; In Canada: Oxford, 1992. 157p. col. ill.
Several challenging, but well-illustrated, tales and poems by famous and less well-known authors about ghosts, the supernatural, and the "scary." Good choice for reading aloud.
SUBJ: Ghosts--Fiction./ Monsters--Fiction./ Horror stories./ Short stories.

Ph-2 4-6/4 $16.99   L   KH570
PARK, BARBARA. Mick Harte was here. Apple Soup/Knopf ISBN 0-679-97088-6; In Canada: Random House, 1995. 89p.
Phoebe, thirteen, recalls her brother Mick, his death in a bicycle accident, and her reactions in a series of flashbacks. He was a typical younger brother, sometimes a pest, sometimes a friend, but his perpetual failure to wear a bicycle safety helmet causes the head injury which leads to his death. Above all, this is a plea for bicycle safety as an appended author's note makes clear. It is, however, a strong portrayal of people any one of us might meet. When bicycle safety talks are given in the schools and libraries, MICK HARTE will be a strong adjunct activity for reading aloud.
SUBJ: Brothers and sisters--Fiction./ Death--Fiction./ Bicycles and bicycling--Safety measures--Fiction.

Ph-2 5-A/6 $14.95   L   KH571
PARK, RUTH. Playing Beatie Bow. Atheneum ISBN 0-689-30889-2, 1982. 196p.
Selectors' Choice, 14th ed.
Set in Sydney, Australia, 14-year-old Abigail is shattered to find her mother reconciling with the husband who left them. Watching neighbor's children play an odd game called "Beatie Bow," she is drawn back in time to Beatie's real family living in a sordid Sydney slum of the 1870s. Her time warp visit to the Bows leaves her more mature and tolerant and when she falls in love with a Bow descendant some years later, finally pieces together the history of Beatie and her family. Although the historical background is unfamiliar, this title, if presented, should prove popular with fantasy fans.
SUBJ: Family life--Fiction./ Time travel--Fiction./ Australia--Fiction.

Ph-1 5-A/3 $14.99   T   KH572
PARTRIDGE, ELIZABETH. Clara and the hoodoo man. Dutton ISBN 0-525-45403-9; In Canada: McClelland & Stewart, 1996. 168p.
A few days in Clara's life are finely detailed in a story set in rural Tennessee in 1900. Readers will learn about superstition, plant and animal life, and medicine (both professional and folk). When her little sister Bessie becomes very ill, her mother blames the hoodoo man for putting a spell on the little girl. Clara takes matters into her own hands and braves her many fears to ask him to treat the child with his herbal remedy despite her mother's anxieties. It is a fascinating, well-written glimpse into the life of a African-American family. Though historical fiction, it is based on interviews the author conducted with one of her patients who told the story. The author's note is particularly interesting in a holding, well-characterized book which is excellent for reading aloud and independent reading. A natural follow-up or prologue to WHERE THE LILIES BLOOM. For multicultural studies.
SUBJ: Mountain life--Tennessee--Fiction./ Afro-Americans--Fiction./ Sisters--Fiction./ Tennessee--Fiction.

Ph-1 5-A/6 $15.89   L   KH573
PATERSON, KATHERINE. Bridge to Terabithia. Illus. by Donna Diamond. Crowell/HarperCollins ISBN 0-690-04635-9, 1977. 128p. ill.
Newbery Medal Award.
Selectors' Choice, 12th ed.
Available from National Library Service for the Blind and Physically Handicapped on sound recording cassette RC12343.
Jess wants to be the fastest runner in the fifth grade but when Leslie comes to the small school he has to yield first place to her. They become fast friends and build a secret place in the woods "like Narnia" but they call it Terabithia. Leslie brings Jess many new experiences including deep grief when he learns that she has drowned. Effective tale of the relationship of the two children and of Jess' reaction to the tragedy, also reflected in the evocative illustrations.
SUBJ: Friendship--Fiction./ Death--Fiction.

Ph-1 5-A/4 $12.95   T   KH574
PATERSON, KATHERINE. Come sing, Jimmy Jo. Lodestar/Dutton ISBN 0-525-67167-6, 1985. 197p.
Selectors' Choice, 15th ed.
Available from National Library Service for the Blind and Physically Handicapped on sound recording cassette RC23271.
Booktalk videocassette available from WETA Television, 1987. 1 1/2" VHS videocassette color (15min) $49.95. (Books from cover to cover) Teacher's guide for $2.50.
Handed down through generations, the Appalachian bluegrass songs taught to eleven-year-old James by his beloved grandmother take on an added luster when James joins his grandfather, parents and uncle in their bluegrass group, The Family. Torn from his grandmother's side, and sent to a city school, he must also cope with his growing fame on TV, where he is called Jimmy Jo. He must deal with the family and school pressures his sudden success has brought. A superb story.
SUBJ: Country music--Fiction./ Musicians--Fiction./ Family life--Fiction.

Ph-1 5-A/6 $3.99   P   KH575
PATERSON, KATHERINE. Flip-flop girl. Penguin ISBN 0-14-037679-8,
1996. 120p.
Selectors' Choice, 20th ed.
Available from the National Library Service for the Blind and
Physically Handicapped on sound recording cassette RC 40003.
"Uprooted following the death of their father, nine-year-old Vinnie
and her five-year-old brother, Mason, cope in different ways--one in
silence--but both with the help of Lupe, the flip-flop girl." (CIP) With
tense plot, strong believable characters, tight description, and
dialogue, Paterson tells the story of three children who face great and
real difficulties. Lupe is another of Paterson's memorable characters.
Though meant for silent reading, the book would also be effective for
reading aloud to fourth graders and above.
SUBJ: Brothers and sisters--Fiction./ Grief--Fiction./ Death--Fiction./
Friendship--Fiction./ Mutism, Elective--Fiction./ Moving, Household--
Fiction.

Ph-1 5-A/5 $13.89   L   KH576
PATERSON, KATHERINE. Great Gilly Hopkins. Crowell/HarperCollins
ISBN 0-690-03838-0; In Canada: HarperCollins, c1978. 148p.
National Book Award.
Newbery Honor Book.
Selectors' Choice, 12th ed.
Available from National Library Service for the Blind and Physically
Handicapped on sound recording cassette RC12172.
Spanish version LA GRAN GILLY HOPKINS available from Santillana
(ISBN 84-204-32229, n.d.).
Eleven-year-old Gilly Hopkins is rebellious, manipulative, and very
bright. Abandoned by her young mother at three, she thrives on
hostility. But her newest foster mother, huge, untidy Maime Trotter,
pours out such unstinting love that she gradually pierces Gilly's
defenses. There are other wonderfully drawn characters in this book
but Gilly and Maime are truly memorable. This is a popular theme
but the author's humor, insight and skill make this book exceptional.
SUBJ: Foster home care--Fiction./ Love--Fiction.

Ph-1 5-A/7 $15.99   T   KH577
PATERSON, KATHERINE. Jip: his story. Lodestar/Dutton ISBN 0-525-
67543-4; In Canada: McClelland & Stewart, 1996. 181p.
A subtle, suspenseful novel based, in part, on a historical incident in
Vermont when the odious Fugitive Slave Law was in effect depicts
Jip, a boy existing in the town's poor house as a virtual slave who
learns that his origins put him in danger. The boy, about 12-14, lives
among the aged poor, the simpleminded, a sometimes dangerous
lunatic, and the superintendents of the poor house--two characters
lazy and mean enough to have been created by Dickens. He is a
friend to all in his innocence and almost too good to be true,
perhaps, the book's major fault. His escape to Canada viscerally
demonstrates the danger of the times and the unbridled power of
slave catchers and those who helped them for profit in a classic battle
between good and evil. Important historical fiction for units on
slavery, the Fugitive Slave Act, and the period of United States
history immediately before the Civil War. For multicultural studies.
SUBJ: Identity--Fiction./ Fugitive slaves--Fiction./ Slavery--Fiction./
Afro-Americans--Fiction.

Ph-1 3-6/6 $16.89   L   KH578
PATERSON, KATHERINE. King's equal. Illus. by Vladimir Vagin.
HarperCollins ISBN 0-06-022497-5; In Canada: HarperCollins, 1992.
64p. col. ill.
Available from the National Library Service for the Blind and
Physically Handicapped on sound recording cassette RC 36149.
In a story that can be read on several levels, an arrogant prince
cannot assume the king's crown until he finds a bride equal to him.
After a year away from court in the far mountains working as a
menial laborer, the prince finds his equal in the daughter of a simple
farmer, Rosamund. With the help of a clever wolf, a happy marriage
takes place. Active and colorful paintings add to the mood. A modern
folktale, good for reading aloud.
SUBJ: Fairy tales./ Princes--Fiction./ Wolves--Fiction.

Ph-1 6-A/7 $15.00   T   KH579
PATERSON, KATHERINE. Lyddie. Lodestar/Dutton ISBN 0-525-67338-5;
In Canada: McClelland & Stewart, 1991. 184p.
Set in the Lowell, Massachusetts, cloth factories in the 1840s, this
story of an impoverished Vermont farm girl takes her from the farm
to work in a Vermont inn, to the terrible factories of Lowell, where
she seeks independence and teaches herself to read. The facts of life
and labor in the mills and the boarding houses ring true in these
"model" factories where the mill hands were enslaved by the
owners. Paterson has succeeded in presenting interesting characters
and a slice of U.S. History about women of the laboring classes and
several reasons why unions developed.
SUBJ: Self-reliance--Fiction./ Work--Fiction./ Factories--Fiction.

Ph-1 6-A/6 $3.50   P   KH580
PATERSON, KATHERINE. Master puppeteer. Illus. by Haru Wells.
HarperCollins ISBN 0-06-440281-9, c1975. 179p. ill.
National Book Award.
Available from the National Library Service for the Blind and Physically
Handicapped on sound recording cassette RC10374.
The city of Osaka is suffering under a terrible drought. A mysterious
bandit Saburo robs the rich and gives rice to the poor but this does
not help Jiro or his family. His father makes puppets for the master
puppeteer, and Jiro runs away and offers himself to work for the
puppeteer. This engrossing mystery of Japan several hundred years
ago pictures a totally different culture and the art of its puppet
theater.
SUBJ: Puppet plays--Fiction./ Japan--History--Fiction./ Droughts--
Fiction.

Ph-1 5-A/6 $14.89   L   KH581
PATERSON, KATHERINE. Sign of the chrysanthemum. Illus. by Peter
Landa. HarperCollins ISBN 0-690-04913-7, c1973, 1991. 132p. ill.
In medieval Japan, a peasant boy buries his mother and leaves for
the great city to find his long-lost father. His mother told him that his
father was a great samurai warrior and that he would know him by a
small chrysanthemum tattooed on his left shoulder. He is befriended
by a renegade samurai, then by a sandalmaker and finally by a
swordsmith. A compelling and exciting story by an author who has
lived and studied in China and Japan.
SUBJ: Japan--History--Fiction./ Samurai--Fiction.

Ph-1 6-A/7 $3.95   P   KH582
PATON WALSH, JILL. Chance child. Farrar, Straus & Giroux ISBN
0-374-41174-3, c1978, 1991. 186p.
Selectors' Choice, 12th ed.
Unwanted, of illegitimate birth, confined by his mother in a closet,
modern day Creep escapes and finds himself in the nineteenth
century, a victim of the brutality of child labor. He finds a
companionship of mutual understanding of abuse with children of the
past and decides to remain there. Artfully interwoven is the
counterplot of Creep's half-brother who searches old Parliamentary
records concerning child labor and there he finds Creep. Paton
Walsh's work is one of the most intensive and instructive novels about
child labor in Britain. It can serve well in history classes - and as an
example of a finely wrought book.
SUBJ: Child labor--Great Britain--Fiction./ Great Britain--History--19th
century--Fiction./ Time travel--Fiction.

Ph-2 4-6/6 $13.00   T   KH583
PATON WALSH, JILL. Green book. Illus. by Lloyd Bloom. Farrar, Straus
& Giroux ISBN 0-374-32778-5, 1982. 74p. ill.
Selectors' Choice, 14th ed.
Book talk videocassette available from WETA Television, 1987. 1/2"
VHS videocassette color (15min) $49.95. (Books from cover to cover)
Teacher's guide available for $2.50.
Pattie's father is part of a picked group of colonists fleeing dying
Earth. Landing on a planet named Shine by Pattie, the adults who
know their lives depend on the resources of this vaguely hostile planet
are tense and fearful. But the children, who barely remember Earth,
delight in discovering the secrets of survival in their new and luminous
world. A short and unusual science fiction book useful for read aloud
and discussion.
SUBJ: Science fiction./ Survival--Fiction.

Ph-2 4-6/4 $11.95   T   KH584
PATTERSON, NANCY RUTH. Shiniest rock of all. Illus. by Karen A.
Jerome. Farrar, Straus & Giroux ISBN 0-374-36805-8; In Canada:
HarperCollins, 1991. 72p b&w illus.
Cursed with an embarrassing speech defect, the inability to pronounce
"R" properly, Robert Morris Reynolds lives in fear of being a
laughing-stock to his peers. Otherwise an average youngster, he tries
to "keep his mouth shut" until, at last, he consents to work with a
speech therapist, a matter of interest (and perphaps encouragement)
to children who have similar problems. Although the characters are
stereotypical at times, readers will identify with Robert, his
experiences, and the people he meets and knows. Would be an
excellent selection in groups where children have speech and language
difficulties--and perhaps as an oral presentation to those who make
fun of others.
SUBJ: Speech disorders--Fiction.

Ph-2 5-A/5 $15.95   T   KH585
PAULSEN, GARY. Call me Francis Tucket. Delacorte ISBN 0-385-32116-
3; In Canada: Bantam Doubleday Dell, 1995. 97p.
Sequel to: MR. TUCKET, Delacorte, 1994.
"Having separated from the one-armed trapper who taught him how
to survive in the wilderness of the Old West, fifteen-year-old Francis
gets lost and continues to have adventures involving dangerous men

and a friendly mule." (CIP) In a series of fast-paced episodes, he rescues two children and finds that caring for them is as involved as protecting himself from the perils of the wilderness.
SUBJ: Frontier and pioneer life--West (U.S.)--Fiction./ West (U.S.)--Fiction./ Mules--Fiction.

Ph-2 6-A/7 $13.95 T KH586

PAULSEN, GARY. Harris and me: a summer remembered. Harcourt Brace ISBN 0-15-292877-4; In Canada: Harcourt Brace c/o Canadian Manda, 1993. 157p.
Basing the story on his life, Paulsen tells of a summer when he is sent to stay with relatives on a farm because of his very bad home life. Now, eleven, he accepts the hard work on the farm as a way of life, but it is his younger cousin, Harris, who is at the center of the story. Harris is a wild daredevil, basically a good person, but someone who is always in trouble and sometimes danger, and who leads the narrator into the same condition. Paulsen has provided a mighty character in Harris and the reminiscence is hilarious. Readers should enjoy the adventures.
SUBJ: Farm life--Fiction./ Cousins--Fiction./ Boys--Fiction.

CE

Ph-1 5-A/6 $16.00 L KH587

PAULSEN, GARY. Hatchet. Bradbury ISBN 0-02-770130-1; In Canada: Collier Macmillan, 1987. 195p.
Newbery Honor book.
Selectors' Choice, 17th ed.
Available from National Library Service for the Blind and Physically Handicapped on sound recording cassette RC30535.
Talking book performed by Peter Coyote available from Bantam Audio (ISBN 0-553-47087-6, 1992). 3 sound cassettes (210min), $17.99.
Surviving fifty-four days in the Canadian wilderness after a plane crash, thirteen-year-old Brian Robeson discovers and develops totally new talents and skills. Armed with only a hatchet, he invents his own technology to make fire, create shelter, and find food. In an intense coming of age tale set in a unique setting, Brian learns to "look" in a new way and, as a result, survives and grows.
SUBJ: Survival--Fiction./ Divorce--Fiction.

Ph-2 5-A/5 $15.95 T KH588

PAULSEN, GARY. Mr. Tucket. Delacorte ISBN 0-385-31169-9; In Canada: Bantam Doubleday Dell, 1994. 166p.
"In 1848, while on a wagon train headed for Oregon, fourteen-year-old Francis Tucket is kidnapped by Pawnee Indians and then falls in with a one-armed trapper who teaches him how to live in the wild." (CIP) Cliff-hanging adventures, constant action, and detailed explanations of hunting, riding, and seeking food and shelter make this eminently readable. Although it appears that no Indian is a good Indian, the book explains how the settlers took land from the Native Americans and changed their ways of life, and one or two of the settlers are not such model individuals, either. Totally lacking in subtlety, the book will, nonetheless, hold readers and give a picture of the Old West, reflecting the thinking of most settlers of the time.
SUBJ: Frontier and pioneer life--West (U.S.)--Fiction./ Pawnee Indians--Fiction./ Indians of North America--Great Plains--Fiction./ Overland journeys to the Pacific--Fiction./ West (U.S.)--Fiction.

Ph-1 5-6/5 $13.89 L KH589

PEARCE, A. PHILIPPA. Tom's midnight garden. Illus. by Susan Einzig. HarperCollins ISBN 0-397-30477-3, c1958, 1991. 229p. ill.
Carnegie Medal.
Book talk videocassette available from WETA Television, 1987 (OPC). 1/2" VHS videocassette color (15min) $49.95. (Books from cover to cover) Teacher's guide available for $2.50.
Prowling through his relatives' home at night, Tom discovers a Victorian garden where none exists in the day. Enchanted by the characters he meets and the activities they engage in, Tom is reluctant to return home. A fascinating and totally believable space and time fantasy for fans of this genre. Try oral presentation.
SUBJ: Fantasy./ Time travel--Fiction.

Ph-2 5-6/6 $11.95 L KH590

PEARCE, A. PHILIPPA. Who's afraid? and other strange stories. Greenwillow ISBN 0-688-06895-2, 1987. 152p.
An old Christmas pudding, a ghost who plays the violin poorly at the top of the apple tree, are among the eleven stories in this spine-tingling collection. The reader is caught up in the other-world aura sketched by the descriptive prose.
SUBJ: Ghosts--Fiction./ Supernatural--Fiction./ Short stories.

Ph-1 5-A/6 $3.99 P KH591

PEARSON, KIT. Sky is falling. Penguin ISBN 0-14-037652-6; In Canada: Penguin, 1995. 248p.
Two British children are sent to Canada for safety at the beginning of World War II. The children, Norah, about ten, and her considerably younger brother, Gavin, must adjust to new people, new ways, new language, and homesickness for their parents and all they know. As they remain in Canada, they adapt. Readers of historical fiction will sympathize with Norah as she grows and changes.
SUBJ: World War, 1939-1945--Evacuation of civilians--Great Britain--Fiction./ Canada--Fiction./ Brothers and sisters--Fiction.

Ph-1 A/6 $3.99 P KH592

PECK, RICHARD. Are you in the house alone? Dell ISBN 0-440-90227-4, 1989. 156p.
Available from National Library Service for the Blind and Physically Handicapped on sound recording cassette RC10446.
Gail had been meeting secretly with Steve at a deserted camp, but they were unaware of a secret watcher. Then she begins to receive obscene phone calls and notes stuck in her locker at school. Finally, the nightmare becomes fact when she admits a classmate to the house where she is baby-sitting and he rapes her. Because of his social position and her own vulnerability to blackmail, she and her family realize she can not bring the case to court. A sensitive story honestly told. For the special reader.
SUBJ: Rape--Fiction.

Ph-2 5-A/3 $14.99 T KH593

PECK, RICHARD. Lost in cyberspace. Dial ISBN 0-8037-1931-0, 1995. 151p.
Available from the National Library Service for the Blind and Physically Handicapped on sound recording cassette RC 42808.
Owing more to Peck's humorous and "ghostly" novels than his realistic, issue-centered ones, this new adventure presents a cast of super-sophisticated young New Yorkers and a computer genius who sends himself and first person narrator, sixth grader Josh, into the past and future while also transporting characters from the past into the present. Humorous, especially in its dialogue and Josh's descriptions, the novel will appeal to reluctant readers.
SUBJ: Time travel--Fiction./ Schools--Fiction./ Brothers and sisters--Fiction.

Ph-1 4-6/6 $9.99 L KH594

PECK, ROBERT NEWTON. Soup. Illus. by Charles Gehm. Knopf ISBN 0-394-92700-1, 1974. 96p. ill.
Available from National Library Service for the Blind and Physically Handicapped on sound recording disc RD07473.
The friendship and mutual troubles of two boys--Soup and Robert--and their boyhood in a rural northern New England town. "Sassing" the teacher, rolling down hill in a barrel, whipping apples, and cheating the store keeper are among the hilarious and serious adventures they have. Episodic but doesn't really need "reading aloud" except perhaps to start it.
Followed by SOUP AND ME (ISBN 0-394-93157-2, 1975, OPC); SOUP FOR PRESIDENT (ISBN 0-394-93675-2, 1978, OPC); SOUP'S DRUM (ISBN 0-394-94251-5, 1980, OPC); SOUP ON WHEELS (ISBN 0-394-94581-6, 1981, OPC); SOUP IN THE SADDLE (ISBN 0-394-95294-4, 1983, OPC); SOUP'S GOAT (ISBN 0-394-96322-9, 1984, OPC); SOUP ON ICE (ISBN 0-394-97613-4, 1985, OPC); and SOUP ON FIRE (Dell ISBN 0-440-40193-3, 1987).
Available from NLSBPH are the following: SOUP IN THE SADDLE on sound recording cassette RC21836; SOUP'S GOAT on sound recording cassette RC22157.
SUBJ: Friendship--Fiction./ Vermont--Fiction.

CE

Ph-1 4-6/7 $15.99 L KH595

PENE DU BOIS, WILLIAM. Twenty-one balloons. Viking ISBN 0-670-73441-1, c1947. 179p. ill.
Newbery Medal Award.
Talking book available from Live Oak Media (ISBN 0-670-73444-6, 1972). 1 sound cassette, $9.95.
Available from National Library Service for the Blind and Physically Handicapped in Braille BRA03561, on sound recording cassette RC23467, as talking book TB01790.
In the fall of 1883 Professor William Waterbury Sherman, weary of 40 years of teaching arithmetic, sets forth from San Francisco on a balloon expedition. What happens in the three weeks between that day and the day he is rescued from the Atlantic Ocean makes up this unbelievable tale, which would be an excellent choice for oral presentation.
SUBJ: Balloons--Fiction./ Voyages and travels--Fiction.

Ph-1 4-6/7 $14.95 T KH596

PENNYPACKER, SARA. Dumbstruck. Illus. by Mary Jane Auch. Holiday House ISBN 0-8234-1123-0, 1994. 149p. ill.
Roald Dahl's ability to name characters, create wild and apt descriptions, broadly draw but sharply define characters, and depict nonsensical situations seems to have been reborn in the hands of

first-time novelist Pennypacker. Plot involves lost parents, cruel operators of an orphanage, orphans, a zany aunt, an ostrich, and a cast of eccentrics. Auch's black and white grotesque art matches the characters and situations perfectly in a book that is sometimes a bit much (a la Dahl), but is always fun. It is good for reading aloud--especially the takeoff on TV game show letter turners--and should be popular with Dahl fans.
SUBJ: Orphans--Fiction./ Humorous stories.

Ph-2 6-A/7 $13.95 T KH597
PEREZ, N. A. Breaker. Houghton Mifflin ISBN 0-395-45537-5, 1988. 206p.
Losing the father to a mining accident causes a great shift in the MacFarlane family as they struggle to survive in Scatter Patch, Pennsylvania, in 1902. Battling terrible working conditions, housing, and prejudice, young Pat MacFarlane, a breaker boy, fights to make his own way in the world. Details of the labor movement at the turn of the century will appeal to mature readers.
SUBJ: Coal mines and mining--Fiction./ Strikes and lockouts--Fiction./ Labor and laboring classes--Fiction./ Pennsylvania--History--1865--Fiction.

Ph-2 5-A/6 $14.95 L KH598
PERKINS, MITALI. Sunita experiment. Joy Street/Little, Brown ISBN 0-316-69943-8; In Canada: Little, Brown, 1993. 179p.
Embarrassed by her East Indian heritage, eighth grader Sunita begins to believe her friends are "normal," but she is not. The interesting details about East Indian customs, foods, and clothing as contrasted to United States life add an extra dimension to a well-developed story. Good for multicultural units.
SUBJ: East Indian Americans--Fiction./ Grandparents--Fiction./ Family life--Fiction./ Friendship--Fiction.

Ph-2 5-6/4 $4.50 P KH599
PETRY, ANN. Tituba of Salem Village. HarperCollins ISBN 0-06-440403-X, 1991. 254p.
Available from National Library Service for the Blind and Physically Handicapped in Braille BRA05545.
Gentle strong hands capable of nursing the sick; of spinning strong even thread; of planting a garden; of caring for livestock; these hands bring Tituba to trial for witchcraft in Salem Village.
SUBJ: Tituba--Fiction./ Afro-Americans--Fiction./ Salem (Mass.)--Fiction./ Witchcraft--Fiction.

Ph-1 3-5/6 $5.99 P KH600
PHILLIPS, MILDRED. Sign in Mendel's window. Illus. by Margot Zemach. Aladdin Paperbacks ISBN 0-689-80979-4; In Canada: Distican, c1985, 1996. unp. col. ill.
Available from National Library Service for the Blind and Physically Handicapped on sound recording cassette RC25696.
Advertising a room for rent in his small shop, Mendel soon discovers that he has a thief living with him. How his wife Molly proves that Tinker is a thief is a tale filled with wit and human kindness. The zestful watercolor illustrations capture the activities of the village in a title suitable for reading aloud.
SUBJ: Robbers and outlaws--Fiction./ Butchers--Fiction./ City and town life--Fiction.

Ph-2 3-5/7 $14.95 L KH601
PICO, FERNANDO. Red comb. Illustrated by Maria Antonia Ordonez. Translated by Argentina Palacios. BridgeWater ISBN 0-8167-3539-5; In Canada: BridgeWater/dist. by Vanwell, 1994. unp. col. ill.
"In mid-nineteenth-century Puerto Rico, an old woman and a young village girl conspire to save a runaway African slave by passing her off as the woman's niece." (CIP) Translated from the Spanish, the tale of life in Puerto Rico during the days of slavery demonstrates the steadfastness of the girl and old Rosa, who passes herself off as a conjure woman to overcome the selfish, Puerto Rican rich man who wants to capture the slave for the rich reward. Historical fiction based, in part, on official records provides background on the history of slavery on the island. Illustrated in full-page color paintings, the story has strong character and setting. Useful for multicultural studies and units on slavery and Puerto Rico.
SUBJ: Fugitive slaves--Fiction./ Blacks--Puerto Rico--Fiction./ Puerto Rico--Fiction.

Ph-1 5-A/7 $3.25 P KH602
PINKWATER, DANIEL MANUS. Fat men from space. Dell ISBN 0-440-44542-6, 1977. 57p. ill.
Available from National Library Service for the Blind and Physically Handicapped on sound recording cassette RC22090.
William has his tooth filled and, in a one-in-a-million accident, his tooth acts as a radio. Furthermore, he begins to hear, and later see, a UFO in which fat men from the planet Spiegel are coming to attack

the earth. But all they want is to eat up all the junk food on earth. A hilarious science-fiction tale.
SUBJ: Food--Fiction./ Unidentified flying objects--Fiction./ Humorous stories.

CE   Ph-1 5-A/6 $4.95 P KH603
PINKWATER, DANIEL MANUS. Hoboken chicken emergency. By D. Manus Pinkwater. Prentice-Hall ISBN 0-671-66447-6, c1977. 83p. ill. Videocassette available from Bonneville Worldwide (ISBN 0-7800-0007-2, 1984). 1/2" VHS videocassette color (58min), $29.95. (WonderWorks.)
Arthur Bobowicz must fetch the family's Thanksgiving turkey but they're all gone. Furthermore, he can't find a bird for dinner anywhere in Hoboken. He meets a mad professor who sells him a live 266-pound chicken. And from that moment, matters go from bad to worse...
SUBJ: Chickens--Fiction./ Humorous stories.

Ph-1 3-6/4 $15.00 T KH604
PINKWATER, DANIEL MANUS. Mush, a dog from space. By Daniel Pinkwater. Atheneum ISBN 0-689-80317-6; In Canada: Distican, 1995. 40p. col. ill.
Kelly Mangiaro wants a pet, any pet, but her parents, who are rarely home, object. When she meets Mush, a talking mushamute dog from planet Growf-Woof-Woof in solar system Arfturus, she meets a talented cook, organizer, and friend. A volume in Pinkwater's Guides to the Galaxy, this sheer nonsensical fantasy will join other delightful silly stories, illustrated in Pinkwater's inimitable style, as a new favorite. Ridiculous.
SUBJ: Dogs--Fiction./ Moving, Household--Fiction./ Humorous stories.

Ph-2 2-5/3 $15.00 T KH605
PINKWATER, DANIEL MANUS. Wallpaper from space. By Daniel Pinkwater. Illus. by Jill Pinkwater. Atheneum ISBN 0-689-80764-3; In Canada: Distican, 1996. 32p. col. ill.
"At bedtime, a young boy (Steve) enters the outer space-patterned wallpaper in his room and has adventures with a band of spacemice." (CIP) The spacemice--Steve is turned into one--have aimless, but amusing, adventures in their search for gumballs. In nine episodes, humorously illustrated in solid marker colors, nothing much happens, but the action is constant and silly. Newly established readers will be able to handle the transitional reader, and Pinkwater fans will, as usual, welcome the slight story.
SUBJ: Outer space--Fiction./ Adventure and adventurers--Fiction./ Humorous stories.

Ph-1 5-A/4 $15.99 T KH606
PINKWATER, JILL. Mister Fred. Dutton ISBN 0-525-44778-4, 1994. 211p.
When their beloved teacher leaves, Mr. Fred (Goldberg Fred) becomes the substitute teacher for a class of ill-behaved sixth graders. Mr. Fred seems to have extraterrestrial powers which quell the rebellious group's activities as narrated by Anya Murray, class president. Is the substitute, who manages to make learning a positive and interesting experience, from our planet or from another galaxy? Humorous science fiction that will make many students wish for a Mister Fred as a teacher--one whose methods might serve as inspiration for teachers, earthlings or otherwise.
SUBJ: Schools--Fiction./ Teachers--Fiction./ Extraterrestrial beings--Fiction./ Extrasensory perception--Fiction./ Humorous stories.

Ph-1 4-6/2 $15.95 L KH607
POLACCO, PATRICIA. Pink and Say. Philomel ISBN 0-399-22671-0; In Canada: Putnam, 1994. unp. col. ill.
When Pink, an African-American soldier, rescues Say, who was left for dead, and takes him home to his mother, their presence poses a threat from Confederate marauders. The heartbreaking story of war and friendship has a troubled ending when Pink's mother is killed and the boys are captured and taken to Andersonville. Historical fiction in picture book format for older audiences especially those who are studying the Civil War. The fictionalized account will be valuable in interdisciplinary units for social studies.
SUBJ: United States--History--Civil War, 1861-1865--Fiction./ Friendship--Fiction.

Ph-1 5-A/4 $13.95 T KH608
POLIKOFF, BARBARA GARLAND. Life's a funny proposition, Horatio. Henry Holt ISBN 0-8050-1972-3; In Canada: Fitzhenry & Whiteside, 1992. 103p.
"When someone dies, the hardest thing to get used to is that they just aren't around anymore," writes twelve-year-old Horatio after the death of his father. He learns to come to terms with the loss and the change in family situation, in part, when his grandfather's dog runs away and dies. Not a gloomy book, it is filled with believable and

real character development and an understanding of life's occurrences as well as how other people and time help, if not cure. A fine reading experience for the mature, more sensitive reader.
SUBJ: Death--Fiction./ Grandfathers--Fiction.

Ph-2 5-6/6 $15.95   T   KH609
POPE, ELIZABETH MARIE. Perilous gard. Illus. by Richard Cuffari. Houghton Mifflin ISBN 0-395-18512-2, 1974. 280p. ill.
Newbery Honor Book.
Available from National Library Service for the Blind and Physically Handicapped on sound recording cassette RC08842.
When Alicia (the beautiful but silly sister) writes an unwise letter to Queen Mary, it is Kate (sensible and clever) who is punished and is sent to be kept in The Perilous Gard--a mysterious castle in a remote and old part of England. The Gard was feared by the local peasants because of its association with the Fairy Folk and heathen magic. Kate is involved in a strange, unbelievable series of events which eventually bring about a resolution of the mystery and the domination of the Fairy Folk.
SUBJ: Fantasy./ Great Britain--History--Tudors, 1485-1603--Fiction.

Ph-1 4-6/4 $14.99   L   KH610
PORTE, BARBARA ANN. Fat Fanny, Beanpole Bertha, and the boys. Illus. by Maxie Chambliss. Orchard ISBN 0-531-08528-7, 1991. 101p. ill.
Peopled with memorable characters reminiscent of the best of Ellen Raskin, this is a complex yet simple telling of the story of two best friends, one whose father is lost in the Bermuda Triangle, and the other who is the untheatrical daughter of secretly divorced parents who are theatrical agents. It speeds along to recount various adventures of the two girls and their families. Even minor characters are well developed in this humorous adventure about offbeat people who seem real.
SUBJ: Humorous stories.

Ph-2 1-3/2 $14.00   L   KH611
PORTE, BARBARA ANN. Turkey drive and other tales. Illus. by Yossi Abolafia. Greenwillow ISBN 0-688-11336-2, 1993. 64p. ill. (Taxicab tales).
Sam and Abigail make up stories about the paintings in their house. Comical illustrations accompany the humorous episodic chapters. Newly established readers familiar with the characters from TAXICAB TALES will enjoy the latest adventures of the quirky family and their dog, Benton.
SUBJ: Storytelling--Fiction./ Family life--Fiction.

Ph-3 3-4/4 $8.95   L   KH612
POWELL, E. SANDY. Daisy. Illus. by Peter J. Thornton. Carolrhoda ISBN 0-87614-449-0, 1991. 32p. ill.
Abandoned by her mother and abused by her father, young Daisy draws her dreams as escape. An observant school tutor notices the marks of physical abuse on Daisy and reports the situation. The story is simple enough for a better second grade reader to understand, and the illustrations give clues to character. This helpful book can be of use to abused children by showing them a way out and will aid the understanding of those who are not abused.
SUBJ: Child abuse--Fiction.

CE   Ph-3 4-7/7 $8.95   P   KH613
POWELL, MARY CURTNER. Queen of the air: the story of Katherine Stinson, 1891-1977. Coldwater Press ISBN 1-880384-07-8, 1993. 121p.
Videocassette available from Coldwater Press (ISBN 1-880384-08-6, 1993). 1/2" VHS videocassette color (26min), $21.95. Includes teacher's guide.
Presents the fictionalized biography of aviatrix Katherine Stinson, her remarkable career in the early years of aviation, and her other accomplishments as a pioneer in several fields. Use in units on women's studies and the history of flight.
SUBJ: Stinson, Katherine--Fiction./ Air pilots--Fiction./ Women air pilots--Fiction.

Ph-2 3-5/6 $6.95   P   KH614
PYLE, HOWARD. King Stork. Illus. by Trina Schart Hyman. Little, Brown ISBN 0-316-72441-6; In Canada: Little, Brown, 1973. 48p col illus.
Following the folkloric theme of kindness being rewarded, a soldier returning from the wars befriends an elderly man and as a result wins and reforms a beautiful princess. Taken from Pyle's THE WONDERCLOCK and illustrated by the award winning artist, this is an unusual tale for telling or reading aloud.
SUBJ: Fairy tales./ Princesses--Fiction.

Ph-2 2-4/3 $14.95   T   KH615
QUATTLEBAUM, MARY. Jazz, Pizzazz, and the silver threads. Illus. by Robin Oz. Delacorte ISBN 0-385-32183-X; In Canada: Bantam

Doubleday Dell, 1996. 120p. ill.
Calvin Hastings, nine, longs for a pet, any pet. When neighbor Jenny, a magician-in-training, acquires a hamster, Pizzazz, Calvin becomes the best friend and protector of the small, active rodent. Through a series of circumstances, many humorous, the creature eventually becomes his. An easy-to-read book with plenty of action.
SUBJ: Hamsters--Fiction./ Pets--Fiction./ Magicians--Fiction.

Ph-2 2-4/4 $14.95   T   KH616
QUATTLEBAUM, MARY. Magic Squad and the dog of great potential. Illus. by Frank Remkiewicz. Delacorte ISBN 0-385-32276-3; In Canada: Bantam Doubleday Dell, 1997. 123p. ill.
Calvin believes he is ordinary, especially when he compares himself to his younger brother and neighbor girl. Then he shows his talent and persistence when he rescues--and trains--a large dog from the pound. Fast paced and humorous, this is a strong transitional reader.
SUBJ: Dogs--Fiction./ Pets--Fiction./ Animals--Treatment--Fiction.

Ph-1 3-5/4 $12.95   L   KH617
RADIN, RUTH YAFFE. All Joseph wanted. Illus. by Deborah Kogan Ray. Macmillan ISBN 0-02-775641-6; In Canada: Maxwell Macmillan, 1991. 80p. ill.
Sixth-grader Joseph often serves as the embarrassed parent to his illiterate mother. She is a fine mother, but her inability to read puts a strain on everyone. Thanks to a program and a sympathetic tutor of adult nonreaders at the local library she does become independent. The book presents an awareness of a too common situation, the reluctance to enter tutoring in adulthood, and possible solutions. Ray's soft black and white illustrations fit the mood nicely. Read aloud to inform youngsters about adult literacy classes and raise discussion.
SUBJ: Literacy--Fiction./ Mothers and sons--Fiction.

Ph-2 4-6/6 $5.99   P   KH618
RASKIN, ELLEN. Figgs and phantoms. Penguin ISBN 0-14-032944-7, 1974. 152p. ill.
Newbery Honor Book.
A fantastic story about a fantastic family: Sister Figg Newton, tap dancer and baton twirler (mother); Truman, the human pretzel (uncle); Romulus, the walking book of knowledge, and Remus, the talking adding machine; and others, not to speak of Uncle Florence the book dealer who was only 4'6" tall. The only person Mona had really loved was Uncle Florence and when he dies and goes to Capri (Figg Family heaven) she tries to follow him. A rewarding reading experience, of mystery and fantasy, both reflected in the off-beat illustrations as well as in the story.
SUBJ: Family life--Fiction./ Fantasy.

Ph-1 5-6/5 $15.95   L   KH619
RASKIN, ELLEN. Westing game. Dutton ISBN 0-525-42320-6, c1978. 163p.
Newbery Medal Award.
Selectors' Choice, 12th ed.
Available from National Library Service for the Blind and Physically Handicapped on sound recording cassette RC12787 and in Braille BR06285.
An eccentric multimillionaire's will requires that his 16 heirs (all mysteriously residents of the same building) solve clues to an ingenious puzzle to gain his fortune. Thirteen-year-old Tabitha-Ruth "Turtle" Wexler leads the chase. The shifting identities of the heirs, a "murder" and the clever twists and turns of a plot that never lags holds the reader enthralled to the very last word. A first-rate entertainment.
SUBJ: Inheritance and succession--Fiction./ Mystery and detective stories.

Ph-1 2-5/5 $14.95   L   KH620
RATZ DE TAGYOS, PAUL. Coney tale. Clarion ISBN 0-395-58834-0, 1992. unp. col. ill.
Selectors' Choice, 19th ed.
Illustrated in vibrant colors which depict scenes reminiscent of Flemish high art, the tale of the town of Conage and its citizens--coneys (rabbits) provides a delightful fantasy. When father and son, Holbun the Elder and Younger, accidentally discover a tree-sized carrot, the mechanical genius of the citizens of Conage comes into play as they remove it and have the feast of all feasts. The art is skillful, humorous, and personalizes the Flemish costumed coneys. Use in art lessons about Flemish paintings.
SUBJ: Rabbits--Fiction./ Carrots--Fiction./ Flanders--Fiction.

Ph-1 1-4/5 $14.95   L   KH621
RATZ DE TAGYOS, PAUL. Showdown at Lonesome Pellet. Clarion ISBN 0-395-67645-2, 1994. unp. col. ill., map.
Lonesome Pellet, a coney town in the Western Territory, is bullied by the mean and ornery Pointy Brothers until one day a stranger wearing

a radish hat comes to town. The quiet stranger engineers a showdown to outsmart the outlaw brothers and wins the respect of the town. Text and marker illustrations imbue the story and its rabbit characters with subtle humor and will have enormous appeal for fans of the Western genre.
SUBJ: West (U.S.)--Fiction./ Rabbits--Fiction.

Ph-1 5-A/5 $24.95 L KH622
RAWLINGS, MARJORIE KINNAN. Yearling. Illus. by N. C. Wyeth. Scribner's ISBN 0-684-18461-3; In Canada: Scribner's, c1938, 1967. 400p. col. ill.
Available from National Library Service for the Blind and Physically Handicapped in Braille BR00547 and talking book TB02864.
Forced to decide the fate of his fawn, Flag, Jody comes to terms with the harsh reality of life in the rugged Florida backwoods of sixty years ago. This reprint of the 1939 edition of the classic story of the Baxter family is suitable as a gift book and is best introduced to today's young people as a read-aloud.
SUBJ: Deer--Fiction./ Florida--Fiction./ Parent and child--Fiction./ Farm life--Florida--Fiction.

Ph-1 4-6/6 $14.95 T KH623
RAWLS, WILSON. Summer of the monkeys. Doubleday ISBN 0-385-11450-8, 1976. 239p.
Available from National Library Service for the Blind and Physically Handicapped on sound recording cassette RC12258.
Jay Berry Lee is a fourteen-year-old farm boy living in Oklahoma in the 1890s. To his delight, a troupe of monkeys and one canny chimpanzee, newly escaped from a circus truck, have fled to his father's farm where Jay, mindful of the large reward for them, sets out in a hilarious pursuit foiled by the monkeys until a storm vanquishes them. Amusing and very well written.
SUBJ: Farm life--Fiction./ Monkeys--Fiction./ Oklahoma--Fiction.

Ph-2 A/4 $5.50 P KH624
RAWLS, WILSON. Where the red fern grows: the story of two dogs and a boy. Bantam Doubleday Dell ISBN 0-553-27429-5; In Canada: Bantam Doubleday Dell, c1961, 1988. 212p.
Available from National Library Service for the Blind and Physically Handicapped in Braille BRA04108 and as talking book TB04333.
Based on a story which first appeared in The Saturday Evening Post, this tells of Billy Colman's great yearning for a pair of coon hounds, how he worked for two long years to save $50 in order to buy them, how he trained and hunted with them. As their fame spread, he won the coveted gold cup in the annual coon-hunt contest but his victory was short-lived. Tragedy awaited the pups.
SUBJ: Dogs--Fiction./ Ozark Mountains--Fiction.

Ph-1 4-6/6 $14.95 T KH625
REGAN, DIAN CURTIS. Monsters in the attic. Illus. by Laura Cornell. Henry Holt ISBN 0-8050-3709-8; In Canada: Fitzhenry & Whiteside, 1995. 182p. ill.
Sequel to: MONSTER OF THE MONTH CLUB, 1994.
The toy monsters Rilla has been receiving as a gift continue to come to life and cause problems and mischief for her. Among the new monsters is a mermaid who takes over the bathtub and causes it to overflow, and an over active sports monster who is entirely too anxious to compete in every sport known to humanity. Funny and well developed, readers should enjoy this--and listeners might, too. For reading aloud.
SUBJ: Monsters--Fiction./ Toys--Fiction.

Ph-1 4-A/6 $14.00 L KH626
REID BANKS, LYNNE. Adventures of King Midas. Illus. by Jos. A. Smith. Morrow ISBN 0-688-10894-6, 1992. 153p. ill.
Retells, with physical descriptions and character details, the story of King Midas set in a more modern, although fairy-tale-like frame. His adventures as he seeks to be freed from the curse of turning everything he touches into gold will amuse, as will Smith's humorous black and white sketches. Try reading aloud.
SUBJ: Midas (Legendary character)--Fiction./ Kings, queens, rulers, etc.--Fiction./ Magic--Fiction.

CE Ph-1 4-6/4 $15.95 T KH627
REID BANKS, LYNNE. Indian in the cupboard. Illus. by Brock Cole. Doubleday ISBN 0-385-17051-3, 1980. 181p. ill.
Selectors' Choice, 14th ed.
Available from National Library Service for the Blind and Physically Handicapped in Braille BR05238.
Talking book available from Listening Library YA 809-3 (ISBN 0-0872-0217-7, 1992). 3 sound cassettes (240min), $19.95.
Omri receives a small cupboard as a birthday present. When his mother gives him a key which locks the cupboard, he finds that the plastic Indian toy he left inside has turned into a tiny human being,

and his friend Patrick doesn't realize that the tiny toys are really human beings and must not be exploited. An exciting and different fantasy.
SUBJ: Indians of North America--Fiction./ Toys--Fiction./ Magic--Fiction.

CE Ph-1 5-A/6 $15.93 L KH628
REID BANKS, LYNNE. Mystery of the cupboard. Illus. by Tom Newsom. Morrow ISBN 0-688-12635-9, 1993. 246p. ill.
Sequel to: SECRET OF THE INDIAN, Doubleday, 1989.
Talking book read by the author available from Listening Library YA 852, 1993 (ISBN 0-8072-7415-1). 1 sound cassette (270min), $29.98.
Explains the origins of the magical cupboard first introduced in THE INDIAN IN THE CUPBOARD. Omri relives the days of pre-World War I London as the miniatures belonging to his great-great-aunt Charlotte become enlivened in the cupboard.
SUBJ: Family life--Fiction./ Magic--Fiction./ Toys--Fiction./ Moving, Household--Fiction.

Ph-1 5-A/6 $15.95 T KH629
REID BANKS, LYNNE. Return of the Indian. Illus. by William Geldart. Doubleday ISBN 0-385-23497-X; In Canada: Doubleday, 1986. 189p. ill.
Available from National Library Service for the Blind and Physically Handicapped in Braille BR7028.
Omri continues to think about the Indian and cowboy he brought to life. Once again he brings Little Bear, his wife Bright Stars, and the tender cowboy, Boone, to life--but it is now the French and Indian War and Little Bear is a participant, as chief. Plastic soldiers, doctors, nurses of World War I, cross time boundaries and work to save the lives of the living miniature figures. Those fascinated with the first book will want to read this somewhat repetitive, but nonetheless gripping, sequel.
In THE SECRET OF THE INDIAN (ISBN 0-385-26292-2, 1989, available from the NLSBPH on sound recording cassette RC 3563), when Patrick travels in time to the wild West and accidently brings back a tornado, the secret of the magical cupboard is almost discovered, and Omri vows never to open it again.
SUBJ: Indians of North America--Fiction./ Toys--Fiction./ Magic--Fiction.

Ph-2 6-A/7 $15.95 T KH630
REISS, KATHRYN. Time windows. Harcourt Brace Jovanovich ISBN 0-15-288205-7; In Canada: Harcourt Brace c/o Canadian Manda, 1991. 260p.
Moving from an apartment in New York City to a large, possibly haunted old home in Massachusetts, thirteen-year-old Miranda, her physician mother, and her historian father encounter a new way of life. A dollhouse in the attic, the exact miniature replica of the house as it was years ago, pulls Miranda into child abuse and death which occurred in the past. The sense of evil is well-developed and will hold the better reader.
SUBJ: Dollhouses--Fiction./ Space and time--Fiction./ Moving, Household--Fiction./ Good and evil--Fiction.

Ph-2 3-5/3 $3.99 P KH631
RICHEMONT, ENID. Magic skateboard. Illus. by Jan Ormerod. Candlewick ISBN 1-56402-449-0; In Canada: Douglas & McIntyre, 1992. 80p. ill.
A tall, strange-looking woman changes Danny's skateboard into a modern magic carpet on which he takes trips to anywhere he wishes--including a visit to the Queen of England's commode, which he uses. Since the time is so near the Christmas holidays, the magic in the fantasy may be connected with the holiday or just a young boy's wishing. Ormerod's black and white silhouettes and line art fit the story and are the only way by which the reader knows Danny is a young, black child.
SUBJ: Magic--Fiction./ Skateboards--Fiction./ Blacks--England--Fiction./ London (England)--Fiction.

Ph-1 5-A/5 $3.99 P KH632
RICHTER, CONRAD. Light in the forest. Fawcett ISBN 0-449-70437-8, 1994. 117p.
True Son became an Indian when he was captured at four from the field of his parents' Pennsylvania frontier farm. He became a real Lenni Lenape and loved the woods and Indian's way of life. When he is forced to return to his parents, he is torn by the conflict between the free Indian life and the restrictions of the settlers.
SUBJ: Pennsylvania--Fiction./ Delaware Indians--Fiction./ Indians of North America--Captivities--Fiction.

Ph-1 5-A/5 $4.99 P KH633
RICHTER, HANS PETER. Friedrich. Translated from the German by Edite Kroll. Puffin/Penguin ISBN 0-14-032205-1, c1970, 1987. 152p.

Batchelder Award, 1972.
Friedrich Schneider is unfortunate enough to be born in 1925, to a Jewish family, and in Germany. He is fortunate in that his best friend, a Gentile boy of the same age, remains a friend though not very helpful at times. Friedrich is interested in life and learning and being part of his country, but as Hitler grows in power, one curtailment after another comes to him. Caught up in man's insanity, Friedrich is dead at seventeen. The style is cold, and the powerful story engages the mature reader.
SUBJ: World War, 1939-1945--Germany--Fiction./ World War, 1939-1945--Jews--Fiction./ Holocaust, Jewish (1939-1945)--Fiction./ Friendship--Fiction.

Ph-2 5-A/4 $15.99   T   KH634
RIDLEY, PHILIP. Kasper in the glitter. Illus. by Chris Riddell. Dutton ISBN 0-525-45799-2; In Canada: McClelland & Stewart, 1997. 204p. ill.
Originally published in Great Britain, Viking U.K., 1994.
Better readers, especially those who have understood Ridley's delightful nonsense in KRINDLEKRAX, will appreciate the strange adventures of Kasper. Son of the self-centered Pumpkin, he is a boy "who has no friends" in a strange world of wastelands, glitter, and gloom. Various unusual, but believable, characters wander in and out of "the nothing" where Kasper lives in a sterile and unhappy future society. Thanks to bravery and adventure, they change the course of that awful and dangerous world. Characters represent various symbolic persons extant in our own world and will intrigue and involve readers in these very fast paced, idiosyncratic adventures. Fascinating for stronger readers of fantasy. Riddell's black and white sketches add to the adventure.
SUBJ: Adventure and adventurers--Fiction./ Humorous stories.

Ph-2 5-6/6 $14.95   T   KH635
ROBERTS, WILLO DAVIS. Don't hurt Laurie! Illus. by Ruth Sanderson. Atheneum ISBN 0-689-30571-0, 1977. 176p. ill.
Keeping the secret of her mother's abuse, even from her stepfather and siblings, Laurie endures repeated episodes that require hospital visits. When she makes friends and life goes well the family moves on until one day when Annabelle's rage escalates to the point that she almost kills Laurie and finally the secret can no longer be contained. This gripping novel deals with child abuse in a realistic manner and fills a need for a timely topic that is frequently discussed.
SUBJ: Child abuse--Fiction.

Ph-2 4-6/5 $13.95   T   KH636
ROBERTS, WILLO DAVIS. Girl with the silver eyes. Atheneum ISBN 0-689-30786-1; In Canada: Collier Macmillan, 1980. 181p.
Available from National Library Service for the Blind and Physically Handicapped in Braille BR04939 and on sound recording cassette RC17387.
Katie's silver eyes are frightening to people unaware of her psychokinetic powers, although a new tenant, Mr. Cooper, seems oddly interested. A chance clue, the support of an understanding elderly friend and her own telepathic powers, help Katie track down three other children with silver eyes--children whose mothers all took an experimental drug during pregancy. Mr. Cooper, it turns out, has located seventeen other children with silver eyes so they know they are no longer alone. For occult fans.
SUBJ: Psychokinesis--Fiction./ Extrasensory perception--Fiction.

TB
Ph-1 4-6 $9.95   OD KH637
ROBERTSON, KEITH. Henry Reed, Inc. (Talking book). Performed by the High Tor Repertory Players. Live Oak Media ISBN 0-670-36799-0, 1973. 1 sound cassette.
The industrious, free-enterprising schemes of Henry Reed unfold in this dramatic presentation, adapted from the book by Keith Robertson, with excellent characterizations, well-conceived sound effects, and musical background. A journal effect is achieved as short musical interludes divide the various time segments. Henry Reed describes the day's activities and the scene then proceeds into playform. Based on the book of the same title.
SUBJ: Humorous stories./ New Jersey--Fiction.

Ph-1 4-6/6 $4.99   P   KH638
ROBERTSON, KEITH. Henry Reed's baby-sitting service. Illus. by Robert McCloskey. Penguin ISBN 0-14-034146-3, c1966. 204p. ill.
Available from National Library Service for the Blind and Physically Handicapped in Braille BR01984 and on talking book TB02113.
Returning to spend the summer in Grover's Corners, New Jersey, Henry and his partner, Midge, establish a company for baby-sitting services. They receive free advertising on the Trenton radio, master the quirks and peculiarities of their "clients," and win a "Business-of-the-Month Award." Fun for everyone.
Other titles in this series HENRY REED, INC. (ISBN 0-14-034144-7, 1989), HENRY REED'S JOURNEY (ISBN 0-14-034145-5, 1989,

OPC), HENRY REED'S BIG SHOW (ISBN 0-670-36839-3, 1970, OPC), and HENRY REED'S THINK TANK (ISBN 0-670-80968-3, 1986, OPC).
Available also from NLSBPH are: HENRY REED, INC. in Braille BRA07226; HENRY REED'S JOURNEY in Braille BR00029 and sound recording cassette RC11316; HENRY REED'S BIG SHOW as talking book TB04003.
SUBJ: Babysitters--Fiction./ New Jersey--Fiction./ Humorous stories.

Ph-2 5-A/5 $14.95   L   KH639
ROBINET, HARRIETTE GILLEM. Mississippi chariot. Atheneum ISBN 0-689-31960-6; In Canada: Maxwell Macmillan, 1994. 117p.
"Jean Karl book."
Includes bibliography.
In Mississippi in 1936, Shortning Bread Jackson, twelve, helps free his falsely convicted father who is serving on a chain gang. Through a series of clever stratagems in the violently racist society in which he lives, he succeeds in having his father released and achieves his goal to have the family go North to a better life. Shortning is a fascinating character--perhaps a bit too wise for his years--but the situation and the "down home expressions" and colorful metaphors skillfully set the scene and rapidly developed plot well. Engaging historical fiction for multicultural studies depicts the troubled race relations during the Great Depression.
SUBJ: Afro-Americans--Fiction./ Race relations--Fiction./ Mississippi--Fiction./ United States--History--1933-1945--Fiction.

Ph-1 4-6/7 $13.89   L   KH640
ROBINSON, BARBARA. Best Christmas pageant ever. Illus. by Judith Gwyn Brown. HarperCollins ISBN 0-06-025044-5, c1972. 80p. ill.
Selectors' Choice, 8th ed.
Available from National Library Service for the Blind and Physically Handicapped in Braille BR05636.
In a Christmas story with a really different twist, the Herdmans--all six of them--are all horrible. They blackmail the other children, threaten to stuff pussywillows in their ears, create havoc wherever they go. When they decide to join Sunday School and become actors in the Christmas pageant, the whole town thinks the end has come. Very funny and really memorable story which ends with surprises all around.
SUBJ: Christmas--Fiction./ Brothers and sisters--Fiction.

Ph-1 3-A/5 $12.89   L   KH641
ROBINSON, BARBARA. Best school year ever. HarperCollins ISBN 0-06-023043-6, 1994. 117p.
Sequel to BEST CHRISTMAS PAGEANT EVER, HarperCollins, 1972.
Selectors' Choice, 20th ed.
Available from the National Library Service for the Blind and Physically Handicapped on sound recording cassette RC 40069.
The several Herdman children, first met some years ago in THE BEST CHRISTMAS PAGEANT EVER, once again cause general discomfort and trouble for everyone with whom they have contact. Readers will especially appreciate unpleasant children being on the receiving end of Herdman actions. The humor is logical and smooth in its development, and every detail is in place because of the strong backgrounds to situations that Robinson supplies. Totally child centered, it is definitely a first choice for reading aloud which will cause listeners to want to read the book themselves.
SUBJ: Schools--Fiction./ Humorous stories.

Ph-2 3-6/4 $13.95   L   KH642
ROBINSON, NANCY K. Veronica the show-off. Four Winds ISBN 0-02-777360-4, c1982. 127p.
Available from National Library Service for the Blind and Physically Handicapped on sound recording cassette RC21774.
Although Veronica is a horrendous little girl, bossy, boastful and sometimes plain mean--younger readers enjoy this book. Veronica's single-parent mother gives her little attention, but a friendly librarian helps her and she acquires two understanding friends. Her wonderful letter to the paper, on behalf of the beleaguered public library, gives her the positive attention she needs.
In VERONICA MEETS HER MATCH (ISBN 0-590-41512-3, 1990, OPC) she meets a new neighbor, Crystal, who has a mysterious past and an imagination as wild as Veronica's own; and in COUNTESS VERONICA (ISBN 0-590-44486-7, c1994, 1996) Veronica decides to be a chess champion and serves as an unwitting marriage broker for her father.
SUBJ: Behavior--Fiction.

Ph-1 4-6/5 $21.80   L   KH643
ROCKWELL, THOMAS. How to eat fried worms. Illus. by Emily Arnold McCully. Watts ISBN 0-531-02631-0, 1973. 115p. ill.
For fifty dollars, Billy takes the bet of eating 15 worms--one a day. His friends and family help him to invent different ways to cook them:

worm pie, worm loaf, Alsatian smothered worms, etc. etc. But his opponents soon learn they may lose their money, and so work to thwart his attempts. Episodic tales based on an idea repulsive to most adults are highly appealing to children, especially reluctant readers.
SUBJ: Humorous stories./ Worms--Fiction./ Food--Fiction.

Ph-2 6-A/6 $7.95   P   KH644
ROCKWOOD, JOYCE. To spoil the sun. Henry Holt ISBN 0-8050-3465-X; In Canada: Fitzhenry & Whiteside, c1976, 1994. 180p., map.
Includes chronology.
Selectors' Choice, 11th ed.
Eleven-year-old Rain Dove tells the story of two generations of Cherokee history at the dawn of exploration of North America. Strongly written, it is an empathetic re-creation of Cherokee life and culture for multicultural studies. Describes the devastating effects of the European diseases which the Spaniards introduced to the indigenous population. Moving historical fiction for the social studies curriculum.
SUBJ: Cherokee Indians--Fiction./ Indians of North America--Fiction./ America--Discovery and exploration--Fiction./ Smallpox--Fiction.

Ph-1 5-A/6 $12.95   L   KH645
RODDA, EMILY. Finders keepers. Illus. by Noela Young. Greenwillow ISBN 0-688-10516-5, 1991. 184p. ill.
Chosen randomly by a computer, Patrick becomes the contestant on what appears to be a television game show. He must find three objects which have been lost in order to win "fabulous" prizes. The objects are in our world, but the show is beyond a time-space fence where lost things are collected. This gentle science fiction fantasy is for readers older than BORROWERS' fans, but the suspense and imaginative writing should appeal to the same audience. Prime for reading aloud.
SUBJ: Lost and found possessions--Fiction./ Time travel--Fiction./ Game shows--Fiction.

CE   Ph-1 4-6/7 $3.95   P   KH646
RODGERS, MARY. Billion for Boris. HarperCollins ISBN 0-06-410075-1, c1974. 211p.
Sequel to: FREAKY FRIDAY.
Kit available from Listening Library SWR18, 1979. 1 sound cassette (38min), 1 paperback book, $14.95. (Soundways to reading)
Available from National Library Service for the Blind and Physically Handicapped in Braille BRA14468.
Annabel Andrews has another strange experience. This time her brother Ape Face mends an old TV set and she and her friend Boris discover that it shows what will happen tomorrow. Boris has decided he must renovate his apartment, while his mother is away in Los Angeles; and to do this he needs a great deal of money. How he earns it, almost, the mind-boggling adventures they have, certainly don't work out as they'd planned. Was it ESP?
SUBJ: Extrasensory perception--Fiction./ Mothers and sons--Fiction./ Brothers and sisters--Fiction.

CE   Ph-1 5-6/5 $13.89   L   KH647
RODGERS, MARY. Freaky Friday. HarperCollins ISBN 0-06-025049-6, c1972. 145p.
Read-along kit available from Listening Library SWR16, 1978. 1 sound cassette (23min), 1 paperback book $15.98. (Soundways to reading).
Spanish version VIERNES EMBRUJADO available from Santillana (ISBN 84-204-36402, 1987).
Annabel Andrews, thirteen-years-old, is a mess, and she's suddenly been forced to recognize this awful truth. One morning, after a particularly harrowing fight with her mother, she writes, "When I woke up this morning, I found I'd turned into my mother." This book is the story of her day in her mother's body and the traumatic results for everyone in her family and circle of friends and acquaintances. Funny--but also searing. Top-notch preteen story.
Followed by: BILLION FOR BORIS.
SUBJ: Mothers and daughters--Fiction./ Family life--Fiction./ Spanish language materials.

Ph-2 5-6/7 $12.89   L   KH648
RODGERS, MARY. Summer switch. HarperCollins ISBN 0-06-025059-3; In Canada: HarperCollins, 1982. 185p.
Available from National Library Service for the Blind and Physically Handicapped on sound recording cassette RC19150.
Benjamin "Ape Face" Andrews, who is on his way to camp, voices a vague wish to be like his father and suddenly finds himself in his father's body heading for a screen conference with the lovely female boss of Galaxy Films. Mr. Andrews, aghast, finds himself at Camp Soonawissakit. The story neatly switches back and forth between the unhappy pair as they struggle with their new roles and at last gratefully resume their own identities. A very funny story.
SUBJ: Humorous stories./ Fathers and sons--Fiction.

Ph-2 4-5/6 $4.50   P   KH649
RODOWSKY, COLBY. Dog days. Illustrated by Kathleen C. Howell. Farrar, Straus & Giroux ISBN 0-374-41818-7; In Canada: HarperCollins, 1993. 131p. ill.
Rosie Riggs, who has the hyperbolic imagination of Mariah Delany (Greenwald), believes that the new dog next door, pet of her favorite author, is the "Super Dog" depicted in the fiction she loves. Reality intervenes and Rosie, her new friend Skinny-bones, and the neighborhood bully manage to become heroes and learn the difference between real life characters and fictional ones. This novel's serious core is wrapped in humor, good characterization and diction.
SUBJ: Dogs--Fiction./ Friendship--Fiction./ Imagination--Fiction.

Ph-1 5-A/7 $15.00   T   KH650
RODOWSKY, COLBY. Hannah in between. Farrar Straus Giroux ISBN 0-374-32837-4; In Canada: HarperCollins, 1994. 152p.
Takes the reader through one year from birthday to birthday as Hannah, age twelve, tries to cope with her mother's alcoholism and the emotional cost to all concerned. The details of hiding the situation from friends, of thinking she is alone, of trying to maintain a "normal" life in the face of her mother's condition ring true. Although it is the contrived device of her mother seeing herself suffering the d.t.'s in Hannah's photographs that convinces her to seek out Alcoholics Annoyomous, the book is otherwise strong. An important book because of its subject, it should be available in every library and Alateen center.
SUBJ: Alcoholism--Fiction./ Family problems--Fiction./ Mothers and daughters--Fiction.

Ph-3 3-5/6 $16.00   T   KH651
ROSE, DEBORAH LEE. Rose horse. Illus. by Greg Shed. Harcourt Brace ISBN 0-15-200068-2; In Canada: Harcourt Brace c/o Canadian Manda, 1995. 60p. ill.
Includes glossary.
Set in Coney Island, New York in 1909, the story, based on fact, describes Lily's visit to see her prematurely born sister at an incubator clinic which is on display for paying customers. While there she learns about a group of Jewish wood-carvers who make carousel animals. The story, interwoven with Jewish holidays, provides an interesting view of the treatment of premature infants, Jewish family life, and a most unusual occupation. Black and white illustrations add to the atmosphere of the period. Historical fiction useful for modern United States history classes and units on Jewish culture.
SUBJ: Merry-go-round--Fiction./ Wood-carving--Fiction./ Jews--Fiction./ Babies--Fiction./ Coney Island (New York, N.Y.)--Fiction.

Ph-1 3-6/7 $13.95   T   KH652
ROSEN, MICHAEL J. Elijah's angel: a story for Chanukah and Christmas. Illus. by Aminah Brenda Lynn Robinson. Harcourt Brace Jovanovich ISBN 0-15-225394-7; In Canada: Harcourt Brace Jovanovich, 1992. unp. col. ill.
Available from the National Library Service for the Blind and Physically Handicapped on sound recording cassette RC 38127.
Elijah, an African-American barber and woodcarver, gives one of his carved angels to Michael, a young Jewish boy, for Christmas. Michael accepts the graven image fearing he has broken Jewish law. However, he makes a menorah for Elijah and learns that friendship transcends religion. Based on the carvings of renowned woodcarver Elijah Pierce, the full-color art, almost primitive in style, will bear repeated examination. This unusual book presents warm and loving characters, people a reader might like to meet. For multicultural studies.
SUBJ: Pierce, Elijah--Fiction./ Wood-carvers--Fiction./ Afro-Americans--Fiction./ Christmas--Fiction./ Hanukkah--Fiction.

Ph-1 4-8/6 $16.00   L   KH653
ROSEN, MICHAEL J. School for Pompey Walker. Illus. by Aminah Brenda Lynn Robinson. Harcourt Brace ISBN 0-15-200114-X; In Canada: Harcourt Brace c/o Canadian Manda, 1995. unp. col. ill.
Available from the National Library Service for the Blind and Physically Handicapped on sound recording cassette RC 42927.
"At the dedication of a school named after him, an old former slave tells the story of his life and how, with the help of a white friend, he managed to save money to build a school for black children in Ohio by being repeatedly sold into and escaping from slavery." (CIP) Based on historical facts and details, Walker's story is a horrifying and inspiring one. The bold, often full-page, illustrations in colored pencils and inks are vibrant and blend well with the text. Excellent choice to use for reading aloud in units about United States history, slavery, and African Americans. Historical fiction for multicultural studies.
SUBJ: Slavery--Fiction./ Schools--Fiction./ Underground railroad--Fiction./ Fugitive slaves--Fiction./ Abolitionists--Fiction./ Afro-Americans--Fiction.

Ph-1 6-A/7 $15.90   L   KH654
ROSENBURG, JOHN M. William Parker: rebel without rights: a novel based on fact. By John Rosenburg. Millbrook ISBN 1-56294-139-9, 1996. 142p. ill., maps.

"William Parker, an escaped slave, defies the United States government in the Christiana (Pennsylvania) Riot of 1851, an event that triggers the biggest treason trial in American history." (CIP) A victim of both slavery and the Fugitive Slave Act, Parker and his times are well delineated in this "novel based on facts." The book is holding, and period illustrations and portraits add to the picture of the constant threat to Parker and others sharing the condition of being either freemen, escaped slaves, or those who aided them. Readers will be relieved when they learn that Parker did escape to Canada via the Underground Railroad. Unfortunately, it is not always clear what is fact and what is not fact. An author note would have remedied this. Historical fiction good for units on United States history, slavery, and the Compromise of 1850.
SUBJ: Parker, Williams--Fiction./ Fugitive slaves--Fiction./ Slavery--Fiction./ Afro-Americans--Fiction./ Riots--Pennsylvania--Christiana--Fiction./ Christiana (Pa.)--Fiction.

Ph-2 4-6/4 $11.95   L   KH655
ROSS, LILLIAN HAMMER. Sarah, also known as Hannah. Illus. by Helen Cogancherry. Whitman ISBN 0-8075-7237-3; In Canada: General, 1994. 63p. ill., map.

"When twelve-year-old Sarah leaves the Ukraine for America in her sister's place, she must use her sister's passport and her sister's name, Hannah." (CIP) The story of Sarah's voyage via train and transatlantic steamer in 1910 allows the reader to meet other emigrants and explores the hardships and worries of the trip, including seasickness, the health check at Ellis Island, and fear of not being met. Although there are problems with the illustrations (Scene on p.8 shows Sarah barefoot, but shoes are mentioned in the text; drawings on p.15 and 22 depict her mother without the head covering typically worn by Jewish women of Eastern Europe.), they do not detract from nor add to the story. Useful historical fiction for units on immigration.
SUBJ: Emigration and immigration--Fiction.

Ph-1 6-A/4 $14.89   L   KH656
ROSTKOWSKI, MARGARET I. After the dancing days. HarperCollins ISBN 0-06-025078-X; In Canada: HarperCollins, 1986. 217p.

Greeting her father at the train station when he returns from serving in World War I, 13-year-old Annie is drawn to the plight of the wounded. At the veterans' hospital where her father, a doctor, works, Annie meets Andrew, a badly burned, bitter young man, whom she helps in his painful adjustment to his new life. An absorbing novel for mature readers centering on a young girl's emergence into womanhood as she grapples with the brutal reality of war.
SUBJ: World War, 1914-1918--United States--Fiction./ Heroes--Fiction./ Physically handicapped--Fiction.

Ph-2 3-5/2 $13.88   L   KH657
RUEPP, KRISTA. Midnight Rider. Illustrated by Ulrike Heyne. Translated by J. Alison James. North-South Books ISBN 1-55858-495-1; In Canada: North-South Books, 1995. 61p. col. ill.

The Midnight Rider is a girl, Charlie, who "borrows" a neighbor's horse for rides at night. One night, during a well described storm, she is thrown. The owner, a dour reclusive old man, is finally brought out of his lonely ways by his association with the girl. Illustrated in moody and effective colors, the small adventure will be good for reading aloud.
SUBJ: Horses--Fiction./ Friendship--Fiction./ Secrets--Fiction.

Ph-2 5-A/6 $3.50   P   KH658
RYAN, MARY C. Me two. Illus. by Rob Sauber. Avon ISBN 0-380-71826-X, 1993. 179p. ill.

Cloning himself accidentally, seventh grader Wilf discovers the advantages and disadvantages of being two people. Various humorous situations ensue, much clever word play, and a reasonable solution make this a good choice for the reader of amusingly light science fiction.
SUBJ: Cloning--Fiction./ Science fiction.

Ph-2 6-A/3 $15.00   T   KH659
RYAN, MARY E. Trouble with perfect. Simon & Schuster ISBN 0-689-80276-5; In Canada: Distican, 1995. 170p.

Continually pressured by his anxious father to be something he is not, Kyle, thirteen, contemplates cheating in math. There is no way the younger boy can compete with his older brother, a high school basketball star, nor can he stand the taunts of the bullies in his class. When he admits to his cheating, he takes the consequences and, with the help of his brother, begins to be his own person as he solves his own dilemma. Young people who suffer parental and group pressure should identify with Kyle. Good choice for reluctant readers.

SUBJ: Self-esteem--Fiction./ Fathers and sons--Fiction./ Alcoholism--Fiction./ Honesty--Fiction.

Ph-1 4-6/6 $5.95   P   KH660
RYLANT, CYNTHIA. Children of Christmas: stories for the season. Illus. by S. D. Schindler. Orchard ISBN 0-531-07042-5, c1987, 1993. 380p. ill.

Choosing the theme of Christmas and six unique characters, Rylant presents vignettes that are poignant and memorable. Skillfully written, this is a valuable addition to holiday collections and oral presentation.
SUBJ: Christmas--Fiction./ Short stories.

Ph-1 6-A/4 $13.95   T   KH661
RYLANT, CYNTHIA. Fine white dust. Bradbury ISBN 0-02-777240-3; In Canada: Collier Macmillan, 1986. 106p.
Newbery Honor Book.
Selectors' Choice, 16th ed.
Available from National Library Service for the Blind and Physically Handicapped in Braille BR 06809 and on sound recording cassette RC 37792.

Struggling to reconcile the power of God with the shallowness of the charismatic "Preacher Man," 13-year-old Pete tells his story of religious conversion and subsequent disillusionment. This is a profound view of a young man's fascination with God, balanced by the true caring of his friend, Rufus, an avowed atheist. The result is a powerful novel about the true nature of religious belief for mature readers.
SUBJ: Religious life--Fiction./ Interpersonal relations--Fiction./ Friendship--Fiction.

Ph-1 3-5/5 $15.00   T   KH662
RYLANT, CYNTHIA. Gooseberry Park. Illus. by Arthur Howard. Harcourt Brace ISBN 0-15-232242-6; In Canada: Harcourt Brace c/o Canadian Manda, 1995. 133p. ill.

"When a storm separates Stumpy the squirrel from her newborn babies, her animal friends come to the rescue." (CIP) A Labrador, hermit crab, owl, and a bat join together in high adventure and manage to save the squirrely brood in a nicely characterized talking-animal fable. The many companions are illustrated in suitably cute black and white sketches, and the story will be just right for reading aloud.
SUBJ: Squirrels--Fiction./ Animals--Fiction.

Ph-1 5-A/7 $14.99   L   KH663
RYLANT, CYNTHIA. Missing May. Orchard ISBN 0-531-08596-1, 1992. 89p.
Newbery Award.
Selectors' Choice, 19th ed.
Available from the National Library Service for the Blind and Physically Handicapped on sound recording cassette RC 36384.

Searching for the strength to continue living after the death of his beloved wife, Ob and his twelve-year-old niece seek the help of a medium to contact May. Although their journey is unsuccessful, they eventually find understanding in signs from nature which remind them of May. With tight prose and a fast-paced plot, Rylant has magically created memorable, living characters. Good for oral presentation.
SUBJ: Death--Fiction./ Grief--Fiction./ West Virginia--Fiction./ Aunts--Fiction.

Ph-1 5-A/7 $14.00   T   KH664
RYLANT, CYNTHIA. Van Gogh Cafe. Harcourt Brace ISBN 0-15-200843-8; In Canada: Harcourt Brace c/o Canadian Manda, 1995. 53p.

Located in an old movie theater in Flowers, Kansas, the Van Gogh Cafe has a magic that transforms the ordinary into a gentle series of extraordinary happenings to all who stop there. Young Clara, ten, and her father may create the moments of magic, but in the mysterious episodes magical muffins appear, an old silent movie star finds his long dead friend, and other magic concerning animals and people rises from the page. The literal reader may be disappointed, but those who still believe that magic can be found almost anywhere will be enchanted by the strong, economical, and intense writing. Try reading aloud.
SUBJ: Restaurants--Fiction./ Magic--Fiction.

Ph-2 5-A/5 $4.99   P   KH665
SACHAR, LOUIS. Dogs don't tell jokes. Knopf ISBN 0-679-83372-2; In Canada: Random House, 1992. 209p.
Available from the National Library Service for the Blind and Physically Handicapped on sound recording cassette RC 35695.

Gary Boone, twelve, nicknamed Goon because of his constant joking and smiling at inappropriate moments, wants to be a stand-up comic. Although he is encouraged and supported by Angeline (of SOMEDAY ANGELINE) and her "family," his parents, teachers, and classmates do not appreciate his smart-aleck attitude. His ultimate triumph as the prizewinner in a school talent show may make this

fast-paced, humorous book (replete with comic routines) a prizewinner among young people.
SUBJ: Self-perception--Fiction./ Schools--Fiction.

CE   Ph-2 3-5/4 $13.00   L   KH666
SACHAR, LOUIS. Wayside School is falling down. Illus. by Joel Schick. Lothrop, Lee & Shepard ISBN 0-688-07868-0, 1989. 179p. ill.
Talking book available from Listening Library YA 858 (ISBN 0-8072-7434-8, 1994). 2 sound cassettes (227min), $16.98.
Thirty stories reveal that Wayside School is decidedly out of the ordinary and Mrs. Jewls' class on the very top floor is probably the zaniest. The slapstick humor which predominates will appeal to middle grade readers.
The first title about this unusual school SIDEWAYS STORIES FROM WAYSIDE SCHOOL (Avon ISBN 0-380-69871-4, c1978, 1996) will be enjoyed by middle graders.
Read-along kit of SIDEWAYS STORIES FROM WAYSIDE SCHOOL is available from Listening Library, YA842 (ISBN 0-8072-7401-1, 1993); illus. by Julie Brinckloe. 1 paperback book, 2 sound cassettes (168min), $20.98; teacher's guide.
SUBJ: Humorous stories./ Schools--Fiction.

                         Ph-1 5-A/6 $4.95   P   KH667
SACHS, MARILYN. Call me Ruth. Beech Tree ISBN 0-688-13737-7, c1982, 1995. 134p.
Originally published by Doubleday, 1982.
"The daughter of a Russian immigrant family, newly arrived in Manhattan in 1908, has conflicting feelings about her mother's increasingly radical union involvement." (CIP) Rifka's (Ruth's) feelings and snobbish shame about her mother's old world ways, dress, and language could take place today among young newcomers to the United States who are experiencing intergenerational conflicts. Thanks to strong characterization and her ability to set a scene, Sachs has created strong historical fiction in which characters emerge as real people. It will be the rare reader who does not want to make Ruth understand how badly she is acting. Use for reading aloud in units on modern United States history, family relations, immigration, and the development of labor unions especially in the garment industry.
SUBJ: Russian Americans--Fiction./ Jews--Fiction./ New York (N.Y.)--Fiction./ Mothers and daughters--Fiction./ Emigration and immigration--Fiction./ Labor unions--Fiction.

                         Ph-1 4-A/5 $3.99   P   KH668
SACHS, MARILYN. Pocket full of seeds. Illus. by Ben Stahl. Puffin ISBN 0-14-036593-1; In Canada: Penguin, c1973, 1994. 137p. ill.
Selectors' Choice, 9th ed.
Based on the girlhood of one of Sachs' friends, the true-to-life events relate the life of Nicole Nieman during the German occupation of France. Because the family was Jewish, her parents were put in a detention camp. Nicole must find places to hide before she, too, becomes a prisoner. The welcome reissue of a powerful book features a girl's war-time memories that would be a strong follow-up for THE DIARY OF A YOUNG GIRL by Anne Frank. Poignant historical fiction for the social studies curriculum.
SUBJ: France--History--German Occupation, 1940-1945--Fiction./ Jews--France--Fiction.

                         Ph-1 5-A/6 $3.99   P   KH669
SACHS, MARILYN. Truth about Mary Rose Puffin ISBN 0-14-037083-8; In Canada: Penguin, 1995. 134p.
Originally published by Doubleday, 1973.
Pursuing family stories about her namesake becomes almost an obsession for Mary Rose Ramirez. When the family moves to New York to live with Grandmother, there is more time to be immersed in family stories. In this strong story of growing and understanding, she soon discovers that not all family members share her perception of her heroine aunt.
SUBJ: Aunts--Fiction./ New York (N.Y.)--Fiction./ Heroes--Fiction./ Self-perception--Fiction./ Interpersonal relations--Fiction.

                         Ph-2 3-5/5 $3.99   P   KH670
SACKS, MARGARET. Themba. Illus. by Wil Clay. Penguin ISBN 0-14-036445-5, 1994. 44p. ill.
Originally published in South Africa as THEMBA FETCHES HIS FATHER, 1985.
Set in the South African countryside far from the city where his father works, this fast-paced story depicts the young black boy Themba as he awaits his father's return after a very long time without him. When he does not arrive, Themba devises a plan to find his father in the city. The perceptions of how someone first sees new and different things are eye-opening.
SUBJ: Fathers and sons--Fiction./ Blacks--South Africa--Fiction.

                         Ph-1 4-A/6 $13.95   T   KH671
SAINT EXUPERY, ANTOINE DE. Little prince. Translated from the French by Katherine Woods. Harcourt Brace Jovanovich ISBN 0-15-246503-0, c1943. 91p. col. ill.
Available from National Library Service for the Blind and Physically Handicapped in Braille BR01431, and on sound recording cassette RD07280.
The little prince lives on a tiny planet with three volcanoes and a lovely flower whose proud selfish speech upsets the prince's little world and sends him searching for the answer to what is truly important in life. A fable of enduring popularity.
SUBJ: Fairy tales./ Interplanetary voyages--Fiction./ Sahara--Fiction.

                         Ph-1 6-A/4 $15.95   T   KH672
SALISBURY, GRAHAM. Under the blood-red sun. Delacorte ISBN 0-385-32099-X; In Canada: Bantam Doubleday Dell, 1994. 246p.
Set in Hawaii at the time of the attack on Pearl Harbor in December 1941, the gripping novel details the experiences of Japanese-American eighth grader Tomi (Tomikazu Nakaji) and attitudes towards those of Japanese origins. Although he and his friends represent many ethnic backgrounds, there are people, too many in power, who treat his family as unwanted, overly different aliens. Characterization and action are clear and understandable and should raise consciousness about people of different backgrounds as they come face-to-face with those who practice prejudice. Historical fiction useful for multicultural studies.
SUBJ: Pearl Harbor (Hawaii), Attack on, 1941--Fiction./ World War, 1939-1945--Fiction./ Japanese Americans--Fiction./ Hawaii--Fiction./ Prejudices--Fiction.

                         Ph-1 5-A/6 $18.00   L   KH673
SALTEN, FELIX. Bambi: a life in the woods. Illus. by Michael J. Woods. Simon & Schuster ISBN 0-671-73937-9; In Canada: Simon & Schuster, 1992. 158p. col. ill.
Brings to life the story of Bambi, a young deer, by showing his place in the forest, the other animals, the seasons, and the constant fear of the great enemy: Him--man as hunter and destroyer. Although heavily anthropomorphized, the moving narration of this classic story closely observes animals, their habits, and their forest. Reissued with watercolor paintings which adequately depict the text. Unfortunately no information about Salten or the translator of the work is given. Story meant to be read aloud.
SUBJ: Deer--Fiction.

                         Ph-1 1-6/7 $4.95   P   KH674
SANDBURG, CARL. Rootabaga stories. Illus. by Michael Hague. Harcourt Brace Jovanovich ISBN 0-15-269065-4, c1922, 1990. 188p. col. ill.
Gimmie the Ax, his son Please Gimme and his daughter Ax me no questions sell everything they have and purchase tickets "to ride where the railroad tracks run off into the sky and never come back" (p5) to Rootabaga country where pigs wear bibs, clowns are baked in ovens, and the Rag Doll and Broom Handle are married with a grand procession. Superbly descriptive and definitely whimsical these 25 stories and the 24 more in ROOTABAGA STORIES: PART TWO (ISBN 0-15-269062-X, 1989) call to be read aloud.
SUBJ: Short stories./ Fantasy.

                         Ph-2 3-5/5 $14.95   L   KH675
SANDERS, SCOTT R. Warm as wool. Illus. by Helen Cogancherry. Bradbury/Macmillan ISBN 0-02-778139-9; In Canada: Maxwell Macmillan, 1992. unp. col. ill.
Making a home in the Ohio wilderness at the beginning of the nineteenth century, Betsy Ward purchases a flock of sheep for wool to spin, weave, and make clothing for her family. Illustrations convey people and pioneer setting well. Use in units on pioneering and frontier living. Accompanies AURORA MEANS DAWN.
SUBJ: Frontier and pioneer life--Fiction./ Ohio--Fiction./ Sheep--Fiction.

                         Ph-1 2-6/4 $12.00   T   KH676
SANFIELD, STEVE. Great turtle drive. Illus. by Dirk Zimmer. Knopf ISBN 0-679-85834-2; In Canada: Random House, 1996. unp. ill.
"Borzoi book."
A delightful tall tale about s...l...o...w turtles and a cowboy who wants to make a fortune herding thousands of them from Texas to market in Kansas City. Told in folksy first person by the herder, the laugh-out-loud humor, aided by imaginative and zesty green, black, and white illustrations, is perfect for reading aloud. Great fun which may inspire creative writing activities about the Old West.
SUBJ: Turtles--Fiction./ Cowboys--Fiction./ Humorous stories.

                         Ph-1 1-3/2 $13.95   T   KH677
SATHRE, VIVIAN. Leroy Potts meets the McCrooks. Illus. by Rowan Barnes-Murphy. Delacorte ISBN 0-385-32192-9; In Canada: Bantam

Doubleday Dell, 1997. 46p. col. ill. (Yearling first choice chapter book).
Beginning readers will welcome the tall tale adventures of Leroy Potts, a cowboy who loses his memory after a lightning strike, and the nasty, mean McCrook brothers, bandits who have Leroy do their dirty work. He is forced to rob a bank, hold up people in a restaurant, and other dastardly deeds. Luckily, he recovers his memory, captures the nasties, and wins both the reward and Miss Hattie Mae, his own true love. Illustrated in bright, active pictures and printed in large type with wide leading, the tale is a prime choice for new readers--and maybe reluctant older ones, too.
SUBJ: Robbers and outlaws--Fiction.

Ph-1 2-4/2 $17.00   L   KH678
SAY, ALLEN. Allison. Houghton Mifflin ISBN 0-395-85895-X, 1997. 32p. col. ill.
"Walter Lorraine books."
Selectors' Choice, 21st ed.
Allison, who appears to be a child of Japanese origins adopted by Caucasian parents, is glowingly illustrated in meticulously drawn watercolors. The art accompanies a lucid text which takes the child and reader through her emotions when she believes she has neither father nor mother despite the obvious love her parents demonstrate. Emotions shown by the characters are very real, and Say's art and text once again illuminate a different corner of humanity. Highly recommended. For multicultural studies.
SUBJ: Adoption--Fiction./ Dolls--Fiction./ Cats--Fiction.

Ph-2 3-5/2 $13.89   L   KH679
SCHECTER, ELLEN. Big idea. Illus. by Bob Dorsey. Hyperion ISBN 0-7868-2085-3, 1996. 76p. ill., map. (West Side kids).
"Bank Street."
Includes directory.
Luz Mendes, eight, works hard and convinces others to turn a trash filled lot into a community garden with the help of a municipal organization, The Green Giants. Although her voice as narrator is not that of an eight-year-old and the constant intrusion of a subplot stops the action, the story is interesting--and heartening. Its setting is in a multiethnic neighborhood where, apparently, everyone is almost friendly with everyone else. An afterword includes advice on how to start a community garden and where to write for help. For multicultural studies.
SUBJ: Community gardens--Fiction./ Gardens--Fiction./ City and town life--New York (N.Y.)--Fiction./ Hispanic Americans--Fiction./ New York (N.Y.)--Fiction.

Ph-1 5-A/3 $6.95   P   KH680
SCHMIDT, ANNIE M. G. Minnie. Translated by Lance Salway. Illus. by Kay Sather. Milkweed Editions ISBN 1-57131-600-0, 1994. 164p. ill.
Translated from the Dutch, Schmidt's book will be a delight even to non cat-lovers. Lively, humorous, and imaginative, the story depicts Minnie the cat who becomes a woman (although the illustrations show a girl). She adopts Mr. Tibbs, an innocent journalist, whose position at the newspaper is saved by the information the town's cats provide him about business, scandal, government, and the town's leading citizen (a not-at-all-nice-person). Active, humorous tale just right for reading aloud. Fun.
SUBJ: Cats--Fiction./ Reporters and reporting--Fiction.

Ph-1 4-A/7 $13.93   L   KH681
SCHNUR, STEVEN. Shadow children. Illus. by Herbert Tauss. Morrow ISBN 0-688-13831-4, 1994. 87p. ill.
Set outside a small farming village in France after World War II, Schnur's book can be read merely as a story or plumbed to its depths to answer the question: How far does responsibility for one's own family extend when faced with the certain deaths of strangers? While visiting with his grandfather, Etienne, eleven, encounters the ghosts of Jewish children who have escaped from the Nazis to the French town. Only he can see the children's ghosts and the ghostly train that takes them to their certain deaths because only he is unaware of how the townspeople sacrificed them to save their own. Misty, black and white charcoal drawings add to the atmosphere of this haunting story--historical fiction holding deep philosophical and ethical questions. Try reading aloud to encourage discussion.
SUBJ: Holocaust, Jewish (1939-1945)--Fiction./ Ghosts--Fiction./ France--Fiction./ Farm life--France--Fiction./ Grandfathers--Fiction.

Ph-2 3-5/4 $17.99   L   KH682
SCHOTTER, RONI. Nothing ever happens on 90th Street. Illus. by Kyrsten Brooker. Orchard ISBN 0-531-08886-3, 1997. unp. col. ill.
"Melanie Kroupa book."
Bright, active collages which illuminate character join with a lively text as Eva brings her multicultural neighborhood together and revives the stores on her city street. Each of her neighbors gives Eva advice on how to write her school assignment, changing her notion that nothing

ever happens on her street. Text is long, but art pushes the enjoyable story, and the illustrations will carry to a group when reading the book aloud.
SUBJ: Authorship--Fiction./ Neighborliness--Fiction.

Ph-1 4-A/5 $14.89   L   KH683
SCHUR, MAXINE ROSE. When I left my village. Illus. by Brian Pinkney. Dial ISBN 0-8037-1562-5, 1996. 64p. ill., map.
Sequel to DAY OF DELIGHT, Dial, 1994.
"An Ethiopian Jewish family leaves their oppressed mountain village to make a difficult and treacherous journey in the hope of reaching freedom in Israel." (CIP) The book provides a brief, but understandable, history of the Jews in Ethiopia and makes clear their situation as virtual prisoners in their ancestral land, a land where they can never hope to own the small farms they work and where they live a feudal existence with the ever-present danger of being sold into slavery. The tension of the journey is omnipresent. Black and white scratchboard illustrations add to the tone and mood of the book. It will be useful for reading aloud and for units dealing with African, Jewish, and modern history. For multicultural studies.
SUBJ: Jews--Ethiopia--Fiction./ Jews--Persecutions--Fiction./ Emigration and immigration--Fiction.

Ph-3 2-4/2 $9.95   T   KH684
SCHWARTZ, AMY. Yossel Zissel and the wisdom of Chelm. Jewish Publication Society ISBN 0-8276-0258-8, 1986. unp. ill.
Fools are scattered all over the world because Yossel Zissel, a "wise man of Chelm," was too lazy to carry home bags of gold. Based on the town of fools found in Jewish folklore, this fanciful pourquoi story is replete with the sardonic humor that marks the original stories.
SUBJ: Humorous stories.

Ph-1 3-6/3 $11.99   L   KH685
SCIESZKA, JON. Knights of the kitchen table. Illus. by Lane Smith. Viking Penguin ISBN 0-670-83622-2; In Canada: Penguin, 1991. 55p. ill.
Cast by a magic book into the days of knights bold and dangerous, the "Time Warp Trio", three modern boys, find themselves in constant end-of-chapter danger in a hilarious, fast-paced book guaranteed to hold even the most bored child.
In THE NOT-SO-JOLLY ROGER (ISBN 0-670-83754-7, 1991) the three meet pirates, sing silly chanteys, and are thoroughly frightened by Blackbeard. The "Time Warp Trio" travels to the Old West in THE GOOD, THE BAD, AND THE GOOFY (ISBN 0-670-84380-6, 1992). Cast back in time 42,000 years in YOUR MOTHER WAS A NEANDERTHAL (ISBN 0-14-036372-6, 1995, available from the NLSBPH on sound recording cassette RC 40670), the trio renew their time-travel adventures--now in prehistory with cave women, mammoths, and without the magic book. In TUT, TUT (ISBN 0-670-84832-8, 1996) the boys and little sister, Anna, visit ancient Egypt.
SUBJ: Time travel--Fiction.

Ph-1 4-6/4 $16.00   L   KH686
SCIESZKA, JON. Stinky Cheese Man and other fairly stupid tales. Illus. by Lane Smith. Viking ISBN 0-670-84487-X; In Canada: Penguin, 1992. unp. col. ill.
Caldecott Honor book, 1993.
Available from the National Library Service for the Blind and Physically Handicapped on sound recording cassette RC 38039.
A creative team of author and illustrator dare the reader to recognize "traditional" fairy tales in new dress. Great for reading aloud and for sparking creative writing assignments.
SUBJ: Fairy tales--Parodies, imitations, etc./ Short stories.

Ph-2 3-5/6 $12.95   L   KH687
SCOTT, ANN HERBERT. Brand is forever. Illus. by Ronald Himler. Clarion ISBN 0-395-60118-5, 1993. 47p. col. ill.
"Despite the fact that Gramp has designed and made a special brand to be her own, Annie is distressed about the upcoming branding of her beloved orphan calf Doodle." (CIP) Presents authentic details of branding time on a ranch and the emotions of young Annie. Himler's watercolors will add to the reader's knowledge of character and setting. Useful for units on ranch and farm life.
SUBJ: Cattle brands--Fiction./ Cattle--Marking--Fiction./ Ranch life--Fiction.

Ph-2 3-5/2 $14.95   L   KH688
SCOTT, ANN HERBERT. Brave as a mountain lion. Illus. by Glo Coalson. Clarion ISBN 0-395-66760-7, 1996. 31p. col. ill.
"Spider is afraid to get up on stage in front of everybody in the school spelling bee, but after listening to his father's advice, decides that he too will try to be as brave as his Shoshoni ancestors." (CIP) Illustrated in dark watercolors which present the settings and characters well, Spider's growing stage fright is well-developed and palpable. Similar in situation and solution to Jukes' LIKE JAKE AND

FICTION

ME. The fear also suffered by an admired adult makes this a very human tale. For multicultural studies.
SUBJ: Courage--Fiction./ Stage fright--Fiction./ Schools--Fiction./ Shoshoni Indians--Fiction./ Indians of North America--Fiction.

CE   Ph-1 5-A/7 $3.99   P   KH689
SEBESTYEN, OUIDA. Words by heart. Delacorte ISBN 0-440-41346-X; In Canada: Bantam Doubleday Dell, 1997. 162p.
Originally published by Little, Brown, 1979.
Available from National Library Service for the Blind and Physically Handicapped on sound recording cassette RC16629.
Videocassette available from Bonneville Worldwide (ISBN 0-7800-0229-6, 1984). 1/2" VHS videocassette color (116min). $29.95. (WonderWorks.)
Bright Lena Sills shared her father's ambition to build a better life in the Oklahoma Territory in the 1890s. As the only African Americans in their small town, they face prejudice and, ultimately, her father's death. Her step-mother who always yearned to "go back home" decides to stay and fight for Ben Sills' dreams in powerful and moving historical fiction. For multicultural studies.
SUBJ: Fathers and daughters--Fiction./ Race relations--Fiction./ Afro-Americans--Fiction.

                          Ph-1 5-A/7 $4.95   P   KH690
SEGAL, JERRY. Place where nobody stopped. Illus. by Dav Pilkey. Morrow ISBN 0-688-12567-0, 1994. 154p. ill.
In the little Russian village, "the place where nobody stopped," Mordecai, a gifted scholar and optimist, his wife and daughter stop with a lonely baker, Yosip, to await passports to emigrate to the U.S. When a shifty relative fails to bring the needed and expensive papers, the family stays, enlarges, grows up, and sees the course of Russian absolutism under the czars, which forced Jews to leave to pursue freer lives. Peopled with characters that Sholom Aleichem might have invented, at once silly and serious, the challenging reading and Chagall-like illustrations will attract the able reader who will look forward to the other books in the projected trilogy.
SUBJ: Soviet Union--Fiction./ Jews--Soviet Union--Fiction.

                          Ph-1 4-6/5 $20.00   L   KH691
SEIDLER, TOR. Wainscott weasel. Illus. by Fred Marcellino. HarperCollins ISBN 0-06-205032-X; In Canada: HarperCollins, 1993. 194p. ill. (some col.).
"Michael di Capua books."
Destined to be a legendary weasel like his father, Bagley Brown Jr. falls in love with a striped bass. With the assistance of many other creatures, he heroically saves the pond inhabitants from the ravaging osprey. The tight, brilliantly characterized animal fantasy adventure is just right for reading aloud.
SUBJ: Weasels--Fiction./ Brothers--Fiction./ Animals--Fiction./ Fantasy.

                          Ph-1 2-4/5 $3.99   P   KH692
SELDEN, GEORGE. Chester Cricket's new home. Illus. by Garth Williams. Delacorte ISBN 0-440-41246-3, 1983. 142p. ill.
Available from National Library Service for the Blind and Physically Handicapped on sound recording cassette RC21690.
Losing his tree stump home, Chester Cricket embarks on a homefinding journey abetted by his bird and animal friends. Having tried a turtle's log, a bird's nest and a chipmunk lair, he finds a new and happy home. A really rich and amusing book with delightful animal characterizations, this is an ideal read-aloud to lower grades with no reference to the previous books in the series necessary.
SUBJ: Crickets--Fiction./ Humorous stories.

                          Ph-2 3-4/5 $3.50   P   KH693
SELDEN, GEORGE. Chester Cricket's pigeon ride. Illus. by Garth Williams. Delacorte ISBN 0-440-41389-3, 1983. 57p. ill.
Available from National Library Service for the Blind and Physically Handicapped on sound recording cassette RC24714.
This flashback to Chester Cricket's first terrifying weeks in New York recounts how homesick he becomes for the sights, smells, and sounds of the country. Venturing from his subway hideaway, he determinedly makes his way to a sycamore tree where he meets a pigeon named Lulu. She takes him on a nighttime aerial view to see the sights. This picture book sized volume is delightfully illustrated and is recommended for reading aloud for a younger audience than that of the famous series.
SUBJ: Crickets--Fiction./ Pigeons--Fiction./ New York (N.Y.)--Fiction.

CE   Ph-1 4-6/6 $15.95   T   KH694
SELDEN, GEORGE. Cricket in Times Square. Illus. by Garth Williams. Farrar, Straus & Giroux ISBN 0-374-31650-3, c1960. 151p. ill.
Newbery Honor Book.
Talking book available from SRA/McGraw-Hill 87-507831, 1971, $17.15.

Available from National Library Service for the Blind and Physically Handicapped in Braille BR05850.
Spanish version available UN GRILLO EN TIMES SQUARE (ISBN 0-374-32790-4, 1992).
Chester, a musical cricket from Connecticut who spends the summer in a New York Subway, is befriended by a mouse, a cat and a boy.
SUBJ: Crickets--Fiction./ New York (N.Y.)--Fiction./ Spanish language materials.

                          Ph-1 4-6/7 $3.95   P   KH695
SELDEN, GEORGE. Genie of Sutton Place. Farrar, Straus & Giroux ISBN 0-374-42530-2, c1973. 175p.
Available from National Library Service for the Blind and Physically Handicapped on sound recording cassette RC07794.
Tim Farr relives the story of a magical summer when his own personal genie, Abdullah, nicknamed "Dooley", does his bidding and works many miracles as well as mix-ups. Set in the present in New York City, it brings to life many unusual characters other than the genie-- Madame Sosostris, Tim's dog Sam, and of course Tim Farr himself. Superb storytelling by a Newbery Prize winner.
SUBJ: Magic--Fiction./ New York (N.Y.)--Fiction.

                          Ph-3 2-4/4 $14.00   T   KH696
SELDEN, GEORGE. Harry Kitten and Tucker Mouse. Illus. by Garth Williams. Farrar, Straus & Giroux ISBN 0-374-32860-9, 1986. 79p. ill.
Meeting for the first time, two young animals become friends; not so unusual, except in this case one is a baby mouse and the other is a kitten. This prequel to A CRICKET IN TIMES SQUARE introduces Harry Kitten and Tucker Mouse and recounts some of their early adventures. Not as fully developed as the main work, this oversized, multi-illustrated introduction to the well-known series may be enjoyed by younger readers.
SUBJ: Mice--Fiction./ Cats--Fiction./ New York (N.Y.)--Fiction.

                          Ph-2 3-5/5 $15.00   T   KH697
SELDEN, GEORGE. Old meadow. Illus. by Garth Williams. Farrar Straus & Giroux ISBN 0-374-35616-5, 1987. 193p. ill.
Hearing that his master, Mr. Budd, is about to be evicted from the Old Meadow, Dubber, the dog, enlists the help of Chester Cricket and all of the meadow inhabitants to create a night of such magic that it makes a difference. The theme of working cooperatively to benefit the community is emphasized, as are environmental issues. Useful as a read aloud for a wide range of ages.
SUBJ: Fantasy./ Animals--Fiction.

                          Ph-2 4-6/5 $4.50   P   KH698
SELDEN, GEORGE. Tucker's countryside. Illus. by Garth Williams. Delacorte ISBN 0-440-40248-4, c1969, 1989. 167p. ill.
Available from National Library Service for the Blind and Physically Handicapped in Braille BRA13238.
Tucker Mouse and Harry Cat are summoned to Connecticut by their friend Chester Cricket to help save the countryside from being developed into apartment complexes.
SUBJ: Fantasy./ Animals--Fiction./ Ecology--Fiction.

                          Ph-2 5-6/6 $24.95   T   KH699
SERRAILLIER, IAN. Silver sword. Illus. by C. Walter Hodges. Phillips ISBN 0-87599-104-1, c1959. 187p. ill.
When the Balicki family is torn apart in Warsaw in 1940, the father is sent to prison, the mother to concentration camp; the three children-- Ruth, Edek, and Bronia--fend as animals in the defeated city until liberation in 1945. How they make their way across Germany and are eventually reunited in Switzerland absorbs lifetimes of hair-raising situations and narrow escapes.
SUBJ: Warsaw (Poland)--Fiction./ World War, 1939-1945--Jews--Fiction./ Poland--German occupation, 1939-1945--Fiction.

                          Ph-2 3-5/5 $12.95   L   KH700
SERVICE, PAMELA F. Stinker from space. Scribner's ISBN 0-684-18910-0, 1988. 83p.
Available from the National Library Service for the Blind and Physically Handicapped on sound recording cassette RC 35275.
Landing unexpectedly in the U.S., Tsynq Yr must find a new body to live in until he can find a way back to his own planet. A skunk provides the body and access to Karen and Jonathan, the children who befriend him and help him gain access to the NASA space shuttle he needs to return home. An unusual and humorous tale appropriate for reading aloud.
Tsynq Yr--still in skunk's clothing, returns to find an object to calm a despot in space in STINKER'S RETURN (ISBN 0-684-19542-9, 1993, available from the NLSBPH on sound recording cassette RC 36488).
SUBJ: Extraterrestrial beings--Fiction./ Skunks--Fiction./ Science fiction.

Ph-1 6-A/6 $4.50   P   KH701
SERVICE, PAMELA F. Weirdos of the universe, unite! Fawcett ISBN
0-449-70429-7, 1992. 136p.
"Jean Karl book."
Two self-proclaimed weirdos Mandy and Owen accidentally summon
five otherworldly beings from various cultures: Baba Yaga, Siegfried,
Coyote, Lung Nu, and the Horned King when they defend earth from
invaders from space. Plot develops swiftly with great humor and
anachronisms that are marvelously funny for example Baba Yaga as a
television addict. Baba Yaga is definitely the hero with her multiplying
tribble-trick (from "Star Trek") and the use of a television remote
control as a weapon against the enemy. Multicultural romp through
space that is highly recommended as an antidote to the usual high
seriousness of science fiction and mythology.
SUBJ: Behavior--Fiction./ Computers--Fiction./ Baba Yaga (Legendary
character)--Fiction./ Fantasy.

Ph-1 5-7/7 $22.00   L   KH702
SEWELL, ANNA. Black Beauty: the autobiography of a horse. Afterword
by Peter Glassman. Illus. by Lucy Kemp-Welch. Books of Wonder/
Morrow ISBN 0-688-14714-3, 1997. 252p. ill. (some col.).
Nineteenth century England depended on horses for recreation, travel,
and commerce. Treatment of horses in these different roles is shown
in this story told by a horse who started life pampered, but who went
from one owner to another, his treatment worsening before the story
draws to a happy conclusion. Pen and ink and occasional full-color
illustrations show the flavor of life in these times.
SUBJ: Horses--Fiction./ Great Britain--History--19th century--Fiction.

Ph-2 2-5/2 $9.99   L   KH703
SHARMAT, MARJORIE WEINMAN. Genghis Khan: a dog star is born.
Illus. by Mitchell Rigie. Random House ISBN 0-679-95406-6; In Canada:
Random House, 1994. 71p. ill. (First stepping stone book).
Sequel to GREAT GENGHIS KHAN LOOK-ALIKE CONTEST,
Random House, 1993.
A cat lover arranges to dognap Duz as he begins his career as a
Hollywood movie star. A humorous transitional reader for mystery
fans.
SUBJ: Dogs--Fiction./ Motion pictures--Production and direction--
Fiction./ Kidnapping--Fiction.

Ph-2 2-5/2 $3.99   P   KH704
SHARMAT, MARJORIE WEINMAN. Genghis Khan: dog-gone
Hollywood. Illus. by Mitchell Rigie. Random House ISBN 0-679-86953-0;
In Canada: Random House, 1995. 71p. ill. (First stepping stone book).
Sequel to GENGHIS KHAN, A DOG STAR IS BORN, Random
House, 1994.
Duz's stardom is in jeopardy when he is accused of biting Billy Brat.
Light, humorous transitional reader perfect for dog and mystery fans.
SUBJ: Dogs--Fiction./ Motion pictures--Production and direction--
Fiction./ Academy Awards (Motion pictures)--Fiction.

Ph-2 4-6/4 $13.89   L   KH705
SHARMAT, MARJORIE WEINMAN. Getting something on Maggie
Marmelstein. Illus. by Ben Shecter. HarperCollins ISBN 0-06-025552-8,
c1971. 101p. ill.
Available from National Library Service for the Blind and Physically
Handicapped on sound recording cassette RC 41779.
Thad Smith dislikes Maggie Marmelstein and she reciprocates. Trouble
is, she knows something juicy about Thad. All during rehearsals for
their play where Thad is the Frog and Maggie is the Princess, he
works on his GSOMM--Get Something on Maggie Marmelstein.
Then, when he succeeds, he doesn't use it.
Followed by MAGGIE MARMELSTEIN FOR PRESIDENT (ISBN
0-06-440079-4, 1975) when both Maggie and Thad run for class
president and MYSTERIOUSLY YOURS, MAGGIE MARMELSTEIN
(ISBN 0-06-025517-X, 1982, OPC) when Maggie becomes the
mystery person gossip columnist for her school paper with the
predictable envious results.
Also available from NLSBPH is MYSTERIOUSLY YOURS, MAGGIE
MARMELSTEIN on sound recording cassette RC23247.
SUBJ: Schools--Fiction.

Ph-1 5-A/7 $13.00   L   KH706
SHREVE, SUSAN. Amy Dunn quits school. Illus. by Diane De Groat.
Tambourine ISBN 0-688-10320-0, 1993. 96p. ill.
Over scheduled and overprotected by her ambitious, loving lawyer
mother, sixth-grader Amy Dunn finally throws in the towel on lessons
in ballet, music, French, and gymnastics. She even skips a day at her
private school when her mother insists she wear a Halloween costume
although Amy has told her that most other sixth graders won't. She
wanders around New York City to places she enjoys and meets some
people who are frightening and others who are not. Amy shows
spunk, and any child whose life is as busy as Amy's will appreciate
her revolt against the perfection her perfect mother expects from her

in this sophisticated, very modern story.
SUBJ: Mothers and daughters--Fiction./ New York (N.Y.)--Fiction.

Ph-3 4-6/6 $2.99   P   KH707
SHREVE, SUSAN. Flunking of Joshua T. Bates. Illus. by Diane De Groat.
Knopf ISBN 0-679-84187-3, c1984, 1993. 82p. ill.
"Bullseye books."
Repeating third grade is the worst thing in Joshua's young life. But his
teacher is supportive and tutors him diligently, his parents are
understanding and he even achieves a stand-off with his former
classmates whose teasing sometimes hits too close to home. The full
page illustrations are very good and this book will be useful for
discussion of attitudes towards peers, teachers and school in general.
SUBJ: Schools--Fiction.

Ph-2 3-5/6 $13.00   L   KH708
SHREVE, SUSAN. Formerly great Alexander family. Illus. by Chris Cart.
Tambourine ISBN 0-688-13551-X, 1995. 91p. ill.
Liam Alexander, ten, is ashamed that his "perfect" family is in the
process of a divorce. Shreve provides strong descriptions of one
boy's emotional state after a divorce, a boy who feels small, wimpish,
and demeaned and who engages in perfectly understandable self-pity.
The solution is a bit fast, but adds to the readability of the story.
SUBJ: Divorce--Fiction./ Fathers and sons--Fiction./ Brothers and
sisters--Fiction.

Ph-3 4-6/6 $12.95   L   KH709
SHREVE, SUSAN. Gift of the girl who couldn't hear. Tambourine ISBN
0-688-10318-9, 1991. 79p.
In order to encourage her friend, Eliza, Lucy, thirteen, who is hearing
impaired tries out for a role in a school musical. Eliza, a gifted singer
who is feeling too insecure to audition, gains confidence in herself as
she helps Lucy learn to sing and understands her courage. Although
the book lacks fine development, it presents an interesting view of
deafness, despite a somewhat moralizing tone.
SUBJ: Deaf--Fiction./ Friendship--Fiction./ Schools--Fiction.

Ph-2 4-6/4 $4.99   P   KH710
SHREVE, SUSAN. Joshua T. Bates takes charge. Illus. by Dan
Andreasen. Random House ISBN 0-679-87039-3; In Canada: Random
House, c1993, 1995. 102p. ill.
Joshua, eleven, has had problems in school and knuckles under to a
gang of bullies in his fifth-grade class. When they torture a new,
smaller classmate, however, Joshua finally rouses to take action and
put a stop to the gang's control. Book questions popularity,
"nerdhood," and what one person can do in the face of unbridled
power. Perhaps it takes Joshua a long time to act, but readers will
understand his dilemma. Discussion-starter that is good for reading
aloud.
SUBJ: Schools--Fiction./ Popularity--Fiction./ Bullies--Fiction.

Ph-2 4-6/6 $13.89   L   KH711
SIEGELSON, KIM L. Terrible, wonderful tellin' at Hog Hammock. By Kim
Siegelson. Illus. by Eric Velasquez. HarperCollins ISBN 0-06-024878-5; In
Canada: HarperCollins, 1996. 89p. ill.
"Jonas wants to keep the memory of his beloved Gullah grandfather
alive by representing his family at the traditional storytelling contest,
even though he feels like a nervous child trying to do a man's job."
(CIP) A gentle book, giving the flavor of Gullah culture and daily life,
shows a boy who assumes a man's mantle, but in his own way, and
succeeds. Those who suffer stage fright might identify with and be
encouraged by this telling. Incorporates some Gullah phrases to add
spice. For multicultural studies.
SUBJ: Gullahs--Fiction./ Grandfathers--Fiction./ Storytelling--Fiction./
Sea Islands--Fiction./ Afro-Americans--Fiction.

Ph-2 5-6/5 $3.50   P   KH712
SINGER, ISAAC BASHEVIS. Naftali the storyteller and his horse, Sus.
Illus. by Margot Zemach. Farrar, Straus & Giroux ISBN 0-374-45487-6;
In Canada: McGraw-Hill Ryerson, 1987. 129p. ill.
Eight tales, seven translations and one original, have been gathered
here by Isaac Singer to show man's dedication to a dream, and also
his foolishness. Household imps are explained and also how people
may be fools but still understand love. A good source for the
storyteller.
SUBJ: Poland--Fiction./ Jews--Folklore./ Jews--Poland--Fiction./ Short
stories.

Ph-1 5-A/6 $22.95   T   KH713
SINGER, ISAAC BASHEVIS. Stories for children. Farrar, Straus &
Giroux ISBN 0-374-37266-7, 1984. 337p.
Available from National Library Service for the Blind and Physically
Handicapped on sound recording cassette RC22928.
Compiling the major portion of this distinguished author's work in a

single volume provides a tremendous resource for young readers and for librarians. Stories from Chelm, from ZLATLEH THE GOAT and from NAFTALI THE STORYTELLER are here as well as additional stories published elsewhere but never in book form. This volume should not supersede the other books by the author, for some children will prefer the individual volumes, but it is a classic edition and a gold mine for storytelling.
SUBJ: Short stories.

Ph-3 5-A/4 $22.50   T   KH714
SIS, PETER. Three golden keys. Doubleday ISBN 0-385-47292-7; In Canada: Bantam Doubleday Dell, 1994. unp. col. ill.
When a man lands in a hot air balloon in the old city of Prague, he finds himself lost in the place of his childhood where he must discover three keys each with an ancient legend attached. Dreamlike, the illustrations and legends are the compelling elements of the book. For the special reader who will appreciate the sophisticated presentation and take the time to pore over the details.
SUBJ: Fairy tales./ Prague (Czech Republic)--Fiction.

Ph-1 6-A/4 $14.00   T   KH715
SKINNER, DAVID. Wrecker. Simon & Schuster ISBN 0-671-79771-9; In Canada: Distican, 1995. 106p.
Narrated in absolutely cold "just the facts, ma'am" diction by Michael, the new kid who has been enlisted by eighth grade genius Theo to "wreck" the school bully, the short novel packs an unforgettable punch. Theo puts together a device, a "mind and soul wrecker" that destroys the mean core of Jeffrey, an incredibly mean person. Theo's other inventions, devices that "find" him and seemingly build themselves, are as amazing as this seemingly amoral mechanistic character is. Chilling and gripping, the fast-paced novel leaves an indelible impression that goes beyond science fiction into phantasmagoria.
SUBJ: Bullies--Fiction./ Inventions--Fiction./ Genius--Fiction./ Schools--Fiction.

Ph-1 5-A/4 $16.00   T   KH716
SKURZYNSKI, GLORIA. Virtual war. Simon & Schuster ISBN 0-689-81374-0; In Canada: Distican, 1997. 152p.
Selectors' Choice, 21st ed.
"In a future world where global contamination has necessitated limited human contact, three young people with unique genetically engineered abilities are teamed up to wage a war in virtual reality." (CIP) Surefire science fiction combined with rapid pace; imaginative details of dress, food, living arrangements, and science; and superb characterization make this title a winner. It is a strong choice for independent reading, for reading aloud, and to use as a discussion starter about the ethics of war and possible futures for our world if we do not guard it well. The author's several positively reviewed nonfiction books about virtual reality and cyberspace have provided excellent background for this work.
SUBJ: Science fiction./ Virtual reality--Fiction./ War--Fiction.

Ph-1 A/6 $3.99   P   KH717
SLEATOR, WILLIAM. Duplicate. Bantam Doubleday Del ISBN 0-553-28284-X, 1990. 154p.
Using his newfound Spee-Dee-Dupe machine to duplicate himself solves 16-year-old David's problem of how to be in two places at once on Sunday night. The fun is fleeting as he and his duplicate struggle to solve everyday problems such as who eats meals, goes to school, and spends time with girlfriend Angela. This page turner will be enjoyed by mature readers. Could also be used to spark discussion of the future--genetics, cloning, medical ethics.
SUBJ: Science fiction.

Ph-1 4-6/4 $13.95   T   KH718
SLEPIAN, JAN. Alfred Summer. Macmillan ISBN 0-02-782920-0; In Canada: Collier Macmillan, 1980. 119p.
Selectors' Choice, 13th ed.
Available from National Library Service for the Blind and Physically Handicapped on sound recording cassette RC21341.
Set in Brooklyn in the 1930s, this perceptive story explores the friendship between Lester, whose speech problems and awkward body movements are caused by cerebral palsy, Alfred, a younger retarded boy, and two neighborhood children, Myron and Claire. The shared excitement of helping Myron build a rowboat in their apartment house basement, and the freedom Lester and Alfred experience away from their protective families, are well portrayed in the unusual and ultimately moving story of four unlikely friends.
SUBJ: Friendship--Fiction./ Physically handicapped--Fiction./ Mentally handicapped--Fiction./ Courage--Fiction.

Ph-1 4-A/4 $13.89   L   KH719
SLOTE, ALFRED. Finding Buck McHenry. HarperCollins ISBN 0-06-021653-0; In Canada: HarperCollins, 1991. 250p.
"Eleven-year-old Jason, believing the school custodian Mack Henry to be Buck McHenry, a famous pitcher from the old Negro League, tries to enlist him as a coach for his Little League team by revealing his identity to the world." (CIP). Less a "Play Ball" baseball story than the story of the treatment players received from white rivals who played against teams in the Negro League, it is also a mystery story and presents lively history and characters from the present--and the past. A "must" for baseball fans, baseball card collectors, and units on the history of sports in the U.S. and African-American history. For multicultural studies.
SUBJ: Baseball--Fiction./ Afro-Americans--Fiction.

Ph-2 5-A/6 $13.99   T   KH720
SMITH, DORIS BUCHANAN. Best girl. Viking Penguin ISBN 0-670-83752-0; In Canada: Penguin, 1993. 144p.
Trying to cope with her strict and seemingly unloving divorced mother, Nealy, eleven, is a child who is a keen observer of nature. She shelters herself and her treasure box under a neighbor's porch until an arson fire destroys much of the house. Her hiding place lost, Nealy confronts herself with the help of adults in the small town. Brilliantly written and strongly characterized, the book requires a sensitive reader to understand why the mother acts as she does and how the girl observes, grows, and encounters her world.
SUBJ: Mothers and daughters--Fiction./ Family problems--Fiction./ Self-acceptance--Fiction.

Ph-1 5-A/5 $4.99   P   KH721
SMITH, DORIS BUCHANAN. Return to Bitter Creek. Penguin ISBN 0-14-032223-X; In Canada: Penguin, 1988. 174p.
Selectors' Choice, 16th ed.
Learning to cope with a large, but somewhat suspicious family, Lacey wonders if she will ever be accepted in the rural community of Bitter Creek. Her unmarried mother's choice of an alternative life style encourages hostility among family members, particularly from grandmother. However, when tragedy strikes, the whole family is able to come to terms with the reality of the situation. A powerful story with great depth and strong feeling.
SUBJ: Family life--Fiction./ Appalachian Region--Fiction./ Mothers and daughters--Fiction./ Unmarried mothers--Fiction.

Ph-1 4-6/4 $13.89   L   KH722
SMITH, DORIS BUCHANAN. Taste of blackberries. Illus. by Charles Robinson. Crowell/HarperCollins ISBN 0-690-80512-8, c1973. 58p. ill.
Jamie, the protagonist's best friend, dies suddenly from bee stings. Guilt lingers after Jamie's death, for everyone ran from the swarming bees but the narrator; he thought Jamie was play acting his pain, so even he left Jamie alone. Acceptance of grief and guilt is the theme and the prose is realistic.
SUBJ: Joy and sorrow--Fiction./ Death--Fiction./ Friendship--Fiction.

Ph-3 2-4/6 $15.95   T   KH723
SMITH, E. BOYD. Farm book. Houghton Mifflin ISBN 0-395-32951-5, c1910, 1982. 55p. ill.
Selectors' Choice, 14th ed.
Bob and Betty's trip to their uncle's New England farm records the seasonal activities of 19th century farm life. Filled with detailed illustrations and information, this old title continues to enthrall children and can be used as a social studies adjunct. A welcome reprint of a classic title.
SUBJ: Farm life--Fiction.

Ph-3 3-6/9 $12.95   L   KH724
SMITH, E. BOYD. Seashore book. Houghton Mifflin ISBN 0-395-38015-4, 1985. 55p. ill. (some col.).
Descriptions of ships and adventures at sea combined with full-page illustrations of ships, ship-building, and adventures along the shore bring an earlier era to life. Though fictionalized and old-fashioned, this may prove useful for social studies classes and have some appeal to those who enjoy the ocean.
SUBJ: Seashore--Fiction./ Sailing--Fiction./ Shipbuilding--Fiction.

Ph-1 2-4/4 $12.89   L   KH725
SMITH, JANICE LEE. Monster in the third dresser drawer and other stories about Adam Joshua. Illus. by Dick Gackenbach. HarperCollins ISBN 0-06-025739-3; In Canada: HarperCollins, 1981. 86p. ill.
Selectors' Choice, 14th ed.
Available from National Library Service for the Blind and Physically Handicapped on sound recording cassette RC31225, and in Braille BR7374.
Six short stories about Adam Joshua deal with such eternal problems of young children as a new baby sister, an imaginary monster in his room, and losing his baby teeth. Told with humor and insight, they

are popular with young readers and are good for reading aloud to lower primary grades.
Followed by THE KID NEXT DOOR AND OTHER HEADACHES (ISBN 0-06-025793-8, 1984). Five more delightful stories about Adam, his friend Nelson, his new dog and a visiting girl called Cynthia. Excellent read aloud. In THE SHOW AND TELL WAR (ISBN 0-06-442006-X, c1988, 1995) more adventures and misadventures face Adam Joshua, his friend, Nelson and his enemy, Elliot, in the new school year. SERIOUS SCIENCE: AN ADAM JOSHUA STORY (ISBN 0-06-020782-5, 1993) presents several wacky, funny projects proving if they can go wrong, they do.
Adam Joshua and his friends suffer outrageous fortune in a school Thanksgiving play - but take revenge through humor in THE TURKEY'S SIDE OF IT: ADAM JOSHUA'S THANKSGIVING (ISBN 0-06-025859-4, 1990); and IT'S NOT EASY BEING GEORGE (ISBN 0-06-025853-5, 1989, OPC) features three humorous episodes starring Adam Joshua's dog, George, as he appears in the school pet show, tries to camp out with the children in the library, and is part of his devoted owner's comedy act for the talent show. In THERE'S A GHOST IN THE COATROOM: ADAM JOSHUA'S CHRISTMAS (ISBN 0-06-022864-4, 1991, OPC). NELSON IN LOVE: AN ADAM JOSHUA VALENTINE'S DAY STORY (ISBN 0-06-020293-9, 1992, OPC). In another funny and charming story THE BABY BLUES: AN ADAM JOSHUA STORY (ISBN 0-06-023643-4, 1994, OPC), Ms. D, heavily pregnant, gives eggs for each member of her class to parent--with hilarious results.
Available from National Library Service for the Blind and Physically Handicapped on sound recording cassette RC31227 is THE SHOW AND TELL WAR, and in Braille BR7217 is THE KID NEXT DOOR AND OTHER HEADACHES.
SUBJ: Family life--Fiction./ Short stories.

Ph-2 3-6/4 $3.99   P   KH726
SMITH, ROBERT KIMMEL. Bobby baseball. Illus. by Alan Tiegreen. Delacorte ISBN 0-440-40417-7, 1991. 165p. ill.
Because he believes himself to be a super player and has some luck as a starting pitcher against three weak Mustang League teams, Bobby Ellis, a.k.a., Bobby Baseball, owner of a horrific temper, mutinies against orders from his coach, who is also his father. Character development and game action will hold readers as Bobby begins to learn a great deal about himself as a person and as a baseball player. Diction/usage glitches cause an occasional hiccup in a work that many boys will enjoy.
SUBJ: Baseball--Fiction./ Fathers and sons--Fiction./ Self-perception--Fiction.

Ph-1 4-A/5 $15.95   L   KH727
SNOW, ALAN. How dogs really work! Little, Brown ISBN 0-316-80261-1; In Canada: Little, Brown, 1993. 32p. col. ill.
First published in Great Britain, HarperCollins.
Includes index.
Snow's hilariously detailed art and tongue-in-cheek text explain the mechanics and mentality of canines--as advanced machines. Sheer fun, a doggy treat.
SUBJ: Dogs--Fiction./ Humorous stories.

Ph-1 4-A/7 $14.95   L   KH728
SNOW, ALAN. Truth about cats. Little, Brown ISBN 0-316-80282-4; In Canada: Little, Brown, 1996. 29p. col. ill.
Includes index.
Like its equally hilarious and original HOW DOGS REALLY WORK!, the new volume provides detailed schematics of felines, their origins (Planet Nip), and their arrival and life on Planet Earth. Great fun--worth several examinations.
SUBJ: Cats--Fiction./ Humorous stories.

Ph-2 4-6/7 $3.95   P   KH729
SNYDER, ZILPHA KEATLEY. Black and blue magic. Illus. by Gene Holtan. Aladdin ISBN 0-689-71848-9; In Canada: Distican, c1966, 1994. 184p. ill.
Harry Houdini Marco (named for the famous magician) is given a liquid which enables him to grow wings and fly. It doesn't work out altogether perfectly, and puts Harry into many bruising and ludicrous situations--always unexpectedly. For reading aloud.
SUBJ: Magic--Fiction./ Flight--Fiction./ San Francisco (Calif.)--Fiction./ Fantasy.

Ph-1 5-A/7 $14.95   T   KH730
SNYDER, ZILPHA KEATLEY. Cat running. Delacorte ISBN 0-385-31056-0; In Canada: Bantam Doubleday Dell, 1994. 168p.
Selectors' Choice, 20th ed.
Set in a small California town during the worst years of the Great Depression, this strong novel centers on Cat Kinsey, the daughter of a middle-class family which is having economic problems. Cat becomes

involved with a classmate who is from one of the "Okie" families. Living in poverty, Zane's family, though down on its luck, has pride. As Zane reveals his hidden dimensions, Cat learns that the word "Okie," filth in the mouths of many, does not truly describe people, and she begins to change her attitude as she learns about herself, her own family, and the people around her. This powerful historical fiction presents an active study of people and times.
SUBJ: Depressions--1929--Fiction./ Family life--Fiction./ California--Fiction.

Ph-1 5-6/6 $14.95   L   KH731
SNYDER, ZILPHA KEATLEY. Egypt game. Illus. by Alton Raible. Atheneum ISBN 0-689-30006-9, c1967. 215p. ill.
Newbery Honor Book.
Available from the National Library Service for the Blind and Physically Handicapped in Braille BRA 02704 and on sound recording cassette RC 37531.
Melanie knows that her new friend, April, will not fit into their school. Within a month, the two girls and other friends convert an abandoned junk yard into an Egyptian temple. When a real murderer roams in the neighborhood, the girls have a winter of excitement.
SUBJ: Egypt--Antiquities--Fiction./ Schools--Fiction./ Girls--Fiction.

Ph-1 6-A/7 $14.00   T   KH732
SNYDER, ZILPHA KEATLEY. Fool's gold. Delacorte ISBN 0-385-30908-2; In Canada: Bantam Doubleday Dell, 1993. 214p.
Available from the National Library Service for the Blind and Physically Handicapped on sound recording cassette RC 38796.
Warned constantly never to play in the abandoned mines in Pyramid Hill, Rudy and Barney are, nevertheless, convinced by their new, daredevil classmate Ty to search for gold. Because of a long-forgotten accident, Rudy, who suffers from claustrophobia and has nightmares about being trapped in a dark place, tries to stop his friends from their foolhardy actions. Rudy must overcome his phobias to save Ty in this strongly characterized novel full of psychological and physical tension.
SUBJ: Friendship--Fiction./ Phobias--Fiction./ Gold mines and mining--Fiction./ Single-parent family--Fiction.

CE   Ph-1 4-6/7 $15.95   L   KH733
SNYDER, ZILPHA KEATLEY. Headless cupid. Illus. by Alton Raible. Atheneum ISBN 0-689-20687-9, c1971. 203p. ill.
Newbery Honor Book.
Available from National Library Service for the Blind and Physically Handicapped in Braille BR13679, on sound recording cassette RC24224, and talking book TB04210.
David and the three younger children settled into the big old house with their father and their new mother Molly. He was apprehensive how Amanda, Molly's daughter whom they didn't know yet, would fit the new household. Amanda turns out to be "a student of the occult" and she decides to put all the children through a series of tests and the rites of initation. David, and even little Blair, are skeptical, especially when they begin to have manifestations of a poltergeist. Strong characterizations, just the right amount of suspense, and a satisfying climax, make this a tense reading or hearing experience.
In THE FAMOUS STANLEY KIDNAPPING CASE (Dell ISBN 0-440-42485-2, 1985) the Stanley family spends a year in Italy where Amanda's chance remarks about her rich father results in the children being kidnapped. Followed by BLAIR'S NIGHTMARE (ISBN 0-689-31022-6, 1984, OPC) in which the family worries about Blair's imaginary dog and discovers that the giant Irish wolfhound is not a dream. Combined, the titles portray, convincingly, a stepfamily beginning to draw closer together.
Eight-year-old Janie Stanley moves front and center when she sets up a detective agency to find missing neighborhood dogs in JANIE'S PRIVATE EYES (Delacorte ISBN 0-385-30146-4, 1989, OPC). BLAIR'S NIGHTMARE is available from NLSBPH on sound recording cassette RC25045.
SUBJ: Stepsisters--Fiction./ Occult sciences--Fiction./ Extrasensory perception--Fiction.

Ph-1 5-A/6 $14.95   T   KH734
SNYDER, ZILPHA KEATLEY. Trespassers. Delacorte ISBN 0-385-31055-2; In Canada: Bantam Doubleday Dell, 1995. 200p.
Having trespassed and explored the empty Hutchinson mansion, which seems haunted by the presence of a long-dead young girl, sixth grader Neely and her little brother become regular visitors when emotionally disturbed Curtis Hutchinson moves in." (CIP) The characters of the children are very clear as is the setting--central coastal California. As the children return time after time to the playroom and discover toys and a dollhouse, readers will follow along to discover if the house is indeed haunted and what relation the old toys have to the past--and the present. Mood, character, the

past, the present, and setting combine to produce a suspenseful novel. Curtis is such a strange, strong character, one who can frighten a reader because he seems to be a person one may have met.
SUBJ: Ghosts--Fiction./ Emotional problems--Fiction.

Ph-2 4-6/7 $14.95   L   KH735
SNYDER, ZILPHA KEATLEY. Witches of Worm. Illus. by Alton Raible. Atheneum ISBN 0-689-30066-2, c1965. 183p. ill.
Newbery Honor Book.
Selectors' Choice, 8th ed.
Jessica is left alone--deserted by Brandon, her only friend, and by her mother who works all day and in the evening goes out with her newest boyfriend. She finds--and is forced to adopt--a kitten which she names Worm and decides must be a witch's cat. Does a witch or maybe even a devil control Worm? She thinks it makes her do dreadful things and think wrong thoughts. Finding out about Worm leads to an unexpected answer to Jessica's problems.
SUBJ: Cats--Fiction./ Witches--Fiction./ Magic--Fiction.

Ph-1 3-5/6 $14.95   T   KH736
SOBOL, DONALD J. Encyclopedia Brown and the case of Pablo's nose. Illus. by Eric Velasquez. Delacorte ISBN 0-385-32184-8; In Canada: Bantam Doubleday Dell, 1996. 71p. ill.
Ten more mysteries to solve with the boy sleuth. The solutions are provided in the back of the book.
SUBJ: Mystery and detective stories.

Ph-1 3-5/6 $13.99   T   KH737
SOBOL, DONALD J. Encyclopedia Brown, boy detective. Lodestar/Dutton ISBN 0-525-67200-1, 1963. 88p. ill.
Available from National Library Service for the Blind and Physically Handicapped on sound recording cassette RC11047.
Young Encyclopedia Brown, whose brain is packed full of all kinds of information, helps his father, the police chief, solve all the crimes in the small town of Idaville. Each title in the series contains ten cases and the answers are found in the back. Appealing format for reluctant readers.
ENCYCLOPEDIA BROWN: BOY DETECTIVE (1963); ...AND THE CASE OF THE SECRET PITCH (ISBN 0-525-67202-8, 1965); ...FINDS THE CLUES (ISBN 0-525-67204-4, 1966); ...GETS HIS MAN (ISBN 0-525-67206-0, 1967); ...SOLVES THEM ALL (ISBN 0-525-67212-5, 1968); ...KEEPS THE PEACE (ISBN 0-525-67208-7, 1969); ...TRACKS THEM DOWN (ISBN 0-525-67214-1, 1971); ...SHOWS THE WAY (ISBN 0-525-67216-8, 1972, OPC); ...SAVES THE DAY (ISBN 0-525-67210-9, 1972); ...TAKES THE CASE (ISBN 0-525-66318-5, 1973); ...LENDS A HAND (ISBN 0-525-67218-4, 1974); ...AND THE CASE OF THE DEAD EAGLES (ISBN 0-525-67220-6, 1975); ...AND THE CASE OF THE MIDNIGHT VISITOR (ISBN 0-525-67221-4, 1977); ...CARRIES ON (Four Winds/Macmillan ISBN 0-02-786190-2, 1980, OPC); ...SETS THE PACE (Four Winds/Macmillan ISBN 0-02-786200-3, 1982); ...AND THE CASE OF THE MYSTERIOUS HANDPRINTS (Morrow ISBN 0-688-04626-6, 1985); ...AND THE CASE OF THE TREASURE HUNT (Morrow ISBN 0-688-06955-X, 1988).
Also available from NLSBPH are: ...AND THE CASE OF THE DEAD EAGLES in Braille BRA14357 and sound recording cassette RC10692; ...AND THE CASE OF THE MIDNIGHT VISITORS on sound recording cassette RC12159; ...GETS HIS MAN in Braille BRA04496 and on sound recording cassette RC11044; ...KEEPS THE PEACE in Braille BR01315; ...LENDS A HAND in Braille BR02645 and on sound recording cassette RC16484; ...SHOWS THE WAY on sound recording cassette RC07745; ...SOLVES THEM ALL in Braille BR02145, on sound recording cassette RC08984; ...TAKES THE CASE in Braille BR02638.
SUBJ: Mystery and detective stories.

Ph-2 6-A/6 $14.95   T   KH738
SOTO, GARY. Baseball in April and other stories. Harcourt Brace Jovanovich ISBN 0-15-205720-X, 1990. 111p.
Includes glossary of Spanish words used in book.
Spanish version available from Lectorum BEISBOL EN ABRIL Y OTRAS HISTORIAS (ISBN 968-16-4838-2, 1995).
Soto's 11 short stories, most with built-in disappointments of young people, especially those in junior high, relate incidents in the lives of Mexican-American youngsters growing up in Fresno, California. Each story is different and each presents, in a tightly woven style, memorable characters in a diction that haunts the mind's ear. Better, more mature readers will appreciate the stories and the variety of experiences which, although set in a Latino frame, will resonate for many young people of all cultures who can identify with the happenings. Try oral presentation for younger groups.
SUBJ: Mexican Americans--California--Fiction./ Short stories./ Spanish language materials.

Ph-2 4-6/5 $14.95   T   KH739
SOTO, GARY. Boys at work. Illus. by Robert Casilla. Delacorte ISBN 0-385-32048-5; In Canada: Bantam Doubleday Dell, 1995. 134p. ill.
Companion to: POOL PARTY, 1993.
"When ten-year-old Rudy breaks an older boy's Discman at a baseball game, he and his friend Alex come up with a variety of ways to make money to pay for a new one." (CIP) The various labors in which they engage provide the humor and suspense in the book, which will also be good for older reluctant readers. However, a glossary of the Spanish words incorporated throughout the text would be helpful, especially for those who have little or no vocabulary in that language. For multicultural studies.
SUBJ: Mexican Americans--California--Fiction./ Friendship--Fiction./ Moneymaking projects--Fiction.

Ph-2 6-A/6 $14.95   T   KH740
SOTO, GARY. Local news. Harcourt Brace Jovanovich ISBN 0-15-248117-6; In Canada: Harcourt Brace Jovanovich c/o Canadian Manda, 1993. 148p.
Includes glossary.
Everyday lives of children--who happen to be Mexican-American--are explicated in 13 short stories dealing with a variety of experiences. Spanish words and phrases flow naturally within the text and can be identified through context or in the glossary. Insightful view of contemporary Hispanic life for multicultural studies.
SUBJ: Mexican Americans--California--Fiction./ Short stories.

Ph-2 4-6/5 $3.50   P   KH741
SOTO, GARY. Pool party. Illus. by Robert Casilla. Delacorte ISBN 0-440-41010-X; In Canada: Bantam Doubleday Dell, c1993, 1995. 104p. ill.
Companion title: BOYS AT WORK, Delacorte, 1995.
Rudy Herrera is invited to a pool party by one of his well-to-do classmates. His loving, hard working and not-so-wealthy Mexican-American family give him many explanations of a pool party, all but one of which is absolutely incorrect. His many (mis)adventures before and during the party, including his acquisition of a very large inner tube which he carries to the party and which everyone enjoys, are amusing and rapid. The Hispanic-English diction is strong and helps create character, although a glossary of Spanish words would help. Rudy is a typical boy--much bravado but appreciative of his family and friends. Try with reluctant readers. For multicultural studies.
SUBJ: Mexican Americans--Fiction./ Family life--Fiction./ California--Fiction.

CE   Ph-2 5-6/5 $13.95   T   KH742
SPEARE, ELIZABETH GEORGE. Witch of Blackbird Pond. Houghton Mifflin ISBN 0-395-07114-3, c1958. 249p.
Newbery Medal Award.
Available from National Library Service for the Blind and Physically Handicapped in Braille BR01427, on sound recording cassette RC22927, and as talking book TB01816.
Kit Tyler on a visit to colonial Connecticut from her home in Barbados becomes friendly with Hannah the witch, teaches a little girl to read, and is thus saved in the ensuing witch-hunt.
SUBJ: Connecticut--Fiction./ Witchcraft--Fiction./ Puritans--Fiction.

CE   Ph-1 5-6/6 $16.00   L   KH743
SPERRY, ARMSTRONG. Call it courage. Macmillan ISBN 0-02-786030-2, c1940. 95p. ill.
Newbery Medal Award.
Talking book available from SRA/McGraw-Hill 87-507913, $17.15.
Spanish version available from Lectorum ESTO ES CORAJE (ISBN 84-279-3228-6, n.d.).
Mafatu, son of a Polynesian chief, is terrified of the vast ocean which claimed his mother's life. In this lean account which encompasses thrilling adventures, he overcomes his fear of the sea in an epic journey which wins him the respect of his people. Try reading aloud. It invariably provokes discussion.
SUBJ: Polynesia--Fiction./ Survival--Fiction./ Courage--Fiction./ Spanish language materials.

Ph-2 5-A/3 $17.99   L   KH744
SPINELLI, JERRY. Crash. Knopf ISBN 0-679-97957-3; In Canada: Random House, 1996. 162p.
"Borzoi book."
Told in the first person by John "Crash" Coogan, a truly unpleasant seventh grader, the narrative shows how he has always been tough and run roughshod over any and all who are different, especially a neighbor, a gentle but tough-minded Quaker boy, Penn. He changes only after his beloved grandfather suffers a stroke, and he begins to learn that Penn's values are worthwhile. It takes Crash most of the book to change, and the reader is left with a fascinating, honest, and not-very-nice portrait of a machismo boy who does, at least, change and becomes more human and less of a bully. Action is rapid, filled

with sports events, and young male attitudes and actions. Meant to be funny because of exaggeration, some may be put off by Crash.
SUBJ: Conduct of life--Fiction./ Friendship--Fiction./ Family life--Fiction.

Ph-1 6-A $12.95   L   KH745
SPOOKY STORIES OF THE SUPERNATURAL. Edited by Pamela Lonsdale. Illus. by Joanna Carey. Prentice-Hall ISBN 0-13-835463-4, 1985. 143p b&w illus.
Selected by a British editor from a ghost story series run on the BBC, these seven original tales are not only unusually high in quality but most are so new they will have fresh appeal to ghost story buffs. The stories deal with possession, hauntings, even an ingenious spirit who breaks into a radio talk show. All are first rate and well written.
SUBJ: Ghosts--Fiction./ Short stories.

Ph-3 5-A/6 $22.00   L   KH746
SPYRI, JOHANNA. Heidi. Illus. by Jessie Willcox Smith. Books of Wonder/Morrow ISBN 0-688-14519-1, 1996. 383p. ill. (some col.).
Heidi, the five-year-old Swiss girl who is sent to live with her stern grandfather high in the Alps, reflects the naivety expected of children in the Victorian age. She is sweet, innocent, and old-fashioned. While staying with an aunt in Frankfurt, she meets Clara, the sickly child who is restored to health during a stay in the Alps. As a period piece the book is interesting and can serve as a replacement copy. However, because of its length and awkward translation, it is probably best used for reading aloud.
SUBJ: Grandfathers--Fiction./ Mountain life--Switzerland--Fiction./ Orphans--Fiction./ Switzerland--Fiction.

Ph-3 2-4/2 $11.95   L   KH747
STANEK, MURIEL. I speak English for my mom. Illus. by Judith Friedman. Whitman ISBN 0-8075-3659-8; In Canada: General, 1989. unp. ill.
Bringing her daughter Lupe to the United States from Mexico was her husband's dying wish, but her life is difficult when Mrs. Gomez speaks no English and must rely on her daughter to transact daily business. When she decides to take English lessons, she and Lupe practice at night. Useful for collections serving Hispanic populations or units studying problems of immigrants.
SUBJ: Mexican Americans--Fiction./ Mothers and daughters--Fiction./ Emigration and immigration--Fiction.

Ph-1 6-A/6 $18.99   L   KH748
STAPLES, SUZANNE FISHER. Shabanu, daughter of the wind. Knopf ISBN 0-394-94815-7; In Canada: Random House, 1989. 240p.
Includes glossary.
Newbery Honor Book, 1990.
Develops, in many dimensions, a loving, contemporary, nomadic family in the Cholistan Desert of Pakistan as the family members are affected by daily and special events and sometimes tragic occurrences. The story centers on Shabanu, the eleven-year-old independent daughter as she grows to young womanhood. Much information about the people and their customs is provided in a non-didactic fashion. A gripping reading experience for the more mature reader and a daring choice for oral reading in history units dealing with nomads and Pakistan.
SUBJ: Cholistan Desert (Pakistan)--Fiction./ Pakistan--Fiction./ Sex role--Fiction.

CE
Ph-1 4-6/6 $14.00   T   KH749
STEIG, WILLIAM. Abel's island. Farrar, Straus & Giroux ISBN 0-374-30010-0; In Canada: HarperCollins, 1976. 117p. ill.
Newbery Honor Book.
Available from National Library Service for the Blind and Physically Handicapped on sound recording cassette RC10693.
Animated 1/2" VHS videocassette color (30min) available from Random House Home Video (ISBN 0-394-89871-0, 1988), $14.95.
Available in Spanish LA ISLA DE ABEL (HarperCollins ISBN 0-374-34286-5, 1992).
Abel and his wife have always been secure in their own mouse world when a great flood dumps Abel on an uninhabited island. He lives there for a year until his wit and courage finally take him back home. He gains a new understanding of the world in this mouse tale of real distinction. Steig's illustrations add to the story.
SUBJ: Mice--Fiction./ Wilderness survival--Fiction./ Islands--Fiction.

Ph-1 4-6/7 $15.00   T   KH750
STEIG, WILLIAM. Dominic. Farrar, Straus & Giroux ISBN 0-374-31822-0, c1972. 145p. ill.
Spanish version DOMINICO available from Mirasol/Farrar Straus Giroux (ISBN 0-374-31823-9, 1994).
Dominic is a spunky young dog who sets out to see the world and experience adventure. He has many dangerous encounters with the wicked, scheming Doomsday Gang, helps many animals in trouble, gains a fortune, becomes a hero, and finally reaches an enchanted garden where he magically awakens from a long sleep the most beautiful dog he has ever seen.
SUBJ: Dogs--Fiction./ Voyages and travels--Fiction./ Spanish language materials.

Ph-1 4-6/6 $12.95   T   KH751
STEIG, WILLIAM. Real thief. Farrar, Straus & Giroux ISBN 0-374-36217-3, c1973. 58p. ill.
Selectors' Choice, 9th ed.
Gawain is an upright, trustworthy goose chosen by King Basil, a bear, to guard the Royal Treasury. When gold, jewels and a famous diamond disappear from the treasure house, Gawain is accused of the theft. Though really innocent he is found guilty but escapes from the courtroom and flies away to hide. Derek, a guilt ridden mouse, is the real culprit; through his efforts the king and townspeople realize that the faithful goose has been wrongly accused.
SUBJ: Geese--Fiction./ Robbers and outlaws--Fiction./ Kings, queens, rulers, etc.--Fiction.

Ph-1 1-A/5 $13.95   T   KH752
STEIG, WILLIAM. Spinky sulks. Farrar, Straus and Giroux ISBN 0-374-38321-9; In Canada: HarperCollins, 1988. unp col illus.
After Spinky's feelings are hurt, he sulks and sulks and sulks. Neither his sister, nor his brother, nor his parents, nor his best friends, all acting sweet and considerate for days can change his mind. As he begins to weaken, Spinky's problem is how can he give in, rejoin the family, and still save his pride. This one is for all ages.
SUBJ: Emotions--Fiction.

Ph-2 4-6/6 $13.89   L   KH753
STERMAN, BETSY. Backyard dragon. By Betsy and Samuel Sterman. Illus. by David Wenzel. HarperCollins ISBN 0-06-020784-1; In Canada: HarperCollins, 1993. 189p. ill.
Bewitched by a wizard, a fifteenth century Welsh dragon finds himself in Owen's twentieth century backyard in New Jersey. Owen must help the dragon, Wyrdryn, return to his time and place, or its monthly meal will decimate the town. With the help of his grandfather and three friends, he manages the humorous complications of moving the dragon to New York City for the Macy's parade. Chapter one, in which Owen flies a dragon kite, is not well integrated into the plot and requires leaps of imagination from readers.
SUBJ: Dragons--Fiction./ Magic--Fiction.

Ph-2 3-5/6 $4.95   P   KH754
STEVENS, CARLA. Trouble for Lucy. Illus. by Ronald Himler. Clarion ISBN 0-89919-523-7, 1979. 80p. ill.
Traveling by wagon train to Oregon in 1843, Lucy Stewart's new fox terrier puppy seems to cause more trouble than her father is willing to handle. The emigrant experience is presented in a realistic way. The hard life on wagon trains will be useful in studies of the Oregon Trail or the Great Migration and could be used in conjunction with SARAH, PLAIN AND TALL, DAKOTA DUGOUT and MY PRAIRIE YEARS.
SUBJ: Frontier and pioneer life--Fiction./ Oregon Trail--Fiction./ Dogs--Fiction.

Ph-1 4-6/6 $14.00   L   KH755
STEVENSON, JAMES. Bones in the cliff. Greenwillow ISBN 0-688-13745-8, 1995. 119p.
Told by his father to watch for a gunman--a large man with a cigar coming to Cutlass Island on the ferry boats--Pete, eleven, is frightened and lonely. Rootie, a neighbor girl with an adventuresome imagination, helps Pete by providing companionship and games and shares his watch for the man hired to kill Pete's alcoholic father. When the gunman arrives, a scene fraught with tension and danger ensues in this well-written, fast paced book which is a good choice for reading aloud. Stevenson paints his scenes and characters with the same skill he uses in his picture books.
SUBJ: Islands--Fiction./ Criminals--Fiction./ Family problems--Fiction./ Friendship--Fiction./ Fathers and sons--Fiction.

Ph-2 2-3/2 $14.93   L   KH756
STEVENSON, JAMES. Yard sale. Greenwillow ISBN 0-688-14127-7, 1996. 32p. col. ill.
Stevenson's whimsical small animals, rendered in watercolor and pen, swap and trade treasures (none in good condition) at the Mud Flat Yard Sale. All in good fun, the heroes of THE MUD FLAT OLYMPICS once again provide humor and a sideways glance at bargains. Short chapters and low reading level make this an appealing transitional reader.
SUBJ: Garage sales--Fiction./ Collectors and collecting--Fiction./ Humorous stories.

Ph-2 6-A/6 $25.00   L   KH757
STEVENSON, ROBERT LOUIS. David Balfour: being memoirs of the
further adventures of David Balfour at home and abroad. Illus. by N. C.
Wyeth. Scribner's ISBN 0-684-19736-7; In Canada: Maxwell Macmillan,
c1952, 1994. 356p. col. ill.
Sequel to KIDNAPPED, Scribner's, 1982.
For those readers who wish to trace David Balfour's adventures first
set forth in KIDNAPPED, this sequel in facsimile of the 1922 edition,
illustrated by N. C. Wyeth, is the edition of choice--but it requires a
very strong reader. Set in the Scottish Highlands, the historical fiction,
adventure story is compelling reading for advanced students.
SUBJ: Adventure and adventurers--Fiction./ Scotland--History--18th
century--Fiction.

Ph-2 5-6/6 $24.95   L   KH758
STEVENSON, ROBERT LOUIS. Kidnapped: being the memoirs of the
adventures of David Balfour in the year 1751. Illus. by N. C. Wyeth.
Scribner's ISBN 0-684-17634-3, 1982. 289p. col. ill.
Available from National Library Service for the Blind and Physically
Handicapped in Braille BRA11966, on sound recording cassette
RC25158, and as talking book TB01987.
This classic adventure story is set in the Scotland of the 1750s.
Orphaned Davie Balfour is true heir to his wicked uncle's fortune but
is kidnapped by his uncle's cohorts and sent to sea. He falls in with
the Jacobite adventurer Alan Breck Stewart and the two share many
adventures until Davie regains his inheritance and Alan, suspected of
a Whig murder, flees the country. A reprint of the 1913 edition with
illustrations by N.C. Wyeth.
SUBJ: Adventure and adventurers--Fiction./ Scotland--Fiction.

Ph-1 5-A/6 $26.00   L   KH759
STEVENSON, ROBERT LOUIS. Treasure Island. Illus. by N. C. Wyeth.
Scribner's ISBN 0-684-17160-0, c1911, 1981. 273p. col. ill. (Treasury of
children's classics).
Available from National Library Service for the Blind and Physically
Handicapped in Braille BRA09965, on sound recording cassette
RC18121, as talking book TB02019.
The classic treasure hunt story and the machinations of the villainous
crew of Black Dog, Long John Silver, and Pew are presented in this
special edition which features distinctive full-color illustrations.
SUBJ: Pirates--Fiction./ Buried treasure--Fiction./ Adventure and
adventurers--Fiction.

TB   Ph-1 5-A $57.25   KH760
STEVENSON, ROBERT LOUIS. Treasure Island (Talking book). Read by
Michael Page. Brilliance Corporation ISBN 1-56100-140-6, 1993. 6
sound cassettes (420min).
ALA notable recording, 1994.
The classic treasure hunt story and the machinations of the villainous
crew of Black Dog, Long John Silver, and Pew are presented in a
rousing narration which recreates their exciting adventures.
SUBJ: Pirates--Fiction./ Buried treasure--Fiction./ Adventure and
adventurers--Fiction.

Ph-2 3-5/6 $14.95   L   KH761
STEWART, ELISABETH J. Bimmi finds a cat. Illustrated by James E.
Ransome. Clarion ISBN 0-395-64652-9, 1996. 33p. col. ill.
Bimmi, "an eight-year-old Creole boy on Galveston Island [Texas]
grieves the death of his cat Crabmeat, but when another lost cat
leads him to a new friend he starts to heal." (CIP) Using some
Creole dialect and syntax, Stewart creates the ambience and life of
Bimmi and his world. Ransome's full-page oil paintings show character
and setting well to produce a deeper dimension of life on Galveston
Island and its people. Text helps readers empathize with Bimmi on the
loss of his beloved cat.
SUBJ: Cats--Fiction./ Lost and found possessions--Fiction./ Death--
Fiction./ Grief--Fiction./ Creoles--Fiction./ Galveston Island (Tex.)--
Fiction.

Ph-2 4-6/4 $13.95   T   KH762
STEWART, ELISABETH J. On the long trail home. Clarion ISBN 0-395-
68361-0, 1994. 106p., map.
Available from National Library Service for the Blind and
Physically Handicapped on sound recording cassette RC 42414.
Meli, nine, and her older brother Tahlikwa escape from a stopping
place on the Cherokee Trail of Tears in 1838. The conditions of the
forced march under the control of the United States Army are
harrowing as is the escape to their home in northwestern North
Carolina from southwestern Kentucky. The historical fiction account is
based on the life of the author's great-grandmother. Afterword
provides factual information about the Cherokee Nation and their
removal from their ancestral lands. Useful in units on Native American
life, multicultural studies, and United States history in the Jacksonian
period.
SUBJ: Cherokee Indians--Fiction./ Indians of North America--Fiction./
Trail of Tears, 1838--Fiction.

Ph-3 5-6/7 $13.89   L   KH763
STOCKTON, FRANK R. Bee-man of Orn. Illus. by Maurice Sendak.
HarperCollins ISBN 0-06-025819-5, c1964, 1987. 44p. col. ill.
Available from National Library Service for the Blind and Physically
Handicapped in Braille BRA01715 and as talking book TB01559.
Having been told by a junior sorceror that he's under a spell, the
bee-man of Orn sets out to discover his original state. The tongue-in-
cheek humor nicely paired with muted detailed watercolors make this
a prime candidate to read aloud.
SUBJ: Magic--Fiction./ Fairy tales.

Ph-2 3-5/7 $14.95   T   KH764
STOCKTON, FRANK R. Griffin and the minor canon. Illus. by Maurice
Sendak. HarperCollins ISBN 0-06-025816-0, c1963, 1986. 56p. col. ill.
Available from National Library Service for the Blind and Physically
Handicapped in Braille BRA05490 and as talking book TB01559.
Having heard about a statue of himself in a town in England, a griffin
(part lion, part eagle) decides to visit it and creates havoc in the
town. The sardonic humor of the text aptly interpreted in Sendak's
pen and ink and watercolor illustrations is best enjoyed when read
aloud to middle graders.
SUBJ: Griffins--Fiction./ Fantasy.

Ph-1 4-6/4 $14.89   L   KH765
STOLZ, MARY. Dog on Barkham Street. Illus. by Leonard Shortall.
HarperCollins ISBN 0-06-025841-1, c1960. 184p. ill.
Available from National Library Service for the Blind and Physically
Handicapped in Braille BRA06031.
Edward, and his friend Rod, want a dog of their own. But Edward's
main problem in life is his next-door neighbor Martin "Fatso"
Hastings, the Bully of Barkham Street. When Edward's traveling uncle
comes to visit, he brings his own dog and eventually problems are
solved.
The same story is told from the point of view of Martin Hastings, the
bully in BULLY OF BARKHAM STREET (ISBN 0-06-025821-7, 1963,
OPC) and in THE EXPLORER OF BARKHAM STREET (ISBN 0-06-
025976-0, 1985, OPC) the former bully begins to reach out to
people around him.
SUBJ: Dogs--Fiction./ Problem children--Fiction.

Ph-1 3-6/6 $12.89   L   KH766
STOLZ, MARY. Go fish. Illus. by Pat Cummings. HarperCollins ISBN
0-06-025822-5; In Canada: HarperCollins, 1991. 74p. ill.
Selectors' Choice, 18th ed.
Presents Thomas and his grandfather, whom readers met in STORM
IN THE NIGHT, in a more advanced first chapter book just right for
quiet reading and hearing. Their day together is detailed and ends
with a story about their African heritage which, one hopes, Thomas
will tell his own grandchildren someday. Cummings' black-and-white
illustrations add to this lovely book about a special grandfather and a
fine, typically curious and sometimes fidgety child of eight. For
multicultural studies.
SUBJ: Grandfathers--Fiction./ Fishing--Fiction./ Mexico, Gulf of--
Fiction./ Afro-Americans--Fiction.

CE   Ph-3 4-6/6 $14.89   L   KH767
STOLZ, MARY. Noonday friends. HarperCollins ISBN 0-06-025946-9,
c1965. 182p. ill.
Newbery Honor Book.
Available from National Library Service for the Blind and Physically
Handicapped in Braille BR00279.
In a warm story about a New York family, its problems and its
friends, Franny wishes she could take lunch to school in a lunch box
or even a paper bag, instead of using the free pass issued needy
children. Jim, her twin, tries begging pop bottles so he can have
spending money.
SUBJ: Family life--Fiction./ New York (N.Y.)--Fiction./ Irish--United
States--Fiction.

Ph-1 3-5/6 $13.89   L   KH768
STOLZ, MARY. Stealing home. HarperCollins ISBN 0-06-021157-1; In
Canada: HarperCollins, 1992. 153p.
Previously introduced in STORM IN THE NIGHT and GO FISH,
Thomas and Grandfather are now older, and their orderly lives
together are disturbed by the possibly permanent visit of Thomas'
great-aunt Linzy, a woman whose compulsions equal Grandfather's.
Much of the story deals with the joy of baseball: in fact, it is almost
a paean to the skill, history, and joy of the game. In time, the lives of
all three clearly delineated characters are bettered as each helps the
other and changes. The novel is filled with quiet love and humor
which derives from the strong characterization of three different
human beings. For reading aloud and for multicultural studies.
SUBJ: Grandfathers--Fiction./ Great-aunts--Fiction./ Afro-Americans--
Fiction./ Old age--Fiction./ Florida--Fiction./ Baseball--Fiction.

Ph-1 4-6/6 $8.95 ea. T   KH769
STORIES FROM ASIA TODAY: COLLECTION FOR YOUNG READERS, BOOKS ONE AND TWO. Weatherhill/dist. by Tuttle ISBN 0-8348-1038-7, 1979. 2v illus. (Asian copublication programme).
Includes Notes on authors and illustrators.
Each anthology features over a dozen stories written by well-known modern authors and illustrated by prominent artists. The stories not only convey the universal experience of childhood, but reveal distinct and important cultural differences. Important to collections not only for social studies units, but for comparative literature studies as well.
SUBJ: Asia--Fiction./ Short stories.

Ph-2 2-5/3 $11.95 L   KH770
STOWE, CYNTHIA. Not-so-normal Norman. Illus. by Cat Bowman Smith. Whitman ISBN 0-8075-5767-6; In Canada: General, 1995. 127p. ill.
Available from the National Library Service for the Blind and Physically Handicapped on sound recording cassette RC 43106.
Norman is a huge tarantula being pet-sat by Anthony who is earning money while his father is out of work due to a back injury. Large, widely leaded type and clear sentences will make this transitional reader accessible to first chapter book readers, and it will also be of interest because of the unusual title character, Norman.
SUBJ: Moneymaking projects--Fiction./ Tarantulas--Fiction./ Family life--Fiction.

Ph-1 5-A/4 $13.95 T   KH771
STRETE, CRAIG KEE. World in Grandfather's hands. Clarion ISBN 0-395-72102-4, 1995. 135p.
"Eleven-year-old Jimmy is upset when he and his mother must move from the pueblo to the city after his father's death, but his grandfather's patient philosophy of life helps Jimmy slowly adjust." (CIP) Told in the first person by Jimmy, the narrative reveals his love for everything in the desert and his shock and dislike for the seamy urban setting. His mother and grandfather help him keep his Native American customs as he learns the ways and lessons of the city. It is a strong portrait of a boy in a world of transition and will be good for multicultural studies and for units on Native Americans in today's world.
SUBJ: Indians of North America--Southwest, New--Fiction./ Grandfathers--Fiction./ Death--Fiction.

Ph-2 5-A/6 $14.89 L   KH772
STRICKLAND, BRAD. Hand of the necromancer. Frontispiece by Edward Gorey. Dial ISBN 0-8037-1830-6, 1996. 168p.
Based on John Bellairs' characters, Johnny, the Professor, and new friend, Sarah, are in danger as Matthews Mergal tries to possess the necromancy of a long gone evil relative, so that he may rule the world. Suspenseful.
SUBJ: Wizards--Fiction./ Magic--Fiction./ Mystery and detective stories.

Ph-3 4-6/3 $2.99 P   KH773
SULLIVAN, ANN. Molly Maguire: wide receiver. Avon ISBN 0-380-76114-9; In Canada: Avon, 1992. 104p.
"Avon Camelot book."
The story has been done before, and it's been done better but not for the younger age group. A girl who is a natural athlete earns a place as a member of the football team and finds unexpected help from the class bully. The humorous story of the wide receiver will catch many a fan. For football enthusiasts, male or female.
SUBJ: Football--Fiction./ Schools--Fiction.

Ph-3 3-5/5 $11.95 L   KH774
SUSSMAN, SUSAN. Hanukkah: eight lights around the world. Illus. by Judith Friedman. Whitman ISBN 0-8075-3145-6, 1988. 37p. ill.
Includes bibliography and glossary.
Traveling around the world to visit contemporary families celebrating Hanukkah, these eight short stories emphasize the common practice of this celebration regardless of where families live. Countries visited are Israel, Mexico, Argentina, U.S., France, India, Morocco, and the U.S.S.R. This is a resource for collections needing information on this holiday, but could also be used in Social Studies class or in places emphasizing multicultural objectives.
SUBJ: Hanukkah--Fiction./ Short stories.

Ph-1 3-6/7 $6.99 P   KH775
SUTCLIFF, ROSEMARY. Minstrel and the dragon pup. Illus. by Emma Chichester Clark. Candlewick ISBN 1-56402-603-5; In Canada: Douglas & McIntyre, c1993, 1996. 45p. col. ill.
Lucky, a baby dragon, leads a happy life with the minstrel who adopted him until he is stolen by a wicked showman. In his grief, the minstrel wanders the kingdom in search of the baby dragon, but his songs have lost their joy. When they are finally reunited, the entire kingdom rejoices. Oil pastel illustrations show hints of the Renaissance. The handsome book is prime for reading aloud.
SUBJ: Dragons--Fiction./ Minstrels--Fiction.

Ph-1 4-6/5 $15.99 T   KH776
TAYLOR, MILDRED D. Friendship. Illus. by Max Ginsburg. Dial ISBN 0-8037-0417-8; In Canada: Fitzhenry & Whiteside, 1987. 53p. ill.
Coretta Scott King Award.
Available from National Library Service for the Blind and Physically Handicapped in Braille BR7258.
Finding themselves at the "forbidden" Wallace store makes the Logan children nervous enough, but witnessing a confrontation between Mr. Tom Bee, an African-American, and the white storekeeper is a total shock. This short, but moving book will give access to the Logans in a smaller--but no less powerful context than "Roll of Thunder," and presents a story appropriate for discussion about life in the 1930s, human rights, prejudice, respect, and decision-making. For multicultural studies.
SUBJ: Afro-Americans--Fiction./ Southern States--Race relations--Fiction./ Race relations--Fiction./ Prejudices--Fiction.

Ph-3 5-6/8 $16.99 T   KH777
TAYLOR, MILDRED D. Let the circle be unbroken. Dial ISBN 0-8037-4748-9, 1981. 432p.
Sequel to ROLL OF THUNDER, HEAR MY CRY.
Coretta Scott King Award.
Available from National Library Service for the Blind and Physically Handicapped in Braille BR06355.
Eleven-year-old Cassie becomes even more aware of the tension between the races. She sees her parents'and other African Americans' constant humiliation at the hands of local white land-owners and is made subtly aware of the interracial sexual relationships when her biracial cousin comes to visit. At the story's end, the Logans have once more survived with their land and pride intact. For multicultural studies.
SUBJ: Afro-Americans--Fiction./ Mississippi--Fiction.

Ph-1 5-A/4 $15.99 T   KH778
TAYLOR, MILDRED D. Mississippi bridge. Illus. by Max Ginsburg. Dial ISBN 0-8037-0426-7, 1990. 62p. ill.
Years of bigotry and a weak bridge over a raging river change the lives of a group of African Americans ordered off a bus in rural Mississippi in the 1930s and cost the lives of white passengers allowed to ride. The slowly unfolding book is seen through the eyes of shy 10-year-old Jeremy Simms, a white boy whose father is violently racist. Another book about the Logan family, this one an excellent choice for oral presentation, with well-developed characters, a taut plot and Ginsburg's black and white illustrations. For multicultural studies.
SUBJ: Race relations--Fiction./ Afro-Americans--Fiction./ Prejudices--Fiction./ Southern States--Race relations--Fiction.

CE   Ph-1 5-6/6 $15.00 T   KH779
TAYLOR, MILDRED D. Roll of thunder, hear my cry. Frontispiece by Jerry Pinkney. Dial ISBN 0-8037-7473-7, c1976. 276p.
Sequel to SONG OF THE TREES.
Newbery Medal Award.
Selectors' Choice, 11th ed.
Talking book available from SRA/McGraw-Hill 87-507851, 1978, $16.00.
Available from National Library Service for the Blind and Physically Handicapped in Braille BR06288 and as sound recording cassette RC10893.
The Logan family, living in the back country of Mississippi during the Depression, experiences economic exploitation, bitter inequality in schooling, and worse during one turbulent year of night-riders and burnings. Rich characterization in a powerful story told in language characteristic of the time and period but not "black English." An unforgettable story, its nearest counterpart is Wilkinson's LUDELL. For multicultural studies.
SUBJ: Afro-Americans--Fiction./ Southern States--Race relations--Fiction./ Depressions--1929--Fiction./ Mississippi--Fiction.

Ph-1 4-6/4 $13.50 T   KH780
TAYLOR, MILDRED D. Song of the trees. Illus. by Jerry Pinkney. Dial ISBN 0-8037-5452-3, 1975. 48p. ill.
Council on Interracial Books for Children Award.
Available from the National Library Service for the Blind and Physically Handicapped on sound recording cassette RC 40146.
The trees on the small Mississippi farm were old and protective to the African-American children, and especially Cassie. While Papa was away (in Depression days) working on the railroad in Louisiana, some white men hood-winked Big Ma out of them and cut them into lumber. The eyeball-to-eyeball encounter between the usurpers and Papa, literally holding dynamite, gains self-respect and time for the family. But the reader is left with Papa's haunting question: "Dear old trees, will you ever sing again?" For multicultural studies.
Followed by ROLL OF THUNDER, HEAR MY CRY.
SUBJ: Trees--Fiction./ Depressions--1929--Fiction./ Afro-Americans--Fiction./ Mississippi--Fiction./ Poverty--Fiction.

Ph-1 5-A/4 $14.89   L   KH781
TAYLOR, MILDRED D. Well: David's story. Dial ISBN 0-8037-1803-9, 1995. 92p.
Selectors' Choice, 20th ed.
Another of the economically written vignettes about the Logan family, this one centers on David, 10, and is set in the early 1900s in Mississippi. The family allows all the neighbors to use their well, the only one with water in the neighborhood. White racist neighbors, the Simms, bully David and his older brother, and the boys must work in the Simms' fields to avoid serious personal harm. Fraught with tension, well-developed characters, and a situation that will evoke empathy and sympathy from readers and listeners, the short powerful historical fiction is a good choice for reading aloud. Use as a discussion starter for units on racism, United States history, multicultural studies, and the ethical questions of right and wrong.
SUBJ: Afro-Americans--Fiction./ Race relations--Fiction./ Southern States--Race relations--Fiction./ Prejudices--Fiction./ Droughts--Fiction.

Ph-1 4-6/5 $15.95   T   KH782
TAYLOR, SYDNEY. All-of-a-kind family. Illus. by Helen John. Taylor Productions ISBN 0-929093-00-3, 1951, 1988. 189p. ill.
Available from National Library Service for the Blind and Physically Handicapped in Braille BR06191, as talking book TB03366, on sound recording cassette RC25019.
The family of five girls and no boys lives on the lower East side of New York City; together they enjoy midnight snacks, go to the library, play in their father's shop, and participate in the family's Jewish festivals.
Followed by: MORE ALL-OF-A-KIND FAMILY (ISBN 0-929093-02-X, 1954); ALL-OF-A-KIND FAMILY UPTOWN (ISBN 0-929093-03-8, 1958); ALL-OF-A-KIND FAMILY DOWNTOWN, illus. by Beth and Joe Krush (ISBN 0-929093-01-1, 1973, OPC); ELLA OF ALL-OF-A-KIND FAMILY, illus. by Meryl Rosner (ISBN 0-929093-04-6, 1978). Also available from NLSBPH are: ALL-OF-A-KIND FAMILY UPTOWN in Braille BRA10115 and as talking book TB03366; ELLA OF ALL-OF-A-KIND FAMILY on sound recording cassette RC14698; MORE ALL-OF-A-KIND FAMILY in Braille BRA10078 and as talking book TB03366.
SUBJ: Jews--United States--Fiction./ New York (N.Y.)--Fiction./ Girls--Fiction./ Family life--Fiction.

Ph-2 5-6/6 $13.95   T   KH783
TAYLOR, THEODORE. Cay. Doubleday ISBN 0-385-07906-0, c1969. 137p.
Jane Addams Book Award.
Available from National Library Service for the Blind and Physically Handicapped in Braille BRA02850, as talking book TB03219, and on sound recording cassette RC34450.
When Philip and his mother flee from Curacao during World War II, their ship is torpedoed by a German submarine. He is marooned on a tiny unknown island, blinded in the shipwreck, alone with a cat and an old black West Indian sailor. In their struggle to survive, Philip learns a great deal from the wise old man. A memorable tale.
SUBJ: Caribbean Area--Fiction./ Blind--Fiction./ Blacks--Fiction.

Ph-2 5-A/5 $3.50   P   KH784
TAYLOR, THEODORE. Teetoncey. Illus. by Richard Cuffari. Avon/Camelot ISBN 0-380-71024-2; In Canada: Avon, c1975. 153p b&w illus.
Teetoncey is the name which Ben and his mother gave to the almost-drowned girl who was washed up on the shores of the Outer Banks of North Carolina on a stormy and tragic night in 1898. Ben must prove to himself and to the men of the Banks that he is as brave as his father was. Teetoncey and the problems of bringing her back to full life bring unexpected consequences to him and his mother. The first of the "Teetoncey" trilogy.
In TEETONCEY AND BEN O'NEAL (ISBN 0-380-71025-0, c1975) the girl's memory returns. She is revealed as an heiress in THE ODYSSEY OF BEN O'NEAL (ISBN 0-380-71026-9, c1977, 1979) however, instead of returning to England she makes an exciting journey with Ben from Norfolk to Barbados and, finally, safely home to the Banks.
SUBJ: North Carolina--Fiction./ Shipwrecks--Fiction.

Ph-2 5-A/5 $13.95   T   KH785
TAYLOR, THEODORE. Timothy of the cay. Harcourt Brace ISBN 0-15-288358-4; In Canada: Harcourt Brace c/o Canadian Manda, 1993. 161p.
Sequel to: THE CAY, Doubleday, 1969.
Available from the National Library Service for the Blind and Physically Handicapped on sound recording cassette RC37644.
Readers of THE CAY will discover how Phillip survived after his rescue and how Timothy became the man he did in the "prequel-sequel." Alternate suspenseful chapters detail the lives of the boy and the man as readers follow Phillip in an operation to restore his sight, Timothy as he grew from orphaned boy to captain of his own boat, and the meeting of the two after a torpedo sank the transport in 1942. THE CAY underwent a great deal of controversy: perhaps the emendation of Timothy will make it less so. A survival story for multicultural studies.
SUBJ: Caribbean Area--Fiction./ Shipwrecks--Fiction./ Survival--Fiction./ Blacks--Caribbean Area--Fiction./ Blind--Fiction./ Physically handicapped--Fiction.

Ph-2 5-A/6 $13.95   L   KH786
TAYLOR, WILLIAM. Agnes the sheep. Scholastic ISBN 0-590-43365-2; In Canada: Scholastic, 1990. 132p.
The delightfully silly adventures of two children, a recalcitrant sheep, a marvelously eccentric, elderly woman, and several nicely developed villains will give readers a good deal of pleasure. The funny, ever-on-the-go novel contains many irreverent mix-ups, unexpected twists and turns, and fast paced action.
SUBJ: Sheep--Fiction.

Ph-2 4-A/7 $14.95   L   KH787
TAYLOR, WILLIAM. Numbskulls. Scholastic ISBN 0-590-22629-0; In Canada: Scholastic, 1995. 120p.
Sequel to KNITWITS, 1994.
Charlie and his two pals sign up with their nasty neighbor, know-it-all Alice, to learn how to be a good speller, a sexy guy, and a rich guy. Much of the humor is based on Alice's conduct and her insane theories of learning. Charlie does become an ace in spelling though his friends do not achieve their wishes. Funny and well characterized, this sequel, like its predecessor, will be enjoyed by stronger readers.
SUBJ: English language--Spelling--Fiction./ Schools--Fiction./ Family life--Fiction.

Ph-1 6-A/6 $14.99   L   KH788
TEMPLE, FRANCES. Grab hands and run. Orchard ISBN 0-531-08630-5, 1993. 165p.
Felipe, twelve, and his family flee their homeland and seek refuge in Canada after his father is killed for his politics in El Salvador. Along the difficult route are many people, some helpful, some greedy, some cruel. A reader can feel the physical and mental strain on the family as they cross borders, hide, and sometimes outwit those who profit from the misery of others. The novel is graphic and should make a reader understand the price of freedom. Good for social studies units on Central America and emigration and immigration.
SUBJ: Salvadorans--Fiction./ Refugees--Fiction./ Aliens, Illegal--Fiction.

Ph-1 6-A/5 $15.99   L   KH789
TEMPLE, FRANCES. Tonight, by sea: a novel. Orchard ISBN 0-531-08749-2, 1995. 152p., map.
"Richard Jackson book."
Includes glossary.
Available from the National Library Service for the Blind and Physically Handicapped on sound recording cassette RC 41398.
Set in contemporary Haiti, the book centers on young Paulie as she, her family, and friends secretly build a boat in which to escape the increasing poverty and government brutality after President Aristide had been deposed by the military. The book is "talky" allowing the author to supply details of Haitian life and history, but the tone, especially the use of Creole, gives it an authentic flavor as we meet the people and travel with them on their arduous journey to Florida. Glossary of Creole words, including some of their histories, adds authenticity. Both sympathy and empathy are developed in this strong novel. Useful in studies of modern history, Haiti, and modern dictatorships and for multicultural studies.
SUBJ: Haiti--History--1986- --Fiction./ Blacks--Haiti--Fiction.

Ph-2 6-A/4 $13.89   L   KH790
THESMAN, JEAN. Nothing grows here. HarperCollins ISBN 0-06-024458-5; In Canada: HarperCollins, 1994. 182p.
The title is a misnomer because something does grow in the unpleasant Seattle apartment house where Maryanne and her mother move after the death of their father and husband. Maryanne, now in the seventh grade in a new school, grows as does her mother. Essentially a character study, the novel introduces readers to real people in real situations who gradually learn to accept change. They are people whom readers might like to meet.
SUBJ: Moving, Household--Fiction./ Apartment houses--Fiction./ Death--Fiction./ Gardens--Fiction.

Ph-2 2-3/6 $17.95   L   KH791
THURBER, JAMES. Great Quillow. Illus. by Steven Kellogg. Harcourt Brace ISBN 0-15-232544-1; In Canada: Harcourt Brace c/o Canadian Manda, 1994. 56p. col. ill. (Harcourt Brace contemporary classic).
A giant is thwarted in his attempts to terrorize a town by the toymaker, affectionately referred to as "the great Quillow." Quillow's storytelling undermines the giant's confidence, and the

toymaker's mechanical blue men push the giant over the edge and send him running from town. Illustrations for the story, beginning and ending with the endpapers, are in the artist's characteristic style with humor and exaggeration well matched to the story.
SUBJ: Fairy tales./ Giants--Fiction.

Ph-1 3-5/5 $14.95   L   KH792
THURBER, JAMES. Many moons. Illus. by Louis Slobodkin. Harcourt Brace Jovanovich ISBN 0-15-251872-X, c1943, 1990. unp. col. ill. Caldecott Medal Award.
Available from the National Library Service for the Blind and Physically Handicapped on sound recording cassette RC 39639.
Princess Lenore says she will recover from her illness if she is given the moon. Only the Court Jester is wise enough to solve this problem.
SUBJ: Princesses--Fiction./ Fairy tales./ Moon--Fiction.

Ph-1 3-5/5 $14.95   L   KH793
THURBER, JAMES. Many moons. Illus. by Marc Simont. Harcourt Brace Jovanovich ISBN 0-15-251872-X, 1990. unp. col. ill.
Simont's newly illustrated edition of the Louis Slobodkin's 1944 Caldecott Medal winner, now appears with whimsical, gentle, active, and well characterized watercolors. The story of the princess whose wish can only be fulfilled by the court jester remains as fresh as ever, a fine choice for oral presentation. The type face is somewhat difficult to read but librarians will want to hold both the Slobodkin and the Simont versions if possible.
SUBJ: Fairy tales./ Moon--Fiction./ Princesses--Fiction.

Ph-1 5-A/7 $14.00   L   KH794
TOLAN, STEPHANIE S. Save Halloween! Morrow ISBN 0-688-12168-3, 1993. 168p.
Torn between her family's religious fundamentalism and her desire to work on the sixth-grade Halloween pageant, Johanna, eleven, follows her own beliefs. The anti-Halloween religious revival her preacher uncle holds in the town tears the residents into distressing factions. During the turmoil, Johanna, who has learned to think for herself, demonstrates a bravery that is reasonable and admirable. Although the novel seems fair-minded and tries to be neutral, it tends to come down on the side of religious freedom because of the hateful factionalism which arises during the crusade. Fine discussion starter for units on the First Amendment. For reading aloud.
SUBJ: Halloween--Fiction./ Christian life--Fiction./ Schools--Fiction./ Theater--Fiction.

Ph-2 5-A/5 $14.00   L   KH795
TOLAN, STEPHANIE S. Who's there? Morrow ISBN 0-688-04611-8, 1994. 235p.
"When fourteen-year-old Drew and her mute younger brother come to live with their father's estranged relatives after their parents' sudden death, they discover that the house is haunted by ghosts and a deadly family secret." (CIP) The suspenseful events and palpably frightening ghosts wrapped in an old family tragedy provide a rapid reading experience which will hold readers of the genre.
SUBJ: Grief--Fiction./ Ghosts--Fiction./ Brothers and sisters--Fiction./ Mutism, Elective--Fiction.

Ph-1 4-6/5 $14.95   T   KH796
TOLKIEN, J. R. R. Hobbit; or, There and back again. Houghton Mifflin ISBN 0-395-07122-4, n.d. 315p. ill.
Available from National Library Service for the Blind and Physically Handicapped in Braille BRA08811, on sound recording cassette RC11497, and as talking book TB01654.
Questing for gold, Bilbo Baggins, a home loving little hobbit, becomes involved with a wizard, dwarfs, and a dragon. He has many strange and exciting adventures in "dungeons deep and caverns old," but finally becomes an "Expert Treasure Hunter". A great story and one many children should have a chance to read or hear.
SUBJ: Fantasy.

Ph-1 6-A/5 $15.99   L   KH797
TOMLINSON, THERESA. Forestwife. Orchard ISBN 0-531-08750-6, 1995. 170p., map.
"In England during the reign of King Richard I, fifteen-year-old Marian escapes an arranged marriage to live with a community of forest folk that includes a daring young outlaw named Robert." (CIP) In this beautifully developed retelling of Robin Hood, the times and people are shown through the eyes and actions of Marian. Better readers will enjoy the romance of the leading characters. Customs, historical backgrounds of the times, characters, and place settings are all strongly developed. Afterword provides the historical basis of the legend.
SUBJ: Maid Marian (Legendary character)--Fiction./ Robin Hood (Legendary character)--Fiction./ Great Britain--History--Richard I, 1189-1199--Fiction.

Ph-2 2-4/2 $13.95   T   KH798
TORNQVIST, RITA. Christmas carp. Translated by Greta Kilburn. Illus. by Marit Tornqvist. R&S/dist. by Farrar, Straus & Giroux ISBN 91-29-59784-6, 1990. 33p. col. ill.
Tomorrow is Christmas Eve, and Thomas, who is spending the holiday with his grandfather in Prague, Czechoslovakia, must purchase a carp to celebrate. As in Cohen's THE CARP IN THE BATHTUB, affection for the fish makes it impossible to kill and eat it. In a story that tells of a Czech Christmas celebration and customs, illustrated in active yet gentle art, both people and places are clear. A good choice for oral presentation that tells of other places and customs.
SUBJ: Christmas--Fiction./ Fishes--Fiction./ Czechoslovakia--Fiction.

SRC   Ph-3 3-5 $12.00   KH799
TORRENCE, JACKIE. My grandmother's treasure (Sound recording cassette). August House Audio ISBN 0-87483-328-0, 1993. 1 sound cassette (57min).
Listeners discover the world in which Jackie Torrence was raised, the love that surrounded her, and the storytellers who impressed her when she was young. For collections on intergenerational relationships, storytelling, and multicultural studies, particularly African-American life in the 1940's and 1950's.
SUBJ: North Carolina--Fiction./ Short stories./ Storytelling--Collections.

Ph-1 4-6/6 $14.95   T   KH800
TRAVERS, P. L. Mary Poppins. Rev. ed. Illus. by Mary Shepard. Harcourt Brace Jovanovich ISBN 0-15-252408-8, c1962. 206p b&w illus.
Available from National Library Service for the Blind and Physically Handicapped in Braille BR00923, and on sound recording cassette RC16951.
Blown into the Banks family's household by the East Wind, Mary Poppins' prim and proper demeanor masks considerable magical ability, much to the amazement and delight of her young charges. The contradictory personality is one of the chief charms of the original story (not at all transferred to the film version). The other popular titles in the series include MARY POPPINS COMES BACK (Buccaneer ISBN 0-89966-392-3, 1987); MARY POPPINS OPEN THE DOOR (Dell ISBN 0-440-40432-0, 1991, OPC); MARY POPPINS IN THE PARK (Dell ISBN 0-440-40452-5, 1991, OPC); and MARY POPPINS IN CHERRY TREE LANE (Delacorte ISBN 0-385-28601-5, 1982). Available from NLSBPH is MARY POPPINS OPENS THE DOOR in Braille BR0934, and MARY POPPINS IN CHERRY TREE LANE in Braille BR7024.
SUBJ: Fantasy./ England--Fiction./ Magic--Fiction.

TB   Ph-2 4-6 $11.00   OD KH801
TRAVERS, P. L. Mary Poppins (Talking book). Narrated by Robert Stephens. Performed by Maggie Smith and others. HarperAudio/ Caedmon ISBN 1-55994-657-1; In Canada: dist. by HarperCollins, n.d. 1 sound cassette.
Based on the book of the same title. A lively reading of excerpts from the adventures of Mary Poppins, flying nanny.
SUBJ: Fantasy.

Ph-2 3-6/6 $5.95   P   KH802
TREASURY OF ANIMAL STORIES. Chosen by Jane Olliver. Illus. by Annabel Spenceley. Kingfisher ISBN 1-85697-831-1, 1992. 157p. ill. (Read-aloud book).
Nineteen animal stories from Aesop to Kipling to Joel Chandler Harris and Ted Hughes, and many anonymous tales from throughout the world are collected. For telling or reading aloud.
SUBJ: Animals--Fiction./ Short stories./ Animals--Folklore./ Folklore.

Ph-3 3-5/6 $5.95   P   KH803
TREASURY OF GIANT AND MONSTER STORIES. Chosen by Jane Olliver. Illus. by Annabel Spenceley. Kingfisher ISBN 1-85697-832-X, 1992. 157p. ill. (Read-aloud book).
Presents 14 modern and classic tales about giants and monsters by such fantasy authors as Nesbit, Mahy, and Madame de Beaumont. For reading aloud.
SUBJ: Giants--Fiction./ Monsters--Fiction./ Short stories./ Giants--Folklore./ Monsters--Folklore./ Folklore.

Ph-2 4-A/6 $5.95   P   KH804
TREASURY OF SPOOKY STORIES. Chosen by Jane Olliver. Illus. by Annabel Spenceley. Kingfisher ISBN 1-85697-830-3, 1992. 157p. ill. (Read-aloud book).
Fourteen modern and traditional stories are designed to cause shivers whether read aloud or read privately. Includes a variety of authors such as Judith Gorog, Susan Price, Jan Mark, the Grimm Brothers, and Ruskin Bond.
SUBJ: Ghosts--Fiction./ Horror stories./ Short stories./ Ghosts--Folklore./ Folklore.

Ph-2 2-4/5 $5.95 P KH805

TREASURY OF STORIES FOR FIVE YEAR OLDS. Chosen by Edward and Nancy Blishen. Illus. by Polly Noakes. Kingfisher ISBN 1-85697-827-3, 1992. 157p. ill. (Read-aloud book).

Twenty-three stories, some originals and others retellings of traditional tales, are meant for reading aloud or telling.
SUBJ: Short stories./ Folklore.

Ph-2 3-5/6 $5.95 P KH806

TREASURY OF STORIES FOR SEVEN YEAR OLDS. Chosen by Edward and Nancy Blishen. Illus. by Patricia Ludlow. Kingfisher ISBN 1-85697-829-X, 1992. 156p. ill. (Read-aloud book).

Collection of 19 modern and traditional stories which are suitable for reading aloud or telling includes WHY NOAH CHOSE THE DOVE, JOHNNY-CAKE, STEADFAST TIN SOLDIER, and THE OLD WOMAN WHO LIVED IN A VINEGAR BOTTLE.
SUBJ: Short stories./ Folklore.

Ph-2 2-4/5 $5.95 P KH807

TREASURY OF STORIES FOR SIX YEAR OLDS. Chosen by Edward and Nancy Blishen. Illus. by Tizzie Knowles. Kingfisher ISBN 1-85697-828-1, 1992. 158p. ill. (Read-aloud book).

Twenty-four modern and traditional stories include works by Philippa Pearce, Joseph Jacobs, Joel Chandler Harris, and Margaret Mahy. For reading aloud or telling.
SUBJ: Short stories./ Folklore.

Ph-2 5-A/6 $4.95 P KH808

TUNIS, JOHN R. Go, team, go! Morrow ISBN 0-688-09286-1, c1954, 1991. 201p.

At the heart of this book about a high school basketball team in a small town in Indiana is the ethical question of star players who break training rules and who revolt against the coach. The attitudes of the young people toward illegal gambling reflect those of many of the town's adults, something Tunis makes clear. Little Tom struggles with his own values, the betrayal of them, and his anguish when his special girl, a cheerleader, upholds the coach and his actions. As usual, Tunis develops excellent play action, character, and tense situations. Book contains some dated references such as prices and wages.
SUBJ: Basketball--Fiction./ High schools--Fiction.

Ph-1 5-A/6 $4.95 P KH809

TUNIS, JOHN R. Highpockets. Morrow ISBN 0-688-09288-8, c1948. 189p.

Playing only for record books and not for the team, star outfielder and hitter Cecil McDade, "Highpockets" is a Jonah to his teammates on the then Brooklyn Dodgers until he injures a boy in an accident. He begins to think about people other than himself and helps his team in a classic baseball book that combines good baseball with real characters. A winner for oral presentation and just-plain-good-reading for baseball fanatics. There is nothing old-fashioned about this older book.
SUBJ: Baseball--Fiction./ Brooklyn Dodgers (Baseball team)--Fiction.

Ph-1 5-A/7 $4.95 P KH810

TUNIS, JOHN R. Kid comes back. Morrow ISBN 0-688-09290-X, c1946, 1990. 245p.

Tunis, an author who respected his readers and the sport of baseball he portrayed so well and truly, brings back "The Kid", Roy Tucker, superstar of the Brooklyn Dodgers from his service in World War II. Injured on a dangerous mission, Roy must be rehabilitated before he can resume his baseball career in a book that is deep in character and full of baseball games that fairly crackle. Newer readers will be amused at peanuts at 10 cents a bag in 1946, but will want to follow "The Kid" and his team. The series should be read in sequence for best understanding of Roy's growth.
SUBJ: Baseball--Fiction./ Brooklyn Dodgers (Baseball team)--Fiction.

Ph-3 5-6/6 $4.95 P KH811

TURNBULL, ANN. Maroo of the winter caves. Clarion ISBN 0-395-54795-4, c1984, 1990. 136p.

Maroo, a girl in the late Ice Age, saves her family from starvation and freezing after her father dies. Intertwined with her long journey to the group's winter camp are details of daily life among this semi-nomadic hunting people. At times tense, the book features a female, unusual in books depicting this era of pre-history. Good for world history units and as a companion for other fictionalized anthropology books.
SUBJ: Prehistoric peobles--Fiction.

Ph-2 5-A/6 $13.95 L KH812

TURNER, ANN. Nettie's trip south. Illus. by Ronald Himler. Macmillan ISBN 0-02-789240-9; In Canada: Collier Macmillan, 1987. unp. ill.
Selectors' Choice, 16th ed.

Inspired by the author's great-grandmother's diary of her trip to

Richmond in 1859, this is a stark look at the ugly realities of slavery as seen through the eyes of a ten-year-old northern girl. Distinguished by sparse prose that reads like poetry, this is a powerful and deeply moving account of slavery in the South just before the Civil War. An excellent resource for the teaching of U.S. history.
SUBJ: Slavery--Fiction.

Ph-1 5-A/4 $15.00 L KH813

TURNER, MEGAN WHALEN. Instead of three wishes. Greenwillow ISBN 0-688-13922-1, 1995. 132p.

Imaginative, humorous, and choice to use for reading aloud, the seven stories involve characters from the "real" world as they engage in interplay with otherworldly characters: leprechauns, the prince of elves (and his earthy TV-watching mother), ghosts--some kindly, some malevolent. The title story develops fascinating people from both worlds, and humor is often created by having one world's objects and ideas enter the other's. Fun and fanciful, it will be a treat and encourage imagination.
SUBJ: Fantasy./ Short stories.

Ph-1 5-A/4 $21.95 T KH814

TWAIN, MARK. Adventures of Tom Sawyer. Illus. by Barry Moser. Morrow ISBN 0-688-07510-X, 1989. 261p col illus. (Books of wonder).

The familiar and beloved adventures of the harum scarum boy is presented in a most attractive edition with 17 sparkling watercolor illustrations. The edition of choice.
SUBJ: Mississippi River--Fiction./ Missouri--Fiction./ Humorous stories.

Ph-1 5-6/6 $13.95 T KH815

UCHIDA, YOSHIKO. Jar of dreams. Atheneum ISBN 0-689-50210-9, 1981. 131p.

Available from National Library Service for the Blind and Physically Handicapped on sound recording cassette RC22368.
Growing up in a close-knit Japanese family in California in the 1930s, Rinko--aware of the prejudice against Japanese--wants to be a real American. Her mother's sister, visiting from Japan, is an embarrassment to her; but this is the summer when she learns the strength of her family and the Japanese-American community. Rinko, a sensitive and intelligent child, is appealing; all the characterizations are excellent. In THE BEST BAD THING (ISBN 0-689-50290-7, 1983), Rinko is sent to help the widowed and very eccentric Mrs. Tata on her California farm and comes to share her woes. Again the support the Japanese-American community gives to each other comes through strongly.
In THE HAPPIEST ENDING (ISBN 0-689-50326-1, 1985) 12-year-old Rinko is determined to arrange people's lives her way but finds that her outspokenness and honesty are not always welcome.
Also available from NLSBPH are: THE BEST BAD THING on sound recording cassette RC22369 and THE HAPPIEST ENDING on sound recording cassette RC25223.
SUBJ: Japanese--United States--Fiction./ Family life--Fiction./ Poverty--Fiction.

Ph-1 5-A/7 $8.95 P KH816

UCHIDA, YOSHIKO. Journey to Topaz. Illus. by Donald Carrick. Creative Arts ISBN 0-916870-85-5, c1971, 1984. 149p. ill.

The bombing of Pearl Harbor by the Japanese in 1941 brings drastic changes to Yuki Sakane's family as Father is taken by the FBI and Yuki, her mother and older brother, Ken, are ultimately shipped to Topaz, a desert concentration camp, along with thousands of other West Coast Japanese Americans. With courage and patience, the family faces many ordeals but manages to maintain their dignity. Based on the author's own childhood experience, this account of the Japanese American evacuation is a sad footnote of U.S. history that should be read by mature, thoughtful readers.
SUBJ: Japanese Americans--Evacuation and relocation, 1942-1945--Fiction./ World War, 1939-1945--Evacuation of civilians--Fiction.

TB

Ph-2 4-6 $17.15 OD KH817

ULLMAN, JAMES RAMSEY. Banner in the sky (Talking book). SRA/McGraw-Hill 87-507885, n.d. 1 sound cassette.

Adapted from the Newbery Honor book of the same title (O.P.)
Available from National Library Service for the Blind and Physically Handicapped in Braille BRA01811, and on sound recording cassette RC18958.
Presents an particularly effective dramatization of the conflict between Rudi and his desire to climb the great mountain and his mother's fears for his safety. His experiences with the great climber Captain Winter, the avalanche on the mountain and the surprising climax tell a story of Rudi's growth from boy into man.
SUBJ: Mountaineering--Fiction./ Switzerland--Fiction./ Matterhorn--Fiction.

Ph-1 4-6/2 $16.95   T   KH818
VALGARDSON, W. D. Sarah and the people of Sand River. Illus. by Ian Wallace. Groundwood/dist. by Publishers Group West ISBN 0-88899-255-6; In Canada: Groundwood/Douglas & McIntyre, 1996. unp. col. ill., map.

Based on the emigration experiences of the Icelanders to New Iceland on the western shore of Lake Winnipeg, Manitoba, Canada, in 1875, the fictionalized story of young, motherless Sarah who must leave her father to learn Canadian ways and language is at once haunting, sad, and finally victorious. Years before, her ancestors had helped a Native American family dying of smallpox, the Sand River Cree woman gave Sarah's grandmother an amulet. Passed down from grandmother to mother to Sarah, the charm protects her in her bitter ordeals and eventually saves her when a raven appears to watch over her and ghostly Cree help her. In a mystical story set in harsh reality, the experience of a group of settlers and their debt to native populations is shown. Illustrations in pencil, watercolors, and gouache add to the mood. Historical fiction for reading aloud and for units on immigrant groups and native populations. A moving story for multicultural studies.
SUBJ: Frontier and pioneer life--Canada--Fiction./ Indians of North America--Canada--Fiction./ Canada--Fiction./ Supernatural--Fiction.

Ph-2 3-5/4 $15.00   L   KH819
VALGARDSON, W. D. Winter rescue. Illus. by Ange Zhang. McElderry ISBN 0-689-80094-0, 1995. unp. col. ill.
Originally published in Canada as THOR, Groundwood Books/ Douglas & McIntyre, 1994.
"While helping his grandfather, an ice fisherman on frigid Lake Winnipeg, Thor becomes a hero even braver than his favorite cartoon superheroes." (CIP) Illustrated in large paintings which show the equipment, the characters, and the cold, the story explains ice fishing, its methods, and dangers while depicting the relationship between boy and man. This intergenerational story will be of special use in areas of great cold and frozen lakes and will give a picture of another way of life--to those who live without frigid climes.
SUBJ: Ice fishing--Fiction./ Fishing--Fiction./ Grandfathers--Fiction./ Heroes--Fiction.

Ph-1 K-A/4 $17.95   L   KH820
VAN ALLSBURG, CHRIS. Jumanji. Houghton Mifflin ISBN 0-395-30448-2, 1981. unp. ill.
Caldecott Award.
Selectors' Choice, 14th ed.
Available from National Library Service for the Blind and Physically Handicapped in Braille BR05317.
This stunning picture book is executed in black and white illustrations of such skill that the reader is literally drawn into the fantasy world of two children who have chanced upon a seemingly harmless board game called Jumanji, A Jungle Adventure Game. Each roll of the dice brings the jungle home to them--a lion on the piano, riotous monkeys in the kitchen, a deadly snake on the mantle. A very original and popular book which appeals to all age levels.
SUBJ: Play--Fiction./ Fantasy.

KIT   Ph-1 K-A $24.95   KH821
VAN ALLSBURG, CHRIS. Jumanji (Kit). Read by Robin Williams. Music composed and conducted by Michael Moss. Houghton Mifflin ISBN 0-395-75411-9, 1995. 1 hardback book, 1 sound cassette (18min.).
"Charlesberry Production."
ALA notable recording, 1996.
"Breathtaking jungle sounds and an exciting musical score by composer Michael Moss enhance [Robin] William's unique rendering of this fabulous tale" (container) of two children who have chanced upon a seemingly harmless board game called Jumanji, A Jungle Adventure Game. Each roll of the dice brings the jungle home to them--a lion on the piano, riotous monkeys in the kitchen, a deadly snake on the mantle. A very original and popular story which appeals to all age levels.
SUBJ: Play--Fiction./ Fantasy.

CE   Ph-1 2-A/5 $17.95   T   KH822
VAN ALLSBURG, CHRIS. Polar express. Houghton Mifflin ISBN 0-395-38949-6, 1985. unp. col. ill.
Caldecott Award.
Selectors' Choice, 16th ed.
Available from National Library Service for the Blind and Physically Handicapped in Braille BR06467 and on sound recording cassette RC23625.
Spanish version EL EXPRESO POLAR (Ekare/dist. by Kane Miller ISBN 980-257-046-X, 1994), $16.95.
After riding through the night on a train to the North Pole, a young boy, selected to choose the first Christmas gift, asks for and receives a bell from the harness of a reindeer. The lyrical prose and richly hued and toned paintings combine to present a powerful story for

reading aloud and as a discussion starter.
SUBJ: North Pole--Fiction./ Santa Claus--Fiction./ Christmas--Fiction./ Spanish language materials.

Ph-2 3-A/3 $17.95   L   KH823
VAN ALLSBURG, CHRIS. Sweetest fig. Houghton Mifflin ISBN 0-395-67346-1, 1993. unp. col. ill.
Spanish version available from Fondo de Cultura Economica HIGO MAS DULCE (ISBN 968-16-4619-3, 1995).
Sepia illustrations with pointillistic detail show the selfish, thoughtless dentist Monsieur Bibot and his long-suffering little dog as the coldhearted dentist receives his just due--the sweet dog his. Given two magical figs by a patient, Bibot's plans are thwarted when Marcel, the pup, eats the second fig and has his dream come true. The finely detailed art will bear much perusal in a commendable book for older readers.
SUBJ: Dreams--Fiction./ Magic--Fiction./ Dogs--Fiction./ Spanish language materials.

Ph-1 4-A/5 $17.95   L   KH824
VAN ALLSBURG, CHRIS. Widow's broom. Houghton Mifflin ISBN 0-395-64051-2, 1992. unp. col. ill.
Selectors' Choice, 19th ed.
Spanish edition available LA ESCOBA DE LA VIUDA (Fondo de Cultura ISBN 968-16-4005-6, 1991).
In a book that can be read on many levels by many ages, the story of a witch's broom found by widow Minna Shaw presents more than meets the casual eye. The exquisite sepia-tone, steel-engraving-like art will bear frequent reexamination. The story can either be a straightforward one of magic or one warning readers about the dangers of witch hunting, censorship, and the like. Van Allsburg's handsome book and multi-layered story is prime for individual perusal and for reading aloud.
SUBJ: Brooms and brushes--Fiction./ Magic--Fiction./ Spanish language materials.

CE   Ph-1 1-5/3 $16.95   T   KH825
VAN ALLSBURG, CHRIS. Wreck of the Zephyr. Houghton Mifflin ISBN 0-395-33075-0, 1983. unp. col. ill.
Selectors' Choice, 14th ed.
Picture available from Peaceable Kingdom Press (18"x24") color poster, $9.95.
Paintings highlighted with textured apricots and lavenders, toned shadows, pointilistic water and night sky dominate this relatively minor story of a wrecked sailboat that lies on a surprisingly high cliff. An old man tells of a boy whose sailboat was wrecked on an island where sailboats can float above waves. Emboldened, the boy dares to fly home above the moonlit clouds but crashes on a cliff. The old man is the boy in this superbly illustrated book more suitable for older readers.
SUBJ: Fantasy./ Sailing--Fiction.

Ph-1 4-A/4 $17.95   L   KH826
VAN ALLSBURG, CHRIS. Wretched stone. Houghton Mifflin ISBN 0-395-53307-4, 1991. unp col illus.
Excerpted from the captain's log of the sailing ship "Rita Anne," Van Allsburg's story with its colorful, imaginative, detailed art tells of a strange, glowing stone that hypnotizes the crew and eventually makes men into mindless, staring apes during a storm at sea. The suspense and the fine art in this allegorical tale may mesmerize readers and open discussion about what the stone represents--if anything.
SUBJ: Sea stories.

Ph-2 5-A/6 $17.00   T   KH827
VANDE VELDE, VIVIAN. Tales from the Brothers Grimm and the Sisters Weird. Illus. by Brad Weinman. Harcourt Brace ISBN 0-15-200220-0; In Canada: Harcourt Brace c/o Canadian Manda, 1995. 128p. ill.
"Jane Yolen books."
For sophisticated readers who know tales from Grimm, the several "fractured" tales herein will provide a humorous--and comparative-- glimpse at parodies of familiar fairy tales. Includes "Red Riding Hood," "Jack and the Beanstalk," and others as well as a few not-very-good poems. Chapter head illustrations give clues to the original stories for those who may need them. Fun. Useful for creative writing classes.
SUBJ: Fairy tales--Parodies, imitations, etc./ Folklore--Parodies, imitations, etc./ Humorous stories.

Ph-2 5-A/5 $14.89   L   KH828
VAN LEEUWEN, JEAN. Bound for Oregon. Illus. by James Watling. Dial ISBN 0-8037-1527-7, 1994. 167p. ill., map.
Narrated in the first person by Mary Ellen Todd, nine, the book, based on her actual diary, depicts the family's trip from Arkansas to

the Oregon Territory in 1852. The six month trek in a covered wagon is full of hardship, disease, hunger, and pleasant and unpleasant interactions with fellow emigrants and Native Americans. Black and white illustrations help summon the overland journey. Sometimes it is difficult to believe that the diction is that of a young girl, but readers will want to follow Mary Ellen and her family to their new home in Oregon. Map and author's source notes included. Historical fiction for units on western settlement.
SUBJ: Todd, Mary Ellen--Fiction./ Oregon Trail--Fiction./ Overland journeys to the Pacific--Fiction.

Ph-2 5-6/6 $2.95 P KH829
VERNE, JULES. 20,000 leagues under the sea. Bantam ISBN 0-553-21252-4, 1980. 384p.
Available from National Library Service for the Blind and Physically Handicapped in Braille BRA09257, on sound recording cassette RC13748, and as talking book TB00594.
A still popular classic which was first published in 1870 in the early days of underwater exploration. Although Verne's vision of a submarine piloted by the mysterious Captain Nemo penetrating the ocean depths might seem not so unusual to today's youngsters, his pursuit of the narwhal and the adventures that ensue are exciting reading.
SUBJ: Sea stories./ Submarine boats--Fiction./ Adventure and adventurers--Fiction.

Ph-2 5-A/4 $12.95 T KH830
VIVELO, JACKIE. Chills run down my spine. Illus. by Jennifer Eachus. DK Publishing ISBN 1-56458-712-6, 1994. 125p. ill.
Gathers nine selections based on traditional ghost stories in an extremely handsome and well-illustrated book. Although not as "chilling" as advertised in the flap copy, there is enough modified terror in the tales to hold readers of the genre. It might be a good choice for reading aloud.
SUBJ: Supernatural--Fiction./ Short stories.

Ph-2 6-A/5 $16.95 L KH831
VOIGT, CYNTHIA. Bad girls. Scholastic ISBN 0-590-60134-2; In Canada: Scholastic, 1996. 277p.
Two fifth grade girls, Mikey and Margalo, are absolutely independent individuals, not the "bad girls" of the title--devious, clever, bright, self-sufficient certainly, but not "bad." They work hard at their friendship, only slightly controlled by their excellent teacher, Mrs. Chemsky. Subtle undertones carry mental action, and readers who are of an independent nature will identify with the girls, and others might, too.
SUBJ: Schools--Fiction./ Friendship--Fiction./ Behavior--Fiction.

Ph-1 5-6/6 $14.95 T KH832
VOIGT, CYNTHIA. Dicey's song. Atheneum ISBN 0-689-30944-9; In Canada: Collier Macmillan, 1982. 196p.
Newbery Award.
Selectors' Choice, 14th ed.
Available from National Library Service for the Blind and Physically Handicapped in Braille BR05473 and on sound recording cassette RC21617.
This fine novel continues the story told in THE HOMECOMING (1981) but can be read independently. Dicey is thirteen and realizing she is not solely responsible for the three younger children, begins to expand her life to embrace other interests. And Gram's real love is becoming evident under her crusty exterior. When Dicey's mentally ill mother dies, the trip north to her bedside brings Dicey and Gram closer and their return to Maryland solidifies their own unique, newly created family.
SUBJ: Brothers and sisters--Fiction./ Family life--Fiction.

Ph-1 6-A/4 $15.95 T KH833
VOIGT, CYNTHIA. Homecoming. Atheneum ISBN 0-689-30833-7; In Canada: Collier Macmillan, 1981. 312p.
Available from National Library Service for the Blind and Physically Handicapped in Braille BR05240 and on sound recording cassette RC19862.
When their mentally ill mother abandons them in a parking lot in Connecticut, thirteen-year-old Dicey is determined to move her sister and brothers on foot down Route 1 to "rich" Aunt Cilla in Bridgeport. But Aunt Cilla has died and Dicey sets out again with the children for an unknown grandmother on the Maryland shore who gives them the home they need. The book is too long but Dicey's ingenuity, courage and persistence give this unusual interest. For the mature reader.
SUBJ: Survival--Fiction./ Family life--Fiction.

Ph-1 5-A/4 $13.95 T KH834
VOS, IDA. Anna is still here. Translated by Terese Edelstein and Inez Smidt. Houghton Mifflin ISBN 0-395-65368-1, 1993. 139p.
After years spent as a "hidden child" protected by strangers from the Nazis, Anna is free. Yet her memories still haunt her, and she remains suspicious of everyone. How she eventually regains hope and trust is a compelling story. Pair with HIDE AND SEEK, Vos' story of Rachel's years in hiding in Holland.
SUBJ: Holocaust survivors--Fiction./ Jews--Netherlands--Fiction./ Netherlands--Fiction.

Ph-2 5-A/4 $13.95 T KH835
VOS, IDA. Hide and seek. Translated by Terese Edelstein and Inez Smidt. Houghton Mifflin ISBN 0-395-56470-0, c1981, 1991. 132p.
Recounts the conditions of hiding from the Nazis through the eyes of Rachel, a young Jewish girl in Holland during World War II. Unlike THE DIARY OF A YOUNG GIRL (Frank), Vos' story, based on her life, details the shocks when the war ended and families learned about those who had been executed during the Holocaust. Told in staccato sentences, a reader can become involved in the lives of the characters in this fictionalized biography that should be of interest to readers of Anne Frank and THE UPSTAIRS ROOM (Reiss).
SUBJ: World War, 1939-1945--Netherlands--Fiction./ World War, 1939-1945--Jews--Rescue--Fiction./ Netherlands--History--German Occupation, 1940-1945--Fiction./ Jews--Netherlands--Fiction.

Ph-1 2-4/4 $13.00 L KH836
WAGGONER, KAREN. Partners. Illus. by Cat Bowman Smith. Simon & Schuster ISBN 0-671-86466-1; In Canada: Distican, 1995. 95p. ill.
"Third-grader Jamie's dream of raising mice as pets is threatened by his sister's ugly cat Caliban, and by his partner and older brother Gordon's notion of selling the baby mice for profit." (CIP) Fortunately, Jamie with the help of a math whiz in his class (a girl) convinces his brother of the economic problems of endless mouse breeding. Characters seem very real, faults and positive attributes are presented in a fair way. For younger children, this might be good for reading aloud.
SUBJ: Mice--Fiction./ Pets--Fiction./ Brothers and sisters--Fiction./ Moneymaking projects--Fiction.

Ph-1 5-A/7 $15.00 T KH837
WALLACE, BARBARA BROOKS. Cousins in the castle. Atheneum ISBN 0-689-80637-X; In Canada: Distican, 1996. 152p.
"Jean Karl book."
Shades of THE LITTLE PRINCESS, SARA CREWE, and other stories of Victorian girls, reportedly orphans, who are in the hands of villains. Amelia, possibly a young orphan, is taken from her comfortable circumstances in England to the United States by her new guardian, Cousin Charlotte, "a stone-cold person," and thereafter made a prisoner in the worst of circumstances in New York. She finds friends, poses as a boy, and eventually is reunited with the good life--and her father and his new bride. The reader with a theatrical bent will find this melodrama well suited for reading aloud.
SUBJ: Adventure and adventurers--Fiction./ Friendship--Fiction./ Orphans--Fiction.

Ph-3 4-6/4 $10.95 L KH838
WALTER, MILDRED PITTS. Have a happy... a novel. Illus. by Carole Byard. Lothrop, Lee & Shepard ISBN 0-688-06923-1, 1989. 106p. ill.
Intermixes the story of Chris's Christmas birthday with the history of the African-American celebration of Kwanzaa and problems at home caused by the father's unemployed state. Although characterization is weak, and didactic elements tend to overwhelm the story line, nonetheless, the information about Kwanzaa and its customs exist in no other fiction for this age group. The book will be useful and serve as a guide to the holiday. For multicultural studies.
SUBJ: Kwanzaa--Fiction./ Afro-Americans--Fiction./ Birthdays--Fiction./ Christmas--Fiction./ Artists--Fiction./ Family life--Fiction.

Ph-1 4-6/6 $13.00 L KH839
WALTER, MILDRED PITTS. Justin and the best biscuits in the world. Illus. by Catherine Stock. Lothrop, Lee & Shepard ISBN 0-688-06645-3, 1986. 122p. ill.
Coretta Scott King Award.
Available from National Library Service for the Blind and Physically Handicapped on sound recording cassette RC26053.
"Suffering in a family full of females, ten-year-old Justin feels that cleaning and keeping house are 'women's work' until he spends some time on his grandfather's ranch" (CIP) and discovers Grandpa also does "women's work." Strong characterization and warm family situations are nicely interwoven with touches of African-American history. The large print format will attract reluctant readers. For multicultural studies.
SUBJ: Sex role--Fiction./ Grandfathers--Fiction./ Ranch life--Fiction./ Family life--Fiction./ Afro-Americans--Fiction.

Ph-1 4-6/3 $13.00   T   KH840
WARNER, SALLY. Dog years. Knopf ISBN 0-679-87147-0; In Canada: Random House, 1995. 153p. ill.
"Borzoi book."
"After his father is imprisoned, twelve-year-old Case switches to a new school, where he makes some important discoveries about friendship and honesty." (CIP) Case's confusion about acting in a wrong way, something he knows is not right, is very human. Enhanced by Case's cartoons about school, the story explores his painful moral dilemma, his feelings about his own selfish father, and the positive support he receives from many people around him, adults and children. Except for the antagonist, popular Tyler--the very stereotype of an indulged, ambitious, and amoral rich boy--characters act, walk, and talk like average youngsters. Good discussion starter about ethics.
SUBJ: Friendship--Fiction./ Schools--Fiction./ Honesty--Fiction./ Prisoners--Fiction.

Ph-1   A/4 $17.00   L   KH841
WATKINS, YOKO KAWASHIMA. My brother, my sister, and I. Bradbury ISBN 0-02-792526-9; In Canada: Maxwell Macmillan, 1994. 275p.
Sequel to SO FAR FROM THE BAMBOO GROVE, Lothrop, Lee & Shepard, 1986.
Available from the National Library Service for the Blind and Physically Handicapped on sound recording cassette RC 40136. Having survived the horrors of World War II in Korea, Yoko and her siblings struggle as refugees in Japan. Their desperate search for their father intensifies when Ko is falsely accused of arson. Based on the author's life, the intensely personal historical fiction captures their despair as well as their strong family bonds. For multicultural studies.
SUBJ: World War, 1939-1945--Refugees--Fiction./ Japan--Fiction./ Refugees--Fiction./ Watkins, Yoko Kawashima--Fiction.

Ph-1 5-A/5 $4.95   P   KH842
WATKINS, YOKO KAWASHIMA. So far from the bamboo grove. Morrow ISBN 0-688-13115-8, c1986, 1994. 183p. map.
Based on the life of the author, the fictionalized autobiography tells in suspenseful detail the events in the life of Yoko, eleven, her mother, and her sister during their flight from Korea to Japan after World War II. Readers will experience sympathy and empathy with the family. Moving historical fiction which shows a little know aspect of World War II in a very human way. For multicultural studies.
SUBJ: Watkins, Yoko Kawashima--Fiction./ Korea--Fiction./ Japan--Fiction./ World War, 1939-1945--Fiction.

Ph-1 5-A/7 $14.00   L   KH843
WAUGH, SYLVIA. Mennyms. Greenwillow ISBN 0-688-13070-4, 1994. 213p.
Selectors' Choice, 20th ed.
"The Mennyms, a family of life-size rag dolls living in a house in England and pretending to be human, see their peaceful existence threatened when the house's owner announces he is coming from Australia for a visit." (CIP) The extended family, although dolls, are so human that this fantasy could almost be a realistic novel. The author carefully builds up character, situation, actions and settings, detail by detail in short, rapidly paced chapters just perfect for reading aloud. The endless round of unvarying activities from decade to decade finally affects the teenager, and it is she, characterized as an adolescent straining at the rein, who causes familial concerns and the family to change.
SUBJ: Dolls--Fiction./ Family life--England--Fiction./ England--Fiction.

Ph-1 5-A/5 $16.00   L   KH844
WAUGH, SYLVIA. Mennyms alone. Greenwillow ISBN 0-688-14702-X, 1996. 192p.
Sequel to: MENNYMS UNDER SIEGE, Greenwillow, 1996.
Sir Magnus, grandsire of the Mennym clan, is pesky, obdurate, and tyrannical, and he now has the feeling that the life-size living rag dolls will meet their deaths within the year. Suspense builds and builds as readers who have come to know the family wonder if they are on the verge of death. When their house is inherited by Kate Penshaw's family, great discoveries take place. The series continues to be well developed and intriguing although it is sometimes difficult to sort out the relationships of the humans. Try reading aloud.
SUBJ: Dolls--Fiction./ Family life--England--Fiction./ England--Fiction.

Ph-1 5-A/5 $15.00   L   KH845
WAUGH, SYLVIA. Mennyms in the wilderness. Greenwillow ISBN 0-688-13820-9, 1995. 255p.
Sequel to MENNYMS, Greenwillow, 1994.
When the family of rag dolls must move, they set up housekeeping in the country. Albert Pond, their landlord, meets and helps them so much that he is integrated into their lives. Resettling, re-establishing their safety, and protecting themselves from outsiders provide

suspense and deeper understanding of the characters met in the first story. Once again, the author has created memorable situations and characters in a strong book which is excellent for reading aloud.
SUBJ: Dolls--Fiction./ Family life--England--Fiction./ England--Fiction.

Ph-1 6-A/6 $16.00   L   KH846
WAUGH, SYLVIA. Mennyms under siege. Greenwillow ISBN 0-688-14372-5, 1996. 220p.
Sequel to MENNYMS IN THE WILDERNESS, Greenwillow, 1995. Mennym readers will welcome the third adventure about the rag dolls brought to life by magic some years ago. Now, because of a snoopy neighbor and Appleby's and Pilbeam's desires to be out of the house and in the world, real trouble falls on the family, including the death of one of the characters. Sir Magnus is more of a dictator, and unhappy events, except the death, are eventually solved. However, a fourth volume is expected, so readers will see if the loss of a family member is permanent.
SUBJ: Dolls--Fiction./ Family life--England--Fiction./ England--Fiction.

Ph-2 6-A/6 $15.00   T   KH847
WESTALL, ROBERT. Christmas spirit: two stories. Illus. by John Lawrence. Farrar, Straus and Giroux ISBN 0-374-31260-5, 1994. 150p. ill.
Presents two lengthy short stories set during the Christmas season, although the holiday is not essential to either. In the first, a ghostly apparition saves a boy and the entire work force of his father's factory from injury and death. In the second, a girl relates a time when she was sent to stay with her uncle, the local vicar. She has a miserable experience but meets with some street children and changes the course of their lives, her uncle's, and her own. For reading aloud.
SUBJ: Christmas--Fiction./ Short stories.

Ph-2 2-4/5 $3.99   P   KH848
WHELAN, GLORIA. Next spring an oriole. Illus. by Pamela Johnson. Random House ISBN 0-394-89125-2; In Canada: Random House, 1987. 60p. ill. (Stepping stone book).
Leaving Virginia behind in 1837, ten-year-old Libby and her parents travel by covered wagon to Michigan where they plan to live amid trees and wildlife. On the way, they help a young Native American girl with measles, meet the La Belle family, and learn the importance of interdependence when faced with a long winter. Transitional reader useful for social studies classes studying pioneer life and emigration.
SUBJ: Frontier and pioneer life--Michigan--Fiction./ Michigan--Fiction./ Indians of North America--Fiction.

Ph-2 4-6/5 $15.00   T   KH849
WHITCHER, SUSAN. Real mummies don't bleed: friendly tales for October nights. Illus. by Andrew Glass. Farrar Straus Giroux ISBN 0-374-36213-0; In Canada: HarperCollins, 1993. 119p. ill.
Five scary stories, each with a different twist, are just right to use for reading aloud--especially on Halloween.
SUBJ: Horror stories./ Short stories.

Ph-1 3-6/6 $11.89   L   KH850
WHITE, E. B. Charlotte's web. Illus. by Garth Williams. HarperCollins ISBN 0-06-026386-5, c1952. 184p. ill.
Newbery Honor Book.
Available from National Library Service for the Blind and Physically Handicapped in Braille BR01318, on sound recording cassette RC07107, and as talking book TB04061.
Also available in Latin TELA CHARLOTTAE (ISBN 0-06-026401-2, 1991, $18.95).
The life of Wilbur, the pig, is saved by a girl who talks to animals and a spider who weaves strange messages.
SUBJ: Pigs--Fiction./ Spiders--Fiction./ Latin language materials./ Fantasy./ Animals--Fiction.

Ph-1 3-6/5 $11.89   L   KH851
WHITE, E. B. Stuart Little. Illus. by Garth Williams. HarperCollins ISBN 0-06-026396-2, c1945. 131p. ill.
Available from National Library Service for the Blind and Physically Handicapped in Braille BR01319 and as talking book TB04487.
Spanish version STUART LITTLE available from Santillana (ISBN 84-204-46696, n.d.).
Into a normal American family there is born a second son, Stuart, whom everyone notices is not much bigger than a mouse. And since he is indeed a mouse, the story of Stuart Little and his adventures are humorous and unusual.
SUBJ: Mice--Fiction./ New York (N.Y.)--Fiction./ Spanish language materials.

Ph-2 3-6/6 $11.89   L   KH852
WHITE, E. B. Trumpet of the swan. Illus. by Edward Frascino. HarperCollins ISBN 0-06-026398-9, c1970. 210p. ill, music.

Laura Ingalls Wilder Award.
Available from National Library Service for the Blind and Physically Handicapped in Braille BRA03553, on sound recording cassette RC23892, as talking book TB04014.
Louis is the one mute cygnet born on the cold Canadian lake to the two great swans. He could not trumpet to attract the love of Serena, the lady of his choice. This tale of a quest, as the cygnet works to pay off his father's debt, is another fine tale--"a paean to courage, to freedom, to love"--by the winner of the Laura Ingalls Wilder Award.
SUBJ: Swans--Fiction.

Ph-1 6-A/6 $16.00 T KH853
WHITE, RUTH. Belle Prater's boy. Farrar Straus Giroux ISBN 0-374-30668-0; In Canada: HarperCollins, 1996. 196p.
Newbery Honor book, 1997.
"Around 5:00 a.m. on a warm Sunday morning in October 1953, my Aunt Belle left her bed and vanished from the face of the earth." (p.3) From that statement unrolls the mystery of where Aunt Belle went and why she left behind her son Woodrow and her husband. Gypsy, twelve, tries to uncover why and how Belle disappeared. When Woodrow, a marvelously conceived character, moves next door, she begins to learn. Better readers will find this well written novel intriguing.
SUBJ: Cousins--Fiction./ Mother and child--Fiction./ Loss (Psychology)--Fiction./ Identity--Fiction.

Ph-2 6/7 $16.00 T KH854
WHITE, RUTH. Sweet Creek Holler. Farrar, Straus & Giroux ISBN 0-374-37360-4; In Canada: HarperCollins, 1988. 215p.
Moving to Sweet Creek Holler in the coal-mining area of Virginia's Appalachian Mountains in 1948, six-year-old Virginia Carol Shortt finds much to observe about small town life. Insights gained are both bitter and sweet as Ginny grows over a six year period, gaining a sense of community and learning how gossip can destroy lives. Well drawn characters and setting will attract mature readers, despite the ending.
SUBJ: Coal mines and mining--Fiction./ Family life--Fiction./ Gossip--Fiction.

Ph-2 5-6/7 $3.95 P KH855
WIBBERLEY, LEONARD. John Treegate's musket. Farrar, Straus & Giroux ISBN 0-374-43788-2; In Canada: HarperCollins, c1959, 1986. 191p.
Originally a royalist, John Treegate finds himself becoming committed to the colonists' view and with his son fights against the British at Bunker Hill. Detail and strong characterization are two of the plusses in this portrayal of one "struggle for liberty, personal and national" and its effect on one family. An excellent resource for studies of the period.
SUBJ: United States--History--Colonial period, ca. 1600-1775--Fiction./ United States--History--Revolution, 1775-1783--Fiction.

Ph-2 4-6/5 $14.95 T KH856
WIELER, DIANA J. To the mountains by morning. By Diana Wieler. Illus. by Ange Zhang. Groundwood/dist. by Publishers Group West ISBN 0-88899-227-0; In Canada: Groundwood/Douglas & McIntyre, 1996. unp. col. ill.
An engaging horse story is told in the third person largely through events in the eyes of Old Bailey, a ten-year-old chestnut quarter horse who lives in a rental stable. When she realizes she must escape to avoid the dog meat factory, she and a young stallion jump the high fences and find freedom. Illustrated in active colored acrylics. Horse lovers will empathize with the equine characters and their unhappy but ultimately triumphant situation.
SUBJ: Horses--Fiction./ Freedom--Fiction.

Ph-2 5-A/6 $17.00 T KH857
WIGGIN, KATE DOUGLAS. Rebecca of Sunnybrook Farm. Afterword by Peter Glassman. Illus. by Helen Mason Grose. Morrow ISBN 0-688-13481-5, 1994. 291p. ill. (some col.). (Books of wonder.)
This facsimile of the classic novel, first published in 1903, is the edition of choice. Modern readers should realize that some of Rebecca's and other characters' ideas about people in other countries are based on some common conceptions of the late nineteenth century. Best for readers of ANNE OF GREEN GABLES, LITTLE WOMEN, etc., i.e., "old-fashioned" stories. For very strong readers.
SUBJ: Aunts--Fiction./ New England--Fiction./ Girls--Fiction.

Ph-1 4-A/4 $14.99 L KH858
WILD, MARGARET. Let the celebrations begin! Illus. by Julie Vivas. Orchard ISBN 0-531-08537-6, 1991. unp. col. ill.
Selectors' Choice, 19th ed.
"Based on a reference to a small collection of stuffed toys made by

Polish women in Belsen for the first children's party held after the liberation..." (jacket), the text and art in this remarkable book speak to readers of a time in recent history when the essential decency of human beings rose above the long night of Nazi concentration camps. Adults gave the little they had to make toys for the child prisoners who had never known either a toy or childhood. Vivas' multi-colored illustrations show individuality returning to the faces of those made faceless by Nazi methods. Truly a celebratory book, it will bring tears to the eyes while lifting the heart.
SUBJ: Concentration camps--Fiction./ Jews--Fiction.

Ph-1 3-6/5 $14.89 L KH859
WILDER, LAURA INGALLS. Farmer boy. Newly illustrated, uniform ed. Illus. by Garth Williams. HarperCollins ISBN 0-06-026421-7, c1953. 371p. ill.
Sequel to: LITTLE HOUSE ON THE PRAIRIE.
Available from National Library Service for the Blind and Physically Handicapped in Braille BR04262, on sound recording cassette RC21019, as talking book TB03302.
As Laura and Mary Ingalls leave the woods of Wisconsin and find new adventures waiting on the Kansas Prairie, Almanzo Wilder is growing up on his father's farm in northern New York. The days are busy for the nine-year-old boy as he is expected to help with the sowing and harvesting of crops, the care of animals and the numerous tasks involved in the management of the farm home and grounds.
SUBJ: Country life--Fiction./ New York (State)--Fiction./ Boys--Fiction.

Ph-1 3-6/4 $14.89 L KH860
WILDER, LAURA INGALLS. Little house in the Big Woods. Illus. by Garth Williams. HarperCollins ISBN 0-06-026431-4, c1953. 237p. ill.
Newbery Honor Books: ON THE BANKS OF PLUM CREEK, BY THE SHORES OF SILVER LAKE, THE LONG WINTER, LITTLE TOWN ON THE PRAIRIE, THESE HAPPY GOLDEN YEARS.
Available from National Library Service for the Blind and Physically Handicapped in Braille BR04442, on a sound recording cassette RC13972, as talking book TB03591.
Available in large print from Windrush/dist. by Cornerstone (ISBN 1-85089-913-4), $14.95.
The first of the nine stories which narrate the life of the author and her family. In this one, Laura lives in a small house in Wisconsin in 1870 after their move from New York State. LITTLE HOUSE ON THE PRAIRIE (ISBN 0-06-026446-2, 1953) follows their move further west as they build a new house in Kansas. ON THE BANKS OF PLUM CREEK (ISBN 0-06-026471-3, 1953) describes their life in a dugout in Minnesota. In BY THE SHORES OF SILVER LAKE (ISBN 0-06-026417-9, 1953) the family moves again to Dakota Territory where they nearly starve and experience extreme cold, also described in THE LONG WINTER (ISBN 0-06-026461-6, 1953). In LITTLE TOWN ON THE PRAIRIE (ISBN 0-06-026451-9, 1953) Laura gets a job and finds a boy friend and quiet Mary is stricken with blindness after an attack of scarlet fever. Finally, in THESE HAPPY GOLDEN YEARS (ISBN 0-06-026481-0, 1953) and THE FIRST FOUR YEARS (ISBN 0-06-026427-6, 1953) Laura and Almanzo start their family together. Also available from NLSBPH are: LITTLE HOUSE ON THE PRAIRIE in Braille BR04237, as talking book TB03592; ON THE BANKS OF PLUM CREEK in Braille BR04261, on sound recording cassette RC21196, as talking book TB01619; BY THE SHORES OF SILVER LAKE in Braille BR04444, as talking book TB03301, on sound recording cassette RC21197; THE LONG WINTER in Braille BR04445, on sound recording cassette RC21198, as talking book TB03304; LITTLE TOWN ON THE PRAIRIE on sound recording cassette RC21199, as talking book TB00591; THOSE HAPPY GOLDEN YEARS in Braille BR04443, on sound recording cassette RC21200, as talking book TB03251; FIRST FOUR YEARS in Braille BRA04837, on sound recording cassette RC21351, as talking book TB03989.
SUBJ: Frontier and pioneer life--Fiction./ Blind--Fiction./ Family life--Fiction./ Girls--Fiction.

Ph-2 4-6/5 $14.89 L KH861
WILKES, MARIA D. Little house in Brookfield. Illus. by Dan Andreasen. HarperCollins ISBN 0-06-026462-4; In Canada: HarperCollins, 1996. 298p. ill. (Little House: the Brookfield years.)
Although overly long, the fictionalized story about Laura Ingalls Wilder's mother, Caroline, provides background about the people of the "Little House" books. Caroline's childhood in the frontier town of Brookfield, Wisconsin, in 1845 serves as a prequel to MacBride's Rocky Ridge years series. Historical fiction for units on frontier and pioneer life.
In LITTLE TOWN AT THE CROSSROADS (ISBN 0-06-026995-2, 1997) the bustling town of Brookfield is growing, and so is six-year-old Caroline, who experiences her first parade and circus.
SUBJ: Ingalls, Caroline Lake Quiner--Fiction./ Wilder, Laura Ingalls--Family--Fiction./ Wisconsin--Fiction./ Frontier and pioneer life--Wisconsin--Fiction./ Family life--Wisconsin--Fiction.

Ph-1 4-A/6 $19.95 T KH862

WILLARD, NANCY. Beauty and the Beast. Wood engravings by Barry Moser. Harcourt Brace Jovanovich ISBN 0-15-206052-9; In Canada: Harcourt Brace c/o Canadian Manda, 1992. 69p. ill.

Showing that old folktales can transcend time, this retelling of Beauty remains true to the classic story, but is set in New York at the turn of the century. Thus, Moser's typically dark wood engravings help set the scene in both time and place, and the costuming of the characters reflects that era. Moser's beast is shown only once in full face, but the description in the text carries the idea of beastliness more deeply. A generous book, this retelling maintains the tension and mystery of the original.
SUBJ: Fairy tales./ New York (N.Y.)--Fiction.

Ph-2 3-5/6 $5.95 P KH863

WILLARD, NANCY. Sailing to Cythera, and other Anatole stories. Illus. by David McPhail. Harcourt Brace Jovanovich ISBN 0-15-269961-9, 1974. 72p. ill.

Three stories tell about the magic adventures which occur to Anatole. In spite of the fact that he appears to be an ordinary little boy, his daily experiences are extraordinary. A visit on a railroad to a town where it never grows dark; running on the air to Norway; and sailing through the wallpaper to encounter the fearful Blimlin. Needs introduction; recommended for reading aloud.
ISLAND OF THE GRASS KING (ISBN 0-15-239083-9, 1979) and UNCLE TERRIBLE (ISBN 0-15-292793-X, 1982, OPC) provide further magical adventures.
SUBJ: Short stories./ Fantasy.

CE   Ph-1 3-5/6 $9.95 T KH864

WILLIAMS, MARGERY. Velveteen Rabbit; or, How toys become real. Illus. by William Nicholson. Doubleday ISBN 0-385-07725-4, 1988. 44p. col. ill.

Talking book narrated by Eva le Gallienne available from SRA/ McGraw-Hill 87-507573, c1975. $15.00.
Available from National Library Services for the Blind and Physically Handicapped in Braille BRA10391, on sound recording cassette RC24614, as talking book TB03990.
A toy rabbit longs to be real but was told this would only happen through the boy's love. When the boy has scarlet fever and his toys must be destroyed, the toy rabbit gets his wish.
SUBJ: Fairy tales./ Rabbits--Fiction./ Toys--Fiction.

Ph-2 4-A/4 $14.93 L KH865

WILLIAMS, VERA B. Scooter. Greenwillow ISBN 0-688-09377-9, 1993. 150p. ill.

Available from the National Library Service for the Blind and Physically Handicapped on sound recording cassette RC 40036.
Readers of Ruth Sawyer's ROLLER SKATES will appreciate this adventure about a girl who scoots around her neighborhood in the city the summer of her parents' divorce. The people she meets and the events in which she participates help her adjust to her new family situation. Dynamically styled illustrations fit the quirky first-person text perfectly. The voice of the child comes across as something new and original, and the art illuminates the experience. It may take book talking or reading aloud to promote it, but the depth of these events and characters will make it worthwhile.
SUBJ: Scooters--Fiction./ Moving, Household--Fiction./ Divorce-- Fiction./ Friendship--Fiction./ Mothers and daughters--Fiction.

Ph-1 4-A/4 $13.89 L KH866

WILLIS, MEREDITH SUE. Secret super powers of Marco. HarperCollins ISBN 0-06-023559-4; In Canada: HarperCollins, 1994. 104p.

Available from the National Library Service for the Blind and Physically Handicapped on sound recording cassette RC 40024.
Reading the first chapters about fourth grader Marco and his obviously disturbed hyperenergetic classmate, Tyrone, a reader may wonder if it is a wise practice to place children with disabilities in the "mainstream." However, as the book develops and the characters reveal more about the conditions and the people on the mean streets of an inner city, the cast of characters leave their stereotypes behind and become very human individuals. Fine discussion starter.
SUBJ: Learning disabilities--Fiction./ City and town life--Fiction./ Friendship--Fiction./ Self-confidence--Fiction.

Ph-2 2-3/2 $14.95 L KH867

WILLNER-PARDO, GINA. When Jane-Marie told my secret. Illus. by Nancy Poydar. Clarion ISBN 0-395-66382-2, 1995. 39p. col. ill.

When best friend Jane-Marie tells Carolyn's secret, their friendship ends and each finds new companions. In the end, all is well when Jane-Marie realizes the importance of secrets and promises. The transitional reader about the ups and downs of friendships will make a good discussion starter.
SUBJ: Secrets--Fiction./ Friendship--Fiction.

Ph-1 4-6/5 $14.95 L KH868

WILSON, JACQUELINE. Elsa, star of the shelter! Illus. by Nick Sharratt. Whitman ISBN 0-8075-1981-2; In Canada: General, 1996. 208p. ill.

Originally published as: THE BED AND BREAKFAST STAR, Doubleday, 1994.
"Noisy, brash, and a troublemaker, ten-year-old Elsa uses her loud voice to warn of a fire at the homeless shelter where she lives with her family." (CIP) The exuberant child is not a troublemaker, only a girl with too much enthusiasm for life. She is helpful to her mother and the two younger children, but she has no place to work off her energy in the crowded one room in a run-down hotel in which five people live. Briticisms are explained in footnotes, but Elsa's conversational tone and the Brit slang give the book a lively aural quality. Black and white cartoon-like sketches are humorous and lively--as is the book.
SUBJ: Homeless persons--Fiction./ Family life--Fiction.

CE   Ph-1 4-6/5 $15.95 L KH869

WINTHROP, ELIZABETH. Castle in the attic. Holiday House ISBN 0-8234-0579-6, 1985. 179p.

Selectors' Choice, 16th ed.
Talking book available from Listening Library YA904 CX (ISBN 0-8072-7628-6, 1996). 2 sound cassettes (210min), $16.98. ALA notable recording, 1997.
Receiving a model of a medieval castle as a farewell gift does not compensate ten-year-old William for the loss of his beloved babysitter Mrs. Phillips. He discovers the castle is indeed magic and as he becomes part of the magic, William discovers his own inner strength and courage in this well-written fantasy with an exciting plot and a surprise ending. It should prove to be popular reading with fans of the genre.
And in BATTLE FOR THE CASTLE (ISBN 0-8234-1010-2, 1993, available from the NLSBPH on sound recording cassette RC 39157, talking book available from Listening Library YA919 ISBN 0-8072-7793-2, 1997 on 3 sound cassettes) those who ventured into the castle in the attic with William will want to join the now twelve-year-old squire as he re-enters Sir Simon's medieval world.
SUBJ: Castles--Fiction./ Knights and knighthood--Fiction./ Fantasy.

Ph-2 5-A/6 $13.99 T KH870

WISLER, G. CLIFTON. Jericho's journey. Lodestar/Dutton ISBN 0-525-67428-4; In Canada: McClelland & Stewart, 1993. 137p.

Available from the National Library Service for the Blind and Physically Handicapped on sound recording cassette RC 38794.
Re-creates the 1852 journey of Jericho Wetherby and his family from Tennessee to Texas. Weather, lack of roads, and many other hardships accompany the group from start to finish. Each family member comes across as an individual in historical fiction based on an actual journey. Unfortunately, no map is provided to follow the journey.
SUBJ: Frontier and pioneer life--Fiction./ Brothers and sisters--Fiction./ Size--Fiction.

Ph-2 5-A/4 $14.99 T KH871

WISLER, G. CLIFTON. Mr. Lincoln's drummer. Lodestar/Dutton ISBN 0-525-67463-2; In Canada: McClelland & Stewart, 1995. 131p.

Signing on as a drummer in the Third Vermont Volunteers during the Civil War, eleven-year-old Willie Johnston experiences the boredom of sitting around waiting and the horrors of several battles. After he is wounded, he works in a military hospital and, to his surprise, is awarded the Congressional Medal of Honor by President Lincoln for not deserting his drum during a retreat. Based on the true story of the youngest recipient of the Medal of Honor, the lively historical fiction will hold readers and teach them a good deal. A map would have been useful.
SUBJ: Johnston, William J.--Fiction./ United States--History--Civil War, 1861-1865--Fiction.

Ph-2 5-A/6 $14.99 T KH872

WISLER, G. CLIFTON. Mustang Flats. Lodestar/Dutton ISBN 0-525-67544-2; In Canada: McClelland & Stewart, 1997. 116p.

"When his father returns from the war in 1865, fourteen-year-old Alby finds his beloved Pa a changed man and can only hope that they will be friends again." (CIP) Told in the first person by Alby (Albert Draper), the novel depicts the nightmarish conditions about Civil War battles and the condition of civilians in Northern Texas. Alby, who has been the "man of the family" for four years, relates the times and hardships during the war and the stranger who his father has become. The gradual reestablishment of a father-son relationship is at the heart of this fast paced historical fiction. Good for reading aloud, the action will hold adventure story readers, especially the details of catching and taming wild mustang horses.
SUBJ: Fathers and sons--Fiction./ Family life--Fiction./ United States--History--Civil War, 1861-1865--Fiction.

FICTION

Ph-1 5-A/7 $3.99 P KH873
WISLER, G. CLIFTON. Red Cap. Penguin ISBN 0-14-036936-8, 1994. 160p.

Available from the National Library Service for the Blind and Physically Handicapped on sound recording cassette RC 36220. Based on events in the life of a young Yankee drummer boy who joins a Union Army regiment in 1862, the story of Ransom Powell develops as he learns the ropes in the army, goes to battle, and is eventually made a Confederate prisoner, first in Libby Prison and then in the notorious Andersonville. Ransom, nicknamed Red Cap, lives through his prison experiences because of the kindness and compassion of both Confederate and Union soldiers. Although the first third of the novel tends to be slow, it picks up as the actual war and prison experiences enter the story. Excellent historical fiction for units on the Civil War, it may need book talking or reading aloud to help readers beyond the dull beginning.
SUBJ: Powell, Ransom J.--Fiction./ United States--History--Civil War, 1861-1865--Prisoners and prisons--Fiction./ Andersonville Prison--Fiction.

Ph-2 5-A/6 $14.89 L KH874
WITHIN REACH: TEN STORIES. Edited by Donald R. Gallo. HarperCollins ISBN 0-06-021441-4; In Canada: HarperCollins, 1993. 179p.

Collects ten stories about active young people, all of whom experience adventure, challenge, or self-doubt. Wise selection of stories with different moods provides variety for middle grade readers.
SUBJ: Short stories.

CE Ph-1 5-6/6 $13.95 L KH875
WOJCIECHOWSKA, MAIA. Shadow of a bull. Illus. by Alvin Smith. Atheneum ISBN 0-689-30042-5, 1964. 165p. ill.
"Glossary of bullfighting terms:" p157-65.
Newbery Medal Award.
Available from National Library Service for the Blind and Physically Handicapped on sound recording cassette RC23786 and as talking book TB00863.
Manolo is expected to fight the bull like his father, a great toreador, but is tormented by his fear of bulls and the probable betrayal of his father's memory.
SUBJ: Bullfights--Fiction./ Spain--Fiction.

Ph-2 4-6/5 $15.95 T KH876
WOJCIECHOWSKI, SUSAN. Christmas miracle of Jonathan Toomey. Illustrated by P. J. Lynch. Candlewick ISBN 1-56402-320-6; In Canada: Candlewick/dist. by Douglas & McIntyre, 1995. unp. col. ill.
Shining watercolor illustrations combine with a tender story about a misanthropic woodcarver, who changes to a more kindly person thanks to the patience and giving natures of the widow McDowell and her young son. They ask him to carve the figures for a creche to replace those they have lost. As seven-year-old Thomas tells the carver what expressions the figures need to have, the hard-hearted man slowly softens. The story will be good for reading aloud and has potential as a play for the holiday season.
SUBJ: Wood-carving--Fiction./ Christmas--Fiction./ Friendship--Fiction.

Ph-2 2-3/5 $14.95 T KH877
WOJCIECHOWSKI, SUSAN. Don't call me Beanhead! Illus. by Susanna Natti. Candlewick ISBN 1-56402-319-2; In Canada: Douglas & McIntyre, 1994. 75p. ill.
Five episodes in the life of Beany, mostly at school with her bossy friend, show her in the midst of her sensible, supportive, and loving family. Good choice for newly established readers.
SUBJ: Family life--Fiction./ Conduct of life--Fiction./ Schools--Fiction.

Ph-3 4-6/6 $3.45 P KH878
WOLITZER, HILMA. Toby lived here. Farrar, Straus & Giroux ISBN 0-374-47924-0, c1978, 1986. 147p.
When their newly widowed young mother has a nervous breakdown, Toby and her younger sister are sent to a foster home. Twelve-year-old Toby is terrified, haunted by visions of her mother as similar to Mr. Rochester's wife in "Jane Eyre", and also bitterly ashamed. The foster parents, calm and experienced, provide security until mother can care for them again. A competent and compassionate view of the effect of mental illness on young children.
SUBJ: Foster home care--Fiction./ Single-parent family--Fiction.

CE Ph-3 3-5/3 $17.95 T KH879
WOOD, DOUGLAS. Old Turtle. Illus. by Cheng-Khee Chee. Pfeifer-Hamilton ISBN 0-938586-48-3, 1992. unp. col. ill.
Talking book available (ISBN 1-57025-083-9, 1995). 1 sound cassette (37min), $11.95. ALA notable recording, 1997.
Haunting telling of how the animals felt about the coming of people into their world. They sensed that the beauty of the earth would be defiled and abused until the people realized that God was in everything and everything was to be loved and respected. A contemporary fable to be used for environmental studies.
SUBJ: God--Fiction./ Nature--Fiction./ Man--Influence on nature--Fiction./ Peace--Fiction./ Fables.

Ph-1 4-6/6 $14.99 L KH880
WOODRUFF, ELVIRA. Dear Levi: letters from the Overland Trail. Illus. by Beth Peck. Knopf ISBN 0-679-94641-1; In Canada: Random House, 1994. 121p. ill., map.
Includes bibliography.
"Twelve-year-old Austin Ives writes letters to his younger brother describing his three-thousand-mile journey from their home in Pennsylvania to Oregon in 1851." (CIP) Based on original diaries of those who braved the long trail, the book recreates the hardships--and occasional pleasures--of the long journey and features good people and bad. The latter are especially dominant in relations with native populations. This historical fiction work is at once interesting and instructive and will be useful for units on United States history dealing with westward expansion.
SUBJ: Overland journeys to the Pacific--Fiction./ Frontier and pioneer life--Fiction./ Letters--Fiction.

Ph-2 5-A/5 $14.95 T KH881
WOODRUFF, ELVIRA. Orphan of Ellis Island: a time-travel adventure. Scholastic ISBN 0-590-48245-9; In Canada: Scholastic, 1997. 124p. map.
Includes glossary and bibliography.
"During a school trip to Ellis Island, Dominic Cantori, a ten-year-old foster child, travels back in time to 1908 Italy and accompanies two young emigrants to America." (CIP) Concentrating on the very hard life of Italian peasants and the near-starvation conditions under which they lived, Dominic's time-space travel to the past is immediate and should be of interest, especially in units about United States immigration. Print in sepia tones adds to the atmosphere, and time travel readers will find a holding book peopled with believable characters.
SUBJ: Ellis Island Immigration Station (New York, N.Y.)--Fiction./ Emigration and immigration--Fiction./ Italian Americans--Fiction./ Time travel--Fiction./ Foster home care--Fiction.

Ph-2 4-6/5 $14.95 L KH882
WRIGHT, BETTY REN. Dollhouse murders. Holiday House ISBN 0-8234-0497-8, 1983. 149p.
Available from National Library Service for the Blind and Physically Handicapped on sound recording cassette RC24318.
Invited by her aunt to visit her in the house owned by her great-grandparents, Amy, and later her retarded sister Louann, discovers a dollhouse that is a replica of this house and contains dollhouse figures that not only move but actually tell the story of an old murder and reveal the true murderer. This is a competent, well-written, undemanding mystery and will appeal to fans of the genre.
SUBJ: Dollhouses--Fiction./ Dolls--Fiction./ Mystery and detective stories.

Ph-1 5-A/6 $13.95 L KH883
WRIGHT, BETTY REN. Ghost in the house. Scholastic ISBN 0-590-43606-6; In Canada: Scholastic, 1991. 164p.
Sarah is alone in the house with her bedridden Great-Aunt Margaret when increasingly frightening and dangerous events are caused by a malevolent ghost who blames Margaret for the death of his daughter. The tension and fear is well developed and will hold readers who are fond of hauntings. Could be used for reading aloud.
SUBJ: Ghosts--Fiction./ Great-aunts--Fiction.

Ph-3 3-5/4 $15.95 T KH884
WU, PRISCILLA. Abacus contest: stories from Taiwan and China. Illus. by Xiano-jun Li. Fulcrum Kids ISBN 1-55591-243-5, 1996. 55p. ill. (World stories).
Includes glossary.
"In a small city in southern Taiwan, six children with a traditional background experience different changes in their outlook." (CIP) The seven stories, the "result of several visits to (the author's) husband's home in Chiai" (p. vii) give a picture of life and behavior of several children. Each tale tends towards the didactic and moral, but they will serve well for use in multicultural studies, even if the flat writing does not inspire.
SUBJ: Taiwan--Fiction./ Family life--Taiwan--Fiction.

Ph-1 6-A/3 $15.99 L KH885
WYNNE-JONES, TIM. Book of changes: stories. Orchard ISBN 0-531-08789-1; In Canada: Douglas & McIntyre, 1995. 143p.
"Melanie Kroupa book."
Available from the National Library Service for the Blind and

Physically Handicapped on sound recording cassette RC 42768. Better readers will appreciate the finely wrought nature of the seven quirky, original, offbeat stories about quirky, original, and offbeat happenings and characters. Each deserves thought while reading and after reading; each is like an interesting puzzle in which readers must pay attention to the clues to thread their way through a maze. Tightly written, but with much within, the stories are like no others, but they certainly can serve as models in creative writing classes for aspiring writers--and quirky, original, and offbeat human beings.
SUBJ: Short stories.

Ph-1 5-A/5 $14.99 L KH886
WYNNE-JONES, TIM. Some of the kinder planets. Orchard ISBN 0-531-08751-4; In Canada: Douglas & McIntyre, 1995. 130p.
"Melanie Kroupa book."
Available from the National Library Service for the Blind and Physically Handicapped on sound recording cassette RC 41359. Nine short stories present eccentric, fascinating characters each involved in something original, different yet understandable to a reader who might identify with their situations. Told in a humorous fashion, the stories have a serious and subtle center developed by the author's smooth, evocative prose and imaginative plots and characters. Try reading aloud, perhaps it will motivate discussion. Readers of Florence Parry Heide's and Elaine L. Konigsburg's short stories will welcome this Canadian writer's offering.
SUBJ: Short stories.

Ph-2 5-6/6 $14.95 T KH887
YARBROUGH, CAMILLE. Shimmershine Queens. Putnam ISBN 0-399-21465-8; In Canada: Putnam, 1989. 142p.
Set in urban slums and an African-American inner-city school, fifth-graders Angie and Michelle try to change themselves and their classmates by reminding them about the slave children who attended school under impossible circumstances. Thanks to a new teacher who tells the children about their heritage, there is a turn around in the story that uses a modest amount of Black English and concludes in what may be a too unrealistic fashion, but is nonetheless uplifting, amid the realities of modern life. For multicultural studies.
SUBJ: Afro-Americans--Fiction./ Schools--Fiction.

Ph-2 3-4/2 $2.99 P KH888
YARBROUGH, CAMILLE. Tamika and the wisdom rings. Illus. by Anna Rich. Random House ISBN 0-679-82749-8; In Canada: Random House, 1994. 101p. ill. (First stepping stone book).
"Tamika finds strength in her family, her friends, and herself as she copes with the murder of her father by drug dealers." (CIP) Though described in easy language, the situation is not at all easy as Tamika and her family face the sudden death of her strong and loving father. The circumstances in which she and her mother and sister find themselves depict the reality of inner city crime, but the plot is hopeful because of the people involved. Large type and wide leading make the book accessible to younger readers. Although this is an African-American family, the family feeling is (or should be) universal. For multicultural studies.
SUBJ: Afro-Americans--Fiction./ Family problems--Fiction.

Ph-1 4-6/5 $15.95 T KH889
YEE, PAUL. Ghost Train. Illus. by Harvey Chan. Groundwood/dist. by Publishers Group West ISBN 0-88899-257-2; In Canada: Groundwood/Douglas & McIntyre, 1996. unp. col. ill.
Yee, author of the acclaimed TALES FROM GOLD MOUNTAIN, now presents a single story, movingly illustrated in dark, but vibrant oils, about the Chinese experience building railroads in western North America. Almost a fantasy, it tells the story of the daughter of a worker who has been killed in a landslide. Choon-yi is very artistic in spite of the fact that she has only one arm. Ghosts direct her to paint the Ghost Train, take a dream trip on it, then burn the painting so that the ghosts of the dead workers can be returned for their final rest in China. Use in multicultural studies, units on Chinese in North America, and units on railroads in the nineteenth century.
SUBJ: Chinese--United States--Fiction./ Migrant labor--Fiction./ Railroads--History--Fiction./ Painting--Fiction.

Ph-1 5-A/7 $15.95 T KH890
YEE, PAUL. Tales from Gold Mountain: stories of the Chinese in the New World. Illus. by Simon Ng. Macmillan ISBN 0-02-793621-X; In Canada: Groundwood, 1989. 64p. col. ill.
Selectors' Choice, 19th ed.
Available from the National Library Service for the Blind and Physically Handicapped on sound recording cassette RC34790.
"Drawing on the real background of the Chinese role in the gold rush, the building of the railway and the settling of the (U.S. & Canadian) west coast in the nineteenth century, Yee has created eight original stories" combining Chinese folklore and life in the New

World." (Jacket) The stories are varied in tone: ghost stories, romances, stories of trickery, but all center on the Chinese immigrant-experience and the too often hard and unfair events as they weighed on individuals. Excellent for oral presentation, fine for better readers, and a prime choice for units on immigration and the Chinese in the land of the Gold Mountain. A gripping creation, with intriguing full page illustrations.
SUBJ: Chinese Americans--Fiction./ Short stories.

Ph-3 A/6 $12.89 L KH891
YEP, LAURENCE. Child of the owl. HarperCollins ISBN 0-06-026743-7, c1977. 217p.
Jane Addams Book Award.
Available from National Library Service for the Blind and Physically Handicapped on sound recording cassette RC11545.
When Barney is beat up by hoodlums and lands in the hospital, he sends his daughter Casey to stay with her uncle and then her grandmother--Chinese Americans. Barney has always thought he would "hit it big" by gambling. Slowly Casey learns about her mother whom she'd never known, her real Chinese name, and begins to understand her Chinese heritage and of her special burden as a "child of the owl." A fine novel for the mature reader.
SUBJ: Chinese--United States--Fiction./ San Francisco (Calif.)--Fiction./ Grandmothers--Fiction.

Ph-1 5-6/6 $14.89 L KH892
YEP, LAURENCE. Dragonwings. HarperCollins ISBN 0-06-026738-0, c1975. 248p.
Newbery Honor Book.
Selectors' Choice, 10th ed.
Available from National Library Service for the Blind and Physically Handicapped on sound recording cassette RC09784.
Moon Shadow, living in a remote Chinese village with his mother and grandmother in 1903, receives a letter from his father in San Francisco and a visit from an uncle urging he be sent to join him in the land of the Golden Mountain. There, Moon Shadow, and Windrider, his father, a very independent and inventive man, survive despite tremendous difficulties and disasters (the 1906 earthquake), while working toward their dream of creating a dragon-like flying machine.
SUBJ: Airplanes--Fiction./ Fathers and sons--Fiction./ Chinese--San Francisco (Calif.)--Fiction.

Ph-2 4-6/4 $13.89 L KH893
YEP, LAURENCE. Later, Gator. Hyperion ISBN 0-7868-2083-7; In Canada: Little, Brown, 1995. 122p.
Teddy, not the world's nicest brother, buys his "perfect" younger brother Bobby a small alligator as a birthday gift in hopes of frightening him. Alas, he finds that the alligator is the best present, and the entire extended Chinese-American family agrees. Complications arise when the boys start exploring garbage cans from many of San Francisco's Chinese restaurants to feed the pet, and rumors spread that the family needs food. Humorous and fast-paced, the book provides an interesting picture of family life in San Francisco's Chinatown. For multicultural studies.
SUBJ: Chinese Americans--Fiction./ Brothers--Fiction./ Alligators--Fiction./ Birthdays--Fiction./ Asian Americans--Fiction.

Ph-2 6-A/6 $5.95 P KH894
YEP, LAURENCE. Serpent's children. HarperTrophy ISBN 0-06-440645-8; In Canada: HarperCollins, c1984, 1996. 277p.
Returning to his village after fighting to oust foreign invaders, Gallant finds his wife dead and his children barely surviving. While he continues to dream of a free China and is tacitly supported by his daughter Cassia, his son Foxfire emigrates sending back money and news that makes Gallant see there is a future, not only a past. Despite a very slow middle section, the title is welcomed for the depiction of the unfamiliar nineteenth century Chinese village life. In MOUNTAIN LIGHT (ISBN 0-06-440667-9, c1985, 1997) Gallant and Cassia encounter a young man whom they befriend during the rebellion against the Manchus and who then goes on to join Foxfire in facing the dangers of the gold fields of California. Provides insights into the problems faced by Chinese immigrants.
SUBJ: China--History--19th century--Fiction./ Family life--China--Fiction.

Ph-2 6-A/6 $12.95 L KH895
YEP, LAURENCE. Star fisher. Morrow ISBN 0-688-09365-5, 1991. 150p.
Joan Lee is 15 when her family moves from Ohio to become the only Chinese-American family in a West Virginia town in the 1920s. They all must face changes, some unpleasant, some surprisingly welcome. Based on Yep's own grandparental family's life in West Virginia, the fictionalized biography presents a slice-of-life view of "strangers in a strange land" who finally succeed. Can be used in multicultural and

U.S. History units.
SUBJ: Chinese Americans--Fiction./ Moving, Household--Fiction./
Prejudices--Fiction.

Ph-1 6-A/7 $3.99 P KH896
YOLEN, JANE. Children of the wolf. Puffin ISBN 0-14-036477-3; In
Canada: Pengiun, c1984, 1993. 136p.
Summoned to a remote jungle village in India, an English missionary
discovers the ghosts the villagers fear are two young girls who have
been raised as wolves. He removes them to his orphanage where a
highly sensitive and intelligent Indian orphan, Mohandas (the narrator
of the story) attempts to befriend them. Mohandas grows in dignity
as he struggles to civilize the doomed children whom the other
orphans hate and fear. It is a book invaluable for reading aloud or
discussion of prejudice, altruism and the loneliness of the true outcast.
SUBJ: Feral children--Fiction./ India--Fiction.

Ph-2 4-6/6 $13.95 T KH897
YOLEN, JANE. Wizard's Hall. Harcourt Brace ISBN 0-15-298132-2; In
Canada: Harcourt Brace c/o Canadian Manda, 1991. 133p.
Henry, known as Thornmallow, enters a school to train wizards and
succeeds working against evil when he remembers his dear old
mother's motto: "We can try." In a humorous book, somewhat akin
to Diana Wynne Jones' stronger fantasies for older readers,
characters, except for the protagonist, are not clearly delineated.
Middle grade fantasy buffs will find WIZARD'S HALL a good place
to stop for a spell.
SUBJ: Fantasy./ Wizards--Fiction./ Magic--Fiction./ Perseverance
(Ethics)--Fiction.

Ph-3 3-5/5 $10.95 T KH898
YORKE, MALCOLM. Miss Butterpat goes wild! Illus. by Margaret
Chamberlain. DK Publishing ISBN 1-56458-200-0, 1993. 32p. col. ill.
(Teachers' secrets).
Tells the tall tale of dull Miss Butterpat, a teacher, and her wild trip
to South America's rain forests. A complete suspension of disbelief
will help readers of this sprightly and colorfully illustrated bit of
nonsense.
SUBJ: Teachers--Fiction./ Adventure and adventurers--Fiction./
Humorous stories.

Ph-1 6-A/6 $13.95 T KH899
YOUNG, RONDER THOMAS. Learning by heart. Houghton Mifflin ISBN
0-395-65369-X, 1993. 172p.
"In the early 1960s, ten-year-old Rachel sees changes in her family
and her small Southern town as she tries to sort out how she feels
about her young black maid, racial prejudice, and her responsibility
for her own life." (CIP) In a very Southern novel, character comes to
the fore. Readers will meet a cast which defies stereotype in deeply
felt and thoughtful episodes. Like Sue Ellen Bridgers and Doris
Buchanan Smith, Young depicts a time and place that can be easily
pictured by the reader who is willing to savor the work. For
multicultural studies.
SUBJ: Southern States--Fiction./ Race relations--Fiction./ Afro-
Americans--Fiction./ Family life--Fiction.

Ph-1 6-A/4 $18.99 L KH900
YOUNG, RONDER THOMAS. Moving Mama to town. Orchard ISBN
0-531-33025-7, 1997. 219p.
"Melanie Kroupa book."
Selectors' Choice, 21st ed.
Daddy has deserted the family, leaving more gambling debts than
they realize, and young Freddy James Johnson, thirteen, takes charge
of his mother and younger brother. Set in Georgia and South
Carolina in 1947, the story is told in the first person through Freddy's
eyes. The diction and creation of setting and character bring a
disparate group of people together as the three move from farm to
town and gradually become a functioning family. People and
situations are holding because of the strong development and
seemingly easy style the author has provided.
SUBJ: Single-parent family--Fiction./ Fathers and sons--Fiction./ Family
life--Georgia--Fiction./ Georgia--Fiction.

Ph-1 6-A/7 $15.00 T KH901
YUMOTO, KAZUMI. Friends. Translated by Cathy Hirano. Farrar Straus
Giroux ISBN 0-374-32460-3; In Canada: HarperCollins, 1996. 170p.
Batchelder Award, 1997.
Three friends, Japanese schoolboys, secretly observe an elderly man
because they think he will die soon, and they are curious about
death. Soon the boys and man begin to know each other and care
for each other. Readers learn about the lives of the boys and the
history of the man: World War II when he was a soldier, a failed
marriage, his guilt about an incident in the war, and much more. As
the old man gently imparts his philosophy of life to the boys, changes
occur in both him and the boys. Their lives become so interwoven that
the boys expand their school boy world and begin to understand life
itself. It will need a mature reader, because there is so much to
contemplate, and it is far beyond a novel to be used for a mere
cultural lesson. For multicultural studies.
SUBJ: Friendship--Fiction./ Old age--Fiction./ Death--Fiction./ Japan--
Fiction.

A. NONNY MOUSE WRITES AGAIN!: POEMS./ 1993/
K-2 KE052 . . . . **811.008**
AAMODT, A/ Wolf pack: tracking wolves in the wild./ 1985/
6/10 KC836 . . . . **599.773**
AAMUNDSEN, NR/ Two short and one long./ 1990/ 4-6/5 KG811 . **FIC**
AARDEMA, V/ Borreguita and the coyote: a tale from Ayutla, Mexico./
1991/ P-2/4 KB514 . . . . **398.24**
How the ostrich got its long neck: a tale from the Akamba of Kenya./
1995/ P-2/6 KB515 . . . . **CE 398.24**
How the ostrich got its long neck (Talking book)./ 1997/
P-2/6 KB515 . . . . **CE 398.24**
Lonely lioness and the ostrich chicks: a Masai tale./ 1996/
K-2/3 KB516 . . . . **398.24**
This for that: a Tonga tale./ 1997/ K-2/2 KB517 . . . . **398.24**
Who's in Rabbit's house? (Videocassette)./ 1995/
K-3 KB518 . . . . **VCR 398.24**
Why mosquitoes buzz in people's ears: a West African tale./ 1975/
1-3/5 KB519 . . . . **CE 398.24**
Why mosquitoes buzz in people's ears: a West African tale (Braille)./
n.d./ 1-3/5 KB519 . . . . **CE 398.24**
Why mosquitoes buzz in people's ears: a West African tale (Sound
recording cassette)./ n.d./ 1-3/5 KB519 . . . . **CE 398.24**
Why mosquitoes buzz in people's ears: a West African tale
(Videocassette)./ n.d./ 1-3/5 KB519 . . . . **CE 398.24**
Why mosquitoes buzz in people's ears (Big book)./ 1993/
1-3/5 KB519 . . . . **CE 398.24**
Why mosquitoes buzz in people's ears (Talking book)./ 1978/
2-4 KB520 . . . . **TB 398.24**
AASENG, N/ American dinosaur hunters./ 1996/ A/9 KC232 . . . . **560**
Meat-eating plants./ 1996/ 5-8/6 KC425 . . . . **583**
Twentieth-century inventors./ 1991/ A/9 KC889 . . . . **609**
ABBEY, CD/ BIOGRAPHY TODAY ARTISTS SERIES: PROFILES OF
INTEREST TO YOUNG READERS./ 1996-/ 4-6 KA453 . . **REF 709.2**
BIOGRAPHY TODAY SCIENTISTS AND INVENTORS SERIES: PROFILES
OF PEOPLE OF INTEREST TO YOUNG PEOPLE./ 1996-/
4-6 KA438 . . . . **REF 509**
BIOGRAPHY TODAY WORLD LEADERS SERIES: PROFILES OF PEOPLE
OF INTEREST TO YOUNG READERS./ 1997-/ 4-6 KA407   **REF 350**
ABBINK, E/ Missions of the Monterey Bay Area./ 1996/
4-6/9 KF075 . . . . **979.4**
ABELS, H/ Bermuda triangle./ 1987/ 4-6/4 KA560 . . . . **001.94**
ABOLAFIA, Y/ Am I beautiful?/ 1992/ P-K/2 KG140 . . . . **E**
Fox tale./ 1991/ K-2/2 KF126 . . . . **E**
Harry's dog./ 1984/ 1-3/2 KG267 . . . . **E**
It's Valentine's Day./ 1983/ K-2 KE007 . . . . **811**
Moving day./ 1996/ P-1/1 KF865 . . . . **E**
My parents think I'm sleeping./ 1985/ 2-5 KE009 . . . . **811**
Stop, thief!/ 1993/ K-2/1 KF866 . . . . **E**
Turkey drive and other tales./ 1993/ 1-3/2 KH611 . . . . **FIC**
ACCORSI, W/ Friendship's first Thanksgiving./ 1992/ P-1/2 KF127 . . **E**
ACKERMAN, D/ Bats: shadows in the night./ 1997/
5-6/7 KC756 . . . . **599.4**
ACKERMAN, K/ Amanecer./ 1994/ K-2/5 KF129 . . . . **E**
Bingleman's Midway./ 1995/ 2-4/5 KF128 . . . . **E**
Brighter garden./ 1990/ 3-6 KD932 . . . . **811**
By the dawn's early light./ 1994/ K-2/5 KF129 . . . . **E**
By the dawn's early light (Sound recording cassette)./ 1997/
K-2/5 KF129 . . . . **E**

Night crossing./ 1994/ 3-4/8 KG812 . . . . **FIC**
Song and dance man./ 1988/ K-2/6 KF130 . . . . **E**
ADA, AF/ Gathering the sun: an alphabet in Spanish and English./ 1997/
1-3 KE122 . . . . **861**
Gold coin./ 1991/ 1-3/4 KF131 . . . . **E**
Mediopollito/Half-Chicken./ 1995/ K-2/2 KB521 . . . . **398.24**
Moneda de oro./ n.d./ 1-3/4 KF131 . . . . **E**
ADAMS, A/ Easter Bunny that overslept./ 1983/ P-K KF587 . . . . . . **E**
ADAMS, BJ/ Go-around dollar./ 1992/ 3-6/3 KA947 . . . . **332.4**
ADAMS, JT/ ALBUM OF AMERICAN HISTORY. Rev. ed./ 1981/
5-6 KA489 . . . . **REF 973**
ADAMS, MA/ Whoopi Goldberg: from street to stardom./ 1993/
4-6/7 KE371 . . . . **B GOLDBERG, W.**
ADAMS, P/ Early loggers and the sawmill./ 1981/ 4-6/6 KD164 . **634.9**
ADAMS, R/ Watership Down./ c1972, 1974/ 6-A/5 KG813 . . . . . **FIC**
Watership Down (Braille)./ n.d./ 6-A/5 KG813 . . . . **FIC**
ADEL, D/ Book that Jack wrote./ 1994/ P-1 KE021 . . . . **811**
ADKINS, J/ Moving heavy things./ 1980/ A/7 KC088 . . . . **531**
ADLER, CS/ That horse Whiskey!/ 1994/ 4-6/5 KG814 . . . . **FIC**
ADLER, DA/ Calculator riddles./ 1995/ 3-6 KD722 . . . . **793.735**
Cam Jansen and the ghostly mystery./ 1996/ 2-4/2 KG815 . . . . . **FIC**
Cam Jansen and the mystery at the haunted house./ 1992/
2-4/3 KG817 . . . . **FIC**
Cam Jansen and the mystery at the monkey house./ 1985/
2-4/3 KG817 . . . . **FIC**
Cam Jansen and the mystery of flight 54./ 1989/ 2-4/3 KG817 . . **FIC**
Cam Jansen and the mystery of the Babe Ruth baseball./ 1982/
2-4/3 KG817 . . . . **FIC**
Cam Jansen and the mystery of the Babe Ruth baseball (Braille)./ n.d./
2-4/3 KG817 . . . . **FIC**
Cam Jansen and the mystery of the carnival prize./ c1984/
2-4/3 KG817 . . . . **FIC**
Cam Jansen and the mystery of the carnival prize (Braille)./ n.d./
2-4/3 KG817 . . . . **FIC**
Cam Jansen and the mystery of the circus clown./ 1983/
2-4/3 KG817 . . . . **FIC**
Cam Jansen and the mystery of the dinosaur bones./ 1981/
2-4/4 KG816 . . . . **CE FIC**
Cam Jansen and the mystery of the dinosaur bones (Braille)./ n.d./
2-4/4 KG816 . . . . **CE FIC**
Cam Jansen and the mystery of the dinosaur bones (Kit)./ 1989/
2-4/4 KG816 . . . . **CE FIC**
Cam Jansen and the mystery of the gold coins./ 1982/
2-4/3 KG817 . . . . **FIC**
Cam Jansen and the mystery of the gold coins (Braille)./ n.d./
2-4/3 KG817 . . . . **FIC**
Cam Jansen and the mystery of the monster movie./ 1984/
2-4/3 KG817 . . . . **FIC**
Cam Jansen and the mystery of the monster movie (Braille)./ n.d./
2-4/3 KG817 . . . . **FIC**
Cam Jansen and the mystery of the stolen diamonds./ 1980/
2-4/3 KG817 . . . . **FIC**
Cam Jansen and the mystery of the stolen diamonds (Braille)./ n.d./
2-4/3 KG817 . . . . **FIC**
Cam Jansen and the mystery of the television dog./ 1981/
2-4/3 KG817 . . . . **FIC**
Cam Jansen and the mystery of the television dog (Braille)./ n.d./
2-4/3 KG817 . . . . **FIC**

Cam Jansen and the mystery of the UFO./ 1980/ 2-4/3 KG817 . . **FIC**
Cam Jansen and the mystery of the UFO (Braille)./ n.d./
2-4/3 KG817 . . . . **FIC**
Christopher Columbus: great explorer./ 1991/
4-5/4 KE301 . . . . **B COLUMBUS, C.**
Easy math puzzles./ 1997/ K-3 KD723 . . . . **793.735**
Fraction fun./ 1996/ 3-6/2 KB952 . . . . **513.2**
George Washington: father of our country./ 1988/
4-5/6 KE587 . . . . **B WASHINGTON, G**
Hilde and Eli: children of the Holocaust./ 1994/ 4-6/5 KE655 . **940.53**
Libro illustrado sobre Cristobal Colon./ 1992/
2-3/4 KE300 . . . . **CE B COLUMBUS, C.**
Libro ilustrado sobre Martin Luther King, Hijo./ 1992/
3-4/4 KE420 . . . . **CE B KING, M.L.**
Libro ilustrado sobre Martin Luther King, Hijo (Kit)./ 1993/
3-4/4 KE420 . . . . **CE B KING, M.L.**
One yellow daffodil: a Hanukkah story./ 1995/ 3-5/4 KG818 . . . . **FIC**
Onion sundaes./ 1994/ 2-3/2 KG819 . . . . **FIC**
Picture book of Anne Frank./ 1993/ 3-4/5 KE351 . . **CE B FRANK, A.**
Picture book of Anne Frank (Kit)./ 1995/
3-4/5 KE351 . . . . **CE B FRANK, A.**
Picture book of Christopher Columbus./ 1991/
2-3/4 KE300 . . . . **CE B COLUMBUS, C.**
Picture book of Christopher Columbus (Kit)./ 1992/
2-3/4 KE300 . . . . **CE B COLUMBUS, C.**
Picture book of Davy Crockett./ 1996/ 2-3/7 KE310 . . **B CROCKETT, D.**
Picture book of Florence Nightingale./ 1992/
2-4/3 KE478 . . . . **B NIGHTINGALE**
Picture book of Jackie Robinson./ 1994/
2-4/6 KE515 . . . . **B ROBINSON, J.**
Picture book of Jesse Owens./ 1992/ 3-4/6 KE486 . . . . **B OWENS, J.**
Picture book of Louis Braille./ 1997/ 2-3/3 KE261 . . . . **B BRAILLE, L.**
Picture book of Martin Luther King, Jr./ 1989/
3-4/4 KE420 . . . . **CE B KING, M.L.**
Picture book of Martin Luther King, Jr. (Kit)./ 1990/
3-4/4 KE420 . . . . **CE B KING, M.L.**
Picture book of Martin Luther King, Jr. (Videocassette)./ 1990/
3-4/4 KE420 . . . . **CE B KING, M.L.**
Picture book of Paul Revere./ 1995/ 2-4/5 KE508 . . . . **B REVERE, P.**
Picture book of Robert E. Lee./ 1994/ 2-5/5 KE429 . . . . . . **B LEE, R.**
Picture book of Simon Bolivar./ 1992/ 3-4/5 KE257 . . **B BOLIVAR, S.**
Picture book of Sitting Bull./ 1993/ 3-4/5 KE540 . . . **B SITTING BULL**
Picture book of Sojourner Truth./ 1994/ 2-5/6 KE572 . . **B TRUTH, S.**
Picture book of Thomas Alva Edison./ 1996/
2-2/3 KE330 . . . . **B EDISON, T.**
Picture book of Thomas Jefferson./ 1990/
2-3/5 KE403 . . . . **B JEFFERSON, T.**
We remember the holocaust./ c1989, 1995/ 5-6/8 KE656 . . . **940.53**
We remember the holocaust (Sound recording cassette)./ 1993,/
5-6/8 KE656 . . . . **940.53**
Young Cam Jansen and the dinosaur game./ 1996/ 1-2/2 KF132 . . . **E**
Young Cam Jansen and the lost tooth./ 1997/ 1-2/2 KF133 . . . . . . **E**
Young Cam Jansen and the missing cookie./ 1996/ 1-2/2 KF134 . . . **E**
ADLERMAN, D/ Africa calling, nighttime falling./ 1996/ P-2 KF135 . . **E**
ADLERMAN, KM/ Africa calling, nighttime falling./ 1996/ P-2 KF135 . **E**
ADOFF, A/ All the colors of the race./ 1982/ 4-6 KD907 . . . . . . **811**
All the colors of the race (Sound recording cassette)./ n.d./
4-6 KD907 . . . . **811**
Black is brown is tan./ 1973/ P-3/3 KF136 . . . . **E**
Eats./ c1979, 1992/ P-A KD908 . . . . **811**
Eats (Braille)./ n.d.,/ P-A KD908 . . . . **811**
Hard to be six./ 1991/ 1-2 KD909 . . . . **811**
In for winter, out for spring./ 1991/ 1-4 KD910 . . . . **811**
Love letters./ 1997/ K-4 KD911 . . . . **811**
AESOP/ AESOP'S FABLE: THE TORTOISE AND THE HARE (CD-ROM)./
1993/ P-A KB522 . . . . **CDR 398.24**
Aesop's fables./ 1988/ 3-4 KB632 . . . . **398.24**
Hare and the Tortoise./ 1996/ P-1/4 KB597 . . . . **398.24**
Lion and the mouse: an Aesop's fable./ 1995/ P-1/5 KB674 . . **398.24**
Sip of Aesop./ 1995/ K-3 KE050 . . . . **811**
AGEE, J/ So many dynamos!: and other palindromes./ 1994/
3-6 KD719 . . . . **793.734**
AGELL, C/ I slide into the white of winter./ 1994/ K-2/3 KF137 . . . . **E**
I wear long green hair in the summer./ 1994/ K-2/2 KF138 . . . . . **E**
Mud makes me dance in the spring./ 1994/ K-2/2 KF139 . . . . . . **E**
Wind spins me around in the fall./ 1994/ K-2/3 KF140 . . . . **E**
AHLBERG, A/ Bear nobody wanted./ c1992, 1995/ 3-6/6 KG821 . . **FIC**
Each peach pear plum: an "I spy" story./ 1978/ P-1/3 KF141 . . **CE E**
Funnybones./ c1980, 1981/ P-3/2 KF142 . . . . **E**
Giant baby./ 1994/ 3-5/7 KG820 . . . . **FIC**
It was a dark and stormy night./ 1993/ 3-5/6 KG822 . . . . **FIC**
AHLBERG, J/ Bear nobody wanted./ c1992, 1995/ 3-6/6 KG821 . . **CE E**
Each peach pear plum: an "I spy" story./ 1978/ P-1/3 KF141 . . **CE E**

Each peach pear plum: an "I spy" story (Videocassette)./ 1992/
P-1/3 KF141 . . . . **CE E**
Funnybones./ c1980, 1981/ P-3/2 KF142 . . . . **E**
It was a dark and stormy night./ 1993/ 3-5/6 KG822 . . . . **FIC**
AHMAD, N/ Cybersurfer: the Owl Internet guide for kids./ 1996/
3-A/8 KA575 . . . . **BC 025.04**
AIELLO, L/ Janice VanCleave's the human body for every kid: easy
activities that make learning science fun./ 1995/ 5-6/8 KC928 . . **612**
AIKEN, J/ Cold Shoulder Road./ 1995/ 5-A/5 KG823 . . . . **FIC**
Cold Shoulder Road (Sound recording cassette)./ 1997/
5-A/5 KG823 . . . . **FIC**
Is underground./ 1993/ 5-A/7 KG824 . . . . **FIC**
Is underground (Sound recording cassette)./ 1996/ 5-A/7 KG824 . **FIC**
Up the chimney down and other stories./ 1987/ 4-6/6 KG825 . . **FIC**
Up the chimney down and other stories (Braille)./ n.d./
4-6/6 KG825 . . . . **FIC**
Wolves of Willoughby Chase./ c1962, 1987/ 5-A/7 KG826 . . **CE FIC**
AITKEN, A/ One in the middle is the green kangaroo./ 1981/
K-3/2 KF238 . . . . **CE E**
AJMERA, M/ Children from Australia to Zimbabwe: a photographic journey
around the world./ 1997/ 2-5/7 KA822 . . . . **305.23**
AKABA, S/ Suho and the white horse: a legend of Mongolia
(Videocassette)./ 1981/ 3-4 KB626 . . . . **VCR 398.24**
ALARCON, FX/ In my family./En mi familia./ 1996/
2-5/6 KA870 . . . . **306.85**
ALBERT, B/ Where does the trail lead?/ 1991/ K-2/3 KF143 . . . . . . **E**
ALBERT, RE/ Alejandro's gift./ 1994/ 1-3/6 KF144 . . . . **E**
ALBOROUGH, J/ Donde esta mi osito?/ 1995/ P-1/2 KF145 . . . . . **E**
Where's my teddy?/ 1992/ P-1/2 KF145 . . . . **E**
ALBYN, CL/ Multicultural cookbook for students./ 1993/
KA299 . . . . **PROF 641.59**
ALCOCK, V/ Haunting of Cassie Palmer./ 1990/ 5-6/6 KG827 . . . **FIC**
Red-eared ghosts./ 1997/ 5-A/4 KG828 . . . . **FIC**
ALCORN, S/ LINCOLN, IN HIS OWN WORDS./ 1993/
A/8 KE907 . . . . **973.7**
ALCOTT, LM/ Jo's boys./ 1984,/ 5-A/7 KG829 . . . . **FIC**
Little men: life at Plumfield with Jo's boys./ c1947, 1982/
5-A/7 KG829 . . . . **FIC**
Little men: life at Plumfield with Jo's boys (Braille)./ n.d.,/
5-A/7 KG829 . . . . **FIC**
Little men: life at Plumfield with Jo's boys (Sound recording cassette)./
n.d.,/ 5-A/7 KG829 . . . . **FIC**
Little men: life at Plumfield with Jo's boys (Talking book)./ n.d.,/
5-A/7 KG829 . . . . **FIC**
Little women (Talking book)./ 1975/ 5-A KG830 . . . . **TB FIC**
Rose in bloom: a sequel to Eight cousins. Uniform ed./ c1876, 1995/
5-6/7 KG831 . . . . **FIC**
Rose in bloom (Braille)./ n.d.,/ 5-6/7 KG831 . . . . **FIC**
ALDEN, P/ Peterson first guide to mammals of North America./ 1987/
4-6/6 KC720 . . . . **599**
ALDERSON, B/ Arabian nights, or, Tales told by Sheherezade during a
thousand nights and one night./ 1995/ 5-A/7 KB253 . . . . **398.2**
ALDOUS, K/ Meet Posy Bates./ 1992/ 3-5/5 KH038 . . . . **FIC**
Posy Bates, again!/ 1994/ 3-5/3 KH039 . . . . **FIC**
ALEXANDER, E/ Fireflies in the night. Rev. ed./ c1991/
P-2/4 KC552 . . . . **595.76**
ALEXANDER, H/ Oksana: my own story./ 1997/
3-6/4 KE247 . . . . **B BAIUL, O.**
ALEXANDER, L/ Arkadians./ 1995/ 5-A/5 KG832 . . . . **FIC**
Arkadians (Sound recording cassette)./ 1997/ 5-A/5 KG832 . . . **FIC**
Beggar Queen./ 1984/ 5-6/6 KG841 . . . . **FIC**
Beggar Queen (Sound recording cassette)./ n.d./ 5-6/6 KG841 . . . **FIC**
Black cauldron./ 1965/ 6-A/6 KG833 . . . . **FIC**
Black cauldron (Braille)./ n.d./ 6-A/6 KG833 . . . . **FIC**
Black cauldron (Sound recording cassette)./ n.d./ 6-A/6 KG833 . **FIC**
Black cauldron (Talking book)./ n.d./ 6-A/6 KG833 . . . . **FIC**
Book of three./ 1964/ 6-A/6 KG833 . . . . **FIC**
Book of three (Braille)./ n.d./ 6-A/6 KG833 . . . . **FIC**
Book of three (Sound recording cassette)./ n.d./ 6-A/6 KG833 . . **FIC**
Book of three (Talking book)./ n.d./ 6-A/6 KG833 . . . . **FIC**
Castle of Llyr./ 1989/ 6-A/6 KG833 . . . . **FIC**
Castle of Llyr (Sound recording cassette)./ 1993/ 6-A/6 KG833 . . **FIC**
Drackenberg adventure./ 1988/ 5-A/5 KG837 . . . . **FIC**
El Dorado adventure./ 1987/ 5-A/5 KG837 . . . . **FIC**
Fortune-tellers./ 1992/ 2-5/5 KG834 . . . . **FIC**
Foundling and other tales of Prydain./ c1973, 1982/
4-A/5 KG835 . . . . **FIC**
High king (Braille)./ n.d./ 6-A/6 KG833 . . . . **FIC**
High king (Talking book)./ n.d./ 6-A/6 KG833 . . . . **FIC**
House Gobbaleen./ 1995/ 3-5/4 KG836 . . . . **FIC**
Illyrian adventure./ 1986/ 5-A/5 KG837 . . . . **FIC**
Illyrian adventure (Sound recording cassette)./ n.d./ 5-A/5 KG837 . **FIC**
Iron ring./ 1997/ 6-A/6 KG838 . . . . **FIC**
Jedera adventure./ 1990/ 5-A/7 KG839 . . . . **FIC**

Jedera adventure (Sound recording cassette)./ n.d./ 5-A/7 KG839 . **FIC**
Kestrel (Sound recording cassette)./ n.d./ 5-6/6 KG841 . . . . **FIC**
Philadelphia adventure./ 1992/ 5-A/5 KG837 . . . . **FIC**
Remarkable journey of Prince Jen./ 1991/ 6-A/6 KG840 . . . . **FIC**
Taran wanderer./ c1967/ 6-A/6 KG833 . . . . **FIC**
Taran wanderer (Braille)./ n.d./ 6-A/6 KG833 . . . . **FIC**
Taran wanderer (Talking book)./ n.d./ 6-A/6 KG833 . . . . . **FIC**
Westmark./ 1982/ 5-6/6 KG841 . . . . **FIC**
Westmark (Braille)./ n.d./ 5-6/6 KG841 . . . . **FIC**
Westmark (Sound recording cassette)./ n.d./ 5-6/6 KG841 . **FIC**
ALEXANDER, M/ How my library grew by Dinah./ 1983/
   K-2/2 KF146 . . . . **E**
You're a genius, Blackboard Bear./ 1995/ K-2/2 KF147 . . . . . **E**
ALEXANDER, RM/ How animals move (CD-ROM)./ 1995/
   4-A KC464 . . . . **CDR 591.47**
ALEXANDER, SH/ Mom's best friend./ 1992/ 2-4/3 KB003 . . . . **362.4**
ALI, A/ Big Bazoohley./ 1995/ 3-6/5 KG973 . . . . **FIC**
ALIKI/ Communication./ 1993/ K-6/4 KA794 . . . . **302.2**
Como se hace un libro./ 1989/ K-3/3 KD345 . . . . **686**
Corn is maize: the gift of the Indians./ c1976/ K-3/3 KD149 . . . **633.1**
Evolution./ 1987/ 3-4/5 KC290 . . . . **576.8**
Fossils tell of long ago. Rev. ed./ 1990/ 1-3/2 KC233 . . . . . . **560**
Fossils tell of long ago. Rev. ed. (Talking book)./ n.d./
   1-3/2 KC233 . . . . **560**
Gods and goddesses of Olympus./ 1994/ 4-5/5 KA733 . . . . . **292**
Hello! Good-bye!/ 1996/ P-1/2 KB244 . . . . **395.4**
How a book is made./ 1986/ K-3/3 KD345 . . . . **686**
I'm growing!/ 1992/ P-1/2 KC943 . . . . **612.6**
Listening walk./ c1961, 1991/ P-1/1 KG495 . . . . **E**
Manners./ 1990/ 1-6/2 KB239 . . . . **395**
Medieval feast./ 1983/ 2-5/5 KB183 . . . . **CE 394.1**
Milk from cow to carton. Rev. ed./ 1992/ 1-3/2 KD236 . . . . . . **637**
Mis cinco sentidos. Ed. rev./ 1995/ K-2/2 KC962 . . . . . . **612.8**
Mummies made in Egypt./ 1979/ 4-6/6 KB173 . . . . **393**
My feet./ 1990/ P-2/2 KC910 . . . . **612**
My five senses. Rev. ed./ 1989/ K-2/2 KC962 . . . . . . **612.8**
My hands. Rev. ed./ 1990/ P-2/2 KC911 . . . . **612**
My visit to the aquarium./ 1993/ 2-4/5 KC582 . . . . **597**
My visit to the dinosaurs. Rev. ed./ c1969, 1985/
   2-4/4 KC242 . . . . **CE 567.9**
My visit to the dinosaurs. Rev. ed. (Big book)./ 1994,/
   2-4/4 KC242 . . . . **CE 567.9**
My visit to the dinosaurs. Rev. ed. (Kit)./ 1985,/
   2-4/4 KC242 . . . . **CE 567.9**
Tabby: a story in pictures./ 1995/ P-1 KF148 . . . . **E**
Those summers./ 1996/ K-2/4 KF149 . . . . **E**
Wild and woolly mammoths. Rev. ed./ 1996/ 1-3/4 KC268 . . . . **569**
Wild and woolly mammoths (Sound recording cassette)./ n.d./
   1-3/4 KC268 . . . . **569**
ALLARD, H/ Miss Nelson has a field day./ 1985/ 1-3/3 KF151 . . . **CE E**
Miss Nelson is back./ 1982/ 1-3/3 KF151 . . . . **CE E**
Miss Nelson is missing./ 1977/ 1-3/3 KF151 . . . . **CE E**
Miss Nelson is missing (Braille)./ n.d./ 1-3/3 KF151 . . . . . . **CE E**
Miss Nelson is missing (Kit)./ 1987/ 1-3/3 KF151 . . . . . . **CE E**
Stupids die./ 1981/ K-2/5 KF152 . . . . **E**
Stupids have a ball./ 1978/ K-2/5 KF152 . . . . **E**
Stupids step out./ 1974/ K-2/5 KF152 . . . . **E**
Stupids take off./ 1989/ K-2/5 KF152 . . . . **E**
ALLEN, J/ Burton and Stanley./ 1996/ 3-5/6 KH568 . . . . **FIC**
Great white man-eating shark: a cautionary tale./ 1989/
   K-4/5 KG056 . . . . **CE E**
ALLEN, LJ/ Rollo and Tweedy and the ghost at Dougal Castle./ 1992/
   1-3/2 KF153 . . . . **CE E**
Rollo and Tweedy and the ghost at Dougal Castle (Kit)./ 1996/
   1-3/2 KF153 . . . . **CE E**
ALLEN, PG/ As long as the rivers flow: the stories of nine Native
   Americans./ 1996/ 6-A/9 KE746 . . . . **970.1**
ALLEN, TB/ Across the wide dark sea: the Mayflower journey./ 1995/
   2-4/4 KG645 . . . . **E**
Chalk box kid./ 1987/ 2-4/2 KG936 . . . . **FIC**
Place called Freedom./ 1997/ 1-3/3 KG390 . . . . **E**
Sewing quilts./ 1994/ 1-3/6 KG628 . . . . **E**
When Artie was little./ 1996/ 1-3/2 KG417 . . . . **E**
ALLEN, VG/ WHEN THEY DON'T ALL SPEAK ENGLISH: INTEGRATING
   THE ESL STUDENT INTO THE REGULAR CLASSROOM./ 1989/
   KA281 . . . . **PROF 428**
ALLES, H/ More errata: another book of historical errors./ 1995/
   3-6/10 KE143 . . . . **909**
ALLEY, R/ Silliest joke book ever./ 1993/ 2-4/5 KD729 . . . . . **793.735**
ALLEY, RW/ Detective Dinosaur./ 1996/ 1-3/2 KG514 . . . . **E**
Know-Nothing birthday./ 1997/ 1-2/1 KG533 . . . . **E**
Who said boo?: Halloween poems for the very young./ 1995/
   P-1 KD920 . . . . **811**

Young Arthur Ashe: brave champion./ 1996/
   2-3/6 KE242 . . . . **CE B ASHE, A.**
ALLISON, L/ Blood and guts: a working guide to your own insides./
   c1976/ 4-6/4 KC912 . . . . **612**
ALLISON, S/ SCIENTISTS: THE LIVES AND WORKS OF 150
   SCIENTISTS./ 1996/ 5-A KA442 . . . . **REF 509**
ALPERT, L/ You and your dad./ 1992/ P-1/2 KA876 . . . . . . **306.874**
ALSOP, P/ Plugging away (Sound recording cassette)./ 1990/
   1-5 KD604 . . . . **SRC 789.3**
ALSTON, E/ Space camp./ 1990/ 4-5/7 KD135 . . . . **629.45**
ALTENDORF, E/ Lyrical life science (Multimedia kit)./ 1995/
   K-A KA295 . . . . **MMK PROF 570**
ALTMAN, LJ/ Amelia's road./ 1993/ 1-3/4 KF154 . . . . **E**
Camino de Amelia./ 1994/ 1-3/4 KF154 . . . . **E**
ALTMAN, S/ Followers of the North Star: rhymes about African American
   heroes, heroines, and historical times./ 1993/ 3-A KD913 . . . . . **811**
ALTSCHULER, F/ One hundred favorite folktales./ c1968/
   KA274 . . . . **PROF 398.2**
AMERICAN ASSOCIATION OF SCHOOL LIBRARIANS/ AASL
   ELECTRONIC LIBRARY. 1997 ed. (CD-ROM)./ 1997/
   KA045 . . . . **CDR PROF 025**
AMERICAN CHEMICAL SOCIETY/ MINDS-ON SCIENCE: FOR PROFIT,
   FOR PLANET (Videodisc)./ 1995/ 5-A KD348 . . . . **VD 687**
MINDS-ON SCIENCE: FOR THE SAKE OF THE NATION (Videodisc)./
   1995/ 5-A KD804 . . . . **VD 303.48**
MINDS-ON SCIENCE: THE IMPACT OF DISCOVERY (Videodisc)./
   1995/ 5-A KB875 . . . . **VD 502**
AMERICAN FAIRY TALES: FROM RIP VAN WINKLE TO THE
   ROOTABAGA STORIES./ 1996/ 4-6/7 KG843 . . . . **FIC**
AMERICAN LIBRARY ASSOC. OFFICE FOR INTELLECTUAL FREEDOM/
   INTELLECTUAL FREEDOM MANUAL. 5th. ed./ 1996/
   KA052 . . . . **PROF 025.2**
AMERICAN LIBRARY ASSOCIATION./ ANGLO-AMERICAN
   CATALOGUING RULES. 2ND ED., 1988 REVISION./ 1988/
   KA056 . . . . **PROF 025.3**
AMERICAN LIBRARY ASSOCIATION. FILING COMMITTEE./ ALA filing
   rules./ 1980/ KA055 . . . . **PROF 025.3**
AMERICAN MUSEUM OF NATURAL HISTORY/ North American Indian./
   1995/ 4-6/8 KE751 . . . . **970.1**
AMERY, H/ First thousand words in Russian./ 1983/ 4-6 KB863 . . **491.7**
AMES, LJ/ Draw 50 airplanes, aircraft and spacecraft./ 1987/
   4-6 KD416 . . . . **743**
Draw 50 animals./ 1974/ 4-6 KD416 . . . . **743**
Draw 50 beasties and yugglies and turnover uglies and things that go
   bump in the night./ 1990/ 4-6 KD416 . . . . **743**
Draw 50 boats, ships, trucks and trains./ 1987/ 4-6 KD416 . . . . **743**
Draw 50 cars, trucks, and motorcycles./ 1986/ 4-6 KD415 . . . . . **743**
Draw 50 dinosaurs./ 1985/ 4-6 KD416 . . . . **743**
Draw 50 dogs./ 1986/ 4-6 KD416 . . . . **743**
Draw 50 horses./ 1986/ 4-6 KD416 . . . . **743**
AMMON, BD/ Handbook for the Newbery Medal and Honor Books,
   1980-1989./ 1991/ KA347 . . . . **PROF 809**
Worth a thousand words: an annotated guide to picture books for older
   readers./ 1996/ KA010 . . . . **PROF 011.62**
AMMON, R/ Amish Christmas./ 1996/ 3-5/4 KG844 . . . . **FIC**
AMOS, SH/ Atlantic and Gulf coasts./ 1985/ A KC345 . . . . . . **577.69**
AMOS, WH/ Atlantic and Gulf coasts./ 1985/ A KC345 . . . . . . **577.69**
ANAYA, R/ Farolitos of Christmas./ 1995/ 3-6/2 KG845 . . . . **FIC**
ANCONA, G/ Aquarium book./ 1991/ 4-6/7 KD246 . . . . **639.3**
Cutters, carvers and the cathedral./ 1995/ 5-6/7 KD392 . . . . . **726.6**
Earth daughter: Alicia of Acoma Pueblo./ 1995/
   2-4/6 KE791 . . . . **970.489**
Handtalk: an ABC of finger spelling and sign language./ c1974, 1984/
   K-A KB823 . . . . **419**
Handtalk birthday: a number and story book in sign language./ 1987/
   K-3 KB824 . . . . **419**
Handtalk school./ 1991/ K-A KB827 . . . . **419**
Handtalk zoo./ 1989/ K-A KB820 . . . . **419**
Man and mustang./ 1992/ 5-6/6 KD197 . . . . **636.1**
Pablo recuerda./ 1993/ 3-6/5 KB193 . . . . **394.26**
Pablo remembers: the Fiesta of the Day of the Dead./ 1993/
   3-6/5 KB193 . . . . **394.26**
Pinata maker./El Pinatero./ 1994/ 3-6/6 KD450 . . . . **745.594**
Powwow./ 1993/ 3-6/6 KB194 . . . . **394.26**
Riverkeeper./ 1990/ 4-6/7 KA958 . . . . **333.91**
Sheep dog./ 1985/ A/8 KD227 . . . . **636.737**
ANDERSEN, B/ Seven brave women./ 1997/ 1-3/2 KF691 . . . . **E**
ANDERSEN, HC/ Emperor's new clothes./ 1991/ P-2/4 KF968 . . . . . **E**
Emperor's new clothes./ 1992/ 1-3/7 KG128 . . . . **E**
Hans Christian Andersen in Central Park (Sound recording cassette)./
   1981/ 4-6 KG846 . . . . **SRC FIC**
Princess and the pea./ 1982/ K-2/2 KG555 . . . . **CE E**
Princess and the pea./ 1996/ K-2/1 KG796 . . . . **E**
Swineherd./ 1995/ 2-5/5 KG847 . . . . **FIC**

Tinderbox. Newly illustrated ed./ 1988/ K-3/5 KF155 . . . . **E**
Twelve tales./ 1994/ 3-6/5 KG848 . . . . **FIC**
Ugly Duckling./ 1994/ P-A/4 KG143 . . . . **E**
Ugly duckling (Videocassette)./ 1977/ 2-5 KG849 . . . . **VCR FIC**
ANDERSEN, Y/ Make your own animated movies and videotapes./ 1991/ 5-A/6 KD515 . . . . **778.5**
ANDERSON, CC/ Jackie Kennedy Onassis: woman of courage./ 1995/ A/7 KE484 . . . . **B ONASSIS, J.**
ANDERSON, D/ Amazingly easy puppet plays: 42 new scripts for one-person puppetry./ 1997/ KA361 . . . . **PROF 812**
Story of football./ 1985/ 4-A/7 KD782 . . . . **796.332**
Story of football (Braille)./ / 4-A/7 KD782 . . . . **796.332**
Story of the Olympics./ 1996/ 4-6/11 KD819 . . . . **796.48**
ANDERSON, DA/ Origin of life on Earth: an African creation myth./ 1991/ 4-5/4 KA730 . . . . **291.2**
ANDERSON, E/ Great getaway./ 1991/ K-2/2 KF426 . . . . **E**
ANDERSON, J/ American family farm./ 1989/ 5-6/8 KD145 . **630.973**
Batboy: an inside look at spring training./ 1996/ 4-6/6 KD793 . . . . **796.357**
Cowboys: roundup on an American ranch./ 1996/ 3-5/6 KF025 . **978**
Earth keepers./ 1993/ A/9 KB044 . . . . **363.7**
First Thanksgiving feast./ 1984/ 2-4/7 KE935 . . . . **974.4**
Juma and the magic jinn./ 1986/ 2-3/4 KF156 . . . . **E**
Pioneer children of Appalachia./ 1986/ 4-6/6 KE974 . . . . **975.4**
ANDERSON, L/ Linnea's almanac./ c1982, 1989/ 2-6/6 KB879 . . . **507**
Linnea's windowsill garden./ c1978, 1988/ 3-5/6 KD173 . . . . . **635.9**
Playing smart: a parent's guide to enriching offbeat learning activities/ 1990/ KA324 . . . . **PROF 790.1**
ANDERSON, MJ/ Charles Darwin: naturalist./ 1994/ 5-A/4 KE314 . . . . **B DARWIN, C.**
Isaac Newton: the greatest scientist of all time./ 1996/ 6-A/7 KE476 . . . . **B NEWTON, I.**
ANDERSON, MK/ Nez Perce./ 1994/ 4-6/7 KE757 . . . . **970.3**
ANDERSON, PP/ Time for bed, the babysitter said./ 1987/ P-2/1 KF157 . . . . **E**
ANDERSON, R/ Bus people./ 1995/ 6-A/6 KG850 . . . . **FIC**
ANDERSON, RC/ Becoming a nation of readers: the report of the Commission on Reading./ 1985/ KA205 . . . . **PROF 372.4**
ANDERSON, W/ Little House guidebook./ 1996/ 3-5/10 KE196 . **917.8**
ANDO, N/ Shin's tricycle./ 1995/ 4-6/4 KE670 . . . . **940.54**
ANDREASEN, D/ Joshua T. Bates takes charge./ c1993, 1995/ 4-6/4 KH710 . . . . **FIC**
Little house in Brookfield./ 1996/ 4-6/5 KH861 . . . . **FIC**
Pony Express!/ 1996/ 4-6/6 KB130 . . . . **383**
ANDREW, I/ Lion and the mouse: an Aesop's fable./ 1995/ P-1/5 KB674 . . . . **398.24**
ANDREWS, S/ Rattlebone Rock./ 1995/ 1-3/3 KF158 . . . . **E**
ANDRONIK, CM/ Kindred spirit: a biography of L. M. Montgomery, creator of Anne of Green Gables./ 1993/ 5-A/6 KE469 . . . . **B MONTGOMERY, L**
ANGELOU, M/ Kofi and his magic./ 1996/ 2-5/3 KE735 . . . . . . **966.7**
My painted house, my friendly chicken, and me./ 1994/ 1-3/2 KE739 . . . . **968**
ANGLUND, JW/ Christmas is a time of giving./ c1961/ P-2 KB230 . . . . **394.266**
ANHOLT, C/ Here come the babies./ / P-K/2 KA826 . . . . . . **305.232**
ANHOLT, L/ Here come the babies./ / P-K/2 KA826 . . . . **305.232**
ANNESLEY, R/ SPIDER SPINS A STORY: FOURTEEN LEGENDS FROM NATIVE AMERICA./ 1997/ 2-5/6 KB371 . . . . **398.2**
ANNO, M/ Animals: selected poems./ 1992/ 2-6 KE135 . . . . . . **895.6**
Anno's counting book./ 1977/ P-2 KB945 . . . . **513**
Anno's counting book (Big book)./ 1992/ P-2 KB945 . . . . **513**
Anno's journey./ 1978/ P-A KF159 . . . . **E**
Anno's magic seeds./ 1995/ P-4/3 KB987 . . . . **513.4**
Anno's magic seeds (Sound recording cassette)./ 1997/ P-4/3 KB987 . . . . **513.4**
Anno's mysterious multiplying jar./ Anno's mysterious multiplying jar./ 1983/ 1983/ P-A/2 KB944 . . . . **512**
P-A/2 KB944 . . . . **512**
ANSARY, MT/ Stamps./ 1997/ 1-3/2 KD507 . . . . **769.56**
ANTHONY, SC/ Facts plus: an almanac of essential information. New 3rd ed./ 1995/ 4-A KA377 . . . . **REF 030**
ANTLE, N/ Good bad cat./ 1985/ P-1/1 KF160 . . . . **E**
Sam's Wild West Show./ 1995/ 1-3/2 KF161 . . . . **E**
Staying cool./ 1997/ 1-3/2 KF162 . . . . **E**
ANTONISHAK, T/ Three River Junction: a story of an Alaskan bald eagle preserve (Kit)./ 1997/ 2-4 KF313 . . . . **KIT E**
ANZOVIN, S/ Famous first facts. 5th ed./ 1997/ 4-6 KA382 . **REF 031**
APFEL, NH/ Orion, the Hunter./ 1995/ A/10 KC047 . . . . **523.8**
Voyager to the planets./ 1991/ 3-6/7 KC022 . . . . **523.4**
APPELHOF, M/ Worms eat my garbage./ 1982/ A/12 KC502 . . . **592**
APPELT, K/ Bayou lullaby./ 1995/ P-2/5 KF163 . . . . **E**
Watermelon Day./ 1996/ K-2/2 KF164 . . . . **E**
APPLE, M/ Sheep in a jeep./ 1986/ K-3/2 KG489 . . . . **E**
Sybil rides for independence./ 1985/ 3-6/4 KE876 . . . . **973.3**
APPLEGATE, K/ Story of two American generals: Benjamin O. Davis, Jr.; Colin L. Powell./ 1995/ 5-6/5 KA981 . . . . **355**
ARABIAN NIGHTS: THEIR BEST-KNOWN TALES./ c1909, 1994/ 5-A/9 KB255 . . . . **398.2**
ARAI, T/ China's bravest girl: the legend of Hua Mu Lan = [Chin kuo ying hsiung Hua Mu-lan]./ 1993/ 3-5/4 KB430 . . . . **398.22**
ARAUJO, FP/ Nekane, the lamina and the bear: a tale of the Basque Pyrenees./ 1993/ 2-3/3 KB256 . . . . **398.2**
ARCELLA, S/ Poetry for young people./ 1995/ 4-6 KE018 . . . . . . **811**
ARCHAMBAULT, J/ Barn dance!/ 1986/ P-3/3 KG071 . . . . **E**
Chicka chicka boom boom./ 1989/ P-1/2 KG073 . . . . **E**
CHICKA CHICKA BOOM BOOM (CD-ROM)./ 1996/ P-2 KF382 . . . . **CDR E**
Chicka chicka boom boom (Kit)./ 1991/ P-1 KG074 . . . . **KIT E**
Ghost-eye tree./ 1985/ K-3/2 KG075 . . . . **E**
Here are my hands./ 1987/ P-1/2 KG076 . . . . **E**
Listen to the rain./ 1988/ P-2 KG077 . . . . **E**
White Dynamite and Curly Kidd./ c1986, 1989/ K-3/2 KG078 . . . . **E**
ARCHBOLD, R/ Exploring the Bismarck./ 1991/ 5-6/7 KE668 . . **940.54**
ARDIZZONE, E/ Likely place./ c1967, 1986/ 4-6/4 KH135 . . . . **FIC**
ARDLEY, N/ Science book of air./ 1991/ 4-6/4 KC102 . . . . **533**
Science book of color./ 1991/ 4-6/4 KC118 . . . . **535.6**
Science book of electricity./ 1991/ 2-5/3 KC129 . . . . **537**
Science book of gravity./ 1992/ K-3/2 KC089 . . . . **531**
Science book of hot and cold./ 1992/ K-3/2 KC126 . . . . **536**
Science book of light./ 1991/ K-3/6 KC105 . . . . **535**
Science book of machines./ 1992/ 4-6/4 KD050 . . . . **621.8**
Science book of magnets./ 1991/ 2-5/2 KC136 . . . . **538**
Science book of motion./ 1992/ K-3/2 KC090 . . . . **531**
Science book of sound./ 1991/ 2-5/3 KC076 . . . . **530**
Science book of things that grow./ 1991/ K-3/3 KC273 . . . . . . **571.2**
Science book of water./ 1991/ 2-4/4 KC091 . . . . **531**
Science book of weather./ 1992/ K-3/3 KC185 . . . . **551.5**
Young person's guide to music./ 1995/ 5-A/8 KD518 . . . . . . **BA 780**
ARGENT, K/ One woolly wombat./ 1985/ P-2/4 KG617 . . . . **E**
ARKHURST, JC/ Adventures of Spider: West African folktales./ c1964, 1992/ 2-3/5 KB524 . . . . **398.24**
ARMBRUSTER, A/ American flag./ 1991/ 4-6/8 KE613 . . . . **929.9**
St. Lawrence Seaway./ 1996/ 2-4/6 KB141 . . . . **386**
ARMSTRONG, C/ Lives and legends of the saints: with paintings from the great museums of the world./ 1995/ 5-A/10 KA716 . . . . **270**
ARMSTRONG, J/ King Crow./ 1995/ 1-3/4 KF165 . . . . **E**
That terrible baby./ 1994/ K-2/3 KF166 . . . . **E**
ARMSTRONG, T/ Dog who dared (Videocassette)./ 1993/ 4-6 KC993 . . . . **VCR 613.8**
ARMSTRONG, WH/ Sounder./ c1969/ 4-A/4 KG851 . . . . **CE FIC**
Sounder (Braille)./ n.d./ 4-A/4 KG851 . . . . **CE FIC**
Sounder (Sound recording cassette)./ n.d./ 4-A/4 KG851 . . . **CE FIC**
Sounder (Talking book)./ Sounder (Talking book)./ n.d./ 1992/ 4-A/4 KG851 . . . . **CE FIC**
4-A/4 KG851 . . . . **CE FIC**
Trueno./ 1996/ 4-A/4 KG851 . . . . **CE FIC**
ARNDT, U/ Fireworks, picnics, and flags./ 1983/ 3-5/8 KE880 . . **973.3**
Holly, reindeer and colored lights: the story of Christmas symbols./ c1971/ 5-6/7 KB231 . . . . **394.266**
Shamrocks, harps, and shillelaghs: the story of the St. Patrick's Day symbols./ c1977/ 5-6/7 KB218 . . . . **394.262**
ARNO, E/ People of the short blue corn: tales and legends of the Hopi Indians./ c1970, 1996/ 1-A/5 KB278 . . . . **398.2**
Tiger's whisker and other tales from Asia and the Pacific./ c1959, 1995/ 3-5/7 KB279 . . . . **398.2**
ARNOLD, C/ Ancient cliff dwellers of Mesa Verde./ 1992/ 5-6/8 KE790 . . . . **970.488**
Ancient cliff dwellers of Mesa Verde (Sound recording cassette)./ 1994/ 5-6/8 KE790 . . . . **970.488**
Bat./ 1996/ 4-6/7 KC757 . . . . **599.4**
Camel./ 1992/ 4-6/7 KC784 . . . . **599.63**
Cheetah./ 1989/ 5-6/9 KC817 . . . . **599.75**
City of the gods: Mexico's ancient city of Teotihuacan./ 1994/ 5-6/7 KE828 . . . . **972**
Dinosaurs all around: an artist's view of the prehistoric world./ 1993/ 3-6/8 KC243 . . . . **567.9**
Dinosaurs down under and other fossils from Australia./ 1990/ 3-6/8 KC240 . . . . **566**
Elephant./ 1993/ 5-6/9 KC808 . . . . **599.67**
Fox./ 1996/ 4-6/7 KC845 . . . . **599.776**
Hippo./ c1989, 1992/ 4-6/7 KC785 . . . . **599.63**
House sparrows everywhere./ 1992/ 4-6/7 KC704 . . . . **598.8**
Killer whale./ 1994/ 4-6/7 KC764 . . . . **599.5**
Koala./ c1987, 1992/ 4-6/8 KC733 . . . . **599.2**
Lion./ 1995/ 5-6/7 KC828 . . . . **599.757**
Llama./ 1988/ 5-6/7 KD210 . . . . **636.2**

On the brink of extinction: the California condor./ 1993/
5-6/8 KD251 . . . . **639.9**
On the brink of extinction: the California condor (Sound recording
cassette)./ 1995/ 5-6/8 KD251 . . . . **639.9**
Ostriches and other flightless birds./ 1990/ 5-6/7 KC690 . . . . **598.5**
Panda./ 1992/ 4-6/7 KC866 . . . . **599.789**
Pets without homes./ 1983/ 1-4/6 KD189 . . . . **636.08**
Prairie dogs./ 1993/ 4-5/4 KC749 . . . . **599.36**
Reindeer./ 1993/ 4-5/4 KD211 . . . . **636.2**
Rhino./ 1995/ 4-6/7 KC801 . . . . **599.66**
Saving the peregrine falcon./ 1990/ 4-6/7 KC708 . . . . . . **598.9**
Sea lion./ 1994/ 4-6/6 KC867 . . . . **599.79**
Snake./ 1991/ 5-6/7 KC632 . . . . **597.96**
Stone Age farmers beside the sea: Scotland's prehistoric village of Skara
Brae./ 1997/ 3-6/8 KE677 . . . . **941.1**
Tule elk./ 1989/ 5-6/8 KC794 . . . . **599.65**
Watch out for sharks!/ 1991/ 4-6/7 KC590 . . . . **597.3**
Watching desert wildlife./ 1994/ 4-6/7 KC361 . . . . . . **578.754**
Zebra./ 1987/ 5-6/8 KC804 . . . . **599.665**
ARNOLD, J/ Carlos and the skunk./Carlos y el zorrillo./ 1997/
1-3/3 KG554 . . . . **E**
ARNOLD, K/ Baba Yaga: a Russian folktale./ 1993/
2-3/3 KB387 . . . . **398.21**
Katya's book of mushrooms./ 1997/ 3-A/6 KC381 . . . . . . **579.6**
ARNOLD, T/ No jumping on the bed!/ 1987/ P-3/5 KF167 . . . . . **E**
ARNOSKY, J/ All about owls./ 1995/ 2-5/4 KC709 . . . . . . **598.9**
Come out, muskrats./ 1989/ P-K/2 KC742 . . . . **599.35**
Crinkleroot's guide to knowing animal habitats./ 1997/
2-5/4 KC471 . . . . **591.5**
Crinkleroot's guide to knowing butterflies and moths./ 1996/
3-5/5 KC557 . . . . **595.78**
Crinkleroot's guide to knowing the birds./ 1992/ 2-5/6 KC644 . . **598**
Crinkleroot's 25 birds every child should know./ 1993/
P-2/3 KC645 . . . . **598**
Every autumn comes the bear./ 1993/ P-2/2 KF168 . . . . **E**
I see animals hiding./ 1995/ 2-4/6 KC465 . . . . **591.47**
Long Spikes: a story./ 1992/ 5-A/6 KG852 . . . . **FIC**
Nearer nature./ 1996/ A/6 KE933 . . . . **974.3**
Otters under water./ 1992/ K-2/2 KC832 . . . . **599.769**
Rabbits and raindrops./ 1997/ P-2/2 KF169 . . . . **E**
Raccoons and ripe corn./ c1987, 1991/ P-2/3 KC831 . . . . **599.76**
Secrets of a wildlife watcher./ c1983, 1991/ 5-6/7 KC580 . . . . . **596**
Watching foxes./ 1985/ P-K/1 KF170 . . . . **E**
Watching water birds./ 1997/ 4-6/6 KC674 . . . . **598.176**
ARNSTEEN, KK/ Putting on a play: the young playwright's guide to
scripting, directing, and performing./ 1996/ 4-6/7 KD687 . . . . **792**
Young author's do-it-yourself book: how to write, illustrate, and produce
your own book./ 1994/ 2-6/4 KD863 . . . . **808**
Young producer's video book: how to write, direct, and shoot your own
video./ 1995/ 3-6/4 KD686 . . . . **791.45**
ARONSON, B/ They came from DNA./ 1993/ 5-A/6 KC278 . . . **572.8**
ARQUETTE, MF/ Children of the Morning Light: Wampanoag tales./ 1994/
4-5/7 KB348 . . . . **398.2**
ARROYO, A/ Boda: a Mexican wedding celebration./ 1996/
1-3/3 KG641 . . . . **E**
ART INSTITUTE OF CHICAGO/ WITH OPEN EYES: IMAGES FROM THE
ART INSTITUTE OF CHICAGO (CD-ROM)./ 1995/
2-A KD368 . . . . **CDR 701**
ARTELL, M/ Basic cartooning with Mike Artell (Videocassette)./ 1995/
3-6 KD408 . . . . **VCR 741.5**
Wackiest nature riddles on earth./ 1992/ 3-6 KD724 . . . . . . **793.735**
ARTZT, AF/ How to use cooperative learning in the mathematics class./
1990/ KA250 . . . . **PROF 372.7**
ARUEGO, J/ Chick and the duckling./ 1972/ P-1/1 KG585 . . . . . **E**
Leo the late bloomer./ 1971/ P-2/2 KF918 . . . . **CE E**
Mushroom in the rain./ c1974, 1987/ P-2/2 KF623 . . . . **E**
Rockabye crocodile./ 1988/ P-K/2 KB525 . . . . **398.24**
We hide, you seek./ 1979/ P-K/1 KF172 . . . . **E**
Whose mouse are you?/ c1970/ P-1/1 KF919 . . . . **CE E**
ASBJORNSEN, PC/ Man who kept house./ 1992/ 2-4/6 KB719 **398.27**
ASCH, F/ Bear shadow./ 1985/ P-2/2 KF173 . . . . **E**
Bear's bargain./ 1989/ P-1/2 KF174 . . . . **CE E**
Bear's bargain (Big book)./ 1992/ P-1/2 KF174 . . . . **CE E**
Happy birthday, moon./ 1982/ P-1/2 KF174 . . . . **CE E**
Happy birthday, moon (Videocassette)./ n.d./ P-1/2 KF174 . . **CE E**
Moonbear's pet./ 1997/ P-K/2 KF175 . . . . **E**
Moongame./ 1987/ P-1/2 KF174 . . . . **CE E**
Moongame (Big book)./ 1992/ P-1/2 KF174 . . . . **CE E**
ASHABRANNER, B/ LION'S WHISKERS: AND OTHER ETHIOPIAN TALES.
Rev. ed./ 1997/ 3-6/7 KB337 . . . . **398.2**
Our beckoning borders: illegal immigration to America./ 1996/
5-6/12 KA924 . . . . **325.73**
Strange and distant shore: Indians of the Great Plains in exile./ 1996/
4-6/7 KF026 . . . . **978**

To seek a better world: the Haitian minority in America./ 1997/
5-6/8 KA836 . . . . **305.8**
ASIMOV, I/ Christopher Columbus: navigator to the New World./ 1991/
4-5/5 KE302 . . . . **B COLUMBUS, C.**
Complete science fair handbook./ 1990/ KA286 . . . . **PROF 507.8**
How did we find out about microwaves?/ 1989/ A/9 KD045 . . **621.381**
How did we find out about microwaves? (Sound recording cassette)./
n.d./ A/9 KD045 . . . . **621.381**
How did we find out about photosynthesis?/ 1989/ 6-A/9 KC277 . . **572**
How did we find out about photosynthesis? (Sound recording cassette)./
1993/ 6-A/9 KC277 . . . . **572**
How did we find out about superconductivity?/ 1988/
5-A/7 KC135 . . . . **537.6**
How did we find out about superconductivity? (Sound recording
cassette)./ n.d./ 5-A/7 KC135 . . . . **537.6**
ASKA, W/ Aska's sea creatures./ 1994/ 3-5 KD914 . . . . **811**
ASSOCIATION FOR LIBRARY SERVICE TO CHILDREN/ NEWBERY AND
CALDECOTT AWARDS: A GUIDE TO THE MEDAL AND HONOR
BOOKS./ n.d./ KA128 . . . . **PER PROF 050**
AT THE CRACK OF THE BAT: BASEBALL POEMS./ 1992/
3-6 KE053 . . . . **811.008**
ATKIN, SB/ Voices from the fields: children of migrant farmworkers tell their
stories./ 1993/ A/6 KA833 . . . . **305.5**
ATKINS, J/ Aani and the tree huggers./ 1995/ 3-5/3 KG853 . . . . . **FIC**
ATKINSON, M/ Snake book./ 1997/ 2-6/6 KC639 . . . . **597.96**
ATWATER, F/ Mr. Popper's penguins./ c1938/ 3-5/4 KG854 . . . **CE FIC**
ATWATER, R/ Mr. Popper's penguins./ c1938/ 3-5/4 KG854 . . **CE FIC**
Mr. Popper's penguins (Sound recording cassette)./ n.d./
3-5/4 KG854 . . . . **CE FIC**
Mr. Popper's penguins (Talking book)./ Mr. Popper's penguins (Talking
book)./ 1975/ n.d./ 3-5/4 KG854 . . . . **CE FIC**
3-5/4 KG854 . . . . **CE FIC**
AUCH, MJ/ Dumbstruck./ 1994/ 4-6/7 KH596 . . . . **FIC**
Eggs mark the spot./ 1996/ K-2/3 KF176 . . . . **CE E**
Eggs mark the spot (Kit)./ 1997/ K-2/3 KF176 . . . . **CE E**
Eggs mark the spot (Videocassette)./ 1997/ K-2/3 KF176 . . . **CE E**
Latchkey dog./ 1994/ 3-5/4 KG855 . . . . **FIC**
AUGUST, L/ In the month of Kislev: a story for Hanukkah./ 1992/
K-2/2 KF820 . . . . **CE E**
AULNOY, MD/ WHITE CAT (Videocassette)./ 1997/
K-2 KB382 . . . . **VCR 398.2**
AVAKIAN, M/ Historical album of Massachusetts./ 1994/
5-6/7 KE936 . . . . **974.4**
Historical album of New York./ 1993/ 5-6/8 KE954 . . . . . . **974.7**
AVERILL, E/ Fire cat./ c1960/ K-2/2 KF177 . . . . **E**
Fire cat (Braille)./ n.d./ K-2/2 KF177 . . . . **E**
Fire cat (Talking book)./ n.d./ K-2/2 KF177 . . . . **E**
AVERY, S/ Extraordinary American Indians./ 1992/ 5-6/7 KE747 . **970.1**
AVI/ Barn./ 1994/ 5-A/3 KG856 . . . . **FIC**
Barn (Sound recording cassette)./ 1997/ 5-A/3 KG856 . . . . . . **FIC**
Beyond the western sea: book one: the escape from home./ 1996/
6-A/5 KG857 . . . . **FIC**
Beyond the western sea: book two: Lord Kirkle's money./ 1996/
6-A/5 KG858 . . . . **FIC**
City of light, city of dark: a comic-book novel./ 1993/
4-6/6 KD409 . . . . **741.5**
Encounter at Easton./ 1980, 1994/ 5-A/6 KG860 . . . . **FIC**
Finding Providence: the story of Roger Williams./ 1997/
2-3/4 KE596 . . . . **B WILLIAMS, R.**
History of Helpless Harry: to which is added a variety of amusing and
entertaining adventures./ c1980, 1995/ 5-A/7 KG859 . . . . **FIC**
Night journeys./ c1979, 1994/ 5-A/6 KG860 . . . . **FIC**
Nothing but the truth: a documentary novel./ 1991/ 6-A/5 KG861 . **FIC**
Nothing but the truth: a documentary novel (Sound recording cassette)./
1993/ 6-A/5 KG861 . . . . **FIC**
Poppy./ 1995/ 3-5/6 KG862 . . . . **FIC**
Punch with Judy./ 1993/ 5-A/6 KG863 . . . . **FIC**
Smugglers' Island./ 1994/ 4-6/5 KG864 . . . . **FIC**
S.O.R. losers./ 1984/ 5-A/6 KG865 . . . . **FIC**
S.O.R. losers (Braille)./ n.d./ 5-A/6 KG865 . . . . **FIC**
S.O.R. losers (Sound recording cassette)./ n.d./ 5-A/6 KG865 . . . **FIC**
Tom, Babette, and Simon: three tales of transformation./ 1995/
3-6/4 KG866 . . . . **FIC**
True confessions of Charlotte Doyle./ 1990/ 5-A/6 KG867 . . . . . **FIC**
True confessions of Charlotte Doyle (Talking book)./ 1992/
5-A/6 KG867 . . . . **FIC**
AVISHAI, S/ Visit to the big house./ 1993/ 3-5/5 KG956 . . . . **FIC**
AXELROD, A/ Pigs in the pantry: fun with math and cooking./ 1997/
1-3/3 KF178 . . . . **E**
Pigs on a blanket./ 1996/ 2-3/2 KF179 . . . . **E**
SONGS OF THE WILD WEST./ 1991/ 2-A KD597 . . . . **789.2**
AXELROD, G/ Songs of nature and environment (Sound recording
cassette)./ 1978/ 1-3 KC293 . . . . **SRC 577**
AYERS, A/ Maxi, the star./ 1993/ P-2/2 KF201 . . . . **E**

Taxi Dog Christmas./ 1994/ P-2/3 KF202 . . . E
AYLESWORTH, J/ Cat and the fiddle and more./ 1992/ P-1 KD915 811
Old black fly./ 1992/ K-2/2 KF180 . . . E
Old black fly (Big book)./ 1995/ K-2/2 KF180 . . . E
Two terrible frights./ 1987/ P-1/3 KF181 . . . E
AYLIFFE, A/ Lucy's picture./ 1995/ P-1/2 KG153 . . . E
AYTO, R/ Lazy Jack./ 1995/ K-2/2 KB301 . . . 398.2
BABB, R/ Kid style nature crafts: 50 terrific things to make with nature's materials./ 1995/ 4-8/6 KD428 . . . 745.5
BABBITT, N/ Bub, or, The very best thing./ 1994/ P-2/2 KF182 . . . E
Cuentos del pobre diablo./ 1994/ 3-5/4 KG869 . . . CE FIC
Devil's other storybook./ 1987/ 5-6/8 KG868 . . . FIC
Devil's storybook./ 1974/ 3-5/4 KG869 . . . CE FIC
Goody Hall./ c1971, 1992/ 5-6/6 KG870 . . . FIC
Goody Hall (Talking book)./ n.d.,/ 5-6/6 KG870 . . . FIC
Knee-Knock Rise./ c1970/ 4-6/6 KG871 . . . CE FIC
Knee-Knock Rise (Talking book)./ Knee-Knock Rise (Talking book)./ n.d./ 1996/ 4-6/6 KG871 . . . CE FIC
4-6/6 KG871 . . . CE FIC
Search for delicious./ c1969/ 4-6/5 KG872 . . . CE FIC
Search for delicious (Talking book)./ Search for delicious (Talking book)./ 1995/ n.d./ 4-6/5 KG872 . . . CE FIC
4-6/5 KG872 . . . CE FIC
Tuck everlasting./ c1975/ 4-6/4 KG873 . . . CE FIC
Tuck everlasting (Kit)./ 1988/ 4-6/4 KG873 . . . CE FIC
Tuck everlasting (Sound recording cassette)./ n.d./ 4-6/4 KG873 . . . CE FIC
Tuck para siempre./ 1991/ 4-6/4 KG873 . . . CE FIC
Tuck para siempre (Sound recording cassette)./ 1993/ 4-6/4 KG873 . . . CE FIC
BACH, JS/ Bigfoot./ 1995/ 3-6/7 KA562 . . . 001.944
BACK, C/ Bean and plant./ 1986/ K-2/2 KC426 . . . 583
Chicken and egg./ 1986/ K-3/2 KC692 . . . 598.6
BACKER, M/ Lady in the box./ 1997/ 1-3/2 KG103 . . . E
BACON, P/ Teammates./ 1990/ 3-6/6 KD798 . . . 796.357
BAD HEART BULL, A/ Life and death of Crazy Horse./ 1996/ 6-A/7 KE307 . . . B CRAZY HORSE
BADEN, R/ And Sunday makes seven./ 1990/ 2-3/2 KB388 . . . 398.21
Y domingo, siete./ 1990/ 2-3/2 KB388 . . . 398.21
BADT, KL/ Good morning, let's eat!/ 1994/ 3-5/7 KB184 . . . 394.1
Greetings!/ 1994/ 3-5/6 KB245 . . . 395.4
Hair there and everywhere./ 1994/ 4-6/6 KB169 . . . 391.5
Pass the bread!/ 1995/ 4-6/6 KD291 . . . 641.8
BAGERT, B/ Poetry for young people./ 1995/ 5-A KD998 . . . 811
BAGNOLD, E/ National Velvet./ c1935, 1985/ 4-A/5 KG874 . . . FIC
National Velvet (Braille)./ n.d.,/ 4-A/5 KG874 . . . FIC
National Velvet (Sound recording cassette)./ n.d.,/ 4-A/5 KG874 . FIC
National Velvet (Talking book)./ n.d.,/ 4-A/5 KG874 . . . FIC
BAHOUS, S/ Sitti and the cats: a tale of friendship./ 1993/ 3-4/7 KB257 . . . 398.2
BAHTI, T/ When clay sings./ c1972, 1987/ 3-5/6 KE748 . . . 970.1
BAILEY, CS/ Miss Hickory./ c1946/ 4-6/4 KG875 . . . CE FIC
Miss Hickory (Sound recording cassette)./ n.d./ 4-6/4 KG875 . CE FIC
Miss Hickory (Talking book)./ 1972/ 4-6/4 KG875 . . . CE FIC
BAILEY, D/ Cycling./ 1990/ 2-4/2 KD826 . . . 796.6
Fishing./ 1990/ K-2/2 KD861 . . . 799.1
Swimming./ 1990/ 2-4/2 KD846 . . . 797.2
Track and field./ 1991/ 1-3/4 KD809 . . . 796.42
BAIUL, O/ Oksana: my own story./ 1997/ 3-6/4 KE247 . B BAIUL, O.
BAKER, A/ Story of King Arthur./ 1997/ 4/7 KB465 . . . 398.22
Uncle Bouqui of Haiti (Talking book)./ 1959/ K-A KB729 . . TB 398.27
BAKER, B/ One Saturday morning./ 1994/ 1-3/1 KF183 . . . E
One Saturday morning (Sound recording cassette)./ 1997/ 1-3/1 KF183 . . . E
Staying with Grandmother./ 1994/ 1-3/1 KF184 . . . E
BAKER, D/ Paul Bunyan (Videocassette)./ 1990/ 3-5 KB447 . . . VCR 398.22
BAKER, DB/ EXPLORERS AND DISCOVERERS: FROM ALEXANDER THE GREAT TO SALLY RIDE./ 1995/ 5-A KA470 . . . REF 910
BAKER, G/ Storytelling, art and technique. 3rd ed./ 1995/ KA244 . . . PROF 372.67
BAKER, J/ Story of rosy dock./ 1995/ K-4/6 KF115 . . . 994
BAKER, K/ BIG FAT HEN./ 1994/ P-1/1 KB793 . . . 398.8
Hide and snake./ 1991/ P-1/2 KF186 . . . E
Who is the beast?/ 1990/ P-K/1 KF187 . . . E
Who is the beast? (Big book)./ 1991/ P-K/1 KF187 . . . E
BAKER, KL/ Floppy teddy bear./ 1995/ P-1/2 KF982 . . . E
Seneca./ 1997/ K-2/2 KF185 . . . E
BAKER, PJ/ My first book of sign./ c1986, 1995/ K-3 KB821 . . . 419
BAKER, SA/ Grandpa is a flyer./ 1995/ 1-3/5 KF188 . . . E
BALDWIN, LE/ Reading crisis: why poor children fall behind./ 1990/ KA219 . . . PROF 372.6
BALKWILL, FR/ Amazing schemes within your genes./ 1993/ 4-8/6 KC288 . . . 576.5
DNA is here to stay./ 1993/ 5-6/7 KC279 . . . 572.8
BALL, D/ Emily Eyefinger./ 1992/ 1-3/2 KG876 . . . FIC
BALL, Z/ Bristle Face./ 1990/ 5-A/6 KG877 . . . FIC
BALLARD, RD/ Exploring the Bismarck./ 1991/ 5-6/7 KE668 . . . 940.54
Exploring the Titanic./ 1988/ 4-6/8 KB025 . . . 363.12
BALLARD, SD/ COUNT ON READING HANDBOOK: TIPS FOR PLANNING READING MOTIVATION PROGRAMS./ 1997/ KA206 . . . PROF 372.4
BALLESTAR, V/ Drawing dinosaurs./ 1996/ 5-A/3 KD418 . . . 743
Painting and coloring dinosaurs./ 1996/ 5-A/3 KD419 . . . 743
BALLINGER, E/ Detective dictionary: a handbook for aspiring sleuths./ 1994/ 4-6/7 KB028 . . . 363.2
BALLONGA, J/ Barmi: a Mediterranean city through the ages./ 1990/ A/11 KA895 . . . 307.76
Lebek: a city of Northern Europe through the ages./ 1991/ A/10 KA896 . . . 307.76
San Rafael: a Central American city through the ages./ 1992/ A/8 KA897 . . . 307.76
BALTUCK, N/ Apples from heaven: multicultural folk tales about stories and storytellers./ 1995/ KA265 . . . PROF 398.2
BANCROFT, B/ Dreamtime: aboriginal stories./ 1994/ 4-5/6 KB506 . . . 398.23
BANCROFT, H/ Animals in winter. Rev. ed./ 1997/ K-2/2 KC482 . . . 591.56
BANEK, YS/ Computer dictionary for kids...and their parents./ 1995/ 4-A/9 KA566 . . . 004
BANG, M/ Chattanooga sludge./ 1996/ 4-6/7 KD081 . . . 628.4
Dawn./ 1983/ 1-3/2 KF189 . . . E
FROM SEA TO SHINING SEA: A TREASURY OF AMERICAN FOLKLORE AND FOLK SONGS./ 1993/ K-6 KD899 . . . 810.8
Goose./ 1996/ P-2/2 KF190 . . . E
Paper crane./ 1985/ K-3/4 KF191 . . . CE E
Paper crane (Braille)./ n.d./ K-3/4 KF191 . . . CE E
Paper crane (Sound recording cassette)./ n.d./ K-3/4 KF191 . . . CE E
Ten, nine, eight./ 1983/ P-K KF192 . . . E
Ten, nine, eight (Big book)./ 1993/ P-K KF192 . . . E
Ten, nine, eight (Board book)./ 1996/ P-K KF192 . . . E
Tye May and the magic brush./ c1981, 1992/ 1-3/2 KF193 . . . E
Wiley and the Hairy Man./ n.d.,/ 1-3/2 KB389 . . . 398.21
Wiley and the Hairy Man: adapted from an American folk tale./ c1976, 1987/ 1-3/2 KB389 . . . 398.21
BANGS, E/ Yankee Doodle. 2nd ed./ c1976, 1996/ P-2 KD557 . 789.2
BANISH, R/ Forever family./ 1992/ 2-4/3 KB011 . . . 362.73
BANKS, K/ Spider spider./ 1996/ P-1/2 KF194 . . . E
BANNATYNE-CUGNET, J/ Prairie alphabet./ 1992/ 2-6/6 KE811 971.2
Prairie year./ 1994/ 4-6/4 KE812 . . . 971.2
BANNERMAN, H/ Sam and the tigers: a new telling of LITTLE BLACK SAMBO./ 1996/ K-3/2 KF966 . . . E
Story of Little Babaji./ 1996/ K-2/2 KF195 . . . E
BANYAI, I/ Re-zoom./ 1995/ 2-A KF196 . . . E
Zoom./ 1995/ P-A KF197 . . . E
BAQUEDANO, E/ Aztec, Inca and Maya./ 1993/ 4-6/9 KE829 . . 972
BARBER, A/ Catkin./ 1996/ 4-6/6 KG878 . . . FIC
Mousehole cat./ 1990/ 4-6/6 KG879 . . . FIC
BARBER, BE/ Saturday at The New You./ 1994/ K-3/3 KF198 . . . E
BARBOSA, RA/ African animal tales./ 1993/ 2-4/6 KB526 . . . 398.24
BARBOUR, K/ MARVELOUS MATH: A BOOK OF POEMS./ 1997/ 1-4 KE071 . . . 811.008
Sip of Aesop./ 1995/ K-3 KE050 . . . 811
BARCHAS, S/ Giant and the rabbit: six bilingual folktales from Hispanic culture (Sound recording cassette)./ 1996/ 2-4 KB258 . . SRC 398.2
Pinata!: bilingual songs for children (Compact disc)./ 1991/ K-6 KD605 . . . SRC 789.3
Pinata!: bilingual songs for children (Sound recording cassette)./ 1991/ K-6 KD605 . . . SRC 789.3
This old man/Este viejito (Sound recording cassette)./ 1997/ K-2 KD606 . . . SRC 789.3
BARCHERS, SI/ Creating and managing the literate classroom./ 1990/ KA218 . . . PROF 372.6
BARE, CS/ Guinea pigs don't read books./ c1985, 1993/ P-2/3 KD177 . . . 636
Never grab a deer by the ear./ 1993/ 4-5/5 KC795 . . . 599.65
Toby the tabby kitten./ 1995/ K-3/2 KD229 . . . 636.8
BARKER, C/ Complete book of children's activities./ 1993/ KA194 . . . PROF 372.13
BARKER, M/ Magical hands./ 1989/ 1-3/5 KF199 . . . E
Magical hands (Sound recording cassette)./ 1994/ 1-3/5 KF199 . . . E
BARKIN, C/ Happy Thanksgiving!/ 1987/ 3-6/6 KB221 . . . 394.264
Holiday handbook./ 1994/ 5-A/7 KA413 . . . REF 394.26
How to write a great school report./ 1983/ 4-6/7 KB088 . . . 371.302
Jobs for kids: the guide to having fun and making money./ 1990/ 5-6/7 KD305 . . . 650.1
New complete babysitter's handbook./ 1995/ 5-6/6 KD302 . . . 649

New complete babysitter's handbook (Sound recording cassette)./ 1997/
   5-6/6 KD302 . . . . **649**
Sincerely yours: how to write great letters./ 1993/
   3-6/7 KD870 . . . . **808.6**
Social smarts: manners for today's kids./ 1996/ 4-6/6 KB243 . . **395.3**
BARKLEY, J/ Sounder./ c1969/ 4-A/4 KG851 . . . . **CE FIC**
BARNARD, B/ North American Indians./ 1996/ 4-6/10 KE755 . **970.1**
BARNES, M/ Ontario./ 1995/ 4-6/10 KE817 . . . . **971.3**
BARNES-MURPHY, R/ Leroy Potts meets the McCrooks./ 1997/
   1-3/2 KH677 . . . . **FIC**
BARNETT, M/ Me and Neesie./ c1975/ K-2/3 KF642 . . . . **E**
BARNHART, CA/ SCOTT FORESMAN BEGINNING DICTIONARY./
   c1983, 1994/ 2-4 KB836 . . . . **423**
BARNHART, CL/ WORLD BOOK DICTIONARY./ 1996/
   5-6 KA432 . . . . **REF 423**
BARNHART, RK/ WORLD BOOK DICTIONARY./ 1996/
   5-6 KA432 . . . . **REF 423**
BARRACCA, D/ Adventures of taxi dog./ 1990/ P-2/2 KF200 . . . . **CE E**
   Aventuras de Maxi, el perro taxista./ 1996/ P-2/2 KF200 . . . . **CE E**
   Maxi, the hero./ 1991/ P-2/2 KF200 . . . . **CE E**
   Maxi, the star./ 1993/ P-2/2 KF201 . . . . **E**
   Taxi Dog Christmas./ 1994/ P-2/3 KF202 . . . . **E**
BARRACCA, S/ Adventures of taxi dog./ 1990/ P-2/2 KF200 . . . . **CE E**
   Maxi, the star./ 1993/ P-2/2 KF201 . . . . **E**
   Taxi Dog Christmas./ 1994/ P-2/3 KF202 . . . . **E**
BARRETT, A/ Random House book of stories from the ballet./ 1994/
   3-6/6 KD696 . . . . **792.8**
BARRETT, J/ Cloudy with a chance of meatballs./ 1978/ P-2/7 KF203 **E**
BARRETT, NS/ Flying machines./ 1994/ 4-6/8 KD104 . . . . . **629.133**
BARRETT, R/ Cloudy with a chance of meatballs./ 1978/ P-2/7 KF203 **E**
   Dust for dinner./ 1995/ 2-5/2 KG625 . . . . **E**
   Ghastlies, goops & pincushions./ 1989/ 4-A KD965 . . . . **811**
BARRETT, SL/ It's all in your head: a guide to understanding your brain
   and boosting your brain power. Rev. ed./ 1992/ A/8 KA633 . . **153**
BARRETT, T/ Growing up in colonial America./ 1995/
   4-6/9 KE869 . . . . **973.2**
   Nat Turner and the slave revolt./ c1993, 1995/
   5-6/6 KE577 . . . . **B TURNER, N.**
BARRON, AE/ Internet and instruction: activities and ideas./ 1996/
   KA047 . . . . **PROF 025.06**
   New technologies for education: a beginner's guide. 3rd ed./ 1997/
   KA176 . . . . **PROF 371.3**
BARRY, P/ Super kids publishing company./ 1990/ KA333 . . **PROF 808**
BARSTOW, B/ Beyond picture books: a guide to first readers. 2nd ed./
   1995/ KA011 . . . . **PROF 011.62**
BARTH, E/ Holly, reindeer and colored lights: the story of Christmas
   symbols./ c1971/ 5-6/7 KB231 . . . . **394.266**
   Holly, reindeer and colored lights: the story of Christmas symbols (Sound
   recording cassette)./ n.d./ 5-6/7 KB231 . . . . **394.266**
   Shamrocks, harps, and shillelaghs: the story of the St. Patrick's Day
   symbols./ c1977/ 5-6/7 KB218 . . . . **394.262**
BARTLETT, A/ Cow, a bee, a cookie, and me./ 1997/ K-2/2 KF768 . . **E**
BARTLETT, J/ Bartlett's familiar quotations: a collection of passages,
   phrases and proverbs traced to sources in ancient and modern literature.
   16th ed./ 1992/ A KA458 . . . . **REF 803**
BARTO, R/ Quick and easy cookbook./ c1981, 1985/ 1-4 KD281 **641.5**
BARTOLETTI, SC/ Growing up in coal country./ 1996/
   4-6/8 KA934 . . . . **331.3**
BARTON, B/ Airplanes./ 1986/ P-1/2 KB155 . . . . **387.7**
   Big machines (Board book)./ 1995/ P KF204 . . . . **BB E**
   Boats./ 1986/ P-1/2 KB151 . . . . **387.2**
   Building a house./ 1981/ P-2/2 KD355 . . . . **690**
   Dinosaurs (Board book)./ 1995/ P KF205 . . . . **BB E**
   Gila monsters meet you at the airport./ 1980/ K-2/2 KG480 . . . . **E**
   I want to be an astronaut./ 1988/ P-2/2 KF206 . . . . **E**
   Jump, frog, jump! New ed./ c1981, 1996/ P-1/1 KF864 . . . . **CE E**
   Machines at work./ 1987/ P-K/2 KF207 . . . . **E**
   Paper airplane book./ c1971/ 3-5/6 KD113 . . . . **629.133**
   Three bears./ 1991/ P-K/1 KB527 . . . . **398.24**
   Tools (Board book)./ 1995/ P KF208 . . . . **BB E**
   Truck song./ 1984/ P-1 KG502 . . . . **CE E**
   Trucks./ 1986/ P-1/2 KB161 . . . . **388.3**
   Zoo animals (Board book)./ 1995/ P KF209 . . . . **BB E**
BARTON, H/ Geography from A to Z: a picture glossary./ 1988/
   3-6 KE150 . . . . **910**
   Maps and globes./ 1985/ 2-5/7 KE169 . . . . **912**
   Rain and hail. Rev. ed./ 1983/ K-3/2 KC188 . . . . **551.5**
   Sewing by hand./ 1994/ 3-5/3 KD297 . . . . **646.2**
BARTON, J/ Baby Duck and the bad eyeglasses./ 1996/ P-K/1 KF717 **E**
   In the rain with Baby Duck./ 1995/ P-1/2 KF718 . . . . **E**
   You're the boss, Baby Duck!/ 1997/ P-1/2 KF722 . . . . **E**
BARTONE, E/ American too./ 1996/ 1-3/3 KF210 . . . . **E**
   Peppe the lamplighter./ 1993/ 1-3/2 KF211 . . . . **E**
BASE, G/ Animalia./ c1986, 1993/ P-A KF212 . . . . **E**

BASH, B/ Ancient ones: the world of the old-growth Douglas fir./ 1994/
   3-6/7 KC435 . . . . **585**
   Desert giant: the world of the saguaro cactus./ 1989/
   2-6/6 KC427 . . . . **583**
   Shadows of night: the hidden world of the Little Brown Bat./ 1993/
   1-3/5 KC758 . . . . **599.4**
   Urban roosts: where birds nest in the city./ 1990/
   3-6/7 KC672 . . . . **598.156**
BASKIN, L/ Animals that ought to be: poems about imaginary pets./ 1996/
   K-3 KD985 . . . . **811**
BASKIN-SALZBERG, A/ Flightless birds./ 1993/ 5-6/7 KC691 . . . **598.5**
BASSETT, J/ It's groundhog day!/ 1987/ K-2/4 KF929 . . . . **E**
BATEMAN, T/ Ring of Truth: an original Irish tale./ 1997/
   1-3/5 KF213 . . . . **E**
BATES, KL/ America the beautiful./ 1993/ K-3 KD558 . . . . . . **789.2**
BATHERMAN, M/ Alphabet tale. New ed., rev. and re-illustrated./ 1994/
   P-K/3 KF599 . . . . **E**
BAUER, CF/ Celebrations: read-aloud holiday and theme book programs./
   1985/ KA342 . . . . **PROF 808.8**
   Leading kids to books through magic./ 1996/ KA066 . . . **PROF 027.62**
   Poetry break: an annotated anthology with ideas for introducing children
   to poetry./ 1995/ KA234 . . . . **PROF 372.64**
   Presenting reader's theater: plays and poems to read aloud./ 1987/
   KA329 . . . . **PROF 792**
   Read for the fun of it: active programming with books for children./
   1992/ KA067 . . . . **PROF 027.62**
   This way to books./ 1983/ KA089 . . . . **PROF 028.5**
BAUER, H/ Hawai'i: the Pacific State. Rev. and updated edition./ 1997/
   5-A/6 KF123 . . . . **996.9**
BAUER, J/ Sticks./ 1996/ 6-A/4 KG880 . . . . **FIC**
BAUER, MD/ Ghost eye./ 1992/ 4-6/6 KG881 . . . . **FIC**
   On my honor./ 1986/ 5-6/7 KG882 . . . . **CE FIC**
   On my honor (Braille)./ n.d./ 5-6/7 KG882 . . . . **CE FIC**
   On my honor (Talking book)./ 1992/ 5-6/7 KG882 . . . . . . **CE FIC**
   Question of trust./ 1994/ 5-A/6 KG883 . . . . **FIC**
BAUM, A/ Calculators./ 1995/ 4-8/9 KB932 . . . . **510**
   Graphs./ 1995/ A/7 KB941 . . . . **511**
BAUM, LF/ Emerald City of Oz./ 1993/ 4-6/7 KG884 . . . . **FIC**
   Mago de Oz./ 1987/ 4-6/6 KG886 . . . . **CE FIC**
   Marvelous land of Oz (Talking book)./ 1993/ 4-6/6 KG886 . . **CE FIC**
   Ozma of Oz./ 1989/ 4-6/7 KG884 . . . . **FIC**
   Patchwork girl of Oz./ 1995/ 4-6/7 KG884 . . . . **FIC**
   Road to Oz./ 1991/ 4-6/7 KG884 . . . . **FIC**
   Road to Oz (Sound recording cassette)./ 1993/ 4-6/7 KG884 . . . **FIC**
   Scarecrow of Oz./ 1997/ 4-6/7 KG885 . . . . **FIC**
   Tik-Tok of Oz./ 1996/ 4-6/7 KG884 . . . . **FIC**
   Wonderful Wizard of Oz./ 1987/ 4-6/6 KG886 . . . . **CE FIC**
   Wonderful Wizard of Oz (Braille)./ n.d./ 4-6/6 KG886 . . . . . **CE FIC**
   Wonderful Wizard of Oz (Talking book)./ n.d./ 4-6/6 KG886 . . **CE FIC**
BAVIERA, R/ Boy called Slow: the true story of Sitting Bull./ 1994/
   3-4/6 KE541 . . . . **B SITTING BULL**
BAWDEN, N/ Carrie's war./ c1973/ 4-6/4 KG887 . . . . **FIC**
   Granny the Pag./ 1996/ 5-A/4 KG888 . . . . **FIC**
   Handful of thieves./ c1967, 1991/ 5-A/5 KG889 . . . . **FIC**
   Handful of thieves (Sound recording cassette)./ 1995,/
   5-A/5 KG889 . . . . **FIC**
   House of secrets./ c1963, 1992/ 5-A/7 KG890 . . . . **FIC**
   Humbug./ 1992/ 5-A/5 KG891 . . . . **FIC**
   Real Plato Jones./ 1993/ 6-A/6 KG892 . . . . **FIC**
   Real Plato Jones (Sound recording cassette)./ 1995/
   6-A/6 KG892 . . . . **FIC**
   Witch's daughter./ c1966, 1991/ 5-A/6 KG893 . . . . **FIC**
BAYLEY, N/ Mousehole cat./ 1990/ 4-6/6 KG879 . . . . **FIC**
BAYLOR, B/ Desert is theirs./ c1975/ 4-6/5 KC362 . . . . . . **578.754**
   When clay sings./ c1972, 1987/ 3-5/6 KE748 . . . . **970.1**
BAYNES, P/ Lion, the witch and the wardrobe./ 1994/
   5-A/6 KH405 . . . . **CE FIC**
   Thanks be to God: prayers from around the world./ 1990/
   3-6 KA712 . . . . **242**
BEACON, M/ MAVIS BEACON TEACHES TYPING! (Microcomputer
   program)./ 1987/ 4-A KD310 . . . . **MCP 652.3**
BEALER, AW/ Only the names remain: the Cherokees and the Trail of
   Tears. 2nd ed./ 1996/ 5-6/8 KE758 . . . . **970.3**
BECHT, LC/ Singing calendar (Sound recording cassette)./ 1984/
   P-1 KC071 . . . . **SRC 529**
BECHTEL, LS/ Trumpeter of Krakow. New ed./ c1966, 1973/
   /7 KH343 . . . . **FIC**
BECK, I/ Owl and the Pussy-cat./ 1996/ P-2 KE105 . . . . **821**
BECKER, J/ Seven little rabbits./ 1973/ P-2/3 KF214 . . . . **E**
BEDARD, M/ Emily./ 1992/ 2-5/2 KF215 . . . . **E**
BEDDOWS, E/ Emperor's panda./ c1986, 1987/ 4-A/8 KH063 . . . . **FIC**
   Joyful noise: poems for two voices./ 1988/ 4-6 KD934 . . . . . . **811**
   Rooster's gift./ 1996/ K-2/3 KF414 . . . . **E**
BEEN, D/ Waking upside down./ 1996/ 1-3/6 KF693 . . . . **E**

BEERS, GK/ YOUR READING: AN ANNOTATED BOOKLIST FOR MIDDLE
SCHOOL AND JUNIOR HIGH. 1995-96 ed./ 1996/
5-A KA373 . . . . **REF 011.62**
BEGAY, S/ Magic of Spider Woman./ 1996/ 4-5/6 KB733 . . . **398.27**
BEHR, J/ Calculator puzzles, tricks and games./ c1976, 1991/
4-6/9 KB930 . . . . **510**
BEHR, S/ Soup should be seen, not heard!: the kids' etiquette book./
c1988, 1990/ 2-6/5 KB247 . . . . **395.5**
BEHRENS, J/ Missions of the central coast./ 1996/ 4-6/9 KF076 . **979.4**
Whales of the world./ 1987/ 3-5/4 KC765 . . . . . . **599.5**
Whalewatch./ 1978/ 2-4/4 KC766 . . . . **599.5**
BEIFUSS, J/ Armadillo Ray./ 1995/ K-2/4 KF216 . . . . . **E**
BEIRNE, B/ Children of the Ecuadorean Highlands./ 1996/
3-6/9 KF112 . . . . **986.6**
BEISNER, M/ Heavenly zoo: legends and tales of the stars./ c1979, 1996/
5-6/8 KB710 . . . . **398.26**
BELL, A/ Seven ravens: a fairy tale./ 1995/ 3-5/7 KB309 . . . . . **398.2**
Twelve dancing princesses: a fairy tale./ 1995/ 3-4/6 KB311 . . **398.2**
BELL, F/ Jenny's corner./ 1995/ 5-A/7 KG894 . . . . . **FIC**
BELLAIRS, J/ Dark secret of Weatherend./ c1984/ 6-A/6 KG895 . . **FIC**
Dark secret of Weatherend (Braille)./ n.d./ 6-A/6 KG895 . . . . . **FIC**
Dark secret of Weatherend (Sound recording cassette)./ n.d./
6-A/6 KG895 . . . . **FIC**
Doom of the haunted opera./ 1995/ 4-6/6 KG896 . . . . . **FIC**
Figure in the shadows./ 1993/ 4-6/5 KG897 . . . . . **FIC**
Ghost in the mirror./ 1993/ 4-6/5 KG897 . . . . . **FIC**
House with a clock in its walls./ c1973/ 4-6/5 KG897 . . . **FIC**
Letter, the witch, and the ring./ c1976/ 4-6/5 KG897 . . . **FIC**
Mansion in the mist./ c1992/ 4-6/6 KG895 . . . . . **FIC**
Treasure of Alpheus Winterborn./ 1997/ 6-A/6 KG895 . . . **FIC**
Treasure of Alpheus Winterborn (Braille)./ n.d./ 6-A/6 KG895 . . . **FIC**
Treasure of Alpheus Winterborn (Sound recording cassette)./ n.d./
6-A/6 KG895 . . . . **FIC**
BELLER, SP/ To hold this ground: a desperate battle at Gettysburg./ 1995/
A/9 KE897 . . . . **973.7**
BELLVILLE, CW/ Airplane book./ 1991/ 4-6/7 KD105 . . . . . **629.133**
Flying in a hot air balloon./ 1993/ 4-6/7 KD852 . . . . . **797.5**
BELTON, S/ May'naise sandwiches and sunshine tea./ 1994/
1-3/3 KF217 . . . . **E**
BEMELMANS, L/ Madeline./ 1962/ P-2/4 KF218 . . . . . **CE E**
Madeline and other Bemelmans (Talking book)./ n.d./ P-2 KF219 . **TB E**
Madeline (Big book)./ 1993/ P-2/4 KF218 . . . . . **CE E**
Madeline (Braille)./ n.d./ P-2/4 KF218 . . . . . **CE E**
Madeline (Kit)./ 1975/ P-2/4 KF218 . . . . . **CE E**
Madeline (Spanish version)./ 1993/ P-2/4 KF218 . . . . . **CE E**
Madeline (Spanish version) (Kit)./ 1997/ P-2/4 KF218 . . . **CE E**
Madeline (Videocassette)./ 1989/ P-2/4 KF218 . . . . . **CE E**
Madeline's rescue./ c1953/ P-2/2 KF220 . . . . . **CE E**
Madeline's rescue (Braille)./ n.d./ P-2/2 KF220 . . . . . **CE E**
Madeline's rescue (Kit)./ 1978/ P-2/2 KF220 . . . . . **CE E**
BEN FRANKLIN BOOK OF EASY AND INCREDIBLE EXPERIMENTS./
1995/ A/8 KB889 . . . . **507.8**
BEN IZZY, J/ Beggar King and other tales from around the world (Sound
recording cassette)./ 1993/ 2-A KB260 . . . . . **SRC 398.2**
Buried treasures: a storyteller's journey (Compact disc)./ 1995/
3-A KB261 . . . . **SRC 398.2**
Buried treasures: a storyteller's journey (Sound recording cassette)./
1995/ 3-A KB261 . . . . **SRC 398.2**
Stories from far away (Sound recording cassette)./ 1991/
3-A KB262 . . . . **SRC 398.2**
BEN-AMI, D/ Tornado./ 1996/ 2-5/3 KG965 . . . . . **FIC**
BEN-ASHER, N/ JUNIOR JEWISH ENCYCLOPEDIA. 11th rev. ed./ 1991/
5-6 KA396 . . . . **REF 296**
BENCHLEY, N/ George, the drummer boy./ c1977/ 1-3/2 KF221 . . . **E**
George, the drummer boy (Braille)./ n.d./ 1-3/2 KF221 . . . . . **E**
Sam the minuteman./ c1969/ 1-3/2 KF222 . . . . . **E**
Sam the minuteman (Talking book)./ n.d./ 1-3/2 KF222 . . . . . **E**
BENDER, R/ A to Z beastly jamboree./ 1996/ K-2 KB830 . . . . . **421**
BENDICK, J/ Caves!: underground worlds./ 1995/ 5-6/6 KC171 **551.44**
Egyptian tombs./ 1989/ 4-6/7 KE632 . . . . . **932**
Sun: our very own star./ 1991/ 1-3/5 KC044 . . . . . **523.7**
Tombs of the ancient Americas./ 1993/ 3-5/8 KB174 . . . . . **393**
BENITEZ, M/ How spider tricked snake./ 1989/ K-1/1 KB528 . . **398.24**
BENJAMIN, A/ Nickel buys a rhyme./ 1993/ P-2 KD916 . . . . . **811**
BENNET, J/ Harry's Mad./ c1984, 1997/ 5-A/7 KH348 . . . . . **FIC**
BENNETT, J/ Danny, the champion of the world./ c1975, 1988/
4-6/6 KH054 . . . . **FIC**
BENNETT, WJ/ BOOK OF VIRTUES FOR YOUNG PEOPLE: A TREASURY
OF GREAT MORAL STORIES./ 1997/ KA343 . . . . **PROF 808.8**
CHILDREN'S BOOK OF VIRTUES./ 1995/ K-3 KD871 . . . . . **808.8**
BENSON, AC/ Connecting kids and the Internet: a handbook for librarians,
teachers, and parents./ 1996/ KA048 . . . . . **PROF 025.06**
BENTLEY, N/ Putting on a play: the young playwright's guide to scripting,
directing, and performing./ 1996/ 4-6/7 KD687 . . . . . **792**

Young author's do-it-yourself book: how to write, illustrate, and produce
your own book./ 1994/ 2-6/4 KD863 . . . . . **808**
Young producer's video book: how to write, direct, and shoot your own
video./ 1995/ 3-6/4 KD686 . . . . . **791.45**
BENTON, M/ Dinosaur and other prehistoric animal factfinder./ 1992/
4-6/7 KC234 . . . . **560**
BENVENUTI/ My everyday Spanish word book./ 1982/ 1-3 KB861 **468**
BERENSTAIN, J/ BERENSTAIN BEARS GET IN A FIGHT. School ed. (CD-
ROM)./ 1995/ K-3 KF223 . . . . . **CDR E**
BERENSTAIN BEARS IN THE DARK. School ed. (CD-ROM)./ 1996/
K-3 KF224 . . . . **CDR E**
Berenstain Bears learn about strangers./ 1985/ K-2/4 KF225 . . . . **CE E**
Berenstain Bears: no girls allowed./ 1986/ K-2/4 KF226 . . . . . **E**
Inside, outside, upside down./ c1968/ K-1/1 KF227 . . . . . **E**
BERENSTAIN, S/ Berenstain Bears and the sitter./ 1981/ K-2/4 KF226 **E**
Berenstain Bears and the spooky old tree./ 1978/ K-1/1 KF227 . . . . **E**
Berenstain Bears and too much birthday./ 1986/ K-2/4 KF226 . . . . **E**
Berenstain Bears get in a fight./ 1982/ K-2/4 KF226 . . . . . **E**
BERENSTAIN BEARS GET IN A FIGHT. School ed. (CD-ROM)./ 1995/
K-3 KF223 . . . . **CDR E**
Berenstain Bears go to camp./ 1982/ K-2/4 KF226 . . . . . **E**
BERENSTAIN BEARS IN THE DARK. School ed. (CD-ROM)./ 1996/
K-3 KF224 . . . . **CDR E**
Berenstain Bears learn about strangers./ 1985/ K-2/4 KF225 . . . **CE E**
Berenstain Bears' moving day./ 1981/ K-2/4 KF226 . . . . . **E**
Berenstain Bears: no girls allowed./ 1986/ K-2/4 KF226 . . . . . **E**
Berenstain Bears visit the dentist./ 1981/ K-2/4 KF226 . . . . . **E**
Inside, outside, upside down./ c1968/ K-1/1 KF227 . . . . . **E**
Los osos Berenstain y demasiada fiesta./ 1993/ K-2/4 KF226 . . . . **E**
Osos Berenstain dia de mudanza./ 1994/ K-2/4 KF226 . . . . . **E**
BERENZY, A/ Frog prince./ 1989/ 3-5/5 KG898 . . . . . **FIC**
Into the sea./ 1996/ 1-3/3 KC618 . . . . . **597.92**
Rapunzel./ 1995/ 2-4/4 KB263 . . . . . **398.2**
BERG, CR/ Gift of the poinsettia./El regalo de la flor de nochebuena./
1995/ 3-5/4 KH507 . . . . **FIC**
BERGER, G/ How's the weather?: a look at weather and how it changes./
1993/ K-5/2 KC187 . . . . . **551.5**
Round and round the money goes: what money is and how we use it./
1993/ 2-4/2 KA948 . . . . . **332.4**
Where are the stars during the day?: a book about stars./ 1993/
1-4/2 KC048 . . . . . **523.8**
Where did your family come from?: a book about immigrants./ 1993/
2-4/2 KA925 . . . . . **325.73**
Whole world in your hands: looking at maps./ 1993/
1-3/2 KE166 . . . . . **912**
BERGER, M/ Germs make me sick! Rev. ed./ 1995/
1-3/5 KD021 . . . . . **616.9**
How's the weather?: a look at weather and how it changes./ 1993/
K-5/2 KC187 . . . . . **551.5**
Oil spill!/ 1994/ 1-4/4 KB057 . . . . . **363.73**
Round and round the money goes: what money is and how we use it./
1993/ 2-4/2 KA948 . . . . . **332.4**
Switch on, switch off./ 1989/ K-3/5 KC130 . . . . . **537**
Where are the stars during the day?: a book about stars./ 1993/
1-4/2 KC048 . . . . . **523.8**
Where did your family come from?: a book about immigrants./ 1993/
2-4/2 KA925 . . . . . **325.73**
Whole world in your hands: looking at maps./ 1993/
1-3/2 KE166 . . . . . **912**
Why I cough, sneeze, shiver, hiccup, and yawn./ 1983/
1-3/2 KC963 . . . . . **612.8**
Why I cough, sneeze, shiver, hiccup, and yawn (Sound recording
cassette)./ n.d./ 1-3/2 KC963 . . . . . **612.8**
BERGIN, DP/ Zero Street (Videocassette)./ 1995/
4-6 KA894 . . . . . **VCR 307.76**
BERGIN, M/ Greek temple./ 1992/ 4-6/7 KE643 . . . . . **938**
Medieval castle./ 1990/ 4-6/8 KE649 . . . . . **940.1**
16th century mosque./ 1994/ 4-A/10 KD391 . . . . . **726**
BERGSTROM, C/ All the best contests for kids, 1996-1997. 5th ed./
1996/ 3-6/7 KD677 . . . . . **790.1**
BERGSTROM, JM/ All the best contests for kids, 1996-1997. 5th ed./
1996/ 3-6/7 KD677 . . . . . **790.1**
BERKOWITZ, RE/ Information problem-solving: the Big Six Skills approach
to library and information skills instruction./ 1990/
KA063 . . . . . **PROF 025.5**
BERLER, R/ Super book of baseball./ 1991/ 4-A/7 KD794 . . . **796.357**
BERLINER, D/ Living in space./ 1993/ 5-6/9 KD139 . . . . . **629.47**
BERMAN, A/ James McNeil Whistler./ 1993/
5-A/7 KE592 . . . . . **B WHISTLER, J.**
BERMAN, M/ Spin, spider, spin: songs for a greater appreciation of nature
(Sound recording cassette)./ 1974/ P-1 KB916 . . . . . **SRC 508**
BERMAN, R/ American bison./ 1992/ 5-6/7 KC790 . . . . . **599.64**
BERNARDIN, J/ Big men, big country: a collection of American tall tales./
1993/ 4-A/7 KB493 . . . . . **398.22**

Giants!: stories from around the world./ 1995/ 4-6/7 KB381 . . . **398.2**
Little folk: stories from around the world./ 1997/ 2-4/6 KB494 **398.22**
BERNHARD, D/ Dragonfly./ 1993/ 2-4/4 KC534 . . . . **595.7**
Eagles: lions of the sky./ 1994/ 3-6/6 KC710 . . . . **598.9**
Girl who wanted to hunt: a Siberian tale./ 1994/ 3-5/3 KB720 **398.27**
Happy New Year!/ 1996/ 1-3/7 KB205 . . . . **394.261**
How Snowshoe Hare rescued the Sun: a tale from the Arctic./ 1993/
1-2/4 KB529 . . . . **398.24**
Reindeer./ 1994/ 4-5/7 KC796 . . . . **599.65**
Ride on mother's back: a day of baby carrying around the world./ 1996/
1-2/7 KB170 . . . . **392.1**
Salamanders./ 1995/ 2-5/6 KC598 . . . . **597.8**
Tree that rains: the flood myth of the Huichol Indians of Mexico./ 1994/
3-4/5 KB699 . . . . **398.26**
Trouble./ 1997/ K-2/3 KB748 . . . . **398.27**
BERNHARD, E/ Dragonfly./ 1993/ 2-4/4 KC534 . . . . **595.7**
Eagles: lions of the sky./ 1994/ 3-6/6 KC710 . . . . **598.9**
Girl who wanted to hunt: a Siberian tale./ 1994/ 3-5/3 KB720 **398.27**
Happy New Year!/ 1996/ 1-3/7 KB205 . . . . **394.261**
How Snowshoe Hare rescued the Sun: a tale from the Arctic./ 1993/
1-2/4 KB529 . . . . **398.24**
Reindeer./ 1994/ 4-5/7 KC796 . . . . **599.65**
Ride on mother's back: a day of baby carrying around the world./ 1996/
1-2/7 KB170 . . . . **392.1**
Salamanders./ 1995/ 2-5/6 KC598 . . . . **597.8**
Tree that rains: the flood myth of the Huichol Indians of Mexico./ 1994/
3-4/5 KB699 . . . . **398.26**
BERNIER-GRAND, CT/ Juan Bobo: four folktales from Puerto Rico./ 1994/
1-2/2 KB427 . . . . **398.22**
BERNSTEIN, JE/ Books to help children cope with separation and loss: an
annotated bibliography. 4th ed./ 1993/ KA025 . . . **PROF 016.1559**
BERNSTEIN, Z/ Mrs. Frisby and the rats of NIMH./ c1971/
4-A/6 KH556 . . . . **FIC**
BERRY, J/ Ajeemah and his son./ 1992/ 6-A/7 KG899 . . . . **FIC**
Ajeemah and his son (Sound recording cassette)./ 1994/
6-A/7 KG899 . . . . **FIC**
BEST, A/ BE A FRIEND: CHILDREN WHO LIVE WITH HIV SPEAK./ 1994/
2-6/2 KA993 . . . . **362.1**
BEST, C/ Red light, green light, Mama and me./ 1995/ K-2/2 KF228 . **E**
BETHIE/ Bethie's really silly songs about animals (Sound recording
cassette)./ 1993/ K-2 KD607 . . . . **SRC 789.3**
BETTELHEIM, B/ Frederick's fables: a Leo Lionni treasury of favorite stories.
Rev. ed./ 1997/ P-2/4 KF993 . . . . **E**
BIAL, R/ Amish home./ 1993/ 5-A/8 KA719 . . . . **289.7**
Corn belt harvest./ 1991/ 4-5/7 KD150 . . . . **633.1**
Frontier home./ 1993/ 4-6/8 KF027 . . . . **978**
Mist over the mountains: Appalachia and its people./ 1997/
4-6/9 KE923 . . . . **974**
Shaker home./ 1994/ 4-6/8 KA717 . . . . **289**
BIANCHI, J/ Snow: learning for the fun of it./ 1992/
5-A/9 KC208 . . . . **551.57**
BIEGEL, MD/ Satchel Paige: the best arm in baseball./ 1992/
3-5/2 KE489 . . . . **B PAIGE, S.**
BIERHORST, J/ Doctor Coyote: a Native American Aesop's fables./ 1987/
3/3 KB530 . . . . **398.24**
Doctor Coyote: a Native American Aesop's fables (Braille)./ n.d./
3/3 KB530 . . . . **398.24**
LIGHTNING INSIDE YOU AND OTHER NATIVE AMERICAN RIDDLES./
1992/ 3-6 KD733 . . . . **793.735**
Monkey's haircut and other stories told by the Maya./ 1986/
3-4/4 KB531 . . . . **398.24**
Mythology of Mexico and Central America./ 1990/
5-A KA392 . . . . **REF 291.1**
Mythology of North America./ 1985/ 5-A KA392 . . . . **REF 291.1**
Mythology of South America./ 1988/ 5-A KA392 . . . . . . **REF 291.1**
On the road of stars: Native American night poems and sleep charms./
1994/ 2-6 KE141 . . . . **897.008**
BIESTY, S/ Barco de guerra del siglo XVIII./ 1995/ 4-6/7 KA988 **359.1**
Del interior de las cosas./ 1995/ 4-A/6 KC880 . . . . **600**
Man-of-war./ 1993/ 4-6/7 KA988 . . . . **359.1**
Stephen Biesty's incredible cross-sections./ 1992/ 4-A/6 KC880 . . **600**
Stephen Biesty's incredible explosions./ 1996/ 5-6/7 KD411 . . **741.6**
BIG FAT HEN./ 1994/ P-1/1 KB793 . . . . **398.8**
BILECK, M/ Rain makes applesauce./ c1964/ P-A/2 KG403 . . . . . . **E**
BILLIN-FRYE, P/ Box can be many things./ 1997/ K-1/2 KG313 . . . . . **E**
Mystery of the Tooth Gremlin./ 1997/ 1-3/2 KH191 . . . . **FIC**
BINCH, C/ Amazing Grace./ 1991/ P-2/4 KF761 . . . . **CE E**
Boundless Grace./ 1995/ 1-3/5 KF762 . . . . **E**
BINGHAM, C/ CRAFTS FOR DECORATION./ 1993/
3-6/7 KD451 . . . . **745.594**
CRAFTS FOR PLAY./ 1993/ 3-6/7 KD445 . . . . **745.592**
BINGHAM, E/ Poetry break: an annotated anthology with ideas for
introducing children to poetry./ 1995/ KA234 . . . . . . **PROF 372.64**

BIRCH, C/ Careful what you wish for (Sound recording cassette)./ 1993/
2-6 KB264 . . . . **SRC 398.2**
Happily-ever-after love stories...more or less (Sound recording cassette)./
1987/ 2-6 KB265 . . . . **SRC 398.2**
Nightmares rising (Sound recording cassette)./ 1984/
3-6 KB266 . . . . **SRC 398.2**
BIRCHMAN, DF/ Jigsaw Jackson./ 1996/ 1-3/3 KF230 . . . . **E**
BIRDSEYE, T/ Air mail to the moon./ 1988/ K-3/5 KF231 . . . . . . **E**
Soap! soap! don't forget the soap!: an Appalachian folktale./ 1993/
K-2/3 KB267 . . . . **398.2**
BIRKBY, RC/ Boy Scout handbook. 10th ed./ 1990/
4-6/6 KB073 . . . . **369.43**
Official Boy Scout handbook (Sound recording cassette)./ n.d./
4-6/6 KB073 . . . . **369.43**
BIRLING, P/ Brooklyn doesn't rhyme./ 1994/ 4-6/6 KG904 . . . . . . **FIC**
Hidden in sand./ 1994/ 3-4/6 KA759 . . . . **294.3**
BIRMINGHAM, C/ Dancing bear./ 1996/ 4-6/5 KH513 . . . . **FIC**
BISHOP, G/ Maui and the Sun: a Maori tale./ 1996/
3-4/3 KB700 . . . . **398.26**
BITTINGER, N/ Blue and the gray./ 1996/ 3-5/3 KF297 . . . . **E**
Matzah that Papa brought home./ 1995/ 1-3/2 KG059 . . . . **E**
BIXENMAN, J/ Dinosaur jokes./ 1991/ 2-4 KD725 . . . . **793.735**
BJORK, C/ Linnea's almanac./ c1982, 1989/ 2-6/6 KB879 . . . . . **507**
Linnea's windowsill garden./ c1978, 1988/ 3-5/6 KD173 . . . . **635.9**
BJORKMAN, S/ Seeds./ 1994/ K-2/2 KG478 . . . . **E**
Stanley and the magic lamp./ 1996/ 2-4/3 KG932 . . . . **FIC**
BLACK, PT/ Social studies readers theatre for children: scripts and script
development./ 1991/ KA224 . . . . **PROF 372.6**
BLACK, WB/ Too many people?/ 1992/ A/7 KA815 . . . . **304.6**
BLACKBURN, GM/ INDEX TO POETRY FOR CHILDREN AND YOUNG
PEOPLE: 1988-1992./ 1994/ 5-6 KA374 . . . . **REF 016.811**
BLACKSTONE, M/ This is baseball./ c1993, 1997/
P-1/2 KD795 . . . . **796.357**
BLACKSTONE, S/ Grandma went to market: a round-the-world counting
rhyme./ 1996/ 1-3/5 KF232 . . . . **E**
BLACKWOOD, A/ Orchestra: an introduction to the world of classical
music./ 1993/ 4-6/8 KD544 . . . . **784.2**
BLADES, A/ Dog came, too: a true story./ 1993/ 1-4/6 KE185 **917.104**
Mary of Mile 18./ 1971/ 1-3/3 KF233 . . . . **CE E**
Mary of Mile 18 (Sound recording cassette)./ n.d./ 1-3/3 KF233 . **CE E**
BLAISDELL, E/ Rhymes and verses: collected poems for children./ 1947/
4-6 KE099 . . . . **821**
BLAKE, Q/ Enormous Crocodile./ c1978, 1993/ 1-3/4 KF444 . . . . . . **E**
Great piratical rumbustification and The librarian and the robbers./
c1978, 1986/ 5-A/7 KH449 . . . . **FIC**
Magic finger./ 1995/ 3-5/3 KH055 . . . . **FIC**
Matilda./ 1988/ 5-A/7 KH056 . . . . **FIC**
McBroom's wonderful one-acre farm: three tall tales./ 1992/
3-6/4 KH124 . . . . **FIC**
Old Mother Hubbard's dog dresses up./ c1989, 1990/
K-3/4 KG774 . . . . **E**
BLAKE, RJ/ Riptide./ 1990/ 1-3/4 KG695 . . . . **E**
BLAKE, W/ Tyger./ 1993/ 1-4 KE096 . . . . **821**
BLAKEY, N/ More mudpies: 101 alternatives to television./ 1994/
A KD424 . . . . **745.5**
Mudpies activity book: recipes for invention./ c1989, 1993/
A KD424 . . . . **745.5**
BLANC, ES/ Berchick./ 1989/ 3-5/5 KG901 . . . . **FIC**
BLANCO, A/ Angel's kite/La estrella de Angel./ 1994/
2-4/6 KG902 . . . . **FIC**
BLANKLEY, K/ King and the tortoise./ 1993/ 2-3/4 KB624 . . . . **398.24**
BLASHFIELD, JF/ Rescuing endangered species./ 1994/
4-6/7 KA961 . . . . **333.95**
Too many people?/ 1992/ A/7 KA815 . . . . **304.6**
BLASS, RJ/ Beyond the bean seed: gardening activities for grades K-6./
1996/ KA202 . . . . **PROF 372.3**
BLASSINGAME, W/ Look-it-up book of presidents. Rev. ed./ 1996/
4-6/7 KE848 . . . . **973**
BLEDSOE, LJ/ Big bike race./ 1995/ 3-6/2 KG903 . . . . **FIC**
BLEDSOE, S/ Colorado./ 1993/ 4-6/7 KF060 . . . . **978.8**
BLEGVAD, E/ Bed-knob and broomstick./ c1957/ 4-6/5 KH553 . . . . **FIC**
Diamond in the window./ c1962, 1973/ 4-6/5 KH385 . . . . **FIC**
Gammage Cup./ c1959/ 5-6/7 KH344 . . . . **FIC**
Tenth good thing about Barney./ c1971/ K-3/2 KG664 . . . . **E**
Twelve tales./ 1994/ 3-6/5 KG848 . . . . **FIC**
BLISHEN, E/ TREASURY OF STORIES FOR FIVE YEAR OLDS./ 1992/
2-4/5 KH805 . . . . **FIC**
TREASURY OF STORIES FOR SEVEN YEAR OLDS./ 1992/
3-5/6 KH806 . . . . **FIC**
TREASURY OF STORIES FOR SIX YEAR OLDS./ 1992/
2-4/5 KH807 . . . . **FIC**
BLISHEN, N/ TREASURY OF STORIES FOR FIVE YEAR OLDS./ 1992/
2-4/5 KH805 . . . . **FIC**

TREASURY OF STORIES FOR SEVEN YEAR OLDS./ 1992/
3-5/6 KH806 . . . . **FIC**
TREASURY OF STORIES FOR SIX YEAR OLDS./ 1992/
2-4/5 KH807 . . . . **FIC**
BLIZZARD, GS/ Come look with me: world of play./ 1993/
3-6/5 KD369 . . . . **701.1**
BLOCH, LM/ OVERLAND TO CALIFORNIA IN 1859: A GUIDE FOR
WAGON TRAIN TRAVELERS./ 1983/ A/12 KF042 . . . . . **978**
BLOCKSMA, D/ Easy-to-make spaceships that really fly./ 1983/
3-5/3 KD140 . . . . **629.47**
BLOCKSMA, M/ Easy-to-make spaceships that really fly./ 1983/
3-5/3 KD140 . . . . **629.47**
BLOOD, CL/ Goat in the rug./ 1990/ K-3/6 KF234 . . . **E**
BLOOM, C/ Story of Sleeping Beauty (Sound recording cassette)./ 1980/
4-6 KB356 . . . . **SRC 398.2**
Tale of Peter Rabbit, and four other stories (Talking book)./ 1984/
P-2 KG279 . . . . **TB E**
BLOOM, L/ Arthur, for the very first time./ 1980/ 4-6/7 KH443 . . . **FIC**
Green book./ 1982/ 4-6/6 KH583 . . . . **FIC**
Like Jake and me./ 1984/ 5-6/7 KH338 . . . . **FIC**
One yellow daffodil: a Hanukkah story./ 1995/ 3-5/4 KG818 . . **FIC**
POEMS FOR JEWISH HOLIDAYS./ 1986/ K-3 KE077 . . . . . **811.008**
BLOOM, S/ Family for Jamie: an adoption story./ 1991/
P-2/2 KF235 . . . . **E**
BLOS, JW/ Brooklyn doesn't rhyme./ 1994/ 4-6/6 KG904 . . . . . **FIC**
Heroine of the Titanic: a tale both true and otherwise of the life of Molly
Brown./ 1991/ 5-6/6 KE265 . . . . **B BROWN, M.**
Nellie Bly's monkey: his remarkable story in his own words./ 1996/
2-5/9 KF236 . . . . **E**
Old Henry./ 1987/ K-3/2 KF237 . . . . **CE E**
Old Henry (Sound recording cassette)./ n.d./ K-3/2 KF237 . . . . . **CE E**
BLOYD, S/ Animal rights./ 1990/ 5-A/8 KA672 . . . . . **179**
BLUE, R/ Colin Powell: straight to the top. Updated ed./ 1997/
3-6/7 KE502 . . . . **B POWELL, C.**
John Muir: saving the wilderness./ 1992/ 5-6/4 KE473 . . **B MUIR, J.**
People of peace./ 1994/ 5-A/7 KA806 . . . . **303.6**
White House kids./ 1995/ 5-6/7 KE849 . . . . **973**
White House kids (Sound recording cassette)./ 1997/
5-6/7 KE849 . . . . **973**
BLUM, R/ Mathemagic./ 1997/ 5-A KD711 . . . . **793.7**
BLUMBERG, R/ Bloomers!./ 1993/ 3-5/6 KA830 . . . . . **305.42**
Commodore Perry in the land of the Shogun./ 1985/
5-A/7 KE706 . . . . **CE 952**
Commodore Perry in the land of the Shogun (Braille)./ n.d./
5-A/7 KE706 . . . . **CE 952**
Commodore Perry in the land of the Shogun (Sound recording cassette)./
n.d./ 5-A/7 KE706 . . . . **CE 952**
Full steam ahead: the race to build a transcontinental railroad./ 1996/
4-6/10 KB137 . . . . **385**
Remarkable voyages of Captain Cook./ 1991/ 5-6/7 KE163 . . **910.92**
Remarkable voyages of Captain Cook (Sound recording cassette)./ 1995/
5-6/7 KE163 . . . . **910.92**
BLUME, J/ Are you there God? It's me, Margaret./ c1970, 1982/
4-6/5 KG905 . . . . **CE FIC**
Are you there God? It's me, Margaret (Braille)./ n.d.,/
4-6/5 KG905 . . . . **CE FIC**
Are you there God? It's me, Margaret (Kit)./ 1985,/
4-6/5 KG905 . . . . **CE FIC**
Ballena./ 1983/ 4-6/3 KG906 . . . . **FIC**
Blubber./ 1974/ 4-6/3 KG906 . . . . **FIC**
Blubber (Braille)./ n.d./ 4-6/3 KG906 . . . . **FIC**
Blubber (Sound recording cassette)./ n.d./ 4-6/3 KG906 . . . . **FIC**
Deenie./ 1973/ 6/4 KG907 . . . . **FIC**
Deenie (Braille)./ n.d./ 6/4 KG907 . . . . **FIC**
Deenie (Sound recording cassette)./ 1993/ 6/4 KG907 . . . . **FIC**
Estas ahi Dios? Soy yo, Margaret./ 1983,/ 4-6/5 KG905 . . . . **CE FIC**
Freckle juice./ 1971/ 2-4/3 KG908 . . . . **CE FIC**
Freckle juice (Braille)./ n.d./ 2-4/3 KG908 . . . . . **CE FIC**
Freckle juice (Kit)./ 1982/ 2-4/3 KG908 . . . . . . **CE FIC**
Freckle juice (Sound recording cassette)./ n.d./ 2-4/3 KG908 . **CE FIC**
Fudge-a-mania./ 1990/ 4-6/3 KG909 . . . . **CE FIC**
Fudge-a-mania (Talking book)./ 1992/ 4-6/3 KG909 . . . **CE FIC**
Here's to you, Rachel Robinson./ 1993/ 6-A/6 KG910 . . . . . **FIC**
It's not the end of the world./ c1972/ 4-6/4 KG911 . . . . . **FIC**
It's not the end of the world (Braille)./ n.d./ 4-6/4 KG911 . . . . . **FIC**
It's not the end of the world (Sound recording cassette)./ n.d./
4-6/4 KG911 . . . . **FIC**
Jugo de pecas./ n.d./ 2-4/3 KG908 . . . . **CE FIC**
One in the middle is the green kangaroo./ 1981/ K-3/2 KF238 . . **CE E**
One in the middle is the green kangaroo (Kit)./ 1983/
K-3/2 KF238 . . . . **CE E**
Otherwise known as Sheila the Great./ 1972/ 4-6/4 KG912 . . . . . **FIC**
Pain and the great one./ 1984/ K-3/4 KF239 . . . . **CE E**
Pain and the great one (Kit)./ 1988/ K-3/4 KF239 . . . . **CE E**

Pain and the great one (Sound recording cassette)./ n.d./
K-3/4 KF239 . . . . **CE E**
Quiza no lo haga./ 1995/ 6-A/5 KG915 . . . . **FIC**
Sheila la magnifica./ 1991/ 4-6/4 KG912 . . . . . . **FIC**
Superfudge./ 1980/ 2-4/2 KG913 . . . . **CE FIC**
Superfudge (Braille)./ n.d./ 2-4/2 KG913 . . . . . . **CE FIC**
Superfudge (Kit)./ 1994/ 2-4/2 KG913 . . . . **CE FIC**
Superfudge (Spanish version)./ 1996/ 2-4/2 KG913 . . . **CE FIC**
Tales of a fourth grade nothing./ 1972/ 2-4/3 KG914 . . . **CE FIC**
Tales of a fourth grade nothing (Braille)./ n.d./ 2-4/3 KG914 . **CE FIC**
Tales of a fourth grade nothing (Sound recording cassette)./ 1996/
2-4/3 KG914 . . . . **CE FIC**
Tales of a fourth grade nothing (Talking book)./ 1996/
2-4/3 KG914 . . . . **CE FIC**
Then again, maybe I won't./ 1971/ 6-A/5 KG915 . . . . . . **FIC**
Then again, maybe I won't (Braille)./ n.d./ 6-A/5 KG915 . . . . **FIC**
BLYTHE, G/ This is the star./ 1996/ 2-3/2 KA703 . . . . . **232.92**
BOBBISH, J/ Trail fever: the life of a Texas cowboy./ 1992/
4-6/5 KH406 . . . . **FIC**
BODART, JR/ BOOKTALK! 5: MORE SELECTIONS FROM THE
BOOKTALKER FOR ALL AGES AND AUDIENCES./ 1993/
KA090 . . . . **PROF 028.5**
BODECKER, NM/ Magic or not?./ c1959, 1985/ 4-6/6 KH094 . . . . **FIC**
Seven-day magic./ c1962/ 4-6/6 KH095 . . . . **FIC**
BODINE, RJ/ Creating the peaceable school: a comprehensive program for
teaching conflict resolution: program guide./ 1994/
KA161 . . . . **PROF 303.6**
Creating the peaceable school: a comprehensive program for teaching
conflict resolution: student manual./ 1994/ KA161 . . . . . **PROF 303.6**
BODKIN, O/ Banshee train./ 1995/ 1-3/4 KF240 . . . . . **E**
BODMER, K/ Indian winter./ 1992/ A/9 KE202 . . . . . **917.804**
BODNAR, JZ/ Wagonload of fish./ 1996/ K-2/5 KB532 . . . **398.24**
BOE, T/ World desk: a student handbook to the Internet. Rev. ed./ 1996/
A/10 KA576 . . . . **025.04**
BOIES, A/ Imani in the belly./ 1994/ 2-3/5 KB431 . . . . . . **398.22**
BOLAM, E/ Little red hen./ 1995/ K-1/2 KG793 . . . . . **E**
Princess and the pea./ 1996/ K-2/1 KG796 . . . . . **E**
Tortoise's flying lesson./ 1995/ P-2/3 KB615 . . . . . **398.24**
BOLAND, J/ Dog named Sam./ 1996/ K-2/2 KF241 . . . . . **E**
BOLICK, NO/ Shaker villages./ 1993/ 5-6/8 KA718 . . . . . **289**
BOLIN, FS/ Poetry for young people./ 1994/ 4-A KD933 . . . . . **811**
Poetry for young people./ 1995/ 4-6 KE018 . . . . . **811**
BOLOGNESE, D/ Buddy: the first seeing eye dog./ 1996/
1-3/3 KB006 . . . . **362.4**
Buffalo Bill and the Pony Express./ 1995/ 1-3/2 KF399 . . . **E**
George, the drummer boy./ c1977/ 1-3/2 KF221 . . . . **E**
Wagon wheels./ 1978/ 1-3/1 KF259 . . . . **CE E**
BOND, F/ Big green pocketbook./ 1993/ P-1/2 KG303 . . . . . **E**
Big red barn./ c1956, 1989/ P-1/3 KF283 . . . . . . **E**
How to think like a scientist: answering questions by the scientific
method./ 1987/ 4-6/6 KB883 . . . . **507**
BOND, M/ Bear called Paddington./ c1958/ 2-4/5 KG916 . . . . . . **FIC**
Bear called Paddington (Braille)./ n.d./ 2-4/5 KG916 . . . . . **FIC**
Bear called Paddington (Large type)./ n.d./ 2-4/5 KG916 . . . **FIC**
Bear called Paddington (Talking book)./ n.d./ 2-4/5 KG916 . . . . **FIC**
Paddington audio collection (Talking book)./ 1978/ 2-4 KG917 **TB FIC**
Paddington on screen./ 1982/ 2-4/5 KG916 . . . . . **FIC**
Paddington takes the test./ 1980/ 2-4/5 KG916 . . . . **FIC**
Paddington's storybook./ 1984/ 3-6/5 KG918 . . . . . **FIC**
Paddington's storybook (Braille)./ n.d./ 3-6/5 KG918 . . . **FIC**
BONNER, R/ Dads are such fun./ 1992/ P-K/1 KG769 . . . . . **E**
BONSALL, CN/ And I mean it, Stanley./ 1974/ 1-2/1 KF242 . . . . **E**
Case of the cat's meow./ 1965/ 1-2/2 KF243 . . . . **CE E**
Case of the double cross./ 1980/ 1-2/2 KF243 . . . . **CE E**
Case of the dumb bells./ 1966/ 1-2/2 KF243 . . . . **CE E**
Case of the hungry stranger./ c1963/ 1-2/2 KF243 . . . **CE E**
Case of the hungry stranger (Kit)./ 1985/ 1-2/2 KF243 . . . **CE E**
Case of the scaredy cats./ 1971/ 1-2/2 KF243 . . . . **CE E**
Case of the scaredy cats (Kit)./ 1991/ 1-2/2 KF243 . . . . **CE E**
Caso del forastero hambriento./ 1996/ 1-2/2 KF243 . . . . **CE E**
Day I had to play with my sister./ c1972/ 1-2/1 KF244 . . . **E**
Go away, dog./ c1963, 1993/ P-1/1 KG177 . . . . . **E**
Mine's the best. Newly illustrated ed./ 1996/ 1-2/1 KF245 . . . **E**
Piggle./ 1973/ P-2/2 KF246 . . . . **E**
Tell me some more./ c1961/ K-2/2 KF247 . . . . . . **E**
Who's a pest?/ c1962/ P-2/2 KF248 . . . . **E**
Who's afraid of the dark?/ 1980/ P-1/1 KF249 . . . . **E**
BONSON, R/ Earth atlas./ 1994/ A/7 KA443 . . . . . **REF 551**
BOOK OF VIRTUES FOR YOUNG PEOPLE: A TREASURY OF GREAT
MORAL STORIES./ 1997/ KA343 . . . . . **PROF 808.8**
BOOKER, CM/ Smilin' island of song (Compact disc)./ 1993/
K-4 KD667 . . . . **SRC 789.4**
Smilin' island of song (Sound recording cassette)./ 1994/
K-4 KD667 . . . . **SRC 789.4**

BOOSS, C/ SCANDINAVIAN FOLK & FAIRY TALES./ 1984/
KA273 . . . . **PROF 398.2**
BOOTH, BD/ Mandy./ 1991/ K-2/5 KF250 . . . . **E**
BOOTH, G/ Possum come a-knockin'./ 1990/ K-2/2 KG642 . . . . . **E**
Wacky Wednesday./ c1974/ 1-2/1 KF961 . . . . **E**
BOOTH, J/ You animal!/ 1996/ 4-6/5 KC913 . . . . **612**
BOOTMAN, C/ Seth and Samona./ 1995/ 4-6/6 KH313 . . . . **FIC**
BORDEN, L/ Little ships: the heroic rescue at Dunkirk in World War II./
1997/ 3-5/3 KF251 . . . . **E**
Paperboy./ 1996/ 1-3/2 KF926 . . . . **E**
BORDERS, SG/ Children talking about books./ 1993/
KA236 . . . . **PROF 372.64**
BORETZ, C/ Careers for computer buffs./ 1991/ 5-6/9 KA567 . . . **004**
Careers for outdoor types./ 1991/ 4-A/8 KA952 . . . . . **333.7**
Careers for wordsmiths./ 1991/ 6-A/7 KA593 . . . . . . **070.4**
BORMAN, JL/ Computer dictionary for kids...and their parents./ 1995/
4-A/9 KA566 . . . . **004**
BORNOFF, N/ Japan./ 1997/ 3-5/10 KE707 . . . . **952**
BORNSTEIN, H/ Night before Christmas: told in sign language: an
adaptation of the original poem "A visit from St. Nicholas" by Clement
C. Moore./ 1994/ K-6 KD917 . . . . **811**
BORNSTEIN, RL/ Mama One, Mama Two./ 1982/ 2-3/1 KG054 . . . **E**
BORON, MP/ Gymnastics./ 1996/ 3-6/6 KD817 . . . . . . **796.44**
Karate and judo./ 1996/ 3-6/6 KD833 . . . . **796.815**
BOROVSKY, P/ Blabbermouths: adapted from a German folktale./ 1992/
3-4/4 KB751 . . . . **398.27**
BORROR, DJ/ Field guide to the insects of America north of Mexico./
1970/ A/12 KA447 . . . . **REF 595.7**
BORTON, L/ Junk pile!/ 1997/ K-2/3 KF252 . . . . **E**
BOSAK, DA/ Science is...2nd ed./ 1991/ KA285 . . . . . **PROF 507.8**
BOSAK, SV/ Science is...2nd ed./ 1991/ KA285 . . . . . **PROF 507.8**
BOSMA, B/ Fairy tales, fables, legends and myths: using folk literature in
your classroom. 2nd ed./ 1992/ KA177 . . . . **PROF 371.3**
BOSTON, D/ Wonder tales from around the world./ 1995/
3-5/6 KB300 . . . . **398.2**
BOSTON, LM/ Children of Green Knowe./ c1955, 1983/
4-A/6 KG919 . . . . **FIC**
Children of Green Knowe (Braille)./ n.d.,/ 4-A/6 KG919 . . . **FIC**
Children of Green Knowe (Sound recording cassette)./ n.d.,/
4-A/6 KG919 . . . . **FIC**
Enemy at Green Knowe./ 1964,/ 4-A/6 KG919 . . . . **FIC**
Enemy at Green Knowe (Sound recording cassette)./ n.d.,/
4-A/6 KG919 . . . . **FIC**
River at Green Knowe./ 1989,/ 4-A/6 KG919 . . . . **FIC**
Stranger at Green Knowe./ c1961, 1983/ 4-A/6 KG919 . . . **FIC**
Stranger at Green Knowe (Sound recording cassette)./ n.d.,/
4-A/6 KG919 . . . . **FIC**
Treasure of Green Knowe (Braille)./ n.d.,/ 4-A/6 KG919 . . **FIC**
Treasure of Green Knowe (Sound recording cassette)./ n.d.,/
4-A/6 KG919 . . . . **FIC**
BOSTON, P/ Children of Green Knowe./ c1955, 1983/
4-A/6 KG919 . . . . **FIC**
BOUCHER, J/ Fire truck nuts and bolts./ 1993/ 4-5/6 KD085 . . . **628.9**
BOURGEOIS, P/ Amazing apple book./ 1990/ 5-6/7 KD264 . . **641.3**
Amazing dirt book./ 1990/ 4-6/6 KD148 . . . . **631.4**
Amazing paper book./ 1989/ 5-6/6 KD332 . . . . **676**
BOURKE, L/ Eye spy: a mysterious alphabet./ 1991/
1-4 KD720 . . . . **793.734**
BOURNE, B/ Exploring space: using Seymour Simon's astronomy books in
the classroom./ 1994/ KA198 . . . . **PROF 372.3**
BOWDEN, M/ Nature for the very young: a handbook of indoor and
outdoor activities./ 1989/ KA199 . . . . **PROF 372.3**
BOWEN, AR/ Head full of notions: a story about Robert Fulton./ 1997/
4-5/8 KE359 . . . . **B FULTON, R.**
World of knowing: a story about Thomas Hopkins Gallaudet./ 1995/
3-5/6 KE361 . . . . **B GALLAUDET, T.**
BOWEN, B/ Gathering: a northwoods counting book./ 1995/
1-3/3 KB953 . . . . **513.2**
BOWEN, G/ Stranded at Plimoth Plantation, 1626./ 1994/
5-6/7 KE870 . . . . **973.2**
BOWERMASTER, J/ Over the top of the world: explorer Will Steger's trek
across the Arctic./ 1997/ 5-6/6 KE219 . . . . **919.8**
BOWERS, V/ British Columbia./ 1995/ 4-6/9 KE809 . . . . **971.1**
BOWLES, D/ What was it like before television?/ 1995/
1-3/2 KD679 . . . . **790.1**
BOWMAN, LW/ Cuckoo child./ 1993/ 4-6/6 KH347 . . . . . **FIC**
Shadows./ 1991/ 4-6/5 KH224 . . . . **FIC**
BOY SCOUTS OF AMERICA/ Big Bear Cub Scout book. Rev. ed./ 1984/
4-5/5 KB074 . . . . **369.43**
Big Bear Cub Scout book. Rev. ed. (Sound recording cassette)./ 1997/
4-5/5 KB074 . . . . **369.43**
Webelos Scout book. Rev. ed./ 1987/ 4-6/3 KB075 . . . . **369.43**
Wolf Cub Scout book. Rev. ed./ 1986/ 3-4/4 KB076 . . . . **369.43**

Wolf Cub Scout book. Rev. ed. (Sound recording cassette)./ 1997/
3-4/4 KB076 . . . . **369.43**
BOYD, CD/ Daddy, Daddy, be there./ 1995/ 1-3/2 KF254 . . . . **E**
BOYLE, B/ My first atlas./ 1994/ K-3/5 KE167 . . . . **912**
BOYLE, D/ Coral reef hideaway: the story of a clown anemonefish./ 1995/
K-2/7 KF255 . . . . **CE E**
Coral reef hideaway: the story of a clown anemonefish (Kit)./ 1995/
K-2/7 KF255 . . . . **CE E**
BRADBURY, R/ Halloween tree./ c1982/ 5-A/7 KG920 . . . . . **FIC**
BRADBY, M/ More than anything else./ 1995/ 1-3/3 KF256 . . . . . **E**
BRADFORD, K/ There will be wolves./ 1992/ 6-A/5 KG921 . . . . . **FIC**
BRADFORD, W/ Homes in the wilderness: a pilgrim's journal of Plymouth
Plantation in 1620./ c1939, 1988/ 5-A/8 KE941 . . . . . . **974.4**
BRADY, AA/ Kwanzaa karamu: cooking and crafts for a Kwanzaa feast./
1995/ 5-6/5 KD284 . . . . **641.59**
BRAEMER, H/ Tropical fish: a complete pet owner's manual./ 1983/
5-6/9 KD247 . . . . **639.3**
BRAINARD, B/ Soup should be seen, not heard!: the kids' etiquette book./
c1988, 1990/ 2-6/5 KB247 . . . . **395.5**
BRAINE, S/ Drumbeat...heartbeat: a celebration of the powwow./ 1995/
5-6/9 KB178 . . . . **394**
BRANDENBERG, A/ Chop, simmer, season./ 1997/ P-1/2 KF257 . . . . **E**
I am me!/ 1996/ P-K/1 KF258 . . . . **E**
BRANDENBURG, J/ Sand and fog: adventures in Southern Africa./ 1994/
5-6/6 KE740 . . . . **968.81**
To the top of the world: adventures with arctic wolves./ 1993/
5-6/6 KC834 . . . . **599.773**
BRANDT, K/ What makes it rain? The story of a raindrop./ 1982/
P-K/2 KC209 . . . . **551.57**
BRANDT, SR/ State flags: including the Commonwealth of Puerto Rico./
1992/ 4-6/7 KE614 . . . . **929.9**
BRANLEY, FM/ Earthquakes./ 1990/ 2-4/4 KC161 . . . . . . **551.22**
Flash, crash, rumble and roll. Rev. ed./ 1985/
1-3/2 KC195 . . . . **CE 551.55**
Flash, crash, rumble and roll. Rev. ed. (Braille)./ n.d./
1-3/2 KC195 . . . . **CE 551.55**
Flash, crash, rumble and roll. Rev. ed. (Kit)./ 1987/
1-3/2 KC195 . . . . **CE 551.55**
Keeping time: from the beginning and into the 21st century./ 1993/
4-6/6 KC067 . . . . **529**
Planets in our solar system. Rev. ed./ 1987/ 2-4/4 KC023 . . . . **523.4**
Rain and hail. Rev. ed./ 1983/ K-3/2 KC188 . . . . . . **551.5**
Snow is falling. Rev. ed./ 1986/ K-1/2 KC210 . . . . . . **551.57**
Snow is falling. Rev. ed. (Sound recording disc)./ n.d./
K-1/2 KC210 . . . . **551.57**
Sunshine makes the season (Braille)./ n.d./ K-2/3 KC057 . . . **525**
Sunshine makes the season. Rev. ed./ 1985/ K-2/3 KC057 . . . **525**
Tornado alert./ 1988/ P-4/3 KC196 . . . . **551.55**
What happened to the dinosaurs?/ 1989/ 2-4/5 KC244 . . . . . **567.9**
BRAREN, LT/ EcoArt!: earth-friendly art and craft experiences for 3-to
9-year olds./ 1993/ K-4 KD425 . . . . **745.5**
Kids' computer creations: using your computer for art and craft fun./
1995/ 3-5 KD434 . . . . **745.5**
Kids garden!: the anytime, anyplace guide to sowing and growing fun./
1996/ 3-5/6 KD167 . . . . **635**
Kids' science book: creative experiences for hands-on fun./ 1995/
P-4/7 KB892 . . . . **507.8**
BRATMAN, F/ Everything you need to know when a parent dies./ 1992/
5-6/9 KA647 . . . . **155.9**
BRATVOLD, G/ Wisconsin./ 1991/ 4-6/7 KF019 . . . . **977.5**
BRAUN, M/ Encyclopedia of Native American tribes./ 1988/
4-A KA483 . . . . **REF 970.4**
Voices of the winds: Native American legends./ 1989/
KA266 . . . . **PROF 398.2**
BRAY, RL/ Martin Luther King./ 1995/ 2-6/7 KE421 . . . **B KING, M.L.**
BREDESON, C/ Presidential Medal of Freedom winners./ 1996/
5-6/10 KE850 . . . . **973**
BREDESON, LG/ Celebrations: read-aloud holiday and theme book
programs./ 1985/ KA342 . . . . **PROF 808.8**
Presenting reader's theater: plays and poems to read aloud./ 1987/
KA329 . . . . **PROF 792**
Read for the fun of it: active programming with books for children./
1992/ KA067 . . . . **PROF 027.62**
BRENNER, B/ EARTH IS PAINTED GREEN: A GARDEN OF POEMS
ABOUT OUR PLANET./ 1994/ 3-6 KD883 . . . . **808.81**
If you were there in 1776./ 1994/ 5-6/6 KE875 . . . . . . **973.3**
Two orphan cubs./ 1989/ K-2/2 KC848 . . . . **599.78**
Wagon wheels./ 1978/ 1-3/1 KF259 . . . . **CE E**
Wagon wheels (Braille)./ n.d./ 1-3/1 KF259 . . . . **CE E**
Wagon wheels (Kit)./ 1995/ 1-3/1 KF259 . . . . **CE E**
BRENNER, F/ Drinking gourd. Newly illustrated ed./ 1993/
1-3/2 KG151 . . . . **E**
BRENNER, M/ Abe Lincoln's hat./ 1994/ 1-3/2 KE439 **B LINCOLN, A.**
BRENT, I/ Complete Just so stories./ 1993/ 3-5/7 KH360 . . . . . . **FIC**

BRESNICK-PERRY, R/ Leaving for America./ 1992/ 1-4/6 KE688 . . **947**
BRETT, J/ Annie and the wild animals./ 1985/ K-3/2 KF260 . . . . **E**
Beauty and the Beast./ 1989/ 4-5/6 KB268 . . . . **398.2**
Berlioz the bear./ 1991/ K-2/2 KF261 . . . . **E**
Berlioz the bear (Sound recording casssette)./ 1994/ K-2/2 KF261 . . **E**
Mitten./ 1989/ K-2/3 KB534 . . . . **398.24**
Mother's Day mice./ 1986/ P-2/2 KF305 . . . . **CE E**
Scary, scary Halloween./ 1986/ P-K/4 KF308 . . . . **E**
St. Patrick's Day in the morning./ 1980/ K-2/2 KF310 . . . . **E**
Town Mouse, Country Mouse./ 1994/ K-3/3 KB535 . . . . **398.24**
Trouble with trolls./ 1992/ P-1/3 KF262 . . . . **E**
TWELVE DAYS OF CHRISTMAS./ 1986/ P-A KD537 . . . . . . **782.28**
Wild Christmas reindeer./ 1990/ K-2/2 KF263 . . . . **E**
BREWER, C/ MANY PEOPLE, MANY WAYS: UNDERSTANDING CULTURES AROUND THE WORLD./ 1995/ 4-A KA402 . . **REF 306**
BREWSTER, H/ Anastasia's album./ 1996/ 5-A/7 KE234 . . . . **B ANASTASIIA**
BREWSTER, P/ Bear and Mrs. Duck./ 1988/ P-1/1 KG744 . . . . **E**
Fannie Farmer junior cookbook. New and rev. ed./ 1993/ A KD280 . . . . **641.5**
BRIDWELL, N/ Buenas acciones de Clifford./ 1978,/ P-2/1 KF264 . **CE E**
Clifford at the circus./ 1985,/ P-2/1 KF264 . . . . **CE E**
Clifford at the circus (Kit)./ 1987,/ P-2/1 KF264 . . . . **CE E**
Clifford el grand perro colorado./ 1988,/ P-2/1 KF264 . . . . **CE E**
Clifford gets a job./ 1985,/ P-2/1 KF264 . . . . **CE E**
Clifford takes a trip./ 1985,/ P-2/1 KF264 . . . . **CE E**
Clifford the big red dog./ c1963, 1985/ P-2/1 KF264 . . . . **CE E**
Clifford the small red puppy./ 1985,/ P-2/1 KF264 . . . . **CE E**
Clifford va de viaje./ 1995,/ P-2/1 KF264 . . . . **CE E**
Clifford, we love you./ 1991,/ P-2/1 KF264 . . . . **CE E**
Clifford's good deeds./ 1985,/ P-2/1 KF264 . . . . **CE E**
Clifford's Halloween./ 1986,/ P-2/1 KF264 . . . . **CE E**
Clifford's sports day./ 1996,/ P-2/1 KF264 . . . . **CE E**
BRIERLEY, L/ LIGHTNING INSIDE YOU AND OTHER NATIVE AMERICAN RIDDLES./ 1992/ 3-6 KD733 . . . . **793.735**
BRIGGS, CS/ At the controls: women in aviation./ 1991/ 6-A/10 KD090 . . . . **629.13**
BRIGGS, R/ Snowman./ 1978/ P-1 KF265 . . . . **CE E**
Snowman (Videocassette)./ n.d./ P-1 KF265 . . . . **CE E**
BRILL, MT/ Allen Jay and the Underground Railroad./ 1993/ 4-6/4 KE898 . . . . **973.7**
Extraordinary young people./ 1996/ 4-A/7 KA823 . . . . **305.23**
BRIMNER, LD/ Brave Mary./ 1996/ K-1/2 KF266 . . . . **E**
E-mail./ 1997/ 2-4/3 KB134 . . . . **384.3**
Merry Christmas, Old Armadillo./ 1995/ K-2/3 KF267 . . . . **E**
Migrant family./ 1992/ 4-6/6 KA834 . . . . **305.5**
World Wide Web./ 1997/ 2-6/6 KA577 . . . . **025.04**
BRINK, CR/ Caddie Woodlawn. New ed./ 1973/ 4-6/6 KG922 . **CE FIC**
Caddie Woodlawn (Talking book)./ n.d./ 4-6/6 KG922 . . . . . **CE FIC**
Goody O'Grumpity./ 1994/ K-3/3 KF268 . . . . **E**
Magical melons./ c1939/ 4-6/6 KG922 . . . . **CE FIC**
Magical melons (Talking book)./ n.d./ 4-6/6 KG922 . . . . **CE FIC**
BRINSTER, R/ Jeff Gordon./ 1997/ 5-6/7 KE373 . . . . **B GORDON, J.**
BRITTAIN, B/ Dr. Dredd's wagon of wonders./ 1987/ 3-6/5 KG923 **FIC**
Mystery of the several sevens./ 1994/ 2-4/4 KG924 . . . . **FIC**
Wish giver./ 1983/ 3-6/7 KG925 . . . . **FIC**
Wish giver (Sound recording cassette)./ n.d./ 3-6/7 KG925 . . . . . **FIC**
Wizards and the monster./ 1994/ 2-4/4 KG926 . . . . **FIC**
BRITTEN, B/ Young person's guide to the orchestra: Benjamin Britten's composition on CD./ 1996/ 4-6/10 KD545 . . . . **BA 784.2**
BROCK, CE/ Railway children./ 1994/ 4-5/7 KH543 . . . . **FIC**
BRODIE, CS/ Bookmark book./ 1996/ KA310 . . . . **PROF 741.6**
EXPLORING THE PLAINS STATES THROUGH LITERATURE./ 1994/ KA041 . . . . **PROF 016.978**
BRODIE, JM/ Sweet words so brave: the story of African American literature./ 1996/ K-6/7 KD906 . . . . **810.9**
BROECK, FV/ Witch's face: a Mexican tale./ 1993/ 3-5/2 KB402 . . . . **398.21**
BROEKEL, R/ Snakes./ 1982/ 2-4/2 KC633 . . . . **597.96**
BRONIN, A/ CALIFORNIA GOLD RUSH: 1849 (Multimedia kit)./ 1991/ 5-A KF079 . . . . **MMK 979.4**
BROOKE, LL/ Golden goose book: a fairy tale picture book./ 1992/ P-3/6 KB269 . . . . **398.2**
Ring o'roses: a nursery rhyme picture book./ 1992/ P-K KB807 . **398.8**
BROOKE, WJ/ Teller of tales./ 1994/ 5-A/5 KG927 . . . . **FIC**
Telling of the tales: five stories./ 1994/ 5-A/7 KG928 . . . . **FIC**
Untold tales./ 1992/ 6-A/7 KG929 . . . . **FIC**
BROOKER, K/ Nothing ever happens on 90th Street./ 1997/ 3-5/4 KH682 . . . . **FIC**
BROOKFIELD, K/ Book./ 1993/ 4-A/9 KA565 . . . . **002**
BROOKS, B/ Nature by design./ 1991/ A/9 KC483 . . . . **591.56**
BROOKS, N/ Tooth fairy./ 1994/ K-1/1 KF665 . . . . **E**
BROSTERMAN, N/ Inventing kindergarten./ 1997/ KA196 . . . . **PROF 372.21**
BROSTROM, DC/ Guide to homeschooling for librarians./ 1995/ KA065 . . . . **PROF 026.371**
BROWER, P/ Missions of the inland valleys./ 1997/ 4-6/9 KF077 **979.4**
BROWN, C/ In the spring./ 1994/ P-1/2 KF269 . . . . **E**
Tractor./ 1995/ K-2/2 KD146 . . . . **631.3**
BROWN, D/ Alabama./ 1994/ 4-6/7 KE996 . . . . **976.1**
Amazing magic tricks./ 1995/ 4-6 KD744 . . . . **793.8**
Kentucky./ 1992/ 4-6/6 KF010 . . . . **976.9**
New Hampshire./ 1993/ 4-6/7 KE930 . . . . **974.2**
Ruth Law thrills a nation./ 1993/ 2-3/4 KE428 . . . . **B LAW, R.**
BROWN, DP/ Sybil rides for independence./ 1985/ 3-6/4 KE876 **973.3**
BROWN, FG/ Daisy and the Girl Scouts: the story of Juliette Gordon Low./ 1996/ 3-6/7 KE448 . . . . **B LOW, J.**
Owls./ 1991/ 5-6/5 KC711 . . . . **598.9**
Special Olympics./ 1992/ 4-A/7 KD759 . . . . **796**
BROWN, G/ Steven Caney's Kids' America./ 1978/ 4-6/7 KE920 . . . . **973.92**
BROWN, J/ Flat Stanley./ c1964, 1989/ 2-4/5 KG931 . . . . **FIC**
Stanley and the magic lamp./ 1996/ 2-4/3 KG932 . . . . **FIC**
BROWN, JG/ Best Christmas pageant ever./ c1972/ 4-6/7 KH640 . . **FIC**
BROWN, K/ Bear for all seasons./ 1995/ K-2/2 KF589 . . . . **E**
Old woman who named things./ 1996/ 1-3/2 KG383 . . . . **E**
Tough Boris./ 1994/ K-2/2 KF573 . . . . **E**
BROWN, L/ Grasslands./ 1985/ A KC330 . . . . **577.4**
BROWN, LK/ Bionic Bunny Show./ 1984/ K-3/5 KF280 . . . . **E**
Dinosaurs alive and well! a guide to good health./ 1990/ K-3/5 KC982 . . . . **613**
Dinosaurs divorce: a guide for changing families./ 1986/ K-3/6 KA888 . . . . **CE 306.89**
Dinosaurs to the rescue!: a guide to protecting our planet./ 1992/ 1-4/4 KB045 . . . . **CE 363.7**
Dinosaurs to the rescue!: a guide to protecting our planet (Sound recording cassette)./ 1995/ 1-4/4 KB045 . . . . **CE 363.7**
Rex and Lilly family time./ 1995/ K-1/1 KF270 . . . . **E**
Vegetable show./ 1995/ P-2/2 KD289 . . . . **641.6**
When dinosaurs die: a guide to understanding death./ 1996/ K-4/5 KA648 . . . . **155.9**
BROWN, M/ Backbone of the king: the story of Paka'a and his son Ku./ 1984/ 5-6/6 KB428 . . . . **398.22**
Backbone of the king: the story of Paka'a and his son Ku (Braille)./ n.d./ 5-6/6 KB428 . . . . **398.22**
Backbone of the king: the story of Paka'a and his son Ku (Talking book)./ n.d./ 5-6/6 KB428 . . . . **398.22**
Cinderella, or the little glass slipper./ 1954/ 1-3/7 KB762 . . . . **398.27**
Dick Whittington and his cat./ c1950, 1988/ 2-4/6 KB498 . . . **398.23**
Dick Whittington and his cat (Braille)./ n.d.,/ 2-4/6 KB498 . . . **398.23**
How the ostrich got its long neck: a tale from the Akamba of Kenya./ 1995/ P-2/6 KB515 . . . . **CE 398.24**
Once a mouse./ c1961/ 1-3/6 KB536 . . . . **CE 398.24**
Once a mouse (Braille)./ n.d./ 1-3/6 KB536 . . . . **CE 398.24**
Once a mouse (Sound recording cassette)./ n.d./ 1-3/6 KB536 . . . . **CE 398.24**
Once a mouse (Talking book)./ n.d./ 1-3/6 KB536 . . . . **CE 398.24**
Sopa de piedras./ 1991/ K-3/2 KB721 . . . . **CE 398.27**
Sopa de piedras (Kit)./ 1992/ K-3/2 KB721 . . . . **CE 398.27**
Stone soup: an old tale./ c1947/ K-3/2 KB721 . . . . **CE 398.27**
Stone soup (Braille)./ n.d./ K-3/2 KB721 . . . . **CE 398.27**
BROWN, MB/ Great Northern diver: the loon./ 1990/ 3-5/6 KC680 . . . . **598.4**
Joshua and the big bad blue crabs./ 1996/ 3-4/5 KG988 . . . . . . **FIC**
Wings along the waterway./ 1992/ 5-6/6 KC675 . . . . **598.176**
Wings along the waterway (Sound recording cassette)./ 1995/ 5-6/6 KC675 . . . . **598.176**
BROWN, MT/ Arthur babysits./ 1992/ K-2/2 KF276 . . . . **CE E**
Arthur babysits (Kit)./ 1996/ K-2/2 KF276 . . . . **CE E**
Arthur babysits (Videocassette)/ n.d./ K-2/2 KF276 . . . . **CE E**
Arthur goes to camp./ 1982/ K-2/2 KF271 . . . . **CE E**
Arthur meets the president./ 1991/ K-2/2 KF276 . . . . **CE E**
Arthur meets the president (Kit)./ 1996/ K-2/2 KF276 . . . . **CE E**
Arthur writes a story./ 1996/ K-2/2 KF272 . . . . **E**
Arthur's April fool./ 1983/ P-3/2 KF273 . . . . **E**
Arthur's April fool (Kit)./ 1995/ P-3/2 KF273 . . . . **E**
Arthur's baby./ 1987/ K-3/2 KF274 . . . . **E**
Arthur's baby (Braille)./ n.d./ K-3/2 KF274 . . . . **E**
Arthur's birthday./ 1989/ K-3/4 KF277 . . . . **CE E**
Arthur's chicken pox./ 1994/ K-2/2 KF276 . . . . **CE E**
Arthur's Christmas./ 1984/ P-3/2 KF273 . . . . **E**
Arthur's eyes./ 1979/ K-2/2 KF276 . . . . **CE E**
Arthur's eyes (Kit)./ 1993/ K-2/2 KF276 . . . . **CE E**
Arthur's eyes (Sound recording cassette)./ 1997/ K-2/2 KF276 . . **CE E**
Arthur's family vacation./ 1993/ K-2/2 KF271 . . . . **CE E**
Arthur's family vacation (Kit)./ 1996/ K-2/2 KF271 . . . . **CE E**
Arthur's first sleepover./ 1994/ K-2/2 KF275 . . . . **E**
Arthur's Halloween./ 1982/ P-3/2 KF273 . . . . **E**

Arthur's Halloween (Kit)./ 1996/ P-3/2 KF273 . . . . **E**
Arthur's new puppy./ 1993/ K-2/2 KF271 . . . . **CE E**
Arthur's new puppy (Sound recording cassette)./ 1997/
  K-2/2 KF271 . . . . **CE E**
Arthur's nose./ c1976/ K-2/2 KF276 . . . . **CE E**
Arthur's pet business./ 1990/ K-2/2 KF276 . . . . **CE E**
Arthur's pet business (Kit)./ 1995/ K-2/2 KF276 . . . . . **CE E**
Arthur's teacher trouble./ 1986/ K-3/4 KF277 . . . . **CE E**
ARTHUR'S TEACHER TROUBLE (CD-ROM)./ 1992/ 1-4 KF171 . **CDR E**
Arthur's teacher trouble (Microcomputer program)./ 1994/
  2-6 KB109 . . . . **MCP 372.6**
Arthur's Thanksgiving./ 1983/ P-3/2 KF273 . . . . **E**
Arthur's tooth./ 1985/ 1-3/2 KF278 . . . . **CE E**
Arthur's tooth (Braille)./ n.d./ 1-3/2 KF278 . . . . **CE E**
Arthur's TV trouble./ 1995/ K-2/2 KF279 . . . . **E**
Arthur's Valentine./ 1980/ P-3/2 KF273 . . . . **E**
Arturo y sus problemas con el profesor./ 1994/ K-3/4 KF277 . **CE E**
Bionic Bunny Show./ 1984/ K-3/5 KF280 . . . . **E**
Dinosaurs alive and well! a guide to good health./ 1990/
  K-3/5 KC982 . . . . **613**
Dinosaurs, beware: a safety guide./ 1982/ P-3/3 KB020 . . . . . **363.1**
Dinosaurs divorce: a guide for changing families./ 1986/
  K-3/6 KA888 . . . . **CE 306.89**
Dinosaurs to the rescue! a guide to protecting our planet./ 1992/
  1-4/4 KB045 . . . . **CE 363.7**
D.W. all wet./ 1988/ P-2/1 KF281 . . . . **E**
D.W. flips./ 1987/ P-2/1 KF281 . . . . **E**
D.W. rides again!/ 1993/ P-2/1 KF281 . . . . **E**
D.W. the picky eater./ 1995/ P-2/1 KF281 . . . . **E**
D.W. the picky eater (Sound recording cassette)./ 1997/
  P-2/1 KF281 . . . . **E**
D.W. thinks big./ 1993/ P-2/1 KF281 . . . . **E**
MARC BROWN'S ARTHUR'S BIRTHDAY. School ed. (CD-ROM)./ 1994/
  K-4 KG062 . . . . **CDR E**
READ-ALOUD RHYMES FOR THE VERY YOUNG./ c1986/
  P-K KE079 . . . . **811.008**
Rex and Lilly family time./ 1995/ K-1/1 KF270 . . . . **E**
SCARED SILLY! A BOOK FOR THE BRAVE./ 1994/ K-3 KD904 . **810.8**
True Francine./ 1987/ 1-2/1 KF282 . . . . **E**
When dinosaurs die: a guide to understanding death./ 1996/
  K-4/5 KA648 . . . . **155.9**
BROWN, MW/ Big red barn./ c1956, 1989/ P-1/3 KF283 . . . **E**
Buenas noches, luna./ 1995/ P-K/1 KF285 . . . . **CE E**
Buenas noches, luna (Kit)./ 1996/ P-K/1 KF285 . . . . **CE E**
Child's good night book./ c1943, 1992/ P/2 KF284 . . . . **E**
Christmas in the barn./ c1952/ P-K KA700 . . . . **232.92**
Christmas in the barn (Sound recording cassette)./ n.d./
  P-K KA700 . . . . **232.92**
Conejito andarin./ 1995/ P-K/2 KF287 . . . . **CE E**
Conejito andarin (Kit)./ 1995/ P-K/2 KF287 . . . . **CE E**
Goodnight moon./ c1947/ P-K/1 KF285 . . . . **CE E**
Goodnight moon (Big book)./ n.d./ P-K/1 KF285 . . . . **CE E**
Goodnight moon (Kit)./ 1984/ P-K/1 KF285 . . . . **CE E**
Goodnight moon (Picture)./ n.d./ P-K/1 KF285 . . . . **CE E**
Goodnight moon. 50th anniversary ed. (Kit)./ 1997/
  P-K/1 KF285 . . . . **CE E**
Gran granero rojo./ 1996,/ P-1/3 KF283 . . . . **E**
Homes in the wilderness: a pilgrim's journal of Plymouth Plantation in
  1620./ c1939, 1988/ 5-A/8 KE941 . . . . **974.4**
Little Donkey close your eyes./ 1995/ P-K/2 KF286 . . . . **E**
Runaway bunny./ c1972/ P-K/2 KF287 . . . . **CE E**
Runaway bunny (Braille)./ n.d./ P-K/2 KF287 . . . . **CE E**
Runaway bunny (Kit)./ 1985/ P-K/2 KF287 . . . . **CE E**
Runaway bunny (Picture)./ n.d./ P-K/2 KF287 . . . . **CE E**
Under the sun and the moon and other poems./ 1993/ P-2 KD918 **811**
BROWN, R/ Alphabet times four: an international ABC: English, Spanish,
  French, German./ 1991/ 2-4 KB819 . . . . **411**
Ben's Christmas carol./ 1996/ 2-3/4 KF567 . . . . **E**
Earth mirth: the ecology riddle book./ 1994/ 2-4 KD741 . . . **793.735**
Gone fishing./ 1984/ P-1/1 KG030 . . . . **E**
Nicky upstairs and down./ c1987, 1994/ P-1/1 KG795 . . . . . . **E**
Our puppy's vacation./ 1987/ P-1/1 KF288 . . . . **E**
Put a fan in your hat!: inventions, contraptions, and gadgets kids can
  build./ 1997/ 5-6/8 KC885 . . . . **608**
Toad./ 1997/ K-2/3 KF289 . . . . **E**
What rhymes with eel?: a word-and-picture flap book./ 1996/
  P-1/2 KG798 . . . . **E**
100 WORDS ABOUT ANIMALS./ 1987/ P-3 KC457 . . . . . **CE 591**
100 WORDS ABOUT MY HOUSE./ 1988/ P-3 KD296 . . . . . . **645**
BROWN, RS/ Queen of the cold-blooded tales./ 1993/
  6-A/6 KG933 . . . . **FIC**
BROWN, S/ Big bike race./ 1995/ 3-6/6 KG903 . . . . **FIC**
BROWN, T/ City by the bay: a magical journey around San Francisco./
  1993/ 1-5/7 KE207 . . . . **917.94**

Konnichiwa!: I am a Japanese-American girl./ 1995/
  3-5/4 KA839 . . . . **305.8**
Someone special, just like you./ 1984/ P-2/6 KA623 . . . . . . **152.4**
BROWNE, A/ Daydreamer./ 1994/ 4-6/6 KH474 . . . . **FIC**
BROWNE, G/ Aircraft: lift-the-flap book./ 1992/ 3-6/5 KD106 **629.133**
BRUCE, TT/ Dirty, rotten, dead?/ 1996/ 4-6/10 KC303 . . . . . **577.1**
BRUCHAC, J/ Between earth and sky: legends of Native American sacred
  places./ 1996/ 5-A/5 KB270 . . . . **398.2**
Boy called Slow: the true story of Sitting Bull./ 1994/
  3-4/6 KE541 . . . . **B SITTING BULL**
Boy who lived with bears: and other Iroquois stories (Talking book)./
  c1990/ 2-4/4 KB537 . . . . **CE 398.24**
Boy who lived with the bears: and other Iroquois stories./ 1995/
  2-4/4 KB537 . . . . **CE 398.24**
Dog people: native dog stories./ 1995/ 4-6/5 KG934 . . . . **FIC**
First strawberries: a Cherokee story./ 1993/ 1-3/4 KB538 . . . **398.24**
Four ancestors: stories, songs, and poems from Native North America./
  1996/ 2-6/3 KB271 . . . . **398.2**
Gluskabe and the four wishes./ 1995/ 3-5/6 KB272 . . . . **398.2**
Gluskabe stories (Sound recording cassette)./ 1990/
  4-5 KB273 . . . . **SRC 398.2**
Great ball game: a Muskogee story./ 1994/ 2-4/2 KB539 . . . **398.24**
Native American animal stories./ 1992/ 4-6/5 KB540 . . . . . . **398.24**
Story of the Milky Way: a Cherokee tale./ 1995/
  2-3/3 KB701 . . . . **398.26**
Thirteen moons on turtle's back: a Native American year of moons./
  1992/ 2-6 KD919 . . . . **811**
BRUSCA, MC/ On the pampas./ 1991/ 3-6/6 KF106 . . . . **982**
Pedro fools the gringo and other tales of a Latin American trickster./
  1995/ 2-4/3 KB429 . . . . **398.22**
Three friends: a counting book./Tres amigos: un cuento para contar./
  1995/ P-2/1 KB954 . . . . **513.2**
When jaguars ate the moon: and other stories about animals and plants
  of the Americas./ 1995/ 2-3/5 KB541 . . . . **398.24**
BRUST, BW/ Amazing paper cuttings of Hans Christian Andersen./ 1994/
  3-5/8 KE235 . . . . **B ANDERSEN, H.**
BRUUN, B/ Brain--what it is, what it does./ 1989/ 3-5/5 KC914 . . **612**
BRUUN, RD/ Brain--what it is, what it does./ 1989/ 3-5/5 KC914 . **612**
BRYAN, A/ ALL NIGHT, ALL DAY: A CHILD'S FIRST BOOK OF
  AFRICAN-AMERICAN SPIRITUALS./ 1991/ K-6 KD554 . . . . . **789.2**
Beat the story-drum, pum-pum./ 1980/ 4-6/4 KB542 . . . . . . **398.24**
Cat's purr./ 1985/ K-3/2 KB543 . . . . **398.24**
CHRISTMAS GIF': AN ANTHOLOGY OF CHRISTMAS POEMS,
  SONGS, AND STORIES WRITTEN BY AND ABOUT AFRICAN-
  AMERICANS./ 1993/ 4-6 KD897 . . . . **810.8**
It's Kwanzaa time!/ 1995/ 2-6/6 KB208 . . . . **394.261**
Lion and the ostrich chicks and other African folk tales./ 1986/
  4-6/3 KB544 . . . . **398.24**
Story of lightning and thunder./ 1993/ K-2/2 KB702 . . . . . . **398.26**
Story of the three kingdoms./ 1995/ 1-3/3 KG165 . . . . **E**
Turtle knows your name./ 1989/ K-3/6 KB545 . . . . **398.24**
WHAT A MORNING! THE CHRISTMAS STORY IN BLACK SPIRITUALS./
  1987/ K-6 KD532 . . . . **782.25**
What a wonderful world./ 1995/ P-2/2 KG692 . . . . **E**
BRYANT, J/ Marjory Stoneman Douglas: voice of the Everglades./ 1992/
  4-5/6 KE324 . . . . **B DOUGLAS, M.**
BRYANT, M/ Bein' with you this way./ 1994/ P-2 KD996 . . . . . **811**
Our people./ 1994/ K-2/5 KA852 . . . . **305.8**
BRYCELEA, C/ Moon and Otter and Frog./ 1995/ 2-4/2 KB715 **398.26**
BUCHANAN, Y/ Follow the drinking gourd: a story of the Underground
  Railroad (Videocassette)./ 1992/ 2-4 KF412 . . . . **VCR E**
Juneteenth jamboree./ 1995/ 1-3/5 KG690 . . . . **E**
BUCHS, T/ Canopy crossing: a story of an Atlantic rainforest (Kit)./ 1997/
  2-4 KC873 . . . . **KIT 599.8**
BUCHWALD, C/ Puppet book: how to make and operate puppets and
  stage a puppet play./ 1990/ KA326 . . . . **PROF 791.5**
BUCK, N/ Oh, cats!/ 1997/ P-1/1 KF290 . . . . **E**
Sid and Sam./ 1996/ P-1/1 KF291 . . . . **E**
BUCKLEY, HE/ Grandfather and I./ 1994/ P-1/1 KF292 . . . . . . **E**
Grandmother and I./ 1994/ P-1/2 KF293 . . . . **E**
BUDBERG, M/ Russian fairy tales (Talking book)./ n.d./
  4-6 KB722 . . . . **TB 398.27**
BUDBILL, D/ Bones on Black Spruce Mountain./ c1978, 1994/
  4-A/5 KG935 . . . . **FIC**
BUDD, J/ Horses./ 1995/ 4-6/7 KD198 . . . . **636.1**
BUEHNER, C/ Escapada de Marvin el mono./ 1997/ P-2/3 KF294 . . . **E**
Escape of Marvin the ape./ 1992/ P-2/3 KF294 . . . . **E**
Fanny's dream./ 1996/ 1-3/4 KF295 . . . . **E**
Fanny's dream (Sound recording cassette)./ 1997/ 1-3/4 KF295 . . **E**
It's a spoon, not a shovel./ 1995/ 2-6/2 KB248 . . . . **395.5**
BUEHNER, M/ Adventures of taxi dog./ 1990/ P-2/2 KF200 . . . . **CE E**
Escape of Marvin the ape./ 1992/ P-2/3 KF294 . . . . **E**
Fanny's dream./ 1996/ 1-3/4 KF295 . . . . **E**
It's a spoon, not a shovel./ 1995/ 2-6/2 KB248 . . . . **395.5**

BUETTER, BM/ Simple puppets from everyday materials./ 1997/ 2-5/3 KD443 . . . . **745.592**
BUETTNER, D/ Sovietrek: a journey by bicycle across Russia./ 1994/ 4-6/8 KE692 . . . . **947.086**
Sovietrek: a journey by bicycle across Russia (Sound recording cassette)./ 1997/ 4-6/8 KE692 . . . . **947.086**
BUFFALO BILL HISTORICAL CENTER/ SONGS OF THE WILD WEST./ 1991/ 2-A KD597 . . . . **789.2**
BUHOLZER, T/ Life of the snail./ 1987/ 4-6/7 KC510 . . . . **594**
BULFINCH, T/ Book of myths: selections from Bulfinch's Age of fable./ c1942/ A/9 KA734 . . . . **292**
Book of myths: selections from Bulfinch's Age of fable (Braille)./ n.d./ A/9 KA734 . . . . **292**
BULL, J/ Audubon Society field guide to North American birds--Eastern Region./ 1994/ 3-6/7 KC647 . . . . **598**
BULLA, CR/ Chalk box kid./ 1987/ 2-4/2 KG936 . . . . . . **FIC**
Chalk box kid (Sound recording cassette)./ 1993/ 2-4/2 KG936 . **FIC**
Daniel's duck./ 1979/ 1-2/1 KF296 . . . . **E**
Pirate's promise./ c1986, 1994/ 2-4/2 KG937 . . . . . . **FIC**
Shoeshine girl./ 1975/ 3-5/2 KG938 . . . . **FIC**
Shoeshine girl (Braille)./ n.d./ 3-5/2 KG938 . . . . . . **FIC**
Squanto: friend of the Pilgrims./ c1954, 1982/ 3/3 KE547 . . . . **B SQUANTO**
Sword in the tree./ c1956/ 3-5/2 KG939 . . . . **FIC**
Sword in the tree (Braille)./ n.d./ 3-5/2 KG939 . . . . . **FIC**
What makes a shadow? Rev. ed./ 1994/ K-2/2 KC106 . . . **CE 535**
What makes a shadow? Rev. ed. (Kit)./ 1996/ K-2/2 KC106 . **CE 535**
White bird./ c1966, 1990/ 1-6/2 KG940 . . . . **FIC**
BULLOCH, I/ I want to be a puppeteer./ 1996/ 3-5/5 KD444 . **745.592**
I want to be an actor./ 1996/ 3-5/5 KD688 . . . . . . **792**
BUMGARNER-KIRBY, C/ Gwendolyn's gifts./ 1991/ 1-3/5 KG491 . . . **E**
BUNTING, E/ Blue and the gray./ 1996/ 3-5/3 KF297 . . . . **E**
Cheyenne again./ 1995/ 3-5/2 KG941 . . . . **FIC**
Dandelions./ 1995/ 3-5/2 KG942 . . . . **E**
Day's work./ 1994/ 1-3/2 KF298 . . . . **E**
Flower garden./ 1994/ P-2/3 KF299 . . . . **E**
Fly away home./ 1991/ K-3/2 KF300 . . . . **E**
Fly away home (Sound recording cassette)./ 1993/ K-3/2 KF300 . . . **E**
Ghost's hour, spook's hour./ 1987/ P-2/2 KF301 . . . . . **E**
Ghost's hour, spook's hour (Braille)./ n.d./ P-2/2 KF301 . . . **E**
Going home./ 1996/ 1-3/2 KF302 . . . . **E**
In-between days./ 1994/ 4-6/4 KG943 . . . . **FIC**
In-between days (Sound recording cassette)./ 1997/ 4-6/4 KG943 . **FIC**
Jane Martin, dog detective./ 1984/ 1-3/1 KF303 . . . . . **E**
Jane Martin, dog detective (Braille)./ n.d./ 1-3/1 KF303 . . . **E**
Jane Martin, dog detective (Sound recording cassette)./ n.d./ 1-3/1 KF303 . . . . **E**
Man who could call down owls./ 1984/ 1-3/2 KF304 . . . . **E**
Man who could call down owls (Sound recording cassette)./ n.d./ 1-3/2 KF304 . . . . **E**
Mother's Day mice./ 1986/ P-2/2 KF305 . . . . **CE E**
Mother's Day mice (Braille)./ n.d./ P-2/2 KF305 . . . . . **CE E**
Mother's Day mice (Kit)./ 1989/ P-2/2 KF305 . . . . . . **CE E**
On Call Back Mountain./ 1997/ 1-3/2 KF306 . . . . . . **E**
Once upon a time./ 1995/ 2-5/3 KE268 . . . . . . **B BUNTING, E.**
Our teacher's having a baby./ 1992/ P-1/2 KF307 . . . . . **E**
Scary, scary Halloween./ 1986/ P-K/4 KF308 . . . . . . **E**
Scary, scary Halloween (Braille)./ n.d./ P-K/4 KF308 . . . . **E**
Smoky night./ 1994/ 2-5/2 KF309 . . . . **E**
Spying on Miss Muller./ 1995/ 6-A/6 KG944 . . . . **FIC**
St. Patrick's Day in the morning./ 1980/ K-2/2 KF310 . . . . **E**
Sunflower house./ 1996/ P-2/2 KF311 . . . . **E**
Train to Somewhere./ 1996/ 3-5/4 KG945 . . . . **FIC**
Train to Somewhere (Sound recording cassette)./ 1997/ 3-5/4 KG945 . . . . **FIC**
Turkey for Thanksgiving./ 1991/ P-2/2 KF312 . . . . . . **E**
BURANDT, H/ Tales from the homeplace: adventures of a Texas farm girl./ 1997/ 5-A/4 KG946 . . . . **FIC**
BURCH, A/ Children's illustrated Bible./ 1994/ 4-6/5 KA676 . . . . . **220**
BURCHARD, P/ Pirate's promise./ c1986, 1994/ 2-4/2 KG937 . . . **FIC**
BURDEN, PJ/ Mogul and me./ 1989/ 5-A/7 KH046 . . . . **FIC**
BURGEL, PH/ Gorillas./ 1993/ 5-6/7 KC874 . . . . . . **599.884**
BURGER, C/ Old Yeller./ c1956/ A/7 KH170 . . . . . . **CE FIC**
BURGER, L/ Red Cross/Red Crescent: when help can't wait./ 1996/ 4-6/8 KA992 . . . . **361.7**
BURGESS, A/ READY...SET...READ!: THE BEGINNING READER'S TREASURY./ 1990/ P-2 KD901 . . . . **810.8**
BURGESS, BH/ Fred Field./ 1994/ 6-A/6 KG947 . . . . . **FIC**
BURGESS, M/ Cry of the wolf./ 1994/ 5-A/7 KG948 . . . . . **FIC**
BURGUNDER, A/ Zoolutions: a mathematical expedition with topics for grades 4 through 8./ c1993, 1996/ KA251 . . . . **PROF 372.7**
BURKE, SS/ Hide and shriek: riddles about ghosts and goblins./ 1991/ 2-5 KD727 . . . . **793.735**

My very own Halloween: a book of cooking and crafts./ 1993/ 3-6/5 KD701 . . . . **793.2**
Summit up: riddles about mountains./ 1994/ 3-6 KD739 . . . . **793.735**
BURKERT, NE/ Snow-White and the seven dwarfs./ 1972/ 3-4/6 KB310 . . . . **398.2**
BURLEIGH, R/ Flight: the journey of Charles Lindbergh./ 1991/ 1-4/2 KD091 . . . . **629.13**
Flight: the journey of Charles Lindbergh./ 1991/ 4-6/3 KD092 . **629.13**
Flight: the journey of Charles Lindbergh (Sound recording cassette)./ 1994/ 1-4/2 KD091 . . . . **629.13**
Who said that?: famous Americans speak./ 1997/ 4-A/7 KA597 . **080**
BURNETT, FH/ Little princess./ c1963/ 5-A/8 KG949 . . . . **FIC**
Sara Crewe./ 1986/ 4-6/7 KG950 . . . . **FIC**
Secret garden./ c1911, 1987/ 3-6/5 KG951 . . . . . . **CE FIC**
Secret garden (Talking book)./ 1997,/ 3-6/5 KG951 . . . . **CE FIC**
BURNHAM, SD/ Three River Junction: a story of an Alaskan bald eagle preserve (Kit)./ 1997/ 2-4 KF313 . . . . . . **KIT E**
BURNIE, D/ Arbol./ 1995/ K-6/7 KC409 . . . . **582.16**
Bird./ 1988/ A/9 KC648 . . . . **598**
Dictionary of nature./ 1994/ 3-A KA445 . . . . . . **REF 570**
Light./ 1992/ 4-A/7 KC107 . . . . **535**
Plant./ 1989/ 3-A/7 KC383 . . . . **580**
Tree./ 1988/ K-6/7 KC409 . . . . **582.16**
BURNINGHAM, J/ Cannonball Simp./ 1994/ K-2/4 KF314 . . . . **E**
Chitty Chitty Bang Bang: the magical car./ c1964, 1989/ 5-6/7 KH128 . . . . **FIC**
Come away from the water, Shirley./ c1977/ P-2/2 KF315 . . . . . **CE E**
Harvey Slumfenburger's Christmas present./ 1993/ K-2/2 KF316 . . **E**
Mr. Gumpy's motor car./ c1973, 1976/ P-2/2 KF317 . . . . **CE E**
Mr. Gumpy's motor car (Braille)./ n.d.,/ P-2/2 KF317 . . . . **CE E**
Mr. Gumpy's outing./ c1970/ P-2/2 KF318 . . . . . . **CE E**
Mr. Gumpy's outing (Big book)./ 1995/ P-2/2 KF318 . . . . **CE E**
Mr. Gumpy's outing (Talking book)./ n.d./ P-2/2 KF318 . . . . **CE E**
BURNS, DL/ Cranberries: fruit of the bogs./ 1994/ 5-6/7 KD157 . . **634**
Sugaring season: making maple syrup./ 1990/ 5-6/7 KD154 . . . **633.6**
Sugaring season: making maple syrup (Sound recording cassette)./ 1993/ 5-6/7 KD154 . . . . **633.6**
BURNS, K/ Black stars in orbit: NASA'S African American astronauts./ 1995/ 3-6/8 KD136 . . . . **629.45**
BURNS, M/ Math for smarty pants./ 1982/ 4-6/5 KB946 . . . . **513**
This book is about time./ 1978/ 4-6/6 KC068 . . . . . . **529**
BURRESS, L/ Battle of the books: literary censorship in the public schools, 1950-1985./ 1989/ KA051 . . . . **PROF 025.2**
BURROWES, AJ/ My steps./ 1996/ P-1/2 KF482 . . . . **E**
BURROWS, WE/ Mission to deep space: Voyagers' journey of discovery./ 1993/ 4-8/11 KC024 . . . . **523.4**
BURSTEIN, CM/ Jewish kids catalog./ 1983/ 4-6/7 KB179 . . . . . **394**
BURT, D/ Birth of a koala./ 1986/ 4-6/8 KC734 . . . . . . **599.2**
BURTON, B/ Moving within the circle: contemporary Native American music and dance./ 1993/ KA316 . . . . . . **BA PROF 789.2**
Moving withing the circle: contemporary Native American music and dance./ 1993/ KA316 . . . . . . **BA PROF 789.2**
BURTON, L/ HOW MUCH IS A MILLION? (Videocassette)./ 1997/ K-1 KB947 . . . . **VCR 513**
BURTON, VL/ Katy and the big snow./ c1943, 1973/ P-1/4 KF319 . . **E**
Katy and the big snow (Braille)./ n.d.,/ P-1/4 KF319 . . . . **E**
Little house./ c1942, 1978/ K-2/2 KF320 . . . . **CE E**
Little house (Braille)./ n.d./ K-2/2 KF320 . . . . . . **CE E**
Maybelle the cable car./ 1997/ K-2/3 KF321 . . . . . . **CE E**
Mike Mulligan and his steam shovel./ c1939/ P-2/6 KF322 . . . **CE E**
Mike Mulligan and his steam shovel (Braille)./ n.d./ P-2/6 KF322 . **CE E**
Mike Mulligan and his steam shovel (Sound recording cassette)./ n.d./ P-2/6 KF322 . . . . **CE E**
Mike Mulligan and his steam shovel (Talking book)./ n.d./ P-2/6 KF322 . . . . **CE E**
Mike Mulligan and his steam shovel (Videocassette)./ 1985/ P-2/6 KF322 . . . . **CE E**
BUSCH, PS/ Backyard safaris: 52 year-round science adventures./ 1995/ P-A/5 KB901 . . . . **508**
BUSH, T/ Grunt!: the primitive cave boy./ 1995/ K-2/2 KF323 . . . . . **E**
BUSHEY, J/ Farming the land, modern farmers and their machines./ 1987/ 4-6/6 KD147 . . . . **631.3**
BUSHNELL, J/ Circus of the wolves./ 1994/ 4-6/5 KG952 . . . . . . **FIC**
BUSSELL, D/ Young dancer./ 1994/ 3-6/8 KD692 . . . . . . **792.8**
BUSSER, M/ King Bobble./ 1996/ 2-3/2 KG953 . . . . **FIC**
On the road with Poppa Whopper./ 1997/ 3-4/2 KG954 . . . . . **FIC**
BUTLER, J/ Sweet words so brave: the story of African American literature./ 1996/ K-6/7 KD906 . . . . **810.9**
BUTTERFIELD, M/ Jets./ 1996/ 4-6/8 KD061 . . . . **623.7**
BUTTERFIELD, N/ Illustrated rules of in-line hockey./ 1996/ 3-6/6 KD772 . . . . **796.21**
BUTTERWORTH, O/ Enormous egg./ c1956/ 3-5/4 KG955 . . . . **FIC**
Visit to the big house./ 1993/ 3-5/5 KG956 . . . . . . **FIC**

BUTTS, ER/ May Chinn: the best medicine./ 1995/
5-A/8 KE288 . . . . B CHINN, M.
BYAM, M/ Armas y armaduras./ n.d./ A/10 KA986 . . . . 355.8
Arms and armor./ 1988/ A/10 KA986 . . . . 355.8
BYARD, C/ Have a happy... a novel./ 1989/ 4-6/4 KH838 . . . . . . FIC
Working cotton./ 1992/ 3-3/2 KG731 . . . . E
BYARS, BC/ Ant plays Bear./ 1997/ K-1/1 KF324 . . . . E
Bingo Brown and the language of love./ 1989/ 5-A/5 KG957 . . . . FIC
Bingo Brown's guide to romance./ 1992/ 5-A/5 KG957 . . . . FIC
Blossom promise./ 1990/ 4-A/4 KG962 . . . . CE FIC
Blossoms and the Green Phantom./ c1987/ 4-A/4 KG962 . . . CE FIC
Blossoms meet the Vulture Lady./ 1986/ 4-A/4 KG962 . . . . CE FIC
Burning questions of Bingo Brown./ 1990/ 5-A/5 KG958 . . . . FIC
Cartoonist./ 1978/ 4-6/3 KG959 . . . . FIC
Dark stairs./ 1994/ 4-6/5 KG960 . . . . CE FIC
Dark stairs: a Herculeah Jones mystery (Talking book)./ 1995/
4-6/5 KG960 . . . . CE FIC
Dark stairs (Sound recording cassette)./ 1997/ 4-6/5 KG960 . CE FIC
Dead letter./ 1996/ 4-6/5 KG960 . . . . CE FIC
Death's door./ 1997/ 4-6/5 KG960 . . . . CE FIC
Golly sisters go West./ 1986/ 1-3/1 KF325 . . . . CE E
Golly sisters go West (Kit)./ 1995/ 1-3/1 KF325 . . . . CE E
Golly sisters go West (Sound recording cassette)./ 1997/
1-3/1 KF325 . . . . CE E
Golly sisters ride again./ 1994/ 1-3/1 KF325 . . . . CE E
Golly sisters ride again (Sound recording cassette)./ 1997/
1-3/1 KF325 . . . . CE E
Hooray for the Golly sisters!/ 1990/ 1-3/1 KF325 . . . . . . CE E
Hooray for the Golly sisters! (Sound recording cassette)./ 1997/
1-3/1 KF325 . . . . CE E
Joy boys./ 1996/ 2-3/1 KF326 . . . . E
McMummy./ 1993/ 5-A/5 KG961 . . . . FIC
My brother, Ant./ 1996/ K-2/1 KF327 . . . . E
Not-just-anybody family./ 1986/ 4-A/4 KG962 . . . . CE FIC
Pinballs./ c1977/ 5-6/3 KG963 . . . . CE FIC
Pinballs (Kit)./ 1988/ 5-6/3 KG963 . . . . CE FIC
Pinballs (Sound recording cassette)./ n.d./ 5-6/3 KG963 . . . CE FIC
Summer of the swans./ c1970/ 5-6/6 KG964 . . . . CE FIC
Summer of the swans (Sound recording cassette)./ n.d./
5-6/6 KG964 . . . . CE FIC
Summer of the swans (Talking book)./ 1972/ 5-6/6 KG964 . . CE FIC
Tarot says beware./ 1995/ 4-6/5 KG960 . . . . CE FIC
Tarot says beware (Talking book)./ 1996/ 4-6/5 KG960 . . . CE FIC
Tornado./ 1996/ 2-5/3 KG965 . . . . FIC
Wanted...Mud Blossom./ 1991/ 4-A/4 KG962 . . . . CE FIC
Wanted...Mud Blossom (Sound recording cassette)./ 1995/
4-A/4 KG962 . . . . CE FIC
Wanted...Mud Blossom (Talking book)./ 1995/ 4-A/4 KG962 . CE FIC
BYRD, R/ Emperor's new clothes./ 1991/ P-2/4 KF968 . . . . . . E
Little swineherd and other tales./ 1996/ 3-6/4 KH136 . . . . . FIC
BYRD, S/ Abraham Lincoln: a man for all the people: a ballad./ 1993/
K-3 KD974 811
Keep on singing: a ballad of Marian Anderson./ 1994/
1-3 KD977 811
Let freedom ring: a ballad of Martin Luther King, Jr./ 1992/
K-2/4 KD978 811
Picture book of Sitting Bull./ 1993/ 3-4/5 KE540 . . . B SITTING BULL
CABLE, A/ I fly./ 1997/ P-1/2 KG343 . . . . E
Me on the map./ 1996/ K-1/1 KE172 912
CAIN, D/ Copier creations: using copy machines to make decals,
silhouettes, flip books, films, and much more!/ 1993/
3-6/7 KD503 760
Science experiments you can eat. Rev. and updated./ 1994/
3-5/7 KB891 . . . . 507.8
CAIRO, J/ Our brother has Down's syndrome: an introduction for children./
1985/ 1-4/6 KB002 . . . . 362.3
CAIRO, S/ Our brother has Down's syndrome: an introduction for
children./ 1985/ 1-4/6 KB002 . . . . 362.3
CAIRO, T/ Our brother has Down's syndrome: an introduction for
children./ 1985/ 1-4/6 KB002 . . . . 362.3
CALABRO, M/ Operation grizzly bear./ 1989/ 5-6/7 KC858 . 599.784
CALHOUN, M/ Cross-country cat./ 1979/ K-2/4 KF331 . . . . E
Flood./ 1997/ 1-3/2 KF332 . . . . E
Henry the sailor cat./ 1994/ K-2/4 KF331 . . . . E
High-wire Henry./ 1991/ K-2/4 KF331 . . . . E
High-wire Henry (Sound recording cassette)./ 1993/ K-2/4 KF331 . . E
Hot-air Henry./ 1981/ K-2/4 KF331 . . . . E
Katie John./ c1960/ 4-6/4 KG966 . . . . FIC
CALLINAN, T/ Let's clean up our act: songs for the earth (Sound recording
cassette)./ 1989/ K-6 KD559 . . . . SRC 789.2
CALLISON, D/ AASL ELECTRONIC LIBRARY. 1997 ed. (CD-ROM)./
1997/ KA045 . . . . CDR PROF 025
CALMENSON, S/ Crazy eights and other card games./ 1994/
3-6/3 KD758 . . . . 795.4
Eentsy, weentsy spider: fingerplays and action rhymes./ 1991/
P-K KD706 . . . . 793.4
GIVE A DOG A BONE: STORIES, POEMS, JOKES, AND RIDDLES
ABOUT DOGS./ 1996/ K-4 KD874 . . . . 808.8
MISS MARY MACK AND OTHER CHILDREN'S STREET RHYMES./
1990/ 2-5 KD766 . . . . 796.1
Pin the tail on the donkey and other party games./ 1993/
K-2/3 KD698 793
Rain or shine activity book: fun things to make and do./ 1997/
3-6 KD699 793
READY...SET...READ!: THE BEGINNING READER'S TREASURY./ 1990/
P-2 KD901 . . . . 810.8
READY...SET...READ--AND LAUGH!: A FUNNY TREASURY FOR
BEGINNING READERS./ 1995/ K-2 KD902 . . . . 810.8
Rosie, a visiting dog's story./ 1994/ 3-6/2 KD216 . . . . 636.7
SCARY BOOK./ 1991/ 2-4/2 KB691 . . . . 398.25
Six sick sheep: 101 tongue twisters./ / 3-5 KB795 . . . . 398.8
YOURS TILL BANANA SPLITS: 201 AUTOGRAPH RHYMES./ 1995/
3-6 KD894 . . . . 808.88
CALVINO, I/ ITALIAN FOLKTALES./ 1980/ 5-6 KA415 . . REF 398.23
CAMERON, A/ Julian, dream doctor./ 1990/ 3-4/4 KG970 . . . . FIC
Julian's glorious summer./ 1987/ 2-4/2 KG967 . . . . FIC
Julian's glorious summer (Braille)./ n.d./ 2-4/2 KG967 . . . . . FIC
More stories Huey tells./ 1997/ 2-4/2 KG968 . . . . FIC
More stories Julian tells./ 1989/ 3-4/4 KG970 . . . . FIC
More stories Julian tells (Braille)./ n.d./ 3-4/4 KG970 . . . . . FIC
Raven and Snipe./ 1991/ 3-4/6 KB546 . . . . 398.24
Raven goes berrypicking./ 1991/ 3-4/6 KB547 . . . . 398.24
Stories Huey tells./ 1995/ 2-4/2 KG969 . . . . FIC
Stories Julian tells./ 1981/ 3-4/4 KG970 . . . . FIC
Stories Julian tells (Braille)./ n.d./ 3-4/4 KG970 . . . . FIC
Stories Julian tells (Sound recording cassette)./ n.d./ 3-4/4 KG970 FIC
CAMERON, S/ Beethoven lives upstairs./ 1994/ 4-6/4 KH549 . . . FIC
David and Goliath./ 1996/ 1-4/6 KA683 222
CAMP, CA/ American astronomers: searchers and wonderers./ 1996/
A/10 KC000 520
CAMPBELL, A/ New York Public Library amazing space: a book of answers
for kids./ 1997/ 3-A/8 KC001 520
CAMPBELL, J/ Cal Ripken, Jr./ 1997/ 5-6/7 KE512 . . . . B RIPKEN, C.
Comeback!: four true stories./ 1992/ 2-4/4 KD765 796
CAMPBELL, PS/ From rice paddies and temple yards: traditional music of
Vietnam./ c1990, 1992/ KA317 . . . . BA PROF 789.2
Roots and branches: a legacy of multicultural music for children./ 1994/
KA320 . . . . BA PROF 789.3
Silent temples, songful hearts: traditional music of Cambodia./ 1991/
KA318 . . . . BA PROF 789.2
CAMPITELLI, S/ Mammolina: a story about Maria Montessori./ 1993/
4-6/6 KE467 . . . . B MONTESSORI, M
CANADY, RJ/ Story stretchers for the primary grades: activities to expand
children's favorite books./ 1992/ KA240 . . . . PROF 372.64
CANDY, J/ Stormalong (Kit)./ 1995/ 2-5 KB470 . . . . . . KIT 398.22
CANEY, S/ Steven Caney's invention book./ 1985/ A/10 KC884 . 608
Steven Caney's Kids' America./ 1978/ 4-6/7 KE920 . . . . 973.92
CANN, H/ Mother and daughter tales./ 1996/ 3-4/6 KB292 . . . 398.2
CANNON, J/ Bat in the boot./ 1996/ 1-3/2 KF333 . . . . E
CANNON, J/ Stelaluna (Spanish version)./ 1993/ K-2/3 KF334 . . . E
Stellaluna./ 1993/ K-2/3 KF334 . . . . E
STELLALUNA (CD-ROM)./ 1996/ K-3 KG550 . . . . CDR E
Stellaluna (Talking book)./ Stellaluna (Talking book)./ 1996/ 1996/
K-2 KF335 . . . . TB E
K-2 KF335 . . . . TB E
Verdi./ 1997/ K-2/3 KF336 . . . . E
CANYON, C/ Did you hear Wind sing your name?: an Oneida song of
spring./ 1995/ K-2/3 KF454 . . . . E
Tree in the ancient forest./ 1995/ K-3/3 KC437 585
CAPLE, K/ Biggest nose./ 1985/ P-2/2 KF337 . . . . E
Biggest nose (Braille)./ n.d./ P-2/2 KF337 . . . . E
Biggest nose (Sound recording cassette)./ n.d./ P-2/2 KF337 . . . . E
CAPON, B/ Plant survival: adapting to a hostile world./ 1994/
A/9 KC397 . . . . 581.4
CAPONIGRO, JP/ Ghost in the house./ 1993/ 5-6/5 KA598 . . . 133.1
CAPOTE, T/ Christmas memory./ c1956, 1989/ 4-A/6 KG971 . CE FIC
Thanksgiving visitor./ 1996/ 5-A/8 KG972 . . . . FIC
CAPPO, M/ World desk: a student handbook to the Internet. Rev. ed./
1996/ A/10 KA576 . . . . 025.04
CAPUCILLI, A/ Biscuit./ 1996/ P-1/1 KF338 . . . . E
Biscuit finds a friend./ 1997/ P-1/1 KF339 . . . . E
CARDEN, G/ From the Brothers Grimm: a contemporary retelling of
American folktales and classic stories./ 1992/ 5-A KB281 . CE 398.2
CAREY, J/ SPOOKY STORIES OF THE SUPERNATURAL./ 1985/
6-A KH745 . . . . FIC
CAREY, P/ Big Bazoohley./ 1995/ 3-6/5 KG973 . . . . FIC
CARLE, E/ Brown bear, brown bear, what do you see?/ 1992/
P-K/1 KG072 . . . . E

Chenille affamee./ 1992/ P-1/6 KF347 . . . . **E**
Do you want to be my friend?/ 1971/ P-K/1 KF340 . . . . **E**
Eric Carle's animals, animals./ 1989/ P-3 KD880 . . . . **808.81**
Eric Carle's dragons dragons and other creatures that never were./ 1991/
K-3 KD881 . . . . **808.81**
From head to toe./ 1997/ P-K/1 KF341 . . . . **E**
Grouchy ladybug. New ed./ 1996/ P-2/2 KF342 . . . . **E**
Have you seen my cat?/ c1973, 1987/ P-1/1 KF343 . . . . **E**
Hole in the dike./ c1974, 1975/ K-2/2 KF640 . . . . **CE E**
House for Hermit Crab./ 1987/ P-2/2 KF344 . . . . **E**
Mariquita malhumorada./ 1996/ P-2/2 KF342 . . . . **E**
Rooster's off to see the world./ 1972/ P-2/2 KF345 . . . . **E**
TODAY IS MONDAY./ 1993/ P-1 KD661 . . . . **789.3**
Very busy spider./ 1985/ P-2/2 KF346 . . . . **E**
Very busy spider (Braille)./ n.d./ P-2/2 KF346 . . . . **E**
Very hungry caterpillar./ 1981/ P-1/6 KF347 . . . . **E**
Very lonely firefly./ 1995/ P-2/2 KF348 . . . . **E**
1, 2, 3 to the zoo./ c1968/ P-K KF349 . . . . **E**
CARLSON, JD/ Historical album of Minnesota./ 1993/
5-6/7 KF020 . . . . **977.6**
CARLSON, L/ EcoArt!: earth-friendly art and craft experiences for 3-to
9-year olds./ 1993/ K-4 KD425 . . . . **745.5**
LITERARY LAURELS: KIDS' EDITION: A READER'S GUIDE TO AWARD-
WINNING CHILDREN'S BOOKS./ 1996/ KA034 . . . **PROF 016.809**
CARLSON, N/ How to lose all your friends./ 1994/ K-2/2 KF350 . . . **E**
Making the team./ 1985/ P-2/2 KF351 . . . . **CE E**
Mysterious valentine./ 1985/ P-2/2 KF351 . . . . **CE E**
Mysterious valentine (Kit)./ 1987/ P-2/2 KF351 . . . . **CE E**
Perfect family./ 1985/ P-2/2 KF351 . . . . **CE E**
Perfect family (Kit)./ 1987/ P-2/2 KF351 . . . . **CE E**
Sit still!/ 1996/ K-2/2 KF352 . . . . **E**
Talent show./ 1985/ P-2/2 KF351 . . . . **CE E**
Visit to Grandma's./ 1991/ P-2/2 KF353 . . . . **E**
Witch lady./ 1985/ P-2/2 KF351 . . . . **CE E**
CARLSON, NS/ Family under the bridge./ c1958/ 3-5/4 KG974 . . . **FIC**
Family under the bridge (Braille)./ n.d./ 3-5/4 KG974 . . . . **FIC**
Family under the bridge (Sound recording cassette)./ n.d./
3-5/4 KG974 . . . . **FIC**
CARLSON, SJ/ First houses: Native American homes and sacred
structures./ 1993/ 6-A/7 KB171 . . . . **392.3**
CARLSTROM, NW/ Better not get wet, Jesse Bear./ 1988/
P-K/4 KF356 . . . . **E**
Happy birthday, Jesse Bear!/ 1994/ P-K/4 KF356 . . . . **E**
How do you say it today, Jesse Bear?/ 1992/ P-K/4 KF356 . . . **E**
How does the wind walk?/ 1993/ P-2/3 KF354 . . . . **E**
I'm not moving, Mama!/ 1990/ P-1/1 KF355 . . . . **E**
Jesse Bear, what will you wear?/ 1986/ P-K/4 KF356 . . . . **E**
Jesse Bear, what will you wear? (Braille)./ n.d./ P-K/4 KF356 . . . . . **E**
Let's count it out, Jesse Bear./ 1996/ P-1/2 KF357 . . . . **E**
Who said boo?: Halloween poems for the very young./ 1995/
P-1 KD920 . . . . **811**
CARMI, G/ Old woman and her pig./ 1992/ K-2/2 KB603 . . . . **398.24**
CARNEGIE LIBRARY SCHOOL ASSOCIATION/ Our holidays in poetry./
1965/ 5-6 KB196 . . . . **394.26**
CARNOVSKY, M/ Russian fairy tales (Talking book)./ n.d./
4-6 KB722 . . . . **TB 398.27**
CAROSELLI, J/ KNOCK AT THE DOOR./ 1992/ KA269 . . **PROF 398.2**
CARPENTER, AS/ L. Frank Baum: royal historian of Oz./ 1992/
4-6/4 KE251 . . . . **B BAUM, L.**
L. Frank Baum: royal historian of Oz (Sound recording cassette)./ 1995/
4-6/4 KE251 . . . . **B BAUM, L.**
CARPENTER, N/ Can you dance, Dalila?/ 1996/ K-2/5 KF932 . . . . . **E**
Lester's dog./ 1993/ 1-3/3 KF716 . . . . **E**
Masai and I./ 1992/ K-2/4 KF934 . . . . **E**
CARPENTER, S/ KIDS PICK THE FUNNIEST POEMS./ 1991/
3-6 KE068 . . . . **811.008**
New adventures of Mother Goose: gentle rhymes for happy times./
1993/ P-3 KD967 . . . . **811**
You're invited to Bruce Lansky's poetry party!/ 1996/ 3-6 KD968 . **811**
CARRADINE, K/ ANNIE OAKLEY (Videocassette)./ 1997/
3-6 KE479 . . . . **VCR B OAKLEY, A.**
CARRICK, C/ Ben and the porcupine./ 1985/ 1-3/4 KF358 . . . . **E**
Foundling./ 1977/ 1-3/4 KF358 . . . . **E**
Left behind./ 1988/ 1-3/2 KF359 . . . . **E**
Melanie./ 1996/ 1-3/2 KF360 . . . . **E**
Patrick's dinosaurs./ 1983/ K-2/4 KF361 . . . . **CE E**
Patrick's dinosaurs (Kit)./ 1987/ K-2/4 KF361 . . . . **CE E**
Sand tiger shark./ c1977/ 4-6/7 KC591 . . . . **597.3**
Two very little sisters./ 1993/ 2-4/5 KC879 . . . . **599.9**
Whaling days./ 1993/ 4-5/6 KD243 . . . . **639.2**
Whaling days (Sound recording cassette)./ 1995/ 4-5/6 KD243 . . **639.2**
What happened to Patrick's dinosaurs?/ 1986/ K-2/4 KF361 . . . . **CE E**
What happened to Patrick's dinosaurs? (Braille)./ n.d./
K-2/4 KF361 . . . . **CE E**

What happened to Patrick's dinosaurs? (Kit)./ 1988/
K-2/4 KF361 . . . . **CE E**
What happened to Patrick's dinosaurs? (Sound recording cassette)./ n.d./
K-2/4 KF361 . . . . **CE E**
CARRICK, D/ Doctor Change./ 1986/ K-3/2 KF410 . . . . **E**
Foundling./ 1977/ 1-3/4 KF358 . . . . **E**
Ghost's hour, spook's hour./ 1987/ P-2/2 KF301 . . . . **E**
Journey to Topaz./ c1971, 1984/ 5-A/7 KH816 . . . . **FIC**
Left behind./ 1988/ 1-3/2 KF359 . . . . **E**
Milk./ 1985/ K-3/4 KD237 . . . . **637**
Patrick's dinosaurs./ 1983/ K-2/4 KF361 . . . . **CE E**
Sand tiger shark./ c1977/ 4-6/7 KC591 . . . . **597.3**
CARRIER, R/ Basketball player./ 1996/ 4-6/3 KG975 . . . . **FIC**
Boxing champion./ 1991/ 4-6/2 KG976 . . . . **FIC**
Champion (French version)./ 1991/ 4-6/2 KG976 . . . . **FIC**
Jonron mas largo./ 1993/ 2-4/4 KG977 . . . . **FIC**
Joueur de basket-ball./ 1996/ 4-6/3 KG975 . . . . **FIC**
Longest home run./ 1993/ 2-4/4 KG977 . . . . **FIC**
Plus long circuit./ 1993/ 2-4/4 KG977 . . . . **FIC**
CARRIGAN, M/ Jimmy Carter: beyond the presidency./ 1995/
5-6/7 KE280 . . . . **B CARTER, J.**
CARRIS, JD/ Aunt Morbelia and the screaming skulls./ 1990/
4-6/5 KG978 . . . . **FIC**
Beware the ravens, Aunt Morbelia./ 1995/ 5-A/5 KG979 . . . . **FIC**
CARROLL, L/ Alice's adventures in Wonderland./ c1865, 1992/
5-A/7 KG980 . . . . **FIC**
Jabberwocky./ 1992/ K-2/3 KE097 . . . . **821**
Through the looking-glass and what Alice found there./ c1872, 1993/
5-A/7 KG981 . . . . **FIC**
CARROLL, P/ Largest dinosaurs./ 1986/ 4-6/6 KC265 . . . . **567.9**
CARROLL-WELDEN, A/ Olde Mother Goose (Kit)./ 1993/
P-K KB805 . . . . **KIT 398.8**
CARROW, RS/ Put a fan in your hat!: inventions, contraptions, and gadgets
kids can build./ 1997/ 5-6/8 KC885 . . . . **608**
CARSER, SX/ Motocross cycles./ 1992/ 4-A/5 KD828 . . . . **796.7**
CARSON, R/ Edge of the sea./ c1955/ A/10 KC367 . . . . **578.77**
Edge of the sea (Braille)./ n.d./ A/10 KC367 . . . . **578.77**
Edge of the sea (Sound recording cassette)./ n.d./
A/10 KC367 . . . . **578.77**
CART, C/ Formerly great Alexander family./ 1995/ 3-5/6 KH708 . . **FIC**
CARTER, A/ Edwin and Emily./ 1995/ 1-3/2 KG733 . . . . **E**
I THOUGHT I'D TAKE MY RAT TO SCHOOL: POEMS FOR SEPTEMBER
TO JUNE./ 1993/ 2-5 KE066 . . . . **811.008**
CARTER, AR/ Battle of Gettysburg./ 1990/ 4-6/7 KE899 . . . . . . **973.7**
Battle of the ironclads: the Monitor and the Merrimack./ 1993/
4-6/8 KE900 . . . . **973.7**
Last stand at the Alamo./ 1990/ 4-6/7 KF001 . . . . **976.4**
CARTER, DA/ Cars! cars! cars!/ 1995/ P-1/1 KG045 . . . . **E**
In a dark, dark wood./ 1991/ P-2/2 KF362 . . . . **E**
There's a square: a book about shapes./ 1996/ P-1/1 KG442 . . . . . **E**
CARTER, GG/ Mac and Marie and the train toss surprise./ 1993/
K-2/2 KF774 . . . . **E**
May'naise sandwiches and sunshine tea./ 1994/ 1-3/3 KF217 . . . . . **E**
CARTWRIGHT, R/ James and the rain./ 1995/ K-2/5 KF938 . . . . **E**
CARUSONE, A/ Don't open the door after the sun goes down: tales of the
real and unreal./ 1994/ 4-6/4 KG982 . . . . **FIC**
CASA, BDL/ Log of Christopher Columbus' first voyage to America in the
year 1492./ c1938, 1989/ 4-6/7 KE741 . . . . **970.01**
CASELEY, J/ Chloe in the know./ 1993/ 3-5/4 KG985 . . . . **FIC**
Dear Annie./ 1991/ K-2/2 KF363 . . . . **E**
Dorothy's darkest days./ 1997/ 3-5/4 KG983 . . . . **FIC**
Grandpa's garden lunch./ 1990/ P-1/2 KF364 . . . . **E**
Harry and Arney./ 1994/ 3-5/6 KG984 . . . . **FIC**
Harry and Willy and Carrothead./ 1991/ K-1/2 KF365 . . . . **E**
Hurricane Harry./ 1991/ 3-5/4 KG985 . . . . **FIC**
Mama, coming and going./ 1994/ 1-3/4 KF366 . . . . **E**
Noisemakers./ 1992/ P-1/2 KF367 . . . . **E**
Priscilla twice./ 1995/ 1-3/2 KF368 . . . . **E**
Slumber party!/ 1996/ 2-3/2 KF369 . . . . **E**
Sophie and Sammy's library sleepover./ 1993/ P-1/4 KF370 . . . . . **E**
Witch Mama./ 1996/ K-2/3 KF371 . . . . **E**
CASELLI, G/ Middle Ages./ 1988/ 5-A/7 KE144 . . . . **909.07**
Roman Empire and the Dark Ages./ 1985/ 5-A/9 KE644 . . . . . **940.1**
Wonders of the world./ 1992/ 4-A/8 KD382 . . . . **720**
CASEY, D/ Weather everywhere./ 1995/ P-2/6 KC189 . . . . **551.5**
CASEY, P/ My cat Jack./ 1996/ P-1/2 KF372 . . . . **E**
CASH, T/ Plastics./ 1990/ 3-5/5 KD327 . . . . **668.4**
101 physics tricks: fun experiments with everyday materials./ 1993/
4-8/7 KC077 . . . . **530**
CASILLA, R/ Boys at work./ 1995/ 4-6/5 KH739 . . . . **FIC**
Jalapeno bagels./ 1996/ 1-3/2 KG742 . . . . **E**
Picture book of Jackie Robinson./ 1994/
2-4/6 KE515 . . . . **B ROBINSON, J.**
Picture book of Jesse Owens./ 1992/ 3-4/6 KE486 . . . . **B OWENS, J.**

Picture book of Simon Bolivar./ 1992/ 3-4/5 KE257 .. **B BOLIVAR, S.**
Pool party./ c1993, 1995/ 4-6/5 KH741 . . . . **FIC**
With my brother/Con mi hermano./ 1991/ P-2/2 KG346 . . . . **E**
CASSEDY, S/ Behind the attic wall./ 1983/ 6-A/5 KG986 . . . **FIC**
Lucie Babbidge's house./ 1993/ 6-A/7 KG987 . . . . **FIC**
Zoomrimes: poems about things that go./ 1993/ 3-6 KD921 . . . . **811**
CASSELS, J/ Prairie dogs./ 1993/ 4-5/4 KC749 . . . . **599.36**
CASSLER, C/ Herbie Jones and the birthday showdown./ 1995/
3-4/3 KH366 . . . . **FIC**
CASTLE, L/ Quetzalcoatl tale of corn./ 1992/ 2-3/5 KB630 . . . **398.24**
CATALANO, D/ Merry Christmas, Old Armadillo./ 1995/
K-2/3 KF267 . . . . **E**
CATALANO, S/ Moon of the gray wolves. New ed./ 1991/
5-6/6 KC835 . . . . **599.773**
CATALANOTTO, P/ Cecil's story./ 1991/ K-3/2 KG042 . . . . . . **E**
Mama is a miner./ 1994/ 2-3/3 KG044 . . . . **E**
CATLETT, E/ Lift every voice and sing./ 1993/ 2-6/5 KD672 . . . **789.44**
CATROW, D/ Million-Dollar Bear./ 1995/ 2-3/2 KF916 . . . . . . **E**
She's wearing a dead bird on her head!/ 1995/ 3-5/5 KH386 . . **FIC**
Who said that?: famous Americans speak./ 1997/ 4-A/7 KA597 . **080**
CAULEY, LB/ Clap your hands./ 1992/ P-K/5 KF373 . . . . **E**
CAVAN, S/ Irish-American experience./ 1993/ 5-6/7 KA840 . . . . **305.8**
CAZET, D/ Fish in his pocket./ 1987/ P-2/2 KF374 . . . . **E**
CECH, J/ First snow, magic snow./ 1992/ 2-4/6 KB390 . . . . . . **398.21**
CECIL, L/ Frog princess./ 1995/ 1-3/2 KB548 . . . . **398.24**
CECIL, R/ Little Red Cowboy Hat./ 1997/ 1-3/3 KG038 . . . . . . **E**
CEDENO, ME/ Cesar Chavez: labor leader./ 1993/
4-5/6 KE287 . . . . **B CHAVEZ, C.**
CENDRARS, B/ Shadow./ 1982/ 3-5 KE120 . . . . **CE 841**
CEPEDA, J/ Gracias, the Thanksgiving turkey./ 1996/ K-2/1 KF430 . . **E**
Old man and his door./ 1996/ K-2/2 KG528 . . . . **E**
CERULLO, MM/ Lobsters: gangsters of the sea./ 1994/
5-6/7 KC518 . . . . **595.3**
CHA, D/ Dia's story cloth./ 1996/ 2-6/6 KE716 . . . . **959.404**
CHADWICK, B/ John Madden./ 1997/ 5-A/7 KE451 . . **B MADDEN, J.**
CHADWICK, KC/ CELEBRATING WOMEN IN MATHEMATICS AND
SCIENCE./ 1996/ A/11 KA439 . . . . **REF 509**
CHAIKIN, M/ Light another candle: the story and meaning of Hanukkah./
c1981, 1987/ 5-6/8 KA770 . . . . **296.4**
Light another candle: the story and meaning of Hanukkah (Sound
recording cassette)./ n.d./ 5-6/8 KA770 . . . . **296.4**
Sound the Shofar./ 1986/ 5-6/8 KA770 . . . . **296.4**
CHALK, G/ Redwall./ 1986/ 5-A/6 KH320 . . . . **FIC**
CHALL, JS/ Reading crisis: why poor children fall behind./ 1990/
KA219 . . . . **PROF 372.6**
CHALLONER, J/ Science book of numbers./ 1992/ K-3/2 KB956 . **513.2**
CHAMBERLAIN, M/ Miss Butterpat goes wild!/ 1993/ 3-5/5 KH898 . **FIC**
Pattysaurus and other tales (Sound recording cassette)./ 1995/
P-3 KF508 . . . . **SRC E**
CHAMBLISS, M/ Fat Fanny, Beanpole Bertha, and the boys./ 1991/
4-6/4 KH610 . . . . **FIC**
Here comes the snow./ 1996/ K-1/2 KG126 . . . . **E**
How I was adopted: Samantha's story./ 1995/ 1-3/2 KB012 . **362.73**
CHAMPION, J/ Emily and Alice./ 1993/ 1-3/2 KF375 . . . . **E**
Emily and Alice again./ 1995/ 1-3/2 KF376 . . . . **E**
Emily and Alice (Sound recording cassette)./ 1997/ 1-3/2 KF375 . **E**
CHAN, H/ Charlotte stories./ 1994/ 2-3/2 KH321 . . . . **FIC**
Ghost Train./ 1996/ 4-6/5 KH889 . . . . **FIC**
CHANDLER, G/ Recycling./ 1996/ 3-6/10 KB053 . . . . **363.72**
CHANG, M/ Cricket warrior: a Chinese tale./ 1994/
2-3/5 KB549 . . . . **398.24**
CHANG, R/ Cricket warrior: a Chinese tale./ 1994/
2-3/5 KB549 . . . . **398.24**
CHANNING, C/ Madeline and other Bemelmans (Talking book)./ n.d./
P-2 KF219 . . . . **TB E**
CHAPMAN, C/ If the shoe fits...how to develop multiple intelligences in the
classroom./ 1993/ KA157 . . . . **PROF 155.4**
Snow on snow on snow./ 1994/ K-3/3 KF377 . . . . **E**
CHAPMAN, G/ Exploring time./ 1995/ 3-6/6 KC069 . . . . **529**
Making books./ 1992/ 3-6/7 KD412 . . . . **741.6**
Maps and mazes: a first guide to mapmaking./ 1993/
K-6/6 KC064 . . . . **526**
CHARLES, NN/ What am I?: looking through shapes at apples and
grapes./ 1994/ P-2/2 KF378 . . . . **E**
CHARLES, R/ CHICKA CHICKA BOOM BOOM (CD-ROM)./ 1996/
P-2 KF382 . . . . **CDR E**
CHARLES, VM/ Hey! What's that sound?/ 1994/ P-1/1 KF379 . . . **E**
CHARLIP, R/ Handtalk: an ABC of finger spelling and sign language./
c1974, 1984/ K-A KB823 . . . . **419**
Handtalk birthday: a number and story book in sign language./ 1987/
K-3 KB824 . . . . **419**
CHARLOT, J/ And now Miguel./ 1953/ 6-A/5 KH382 . . . . **CE FIC**
Child's good night book./ c1943, 1992/ P/2 KF284 . . . . **E**

CHARNER, K/ GIANT ENCYCLOPEDIA OF CIRCLE TIME AND GROUP
ACTIVITIES FOR CHILDREN 3 TO 6: OVER 600 FAVORITE CIRCLE
TIME ACTIVITES CREATED BY TEACHERS/ 1996/
KA197 . . . . **PROF 372.21**
CHARTIER, N/ Keep looking./ 1989/ P-3/2 KC728 . . . . **599**
Night letters./ 1996/ K-3/3 KG018 . . . . **E**
CHASE, HM/ Chase's calendar of annual events: special days, weeks and
months./ 1958-/ KA264 . . . . **PROF 394.2**
CHASE, R/ Grandfather tales: American-English folk tales./ c1948/
K-A/4 KB723 . . . . **398.27**
Grandfather tales: American-English folk tales (Talking book)./ n.d./
K-A/4 KB723 . . . . **398.27**
Jack tales./ c1943/ K-A/3 KB724 . . . . **398.27**
Jack tales (Braille)./ n.d./ K-A/3 KB724 . . . . **398.27**
Richard Chase tells three "Jack" tales from the Southern Appalachians
(Sound recording cassette)./ n.d./ K-A KB725 . . . . **SRC 398.27**
CHASE, WD/ Chase's calendar of annual events: special days, weeks and
months./ 1958-/ KA264 . . . . **PROF 394.2**
CHASEMORE, R/ Tanks./ 1996/ 4-6/8 KD060 . . . . **623.7**
CHATTON, B/ Using poetry across the curriculum: a whole language
approach./ 1993/ KA237 . . . . **PROF 372.64**
CHEE, C/ Old Turtle./ 1992/ 3-5/3 KH879 . . . . **CE FIC**
CHEESE, C/ WALKING THE BRIDGE OF YOUR NOSE./ 1995/
2-4 KE113 . . . . **821.008**
CHENG, YZ/ China's long march: 6,000 miles of danger./ 1988/
A/6 KE702 . . . . **951.04**
CHERIPKO, J/ Voices of the river: adventures on the Delaware./ 1996/
5-A/5 KE962 . . . . **974.9**
CHERNOFF, GT/ Easy costumes you don't have to sew./ c1975/
P-A/4 KD298 . . . . **646.4**
CHERRY, L/ Great kapok tree: a tale of the Amazon rain forest./ 1990/
2-3/4 KF380 . . . . **E**
Great kapok tree (Videocassette)./ 1996/ 2-3 KF381 . . . . . **VCR E**
If I were in charge of the world and other worries./ 1981/
2-4 KE037 . . . . **811**
River ran wild: an environmental history./ 1992/ 4-6/6 KE937 . . **974.4**
When I'm sleepy./ 1996/ P-K/8 KF776 . . . . **E**
CHESS, V/ Ghosts!: ghostly tales from folklore./ 1991/
1-2/2 KB692 . . . . **CE 398.25**
Rolling Harvey down the hill./ 1980/ 1-4 KE015 . . . . **CE 811**
Tales for the perfect child./ 1985/ 2-5/2 KH233 . . . . **FIC**
This for that: a Tonga tale./ 1997/ K-2/2 KB517 . . . . **398.24**
CHESSARE, M/ Zoomrimes: poems about things that go./ 1993/
3-6 KD921 . . . . **811**
CHESTER, J/ Penguins of the Antarctic (Picture)./ 1995/
4-6 KC685 . . . . **PIC 598.47**
Penguins of the world (Picture)./ 1995/ 3-6 KC686 . . . . **PIC 598.47**
CHESTERMAN, CW/ Audubon Society field guide to North American rocks
and minerals./ 1978/ 3-6 KC225 . . . . **552**
CHESWORTH, M/ Keep 'em laughing: jokes to amuse and annoy your
friends./ 1996/ 3-6 KD736 . . . . **793.735**
Olympics!/ 1996/ P-2/4 KD820 . . . . **796.48**
Putting on the brakes: young people's guide to understanding attention/
1991/ 5-6/7 KD041 . . . . **618.92**
CHEWNING, R/ Where does the garbage go? Rev. ed./ 1994/
2-3/3 KD083 . . . . **628.4**
CHIASSON, J/ African journey./ 1987/ A/11 KE725 . . . . **960**
CHICHESTER-CLARK, E/ Time and the clockmice etcetera./ 1994/
3-A/8 KH077 . . . . **FIC**
CHICOINE, S/ Spain: bridge between continents./ 1997/
4-6/7 KE686 . . . . **946**
CHIEFTAINS (MUSICAL GROUP)./ Tailor of Gloucester (Videocassette)./
1988/ 1-3 KG271 . . . . **VCR E**
CHIEN, J/ Kids garden!: the anytime, anyplace guide to sowing and
growing fun./ 1996/ 3-5/6 KD167 . . . . **635**
CHILCOAT, GW/ Children of Topaz: the story of a Japanese-American
internment camp: based on a classroom diary./ 1996/
5-6/8 KE667 . . . . **940.53**
CHILD, J/ Rise of Islam./ 1995/ 5-A/6 KA784 . . . . **297**
CHILDREN'S BOOK OF VIRTUES./ 1995/ K-3 KB871 . . . . . . **808.8**
CHILDREN'S SCHOOL OF SCIENCE (WOODS HOLE, MASS.)/
Invertebrate zoology./ 1993/ 5-6/8 KC503 . . . . **592**
CHILDRESS, M/ Joshua and the big bad blue crabs./ 1996/
3-4/5 KG988 . . . . **FIC**
CHIN, C/ China's bravest girl: the legend of Hua Mu Lan = [Chin kuo ying
hsiung Hua Mu-lan]./ 1993/ 3-5/4 KB430 . . . . **398.22**
CHINESE MOTHER GOOSE RHYMES./ c1968, 1989/ P-3 KB794 **398.8**
CHIN-LEE, C/ A is for Asia./ 1997/ K-3/8 KE700 . . . . **950**
CHINN, K/ Sam and the lucky money./ 1995/ 1-3/4 KF383 . . . . . **E**
CHOCOLATE, DMN/ Imani in the belly./ 1994/ 2-3/5 KB431 . . **398.22**
My first Kwanzaa book./ 1992/ 2-4/2 KB206 . . . . **394.261**
CHOI, Y/ Nim and the war effort./ 1997/ 2-4/5 KH391 . . . . . . **FIC**
CHORAO, K/ CHRISTMAS STORY./ 1996/ 2-3/4 KA701 . . . . **232.92**
Good-bye book./ 1988/ P-2/2 KG662 . . . . **E**

I'm terrific./ 1977/ P-1/3 KG481 . . . . E
My mama says there aren't any zombies, ghosts, vampires, creatures,
    demons, monsters, fiends, goblins, or things./ 1973/ P-3/4 KG663 . E
POLLITOS DICEN: JUEGOS, RIMAS Y CANCIONES INFANTILES DE
    PAISES DE HABLA HISPANA./THE BABY CHICKS SING:
    TRADITIONAL GAMES, NURSERY/ 1994/ P-1/2 KD584 . . . . **789.2**
CHRIST CHURCH CATHEDRAL CHOIR, OXFORD/ Savior is born (Kit)./
    1992/ 3-5 KA705 . . . . **KIT 232.92**
CHRISTELOW, E/ Don't wake up Mama!/ 1992/ P-K/2 KF384 . . . . . E
Don't wake up Mama! (Sound recording cassette)./ 1995/
    P-K/2 KF384 . . . . E
Five little monkeys sitting in a tree./ 1991/ P-K/2 KF384 . . . . . E
Five little monkeys with nothing to do./ 1996/ P-2/2 KF385 . . . . E
Five-dog night./ 1993/ 1-3/3 KF386 . . . . E
Gertrude, the bulldog detective./ 1992/ K-2/3 KF387 . . . . E
Great pig escape./ 1994/ 1-3/2 KF388 . . . . E
No room for Francie./ 1995/ 2-3/2 KH440 . . . . FIC
Robbery at the Diamond Dog Diner./ 1986/ K-3/4 KF389 . . . . CE E
Robbery at the Diamond Dog Diner (Kit)./ 1989/ K-3/4 KF389 . CE E
Two terrible frights./ 1987/ P-1/3 KF181 . . . . E
What do authors do?/ 1995/ 2-4/2 KD866 . . . . **808.06**
CHRISTENSEN, B/ Breaking into print: before and after the invention of the
    printing press./ 1996/ 3-5/5 KD346 . . . . **686.2**
Putting the world to sleep./ 1995/ P-2/2 KG606 . . . . E
CHRISTIAN, MB/ Hats are for watering horses: why the cowboy dressed
    that way./ 1993/ 4-6/4 KB163 . . . . **391**
Toady and Dr. Miracle./ 1997/ 1-3/2 KF390 . . . . E
CHRISTIANA, D/ Fat man in a fur coat and other bear stories./ 1984/
    5-6/5 KC855 . . . . **599.78**
Gold and silver, silver and gold./ 1988/ 4-6/6 KE628 . . . . . **930.1**
Mouse bride./ 1995/ P-2/2 KB552 . . . . **398.24**
CHRISTIANSEN, C/ Ice horse./ 1993/ 2-3/6 KF391 . . . . E
Sky tree portfolio: science and art (Picture)./ 1995/
    2-6 KC410 . . . . **PIC 582.16**
Sky tree: seeing science through art./ 1995/ 2-6 KC410 . . **PIC 582.16**
CHRISTIANSEN, CB/ Snowman on Sycamore Street./ 1996/
    2-3/2 KG989 . . . . FIC
CHRISTMAS GIF': AN ANTHOLOGY OF CHRISTMAS POEMS, SONGS,
    AND STORIES WRITTEN BY AND ABOUT AFRICAN-AMERICANS./
    1993/ 4-6 KD897 . . . . **810.8**
CHRISTOPHER, J/ City of gold and lead./ 1989/ 4-6/6 KG991 . . . FIC
City of gold and lead (Talking book)./ n.d./ 4-6/6 KG991 . . . . . FIC
Dusk of Demons./ 1994/ 5-A/4 KG990 . . . . FIC
Pool of fire./ 1968/ 4-6/6 KG991 . . . . FIC
Pool of fire (Braille)./ n.d./ 4-6/6 KG991 . . . . FIC
Pool of fire (Talking book)./ n.d./ 4-6/6 KG991 . . . . FIC
White Mountains./ 1967/ 4-6/6 KG991 . . . . FIC
White Mountains (Braille)./ n.d./ 4-6/6 KG991 . . . . FIC
White Mountains (Sound recording cassette)./ n.d./ 4-6/6 KG991 . FIC
White Mountains (Talking book)./ n.d./ 4-6/6 KG991 . . . . FIC
CHRISTOPHER, M/ At the plate with...Ken Griffey Jr./ 1997/
    3-6/6 KE380 . . . . B GRIFFEY, K. JR
In the huddle with...Steve Young./ 1996/ 3-5/8 KE606 . B YOUNG, S.
On the court with...Michael Jordan./ 1996/
    4-6/8 KE409 . . . . CE B JORDAN, M.
On the court with...Michael Jordan (Talking book)./ 1997/
    4-6/8 KE409 . . . . CE B JORDAN, M.
On the ice with...Wayne Gretzky./ 1997/
    3-6/7 KE379 . . . . B GRETZKY, W.
On the mound with...Greg Maddux./ 1997/
    3-5/7 KE452 . . . . B MADDUX, G.
CHUNG, C/ Poetry for young people./ 1994/ 4-A KD933 . . . . . . **811**
CHWAST, J/ Starlight and candles: the joys of the Sabbath./ 1995/
    1-3/2 KG061 . . . . E
CHWAST, S/ Alphabet parade./ 1994/ K-2 KF392 . . . . E
CIARDI, J/ Monster den: or look what happened at my house - and to it./
    c1966, 1991/ 3-6 KD922 . . . . **811**
You know who./ c1964, 1991/ 3-5 KD923 . . . . **811**
You know who, John J. Plenty and Fiddler Dan, and other poems (Kit)./
    n.d./ 3-5 KD924 . . . . **Kit 811**
You know who, John J. Plenty and Fiddler Dan, and other poems (Talking
    book)./ n.d./ 3-5 KD924 . . . . **Kit 811**
CIESLAWSKI, S/ AT THE CRACK OF THE BAT: BASEBALL POEMS./
    1992/ 3-6 KE053 . . . . **811.008**
CINCINNATI ZOO/ Rhino comes to America./ 1993/
    5-6/7 KC802 . . . . **599.66**
CIVARDI, A/ Things people do./ 1986/ 2-6/6 KA940 . . . . **331.7**
CLARK, AN/ In my mother's house./ c1941, 1991/ 1-4 KE759 . . **970.3**
CLARK, B/ Janice VanCleave's math for every kid: easy activities that make
    learning math fun./ 1991/ 4-6/6 KB933 . . . . **510**
CLARK, D/ Peculiar zoo./ 1993/ K-2 KD999 . . . . **811**
CLARK, EC/ Frog princess./ 1995/ 1-3/2 KB548 . . . . **398.24**
Greek myths./ 1993/ 4-6/6 KA748 . . . . **292**
Minstrel and the dragon pup./ c1993, 1996/ 3-6/7 KH775 . . . . . FIC

SOMETHING RICH AND STRANGE: A TREASURY OF SHAKESPEARE'S
    VERSE./ 1995/ 6-A KE118 . . . . **822.3**
CLARK, EE/ Voices of the winds: Native American legends./ 1989/
    KA266 . . . . **PROF 398.2**
CLARK, P/ BROADWAY KIDS SING BROADWAY (Compact disc)./ 1994/
    2-6 KD528 . . . . **CD 782.1**
CLARK, W/ Off the map: the journals of Lewis and Clark./ 1993/
    4-6/7 KE201 . . . . **917.804**
CLARKE, B/ Amphibian./ 1993/ 5-6/9 KC599 . . . . **597.8**
CLARKE, G/ E I E I O: the story of Old MacDonald, who had a farm./
    1993/ K-1 KF393 . . . . E
CLASSROOM CONNECT/ Educator's Internet companion: CLASSROOM
    CONNECT's complete guide to educational resources on the Internet.
    4th ed./ 1996/ KA049 . . . . **BC PROF 025.06**
CLAY, W/ I am Rosa Parks./ 1997/ 1-2/4 KE491 . . . . . B PARKS, R.
Little Eight John./ 1992/ 2-3/2 KB783 . . . . **398.27**
Real McCoy: the life of an African-American inventor./ c1993, 1995/
    4-6/7 KE462 . . . . **B MCCOY, E.**
Tailypo!/ 1991/ 4-5/4 KB421 . . . . **398.21**
Themba./ 1994/ 3-5/5 KH670 . . . . FIC
CLEARY, B/ Beezus and Ramona./ 1955/ 2-5/3 KG992 . . . . FIC
Beezus and Ramona (Braille)./ n.d./ 2-5/3 KG992 . . . . FIC
Dear Mr. Henshaw./ 1983/ 4-A/4 KG993 . . . . FIC
Dear Mr. Henshaw (Braille)./ n.d./ 4-A/4 KG993 . . . . FIC
Dear Mr. Henshaw (Sound recording cassette)./ n.d./
    4-A/4 KG993 . . . . FIC
Ellen Tebbits./ 1951/ 2-4/3 KG994 . . . . FIC
Ellen Tebbits (Braille)./ n.d./ 2-4/3 KG994 . . . . FIC
Girl from Yamhill./ 1988/ 5-6/7 KE292 . . . . B CLEARY, B.
Growing-up feet./ 1987/ P-3/1 KF394 . . . . E
Growing-up feet (Sound recording cassette)./ 1993/ P-3/1 KF394 . . E
Henry and Beezus./ c1952/ 2-5/3 KG995 . . . . CE FIC
Henry and Beezus (Braille)./ n.d./ 2-5/3 KG995 . . . . CE FIC
Henry and Beezus (Talking book)./ Henry and Beezus (Talking book)./
    n.d./ 1997/ 2-5/3 KG995 . . . . CE FIC
    2-5/3 KG995 . . . . CE FIC
Henry and Ribsy./ 1957/ 3-5/4 KG996 . . . . FIC
Henry and Ribsy (Braille)./ n.d./ 3-5/4 KG996 . . . . FIC
Henry and Ribsy (Talking book)./ n.d./ 3-5/4 KG996 . . . . FIC
Henry and the paper route./ 1954/ 3-5/4 KG996 . . . . FIC
Henry and the paper route (Braille)./ n.d./ 3-5/4 KG996 . . . . . FIC
Henry Huggins./ 1950/ 3-5/4 KG996 . . . . FIC
Henry Huggins (Braille)./ n.d./ 3-5/4 KG996 . . . . FIC
Henry Huggins (Sound recording cassette)./ 1993/ 3-5/4 KG996 . . FIC
Henry Huggins (Spanish version)./ 1996/ 3-5/4 KG996 . . . . . . FIC
Janet's thingamajigs./ 1987,/ P/2 KF396 . . . . E
Janet's thingamajigs (Braille)./ n.d.,/ P/2 KF396 . . . . E
Mouse and the motorcycle./ 1965/ 3-5/5 KG997 . . . . CE FIC
Mouse and the motorcycle (Braille)./ n.d./ 3-5/5 KG997 . . . . CE FIC
Mouse and the motorcycle (Sound recording cassette)./ n.d./
    3-5/5 KG997 . . . . CE FIC
Mouse and the motorcycle (Talking book)./ Mouse and the motorcycle
    (Talking book)./ n.d./ 1995/ 3-5/5 KG997 . . . . CE FIC
    3-5/5 KG997 . . . . CE FIC
Muggie Maggie./ 1990/ 3-5/5 KG998 . . . . FIC
Otis Spofford./ 1953/ 3-5/6 KG999 . . . . FIC
Otis Spofford (Braille)./ n.d./ 3-5/6 KG999 . . . . FIC
Petey's bedtime story./ 1993/ 2-3/3 KF395 . . . . E
Querido Senor Henshaw./ 1986/ 4-A/4 KG993 . . . . FIC
Ralph S. Mouse./ 1982/ 3-5/5 KG997 . . . . CE FIC
Ralph S. Mouse (Braille)./ n.d./ 3-5/5 KG997 . . . . CE FIC
Ralph S. Mouse (Sound recording cassette)./ n.d./
    3-5/5 KG997 . . . . CE FIC
Ralph S. Mouse (Talking book)./ Ralph S. Mouse (Talking book)./ n.d./
    1995/ 3-5/5 KG997 . . . . CE FIC
    3-5/5 KG997 . . . . CE FIC
Ralph S. Mouse (Videocassette)./ 1990/ 3-5 KH000 . . . . **VCR FIC**
Ramona and her father./ 1977/ 3-5/7 KH001 . . . . FIC
Ramona and her father (Braille)./ n.d./ 3-5/7 KH001 . . . . FIC
Ramona and her father (Sound recording cassette)./ n.d./
    3-5/7 KH001 . . . . FIC
Ramona and her mother./ 1979/ 3-5/6 KH002 . . . . CE FIC
Ramona and her mother (Sound recording cassette)./ n.d./
    3-5/6 KH002 . . . . CE FIC
Ramona Empieza el curso./ 1989/ 3-5/5 KH004 . . . . CE FIC
Ramona forever./ 1984/ 3-5/6 KH003 . . . . FIC
Ramona forever (Braille)./ n.d./ 3-5/6 KH003 . . . . FIC
Ramona forever (Sound recording cassette)./ n.d./ 3-5/6 KH003 . . FIC
Ramona la chinche./ 1984/ 3-5/5 KH006 . . . . FIC
Ramona Quimby, age 8./ 1981/ 3-5/5 KH004 . . . . CE FIC
Ramona Quimby, age 8 (Braille)./ n.d./ 3-5/5 KH004 . . . . . CE FIC
Ramona Quimby, age 8 (Talking book)./ 1981/ 3-5/5 KH004 . CE FIC
Ramona the brave./ 1975/ 3-5/6 KH005 . . . . FIC
Ramona the brave (Braille)./ n.d./ 3-5/6 KH005 . . . . FIC

Ramona the pest./ c1968/ 3-5/5 KH006 . . . . **FIC**
Ramona the pest (Braille)./ n.d./ 3-5/5 KH006 . . . . **FIC**
Ramona the pest (Sound recording cassette)./ n.d./ 3-5/5 KH006 . **FIC**
Ramona the pest (Talking book)./ n.d./ 3-5/5 KH006 . . . . . . **FIC**
Ramona y su madre./ 1989/ 3-5/6 KH002 . . . . **CE FIC**
Ramona y su padre./ 1987/ 3-5/7 KH001 . . . . **FIC**
Real hole./ c1960, 1986/ P/2 KF396 . . . . **E**
Real hole (Braille)./ n.d., P/2 KF396 . . . . **E**
Real hole (Sound recording cassette)./ n.d., P/2 KF396 . . . . **E**
Ribsy./ 1964/ 2-5/3 KG995 . . . . **CE FIC**
Ribsy (Braille)./ n.d./ 2-5/3 KG995 . . . . **CE FIC**
Ribsy (Talking book)./ n.d./ 2-5/3 KG995 . . . . **CE FIC**
Runaway Ralph./ 1977/ 3-5/5 KG997 . . . . **CE FIC**
Runaway Ralph (Braille)./ n.d./ 3-5/5 KG997 . . . . **CE FIC**
Runaway Ralph (Sound recording cassette)./ n.d./
   3-5/5 KG997 . . . . **CE FIC**
Runaway Ralph (Talking book)./ Runaway Ralph (Talking book)./ 1995/
   n.d./ 3-5/5 KG997 . . . . **CE FIC**
   3-5/5 KG997 . . . . **CE FIC**
Socks./ c1973/ 3-4/6 KH007 . . . . **FIC**
Socks (Sound recording cassette)./ n.d./ 3-4/6 KH007 . . . **FIC**
Strider./ 1991/ 5-A/4 KH008 . . . . **FIC**
Strider (Sound recording cassette)./ 1993/ 5-A/4 KH008 . . . . . . **FIC**
Two dog biscuits./ c1961, 1986/ P/2 KF396 . . . . **E**
Two dog biscuits (Braille)./ n.d., P/2 KF396 . . . . **E**
CLEAVER, B/ Where the lilies bloom./ c1969/ 5-6/6 KH009 . . . **FIC**
CLEAVER, V/ Where the lilies bloom./ c1969/ 5-6/6 KH009 . . . . **FIC**
   Where the lilies bloom (Sound recording cassette)./ n.d./
   5-6/6 KH009 . . . . **FIC**
CLEMENT, F/ Boy who drew cats: a Japanese folktale./ 1993/
   2-4/4 KB609 . . . . **398.24**
CLEMENT, R/ Counting on Frank./ 1991/ 1-6/5 KB927 . . . . **510**
CLEMENTS, G/ Truth about castles./ c1988, 1990/ 3-6/6 KE645   **940.1**
CLEMENTSON, J/ How the animals got their colors: animal myths from
   around the world./ 1992/ 2-4/4 KB640 . . . . **398.24**
CLIFTON, L/ Everett Anderson's Christmas coming./ 1991/
   P-1 KD925 . . . . **811**
CLIMO, S/ Atalanta's race: a Greek myth./ 1995/ 3-6/4 KA735 . . **292**
   City! Washington, D.C./ 1991/ 4-6/7 KE193 . . . . **917.53**
   Cobweb Christmas./ 1982/ K-2/5 KF397 . . . . **E**
   Cobweb Christmas (Braille)./ n.d./ K-2/5 KF397 . . . . . . **E**
   Irish Cinderlad./ 1996/ 2-4/3 KB275 . . . . **398.2**
   Korean Cinderella./ 1993/ 2-4/5 KB726 . . . . **398.27**
   Little red ant and the great big crumb: a Mexican fable./ 1995/
   1-3/2 KF398 . . . . **E**
   Stolen thunder: a Norse myth./ 1994/ 4-5/5 KA755 . . . . **293**
   Treasury of princesses: princess tales from around the world./ 1996/
   3-5/6 KB432 . . . . **398.22**
CLUTTON-BROCK, J/ Caballos./ 1995/ 4-6/8 KD199 . . . . **636.1**
   Dog./ 1991/ A/8 KD217 . . . . **636.7**
   Horses./ 1992/ 4-6/8 KD199 . . . . **636.1**
COALSON, G/ Brave as a mountain lion./ 1996/ 3-5/2 KH688 . . . **FIC**
   Hi./ 1994/ P-K/2 KG422 . . . . **E**
   On mother's lap./ c1972, 1992/ P-K/2 KG423 . . . . **E**
COATSWORTH, E/ Cat who went to heaven. New ed./ c1958/
   A/6 KH010 . . . . **CE FIC**
   Cat who went to heaven (Talking book)./ n.d./ A/6 KH010 . . **CE FIC**
COBB, J/ Light action!: amazing experiments with optics./ 1993/
   2-6/7 KC108 . . . . **535**
COBB, T/ Light action!: amazing experiments with optics./ 1993/
   2-6/7 KC108 . . . . **535**
COBB, V/ Bet you can!: science possibilities to fool you./ 1990/
   4-A/7 KD745 . . . . **793.8**
   Bet you can't: science impossibilities to fool you./ 1980/
   5-6/6 KB880 . . . . **507**
   Bet you can't: science impossibilities to fool you (Sound recording
   cassette)./ n.d./ 5-6/6 KB880 . . . . **507**
   Light action!: amazing experiments with optics./ 1993/
   2-6/7 KC108 . . . . **535**
   Lots of rot./ 1981/ K-3/3 KC302 . . . . **577.1**
   More science experiments you can eat./ 1979/ A/7 KB890 . . **507.8**
   Science experiments you can eat. Rev. and updated./ 1994/
   3-5/7 KB891 . . . . **507.8**
   This place is lonely./ 1991/ 3-6/7 KF116 . . . . **994**
   This place is wet./ 1989/ 3-6/6 KC287 . . . . **574.5**
   Wanna bet?: science challenges to fool you./ 1993/
   4-6/6 KD746 . . . . **793.8**
   Why doesn't the earth fall up?/ 1988/ 4-6/5 KC092 . . . . . **531**
COBLEIGH, C/ Poetry for young people./ 1995/ 5-A KD998 . . . . **811**
COCHRAN, P/ OUR CHANGING EARTH (Videocassette)./ 1991/
   3-5 KC153 . . . . **VCR 551**
COCHRANE, K/ Internet./ 1995/ 4-6/8 KA570 . . . . **004.67**
COCHRANE, PA/ Purely Rosie Pearl./ 1996/ 4-6/6 KH011 . . . . . **FIC**
COCKE, W/ Historical album of Virginia./ 1995/ 4-6/7 KE976 . **975.5**

Historical album of Washington./ 1995/ 4-6/7 KF092 . . . . . . **979.7**
COCONIS, T/ Summer of the swans./ c1970/ 5-6/6 KG964 . . . **CE FIC**
COE, A/ Here is the southwestern desert./ 1995/ P-3/3 KF066 . . **979.1**
COERR, E/ Buffalo Bill and the Pony Express./ 1995/ 1-3/2 KF399 . . **E**
   Chang's paper pony./ 1988/ 2-3/2 KF400 . . . . **E**
   Josefina story quilt./ 1986/ 1-3/2 KF401 . . . . **CE E**
   Josefina story quilt (Braille)./ n.d./ 1-3/2 KF401 . . . . . **CE E**
   Josefina story quilt (Kit)./ 1995/ 1-3/2 KF401 . . . . **CE E**
   Josefina y la colcha de retazos./ 1995/ 1-3/2 KF401 . . . . **CE E**
   Sadako./ 1993/ 3-6/4 KA994 . . . . **CE 362.1**
   Sadako and the thousand paper cranes (Videocassette)./ 1990/
   3-6/4 KA994 . . . . **CE 362.1**
COFFELT, N/ Dog who cried woof./ 1995/ K-2/3 KF402 . . . . . . **E**
   Good night, Sigmund./ 1992/ P-1/2 KF403 . . . . **E**
COGANCHERRY, H/ I am not a crybaby./ 1989/ P-4/2 KA644 . **155.4**
   Millie Cooper and friends./ 1995/ 3-4/7 KH247 . . . . **FIC**
   Sarah, also known as Hannah./ 1994/ 4-6/4 KH655 . . . . . **FIC**
   Warm as wool./ 1992/ 3-5/5 KH675 . . . . **FIC**
   Who is a stranger and what should I do?/ 1985/ 1-3/6 KB021 . **363.1**
   Words in our hands./ 1980/ 4-6/5 KH413 . . . . **FIC**
COHAT, E/ Seashore./ 1995/ 1-4/4 KC366 . . . . **578.769**
COHEN, B/ Molly y los peregrinos./ 1995/ 1-3/4 KH012 . . . **CE FIC**
   Molly's pilgrim./ 1983/ 1-3/4 KH012 . . . . **CE FIC**
   Molly's pilgrim (Braille)./ n.d./ 1-3/4 KH012 . . . . . . **CE FIC**
   Molly's pilgrim (Sound recording cassette)./ n.d./ 1-3/4 KH012 . **CE FIC**
   Molly's pilgrim (Videocassette)./ 1985/ 1-3/4 KH012 . . . **CE FIC**
   Robin Hood and Little John./ 1995/ 2-4/4 KB433 . . . . **398.22**
   Thank you, Jackie Robinson!/ 1997/ 4-A/4 KH013 . . . . **FIC**
COHEN, D/ Ghost in the house./ 1993/ 5-6/5 KA598 . . . . . . **133.1**
   Ghostly warnings./ 1996/ 4-6/7 KA599 . . . . **133.1**
   Ghosts of the deep./ 1993/ 4-6/7 KA600 . . . . **133.1**
   Ghosts of War./ 1990/ 4-A/6 KA601 . . . . **133.1**
   Great ghosts./ 1990/ 4-6/4 KA602 . . . . **133.1**
   Young ghosts. Rev ed./ c1978, 1994/ 4-A/9 KA603 . . . . . **133.1**
COHEN, JH/ Superstars of women's gymnastics./ 1997/
   4-6/7 KD815 . . . . **796.44**
COHEN, M/ Don't eat too much turkey!/ 1987/ K-1/2 KF405 . . . . **CE E**
   Liar, liar, pants on fire!/ 1985/ K-1/2 KF405 . . . . **CE E**
   No good in art./ 1980/ K-1/2 KF405 . . . . **CE E**
   Real-skin rubber monster mask./ 1990/ K-1/2 KF404 . . . . **CE E**
   Real-skin rubber monster mask (Videocassette)./ 1991/
   K-1/2 KF404 . . . . **CE E**
   See you in second grade!/ 1989/ K-1/2 KF404 . . . . **CE E**
   See you in the second grade (Videocassette)./ 1991/
   K-1/2 KF404 . . . . **CE E**
   When will I read?/ 1977/ K-1/2 KF405 . . . . **CE E**
   Will I have a friend?/ c1967/ K-1/2 KF405 . . . . **CE E**
COHEN, N/ Jackie Joyner-Kersee./ 1992/
   4-6/6 KE412 . . . . **B JOYNER-KERSEE**
COHEN, S/ Basketball player./ 1996/ 4-6/3 KG975 . . . . **FIC**
   Boxing champion./ 1991/ 4-6/2 KG976 . . . . **FIC**
   Longest home run./ 1993/ 2-4/4 KG977 . . . . **FIC**
COHN, AL/ FROM SEA TO SHINING SEA: A TREASURY OF AMERICAN
   FOLKLORE AND FOLK SONGS./ 1993/ K-6 KD899 . . . . . . **810.8**
COHN, D/ Christmas menorahs: how a town fought hate./ 1995/
   3-6/5 KA818 . . . . **305**
COILEY, J/ Train./ 1992/ 5-6/8 KD072 . . . . **625.1**
COLANDO, C/ Kid style nature crafts: 50 terrific things to make with
   nature's materials./ 1995/ 4-8/6 KD428 . . . . **745.5**
COLBERT, M/ Discovering dinosaur babies./ 1991/ 3-6/5 KC262 . **567.9**
COLBORN, C/ What do children read next?: a reader's guide to fiction for
   children./ 1997/ KA031 . . . . **PROF 016.80883**
COLE, B/ Drop dead./ 1996/ 2-4/2 KF406 . . . . **E**
   Giant's toe./ 1986/ P-2/2 KF407 . . . . **E**
   Indian in the cupboard./ 1980/ 4-6/4 KH627 . . . . **CE FIC**
   Winter wren./ 1984/ K-3/2 KF408 . . . . **E**
COLE, H/ Barefoot: escape on the Underground Railroad./ 1997/
   1-3/3 KF510 . . . . **E**
   Four famished foxes and Fosdyke./ 1995/ 1-3/3 KF511 . . . . . **E**
   Jack's garden./ 1995/ K-3/3 KF409 . . . . **E**
   Livingstone Mouse./ 1996/ K-2/2 KF512 . . . . **E**
   Some smug slug./ 1996/ P-2/3 KF513 . . . . **E**
   Zipping, zapping, zooming bats./ 1995/ 1-3/4 KC759 . . . . **599.4**
COLE, J/ Autobus magico dentro de un huracan./ 1996/
   2-4/4 KC197 . . . . **551.55**
   Autobus magico en el cuerpo humano./ 1990/ 2-5/5 KC916 . . **612**
   Autobus magico en el fondo del mar./ 1994/ 2-4/5 KC495 . **591.77**
   Autobus magico en el interior de la tierra./ 1993/ 2-4/3 KC152 . **551**
   Autobus magico en el sistema solar./ 1992/ 2-6/4 KC008 . . **523.2**
   Autobus magico en tiempos de los dinosaurios./ 1995/
   2-4/3 KC245 . . . . **567.9**
   Autobus magico viaja por el agua./ 1992/ 2-3/4 KD079 . . . **628.1**
   Cat's body./ 1982/ 4-6/6 KC818 . . . . **599.75**
   Chick hatches./ 1977/ P-2/3 KC694 . . . . **598.6**

Crazy eights and other card games./ 1994/ 3-6/3 KD758 .... **795.4**
Cuts, breaks, bruises and burns: how your body heals./ 1985/ 4-6/6 KC932 .... **612.1**
Doctor Change./ 1986/ K-3/2 KF410 .... **E**
Doctor Change (Sound recording cassette)./ n.d./ K-3/2 KF410 .... **E**
Eentsy, weentsy spider: fingerplays and action rhymes./ 1991/ P-K KD706 .... **793.4**
Evolution./ 1987/ 3-4/5 KC290 .... **576.8**
Fish hatches./ c1978/ P-A/3 KC596 .... **597.5**
Frog's body./ 1980/ P-A/6 KC600 .... **597.8**
GIVE A DOG A BONE: STORIES, POEMS, JOKES, AND RIDDLES ABOUT DOGS./ 1996/ K-4 KD874 .... **808.8**
Horse's body./ 1981/ 4-6/7 KC805 .... **599.665**
How I was adopted: Samantha's story./ 1995/ 1-3/2 KB012 . **362.73**
How you were born. Rev. and expanded ed./ 1993/ K-3/4 KC945 .... **612.6**
Human body: how we evolved./ 1987/ 5-6/7 KC915 ...... **612**
Hungry, hungry sharks./ 1986/ 1-3/2 KC592 .... **597.3**
Insect's body./ 1984/ 5-6/7 KC536 .... **595.7**
Magic School Bus at the waterworks./ 1986/ 2-3/4 KD079 ... **628.1**
Magic School Bus at the waterworks (Big book)./ 1986/ 2-3/4 KD079 .... **628.1**
Magic School Bus in the time of the dinosaurs./ 1994/ 2-4/3 KC245 .... **567.9**
Magic School Bus inside a beehive./ 1996/ 2-4/2 KC570 ... **595.79**
Magic School Bus inside a hurricane./ 1995/ 2-4/4 KC197 ... **551.55**
Magic School Bus inside the earth./ 1987/ 2-4/3 KC152 ...... **551**
Magic School Bus inside the human body./ 1989/ 2-5/5 KC916 ... **612**
Magic School Bus lost in the solar system./ 1990/ 2-6/4 KC008 **523.2**
Magic School Bus on the ocean floor./ 1992/ 2-4/5 KC495 . **591.77**
MISS MARY MACK AND OTHER CHILDREN'S STREET RHYMES./ 1990/ 2-5 KD766 .... **796.1**
My new kitten./ 1995/ P-1/2 KD230 .... **636.8**
My puppy is born. Rev. and expanded ed./ 1991/ P-2/2 KD218 .... **636.7**
Pin the tail on the donkey and other party games./ 1993/ K-2/3 KD698 .... **793**
Rain or shine activity book: fun things to make and do./ 1997/ 3-6 KD699 .... **793**
READY...SET...READ!: THE BEGINNING READER'S TREASURY./ 1990/ P-2 KD901 .... **810.8**
READY...SET...READ--AND LAUGH!: A FUNNY TREASURY FOR BEGINNING READERS./ 1995/ K-2 KD902 .... **810.8**
Riding Silver Star./ 1996/ 3-5/2 KD854 .... **798.2**
SCARY BOOK./ 1991/ 2-4/2 KB691 .... **398.25**
Six sick sheep: 101 tongue twisters./ / 3-5 KB795 .... **398.8**
YOURS TILL BANANA SPLITS: 201 AUTOGRAPH RHYMES./ 1995/ 3-6 KD894 .... **808.88**
COLE, MD/ Walt Disney: creator of Mickey Mouse./ 1996/ 4-6/8 KE322 .... **B DISNEY, W.**
COLE, N/ Blast off!: a space counting book./ 1994/ P-3/6 KD131 .... **629.43**
COLE, RM/ Zany knock knocks./ 1993/ 3-6 KD726 .... **793.735**
COLE, S/ When the tide is low./ 1985/ P-2/3 KF411 .... **E**
COLE, W/ ZOOFUL OF ANIMALS./ 1992/ K-4 KE090 ..... **811.008**
COLEMAN, E/ White socks only./ 1996/ 3-4/4 KH014 .... **FIC**
COLEN, K/ Peas and honey: recipes for kids (with a pinch of poetry)./ 1995/ 3-6 KD269 .... **641.5**
COLES, R/ Story of Ruby Bridges./ 1995/ 2-5/4 KA902 ...... **323.1**
Story of Ruby Bridges (Sound recording cassette)./ 1997/ 2-5/4 KA902 .... **323.1**
COLGATE, B/ Silly Willy workout (Compact disc)./ 1996/ P-1 KD609 .... **SRC 789.3**
Silly Willy workout (Sound recording cassette)./ 1994/ P-1 KD609 .... **SRC 789.3**
COLLIER, C/ Jump ship to freedom./ 1981/ 5-6/5 KH015 .... **FIC**
My brother Sam is dead./ 1974/ 5-6/5 KH016 .... **FIC**
War comes to Willy Freeman./ 1983/ 5-6/6 KH017 .... **FIC**
COLLIER, JL/ Jump ship to freedom./ 1981/ 5-6/5 KH015 .... **FIC**
My brother Sam is dead./ 1974/ 5-6/5 KH016 .... **FIC**
War comes to Willy Freeman./ 1983/ 5-6/6 KH017 .... **FIC**
COLLIER, L/ MAJOR AUTHORS AND ILLUSTRATORS FOR CHILDREN AND YOUNG ADULTS: A SELECTION OF SKETCHES FROM SOMETHING ABOUT THE AUTHOR./ 1993/ KA464 .... **REF 809**
COLLINS, D/ Good morning, Mr. President: a story about Carl Sandburg./ 1988/ 4-6/6 KE531 .... **B SANDBURG, C.**
COLLINS, DR/ J.R.R. Tolkien: master of fantasy./ 1992/ 6-A/6 KE567 .... **B TOLKIEN, J.**
Pioneer plowmaker: a story about John Deere./ 1990/ 5-6/6 KE317 .... **B DEERE, J.**
COLLINS, H/ Kids' summer handbook./ 1994/ 3-6/6 KD678 .... **790.1**
Pioneer sampler: the daily life of a pioneer family in 1840./ 1995/ 4-6/6 KF031 .... **978**

COLLINS, JL/ John Brown and the fight against slavery./ 1991/ 3-5/6 KE263 .... **B BROWN, J.**
COLLINS, P/ STORIES AND READERS: NEW PERSPECTIVES ON LITERATURE IN THE ELEMENTARY CLASSROOM./ 1992/ KA241 .... **PROF 372.64**
COLLINS, PL/ Waiting for baby Joe./ 1990/ K-3/2 KD038 ... **618.92**
COLMAN, P/ Madam C.J. Walker: building a business empire./ 1994/ 4-6/7 KE583 .... **B WALKER, C.J.**
Mother Jones and the march of the mill children./ 1994/ 4-6/7 KA935 .... **331.3**
Rosie the Riveter: women working on the home front in World War II./ 1995/ 5-A/7 KA938 .... **331.4**
Toilets, bathtubs, sinks, and sewers: a history of the bathroom./ 1994/ 5-6/5 KD294 .... **643**
COLON, R/ Celebration!/ 1997/ 1-3/3 KG604 .... **E**
COLUM, P/ Children's Homer: The Adventures of Odysseus and Tale of Troy./ 1982/ A/6 KE123 .... **883**
Children's Homer: The Adventures of Odysseus and Tale of Troy (Braille)./ n.d./ A/6 KE123 .... **883**
Golden fleece and the heroes who lived before Achilles./ c1949/ 5-6/6 KA736 .... **292**
Golden fleece and the heroes who lived before Achilles (Sound recording cassette)./ n.d./ 5-6/6 KA736 .... **292**
COLUMBUS, C/ Log of Christopher Columbus' first voyage to America in the year 1492./ c1938, 1989/ 4-6/7 KE741 .... **970.01**
COMAN, C/ What Jamie saw./ 1995/ 5-A/6 KH018 .... **FIC**
COMES, P/ Barmi: a Mediterranean city through the ages./ 1990/ A/11 KA895 .... **307.76**
COMMIRE, A/ SOMETHING ABOUT THE AUTHOR./ 1971-/ 5-6 KA465 .... **REF 809**
WORLD LEADERS: PEOPLE WHO SHAPED THE WORLD./ 1994/ 5-A KA408 .... **REF 350**
COMPTON, J/ Ashpet: an Appalachian tale./ 1994/ 2-3/4 KB727 .... **398.27**
Sody sallyratus./ / K-3/3 KB550 .... **398.24**
COMPTON, K/ Ashpet: an Appalachian tale./ 1994/ 2-3/4 KB727 .... **398.27**
Sody sallyratus./ / K-3/3 KB550 .... **398.24**
CONE, M/ Come back, salmon: how a group of dedicated kids adopted Pigeon Creek and brought it back to life./ 1992/ 4-6/6 KD248 .... **639.3**
Come back, salmon: how a group of dedicated kids adopted Pigeon Creek and brought it back to life (Sound recording cassette)./ 1995/ 4-6/6 KD248 .... **639.3**
CONE, P/ Wildfire./ 1997/ 4-A/6 KB040 .... **363.37**
CONFORD, E/ Frog Princess of Pelham./ 1997/ 4-A/3 KH019 .... **FIC**
CONLY, JL/ Racso and the rats of NIMH./ 1986/ 5-6/6 KH020 .... **FIC**
Racso and the rats of NIMH (Braille)./ n.d./ 5-6/6 KH020 .... **FIC**
Racso and the rats of NIMH (Sound recording cassette)./ n.d./ 5-6/6 KH020 .... **FIC**
Trout summer./ 1995/ 6-A/5 KH021 .... **FIC**
Trout summer (Sound recording cassette)./ 1997/ 6-A/5 KH021 .. **FIC**
CONNELL, K/ These lands are ours: Tecumseh's fight for the Old Northwest./ 1993/ 5-6/7 KE559 .... **B TECUMSEH**
CONNELLY, B/ Follow the drinking gourd: a story of the Underground Railroad (Videocassette)./ 1992/ 2-4 KF412 .... **VCR E**
CONNER, E/ Amazing world of ants./ 1982/ 2-4/2 KC579 . **CE 595.79**
CONNOLLY, M/ Dragsters./ 1992/ 4-A/4 KD829 .... **796.7**
CONRAD, P/ Call me Ahnighito./ 1995/ 2-5/2 KF413 .... **E**
Our house: the stories of Levittown./ 1995/ 4-6/7 KH022 .... **FIC**
Prairie songs./ 1985/ 5-A/7 KH023 .... **FIC**
Rooster's gift./ 1996/ K-2/3 KF414 .... **E**
Tub Grandfather./ 1993/ 1-3/4 KF415 .... **E**
Tub people./ 1989/ 1-3/4 KF416 .... **CE E**
Tub people (Kit)./ 1996/ 1-3/4 KF416 .... **CE E**
CONWAY, DC/ Northern lights: a Hanukkah story./ 1994/ 1-3/4 KF417 .... **E**
COOK, D/ Abe Lincoln's hat./ 1994/ 1-3/2 KE439 .... **B LINCOLN, A.**
Bravest dog ever: the true story of Balto./ 1989/ 1-3/2 KD223 . **636.7**
White bird./ c1966, 1990/ 1-6/2 KG940 .... **FIC**
COOK, DF/ Kids' multicultural cookbook: food and fun around the world./ 1995/ 3-5 KD285 .... **641.59**
COOK, S/ Nettie Jo's friends./ 1989/ 1-3/4 KG108 .... **E**
COOMBS, KM/ Flush!: treating wastewater./ 1995/ 5-6/10 KD080 .... **628.3**
COONEY, B/ Christmas in the barn./ c1952/ P-K KA700 . **232.92**
Eleanor./ 1996/ 4-5/7 KE520 .... **B ROOSEVELT, E.**
Emily./ 1992/ 2-5/2 KF215 .... **E**
Hattie and the wild waves./ 1990/ 1-3/5 KF418 .... **E**
Letting Swift River go./ 1992/ 1-3/5 KG777 .... **E**
Miss Rumphius./ 1982/ K-3/5 KF419 .... **E**
Miss Rumphius (Kit)./ 1994/ K-3 KF420 .... **KIT E**
Ox-cart man./ 1979/ K-3/7 KF663 .... **CE E**

Remarkable Christmas of the cobbler's sons./ 1994/
1-3/4 KB416 . . . . **398.21**
Roxaboxen./ 1991/ K-3/2 KG110 . . . . **CE E**
Senorita Emilia./ n.d./ K-3/5 KF419 . . . . **E**
Seven little rabbits./ 1973/ P-2/3 KF214 . . . . **E**
Story of Holly and Ivy./ 1985/ 3-5/4 KH179 . . . . **FIC**
TORTILLITAS PARA MAMA AND OTHER SPANISH NURSERY
RHYMES./ 1981/ 1-3 KB816 . . . . **398.8**
Year of the perfect Christmas tree./ 1988/ K-3/6 KF771 . . . . **E**
COONEY, MP/ CELEBRATING WOMEN IN MATHEMATICS AND
SCIENCE./ 1996/ A/11 KA439 . . . . **REF 509**
COOPER, AJ/ Dream quest./ 1987/ 5-A/4 KH024 . . . . **FIC**
COOPER, C/ Matter./ 1992/ 4-A/9 KC078 . . . . **530**
COOPER, E/ Country fair./ 1997/ 1-3/3 KF421 . . . . **E**
COOPER, F/ Brown honey in broomwheat tea: poems./ 1993/
K-6 KE031 . . . . **811**
Chita's Christmas tree./ 1989/ 2-4/5 KF773 . . . . **E**
Coming home: from the life of Langston Hughes./ 1994/
3-5/6 KE394 . . . . **B HUGHES, L.**
Daddy, Daddy, be there./ 1995/ 1-3/2 KF254 . . . . **E**
Gingerbread days: poems./ 1995/ K-4 KE032 . . . . **811**
Girl who loved caterpillars: a twelfth-century tale from Japan./ 1992/
2-4/5 KG132 . . . . **E**
Grandpa's face./ 1988/ K-1/2 KF641 . . . . **E**
HOW SWEET THE SOUND: AFRICAN-AMERICAN SONGS FOR
CHILDREN./ 1995/ K-6 KD571 . . . . **CE 789.2**
Ma Dear's aprons./ 1997/ 3-5/4 KH492 . . . . **FIC**
Mandela: from the life of the South African statesman./ 1996/
3-6/7 KE457 . . . . **B MANDELA, N.**
Meet Danitra Brown./ 1994/ 2-4 KD949 . . . . **811**
One April morning: children remember the Oklahoma City bombing./
1996/ 2-6/6 KF006 . . . . **976.6**
PASS IT ON: AFRICAN-AMERICAN POETRY FOR CHILDREN./ 1993/
1-3 KE075 . . . . **811.008**
Pulling the lion's tail./ 1995/ 1-3/6 KF937 . . . . **E**
When Africa was home./ 1991/ K-3/2 KG729 . . . . **E**
COOPER, H/ Boy who wouldn't go to bed./ 1997/ P-1/2 KF422 . . . . **E**
COOPER, J/ Buddy Love: now on video./ 1995/ 5-A/4 KH025 . . . . **FIC**
Dead Sea Scrolls./ 1997/ 6-A/8 KA768 . . . . **296.1**
COOPER, K/ Too many rabbits and other fingerplays about animals,
nature, weather, and the universe./ 1995/ P-1 KD707 . . . . . . **793.4**
Where in the world are you? a guide to looking at the world./ 1990/
4-6/7 KE145 . . . . **910**
COOPER, M/ Anthony Reynoso: born to rope./ 1996/
3-4/4 KA841 . . . . **305.8**
Lion dancer: Ernie Wan's Chinese New Year./ 1990/
1-4/2 KB217 . . . . **394.261**
COOPER, ML/ Bound for the promised land.: the great black migration./
1995/ 6-A/9 KE851 . . . . **973**
Klondike fever./ 1989/ 5-6/6 KE823 . . . . **971.9**
COOPER, S/ Boggart./ 1993/ 6-A/7 KH026 . . . . **CE FIC**
Boggart and the monster./ 1997/ 5-A/6 KH027 . . . . **FIC**
Boggart (Sound recording cassette)./ 1994/ 6-A/7 KH026 . . . **CE FIC**
Boggart (Talking book)./ 1994/ 6-A/7 KH026 . . . . **CE FIC**
Danny and the kings./ 1993/ 2-4/2 KF423 . . . . **E**
Greenwitch./ 1974/ A/5 KH028 . . . . **FIC**
Greenwitch (Braille)./ n.d./ A/5 KH028 . . . . **FIC**
Greenwitch (Large type)./ 1988/ A/5 KH028 . . . . **FIC**
Greenwitch (Sound recording cassette)./ n.d./ A/5 KH028 . . . . . **FIC**
Over sea, under stone./ 1966/ A/5 KH028 . . . . **FIC**
Over sea, under stone (Large type)./ 1988/ A/5 KH028 . . . . . . **FIC**
Over sea, under stone (Sound recording cassette)./ n.d./
A/5 KH028 . . . . **FIC**
Selkie girl./ 1986/ 3-4/6 KB551 . . . . **CE 398.24**
Selkie girl (Sound recording cassette)./ n.d./ 3-4/6 KB551 . **CE 398.24**
Selkie girl (Videocassette)./ 1991/ 3-4/6 KB551 . . . . . . **CE 398.24**
Silver on the tree./ 1977/ A/5 KH028 . . . . **FIC**
Silver on the tree (Large type)./ n.d./ A/5 KH028 . . . . **FIC**
Silver on the tree (Sound recording cassette)./ n.d./ A/5 KH028 . . **FIC**
Tam Lin./ 1991/ 3-4/4 KB276 . . . . **398.2**
COOPER, SJ/ Dance in your pants: great songs for little kids to dance to
(Sound recording cassette)./ 1988/ K-3 KD620 . . . . **SRC 789.3**
David Jack... live!: Makin' music, makin' friends (Videocassette)./ 1991/
P-2 KD621 . . . . **VCR 789.3**
Gotta hop (Sound recording cassette)./ 1990/ K-3 KD622 . . . **SRC 789.3**
COPELAND, E/ Milton, my father's dog./ 1994/ 1-3/3 KF424 . . . . . **E**
COPELAND, S/ NOAH'S ARK (Videocassette)./ c1989, 1996/
P-2 KA682 . . . . **VCR 221.9**
COPSEY, SE/ Children just like me./ 1995/ 2-6/6 KA825 . . . . . **305.23**
CORBALIS, J/ Porcellus, the flying pig./ 1988/ 2-4/5 KH029 . . . . . **FIC**
CORBEIL, J/ Facts on File visual dictionary./ 1986/
6-A KA390 . . . . **REF 031.02**
CORBELLA, L/ Oceans atlas./ 1994/ 4-A/6 KC173 . . . . **551.46**
Space atlas./ 1992/ 3-6/6 KC002 . . . . **520**

CORBETT, S/ Hockey trick./ 1974/ 4-5/4 KH030 . . . . **FIC**
Lemonade trick./ 1960/ 4-5/4 KH030 . . . . **FIC**
Shake, rattle, and strum./ 1995/ 3-6/6 KD542 . . . . **784.19**
CORBIN, CL/ Knights./ 1989/ 4-6/4 KE646 . . . . **940.1**
CORBY, J/ Shadowgraphs anyone can make./ 1991/ K-6 KD753 . . **793.9**
CORDIER, MH/ Understanding American history through children's
literature: instructional units and activities for grades K-8./ 1994/
KA263 . . . . **PROF 372.89**
COREY, D/ Will there be a lap for me?/ 1992/ P-1/2 KF425 . . . . . **E**
COREY, M/ Spaghetti factory./ 1990/ 3-4/7 KD319 . . . . **664**
CORNELL, L/ Ghost on Saturday night./ 1997/ 3-5/4 KH122 . . . . **FIC**
Monsters in the attic./ 1995/ 4-6/6 KH625 . . . . **FIC**
Traveling backward./ 1994/ 4-6/4 KH134 . . . . **FIC**
CORNI, F/ Lebek: a city of Northern Europe through the ages./ 1991/
A/10 KA896 . . . . **307.76**
CORONADA, R/ Cooking the African way./ 1988/
4-6/8 KD286 . . . . **641.59**
Cooking the Caribbean way./ 1988/ 4-6/8 KD286 . . . . **641.59**
Cooking the French way./ 1982/ 4-6/8 KD286 . . . . **641.59**
Cooking the German way./ 1988/ 4-6/8 KD286 . . . . **641.59**
Cooking the Greek way./ 1984/ 4-6/8 KD286 . . . . **641.59**
Cooking the Hungarian way./ 1986/ 4-6/8 KD286 . . . . **641.59**
Cooking the Indian way./ 1985/ 4-6/8 KD286 . . . . **641.59**
Cooking the Irish way./ 1996/ 4-6/8 KD286 . . . . **641.59**
Cooking the Israeli way./ 1986/ 4-6/8 KD286 . . . . **641.59**
Cooking the Italian way./ 1982/ 4-6/8 KD286 . . . . **641.59**
Cooking the Japanese way./ 1983/ 4-6/8 KD286 . . . . **641.59**
Cooking the Korean way./ 1988/ 4-6/8 KD286 . . . . **641.59**
Cooking the Lebanese way./ 1985/ 4-6/8 KD286 . . . . **641.59**
Cooking the Mexican way./ 1982/ 4-6/8 KD286 . . . . **641.59**
Cooking the Polish way./ 1984/ 4-6/8 KD286 . . . . **641.59**
Cooking the Russian way./ 1986/ 4-6/8 KD286 . . . . **641.59**
Cooking the Thai way./ 1986/ 4-6/8 KD286 . . . . **641.59**
Cooking the Vietnamese way./ 1985/ 4-6/8 KD286 . . . . **641.59**
CORRAIN, L/ Giotto and medieval art: the lives and works of the medieval
artists./ 1995/ 4-A/9 KD494 . . . . **759.5**
CORVAISIER, L/ Gollo and the lion./ 1995/ 2-4/4 KB628 . . . . **398.24**
CORWIN, JH/ Asian crafts./ 1992/ 4-A/7 KD426 . . . . **745.5**
Latin American and Caribbean crafts./ 1992/ 4-A/5 KD427 . . . **745.5**
COSGRAVE, JO/ Log of Christopher Columbus' first voyage to America in
the year 1492./ c1938, 1989/ 4-6/7 KE741 . . . . **970.01**
COSNER, S/ Rubber./ 1986/ 5-6/9 KD337 . . . . **678**
COSSI, O/ Great getaway./ 1991/ K-2/2 KF426 . . . . **E**
COSTAS/ Greek myths: gods, heroes and monsters, their sources, their
stories and their meanings./ 1988/ 6-A KA395 . . . . **REF 292**
COSTELLO, RB/ MACMILLAN DICTIONARY FOR CHILDREN. 3rd. rev.
ed./ 1997/ 2-4 KA425 . . . . **REF 423**
COTE, N/ Fireflies, peach pies and lullabies./ 1995/ 1-3/5 KF933 . . . **E**
Palm trees./ 1993/ K-2/4 KF427 . . . . **E**
COTTERELL, A/ Ancient China./ 1994/ 4-A/10 KE629 . . . . **931**
COTTONWOOD, J/ Adventures of Boone Barnaby./ 1992/
6-A/5 KH031 . . . . **FIC**
Babcock./ 1996/ 6-A/3 KH032 . . . . **FIC**
Danny ain't./ 1992/ 6-A/6 KH033 . . . . **FIC**
Quake!: a novel./ 1995/ 5-A/5 KH034 . . . . **FIC**
COUCH, G/ Aladdin and the magic lamp (Kit)./ 1995/
3-5 KB333 . . . . **KIT 398.2**
COUPER, H/ Space atlas./ 1992/ 3-6/6 KC002 . . . . **520**
COURLANDER, H/ Cow-tail switch and other West African stories./ c1947,
1987/ 4-6/7 KB728 . . . . **398.27**
Fire on the mountain and other stories from Ethiopia and Eritrea./ c1950,
1995/ 3-6/6 KB277 . . . . **398.2**
People of the short blue corn: tales and legends of the Hopi Indians./
c1970, 1996/ 1-A/5 KB278 . . . . **398.2**
Tiger's whisker and other tales from Asia and the Pacific./ c1959, 1995/
3-5/7 KB279 . . . . **398.2**
Uncle Bouqui of Haiti (Talking book)./ 1959/ K-A KB729 . . **TB 398.27**
COUSTEAU SOCIETY/ ADVENTURE IN THE AMAZON./ 1992/
4-6/7 KE211 . . . . **918.1**
COVILLE, B/ Aliens ate my homework./ 1993/ 4-6/5 KH035 . . . . . **FIC**
Jeremy Thatcher, dragon hatcher: a magic shop book./ 1991/
4-A/4 KH036 . . . . **CE FIC**
Jeremy Thatcher, dragon hatcher (Talking book)./ 1995/
4-A/4 KH036 . . . . **CE FIC**
William Shakespeare's A midsummer night's dream./ 1996/
4-6/4 KE114 . . . . **822.3**
COVILLE, K/ Aliens ate my homework./ 1993/ 4-6/5 KH035 . . . . . **FIC**
COWAN, P/ Torah is written./ 1986/ 5-6/7 KA782 . . . . **296.6**
COWCHER, H/ Antarctica./ 1990/ 1-3/4 KC500 . . . . **591.998**
Antartida./ 1993/ 1-3/4 KC500 . . . . **591.998**
Bosque tropical./ 1992/ 2-4/4 KF428 . . . . **E**
Rain forest./ c1988, 1990/ 2-4/4 KF428 . . . . **E**
Tigresa./ 1993/ 1-3/6 KC827 . . . . **599.756**
Tigress./ 1991/ 1-3/6 KC827 . . . . **599.756**

COWEN-FLETCHER, J/ It takes a village./ 1994/ K-2/2 KF429 . . . . . **E**
COWLEY, J/ Gracias, the Thanksgiving turkey./ 1996/ K-2/1 KF430 . **E**
  Mouse bride./ 1995/ P-2/2 KB552 . . . . **398.24**
COX, C/ Fiery vision: the life and death of John Brown./ 1997/
  5-A/8 KE264 . . . . **B BROWN, J.**
  Mark Twain: America's humorist, dreamer, prophet./ 1995/
  6-A/8 KE579 . . . . **B TWAIN, M.**
CRAFT, MC/ Cupid and Psyche./ 1996/ 4-5/6 KA737 . . . . . . **292**
CRAIG, H/ Angelina and the princess./ 1984/ P-2/5 KF764 . . . . **E**
  Porcellus, the flying pig./ 1988/ 2-4/5 KH029 . . . . **FIC**
CRAIG, MJ/ Three wishes./ c1968, 1986/ 2/2 KB730 . . . . **398.27**
CRAIG, R/ Get it together: math problems for groups, grades 4-12./
  1989/ KA290 . . . . **PROF 510**
CRAIGHEAD, C/ Eagle and the river./ 1994/ 5-6/7 KC339 . . . . **577.6**
CRAMPTON, P/ Lion family book./ 1995/ 3-6/6 KC830 . . . . **599.757**
CRAMPTON, WG/ Flag./ 1989/ 5-A/8 KE616 . . . . **929.9**
CRARY, E/ Finders, keepers?/ 1987/ 3-6/2 KA670 . . . . **177**
CRAWFORD, DK/ Creating the peaceable school: a comprehensive
  program for teaching conflict resolution: program guide./ 1994/
  KA161 . . . . **PROF 303.6**
CRAWLEY, A/ KINGFISHER FIRST DICTIONARY./ 1995/
  1-2 KA424 . . . . **REF 423**
CREAGH, C/ Reptiles./ 1996/ 3-6/8 KC613 . . . . **597.9**
  Things with wings./ 1996/ 4-6/5 KC445 . . . . **591**
CREECH, S/ Walk two moons./ 1994/ 5-A/5 KH037 . . . . **FIC**
CREIGHTON, S/ LITERARY LAURELS: KIDS' EDITION: A READER'S
  GUIDE TO AWARD-WINNING CHILDREN'S BOOKS./ 1996/
  KA034 . . . . **PROF 016.809**
CRESPO, G/ Village basket weaver./ 1996/ 2-3/6 KG029 . . . . **E**
CRESSWELL, H/ Meet Posy Bates./ 1992/ 3-5/5 KH038 . . . . **FIC**
  Posy Bates, again!/ 1994/ 3-5/3 KH039 . . . . **FIC**
  Watchers: a mystery at Alton Towers./ 1994/ 5-A/3 KH040 . . . . **FIC**
CRESWICK, P/ Robin Hood./ 1984/ 6/6 KB434 . . . . **398.22**
  Robin Hood (Braille)./ n.d./ 6/6 KB434 . . . . **398.22**
  Robin Hood (Sound recording cassette)./ n.d./ 6/6 KB434 . . . **398.22**
  Robin Hood (Talking book)./ n.d./ 6/6 KB434 . . . . **398.22**
CREW, L/ Nekomah Creek./ 1991/ 4-A/5 KH041 . . . . **FIC**
  Nekomah Creek Christmas./ 1994/ 4-6/4 KH042 . . . . **FIC**
CREWS, D/ Bicycle race./ 1985/ K-2/2 KF431 . . . . **E**
  Bigmama's./ 1991/ K-2/2 KE309 . . . . **CE B CREWS, D.**
  Bigmama's (Videocassette)./ 1993/ K-2/2 KE309 . . . **CE B CREWS, D.**
  Carousel./ 1982/ P-K KF432 . . . . **E**
  Each orange had 8 slices: a counting book./ 1992/
  P-1/2 KB989 . . . . **513.5**
  Flying./ 1986/ P-1 KD093 . . . . **629.13**
  Freight train./ 1978/ P-K KF433 . . . . **E**
  Freight train (Board book)./ 1996/ P-K KF433 . . . . **E**
  Harbor./ 1982/ P-1 KD062 . . . . **623.8**
  Parade./ 1983/ P-2/4 KB188 . . . . **394.2**
  Sail away./ 1995/ P-2/2 KF434 . . . . **E**
  School bus./ 1984/ P-2/1 KF435 . . . . **E**
  Shortcut./ 1992/ K-2/2 KF436 . . . . **E**
  Ten black dots. Rev. and redesigned ed./ c1968, 1986/
  P-2/2 KF437 . . . . **E**
  Tomorrow's alphabet./ 1996/ K-2/2 KG479 . . . . **E**
  Truck./ 1980/ P-K KF438 . . . . **CE E**
  Truck (Big book)./ 1992/ P-K KF438 . . . . **CE E**
CRIBB, J/ Money./ 1990/ 4-6/8 KA949 . . . . **332.4**
CRISMAN, R/ Racing the Iditarod Trail./ 1993/ 5-6/7 KD858 . . . **798.8**
CRISPINO, E/ Van Gogh./ 1996/ 6-A/12 KD499 . . . . **759.9492**
CROFFORD, E/ Frontier surgeons: a story about the Mayo Brothers./
  1989/ 5-6/6 KC899 . . . . **610.69**
CROFT, DJ/ Activities handbook for teachers of young children. 5th ed./
  1990/ KA191 . . . . **PROF 372.1**
CROLL, C/ Clara and the bookwagon./ 1988/ 1-3/1 KF967 . . . . **E**
  Switch on, switch off./ 1989/ K-3/5 KC130 . . . . **537**
  Too many Babas./ c1979, 1994/ K-2/2 KF439 . . . . **E**
CRONKITE, W/ DREAM IS ALIVE: A WINDOW SEAT ON THE SPACE
  SHUTTLE (Videocassette)./ 1985/ 5-6 KD134 . . . . . **VCR 629.44**
CROSS, G/ Great American elephant chase./ 1993/ 6-A/6 KH043 . **FIC**
  New world./ 1995/ 6-A/5 KH044 . . . . **FIC**
  Wolf./ 1991/ A/6 KH045 . . . . **FIC**
CROSS, V/ Movie magic./ 1995/ 4-6/8 KD683 . . . . **791.43**
CRUM, R/ Eagle drum: on the powwow trail with a young grass dancer./
  1994/ 5-A/5 KB197 . . . . **394.26**
CRUZ, R/ Alexander and the terrible, horrible, no good, very bad day./
  c1972/ P-3/7 KG657 . . . . **CE E**
  Alexander, who used to be rich last Sunday./ c1978/
  P-3/5 KG659 . . . . **CE E**
  Baseball fever./ 1981/ 4-6/6 KH297 . . . . **FIC**
CRYSTAL, B/ Horton hatches the egg./If I ran the circus (Videocassette)./
  1992/ P-3 KD694 . . . . **VCR E**
CUFFARI, R/ Cartoonist./ 1978/ 4-6/3 KG959 . . . . **FIC**

Hunter's stew and hangtown fry: what pioneer America ate and why./
  c1977/ A/11 KD275 . . . . **641.5**
  Perilous gard./ 1974/ 5-6/6 KH609 . . . . **FIC**
  Slumps, grunts, and snickerdoodles: what Colonial America ate and why./
  1975/ A/9 KD276 . . . . **641.5**
  Teetoncey./ c1975/ 3-A/5 KH784 . . . . **FIC**
  Thank you, Jackie Robinson/ 1997/ 4-A/4 KH013 . . . . **FIC**
CULLINAN, BE/ CHILDREN'S LITERATURE IN THE CLASSROOM:
  WEAVING CHARLOTTE'S WEB./ 1989/ KA238 . . . . **PROF 372.64**
  Literature and the child. 3rd ed./ 1993/ KA348 . . . . . . **PROF 809**
  Read to me: raising kids who love to read./ 1992/ KA301 . **PROF 649**
CUMMING, P/ Mogul and me./ 1989/ 5-A/7 KH046 . . . . **FIC**
CUMMINGS, EE/ Hist whist./ c1923, 1989/ 2-6 KD926 . . . . **811**
CUMMINGS, P/ Go fish./ 1991/ 3-6/6 KH766 . . . . **FIC**
  My mama needs me./ 1983/ P-2/1 KG685 . . . . **E**
  Storm in the night./ 1988/ K-3/4 KG578 . . . . **E**
CUMMINGS, RW/ School survival guide for kids with LD (Learning
  differences)./ 1991/ 4-6/4 KB093 . . . . **371.92**
  Survival guide for kids with LD (Learning differences)./ 1990/
  4-6/4 KB094 . . . . **371.92**
CUMPIAN, C/ Latino rainbow: poems about Latino Americans./ 1994/
  3-6 KD927 . . . . **811**
CUNNINGHAM, AM/ Ryan White: my own story./ 1991/
  5-A/5 KE594 . . . . **B WHITE, R.**
CUNNINGHAM, S/ LITERARY LAURELS: KIDS' EDITION: A READER'S
  GUIDE TO AWARD-WINNING CHILDREN'S BOOKS./ 1996/
  KA034 . . . . **PROF 016.809**
CUPPLES, P/ Hands on, thumbs up: secret handshakes, fingerprints, sign
  languages, and more handy ways to have fun with hands./ 1993/
  5-6/5 KC904 . . . . **611**
CURLEE, L/ Ships of the air./ 1996/ 5-6/8 KD107 . . . . **629.133**
CURRIE, R/ Full speed ahead: stories and activities for children on
  transportation./ 1988/ KA223 . . . . **PROF 372.6**
  Mudluscious: stories and activities featuring food for preschool children./
  1986/ KA201 . . . . **PROF 372.3**
CURRIE, S/ We have marched together: the working children's crusade./
  1997/ 5-6/8 KA936 . . . . **331.3**
CURRY, BK/ Sweet words so brave: the story of African American
  literature./ 1996/ K-6/7 KD906 . . . . **810.9**
CURRY, JL/ Big Smith snatch./ 1989/ 5-A/6 KH047 . . . . **FIC**
  Christmas Knight./ 1993/ 2-5/3 KB435 . . . . **398.22**
  Great Smith house hustle./ 1993/ 5-A/6 KH047 . . . . **FIC**
  Robin Hood and his Merry Men./ 1994/ 3-5/3 KB436 . . . . . **398.22**
  Robin Hood in the greenwood./ 1995/ 3-5/3 KB437 . . . . . . **398.22**
CURTIS, CP/ Watsons go to Birmingham--1963: a novel./ 1995/
  6-A/7 KH048 . . . . **CE FIC**
  Watsons go to Birmingham--1963: a novel (Sound recording cassette)./
  1997/ 6-A/7 KH048 . . . . **CE FIC**
  Watsons go to Birmingham--1963 (Talking book)./ 1996/
  6-A/7 KH048 . . . . **CE FIC**
CUSH, C/ Artists who created great works./ 1995/ 4-A/8 KD377 **709.2**
CUSHMAN, D/ Aunt Eater's mystery Christmas./ 1995/ 1-2/2 KF440 . **E**
  Aunt Eater's mystery vacation./ 1992/ 1-3/2 KF441 . . . . **E**
  Halloween mice!/ 1995/ P-1/3 KG336 . . . . **E**
CUSHMAN, J/ Do you wanna bet?: your chance to find out about
  probability./ 1991/ 4-6/4 KB997 . . . . **519.2**
CUSHMAN, K/ Ballad of Lucy Whipple./ 1996/ 5-A/7 KH049 . **CE FIC**
  Ballad of Lucy Whipple (Talking book)./ 1997/ 5-A/7 KH049 . **CE FIC**
  Catherine, called Birdy./ 1994/ 6-A/6 KH050 . . . . **CE FIC**
  Catherine, called Birdy (Sound recording casssette)./ 1997/
  6-A/6 KH050 . . . . **CE FIC**
  Catherine, called Birdy (Talking book)./ 1996/ 6-A/6 KH050 . **CE FIC**
  Midwife's apprentice./ 1995/ 6-A/5 KH051 . . . . **CE FIC**
  Midwife's apprentice (Talking book)./ 1996/ 6-A/5 KH051 . . . **CE FIC**
CUTCHINS, J/ Are those animals real?: how museums prepare wildlife
  exhibits. Rev. & updated ed./ 1995/ 3-A/7 KC443 . . . . . . **590.75**
  Scaly babies: reptiles growing up./ 1988/ 5-6/6 KC615 . . . . **597.9**
CUTLER, J/ Mr. Carey's garden./ 1996/ K-2/3 KF442 . . . . **E**
  My wartime summers./ 1994/ 5-A/4 KH052 . . . . **FIC**
  Spaceman./ 1997/ 4-A/2 KH053 . . . . **FIC**
CWIKLIK, R/ Bill Clinton: president of the 90s. Rev. ed./ 1997/
  5-6/8 KE296 . . . . **B CLINTON, B.**
  Malcolm X and black pride./ 1991/ 5-6/6 KE455 . . . **B MALCOLM X**
CYMERMAN, JE/ How's the weather?: a look at weather and how it
  changes./ 1993/ K-5/2 KC187 . . . . **551.5**
CZECH, KP/ Snapshot: America discovers the camera./ 1996/
  5-6/10 KD509 . . . . **770**
CZERNECKI, S/ Cricket's cage: a Chinese folktale./ 1997/
  K-3/7 KB553 . . . . **398.24**
  Hummingbirds' gift./ 1994/ 1-3/7 KF443 . . . . **E**
  Pancho's pinata./ 1992/ 2-4/7 KB703 . . . . **398.26**
DABCOVICH, L/ Maisie./ 1995/ 1-3/4 KG405 . . . . **E**
  Night ones./ 1991/ P-K/2 KF650 . . . . **E**
  Polar bear son: an Inuit tale./ 1997/ K-2/4 KB554 . . . . **398.24**

DAHL, L/ James and the giant peach: the book and movie scrapbook./ 1996/ 3-6/6 KD684 . . . . **791.43**
DAHL, R/ Boy: tales of childhood./ 1984/ 5-6/6 KE312 . . . **B DAHL, R.**
Boy: tales of childhood (Large type)./ n.d./ 5-6/6 KE312 . **B DAHL, R.**
Cocodrilo enorme./ n.d.,/ 1-3/4 KF444 . . . . **E**
Danny, the champion of the world./ c1975, 1988/ 4-6/6 KH054 . . . **FIC**
Enormous Crocodile./ c1978, 1993/ 1-3/4 KF444 . . . . **E**
Enormous crocodile; and, The magic finger (Talking book)./ 1980/ K-3 KF445 . . . . **TB E**
Going solo./ 1986/ 5-6/6 KE312 . . . . **B DAHL, R.**
Going solo (Sound recording cassette)./ n.d./ 5-6/6 KE312 . . . . **B DAHL, R.**
Magic finger./ 1995/ 3-5/3 KH055 . . . . **FIC**
Matilda./ 1988/ 5-A/7 KH056 . . . . **FIC**
Matilda (Sound recording cassette)./ n.d./ 5-A/7 KH056 . . . . **FIC**
Matilda (Spanish version)./ 1995/ 5-A/7 KH056 . . . . **FIC**
DAILEY, S/ Putting the world in a nutshell: the art of the formula tale./ 1994/ KA337 . . . . **PROF 808.5**
DAILY, R/ Code talkers: American Indians in World War II./ 1995/ 4-6/9 KE669 . . . . **940.54**
DAKOS, K/ Don't read this book, whatever you do!: more poems about school./ 1993/ 4-6 KD928 . . . . **811**
If you're not here, please raise your hand: poems about school./ 1990/ 2-5 KD929 . . . . **811**
DALE, P/ Ten out of bed./ 1994/ P-1/2 KF446 . . . . **E**
DALE, S/ Tales from the homeplace: adventures of a Texas farm girl./ 1997/ 5-A/4 KG946 . . . . **FIC**
DALGLIESH, A/ Bears on Hemlock Mountain./ c1952, 1990/ 1-4/4 KH057 . . . . **FIC**
Coraje de Sarah Noble./ n.d.,/ 3-5/3 KH058 . . . . **CE FIC**
Courage of Sarah Noble./ c1954, 1987/ 3-5/3 KH058 . . . . **CE FIC**
Courage of Sarah Noble (Braille)./ n.d./ 3-5/3 KH058 . . . . **CE FIC**
Courage of Sarah Noble (Sound recording cassette)./ n.d.,/ 3-5/3 KH058 . . . . **CE FIC**
Courage of Sarah Noble (Talking book)./ 1978/ 3-5/3 KH058 . . . . **CE FIC**
Thanksgiving story./ c1954/ 3-6/4 KB222 . . . . **394.264**
Thanksgiving story (Braille)./ n.d./ 3-6/4 KB222 . . . . . . **394.264**
DALLINGER, J/ Grasshoppers./ c1981, 1990/ K-2/3 KC537 . . . . **595.7**
DALY, N/ My dad./ 1995/ 1-4/5 KF447 . . . . **E**
Not so fast, Songololo./ 1986/ K-3/2 KF448 . . . . **CE E**
Not so fast, Songololo (Braille)./ n.d./ K-3/2 KF448 . . . . **CE E**
Not so fast, Songololo (Videocassette)./ 1992/ K-3/2 KF448 . . . . **CE E**
Red light, green light, Mama and me./ 1995/ K-2/2 KF228 . . . . . . **E**
Somewhere in Africa./ 1992/ K-2/4 KG129 . . . . **E**
DALY, W/ Bonnie Blair: power on ice./ 1996/ 4-6/6 KE255 . . . . **B BLAIR, B.**
DAMON, D/ When this cruel war is over: the Civil War home front./ 1996/ 5-6/10 KE902 . . . . **973.7**
DANIEL, A/ Bunnicula: a rabbit-tale mystery./ 1979/ 3-6/5 KH285 . . **FIC**
Grand escape./ 1993/ 3-6/7 KH536 . . . . **FIC**
Rabbit-Cadabra!/ 1993/ K-3/3 KF779 . . . . **E**
Story of Canada./ 1992/ 5-A/7 KE804 . . . . **971**
DANNER, B/ Alexander and the terrible, horrible, no good, very bad day and other stories and poems (Talking book)./ 1984/ P-3 KG658 . . . . **TB E**
DANZIGER, P/ Ambar en cuarto y sin su amigo./ 1995/ 2-4/4 KH059 . . . . **FIC**
Amber Brown goes fourth./ 1995/ 2-4/4 KH059 . . . . **FIC**
Amber Brown goes fourth (Sound recording cassette)./ 1997/ 2-4/4 KH059 . . . . **FIC**
Amber Brown is not a crayon./ 1994/ 2-4/6 KH060 . . . . **FIC**
Amber Brown wants extra credit./ 1996/ 2-4/4 KH061 . . . . **FIC**
Forever Amber Brown./ 1996/ 2-4/4 KH062 . . . . **FIC**
Sequiremos siendo amigos./ 1994/ 2-4/6 KH060 . . . . **FIC**
DARBY, J/ Dwight D. Eisenhower: a man called Ike./ 1989/ 5-6/6 KE335 . . . . **B EISENHOWER, D**
DARLING, DJ/ Could you ever build a time machine?/ 1991/ 4-A/7 KC082 . . . . **530.1**
Could you ever meet an alien?/ 1990/ A/7 KC291 . . . . . . **576.8**
Making light work: the science of optics./ 1991/ 6-A/8 KC109 . . **535**
Sounds interesting: the science of acoustics./ 1991/ 6-A/8 KC103 **534**
DARLING, K/ Amazon ABC./ 1996/ K-5/3 KC499 . . . . **591.981**
Bet you can!: science possibilities to fool you./ 1990/ 4-A/7 KD745 . . . . **793.8**
Bet you can't: science impossibilities to fool you./ 1980/ 5-6/6 KB880 . . . . **507**
Komodo dragon: on location./ 1997/ 4-6/7 KC625 . . . . . . **597.95**
Manatee: on location./ 1991/ 5-6/7 KC779 . . . . **599.55**
Tasmanian devil: on location./ 1992/ 5-6/6 KC735 . . . . **599.2**
Walrus: on location./ 1991/ 5-6/6 KC868 . . . . **599.79**
Wanna bet?: science challenges to fool you./ 1993/ 4-6/6 KD746 . . . . **793.8**
DARLING, L/ Beezus and Ramona./ 1955/ 2-5/3 KG992 . . . . **FIC**

Ellen Tebbits./ 1951/ 2-4/3 KG994 . . . . **FIC**
Henry and Beezus./ c1952/ 2-5-/3 KG995 . . . . **CE FIC**
Henry Huggins./ 1950/ 3-5/4 KG996 . . . . **FIC**
Mouse and the motorcycle./ 1965/ 3-5/5 KG997 . . . . **CE FIC**
Otis Spofford./ 1953/ 3-5/6 KG999 . . . . **FIC**
Ramona the pest./ c1968/ 3-5/5 KH006 . . . . **FIC**
DARWIN, B/ Socks./ c1973/ 3-4/6 KH007 . . . . **FIC**
DASH, J/ We shall not be moved: the women's factory strike of 1909./ 1996/ 6-A/8 KA939 . . . . **331.4**
DAUGHERTY, J/ Landing of the Pilgrims./ c1950/ 4-6/7 KE938 . **974.4**
D'AULAIRE, EP/ Abraham Lincoln./ c1957, 1993/ 3-4/4 KE440 . . . . **CE B LINCOLN, A.**
Benjamin Franklin./ c1950/ 2-4/6 KE354 . . . . . **B FRANKLIN, B.**
D'Aulaires' trolls./ c1972, 1993/ 4-6/6 KB280 . . . . **398.2**
Ingri and Edgar Parin d'Aulaire's Book of Greek myths./ c1962/ 2-6/7 KA738 . . . . **CE 292**
D'AULAIRE, I/ Abraham Lincoln./ c1957, 1993/ 3-4/4 KE440 . . . . **CE B LINCOLN, A.**
Abraham Lincoln (Braille)./ n.d./ 3-4/4 KE440 . . . **CE B LINCOLN, A.**
Abraham Lincoln (Sound recording cassette)./ n.d.,/ 3-4/4 KE440 . . . . **CE B LINCOLN, A.**
Benjamin Franklin./ c1950/ 2-4/6 KE354 . . . . . **B FRANKLIN, B.**
D'Aulaires' trolls./ c1972, 1993/ 4-6/6 KB280 . . . . **398.2**
Ingri and Edgar d'Aulaire's book of Greek myths (Sound recording cassette)./ n.d./ 2-6/7 KA738 . . . . **CE 292**
Ingri and Edgar Parin d'Aulaire's Book of Greek myths./ c1962/ 2-6/7 KA738 . . . . **CE 292**
DAVALOS, F/ Punia and the King of Sharks: a Hawaiian folktale./ 1997/ 2-3/3 KB672 . . . . **398.24**
DAVENPORT, T/ Ashpet: an American Cinderella (Videocassette)./ 1989/ 5-A KB281 . . . . **CE 398.2**
Bearskin; or, The man who didn't wash for seven years (Videocassette)./ 1983/ 5-A KB281 . . . . **CE 398.2**
Bristlelip (Videocassette)./ 1982/ 5-A KB281 . . . . **CE 398.2**
Frog king; and, The making of the frog king (Videocassette)./ 1981/ 5-A KB281 . . . . **CE 398.2**
From the Brothers Grimm: a contemporary retelling of American folktales and classic stories./ 1992/ 5-A KB281 . . . . **CE 398.2**
Goose girl (Videocassette)./ 1984/ 5-A KB281 . . . . **CE 398.2**
Hansel and Gretel: an Appalachian version (Videocassette)./ 1975/ 5-A KB281 . . . . **CE 398.2**
Jack and the dentist's daughter (Videocassette)./ 1984/ 5-A KB281 . . . . **CE 398.2**
Mutzmag: an Appalachian folktale (Videocassette)/ 1993/ 5-A KB281 . . . . **CE 398.2**
Rapunzel, Rapunzel (Videocassette)./ 1978/ 5-A KB281 . . . . **CE 398.2**
Soldier Jack; or, The man who caught Death in a sack (Videocassette)/ 1988/ 5-A KB281 . . . . **CE 398.2**
DAVIDSON, JL/ COUNTERPOINT AND BEYOND: A RESPONSE TO BECOMING A NATION OF READERS./ 1988/ KA207 . **PROF 372.4**
DAVIDSON, R/ Take a look: an introduction to the experience of art./ 1994/ 5-6/7 KD364 . . . . **701**
DAVIE, H/ Animals in winter. Rev. ed./ 1997/ K-2/2 KC482 . . . **591.56**
Great buffalo race: how the buffalo got its hump: a Seneca tale./ 1994/ 3-4/6 KB564 . . . . **398.24**
What lives in a shell?/ 1994/ P-1/2 KC517 . . . . **594**
DAVIES, N/ Big blue whale./ 1997/ K-4/3 KC767 . . . . **599.5**
DAVIS, B/ Black heroes of the American revolution./ 1976/ 5-6/10 KE877 . . . . **973.3**
DAVIS, D/ Jack and the animals: an Appalachian folktale./ 1995/ 2-4/5 KB555 . . . . **398.24**
DAVIS, L/ Baby whales drink milk./ 1994/ 1-3/2 KC768 . . . . . . **599.5**
DAVIS, N/ My bike./ 1994/ K-2/3 KF821 . . . . **E**
DAVIS, O/ Escape to freedom: a play about young Frederick Douglass./ c1976, 1990/ A-6 KE091 . . . . **812**
JACOB LAWRENCE: THE GLORY OF EXPRESSION (Videocassette)./ 1995/ 5-A KD487 . . . . **VCR 759.13**
DAVIS, RG/ LION'S WHISKERS: AND OTHER ETHIOPIAN TALES. Rev. ed./ 1997/ 3-6/7 KB337 . . . . **398.2**
DAVOL, MW/ Batwings and the curtain of night./ 1997/ 1-3/2 KF449 . . . . **E**
How Snake got his hiss: an original tale./ 1996/ K-2/2 KF450 . . . . . **E**
DAWSON, ML/ Over here it's different: Carolina's story./ 1993/ 5-6/7 KA842 . . . . **305.8**
DAY, A/ Frank and Ernest on the road./ 1994/ 2-3/2 KF451 . . . . . . **E**
Frank and Ernest play ball./ 1990/ 2-3/4 KF452 . . . . **E**
DAY, D/ Aska's sea creatures./ 1994/ 3-5 KD914 . . . . **811**
Emperor's panda./ c1986, 1987/ 4-A/8 KH063 . . . . **FIC**
DAY, J/ Let's make magic./ 1992/ 3-6 KD747 . . . . **793.8**
DAY, JA/ Peterson first guide to clouds and weather./ 1991/ 3-6/A KC211 . . . . **551.57**
DAY, N/ Horseshoe crab./ 1992/ 5-6/7 KC524 . . . . **595.4**
DAY, NY/ Kancil and the crocodiles: a tale from Malaysia./ 1996/ 2-3/2 KB556 . . . . **398.24**

DAYRELL, E/ Why the sun and the moon live in the sky: an African folktale./ c1968/ K-3/6 KB704 . . . . **CE 398.26**
Why the sun and the moon live in the sky (Videocassette)./ n.d./ K-3/6 KB704 . . . . **CE 398.26**
DE ANGELI, M/ Door in the wall./ c1949, 1989/ 4-6/6 KH064 . . . **FIC**
DE BEAUMONT, ML/ Beauty and the Beast./ 1990/ 4-5/6 KB282 . . . . **398.2**
DE BEER, H/ King Bobble./ 1996/ 2-3/2 KG953 . . . . **FIC**
On the road with Poppa Whopper./ 1997/ 3-4/2 KG954 . . . . **FIC**
DE BOURGOING, P/ Colors./ 1991/ K-3/2 KC121 . . . . **535.6**
Egg./ 1992/ P-3/2 KC281 . . . . **573.6**
Fruit./ 1992/ P-3/2 KD159 . . . . **634**
Ladybug and other insects./ 1991/ K-3/4 KC538 . . . . . . **595.7**
DE BRUNHOFF, J/ Babar and his children./ c1938, 1989/ P-2/3 KF453 . . . . **E**
Story of Babar, the little elephant./ c1937, 1960/ P-2/3 KF453 . . . . **E**
Story of Babar, the little elephant (Braille)./ n.d.,/ P-2/3 KF453 . . . **E**
Story of Babar, the little elephant (Sound recording cassette)./ n.d.,/ P-2/3 KF453 . . . . **E**
DE COLORES AND OTHER LATIN-AMERICAN FOLK SONGS FOR CHILDREN./ 1994/ K-3 KD561 . . . . **789.2**
DE COTEAU ORIE, S/ Did you hear Wind sing your name?: an Oneida song of spring./ 1995/ K-2/3 KF454 . . . . **E**
DE GROAT, D/ All about Sam./ 1988/ 3-5/4 KH421 . . . . **FIC**
Amy Dunn quits school./ 1993/ 5-A/7 KH706 . . . . **FIC**
Flunking of Joshua T. Bates./ c1984, 1993/ 4-6/6 KH707 . . . **FIC**
Our teacher's having a baby./ 1992/ P-1/2 KF307 . . . . **E**
Roses are pink, your feet really stink./ 1996/ K-2/2 KF457 . . . **E**
Some days, other days./ 1994/ K-2/2 KG234 . . . . **E**
Turkey for Thanksgiving./ 1991/ P-2/2 KF312 . . . . **E**
DE HUGO, P/ Seashore./ 1995/ 1-4/4 KC366 . . . . **578.769**
DE LA MARE, W/ Rhymes and verses: collected poems for children./ 1947/ 4-6 KE099 . . . . **821**
Turnip./ 1992/ 3-5/6 KB557 . . . . **398.24**
DE MELLO VIANNA, F/ WEBSTER'S NEW WORLD CHILDREN'S DICTIONARY. New ed./ 1997/ 3-5 KB838 . . . . **423**
DE PAOLA, T/ Abuelita de arriba y la Abueita de abajo./ 1991,/ K-3/6 KF475 . . . . **E**
Art lesson./ 1989/ K-2/4 KF464 . . . . **CE E**
Art lesson (Kit)./ 1991/ K-2/4 KF464 . . . . **CE E**
Baby sister./ 1996/ K-2/2 KF465 . . . . **E**
Big Anthony and the magic ring./ 1979/ 1-3/5 KF466 . . . . . . **E**
BIG ANTHONY'S MIXED-UP MAGIC (CD-ROM)./ 1996/ K-2 KF229 . . . . **CDR E**
Can't you make them behave, King George?/ c1977/ 5-6/7 KE365 . . . . **CE B GEORGE III**
Charlie needs a cloak./ 1982/ P-2/3 KD299 . . . . **CE 646.4**
Charlie needs a cloak (Braille)./ n.d./ P-2/3 KD299 . . . . . **CE 646.4**
Charlies needs a cloak (Videocassette)./ n.d./ P-2/3 KD299 . . **CE 646.4**
Christopher: the holy giant./ 1994/ 2-3/4 KB438 . . . . **398.22**
Clown of God./ 1978/ K-3/6 KF467 . . . . **CE E**
Clown of God (Videocassette)./ n.d./ K-3/6 KF467 . . . . **CE E**
Comic adventures of Old Mother Hubbard and her dog./ 1981/ P-2 KB802 . . . . **398.8**
Days of the blackbird: a tale of northern Italy./ 1997/ 1-3/6 KF468 . **E**
Eagle and the rainbow: timeless tales from Mexico./ 1997/ 4-5/7 KB339 . . . . **398.2**
Early American Christmas./ 1987/ K-3/5 KF469 . . . . **E**
Family Christmas tree book./ c1980, 1984/ 2-4/6 KB234 . . . **394.266**
Favorite nursery tales./ 1986/ P-1 KB796 . . . . **398.8**
Favorite nursery tales (Sound recording cassette)./ n.d./ P-1 KB796 . . . . **398.8**
Fin M'Coul: the giant of Knockmany Hill./ 1981/ 1-3/4 KB392 . **398.21**
First Christmas./ 1984/ P-4/7 KA702 . . . . **232.92**
GOOD MORNING TO YOU, VALENTINE: POEMS FOR VALENTINE'S DAY./ c1976, 1993/ K-6 KE061 . . . . **811.008**
Hunter and the animals: a wordless picture book./ 1981/ K-1 KF470 . **E**
Jamie O'Rourke and the big potato: an Irish folktale./ 1992/ P-3/4 KB393 . . . . **398.21**
Jamie O'Rourke and the big potato: an Irish folktale (Sound recording cassette)./ 1995/ P-3/4 KB393 . . . . **398.21**
Kids' cat book./ 1979/ K-2/2 KD231 . . . . **636.8**
Knight and the dragon./ 1980/ K-2/5 KF471 . . . . **E**
Lady of Guadalupe./ 1980/ 1-4/6 KA698 . . . . **232.91**
Legend of the Bluebonnet: an old tale of Texas./ 1983/ 2-4/4 KB558 . . . . **CE 398.24**
Legend of the Indian Paintbrush./ 1988/ 2-4/4 KB558 . . . . **CE 398.24**
Legend of the Persian carpet./ 1993/ 2-3/6 KB285 . . . . **398.2**
Leyenda de la Flor el Conejo: una antigua leyenda de Texas./ 1993/ 2-4/4 KB558 . . . . **CE 398.24**
Leyenda del pincel Indio./ 1988/ 2-4/4 KB558 . . . . **CE 398.24**
Libro de las arena movedizas./ 1993/ K-3/2 KC226 . . . . **552**
Libro de las palomitas de maiz./ 1993/ 2-4/6 KD290 . . . . . . **641.6**

Little Grunt and the big egg: a prehistoric fairy tale./ 1990/ K-2/2 KF472 . . . . **E**
Mary: the mother of Jesus./ 1995/ 3-6/5 KA699 . . . . **232.91**
Merry Christmas, Strega Nona./ 1986/ K-3/5 KF473 . . . . **E**
Merry Christmas, Strega Nona (Talking book)./ 1991/ K-3 KF474 . . . . **TB E**
Mice squeak, we speak: a poem./ 1997/ P-1/3 KE022 . . . . **811**
Miracles of Jesus./ 1987/ 5-6/7 KA695 . . . . **232.9**
Nana upstairs and Nana downstairs./ c1973, 1978/ K-3/6 KF475 . . **E**
Now one foot, now the other./ 1981/ K-3/5 KF476 . . . . **E**
Nuestra Senora de Guadalupe./ 1980/ 1-4/6 KA698 . . . . . . **232.91**
Oliver Button is a sissy./ 1979/ K-2/2 KF477 . . . . **E**
Pancakes for breakfast./ 1978/ 1-2 KF478 . . . . **E**
Parables of Jesus./ 1987/ 5-6/7 KA695 . . . . **232.9**
Pasito...y otro pasito./ 1986/ K-3/5 KF476 . . . . **E**
Patrick: patron saint of Ireland./ 1992/ 2-4/4 KE492 . **B PATRICK, ST.**
Popcorn book./ c1978/ 2-4/6 KD290 . . . . **641.6**
Quicksand book./ c1977/ K-3/2 KC226 . . . . **552**
Quilt story./ 1985/ P-3/2 KF840 . . . . **E**
Shh! We're writing the Constitution./ 1987/ 3-6/6 KA971 . **CE 342.73**
Simple pictures are best./ c1977/ K-3/6 KG724 . . . . **E**
Spooky Halloween party./ 1981/ 1-3/2 KG287 . . . . **E**
Strega Nona: an old tale./ 1975/ 1-4/6 KB394 . . . . **CE 398.21**
Strega Nona: an old tale (Videocassette)./ 1978/ 1-4/6 KB394 . . . . **CE 398.21**
Strega Nona (Big book)./ 1992/ 1-4/6 KB394 . . . . **CE 398.21**
Strega Nona meets her match./ 1993/ 1-3/2 KF479 . . . . **E**
Strega Nonna (Kit)./ 1993/ 1-4/6 KB394 . . . . **CE 398.21**
Tale of Rabbit and Coyote./ 1994/ 2-3/2 KB596 . . . . **398.24**
Tom./ 1993/ K-2/2 KF480 . . . . **E**
TOMIE DE PAOLA'S BOOK OF POEMS./ 1988/ K-3 KD891 . **808.81**
Tomie De Paola's Mother Goose./ 1985/ P-1 KB796 . . . . . . **398.8**
Tomie de Paola's Mother Goose (Braille)./ n.d./ P-1 KB796 . . . **398.8**
Tony's bread./ 1989/ K-3/5 KB500 . . . . **398.23**
Tony's bread (Sound recording cassette)./ 1993/ K-3/5 KB500 . **398.23**
Tyrannosaurus game./ c1976/ K-2/6 KF931 . . . . **CE E**
Watch out for the chicken feet in your soup./ 1974/ K-2/2 KF481 . **E**
DE REGNIERS, BS/ David and Goliath./ 1996/ 1-4/6 KA683 . . . **222**
Little house of your own./ c1954/ K-1/4 KF483 . . . . **E**
Little Sister and the Month Brothers./ c1976, 1994/ 2-3/2 KB501 . . . . **398.23**
Red Riding Hood./ c1972, 1990/ P-2 KB732 . . . . **CE 398.27**
Way I feel--sometimes./ 1988/ 1-4 KD931 . . . . **811**
DE RUIZ, DC/ Causa: the migrant farmworkers' story./ 1993/ 4-6/6 KA944 . . . . **331.88**
DE SEVE, P/ Finn McCoul (Videocassette)./ 1991/ 3-5 KB445 . . . . **VCR 398.22**
DEAN, J/ Year on Monhegan Island./ 1995/ 4-6/8 KE926 . . . . . **974.1**
Year on Monhegan Island (Sound recording cassette)./ 1997/ 4-6/8 KE926 . . . . **974.1**
DEARMOND, D/ Seal oil lamp./ 1988/ 5-6/6 KB499 . . . . . . **398.23**
DEBECK, S/ APPLES (Videocassette)./ 1996/ 3-5 KD156 . . . . **VCR 634**
CANADA'S MAPLE TREE: THE STORY OF THE COUNTRY'S EMBLEM (Videocassette)./ 1995/ 1-4 KE615 . . . . **VCR 929.9**
Dinosaurs! (Videocassette)./ 1989/ 2-5 KC246 . . . . . . **VCR 567.9**
DECLEMENTS, B/ Pickle song./ 1993/ 4-6/4 KH065 . . . . **FIC**
DEEM, JM/ How to find a ghost./ 1988/ 4-A/7 KA604 . . . . . . **133.1**
How to hunt buried treasure./ 1992/ 4-6/8 KD058 . . . . **622**
How to make a mummy talk./ 1995/ 4-6/8 KB175 . . . . **393**
DEFELICE, CC/ Apprenticeship of Lucas Whitaker./ 1998/ 5-A/6 KH066 . . . . **CE FIC**
Apprenticeship of Lucas Whitaker (Talking book)./ 1997/ 5-A/6 KH066 . . . . **CE FIC**
Dancing skeleton./ 1996/ 3-6/6 KB684 . . . . **CE 398.25**
Dancing skeleton (Videocassette)./ 1991/ 3-6/6 KB684 . . . **CE 398.25**
Lostman's River./ 1994/ 4-A/6 KH067 . . . . **FIC**
Willy's silly grandma./ 1997/ 1-3/2 KF455 . . . . **E**
DEFOE, D/ Robinson Crusoe./ 1983/ 5-A/7 KH068 . . . . **FIC**
DEGEN, B/ Jamberry./ 1983/ P-2 KF456 . . . . **CE E**
Jamberry (Kit)./ 1996/ P-2 KF456 . . . . **CE E**
Jesse Bear, what will you wear?/ 1986/ P-K/4 KF356 . . . . **E**
Josefina story quilt./ 1986/ 1-3/2 KF401 . . . . **CE E**
Let's count it out, Jesse Bear./ 1996/ P-1/2 KF357 . . . . **E**
Magic School Bus at the waterworks./ 1986/ 2-3/4 KD079 . . . **628.1**
Magic School Bus in the time of the dinosaurs./ 1994/ 2-4/3 KC245 . . . . **567.9**
Magic School Bus inside a beehive./ 1996/ 2-4/2 KC570 . . . **595.79**
Magic School Bus inside a hurricane./ 1995/ 2-4/4 KC197 . . **551.55**
Magic School Bus inside the human body./ 1989/ 2-5/5 KC916 . **612**
Magic School Bus lost in the solar system./ 1990/ 2-6/6 KC008 . **523.2**
Magic School Bus on the ocean floor./ 1992/ 2-4/5 KC495 . **591.77**
DEJOHN, M/ Daisy and the Girl Scouts: the story of Juliette Gordon Low./ 1996/ 3-6/7 KE448 . . . . **B LOW, J.**
DEJONG, M/ Shadrach./ c1953/ 2-3/5 KH069 . . . . **FIC**

Shadrach (Talking book)./ n.d./ 2-3/5 KH069 . . . . **FIC**
Wheel on the school./ c1954/ 4-6/3 KH070 . . . . **FIC**
Wheel on the school (Braille)./ n.d./ 4-6/3 KH070 . . . . . . **FIC**
Wheel on the school (Sound recording cassette)./ n.d./
4-6/3 KH070 . . . . **FIC**
DELACRE, L/ ARROZ CON LECHE: POPULAR SONGS AND RHYMES
FROM LATIN AMERICA./ 1989/ P-3 KD556 . . . . **789.2**
Bossy gallito/el gallo de bodas: a traditional Cuban folktale./ 1994/
K-2/4 KB577 . . . . **398.24**
De oro y esmeraldas: mitos, leyendas y cuentos populares de
Latinoamerica./ 1996/ 4-5/6 KB283 . . . . **398.2**
Golden tales: myths, legends, and folktales from Latin America./ 1996/
4-5/6 KB283 . . . . **398.2**
LAS NAVIDADES: POPULAR CHRISTMAS SONGS FROM LATIN
AMERICA./ 1990/ K-3 KD580 . . . . **789.2**
Senor Cat's romance and other favorite stories from Latin America./
1997/ K-2/3 KB303 . . . . **398.2**
Vejigante masquerader./ 1993/ 1-3/4 KF458 . . . . **E**
DELAFOSSE, C/ Birds./ 1993/ 2-4/4 KC652 . . . . **598**
DELANEY, A/ Pearl's first prize plant./ 1997/ K-2/1 KF459 . . . . **E**
DELANEY, M/ Natalie Spitzer's turtles./ 1992/ 1-3/2 KG741 . . . . . **E**
DEMAREST, CL/ Butterfly jar./ 1989/ 2-6 KD991 . . . . **811**
SCARY BOOK./ 1991/ 2-4/2 KB691 . . . . **398.25**
What would Mama do?/ 1995/ K-2/2 KF526 . . . . **E**
DEMI/ Buddha./ 1996/ 2-6/6 KA758 . . . . **294.3**
Grass sandals: the travels of Basho./ 1997/ 1-4/5 KE136 . . . . **895.6**
Light another candle: the story and meaning of Hanukkah./ c1981, 1987/
5-6/8 KA770 . . . . **296.4**
Magic gold fish: a Russian folktale./ 1995/ 3-5/2 KB284 . . . . **398.2**
One grain of rice: a mathematical folktale./ 1997/
3-6/6 KB731 . . . . **398.27**
DEMING, AG/ Who is tapping at my window?/ c1988, 1994/
P-K KD930 . . . . **811**
Who is tapping at my window? (Big book)./ c1988, 1994/
P-K KD930 . . . . **811**
DEMUTH, J/ Busy at day care head to toe./ 1996/ P-K/2 KF460 . . . **E**
DEMUTH, P/ Busy at day care head to toe./ 1996/ P-K/2 KF460 . . . **E**
DENNIS, W/ Born to trot./ c1950, 1993/ 5-A/5 KH241 . . . . . **FIC**
Brighty of the Grand Canyon./ c1953, 1991/ 4-5/5 KH242 . . **CE FIC**
King of the wind./ c1948, 1990/ 4-6/5 KH243 . . . . **CE FIC**
Misty of Chincoteague./ c1947/ 3-5/4 KH244 . . . . **CE FIC**
White stallion of Lipizza./ c1964, 1990/ 4-6/6 KH246 . . . . . **FIC**
DENSLOW, SP/ On the trail with Miss Pace./ 1995/ 1-3/2 KF461 . . . **E**
Radio boy./ 1995/ 1-3/7 KF462 . . . . **E**
DENSLOW, WW/ Wonderful Wizard of Oz./ 1987/
4-6/6 KG886 . . . . **CE FIC**
DENTON, KM/ Would they love a lion?/ 1995/ P-1/1 KF463 . . . . **E**
DENVER MUSEUM OF NATURAL HISTORY/ Taking time out: recreation
and play./ 1996/ 5-A/7 KA865 . . . . **306.4**
Worlds of belief: religion and spirituality./ 1995/ 4-A/10 KA728 . **291**
DEPAUW, SA/ Don't-give-up Kid and learning differences. 2nd ed./ 1996/
K-3/2 KB095 . . . . **371.92**
DERANEY, MJ/ Molly's pilgrim./ 1983/ 1-3/4 KH012 . . . . . **CE FIC**
DERBY, S/ Jacob and the stranger./ 1994/ 3-5/4 KH071 . . . . . **FIC**
My steps./ 1996/ P-1/2 KF482 . . . . **E**
DEROSA, D/ Soccer circus./ 1993/ 3-5/5 KH169 . . . . **FIC**
DESIMINI, L/ Heron Street./ 1989/ 1-3/3 KG626 . . . . **E**
Love letters./ 1997/ K-4 KD911 . . . . **811**
Magic weaver of rugs: a tale of the Navajo./ 1994/
2-4/3 KB627 . . . . **398.24**
DESPAIN, P/ Eleven nature tales: a multicultural journey./ 1996/
3-5/7 KB286 . . . . **398.2**
Eleven turtle tales: adventure tales from around the world./ 1994/
2-3/4 KB559 . . . . **398.24**
Strongheart Jack and the beanstalk./ 1995/ 2-5/3 KB287 . . . . **398.2**
Tales to tell from around the world. Vol. 1 (Sound recording cassette)./
1995/ K-2 KB288 . . . . **SRC 398.2**
Tales to tell from around the world. Vol. 2 (Sound recording cassette)./
1995/ K-2 KB288 . . . . **SRC 398.2**
DETROIT INSTITUTE OF ARTS/ Catalogue of color reproductions./ n.d./
KA307 . . . . **PROF 703**
DEWEY, A/ Chick and the duckling./ 1972/ P-1/1 KG585 . . . . . . **E**
Mushroom in the rain./ c1974, 1987/ P-2/2 KF623 . . . . **E**
Naming colors./ 1995/ 4-8/8 KC120 . . . . **535.6**
Rockabye crocodile./ 1988/ P-K/2 KB525 . . . . **398.24**
We hide, you seek./ 1979/ P-K/1 KF172 . . . . **E**
DEWEY, JO/ Case of the mummified pigs and other mysteries in nature./
1995/ 4-A/9 KB911 . . . . **508**
Cowgirl dreams: a western childhood./ 1995/
3-4/4 KE320 . . . . **B DEWEY, J.**
Rattlesnake dance: true tales, mysteries, and rattlesnake ceremonies./
1997/ 4-6/4 KC634 . . . . **597.96**
Wildlife rescue: the work of Dr. Kathleen Ramsay./ 1994/
4-6/7 KD252 . . . . **639.9**

DEWEY, M/ Abridged Dewey decimal classification and relative index. Ed.
13./ 1997/ KA058 . . . . **PROF 025.4**
DEXTER, C/ Doll who knew the future./ 1994/ 4-6/6 KH072 . . . . **FIC**
Gertie's green thumb./ 1995/ 3-5/4 KH073 . . . . **FIC**
DEXTER, R/ Young Arthur Ashe: brave champion./ 1996/
2-3/6 KE242 . . . . **CE B ASHE, A.**
Young Arthur Ashe: brave champion (Talking book)./ 1996/
2-3/6 KE242 . . . . **CE B ASHE, A.**
DI CAGNO, G/ Michelangelo./ 1996/ 6-A/12 KD378 . . . . **709.2**
DI FIORI, L/ Toad for Tuesday./ 1974/ 1-3/3 KF528 . . . . **CE E**
DI PIAZZA, D/ Arkansas./ 1994/ 4-6/7 KF007 . . . . **976.7**
DIAKITE, BW/ Hunterman and the crocodile: a West African folktale./
1997/ 2-3/5 KB560 . . . . **398.24**
DIAMOND, D/ Beat the turtle drum./ c1976, 1994/ 5-6/4 KH198 . . **FIC**
Bridge to Terabithia./ 1977/ 5-A/6 KH573 . . . . **FIC**
DIANE GOODE'S BOOK OF SCARY STORIES AND SONGS./ 1994/
2-5/5 KB685 . . . . **398.25**
DIANOV, A/ Melanie./ 1996/ 1-3/2 KF360 . . . . **E**
DIAZ, D/ Going home./ 1996/ 1-3/2 KF302 . . . . **E**
Neighborhood odes: poems./ 1992/ 3-A KE029 . . . . **811**
Smoky night./ 1994/ 2-5/2 KF309 . . . . **E**
Wilma unlimited: how Wilma Rudolph became the world's fastest woman./
1996/ 3-5/7 KE527 . . . . **B RUDOLPH, W.**
DICKENS, C/ Christmas Carol in prose, being a ghost story of Christmas./
1983/ 4-6/5 KH074 . . . . **CE FIC**
Christmas Carol in prose, being a ghost story of Christmas (Braille)./ n.d./
4-6/5 KH074 . . . . **CE FIC**
DICKER, EB/ Sign language talk./ 1989/ 5-A/9 KB825 . . . . **419**
DICKINSON, E/ Brighter garden./ 1990/ 3-6 KD932 . . . . **811**
Poetry for young people./ 1994/ 4-A KD933 . . . . **811**
DICKINSON, P/ Bone from a dry sea./ 1993/ 6-A/7 KH075 . . . . **FIC**
Chuck and Danielle./ 1996/ 4-6/7 KH076 . . . . **FIC**
Time and the clockmice etcetera./ 1994/ 3-A/8 KH077 . . . . . **FIC**
DICKINSON, T/ Exploring the sky by day: the equinox guide to weather
and the atmosphere./ 1988/ 3-A/7 KC217 . . . . **551.6**
DICKS, JT/ Little seven-colored horse: a Spanish American folktale./ 1995/
3-5/5 KB648 . . . . **398.24**
DIEHN, G/
Kid style nature crafts: 50 terrific things to make with nature's materials./
Kid style nature crafts: 50 terrific things to make with nature's
materials./ 1995/ 1995/ 4-8/6 KD428 . . . . **745.5**
4-8/6 KD428 . . . . **745.5**
Nature crafts for kids./ 1992/ 4-6/6 KD429 . . . . **745.5**
DIETL, U/ Plant-and-grow project book./ 1993/ P-4/5 KC384 . . . . **580**
DILLON, D/ Songs and stories from Uganda./ c1974, 1987/
KA319 . . . . **BA PROF 789.2**
Why mosquitoes buzz in people's ears: a West African tale./ 1975/
1-3/5 KB519 . . . . **CE 398.24**
DILLON, L/ Songs and stories from Uganda./ c1974, 1987/
KA319 . . . . **BA PROF 789.2**
Why mosquitoes buzz in people's ears: a West African tale./ 1975/
1-3/5 KB519 . . . . **CE 398.24**
DIMIDJIAN, VJ/ Early childhood at risk: actions and advocacy for young
children./ 1989/ KA190 . . . . **PROF 372**
DINN, S/ Hearts of gold: a celebration of Special Olympics and its
heroes./ 1996/ 4-6/9 KD760 . . . . **796**
DINNER, SH/ Nothing to be ashamed of: growing up with mental illness in
your family./ 1989/ 5-6/9 KD020 . . . . **616.89**
DIPPOLD, J/ Troy Aikman: quick-draw quarterback./ 1994/
4-6/6 KE230 . . . . **B AIKMAN, T.**
DISALVO-RYAN, D/ Christmas Knight./ 1993/ 2-5/3 KB435 . . . **398.22**
City green./ 1994/ 1-3/3 KF484 . . . . **E**
Growing-up feet./ 1987/ P-3/1 KF394 . . . . **E**
Nina, Nina ballerina./ 1993/ P-1/1 KG189 . . . . **E**
Real hole./ c1960, 1986/ P/2 KF396 . . . . **E**
True Blue./ 1996/ 2-4/2 KH098 . . . . **FIC**
Uncle Willie and the soup kitchen./ 1991/ 1-3/2 KF485 . . . . **E**
You want women to vote, Lizzie Stanton?/ 1995/
3-6/5 KE549 . . . . **B STANTON, E.**
DIVITO, A/ Striking it rich: the story of the California gold rush./ 1996/
2-4/6 KF082 . . . . **979.4**
DIXON, A/ Clay./ 1990/ K-5/4 KC230 . . . . **553.6**
Paper./ 1991/ 3-5/6 KD333 . . . . **676**
DIXON, T/ Berchick./ 1989/ 3-5/5 KG901 . . . . **FIC**
Heroine of the Titanic: a tale both true and otherwise of the life of Molly
Brown./ 1991/ 5-6/6 KE265 . . . . **B BROWN, M.**
DOCKRAY, T/ MicroAliens: dazzling journeys with an electron microscope./
1993/ 3-A/7 KC376 . . . . **579**
DODDS, DA/ Color box./ 1992/ P-K/1 KF486 . . . . **E**
DODSON, B/ Supergrandpa./ 1991/ K-3/5 KG416 . . . . **E**
DODSON, P/ Alphabet of dinosaurs./ 1995/ 1-6/5 KC248 . . . . **567.9**
DOHERTY, B/ Street child./ 1994/ 5-A/6 KH078 . . . . **FIC**
DOHERTY, CA/ Golden Gate Bridge./ 1995/ 5-6/8 KD067 . . . . . **624**
DOHERTY, KM/ Golden Gate Bridge./ 1995/ 5-6/8 KD067 . . . . . **624**

DOHERTY, P/ Cheshire cat and other eye-popping experiments on how we see the world./ 1995/ 4-A/5 KA612 .... **152.14**

Cool hot rod and other electrifying experiments on energy and matter./ 1996/ 4-A/5 KC093 .... **531**

Magic wand and other bright experiments on light and color./ 1995/ 4-A/5 KC110 .... **535**

Spinning blackboard and other dynamic experiments on force and motion./ 1996/ 4-A/5 KC094 .... **531**

DOLAN, EF/ America in World War I./ 1996/ 5-A/7 KE651 ... **940.3**

American revolution: how we fought the War of Independence./ 1995/ 4-6/8 KE879 .... **973.3**

DOLL, CA/ EXPLORING THE PACIFIC STATES THROUGH LITERATURE./ 1994/ KA042 .... **PROF 016.9795**

Nonfiction books for children: activities for thinking, learning and doing./ 1990/ KA072 .... **PROF 027.8**

DOLPHIN BIOLOGY RESEARCH INSTITUTE/ Dolphin man: exploring the world of dolphins./ 1995/ 5-6/11 KC776 .... **599.5**

DOMANSKA, J/ Trumpeter of Krakow. New ed./ c1966, 1973/ /7 KH343 .... **FIC**

DOMM, J/ What's the difference between apes and monkeys and other living things?/ 1995/ 4-6/7 KC271 .... **571**

What's the difference between lenses and prisms and other scientific things?/ 1995/ 4-6/7 KB872 .... **500**

DONATO, MA/ Squanto and the first Thanksgiving (Kit)./ 1996/ 2-6 KE548 .... **KIT B SQUANTO**

DONEY, TLW/ Red Bird./ 1996/ 1-3/4 KG145 .... **E**

Sleeping Beauty: the ballet story./ 1994/ 1-5/7 KD695 ...... **792.8**

DONNELLY, L/ Dinosaur day./ 1987/ P-2/1 KF487 .... **E**

DONOHUE, D/ Dear Daddy./ 1995/ K-2/2 KG406 .... **E**

DOOLING, M/ Thomas Jefferson: a picture book biography./ 1994/ 3-5/5 KE404 .... **B JEFFERSON, T.**

DOPPERT, M/ Streets are free. Rev. ed./ 1995/ 3-4/5 KH383 .... **FIC**

DORIS, E/ Invertebrate zoology./ 1993/ 5-6/8 KC503 .... **592**

DORRIS, M/ Guests./ 1994/ 5-A/7 KH079 .... **FIC**

Morning Girl./ 1992/ 6-A/7 KH080 .... **FIC**

Morning Girl (Sound recording cassette)./ 1995/ 6-A/7 KH080 .. **FIC**

Sees Behind Trees./ 1996/ 5-A/4 KH081 .... **FIC**

Tainos./ 1995/ 6-A/7 KH080 .... **FIC**

DORROS, A/ Abuela./ 1991/ P-2/2 KF488 .... **E**

Abuela (Spanish version)./ 1995/ P-2/2 KF488 .... **E**

Abuela (Videocassette)./ 1994/ P-2 KF489 .... **VCR E**

Ant cities./ 1987/ 1-4/4 KC571 .... **595.79**

Ciudades de hormigas./ 1995/ 1-4/4 KC571 .... **595.79**

Esta es mi casa./ 1993/ 1-3/2 KD393 .... **728**

Feel the wind./ 1989/ P-2/2 KC190 .... **551.5**

Isla./ 1995/ K-2/2 KF490 .... **E**

Isla (Spanish version)./ 1995/ K-2/2 KF490 .... **E**

Por fin es Carnaval./ 1991/ 1-3/4 KF492 .... **E**

Radio Man: a story in English and Spanish./Don Radio: un cuento en Ingles y Espanol./ 1993/ 2-5/2 KF491 .... **E**

This is my house./ 1992/ 1-3/2 KD393 .... **728**

Tonight is Carnaval./ 1991/ 1-3/4 KF492 .... **E**

DORSEY, B/ Big idea./ 1996/ 3-5/2 KH679 .... **FIC**

Don't call me Slob-o./ 1996/ 3-5/2 KH565 .... **FIC**

DOTY, R/ Jobs for kids: the guide to having fun and making money./ 1990/ 5-6/7 KD305 .... **650.1**

Making waves: finding out about rhythmic motion./ 1994/ 5-A/7 KC081 .... **530**

Mirrors: finding out about the properties of light./ 1992/ 5-6/8 KC116 .... **535**

Shadow play: making pictures with light and lenses./ 1995/ 4-8/7 KC117 .... **535**

Tales of a fourth grade nothing./ 1972/ 2-4/3 KG914 ...... **CE FIC**

Wheels at work: building and experimenting with models of machines./ 1986/ 5-6/8 KD054 .... **621.8**

DOW, L/ Incredible plants./ 1997/ A/7 KC385 .... **580**

DOWDEN, AO/ Blossom on the bough: a book of trees./ c1975, 1994/ 5-8/9 KC411 .... **582.16**

DOWNING, J/ Magpies' nest./ 1995/ 1-3/3 KB567 .... **398.24**

Mr. Griggs' work./ c1989, 1993/ P-2/6 KG376 .... **E**

Robin Hood in the greenwood./ 1995/ 3-5/3 KB437 .... **398.22**

DOYLE, AC/ Adventures of Sherlock Holmes./ 1992/ 6-A/7 KH082 . **FIC**

DOYLE, B/ Uncle Ronald./ 1997/ 5-A/5 KH083 .... **FIC**

DR. JOHN (MUSICAL GROUP)/ Brer Rabbit and Boss Lion (Kit)./ 1996/ 3-A KB599 .... **KIT 398.24**

DRAANEN, WV/ How I survived being a girl./ 1997/ 4-A KH084 .. **FIC**

DRAGON POEMS./ 1991/ K-A KE055 .... **811.008**

DRAGONWAGON, C/ Alligator arrived with apples, a potluck alphabet feast./ 1987/ K-2/5 KF494 .... **E**

Annie flies the birthday bike./ 1993/ K-2/2 KF495 .... **E**

Itch book./ 1990/ K-3 KF496 .... **E**

DRAKE, J/ Kids' summer handbook./ 1994/ 3-6/6 KD678 ..... **790.1**

DRAPER, R/ Georgia O'Keeffe./ 1996/ 2-3/2 KE482 .. **B O'KEEFFE, G.**

DRATH, B/ When someone dies./ 1992/ K-3/4 KA649 .... **155.9**

DRESCHER, H/ Simon's book./ 1983/ K-2/6 KF497 .... **CE E**

DRESCHER, J/ Bubbles./ 1979/ 4-6/8 KC085 .... **530.4**

DREW, H/ My first music book./ 1993/ 2-4/2 KD543 ...... **784.192**

DREYER, SS/ BEST OF BOOKFINDER: A GUIDE TO CHILDREN'S LITERATURE ABOUT INTERESTS AND CONCERNS OF YOUTH AGED 2-18./ 1992/ KA083 .... **PROF 028.1**

DRIEMEN, JE/ Winston Churchill: an unbreakable spirit./ 1990/ 5-6/7 KE290 .... **B CHURCHILL, W.**

DRUCKER, M/ Family treasury of Jewish holidays./ 1994/ 2-6/6 KA772 .... **296.4**

DUBANEVICH, A/ Pig William./ 1985/ P-2/1 KF498 .... **E**

DUBOIS, ML/ Abenaki Captive./ 1994/ 6-A/6 KH085 .... **FIC**

DUBOSQUE, D/ Draw! cars. Rev. ed./ 1997/ 4-A/5 KD417 .... **743**

Learn to draw 3-D./ 1992/ 5-A/7 KD414 .... **742**

DUBOWSKI, CE/ Pirate School./ 1996/ 1-3/2 KF499 .... **E**

DUBOWSKI, M/ Pirate School./ 1996/ 1-3/2 KF499 .... **E**

DUENSING, E/ Talking to fireflies, shrinking the moon: nature activities for all ages./ 1997/ KA288 .... **PROF 508**

DUFFEY, B/ Camp Knock Knock./ 1996/ 1-3/2 KF500 .... **E**

Lucky Christmas./ 1994/ 3-5/4 KH086 .... **FIC**

Utterly yours, Booker Jones./ 1995/ 4-6/5 KH087 .... **FIC**

Virtual Cody./ 1997/ 1-4/2 KH088 .... **FIC**

DUFFY, DM/ Theodoric's rainbow./ 1995/ 3-6/4 KH380 ...... **FIC**

DUGAN, B/ Loop the loop./ 1992/ 1-3/4 KF501 .... **E**

Loop the loop (Sound recording cassette)./ 1997/ 1-3/4 KF501 .... **E**

DUGAN, K/ Christmas around the world./ 1995/ 3-6/7 KB237 **394.266**

Jacks around the world./ 1996/ 3-6/10 KD770 .... **796.2**

DUGGLEBY, J/ Artist in overalls: the life of Grant Wood./ 1995/ 5-A/6 KE599 .... **B WOOD, G.**

DUGIN, A/ Dragon feathers./ 1993/ 4-5/7 KB289 .... **398.2**

DUGINA, O/ Dragon feathers./ 1993/ 4-5/7 KB289 .... **398.2**

DUKE, K/ Archaeologists dig for clues./ 1997/ 2-4/3 KE623 .... **930.1**

One Saturday morning./ 1994/ 1-3/1 KF183 .... **E**

DUNBAR, F/ Camp Knock Knock./ 1996/ 1-3/2 KF500 .... **E**

DUNBAR, J/ This is the star./ 1996/ 2-3/2 KA703 .... **232.92**

DUNCAN, AF/ National Civil Rights Museum celebrates everyday people./ 1995/ 3-6/8 KA903 .... **323.1**

DUNCAN, BK/ Explore the wild: a nature search-and-find book./ 1996/ 2-6/7 KC358 .... **578.7**

DUNCAN, L/ Magic of Spider Woman./ 1996/ 4-5/6 KB733 ... **398.27**

Third eye./ 1984/ A/5 KH089 .... **FIC**

DUNLAP, J/ Birds in the bushes: a story about Margaret Morse Nice./ 1996/ 3-5/9 KE477 .... **B NICE, M.**

Eye on the wild: a story about Ansel Adams./ 1995/ 3-6/7 KE225 .... **B ADAMS, A.**

DUNN, A/ Skyscrapers./ 1993/ 3-6/7 KD383 .... **720**

DUNN, AB/ Trouble with school: a family story about learning disabilities./ 1993/ KA184 .... **PROF 371.9**

DUNN, KB/ Trouble with school: a family story about learning disabilities./ 1993/ KA184 .... **PROF 371.9**

DUNPHY, M/ Here is the Arctic winter./ 1993/ K-4/2 KC731 .. **599.17**

Here is the southwestern desert./ 1995/ P-3/3 KF066 ...... **979.1**

DUNTZE, D/ Twelve dancing princesses: a fairy tale./ 1995/ 3-4/6 KB311 .... **398.2**

DUPASQUIER, P/ Country far away./ 1988/ K-3/1 KF638 .... **E**

DUPLACEY, J/ Amazing forwards./ 1996/ 4-6/6 KD838 ...... **796.962**

Great goalies./ 1996/ 4-6/6 KD839 .... **796.962**

Top rookies./ 1996/ 4-6/6 KD840 .... **796.962**

DUPONT, P/ Cheetah: fast as lightning./ 1992/ 1-4/5 KC819 .. **599.75**

DUVOISIN, R/ Hide and seek fog./ c1965/ K-2 KG615 .... **E**

Petunia./ c1950/ K-2/3 KF502 .... **CE E**

Petunia (Braille)./ n.d./ K-2/3 KF502 .... **CE E**

Petunia (Talking book)./ n.d./ K-2/3 KF502 .... **CE E**

Petunia (Videocassette)./ 1985/ K-2/3 KF502 .... **CE E**

Petunia's Christmas./ c1952/ K-2/3 KF502 .... **CE E**

DYER, J/ Animal crackers: a delectable collection of pictures, poems, and lullabies for the very young./ 1996/ P-1 KD882 .... **808.81**

Piggins./ 1987/ K-3/4 KG779 .... **E**

TALKING LIKE THE RAIN: A FIRST BOOK OF POEMS./ 1992/ P-2 KE112 .... **821.008**

Time for bed./ 1993/ P-1/2 KF572 .... **E**

DYGARD, TJ/ Backfield package./ 1992/ 6-A/7 KH090 .... **FIC**

Forward pass./ 1989/ 5-A/7 KH091 .... **FIC**

Game plan./ 1993/ 5-A/8 KH092 .... **FIC**

Infield hit./ 1995/ 5-A/7 KH093 .... **FIC**

EACHUS, J/ Chills run down my spine./ 1994/ 5-A/4 KH830 ... **FIC**

EAGER, E/ Half magic./ c1954, 1982/ 4-6/6 KH094 .... **FIC**

Knight's castle./ c1956, 1984/ 4-6/6 KH094 .... **FIC**

Knight's castle (Sound recording cassette)./ n.d./ 4-6/6 KH094 ... **FIC**

Magic or not?/ c1959, 1985/ 4-6/6 KH094 .... **FIC**

Magic or not? (Sound recording cassette)./ n.d./ 4-6/6 KH094 ... **FIC**

Seven-day magic./ c1962/ 4-6/6 KH095 .... **FIC**

Seven-day magic (Braille)./ n.d./ 4-6/6 KH095 .... **FIC**

Seven-day magic (Sound recording cassette)./ n.d./ 4-6/6 KH095 . **FIC**

Time garden./ c1958,/ 4-6/6 KH094 . . . . **FIC**
Well wishers (Sound recording cassette)./ n.d.,/ 4-6/6 KH094 . . . . **FIC**
EAGLE, E/ Gertie's green thumb./ 1995/ 3-5/4 KH073 . . . . **FIC**
Patakin: world tales of drums and drummers./ 1994/
5-6/6 KB321 . . . . **398.2**
EAGLE WALKING TURTLE/ Full moon stories: thirteen Native American
legends./ 1997/ 3-5/7 KH096 . . . . **FIC**
EARLE, A/ Zipping, zapping, zooming bats./ 1995/ 1-3/4 KC759 **599.4**
EARLY, M/ Sleeping Beauty./ 1993/ 2-5/5 KB290 . . . . **398.2**
William Tell./ 1991/ 4-6/6 KB440 . . . . **398.22**
William Tell (Sound recording cassette)./ 1994/ 4-6/6 KB440 . . **398.22**
EARTH IS PAINTED GREEN: A GARDEN OF POEMS ABOUT OUR
PLANET./ 1994/ 3-6 KB883 . . . . **808.81**
EASTERLING, B/ Prize in the snow./ 1994/ 2-3/4 KF503 . . . . **E**
EASTMAN, P/ CAT IN THE HAT BEGINNER BOOK DICTIONARY./
c1964, 1984/ 1-2 KB833 . . . . **423**
EASTMAN, PD/ Are you my mother?/ c1960/ P-1/1 KF504 . . . . **E**
Are you my mother? (Braille)./ n.d./ P-1/1 KF504 . . . . **E**
Are you my mother? plus two more P.D. Eastman classics
(Videocassette)./ 1991/ P-1 KF505 . . . . **VCR E**
Are you my mother? (Sound recording cassette)./ n.d./ P-1/1 KF504 **E**
Are you my mother? (Talking book)./ n.d./ P-1/1 KF504 . . . . **E**
Best nest (Videocassette)./ / P-1 KF505 . . . . **VCR E**
Corre, perro, corre!/ 1992/ P-1/1 KF506 . . . . **E**
Fish out of water./ c1961/ K-2/2 KG209 . . . . **E**
Go, dog, go!/ c1961/ P-1/1 KF506 . . . . **E**
Go, dog, go! (Videocassette)./ / P-1 KF505 . . . . **VCR E**
Robert the rose horse./ 1962/ K-2/1 KF696 . . . . **E**
Sam and the firefly./ c1958/ P-1/1 KF507 . . . . **E**
ECKERT, AW/ Incident at Hawk's Hill./ 1971/ 6-A/7 KH097 . . . . . **FIC**
Incident at Hawk's Hill (Braille)./ n.d./ 6-A/7 KH097 . . . . **FIC**
Incident at Hawk's Hill (Sound recording cassette)./ 1996/
6-A/7 KH097 . . . . **FIC**
EDELSON, W/ Baker's dozen: a Saint Nicholas tale./ 1995/
K-2/4 KB487 . . . . **398.22**
EDELSTEIN, T/ Hide and seek./ c1981, 1991/ 5-A/4 KH835 . . . . . **FIC**
EDENS, C/ Glorious Mother Goose./ 1988/ P-K KB803 . . . . **398.8**
EDGECOMB, D/ Pattysaurus and other tales (Sound recording cassette)./
1995/ P-3 KF508 . . . . **SRC E**
EDMONDS, M/ Voices of the winds: Native American legends./ 1989/
KA266 . . . . **PROF 398.2**
EDUCATIONAL SOFTWARE PREVIEW GUIDE CONSORTIUM/
EDUCATIONAL SOFTWARE PREVIEW GUIDE./ 1982-/
KA107 . . . . **PER PROF 050**
EDWARDS, C/ Young inline skater./ 1996/ 3-6/6 KD771 . . . . . **796.21**
EDWARDS, FB/ Ottawa: a kid's eye view./ 1993/ 5-6/8 KE818 . . **971.3**
Snow: learning for the fun of it./ 1992/ 5-A/9 KC208 . . . . . . **551.57**
EDWARDS, M/ Alef-bet: a Hebrew alphabet book./ 1992/
1-3 KB864 . . . . **492.4**
Chicken man./ 1991/ K-2/2 KF509 . . . . **E**
EDWARDS, PD/ Barefoot: escape on the Underground Railroad./ 1997/
1-3/3 KF510 . . . . **E**
Four famished foxes and Fosdyke./ 1995/ 1-3/3 KF511 . . . . **E**
Livingstone Mouse./ 1996/ K-2/2 KF512 . . . . **E**
Some smug slug./ 1996/ P-2/3 KF513 . . . . **E**
EGAN, T/ Burnt toast on Davenport Street./ 1997/ 1-3/2 KF514 . . . **E**
Macmillan book of baseball stories./ 1992/ 4-A/5 KD796 . . **796.357**
EGIELSKI, R/ Call me Ahnighito./ 1995/ 2-5/2 KF413 . . . . **E**
Hey, Al./ 1986/ 1-3/3 KG781 . . . . **E**
Louis the fish./ 1980/ K-3/4 KG782 . . . . **E**
Oh, brother./ 1989/ 1-4/5 KG783 . . . . **E**
Telling of the tales: five stories./ 1994/ 5-A/7 KG928 . . . . **FIC**
Tub Grandfather./ 1993/ 1-3/4 KF415 . . . . **E**
Tub people./ 1989/ 1-3/4 KF416 . . . . **CE E**
EGOFF, S/ New republic of childhood: a critical guide to Canadian
children's literature in/ 1990/ KA349 . . . . **PROF 809**
EHLERT, L/ Chicka chicka boom boom./ 1989/ P-1/2 KG073 . . . . . . **E**
CHICKA CHICKA BOOM BOOM (CD-ROM)./ 1996/
P-2 KF382 . . . . **CDR E**
Chicka chicka boom boom (Kit)./ 1991/ P-1 KG074 . . . . . . **KIT E**
Color farm./ 1990/ P-K KF515 . . . . **E**
Color zoo./ 1989/ P-1/2 KF516 . . . . **E**
Crocodile smile: 10 songs of the Earth as the animals see it./ 1994/
P-2 KD665 . . . . **BA 789.3**
Cuckoo: a Mexican folktale./Cucu: un cuento folklorico mexicano./ 1997/
P-2/3 KB561 . . . . **398.24**
Feathers for lunch./ 1990/ P-1/2 KF517 . . . . **E**
Feathers for lunch (Big book)./ 1993/ P-1/2 KF517 . . . . **E**
Fish eyes: a book you can count on./ 1990/ P-K/1 KF518 . . . . **E**
Mole's hill: a woodland tale./ 1994/ K-2/3 KB562 . . . . **398.24**
Moon rope: a Peruvian folktale/Un lazo a la luna: una leyenda Peruana./
1992/ 1-3/2 KB563 . . . . **398.24**
Nuts to you!/ 1993/ P-2/2 KF519 . . . . **E**
Pair of socks./ 1996/ P-1/2 KA634 . . . . **153.14**

Plumas para almorzar./ 1996/ P-1/2 KF517 . . . . **E**
Red leaf, yellow leaf./ 1991/ P-1/4 KC412 . . . . **582.16**
Snowballs./ 1995/ P-2/2 KF520 . . . . **E**
Under my nose./ 1996/ 3-6/2 KE333 . . . . **B EHLERT, L.**
EHRLICH, A/ Parents in the pigpen, pigs in the tub./ 1993/
K-2/1 KF521 . . . . **E**
EINZIG, S/ Tom's midnight garden./ c1958, 1991/ 5-6/5 KH589 . . . **FIC**
EISEN, A/ TREASURY OF CHILDREN'S LITERATURE./ 1992/
P-3 KD879 . . . . **808.8**
EISENBERG, L/ Batty riddles./ 1993/ K-3 KD728 . . . . **793.735**
EISENBERG, MB/ Information problem-solving: the Big Six Skills approach
to library and information skills instruction./ 1990/
KA063 . . . . **PROF 025.5**
EISLER, C/ Cats know best./ 1988/ P-1/1 KD232 . . . . **636.8**
EISS, HE/ Dictionary of language games, puzzles, and amusements./
1986/ 4-6 KA455 . . . . **REF 793.734**
EKOOMIAK, N/ Arctic memories./ c1988, 1990/ 2-6/4 KF125 . . . **998**
ELDON, D/ Lyrical life science (Multimedia kit)./ 1995/
K-A KA295 . . . . **MMK PROF 570**
ELIOT, TS/ Old possum's book of practical cats./ 1982/ 4-A KE100 **821**
ELISH, D/ Harriet Tubman and the Underground Railroad./ 1993/
4-6/4 KE574 . . . . **B TUBMAN, H.**
James Meredith and school desegregation./ 1994/
4-5/7 KE463 . . . . **B MEREDITH, J.**
ELKIN, J/ Mighty Mountain and the three strong women./ 1990/
3-5/5 KB316 . . . . **398.2**
ELLIOTT, D/
Crawdads, doodlebugs and creasy greens: songs, stories and lore
celebrating the natural world (Sound recording cassette)./ Crawdads,
doodlebugs and creasy greens: songs, stories and lore celebrating the
natural world (Compact disc)./ 1995/ 1996/ 3-5 KB291 . . **CD 398.2**
3-5 KB291 . . . . **CD 398.2**
ELLIOTT, L/ Guide to night sounds (Compact disc)./ 1992/
3-6 KC484 . . . . **SRC 591.59**
Guide to night sounds (Sound recording cassette)./ 1992/
3-6 KC484 . . . . **SRC 591.59**
ELLIS, JD/ Fiesta!: Mexico's greatest celebrations./ 1992/
4-6/7 KB203 . . . . **394.26**
Winter solstice./ 1994/ 3-5/6 KB211 . . . . **394.261**
ELLIS, VF/ Wynton Marsalis./ 1997/ 5-A/10 KE459 . **B MARSALIS, W.**
ELSTE, J/ True Blue./ 1996/ 2-4/2 KH098 . . . . **FIC**
ELTING, M/ Math fun with a pocket calculator./ 1992/
4-A/4 KD713 . . . . **793.7**
Math fun with tricky lines and shapes./ 1992/ 4-A/5 KD714 . . . **793.7**
Test your luck./ 1992/ 5-6/4 KB998 . . . . **519.2**
ELYA, SM/ Say hola to Spanish./ 1996/ K-2/3 KB862 . . . . **468.1**
EMBERLEY, E/ Go away, big green monster!/ 1992/ P-1/2 KF522 . . . **E**
EMBERLEY, M/ Happy birth day!/ 1996/ P-2/3 KF676 . . . . **E**
It's perfectly normal: a book about changing bodies, growing up, sex, and
sexual health./ 1994/ 5-6/6 KC949 . . . . **612.6**
Ruby./ 1990/ 1-3/3 KF523 . . . . **E**
Welcome back, Sun./ 1993/ 1-3/3 KF524 . . . . **E**
EMBERLEY, R/ Let's go: a book in two languages./Vamos: un libro en dos
lenguas./ 1993/ K-2/2 KB857 . . . . **463**
My house: a book in two languages/Mi Casa: un libro en dos lenguas./
1990/ K-2 KB858 . . . . **463**
Taking a walk/Caminando./ c1990/ K-2 KB858 . . . . **463**
Three cool kids./ 1995/ P-1/3 KF525 . . . . **E**
Three cool kids (Sound recording cassette)./ 1997/ P-1/3 KF525 . . . **E**
EMMERT, M/ I'm the big sister now./ 1989/ 3-5/5 KD039 . . . . **618.92**
EMMOND, K/ Manitoba./ 1992/ 5-A/8 KE816 . . . . **971.27**
EMORY, J/ Dirty, rotten, dead?/ 1996/ 4-6/10 KC303 . . . . **577.1**
ENDERLE, JR/ What would Mama do?/ 1995/ K-2/2 KF526 . . . . . . **E**
ENDICOTT, J/ Listen to the rain./ 1988/ P-2 KG077 . . . . **E**
ENGEL, T/ We'll never forget you, Roberto Clemente./ 1997/
2-4/2 KE293 . . . . **B CLEMENTE, R.**
ENGFER, L/ Maine./ 1991/ 4-6/7 KE927 . . . . **974.1**
ENGLANDER, K/ Streets are free. Rev. ed./ 1995/ 3-4/5 KH383 . . **FIC**
ENGLISH, JA/ Mission: Earth: voyage to the home planet./ 1996/
4-A/8 KC145 . . . . **550**
ENGLISH, K/ Neeny coming, Neeny going./ 1996/ 1-3/2 KF527 . . . . **E**
ENRIGHT, E/ Saturdays./ c1941, 1988/ 4-6/5 KH099 . . . . **FIC**
Saturdays (Braille)./ n.d./ 4-6/5 KH099 . . . . **FIC**
Thimble summer./ 1966/ 4-6/6 KH100 . . . . **CE FIC**
Thimble summer (Sound recording cassette)./ n.d./
4-6/6 KH100 . . . . **CE FIC**
Thimble summer (Talking book)./ Thimble summer (Talking book)./ n.d./
1966/ 4-6/6 KH100 . . . . **CE FIC**
4-6/6 KH100 . . . . **CE FIC**
EPPLE, W/ Barn owls./ 1992/ 4-6/5 KC713 . . . . **598.9**
EPSTEIN-KRAVIS, A/ Happy to be me (Sound recording cassette)./ 1993/
P-1 KA638 . . . . **SRC 155.2**
Tot's tunes (Sound recording cassette)./ c1987, 1990/
P-1 KD610 . . . . **SRC 789.3**

ERICKSON, RE/ Toad for Tuesday./ 1974/ 1-3/3 KF528 . . . . **CE E**
Toad for Tuesday (Braille)./ n.d./ 1-3/3 KF528 . . . . **CE E**
Toad for Tuesday (Kit)./ 1981/ 1-3/3 KF528 . . . . **CE E**
Toad for Tuesday (Sound recording cassette)./ n.d./ 1-3/3 KF528 . . . . **CE E**
ERICKSON, T/ Get it together: math problems for groups, grades 4-12./ 1989/ KA290 . . . . **PROF 510**
ERLBACH, A/ Best friends book: true stories about real best friends.../ 1995/ 5-A/4 KA656 . . . . **158**
Peanut butter./ 1994/ 4-6/7 KD265 . . . . **641.3**
Sidewalk games around the world./ 1997/ 2-5/6 KD769 . . . . . **796.2**
ERNST, LC/ Ginger jumps./ 1990/ K-3/4 KF529 . . . . **E**
Letters are lost!/ 1996/ P-K/2 KF530 . . . . **E**
Little Red Riding Hood: a newfangled prairie tale./ 1995/ K-2/4 KF531 . . . . **E**
Luckiest kid on the planet./ 1994/ 1-3/2 KF532 . . . . **E**
Potato: a tale from the Great Depression./ 1997/ K-3/2 KF980 . . . . **E**
Squirrel Park./ 1993/ K-2/5 KF533 . . . . **E**
Walter's tail./ 1992/ P-2/3 KF534 . . . . **E**
Zinnia and Dot./ 1992/ P-1/2 KF535 . . . . **E**
Zinnia and Dot (Sound recording cassette)./ 1994/ P-1/2 KF535 . . . **E**
ESBENSEN, BJ/ Baby whales drink milk./ 1994/ 1-3/2 KC768 . . **599.5**
Great buffalo race: how the buffalo got its hump: a Seneca tale./ 1994/ 3-4/6 KB564 . . . . **398.24**
Great Northern diver: the loon./ 1990/ 3-5/6 KC680 . . . . **598.4**
Great Northern diver: the loon (Sound recording cassette)./ 1993/ 3-5/6 KC680 . . . . **598.4**
Sponges are skeletons./ 1993/ 1-3/2 KC508 . . . . **593.4**
ESPELAND, P/ Bringing out the best: a resource guide for parents of young gifted children. Rev. and updated./ 1991/ KA189 . . . . **PROF 371.95**
How to help your child with homework: every caring parent's guide to encouraging good study habits and ending the Homework Wars: for parents/ 1997/ KA181 . . . . **PROF 371.3**
Playing smart: a parent's guide to enriching offbeat learning activities/ 1990/ KA324 . . . . **PROF 790.1**
School survival guide for kids with LD (Learning differences)./ 1991/ 4-6/4 KB093 . . . . **371.92**
Stick up for yourself!: every kid's guide to personal power and positive self-esteem./ 1990/ 6-A/6 KA659 . . . . **158**
ESSLEY, R/ Angels in the dust./ 1997/ 2-3/2 KG315 . . . . **E**
ESTERL, A/ Okino and the whales./ 1995/ 3-5/3 KH101 . . . . **FIC**
ESTES, E/ Hundred dresses./ c1944/ 2-4/6 KH102 . . . . **FIC**
Hundred dresses (Braille)./ n.d./ 2-4/6 KH102 . . . . **FIC**
Hundred dresses (Sound recording cassette)./ 1997/ 2-4/6 KH102 . **FIC**
Moffat museum./ 1983/ 3-5/3 KH103 . . . . **FIC**
Moffat museum (Braille)./ n.d./ 3-5/3 KH103 . . . . **FIC**
Moffat museum (Sound recording cassette)./ n.d./ 3-5/3 KH103 . . **FIC**
Moffats./ c1941/ 3-5/3 KH103 . . . . **FIC**
Moffats (Braille)./ n.d./ 3-5/3 KH103 . . . . **FIC**
Moffats (Sound recording cassette)./ n.d./ 3-5/3 KH103 . . . . **FIC**
Moffats (Talking book)./ n.d./ 3-5/3 KH103 . . . . **FIC**
ETS, MH/ Gilberto and the wind./ c1963/ P-1/2 KF536 . . . . **CE E**
Gilberto and the wind (Kit)./ 1996/ P-1/2 KF536 . . . . **CE E**
Gilberto and the wind (Sound recording cassette)./ n.d./ P-1/2 KF536 . . . . **CE E**
Gilberto y el viento./ 1995/ P-1/2 KF536 . . . . **CE E**
Gilberto y el viento (Kit)./ 1996/ P-1/2 KF536 . . . . **CE E**
In the forest./ c1944, 1976/ P-1/2 KF537 . . . . **E**
In the forest (Braille)./ n.d.,/ P-1/2 KF537 . . . . **E**
Nine days to Christmas./ c1959/ 1-3/2 KF538 . . . . **E**
Nine days to Christmas (Sound recording cassette)./ n.d./ 1-3/2 KF538 . . . . **E**
Nueve dias para navidad./ 1991/ 1-3/2 KF538 . . . . **E**
Play with me./ c1955/ P-1/2 KF539 . . . . **CE E**
Play with me (Braille)./ n.d./ P-1/2 KF539 . . . . **CE E**
Play with me (Talking book)./ n.d./ P-1/2 KF539 . . . . **CE E**
ETTLINGER, D/ Janice VanCleave's rocks and minerals: mind-boggling experiments you can turn into science fair projects./ 1996/ 4-6/8 KC228 . . . . **552**
EUVREMER, T/ Toby, where are you?/ 1997/ P-1/2 KG546 . . . . **E**
EVANS, D/ Classroom at the end of the hall./ 1996/ 3-5/4 KH104 . **FIC**
MONSTER SOUP AND OTHER SPOOKY POEMS./ 1992/ K-3 KD986 . . . . **811**
EVANS, GB/ Riverside Shakespeare./ 1974/ A KA468 . . . . **REF 822.3**
EVANS, IH/ BREWER'S DICTIONARY OF PHRASE AND FABLE. 15th ed./ 1995/ 5-6 KA459 . . . . **REF 803**
EVANS, J/ Camping and survival./ 1992/ 4-A/6 KD825 . . . . . **796.54**
Horseback riding./ 1992/ 4-A/6 KD855 . . . . **798.2**
Skiing./ 1992/ 5-A/7 KD837 . . . . **796.93**
Whitewater kayaking./ 1992/ 4-A/7 KD845 . . . . **797.1**
EVANS, M/ Guinea pigs./ 1992/ 3-6/6 KD178 . . . . **636**
Rabbit./ 1992/ 3-6/4 KD179 . . . . **636**
EVANS, R/ Inktomi and the ducks and other Assiniboin trickster stories (Talking book)./ 1994/ 3-5 KB441 . . . . **TB 398.22**
EVERETT, P/ One that got away./ 1992/ K-2/2 KF540 . . . . **E**
EVERNDEN, M/ Of swords and sorcerers: the adventures of King Arthur and his knights./ 1993/ 4-5/6 KB452 . . . . **398.22**
EVERSOLE, R/ Flute player./La Flautista./ 1995/ K-2/2 KF541 . . . . . **E**
EVETTS-SECKER, J/ Mother and daughter tales./ 1996/ 3-4/6 KB292 . . . . **398.2**
EWART, C/ Dwarf, the giant, and the unicorn: a tale of King Arthur./ 1996/ 3-5/4 KB443 . . . . **398.22**
Legend of the Persian carpet./ 1993/ 2-3/6 KB285 . . . . **398.2**
Time train./ 1994/ 1-3/2 KF551 . . . . **E**
EWING, C/ Moose and friends./ 1993/ 1-3/2 KF947 . . . . **E**
Phoebe's parade./ 1994/ K-2/2 KG138 . . . . **E**
EXPLORATORIUM TEACHER INSTITUTE (SAN FRANCISCO, CALIF.)/ Cheshire cat and other eye-popping experiments on how we see the world./ 1995/ 4-A/5 KA612 . . . . **152.14**
Cool hot rod and other electrifying experiments on energy and matter./ 1996/ 4-A/5 KC093 . . . . **531**
Magic wand and other bright experiments on light and color./ 1995/ 4-A/5 KC110 . . . . **535**
Spinning blackboard and other dynamic experiments on force and motion./ 1996/ 4-A/5 KC094 . . . . **531**
EXTRA INNINGS: BASEBALL POEMS./ 1993/ 3-6 KE056 . . . **811.008**
FABER, D/ Calamity Jane: her life and her legend./ 1992/ 4-6/8 KE274 . . . . **B CALAMITY JANE**
Great lives: nature and the environment./ 1991/ 5-A/7 KB903 . . **508**
FABER, H/ Great lives: nature and the environment./ 1991/ 5-A/7 KB903 . . . . **508**
FACKLAM, H/ Bacteria./ 1994/ 5-A/9 KC378 . . . . **579.3**
Spare parts for people./ 1987/ A/9 KD035 . . . . **617**
Viruses./ 1994/ 5-A/8 KC377 . . . . **579.2**
FACKLAM, M/ And then there was one: the mysteries of extinction./ 1990/ 5-6/7 KC488 . . . . **591.68**
Bacteria./ 1994/ 5-A/9 KC378 . . . . **579.3**
Creepy, crawly caterpillars./ 1996/ 4-6/6 KC559 . . . . **595.78**
Spare parts for people./ 1987/ A/9 KD035 . . . . **617**
Viruses./ 1994/ 5-A/8 KC377 . . . . **579.2**
FACKLAM, P/ Creepy, crawly caterpillars./ 1996/ 4-6/6 KC559 **595.78**
FADDEN, DK/ Native American animal stories./ 1992/ 4-6/5 KB540 . . . . **398.24**
FADDEN, JK/ Native American animal stories./ 1992/ 4-6/5 KB540 . . . . **398.24**
FAIR, J/ Black bear magic for kids./ 1991/ 4-5/5 KC849 . . . . . **599.78**
FALKOF, L/ Lyndon B. Johnson, 36th president of the United states./ 1989/ 6-A/9 KE406 . . . . **B JOHNSON, L.**
FALWELL, C/ New moon./ 1996/ P-2/2 KG490 . . . . **E**
We have a baby./ 1993/ P-K/1 KF542 . . . . **E**
FAMILIES: POEMS CELEBRATING THE AFRICAN AMERICAN EXPERIENCE./ 1994/ K-3 KE057 . . . . **811.008**
FANELLI, S/ My map book./ 1995/ K-2 KF543 . . . . **E**
FANG, L/ Ch'i-lin purse: a collection of ancient Chinese stories./ 1995/ 4-6/5 KB295 . . . . **398.2**
FARANDA, B/ Pizza!/ 1989/ 3-4/2 KD292 . . . . **641.8**
FARB, N/ Galapagos: islands of change./ 1995/ 4-A/8 KF113 . . **986.6**
FARIS, K/ Arctic whales and whaling./ 1988/ 5-6/6 KC771 . . . . **599.5**
FARJEON, E/ Cats sleep anywhere./ 1996/ K-3 KE101 . . . . **821**
Morning has broken./ 1996/ P-2 KD611 . . . . **789.3**
FARLEY, CJ/ Mr. Pak buys a story./ 1997/ K-3/2 KB734 . . . . . **398.27**
FARLEY, W/ Black Stallion./ c1941, 1994/ 4-6/5 KH105 . . . . **FIC**
Black Stallion and Flame./ c1960, 1991/ 4-6/5 KH105 . . . . **FIC**
Black Stallion (Braille)./ n.d.,/ 4-6/5 KH105 . . . . **FIC**
Black Stallion mystery./ c1957, 1992/ 4-6/5 KH105 . . . . **FIC**
Black Stallion's ghost./ c1969, 1995/ 4-6/5 KH105 . . . . **FIC**
Man O'War./ c1962/ 5-6/6 KH106 . . . . **FIC**
Young Black Stallion./ 1991,/ 4-6/5 KH105 . . . . **FIC**
FARMER, LSJ/ Cooperative learning activities in the library media center./ 1991/ KA073 . . . . **PROF 027.8**
Creative partnerships: librarians and teachers working together./ 1993/ KA074 . . . . **PROF 027.8**
I speak HyperCard./ 1992/ 3-A KA573 . . . . **005.265**
FARMER, N/ Do you know me./ 1993/ 4-A/5 KH107 . . . . **FIC**
Ear, the Eye and the Arm: a novel./ 1994/ 6-A/4 KH108 . . . . **FIC**
Girl named Disaster./ 1996/ 6-A/5 KH109 . . . . **FIC**
Warm Place./ 1995/ 4-A/3 KH110 . . . . **FIC**
FARNSWORTH, B/ Grandpa is a flyer./ 1995/ 1-3/5 KF188 . . . . . . **E**
FARRAND, J/ Audubon Society field guide to North American birds-- Eastern Region./ 1994/ 3-6/7 KC647 . . . . **598**
FARRELL, DL/ Glues, brews, and goos: recipes and formulas for almost any classroom project./ 1996/ KA216 . . . . **PROF 372.5**
FARRELL, K/ TALKING TO THE SUN: AN ILLUSTRATED ANTHOLOGY OF POEMS FOR YOUNG PEOPLE./ 1985/ 6-A KE087 . . . . . **811.008**
FARRELL, M/ Marrying Malcolm Murgatroyd./ 1995/ 5-A/4 KH111 . **FIC**
FARRIS, PJ/ Young Mouse and Elephant: an East African folktale./ 1996/ K-2/4 KB565 . . . . **398.24**

FARROW, M/ BEAUTY AND THE BEAST (Videocassette)./ c1989, 1996/
 K-3 KB259 . . . . **VCR 398.2**
 PEGASUS (Videocassette)./ 1990/ 3-6 KA749 . . . . **VCR 292**
FASICK, AM/ LANDS OF PLEASURE: ESSAYS ON LILLIAN H. SMITH
 AND THE DEVELOPMENT OF/ 1990/ KA044 . . . . **PROF 020**
FASSLER, J/ Howie helps himself./ 1974, c1975/ K-2/4 KF544 . . . . . **E**
 Howie helps himself (Sound recording cassette)./ n.d.,/ K-2/4 KF544 **E**
FECHNER, A/ Kitten who couldn't purr./ 1991/ P-K/1 KG611 . . . . . **E**
FECKO, MB/ Cataloging nonbook resources: a how-to-do-it manual for
 librarians./ 1993/ KA057 . . . . **PROF 025.3**
FEELINGS, ML/ Jambo means hello: Swahili alphabet book./ 1974/
 1-3/7 KF545 . . . . **E**
FEELINGS, T/ Jambo means hello: Swahili alphabet book./ 1974/
 1-3/7 KF545 . . . . **E**
 SOUL LOOKS BACK IN WONDER./ 1993/ 4-A KE084 . . . . **811.008**
 To be a slave./ c1968/ A/7 KA928 . . . . **326**
FEENEY, S/ A is for aloha./ 1980/ K-3 KF546 . . . . **E**
 Hawaii is a rainbow./ 1985/ P-6 KF121 . . . . **996**
FEHR, KS/ Monica Seles: returning champion./ 1997/
 4-6/10 KE533 . . . . **B SELES, M.**
FEIFFER, J/ Man in the ceiling./ 1993/ 5-A/7 KH112 . . . . **FIC**
FELDMAN, EB/ Animals don't wear pajamas: a book about sleeping./
 1992/ P-2/6 KC473 . . . . **591.5**
FELTS, S/ Blue whale./ 1993/ 3-5/7 KC772 . . . . **599.5**
FENTON, AD/ Reference books for children, 4th ed./ 1992/
 KA021 . . . . **PROF 011.62**
FERGUSON, A/ Tumbleweed Christmas./ 1996/ 1-3/3 KF547 . . . . . **E**
FERRER, IE/ Feliz nochebuena, feliz navidad: Christmas feasts of the
 Hispanic Caribbean./ c1994, 1996/ 5-A/7 KB238 . . . . **394.266**
FERRIS, H/ Favorite poems, old and new, selected for boys and girls./
 c1957/ 5-6 KA467 . . . . **REF 811.008**
FERRIS, J/ What I had was singing: the story of Marian Anderson./ 1994/
 5-A/6 KE236 . . . . **B ANDERSON, M.**
FEW, R/ Macmillan animal encyclopedia for children./ 1991/
 5-6/7 KC446 . . . . **591**
FIAMMENGHI, G/ Occasional cow./ 1989/ 5-6/8 KH284 . . . . **FIC**
 Stay in line./ 1996/ K-2/2 KG516 . . . . **E**
FIAROTTA, N/ Papercrafts around the world./ 1996/
 2-6/6 KD440 . . . . **745.54**
FIAROTTA, P/ Papercrafts around the world./ 1996/
 2-6/6 KD440 . . . . **745.54**
FIELD, EW/ Newbery Medal books: 1922-1955: with their authors'
 acceptance papers, biographies, and related materials chiefly from the
 Horn/ c1957/ KA353 . . . . **PROF 809**
FIELD, R/ General store./ c1926, 1988/ P-3 KF548 . . . . **E**
 Prayer for a child./ 1973/ K-3/4 KA713 . . . . **242**
FIELD, S/ LITTLE BOOK OF LOVE./ 1995/ 4-6 KD886 . . . . . . **808.81**
FIENBERG, A/ Vico y boa./ 1992/ 5-6/7 KH113 . . . . **FIC**
 Wiggy and Boa./ c1988, 1990/ 5-6/7 KH113 . . . . **FIC**
FIESER, S/ Sabbath lion: a Jewish folktale from Algeria./ 1992/
 4-6/6 KB511 . . . . **398.23**
 Silk Route: 7,000 miles of history./ c1995, 1996/ 4-6/6 KE701 . . **950**
 Wonder child and other Jewish fairy tales./ 1996/ 2-4/5 KB369 **398.2**
FILBIN, D/ Arizona./ 1991/ 4-6/7 KF067 . . . . **979.1**
FILLING, G/ TAKE ME TO YOUR LITER: SCIENCE AND MATH JOKES./
 1991/ 3-6 KD740 . . . . **793.735**
FINE, H/ Piggie Pie!/ 1995/ 1-5/2 KG207 . . . . **E**
FINE, JC/ Free spirits in the sky./ 1994/ 2-5/7 KD853 . . . . **797.5**
FINKELSTEIN, NH/ Other 1492: Jewish settlement in the new world./
 1992/ 5-6/8 KE687 . . . . **946**
FIORE, PM/ HAND IN HAND: AN AMERICAN HISTORY THROUGH
 POETRY./ 1994/ 2-6 KE063 . . . . **811.008**
FIRTH, B/ Can't you sleep, Little Bear? 2nd ed./ c1988, 1992/
 P-K/3 KG674 . . . . **E**
 Let's go home, Little Bear./ 1993/ P-K/3 KG676 . . . . **E**
 You and me, Little Bear./ 1996/ P-K/1 KG677 . . . . **E**
FISCHER, H/ Puss in boots: a fairy tale./ 1996/ K-3/5 KB634 . . **398.24**
FISCHER-NAGEL, A/ Fir trees./ 1989/ 3-6/7 KC436 . . . . **585**
 Housefly./ 1990/ 5-6/7 KC556 . . . . **595.77**
 Life of the honeybee./ 1986/ 4-6/7 KC572 . . . . **595.79**
 Life of the ladybug./ 1986/ 5-6/9 KC551 . . . . **595.76**
 Look through the mouse hole./ 1989/ 4-6/6 KC743 . . . . . . **599.35**
FISCHER-NAGEL, H/ Fir trees./ 1989/ 3-6/7 KC436 . . . . **585**
 Housefly./ 1990/ 5-6/7 KC556 . . . . **595.77**
 Life of the honeybee./ 1986/ 4-6/7 KC572 . . . . **595.79**
 Life of the ladybug./ 1986/ 5-6/9 KC551 . . . . **595.76**
 Look through the mouse hole./ 1989/ 4-6/6 KC743 . . . . . . **599.35**
FISCHMAN, S/ Boxing champion./ 1991/ 4-6/2 KG976 . . . . **FIC**
 Longest home run./ 1993/ 2-4/4 KG977 . . . . **FIC**
FISHER, AL/ Story of Easter./ 1997/ 2-3/2 KA714 . . . . **263**
FISHER, C/ Be ready at eight./ 1996/ 1-2/1 KG212 . . . . **E**
 Calculator riddles./ 1995/ 3-6 KD722 . . . . **793.735**
 Easy math puzzles./ 1997/ K-3 KD723 . . . . **793.735**
 Let's make magic./ 1992/ 3-6 KD747 . . . . **793.8**

School mouse./ 1995/ 3-5/7 KH353 . . . . **FIC**
FISHER, GL/ School survival guide for kids with LD (Learning differences)./
 1991/ 4-6/4 KB093 . . . . **371.92**
 Survival guide for kids with LD (Learning differences)./ 1990/
 4-6/4 KB094 . . . . **371.92**
FISHER, LE/ Cabinetmakers./ 1997/ 3-6/7 KD343 . . . . **684.1**
 Cyclops./ 1991/ 1-6/4 KA739 . . . . **292**
 Festivals./ 1996/ 3-6 KD976 . . . . **811**
 Gandhi./ 1995/ 3-6/8 KE362 . . . . **B GANDHI, M.**
 Glassmakers./ 1997/ 3-6/7 KD323 . . . . **666**
 Great Wall of China./ 1986/ 3-6/3 KE630 . . . . **931**
 Great Wall of China (Sound recording cassette)./ n.d./
 3-6/3 KE630 . . . . **931**
 Gutenberg./ 1993/ 5-A/8 KE382 . . . . **B GUTENBERG, J.**
 Kinderdike./ 1994/ 2-4/3 KB395 . . . . **398.21**
 Moses./ 1995/ 3-4/3 KA677 . . . . **221.9**
 Olympians: great gods and goddesses of Ancient Greece./ 1984/
 5-6/7 KA740 . . . . **292**
 Prince Henry the Navigator./ 1990/ 4-6/6 KE387 . **B HENRY, PRINCE**
 Schoolmasters./ 1997/ 3-6/7 KB083 . . . . **371.1**
 Stars and Stripes: our national flag./ 1993/ 3-6/7 KE617 . . . . **929.9**
 Statue of Liberty./ 1985/ 5-6/7 KD400 . . . . **735**
 Tanners./ c1966, 1986/ 5-6/7 KD331 . . . . **675**
 Theseus and the Minotaur./ 1988/ 5-6/6 KA741 . . . . **292**
 Three princes: a tale from the Middle East./ 1994/
 2-3/4 KB461 . . . . **398.22**
 Tower of London./ 1987/ 3-6/7 KE679 . . . . **942**
 White House./ 1989/ 5-6/8 KE970 . . . . **975.3**
 White House (Sound recording cassette)./ n.d./ 5-6/8 KE970 . **975.3**
 William Tell./ 1996/ 3-5/4 KB442 . . . . **398.22**
FITTIPALDI, C/ African animal tales./ 1993/ 2-4/6 KB526 . . . . . **398.24**
FITZGERALD, J/ Ten small tales./ 1994/ P-1/2 KB338 . . . . **398.2**
FITZHUGH, L/ Harriet the spy./ c1964/ 3-5/4 KH114 . . . . **FIC**
 Harriet the spy (Braille)./ n.d./ 3-5/4 KH114 . . . . **FIC**
 Harriet the spy (Sound recording cassette)./ n.d./ 3-5/4 KH114 . . . **FIC**
 Harriet the spy (Talking book)./ n.d./ 3-5/4 KH114 . . . . **FIC**
 Long secret./ c1965/ 3-5/4 KH114 . . . . **FIC**
 Long secret (Talking book)./ n.d./ 3-5/4 KH114 . . . . **FIC**
FITZ-RANDOLPH, J/ Mummies, dinosaurs, moon rocks: how we know how
 old things are./ 1996/ 4-6/9 KE625 . . . . **930.1**
FIVE LITTLE DUCKS: AN OLD RHYME./ 1995/ P-1/1 KB797 . . . **398.8**
FLACK, JD/ Inventing, inventions, and inventors: a teaching resource book./
 1989/ KA297 . . . . **PROF 607**
FLACK, M/ Ask Mr. Bear./ c1932/ P-1/2 KF549 . . . . **CE E**
 Ask Mr. Bear (Kit)./ 1990/ P-1/2 KF549 . . . . **CE E**
 Country bunny and the little gold shoes, as told to Jenifer./ c1939/
 P-K/7 KF723 . . . . **E**
 Historia de Ping./ 1996/ P-1/6 KF550 . . . . **CE E**
 Story about Ping./ c1933/ P-1/6 KF550 . . . . **CE E**
 Story about Ping (Braille)./ n.d./ P-1/6 KF550 . . . . **CE E**
 Story about Ping (Kit)./ 1993/ P-1/6 KF550 . . . . **CE E**
 Story about Ping (Talking book)./ n.d./ P-1/6 KF550 . . . . . **CE E**
 Story about Ping (Videocassette)./ 1956/ P-1/6 KF550 . . . . **CE E**
FLANAGAN, A/ Busy day at Mr. Kang's grocery store./ 1996/
 1-3/2 KB126 . . . . **381**
FLEISCHMAN, P/ Borning room./ 1991/ 6-A/5 KH115 . . . . **FIC**
 Borning room (Sound recording cassette)./ 1994/ 6-A/5 KH115 . . **FIC**
 Bull Run./ 1993/ 5-A/5 KH116 . . . . **FIC**
 Bull Run (Sound recording cassette)./ 1995/ 5-A/5 KH116 . . . **FIC**
 Copier creations: using copy machines to make decals, silhouettes, flip
 books, films, and much more!/ 1993/ 3-6/7 KD503 . . . . **760**
 Half-a-Moon Inn./ c1980, 1991/ 6/7 KH117 . . . . **FIC**
 Half-a-Moon Inn (Braille)./ n.d.,/ 6/7 KH117 . . . . **FIC**
 Joyful noise: poems for two voices./ 1988/ 4-6 KD934 . . . . . . **811**
 Joyful noise: poems for two voices (Sound recording cassette)./ n.d./
 4-6 KD934 . . . . **811**
 Seedfolks./ 1997/ 5-A/5 KH118 . . . . **FIC**
 Time train./ 1994/ 1-3/2 KF551 . . . . **E**
FLEISCHMAN, S/ Abracadabra kid: a writer's life./ 1996/
 3-A/7 KE344 . . . . **B FLEISCHMAN, S**
 By the Great Horn Spoon!/ c1963/ 4-6/4 KH119 . . . . **FIC**
 By the Great Horn Spoon! (Sound recording cassette)./ n.d./
 4-6/4 KH119 . . . . **FIC**
 Chancy and the Grand Rascal./ c1966, 1997/ 4-6/5 KH120 . . . **FIC**
 Chancy and the Grand Rascal (Sound recording cassette)./ n.d.,/
 4-6/5 KH120 . . . . **FIC**
 Ghost in the noonday sun./ 1965/ 5-A/7 KH121 . . . . **FIC**
 Ghost on Saturday night./ 1997/ 3-5/4 KH122 . . . . **FIC**
 Ghost on Saturday night (Sound recording cassette)./ n.d./
 3-5/4 KH122 . . . . **FIC**
 Here comes McBroom!: three more tall tales./ 1992/ 3-6/4 KH124 . **FIC**
 Jim Ugly./ 1992/ 4-A/6 KH123 . . . . **FIC**
 Jim Ugly (Sound recording cassette)./ 1995/ 4-A/6 KH123 . . . . . **FIC**

McBroom's wonderful one-acre farm: three tall tales./ 1992/
3-6/4 KH124 . . . . **FIC**
Midnight horse./ 1990/ 5-A/4 KH125 . . . . **FIC**
Mr. Mysterious and Company./ c1962, 1997/ 3-6/6 KH126 . . . . . **FIC**
Scarebird./ 1987/ 1-3/5 KF552 . . . . **E**
13th floor: a ghost story./ 1995/ 5-A/6 KH127 . . . . **CE FIC**
13th floor: a ghost story (Talking book)./ 1995/ 5-A/6 KH127 . . **CE FIC**
FLEISHER, P/ Ecology A to Z./ 1992/ 6-A KA410 . . . . **REF 363.7**
Our oceans: experiments and activities in marine science./ 1995/
4-6/7 KC172 . . . . **551.46**
FLEISHMAN, S/ Memoirs of Andrew Sherburne: patriot and privateer of
the American Revolution./ 1993/ 5-A/8 KE886 . . . . **973.3**
FLEMING, A/ What, me worry?: how to hang in when your problems stress
you out./ 1992/ 4-6/8 KA624 . . . . **152.4**
FLEMING, C/ Women of the lights./ 1996/ 4-6/6 KB148 . . . . . . **387.1**
FLEMING, D/ Barnyard banter./ 1994/ P-1/3 KF553 . . . . **E**
Count!/ 1992/ P-K KF554 . . . . **E**
In the small, small pond./ 1993/ P-2/1 KF555 . . . . **E**
In the tall, tall grass./ 1991/ P-K/1 KF556 . . . . **E**
Lunch./ 1992/ P-K/2 KF557 . . . . **E**
Time to sleep./ 1997/ P-1/2 KF558 . . . . **E**
Where once there was a wood./ 1996/ 1-4/3 KD253 . . . . . . **639.9**
FLEMING, I/ Chitty Chitty Bang Bang: the magical car./ c1964, 1989/
5-6/7 KH128 . . . . **FIC**
FLETCHER, N/ Penguin./ 1993/ P-1/2 KC687 . . . . **598.47**
FLETCHER, R/ Fig pudding./ 1995/ 5-A/4 KH129 . . . . **FIC**
FLIGHT, N/ British Columbia./ 1994/ 5-A/9 KE810 . . . . **971.1**
FLOCA, B/ City of light, city of dark: a comic-book novel./ 1993/
4-6/6 KD409 . . . . **741.5**
Jenius: the amazing guinea pig./ 1996/ 2-4/5 KH349 . . . . . **FIC**
Poppy./ 1995/ 3-5/6 KG862 . . . . **FIC**
FLOOD, NB/ From the mouth of the monster eel: stories from Micronesia./
1996/ 2-5/5 KB296 . . . . **398.2**
FLORA, J/ Fabulous Firework Family./ 1994/ 1-3/4 KF559 . . . . . **E**
FLORCZAK, R/ Rainbow bridge: inspired by a Chumash tale./ 1995/
3-5/4 KB675 . . . . **398.24**
FLORIAN, D/ Auto mechanic./ 1994/ P-2/3 KD128 . . . . . . **629.28**
Beast feast./ 1994/ K-3 KD935 . . . . **811**
Bing bang boing./ 1994/ 3-6 KD936 . . . . **811**
Chef./ 1992/ K-2/5 KD270 . . . . **641.5**
City street./ 1990/ P-1 KA893 . . . . **307.3**
Discovering seashells./ 1986/ 4-5/7 KC511 . . . . **594**
Fisher./ 1994/ 1-3/5 KD244 . . . . **639.2**
In the swim: poems and paintings./ 1997/ 1-3 KD937 . . . . . . **811**
Monster Motel: poems and paintings./ 1993/ 4-6 KD938 . . . . . **811**
Nature walk./ 1989/ P-1 KB922 . . . . **508.3**
On the wing: bird poems and paintings./ 1996/ 1-4 KD939 . . . . **811**
Painter./ 1993/ 1-2/4 KD464 . . . . **750**
Summer day./ 1988/ P-1/1 KF560 . . . . **E**
Very scary./ 1995/ P-2/3 KF842 . . . . **E**
Winter day./ 1987/ P-1/1 KF560 . . . . **E**
FLOURNOY, V/
Celie and the harvest fiddler./ Celie and the harvest fiddler./ 1995/
1995/ 2-4/6 KH130 . . . . **FIC**
2-4/6 KH130 . . . . **FIC**
Patchwork quilt./ 1985/ K-3/5 KF561 . . . . **E**
Patchwork quilt (Braille)./ n.d./ K-3/5 KF561 . . . . **E**
Tanya's reunion./ 1995/ K-3/3 KF562 . . . . **E**
FOA, M/ Odin's family: myths of the Vikings./ 1996/
3-A/6 KA757 . . . . **293**
SONGS ARE THOUGHTS: POEMS OF THE INUIT./ 1995/
4-6 KE140 . . . . **897**
FODEMSKI, LC/ Connecting kids and the Internet: a handbook for
librarians, teachers, and parents./ 1996/ KA048 . . . . . **PROF 025.06**
FOLKENS, P/ Great whales: the gentle giants./ 1993/
4-5/4 KC773 . . . . **599.5**
FOLKTELLERS/ Stories for the road (Sound recording cassette)./ 1992/
5-A KB297 . . . . **SRC 398.2**
Storytelling: tales and techniques (Videocassette)./ 1994/
KA245 . . . . **VCR PROF 372.67**
Tales to grow on (Sound recording cassette)./ c1981/
K-3 KB298 . . . . **SRC 398.2**
FOLSOM, M/
Easy as pie: a guessing game of sayings./ Easy as pie: a guessing game
of sayings./ 1985/ 1985/ 1-3/3 KF564 . . . . **E**
1-3/3 KF564 . . . . **E**
FONG, A/ Made in China: ideas and inventions from Ancient China./
1996/ 4-6/6 KE631 . . . . **931**
FONTANEL, B/ Penguin: a funny bird./ 1992/ 1-4/4 KC688 . . . **598.47**
FONTEYN, M/ Swan Lake./ 1989/ 4-6/7 KD693 . . . . **CE 792.8**
Swan Lake (Kit)./ 1991/ 4-6/7 KD693 . . . . **CE 792.8**
FOR LAUGHING OUT LOUD: POEMS TO TICKLE YOUR FUNNYBONE./
1991/ K-5 KE058 . . . . **811.008**
/ 1993/ K-5 KE058 . . . . **811.008**

FOR LAUGHING OUT LOUDER: MORE POEMS TO TICKLE YOUR
FUNNYBONE./ 1995/ K-5 KE059 . . . . **811.008**
FORBES, E/ America's Paul Revere./ c1946/ A/7 KE509 . **B REVERE, P.**
America's Paul Revere (Braille)./ n.d./ A/7 KE509 . . . . . **B REVERE, P.**
Johnny Tremain: a novel for old and young./ c1943, 1971/
4-6/6 KH131 . . . . **CE FIC**
Johnny Tremain: a novel for old and young (Braille)./ n.d.,/
4-6/6 KH131 . . . . **CE FIC**
Johnny Tremain: a novel for old and young (Sound recording cassette)./
n.d.,/ 4-6/6 KH131 . . . . **CE FIC**
Johnny Tremain: a novel for old and young (Talking book)./ Johnny
Tremain: a novel for old and young (Talking book)./ 1970/, n.d.,/
4-6/6 KH131 . . . . **CE FIC**
4-6/6 KH131 . . . . **CE FIC**
FORD, B/ Automobile./ 1987/ 5-6/8 KD114 . . . . **629.222**
Howard Carter: searching for King Tut./ 1995/
A/9 KE279 . . . . **B CARTER, H.**
Hunter who was king and other African tales./ 1994/
K-3/4 KB299 . . . . **398.2**
Most wonderful movie in the world./ 1996/ 6-A/4 KH132 . . . . . **FIC**
FORD, G/ Hunter who was king and other African tales./ 1994/
K-3/4 KB299 . . . . **398.2**
Story of Ruby Bridges./ 1995/ 2-5/4 KA902 . . . . **323.1**
FORD, M/ Little elephant./ 1994/ P-K/1 KF565 . . . . **E**
Sunflower./ 1995/ P-1/1 KF566 . . . . **E**
FOREMAN, M/ Arabian nights, or, Tales told by Sheherezade during a
thousand nights and one night./ 1995/ 5-A/7 KB253 . . . **398.2**
Little ships: the heroic rescue at Dunkirk in World War II./ 1997/
3-5/3 KF251 . . . . **E**
Michael Foreman's Mother Goose./ 1991/ P-1 KB804 . . . . . . **398.8**
Robin of Sherwood./ 1996/ 5-A/6 KH514 . . . . **FIC**
War boy: a country childhood./ 1990/
4-A/6 KE347 . . . . **B FOREMAN, M.**
FOREST, H/ Songspinner: folktales and fables sung and told (Sound
recording cassette)./ 1982/ 2-4 KB735 . . . . **SRC 398.27**
Tales of womenfolk (Sound recording cassette)./ 1985/
2-4 KB735 . . . . **SRC 398.27**
Woman who flummoxed the fairies: an old tale from Scotland./ 1990/
3-4/5 KB396 . . . . **398.21**
Wonder tales from around the world./ 1995/ 3-5/6 KB300 . . . **398.2**
FORNARI, G/ Body atlas./ 1993/ A/7 KC905 . . . . **611**
Inside the body: a lift-the-flap book./ 1996/ 5-6/7 KC902 . . . . **611**
FORRESTER, S/ Sound the jubilee./ 1995/ 5-A/4 KH133 . . . . . **FIC**
Sound the jubilee (Sound recording cassette)./ 1997/
5-A/6 KH133 . . . . **FIC**
FORSHAW, J/ Birding./ c1994, 1995/ 5-6/8 KA448 . . . . . . **REF 598**
FORSYTH, A/ How monkeys make chocolate: foods and medicines from the
rainforest./ 1995/ 4-8/7 KC402 . . . . **581.6**
FORSYTH, EH/ Know about AIDS. 3rd ed./ 1994/
5-6/8 KD030 . . . . **616.97**
FORTNUM, P/ Bear called Paddington./ c1958/ 2-4/5 KG916 . . . . **FIC**
Paddington's storybook./ 1984/ 3-6/5 KG918 . . . . **FIC**
FORWARD, T/ Ben's Christmas carol./ 1996/ 2-3/4 KF567 . . . . . . **E**
Traveling backward./ 1994/ 4-6/4 KH134 . . . . **FIC**
FOSTER, J/ DRAGON POEMS./ 1991/ K-A KE055 . . . . **811.008**
Magpies' nest./ 1995/ 1-3/3 KB567 . . . . **398.24**
FOSTER, K/ CRAFTS FOR DECORATION./ 1993/
3-6/7 KD451 . . . . **745.594**
CRAFTS FOR PLAY./ 1993/ 3-6/7 KD445 . . . . **745.592**
FOUDRAY, RS/ NEWBERY AND CALDECOTT MEDALISTS AND HONOR
BOOK WINNERS: BIBLIOGRAPHIES AND RESOURCE MATERIAL
THROUGH 1991. 2nd ed./ 1992/ KA004 . . . . **PROF 011**
FOUNTAIN, JF/ Subject headings for school and public libraries: an
LCSH/Sears companion. 2nd ed./ 1996/ KA059 . . . . . **PROF 025.4**
FOWLER, A/ Como sabes que es otono?/ 1992/ P-2/2 KB917 . . **508.2**
Como sabes que es otono? (Big book)./ 1992/ P-2/2 KB917 . . **508.2**
Como sabes que es primavera?/ 1994/ P-2/2 KB917 . . . . . . **508.2**
Como sabes que es verano?/ 1992/ P-2/2 KB917 . . . . **508.2**
Como sabes que es verano? (Big book)./ 1992/ P-2/2 KB917 . . **508.2**
Gracias a las vacas (Big book)./ 1992/ K-2/2 KD238 . . . . . . **637**
How do you know it's fall?/ 1992/ P-2/2 KB917 . . . . **508.2**
How do you know it's fall? (Big book)./ 1992/ P-2/2 KB917 . . **508.2**
How do you know it's spring?/ 1991/ P-2/2 KB917 . . . . **508.2**
How do you know it's spring? (Big book)./ 1991/ P-2/2 KB917 . . **508.2**
How do you know it's summer?/ 1992/ P-2/2 KB917 . . . . . . **508.2**
How do you know it's summer? (Big book)./ 1992/
P-2/2 KB917 . . . . **508.2**
How do you know it's winter?/ 1991/ P-2/2 KB917 . . . . **508.2**
How do you know it's winter? (Big book)./ 1991/ P-2/2 KB917 . . **508.2**
It could still be water./ 1992/ P-2/2 KC231 . . . . **553.7**
It could still be water (Big book)./ 1992/ P-2/2 KC231 . . . . . **553.7**
Library of Congress./ 1996/ 3-6/11 KA587 . . . . **027.5**
Thanks to cows./ 1992/ K-2/2 KD238 . . . . **637**
Thanks to cows (Big book)./ 1992/ K-2/2 KD238 . . . . **637**

Y aun podria ser agua./ 1993/ P-2/2 KC231 . . . .   **553.7**
FOWLER, J/ I'll see you when the moon is full./ 1994/ K-2/2 KF568 . . **E**
FOWLER, SG/ I'll see you when the moon is full./ 1994/
K-2/2 KF568 . . . . **E**
FOX, D/ GO IN AND OUT THE WINDOW: AN ILLUSTRATED
SONGBOOK FOR YOUNG PEOPLE./ 1987/ 2-A KD564 . . .   **789.2**
SONGS OF THE WILD WEST./ 1991/ 2-A KD597 . . . .   **789.2**
FOX, M/ Guillermo Jorge Manuel Jose./ n.d./ K-3/6 KF574 . . . . **E**
Hattie and the fox./ 1987/ P-2/2 KF569 . . . . **E**
Hattie and the fox (Big book)./ 1988/ P-2/2 KF569 . . . . **E**
Mem Fox reads (Talking book)./ 1992/ P-2 KF570 . . . . **TB E**
Possum magic./ c1983, 1990/ P-2/4 KF571 . . . . **E**
Time for bed./ 1993/ P-1/2 KF572 . . . . **E**
Time for bed (Big book)./ 1996/ P-1/2 KF572 . . . . **E**
Tough Boris./ 1994/ K-2/2 KF573 . . . . **E**
Whoever you are./ 1997/ P-1/1 KA843 . . . . **305.8**
Wilfrid Gordon McDonald Partridge./ 1985/ K-3/6 KF574 . . . . . . **E**
Wilfrid Gordon McDonald Partridge (Big book)./ 1995/
K-3/6 KF574 . . . . **E**
FOX, P/ Likely place./ c1967, 1986/ 4-6/4 KH135 . . . . **FIC**
Little swineherd and other tales./ 1996/ 3-6/4 KH136 . . . . **FIC**
Monkey island./ 1991/ 6-A/6 KH137 . . . . **FIC**
Monkey island (Sound recording cassette)./ 1993/ 6-A/6 KH137 . **FIC**
One-eyed cat./ 1984/ A/7 KH138 . . . . **FIC**
One-eyed cat (Sound recording cassette)./ n.d./ A/7 KH138 . . . . **FIC**
Slave dancer: a novel./ c1973/ 5-6/6 KH139 . . . . **CE FIC**
Slave dancer: a novel (Braille)./ n.d./ 5-6/6 KH139 . . . . **CE FIC**
Slave dancer: a novel (Sound recording cassette)./ n.d./
5-6/6 KH139 . . . . **CE FIC**
Slave dancer: a novel (Talking book)./ 1996/ 5-6/6 KH139 . . **CE FIC**
Stone-faced boy./ 1987/ 4-6/3 KH140 . . . . **FIC**
Stone-faced boy (Braille)./ n.d./ 4-6/3 KH140 . . . . **FIC**
Western wind: a novel./ 1993/ 5-A/5 KH141 . . . . **FIC**
Western wind: a novel (Sound recording cassette)./ 1995/
5-A/5 KH141 . . . . **FIC**
FOX-DAVIES, S/ Little Beaver and The Echo./ 1990/ P-K/1 KG049 . . **E**
FRADIN, DB/ Arkansas./ 1994/ 4-6/4 KF008 . . . . **976.7**
Colorado./ 1993/ 3-6/3 KF061 . . . . **978.8**
Connecticut./ 1994/ 4-6/4 KE952 . . . . **974.6**
Delaware./ 1994/ 4-6/3 KE968 . . . . **975.1**
Earth./ 1989/ 4-5/4 KC058 . . . . **525**
Georgia Colony./ 1989/ 5-6/7 KE988 . . . . **975.8**
Hiawatha: messenger of peace./ 1992/ 5-6/7 KE389 . . **B HIAWATHA**
Indiana./ 1994/ 4-6/3 KF014 . . . . **977.2**
Louisiana./ 1995/ 4-6/4 KF000 . . . . **976.3**
Maine./ 1994/ 4-6/4 KE928 . . . . **974.1**
Maryland./ 1994/ 4-6/3 KE969 . . . . **975.2**
Minnesota./ 1994/ 4-6/3 KF021 . . . . **977.6**
Missouri./ 1994/ 4-6/4 KF023 . . . . **977.8**
New Hampshire Colony./ 1988/ 5-6/9 KE931 . . . . **974.2**
New Jersey Colony./ 1991/ 5-6/7 KE963 . . . . **974.9**
New York./ 1993/ 4-6/3 KE955 . . . . **974.7**
New York Colony./ 1988/ 5-6/8 KE956 . . . . **974.7**
North Carolina Colony./ 1991/ 5-6/7 KE982 . . . . **975.6**
North Dakota./ 1994/ 4-6/3 KF057 . . . . **978.4**
Oklahoma./ 1995/ 4-6/4 KF005 . . . . **976.6**
Oregon./ 1995/ 4-6/4 KF089 . . . . **979.5**
Pennsylvania Colony./ 1988/ 5-6/7 KE959 . . . . **974.8**
Rhode Island Colony./ 1989/ 5-6/7 KE951 . . . . **974.5**
South Carolina./ 1992/ 4-6/5 KE984 . . . . **975.7**
South Carolina Colony./ 1992/ A/7 KE985 . . . . **975.7**
South Dakota./ 1995/ 4-6/7 KF056 . . . . **978.3**
Tennessee./ 1992/ 4-6/2 KF009 . . . . **976.8**
Vermont./ 1993/ 4-6/4 KE934 . . . . **974.3**
Virginia Colony./ 1986/ A/10 KE977 . . . . **975.5**
Washington./ 1994/ 4-6/4 KF093 . . . . **979.7**
West Virginia./ 1994/ 4-6/7 KE975 . . . . **975.4**
FRADIN, JB/ Arkansas./ 1994/ 4-6/4 KF008 . . . . **976.7**
Connecticut./ 1994/ 4-6/4 KE952 . . . . **974.6**
Delaware./ 1994/ 4-6/3 KE968 . . . . **975.1**
Indiana./ 1994/ 4-6/3 KF014 . . . . **977.2**
Louisiana./ 1995/ 4-6/4 KF000 . . . . **976.3**
Minnesota./ 1994/ 4-6/3 KF021 . . . . **977.6**
Missouri./ 1994/ 4-6/4 KF023 . . . . **977.8**
North Dakota./ 1994/ 4-6/3 KF057 . . . . **978.4**
Oklahoma./ 1995/ 4-6/4 KF005 . . . . **976.6**
Oregon./ 1995/ 4-6/4 KF089 . . . . **979.5**
South Dakota./ 1995/ 4-6/7 KF056 . . . . **978.3**
Washington./ 1994/ 4-6/4 KF093 . . . . **979.7**
West Virginia./ 1994/ 4-6/7 KE975 . . . . **975.4**
FRADON, D/ King's fool: a book about medieval and renaissance fools./
1993/ 4-6/7 KE647 . . . . **940.1**
FRAME, P/ Katie John./ c1960/ 4-6/4 KG966 . . . . **FIC**

FRAMPTON, D/ Miro in the Kingdom of the Sun./ 1996/
3-4/5 KB505 . . . . **398.23**
Of swords and sorcerers: the adventures of King Arthur and his knights./
1993/ 4-5/6 KB452 . . . . **398.22**
FRANCIS, J/ Bicycling./ 1996/ 3-6/6 KD827 . . . . **796.6**
FRANK, A/ Diary of a young girl./ c1967/ 4-6/6 KE352 . **B FRANK, A.**
Diary of a young girl (Braille)./ n.d./ 4-6/6 KE352 . . . . **B FRANK, A.**
Diary of a young girl (Sound recording cassette)./ n.d./
4-6/6 KE352 . . . . **B FRANK, A.**
Diary of a young girl (Talking book)./ n.d./
4-6/6 KE352 . . . . **B FRANK, A.**
FRANK, J/ SNOW TOWARD EVENING: A YEAR IN A RIVER VALLEY:
NATURE POEMS./ 1995/ 2-6 KE082 . . . . **811.008**
FRANKLIN INSTITUTE (PHILADELPHIA, PA.). SCIENCE MUSEUM./ BEN
FRANKLIN BOOK OF EASY AND INCREDIBLE EXPERIMENTS./ 1995/
A/8 KB889 . . . . **507.8**
FRANKLIN, KL/ Iguana Beach./ 1997/ P-1/2 KF575 . . . . **E**
Wolfhound./ 1996/ 1-3/3 KF576 . . . . **E**
FRANSWORTH, B/ Christmas menorahs: how a town fought hate./ 1995/
3-6/5 KA818 . . . . **305**
FRASCINO, E/ Trumpet of the swan./ c1970/ 3-6/6 KH852 . . . . . **FIC**
FRASER, D/ David and Goliath (Videocassette)./ 1992/
2-4 KA686 . . . . **VCR 222**
FRASER, MA/ Holiday origami./ 1995/ 3-6 KD403 . . . . **736**
In search of the Grand Canyon./ 1995/ 3-5/6 KF068 . . . . . . **979.1**
Ten mile day and the building of the transcontinental railroad./ c1993,
1996/ 5-6/7 KB139 . . . . **385**
FRASIER, D/ On the day you were born./ 1991/ P-3/5 KF577 . . . . **E**
ON THE DAY YOU WERE BORN (Videocassette)./ 1996/
P-A KG192 . . . . **VCR E**
FRAZEE, M/ That Kookoory!/ 1995/ K-2/3 KF588 . . . . **E**
FREDEEN, C/ Kansas./ 1992/ 4-6/5 KF053 . . . . **978.1**
New Jersey./ 1993/ 4-6/5 KE964 . . . . **974.9**
South Carolina./ 1991/ 4-6/6 KE986 . . . . **975.7**
FREDERICK, R/ Dog who dared (Videocassette)./ 1993/
4-6 KC993 . . . . **VCR 613.8**
FREDERICKS, AD/ Complete guide to thematic units: creating the integrated
curriculum./ 1995/ KA195 . . . . **PROF 372.19**
Complete science fair handbook./ 1990/ KA286 . . . . . . **PROF 507.8**
Frantic frogs and other frankly fractured folktales for readers theatre./
1993/ KA362 . . . . **PROF 812**
Social studies through children's literature: an integrated approach./
1991/ KA260 . . . . **PROF 372.83**
FREDERICKS, PD/ Complete science fair handbook./ 1990/
KA286 . . . . **PROF 507.8**
FREDERICKS, RN/ Social studies through children's literature: an integrated
approach./ 1991/ KA260 . . . . **PROF 372.83**
FREEDMAN, D/ MATH FOR THE VERY YOUNG: A HANDBOOK OF
ACTIVITIES FOR PARENTS AND TEACHERS./ 1995/
KA254 . . . . **PROF 372.7**
FREEDMAN, R/ Buffalo hunt./ 1988/ 4-6/7 KE787 . . . . **970.48**
Children of the wild west./ 1983/ 4-6/8 KA824 . . . . **305.23**
Children of the wild west (Sound recording cassette)./ n.d./
4-6/8 KA824 . . . . **305.23**
Cowboys of the wild west./ 1985/ 5-A/7 KF029 . . . . **978**
Eleanor Roosevelt: a life of discovery./ 1993/
6-A/7 KE521 . . . . **B ROOSEVELT, E.**
Franklin Delano Roosevelt./ 1990/ 6-A/7 KE522 . . . **B ROOSEVELT, F.**
Indian chiefs./ 1987/ 5-6/8 KE749 . . . . **970.1**
Indian winter./ 1992/ A/9 KE202 . . . . **917.804**
Kids at work: Lewis Hine and the crusade against child labor./ 1994/
5-A/8 KA937 . . . . **331.3**
Life and death of Crazy Horse./ 1996/
6-A/7 KE307 . . . . **B CRAZY HORSE**
Lincoln, a photobiography./ 1987/ A/11 KE441 . . . . **B LINCOLN, A.**
Out of darkness: the story of Louis Braille./ 1997/
3-5/6 KE262 . . . . **B BRAILLE, L.**
Wright brothers: how they invented the airplane./ 1991/
A/7 KD094 . . . . **629.13**
Wright brothers: how they invented the airplane (Sound recording
cassette)./ 1993/ A/7 KD094 . . . . **629.13**
FREEMAN, B/ Tales to grow on (Sound recording cassette)./ c1981/
K-3 KB298 . . . . **SRC 398.2**
FREEMAN, D/ Bolsillo para Corduroy./ 1992/ P-2/2 KF581 . . . . **CE E**
Bolsillo para Corduroy (Kit)./ 1992/ P-2/2 KF581 . . . . **CE E**
Corduroy./ Corduroy./ c1968/ 1988/ P-2/2 KF578 . . . . . . **CE E**
P-2/2 KF578 . . . . **CE E**
Corduroy (Kit)./ 1982/ P-2/2 KF578 . . . . **CE E**
Corduroy (Talking book)./ n.d./ P-2/2 KF578 . . . . **CE E**
Corduroy (Videocassette)./ n.d./ P-2/2 KF578 . . . . **CE E**
Dandelion./ c1964/ K-1/2 KF579 . . . . **CE E**
Dandelion (Kit)./ 1982/ K-1/2 KF579 . . . . **CE E**
Norman the doorman./ c1959/ K-1/7 KF580 . . . . **CE E**
Norman the doorman (Talking book)./ n.d./ K-1/7 KF580 . . . . **CE E**

Norman the doorman (Videocassette)./ n.d./ K-1/7 KF580 . . . . . **CE E**
Pet of the Met./ c1953/ 1-2/7 KF582 . . . . **CE E**
Pocket for Corduroy./ 1978/ P-2/2 KF581 . . . . **CE E**
Pocket for Corduroy (Braille)./ n.d./ P-2/2 KF581 . . . . **CE E**
FREEMAN, J/ Books kids will sit still for: the complete read-aloud guide.
  2nd ed./ 1990/ KA015 . . . . **PROF 011.62**
FREEMAN, L/ Pet of the Met./ c1953/ 1-2/7 KF582 . . . . **E**
Talking to Faith Ringgold./ 1996/ 4-6/6 KD379 . . . . **709.2**
FREEMAN, M/ FOLLOW THE DRINKING GOURD./ 1993/
  2-4 KF563 . . . . **BA E**
Follow the drinking gourd: a story of the Underground Railroad
  (Videocassette)./ 1992/ 2-4 KF412 . . . . **VCR E**
Savior is born (Kit)./ 1992/ 3-5 KA705 . . . . **KIT 232.92**
FREEMAN, S/ Cuckoo's child./ 1996/ 5-A/5 KH142 . . . . **FIC**
FRENCH, F/ Anancy and Mr. Dry-Bone./ 1991/ K-2/2 KF583 . . . . . . **E**
Lord of the animals: a Miwok Indian creation myth./ 1997/
  K-3/4 KB568 . . . . **398.24**
Pepi and the secret names./ 1995/ 2-3/6 KG683 . . . . **E**
FRENCH, V/ Lazy Jack./ 1995/ K-2/2 KB301 . . . . **398.2**
Red Hen and Sly Fox./ 1995/ P-2/2 KF584 . . . . **E**
FREY, PD/ EXPLORING THE NORTHEAST STATES THROUGH
  LITERATURE./ 1994/ KA036 . . . . **PROF 016.974**
FRICKER, S/ Creature features./ 1997/ 3-6/6 KC447 . . . . **591**
FRIEDMAN, A/ Cloak for the dreamer./ 1995/ 1-3/6 KF585 . . . . . . **E**
FRIEDMAN, IR/ How my parents learned to eat./ 1984/ 1-3/2 KF586 . **E**
How my parents learned to eat (Sound recording cassette)./ n.d./
  1-3/2 KF586 . . . . **E**
FRIEDMAN, J/ Hanukkah: eight lights around the world./ 1988/
  3-5/5 KH774 . . . . **FIC**
I speak English for my mom./ 1989/ 2-4/2 KH747 . . . . **FIC**
Losing Uncle Tim./ 1989/ 3-5/4 KH336 . . . . **FIC**
FRIEDMAN, LB/ Teaching thinking skills: English/language arts./ 1987/
  KA280 . . . . **PROF 428**
FRIEDMANN, S/ Macmillan book of baseball stories./ 1992/
  4-A/5 KD796 . . . . **796.357**
FRIEDRICH, O/ Easter Bunny that overslept./ 1983/ P-K KF587 . . . . **E**
FRIEDRICH, P/ Easter Bunny that overslept./ 1983/ P-K KF587 . . . . **E**
FRISCH, C/ Wyoming./ 1994/ 4-6/7 KF059 . . . . **978.7**
FRISKEY, M/ Birds we know./ 1981/ P-2/2 KC649 . . . . **598**
FRITZ, J/ And then what happened, Paul Revere?/ c1973/
  5-6/6 KE510 . . . . **CE B REVERE, P.**
And then what happened, Paul Revere? (Sound recording cassette)./
  n.d./ 5-6/6 KE510 . . . . **CE B REVERE, P.**
And then what happened, Paul Revere? (Talking book)./ 1977/
  5-6/6 KE510 . . . . **CE B REVERE, P.**
Around the world in 100 years: from Henry the Navigator to Magellan./
  1994/ 5-A/7 KE164 . . . . **910.92**
Around the world in 100 years: from Henry the Navigator to Megellan
  (Sound recording cassette)./ 1996/ 5-A/7 KE164 . . . . **910.92**
Bully for you, Teddy Roosevelt!/ 1991/
  5-6/6 KE523 . . . . **B ROOSEVELT, T.**
Bully for you, Teddy Roosevelt (Sound recording cassette)./ 1993/
  5-6/6 KE523 . . . . **B ROOSEVELT, T.**
Cabin faced west./ c1958/ 4-6/6 KH143 . . . . **FIC**
Can't you make them behave, King George?/ c1977/
  5-6/7 KE365 . . . . **CE B GEORGE III**
Can't you make them behave, King George? (Talking book)./ 1977/
  5-6/7 KE365 . . . . **CE B GEORGE III**
China homecoming./ 1985/ 4-6/7 KE703 . . . . **951.05**
China homecoming (Sound recording cassette)./ n.d./
  4-6/7 KE703 . . . . **951.05**
China's long march: 6,000 miles of danger./ 1988/ A/6 KE702 **951.04**
Double life of Pocahontas./ 1983/ 5-6/6 KE500 . . . . **B POCAHONTAS**
Double life of Pocahontas (Sound recording cassette)./ n.d./
  5-6/6 KE500 . . . . **B POCAHONTAS**
Early thunder./ c1967, 1987/ 5-A/6 KH144 . . . . **FIC**
Early thunder (Talking book)./ n.d., 5-A/6 KH144 . . . . **FIC**
Great little Madison./ 1989/ 5-A/8 KE453 . . . . . . **B MADISON, J.**
Harriet Beecher Stowe and the Beecher preachers./ 1994/
  6-A/7 KE556 . . . . **B STOWE, H.**
Homesick: my own story./ 1982/ 4-A/4 KH145 . . . . **FIC**
Homesick; my own story (Sound recording cassette)./ n.d./
  4-A/4 KH145 . . . . **FIC**
Make way for Sam Houston./ 1986/ 6/7 KE392 . . . **B HOUSTON, S.**
Make way for Sam Houston (Sound recording cassette)./ n.d./
  6/7 KE392 . . . . **B HOUSTON, S.**
Shh! We're writing the Constitution./ 1987/ 3-6/6 KA971 . **CE 342.73**
Stonewall./ 1979/ 5-A/8 KE399 . . . . **B JACKSON, T.**
Stonewall (Sound recording cassette)./ n.d./
  5-A/8 KE399 . . . . **B JACKSON, T.**
What's the big idea, Ben Franklin?/ c1976/
  5-6/7 KE355 . . . . **CE B FRANKLIN, B.**
What's the big idea, Ben Franklin? (Kit)./ 1977/
  5-6/7 KE355 . . . . **CE B FRANKLIN, B.**

What's the big idea, Ben Franklin? (Sound recording cassette)./ n.d./
  5-6/7 KE355 . . . . **CE B FRANKLIN, B.**
What's the big idea, Ben Franklin? (Talking book)./ 1977/
  5-6/7 KE355 . . . . **CE B FRANKLIN, B.**
What's the big idea, Ben Franklin? (Videocassette)./ 1993/
  5-6/7 KE355 . . . . **CE B FRANKLIN, B.**
Where do you think you're going, Christopher Columbus?/ 1980/
  4-6/6 KE303 . . . . **CE B COLUMBUS, C.**
Where do you think you're going, Christopher Columbus? (Sound
  recording cassette)./ n.d./ 4-6/6 KE303 . . . . **CE B COLUMBUS, C.**
Where do you think you're going, Christopher Columbus? (Talking book)./
  1982/ 4-6/6 KE303 . . . . **CE B COLUMBUS, C.**
Where do you think you're going, Christopher Columbus?
  (Videocassette)./ 1991/ 4-6/6 KE303 . . . . . . **CE B COLUMBUS, C.**
Where was Patrick Henry on the 29th of May?/ c1975, 1982/
  5-6/7 KE386 . . . . **CE B HENRY, P.**
Where was Patrick Henry on the 29th of May? (Sound recording
  cassette)./ n.d./ 5-6/7 KE386 . . . . **CE B HENRY, P.**
Where was Patrick Henry on the 29th of May? (Talking book)./ 1977,/
  5-6/7 KE386 . . . . **CE B HENRY, P.**
Who's that stepping on Plymouth Rock?/ c1975/
  3-5/5 KE940 . . . . **CE 974.4**
Who's that stepping on Plymouth Rock? (Talking book)./ 1982/
  3-5/5 KE940 . . . . **CE 974.4**
Why don't you get a horse, Sam Adams?/ c1974/
  3-5/7 KE227 . . . . **CE B ADAMS, S.**
Will you sign here, John Hancock?/ c1976, 1997/
  5-6/7 KE383 . . . . **CE B HANCOCK, J.**
Will you sign here, John Hancock? (Sound recording cassette)./ n.d.,/
  5-6/7 KE383 . . . . **CE B HANCOCK, J.**
Will you sign here, John Hancock? (Talking book)./ 1977,/
  5-6/7 KE383 . . . . **CE B HANCOCK, J.**
You want women to vote, Lizzie Stanton?/ 1995/
  3-6/5 KE549 . . . . **B STANTON, E.**
FROEHLICH, MW/ That Kookoory!/ 1995/ K-2/3 KF588 . . . . **E**
FROESE, DL/ Wise washerman: a folktale from Burma./ 1996/
  K-2/7 KB569 . . . . **398.24**
FROG INSIDE MY HAT: A FIRST BOOK OF POEMS./ 1993/
  P-1 KD884 . . . . **808.81**
FROMENTAL, J/ Broadway chicken./ 1995/ 5-A/7 KH146 . . . . **FIC**
FROST, MP/ Mexican Revolution./ 1997/ 5-A/11 KE830 . . . . **972**
FROST, R/ Poetry for young people./ 1994/ 4-A KD940 . . . . **811**
Stopping by the woods on a snowy evening./ 1978/ P-A KD941 . . **811**
Swinger of birches: poems of Robert Frost for young people./ 1982/
  3-6 KD942 . . . . **811**
You come too: favorite poems for young readers./ c1959, 1987/
  5-6 KD943 . . . . **811**
You come too: favorite poems for young readers (Braille)./ n.d.,/
  5-6 KD943 . . . . **811**
FROUD, B/ Are all the giants dead?/ c1975, 1997/ 4-A/5 KH552 . . **FIC**
FUCHS, B/ Carolina shout!/ 1995/ 1-5/3 KG411 . . . . **E**
FUCHS, DM/ Bear for all seasons./ 1995/ K-2/2 KF589 . . . . **E**
FUENMAYOR, M/ Spirit of Tio Fernando: a Day of the Dead story./ El
  espiritu de tio Fernando: una historia del Dia de los Muertos./ 1995/
  1-3/5 KH404 . . . . **FIC**
FUGE, C/ Sam's sneaker search./ 1997/ P-2/3 KG186 . . . . **E**
FUJIYAMA, K/ JAPANESE FAIRY TALES./ 1992/ 2-4/7 KB322 . . **398.2**
FULWEILER, J/ Iron dragon never sleeps./ 1995/ 3-5/2 KH381 . . . **FIC**
FUNAI, M/ Dolphin./ c1975/ K-2/2 KC778 . . . . **599.53**
FUSETTI, L/ Hyperactive child book./ 1994/ KA303 . . . . **PROF 649**
GABB, M/ Human body./ c1991, 1992/ 5-6/6 KC918 . . . . **612**
GABER, S/ Bit by bit./ 1995/ K-2/2 KB772 . . . . **398.27**
GACKENBACH, D/ Mag the magnificent./ 1985/ K-2/2 KF590 . . . . . **E**
Monster in the third dresser drawer and other stories about Adam
  Joshua./ 1981/ 2-4/4 KH725 . . . . **FIC**
GAEDDERT, L/ Breaking free./ 1994/ 5-A/5 KH147 . . . . **FIC**
Breaking free (Sound recording cassette)./ 1997/ 5-A/5 KH147 . . . **FIC**
Hope./ 1995/ 5-A/6 KH148 . . . . **FIC**
GAG, W/ ABC bunny./ c1933, 1997/ P-K KF591 . . . . **E**
ABC bunny (Talking book)./ n.d., P-K KF591 . . . . **E**
Millions of cats./ c1928/ P-1/6 KF592 . . . . **CE E**
Millions of cats (Braille)./ n.d./ P-1/6 KF592 . . . . **CE E**
Millions of cats (Videocassette)./ 1985/ P-1/6 KF592 . . . . . . **CE E**
GAGE, W/ My stars, it's Mrs. Gaddy!: the three Mrs. Gaddy stories./
  1991/ 1-3/2 KF593 . . . . **E**
GAGNE, KD/ Books to help children cope with separation and loss: an
  annotated bibliography. 4th ed./ 1993/ KA025 . . . **PROF 016.1559**
GAGNON, A/ Guidelines for children's services./ 1989/
  KA068 . . . . **PROF 027.62**
GAINER, C/ MathArts: exploring math through art for 3 to 6 year olds./
  1996/ KA253 . . . . **PROF 372.7**
GALDONE, P/ Gingerbread boy./ 1975/ P-2/4 KB736 . . . . **CE 398.27**
Henny Penny./ c1968/ P-K/2 KF594 . . . . **CE E**
Henny Penny (Big book)./ 1992/ P-K/2 KF594 . . . . **CE E**

Henny Penny (Kit)./ n.d./ P-K/2 KF594 . . . . **CE E**
King of the cats./ 1980/ 1-3/2 KB595 . . . . **CE 398.24**
Lemonade trick./ 1960/ 4-5/4 KH030 . . . . **FIC**
Little red hen./ c1973/ P-K/2 KF595 . . . . **CE E**
Little red hen (Braille)./ n.d./ P-K/2 KF595 . . . . . . **CE E**
Little red hen (Videocassette)./ 1991/ P-K/2 KF595 . . **CE E**
Magic porridge pot./ c1976/ P-2/4 KF596 . . . . **E**
Magic porridge pot (Braille)./ n.d./ P-2/4 KF596 . . . **E**
Sword in the tree./ c1956/ 3-5/2 KG939 . . . . **FIC**
Three little kittens./ 1986/ P-1/5 KB798 . . . . **398.8**
Three little kittens (Braille)./ n.d./ P-1/5 KB798 . . . **398.8**
GALL, SB/ ASIAN AMERICAN BIOGRAPHY./ 1995/
    5-A/11 KA399 . . . . **REF 305.8**
GALLANT, RA/ Before the sun dies: the story of evolution./ 1989/
    A/11 KC292 . . . . **576.8**
GALLIMARD JEUNESSE/ Birds./ 1993/ 2-4/4 KC652 . . . . **598**
Colors./ 1991/ K-3/2 KC121 . . . . **535.6**
Egg./ 1992/ P-3/2 KC281 . . . . **573.6**
Fruit./ 1992/ P-3/2 KD159 . . . . **634**
Ladybug and other insects./ 1991/ K-3/4 KC538 . . . . **595.7**
Seashore./ 1995/ 1-4/4 KC366 . . . . **578.769**
GALLINA, J/ A to Z, the animals and me (Compact disc)./ 1993/
    P-1 KD612 . . . . **SRC 789.3**
A to Z, the animals and me (Sound recording cassette)./ 1993/
    P-1 KD612 . . . . **SRC 789.3**
Alphabet in action: consonants and vowels taught through song and motor
    activities (Sound recording cassette)./ 1978/ K-2 KB102 . . **SRC 372.4**
Feelin' good (Sound recording cassette)./ 1981/ 1-3 KC983 . **SRC 613**
GALLINA, M/ A to Z, the animals and me (Sound recording cassette)./
    1993/ P-1 KD612 . . . . **SRC 789.3**
Alphabet in action: consonants and vowels taught through song and motor
    activities (Sound recording cassette)./ 1978/ K-2 KB102 . . **SRC 372.4**
GALLO, DR/ WITHIN REACH: TEN STORIES./ 1993/
    5-A/6 KH874 . . . . **FIC**
GALOUCHKO, AG/ Mala: a women's folktale./ 1996/
    3-5/2 KB718 . . . . **398.26**
GALT, MF/ Up to the plate: the All American Girls Professional Baseball
    League./ 1995/ 4-6/6 KD797 . . . . **796.357**
GAMMELL, S/ Air mail to the moon./ 1988/ K-3/5 KF231 . . . . **E**
Come a tide./ 1990/ K-3/2 KG043 . . . . **E**
Great dimpole oak./ 1987/ 3-6/6 KH411 . . . . **FIC**
HALLOWEEN POEMS./ 1989/ K-4 KE062 . . . . **811.008**
Monster mama./ 1993/ K-2/4 KG354 . . . . **E**
Monster mama (Videocassette)./ 1996/ K-2 KG355 . . . **VCR E**
Old black fly./ 1992/ K-2/2 KF180 . . . . **E**
Old Henry./ 1987/ K-3/2 KF237 . . . . **CE E**
Relatives came./ 1985/ K-3/8 KG385 . . . . **E**
Scary stories to tell in the dark./ 1981/ 4-A/3 KB694 . . . . **CE 398.25**
Song and dance man./ 1988/ K-2/6 KF130 . . . . **E**
Stonewall./ 1979/ 5-A/8 KE399 . . . . **B JACKSON, T.**
THANKSGIVING POEMS./ 1985/ K-6 KE089 . . . . . . **811.008**
Thunder at Gettysburg./ c1975, 1990/ 4-6/4 KE903 . . . **973.7**
Will's mammoth./ 1989/ 1-3/2 KG080 . . . . **CE E**
GAN, G/ Communication./ 1997/ 5-6/9 KA795 . . . . . . **302.2**
GANERI, A/ Creature features./ 1997/ 3-6/6 KC447 . . . . **591**
Funny bones./ 1997/ 3-6/6 KC903 . . . . **611**
Oceans atlas./ 1994/ 4-A/6 KC173 . . . . **551.46**
Out of the ark: stories from the world's religions./ 1996/
    3-6/5 KA729 . . . . **291.1**
Religions explained: a beginner's guide to world faiths./ 1997/
    3-5/9 KA723 . . . . **291**
Story of time and clocks./ 1996/ 4-6/8 KC070 . . . . . . **529**
What do we know about Hinduism?/ 1995/ 5-A/9 KA762 . . . . **294.5**
What's inside us?/ 1995/ 5-6/8 KC919 . . . . **612**
Young person's guide to the orchestra: Benjamin Britten's composition on
    CD./ 1996/ 4-6/10 KD545 . . . . **BA 784.2**
GANN, M/ New Brunswick./ 1995/ 5-A/9 KE820 . . . . . **971.5**
GANNETT, RC/ My father's dragon./ c1948, 1986/ 3-5/6 KH149 . . **FIC**
GANNETT, RS/ Dragons of Blueland./ 1963/ 3-5/6 KH149 . . . . . . **FIC**
Elmer and the dragon./ c1950, 1987/ 3-5/6 KH149 . . . . **FIC**
Elmer and the dragon (Braille)./ n.d., 3-5/6 KH149 . . . . . . **FIC**
Elmer and the dragon (Talking book)./ n.d., 3-5/6 KH149 . . . . **FIC**
My father's dragon./ c1948, 1986/ 3-5/6 KH149 . . . . **FIC**
My father's dragon (Braille)./ n.d./ 3-5/6 KH149 . . . . . . **FIC**
My father's dragon (Sound recording cassette)./ n.d.,/
    3-5/6 KH149 . . . . **FIC**
My father's dragon (Talking book)./ n.d., 3-5/6 KH149 . . . . . **FIC**
GANS, R/ How do birds find their way?/ 1996/ 3-4/2 KC673 . **598.156**
GANTOS, J/ Happy birthday Rotten Ralph./ 1990/ K-2/3 KF597 . . . **E**
Heads or tails: stories from the sixth grade./ 1994/ 5-A/4 KH150 . **FIC**
Jack's new power: stories from a Caribbean year./ 1995/
    5-A/4 KH151 . . . . **FIC**
Rotten Ralph./ 1976/ K-2/3 KF597 . . . . **E**
Rotten Ralph's show and tell./ 1989/ K-2/3 KF597 . . . . **E**

GARAY, L/ Pedrito's Day./ 1997/ 1-3/2 KF598 . . . . **E**
GARCIA, S/ Snapshots from the wedding./ 1997/ K-2/2 KG529 . . . . **E**
GARDINER, JR/ General Butterfingers./ c1986, 1993/ 4-6/6 KH152 **FIC**
GARDINER, L/ North American Indian./ 1995/ 4-6/8 KE751 . . . **970.1**
GARDNER, B/ Guess what?/ 1985/ K-3 KB904 . . . . **508**
GARDNER, JM/ Henry Moore: from bones and stones to sketches and
    sculptures./ 1993/ 3-6/6 KD397 . . . . **730**
GARDNER, M/ Codes, ciphers and secret writing./ c1972, 1984/
    5-6/8 KD308 . . . . **652**
GARDNER, R/ Science in your backyard./ 1987/ A/6 KB881 . . . . **507**
GARDNER-LOULAN, J/ Period: revised and updated with a parents'
    guide./ 1991/ 5-6/7 KC947 . . . . **612.6**
GARELICK, M/ Two orphan cubs./ 1989/ K-2/2 KC848 . . . . . **599.78**
GARLAND, S/ Vietnam: rebuilding a nation:/ 1990/ 5-6/7 KE717 **959.7**
GARNETT, R/ Five notable inventors./ 1995/ 3-5/4 KB892 . . . . **609**
GARNS, A/ Astronauts are sleeping./ 1996/ K-2/3 KG535 . . . . . **E**
GARRAMONE, R/ Zany knock knocks./ 1993/ 3-6 KD726 . . . **793.735**
GARRICK, J/ George Washington: father of our country./ 1988/
    4-5/6 KE587 . . . . **B WASHINGTON, G**
GARTEN, J/ Alphabet tale. New ed., rev. and re-illustrated./ 1994/
    P-K/3 KF599 . . . . **E**
GARZA, CL/ Family pictures: Cuadros de familia./ 1990/
    2-5/6 KA866 . . . . **306.85**
GATES, F/ Owl eyes./ 1994/ 1-3/4 KB570 . . . . **398.24**
GATES, L/ This way to books./ 1983/ KA089 . . . . . . **PROF 028.5**
GATES, P/ Nature got there first./ 1995/ 4-8/10 KB905 . . . . . . **508**
GATH, T/ SCIENCE BOOKS AND FILMS' BEST BOOKS FOR CHILDREN,
    1992-1995./ 1996/ KA028 . . . . **PROF 016.5**
GAUCH, PL/ Christina Katerina and the time she quit the family./ 1987/
    K-2/6 KF600 . . . . **E**
Noah./ 1994/ K-2/4 KA684 . . . . **222**
This time, Tempe Wick?/ c1974, 1992/ 3-5/7 KH153 . . . . . **FIC**
This time, Tempe Wick? (Sound recording cassette)./ n.d.,/
    3-5/7 KH153 . . . . **FIC**
Thunder at Gettysburg./ c1975, 1990/ 4-6/4 KE903 . . . . **973.7**
GAUDISZ, J/ Story of sculpture./ 1995/ 4-A/9 KD399 . . . . . . **730**
GAUTHIER, G/ My life among the aliens./ 1996/ 4-6/5 KH154 . . **FIC**
GAVER, MV/ Braided cord: memoirs of a school librarian./ 1988/
    KA368 . . . . **PROF B GAVER, M**
GAY, M/ Rumpelstiltskin./ 1997/ K-2/2 KB308 . . . . **398.2**
GAZSI, ES/ Seven ravens./ 1994/ 2-3/6 KB302 . . . . **398.2**
GEE, M/ Fire-raiser./ 1992/ 6-A/6 KH155 . . . . **FIC**
GEERE, CL/ Lost in the barrens./ 1962/ 5-6/6 KH518 . . . . . . **FIC**
GEHM, C/ Soup./ 1974/ 4-6/6 KH594 . . . . **FIC**
GEHRET, J/ Don't-give-up Kid and learning differences. 2nd ed./ 1996/
    K-3/2 KB095 . . . . **371.92**
GEIGER, E/ TNT: two hundred and ninety-two activites for literature and
    language arts!/ 1989/ KA222 . . . . **PROF 372.6**
GEISERT, A/ After the flood./ 1994/ K-2/3 KF601 . . . . **E**
Etcher's studio./ 1997/ 2-5/2 KF602 . . . . **E**
Haystack./ 1995/ K-3/5 KD153 . . . . **633.2**
Pigs from A to Z./ 1986/ 1-3/3 KF603 . . . . **E**
Pigs from 1 to 10./ 1992/ 1-3/3 KF604 . . . . **E**
Roman numerals I to MM./Numerabilia romana uno ad duo mila: liber de
    difficillimo computando numerum./ 1996/ K-4/3 KB988 . . . . **513.5**
GEISERT, B/ Haystack./ 1995/ K-3/5 KD153 . . . . **633.2**
GELDART, W/ Return of the Indian./ 1986/ 5-A/6 KH629 . . . . **FIC**
GELLMAN, M/ God's mailbox: more stories about stories in the Bible./
    1996/ 4-6/6 KA678 . . . . **221.9**
How do you spell God?: answers to the big questions from around the
    world./ 1995/ 5-A/4 KA724 . . . . **291**
GEORGE, JC/ Dear Rebecca, winter is here./ 1993/ 1-3/3 KF605 . . . **E**
Everglades./ 1995/ 2-5/7 KE991 . . . . **975.9**
Everglades (Sound recording cassette)./ 1997/ 2-5/7 KE991 . **975.9**
First Thanksgiving./ 1993/ 4-6/6 KB223 . . . . **394.264**
Julie./ 1994/ 5-A/3 KH156 . . . . **FIC**
Julie of the wolves./ c1972/ 6-A/6 KH157 . . . . **CE FIC**
Julie of the wolves (Braille)./ n.d./ 6-A/6 KH157 . . . . . **CE FIC**
Julie of the wolves (Talking book)./ 1977/ 6-A/6 KH157 . . . . **CE FIC**
Julie of the wolves (Talking book)./ 1993/ 6-A KH158 . . . . **TB FIC**
Julie (Sound recording cassette)./ 1996/ 5-A/3 KH156 . . . . . . **FIC**
Moon of the gray wolves. New ed./ 1991/ 5-6/6 KC835 . . . **599.773**
My side of the mountain./ c1959/ 5-6/6 KH159 . . . . **FIC**
My side of the mountain (Braille)./ n.d./ 5-6/6 KH159 . . . . **FIC**
My side of the mountain (Sound recording cassette)./ n.d./
    5-6/6 KH159 . . . . **FIC**
One day in the tropical rain forest./ 1990/ 4-6/6 KC315 . . . . **577.34**
Tarantula in my purse and 172 other wild pets./ 1996/
    4-6/4 KE366 . . . . **B GEORGE, J.**
Vulpes, the red fox./ c1948, 1996/ 5-A/5 KH160 . . . . **FIC**
Who really killed Cock Robin?: an ecological mystery./ c1971, 1991/
    5-A/7 KH161 . . . . **FIC**
GEORGE, JL/ Vulpes, the red fox./ c1948, 1996/ 5-A/5 KH160 . . . **FIC**

GEORGE, LB/ Around the pond: who's been here?/ 1996/
K-2/2 KF606 . . . . 1989/ 1-3/3 KF608 . . . . **E**
Box turtle at Long Pond./ 1989/ 1-3/3 KF608 . . . . **E**
In the snow: who's been here?/ 1995/ 1-3/2 KF607 . . . . **E**
GEORGE, WT/ Box turtle at Long Pond./ 1989/ 1-3/3 KF608 . . . . . **E**
GERBER, MJ/ Wings to fly./ 1997/ 5-A/5 KH419 . . . . **FIC**
GERHOLDT, JE/ Frogs./ 1994/ 3-5/5 KC601 . . . . **597.8**
Tree frogs./ 1994/ 3-5/5 KC602 . . . . **597.8**
GERINGER, L/ Pomegranate seeds: a classic Greek myth./ 1995/
3-6/5 KA742 . . . . **292**
Seven ravens./ 1994/ 2-3/6 KB302 . . . . **398.2**
Three hat day./ 1985/ P-3/2 KF609 . . . . **E**
Three hat day (Sound recording cassette)./ n.d./ P-3/2 KF609 . . . . **E**
GERSHATOR, D/ Bread is for eating./ 1995/ P-2/2 KF610 . . . . **E**
GERSHATOR, P/ Bread is for eating./ 1995/ P-2/2 KF610 . . . . **E**
Iroko-man: a Yoruba folktale./ 1994/ 2-3/6 KB397 . . . . . **398.21**
Rata-pata-scata-fata: a Caribbean story./ 1994/ K-2/2 KF611 . . . **E**
Sambalena show-off./ 1995/ 1-3/2 KF612 . . . . **E**
Sweet, sweet fig banana./ 1996/ K-2/2 KF613 . . . . **E**
Tukama Tootles the flute: a tale from the Antilles./ 1994/
K-2/5 KB398 . . . . **398.21**
GERSON, M/ People of corn: a Mayan story./ 1995/
2-4/3 KB399 . . . . **398.21**
Why the sky is far away: a Nigerian folktale./ 1992/
2-4/5 KB705 . . . . **398.26**
GERSTEIN, M/ Behind the couch./ 1996/ 2-4/3 KH162 . . . . . . **FIC**
Something queer at the scary movie./ 1995/ 3-5/3 KH403 . . . . **FIC**
Something queer is going on (a mystery)./ C1973/ 1-3/3 KF972 . . **CE E**
GETER, T/ White socks only./ 1996/ 3-4/4 KH014 . . . . **FIC**
GETZ, D/ Frozen man./ 1994/ 4-6/7 KE638 . . . . **937**
GHAZI, SH/ Ramadan./ 1996/ 3-5/7 KA785 . . . . **297**
GHERMAN, B/ E.B. White: some writer!/ 1992/
6-A/8 KE593 . . . . **B WHITE, E.B.**
E.B. White: some writer! (Sound recording cassette)./ 1995/
6-A/8 KE593 . . . . **B WHITE, E.B.**
GHIGNA, C/ Tickle Day: poems from Father Goose./ 1994/
P-1 KD944 . . . . **811**
GIAGNOCAVO, G/ Educator's Internet companion: CLASSROOM
CONNECT's complete guide to educational resources on the Internet.
4th ed./ 1996/ KA049 . . . . **BC PROF 025.06**
GIANNINI, E/ Caterina, the clever farm girl: a tale from Italy./ 1996/
2-4/3 KB357 . . . . **398.2**
GIBBONS, G/ Beacons of light: lighthouses./ 1990/ 3-6/6 KB149 **387.1**
Beacons of light: lighthouses (Sound recording cassette)./ 1993/
3-6/6 KB149 . . . . **387.1**
Bicycle book./ 1995/ 2-5/3 KD124 . . . . **629.227**
Boat book./ 1983/ P-2/3 KB152 . . . . **387.2**
Catch the wind!: all about kites./ 1989/ 1-3/4 KD108 . . . . **629.133**
Cats./ 1996/ K-3/3 KC821 . . . . **599.75**
Caves and caverns./ 1993/ K-6/6 KC166 . . . . **551.4**
Check it out!: the book about libraries./ 1985/ 1-3/3 KA585 . . **CE 027**
Click!: a book about cameras and taking pictures./ 1997/
2-4/5 KD512 . . . . **771**
Deserts./ 1996/ K-3/4 KC363 . . . . **578.754**
Dinosaurs./ 1987/ P-2/4 KC249 . . . . **CE 567.9**
Dinosaurs (Kit)./ 1988/ P-2/4 KC249 . . . . **CE 567.9**
Emergency!/ 1994/ P-1/6 KB032 . . . . **363.3**
Farming./ 1988/ K-3/2 KD143 . . . . **630**
Fill it up! All about service stations./ 1985/ K-3/4 KD129 . . . **629.28**
Fire! Fire!/ 1984/ P-2/4 KD086 . . . . **628.9**
Fire! Fire! (Sound recording cassette)./ n.d./ P-2/4 KD086 . . . . **628.9**
Flying./ 1986/ K-2/2 KD095 . . . . **629.13**
Frogs./ 1993/ K-3/3 KC603 . . . . **597.8**
From seed to plant./ 1991/ K-3/4 KC398 . . . . **581.4**
Great St. Lawrence Seaway./ 1992/ 2-5/6 KB142 . . . . . . **386**
Great St. Lawrence Seaway (Sound recording cassette)./ 1995/
2-5/6 KB142 . . . . **386**
Gulls...gulls...gulls..../ 1997/ K-4/3 KC676 . . . . **598.3**
Halloween./ 1984/ P-2/7 KB224 . . . . **CE 394.264**
Halloween (Kit)./ 1984/ P-2/7 KB224 . . . . **CE 394.264**
Halloween (Videocassette)./ 1993/ P-2/7 KB224 . . . . . . **CE 394.264**
Honey makers./ 1997/ 3-5/6 KC573 . . . . **595.79**
Milk makers./ 1985/ K-3/6 KD239 . . . . **637**
Milk makers (Braille)./ n.d./ K-3/6 KD239 . . . . **637**
Monarch butterfly./ 1989/ K-2/4 KC560 . . . . **595.78**
Moon book./ 1997/ K-6/4 KC019 . . . . **523.3**
Nature's green umbrella: tropical rain forests./ 1994/
2-6/5 KC316 . . . . **577.34**
New road!/ 1983/ 1-3/4 KD078 . . . . **625.7**
Pirates: robbers of the high seas./ 1993/ 2-4/7 KE154 . . . . **910.4**
Planet Earth/inside out./ 1995/ 3-6/6 KC146 . . . . **550**
Planets./ 1993/ 2-4/4 KC025 . . . . **523.4**
Prehistoric animals./ 1988/ P-3/5 KC241 . . . . **566**
Puff...flash...bang!: a book about signals./ 1993/ 1-4/4 KA796 **302.2**

Puffins are back!/ 1991/ 2-4/5 KC677 . . . . **598.3**
Reasons for seasons./ 1995/ P-4/5 KC059 . . . . **525**
Say woof!: the day of a country veterinarian./ 1992/
P-2/2 KD194 . . . . **636.089**
Sea turtles./ 1995/ 2-4/6 KC617 . . . . **597.92**
Sharks./ 1992/ P-3/3 KC593 . . . . **597.3**
Spiders./ 1993/ 1-3/4 KC525 . . . . **595.4**
St. Patrick's Day./ 1994/ 2-5/2 KB219 . . . . **394.262**
Stargazers./ 1992/ K-2/4 KC049 . . . . **523.8**
Sun up, sun down./ 1983/ P-2/2 KC045 . . . . **523.7**
Sun up, sun down (Braille)./ n.d./ P-2/2 KC045 . . . . **523.7**
Sun up, sun down (Sound recording cassette)./ n.d./
P-2/2 KC045 . . . . **523.7**
Sunken treasure./ 1988/ 4-6/6 KE194 . . . . **917.59**
Thanksgiving Day./ 1983/ P-2/4 KB225 . . . . **CE 394.264**
Thanksgiving Day (Kit)./ 1984/ P-2/4 KB225 . . . . **CE 394.264**
Thanksgiving Day (Videocassette)./ 1993/ P-2/4 KB225 . . **CE 394.264**
Tool book./ 1982/ P-K/2 KD055 . . . . **621.9**
Trains./ 1987/ 1-3/3 KD073 . . . . **625.1**
Trucks./ 1981/ P-1/1 KD117 . . . . **629.224**
Tunnels./ c1984, 1987/ K-2/2 KD069 . . . . **624.1**
Up goes the skyscraper!/ 1986/ K-3/6 KD356 . . . . **690**
Valentine's Day./ 1986/ 1-6/5 KB207 . . . . **CE 394.261**
Valentine's Day (Kit)./ 1986/ 1-6/5 KB207 . . . . **CE 394.261**
Weather forecasting./ 1987/ 2-4/7 KC224 . . . . **551.63**
Weather words and what they mean./ 1990/ K-4/4 KC218 . **551.6**
Whales./ 1991/ K-4/3 KC769 . . . . **599.5**
Zoo./ 1991/ K-2/4 KC441 . . . . **CE 590.73**
Zoo (Kit)./ n.d./ K-2/4 KC441 . . . . **CE 590.73**
GIBBS, J/ Backyard almanac./ 1996/ 3-A/7 KB915 . . . . . . **508**
GIBLIN, JC/ Be seated: a book about chairs./ 1993/ 4-A/7 KD463 **749**
Be seated: a book about chairs (Sound recording cassette)./ 1996/
4-A/7 KD463 . . . . **749**
Dwarf, the giant, and the unicorn: a tale of King Arthur./ 1996/
3-5/4 KB443 . . . . **398.22**
Fireworks, picnics, and flags./ 1983/ 3-5/8 KE880 . . . . . . **973.3**
Fireworks, picnics, and flags (Braille)./ n.d./ 3-5/8 KE880 . . . **973.3**
From hand to mouth, or how we invented knives, forks, spoons, and
chopsticks & the table manners to go with them./ 1987/
5-6/8 KB185 . . . . **394.1**
Riddle of the Rosetta Stone: key to ancient Egypt./ 1990/
5-A/7 KB865 . . . . **493**
Riddle of the Rosetta Stone: key to ancient Egypt (Sound recording
cassette)./ 1993/ 5-A/7 KB865 . . . . **493**
Thomas Jefferson: a picture book biography./ 1994/
3-5/5 KE404 . . . . **B JEFFERSON, T.**
Truth about unicorns./ c1991, 1996/ 5-A/7 KB571 . . . . . . **398.24**
Truth about unicorns (Sound recording cassette)./ 1993,/
5-A/7 KB571 . . . . **398.24**
When plague strikes: the Black Death, smallpox, AIDS./ 1995/
A/11 KD010 . . . . **614.4**
GIBSON, M/ David and Goliath (Videocassette)./ 1992/
2-4 KA686 . . . . **VCR 222**
GIECK, C/ Bald eagle magic for kids./ 1991/ 5-6/6 KC714 . . **598.9**
GIFALDI, D/ Gregory, Maw, and the Mean One./ 1992/
5-A/7 KH163 . . . . **FIC**
GIFF, PR/ All about Stacy./ 1988/ 1-2/2 KF614 . . . . **CE E**
All about Stacy (Kit)./ 1994/ 1-2/2 KF614 . . . . **CE E**
B-E-S-T friends./ 1988/ 1-2/2 KF614 . . . . **CE E**
B-E-S-T friends (Kit)./ 1994/ 1-2/2 KF614 . . . . **CE E**
Fourth-grade celebrity./ 1981/ 4-6/6 KH164 . . . . **FIC**
Garbage juice for breakfast./ 1989/ 2-3/2 KF615 . . . . . . **E**
Girl who knew it all./ 1984/ 4-6/6 KH164 . . . . **FIC**
Left-handed shortstop./ 1980/ 4-6/6 KH164 . . . . **FIC**
Lily's crossing./ 1997/ 5-A/5 KH165 . . . . **FIC**
Powder puff puzzle./ 1987/ 2-3/2 KF615 . . . . **E**
Rat teeth./ c1984/ 3-5/3 KH166 . . . . **FIC**
Stacy says good-bye./ 1989/ 1-2/2 KF614 . . . . **CE E**
Stacy says good-bye (Kit)./ 1994/ 1-2/2 KF614 . . . . **CE E**
Today was a terrible day./ 1980/ 1-2/2 KF616 . . . . **CE E**
Today was a terrible day (Kit)./ 1993/ 1-2 KF617 . . . . . . **KIT E**
Today was a terrible day (Videocassette)./ 1988/ 1-2/2 KF616 . . **CE E**
Winter worm business./ 1981/ 4-6/6 KH164 . . . . **FIC**
GIGANTI, JR., P/ Each orange had 8 slices: a counting book./ 1992/
P-1/2 KB989 . . . . **513.5**
Each orange had 8 slices: a counting book (Big book)./ 1994/
P-1/2 KB989 . . . . **513.5**
GILBERT, A/ MAXFIELD PARRISH: A TREASURY OF ART AND
CHILDREN'S LITERATURE./ 1995/ K-6 KD413 . . . . . . **741.6**
GILBERT, S/ Hawk Hill./ 1996/ 4-6/4 KH167 . . . . **FIC**
GILBERT, Y/ Per and the Dala horse./ 1995/ 1-3/6 KF724 . . **E**
GILCHRIST, JS/ Everett Anderson's Christmas coming./ 1991/
P-1 KD925 . . . . **811**
Nathaniel talking./ 1988/ K-6 KD948 . . . . **811**

GILLEECE, D/ Little house on Rocky Ridge./ 1993/ 4-6/6 KH436 . . . **FIC**

GILLEN, PB/ My first book of sign./ c1986, 1995/ K-3 KB821 . . . **419**

GILLESPIE, JT/ Administering the school library media center. 3rd ed./ 1992/ KA077 . . . . **PROF 027.8**

Best books for children: preschool through grade 6. 5th ed./ 1994/ KA084 . . . . **PROF 028.1**

Introducing bookplots 3: a book talk guide for use with readers ages 8--12./ 1988/ KA092 . . . . **PROF 028.5**

Introducing more books: a guide for the middle grades./ 1978/ KA092 . . . . **PROF 028.5**

Juniorplots: a book talk manual for teachers and librarians./ 1967/ KA091 . . . . **PROF 028.5**

Juniorplots 3: a book talk guide for use with readers ages 12-16./ 1987/ KA091 . . . . **PROF 028.5**

Juniorplots 4: a book talk guide for use with readers ages 12-16./ 1993/ KA091 . . . . **PROF 028.5**

Middleplots 4: a book talk guide for use with readers ages 8-12./ 1994/ KA092 . . . . **PROF 028.5**

More juniorplots: a guide for teachers and librarians./ 1977/ KA091 . . . . **PROF 028.5**

Newbery companion: booktalk and related materials for Newbery Medal and Honor Books./ 1996/ KA035 . . . . . **PROF 016.813**

GILLILAND, JH/ Day of Ahmed's secret./ 1990/ 1-3/4 KF694 . . . . . . **E**

Not in the house, Newton!/ 1995/ P-2/2 KF618 . . . . **E**

River./ 1993/ K-3/3 KC317 . . . . **577.34**

Sami and the time of the troubles./ 1992/ 2-4/4 KF695 . . . . **E**

GILLMAN, A/ Radio boy./ 1995/ 1-3/7 KF462 . . . . **E**

Take me out to the ballgame./ 1992/ K-2 KD639 . . . . **789.3**

Toad or frog, swamp or bog?: a big book of nature's confusables./ 1994/ K-4/4 KB906 . . . . **508**

GILMAN, P/ Gypsy princess./ 1997/ K-2/3 KF619 . . . . **E**

Something from nothing: adapted from a Jewish folktale./ 1993/ 1-3/3 KB737 . . . . **398.27**

GILMORE, R/ Lights for Gita./ 1994/ 1-3/5 KF620 . . . . **E**

GILSON, J/ Hobie Hanson, greatest hero of the mall./ 1989/ KH168 . . . . **FIC**

Hobie Hanson, you're weird./ 1987/ 3-5/6 KH168 . . . . **FIC**

Soccer circus./ 1993/ 3-5/5 KH169 . . . . **FIC**

Soccer circus (Sound recording cassette)./ 1996/ 3-5/5 KH169 . . . **FIC**

Sticks and stones and skeleton bones./ 1991/ 3-5/6 KH168 . . . . . **FIC**

GINSBURG, M/ Across the stream./ 1982/ P-K/2 KF621 . . . . **E**

Asleep, asleep./ 1992/ P/1 KF622 . . . . **E**

Chick and the duckling./ 1972/ P-1/1 KG585 . . . . **E**

Friendship./ 1987/ 4-6/5 KH776 . . . . **FIC**

Kate Shelley: bound for legend./ 1995/ 3-5/5 KE539 . **B SHELLEY, K.**

King who tried to fry an egg on his head: based on a Russian tale./ 1994/ 2-4/6 KB444 . . . . **398.22**

Mississippi bridge./ 1990/ 5-A/4 KH778 . . . . **FIC**

Mushroom in the rain./ c1974, 1987/ P-2/2 KF623 . . . . **E**

Sun's asleep behind the hill./ 1982/ P-K/1 KF624 . . . . **E**

GIOVANNI, N/ Knoxville, Tennessee./ 1994/ P-1/2 KD945 . . . . . **811**

Spin a soft black song. Rev. ed./ c1971, 1985/ 1-4 KD946 . . . . **811**

GIOVANOPOULOS, P/ Learning to say goodbye: when a parent dies./ c1976/ 5-6/7 KA651 . . . . **155.9**

GIPSON, F/ Old Yeller./ c1956/ A/7 KH170 . . . . **CE FIC**

Old Yeller (Braille)./ n.d./ A/7 KH170 . . . . **CE FIC**

Old Yeller (Sound recording cassette)./ n.d./ A/7 KH170 . . . . **CE FIC**

Old Yeller (Talking book)./ Old Yeller (Talking book)./ n.d./ 1973/ A/7 KH170 . . . . **CE FIC**
A/7 KH170 . . . . **CE FIC**

GIRARD, LW/ Who is a stranger and what should I do?/ 1985/ 1-3/4 KB021 . . . . **363.1**

You were born on your very first birthday./ 1982/ P/2 KC948 . **612.6**

GIRL SCOUTS OF THE UNITED STATES OF AMERICA/ Brownie Scout handbook./ 1993/ 1-3 KB078 . . . . **369.463**

Junior Girl Scout handbook./ 1994/ 4-6 KB079 . . . . **369.463**

Junior Girl Scout handbook (Braille)./ n.d./ 4-6 KB079 . . . . . **369.463**

Junior Girl Scout handbook (Sound recording cassette)./ n.d./ 4-6 KB079 . . . . **369.463**

GIRL TECH/ TECH GIRL'S INTERNET ADVENTURE./ 1997/ 4-A KA580 . . . . **BC 025.04**

GIROUARD, P/ Test your luck./ 1992/ 5-6/4 KB998 . . . . **519.2**

GIVE A DOG A BONE: STORIES, POEMS, JOKES, AND RIDDLES ABOUT DOGS./ 1996/ K-4 KD874 . . . . **808.8**

GLANZMAN, LS/ Pippi Longstocking./ c1950, 1978/ 3-5/4 KH407 . . . . **CE FIC**

GLASER, B/ Action alphabet./ 1985/ 1-3 KG171 . . . . **E**

GLASER, L/ Compost!: growing gardens from your garbage./ 1996/ P-K/3 KD166 . . . . **635**

Rosie's birthday rat./ 1996/ 1-3/2 KH171 . . . . **FIC**

GLASS, A/ Ananse's feast: an Ashanti tale./ 1997/ K-2/3 KB622 . . . . **398.24**

Don't open the door after the sun goes down: tales of the real and unreal./ 1994/ 4-6/4 KG982 . . . . **FIC**

Dr. Dredd's wagon of wonders./ 1987/ 3-6/5 KG923 . . . . **FIC**

Folks call me Appleseed John./ 1995/ 3-5/6 KH172 . . . . **FIC**

Folks call me Appleseed John (Sound recording cassette)./ 1997/ 3-5/6 KH172 . . . . **FIC**

Lavender./ 1995/ 2-3/2 KH251 . . . . **FIC**

Real mummies don't bleed: friendly tales for October nights./ 1993/ 4-6/5 KH849 . . . . **FIC**

Soap! soap! don't forget the soap!: an Appalachian folktale./ 1993/ K-2/3 KB267 . . . . **398.2**

Wish giver./ 1983/ 3-6/7 KG925 . . . . **FIC**

GLASS, H/ Children's all-time Mother Goose favorites (Sound recording cassette)./ 1989/ KA275 . . . . **SRC PROF 398.8**

Fingerplays and footplays (Videocassette)./ 1997/ P-K KD708 . . . . **VCR 793.4**

GLASSER, RP/ Alexander, who's not (Do you hear me? I mean it!) going to move./ 1995/ 1-3/2 KG660 . . . . **E**

GLASSMAN, P/ Wizard next door./ 1993/ K-2/2 KF625 . . . . **E**

GLAZER, T/ Merry Christmas, Strega Nona (Talking book)./ 1991/ K-3 KF474 . . . . **TB E**

GLEESON, B/ Anansi (Kit)./ 1992/ 3-5 KB572 . . . . **KIT 398.24**

Anansi (Videocassette)./ 1991/ 3-5 KB572 . . . . **VCR 398.24**

Finn McCoul (Kit)./ 1995/ 3-5 KB445 . . . . **VCR 398.22**

Finn McCoul (Videocassette)./ 1991/ 3-5 KB445 . . . . . . **VCR 398.22**

Joseph and his brothers (Videocassette)./ 1993/ 5-6 KA685 . **VCR 222**

Koi and the kola nuts (Kit)./ 1992/ 2-5 KB446 . . . . . . **KIT 398.24**

Paul Bunyan (Videocassette)./ 1990/ 3-5 KB447 . . . . . **VCR 398.22**

Savior is born (Kit)./ Savior is born (Kit)./ 1992/ 1992/ 3-5 KA705 . . . . **KIT 232.92**
3-5 KA705 . . . . **KIT 232.92**

GLEITZMAN, M/ Blabber mouth./ 1995/ 3-5/4 KH173 . . . . **FIC**

Blabber mouth (Sound recording cassette)./ 1997/ 3-5/4 KH173 . . **FIC**

Misery guts./ 1993/ 5-A/7 KH174 . . . . **FIC**

Puppy fat./ 1995/ 5-A/5 KH175 . . . . **FIC**

Sticky Beak./ 1995/ 3-5/4 KH176 . . . . **FIC**

Sticky Beak (Sound recording cassette)./ 1997/ 3-5/4 KH176 . . . . **FIC**

Worry warts./ 1993/ 5-A/7 KH174 . . . . **FIC**

GLICKMAN, S/ NATIVE NORTH AMERICAN BIOGRAPHY./ 1996/ 6-A KA481 . . . . **REF 970.1**

GLOVER, D/ Brer Rabbit and Boss Lion (Kit)./ 1996/ 3-A KB599 . . . . **KIT 398.24**

BRER RABBIT AND BOSS LION (Talking book)./ 1992/ 3-A KB533 . . . . **TB 398.24**

TALKING EGGS (Videocassette)./ 1993/ 2-5 KB420 . . . . **VCR 398.21**

GOBLE, P/ Adopted by the eagles: a Plains Indian story of friendship and treachery./ 1994/ 2-5/4 KB706 . . . . **398.26**

Beyond the ridge./ 1989/ 2-4/4 KH177 . . . . **FIC**

Beyond the ridge (Sound recording cassette)./ 1993/ 2-4/4 KH177 . . . . **FIC**

Brave Eagle's account of the Fetterman Fight, 21 December 1866./ c1972, 1992/ 5-6/6 KE913 . . . . **973.8**

Crow Chief: a Plains Indian story./ 1992/ 3-4/4 KB573 . . . . . **398.24**

Crow Chief: a Plains Indian story (Sound recording cassette)./ 1995/ 3-4/4 KB573 . . . . **398.24**

Death of the iron horse./ 1987/ K-3/2 KF626 . . . . **E**

Dream wolf./ 1990/ K-3/4 KF627 . . . . **E**

Dream wolf (Sound recording cassette)./ 1994/ K-3/4 KF627 . . . . **E**

Girl who loved wild horses./ 1978/ K-3/4 KF628 . . . . **CE E**

Girl who loved wild horses (Sound recording cassette)./ 1995/ K-3/4 KF628 . . . . **CE E**

Girl who loved wild horses (Videocassette)./ 1988/ K-3/4 KF628 . **CE E**

Great race of the birds and animals./ 1991/ 3-5/4 KB574 . . . **398.24**

Lost children: the boys who were neglected./ 1993/ 3-5/5 KB707 . . . . **398.26**

Love flute./ 1992/ 3-5/6 KB738 . . . . **CE 398.27**

Love flute (Kit)./ 1992/ 3-5/6 KB738 . . . . **CE 398.27**

Love flute (Videocassette)./ 1993/ 3-5/6 KB738 . . . . . . **CE 398.27**

Red Hawk's account of Custer's last battle; the Battle of the Little Bighorn, 25 June 1876./ c1969, 1992/ 5-6/6 KE914 . . . . **973.8**

Remaking the earth: a creation story from the Great Plains of North America./ 1996/ 3-5/7 KB448 . . . . **398.22**

Return of the buffaloes: a Plains Indian story about famine and renewal of the Earth./ 1996/ 3-5/3 KB575 . . . . **398.24**

GODDEN, R/ Listen to the nightingale./ c1992, 1994/ 5-A/4 KH178 . . . . **FIC**

Listen to the nightingale (Sound recording cassette)./ 1995,/ 5-A/6 KH178 . . . . **FIC**

Story of Holly and Ivy./ 1985/ 3-5/4 KH179 . . . . **FIC**

Story of Holly and Ivy (Braille)./ n.d./ 3-5/4 KH179 . . . . **FIC**

Story of Holly and Ivy (Sound recording cassette)./ n.d./ 3-5/4 KH179 . . . . **FIC**

GODKIN, C/ Wolf Island./ 1993/ 3-5/4 KC334 . . . . **577.5**

GOEDECKE, CJ/ Wind warrior: the training of a Karate champion./ 1992/ 4-6/5 KD831 . . . . **796.815**

GOENNEL, H/ Odds and evens: a numbers book./ 1994/
P-1/2 KB957 . . . . **513.2**
GOFFE, T/ Legend of Slappy Hooper: an American tall tale./ 1993/
3-5/3 KB489 . . . . **398.22**
GOFFSTEIN, MB/ Goldie, the dollmaker./ 1969/ 3-6/6 KH180 . . . . **FIC**
GOLD, A/ Andrew Gold's Halloween howls (Compact disc)./ 1996/
K-2 KB226 . . . . **CD 394.264**
Andrew Gold's Halloween howls (Sound recording cassette)./ 1996/
K-2 KB226 . . . . **CD 394.264**
GOLD, R/ Happy to be me (Sound recording cassette)./ 1993/
P-1 KA638 . . . . **SRC 155.2**
GOLD, SD/ Indian treaties./ 1997/ 5-6/10 KA904 . . . . **323.1**
GOLDBERG, MH/ Blunder book: colossal errors, minor mistakes, and
surprising slipups that/ 1984/ 5-A/9 KA556 . . . . **001.9**
Blunder book: colossal errors, minor mistakes, and surprising slipups that
have changed the course of history (Braille)./ n.d./
5-A/9 KA556 . . . . **001.9**
GOLDBERG, W/ Koi and the kola nuts (Kit)./ 1992/
2-5 KB446 . . . . **KIT 398.22**
GOLDENSTERN, J/ Lost cities./ 1996/ 3-6/7 KE624 . . . . **930.1**
GOLDIN, BD/ Bat mitzvah: a Jewish girl's coming of age./ 1995/
5-A/10 KA773 . . . . **296.4**
Coyote and the fire stick: a Pacific Northwest Indian tale./ 1996/
2-4/2 KB576 . . . . **398.24**
Magician's visit: a Passover tale./ 1993/ K-3/5 KF629 . . . . **E**
World's birthday: a Rosh Hashanah story./ 1990/ 2-3/2 KH181 . . **FIC**
GOLDSEN, L/ Colors./ 1991/ K-3/2 KC121 . . . . **535.6**
Egg./ 1992/ P-3/2 KC281 . . . . **573.6**
Fruit./ 1992/ P-3/2 KD159 . . . . **634**
Ladybug and other insects./ 1991/ K-3/4 KC538 . . . . **595.7**
GOLDSMITH, S/ Man who loved machines (Videocassette)./ 1983/
3-A KC127 . . . . **VCR 536**
GOLDSTEIN, BS/ INNER CHIMES: POEMS ON POETRY./ 1992/
2-6 KD885 . . . . **808.81**
GOLDSTEIN, N/ Rebuilding prairies and forests./ 1994/
4-6/7 KA955 . . . . **333.74**
GOLEMBE, C/ Creation: a poem./ 1993/ 1-6 KD957 . . . . **811**
People of corn: a Mayan story./ 1995/ 2-4/3 KB399 . . . . . . **398.21**
Why the sky is far away: a Nigerian folktale./ 1992/
2-4/5 KB705 . . . . **398.26**
Woman in the moon: a story from Hawaii./ 1996/
K-2/6 KB474 . . . . **398.22**
GOLENBOCK, P/ Teammates./ 1990/ 3-6/6 KD798 . . . . **796.357**
GOLUB, J/ FOCUS ON COLLABORATIVE LEARNING: CLASSROOM
PRACTICES IN TEACHING ENGLISH./ 1988/ KA221 . . . **PROF 372.6**
GOMI, T/ Who hid it?./ 1991/ P-K/2 KF630 . . . . **E**
GONZALES, E/ Farolitos of Christmas./ 1995/ 3-6/2 KG845 . . . . . **FIC**
GONZALEZ, LM/ Bossy gallito/el gallo de bodas: a traditional Cuban
folktale./ 1994/ K-2/4 KB577 . . . . **398.24**
Senor Cat's romance and other favorite stories from Latin America./
1997/ K-2/3 KB303 . . . . **398.2**
GOOCH, R/ Traditional crafts from Africa./ 1996/ 4-6/7 KD422 . . **745**
Traditional crafts from Mexico and Central America./ 1996/
3-6/5 KD438 . . . . **745.5**
GOOD MORNING TO YOU, VALENTINE: POEMS FOR VALENTINE'S
DAY./ c1976, 1993/ K-6 KE061 . . . . **811.008**
GOODALL, J/ Chimpanzee family book./ 1997/ 4-6/6 KC878 **599.885**
GOODALL, JS/ Story of a castle./ 1986/ 2-6 KE680 . . . . **942**
Story of a main street./ 1987/ K-3 KF631 . . . . **E**
GOODE, D/ DIANE GOODE'S AMERICAN CHRISTMAS./ 1997/
K-A KD898 . . . . **810.8**
DIANE GOODE'S BOOK OF SCARY STORIES AND SONGS./ 1994/
2-5/5 KB685 . . . . **398.25**
DIANE GOODE'S BOOK OF SILLY STORIES AND SONGS./ 1992/
K-3 KD872 . . . . **808.8**
House Gobbaleen./ 1995/ 3-5/4 KG836 . . . . **FIC**
Watch the stars come out./ c1985, 1995/ K-2/2 KF969 . . . . **E**
When I was young in the mountains./ 1982/ K-3/6 KG387 . . . . **CE E**
Where's our mama?/ 1991/ P-2/2 KF632 . . . . **E**
GOODE, E/ LETTERS FOR OUR CHILDREN: FIFTY AMERICANS SHARE
LESSONS IN LIVING./ 1996/ KA158 . . . . **PROF 170**
GOODELL, J/ Mouse called Wolf./ 1997/ 3-5/3 KH351 . . . . **FIC**
GOODMAN, SE/ Bats, bugs, and biodiversity: adventures in the
Amazonian rain forest./ 1995/ 3-6/7 KC318 . . . . **577.34**
GOODRICH, D/ Bookmark book./ 1996/ KA310 . . . . **PROF 741.6**
GOODSMITH, L/ Children of Mauritania: days in the desert and by the
river shore./ 1993/ 4-6/6 KE733 . . . . **966.1**
GOODWILL SPIRITUAL CHOIR/ African-American folk songs and rhythms
(Sound recording cassette)./ c1960, 1992/ K-6 KD572 . . **SRC 789.2**
GOOR, N/ Insect metamorphosis from egg to adult./ 1990/
4-6/6 KC539 . . . . **595.7**
Shadows: here, there, and everywhere./ 1981/ 1-3/5 KC111 . . . **535**
Williamsburg: cradle of the revolution./ 1994/ 5-A/7 KE978 . . **975.5**

GOOR, R/ Insect metamorphosis from egg to adult./ 1990/
4-6/6 KC539 . . . . **595.7**
Shadows: here, there, and everywhere./ 1981/ 1-3/5 KC111 . . . **535**
Williamsburg: cradle of the revolution./ 1994/ 5-A/7 KE978 . . . **975.5**
GORBACHEV, V/ Young Mouse and Elephant: an East African folktale./
1996/ K-2/4 KB565 . . . . **398.24**
GORDH, B/ Morning, noon and nighttime tales (Sound recording
cassette)./ 1993/ K-2 KD565 . . . . **SRC 789.2**
GORDON, G/ Anthony Reynoso: born to rope./ 1996/
3-4/4 KA841 . . . . **305.8**
My two worlds./ 1993/ 3-6/4 KA844 . . . . **305.8**
GORDON, JR/ Hide and shriek: riddles about ghosts and goblins./ 1991/
2-5 KD727 . . . . **793.735**
GORDON, L/ Messipes: a microwave cookbook of deliciously messy
masterpieces./ 1996/ 3-6 KD271 . . . . **641.5**
GORDON, R/ PEELING THE ONION: AN ANTHOLOGY OF POEMS./
1993/ A KD888 . . . . **808.81**
GORE, L/ I am king!/ 1994/ K-1/1 KG205 . . . . **E**
Jacob and the stranger./ 1994/ 3-5/4 KH071 . . . . **FIC**
Pomegranate seeds: a classic Greek myth./ 1995/ 3-6/5 KA742 . **292**
GOREY, E/ Doom of the haunted opera./ 1995/ 4-6/6 KG896 . . . . **FIC**
House with a clock in its walls./ c1973/ 4-6/5 KG897 . . . . **FIC**
Monster den: or look what happened at my house - and to it./ c1966,
1991/ 3-6 KD922 . . . . **811**
Old possum's book of practical cats./ 1982/ 4-A KE100 . . . . . . **821**
Red Riding Hood./ c1972, 1990/ P-2 KB732 . . . . **CE 398.27**
Shrinking of Treehorn./ c1971/ 3-A/6 KH232 . . . . **CE FIC**
You know who./ c1964, 1991/ 3-5 KD923 . . . . **811**
GORK/ Bicycling./ 1996/ 3-6/6 KD827 . . . . **796.6**
GORMAN, C/ Miraculous makeover of Lizard Flanagan./ c1994, 1996/
5-A/3 KH182 . . . . **FIC**
GORMAN, M/ ANGLO-AMERICAN CATALOGUING RULES. 2ND ED.,
1988 REVISION./ 1988/ KA056 . . . . **PROF 025.3**
GORMLEY, B/ First Ladies: women who called the White House home./
1997/ 4-6/9 KE852 . . . . **973**
GOROG, J/ In a creepy, creepy place and other scary stories./ 1996/
4-6/4 KH183 . . . . **FIC**
In a messy, messy room./ 1990/ 4-6/6 KH184 . . . . **FIC**
Please do not touch: a collection of stories./ c1993, 1995/
6-A/7 KH185 . . . . **FIC**
GOROSH, E/ Subject index for children & young people to Canadian
poetry in English. 2nd ed./ 1986/ A KA375 . . . . **REF 016.811**
GORRELL, GK/ North Star to freedom: the story of the Underground
Railroad./ 1997/ 5-6/8 KE905 . . . . **973.7**
GORSLINE, DW/ Little men: life at Plumfield with Jo's boys./ c1947,
1982/ 5-A/7 KG829 . . . . **FIC**
GORTON, J/ My new sandbox./ 1996/ P-1/1 KF822 . . . . **E**
GOSS, C/ It's Kwanzaa time!/ 1995/ 2-6/6 KB208 . . . . **394.261**
GOSS, L/ It's Kwanzaa time!/ 1995/ 2-6/6 KB208 . . . . **394.261**
It's Kwanzaa time! (Sound recording cassette)./ 1997/
2-6/6 KB208 . . . . **394.261**
GOTTLIEB, D/ Watermelon Day./ 1996/ K-2/2 KF164 . . . . **E**
GOUCK, M/ Great Barrier Reef./ 1993/ 3-6/5 KF119 . . . . **994.3**
Mountain lions./ 1993/ 3-5/5 KC829 . . . . **599.757**
GOULDTHORPE, P/ Wonder thing./ 1996/ P-2 KC181 . . . . . . **551.48**
GRABOWSKI, J/ Stan Musial./ 1993/ 5-A/7 KE474 . . . . **B MUSIAL, S.**
GRACE, CO/ I want to be... a veterinarian./ 1997/
5-6/9 KD195 . . . . **636.089**
I want to be... an astronaut./ 1997/ 5-6/9 KD137 . . . . **629.45**
GRACE, ES/ Elephants./ 1993/ 5-6/8 KC810 . . . . **599.67**
GRAEF, R/ Dance at Grandpa's./ 1994/ K-3/4 KG719 . . . . **E**
Winter days in the Big Woods./ 1994/ K-3/4 KG720 . . . . **E**
GRAFF, NP/ Where the river runs: a portrait of a refugee family./ 1993/
4-6/7 KA845 . . . . **305.8**
GRAHAM, H/ Boy and his bear./ 1996/ 5-A/5 KH186 . . . . **FIC**
GRAHAM, J/ Crime-fighting./ 1995/ 5-6/7 KB029 . . . . **363.2**
Fakes and forgeries./ 1995/ A/8 KA557 . . . . **001.9**
GRAHAM, K/ Recycling./ 1996/ 3-6/10 KB053 . . . . **363.72**
GRAHAM, M/ Dream jar./ 1996/ 2-3/5 KG291 . . . . **E**
My father's hands./ 1996/ 3-6/4 KG366 . . . . **E**
GRAHAM, MB/ Be nice to spiders./ c1967/ P-2/3 KF633 . . . . **E**
Be nice to spiders (Talking book)./ n.d./ P-2/3 KF633 . . . . **E**
Harry the dirty dog./ c1956/ P-2/2 KG800 . . . . **CE E**
GRAHAM, S/ Dear old Donegal./ 1996/ 1-3/2 KD566 . . . . . . **789.2**
GRAHAM-BARBER, L/ Doodle Dandy!: the complete book of Independence
Day words./ 1992/ 5-A/A KB220 . . . . **394.263**
Doodle Dandy!: the complete book of Independence Day words (Sound
recording cassette)./ 1996/ 5-A/A KB220 . . . . **394.263**
Ho Ho Ho!: the complete book of Christmas words./ 1993/
2-6/8 KB235 . . . . **394.266**
Mushy! the complete book of Valentine words./ 1991/
5-6/8 KB209 . . . . **394.261**
Toad or frog, swamp or bog?: a big book of nature's confusables./
1994/ K-4/4 KB906 . . . . **508**

GRAHAME, K/ Reluctant dragon./ c1938/ 3-6/7 KH187 . . . . . **CE FIC**
Reluctant dragon./ 1983/ 3-6/6 KH188 . . . . **CE FIC**
Reluctant dragon (Braille)./ n.d./ 3-6/7 KH187 . . . . **CE FIC**
Reluctant dragon (Sound recording cassette)./ n.d./
3-6/7 KH187 . . . . **CE FIC**
Reluctant dragon (Videocassette)./ 1981/ 3-6/7 KH187 . . . . **CE FIC**
Wind in the willows./ 1980/ 5-6/8 KH189 . . . . **FIC**
Wind in the willows (Braille)./ n.d./ 5-6/8 KH190 . . . . **FIC**
Wind in the willows (Sound recording cassette)./ n.d./
5-6/8 KH190 . . . . **FIC**
Wind in the willows (Talking book)./ n.d./ 5-6/8 KH190 . . . **FIC**
Wind in the willows. 75th anniversary edition./ 1983/
5-6/8 KH190 . . . . **FIC**
GRALLA, P/ Online kids: a young surfer's guide to cyberspace./ 1996/
3-A/4 KA578 . . . . **025.04**
GRAMATKY, H/ Little Toot./ 1981/ P-1/4 KF634 . . . . **CE E**
Little Toot (Braille)./ n.d./ P-1/4 KF634 . . . . **CE E**
GRANDPRE, M/ Batwings and the curtain of night./ 1997/
1-3/2 KF449 . . . . **E**
GRANFIELD, L/ Cowboy: an album./ 1994/ 5-A/8 KF030 . . . . . **978**
Extra! extra!: the who, what, where, when and why of newspapers./
1994/ 3-6/5 KA596 . . . . **071**
In Flanders Fields: the story of the poem by John McCrae./ 1995/
4-6/7 KD947 . . . . **811**
GRANGER, N/ Stamp collecting./ 1994/ 4-6/8 KD508 . . . . . . **769.56**
GRANT, L/ Shoeshine girl./ 1975/ 3-5/2 KG938 . . . . **FIC**
GRAUBART, CB/ World desk: a student handbook to the Internet. Rev.
ed./ 1996/ A/10 KA576 . . . . **025.04**
GRAVES, BB/ Mystery of the Tooth Gremlin./ 1997/ 1-3/2 KH191 . **FIC**
GRAVES, R/ Big green book./ c1962, 1990/ 3-6/4 KH192 . . . **FIC**
GRAVETT, C/ Knight./ 1993/ 4-A/7 KE648 . . . . **940.1**
GRAVOIS, JM/ Quickly, Quigley./ 1994/ P-1/2 KF635 . . . . . . **E**
GRAY, EJ/ Adam of the road./ c1942, 1970/ 5-6/6 KH194 . . . **CE FIC**
Adam of the road (Braille)./ n.d./ 5-6/6 KH194 . . . . **CE FIC**
Adam of the road (Sound recording cassette)./ n.d./
5-6/6 KH194 . . . . **CE FIC**
Adam of the road (Talking book)./ Adam of the road (Talking book)./
n.d.,/ 1980,/ 5-6/6 KH194 . . . . **CE FIC**
GRAY, L/ Falcon's egg./ 1995/ 5-A/6 KH195 . . . . **FIC**
GRAY, LM/ Is there room on the feather bed?/ 1997/ K-2/4 KF636 . . **E**
Small Green Snake./ 1994/ P-2/6 KF637 . . . . **E**
GRAY, N/ Country far away./ 1988/ K-3/1 KF638 . . . . **E**
GREEN, AC/ Sibling rivalry: brothers and sisters at odds./ 1994/
5-A/6 KA885 . . . . **306.875**
GREEN CHILI JAM BAND/ Magic bike (Sound recording cassette)./ 1991/
P-3 KD613 . . . . **SRC 789.3**
Starfishing (Compact disc)./ 1993/ P-2 KD614 . . . . **SRC 789.3**
Starfishing (Sound recording cassette)./ 1993/ P-2 KD614 . **SRC 789.3**
GREEN, CJ/ Emmy./ 1992/ 6-A/5 KH196 . . . . **FIC**
GREEN, CR/ Babe Didrikson Zaharias./ 1993/
4-5/4 KE608 . . . . **B ZAHARIAS, B.**
Brigham Young: pioneer and Mormon leader./ 1996/
5-6/8 KE605 . . . . **B YOUNG, B.**
John C. Fremont: soldier and pathfinder./ 1996/
5-6/4 KE357 . . . . **B FREMONT, J.**
Kit Carson: frontier scout./ 1996/ 5-6/7 KE277 . . . . . **B CARSON, K.**
Mysterious mind powers./ 1993/ 4-6/3 KA609 . . . . **133.8**
Recalling past lives./ 1993/ 4-6/3 KA611 . . . . **133.9**
Seeing the unseen./ 1993/ 4-6/5 KA610 . . . . **133.8**
Zebulon Pike: explorer of the Southwest./ 1996/
5-6/8 KE497 . . . . **B PIKE, Z.**
GREEN, J/ Noah./ 1994/ K-2/4 KA684 . . . . **222**
GREEN, K/ Number of animals./ 1993/ P-2/3 KG770 . . . . . . **E**
GREEN, L/ Young rider./ 1993/ 3-8/8 KD856 . . . . **798.2**
GREEN, N/ Advice for a frog./ 1995/ 3-5 KE019 . . . . **811**
GREEN, NB/ Hole in the dike./ c1974, 1975/ K-2/2 KF640 . . . **CE E**
Hole in the dike (Braille)./ n.d./ K-2/2 KF640 . . . . **CE E**
GREENAWAY, F/ Snake book./ 1997/ 2-6/6 KC639 . . . . . . **597.96**
GREENBERG, KE/ Out of the gang./ 1992/ 4-6/6 KB071 . . . . . **364.1**
Steven Jobs and Stephen Wozniak: creating the Apple computer./ 1994/
4-6/7 KD046 . . . . **621.39**
Zack's story: growing up with same-sex parents./ 1996/
4-6/4 KA877 . . . . **306.874**
GREENBERG, L/ AIDS: how it works in the body./ 1992/
A/8 KD028 . . . . **616.97**
GREENBERG, MH/ NEWBERY HALLOWEEN: A DOZEN SCARY STORIES
BY NEWBERY AWARD-WINNING AUTHORS./ 1993/
5-6/5 KH548 . . . . **FIC**
GREENE, B/ Summer of my German soldier./ c1973, 1993/
A/8 KH197 . . . . **FIC**
GREENE, C/ Eugene Field: the children's poet./ 1994/
2-4/4 KE343 . . . . **B FIELD, E.**

Johann Sebastian Bach: great man of music./ 1992/
2-4/2 KE246 . . . . **B BACH, J.**
John Philip Sousa: the march king./ 1992/ 2-4/2 KE544 . . **B SOUSA, J.**
Margarete Steiff: toy maker./ 1993/ 2-3/2 KE550 . . . **B STEIFF, M.**
Robert Louis Stevenson: author of A CHILD'S GARDEN OF VERSES./
1994/ 2-4/4 KE554 . . . . **B STEVENSON, R.**
Roy Campanella: major-league champion./ 1994/
1-2/2 KE275 . . . . **B CAMPANELLA, R**
Rudyard Kipling: author of the "Jungle books."/ 1994/
3-6/2 KE424 . . . . **B KIPLING, R.**
GREENE, CC/ Beat the turtle drum./ c1976, 1994/ 5-6/4 KH198 . . **FIC**
Beat the turtle drum (Sound recording cassette)./ n.d.,/
5-6/4 KH198 . . . . **FIC**
GREENE, E/ Billy Beg and his bull: an Irish tale./ 1994/
2-4/5 KB304 . . . . **398.2**
GREENE, JD/ Maya./ 1992/ 4-6/7 KE843 . . . . **972.81**
What his father did./ 1992/ 2-4/5 KB305 . . . . **398.2**
GREENE, L/ Sign language talk./ 1989/ 5-A/9 KB825 . . . . . . **419**
GREENFELD, H/ Hidden children./ 1993/ A/7 KE657 . . . . . **940.53**
Hidden children (Sound recording cassette)./ 1997/
A/7 KE657 . . . . **940.53**
Marc Chagall./ 1990/ 6-A/8 KE284 . . . . **B CHAGALL, M.**
GREENFIELD, E/ Grandpa's face./ 1988/ K-1/2 KF641 . . . . . . **E**
Koya DeLaney and the good girl blues./ c1992, 1995/
4-6/6 KH199 . . . . **FIC**
Me and Neesie./ c1975/ K-2/3 KF642 . . . . **E**
Nathaniel talking./ 1988/ K-6 KD948 . . . . **811**
GREENLEE, S/ When someone dies./ 1992/ K-3/4 KA649 . . . . **155.9**
GREENSPUN, AA/ Daddies./ 1991/ 1-3/4 KA878 . . . . **306.874**
GREENSTEIN, E/ Mrs. Rose's garden./ 1996/ K-2/3 KF643 . . . **E**
GREENWALD, S/ Rosy Cole: she grows and graduates./ 1997/
3-5/4 KH200 . . . . **FIC**
Rosy Cole: she walks in beauty./ 1994/ 3-6/3 KH201 . . . **FIC**
GREENWAY, S/ Can you see me?/ 1992/ K-2/4 KC461 . . . . . **591.4**
Two's company./ 1997/ K-2/3 KB845 . . . . **428.1**
Whose baby am I?/ 1992/ K-2/4 KC458 . . . . **591.3**
GREENWOOD, B/ Pioneer sampler: the daily life of a pioneer family in
1840./ 1995/ 4-6/6 KF031 . . . . **978**
GREENWOOD, PD/ What about my goldfish?/ 1993/ 1-3/2 KF644 . **E**
GREESON, J/ Name that book! Questions and answers on outstanding
children's books./ 1996/ KA350 . . . . **PROF 809**
GREGORY, C/ Cynthia Gregory dances Swan Lake./ 1990/
4-A/7 KD694 . . . . **792.8**
GREGORY, K/ Earthquake at dawn./ 1992/ 5-A/6 KH202 . . . . **FIC**
GRIEGO, MC/ TORTILLITAS PARA MAMA AND OTHER SPANISH
NURSERY RHYMES./ 1981/ 1-3 KB816 . . . . **398.8**
GRIEHL, K/ Snakes: giant snakes and non-venomous snakes in the
terrarium./ 1984/ A/9 KD249 . . . . **639.3**
GRIER, K/ Discover: investigate the mysteries of history with 40 practical/
1990/ 3-6/6 KA592 . . . . **069**
GRIESE, AA/ Way of our people./ 1997/ 5-6/5 KH203 . . . . . **FIC**
GRIFALCONI, A/ Darkness and the butterfly./ 1987/ K-2/4 KF645 . . **E**
Jasmine's parlour day./ 1994/ 1-3/3 KF856 . . . . **E**
Village of round and square houses./ 1986/ 3-4/6 KB739 . **CE 398.27**
Village of round and square houses (Videocassette)./ 1989/
3-4/6 KB739 . . . . **CE 398.27**
GRIFFIN-PIERCE, T/ Encyclopedia of Native America./ 1995/
5-A KA480 . . . . **REF 970.1**
GRIFFITH, G/ Jumping the broom./ 1994/ K-3/5 KG771 . . . . . **E**
Picture book of Sojourner Truth./ 1994/ 2-5/6 KE572 . . . **B TRUTH, S.**
Wagon train: a family goes West in 1865./ 1995/ 4-6/3 KF052 . **978**
GRIFFITH, HV/ Caitlin's Holiday./ 1990/ 4-6/4 KH204 . . . . . **FIC**
Emily and the enchanted frog./ 1989/ 2-4/2 KF646 . . . . . . **E**
Grandaddy and Janetta./ 1993/ 1-4/1 KF647 . . . . **E**
Grandaddy and Janetta (Sound recording cassette)./ 1995/
1-4/1 KF647 . . . . **E**
Grandaddy's place./ 1987/ 1-4/1 KF647 . . . . **E**
Grandaddy's place (Sound recording cassette)./ 1997/ 1-4/1 KF647 . **E**
Grandaddy's stars./ 1995/ 1-4/2 KF648 . . . . **E**
Grandaddy's stars (Sound recording cassette)./ 1997/ 1-4/2 KF648 . **E**
Mine will, said John. New ed./ 1992/ P-2/2 KF649 . . . . . . **E**
GRIMES, N/ Meet Danitra Brown./ 1994/ 2-4 KD949 . . . . . . **811**
GRIMES, T/ Where the wild things are and other stories (Talking book)./
1977/ P-2 KG437 . . . . **TB E**
GRIMM, J/ Bremen-Town musicians./ 1998/ 1-3/4 KB636 . . . . **398.24**
Frog prince./ c1974, 1993/ P-3/2 KB376 . . . . **398.2**
From the Brothers Grimm: a contemporary retelling of American folktales
and classic stories./ 1992/ 5-A KB281 . . . . **CE 398.2**
Golden goose./ 1995/ K-3/2 KB650 . . . . **398.24**
Goose girl: a story from the Brothers Grimm./ 1995/
3-5/5 KB328 . . . . **398.2**
Hansel and Gretel./ 1990/ 2-4/4 KB340 . . . . **398.2**
Hansel and Gretel: a tale from the Brothers Grimm./ 1984/
5/6 KB740 . . . . **CE 398.27**

Hansel and Gretel: a tale from the Brothers Grimm (Sound recording cassette)./ n.d./ 5/6 KB740 . . . . **CE 398.27**
Iron John./ 1994/ 4-5/4 KB330 . . . . **398.2**
Juniper tree and other tales from Grimm./ c1973, 1992/ 5-A/7 KB306 . . . . **398.2**
Little Red Riding Hood./ 1983/ 1-4/6 KB741 . . . . . . **CE 398.27**
Little Red Riding Hood (Braille)./ n.d./ 1-4/6 KB741 . **CE 398.27**
Rapunzel./ 1982/ 2-4/4 KB307 . . . . **398.2**
Rumpelstiltskin./ 1986/ 1-4/7 KB385 . . . . **CE 398.2**
Rumpelstiltskin./ 1997/ K-2/2 KB308 . . . . **398.2**
Seven ravens./ 1994/ 2-3/6 KB302 . . . . **398.2**
Seven ravens: a fairy tale./ 1995/ 3-5/7 KB309 . . . . . **398.2**
Shoemaker and the elves./ 1991/ 2-4/4 KB359 . . . . . . **398.2**
Snow-White and the seven dwarfs./ 1972/ 3-4/6 KB310 . **398.2**
Turnip./ 1992/ 3-5/6 KB557 . . . . **398.24**
Twelve dancing princesses: a fairy tale./ 1995/ 3-4/6 KB311 . . **398.2**
Wolf and the seven little kids: a fairy tale./ 1995/ 1-2/4 KB579 . . . . **398.24**
GRIMM, W/ Bremen-Town musicians./ 1998/ 1-3/4 KB636 . . . **398.24**
Frog prince./ c1974, 1993/ P-3/2 KB376 . . . . **398.2**
From the Brothers Grimm: a contemporary retelling of American folktales and classic stories./ 1992/ 5-A KB281 . . . . **CE 398.2**
Golden goose./ 1995/ K-3/2 KB650 . . . . **398.24**
Goose girl: a story from the Brothers Grimm./ 1995/ 3-5/5 KB328 . . . . **398.2**
Hansel and Gretel./ 1990/ 2-4/4 KB340 . . . . **398.2**
Hansel and Gretel: a tale from the Brothers Grimm./ 1984/ 5/6 KB740 . . . . **CE 398.27**
Iron John./ 1994/ 4-5/4 KB330 . . . . **398.2**
Juniper tree and other tales from Grimm./ c1973, 1992/ 5-A/7 KB306 . . . . **398.2**
Little Red Riding Hood./ 1983/ 1-4/6 KB741 . . . . . . **CE 398.27**
Rapunzel./ 1982/ 2-4/4 KB307 . . . . **398.2**
Rumpelstiltskin./ 1986/ 1-4/7 KB385 . . . . **CE 398.2**
Rumpelstiltskin./ 1997/ K-2/2 KB308 . . . . **398.2**
Seven ravens./ 1994/ 2-3/6 KB302 . . . . **398.2**
Seven ravens: a fairy tale./ 1995/ 3-5/7 KB309 . . . . . **398.2**
Shoemaker and the elves./ 1991/ 2-4/4 KB359 . . . . . . **398.2**
Snow-White and the seven dwarfs./ 1972/ 3-4/6 KB310 . **398.2**
Turnip./ 1992/ 3-5/6 KB557 . . . . **398.24**
Twelve dancing princesses: a fairy tale./ 1995/ 3-4/6 KB311 . . **398.2**
Wolf and the seven little kids: a fairy tale./ 1995/ 1-2/4 KB579 . . . . **398.24**
GRINDE, L/ MANY PEOPLE, MANY WAYS: UNDERSTANDING CULTURES AROUND THE WORLD./ 1995/ 4-A KA402 . . **REF 306**
GRISEWOOD, J/ KINGFISHER FIRST DICTIONARY./ 1995/ 1-2 KA424 . . . . **REF 423**
GRONER, J/ Miracle meals, eight nights of food 'n fun for Chanukah./ 1987/ 4-5 KD288 . . . . **641.59**
GROSE, HM/ Rebecca of Sunnybrook Farm./ 1994/ 5-A/6 KH857 . **FIC**
GROSS, RB/ Snakes. Rev. ed./ 1990/ 4-6/4 KC636 . . . . **597.96**
GROSSMAN, P/ Night ones./ 1991/ P-K/2 KF650 . . . . . **E**
GROVER, R/ AASL ELECTRONIC LIBRARY. 1997 ed. (CD-ROM)./ 1997/ KA045 . . . . **CDR PROF 025**
GRYSKI, C/ Hands on, thumbs up: secret handshakes, fingerprints, sign languages, and more handy ways to have fun with hands./ 1993/ 5-6/5 KC904 . . . . **611**
GUARINO, D/ Is your mama a llama?/ 1989/ P-1/2 KF651 . . . . **E**
Is your mama a llama? (Big book)./ 1992/ P-1/2 KF651 . . . **E**
Tu mama es una llama?/ 1993/ P-1/2 KF651 . . . . **E**
GUARNACCIA, S/ Anansi (Kit)./ 1992/ 3-5 KB572 . . . . **KIT 398.24**
GUBACK, G/ Luka's quilt./ 1994/ 1-3/2 KF652 . . . . **E**
GUCCIONE, LD/ Come morning./ 1995/ 4-6/3 KH205 . . . . **FIC**
GUERNSEY, JB/ Sand and fog: adventures in Southern Africa./ 1994/ 5-6/6 KE740 . . . . **968.81**
To the top of the world: adventures with arctic wolves./ 1993/ 5-6/7 KC834 . . . . **599.773**
GUEVARA, S/ Chato's kitchen./ c1995, 1997/ 1-3/5 KG527 . . . . . **E**
GUIBERSON, BZ/ Into the sea./ 1996/ 1-3/3 KC618 . . . . . **597.92**
Lighthouses: watchers at sea./ 1995/ 5-6/8 KB150 . . . . **387.1**
GUNDERSHEIMER, K/ Happy winter./ 1982/ P-1/3 KF653 . . . . . . **E**
Special trade./ 1978/ P-3/4 KG754 . . . . **E**
GUNNING, M/ Not a copper penny in me house: poems from the Caribbean./ 1993/ P-3 KD950 . . . . **811**
GUNNING, TG/ Dream planes./ 1992/ 5-6/7 KD109 . . . . . **629.133**
Dream trains./ 1992/ 4-6/6 KD074 . . . . **625.1**
GUTELLE, A/ Kirby Puckett's baseball games./ 1996/ 3-6/7 KD801 . . . . **796.357**
GUTHRIE, D/ How to write, recite, and delight in all kinds of poetry./ 1996/ 3-6 KD867 . . . . **808.06**
Putting on a play: the young playwright's guide to scripting, directing, and performing./ 1996/ 4-6/7 KD687 . . . . **792**
Rose for Abby./ 1988/ 2-4/5 KF654 . . . . **E**

Young author's do-it-yourself book: how to write, illustrate, and produce your own book./ 1994/ 2-6/4 KD863 . . . . **808**
Young producer's video book: how to write, direct, and shoot your own video./ 1995/ 3-6/4 KD686 . . . . **791.45**
GUTHRIE, F/ African animal tales./ 1993/ 2-4/6 KB526 . . . . . . **398.24**
GUTHRIE, W/ Nursery days (Compact disc)./ 1992/ P-1 KD567 . . . . **CD 789.2**
GUTIERREZ, R/ Causa: the migrant farmworkers' story./ 1993/ 4-6/6 KA944 . . . . **331.88**
GUTMAN, B/ Frank Thomas: power hitter./ 1996/ 3-5/6 KE563 . . . . **B THOMAS, F.**
Gail Devers./ 1996/ 5-6/6 KE319 . . . . **B DEVERS, G.**
Grant Hill: basketball's high flier./ 1996/ 5-6/7 KE390 . . **B HILL, G.**
Hakeem Olajuwon: superstar center./ 1995/ 4-5/6 KE483 . . . . **B OLAJUWON, H.**
Hazards at home./ 1996/ 5-6/7 KB022 . . . . **363.1**
Jim Eisenreich./ 1996/ 3-5/6 KE336 . . . . **B EISENREICH, J**
Julie Krone./ 1996/ 5-6/5 KE425 . . . . **B KRONE, J.**
Michael Jordan: basketball to baseball and back. Rev. ed./ 1995/ 4-6/8 KE410 . . . . **B JORDAN, M.**
Steve Young: NFL passing wizard./ 1996/ 4-6/7 KE607 . . . . **B YOUNG, S.**
GUTMAN, D/ Taking flight: my story./ 1995/ 3-6/6 KD101 . . . **629.13**
GUY, GF/ Fiesta!/ 1996/ P-1/1 KF655 . . . . **E**
GWYNNE, F/ Pondlarker./ 1990/ K-2/5 KF656 . . . . **E**
HAARHOFF, D/ Desert December./ 1992/ 3-5/4 KH206 . . . . . **FIC**
HAAS, D/ Burton and the giggle machine./ 1992/ 4-6/5 KH207 . . . **FIC**
Burton's zoom zoom va-rooom machine./ 1996/ 4-6/5 KH207 . . . . **FIC**
HAAS, I/ Little house of your own./ c1954/ K-1/4 KF483 . . . . . **E**
HAAS, J/ Be well, Beware./ 1996/ 3-5/2 KH208 . . . . **FIC**
Be well, Beware (Sound recording cassette)./ 1997/ 3-5/2 KH208 . **FIC**
Beware the mare./ 1993/ 3-5/4 KH209 . . . . **FIC**
Beware the mare (Sound recording cassette)./ 1997/ 3-5/4 KH209 . . . . **FIC**
Safe horse, safe rider: a young rider's guide to responsible horsekeeping./ 1994/ 5-6/6 KD200 . . . . **636.1**
Sugaring./ 1996/ K-2/2 KF657 . . . . **E**
Uncle Daney's way./ 1994/ 4-6/4 KH210 . . . . **FIC**
HAAS, MS/ Story of Babar, the little elephant./ c1937, 1960/ P-2/3 KF453 . . . . **E**
HAAS, SO/ Daddy's chair./ 1991/ P-2/2 KF944 . . . . **E**
Listening to crickets: a story about Rachel Carson./ 1993/ 5-6/6 KE278 . . . . **B CARSON, R.**
Northern lights: a Hanukkah story./ 1994/ 1-3/4 KF417 . . . . **E**
HABAN, RD/ How proudly they wave: flags of the fifty states./ 1989/ 5-6/8 KE619 . . . . **929.9**
HADDIX, MP/ Running out of time./ 1995/ 5-A/5 KH211 . . . . . **FIC**
HADER, B/ Big snow./ 1948/ K-2/5 KF658 . . . . **E**
Big snow (Braille)./ n.d./ K-2/5 KF658 . . . . **E**
HADER, E/ Big snow./ 1948/ K-2/5 KF658 . . . . **E**
HADITHI, M/ Crafty chameleon./ c1987, 1995/ P-2/7 KF659 . . . . **E**
Hot Hippo./ 1986/ K-3/4 KF660 . . . . **CE E**
Hot Hippo (Braille)./ n.d./ K-3/4 KF660 . . . . **CE E**
Hot Hippo (Videocassette)./ n.d./ K-3/4 KF660 . . . . . . **CE E**
HAERINGEN, AV/ Tales of the wicked witch./ 1995/ 3-5/3 KH379 . **FIC**
HAFER, JC/ Come sign with us: sign language activities for children. 2nd. ed./ 1996/ KA279 . . . . **PROF 419**
HAFNER, M/ Candy witch./ 1979/ K-1/6 KF927 . . . . **E**
Daddy, could I have an elephant?/ 1996/ K-2/2 KG755 . . . . . **E**
Germs make me sick! Rev. ed./ 1995/ 1-3/5 KD021 . . . . **616.9**
Hanukkah!/ 1993/ K-2/2 KA779 . . . . **296.4**
Happy Father's Day./ 1988/ K-2/2 KF928 . . . . **E**
It's Halloween./ c1977/ 1-3 KE004 . . . . **811**
It's Thanksgiving./ 1982/ 1-3 KE006 . . . . **CE 811**
Lunch bunnies./ 1996/ K-2/2 KF946 . . . . **E**
Mind your manners!/ , 1994/ 1-3 KB250 . . . . **395.5**
My stars, it's Mrs. Gaddy!: the three Mrs. Gaddy stories./ 1991/ 1-3/2 KF593 . . . . **E**
Passover magic./ 1995/ K-2/2 KG410 . . . . **E**
Rainy rainy Saturday./ 1980/ 1-3 KE013 . . . . **811**
HAGERMAN, J/ Bookworks: making books by hand./ 1995/ 3-6/5 KD437 . . . . **745.5**
Say it with music: a story about Irving Berlin./ 1994/ 4-5/5 KE252 . . . . **B BERLIN, I.**
HAGUE, M/ CHILDREN'S BOOK OF VIRTUES./ 1995/ K-3 KD871 . . . . **808.8**
Owl and the Pussy-cat and other nonsense poems./ 1995/ 3-6 KE106 . . . . **821**
RAINBOW FAIRY BOOK./ 1993/ 2-6/8 KB360 . . . . . . **398.2**
Reluctant dragon./ 1983/ 3-6/6 KH188 . . . . **CE FIC**
Rootabaga stories./ c1922, 1990/ 1-6/7 KH674 . . . . **FIC**
SLEEP, BABY, SLEEP: LULLABIES AND NIGHT POEMS./ 1994/ P-K KD889 . . . . **808.81**
Twinkle, twinkle, little star./ 1992/ P-K KE111 . . . . **821**

Wind in the willows./ 1980/ 5-6/8 KH189 . . . . **FIC**
HAHN, D/ Animation magic: a behind-the-scenes look at how an animated
　film is made./ 1996/ 4-6/9 KD685 . . . . **791.43**
HALE, C/ Juan Bobo and the pig: a Puerto Rican folktale./ 1993/
　2-4/2 KB763 . . . . **398.27**
HALE, JG/ How mountains are made./ 1995/ 2-4/4 KC170 . . . . **551.43**
Through moon and stars and night skies./ 1990/ P-2/1 KG629 . . **CE E**
HALEBIAN, C/ Out of the gang./ 1992/ 4-6/6 KB071 . . . . **364.1**
HALEY, GE/ Mountain Jack tales./ 1992/ 4-6/6 KB449 . . . . . **398.22**
Story, a story: an African tale./ c1970/ 3-5/5 KB580 . . . . **CE 398.24**
Story, a story: an African tale (Braille)./ n.d./ 3-5/5 KB580 **CE 398.24**
Story, a story: an African tale (Sound recording cassette)./ 1997/
　3-5/5 KB580 . . . . **CE 398.24**
Story, a story: an African tale (Talking book)./ Story, a story: an African
　tale (Talking book)./ 1993/ n.d./ 3-5/5 KB580 . . . .
　3-5/5 KB580 . . . . **CE 398.24**
Story, a story: an African tale (Videocassette)./ n.d./
　3-5/5 KB580 . . . . **CE 398.24**
Two bad boys: a very old Cherokee tale./ 1996/ 2-5/5 KB742 **398.27**
HALKIN, H/ Island on Bird Street./ 1983/ 5-A/6 KH566 . . . . . . **FIC**
Man from the other side./ 1991/ 5-A/6 KH567 . . . . **FIC**
HALL, A/ Stories from the sea./ 1996/ K-3/3 KB508 . . . . . . **398.23**
HALL, D/ Celebrate! in South Asia./ 1996/ 2-5/11 KB191 . . . . **394.2**
Celebrate! in Southeast Asia./ 1996/ 2-5/11 KB192 . . . . . . **394.2**
I am the dog, I am the cat./ 1994/ K-3/3 KF661 . . . . **E**
Lucy's Christmas./ 1994/ 1-3/6 KF662 . . . . **E**
Ox-cart man./ 1979/ K-3/7 KF663 . . . . **CE E**
Ox-cart man (Braille)./ n.d./ K-3/7 KF663 . . . . **CE E**
Ox-cart man (Kit)./ 1984/ K-3/7 KF663 . . . . **CE E**
Ox-cart man (Sound recording cassette)./ n.d./ K-3/7 KF663 . . **CE E**
Ox-cart man (Videocassette)./ 1992/ K-3/7 KF663 . . . . **CE E**
When Willard met Babe Ruth./ 1996/ 4-6/6 KH212 . . . . **FIC**
HALL, E/ Thunder rolling in the mountains./ 1992/ 5-A/5 KH563 . . . **FIC**
HALL, K/ Batty riddles./ 1993/ K-3 KD728 . . . . **793.735**
I'm not scared./ 1994/ K-1/1 KF664 . . . . **E**
Tooth fairy./ 1994/ K-1/1 KF665 . . . . **E**
HALL, MW/ July is a mad mosquito./ 1994/ P-3 KD972 . . . . **811**
Weather: poems./ 1994/ K-3 KE064 . . . . **811.008**
HALL, NA/ POLLITOS DICEN: JUEGOS, RIMAS Y CANCIONES
　INFANTILES DE PAISES DE HABLA HISPANA./THE BABY CHICKS
　SING: TRADITIONAL GAMES, NURSERY/ 1994/
　P-1/2 KD584 . . . . **789.2**
HALL, WE/ Adventures of High John the Conqueror./ 1989/
　3-6/5 KB480 . . . . **398.22**
HALL, Z/ Apple pie tree./ 1996/ 1-4/2 KC413 . . . . **582.16**
It's pumpkin time!/ 1996/ P-2/3 KF666 . . . . **E**
HALLENSLEBEN, G/ Spider spider./ 1996/ P-1/2 KF194 . . . . **E**
HALLOWEEN POEMS./ 1989/ K-4 KE062 . . . . **811.008**
HALLUM, R/ Children's all-time Mother Goose favorites (Sound recording
　cassette)./ 1997/ KA275 . . . . **SRC PROF 398.8**
Fingerplays and footplays (Videocassette)./ 1997/
　P-K KD708 . . . . **VCR 793.4**
HALPERIN, WA/ Homeplace./ 1995/ 1-3/3 KG493 . . . . **E**
Hunting the white cow./ 1993/ 1-3/2 KG474 . . . . **E**
HALPERN, NA/ Kids and the environment: taking responsibility for our
　surroundings (Microcomputer program)./ 1994/
　1-5 KB046 . . . . **CDR 363.7**
HALPERN, S/ Apple pie tree./ 1996/ 1-4/2 KC413 . . . . **582.16**
It's pumpkin time!/ 1994/ P-2/3 KF666 . . . . **E**
No, no, Titus!/ 1997/ P-1/2 KG083 . . . . **E**
HALSEY, M/ 3 pandas planting./ 1994/ P-1/2 KB958 . . . . **513.2**
HALSTEAD, V/ TEN-SECOND RAINSHOWERS: POEMS BY YOUNG
　PEOPLE./ 1996/ 3-6 KE088 . . . . **811.008**
HALTON, CM/ Those amazing eels./ 1990/ 5-6/7 KC597 . . . . . **597.5**
Those amazing leeches./ 1989/ 5-6/9 KC504 . . . . **592**
HAMANAKA, S/ All the colors of the earth./ 1994/ P-2/4 KF667 . . . **E**
Class clown./ 1987/ 2-4/4 KH298 . . . . **FIC**
Journey: Japanese Americans, racism, and renewal./ 1990/
　5-6/7 KE854 . . . . **973**
Peace crane./ 1995/ 1-3/4 KF668 . . . . **E**
Screen of frogs: an old tale./ 1993/ 2-4/4 KB581 . . . . **398.24**
Sofie's role./ 1992/ P-2/2 KF692 . . . . **E**
Teacher's pet./ 1988/ 3-5/4 KH305 . . . . **FIC**
HAMILTON, M/ Haunting tales: live from the Culbertson Mansion State
　Historic Site (Sound recording cassette)./ 1996/
　2-4 KB686 . . . . **SRC 398.25**
SOME DOG AND OTHER KENTUCKY WONDERS (Sound recording
　cassette)./ 1992/ 3-4 KB370 . . . . **SRC 398.2**
HAMILTON, V/ Cousins./ 1990/ 6-A/5 KH213 . . . . **FIC**
Drylongso./ 1992/ 4-6/4 KH214 . . . . **FIC**
Her stories: African-American folktales, fairy tales, and true tales./ 1995/
　4-6/3 KB312 . . . . **398.2**
House of Dies Drear./ c1968/ 4-6/5 KH215 . . . . **CE FIC**
House of Dies Drear (Braille)./ n.d./ 4-6/5 KH215 . . . . **CE FIC**

House of Dies Drear (Talking book)./ n.d./ 4-6/5 KH215 . . . . **CE FIC**
House of Dies Drear (Videocassette)./ c1984/ 4-6/5 KH215 . . **CE FIC**
In the beginning: creation stories from around the world./ 1988/
　5-6/4 KA731 . . . . **291.2**
Many thousand gone: African Americans from slavery to freedom./
　1993/ 4-6/7 KA927 . . . . **326**
M.C. Higgins, the great./ 1974/ A/4 KH216 . . . . **FIC**
M.C. Higgins, the great (Braille)./ n.d./ A/4 KH216 . . . . **FIC**
Mystery of Drear House./ 1987/ 4-6/5 KH215 . . . . **CE FIC**
Plain City./ 1993/ 6-A/5 KH217 . . . . **FIC**
Plain City (Sound recording cassette)./ 1995/ 6-A/5 KH217 . . . . **FIC**
Planet of Junior Brown./ c1971/ A/6 KH218 . . . . **CE FIC**
Planet of Junior Brown (Talking book)./ 1975/ A/6 KH218 . . . **CE FIC**
Primos./ 1995/ 6-A/5 KH213 . . . . **FIC**
When birds could talk and bats could sing: the adventures of Bruh
　Sparrow, Sis Wren, and their friends./ 1996/ 2-5/2 KB582 . **398.24**
Willie Bea and the time the Martians landed./ 1983/ 5-6/3 KH219 **FIC**
Willie Bea and the time the Martians landed (Sound recording cassette)./
　n.d./ 5-6/3 KH219 . . . . **FIC**
Zeely./ c1967/ 4-A/4 KH220 . . . . **FIC**
Zeely (Braille)./ n.d./ 4-A/4 KH220 . . . . **FIC**
Zeely (Talking book)./ n.d./ 4-A/4 KH220 . . . . **FIC**
HAMLIN, J/ Howard Carter: searching for King Tut./ 1995/
　A/9 KE279 . . . . **B CARTER, H.**
Jack Horner: living with dinosaurs./ 1994/
　5-A/8 KE391 . . . . **B HORNER, J.**
Living fossils: animals that have withstood the test of time./ 1997/
　4-A/9 KC453 . . . . **591**
May Chinn: the best medicine./ 1995/ 5-A/8 KE288 . . . **B CHINN, M.**
HAMM, DJ/ Grandma drives a motor bed./ 1987/ P-3/2 KF669 . . . . **E**
Grandma drives a motor bed (Sound recording cassette)./ n.d./
　P-3/2 KF669 . . . . **E**
Laney's lost momma./ 1991/ P-1/2 KF670 . . . . **E**
HAMMEL, P/ Popcorn shop./ 1993/ P-2/2 KG035 . . . . **E**
HAMMERSTEIN, O/ Sound of music. Selections. 2nd ed. (Sound recording
　cassette)./ 1965/ K-A KD531 . . . . **SRC 782.1**
HAMMETT, CT/ PRESCHOOL ACTION TIME (Sound recording cassette)./
　1988/ P KD650 . . . . **SRC 789.3**
HAMMOND, G/ Raven and Snipe./ 1991/ 3-4/6 KB546 . . . . . **398.24**
Raven goes berrypicking./ 1991/ 3-4/6 KB547 . . . . **398.24**
HAMMOND, T/ Sports./ 1988/ 4-A/8 KD761 . . . . **796**
HAN, OS/ Kongi and Potgi: a Cinderella story from Korea./ 1996/
　K-3/5 KB313 . . . . **398.2**
HAN, SC/ Rabbit's escape/Kusa ilsaenghan tookki./ 1995/
　P-2/3 KB583 . . . . **398.24**
HANCOCK, H/ Koi and the kola nuts (Kit)./ 1992/
　2-5 KB446 . . . . **KIT 398.22**
HANCOCK, L/ Northwest Territories./ 1993/ 5-6/8 KE824 . . . . . **971.9**
Nunavut./ 1995/ 4-6/7 KE825 . . . . **971.9**
HAND IN HAND: AN AMERICAN HISTORY THROUGH POETRY./ 1994/
　2-6 KE063 . . . . **811.008**
HANDELSMAN, J/ Who's that stepping on Plymouth Rock?/ c1975/
　3-5/5 KE940 . . . . **CE 974.4**
HANKIN, R/ What was it like before television?/ 1995/
　1-3/2 KD679 . . . . **790.1**
HANNA, C/ Hard to be six./ 1991/ 1-2 KD909 . . . . **811**
HANNA, J/ AMAZING ANIMALS (Videocassette)./ 1994/
　3-6 KD188 . . . . **VCR 636.008**
HIMALAYAN ADVENTURE (Videocassette)./ 1994/
　K-6 KE712 . . . . **VCR 954.96**
HANSARD, P/ Jig, Fig, and Mrs. Pig./ 1995/ P-2/3 KB584 . . . **398.24**
HANSEN, E/ Guinea pigs./ 1992/ 4-6/6 KD181 . . . . **636**
HANSON, PE/ Buttons for General Washington./ 1986/
　4-6/4 KE885 . . . . **973.3**
HANSON, R/ I pledge allegiance./ 1990/ 2-5/4 KA909 . . . . **CE 323.6**
HARGROVE, J/ Pigeons and doves./ 1992/ 4-6/4 KC696 . . . . . . **598.6**
HARITON, A/ Compost!: growing gardens from your garbage./ 1996/
　P-K/3 KD166 . . . . **635**
HARLEY, B/ Come on out and play (Sound recording cassette)./ 1990,/
　1-3 KF671 . . . . **SRC E**
Dinosaurs never say please and other stories (Sound recording cassette)./
　c1987, 1989/ 1-3 KF671 . . . . **SRC E**
Grownups are strange (Sound recording cassette)./ 1990,/
　1-3 KF671 . . . . **SRC E**
I'M GONNA LET IT SHINE: A GATHERING OF VOICES FOR
　FREEDOM (Sound recording cassette)./ 1990/
　3-6 KD619 . . . . **SRC 789.3**
Lunchroom tales: a natural history of the cafetorium (Compact disc)./
　1996/ 2-4 KD615 . . . . **SRC 789.3**
Lunchroom tales: a natural history of the cafetorium (Sound recording
　cassette)./ 1996/ 2-4 KD615 . . . . **SRC 789.3**
Sitting down to eat./ 1996/ P-2/2 KF672 . . . . **E**
HARMS, JM/ Picture books to enhance the curriculum./ 1996/
　KA016 . . . . **PROF 011.62**

HARNESS, C/ Abe Lincoln goes to Washington 1837-1865./ 1997/
2-4/7 KE443 . . . . **B LINCOLN, A.**
Amazing impossible Erie Canal./ 1995/ 3-6/8 KB143 . . . . **386**
They're off!: the story of the Pony Express./ 1996/ 2-5/8 KB129 . **383**
Young Abe Lincoln: the frontier days, 1809-1837./ 1996/
2-4/5 KE442 . . . . **B LINCOLN, A.**
Young John Quincy./ 1994/ 3-5/6 KE226 . . . . **B ADAMS, J.Q.**
HARPER, I/ My cats Nick and Nora./ 1995/ P-1/2 KF673 . . . . **E**
My dog Rosie./ 1994/ P-1/1 KF674 . . . . **E**
Our new puppy./ 1996/ P-2/1 KF675 . . . . **E**
HARPER, M/ Subject index for children & young people to Canadian
poetry in English. 2nd ed./ 1986/ A KA375 . . . . **REF 016.811**
HARRINGTON, DJ/ Top 10 women tennis players./ 1995/
3-6/7 KD790 . . . . **796.342**
HARRIS, A/ Painting: a young artist's guide./ 1993/
5-6/8 KD470 . . . . **751.4**
HARRIS, AW/ Great Voyager adventure: a guided tour through the solar
system./ 1990/ A/9 KC026 . . . . **523.4**
HARRIS, J/ Curious George and other stories about Curious George
(Talking book)./ 1973/ P-2 KG323 . . . . **TB E**
Little women (Talking book)./ 1975/ 5-A KG830 . . . . **TB FIC**
Three little javelinas./ 1992/ K-2/4 KG039 . . . . **E**
Tortoise and the jackrabbit./ 1994/ K-2/3 KG040 . . . . **E**
Way of the ferret: finding and using educational resources on the Internet.
2nd. ed./ 1995/ KA046 . . . . **PROF 025.04**
HARRIS, JC/ Brer Rabbit and Boss Lion (Kit)./ 1996/
3-A KB599 . . . . **KIT 398.24**
Jump! The adventures of Brer Rabbit./ 1997/ 3-4/6 KB585 . . **398.24**
Jump! The adventures of Brer Rabbit (Sound recording cassette)./ n.d./
3-4/6 KB585 . . . . **398.24**
HARRIS, L/ Caribou./ 1988/ 4-5/8 KC797 . . . . **599.65**
Hockey./ 1994/ 3-6/4 KD841 . . . . **796.962**
HARRIS, LL/ BIOGRAPHY FOR BEGINNERS: SKETCHES FOR EARLY
READERS./ 1995/ 3-5 KA476 . . . . **REF 920**
BIOGRAPHY TODAY ARTISTS SERIES: PROFILES OF INTEREST TO
YOUNG READERS./ 1996/ 4-6 KA453 . . . . **REF 709.2**
BIOGRAPHY TODAY AUTHOR SERIES: PROFILES OF PEOPLE OF
INTEREST TO YOUNG READERS./ 1996-/ 4-6 KA461 . . . **REF 809**
BIOGRAPHY TODAY SCIENTISTS AND INVENTORS SERIES: PROFILES
OF PEOPLE OF INTEREST TO YOUNG PEOPLE./ 1996-/
4-6 KA438 . . . . **REF 509**
BIOGRAPHY TODAY SPORTS SERIES: PROFILES OF PEOPLE OF
INTEREST TO YOUNG READERS./ 1996-/ 4-6 KA456 . . . **REF 796**
BIOGRAPHY TODAY WORLD LEADERS SERIES: PROFILES OF PEOPLE
OF INTEREST TO YOUNG READERS./ 1997-/ 4-6 KA407 **REF 350**
HARRIS, RH/ Happy birth day!/ 1996/ P-2/3 KF676 . . . . **E**
It's perfectly normal: a book about changing bodies, growing up, sex, and
sexual health./ 1994/ 5-6/6 KC949 . . . . **612.6**
HARRIS, W/ Going home./ 1993/ 1-3/3 KG716 . . . . **E**
HARRISON, B/ Twilight struggle: the life of John Fitzgerald Kennedy./
1992/ 6-A/8 KE418 . . . . **B KENNEDY, J.**
HARRISON, DL/ Somebody catch my homework./ 1993/
2-6 KD951 . . . . **811**
HARRISON, P/ Claude Monet./ 1996/ 4-6/7 KE466 . . . . **B MONET, C.**
Vincent van Gogh./ 1996/ 4-6/7 KE369 . . . . **B GOGH, V.**
HARRISON, T/ O Canada./ 1993/ 3-6/6 KE802 . . . . **971**
HARSTE, JC/ New policy guidelines for reading: connecting research and
practice./ 1989/ KA208 . . . . **PROF 372.4**
HARSTON, J/ Dick Rutan and Jeana Yeager: flying non-stop around the
world./ 1994/ 5-6/6 KD099 . . . . **629.13**
HART, A/ Kids garden!: the anytime, anyplace guide to sowing and
growing fun./ 1996/ 3-5/6 KD167 . . . . **635**
HART, G/ Ancient Egypt./ 1990/ 5-6/8 KE633 . . . . **932**
Antiguo Egipto./ n.d./ 5-6/8 KE633 . . . . **932**
HART, M/ Aladdin and the magic lamp (Kit)./ 1995/
3-5 KB333 . . . . **KIT 398.2**
HART, PS/ Up in the air: the story of Bessie Coleman./ 1996/
4-6/8 KE299 . . . . **B COLEMAN, B.**
HART, TL/ Creative ideas for library media center facilities./ 1990/
KA075 . . . . **PROF 027.8**
HARTELIUS, MA/ Easy costumes you don't have to sew./ c1975/
P-A/4 KD298 . . . . **646.4**
HARTMAN, T/ How do you spell God?: answers to the big questions from
around the world./ 1995/ 5-A/4 KA724 . . . . **291**
HARTMAN, V/ Silliest joke book ever./ 1993/ 2-4/5 KD729 . **793.735**
HARTMANN, J/ Let's read together and other songs for sharing and caring
(Sound recording cassette)./ 1991/ P-2 KD616 . . . . **SRC 789.3**
Make a friend, be a friend: songs for growing up and growing together
with friends (Sound recording cassette)./ 1990/
K-5 KD617 . . . . **SRC 789.3**
One voice for children (Videocassette)./ 1993/ K-4 KD618 . **VCR 789.3**
HARTMANN, W/ One sun rises: an African wildlife counting book./ 1994/
P-2/3 KB959 . . . . **513.2**
HARTWIG, M/ Gorillas./ 1993/ 5-6/7 KC874 . . . . **599.884**

HARVEY, B/ Cassie's journey: going West in the 1860s./ 1988/
1-3/5 KF677 . . . . **E**
Cassie's journey: going West in the 1860s (Sound recording cassette)./
n.d./ 1-3/5 KF677 . . . . **E**
Immigrant girl: Becky of Eldridge Street./ 1987/ 3-5/5 KH221 . . . . **FIC**
My prairie Christmas./ 1990/ 2-4/4 KH222 . . . . **FIC**
HARVEY, D/ Secret elephant of Harlan Kooter./ 1992/
4-A/6 KH223 . . . . **FIC**
Secret elephant of Harlan Kooter (Sound recording cassette)./ 1995/
4-A/6 KH223 . . . . **FIC**
HARVEY, I/ Tanks./ 1996/ 4-6/8 KD060 . . . . **623.7**
HARVEY, L/ Head full of notions: a story about Robert Fulton./ 1997/
4-5/8 KE359 . . . . **B FULTON, R.**
HARVEY, M/ Fall of the Soviet Union./ 1995/ 5-A/7 KE689 . . . . . **947**
HARVEY, P/ Math fun with tricky lines and shapes./ 1992/
4-A/5 KD714 . . . . **793.7**
HARVILL, K/ Jack and the animals: an Appalachian folktale./ 1995/
2-4/5 KB555 . . . . **398.24**
Sitting down to eat./ 1996/ P-2/2 KF672 . . . . **E**
HASELEY, D/ Shadows./ 1991/ 4-6/5 KH224 . . . . **FIC**
HASKINS, J/ Headless haunt and other African-American ghost stories./
1994/ 4-5/4 KB687 . . . . **398.25**
I am Rosa Parks./ 1997/ 1-2/4 KE491 . . . . **B PARKS, R.**
One more river to cross: the stories of twelve Black Americans./ 1992/
5-A/7 KA847 . . . . **305.8**
One more river to cross: the stories of twelve Black Americans (Sound
recording cassette)./ 1995/ 5-A/7 KA847 . . . . **305.8**
Outward dreams: black inventors and their inventions./ 1991/
A/10 KC890 . . . . **609**
Rosa Parks: my story./ 1992/ 6-A/5 KE490 . . . . **B PARKS, R.**
HASLER, E/ Winter magic./ 1989/ K-3/4 KF678 . . . . **E**
HASS, M/ Beware the mare./ 1993/ 3-5/4 KH209 . . . . **FIC**
HASTINGS, S/ Children's illustrated Bible./ 1994/ 4-6/5 KA676 . . **220**
Reynard the Fox./ 1991/ 2-3/6 KB586 . . . . **398.24**
Sir Gawain and the green knight./ 1981/ 6/6 KB450 . . . . . **398.22**
HATCH, JM/ AMERICAN BOOK OF DAYS. 3rd ed./ 1978/
4-6 KA412 . . . . **REF 394.2**
HATFIELD, JT/ America's religions: an educator's guide to beliefs and
practices./ 1997/ KA160 . . . . **PROF 200**
HATHORN, L/ Wonder thing./ 1996/ P-2 KC181 . . . . **551.48**
HATRICK, G/ Masks./ 1996/ 6-A/3 KH225 . . . . **FIC**
HAUGAARD, EC/ Boy and the Samurai./ 1991/ 6-A/6 KH226 . **CE FIC**
Boy and the Samurai (Talking book)./ 1993/ 6-A/6 KH226 . . **CE FIC**
Little fishes./ c1967, 1987/ A/6 KH227 . . . . **FIC**
Little fishes (Braille)./ n.d.,/ A/6 KH227 . . . . **FIC**
Little fishes (Talking book)./ n.d.,/ A/6 KH227 . . . . **FIC**
Samurai's tale./ 1984/ 6-A/5 KH228 . . . . **FIC**
Samurai's tale (Sound recording cassette)./ n.d./ 6-A/5 KH228 . . . **FIC**
HAUMAN, D/ Little engine that could./ c1961/ P-K/4 KG246 . . . . **CE E**
HAUMAN, G/ Little engine that could./ c1961/ P-K/4 KG246 . . . . **CE E**
HAUSHERR, R/ Children and the AIDS virus: a book for children, parents,
and teachers./ 1989/ 2-4/7 KD029 . . . . **616.97**
One-room school at Squabble Hollow./ 1988/ 3-6/7 KB084 . **371.19**
What food is this?/ 1994/ K-2/2 KD266 . . . . **641.3**
HAUSMAN, G/ Eagle boy: a traditional Navajo legend./ 1996/
3-4/5 KB587 . . . . **398.24**
How Chipmunk got tiny feet: Native American animal origin stories./
1995/ K-3/3 KB588 . . . . **398.24**
HAUTZIG, D/ Aladdin and the magic lamp./ 1993/ 1-2/2 KB314 . **398.2**
At the supermarket./ 1994/ 1-4/6 KB127 . . . . **381**
Pedal power: how a mountain bike is made./ 1996/
5-6/6 KD125 . . . . **629.227**
HAUTZIG, E/ Endless steppe: growing up in Siberia./ c1968/
5-6/4 KE658 . . . . **940.53**
Endless steppe: growing up in Siberia (Sound recording cassette)./ n.d./
5-6/4 KE658 . . . . **940.53**
Endless steppe: growing up in Siberia (Talking book)./ n.d./
5-6/4 KE658 . . . . **940.53**
HAVARD, C/ Fox: playful prowler./ 1995/ 3-5/4 KC842 . . . . **599.775**
HAVEN, K/ Amazing American women: 40 fascinating 5-minute reads./
1995/ KA166 . . . . **PROF 305.4**
Fathers and sons (Sound recording cassette)./ 1991/ 1-4 KF679 **SRC E**
HAVILL, J/ Jamaica and Brianna./ 1993/ K-2/2 KF680 . . . . **E**
Jamaica's blue marker./ 1995/ K-1/2 KF681 . . . . **E**
Jamaica's find./ 1986/ K-2/2 KF682 . . . . **E**
Treasure nap./ 1992/ P-1/2 KF683 . . . . **E**
HAWES, J/ Fireflies in the night. Rev. ed./ c1991/ P-2/4 KC552 **595.76**
HAWKES, K/ Boogie Bones./ 1997/ K-2/3 KG034 . . . . **E**
By the light of the Halloween moon./ 1993/ 1-3/3 KG582 . . . . . **E**
Librarian who measured the earth./ 1994/
4-A/6 KE339 . . . . **B ERATOSTHENES**
Turnip./ 1992/ 3-5/6 KB557 . . . . **398.24**
HAWKINS, H/ Be a friend: the story of African American music in song,
words and pictures./ 1994/ K-3 KD670 . . . . **BA 789.4**

HAWKINS, L/ Figment, your dog, speaking./ 1991/ 5-A/4 KH229 . . **FIC**
Figment, your dog, speaking (Sound recording cassette)./ 1995/
5-A/4 KH229 . . . . **FIC**
HAYDEN, CD/ VENTURE INTO CULTURES: A RESOURCE BOOK OF
MULTICULTURAL MATERIALS AND PROGRAMS./ 1992/
KA024 . . . . **PROF 011.62**
HAYDEN, RC/ 11 African-American doctors. Rev. and expanded ed./
1992/ 5-6/8 KC900 . . . . **610.69**
7 African-American scientists. Rev. and expanded ed./ 1992/
6-A/6 KB923 . . . . **509**
9 African-American inventors. Rev. and expanded ed./ 1992/
6-A/7 KC891 . . . . **609**
HAYES, J/ Spoon for every bite./ 1996/ 2-4/4 KF684 . . . . **E**
Tales from the Southwest (Sound recording cassette)./ 1984/
4-5 KB502 . . . . **SRC 398.23**
Watch out for clever women!/Cuidado con las mujeres astutas!: Hispanic
folktales./ 1994/ 2-5/4 KB315 . . . . **398.2**
HAYES, S/ Eat up, Gemma./ 1988/ P-2/2 KF685 . . . . **E**
Happy Christmas Gemma./ 1986/ P-1/2 KF686 . . . . **E**
HAYS, M/ Hundredth name./ c1995, 1997/ 2-3/2 KG194 . . . . . **E**
Jackie Robinson./ 1996/ 5-6/6 KE516 . . . . **B ROBINSON, J.**
Pedro and the monkey./ 1996/ 3-4/2 KB649 . . . . **398.24**
Storm./ 1993/ P-1/2 KG174 . . . . **E**
HAYWARD, L/ First Thanksgiving./ 1990/ 1-4/2 KB227 . . **CE 394.264**
HAYWOOD, C/ "B" is for Betsy./ c1939/ 2-3/3 KH230 . . . . . . **FIC**
"B" is for Betsy (Braille)./ n.d./ 2-3/3 KH230 . . . . **FIC**
"B" is for Betsy (Sound recording cassette)./ n.d./ 2-3/3 KH230 . **FIC**
Betsy and Billy./ c1941/ 2-3/3 KH230 . . . . **FIC**
Betsy and Billy (Braille)./ n.d./ 2-3/3 KH230 . . . . **FIC**
Betsy and the boys./ c1945/ 2-3/3 KH230 . . . . **FIC**
Betsy and the boys (Braille)./ n.d./ 2-3/3 KH230 . . . . **FIC**
Betsy and the boys (Sound recording cassette)./ n.d./
2-3/3 KH230 . . . . **FIC**
HAZARD, P/ Books, children and men. 5th ed./ 1983/
KA351 . . . . **PROF 809**
HAZELAAR, C/ Zoo dreams./ 1997/ P-1/3 KF687 . . . . **E**
HAZELL, R/ Heroes: great men through the ages./ 1997/
3-A/9 KA828 . . . . **305.3**
Heroines: great women through the ages./ 1996/
4-A/10 KA829 . . . . **305.4**
HAZEN, BS/ Mommy's office./ 1992/ P-2/2 KF688 . . . . **E**
Tight times./ 1983/ K-2/1 KF689 . . . . **E**
HEAGY, W/ J.R.R. Tolkien: master of fantasy./ 1992/
6-A/6 KE567 . . . . **B TOLKIEN, J.**
HEALE, J/ Ugly Duckling./ 1994/ P-A/4 KG143 . . . . **E**
HEARN, DD/ Bad Luck Boswell./ 1995/ 1-3/5 KF690 . . . . **E**
HEARNE, B/ Best in children's books: the University of Chicago guide to
children's literature./ 1991/ KA023 . . . . **PROF 011.62**
Seven brave women./ 1997/ 1-3/2 KF691 . . . . **E**
HEATH, A/ Sofie's role./ 1992/ P-2/2 KF692 . . . . **E**
HECKMAN, D/ Alexander and the terrible, horrible, no good, very bad
day and other stories and poems (Talking book)./ 1984/
P-3 KG658 . . . . **TB E**
Angelina Ballerina and other stories (Talking book)./ 1986/
P-2 KF765 . . . . **TB E**
Paddington audio collection (Talking book)./ 1978/ 2-4 KG917 **TB FIC**
HECKMAN, P/ Waking upside down./ 1996/ 1-3/6 KF693 . . . . **E**
HEDLUND, I/ Mighty Mountain and the three strong women./ 1990/
3-5/5 KB316 . . . . **398.2**
HEFNER, CR/ Literature-based science: children's books and activities to
enrich the K-5 curriculum./ 1995/ KA200 . . . . **PROF 372.3**
HEHNER, B/ Looking at insects./ 1992/ 4-6/5 KC550 . . . . **595.7**
HEIDE, FP/ Day of Ahmed's secret./ 1990/ 1-3/4 KF694 . . . . **E**
Sami and the time of the troubles./ 1992/ 2-4/4 KF695 . . . . . **E**
Shrinking of Treehorn./ c1971/ 3-A/6 KH232 . . . . **CE FIC**
Shrinking of Treehorn (Kit)./ 1983/ 3-A/6 KH232 . . . . . **CE FIC**
Shrinking of Treehorn (Sound recording cassette)./ 1997/
3-A/6 KH232 . . . . **CE FIC**
Tales for the perfect child./ 1985/ 2-5/2 KH233 . . . . **FIC**
Tales for the perfect child (Braille)./ n.d./ 2-5/2 KH233 . . . . **FIC**
HEILBRONER, J/ Robert the rose horse./ 1962/ K-2/1 KF696 . . . . . **E**
HEILIGMAN, D/ From caterpillar to butterfly./ 1996/
K-2/2 KC561 . . . . **595.78**
HEINE, H/ Pigs' wedding./ c1978, 1986/ P-2/6 KF697 . . . . . . **CE E**
HEINRICHS, A/ Alaska./ 1990/ 4-6/7 KF096 . . . . **979.8**
Alaska (Sound recording cassette)./ 1993/ 4-6/7 KF096 . . . **979.8**
Arizona./ 1991/ 4-6/7 KF070 . . . . **979.1**
Arizona (Sound recording cassette)./ 1993/ 4-6/7 KF070 . . . **979.1**
Montana./ 1991/ 5-6/8 KF058 . . . . **978.6**
Montana (Sound recording cassette)./ 1993/ 5-6/8 KF058 . . . **978.6**
Rhode Island./ 1990/ 4-6/9 KE932 . . . . **974.2**
Rhode Island (Sound recording cassette)./ 1993/ 4-6/9 KE932 . **974.2**
HEINS, E/ Cat and the cook and other fables of Krylov./ 1995/
3-5/6 KH234 . . . . **FIC**

HEINZ, BJ/ Kayuktuk: an Arctic quest./ 1996/ 4-A/3 KH235 . . . . . **FIC**
HEITZEG, S/ ON THE DAY YOU WERE BORN (Videocassette)./ 1996/
P-A KG192 . . . . **VCR E**
HELFMAN, E/ On being Sarah./ 1993/ 5-A/6 KH236 . . . . **FIC**
HELLDORFER, MC/ Mapmaker's daughter./ 1991/ 2-3/3 KF698 . . . . **E**
HELLER, J/ Enchanted horse./ 1993/ 4-6/7 KH525 . . . . **FIC**
King Arthur: the legends of Camelot./ 1993/ 5-A/7 KB471 . . . **398.22**
HELLER, N/ This little piggy./ 1997/ P-1/2 KF699 . . . . **E**
HELLER, R/ Cache of jewels and other collective nouns./ c1987, 1989/
P-3 KB846 . . . . **428.1**
Chickens aren't the only ones./ 1981/ P-K KC282 . . . . **573.6**
Fine lines./ 1996/ 4-6/2 KE385 . . . . **B HELLER, R.**
King Solomon and the bee./ 1994/ 2-3/4 KB475 . . . . . . **398.22**
Korean Cinderella./ 1993/ 2-4/5 KB726 . . . . **398.27**
Las gallinas no son las unicas./ 1992/ P-K KC282 . . . . **573.6**
Many luscious lollipops: a book about adjectives./ 1989/
1-3 KB851 . . . . **428.2**
Up, up and away: a book about adverbs./ 1991/ 1-3 KB852 . . **428.2**
HELLER, S/ Stellaluna (Talking book)./ 1996/ K-2 KF335 . . . . **TB E**
HELLWEG, P/ FACTS ON FILE STUDENT'S THESAURUS./ 1991/
5-A KA420 . . . . **REF 423**
HELMER, J/ Amazing world of butterflies and moths./ 1982/
2-4/4 KC566 . . . . **CE 595.78**
HELMS, D/ Swimming./ 1996/ 3-6/6 KD850 . . . . **797.2**
HELTSHE, MA/ Multicultural explorations: joyous journeys with books./
1991/ KA262 . . . . **PROF 372.89**
HENBEST, N/ Space atlas./ 1992/ 3-6/6 KC002 . . . . **520**
HENDERSON, A/ Pretend soup and other real recipes: a cookbook for
preschoolers and up./ 1994/ P-3 KD272 . . . . **641.5**
HENDERSON, D/ Dinosaur tree./ 1994/ 3-6/5 KC235 . . . . **560**
How dinosaurs came to be./ 1996/ 4-A/6 KC251 . . . . **567.9**
Keep Ms. Sugarman in the fourth grade./ 1992/ 3-5/5 KH402 . . **FIC**
Living with dinosaurs./ 1991/ 3-6/5 KC252 . . . . **567.9**
HENDERSON, G/ Joseph and his brothers (Videocassette)./ 1993/
5-6 KA685 . . . . **VCR 222**
HENDERSON, K/ Great Lakes./ 1989/ 4-5/6 KC182 . . . . **551.48**
Year in the city./ 1996/ K-2/2 KF700 . . . . **E**
HENDRY, L/ Amazing apple book./ 1990/ 5-6/7 KD264 . . . . . . **641.3**
Amazing paper book./ 1989/ 5-6/6 KD332 . . . . **676**
HENEGHAN, J/ Wish me luck./ 1997/ 6-A/5 KH237 . . . . **FIC**
HENKES, K/ Biggest boy./ 1995/ P/2 KF701 . . . . **E**
Chester's way./ 1988/ K-2/5 KF702 . . . . **E**
Chester's way (Sound recording cassette)./ n.d./ K-2/5 KF702 . . **E**
Chrysanthemum./ 1991/ K-2/2 KF703 . . . . **E**
Chrysanthemum (Sound recording cassette)./ 1995/ K-2/2 KF703 . . **E**
Good-bye, Curtis./ 1995/ P-2/2 KF704 . . . . **E**
Grandpa and Bo./ 1986/ P-2/2 KF705 . . . . **E**
Jessica./ 1989/ K-1/2 KF706 . . . . **E**
Julius, the baby of the world./ 1990/ K-3/2 KF707 . . . . **E**
Lilly's purple plastic purse./ 1996/ K-2/2 KF708 . . . . **E**
Owen./ 1993/ P-2/2 KF709 . . . . **E**
Owen (Videocassette)./ 1995/ P-2 KF710 . . . . **VCR E**
Protecting Marie./ 1995/ 5-A/6 KH238 . . . . **FIC**
Sheila Rae, the brave./ 1987/ P-2/4 KF711 . . . . **E**
Sun and spoon./ 1997/ 5-A/6 KH239 . . . . **FIC**
Weekend with Wendell./ 1986/ P-2/2 KF712 . . . . **E**
Words of stone./ 1992/ 5-A/6 KH240 . . . . **FIC**
HENNESSY, BG/ First night./ 1993/ P-2/3 KA706 . . . . **232.92**
Olympics!/ 1996/ P-2/4 KD820 . . . . **796.48**
School days./ 1990/ P-1/3 KF713 . . . . **E**
HENRY, M/ Born to trot./ c1950, 1993/ 5-A/5 KH241 . . . . **FIC**
Brighty of the Grand Canyon./ c1953, 1991/ 4-5/5 KH242 . . **CE FIC**
Brighty of the Grand Canyon (Braille)./ n.d./ 4-5/5 KH242 . . **CE FIC**
Brighty of the Grand Canyon (Talking book)./ n.d./
4-5/5 KH242 . . . . **CE FIC**
King of the wind./ c1948, 1990/ 4-6/5 KH243 . . . . **CE FIC**
King of the wind (Braille)./ n.d./ 4-6/5 KH243 . . . . **CE FIC**
King of the wind (Sound recording cassette)./ n.d./
4-6/5 KH243 . . . . **CE FIC**
King of the wind (Talking book)./ 1971, 4-6/5 KH243 . . . . **CE FIC**
Misty of Chincoteague./ c1947/ 3-5/4 KH244 . . . . **CE FIC**
Misty of Chincoteague (Braille)./ n.d./ 3-5/4 KH244 . . . . . **CE FIC**
Misty of Chincoteague (Sound recording cassette)./ n.d./
3-5/4 KH244 . . . . **CE FIC**
Misty of Chincoteague (Videocassette)./ 1988/ 3-5/4 KH244 . **CE FIC**
Mustang, wild spirit of the West./ c1966, 1992/ 5-6/5 KH245 . . **FIC**
Mustang, wild spirit of the West (Braille)./ n.d./ 5-6/5 KH245 . . . **FIC**
Mustang, wild spirit of the West (Sound recording cassette)./ n.d./
5-6/5 KH245 . . . . **FIC**
Sea-Star: orphan of Chincoteague./ 1970/ 3-5/4 KH244 . . . . **CE FIC**
Stormy, Misty's foal./ 1963/ 3-5/4 KH244 . . . . **CE FIC**
Stormy, Misty's foal (Braille)./ n.d./ 3-5/4 KH244 . . . . **CE FIC**
Stormy, Misty's foal (Sound recording cassette)./ n.d./
3-5/4 KH244 . . . . **CE FIC**

Stormy, Misty's foal (Talking book)./ n.d./ 3-5/4 KH244 .... **CE FIC**
White stallion of Lipizza./ c1964, 1994/ 4-6/6 KH246 .... **FIC**
HENTERLY, J/ Young Guinevere./ 1993/ 3-4/6 KB482 ...... **398.22**
Young Lancelot./ 1996/ 4-5/6 KB483 .... **398.22**
HEO, Y/ A is for Asia./ 1997/ K-3/8 KE700 .... **950**
Green frogs: a Korean folktale./ 1996/ P-2/2 KB589 ...... **398.24**
Lonely lioness and the ostrich chicks: a Masai tale./ 1996/ K-2/3 KB516 .... **398.24**
Rabbit's escape/Kusa ilsaenghan tookki./ 1995/ P-2/3 KB583 . **398.24**
HEPLER, S/ Blue pages: resources for teachers from Invitations. Updated, expanded, and rev./ 1994/ KA026 .... **PROF 016.372**
HEPWORTH, C/ ANTics!: an alphabetical anthology./ 1992/ 2-6 KB831 .... **421**
HERB, AM/ Beyond the Mississippi: early westward expansion of the United States./ 1996/ 4-6/10 KF032 .... **978**
HERMAN, C/ Millie Cooper and friends./ 1995/ 3-4/7 KH247 .... **FIC**
HERMAN, RA/ Pal the pony./ 1996/ K-1/2 KF714 .... **E**
HERMANN, S/ Geronimo: Apache freedom fighter./ 1997/ 5-6/12 KE367 .... **B GERONIMO**
R.C. Gorman: Navajo artist./ 1995/ 3-5/3 KE375 . . **B GORMAN, R.C.**
HERMES, J/ Children of Bolivia./ 1996/ 4-6/10 KF108 .... **984**
Children of India./ 1993/ 4-6/6 KE711 .... **954**
Children of Micronesia./ 1994/ 4-6/9 KF122 .... **996.5**
Children of Morocco./ 1995/ 3-6/7 KE730 .... **964**
HERMES, P/ Heads, I win./ 1989/ 5-6/3 KH248 .... **FIC**
Kevin Corbett eats flies./ 1989/ 5-6/3 KH248 .... **FIC**
Nothing but trouble, trouble, trouble./ 1995/ 4-6/6 KH249 ...... **FIC**
Nothing but trouble, trouble, trouble (Sound recording cassette)./ 1997/ 4-6/6 KH249 .... **FIC**
Someone to count on: a novel./ 1993/ 6-A/7 KH250 .... **FIC**
Someone to count on: a novel (Sound recording cassette)./ 1996/ 6-A/7 KH250 .... **FIC**
HERNANDEZ, X/ Barmi: a Mediterranean city through the ages./ 1990/ A/11 KA895 .... **307.76**
Lebek: a city of Northern Europe through the ages./ 1991/ A/10 KA896 .... **307.76**
San Rafael: a Central American city through the ages./ 1992/ A/8 KA897 .... **307.76**
HEROLD, MR/ Very important day./ 1995/ K-3/2 KF715 .... **E**
Very important day (Sound recording cassette)./ 1997/ K-3/2 KF715 **E**
HERRERA, V/ In my mother's house./ c1941, 1991/ 1-4 KE759 . . **970.3**
HERSHBERGER, P/ Make costumes!: for creative play./ 1992/ 4-6/2 KD300 .... **646.4**
HERZOG, G/ Cow-tail switch and other West African stories./ c1947, 1987/ 4-6/7 KB728 .... **398.27**
HESLEWOOD, J/ History of Western painting: a young person's guide./ 1996/ 4-6/8 KD483 .... **759**
History of Western sculpture: a young person's guide./ 1996/ 4-6/9 KD398 .... **730**
HESS, M/ Hercules: the man, the myth, the hero./ 1997/ 5-6/4 KA747 .... **292**
HESS, RD/ Activities handbook for teachers of young children. 5th ed./ 1990/ KA191 .... **PROF 372.1**
HESSE, K/ Lavender./ 1995/ 2-3/2 KH251 .... **FIC**
Lester's dog./ 1993/ 1-3/3 KF716 .... **E**
Lester's dog (Sound recording cassette)./ 1995/ 1-3/3 KF716 ..... **E**
Music of dolphins./ 1996/ 5-A/3 KH252 .... **FIC**
Sable./ 1994/ 3-5/4 KH253 .... **FIC**
HEST, A/ Baby Duck and the bad eyeglasses./ 1996/ P-K/1 KF717 . . **E**
In the rain with Baby Duck./ 1995/ P-1/2 KF718 .... **E**
Jamaica Louise James./ 1996/ K-2/2 KF719 .... **E**
Nana's birthday party./ 1993/ 1-3/4 KF720 .... **E**
Purple coat./ 1986/ K-3/4 KF721 .... **E**
You're the boss, Baby Duck!/ 1997/ P-1/2 KF722 .... **E**
HEWITT, K/ Flower garden./ 1994/ P-2/3 KF299 .... **E**
Lives of the musicians: good times, bad times (and what the neighbors thought)./ 1993/ 5-A/6 KD520 .... **780**
Sunflower house./ 1996/ P-2/2 KF311 .... **E**
HEWITT, M/ One proud summer./ 1981/ A/7 KH254 .... **FIC**
HEWLETT, J/ I speak HyperCard./ 1992/ 3-A KA573 ...... **005.265**
HEYER, C/ Easter story./ 1990/ 5-6/5 KA710 .... **232.96**
HEYMSFELD, C/ Coaching Ms. Parker./ 1992/ 2-4/4 KH255 ..... **FIC**
HEYWARD, DB/ Country bunny and the little gold shoes, as told to Jenifer./ c1939/ P-K/7 KF723 .... **E**
Country bunny and the little gold shoes, as told to Jenifer (Braille)./ n.d./ P-K/7 KF723 .... **E**
HICKMAN, J/ CHILDREN'S LITERATURE IN THE CLASSROOM: WEAVING CHARLOTTE'S WEB./ 1989/ KA238 .... **PROF 372.64**
Jericho: a novel./ 1994/ 6-A/7 KH256 .... **FIC**
HICKMAN, PM/ Birdwise: forty fun feats for finding out about our feathered friends./ 1988/ 4-6/6 KC650 .... **598**
Bugwise: thirty incredible insect investigations and arachnid activities./ c1990, 1991/ 4-6/7 KC540 .... **595.7**
HICKOX, R/ Per and the Dala horse./ 1995/ 1-3/6 KF724 .... **E**
Zorro and Quwi: tales of a trickster guinea pig./ 1997/ 1-3/3 KB590 .... **398.24**
HICYILMAZ, G/ Frozen waterfall./ 1994/ 6-A/6 KH257 .... **FIC**
HIDAKA, M/ Girl from the snow country./ 1986/ K-2/4 KF725 ..... **E**
HIGGINSON, WJ/ WIND IN THE LONG GRASS: A COLLECTION OF HAIKU./ 1991/ 2-5 KD892 .... **808.81**
HIGHTOWER, S/ Twelve snails to one lizard: a tale of mischief and measurement./ 1997/ 1-3/2 KF726 .... **E**
HIGHWATER, J/ Anpao: an American Indian odyssey./ c1977, 1992/ 5-6/5 KB743 .... **398.27**
HILDICK, EW/ Case of the weeping witch./ 1992/ 3-6/5 KH258 . . . **FIC**
Case of the weeping witch (Sound recording cassette)./ 1997/ 3-6/5 KH258 .... **FIC**
HILL, A/ Burnt stick./ 1995/ 4-A/7 KH259 .... **FIC**
Quickly, Quigley./ 1994/ P-1/2 KF635 .... **E**
HILL, D/ Take it easy./ 1997/ 6-A/4 KH260 .... **FIC**
HILL, E/ Ki con dau roi nhi./ / P-2/2 KF728 .... **E**
Where's Spot? Sign language edition./ 1987/ P-2/2 KF728 ...... **E**
HILL, ES/ Evan's corner./ c1967, 1991/ K-2/2 KF727 .... **E**
HILL, K/ Toughboy and sister./ 1990/ 4-6/6 KH261 .... **FIC**
Winter camp./ 1993/ 5-A/6 KH262 .... **FIC**
Winter camp (Sound recording cassette)./ 1996/ 5-A/6 KH262 . . . **FIC**
HILLENBRAND, W/ Coyote and the fire stick: a Pacific Northwest Indian tale./ 1996/ 2-4/2 KB576 .... **398.24**
House that Drac built./ 1995/ 1-3/3 KG503 .... **E**
I'm the best!/ 1991/ K-2/1 KG482 .... **E**
King who tried to fry an egg on his head: based on a Russian tale./ 1994/ 2-4/6 KB444 .... **398.22**
Tale of Ali Baba and the forty thieves: a story from the Arabian Nights./ 1996/ 3-4/6 KB332 .... **398.2**
HILLER, I/ Introducing mammals to young naturalists: from Texas Parks & Wildlife Magazine./ 1990/ A/7 KC721 .... **599**
Young naturalist, from Texas Parks and Wildlife Magazine./ 1983/ 3-A/9 KB907 .... **508**
HILLERICH, RL/ American Heritage picture dictionary./ 1994/ P-1 KA423 .... **REF 423**
HILLERMAN, A/ Done in the sun, solar projects for children./ 1983/ 2-4/7 KD048 .... **621.47**
HILLMAN, LE/ Nature puzzlers./ 1989/ KA289 .... **PROF 508**
HILTON, J/ PHOTOGRAPHY./ 1994/ 5-A/7 KD514 .... **771**
HILTON, S/ Miners, merchants, and maids./ 1995/ 4-6/8 KF033 . . **978**
HIMLER, R/ Apaches./ 1997/ 4-6/5 KE768 .... **970.3**
Brand is forever./ 1993/ 3-5/6 KH687 .... **FIC**
Cherokees./ 1996/ 4-6/5 KE769 .... **970.3**
Cheyennes./ 1996/ 4-6/6 KE770 .... **970.3**
Dakota dugout./ 1985/ 1-3/6 KG624 .... **E**
Day's work./ 1994/ 1-3/2 KF298 .... **E**
Fly away home./ 1991/ K-3/2 KF300 .... **E**
Hopis./ 1995/ 4-6/7 KE771 .... **970.3**
Iroquois./ 1995/ 4-6/5 KE772 .... **970.3**
Katie's trunk./ 1992/ 3-5/3 KG627 .... **E**
Navajos./ 1993/ 4-6/6 KE773 .... **970.3**
Nettie's trip south./ 1987/ 5-A/6 KH812 .... **FIC**
Nez Perce./ 1994/ 4-6/7 KE774 .... **970.3**
Seminoles./ 1994/ 4-6/7 KE775 .... **970.3**
Sioux./ 1993/ 4-6/5 KE776 .... **970.3**
Squish!: a wetland walk./ 1994/ P-2/3 KC342 .... **577.68**
Train to Somewhere./ 1996/ 3-5/4 KG945 .... **FIC**
Trouble for Lucy./ 1979/ 3-5/6 KH754 .... **FIC**
HIMMELMAN, J/ Buzby./ 1992/ K-2/2 KF731 .... **CE E**
Buzby to the rescue./ 1995/ K-2/2 KF732 .... **E**
Clover County carrot contest./ 1991/ 1-3/1 KF729 .... **E**
Day-off machine./ 1990/ 1-3/1 KF729 .... **E**
Great leaf blast-off./ 1990/ 1-3/1 KF729 .... **E**
Super camper caper./ 1991/ 1-3/1 KF729 .... **E**
HINES, AG/ What Joe saw./ 1994/ K-2/3 KF730 .... **E**
HINOJOSA, T/ Cada nino./Every child (Compact disc)./ 1996/ 2-6 KD568 .... **CD 789.2**
Cada nino./Every child (Sound recording cassette)./ 1995/ 2-6 KD568 .... **CD 789.2**
HINTON, SE/ Puppy sister./ 1995/ 3-5/4 KH263 .... **FIC**
HINTZ, M/ Farewell, John Barleycorn: prohibition in the United States./ 1996/ 5-6/12 KB043 .... **363.4**
HIREZAKI, E/ Grandfather Cherry-Blossom./ 1993/ 2-3/3 KB753 **398.27**
HIRSCHFELD, R/ Kids' science book: creative experiences for hands-on fun./ 1995/ P-4/7 KB892 .... **507.8**
HIRSCHFELDER, AB/ RISING VOICES: WRITINGS OF YOUNG NATIVE AMERICANS./ 1992/ 5-A/7 KD903 .... **810.8**
HIRSCHI, R/ What is a cat?/ 1991/ K-4/2 KD233 .... **636.8**
HISCOCK, B/ Big rivers: the Missouri, the Mississipi, and the Ohio./ 1997/ 3-6/6 KC183 .... **551.48**
Big storm./ 1993/ 4-6/6 KC198 .... **551.55**
Big tree./ 1991/ 1-5/6 KC414 .... **582.16**

Mummies, dinosaurs, moon rocks: how we know how old things are./ 1996/ 4-6/9 KE625 . . . . 930.1
Tundra, the Arctic land./ 1986/ 4-A/7 KC335 . . . . 577.5
/ 1993/ 2-3/4 KA688 222
HITCHCOCK, S/ Day Sun was stolen./ 1995/ K-2/5 KB712 . . . 398.26
HITE, S/ Dither Farm: a novel./ 1992/ 5-A/7 KH265 . . . . FIC
Dither Farm: a novel (Sound recording cassette)./ 1996/ 5-A/7 KH265 . . . . FIC
Even break./ 1995/ 5-A/6 KH266 . . . . FIC
HO, M/ Hush!: a Thai lullaby./ 1996/ P-1 KD952 811
MAPLES IN THE MIST: CHILDREN'S POEMS FROM THE TANG DYNASTY./ 1996/ K-3 KE133 895
HOBAN, J/ Buzby./ 1992/ K-2/2 KF731 . . . . CE E
Buzby (Kit)./ 1996/ K-2/2 KF731 . . . . CE E
Buzby to the rescue./ 1995/ K-2/2 KF732 . . . . E
HOBAN, L/ Arthur's camp-out./ 1993/ 1-3/2 KF734 . . . . CE E
Arthur's camp-out (Kit)./ 1996/ 1-3/2 KF734 . . . . CE E
Arthur's Christmas cookies./ 1972/ 1-3/2 KF734 . . . . CE E
Arthur's funny money./ 1981/ 1-3/2 KF733 . . . . E
Arthur's great big valentine./ 1989/ 1-3/2 KF734 . . . . CE E
Arthur's Halloween costume./ 1984/ 1-3/2 KF734 . . . . CE E
Arthur's Halloween costume (Braille)./ n.d./ 1-3/2 KF734 . . . . CE E
Arthur's honey bear./ c1964/ 1-3/2 KF734 . . . . CE E
Arthur's honey bear (Braille)./ n.d./ 1-3/2 KF734 . . . . CE E
Arthur's honey bear (Kit)./ 1986/ 1-3/2 KF734 . . . . CE E
Arthur's loose tooth./ 1985/ 1-3/2 KF734 . . . . CE E
Arthur's loose tooth (Braille)./ n.d./ 1-3/2 KF734 . . . . CE E
Arthur's pen pal./ c1976/ 1-3/2 KF735 . . . . E
Arthur's pen pal (Braille)./ n.d./ 1-3/2 KF735 . . . . E
Arthur's prize reader./ 1978/ 1-3/2 KF734 . . . . CE E
Arthur's prize reader (Braille)./ n.d./ 1-3/2 KF734 . . . . CE E
Arthur's prize reader (Kit)./ 1985/ 1-3/2 KF734 . . . . CE E
Big little otter (Board book)./ 1997/ P/1 KF736 . . . . BB E
Big seed./ 1993/ 1-3/2 KF775 . . . . E
Birthday for Frances./ c1968, 1995/ P-1/2 KF740 . . . . E
Case of the two masked robbers./ 1988/ K-2/1 KF737 . . . . E
New neighbors for Nora./ c1979, 1991/ 2-4/6 KH299 . . . . FIC
Nora and Mrs. Mind-your-own business./ c1977, 1991/ 2-4/4 KH300 . . . . FIC
Russell Sprouts./ 1987/ 2-4/4 KH303 . . . . FIC
See you in second grade!/ 1989/ K-1/2 KF404 . . . . CE E
Silly Tilly and the Easter Bunny./ / K-2/2 KF738 . . . . E
Silly Tilly's Thanksgiving dinner./ 1990/ K-2/2 KF738 . . . . E
Superduper Teddy./ c1980, 1990/ 2-4/4 KH304 . . . . FIC
Will I have a friend?/ c1967/ K-1/2 KF405 . . . . CE E
HOBAN, R/ Baby sister for Frances (Kit)./ 1977/ P-1/2 KF739 . . . CE E
Baby sister for Frances. Newly ill. ed./ 1993/ P-1/2 KF739 . . . . CE E
Baby sister for Frances (Sound recording cassette)./ 1995/ P-1/2 KF739 . . . . CE E
Bargain for Frances. Newly ill. ed./ 1992/ P-1/2 KF739 . . . . CE E
Bargain for Frances (Sound recording cassette)./ n.d./ P-1/2 KF739 . . . . CE E
Bargain for Frances (Talking book)./ n.d./ P-1/2 KF739 . . . . CE E
Bedtime for Frances. Newly ill. ed./ 1995/ P-1/2 KF739 . . . . CE E
Best friends for Frances. Newly ill. ed./ 1994/ P-1/2 KF739 . . . . CE E
Best friends for Frances (Talking book)./ n.d./ P-1/2 KF739 . . . . CE E
Birthday for Frances./ c1968, 1995/ P-1/2 KF740 . . . . E
Bread and jam for Frances (Big book)./ 1993/ P-1/2 KF739 . . . . CE E
Bread and jam for Frances (Braille)./ n.d./ P-1/2 KF739 . . . . CE E
Bread and jam for Frances. Newly ill. ed./ 1993/ P-1/2 KF739 . . CE E
Gran negocio de Francisca./ 1996/ P-1/2 KF739 . . . . CE E
Hora de acostarse de Francisca./ 1996/ P-1/2 KF739 . . . . CE E
Nueva hermanita de Francisca./ 1997/ P-1/2 KF739 . . . . CE E
Pan y mermelada para Francisca./ 1995/ P-1/2 KF739 . . . . CE E
HOBAN, T/ All about where./ 1991/ P-1 KB853 . . . . 428.2
Children's zoo./ 1985/ P-K KC448 591
Circles, triangles, and squares./ 1974/ P-1 KB990 516
Colors everywhere./ 1995/ P-1 KC122 . . . . 535.6
Count and see./ c1972/ P KF741 . . . . E
Dig, drill, dump, fill./ 1975/ P-2 KD122 . . . . 629.225
Dots, spots, speckles, and stripes./ 1987/ P-A KA613 . . . . 152.14
Exactly the opposite./ 1990/ P-1 KB847 . . . . 428.1
I read signs./ 1983/ P-1 KA800 . . . . 302.23
I read symbols./ 1983/ P-1 KA797 . . . . 302.2
Is it red? Is it yellow? Is it blue? An adventure in color./ 1978/ P KA614 . . . . 152.14
Is it rough? Is it smooth? Is it shiny?/ 1984/ P-1 KF742 . . . . E
Just look./ 1996/ P-2 KA615 . . . . 152.14
Little elephant./ 1994/ P-K/1 KF565 . . . . E
Look book./ 1997/ P-K KD516 779
Look! look! look!/ 1988/ P-3 KA616 . . . . 152.14
Look up, look down./ 1992/ P-1 KF743 . . . . E
Of colors and things./ 1989/ P-K KC123 . . . . 535.6
One little kitten./ 1979/ P-K/1 KF744 . . . . E
Over, under and through, and other spatial concepts./ 1973/ P-K KF745 . . . . E
Push, pull, empty, full: a book of opposites./ c1972/ P-K KF746 . . . . E
Shadows and reflections./ 1990/ P-6 KC112 535
Shapes and things./ c1970/ P-1 KA617 . . . . 152.14
Shapes, shapes, shapes./ 1986/ 2-6 KB991 516
Spirals, curves, fanshapes and lines./ 1992/ P-2 KB992 516
Take another look./ 1981/ P-A KA618 . . . . 152.14
Where is it?/ c1972/ P-K/1 KF747 . . . . E
26 letters and 99 cents./ 1987/ P-2 KF748 . . . . E
HOBBS, W/ Ghost canoe./ 1997/ 5-A/6 KH267 . . . . FIC
HOBERMAN, MA/ MY SONG IS BEAUTIFUL: POEMS AND PICTURES IN MANY VOICES./ 1994/ 1-4 KD887 . . . . 808.81
HOBSON, S/ Chicken Little./ 1994/ P-2/2 KF749 . . . . E
Red Hen and Sly Fox./ 1995/ P-2/2 KF584 . . . . E
HOCKERMAN, D/ Rose for Abby./ 1988/ 2-4/5 KF654 . . . . E
HODGES, CW/ Silver sword./ c1959/ 5-6/6 KH699 . . . . FIC
HODGES, M/ Brother Francis and the friendly beasts./ 1991/ 3-5/5 KE349 . . . . B FRANCIS, ST.
Hero of Bremen./ 1993/ 3-5/6 KB451 . . . . 398.22
Hidden in sand./ 1994/ 3-4/6 KA759 . . . . 294.3
Molly Limbo./ 1996/ K-3/3 KB688 . . . . 398.25
Of swords and sorcerers: the adventures of King Arthur and his knights./ 1993/ 4-5/6 KB452 . . . . 398.22
Saint George and the dragon: a golden legend./ 1984/ 5/7 KB453 . . . . CE 398.22
Saint George and the dragon: a golden legend (Sound recording cassette)./ n.d./ 5/7 KB453 . . . . CE 398.22
Saint Patrick and the peddler./ 1993/ 3-4/5 KB454 . . . . 398.22
True tale of Johnny Appleseed./ 1997/ 2-4/6 KE238 . . . . B APPLESEED, J.
HOESTLANDT, J/ Star of fear, star of hope./ 1995/ 3-5/5 KH268 . FIC
HOFER, A/ Lion family book./ 1995/ 3-6/6 KC830 . . . . 599.757
HOFF, MK/ Our endangered planet: atmosphere./ 1995/ 4-6/8 KB061 . . . . 363.73
Our endangered planet: groundwater./ 1991/ 5-6/8 KA959 . . 333.91
Our endangered planet: life on land./ 1992/ 5-6/8 KA962 . . . 333.95
Our endangered planet: oceans./ 1992/ 5-6/8 KA959 . . . . 333.91
Our endangered planet: rivers and lakes./ 1991/ 5-6/8 KB062 363.73
HOFF, S/ Arturo's baton./ 1995/ K-2/2 KF750 . . . . E
Barkley./ c1975/ K-2/1 KF751 . . . . E
Barkley (Braille)./ n.d./ K-2/1 KF751 . . . . E
Captain Cat: story and pictures./ 1993/ K-2/2 KF752 . . . . E
Danny and the dinosaur./ c1958/ K-2/2 KF753 . . . . CE E
Danny and the dinosaur (Braille)./ n.d./ K-2/2 KF753 . . . . CE E
Danny and the dinosaur go to camp./ 1996/ K-2/2 KF754 . . . . E
Danny and the dinosaur (Kit)./ 1985/ K-2/2 KF753 . . . . CE E
Grizzwold./ c1963/ K-2/2 KF755 . . . . E
Happy birthday, Danny and the dinosaur!/ 1995/ K-1/2 KF756 . . . . E
Horse in Harry's room./ c1970/ K-2/2 KF757 . . . . E
Julius./ c1959/ K-1/1 KF758 . . . . E
Julius (Braille)./ n.d./ K-1/1 KF758 . . . . E
Mrs. Brice's mice./ 1988/ K-2/2 KF759 . . . . E
Rooftop mystery./ c1968/ 1-2/1 KF979 . . . . E
Who will be my friends?/ c1960/ K-1/1 KF760 . . . . E
HOFFMAN, C/ Sewing by hand./ 1994/ 3-5/3 KD297 . . . . 646.2
HOFFMAN, D/ Horton hears a Who!/Thidwick the big-hearted moose (Videocassette)./ 1992/ P-3 KG458 . . . . VCR E
HOFFMAN, M/ Amazing Grace./ 1991/ P-2/4 KF761 . . . . CE E
Amazing Grace (Videocassette)./ Amazing Grace (Videocassette)./ 1996/ 1994/ P-2/4 KF761 . . . . CE E
P-2/4 KF761 . . . . CE E
Asombrosa Graciela./ 1996/ P-2/4 KF761 . . . . CE E
Boundless Grace./ 1995/ 1-3/5 KF762 . . . . E
Earth, fire, water, air./ 1995/ 2-6/7 KA814 . . . . 304.2
Four-legged ghosts./ 1995/ 2-4/6 KH269 . . . . FIC
HOFFMAN, R/ JANE YOLEN'S MOTHER GOOSE SONGBOOK./ 1992/ KA277 . . . . PROF 398.8
HOFSINDE, R/ Indian sign language./ c1956/ 2-4/4 KA798 . . . . 302.2
HOGARTH, GA/ ILLUSTRATORS OF CHILDREN'S BOOKS, 1967-1976./ 1978/ KA311 . . . . PROF 741.6
HOGROGIAN, N/ Always room for one more./ 1965/ K-2/7 KB760 . . . . 398.27
Buen dia./ 1997/ P-2/5 KF763 . . . . CE E
Contest./ c1976/ 3-5/5 KB744 . . . . 398.27
First Christmas./ 1995/ K-2/5 KA707 . . . . 232.92
One fine day./ c1971/ P-2/5 KF763 . . . . CE E
One fine day (Kit)./ 1973/ P-2/5 KF763 . . . . CE E
One fine day (Talking book)./ n.d./ P-2/5 KF763 . . . . CE E
HOIG, S/ People of the sacred arrows: the Southern Cheyenne today./ 1992/ 6-A/7 KE781 . . . . 970.466
HOLABIRD, K/ Angelina and Alice./ 1987/ P-2/5 KF764 . . . . E
Angelina and the princess./ 1984/ P-2/5 KF764 . . . . E
Angelina Ballerina./ 1983/ P-2/5 KF764 . . . . E

Angelina Ballerina and other stories (Talking book)./ 1986/ P-2 KF765 . . . . **TB E**
Angelina ice skates./ 1993/ P-2/5 KF764 . . . . **E**
Angelina on stage./ 1986/ P-2/5 KF764 . . . . **E**
Angelina's baby sister./ 1991/ P-2/5 KF764 . . . . **E**
Angelina's birthday surprise./ 1989/ P-2/5 KF764 . . . . **E**
Angelina's Christmas./ 1985/ P-2/5 KF764 . . . . **E**
Angelina's Christmas (Braille)./ n.d./ P-2/5 KF764 . . . . **E**
Angelina's Christmas (Sound recording cassette)./ n.d./ P-2/5 KF764 **E**
HOLLAND, I/ Journey home./ 1993/ 6-A/6 KH270 . . . . **FIC**
Journey home (Sound recording cassette)./ 1993/ 6-A/6 KH270 **FIC**
HOLLING, HC/ Minn of the Mississippi./ c1951/ 5-6/6 KC619 . . **597.92**
Minn of the Mississippi (Braille)./ n.d./ 5-6/6 KC619 . . . . . . **597.92**
Paddle-to-the-sea./ c1941/ 4-6/5 KH271 . . . . **FIC**
Pagoo./ 1957/ 5-6/4 KC519 . . . . **595.3**
Pagoo (Sound recording cassette)./ n.d./ 5-6/4 KC519 . . . . . **595.3**
Seabird./ c1948/ 5-6/5 KH272 . . . . **FIC**
Seabird (Braille)./ n.d./ 5-6/5 KH272 . . . . **FIC**
Seabird (Sound recording cassette)./ n.d./ 5-6/5 KH272 . . . . **FIC**
Tree in the trail./ c1942/ 5-6/5 KH273 . . . . **FIC**
Tree in the trail (Braille)./ n.d./ 5-6/5 KH273 . . . . **FIC**
Tree in the trail (Sound recording cassette)./ n.d./ 5-6/5 KH273 . . **FIC**
HOLM, C/ Christmas memory./ c1956, 1989/ 4-A/6 KG971 . . . **CE FIC**
Merry Christmas, Strega Nona (Talking book)./ 1991/ K-3 KF474 . . . . **TB E**
HOLM, SL/ Crafts for Christmas./ 1995/ 3-5 KD452 . . . . . . **745.594**
Crafts for Easter./ 1995/ 3-5 KD453 . . . . **745.594**
Crafts for Halloween./ 1994/ 3-5 KD454 . . . . **745.594**
Crafts for Hanukkah./ 1996/ 3-6 KD455 . . . . **745.594**
Crafts for Kwanzaa./ 1994/ 3-6 KD456 . . . . **745.594**
Crafts for Thanksgiving./ 1995/ 3-5 KD457 . . . . **745.594**
Every day is Earth Day: a craft book./ 1995/ K-3/5 KD442 . . **745.58**
Sidewalk games around the world./ 1997/ 2-5/6 KD769 . . . . **796.2**
HOLMAN, F/ Runaway (Videocassette)./ 1989/ 6-A/7 KH274 . **CE FIC**
Slake's limbo./ 1974/ 6-A/7 KH274 . . . . **CE FIC**
HOLMES, S/ Complete fairy tales of Charles Perrault./ 1993/ 3-4/6 KB355 . . . . **398.2**
HOLT, D/ Grandfather's greatest hits (Compact disc)./ 1991/ K-4 KD569 . . . . **SRC 789.2**
Grandfather's greatest hits (Sound recording cassette)./ 1991/ K-4 KD569 . . . . **SRC 789.2**
Hogaphone and other stories (Videocassette)./ 1991/ 2-6 KH275 . . . . **VCR FIC**
I got a bullfrog: folksongs for the fun of it (Compact disc)./ 1994/ 2-4 KD570 . . . . **SRC 789.2**
I got a bullfrog: folksongs for the fun of it (Sound recording cassette)./ 1994/ 2-4 KD570 . . . . **SRC 789.2**
READY-TO-TELL TALES: SURE-FIRE STORIES FROM AMERICA'S FAVORITE STORYTELLERS./ 1994/ KA272 . . . . **PROF 398.2**
Stellaluna (Talking book)./ 1996/ K-2 KF335 . . . . **TB E**
Why the dog chases the cat: great animal stories (Sound recording cassette)./ 1994/ 1-3 KB591 . . . . **SRC 398.24**
HOLTAN, G/ Black and blue magic./ c1966, 1994/ 4-6/7 KH729 . . **FIC**
HOLUB, J/ I'm not scared./ 1994/ K-1/1 KF664 . . . . **E**
HOM, N/ Judge Rabbit and the tree spirit: a folktale from Cambodia./ 1991/ 3-4/4 KB655 . . . . **398.24**
Nine-in-one, grr! grr! a folktale from the Hmong people of Laos./ 1989/ P-3/4 KB677 . . . . **398.24**
HONDA, T/ Wild horse winter./ 1992/ K-3/4 KC806 . . . . . . **599.665**
HONEYCUTT, N/ All new Jonah Twist./ 1987/ 3-5/4 KH277 . . **FIC**
Best-laid plans of Jonah Twist./ 1988/ 3-5/4 KH277 . . . . **FIC**
Juliet Fisher and the foolproof plan./ 1992/ 3-5/4 KH277 . . . **FIC**
Twilight in Grace Falls./ 1997/ 6-A/6 KH278 . . . . **FIC**
HONG, LT/ Empress and the silkworm./ 1995/ 1-3/6 KF766 . . . . **E**
Empress and the silkworm (Sound recording cassette)./ 1997/ 1-3/6 KF766 . . . . **E**
Two of everything./ 1993/ 2-3/4 KB317 . . . . **398.2**
HOOKER, R/ Matthew the cowboy./ 1990/ K-2/2 KF767 . . . . . . **E**
HOOKS, WH/ Freedom's fruit./ 1996/ 4-6/3 KH279 . . . . **FIC**
Snowbear Whittington: an Appalachian Beauty and the Beast./ 1994/ 2-3/4 KB318 . . . . **398.2**
Three little pigs and the fox./ 1989/ 2-4/5 KB592 . . . . **398.24**
HOOPER, M/ Cow, a bee, a cookie, and me./ 1997/ K-2/2 KF768 . **E**
HOOPER, T/ Electricity./ 1994/ 5-6/11 KC131 . . . . **537**
Genetics./ 1994/ 5-6/9 KC289 . . . . **576.5**
HOOPES, LL/ Unbeatable bread./ 1996/ K-2/3 KF769 . . . . **E**
HOOVER, HM/ Only child./ 1992/ 5-A/5 KH280 . . . . **FIC**
Winds of Mars./ 1995/ 6-A/4 KH281 . . . . **FIC**
HOPKINS, D/ My first atlas./ 1994/ K-3/5 KE167 . . . . **912**
HOPKINS, LB/ Been to yesterdays: poems of a life./ 1995/ 3-6 KD953 . . . . **811**
EXTRA INNINGS: BASEBALL POEMS./ 1993/ 3-6 KE056 . . **811.008**
GOOD BOOKS, GOOD TIMES!./ 1990/ K-3 KE060 . . . . . . **811.008**

GOOD MORNING TO YOU, VALENTINE: POEMS FOR VALENTINE'S DAY./ c1976, 1993/ K-6 KE061 . . . . **811.008**
HAND IN HAND: AN AMERICAN HISTORY THROUGH POETRY./ 1994/ 2-6 KE063 . . . . **811.008**
MARVELOUS MATH: A BOOK OF POEMS./ 1997/ 1-4 KE071 . . . . **811.008**
OPENING DAYS: SPORTS POEMS./ 1996/ 3-6 KE074 . . . . **811.008**
Weather: poems./ 1994/ K-3 KE064 . . . . **811.008**
HOPKINSON, D/ Birdie's lighthouse./ 1997/ 3-5/3 KH282 . . . . **FIC**
Sweet Clara and the freedom quilt./ 1993/ 1-3/4 KF770 . . . . . **E**
HOPPING, LJ/ Wild weather. Tornadoes!./ 1994/ 2-6/3 KC199 . **551.55**
HORENSTEIN, H/ Sam goes trucking./ 1989/ 2-3/3 KD118 . . **629.224**
HORIO, S/ Monkey and the crab./ 1985/ 3/3 KB598 . . . . . . **398.24**
HORN BOOK MAGAZINE/ Newbery and Caldecott medal books, 1966-1975: with acceptance papers & related material chiefly from the/ 1975/ KA352 . . . . **PROF 809**
Newbery and Caldecott medal books, 1976-1985./ 1986/ KA352 . . . . **PROF 809**
Newbery Medal books: 1922-1955: with their authors' acceptance papers, biographies, and related materials chiefly from the Horn/ c1957/ KA353 . . . . **PROF 809**
HORNE, D/ Young Merlin./ c1990, 1996/ 4-5/6 KB484 . . . . . **398.24**
HORNING, KT/ From cover to cover: evaluating and reviewing children's books./ 1997/ KA085 . . . . **PROF 028.1**
HORNSBY, JR., A/ Chronology of African-American history: significant events and people from 1619 to the present./ 1997/ KA490 . . . . **REF 973**
HOROSKO, M/ Sleeping Beauty: the ballet story./ 1994/ 1-5/7 KD695 . . . . **792.8**
HORROX, R/ Exploring time./ 1995/ 3-6/6 KC069 . . . . **529**
HORTON, B/ Lyrical life science (Multimedia kit)./ 1995/ K-A KA295 . . . . **MMK PROF 570**
Lyrical life science. Vol. 2: mammals, ecology and biomes (Multimedia kit)./ 1996/ K-A KA295 . . . . **MMK PROF 570**
HORVATH, P/ Happy yellow car./ 1994/ 4-6/6 KH283 . . . . **FIC**
Occasional cow./ 1989/ 5-6/8 KH284 . . . . **FIC**
HOSHINO, M/ Grizzly bear family book./ 1994/ 4-6/6 KC859 . . . . **599.784**
HOUSTON, G/ My great-aunt Arizona./ 1992/ 3-5/4 KE393 . . . **B HUGHES, A.**
Year of the perfect Christmas tree./ 1988/ K-3/6 KF771 . . . . . . **E**
/ 1995/ K-6 KD571 . . . . **CE 789.2**
HOW SWEET THE SOUND: AFRICAN-AMERICAN SONGS FOR CHILDREN./ 1995/ K-6 KD571 . . . . **CE 789.2**
HOWARD, A/ Gooseberry Park./ 1995/ 3-5/5 KH662 . . . . **FIC**
Mr. Putter and Tabby bake the cake./ 1994/ 1-3/2 KG377 . . . . **E**
Mr. Putter and Tabby fly the plane./ 1997/ K-2/2 KG378 . . . . . **E**
Mr. Putter and Tabby pick the pears./ 1995/ 1-3/2 KG379 . . . . **E**
Mr. Putter and Tabby pour the tea./ 1994/ 1-3/2 KG380 . . . . . **E**
Mr. Putter and Tabby row the boat./ 1997/ K-2/2 KG381 . . . . . **E**
Mr. Putter and Tabby walk the dog./ 1994/ 1-3/2 KG382 . . . . . **E**
HOWARD, DE/ Soccer stars./ 1994/ 3-6/6 KD788 . . . . **796.334**
HOWARD, E/ Big seed./ 1993/ 1-3/2 KF775 . . . . **E**
HOWARD, EF/ Aunt Flossie's hats (and crab cakes later)./ 1991/ 1-3/2 KF772 . . . . **E**
Chita's Christmas tree./ 1989/ 2-4/5 KF773 . . . . **E**
Mac and Marie and the train toss surprise./ 1993/ K-2/2 KF774 . . **E**
HOWARD, JR/ Cuando tengo sueno./ 1996/ P-K/8 KF776 . . . . . **E**
When I'm sleepy./ 1996/ P-K/8 KF776 . . . . **E**
HOWARD, K/ Cloak for the dreamer./ 1995/ 1-3/6 KF585 . . . . . **E**
Mediopollito/Half-Chicken./ 1995/ K-2/2 KB521 . . . . **398.24**
Zorro and Quwi: tales of a trickster guinea pig./ 1997/ 1-3/3 KB590 . . . . **398.24**
HOWARD, P/ Year in the city./ 1996/ K-2/2 KF700 . . . . **E**
HOWARD, R/ Beauty and the Beast./ 1990/ 4-5/6 KB282 . . . . . **398.2**
HOWE, D/ Bonicula./ 1992/ 3-6/5 KH285 . . . . **FIC**
Bunnicula: a rabbit-tale mystery./ 1979/ 3-6/5 KH285 . . . . . . **FIC**
Bunnicula: a rabbit-tale mystery (Braille)./ n.d./ 3-6/5 KH285 . . **FIC**
Bunnicula: a rabbit-tale mystery (Sound recording cassette)./ n.d./ 3-6/5 KH285 . . . . **FIC**
Celery stalks at midnight./ 1983/ 3-6/5 KH285 . . . . **FIC**
Celery stalks at midnight (Braille)./ n.d./ 3-6/5 KH285 . . . . . **FIC**
Celery stalks at midnight (Sound recording cassette)./ n.d./ 3-6/5 KH285 . . . . **FIC**
Howliday Inn./ 1982/ 3-6/5 KH285 . . . . **FIC**
Howliday Inn (Braille)./ n.d./ 3-6/5 KH285 . . . . **FIC**
Return to Howliday Inn./ 1992/ 3-6/5 KH285 . . . . **FIC**
HOWE, J/ Bunnicula: a rabbit-tale mystery./ 1979/ 3-6/5 KH285 . . **FIC**
Creepy-crawly birthday./ 1991/ K-3/3 KF780 . . . . **E**
Hot fudge./ 1990/ K-3/2 KF777 . . . . **E**
I wish I were a butterfly./ 1987/ K-3/2 KF778 . . . . **E**
Knight with the lion: the story of Yvain./ 1996/ 5-6/6 KB455 . **398.22**
Rabbit-Cadabra!./ 1993/ K-3/3 KF779 . . . . **E**
Scared silly: a Halloween treat./ 1989/ K-3/3 KF780 . . . . **E**

There's a monster under my bed./ 1986/ P-2/2 KF781 . . . . **E**
There's a monster under my bed (Braille)./ n.d./ P-2/2 KF781 . . . . . **E**
When you go to kindergarten. Rev. and updated ed./ 1994/
P-K/2 KB097 . . . . **372.21**
HOWELL, F/ Spirit walker: poems./ 1993/ 6-A KE046 . . . . **811**
HOWELL, KC/ Singing green: new and selected poems for all seasons./
1992/ 3-A KD984 . . . . **811**
HOWELL, S/ Birding./ c1994, 1995/ 5-6/8 KA448 . . . . **REF 598**
HOWELL, T/ Favorite Norse myths./ 1996/ 4-6/6 KA756 . . . . . . **293**
Maiden on the moor./ 1995/ 4-6/3 KB418 . . . . **398.21**
MERMAID TALES FROM AROUND THE WORLD./ 1993/
3-5/5 KB405 . . . . **398.21**
HOWLAND, N/ ABCDrive!: a car trip alphabet./ 1994/ P-1/1 KF782 . **E**
HOYT-GOLDSMITH, D/ Apache rodeo./ 1995/ 4-6/7 KE798 . **970.491**
Arctic hunter./ 1992/ 3-6/6 KF097 . . . . **979.8**
Celebrating Hanukkah./ 1996/ 3-4/7 KA775 . . . . **296.4**
Celebrating Kwanzaa./ 1993/ 4-6/7 KB210 . . . . **394.261**
Cherokee summer./ 1993/ 3-5/5 KE782 . . . . **970.466**
Day of the Dead: a Mexican-American celebration./ 1994/
4-6/7 KB198 . . . . **394.26**
Hoang Anh: a Vietnamese-American boy./ 1992/ 3-6/6 KA849 . **305.8**
Potlatch: a Tsimshian celebration./ 1997/ 2-5/9 KB189 . . . . . **394.2**
Pueblo storyteller./ 1991/ 3-6/6 KE792 . . . . **970.489**
HRU, D/ Magic moonberry jump ropes./ 1996/ K-2/2 KF783 . . . . . **E**
HSU-FLANDERS, L/ Dumpling soup./ 1993/ 1-3/2 KG312 . . . . **E**
HU, Y/ MAKE A JOYFUL SOUND: POEMS FOR CHILDREN BY
AFRICAN-AMERICAN POETS./ 1991/ 1-6 KE070 . . . . **811.008**
Vanished!: the mysterious disappearance of Amelia Earhart./ 1996/
2-4/7 KE328 . . . . **B EARHART, A.**
HUANG, B/ Mr. Pak buys a story./ 1997/ K-3/2 KB734 . . . . . **398.27**
HUBBARD, BJ/ America's religions: an educator's guide to beliefs and
practices./ 1997/ KA160 . . . . **PROF 200**
HUBBARD, J/ Lives turned upside down: homeless children in their own
words and photographs./ 1996/ 3-6/4 KB009 . . . . **362.5**
HUBBARD, W/ Moles and the Mireuk: a Korean folktale./ 1993/
K-2/4 KB605 . . . . **398.24**
HUBBARDS (MUSICAL GROUP)/ Olde Mother Goose (Kit)./ 1993/
P-K KB805 . . . . **KIT 398.8**
HUBBELL, P/ Camel caravan./ 1996/ P-1/3 KG335 . . . . **E**
HUCK, CS/ Princess Furball./ 1989/ 3-4/6 KB745 . . . . . . **CE 398.27**
Princess Furball (Kit)./ 1993/ 3-4/6 KB745 . . . . **CE 398.27**
Princess Furball (Talking book)./ 1993/ 3-4/6 KB745 . . . . **CE 398.27**
Princess Furball (Videocassette)./ 1993/ 3-4/6 KB745 . . . . **CE 398.27**
Toads and diamonds./ 1996/ 2-3/3 KB319 . . . . **398.2**
HUDSON, CW/ HOW SWEET THE SOUND: AFRICAN-AMERICAN
SONGS FOR CHILDREN./ 1995/ K-6 KD571 . . . . **CE 789.2**
HUDSON, J/ Sweetgrass./ 1989/ 6-A/5 KH286 . . . . **FIC**
HUDSON, W/ Five notable inventors./ 1995/ 3-5/4 KC892 . . . . . **609**
HOW SWEET THE SOUND: AFRICAN-AMERICAN SONGS FOR
CHILDREN./ 1995/ K-6 KD571 . . . . **CE 789.2**
IN PRAISE OF OUR FATHERS AND OUR MOTHERS: A BLACK FAMILY
TREASURY BY OUTSTANDING AUTHORS AND ARTISTS./ 1997/
3-6 KA867 . . . . **306.85**
PASS IT ON: AFRICAN-AMERICAN POETRY FOR CHILDREN./ 1993/
1-3 KE075 . . . . **811.008**
HUFF, BA/ Greening the city streets: the story of community gardens./
1990/ 5-6/7 KD168 . . . . **635**
HUFFMAN, T/ Alcohol--what it is, what it does./ c1977/
1-3/5 KD002 . . . . **613.81**
Allergies - what they are, what they do./ 1991/ 3-5/6 KD033 . **616.97**
HUGHES, A/ Van Gogh./ 1994/ 6-A/9 KE370 . . . . **B GOGH, V.**
HUGHES, L/ Dream keeper and other poems, including seven additional
poems./ 1994/ 4-6 KD954 . . . . **811**
Story of jazz (Sound recording cassette)./ 1954/
5-6 KD673 . . . . **SRC 789.5**
HUGHES, M/ Golden Aquarians./ 1995/ 5-A/6 KH287 . . . . **FIC**
Invitation to the game./ 1993/ 6-A/6 KH288 . . . . **FIC**
Invitation to the game (Sound recording cassette)./ 1996/
6-A/6 KH288 . . . . **FIC**
HUGHES, ME/ Mario Lemieux: beating the odds./ 1996/
4-6/9 KE433 . . . . **B LEMIEUX, M.**
HUGHES, S/ Alfie gets in first./ 1987/ P-K/2 KF784 . . . . **E**
Alfie gets in first (Braille)./ n.d./ P-K/2 KF784 . . . . **E**
Big Alfie and Annie Rose storybook./ 1988/ P-3/6 KF785 . . . . **E**
Big Alfie out of doors storybook./ 1992/ P-3/6 KF785 . . . . **E**
Bouncing./ 1995/ P/2 KF786 . . . . **E**
Chatting./ 1996/ P-1/2 KF787 . . . . **E**
Dogger./ c1978/ P-2/3 KF788 . . . . **E**
Hiding./ 1996/ P-K/2 KF789 . . . . **E**
Nursery collection./ c1986, 1994/ P/2 KF790 . . . . **E**
Rhymes for Annie Rose./ 1995/ P-K KF102 . . . . **821**
HUGHES, T/ Iron giant: a story in five nights./ 1988/ 3-6/3 KH289 . **FIC**
Iron giant: a story in five nights (Sound recording cassette)./ n.d./
3-6/3 KH289 . . . . **FIC**

Tales of the early world./ 1991/ 4-A/5 KH290 . . . . **FIC**
Tales of the early world (Sound recording cassette)./ 1994/
4-A/5 KH290 . . . . **FIC**
HULL, R/ Alphabet from Z to A: (with much confusion on the way)./ 1994/
2-5 KE036 . . . . **811**
Cat and the fiddle and more./ 1992/ P-1 KD915 . . . . **811**
Sad underwear and other complications: more poems for children and
their parents./ 1995/ 2-4 KE038 . . . . **811**
HULME, JN/ How to write, recite, and delight in all kinds of poetry./
1996/ 3-6 KD867 . . . . **808.06**
Sea squares./ 1991/ K-3/3 KB960 . . . . **513.2**
Sea sums./ 1996/ P-2/3 KB961 . . . . **513.2**
HULPACH, V/ Ahaiyute and Cloud Eater./ 1996/ 3-4/5 KB708 . **398.26**
HUNG, G/ Science dictionary of the human body./ 1992/
4-6/7 KC906 . . . . **611**
HUNT, I/ Across five Aprils./ 1984/ 5-A/5 KH291 . . . . **CE FIC**
Across five Aprils (Braille)./ n.d./ 5-A/5 KH291 . . . . **CE FIC**
Across five Aprils (Sound recording cassette)./ n.d./
5-A/5 KH291 . . . . **CE FIC**
Across five Aprils (Talking book)./ Across five Aprils (Talking book)./
n.d./ 1973/ 5-A/5 KH291 . . . . **CE FIC**
5-A/5 KH291 . . . . **CE FIC**
Up a road slowly./ 1993/ A/7 KH292 . . . . **CE FIC**
HUNT, J/ First look at animals with horns./ 1989/ 1-3/2 KC792 **599.64**
First look at ducks, geese, and swans./ 1990/ 1-3/2 KC683 . . **598.4**
Keep looking./ 1989/ P-3/2 KC728 . . . . **599**
Mapmaker's daughter./ 1991/ 2-3/3 KF698 . . . . **E**
HUNT, T/ Puppetry in early childhood education./ 1982/
KA327 . . . . **PROF 791.5**
HUNTER, H/ THREE BILLY GOATS GRUFF; AND, THE THREE LITTLE PIGS
(Videocassette)./ 1989/ P-K KB665 . . . . **VCR 398.24**
HUNTER, M/ Gilly Martin the Fox./ 1994/ 3-4/7 KB593 . . . . . **398.24**
Stranger came ashore./ c1975/ A/7 KH293 . . . . **FIC**
Third eye./ 1991/ A/7 KH294 . . . . **FIC**
Third eye (Sound recording cassette)./ n.d./ A/7 KH294 . . . . . **FIC**
Walking stones./ 1996/ 6-A/8 KH295 . . . . **FIC**
HURD, C/ Goodnight moon./ c1947/ P-K/1 KF285 . . . . **CE E**
Runaway bunny./ c1972/ P-K/2 KF287 . . . . **CE E**
HURD, ET/ I dance in my red pajamas./ 1982/ K-1/2 KF791 . . . . . **E**
HURD, T/ Art dog./ 1996/ 1-3/2 KF792 . . . . **E**
Mama don't allow./ 1984/ K-3/2 KF793 . . . . **CE E**
Mama don't allow (Talking book)./ 1984/ K-3/2 KF793 . . . . . **CE E**
Mama don't allow (Videocassette)./ 1989/ K-3/2 KF793 . . . . . **CE E**
MAMA NO QUIERE (Videocassette)./ 1989/ K-3/2 KF793 . . . . **CE E**
HURT, J/ Aladdin and the magic lamp (Kit)./ 1995/
3-5 KB333 . . . . **KIT 398.2**
HURWITZ, J/ Aldo Applesauce./ 1979/ 4-6/6 KH296 . . . . **FIC**
Aldo Applesauce (Sound recording cassette)./ n.d./ 4-6/6 KH296 . **FIC**
Aldo Ice Cream./ 1981/ 4-6/6 KH296 . . . . **FIC**
Aldo Ice Cream (Braille)./ n.d./ 4-6/6 KH296 . . . . **FIC**
Aldo Ice Cream (Sound recording cassette)./ n.d./ 4-6/6 KH296 . . **FIC**
Aldo Peanut Butter./ 1990/ 4-6/6 KH296 . . . . **FIC**
Baseball fever./ 1981/ 4-6/6 KH297 . . . . **FIC**
Baseball fever (Sound recording cassette)./ n.d./ 4-6/6 KH297 . . . **FIC**
BIRTHDAY SURPRISES: TEN GREAT STORIES TO UNWRAP./ 1995/
5-A/6 KG900 . . . . **FIC**
Class clown./ 1987/ 2-4/4 KH298 . . . . **FIC**
Class president./ 1990/ 2-4/4 KH298 . . . . **FIC**
Class president (Sound recording cassette)./ 1994/ 2-4/4 KH298 . . **FIC**
E is for Elisa./ 1991/ 2-4/4 KH303 . . . . **FIC**
E is for Elisa (Sound recording cassette)./ 1994/ 2-4/4 KH303 . . . **FIC**
Elisa in the middle./ 1995/ 2-4/4 KH303 . . . . **FIC**
Leonard Bernstein: a passion for music./ 1993/
5-A/7 KE253 . . . . **B BERNSTEIN, L.**
Make room for Elisa./ 1993/ 2-4/4 KH303 . . . . **FIC**
Much ado about Aldo./ c1978/ 4-6/6 KH296 . . . . **FIC**
New neighbors for Nora./ c1979, 1991/ 2-4/6 KH299 . . . . . . **FIC**
New shoes for Silvia./ 1993/ K-2/2 KF794 . . . . **E**
Nora and Mrs. Mind-your-own business./ c1977, 1991/
2-4/4 KH300 . . . . **FIC**
Ozzie on his own./ 1995/ 3-5/4 KH301 . . . . **FIC**
Ozzie on his own (Sound recording cassette)./ 1997/
3-5/4 KH301 . . . . **FIC**
Roz and Ozzie./ 1992/ 3-5/5 KH302 . . . . **FIC**
Roz and Ozzie (Sound recording cassette)./ 1995/ 3-5/5 KH302 . . **FIC**
Russell and Elisa./ 1989/ 2-4/4 KH303 . . . . **FIC**
Russell Sprouts./ 1987/ 2-4/4 KH303 . . . . **FIC**
School spirit./ 1994/ 2-4/4 KH298 . . . . **FIC**
School's out./ 1991/ 2-4/4 KH298 . . . . **FIC**
Superduper Teddy./ c1980, 1990/ 2-4/4 KH304 . . . . **FIC**
Teacher's pet./ 1988/ 3-5/4 KH305 . . . . **FIC**
HUSAIN, S/ What do we know about Islam?/ 1996/ 4-6/9 KA786 **297**
HUTCHINS, HJ/ Anastasia Morningstar and the crystal butterfly. Rev. ed./
1984/ 4-6/6 KH306 . . . . **FIC**

AUTHOR/ILLUSTRATOR INDEX

Cat of Artimus Pride./ 1991/ 3-5/6 KH307 . . . . **FIC**
Prince of Tarn./ 1997/ 4-6/5 KH308 . . . . **FIC**
Tess./ 1995/ 3-5/4 KH309 . . . . **FIC**
Three and many wishes of Jason Reid./ 1988/ 4-6/6 KH310 . . **FIC**
Three and many wishes of Jason Reid (Sound recording cassette)./ 1993/
4-6/6 KH310 . . . . **FIC**
Within a painted past./ 1994/ 5-A/4 KH311 . . . . **FIC**
HUTCHINS, P/ Changes, changes./ c1971/ P-1 KF795 . . . . **CE E**
Don't forget the bacon!/ c1976, 1987/ P-2/3 KF796 . . . . . . **CE E**
Don't forget the bacon! (Big book)./ 1994/ P-2/3 KF796 . . . . **CE E**
Don't forget the bacon! (Kit)./ 1992/ P-2/3 KF796 . . . . **CE E**
Doorbell rang./ 1986/ P-2/2 KF797 . . . . **CE E**
Doorbell rang (Big book)./ 1994/ P-2/2 KF797 . . . . **CE E**
Doorbell rang (Braille)./ n.d./ P-2/2 KF797 . . . . **CE E**
Good-night owl./ c1972/ P-2/3 KF798 . . . . **CE E**
Little Pink Pig./ 1994/ P-1/2 KF799 . . . . **E**
Llaman a la puerta./ 1994/ P-2/2 KF797 . . . . **CE E**
Llaman a la puerta (Kit)./ 1996/ P-2/2 KF797 . . . . **CE E**
One hunter./ 1982/ P-K KF800 . . . . **E**
One-Eyed Jake./ c1979, 1994/ K-2/4 KF801 . . . . **E**
Paseo de Rosie./ 1997/ P-1/1 KF802 . . . . **CE E**
Rosie's walk./ c1968/ P-1/1 KF802 . . . . **CE E**
Rosie's walk (Big book)./ 1992/ P-1/1 KF802 . . . . **CE E**
Rosie's Walk (Kit)./ 1992/ P-1/1 KF802 . . . . **CE E**
Rosie's walk (Videocassette)./ 1986/ P-1/1 KF802 . . . . **CE E**
Shrinking mouse./ 1997/ P-K/1 KF803 . . . . **E**
Silly Billy!/ 1992/ P-2/2 KF806 . . . . **CE E**
Tale of Thomas Mead./ 1980/ 1-2/2 KF804 . . . . **CE E**
Tidy Titch./ 1991/ P-2/2 KF808 . . . . **E**
Titch and Daisy./ 1996/ P-K/2 KF805 . . . . **E**
Very worst monster./ 1985/ P-2/2 KF806 . . . . **CE E**
Very worst monster (Kit)./ 1988/ P-2/2 KF806 . . . . **CE E**
Where's the baby?/ 1988/ P-2/2 KF806 . . . . **CE E**
Which witch is which?/ 1989/ P-1/2 KF807 . . . . **E**
You'll soon grow into them, Titch./ 1983/ P-2/2 KF808 . . . . . **E**
HUTCHINSON, S/ Snap!/ 1996/ K-2/2 KG651 . . . . **E**
HUTTON, W/ Cricket warrior: a Chinese tale./ 1994/
2-3/5 KB549 . . . . **398.24**
Moses in the bulrushes./ 1986/ P-2/6 KA679 . . . . **221.9**
Persephone./ 1994/ 5-6/5 KA744 . . . . **292**
Perseus./ 1993/ 5-6/4 KA745 . . . . **292**
Selkie girl./ 1986/ 3-4/6 KB551 . . . . **CE 398.24**
Tam Lin./ 1991/ 3-4/4 KB276 . . . . **398.2**
Theseus and the Minotaur./ 1989/ 5-6/6 KA746 . . . . **292**
Tinderbox. Newly illustrated ed./ 1988/ K-3/5 KF155 . . . . . . **E**
Trojan horse./ 1992/ 2-5/5 KE124 . . . . **883**
Trojan horse (Sound recording cassette)./ 1995/ 2-5/5 KE124 . . . **883**
HUYNH, QN/ Land I lost: adventures of a boy in Vietnam./ 1982/
5-6/7 KE718 . . . . **959.7**
Land I lost: adventures of a boy in Vietnam (Sound recording cassette)./
n.d./ 5-6/7 KE718 . . . . **959.7**
HYATT, PR/ Coast to coast with Alice./ 1995/ 4-6/5 KH312 . . . . . **FIC**
HYDE, L/ Meeting death./ 1989/ A/7 KA891 . . . . **306.9**
HYDE, MO/ Kids in and out of trouble./ 1995/ A/8 KB072 . . . **364.36**
Know about AIDS. 3rd ed./ 1994/ 5-6/8 KD030 . . . . **616.97**
Meeting death./ 1989/ A/7 KA891 . . . . **306.9**
HYMAN, M/ Broadway chicken./ 1995/ 5-A/7 KH146 . . . . **FIC**
HYMAN, TS/ Adventures of Hershel of Ostropol./ 1995/
2-4/7 KB459 . . . . **398.22**
Caddie Woodlawn. New ed./ 1973/ 4-6/6 KG922 . . . . **CE FIC**
Child's Christmas in Wales./ 1985/ P-A/8 KE119 . . . . **828**
Christmas Carol in prose, being a ghost story of Christmas./ 1983/
4-6/5 KH074 . . . . **CE FIC**
Fortune-tellers./ 1992/ 2-5/5 KG834 . . . . **FIC**
Ghost eye./ 1992/ 4-6/6 KG881 . . . . **FIC**
Haunts: five hair-raising tales./ 1996/ 4-6/4 KH495 . . . . . . **FIC**
Iron John./ 1994/ 4-5/4 KB330 . . . . **398.2**
King Stork./ 1973/ 3-5/6 KH614 . . . . **FIC**
Little Red Riding Hood./ 1983/ 1-4/6 KB741 . . . . **CE 398.27**
Rapunzel./ 1982/ 2-4/4 KB307 . . . . **398.2**
Saint George and the dragon: a golden legend./ 1984/
5/7 KB453 . . . . **CE 398.22**
Swan Lake./ 1989/ 4-6/7 KD693 . . . . **CE 792.8**
Tight times./ 1983/ K-2/1 KF689 . . . . **E**
Why don't you get a horse, Sam Adams?/ c1974/
3-5/7 KE227 . . . . **CE B ADAMS, S.**
Will you sign here, John Hancock?/ c1976, 1997/
5-6/7 KE383 . . . . **CE B HANCOCK, J.**
HYPPOLITE, J/ Seth and Samona./ 1995/ 4-6/6 KH313 . . . . . . **FIC**
I SAW ESAU: THE SCHOOLCHILD'S POCKET BOOK./ 1992/
KA276 . . . . **PROF 398.8**
I THOUGHT I'D TAKE MY RAT TO SCHOOL: POEMS FOR SEPTEMBER
TO JUNE./ 1993/ 2-5 KE066 . . . . **811.008**
INCISA, M/ Forgetful wishing well./ 1985/ 4-6 KD963 . . . . . . **811**

INGPEN, R/ Peace begins with you./ 1990/ P-2/5 KA812 . . . . . **303.6**
INGRAHAM, E/ Cross-country cat./ 1979/ K-2/4 KF331 . . . . **E**
Flood./ 1997/ 1-3/2 KF332 . . . . **E**
INNER CHIMES: POEMS ON POETRY./ 1992/ 2-6 KD885 . . . **808.81**
IRIZARRY, C/ Mexico. Rev. ed./ 1994/ A/11 KE831 . . . . **972**
IRVING, J/ Full speed ahead: stories and activities for children on
transportation./ 1988/ KA223 . . . . **PROF 372.6**
Mudluscious: stories and activities featuring food for preschool children./
1986/ KA201 . . . . **PROF 372.3**
IRVING, W/ Legend of Sleepy Hollow./ c1928, 1990/
6-A/9 KH314 . . . . **FIC**
Rip Van Winkle./ 1987/ 4-A/9 KH315 . . . . **FIC**
Rip Van Winkle; and, The Legend of Sleepy Hollow (Talking book)./
1986/ 5-6 KH316 . . . . **TB FIC**
Rip Van Winkle (Braille)./ n.d./ 4-A/9 KH315 . . . . **FIC**
Rip Van Winkle (Sound recording cassette)./ n.d./ 4-A/9 KH315 . . **FIC**
ISAACS, A/ Swamp Angel./ 1994/ 2-5/6 KF810 . . . . **E**
ISAACSON, P/ Short walk around the Pyramids and through the world of
art./ 1993/ 5-A/6 KD363 . . . . **700**
ISADORA, R/ At the crossroads./ 1991/ K-2/1 KF811 . . . . **E**
At the crossroads (Videocassette)./ 1996/ K-2 KF812 . . . . . . **VCR E**
Ben's trumpet./ c1979/ 1-3/3 KF813 . . . . **E**
City seen from A to Z./ 1983/ P-1 KF814 . . . . **E**
Flossie and the fox./ 1986/ K-3/2 KG105 . . . . **CE E**
Lili at ballet./ 1993/ P-2/2 KF815 . . . . **E**
Lili backstage./ 1997/ K-2/3 KF816 . . . . **E**
Over the green hills./ 1992/ 1-3/2 KF817 . . . . **E**
Seeing is believing./ 1979/ K-2/2 KG496 . . . . **E**
White stallion./ 1982/ 1-3/2 KG497 . . . . **E**
Young Mozart./ 1997/ 2-3/6 KE472 . . . . **B MOZART, W.**
ISENBART, H/ Birth of a foal./ 1986/ 3-6/5 KD201 . . . . **636.1**
ITO, T/ California gold rush./ 1997/ 5-6/11 KF080 . . . . **979.4**
ITO, Y/ Jojofu./ 1996/ 1-4/5 KB670 . . . . **398.24**
Lily and the wooden bowl./ 1994/ 3-5/7 KB366 . . . . **398.2**
ITZKOFF, SW/ Children learning to read: a guide for parents and
teachers./ 1996/ KA209 . . . . **PROF 372.4**
IVERS, KS/ Internet and instruction: activities and ideas./ 1996/
KA047 . . . . **PROF 025.06**
IVORY, LA/ Cats know best./ 1988/ P-1/1 KD232 . . . . **636.8**
IZUKI, S/ Believers in America: poems about Americans of Asian and Pacific
islander descent./ 1994/ 3-6 KD955 . . . . **811**
JACK, D/ Dance in your pants: great songs for little kids to dance to
(Sound recording cassette)./ 1988/ K-3 KD620 . . . . **SRC 789.3**
David Jack... live!: Makin' music, makin' friends (Videocassette)./ 1991/
P-2 KD621 . . . . **VCR 789.3**
Gotta hop (Sound recording cassette)./ 1990/ K-3 KD622 . **SRC 789.3**
JACKSON, A/ Blowing bubbles with the enemy./ 1993/
4-6/5 KH317 . . . . **FIC**
JACKSON, E/ Brown cow, green grass, yellow mellow sun./ 1995/
P-1/2 KF818 . . . . **E**
Impossible riddle./ 1995/ K-3/4 KF819 . . . . **E**
Precious gift: a Navaho creation myth./ 1996/ 2-3/2 KB594 . . **398.24**
Winter solstice./ 1994/ 3-5/6 KB211 . . . . **394.261**
JACKSON, I/ Somebody's new pajamas./ 1996/ 3-5/4 KH318 . . . . **FIC**
Somebody's new pajamas (Sound recording cassette)./ 1997/
3-5/4 KH318 . . . . **FIC**
JACKSON, J/ WHITE CAT (Videocassette)./ 1997/
K-2 KB382 . . . . **VCR 398.2**
JACKSON, L/ Newfoundland and Labrador./ 1995/ 4-6/8 KE822 . . **971.8**
JACKSON, S/ Do you know me./ 1993/ 4-A/5 KH107 . . . . **FIC**
Great Aunt Martha./ 1995/ 1-3/2 KF853 . . . . **E**
Willy's silly grandma./ 1997/ 1-3/2 KF455 . . . . **E**
JACOB, M/ Boy who lived with the bears: and other Iroquois stories./
1995/ 2-4/4 KB537 . . . . **CE 398.24**
Dog people: native dog stories./ 1995/ 4-6/5 KG934 . . . . . **FIC**
How Rabbit tricked Otter and other Cherokee trickster stories./ 1994/
2-4/6 KB641 . . . . **CE 398.24**
How Turtle's back was cracked: a traditional Cherokee tale./ 1995/
4-5/5 KB642 . . . . **398.24**
Legend of the Windigo: a tale from native North America./ 1996/
2-3/6 KB410 . . . . **398.21**
JACOBI, K/ Half-a-Moon Inn./ c1980, 1991/ 6/7 KH117 . . . . . . **FIC**
JACOBS, F/ Sam the sea cow./ 1991/ 1-3/2 KC780 . . . . **599.55**
JACOBS, J/ King of the cats./ 1980/ 1-3/2 KB595 . . . . . . **CE 398.24**
JACOBS, L/ Letting off steam./ 1989/ 4-A/7 KC156 . . . . **551.2**
JACOBS, PS/ James Printer: a novel of rebellion./ 1997/
5-A/6 KH319 . . . . **FIC**
JACOBS, VA/ Reading crisis: why poor children fall behind./ 1990/
KA219 . . . . **PROF 372.6**
JACOBS, WJ/ Ellis Island: new hope in a new land./ 1990/
3-6/6 KA919 . . . . **325**
Ellis Island: new hope in a new land (Sound recording cassette)./ 1993/
3-6/6 KA919 . . . . **325**
Great lives: human rights./ 1990/ 6-A/7 KA900 . . . . **323**

Mother Teresa: helping the poor./ 1991/
4-6/6 KE561 . . . . **B TERESA,MOTHER**
JACOBSON, D/ Three wishes./ c1993, 1996/ P-1/1 KG797 . . . . **E**
JACQUES, B/ Redwall./ 1986/ 5-A/6 KH320 . . . . **FIC**
JACQUES, L/ At home in the rain forest./ 1991/ K-4/6 KC328 **577.34**
JAFFE, N/ Golden flower: a Taino myth from Puerto Rico./ 1996/
2-4/5 KB503 . . . . **398.23**
In the month of Kislev: a story for Hanukkah./ 1992/
K-2/2 KF820 . . . . **CE E**
In the month of Kislev: a story for Hanukkah (Sound recording cassette)./
1995/ K-2/2 KF820 . . . . **CE E**
In the month of Kislev (Videocassette)./ 1993/ K-2/2 KF820 . . . **CE E**
Older brother, younger brother: a Korean folktale./ 1995/
3-4/6 KB320 . . . . **398.2**
Patakin: world tales of drums and drummers./ 1994/
5-6/6 KB321 . . . . **398.2**
Voice for the people: the life and work of Harold Courlander./ 1997/
KA367 . . . . **PROF B COURLAND**
JAKOB, D/ My bike./ 1994/ K-2/3 KF821 . . . . **E**
My new sandbox./ 1996/ P-1/1 KF822 . . . . **E**
JAKOBSEN, K/ Johnny Appleseed./ 1990/ K-3 KD973 . . . . . . **811**
My New York./ 1993/ 2-5/3 KE957 . . . . **974.7**
JAKUBISZYN, A/ Puppet book: how to make and operate puppets and
stage a puppet play./ 1990/ KA326 . . . . **PROF 791.5**
JAM, T/ Charlotte stories./ 1994/ 2-3/2 KH321 . . . . **FIC**
JAMES, A/ Dog in, cat out./ 1993/ P-1/1 KG359 . . . . **E**
Wiggy and Boa./ c1988, 1990/ 5-6/7 KH113 . . . . **FIC**
JAMES, B/ Mary Ann./ 1994/ K-2/3 KF823 . . . . **E**
No more animals!/ 1995/ 1-3/2 KH502 . . . . **FIC**
SLAM DUNK: BASKETBALL POEMS./ 1995/ 4-6 KE081 . . . **811.008**
JAMES, D/ I want to be a puppeteer./ 1996/ 3-5/5 KD444 . . **745.592**
I want to be an actor./ 1996/ 3-5/5 KD688 . . . . **792**
Play with paint./ 1993/ K-2/3 KD465 . . . . **750**
Play with paper./ 1993/ K-2/3 KD441 . . . . **745.54**
JAMES, DL/ Singing calendar (Sound recording cassette)./ 1984/
P-1 KC071 . . . . **SRC 529**
JAMES, E/ Happy Thanksgiving!/ 1987/ 3-6/6 KB221 . . . . . **394.264**
Holiday handbook./ 1994/ 5-A/7 KA413 . . . . **REF 394.26**
How to write a great school report./ 1983/ 4-6/7 KB088 . . **371.302**
Jobs for kids: the guide to having fun and making money./ 1990/
5-6/7 KD305 . . . . **650.1**
New complete babysitter's handbook./ 1995/ 5-6/6 KD302 . . . . **649**
Sincerely yours: how to write great letters./ 1993/
3-6/7 KD870 . . . . **808.6**
Social smarts: manners for today's kids./ 1996/ 4-6/6 KB243 . **395.3**
JAMES, J/ Medieval cathedral./ 1991/ 6-A/9 KD390 . . . . **726**
Roman villa./ 1992/ 4-6/7 KE641 . . . . **937**
Shakespeare's theater./ 1994/ 4-A/7 KD689 . . . . **792**
JAMES, JA/ King Bobble./ 1996/ 2-3/2 KG953 . . . . **FIC**
On the road with Poppa Whopper./ 1997/ 3-4/2 KG954 . . . . . **FIC**
JAMES, M/ Frankenlouse./ 1994/ 6-A/6 KH322 . . . . **FIC**
Shoebag./ 1992/ 6-A/6 KH323 . . . . **FIC**
Shoebag returns./ 1996/ 6-A/6 KH324 . . . . **FIC**
JAMES, S/ Ancient Rome./ 1990/ 5-6/8 KE639 . . . . **937**
Antigua Roma./ n.d./ 5-6/8 KE639 . . . . **937**
Leon and Bob./ 1997/ K-2/2 KF824 . . . . **E**
Wild woods./ 1996/ P-2/2 KF825 . . . . **E**
JANE YOLEN'S MOTHER GOOSE SONGBOOK./ 1992/
KA277 . . . . **PROF 398.8**
JANECZKO, PB/ Loads of codes and secret ciphers./ 1984/
A/7 KD309 . . . . **652**
PLACE MY WORDS ARE LOOKING FOR: WHAT POETS SAY ABOUT
AND THROUGH THEIR WORK./ 1990/ 3-A KE076 . . . . **811.008**
JANIAK, W/ Basic skills for young children (Sound recording cassette)./
c1980, 1990/ P-K KD623 . . . . **SRC 789.3**
JANSSON, T/ Comet in Moominland./ c1946, 1992/ 3-6/7 KH325 . **FIC**
Comet in Moominland (Sound recording cassette)./ 1997,/
3-6/7 KH325 . . . . **FIC**
Finn Family Moomintroll./ c1948, 1990/ 3-6/7 KH325 . . . . . . **FIC**
Finn Family Moomintroll (Large print)./ 1989,/ 3-6/7 KH325 . . . . **FIC**
Moominland midwinter./ c1958, 1992/ 3-6/7 KH325 . . . . . . **FIC**
Moominland midwinter (Sound recording cassette)./ 1997,/
3-6/7 KH325 . . . . **FIC**
Moominpappa at sea./ 1993,/ 3-6/7 KH325 . . . . **FIC**
Moominpappa at sea (Sound recording cassette)./ 1997,/
3-6/7 KH325 . . . . **FIC**
Moominpappa's memoirs./ 1994/ 3-6/7 KH325 . . . . **FIC**
Moominpappa's memoirs (Sound recording cassette)./ 1997,/
3-6/7 KH325 . . . . **FIC**
Moominsummer madness./ c1954, 1991/ 3-6/7 KH325 . . . . . **FIC**
Tales from Moominvalley./ c1964, 1995/ 3-6/7 KH325 . . . . . **FIC**
JAPANESE FAIRY TALES./ 1992/ 2-4/7 KB322 . . . . **398.2**
JAQUES, F/ Old Peter's Russian tales./ 1975/ 5-6/6 KB766 . . **398.27**
JARNER, B/ Chicken and egg./ 1986/ K-3/2 KC692 . . . . **598.6**

JARRELL, R/ Animal family./ 1995/ 5-A/6 KH326 . . . . **FIC**
Animal family (Braille)./ n.d./ 5-A/6 KH326 . . . . **FIC**
Animal family (Sound recording cassette)./ n.d./ 5-A/6 KH326 . . . **FIC**
Animal family (Talking book)./ n.d./ 5-A/6 KH326 . . . . **FIC**
Bat-poet./ 1996/ 4-A/6 KH327 . . . . **FIC**
Snow-White and the seven dwarfs./ 1972/ 3-4/6 KB310 . . . . **398.2**
JARROW, G/ Naked mole-rats./ 1996/ 4-6/7 KC744 . . . . . **599.35**
JASPERSOHN, W/ Cookies./ 1993/ 3-5/8 KD320 . . . . **664**
Cranberries./ 1991/ 4-5/6 KD160 . . . . **634**
JAY, LA/ Sea turtle journey: the story of a loggerhead turtle./ 1995/
K-2/5 KF826 . . . . **CE E**
Sea turtle journey: the story of a loggerhead turtle (Kit)./ 1995/
K-2/5 KF826 . . . . **CE E**
JEDROSZ, A/ Eyes./ 1992/ 5-6/6 KC965 . . . . **612.8**
JEFFERS, S/ Hiawatha./ 1983/ P-A KD979 . . . . **CE 811**
McDuff comes home./ 1997/ K-2/2 KG705 . . . . **E**
McDuff moves in./ 1997/ K-2/2 KG706 . . . . **E**
Stopping by the woods on a snowy evening./ 1978/ P-A KD941 . **811**
JEFFREY, LS/ American inventors of the 20th century./ 1996/
4-6/12 KC894 . . . . **609**
Great American businesswomen./ 1996/ 5-6/7 KD315 . . . . . **658.4**
JENKINS, DR/ I wanted to know all about God./ 1994/
K-2/2 KA694 . . . . **231**
JENKINS, E/ African-American folk songs and rhythms (Sound recording
cassette)./ c1960, 1992/ K-6 KD572 . . . . **SRC 789.2**
And one and two and other songs for pre-school and primary children
(Compact disc)./ 1995/ P-K KD624 . . . . **CD 789.3**
And one and two and other songs for pre-school and primary children
(Sound recording cassette)./ 1990/ P-K KD624 . . . . **CD 789.3**
Call and response: rhythmic group singing (Sound recording cassette)./
1990/ K-3 KD625 . . . . **SRC 789.3**
Come dance by the ocean (Compact disc)./ 1991/
P-2 KD626 . . . . **SRC 789.3**
Come dance by the ocean (Sound recording cassette)./ 1991/
P-2 KD626 . . . . **SRC 789.3**
Counting games and rhythms for the little ones, vol. 1 (Sound recording
cassette)./ c1964, 1990/ P-2 KB948 . . . . **SRC 513**
Ella Jenkins live!: at the Smithsonian (Videocassette)./ 1991/
P-K KD627 . . . . **VCR 789.3**
Growing up with Ella Jenkins: rhythms songs and rhymes (Sound
recording cassette)./ 1990/ P-2 KD628 . . . . **SRC 789.3**
Holiday times (Compact disc)./ 1996/ P-3 KB199 . . . . . . **CD 394.26**
Holiday times (Sound recording cassette)./ 1996/
P-3 KB199 . . . . **CD 394.26**
Jambo and other call and response songs and chants (Sound recording
cassette)./ 1990/ K-3 KD573 . . . . **SRC 789.2**
Long time to freedom (Sound recording cassette)./ c1969, 1992/
K-A KD574 . . . . **SRC 789.2**
Multicultural children's songs (Compact disc)./ 1995/
K-2 KD629 . . . . **CD 789.3**
Multicultural children's songs (Sound recording cassette)./ 1995/
K-2 KD629 . . . . **CD 789.3**
Rhythm and game songs for the little ones (Sound recording cassette)./
1990/ P-K KD630 . . . . **SRC 789.3**
Songs and rhythms from near and far (Compact disc)./ 1997,/
K-2 KD575 . . . . **SRC 789.2**
Songs and rhythms from near and far (Sound recording cassette)./
c1964, 1992/ K-2 KD575 . . . . **SRC 789.2**
Songs children love to sing (Compact disc)./ 1996/
K-3 KD631 . . . . **CD 789.3**
Songs children love to sing (Sound recording cassette)./ 1996/
K-3 KD631 . . . . **CD 789.3**
This is rhythm (Compact disc)./ 1994/ K-2 KD632 . . . . . . **CD 789.3**
This is rhythm (Sound recording cassette)./ 1994/
K-2 KD632 . . . . **CD 789.3**
Travellin' with Ella Jenkins: a bilingual journey (Compact disc)./ 1989/
K-2 KD576 . . . . **CD 789.2**
Travellin' with Ella Jenkins: a bilingual journey (Sound recording
cassette)./ 1989/ K-2 KD576 . . . . **CD 789.2**
We are America's children (Compact disc)./ 1989/
1-6 KD577 . . . . **CD 789.2**
We are America's children (Sound recording cassette)./ 1989/
1-6 KD577 . . . . **CD 789.2**
You'll sing a song and I'll sing a song (Compact disc)./ 1989,/
P-2 KD633 . . . . **SRC 789.3**
You'll sing a song and I'll sing a song (Sound recording cassette)./
c1966, 1989/ P-2 KD633 . . . . **SRC 789.3**
JENKINS, J/ Pond water zoo: an introduction to microscopic life./ 1996/
6-A/8 KC372 . . . . **579**
JENKINS, L/ Man who knew too much: a moral tale from the Baila of
Zambia./ 1994/ 4-5/3 KB607 . . . . **398.24**
Sambalena show-off./ 1995/ 1-3/2 KF612 . . . . **E**
JENKINS, PB/ Nest full of eggs./ 1995/ K-2/2 KC705 . . . . . . **598.8**
JENKINS, S/ Biggest, strongest, fastest./ 1995/ K-4/3 KC449 . . . . **591**

Elephants swim./ 1995/ P-2/3 KC466 . . . . **591.47**
Flip-flap./ 1995/ P-K/2 KA619 . . . . **152.14**
Looking down./ 1995/ K-3 KF827 . . . . **E**
Storytelling: learning and sharing (Videocassette)./ 1995/
KA246 . . . . **VCR PROF 372.67**
JENKINS, WA/ In other words: a beginning thesaurus./ 1987/
4-6 KA429 . . . . **REF 423**
JENNESS, A/ Families: a celebration of diversity, commitment, and love./
1990/ 4-6/5 KA868 . . . . **306.85**
In two worlds: a Yup'ik Eskimo family./ 1989/ 5-6/7 KF098 . . . **979.8**
JENNESS, D/ Indians of Canada. 7th ed./ 1977/
A/12 KA485 . . . . **REF 971**
JENNINGS, J/ Long shots: they beat the odds./ 1990/
5-6/6 KD762 . . . . **796**
JENNINGS, S/ Jeremiah and Mrs. Ming./ 1990/ K-2/2 KF828 . . . . . **E**
Jeremiah and Mrs. Ming (Big book)./ 1990/ K-2/2 KF828 . . . . **E**
JENNY, C/ Toady and Dr. Miracle./ 1997/ 1-3/2 KF390 . . . . **E**
JENSON, LB/ Fishermen of Nova Scotia./ 1980/ A/9 KD245 . . . . **639.2**
JENSSEN, H/ Jets./ 1996/ 4-6/8 KD061 . . . . **623.7**
JERAM, A/ I love guinea pigs./ 1995/ K-4/3 KD183 . . . . **636**
My hen is dancing./ c1994, 1996/ K-2/2 KD215 . . . . **636.5**
JEROME, KA/ Shiniest rock of all./ 1991/ 4-6/4 KH584 . . . . . . **FIC**
St. Patrick's Day shamrock mystery./ 1995/ 2-4/3 KH457 . . . . . . **FIC**
JESPERSEN, J/ Mummies, dinosaurs, moon rocks: how we know how old
things are./ 1996/ 4-6/9 KE625 . . . . **930.1**
JOHN, D/ BRER RABBIT AND BOSS LION (Talking book)./ 1992/
3-A KB533 . . . . **TB 398.24**
JOHN, H/ All-of-a-kind family./ 1951, 1988/ 4-6/5 KH782 . . . . . **FIC**
JOHNSON, A/ Joshua by the sea (Board book)./ 1994/
P/2 KF829 . . . . **BB E**
Joshua's night whispers (Board book)./ 1994/ P/2 KF830 . . . . **BB E**
Julius./ 1993/ P-2/2 KF831 . . . . **E**
Julius (Sound recording cassette)./ 1995/ P-2/2 KF831 . . . . **E**
One of three./ 1991/ P-1/2 KF832 . . . . **E**
Rain feet (Board book)./ 1994/ P/2 KF833 . . . . **BB E**
When I am old with you./ 1990/ P-2/6 KF834 . . . . **E**
JOHNSON, C/ Carrot seed./ c1945/ P-2/2 KF920 . . . . **CE E**
Harold and the purple crayon./ c1955, 1994/ P-2/2 KF835 . . . **CE E**
Harold and the purple crayon (Talking book)./ n.d.,/
P-2/2 KF835 . . . . **CE E**
Harold and the purple crayon (Videocassette)./ 1985,/
P-2/2 KF835 . . . . **CE E**
Harold y el lapiz color morado./ 1995/ P-2/2 KF835 . . . . **CE E**
Harold's ABC./ 1963,/ P-2/2 KF835 . . . . **CE E**
Harold's fairy tale: further adventures with the purple crayon./ c1984,
1994/ P-2/2 KF835 . . . . **CE E**
Harold's trip to the sky./ 1957,/ P-2/2 KF835 . . . . **CE E**
Picture for Harold's room./ 1960,/ P-2/2 KF835 . . . . **CE E**
Picture for Harold's room (Videocassette)./ n.d.,/ P-2/2 KF835 . . **CE E**
Rainy day./ 1993/ P-2/6 KC214 . . . . **551.57**
JOHNSON, D/ What will Mommy do when I'm at school?/ 1990/
K-1/2 KF836 . . . . **E**
JOHNSON, E/ CONVERSATION WITH MAGIC (Videocassette)./ 1992/
4-6 KD026 . . . . **VCR 616.97**
JOHNSON, J/ How big is a whale?/ 1995/ 2-5/5 KC462 . . . . . **591.4**
Simon and Schuster children's guide to insects and spiders./ 1996/
5-6/7 KC542 . . . . **595.7**
JOHNSON, JW/ Creation./ 1994/ K-3 KD956 . . . . **811**
Creation: a poem./ 1993/ 1-6 KD957 . . . . **811**
Lift every voice and sing./ 1993/ 2-6/5 KD672 . . . . **789.44**
JOHNSON, K/ Worm's eye view: make your own wildlife refuge./ 1991/
2-4/5 KC294 . . . . **577**
JOHNSON, L/ Granddaddy's gift./ 1997/ 1-3/2 KG146 . . . . **E**
Knoxville, Tennessee./ 1994/ P-1/2 KD945 . . . . **811**
Train./ 1996/ K-3/2 KG599 . . . . **E**
JOHNSON, M/ Black pearl./ c1967/ 5-6/5 KH557 . . . . **CE FIC**
Little fishes./ c1967, 1987/ A/6 KH227 . . . . **FIC**
Wanna bet?: science challenges to fool you./ 1993/
4-6/6 KD746 . . . . **793.8**
JOHNSON, N/ Battle of Lexington and Concord./ 1992/
4-6/7 KE881 . . . . **973.3**
JOHNSON, P/ And then there was one: the mysteries of extinction./
1990/ 5-6/7 KC488 . . . . **591.68**
Next spring an oriole./ 1987/ 2-4/5 KH848 . . . . **FIC**
Reindeer./ 1993/ 4-5/4 KD211 . . . . **636.2**
JOHNSON, PB/ Farmers' market./ 1997/ P-1/2 KF837 . . . . **E**
Insects are my life./ 1995/ 1-3/2 KG097 . . . . **E**
Saint Patrick and the peddler./ 1993/ 3-4/5 KB454 . . . . **398.22**
JOHNSON, RL/ Braving the frozen frontier: women working in Antarctica./
1997/ 4-6/6 KE214 . . . . **919.8**
Investigating the ozone hole./ 1993/ A/10 KC191 . . . . **551.5**
Science on the ice: an Antarctic journal./ 1995/ 5-A/7 KE215 . . **919.8**
JOHNSON, S/ Alphabet city./ 1995/ K-A KF838 . . . . **E**
Frog Prince, continued./ 1991/ 1-3/4 KG419 . . . . **E**

That's fresh!: seasonal recipes for young cooks./ 1995/
5-6 KD277 . . . . **641.5**
JOHNSON, SA/ Albatrosses of Midway Island./ 1990/
5-6/7 KC681 . . . . **598.4**
Apple trees./ 1983/ 4-6/9 KD161 . . . . **634**
Bats./ 1985/ 4-6/9 KC760 . . . . **599.4**
Beekeeper's year./ 1994/ 5-6/6 KD240 . . . . **638**
Crabs./ 1982/ 4-6/7 KC520 . . . . **595.3**
Elephant seals./ 1989/ 5-6/7 KC869 . . . . **599.79**
Ferrets./ 1997/ 5-6/10 KD182 . . . . **636**
Fireflies./ 1986/ A/10 KC553 . . . . **595.76**
Hermit crabs./ 1989/ A/7 KC521 . . . . **595.3**
How leaves change./ 1986/ 4-6/9 KC399 . . . . **581.4**
Inside an egg./ 1982/ 4-6/8 KC695 . . . . **598.6**
Ladybugs./ 1983/ A/11 KC554 . . . . **595.76**
Manada de lobos: siguiendo las huellas de los lobos en su entorno
natural./ 1993/ 6/10 KC836 . . . . **599.773**
Morning glories./ 1985/ 4-6/7 KC428 . . . . **583**
Mosses./ 1983/ 6/8 KC438 . . . . **588**
Raptor rescue!: an eagle flies free./ 1995/ 5-6/7 KD254 . . . . **639.9**
Silkworms./ 1982/ 4-6/8 KD241 . . . . **638**
Snails./ 1982/ 4-6/7 KC512 . . . . **594**
Tree frogs./ 1986/ 5-6/7 KC604 . . . . **597.8**
Wasps./ 1984/ 5-6/8 KC574 . . . . **595.79**
Water insects./ 1989/ A/7 KC543 . . . . **595.7**
Wheat./ 1990/ 5-6/7 KD151 . . . . **633.1**
Wolf pack: tracking wolves in the wild./ 1985/ 6/10 KC836 . . **599.773**
JOHNSON, ST/ Samurai's daughter: a Japanese legend./ 1992/
3-4/6 KB365 . . . . **398.2**
Snow wife./ 1993/ 3-9/5 KB414 . . . . **398.21**
Tie man's miracle: a Chanukah tale./ 1995/ 2-3/4 KG409 . . . . **E**
JOHNSTON, A/ Girls speak out: finding your true self./ 1997/
A/6 KA646 . . . . **155.5**
JOHNSTON, G/ Are those animals real?: how museums prepare wildlife
exhibits. Rev. & updated ed./ 1995/ 3-A/7 KC443 . . . . . . **590.75**
Scaly babies: reptiles growing up./ 1988/ 5-6/6 KC615 . . . . . **597.9**
JOHNSTON, J/ Alaska./ 1994/ 4-6/7 KF099 . . . . **979.8**
Washington, D.C./ 1993/ 4-6/7 KE971 . . . . **975.3**
JOHNSTON, M/ LANDS OF PLEASURE: ESSAYS ON LILLIAN H. SMITH
AND THE DEVELOPMENT OF/ 1990/ KA044 . . . . **PROF 020**
JOHNSTON, T/ Cowboy and the black-eyed pea./ 1992/
K-2/5 KF839 . . . . **E**
Ghost of Nicholas Greebe./ 1996/ 3-5/6 KH328 . . . . **FIC**
My Mexico--Mexico mio./ 1996/ K-3 KD958 . . . . **811**
Quilt story./ 1985/ P-3/2 KF840 . . . . **E**
Soup bone./ 1990/ K-2/2 KF841 . . . . **E**
Tale of Rabbit and Coyote./ 1994/ 2-3/2 KB596 . . . . **398.24**
Very scary./ 1995/ P-2/3 KF842 . . . . **E**
Wagon./ 1996/ 2-5/5 KF843 . . . . **E**
JOHNSTONE, L/ Silly science: strange and startling projects to amaze your
family and friends./ 1995/ 3-8/7 KB893 . . . . **507.8**
JONAS, A/ Aardvarks, disembark!/ 1990/ 2-A/4 KA963 . . . . . **333.95**
Color dance./ 1989/ P-1/1 KF844 . . . . **E**
Holes and peeks./ 1984/ P-K/1 KF845 . . . . **E**
Quilt./ 1984/ K-1/2 KF846 . . . . **E**
Round trip./ 1983/ K-2/2 KF847 . . . . **CE E**
Round trip (Kit)./ 1992/ K-2/2 KF847 . . . . **CE E**
Splash!/ 1995/ P-2/1 KF848 . . . . **E**
Trek./ 1985/ P-2/4 KF849 . . . . **E**
When you were a baby./ 1982/ P-K/2 KF850 . . . . **E**
13th clue./ 1992/ 1-2/1 KF851 . . . . **E**
JONES, B/ CHILD'S SEASONAL TREASURY./ 1996/
KA193 . . . . **PROF 372.13**
JONES, BF/ Teaching thinking skills: English/language arts./ 1987/
KA280 . . . . **PROF 428**
JONES, C/ Hare and the Tortoise./ 1996/ P-1/4 KB597 . . . . . **398.24**
THIS OLD MAN./ 1990/ P-1 KD602 . . . . **789.2**
JONES, CF/ Accidents may happen./ 1996/ 4-A/9 KC895 . . . . . . **609**
JONES, DB/ Children's literature awards and winners: a directory of prizes,
authors, and illustrators. 3rd ed./ 1994/ KA354 . . . . **PROF 809**
JONES, DW/ Archer's goon./ 1984/ A/6 KH329 . . . . **FIC**
Aunt Maria./ 1991/ 6-A/6 KH330 . . . . **FIC**
Cart and cwidder./ c1977, 1995/ 6-A/6 KH331 . . . . **FIC**
Castle in the air./ 1991/ 6-A/7 KH332 . . . . **FIC**
Crown of Dalemark./ 1995/ 6-A/6 KH331 . . . . **FIC**
Drowned Ammet./ c1978, 1995/ 6-A/6 KH331 . . . . **FIC**
Howl's moving castle./ 1986/ A/7 KH333 . . . . **FIC**
Spellcoats./ c1979, 1995/ 6-A/6 KH331 . . . . **FIC**
Stopping for a spell: three fantasies./ 1993/ 3-9/4 KH334 . . . . **FIC**
Witch week. New ed./ c1982, 1993/ 6-A/6 KH335 . . . . **FIC**
JONES, G/ My first book of how things are made: crayons, jeans, peanut
butter, guitars, and more./ 1995/ K-5/7 KD328 . . . . **670**
JONES, JE/ NOAH'S ARK (Videocassette)./ c1989, 1996/
P-2 KA682 . . . . **VCR 221.9**

JONES, JN/ These lands are ours: Tecumseh's fight for the Old Northwest./ 1993/ 5-6/7 KE559 . . . . **B TECUMSEH**
JONES, LC/ Things that go bump in the night./ c1959, 1983/ A/9 KA605 . . . . 133.1
JONES, M/ Jump! The adventures of Brer Rabbit./ 1997/ 3-4/6 KB585 . . . . 398.24
JONES, R/ 500 five minute games: quick and easy activities for 3-6 year olds./ 1995/ KA325 . . . . **PROF 790.1**
JONES, RC/ Down at the bottom of the deep dark sea./ 1991/ P-K/2 KF852 . . . . E
Great Aunt Martha./ 1995/ 1-3/2 KF853 . . . . E
President has been shot!: true stories of the attacks on ten U.S. presidents./ 1996/ 6-A/9 KE855 973
JONES, RF/ Jake: a Labrador puppy at work and play./ 1992/ 2-5/5 KD228 . . . . 636.752
JONES, TD/ Mission: Earth: voyage to the home planet./ 1996/ 4-A/8 KC145 550
JOOSSE, BM/ Mama, do you love me?/ 1991/ P-1/2 KF854 . . . . . E
JORDAN, HJ/ Como crece una semilla./ 1996/ P-2/1 KC387 . 580
How a seed grows. Rev. ed./ 1992/ P-2/1 KC387 580
JORDAN, M/ Losing Uncle Tim./ 1989/ 3-5/4 KH336 . . . . FIC
JORDAN-WONG, J/ Forever family./ 1992/ 2-4/3 KB011 . . . . 362.73
JORGENSEN, D/ Tailor of Gloucester (Videocassette)./ 1988/ 1-3 KG271 . . . . VCR E
Tale of Mr. Jeremy Fisher./ 1989/ K-2/7 KG275 . . . . E
THREE BILLY GOATS GRUFF; AND, THE THREE LITTLE PIGS (Videocassette)./ 1989/ P-K KB665 . . . . **VCR 398.24**
JORGENSON, L/ Grand trees of America: our state and champion trees./ 1992/ 3-6/6 KC415 . . . . 582.16
JOSEPH, L/ Island Christmas./ 1992/ 1-3/2 KF855 . . . . E
Island Christmas (Sound recording cassette)./ 1994/ 1-3/2 KF855 . . E
Jasmine's parlour day./ 1994/ 1-3/3 KF856 . . . . E
Mermaid's twin sister: more stories from Trinidad./ 1994/ 3-4/5 KB323 . . . . 398.2
JOSEPHSON, JP/ Jesse Owens: track and field legend./ 1997/ 5-A/8 KE487 . . . . B OWENS, J.
JOUDREY, K/ Trees./ 1995/ 3-6/3 KC421 . . . . 582.16
JOYCE, W/ Bently and egg./ 1992/ 1-3/4 KF857 . . . . E
Bently and egg (Sound recording cassette)./ 1994/ 1-3/4 KF857 . . . E
Buddy: based on the true story of Gertrude Lintz./ 1997/ 5-A/5 KH337 . . . . FIC
Day with Wilbur Robinson./ 1990/ 1-3/4 KF858 . . . . E
Dinosaur Bob and his adventures with the family Lazardo./ 1988/ K-3/3 KF859 . . . . E
George shrinks./ 1985/ P-2/2 KF860 . . . . E
Leaf Men and the brave good bugs./ 1996/ 1-3/3 KF861 . . . . E
Santa calls./ 1993/ 2-4/4 KF862 . . . . CE E
Shoes./ 1986/ P-K/4 KG745 . . . . CE E
JUBA THIS AND JUBA THAT./ 1995/ KA366 . . . . **PROF 820.8**
/ n.d./ KA366 . . . . **PROF 820.8**
JUBB, KJ/ Flashy fantastic rain forest frogs./ 1997/ 4-6/4 KC607 597.8
JUDSON, K/ Ronald Reagan./ 1997/ 6-A/10 KE504 . . . B REAGAN, R.
JUKES, M/ Like Jake and me./ 1984/ 5-6/7 KH338 . . . . FIC
Like Jake and me (Sound recording cassette)./ n.d./ 5-6/7 KH338 . FIC
JULIVERT, A/ Fascinating world of frogs and toads./ 1993/ 4-6/6 KC605 . . . . 597.8
JUNIOR LEAGUE OF SAN FRANCISCO/ City by the bay: a magical journey around San Francisco./ 1993/ 1-5/7 KE207 . . . . . . 917.94
JURENKA, NEA/ Beyond the bean seed: gardening activities for grades K-6./ 1996/ KA202 . . . . **PROF 372.3**
JUSTER, N/ Otter nonsense./ 1994/ 3-6 KD721 . . . . 793.734
Phantom tollbooth (Braille)./ n.d./ 4-6/6 KH339 . . . . . CE FIC
Phantom tollbooth (Sound recording cassette)./ n.d./ 4-6/6 KH339 . . . . CE FIC
Phantom tollbooth. Special 35th anniversary ed./ 1996/ 4-6/6 KH339 . . . . CE FIC
Phantom tollbooth (Talking book)./ n.d./ 4-6/6 KH339 . . . . . CE FIC
KADODWALA, D/ Holi./ 1997/ 4-6/7 KA763 . . . . 294.5
KAHL, JD/ Storm warning: tornadoes and hurricanes./ 1993/ 4-7/8 KC200 . . . . 551.55
Thunderbolt: learning about lightning./ 1993/ 4-6/9 KC207 . . . 551.56
Weatherwise: learning about the weather./ 1992/ 4-6/6 KC219 . 551.6
Wet weather: rain showers and snowfall./ 1992/ 4-6/7 KC212 . 551.57
KAHN, M/ Mi libro de palabras Inglesas de todos los dias./ 1982/ 1-3 KB843 428
My everyday Spanish word book./ 1982/ 1-3 KB861 468
KALAN, R/ Jump, frog, jump! (Big book)./ 1996/ P-1/1 KF864 . CE E
Jump, frog, jump! New ed./ c1981, 1995/ P-1/1 KF864 . . . . . E
Moving day./ 1996/ P-1/1 KF865 . . . . E
Salta, ranita, salta!/ 1994/ P-1/1 KF864 . . . . CE E
Salta, ranita, salta! (Kit)./ 1996/ P-1/1 KF864 . . . . CE E
Stop, thief!/ 1993/ K-2/1 KF866 . . . . E
KALAS, S/ Polar bear family book./ 1996/ 4-6/4 KC862 . . . . 599.786

KALLEVIG, CP/ Holiday folding stories: storytelling and origami together for holiday fun./ 1992/ KA309 . . . . **PROF 736**
KALMAN, B/ Arctic animals./ 1988/ 4-6/8 KC501 . . . . . . 591.998
Arctic whales and whaling./ 1988/ 5-6/6 KC771 . . . . . . 599.5
Colonial crafts./ 1992/ 4-5/6 KD338 680
Early artisans./ 1983/ 4-A/8 KD430 . . . . 745.5
Early pleasures and pastimes./ 1983/ 4-A/8 KD680 . . . . . 790.1
Fun with my friends./ 1985/ P-1/2 KA658 158
Giraffes./ 1997/ 3-5/7 KC788 . . . . 599.638
Home crafts./ 1990/ 3-6/6 KD431 . . . . 745.5
Kitchen./ 1990/ 4-5/5 KD295 643
Koala is not a bear!/ 1997/ 3-5/3 KC738 . . . . 599.2
Pioneer projects./ 1997/ 3-5/6 KD432 . . . . 745.5
Web weavers and other spiders./ 1997/ 3-5/5 KC526 . . . . . 595.4
18th century clothing./ 1993/ 4-6/6 KB164 391
19th century clothing./ 1993/ 4-6/6 KB164 391
KALMAN, M/ Chicken soup, boots./ 1993/ P-K/3 KA941 . . . . 331.7
Ooh-la-la (Max in love)./ 1991/ 4-A/3 KH340 . . . . FIC
Sayonara, Mrs. Kackleman./ 1989/ 1-3/3 KF867 . . . . E
KAMERMAN, SE/ PLAYS FROM FAVORITE FOLK TALES./ 1987/ 3-6 KE094 . . . . 812.008
PLAYS OF BLACK AMERICANS: THE BLACK EXPERIENCE IN AMERICA, DRAMATIZED FOR YOUN PEOPLE. New expanded ed./ 1994/ 4-6 KE095 . . . . 812.008
KAMINSKI, R/ Children's traditional games: games from 137 countries and cultures./ 1995/ KA331 . . . . **PROF 796**
KANDOIAN, E/ RAINY DAY RHYMES./ 1992/ 1-3 KE078 . . . 811.008
KANE, JN/ Famous first facts. 5th ed./ 1997/ 4-6 KA382 . . . **REF 031**
KANE, R/ Fire on the mountain and other stories from Ethiopia and Eritrea./ c1950, 1995/ 3-6/6 KB277 . . . . 398.2
KANER, E/ Balloon science./ 1989/ 2-6/6 KC079 530
KANG, J/ Star of fear, star of hope./ 1995/ 3-5/5 KH268 . . . . . FIC
KANI, S/ Monkey and the crab./ 1985/ 3/3 KB598 . . . . 398.24
KAPLAN, A/ Careers for computer buffs./ 1991/ 5-6/9 KA567 . . . 004
Careers for outdoor types./ 1991/ 4-A/8 KA952 . . . . 333.7
Careers for wordsmiths./ 1991/ 6-A/7 KA593 . . . . 070.4
KAPLAN, M/ Earth words: a dictionary of the environment./ 1995/ 3-6/9 KB067 . . . . 363.73
KAPPELER, M/ Big cats./ 1991/ 5-6/7 KC822 . . . . 599.75
Dogs: wild and domestic./ 1991/ 5-6/6 KD220 . . . . 636.7
Owls./ 1991/ 5-6/6 KC715 . . . . 598.9
KARAS, GB/ Dog named Sam./ 1996/ K-2/2 KF241 . . . . E
Don't read this book, whatever you do!: more poems about school./ 1993/ 4-6 KD928 811
Flute player./La Flautista./ 1995/ K-2/2 KF541 . . . . E
Home on the bayou: a cowboy's story./ 1996/ K-2/2 KF868 . . . . . E
If you're not here, please raise your hand: poems about school./ 1990/ 2-5 KD929 811
Math fun with a pocket calculator./ 1992/ 4-A/4 KD713 . . . . . 793.7
Mr. Carey's garden./ 1996/ K-2/3 KF442 . . . . E
Nobody's mother is in second grade./ 1992/ K-2/2 KG293 . . . . . E
On the trail with Miss Pace./ 1995/ 1-3/2 KF461 . . . . E
Puddles./ 1997/ P-1/3 KG027 . . . . E
Saving Sweetness./ 1996/ 1-3/4 KG538 . . . . E
Sid and Sam./ 1996/ P-1/1 KF291 . . . . E
Sleepless Beauty./ 1996/ 2-3/3 KG142 . . . . E
KARDALEFF, PP/ Literature-based social studies: children's books and activities to enrich the K-5/ 1991/ KA261 . . . . **PROF 372.83**
KARLIN, N/ I see, you saw./ 1997/ P-1/1 KF869 . . . . E
KARLSBERG, E/ Eating pretty./ 1991/ 5-A/7 KC985 . . . . 613.2
KARPINSKI, JE/ Laurie tells./ 1994/ 3-6/4 KH420 . . . . FIC
KARPISEK, ME/ Policymaking for school library media programs./ 1989/ KA050 . . . . **PROF 025.1**
KARR, K/ Cave./ 1994/ 5-A/4 KH341 . . . . FIC
Oh, those Harper girls!; or Young and dangerous./ 1992/ 5-A/Y KH342 . . . . FIC
KASAMATSU, S/ Inch-high samurai./ 1993/ 3-4/4 KB754 . . . . 398.27
KASZA, K/ Estofado del lobo./ 1991/ P-2/2 KF870 . . . . E
Wolf's chicken stew./ 1987/ P-2/2 KF870 . . . . E
KATAN, NJ/ Hieroglyphs, the writing of ancient Egypt./ 1981/ 5-6/9 KB866 493
KATZ, B/ Could we be friends?: poems for pals./ 1997/ 1-3 KD959 811
KATZ, D/ Blood and guts: a working guide to your own insides./ c1976/ 4-6/6 KC912 612
KATZ, WL/ Black women of the Old West./ 1995/ 5-6/9 KF036 . . 978
Breaking the chains: African-American slave resistance./ 1990/ A/8 KE966 975
KATZEN, M/ Pretend soup and other real recipes: a cookbook for preschoolers and up./ 1994/ P-3 KD272 . . . . 641.5
KAUFMAN, G/ Stick up for yourself!: every kid's guide to personal power and positive self-esteem./ 1990/ 6-A/6 KA659 158
KAULA, EM/ African village folktales, vols 1-3 (Talking book)./ n.d./ 4-6 KB746 . . . . TB 398.27
KAVANAGH, J/ Robert E. Lee./ 1995/ 4-5/6 KE430 . . . . . . B LEE, R.

KAZUKO/ What will the weather be like today?/ 1990/
  P-1/2 KC221 . . . . 551.6
KAZUNAS, C/ Internet for kids./ 1997/ 2-4/7 KA571 . . . . . . 004.67
KAZUNAS, T/ Internet for kids./ 1997/ 2-4/7 KA571 . . . . . . 004.67
KEATES, C/ Dinosaur./ 1989/ 3-A/7 KC258 . . . . 567.9
KEATING, E/ Careers for computer buffs./ 1991/ 5-6/9 KA567 . . 004
  Careers for outdoor types./ 1991/ 4-A/8 KA952 . . . . . 333.7
  Careers for wordsmiths./ 1991/ 6-A/7 KA593 . . . . 070.4
KEATS, EJ/ Dia de nieve./ 1991/ P-2/2 KF878 . . . . CE E
  Dia de nieve (Kit)./ 1991/ P-2/2 KF878 . . . . CE E
  Ezra Jack Keats Library (Videocassette)./ 1992/ P-2 KF871 . . . VCR E
  Goggles!/ c1969, 1971/ K-2/2 KF872 . . . . CE E
  Goggles! (Braille)./ n.d.,/ K-2/2 KF872 . . . . CE E
  Goggles! (Talking book)./ n.d./ K-2/2 KF872 . . . . CE E
  Goggles! (Videocassette)./ 1974/ K-2/2 KF872 . . . . . . CE E
  Hi, cat!/ c1970, 1988/ P-2/2 KF873 . . . . CE E
  Hi, cat! (Kit)./ 1990/ P-2/2 KF873 . . . . CE E
  Letter to Amy./ c1968/ P-2/2 KF874 . . . . CE E
  Letter to Amy (Braille)./ n.d./ P-2/2 KF874 . . . . CE E
  Letter to Amy (Videocassette)./ 1973/ P-2/2 KF874 . . . . CE E
  Maggie and the pirate./ 1979/ P-2/2 KF875 . . . . E
  Maggie and the pirate (Braille)./ n.d./ P-2/2 KF875 . . . E
  Pet show./ 1987/ P-2/2 KF876 . . . . CE E
  Pet show (Kit)./ 1992/ P-2/2 KF876 . . . . CE E
  Pet show (Talking book)./ n.d./ P-2/2 KF876 . . . . CE E
  Pet show (Videocassette)./ 1992/ P-2/2 KF876 . . . . . . CE E
  Peter's chair./ c1967/ P-2/2 KF877 . . . . CE E
  Peter's chair (Big book)./ 1993/ P-2/2 KF877 . . . . . . CE E
  Peter's chair (Braille)./ n.d./ P-2/2 KF877 . . . . CE E
  Peter's chair (Kit)./ 1995/ P-2/2 KF877 . . . . CE E
  Peter's chair (Videocassette)./ 1969/ P-2/2 KF877 . . . . CE E
  Silba por Willie./ 1992,/ P-2/3 KF880 . . . . CE E
  Silla de Pedro./ 1996/ P-2/2 KF877 . . . . CE E
  Snowy day./ c1962, 1963/ P-2/2 KF878 . . . . CE E
  Snowy day (Braille)./ n.d.,/ P-2/2 KF878 . . . . CE E
  Snowy day (Kit)./ 1974/ P-2/2 KF878 . . . . CE E
  Snowy day (Videocassette)./ ,/ P-2/2 KF878 . . . . CE E
  Trip./ c1978/ K-2/2 KF879 . . . . CE E
  Trip (Videocassette)./ 1979/ K-2/2 KF879 . . . . CE E
  Whistle for Willie./ c1964, 1977/ P-2/3 KF880 . . . . . . CE E
  Whistle for Willie (Kit)./ 1975,/ P-2/3 KF880 . . . . . . CE E
  Whistle for Willie (Talking book)./ n.d.,/ P-2/3 KF880 . CE E
  Whistle for Willie (Videocassette)./ 1965,/ P-2/3 KF880 . CE E
KEEGAN, M/ Pueblo boy: growing up in two worlds./ 1991/
  4-6/5 KE793 . . . . 970.489
KEEGAN, S/ Biz kids' guide to success: money-making ideas for young
  entrepreneurs./ 1992/ 5-6/6 KD307 . . . . 650.1
KEELER, PA/ Our oceans: experiments and activities in marine science./
  1995/ 4-6/7 KC172 . . . . 551.46
  Unraveling fibers./ 1995/ 4-6/4 KD335 677
KEENE, AT/ Earthkeepers: observers and protectors of nature./ 1994/
  5-A KA436 . . . . REF 508
KEENS-DOUGLAS, R/ Diablesse and the baby: a Caribbean folktale./
  1994/ 3-4/4 KB324 . . . . 398.2
KEHRET, P/ Small steps: the year I got polio./ 1996/
  2-5/5 KE414 . . . . B KEHRET, P.
KEITH, E/ House of Dies Drear./ c1968/ 4-6/5 KH215 . . . . . CE FIC
  Slave dancer: a novel./ c1973/ 5-6/6 KH139 . . . . CE FIC
KELLEHER, K/ Turtles./ 1982/ P-K/1 KC621 . . . . 597.92
KELLER, C/ PLANET OF THE GRAPES: SHOW BIZ JOKES AND
  RIDDLES./ 1992/ 3-6 KD737 . . . . 793.735
  TAKE ME TO YOUR LITER: SCIENCE AND MATH JOKES./ 1991/
  3-6 KD740 . . . . 793.735
KELLER, H/ Be a friend to trees./ 1994/ P-2/3 KC416 . . . . . CE 582.16
  Best bug parade./ 1996/ P-1/1 KG163 . . . . E
  From tadpole to frog./ 1994/ K-2/2 KC608 . . . . CE 597.8
  Geraldine first./ 1996/ K-2/2 KF881 . . . . E
  Geraldine's big snow./ 1988/ P-2/4 KF882 . . . . E
  Grandfather's dream./ 1994/ K-2/2 KF883 . . . . E
  Harry and Tuck./ 1993/ K-1/2 KF884 . . . . E
  Island baby./ 1992/ P-2/3 KF885 . . . . E
  Octopus is amazing./ 1990/ 1-3/4 KC514 594
  Rosata./ 1995/ K-2/2 KF886 . . . . E
  Snakes are hunters./ 1988/ 2-4/3 KC637 . . . . 597.96
  Snow is falling. Rev. ed./ 1986/ K-1/2 KC210 . . . . . . 551.57
  Sponges are skeletons./ 1993/ 1-3/2 KC508 . . . . 593.4
  Story of my life./ c1988, 1990/ 6-A/8 KE416 . . . . B KELLER, H.
  What's it like to be a fish?/ 1996/ K-3/3 KC585 597
  Who eats what?: food chains and food webs./ 1995/
  K-3/2 KC295 577
  Why I cough, sneeze, shiver, hiccup, and yawn./ 1983/
  1-3/2 KC963 . . . . 612.8
  You're aboard spaceship Earth./ 1996/ 1-3/3 KC147 550

KELLER, K/ First children: growing up in the White House./ 1996/
  A/9 KE856 973
  Seven loaves of bread./ 1993/ 1-3/2 KG758 . . . . E
KELLER, G/ Christmas of the reddle moon./ 1994/ 1-3/4 KF975 . . . . E
  Red heels./ 1996/ 3-5/6 KG393 . . . . E
KELLEY, P/ Illustrated rules of softball./ 1996/ 3-6/6 KD803 . . 796.357
KELLEY, T/ Cuts, breaks, bruises and burns: how your body heals./ 1985/
  4-6/6 KC932 . . . . 612.1
  How to find a ghost./ 1988/ 4-A/7 KA604 . . . . 133.1
  How to hunt buried treasure./ 1992/ 4-6/8 KD058 622
  How to make a mummy talk./ 1995/ 4-6/8 KB175 393
  I've got chicken pox./ 1994/ K-3/2 KF887 . . . . E
  Look at your eyes. Rev. ed./ 1992/ P-1/2 KC978 . . . . . 612.8
  Three stories you can read to your cat./ 1997/ K-2/2 KG137 . E
KELLOGG, S/ Best friends./ 1986/ K-3/2 KF888 . . . . E
  Best friends (Sound recording cassette)./ n.d./ K-3/2 KF888 . . . . E
  Chicken Little./ 1985/ K-3/5 KF889 . . . . CE E
  Chicken Little (Kit)./ 1989/ K-3/5 KF889 . . . . CE E
  Day Jimmy's boa ate the wash./ 1980/ K-2/2 KG176 . . . CE E
  Great Quillow./ 1994/ 2-3/6 KH791 . . . . FIC
  How much is a million?/ 1985/ K-1/2 KB950 513
  If you made a million./ 1989/ 2-5/5 KA946 . . . . 332.024
  Is your mama a llama?/ 1989/ P-1/2 KF651 . . . . E
  Island of the skog./ c1973/ K-3/5 KF890 . . . . CE E
  Island of the skog (Videocassette)./ 1985/ K-3/5 KF890 . . CE E
  Jack and the beanstalk./ 1991/ 2-3/4 KB325 . . . . 398.2
  Mike Fink./ 1992/ 3-4/5 KB456 . . . . 398.22
  Much bigger than Martin./ c1976/ K-2/2 KF891 . . . . . . E
  Mystery of the missing red mitten./ 1974/ P-2/2 KF892 . . E
  Mystery of the stolen blue paint./ 1982/ P-1/2 KF893 . . . E
  Parents in the pigpen, pigs in the tub./ 1993/ K-2/6 KF521 . . . E
  Paul Bunyan, a tall tale./ 1984/ 4-6/7 KB457 . . . . 398.22
  Paul Bunyan, a tall tale (Big book)./ 1993/ 4-6/7 KB457 . . 398.22
  Paul Bunyan: un cuento fantastico./ 1994/ 4-6/7 KB457 . . . . . 398.22
  Pecos Bill./ 1986/ 4-6/7 KB457 . . . . 398.22
  Pecos Bill (Sound recording cassette)./ n.d./ 4-6/7 KB457 . . 398.22
  Pecos Bill: un cuento fantastico./ 1995/ 4-6/7 KB457 . . . 398.22
  Pinkerton, behave./ 1979/ P-2/2 KF894 . . . . CE E
  Pollita Pequenita./ 1991/ K-3/5 KF889 . . . . CE E
  Prehistoric Pinkerton./ 1987/ P-3/5 KF895 . . . . E
  Rattlebang picnic./ 1994/ K-2/5 KG057 . . . . E
  Rose for Pinkerton./ 1984/ P-2/2 KF894 . . . . CE E
  Sally Ann Thunder Ann Whirlwind Crockett: a tall tale./ 1995/
  2-5/5 KB458 . . . . 398.22
  SNUFFLES AND SNOUTS: POEMS./ 1995/ P-2 KE083 . . . . 811.008
  Tallyho, Pinkerton./ 1982/ P-2/2 KF894 . . . . CE E
  Wizard next door./ 1993/ K-2/2 KF625 . . . . E
  Yankee Doodle. 2nd ed./ c1976, 1996/ P-2 KD557 . . . . 789.2
KELLY, EP/ Trumpeter of Krakow. New ed./ c1966, 1973/
  /7 KH343 . . . . FIC
  Trumpeter of Krakow. New. ed. (Sound recording cassette)./ n.d.,/
  /7 KH343 . . . . FIC
  Trumpeter of Krakow. New ed. (Talking book)./ n.d.,/ /7 KH343 . . FIC
KELLY, J/ Superstars of women's basketball./ 1997/
  4-6/7 KD775 . . . . 796.323
KELLY, K/ Everything you need to know about math homework./ 1994/
  4-10/7 KB934 510
KELLY, L/ Carol for Christmas./ 1994/ K-3/5 KG612 . . . . . . E
  Flower of Sheba./ 1994/ 1-2/2 KA687 222
  Old Bet and the start of the American circus./ 1993/
  4-6/6 KD682 . . . . 791.3
  Sam the sea cow./ 1991/ 1-3/2 KC780 . . . . 599.55
  Warrior maiden: a Hopi legend./ 1992/ 1-2/2 KB485 . . . 398.22
KELLY, MA/ Child's book of wildflowers./ 1992/ 3-5/5 KC405 . . 582.13
KELLY, SM/ Lots of dads./ 1997/ P-1/2 KA881 . . . . 306.874
  Lots of moms./ 1996/ P-1/1 KA882 . . . . 306.874
KEMP-WELCH, L/ Black Beauty: the autobiography of a horse./ 1997/
  5-7/7 KH702 . . . . FIC
KENDA, M/ Cooking wizardry for kids./ 1990/ 5-6 KD273 . . . . 641.5
KENDALL, C/ Gammage Cup./ c1959/ 5-6/7 KH344 . . . . FIC
  Gammage Cup (Braille)./ n.d./ 5-6/7 KH344 . . . . FIC
  Gammage Cup (Talking book)./ n.d./ 5-6/7 KH344 . . . . . FIC
KENDALL, ME/ Nellie Bly: reporter for the world./ 1992/
  4-6/5 KE256 . . . . B BLY, N.
KENDALL, R/ Eskimo boy: life in an Inupiaq Eskimo village./ 1992/
  3-6/6 KF100 . . . . 979.8
  Russian girl: life in an old Russian town./ 1994/ 3-6/5 KE690 . . . 947
KENNA, K/ People apart./ 1995/ 4-6/7 KA720 . . . . 289.7
KENNAWAY, A/ Crafty chameleon./ c1987, 1995/ P-2/7 KF659 . . . . E
  Hot Hippo./ 1986/ K-3/4 KF660 . . . . CE E
KENNEDY, DM/ I THOUGHT I'D TAKE MY RAT TO SCHOOL: POEMS
  FOR SEPTEMBER TO JUNE./ 1993/ 2-5 KE066 . . . . 811.008
  TALKING LIKE THE RAIN: A FIRST BOOK OF POEMS./ 1992/
  P-2 KE112 . . . . 821.008

KENNEDY, P/ Christmas celebration: traditions and customs from around
the world./ 1992/ 4-6/7 KB236 . . . . **394.266**
Hyperactive child book./ 1994/ KA303 . . . . **PROF 649**
KENNEDY, S/ Irish folk tales for children (Compact disc)./ 1996/
3-5 KB326 . . . . **CD 398.2**
Irish folk tales for children (Sound recording cassette)./ 1996/
3-5 KB326 . . . . **CD 398.2**
KENNEDY, XJ/ Beasts of Bethlehem./ 1992/ 1-6 KD960 . . . . **811**
Brats./ 1986/ 3-6 KD961 . . . . **811**
Drat these brats!/ 1993/ 3-6 KD962 . . . . **811**
Forgetful wishing well./ 1985/ 4-6 KD963 . . . . **811**
Fresh brats./ 1990/ 3-6 KD964 . . . . **811**
Ghastlies, goops & pincushions./ 1989/ 4-A KD965 . . . . . . **811**
TALKING LIKE THE RAIN: A FIRST BOOK OF POEMS./ 1992/
P-2 KE112 . . . . **821.008**
KENOWER, FC/ Cub Scout fun book./ c1956, 1986/
2-4/6 KB077 . . . . **369.43**
KENOWER, FT/ Cub Scout fun book./ c1956, 1986/
2-4/6 KB077 . . . . **369.43**
KENT, D/ Dublin./ 1997/ 3-5/8 KE678 . . . . **941.8**
Iowa./ 1991/ 5-6/8 KF022 . . . . **977.7**
Iowa (Sound recording cassette)./ 1993/ 5-6/8 KF022 . . . . **977.7**
Mexico: rich in spirit and tradition./ 1996/ 3-5/7 KE832 . . **972**
New York City./ 1996/ 3-5/8 KE958 . . . . **974.7**
Puerto Rico./ 1992/ 5-6/6 KE847 . . . . **972.95**
Puerto Rico (Sound recording cassette)./ 1993/ 5-6/6 KE847 . **972.95**
Titanic./ 1993/ 4-6/7 KB026 . . . . **363.12**
Tokyo./ 1996/ 3-5/8 KE709 . . . . **952**
Vietnam Women's Memorial./ 1995/ 4-6/7 KE720 . . . . **959.704**
KENT, J/ Caterpillar and the polliwog./ 1982/ K-2/4 KF896 . . . . . **CE E**
Caterpillar and the polliwog (Videocassette)./ n.d./ K-2/4 KF896 . . **CE E**
Easy as pie: a guessing game of sayings./ 1985/ 1-3/3 KF564 . . . . **E**
KENT, Z/ George Bush: forty-first president of the United States./ 1989/
5-6/8 KE272 . . . . **B BUSH, G.**
Idaho./ 1990/ 4-6/9 KF091 . . . . **979.6**
Idaho (Sound recording cassette)./ 1993/ 4-6/9 KF091 . . . . **979.6**
Kansas./ 1990/ 4-6/9 KF054 . . . . **978.1**
Persian Gulf War: "the mother of all battles."/ 1994/
6-A/6 KE715 . . . . **956.7044**
Persian Gulf War: "the mother of all battles" (Sound recording
cassette)./ 1997/ 6-A/6 KE715 . . . . **956.7044**
Williamsburg./ 1992/ 4-6/5 KE871 . . . . **973.2**
KENTLEY, E/ Boat./ 1992/ 5-6/7 KD063 . . . . **623.8**
KENYON, MP/ Home schooling from scratch./ 1996/
KA175 . . . . **PROF 371.04**
KERBY, M/ Amelia Earhart: courage in the sky./ 1990/
3-4/5 KE327 . . . . **B EARHART, A.**
KERROD, R/ Amazing flying machines./ 1992/ 4-6/6 KD110 . . **629.133**
Story of space exploration (Picture)./ 1994/ 4-6 KC027 . . . **PIC 523.4**
KERVEN, R/ Id-ul-Fitr./ 1997/ 3-5/7 KA787 . . . . **297**
KESSLER, B/ Brer Rabbit and Boss Lion (Kit)./ 1996/
3-A KB599 . . . . **KIT 398.24**
KESSLER, E/ Stan the hot dog man./ 1990/ 1-2/1 KF897 . . . . **E**
KESSLER, L/ Aqui viene el ponchado (Braille)./ n.d./ 1-2/2 KF898 . **CE E**
Aqui viene el que se poncha!/ 1995/ 1-2/2 KF898 . . . . **CE E**
Big mile race./ 1983/ K-3/2 KF901 . . . . **E**
Here comes the strikeout./ c1965/ 1-2/2 KF898 . . . . **CE E**
Here comes the strikeout (Braille)./ n.d./ 1-2/2 KF898 . . . . . **CE E**
Here comes the strikeout (Kit)./ n.d./ 1-2/2 KF898 . . . . **CE E**
Kick, pass, and run./ c1966/ 1-2/2 KF899 . . . . **E**
Kick, pass, and run (Braille)./ n.d./ 1-2/2 KF899 . . . . **E**
Last one in is a rotten egg./ c1969/ 1-2/1 KF900 . . . . **E**
Last one in is a rotten egg (Talking book)./ n.d./ 1-2/1 KF900 . . . **E**
Old Turtle's soccer team./ 1988/ K-3/2 KF901 . . . . **E**
Old Turtle's 90 knock-knocks, jokes, and riddles./ 1991/
2-4 KD730 . . . . **793.735**
Stan the hot dog man./ 1990/ 1-2/1 KF897 . . . . **E**
Ultimo en tirarse es un miedoso./ 1995/ 1-2/1 KF900 . . . . **E**
KETCHUM, L/ Gold rush./ 1996/ 4-6/6 KF081 . . . . **979.4**
KETTELKAMP, L/ ETs and UFOs: are they real?/ 1996/
4-6/8 KA558 . . . . **001.9**
Living in space./ 1993/ A/8 KD130 . . . . **629.4**
KHALSA, DK/ I want a dog./ 1987/ P-2/5 KF902 . . . . **E**
Tales of a gambling grandma./ 1986/ 3-5/6 KH345 . . . . **FIC**
KHERDIAN, D/ Road from home: the story of an Armenian girl./ 1979/
5-6/6 KE698 . . . . **949.6**
KIDDEL-MONROE, J/ Odyssey of Homer./ c1952, 1992/
5-A/7 KE126 . . . . **883**
KIDDER, T/ Among schoolchildren./ 1989/ KA192 . . . . **PROF 372.11**
Among schoolchildren (Sound recording cassette)./ n.d./
KA192 . . . . **PROF 372.11**
KIEFFER, C/ Lemon drop jar./ 1992/ P-2/2 KG711 . . . . **E**
You were born on your very first birthday./ 1982/ P/2 KC948 . **612.6**
KIEFTE, KD/ Chuck and Danielle./ 1996/ 4-6/7 KH076 . . . . **FIC**

Cricket never does: a collection of haiku and tanka./ 1997/
3-6 KD975 . . . . **811**
Yang the third and her impossible family./ 1995/ 3-6/5 KH527 . . . **FIC**
Yang the youngest and his terrible ear./ 1994/ 5-A/5 KH528 . . . . **FIC**
KIESLER, K/ Into the deep forest with Henry David Thoreau./ 1995/
5-A/7 KE929 . . . . **974.1**
Out of darkness: the story of Louis Braille./ 1997/
3-5/6 KE262 . . . . **B BRAILLE, L.**
KILBURN, G/ Christmas carp./ 1990/ 2-4/2 KH798 . . . . **FIC**
KIM, HC/ Iroko-man: a Yoruba folktale./ 1994/ 2-3/6 KB397 . . **398.21**
KIM, JU/ Could we be friends?: poems for pals./ 1997/ 1-3 KD959 **811**
KIM, M/ Blue whale./ 1993/ 3-5/7 KC772 . . . . **599.5**
Mountain gorilla./ 1993/ 4-5/8 KC875 . . . . **599.884**
KIMMEL, EA/ Adventures of Hershel of Ostropol./ 1995/
2-4/7 KB459 . . . . **398.22**
Adventures of Hershel of Ostropol (Sound recording cassette)./ 1997/
2-4/7 KB459 . . . . **398.22**
Anansi and the moss-covered rock./ 1988/ 1-2/4 KB600 . . **CE 398.24**
Anansi and the moss-covered rock (Kit)./ 1991/
1-2/4 KB600 . . . . **CE 398.24**
Anansi and the talking melon./ 1994/ 2-3/2 KB601 . . . . **CE 398.24**
Anansi and the talking melon (Kit)./ 1995/ 2-3/2 KB601 . . **CE 398.24**
Anansi and the talking melon (Videocassette)./ 1994/
2-3/2 KB601 . . . . **CE 398.24**
Anansi goes fishing./ 1991, c1992/ K-2/2 KB602 . . . . . **CE 398.24**
Anansi goes fishing (Kit)./ 1993/ K-2/2 KB602 . . . . . . **CE 398.24**
Anansi goes fishing (Sound recording cassette)./ 1995,/
K-2/2 KB602 . . . . **CE 398.24**
Anansi goes fishing (Videocassette)./ 1992,/ K-2/2 KB602 . **CE 398.24**
Bar mitzvah: a Jewish boy's coming of age./ 1995/
5-A/7 KA776 . . . . **296.4**
Bearhead: a Russian folktale./ 1991/ 2-4/4 KB327 . . . . . . **398.2**
Bernal and Florinda: a Spanish tale./ 1994/ 2-4/3 KF903 . . . . . **E**
Billy Lazroe and the King of the Sea: a tale of the Northwest./ 1996/
4-5/5 KB460 . . . . **398.22**
Boots and his brothers: a Norwegian tale./ 1992/
2-4/2 KB400 . . . . **398.21**
Boots and his brothers: a Norwegian tale (Sound recording cassette)./
1995/ 2-4/2 KB400 . . . . **398.21**
Count Silvernose: a story from Italy./ 1996/ 3-5/5 KB504 . . **398.23**
Days of awe: stories for Rosh Hashanah and Yom Kippur./ 1991/
4-6/5 KA777 . . . . **296.4**
Goose girl: a story from the Brothers Grimm./ 1995/
3-5/5 KB328 . . . . **398.2**
I-know-not-what, I-know-not-where: a Russian tale./ 1994/
3-4/6 KB329 . . . . **398.2**
Iron John./ 1994/ 4-5/4 KB330 . . . . **398.2**
Magic dreidels: a Hanukkah story./ 1996/ K-3/2 KF904 . . . . **E**
Old woman and her pig./ 1992/ K-2/2 KB603 . . . . **398.24**
One Eye, Two Eyes, Three Eyes: a Hutzul tale./ 1996/
2-4/7 KB401 . . . . **398.21**
Rimonah of the Flashing Sword: a North African tale./ 1995/
3-4/4 KB331 . . . . **398.2**
Tale of Ali Baba and the forty thieves: a story from the Arabian Nights./
1996/ 3-4/6 KB332 . . . . **398.2**
Three princes: a tale from the Middle East./ 1994/
2-3/4 KB461 . . . . **398.22**
Witch's face: a Mexican tale./ 1993/ 3-5/2 KB402 . . . . **398.21**
KINCHER, J/ First honest book about lies./ 1992/ KA159 . . **PROF 177**
KINDERSLEY, A/ Children just like me./ 1995/ 2-6/8 KA825 . . . **305.23**
KINDERSLEY, B/ Children just like me./ 1995/ 2-6/8 KA825 . . . **305.23**
KING, A/ Bookworks: making books by hand./ 1995/
3-6/5 KD437 . . . . **745.5**
KING, D/ My first photography book./ 1994/ 3-6/3 KD513 . . . . **771**
Snake book./ 1997/ 2-6/6 KC639 . . . . **597.96**
KING, DC/ Egypt: ancient traditions, modern hopes./ 1997/
4-6/7 KE634 . . . . **932**
Freedom of assembly./ 1997/ 4-6/7 KA972 . . . . **342.73**
Right to speak out./ 1997/ 4-6/7 KA973 . . . . **342.73**
KING, E/ Backyard sunflower./ 1993/ 1-4/4 KD174 . . . . . . **635.9**
Chile fever: a celebration of peppers./ 1995/ 5-6/6 KD267 . . **641.3**
Pumpkin patch./ 1990/ 1-4/4 KD169 . . . . **635**
KING, N/ You animal!/ 1996/ 4-6/5 KC913 . . . . **612**
KING, S/ Shannon: an Ojibway dancer./ 1993/ 4-6/4 KE784 . **970.476**
KINGMAN, L/ ILLUSTRATORS OF CHILDREN'S BOOKS, 1967-1976./
1978/ KA311 . . . . **PROF 741.6**
Newbery and Caldecott medal books, 1966-1975: with acceptance papers
& related material chiefly from the/ 1975/ KA352 . . . . **PROF 809**
KINGSLEY, B/ Young person's guide to the orchestra: Benjamin Britten's
composition on CD./ 1996/ 4-6/10 KD545 . . . . **BA 784.2**
KING-SMITH, D/ Ace: the very important pig./ c1990/
2-5/5 KH346 . . . . **CE FIC**
Babe: the gallant pig./ 1994/ 2-5/5 KH346 . . . . **CE FIC**
Babe: the sheep-pig (Talking book)./ c1986/ 2-5/5 KH346 . . . **CE FIC**

Cuckoo child./ 1993/ 4-6/6 KH347 . . . . FIC
Cuckoo child (Sound recording cassette)./ 1995/ 4-6/6 KH347 . . . FIC
Harry's Mad./ c1984, 1997/ 5-A/7 KH348 . . . . FIC
I love guinea pigs./ 1995/ K-4/3 KD183 636
I love guinea pigs (Sound recording cassette)./ 1997/
   K-4/3 KD183 636
Jenius: the amazing guinea pig./ 1996/ 2-4/5 KH349 . . . . FIC
Lady Daisy (Talking book)./ 1995/ 4-6 KH350 . . . . TB FIC
Mouse called Wolf./ 1997/ 3-5/3 KH351 . . . . FIC
Mr. Potter's pet./ 1996/ 3-5/2 KH352 . . . . FIC
School mouse./ 1995/ 3-5/7 KH353 . . . . FIC
Sophie hits six./ 1993/ 2-4/6 KH354 . . . . FIC
Sophie in the saddle./ 1996/ 3-5/6 KH355 . . . . FIC
Sophie's Lucky./ 1996/ 3-4/8 KH356 . . . . FIC
Sophie's Tom./ c1991, 1994/ 3-5/5 KH357 . . . . FIC
Three terrible trins./ 1994/ 3-5/6 KH358 . . . . CE FIC
Three terrible trins (Talking book)./ 1996/ 3-5/6 KH358 . . . . CE FIC
KINKADE, S/ Children of the Philippines./ 1996/ 3-6/8 KE722 . . 959.9
KINSEY, H/ Bear that heard crying./ 1993/ 2-3/2 KF905 . . . . E
KINSEY-WARNOCK, N/ Bear that heard crying./ 1993/ 2-3/2 KF905   E
When spring comes./ 1993/ P-2/3 KF906 . . . . E
KIPLING, R/ Beginning of the armadillos./ 1995/ 3-5/8 KH359 . . . FIC
Complete Just so stories./ 1993/ 3-5/7 KH360 . . . . FIC
How the rhinoceros got his skin; and, How the camel got his hump
   (Videocassette)./ 1987/ 2-5 KH361 . . . . VCR FIC
How the rhinoceros got his skin (Kit)./ 1988/ 3-5 KH362 . . . . KIT FIC
Jungle book: the Mowgli stories./ 1995/ 6-A/7 KH363 . . . . . . FIC
Rikki-Tikki-Tavi and Wee Willie Winkie (Talking book)./ n.d./
   4-6 KH364 . . . . TB FIC
KIRCHNER, AB/ In days gone by: folklore and traditions of the
   Pennsylvania Dutch./ 1996/ KA268 . . . . PROF 398.2
Multicultural explorations: joyous journeys with books./ 1991/
   KA262 . . . . PROF 372.89
KIRILENKO, K/ First thousand words in Russian./ 1983/
   4-6 KB863 . . . . 491.7
KIRK, D/ Lucky's 24-hour garage./ 1996/ K-2/4 KF907 . . . . E
Trash trucks./ 1997/ K-2/3 KF908 . . . . E
KIRK, E/ In days gone by: folklore and traditions of the Pennsylvania
   Dutch./ 1996/ KA268 . . . . PROF 398.2
KIRMSE, M/ Lassie come-home./ 1978/ 4-6/5 KH370 . . . . FIC
KIRSTEIN, L/ Puss in boots./ c1992, 1994/ 3-4/6 KB604 . . . . . 398.24
KITAMURA, S/ UFO diary./ 1989/ K-2/2 KF909 . . . . E
KITE, P/ Down in the sea: the jellyfish./ 1993/ 3-5/4 KC509 . . . . 593.5
Down in the sea: the octopus./ 1993/ 3-5/4 KC513 594
KIUCHI, T/ Mysterious tales of Japan./ 1996/ 3-5/3 KB690 . . . 398.25
Seasons and Someone./ 1994/ K-3/5 KF935 . . . . E
Tsubu the little snail./ 1995/ 3-5/4 KB673 . . . . 398.24
KJELGAARD, J/ Big Red: the story of a champion Irish setter and a
   trapper's son who grew up together, roaming the wilderness. New ed./
   c1945, 1956/ 6-A/7 KH365 . . . . FIC
Big Red: the story of a champion Irish setter and a trapper's son who
   grew up together, roaming the wilderness. New ed. (Braille)./ Big Red:
   the story of a champion Irish setter and a trapper's son who grew up
   together, roaming the wilderness. New ed. (Sound recording cassette)./
   n.d.,/ n.d./ 6-A/7 KH365 . . . . FIC
   6-A/7 KH365 . . . . FIC
KLAUSNER, J/ Sequoyah's gift: a portrait of the Cherokee leader./ 1993/
   5-6/7 KE535 . . . . B SEQUOYAH
KLEIN, M/ Do people grow on family trees?: genealogy for kids and other
   beginners: the official Ellis Island handbook./ 1991/
   5-A/7 KE610 929
KLEIN, T/ Loon magic for kids./ c1989, 1991/ 3-5/5 KC651 598
KLEVEN, E/ Abuela./ 1991/ P-2/2 KF488 . . . . E
B is for Bethlehem: a Christmas alphabet./ 1990/ K-3 KE043 811
City by the bay: a magical journey around San Francisco./ 1993/
   1-5/7 KE207 . . . . 917.94
DE COLORES AND OTHER LATIN-AMERICAN FOLK SONGS FOR
   CHILDREN./ 1994/ K-3 KD561 . . . . 789.2
Hooray! A pinata!/ 1996/ K-2/2 KF910 . . . . E
Isla./ 1995/ K-2/2 KF490 . . . . E
Viva! Una pinata!/ 1996/ K-2/2 KF910 . . . . E
KLINE, MP/ Kids' multicultural cookbook: food and fun around the world./
   1995/ 3-5 KD285 . . . . 641.59
KLINE, S/ Herbie Jones and Hamburger Head./ 1989/
   3-4/2 KH367 . . . . FIC
Herbie Jones and the birthday showdown./ 1995/ 3-4/3 KH366 . . FIC
Herbie Jones and the class gift./ 1989/ 3-4/2 KH367 . . . . . . FIC
Horrible Harry and the green slime./ 1989/ 2-4/2 KH368 . . . . . FIC
Horrible Harry and the green slime (Sound recording cassette)./ 1995/
   2-4/2 KH368 . . . . FIC
Horrible Harry's secret./ 1990/ 2-4/2 KH368 . . . . FIC
Mary Marony hides out./ 1993/ 1-3/4 KH369 . . . . FIC
KLINTING, L/ Bruno the baker./ 1997/ P-2/2 KF911 . . . . E
Bruno the carpenter./ 1996/ K-2/2 KF912 . . . . E
Bruno the tailor./ 1996/ K-2/2 KF913 . . . . E
KNAPP, H/ One potato, two potato: the folklore of American children./
   1978/ KA278 . . . . PROF 398.8
KNAPP, M/ One potato, two potato: the folklore of American children./
   1978/ KA278 . . . . PROF 398.8
KNAPP, R/ Chris Webber: star forward./ 1997/
   5-6/7 KE590 . . . . B WEBBER, C.
Top 10 basketball centers./ 1994/ 3-6/4 KD776 . . . . 796.323
Top 10 basketball scorers./ 1994/ 3-6/4 KD777 . . . . 796.323
Top 10 hockey scorers./ 1994/ 4-6/5 KD842 . . . . 796.962
KNEEN, M/ Milly and Tilly: the story of a town mouse and a country
   mouse./ 1997/ K-2/2 KB661 . . . . 398.24
KNIGHT, AS/ Way west: journal of a pioneer woman./ 1993/
   5-6/5 KE197 . . . . 917.8
Way west: journal of a pioneer woman (Sound recording cassette)./
   1996/ 5-6/5 KE197 . . . . 917.8
KNIGHT, CG/ Searching for Laura Ingalls: a reader's journey./ 1993/
   3-6/6 KE198 . . . . 917.8
KNIGHT, E/ Lassie come-home./ 1978/ 4-6/5 KH370 . . . . FIC
Lassie come-home (Sound recording cassette)./ n.d./ 4-6/5 KH370 . FIC
Lassie come-home (Talking book)./ n.d./ 4-6/5 KH370 . . . . . FIC
KNIGHT, H/ Beauty and the Beast./ 1990/ 4-5/6 KB282 . . . . . 398.2
KNIGHT, L/ Sierra Club book of great mammals./ 1992/
   5-6/7 KC722 599
KNIGHT, M/ Searching for Laura Ingalls: a reader's journey./ 1993/
   3-6/6 KE198 . . . . 917.8
KNIGHT, MB/ Welcoming babies./ 1994/ P-1/2 KA875 . . . . . . 306.87
KNOCK AT THE DOOR./ 1992/ KA269 . . . . PROF 398.2
KNOWLES, T/ TREASURY OF STORIES FOR SIX YEAR OLDS./ 1992/
   2-4/5 KH807 . . . . FIC
KNOWLTON, J/ Geography from A to Z: a picture glossary./ 1988/
   3-6 KE150 910
Mapas y globos terraqueos./ 1996/ 2-5/7 KE169 912
Maps and globes./ 1985/ 2-5/7 KE169 912
KNUTSON, B/ Faxing friends; a resource guide for forming international
   friendships among students, age 5-9./ 1992/ KA173 . PROF 370.117
Kwanzaa karamu: cooking and crafts for a Kwanzaa feast./ 1995/
   5-6/5 KD284 . . . . 641.59
KNUTSON, K/ Ska-tat!/ 1993/ P-2/3 KF914 . . . . E
KOBER, N/ Mapping a changing world./ 1996/ A/12 KC065 526
KOBRIN, B/ Eyeopeners II: children's books to answer children's questions
   about the world around them./ 1995/ KA355 . . . . PROF 809
KOCH, K/ TALKING TO THE SUN: AN ILLUSTRATED ANTHOLOGY OF
   POEMS FOR YOUNG PEOPLE./ 1985/ 6-A KE087 . . . . . 811.008
Wishes, lies, and dreams: teaching children to write poetry./ c1970,
   1980/ KA346 . . . . PROF 808.81
KOCH, M/ World water watch./ 1993/ K-2/4 KD255 . . . . 639.9
KODAMA, T/ Shin's tricycle./ 1995/ 4-6/4 KE670 . . . . 940.54
KOEPPEN, P/ Swinger of birches: poems of Robert Frost for young
   people./ 1982/ 3-6 KD942 811
KOERTGE, R/ Harmony Arms./ 1994/ A/5 KH371 . . . . FIC
KOHL, MAF/ MathArts: exploring math through art for 3 to 6 year olds./
   1996/ KA253 . . . . PROF 372.7
KOHLER, FW/ Tropical fish: a complete pet owner's manual./ 1983/
   5-6/9 KD247 . . . . 639.3
Turtles: everything about purchase, care, nutrition and diseases./ 1983/
   5-6/9 KD250 . . . . 639.3
KONIGSBURG, EL/ Altogether, one at a time./ c1971/ A/6 KH372 . FIC
From the mixed-up files of Mrs. Basil E. Frankweiler./ c1967/
   4-6/7 KH373 . . . . CE FIC
From the mixed-up files of Mrs. Basil E. Frankweiler (Braille)./ n.d./
   4-6/7 KH373 . . . . CE FIC
From the mixed-up files of Mrs. Basil E. Frankweiler (Kit)./ 1988/
   4-6/7 KH373 . . . . CE FIC
From the mixed-up files of Mrs. Basil E. Frankweiler (Sound recording
   cassette)./ n.d./ 4-6/7 KH373 . . . . CE FIC
From the mixed-up files of Mrs. Basil E. Frankweiler (Talking book)./ n.d./
   4-6/7 KH373 . . . . CE FIC
Jennifer, Hecate, Macbeth, William McKinley, and me, Elizabeth./ c1967/
   3-6/4 KH374 . . . . CE FIC
Jennifer, Hecate, Macbeth, William McKinley, and me, Elizabeth (Talking
   book)./ n.d./ 3-6/4 KH374 . . . . CE FIC
T-backs, T-shirts, COAT, and suit./ 1993/ 6-A/7 KH375 . . . . FIC
T-backs, T-shirts, COAT, and suit (Sound recording cassette)./ 1995/
   6-A/7 KH375 . . . . FIC
Throwing shadows./ 1979/ 5-6/6 KH376 . . . . FIC
Throwing shadows (Braille)./ n.d./ 5-6/6 KH376 . . . . FIC
Throwing shadows (Sound recording cassette)./ n.d./
   5-6/6 KH376 . . . . FIC
View from Saturday./ 1996/ 5-A/7 KH377 . . . . FIC
KOPLOW, L/ Tanya and the Tobo Man/Tanya y el Hombre Tobo: a story
   in English and Spanish for children entering therapy/ 1991/
   K-2/2 KD040 . . . . 618.92

KORMAN, B/ D- poems of Jeremy Bloom: a collection of poems about
  school, homework, and life (sort of)./ 1992/ 4-A KD966 . . . . . **811**
KORMAN, G/ D- poems of Jeremy Bloom: a collection of poems about
  school, homework, and life (sort of)./ 1992/ 4-A KD966 . . . . . **811**
Go jump in the pool!/ 1979/ 5-A/7 KH378 . . . . **FIC**
Something fishy at Macdonald Hall./ 1995/ 5-A/7 KH378 . . . . . . **FIC**
This can't be happening at Macdonald Hall!/ 1978/ 5-A/7 KH378 . **FIC**
Zucchini warriors./ 1991/ 5-A/7 KH378 . . . . **FIC**
KORS, E/ How did we find out about microwaves?/ 1989/
  A/9 KD045 . . . . **621.381**
How did we find out about photosynthesis?/ 1989/ 6-A/9 KC277 **572**
How did we find out about superconductivity?/ 1988/
  5-A/7 KC135 . . . . **537.6**
Two orphan cubs./ 1989/ K-2/2 KC848 . . . . **599.78**
KOSCIELNIAK, B/ Geoffrey Groundhog predicts the weather./ 1995/
  K-2/2 KF915 . . . . **E**
KOSHKIN, A/ Atalanta's race: a Greek myth./ 1995/ 3-6/4 KA735 **292**
Stolen thunder: a Norse myth./ 1994/ 4-5/5 KA755 . . . . **293**
KOSLOW, P/ Dahomey: the warrior kings./ 1997/ 6-A/9 KE736 . **966.9**
Yorubaland: the flowering of genius./ 1996/ 6-A/12 KE726 . . . **960**
KOTTKE, L/ Paul Bunyan (Videocassette)./ 1990/
  3-5 KB447 . . . . **VCR 398.22**
KOTZWINKLE, W/ Million-Dollar Bear./ 1995/ 2-3/2 KF916 . . . . . **E**
KOVALSKI, M/ Cake that Mack ate./ 1986/ P-1/1 KG334 . . . . . . **E**
Pizza for breakfast./ 1991/ K-2/2 KF917 . . . . **E**
KRAAN, H/ Tales of the wicked witch./ 1995/ 3-5/3 KH379 . . . . **FIC**
Wicked witch is at it again./ 1997/ 3-5/3 KH379 . . . . **FIC**
KRAMER, B/ Ken Griffey Junior: all-around all-star./ 1996/
  4-5/4 KE381 . . . . **B GRIFFEY, K. JR**
KRAMER, J/ Bo Jackson./ 1996/ 4-5/6 KE398 . . . . . **B JACKSON, B.**
Jim Abbott./ 1996/ 4-5/6 KE223 . . . . **B ABBOTT, J.**
Lee Trevino./ 1996/ 5-6/6 KE570 . . . . **B TREVINO, L.**
KRAMER, S/ Tiger Woods: golfing to greatness./ 1997/
  2-6/6 KE600 . . . . **B WOODS, T.**
KRAMER, SA/ Ty Cobb: bad boy of baseball./ 1995/
  2-4/4 KE298 . . . . **B COBB, T.**
KRAMER, SP/ Avalanche./ 1991/ 3-6/6 KC213 . . . . **551.57**
How to think like a scientist: answering questions by the scientific
  method./ 1987/ 4-6/6 KB883 . . . . **507**
Theodoric's rainbow./ 1995/ 3-6/4 KH380 . . . . **FIC**
Tornado./ 1992/ 3-6/6 KC201 . . . . **551.55**
KRANZ, R/ Biographical dictionary of Black Americans./ 1992/
  KA401 . . . . **REF 305.8**
Straight talk about child abuse./ 1991/ A/10 KB017 . . . . . . **362.76**
KRASHEN, S/ Power of reading: insights from the research./ 1993/
  KA082 . . . . **PROF 028**
KRAULIS, JA/ Ottawa: a kid's eye view./ 1993/ 5-6/8 KE818 . . **971.3**
KRAUS, R/ Come out and play, little mouse./ 1986/ P-1/1 KF919 . **CE E**
Leo the late bloomer./ 1971/ P-2/2 KF918 . . . . **CE E**
Where are you going little mouse?/ 1986/ P-1/1 KF919 . . . . **CE E**
Whose mouse are you?/ c1970/ P-1/1 KF919 . . . . **CE E**
KRAUSS, R/ Carrot seed./ c1945/ P-2/2 KF920 . . . . **CE E**
Carrot seed (Big book)./ 1978/ P-2/2 KF920 . . . . **CE E**
Carrot seed (Kit)./ 1990/ P-2/2 KF920 . . . . **CE E**
Dia feliz./ 1995/ P-2/2 KF921 . . . . **E**
Happy day./ c1945, 1949/ P-2/2 KF921 . . . . **E**
Hole is to dig: a first book of first definitions./ c1952/
  P-2/2 KF922 . . . . **CE E**
Hole is to dig: a first book of first definitions (Braille)./ n.d./
  P-2/2 KF922 . . . . **CE E**
Hole is to dig: a first book of first definitions (Kit)./ 1990/
  P-2/2 KF922 . . . . **CE E**
Very special house./ c1953/ P-1/1 KF923 . . . . **E**
KRAUTWURST, T/ Kid style nature crafts: 50 terrific things to make with
  nature's materials./ 1995/ 4-8/6 KD428 . . . . **745.5**
Nature crafts for kids./ 1992/ 4-6/6 KD429 . . . . **745.5**
KREISCHER, EK/ Maria Montoya Martinez: master potter./ 1995/
  5-6/3 KE461 . . . . **B MARTINEZ, M.**
KREISLER, K/ Faces./ 1994/ P-1/2 KC924 . . . . **612**
Nature spy./ 1992/ P-1/4 KB912 . . . . **508**
Ocean day./ 1993/ P-2/3 KG357 . . . . **E**
KRENINA, K/ Magic dreidels: a Hanukkah story./ 1996/ K-3/2 KF904 **E**
KRENSKY, S/ Breaking into print: before and after the invention of the
  printing press./ 1996/ 3-5/5 KD346 . . . . **686.2**
Dinosaurs, beware: a safety guide./ 1982/ P-3/3 KB020 . . . . . **363.1**
Iron dragon never sleeps./ 1995/ 3-5/2 KH381 . . . . **FIC**
Lionel and Louise./ 1997/ K-2/2 KF924 . . . . **E**
Lionel at large./ 1986/ K-2/2 KF924 . . . . **E**
Lionel at large (Braille)./ n.d./ K-2/2 KF924 . . . . **E**
Lionel in the winter./ 1996/ K-2/2 KF924 . . . . **E**
Striking it rich: the story of the California gold rush./ 1996/
  2-4/5 KF082 . . . . **979.4**
Three blind mice mystery./ 1995/ 1-3/2 KF925 . . . . **E**
Witch hunt: it happened in Salem Village./ 1989/ 3-5/4 KA606 . **133.4**

KRISHNASWAMI, U/ Broken tusk: stories of the Hindu god Ganesha./
  1996/ 3-4/4 KA764 . . . . **294.5**
KROEGER, MK/ Paperboy./ 1996/ 1-3/2 KF926 . . . . **E**
KROLL, E/ Friedrich./ c1970, 1987/ 5-A/5 KH633 . . . . **FIC**
KROLL, S/ Candy witch./ 1979/ K-1/6 KF927 . . . . **E**
Ellis Island: doorway to freedom./ 1995/ 2-4/10 KA920 . . . . **325**
Happy Father's Day./ 1988/ K-2/2 KF928 . . . . **E**
It's groundhog day!/ 1987/ K-2/4 KF929 . . . . **E**
Lewis and Clark: explorers of the American West./ 1994/
  4-6/6 KE203 . . . . **917.804**
One tough turkey: a Thanksgiving story./ 1982/ K-2/2 KF930 . . **E**
Pony Express!/ 1996/ 4-6/6 KB130 . . . . **383**
Tyrannosaurus game./ c1976/ K-2/6 KF931 . . . . **CE E**
Tyrannosaurus game (Kit)./ 1986/ K-2/6 KF931 . . . . **CE E**
KROLL, VL/ Can you dance, Dalila?/ 1996/ K-2/5 KF932 . . . . . **E**
Fireflies, peach pies and lullabies./ 1995/ 1-3/5 KF933 . . . . **E**
I wanted to know all about God./ 1994/ K-2/2 KA694 . . . . . **231**
Masai and I./ 1992/ K-2/4 KF934 . . . . **E**
Seasons and Someone./ 1994/ K-3/5 KF935 . . . . **E**
KRONENWETTER, M/ Congress of the United States./ 1996/
  5-A/10 KA932 . . . . **328.73**
Supreme Court of the United States./ 1996/ 5-A/10 KA978 . . . **347.73**
KROPP, P/ Raising a reader: make your child a reader for life./ c1993,
  1996/ KA182 . . . . **PROF 371.3028**
KRULIK, NE/ Birds./ 1993/ 2-4/4 KC652 . . . . **598**
KRULL, K/ Bridges to change: how kids live on a South Carolina Sea
  Island./ 1995/ 4-6/7 KE987 . . . . **975.7**
Lives of the musicians: good times, bad times (and what the neighbors
  thought) (Sound recording cassette)./ Lives of the musicians: good
  times, bad times (and what the neighbors thought)./ 1993/ 1995/
  5-A/6 KD520 . . . . **780**
  5-A/6 KD520 . . . . **780**
Maria Molina and the Days of the Dead./ 1994/ 2-4/4 KF936 . . . . **E**
One nation, many tribes: how kids live in Milwaukee's Indian community./
  1995/ 4-6/7 KE783 . . . . **970.475**
V is for victory: America remembers World War II./ 1995/
  A/7 KE659 . . . . **940.53**
Wilma unlimited: how Wilma Rudolph became the world's fastest woman./
  1996/ 3-5/7 KE527 . . . . **B RUDOLPH, W.**
KRUMGOLD, J/ And now Miguel./ 1953/ 6-A/5 KH382 . . . . . **CE FIC**
And now Miguel (Braille)./ n.d./ 6-A/5 KH382 . . . . **CE FIC**
And now Miguel (Sound recording cassette)./ n.d./
  6-A/5 KH382 . . . . **CE FIC**
And now Miguel (Talking book)./ n.d./ 6-A/5 KH382 . . . . . **CE FIC**
KRUPINSKI, L/ Dear Rebecca, winter is here./ 1993/ 1-3/3 KF605 . . . **E**
How a seed grows. Rev. ed./ 1992/ P-2/1 KC387 . . . . **580**
Irish Cinderlad./ 1996/ 2-4/3 KB275 . . . . **398.2**
Why do leaves change color?/ 1994/ P-4/2 KC400 . . . . . **CE 581.4**
KRUPP, EC/ Big dipper and you./ 1989/ 1-6/4 KC050 . . . . . . **523.8**
Moon and you./ 1993/ 4-6/4 KC020 . . . . **523.3**
KRUPP, RR/ Let's go traveling./ 1992/ 3-5/4 KE155 . . . . . . **910.4**
Let's go traveling in Mexico./ 1996/ 2-4/6 KE187 . . . . **917.2**
Moon and you./ 1993/ 4-6/4 KC020 . . . . **523.3**
KRUSH, B/ Borrowers./ c1953, 1989/ 4-6/6 KH554 . . . . . . **CE FIC**
KRUSH, J/ Borrowers./ c1953, 1989/ 4-6/6 KH554 . . . . . . **CE FIC**
KRYKORKA, V/ Baseball bats for Christmas./ 1990/ 4-6/4 KH384 . . **FIC**
Promise is a promise./ 1988/ 3-5/2 KH519 . . . . **FIC**
KRYLOV, IA/ Cat and the cook and other fables of Krylov./ 1995/
  3-5/6 KH234 . . . . **FIC**
KUBINYI, L/ Cat mummies./ 1996/ 3-6/9 KE637 . . . . **932**
KUCHERA, K/ Your skin and mine. Rev. ed./ 1991/ K-2/2 KC960 . . **612.7**
KUDLINSKI, KV/ Animal tracks and traces./ 1991/ 3-4/4 KC475 . **591.5**
KUHN, B/ Big Red: the story of a champion Irish setter and a trapper's son
  who grew up together, roaming the wilderness. New ed./ c1945,
  1956/ 6-A/7 KH365 . . . . **FIC**
KUHN, D/ More than just a flower garden./ 1990/ 4-5/6 KD175 **635.9**
More than just a vegetable garden./ 1990/ 4-5/5 KD170 . . . . . **635**
My first book of nature: how living things grow./ 1993/
  P-2/4 KC276 . . . . **571.8**
Turtle's day./ 1994/ P-2/4 KC620 . . . . **597.92**
KUI, W/ Wise washerman: a folktale from Burma./ 1996/
  K-2/7 KB569 . . . . **398.24**
KUKLIN, S/ Fighting fires./ 1993/ K-3/5 KD087 . . . . **628.9**
Fireworks: the science, the art, and the magic./ 1996/
  5-6/6 KD317 . . . . **662**
From head to toe: how a doll is made./ 1994/ 4-6/6 KD350 . . . **688.7**
Going to my gymnastics class./ 1991/ 3-5/4 KD816 . . . . . . **796.44**
Going to my nursery school./ 1990/ P-3/2 KB098 . . . . **372.21**
How my family lives in America./ 1992/ 1-3/5 KA850 . . . . . **305.8**
Kodomo: children of Japan./ 1995/ 3-5/6 KE710 . . . . **952.04**
Taking my cat to the vet./ 1988/ P-K/4 KD234 . . . . **636.8**
When I see my doctor./ 1988/ P-K/4 KC901 . . . . **610.69**
KULLING, M/ Vanished!: the mysterious disappearance of Amelia Earhart./
  1996/ 2-4/7 KE328 . . . . **B EARHART, A.**

KUNHARDT, E/ Honest Abe./ 1993/ 1-3/4 KE444 . . . **B LINCOLN, A.**
KUNKEL, D/ MicroAliens: dazzling journeys with an electron microscope./
1993/ 3-A/7 KC376 . . . . **579**
KUNSTLER, JH/ Aladdin and the magic lamp (Kit)./ 1995/
3-5 KB333 . . . . **KIT 398.2**
Johnny Appleseed (Videocassette)./ 1992/
2-5 KE239 . . . . **VCR B APPLESEED, J.**
KURELEK, W/ Lumberjack./ 1974/ 4-6/6 KD165 . . . . **634.9**
Northern Nativity: Christmas dreams of a prairie boy./ c1976/
4-6/7 KA708 . . . . **CE 232.92**
Prairie boy's summer./ 1975/ 3-5/7 KE813 . . . . **971.2**
Prairie boy's winter./ c1973/ 3-6/7 KE814 . . . . **CE 971.2**
KUROKAWA, M/ Dinosaur Valley./ 1992/ 2-6/6 KC250 . . . . . **567.9**
KURTZ, J/ Fire on the mountain./ 1994/ 2-4/6 KB747 . . . . . . **398.2**
Miro in the Kingdom of the Sun./ 1996/ 3-4/5 KB505 . . . . . . **398.23**
Pulling the lion's tail./ 1995/ 1-3/6 KF937 . . . . **E**
Trouble./ 1997/ K-2/3 KB748 . . . . **398.27**
KURUSA/ Streets are free. Rev. ed./ 1995/ 3-4/5 KH383 . . . . **FIC**
KUSKIN, K/ Great miracle happened there: a Chanukah story./ c1993,
1995/ 3-4/4 KA778 . . . . **296.4**
James and the rain./ 1995/ K-2/5 KF938 . . . . **E**
Philharmonic gets dressed./ 1982/ K-3/5 KF939 . . . . **E**
Roar and more./ c1956, 1990/ P-1 KF940 . . . . **E**
Thoughts, pictures, and words./ 1995/ 2-5/6 KE426 . . **B KUSKIN, K.**
KUSUGAK, M/ Baseball bats for Christmas./ 1990/ 4-6/4 KH384 . . **FIC**
Promise is a promise./ 1988/ 3-5/2 KH519 . . . . **FIC**
KWITZ, MD/ Little Vampire and the Midnight Bear./ 1995/
1-3/2 KF941 . . . . **E**
KWON, HH/ Moles and the Mireuk: a Korean folktale./ 1993/
K-2/4 KB605 . . . . **398.24**
LA PIERRE, Y/ Mapping a changing world./ 1996/ A/12 KC065 . . **526**
LABASTIDA, A/ Nine days to Christmas./ c1959/ 1-3/2 KF538 . . . **E**
LABONTE, G/ Leeches, lampreys, and other cold-blooded bloodsuckers./
1991/ 5-6/7 KC505 . . . . **592**
Tarantula./ 1991/ 5-6/7 KC527 . . . . **595.4**
LACAPA, M/ Antelope Woman: an Apache folktale./ 1992/
2-4/5 KB606 . . . . **398.24**
LACE, WW/ Top 10 football quarterbacks./ 1994/
3-6/4 KD783 . . . . **796.332**
Top 10 football rushers./ 1994/ 3-6/4 KD784 . . . . . . **796.332**
LACEY, EA/ What's the difference?: a guide to some familiar animal look-
alikes./ 1993/ 5-6/8 KC450 . . . . **591**
LADOUX, RC/ Georgia./ 1991/ 4-6/7 KE989 . . . . **975.8**
LADWIG, T/ Morning has broken./ 1996/ P-2 KD611 . . . . . **789.3**
PSALM TWENTY-THREE./ 1997/ P-A/3 KA691 . . . . **223**
LAFFERTY, P/ Force and motion./ 1992/ 4-A/7 KC095 . . . . . **531**
LAFRANCE, M/ Diablesse and the baby: a Caribbean folktale./ 1994/
3-4/4 KB324 . . . . **398.2**
LAI, E/ SCIENCE ACTIVITIES FOR YOUNG PEOPLE./ 1983/
5-A/9 KB884 . . . . **507**
LAKIN, P/ Dad and me in the morning./ 1994/ 1-3/2 KF942 . . . . . . **E**
Palace of stars./ 1993/ 1-3/3 KF943 . . . . **E**
LAMARCHE, J/ Mandy./ 1991/ K-2/5 KF250 . . . . **E**
Rainbabies./ 1992/ 2-3/5 KG127 . . . . **E**
LAMB, C/ Tales from Shakespeare./ 1979/ A/9 KE115 . . . . . **822.3**
Tales from Shakespeare (Braille)./ n.d/ A/9 KE115 . . . . . **822.3**
Tales from Shakespeare (Sound recording cassette)./ n.d./
A/9 KE115 . . . . **822.3**
LAMB, M/ Tales from Shakespeare./ 1979/ A/9 KE115 . . . . . **822.3**
LAMB, N/ One April morning: children remember the Oklahoma City
bombing./ 1996/ 2-6/6 KF006 . . . . **976.6**
LAMB, SC/ Caitlin's Holiday./ 1990/ 4-6/4 KH204 . . . . . . **FIC**
Emily and the enchanted frog./ 1989/ 2-4/2 KF646 . . . . **E**
My great-aunt Arizona./ 1992/ 3-5/4 KE393 . . . . **B HUGHES, A.**
Prairie primer A to Z./ 1996/ 1-3/3 KG583 . . . . **E**
LAMBASE, B/ Garden of happiness./ 1996/ 1-3/2 KG593 . . . . **E**
LAMBERT, D/ Children's animal atlas: how animals have evolved, where
they live today, why so many are in danger./ 1992/
5-6/8 KC496 . . . . **591.9**
LAMBERT, PL/ Magic pencil: teaching children creative writing: exercises
and activities for children, their parents, and their teachers./ 1994/
KA228 . . . . **PROF 372.6**
LAMBORN, F/ Pippi Longstocking./ c1950, 1978/ 3-5/4 KH407 **CE FIC**
LAMPRELL, K/ Scaly things./ 1996/ 4-6/5 KC616 . . . . . . **597.9**
LAMPTON, C/ Earthquake./ 1991 5-6/7 KC162 . . . . **551.22**
Hurricane./ 1991/ 4-6/7 KC202 . . . . **551.55**
Volcano./ 1991/ 4-6/7 KC157 . . . . **551.21**
LAMUT, S/ This little piggy./ 1997/ P-1/2 KF699 . . . . **E**
LANDA, P/ Sign of the chrysanthemum./ c1973, 1991/
5-A/4 KH581 . . . . **FIC**
LANDAU, E/ Cherokees./ 1992/ 4-6/7 KE760 . . . . **970.3**
Sibling rivalry: brothers and sisters at odds./ 1994/
5-A/6 KA885 . . . . **306.875**

State birds: including the Commonwealth of Puerto Rico./ 1992/
4-6/8 KC653 . . . . **598**
State flowers: including the Commonwealth of Puerto Rico./ 1992/
3-6/8 KC406 . . . . **582.13**
LANDE, A/ THREE BILLY GOATS GRUFF; AND, THE THREE LITTLE PIGS
(Videocassette)./ 1989/ P-K KB665 . . . . **VCR 398.24**
LANFREDI, J/ Year you were born, 1983./ 1992/
4-6/7 KE922 . . . . **973.927**
LANG, A/ Flying ship./ 1995/ K-3/6 KB749 . . . . **398.27**
RAINBOW FAIRY BOOK./ 1993/ 2-6/8 KB360 . . . . **398.2**
LANGFORD, A/ Whales: the gentle giants./ 1989/ 1-3/2 KC774 . **599.5**
LANGLEY, J/ My first dictionary./ 1993/ P-2 KB835 . . . . . . **423**
LANGSLEY, E/ Gymnastics./ 1996/ 3-6/6 KD817 . . . . **796.44**
LANGSTAFF, J/ Frog went a-courtin'./ c1955/ P-3 KD579 . . . **CE 789.2**
Frog went a-courtin' (Kit)./ 1965/ P-3 KD579 . . . . . . **CE 789.2**
Frog went a-courtin' (Videocassette)./ 1965/ P-3 KD579 . . . **CE 789.2**
Let's sing!: John Langstaff sings with children, ages 3-7. Teacher's guide./
1997/ KA314 . . . . **VCR PROF 780**
Let's sing!: John Langstaff sings with children, ages 3-7 (Videocassette)./
1997/ KA314 . . . . **VCR PROF 780**
Making music with children, ages 3-7 (Videocassette)./ 1995/
KA315 . . . . **VCR PROF 780**
WHAT A MORNING! THE CHRISTMAS STORY IN BLACK SPIRITUALS./
1987/ K-6 KD532 . . . . **782.25**
LANGTON, J/ Diamond in the window./ c1962, 1973/
4-6/5 KH385 . . . . **FIC**
Diamond in the window (Braille)./ n.d.,/ 4-6/5 KH385 . . . . . **FIC**
LANKFORD, MD/ Christmas around the world./ 1995/
3-6/7 KB237 . . . . **394.266**
Jacks around the world./ 1996/ 3-6/10 KD770 . . . . **796.2**
Quinceanera: a Latina's journey to womanhood./ 1994/
5-6/7 KA715 . . . . **265**
Successful field trips./ 1992/ KA178 . . . . **PROF 371.3**
LANSKY, B/ KIDS PICK THE FUNNIEST POEMS./ 1991/
3-6 KE068 . . . . **811.008**
New adventures of Mother Goose: gentle rhymes for happy times./
1993/ P-3 KD967 . . . . **811**
You're invited to Bruce Lansky's poetry party!/ 1996/ 3-6 KD968 . **811**
LANTON, S/ Daddy's chair./ 1991/ P-2/2 KF944 . . . . **E**
LANZEN, CD/ BIOGRAPHY TODAY SPORTS SERIES: PROFILES OF
PEOPLE OF INTEREST TO YOUNG READERS./ 1996-/
4-6 KA456 . . . . **REF 796**
LAPOINTE, C/ Out of sight! Out of mind!/ 1995/ 1-3/1 KF945 . . . . **E**
LARIOS, R/ Causa: the migrant farmworkers' story./ 1993/
4-6/6 KA944 . . . . **331.88**
LAROCHE, G/ Color box./ 1992/ P-K/1 KF486 . . . . **E**
LARRY, C/ Peboan and Seegwun./ 1993/ 2-3/4 KB709 . . . . . **398.26**
LARSEN, T/ Polar bear family book./ 1996/ 4-6/4 KC862 . . . **599.786**
LASCOM, A/ What is a bird?/ 1993/ 4-6/6 KC665 . . . . **598**
What is an insect?/ 1993/ 4-6/6 KC548 . . . . **595.7**
LASKER, J/ All kinds of families./ c1976/ 1-3/5 KA873 . . . . . **306.85**
Cobweb Christmas./ 1982/ K-2/5 KF397 . . . . **E**
Howie helps himself./ 1974, c1975/ K-2/4 KF544 . . . . **E**
LASKY, K/ Days of the Dead./ 1994/ 5-6/6 KB200 . . . . . . **394.26**
Hercules: the man, the myth, the hero./ 1997/ 5-6/4 KA747 . . . . **292**
Librarian who measured the earth./ 1994/
4-A/6 KE339 . . . . **B ERATOSTHENES**
Lunch bunnies./ 1996/ K-2/2 KF946 . . . . **E**
Searching for Laura Ingalls: a reader's journey./ 1993/
3-6/6 KE198 . . . . **917.8**
She's wearing a dead bird on her head!/ 1995/ 3-5/5 KH386 . . . **FIC**
Sugaring time./ 1983/ 4-6/9 KD155 . . . . **CE 633.6**
Sugaring time (Videocassette)./ 1989/ 4-6/9 KD155 . . . . . **CE 633.6**
Surtsey: the newest place on earth./ 1992/ A/7 KE697 . . . . . **949.12**
LATHAM, JL/ Carry on, Mr. Bowditch./ c1955/
5-A/3 KE260 . . . . **CE B BOWDITCH, N.**
Carry on, Mr. Bowditch (Talking book)./ 1971/
5-A/3 KE260 . . . . **CE B BOWDITCH, N.**
LATIMER, J/ Irish piper./ 1991/ 3-5/6 KB463 . . . . **398.22**
Moose and friends./ 1993/ 1-3/2 KF947 . . . . **E**
LATROBE, KH/ EXPLORING THE GREAT LAKES STATES THROUGH
LITERATURE./ 1994/ KA039 . . . . **PROF 016.977**
Readers theatre for children: scripts and script development./ 1990/
KA339 . . . . **PROF 808.5**
LATTIMORE, DN/ Arabian nights: three tales./ 1995/
3-5/6 KB334 . . . . **398.2**
Flame of peace, a tale of the Aztecs./ 1987/ 2-3/2 KF948 . . . . . **E**
Frida Maria: a story of the old Southwest./ 1994/ 1-3/2 KF949 . . . **E**
Gittel's hands./ 1996/ K-2/2 KG506 . . . . **E**
Punga, the goddess of ugly./ 1993/ 3-5/4 KF950 . . . . **E**
LAUBER, P/ Be a friend to trees./ 1994/ P-2/2 KC416 . . . **CE 582.16**
Be a friend to trees (Kit)./ 1996/ P-2/3 KC416 . . . . . **CE 582.16**
Dinosaurs walked here and other stories fossils tell./ 1987/
4-6/6 KC236 . . . . **560**

Dinosaurs walked here and other stories fossils tell (Braille)./ n.d./
4-6/6 KC236 . . . . **560**
Flood: wrestling with the Mississippi./ 1996/ 4-6/4 KB035 . . . **363.34**
Great whales: the gentle giants./ 1993/ 4-5/4 KC773 . . . . **599.5**
How dinosaurs came to be./ 1996/ 4-A/6 KC251 . . . . **567.9**
How we learned the earth is round./ c1990, 1992/ K-3/2 KC060 . . **525**
Hurricanes: Earth's mightiest storms./ 1996/ 3-6/6 KC203 . . . . **551.55**
Journey to the planets. 4th ed./ 1993/ 4-6/6 KC028 . . . . **523.4**
Living with dinosaurs./ 1991/ 3-6/5 KC252 . . . . **567.9**
Living with dinosaurs (Sound recording cassette)./ 1994/
3-6/5 KC252 . . . . **567.9**
News about dinosaurs./ 1989/ P-A/7 KC253 . . . . **567.9**
News about dinosaurs (Sound recording cassette)./ 1993/
P-A/7 KC253 . . . . **567.9**
Octopus is amazing./ 1990/ 1-3/4 KC514 . . . . **594**
Snakes are hunters./ 1993/ 2-4/3 KC637 . . . . **597.96**
Tales mummies tell./ 1985/ 4-6/8 KE626 . . . . **930.1**
Volcano: the eruption and healing of Mount St. Helens./ 1986/
P-A/6 KC158 . . . . **CE 551.21**
What do you see and how do you see it?: exploring light, color, and
vision./ 1994/ 1-6/4 KC113 . . . . **535**
Who eats what?: food chains and food webs./ 1995/
K-3/2 KC295 . . . . **577**
You're aboard spaceship Earth./ 1996/ 1-3/3 KC147 . . . . . . **550**
LAUGHLIN, MK/ Literature-based reading: children's books and activities to
enrich the K-5/ 1990/ KA210 . . . . **PROF 372.4**
Literature-based social studies: children's books and activities to enrich the
K-5/ 1991/ KA261 . . . . **PROF 372.83**
Readers theatre for children: scripts and script development./ 1990/
KA339 . . . . **PROF 808.5**
Social studies readers theatre for children: scripts and script
development./ 1991/ KA224 . . . . **PROF 372.6**
LAUKEL, HG/ Desert fox family book./ 1996/ 3-6/7 KC846 . . **599.776**
LAURENT, R/ Leading kids to books through magic./ 1996/
KA066 . . . . **PROF 027.62**
LAUTURE, D/ Running the road to ABC./ 1996/ 1-3/4 KF951 . . . . . **E**
LAVALLEE, B/ Mama, do you love me?/ 1991/ P-1/2 KF854 . . . . . **E**
This place is lonely./ 1991/ 3-6/7 KF116 . . . . **994**
This place is wet./ 1989/ 3-6/6 KC287 . . . . **574.5**
Uno, dos, tres: one, two, three./ 1996/ P-1/3 KG155 . . . . **E**
LAVENDER, DS/ Santa Fe Trail./ 1995/ A/6 KF037 . . . . **978**
Snowbound: the tragic story of the Donner Party./ 1996/
5-6/6 KF038 . . . . **978**
LAVIES, B/ Compost critters./ 1993/ 5-6/7 KC336 . . . . **577.5**
Gathering of garter snakes./ 1993/ 4-6/7 KC638 . . . . **597.96**
Gathering of garter snakes (Sound recording cassette)./ 1995/
4-6/7 KC638 . . . . **597.96**
Mangrove wilderness: nature's nursery./ 1994/ K-3/7 KC341 . **577.68**
Monarch butterflies: mysterious travelers./ 1992/ 5-6/7 KC562 **595.78**
LAWLOR, L/ Real Johnny Appleseed./ 1995/
5-6/8 KE240 . . . . **B APPLESEED, J.**
LAWLOR, V/ I WAS DREAMING TO COME TO AMERICA: MEMORIES
FROM THE ELLIS ISLAND ORAL HISTORY PROJECT./ 1995/
4-6/7 KA916 . . . . **325**
LAWRENCE, A/ Chess for children./ 1993/ 4-A/8 KD756 . . . . . **794.1**
LAWRENCE, J/ Christmas spirit: two stories./ 1994/ 6-A/6 KH847 . . **FIC**
Great migration: an American story./ 1993/ K-5/7 KD488 . . . **759.13**
Harriet and the Promised Land./ 1993/ K-3 KD969 . . . . **811**
Toussaint L'Ouverture: the fight for Haiti's freedom./ 1996/
4-A/8 KE569 . . . . **B TOUSSAINT**
LAWRENCE, RD/ Wolves./ 1990/ 5-6/7 KC837 . . . . **599.773**
LAWSON, J/ If pigs could fly./ 1989/ 5-A/6 KH387 . . . . **FIC**
LAWSON, R/ Adam of the road./ c1942, 1970/ 5-6/6 KH194 . **CE FIC**
Ben and me: a new and astonishing life of Benjamin Franklin, as written/
c1939/ 3-5/5 KH388 . . . . **FIC**
Ben and me: a new and astonishing life of Benjamin Franklin, as written
by his good mouse Amos; lately discovered (Talking book)./ Ben and
me: a new and astonishing life of Benjamin Franklin, as written by his
good mouse Amos; lately discovered (Braille)./ n.d./ n.d./
3-5/5 KH388 . . . . **FIC**
3-5/5 KH388 . . . . **FIC**
Mr. Popper's penguins./ c1938/ 3-5/4 KG854 . . . . **CE FIC**
Mr. Revere and I: being an account of certain episodes in the career of
Paul/ c1953/ 5-6/7 KH389 . . . . **FIC**
Mr. Revere and I: (Braille)./ n.d./ 5-6/7 KH389 . . . . **FIC**
Mr. Revere and I: (Talking Book)./ n.d./ 5-6/7 KH389 . . . . . . **FIC**
Rabbit Hill./ c1944, 1962/ 4-6/7 KH390 . . . . **CE FIC**
Rabbit Hill (Braille)./ n.d./ 4-6/7 KH390 . . . . **CE FIC**
Rabbit Hill (Kit)./ 1972/ 4-6/7 KH390 . . . . **CE FIC**
Rabbit Hill (Sound recording cassette)./ n.d./ 4-6/7 KH390 . . **CE FIC**
Rabbit Hill (Talking book)./ n.d./ 4-6/7 KH390 . . . . **CE FIC**
Story of Ferdinand./ c1936/ P-1/3 KF953 . . . . **CE E**
They were strong and good./ c1940/ 4-6 KE891 . . . . **973.4**

LAZEAR, DG/ Seven pathways of learning: teaching students and parents
about multiple intelligences./ 1994/ KA174 . . . . **PROF 370.15**
LAZO, C/ Mahatma Gandhi./ 1993/ 4-6/7 KE363 . . . . . **B GANDHI, M.**
LE GUIN, UK/ Farthest shore./ 1987,/ 6-A/7 KH392 . . . . **FIC**
Tehanu: the last book of Earthsea./ 1990/ 6-A/7 KH392 . . . . . . **FIC**
Wizard of Earthsea./ c1968, 1991/ 6-A/7 KH392 . . . . **FIC**
Wizard of Earthsea (Sound recording cassette)./ n.d./
6-A/7 KH392 . . . . **FIC**
Wizard of Earthsea (Talking book)./ n.d./ 6-A/7 KH392 . . . . . . **FIC**
LEAF, H/ JUNIOR JEWISH ENCYCLOPEDIA. 11th rev. ed./ 1991/
5-6 KA396 . . . . **REF 296**
LEAF, M/ Cuento de Ferdinado./ 1988/ P-1/3 KF953 . . . . **CE E**
Cuento de Ferdinando (Kit)./ 1990/ P-1/3 KF953 . . . . **CE E**
Eyes of the dragon./ 1987/ K-3/5 KF952 . . . . **E**
Four-and-twenty watchbirds./ c1939, 1990/ P-3/6 KB240 . . . . **395**
Manners can be fun. Rev. ed./ 1985/ 1-3/4 KB249 . . . . **395.5**
Story of Ferdinand./ c1936/ P-1/3 KF953 . . . . **CE E**
Story of Ferdinand (Braille)./ n.d./ P-1/3 KF953 . . . . **CE E**
Story of Ferdinand (Kit)./ 1978/ P-1/3 KF953 . . . . **CE E**
Story of Ferdinand (Sound recording cassette)./ n.d./
P-1/3 KF953 . . . . **CE E**
Story of Ferdinand (Talking book)./ n.d./ P-1/3 KF953 . . . . . **CE E**
LEAHY, CW/ Peterson first guide to insects of North America./ 1987/
5-6/8 KC544 . . . . **595.7**
LEAR, E/ Daffy down dillies: silly limericks./ 1992/ K-A KE103 . . . **821**
Nonsense songs./ 1997/ K-3 KE104 . . . . **821**
Owl and the Pussy-cat./ 1996/ P-2 KE105 . . . . **821**
Owl and the Pussy-cat and other nonsense poems./ 1995/
3-6 KE106 . . . . **821**
LEAVITT, J/ Easy carpentry projects for children./ c1959, 1986/
5-6/4 KD340 . . . . **684**
LECHNER, S/ Followers of the North Star: rhymes about African American
heroes, heroines, and historical times./ 1993/ 3-A KD913 . . . **811**
LECHON, D/ Desert is my mother./El desierto es mi madre./ 1994/
K-3 KD989 . . . . **811**
Gift of the poinsettia./El regalo de la flor de nochebuena./ 1995/
3-5/4 KH507 . . . . **FIC**
LECOURT, N/ Abracadabra to zigzag: an alphabet book./ 1991/
K-3 KF954 . . . . **E**
LEDER, D/ I was so mad./ 1974/ P-2/2 KA630 . . . . **152.4**
Julian's glorious summer./ 1987/ 2-4/2 KG967 . . . . **FIC**
LEE, A/ Black ships before Troy: the story of the Iliad./ 1993/
5-A/8 KE127 . . . . **883**
Wanderings of Odysseus: the story of the Odyssey./ 1996/
5-A/7 KE128 . . . . **883**
LEE, D/ ALLIGATOR PIE (Videocassette)./ 1993/ P-2 KD912 . **VCR 811**
Baseball saved us./ 1993/ 4-A/6 KH500 . . . . **FIC**
Dinosaur dinner (with a slice of alligator pie): favorite poems./ 1997/
K-3 KD970 . . . . **811**
Heroes./ 1995/ 3-5/4 KH501 . . . . **FIC**
Passage to freedom: the Sugihara story./ 1997/ 3-6/4 KE662 . **940.53**
LEE, HV/ In the snow./ 1995/ 1-3/2 KF955 . . . . **E**
LEE, J/ Anne of Green Gables./ c1908, 1983/ 4-A/6 KH503 . . . . . **FIC**
LEE, JM/ Ch'i-lin purse: a collection of ancient Chinese stories./ 1995/
4-6/5 KB295 . . . . **398.2**
Silent Lotus./ 1991/ P-2/4 KF956 . . . . **E**
LEE, K/ Sea turtle journey: the story of a loggerhead turtle./ 1995/
K-2/5 KF826 . . . . **CE E**
LEE, M/ Nim and the war effort./ 1997/ 2-4/5 KH391 . . . . **FIC**
LEEDY, L/ Blast off to Earth!: a look at geography./ 1992/
1-4/4 KE151 . . . . **910**
Fraction action./ 1994/ 2-4/2 KB963 . . . . **513.2**
How humans make friends./ 1996/ K-3/3 KA660 . . . . **158**
Messages in the mailbox: how to write a letter./ 1991/
2-5/2 KB246 . . . . **395.4**
Mission: addition./ 1997/ K-3/2 KB964 . . . . **513.2**
Monster money book./ 1992/ 1-3/2 KF957 . . . . **E**
Postcards from Pluto: a tour of the solar system./ 1993/
1-6/3 KC012 . . . . **523.2**
Who's who in my family./ 1995/ K-2/2 KA869 . . . . **306.85**
2 x 2 = boo!: a set of spooky multiplication stories./ 1995/
1-3/2 KB965 . . . . **513.2**
LEER, R/ Spoon for every bite./ 1996/ 2-4/4 KF684 . . . . **E**
LEHMAN, B/ Abracadabra to zigzag: an alphabet book./ 1991/
K-3 KF954 . . . . **E**
LEHTINEN, R/ Grandchildren of the Incas./ 1991/ 4-6/6 KF110 . . **985**
LEINER, K/ First children: growing up in the White House./ 1996/
A/9 KE856 . . . . **973**
LEMIEUX, M/ Winter magic./ 1989/ K-3/4 KF678 . . . . **E**
LEMKE, N/ Missions of the Southern Coast./ 1996/ 4-6/9 KF083 **979.4**
L'ENGLE, M/ Arruga en el tiempo./ n.d./ 4-6/6 KH394 . . . . . . **CE FIC**
Glorious impossible./ 1990/ 4-A/6 KA697 . . . . **232.9**
Wind in the door./ c1973/ 5-6/7 KH393 . . . . **FIC**

Wind in the door (Sound recording cassette)./ 1997/
5-6/7 KH393 . . . . **FIC**
Wrinkle in time./ c1962/ 4-6/6 KH394 . . . . **CE FIC**
Wrinkle in time (Braille)./ n.d./ 4-6/6 KH394 . . . . **CE FIC**
Wrinkle in time (Sound recording cassette)./ n.d./
4-6/6 KH394 . . . . **CE FIC**
LENT, B/ Tikki Tikki Tembo./ 1967/ P-2/5 KB759 . . . . 398.27
Why the sun and the moon live in the sky: an African folktale./ c1968/
K-3/6 KB704 . . . . **CE 398.26**
LEONARD, R/ Cowboys./ 1991/ 4-6/6 KF039 978
Latino rainbow: poems about Latino Americans./ 1994/
3-6 KD927 811
Story of Sacajawea: guide to Lewis and Clark./ 1995/
5-6/6 KE529 . . . . **B SACAGAWEA**
LEONARD, T/ Under the sun and the moon and other poems./ 1993/
P-2 KD918 811
LEPTHIEN, EU/ Beavers./ 1992/ 3-5/5 KC754 . . . . 599.37
Buffalo./ 1989/ 3-5/5 KC791 . . . . 599.64
Elk./ 1994/ 4-6/5 KC798 . . . . 599.65
Manatees./ 1991/ 5-6/7 KC781 . . . . 599.55
Polar bears./ 1991/ 2-4/5 KC863 . . . . 599.786
Squirrels./ 1992/ 4-6/4 KC751 . . . . 599.36
Wolves./ 1991/ 2-4/5 KC838 . . . . 599.773
Woodchucks./ 1992/ 3-4/4 KC752 . . . . 599.36
Zebras./ 1994/ 3-5/4 KC807 . . . . 599.665
LERNER, C/ Backyard birds of summer./ 1996/ 5-6/7 KC654 598
Cactus./ 1992/ 5-6/7 KC429 583
Moonseed and mistletoe: a book of poisonous wild plants./ 1988/
4-A/6 KC403 . . . . 581.6
Plant families./ 1989/ A/7 KC388 580
Plants that make you sniffle and sneeze./ 1993/ 5-6/9 KC404 . . 581.6
LESHAN, E/ Grandparents: a special kind of love./ 1984/
4-6/9 KA879 . . . . 306.874
Learning to say goodbye: when a parent dies./ c1976/
5-6/7 KA651 . . . . 155.9
Learning to say goodbye: when a parent dies (Sound recording
cassette)./ n.d./ 5-6/7 KA651 . . . . 155.9
LESHER, S/ MATH FOR THE VERY YOUNG: A HANDBOOK OF
ACTIVITIES FOR PARENTS AND TEACHERS./ 1995/
KA254 . . . . **PROF 372.7**
LESIEG, T/ Eye book./ c1968/ 1-2/1 KF958 . . . . E
Ten apples up on top!/ c1961/ 1-2/1 KF959 . . . . E
Tooth book./ 1981/ K-2/2 KF960 . . . . E
Wacky Wednesday./ c1974/ 1-2/1 KF961 . . . . E
LESLAU, W/ Fire on the mountain and other stories from Ethiopia and
Eritrea./ c1950, 1995/ 3-6/6 KB277 . . . . 398.2
LESLIE, C/ Story of the treasure seekers./ 1986/ 5-6/7 KH544 . . . . FIC
LESLIE, CW/ Nature all year long./ 1991/ 1-5/6 KB908 508
LESSAC, F/ Caribbean alphabet./ 1994/ 1-3 KF962 . . . . E
Chalk doll./ c1989, 1993/ 1-3/2 KG263 . . . . E
Distant talking drum: poems from Nigeria./ 1995/ K-2 KE139 . . . 896
Not a copper penny in me house: poems from the Caribbean./ 1993/
P-3 KD950 811
O Christmas tree./ 1996/ 1-3/4 KG298 . . . . E
Wonderful Towers of Watts./ 1994/ 2-4/6 KD387 725
LESSEM, D/ Dinosaur worlds: new dinosaurs, new discoveries./ 1996/
4-6/6 KC254 . . . . 567.9
Iceman./ 1994/ 4-6/6 KE640 937
Inside the amazing Amazon./ 1995/ 2-6/7 KC319 . . . . 577.34
Jack Horner: living with dinosaurs./ 1994/
5-A/8 KE391 . . . . **B HORNER, J.**
Jack Horner: living with dinosaurs (Sound recording cassette)./ 1996/
5-A/8 KE391 . . . . **B HORNER, J.**
LESSER, C/ What a wonderful day to be a cow./ 1995/ K-2/3 KF963 E
LESSER, R/ Hansel and Gretel: a tale from the Brothers Grimm./ 1984/
5/6 KB740 . . . . **CE 398.27**
LESTER, H/ Author: a true story./ 1997/ 2-5/2 KE436 . . . **B LESTER, H.**
Listen Buddy./ 1995/ K-2/2 KF964 . . . . E
Princess Penelope's parrot./ 1996/ K-2/2 KF965 . . . . E
LESTER, J/ Further tales of Uncle Remus: the misadventures of Brer Rabbit,
Brer Fox, Brer Wolf, the Doodang, and other creatures./ 1990/
4-5/5 KB608 . . . . 398.24
How many spots does a leopard have? and other tales./ c1989, 1994/
5-6/6 KB335 . . . . 398.2
John Henry./ 1994/ 2-5/4 KB464 . . . . 398.22
Last tales of Uncle Remus./ 1994/ 4-5/5 KB608 . . . . 398.24
Long journey home: stories from Black history./ c1972, 1993/
6-A/6 KH395 . . . . FIC
Man who knew too much: a moral tale from the Baila of Zambia./ 1994/
4-5/3 KB607 . . . . 398.24
More tales of Uncle Remus./ 1987/ 4-5/5 KB608 . . . . 398.24
Sam and the tigers: a new telling of LITTLE BLACK SAMBO./ 1996/
K-3/2 KF966 . . . . E

Tales of Uncle Remus: the adventures of Brer Rabbit./ 1987/
4-5/5 KB608 . . . . 398.24
Tales of Uncle Remus: the adventures of Brer Rabbit (Sound recording
cassette)./ n.d./ 4-5/5 KB608 . . . . 398.24
To be a slave./ c1968/ A/7 KA928 326
To be a slave (Braille)./ n.d./ A/7 KA928 326
LE-TAN, P/ Puss in Boots (Kit)./ 1992/ 1-4 KB620 . . . . . . **KIT 398.24**
LETTOW, L/ Picture books to enhance the curriculum./ 1996/
KA016 . . . . **PROF 011.62**
LEVERICH, K/ Barmi: a Mediterranean city through the ages./ 1990/
A/11 KA895 . . . . 307.76
Lebek: a city of Northern Europe through the ages./ 1991/
A/10 KA896 . . . . 307.76
San Rafael: a Central American city through the ages./ 1992/
A/8 KA897 . . . . 307.76
LEVERT, M/ Jeremiah and Mrs. Ming./ 1990/ K-2/2 KF828 . . . . E
LEVERT, S/ Hillary Rodham Clinton, first lady./ 1994/
4-6/9 KE297 . . . . **B CLINTON, H.**
LEVEY, JS/ MACMILLAN FIRST DICTIONARY./ 1990/ K-2 KB834 . 423
LEVIN, B/ Fire in the wind./ 1995/ 5-A/4 KH396 . . . . FIC
LEVINE, AA/ Boy who drew cats: a Japanese folktale./ 1993/
2-4/4 KB609 . . . . 398.24
LEVINE, CA/ Riddles to tell your cat./ 1992/ 2-5 KD732 . . . . 793.735
LEVINE, GC/ Ella enchanted./ 1997/ 5-A/5 KH397 . . . . FIC
LEVINE, M/ Macmillan book of baseball stories./ 1992/
4-A/5 KD796 . . . . 796.357
LEVINE, S/ Everyday science: fun and easy projects for making practical
things./ 1995/ 3-8/7 KB893 . . . . 507.8
Silly science: strange and startling projects to amaze your family and
friends./ 1995/ 3-8/7 KB893 . . . . 507.8
LEVINSON, NS/ Clara and the bookwagon./ 1988/ 1-3/1 KF967 . . . E
Snowshoe Thompson./ 1992/ K-3/2 KE564 . . . . . . **B THOMPSON, S.**
LEVINSON, R/ Emperor's new clothes./ 1991/ P-2/4 KF968 . . . . . . E
Mira como salen las estrellas./ 1992/ K-2/2 KF969 . . . . E
Watch the stars come out./ c1985, 1995/ K-2/2 KF969 . . . . . . E
LEVITIN, S/ Annie's promise./ ,/ 5-A/5 KH398 . . . . FIC
Journey to America./ c1970, 1993/ 5-A/5 KH398 . . . . FIC
Journey to America (Talking book)./ n.d.,/ 5-A/5 KH398 . . . . . FIC
Man who kept his heart in a bucket./ 1991/ K-2/3 KF970 . . . . E
Silver days./ 1992,/ 5-A/5 KH398 . . . . FIC
LEVITT, MJ/ Tales of an October moon: haunting stories from New
England (Sound recording cassette)./ 1992/ 4-6 KH399 . . . **SRC FIC**
LEVITT, S/ Bingo, the best dog in the world./ 1991/ K-1/1 KG510 . . E
Mighty Movers./ 1994/ K-2/2 KF971 . . . . E
LEVOY, M/ Witch of Fourth Street, and other stories./ c1972/
4-6/7 KH400 . . . . FIC
Witch of Fourth Street and other stories (Kit)./ 1978/
4-6 KH401 . . . . **KIT FIC**
LEVY, E/ Keep Ms. Sugarman in the fourth grade./ 1992/
3-5/5 KH402 . . . . FIC
Keep Ms. Sugarman in the fourth grade (Sound recording cassette)./
1995/ 3-5/5 KH402 . . . . FIC
Something queer at the haunted school./ 1982/ 1-3/3 KF972 . . **CE E**
Something queer at the haunted school (Kit)./ n.d./ 1-3/3 KF972 . **CE E**
Something queer at the lemonade stand./ 1982/ 1-3/3 KF972 . . . **CE E**
Something queer at the scary movie./ 1995/ 3-5/3 KH403 . . . . FIC
Something queer in outer space./ 1993/ 1-3/3 KF972 . . . . . **CE E**
Something queer is going on (a mystery)./ C1973/ 1-3/3 KF972 . **CE E**
Something queer is going on (a mystery) (Kit)./ 1983/
1-3/3 KF972 . . . . **CE E**
LEVY, J/ Spirit of Tio Fernando: a Day of the Dead story./El espiritu de tio
Fernando: una historia del Dia de los Muertos./ 1995/
1-3/5 KH404 . . . . FIC
LEWIN, B/ Booby hatch./ 1995/ K-2/2 KF973 . . . . E
Classroom pet./ 1995/ K-1/2 KG046 . . . . E
Doodle Dandy!: the complete book of Independence Day words./ 1992/
5-A/A KB220 . . . . 394.263
Ho Ho Ho!: the complete book of Christmas words./ 1993/
2-6/8 KB235 . . . . 394.266
M.C. Turtle and the Hip Hop Hare: a nursery rap./ 1997/
2-3/2 KG665 . . . . E
Mushy! the complete book of Valentine words./ 1991/
5-6/8 KB209 . . . . 394.261
Somebody catch my homework./ 1993/ 2-6 KD951 811
LEWIN, T/ Ali, child of the desert./ 1997/ K-3/3 KG019 . . . . . . E
Always Prayer Shawl./ 1994/ 2-4/2 KG184 . . . . E
Amazon boy./ 1993/ K-2/5 KF974 . . . . E
American too./ 1996/ 1-3/3 KF210 . . . . E
Brother Francis and the friendly beasts./ 1991/
3-5/5 KE349 . . . . **B FRANCIS, ST.**
Cowboy country./ 1993/ 3-6/3 KF049 978
Day of Ahmed's secret./ 1990/ 1-3/4 KF694 . . . . E
Fair!/ 1997/ 1-3/6 KB180 394
Island of the Blue Dolphins./ c1960, 1990/ 5-6/6 KH560 . . . . . . FIC

Lost moose./ 1995/ K-2/2 KG517 . . . . E
Market!/ 1996/ 1-3/6 KB128 381
National Velvet./ c1935, 1985/ 4-A/5 KG874 . . . . FIC
Paperboy./ 1996/ 1-3/2 KF926 . . . . E
Peppe the lamplighter./ 1993/ 1-3/2 KF211 . . . . E
Potato man./ 1991/ K-3/5 KG098 . . . . E
Reindeer people./ 1994/ 4-6/6 KE695 . . . . 948.97
Sacred river./ 1995/ 4-6/6 KA765 . . . . 294.5
Sami and the time of the troubles./ 1992/ 2-4/4 KF695 . . . . . . E
Sea watch: a book of poetry./ 1996/ 4-6 KE049 811
LEWINGTON, A/ Atlas of rain forests./ 1997/ 3-6/7 KC321 . 577.34
LEWIS, BA/ Kid's guide to social action: how to solve the social problems
  you choose--and turn creative thinking into positive action./ 1991/
  3-6/6 KA991 . . . . 361.2
LEWIS, CS/ Caballo y su jinete./ 1995/ 5-A/6 KH405 . . . . . . CE FIC
Chronicles of Narnia super-sound book (Talking book)./ 1993/
  5-A/6 KH405 . . . . CE FIC
Horse and his boy./ 1994/ 5-A/6 KH405 . . . . CE FIC
Horse and his boy (Braille)./ n.d./ 5-A/6 KH405 . . . . . . CE FIC
Horse and his boy (Sound recording cassette)./ n.d./
  5-A/6 KH405 . . . . CE FIC
Horse and his boy (Talking book)./ n.d./ 5-A/6 KH405 . . . CE FIC
Last battle./ 1994/ 5-A/6 KH405 . . . . CE FIC
Last battle (Braille)./ n.d./ 5-A/6 KH405 . . . . CE FIC
Last battle (Sound recording cassette)./ n.d./ 5-A/6 KH405 . CE FIC
Last battle (Talking book)./ n.d./ 5-A/6 KH405 . . . . CE FIC
Leon, la bruja, y el armario./ n.d./ 5-A/6 KH405 . . . . . . CE FIC
Lion, the witch and the wardrobe./ 1994/ 5-A/6 KH405 . . . CE FIC
Lion, the witch and the wardrobe (Braille)./ n.d./ 5-A/6 KH405 CE FIC
Lion, the witch and the wardrobe (Sound recording cassette)./ n.d./
  5-A/6 KH405 . . . . CE FIC
Lion, the witch and the wardrobe (Talking book)./ n.d./
  5-A/6 KH405 . . . . CE FIC
Lion, the witch and the wardrobe (Videocassette)./ 1988/
  5-A/6 KH405 . . . . CE FIC
Magician's nephew./ 1994/ 5-A/6 KH405 . . . . CE FIC
Magician's nephew (Braille)./ n.d./ 5-A/6 KH405 . . . . . . CE FIC
Magician's nephew (Sound recording cassette)./ 1994/
  5-A/6 KH405 . . . . CE FIC
Magician's nephew (Talking book)./ n.d./ 5-A/6 KH405 . . . . CE FIC
Prince Caspian and the Voyage of the Dawn Treader (Videocassette)./
  1989/ 5-A/6 KH405 . . . . CE FIC
Prince Caspian (Braille)./ n.d./ 5-A/6 KH405 . . . . CE FIC
Prince Caspian (Sound recording cassette)./ n.d./
  5-A/6 KH405 . . . . CE FIC
Prince Caspian (Talking book)./ n.d./ 5-A/6 KH405 . . . . . . CE FIC
Prince Caspian: the return to Narnia./ 1994/ 5-A/6 KH405 . . . CE FIC
Principe Caspio./ 1995/ 5-A/6 KH405 . . . . CE FIC
Sillon de plata./ n.d./ 5-A/6 KH405 . . . . CE FIC
Silver chair./ 1994/ 5-A/6 KH405 . . . . CE FIC
Silver chair (Braille)./ n.d./ 5-A/6 KH405 . . . . CE FIC
Silver chair (Sound recording cassette)./ n.d./ 5-A/6 KH405 . CE FIC
Silver chair (Talking book)./ n.d./ 5-A/6 KH405 . . . . CE FIC
Silver chair (Videocassette)./ 1990/ 5-A/6 KH405 . . . . . . CE FIC
Ultima batalla./ n.d./ 5-A/6 KH405 . . . . CE FIC
Viaje del Amanecer./ n.d./ 5-A/6 KH405 . . . . CE FIC
Voyage of the Dawn Treader./ 1994/ 5-A/6 KH405 . . . . . . CE FIC
Voyage of the Dawn Treader (Braille)./ n.d./ 5-A/6 KH405 . . CE FIC
Voyage of the Dawn Treader (Sound recording cassette)./ n.d./
  5-A/6 KH405 . . . . CE FIC
Voyage of the Dawn Treader (Talking book)./ n.d./
  5-A/6 KH405 . . . . CE FIC
LEWIS, IM/ Why ostriches don't fly and other tales from the African bush./
  1997/ 4-6/6 KB336 . . . . 398.2
LEWIS, JP/ Black swan/white crow: haiku./ 1995/ 3-6 KD971 811
Christmas of the reddle moon./ 1994/ 1-3/4 KF975 . . . . E
July is a mad mosquito./ 1994/ P-3 KD972 811
LEWIS, K/ My friend Harry./ 1995/ P-1/2 KF976 . . . . E
LEWIS, KR/ Literature-based science: children's books and activities to
  enrich the K-5 curriculum./ 1995/ KA200 . . . . PROF 372.3
LEWIS, M/ Off the map: the journals of Lewis and Clark./ 1993/
  4-6/7 KE201 . . . . 917.804
LEWIS, PO/ Davy's dream./ 1988/ 1-3/3 KF977 . . . . E
P. Bear's New Year's party!: a counting book./ 1989/ K-1/3 KF978 . E
Storm boy./ 1995/ 2-4/3 KB610 . . . . 398.24
LEWIS, S/ Get your teddy ready (Videocassette)./ 1994/
  P-2 KD681 . . . . VCR 790.1
Let's play games (Videocassette)./ 1994/ P-2 KD709 . . . . VCR 793.4
LEXAU, JM/ Rooftop mystery./ c1968/ 1-2/1 KF979 . . . . E
Rooftop mystery (Braille)./ n.d./ 1-2/1 KF979 . . . . E
LIEBERMAN, S/ Intrepid birdmen: the fighter pilots of World War I (Sound
  recording cassette)./ 1993/ A KE654 . . . . SRC 940.4
LIED, K/ Potato: a tale from the Great Depression./ 1997/
  K-3/2 KF980 . . . . E

LIFE, K/ Muggie Maggie./ 1990/ 3-5/5 KG998 . . . . FIC
LIGASAN, D/ Caravan./ 1995/ 3-5/6 KH480 . . . . FIC
LIGHTFOOT, DJ/ Trail fever: the life of a Texas cowboy./ 1992/
  4-6/5 KH406 . . . . FIC
Trail fever: the life of a Texas cowboy (Sound recording cassette)./
  1995/ 4-6/5 KH406 . . . . FIC
LIGHTFOOT, M/ Cartooning for kids./ 1993/ 3-6/5 KD410 . . . . 741.5
LIGHTNING INSIDE YOU AND OTHER NATIVE AMERICAN RIDDLES./
  1992/ 3-6 KD733 . . . . 793.735
LILLEGARD, D/ Nevada./ 1990/ 4-6/9 KF074 . . . . 979.3
Nevada (Sound recording cassette)./ 1993/ 4-6/9 KF074 . . . . 979.3
LILLIE, P/ Everything has a place./ 1993/ P-K/1 KF981 . . . . E
Floppy teddy bear./ 1995/ P-1/2 KF982 . . . . E
LILLY, C/ Escape from slavery: five journeys to freedom./ 1991/
  4-6/4 KE863 973
LIMA, CW/ A to zoo: subject access to children's picture books. 5th ed./
  1998/ KA017 . . . . PROF 011.62
LIMA, JA/ A to zoo: subject access to children's picture books. 5th ed./
  1998/ KA017 . . . . PROF 011.62
LINCH, T/ This and that./ 1996/ P-1/2 KG586 . . . . E
LINCOLN, A/ Gettysburg Address./ 1995/ 4-6/6 KE906 . . . . . . 973.7
LINCOLN, IN HIS OWN WORDS./ 1993/ A/8 KE907 . . . . . . 973.7
LINCOLN, M/ Amazing boats./ 1992/ 3-5/5 KD064 . . . . 623.8
LINDBERGH, R/ Johnny Appleseed./ 1990/ K-3 KD973 811
Nobody owns the sky: the story of "Brave Bessie" Coleman./ 1996/
  1-3/2 KF983 . . . . E
LINDBLAD, L/ Serengeti migration: Africa's animals on the move./ 1994/
  5-6/10 KC497 . . . . 591.96
LINDBLOM, S/ Fly the hot ones./ 1991/ A/8 KD103 . . . . . . 629.132
LINDEN, AM/ One smiling grandma: a Caribbean counting book./ 1995/
  P-1/2 KF984 . . . . E
LINDGREN, A/ Lotta's Christmas surprise./ c1977, 1990/
  1-2/2 KF985 . . . . E
Pippi goes on board./ 1957/ 3-5/4 KH407 . . . . CE FIC
Pippi goes on board (Braille)./ n.d./ 3-5/4 KH407 . . . . . . CE FIC
Pippi goes on board (Talking book)./ n.d./ 3-5/4 KH407 . . . CE FIC
Pippi in the South Seas./ c1959/ 3-5/4 KH407 . . . . CE FIC
Pippi in the South Seas (Talking book)./ n.d./ 3-5/4 KH407 . . CE FIC
Pippi Longstocking./ c1950, 1978/ 3-5/4 KH407 . . . . CE FIC
Pippi Longstocking (Braille)./ n.d./ 3-5/4 KH407 . . . . . . CE FIC
Pippi Longstocking (Large type)./ 1987/ 3-5/4 KH407 . . . . CE FIC
Pippi Longstocking (Sound recording cassette)./ n.d./
  3-5/4 KH407 . . . . CE FIC
Pippi Longstocking (Talking book)./ Pippi Longstocking (Talking book)./
  n.d./ 1973/ 3-5/4 KH407 . . . . CE FIC
  3-5/4 KH407 . . . . CE FIC
Tomten./ c1965, 1997/ K-2/3 KF986 . . . . CE E
Tomten and the fox./ 1965/ K-2/3 KF986 . . . . CE E
Tomten (Videocassette)./ 1982/ K-2/3 KF986 . . . . CE E
LINDLEY, M/ Lizard in the jungle./ 1988/ 5-6/7 KC626 . . . . 597.95
LINDOP, L/ Athletes./ 1996/ 4-6/7 KD763 796
Political leaders./ 1996/ 6-A/12 KA899 320
LINDSAY, W/ Tyrannosaurus./ 1992/ 5-6/9 KC255 . . . . 567.9
LINDSEY, T/ Birding./ c1994, 1995/ 5-6/8 KA448 . . . . . . REF 598
LING, B/ Fattest, tallest, biggest snowman ever./ 1997/ K-2/2 KF987 . E
Maya Lin./ 1997/ 4-6/10 KE437 . . . . B LIN, M.
LING, M/ Snake book./ 1997/ 2-6/6 KC639 . . . . 597.96
LINK, M/ Goat in the rug./ 1990/ K-3/6 KF234 . . . . E
LINN, D/ Ghostly warnings./ 1996/ 4-6/7 KA599 . . . . 133.1
LINTON, P/ Young dancer./ 1994/ 3-6/8 KD692 . . . . 792.8
LIONNI, L/ Alexander and the wind-up mouse./ 1987/ P-1/4 KF988 . E
Alexander and the wind-up mouse (Braille)./ n.d./ P-1/4 KF988 . . . E
Alexander and the wind-up mouse (Talking book)./ n.d./
  P-1/4 KF988 . . . . E
Alexander and the wind-up mouse (Videocassette)./ 1985/
  P-2 KF994 . . . . VCR E
Alphabet tree./ c1968, 1990/ 1-2/3 KF989 . . . . E
Color of his own./ c1975, 1997/ K-2/5 KF990 . . . . E
Extraordinary egg./ 1994/ 1-3/2 KF991 . . . . E
Frederick./ c1967/ P-2/2 KF992 . . . . E
Frederick (Braille)./ n.d./ P-2/2 KF992 . . . . E
Frederick (Videocassette)./ 1985/ P-2 KF994 . . . . VCR E
Frederick's fables: a Leo Lionni treasury of favorite stories. Rev. ed./
  1997/ P-2/4 KF993 . . . . E
Frederick's fables: a Leo Lionni treasury of favorite stories (Sound
  recording cassette)./ n.d./ P-2/4 KF993 . . . . E
Leo Lionni's Caldecotts (Videocassette)./ 1985/ P-2 KF994 . . . VCR E
Swimmy./ c1968/ K-2/6 KF995 . . . . E
Swimmy (Videocassette)./ 1985/ P-2 KF994 . . . . VCR E
LION'S WHISKERS: AND OTHER ETHIOPIAN TALES. REV. ED./ 1997/
  3-6/7 KB337 . . . . 398.2
LIPPINCOTT, GA/ Jeremy Thatcher, dragon hatcher: a magic shop book./
  1991/ 4-A/4 KH036 . . . . CE FIC

LIPSYTE, R/ Jim Thorpe: 20th-century jock./ /
    6-A/7 KE566 . . . . **B THORPE, J.**
Joe Louis: a champ for all America./ 1994/ 4-6/6 KE447 . **B LOUIS, J.**
Michael Jordan: a life above the rim./ 1994/
    4-6/7 KE411 . . . . **B JORDAN, M.**
LIPTAK, K/ North American Indian ceremonies./ 1992/
    4-6/7 KA790 . . . . **299**
North American Indian sign language./ 1990/ 4-A/5 KB826 . . . . **419**
Saving our wetlands and their wildlife./ 1991/ 4-6/8 KA960 . . **333.91**
LIPTON, GC/ Beginning Spanish bilingual dictionary: a beginner's guide in
    words and pictures. 2nd rev. ed./ 1989/ 3-A KB859 . . . . **463**
LISI, V/ Snowbear Whittington: an Appalachian Beauty and the Beast./
    1994/ 2-3/4 KB318 . . . . **398.2**
LISKER, E/ Just rewards, or, Who is that man in the moon and what's he
    doing up there anyway?/ 1996/ K-2/4 KB713 . . . . **398.26**
Punch with Judy./ 1993/ 5-A/6 KG863 . . . . **FIC**
Strudel, strudel, strudel./ 1995/ 2-3/4 KB773 . . . . . . **398.27**
LISKER, SO/ Freckle juice./ 1971/ 2-4/3 KG908 . . . . **CE FIC**
Leonard Bernstein: a passion for music./ 1993/
    5-A/7 KE253 . . . . **B BERNSTEIN, L.**
LISLE, JT/ Afternoon of the elves./ 1989/ 6-A/6 KH408 . . . . . **FIC**
Forest./ 1993/ 5-A/7 KH409 . . . . **FIC**
Forest (Sound recording cassette)./ 1995/ 5-A/7 KH409 . . . . . **FIC**
Gold dust letters./ 1994/ 4-6/7 KH410 . . . . **FIC**
Gold dust letters (Sound recording cassette)./ 1996/ 4-6/7 KH410 **FIC**
Great dimpole oak./ 1987/ 5-6/6 KH411 . . . . **FIC**
Looking for Juliette./ 1994/ 4-6/6 KH412 . . . . **FIC**
Looking for Juliette (Sound recording cassette)./ 1996/
    4-6/6 KH412 . . . . **FIC**
LISOWSKI, G/ Witch of Fourth Street, and other stories./ c1972/
    4-6/7 KH400 . . . . **FIC**
LIST, BA/ Milestones in science and technology: the ready reference guide
    to discoveries, inventions, and/ 1994/ 5-A KA441 . . . . . . **REF 509**
LISTER, R/ Story of King Arthur./ 1997/ 4/7 KB465 . . . . . . **398.22**
LITCHFIELD, AB/ Words in our hands./ 1980/ 4-6/5 KH413 . . . . . **FIC**
LITKE, R/ Ice hockey./ 1997/ 3-6/8 KD843 . . . . **796.962**
LITTLE BOOK OF LOVE./ 1995/ 4-6 KD886 . . . . **808.81**
LITTLE, JR., EL/ Audubon Society field guide to North American trees,
    Eastern Region./ 1980/ 3-6 KC417 . . . . **582.16**
Audubon Society field guide to North American trees, Western Region./
    1980/ 3-6 KC417 . . . . **582.16**
LITTLE, J/ Mine for keeps./ c1962, 1994/ 5-A/5 KH414 . . . . **FIC**
Revenge of the small Small./ 1992/ 1-3/2 KF996 . . . . **E**
LITTLE, MO/ Yoshiko and the foreigner./ 1996/ 3-5/2 KF997 . . . . **E**
LITTLECHILD, G/ This land is my land./ 1993/ 2-A/4 KE803 . . . . . **971**
LITTLEFIELD, H/ Fire at the Triangle Factory./ 1996/ 2-5/1 KF998 . . . **E**
LIU, SW/ Magical starfruit tree: a Chinese folktale./ 1993/
    2-3/6 KB784 . . . . **398.27**
LIVELY, P/ Ghost of Thomas Kempe./ c1973/ 4-6/7 KH415 . . . . . . **FIC**
LIVINGSTON, MC/ Abraham Lincoln: a man for all the people: a ballad./
    1993/ K-3 KD974 . . . . **811**
Cricket never does: a collection of haiku and tanka./ 1997/
    3-6 KD975 . . . . **811**
Festivals./ 1996/ 3-6 KD976 . . . . **811**
HALLOWEEN POEMS./ 1989/ K-4 KE062 . . . . **811.008**
I LIKE YOU, IF YOU LIKE ME: POEMS OF FRIENDSHIP./ 1987/
    3-A KE065 . . . . **811.008**
Keep on singing: a ballad of Marian Anderson./ 1994/
    1-3 KD977 . . . . **811**
Let freedom ring: a ballad of Martin Luther King, Jr./ 1992/
    K-2/4 KD978 . . . . **811**
LOTS OF LIMERICKS./ 1991/ 3-6 KE069 . . . . **811.008**
Poem-making: ways to begin writing poetry./ 1991/
    5-6/7 KD868 . . . . **808.1**
POEMS FOR JEWISH HOLIDAYS./ 1986/ K-3 KE077 . . . . . **811.008**
RIDDLE-ME RHYMES./ 1994/ 3-5 KD738 . . . . **793.735**
ROLL ALONG: POEMS ON WHEELS./ 1993/ 4-A KE080 . . **811.008**
THANKSGIVING POEMS./ 1985/ K-6 KE089 . . . . **811.008**
LIVITIN, J/ SUPER SITTERS: A TRAINING COURSE (Videocassette)./
    1988/ 5-A KD304 . . . . **VCR 649**
LIVO, LJ/ Of bugs and beasts: fact, folklore, and activities./ 1995/
    KA296 . . . . **PROF 591**
LIVO, NJ/ Of bugs and beasts: fact, folklore, and activities./ 1995/
    KA296 . . . . **PROF 591**
Storytelling activities./ 1987/ KA247 . . . . **PROF 372.67**
Storytelling folklore sourcebook./ 1991/ KA340 . . . . . . **PROF 808.5**
LLEWELLYN, C/ My first book of time./ 1992/ K-3/2 KC072 . . . . **529**
LLOYD, M/ Gingerbread doll./ 1993/ 1-3/5 KG602 . . . . **E**
How we learned the earth is round./ c1990, 1992/ K-3/2 KC060 **525**
Little old lady who was not afraid of anything./ 1986/
    P-2/4 KG730 . . . . **CE E**
Military badges and insignia./ 1995/ 4-8/12 KA984 . . . . . . **355.1**
LO TURCO, L/ Great Pyramid./ 1996/ 4-6/6 KE635 . . . . **932**
LOBEL, A/ Alison's zinnia./ 1990/ P-2/2 KF999 . . . . **E**

Arnold Lobel book of Mother Goose./ 1997/ P-1 KB800 . . . . . **398.8**
Arnold Lobel video showcase (Videocassette)./ 1985/
    1-3 KG000 . . . . **VCR E**
Cat and the cook and other fables of Krylov./ 1995/
    3-5/6 KH234 . . . . **FIC**
Days with Frog and Toad./ 1979/ K-2/1 KG001 . . . . **E**
Dias con Sapo y Sepo./ 1995/ K-2/1 KG001 . . . . **E**
Fables./ 1980/ 3-A/5 KH416 . . . . **FIC**
Fabulas./ 1980/ 3-A/5 KH416 . . . . **FIC**
Frog and Toad all year./ c1976/ K-2/1 KG002 . . . . **CE E**
Frog and Toad all year (Braille)./ n.d./ K-2/1 KG002 . . . . . . **CE E**
Frog and Toad all year (Kit)./ 1985/ K-2/1 KG002 . . . . . . **CE E**
Frog and Toad are friends./ c1972/ K-2/2 KG003 . . . . . . **CE E**
Frog and Toad are friends (Kit)./ 1985/ K-2/2 KG003 . . . . . **CE E**
Frog and Toad together./ c1972/ K-2/2 KG004 . . . . **CE E**
Frog and Toad together (Kit)./ 1985/ K-2/2 KG004 . . . . . . **CE E**
Frog and Toad together (Talking book)./ n.d./ K-2/2 KG004 . . **CE E**
Grasshopper on the road./ 1978/ K-2/2 KG005 . . . . **CE E**
Grasshopper on the road (Braille)./ n.d./ K-2/2 KG005 . . . . **CE E**
Grasshopper on the road (Kit)./ 1991/ K-2/2 KG005 . . . . . **CE E**
Headless Horseman rides tonight: more poems to trouble your sleep./
    1980/ 2-4 KE003 . . . . **811**
Hildilid's night./ c1971, 1986/ K-3/6 KG365 . . . . **E**
Mangaboom./ 1997/ 1-3/3 KG264 . . . . **E**
Ming Lo moves the mountain./ 1982/ K-2/1 KG006 . . . . . . **CE E**
Ming Lo moves the mountain (Braille)./ n.d./ K-2/1 KG006 . . **CE E**
Ming Lo moves the mountain (Videocassette)./ 1993/
    K-2/1 KG006 . . . . **CE E**
Mouse soup./ c1977/ K-2/1 KG007 . . . . **CE E**
Mouse soup (Braille)./ n.d./ K-2/1 KG007 . . . . **CE E**
Mouse soup (Kit)./ 1986/ K-2/1 KG007 . . . . **CE E**
Mouse soup (Sound recording cassette)./ n.d./ K-2/1 KG007 . . . **CE E**
Mouse tales./ c1972/ K-2/2 KG008 . . . . **CE E**
Mouse tales (Kit)./ 1985/ K-2/2 KG008 . . . . **CE E**
Nightmares: poems to trouble your sleep./ c1976/ 3-5 KE011 . . . **811**
On Market Street./ On Market Street./ 1981/ 1981/ P-1/6 KG009   **E**
    P-1/6 KG009
On Market Street (Big book)./ 1986/ P-1/6 KG009 . . . . **E**
Owl at home./ c1975/ K-2/1 KG010 . . . . **E**
Owl at home (Sound recording cassette)./ n.d./ K-2/1 KG010 . . . **E**
Princess Furball./ 1989/ 3-4/6 KB745 . . . . **CE 398.27**
Random House book of Mother Goose (Sound recording cassette)./ n.d./
    P-1 KB800 . . . . **398.8**
Rose in my garden./ Rose in my garden./ 1984/ 1984/ K-3 KG011 . **E**
    K-3 KG011
Rose in my garden (Sound recording cassette)./ n.d./ K-3 KG011 . . **E**
Sam the minuteman./ c1969/ 1-3/2 KF222 . . . . **E**
Sapo y Sepo inseparables./ n.d./ K-2/2 KG004 . . . . **CE E**
Sapo y Sepo son amigos./ n.d./ K-2/2 KG003 . . . . **CE E**
Sapo y Sepo un ano entero./ n.d./ K-2/1 KG002 . . . . **CE E**
Small pig./ c1969/ K-2/2 KG012 . . . . **E**
Small pig (Braille)./ n.d./ K-2/2 KG012 . . . . **E**
Tales of Oliver Pig./ 1979/ K-2/1 KG649 . . . . **CE E**
Three hat day./ 1985/ P-3/2 KF609 . . . . **E**
Toads and diamonds./ 1996/ 2-3/3 KB319 . . . . **398.2**
Treeful of pigs./ Treeful of pigs./ 1979/ 1979/ P-2/4 KG013 . . . . **E**
    P-2/4 KG013
Tyrannosaurus was a beast: dinosaur poems./ c1988, 1992/
    1-5 KE017 . . . . **CE 811**
Uncle Elephant./ 1981/ K-1/1 KG014 . . . . **E**
Zoo for Mister Muster./ c1962/ P-1/5 KG015 . . . . **E**
LOBERG, MK/ Social studies readers theatre for children: scripts and script
    development./ 1991/ KA224 . . . . **PROF 372.6**
LOBOS (MUSICAL GROUP)./ ANNIE OAKLEY (Videocassette)./ 1997/
    3-6 KE479 . . . . **VCR B OAKLEY, A.**
LOCKER, T/ Between earth and sky: legends of Native American sacred
    places./ 1996/ 5-A/5 KB270 . . . . **398.2**
First Thanksgiving./ 1993/ 4-6/6 KB223 . . . . **394.264**
Ice horse./ 1993/ 2-3/6 KF391 . . . . **E**
Sky tree portfolio: science and art (Picture)./ 1995/
    2-6 KC410 . . . . **PIC 582.16**
SNOW TOWARD EVENING: A YEAR IN A RIVER VALLEY: NATURE
    POEMS./ 1995/ 2-6 KE082 . . . . **811.008**
Thirteen moons on turtle's back: a Native American year of moons./
    1992/ 2-6 KD919 . . . . **811**
Where the river begins./ 1984/ K-3/5 KG016 . . . . **E**
LOCKHART, G/ Weather companion./ 1988/ KA293 . . . . . **PROF 551.5**
LODGE, B/ Grandma went to market: a round-the-world counting rhyme./
    1996/ 1-3/5 KF232 . . . . **E**
SONGS FOR SURVIVAL: SONGS AND CHANTS FROM TRIBAL
    PEOPLES AROUND THE WORLD./ 1996/ 1-6 KD596 . . . . **789.2**
LOEHLE, R/ 11 African-American doctors. Rev. and expanded ed./ 1992/
    5-6/8 KC900 . . . . **610.69**

7 African-American scientists. Rev. and expanded ed./ 1992/
6-A/6 KB923 . . . . **509**
9 African-American inventors. Rev. and expanded ed./ 1992/
6-A/7 KC891 . . . . **609**
LOEPER, JJ/ Going to school in 1776./ 1973/ 4-6/8 KB123 . . **372.973**
Going to school in 1876./ 1984/ 3-6/7 KB124 . . . . **372.973**
LOERTSCHER, DV/ Taxonomies of the school library media program./
1988/ KA076 . . . . **PROF 027.8**
LOERTSCHER, M/ Taxonomies of the school library media program./
1988/ KA076 . . . . **PROF 027.8**
LOEWENSTEIN, B/ REAL MOTHER GOOSE BOOK OF AMERICAN
RHYMES./ 1993/ P-2 KB811 . . . . **398.8**
LOEWER, HP/ Pond water zoo: an introduction to microscopic life./ 1996/
6-A/8 KC372 . . . . **579**
LOFTS, P/ Wombat stew./ c1984/ P-2/4 KG652 . . . . **E**
LOH, M/ Tucking mommy in./ 1987/ P-2/2 KG017 . . . . **E**
LOHSTOETER, L/ Christmas surprise for Chabelita./ 1993/
1-3/2 KG206 . . . . **E**
Iguana Beach./ 1997/ P-1/2 KF575 . . . . **E**
LOMAS GARZA, C/ In my family./En mi familia./ 1996/
2-5/6 KA870 . . . . **306.85**
LOMASK, M/ Great lives: invention and technology./ 1991/
5-A/9 KC896 . . . . **609**
LOMONACO, P/ Night letters./ 1996/ K-3/3 KG018 . . . . **E**
LONDON, J/ Ali, child of the desert./ 1997/ K-3/3 KG019 . . . . . **E**
Fire race: a Karuk Coyote tale about how fire came to the people./
1993/ 3-4/4 KB611 . . . . **398.24**
Fireflies, fireflies, light my way./ 1996/ P-2/2 KG020 . . . . **E**
Froggy gets dressed./ 1992/ P-K/2 KG021 . . . . **E**
Froggy gets dressed (Big book)./ 1995/ P-K/2 KG021 . . . . . . **E**
Froggy goes to school./ 1996/ P-1/2 KG022 . . . . **E**
Froggy se viste./ 1997/ P-K/2 KG021 . . . . **E**
Gray Fox./ c1993, 1995/ K-2/5 KG023 . . . . **E**
Let's go, Froggy!/ 1994/ P-K/2 KG024 . . . . **E**
Lion who had asthma./ 1992/ P-2/2 KG025 . . . . **E**
Owl who became the moon./ 1993/ P-2/3 KG026 . . . . **E**
Puddles./ 1997/ P-1/3 KG027 . . . . **E**
Red wolf country./ 1996/ K-3/4 KG028 . . . . **E**
Thirteen moons on turtle's back: a Native American year of moons./
1992/ 2-6 KD919 . . . . **811**
Village basket weaver./ 1996/ 2-3/6 KG029 . . . . **E**
White Fang./ c1905, 1985/ 6-A/6 KH417 . . . . **FIC**
White Fang (Braille)./ n.d./ 6-A/6 KH417 . . . . **FIC**
White Fang (Sound recording cassette)./ n.d.,/ 6-A/6 KH417 . . . . **FIC**
White Fang (Talking book)./ n.d.,/ 6-A/6 KH417 . . . . **FIC**
LONG, E/ Gone fishing./ 1984/ P-1/1 KG030 . . . . **E**
LONG, JF/ Bee and the dream: a Japanese tale./ 1996/
2-3/2 KB612 . . . . **398.24**
LONG, L/ Domino addition./ 1996/ P-2/2 KB966 . . . . **513.2**
Sumemos con el domino./ 1997/ P-2/2 KB966 . . . . **513.2**
LONG, M/ Any bear can wear glasses: the spectacled bear and other
curious creatures./ 1995/ 4-6/6 KC451 . . . . **591**
LONG, S/ Alejandro's gift./ 1994/ 1-3/6 KF144 . . . . **E**
Any bear can wear glasses: the spectacled bear and other curious
creatures./ 1995/ 4-6/6 KC451 . . . . **591**
Fire race: a Karuk Coyote tale about how fire came to the people./
1993/ 3-4/4 KB611 . . . . **398.24**
Hawk Hill./ 1996/ 4-6/4 KH167 . . . . **FIC**
LONG, T/ Any bear can wear glasses: the spectacled bear and other
curious creatures./ 1995/ 4-6/6 KC451 . . . . **591**
LONGFELLOW, HW/ Hiawatha./ 1983/ P-A KD979 . . . . **CE 811**
Hiawatha (Braille)./ n.d./ P-A KD979 . . . . **CE 811**
Hiawatha (Sound recording cassette)./ n.d./ P-A KD979 . . . . . **CE 811**
Hiawatha (Spanish version)./ 1996/ P-A KD979 . . . . **CE 811**
Hiawatha (Videocassette)./ 1995/ P-A KD979 . . . . **CE 811**
Paul Revere's ride./ 1990/ 3-A KD980 . . . . **CE 811**
Paul Revere's ride (Videocassette)./ 1992/ 3-A KD980 . . . . . **CE 811**
LONSDALE, P/ SPOOKY STORIES OF THE SUPERNATURAL./ 1985/
6-A KH745 . . . . **FIC**
LOOMIS, C/ In the diner./ 1994/ P-2/2 KG031 . . . . **E**
LOPEZ, B/ Period: revised and updated with a parents' guide./ 1991/
5-6/7 KC947 . . . . **612.6**
LOPEZ ESCRIVA, A/ Abuelo y los tres osos./Abuelo and the three bears./
1997/ K-2/2 KG598 . . . . **E**
LOPEZ, L/ Birthday swap./ 1997/ K-2/2 KG032 . . . . **E**
Say hola to Spanish./ 1996/ K-2/3 KB862 . . . . **468.1**
LOPSHIRE, R/ Put me in the zoo./ c1960/ K-1/1 KG033 . . . . **E**
Put me in the zoo (Braille)./ n.d./ K-1/1 KG033 . . . . **E**
Put me in the zoo (Sound recording cassette)./ n.d./ K-1/1 KG033 . **E**
LORD, T/ Amazing bikes./ 1992/ 3-5/6 KD126 . . . . **629.227**
LOREDO, E/ Boogie Bones./ 1997/ K-2/3 KG034 . . . . **E**
LORIA, S/ Pablo Picasso./ 1995/ 4-A/12 KD490 . . . . **759.4**
LOTS OF LIMERICKS./ 1991/ 3-6 KE069 . . . . **811.008**
LOTTRIDGE, CB/ Ten small tales./ 1994/ P-1/2 KB338 . . . . **398.2**

Ticket to Canada./ 1996/ 4-A/5 KH418 . . . . **FIC**
Wings to fly./ 1997/ 5-A/5 KH419 . . . . **FIC**
LOTU, D/ Running the road to ABC./ 1996/ 1-3/4 KF951 . . . . . **E**
LOTURCO, L/ Shaker villages./ 1993/ 5-6/6 KA718 . . . . **289**
LOTZ, J/ Nova Scotia./ 1992/ 5-A/8 KE821 . . . . **971.6**
LOUCHARD, R/ Hey, Ludwig!: classical piano solos for playful times (Sound
recording cassette)./ 1993/ P-3 KD675 . . . . **SRC 789.8**
Hey, Ludwig! (Compact disc)./ 1993/ P-3 KD675 . . . . **SRC 789.8**
LOUGHEED, R/ Mustang, wild spirit of the West./ c1966, 1992/
5-6/5 KH245 . . . . **FIC**
LOUIE, A/ Yeh-Shen, a Cinderella story from China./ c1982, 1990/
3-5/6 KB750 . . . . **398.27**
LOURIE, P/ Everglades: Buffalo Tiger and the river of grass./ c1994,
1998/ 4-6/6 KE992 . . . . **975.9**
Hudson River: an adventure from the mountains to the sea./ 1992/
4-6/6 KE192 . . . . **917.47**
Yukon River: an adventure to the gold fields of the Klondike./ 1992/
4-6/6 KE210 . . . . **917.98**
LOVE, A/ Kids' summer handbook./ 1994/ 3-6/6 KD678 . . . . . **790.1**
LOW, A/ Popcorn shop./ 1993/ P-2/2 KG035 . . . . **E**
SPOOKY STORIES FOR A DARK AND STORMY NIGHT./ 1994/
2-4/4 KB695 . . . . **398.25**
LOW, J/ Mice twice./ 1980/ P-2/2 KG036 . . . . **E**
LOW, W/ Chinatown./ 1997/ K-2/3 KG037 . . . . **E**
King, the princess, and the tinker./ 1992/ 3-5/4 KH483 . . . . . **FIC**
LOWELL, S/ Little Red Cowboy Hat./ 1997/ 1-3/3 KG038 . . . . . **E**
Three little javelinas./ 1992/ K-2/4 KG039 . . . . **E**
Tortoise and the jackrabbit./ 1994/ K-2/3 KG040 . . . . **E**
Tres pequenos jabalies./The three little javelinas./ 1996/
K-2/4 KG039 . . . . **E**
LOWERY, L/ Georgia O'Keeffe./ 1996/ 2-3/2 KE482 . **B O'KEEFFE, G.**
Laurie tells./ 1994/ 3-6/4 KH420 . . . . **FIC**
Wilma Mankiller./ 1996/ 2-3/4 KE458 . . . . . **B MANKILLER, W.**
LOWRY, L/ All about Sam./ 1988/ 3-5/4 KH421 . . . . **FIC**
All about Sam (Sound recording cassette)./ n.d./ 3-5/4 KH421 . . . **FIC**
Anastasia, absolutely./ 1995/ 4-A/6 KH422 . . . . **FIC**
Anastasia again./ 1981/ 4-6/7 KH424 . . . . **FIC**
Anastasia again (Braille)./ n.d./ 4-6/7 KH424 . . . . **FIC**
Anastasia again (Sound recording cassette)./ n.d./ 4-6/7 KH424 . . . **FIC**
Anastasia ask your analyst./ 1984/ 4-6/7 KH424 . . . . **FIC**
Anastasia ask your analyst (Braille)./ n.d./ 4-6/7 KH424 . . . . . **FIC**
Anastasia ask your analyst (Sound recording cassette)./ n.d./
4-6/7 KH424 . . . . **FIC**
Anastasia at this address./ 1991/ 4-6/6 KH425 . . . . **FIC**
Anastasia at your service./ 1982/ 4-6/7 KH424 . . . . **FIC**
Anastasia at your service (Braille)./ n.d./ 4-6/7 KH424 . . . . . **FIC**
Anastasia at your service (Sound recording cassette)./ n.d./
4-6/7 KH424 . . . . **FIC**
Anastasia has the answers./ 1986/ 4-6/7 KH423 . . . . **FIC**
Anastasia has the answers (Sound recording cassette)./ n.d./
4-6/7 KH423 . . . . **FIC**
Anastasia Krupnik./ 1979/ 4-6/7 KH424 . . . . **FIC**
Anastasia Krupnik (Braille)./ n.d./ 4-6/7 KH424 . . . . **FIC**
Anastasia Krupnik (Sound recording cassette)./ n.d./ 4-6/7 KH424 . **FIC**
Anastasia Krupnik (Spanish version)./ 1995/ 4-6/7 KH424 . **FIC**
Anastasia on her own./ 1985/ 4-6/6 KH425 . . . . **FIC**
Anastasia on her own (Braille)./ n.d./ 4-6/6 KH425 . . . . . . **FIC**
Anastasia on her own (Sound recording cassette)./ n.d./
4-6/6 KH425 . . . . **FIC**
Anastasia's chosen career./ 1987/ 4-6/6 KH425 . . . . **FIC**
Attaboy, Sam!/ 1992/ 3-5/4 KH421 . . . . **FIC**
Attaboy, Sam! (Sound recording cassette)./ 1993/ 3-5/4 KH421 . . **FIC**
Giver./ 1993/ 5-A/6 KH426 . . . . **FIC**
Giver (Sound recording cassette)./ 1995/ 5-A/6 KH426 . . . . . **FIC**
Number the stars./ 1989/ 5-6/6 KH427 . . . . **FIC**
See you around, Sam!/ 1996/ 3-6/6 KH428 . . . . **FIC**
LUBIN, L/ Racso and the rats of NIMH./ 1986/ 5-6/6 KH020 . . . . . **FIC**
LUCHT, I/ Red poppy./ 1995/ 1-4/5 KC430 . . . . **583**
LUDLOW, P/ TREASURY OF STORIES FOR SEVEN YEAR OLDS./ 1992/
3-5/6 KH806 . . . . **FIC**
LUDWIG, W/ Cowboy and the black-eyed pea./ 1992/ K-2/5 KF839 . **E**
LUENN, N/ Nessa's fish./ 1990/ K-2/2 KG041 . . . . **CE E**
Nessa's fish (Sound recording cassette)./ 1993/ K-2/2 KG041 . . **CE E**
Nessa's fish (Videocassette)./ 1993/ K-2/2 KG041 . . . . **CE E**
Pesca de Nessa./ 1994/ K-2/2 KG041 . . . . **CE E**
Squish!: a wetland walk./ 1994/ P-2/3 KC342 . . . . **577.68**
LUMPKIN, S/ Big cats./ 1993/ 5-6/6 KC823 . . . . **599.75**
Small cats./ 1993/ 5-6/8 KC824 . . . . **599.75**
LUNDELL, M/ Girl named Helen Keller./ 1995/
1-2/1 KE417 . . . . **B KELLER, H.**
LUNN, J/ Story of Canada./ 1992/ 5-A/7 KE804 . . . . **971**
LURIE, A/ Heavenly zoo: legends and tales of the stars./ c1979, 1996/
5-6/8 KB710 . . . . **398.26**

LURIE, J/ Allison's story: a book about homeschooling./ 1996/
2-5/2 KD303 . . . . **649**
LUTZEIER, E/ Coldest winter./ 1991/ 6-A/7 KH429 . . . . **FIC**
LYNCH, A/ Great buildings./ 1996/ 4-6/12 KD386 . . . . **720.9**
LYNE, S/ TEN-SECOND RAINSHOWERS: POEMS BY YOUNG PEOPLE./
1996/ 3-6 KE088 . . . . **811.008**
LYNN, RN/ Fantasy literature for children and young adults: an annotated
bibliography. 4th ed./ 1994/ KA032 . . . . **PROF 016.80883**
LYNN, S/ Play with paint./ 1993/ K-2/3 KD465 . . . . **750**
Play with paper./ 1993/ K-2/3 KD441 . . . . **745.54**
LYON, GE/ Cecil's story./ 1991/ K-3/2 KG042 . . . . **E**
Come a tide./ 1990/ K-3/2 KG043 . . . . **E**
Mama is a miner./ 1994/ 2-3/3 KG044 . . . . **E**
Wordful child./ 1996/ 4-5/4 KE450 . . . . **B LYON, G. E.**
LYONS, ME/ Letters from a slave girl: the story of Harriet Jacobs./ 1992/
4-6/4 KH430 . . . . **FIC**
RAW HEAD, BLOODY BONES: AFRICAN-AMERICAN TALES OF THE
SUPERNATURAL./ 1991/ 4-6/4 KB361 . . . . **398.2**
Sorrow's kitchen: the life and folklore of Zora Neale Hurston./ 1990/
6-A/6 KE396 . . . . **B HURSTON, Z.**
Starting home: the story of Horace Pippin, painter./ 1993/
5-A/5 KE499 . . . . **B PIPPIN, H.**
LYTLE, J/ Robin Hood and his Merry Men./ 1994/ 3-5/3 KB436   **398.22**
MA, W/ Older brother, younger brother: a Korean folktale./ 1995/
3-4/6 KB320 . . . . **398.2**
MACAULAY, D/ Baaa./ 1985/ 5-A/7 KH431 . . . . **FIC**
Black and white./ 1990/ 3-A/5 KH432 . . . . **FIC**
Castle./ 1977/ A/9 KD059 . . . . **CE 623**
Cathedral: the story of its construction./ c1973/ 5-6/6 KD388 . . . **726**
Cathedral (Videocassette)./ 1986/ 6-A KD389 . . . . **VCR 726**
Mill./ 1983/ A/9 KD336 . . . . **677**
Mill (Sound recording cassette)./ n.d./ A/9 KD336 . . . . **677**
Pyramid./ 1975/ A/10 KD357 . . . . **CE 690**
Pyramid (Videocassette)./ 1988/ A/10 KD357 . . . . **CE 690**
Ship./ 1993/ 5-6/8 KH433 . . . . **FIC**
Shortcut./ 1995/ 3-A/3 KH434 . . . . **FIC**
Underground./ 1976/ A/10 KD070 . . . . **624.1**
Way things work./ 1988/ A/11 KC881 . . . . **600**
Way things work (CD-ROM)./ 1996/ 3-A KC882 . . . . **CDR 600**
Why the chicken crossed the road./ 1987/ 4-A/7 KH435 . . . . . . **FIC**
MACBRIDE, RL/ In the land of the big red apple./ 1995/
4-6/6 KH436 . . . . **FIC**
In the land of the big red apple (Sound recording cassette)./ 1997/
4-6/6 KH436 . . . . **FIC**
Little farm in the Ozarks./ 1994/ 4-6/6 KH436 . . . . **FIC**
Little house on Rocky Ridge./ 1993/ 4-6/6 KH436 . . . . **FIC**
Little town in the Ozarks./ 1996/ 4-6/6 KH436 . . . . **FIC**
On the other side of the hill./ 1995/ 4-6/6 KH436 . . . . **FIC**
MACCARONE, G/ Cars! cars! cars!/ 1995/ P-1/1 KG045 . . . . **E**
Classroom pet./ 1995/ K-1/2 KG046 . . . . **E**
Pizza party!/ 1994/ P-1/1 KG047 . . . . **E**
MACCARTHY, P/ Five sisters./ 1997/ 4-6/7 KH446 . . . . **FIC**
MACCLINTOCK, D/ Animals observed: a look at animals in art./ 1993/
4-A/7 KD372 . . . . **704.9**
MACCOMBIE, T/ Stegosaurs: the solar-powered dinosaurs./ 1992/
3-6/8 KC260 . . . . **567.9**
MACDONALD, A/ Cousin Ruth's tooth./ 1996/ K-2/2 KG048 . . . . . **E**
Little Beaver and The Echo./ 1990/ P-K/1 KG049 . . . . **E**
No more nice./ 1996/ 4-6/6 KH437 . . . . **FIC**
No more nice./ 1996/ 3-5/6 KH438 . . . . **FIC**
Rachel Fister's blister./ 1990/ K-2/2 KG050 . . . . **E**
MACDONALD, F/ Greek temple./ 1992/ 4-6/7 KE643 . . . . **938**
Medieval castle./ 1990/ 4-6/8 KE649 . . . . **940.1**
Medieval cathedral./ 1991/ 6-A/9 KD390 . . . . **726**
16th century mosque./ 1994/ 4-A/10 KD391 . . . . **726**
MACDONALD, G/ Light princess./ 1977/ 4-5/5 KH439 . . . . **FIC**
Light princess (Braille)./ n.d./ 4-5/5 KH439 . . . . **FIC**
Light princess (Sound recording cassette)./ n.d./ 4-5/5 KH439 . . . **FIC**
Light princess (Talking book)./ n.d./ 4-5/5 KH439 . . . . **FIC**
MACDONALD, K/ Anne of Green Gables cookbook./ 1986/
5-6/7 KD274 . . . . **641.5**
MACDONALD, M/ No room for Francie./ 1995/ 2-3/2 KH440 . . . . **FIC**
MACDONALD, MR/ Celebrate the world: twenty tellable folktales for
multicultural festivals./ 1994/ KA270 . . . . **PROF 398.2**
Peace tales: world folktales to talk about./ 1992/ KA271 **PROF 398.2**
Skit book: 101 skits from kids./ 1990/ 3-6 KE092 . . . . **812**
Storyteller's sourcebook: a subject, title, and motif index to folklore
collections for children./ 1982/ 4-6 KA027 . . . . . . **PROF 016.3982**
MACDONALD, RE/ Ghosts of Austwick Manor./ c1983, 1991/
4-A/5 KH441 . . . . **FIC**
MACDONALD, S/ Alphabatics./ 1986/ P-2 KG051 . . . . **E**
Alphabatics (Braille)./ n.d./ P-2 KG051 . . . . **E**
Peck slither and slide./ 1997/ P-2/1 KC452 . . . . **591**
Sea shapes./ 1994/ P-2 KB993 . . . . **516**

MACHOTKA, H/ Breathtaking noses./ 1992/ 3-5/6 KC280 . . . . . **573.2**
Terrific tails./ 1994/ 3-5/7 KC272 . . . . **571.1**
MACHT, NL/ Lou Gehrig./ 1993/ 5-A/7 KE364 . . . . . . **B GEHRIG, L.**
Muhammad Ali./ 1994/ 4-6/6 KE233 . . . . **B ALI, M.**
Roberto Clemente./ 1994/ 5-A/7 KE294 . . . . **B CLEMENTE, R.**
Roberto Clemente (Spanish version)./ 1995/
5-A/7 KE294 . . . . **B CLEMENTE, R.**
Sandra Day O'Connor./ 1992/ 4-5/8 KE481 . . . . . **B O'CONNOR, S.**
MACK, S/ 10 bears in my bed: a goodnight countdown./ 1974/
P-1/1 KG052 . . . . **E**
MACKAY, C/ One proud summer./ 1981/ A/7 KH254 . . . . **FIC**
Touching all the bases: baseball for kids of all ages./ c1994, 1996/
4-6/7 KD799 . . . . **796.357**
MACKAY, DA/ Stone-faced boy./ 1987/ 4-6/3 KH140 . . . . **FIC**
MACKAY, K/ Ontario./ 1992/ 5-A/8 KE819 . . . . **971.3**
MACKEN, W/ Flight of the doves./ 1992/ 5-A/3 KH442 . . . . **FIC**
MACKLIN, R/ Songs of nature and environment (Sound recording
cassette)./ 1978/ 1-3 KC293 . . . . **SRC 577**
MACK-WILLIAMS, K/ Food and our history./ 1995/
5-6/7 KD287 . . . . **641.59**
MACLACHLAN, P/ All the places to love./ 1994/ 1-4/5 KG053 . . . . **E**
Arthur, for the very first time./ 1980/ 4-6/7 KH443 . . . . **FIC**
Arthur, for the very first time (Sound recording cassette)./ n.d./
4-6/7 KH443 . . . . **FIC**
Mama One, Mama Two./ 1982/ 2-3/1 KG054 . . . . **E**
Sarah, plain and tall./ 1985/ 3-5/4 KH444 . . . . **CE FIC**
Sarah, plain and tall (Sound recording cassette)./ n.d./
3-5/4 KH444 . . . . **CE FIC**
Sarah, plain and tall (Talking book)./ 1986/ 3-5/4 KH444 . . . **CE FIC**
Sarah, sencilla y alta./ n.d./ 3-5/4 KH444 . . . . **CE FIC**
Skylark./ 1994/ 3-5/3 KH445 . . . . **FIC**
Three Names./ 1991/ 2-3/5 KG055 . . . . **E**
Three Names (Sound recording cassette)./ 1994/ 2-3/5 KG055 . . . . **E**
MACMAHON, J/ Deserts./ 1985/ A KC338 . . . . **577.54**
MACMILLAN, D/ Elephants: our last land giants./ 1993/
5-6/8 KC811 . . . . **599.67**
Missions of the Los Angeles Area./ 1996/ 4-6/9 KF084 . . . . . . **979.4**
MACNOW, G/ Shaquille O'Neal: star center./ 1996/
4-5/6 KE485 . . . . **B O'NEAL, S.**
MACQUITTY, M/ Desert./ 1994/ 4-6/7 KC364 . . . . **578.754**
Ocean./ 1995/ 2-6/7 KC174 . . . . **551.46**
MACY, S/ Winning ways: a photohistory of American women in sports./
1996/ 4-6/12 KD764 . . . . **796**
MADARAS, A/ What's happening to my body? Book for girls. Rev. ed./
1983/ 5-6/9 KC952 . . . . **612.6**
MADARAS, L/ What's happening to my body? Book for girls. Rev. ed./
1983/ 5-6/9 KC952 . . . . **612.6**
MADDEN, D/ Drop of blood. Rev. ed./ 1989/ K-2/2 KC936 . . . . **612.1**
Planets in our solar system. Rev. ed./ 1987/ 2-4/4 KC023 . . . . **523.4**
MADISON, A/ Drugs and you. Rev. ed./ 1990/ 5-6/7 KC999 . . . . **613.8**
MADO, M/ Animals: selected poems./ 1992/ 2-6 KE135 . . . . . **895.6**
MADRIGAL, AH/ Eagle and the rainbow: timeless tales from Mexico./
1997/ 4-5/9 KB339 . . . . **398.2**
MAESTRO, B/ All aboard overnight: a book of compound words./ 1992/
P-3/3 KB848 . . . . **428.1**
Bats: night fliers./ 1994/ 1-4/6 KC761 . . . . **599.4**
Coming to America: the story of immigration./ 1996/
1-3/8 KA921 . . . . **325**
Discovery of the Americas./ 1991/ 2-6/8 KE183 . . . . **917.04**
Discovery of the Americas: activities book./ 1992/
2-6/8 KE183 . . . . **917.04**
Discovery of the Americas (Sound recording cassette)./ 1994/
2-6/8 KE183 . . . . **917.04**
Exploration and conquest: the Americas after Columbus: 1500 - 1620./
1994/ 2-6/7 KE184 . . . . **917.04**
Ferryboat./ 1986/ P-3/2 KB144 . . . . **386**
How do apples grow?/ 1992/ K-2/4 KC418 . . . . **582.16**
More perfect union: the story of our constitution./ 1987/
4-6/8 KA974 . . . . **342.73**
Story of money./ 1993/ 3-6/5 KA950 . . . . **332.4**
Story of religion./ 1996/ 3-4/9 KA725 . . . . **291**
Story of the Statue of Liberty./ 1986/ P-3/6 KD401 . . . . **735**
Take a look at snakes./ 1992/ 3-5/6 KC640 . . . . **597.96**
Voice of the people: American democracy in action./ 1996/
4-6/8 KA915 . . . . **324.973**
Why do leaves change color?/ 1994/ P-4/2 KC400 . . . . . . **CE 581.4**
Why do leaves change color? (Kit)./ 1996/ P-4/2 KC400 . . . **CE 581.4**
MAESTRO, G/ All aboard overnight: a book of compound words./ 1992/
P-3/3 KB848 . . . . **428.1**
Bats: night fliers./ 1994/ 1-4/6 KC761 . . . . **599.4**
Discovery of the Americas./ 1991/ 2-6/8 KE183 . . . . **917.04**
Exploration and conquest: the Americas after Columbus: 1500 - 1620./
1994/ 2-6/7 KE184 . . . . **917.04**
Ferryboat./ 1986/ P-3/2 KB144 . . . . **386**

How do apples grow?/ 1992/ K-2/4 KC418 . . . . **582.16**
It figures!: fun figures of speech./ 1993/ 5-A/8 KD865 . . . . **808**
More perfect union: the story of our constitution./ 1987/
4-6/8 KA974 . . . . **342.73**
More science experiments you can eat./ 1979/ A/7 KB890 . . . . **507.8**
Our patchwork planet: the story of plate tectonics./ 1995/
A/7 KC155 . . . . **551.1**
Riddle City, USA!: a book of geography riddles./ 1994/
2-6 KD734 . . . . **793.735**
Story of money./ 1993/ 3-6/5 KA950 . . . . **332.4**
Story of religion./ 1996/ 3-4/9 KA725 . . . . **291**
Story of the Statue of Liberty./ 1986/ P-3/6 KD401 . . . . **735**
Superdupers! really funny real words./ 1989/ 3-6/6 KB850 . . . . **428.1**
Take a look at snakes./ 1992/ 3-5/6 KC640 . . . . **597.96**
Tornado alert./ 1988/ P-4/3 KC196 . . . . **551.55**
Voice of the people: American democracy in action./ 1996/
4-6/8 KA915 . . . . **324.973**
MAESTRO, M/ Riddle City, USA!: a book of geography riddles./ 1994/
2-6 KD734 . . . . **793.735**
MAGARIL, M/ Feather merchants and other tales of the fools of Chelm./
1991/ 6-A/7 KB510 . . . . **398.23**
MAGEE, D/ All aboard ABC./ 1990/ K-2/2 KD075 . . . . **625.1**
MAGUIRE, K/ Eye on the wild: a story about Ansel Adams./ 1995/
3-6/7 KE225 . . . . **B ADAMS, A.**
MAHLER, J/ Itch book./ 1990/ K-3 KF496 . . . . **E**
MAHY, M/ Five sisters./ 1997/ 4-6/7 KH446 . . . . **FIC**
Fortune branches out./ c1994, 1995/ 3-5/4 KH447 . . . . **FIC**
Good Fortunes gang./ Good Fortunes gang./ 1995/ 1993/
3-5/7 KH448 . . . . **FIC**
3-5/7 KH448 . . . . **FIC**
Great piratical rumbustification and The librarian and the robbers./
c1978, 1986/ 5-A/7 KH449 . . . . **FIC**
Great piratical rumbustification and The librarian and the robbers (Sound
recording cassette)./ n.d., / 5-A/7 KH449 . . . . **FIC**
Great white man-eating shark: a cautionary tale./ 1989/
K-4/5 KG056 . . . . **CE E**
Great white man-eating shark: a cautionary tale (Kit)./ 1992/
K-4/5 KG056 . . . . **CE E**
Great white man-eating shark: a cautionary tale (Videocassette)./ 1991/
K-4/5 KG056 . . . . **CE E**
Greatest show off earth./ 1994/ 4-A/7 KH450 . . . . **CE FIC**
Greatest show off earth (Sound recording cassette)./ 1997/
4-A/7 KH450 . . . . **CE FIC**
Greatest show off earth (Talking book)./ 1995/ 4-A/7 KH450 **CE FIC**
Haunting./ 1982/ 5-A/6 KH451 . . . . **CE FIC**
Haunting (Braille)./ n.d./ 5-A/6 KH451 . . . . **CE FIC**
Haunting of Barney Palmer (Videocassette)./ c1986/
5-A/6 KH451 . . . . **CE FIC**
Haunting (Sound recording cassette)./ n.d./ 5-A/6 KH451 . . . **CE FIC**
Horrible story and others (Talking book)./ 1992/ 3-A KH452 . . **TB FIC**
My mysterious world./ 1995/ 2-4/6 KE454 . . . . **B MAHY, M.**
Rattlebang picnic./ 1994/ K-2/5 KG057 . . . . **E**
Rattlebang picnic (Sound recording cassette)./ 1997/ K-2/5 KG057 . **E**
Tall story and other tales./ 1992/ 4-6/4 KH453 . . . . **FIC**
Tingleberries, tuckertubs and telephones: a tale of love and ice-cream./
1996/ 3-6/5 KH454 . . . . **FIC**
Underrunners./ 1992/ 6-A/6 KH455 . . . . **FIC**
MAI, VD/ Sky legends of Vietnam./ 1993/ 3-5/7 KB717 . . . . **398.26**
MAIONE, HH/ Onion sundaes./ 1994/ 2-3/2 KG819 . . . . **FIC**
MAIR, J/ Ocean of story: fairy tales from India./ 1996/
4-6/5 KB353 . . . . **398.2**
MAITLAND, A/ Ghost of Thomas Kempe./ c1973/ 4-6/7 KH415 . . . **FIC**
MAJOR, JS/ Silk Route: 7,000 miles of history./ c1995, 1996/
4-6/6 KE701 . . . . **950**
MAKI, C/ Snowflakes, sugar, and salt: crystals up close./ 1993/
P-2/5 KC143 . . . . **548**
MALAND, N/ Big blue whale./ 1997/ K-4/3 KC767 . . . . **599.5**
MALCOLM, AH/ Land and people of Canada./ 1991/
A/10 KE805 . . . . **971**
MALICK, N/ Sitti and the cats: a tale of friendship./ 1993/
3-4/7 KB257 . . . . **398.2**
MALINOWSKI, S/ NATIVE NORTH AMERICAN BIOGRAPHY./ 1996/
6-A KA481 . . . . **REF 970.1**
MALLAN, K/ Children as storytellers./ 1992/ KA341 . . . . . **PROF 808.5**
MALONE, NL/ Earrings!/ 1990/ 1-3/2 KG661 . . . . **E**
King of the playground./ 1991/ K-3/2 KG167 . . . . **E**
MALONE, P/ Adventures of Odysseus./ 1997/ 3-6/5 KE125 . . . . **883**
MANLEY, M/ Martin Manley's basketball heaven./ 1987-/
4-A KD778 . . . . **796.323**
MANN, E/ Brooklyn Bridge./ 1996/ 5-6/5 KD068 . . . . **624**
Great Pyramid./ 1991/ 4-6/6 KE635 . . . . **932**
MANN, P/ Frog Princess?/ 1995/ 1-3/2 KG058 . . . . **E**
MANNING, G/ WHOLE LANGUAGE: BELIEFS AND PRACTICES, K-8./
1989/ KA233 . . . . **PROF 372.6**

MANNING, M/ Think of a beaver./ 1993/ K-2/4 KC755 . . . . . **599.37**
WHOLE LANGUAGE: BELIEFS AND PRACTICES, K-8./ 1989/
KA233 . . . . **PROF 372.6**
MANSON, A/ Dog came, too: a true story./ 1993/
1-4/6 KE185 . . . . **917.104**
MANSON, C/ Tree in the wood: an old nursery song./ 1993/
P-1/2 KB801 . . . . **398.8**
MANTELL, P/ Kids garden!: the anytime, anyplace guide to sowing and
growing fun./ 1996/ 3-5/6 KD167 . . . . **635**
MANTINBAND, G/ Blabbermouths: adapted from a German folktale./
1992/ 3-4/4 KB751 . . . . **398.27**
MANUSHKIN, F/ Matzah that Papa brought home./ 1995/
1-3/2 KG059 . . . . **E**
Peeping and sleeping./ 1994/ P-2/2 KG060 . . . . **E**
Starlight and candles: the joys of the Sabbath./ 1995/ 1-3/2 KG061 **E**
MARCELLINO, F/ Puss in boots./ 1990/ 3-4/4 KB633 . . . . **398.24**
Story of Little Babaji./ 1996/ K-2/2 KF195 . . . . **E**
Wainscott weasel./ 1993/ 4-6/5 KH691 . . . . **FIC**
MARCHESI, S/ Night before Christmas: told in sign language: an
adaptation of the original poem "A visit from St. Nicholas" by Clement
C. Moore./ 1994/ K-6 KD917 . . . . **811**
Story of Junipero Serra: brave adventurer./ 1996/
4-6/7 KE536 . . . . **B SERRA, J.**
MARGESON, SM/ Viking./ 1994/ 4-6/7 KE693 . . . . **948**
MARGOLIES, BA/ Kanu of Kathmandu: a journey in Nepal./ 1992/
3-5/6 KE713 . . . . **954.96**
Rehema's journey: a visit in Tanzania./ c1990/ 3-6/4 KE180 . . **916.78**
MARGOLIN, M/ NATIVE WAYS: CALIFORNIA INDIAN STORIES AND
MEMORIES./ 1995/ 5-A/6 KE800 . . . . **970.494**
MARINO, J/ Day that Elvis came to town./ 1993/ 6-A/6 KH456 . . . **FIC**
MARITZ, N/ One sun rises: an African wildlife counting book./ 1994/
P-2/3 KB959 . . . . **513.2**
Somewhere in Africa./ 1992/ K-2/4 KG129 . . . . **E**
MARK, J/ Tale of Tobias./ 1996/ 1-3/2 KA693 . . . . **229**
MARKHAM, L/ Colombia: the gateway to South America./ 1997/
4-6/7 KF111 . . . . **986.1**
MARKHAM, MM/ St. Patrick's Day shamrock mystery./ 1995/
2-4/3 KH457 . . . . **FIC**
MARKLE, S/ Creepy spooky science./ 1996/ 3-6/8 KB894 . . . . . **507.8**
Digging deeper: investigations into rocks, shocks, quakes, and other
earthly/ 1987/ 4-6/9 KC148 . . . . **550**
Icky squishy science./ 1996/ 4-8/6 KB895 . . . . **507.8**
Math mini-mysteries./ 1993/ 3-6/7 KB928 . . . . **510**
Measuring up!: experiments, puzzles, and games exploring measurement./
1995/ 5-6/6 KC086 . . . . **530.8**
Outside and inside birds./ 1994/ 4-6/5 KC655 . . . . **598**
Outside and inside sharks./ 1996/ 4-6/5 KC594 . . . . **597.3**
Outside and inside snakes./ 1995/ 4-6/4 KC641 . . . . **597.96**
Outside and inside spiders./ 1994/ 5-6/4 KC528 . . . . **595.4**
Outside and inside trees./ 1993/ 3-6/6 KC419 . . . . **582.16**
Outside and inside you./ 1991/ 4-6/6 KC921 . . . . **612**
Pioneering ocean depths./ 1995/ 4-A/8 KC175 . . . . **551.46**
Power up: experiments, puzzles, and games exploring electricity./ 1989/
3-6/7 KC133 . . . . **537**
Rainy day./ 1993/ P-2/6 KC214 . . . . **551.57**
Science to the rescue./ 1994/ 6-A/8 KB896 . . . . **507.8**
MARKS, A/ RING-A-RING O' ROSES AND A DING, DONG, BELL: A
BOOK OF NURSERY RHYMES./ 1991/ P-K/2 KB813 . . . . **398.8**
MARKS, DF/ Glues, brews, and goos: recipes and formulas for almost any
classroom project./ 1996/ KA216 . . . . **PROF 372.5**
MARQUARDT, M/ Wilbur and Orville and the flying machine./ 1989/
1-3/1 KD096 . . . . **629.13**
MARRIN, A/ Aztecs and Spaniards: Cortes and the conquest of Mexico./
1986/ 5-6/7 KE833 . . . . **972**
Aztecs and Spaniards: Cortes and the conquest of Mexico (Braille)./ n.d./
5-6/7 KE833 . . . . **972**
Inca and Spaniard: Pizarro and the conquest of Peru./ 1989/
A/8 KF109 . . . . **985**
Spanish-American War./ 1991/ A/7 KE915 . . . . **973.8**
Struggle for a continent: the French and Indian wars 1690-1760./ 1987/
5-6/8 KE872 . . . . **973.2**
Victory in the Pacific./ 1983/ 4-6/7 KE671 . . . . **940.54**
War for independence: the story of the American Revolution./ 1988/
5-6/9 KE882 . . . . **973.3**
Yanks are coming: the United States in the First World War./ 1986/
A/7 KE652 . . . . **940.3**
MARSALIS, B/ David and Goliath (Videocassette)./ 1992/
2-4 KA686 . . . . **VCR 222**
MARSCHALL, K/ On board the Titanic./ 1996/ 4-A/6 KB027 . . . **363.12**
MARSHALL, E/ Four on the shore./ 1985/ K-3/1 KG066 . . . . . **CE E**
Fox all week./ c1984/ K-2/1 KG064 . . . . **CE E**
Fox and his friends./ 1994/ K-2/1 KG064 . . . . **CE E**
Fox and his friends (Kit)./ 1985/ K-2/1 KG064 . . . . **CE E**
Fox at school (Kit)./ 1983/ K-2/1 KG064 . . . . **CE E**

Fox in love./ 1994/ K-2/1 KG064 . . . . **CE E**
Fox in love (Kit)./ 1982/ K-2/1 KG064 . . . . **CE E**
Fox on stage./ 1993/ K-2/1 KG064 . . . . **CE E**
Fox on wheels (Kit)./ 1983/ K-2/1 KG064 . . . . **CE E**
Pandilla en la orilla./ n.d./ K-3/1 KG066 . . . . **CE E**
Space case./ 1980/ P-2/4 KG065 . . . . **E**
Three by the sea./ 1981/ K-3/1 KG066 . . . . **CE E**
Three by the sea (Braille)./ n.d./ K-3/1 KG066 . . . . **CE E**
Three by the sea (Kit)./ 1984/ K-3/1 KG066 . . . . **CE E**
Three by the sea (Sound recording cassette)./ n.d./
    K-3/1 KG066 . . . . **CE E**
Three up a tree./ 1986/ K-3/1 KG066 . . . . **CE E**
Tres en un arbol./ n.d./ K-3/1 KG066 . . . . **CE E**
Zorro y sus amigos./ 1996/ K-2/1 KG064 . . . . **CE E**
MARSHALL, EG/ INDEPENDENCE: BIRTH OF A FREE NATION
    (Videocassette)./ 1976/ A KE890 . . . . **VCR 973.4**
MARSHALL, J/ Fox and his friends./ 1994/ K-2/1 KG064 . . . **CE E**
Fox be nimble./ 1990,/ K-3/2 KG067 . . . . **E**
Fox on the job./ c1988, 1990/ K-3/2 KG067 . . . . **E**
Fox outfoxed./ 1992,/ K-2/2 KG067 . . . . **E**
Frog prince./ c1974, 1993/ P-3/2 KB376 . . . . **398.2**
George and Martha./ c1972/ P-2/3 KG068 . . . . **CE E**
George and Martha back in town./ 1984/ P-2/3 KG068 . . . **CE E**
George and Martha encore./ 1973/ P-2/3 KG068 . . . . **CE E**
George and Martha (Kit)./ 1987/ P-2/3 KG068 . . . . **CE E**
George and Martha one fine day./ 1978/ P-2/3 KG068 . . . **CE E**
George and Martha rise and shine./ 1976/ P-2/3 KG068 . . **CE E**
George and Martha 'round and 'round./ 1988/ P-2/3 KG068 . **CE E**
Hansel and Gretel./ 1990/ 2-4/4 KB340 . . . . **398.2**
Miss Nelson is missing./ 1977/ 1-3/3 KF151 . . . . **CE E**
OLD MOTHER HUBBARD AND HER WONDERFUL DOG./ 1991/
    P-K KB809 . . . . **398.8**
Rats on the range and other stories./ 1993/ 1-4/2 KH458 . . . . **FIC**
Rats on the roof and other stories./ 1991/ 1-4/2 KH459 . . . . **FIC**
Rats on the roof and other stories (Sound recording cassette)./ 1993/
    1-4/2 KH459 . . . . **FIC**
Space case./ 1980/ P-2/4 KG065 . . . . **E**
Stupids step out./ 1974/ K-2/5 KF152 . . . . **E**
Three by the sea./ 1981/ K-3/1 KG066 . . . . **CE E**
Three little pigs./ 1989/ K-2/2 KB613 . . . . **CE 398.24**
Three little pigs (Videocassette)./ 1992/ K-2/2 KB613 . . . . **CE 398.24**
MARSTALL, B/ Extraordinary life: the story of a monarch butterfly./ 1997/
    5-6/6 KC564 . . . . **595.78**
Fire in the forest: a cycle of growth and renewal./ 1995/
    A/8 KC305 . . . . **577.2**
Lady and the spider./ 1986/ 1-3/2 KG114 . . . . **E**
MARSTON, HI/ Big rigs. Rev. and updated ed./ 1993/
    K-5/4 KD119 . . . . **629.224**
MARTCHENKO, M/ Matthew and the midnight pilot./ 1997/
    1-2/3 KG156 . . . . **E**
MARTELL, H/ Kingfisher book of the ancient world: from the Ice Age to the
    fall of Rome./ 1995/ 4-6/10 KE621 . . . . **930**
MARTIN, AM/ Rachel Parker, kindergarten show-off./ 1992/
    K-2/1 KG069 . . . . **E**
MARTIN, AT/ Famous seaweed soup./ 1993/ P-2/4 KG070 . . . **E**
MARTIN, JR., B/ Barn dance!/ 1986/ P-3/3 KG071 . . . . **E**
Brown bear, brown bear, what do you see?/ 1992/ P-K/1 KG072 . . **E**
Chicka chicka boom boom./ 1989/ P-1/2 KG073 . . . . **E**
Chicka chicka boom boom (Kit)./ 1991/ P-1 KG074 . . . . **KIT E**
Ghost-eye tree./ 1985/ K-3/2 KG075 . . . . **E**
Here are my hands./ 1987/ P-1/2 KG076 . . . . **E**
Listen to the rain./ 1988/ P-2 KG077 . . . . **E**
Polar bear, polar bear, what do you hear?/ 1991/ P-K/1 KG072 . . **E**
Polar bear, polar bear, what do you hear? (Big book)./ 1992/
    P-K/1 KG072 . . . . **E**
White Dynamite and Curly Kidd./ c1986, 1989/ K-3/2 KG078 . . **E**
MARTIN, F/ Jig, Fig, and Mrs. Pig./ 1995/ P-2/3 KB584 . . . **398.24**
MARTIN, G/ ITALIAN FOLKTALES./ 1980/ 5-6 KA415 . . . **REF 398.23**
MARTIN, J/ Living fossils: animals that have withstood the test of time./
    1997/ 4-A/9 KC453 . . . . **591**
MARTIN, JB/ Grandmother Bryant's pocket./ 1996/ 1-4/3 KG079 . . . **E**
MARTIN, JH/ Day in the life of a carpenter./ 1985/
    4-6/7 KD362 . . . . **CE 694**
MARTIN, JR., B/ CHICKA CHICKA BOOM BOOM (CD-ROM)./ 1996/
    P-2 KF382 . . . . **CDR E**
MARTIN, R/ Boy who lived with the seals./ 1993/ 2-4/6 KB614 . . **398.24**
Foolish rabbit's big mistake./ 1985/ 3-4/4 KA760 . . . . **294.3**
Ghostly tales of Japan (Sound recording cassette)./ 1989/
    3-6 KB689 . . . . **SRC 398.25**
Mysterious tales of Japan./ 1996/ 3-5/3 KB690 . . . . **398.25**
Rafe Martin tells his children's books (Talking book)./ 1994/
    K-4 KB341 . . . . **TB 398.2**
Rough-face girl./ 1992/ 3-5/4 KB752 . . . . **398.27**
Will's mammoth./ 1989/ 1-3/2 KG080 . . . . **CE E**

Will's mammoth (Videocassette)./ 1991/ 1-3/2 KG080 . . . . **CE E**
MARTIN, SC/ Comic adventures of Old Mother Hubbard and her dog./
    1981/ P-2 KB802 . . . . **398.8**
MARTINET, J/ Year you were born, 1981./ 1994/
    4-6/7 KE922 . . . . **973.927**
Year you were born, 1982./ 1994/ 4-6/7 KE922 . . . . **973.927**
Year you were born, 1983./ 1992/ 4-6/7 KE922 . . . . **973.927**
Year you were born, 1984./ 1992/ 4-6/7 KE922 . . . . **973.927**
Year you were born, 1985./ 1992/ 4-6/7 KE922 . . . . **973.927**
Year you were born, 1986./ 1993/ 4-6/7 KE922 . . . . **973.927**
Year you were born, 1987./ 1993/ 4-6/7 KE922 . . . . **973.927**
Year you were born, 1988./ 1995/ 4-6/7 KE922 . . . . **973.927**
Year you were born, 1989./ 1996/ 4-6/7 KE922 . . . . **973.927**
MARTINEZ, AC/ Woman who outshone the sun: the legend of Lucia
    Zenteno./La mujer que brillaba aun mas que el sol: la leyenda de Lucia
    Zenteno./ 1991/ 3-5/5 KB403 . . . . **398.21**
MARTINEZ, E/ Too many tamales./ 1993/ K-3/3 KG530 . . . . **E**
MARTINEZ, JC/ Dragons and prehistoric monsters./ 1996/
    3-6/3 KD447 . . . . **745.592**
Drawing dinosaurs./ 1996/ 5-A/3 KD418 . . . . **743**
Modeling dinosaurs./ 1996/ 3-6/3 KD448 . . . . **745.592**
Monsters and extraterrestrials./ 1996/ 3-6/3 KD449 . . . . . **745.592**
Painting and coloring dinosaurs./ 1996/ 5-A/3 KD419 . . . . . **743**
MARTINEZ, MG/ BOOK TALK AND BEYOND: CHILDREN AND
    TEACHERS RESPOND TO LITERATURE./ 1995/
    KA235 . . . . **PROF 372.64**
MARTINEZ, S/ Weapons and warfare: from the stone age to the space
    age./ 1996/ 4-6/8 KA983 . . . . **355.02**
MARTINO, T/ Pizza!/ 1989/ 3-4/2 KD292 . . . . **641.8**
MARTINS, G/ Spin a soft black song. Rev. ed./ c1971, 1985/
    1-4 KD946 . . . . **811**
MARTORELL, A/ Song of el coqui and other tales of Puerto Rico./ 1995/
    3-4/3 KB621 . . . . **398.24**
MARUKI, T/ Hiroshima no pika./ 1982/ 4-6/5 KE672 . . . . **940.54**
MARVELOUS MATH: A BOOK OF POEMS./ 1997/
    1-4 KE071 . . . . **811.008**
MARX, T/ Echoes of World War II./ 1994/ A/7 KE660 . . . . . . **940.53**
MARZOLLO, J/ Happy Birthday, Martin Luther King./ 1993/
    1-5/5 KE422 . . . . **B KING, M.L.**
I spy Christmas: a book of picture riddles./ 1992/ P-2 KD715 . **793.73**
I spy school days: a book of picture riddles./ 1995/
    K-3/3 KD717 . . . . **793.73**
I'm a seed./ 1996/ K-2/1 KG080 . . . . **E**
I'm tyrannosaurus!: a book of dinosaur rhymes./ 1993/
    K-2/3 KD981 . . . . **811**
Pretend you're a cat./ 1990/ P-1 KG082 . . . . **E**
MASON, C/ Wild fox: a true story./ 1993/ 4-5/5 KC843 . . . **599.775**
MASSEY, C/ My first Kwanzaa book./ 1992/ 2-4/2 KB206 . . **394.261**
MASTERS, SR/ Libby Bloom./ 1995/ 3-5/6 KH460 . . . . **FIC**
MASUREL, C/ No, no, Titus!/ 1997/ P-1/2 KG083 . . . . **E**
MATH FOR THE VERY YOUNG: A HANDBOOK OF ACTIVITIES FOR
    PARENTS AND TEACHERS./ 1995/ KA254 . . . . . **PROF 372.7**
MATHERS, D/ Brain./ 1992/ 5-6/6 KC966 . . . . **612.8**
Ears./ 1992/ 5-6/6 KC967 . . . . **612.8**
MATHERS, P/ Borreguita and the coyote: a tale from Ayutla, Mexico./
    1991/ P-2/4 KB514 . . . . **398.24**
Grandmother Bryant's pocket./ 1996/ 1-4/3 KG079 . . . . **E**
Tell me a season./ 1997/ P-1/1 KG500 . . . . **E**
MATHEWS, J/ Oh, how waffle!: riddles you can eat./ 1993/
    2-6 KD735 . . . . **793.735**
MATHEWS, SS/ Sad Night: the story of an Aztec victory and a Spanish
    loss./ 1994/ 4-6/6 KE834 . . . . **972**
MATHIS, MB/ Night gliders./ 1996/ P-2/2 KG367 . . . . **E**
What a wonderful day to be a cow./ 1995/ K-2/3 KF963 . . . . . **E**
MATHIS, SB/ Hundred penny box./ 1975/ 4-6/4 KH461 . . . . **CE FIC**
Hundred penny box (Sound recording cassette)./ n.d./
    4-6/4 KH461 . . . . **CE FIC**
Hundred penny box (Talking book)./ 1977/ 4-6/4 KH461 . . . **CE FIC**
Hundred penny box (Videocassette)./ 1979/ 4-6/4 KH461 . . . **CE FIC**
MATSEN, B/ Raptors, fossils, fins, and fangs: a prehistoric creature
    feature./ 1996/ 3-6/6 KC239 . . . . **560**
MATSICK, A/ ...If you lived at the time of the Civil War./ 1994/
    3-5/6 KE908 . . . . **973.7**
Mirror magic./ 1991/ 3-5/6 KC114 . . . . **535**
MATTHEWS, D/ Arctic foxes./ 1995/ 4-6/4 KC847 . . . . . . **599.776**
Arctic summer./ 1993/ 5-6/3 KC732 . . . . **599.17**
Harp seal pups./ 1997/ 4-6/3 KC870 . . . . **599.79**
MATTHEWS, M/ Magid fasts for Ramadan./ 1996/ 4-6/4 KH462 . . **FIC**
MATTHEWS, R/ Explorer./ 1991/ 4-6/8 KE152 . . . . **910**
Record breakers of the air./ 1990/ 2-4/6 KA590 . . . . **031.02**
Record breakers of the land./ 1990/ 2-4/6 KA590 . . . . . . **031.02**
Record breakers of the sea./ 1990/ 2-4/6 KA590 . . . . **031.02**
MAURER, R/ Rocket!: how a toy launched the space age./ 1995/
    5-6/10 KD047 . . . . **621.43**

MAVOR, S/
You and me: poems of friendship./ You and me: poems of friendship./
1997/ 1997/ K-2 KE072 . . . . **811.008**
K-2 KE072 . . . . **811.008**
MAX, J/ SPIDER SPINS A STORY: FOURTEEN LEGENDS FROM NATIVE
AMERICA./ 1997/ 2-5/6 KB371 . . . . **398.2**
MAXFIELD PARRISH: A TREASURY OF ART AND CHILDREN'S
LITERATURE./ 1995/ K-6 KD413 . . . . **741.6**
MAYER, B/ Brer Rabbit and Boss Lion (Kit)./ 1996/
3-A KB599 . . . . **KIT 398.24**
MAYER, EL/ Let's sing!: John Langstaff sings with children, ages 3-7
(Videocassette)./ 1997/ KA314 . . . . **VCR PROF 780**
Making music with children, ages 3-7 (Videocassette)./ 1995/
KA315 . . . . **VCR PROF 780**
MAYER, M/ Baba Yaga and Vasilisa the Brave./ 1994/
3-5/5 KB466 . . . . **398.22**
Boy, a dog and a frog./ c1967/ P-1 KG084 . . . . **CE E**
Boy, a dog and a frog (Videocassette)./ 1981/ P-1 KG084 . **CE E**
Frog goes to dinner./ 1974/ P-1 KG084 . . . . **CE E**
Frog on his own./ 1973/ P-1 KG084 . . . . **CE E**
Frog where are you?/ 1969/ P-1 KG084 . . . . **CE E**
JUST GRANDMA AND ME (CD-ROM)./ 1992/ P-2 KF863 . . . **CDR E**
MERCER MAYER'S LITTLE MONSTER AT SCHOOL. School ed. (CD-
ROM)./ 1994/ K-3 KG130 . . . . **CDR E**
One frog too many./ 1975/ P-1 KG084 . . . . **CE E**
There's an alligator under my bed./ 1987/ P-2/2 KG085 . . **E**
Turandot./ 1995/ 3-5/5 KB342 . . . . **398.2**
MAYERS, FC/ FOLK ART COUNTING BOOK./ 1992/
P-3/1 KD420 . . . . **745**
MAYNARD, C/ Jobs people do./ 1997/ P-1/4 KA942 . . . . . . **331.7**
MAYNARD, T/ Rhino comes to America./ 1993/ 5-6/7 KC802 . **599.66**
Saving endangered mammals: a field guide to some of the earth's rarest
animals (Sound recording cassette)./ Saving endangered mammals: a
field guide to some of the earth's rarest animals./ 1995/ 1992/
5-6/8 KC489 . . . . **591.68**
5-6/8 KC489 . . . . **591.68**
MAYO, E/ SMITHSONIAN BOOK OF THE FIRST LADIES: THEIR LIVES,
TIMES, AND ISSUES./ 1996/ 6-A/9 KE866 . . . . **973**
MAYO FOUNDATION FOR MEDICAL EDUCATION AND RESEARCH/
WHAT IS A BELLYBUTTON?: FUN AND INTERACTIVE QUESTIONS
AND ANSWERS ABOUT THE HUMAN BODY (CD-ROM)./ 1994/
2-6 KC930 . . . . **CDR 612**
MAYO, M/ Magical tales from many lands./ 1993/ 4-5/6 KB343 **398.2**
Tortoise's flying lesson./ 1995/ P-2/3 KB615 . . . . **398.24**
MAYO, T/ Illustrated rules of in-line hockey./ 1996/
3-6/6 KD772 . . . . **796.21**
MAZE, S/ I want to be... a veterinarian./ 1997/ 5-6/9 KD195 . **636.089**
I want to be... an astronaut./ 1997/ 5-6/9 KD137 . . . . **629.45**
MAZER, A/ Accidental witch./ 1995/ 3-5/4 KH463 . . . . **FIC**
MAZER, H/ Island keeper./ 1981/ A/6 KH464 . . . . **FIC**
Last mission./ c1979, 1986/ A/6 KH465 . . . . **FIC**
MAZZOLA, F/ Crayon counting book./ 1996/ P-1/3 KB982 . . . **513.2**
MAZZOLA, F/ Counting is for the birds./ 1997/ K-3/3 KB968 . . **513.2**
MCCAFFREY, A/ Dragondrums./ 1980,/ 6-A/6 KH466 . . . . . **FIC**
Dragondrums (Braille)./ n.d.,/ 6-A/6 KH466 . . . . **FIC**
Dragondrums (Sound recording cassette)./ n.d.,/ 6-A/6 KH466 . . . **FIC**
Dragonsinger./ 1977,/ 6-A/6 KH466 . . . . **FIC**
Dragonsinger (Braille)./ n.d.,/ 6-A/6 KH466 . . . . **FIC**
Dragonsinger (Sound recording cassette)./ n.d.,/ 6-A/6 KH466 . . **FIC**
Dragonsong./ c1976, 1986/ 6-A/6 KH466 . . . . **FIC**
MCCALL, FX/ Unraveling fibers./ 1995/ 4-6/4 KD335 . . . . . . **677**
MCCALL, MR/ EUREKA!/ 1995/ 4-7 KA451 . . . . **REF 608**
WOMEN'S ALMANAC./ 1997/ 5-A KA397 . . . . **REF 305.4**
MCCARTHY, RF/ Grandfather Cherry-Blossom./ 1993/
2-3/3 KB753 . . . . **398.27**
Inch-high samurai./ 1993/ 3-4/4 KB754 . . . . **398.27**
Moon princess./ 1993/ 3-4/4 KB404 . . . . **398.21**
MCCARTY, P/ Frozen man./ 1994/ 4-6/7 KE638 . . . . **937**
MCCAUGHREAN, G/ Golden hoard: myths and legends of the world./
1996/ 2-5/7 KB344 . . . . **398.2**
Greek myths./ 1993/ 4-6/6 KA748 . . . . **292**
Random House book of stories from the ballet./ 1994/
3-6/6 KD696 . . . . **792.8**
Silver treasure: myths and legends of the world./ 1996/
K-6/6 KB345 . . . . **398.2**
MCCLINTOCK, B/ Fantastic drawings of Danielle./ 1996/
3-5/4 KH467 . . . . **FIC**
WHITE CAT (Videocassette)./ 1997/ K-2 KB382 . . . . **VCR 398.2**
MCCLINTOCK, M/ Stop that ball./ c1959, 1987/ K-2/1 KG086 . . . . **E**
MCCLOSKEY, R/ Abran paso a los patitos./ 1996/ P-1/4 KG089 . **CE E**
Blueberries for Sal./ c1948/ P-2/7 KG087 . . . . **CE E**
Blueberries for Sal (Braille)./ n.d./ P-2/7 KG087 . . . . . . **CE E**
Blueberries for Sal (Kit)./ 1993/ P-2/7 KG087 . . . . **CE E**

Blueberries for Sal (Sound recording cassette)./ n.d./
P-2/7 KG087 . . . . **CE E**
Blueberries for Sal (Videocassette)./ n.d./ P-2/7 KG087 . . . . **CE E**
Burt Dow, deep-water man: a tale of the sea in the classic tradition./
c1963/ P-A/6 KH468 . . . . **CE FIC**
Burt Dow, deep-water man: a tale of the sea in the classic tradition (Kit)./
1990/ P-A/6 KH468 . . . . **CE FIC**
Burt Dow, deep-water man: a tale of the sea in the classic tradition
(Videocassette)./ 1990/ P-A/6 KH468 . . . . **CE FIC**
Centerburg tales./ 1951/ 3-6/5 KH470 . . . . **CE FIC**
Centerburg tales (Braille)./ n.d./ 3-6/5 KH470 . . . . . . **CE FIC**
Doughnuts (Videocassette)./ 1984/ 2-6 KH469 . . . . . . **VCR FIC**
Henry Reed's baby-sitting service./ c1966/ 4-6/6 KH638 . . . . **FIC**
Homer Price./ c1943/ 3-6/5 KH470 . . . . **CE FIC**
Homer Price (Kit)./ 1973/ 3-6/5 KH470 . . . . **CE FIC**
Homer Price (Sound recording cassette)./ n.d./ 3-6/5 KH470 . **CE FIC**
Homer Price stories (Talking book)./ n.d./ 3-6 KH471 . . . . **TB FIC**
Homer Price (Talking book)./ n.d./ 3-6/5 KH470 . . . . . . **CE FIC**
Journey cake, ho./ c1953, 1989/ P-3/5 KB776 . . . . **398.27**
Lentil./ c1940/ 1-3/6 KG088 . . . . **CE E**
Lentil (Braille)./ n.d./ 1-3/6 KG088 . . . . **CE E**
Lentil (Talking book)./ n.d./ 1-3/6 KG088 . . . . **CE E**
Lentil (Videocassette)./ 1965/ 1-3/6 KG088 . . . . **CE E**
Make way for ducklings./ c1941, 1963/ P-1/4 KG089 . . . . **CE E**
Make way for ducklings (Braille)./ n.d.,/ P-1/4 KG089 . . . . **CE E**
Make way for ducklings (Kit)./ 1975,/ P-1/4 KG089 . . . . . **CE E**
Make way for ducklings (Sound recording cassette)./ 1997,/
P-1/4 KG089 . . . . **CE E**
Make way for ducklings (Talking book)./ n.d.,/ P-1/4 KG089 . . . **CE E**
Make way for ducklings (Videocassette)./ 1985,/ P-1/4 KG089 . **CE E**
One morning in Maine./ c1952, 1962/ 1-3/6 KG090 . . . . . **CE E**
One morning in Maine (Braille)./ n.d.,/ 1-3/6 KG090 . . . . . **E**
Time of wonder./ c1957, 1962/ P-A/6 KG091 . . . . **CE E**
Time of wonder (Braille)./ n.d.,/ P-A/6 KG091 . . . . **CE E**
Time of wonder (Videocassette)./ n.d./ P-A/6 KG091 . . . . . **CE E**
MCCLOSKEY-PADGETT, P/ REAL MOTHER GOOSE BOOK OF
AMERICAN RHYMES./ 1993/ P-2 KB811 . . . . **398.8**
MCCLUNG, RM/ Hugh Glass, mountain man./ 1993/ 6-A/7 KH472 . **FIC**
Hugh Glass, mountain man (Sound recording cassette)./ 1994/
6-A/7 KH472 . . . . **FIC**
Old Bet and the start of the American circus./ 1993/
4-6/6 KD682 . . . . **791.3**
MCCONNAUGHEY, BH/ Pacific coast./ 1985/ A KC296 . . . . . **577**
MCCONNAUGHEY, E/ Pacific coast./ 1985/ A KC296 . . . . . **577**
MCCORD, KG/ Don't be afraid, Amanda./ 1992/ 2-4/4 KH504 . . . **FIC**
MCCORMICK, DJ/ Paul Bunyan swings his axe./ c1936, 1962/
4-6/6 KB467 . . . . **398.22**
Paul Bunyan swings his axe (Braille)./ n.d.,/ 4-6/6 KB467 . . . . **398.22**
Tall timber tales: more Paul Bunyan stories./ c1939/
4-6/6 KB468 . . . . **398.22**
MCCOY, BF/ Believers in America: poems about Americans of Asian and
Pacific islander descent./ 1994/ 3-6 KD955 . . . . **811**
MCCRAE, J/ In Flanders Fields: the story of the poem by John McCrae./
1995/ 4-6/7 KD947 . . . . **811**
MCCREARY, J/ Round and round the money goes: what money is and how
we use it./ 1993/ 2-4/2 KA948 . . . . **332.4**
MCCUE, L/ Puppy who wanted a boy./ c1958, 1986/ 1-3/2 KG603 . **E**
MCCULLOUGH-BRABSON, E/ Roots and branches: a legacy of
multicultural music for children./ 1994/ KA320 . . . . **BA PROF 789.3**
MCCULLY, EA/ Annie flies the birthday bike./ 1993/ K-2/2 KF495 . . . **E**
Ballot box battle./ 1996/ 1-3/2 KH473 . . . . **FIC**
Black is brown is tan./ 1973/ P-3/3 KF136 . . . . **E**
Boston coffee party./ 1988/ K-3/2 KG306 . . . . **E**
How to eat fried worms./ 1973/ 4-6/5 KH643 . . . . **FIC**
I dance in my red pajamas./ 1982/ K-1/2 KF791 . . . . **E**
Little Kit or, The Industrious Flea Circus girl./ 1995/ 2-4/4 KG092 . . **E**
Lulu and the witch baby./ 1986/ K-3/2 KG188 . . . . **E**
Mirette on the high wire./ 1992/ 1-3/2 KG093 . . . . **E**
Mirette on the high wire (Sound recording cassette)./ 1994/
1-3/2 KG093 . . . . **E**
Picnic./ 1984/ P-2 KG094 . . . . **CE E**
Picnic (Videocassette)./ 1991/ P-2 KG094 . . . . **CE E**
Pirate queen./ 1995/ 3-5/5 KE156 . . . . **910.4**
Pizza party!/ 1994/ P-1/1 KG047 . . . . **E**
School./ 1987/ P-K KG095 . . . . **E**
MCCURDY, M/ AMERICAN FAIRY TALES: FROM RIP VAN WINKLE TO
THE ROOTABAGA STORIES./ 1996/ 4-6/7 KG843 . . . . . **FIC**
Beasts of Bethlehem./ 1992/ 1-6 KD960 . . . . **811**
Gettysburg Address./ 1995/ 4-6/6 KE906 . . . . **973.7**
Lucy's Christmas./ 1994/ 1-3/6 KF662 . . . . **E**
Seasons sewn: a year in patchwork./ 1996/ 3-6/7 KD462 . . . **746.46**
Way west: journal of a pioneer woman./ 1993/ 5-6/6 KE197 . **917.8**
MCCUTCHEON, J/ Family garden (Sound recording cassette)./ 1993/
P-3 KD581 . . . . **SRC 789.2**

Happy adoption day!/ 1996/ 2-4/3 KD637 . . . . **789.3**
John McCutcheon's four seasons: wintersongs (Compact disc)./ 1995/ K-3 KD638 . . . . **CD 789.3**
John McCutcheon's four seasons: wintersongs (Sound recording cassette)./ 1995/ K-3 KD638 . . . . **CD 789.3**
MCDERMOTT, D/ Flying ship./ 1995/ K-3/6 KB749 . . . . **398.27**
Gilly Martin the Fox./ 1994/ 3-4/7 KB593 . . . . **398.24**
MCDERMOTT, G/ Anansi the spider: a tale from the Ashanti./ c1972/ 1-3/2 KB616 . . . . **398.24**
Anansi the spider: a tale from the Ashanti (Braille)./ n.d./ 1-3/2 KB616 . . . . **398.24**
Anansi the spider: a tale from the Ashanti (Sound recording cassette)./ n.d./ 1-3/2 KB616 . . . . **398.24**
Arrow to the sun./ 1974/ 2-4/3 KB711 . . . . **CE 398.26**
Coyote: a trickster tale from the American Southwest./ 1994/ P-2/2 KB617 . . . . **398.24**
Daniel O'Rourke: an Irish tale./ 1986/ 2/2 KB755 . . . . . **398.27**
Flecha al sol./ 1991/ 2-4/3 KB711 . . . . **CE 398.26**
Papagayo the mischief maker./ 1992/ P-2/5 KG096 . . . . **E**
Raven: a trickster tale from the Pacific Northwest./ 1993/ 1-3/3 KB618 . . . . **398.24**
Stonecutter (Videocassette)./ 1976/ 2-4 KB756 . . . . **VCR 398.27**
Tim O'Toole and the weefolk./ 1992/ 2/2 KB755 . . . . **398.27**
Zomo the rabbit: a trickster tale from West Africa./ 1992/ K-2/1 KB619 . . . . **398.24**
Zomo the Rabbit: a trickster tale from West Africa. (Big book)./ 1996/ K-2/1 KB619 . . . . **398.24**
MCDERMOTT, M/ Truth about unicorns./ c1991, 1996/ 5-A/7 KB571 . . . . **398.24**
MCDONALD, J/ Rip Van Winkle; and, The Legend of Sleepy Hollow (Talking book)./ 1986/ 5-6 KH316 . . . . **TB FIC**
MCDONALD, K/ Divers./ 1992/ 4-6/8 KD847 . . . . **797.2**
MCDONALD, M/ Great pumpkin switch./ 1992/ K-3/5 KG098 . . . . . **E**
How Snake got his hiss: an original tale./ 1996/ K-2/2 KF450 . . . . . **E**
Insects are my life./ 1995/ 1-3/2 KG097 . . . . **E**
Is this a house for hermit crab?/ 1990/ P-1/3 KC522 . . . . **595.3**
Potato man./ 1991/ K-3/5 KG098 . . . . **E**
MCDONALD, MA/ Flying squirrels./ 1993/ 1-5/5 KC753 . . . . . **599.36**
MCDONALD, MR/ FOLKLORE OF WORLD HOLIDAYS./ 1992/ 4-6 KA414 . . . . **REF 394.26**
MCDONNELL, F/ Flora McDonnell's ABC./ 1997/ P-K/3 KG099 . . . . **E**
I love animals./ 1994/ P-1/2 KG100 . . . . **E**
I love animals (Big book)./ 1996/ P-1/2 KG100 . . . . **E**
I love boats./ 1995/ P-1/3 KG101 . . . . **E**
MCDONOUGH, YZ/ Eve and her sisters: women of the Old Testament./ 1994/ 3-4/7 KA680 . . . . **221.9**
MCELMEEL, DL/ Author a month (for pennies)./ 1988/ KA069 . . . . **PROF 027.62**
Latest and greatest read-alouds./ 1994/ KA239 . . . . . . **PROF 372.64**
McElmeel booknotes: literature across the curriculum./ 1993/ KA225 . . . . **PROF 372.6**
MCELMEEL, SL/ Author a month (for dimes)./ 1993/ KA069 . . . . **PROF 027.62**
Author a month (for nickels)./ 1990/ KA069 . . . . **PROF 027.62**
Author a month (for pennies)./ 1988/ KA069 . . . . **PROF 027.62**
Great new nonfiction reads./ 1995/ KA086 . . . . **PROF 028.1**
Latest and greatest read-alouds./ 1994/ KA239 . . . . . . **PROF 372.64**
McElmeel booknotes: literature across the curriculum./ 1993/ KA225 . . . . **PROF 372.6**
MCEWAN, I/ Daydreamer./ 1994/ 4-6/6 KH474 . . . . **FIC**
MCFARLANE, B/ Hockey for kids: heroes, tips, and facts./ 1996/ 4-6/7 KD844 . . . . **796.962**
MCFERRIN, B/ How the rhinoceros got his skin; and, How the camel got his hump (Videocassette)./ 1987/ 2-5 KH361 . . . . **VCR FIC**
MCGAW, L/ Discovering the Iceman: what was it like to find a 5,300-year-old mummy?/ 1997/ 3-5/4 KE642 . . . . **937**
Polar, the Titanic bear./ 1994/ 4-6/7 KE158 . . . . **910.4**
MCGEE, R/ GROARK LEARNS ABOUT BULLYING (Videocassette)./ 1996/ 1-3 KA810 . . . . **VCR 303.6**
GROARK LEARNS ABOUT PREJUDICE (Videocassette)./ 1996/ 1-3 KA819 . . . . **VCR 305**
GROARK LEARNS TO WORK OUT CONFLICTS (Videocassette)./ 1996/ 1-3 KA811 . . . . **VCR 303.6**
MCGEORGE, CW/ Boomer's big day./ 1994/ K-2/2 KG102 . . . . . . **E**
MCGINLEY-NALLY, S/ First snow, magic snow./ 1992/ 2-4/6 KB390 . . . . **398.21**
Pigs in the pantry: fun with math and cooking./ 1997/ 1-3/3 KF178 . **E**
Pigs on a blanket./ 1996/ 2-3/2 KF179 . . . . **E**
MCGLATHERY, G/ Of bugs and beasts: fact, folklore, and activities./ 1995/ KA296 . . . . **PROF 591**
MCGOVERN, A/ Down under, down under: diving adventures on the Great Barrier Reef./ 1989/ 3-6/5 KF120 . . . . **994.3**
Lady in the box./ 1997/ 1-3/2 KG103 . . . . **E**
MCGOWEN, T/ World War I./ 1993/ 4-6/8 KE653 . . . . **940.3**

World War II./ 1993/ 4-6/8 KE673 . . . . **940.54**
MCGRAW, EJ/ Moorchild./ 1996/ 5-A/6 KH475 . . . . **FIC**
MCGUIRE, K/ Woodworking for kids: 40 fabulous, fun and useful things for kids to make./ 1993/ 5-A KD341 . . . . **684**
MCGUIRE, R/ Night becomes day./ 1994/ 1-3/1 KG104 . . . . **E**
MCHUGH, C/ Animals./ 1993/ 4-A/7 KD373 . . . . **704.9**
Faces./ 1993/ 4-A/7 KD374 . . . . **704.9**
Water./ 1993/ 4-A/7 KD375 . . . . **704.9**
MCINERNEY, C/ Tracking the facts: how to develop research skills./ 1990/ 5-A/6 KB089 . . . . **371.302**
MCINTOSH, J/ Archeology./ 1994/ 4-A/11 KE627 . . . . **930.1**
MCKAY, H/ Amber cat./ 1997/ 5-8/6 KH476 . . . . **FIC**
Dog Friday./ 1995/ 4-A/7 KH477 . . . . **FIC**
Exiles./ 1992/ 6-A/7 KH478 . . . . **FIC**
Exiles at home./ 1994/ 5-A/7 KH479 . . . . **FIC**
Exiles (Sound recording cassette)./ 1995/ 6-A/7 KH478 . . . . **FIC**
MCKAY, JR., L/ Caravan./ 1995/ 3-5/6 KH480 . . . . **FIC**
MCKEATING, E/ Ozzie on his own./ 1995/ 3-5/4 KH301 . . . . **FIC**
Roz and Ozzie./ 1992/ 3-5/5 KH302 . . . . **FIC**
MCKENNA, CO/ Good grief, third grade./ 1993/ 3-4/4 KH481 . . . **FIC**
Valentine's Day can be murder./ 1996/ 3-5/4 KH482 . . . . **FIC**
MCKENZIE, EK/ King, the princess, and the tinker./ 1992/ 3-5/4 KH483 . . . . **FIC**
Stargone John./ 1990/ 3-5/5 KH484 . . . . **FIC**
MCKIE, R/ Eye book./ c1968/ 1-2/1 KF958 . . . . **E**
Ten apples up on top!/ c1961/ 1-2/1 KF959 . . . . **E**
Tooth book./ 1981/ K-2/2 KF960 . . . . **E**
MCKINLEY, R/ Beauty: a retelling of the story of Beauty and the Beast./ 1978/ 6-A/6 KH485 . . . . **FIC**
Beauty: a retelling of the story of Beauty and the Beast (Braille)./ n.d./ 6-A/6 KH485 . . . . **FIC**
Beauty: a retelling of the story of Beauty and the Beast (Sound recording cassette)./ n.d./ 6-A/6 KH485 . . . . **FIC**
Blue sword./ 1982/ A/7 KH486 . . . . **FIC**
Blue sword (Sound recording cassette)./ n.d./ A/7 KH486 . . . . . . **FIC**
Door in the hedge./ 1981/ 4-6/6 KH487 . . . . **FIC**
Hero and the crown./ 1984/ 5-A/7 KH488 . . . . **FIC**
Hero and the crown (Sound recording cassette)./ n.d./ 5-A/7 KH488 . . . . **FIC**
Knot in the grain and other stories./ 1994/ 6-A/7 KH489 . . . . . . **FIC**
Outlaws of Sherwood./ 1988/ A/8 KH490 . . . . **FIC**
MCKISSACK, F/ African-American scientists./ 1994/ 4-6/7 KB924 . **509**
Carter G. Woodson: the father of black history./ 1991/ 3-6/2 KE601 . . . . **B WOODSON, C.**
Christmas in the big house, Christmas in the quarters./ 1994/ 4-A/6 KE967 . . . . **975**
Mary Church Terrell: leader for equality./ 1991/ 3-6/2 KE562 . . . . **B TERRELL, M.**
Mary McLeod Bethune./ 1992/ 4-6/5 KE254 . . . . . . **B BETHUNE, M.**
Paul Robeson: a voice to remember./ 1992/ 2-5/2 KE514 . . . . **B ROBESON, P.**
Rebels against slavery: American slave revolts./ 1996/ 4-6/7 KA929 . . . . **326**
Royal kingdoms of Ghana, Mali, and Songhay: life in medieval Africa./ c1994, 1995/ A/8 KE734 . . . . **966.2**
Satchel Paige: the best arm in baseball./ 1992/ 3-5/2 KE489 . . . . **B PAIGE, S.**
Sojourner Truth: ain't I a woman?/ 1992/ 6-A/7 KE573 . . **B TRUTH, S.**
MCKISSACK, JR., F/ Black diamond: the story of the Negro baseball leagues./ 1994/ 4-6/7 KD800 . . . . **796.357**
MCKISSACK, P/ African-American scientists./ 1994/ 4-6/7 KB924 . **509**
Black diamond: the story of the Negro baseball leagues./ 1994/ 4-6/7 KD800 . . . . **796.357**
Carter G. Woodson: the father of black history./ 1991/ 3-6/2 KE601 . . . . **B WOODSON, C.**
Christmas in the big house, Christmas in the quarters./ Christmas in the big house, Christmas in the quarters./ 1997/ 1994/ 4-A/6 KE967 . . . . **975**
4-A/6 KE967 . . . . **975**
Dark-thirty: Southern tales of the supernatural./ 1992/ 5-A/6 KH491 . . . . **FIC**
Dark-thirty: Southern tales of the supernatural (Sound recording cassette)./ 1994/ 5-A/6 KH491 . . . . **FIC**
Flossie and the fox./ 1986/ K-3/2 KG105 . . . . **CE E**
Flossie and the fox (Videocassette)./ 1992/ K-3/2 KG105 . . . . . **CE E**
Ma Dear's aprons./ 1997/ 3-5/4 KH492 . . . . **FIC**
Mary Church Terrell: leader for equality./ 1991/ 3-6/2 KE562 . . . . **B TERRELL, M.**
Mary McLeod Bethune./ 1992/ 4-6/5 KE254 . . . . . . **B BETHUNE, M.**
Million fish...more or less./ c1992, 1996/ 1-3/4 KG106 . . . . **E**
Mirandy and Brother Wind./ 1988/ 1-3/6 KG107 . . . . **CE E**
Nettie Jo's friends./ 1989/ 1-3/4 KG108 . . . . **E**
Paul Robeson: a voice to remember./ 1992/ 2-5/2 KE514 . . . . **B ROBESON, P.**

Rebels against slavery: American slave revolts./ 1996/
4-6/7 KA929 . . . . **326**
Royal kingdoms of Ghana, Mali, and Songhay: life in medieval Africa./
c1994, 1995/ A/8 KE734 . . . . **966.2**
Satchel Paige: the best arm in baseball./ 1992/
3-5/2 KE489 . . . . **B PAIGE, S.**
Sojourner Truth: ain't I a woman?/ 1992/ 6-A/7 KE573 . . **B TRUTH, S.**
MCLAIN, G/ Indian way: learning to communicate with Mother Earth./
1990/ 2-6/6 KE750 . . . . **970.1**
MCLANATHAN, R/ Leonardo da Vinci./ 1990/ 6-A/6 KD495 . . . **759.5**
MCLEOD, EW/ Bear's bicycle./ c1975, 1986/ P-2/2 KG109 . . . . . **CE E**
Bear's bicycle (Kit)./ 1977,/ P-2/2 KG109 . . . . **CE E**
MCLERRAN, A/ Roxaboxen./ 1991/ K-3/2 KG110 . . . . **CE E**
Roxaboxen (Videocassette)./ 1991/ K-3/2 KG110 . . . . . . **CE E**
MCLOONE, M/ George Washington Carver: a photo-illustrated
biography./ 1997/ 2-4/5 KE282 . . . . **B CARVER, G.**
MCMAHON, P/ Chi-hoon: a Korean girl./ c1993, 1998/
3-5/6 KE705 . . . . **951.95**
Listen for the bus: David's story./ 1995/ 1-3/3 KB004 . . . . **362.4**
Summer tunes: a Martha's Vineyard vacation./ 1996/
2-5/7 KB005 . . . . **362.4**
MCMANNERS, H/ Outdoor adventure handbook./ 1996/
4-6/6 KC823 . . . . **796.5**
MCMILLAN, B/ Dry or wet?/ 1988/ P-1 KB844 . . . . **428**
Eating fractions./ 1991/ P-2/1 KB969 . . . . **513.2**
Growing colors./ 1988/ P-1 KC124 . . . . **535.6**
Jelly beans for sale./ 1996/ K-3/2 KA951 . . . . **332.4**
Mouse views: what the class pet saw./ 1993/ K-3/1 KG111 . . . . . **E**
Nights of the pufflings./ 1995/ 1-3/6 KC678 . . . . **598.3**
Sense suspense: a guessing game for the five senses./ 1994/
P-2 KC968 . . . . **612.8**
Summer ice: life along the Antarctic Peninsula./ 1995/
A/8 KE216 . . . . **919.8**
Weather sky./ 1991/ 5-A/7 KC220 . . . . **551.6**
MCMULLAN, K/ If you were my bunny./ 1996/ P-K/3 KG112 . . . . . **E**
MCNAUGHTON, C/ Captain Abdul's pirate school./ 1994/
1-3/3 KG113 . . . . **E**
Making friends with Frankenstein: a book of monstrous poems and
pictures./ 1994/ K-3 KE107 . . . . **821**
MCNEESE, T/ Panama Canal./ 1997/ 5-6/11 KB145 . . . . **386**
MCNEIL, H/ Hyena and the moon: stories to listen to from Kenya (Talking
book)./ 1995/ 5-6 KB346 . . . . **TB 398.2**
Hyena and the moon: stories to tell from Kenya./ 1994/
5-6/7 KB347 . . . . **398.2**
MCNEIL, K/ COWBOY SONGS (Sound recording cassette)./ 1992/
4-A KD560 . . . . **SRC 789.2**
MCNEIL, R/ COWBOY SONGS (Sound recording cassette)./ 1992/
4-A KD560 . . . . **SRC 789.2**
MCNULTY, F/ How to dig a hole to the other side of the world./ c1979,
1990/ 2-4/6 KC154 . . . . **CE 551.1**
How to dig a hole to the other side of the world (Kit)./ 1991,/
2-4/6 KC154 . . . . **CE 551.1**
Lady and the spider./ 1986/ 1-3/2 KG114 . . . . **E**
Snake in the house./ 1994/ 1-3/2 KG115 . . . . **E**
MCPHAIL, D/ Bear's bicycle./ c1975, 1986/ P-2/2 KG109 . . . . **CE E**
Bear's toothache./ c1972/ K-2/2 KG116 . . . . **CE E**
Bear's toothache (Braille)./ n.d./ K-2/2 KG116 . . . . **CE E**
Bear's toothache (Kit)./ 1980/ K-2/2 KG116 . . . . **CE E**
Cerdos a montones, cerdos a granel!/ 1996/ P-2/2 KG122 . . . . . **E**
Edward and the pirates./ 1997/ K-2/3 KG117 . . . . **E**
Farm morning./ c1985, 1991/ P-1/2 KG118 . . . . **E**
If you were my bunny./ 1996/ P-K/3 KG112 . . . . **E**
Lost!/ 1990/ P-1/2 KG119 . . . . **E**
Moony B. Finch, the fastest draw in the West./ 1994/ 1-3/4 KG120 **E**
Pigs ahoy!/ 1995/ P-2/3 KG121 . . . . **E**
Pigs aplenty, pigs galore!/ 1993/ P-2/2 KG122 . . . . **E**
Pigs aplenty, pigs galore! (Sound recording cassette)./ 1995/
P-2/2 KG122 . . . . **E**
Sailing to Cythera, and other Anatole stories./ 1974/
3-5/6 KH863 . . . . **FIC**
Why a disguise?/ 1996/ K-2/2 KG182 . . . . **E**
MCPHERSON, SS/ Ordinary genius: the story of Albert Einstein./ 1995/
5-A/6 KE334 . . . . **B EINSTEIN, A.**
Peace and bread: the story of Jane Addams./ 1993/
4-6/5 KE228 . . . . **B ADDAMS, J.**
Rooftop astronomer: a story about Maria Mitchell./ 1990/
4-5/6 KE465 . . . . **B MITCHELL, M.**
TV's forgotten hero: the story of Philo Farnsworth./ 1996/
5-A/9 KE342 . . . . **B FARNSWORTH, P**
MCVEY, V/ Sierra Club kid's guide to planet care and repair./ 1993/
4-6/7 KB048 . . . . **363.7**
MEACHUM, V/ Jane Goodall: protector of chimpanzees./ 1997/
5-A/7 KE372 . . . . **B GOODALL, J.**

Steven Spielberg: Hollywood filmmaker./ 1996/
4-6/8 KE545 . . . . **B SPIELBERG, S.**
MEAD, A/ Junebug./ 1995/ 5-A/5 KH493 . . . . **FIC**
MEADE, H/ Hush!: a Thai lullaby./ 1996/ P-1 KD952 . . . . **811**
Rata-pata-scata-fata: a Caribbean story./ 1994/ K-2/2 KF611 . . . . . **E**
Sleep, sleep, sleep: a lullaby for little ones around the world./ 1995/
P-2/3 KG644 . . . . **E**
Small Green Snake./ 1994/ P-2/6 KF637 . . . . **E**
MEBANE, RC/ Environmental experiments about air./ 1993/
5-6/7 KD084 . . . . **628.5**
Environmental experiments about water./ 1993/ 5-6/7 KB066 . . . **363.73**
MECC/ AFRICA TRAIL (CD-ROM)./ 1995/ 4-A KE723 . . . . . **CDR 960**
BIG ANTHONY'S MIXED-UP MAGIC (CD-ROM)./ 1996/
K-2 KF229 . . . . **CDR E**
OREGON TRAIL II (CD-ROM)./ 1994/ 4-A KE745 . . . . . **CDR 970.04**
STORYBOOK WEAVER DELUXE (CD-ROM)./ 1995/
1-5 KB118 . . . . **CDR 372.6**
WRITING ALONG THE OREGON TRAIL (Microcomputer program)./
1994/ 4-A KB121 . . . . **MCP 372.6**
MEDDAUGH, S/ Hog-eye./ 1995/ K-3/2 KG123 . . . . **E**
Martha blah blah./ 1996/ K-2/2 KG124 . . . . **E**
That terrible baby./ 1994/ K-2/3 KF166 . . . . **E**
Way I feel--sometimes./ 1988/ 1-4 KD931 . . . . **811**
Witches' supermarket./ 1991/ 1-3/2 KG125 . . . . **E**
MEDEARIS, AS/ Adventures of Sugar and Junior./ 1995/
2-3/2 KH494 . . . . **FIC**
Dance./ 1997/ 4-6/11 KD704 . . . . **793.3**
Dare to dream: Coretta Scott King and the civil rights movement./ 1994/
3-5/3 KE419 . . . . **B KING, C.S.**
Dare to dream: Coretta Scott King and the civil rights movement (Sound
recording cassette)./ 1997/ 3-5/3 KE419 . . . . **B KING, C.S.**
Haunts: five hair-raising tales./ 1996/ 4-6/4 KH495 . . . . **FIC**
Here comes the snow./ 1996/ K-1/2 KG126 . . . . **E**
Little Louis and the jazz band: the story of Louis "Satchmo" Armstrong./
1994/ 2-4/6 KE241 . . . . **B ARMSTRONG, L.**
Music./ 1997/ 4-6/11 KD521 . . . . **780**
Our people./ 1994/ K-2/5 KA852 . . . . **305.8**
Singing man: adapted from a West African folktale./ 1994/
4-5/6 KB757 . . . . **398.27**
MEDEARIS, M/ Dance./ 1997/ 4-6/11 KD704 . . . . **793.3**
Music./ 1997/ 4-6/11 KD521 . . . . **780**
MEDICINE STORY/ Children of the Morning Light: Wampanoag tales./
1994/ 4-5/7 KB348 . . . . **398.2**
MEDLOCK, S/ EXTRA INNINGS: BASEBALL POEMS./ 1993/
3-6 KE056 . . . . **811.008**
OPENING DAYS: SPORTS POEMS./ 1996/ 3-6 KE074 . . . . **811.008**
MEGAN, T/ Pattysaurus and other tales (Sound recording cassette)./
1995/ P-3 KF508 . . . . **SRC E**
MEIGS, C/ Invincible Louisa./ 1933/ 5-6/8 KE232 . . . . . **B ALCOTT, L.**
Invincible Louisa (Braille)./ n.d./ 5-6/8 KE232 . . . . . . **B ALCOTT, L.**
Invincible Louisa (Sound recording cassette)./ n.d./
5-6/8 KE232 . . . . **B ALCOTT, L.**
Invincible Louisa (Talking book)./ n.d./ 5-6/8 KE232 . . . **B ALCOTT, L.**
MEINBACH, AM/ Complete guide to thematic units: creating the integrated
curriculum./ 1995/ KA195 . . . . **PROF 372.19**
MEISEL, P/ I am really a princess./ 1993/ 1-3/3 KG494 . . . . . . **E**
Kirby Puckett's baseball games./ 1996/ 3-6/3 KD801 . . . . . . **796.357**
Max and Maggie in spring./ 1995/ K-1/1 KG208 . . . . **E**
MELMED, LK/ Rainbabies./ 1992/ 2-3/5 KG127 . . . . **E**
MELTON, D/ Written & illustrated by... a revolutionary two-brain approach
for teaching students how to write and illustrate amazing books./ 1985/
KA226 . . . . **PROF 372.6**
MELTZER, M/ American revolutionaries: a history in their own words--
1750-1800./ 1993/ 5-6/8 KE883 . . . . **973.3**
Black Americans: a history in their own words 1619-1983./ 1984/
5-6/9 KE857 . . . . **973**
Gold: the true story of why people search for it, mine it, trade it, steal it,
mint it, hoard it, shape it, wear it, fight and kill for it./ 1993/
4-8/7 KC229 . . . . **553.4**
Hold your horses: a feedbag full of fact and fable./ 1995/
5-6/7 KD202 . . . . **636.1**
LINCOLN, IN HIS OWN WORDS./ 1993/ A/8 KE907 . . . . . . **973.7**
Never to forget: the Jews of the Holocaust./ c1976/
A/7 KE674 . . . . **940.54**
Never to forget: the Jews of the Holocaust (Sound recording cassette)./
n.d./ A/7 KE674 . . . . **940.54**
Rescue: the story of how Gentiles saved Jews in the Holocaust./ 1988/
5-A/7 KE661 . . . . **940.53**
Weapons and warfare: from the stone age to the space age./ 1996/
4-6/8 KA983 . . . . **355.02**
MENDELSON, ST/ Emperor's new clothes./ 1992/ 1-3/7 KG128 . . . . **E**
MENDLER, AN/ Smiling at yourself: educating young children about stress
and self-esteem./ 1990/ KA304 . . . . **PROF 649**
MENNEN, I/ Somewhere in Africa./ 1992/ K-2/4 KG129 . . . . **E**

MERKIN, R/ Leagues apart: the men and times of the Negro baseball leagues./ 1995/ 2-4/7 KD802 . . . . **796.357**

MERMAID TALES FROM AROUND THE WORLD./ 1993/ 3-5/5 KB405 . . . . **398.21**

MERRIAM, E/ Halloween A B C./ 1987/ P-A KD982 . . . . **811**
Higgle wiggle: happy rhymes./ 1994/ P-1 KD983 . . . . **811**
Hole story./ 1995/ P-1/2 KG131 . . . . **E**
Singing green: new and selected poems for all seasons./ 1992/ 3-A KD984 . . . . **811**

MERRILL, J/ Girl who loved caterpillars: a twelfth-century tale from Japan./ 1992/ 2-4/5 KG132 . . . . **E**

MERRIMAN, R/ Tale of Tobias./ 1996/ 1-3/2 KA693 . . . . **229**

MERYMAN, R/ Andrew Wyeth./ 1991/ 6-A/7 KE602 . . . **B WYETH, A.**

MESSIER, L/ Fireflies, fireflies, light my way./ 1996/ P-2/2 KG020 . . . **E**

METAXAS, E/ David and Goliath (Kit)./ 1996/ 2-4 KA686 . . . **VCR 222**
David and Goliath (Talking book)./ 1996/ 2-4 KA686 . . . . **VCR 222**
David and Goliath (Videocassette)./ 1992/ 2-4 KA686 . . . . **VCR 222**
Jack and the beanstalk./ K-2 KB349 . . . . **VCR 398.2**
Jack and the beanstalk (Kit)./ 1997/ K-2 KB349 . . . . . . **VCR 398.2**
Jack and the beanstalk (Videocassette)./ 1991/ K-2 KB349 . **VCR 398.2**
Peachboy (Kit)./ 1995/ 2-5 KB469 . . . . **VCR 398.22**
Peachboy (Videocassette)./ 1991/ 2-5 KB469 . . . . . . **VCR 398.22**
Puss in Boots (Kit)./ 1992/ 1-4 KB620 . . . . **KIT 398.24**
Squanto and the first Thanksgiving (Kit)./ 1996/ 2-6 KE548 . . . . **KIT B SQUANTO**
Stormalong (Kit)./ 1995/ 2-5 KB470 . . . . **KIT 398.22**
Stormalong (Videocassette)./ 1992/ 2-5 KB470 . . . . . **KIT 398.22**
WHITE CAT (Videocassette)./ 1997/ K-2 KB382 . . . . . **VCR 398.2**

METROPOLITAN MUSEUM OF ART (NEW YORK, N.Y.)/ GO IN AND OUT THE WINDOW: AN ILLUSTRATED SONGBOOK FOR YOUNG PEOPLE./ 1987/ 2-A KD564 . . . . **789.2**
Inside the museum: a children's guide to the Metropolitan Museum of Art./ 1993/ 2-A/7 KD376 . . . . **708**
SONGS OF THE WILD WEST./ 1991/ 2-A KD597 . . . . **789.2**
TALKING TO THE SUN: AN ILLUSTRATED ANTHOLOGY OF POEMS FOR YOUNG PEOPLE./ 1985/ 6-A KE087 . . . . **811.008**
What makes a Bruegel a Bruegel?/ 1993/ 5-A/8 KD502 . . . **759.9493**
What makes a Cassatt a Cassatt?/ 1994/ 5-A/7 KD489 . . . . **759.13**
What makes a Degas a Degas?/ 1993/ 5-A/7 KD491 . . . . . . **759.4**
What makes a Goya a Goya?/ 1994/ 5-A/7 KD498 . . . . . . **759.6**
What makes a Leonardo a Leonardo?/ 1994/ 5-A/7 KD496 . . . **759.5**
What makes a Monet a Monet?/ 1993/ 5-A/7 KD492 . . . . . **759.4**
What makes a Picasso a Picasso?/ 1994/ 5-A/7 KD493 . . . . **759.4**
What makes a Raphael a Raphael?/ 1993/ 5-A/7 KD497 . . . . **759.5**
What makes a Rembrandt a Rembrandt?/ 1993/ 5-A/7 KD500 . . . . **759.9492**

METS, M/ Baseball birthday party./ 1995/ 1-3/2 KG286 . . . . **E**
Brave Mary./ 1996/ K-1/2 KF266 . . . . **E**

METTLER, R/ Birds./ 1993/ 2-4/4 KC652 . . . . **598**
Egg./ 1992/ P-3/2 KC281 . . . . **573.6**

MEYER, SE/ Edgar Degas./ 1994/ 6-A/9 KE318 . . . . . . **B DEGAS, E.**
Mary Cassatt./ 1990/ 6-A/8 KE283 . . . . **B CASSATT, M.**

MEYEROWITZ, R/ Paul Bunyan (Videocassette)./ 1990/ 3-5 KB447 . . . . **VCR 398.22**

MICHAEL, D/ How skyscrapers are made./ 1987/ A/10 KD358 . . **690**

MICHAELS, S/ Kid's guide to social action: how to solve the social problems you choose--and turn creative thinking into positive action./ 1991/ 3-6/6 KA991 . . . . **361.2**

MICHELS, P/ Day in the life of a beekeeper./ 1990/ 4-5/6 KD242 **638**

MICHELSON, R/ Animals that ought to be: poems about imaginary pets./ 1996/ K-3 KD985 . . . . **811**

MICHIKO, E/ Animals: selected poems./ 1992/ 2-6 KE135 . . . . . **895.6**

MICHL, R/ Day on the river./ 1986/ 1-3/4 KG133 . . . . **E**

MICKLETHWAIT, L/ Child's book of art: great pictures, first words./ 1993/ P-1 KD366 . . . . **701**
I spy a freight train: transportation in art./ 1996/ P-2/2 KD473 . . **758**
I spy a lion: animals in art./ 1994/ P-2/2 KD474 . . . . **758**
I spy: an alphabet in art./ 1992/ P-2/2 KD484 . . . . **759**
I spy two eyes: numbers in art./ 1993/ P-A KB970 . . . . **513.2**
Spot a cat./ 1995/ K-2/2 KD466 . . . . **750**
Spot a dog./ 1995/ K-2/1 KD467 . . . . **750**

MICUCCI, C/ Life and times of the apple./ 1992/ 3-5/5 KD162 . . **634**
Life and times of the honeybee./ 1995/ 4-6/6 KC576 . . . . . **595.79**
Life and times of the peanut./ 1997/ 3-6/11 KD268 . . . . . . **641.3**

MIKOLAYCAK, C/ Bearhead: a Russian folktale./ 1991/ 2-4/4 KB327 . . . . **398.2**
He is risen: the Easter story./ 1985/ 5-6/7 KA711 . . . . **232.96**
Hero of Bremen./ 1993/ 3-5/6 KB451 . . . . **398.22**
Juma and the magic jinn./ 1986/ 2-3/4 KF156 . . . . **E**
Man who could call down owls./ 1984/ 1-3/2 KF304 . . . . **E**
Peter and the wolf./ 1982/ P-3/4 KD676 . . . . **CE 789.8**
Tam Lin./ 1990/ 3-4/4 KB384 . . . . **398.2**

MILES, B/ Hey! I'm reading!: a how-to-read book for beginners./ 1995/ P-1/2 KB103 . . . . **372.4**

MILES, E/ Molly Limbo./ 1996/ K-3/3 KB688 . . . . **398.25**

MILES, M/ Ani y la anciana./ 1992/ 4-6/4 KH496 . . . . **FIC**
Annie and the old one./ c1971/ 4-6/4 KH496 . . . . **FIC**
Annie and the old one (Braille)./ n.d./ 4-6/4 KH496 . . . . **FIC**

MILES, W/ Black stars in orbit: NASA'S African American astronauts./ 1995/ 3-6/8 KD136 . . . . **629.45**

MILHOUS, K/ Egg tree./ c1950, 1992/ 1-3/4 KG134 . . . . **E**

MILLAR, HR/ Enchanted castle./ c1907, 1985/ 5-6/7 KH541 . . . . . **FIC**

MILLER, BM/ Newbery Medal books: 1922-1955: with their authors' acceptance papers, biographies, and related materials chiefly from the Horn/ c1957/ KA353 . . . . **PROF 809**

MILLER, EB/ Internet resource directory for K-12 teachers and librarians./ 1994-/ KA179 . . . . **PROF 371.3**

MILLER, J/ SEARS LIST OF SUBJECT HEADINGS. 16th ed./ 1997/ KA061 . . . . **PROF 025.4**

MILLER, L/ Christopher Columbus: great explorer./ 1991/ 4-5/4 KE301 . . . . **B COLUMBUS, C.**
Hats are for watering horses: why the cowboy dressed that way./ 1993/ 4-6/4 KB163 . . . . **391**

MILLER, M/ MATH FOR THE VERY YOUNG: A HANDBOOK OF ACTIVITIES FOR PARENTS AND TEACHERS./ 1995/ KA254 . . . . **PROF 372.7**
Mis cinco sentidos./ 1995/ P-1/2 KC969 . . . . **612.8**
My five senses./ 1994/ P-1/2 KC969 . . . . **612.8**
Now I'm big./ 1996/ P/2 KG135 . . . . **E**
Where does it go?/ 1992/ P-K/1 KG136 . . . . **E**
Who uses this?/ 1990/ P-K KA943 . . . . **331.7**
Whose hat?/ 1988/ P-K KB166 . . . . **391.4**
Whose shoe?/ 1991/ P-K KB166 . . . . **391.4**

MILLER, MB/ Handtalk: an ABC of finger spelling and sign language./ c1974, 1984/ K-A KB823 . . . . **419**
Handtalk birthday: a number and story book in sign language./ 1987/ K-3 KB824 . . . . **419**
Handtalk school./ 1991/ K-A KB827 . . . . **419**
Handtalk zoo./ 1989/ K-A KB820 . . . . **419**

MILLER, RH/ Buffalo Soldiers./ 1991/ 4-6/6 KF039 . . . . **978**
Cowboys./ 1991/ 4-6/6 KF039 . . . . **978**

MILLER, SS/ Three stories you can read to your cat./ 1997/ K-2/2 KG137 . . . . **E**

MILLER, TR/ Taking time out: recreation and play./ 1996/ 5-A/7 KA865 . . . . **306.4**

MILLER-LACHMANN, L/ Our family, our friends, our world: an annotated guide to significant multicultural books for/ 1992/ KA020 . . . . **PROF 011.62**

MILLEVOIX, F/ Sweet, sweet fig banana./ 1996/ K-2/2 KF613 . . . **E**

MILLS, C/ Phoebe's parade./ 1994/ K-2/2 KG138 . . . . **E**

MILLS, LA/ Book of little folk: faery stories and poems from around the world./ 1997/ 1-4 KD875 . . . . **808.8**
Rag coat./ 1991/ 2-3/4 KG139 . . . . **E**
Rag coat (Sound recording cassette)./ 1994/ 2-3/4 KG139 . . . . . **E**
Tatterhood and the hobgoblins: a Norwegian folktale./ 1993/ 3-4/6 KB350 . . . . **398.2**

MILLS, P/ On an island in the bay./ 1994/ 2-4/3 KE979 . . . . . **975.5**

MILNE, AA/ House at Pooh Corner./ c1956/ K-6/3 KH497 . . . . . **FIC**
House at Pooh Corner (Braille)./ n.d./ K-6/3 KH497 . . . . **FIC**
House at Pooh Corner (Sound recording cassette)./ n.d./ K-6/3 KH497 . . . . **FIC**
House at Pooh Corner (Talking book)./ n.d./ K-6/3 KH497 . . . . **FIC**
Winnie-the-Pooh./ 1974/ K-6/3 KH498 . . . . **FIC**
Winnie-the-Pooh (Braille)./ n.d./ K-6/3 KH498 . . . . **FIC**
Winnie-the-Pooh (Sound recording cassette)./ n.d./ K-6/3 KH498 . . **FIC**
Winnie-the-Pooh (Talking book)./ n.d./ K-6/3 KH498 . . . . . . **FIC**
World of Christopher Robin: the complete When we were very young and Now we are six./ c1958/ P-2 KE108 . . . . **821**
World of Christopher Robin: the complete When we were very young and Now we are six (Braille)./ World of Christopher Robin: the complete When we were very young and Now we are six (Sound recording cassette)./ World of Christopher Robin: the complete When we were very young and Now we are six (Talking book)./ n.d./ n.d./ n.d./ P-2 KE108 . . . . **821**
P-2 KE108 . . . . **821**
P-2 KE108 . . . . **821**
World of Pooh: the complete "Winnie-the-Pooh" and "The House at Pooh Corner."/ c1957/ K-6/3 KH499 . . . . **FIC**
World of Pooh: the complete "Winnie-the-Pooh" and "The House at Pooh Corner" (Sound recording cassette)./ n.d./ K-6/3 KH499 . . **FIC**
World of Pooh: the complete "Winnie-the-Pooh" and "The House at Pooh Corner" (Talking book)./ n.d./ K-6/3 KH499 . . . . **FIC**

MILNER, A/ Dinosaur./ 1989/ 3-A/7 KC258 . . . . **567.9**

MILORD, S/ Hands around the world: 365 creative ways to build cultural awareness and global respect./ 1992/ KA167 . . . . **PROF 306**
Kids' nature book: 365 indoor/outdoor activities and experiences. Rev. ed./ 1996/ 4/6 KB910 . . . . **508**

MILTON, J/ Whales: the gentle giants./ 1989/ 1-3/2 KC774 . . . **599.5**

MINARIK, EH/ Am I beautiful?/ 1992/ P-K/2 KG140 . . . . E
Amigos de Osito./ n.d./ P-1/2 KG141 . . . . CE E
Father Bear comes home./ 1959/ P-1/2 KG141 . . . . CE E
Father Bear comes home (Kit)./ 1995/ P-1/2 KG141 . . . CE E
Father Bear comes home (Talking book)./ n.d./ P-1/2 KG141 . . . CE E
Kiss for Little Bear./ 1968/ P-1/2 KG141 . . . . CE E
Kiss for Little Bear (Kit)./ 1991/ P-1/2 KG141 . . . . CE E
Little Bear./ c1961/ P-1/2 KG141 . . . . CE E
Little Bear (Braille)./ n.d./ P-1/2 KG141 . . . . CE E
Little Bear (Kit)./ 1986/ P-1/2 KG141 . . . . CE E
Little Bear (Talking book)./ n.d./ P-1/2 KG141 . . . . CE E
Little Bear's friend./ 1960/ P-1/2 KG141 . . . . CE E
Little Bear's friend (Braille)./ n.d./ P-1/2 KG141 . . . . . CE E
Little Bear's friend (Kit)./ 1990/ P-1/2 KG141 . . . . CE E
Little Bear's visit./ 1961/ P-1/2 KG141 . . . . CE E
Little Bear's visit (Braille)./ n.d./ P-1/2 KG141 . . . . . . CE E
Little Bear's visit (Kit)./ 1961/ P-1/2 KG141 . . . . CE E
Osito./ n.d./ P-1/2 KG141 . . . . CE E
Papa Oso vuelve a casa./ n.d./ P-1/2 KG141 . . . . CE E
Visita de Osito./ 1994/ P-1/2 KG141 . . . . CE E
MING-YI, Y/ Long-haired girl: a Chinese legend./ 1995/
   2-3/4 KB409 . . . . 398.21
MINNESOTA ORCHESTRA/ ON THE DAY YOU WERE BORN
   (Videocassette)./ 1996/ P-A KG192 . . . . VCR E
MINOR, W/ Everglades./ 1995/ 2-5/7 KE991 . . . . 975.9
Julie./ 1994/ 5-A/3 KH156 . . . . FIC
Sierra./ 1991/ 2-6 KE023 811
MINTERS, F/ Sleepless Beauty./ 1996/ 2-3/3 KG142 . . . E
MINTZ, B/ Hieroglyphs, the writing of ancient Egypt./ 1981/
   5-6/9 KB866 493
MIROCHA, P/ How do birds find their way?/ 1996/
   3-4/2 KC673 . . . . 598.156
Oil spill!/ 1994/ 1-4/4 KB057 . . . . 363.73
MISH, M/ Kid's eye view of ecology (Videocassette)./ 1991/
   3-6 KB049 . . . . VCR 363.7
Kid's eye view of the environment (Sound recording cassette)/ 1989/
   P-2 KB050 . . . . SRC 363.7
MISS MARY MACK AND OTHER CHILDREN'S STREET RHYMES./ 1990/
   2-5 KD766 . . . . 796.1
MISTRY, N/ Illustrated book of myths: tales and legends of the world./
   1995/ 5-A KA394 . . . . REF 291.1
MITCHELL, A/ Ugly Duckling./ 1994/ P-A/4 KG143 . . . . . . E
MITCHELL, B/ Down Buttermilk Lane./ 1993/ 1-3/2 KG144 . . . . . . E
Good morning, Mr. President: a story about Carl Sandburg./ 1988/
   4-6/6 KE531 . . . . B SANDBURG, C.
Raggin', a story about Scott Joplin./ 1987/ A/8 KE407 . B JOPLIN, S.
Red Bird./ 1996/ 1-3/4 KG145 . . . . E
We'll race you, Henry: a story about Henry Ford./ 1986/
   4-5/3 KE346 . . . . B FORD, H.
Wizard of sound: a story about Thomas Edison./ 1991/
   4-6/6 KE331 . . . . B EDISON, T.
MITCHELL, H/ Rooftop astronomer: a story about Maria Mitchell./ 1990/
   4-5/6 KE465 . . . . B MITCHELL, M.
Wizard of sound: a story about Thomas Edison./ 1991/
   4-6/6 KE331 . . . . B EDISON, T.
MITCHELL, JS/ Abridged Dewey decimal classification and relative index.
   Ed. 13./ 1997/ KA058 . . . . PROF 025.4
MITCHELL, K/ Aladdin and the magic lamp./ 1993/ 1-2/2 KB314 398.2
MITCHELL, M/ Books, children and men. 5th ed./ 1983/
   KA351 . . . . PROF 809
MITCHELL, MK/ Granddaddy's gift./ 1997/ 1-3/2 KG146 . . . . E
Uncle Jed's barbershop./ 1993/ 1-3/4 KG147 . . . . E
MITCHELL, R/ Joshua by the sea (Board book)./ 1994/
   P/2 KF829 . . . . BB E
Joshua's night whispers (Board book)./ 1994/ P/2 KF830 . . . . . BB E
Rain feet (Board book)./ 1994/ P/2 KF833 . . . . BB E
MITCHLEY, R/ Horrible story and others (Talking book)./ 1992/
   3-A KH452 . . . . TB FIC
MITGUTSCH, A/ From tree to table./ 1981/ P-2/2 KD329 674
MITRA, A/ Christmas Witch: an Italian legend./ 1993/
   1-3/2 KB507 . . . . 398.23
MIYAKE, Y/ Owl eyes./ 1994/ 1-3/4 KB570 . . . . 398.24
What makes it rain? The story of a raindrop./ 1982/
   P-K/2 KC209 . . . . 551.57
MOCHIZUKI, K/ Baseball saved us./ 1993/ 4-A/6 KH500 . . . . . . FIC
Beisbol nos salvo./ 1995/ 4-A/6 KH500 . . . . FIC
Heroes./ 1995/ 3-5/4 KH501 . . . . FIC
Passage to freedom: the Sugihara story./ 1997/ 3-6/4 KE662 . 940.53
MODELL, F/ Look out, it's April Fools' Day./ 1985/ K-2/2 KG148 . . . E
MOE, JE/ Man who kept house./ 1992/ 2-4/6 KB719 . . . . 398.27
MOEHLMAN, PDR/ Jackal woman: exploring the world of jackals./ 1993/
   5-6/6 KC833 . . . . 599.77
MOFFATT, J/ I'm a seed./ 1996/ K-2/1 KG081 . . . . E

Too many rabbits and other fingerplays about animals, nature, weather,
   and the universe./ 1995/ P-1 KD707 . . . . 793.4
Who stole the cookies?/ 1996/ P-1/1 KG149 . . . . E
MOHL, R/ Planetary taxi (CD-ROM)./ 1993/ 4-A KC013 . . . CDR 523.2
MOHR, N/ Cancion del coqui y otros cuentos de Puerto Rico./ 1995/
   3-4/3 KB621 . . . . 398.24
Song of el coqui and other tales of Puerto Rico./ 1995/
   3-4/3 KB621 . . . . 398.24
MOLLEL, TM/ Ananse's feast: an Ashanti tale./ 1997/
   K-2/3 KB622 . . . . 398.24
Big boy./ 1995/ K-2/3 KG150 . . . . E
Flying tortoise: an Igbo tale./ 1994/ 2-3/3 KB623 . . . . 398.24
King and the tortoise./ 1993/ 2-3/4 KB624 . . . . 398.24
Orphan boy: a Maasai story./ 1990/ 4-5/4 KB406 . . . . . . 398.21
Orphan boy: a Maasai story (Sound recording cassette)./ 1994/
   4-5/4 KB406 . . . . 398.21
Rhinos for lunch and elephants for supper!: a Masai tale./ 1991/
   P-3/4 KB625 . . . . 398.24
MONFRIED, L/ No more animals!/ 1995/ 1-3/2 KH502 . . . . . FIC
MONJO, FN/ Drinking gourd (Braille)./ n.d./ 1-3/2 KG151 . . . . . . E
Drinking gourd. Newly illustrated ed./ 1993/ 1-3/2 KG151 . . . . . . E
Osa menor: una historia del ferrocarril subterraneo./ 1997/
   1-3/2 KG151 . . . . E
MONROE, JG/ First houses: Native American homes and sacred
   structures./ 1993/ 6-A/7 KB171 . . . . 392.3
MONSON, AM/ Wanted: best friend./ 1997/ K-2/2 KG152 . . . . . E
MONSTER SOUP AND OTHER SPOOKY POEMS./ 1992/
   K-3 KD986 811
MONTEZINOS, NS/ Joe Joe./ 1993/ P-K/1 KG440 . . . . E
MONTGOMERY, LM/ Anne of Avonlea./ 1976,/ 4-A/6 KH503 . . . FIC
Anne of Avonlea (Braille)./ n.d./ 4-A/6 KH503 . . . . FIC
Anne of Avonlea (Sound recording cassette)./ n.d./ 4-A/6 KH503 . . FIC
Anne of Green Gables./ c1908, 1983/ 4-A/6 KH503 . . . FIC
Anne of Green Gables (Braille)./ n.d./ 4-A/6 KH503 . . . FIC
Anne of Ingleside./ 1981/ 4-A/6 KH503 . . . . FIC
Anne of Ingleside (Sound recording cassette)./ n.d.,/
   4-A/6 KH503 . . . . FIC
Anne of the island./ 1976/ 4-A/6 KH503 . . . . FIC
Anne of the island: an Anne of Green Gables story./ 1992,/
   4-A/6 KH503 . . . . FIC
Anne of the island (Braille)./ n.d.,/ 4-A/6 KH503 . . . . . FIC
Anne of the island (Sound recording cassette)./ n.d.,/
   4-A/6 KH503 . . . . FIC
Anne of Windy Poplars./ 1981/ 4-A/6 KH503 . . . . FIC
Anne of Windy Poplars (Braille)./ n.d.,/ 4-A/6 KH503 . . . FIC
Anne of Windy Poplars (Sound recording cassette)./ n.d.,/
   4-A/6 KH503 . . . . FIC
Anne's house of dreams./ 1981/ 4-A/6 KH503 . . . . FIC
Anne's house of dreams (Braille)./ n.d.,/ 4-A/6 KH503 . . FIC
Anne's house of dreams (Sound recording cassette)./ n.d.,/
   4-A/6 KH503 . . . . FIC
Rainbow Valley./ 1985,/ 4-A/6 KH503 . . . . FIC
Rilla of Ingleside./ 1985,/ 4-A/6 KH503 . . . . FIC
Rilla of Ingleside (Sound recording cassette)./ 1993,/
   4-A/6 KH503 . . . . FIC
MONTGOMERY, PK/ Bookmark book./ 1996/ KA310 . . . PROF 741.6
MONTIJO, Y/ NATIVE WAYS: CALIFORNIA INDIAN STORIES AND
   MEMORIES./ 1995/ 5-A/6 KE800 . . . . 970.494
MOODIE, F/ Nabulela: a South Africa folk tale./ 1997/
   2-4/4 KB758 . . . . 398.27
MOODY INSTITUTE OF SCIENCE/ MICROORGANISMS: THE INVISIBLE
   WORLD (Videocassette)./ 1995/ 4-8 KC373 . . . . . VCR 579
MOON, N/ Lucy's picture./ 1995/ P-1/2 KG153 . . . . E
MOONEY, W/ READY-TO-TELL TALES: SURE-FIRE STORIES FROM
   AMERICA'S FAVORITE STORYTELLERS./ 1994/
   KA272 . . . . PROF 398.2
Why the dog chases the cat: great animal stories (Sound recording
   cassette)./ 1994/ 1-3 KB591 . . . . SRC 398.24
MOORE, A/ Broken Arrow boy./ 1990/ 3-6/6 KA996 . . . . . . 362.1
MOORE, C/ FROG INSIDE MY HAT: A FIRST BOOK OF POEMS./
   1993/ P-1 KD884 . . . . 808.81
Story of Canada./ 1992/ 5-A/7 KE804 971
Tickle Day: poems from Father Goose./ 1994/ P-1 KD944 811
MOORE, CC/ Grandma Moses Night before Christmas./ 1991/
   P-A KD987 811
Night before Christmas: told in sign language: an adaptation of the
   original poem "A visit from St. Nicholas" by Clement C. Moore./
   1994/ K-6 KD917 811
Twas the night before Christmas: a visit from St. Nicholas./ c1912, 1992/
   P-A KD988 811
MOORE, E/ Buddy: the first seeing eye dog./ 1996/
   1-3/3 KB006 . . . . 362.4
Grandma's house./ 1985/ K-2/4 KG154 . . . . E
Grandma's promise./ 1988/ K-2/4 KG154 . . . . E

MOORE, K/ ...If you lived at the time of the Civil War./ 1994/
  3-5/6 KE908 .... **973.7**
MOORE, L/ Don't be afraid, Amanda./ 1992/ 2-4/4 KH504 ..... **FIC**
  Don't be afraid, Amanda (Sound recording cassette)./ 1994/
  2-4/4 KH504 .... **FIC**
  I'll meet you at the cucumbers./ 1988/ 2-4/5 KH505 .... **FIC**
  SUNFLAKES: POEMS FOR CHILDREN./ 1992/ P-2 KE086 .. **811.008**
MOORE, M/ Under the mermaid angel./ 1995/ 6-A/5 KH506 ... **FIC**
MOORE, Y/ Prairie alphabet./ 1992/ 2-6/6 KE811 .... **971.2**
  Prairie year./ 1994/ 4-6/4 KE812 .... **971.2**
MORA, FX/ Listen to the desert/Oye al desierto./ 1994/
  P-1 KD990 .... **811**
  Little red ant and the great big crumb: a Mexican fable./ 1995/
  1-3/2 KF398 .... **E**
MORA, P/ Desert is my mother./El desierto es mi madre./ 1994/
  K-3 KD989 .... **811**
  Gift of the poinsettia./El regalo de la flor de nochebuena./ 1995/
  3-5/4 KH507 .... **FIC**
  Listen to the desert/Oye al desierto./ 1994/ P-1 KD990 ...... **811**
  Uno, dos, tres: one, two, three./ 1996/ P-1/3 KG155 .... **E**
MORALES, R/ Angel's kite/La estrella de Angel./ 1994/
  2-4/6 KG902 .... **FIC**
MORENO, RK/ Fiesta!/ 1996/ P-1/1 KF655 .... **E**
MOREY, W/ Gentle Ben (Braille)./ n.d.,/ 5-A/6 KH508 .... **FIC**
  Gentle Ben. Reissued./ c1965, 1997/ 5-A/6 KH508 .... **FIC**
  Gentle Ben (Sound recording cassette)./ n.d.,/ 5-A/6 KH508 .. **FIC**
  Home is the North./ c1967, 1990/ 5-A/5 KH509 .... **FIC**
  Kavik, the wolf dog./ c1968/ 4-6/6 KH510 .... **FIC**
  Scrub dog of Alaska./ c1971, 1989/ 5-A/6 KH511 .... **FIC**
MORGAN, A/ Matthew and the midnight pilot./ 1997/ 1-2/3 KG156 **E**
MORGAN, M/ Animal tracks and traces./ 1991/ 3-4/4 KC475 .. **591.5**
  Bloomers!./ 1993/ 3-5/6 KA830 .... **305.42**
  Hannah and Jack./ 1996/ K-2/2 KG170 .... **E**
MORGAN, P/ Squiggle./ 1996/ P-2/3 KG402 .... **E**
MORGAN, T/ Junior Seau: high-voltage linebacker./ 1997/
  5-A/10 KE532 .... **B SEAU, J.**
MORGUI, E/ Monsters and extraterrestrials./ 1996/
  3-6/3 KD449 .... **745.592**
MORIN, A/ Newspaper theatre: creative play production for low budgets
  and no budgets./ 1989/ KA330 .... **PROF 792**
MORIN, P/ Orphan boy: a Maasai story./ 1990/ 4-5/4 KB406 . **398.21**
MORITY, C/ CURRENT BIOGRAPHY YEARBOOK./ 1967-/
  5-6 KA477 .... **REF 920**
MORLEY, J/ Roman villa./ 1992/ 4-6/7 KE641 .... **937**
  Shakespeare's theater./ 1994/ 4-A/7 KD689 .... **792**
MORONEY, L/ Elinda who danced in the sky: an Estonian folktale./ 1990/
  3-5/5 KB407 .... **398.21**
MORPURGO, M/ Butterfly lion./ 1997/ 5-A/5 KH512 .... **FIC**
  Dancing bear./ 1996/ 4-6/5 KH513 .... **FIC**
  Robin of Sherwood./ 1996/ 5-A/6 KH514 .... **FIC**
  Waiting for Anya./ 1991/ 5-A/7 KH515 .... **FIC**
  Wreck of the Zanzibar./ 1995/ 4-6/3 KH516 .... **FIC**
MORRILL, L/ Fourth-grade celebrity./ 1981/ 4-6/6 KH164 .... **FIC**
  Hot fudge./ 1990/ K-3/2 KF777 .... **E**
  Lucky Christmas./ 1994/ 3-5/4 KH086 .... **FIC**
  Rat teeth./ c1984/ 3-5/3 KH166 .... **FIC**
  Scared silly: a Halloween treat./ 1989/ K-3/3 KF780 ..... **E**
MORRIS, A/ Bread, bread, bread./ 1989/ K-2/2 KD293 ..... **641.8**
  Chico karateka./ 1996/ 2-4/5 KD832 .... **796.815**
  Hats, hats, hats./ 1989/ 1-4/1 KB167 .... **391.4**
  Houses and homes./ 1992/ 2-4/6 KD394 .... **728**
  How teddy bears are made: a visit to the Vermont Teddy Bear factory./
  1994/ K-2/3 KD351 .... **688.7**
  Karate boy./ 1996/ 2-4/5 KD832 .... **796.815**
  Loving./ 1990/ 1-3/2 KA880 .... **306.874**
  Tools./ 1992/ P-2/2 KD056 .... **621.9**
MORRIS, BJ/ Administering the school library media center. 3rd ed./
  1992/ KA077 .... **PROF 027.8**
MORRIS, C/ HARCOURT BRACE STUDENT THESAURUS. 2nd ed./ 1994/
  4-6 KA422 .... **REF 423**
MORRIS, J/ Bears, bears, and more bears./ 1995/ P/1 KC850 . **599.78**
  Out of the ark: stories from the world's religions./ 1996/
  3-6/5 KA729 .... **291.1**
MORRIS, RA/ Dolphin./ c1975/ K-2/2 KC778 .... **599.53**
  Dolphin (Braille)./ n.d./ K-2/2 KC778 .... **599.53**
MORRIS, RB/ ENCYCLOPEDIA OF AMERICAN HISTORY. 7th ed./ 1992/
  5-6 KA495 .... **REF 973.03**
MORRISON, K/ MATH FOR THE VERY YOUNG: A HANDBOOK OF
  ACTIVITIES FOR PARENTS AND TEACHERS./ 1995/
  KA254 .... **PROF 372.7**
MORRISON, L/ AT THE CRACK OF THE BAT: BASEBALL POEMS./
  1992/ 3-6 KE053 .... **811.008**
  SLAM DUNK: BASKETBALL POEMS./ 1995/ 4-6 KE081 ... **811.008**
MORRISON, SD/ Passenger pigeon./ 1989/ 4-6/4 KC656 ..... **598**

MORROW, H/ On to Oregon./ c1954/ 5-6/4 KH517 .... **FIC**
  On to Oregon (Talking book)./ n.d./ 5-6/4 KH517 .... **FIC**
MORTIMER, A/ Cats sleep anywhere./ 1996/ K-3 KE101 .... **821**
MOSEL, A/ Tikki Tikki Tembo./ 1967/ P-2/5 KB759 .... **398.27**
  Tikki Tikki Tembo (Big book)./ 1992/ P-2/5 KB759 ...... **398.27**
  Tikki Tikki Tembo (Talking book)./ n.d./ P-2/5 KB759 ... **398.27**
MOSER, B/ Adventures of Sherlock Holmes./ 1992/ 6-A/7 KH082 .. **FIC**
  Adventures of Tom Sawyer./ 1989/ 5-A/4 KH814 .... **FIC**
  Appalachia: the voices of sleeping birds./ 1991/ 3-6/6 KE925 ... **974**
  Bingleman's Midway./ 1995/ 2-4/5 KF128 .... **E**
  Eagle boy: a traditional Navajo legend./ 1996/ 3-4/5 KB587 . **398.24**
  I am the dog, I am the cat./ 1994/ K-3/3 KF661 .... **E**
  In the beginning: creation stories from around the world./ 1988/
  5-6/4 KA731 .... **291.2**
  Jump! The adventures of Brer Rabbit./ 1997/ 3-4/6 KB585 ... **398.24**
  My cats Nick and Nora./ 1995/ P-1/2 KF673 .... **E**
  My dog Rosie./ 1994/ P-1/1 KF674 .... **E**
  On Call Back Mountain./ 1997/ 1-3/2 KF306 .... **E**
  Our new puppy./ 1996/ P-2/1 KF675 .... **E**
  Sky dogs./ 1990/ 2-3/6 KG780 .... **E**
  Tucker Pfeffercorn: an old story retold./ 1994/ 2-3/5 KB351 .. **398.2**
  When birds could talk and bats could sing: the adventures of Bruh
  Sparrow, Sis Wren, and their friends./ 1996/ 2-5/2 KB582 . **398.24**
  When Willard met Babe Ruth./ 1996/ 4-6/6 KH212 .... **FIC**
MOSER, C/ Eagle boy: a traditional Navajo legend./ 1996/
  3-4/5 KB587 .... **398.24**
MOSES, G/ Grandma Moses Night before Christmas./ 1991/
  P-A KD987 .... **811**
MOSS, C/ Little big ears; the story of Ely./ 1997/ K-4/6 KC812 **599.67**
MOSS, J/ Butterfly jar./ 1989/ 2-6 KD991 .... **811**
  PEOPLES OF THE WORLD: NORTH AMERICANS./ 1991/
  6-A KA479 .... **REF 970.004**
MOSS, L/ Zin! zin! zin! a violin./ 1995/ K-3/3 KG157 .... **E**
MOSS, M/ Jumanji (Kit)./ 1995/ K-A KH821 .... **KIT FIC**
  Mel's Diner./ 1994/ K-2/2 KG158 .... **E**
MOSS, T/ I want to be./ 1993/ 1-4/3 KG159 .... **E**
MOST, B/ Dinosaur questions./ 1995/ K-4/7 KC257 ...... **567.9**
  Hippopotamus hunt./ 1994/ 1-3/2 KG160 .... **E**
MOTHER GOOSE/ Children's all-time Mother Goose favorites (Sound
  recording cassette)./ 1989/ KA275 .... **SRC PROF 398.8**
  Glorious Mother Goose./ 1988/ P-K KB803 .... **398.8**
  Michael Foreman's Mother Goose./ 1991/ P-1 KB804 ..... **398.8**
  MY VERY FIRST MOTHER GOOSE./ 1996/ P-K/2 KB808 .. **398.8**
  OLD MOTHER HUBBARD AND HER WONDERFUL DOG./ 1991/
  P-K KB809 .... **398.8**
  Olde Mother Goose (Kit)./ 1993/ P-K KB805 .... **KIT 398.8**
  Real Mother Goose./ c1944, 1994/ P-2 KB806 .... **398.8**
  Real Mother Goose (Braille)./ n.d.,/ P-2 KB806 .... **398.8**
  Real Mother Goose (Talking book)./ n.d.,/ P-2 KB806 .... **398.8**
  Ring o'roses: a nursery rhyme picture book./ 1992/ P-K KB807 . **398.8**
MOTT, EC/ Dancing rainbows: a Pueblo boy's story./ 1996/
  2-4/2 KE794 .... **970.489**
MOUND, L/ Insect./ 1990/ 5-6/8 KC545 .... **595.7**
MOUNT, E/ Milestones in science and technology: the ready reference
  guide to discoveries, inventions, and/ 1994/ 5-A KA441 .. **REF 509**
MOUNTFORD, C/ Kids can type too!/ c1985, 1987/ 4-6 KD311 . **652.3**
MOURT'S RELATION/ Homes in the wilderness: a pilgrim's journal of
  Plymouth Plantation in 1620./ c1939, 1988/ 5-A/8 KE941 ... **974.4**
MOWAT, F/ Lost in the barrens./ 1962/ 5-6/6 KH518 .... **FIC**
  Lost in the barrens (Braille)./ n.d./ 5-6/6 KH518 .... **FIC**
MOXLEY, S/ Arabian nights./ 1994/ 5-6/6 KB358 .... **398.2**
  / 1987/ P-3 KC457 .... **CE 591**
  / 1987/ P-3 KD296 .... **645**
MUELLER, V/ Halloween mask for Monster./ 1986/ P-1/1 KG162 ... **E**
MUFSON, S/ Straight talk about child abuse./ 1991/
  A/10 KB017 .... **362.76**
MUGNAINI, J/ Halloween tree./ c1982/ 5-A/7 KG920 .... **FIC**
MUHLBERGER, R/ What makes a Bruegel a Bruegel?/ 1993/
  5-A/8 KD502 .... **759.9493**
  What makes a Cassatt a Cassatt?/ 1994/ 5-A/7 KD489 ... **759.13**
  What makes a Degas a Degas?/ 1993/ 5-A/7 KD491 ...... **759.4**
  What makes a Goya a Goya?/ 1994/ 5-A/7 KD498 ...... **759.6**
  What makes a Leonardo a Leonardo?/ 1994/ 5-A/7 KD496 ... **759.5**
  What makes a Monet a Monet?/ 1993/ 5-A/7 KD492 ...... **759.4**
  What makes a Picasso a Picasso?/ 1994/ 5-A/7 KD493 .... **759.4**
  What makes a Raphael a Raphael?/ 1993/ 5-A/7 KD497 ... **759.5**
  What makes a Rembrandt a Rembrandt?/ 1993/
  5-A/7 KD500 .... **759.9492**
MUIR, H/ LAROUSSE DICTIONARY OF SCIENTISTS./ 1996/
  5-A KA440 .... **REF 509**
MULLINEAUX, L/ Creating and managing the literate classroom./ 1990/
  KA218 .... **PROF 372.6**
MULLINS, P/ Hattie and the fox./ 1987/ P-2/2 KF569 .... **E**

MUNOZ, O/ Beginning Spanish bilingual dictionary: a beginner's guide in words and pictures. 2nd rev. ed./ 1989/ 3-A KB859 . . . . **463**

MUNOZ, R/ King Island Christmas./ 1985/ K-3/5 KG347 . . . . **E**

Runaway mittens./ 1988/ P-2/4 KG348 . . . . **E**

MUNRO, R/ Inside-outside book of London./ c1989, 1996/ 2-A KE681 . . . . **942.1**

Inside-outside book of Paris./ 1992/ 2-6/8 KE684 . . . . **944**

MUNSCH, R/ Promise is a promise./ 1988/ 3-5/2 KH519 . . . . **FIC**

MUNSINGER, L/ Halloween mask for Monster./ 1986/ P-1/1 KG162 . **E**

Listen Buddy./ 1995/ K-2/2 KF964 . . . . **E**

Princess Penelope's parrot./ 1996/ K-2/2 KF965 . . . . **E**

Three blind mice mystery./ 1995/ 1-3/2 KF925 . . . . **E**

Wanted: best friend./ 1997/ K-2/2 KG152 . . . . **E**

Week of raccoons./ 1988/ K-2/5 KG710 . . . . **E**

ZOOFUL OF ANIMALS./ 1992/ K-4 KE090 . . . . **811.008**

MUNSON, HR/ Science experiences with everyday things./ 1988/ KA283 . . . . **PROF 507**

MURDOCH, DH/ Cowboy./ 1993/ 4-A/8 KF040 . . . . **978**

North American Indian./ 1995/ 4-6/8 KE751 . . . . **970.1**

MURDOCH, EC/ Robert E. Lee./ 1995/ 4-5/6 KE430 . . . . **B LEE, R.**

MURIE, OJ/ Field guide to animal tracks. 2nd ed./ 1974/ A/8 KC476 . . . . **591.5**

MURPHY, B/ Experiment with water./ 1991/ K-3/4 KC101 . . . . . . **532**

MURPHY, CR/ Child's Alaska./ 1994/ 3-5/8 KF101 . . . . **979.8**

Prince and the Salmon People./ 1993/ 4-6/7 KB352 . . . . **398.2**

MURPHY, J/ Across America on an emigrant train./ 1993/ 6-A/8 KB140 . . . . **385**

Boys' war: Confederate and Union soldiers talk about the Civil War./ 1990/ 5-6/7 KE909 . . . . **973.7**

Boys' war: Confederate and Union soldiers talk about the Civil War (Sound recording cassette)./ 1993/ 5-6/7 KE909 . . . . . . **973.7**

Great fire./ 1995/ A/7 KF015 . . . . **977.3**

Into the deep forest with Henry David Thoreau./ 1995/ 5-A/7 KE929 . . . . **974.1**

Jeffrey Strangewords./ 1994/ 4-5/7 KH520 . . . . **FIC**

Long road to Gettysburg./ 1992/ 5-A/7 KE910 . . . . **973.7**

Songs about insects, bugs and squiggly things (Compact disc)./ 1993/ P-2 KC546 . . . . **SRC 595.7**

Songs about insects, bugs and squiggly things (Sound recording cassette)./ 1993/ P-2 KC546 . . . . **SRC 595.7**

Songs for you and me: kids learn about feelings and emotions (Sound recording cassette)./ n.d./ K-1 KA629 . . . . **SRC 152.4**

Young patriot: the American Revolution as experienced by one boy./ 1996/ 5-A/9 KE884 . . . . **973.3**

MURPHY, SJ/ Best bug parade./ 1996/ P-1/1 KG163 . . . . **E**

Best vacation ever./ 1997/ K-2/2 KG164 . . . . **E**

Pair of socks./ 1996/ P-1/1 KA634 . . . . **153.14**

Too many kangaroo things to do!/ 1996/ P-3/2 KB974 . . . . . **513.2**

MURPHY, VR/ Across the plains in the Donner Party./ 1996/ 5-6/7 KF041 . . . . **978**

MURRAY, P/ Amazon./ 1994/ 3-6/7 KE212 . . . . **918.1**

Everglades./ 1993/ 3-6/6 KE195 . . . . **917.59**

Hummingbirds./ 1993/ 3-5/6 KC700 . . . . **598.7**

Parrots./ 1993/ 3-5/7 KC701 . . . . **598.7**

Porcupines./ 1994/ 1-4/6 KC745 . . . . **599.35**

Sahara./ 1994/ 3-6/6 KE731 . . . . **966**

MUSGROVE, M/ Ashanti to Zulu: African traditions./ c1976/ 4-6/6 KE727 . . . . **960**

MY VERY FIRST MOTHER GOOSE./ 1996/ P-K/2 KB808 . . . . . **398.8**

MYERS, A/ Cheyenne./ 1992/ 4-6/7 KE761 . . . . **970.3**

Rosie's tiger./ 1994/ 4-A/4 KH521 . . . . **FIC**

MYERS, C/ Harlem: a poem./ 1997/ 3-6 KD994 . . . . **811**

MYERS, CA/ Galapagos: islands of change./ 1995/ 4-A/8 KF113 . . . . **986.6**

MYERS, J/ What makes popcorn pop?: and other questions about the world around us./ c1991, 1994/ 3-6/7 KB868 . . . . **500**

MYERS, LB/ Galapagos: islands of change./ 1995/ 4-A/8 KF113 **986.6**

MYERS, WD/ Brown angels: an album of pictures and verse./ 1993/ K-6 KD992 . . . . **811**

Glorious angels: a celebration of children./ 1995/ K-6 KD993 . . . **811**

Glory Field./ 1994/ 6-A/6 KH522 . . . . **FIC**

Glory Field (Sound recording cassette)./ 1996/ 6-A/6 KH522 . . . . **FIC**

Harlem: a poem./ 1997/ 3-6 KD994 . . . . **811**

Malcolm X: by any means necessary: a biography./ 1993/ 6-A/8 KE456 . . . . **B MALCOLM X**

Now is your time!: the African-American struggle for freedom./ 1991/ A/7 KE858 . . . . **973**

Now is your time!: the African-American struggle for freedom (Sound recording cassette)./ 1993/ A/7 KE858 . . . . **973**

Place called heartbreak: a story of Vietnam./ 1993/ 5-6/6 KE721 . . . . **959.704**

Righteous revenge of Artemis Bonner./ 1994/ 5-A/7 KH523 . . . . . **FIC**

Story of the three kingdoms./ 1995/ 1-3/3 KG165 . . . . **E**

Story of the three kingdoms (Sound recording cassette)./ 1997/ 1-3/3 KG165 . . . . **E**

Toussaint L'Ouverture: the fight for Haiti's freedom./ 1996/ 4-A/8 KE569 . . . . **B TOUSSAINT**

Young landlords./ c1979/ 5-6/6 KH524 . . . . **FIC**

Young landlords (Sound recording cassette)./ n.d./ 5-6/6 KH524 . . **FIC**

NABB, M/ Enchanted horse./ 1993/ 4-6/7 KH525 . . . . **FIC**

NADEN, CJ/ Best books for children: preschool through grade 6. 5th ed./ 1994/ KA084 . . . . **PROF 028.1**

Colin Powell: straight to the top. Updated ed./ 1997/ 3-6/7 KE502 . . . . **B POWELL, C.**

John Muir: saving the wilderness./ 1992/ 5-6/4 KE473 . . **B MUIR, J.**

Juniorplots 4: a book talk guide for use with readers ages 12-16./ 1993/ KA091 . . . . **PROF 028.5**

Middleplots 4: a book talk guide for use with readers ages 8-12./ 1994/ KA092 . . . . **PROF 028.5**

Newbery companion: booktalk and related materials for Newbery Medal and Honor Books./ 1996/ KA035 . . . . **PROF 016.813**

People of peace./ 1994/ 5-A/7 KA806 . . . . **303.6**

White House kids./ 1995/ 5-6/7 KA849 . . . . **973**

NAGDA, AW/ Canopy crossing: a story of an Atlantic rainforest (Kit)./ 1997/ 2-4 KC873 . . . . **KIT 599.8**

NAGEL, R/ HISPANIC AMERICAN BIOGRAPHY./ 1995/ 5-A KA400 . . . . **REF 305.8**

WORLD LEADERS: PEOPLE WHO SHAPED THE WORLD./ 1994/ 5-A KA408 . . . . **REF 350**

NAGY, WE/ Teaching vocabulary to improve reading comprehension./ 1988/ KA211 . . . . **PROF 372.4**

NAIDOO, B/ No turning back: a novel of South Africa./ 1997/ 6-A/6 KH526 . . . . **FIC**

NAKAMURA, J/ MAJOR AUTHORS AND ILLUSTRATORS FOR CHILDREN AND YOUNG ADULTS: A SELECTION OF SKETCHES FROM SOMETHING ABOUT THE AUTHOR./ 1993/ KA464 . . . . **REF 809**

SOMETHING ABOUT THE AUTHOR AUTOBIOGRAPHY SERIES./ 1986-/ 4-6 KA466 . . . . **REF 809**

NAMIOKA, L/ Yang the third and her impossible family./ 1995/ 3-6/6 KH527 . . . . **FIC**

Yang the youngest and his terrible ear./ 1994/ 5-A/5 KH528 . . . . **FIC**

NANNY, M/ Planetary taxi (CD-ROM)./ 1993/ 4-A KC013 . **CDR 523.2**

NANTON, I/ British Columbia./ 1994/ 5-A/9 KE810 . . . . **971.1**

NAPOLI, DJ/ Bravest thing./ 1995/ 3-5/6 KH529 . . . . **FIC**

Jimmy, the pickpocket of the palace./ 1995/ 3-A/3 KH530 . . . . . **FIC**

Prince of the pond: otherwise known as De Fawg Pin./ 1992/ 3-A/3 KH531 . . . . **FIC**

NARAHASHI, K/ I have a friend./ 1987/ P-2/2 KG166 . . . . **CE E**

Magic purse./ 1993/ 2-4/4 KB379 . . . . **398.2**

Rain talk./ 1990/ P-1/4 KG441 . . . . **E**

What's what?: a guessing game./ 1996/ P-1/2 KG443 . . . . **E**

Who said red?/ 1988/ P-K/2 KG444 . . . . **E**

NARDI, TJ/ Karate and judo./ 1996/ 3-6/6 KD833 . . . . **796.815**

NASTA, V/ Plane song./ 1993/ 3-6 KD112 . . . . **629.133**

NATCHEV, A/ Hobyahs./ 1996/ 3-4/6 KB647 . . . . **398.24**

Tom, Babette, and Simon: three tales of transformation./ 1995/ 3-6/4 KG866 . . . . **FIC**

Wagonload of fish./ 1996/ K-2/5 KB532 . . . . **398.24**

Wet world./ 1995/ P-1/3 KG508 . . . . **E**

NATIONAL ACADEMY OF SCIENCES (U.S.)/ RESOURCES FOR TEACHING ELEMENTARY SCHOOL SCIENCE./ 1996/ KA203 . . . . **PROF 372.3**

NATIONAL COUNCIL OF TEACHERS OF MATHEMATICS/ NEW DIRECTIONS FOR ELEMENTARY SCHOOL MATHEMATICS, 1989 YEARBOOK./ 1989/ KA255 . . . . **PROF 372.7**

NATIONAL GALLERY (GREAT BRITAIN)/ HARK! THE HERALD ANGELS SING./ 1993/ K-6 KD534 . . . . **782.28**

NATIONAL GALLERY OF ART (U.S.)/ Catalogue of color reproductions: books and catalogues, educational materials./ n.d./ KA308 . . . . **PROF 703**

NATIONAL GEOGRAPHIC SOCIETY/ NATIONAL GEOGRAPHIC PICTURE ATLAS OF OUR FIFTY STATES./ 1994/ 4-A KA475 . . . **REF 912.73**

NATIONAL MUSEUM OF AMERICAN ART, SMITHSONIAN INSTITUTE/ CELEBRATE AMERICA IN POETRY AND ART./ 1994/ 3-6 KE054 . . . . **811.008**

NATIONAL MUSEUM OF AMERICAN HISTORY (U.S.)/ MINDS-ON SCIENCE: FOR PROFIT, FOR PLANET (Videodisc)./ 1995/ 5-A KD348 . . . . **VD 687**

MINDS-ON SCIENCE: FOR THE SAKE OF THE NATION (Videodisc)./ 1995/ 5-A KA804 . . . . **VD 303.48**

MINDS-ON SCIENCE: THE IMPACT OF DISCOVERY (Videodisc)./ 1995/ 5-A KB875 . . . . **VD 502**

NATIONAL RESEARCH COUNCIL (U.S.)/ NATIONAL SCIENCE EDUCATION STANDARDS: OBSERVE, INTERACT, CHANGE, LEARN./ 1996/ KA284 . . . . **PROF 507**

NATIONAL SCIENCE RESOURCE CENTER (U.S.)/ RESOURCES FOR TEACHING ELEMENTARY SCHOOL SCIENCE./ 1996/ KA203 . . . . **PROF 372.3**
NATIONAL STORYTELLING ASSOCIATION (U.S.)/ MANY VOICES: TRUE TALES FROM AMERICA'S PAST./ 1995/ KA371 . . . . . . **PROF 973**
NATIVITY./ 1996/ 3-5/5 KA709 . . . . **232.92**
NATTI, S/ Cam Jansen and the ghostly mystery./ 1996/ 2-4/2 KG815 . . . . **FIC**
Cam Jansen and the mystery of the dinosaur bones./ 1981/ 2-4/4 KG816 . . . . **CE FIC**
Cam Jansen and the mystery of the stolen diamonds./ 1980/ 2-4/3 KG817 . . . . **FIC**
Don't call me Beanhead!/ 1994/ 2-3/5 KH877 . . . . **FIC**
Lionel at large./ 1986/ K-2/2 KF924 . . . . **E**
Today was a terrible day./ 1980/ 1-2/2 KF616 . . . . . . **CE E**
Today was a terrible day (Kit)./ 1993/ 1-2 KF617 . . . . . . **KIT E**
Young Cam Jansen and the dinosaur game./ 1996/ 1-2/2 KF132 . . . **E**
Young Cam Jansen and the lost tooth./ 1997/ 1-2/2 KF133 . . . . . . **E**
Young Cam Jansen and the missing cookie./ 1996/ 1-2/2 KF134 . . . **E**
NAVASKY, B/ FESTIVAL IN MY HEART: POEMS BY JAPANESE CHILDREN./ 1993/ 3-A KE134 . . . . **895.6**
NAYLOR, AP/ Children talking about books./ 1993/ KA236 . . . . **PROF 372.64**
NAYLOR, PR/ Agony of Alice./ 1985/ 5-6/6 KH532 . . . . **FIC**
Agony of Alice (Sound recording cassette)./ n.d./ 5-6/6 KH532 . . **FIC**
Alice in April./ 1993/ 6-A/6 KH533 . . . . **FIC**
Alice in rapture, sort of./ 1989/ 6-A/6 KH533 . . . . **FIC**
Alice the brave./ 1995/ 6-A/6 KH533 . . . . **FIC**
All but Alice./ 1992/ 6-A/6 KH533 . . . . **FIC**
All but Alice (Sound recording cassette)./ 1993/ 6-A/6 KH533 . . . **FIC**
Beetles, lightly toasted./ 1987/ 5-6/6 KH534 . . . . **FIC**
Bernie and the Bessledorf ghost./ 1990/ 4-6/5 KH535 . . . . . **FIC**
Bodies in the Bessledorf Hotel./ 1988/ 4-6/5 KH535 . . . . . . **FIC**
Face in the Bessledorf Funeral Parlor./ 1993/ 4-6/5 KH535 . . . **FIC**
Grand escape./ 1993/ 3-6/7 KH536 . . . . **FIC**
King of the playground./ 1991/ K-3/2 KG167 . . . . **E**
Reluctantly Alice./ 1991/ 6-A/6 KH533 . . . . **FIC**
Reluctantly Alice (Sound recording cassette)./ 1993/ 6-A/6 KH533 . **FIC**
Saving Shiloh./ 1997/ 4-A/4 KH537 . . . . **FIC**
Shiloh./ 1991/ 4-6/6 KH538 . . . . **CE FIC**
Shiloh season./ 1996/ 4-A/4 KH539 . . . . **CE FIC**
Shiloh (Sound recording cassette)./ 1993/ 4-6/6 KH538 . . . . **CE FIC**
Shiloh (Talking book)./ 1992/ 4-6/6 KH538 . . . . **CE FIC**
N.E. THING ENTERPRISES/ MAGIC EYE: A NEW WAY OF LOOKING AT THE WORLD./ 1993/ 3-A KA620 . . . . **152.14**
NEEDHAM, JM/ One on a web: counting animals at home./ 1997/ P-2/3 KC456 . . . . **591**
NEILL, JR/ Road to Oz./ 1991/ 4-6/7 KG884 . . . . **FIC**
Scarecrow of Oz./ 1997/ 4-6/7 KG885 . . . . **FIC**
NEITZEL, S/ Dress I'll wear to the party./ 1992/ P-2/2 KG168 . . . . . **E**
Jacket I wear in the snow./ 1989/ P-2/2 KG168 . . . . **E**
Jacket I wear in the snow (Big book)./ 1997/ P-2/2 KG168 . . . . **E**
We're making breakfast for Mother./ 1997/ P-1/2 KG169 . . . . . . **E**
NELSON, A/ Canto familiar./ 1995/ 4-6 KE028 . . . . **811**
NELSON, EL/ Everybody sing and dance./ 1989/ KA321 . . . . **CE PROF 789.3**
Everybody sing and dance (Sound recording cassette)./ 1989/ KA321 . . . . **CE PROF 789.3**
NELSON, RW/ Selma, Lord, Selma: girlhood memories of the civil-rights days./ c1980, 1997/ A/7 KA906 . . . . **323.1**
NELSON, T/ Earthshine: a novel./ 1994/ 6-A/4 KH540 . . . . **FIC**
NELSON, VM/ Zoolutions: a mathematical expedition with topics for grades 4 through 8./ c1993, 1996/ KA251 . . . . **PROF 372.7**
NESBIT, E/ Enchanted castle./ c1907, 1985/ 5-6/7 KH541 . . . . . **FIC**
Enchanted castle./ 1992/ 5-A/6 KH542 . . . . **FIC**
Enchanted castle (Braille)./ n.d.,/ 5-6/7 KH541 . . . . **FIC**
Enchanted castle (Sound recording cassette)./ n.d.,/ 5-6/7 KH541 . **FIC**
Railway children./ 1994/ 4-5/7 KH543 . . . . **FIC**
Railway children (Large type)./ 1988/ 4-5/7 KH543 . . . . **FIC**
Story of the treasure seekers./ 1986/ 5-6/7 KH544 . . . . **FIC**
Wouldbegoods./ 1985/ 5-6/7 KH544 . . . . **FIC**
NESBITT, J/ Tall story and other tales./ 1992/ 4-6/4 KH453 . . . . . **FIC**
NESS, C/ Ocean of story: fairy tales from India./ 1996/ 4-6/5 KB353 . . . . **398.2**
NESS, E/ TOM TIT TOT: AN ENGLISH FOLK TALE./ c1965, 1997/ P-3/6 KB378 . . . . **398.2**
NETHERY, M/ Hannah and Jack./ 1996/ K-2/2 KG170 . . . . . . **E**
NEUFELD, J/ Edgar Allan: a novel./ c1968/ 4-A/5 KH545 . . . . . . **FIC**
Edgar Allan: a novel (Braille)./ n.d./ 4-A/5 KH545 . . . . **FIC**
Gaps in stone walls./ 1996/ 6-A/7 KH546 . . . . **FIC**
NEUMEIER, M/ Action alphabet./ 1985/ 1-3 KG171 . . . . **E**
NEVILLE, EC/ It's like this, Cat./ c1963/ 5-6/6 KH547 . . . . . **CE FIC**
It's like this, Cat (Braille)./ n.d./ 5-6/6 KH547 . . . . **CE FIC**

It's like this, Cat (Sound recording cassette)./ n.d./ 5-6/6 KH547 . . . . **CE FIC**
It's like this, Cat (Talking book)./ It's like this, Cat (Talking book)./ 1970/ n.d./ 5-6/6 KH547 . . . . **CE FIC**
5-6/6 KH547 . . . . **CE FIC**
NEWBIGGING, M/ Cybersurfer: the Owl Internet guide for kids./ 1996/ 3-A/8 KG177 . . . . **BC 025.04**
NEWFELDT, V/ WEBSTER'S NEW WORLD CHILDREN'S DICTIONARY. New ed./ 1997/ 3-5 KB838 . . . . **423**
NEWKIRK, I/ Kids can save the animals!: 101 easy things to do./ 1991/ 3-6/7 KA673 . . . . **179**
NEWMAN, CM/ How to use cooperative learning in the mathematics class./ 1990/ KA250 . . . . **PROF 372.7**
NEWMAN, L/ Too far away to touch./ 1995/ 1-3/6 KG172 . . . . . . **E**
NEWMAN, R/ All aboard ABC./ 1990/ K-2/2 KD075 . . . . **625.1**
NEWMAN, SP/ Incas./ 1992/ 5-6/7 KF103 . . . . **980.3**
Inuits./ 1993/ 4-6/7 KF102 . . . . **979.8**
NEWSOM, C/ Kevin Corbett eats flies./ 1989/ 5-6/3 KH248 . . . . . **FIC**
NEWSOM, T/ Mystery of the cupboard./ 1993/ 5-A/6 KH628 . **CE FIC**
NEWTON, J/ Frog Princess?/ 1995/ 1-3/2 KG058 . . . . **E**
NG, S/ Tales from Gold Mountain: stories of the Chinese in the New World./ 1989/ 5-A/7 KH890 . . . . **FIC**
NGUYEN, PT/
From rice paddies and temple yards: traditional music of Vietnam./ From rice paddies and temple yards: traditional music of Vietnam./ c1990, 1992/ 1992,/ KA317 . . . . **BA PROF 789.2**
KA317 . . . . **BA PROF 789.2**
NIC LEODHAS, S/ Always room for one more./ 1965/ K-2/7 KB760 . . . . **398.27**
Always room for one more (Braille)./ n.d./ K-2/7 KB760 . . . . **398.27**
NICHOL, B/ Beethoven lives upstairs./ 1994/ 4-6/4 KH549 . . . . . . **FIC**
Beethoven lives upstairs (Talking book)./ Beethoven lives upstairs (Talking book)./ 1991/ 1991/ 4-6 KH550 . . . . **VCR FIC**
4-6 KH550 . . . . **VCR FIC**
Beethoven lives upstairs (Videocassette)./ 1992/ 4-6 KH550 . **VCR FIC**
Beethoven vive arriba./ 1996/ 4-6/4 KH549 . . . . **FIC**
NICHOLSON, D/ Wild boars./ 1987/ 5-6/9 KC786 . . . . **599.63**
NICHOLSON, J/ How the rhinoceros got his skin; and, How the camel got his hump (Videocassette)./ 1987/ 2-5 KH361 . . . . . . **VCR FIC**
NICHOLSON, W/ Velveteen Rabbit; or, How toys become real./ 1988/ 3-5/6 KH864 . . . . **CE FIC**
NICKLES, G/ Giraffes./ 1997/ 3-5/7 KC788 . . . . **599.638**
NIELSEN, NJ/ Carnivorous plants./ 1992/ 1-6/6 KC431 . . . . **583**
NIERING, WA/ Audubon Society field guide to North American wildflowers, Eastern Region./ 1979/ 3-6 KC407 . . . . . **582.13**
NIEVES, ER/ Juan Bobo: four folktales from Puerto Rico./ 1994/ 1-2/2 KB427 . . . . **398.22**
NIKOLA-LISA, W/ Alegria de ser tu y yo./ 1996/ P-2 KD996 . . . . **811**
Bein' with you this way./ 1994/ P-2 KD996 . . . . **811**
One hole in the road./ 1996/ P-K/2 KG173 . . . . **E**
Storm./ 1993/ P-1/2 KG174 . . . . **E**
NIMMO, J/ Griffin's castle./ 1997/ 6-A/5 KH551 . . . . **FIC**
NIRGIOTIS, N/ No more dodos: how zoos help endangered wildlife./ 1996/ A/6 KD256 . . . . **639.9**
NIRGIOTIS, T/ No more dodos: how zoos help endangered wildlife./ 1996/ A/6 KD256 . . . . **639.9**
NITTA, K/ Twisters!/ 1996/ 2-4/3 KC204 . . . . **551.55**
NOAKES, P/ TREASURY OF STORIES FOR FIVE YEAR OLDS./ 1992/ 2-4/5 KH805 . . . . **FIC**
NOBLE, TH/ Apple tree Christmas./ 1984/ K-3/6 KG175 . . . . . . **E**
Day Jimmy's boa ate the wash./ 1980/ K-2/2 KG176 . . . . **CE E**
Day Jimmy's boa ate the wash (Braille)./ n.d./ K-2/2 KG176 . . . **CE E**
Day Jimmy's boa ate the wash (Videocassette)./ 1992/ K-2/2 KG176 . . . . **CE E**
Dia que la boa de Jimmy se comio la ropa./ 1997/ K-2/2 KG176 . . . . **CE E**
Jimmy's boa and the big splash birthday bash./ 1989/ K-2/2 KG176 . . . . **CE E**
Jimmy's boa bounces back./ 1984/ K-2/2 KG176 . . . . . . **CE E**
Jimmy's boa bounces back (Braille)./ n.d./ K-2/2 KG176 . . . . **CE E**
NODELMAN, P/ TOUCHSTONES: REFLECTIONS ON THE BEST IN CHILDREN'S LITERATURE, VOL. 1./ 1985/ KA359 . . . . . **PROF 809**
NODSET, JL/ Go away, dog./ c1963, 1993/ P-1/1 KG177 . . . . **E**
NOFSINGER, R/ Pigeons and doves./ 1992/ 4-6/4 KC696 . . . . . **598.6**
NOLAN, D/ Dinosaur dream./ 1990/ 2-3/5 KG178 . . . . **E**
William Shakespeare's A midsummer night's dream./ 1996/ 4-6/4 KE114 . . . . **822.3**
Wings./ c1991, 1997/ 5-6/4 KA754 . . . . **292**
NOLL, CK/ BEN FRANKLIN BOOK OF EASY AND INCREDIBLE EXPERIMENTS./ 1995/ A/8 KB889 . . . . **507.8**
NOLL, S/ Sunflower./ 1995/ P-1/1 KF566 . . . . **E**
Surprise!/ 1997/ P-K/2 KG179 . . . . **E**
NOONAN, J/ Nineteenth-century inventors./ 1992/ 5-6/7 KC897 . **609**

NOONAN, W/ Bigfoot and other legendary creatures./ 1992/
4-6/6 KA564 . . . . **001.944**
NOREIKA, R/ Moon for seasons./ 1994/ 3-6 KE034 . . . . **811**
NOREY, V/ Read-aloud handbook. 4th ed./ 1995/
KA242 . . . . **PROF 372.64**
NORMAN, D/ Dinosaur./ 1989/ 3-A/7 KC258 . . . . **567.9**
NORMILE, D/
Gymnastics./ Gymnastics./ 1996/ 1996/ 3-6/6 KD817 . . . . . **796.44**
3-6/6 KD817 . . . . **796.44**
NORTON, M/ Are all the giants dead?/ c1975, 1997/
4-A/5 KH552 . . . . **FIC**
Are all the giants dead? (Braille)./ n.d., 4-A/5 KH552 . . . . **FIC**
Bed-knob and broomstick./ c1957/ 4-6/5 KH553 . . . . **FIC**
Bed-knob and broomstick (Braille)./ n.d./ 4-6/5 KH553 . . . . . **FIC**
Borrowers./ c1953, 1989/ 4-6/6 KH554 . . . . **CE FIC**
Borrowers afield./ 1970/, 4-6/6 KH554 . . . . **CE FIC**
Borrowers afield (Braille)./ n.d., 4-6/6 KH554 . . . . **CE FIC**
Borrowers afloat./ 1955/, 4-6/6 KH554 . . . . **CE FIC**
Borrowers afloat (Sound recording cassette)./ 1997,/
4-6/6 KH554 . . . . **CE FIC**
Borrowers aloft./ 1961/, 4-6/6 KH554 . . . . **CE FIC**
Borrowers aloft (Braille)./ n.d., 4-6/6 KH554 . . . . **CE FIC**
Borrowers aloft (Sound recording cassette)./ 1997/
4-6/6 KH554 . . . . **CE FIC**
Borrowers avenged./ 1986/, 4-6/6 KH554 . . . . **CE FIC**
Borrowers avenged (Braille)./ n.d., 4-6/6 KH554 . . . . **CE FIC**
Borrowers avenged (Sound recording cassette)./ n.d.,/
4-6/6 KH554 . . . . **CE FIC**
Borrowers (Braille)./ n.d., 4-6/6 KH554 . . . . **CE FIC**
Borrowers (Sound recording cassette)./ n.d., 4-6/6 KH554 . . **CE FIC**
NORWORTH, J/ Take me out to the ballgame./ 1992/
K-2 KD639 . . . . **789.3**
NOTTINGHAM, T/ Chess for children./ 1993/ 4-A/8 KD756 . . . **794.1**
NOURSE, AE/ Virus invaders./ 1992/ A/10 KD012 . . . . **616**
NOVAK, J/ Where in the world are you? a guide to looking at the world./
1990/ 4-6/7 KE145 . . . . **910**
NOVAK, M/ Mouse TV./ 1994/ K-2/3 KG180 . . . . **E**
Newt./ 1996/ 1-3/2 KG181 . . . . **E**
Twelve snails to one lizard: a tale of mischief and measurement./ 1997/
1-3/2 KF726 . . . . **E**
NOVOSAD, C/ NYSTROM DESK ATLAS./ 1994/ 5-A KA474 **REF 912**
NRBQ (MUSICAL GROUP)/ Stormalong (Kit)./ 1995/
2-5 KB470 . . . . **KIT 398.22**
NUMEROFF, LJ/ Why a disguise?/ 1996/ K-2/2 KG182 . . . . **E**
NUNES, S/ Last dragon./ 1995/ 2-3/3 KG183 . . . . **E**
NURMI, KE/ Grandchildren of the Incas./ 1991/ 4-6/6 KF110 . . . . **985**
NURSERY TALES AROUND THE WORLD./ 1996/ P-2/7 KB354 . **398.2**
NYE, NS/ TREE IS OLDER THAN YOU ARE: A BILINGUAL GATHERING
OF POEMS AND STORIES FROM MEXICO WITH PAINTINGS BY
MEXICAN ARTISTS./ 1995/ 5-A KE121 . . . . **860.9**
O, N/ Carter G. Woodson: the father of black history./ 1991/
3-6/2 KE601 . . . . **B WOODSON, C.**
Mary Church Terrell: leader for equality./ 1991/
3-6/2 KE562 . . . . **B TERRELL, M.**
OBERMAN, S/ Always Prayer Shawl./ 1994/ 2-4/2 KG184 . . . . **E**
White stone in the castle wall./ 1995/ 4-6/2 KH555 . . . . **FIC**
OBLIGADO, L/ Chocolate cow./ 1993/ K-2/2 KG185 . . . . **E**
O'BRIEN, AS/ Jamaica and Brianna./ 1993/ K-2/2 KF680 . . . . . . **E**
Jamaica's blue marker./ 1995/ K-1/2 KF681 . . . . **E**
Jamaica's find./ 1986/ K-2/2 KF682 . . . . **E**
Princess and the beggar: a Korean folktale./ 1993/
3-4/6 KB761 . . . . **398.27**
Welcoming babies./ 1994/ P-1/2 KA875 . . . . **306.87**
O'BRIEN, C/ Sam's sneaker search./ 1997/ P-2/3 KG186 . . . . **E**
O'BRIEN, J/ Accidents may happen./ 1996/ 4-A/9 KC895 . . . . . **609**
Daffy down dillies: silly limericks./ 1992/ K-A KE103 . . . . . . **821**
Dear old Donegal./ 1996/ 1-3/2 KD766 . . . . **789.2**
Fast Freddie Frog and other tongue-twister rhymes./ 1993/
2-6 KB812 . . . . **398.8**
Irish piper./ 1991/ 3-5/6 KB463 . . . . **398.22**
This is baseball./ c1993, 1997/ P-1/2 KD795 . . . . **796.357**
TWELVE DAYS OF CHRISTMAS./ 1993/ P-A KD538 . . . . . **782.28**
What his father did./ 1992/ 2-4/5 KB305 . . . . **398.2**
O'BRIEN, RC/ Mrs. Frisby and the rats of NIMH./ c1971/
4-A/6 KH556 . . . . **FIC**
Mrs. Frisby and the rats of NIMH (Braille)./ n.d./ 4-A/6 KH556 . **FIC**
Mrs. Frisby and the rats of NIMH (Sound recording cassette)./ n.d./
4-A/6 KH556 . . . . **FIC**
Mrs. Frisby and the rats of NIMH (Talking book)./ n.d./
4-A/6 KH556 . . . . **FIC**
Senora a Frisby y las ratas de nimh./ 1985/ 4-A/6 KH556 . . . . . **FIC**
O'BRIEN, TC/ PUZZLE TANKS: A GAME OF NUMBERS AND LOGIC
(Microcomputer program)./ 1984/ 3-A KB940 . . . . **MCP 511**

OCHOA, G/ Fall of Quebec and the French and Indian War./ 1990/
5-6/7 KE873 . . . . **973.2**
OCHS, CP/ When I'm alone./ 1993/ P-2/4 KG187 . . . . **E**
OCKENGA, S/ World of wonders: a trip through numbers./ 1988/
3-A/3 KB975 . . . . **513.2**
O'CONNOR, B/ Mammolina: a story about Maria Montessori./ 1993/
4-6/6 KE467 . . . . **B MONTESSORI, M**
O'CONNOR, J/ Comeback!: four true stories./ 1992/ 2-4/3 KD765 **796**
Lulu and the witch baby./ 1986/ K-3/2 KG188 . . . . **E**
Nina, Nina ballerina./ 1993/ P-1/1 KG189 . . . . **E**
O'CONNOR, J/ Feather book./ 1990/ 5-6/6 KC670 . . . . **598.147**
Herring gull./ 1992/ 5-6/5 KC657 . . . . **598**
O'CONOR, J/ Coaching Ms. Parker./ 1992/ 2-4/4 KH255 . . . . . . **FIC**
ODA, K/ Moon princess./ 1993/ 3-4/4 KB404 . . . . **398.21**
O'DELL, S/ Black pearl./ c1967/ 5-6/5 KH557 . . . . **CE FIC**
Black pearl (Braille)./ n.d./ 5-6/5 KH557 . . . . **CE FIC**
Black pearl (Talking book)./ n.d./ 5-6/5 KH557 . . . . **CE FIC**
Captive./ 1979/ 6-A/6 KH558 . . . . **FIC**
Cruise of the Arctic Star./ c1973/ 5-6/6 KE208 . . . . **917.94**
Island of the Blue Dolphins./ c1960/ 5-6/6 KH559 . . . . **FIC**
Island of the Blue Dolphins./ c1960, 1990/ 5-6/6 KH560 . . . . . **FIC**
Island of the Blue Dolphins (Braille)./ n.d./ 5-6/6 KH559 . . . . **FIC**
Island of the Blue Dolphins (Sound recording cassette)./ n.d./
5-6/6 KH559 . . . . **FIC**
Island of the Blue Dolphins (Talking book)./ n.d./ 5-6/6 KH559 . . **FIC**
Negra perla./ n.d./ 5-6/5 KH557 . . . . **CE FIC**
Sarah Bishop./ 1980/ 5-6/5 KH561 . . . . **FIC**
Sarah Bishop (Braille)./ n.d./ 5-6/5 KH561 . . . . **FIC**
Sarah Bishop (Sound recording cassette)./ n.d./ 5-6/5 KH561 . . . **FIC**
Sing down the moon./ c1970/ 5-6/3 KH562 . . . . **CE FIC**
Sing down the moon (Sound recording cassette)./ n.d./
5-6/3 KH562 . . . . **CE FIC**
Sing down the moon (Talking book)./ Sing down the moon (Talking
book)./ 1973/ n.d./ 5-6/3 KH562 . . . . **CE FIC**
5-6/3 KH562 . . . . **CE FIC**
Sing down the moon (Videocassette)./ 1986/ 5-6/3 KH562 . . **CE FIC**
Thunder rolling in the mountains./ 1992/ 5-A/5 KH563 . . . . . . **FIC**
Thunder rolling in the mountains (Sound recording cassette)./ 1996/
5-A/5 KH563 . . . . **FIC**
Zia./ 1976/ 6-A/7 KH564 . . . . **CE FIC**
Zia (Talking book)./ 1993/ 6-A/7 KH564 . . . . **CE FIC**
OECHSLI, K/ Scruffy./ 1988/ K-3/1 KG217 . . . . **E**
OGBURN, JK/ Noise lullaby./ 1995/ P-2/2 KG190 . . . . **E**
OGDEN, B/ Pal the pony./ 1996/ K-1/2 KF714 . . . . **E**
OHI, R/ Cat of Artimus Pride./ 1991/ 3-5/5 KH307 . . . . **FIC**
Prince of Tarn./ 1997/ 4-6/5 KH308 . . . . **FIC**
Tess./ 1995/ 3-5/4 KH309 . . . . **FIC**
Within a painted past./ 1994/ 5-A/4 KH311 . . . . **FIC**
OHLSSON, I/ Celebration: the story of American holidays./ 1993/
4-6/7 KB201 . . . . **394.26**
It happened in America: true stories from the fifty states./ 1992/
4-A/7 KE861 . . . . **973**
OKIE, S/ To space and back./ 1986/ 4-6/7 KD138 . . . . **629.45**
OLALEYE, I/ Distant talking drum: poems from Nigeria./ 1995/
K-2 KE139 . . . . **896**
Distant talking drum: poems from Nigeria (Sound recording cassette)./
1997/ K-2 KE139 . . . . **896**
OLD MOTHER HUBBARD AND HER WONDERFUL DOG./ 1991/
P-K KB809 . . . . **398.8**
OLD, WC/ Duke Ellington: giant of jazz./ 1996/
5-A/9 KE338 . . . . **B ELLINGTON, D.**
OLDER, J/ Cow./ 1997/ P-4/2 KD214 . . . . **636.2**
O'LEARY, D/ They came from DNA./ 1993/ 5-A/6 KC278 . . . . . **572.8**
OLESEN, J/ Chicken and egg./ 1986/ K-3/2 KC692 . . . . **598.6**
Snail./ 1986/ 2-4/2 KC515 . . . . **594**
OLIVERA, F/ Woman who outshone the sun: the legend of Lucia Zenteno./
La mujer que brillaba aun mas que el sol: la leyenda de Lucia Zenteno./
1991/ 3-5/5 KB403 . . . . **398.21**
OLIVIERO, J/ Day Sun was stolen./ 1995/ K-2/5 KB712 . . . . . **398.26**
OLLIVER, J/ TREASURY OF ANIMAL STORIES./ 1992/
3-6/6 KH802 . . . . **FIC**
TREASURY OF GIANT AND MONSTER STORIES./ 1992/
3-5/6 KH803 . . . . **FIC**
TREASURY OF SPOOKY STORIES./ 1992/ 4-A/6 KH804 . . . . . . **FIC**
OLMSTEAD, N/ Audubon Society field guide to North American
wildflowers, Eastern Region./ 1979/ 3-6 KC407 . . . . **582.13**
OLSEN, ML/ More creative connections: literature and the reading
program, grades 4-6./ 1993/ KA212 . . . . **PROF 372.4**
OLSON, NB/ Cataloging of audiovisual materials and other special
materials: a manual based on AACR2. New 4th ed./ 1998/
KA060 . . . . **PROF 025.4**
OLSON, S/ Johnny Appleseed (Videocassette)./ 1992/
2-5 KE239 . . . . **VCR B APPLESEED, J.**

OLSZEWSKI-KUBILIUS, P/ PATTERNS OF INFLUENCE ON GIFTED LEARNERS: THE HOME, SELF, AND THE SCHOOL./ 1989/ KA188 . . . . **PROF 371.95**

O'MALLEY, K/ Too many kangaroo things to do!/ 1996/ P-3/2 KB974 . . . . **513.2**

What's for lunch?/ 1994/ P-1/2 KG407 . . . . **E**

Who killed Cock Robin?/ 1993/ 1-3/2 KG191 . . . . **E**

/ 1990/ P-3 KC457 . . . . **CE 591**

ONO, K/ Bee and the dream: a Japanese tale./ 1996/ 2-3/2 KB612 . . . . **398.24**

ONYEFULU, I/ A is for Africa./ 1993/ 2-4/5 KE178 . . . . **916**

Emeka's gift: an African counting story./ 1995/ 1-4/5 KE728 . . **960**

Ogbo: sharing life in an African village./ 1996/ 3-5/6 KE737 . . **966.9**

ONYSHKEWYCH, Z/ Jenny's corner./ 1995/ 5-A/7 KG894 . . . . . **FIC**

OODGEROO/ Dreamtime: aboriginal stories./ 1994/ 4-5/6 KB506 . . . . **398.23**

OPENING DAYS: SPORTS POEMS./ 1996/ 3-6 KE074 . . . . . **811.008**

OPIE, IA/ I SAW ESAU: THE SCHOOLCHILD'S POCKET BOOK./ 1992/ KA276 . . . . **PROF 398.8**

MY VERY FIRST MOTHER GOOSE./ 1996/ P-K/2 KB808 . . . . **398.8**

OXFORD DICTIONARY OF NURSERY RHYMES./ 1997/ 5-6 KA416 . . . . **REF 398.8**

OPIE, P/ I SAW ESAU: THE SCHOOLCHILD'S POCKET BOOK./ 1992/ KA276 . . . . **PROF 398.8**

OXFORD DICTIONARY OF NURSERY RHYMES./ 1997/ 5-6 KA416 . . . . **REF 398.8**

OPPENHEIM, J/ Christmas Witch: an Italian legend./ 1993/ 1-3/2 KB507 . . . . **398.23**

Have you seen trees?/ 1995/ P-2/3 KC420 . . . . . . **582.16**

You can't catch me!/ 1986/ P-1 KG193 . . . . **E**

You can't catch me! (Sound recording cassette)./ n.d./ P-1 KG193 . . **E**

OPPENHEIM, SL/ And the Earth trembled: the creation of Adam and Eve./ 1996/ 5-6/3 KA788 . . . . **297**

Hundredth name./ c1995, 1997/ 2-3/2 KG194 . . . . **E**

Iblis./ 1994/ 4-5/4 KA789 . . . . **297**

OREGON PUPPET THEATRE/ MAKING AND USING PUPPETS IN THE PRIMARY GRADES (Videocassette)./ 1992/ K-6 KD446 . . . . **VCR 745.592**

ORGEL, D/ Don't call me Slob-o./ 1993/ 3-5/2 KH565 . . . **FIC**

Flower of Sheba./ 1994/ 1-2/2 KA687 . . . . **222**

ORLANDO, L/ Multicultural game book: more than 70 traditional games from 30 countries./ 1993/ KA323 . . . . . . **PROF 790.1**

ORLEV, U/ Island on Bird Street./ 1983/ 5-A/6 KH566 . . . . **FIC**

Island on Bird Street (Sound recording cassette)./ n.d./ 5-A/6 KH566 . . . . **FIC**

Man from the other side./ 1991/ 5-A/6 KH567 . . . . **FIC**

Man from the other side (Sound recording cassette)./ 1995/ 5-A/6 KH567 . . . . **FIC**

ORLICK, T/ Free to feel great: teaching children to excel at living./ 1993/ KA305 . . . . **PROF 649**

ORMAI, S/ Bet you can!: science possibilities to fool you./ 1990/ 4-A/7 KD745 . . . . **793.8**

ORMEROD, J/ Eat up, Gemma./ 1988/ P-2/2 KF685 . . . . **E**

Grandfather and I./ 1994/ P-1/1 KF292 . . . . **E**

Grandmother and I./ 1994/ P-1/2 KF293 . . . . **E**

Happy Christmas Gemma./ 1986/ P-1/2 KF686 . . . . **E**

Magic skateboard./ 1992/ 3-5/3 KH631 . . . . **FIC**

Moonlight./ 1982/ P-1 KG195 . . . . **E**

SUNFLAKES: POEMS FOR CHILDREN./ 1992/ P-2 KE086 . . **811.008**

Sunshine./ 1981/ P-1 KG196 . . . . **E**

When we went to the zoo./ 1991/ P-2/3 KC442 . . . . **590.73**

101 things to do with a baby./ 1984/ P-K KG197 . . . . **E**

O'ROURKE, F/ Burton and Stanley./ 1996/ 3-5/6 KH568 . . . . **FIC**

OROZCO, J/ DE COLORES AND OTHER LATIN-AMERICAN FOLK SONGS FOR CHILDREN./ 1994/ K-3 KD561 . . . . **789.2**

ORR, K/ My grandpa and the sea./ 1990/ K-2/2 KG198 . . . . **E**

Story of a dolphin./ 1993/ 1-3/6 KG199 . . . . **E**

ORR, R/ Bird atlas./ 1993/ 4-6/9 KA449 . . . . **REF 598**

Richard Orr's nature cross-sections./ 1995/ 2-A/8 KC359 . . . . . **578.7**

ORTIZ, G/ WORLD OF CHILDREN'S SONGS./ 1993/ KA322 . . . . **PROF 789.3**

ORWIG, GW/ New technologies for education: a beginner's guide. 3rd ed./ 1997/ KA176 . . . . **PROF 371.3**

OSBORNE, MP/ Favorite Norse myths./ 1996/ 4-6/6 KA756 . . . . **293**

MERMAID TALES FROM AROUND THE WORLD./ 1993/ 3-5/5 KB405 . . . . **398.21**

One world, many religions: the ways we worship./ 1996/ 4-A/7 KA726 . . . . **291**

OSEKI, I/ Growing rock: a Southwest Native American tale (Kit)./ 1993/ P-1 KB638 . . . . **KIT 398.24**

O'SHAUGHNESSY, T/ Third planet: exploring the earth from space./ 1994/ 2-8/7 KC062 . . . . **525**

Voyager: an adventure to the edge of the solar system./ 1992/ 3-6/7 KC030 . . . . **523.4**

OSINSKI, A/ Woodrow Wilson: twenty-eighth President of the United States./ 1989/ 5-A/8 KE597 . . . . **B WILSON, W.**

OSINSKI, C/ Busy day at Mr. Kang's grocery store./ 1996/ 1-3/2 KB126 . . . . **381**

OSLER, R/ LANDS OF PLEASURE: ESSAYS ON LILLIAN H. SMITH AND THE DEVELOPMENT OF/ 1990/ KA044 . . . . **PROF 020**

OSOFSKY, A/ Dreamcatcher./ 1992/ K-2/5 KG200 . . . . **E**

Free to dream: the making of a poet: Langston Hughes./ 1996/ 6-A/7 KE395 . . . . **B HUGHES, L.**

My Buddy./ 1992/ K-2/2 KG201 . . . . **E**

OSTROW, V/ All about asthma./ 1989/ 5-6/7 KD015 . . . . **616.2**

OSTROW, W/ All about asthma./ 1989/ 5-6/7 KD015 . . . . **616.2**

OTANI, J/ What makes a shadow? Rev. ed./ 1994/ K-2/2 KC106 . . . . **CE 535**

OTERO, B/ Headless haunt and other African-American ghost stories./ 1994/ 4-5/4 KB687 . . . . **398.25**

OTFINOSKI, S/ Blizzards./ 1994/ 4-6/7 KB036 . . . . . . **363.34**

OTSUKA, Y/ Suho and the white horse: a legend of Mongolia (Videocassette)./ 1981/ 3-4 KB626 . . . . . . **VCR 398.24**

OTTO, C/ Raccoon at Clear Creek Road./ 1995/ K-2/3 KG202 . . **CE E**

Raccoon at Clear Creek Road (Kit)./ 1995/ K-2/3 KG202 . . . . . **CE E**

OUGHTON, J/ Magic weaver of rugs: a tale of the Navajo./ 1994/ 2-4/3 KB627 . . . . **398.24**

OVERBECK, C/ Ants./ 1982/ 4-6/7 KC577 . . . . **595.79**

Carnivorous plants./ 1982/ 3-5/6 KC432 . . . . **583**

How seeds travel./ 1982/ 2-4/6 KC389 . . . . **580**

OWEN, M/ Animal rights: yes or no?/ 1993/ 6-A/9 KA674 . . . . . **179**

OWENS, G/ I'm the big sister now./ 1989/ 3-5/5 KD039 . . . . **618.92**

OWENS, MB/ Animals don't wear pajamas: a book about sleeping./ 1992/ P-2/6 KC473 . . . . **591.5**

Counting cranes./ 1993/ P-4/3 KB976 . . . . **513.2**

Prize in the snow./ 1994/ 2-3/4 KF503 . . . . **E**

OWENS, P/ Classroom newspaper workshop (CD-ROM)./ 1995/ 4-A KA594 . . . . **CDR 070.4**

Research paper writer (Microcomputer program)./ c1990/ 5-A KB090 . . . . **MCP 371.302**

OWENS, TS/ Collecting baseball cards./ 1993/ 4-A/7 KD505 . . . **769**

OXENBURY, H/ Farmer duck./ 1992/ P-1/2 KG675 . . . . **E**

Grandma and grandpa./ c1984, 1993/ P-K/2 KG203 . . . . **E**

Three little wolves and the big bad pig./ 1993/ P-3/4 KG619 . . . . . **E**

We're going on a bear hunt./ 1989/ P-2/2 KB814 . . . . . . **398.8**

OXFORD SCIENTIFIC FILMS/ LIFE CYCLE OF THE HONEYBEE (Videocassette)./ c1976, 1986/ 3-6 KC575 . . . . **VCR 595.79**

Lizard in the jungle./ 1988/ 5-6/7 KC626 . . . . **597.95**

OXLADE, C/ Science magic with air./ 1994/ 4-A/6 KD748 . . . . **793.8**

Science magic with light./ 1994/ 3-6/5 KD749 . . . . . . **793.8**

Science magic with magnets./ 1995/ 3-6/6 KD750 . . . . . **793.8**

Science magic with shapes and materials./ 1995/ 3-6/5 KD751 . . **793.8**

OYONO, E/ Gollo and the lion./ 1995/ 2-4/4 KB628 . . . . **398.24**

OZ, R/ Jazz, Pizzazz, and the silver threads./ 1996/ 2-4/3 KH615 . **FIC**

PACKARD, M/ Christmas kitten./ 1994/ K-1/1 KG204 . . . . **E**

I am king!/ 1994/ K-1/1 KG205 . . . . **E**

PAIGE, D/ Day in the life of a sports therapist./ 1985/ 3-5/6 KC989 . . . . **613.7**

Day in the life of a zoo veterinarian./ 1985/ 2-5/6 KD196 . . . . **CE 636.089**

PAINTBRUSH DIPLOMACY (EXCHANGE PROGRAM)/ WORLD IN OUR HANDS: IN HONOR OF THE FIFTIETH ANNIVERSARY OF THE UNITED NATIONS./ 1995/ 5-A/8 KA970 . . . . **341.23**

PALACIOS, A/ Christmas surprise for Chabelita./ 1993/ 1-3/2 KG206 . **E**

Sorpresa de Navidad para Chabelita./ 1994/ 1-3/2 KG206 . . . . . . **E**

PALATINI, M/ Piggie Pie!/ 1995/ 1-5/2 KG207 . . . . **E**

PALAZZO-CRAIG, J/ Max and Maggie in autumn./ 1994/ K-1/1 KG208 . . . . **E**

Max and Maggie in spring./ 1995/ K-1/1 KG208 . . . . **E**

Max and Maggie in summer./ 1994/ K-1/1 KG208 . . . . **E**

Max and Maggie in winter./ 1995/ K-1/1 KG208 . . . . **E**

Turtles./ 1982/ P-K/1 KC621 . . . . **597.92**

PALIN, M/ Jack and the beanstalk (Videocassette)./ 1991/ K-2 KB349 . . . . **VCR 398.2**

PALLAS, N/ Calculator puzzles, tricks and games./ c1976, 1991/ 4-6/9 KB930 . . . . **510**

PALLOTTA, J/ Crayon counting book./ 1996/ P-1/3 KB982 . . . . **513.2**

PALMATIER, RA/ Speaking of animals: a dictionary of animal metaphors./ 1995/ 6-A KA427 . . . . **REF 423**

PALMER, H/ Can a cherry pie wave goodbye? (Compact disc)./ 1991/ P-K KD641 . . . . **SRC 789.3**

Can a cherry pie wave goodbye?: songs for learning through music and movement (Sound recording cassette)./ 1991/ P-K KD641 **SRC 789.3**

Child's world of lullabies: multicultural songs for quiet times (Sound recording cassette)./ 1993/ P-2 KD642 . . . . **SRC 789.3**

Child's world of lullabies: multicultural songs for quiet times (Compact disc)./ 1993/ P-2 KD642 . . . . **SRC 789.3**

Fish out of water./ c1961/ K-2/2 KG209 . . . . **E**

Fish out of water (Sound recording cassette)./ n.d./ K-2/2 KG209 . . **E**
Getting to know myself (Compact disc)./ 1972/ P-1 KA641 **SRC 155.2**
Getting to know myself (Sound recording cassette)./ 1972/
  P-1 KA641 . . . . **SRC 155.2**
Learning basic skills (Videocassette)./ 1986/ P-1 KD700 . . . . **VCR 793**
Math readiness--vocabulary and concepts (Sound recording cassette)./
  n.d./ 1-3 KB931 . . . . **SRC 510**
Sammy and other songs from "Getting to know myself"
  (Videocassette)./ 1993/ P-1 KD643 . . . . **VCR 789.3**
Singing multiplication tables (Sound recording cassette)./ 1971/
  2-4 KB977 . . . . **SRC 513.2**
So big: activity songs for little ones (Compact disc)./ 1994/
  P-2 KD644 . . . . **CD 789.3**
Stepping out with Hap Palmer (Videocassette)./ 1994/
  P-2 KD645 . . . . **VCR 789.3**
PALMER, P/ Singing multiplication tables (Sound recording cassette)./
  1971/ 2-4 KB977 . . . . **SRC 513.2**
PANIK, S/ Quetzalcoatl tale of corn./ 1992/ 2-3/5 KB630 . . . **398.24**
PANTALEONI, H/ Songs and stories from Uganda./ c1974, 1987/
  KA319 . . . . **BA PROF 789.2**
PANZER, N/ CELEBRATE AMERICA IN POETRY AND ART./ 1994/
  3-6 KE054 . . . . **811.008**
PAPARONE, P/ FIVE LITTLE DUCKS: AN OLD RHYME./ 1995/
  P-1/1 KB797 . . . . **398.8**
Nobody owns the sky: the story of "Brave Bessie" Coleman./ 1996/
  1-3/2 KF983 . . . . **E**
PAPERT, S/ Children's machine: rethinking school in the age of the
  computer./ 1993/ KA180 . . . . **PROF 371.3**
PARE, MA/ Sports stars./ 1994/ 5-A KA457 . . . . **REF 796**
Sports stars. Series 2./ 1996/ 5-A KA457 . . . . **REF 796**
PARENT, M/ Tails and childhood (Sound recording cassette)./ 1985/
  K-3 KB629 . . . . **SRC 398.24**
PARISH, H/ Bravo, Amelia Bedelia!/ 1997/ 1-2/2 KG210 . . . . **E**
PARISH, P/ Amelia Bedelia goes camping./ 1985/ 1-3/2 KG214 . . **CE E**
Amelia Bedelia's family album./ 1988/ K-3/4 KG211 . . . . **E**
Be ready at eight./ 1996/ 1-2/1 KG212 . . . . **E**
Come back, Amelia Bedelia. Newly illustrated ed./ 1995/
  K-2/2 KG213 . . . . **E**
Good work, Amelia Bedelia./ c1976/ 1-3/2 KG214 . . . . **CE E**
Merry Christmas, Amelia Bedelia./ 1987/ 1-3/2 KG214 . . . . **CE E**
Merry Christmas, Amelia Bedelia (Kit)./ 1987/ 1-3/2 KG214 . . . . **CE E**
Mind your manners!/ , 1994/ 1-3 KB250 . . . . **395.5**
No more monsters for me!/ 1981/ K-1/1 KG215 . . . . **E**
Play ball, Amelia Bedelia./ 1996/ 1-3/2 KG216 . . . . **E**
Scruffy./ 1988/ K-3/1 KG217 . . . . **E**
Teach us, Amelia Bedelia./ 1977/ 1-3/2 KG214 . . . . **CE E**
Thank you, Amelia Bedelia (Kit)./ 1995/ 1-3/2 KG218 . . . . **CE E**
Thank you, Amelia Bedelia. Rev. ed./ 1993/ 1-3/2 KG218 . . . . . **CE E**
PARK, B/ Mick Harte was here./ 1995/ 4-6/4 KH570 . . . . **FIC**
PARK, R/ Playing Beatie Bow./ 1982/ 5-A/4 KH571 . . . . **FIC**
PARKE, M/ Quetzalcoatl tale of corn./ 1992/ 2-3/5 KB630 . . . **398.24**
PARKER, D/ Sign for friends (Videocassette)./ 1991/
  3-5 KB828 . . . . **VCR 419**
PARKER, NW/ Barbara Frietchie./ 1992/ 1-3 KE040 . . . . **811**
Bugs./ 1987/ 4-5/6 KC547 . . . . **595.7**
Frogs, toads, lizards and salamanders./ 1990/ 5-6/7 KC606 . . . **597.8**
General store./ c1926, 1988/ P-3 KF548 . . . . **E**
Goat in the rug./ 1990/ K-3/6 KF234 . . . . **E**
Jacket I wear in the snow./ 1989/ P-2/2 KG168 . . . . **E**
Locks, crocs, and skeeters: the story of the Panama Canal./ 1996/
  3-5/7 KB147 . . . . **386**
Money, money, money: the meaning of the art and symbols on United
  States paper currency./ 1995/ 3-6/11 KD506 . . . . **769.5**
We're making breakfast for Mother./ 1997/ P-1/2 KG169 . . . . **E**
PARKER, RA/ Circus of the wolves./ 1994/ 4-6/5 KG952 . . . . . . **FIC**
Dancing skeleton./ 1996/ 3-6/6 KB684 . . . . **CE 398.25**
Grandfather Tang's story./ 1990/ 2-3/4 KG613 . . . . **E**
Great miracle happened there: a Chanukah story./ c1993, 1995/
  3-4/4 KA778 . . . . **296.4**
Magician's visit: a Passover tale./ 1993/ K-3/5 KF629 . . . . **E**
Monkey's haircut and other stories told by the Maya./ 1986/
  3-4/4 KB531 . . . . **398.24**
PARKER, S/ Body and how it works./ 1992/ A/6 KC923 . . . . . **612**
Body atlas./ 1993/ A/ KC905 . . . . **611**
Ear and hearing. Rev. ed./ 1989/ 5-6/8 KC971 . . . . . **612.8**
Electricity./ 1992/ 4-A/9 KC134 . . . . **537**
Eye and seeing. Rev. ed./ 1989/ A/8 KC972 . . . . **612.8**
Fish./ 1990/ 5-6/7 KC584 . . . . **597**
Food and digestion. Rev. ed./ 1990/ 5-6/8 KC940 . . . . **612.3**
Heart and blood. Rev. ed./ 1989/ 5-6/8 KC933 . . . . **612.1**
Lungs and breathing. Rev. ed./ 1989/ 5-6/8 KC934 . . . . . **612.1**
Mammal./ 1989/ 4-6/7 KC725 . . . . **599**
Peces./ 1995/ 5-6/7 KC584 . . . . **597**
Pond and river./ 1988/ 1-6/7 KC340 . . . . **577.63**

Skeleton./ 1988/ 5-6/8 KC285 . . . . **573.7**
Skeleton and movement. Rev. ed./ 1989/ 5-6/7 KC958 . . . . . . **612.7**
PARKER, SJ/ Owen (Videocassette)./ 1995/ P-2 KF710 . . . . **VCR E**
PARKINS, D/ Aunt Nancy and Old Man Trouble./ 1996/
  K-3/6 KG350 . . . . **E**
Sophie hits six./ 1993/ 2-4/6 KH354 . . . . **FIC**
Sophie in the saddle./ 1996/ 3-5/6 KH355 . . . . **FIC**
Sophie's Lucky./ 1996/ 3-4/8 KH356 . . . . **FIC**
Sophie's Tom./ c1991, 1994/ 3-5/5 KH357 . . . . **FIC**
PARKS, MM/ Holiday handbook./ 1994/ 5-A/7 KA413 . . . **REF 394.26**
PARKS, R/ Dear Mrs. Parks: a dialogue with today's youth./ 1996/
  5-6/6 KA901 . . . . **323**
I am Rosa Parks./ 1997/ 1-2/4 KE491 . . . . **B PARKS, R.**
Rosa Parks: my story./ 1992/ 6-A/5 KE490 . . . . **B PARKS, R.**
PARKS, VD/ Jump! The adventures of Brer Rabbit./ 1997/
  3-4/6 KB585 . . . . **398.24**
PARMS, CA/ Marriage of the rain goddess: a South African myth./ 1996/
  4-5/5 KB424 . . . . **398.21**
PARNALL, P/ Annie and the old one./ c1971/ 4-6/4 KH496 . . . . . **FIC**
Desert is theirs./ c1975/ 4-6/5 KC362 . . . . **578.754**
Feet!/ 1988/ P-2/1 KG219 . . . . **E**
Kavik, the wolf dog./ c1968/ 4-6/6 KH510 . . . . **FIC**
PARNWELL, EC/ Oxford picture dictionary of American English. English/
  Spanish ed./ c1978, 1988/ 4-6 KB860 . . . . **463**
PARRAMON, JM/ El gusto./ 1985/ P-1/2 KC975 . . . . **612.8**
El oido./ 1985/ P-1/1 KC973 . . . . **612.8**
El tacto./ 1985/ P-1/2 KC976 . . . . **612.8**
Hearing./ 1985/ P-1/1 KC973 . . . . **612.8**
Sight./ 1985/ P-1/1 KC974 . . . . **612.8**
Taste./ 1985/ P-1/2 KC975 . . . . **612.8**
Touch./ 1985/ P-1/2 KC976 . . . . **612.8**
Vista./ 1985/ P-1/1 KC974 . . . . **612.8**
PARRISH, M/ ARABIAN NIGHTS: THEIR BEST-KNOWN TALES./ c1909,
  1994/ 5-A/9 KB255 . . . . **398.2**
MAXFIELD PARRISH: A TREASURY OF ART AND CHILDREN'S
  LITERATURE./ 1995/ K-6 KD413 . . . . **741.6**
PARSONS, A/ Amazing birds./ 1990/ 3-6/5 KC658 . . . . **598**
Amazing mammals./ 1990/ 2-6/6 KC726 . . . . **599**
Amazing snakes./ 1990/ 2-6/5 KC642 . . . . **597.96**
Amazing spiders./ 1990/ 2-6/6 KC695 . . . . **595.4**
PARTON, S/ Story of Frederick Douglass: voice of freedom./ 1996/
  3-5/3 KE326 . . . . **B DOUGLASS, F.**
PARTRIDGE, E/ Clara and the hoodoo man./ 1996/ 5-A/3 KH572 . **FIC**
PASCHKIS, J/ Happy adoption day!/ 1996/ 2-4/3 KD637 . . . . . **789.3**
PASCO, D/ Prince and the Salmon People./ 1993/ 4-6/7 KB352 . **398.2**
PASCOE, E/ Butterflies and moths./ 1997/ 4-6/6 KC563 . . . **595.78**
Earthworms./ 1997/ 4-6/4 KC506 . . . . **592**
First facts about the presidents./ 1996/ 3-6/8 KE860 . . . . . **973**
Mexico and the United States: cooperation and conflict./ 1996/
  6-A/11 KA805 . . . . **303.48**
Right to vote./ 1997/ 4-6/12 KA910 . . . . **324.6**
PASS IT ON: AFRICAN-AMERICAN POETRY FOR CHILDREN./ 1993/
  1-3 KE075 . . . . **811.008**
PATENT, DH/ African elephants: giants of the land./ 1991/
  4-6/6 KC813 . . . . **599.67**
Appaloosa horses./ 1988/ 4-6/7 KD203 . . . . **636.1**
Biodiversity./ 1996/ 5-6/9 KA964 . . . . **333.95**
Buffalo: the American Bison today./ 1986/ 5-6/8 KA965 . . . **333.95**
Eagles of America./ 1995/ 4-6/6 KC716 . . . . **598.9**
Feathers./ 1992/ 5-6/6 KC671 . . . . **598.147**
Flashy fantastic rain forest frogs./ 1997/ 4-6/4 KC607 . . . . . . **597.8**
Gray wolf, red wolf./ 1990/ 5-6/8 KC839 . . . . **599.773**
Hugger to the rescue./ 1994/ 3-6/5 KD226 . . . . **636.73**
Killer whales./ 1993/ 4-6/6 KC775 . . . . **599.5**
Looking at bears./ 1994/ 5-6/6 KC851 . . . . **599.78**
Looking at penguins./ 1993/ 5-6/5 KC689 . . . . **598.47**
Nutrition: what's in the food we eat./ 1992/ 4-6/6 KC941 . . . . **612.3**
Ospreys./ 1993/ A/7 KC717 . . . . **598.9**
Pelicans./ 1992/ 5-6/8 KC682 . . . . **598.4**
Places of refuge: our national wildlife refuge system./ Places of refuge:
  our national wildlife refuge system./ 1997/ 1992/
  4-6/7 KA966 . . . . **333.95**
  4-6/7 KA966 . . . . **333.95**
Quetzal: sacred bird of the cloud forest./ 1996/ 3-6/6 KC702 . **598.7**
Way of the grizzly./ 1987/ 5-6/8 KC860 . . . . **599.784**
West by covered wagon: retracing the pioneer trails./ 1995/
  2-4/8 KF043 . . . . **978**
Where the bald eagles gather./ 1984/ 5-6/7 KC718 . . . . . . **598.9**
Where the wild horses roam./ 1989/ 5-6/7 KD257 . . . . **639.9**
Whooping crane: a comeback story./ 1988/ A/9 KD258 . . . . **639.9**
Whooping crane (Sound recording cassette)./ n.d./ A/9 KD258 . **639.9**
Why mammals have fur./ 1995/ 4-6/6 KC727 . . . . **599**
Wild turkey, tame turkey./ 1989/ 5-6/7 KC697 . . . . **598.6**

Wild turkey, tame turkey (Sound recording cassette)./ 1993/ 5-6/7 KC697 . . . . 598.6
PATERSON, AJ/ How glass is made./ 1985/ 5-6/9 KD324 666
PATERSON, B/ Little green thumbs./ 1996/ 3-5/4 KD176 . . . . . 635.9
PATERSON, D/ Thumbs up, Rico!/ 1994/ 1-3/2 KG601 . . . . E
PATERSON, K/ Bridge to Terabithia./ 1977/ 5-A/6 KH573 . . . . . . FIC
Come sing, Jimmy Jo./ 1985/ 5-A/4 KH574 . . . . FIC
Come sing, Jimmy Jo (Sound recording cassette)./ n.d./ 5-A/4 KH574 . . . . FIC
Flip-flop girl./ 1996/ 5-A/6 KH575 . . . . FIC
Flip-flop girl (Sound recording cassette)./ 1996/ 5-A/6 KH575 . . . FIC
Gran gilly Hopkins./ n.d./ 5-A/5 KH576 . . . . FIC
Great Gilly Hopkins./ c1978/ 5-A/5 KH576 . . . . FIC
Great Gilly Hopkins (Sound recording cassette)./ n.d./ 5-A/5 KH576 . . . . FIC
Jip: his story./ 1996/ 5-A/7 KH577 . . . . FIC
King's equal./ 1992/ 3-6/6 KH578 . . . . FIC
King's equal (Sound recording cassette)./ 1994/ 3-6/6 KH578 . . . . FIC
Lyddie./ 1991/ 6-A/7 KH579 . . . . FIC
Master puppeteer./ c1975/ 6-A/6 KH580 . . . . FIC
Master puppeteer (Sound recording cassette)./ n.d./ 6-A/6 KH580 . FIC
Sign of the chrysanthemum./ c1973, 1991/ 5-A/6 KH581 . . . . FIC
Tale of the mandarin ducks./ 1990/ 2-3/6 KB631 . . . . 398.24
PATON, J/ KINGFISHER CHILDREN'S ENCYCLOPEDIA. REV. ED./ 1992/ KA383 . . . . REF 031
PATON WALSH, J/ Chance child./ c1978, 1991/ 6-A/7 KH582 . . . FIC
Green book./ 1982/ 4-6/6 KH583 . . . . FIC
PATRICK, DL/ Red dancing shoes./ 1993/ P-1/2 KG220 . . . . E
PATRICK, P/ Amish Christmas./ 1996/ 3-5/4 KG844 . . . . FIC
PATRICK-WEXLER, D/ Barbara Jordan./ 1996/ 4-6/8 KE408 . . . . B JORDAN, B.
Walter Dean Myers./ 1996/ 5-6/6 KE475 . . . . B MYERS, W.
PATTERSON, F/ Koko's kitten./ 1985/ 3-5/6 KC877 . . . . 599.884
Koko's kitten (Braille)./ n.d./ 3-5/6 KC877 . . . . 599.884
PATTERSON, G/ Jonah and the whale./ 1992/ P-2/4 KA692 224
PATTERSON, L/ Indian terms of the Americas./ 1994/ 5-A KA478 . . . . REF 970.004
PATTERSON, NR/ Shiniest rock of all./ 1991/ 4-6/4 KH584 . . . . . . FIC
PATTON, D/ Armadillos./ 1996/ 4-6/9 KC739 . . . . 599.3
Flamingos./ 1996/ 4-6/7 KC679 . . . . 598.3
Iguanas./ 1996/ 4-6/7 KC627 . . . . 597.95
PATZ, N/ Family treasury of Jewish holidays./ 1994/ 2-6/6 KA772 . . . . 296.4
PAUL, AW/ Seasons sewn: a year in patchwork./ 1996/ 3-6/7 KD462 . . . . 746.46
PAUL, K/ DRAGON POEMS./ 1991/ K-A KE055 . . . . 811.008
PAULSEN, G/ Call me Francis Tucket./ 1995/ 5-A/5 KH585 . . . . . . FIC
Dogteam./ 1993/ 1-3/4 KG221 . . . . E
Harris and me: a summer remembered./ 1993/ 6-A/7 KH586 . . . . FIC
Hatchet./ 1987/ 5-A/6 KH587 . . . . CE FIC
Hatchet (Sound recording cassette)./ n.d./ 5-A/6 KH587 . . . . CE FIC
Hatchet (Talking book)./ 1992/ 5-A/6 KH587 . . . . CE FIC
Mr. Tucket./ 1994/ 5-A/5 KH588 . . . . FIC
Puppies, dogs, and blue northers: reflections on being raised by a pack of sled dogs./ 1996/ 3-6/7 KD859 . . . . 798.8
Woodsong./ 1990/ 5-A/6 KD824 . . . . 796.5
Woodsong (Sound recording cassette)./ 1993/ 5-A/6 KD824 . . 796.5
Worksong./ 1997/ K-2/2 KG222 . . . . E
PAULSEN, RW/ Dogteam./ 1993/ 1-3/4 KG221 . . . . E
Worksong./ 1997/ K-2/2 KG222 . . . . E
PAXTON, T/ Aesop's fables./ 1988/ 3-4 KB632 . . . . 398.24
Aesop's fables (Sound recording cassette)./ n.d./ 3-4 KB632 . . 398.24
Belling the cat and other Aesop's fables./ 1990/ 3-4 KB632 . . 398.24
Belling the cat and other Aesop's fables (Sound recording cassette)./ 1993/ 3-4 KB632 . . . . 398.24
PEACE CHILD INTERNATIONAL/ WORLD IN OUR HANDS: IN HONOR OF THE FIFTIETH ANNIVERSARY OF THE UNITED NATIONS./ 1995/ 5-A/8 KA970 . . . . 341.23
PEALE, CW/ Ingenious Mr. Peale: painter, patriot and man of science./ 1996/ 6-A/8 KE493 . . . . B PEALE, C.
PEARCE, AP/ Tom's midnight garden./ c1958, 1991/ 5-6/5 KH589 . FIC
Who's afraid? and other strange stories./ 1987/ 5-6/6 KH590 . . . FIC
PEARSE, P/ See how you grow./ 1988/ K-3/5 KC954 . . . . 612.6
PEARSON, K/ Sky is falling./ 1995/ 5-A/6 KH591 . . . . FIC
PEARSON, TC/ School days./ 1990/ P-1/3 KF713 . . . . E
PECK, B/ Christmas memory./ c1956, 1989/ 4-A/6 KG971 . . . . CE FIC
Dear Levi: letters from the Overland Trail./ 1994/ 4-6/6 KH880 . . FIC
House on Maple Street./ 1987/ K-3/4 KG292 . . . . E
Thanksgiving visitor./ 1996/ 5-A/8 KG972 . . . . FIC
PECK, R/ Are you in the house alone?/ 1989/ A/6 KH592 . . . . FIC
Are you in the house alone? (Sound recording cassette)./ n.d./ A/6 KH592 . . . . FIC
Lost in cyberspace./ 1995/ 5-A/3 KH593 . . . . FIC
Lost in cyberspace (Sound recording cassette)./ 1997/ 5-A/3 KH593 . . . . FIC
PECK, RN/ Soup./ 1974/ 4-6/6 KH594 . . . . FIC
Soup in the saddle (Sound recording cassette)./ n.d./ 4-6/6 KH594 . . . . FIC
Soup (Sound recording disc)./ n.d./ 4-6/6 KH594 . . . . FIC
Soup's goat (Sound recording cassette)./ n.d./ 4-6/6 KH594 . . . . FIC
PEDERSEN, J/ On the road of stars: Native American night poems and sleep charms./ 1994/ 2-6 KE141 . . . . 897.008
Seedfolks./ 1997/ 5-A/5 KH118 . . . . FIC
PEDERSON, J/ NYSTROM DESK ATLAS./ 1994/ 5-A KA474 . REF 912
PEET, B/ Ant and the elephant./ c1972/ K-3/5 KG223 . . . . E
Big bad Bruce./ 1977/ K-3/3 KG224 . . . . E
Bill Peet: an autobiography./ 1989/ 6-A/8 KE494 . . . . B PEET, B.
Bill Peet: an autobiography (Sound recording cassette)./ n.d./ 6-A/8 KE494 . . . . B PEET, B.
Capyboppy./ c1966/ 1-3/8 KC746 . . . . 599.35
Cowardly Clyde./ 1979/ K-2/6 KG225 . . . . E
Encore for Eleanor./ 1981/ K-2/7 KG226 . . . . E
Farewell to Shady Glade./ c1966/ K-2 KG227 . . . . E
Jennifer and Josephine./ c1967/ K-2/7 KG228 . . . . E
Jethro and Joel were a troll./ 1987/ 1-3/4 KG229 . . . . E
Wump World./ c1970/ 1-3/7 KG230 . . . . E
Zella, Zack and Zodiac./ 1986/ K-3/4 KG231 . . . . E
Zella, Zack and Zodiac (Sound recording cassette)./ n.d./ K-3/4 KG231 . . . . E
PELLANT, C/ Eyewitness handbook of rocks and minerals./ 1992/ A/10 KC144 549
PELLEGRINI, N/ Families are different./ 1991/ P-1/2 KG232 . . . . . . E
PELLETIER, D/ Graphic alphabet./ 1996/ 2-4/2 KB832 421
PELLOWSKI, A/ Family storytelling handbook./ 1987/ KA070 . . . . PROF 027.62
Story vine: a source book of unusual and easy-to-tell stories from/ 1984/ KA248 . . . . PROF 372.67
Storytelling handbook: a young people's collection of unusual tales and helpful hints on how to tell them./ 1995/ KA249 . . . . PROF 372.67
PELS, W/ Turandot./ 1995/ 3-5/5 KB342 . . . . 398.2
PELTA, K/ California./ 1994/ 4-6/7 KF085 . . . . 979.4
Discovering Christopher Columbus./ 1991/ A/6 KE742 . . . . . . 970.01
Discovering Christopher Columbus: how history is invented (Sound recording cassette)./ 1993/ A/6 KE742 . . . . 970.01
PEMBLETON, S/ Armadillo./ 1992/ 5-6/7 KC740 . . . . 599.3
PENA, N/ TUN-TA-CA-TUN: MORE STORIES AND POEMS IN ENGLISH AND SPANISH FOR CHILDREN./ 1986/ K-6 KD905 . . . . 810.8
PENA, SC/ TUN-TA-CA-TUN: MORE STORIES AND POEMS IN ENGLISH AND SPANISH FOR CHILDREN./ 1986/ K-6 KD905 . . . . 810.8
PENE DU BOIS, W/ My grandson Lew./ c1974/ K-2/2 KG805 . . . . . E
Twenty-one balloons./ c1947/ 4-6/7 KH595 . . . . CE FIC
Twenty-one balloons (Braille)./ n.d./ 4-6/7 KH595 . . . . CE FIC
Twenty-one balloons (Sound recording cassette)./ n.d./ 4-6/7 KH595 . . . . CE FIC
Twenty-one balloons (Talking book)./ Twenty-one balloons (Talking book)./ 1972/ n.d./ 4-6/7 KH595 . . . . CE FIC
4-6/7 KH595 . . . . CE FIC
William's doll./ c1972/ P-2/4 KG810 . . . . E
PENHALE, D/ Coyotes in the crosswalk: true tales of animal life in the wilds...of the city!/ 1995/ 4-6/6 KC494 . . . . 591.75
Sky dancers: the amazing world of North American birds./ 1995/ 4-5/5 KC667 598
PENNER, LR/ Celebration: the story of American holidays./ 1993/ 4-6/7 KB201 . . . . 394.26
Eating the plates: a Pilgrim book of food and manners./ 1991/ 3-6/4 KB186 . . . . 394.1
Native American feast./ 1994/ 4-6/6 KB187 . . . . 394.1
Pilgrims at Plymouth./ 1996/ 1-3/2 KE943 . . . . 974.4
Twisters!/ 1996/ 2-4/3 KC204 . . . . 551.55
PENNINGTON, D/ Itse Selu: Cherokee harvest festival./ 1994/ K-3/6 KB190 . . . . 394.2
PENNYPACKER, S/ Dumbstruck./ 1994/ 4-6/7 KH596 . . . . FIC
PEOPLES OF THE WORLD: NORTH AMERICANS./ 1991/ 6-A KA479 . . . . REF 970.004
PEPPER, D/ OXFORD BOOK OF SCARYTALES./ 1992/ 6-A/7 KH569 . . . . FIC
PERCY, G/ Reynard the Fox./ 1991/ 2-3/6 KB586 . . . . 398.24
PERETZ, I/ Magician's visit: a Passover tale./ 1993/ K-3/5 KF629 . . . E
PEREZ, NA/ Breaker./ 1988/ 6-A/7 KH597 . . . . FIC
PEREZ-STABLE, MA/ Understanding American history through children's literature: instructional units and activities for grades K-8./ 1994/ KA263 . . . . PROF 372.89
PERHAM, M/ King Arthur: the legends of Camelot./ 1993/ 5-A/7 KB471 . . . . 398.22
PERKINS, LR/ Home lovely./ 1995/ K-2/5 KG233 . . . . E
PERKINS, M/ Sunita experiment./ 1993/ 5-A/6 KH598 . . . . FIC

PERL, L/ Don't sing before breakfast, don't sleep in the moonlight: everyday superstitions and how they began./ 1988/ 4-A/8 KA559 . . . . **001.9**
Don't sing before breakfast, don't sleep in the moonlight: everyday superstitions and how they began (Sound recording cassette)./ n.d./ 4-A/8 KA559 . . . . **001.9**
Hunter's stew and hangtown fry: what pioneer America ate and why./ c1977/ A/11 KD275 . . . . **641.5**
It happened in America: true stories from the fifty states./ 1992/ 4-A/7 KE861 . . . . **973**
Mummies, tombs, and treasure: secrets of ancient Egypt./ 1987/ 5-A/8 KE636 . . . . **932**
Pinatas and paper flowers, holidays of the Americas in English and Spanish/ Pinatas y flores de papel, fiestas de las Americas en ingles/ 1983/ 4-6/6 KB202 . . . . **394.26**
Slumps, grunts, and snickerdoodles: what Colonial America ate and why./ 1975/ A/9 KD276 . . . . **641.5**
Slumps, grunts, and snickerdoodles: what Colonial America ate and why (Braille)./ n.d./ A/9 KD276 . . . . **641.5**
PEROLS, S/ Colors./ 1991/ K-3/2 KC121 . . . . **535.6**
Ladybug and other insects./ 1991/ K-3/4 KC538 . . . . . **595.7**
PERRAULT, C/ Cinderella./ 1994/ 2-4/6 KB364 . . . . . **398.2**
Cinderella, or the little glass slipper./ 1954/ 1-3/7 KB762 . . . **398.27**
Cinderella, or the little glass slipper (Braille)./ n.d./ 1-3/7 KB762 . . . . **398.27**
Complete fairy tales of Charles Perrault./ 1993/ 3-4/6 KB355 . . **398.2**
Gato con botas./ 1990/ 3-4/4 KB633 . . . . **398.24**
Puss in boots./ 1990/ 3-4/4 KB633 . . . . **398.24**
Puss in boots: a fairy tale./ 1996/ K-3/5 KB634 . . . . . **398.24**
Story of Sleeping Beauty (Sound recording cassette)./ 1980/ 4-6 KB356 . . . . **SRC 398.2**
PERRONE, D/ Mermaid's twin sister: more stories from Trinidad./ 1994/ 3-4/5 KB323 . . . . **398.2**
PERRY, PJ/ Guide to math materials: resources to support the NCTM standards./ 1997/ KA256 . . . . **PROF 372.7**
World's regions and weather: linking fiction to nonfiction./ 1996/ KA294 . . . . **PROF 551.6**
PERRY, R/ LOTS OF LIMERICKS./ 1991/ 3-6 KE069 . . . . . . **811.008**
RIDDLE-ME RHYMES./ 1994/ 3-5 KD738 . . . . **793.735**
PERRY, SK/ Playing smart: a parent's guide to enriching offbeat learning activities/ 1990/ KA324 . . . . **PROF 790.1**
PERTZOFF, A/ In-between days./ 1994/ 4-6/4 KG943 . . . . **FIC**
Three Names./ 1991/ 2-3/5 KG055 . . . . **E**
PESCIO, C/ Rembrandt and seventeenth-century Holland./ 1995/ 4-A/12 KD501 . . . . **759.9492**
PETER, PAUL & MARY/ Peter, Paul and Mommy, too (Compact disc)./ 1993/ P-3 KD583 . . . . **CD 789.2**
PETERS, B/ African village folktales, vols 1-3 (Talking book)./ n.d./ 4-6 KB746 . . . . **TB 398.27**
PETERS, LW/ Serengeti./ 1989/ 4-6/6 KE738 . . . . **967.8**
PETERS, RM/ Clambake: a Wampanoag tradition./ 1992/ 4-6/5 KE780 . . . . **970.444**
PETERSEN, P/ Moose./ 1994/ 3-6/6 KC800 . . . . **599.65**
PETERSEN, PJ/ Some days, other days./ 1994/ K-2/2 KG234 . . . . . **E**
PETERSHAM, M/
Circus baby./ Circus baby./ c1950/ c1950/ P-2/3 KG235 . . . . . **CE E**
P-2/3 KG235 . . . . **CE E**
Circus baby (Videocassette)./ 1965/ P-2/3 KG235 . . . . . **CE E**
Rooster crows: a book of American rhymes and jingles./ Rooster crows: a book of American rhymes and jingles./ c1945/ c1945/
K-2 KB810 . . . . **398.8**
K-2 KB810 . . . . **398.8**
Rooster crows: a book of American rhymes and jingles (Braille)./ n.d./ K-2 KB810 . . . . **398.8**
Rooster crows: a book of American rhymes and jingles (Sound recording cassette)./ n.d./ K-2 KB810 . . . . **398.8**
PETERSON, CS/ Reference books for children, 4th ed./ 1992/ KA021 . . . . **PROF 011.62**
PETERSON, J/ Caterina, the clever farm girl: a tale from Italy./ 1996/ 2-4/3 KB357 . . . . **398.2**
PETERSON, JW/ I have a sister--my sister is deaf./ c1977/ 2-4/4 KB007 . . . . **362.4**
PETERSON, M/ Argentina: a wild west heritage. New ed./ 1997/ 5-6/8 KF107 . . . . **982**
PETERSON, PR/ Know it all: resource book for kids./ 1989/ 4-A/6 KA591 . . . . **031.02**
PETERSON, R/ Argentina: a wild west heritage. New ed./ 1997/ 5-6/8 KF107 . . . . **982**
PETERSON, RT/ Field guide to the birds: a completely new guide to all birds of eastern and central/ 1980/ 4-6/7 KC659 . . . . . . **598**
Field guide to western birds. 3rd ed./ 1990/ 4-6/7 KC660 . . **598**
PETRY, A/ Harriet Tubman: conductor on the Underground Railroad./ c1955, 1996/ A/7 KE575 . . . . **B TUBMAN, H.**
Tituba of Salem Village./ 1991/ 5-6/4 KH599 . . . . **FIC**

Tituba of Salem Village (Braille)./ n.d./ 5-6/4 KH599 . . . . **FIC**
PETTIT, J/ Maya Angelou: journey of the heart./ 1996/ 4-6/8 KE237 . . . . **B ANGELOU, M.**
Place to hide./ 1993/ 5-A/7 KE663 . . . . **940.53**
PFEFFER, W/ From tadpole to frog./ 1994/ K-2/2 KC608 . . . **CE 597.8**
From tadpole to frog (Kit)./ 1996/ K-2/2 KC608 . . . . **CE 597.8**
What's it like to be a fish?/ 1996/ K-3/2 KC585 . . . . **597**
PFEIFER, KB/ Henry O. Flipper./ 1993/ 4-6/9 KE345 . . **B FLIPPER, H.**
PFLAUM, R/ Marie Curie and her daughter Irene./ 1993/ 6-A/8 KC139 . . . . **539.7**
PHI DELTA KAPPA EDUCATIONAL FOUNDATION/ Fastback series./ 1972/ KA172 . . . . **PROF 370.11**
PHILIP, N/ Adventures of Odysseus./ 1997/ 3-6/5 KE125 . . . . . . **883**
AMERICAN FAIRY TALES: FROM RIP VAN WINKLE TO THE ROOTABAGA STORIES./ 1996/ 4-6/7 KG843 . . . . **FIC**
Arabian nights./ 1994/ 5-6/6 KB358 . . . . **398.2**
Illustrated book of myths: tales and legends of the world./ 1995/ 5-A KA394 . . . . **REF 291.1**
Ocean of story: fairy tales from India./ 1996/ 4-6/5 KB353 . . . **398.2**
Odin's family: myths of the Vikings./ 1996/ 3-A/6 KA757 . . . **293**
SONGS ARE THOUGHTS: POEMS OF THE INUIT./ 1995/ 4-6 KE140 . . . . **897**
PHILLIPS, L/ Balloon science./ 1989/ 2-6/6 KC079 . . . . . . **530**
Keep 'em laughing: jokes to amuse and annoy your friends./ 1996/ 3-6 KD736 . . . . **793.735**
PHILLIPS, M/ Sign in Mendel's window./ c1985, 1996/ 3-5/6 KH600 . . . . **FIC**
Sign in Mendel's window (Sound recording cassette)./ n.d./ 3-5/6 KH600 . . . . **FIC**
PHILLIPS, RB/ Mudluscious: stories and activities featuring food for preschool children./ 1986/ KA201 . . . . **PROF 372.3**
PICARD, BL/ Odyssey of Homer./ c1952, 1992/ 5-A/7 KE126 . . . **883**
PICKERING, M/ Picture reference atlas./ 1996/ 2-4/3 KE171 . . . **912**
PICO, F/ Red comb./ 1994/ 3-5/7 KH601 . . . . **FIC**
PIERS, H/ Taking care of your gerbils./ 1993/ 3-5/6 KD184 . . . **636**
PILGRIM VOICES: OUR FIRST YEAR IN THE NEW WORLD./ 1995/ 3-6/7 KE944 . . . . **974.4**
PILKEY, D/ Dog breath: the horrible trouble with Hally Tosis./ 1994/ 2-3/3 KG236 . . . . **E**
Hallo-wiener./ 1995/ K-2/2 KG237 . . . . **E**
Hallo-wiener (Sound recording cassette)./ 1997/ K-2/2 KG237 . . . . **E**
Julius./ 1993/ P-2/2 KF831 . . . . **E**
Paperboy./ 1996/ K-2/2 KG238 . . . . **E**
Place where nobody stopped./ 1994/ 5-A/7 KH690 . . . . . . **FIC**
PINCUS, H/ Tell me a Mitzi./ c1970/ K-3/6 KG426 . . . . **E**
PINDAL, K/ Peep and the big wide world (Videocassette)./ 1991/ P-2 KG239 . . . . **VCR E**
PINDER, M/
People with one heart (Talking book)./ People with one heart (Talking book)./ 1996/ 1996/ P-1 KD876 . . . . **TB 808.8**
P-1 KD876 . . . . **TB 808.8**
Planet with one mind: stories from around the world for the child within us all (Talking book)./ Planet with one mind: stories from around the world for the child within us all (Talking book)./ 1995/ 1995/ 1-4 KD877 . . . . **TB 808.8**
1-4 KD877 . . . . **TB 808.8**
PINE, J/ Trees./ 1995/ 3-6/3 KC421 . . . . **582.16**
PINKNEY, AD/ Alvin Ailey./ 1993/ 2-4/5 KE231 . . . . . **B AILEY, A.**
Bill Pickett: rodeo-ridin' cowboy./ 1996/ 2-5/7 KE496 . . . **B PICKETT, B.**
Dear Benjamin Banneker./ 1994/ 4-6/6 KE249 . . . . **B BANNEKER, B.**
Dear Benjamin Banneker (Sound recording cassette)./ 1997/ 4-6/6 KE249 . . . . **B BANNEKER, B.**
Seven candles for Kwanzaa./ 1993/ 2-6/7 KB214 . . . . . . **394.261**
PINKNEY, GJ/ Back home./ 1992/ 1-3/4 KG240 . . . . **E**
Sunday outing./ 1994/ 1-3/2 KG241 . . . . **E**
PINKNEY, J/ Adventures of Spider: West African folktales./ c1964, 1992/ 2-3/5 KB524 . . . . **398.24**
Back home./ 1992/ 1-3/4 KG240 . . . . **E**
Drylongso./ 1992/ 4-6/4 KH214 . . . . **FIC**
Hired hand: an African-American folktale./ 1997/ 3-4/3 KB412 . **398.21**
I want to be./ 1993/ 1-4/3 KG159 . . . . **E**
In for winter, out for spring./ 1991/ 1-4 KD910 . . . . **811**
John Henry./ 1994/ 2-5/4 KB464 . . . . **398.22**
Jungle book: the Mowgli stories./ 1995/ 6-A/7 KH363 . . . . . **FIC**
Man who kept his heart in a bucket./ 1991/ K-2/3 KF970 . . . . **E**
Mirandy and Brother Wind./ 1988/ 1-3/6 KG107 . . . . **CE E**
New shoes for Silvia./ 1993/ K-2/2 KF794 . . . . **E**
Patchwork quilt./ 1985/ K-3/5 KF561 . . . . **E**
Pretend you're a cat./ 1990/ P-1 KG082 . . . . **E**
Sam and the tigers: a new telling of LITTLE BLACK SAMBO./ 1996/ K-3/2 KF966 . . . . **E**
Song of the trees./ 1975/ 4-6/4 KH780 . . . . **FIC**
Starlit somersault downhill./ 1993/ K-2/3 KG725 . . . . **E**
Sunday outing./ 1994/ 1-3/2 KG241 . . . . **E**

Tales of Uncle Remus: the adventures of Brer Rabbit./ 1987/
  4-5/5 KB608 . . . . **398.24**
Talking eggs./ 1989/ 3-5/5 KB415 . . . . **CE 398.21**
Tanya's reunion./ 1995/ K-3/3 KF562 . . . . **E**
PINKNEY, JB/ Adventures of Sparrowboy./ 1997/ K-2/3 KG242 . . . . **E**
Alvin Ailey./ 1993/ 2-4/5 KE231 . . . . **B AILEY, A.**
Bill Pickett: rodeo-ridin' cowboy./ 1996/ 2-5/7 KE496 . . **B PICKETT, B.**
Boy and the ghost./ 1989/ 2-3/6 KG392 . . . . **E**
Cut from the same cloth: American women of myth, legend, and tall tale./
  1993/ 5-6/6 KB481 . . . . **398.22**
Dark-thirty: Southern tales of the supernatural./ 1992/
  5-A/6 KH491 . . . . **FIC**
Elephant's wrestling match./ 1992/ P-2/4 KB652 . . . . **398.24**
Faithful friend./ 1995/ 4-6/5 KB411 . . . . **398.21**
Happy Birthday, Martin Luther King./ 1993/
  1-5/5 KE422 . . . . **B KING, M.L.**
JoJo's flying side kick./ 1995/ K-3/2 KG243 . . . . **E**
JoJo's flying side kick (Sound recording cassette)./ 1997/
  K-3/2 KG243 . . . . **E**
Wiley and the Hairy Man./ 1996/ K-3/4 KB417 . . . . **398.21**
PINKWATER, DM/ Aunt Lulu./ 1991/ P-2/2 KG244 . . . . **E**
Doodle flute./ 1991/ 1-3/2 KG245 . . . . **E**
Fat men from space./ 1977/ 5-A/7 KH602 . . . . **FIC**
Fat men from space (Sound recording cassette)./ n.d./
  5-A/7 KH602 . . . . **FIC**
Hoboken chicken emergency./ c1977/ 5-A/6 KH603 . . . . **CE FIC**
Hoboken chicken emergency (Videocassette)./ c1984/
  5-A/6 KH603 . . . . **CE FIC**
Mush, a dog from space./ 1995/ 3-6/4 KH604 . . . . **FIC**
Wallpaper from space./ 1996/ 2-5/3 KH605 . . . . **FIC**
PINKWATER, J/ Mister Fred./ 1994/ 5-A/4 KH606 . . . . **FIC**
Wallpaper from space./ 1996/ 2-5/3 KH605 . . . . **FIC**
PINOL, R/ Dragons and prehistoric monsters./ 1996/
  3-6/3 KD447 . . . . **745.592**
Modeling dinosaurs./ 1996/ 3-6/3 KD448 . . . . **745.592**
PINOLA, L/ Fire race: a Karuk Coyote tale about how fire came to the
  people./ 1993/ 3-4/4 KB611 . . . . **398.24**
PINTO, VJ/ Aani and the tree huggers./ 1995/ 3-5/3 KG853 . . . . **FIC**
PIPE, J/ In the footsteps of the werewolf./ 1996/ 4-6/7 KB635 . **398.24**
PIPER, W/ Little engine that could./ c1961/ P-K/4 KG246 . . . . . **CE E**
Little engine that could (Braille)./ n.d./ P-K/4 KG246 . . . . . . **CE E**
Little engine that could (Kit)./ 1985/ P-K/4 KG246 . . . . **CE E**
Little engine that could (Talking book)./ n.d./ P-K/4 KG246 . . . **CE E**
PIRNER, CW/ Even little kids get diabetes./ 1991/ K-2/2 KD017 . **616.4**
PITKANEN, MA/ Grandchildren of the Incas./ 1991/ 4-6/6 KF110 . **985**
Grandchildren of the Vikings./ 1996/ 4-6/8 KE694 . . . . **948**
PITRE, F/ Juan Bobo and the pig: a Puerto Rican folktale./ 1993/
  2-4/2 KB763 . . . . **398.27**
PIZZO, PA/ BE A FRIEND: CHILDREN WHO LIVE WITH HIV SPEAK./
  1994/ 2-6/2 KA993 . . . . **362.1**
PLACE, F/ Wreck of the Zanzibar./ 1995/ 4-6/3 KH516 . . . . **FIC**
PLANET OF THE GRAPES: SHOW BIZ JOKES AND RIDDLES./ 1992/
  3-6 KD737 . . . . **793.735**
PLATT, R/ Man-of-war./ 1993/ 4-6/7 KA988 . . . . **359.1**
Pirate./ 1994/ 4-A/7 KE157 . . . . **910.4**
Stephen Biesty's incredible explosions./ 1996/ 5-6/7 KD411 . . **741.6**
PLECAS, J/ Outside dog./ 1993/ P-2/2 KG266 . . . . **CE E**
Peeping and sleeping./ 1994/ P-2/2 KG060 . . . . **E**
Rattlebone Rock./ 1995/ 1-3/3 KF158 . . . . **E**
What about my goldfish?./ 1993/ 1-3/2 KF644 . . . . **E**
PLOSKI, HA/ AFRICAN AMERICAN ALMANAC. 7th ed./ 1997/
  5-A KA486 . . . . **REF 973**
PLOURDE, L/ Pigs in the mud in the middle of the rud./ 1997/
  K-2/2 KG247 . . . . **E**
PLUCKROSE, H/ Seashore./ 1994/ P-2/4 KC347 . . . . **577.69**
Trees./ 1994/ P-2/4 KC422 . . . . **582.16**
Under the ground./ 1994/ P-2/4 KC360 . . . . **578.75**
Weather./ 1994/ P-2/4 KC192 . . . . **551.5**
PLUME, I/ Bremen-Town musicians./ 1998/ 1-3/4 KB636 . . . . . **398.24**
Shoemaker and the elves./ 1991/ 2-4/4 KB359 . . . . **398.2**
Sleepy book./ c1958, 1988/ P-1 KC481 . . . . **591.5**
PLUNKETT, SH/ Kongi and Potgi: a Cinderella story from Korea./ 1996/
  K-3/5 KB313 . . . . **398.2**
PODELL, J/ Famous first facts. 5th ed./ 1997/ 4-6 KA382 . . . . **REF 031**
PODWAL, M/ Book of tens./ 1994/ 5-6/7 KA769 . . . . **296.1**
Golem: a giant made of mud./ 1995/ 4-6/7 KB408 . . . . **398.21**
POE, EA/ Annabel Lee./ 1987/ 3-6 KD997 . . . . **811**
Poetry for young people./ 1995/ 5-A KD998 . . . . **811**
POEMS FOR JEWISH HOLIDAYS./ 1986/ K-3 KE077 . . . . . . **811.008**
POGANY, W/ Children's Homer: The Adventures of Odysseus and Tale of
  Troy./ 1982/ A/6 KE123 . . . . **883**
Golden fleece and the heroes who lived before Achilles./ c1949/
  5-6/6 KA736 . . . . **292**

POLACCO, P/ Aunt Chip and the great Triple Creek Dam affair./ 1996/
  2-4/2 KG248 . . . . **E**
Babushka Baba Yaga./ 1993/ 1-3/5 KG249 . . . . **E**
Babushka's Mother Goose./ 1995/ P-2/3 KD878 . . . . **808.8**
Bee tree./ 1993/ K-2/3 KG250 . . . . **E**
Chicken Sunday./ 1992/ 1-3/2 KG251 . . . . **E**
Dream keeper (Videocassette)./ 1996/
  2-4 KE501 . . . . **VCR B POLACCO, P.**
Keeping quilt./ 1988/ K-3/6 KG252 . . . . **CE E**
Keeping quilt (Videocassette)./ 1993/ K-3/6 KG252 . . . . **CE E**
Mrs. Katz and Tush./ 1992/ 1-3/2 KG253 . . . . **E**
Mrs. Katz and Tush (Sound recording cassette)./ 1994/
  1-3/2 KG253 . . . . **E**
My ol' man./ 1995/ 1-3/3 KG254 . . . . **E**
My rotten redheaded older brother./ 1994/ 1-3/3 KG255 . . . . **E**
My rotten redheaded older brother (Sound recording cassette)./ 1997/
  1-3/3 KG255 . . . . **E**
Pink and Say./ 1994/ 4-6/2 KH607 . . . . **FIC**
Rechenka's eggs./ 1988/ 1-3/5 KG256 . . . . **CE E**
Rechenka's eggs (Videocassette)./ 1991/ 1-3/5 KG256 . . . . . . **CE E**
Some birthday!/ 1991/ K-2/4 KG257 . . . . **E**
Thunder cake./ 1990/ 1-3/4 KG258 . . . . **CE E**
Thunder cake (Videocassette)./ 1990/ 1-3/4 KG258 . . . . **CE E**
Tikvah means hope./ 1994/ 1-3/2 KG259 . . . . **E**
Trees of the dancing goats./ 1996/ 1-3/3 KG260 . . . . **E**
Uncle Vova's tree./ 1989/ 1-3/6 KG261 . . . . **E**
POLANSKY, DS/ I like dessert (Sound recording cassette)./ 1987/
  K-6 KD647 . . . . **SRC 789.3**
POLETTE, N/ ABC's of books and thinking skills./ 1987/
  KA156 . . . . **PROF 153.4**
Brain power through picture books: help children develop with books that
  stimulate specific/ 1992/ KA227 . . . . **PROF 372.6**
POLIKOFF, BG/ Life's a funny proposition, Horatio./ 1992/
  5-A/4 KH608 . . . . **FIC**
POLIS, GA/ Scorpion man: exploring the world of scorpions./ 1994/
  5-6/8 KC530 . . . . **595.4**
POLISAR, BL/ Barry's scrapbook: a window into art (Videocassette)./
  1994/ 1-4 KD367 . . . . **VCR 701**
Family concert (Compact disc)./ 1993/ 1-6 KD648 . . . . **CD 789.3**
Family concert (Sound recording cassette)./ 1993/
  1-6 KD648 . . . . **CD 789.3**
Old dogs, new tricks (Compact disc)./ / P-3 KD649 . . . . . **SRC 789.3**
Old dogs, new tricks (Sound recording cassette)./ 1993/
  P-3 KD649 . . . . **SRC 789.3**
Peculiar zoo./ 1993/ K-2 KD999 . . . . **811**
POLITI, L/ Song of the swallows./ c1949, 1987/ K-3/6 KG262 . . . **CE E**
Song of the swallows (Braille)./ n.d./ K-3/6 KG262 . . . . **CE E**
POLLACK, JS/ Shirley Chisholm./ 1994/
  5-6/10 KE289 . . . . **B CHISHOLM, S.**
POLLARD, N/ REAL MOTHER GOOSE BOOK OF AMERICAN RHYMES./
  1993/ P-2 KB811 . . . . **398.8**
POLLINGER, G/ SOMETHING RICH AND STRANGE: A TREASURY OF
  SHAKESPEARE'S VERSE./ 1995/ 6-A KE118 . . . . **822.3**
POLLITOS DICEN: JUEGOS, RIMAS Y CANCIONES INFANTILES DE
  PAISES DE HABLA HISPANA./THE BABY CHICKS SING:
  TRADITIONAL GAMES, NURSERY/ 1994/ P-1/2 KD584 . . . . **789.2**
POLLOCK, P/ Turkey girl: a Zuni Cinderella story./ 1996/
  2-4/6 KB764 . . . . **398.27**
POLLOCK, S/ Atlas of endangered animals./ 1993/
  5-6/7 KC491 . . . . **591.68**
POLONSKY, L/ MATH FOR THE VERY YOUNG: A HANDBOOK OF
  ACTIVITIES FOR PARENTS AND TEACHERS./ 1995/
  KA254 . . . . **PROF 372.7**
POMERANTZ, C/ Chalk doll./ c1989, 1993/ 1-3/2 KG263 . . . . **E**
Mangaboom./ 1997/ 1-3/3 KG264 . . . . **E**
One duck, another duck./ 1984/ P-1/1 KG265 . . . . **E**
Outside dog./ 1993/ P-2/2 KG266 . . . . **CE E**
Outside dog (Kit)./ 1996/ P-2/2 KG266 . . . . **CE E**
Outside dog (Sound recording cassette)./ 1996/ P-2/2 KG266 . . **CE E**
PONCET, S/ Antarctic encounter: destination South Georgia./ 1995/
  4-6/6 KE217 . . . . **919.8**
PONDISCIO, R/ Kids on-line: 150 ways for kids to surf the net for fun and
  information./ 1995/ 3-6/6 KA572 . . . . **004.67**
PONTY, JL/ Puss in Boots (Kit)./ 1992/ 1-4 KB620 . . . . **KIT 398.24**
POPE, EM/ Perilous gard./ 1974/ 5-6/6 KH609 . . . . **FIC**
Perilous gard (Sound recording cassette)./ n.d./ 5-6/6 KH609 . . . **FIC**
POPP, KW/ Princess Florecita and the iron shoes: a Spanish fairy tale./
  1995/ 3-4/5 KB372 . . . . **398.2**
PORTE, BA/ Fat Fanny, Beanpole Bertha, and the boys./ 1991/
  4-6/4 KH610 . . . . **FIC**
Harry gets an uncle./ 1991/ 1-3/2 KG267 . . . . **E**
Harry in trouble./ 1989/ 1-3/2 KG267 . . . . **E**
Harry's birthday./ 1994/ 1-3/2 KG267 . . . . **E**
Harry's dog./ 1984/ 1-3/2 KG267 . . . . **E**

Harry's pony./ 1997/ 1-3/2 KG267 . . . . **E**
Turkey drive and other tales./ 1993/ 1-3/2 KH611 . . . . **FIC**
PORTER, F/ Place called heartbreak: a story of Vietnam./ 1993/
5-6/6 KE721 . . . . **959.704**
PORTER, JL/ Allen Jay and the Underground Railroad./ 1993/
4-6/4 KE898 . . . . **973.7**
Wilma Mankiller./ 1996/ 2-3/4 KE458 . . . . **B MANKILLER, W.**
PORTMAN, DJ/ Teaching physics with toys: activities for grades K-9./
1995/ KA204 . . . . **PROF 372.3**
POSELL, E/ Horses./ 1981/ 1-3/4 KD204 . . . . **636.1**
POTH, J/ Teaching physics with toys: activities for grades K-9./ 1995/
KA204 . . . . **PROF 372.3**
POTTER, B/ Cuento de Juanito Raton de la Ciudad./ 1988/
P-2/8 KG274 . . . . **E**
Cuento de la Oca Carlota./ 1988/ P-2/6 KG273 . . . . **E**
CUENTO DE LOS DOS MALVADOS RATONES./ 1988,/
P-2/6 KG284 . . . . **E**
Cuento del Conejito Benjamin./ 1988,/ P-2/8 KG272 . . . . **E**
Cuento del Gato Tomas./ 1988/ P-2/7 KG283 . . . . **E**
El Cuento de Pedro, el Conejo./ n.d.,/ P-2/6 KG278 . . . . **E**
Hill top tales./ c1907, 1987/ P-2/2 KG268 . . . . **E**
L'Histoire de Pierre Lapin./ n.d.,/ P-2/6 KG278 . . . . **E**
Story of Miss Moppet./ 1987/ K-2/4 KG269 . . . . **E**
Story of Miss Moppet (Sound recording cassette)./ n.d.,/
K-2/4 KG269 . . . . **E**
Tailor of Gloucester./ c1931, 1987/ P-3/7 KG270 . . . . **E**
Tailor of Gloucester (Sound recording cassette)./ n.d.,/
P-3/7 KG270 . . . . **E**
Tailor of Gloucester (Talking book)./ 1988/ 1-3 KG271 . . . . . **VCR E**
Tailor of Gloucester (Videocassette)./ 1988/ 1-3 KG271 . . . . **VCR E**
Tale of Benjamin Bunny./ c1932, 1987/ P-2/8 KG272 . . . . . . **E**
Tale of Jemima Puddle-Duck./ c1936, 1987/ P-2/6 KG273 . . . . **E**
Tale of Jemima Puddle-Duck (Braille)./ n.d.,/ P-2/6 KG273 . . . . **E**
Tale of Jemima Puddle-Duck (Large type)./ 1996,/ P-2/6 KG273 . . . **E**
Tale of Jemima Puddle-Duck (Sound recording cassette)./ n.d.,/
P-2/6 KG273 . . . . **E**
Tale of Johnny Town-Mouse./ c1946, 1987/ P-2/8 KG274 . . . . . **E**
Tale of Mr. Jeremy Fisher./ 1989/ K-2/7 KG275 . . . . **E**
Tale of Mrs. Tiggy-Winkle./ c1905, 1987/ P-2/7 KG276 . . . . . **E**
Tale of Mrs. Tittlemouse./ c1938, 1987/ P-2/7 KG277 . . . . . . **E**
Tale of Mrs. Tittlemouse (Sound recording cassette)./ n.d.,/
P-2/7 KG277 . . . . **E**
Tale of Peter Rabbit./ n.d., 1987/ P-2/6 KG278 . . . . **E**
Tale of Peter Rabbit, and four other stories (Talking book)./ 1984/
P-2 KG279 . . . . **TB E**
Tale of Peter Rabbit (Big book)./ c1902, 1993/ P-2/6 KG278 . . . **E**
Tale of Peter Rabbit (Braille)./ n.d.,/ P-2/6 KG278 . . . . **E**
Tale of Peter Rabbit (Sound recording cassette)./ n.d.,/
P-2/6 KG278 . . . . **E**
Tale of Peter Rabbit (Talking book)./ n.d.,/ P-2/6 KG278 . . . . **E**
Tale of Squirrel Nutkin./ c1931, 1987/ P-2/7 KG280 . . . . . . **E**
Tale of Squirrel Nutkin (Sound recording cassette)./ n.d.,/
P-2/7 KG280 . . . . **E**
Tale of the Flopsy Bunnies./ c1937, 1987/ P-2/7 KG281 . . . . . **E**
Tale of the Flopsy Bunnies (Sound recording cassette)./ n.d.,/
P-2/7 KG281 . . . . **E**
Tale of the pie and the patty-pan./ c1933, 1987/ K-2/5 KG282 . . . **E**
Tale of Tom Kitten./ c1935/ P-2/7 KG283 . . . . **E**
Tale of two bad mice./ c1932, 1987/ P-2/6 KG284 . . . . **E**
POWELL, C/ Bold carnivore: an alphabet of predators./ 1995/
P-5/5 KC454 . . . . **591**
POWELL, ES/ Daisy./ 1991/ 3-4/4 KH612 . . . . **FIC**
Washington./ 1993/ 4-6/6 KF094 . . . . **979.7**
POWELL, MC/ Queen of the air: the story of Katherine Stinson, 1891--
1977./ 1993/ 4-7/7 KH613 . . . . **CE FIC**
Queen of the air: the story of Katherine Stinson, 1891-1977
(Videocassette)./ 1993/ 4-7/7 KH613 . . . . **CE FIC**
POWERS, T/ Steven Spielberg: master storyteller./ 1997/
5-A/7 KE546 . . . . **B SPIELBERG, S.**
POWZYK, J/ Child's book of wildflowers./ 1992/ 3-5/5 KC405 . **582.13**
River./ 1993/ K-3/3 KC317 . . . . **577.34**
Tyrannosaurus rex and its kin: the Mesozoic monsters./ 1989/
3-6/8 KC261 . . . . **567.9**
POYDAR, N/ Adventures of Sugar and Junior./ 1995/
2-3/2 KH494 . . . . **FIC**
Busy Bea./ 1994/ P-1/2 KG285 . . . . **E**
In the diner./ 1994/ P-2/2 KG031 . . . . **E**
Rachel Parker, kindergarten show-off./ 1992/ K-2/1 KG069 . . . . **E**
Rosie's birthday rat./ 1996/ 1-3/2 KH171 . . . . **FIC**
When Jane-Marie told my secret./ 1995/ 2-3/2 KH867 . . . . . **FIC**
Will there be a lap for me?/ 1992/ P-1/2 KF425 . . . . **E**
POYNTER, M/ Killer asteroids./ 1996/ 6-8/6 KC036 . . . . . **523.44**
Marie Curie: discoverer of radium./ 1994/ 4-6/4 KE311 . **B CURIE, M.**
PRAGER, A/ Baseball birthday party./ 1995/ 1-3/2 KG286 . . . . **E**

Spooky Halloween party./ 1981/ 1-3/2 KG287 . . . . **E**
PRATT, KJ/ Paseo por el bosque liuvio./A walk in the rainforest./ 1993/
K-6/7 KC322 . . . . **577.34**
Walk in the rainforest./ 1992/ K-6/7 KC322 . . . . **577.34**
PREISS, B/ BEST CHILDREN'S BOOKS IN THE WORLD: A TREASURY OF
ILLUSTRATED STORIES./ 1996/ KA336 . . . . **PROF 808.3**
PRELUTSKY, J/ A. NONNY MOUSE WRITES AGAIN!: POEMS./ 1993/
K-2 KE052 . . . . **811.008**
Baby uggs are hatching./ 1982/ 1-3 KE000 . . . . **811**
Baby uggs are hatching (Braille)./ n.d./ 1-3 KE000 . . . . . . **811**
Beneath a blue umbrella./ 1990/ K-2 KE001 . . . . **811**
Dinosaur dinner (with a slice of alligator pie): favorite poems./ 1997/
K-3 KD970 . . . . **811**
Dragons are singing tonight./ 1993/ 2-4 KE002 . . . . **811**
Dragons are singing tonight (Sound recording cassette)./ 1995/
2-4 KE002 . . . . **811**
FOR LAUGHING OUT LOUD: POEMS TO TICKLE YOUR FUNNYBONE./
1991/ K-5 KE058 . . . . **811.008**
FOR LAUGHING OUT LOUDER: MORE POEMS TO TICKLE YOUR
FUNNYBONE./ 1995/ K-5 KE059 . . . . **811.008**
Headless Horseman rides tonight: more poems to trouble your sleep./
1980/ 2-4 KE003 . . . . **811**
It's Halloween./ c1977/ 1-3 KE004 . . . . **811**
It's Halloween (Braille)./ n.d./ 1-3 KE004 . . . . **811**
It's snowing! It's snowing!/ 1984/ K-3 KE005 . . . . **811**
It's Thanksgiving./ 1982/ 1-3 KE006 . . . . **CE 811**
It's Thanksgiving (Braille)./ n.d./ 1-3 KE006 . . . . **CE 811**
It's Thanksgiving (Sound recording cassette)./ n.d./ 1-3 KE006 . **CE 811**
It's Valentine's Day./ 1983/ K-2 KE007 . . . . **811**
Monday's troll: poems./ 1996/ K-4 KE008 . . . . **CE 811**
Monday's troll: poems (Talking book)./ 1996/ K-4 KE008 . . . . **CE 811**
My parents think I'm sleeping./ 1985/ 2-5 KE009 . . . . **811**
New kid on the block./ 1984/ 2-6 KE010 . . . . **811**
NEW KID ON THE BLOCK (CD-ROM)./ 1993/ K-A KD995 . **CDR 811**
New kid on the block (Sound recording cassette)./ n.d./
2-6 KE010 . . . . **CE 811**
New kid on the block (Talking book)./ 1986/ 2-6 KE010 . . . . **CE 811**
Nightmares: poems to trouble your sleep./ c1976/ 3-5 KE011 . . . **811**
Nightmares: poems to trouble your sleep (Sound recording cassette)./
n.d./ 3-5 KE011 . . . . **811**
Pizza the size of the sun: poems./ 1996/ K-A KE012 . . . . . . **811**
Rainy rainy Saturday./ 1980/ 1-3 KE013 . . . . **811**
READ-ALOUD RHYMES FOR THE VERY YOUNG./ c1986/
P-K KE079 . . . . **811.008**
Ride a purple pelican./ 1986/ P-3 KE014 . . . . **811**
Ride a purple pelican (Braille)./ n.d./ P-3 KE014 . . . . **811**
Rolling Harvey down the hill./ 1980/ 1-4 KE015 . . . . **CE 811**
Rolling Harvey down the hill (Talking book)./ 1993/
1-4 KE015 . . . . **CE 811**
Something big has been here (Talking book)./ 1991/
K-4 KE016 . . . . **TB 811**
Tyrannosaurus was a beast: dinosaur poems./ c1988, 1992/
1-5 KE017 . . . . **CE 811**
Tyrannosaurus was a beast: dinosaur poems (Big book)./ 1992,/
1-5 KE017 . . . . **CE 811**
Tyrannosaurus was a beast: dinosaur poems (Kit)./ 1988,/
1-5 KE017 . . . . **CE 811**
PRESILLA, ME/ Feliz nochebuena, feliz navidad: Christmas feasts of the
Hispanic Caribbean./ c1994, 1996/ 5-A/7 KB238 . . . . . . **394.266**
Life around the lake./ 1996/ 2-6/8 KE837 . . . . **972**
Mola: Cuna life stories and art./ 1996/ 3-5/7 KA832 . . . . **305.48**
PRESS, P/ Indians of the Northwest: traditions, history, legends, and life./
1997/ 4-6/9 KE762 . . . . **970.3**
PRICE, A/ MIDDLE AND JUNIOR HIGH SCHOOL LIBRARY CATALOG.
7th ed./ 1995/ KA019 . . . . **PROF 011.62**
PRICE, L/ Aida./ 1990/ 4-A/6 KD530 . . . . **782.1**
PRICEMAN, M/ A. NONNY MOUSE WRITES AGAIN!: POEMS./ 1993/
K-2 KE052 . . . . **811.008**
Cousin Ruth's tooth./ 1996/ K-2/2 KG048 . . . . **E**
FOR LAUGHING OUT LOUD: POEMS TO TICKLE YOUR FUNNYBONE./
1991/ K-5 KE058 . . . . **811.008**
FOR LAUGHING OUT LOUDER: MORE POEMS TO TICKLE YOUR
FUNNYBONE./ 1995/ K-5 KE059 . . . . **811.008**
How to make an apple pie and see the world./ 1994/ K-2/3 KG288 **E**
Rachel Fister's blister./ 1990/ K-2/2 KG050 . . . . **E**
Zin! zin! zin! a violin./ 1995/ K-3/3 KG157 . . . . **E**
PRICHETT, S/ PILGRIM VOICES: OUR FIRST YEAR IN THE NEW
WORLD./ 1995/ 3-6/7 KE944 . . . . **974.4**
PRIESTLEY., A/ Lights for Gita./ 1994/ 1-3/5 KF620 . . . . **E**
PRIMAVERA, E/ Christina Katerina and the time she quit the family./
1987/ K-2/6 KF600 . . . . **E**
Grandma's house./ 1985/ K-2/4 KG154 . . . . **E**
Make way for Sam Houston./ 1986/ 6/7 KE392 . . . **B HOUSTON, S.**

PRINCE, A/ Moon rope: a Peruvian folktale/Un lazo a la luna: una leyenda
Peruana./ 1992/ 1-3/2 KB563 . . . . **398.24**
PRINGLE, LP/ Antarctica: the last unspoiled continent./ 1992/
4-6/6 KE218 . . . . **919.8**
Batman: exploring the world of bats./ 1991/ 5-A/9 KC762 . . . . **599.4**
Bearman: exploring the world of black bears./ 1989/
5-6/7 KC852 . . . . **599.78**
Coral reefs: Earth's undersea treasures./ 1995/ 5-6/7 KC351 **577.7**
Dolphin man: exploring the world of dolphins./ 1995/
5-6/11 KC776 . . . . **599.5**
Extraordinary life: the story of a monarch butterfly./ 1997/
5-6/6 KC564 . . . . **595.78**
Fire in the forest: a cycle of growth and renewal./ 1995/
A/8 KC305 . . . . **577.2**
Jackal woman: exploring the world of jackals./ 1993/
5-6/6 KC833 . . . . **599.77**
Killer bees. Rev. ed./ 1990/ A/8 KC578 . . . . **595.79**
Oil spills: damage, recovery, and prevention./ 1993/
5-6/9 KB065 . . . . **363.73**
Scorpion man: exploring the world of scorpions./ 1994/
5-6/8 KC530 . . . . **595.4**
Smoking: a risky business./ 1996/ 4-6/9 KA998 . . . . **362.29**
PRITCHARD, M/ COOPERATION (Videocassette)./ 1990/
4-6 KA655 . . . . **VCR 158**
PROKOFIEV, S/ Peter and the wolf./ 1982/ P-3/4 KD676 . . . **CE 789.8**
PROVENSEN, A/ Glorious flight: across the channel with Louis Bleriot./
1983/ K-2/4 KD098 . . . . **CE 629.13**
Glorious flight: across the channel with Louis Bleriot (Kit)./ n.d./
K-2/4 KD098 . . . . **CE 629.13**
Glorious flight: across the channel with Louis Bleriot (Videocassette)./
n.d./ K-2/4 KD098 . . . . **CE 629.13**
Leonardo da Vinci./ 1984/ 4-6/7 KE434 . . . . **B LEONARDO**
My fellow Americans: a family album./ 1995/ 3-6/9 KE862 **973**
Our animal friends at Maple Hill Farm./ 1974/ K-2/4 KG290 . . . . . **E**
Owl and three pussycats./ 1994/ K-2/5 KG289 . . . . **E**
Year at Maple Hill Farm./ 1978/ K-2/4 KG290 . . . . **E**
PROVENSEN, M/ Glorious flight: across the channel with Louis Bleriot./
1983/ K-2/4 KD098 . . . . **CE 629.13**
Leonardo da Vinci./ 1984/ 4-6/7 KE434 . . . . **B LEONARDO**
Owl and three pussycats./ 1994/ K-2/5 KG289 . . . . **E**
Year at Maple Hill Farm./ 1978/ K-2/4 KG290 . . . . **E**
PRYOR, B/ Dream jar./ 1996/ 2-3/5 KG291 . . . . **E**
House on Maple Street./ 1987/ K-3/4 KG292 . . . . **E**
PSALM TWENTY-THREE./ 1997/ P-A/3 KA691 . . . . **223**
PUCKETT, K/ Kirby Puckett's baseball games./ 1996/
3-6/3 KD801 . . . . **796.357**
PUIG, J/ Hearing./ 1985/ P-1/1 KC973 . . . . **612.8**
Sight./ 1985/ P-1/1 KC974 . . . . **612.8**
Taste./ 1985/ P-1/2 KC975 . . . . **612.8**
Touch./ 1985/ P-1/2 KC976 . . . . **612.8**
PULVER, H/ Tracking the facts: how to develop research skills./ 1990/
5-A/9 KB089 . . . . **371.302**
PULVER, R/ Nobody's mother is in second grade./ 1992/
K-2/2 KG293 . . . . **E**
PUSHKIN, AS/ Magic gold fish: a Russian folktale./ 1995/
3-5/2 KB284 . . . . **398.2**
PUTNAM, J/ Mummy./ 1993/ 4-6/8 KB176 . . . . **393**
Pyramid./ 1994/ 4-A/7 KD359 . . . . **690**
PYLE, H/ King Stork./ 1973/ 3-5/6 KH614 . . . . **FIC**
Story of King Arthur and his knights./ c1933, 1984/
A/9 KB472 . . . . **398.22**
Story of King Arthur and his knights (Braille)./ n.d./
A/9 KB472 . . . . **398.22**
Story of King Arthur and his knights (Talking book)./ n.d.,/
A/9 KB472 . . . . **398.22**
Story of Sir Launcelot and his champions./ c1984, 1991/
A/9 KB472 . . . . **398.22**
Story of the Champions of the Round Table./ 1984,/
A/9 KB472 . . . . **398.22**
Story of the Grail and the passing of Arthur./ 1984,/
A/9 KB472 . . . . **398.22**
Swan Maiden./ 1994/ 2-4/6 KG294 . . . . **E**
QUACKENBUSH, M/ Period: revised and updated with a parents' guide./
1991/ 5-6/7 KC947 . . . . **612.6**
Smiling at yourself: educating young children about stress and self-
esteem./ 1990/ KA304 . . . . **PROF 649**
QUACKENBUSH, R/ Arthur Ashe and his match with history./ 1994/
3-5/7 KE243 . . . . **B ASHE, A.**
James Madison and Dolley Madison and their times./ 1992/
4-5/7 KE894 . . . . **973.5**
Mark Twain? What kind of name is that?: a story of Samuel Langhorne
Clemens./ 1984/ 6/8 KE580 . . . . **B TWAIN, M.**
Where did your family come from?: a book about immigrants./ 1993/
2-4/2 KA925 . . . . **325.73**

Whole world in your hands: looking at maps./ 1993/
1-3/2 KE166 . . . . **912**
QUATTLEBAUM, M/ Jazz, Pizzazz, and the silver threads./ 1996/
2-4/3 KH615 . . . . **FIC**
Magic Squad and the dog of great potential./ 1997/
2-4/4 KH616 . . . . **FIC**
QUAYLE, A/ Rikki-Tikki-Tavi and Wee Willie Winkie (Talking book)./ n.d./
4-6 KH364 . . . . **TB FIC**
QUEEN, JA/ Complete karate./ 1993/ 4-6/6 KD834 . . . . **796.815**
QUILLER-COUCH, A/ Beauty and the Beast./ 1989/ 4-5/6 KB268 **398.2**
QUIMBY, H/ ILLUSTRATORS OF CHILDREN'S BOOKS, 1967-1976./
1978/ KA311 . . . . **PROF 741.6**
QUINLAN, P/ My dad takes care of me./ 1987/ 1-3/2 KG295 . . . . . **E**
QUINLAN, SE/ Case of the mummified pigs and other mysteries in nature./
1995/ 4-A/7 KB911 . . . . **508**
QUINN, PO/ Putting on the brakes: young people's guide to understanding
attention./ 1991/ 5-6/7 KD041 . . . . **618.92**
QUIRI, PR/ Algonquians./ 1992/ 4-6/6 KE763 . . . . **970.3**
White House./ 1996/ 4-6/10 KE972 . . . . **975.3**
RABE, B/ Where's Chimpy?/ 1988/ P-2/2 KG296 . . . . . . **E**
RABIN, S/ Casey over there./ 1994/ 2-4/4 KG297 . . . . . . **E**
RACKHAM, A/ Legend of Sleepy Hollow./ c1928, 1990/
6-A/9 KH314 . . . . **FIC**
RADENCICH, MC/ How to help your child with homework: every caring
parent's guide to encouraging good study habits and ending the
Homework Wars: for parents/ 1997/ KA181 . . . . . **PROF 371.3**
RADER, L/ Turnip./ 1996/ K-1/1 KB683 . . . . **398.24**
RADFORD, D/ Cargo machines and what they do./ 1992/
P-2/4 KD089 . . . . **629.04**
RADIN, RY/ All Joseph wanted./ 1991/ 3-5/4 KH617 . . . . **FIC**
RADLEY, G/ RAINY DAY RHYMES./ 1992/ 1-3 KE078 . . . . . **811.008**
RAFFI/ Raffi's Christmas album (Sound recording cassette)./ 1983/
P-3 KD535 . . . . **SRC 782.28**
Rise and shine (Sound recording cassette)./ c1982/
P-5 KD652 . . . . **SRC 789.3**
Wheels on the bus./ c1988, 1990/ P-2 KD653 . . . . . . **789.3**
RAFFO, D/ Football./ 1994/ 3-6/4 KD785 . . . . **796.332**
RAGAZA, A/ Lives of notable Asian Americans: business, politics, science./
1995/ 6-A/7 KA856 . . . . **305.8**
RAGLIN, T/ How the rhinoceros got his skin; and, How the camel got his
hump (Videocassette)./ 1987/ 2-5 KH361 . . . . . . **VCR FIC**
How the rhinoceros got his skin (Kit)./ 1988/ 3-5 KH362 . . . . **KIT FIC**
RAHAMAN, V/ O Christmas tree./ 1996/ 1-3/4 KG298 . . . . . **E**
RAHM, DL/ Red Cross/Red Crescent: when help can't wait./ 1996/
4-6/8 KA992 . . . . **361.7**
RAHN, JE/ Plants up close./ 1981/ 4-6/6 KC391 . . . . . . **580**
RAIBLE, A/ Egypt game./ c1967/ 5-6/6 KH731 . . . . **FIC**
Headless cupid./ c1971/ 4-6/7 KH733 . . . . **CE FIC**
Witches of Worm./ c1965/ 4-6/7 KH735 . . . . **FIC**
RAINES, SC/ More story stretchers: more activities to expand children's
favorite books./ 1991/ KA240 . . . . **PROF 372.64**
Story stretchers for the primary grades: activities to expand children's
favorite books./ 1992/ KA240 . . . . **PROF 372.64**
450 more story stretchers for the primary grades: activities to expand
children's favorite books./ 1994/ KA240 . . . . . . **PROF 372.64**
RAINEY, R/ Monster factory./ 1993/ 3-6/8 KD895 . . . . **809.3**
RAINIS, KG/ Exploring with a magnifying glass./ 1991/
6-A/7 KB897 . . . . **507.8**
RAINY DAY RHYMES./ 1992/ 1-3 KE078 . . . . **811.008**
RAMSTAD, RL/ Birds in the bushes: a story about Margaret Morse Nice./
1996/ 3-5/9 KE477 . . . . **B NICE, M.**
RAND, G/ Aloha, Salty!/ 1996/ 1-3/3 KG299 . . . . **E**
Prince William./ 1992/ 2-3/4 KG300 . . . . **E**
Salty dog./ 1991/ 2-3/5 KG301 . . . . **E**
Willie takes a hike./ 1996/ K-2/3 KG302 . . . . **E**
RAND, T/ Aloha, Salty!/ 1996/ 1-3/3 KG299 . . . . **E**
Barn dance!/ 1986/ P-3/3 KG071 . . . . **E**
Bear that heard crying./ 1993/ 2-3/2 KF905 . . . . **E**
Football that won.../ 1996/ K-2/2 KD786 . . . . **796.332**
Ghost-eye tree./ 1985/ K-3/2 KG075 . . . . **E**
Here are my hands./ 1987/ P-1/2 KG076 . . . . **E**
In the palace of the Ocean King./ 1995/ 2-3/5 KG509 . . . . . **E**
My Buddy./ 1992/ K-2/2 KG201 . . . . **E**
Owl who became the moon./ 1993/ P-2/3 KG026 . . . . . . **E**
Paul Revere's ride./ 1990/ 3-A KD980 . . . . **CE 811**
Prince William./ 1992/ 2-3/4 KG300 . . . . **E**
Salty dog./ 1991/ 2-3/5 KG301 . . . . **E**
Snake in the house./ 1994/ 1-3/2 KG115 . . . . **E**
White Dynamite and Curly Kidd./ c1986, 1989/ K-3/2 KG078 . . . . **E**
Willie takes a hike./ 1996/ K-2/3 KG302 . . . . **E**
RANDOLPH, SG/ Shaker villages./ 1993/ 5-6/6 KA718 . . . . **289**
RANKIN, L/ Handmade alphabet./ 1991/ K-3 KB829 . . . . . **419**
RANSOM, CF/ Big green pocketbook./ 1993/ P-1/2 KG303 . . . . . **E**

Listening to crickets: a story about Rachel Carson./ 1993/
5-6/6 KE278 . . . . **B CARSON, R.**
Shooting star summer./ 1992/ K-2/2 KG304 . . . . **E**
When the whippoorwill calls./ 1995/ 1-3/2 KG305 . . . . . . **E**
RANSOME, A/ Fool of the world and the flying ship: a Russian tale./
c1968/ 2-5/5 KB765 . . . . **398.27**
Fool of the world and the flying ship: a Russian tale (Braille)./ n.d./
2-5/5 KB765 . . . . **398.27**
Fool of the world and the flying ship: a Russian tale (Sound recording
cassette)./ n.d./ 2-5/5 KB765 . . . . **398.27**
Old Peter's Russian tales./ 1975/ 5-6/6 KB766 . . . . **398.27**
Old Peter's Russian tales (Sound recording cassette)./ n.d./
5-6/6 KB766 . . . . **398.27**
Tontimundo y el barco volador./ 1991/ 2-5/5 KB765 . . . . . **398.27**
RANSOME, J/ Aunt Flossie's hats (and crab cakes later)./ 1991/
1-3/2 KF772 . . . . **E**
Bonesy and Isabel./ 1995/ 2-3/6 KG352 . . . . **E**
Celie and the harvest fiddler./ 1995/ 2-4/6 KH130 . . . . . **FIC**
Freedom's fruit./ 1996/ 4-6/3 KH279 . . . . **FIC**
Old dog. Rev. and newly illustrated ed./ 1995/ K-2/2 KG806 . . . . . **E**
Sweet Clara and the freedom quilt./ 1993/ 1-3/4 KF770 . . . **E**
Uncle Jed's barbershop./ 1993/ 1-3/4 KG147 . . . . **E**
RAPHAEL, L/ Stick up for yourself!: every kid's guide to personal power
and positive self-esteem./ 1990/ 6-A/6 KA659 . . . . . . **158**
RAPPAPORT, D/ Boston coffee party./ 1988/ K-3/2 KG306 . . . . **E**
Escape from slavery: five journeys to freedom./ 1991/
4-6/4 KE863 . . . . **973**
Long-haired girl: a Chinese legend./ 1995/ 2-3/4 KB409 . . . **398.21**
Long-haired girl: a Chinese legend (Sound recording cassette)./ 1997/
2-3/4 KB409 . . . . **398.21**
New king./ 1995/ 4-A/3 KB473 . . . . **398.22**
New king (Sound recording cassette)./ 1997/ 4-A/3 KB473 . . **398.22**
RASCHKA, C/ Yo! Yes?./ 1993/ P-3/1 KG307 . . . . **E**
RASKIN, E/ Figgs and phantoms./ 1974/ 4-6/6 KH618 . . . . . **FIC**
Nothing ever happens on my block./ c1966/ K-2/2 KG308 . . **FIC**
Westing game./ c1978/ 5-6/5 KH619 . . . . **FIC**
Westing game (Braille)./ n.d./ 5-6/5 KH619 . . . . **FIC**
Westing game (Sound recording cassette)./ n.d./ 5-6/5 KH619 . . . **FIC**
RATHJEN, D/ Cheshire cat and other eye-popping experiments on how we
see the world./ 1995/ 4-A/5 KA612 . . . . **152.14**
Cool hot rod and other electrifying experiments on energy and matter./
1996/ 4-A/5 KC093 . . . . **531**
Magic wand and other bright experiments on light and color./ 1995/
4-A/5 KC110 . . . . **535**
Spinning blackboard and other dynamic experiments on force and
motion./ 1996/ 4-A/5 KC094 . . . . **531**
RATHMANN, P/ Good night, Gorilla./ 1994/ K-2/1 KG309 . . . . . . **E**
Officer Buckle and Gloria./ 1995/ K-2/3 KG310 . . . . **E**
Ruby the copycat./ 1991/ K-2/2 KG311 . . . . **E**
RATTIGAN, JK/ Dumpling soup./ 1993/ 1-3/2 KG312 . . . . . . **E**
Woman in the moon: a story from Hawaii./ 1996/
K-2/6 KB474 . . . . **398.22**
RATZ DE TAGYOS, P/ Coney tale./ 1992/ 2-5/5 KH620 . . . . . . **FIC**
Showdown at Lonesome Pellet./ 1994/ 1-4/5 KH621 . . . . . **FIC**
RAU, DM/ Box can be many things./ 1997/ K-1/2 KG313 . . . . . . **E**
Robin at Hickory Street./ 1995/ K-2/3 KG314 . . . . **CE E**
Robin at Hickory Street (Kit)./ 1995/ K-2/3 KG314 . . . . . **CE E**
RAVEN, M/ Angels in the dust./ 1997/ 3-5/6 KG315 . . . . . **E**
RAWLINGS, MK/ Yearling./ c1938, 1967/ 5-A/5 KH622 . . . . **FIC**
Yearling (Braille)./ n.d., 5-A/5 KH622 . . . . **FIC**
Yearling (Talking book)./ n.d., 5-A/5 KH622 . . . . **FIC**
RAWLINS, D/ My place./ 1992/ 5-6/3 KF118 . . . . **994**
Tucking mommy in./ 1987/ P-2/2 KG017 . . . . **E**
RAWLS, W/ Summer of the monkeys./ 1976/ 4-6/6 KH623 . . . **FIC**
Summer of the monkeys (Sound recording cassette)./ n.d./
4-6/6 KH623 . . . . **FIC**
Where the red fern grows: the story of two dogs and a boy./ c1961,
1988/ A/4 KH624 . . . . **FIC**
Where the red fern grows: the story of two dogs and a boy (Braille)./
n.d./ A/4 KH624 . . . . **FIC**
Where the red fern grows: the story of two dogs and a boy (Talking
book)./ n.d./ A/4 KH624 . . . . **FIC**
RAY, D/ Behind the blue and gray: the soldier's life in the Civil War./
1991/ 5-A/7 KE911 . . . . **973.7**
Robin Hood and Little John./ 1995/ 2-4/4 KB433 . . . . **398.22**
RAY, DK/ All Joseph wanted./ 1991/ 3-5/4 KH617 . . . . . . **FIC**
Cassie's journey: going West in the 1860s./ 1988/ 1-3/5 KF677 . . . **E**
Chang's paper pony./ 1988/ 2-3/2 KF400 . . . . **E**
Hist whist./ c1923, 1989/ 2-6 KD926 . . . . **811**
How does the wind walk?/ 1993/ P-2/3 KF354 . . . . **E**
I have a sister--my sister is deaf./ c1977/ 2-4/4 KB007 . . . . . **362.4**
Immigrant girl: Becky of Eldridge Street./ 1987/ 3-5/5 KH221 . . . . **FIC**
My prairie Christmas./ 1990/ 2-4/4 KH222 . . . . **FIC**
RAY, J/ Earth, fire, water, air./ 1995/ 2-6/7 KA814 . . . . **304.2**

Fun magic with things around the house (Videocassette)./ 1995/
3-6 KD752 . . . . **VCR 793.8**
Magical tales from many lands./ 1993/ 4-5/6 KB343 . . . . . **398.2**
STORY OF THE CREATION: WORDS FROM GENESIS./ 1993/
2-3/4 KA688 . . . . **222**
RAY, ML/ Mud./ 1996/ P-2/2 KG316 . . . . **E**
RAYEVSKY, R/ Aesop's fables./ 1988/ 3-4 KB632 . . . . **398.24**
Bernal and Florinda: a Spanish tale./ 1994/ 2-4/3 KF903 . . . . . . **E**
RAYMOND, L/ Jacques Cousteau: champion of the sea./ 1992/
4-6/7 KE305 . . . . **B COUSTEAU, J.**
Marjory Stoneman Douglas: voice of the Everglades./ 1992/
4-5/6 KE324 . . . . **B DOUGLAS, M.**
RAYMOND, V/ Brown cow, green grass, yellow mellow sun./ 1995/
P-1/2 KF818 . . . . **E**
RAYNER, M/ Babe: the gallant pig./ 1994/ 2-5/5 KH346 . . . **CE FIC**
Garth Pig and the ice cream lady./ 1977/ K-2/4 KG317 . . . **E**
Garth Pig and the ice cream lady (Braille)./ n.d./ K-2/4 KG317 . . . . **E**
Garth Pig and the ice cream lady (Sound recording cassette)./ n.d./
K-2/4 KG317 . . . . **E**
Mr. and Mrs. Pig's evening out./ c1976/ K-2/4 KG317 . . . . . **E**
Mr. and Mrs. Pig's evening out (Braille)./ n.d./ K-2/4 KG317 . . . **E**
Mrs. Pig's bulk buy./ 1981/ K-2/4 KG317 . . . . **E**
RAYSON, A/ Hawai'i: the Pacific State. Rev. and updated edition./ 1997/
5-A/6 KF123 . . . . **996.9**
RAYYAN, O/ Count Silvernose: a story from Italy./ 1996/
3-5/5 KB504 . . . . **398.23**
Ramadan./ 1996/ 3-5/7 KA785 . . . . **297**
Rimonah of the Flashing Sword: a North African tale./ 1995/
3-4/4 KB331 . . . . **398.2**
Ring of Truth: an original Irish tale./ 1997/ 1-3/5 KF213 . . . . **E**
REA, JG/ Atariba and Niguayona: a story from the Taino people of Puerto
Rico./ c1976, 1988/ 4-5/5 KB769 . . . . **398.27**
READ BY AUGUSTA BAKER./ Uncle Bouqui of Haiti (Talking book)./
1959/ K-A KB729 . . . . **TB 398.27**
READHEAD, L/ Gymnastics./ 1996/ 3-6/8 KD818 . . . . **796.44**
REASONER, C/ Night owl and the rooster: a Haitian legend./ 1995/
K-2/6 KB637 . . . . **CE 398.24**
Night owl and the rooster: a Haitian legend (Talking book)./ 1996/
K-2/6 KB637 . . . . **CE 398.24**
REDENBAUGH, VJ/ When I'm alone./ 1993/ P-2/4 KG187 . . . . . **E**
REDGRAVE, L/ HERE WE GO AGAIN! (Videocassette)./ 1986/
1-4 KB157 . . . . **VCR 388**
HERE WE GO. VOL. 1 (Videocassette)./ 1986/ 1-4 KB158 . **VCR 388**
Napping house and other stories (Talking book)./ 1987/
P-3 KG765 . . . . **TB E**
REDIGER, P/ Great African Americans in music./ 1996/
3-6/8 KD524 . . . . **780**
REDMOND, I/ Elephant./ 1993/ 4-6/7 KC815 . . . . **599.67**
REED, GJ/ Dear Mrs. Parks: a dialogue with today's youth./ 1996/
5-6/6 KA901 . . . . **323**
REED, JF/ Across the plains in the Donner Party./ 1996/
5-6/7 KF041 . . . . **978**
REED-JONES, C/ Tree in the ancient forest./ 1995/ K-3/3 KC437 . **585**
REEF, C/ Black fighting men: a proud history./ 1994/ 5-6/6 KA982 . **355**
Jacques Cousteau: champion of the sea./ 1992/
4-6/7 KE305 . . . . **B COUSTEAU, J.**
Monticello./ 1991/ 3-5/6 KE892 . . . . **973.4**
REES, E/ Fast Freddie Frog and other tongue-twister rhymes./ 1993/
2-6 KB812 . . . . **398.8**
REEVE, P/ Amazing magic tricks./ 1995/ 4-6 KD744 . . . . . . **793.8**
REGAN, DC/ Monsters in the attic./ 1995/ 4-6/6 KH625 . . . . . **FIC**
REGAN, L/ Welcome to the green house./ 1993/ K-3/4 KC329 . **577.34**
REGAN-BLAKE, C/ Tales to grow on (Sound recording cassette)./ c1981/
K-3 KB298 . . . . **SRC 398.2**
REGGUINTI, G/ Sacred harvest: Ojibway wild rice gathering./ 1992/
4-6/6 KE785 . . . . **970.476**
REHDER, HA/ Audubon Society field guide to North American seashells./
1981/ 3-6 KC516 . . . . **594**
REICHMAN, H/ Censorship and selection: issues and answers for schools.
Rev. ed./ 1993/ KA053 . . . . **PROF 025.2**
REID BANKS, L/ Adventures of King Midas./ 1992/ 4-A/6 KH626 . . **FIC**
Indian in the cupboard./ 1980/ 4-6/4 KH627 . . . . **CE FIC**
Indian in the cupboard (Braille)./ n.d./ 4-6/4 KH627 . . . . **CE FIC**
Indian in the cupboard (Talking book)./ 1992/ 4-6/4 KH627 . . **CE FIC**
Mystery of the cupboard./ 1993/ 5-A/6 KH628 . . . . **CE FIC**
Mystery of the cupboard (Talking book)./ 1993/ 5-A/6 KH628 **CE FIC**
Return of the Indian./ 1986/ 5-A/6 KH629 . . . . **FIC**
Return of the Indian (Braille)./ n.d./ 5-A/6 KH629 . . . . **FIC**
Secret of the Indian./ 1989/ 5-A/6 KH629 . . . . **FIC**
Secret of the Indian (Sound recording cassette)./ 1994/
5-A/6 KH629 . . . . **FIC**
REID, R/ Children's jukebox: a subject guide to musical recordings and
programming ideas for songsters ages one to twelve./ 1995/
KA029 . . . . **PROF 016.7893**

REIDEL, M/ From egg to bird./ 1981/ P-2/2 KC661 . . . . **598**
From egg to butterfly./ 1981/ P-2/5 KC565 . . . . **595.78**
REISBERG, M/ Leaving for America./ 1992/ 1-4/6 KE688 . . . . . . **947**
REISBERG, V/ Elinda who danced in the sky: an Estonian folktale./ 1990/ 3-5/5 KB407 . . . . **398.21**
REISER, L/ Beach feet./ 1996/ P-3/2 KG318 . . . . **E**
Surprise family./ 1994/ P-2/2 KG319 . . . . **E**
Two mice in three fables./ 1995/ P-2/3 KG320 . . . . **E**
REISS, J/ Journey back./ c1976/ 5-6/5 KE506 . . . . **B REISS, J.**
Upstairs room./ c1972/ 5-6/5 KE506 . . . . **B REISS, J.**
REISS, JJ/ Numbers./ c1971/ P-1 KG321 . . . . **E**
Shapes./ c1974/ P-1 KB994 . . . . **516**
REISS, K/ Time windows./ 1991/ 6-A/7 KH630 . . . . **FIC**
REMKIEWICZ, F/ Froggy gets dressed./ 1992/ P-K/2 KG021 . . . . . . **E**
Froggy goes to school./ 1996/ P-1/2 KG022 . . . . **E**
Horrible Harry and the green slime./ 1989/ 2-4/2 KH368 . . . . **FIC**
Joy boys./ 1996/ 2-3/1 KF326 . . . . **E**
Let's go, Froggy!/ 1994/ P-K/2 KG024 . . . . **E**
Magic Squad and the dog of great potential./ 1997/ 2-4/4 KH616 . . . . **FIC**
RENBERG, DH/ King Solomon and the bee./ 1994/ 2-3/4 KB475 . . . . **398.22**
RENDEIRO, C/ Been to yesterdays: poems of a life./ 1995/ 3-6 KD953 . . . . **811**
RENDON, MR/ Powwow summer: a family celebrates the circle of life./ 1996/ 1-3/3 KB181 . . . . **394**
RENFRO, N/ Puppetry in early childhood education./ 1982/ KA327 . . . . **PROF 791.5**
Puppetry, language, and the special child: discovering alternate languages./ 1984/ KA328 . . . . **PROF 791.5**
RENNERT, RS/ Henry Aaron./ 1993/ 5-A/9 KE222 . . . **B AARON, H.**
REX, M/ Fattest, tallest, biggest snowman ever./ 1997/ K-2/2 KF987 . **E**
REX-JOHNSON, B/ That's fresh!: seasonal recipes for young cooks./ 1995/ 5-6 KD277 . . . . **641.5**
REY, H/ Curious George flies a kite./ c1958/ P-2/1 KG328 . . . . **E**
Curious George goes to the hospital./ c1966/ P-2/2 KG329 . . . . . . **E**
REY, HA/ Curious George./ c1941/ P-2/2 KG322 . . . . **E**
Curious George and other stories about Curious George (Talking book)./ 1973/ P-2 KG323 . . . . **TB E**
Curious George (Big book)./ 1994/ P-2/2 KG322 . . . . **E**
Curious George (Braille)./ n.d./ P-2/2 KG322 . . . . **E**
Curious George gets a medal./ 1957/ P-2/2 KG324 . . . . **E**
Curious George gets a medal (Braille)./ n.d./ P-2/2 KG324 . . . . . . **E**
Curious George learns the alphabet./ c1963/ P-2/2 KG325 . . . . . . **E**
Curious George learns the alphabet (Sound recording cassette)./ n.d./ P-2/2 KG325 . . . . **E**
Curious George rides a bike./ c1952/ P-2/1 KG326 . . . . **CE E**
Curious George rides a bike (Kit)./ 1993/ P-2/1 KG326 . . . . . . **CE E**
Curious George rides a bike (Videocassette)./ 1985/ P-2/1 KG326 . . . . **CE E**
Curious George (Sound recording cassette)./ n.d./ P-2/2 KG322 . . . **E**
Curious George takes a job./ c1947/ P-2/3 KG327 . . . . **E**
Curious George takes a job (Braille)./ n.d./ P-2/3 KG327 . . . . **E**
Curious George (Talking book)./ n.d./ P-2/2 KG322 . . . . **E**
Find the constellations. Rev. ed./ 1976/ 4-6/6 KC052 . . . . **523.8**
Jorge el Curioso./ n.d./ P-2/2 KG322 . . . . **E**
Stars: a new way to see them./ c1967/ 4-6/8 KC053 . . . . **523.8**
REY, M/ Curious George flies a kite./ c1958/ P-2/1 KG328 . . . . **E**
Curious George flies a kite (Braille)./ n.d./ P-2/1 KG328 . . . . **E**
Curious George goes to the hospital./ c1966/ P-2/2 KG329 . . . . . . **E**
Curious George goes to the hospital (Braille)./ n.d./ P-2/2 KG329 . . **E**
REYNOLDS, J/ Amazon Basin: vanishing cultures./ 1993/ 3-6/7 KF104 . . . . **981**
Down under: vanishing cultures./ 1992/ 3-6/6 KF117 . . . . **994**
Far north: vanishing cultures./ 1992/ 3-6/6 KE696 . . . . **948.97**
Frozen land: vanishing cultures./ 1993/ 3-6/6 KE827 . . . . **971.9**
Himalaya: vanishing cultures./ 1991/ 4-6/7 KE714 . . . . **954.96**
Mongolia: vanishing cultures./ 1994/ 4-6/7 KE704 . . . . **951.7**
Sahara: vanishing cultures./ 1991/ 4-6/6 KE732 . . . . **966**
RHODES, T/ Hummingbirds' gift./ 1994/ 1-3/7 KF443 . . . . **E**
Pancho's pinata./ 1992/ 2-4/7 KB703 . . . . **398.26**
RICE, E/ Benny bakes a cake./ c1981, 1993/ P-2/2 KG330 . . . . **E**
RICE, M/ Complete book of children's activities./ 1993/ KA194 . . . . **PROF 372.13**
RICH, A/ Dare to dream: Coretta Scott King and the civil rights movement./ 1994/ 3-5/3 KE419 . . . . **B KING, C.S.**
Little Louis and the jazz band: the story of Louis "Satchmo" Armstrong./ 1994/ 2-4/6 KE241 . . . . **B ARMSTRONG, L.**
Microsoft composer collection (CD-ROM)./ 1994/ 4-A KD525 . . . . **CDR 780**
Saturday at The New You./ 1994/ K-3/3 KF198 . . . . **E**
Tamika and the wisdom rings./ 1994/ 3-4/2 KH888 . . . . **FIC**
RICHARDSON, J/ Inside the museum: a children's guide to the Metropolitan Museum of Art./ 1993/ 2-A/7 KD376 . . . . **708**
Science dictionary of the human body./ 1992/ 4-6/7 KC906 . . . . **611**
RICHARDSON, M/ Secret elephant of Harlan Kooter./ 1992/ 4-A/6 KH223 . . . . **FIC**
RICHARDSON, SK/ Magazines for children, a guide for parents, teachers, and librarians./ 1983/ KA022 . . . . **PROF 011.62**
RICHEMONT, E/ Magic skateboard./ 1992/ 3-5/3 KH631 . . . . **FIC**
RICHEY, D/ Eating pretty./ 1991/ 5-A/7 KC985 . . . . **613.2**
RICHMOND, J/ Three and many wishes of Jason Reid./ 1988/ 4-6/6 KH310 . . . . **FIC**
RICHMOND, R/ Story in a picture: animals in art./ 1993/ 4-A/7 KD475 . . . . **758**
Story in a picture: children in art./ 1992/ 3-6/7 KD471 . . . . **757**
RICHTER, C/ Light in the forest./ 1994/ 5-A/5 KH632 . . . . **FIC**
RICHTER, HP/ Friedrich./ c1970, 1987/ 5-A/5 KH633 . . . . **FIC**
RICHTER, M/ PLANET OF THE GRAPES: SHOW BIZ JOKES AND RIDDLES./ 1992/ 3-6 KD737 . . . . **793.735**
RICKARBY, LA/ Ulysses S. Grant and the strategy of victory./ 1991/ 6-A/6 KE377 . . . . **B GRANT, U.**
RIDDELL, C/ Kasper in the glitter./ 1997/ 5-A/4 KH634 . . . . **FIC**
RIDDELL, E/ Senses: a lift-the-flap body book./ 1993/ 1-3/4 KC977 . . . . **612.8**
RIDDLE-ME RHYMES./ 1994/ 3-5 KD738 . . . . **793.735**
RIDE, S/ Third planet: exploring the earth from space./ 1994/ 2-8/7 KC062 . . . . **525**
To space and back./ 1986/ 4-6/7 KD138 . . . . **629.45**
Voyager: an adventure to the edge of the solar system./ 1992/ 3-6/7 KC030 . . . . **523.4**
Voyager: an adventure to the edge of the solar system (Sound recording cassette)./ 1996/ 3-6/7 KC030 . . . . **523.4**
RIDLEY, P/ Kasper in the glitter./ 1997/ 5-A/4 KH634 . . . . **FIC**
RIETZ, SA/ Storytelling activities./ 1987/ KA247 . . . . **PROF 372.67**
Storytelling folklore sourcebook./ 1991/ KA340 . . . . **PROF 808.5**
RIGG, P/ WHEN THEY DON'T ALL SPEAK ENGLISH: INTEGRATING THE ESL STUDENT INTO THE REGULAR CLASSROOM./ 1989/ KA281 . . . . **PROF 428**
RIGGIO, A/ Secret signs: along the Underground Railroad./ 1997/ 2-3/2 KG331 . . . . **E**
RIGGLE, J/ Beyond picture books: a guide to first readers. 2nd ed./ 1995/ KA011 . . . . **PROF 011.62**
RIGIE, M/ Genghis Khan: a dog star is born./ 1994/ 2-5/2 KH703 . **FIC**
Genghis Khan: dog-gone Hollywood./ 1995/ 2-5/2 KH704 . . . . . . **FIC**
RILEY, GB/ Wah Ming Chang: artist and master of special effects./ 1995/ 5-6/6 KE285 . . . . **B CHANG, W.**
RILEY, J/
Prairie cabin: a Norwegian pioneer woman's story (Videocassette)./
Prairie cabin: a Norwegian pioneer woman's story (Videocassette)./ 1991/ 1991/ A KF012 . . . . **VCR 977**
A KF012 . . . . **VCR 977**
WOMEN IN POLICING (Videocassette)./ 1994/ 5-6 KB030 . . . . **VCR 363.2**
RILEY, LC/ Elephants swim./ 1995/ P-2/3 KC466 . . . . **591.47**
RING, E/ Henry David Thoreau: in step with nature./ 1993/ 2-5/3 KE565 . . . . **B THOREAU, H.**
What rot!: nature's mighty recycler./ 1996/ 1-3/3 KC304 . . . . . **577.1**
RINGGOLD, F/ Dinner at Aunt Connie's house./ 1993/ 2-4/5 KG332 **E**
My dream of Martin Luther King./ 1995/ 3-5/7 KE423 . **B KING, M.L.**
Talking to Faith Ringgold./ 1996/ 4-6/6 KD379 . . . . **709.2**
Tar beach./ 1991/ 2-3/4 KG333 . . . . **E**
RIORDAN, J/ Stories from the sea./ 1996/ K-3/3 KB508 . . . . . **398.23**
RISHEL, M/ Nature for the very young: a handbook of indoor and outdoor activities./ 1989/ KA199 . . . . **PROF 372.3**
RITCHIE, D/ Frontier life./ 1996/ 5-6/9 KF045 . . . . **978**
Kid's cuisine./ 1988/ 4-6 KD278 . . . . **641.5**
RITTER, LS/ Leagues apart: the men and times of the Negro baseball leagues./ 1995/ 2-4/7 KD802 . . . . **796.357**
RITZ, K/ Ellis Island: doorway to freedom./ 1995/ 2-4/10 KA920 . **325**
Frontier surgeons: a story about the Mayo Brothers./ 1989/ 5-6/6 KC899 . . . . **610.69**
Hilde and Eli: children of the Holocaust./ 1994/ 4-6/5 KE655 . **940.53**
Picture book of Anne Frank./ 1993/ 3-4/5 KE351 . . **CE B FRANK, A.**
RIUS, M/ Hearing./ 1985/ P-1/1 KC973 . . . . **612.8**
Sight./ 1985/ P-1/1 KC974 . . . . **612.8**
Taste./ 1985/ P-1/2 KC975 . . . . **612.8**
Touch./ 1985/ P-1/2 KC976 . . . . **612.8**
RIVERS, A/ In two worlds: a Yup'ik Eskimo family./ 1989/ 5-6/7 KF098 . . . . **979.8**
ROACH, MK/ In the days of the Salem witchcraft trials./ 1996/ 3-6/10 KE945 . . . . **974.4**
ROALF, P/ Cats./ 1992/ 5-A/8 KD476 . . . . **758**
Circus./ 1993/ 5-A/8 KD477 . . . . **758**
Dancers./ 1992/ 5-A/7 KD478 . . . . **758**
Families./ 1992/ 5-A/7 KD472 . . . . **757**
Flowers./ 1993/ 5-A/8 KD479 . . . . **758**
Horses./ 1992/ 5-A/8 KD480 . . . . **758**

Landscapes./ 1992/ 5-A/8 KD481 . . . . **758**
Seascapes./ 1992/ 5-A/7 KD482 . . . . **758**
ROBART, R/ Cake that Mack ate./ 1986/ P-1/1 KG334 . . . . **E**
ROBB, L/ SNUFFLES AND SNOUTS: POEMS./ 1995/
P-2 KE083 . . . . **811.008**
ROBBINS, K/ Power machines./ c1993, 1997/ K-4/6 KD051 . . . . **621.8**
ROBBINS, R/ Baboushka and the three kings./ c1960/
2-4/6 KB509 . . . . **398.23**
Baboushka and the three kings (Braille)./ n.d./ 2-4/6 KB509 . . **398.23**
Baboushka and the three kings (Sound recording cassette)./ n.d./
2-4/6 KB509 . . . . **398.23**
ROBBINS, S/ Growing rock: a Southwest Native American tale (Kit)./
1993/ P-1 KB638 . . . . **KIT 398.24**
ROBERTS, B/ Camel caravan./ 1996/ P-1/3 KG335 . . . . **E**
Halloween mice!/ 1995/ P-1/3 KG336 . . . . **E**
ROBERTS, JL/ Booker T. Washington: educator and leader./ 1995/
4-6/5 KE586 . . . . **B WASHINGTON, B**
ROBERTS, T/ THREE BILLY GOATS GRUFF; AND, THE THREE LITTLE
PIGS (Videocassette)./ 1989/ P-K KB665 . . . . **VCR 398.24**
ROBERTS, WD/ Don't hurt Laurie!/ 1977/ 5-6/6 KH635 . . . . **FIC**
Girl with the silver eyes./ 1980/ 4-6/5 KH636 . . . . **FIC**
Girl with the silver eyes (Braille)./ n.d./ 4-6/5 KH636 . . . . . . **FIC**
Girl with the silver eyes (Sound recording cassette)./ n.d./
4-6/5 KH636 . . . . **FIC**
ROBERTSON, D/ Super kids publishing company./ 1990/
KA333 . . . . **PROF 808**
ROBERTSON, K/ Henry Reed, Inc./ 1989/ 4-6/6 KH638 . . . . **FIC**
Henry Reed, Inc. (Braille)./ n.d./ 4-6/6 KH638 . . . . **FIC**
Henry Reed, Inc. (Talking book)./ 1973/ 4-6 KH637 . . . . . **TB FIC**
Henry Reed's baby-sitting service./ c1966/ 4-6/6 KH638 . . . . . **FIC**
Henry Reed's baby-sitting service (Braille)./ n.d./ 4-6/6 KH638 . . **FIC**
Henry Reed's baby-sitting service (Talking book)./ n.d./
4-6/6 KH638 . . . . **FIC**
Henry Reed's big show (Talking book)./ n.d./ 4-6/6 KH638 . . . . **FIC**
Henry Reed's journey (Braille)./ n.d./ 4-6/6 KH638 . . . . **FIC**
Henry Reed's journey (Sound recording cassette)./ n.d./
4-6/6 KH638 . . . . **FIC**
ROBERTUS, PM/ Dog who had kittens./ 1991/ K-1/4 KG337 . . . . **CE E**
Dog who had kittens (Kit)./ 1992/ K-1/4 KG337 . . . . **CE E**
Dog who had kittens (Videocassette)./ 1992/ K-1/4 KG337 . . . . **CE E**
ROBINET, HG/ Mississippi chariot./ 1994/ 5-A/5 KH639 . . . . **FIC**
ROBINS, J/ Addie meets Max./ 1985/ K-2/1 KG338 . . . . **E**
Addie's bad day./ 1993/ K-1/2 KG339 . . . . **E**
ROBINSON, ABL/ Elijah's angel: a story for Chanukah and Christmas./
1992/ 3-6/7 KH652 . . . . **FIC**
School for Pompey Walker./ 1995/ 4-8/6 KH653 . . . . **FIC**
ROBINSON, AJ/ Here is the Arctic winter./ 1993/ K-4/2 KC731 **599.17**
ROBINSON, B/ Best Christmas pageant ever./ c1972/ 4-6/7 KH640 **FIC**
Best Christmas pageant ever (Braille)./ n.d./ 4-6/7 KH640 . . . . **FIC**
Best school year ever./ 1994/ 3-A/5 KH641 . . . . **FIC**
Best school year ever (Sound recording cassette)./ 1997/
3-A/5 KH641 . . . . **FIC**
ROBINSON, C/ Grandma drives a motor bed./ 1987/ P-3/2 KF669 . **E**
Journey to America./ c1970, 1993/ 5-A/5 KH398 . . . . **FIC**
Nekomah Creek./ 1991/ 4-A/5 KH041 . . . . **FIC**
Nekomah Creek Christmas./ 1994/ 4-6/4 KH042 . . . . **FIC**
Taste of blackberries./ c1973/ 4-6/4 KH722 . . . . **FIC**
ROBINSON, F/ FROG INSIDE MY HAT: A FIRST BOOK OF POEMS./
1993/ P-1 KD884 . . . . **808.81**
Oh, how waffle!: riddles you can eat./ 1993/ 2-6 KD735 . . **793.735**
Space probes to the planets./ 1993/ 2-5/5 KC031 . . . . **523.4**
ROBINSON, K/ Mysterious mind powers./ 1993/ 4-6/3 KA609 . . **133.8**
Recalling past lives./ 1993/ 4-6/3 KA611 . . . . **133.9**
Seeing the unseen./ 1993/ 4-6/3 KA610 . . . . **133.8**
ROBINSON, NK/ Veronica the show-off./ c1982/ 3-6/4 KH642 . . . **FIC**
ROBISON, N/ Buffalo Bill./ 1991/ 5-6/6 KE267 . . . . **B BUFFALO BILL**
ROBSON, P/ Exploring time./ 1995/ 3-6/6 KC069 . . . . **529**
Making books./ 1992/ 3-6/7 KD412 . . . . **741.6**
Maps and mazes: a first guide to mapmaking./ 1993/
K-6/6 KC064 . . . . **526**
ROBY, C/ When learning is tough: kids talk about their learning
disabilities./ 1994/ 4-6/6 KB096 . . . . **371.92**
ROCHELLE, B/ Witnesses to freedom: young people who fought for civil
rights./ 1993/ 5-6/7 KA905 . . . . **323.1**
ROCKWELL, AF/ Acorn tree and other folktales./ 1995/
P-2/2 KB362 . . . . **398.2**
At the beach./ 1987/ P-3/3 KG340 . . . . **E**
Cars./ 1992/ P/1 KD115 . . . . **629.222**
Ducklings and pollywogs./ 1994/ K-2/3 KG341 . . . . **E**
Fire engines./ 1986/ P/3 KD088 . . . . **628.9**
First snowfall./ 1987/ P-1/2 KG342 . . . . **E**
I fly./ 1997/ P-1/2 KG343 . . . . **E**
Machines./ c1972/ K-2/3 KD052 . . . . **621.8**
Once upon a time this morning./ 1997/ P-K/2 KG344 . . . . **E**

One-eyed giant and other monsters from the Greek myths./ 1996/
2-5/6 KA750 . . . . **292**
Our yard is full of birds./ 1992/ K-2/4 KC662 . . . . **598**
Pots and pans./ 1993/ P/3 KD279 . . . . **641.5**
Robber baby: stories from the Greek myths./ 1994/ 3-6/6 KA751 **292**
Show and tell day./ 1997/ P-K/2 KG345 . . . . **E**
Toolbox./ 1990/ P-K/3 KD057 . . . . **621.9**
Toolbox (Braille)./ n.d./ P-K/3 KD057 . . . . **621.9**
What we like./ 1992/ P KB849 . . . . **428.1**
ROCKWELL, H/ At the beach./ 1987/ P-3/3 KG340 . . . . **E**
First snowfall./ 1987/ P-1/2 KG342 . . . . **E**
Machines./ c1972/ K-2/3 KD052 . . . . **621.8**
My dentist./ 1975/ P-1/2 KD037 . . . . **617.6**
My dentist (Braille)./ n.d./ P-1/2 KD037 . . . . **617.6**
Toolbox./ 1990/ P-K/3 KD057 . . . . **621.9**
ROCKWELL, L/ Ducklings and pollywogs./ 1994/ K-2/3 KG341 . . . **E**
Nest full of eggs./ 1995/ K-2/2 KC705 . . . . **598.8**
Our yard is full of birds./ 1992/ K-2/4 KC662 . . . . **598**
Pots and pans./ 1993/ P/3 KD279 . . . . **641.5**
Show and tell day./ 1997/ P-K/2 KG345 . . . . **E**
ROCKWELL, T/ How to eat fried worms./ 1973/ 4-6/5 KH643 . . . **FIC**
ROCKWOOD, J/ To spoil the sun./ c1976, 1994/ 6-A/6 KH644 . . . **FIC**
ROCKWOOD, R/ New book of dinosaurs./ 1997/ K-6/9 KC266 . **567.9**
RODANAS, K/ Dance of the sacred circle: a Native American tale./ 1994/
3-4/5 KB639 . . . . **398.24**
Dragonfly's tale./ 1992/ 2-3/4 KB767 . . . . **398.27**
Eagle's song: a tale from the Pacific Northwest./ 1995/
3-4/5 KB768 . . . . **398.27**
Only the names remain: the Cherokees and the Trail of Tears. 2nd ed./
1996/ 5-6/8 KE758 . . . . **970.3**
RODDA, E/ Finders keepers./ 1991/ 5-A/6 KH645 . . . . **FIC**
RODGERS, M/ Billion for Boris./ c1974/ 4-6/7 KH646 . . . . . . **CE FIC**
Billion for Boris (Braille)./ n.d./ 4-6/7 KH646 . . . . **CE FIC**
Billion for Boris (Kit)./ 1979/ 4-6/7 KH646 . . . . **CE FIC**
Freaky Friday./ c1972/ 5-6/5 KH647 . . . . **CE FIC**
Freaky Friday (Kit)./ 1978/ 5-6/5 KH647 . . . . **CE FIC**
Summer switch./ 1982/ 5-6/7 KH648 . . . . **FIC**
Summer switch (Sound recording cassette)./ n.d./ 5-6/7 KH648 . . **FIC**
Viernes embrujado./ 1987/ 5-6/5 KH647 . . . . **CE FIC**
RODGERS, MM/ Our endangered planet: air./ 1995/
4-6/8 KB069 . . . . **363.73**
Our endangered planet: Antarctica./ 1992/ 5-6/8 KE221 . . . . **919.8**
Our endangered planet: atmosphere./ 1995/ 4-6/8 KB061 . . . **363.73**
Our endangered planet: groundwater./ 1991/ 5-6/8 KA959 . . **333.91**
Our endangered planet: life on land./ 1992/ 5-6/8 KA962 . . **333.95**
Our endangered planet: population growth./ 1990/
5-6/9 KA816 . . . . **304.6**
Our endangered planet: rivers and lakes./ 1991/ 5-6/8 KB062 **363.73**
RODGERS, R/ Sound of music. Selections. 2nd ed. (Sound recording
cassette)./ 1965/ K-A KD531 . . . . **SRC 782.1**
RODOWSKY, C/ Dog days./ 1993/ 4-5/6 KH649 . . . . **FIC**
Hannah in between./ 1994/ 5-A/7 KH650 . . . . **FIC**
RODRIGUEZ, J/ Gloria Estefan./ 1996/ 5-6/6 KE340 . . . **B ESTEFAN, G.**
ROE, E/ With my brother/Con mi hermano./ 1991/ P-2/2 KG346 . . . **E**
ROESSEL, M/ Kinaalda: a Navajo girl grows up./ 1993/
4-6/5 KE789 . . . . **970.48**
Songs from the loom: a Navajo girl learns to weave./ 1995/
4-6/6 KE799 . . . . **970.491**
ROFES, EE/ KID'S BOOK ABOUT DEATH AND DYING./ 1985/
4-6/6 KA650 . . . . **155.9**
ROFFE, M/ Sun: our very own star./ 1991/ 1-3/5 KC044 . . . . . **523.7**
ROGASKY, B/ Rapunzel./ 1982/ 2-4/4 KB307 . . . . **398.2**
Smoke and ashes: the story of the Holocaust./ 1988/
A/8 KE664 . . . . **940.53**
ROGERS, J/ King Island Christmas./ 1985/ K-3/5 KG347 . . . . **E**
MONSTER SOUP AND OTHER SPOOKY POEMS./ 1992/
K-3 KD986 . . . . **811**
Not-just-anybody family./ 1986/ 4-A/4 KG962 . . . . **CE FIC**
Puppy sister./ 1995/ 3-5/4 KH263 . . . . **FIC**
Runaway mittens./ 1988/ P-2/4 KG348 . . . . **E**
ROGERS, L/ Bearman: exploring the world of black bears./ 1989/
5-6/7 KC852 . . . . **599.78**
ROGERS, P/ What will the weather be like today?/ 1990/
P-1/2 KC221 . . . . **551.6**
ROGERS, S/ What can one little person do? (Compact disc)./ 1992/
P-2 KD654 . . . . **SRC 789.3**
What can one little person do? (Sound recording cassette)./ 1992/
P-2 KD654 . . . . **SRC 789.3**
ROGINSKI, J/ Behind the covers: interviews with authors and illustrators of
books for/ 1985/ KA335 . . . . **PROF 808.06**
Behind the covers: interviews with authors and illustrators of books for
children and young adults, Vol. II./ 1989/ KA335 . . . . **PROF 808.06**
ROHMANN, E/ King Crow./ 1995/ 1-3/4 KF165 . . . . **E**
Time flies./ 1994/ 1-3 KG349 . . . . **E**

ROHMER, H/ Atariba and Niguayona: a story from the Taino people of
Puerto Rico./ c1976, 1988/ 4-5/5 KB769 . . . . **398.27**
Atariba and Niguayona: a story from the Taino people of Puerto Rico
(Braille)./ n.d.,/ 4-5/5 KB769 . . . . **398.27**
Atariba and Niguayona: a story from the Taino people of Puerto Rico
(Sound recording cassette)./ n.d.,/ 4-5/5 KB769 . . . . **398.27**
In my family./En mi familia./ 1996/ 2-5/6 KA870 . . . . **306.85**
Uncle Nacho's hat: a folktale from Nicaragua/El sombrero de Tio Nacho:
un cuento de Nicaragua./ 1989/ 2-4/2 KB770 . . . . **398.27**
Woman who outshone the sun: the legend of Lucia Zenteno./La mujer que
brillaba aun mas que el sol: la leyenda de Lucia Zenteno./ 1991/
3-5/5 KB403 . . . . **398.21**
ROJANKOVSKY, F/ Cabin faced west./ c1958/ 4-6/6 KH143 . . . . . **FIC**
Frog went a-courtin'./ c1955/ P-3 KD579 . . . . **CE 789.2**
ROLAND-ENTWISTLE, T/ More errata: another book of historical errors./
1995/ 3-6/10 KE143 . . . . **909**
ROLLINS, CH/ CHRISTMAS GIF': AN ANTHOLOGY OF CHRISTMAS
POEMS, SONGS, AND STORIES WRITTEN BY AND ABOUT
AFRICAN-AMERICANS./ 1993/ 4-6 KD897 . . . . **810.8**
ROLPH, M/ Amazing schemes within your genes./ 1993/
4-8/6 KC288 . . . . **576.5**
DNA is here to stay./ 1993/ 5-6/7 KC279 . . . . **572.8**
ROMEI, F/ Story of sculpture./ 1995/ 4-A/9 KD399 . . . . **730**
ROOP, C/ Buttons for General Washington./ 1986/ 4-6/4 KE885 **973.3**
Keep the lights burning, Abbie./ 1985/
1-3/1 KE270 . . . . **CE B BURGESS, A.**
Off the map: the journals of Lewis and Clark./ 1993/
4-6/7 KE201 . . . . **917.804**
PILGRIM VOICES: OUR FIRST YEAR IN THE NEW WORLD./ 1995/
3-6/7 KE944 . . . . **974.4**
ROOP, P/ Buttons for General Washington./ 1986/ 4-6/4 KE885 **973.3**
Buttons for General Washington (Braille)./ n.d./ 4-6/4 KE885 . . **973.3**
Keep the lights burning, Abbie./ 1985/
1-3/1 KE270 . . . . **CE B BURGESS, A.**
Keep the lights burning, Abbie (Kit)./ 1989/
1-3/1 KE270 . . . . **CE B BURGESS, A.**
Off the map: the journals of Lewis and Clark./ 1993/
4-6/7 KE201 . . . . **917.804**
PILGRIM VOICES: OUR FIRST YEAR IN THE NEW WORLD./ 1995/
3-6/7 KE944 . . . . **974.4**
ROOT, B/ My first dictionary./ 1993/ P-2 KB835 . . . . **423**
ROOT, KB/ Billy Beg and his bull: an Irish tale./ 1994/
2-4/5 KB304 . . . . **398.2**
Birdie's lighthouse./ 1997/ 3-5/3 KH282 . . . . **FIC**
Boots and his brothers: a Norwegian tale./ 1992/
2-4/2 KB400 . . . . **398.21**
In a creepy, creepy place and other scary stories./ 1996/
4-6/4 KH183 . . . . **FIC**
In a messy, messy room./ 1990/ 4-6/6 KH184 . . . . **FIC**
Junk pile!/ 1997/ K-2/3 KF252 . . . . **E**
Palace of stars./ 1993/ 1-3/3 KF943 . . . . **E**
Toll-bridge troll./ 1995/ 1-3/2 KG759 . . . . **E**
True tale of Johnny Appleseed./ 1997/
2-4/6 KE238 . . . . **B APPLESEED, J.**
When the whippoorwill calls./ 1995/ 1-3/2 KG305 . . . . **E**
ROOT, P/ Aunt Nancy and Old Man Trouble./ 1996/ K-3/6 KG350 . **E**
Coyote and the magic words./ 1993/ P-2/2 KG351 . . . . . . **E**
RORER, A/ Maybe I will do something./ 1993/ 4-5/6 KB669 . . **398.24**
ROSE, DL/ Rose horse./ 1995/ 3-5/6 KH651 . . . . **FIC**
ROSE, DS/ There's a monster under my bed./ 1986/ P-2/2 KF781 . . . **E**
ROSE, S/ CDs, SUPER GLUE, AND SALSA: HOW EVERYDAY PRODUCTS
ARE MADE./ 1995/ 5-A KA452 . . . . **REF 670**
HISPANIC AMERICAN BIOGRAPHY./ 1995/ 5-A KA400 . . **REF 305.8**
ROSE, T/ Banshee train./ 1995/ 1-3/4 KF240 . . . . **E**
ROSEN, M/ How the animals got their colors: animal myths from around
the world./ 1992/ 2-4/4 KB640 . . . . **398.24**
Michael Rosen's ABC./ 1996/ 2-4 KE109 . . . . **821**
Vamos a cazar un oso./ n.d./ P-2/2 KB814 . . . . **398.8**
WALKING THE BRIDGE OF YOUR NOSE./ 1995/
2-4 KE113 . . . . **821.008**
We're going on a bear hunt./ 1989/ P-2/2 KB814 . . . . **398.8**
We're going on a bear hunt (Sound recording cassette)./ 1993/
P-2/2 KB814 . . . . **398.8**
ROSEN, MJ/ Bonesy and Isabel./ 1995/ 2-3/6 KG352 . . . . **E**
Elijah's angel: a story for Chanukah and Christmas./ 1992/
3-6/7 KH652 . . . . **FIC**
Elijah's angel: a story for Chanukah and Christmas (Sound recording
cassette)./ 1995/ 3-6/7 KH652 . . . . **FIC**
HOME./ 1992/ K-6 KD900 . . . . **810.8**
School for Pompey Walker./ 1995/ 4-8/6 KH653 . . . . **FIC**
School for Pompey Walker (Sound recording cassette)./ 1997/
4-8/6 KH653 . . . . **FIC**
ROSENBERG, L/ Big and little alphabet./ 1997/ K-2/2 KG353 . . . . **E**
Monster mama./ 1993/ K-2/4 KG354 . . . . **E**

Monster mama (Videocassette)./ 1996/ K-2 KG355 . . . . **VCR E**
ROSENBERG, MB/ Brothers and sisters./ 1991/ 1-4/4 KA887 . **306.875**
Finding a way: living with exceptional brothers and sisters./ 1988/
4-6/8 KB008 . . . . **362.4**
Growing up adopted./ 1989/ 5-6/7 KB013 . . . . **362.73**
Hiding to survive: stories of Jewish children rescued from the Holocaust./
1994/ A/6 KE665 . . . . **940.53**
Living with a single parent./ 1992/ 4-6/6 KA872 . . . . **306.85**
ROSENBERRY, V/ Big and little alphabet./ 1997/ K-2/2 KG353 . . . . **E**
Savitri: a tale of ancient India./ 1992/ 3-4/4 KA766 . . . . . . **294.5**
ROSENBLUM, R/ Old synagogue./ 1989/ 3-6/7 KA783 . . . . . . **296.6**
Old synagogue (Sound recording cassette)./ n.d./ 3-6/7 KA783 **296.6**
ROSENBURG, JM/ William Parker: rebel without rights: a novel based on
fact./ 1996/ 6-A/7 KH654 . . . . **FIC**
ROSENTHAL, B/ Track and field./ 1994/ 3-6/4 KD810 . . . . . . **796.42**
ROSENTHAL, M/ Bears./ 1983/ 2-4/2 KC853 . . . . **599.78**
Where on earth: a geografunny guide to the globe./ 1992/
4-6/6 KE153 . . . . **910**
ROSENTHAL, P/ Where on earth: a geografunny guide to the globe./
1992/ 4-6/6 KE153 . . . . **910**
ROSER, NL/ BOOK TALK AND BEYOND: CHILDREN AND TEACHERS
RESPOND TO LITERATURE./ 1995/ KA299 . . . . . **PROF 372.64**
ROSNER, R/ All alone after school./ 1985/ 2-3/2 KG536 . . . . . . **E**
ROSS, G/ How Rabbit tricked Otter and other Cherokee animal stories
(Talking book)./ c1991/ 2-4/6 KB641 . . . . **CE 398.24**
How Rabbit tricked Otter and other Cherokee trickster stories./ 1994/
2-4/6 KB641 . . . . **CE 398.24**
How Turtle's back was cracked: a traditional Cherokee tale./ 1995/
4-5/5 KB642 . . . . **398.24**
How Turtle's back was cracked: a traditional Cherokee tale (Sound
recording cassette)./ 1997/ 4-5/5 KB642 . . . . **398.24**
Legend of the Windigo: a tale from native North America./ 1996/
2-3/6 KB410 . . . . **398.21**
Story of the Milky Way: a Cherokee tale./ 1995/
2-3/3 KB701 . . . . **398.26**
ROSS, K/ Crafts for Christmas./ 1995/ 3-5 KD452 . . . . **745.594**
Crafts for Easter./ 1995/ 3-5 KD453 . . . . **745.594**
Crafts for Halloween./ 1994/ 3-5 KD454 . . . . **745.594**
Crafts for Hanukkah./ 1996/ 3-6 KD455 . . . . **745.594**
Crafts for Kwanzaa./ 1994/ 3-6 KD456 . . . . **745.594**
Crafts for Thanksgiving./ 1995/ 3-5 KD457 . . . . **745.594**
Every day is Earth Day: a craft book./ 1995/ K-3/5 KD442 . . **745.58**
ROSS, LH/ Sarah, also known as Hannah./ 1994/ 4-6/4 KH655 . . **FIC**
ROSS, S/ Shakespeare and Macbeth: the story behind the play./ 1994/
5-A/7 KE116 . . . . **822.3**
ROSS, T/ Amber Brown goes fourth./ 1995/ 2-4/4 KH059 . . . . . **FIC**
Amber Brown is not a crayon./ 1994/ 2-4/6 KH060 . . . . . . **FIC**
Amber Brown wants extra credit./ 1996/ 2-4/4 KH061 . . . . . **FIC**
Forever Amber Brown./ 1996/ 2-4/4 KH062 . . . . **FIC**
ROSTKOWSKI, MI/ After the dancing days./ 1986/ 6-A/4 KH656 . . **FIC**
ROTH, R/ Tiger Woman./ 1995/ 1-3/6 KB789 . . . . **398.27**
ROTH, SL/ Biggest frog in Australia./ 1996/ 2-3/2 KB643 . . . . **398.24**
Brave Martha and the dragon./ 1996/ 2-4/4 KB476 . . . . . . **398.22**
Great ball game: a Muskogee story./ 1994/ 2-4/2 KB539 . . . **398.24**
My love for you./ 1997/ P-1/2 KG356 . . . . **E**
ROTHAUS, D/ Moray eels./ 1996/ 4-6/8 KC586 . . . . **597**
Warthogs./ 1995/ 4-6/8 KC787 . . . . **599.63**
ROTHENBERG, J/ Yettele's feathers./ 1995/ 2-4/3 KB771 . . . . **398.27**
ROTHLEIN, L/ Complete guide to thematic units: creating the integrated
curriculum./ 1995/ KA195 . . . . **PROF 372.19**
ROTHMAN, M/ Inside the amazing Amazon./ 1995/
2-6/7 KC319 . . . . **577.34**
Lizard in the sun./ 1990/ 1-3/5 KC628 . . . . **597.95**
ROTNER, S/ Action alphabet./ 1996/ K-2/2 KB854 . . . . **428.2**
Faces./ Faces./ 1994/ 1994/ P-1/2 KC924 . . . . **612**
P-1/2 KC924 . . . . **612**
Lots of dads./ 1997/ P-1/2 KA881 . . . . **306.874**
Lots of moms./ 1996/ P-1/1 KA882 . . . . **306.874**
Nature spy./ 1992/ P-1/4 KB912 . . . . **508**
Ocean day./ 1993/ P-2/3 KG357 . . . . **E**
Wheels around./ 1995/ P-2/3 KD053 . . . . **621.8**
ROTTER, C/ Walruses./ 1993/ 3-5/3 KC871 . . . . **599.79**
ROUCHER, N/ Talking to Faith Ringgold./ 1996/ 4-6/6 KD379 . . **709.2**
ROUGHSEY, D/ Giant devil dingo (Videocassette)./ n.d./
1-3 KA791 . . . . **VCR 299**
ROUNDS, G/ Cowboys./ 1991/ P-K/6 KF047 . . . . **978**
I know an old lady who swallowed a fly./ 1990/ K-3 KD586 . . **789.2**
Ol' Paul, the mighty logger: being a true account of the seemingly
incredible exploits/ 1976/ 4-6/7 KB477 . . . . **398.22**
Once we had a horse./ 1996/ K-2/3 KG358 . . . . **E**
Sod houses on the Great Plains./ 1995/ 2-6/7 KD361 . . . . . **693**
Sod houses on the Great Plains (Sound recording cassette)./ 1997/
2-6/7 KD361 . . . . **693**
Three billy goats Gruff./ 1993/ P-1/2 KB644 . . . . **398.24**

Three little pigs and the big bad wolf./ 1992/ K-3/4 KB645 . . **398.24**
ROUSE, J/ Young swimmer./ 1997/ 3-6/6 KD848 . . . . **797.2**
ROUTMAN, R/ Blue pages: resources for teachers from Invitations.
  Updated, expanded, and rev./ 1994/ KA026 . . . . . . **PROF 016.372**
  Invitations: changing as teachers and learners K-12. Updated, expanded,
  and rev. resources and Blue pages./ c1991, 1994/
  KA214 . . . . **PROF 372.4**
ROWAN, JP/ Prairies and grasslands./ 1983/ 3-6/4 KC331 . . . . **577.4**
ROWDEN, R/ Kid's cuisine./ 1988/ 4-6 KD278 . . . . **641.5**
ROWE, JA/ Beginning of the armadillos./ 1995/ 3-5/8 KH359 . . . . **FIC**
  Gingerbread Man: an old English folktale./ 1996/ P-K/2 KB363 . **398.2**
ROWEN, L/ Beyond winning: sports and games all kids want to play./
  1990/ KA332 . . . . **PROF 796.1**
ROWLAND, D/ Story of Sacajawea: guide to Lewis and Clark./ 1995/
  5-6/6 KE529 . . . . **B SACAGAWEA**
ROWLAND-WARNE, L/ Costume./ 1992/ 4-6/8 KB165 . . . . **391**
ROYAL ACADEMY OF ARTS (GREAT BRITAIN)./ Painting: a young artist's
  guide./ 1993/ 5-6/8 KD470 . . . . **751.4**
ROYSTON, A/ Cars./ 1991/ P-2/2 KD116 . . . . **629.222**
  Diggers and dump trucks./ 1991/ P-2/4 KD123 . . . . . . **629.225**
  Dinosaurs./ 1991/ K-2/4 KC259 . . . . **567.9**
  Jungle animals./ 1991/ P-2/4 KC493 . . . . **591.734**
  Senses: a lift-the-flap body book./ 1993/ 1-3/4 KC977 . . . . **612.8**
ROZAKIS, L/ Dick Rutan and Jeana Yeager: flying non-stop around the
  world./ 1994/ 5-6/6 KD099 . . . . **629.13**
ROZENS, A/ Floods./ 1994/ 4-6/7 KB037 . . . . **363.34**
RUBALCABA, J/ Uncegila's seventh spot: a Lakota legend./ 1995/
  3-5/3 KB478 . . . . **398.22**
RUBEL, D/ Scholastic encyclopedia of the presidents and their times.
  Updated ed./ 1997/ 4-A KA492 . . . . **REF 973**
  Science./ 1995/ 4-6/7 KB877 . . . . **503**
  United States in the 19th century./ 1996/ 4-A/8 KE895 . . . . . **973.5**
  United States in the 20th century./ 1995/ 4-A/8 KE916 . . . . . **973.9**
RUBEL, N/ Batty riddles./ 1993/ K-3 KD728 . . . . **793.735**
  Rotten Ralph./ 1976/ K-2/3 KF597 . . . . **E**
RUBENSTEIN, L/ Invertebrate zoology./ 1993/ 5-6/8 KC503 . . . . **592**
RUBINSTEIN, G/ Dog in, cat out./ 1993/ P-1/1 KG359 . . . . **E**
RUDEEN, K/ Jackie Robinson./ 1996/ 5-6/6 KE516 . **B ROBINSON, J.**
RUDMAN, MK/ Books to help children cope with separation and loss: an
  annotated bibliography. 4th ed./ 1993/ KA025 . . . **PROF 016.1559**
RUDOLPH, M/ How a shirt grew in the field./ 1992/ K-2/2 KG636 . . **E**
RUDY, LJ/ BEN FRANKLIN BOOK OF EASY AND INCREDIBLE
  EXPERIMENTS./ 1995/ A/8 KB889 . . . . **507.8**
RUEPP, K/ Midnight Rider./ 1995/ 3-5/2 KH657 . . . . **FIC**
RUFFINS, R/ Koi and the kola nuts (Kit)./ 1992/ 2-5 KB446 . **KIT 398.22**
  Running the road to ABC./ 1996/ 1-3/4 KF951 . . . . **E**
RUSH, B/ Diamond tree: Jewish tales from around the world./ 1991/
  3-4/6 KB368 . . . . **398.2**
  Sabbath lion: a Jewish folktale from Algeria./ 1992/
  4-6/6 KB511 . . . . **398.23**
  Wonder child and other Jewish fairy tales./ 1996/ 2-4/5 KB369 **398.2**
RUSSELL, L/ One smiling grandma: a Caribbean counting book./ 1995/
  P-1/1 KF984 . . . . **E**
RUSSELL, M/ Along the Santa Fe Trail: Marion Russell's own story./
  1993/ 4-6/7 KE199 . . . . **917.8**
RUSSO, M/ Good-bye, Curtis./ 1995/ P-2/2 KF704 . . . . **E**
  Grandpa Abe./ 1996/ K-2/2 KG360 . . . . **E**
  I don't want to go back to school./ 1994/ 1-3/2 KG361 . . . . . . **E**
  Line up book./ 1986/ P-1/1 KG362 . . . . **E**
  Tree almanac: a year-round activity guide./ 1993/
  3-6/6 KC423 . . . . **582.16**
  Under the table./ 1997/ P-K/2 KG363 . . . . **E**
RUSSO, S/ Eats./ c1979, 1992/ P-A KD908 . . . . **811**
RUURS, M/ Emma's eggs./ 1996/ P-2/2 KG364 . . . . **E**
RYAN, CD/ Hildilid's night./ c1971, 1986/ K-3/6 KG365 . . . . . . **FIC**
  Hildilid's night (Talking book)./ n.d./ K-3/6 KG365 . . . . **E**
RYAN, M/ How to read and write poems./ 1991/ 4-6/7 KD869 . **808.1**
RYAN, MC/ Me two./ 1993/ 5-A/6 KH658 . . . . **FIC**
RYAN, ME/ Trouble with perfect./ 1995/ 6-A/3 KH659 . . . . **FIC**
RYAN, PM/ Crayon counting book./ 1996/ P-1/3 KB982 . . . . . **513.2**
RYAN, S/ Coming to America: the story of immigration./ 1996/
  1-3/8 KA921 . . . . **325**
RYBOLT, TR/ Environmental experiments about air./ 1993/
  5-6/7 KD084 . . . . **628.5**
  Environmental experiments about water./ 1993/ 5-6/7 KB066 . **363.73**
RYDBERG., V/ Tomten./ c1965, 1997/ K-2/3 KF986 . . . . **CE E**
RYDEN, H/ Joey: the story of a baby kangaroo./ 1994/
  2-5/4 KC737 . . . . **599.2**
  Your cat's wild cousins./ 1991/ 4-6/5 KC825 . . . . **599.75**
RYDER, J/ Lizard in the sun./ 1990/ 1-3/5 KC628 . . . . **597.95**
  My father's hands./ 1994/ K-2 KG366 . . . . **E**
  Night gliders./ 1996/ P-2/2 KG367 . . . . **E**
RYLANT, C/ Appalachia: the voices of sleeping birds./ 1991/
  3-6/6 KE925 . . . . **974**

Birthday presents./ 1991/ P-1/2 KG368 . . . . **E**
Bookshop dog./ 1996/ K-2/2 KG369 . . . . **E**
Children of Christmas: stories for the season./ c1987, 1993/
  4-6/6 KH660 . . . . **FIC**
Everyday children (Board book)./ 1993/ P-K/2 KG370 . . . . . . **BB E**
Everyday garden (Board book)./ 1993/ P-K/2 KG371 . . . . **BB E**
Everyday house (Board book)./ 1993/ P-K/2 KG372 . . . . **BB E**
Everyday pets (Board book)./ 1993/ P-K/2 KG373 . . . . **BB E**
Everyday town (Board book)./ 1993/ P-K/2 KG374 . . . . **BB E**
Fine white dust./ 1986/ 6-A/4 KH661 . . . . **FIC**
Fine white dust (Braille)./ n.d./ 6-A/4 KH661 . . . . **FIC**
Fine white dust (Sound recording cassette)./ 1995/ 6-A/4 KH661 . **FIC**
Gooseberry Park./ 1995/ 3-5/5 KH662 . . . . **FIC**
Henry and Mudge and the bedtime thumps./ 1991/
  K-3/2 KG375 . . . . **CE E**
Henry and Mudge and the best day of all./ 1995/ K-3/2 KG375 . **CE E**
Henry and Mudge and the careful cousin./ 1994/ K-3/2 KG375 . **CE E**
Henry and Mudge and the careful cousin (Sound recording cassette)./
  1997/ K-3/2 KG375 . . . . **CE E**
Henry and Mudge and the forever sea./ 1989/ K-3/2 KG375 . . **CE E**
Henry and Mudge and the happy cat./ 1990/ K-3/2 KG375 . . . . **CE E**
Henry and Mudge and the long weekend./ 1992/ K-3/2 KG375 . **CE E**
Henry and Mudge and the wild wind./ 1993/ K-3/2 KG375 . . . **CE E**
Henry and Mudge get the cold shivers./ 1989/ K-3/2 KG375 . . **CE E**
Henry and Mudge in puddle trouble./ 1990/ K-3/2 KG375 . . . **CE E**
Henry and Mudge in puddle trouble (Braille)./ n.d./
  K-3/2 KG375 . . . . **CE E**
Henry and Mudge in puddle trouble (Videocassette)./ 1987/
  K-3/2 KG375 . . . . **CE E**
Henry and Mudge in the green time./ 1987/ K-3/2 KG375 . . . **CE E**
Henry and Mudge in the green time (Braille)./ n.d./
  K-3/2 KG375 . . . . **CE E**
Henry and Mudge in the sparkle days./ 1988/ K-3/2 KG375 . . . **CE E**
Henry and Mudge in the sparkle days (Videocassette)./ 1989/
  K-3/2 KG375 . . . . **CE E**
Henry and Mudge take the big test./ 1991/ K-3/2 KG375 . . . . **CE E**
Henry and Mudge: the first book./ 1987/ K-3/2 KG375 . . . . . **CE E**
Henry and Mudge: the first book (Braille)./ n.d./ K-3/2 KG375 . . **CE E**
Henry and Mudge under the yellow moon./ 1997/ K-3/2 KG375 . **CE E**
Henry and Mudge under the yellow moon (Braille)./ n.d./
  K-3/2 KG375 . . . . **CE E**
Henry and Mudge under the yellow moon (Sound recording cassette)./
  n.d./ K-3/2 KG375 . . . . **CE E**
Henry and Mudge under the yellow moon (Videocassette)./ 1989/
  K-3/2 KG375 . . . . **CE E**
Henry y Mudge con barro hasta el rabo./ 1996/ K-3/2 KG375 . . **CE E**
Henry y Mudge: el primer libro de sus aventuras./ 1996/
  K-3/2 KG375 . . . . **CE E**
Henry y mudge y el mejor dia del ano./ 1997/ K-3/2 KG375 . . . **CE E**
Missing May./ 1992/ 5-A/7 KH663 . . . . **FIC**
Missing May (Sound recording cassette)./ 1994/ 5-A/7 KH663 . . . **FIC**
Mr. Griggs' work./ c1989, 1993/ P-2/6 KG376 . . . . **E**
Mr. Putter and Tabby bake the cake./ 1994/ 1-3/2 KG377 . . . . . **E**
Mr. Putter and Tabby bake the cake (Sound recording cassette)./ 1997/
  1-3/2 KG377 . . . . **E**
Mr. Putter and Tabby fly the plane./ 1997/ K-2/2 KG378 . . . . . . **E**
Mr. Putter and Tabby pick the pears./ 1995/ 1-3/2 KG379 . . . . . **E**
Mr. Putter and Tabby pour the tea./ 1994/ 1-3/2 KG380 . . . . . . **E**
Mr. Putter and Tabby row the boat./ 1997/ K-2/2 KG381 . . . . . . **E**
Mr. Putter and Tabby walk the dog./ 1994/ 1-3/2 KG382 . . . . . . **E**
Old woman who named things./ 1996/ 1-3/2 KG383 . . . . **E**
Poppleton./ 1997/ K-2/2 KG384 . . . . **E**
Relatives came./ 1985/ K-3/8 KG385 . . . . **E**
Relatives came (Braille)./ n.d./ K-3/8 KG385 . . . . **E**
Silver packages: an Appalachian Christmas story./ 1997/
  1-3/2 KG386 . . . . **E**
Van Gogh Cafe./ 1995/ 5-A/7 KH664 . . . . **FIC**
When I was young in the mountains./ 1982/ K-3/6 KG387 . . . . . **CE E**
When I was young in the mountains (Talking book)./ 1983/
  K-3/6 KG387 . . . . **CE E**
SAARI, P/ EXPLORERS AND DISCOVERERS: FROM ALEXANDER THE
  GREAT TO SALLY RIDE./ 1995/ 5-A KA470 . . . . **REF 910**
SCIENTISTS: THE LIVES AND WORKS OF 150 SCIENTISTS./ 1996/
  5-A KA442 . . . . **REF 509**
SABBETH, C/ Kids' computer creations: using your computer for art and
  craft fun./ 1995/ 3-5 KD434 . . . . **745.5**
SABIN, F/ Amazing world of ants./ 1982/ 2-4/4 KC579 . . **CE 595.79**
  Amazing world of ants (Kit)./ 1983/ 2-4/2 KC579 . . . . . **CE 595.79**
SABIN, L/ Amazing world of butterflies and moths./ 1982/
  2-4/4 KC566 . . . . **CE 595.78**
  Amazing world of butterflies and moths (Kit)./ 1983/
  2-4/4 KC566 . . . . **CE 595.78**
SABUDA, R/ Arthur and the sword./ 1995/ 3-5/5 KB479 . . . . . **398.22**
  Saint Valentine./ 1992/ 4-6/4 KE581 . . . . **B VALENTINE, ST.**

Saint Valentine (Sound recording cassette)./ 1995/
   4-6/4 KE581 . . . . **B VALENTINE,ST.**
Tutankhamen's gift./ 1994/ 2-4/3 KE578 . . . . . . **B TUTANKHAMEN**
SACHAR, L/ Dogs don't tell jokes./ 1992/ 5-A/5 KH665 . . . . **FIC**
Dogs don't tell jokes (Sound recording cassette)./ 1994/
   5-A/5 KH665 . . . . **FIC**
Sideways arithmetic from Wayside School./ 1989/ 3-6/6 KD712 **793.7**
Sideways stories from Wayside School./ c1978/ 3-5/4 KH666 **CE FIC**
Sideways stories from Wayside School (Kit)./ 1993/
   3-5/4 KH666 . . . . **CE FIC**
Wayside School is falling down./ 1989/ 3-5/4 KH666 . . . . . . **CE FIC**
Wayside School is falling down (Talking book)./ 1994/
   3-5/4 KH666 . . . . **CE FIC**
SACHS, M/ Call me Ruth./ c1982, 1995/ 5-A/6 KH667 . . . . **FIC**
Pocket full of seeds./ c1973, 1994/ 4-A/5 KH668 . . . . **FIC**
Truth about Mary Rose./ 1995/ 5-A/6 KH669 . . . . **FIC**
SACKS, M/ Themba./ 1994/ 3-5/5 KH670 . . . . **FIC**
SACRE, A/ Looking for Papito: family stories from Latin America (Sound
   recording cassette)./ 1996/ 1-6 KA857 . . . . **SRC 305.8**
SADOWSKI, W/ Grandma Essie's covered wagon./ 1993/
   2-4/4 KG726 . . . . **E**
SAINT EXUPERY, AD/ Little prince./ c1943/ 4-A/6 KH671 . . . . . . **FIC**
Little prince (Braille)./ n.d./ 4-A/6 KH671 . . . . **FIC**
Little prince (Sound recording cassette)./ n.d./ 4-A/6 KH671 . . . **FIC**
SAINT JAMES, S/ Gifts of Kwanzaa./ 1994/ 1-4/2 KB216 . . **394.261**
Neeny coming, Neeny going./ 1996/ 1-3/2 KF527 . . . . **E**
Snow on snow on snow./ 1994/ K-3/3 KF377 . . . . **E**
Tukama Tootles the flute: a tale from the Antilles./ 1994/
   K-2/5 KB398 . . . . **398.21**
SAKAMOTO, R/ Peachboy (Videocassette)./ 1991/
   2-5 KB469 . . . . **VCR 398.22**
SALAZAR, D/ BEHIND THE MASK. Rev. ed. (Videocassette)./ 1987/
   1-3 KA817 . . . . **VCR 305**
SALISBURY, G/ Under the blood-red sun./ 1994/ 6-A/4 KH672 . . . **FIC**
SALK, L/ SUPER SITTERS: A TRAINING COURSE (Videocassette)./ 1988/
   5-A KD304 . . . . **VCR 649**
SALMON, S/ POWER UP YOUR LIBRARY: CREATING THE NEW
   ELEMENTARY SCHOOL LIBRARY PROGRAM./ 1996/
   KA078 . . . . **PROF 027.8**
SALTEN, F/ Bambi: a life in the woods./ 1992/ 5-A/6 KH673 . . . . . **FIC**
SALTZBERG, B/ Show-and-tell./ 1994/ K-2/2 KG388 . . . . **E**
SALVI, F/ Impressionists: the origins of modern painting./ 1994/
   6-A/9 KD485 . . . . **759.05**
SALZBERG, A/ Flightless birds./ 1993/ 5-6/7 KC691 . . . . **598.5**
SALZMAN, M/ Kids on-line: 150 ways for kids to surf the net for fun and
   information./ 1995/ 3-6/6 KA572 . . . . **004.67**
SAM, S/
Silent temples, songful hearts: traditional music of Cambodia./ Silent
   temples, songful hearts: traditional music of Cambodia./ 1991/ 1991/
   KA318 . . . . **BA PROF 789.2**
   KA318 . . . . **BA PROF 789.2**
SAM, Y/ Silent temples, songful hearts: traditional music of Cambodia./
   1991/ KA318 . . . . **BA PROF 789.2**
SAMPSON, M/ Football that won.../ 1996/ K-2/2 KD786 . . . **796.332**
SAMTON, SW/ Jamaica Louise James./ 1996/ K-2/2 KF719 . . . . . . **E**
World from my window./ c1985, 1991/ P-K/2 KG389 . . . . **E**
SAMUELS, BG/ YOUR READING: AN ANNOTATED BOOKLIST FOR
   MIDDLE SCHOOL AND JUNIOR HIGH. 1995-96 ed./ 1996/
   5-A KA373 . . . . **REF 011.62**
SAN JOSE, C/ Cinderella./ 1994/ 2-4/6 KB364 . . . . **398.2**
SAN SOUCI, D/ Gifts of Wali Dad: a tale of India and Pakistan./ 1995/
   2-3/2 KB488 . . . . **398.22**
Jigsaw Jackson./ 1996/ 1-3/3 KF230 . . . . **E**
Red wolf country./ 1996/ K-3/4 KG028 . . . . **E**
Sootface: an Ojibwa Cinderella story./ 1994/ 1-3/6 KB774 . . **398.27**
SAN SOUCI, RD/ Boy and the ghost./ 1989/ 2-3/6 KG392 . . . . **E**
Cut from the same cloth: American women of myth, legend, and tall tale./
   1993/ 5-6/6 KB481 . . . . **398.22**
Faithful friend./ 1995/ 4-6/5 KB411 . . . . **398.21**
Hired hand: an African-American folktale./ 1997/ 3-4/3 KB412 **398.21**
Hobyahs./ 1996/ 3-4/6 KB647 . . . . **398.24**
Huevos hablantes./ 1996/ 3-5/5 KB415 . . . . **CE 398.27**
Kate Shelley: bound for legend./ 1995/ 3-5/5 KE539 . **B SHELLEY, K.**
Little seven-colored horse: a Spanish American folktale./ 1995/
   3-5/5 KB648 . . . . **398.24**
N.C. Wyeth's pilgrims./ 1991/ 4-6/7 KE946 . . . . **974.4**
Nicholas Pipe./ 1997/ 2-5/6 KB413 . . . . **398.21**
Pedro and the monkey./ 1996/ 3-4/2 KB649 . . . . **398.24**
Red heels./ 1996/ 3-5/6 KG393 . . . . **E**
Samurai's daughter: a Japanese legend./ 1992/ 3-4/6 KB365 . . **398.2**
Snow wife./ 1993/ 3-9/5 KB414 . . . . **398.21**
Sootface: an Ojibwa Cinderella story./ 1994/ 1-3/6 KB774 . . . **398.27**
Sukey and the mermaid./ 1992/ 3-4/6 KB775 . . . . **398.27**

Sukey and the mermaid (Sound recording cassette)./ 1997/
   3-4/6 KB775 . . . . **398.27**
Talking eggs./ 1989/ 3-5/5 KB415 . . . . **CE 398.21**
Talking eggs (Videocassette)./ 1991/ 3-5/5 KB415 . . . . . **CE 398.21**
Young Guinevere./ 1993/ 3-4/6 KB482 . . . . **398.22**
Young Lancelot./ 1996/ 4-5/6 KB483 . . . . **398.22**
Young Merlin./ c1990, 1996/ 4-5/6 KB484 . . . . **398.22**
SANCHEZ, EO/ Amelia's road./ 1993/ 1-3/4 KF154 . . . . **E**
Golden flower: a Taino myth from Puerto Rico./ 1996/
   2-4/5 KB503 . . . . **398.23**
Maria Molina and the Days of the Dead./ 1994/ 2-4/4 KF936 . . . . **E**
SANCHEZ SANCHEZ, I/ Dragons and prehistoric monsters./ 1996/
   3-6/3 KD447 . . . . **745.592**
Drawing dinosaurs./ 1996/ 5-A/3 KD418 . . . . **743**
Dreadful creatures./ 1996/ 3-6/3 KD449 . . . . **745.592**
Modeling dinosaurs./ 1996/ 3-6/3 KD448 . . . . **745.592**
Monsters and extraterrestrials./ 1996/ 3-6/3 KD449 . . . . . **745.592**
Painting and coloring dinosaurs./ 1996/ 5-A/3 KD419 . . . . . . **743**
SANDBURG, C/ Poetry for young people./ 1995/ 4-6 KE018 . . . . . **811**
Rootabaga stories./ c1922, 1990/ 1-6/7 KH674 . . . . **FIC**
Rootabaga stories: part two./ 1990/, 1-6/7 KH674 . . . . **FIC**
SANDELSON, R/ Ball sports./ 1991/ 4-6/8 KD777 . . . . **796.3**
Ice sports./ 1991/ 4-6/7 KD835 . . . . **796.9**
Track athletics./ 1991/ 4-6/7 KD811 . . . . **796.42**
SANDEMAN, A/ Babies./ 1996/ 2-5/6 KC955 . . . . **612.6**
SANDERS, E/ What's your name?: from Ariel to Zoe./ 1995/
   K-3/2 KE611 . . . . **929.4**
SANDERS, M/ What's your name?: from Ariel to Zoe./ 1995/
   K-3/2 KE611 . . . . **929.4**
SANDERS, SR/ Place called Freedom./ 1997/ 1-3/3 KG390 . . . . . . **E**
Warm as wool./ 1992/ 3-5/5 KH675 . . . . **FIC**
SANDERSON, R/ Don't hurt Laurie!/ 1977/ 5-6/6 KH635 . . . . **FIC**
Papa Gatto: an Italian fairy tale./ 1995/ 3-4/6 KB646 . . . . . **398.24**
Treasury of princesses: princess tales from around the world./ 1996/
   3-5/6 KB432 . . . . **398.22**
SANDFORD, J/ Down Buttermilk Lane./ 1993/ 1-3/2 KG144 . . . . . **E**
Good bad cat./ 1985/ P-1/1 KF160 . . . . **E**
Noise lullaby./ 1995/ P-2/2 KG190 . . . . **E**
SANDIN, J/ Daniel's duck./ 1979/ 1-2/1 KF296 . . . . **E**
Long way to a new land./ 1981/ 1-3/2 KG391 . . . . **E**
Long way westward./ 1989/ 1-3/2 KG391 . . . . **E**
Snowshoe Thompson./ 1992/ K-3/2 KE564 . . . . . **B THOMPSON, S.**
SANDLER, MW/ Immigrants./ 1995/ 5-A/7 KA922 . . . . **325**
Presidents./ 1995/ 5-A/8 KE864 . . . . **973**
SANDS, D/ African village folktales, vols 1-3 (Talking book)./ n.d./
   4-6 KB746 . . . . **TB 398.27**
SANDVED, KB/ Butterfly alphabet./ 1996/ 3-6/6 KC567 . . . . . **595.78**
SANFIELD, S/ Adventures of High John the Conqueror./ 1989/
   3-6/5 KB480 . . . . **398.22**
Bit by bit./ 1995/ K-2/2 KB772 . . . . **398.27**
Feather merchants and other tales of the fools of Chelm./ 1991/
   6-A/7 KB510 . . . . **398.23**
Great turtle drive./ 1996/ 2-6/4 KH676 . . . . **FIC**
Just rewards, or, Who is that man in the moon and what's he doing up
   there anyway?/ 1996/ K-2/4 KB713 . . . . **398.26**
Strudel, strudel, strudel./ 1995/ 2-3/4 KB773 . . . . **398.27**
SANFORD, WR/ Babe Didrikson Zaharias./ 1993/
   4-5/4 KE608 . . . . **B ZAHARIAS, B.**
Brigham Young: pioneer and Mormon leader./ 1996/
   5-6/8 KE605 . . . . **B YOUNG, B.**
John C. Fremont: soldier and pathfinder./ 1996/
   5-6/4 KE357 . . . . **B FREMONT, J.**
Kit Carson: frontier scout./ 1996/ 5-6/7 KE277 . . . . . **B CARSON, K.**
Mysterious mind powers./ 1993/ 4-6/3 KA609 . . . . **133.8**
Recalling past lives./ 1993/ 4-6/3 KA611 . . . . **133.9**
Seeing the unseen./ 1993/ 4-6/5 KA610 . . . . **133.8**
Zebulon Pike: explorer of the Southwest./ 1996/
   5-6/8 KE497 . . . . **B PIKE, Z.**
SANGPHET, T/ Silent temples, songful hearts: traditional music of
   Cambodia./ 1991/ KA318 . . . . **BA PROF 789.2**
SANTELLA, A/ Jackie Robinson breaks the color line./ 1996/
   4-6/6 KE517 . . . . **B ROBINSON, J.**
SANTINI, D/ Cinderella./ 1994/ 2-4/6 KB364 . . . . **398.2**
SANTORO, C/ Giraffes, the sentinels of the savannas./ 1989/
   5-6/8 KC789 . . . . **599.638**
Hominids: a look back at our ancestors./ 1988/ 4-A/8 KC269 . . **569.9**
SANTUCCI, JA/ America's religions: an educator's guide to beliefs and
   practices./ 1997/ KA160 . . . . **PROF 200**
SAPP, J/ We've all got stories: songs from the Dream Project (Compact
   disc)./ 1996/ K-6 KD655 . . . . **CD 789.3**
We've all got stories: songs from the Dream Project (Sound recording
   cassette)./ 1996/ K-6 KD655 . . . . **CD 789.3**
SATHER, K/ Minnie./ 1994/ 5-A/3 KH680 . . . . **FIC**
SATHRE, V/ Leroy Potts meets the McCrooks./ 1997/ 1-3/2 KH677 . **FIC**

Mouse chase./ 1995/ P-1/2 KG394 . . . . E
SATTLER, HR/ Book of North American owls./ 1995/
  5-6/6 KC719 . . . . **598.9**
Earliest Americans./ 1993/ 5-A/8 KE743 . . . . **970.01**
Earliest Americans (Sound recording cassette)./ 1995/
  5-A/8 KE743 . . . . **970.01**
Giraffes, the sentinels of the savannas./ 1989/ 5-6/8 KC789 . **599.638**
Hominids: a look back at our ancestors./ 1988/ 4-A/8 KC269 . . **569.9**
New illustrated dinosaur dictionary. Rev. ed./ c1983, 1990/
  3-6 KA444 . . . . **REF 567.9**
Our patchwork planet: the story of plate tectonics./ 1995/
  A/7 KC155 . . . . **551.1**
Recipes for art and craft material. Newly rev./ c1973, 1994/
  4-6/6 KD435 . . . . **745.5**
Stegosaurs: the solar-powered dinosaurs./ 1992/ 3-6/8 KC260 . **567.9**
Tyrannosaurus rex and its kin: the Mesozoic monsters./ 1989/
  3-6/8 KC261 . . . . **567.9**
SAUBER, R/ Goose girl: a story from the Brothers Grimm./ 1995/
  3-5/5 KB328 . . . . **398.2**
I-know-not-what, I-know-not-where: a Russian tale./ 1994/
  3-4/6 KB329 . . . . **398.2**
Me two./ 1993/ 5-A/6 KH658 . . . . **FIC**
Swan Maiden./ 1994/ 2-4/6 KG294 . . . . E
SAUL, W/ Exploring space: using Seymour Simon's astronomy books in the
  classroom./ 1994/ KA198 . . . . **PROF 372.3**
SAULNIER, KL/ Night before Christmas: told in sign language: an
  adaptation of the original poem "A visit from St. Nicholas" by Clement
  C. Moore./ 1994/ K-6 KD917 811
SAUNDERS, J/ Bringing out the best: a resource guide for parents of
  young gifted children. Rev. and updated./ 1991/
  KA189 . . . . **PROF 371.95**
SAUNDERSON, J/ Heart and lungs./ 1992/ 5-6/6 KC935 . . . . . **612.1**
Muscles and bones./ 1992/ 5-6/5 KC959 . . . . **612.7**
SAUVANT, H/ Seven ravens: a fairy tale./ 1995/ 3-5/7 KB309 . . **398.2**
SAVADIER, E/ Treasure nap./ 1992/ P-1/2 KF683 . . . . E
SAVAGE, J/ Andre Agassi: reaching the top--again./ 1997/
  4-5/7 KE229 . . . . **B AGASSI, A.**
Barry Bonds: Mr. Excitement./ 1997/ 4-6/3 KE258 . . . . **B BONDS, B.**
Kristi Yamaguchi: pure gold./ 1993/
  3-5/7 KE603 . . . . **B YAMAGUCHI, K.**
Mike Piazza: hard-hitting catcher./ 1997/ 4-6/7 KE495 . **B PIAZZA, M.**
SAWYER, R/ Journey cake, ho./ c1953, 1989/ P-3/5 KB776 . . **398.27**
Remarkable Christmas of the cobbler's sons./ 1994/
  1-3/4 KB416 . . . . **398.21**
SAY, A/ Allison./ 1997/ 2-4/2 KH678 . . . . **FIC**
Bicycle man./ 1982/ K-3/4 KG395 . . . . E
Boy of the three-year nap./ 1988/ K-3/6 KG525 . . . . E
El Chino./ 1990/ 3-5/4 KE598 . . . . **B WONG, B.**
Emma's rug./ 1996/ 1-3/3 KG396 . . . . E
Grandfather's journey./ 1993/ 2-4/5 KG397 . . . . E
How my parents learned to eat./ 1984/ 1-3/2 KF586 . . . . E
Lost lake./ 1989/ 1-3/2 KG398 . . . . E
River dream./ 1988/ K-3/4 KG399 . . . . E
Tree of cranes./ 1991/ 1-3/4 KG400 . . . . E
Under the cherry blossom tree: an old Japanese tale./ 1997/
  P-1/5 KB777 . . . . **398.27**
SAYLES, E/ Night crossing./ 1994/ 3-4/8 KG812 . . . . **FIC**
Not in the house, Newton!/ 1995/ P-2/2 KF618 . . . . E
SCALZO, JL/ LETTERS FOR OUR CHILDREN: FIFTY AMERICANS SHARE
  LESSONS IN LIVING./ 1996/ KA158 . . . . **PROF 170**
SCHACHNER, JB/ Jimmy, the pickpocket of the palace./ 1995/
  3-A/3 KH530 . . . . **FIC**
Prince of the pond: otherwise known as De Fawg Pin./ 1992/
  3-A/3 KH531 . . . . **FIC**
Staying with Grandmother./ 1994/ 1-3/1 KF184 . . . . E
Willy and May./ 1995/ 1-3/5 KG401 . . . . E
SCHAEFER, CL/ Squiggle./ 1996/ P-2/3 KG402 . . . . E
SCHAEFER, VJ/ Peterson first guide to clouds and weather./ 1991/
  3-6/A KC211 . . . . **551.57**
SCHAFER, S/ Galapagos tortoise./ 1992/ 5-6/7 KC622 . . . . . **597.92**
Komodo dragon./ c1992, 1996/ 5-6/5 KC629 . . . . **597.95**
SCHAFFER, A/ How now, brown cow?/ 1994/ 1-3 KE020 811
SCHANZER, R/ How we crossed the West: the adventures of Lewis and
  Clark./ 1997/ 3-6/7 KE205 . . . . **917.804**
SCHATELL, B/ Lots of rot./ 1981/ K-3/3 KC302 . . . . **577.1**
SCHECTER, D/ In my family./En mi familia./ 1996/
  2-5/6 KA870 . . . . **306.85**
Woman who outshone the sun: the legend of Lucia Zenteno./La mujer que
  brillaba aun mas que el sol: la leyenda de Lucia Zenteno./ 1991/
  3-5/5 KB403 . . . . **398.21**
SCHECTER, E/ Big idea./ 1996/ 3-5/2 KH679 . . . . **FIC**
Flower of Sheba./ 1994/ 1-2/2 KA687 222
Warrior maiden: a Hopi legend./ 1992/ 1-2/2 KB485 . . . . . **398.22**
SCHEER, J/ Rain makes applesauce./ c1964/ P-A/2 KG403 . . . . E

SCHEMENAUER, E/ Canada./ 1994/ 4-6/4 KE806 971
SCHERTLE, A/ Advice for a frog./ 1995/ 3-5 KE019 811
How now, brown cow?/ 1994/ 1-3 KE020 811
Jeremy Bean's St. Patrick's Day./ 1987/ K-2/4 KG404 . . . . E
Maisie./ 1995/ 1-3/4 KG405 . . . . E
SCHEURMANN, I/ Tropical fish: a complete pet owner's manual./ 1983/
  5-6/9 KD247 . . . . **639.3**
SCHICK, E/ Navajo ABC: a Dine alphabet book./ 1995/
  2-4 KE797 . . . . **970.49**
SCHICK, J/ Wayside School is falling down./ 1989/
  3-5/4 KH666 . . . . **CE FIC**
SCHILLER, A/ In other words: a beginning thesaurus./ 1987/
  4-6 KA429 . . . . **REF 423**
SCHINDEL, J/ Dear Daddy./ 1995/ K-2/2 KG406 . . . . E
What's for lunch?/ 1994/ P-1/2 KG407 . . . . E
SCHINDLER, SD/ Big pumpkin./ 1992/ P-2/2 KG504 . . . . E
Children of Christmas: stories for the season./ c1987, 1993/
  4-6/6 KH660 . . . . **FIC**
Don't fidget a feather!/ 1994/ P-2/2 KG505 . . . . E
EARTH IS PAINTED GREEN: A GARDEN OF POEMS ABOUT OUR
  PLANET./ 1994/ 3-6 KD883 . . . . **808.81**
Ghost of Nicholas Greebe./ 1996/ 3-5/6 KH328 . . . . **FIC**
Is this a house for hermit crab?/ 1990/ P-1/3 KC522 . . . . . . **595.3**
Little Vampire and the Midnight Bear./ 1995/ 1-3/2 KF941 . . . . . E
Pilgrims at Plymouth./ 1996/ 1-3/2 KE943 . . . . **974.4**
Three little pigs and the fox./ 1989/ 2-4/5 KB592 . . . . . . **398.24**
SCHLAGER, N/ CDs, SUPER GLUE, AND SALSA: HOW EVERYDAY
  PRODUCTS ARE MADE./ 1995/ 5-A KA452 . . . . . . **REF 670**
SCHLEIN, M/ Discovering dinosaur babies./ 1991/ 3-6/5 KC262 . . **567.9**
SCHLICHTING, M/ MARK SCHLICHTING'S HARRY AND THE HAUNTED
  HOUSE. School ed. (CD-ROM)./ 1994/ K-3 KG063 . . . . . . **CDR E**
SCHLISSEL, L/ Black frontiers: a history of African American heroes in the
  Old West./ 1995/ 4-6/8 KF048 978
SCHLOSS, M/ Venus./ 1991/ 4-6/8 KC033 . . . . **523.42**
SCHMID, E/ Water's journey./ 1989/ 2-4/7 KG408 . . . . E
SCHMIDT, A/ Bears and their forest cousins./ 1991/
  5-6/7 KC854 . . . . **599.78**
SCHMIDT, AMG/ Minnie./ 1994/ 5-A/3 KH680 . . . . **FIC**
SCHMIDT, CR/ Bears and their forest cousins./ 1991/
  5-6/7 KC854 . . . . **599.78**
SCHMIDT, GD/ Poetry for young people./ 1994/ 4-A KD940 811
SCHMIDT, J/ In the village of the elephants./ 1994/
  4-6/6 KC816 . . . . **599.67**
Two lands, one heart: an American boy's journey to his mother's
  Vietnam./ 1995/ 1-3/7 KE719 . . . . **959.7**
SCHMIDT, KL/ Nickel buys a rhyme./ 1993/ P-2 KD916 811
SCHMITT, J/ Smart spending: a young consumer's guide./ 1989/
  5-6/8 KD262 640
SCHMITTROTH, L/ EUREKA!/ 1995/ 4-7 KA451 . . . . . . **REF 608**
WOMEN'S ALMANAC./ 1997/ 5-A KA397 . . . . **REF 305.4**
SCHNAKENBERG, R/ Scottie Pippen: reluctant superstar./ 1997/
  4-6/6 KE498 . . . . **B PIPPEN, S.**
SCHNEIDER, RM/ Add it, dip it, fix it: a book of verbs./ 1995/
  K-2/2 KB855 . . . . **428.2**
SCHNEIDER, C/ Amazing spiders./ 1989/ 4-6/6 KC531 . . . . . . **595.4**
Apple tree through the year./ c1982, 1987/ 5-6/7 KD163 634
Chameleons./ 1989/ 5-6/7 KC630 . . . . **597.95**
Chameleons (Sound recording cassette)./ 1993/ 5-6/7 KC630 . **597.95**
On the trail of the fox./ 1986/ 4-6/8 KC844 . . . . **599.775**
SCHNUR, S/ Shadow children./ 1994/ 4-A/7 KH681 . . . . **FIC**
Tie man's miracle: a Chanukah tale./ 1995/ 2-3/4 KG409 . . . . . . E
SCHOBERLE, C/ Creepy spooky science./ 1996/ 3-6/8 KB894 . . . **507.8**
Icky squishy science./ 1996/ 4-8/6 KB895 . . . . **507.8**
SCHOENHERR, J/ Gentle Ben. Reissued./ c1965, 1997/
  5-A/6 KH508 . . . . **FIC**
Incident at Hawk's Hill./ 1971/ 6-A/7 KH097 . . . . **FIC**
Julie of the wolves./ c1972/ 6-A/6 KH157 . . . . **CE FIC**
Owl moon./ 1987/ P-3/2 KG778 . . . . **CE E**
Pigs in the mud in the middle of the rud./ 1997/ K-2/2 KG247 . . . E
SCHOLDER, F/ Anpao: an American Indian odyssey./ c1977, 1992/
  5-6/5 KB743 . . . . **398.27**
SCHOLES, K/ Peace begins with you./ 1990/ P-2/5 KA812 . . . . **303.6**
SCHON, I/ Hispanic heritage, series II./ 1985/ KA043 . . . **PROF 016.98**
Hispanic heritage, series III./ 1988/ KA043 . . . . **PROF 016.98**
Latino heritage, series V./ 1995/ KA043 . . . . **PROF 016.98**
SCHORIES, P/ Biscuit./ 1996/ P-1/1 KF338 . . . . E
Biscuit finds a friend./ 1997/ P-1/1 KF339 . . . . E
SCHOTT, JA/ Will Rogers./ 1996/ 1-3/2 KE519 . . . . . **B ROGERS, W.**
SCHOTTER, R/ Hanukkah!/ 1993/ K-2/2 KA779 . . . . **296.4**
Nothing ever happens on 90th Street./ 1997/ 3-5/4 KH682 . . . . **FIC**
Passover magic./ 1995/ K-2/2 KG410 . . . . E
SCHRODER, R/ King Bobble./ 1996/ 2-3/2 KG953 . . . . **FIC**
On the road with Poppa Whopper./ 1997/ 3-4/2 KG954 . . . . **FIC**
SCHROEDER, A/ Carolina shout!/ 1995/ 1-5/3 KG411 . . . . E

Lily and the wooden bowl./ 1994/ 3-5/7 KB366 . . . . **398.2**
Smoky Mountain Rose: an Appalachian Cinderella./ 1997/
2-3/4 KB367 . . . . **398.2**
SCHRUMPF, F/ Creating the peaceable school: a comprehensive program
for teaching conflict resolution: program guide./ 1994/
KA161 . . . . **PROF 303.6**
SCHUETT, S/ When spring comes./ 1993/ P-2/3 KF906 . . . . **E**
SCHULZ, A/ North Carolina./ 1993/ 4-6/7 KE983 . . . . **975.6**
SCHUMAKER, W/ Mouse chase./ 1995/ P-1/2 KG394 . . . . **E**
SCHUMAN, M/ Harry S. Truman./ 1997/
5-A/9 KE571 . . . . **B TRUMAN, H.**
SCHUMM, JS/ How to help your child with homework: every caring
parent's guide to encouraging good study habits and ending the
Homework Wars: for parents/ 1997/ KA181 . . . . **PROF 371.3**
SCHUR, MR/ Day of delight: a Jewish Sabbath in Ethiopia./ 1994/
1-3/4 KG412 . . . . **E**
When I left my village./ 1996/ 4-A/5 KH683 . . . . **FIC**
SCHUTZ, WE/ How to attract, house and feed birds./ c1974/
3-6 KC663 . . . . **598**
How to attract, house and feed birds (Sound recording cassette)./ n.d./
3-6 KC663 . . . . **598**
SCHUTZER, D/ Million fish...more or less./ c1992, 1996/
1-3/4 KG106 . . . . **E**
SCHWABACHER, M/ Superstars of women's tennis./ 1997/
4-6/7 KD791 . . . . **796.342**
SCHWALBE, M/ SCIENCE ACTIVITIES FOR YOUNG PEOPLE./ 1983/
5-A/9 KB884 . . . . **507**
SCHWARTZ, A/ Annabelle Swift, Kindergartner./ 1988/
P-2/1 KG413 . . . . **CE E**
Annabelle Swift: Kindergartner (Kit)./ 1996/ P-2/1 KG413 . . . . . **CE E**
Fat man in a fur coat and other bear stories./ 1984/
5-6/5 KC855 . . . . **599.78**
Fat man in a fur coat and other bear stories (Sound recording cassette)./
n.d./ 5-6/5 KC855 . . . . **599.78**
Ghosts!: ghostly tales from folklore./ 1991/ 1-2/2 KB692 . . **CE 398.25**
Ghosts!: ghostly tales from folklore (Kit)./ 1995/
1-2/2 KB692 . . . . **CE 398.25**
Gold and silver, silver and gold./ 1988/ 4-6/6 KE628 . . . . **930.1**
How I captured a dinosaur./ c1989, 1993/ P-2/2 KG418 . . . . . . **E**
In a dark, dark room and other scary stories./ 1984/
K-3/1 KB693 . . . . **398.25**
Jane Martin, dog detective./ 1984/ 1-3/1 KF303 . . . . **E**
More scary stories to tell in the dark./ c1986/
4-A/3 KB694 . . . . **CE 398.25**
Nana's birthday party./ 1993/ 1-3/4 KF720 . . . . **E**
Oma and Bobo./ 1987/ K-3/2 KG414 . . . . **E**
Purple coat./ 1986/ K-3/4 KF721 . . . . **E**
Scary stories to tell in the dark./ 1981/ 4-A/3 KB694 . . . . **CE 398.25**
Scary stories to tell in the dark (Braille)./ n.d./
4-A/3 KB694 . . . . **CE 398.25**
Scary stories to tell in the dark (Sound recording cassette)./ n.d./
4-A/3 KB694 . . . . **CE 398.25**
Scary stories to tell in the dark (Talking book)./ 1986/
4-A/3 KB694 . . . . **CE 398.25**
Scary stories 3: more tales to chill your bones./ 1991/
4-A/3 KB694 . . . . **CE 398.25**
Teeny tiny baby./ 1994/ P-2/2 KG415 . . . . **E**
Yossel Zissel and the wisdom of Chelm./ 1986/ 2-4/2 KH684 . . . . **FIC**
SCHWARTZ, C/ Sea squares./ 1991/ K-3/3 KB960 . . . . **513.2**
Sea sums./ 1996/ P-2/3 KB961 . . . . **513.2**
SCHWARTZ, DM/ How much is a million?/ 1985/ K-1/2 KB950 . . . **513**
How much is a million? (Big book)./ 1994/ K-1/2 KB950 . . . . . **513**
HOW MUCH IS A MILLION? (Videocassette)./ 1997/
K-1 KB947 . . . . **VCR 513**
If you made a million./ 1989/ 2-5/5 KA946 . . . . **332.024**
Supergrandpa./ 1991/ K-3/5 KG416 . . . . **E**
Yanomami: people of the Amazon./ 1995/ 4-6/7 KF105 . . . . . . **981**
SCHWARTZ, G/ Rembrandt./ 1992/ 6-A/7 KE507 . . . **B REMBRANDT**
SCHWARTZ, H/ Diamond tree: Jewish tales from around the world./
1991/ 3-4/6 KB368 . . . . **398.2**
Diamond tree: Jewish tales from around the world (Sound recording
cassette)./ 1994/ 3-4/6 KB368 . . . . **398.2**
How I captured a dinosaur./ c1989, 1993/ P-2/2 KG418 . . . . **E**
Next year in Jerusalem: 3000 years of Jewish stories./ 1996/
3-6/7 KA780 . . . . **296.4**
Next year in Jerusalem: 3000 years of Jewish stories (Sound
recording cassette)./ 1997/ 3-6/7 KA780 . . . . **296.4**
Sabbath lion: a Jewish folktale from Algeria./ 1992/
4-6/6 KB511 . . . . **398.23**
Wonder child and other Jewish fairy tales./ 1996/ 2-4/5 KB369 **398.2**
SCHWARTZ, HB/ When Artie was little./ 1996/ 1-3/2 KG417 . . . . **E**
SCHWARTZ, JR/ May Chinn: the best medicine./ 1995/
5-A/8 KE288 . . . . **B CHINN, M.**

SCHWARTZ, P/ Carolyn's story: a book about an adopted girl./ 1996/
3-6/6 KB014 . . . . **362.73**
SCHWENINGER, A/ Oliver Pig at school./ 1994/ K-2/1 KG648 . . **CE E**
SCIESZKA, J/ Book that Jack wrote./ 1994/ P-1 KE021 . . . . **811**
Frog Prince, continued./ 1991/ 1-3/4 KG419 . . . . **E**
Frog Prince, continued (Sound recording cassette)./ 1993/
1-3/4 KG419 . . . . **E**
Good, the bad, and the goofy./ 1992/ 3-6/3 KH685 . . . . **FIC**
Knights of the kitchen table./ 1991/ 3-6/3 KH685 . . . . **FIC**
Math curse./ 1995/ 2-5/3 KG420 . . . . **E**
Math curse (Sound recording cassette)./ 1997/ 2-5/3 KG420 . . . . . **E**
Not-so-jolly Roger./ 1991/ 3-6/3 KH685 . . . . **FIC**
Stinky Cheese Man and other fairly stupid tales./ 1992/
4-6/4 KH686 . . . . **FIC**
Stinky Cheese Man and other fairly stupid tales (Sound recording
cassette)./ 1995/ 4-6/4 KH686 . . . . **FIC**
True story of the 3 little pigs./ 1989/ K-3/2 KG421 . . . . . **CE E**
Tut, tut./ 1996/ 3-6/3 KH685 . . . . **FIC**
Verdadera historia de los tres cerditos!/ 1991/ K-3/2 KG421 . . . **CE E**
Verdadera historia de los tres cerditos (Kit)./ 1997/
K-3/2 KG421 . . . . **CE E**
Your mother was a Neanderthal./ 1995/ 3-6/3 KH685 . . . . . **FIC**
Your mother was a neanderthal (Sound recording cassette)./ 1997/
3-6/3 KH685 . . . . **FIC**
SCOBEY, J/ Fannie Farmer junior cookbook. New and rev. ed./ 1993/
A KD280 . . . . **641.5**
SCOTT, A/ Come on everybody! Let's go to the fair (Kit)./ 1991/
P KB182 . . . . **KIT 394**
SCOTT, AH/ Brand is forever./ 1993/ 3-5/6 KH687 . . . . **FIC**
Brave as a mountain lion./ 1996/ 3-5/2 KH688 . . . . **FIC**
Cowboy country./ 1993/ 3-6/3 KF049 . . . . **978**
Hi./ 1994/ P-K/2 KG422 . . . . **E**
On mother's lap./ c1972, 1992/ P-K/2 KG423 . . . . **E**
On mother's lap (Braille)./ n.d./ P-K/2 KG423 . . . . **E**
One good horse: a cowpuncher's counting book./ 1990/
K-2/2 KG424 . . . . **E**
SCOTT, E/ Adventure in space: the flight to fix the Hubble./ 1995/
A/7 KC006 . . . . **522**
SCOTT, G/ Labor Day./ 1982/ 2-3/2 KB228 . . . . **394.264**
SCOTT, H/ Winnie-the-Pooh./ 1974/ K-6/3 KH498 . . . . **FIC**
SCOTT, WR/ Homes in the wilderness: a pilgrim's journal of Plymouth
Plantation in 1620./ c1939, 1988/ 5-A/8 KE941 . . . . . . **974.4**
SCRACE, C/ X-ray picture book of dinosaurs and other prehistoric
creatures./ 1995/ 4-8/7 KC264 . . . . **567.9**
SCRUGGS, J/ Ants (Compact disc)./ 1994/ K-3 KD657 . . . **CD 789.3**
Ants (Sound recording cassette)./ 1994/ K-3 KD657 . . . . . . **CD 789.3**
SEABROOK, E/ Cabbage and kings./ 1997/ 1-3/2 KG425 . . . . . . **E**
SEAGO, B/ GREEDY CAT (Videocassette)./ 1987/
K-3 KB578 . . . . **VCR 398.24**
VILLAGE STEW (Videocassette)./ 1987/ K-3 KB782 . . . . **VCR 398.27**
SEAVER, JE/ Captured by Indians: the life of Mary Jemison./ 1995/
5-A/8 KE405 . . . . **B JEMISON, M.**
SEBESTA, SL/ USING LITERATURE IN THE ELEMENTARY CLASSROOM.
Rev. ed./ 1989/ KA243 . . . . **PROF 372.64**
SEBESTYEN, O/ Words by heart./ 1997/ 5-A/7 KH689 . . . . . **CE FIC**
Words by heart (Sound recording cassette)./ n.d./
5-A/7 KH689 . . . . **CE FIC**
Words by heart (Videocassette)./ 1984/ 5-A/7 KH689 . . . . . **CE FIC**
SEEGER, P/ Abiyoyo: based on a South African lullaby and folk story./
1986/ 2-5 KD587 . . . . **789.2**
Abiyoyo: based on a South African lullaby and folk story (Braille)./ n.d./
2-5 KD587 . . . . **789.2**
Pete Seeger's family concert (Videocassette)./ 1992/
K-3 KD588 . . . . **VCR 789.2**
Song and play time (Sound recording cassette)./ 1990/
K-3 KD589 . . . . **SRC 789.2**
SEELEY, LL/ Four-legged ghosts./ 1995/ 2-4/6 KH269 . . . . . **FIC**
SEGAL, J/ Place where nobody stopped./ 1994/ 5-A/7 KH690 . . . **FIC**
SEGAL, L/ Juniper tree and other tales from Grimm./ c1973, 1992/
5-A/7 KB306 . . . . **398.2**
Tell me a Mitzi./ c1970/ K-3/6 KG426 . . . . **E**
Tell me a Mitzi (Braille)./ n.d./ K-3/6 KG426 . . . . **E**
Tell me a Trudy./ c1977, 1981/ K-3/4 KG427 . . . . **E**
SEIDEN, A/ Baseball./ 1994/ 3-6/3 KD808 . . . . **796.357**
Basketball./ 1994/ 3-6/4 KD781 . . . . **796.323**
Bicycling./ 1996/ 3-6/6 KD827 . . . . **796.6**
Football./ 1994/ 3-6/4 KD785 . . . . **796.332**
Hockey./ 1994/ 3-6/4 KD841 . . . . **796.962**
Karate and judo./ 1996/ 3-6/6 KD833 . . . . **796.815**
Soccer./ 1994/ 3-6/4 KD789 . . . . **796.334**
Swimming./ 1996/ 3-6/6 KD850 . . . . **797.2**
Track and field./ 1994/ 3-6/4 KD810 . . . . **796.42**
Trucks (Board book)./ 1983/ P KG428 . . . . **BB E**
SEIDLER, T/ Wainscott weasel./ 1993/ 4-6/5 KH691 . . . . **FIC**

SEILER, B/ How the west was one + three x four (Microcomputer program)./ c1987, 1989/ 4-A KB951 . . . . **MCP 513**
SEIXAS, JS/ Alcohol--what it is, what it does./ c1977/ 1-3/5 KD002 . . . . **613.81**
Allergies - what they are, what they do./ 1991/ 3-5/6 KD033 . **616.97**
Living with a parent who drinks too much./ 1979/ 4-6/7 KB000 . . . . **362.292**
SELDEN, G/ Chester Cricket's new home./ 1983/ 2-4/5 KH692 . . . . **FIC**
Chester Cricket's new home (Sound recording cassette)./ n.d./ 2-4/5 KH692 . . . . **FIC**
Chester Cricket's pigeon ride./ 1983/ 3-4/5 KH693 . . . . **FIC**
Chester Cricket's pigeon ride (Sound recording cassette)./ n.d./ 3-4/5 KH693 . . . . **FIC**
Cricket in Times Square./ c1960/ 4-6/6 KH694 . . . . **CE FIC**
Cricket in Times Square (Braille)./ n.d./ 4-6/6 KH694 . . . . . . **CE FIC**
Cricket in Times Square (Talking book)./ 1971/ 4-6/6 KH694 . **CE FIC**
Genie of Sutton Place./ c1973/ 4-6/7 KH695 . . . . **FIC**
Genie of Sutton Place (Sound recording cassette)./ n.d./ 4-6/7 KH695 . . . . **FIC**
Harry Kitten and Tucker Mouse./ 1986/ 2-4/4 KH696 . . . . **FIC**
Old meadow./ 1987/ 3-5/5 KH697 . . . . **FIC**
Tucker's countryside./ c1969, 1989/ 4-6/5 KH698 . . . . **FIC**
Tucker's countryside (Braille)./ n.d.,/ 4-6/5 KH698 . . . . **FIC**
SELSAM, ME/ Egg to chick. Rev. ed./ 1970/ P-2/2 KC698 . . . . **598.6**
First look at animals with horns./ 1989/ 1-3/2 KC792 . . . . . . **599.64**
First look at ducks, geese, and swans./ 1990/ 1-3/2 KC683 . . . **598.4**
Keep looking./ 1989/ P-3/2 KC728 . . . . **599**
SELTZER, I/ Man who tricked a ghost./ 1993/ 1-3/4 KB697 . . . **398.25**
Tree of dreams: ten tales from the garden of night./ 1995/ 4-6/3 KB790 . . . . **398.27**
SELTZER, M/ Riddles to tell your cat./ 1992/ 2-5 KD732 . . . . **793.735**
SELVEN, M/ Broken tusk: stories of the Hindu god Ganesha./ 1996/ 3-4/4 KA764 . . . . **294.5**
SELZNICK, B/ Our house: the stories of Levittown./ 1995/ 4-6/7 KH022 . . . . **FIC**
SENDAK, M/ Alligators all around: an alphabet./ c1962/ P-1 KG429 . . . . **CE E**
Alligators all around: an alphabet (Videocassette)./ 1976/ P-1 KG429 . . . . **CE E**
Bat-poet./ 1996/ 4-A/6 KH327 . . . . **FIC**
Bee-man of Orn./ c1964, 1987/ 5-6/7 KH763 . . . . **FIC**
Big green book./ c1962, 1990/ 3-6/4 KH192 . . . . **FIC**
Caldecott and Co.: notes on books & pictures./ 1988/ KA356 . . . . **PROF 809**
Chicken soup with rice: a book of months./ c1962/ P-1 KG430 . . **CE E**
Chicken soup with rice: a book of months (Big book)./ 1992/ P-1 KG430 . . . . **CE E**
Chicken soup with rice: a book of months (Kit)./ / P-1 KG430 . . . **CE E**
Chicken soup with rice; a book of months (Videocassette)./ 1976/ P-1 KG430 . . . . **CE E**
Cocina de noche./ 1997/ K-3/3 KG432 . . . . **CE E**
Cocina de noche (Videocassette)./ 1993/ K-3/3 KG432 . . . . **CE E**
Donde viven los monstruos./ 1996,/ P-3/2 KG438 . . . . **CE E**
Donde viven los monstruos (Videocassette)./ 1993,/ P-3/2 KG438 . . . . **CE E**
Griffin and the minor canon./ c1963, 1986/ 3-5/7 KH764 . . . . . . **FIC**
Hector Protector and As I went over the water: two nursery rhymes with pictures./ c1965, 1990/ P-K KB815 . . . . **398.8**
Higglety pigglety pop, or, There must be more to life./ c1967/ 1-3/6 KG431 . . . . **E**
Higglety pigglety pop, or, There must be more to life (Braille)./ n.d./ 1-3/6 KG431 . . . . **E**
Hole is to dig: a first book of first definitions./ c1952/ P-2/2 KF922 . . . . **CE E**
I SAW ESAU: THE SCHOOLCHILD'S POCKET BOOK./ 1992/ KA276 . . . . **PROF 398.8**
In the night kitchen./ c1970/ K-3/3 KG432 . . . . **CE E**
In the night kitchen (Picture)./ n.d./ K-3/3 KG432 . . . . **CE E**
In the night kitchen (Talking Book)./ n.d./ K-3/3 KG432 . . . . **CE E**
In the night kitchen (Videocassette)./ n.d./ K-3/3 KG432 . . . . . . **CE E**
Juniper tree and other tales from Grimm./ c1973, 1992/ 5-A/7 KB306 . . . . **398.2**
Let's be enemies./ c1961/ P-1/2 KG632 . . . . **E**
Light princess./ 1977/ 4-5/5 KH439 . . . . **FIC**
Little Bear./ c1961/ P-1/2 KG141 . . . . **CE E**
Maurice Sendak Library (Videocassette)./ 1992/ P-2 KG433 . . . **VCR E**
Mr. Rabbit and the lovely present./ c1962/ P-2/2 KG804 . . . . . **CE E**
Nutshell library (Videocassette)./ 1987/ P-2 KG434 . . . . **VCR E**
One was Johnny: a counting book./ c1962/ P-1 KG435 . . . . **CE E**
One was Johnny: a counting book (Videocassette)./ 1976/ P-1 KG435 . . . . **CE E**
Pierre: a cautionary tale in five chapters and a prologue./ c1962/ P-1 KG436 . . . . **CE E**
Pierre: a cautionary tale in five chapters and a prologue (Videocassette)./ 1976/ P-1 KG436 . . . . **CE E**
Shadrach./ c1953/ 2-3/5 KH069 . . . . **FIC**
Very special house./ c1953/ P-1/1 KF923 . . . . **E**
Wheel on the school./ c1954/ 4-6/3 KH070 . . . . **FIC**
Where the wild things are and other stories (Talking book)./ 1977/ P-2 KG437 . . . . **TB E**
Where the wild things are (Braille)./ n.d.,/ P-3/2 KG438 . . . . . . **CE E**
Where the wild things are (Picture)./ n.d.,/ P-3/2 KG438 . . . . . . **CE E**
Where the wild things are (Sound recording cassette)./ n.d.,/ P-3/2 KG438 . . . . **CE E**
Where the wild things are (Talking book)./ n.d.,/ P-3/2 KG438 . . **CE E**
Where the wild things are (Videocassette)./ 1985,/ P-3/2 KG438 **CE E**
Where the wild things are. 25th anniv. ed./ c1963, 1988/ P-3/2 KG438 . . . . **CE E**
SENIOR, K/ X-ray picture book of dinosaurs and other prehistoric creatures./ 1995/ 4-8/7 KC264 . . . . **567.9**
SENISI, EB/ Secrets./ 1995/ K-2/2 KA643 . . . . **155.4**
SEREDY, K/ White stag./ c1937/ 5-6/7 KB486 . . . . **398.22**
White stag (Braille)./ n.d./ 5-6/7 KB486 . . . . **398.22**
White stag (Sound recording cassette)./ n.d./ 5-6/7 KB486 . . **398.22**
White stag (Talking book)./ n.d./ 5-6/7 KB486 . . . . **398.22**
SERFOZO, M/ Benjamin Bigfoot./ 1993/ P-K/2 KG439 . . . . **E**
Joe Joe./ 1993/ P-K/1 KG440 . . . . **E**
Rain talk./ 1990/ P-1/4 KG441 . . . . **E**
There's a square: a book about shapes./ 1996/ P-1/1 KG442 . . . . . **E**
What's what?: a guessing game./ 1996/ P-1/2 KG443 . . . . **E**
Who said red?/ 1988/ P-K/2 KG444 . . . . **E**
SERGIO/ Rembrandt and seventeenth-century Holland./ 1995/ 4-A/12 KD501 . . . . **759.9492**
SERRAILLIER, I/ Silver sword./ c1959/ 5-6/6 KH699 . . . . **FIC**
SERVICE, PF/ Stinker from space./ 1988/ 3-5/5 KH700 . . . . **FIC**
Stinker from space (Sound recording cassette)./ 1993/ 3-5/5 KH700 . . . . **FIC**
Stinker's return./ 1993/ 3-5/5 KH700 . . . . **FIC**
Stinker's return (Sound recording cassette)./ 1994/ 3-5/5 KH700 . . **FIC**
Weirdos of the universe, unite!/ 1992/ 6-A/6 KH701 . . . . **FIC**
SERWADDA, WM/
Songs and stories from Uganda./ Songs and stories from Uganda./ 1987,/ c1974, 1987/ KA319 . . . . **BA PROF 789.2**
KA319 . . . . **BA PROF 789.2**
SETZER, PM/ Come sign with us: sign language activities for children. 2nd. ed./ 1996/ KA279 . . . . **PROF 419**
SEUSS, D/ And to think that I saw it on Mulberry Street./ c1937, 1964/ K-2/2 KG445 . . . . **E**
And to think that I saw it on Mulberry Street (Talking book)./ n.d.,/ K-2/2 KG445 . . . . **E**
Bartholomew and the oobleck./ c1949/ P-3/6 KG446 . . . . **E**
Bartholomew and the oobleck (Videocassette)./ 1985/ 1-3 KG450 . . . . **VCR E**
Butter battle book./ 1984/ K-3/5 KG447 . . . . **E**
Butter battle book (Braille)./ n.d./ K-3/5 KG447 . . . . **E**
Butter battle book (Sound recording cassette)./ n.d./ K-3/5 KG447 . **E**
Cat in the hat./ c1957/ P-2/1 KG448 . . . . **CE E**
Cat in the hat comes back./ 1958/ P-2/1 KG448 . . . . **CE E**
Cat in the Hat gets grinched (Videocassette)./ 1982/ K-2 KG449 . . . . **VCR E**
Dr. Seuss' Caldecotts (Videocassette)./ 1985/ 1-3 KG450 . . . . **VCR E**
Dr. Seuss's ABC./ c1963/ P-2/2 KG451 . . . . **CE E**
Dr. Seuss's ABC (Talking book)./ n.d./ P-2/2 KG451 . . . . **CE E**
Foot book./ c1968/ P-1/1 KG452 . . . . **E**
Fox in socks./ c1965/ P-2/2 KG453 . . . . **E**
Gato ensombrerado (Kit)./ 1993/ P-2/1 KG448 . . . . **CE E**
Green eggs and ham./ 1960/ P-2/1 KG454 . . . . **CE E**
GREEN EGGS AND HAM. School ed. (CD-ROM)./ 1996/ K-2 KF639 . . . . **CDR E**
Green eggs and ham (Videocassette)./ n.d./ P-2/1 KG454 . . . . . **CE E**
Hop on pop./ c1963/ P-1/1 KG455 . . . . **E**
Hop on pop (Braille)./ n.d./ P-1/1 KG455 . . . . **E**
Horton hatches the egg./ c1940/ P-3/3 KG456 . . . . **CE E**
Horton hatches the egg (Braille)./ n.d./ P-3/3 KG456 . . . . **CE E**
Horton hatches the egg./If I ran the circus (Videocassette)./ 1992/ P-3 KG457 . . . . **VCR E**
Horton hears a Who./ 1954/ P-3/3 KG456 . . . . **CE E**
Horton hears a Who (Braille)./ n.d./ P-3/3 KG456 . . . . **CE E**
Horton hears a Who (Kit)./ 1990/ P-3/3 KG456 . . . . **CE E**
Horton hears a Who!/Thidwick the big-hearted moose (Videocassette)./ 1992/ P-3 KG458 . . . . **VCR E**
How the Grinch stole Christmas./ c1957/ P-3 KG459 . . . . **E**
How the Grinch stole Christmas (Braille)./ n.d./ P-3 KG459 . . . . **E**
How the Grinch stole Christmas (Sound recording cassette)./ n.d./ P-3 KG459 . . . . **E**
Huevos verdes con jamon./ 1992/ P-2/1 KG454 . . . . **CE E**
Hunches in bunches./ 1982/ K-3/2 KG460 . . . . **E**

I am not going to get up today!/ 1987/ 1-3/2 KG461 . . . . **E**
I am not going to get up today! (Braille)./ n.d./ 1-3/2 KG461 . . . . **E**
I am not going to get up today! plus three more Dr. Seuss classics
   (Videocassette)./ 1991/ 1-3 KG462 . . . . **VCR E**
I can read with my eyes shut./ 1978/ P-2/2 KG463 . . . . **E**
If I ran the circus./ c1956/ P-3/4 KG464 . . . . **E**
If I ran the circus (Braille)./ n.d./ P-3/4 KG464 . . . . **E**
If I ran the zoo./ 1950/ P-3/5 KG465 . . . . **E**
If I ran the zoo (Braille)./ n.d./ P-3/5 KG465 . . . . **E**
If I ran the zoo (Sound recording cassette)./ 1993/ P-3/5 KG465 . . **E**
If I ran the zoo (Talking book)./ n.d./ P-3/5 KG465 . . . . **E**
If I ran the zoo (Videocassette)./ 1985/ 1-3 KG450 . . . . **VCR E**
Lorax./ c1971/ P-3/3 KG466 . . . . **CE E**
Lorax (Kit)./ 1992/ P-3/3 KG466 . . . . **CE E**
Lorax (Sound recording cassette)./ n.d./ P-3/3 KG466 . . **CE E**
Lorax (Spanish version)./ 1993/ P-3/3 KG466 . . . . . . **CE E**
McElligot's pool./ c1947/ P-3 KG467 . . . . **E**
McElligot's pool (Braille)./ n.d./ P-3 KG467 . . . . **E**
McElligot's pool (Videocassette)./ 1985/ 1-3 KG450 . . . . **VCR E**
My many colored days./ 1996/ K-2/2 KG468 . . . . **E**
Oh, cuan lejos llegaras!/ 1993/ 1-3/2 KG469 . . . . **E**
Oh, the places you'll go!/ 1990/ 1-3/2 KG469 . . . . **E**
Oh, the places you'll go! (Sound recording cassette)./ n.d./
   1-3/2 KG469 . . . . **E**
On beyond zebra./ 1955/ P-3/6 KG470 . . . . **E**
One fish, two fish, red fish, blue fish./ c1960/ P-1/1 KG471 . . . . **E**
One fish, two fish, red fish, blue fish (Braille)./ n.d./ P-1/1 KG471 . . **E**
One fish, two fish, red fish, blue fish (Sound recording cassette)./ n.d./
   P-1/1 KG471 . . . . **E**
Yertle the turtle, and other stories./ c1958/ P-3/3 KG472 . . . . . **CE E**
Yertle the turtle, and other stories (Sound recording cassette)./ 1993/
   P-3/3 KG472 . . . . **CE E**
Yertle the turtle, and other stories (Videocassette)./ 1992/
   P-3/3 KG472 . . . . **CE E**
500 hats of Bartholomew Cubbins./ c1938, 1989/ P-A/6 KG473 . . . **E**
500 hats of Bartholomew Cubbins (Braille)./ n.d./ P-A/6 KG473 . . . **E**
500 hats of Bartholomew Cubbins (Talking book)./ n.d./
   P-A/6 KG473 . . . . **E**
SEUSS, DR./ DR. SEUSS'S ABC (CD-ROM)./ 1995/ P-2 KF493 . . **CDR E**
SEVERANCE, JB/ Winston Churchill: soldier, statesman, artist./ 1996/
   6-A/10 KE291 . . . . **B CHURCHILL, W.**
SEVERANCE, L/ Cow./ 1997/ P-4/2 KD214 . . . . **636.2**
SEWALL, M/ People of the breaking day./ 1990/ 3-6/5 KA858 . **305.8**
People of the breaking day (Sound recording cassette)./ 1993/
   3-6/5 KA858 . . . . **305.8**
Pilgrims of Plimoth./ 1986/ 4-6/7 KE947 . . . . **CE 974.4**
Pilgrims of Plimoth (Videocassette)./ 1990/ 4-6/7 KE947 . . . **CE 974.4**
Sable./ 1994/ 3-5/4 KH253 . . . . **FIC**
Sarah, plain and tall./ 1985/ 3-5/4 KH444 . . . . **CE FIC**
Thunder from the clear sky./ 1995/ 4-6/7 KE874 . . . . . . **973.2**
SEWELL, A/ Black Beauty: the autobiography of a horse./ 1997/
   5-7/7 KH702 . . . . **FIC**
SEWELL, H/ Bears on Hemlock Mountain./ c1952, 1990/
   1-4/4 KH057 . . . . **FIC**
Book of myths: selections from Bulfinch's Age of fable./ c1942/
   A/9 KA734 . . . . **292**
Thanksgiving story./ c1954/ 3-6/4 KB222 . . . . **394.264**
SEYMOUR, T/ Hunting the white cow./ 1993/ 1-3/2 KG474 . . . . . **E**
SEYMOUR, TVN/ Gift of Changing Woman./ 1993/ 6-A/7 KA792 . **299**
SHACHAT, A/ You can't catch me!/ 1986/ P-1 KG193 . . . . **E**
SHAFFER, T/ Singing man: adapted from a West African folktale./ 1994/
   4-5/6 KB757 . . . . **398.27**
SHAHAN, S/ Barnacles eat with their feet: delicious facts about the tide
   pool food chain./ 1996/ 3-6/5 KC348 . . . . **577.69**
Dashing through the snow: the story of the Jr. Iditarod./ 1997/
   4-6/7 KD860 . . . . **798.8**
SHAKESPEARE, W/ Riverside Shakespeare./ 1974/
   A KA468 . . . . **REF 822.3**
SHAKESPEARE FOR CHILDREN (Sound recording cassette)./ 1995/
   4-6 KE117 . . . . **SRC 822.3**
SOMETHING RICH AND STRANGE: A TREASURY OF SHAKESPEARE'S
   VERSE./ 1995/ 6-A KE118 . . . . **822.3**
Tales from Shakespeare./ 1979/ A/9 KE115 . . . . **822.3**
William Shakespeare's A midsummer night's dream./ 1996/
   4-6/4 KE114 . . . . **822.3**
SHANNON, D/ Amazing Christmas extravaganza./ 1995/
   2-5/6 KG475 . . . . **E**
Boy who lived with the seals./ 1993/ 2-4/6 KB614 . . . . . **398.24**
Bunyans./ 1996/ 1-5/6 KG760 . . . . **E**
How Georgie Radbourn saved baseball./ 1994/ 2-5/6 KG476 . . . . **E**
How many spots does a leopard have? and other tales./ c1989, 1994/
   5-6/6 KB335 . . . . **398.2**
Nicholas Pipe./ 1997/ 2-5/6 KB413 . . . . **398.21**
Rough-face girl./ 1992/ 3-5/4 KB752 . . . . **398.27**

Sacred places./ 1996/ 3-6 KE048 . . . . **811**
SHANNON, G/ April showers./ 1995/ P-1/2 KG477 . . . . **E**
KNOCK AT THE DOOR./ 1992/ KA269 . . . . . . **PROF 398.2**
More stories to solve: fifteen folktales from around the world./ 1991/
   5-6/6 KB714 . . . . **398.26**
Seeds./ 1994/ K-2/2 KG478 . . . . **E**
SPRING: A HAIKU STORY./ 1996/ 1-6 KE137 . . . . **895.6**
Still more stories to solve: fourteen folktales from around the world./
   1994/ 5-6/6 KB714 . . . . **398.26**
Stories to solve./ 1985/ 5-6/6 KB714 . . . . **398.26**
Stories to solve (Sound recording cassette)./ n.d./
   5-6/6 KB714 . . . . **398.26**
Tomorrow's alphabet./ 1996/ K-2/2 KG479 . . . . **E**
SHAPIRO, A/ Let's clean up our act: songs for the earth (Sound recording
   cassette)./ 1989/ K-6 KD559 . . . . **SRC 789.2**
Mice squeak, we speak: a poem./ 1997/ P-1/3 KE022 . . . . **811**
SHARKEY, PB/ Newbery and Caldecott Medal and Honor books in other
   media./ 1992/ KA087 . . . . **PROF 028.1**
SHARMAT, C/ Nate the Great and the crunchy Christmas./ 1996/
   2-4/2 KG485 . . . . **E**
Nate the Great and the tardy tortoise./ 1995/ 1-3/2 KG487 . . . . . **E**
SHARMAT, M/ Gregory, the terrible eater./ 1980/ K-2/4 KG488 . . . **E**
SHARMAT, MW/ Genghis Khan: a dog star is born./ 1994/
   2-5/2 KH703 . . . . **FIC**
Genghis Khan: dog-gone Hollywood./ 1995/ 2-5/2 KH704 . . . . . **FIC**
Getting something on Maggie Marmelstein./ c1971/ 4-6/4 KH705 . **FIC**
Getting something on Maggie Marmelstein (Sound recording cassette)./
   1997/ 4-6/4 KH705 . . . . **FIC**
Gila monsters meet you at the airport./ 1980/ K-2/2 KG480 . . . . . **E**
I'm terrific./ 1977/ P-1/3 KG481 . . . . **E**
I'm the best!/ 1991/ K-2/1 KG482 . . . . **E**
Maggie Marmelstein for president./ 1975/ 4-6/4 KH705 . . . . . . **FIC**
Mitchell is moving./ 1978/ K-3/1 KG483 . . . . **E**
Mysteriously yours, Maggie Marmelstein (Sound recording cassette)./
   n.d./ 4-6/4 KH705 . . . . **FIC**
Nate the Great./ c1972/ 1-3/2 KG484 . . . . **CE E**
Nate the Great and the crunchy Christmas./ 1996/ 2-4/2 KG485 . . **E**
Nate the Great and the fishy prize (Braille)./ n.d./ 1-3/2 KG484 . **CE E**
Nate the Great and the Halloween hunt./ 1990/ 1-3/2 KG484 . **CE E**
Nate the Great and the lost list./ 1981/ 1-3/2 KG484 . . . . **CE E**
Nate the Great and the lost list (Braille)./ n.d./ 1-3/2 KG484 . **CE E**
Nate the Great and the missing key (Kit)./ 1989/ 1-3/2 KG484 . **CE E**
Nate the Great and the phony clue./ 1981/ 1-3/2 KG484 . . . . **CE E**
Nate the Great and the pillowcase./ 1993./ 1-3/1 KG486 . . . . . **E**
Nate the Great and the snowy trail (Braille)./ n.d./ 1-3/2 KG484 . **CE E**
Nate the Great and the stolen base./ 1992/ 1-3/2 KG484 . . . **CE E**
Nate the Great and the tardy tortoise./ 1995/ 1-3/2 KG487 . . . **CE E**
Nate the Great (Braille)./ n.d./ 1-3/2 KG484 . . . . **CE E**
Nate the Great goes undercover./ c1974/ 1-3/2 KG484 . . . . **CE E**
Nate the Great goes undercover (Braille)./ n.d./ 1-3/2 KG484 . **CE E**
Nate the Great goes undercover (Kit)./ 1995/ 1-3/2 KG484 . **CE E**
Nate the Great stalks stupidweed./ 1989/ 1-3/2 KG484 . . . **CE E**
SHARP, PT/ EXPLORING THE SOUTHWEST STATES THROUGH
   LITERATURE./ 1994/ KA038 . . . . **PROF 016.976**
SHARRATT, N/ Elsa, star of the shelter!/ 1996/ 4-6/5 KH868 . . . . **FIC**
SHATTUCK, CH/ Riverside Shakespeare./ 1974/ A KA468 . . **REF 822.3**
SHAW, N/ Sheep in a jeep./ 1986/ K-3/2 KG489 . . . . **E**
Sheep in a shop./ 1991/ K-3/2 KG489 . . . . **E**
Sheep in a shop (Sound recording cassette)./ 1994/ K-3/2 KG489 . **E**
Sheep on a ship./ 1989/ K-3/2 KG489 . . . . **E**
Sheep out to eat./ 1992/ K-3/2 KG489 . . . . **E**
Sheep out to eat (Sound recording cassette)./ 1994/ K-3/2 KG489 . **E**
SHAW-SMITH, E/ Bread is for eating./ 1995/ P-2/2 KF610 . . . . . **E**
SHEA, PD/ New moon./ 1996/ P-2/2 KG490 . . . . **E**
SHEARER, BF/ State names, seals, flags, and symbols: a historical guide.
   Rev. and expanded ed./ 1994/ 4-A KA493 . . . . . . **REF 973**
SHEARER, BS/ State names, seals, flags, and symbols: a historical guide.
   Rev. and expanded ed./ 1994/ 4-A KA493 . . . . . . **REF 973**
SHECTER, B/ Getting something on Maggie Marmelstein./ c1971/
   4-6/4 KH705 . . . . **FIC**
Hating book./ c1969, 1989/ K-2/2 KG801 . . . . **E**
SHED, G/ Casey over there./ 1994/ 2-4/4 KG297 . . . . **E**
Dandelions./ 1995/ 3-5/2 KG942 . . . . **FIC**
Rose horse./ 1995/ 3-5/6 KH651 . . . . **FIC**
SHEEHAN, P/ Gwendolyn's gifts./ 1991/ 1-3/5 KG491 . . . . **E**
SHEEN, M/ DOG (Videocassette)./ 1994/ 3-6 KD219 . . . . . **VCR 636.7**
MAMMAL (Videocassette)./ 1996/ 5-6 KC723 . . . . . **VCR 599**
SHEFELMAN, J/ Peddler's dream./ 1992/ 1-3/2 KG492 . . . . **E**
SHEFELMAN, T/ Peddler's dream./ 1992/ 1-3/2 KG492 . . . . **E**
SHELBY, A/ Homeplace./ 1995/ 1-3/3 KG493 . . . . **E**
SHELNUTT, E/ Magic pencil: teaching children creative writing: exercises
   and activities for children, their parents, and their teachers./ 1994/
   KA228 . . . . **PROF 372.6**

SHEMIE, B/ Mounds of earth and shell: the Southeast./ 1993/
4-6/7 KB172 . . . . **392.3**
SHENTON, E/ On to Oregon./ c1954/ 5-6/4 KH517 . . . . **FIC**
SHEPARD, A/ Baker's dozen: a Saint Nicholas tale./ 1995/
K-2/4 KB487 . . . . **398.22**
Gifts of Wali Dad: a tale of India and Pakistan./ 1995/
2-3/2 KB488 . . . . **398.22**
Legend of Slappy Hooper: an American tall tale./ 1993/
3-5/3 KB489 . . . . **398.22**
Savitri: a tale of ancient India./ 1992/ 3-4/4 KA766 . . . . **294.5**
STORIES ON STAGE: SCRIPTS FOR READER'S THEATER./ 1993/
KA363 . . . . **PROF 812**
SHEPARD, EH/ Reluctant dragon./ c1938/ 3-6/7 KH187 . . . . . **CE FIC**
Wind in the willows. 75th anniversary edition./ 1983/
5-6/8 KH190 . . . . **FIC**
SHEPARD, M/ Mary Poppins. Rev. ed./ c1962/ 4-6/6 KH800 . . . . . **FIC**
SHEPHARD, MT/ Maria Montessori: teacher of teachers./ 1996/
A/9 KE468 . . . . **B MONTESSORI, M**
SHEPHERD, DW/ Auroras: light shows in the night sky./ 1995/
4-8/6 KC137 . . . . **538**
Aztecs./ 1992/ 4-6/7 KE838 . . . . **972**
SHERBURNE, A/ Memoirs of Andrew Sherburne: patriot and privateer of
the American Revolution./ 1993/ 5-A/8 KE886 . . . . **973.3**
SHERMAN, GW/ Handbook for the Newbery Medal and Honor Books,
1980-1989./ 1991/ KA347 . . . . **PROF 809**
Worth a thousand words: an annotated guide to picture books for older
readers./ 1990/ KA010 . . . . **PROF 011.62**
SHERMAN, PW/ Naked mole-rats./ 1996/ 4-6/7 KC744 . . . . . **599.35**
SHERROW, V/ American Indian children of the past./ 1997/
3-6/7 KE764 . . . . **970.3**
Freedom of worship./ 1997/ 4-6/12 KA908 . . . . **323.44**
Phillis Wheatley./ 1992/ 4-6/7 KE591 . . . . **B WHEATLEY, P.**
Porcupine./ 1991/ 5-6/6 KC747 . . . . **599.35**
SHETTERLY, R/ What's the difference?: a guide to some familiar animal
look-alikes./ 1993/ 5-6/8 KC450 . . . . **591**
SHIELDS, CD/ I am really a princess./ 1993/ 1-3/3 KG494 . . . . **FIC**
SHIMIN, S/ Zeely./ c1967/ 4-A/4 KH220 . . . . **FIC**
SHIPTON, A/ Brass./ 1994/ 4-A/7 KD553 . . . . **788.9**
Percussion./ 1994/ 4-6/7 KD547 . . . . **786.8**
Singing./ 1994/ 4-6/7 KD527 . . . . **782**
Strings./ 1994/ 4-6/7 KD548 . . . . **787**
Woodwinds./ 1994/ 4-6/7 KD550 . . . . **788.2**
SHIRLEY, D/ Diego Rivera./ 1995/ 5-6/7 KE513 . . . . . . **B RIVERA, D.**
SHIRLEY, J/ L. Frank Baum: royal historian of Oz./ 1992/
4-6/4 KE251 . . . . **B BAUM, L.**
SHLICHTA, J/ Eleven nature tales: a multicultural journey./ 1996/
3-5/7 KB286 . . . . **398.2**
Eleven turtle tales: adventure tales from around the world./ 1994/
2-3/4 KB559 . . . . **398.24**
Strongheart Jack and the beanstalk./ 1995/ 2-5/3 KB287 . . . . **398.2**
SHONE, R/ New book of dinosaurs./ 1997/ K-6/9 KC266 . . . . . **567.9**
SHORE, J/ Birdwise: forty fun feats for finding out about our feathered
friends./ 1988/ 4-6/6 KC650 . . . . **598**
Bugwise: thirty incredible insect investigations and arachnid activities./
c1990, 1991/ 4-6/7 KC540 . . . . **595.7**
SHORTALL, L/ Dog on Barkham Street./ c1960/ 4-6/4 KH765 . . . . **FIC**
SHOWERS, P/ Drop of blood. Rev. ed./ 1989/ K-2/2 KC936 . . . **612.1**
Drop of blood. Rev. ed. (Talking book)./ n.d./ K-2/2 KC936 . . . **612.1**
Listening walk./ c1961, 1991/ P-1/1 KG495 . . . . **E**
Look at your eyes. Rev. ed./ 1992/ P-1/1 KC978 . . . . **612.8**
Sleep is for everyone (Braille)./ n.d./ K-2/3 KC979 . . . . **612.8**
Sleep is for everyone. Newly illustrated ed./ 1997/
K-2/3 KC979 . . . . **612.8**
Sleep is for everyone (Sound recording cassette)./ n.d./
K-2/3 KC979 . . . . **612.8**
Sonidos a mi alrededor./ 1996,/ P-1/1 KG495 . . . . **E**
What happens to a hamburger? Rev. ed./ 1985/ K-2/3 KC942 . **612.3**
Where does the garbage go? Rev. ed./ 1994/ 2-3/3 KD083 . . **628.4**
Your skin and mine. Rev. ed./ 1991/ K-2/2 KC960 . . . . **612.7**
SHRADER, CN/ Gluskabe and the four wishes./ 1995/
3-5/6 KB272 . . . . **398.2**
SHREVE, S/ Amy Dunn quits school./ 1993/ 5-A/7 KH706 . . . . **FIC**
Flunking of Joshua T. Bates./ c1984, 1993/ 4-6/6 KH707 . . . . . **FIC**
Formerly great Alexander family./ 1995/ 3-5/6 KH708 . . . . **FIC**
Gift of the girl who couldn't hear./ 1991/ 4-6/6 KH709 . . . . . . **FIC**
Joshua T. Bates takes charge./ c1993, 1995/ 4-6/4 KH710 . . . . **FIC**
SHUB, E/ Mazel and Shlimazel; or, The milk of a lioness./ 1967/
4-6/6 KB779 . . . . **398.27**
Seeing is believing./ 1979/ K-2/2 KG496 . . . . **E**
White stallion./ 1982/ 1-3/2 KG497 . . . . **E**
White stallion (Braille)./ n.d./ 1-3/2 KG497 . . . . **E**
White stallion (Sound recording cassette)./ n.d./ 1-3/2 KG497 . . . . . **E**
SHULEVITZ, U/ Dawn./ 1974/ K-2/2 KG498 . . . . **E**

Diamond tree: Jewish tales from around the world./ 1991/
3-4/6 KB368 . . . . **398.2**
Fool of the world and the flying ship: a Russian tale./ c1968/
2-5/5 KB765 . . . . **398.27**
Golden goose./ 1995/ K-3/2 KB650 . . . . **398.24**
Rain, rain rivers./ c1969, 1998/ P-2/2 KG499 . . . . **E**
Tesoro./ 1992/ 2-4/4 KB778 . . . . **398.27**
Treasure./ 1978/ 2-4/4 KB778 . . . . **398.27**
SHULTE, AP/ NEW DIRECTIONS FOR ELEMENTARY SCHOOL
MATHEMATICS, 1989 YEARBOOK./ 1989/ KA255 . . . **PROF 372.7**
SHUTE, L/ Jeremy Bean's St. Patrick's Day./ 1987/ K-2/4 KG404 . . . **E**
Rabbit wishes./ 1995/ K-2/2 KB651 . . . . **398.24**
SIDDALS, MM/ Tell me a season./ 1997/ P-1/1 KG500 . . . . **E**
SIDJAKOV, N/ Baboushka and the three kings./ c1960/
2-4/6 KB509 . . . . **398.23**
SIEBEL, F/ Tell me some more./ c1961/ K-2/2 KF247 . . . . **E**
SIEBERT, D/ Plane song./ 1993/ 3-6 KD112 . . . . **629.133**
Sierra./ 1991/ 2-6 KE023 . . . . **811**
Train song./ 1990/ P-3 KG501 . . . . **E**
Truck song./ 1984/ P-1 KG502 . . . . **CE E**
Truck song (Braille)./ n.d./ P-1 KG502 . . . . **CE E**
Truck song (Kit)./ n.d./ P-1 KG502 . . . . **CE E**
Truck song (Videocassette)./ 1992/ P-1 KG502 . . . . **CE E**
SIEGAL, A/ Upon the head of the goat: a childhood in Hungary 1939--
1944./ 1981/ 4-6/8 KE691 . . . . **CE 947.084**
SIEGELSON, KL/ Terrible, wonderful tellin' at Hog Hammock./ 1996/
4-6/6 KH711 . . . . **FIC**
SIEGEN-SMITH, N/ SONGS FOR SURVIVAL: SONGS AND CHANTS
FROM TRIBAL PEOPLES AROUND THE WORLD./ 1996/
1-6 KD596 . . . . **789.2**
SIEGL, H/ LION'S WHISKERS: AND OTHER ETHIOPIAN TALES. Rev. ed./
1997/ 3-6/7 KB337 . . . . **398.2**
SIEMENS, D/ Elephants./ 1993/ 5-6/8 KC810 . . . . **599.67**
SIERRA, FJ/ My Mexico--Mexico mio./ 1996/ K-3 KD958 . . . . . . **811**
SIERRA, J/ Children's traditional games: games from 137 countries and
cultures./ 1995/ KA331 . . . . **PROF 796**
Elephant's wrestling match./ 1992/ P-2/4 KB652 . . . . **398.24**
House that Drac built./ 1995/ 1-3/3 KG503 . . . . **E**
NURSERY TALES AROUND THE WORLD./ 1996/ P-2/7 KB354 **398.2**
Wiley and the Hairy Man./ 1996/ K-3/4 KB417 . . . . **398.21**
SIKORA, F/ Selma, Lord, Selma: girlhood memories of the civil-rights
days./ c1980, 1997/ A/7 KA906 . . . . **323.1**
SILBERG, J/ 500 five minute games: quick and easy activities for 3-6 year
olds./ 1995/ KA325 . . . . **PROF 790.1**
SILL, C/ About birds: a guide for children./ 1991/ K-2/1 KC664 . . . **598**
SILL, J/ About birds: a guide for children./ 1991/ K-2/1 KC664 . . **598**
SILLS, L/ Inspirations: stories about women artists./ 1989/
5-A/7 KD486 . . . . **759.1**
Visions: stories about women artists./ 1993/ 4-A/6 KD380 . . . . **709.2**
SILVA, S/ Gathering the sun: an alphabet in Spanish and English./ 1997/
1-3 KE122 . . . . **861**
SILVERMAN, E/ Big pumpkin./ 1992/ P-2/2 KG504 . . . . **E**
Big pumpkin (Sound recording cassette)./ 1995/ P-2/2 KG504 . . . . . **E**
Don't fidget a feather!/ 1994/ P-2/2 KG505 . . . . **E**
Don't fidget a feather! (Sound recording cassette)./ 1997/
P-2/2 KG505 . . . . **E**
Gittel's hands./ 1996/ K-2/2 KG506 . . . . **E**
SILVERMAN, J/ African roots./ 1994/ 5-A KD590 . . . . **789.2**
Blues./ 1994/ 5-A KD671 . . . . **789.43**
Children's songs./ 1993/ 5-A KD591 . . . . **789.2**
Christmas songs./ 1993/ 5-A KD536 . . . . **782.28**
Slave songs./ 1994/ 5-A KD592 . . . . **789.2**
Songs of protest and civil rights./ 1992/ 5-A KD593 . . . . **789.2**
SILVERSTEIN, A/ Dogs: all about them./ 1986/ 5-6/7 KD221 . . . **636.7**
Fungi./ 1996/ 4-8/8 KC380 . . . . **579.5**
Monerans and protists./ 1996/ A/11 KC374 . . . . **579**
Plants./ 1996/ 5-A/7 KC392 . . . . **580**
Vertebrates./ 1996/ A/9 KC581 . . . . **596**
SILVERSTEIN, RA/ Fungi./ 1996/ 4-8/8 KC380 . . . . **579.5**
Monerans and protists./ 1996/ A/11 KC374 . . . . **579**
Plants./ 1996/ 5-A/7 KC392 . . . . **580**
Vertebrates./ 1996/ A/9 KC581 . . . . **596**
SILVERSTEIN, S/ Falling up: poems and drawings./ 1996/
P-A KE024 . . . . **811**
Falling up: poems and drawings (Sound recording cassette)./ 1997/
P-A KE024 . . . . **811**
Light in the attic./ 1981/ P-A KE025 . . . . **811**
Light in the attic (Braille)./ n.d./ P-A KE025 . . . . **811**
Light in the attic (Sound recording cassette)./ n.d./ P-A KE025 . . **811**
Where the sidewalk ends: the poems and drawings of Shel Silverstein./
c1974/ P-A KE026 . . . . **811**
Where the sidewalk ends: the poems and drawings of Shel Silverstein
(Braille)./ n.d./ P-A KE026 . . . . **811**

Where the sidewalk ends: the poems and drawings of Shel Silverstein (Sound recording cassette)./ 1993/ P-A KE026 . . . . **811**
SILVERSTEIN, VB/ Dogs: all about them./ 1986/ 5-6/7 KD221 . . **636.7**
Fungi./ 1996/ 4-8/8 KC380 . . . . **579.5**
Monerans and protists./ 1996/ A/11 KC374 . . . . **579**
Plants./ 1996/ 5-A/7 KC392 . . . . **580**
Vertebrates./ 1996/ A/9 KC581 . . . . **596**
SILVERTHORNE, E/ Fiesta!: Mexico's greatest celebrations./ 1992/ 4-6/7 KB203 . . . . **394.26**
SIMMONS, A/ Ben Carson./ 1996/ 4-6/7 KE276 . . . . **B CARSON, B.**
John Lucas./ 1996/ 5-A/7 KE449 . . . . **B LUCAS, J.**
SIMMONS, CW/ Becoming myself: true stories about learning from life./ 1994/ 5-A/6 KA664 . . . . **158**
SIMMONS, T/ STORYTELLING TIME IS HERE (Sound recording cassette)./ 1992/ 2-4 KB374 . . . . **SRC 398.2**
SIMMS, L/ Moon and Otter and Frog./ 1995/ 2-4/2 KB715 . . **398.26**
SIMON, C/ One happy classroom./ 1997/ K-1/2 KG507 . . . . **E**
Seiji Ozawa: symphony conductor./ 1992/ 4-5/6 KE488 . . . . **B OZAWA, S.**
SIMON, HW/ 100 great operas and their stories. Rev. ed./ c1957, 1989/ 4-A KA454 . . . . **REF 792.5**
SIMON, N/ All kinds of families./ c1976/ 1-3/5 KA873 . . . . . **306.85**
I am not a crybaby./ 1989/ P-4/2 KA644 . . . . **155.4**
I was so mad./ 1974/ P-2/2 KA630 . . . . **152.4**
Story of Passover./ 1997/ 2-4/3 KA781 . . . . **296.4**
Wet world./ 1995/ P-1/3 KG508 . . . . **E**
SIMON, S/ Autumn across America./ 1993/ 4-6/7 KB918 . . . . . **508.2**
Big cats./ 1991/ 4-6/6 KC826 . . . . **599.75**
Brain: our nervous system./ 1997/ 5-6/6 KC980 . . . . **612.8**
Comets, meteors, and asteroids./ 1994/ 4-6/7 KC043 . . . . **523.6**
Deserts./ 1990/ 1-5/7 KC167 . . . . **551.4**
Earth words: a dictionary of the environment./ 1995/ 3-6/9 KB067 . . . . **363.73**
Earthquakes./ 1991/ 3-6/7 KC163 . . . . **551.22**
Exploring space: using Seymour Simon's astronomy books in the classroom./ 1994/ KA198 . . . . **PROF 372.3**
Heart: our circulatory system./ 1996/ 5-A/6 KC937 . . . . **612.1**
How to be an ocean scientist in your own home./ 1988/ 5-A/5 KC176 . . . . **551.46**
How to be an ocean scientist in your own home (Sound recording cassette)./ n.d./ 5-A/5 KC176 . . . . **551.46**
Icebergs and glaciers./ 1987/ 3-6/7 KC165 . . . . **551.3**
Jupiter./ 1985/ 3-6/7 KC038 . . . . **523.45**
Largest dinosaurs./ 1986/ 4-6/6 KC265 . . . . **567.9**
Mars./ 1987/ 4-A/8 KC035 . . . . **523.43**
Mercury./ 1992/ 3-6/7 KC032 . . . . **523.41**
Mirror magic./ 1991/ 3-5/6 KC114 . . . . **535**
Moon./ 1984/ K-4/4 KC021 . . . . **523.3**
Mountains./ 1994/ 4-6/7 KC168 . . . . **551.4**
Neptune./ 1991/ 4-6/8 KC041 . . . . **523.48**
Oceans./ 1990/ 3-6/7 KC177 . . . . **551.46**
Optical illusion book./ c1976, 1984/ 4-6/5 KC115 . . . . **535**
Our solar system./ 1992/ 4-8/7 KC015 . . . . **523.2**
Paper airplane book./ c1971/ 3-5/6 KD113 . . . . **629.133**
Saturn./ 1985/ 3-6/6 KC039 . . . . **523.46**
Sharks./ 1995/ 5-6/7 KC595 . . . . **597.3**
Snakes./ 1992/ 4-6/6 KC643 . . . . **597.96**
Spring across America./ 1996/ 5-8/7 KB919 . . . . **508.2**
STAR WALK./ 1995/ 4-8 KE085 . . . . **811.008**
Stars./ 1986/ 4-6/6 KC054 . . . . **523.8**
Storms./ 1989/ 2-6/7 KC205 . . . . **551.55**
Strange mysteries from around the world. Rev. ed./ 1997/ 4-6/7 KA561 . . . . **001.94**
Sun./ 1986/ P-A/7 KC046 . . . . **523.7**
Uranus./ 1987/ 4-6/6 KC040 . . . . **523.47**
Venus./ 1992/ 3-6/8 KC034 . . . . **523.42**
Volcanoes./ 1988/ 3-6/6 KC159 . . . . **551.21**
Weather./ 1993/ 3-6/7 KC193 . . . . **551.5**
Whales./ 1989/ 5-6/6 KC777 . . . . **599.51**
Wild babies./ 1997/ 3-5/6 KC459 . . . . **591.3**
Wildfires./ 1996/ 3-6/7 KB041 . . . . **363.37**
Winter across America./ 1994/ 4-6/6 KB920 . . . . **508.2**
Wolves./ 1993/ 4-6/7 KC840 . . . . **599.773**
SIMONT, M/ Ant plays Bear./ 1997/ K-1/1 KF324 . . . . **E**
Happy day./ c1945, 1949/ P-2/2 KF921 . . . . **E**
How to dig a hole to the other side of the world./ c1979, 1990/ 2-4/6 KC154 . . . . **CE 551.1**
Many moons./ 1990/ 3-5/5 KH793 . . . . **FIC**
My brother, Ant./ 1996/ K-2/1 KF327 . . . . **E**
Nate the Great./ c1972/ 1-3/2 KG484 . . . . **CE E**
Nate the Great and the crunchy Christmas./ 1996/ 2-4/2 KG485 . . **E**
Nate the Great and the pillowcase./ 1993./ 1-3/1 KG486 . . . . **E**
Nate the Great and the tardy tortoise./ 1995/ 1-3/2 KG487 . . . . . **E**
No more monsters for me!/ 1981/ K-1/1 KG215 . . . . **E**
Philharmonic gets dressed./ 1982/ K-3/5 KF939 . . . . **E**
Playing right field./ 1995/ K-2/3 KG694 . . . . **E**
Tree is nice./ c1956/ K-2/2 KG633 . . . . **E**
What happened to the dinosaurs?/ 1989/ 2-4/5 KC244 . . . . . . **567.9**
SIMS, B/ All about asthma./ 1989/ 5-6/7 KD015 . . . . **616.2**
All about Stacy./ 1988/ 1-2/2 KF614 . . . . **CE E**
Mary Marony hides out./ 1993/ 1-3/4 KH369 . . . . **FIC**
Powder puff puzzle./ 1987/ 2-3/2 KF615 . . . . **E**
Where are the stars during the day?: a book about stars./ 1993/ 1-4/2 KC048 . . . . **523.8**
SINCLAIR, J/ Mathemagic./ 1997/ 5-A KD711 . . . . **793.7**
SINGER, BR/ RISING VOICES: WRITINGS OF YOUNG NATIVE AMERICANS./ 1992/ 5-A/7 KD903 . . . . **810.8**
SINGER, D/ Structures that changed the way the world looked./ 1995/ 4-A/9 KD384 . . . . **720**
SINGER, IB/ Mazel and Shlimazel; or, The milk of a lioness./ 1967/ 4-6/6 KB779 . . . . **398.27**
Naftali the storyteller and his horse, Sus./ 1987/ 5-6/5 KH712 . . . **FIC**
Stories for children./ 1984/ 5-A/6 KH713 . . . . **FIC**
Stories for children (Sound recording cassette)./ n.d./ 5-A/6 KH713 . . . . **FIC**
SINGER, M/ All we needed to say: poems about school from Tanya and Sophie./ 1996/ 3-6 KE027 . . . . **811**
En el palacio del Rey del Oceano./ 1995/ 2-3/5 KG509 . . . . **E**
In the palace of the Ocean King./ 1995/ 2-3/5 KG509 . . . . **E**
Maiden on the moor./ 1995/ 4-6/3 KB418 . . . . **398.21**
SINNOTT, S/ Extraordinary Asian Pacific Americans./ 1993/ 5-A/8 KA859 . . . . **305.8**
Extraordinary Hispanic Americans./ 1991/ 5-A/7 KA860 . . . . . **305.8**
Extraordinary Hispanic Americans (Sound recording cassette)./ 1995/ 5-A/7 KA860 . . . . **305.8**
SIRACUSA, C/ Bingo, the best dog in the world./ 1991/ K-1/1 KG510 . . . . **E**
Mike and Tony: best friends./ 1987/ K-2/1 KG794 . . . . **E**
SIRCH, WA/ Eco-women: protectors of the earth./ 1996/ 4-6/7 KA953 . . . . **333.7**
SIRETT, D/ My first paint book./ 1994/ 3-6/7 KD436 . . . . **745.5**
SIRVAITIS, K/ Florida./ 1994/ 4-6/7 KE993 . . . . **975.9**
Michigan./ 1994/ 4-6/7 KF017 . . . . **977.4**
Utah./ 1991/ 4-6/6 KF073 . . . . **979.2**
Virginia./ 1991/ 4-6/6 KE981 . . . . **975.5**
SIS, P/ Dragons are singing tonight./ 1993/ 2-4 KE002 . . . . **811**
Ghost in the noonday sun./ 1965/ 5-A/7 KH121 . . . . **FIC**
Going up! A color counting book./ 1989/ P-2 KG511 . . . . **E**
Midnight horse./ 1990/ 5-A/4 KH125 . . . . **FIC**
Monday's troll: poems./ 1996/ K-4 KE008 . . . . **CE 811**
Scarebird./ 1987/ 1-3/5 KF552 . . . . **E**
Starry messenger: a book depicting the life of a famous scientist, mathematician, astronomer, philosopher, physicist: Galileo/ 1996/ 3-6/6 KE360 . . . . **CE B GALILEO**
Starry messenger: a book depicting the life of a famous scientist, mathematician, astronomer, philosopher, physicist Galileo Galilei (Talking book)./ 1997/ 3-6/6 KE360 . . . . **CE B GALILEO**
Stories to solve./ 1985/ 5-6/6 KB714 . . . . **398.26**
Three golden keys./ 1994/ 5-A/4 KH714 . . . . **FIC**
Waving: a counting book./ 1988/ P-2 KG512 . . . . **E**
13th floor: a ghost story./ 1995/ 5-A/6 KH127 . . . . **CE FIC**
SISULU, E/ Day Gogo went to vote: South Africa, April 1994./ 1996/ 1-3/2 KG513 . . . . **E**
SITA, L/ Indians of the Great Plains: traditions, history, legends, and life./ 1997/ 4-6/8 KE765 . . . . **970.3**
Indians of the Northeast: traditions, history, legends, and life./ 1997/ 4-6/9 KE766 . . . . **970.3**
Indians of the Southwest: traditions, history, legends, and life./ 1997/ 4-6/9 KE767 . . . . **970.3**
Worlds of belief: religion and spirituality./ 1995/ 4-A/10 KA728 . **291**
SIY, A/ Arctic National Wildlife Refuge./ 1991/ 6-A/6 KC337 . . **577.5**
Brazilian rain forest./ 1992/ 4-6/6 KC326 . . . . **577.34**
Great Astrolabe Reef./ 1992/ 4-6/7 KC352 . . . . **577.7**
SKIDMORE, S/ Poison! beware! be an ace poison spotter./ 1991/ 3-6/5 KD011 . . . . **615.9**
SKIERA-ZUCEK, L/ Save the animals, save the earth: songs about endangered animals and the earth/ 1991/ K-4 KD658 . . . **SRC 789.3**
SKINER, L/ Extraordinary American Indians./ 1992/ 5-6/7 KE747 **970.1**
SKINNER, D/ Wrecker./ 1995/ 6-A/4 KH715 . . . . **FIC**
SKOFIELD, J/ Detective Dinosaur./ 1996/ 1-3/2 KG514 . . . . **E**
SKURZYNSKI, G/ Get the message: telecommunications in your high-tech world./ 1993/ A/8 KD044 . . . . **621.38**
Here comes the mail./ 1992/ 1-4/4 KB133 . . . . **383**
Know the score: video games in your high-tech world./ 1994/ 3-6/8 KD757 . . . . **794.8**
Robots: your high-tech world./ 1990/ 5-6/8 KD141 . . . . **629.8**
Virtual war./ 1997/ 5-A/4 KH716 . . . . **FIC**
Zero gravity./ 1994/ 3-6/5 KC100 . . . . **531**

SLABY, RG/ Early violence prevention: tools for teachers of young
children./ 1995/ KA162 . . . . **PROF 303.6**
SLAM DUNK: BASKETBALL POEMS./ 1995/ 4-6 KE081 . . . . **811.008**
SLATE, J/ Miss Bindergarten gets ready for kindergarten./ 1996/
P-K/2 KG515 . . . . **E**
SLATER, T/ Stay in line./ 1996/ K-2/2 KG516 . . . . **E**
SLAUGHTER, JP/ Beyond storybooks: young children and the shared book
experience./ 1993/ KA215 . . . . **PROF 372.4**
SLAVIN, B/ Cat came back: a traditional song./ 1992/
P-2/2 KD594 . . . . **789.2**
Extra! extra!: the who, what, where, when and why of newspapers./
1994/ 3-6/5 KA596 . . . . **071**
Hockey for kids: heroes, tips, and facts./ 1996/ 4-6/7 KD844 **796.962**
Touching all the bases: baseball for kids of all ages./ c1994, 1996/
4-6/7 KD799 . . . . **796.357**
SLEATOR, W/ Duplicate./ 1990/ A/6 KH717 . . . . **FIC**
SLEPIAN, J/ Alfred Summer./ 1980/ 4-6/4 KH718 . . . . **FIC**
Alfred Summer (Sound recording cassette)./ n.d./ 4-6/4 KH718 . . . **FIC**
Lost moose./ 1995/ K-2/2 KG517 . . . . **E**
SLIER, D/ MAKE A JOYFUL SOUND: POEMS FOR CHILDREN BY
AFRICAN-AMERICAN POETS./ 1991/ 1-6 KE070 . . . . . . **811.008**
REAL MOTHER GOOSE BOOK OF AMERICAN RHYMES./ 1993/
P-2 KB811 . . . . **398.8**
SLOAT, R/ Hungry giant of the tundra./ 1993/ K-3/5 KB419 . . **398.21**
SLOAT, T/ Hungry giant of the tundra./ 1993/ K-3/5 KB419 . . **398.21**
Sody sallyratus./ 1997/ 1-3/5 KB653 . . . . **398.24**
SLOBODKIN, L/ Hundred dresses./ c1944/ 2-4/6 KH102 . . . . **FIC**
Many moons./ c1943, 1990/ 3-5/5 KH792 . . . . **FIC**
Moffats./ c1941/ 3-5/3 KH103 . . . . **FIC**
SLOBODKINA, E/ Caps for sale: a tale of a peddler, some monkeys &
their monkey business (Big book)./ 1996/ P-2/1 KG519 . . . . . **CE E**
Caps for sale: a tale of a peddler, some monkeys & their monkey business
(Kit)./ 1987/ P-2/1 KG519 . . . . **CE E**
Caps for sale: a tale of a peddler, some monkeys & their monkey business
(Videocassette)./ n.d./ P-2/1 KG519 . . . . **CE E**
Caps for sale: a tale of a peddler, some monkeys and their monkey
business./ c1947/ P-2/1 KG519 . . . . **CE E**
Caps for sale: a tale of a peddler, some monkeys and their monkey
business (Kit)./ 1995/ P-2/1 KG519 . . . . **CE E**
Venden gorras: la historia de un vendedor ambulante, unos monos y sus
travesuras./ Venden gorras: la historia de un vendedor ambulante, unos
monos y sus travesuras (Kit)./ 1995/ 1995/ P-2/1 KG519 . . . . **CE E**
P-2/1 KG519 . . . . **CE E**
SLONECKI, C/ Children's songs around the world (Compact disc)./ 1989/
K-3 KD595 . . . . **SRC 789.2**
Children's songs around the world (Sound recording cassette)./ 1989/
K-3 KD595 . . . . **SRC 789.2**
Dog ate my homework: social skills for today (Compact disc)./ 1995/
1-3 KB242 . . . . **SRC 395**
Dog ate my homework: social skills for today (Sound recording
cassette)./ 1995/ 1-3 KB242 . . . . **SRC 395**
SLOTE, A/ Finding Buck McHenry./ 1991/ 4-A/4 KH719 . . . . **FIC**
SLOVENZ-LOW, M/ Lion dancer: Ernie Wan's Chinese New Year./ 1990/
1-4/2 KB217 . . . . **394.261**
SMALL, D/ Fenwick's suit./ 1996/ K-2/2 KG520 . . . . **E**
Gardener./ 1997/ K-3/2 KG571 . . . . **E**
Hoover's bride./ 1995/ 1-3/5 KG521 . . . . **E**
Imogene's antlers./ 1985/ P-2/6 KG522 . . . . **CE E**
Imogene's antlers (Kit)./ 1994/ P-2/6 KG522 . . . . **CE E**
Library./ 1995/ K-3/3 KG572 . . . . **CE E**
Petey's bedtime story./ 1993/ 2-3/3 KF395 . . . . **E**
Ruby Mae has something to say./ 1992/ 1-3/4 KG523 . . . . **E**
SMIDT, I/ Hide and seek./ c1981, 1991/ 5-A/4 KH835 . . . . . **FIC**
SMITH, A/ Historical album of Kentucky./ 1995/ 4-6/7 KF011 . . **976.9**
Shadow of a bull./ 1964/ 5-6/6 KH875 . . . . **CE FIC**
SMITH, AG/ What time is it?/ 1992/ 4-A/8 KC073 . . . . **529**
SMITH, BC/ Women win the vote./ 1989/ 5-A/5 KA911 . . . . **324.6**
SMITH, C/ Historical album of New York./ 1993/ 5-6/8 KE954 . **974.7**
SMITH, CB/ General Butterfingers./ c1986, 1993/ 4-6/6 KH152 . . . **FIC**
Latchkey dog./ 1994/ 3-5/4 KG855 . . . . **FIC**
Matthew the cowboy./ 1990/ K-2/2 KF767 . . . . **E**
No more nice./ 1996/ 4-6/6 KH437 . . . . **FIC**
No more nice./ 1996/ 3-5/6 KH438 . . . . **FIC**
Not-so-normal Norman./ 1995/ 2-5/3 KH770 . . . . **FIC**
Partners./ 1995/ 2-4/4 KH836 . . . . **FIC**
SMITH, D/ Holidays and festivals activities./ 1994/
1-6/6 KD458 . . . . **745.594**
SMITH, DB/ Best girl./ 1993/ 5-A/6 KH720 . . . . **FIC**
Return to Bitter Creek./ 1988/ 5-A/5 KH721 . . . . **FIC**
Taste of blackberries./ c1973/ 4-6/4 KH722 . . . . **FIC**
SMITH, EB/ Farm book./ c1910, 1982/ 2-4/6 KH723 . . . . . **FIC**
Seashore book./ 1985/ 3-6/9 KH724 . . . . **FIC**
SMITH, HM/ CORETTA SCOTT KING AWARDS BOOK: FROM VISION
TO REALITY./ 1994/ KA008 . . . . **PROF 011.008**

SMITH, J/ Peachboy (Videocassette)./ 1991/ 2-5 KB469 . . **VCR 398.22**
SMITH, JA/ How do you spell God?: answers to the big questions from
around the world./ 1995/ 5-A/4 KA724 . . . . **291**
SMITH, JH/ Most rugged all-terrain vehicles./ 1995/
5-6/6 KD830 . . . . **796.7**
SMITH, JL/ Kid next door and other headaches./ 1984/
2-4/4 KH725 . . . . **FIC**
Kid next door and other headaches (Braille)./ n.d./ 2-4/4 KH725 . . . **FIC**
Monster in the third dresser drawer and other stories about Adam
Joshua./ 1981/ 2-4/4 KH725 . . . . **FIC**
Monster in the third dresser drawer and other stories about Adam Joshua
(Braille)./ n.d./ 2-4/4 KH725 . . . . **FIC**
Monster in the third dresser drawer and other stories about Adam Joshua
(Sound recording cassette)./ n.d./ 2-4/4 KH725 . . . . **FIC**
Serious science: an Adam Joshua story./ 1993/ 2-4/4 KH725 . . . . **FIC**
Show and tell war./ c1988/ 2-4/4 KH725 . . . . **FIC**
Show and tell war (Sound recording cassette)./ n.d./
2-4/4 KH725 . . . . **FIC**
Turkey's side of it: Adam Joshua's Thanksgiving./ 1990/
2-4/4 KH725 . . . . **FIC**
SMITH, JW/ Child's garden of verses./ 1905/ P-2 KE110 . . . . . . **821**
Heidi./ 1996/ 5-A/6 KH746 . . . . **FIC**
Twas the night before Christmas: a visit from St. Nicholas./ c1912, 1992/
P-A KD988 . . . . **811**
SMITH, JY/ State names, seals, flags, and symbols: a historical guide. Rev.
and expanded ed./ 1994/ 4-A KA493 . . . . **REF 973**
SMITH, KS/ Historical album of Kentucky./ 1995/ 4-6/7 KF011 . . **976.9**
SMITH, L/ Glasses: who needs 'em?./ 1991/ 2-3/3 KG524 . . . . . . **E**
Halloween A B C./ 1987/ P-A KD982 . . . . **811**
Knights of the kitchen table./ 1991/ 3-6/3 KH685 . . . . **FIC**
Math curse./ 1995/ 2-5/3 KG420 . . . . **E**
Stinky Cheese Man and other fairly stupid tales./ 1992/
4-6/4 KH686 . . . . **FIC**
True story of the 3 little pigs./ 1989/ K-3/2 KG421 . . . . **CE E**
Unreluctant years: a critical approach to children's literature./ c1953,
1991/ KA357 . . . . **PROF 809**
SMITH, M/ Let's get a pet./ c1993, 1996/ K-3/2 KD193 . . . . **636.088**
Mary Poppins (Talking book)./ n.d./ 4-6 KH801 . . . . **TB FIC**
SMITH, NA/ ARABIAN NIGHTS: THEIR BEST-KNOWN TALES./ c1909,
1994/ 5-A/9 KB255 . . . . **398.2**
SMITH, P/ JAPANESE FAIRY TALES./ 1992/ 2-4/7 KB322 . . . **398.2**
Superstars of women's figure skating./ 1997/ 4-6/7 KD836 . . **796.91**
SMITH, PC/ As long as the rivers flow: the stories of nine Native
Americans./ 1996/ 6-A/9 KE746 . . . . **970.1**
SMITH, R/ Stories Huey tells./ 1995/ 2-4/2 KG969 . . . . **FIC**
SMITH, RK/ Bobby baseball./ 1991/ 3-6/4 KH726 . . . . **FIC**
SMITH, RM/ Celebrate the world: twenty tellable folktales for multicultural
festivals./ 1994/ KA270 . . . . **PROF 398.2**
SMITH, SG/ EXPLORING THE MOUNTAIN STATES THROUGH
LITERATURE./ 1994/ KA040 . . . . **PROF 016.978**
SMITH, W/ Greatest show off earth./ 1994/ 4-A/7 KH450 . . . **CE FIC**
SMITHSONIAN INSTITUTION/ BLUE PLANET (Videocassette)./ 1993/
5-A KB058 . . . . **VCR 363.73**
MINDS-ON SCIENCE: FOR PROFIT, FOR PLANET (Videodisc)./ 1995/
5-A KD348 . . . . **VD 687**
MINDS-ON SCIENCE: FOR THE SAKE OF THE NATION (Videodisc)./
1995/ 5-A KA804 . . . . **VD 303.48**
MINDS-ON SCIENCE: THE IMPACT OF DISCOVERY (Videodisc)./
1995/ 5-A KB875 . . . . **VD 502**
RESOURCES FOR TEACHING ELEMENTARY SCHOOL SCIENCE./
1996/ KA203 . . . . **PROF 372.3**
SMITHSONIAN BOOK OF THE FIRST LADIES: THEIR LIVES, TIMES,
AND ISSUES./ 1996/ 6-A/9 KE866 . . . . **973**
SMOLINSKI, J/ Holiday origami./ 1995/ 3-6 KD403 . . . . **736**
SMOOTHEY, M/ Calculators./ 1995/ 4-8/9 KB932 . . . . **510**
Graphs./ 1995/ A/7 KB941 . . . . **511**
SNEDDEN, R/ What is a bird?/ 1993/ 4-6/6 KC665 . . . . **598**
What is an insect?/ 1993/ 4-6/6 KC548 . . . . **595.7**
Yuck!: a big book of little horrors./ 1996/ 3-8/7 KC375 . . . . . **579**
SNEED, B/ Smoky Mountain Rose: an Appalachian Cinderella./ 1997/
2-3/4 KB367 . . . . **398.2**
Unbeatable bread./ 1996/ K-2/3 KF769 . . . . **E**
SNEVE, V/ Apaches./ 1997/ 4-6/5 KE768 . . . . **970.3**
Cherokees./ 1996/ 4-6/5 KE769 . . . . **970.3**
Cheyennes./ 1996/ 4-6/6 KE770 . . . . **970.3**
Hopis./ 1995/ 4-6/7 KE771 . . . . **970.3**
Iroquois./ 1995/ 4-6/5 KE772 . . . . **970.3**
Navajos./ 1993/ 4-6/6 KE773 . . . . **970.3**
Nez Perce./ 1994/ 4-6/7 KE774 . . . . **970.3**
Seminoles./ 1994/ 4-6/7 KE775 . . . . **970.3**
Sioux./ 1993/ 4-6/5 KE776 . . . . **970.3**
SNODGRASS, ME/ BLACK HISTORY MONTH RESOURCE BOOK./
1993/ KA370 . . . . **PROF 973**
Indian terms of the Americas./ 1994/ 5-A KA478 . . . . . . **REF 970.004**

SNOW, A/ How dogs really work!/ 1993/ 4-A/5 KH727 . . . . **FIC**
Truth about cats./ 1996/ 4-A/7 KH728 . . . . **FIC**
SNOW, K/ Subject index for children & young people to Canadian poetry in English. 2nd ed./ 1986/ A KA375 . . . . **REF 016.811**
SNOW TOWARD EVENING: A YEAR IN A RIVER VALLEY: NATURE POEMS./ 1995/ 2-6 KE082 . . . . **811.008**
SNUFFLES AND SNOUTS: POEMS./ 1995/ P-2 KE083 . . . **811.008**
SNYDER, D/ Boy of the three-year nap./ 1988/ K-3/6 KG525 . . . . **E**
Siesta de tres anos./ 1995/ K-3/6 KG525 . . . . **E**
SNYDER, J/ Robin at Hickory Street./ 1995/ K-2/3 KG314 . . . . . **CE E**
SNYDER, ZK/ Black and blue magic./ c1966, 1994/ 4-6/7 KH729 . **FIC**
Blair's nightmare (Sound recording cassette)./ n.d./
   4-6/7 KH733 . . . . **CE FIC**
Cat running./ 1994/ 5-A/7 KH730 . . . . **FIC**
Egypt game./ c1967/ 5-6/6 KH731 . . . . **FIC**
Egypt game (Braille)./ n.d./ 5-6/6 KH731 . . . . **FIC**
Egypt game (Sound recording cassette)./ 1995/ 5-6/6 KH731 . . . **FIC**
Famous Stanley kidnapping case./ 1985/ 4-6/7 KH733 . . . . . **CE FIC**
Fool's gold./ 1993/ 6-A/7 KH732 . . . . **FIC**
Fool's gold (Sound recording cassette)./ 1995/ 6-A/7 KH732 . . . **FIC**
Headless cupid./ c1971/ 4-6/7 KH733 . . . . **CE FIC**
Headless cupid (Braille)./ n.d./ 4-6/7 KH733 . . . . **CE FIC**
Headless cupid (Sound recording cassette)./ n.d./
   4-6/7 KH733 . . . . **CE FIC**
Headless cupid (Talking book)./ n.d./ 4-6/7 KH733 . . . . . . **CE FIC**
Trespassers./ 1995/ 5-A/6 KH734 . . . . **FIC**
Witches of Worm./ c1965/ 4-6/7 KH735 . . . . **FIC**
SO, M/ Wishbones: a folk tale from China./ 1993/ 2-3/6 KB383 **398.2**
SOBOL, DJ/ Encyclopedia Brown and the case of Pablo's nose./ 1996/
   3-5/6 KH736 . . . . **FIC**
Encyclopedia Brown and the case of the dead eagles./ 1975/
   3-5/6 KH737 . . . . **FIC**
Encyclopedia Brown and the case of the dead eagles (Braille)./ n.d./
   3-5/6 KH737 . . . . **FIC**
Encyclopedia Brown and the case of the dead eagles (Sound recording
   cassette)./ n.d./ 3-5/6 KH737 . . . . **FIC**
Encyclopedia Brown and the case of the midnight visitor./ 1977/
   3-5/6 KH737 . . . . **FIC**
Encyclopedia Brown and the case of the midnight visitor (Sound recording
   cassette)./ n.d./ 3-5/6 KH737 . . . . **FIC**
Encyclopedia Brown and the case of the mysterious handprints./ 1985/
   3-5/6 KH737 . . . . **FIC**
Encyclopedia Brown and the case of the secret pitch./ 1965/
   3-5/6 KH737 . . . . **FIC**
Encyclopedia Brown and the case of the treasure hunt./ 1988/
   3-5/6 KH737 . . . . **FIC**
Encyclopedia Brown, boy detective./ 1963/ 3-5/6 KH737 . . . . . . **FIC**
Encyclopedia Brown: boy detective (Sound recording cassette)./ n.d./
   3-5/6 KH737 . . . . **FIC**
Encyclopedia Brown finds the clues./ 1966/ 3-5/6 KH737 . . . . . **FIC**
Encyclopedia Brown gets his man./ 1967/ 3-5/6 KH737 . . . . . . **FIC**
Encyclopedia Brown gets his man (Braille)./ n.d./ 3-5/6 KH737 . . . **FIC**
Encyclopedia Brown gets his man (Sound recording cassette)./ n.d./
   3-5/6 KH737 . . . . **FIC**
Encyclopedia Brown keeps the peace./ 1969/ 3-5/6 KH737 . . . . . **FIC**
Encyclopedia Brown keeps the peace (Braille)./ n.d./ 3-5/6 KH737 . **FIC**
Encyclopedia Brown lends a hand./ 1974/ 3-5/6 KH737 . . . . . . **FIC**
Encyclopedia Brown lends a hand (Braille)./ n.d./ 3-5/6 KH737 . . . **FIC**
Encyclopedia Brown lends a hand (Sound recording cassette)./ n.d./
   3-5/6 KH737 . . . . **FIC**
Encyclopedia Brown saves the day./ 1972/ 3-5/6 KH737 . . . . . . **FIC**
Encyclopedia Brown sets the pace./ 1982/ 3-5/6 KH737 . . . . . . **FIC**
Encyclopedia Brown shows the way (Sound recording cassette)./ n.d./
   3-5/6 KH737 . . . . **FIC**
Encyclopedia Brown solves them all./ 1968/ 3-5/6 KH737 . . . . . **FIC**
Encyclopedia Brown solves them all (Braille)./ n.d./ 3-5/6 KH737 . . **FIC**
Encyclopedia Brown solves them all (Sound recording cassette)./ n.d./
   3-5/6 KH737 . . . . **FIC**
Encyclopedia Brown takes the case./ 1973/ 3-5/6 KH737 . . . . . . **FIC**
Encyclopedia Brown takes the case (Braille)./ n.d./ 3-5/6 KH737 . . **FIC**
Encyclopedia Brown tracks them down./ 1971/ 3-5/6 KH737 . . . . **FIC**
SOENTPIET, CK/ Around town./ 1994/ K-2/3 KA898 . . . . . **307.76**
Last dragon./ 1995/ 2-3/3 KG183 . . . . **E**
More than anything else./ 1995/ 1-3/3 KF256 . . . . **E**
Silver packages: an Appalachian Christmas story./ 1997/
   1-3/2 KG386 . . . . **E**
SOFILAS, M/ Burnt stick./ 1995/ 4-A/7 KH259 . . . . **FIC**
SOGABE, A/ Cinnamon, mint, and mothballs: a visit to Grandmother's
   house./ 1993/ K-3 KE033 . . . . **811**
SOLGA, K/ Draw!/ 1991/ 2-6/4 KD405 . . . . **741.2**
Make cards!/ 1992/ 1-5/5 KD459 . . . . **745.594**
Make prints!/ 1991/ 2-6/4 KD504 . . . . **760**
Paint!/ 1991/ 2-6/4 KD370 . . . . **702.8**
SOLOMON, D/ How come?./ 1993/ 4-8/6 KB874 . . . . **500**

SOMAN, D/ Mommy's office./ 1992/ P-2/2 KF688 . . . . **E**
One of three./ 1991/ P-1/2 KF832 . . . . **E**
Somebody's new pajamas./ 1996/ 3-5/4 KH318 . . . . **FIC**
When I am old with you./ 1990/ P-2/6 KF834 . . . . **E**
SOMETHING RICH AND STRANGE: A TREASURY OF SHAKESPEARE'S
   VERSE./ 1995/ 6-A KE118 . . . . **822.3**
SONGS ARE THOUGHTS: POEMS OF THE INUIT./ 1995/
   4-6 KE140 . . . . **897**
SONGS FOR SURVIVAL: SONGS AND CHANTS FROM TRIBAL PEOPLES
   AROUND THE WORLD./ 1996/ 1-6 KD596 . . . . **789.2**
SONNEBORN, L/ Clara Barton./ 1992/ 4-6/6 KE250 . . **B BARTON, C.**
SOREL, E/ Jack and the beanstalk (Videocassette)./ 1991/
   K-2 KB349 . . . . **VCR 398.2**
SORENSEN, H/ Fourth of July on the plains./ 1997/ 2-5/2 KG647 . . **E**
Gift of the tree./ c1972, 1992/ K-4/6 KC312 . . . . **577.3**
New Hope./ 1995/ 1-4/4 KG526 . . . . **E**
Poetry for young people./ 1994/ 4-A KD940 . . . . **811**
SORENSEN, SO/ Man who kept house./ 1992/ 2-4/6 KB719 . . **398.27**
SOSA, M/ SCIENCE BOOKS AND FILMS' BEST BOOKS FOR CHILDREN,
   1992-1995./ 1996/ KA028 . . . . **PROF 016.5**
SOTO, G/ Baseball in April and other stories./ 1990/ 6-A/6 KH738 **FIC**
Beisbol en Abril y otras historias./ 1995/ 6-A/6 KH738 . . . . . . **FIC**
Boys at work./ 1995/ 4-6/5 KH739 . . . . **FIC**
Canto familiar./ 1995/ 4-6 KE028 . . . . **811**
Chato y su cena./ 1995,/ 1-3/5 KG527 . . . . **E**
Chato's kitchen./ c1995, 1997/ 1-3/5 KG527 . . . . **E**
Chato's kitchen (Sound recording cassette)./ 1997,/ 1-3/5 KG527 . **E**
Life around the lake./ 1996/ 2-6/8 KE837 . . . . **972**
Local news./ 1993/ 6-A/6 KH740 . . . . **FIC**
Neighborhood odes: poems./ 1992/ 3-A KE029 . . . . **811**
Old man and his door./ 1996/ K-2/2 KG528 . . . . **E**
Pool party./ c1993, 1995/ 4-6/5 KH741 . . . . **FIC**
Snapshots from the wedding./ 1997/ K-2/2 KG529 . . . . **E**
Too many tamales./ 1993/ K-3/3 KG530 . . . . **E**
SOTZEK, H/ Koala is not a bear!/ 1997/ 3-5/3 KC738 . . . . . **599.2**
SOUCIE, G/ What's the difference between apes and monkeys and other
   living things?/ 1995/ 4-6/7 KC271 . . . . **571**
What's the difference between lenses and prisms and other scientific
   things?/ 1995/ 4-6/7 KB872 . . . . **500**
SOUHAMI, J/ Leopard's drum: an Asante tale from West Africa./ 1995/
   P-1/2 KB654 . . . . **398.24**
SOUL LOOKS BACK IN WONDER./ 1993/ 4-A KE084 . . . . . **811.008**
SOUZA, DM/ Catch me if you can./ 1992/ 4-6/6 KC631 . . . . **597.95**
Hurricanes./ 1996/ 4-6/7 KC206 . . . . **551.55**
Northern lights./ 1994/ 6-A/7 KC138 . . . . **538**
Powerful waves./ 1992/ 3-6/5 KC180 . . . . **551.47**
SOWLER, S/ Amazing armored animals./ 1992/ 4-6/6 KC467 . . **591.47**
Asombrosos animales acorazados./ 1995/ 4-6/6 KC467 . . . . **591.47**
SPAGNOLI, C/ Judge Rabbit and the tree spirit: a folktale from
   Cambodia./ 1991/ 3-4/4 KB655 . . . . **398.24**
Nine-in-one, grr! grr! a folktale from the Hmong people of Laos./ 1989/
   P-3/4 KB677 . . . . **398.24**
SPANFELLER, J/ Where the lilies bloom./ c1969/ 5-6/6 KH009 . . . . **FIC**
SPATT, LE/ Behind the scenes at the ballet: rehearsing and performing
   "The Sleeping Beauty"/ 1995/ 4-6/9 KD697 . . . . **792.8**
SPEARE, EG/ Witch of Blackbird Pond./ c1958/ 5-6/5 KH742 . **CE FIC**
Witch of Blackbird Pond (Braille)./ n.d./ 5-6/5 KH742 . . . . . **CE FIC**
Witch of Blackbird Pond (Sound recording cassette)./ n.d./
   5-6/5 KH742 . . . . **CE FIC**
Witch of Blackbird Pond (Talking book)./ n.d./ 5-6/5 KH742 . **CE FIC**
SPEDDEN, DCS/ Polar, the Titanic bear./ 1994/ 4-6/7 KE158 . **910.4**
SPEIDEL, S/ Coyote and the magic words./ 1993/ P-2/2 KG351 . . . . **E**
Evan's corner./ c1967, 1991/ K-2/2 KF727 . . . . **E**
WIND IN THE LONG GRASS: A COLLECTION OF HAIKU./ 1991/
   2-5 KD892 . . . . **808.81**
SPEIRS, J/ GIVE A DOG A BONE: STORIES, POEMS, JOKES, AND
   RIDDLES ABOUT DOGS./ 1996/ K-4 KD874 . . . . **808.8**
SPELLENBERG, R/ Audubon Society field guide to North American
   wildflowers, Western Region./ 1979/ 3-6 KC408 . . . . **582.13**
SPENCE, J/ Steven Jobs and Stephen Wozniak: creating the Apple
   computer./ 1994/ 4-6/9 KD046 . . . . **621.39**
SPENCELEY, A/ TREASURY OF ANIMAL STORIES./ 1992/
   3-6/6 KH802 . . . . **FIC**
TREASURY OF GIANT AND MONSTER STORIES./ 1992/
   3-5/6 KH803 . . . . **FIC**
TREASURY OF SPOOKY STORIES./ 1992/ 4-A/6 KH804 . . . . . . **FIC**
SPERRY, A/ Call it courage./ c1940/ 5-6/6 KH743 . . . . **CE FIC**
Call it courage (Talking book)./ n.d./ 5-6/6 KH743 . . . . **CE FIC**
Esto es coraje./ n.d./ 5-6/6 KH743 . . . . **CE FIC**
SPIER, P/ Dreams./ 1986/ P-2 KG531 . . . . **E**
NOAH'S ARK./ c1977/ P-2 KA681 . . . . **221.9**
NOAH'S ARK (Videocassette)./ c1989, 1996/ P-2 KA682 . **VCR 221.9**
Peter Spier's circus!/ 1992/ P-2/4 KG532 . . . . **E**
SPIES, KB/ Earthquakes./ 1994/ 4-6/7 KB038 . . . . **363.34**

SPILLMAN, CV/ Integrating language arts through literature in elementary classrooms./ 1996/ KA229 .... **PROF 372.6**
SPINELLI, J/ Crash./ 1996/ 5-A/3 KH744 .... **FIC**
SPIRN, M/ Know-Nothing birthday./ 1997/ 1-2/1 KG533 ...... **E**
SPIRT, DL/ Administering the school library media center. 3rd ed./ 1992/ KA077 .... **PROF 027.8**
SPIVAK, D/ Grass sandals: the travels of Basho./ 1997/ 1-4/5 KE136 .... **895.6**
SPOHN, K/ Dog and Cat shake a leg./ 1996/ K-2/1 KG534 ...... **E**
SPOOKY STORIES FOR A DARK AND STORMY NIGHT./ 1994/ 2-4/4 KB695 .... **398.25**
SPOOKY STORIES OF THE SUPERNATURAL./ 1985/ 6-A KH745 .. **FIC**
SPORN, M/ TALKING EGGS (Videocassette)./ 1993/ 2-5 KB420 .... **VCR 398.21**
SPRING: A HAIKU STORY./ 1996/ 1-6 KE137 .... **895.6**
SPRINGER, H/ First look at animals with horns./ 1989/ 1-3/2 KC792 .... **599.64**
First look at ducks, geese, and swans./ 1990/ 1-3/2 KC683 ... **598.4**
SPRINGETT, M/ Wise old woman./ 1994/ 2-4/5 KB492 .... **398.22**
SPURLL, B/ Emma's eggs./ 1996/ P-2/2 KG364 .... **E**
Flying tortoise: an Igbo tale./ 1994/ 2-3/3 KB623 .... **398.24**
Rhinos for lunch and elephants for supper!: a Masai tale./ 1991/ P-3/4 KB625 .... **398.24**
SPYRI, J/ Heidi./ 1996/ 5-A/6 KH746 .... **FIC**
SQUIRE, A/ Understanding man's best friend: why dogs look and act the way they do./ 1991/ 5-6/7 KD222 .... **636.7**
101 questions and answers about pets and people./ 1988/ 5-6/7 KD192 .... **636.088**
ST. GEORGE, J/ Crazy Horse./ 1994/ A/9 KE308 .. **B CRAZY HORSE**
To see with the heart: the life of Sitting Bull./ 1996/ 5-A/6 KE542 .... **B SITTING BULL**
ST. PIERRE, S/ Our national anthem./ 1992/ 4-A/6 KD598 ...... **789.2**
STAERMOSE, R/ Tingleberries, tuckertubs and telephones: a tale of love and ice-cream./ 1996/ 3-6/5 KH454 .... **FIC**
STAFFORD, P/ Your two brains./ 1986/ 5-6/8 KC981 .... **612.8**
STAHL, B/ Pocket full of seeds./ c1973, 1994/ 4-A/5 KH668 ...... **FIC**
STALLCUP, R/ Birding./ c1994, 1995/ 5-6/8 KA448 .... **REF 598**
STALLINGS, D/ Of bugs and beasts: fact, folklore, and activities./ 1995/ KA296 .... **PROF 591**
STAMMEN, JEM/ Wild fox: a true story./ 1993/ 4-5/5 KC843 .... **599.775**
STANDIFORD, N/ Astronauts are sleeping./ 1996/ K-2/3 KG535 ... **E**
Bravest dog ever: the true story of Balto./ 1989/ 1-3/2 KD223 . **636.7**
STANEK, LW/ Whole language: literature, learning, and literacy: a workshop in print./ 1993/ KA230 .... **PROF 372.6**
STANEK, M/ All alone after school./ 1985/ 2-3/2 KG536 .... **E**
I speak English for my mom./ 1989/ 2-4/2 KH747 .... **FIC**
We came from Vietnam./ 1985/ 4-6/7 KA861 .... **305.8**
STANGL, J/ Recycling activities for the primary grades./ 1993/ KA313 .... **PROF 745.5**
STANLEY, D/ Bard of Avon: the story of William Shakespeare./ 1992/ 4-6/7 KE538 .... **B SHAKESPEARE**
Charles Dickens: the man who had great expectations./ 1993/ 5-6/7 KE321 .... **B DICKENS, C.**
Cleopatra./ c1974/ 4-6/6 KE295 .... **B CLEOPATRA**
Good Queen Bess: the story of Elizabeth I of England./ 1990/ 6-A/7 KE337 .... **B ELIZABETH I**
Good Queen Bess: the story of Elizabeth I of England (Sound recording cassette)./ 1993/ 6-A/7 KE337 .... **B ELIZABETH I**
Last princess: the story of Princess Kaiulani of Hawaii./ 1991/ 5-6/7 KE413 .... **B KAIULANI**
Leonardo da Vinci./ 1996/ 5-A/8 KE435 .... **B LEONARDO**
Petrosinella: a Neapolitan Rapunzel./ 1995/ 2-4/6 KB780 ... **398.27**
Rumpelstiltskin's daughter./ 1997/ 2-5/3 KG537 .... **E**
Saving Sweetness./ 1996/ 1-3/4 KG538 .... **E**
Shaka, king of the Zulus./ 1988/ 4-6/6 KE537 .... **B SHAKA, KING**
True adventure of Daniel Hall./ 1995/ 5-6/7 KE159 .... **910.4**
STANLEY, F/ Last princess: the story of Princess Kaiulani of Hawaii./ 1991/ 5-6/7 KE413 .... **B KAIULANI**
STANLEY, J/ Children of the Dust Bowl: the true story of the school at Weedpatch Camp./ 1992/ 5-A/7 KA835 .... **305.5**
I am an American: a true story of Japanese internment./ 1994/ 5-A/8 KE666 .... **940.53**
STANLEY, L/ Be a friend: the story of African American music in song, words and pictures./ 1994/ K-3 KD670 .... **BA 789.4**
STAPLES, SF/ Shabanu, daughter of the wind./ 1989/ 6-A/6 KH748 .... **FIC**
STAUB, FJ/ America's prairies./ 1994/ 4-6/7 KC332 .... **577.4**
Children of Cuba./ 1996/ 4-6/8 KE846 .... **972.91**
Children of the Sierra Madre./ 1996/ 4-6/8 KE839 .... **972**
Children of Yucatan./ 1996/ 4-6/7 KE840 .... **972**
Mountain goats./ 1994/ 3-5/2 KC793 .... **599.64**
Yellowstone's cycle of fire./ 1993/ 4-6/8 KC306 .... **577.2**
STAUB, L/ Whoever you are./ 1997/ P-1/1 KA843 .... **305.8**

STEARNS, PH/ Graph Club with Fizz and Martina (Microcomputer program)./ 1993/ K-4 KB942 .... **MCP 511**
STEDMAN, N/ Common cold and influenza./ 1986/ A/10 KD016 .... **616.2**
STEELE, P/ Boats./ 1991/ 4-6/6 KD065 .... **623.8**
Castles./ 1995/ 4-6/7 KE650 .... **940.1**
Insects./ 1991/ 4-6/6 KC549 .... **595.7**
Pirates./ 1997/ 3-6/7 KE160 .... **910.4**
Planes./ 1991/ 4-6/6 KD100 .... **629.13**
Rain: causes and effects./ 1991/ 3-6/7 KC215 .... **551.57**
Snow: causes and effects./ 1991/ 3-6/7 KC216 .... **551.57**
STEELE, RG/ Dad and me in the morning./ 1994/ 1-3/2 KF942 ... **E**
STEFFENS, B/ Loch Ness Monster./ 1995/ 3-6/9 KA563 .... **001.944**
STEFOFF, R/ Al Gore, vice president./ 1994/ 4-5/6 KE374 .... **B GORE, A.**
Children of the westward trail./ 1996/ 4-6/8 KF050 .... **978**
Lewis and Clark./ 1992/ 5-6/5 KE206 .... **917.804**
Scientific explorers: travels in search of knowledge./ 1992/ 6-A/9 KB925 .... **509**
STEGER, W/ Over the top of the world: explorer Will Steger's trek across the Arctic./ 1997/ 5-6/6 KE219 .... **919.8**
STEIG, J/ Consider the lemming./ 1988/ K-6 KE030 .... **811**
Consider the lemming (Sound recording cassette)./ n.d./ K-6 KE030 .... **811**
STEIG, W/ Abel's island./ 1976/ 4-6/6 KH749 .... **CE FIC**
Abel's island (Sound recording cassette)./ n.d./ 4-6/6 KH749 . **CE FIC**
Abel's island (Videocassette)./ 1988/ 4-6/6 KH749 .... **CE FIC**
Amazing bone./ 1976/ 1-3/5 KG539 .... **CE E**
Amazing bone (Kit)./ c1986/ 1-3/5 KG539 .... **CE E**
Amazing bone (Sound recording cassette)./ n.d./ 1-3/5 KG539 .. **CE E**
Amazing bone (Videocassette)./ 1986/ 1-3/5 KG539 .... **CE E**
Amos and Boris./ c1971/ 1-3/7 KG540 .... **CE E**
Brave Irene./ 1986/ K-3/3 KG541 .... **CE E**
Brave Irene (Sound recording cassette)./ n.d./ K-3/3 KG541 .... **CE E**
Brave Irene (Videocassette)./ 1990/ K-3/3 KG541 .... **CE E**
Consider the lemming./ 1988/ K-6 KE030 .... **811**
Doctor De Soto./ 1982/ P-3/4 KG542 .... **CE E**
Doctor De Soto (Braille)./ n.d./ P-3/4 KG542 .... **CE E**
Doctor De Soto goes to Africa./ 1992/ P-3/4 KG542 ...... **CE E**
Doctor De Soto goes to Africa (Kit)./ 1995/ P-3/4 KG542 ..... **CE E**
Doctor De Soto goes to Africa (Sound recording cassette)./ 1995/ P-3/4 KG542 .... **CE E**
Doctor De Soto (Kit)./ 1993/ P-3/4 KG542 .... **CE E**
Doctor De Soto (Spanish version)./ 1991/ P-3/4 KG542 ..... **CE E**
Doctor De Soto (Spanish version) (Videocassette)./ 1993/ P-3/4 KG542 .... **CE E**
Doctor De Soto (Talking book)./ 1993/ P-3/4 KG542 ...... **CE E**
Doctor De Soto (Videocassette)./ 1986/ P-3/4 KG542 ...... **CE E**
Dominic./ c1972/ 4-6/7 KH750 .... **FIC**
Dominico./ 1994/ 4-6/7 KH750 .... **FIC**
Farmer Palmer's wagon ride./ c1974, 1992/ K-3/6 KG543 ...... **E**
Hueso prodigioso./ 1993/ 1-3/5 KG539 .... **CE E**
Irene, la valiente./ 1991/ K-3/3 KG541 .... **CE E**
Isla de Abel./ 1992/ 4-6/6 KH749 .... **CE FIC**
Real thief./ c1973/ 4-6/6 KH751 .... **FIC**
Silvestre y la piedrecita magica./ 1990/ K-2/6 KG544 ...... **CE E**
Silvestre y la piedrecita magica (Kit)./ 1992/ K-2/6 KG544 .... **CE E**
Spinky sulks./ 1988/ 1-A/5 KH752 .... **FIC**
Sylvester and the magic pebble./ c1969, 1988/ K-2/6 KG544 .. **CE E**
Sylvester and the magic pebble (Videocassette)./ 1992/ K-2 KG545 .... **VCR E**
Toby, where are you?/ 1997/ P-1/2 KG546 .... **E**
Toy brother./ 1996/ 2-5/6 KG547 .... **E**
William Steig library (Videocassette)./ 1995/ 1-3 KG548 ..... **VCR E**
Zeke Pippin./ 1994/ 1-3/6 KG549 .... **E**
STEIN, RC/ Assassination of John F. Kennedy./ 1992/ 5-6/7 KE921 .... **973.922**
Declaration of Independence./ 1995/ 5-A/7 KE887 .... **973.3**
Great Depression. Rev. ed./ 1993/ 4-6/7 KE918 .... **973.917**
London./ 1996/ 3-5/8 KE682 .... **942.1**
Montgomery bus boycott. Rev. ed./ 1993/ 5-6/6 KE998 ..... **976.1**
Paris./ 1996/ 3-5/8 KE685 .... **944**
United Nations. Rev. ed./ 1994/ 4-6/7 KA969 .... **341.23**
United States of America./ 1994/ 4-A/9 KE867 .... **973**
STEIN, S/ Oh, baby!/ 1993/ P-K/3 KA827 .... **305.232**
Science book./ 1979/ 2-A/5 KB873 .... **500**
STEINS, R/ Our elections./ 1994/ 5-6/7 KA912 .... **324.6**
Our national capital./ 1994/ 4-6/9 KE973 .... **975.3**
STEIRNAGLE, M/ Billy Lazroe and the King of the Sea: a tale of the Northwest./ 1996/ 4-5/5 KB460 .... **398.22**
STEMPLE, A/ JANE YOLEN'S MOTHER GOOSE SONGBOOK./ 1992/ KA277 .... **PROF 398.8**
STEPHENS, R/ Mary Poppins (Talking book)./ n.d./ 4-6 KH801 . **TB FIC**
STEPTOE, J/ All the colors of the race./ 1982/ 4-6 KD907 ...... **811**

Baby says./ 1988/ P-K KG551 . . . . E
Mufaro's beautiful daughters: an African tale./ 1987/
K-3/5 KG552 . . . . **CE E**
Mufaro's beautiful daughters: an African tale (Videocassette)./ 1988/
K-3/5 KG552 . . . . **CE E**
Stevie./ c1969/ K-3/3 KG553 . . . . E
Stevie (Spanish version)./ 1996/ K-3/3 KG553 . . . . E
Stevie (Talking book)./ n.d./ K-3/3 KG553 . . . . E
Story of Jumping Mouse: a Native American legend./ 1984/
4-5/5 KB656 . . . . **CE 398.24**
Story of Jumping Mouse: a native American legend (Sound recording
cassette)./ n.d./ 4-5/5 KB656 . . . . **CE 398.24**
STERMAN, B/ Backyard dragon./ 1993/ 4-6/6 KH753 . . . . . . **FIC**
STERMAN, S/ Backyard dragon./ 1993/ 4-6/6 KH753 . . . . . . **FIC**
STERN, JM/ Putting on the brakes: young people's guide to understanding
attention./ 1991/ 5-6/7 KD041 . . . . **618.92**
STEVENS, B/ Frank Thompson: her Civil War story./ 1992/
6-A/7 KE332 . . . . **B EDMONDS, S.**
STEVENS, BS/ Colonial American craftspeople./ 1993/
5-6/8 KD339 . . . . **680**
STEVENS, C/ Book of your own: keeping a diary or journal./ 1993/
5-A/9 KD864 . . . . **808**
Trouble for Lucy./ 1979/ 3-5/6 KH754 . . . . **FIC**
STEVENS, J/ Anansi and the moss-covered rock./ 1988/
1-2/4 KB600 . . . . **CE 398.24**
Anansi and the talking melon./ 1994/ 2-3/2 KB601 . . **CE 398.24**
Anansi goes fishing./ 1991, c1992/ K-2/2 KB602 . . . **CE 398.24**
Coyote steals the blanket: a Ute tale./ 1993/ 2-4/2 KB657 . . **398.24**
Coyote steals the blanket: a Ute tale (Sound recording cassette)./ 1995/
2-4/2 KB657 . . . . **398.24**
Dog who had kittens./ 1991/ K-1/4 KG337 . . . . **CE E**
How the Manx cat lost its tail./ 1990/ 2-3/4 KB658 . . . . **398.24**
Old bag of bones: a coyote tale./ 1996/ 1-3/2 KB659 . . . **398.24**
Princess and the pea./ 1982/ K-2/2 KG555 . . . . **CE E**
Princess and the pea (Kit)./ 1996/ K-2/2 KG555 . . . . . . **CE E**
Tops and bottoms./ 1995/ K-2/2 KB660 . . . . **398.24**
STEVENS, JR/ Carlos and the skunk./Carlos y el zorrillo./ 1997/
1-3/3 KG554 . . . . E
STEVENS, L/ Clown games./ 1993/ P-1/1 KG791 . . . . E
STEVENS, SH/ Classroom success for the LD and ADHD child./ 1997/
KA186 . . . . **PROF 371.92**
STEVENSON, H/ Grandpa's house./ 1994/ P-1/2 KG556 . . . . . . E
STEVENSON, J/ All aboard!/ 1995/ 1-3/2 KG557 . . . . E
Baby uggs are hatching./ 1982/ 1-3 KE000 . . . . **811**
Bones in the cliff./ 1995/ 4-6/6 KH755 . . . . **FIC**
Could be worse./ c1977, 1987/ K-3/4 KG558 . . . . **CE E**
Don't you know there's a war on?/ 1992/
K-3/2 KE552 . . . . **B STEVENSON, J.**
Don't you know there's a war on? (Sound recording cassette)./ 1994/
K-3/2 KE552 . . . . **B STEVENSON, J.**
Flying Acorns./ 1993/ 1-3/3 KG559 . . . . E
Fried feathers for Thanksgiving./ 1986/ P-2/2 KG560 . . . . . . E
Fun no fun./ 1994/ 3-4/4 KE551 . . . . **B STEVENSON, J.**
Grandaddy's place./ 1987/ 1-4/1 KF647 . . . . E
Grandaddy's stars./ 1995/ 1-4/2 KF648 . . . . E
Higher on the door./ 1987/ 3-4/4 KE553 . . . . . **B STEVENSON, J.**
I am not going to get up today!/ 1987/ 1-3/2 KG461 . . . . . . E
I had a lot of wishes./ 1995/ 3-4/4 KE551 . . . . **B STEVENSON, J.**
I know a lady./ 1984/ K-2/6 KG802 . . . . E
July./ 1990/ 3-4/4 KE551 . . . . **B STEVENSON, J.**
Loop the loop./ 1992/ 1-3/4 KF501 . . . . E
Mud Flat mystery./ 1997/ 1-3/2 KG561 . . . . E
Mud Flat Olympics./ 1994/ 1-3/2 KG562 . . . . E
Mud Flat Olympics (Sound recording cassette)./ 1997/
1-3/2 KG562 . . . . E
National worm day./ 1990/ K-2/1 KG563 . . . . E
New kid on the block./ 1984/ 2-6 KE010 . . . . **CE 811**
Night after Christmas./ 1981/ K-2/2 KG564 . . . . **CE E**
Oldest elf./ 1996/ P-2/2 KG565 . . . . E
Pizza the size of the sun: poems./ 1996/ K-A KE012 . . . . . . **811**
Rolling Rose./ 1992/ P-K/2 KG566 . . . . E
Rolling Rose (Sound recording cassette)./ 1995/ P-K/2 KG566 . . . E
Sea View Hotel./ c1978, 1994/ K-3/3 KG567 . . . . E
That terrible Halloween night./ 1988/ K-3/4 KG558 . . . . . . **CE E**
Village full of valentines./ 1995/ 1-3/2 KG568 . . . . E
We hate rain!/ 1988/ P-3/2 KG569 . . . . E
What's under my bed./ 1983/ K-3/4 KG558 . . . . **CE E**
What's under my bed (Videocassette)./ n.d./ K-3/4 KG558 . . . **CE E**
When I was nine./ 1986/ 3-4/4 KE551 . . . . **B STEVENSON, J.**
Worse than the worst./ 1994/ K-3/4 KG570 . . . . E
Worst goes South./ 1995/ K-3/4 KG570 . . . . E
Worst person in the world./ c1978/ K-3/4 KG570 . . . . E
Yard sale./ 1996/ 2-3/2 KH756 . . . . **FIC**
STEVENSON, RL/ Child's garden of verses./ 1905/ P-2 KE110 . . . **821**

CHILD'S GARDEN OF VERSES AND A POTPOURRI OF POETRY: AN
INTRODUCTION TO GREAT POETS (Sound recording cassette)./ n.d./
2-6 KE098 . . . . **SRC 821**
Child's garden of verses (Braille)./ n.d./ P-2 KE110 . . . . **821**
Child's garden of verses (Talking book)./ n.d./ P-2 KE110 . . . . . **821**
David Balfour: being memoirs of the further adventures of David Balfour
at home and abroad./ c1952, 1994/ 6-A/6 KH757 . . . . . **FIC**
Kidnapped: being the memoirs of the adventures of David Balfour/ 1982/
5-6/6 KH758 . . . . **FIC**
Kidnapped: being the memoirs of the adventures of David Balfour in the
year 1751 (Sound recording cassette)./ Kidnapped: being the memoirs
of the adventures of David Balfour in the year 1751 (Talking book)./
Kidnapped: being the memoirs of the adventures of David Balfour in the
year 1751 (Braille)./ n.d/ n.d./ n.d./ 5-6/6 KH758 . . . . **FIC**
5-6/6 KH758 . . . . **FIC**
5-6/6 KH758 . . . . **FIC**
Treasure Island./ c1911, 1981/ 5-A/6 KH759 . . . . **FIC**
Treasure Island (Braille)./ n.d, 5-A/6 KH759 . . . . **FIC**
Treasure Island (Sound recording cassette)./ n.d., 5-A/6 KH759 . . **FIC**
Treasure Island (Talking book)./ n.d,/ 5-A/6 KH759 . . . . . . **FIC**
Treasure Island (Talking book)./ 1993/ 5-A KH760 . . . . . **TB FIC**
STEVENSON, S/ Birthday presents./ 1991/ P-1/2 KG368 . . . . . . E
Emily and Alice./ 1993/ 1-3/2 KF375 . . . . E
Emily and Alice again./ 1995/ 1-3/2 KF376 . . . . E
Henry and Mudge: the first book./ 1987/ K-3/2 KG375 . . . . **CE E**
Once upon a time this morning./ 1997/ P-K/2 KG344 . . . . E
STEWART, D/ Itse Selu: Cherokee harvest festival./ 1994/
K-3/6 KB190 . . . . **394.2**
STEWART, DA/ Jack and the beanstalk (Videocassette)./ 1991/
K-2 KB349 . . . . **VCR 398.2**
STEWART, EJ/ Bimmi finds a cat./ 1996/ 3-5/6 KH761 . . . . . . **FIC**
On the long trail home./ 1994/ 4-6/4 KH762 . . . . **FIC**
On the long trail home (Sound recording cassette)./ 1997/
4-6/4 KH762 . . . . **FIC**
STEWART, G/ Folk dance fun: simple folk songs and dances (Sound
recording cassette)./ 1984/ 2-6 KD705 . . . . **SRC 793.3**
Good morning exercises for kids (Sound recording cassette)./ 1987/
P-3 KC991 . . . . **SRC 613.7**
Multicultural rhythm stick fun (Compact disc)./ 1992/
P-2 KD768 . . . . **SRC 796.1**
Multicultural rhythm stick fun (Sound recording cassette)./ 1992/
P-2 KD768 . . . . **SRC 796.1**
Pre-K hooray! (Sound recording cassette)./ 1993/
P-K KD659 . . . . **SRC 789.3**
Preschool favorites (Sound recording cassette)./ 1990/
P-K KD660 . . . . **SRC 789.3**
STEWART, GB/ Appaloosa horse./ 1995/ 4-5/6 KD205 . . . **636.1**
Arabian horse./ 1995/ 4-6/5 KD206 . . . . **636.1**
Quarter horse./ 1995/ 4-6/5 KD207 . . . . **636.1**
Thoroughbred horse: born to run./ 1995/ 4-6/5 KD208 . . . **636.1**
STEWART, GR/ Pioneers go west./ c1982, 1997/ 4-6/7 KF051 . . **978**
STEWART, J/ Kid's cuisine./ 1988/ 4-6 KD278 . . . . **641.5**
STEWART, MW/ Homes in the wilderness: a pilgrim's journal of Plymouth
Plantation in 1620./ c1939, 1988/ 5-A/8 KE941 . . . . . . **974.4**
STEWART, N/ Rhythm of the rocks: a multicultural musical journey (Sound
recording cassette)./ 1993/ K-2 KD599 . . . . **SRC 789.2**
Rhythm of the rocks songbook: a multicultural musical journey.../ 1994/
K-2 KD600 . . . . **789.2**
STEWART, S/ Gardener./ 1997/ K-3/2 KG571 . . . . E
Library./ 1995/ K-3/3 KG572 . . . . **CE E**
Library (Kit)./ 1996/ K-3/3 KG572 . . . . **CE E**
Library (Videocassette)./ 1996/ K-3/3 KG572 . . . . **CE E**
STEWART, W/ Aung San Suu Kyi: fearless voice of Burma./ 1997/
5-A/7 KE244 . . . . **B AUNG SAN SUU**
14th Dalai Lama: spiritual leader of Tibet./ 1996/
5-A/10 KA761 . . . . **294.3**
STEWIG, JW/ Looking at picture books./ 1995/ KA312 . . **PROF 741.6**
Princess Florecita and the iron shoes: a Spanish fairy tale./ 1995/
3-4/5 KB372 . . . . **398.2**
USING LITERATURE IN THE ELEMENTARY CLASSROOM. Rev. ed./
1989/ KA243 . . . . **PROF 372.64**
STILZ, CC/ Grandma Buffalo, May, and me./ 1995/ 1-3/3 KG573 . . E
STIRLING, I/ Bears./ 1992/ 5-A/7 KC857 . . . . **599.78**
STOBEROCK, M/ Storytelling handbook: a young people's collection of
unusual tales and helpful hints on how to tell them./ 1995/
KA249 . . . . **PROF 372.67**
STOCK, C/ Birthday present./ / P-K/2 KG574 . . . . E
By the dawn's early light./ 1994/ K-2/5 KF129 . . . . E
Christmas time./ / P-K/2 KG574 . . . . E
Easter surprise./ / P-K/2 KG574 . . . . E
Galimoto./ 1990/ 1-2/2 KG727 . . . . **CE E**
Halloween monster./ 1990/ P-K/2 KG574 . . . . E
Island Christmas./ 1992/ 1-3/2 KF855 . . . . E
Justin and the best biscuits in the world./ 1986/ 4-6/6 KH839 . . . **FIC**

Nellie Bly's monkey: his remarkable story in his own words./ 1996/
2-5/9 KF236 . . . . **E**
Tap-tap./ 1994/ K-2/2 KG728 . . . . **CE E**
Thanksgiving treat./ / P-K/2 KG574 . . . . **E**
Tiger called Thomas./ c1963, 1988/ K-2/4 KG808 . . . . **E**
Too far away to touch./ 1995/ 1-3/6 KG172 . . . . **E**
Very important day./ 1995/ K-3/2 KF715 . . . . **E**
Where are you going Manyoni?/ 1993/ K-3/3 KG575 . . . . **E**
STOCKTON, FR/ Bee-man of Orn./ c1964, 1987/ 5-6/7 KH763 . . . **FIC**
Bee-man of Orn (Braille)./ n.d.,/ 5-6/7 KH763 . . . . **FIC**
Bee-man of Orn (Talking book)./ n.d.,/ 5-6/7 KH763 . . . . **FIC**
Griffin and the minor canon./ c1963, 1986/ 3-5/7 KH764 . . . . **FIC**
Griffin and the minor canon (Braille)./ n.d.,/ 3-5/7 KH764 . . . **FIC**
Griffin and the minor canon (Talking book)./ n.d.,/ 3-5/7 KH764 . . **FIC**
STOEKE, JM/ Hat for Minerva Louise./ 1994/ P-K/2 KG576 . . . . . **E**
Minerva Louise at school./ 1996/ P-1/2 KG577 . . . . **E**
STOKER, W/ Nevada./ 1990/ 4-6/9 KF074 . . . . **979.3**
STOKES, DW/ Guide to nature in winter, northeast and north central North
America./ c1976, 1979/ 6-A/8 KB921 . . . . **508.2**
STOLL, DR/ MAGAZINES FOR KIDS AND TEENS: Rev. ed./ 1997/
KA018 . . . . **PROF 011.62**
STOLTZ, WJ/ Come walk with me (Videocassette)./ 1994/
P-3 KC309 . . . . **VCR 577.3**
STOLZ, M/ Dog on Barkham Street./ c1960/ 4-6/4 KH765 . . . . . **FIC**
Dog on Barkham Street (Braille)./ n.d./ 4-6/4 KH765 . . . . **FIC**
Go fish./ 1991/ 3-6/6 KH766 . . . . **FIC**
Noonday friends./ c1965/ 4-6/6 KH767 . . . . **CE FIC**
Noonday friends (Braille)./ n.d./ 4-6/6 KH767 . . . . **CE FIC**
Stealing home./ 1992/ 3-5/6 KH768 . . . . **FIC**
Storm in the night./ 1988/ K-3/4 KG578 . . . . **E**
STONE, J/ Julian Messner illustrated dictionary of science./ 1986/
4-6/9 KB878 . . . . **503**
STONE, LM/ Grizzlies./ 1993/ 5-6/6 KC861 . . . . **599.784**
Pelican./ 1990/ 5-6/6 KC684 . . . . **598.4**
Temperate forests./ 1989/ 4-6/9 KC310 . . . . **577.3**
STORY OF THE CREATION: WORDS FROM GENESIS./ 1993/
2-3/4 KA688 . . . . **222**
STOTTER, R/ Origami stories (Videocassette)./ 1993/
1-3 KB122 . . . . **VCR 372.67**
STOWE, C/ Not-so-normal Norman./ 1995/ 2-5/3 KH770 . . . . . . **FIC**
Not-so-normal Norman (Sound recording cassette)./ 1997/
2-5/3 KH770 . . . . **FIC**
STRAUB, DG/ AFRICAN AMERICAN VOICES./ 1996/
5-A KA487 . . . . **REF 973**
NATIVE NORTH AMERICAN VOICES./ 1997/ 5-A KA482 . **REF 970.1**
STREEP, M/ Tailor of Gloucester (Videocassette)./ 1988/
1-3 KG271 . . . . **VCR E**
STREET, J/ Animal fare: poems./ 1994/ K-3 KE047 . . . . **811**
STREISSGUTH, T/ Say it with music: a story about Irving Berlin./ 1994/
4-5/5 KE252 . . . . **B BERLIN, I.**
STRETE, CK/ They thought they saw him./ 1996/ K-2/2 KG579 . . . . **E**
World in Grandfather's hands./ 1995/ 5-A/4 KH771 . . . . **FIC**
STRICKLAND, B/ Doom of the haunted opera./ 1995/
4-6/6 KG896 . . . . **FIC**
Hand of the necromancer./ 1996/ 5-A/6 KH772 . . . . **FIC**
STRICKLAND, MR/ FAMILIES: POEMS CELEBRATING THE AFRICAN
AMERICAN EXPERIENCE./ 1994/ K-3 KE057 . . . . **811.008**
STRINGER, L/ Mud./ 1996/ P-2/2 KG316 . . . . **E**
STROMOSKI, R/ Trouble with school: a family story about learning
disabilities./ 1993/ KA184 . . . . **PROF 371.9**
STROUD, VA/ Doesn't Fall Off His Horse./ 1994/ 2-3/4 KG580 . . **E**
Path of the Quiet Elk: a Native American alphabet book./ 1996/
3-6/9 KA793 . . . . **299**
Story of the Milky Way: a Cherokee tale./ 1995/
2-3/3 KB701 . . . . **398.26**
STRUGNELL, A/ Mountain gorilla./ 1993/ 4-5/8 KC875 . . . . **599.884**
Stories Julian tells./ 1981/ 3-4/4 KG970 . . . . **FIC**
STRUTHERS, S/ Angelina Ballerina and other stories (Talking book)./
1986/ P-2 KF765 . . . . **TB E**
STUART, D/ Astonishing armadillo./ 1993/ 5-6/7 KC741 . . . . . . **599.3**
Bats: mysterious flyers of the night./ 1994/ 5-6/8 KC763 . . . . . **599.4**
STURGES, P/ Marushka and the Month Brothers: a folktale./ 1996/
1-3/4 KB513 . . . . **398.23**
Ten flashing fireflies./ 1995/ K-2/2 KG581 . . . . **E**
STUTSON, C/ By the light of the Halloween moon./ 1993/
1-3/3 KG582 . . . . **E**
Prairie primer A to Z./ 1996/ 1-3/3 KG583 . . . . **E**
SUBLETT, A/ Illustrated rules of softball./ 1996/ 3-6/6 KD803 **796.357**
SULLIVAN, A/ Molly Maguire: wide receiver./ 1992/ 4-6/3 KH773 . **FIC**
SULLIVAN, C/ CHILDREN OF PROMISE: AFRICAN-AMERICAN
LITERATURE AND ART FOR YOUNG PEOPLE./ 1991/
3-A/7 KD896 . . . . **810.8**
IMAGINARY GARDENS: AMERICAN POETRY AND ART FOR YOUNG
PEOPLE./ 1989/ 4-A KE067 . . . . **811.008**

SULLIVAN, G/ Alamo!/ 1997/ 4-6/10 KF002 . . . . **976.4**
All about football./ 1987/ 4-6/6 KD787 . . . . **796.332**
Black artists in photography, 1840-1940./ 1996/ 5-6/12 KD510 . **770**
Glovemen: twenty-seven of baseball's greatest./ 1996/
4-6/8 KD804 . . . . **796.357**
How an airport really works./ 1993/ 5-6/8 KB156 . . . . **387.7**
In-line skating: a complete guide for beginners./ 1993/
4-6/6 KD773 . . . . **796.21**
Pitchers: twenty-seven of baseball's greatest./ 1994/
5-A/6 KD805 . . . . **796.357**
Sluggers: twenty-seven of baseball's greatest./ 1991/
5-A/6 KD806 . . . . **796.357**
SULLIVAN, MJ/ Mark Messier: star center./ 1997/
5-A/7 KE464 . . . . **B MESSIER, M.**
Top 10 baseball pitchers./ 1994/ 3-6/4 KD807 . . . . **796.357**
SULLY, T/ Tumbleweed Christmas./ 1996/ 1-3/3 KF547 . . . . **E**
SUMMERS, K/ Milly and Tilly: the story of a town mouse and a country
mouse./ 1997/ K-2/2 KB661 . . . . **398.24**
SUMNERS, C/ Toys in space: exploring science with the astronauts./
1997/ KA282 . . . . **PROF 500.5**
SUNFLAKES: POEMS FOR CHILDREN./ 1992/ P-2 KE086 . . . . **811.008**
SUNSERI, M/ Rhythm of the rocks: a multicultural musical journey (Compact
disc)./ 1996/ K-2 KD599 . . . . **SRC 789.2**
Rhythm of the rocks: a multicultural musical journey (Sound recording
cassette)./ 1993/ K-2 KD599 . . . . **SRC 789.2**
Rhythm of the rocks songbook: a multicultural musical journey.../ 1994/
K-2 KD600 . . . . **789.2**
SUPER, N/ Daniel "Chappie" James./ 1992/
5-A/6 KE401 . . . . **B JAMES, D.**
SUPRANER, R/ Quick and easy cookbook./ c1981, 1985/
1-4 KD281 . . . . **641.5**
SURAT, MM/ Angel child, dragon child./ c1983, 1989/ 1-3/2 KG584 **E**
Angel child, dragon child (Sound recording cassette)./ 1995,/
1-3/2 KG584 . . . . **E**
SUSSMAN, S/ Hanukkah: eight lights around the world./ 1988/
3-5/5 KH774 . . . . **FIC**
SUTCLIFF, R/ Black ships before Troy: the story of the Iliad./ 1993/
5-A/8 KE127 . . . . **883**
Minstrel and the dragon pup./ c1993, 1996/ 3-6/7 KH775 . . . . . **FIC**
Wanderings of Odysseus: the story of the Odyssey./ 1996/
5-A/7 KE128 . . . . **883**
SUTEEV, V/ Chick and the duckling./ 1972/ P-1/1 KG585 . . . . . . **E**
Mushroom in the rain./ c1974, 1987/ P-2/2 KF623 . . . . **E**
SUTHERLAND, Z/ Best in children's books: the University of Chicago guide
to children's literature,/ 1991/ KA023 . . . . **PROF 011.62**
Children and books. 9th ed./ 1997/ KA358 . . . . **PROF 809**
SUTTON, R/ Best in children's books: the University of Chicago guide to
children's literature,/ 1991/ KA023 . . . . **PROF 011.62**
SUTTON, WK/ ADVENTURING WITH BOOKS: A BOOKLIST FOR PRE-K-
GRADE 6. 1997 ed./ 1997/ KA009 . . . . **PROF 011.62**
SUZUKI, D/ Connections: finding out about the environment (Sound
recording cassette)./ 1990/ P-2 KC297 . . . . **SRC 577**
Looking at insects./ 1992/ 4-6/5 KC550 . . . . **595.7**
SALAMANDERS (Videocassette)./ 1985/ 5-6 KC609 . . . . . **VCR 597.8**
SWAIN, G/ Bookworks: making books by hand./ 1995/
3-6/5 KD437 . . . . **745.5**
Pennsylvania./ 1994/ 4-6/7 KE960 . . . . **974.8**
SWANSON, D/ Coyotes in the crosswalk: true tales of animal life in the
wilds...of the city!/ 1995/ 4-6/6 KC494 . . . . **591.75**
Safari beneath the sea: the wonder world of the North Pacific coast./
1994/ 4-6/7 KC370 . . . . **578.77**
Sky dancers: the amazing world of North American birds./ 1995/
4-5/5 KC667 . . . . **598**
SWANSON, J/ I pledge allegiance./ 1990/ 2-5/4 KA909 . . . **CE 323.6**
I pledge allegiance (Kit)./ 1991/ 2-5/4 KA909 . . . . **CE 323.6**
Summit up: riddles about mountains./ 1994/ 3-6 KD739 . . . . **793.735**
SWANSON, M/ American Heritage picture dictionary./ 1994/
P-1 KA423 . . . . **REF 423**
SWEAT, L/ Amelia Bedelia's family album./ 1988/ K-3/4 KG211 . . . . **E**
Bravo, Amelia Bedelia!/ 1997/ 1-2/2 KG210 . . . . **E**
Family storytelling handbook./ 1987/ KA070 . . . . **PROF 027.62**
Good work, Amelia Bedelia./ c1976/ 1-3/2 KG214 . . . . **CE E**
One good horse: a cowpuncher's counting book./ 1990/
K-2/2 KG424 . . . . **E**
Story vine: a source book of unusual and easy-to-tell stories from/ 1984/
KA248 . . . . **PROF 372.67**
SWEENEY, J/ Me on the map./ 1996/ K-1/1 KE172 . . . . **912**
SWEET, M/ Snowman on Sycamore Street./ 1996/ 2-3/2 KG989 . . **FIC**
SWENTZELL, R/ Children of clay: a family of Pueblo potters./ 1992/
4-6/6 KE795 . . . . **970.489**
SWISHER, CL/ Literature-based reading: children's books and activities to
enrich the K-5/ 1990/ KA210 . . . . **PROF 372.4**
SWITZER, E/ Greek myths: gods, heroes and monsters, their sources, their
stories and their meanings./ 1988/ 6-A KA395 . . . . **REF 292**

SWOPE, S/ Katya's book of mushrooms./ 1997/ 3-A/6 KC381 . . **579.6**

SYKES, J/ This and that./ 1996/ P-1/2 KG586 . . . . **E**

SYMONS, RD/ Grandfather Symons' homestead book./ 1981/
3-5/6 KE815 . . . . **971.2**

SYNARSKI, S/ Messipes: a microwave cookbook of deliciously messy
masterpieces./ 1996/ 3-6 KD271 . . . . **641.5**

SYVERSON-STORK, J/ POLLITOS DICEN: JUEGOS, RIMAS Y
CANCIONES INFANTILES DE PAISES DE HABLA HISPANA./THE
BABY CHICKS SING: TRADITIONAL GAMES, NURSERY/ 1994/
P-1/2 KD584 . . . . **789.2**

SZABO, C/ Sky pioneer: a photobiography of Amelia Earhart./ 1997/
4-6/12 KE329 . . . . **B EARHART, A.**

SZPURA, B/ Libby Bloom./ 1995/ 3-5/6 KH460 . . . . **FIC**

TABACK, S/ Jason's bus ride./ c1987, 1993/ K-2/1 KG792 . . . . . . **E**

LAUGHING TOGETHER: GIGGLES AND GRINS FROM AROUND THE
GLOBE./ c1977, 1992/ 3-A KD731 . . . . **793.735**

Sam's Wild West Show./ 1995/ 1-3/2 KF161 . . . . **E**

Who said moo?/ 1996/ P-1/2 KG799 . . . . **E**

TAFURI, N/ Across the stream./ 1982/ P-K/2 KF621 . . . . **E**

Asleep, asleep./ 1992/ P/1 KF622 . . . . **E**

Biggest boy./ 1995/ P/2 KF701 . . . . **E**

Do not disturb./ 1987/ P-2 KG587 . . . . **E**

Early morning in the barn./ 1983/ P KG588 . . . . **E**

Everything has a place./ 1993/ P-K/1 KF981 . . . . **E**

Follow me!/ 1990/ P-2 KG589 . . . . **E**

Have you seen my duckling?/ 1984/ P-K/1 KG590 . . . . **E**

Have you seen my duckling? (Board book)./ 1996/ P-K/1 KG590 . . **E**

Spots, feathers, and curly tails./ 1988/ P-K/1 KD185 . . . . **636**

This is the farmer./ 1994/ P-1/1 KG591 . . . . **E**

Who's counting?/ 1986/ P-K KG592 . . . . **E**

TAHA, K/ Name that book! Questions and answers on outstanding
children's books./ 1996/ KA350 . . . . **PROF 809**

TAIT, L/ White stone in the castle wall./ 1995/ 4-6/2 KH555 . . . . **FIC**

TAJ MAHAL (MUSICAL GROUP)/ FOLLOW THE DRINKING GOURD./
1993/ 2-4 KF563 . . . . **BA E**

Follow the drinking gourd: a story of the Underground Railroad
(Videocassette)./ 1992/ 2-4 KF412 . . . . **VCR E**

TAKE ME TO YOUR LITER: SCIENCE AND MATH JOKES./ 1991/
3-6 KD740 . . . . **793.735**

TALAB, RS/ Commonsense copyright: a guide to the new technologies./
1986/ KA169 . . . . **PROF 346.73**

TALBOTT, H/ King Arthur and the Round Table./ 1995/
4-5/6 KB490 . . . . **398.22**

TALKING LIKE THE RAIN: A FIRST BOOK OF POEMS./ 1992/
P-2 KE112 . . . . **821.008**

TAMAR, E/ Garden of happiness./ 1996/ 1-3/2 KG593 . . . . **E**

TAMES, R/ Ancient Olympics./ 1996/ 3-6/8 KD821 . . . . **796.48**

Modern Olympics./ 1996/ 3-6/8 KD822 . . . . **796.48**

TANAKA, S/ Discovering the Iceman: what was it like to find a 5,300-
year-old mummy?/ 1997/ 3-5/4 KE642 . . . . **937**

On board the Titanic./ 1996/ 4-A/6 KB027 . . . . **363.12**

TANNER, T/ Off the map: the journals of Lewis and Clark./ 1993/
4-6/7 KE201 . . . . **917.804**

TAPAHONSO, L/ Navajo ABC: a Dine alphabet book./ 1995/
2-4 KE797 . . . . **970.49**

TARCOV, EH/ Frog prince./ c1974, 1993/ P-3/2 KB376 . . . . . **398.2**

TASHJIAN, V/ JUBA THIS AND JUBA THAT./ 1995/
KA366 . . . . **PROF 820.8**

TASSIA, MR/ In days gone by: folklore and traditions of the Pennsylvania
Dutch./ 1996/ KA268 . . . . **PROF 398.2**

TATE GALLERY/ Drawing: a young artist's guide./ 1994/
3-6/6 KD406 . . . . **741.2**

TAUSS, H/ Shadow children./ 1994/ 4-A/7 KH681 . . . . **FIC**

TAYLOR, B/ Arctic and Antarctic./ 1995/ 3-6/7 KE220 . . . . . **919.8**

Be an inventor./ 1987/ 5-6/7 KC888 . . . . **608**

Bird atlas./ 1993/ 4-6/9 KA449 . . . . **REF 598**

Incredible plants./ 1997/ 3-8/8 KC393 . . . . **580**

TAYLOR, BAP/ Teaching physics with toys: activities for grades K-9./
1995/ KA204 . . . . **PROF 372.3**

TAYLOR, CJ/ Deux-Plumes et la solitude disparue./ 1990/
3-4/2 KB716 . . . . **398.26**

Ghost and Lone Warrior: an Arapaho legend./ 1991/
2-5/4 KB696 . . . . **398.25**

Guerrier-Solitaire et le fantome./ 1991/ 2-5/4 KB696 . . . . . **398.25**

How Two-Feather was saved from loneliness: an Abenaki legend./ 1990/
3-4/2 KB716 . . . . **398.26**

How we saw the world: nine Native stories of the way things began./
1993/ 4-5/4 KB377 . . . . **398.2**

TAYLOR, CM/ Camel caravan./ 1996/ P-1/3 KG335 . . . . **E**

TAYLOR, D/ You and your cat./ 1986/ 5-A KD235 . . . . **636.8**

You and your dog./ 1986/ 5-A KD224 . . . . **636.7**

TAYLOR, HP/ Coyote and the laughing butterflies./ 1995/
2-3/5 KB662 . . . . **398.24**

TAYLOR, J/ Twinkle, twinkle, little star./ 1992/ P-K KE111 . . . . . **821**

TAYLOR, MD/ Friendship./ 1987/ 4-6/5 KH776 . . . . **FIC**

Friendship (Braille)./ n.d./ 4-6/5 KH776 . . . . **FIC**

Let the circle be unbroken./ 1981/ 5-6/8 KH777 . . . . **FIC**

Let the circle be unbroken (Braille)./ n.d./ 5-6/8 KH777 . . . . . **FIC**

Mississippi bridge./ 1990/ 5-A/4 KH778 . . . . **FIC**

Roll of thunder, hear my cry./ c1976/ 5-6/6 KH779 . . . . . **CE FIC**

Roll of thunder, hear my cry (Braille)./ n.d./ 5-6/6 KH779 . . . **CE FIC**

Roll of thunder, hear my cry (Sound recording cassette)./ n.d./
5-6/6 KH779 . . . . **CE FIC**

Roll of thunder, hear my cry (Talking book)./ 1978/
5-6/6 KH779 . . . . **CE FIC**

Song of the trees./ 1975/ 4-6/4 KH780 . . . . **FIC**

Song of the trees (Sound recording cassette)./ 1996/
4-6/4 KH780 . . . . **FIC**

Well: David's story./ 1995/ 5-A/4 KH781 . . . . **FIC**

TAYLOR, MW/ MADAM C.J. WALKER (Videocassette)./ 1992/
5-A KE584 . . . . **VCR B WALKER, C.J.**

TAYLOR, PD/ Fossil./ 1990/ 4-A/9 KC237 . . . . **560**

TAYLOR, S/ All-of-a-kind family./ 1951, 1988/ 4-6/5 KH782 . . . . **FIC**

All-of-a-kind family (Braille)./ n.d./ 4-6/5 KH782 . . . . **FIC**

All-of-a-kind family (Sound recording cassette)./ n.d./
4-6/5 KH782 . . . . **FIC**

All-of-a-kind family (Talking book)./ n.d./ 4-6/5 KH782 . . . . . **FIC**

All-of-a-kind family uptown./ 1958/ 4-6/5 KH782 . . . . **FIC**

All-of-a-kind family uptown (Braille)./ n.d./ 4-6/5 KH782 . . . . . **FIC**

All-of-a-kind family uptown (Talking book)./ n.d./ 4-6/5 KH782 . . **FIC**

Ella of all-of-a-kind family./ 1978/ 4-6/5 KH782 . . . . **FIC**

Ella of all-of-a-kind family (Sound recording cassette)./ n.d./
4-6/5 KH782 . . . . **FIC**

More all-of-a-kind family./ 1954, 4-6/5 KH782 . . . . **FIC**

More all-of-a-kind family (Braille)./ n.d./ 4-6/5 KH782 . . . . . **FIC**

More all-of-a-kind family (Talking book)./ n.d., 4-6/5 KH782 . . . **FIC**

TAYLOR, T/ Cay./ c1969/ 5-6/6 KH783 . . . . **FIC**

Cay (Braille)./ n.d./ 5-6/6 KH783 . . . . **FIC**

Cay (Sound recording cassette)./ 1993/ 5-6/6 KH783 . . . . . . **FIC**

Cay (Talking book)./ n.d./ 5-6/6 KH783 . . . . **FIC**

Odyssey of Ben O'Neal./ c1977/ 5-A/5 KH784 . . . . **FIC**

Teetoncey./ c1975/ 5-A/5 KH784 . . . . **FIC**

Teetoncey and Ben O'Neal./ c1975/ 5-A/5 KH784 . . . . **FIC**

Timothy of the cay./ 1993/ 5-A/5 KH785 . . . . **FIC**

Timothy of the cay (Sound recording cassette)./ 1995/
5-A/5 KH785 . . . . **FIC**

TAYLOR, W/ Agnes the sheep./ 1990/ 5-A/6 KH786 . . . . **FIC**

Numbskulls./ 1995/ 4-A/7 KH787 . . . . **FIC**

TCHAIKOVSKY, PI/ Sleeping Beauty: the ballet story./ 1994/
1-5/7 KD695 . . . . **792.8**

Story of Sleeping Beauty (Sound recording cassette)./ 1980/
4-6 KB356 . . . . **SRC 398.2**

TEAGUE, M/ Field beyond the outfield./ 1992/ K-2/2 KG594 . . . . . **E**

Flying Dragon Room./ 1996/ 2-4/3 KG761 . . . . **E**

Mr. Potter's pet./ 1996/ 3-5/2 KH352 . . . . **FIC**

Pigsty./ 1994/ K-2/2 KG595 . . . . **E**

Poppleton./ 1997/ K-2/2 KG384 . . . . **E**

Secret shortcut./ 1996/ 1-3/2 KG596 . . . . **E**

Three terrible trins./ 1994/ 3-5/6 KH358 . . . . **CE FIC**

TECKENTRUP, B/ Kancil and the crocodiles: a tale from Malaysia./ 1996/
2-3/2 KB556 . . . . **398.24**

TEETERS, P/ Jules Verne: the man who invented tomorrow./ 1992/
5-A/6 KE582 . . . . **B VERNE, J.**

Jules Verne: the man who invented tomorrow (Sound recording cassette)./
1995/ 5-A/6 KE582 . . . . **B VERNE, J.**

TEIRSTEIN, MA/ Baseball./ 1994/ 3-6/3 KD808 . . . . **796.357**

TEJIMA, K/ Fox's dream./ 1987/ P-2/4 KG597 . . . . **E**

Sueno del Zorro./ 1989/ P-2/4 KG597 . . . . **E**

TELANDER, T/ Caves!: underground worlds./ 1995/
5-6/6 KC171 . . . . **551.44**

TELLO, J/ Abuelo y los tres osos./Abuelo and the three bears./ 1997/
K-2/2 KG598 . . . . **E**

TEMKO, F/ Origami for beginners: the creative world of paperfolding./
1991/ 4-6/4 KD404 . . . . **736**

Traditional crafts from Africa./ 1996/ 4-6/7 KD422 . . . . **745**

Traditional crafts from Mexico and Central America./ 1996/
3-6/5 KD438 . . . . **745.5**

TEMPLE, C/ STORIES AND READERS: NEW PERSPECTIVES ON
LITERATURE IN THE ELEMENTARY CLASSROOM./ 1992/
KA241 . . . . **PROF 372.64**

Train./ 1996/ K-3/2 KG599 . . . . **E**

TEMPLE, F/ Grab hands and run./ 1993/ 6-A/6 KH788 . . . . **FIC**

Tiger soup: an Anansi story from Jamaica./ 1994/
2-3/2 KB663 . . . . **398.24**

Tiger soup: an Anansi story from Jamaica (Sound recording cassette)./
1996/ 2-3/2 KB663 . . . . **398.24**

Tonight, by sea: a novel./ 1995/ 6-A/5 KH789 . . . . **FIC**

Tonight, by sea: a novel (Sound recording cassette)./ 1997/
6-A/5 KH789 . . . . **FIC**
TENNIEL, J/ Alice's adventures in Wonderland./ c1865, 1992/
5-A/7 KG980 . . . . **FIC**
Through the looking-glass and what Alice found there./ c1872, 1993/
5-A/7 KG981 . . . . **FIC**
TEN-SECOND RAINSHOWERS: POEMS BY YOUNG PEOPLE./ 1996/
3-6 KE088 . . . . **811.008**
TERBAN, M/ Checking your grammar./ 1993/ 5-A KB856 . **428.2**
It figures!: fun figures of speech./ 1993/ 5-A/8 KD865 . . . . . . **808**
Scholastic dictionary of idioms./ 1996/ 4-6 KA431 . . . . **REF 423**
Superdupers! really funny real words./ 1989/ 3-6 KB850 . . . . . **428.1**
TERDAL, L/ Hyperactive child book./ 1994/ KA303 . . . . . **PROF 649**
TERLSON, C/ Amazing dirt book./ 1990/ 4-6/6 KD148 . . . . . . **631.4**
TERRIS, D/ Twilight struggle: the life of John Fitzgerald Kennedy./ 1992/
6-A/8 KE418 . . . . **B KENNEDY, J.**
TESAR, J/ New view almanac: the first all-visual resource of vital facts and
statistics! Premiere edition./ 1996/ 4-A KA391 . . . . **REF 031.02**
TESSLER, SG/ What would Mama do?/ 1995/ K-2/2 KF526 . . . . . . **E**
TESTA, M/ Thumbs up, Rico!/ 1994/ 1-3/2 KG601 . . . . **E**
TEWS, S/ Gingerbread doll./ 1993/ 1-3/5 KG602 . . . . **E**
THALER, M/ Earth mirth: the ecology riddle book./ 1994/
2-4 KD741 . . . . **793.735**
THANKSGIVING POEMS./ 1985/ K-6 KE089 . . . . **811.008**
/ n.d./ K-6 KE089 . . . . **811.008**
THAYER, J/ Puppy who wanted a boy./ c1958, 1986/ 1-3/2 KG603 . **E**
Puppy who wanted a boy (Sound recording cassette)./ n.d.,/
1-3/2 KG603 . . . . **E**
THEIL, S/ OKLAHOMA LAND RUSH (Multimedia kit)./ 1993/
5-A KE997 . . . . **MMK 976.1**
THESMAN, J/ Nothing grows here./ 1994/ 6-A/4 KH790 . . . . . . **FIC**
THIELE, B/ What a wonderful world./ 1995/ P-2/2 KG692 . . . . **E**
THIS OLD MAN./ 1990/ P-1 KD602 . . . . **789.2**
THOMAS, BS/ Thank you, Amelia Bedelia. Rev. ed./ 1993/
1-3/2 KG218 . . . . **CE E**
THOMAS, D/ Child's Christmas in Wales./ 1985/ P-A/8 KE119 . . . **828**
Child's Christmas in Wales (Sound recording cassette)./ n.d./
P-A/8 KE119 . . . . **828**
THOMAS, E/ Children's illustrated Bible./ 1994/ 4-6/5 KA676 . . . **220**
THOMAS, JC/ Brown honey in broomwheat tea: poems./ 1993/
K-6 KE031 . . . . **811**
Brown honey in broomwheat tea: poems (Sound recording cassette)./
1996/ K-6 KE031 . . . . **811**
Gingerbread days: poems./ 1995/ K-4 KE032 . . . . **811**
THOMAS, JL/ Play, learn, and grow: an annotated guide to the best books
and materials for very young children./ 1992/ KA088 . . **PROF 028.1**
THOMAS, JR/ Celebration!/ 1997/ 1-3/3 KG604 . . . . **E**
THOMAS, P/ Stand back, said the elephant, I'm going to sneeze!/ c1971,
1990/ K-3/2 KG605 . . . . **E**
THOMAS, RL/ Primaryplots: a book talk guide for use with readers age 4--
8./ 1989/ KA093 . . . . **PROF 028.5**
Primaryplots 2: a book talk guide for use with readers ages 4-8./ 1993/
KA093 . . . . **PROF 028.5**
THOMAS, SM/ Putting the world to sleep./ 1995/ P-2/2 KG606 . . . **E**
THOMASON, D/ Lessons from the animal people (Compact disc)./ 1996/
2-5 KB664 . . . . **SRC 398.24**
Lessons from the animal people (Sound recording cassette)./ 1996/
2-5 KB664 . . . . **SRC 398.24**
WOPILA--A GIVEAWAY: LAKOTA STORIES (Sound recording cassette)./
1993/ 3-5 KB676 . . . . **SRC 398.24**
THOMPSON, E/ Virtual Cody./ 1997/ 1-4/2 KH088 . . . . **FIC**
WHITE CAT (Videocassette)./ 1997/ K-2 KB382 . . . . . . **VCR 398.2**
THOMPSON, I/ Audubon Society field guide to North American fossils./
1982/ 4-6 KC238 . . . . **560**
Babies./ 1996/ 2-5/6 KC955 . . . . **612.6**
THOMPSON, J/ Christmas in the big house, Christmas in the quarters./
1994/ 4-A/6 KE967 . . . . **975**
Dead Sea Scrolls./ 1997/ 6-A/8 KA768 . . . . **296.1**
THOMPSON, M/ Real Johnny Appleseed./ 1995/
5-6/8 KE240 . . . . **B APPLESEED, J.**
THOMPSON, S/ One hundred favorite folktales./ c1968/·
KA274 . . . . **PROF 398.2**
THOMPSON, T/ Biz kids' guide to success: money-making ideas for young
entrepreneurs./ 1992/ 5-6/6 KD307 . . . . **650.1**
THOMPSON, VL/ Hawaiian legends of tricksters and riddlers./ c1969,
1991/ 4-5/4 KB491 . . . . **398.22**
Hawaiian tales of heroes and champions./ c1971, 1986/
4-5/4 KB491 . . . . **398.22**
THOMPSON, W/ Claude Debussy./ 1993/
6-A/9 KE316 . . . . **B DEBUSSY, C.**
Pyotr Ilyich Tchaikovsky./ 1993/ 6-A/8 KE558 . **B TCHAIKOVSKY, P**
THOMSON, P/ Auks, rocks and the odd dinosaur: inside stories from the
Smithsonian's Museum of Natural History./ 1985/ 3-A/7 KB914 **508**

Auks, rocks and the odd dinosaur: inside stories from the Smithsonian's
Museum of Natural History (Sound recording cassette)./ n.d./
3-A/7 KB914 . . . . **508**
Katie Henio: Navajo sheepherder./ 1995/ 5-6/6 KE796 . . . . **970.489**
THOMSON, R/ Rice./ 1990/ 3-5/4 KD152 . . . . **633.1**
THORNBURGH, RM/ One happy classroom./ 1997/ K-1/2 KG507 . . **E**
THORNDIKE, E/ SCOTT FORESMAN BEGINNING DICTIONARY./ c1983,
1994/ 2-4 KB836 . . . . **423**
THORNHILL, J/ Tree in a forest./ 1992/ 3-5/6 KC311 . . . . **577.3**
Wild in the city./ 1996/ P-2/5 KC478 . . . . **591.5**
Wildlife A-B-C: a nature alphabet book./ 1990/ P-2/3 KC498 . **591.97**
Wildlife 1 2 3: a nature counting book./ 1989/ P-2 KC455 . . . **591**
THORNLEY, S/ Emmitt Smith: relentless rusher./ 1997/
4-6/7 KE543 . . . . **B SMITH, E.**
THORNTON, PJ/ Daisy./ 1991/ 3-4/4 KH612 . . . . **FIC**
THREADGALL, C/ Proud rooster and the fox./ 1992/ P-1/4 KG607 . **E**
THURBER, J/ Great Quillow./ 1994/ 2-3/6 KH791 . . . . **FIC**
Many moons./ c1943, 1990/ 3-5/5 KH792 . . . . **FIC**
Many moons./ 1990/ 3-5/5 KH793 . . . . **FIC**
Many moons (Sound recording cassette)./ 1996,/ 3-5/5 KH792 . **FIC**
TIBO, G/ Annabel Lee./ 1987/ 3-6 KD997 . . . . **811**
TIEGREEN, A/ Bobby baseball./ 1991/ 3-6/4 KH726 . . . . **FIC**
Crazy eights and other card games./ 1994/ 3-6/3 KD758 . . . **795.4**
Eentsy, weentsy spider: fingerplays and action rhymes./ 1991/
P-K KD706 . . . . **793.4**
MISS MARY MACK AND OTHER CHILDREN'S STREET RHYMES./
1990/ 2-5 KD766 . . . . **796.1**
Pin the tail on the donkey and other party games./ 1993/
K-2/3 KD698 . . . . **793**
Rain or shine activity book: fun things to make and do./ 1997/
3-6 KD699 . . . . **793**
Ramona and her father./ 1977/ 3-5/7 KH001 . . . . **FIC**
Ramona and her mother./ 1979/ 3-5/6 KH002 . . . . **CE FIC**
Ramona forever./ 1984/ 3-5/6 KH003 . . . . **FIC**
Ramona Quimby, age 8./ 1981/ 3-5/5 KH004 . . . . **CE FIC**
Ramona the brave./ 1975/ 3-7 KH005 . . . . **FIC**
Six sick sheep: 101 tongue twisters./ / 3-5 KB795 . . . . . . **398.8**
YOURS TILL BANANA SPLITS: 201 AUTOGRAPH RHYMES./ 1995/
3-6 KD894 . . . . **808.88**
TIGER, S/ Diabetes./ 1987/ A/9 KD018 . . . . **616.4**
TILLER, R/ Cinnamon, mint, and mothballs: a visit to Grandmother's house./
1993/ K-3 KE033 . . . . **811**
TILLEY, D/ Dinosaur dinner (with a slice of alligator pie): favorite poems./
1997/ K-3 KD970 . . . . **811**
God's mailbox: more stories about stories in the Bible./ 1996/
4-6/6 KA678 . . . . **221.9**
TIME-LIFE/ WHAT IS A BELLYBUTTON?: FIRST QUESTIONS AND
ANSWERS ABOUT THE HUMAN BODY./ 1993/ P-K/2 KC929 **612**
TIMMONS, D/ Indian terms of the Americas./ 1994/
5-A KA478 . . . . **REF 970.004**
TINZMANN, M/ Teaching thinking skills: English/language arts./ 1987/
KA280 . . . . **PROF 428**
TITHERINGTON, J/ It's snowing! It's snowing!/ 1984/ K-3 KE005 . **811**
Place for Ben./ 1987/ P-2/2 KG608 . . . . **E**
Pumpkin pumpkin./ 1986/ P-2/1 KG609 . . . . **E**
Pumpkin pumpkin (Big book)./ 1990/ P-2/1 KG609 . . . . **E**
Where are you going, Emma?/ 1988/ P-K/3 KG610 . . . . **E**
TITUS, E/ Kitten who couldn't purr./ 1991/ P-K/1 KG611 . . . . . . **E**
TOBIN, N/ Fraction fun./ 1996/ 2-5/2 KB952 . . . . **513.2**
TODAY IS MONDAY./ 1993/ P-1 KD661 . . . . **789.3**
TODDY, I/ Cheyenne again./ 1995/ 3-5/2 KG941 . . . . **FIC**
Uncegila's seventh spot: a Lakota legend./ 1995/ 3-5/3 KB478 **398.22**
TOFT, L/ More stories Huey tells./ 1997/ 2-4/2 KG968 . . . . . . **FIC**
TOLAN, SS/ Save Halloween!/ 1993/ 5-A/7 KH794 . . . . **FIC**
Who's there?/ 1994/ 5-A/5 KH795 . . . . **FIC**
TOLKIEN, JRR/ Hobbit; or, There and back again./ n.d./
4-6/5 KH796 . . . . **FIC**
Hobbit; or, There and back again (Braille)./ n.d/ 4-6/5 KH796 . . . **FIC**
Hobbit; or, There and back again (Sound recording cassette)./ n.d./
4-6/5 KH796 . . . . **FIC**
Hobbit; or, There and back again (Talking book)./ n.d./
4-6/5 KH796 . . . . **FIC**
TOM SNYDER PRODUCTIONS/ CLASSROOM STOREWORKS
(Microcomputer program)./ 1997/ 2-5 KD313 . . . . **MCP 658**
COLONIZATION (Microcomputer program)./ 1986/
5-A KA667 . . . . **MCP 172**
ENVIRONMENT (Microcomputer program)./ 1990/
5-A KB059 . . . . **MCP 363.73**
EUROPE INSPIRER (CD-ROM)./ 1997/ 4-A KE177 . . . . **CDR 914**
GETTING TO THE HEART OF IT (Videocassette)./ 1993/
5-A KA809 . . . . **VCR 303.6**
GRAPH ACTION (Microcomputer program)./ 1996/
4-A KB936 . . . . **MCP 511**
GRAPH ACTION PLUS (CD-ROM)./ 1996/ 4-A KB937 . . . . **CDR 511**

GREAT OCEAN RESCUE (CD-ROM)./ 1996/ 3-A KC349 . **CDR 577.7**
GREAT SOLAR SYSTEM RESCUE (CD-ROM)./ 1996/
 5-A KC009 . . . . **CDR 523.2**
GREAT SOLAR SYSTEM RESCUE (Videodisc)./ 1992/
 5-A KC010 . . . . **VD 523.2**
IMMIGRATION (Microcomputer program)./ 1996/
 5-A KA917 . . . . **MCP 325**
INTERNATIONAL INSPIRER (Microcomputer program)./ 1990/
 5-A KE149 . . . . **MCP 910**
Kids and the environment: taking responsibility for our surroundings
 (Microcomputer program)./ 1994/ 1-5 KB046 . . . . **CDR 363.7**
MINDS-ON SCIENCE: FOR PROFIT, FOR PLANET (Videodisc)./ 1995/
 5-A KD348 . . . . **VD 687**
MINDS-ON SCIENCE: FOR THE SAKE OF THE NATION (Videodisc)./
 1995/ 5-A KA804 . . . . **VD 303.48**
MINDS-ON SCIENCE: THE IMPACT OF DISCOVERY (Videodisc)./
 1995/ 5-A KB875 . . . . **VD 502**
NATIONAL INSPIRER (Microcomputer program)./ 1997/
 5-A KE190 . . . . **MCP 917.3**
NEIGHBORHOOD MAPMACHINE (Microcomputer program)./ 1997/
 1-5 KC066 . . . . **MCP 526**
ON THE PLAYGROUND (Microcomputer program)./ 1988/
 1-6 KA662 . . . . **MCP 158**
RAINFOREST RESEARCHERS (CD-ROM)./ 1996/
 5-A KC323 . . . . **CDR 577.34**
Research paper writer (Microcomputer program)./ c1990/
 5-A KB090 . . . . **MCP 371.302**
REVOLUTIONARY WARS: CHOOSING SIDES (Microcomputer
 program)./ 1986/ 5-A KA668 . . . . **MCP 172**
SUBSTANCE ABUSE (Microcomputer program)./ 1992/
 4-A KD000 . . . . **MCP 613.8**
TAKING RESPONSIBILITY (Microcomputer program)./ 1988/
 1-6 KA665 . . . . **MCP 158**
TIMELINER: HISTORY IN PERSPECTIVE (Microcomputer program)./
 1986/ K-A KE142 . . . . **MCP 902**
TOM TIT TOT: AN ENGLISH FOLK TALE./ c1965, 1997/
 P-3/6 KB378 . . . . **398.2**
TOMB, H/ MicroAliens: dazzling journeys with an electron microscope./
 1993/ 3-A/7 KC376 . . . . **579**
TOMES, M/ And then what happened, Paul Revere?/ c1973/
 5-6/6 KE510 . . . . **CE B REVERE, P.**
Homesick: my own story./ 1982/ 4-A/4 KH145 . . . . **FIC**
Little Sister and the Month Brothers./ c1976, 1994/
 2-3/2 KB501 . . . . **398.23**
Soup bone./ 1990/ K-2/2 KF841 . . . . **E**
This time, Tempe Wick?/ c1974, 1992/ 3-5/7 KH153 . . . . . **FIC**
Ty's one-man band./ c1980, 1987/ 1-3/2 KG686 . . . . **E**
What's the big idea, Ben Franklin?/ c1976/
 5-6/7 KE355 . . . . **CE B FRANKLIN, B.**
Where do you think you're going, Christopher Columbus?/ 1980/
 4-6/6 KE303 . . . . **CE B COLUMBUS, C.**
Where was Patrick Henry on the 29th of May?/ c1975, 1982/
 5-6/7 KE386 . . . . **CE B HENRY, P.**
TOMLINSON, T/ Forestwife./ 1995/ 6-A/5 KH797 . . . . **FIC**
TOMPERT, A/ Carol for Christmas./ 1994/ K-3/5 KG612 . . . . **E**
Grandfather Tang's story./ 1990/ 2-3/4 KG613 . . . . **E**
TOPAL, CW/ Children and painting./ 1992/ KA217 . . . . . **PROF 372.5**
TOPPER, F/ Historical album of New Jersey./ 1995/
 4-6/7 KE965 . . . . **974.9**
TORNQVIST, M/ Christmas carp./ 1990/ 2-4/2 KH798 . . . . **FIC**
TORNQVIST, R/ Christmas carp./ 1990/ 2-4/2 KH798 . . . . **FIC**
TORRENCE, J/ Brer Rabbit stories (Sound recording cassette)./ 1984/
 4-5 KB666 . . . . **SRC 398.24**
Classic children's tales (Compact disc)./ 1989/ P-1 KB667 . **SRC 398.24**
Classic children's tales (Sound recording cassette)./ 1989/
 P-1 KB667 . . . . **SRC 398.24**
My grandmother's treasure (Sound recording cassette)./ 1993/
 3-5 KH799 . . . . **SRC FIC**
Story lady (Sound recording cassette)./ 1982/ 4-6 KB781   **SRC 398.27**
Traditions: a potpourri of tales (Sound recording cassette)./ 1994/
 2-3 KB668 . . . . **SRC 398.24**
TORRES, L/ Sancocho del sabado./ 1995/ K-2/5 KG614 . . . . **E**
Saturday sancocho./ 1995/ K-2/5 KG614 . . . . **E**
TORTILLITAS PARA MAMA AND OTHER SPANISH NURSERY RHYMES./
 1981/ 1-3 KB816 . . . . **398.8**
TOWER, CC/ Homeless students./ 1989/ KA183 . . . . . . **PROF 371.826**
TOWLE, W/ Real McCoy: the life of an African-American inventor./ c1993,
 1995/ 4-6/7 KE462 . . . . **B MCCOY, E.**
TOWNSEND, B/ Anfernee Hardaway: basketball's lucky penny./ 1997/
 3-5/6 KE384 . . . . **B HARDAWAY, A.**
TOYNTON, E/ Growing up in America, 1830-1860./ 1995/
 A/7 KA896 . . . . **973.5**
TRACHOK, C/ Raccoon at Clear Creek Road./ 1995/
 K-2/3 KG202 . . . . **CE E**

TRACQUI, V/ Cheetah: fast as lightning./ 1992/ 1-4/5 KC819 . **599.75**
Polar bear: master of the ice./ 1994/ 3-5/4 KC865 . . . . **599.786**
TRAFTON, PR/ NEW DIRECTIONS FOR ELEMENTARY SCHOOL
 MATHEMATICS, 1989 YEARBOOK./ 1989/ KA255 . . . **PROF 372.7**
TRAPANI, I/ Itsy bitsy spider./ 1996/ P-1/2 KD662 . . . . **789.3**
TRAVERS, B/ EUREKA!/ 1995/ 4-7 KA451 . . . . **REF 608**
TRAVERS, PL/ Mary Poppins comes back./ 1987/ 4-6/6 KH800 . . . **FIC**
Mary Poppins in Cherry Tree Lane./ 1982/ 4-6/6 KH800 . . . . . . **FIC**
Mary Poppins in Cherry Tree Lane (Braille)./ n.d./ 4-6/6 KH800 . **FIC**
Mary Poppins opens the door (Braille)./ n.d./ 4-6/6 KH800 . . . **FIC**
Mary Poppins. Rev. ed./ c1962/ 4-6/6 KH800 . . . . **FIC**
Mary Poppins. Rev. ed. (Braille)./ n.d./ 4-6/6 KH800 . . . . . . **FIC**
Mary Poppins. Rev. ed. (Sound recording cassette)./ n.d./
 4-6/6 KH800 . . . . **FIC**
Mary Poppins (Talking book)./ n.d./ 4-6 KH801 . . . . **TB FIC**
TREASURY OF ANIMAL STORIES./ 1992/ 3-6/6 KH802 . . . . **FIC**
TREASURY OF GIANT AND MONSTER STORIES./ 1992/
 3-5/6 KH803 . . . . **FIC**
TREASURY OF SPOOKY STORIES./ 1992/ 4-A/6 KH804 . . . . **FIC**
TREASURY OF STORIES FOR FIVE YEAR OLDS./ 1992/
 2-4/5 KH805 . . . . **FIC**
TREASURY OF STORIES FOR SEVEN YEAR OLDS./ 1992/
 3-5/6 KH806 . . . . **FIC**
TREASURY OF STORIES FOR SIX YEAR OLDS./ 1992/
 2-4/5 KH807 . . . . **FIC**
TREGO HILL, V/ Watch out for clever women!/Cuidado con las mujeres
 astutas!./ 1994/ 2-5/4 KB315 . . . . **398.2**
TRELEASE, J/ HEY! LISTEN TO THIS: STORIES TO READ ALOUD./ 1992/
 KA338 . . . . **PROF 808.5**
Read-aloud handbook. 4th ed./ 1995/ KA242 . . . . . **PROF 372.64**
TRESSELT, A/ Gift of the tree./ c1972, 1992/ K-4/6 KC312 . . . . **577.3**
Gift of the tree (Sound recording cassette)./ 1996,/
 K-4/6 KC312 . . . . **577.3**
Hide and seek fog./ c1965/ K-2 KG615 . . . . **E**
Wake up, city!/ c1957, 1990/ 1-3/5 KG616 . . . . **E**
Wake up, city! (Sound recording cassette)./ 1993/ 1-3/5 KG616 . . **E**
TRIMBLE, S/ Village of blue stone./ 1990/ 4-6/6 KF063 . . . . . **979**
TRIMM, WJ/ Backyard safaris: 52 year-round science adventures./ 1995/
 P-A/5 KB901 . . . . **508**
TRINCA, R/ One woolly wombat./ 1985/ P-2/4 KG617 . . . . **E**
TRIPP, W/ Come back, Amelia Bedelia. Newly illustrated ed./ 1995/
 K-2/1 KG213 . . . . **E**
Play ball, Amelia Bedelia./ 1996/ 1-3/2 KG216 . . . . **E**
Stand back, said the elephant, I'm going to sneeze!/ c1971, 1990/
 K-3/2 KG605 . . . . **E**
TRIVAS, I/ Emma's Christmas: an old song./ 1988/ P-3/6 KG618 . . . **E**
Girl named Helen Keller./ 1995/ 1-2/1 KE417 . . . . **B KELLER, H.**
Pain and the great one./ 1984/ K-3/4 KF239 . . . . **CE E**
TRIVIZAS, E/ Three little wolves and the big bad pig./ 1993/
 P-3/4 KG619 . . . . **E**
Tres lobitos y el cochino feroz./ 1995/ P-3/4 KG619 . . . . **E**
TROLL, R/ Raptors, fossils, fins, and fangs: a prehistoric creature feature./
 1996/ 3-6/6 KC239 . . . . **560**
TROOST, E/ BEAUTY AND THE BEAST (Videocassette)./ c1989, 1996/
 K-3 KB259 . . . . **VCR 398.2**
Owen (Videocassette)./ 1995/ P-2 KF710 . . . . **VCR E**
PEGASUS (Videocassette)./ 1990/ 3-6 KA749 . . . . **VCR 292**
TROWER, B/ Anastasia Morningstar and the crystal butterfly. Rev. ed./
 1984/ 4-6/6 KH306 . . . . **FIC**
TRUESDELL, S/ Addie meets Max./ 1985/ K-2/1 KG338 . . . . **E**
Addie's bad day./ 1993/ K-1/2 KG339 . . . . **E**
Golly sisters go West./ 1986/ 1-3/1 KF325 . . . . **CE E**
TRUMBLE, K/ Cat mummies./ 1996/ 3-6/9 KE637 . . . . **932**
TRYON, L/ Albert's alphabet./ 1991/ P-1 KG620 . . . . **E**
Albert's ballgame./ 1996/ P-1 KG620 . . . . **E**
Albert's field trip./ 1993/ P-1 KG620 . . . . **E**
Albert's play./ 1992/ P-1 KG620 . . . . **E**
Albert's Thanksgiving./ 1994/ K-2/2 KG621 . . . . **E**
TSENG, J/ MAPLES IN THE MIST: CHILDREN'S POEMS FROM THE
 TANG DYNASTY./ 1996/ K-3 KE133 . . . . **895**
TSENG, M/ MAPLES IN THE MIST: CHILDREN'S POEMS FROM THE
 TANG DYNASTY./ 1996/ K-3 KE133 . . . . **895**
TUCKER, JC/ Roots and branches: a legacy of multicultural music for
 children./ 1994/ KA320 . . . . **BA PROF 789.3**
TUCKER, JS/ Come look with me: discovering photographs with children./
 1994/ K-6/5 KD511 . . . . **770**
TUDOR, T/ Brighter garden./ 1990/ 3-6 KD932 . . . . **811**
Little princess./ c1963/ 5-A/8 KG949 . . . . **FIC**
Secret garden./ c1911, 1987/ 3-6/5 KG951 . . . . **CE FIC**
Time to keep: the Tasha Tudor book of holidays./ 1996/
 P-A/4 KB204 . . . . **394.26**
TUNG, JD/ Chinese-American experience./ 1993/ 5-6/8 KA864 . **305.8**
TUNIS, E/ Frontier living./ c1961/ 5-6/9 KE893 . . . . **973.4**
Frontier living (Talking book)./ n.d./ 5-6/9 KE893 . . . . **973.4**

Indians. Rev. ed./ 1979/ 4-6/7 KE754 . . . . **970.1**
TUNIS, JR/ Go, team, go!/ c1954, 1991/ 5-A/6 KH808 . . . . **FIC**
Highpockets./ c1948/ 5-A/6 KH809 . . . . **FIC**
Kid comes back./ c1946, 1990/ 5-A/7 KH810 . . . . **FIC**
TUNNELL, MO/ Children of Topaz: the story of a Japanese-American
    internment camp: based on a classroom diary./ 1996/
    5-6/8 KE667 . . . . **940.53**
TUNNEY, L/ Your two brains./ 1986/ 5-6/8 KC981 . . . . **612.8**
TUN-TA-CA-TUN: MORE STORIES AND POEMS IN ENGLISH AND
    SPANISH FOR CHILDREN./ 1986/ K-6 KD905 . . . . **810.8**
TURK, R/ Ray Charles: soul man./ 1996/ 5-A/8 KE286 **B CHARLES, R.**
TURKLE, B/ Do not open./ 1981/ K-2/2 KG622 . . . . **E**
Do not open (Braille)./ n.d./ K-2/2 KG622 . . . . **E**
Rachel and Obadiah./ 1978/ K-3/5 KG623 . . . . **E**
Rachel and Obadiah (Braille)./ n.d./ K-3/5 KG623 . . . . **E**
Thy friend, Obadiah./ c1969/ K-3/5 KG623 . . . . **E**
Thy friend, Obadiah (Braille)./ n.d./ K-3/5 KG623 . . . . **E**
TURLEY, P/ Armadillo Ray./ 1995/ K-2/4 KF216 . . . . **E**
TURNBULL, A/ Maroo of the winter caves./ c1984, 1990/
    5-6/6 KH811 . . . . **FIC**
TURNER, A/ Dakota dugout./ 1985/ 1-3/6 KG624 . . . . **E**
Dust for dinner./ 1995/ 2-5/2 KG625 . . . . **E**
Heron Street./ 1989/ 1-3/3 KG626 . . . . **E**
Katie's trunk./ 1992/ 3-5/3 KG627 . . . . **E**
Moon for seasons./ 1994/ 3-6 KE034 . . . . **811**
Nettie's trip south./ 1987/ 5-A/6 KH812 . . . . **FIC**
Sewing quilts./ 1994/ 1-3/6 KG628 . . . . **E**
Through moon and stars and night skies./ 1990/ P-2/1 KG629 . **CE E**
Through moon and stars and night skies (Kit)./ 1995/
    P-2/1 KG629 . . . . **CE E**
TURNER, BC/ HARK! THE HERALD ANGELS SING./ 1993/
    K-6 KD534 . . . . **782.28**
Living clarinet./ 1996/ 4-6/12 KD552 . . . . **BA 788.6**
Living flute./ 1996/ 4-6/11 KD551 . . . . **BA 788.3**
Living piano./ 1996/ 4-6/12 KD546 . . . . **BA 786.2**
Living violin./ 1996/ 4-6/12 KD549 . . . . **BA 787.2**
TURNER, M/ Come on everybody! Let's go to the fair (Kit)./ 1991/
    P KB182 . . . . **KIT 394**
TURNER, MW/ Instead of three wishes./ 1995/ 5-A/4 KH813 . . . . . **FIC**
TURNER, P/ War between the Vowels and the Consonants./ 1996/
    1-3/3 KG630 . . . . **E**
TURNER, R/ Dorothea Lange./ 1994/ 5-A/7 KE427 . . . . **B LANGE, D.**
Faith Ringgold./ 1993/ 4-A/7 KE511 . . . . **B RINGGOLD, F.**
Texas traditions: the culture of the Lone Star State./ 1996/
    4-6/10 KF003 . . . . **976.4**
TURNER, W/ War between the Vowels and the Consonants./ 1996/
    1-3/3 KG630 . . . . **E**
TUTEN-PUCKETT, KE/ My name in books: a guide to character names in
    children's literature./ 1993/ KA360 . . . . **PROF 809**
TUTTLE, MD/ Batman: exploring the world of bats./ 1991/
    5-A/9 KC762 . . . . **599.4**
TWAIN, M/ Adventures of Tom Sawyer./ 1989/ 5-A/4 KH814 . . . . **FIC**
TWELVE DAYS OF CHRISTMAS./ 1986/ P-A KD537 . . . . **782.28**
TWELVE DAYS OF CHRISTMAS./ 1993/ P-A KD538 . . . . **782.28**
TWIST, C/ Charles Darwin: on the trail of evolution./ 1994/
    5-8/8 KE315 . . . . **B DARWIN, C.**
TYRRELL, EQ/ Hummingbirds: jewels in the sky./ 1992/
    5-6/5 KC703 . . . . **598.7**
TYRRELL, F/ Woodland Christmas: twelve days of Christmas in the North
    Woods./ 1996/ K-2 KD541 . . . . **782.28**
UB40 (MUSICAL GROUP)/ Anansi (Kit)./ 1992/ 3-5 KB572 **KIT 398.24**
UCHIDA, Y/ Best bad thing./ 1983/ 5-6/6 KH815 . . . . **FIC**
Best bad thing (Sound recording cassette)./ n.d./ 5-6/6 KH815 . . . **FIC**
Bracelet./ 1993/ 2-5/3 KG631 . . . . **E**
Happiest ending./ 1985/ 5-6/6 KH815 . . . . **FIC**
Happiest ending (Sound recording cassette)./ n.d./ 5-6/6 KH815 . . **FIC**
Jar of dreams./ 1981/ 5-6/6 KH815 . . . . **FIC**
Jar of dreams (Sound recording cassette)./ n.d./ 5-6/6 KH815 . . . **FIC**
Journey to Topaz./ c1971, 1984/ 5-A/7 KH816 . . . . **FIC**
Magic purse./ 1993/ 2-4/4 KB379 . . . . **398.2**
Wise old woman./ 1994/ 2-4/5 KB492 . . . . **398.22**
UDE, W/ Maybe I will do something./ 1993/ 4-5/6 KB669 . . . . **398.24**
UDRY, JM/ Arbol es hermoso./ 1995/ K-2/2 KG633 . . . . **E**
Let's be enemies./ c1961/ P-1/2 KG632 . . . . **E**
Tree is nice./ c1956/ K-2/2 KG633 . . . . **E**
Tree is nice (Braille)./ n.d./ K-2/2 KG633 . . . . **E**
UDVARDY, MD/ Audubon Society field guide to North American birds--
    Western Region./ 1977/ 3-6/7 KC668 . . . . **598**
ULALI/ Lessons from the animal people (Sound recording cassette)./ 1996/
    2-5 KB664 . . . . **SRC 398.24**
ULLMAN, JR/ Banner in the sky (Braille)./ n.d./ 4-6 KH817 . . . . **TB FIC**
Banner in the sky (Sound recording cassette)./ n.d./ 4-6 KH817 **TB FIC**
Banner in the sky (Talking book)./ n.d./ 4-6 KH817 . . . . . **TB FIC**
ULLMAN, T/ Puss in Boots (Kit)./ 1992/ 1-4 KB620 . . . . . **KIT 398.24**

ULRICH, G/ Emily Eyefinger./ 1992/ 1-3/2 KG876 . . . . **FIC**
UNGERER, T/ Crictor./ c1958/ K-2 KG634 . . . . **E**
Flat Stanley./ c1964, 1989/ 2-4/5 KG931 . . . . **FIC**
Tomi Ungerer Library (Videocassette)./ 1993/ K-2 KG635 . . . . **VCR E**
UNITED NATIONS CHILDREN'S FUND/ Children just like me./ 1995/
    2-6/8 KA825 . . . . **305.23**
UNITED STATES. BUREAU OF PUBLIC AFFAIRS, DEPT. OF STATE./
    Background notes of the countries of the world./ n.d./
    4-6 KA404 . . . . **REF 310**
UNWIN, D/ New book of dinosaurs./ 1997/ K-6/9 KC266 . . . . . **567.9**
UPDIKE, J/ Helpful alphabet of friendly objects: poems./ 1995/
    P-1 KE035 . . . . **811**
URBANIK, MK/ Curriculum planning and teaching using the library media
    center./ 1989/ KA064 . . . . **PROF 025.5**
URBANOVIC, J/ It's all in your head: a guide to understanding your brain
    and boosting your brain power. Rev. ed./ 1992/ A/8 KA633 . . **153**
Survival guide for kids with LD (Learning differences)./ 1990/
    4-6/4 KB094 . . . . **371.92**
USHINSKY, K/ How a shirt grew in the field./ 1992/ K-2/2 KG636 . . **E**
USTINOV, P/ Peep and the big wide world (Videocassette)./ 1991/
    P-2 KG239 . . . . **VCR E**
VAES, A/ Puss in boots./ c1992, 1994/ 3-4/6 KB604 . . . . . . **398.24**
VAGIN, V/ King's equal./ 1992/ 3-6/6 KH578 . . . . **FIC**
VALERI, M/ Mi casa es su casa/my house is your house: a bi-lingual
    musical journey through Latin America (Sound recording cassette)./
    1991/ K-3 KD663 . . . . **SRC 789.3**
VALET, PM/ Colors./ 1991/ K-3/2 KC121 . . . . **535.6**
Fruit./ 1992/ P-3/2 KD159 . . . . **634**
VALGARDSON, WD/ Sarah and the people of Sand River./ 1996/
    4-6/2 KH818 . . . . **FIC**
Winter rescue./ 1995/ 3-5/4 KH819 . . . . **FIC**
VAN ALLSBURG, C/ Bad day at Riverbend./ 1995/ 1-3/3 KG637 . . . **E**
Escoba de la viuda./ 1993/ 4-A/5 KH824 . . . . **FIC**
Expreso polar./ 1994/ 2-A/5 KH822 . . . . **CE FIC**
Garden of Abdul Gasazi./ 1979/ 1-3/5 KG638 . . . . **CE E**
Garden of Abdul Gasazi (Sound recording cassette)./ 1993/
    1-3/5 KG638 . . . . **CE E**
Garden of Abdul Gasazi (Talking book)./ 1983/ 1-3/5 KG638 . . **CE E**
Higo mas dulce./ 1995/ 3-A/3 KH823 . . . . **FIC**
Jumanji./ 1981/ K-A/4 KH820 . . . . **FIC**
Jumanji (Braille)./ n.d./ K-A/4 KH820 . . . . **FIC**
Jumanji (Kit)./ 1995/ K-A KH821 . . . . **KIT FIC**
Polar express./ 1985/ 2-A/5 KH822 . . . . **CE FIC**
Polar express (Braille)./ n.d./ 2-A/5 KH822 . . . . **CE FIC**
Polar express (Sound recording cassette)./ n.d./ 2-A/5 KH822 **CE FIC**
Sweetest fig./ 1993/ 3-A/3 KH823 . . . . **FIC**
Two bad ants./ 1988/ 1-3/4 KG639 . . . . **E**
Widow's broom./ 1992/ 4-A/5 KH824 . . . . **FIC**
Wreck of the Zephyr./ 1983/ 1-5/3 KH825 . . . . **CE FIC**
Wreck of the Zephyr (Picture)./ n.d./ 1-5/3 KH825 . . . . . . **CE FIC**
Wretched stone./ 1991/ 4-A/4 KH826 . . . . **FIC**
Z was zapped./ 1987/ 2-A KG640 . . . . **E**
VAN DAM, L/ PEOPLES OF THE WORLD: NORTH AMERICANS./ 1991/
    6-A KA479 . . . . **REF 970.004**
VAN DER ROL, R/ Anne Frank, beyond the diary: a photographic
    remembrance./ 1993/ 6-A/7 KE353 . . . . **B FRANK, A.**
VAN GELDER, RG/ Animals in winter. Rev. ed./ 1997/
    K-2/2 KC482 . . . . **591.56**
VAN HAGE, MA/ Little green thumbs./ 1996/ 3-5/4 KD176 . . . **635.9**
VAN KAMPEN, V/ My dad takes care of me./ 1987/ 1-3/2 KG295 . **E**
VAN LAAN, N/ Boda: a Mexican wedding celebration./ 1996/
    1-3/2 KG641 . . . . **E**
Possum come a-knockin'./ 1990/ K-2/2 KG642 . . . . **E**
Round and round again./ 1994/ P-2/3 KG643 . . . . **E**
Sleep, sleep, sleep: a lullaby for little ones around the world./ 1995/
    P-2/3 KG644 . . . . **E**
VAN LEEUWEN, J/ Across the wide dark sea: the Mayflower journey./
    1995/ 2-4/4 KG645 . . . . **E**
Amanda Pig and her big brother, Oliver./ 1994/ K-2/1 KG648 . . **CE E**
Amanda Pig and her big brother, Oliver (Kit)./ 1984/
    K-2/1 KG648 . . . . **CE E**
Amanda Pig on her own./ 1991/ K-2/1 KG648 . . . . **CE E**
Amanda Pig, schoolgirl./ 1997/ K-2/1 KG648 . . . . **CE E**
Bound for Oregon./ 1994/ 5-A/5 KH828 . . . . **FIC**
Cuentos del cerdito Oliver./ 1996/ K-2/1 KG649 . . . . **CE E**
Emma Bean./ 1993/ K-2/2 KG646 . . . . **E**
Fourth of July on the plains./ 1997/ 2-5/2 KG647 . . . . **E**
More tales of Amanda Pig./ 1985/ K-2/1 KG648 . . . . **CE E**
Oliver, Amanda, and Grandmother Pig./ c1987/ K-2/1 KG648 . . **CE E**
Oliver and Amanda and the big snow./ 1995/ K-2/1 KG648 . . **CE E**
Oliver and Amanda's Christmas./ 1989/ K-2/1 KG648 . . . . . **CE E**
Oliver and Amanda's Halloween./ 1992/ K-2/1 KG648 . . . . . **CE E**
Oliver Pig at school./ 1994/ K-2/1 KG648 . . . . **CE E**
Tales of Amanda Pig./ 1994/ K-2/1 KG648 . . . . **CE E**

Tales of Amanda Pig (Braille)./ n.d./ K-2/1 KG648 . . . . **CE E**
Tales of Oliver Pig./ 1979/ K-2/1 KG649 . . . . **CE E**
Tales of Oliver Pig (Kit)./ 1983/ K-2/1 KG649 . . . . **CE E**
VAN MANENS/ We recycle and other songs for Earth keepers (Sound
recording cassette)./ 1990/ K-4 KD664 . . . . **SRC 789.3**
VAN METER, V/ Taking flight: my story./ 1995/ 3-6/6 KD101 . **629.13**
Taking flight: my story (Sound recording cassette)./ 1997/
3-6/6 KD101 . . . . **629.13**
VAN NUTT, R/ Junior thunder lord./ 1994/ 2-4/3 KB425 . . . . **398.21**
Savior is born (Kit)./ 1992/ 3-5 KA705 . . . . **KIT 232.92**
VAN ORDEN, P/ Collection program in schools: concepts, practices, and
information sources. 2nd ed./ 1995/ KA054 . . . . **PROF 025.2**
VAN ROSE, S/ Earth atlas./ 1994/ A/7 KA443 . . . . **REF 551**
Volcano and earthquake./ 1992/ 3-6/7 KC160 . . . . . . **551.21**
VAN RYNBACH, I/ Five little pumpkins./ 1995/ P-K/2 KB817 . . . **398.8**
VAN WRIGHT, C/ MAKE A JOYFUL SOUND: POEMS FOR CHILDREN BY
AFRICAN-AMERICAN POETS./ 1991/ 1-6 KE070 . . . . . . **811.008**
Vanished!: the mysterious disappearance of Amelia Earhart./ 1996/
2-4/7 KE328 . . . . **B EARHART, A.**
VAN ZYLE, J/ Kayuktuk: an Arctic quest./ 1996/ 4-A/3 KH235 . . . . **FIC**
VANCIL, M/ NBA basketball basics./ 1995/ 5-6/6 KD779 . . . **796.323**
VANCLEAVE, JP/ Biology for every kid: 101 easy experiments that really
work./ 1989/ P-4/8 KC270 . . . . **570**
Janice VanCleave's guide to the best science fair projects./ 1997/
3-6 KB899 . . . . **507.8**
Janice VanCleave's math for every kid: easy activities that make learning
math fun./ 1991/ 4-6/6 KB933 . . . . **510**
Janice VanCleave's oceans for every kid: easy activities that make learning
science fun./ 1996/ 3-6/8 KC178 . . . . **551.46**
Janice VanCleave's rocks and minerals: mind-boggling experiments you
can turn into science fair projects./ 1996/ 4-6/8 KC228 . . . . . **552**
Janice VanCleave's the human body for every kid: easy activities that
make learning science fun./ 1995/ 5-6/8 KC928 . . . . **612**
VANDE VELDE, V/ Tales from the Brothers Grimm and the Sisters Weird./
1995/ 5-A/6 KH827 . . . . **FIC**
VANDERBEEK, D/ Stormalong (Kit)./ 1995/ 2-5 KB470 . . . **KIT 398.22**
VANDERHEYDEN-TRESCONY, C/ Faxing friends; a resource guide for
forming international friendships among students, age 5-9./ 1992/
KA173 . . . . **PROF 370.117**
VANTASSEL-BASKA, JL/ PATTERNS OF INFLUENCE ON GIFTED
LEARNERS: THE HOME, SELF, AND THE SCHOOL./ 1989/
KA188 . . . . **PROF 371.95**
VARLEY, S/ Badger's parting gifts./ 1984/ 1-3/7 KG650 . . . . **E**
VAUGHAN, MK/ Snap!/ 1996/ K-2/2 KG651 . . . . **E**
Wombat stew./ c1984/ P-2/4 KG652 . . . . **E**
VECCHIONE, G/ 100 amazing make-it-yourself science fair projects./
1995/ KA287 . . . . **PROF 507.8**
VELASQUEZ, E/ Encyclopedia Brown and the case of Pablo's nose./ 1996/
3-5/6 KH736 . . . . **FIC**
Tanya and the Tobo Man/Tanya y el Hombre Tobo: a story in English
and Spanish for children entering therapy/ 1991/
K-2/2 KD040 . . . . **618.92**
Terrible, wonderful tellin' at Hog Hammock./ 1996/ 4-6/6 KH711 . **FIC**
VELTZE, L/ EXPLORING THE SOUTHEAST STATES THROUGH
LITERATURE./ 1994/ KA037 . . . . **PROF 016.975**
VENEZIA, M/ Aaron Copland./ 1995/ 5-6/7 KE304 . . **B COPLAND, A.**
Francisco Goya./ 1991/ 4-5/6 KE376 . . . . **B GOYA, F.**
George Gershwin./ 1994/ 4-6/7 KE368 . . . . **B GERSHWIN, G.**
Henri de Toulouse-Lautrec./ 1995/ 4-6/8 KE568 . . **B TOULOUSE-LAUT**
Igor Stravinsky./ 1996/ 5-6/7 KE557 . . . . **B STRAVINSKY, I**
Salvador Dali./ 1993/ 4-6/7 KE313 . . . . **B DALI, S.**
VENNEMA, P/ Bard of Avon: the story of William Shakespeare./ 1992/
4-6/7 KE538 . . . . **B SHAKESPEARE**
Charles Dickens: the man who had great expectations./ 1993/
5-6/7 KE321 . . . . **B DICKENS, C.**
Cleopatra./ 1994/ 4-6/6 KE295 . . . . **B CLEOPATRA**
Good Queen Bess: the story of Elizabeth I of England./ 1990/
6-A/7 KE337 . . . . **B ELIZABETH I**
Shaka, king of the Zulus./ 1988/ 4-6/6 KE537 . . . . **B SHAKA, KING**
VENTI, AB/ Around the world in 100 years: from Henry the Navigator to
Magellan./ 1994/ 5-A/7 KE164 . . . . **910.92**
VENTURA, P/ Houses: structures, methods, and ways of living./ 1993/
4-A/9 KD395 . . . . **728**
VERHOEVEN, R/ Anne Frank, beyond the diary: a photographic
remembrance./ 1993/ 6-A/7 KE353 . . . . **B FRANK, A.**
VERMEULEN, L/ Desert December./ 1992/ 3-5/4 KH206 . . . . . . **FIC**
VERNE, J/ 20,000 leagues under the sea./ 1980/ 5-6/6 KH829 . . . **FIC**
20,000 leagues under the sea (Braille)./ n.d./ 5-6/6 KH829 . . . . . **FIC**
20,000 leagues under the sea (Sound recording cassette)./ n.d./
5-6/6 KH829 . . . . **FIC**
20,000 leagues under the sea (Talking book)./ n.d./ 5-6/6 KH829 . **FIC**
VERRIER, J/ Swimming and diving./ 1996/ 3-6/8 KD849 . . . . . **797.2**
VERSOLA, AR/ Children from Australia to Zimbabwe: a photographic
journey around the world./ 1997/ 2-5/7 KA822 . . . . **305.23**

VICTOR, M/ Peas and honey: recipes for kids (with a pinch of poetry)./
1995/ 3-6 KD269 . . . . **641.5**
VIESTI, JF/ Celebrate! in South Asia./ 1996/ 2-5/11 KB191 . . . . **394.2**
Celebrate! in Southeast Asia./ 1996/ 2-5/11 KB192 . . . . . . **394.2**
VIGIL, A/ Corn woman: audio stories and legends of the Hispanic
Southwest/La mujer del maiz: cuentos y leyendas del sudoeste Hispano
(Talking book)./ 1995/ 5-6/4 KB380 . . . . **CE 398.2**
Corn woman: stories and legends of the Hispanic Southwest/La mujer del
maiz: cuentos y leyendas del sudoeste Hispano./ 1994/
5-6/4 KB380 . . . . **CE 398.2**
Teatro!: Hispanic plays for young people./ 1996/ KA364 . . **PROF 812**
VIGNA, J/ I wish Daddy didn't drink so much./ 1988/ P-3/2 KG653 . **E**
When Eric's mom fought cancer./ 1993/ 1-3/3 KG654 . . . . **E**
VINCENT, G/ Ernest and Celestine./ 1982/ P-2/1 KG656 . . . . **E**
Ernest and Celestine at the circus./ 1988/ P-2/2 KG655 . . . . **E**
Ernest and Celestine's picnic./ 1982/ P-2/1 KG656 . . . . **E**
Where are you, Ernest and Celestine?/ 1986/ P-2/1 KG656 . . . . . . **E**
VIOLA, HJ/ North American Indians./ 1996/ 4-6/10 KE755 . . . . **970.1**
VIORST, J/ Alexander and the terrible, horrible, no good, very bad day./
c1972/ P-3/7 KG657 . . . . **CE E**
Alexander and the terrible, horrible, no good, very bad day and other
stories and poems (Talking book)./ 1984/ P-3 KG658 . . . . **TB E**
Alexander and the terrible, horrible, no good, very bad day (Sound
recording cassette)./ n.d./ P-3/7 KG657 . . . . **CE E**
Alexander and the terrible, horrible, no good, very bad day (Talking
book)./ n.d./ P-3/7 KG657 . . . . **CE E**
Alexander, que de ninguna manera (le oyen? lo dice en serio!) se va a
mudar./ 1995/ 1-3/2 KG660 . . . . **E**
Alexander, que era rico el domingo pasado./ 1989/
P-3/5 KG659 . . . . **CE E**
Alexander, que era rico el domingo pasado (Kit)./ 1991/
P-3/5 KG659 . . . . **CE E**
Alexander, who used to be rich last Sunday./ c1978/
P-3/5 KG659 . . . . **CE E**
Alexander, who's not (Do you hear me? I mean it!) going to move./
1995/ 1-3/2 KG660 . . . . **E**
Alexander y el dia terrible, horrible, espantoso, horroroso./ 1989/
P-3/7 KG657 . . . . **CE E**
Alexander y el dia terrible, horrible, espantoso, horroroso (Kit)./ 1991/
P-3/7 KG657 . . . . **CE E**
Alphabet from Z to A: (with much confusion on the way)./ 1994/
2-5 KE036 . . . . **811**
Earrings!/ 1990/ 1-3/2 KG661 . . . . **E**
Good-bye book./ 1988/ P-2/2 KG662 . . . . **E**
If I were in charge of the world and other worries./ 1981/
2-4 KE037 . . . . **811**
In I were in charge of the world and other worries (Sound recording
cassette)./ n.d./ 2-4 KE037 . . . . **811**
My mama says there aren't any zombies, ghosts, vampires, creatures,
demons, monsters, fiends, goblins, or things./ 1973/ P-3/4 KG663 . **E**
Sad underwear and other complications: more poems for children and
their parents./ 1995/ 2-4 KE038 . . . . **811**
Tenth good thing about Barney./ c1971/ K-3/2 KG664 . . . . **E**
VISHAKA/ Our most dear friend: Bhagavad-gita for children./ 1996/
2-5/5 KA767 . . . . **294.5**
VITALE, S/ NURSERY TALES AROUND THE WORLD./ 1996/
P-2/7 KB354 . . . . **398.2**
Story of Easter./ 1997/ 2-3/2 KA714 . . . . **263**
When the wind stops. Rev. and newly illustrated ed./ 1995/
K-2/4 KG809 . . . . **E**
VITARELLI, M/ From the mouth of the monster eel: stories from
Micronesia./ 1996/ 2-5/5 KB296 . . . . **398.2**
VIVAS, J/ I went walking./ 1990/ P-1/1 KG732 . . . . **CE E**
Let the celebrations begin!/ 1991/ 4-A/4 KH858 . . . . **FIC**
Let's eat!/ 1997/ P-2/1 KG786 . . . . **E**
Our granny./ 1994/ P-2 KG717 . . . . **E**
Possum magic./ c1983, 1990/ P-2/4 KF571 . . . . **E**
Wilfrid Gordon McDonald Partridge./ 1985/ K-3/6 KF574 . . . . . . **E**
VIVELO, J/ Chills run down my spine./ 1994/ 5-A/4 KH830 . . . . . . **FIC**
VO, DM/ Angel child, dragon child./ c1983, 1989/ 1-3/2 KG584 . . . **E**
Land I lost: adventures of a boy in Vietnam./ 1982/
5-6/7 KE718 . . . . **959.7**
VOGEL, CG/ Great Midwest flood./ 1995/ 4-6/9 KB034 . . . . . **363.3**
Shock waves through Los Angeles: the Northridge earthquake./ 1996/
3-6/10 KB039 . . . . **363.34**
VOGT, G/ Search for the killer asteroid./ 1994/ A/8 KC037 . . . **523.44**
Viking and the Mars landing./ 1991/ A/10 KD132 . . . . **629.43**
VOIGT, C/ Bad girls./ 1996/ 6-A/5 KH831 . . . . **FIC**
Dicey's song./ 1982/ 5-6/6 KH832 . . . . **FIC**
Dicey's song (Braille)./ n.d./ 5-6/6 KH832 . . . . **FIC**
Dicey's song (Sound recording cassette)./ n.d./ 5-6/6 KH832 . . . **FIC**
Homecoming./ 1981/ 6-A/4 KH833 . . . . **FIC**
Homecoming (Braille)./ n.d./ 6-A/4 KH833 . . . . **FIC**
Homecoming (Sound recording cassette)./ n.d./ 6-A/4 KH833 . . . . **FIC**

VOJTECH, A/ First strawberries: a Cherokee story./ 1993/
1-3/4 KB538 . . . . **398.24**
Marushka and the Month Brothers: a folktale./ 1996/
1-3/4 KB513 . . . . **398.23**
Ten flashing fireflies./ 1995/ K-2/2 KG581 . . . . **E**
VON SCHMIDT, E/ By the Great Horn Spoon!/ c1963/
4-6/4 KH119 . . . . **FIC**
Chancy and the Grand Rascal./ c1966, 1997/ 4-6/5 KH120 . . . . . **FIC**
Mr. Mysterious and Company./ c1962, 1997/ 3-6/6 KH126 . . . . . **FIC**
VOS, I/ Anna is still here./ 1993/ 5-A/4 KH834 . . . . **FIC**
Hide and seek./ c1981, 1991/ 5-A/4 KH835 . . . . **FIC**
VOZAR, D/ M.C. Turtle and the Hip Hop Hare: a nursery rap./ 1997/
2-3/2 KG665 . . . . **E**
VUONG, LD/ Sky legends of Vietnam./ 1993/ 3-5/7 KB717 . . . **398.26**
WABER, B/ Funny, funny Lyle./ 1987/ P-2/3 KG667 . . . . **E**
Gina./ 1995/ 1-3/2 KG666 . . . . **E**
House on East 88th Street./ c1962/ P-2/3 KG667 . . . . **E**
Ira says goodbye./ 1988/ K-2/2 KG668 . . . . **CE E**
Ira says goodbye (Kit)./ 1991/ K-2/2 KG668 . . . . **CE E**
Ira says goodbye (Videocassette)./ 1989/ K-2/2 KG668 . . . . **CE E**
Ira sleeps over./ c1972/ K-2/2 KG668 . . . . **CE E**
Ira sleeps over (Kit)./ 1984/ K-2/2 KG668 . . . . **CE E**
Ira sleeps over (Videocassette)./ 1992/ K-2/2 KG668 . . . . . **CE E**
Lovable Lyle./ 1977/ P-2/3 KG672 . . . . **CE E**
Lovable Lyle (Braille)./ n.d./ P-2/3 KG672 . . . . **CE E**
Lyle and the birthday party./ c1966/ P-2/3 KG669 . . . . **E**
Lyle at the office./ 1994/ K-2/3 KG670 . . . . **E**
Lyle at the office (Sound recording cassette)./ 1997/ K-2/3 KG670 . **E**
Lyle finds his mother./ 1974/ P-2/3 KG671 . . . . **E**
Lyle, Lyle, crocodile./ c1965/ P-2/3 KG672 . . . . **CE E**
Lyle, Lyle, crocodile (Kit)./ 1987/ P-2/3 KG672 . . . . **CE E**
Quique duerme fuera de casa./ 1991/ K-2/2 KG668 . . . . . . **CE E**
You look ridiculous said the rhinoceros to the hippopotamus./ c1966/
1-2/2 KG673 . . . . **E**
WADDELL, M/ Can't you sleep, Little Bear? 2nd ed./ c1988, 1992/
P-K/3 KG674 . . . . **E**
Farmer duck./ 1992/ P-1/2 KG675 . . . . **E**
Farmer duck (Big book)./ 1996/ P-1/2 KG675 . . . . **E**
Let's go home, Little Bear./ 1993/ P-K/3 KG676 . . . . **E**
You and me, Little Bear./ 1996/ P-K/1 KG677 . . . . **E**
WADE, B/ Chess for children./ 1993/ 4-A/8 KD756 . . . . **794.1**
WADSWORTH, E/ World of knowing: a story about Thomas Hopkins
Gallaudet./ 1995/ 3-5/6 KE361 . . . . **B GALLAUDET, T.**
WADSWORTH, G/ Along the Santa Fe Trail: Marion Russell's own story./
1993/ 4-6/7 KE199 . . . . **917.8**
John Burroughs, the sage of Slabsides./ 1997/
A/7 KE271 . . . . **B BURROUGHS, J.**
Laura Ingalls Wilder: storyteller of the prairie./ 1997/
4-A/5 KE595 . . . . **B WILDER, L.**
One on a web: counting animals at home./ 1997/ P-2/3 KC456 . **591**
WAGGONER, K/ Partners./ 1995/ 2-4/4 KH836 . . . . **FIC**
WAHL, J/ Little Eight John./ 1992/ 2-3/2 KB783 . . . . **398.27**
Tailypo!/ 1991/ 4-5/4 KB421 . . . . **398.21**
WAITE, MP/ Jojofu./ 1996/ 1-4/5 KB670 . . . . **398.24**
WAKAN, N/ Haiku: one breath poetry./ 1993/ 5-A KE138 . . . . **895.6**
WALDHERR, K/ Book of goddesses./ 1995/ 4-6/8 KA732 . . . . **291.2**
Persephone and the pomegranate: a myth from Greece./ 1993/
4-6/6 KA753 . . . . **292**
Wolfhound./ 1996/ 1-3/3 KF576 . . . . **E**
WALDMAN, C/ Encyclopedia of Native American tribes./ 1988/
4-A KA483 . . . . **REF 970.4**
WALDMAN, N/ America the beautiful./ 1993/ K-3 KD558 . . . . **789.2**
And the Earth trembled: the creation of Adam and Eve./ 1996/
5-6/3 KA788 . . . . **297**
Bayou lullaby./ 1995/ P-2/5 KF163 . . . . **E**
Gold coin./ 1991/ 1-3/4 KF131 . . . . **E**
Nessa's fish./ 1990/ K-2/2 KG041 . . . . **CE E**
Next year in Jerusalem: 3000 years of Jewish stories./ 1996/
3-6/7 KA780 . . . . **296.4**
Quetzal: sacred bird of the cloud forest./ 1996/ 3-6/6 KC702 . **598.7**
Tyger./ 1993/ 1-4 KE096 . . . . **821**
WALKER, BB/ Teaching thinking skills: English/language arts./ 1987/
KA280 . . . . **PROF 428**
WALKER, BK/ LAUGHING TOGETHER: GIGGLES AND GRINS FROM
AROUND THE GLOBE./ c1977, 1992/ 3-A KD731 . . . **793.735**
TREASURY OF TURKISH FOLKTALES FOR CHILDREN./ 1988/
4-5/7 KB512 . . . . **398.23**
WALKER, BM/ Little House cookbook: frontier foods from Laura Ingalls
Wilder's classic stories. New ed./ 1995/ 4-6/9 KD282 . . . **641.5**
Little House cookbook: frontier foods from Laura Ingalls Wilder's classic
stories (Sound recording cassette)./ n.d./ 4-6/9 KD282 . . . **641.5**
WALKER, C/ Waterskiing and kneeboarding./ 1992/
4-A/7 KD851 . . . . **797.3**
WALKER, L/ Carpentry for children./ 1985/ 4-6/8 KD342 . . . **684**

WALKER, ML/ WORLD OF CHILDREN'S SONGS./ 1993/
KA322 . . . . **PROF 789.3**
WALKER, PR/ Big men, big country: a collection of American tall tales./
1993/ 4-A/7 KB493 . . . . **398.22**
Bigfoot and other legendary creatures./ 1992/ 4-6/6 KA564 . **001.944**
Giants!: stories from around the world./ 1995/ 4-6/7 KB381 . **398.2**
Little folk: stories from around the world./ 1997/ 2-4/6 KB494 **398.22**
WALKER, R/ Children's atlas of the human body: actual size bones,
muscles, and organs in full color./ 1994/ 5-6/6 KC908 . . . . . . **611**
WALKER, SM/ Rhinos./ 1996/ 4-6/7 KC803 . . . . **599.66**
Water up, water down: the hydrologic cycle./ 1992/
4-6/7 KC184 . . . . **551.48**
WALKING THE BRIDGE OF YOUR NOSE./ 1995/ 2-4 KE113 . **821.008**
WALL, LM/ Judge Rabbit and the tree spirit: a folktale from Cambodia./
1991/ 3-4/4 KB655 . . . . **398.24**
WALLACE, BB/ Cousins in the castle./ 1996/ 5-A/7 KH837 . . . . . . **FIC**
WALLACE, I/ Sarah and the people of Sand River./ 1996/
4-6/2 KH818 . . . . **FIC**
WALLACE, K/ My hen is dancing./ c1994, 1996/ K-2/2 KD215 . **636.5**
Think of a beaver./ 1993/ K-2/4 KC755 . . . . **599.37**
WALLACE, MD/ America's deserts: guide to plants and animals./ 1996/
2-A/10 KC365 . . . . **578.754**
WALLIS, D/ Something nasty in the cabbages./ 1991/
2-4/3 KB671 . . . . **398.24**
WALLNER, A/ Alcott family Christmas./ 1996/ 1-3/2 KG678 . . . . . . **E**
Beatrix Potter./ 1995/ 3-5/4 KA369 . . . . **PROF B POTTER, B**
Betsy Ross./ 1994/ 3-4/6 KE526 . . . . **B ROSS, B.**
WALPOLE, B/ Water./ 1990/ K-2/5 KC141 . . . . **546**
WALSH, C/ LITTLE BOOK OF LOVE./ 1995/ 4-6 KD886 . . . . **808.81**
WALSH, ES/ Hop jump./ 1993/ P-K/2 KG679 . . . . **E**
Mouse paint./ 1989/ P-1/2 KG680 . . . . **E**
Samantha./ 1996/ K-2/2 KG681 . . . . **E**
You silly goose./ 1992/ P-K/2 KG682 . . . . **E**
WALSH, JP/ Pepi and the secret names./ 1995/ 2-3/6 KG683 . . **E**
Pepi and the secret names (Sound recording cassette)./ 1997/
2-3/6 KG683 . . . . **E**
WALTER, MP/ Brother to the wind./ 1985/ 1-3/2 KG684 . . . . . **E**
Have a happy... a novel./ 1989/ 4-6/4 KH838 . . . . **FIC**
Justin and the best biscuits in the world./ 1986/ 4-6/6 KH839 . **FIC**
Justin and the best biscuits in the world (Sound recording cassette)./ n.d./
4-6/6 KH839 . . . . **FIC**
My mama needs me./ 1983/ P-2/1 KG685 . . . . **E**
Ty's one-man band./ c1980, 1987/ 1-3/2 KG686 . . . . **E**
WALTON, R/ Noah's square dance./ 1995/ K-2/3 KG687 . . . . **E**
WANG, RC/ Magical starfruit tree: a Chinese folktale./ 1993/
2-3/6 KB784 . . . . **398.27**
WARD, J/ FAMILIES: POEMS CELEBRATING THE AFRICAN AMERICAN
EXPERIENCE./ 1994/ K-3 KE057 . . . . **811.008**
WARD, L/ Biggest bear./ c1952/ 1-3/3 KG688 . . . . **CE E**
Biggest bear (Braille)./ n.d./ 1-3/3 KG688 . . . . **CE E**
Biggest bear (Kit)./ 1993/ 1-3/3 KG688 . . . . **CE E**
Biggest bear (Talking book)./ n.d./ 1-3/3 KG688 . . . . **CE E**
Cat who went to heaven. New ed./ c1958/ A/6 KH010 . . . **CE FIC**
Early thunder./ c1967, 1987/ 5-A/6 KH144 . . . . **FIC**
Johnny Tremain: a novel for old and young./ c1943, 1971/
4-6/6 KH131 . . . . **CE FIC**
WARD, ME/ AUTHORS OF BOOKS FOR YOUNG PEOPLE. 3RD ED./
1990/ 5-A KA460 . . . . **REF 809**
WARD, SG/ Laney's lost momma./ 1991/ P-1/2 KF670 . . . . . . **E**
WARD, T/ Field./ 1996/ 3-6/8 KD812 . . . . **796.42**
Track./ 1996/ 3-6/8 KD813 . . . . **796.42**
WARDLAW, L/ Punia and the King of Sharks: a Hawaiian folktale./ 1997/
2-3/3 KB672 . . . . **398.24**
WARHOLA, J/ Hurricane City./ 1993/ K-2/2 KG691 . . . . **E**
Mystery of the several sevens./ 1994/ 2-4/4 KG924 . . . . . . **FIC**
Wizards and the monster./ 1994/ 2-4/4 KG926 . . . . **FIC**
WARNER, JF/ U.S. Marine Corps./ 1991/ 5-6/7 KA990 . . . . **359.9**
U.S. Marine Corps (Sound recording cassette)./ 1995/
5-6/7 KA990 . . . . **359.9**
WARNER, S/ Dog years./ 1995/ 4-6/3 KH840 . . . . **FIC**
WARREN, A/ Orphan train rider: one boy's true story./ 1996/
4-6/8 KB015 . . . . **362.73**
WARREN, S/ Cities in the sand: the ancient civilizations of the Southwest./
1992/ 5-6/8 KF064 . . . . **979**
WARTER, F/ ANNIE OAKLEY (Videocassette)./ 1997/
3-6 KE479 . . . . **VCR B OAKLEY, A.**
WASHINGTON, D/ Anansi (Kit)./ 1992/ 3-5 KB572 . . . . . **KIT 398.24**
WASSON, DC/ That's fresh!: seasonal recipes for young cooks./ 1995/
5-6 KD277 . . . . **641.5**
WATERS, E/ Painting: a young artist's guide./ 1993/
5-6/8 KD470 . . . . **751.4**
WATERS, JF/ Deep-sea vents: living worlds without sun./ 1994/
4-6/7 KC179 . . . . **551.46**

WATERS, K/ Lion dancer: Ernie Wan's Chinese New Year./ 1990/
1-4/2 KB217 . . . . **394.261**
Samuel Eaton's day: a day in the life of a Pilgrim boy./ 1993/
3-5/6 KE948 . . . . **974.4**
Sarah Morton's day: a day in the life of a Pilgrim girl./ 1989/
3-5/3 KE949 . . . . **974.4**
Tapenum's day: a Wampanoag Indian boy in pilgrim times./ 1996/
3-5/2 KE950 . . . . **974.4**
WATKINS, J/ Programming author visits./ 1996/ KA071 . **PROF 027.62**
WATKINS, YK/ My brother, my sister, and I./ 1994/ A/4 KH841 . . **FIC**
My brother, my sister, and I (Sound recording cassette)./ 1996/
A/4 KH841 . . . . **FIC**
So far from the bamboo grove./ c1986, 1994/ 5-A/5 KH842 . . . . **FIC**
WATLING, J/ Along the Santa Fe Trail: Marion Russell's own story./
1993/ 4-6/7 KE199 . . . . **917.8**
Bound for Oregon./ 1994/ 5-A/5 KH828 . . . . **FIC**
Finding Providence: the story of Roger Williams./ 1997/
2-3/4 KE596 . . . . **B WILLIAMS, R.**
First Thanksgiving./ 1990/ 1-4/2 KB227 . . . . **CE 394.264**
Witch hunt: it happened in Salem Village./ 1989/ 3-5/4 KA606 . **133.4**
Women of the lights./ 1996/ 4-6/6 KB148 . . . . **387.1**
WATSON, A/ FOLK ART COUNTING BOOK./ 1992/
P-3/1 KD420 . . . . **745**
WATSON, B/ Charles Darwin: on the trail of evolution./ 1994/
5-8/8 KE315 . . . . **B DARWIN, C.**
WATSON, C/ AppleBet; an ABC./ 1982/ P-1 KG689 . . . . **E**
WATSON, DJ/ Ideas and insights: language arts in the elementary school./
1987/ KA232 . . . . **PROF 372.6**
WATSON, L/ Warriors, warthogs, and wisdom: growing up in Africa./
1997/ 4-6/7 KE589 . . . . **B WATSON, L.**
WATSON, W/ AppleBet; an ABC./ 1982/ P-1 KG689 . . . . **E**
Doctor Coyote: a Native American Aesop's fables./ 1987/
3/3 KB530 . . . . **398.24**
Sleep is for everyone. Newly illustrated ed./ 1997/
K-2/3 KC979 . . . . **612.8**
WATTS, B/ Birds' nest./ 1986/ 2-5/2 KC706 . . . . **598.8**
Butterfly and caterpillar./ 1985/ 2-4/4 KC568 . . . . . **595.78**
Hamster./ 1986/ 2-4/2 KC748 . . . . **599.35**
Ladybug./ 1987/ 3-5/4 KC555 . . . . **595.76**
Mushroom./ 1986/ K-2/2 KC382 . . . . **579.6**
PHOTOGRAPHY./ 1994/ 5-A/7 KD514 . . . . **771**
Potato./ 1987/ 2-4/2 KD172 . . . . **635**
Wolf and the seven little kids: a fairy tale./ 1995/
1-2/4 KB579 . . . . **398.24**
WATTS, J/ Brats./ 1986/ 3-6 KD961 . . . . **811**
Drat these brats!/ 1993/ 3-6 KD962 . . . . **811**
Fresh brats./ 1990/ 3-6 KD964 . . . . **811**
WAUGH, CG/ NEWBERY HALLOWEEN: A DOZEN SCARY STORIES BY
NEWBERY AWARD-WINNING AUTHORS./ 1993/
5-6/5 KH548 . . . . **FIC**
WAUGH, S/ Mennyms./ 1994/ 5-A/7 KH843 . . . . **FIC**
Mennyms alone./ 1996/ 5-A/5 KH844 . . . . **FIC**
Mennyms in the wilderness./ 1995/ 5-A/5 KH845 . . . . **FIC**
Mennyms under siege./ 1996/ 6-A/6 KH846 . . . . **FIC**
WAX, W/ Say no and know why: kids learn about drugs./ 1992/
5-6/5 KA999 . . . . **362.29**
WEATHERFORD, CB/ Juneteenth jamboree./ 1995/ 1-3/5 KG690 . . . **E**
WEAVER, S/ Peachboy (Videocassette)./ 1991/ 2-5 KB469 **VCR 398.22**
WEBB, LS/ Multicultural cookbook for students./ 1993/
KA299 . . . . **PROF 641.59**
WEBB, PH/ Shadowgraphs anyone can make./ 1991/ K-6 KD753 **793.9**
WEBB, S/ Selma, Lord, Selma: girlhood memories of the civil-rights days./
c1980, 1997/ A/7 KA906 . . . . **323.1**
WEBER, J/ Keeping time: from the beginning and into the 21st century./
1993/ 4-6/6 KC067 . . . . **529**
WEBER, L/ Backyard almanac./ 1996/ 3-A/7 KB915 . . . . **508**
WEBSTER, D/ Science in your backyard./ 1987/ A/6 KB881 . . . . **507**
WEEKS, S/ Crocodile smile: 10 songs of the Earth as the animals see it./
1994/ P-2 KD665 . . . . **BA 789.3**
Hurricane City./ 1993/ K-2/2 KG691 . . . . **E**
WEGNER, F/ Giant baby./ 1994/ 3-5/7 KG820 . . . . **FIC**
WEIDHORN, M/ Jackie Robinson./ 1993/
6-A/7 KE518 . . . . **B ROBINSON, J.**
WEIHS, E/ Bar mitzvah: a Jewish boy's coming of age./ 1995/
5-A/7 KA776 . . . . **296.4**
Bat mitzvah: a Jewish girl's coming of age./ 1995/
5-A/10 KA773 . . . . **296.4**
Days of awe: stories for Rosh Hashanah and Yom Kippur./ 1991/
4-6/5 KA777 . . . . **296.4**
Don't sing before breakfast, don't sleep in the moonlight: everyday
superstitions and how they began./ 1988/ 4-A/8 KA559 . . . . **001.9**
How a shirt grew in the field./ 1992/ K-2/2 KG636 . . . . **E**
Mummies, tombs, and treasure: secrets of ancient Egypt./ 1987/
5-A/8 KE636 . . . . **932**

Story of Passover./ 1997/ 2-4/3 KA781 . . . . **296.4**
Two very little sisters./ 1993/ 2-4/5 KC879 . . . . **599.9**
WEIL, A/ Michael Dorris./ 1997/ 6-A/7 KE323 . . . . . . **B DORRIS, M.**
WEIMER, TE/ Fingerplays and action chants: volume 1: animals./ 1995/
P-1 KD710 . . . . **BA 793.4**
Fingerplays and action chants: volume 1: animals (Sound recording
cassette)./ 1986/ P-1 KD710 . . . . **BA 793.4**
Fingerplays and action chants, volume 2: family and friends./ 1996/
P-1 KD710 . . . . **BA 793.4**
Fingerplays and action chants, volume 2 (Sound recording cassette)./
1986/ P-1 KD710 . . . . **BA 793.4**
WEINER, E/ Story of Frederick Douglass: voice of freedom./ 1996/
3-5/3 KE326 . . . . **B DOUGLASS, F.**
WEINMAN, B/ Tales from the Brothers Grimm and the Sisters Weird./
1995/ 5-A/6 KH827 . . . . **FIC**
WEINMAN, R/ Nate the Great and the pillowcase./ 1993/
1-3/1 KG486 . . . . **E**
WEISGARD, L/ Courage of Sarah Noble./ c1954, 1987/
3-5/3 KH058 . . . . **CE FIC**
Favorite poems, old and new, selected for boys and girls./ c1957/
5-6 KA467 . . . . **REF 811.008**
WEISS, AE/ Lies, deception and truth./ 1988/ 6-A/9 KA671 . . . . **177**
WEISS, E/ It's like this, Cat./ c1963/ 5-6/6 KH547 . . . . **CE FIC**
Very noisy girl./ 1991/ K-2/2 KG747 . . . . **E**
WEISS, GD/ What a wonderful world./ 1995/ P-2/2 KG692 . . . . . **E**
WEISS, H/ Maps: getting from here to there./ 1991/ 3-6/6 KE173 **912**
Strange and wonderful aircraft./ 1995/ 4-6/6 KD102 . . . . . . **629.13**
WEISS, J/ ANIMAL TALES (Sound recording cassette)./ 1990/
P-2 KB523 . . . . **SRC 398.24**
ARABIAN NIGHTS (Sound recording cassette)./ 1991/
4-5 KB254 . . . . **SRC 398.2**
FAIRYTALE FAVORITES IN STORY AND SONG (Sound recording
cassette)./ 1993/ K-3 KB294 . . . . **SRC 398.2**
GREEK MYTHS (Sound recording cassette)./ 1989/
5-6 KA743 . . . . **SRC 292**
KING ARTHUR AND HIS KNIGHTS (Sound recording cassette)./ 1991/
5-6 KB462 . . . . **SRC 398.22**
SHAKESPEARE FOR CHILDREN (Sound recording cassette)./ 1995/
4-6 KE117 . . . . **SRC 822.3**
SHE AND HE: ADVENTURES IN MYTHOLOGY (Sound recording
cassette)./ 1991/ 5-6 KA752 . . . . **SRC 292**
TALES FROM CULTURES FAR AND NEAR (Sound recording cassette)./
1990/ 3-4 KB375 . . . . **SRC 398.2**
WEISS, N/ Stone men./ 1993/ K-2/2 KG693 . . . . **E**
WEISSMAN, B/ From caterpillar to butterfly./ 1996/
K-2/2 KC561 . . . . **595.78**
WEISSMAN, J/ Joining hands with other lands: multicultural songs and
games (Sound recording cassette)./ 1993/ K-3 KD666 . . **SRC 789.3**
Joining hands with other lands: multicultural songs and games (Compact
disc)./ 1994/ K-3 KD666 . . . . **SRC 789.3**
WEISSMAN, P/ Great Voyager adventure: a guided tour through the solar
system./ 1990/ A/9 KC026 . . . . **523.4**
WELCH, W/ Playing right field./ 1995/ K-2/3 KG694 . . . . **E**
WELLER, FW/ Riptide./ 1990/ 1-3/4 KG695 . . . . **E**
WELLINGTON, M/ Who is tapping at my window?/ c1988, 1994/
P-K KD930 . . . . **811**
WELLS, H/ Master puppeteer./ c1975/ 6-A/6 KH580 . . . . **FIC**
WELLS, R/ Bunny cakes./ 1997/ P-1/2 KG696 . . . . **E**
Eduardo cumpleanos en la piscina./ 1996/ P-K/2 KG697 . . . . **E**
Eduardo: el primer dia de colegio./ 1997/ P-K/2 KG698 . . . . **E**
Edward in deep water./ 1995/ P-K/2 KG697 . . . . **E**
Edward unready for school./ 1995/ P-K/2 KG698 . . . . **E**
Edward's overwhelming overnight./ 1995/ P-1/2 KG699 . . . . . **E**
Farmer and the Poor God: a folktale from Japan./ 1996/
2-4/3 KB785 . . . . **398.27**
Max and Ruby's first Greek myth: Pandora's box./ 1993/
P-1/3 KG700 . . . . **E**
Max and Ruby's Midas: another Greek myth./ 1995/ P-1/3 KG701 . **E**
Max's chocolate chicken./ 1989/ P-2/2 KG702 . . . . **CE E**
Max's chocolate chicken (Videocassette)./ 1991/ P-2/2 KG702 . . **CE E**
Max's Christmas./ 1986/ P-1/2 KG703 . . . . **CE E**
Max's Christmas (Videocassette)./ n.d./ P-1/2 KG703 . . . . . . **CE E**
Max's first word (Board book)./ 1979/ P/1 KG704 . . . . **BB E**
Max's new suit./ 1979/ P/1 KG704 . . . . **BB E**
Max's ride./ 1979/ P/1 KG704 . . . . **BB E**
McDuff comes home./ 1997/ K-2/2 KG705 . . . . **E**
McDuff moves in./ 1997/ K-2/2 KG706 . . . . **E**
MY VERY FIRST MOTHER GOOSE./ 1996/ P-K/2 KB808 . . . . **398.8**
Noisy Nora./ 1997/ K-1/4 KG707 . . . . **CE E**
Noisy Nora (Big book)./ 1979/ K-1/4 KG707 . . . . **CE E**
Noisy Nora (Kit)./ 1993/ K-1/4 KG707 . . . . **CE E**
Noisy Nora (Videocassette)./ 1993/ K-1 KG708 . . . . **VCR E**
Nora la revoltosa./ 1997/ K-1/4 KG707 . . . . **CE E**
Tell me a Trudy./ c1977, 1981/ K-3/4 KG427 . . . . **E**

WELLS, RE/ Is a blue whale the biggest thing there is?/ 1993/
K-2/2 KC087 . . . . **530.8**
What's smaller than a pygmy shrew?/ 1995/ 3-6/5 KC140 . . . . **539.7**
WELLS, RS/ Dolphin man: exploring the world of dolphins./ 1995/
5-6/11 KC776 . . . . **599.5**
WELTON, J/ Drawing: a young artist's guide./ 1994/
3-6/6 KD406 . . . . **741.2**
WENZEL, D/ Backyard dragon./ 1993/ 4-6/6 KH753 . . . . **FIC**
WEST, K/ Warriors, warthogs, and wisdom: growing up in Africa./ 1997/
4-6/7 KE589 . . . . **B WATSON, L.**
WEST, R/ My very own Halloween: a book of cooking and crafts./ 1993/
3-6/5 KD701 . . . . **793.2**
WESTALL, R/ Christmas spirit: two stories./ 1994/ 6-A/6 KH847 . . . **FIC**
WESTCOTT, NB/ Best vacation ever./ 1997/ K-2/2 KG164 . . . . **E**
Even little kids get diabetes./ 1991/ K-2/2 KD017 . . . . **616.4**
Famous seaweed soup./ 1993/ P-2/4 KG070 . . . . **E**
I know an old lady who swallowed a fly./ 1980/ P-3 KE039 . . **CE 811**
Is there room on the feather bed?/ 1997/ K-2/4 KF636 . . . . **E**
JUBA THIS AND JUBA THAT./ 1995/ KA366 . . . . **PROF 820.8**
Lady with the alligator purse./ 1988/ P-1 KB818 . . . . **398.8**
Lion who had asthma./ 1992/ P-2/2 KG025 . . . . **E**
NEVER TAKE A PIG TO LUNCH AND OTHER POEMS ABOUT THE FUN
OF EATING./ 1994/ 1-4 KE073 . . . . **811.008**
Oh, cats!/ 1997/ P-1/1 KF290 . . . . **E**
Round and round again./ 1994/ P-2/3 KG643 . . . . **E**
What's alive?/ 1995/ 1-3/2 KC301 . . . . **577**
WESTON, M/ Bet you can't: science impossibilities to fool you./ 1980/
5-6/6 KB880 . . . . **507**
Do you wanna bet?: your chance to find out about probability./ 1991/
4-6/4 KB997 . . . . **519.2**
Math for smarty pants./ 1982/ 4-6/5 KB946 . . . . **513**
New complete babysitter's handbook./ 1995/ 5-6/6 KD302 . . . . **649**
Sierra Club kid's guide to planet care and repair./ 1993/
4-6/7 KB048 . . . . **363.7**
Social smarts: manners for today's kids./ 1996/ 4-6/6 KB243 . . **395.3**
This book is about time./ 1978/ 4-6/6 KC068 . . . . **529**
WESTRAY, K/ Color sampler./ 1993/ 1-6/5 KC125 . . . . **535.6**
Picture puzzler./ 1994/ 1-6/7 KA621 . . . . **152.14**
WEXLER, J/ Fish hatches./ c1978/ P-A/3 KC596 . . . . **597.5**
Pet gerbils./ 1990/ 4-6/7 KD186 . . . . **636**
Pet hamsters./ 1992/ 4-6/7 KD187 . . . . **636**
Queen Anne's lace./ 1994/ 2-6/6 KC433 . . . . **583**
WHALLEY, P/ Butterfly and moth./ 1988/ A/10 KC569 . . . . **595.78**
WHAT A MORNING! THE CHRISTMAS STORY IN BLACK SPIRITUALS./
1987/ K-6 KD532 . . . . **782.25**
WHAYNE, SS/ Night creatures./ 1993/ 4-6/5 KC479 . . . . **591.5**
WHEATLEY, N/ My place./ 1992/ 5-6/3 KF118 . . . . **994**
WHEELER, C/ Bookstore cat./ 1994/ K-2/2 KG709 . . . . **E**
WHEELER, J/ Wild weather. Tornadoes!/ 1994/ 2-6/3 KC199 . . **551.55**
WHELAN, G/ Next spring an oriole./ 1987/ 2-4/5 KH848 . . . . . **FIC**
Week of raccoons./ 1988/ K-2/5 KG710 . . . . **E**
WHIPPLE, L/ Eric Carle's animals, animals./ 1989/ P-3 KD880 . . **808.81**
Eric Carle's dragons dragons and other creatures that never were./ 1991/
K-3 KD881 . . . . **808.81**
WHITAKER, JO/ Audubon Society field guide to North American mammals.
Rev. & expanded./ 1996/ 3-6 KC730 . . . . **599.097**
WHITCHER, S/ Real mummies don't bleed: friendly tales for October
nights./ 1993/ 4-6/5 KH849 . . . . **FIC**
WHITE, DJ/ Homeless students./ 1989/ KA183 . . . . . . **PROF 371.826**
WHITE, EB/ Charlotte's web./ c1952/ 3-6/6 KH850 . . . . **FIC**
Charlotte's web (Braille)./ n.d./ 3-6/6 KH850 . . . . **FIC**
Charlotte's web (Sound recording cassette)./ n.d./ 3-6/6 KH850 . . **FIC**
Charlotte's web (Talking book)./ n.d./ 3-6/6 KH850 . . . . . . **FIC**
Stuart Little./ c1945/ 3-6/5 KH851 . . . . **FIC**
Stuart Little (Braille)./ n.d./ 3-6/5 KH851 . . . . **FIC**
Stuart Little (Spanish version)./ n.d./ 3-6/5 KH851 . . . . . . **FIC**
Stuart Little (Talking book)./ n.d./ 3-6/5 KH851 . . . . **FIC**
Tela Charlottae./ 1991/ 3-6/6 KH850 . . . . **FIC**
Trumpet of the swan./ c1970/ 3-6/6 KH852 . . . . **FIC**
Trumpet of the swan (Braille)./ n.d./ 3-6/6 KH852 . . . . **FIC**
Trumpet of the swan (Sound recording cassette)./ n.d./
3-6/6 KH852 . . . . **FIC**
Trumpet of the swan (Talking book)./ n.d./ 3-6/6 KH852 . . . . . **FIC**
WHITE, FM/ Story of Junipero Serra: brave adventurer./ 1996/
4-6/7 KE536 . . . . **B SERRA, J.**
WHITE, N/ Kids' science book: creative experiences for hands-on fun./
1995/ P-4/7 KB892 . . . . **507.8**
WHITE, R/ Belle Prater's boy./ 1996/ 6-A/6 KH853 . . . . **FIC**
Ryan White: my own story./ 1991/ 5-A/5 KE594 . . . . . **B WHITE, R.**
Sweet Creek Holler./ 1988/ 6/7 KH854 . . . . **FIC**
WHITE, RE/ Field guide to the insects of America north of Mexico./ 1970/
A/12 KA447 . . . . **REF 595.7**
WHITE, S/ Welcome home!/ 1995/ 4-6/6 KD396 . . . . **728**

WHITE, TN/ Missions of the San Francisco Bay Area./ 1996/
4-6/9 KF087 . . . . **979.4**
WHITELAW, N/ Theodore Roosevelt takes charge./ 1992/
5-A/7 KE525 . . . . **B ROOSEVELT, T.**
Theodore Roosevelt takes charge (Sound recording cassette)./ 1995/
5-A/7 KE525 . . . . **B ROOSEVELT, T.**
WHITELEY, S/ REFERENCE BOOKS BULLETIN, 1994-1995: A
COMPILATION OF EVALUATIONS APPEARING IN "REFERENCE
BOOKS/ 1995/ KA006 . . . . **PROF 011**
WHITIN, DJ/ It's the story that counts: more children's books for
mathematical learning, K-6./ 1995/ KA258 . . . . **PROF 372.7**
WHITING, C/ Oh, how waffle!: riddles you can eat./ 1993/
2-6 KD735 . . . . **793.735**
WHITMAN, S/ Get up and go!: the history of American road travel./
1996/ 4-A/10 KB160 . . . . **388.1**
Uncle Sam wants you!: military men and women of World War II./ 1993/
A/8 KE675 . . . . **940.54**
V is for victory: the American home front during World War II./ 1993/
5-6/8 KE919 . . . . **973.917**
WHITNEY, S/ Western forests./ 1985/ A KC313 . . . . **577.3**
WHITTIER, JG/ Barbara Frietchie./ 1992/ 1-3 KE040 . . . . **811**
WHYTE, M/ Boomer's big day./ 1994/ K-2/2 KG102 . . . . **E**
WIBBERLEY, L/ John Treegate's musket./ c1959, 1986/
5-6/7 KH855 . . . . **FIC**
WIBERG, H/ Tomten./ c1965, 1997/ K-2/3 KF986 . . . . **CE E**
WICK, W/ Drop of water: a book of science and wonder./ 1997/
K-6/6 KC142 . . . . **546**
I spy Christmas: a book of picture riddles./ 1992/ P-2 KD715 . **793.73**
I spy fantasy: a book of picture riddles./ 1994/ K-3/3 KD716 . **793.73**
I spy school days: a book of picture riddles./ 1995/
K-3/3 KD717 . . . . **793.73**
I spy spooky night: a book of picture riddles./ 1996/
P-3/5 KD718 . . . . **793.73**
WICKHAM, M/ Superstars of women's track and field./ 1997/
4-6/7 KD814 . . . . **796.42**
WICKSTROM, S/ Hey! I'm reading!: a how-to-read book for beginners./
1995/ P-1/2 KB103 . . . . **372.4**
Wheels on the bus./ c1988, 1990/ P-2 KD653 . . . . **789.3**
WICKSTROM, T/ I'm not moving, Mama!/ 1990/ P-1/1 KF355 . . . . **E**
Noah's square dance./ 1995/ K-2/3 KG687 . . . . **E**
WIDMAN, C/ Lemon drop jar./ 1992/ P-2/2 KG711 . . . . **E**
WIELER, DJ/ To the mountains by morning./ 1996/ 4-6/5 KH856 . . **FIC**
WIENER, LS/ BE A FRIEND: CHILDREN WHO LIVE WITH HIV SPEAK./
1994/ 2-6/2 KA993 . . . . **362.1**
WIESE, K/ Story about Ping./ c1933/ P-1/6 KF550 . . . . **CE E**
WIESNER, D/ Hurricane./ 1990/ K-2/2 KG712 . . . . **E**
June 29, 1999./ 1992/ 1-5/4 KG713 . . . . **E**
Rainbow people./ c1989, 1991/ 5-A/4 KB788 . . . . **398.27**
Tuesday./ 1991/ P-3 KG714 . . . . **E**
WIGGIN, KD/ ARABIAN NIGHTS: THEIR BEST-KNOWN TALES./ c1909,
1994/ 5-A/9 KB255 . . . . **398.2**
Rebecca of Sunnybrook Farm./ 1994/ 5-A/6 KH857 . . . . **FIC**
WIJNGAARD, J/ Emma Bean./ 1993/ K-2/2 KG646 . . . . **E**
Esther's story./ 1996/ 4-A/4 KA690 . . . . **222**
NATIVITY./ 1996/ 3-5/5 KA709 . . . . **232.92**
Sir Gawain and the green knight./ 1981/ 6/6 KB450 . . . . . . **398.22**
WIKLAND, I/ Lotta's Christmas surprise./ c1977, 1990/ 1-2/2 KF985 . **E**
WIKLER, A/ Alfonse, where are you?/ 1996/ P-K/1 KG715 . . . . . . **E**
WIKLER, M/ Miracle meals, eight nights of food 'n fun for Chanukah./
1987/ 4-5 KD288 . . . . **641.59**
WILCOX, C/ Mummies and their mysteries./ 1993/ 5-6/6 KB177 . . **393**
Powerhouse: inside a nuclear power plant./ 1996/
5-A/11 KD049 . . . . **621.48**
WILCOX, S/ Of bugs and beasts: fact, folklore, and activities./ 1995/
KA296 . . . . **PROF 591**
WILD, M/ Going home./ 1993/ 1-3/3 KG716 . . . . **E**
Let the celebrations begin!/ 1991/ 4-A/4 KH858 . . . . **FIC**
Our granny./ 1994/ P-2 KG717 . . . . **E**
Toby./ 1994/ 1-3/3 KG718 . . . . **E**
WILDE, S/ It's the story that counts: more children's books for mathematical
learning, K-6./ 1995/ KA258 . . . . **PROF 372.7**
WILDER, LI/ By the shores of Silver Lake./ 1953/ 3-6/4 KH860 . . . . **FIC**
By the shores of Silver Lake (Braille)./ n.d./ 3-6/4 KH860 . . . . . . **FIC**
By the shores of Silver Lake (Sound recording cassette)./ n.d./
3-6/4 KH860 . . . . **FIC**
By the shores of Silver Lake (Talking book)./ n.d./ 3-6/4 KH860 . . **FIC**
Dance at Grandpa's./ 1994/ K-3/4 KG719 . . . . **E**
Farmer boy./ c1953/ 3-6/5 KH859 . . . . **FIC**
Farmer boy (Braille)./ n.d./ 3-6/5 KH859 . . . . **FIC**
Farmer boy (Sound recording cassette)./ n.d./ 3-6/5 KH859 . . . . **FIC**
Farmer boy (Talking book)./ n.d./ 3-6/5 KH859 . . . . **FIC**
First four years./ 1953/ 3-6/4 KH860 . . . . **FIC**

First four years (Braille)./ n.d./ 3-6/4 KH860 . . . . **FIC**
First four years (Sound recording cassette)./ n.d./ 3-6/4 KH860 . . . **FIC**
First four years (Talking book)./ n.d./ 3-6/4 KH860 . . . . **FIC**
Little house in the Big Woods./ c1953/ 3-6/4 KH860 . . . . **FIC**
Little house in the Big Woods (Braille)./ n.d./ 3-6/4 KH860 . . . . . . **FIC**
Little house in the Big Woods (Large type)./ n.d./ 3-6/4 KH860 . . . **FIC**
Little house in the Big Woods (Sound recording cassette)./ n.d./ 3-6/4 KH860 . . . . **FIC**
Little house in the Big Woods (Talking book)./ n.d./ 3-6/4 KH860 . **FIC**
Little house on the prairie./ 1954/ 3-6/4 KH860 . . . . **FIC**
Little house on the prairie (Braille)./ n.d./ 3-6/4 KH860 . . . . **FIC**
Little house on the prairie (Talking book)./ n.d./ 3-6/4 KH860 . . . . **FIC**
Little town on the prairie./ 1953/ 3-6/4 KH860 . . . . **FIC**
Little town on the prairie (Sound recording cassette)./ n.d./ 3-6/4 KH860 . . . . **FIC**
Little town on the prairie (Talking book)./ n.d./ 3-6/4 KH860 . . . . **FIC**
Long winter./ 1953/ 3-6/4 KH860 . . . . **FIC**
Long winter (Braille)./ n.d./ 3-6/4 KH860 . . . . **FIC**
Long winter (Sound recording cassette)./ n.d./ 3-6/4 KH860 . . . . . **FIC**
Long winter (Talking book)./ n.d./ 3-6/4 KH860 . . . . **FIC**
On the banks of Plum Creek./ 1953/ 3-6/4 KH860 . . . . **FIC**
On the banks of Plum Creek (Braille)./ n.d./ 3-6/4 KH860 . . . . . . **FIC**
On the banks of Plum Creek (Sound recording cassette)./ n.d./ 3-6/4 KH860 . . . . **FIC**
On the banks of Plum Creek (Talking book)./ n.d./ 3-6/4 KH860 . . **FIC**
These happy golden years./ 1953/ 3-6/4 KH860 . . . . **FIC**
Those happy golden years (Braille)./ n.d./ 3-6/4 KH860 . . . . **FIC**
Those happy golden years (Sound recording cassette)./ n.d./ 3-6/4 KH860 . . . . **FIC**
Those happy golden years (Talking book)./ n.d./ 3-6/4 KH860 . . . **FIC**
Winter days in the Big Woods./ 1994/ K-3/4 KG720 . . . . **E**
WILDSMITH, B/ Brian Wildsmith's ABC./ 1995/ P-1 KG721 . . . . **E**
Fishes./ 1985/ P KC587 . . . . **597**
Professor Noah's spaceship./ 1980/ K-2/5 KG722 . . . . **E**
Saint Francis./ 1996/ 2-4/2 KE350 . . . . **B FRANCIS, ST.**
Sara Crewe./ 1986/ 4-6/7 KG950 . . . . **FIC**
WILHELM, H/ Higgle wiggle: happy rhymes./ 1994/ P-1 KD983 . . . **811**
I'm tyrannosaurus!: a book of dinosaur rhymes./ 1993/ K-2/3 KD981 . . . . **811**
Royal raven./ 1996/ K-2/2 KG723 . . . . **E**
WILK, B/ Letter from an Apache: a true story (Videocassette)./ 1983/ 4-6 KE777 . . . . **VCR 970.3**
WILKE, H/ Turtles: everything about purchase, care, nutrition and diseases./ 1983/ 5-6/9 KD250 . . . . **639.3**
WILKER, J/ Harlem Globetrotters./ 1997/ 5-6/10 KD780 . . . . **796.323**
WILKES, A/ Mi primer libro de palabras en Espanol./ 1993/ P-2 KB839 . . . . **423**
Mon premier livre de mots en Francais./ 1993/ P-2 KB839 . . . . . **423**
My first Christmas activity book./ 1994/ 3-6 KD460 . . . . . . **745.594**
My first word book./ 1991/ P-2 KB839 . . . . **423**
WILKES, MD/ Little house in Brookfield./ 1996/ 4-6/5 KH861 . . . . . **FIC**
Little town at the crossroads./ 1997/ 4-6/5 KH861 . . . . **FIC**
WILKES, S/ One day we had to run!: refugee children tell their stories in words and paintings./ 1994/ 4-A/5 KB019 . . . . **362.87**
WILKINSON, P/ Amazing buildings./ 1993/ 4-A/9 KD385 . . . . . . **720**
Building./ 1995/ 5-6/7 KD360 . . . . **690**
WILLARD, N/ Beauty and the Beast./ 1992/ 4-A/6 KH862 . . . . **FIC**
Island of the grass king./ 1979/ 3-5/6 KH863 . . . . **FIC**
Sailing to Cythera, and other Anatole stories./ 1974/ 3-5/6 KH863 . . . . **FIC**
Simple pictures are best./ c1977/ K-3/6 KG724 . . . . **E**
Sorcerer's apprentice./ 1993/ 2-5 KE041 . . . . **811**
Starlit somersault downhill./ 1993/ K-2/3 KG725 . . . . **E**
Visit to William Blake's inn: poems for innocent and experienced travelers./ 1981/ 5-A KE042 . . . . **CE 811**
Visit to William Blake's inn: poems for innocent and experienced travelers (Braille)./ n.d./ 5-A KE042 . . . . **CE 811**
Visit to William Blake's inn: poems for innocent and experienced travelers (Sound recording cassette)./ n.d./ 5-A KE042 . . . . **CE 811**
WILLEY, B/ Golden hoard: myths and legends of the world./ 1996/ 2-5/7 KB344 . . . . **398.2**
Michael Rosen's ABC./ 1996/ 2-4 KE109 . . . . **821**
Nonsense songs./ 1997/ K-3 KE104 . . . . **821**
Silver treasure: myths and legends of the world./ 1996/ K-6/6 KB345 . . . . **398.2**
WILLIAMS, CA/ Tsubu the little snail./ 1995/ 3-5/4 KB673 . . . . **398.24**
WILLIAMS, D/ Grandma Essie's covered wagon./ 1993/ 2-4/4 KG726 . . . . **E**
WILLIAMS, G/ Bedtime for Frances. Newly ill. ed./ 1995/ P-1/2 KF739 . . . . **CE E**
Beneath a blue umbrella./ 1990/ K-2 KE001 . . . . **811**
Charlotte's web./ c1952/ 3-6/6 KH850 . . . . **FIC**
Chester Cricket's new home./ 1983/ 2-4/5 KH692 . . . . **FIC**
Chester Cricket's pigeon ride./ 1983/ 3-4/5 KH693 . . . . **FIC**
Cricket in Times Square./ c1960/ 4-6/6 KH694 . . . . **CE FIC**
Family under the bridge./ c1958/ 3-5/4 KG974 . . . . **FIC**
Farmer boy./ c1953/ 3-6/5 KH859 . . . . **FIC**
Harry Kitten and Tucker Mouse./ 1986/ 2-4/4 KH696 . . . . **FIC**
Little House cookbook: frontier foods from Laura Ingalls Wilder's classic stories. New ed./ 1995/ 4-6/9 KD282 . . . . **641.5**
Little house in the Big Woods./ c1953/ 3-6/4 KH860 . . . . **FIC**
Old meadow./ 1987/ 3-5/5 KH697 . . . . **FIC**
Over and over./ c1957/ P-2/2 KG807 . . . . **E**
Ride a purple pelican./ 1986/ P-3 KE014 . . . . **811**
Stuart Little./ c1945/ 3-6/5 KH851 . . . . **FIC**
Tucker's countryside./ c1969, 1989/ 4-6/5 KH698 . . . . **FIC**
WILLIAMS, J/ AFRICAN AMERICAN ALMANAC. 7th ed./ 1997/ 5-A KA486 . . . . **REF 973**
Christmas kitten./ 1994/ K-1/1 KG204 . . . . **E**
Stringbean's trip to the shining sea./ 1988/ K-A/2 KG739 . . . . **E**
WILLIAMS, JK/ Amish./ 1996/ 5-A/9 KA721 . . . . **289.7**
WILLIAMS, KL/ Galimoto./ 1990/ 1-2/2 KG727 . . . . **CE E**
Galimoto (Kit)./ 1993/ 1-2/2 KG727 . . . . **CE E**
Galimoto (Videocassette)./ 1993/ 1-2/2 KG727 . . . . **CE E**
Tap-tap./ 1994/ K-2/2 KG728 . . . . **CE E**
Tap-tap (Kit)./ 1996/ K-2/2 KG728 . . . . **CE E**
When Africa was home./ 1991/ K-3/2 KG729 . . . . **E**
WILLIAMS, L/ Little old lady who was not afraid of anything./ 1986/ P-2/4 KG730 . . . . **CE E**
Little old lady who was not afraid of anything (Kit)./ 1995/ P-2/4 KG730 . . . . **CE E**
Viejecita que no le tenia miedo a nada./ 1996/ P-2/4 KG730 . . . **CE E**
WILLIAMS, M/ Iliad and the Odyssey./ 1996/ 3-6/8 KE129 . . . . . **883**
Joseph and his magnificent coat of many colors./ 1992/ 2-4/5 KA689 . . . . **222**
Velveteen Rabbit; or, How toys become real./ 1988/ 3-5/6 KH864 . . . . **CE FIC**
Velveteen Rabbit; or, How toys become real (Braille)./ n.d./ 3-5/6 KH864 . . . . **CE FIC**
Velveteen Rabbit; or, How toys become real (Sound recording cassette)./ n.d./ 3-5/6 KH864 . . . . **CE FIC**
Velveteen Rabbit; or, How toys become real (Talking book)./ Velveteen Rabbit; or, How toys become real (Talking book)./ n.d./ c1975/ 3-5/6 KH864 . . . . **CE FIC**
3-5/6 KH864 . . . . **CE FIC**
WILLIAMS, PS/ Cooking wizardry for kids./ 1990/ 5-6 KD273 . . **641.5**
WILLIAMS, R/ Good grief, third grade./ 1993/ 3-4/4 KH481 . . . . . **FIC**
Herbie Jones and the class gift./ 1989/ 3-4/2 KH367 . . . . **FIC**
Jumanji (Kit)./ 1995/ K-A KH821 . . . . **KIT FIC**
Lewis and Clark: explorers of the American West./ 1994/ 4-6/6 KE203 . . . . **917.804**
WILLIAMS, S/ Edwin and Emily./ 1995/ 1-3/2 KG733 . . . . **E**
I went walking./ 1990/ P-1/1 KG732 . . . . **CE E**
I went walking (Big book)./ 1991/ P-1/1 KG732 . . . . **CE E**
Made in China: ideas and inventions from Ancient China./ 1996/ 4-6/6 KE631 . . . . **931**
Sali de paseo./ 1995/ P-1/1 KG732 . . . . **CE E**
Sali de paseo (Kit)./ 1996/ P-1/1 KG732 . . . . **CE E**
WILLIAMS, SA/ Working cotton./ 1992/ 1-3/2 KG731 . . . . **E**
WILLIAMS, VB/ Algo especial para mi./ 1994/ P-3/2 KG738 . . . . . . **E**
Chair for my mother./ 1982/ P-3/3 KG734 . . . . **E**
Chair for my mother (Big book)./ 1992/ P-3/3 KG734 . . . . **E**
Cherries and cherry pits./ c1965, 1984/ K-3/2 KG735 . . . . **E**
More more more, said the baby./ 1990/ P-K/2 KG736 . . . . **E**
Music, music for everyone./ 1984/ P-3/4 KG737 . . . . **E**
Music, music for everyone (Sound recording cassette)./ n.d./ P-3/4 KG737 . . . . **E**
Musica para todo el mundo!/ 1995/ P-3/4 KG737 . . . . **E**
Scooter./ 1993/ 4-A/4 KH865 . . . . **FIC**
Scooter (Sound recording cassette)./ 1996/ 4-A/4 KH865 . . . . . . **FIC**
Sillon para mi mama./ 1994/ P-3/3 KG734 . . . . **E**
Sillon para mi mama (Kit)./ 1994/ P-3/3 KG734 . . . . **E**
Something special for me./ 1983/ P-3/2 KG738 . . . . **E**
Stringbean's trip to the shining sea./ 1988/ K-A/2 KG739 . . . . **E**
Three days on a river in a red canoe./ 1981/ K-3/5 KG740 . . . . . . **E**
WILLIAMS-ELLIS, A/ Russian fairy tales (Talking book)./ n.d./ 4-6 KB722 . . . . **TB 398.27**
WILLIAMSON, RA/ First houses: Native American homes and sacred structures./ 1993/ 6-A/7 KB171 . . . . **392.3**
WILLIS, MS/ Secret super powers of Marco./ 1994/ 4-A/4 KH866 . **FIC**
Secret super powers of Marco (Sound recording cassette)./ 1996/ 4-A/4 KH866 . . . . **FIC**
WILLIS, NC/ Robins in your backyard./ 1996/ K-3/5 KC707 . . . . **598.8**
WILLIS, T/ Healing the land./ 1994/ 4-6/7 KA954 . . . . **333.73**
WILLNER-PARDO, G/ Natalie Spitzer's turtles./ 1992/ 1-3/2 KG741 . **E**
When Jane-Marie told my secret./ 1995/ 2-3/2 KH867 . . . . **FIC**
WILLOW, D/ At home in the rain forest./ 1991/ K-4/6 KC328 . **577.34**
Dentro de la selva tropical./ 1993/ K-4/6 KC328 . . . . **577.34**

WILLS, CA/ Historical album of Alabama./ 1995/ 4-6/7 KE999 . . **976.1**
Historical album of California./ 1994/ 4-6/7 KF088 . . . . **979.4**
Historical album of Colorado./ 1996/ 4-6/7 KF062 . . . . **978.8**
Historical album of Connecticut./ 1995/ 4-6/7 KE953 . . . . . . **974.6**
Historical album of Florida./ 1994/ 4-6/7 KE994 . . . . **975.9**
Historical album of Illinois./ 1994/ 4-6/7 KF016 . . . . **977.3**
Historical album of Michigan./ 1996/ 4-6/7 KF018 . . . . **977.4**
Historical album of Nebraska./ 1994/ 4-6/7 KF055 . . . . **978.2**
Historical album of New Jersey./ 1995/ 4-6/7 KE965 . . . . . . **974.9**
Historical album of Ohio./ 1996/ 4-6/7 KF013 . . . . **977.1**
Historical album of Oregon./ 1995/ 4-6/7 KF090 . . . . **979.5**
Historical album of Pennsylvania./ 1996/ 4-6/7 KE961 . . . . . . **974.8**
Historical album of Texas./ 1995/ 4-6/7 KF004 . . . . **976.4**
WILMER, I/ B is for Bethlehem: a Christmas alphabet./ 1990/
K-3 KE043 . . . . **811**
WILNER, B/ Soccer./ 1994/ 3-6/4 KD789 . . . . **796.334**
Superstars of women's golf./ 1997/ 4-6/7 KD792 . . . . **796.352**
Swimming./ 1996/ 3-6/6 KD850 . . . . **797.2**
WILSON, BK/ Wishbones: a folk tale from China./ 1993/
2-3/6 KB383 . . . . **398.2**
WILSON, G/ PEOPLES OF THE WORLD: NORTH AMERICANS./ 1991/
6-A KA479 . . . . **REF 970.004**
SPOOKY STORIES FOR A DARK AND STORMY NIGHT./ 1994/
2-4/4 KB695 . . . . **398.25**
WILSON, J/ Elsa, star of the shelter!/ 1996/ 4-6/5 KH868 . . . . . . **FIC**
In Flanders Fields: the story of the poem by John McCrae./ 1995/
4-6/7 KD947 . . . . **811**
Ingenious Mr. Peale: painter, patriot and man of science./ 1996/
6-A/8 KE493 . . . . **B PEALE, C.**
Revenge of the small Small./ 1992/ 1-3/2 KF996 . . . . **E**
WILSON, K/ Origin of life on Earth: an African creation myth./ 1991/
4-5/4 KA730 . . . . **291.2**
WILSON, L/ Daily life in a Victorian house./ 1993/
3-6/7 KE676 . . . . **941.081**
WILSON, LL/ Salem witch trials./ 1997/ A/7 KA607 . . . . **133.4**
WILSON, PP/ Professional collection for elementary educators./ 1996/
KA079 . . . . **PROF 027.8**
WILSON, RM/ Come sign with us: sign language activities for children.
2nd. ed./ 1996/ KA279 . . . . **PROF 419**
WILSON, S/ Sledding./ 1989/ P-K/2 KG746 . . . . **E**
WILSON, SR/ Day Gogo went to vote: South Africa, April 1994./ 1996/
1-3/2 KG513 . . . . **E**
WILSON, T/ Pedro fools the gringo and other tales of a Latin American
trickster./ 1995/ 2-4/3 KB429 . . . . **398.22**
Three friends: a counting book./Tres amigos: un cuento para contar./
1995/ P-2/1 KB954 . . . . **513.2**
When jaguars ate the moon: and other stories about animals and plants
of the Americas./ 1995/ 2-3/5 KB541 . . . . **398.24**
WIMMER, M/ All the places to love./ 1994/ 1-4/5 KG053 . . . . **E**
Bully for you, Teddy Roosevelt!/ 1991/
5-6/6 KE523 . . . . **B ROOSEVELT, T.**
Flight: the journey of Charles Lindbergh./ 1991/ 1-4/2 KD091 **629.13**
Flight: the journey of Charles Lindbergh./ 1991/ 4-6/3 KD092 . **629.13**
Train song./ 1990/ P-3 KG501 . . . . **E**
WINCH, R/ Raptor rescue!: an eagle flies free./ 1995/
5-6/7 KD254 . . . . **639.9**
WINCKLER, S/ Nuestro planeta en peligro: la Antartida./ 1993/
5-6/8 KE221 . . . . **919.8**
Our endangered planet: Antarctica./ 1992/ 5-6/8 KE221 . . . . **919.8**
Our endangered planet: population growth./ 1990/
5-6/9 KA816 . . . . **304.6**
WIND IN THE LONG GRASS: A COLLECTION OF HAIKU./ 1991/
2-5 KD892 . . . . **808.81**
WINFIELD, A/ Impossible riddle./ 1995/ K-3/4 KF819 . . . . **E**
WING, N/ Jalapeno bagels./ 1996/ 1-3/2 KG742 . . . . **E**
WINKEL, L/ SUBJECT HEADINGS FOR CHILDREN: A LIST OF SUBJECT
HEADINGS USED BY THE LIBRARY OF CONGRESS WITH DEWEY
NUMBERS ADDED. 2nd ed./ 1998/ KA062 . . . . **PROF 025.4**
WINKLER, PW/ ANGLO-AMERICAN CATALOGUING RULES. 2ND ED.,
1988 REVISION./ 1988/ KA056 . . . . **PROF 025.3**
WINNER, C/ Salamanders./ 1993/ A/7 KC611 . . . . **597.8**
Sunflower family./ 1996/ 3-6/7 KC434 . . . . **583**
WINTER, J/ Cowboy Charlie: the story of Charles M. Russell./ 1995/
2-5/4 KE528 . . . . **B RUSSELL, C.**
Josefina./ 1996/ 1-3/6 KG743 . . . . **E**
World's birthday: a Rosh Hashanah story./ 1990/ 2-3/2 KH181 . . **FIC**
WINTER, R/ Microsoft composer collection (CD-ROM)./ 1994/
4-A KD525 . . . . **CDR 780**
WINTERS, J/ Paul Bunyan (Videocassette)./ 1990/
3-5 KB447 . . . . **VCR 398.22**
WINTHER, B/ Plays from African tales: one-act, royalty-free dramatizations
for young people, from stories and folktales of Africa./ 1992/
4-A KE093 . . . . **812**
WINTHROP, E/ Battle for the castle./ 1993/ 4-6/5 KH869 . . . . **CE FIC**

Battle for the castle (Sound recording cassette)./ 1995/
4-6/5 KH869 . . . . **CE FIC**
Battle for the castle (Talking book)./ 1997/ 4-6/5 KH869 . . . . **CE FIC**
Bear and Mrs. Duck./ 1988/ P-1/1 KG744 . . . . **E**
Bear's Christmas surprise./ 1991/ P-1/1 KG744 . . . . **E**
Castle in the attic./ 1985/ 4-6/5 KH869 . . . . **CE FIC**
Castle in the attic (Talking book)./ 1996/ 4-6/5 KH869 . . . . . **CE FIC**
He is risen: the Easter story./ 1985/ 5-6/7 KA711 . . . . **232.96**
Shoes./ 1986/ P-K/4 KG745 . . . . **CE E**
Shoes (Big book)./ 1993/ P-K/4 KG745 . . . . **CE E**
Shoes (Kit)./ 1996/ P-K/4 KG745 . . . . **CE E**
Shoes (Sound recording cassette)./ n.d./ P-K/4 KG745 . . . . . . **CE E**
Sledding./ 1989/ P-K/2 KG746 . . . . **E**
Very noisy girl./ 1991/ K-2/2 KG747 . . . . **E**
WISEMAN, B/ Morris and Boris./ c1974, 1991/ K-2/1 KG748 . . . . **E**
Morris and Boris at the circus./ 1988,/ K-2/1 KG748 . . . . . . **E**
Morris and Boris (Braille)./ n.d.,/ K-2/1 KG748 . . . . **E**
Morris goes to school./ 1970/ K-2/2 KG749 . . . . **E**
Morris has a cold./ c1978, 1997/ K-2/1 KG748 . . . . **E**
Morris the Moose./ 1989/ K-2/2 KG750 . . . . **CE E**
Morris the Moose (Kit)./ 1996/ K-2/2 KG750 . . . . **CE E**
WISLER, GC/ Jericho's journey./ 1993/ 5-A/6 KH870 . . . . **FIC**
Jericho's journey (Sound recording cassette)./ 1995/ 5-A/6 KH870 **FIC**
Mr. Lincoln's drummer./ 1995/ 5-A/4 KH871 . . . . **FIC**
Mustang Flats./ 1997/ 5-A/6 KH872 . . . . **FIC**
Red Cap./ 1994/ 5-A/7 KH873 . . . . **FIC**
Red Cap (Sound recording cassette)./ 1994/ 5-A/7 KH873 . . . . . **FIC**
WISNEWSKI, A/ BOOK OF VIRTUES FOR YOUNG PEOPLE: A
TREASURY OF GREAT MORAL STORIES./ 1997/
KA343 . . . . **PROF 808.8**
WISNIEWSKI, D/ Elfwyn's saga./ 1990/ 4-6/6 KB422 . . . . **398.21**
Golem./ 1996/ 2-6/5 KB423 . . . . **398.21**
Rain player./ 1991/ 2-3/4 KG751 . . . . **CE E**
Rain player (Kit)./ 1996/ 2-3/4 KG751 . . . . **CE E**
Sundiata: Lion King of Mali./ 1992/ 3-5/4 KB495 . . . . **398.22**
Warrior and the wise man./ 1989/ 1-3/5 KG752 . . . . **E**
Wave of the Sea-Wolf./ 1994/ 1-3/6 KG753 . . . . **E**
WITHERS, T/ Basketball./ 1994/ 3-6/4 KD781 . . . . **796.323**
WITSCHONKE, A/ Brooklyn Bridge./ 1996/ 5-6/5 KD068 . . . . . . **624**
WITTE, M/ Otter nonsense./ 1994/ 3-6 KD721 . . . . **793.734**
WITTMAN, S/ Special trade./ 1978/ P-3/4 KG754 . . . . **E**
WITTSTOCK, LW/ Ininatig's gift of sugar: traditional native sugarmaking./
c1993/ 3-6/3 KE786 . . . . **970.476**
WOJCIECHOWSKA, M/ Shadow of a bull./ 1964/
5-6/6 KH875 . . . . **CE FIC**
Shadow of a bull (Sound recording cassette)./ n.d./
5-6/6 KH875 . . . . **CE FIC**
Shadow of a bull (Talking book)./ n.d./ 5-6/6 KH875 . . . . . . **CE FIC**
WOJCIECHOWSKI, S/ Christmas miracle of Jonathan Toomey./ 1995/
4-6/5 KH876 . . . . **FIC**
Don't call me Beanhead!/ 1994/ 2-3/5 KH877 . . . . **FIC**
WOLF, B/ Homeless./ 1995/ 4-6/4 KB010 . . . . **362.5**
WOLF, J/ Daddy, could I have an elephant?/ 1996/ K-2/2 KG755 . . **E**
WOLF, K/ Full speed ahead: stories and activities for children on
transportation./ 1988/ KA223 . . . . **PROF 372.6**
WOLFF, A/ Goody O'Grumpity./ 1994/ K-3/3 KF268 . . . . **E**
How Chipmunk got tiny feet: Native American animal origin stories./
1995/ K-3/3 KB588 . . . . **398.24**
Little Donkey close your eyes./ 1995/ P-K/2 KF286 . . . . **E**
Miss Bindergarten gets ready for kindergarten./ 1996/ P-K/2 KG515 **E**
Stella and Roy./ 1993/ P-1/3 KG756 . . . . **E**
Year of beasts./ 1986/ P-K/1 KG757 . . . . **E**
WOLFF, B/ Egg to chick. Rev. ed./ 1970/ P-2/2 KG698 . . . . . . **598.6**
WOLFF, F/ Seven loaves of bread./ 1993/ 1-3/2 KG758 . . . . **E**
WOLFF, PR/ Toll-bridge troll./ 1995/ 1-3/2 KG759 . . . . **E**
WOLFMAN, I/ Do people grow on family trees?: genealogy for kids and
other beginners: the official Ellis Island handbook./ 1991/
5-A/7 KE610 . . . . **929**
WOLF-SAMPATH, G/ Mala: a women's folktale./ 1996/
3-5/2 KB718 . . . . **398.26**
WOLFSON, M/ Marriage of the rain goddess: a South African myth./
1996/ 4-5/5 KB424 . . . . **398.21**
WOLITZER, H/ Toby lived here./ c1978, 1986/ 4-6/6 KH878 . . . . . **FIC**
WOLK-STANLEY, J/ New York Public Library amazing space: a book of
answers for kids./ 1997/ 3-A/8 KC001 . . . . **520**
WOLKSTEIN, D/ Esther's story./ 1996/ 4-A/4 KA690 . . . . **222**
Hans Christian Andersen in Central Park (Sound recording cassette)./
1981/ 4-6 KG846 . . . . **SRC FIC**
White Wave: a Chinese tale. Rev. ed./ 1996/ 1-3/2 KB786 . . . . **398.27**
WOLLARD, K/ How come?/ 1993/ 4-8/6 KB874 . . . . **500**
WOLPERT, T/ Wolf magic for kids./ c1990, 1991/
5-6/5 KC841 . . . . **599.773**
WONG, JS/ Good luck gold and other poems./ 1994/ 5-6 KE044 **811**
Suitcase of seaweed and other poems./ 1996/ 5-A KE045 . . . . . **811**

WOOD, A/ Bunyans./ 1996/ 1-5/6 KG760 . . . . E
  Flying Dragon Room./ 1996/ 2-4/3 KG761 . . . . E
  Heckedy peg./ 1987/ K-3/3 KG762 . . . . E
  King Bidgood's in the bathtub./ 1985/ P-2/1 KG763 . **CE E**
  King Bidgood's in the bathtub (Big book)./ 1993/ P-2/1 KG763 . **CE E**
  King Bidgood's in the bathtub (Sound recording cassette)./ n.d./
    P-2/1 KG763 . . . . **CE E**
  King Bidgood's in the bathtub (Videocassette)./ 1988/
    P-2/1 KG763 . . . . **CE E**
  Napping house./ 1984/ P-2/7 KG764 . . . . **CE E**
  Napping house and other stories (Talking book)./ 1987/
    P-3 KG765 . . . . **TB E**
  Napping house (Big book)./ 1991/ P-2/7 KG764 . . . . **CE E**
  Napping house (Braille)./ n.d./ P-2/7 KG764 . . . . **CE E**
  Napping house (Videocassette)./ 1986/ P-2/7 KG764 . . . **CE E**
  Piggies./ 1991/ P-K/1 KG768 . . . . E
  Rainbow bridge: inspired by a Chumash tale./ 1995/
    3-5/4 KB675 . . . . **398.24**
  Silly Sally./ 1992/ P-K/2 KG766 . . . . E
  Weird parents./ 1990/ K-2/4 KG767 . . . . E
WOOD, AJ/ Lion and the mouse: an Aesop's fable./ 1995/
  P-1/5 KB674 . . . . **398.24**
WOOD, D/ Heckedy peg./ 1987/ K-3/3 KG762 . . . . **CE E**
  King Bidgood's in the bathtub./ 1985/ P-2/1 KG763 . . . **CE E**
  Napping house./ 1984/ P-2/7 KG764 . . . . **CE E**
  Old Turtle./ 1992/ 3-5/3 KH879 . . . . **CE FIC**
  Old Turtle (Talking book)./ 1995/ 3-5/3 KH879 . . . . **CE FIC**
  Piggies./ 1991/ P-K/1 KG768 . . . . E
WOOD, J/ Caves: an underground wonderland./ 1991/
  4-6/7 KC169 . . . . **551.4**
  Dads are such fun./ 1992/ P-K/1 KG769 . . . . E
  Jakki Wood's animal hullabaloo: a wildlife noisy book./ 1995/
    P-K KC485 . . . . **591.59**
WOOD, L/ Fires./ 1994/ 4-6/7 KB042 . . . . **363.37**
WOOD, N/ Spirit walker: poems./ 1993/ 6-A KE046 . . . . . . **811**
WOOD, T/ Aztecs./ 1992/ 5-6/7 KE842 . . . . **972**
  Two lands, one heart: an American boy's journey to his mother's
    Vietnam./ 1995/ 1-3/7 KE719 . . . . **959.7**
WOODEN, B/ Followers of the North Star: rhymes about African American
  heroes, heroines, and historical times./ 1993/ 3-A KD913 . . . . . **811**
WOODING, S/ I'll meet you at the cucumbers./ 1988/
  2-4/5 KH505 . . . . **FIC**
WOODRUFF, E/ Dear Levi: letters from the Overland Trail./ 1994/
  4-6/6 KH880 . . . . **FIC**
  Orphan of Ellis Island: a time-travel adventure./ 1997/
    5-A/5 KH881 . . . . **FIC**
WOODS, K/ Little prince./ c1943/ 4-A/6 KH671 . . . . **FIC**
WOODS, M/ How big is a whale?./ 1995/ 2-5/5 KC462 . . . . **591.4**
WOODS, MJ/ Bambi: a life in the woods./ 1992/ 5-A/6 KH673 . . . **FIC**
WOODS, ML/ Sky tree portfolio guide: an interdisciplinary environmental
  curriculum./ 1995/ 2-6 KC424 . . . . **582.16**
WOODWORTH, V/ Animal jokes./ 1993/ 2-4 KD742 . . . . **793.735**
  Dinosaur jokes./ 1991/ 2-4 KD725 . . . . **793.735**
  Fairy tale jokes./ 1993/ 2-4 KD743 . . . . **793.735**
WOODYARD, S/ Music and song./ 1995/ 3-6/7 KD526 . . . . . . **780**
WORLD OF CHILDREN'S SONGS./ 1993/ KA322 . . . . . **PROF 789.3**
WORLD PATROL KIDS/ Earth tunes (Compact disc)./ 1995/
  3-6 KC300 . . . . **VCR 577**
  Earth tunes for kids (Videocassette)./ 1994/ 3-6 KC300 . . . . **VCR 577**
  Earth tunes (Sound recording cassette)./ 1995/ 3-6 KC300 . . **VCR 577**
WORMELL, C/ Number of animals./ 1993/ P-2/3 KG770 . . . . E
WRIGHT, BF/ Real Mother Goose./ c1944, 1994/ P-2 KB806 . . . **398.8**
WRIGHT, BR/ Dollhouse murders./ 1983/ 4-6/5 KH882 . . . . . **FIC**
  Dollhouse murders (Sound recording cassette)./ n.d./ 4-6/5 KH882 **FIC**
  Ghost in the house./ 1991/ 5-A/6 KH883 . . . . **FIC**
WRIGHT, CC/ Jumping the broom./ 1994/ K-3/5 KG771 . . . . E
  Wagon train: a family goes West in 1865./ 1995/ 4-6/3 KF052 . **978**
WRIGHT, D/ Facts on File children's atlas./ 1997/ 4-6 KE176 . . . . **912**
WRIGHT, DA/ One-person puppet plays./ 1990/ KA365 . . . **PROF 812**
WRIGHT, J/ Facts on File children's atlas./ 1997/ 4-6 KE176 . . . . **912**
  One-person puppet plays./ 1990/ KA365 . . . . **PROF 812**
WRIGHT, JR/ Bugs!/ 1987/ 4-5/6 KC547 . . . . **595.7**
  Frogs, toads, lizards and salamanders./ 1990/ 5-6/7 KC606 . . **597.8**
WRIGHT, K/ Challenge of technology: action strategies for the school
  library media specialist./ 1993/ KA080 . . . . **PROF 027.8**
WRIGHT, R/ Knights: facts, things to make, activities./ 1991/
  4-A/8 KD439 . . . . **745.5**
WRIGHT-FRIERSON, V/ Desert scrapbook: dawn to dusk in the Sonoran
  Desert./ 1996/ 3-5/7 KF072 . . . . **979.1**
  Down at the bottom of the deep dark sea./ 1991/ P-K/2 KF852 . . . E
  When the tide is low./ 1985/ P-2/3 KF411 . . . . E
WU, DY/ Chinese-American experience./ 1993/ 5-6/8 KA864 . . **305.8**
WU, N/ Beneath the waves: exploring the hidden world of the kelp forest./
  1992/ 3-6/7 KC353 . . . . **577.7**

City under the sea: life in a coral reef./ 1996/ 4-6/8 KC354 . . . **577.7**
  Fish faces./ c1993, 1997/ 1-6/3 KC588 . . . . **597**
WU, P/ Abacus contest: stories from Taiwan and China./ 1996/
  3-5/4 KH884 . . . . **FIC**
WUKOVITS, JF/ Annie Oakley./ 1997/ 5-6/8 KE480 . . **B OAKLEY, A.**
  Jesse James./ 1997/ 4-6/10 KE402 . . . . **B JAMES, J.**
WYATT, V/ Amazing dirt book./ 1990/ 4-6/6 KD148 . . . . . . **631.4**
  Weather watch./ 1990/ 3-6/6 KC222 . . . . **551.6**
WYETH, J/ Cabbage and kings./ 1997/ 1-3/2 KG425 . . . . E
WYETH, NC/ David Balfour: being memoirs of the further adventures of
  David Balfour at home and abroad./ c1952, 1994/
    6-A/6 KH757 . . . . **FIC**
  Kidnapped: being the memoirs of the adventures of David Balfour/ 1982/
    5-6/6 KH758 . . . . **FIC**
  N.C. Wyeth's pilgrims./ 1991/ 4-6/7 KE946 . . . . **974.4**
  Rip Van Winkle./ 1987/ 4-A/9 KH315 . . . . **FIC**
  Robin Hood./ 1984/ 6/6 KB434 . . . . **398.22**
  Robinson Crusoe./ 1983/ 5-A/7 KH068 . . . . **FIC**
  Treasure Island./ c1911, 1981/ 5-A/6 KH759 . . . . **FIC**
  Yearling./ c1938, 1967/ 5-A/5 KH622 . . . . **FIC**
WYLER, R/ Math fun with a pocket calculator./ 1992/
  4-A/4 KD713 . . . . **793.7**
  Math fun with tricky lines and shapes./ 1992/ 4-A/5 KD714 . . **793.7**
  Science fun with mud and dirt./ 1986/ K-4/2 KB887 . . . . . . **507**
  Starry sky./ 1989/ P-2/2 KC056 . . . . **523.8**
  Test your luck./ 1992/ 5-6/4 KB998 . . . . **519.2**
WYNAR, BS/ RECOMMENDED REFERENCE BOOKS FOR SMALL AND
  MEDIUM-SIZED LIBRARIES AND MEDIA CENTERS./ 1981-/
  KA005 . . . . **PROF 011**
WYNAR, CG/ Guide to reference books for school media centers. 4th ed./
  1992/ KA007 . . . . **PROF 011**
WYNDHAM, R/ CHINESE MOTHER GOOSE RHYMES./ c1968, 1989/
  P-3 KB794 . . . . **398.8**
WYNNE-JONES, T/ Book of changes: stories./ 1995/ 6-A/3 KH885 **FIC**
  Book of changes: stories (Sound recording cassette)./ 1997/
    6-A/3 KH885 . . . . **FIC**
  Some of the kinder planets./ 1995/ 5-A/5 KH886 . . . . **FIC**
  Some of the kinder planets (Sound recording cassette)./ 1997/
    5-A/5 KH886 . . . . **FIC**
XIONG, B/ Nine-in-one, grr! grr! a folktale from the Hmong people of
  Laos./ 1989/ P-3/4 KB677 . . . . **398.24**
YAAKOV, J/ MIDDLE AND JUNIOR HIGH SCHOOL LIBRARY CATALOG.
  7th ed./ 1995/ KA019 . . . . **PROF 011.62**
YACCARINO, D/ One hole in the road./ 1996/ P-K/2 KG173 . . . . . E
YAMASHITA, K/ Paws, wings, and hooves: mammals on the move./ 1993/
  2-5/2 KC468 . . . . **591.47**
YAN, A/ Young person's guide to the orchestra: Benjamin Britten's
  composition on CD./ 1996/ 4-6/10 KD545 . . . . **BA 784.2**
YANG, M/ Shell woman and the king: a Chinese folktale./ 1993/
  3-5/5 KB496 . . . . **398.22**
YARBROUGH, C/ Shimmershine Queens./ 1989/ 5-6/6 KH887 . . . . **FIC**
  Tamika and the wisdom rings./ 1994/ 3-4/2 KH888 . . . . . . **FIC**
YARDLEY, J/ Bracelet./ 1993/ 2-5/3 KG631 . . . . E
YARDLEY, T/ Poison! beware! be an ace poison spotter./ 1991/
  3-6/5 KD011 . . . . **615.9**
YASHIMA, T/ Crow Boy./ 1955/ 1-3/3 KG772 . . . . **CE E**
  Crow Boy (Braille)./ n.d./ 1-3/3 KG772 . . . . **CE E**
  Crow Boy (Kit)./ 1985/ 1-3/3 KG772 . . . . **CE E**
  Crow Boy (Talking book)./ n.d./ 1-3/3 KG772 . . . . **CE E**
  Umbrella./ c1958/ P-K/2 KG773 . . . . **CE E**
  Umbrella (Kit)./ 1985/ P-K/2 KG773 . . . . **CE E**
  Umbrella (Talking book)./ n.d./ P-K/2 KG773 . . . . **CE E**
YATES, E/ Amos Fortune, free man./ c1950/
  A/7 KE348 . . . . **B FORTUNE, A.**
  Amos Fortune, free man (Braille)./ n.d./ A/7 KE348 . **B FORTUNE, A.**
  Amos Fortune, free man (Sound recording cassette)./ n.d./
    A/7 KE348 . . . . **B FORTUNE, A.**
  Amos Fortune, free man (Talking book)./ n.d./
    A/7 KE348 . . . . **B FORTUNE, A.**
  Prudence Crandall: woman of courage. 2nd ed./ 1996/
    6-A/6 KE306 . . . . **B CRANDALL, P.**
YEE, P/ Ghost Train./ 1996/ 4-6/5 KH889 . . . . **FIC**
  Tales from Gold Mountain: stories of the Chinese in the New World./
    1989/ 5-A/7 KH890 . . . . **FIC**
  Tales from Gold Mountain: stories of the Chinese in the New World
    (Sound recording cassette)./ 1993/ 5-A/7 KH890 . . . . **FIC**
YEKTAI, N/ Bears at the beach: counting 10 to 20./ 1996/
  P-1 KB985 . . . . **513.2**
YEOMAN, J/ Old Mother Hubbard's dog dresses up./ c1989, 1990/
  K-3/4 KG774 . . . . E
  Old Mother Hubbard's dog learns to play./ 1990/ K-3/4 KG774 . . E
  Old Mother Hubbard's dog needs a doctor./ 1990/ K-3/4 KG774 . . E
  Old Mother Hubbard's dog takes up sport./ 1990, K-3/4 KG774 . . E
YEP, L/ Child of the owl./ c1977/ A/6 KH891 . . . . **FIC**

Child of the owl (Sound recording cassette)./ n.d./ A/6 KH891 . . . **FIC**
City of dragons./ 1995/ 1-3/5 KG775 . . . . **E**
Dragonwings./ c1975/ 5-6/6 KH892 . . . . **FIC**
Dragonwings (Sound recording cassette)./ n.d./ 5-6/6 KH892 . . . **FIC**
Junior thunder lord./ 1994/ 2-4/3 KB425 . . . . **398.21**
Khan's daughter: a Mongolian folktale./ 1997/ 2-4/6 KB787 . . **398.27**
Later, Gator./ 1995/ 4-6/4 KH893 . . . . **FIC**
Lost garden./ 1996/ 5-A/7 KE604 . . . . **B YEP, L.**
Man who tricked a ghost./ 1993/ 1-3/4 KB697 . . . . **398.25**
Mountain light./ c1985, 1997/ 6-A/6 KH894 . . . . **FIC**
Rainbow people./ 1989, 1991/ 5-A/4 KB788 . . . . **398.27**
Serpent's children./ c1984, 1996/ 6-A/6 KH894 . . . . **FIC**
Shell woman and the king: a Chinese folktale./ 1993/
    3-5/5 KB496 . . . . **398.22**
Star fisher./ 1991/ 6-A/6 KH895 . . . . **FIC**
Tiger Woman./ 1995/ 1-3/6 KB789 . . . . **398.27**
Tree of dreams: ten tales from the garden of night./ 1995/
    4-6/3 KB790 . . . . **398.27**
YEPSEN, R/ City trains: moving through America's cities by rail./ 1993/
    5-6/7 KB162 . . . . **388.4**
Smarten up! how to increase your brain power./ 1990/
    6-A/7 KA645 . . . . **155.42**
YOLEN, J/ All in the woodland early: an ABC book./ c1979, 1991/
    K-1/3 KG776 . . . . **E**
Animal fare: poems./ 1994/ K-3 KE047 . . . . **811**
Children of the wolf./ c1984, 1993/ 6-A/7 KH896 . . . . **FIC**
Emperor and the kite./ 1988/ 2-3/6 KB791 . . . . **398.27**
Emperor and the kite (Braille)./ n.d./ 2-3/6 KB791 . . . . . . **398.27**
FAVORITE FOLKTALES FROM AROUND THE WORLD./ 1986/
    KA267 . . . . **PROF 398.2**
JANE YOLEN'S MOTHER GOOSE SONGBOOK./ 1992/
    KA277 . . . . **PROF 398.8**
Letting Swift River go./ 1992/ 1-3/5 KG777 . . . . **E**
Letting Swift River go (Sound recording cassette)./ 1994/
    1-3/5 KG777 . . . . **E**
Owl moon./ 1987/ P-3/2 KG778 . . . . **CE E**
Owl moon (Videocassette)./ 1989/ P-3/2 KG778 . . . . **CE E**
Picnic with Piggins./ c1988/ K-3/4 KG779 . . . . **E**
Piggins./ 1987/ K-3/4 KG779 . . . . **E**
Piggins and the royal wedding./ 1988/ K-3/4 KG779 . . . . **E**
Sacred places./ 1996/ 3-6 KE048 . . . . **811**
Sea watch: a book of poetry./ 1996/ 4-6 KE049 . . . . **811**
Sip of Aesop./ 1995/ K-3 KE050 . . . . **811**
Sky dogs./ 1990/ 2-3/6 KG780 . . . . **E**
Sky dogs (Sound recording cassette)./ 1993/ 2-3/6 KG780 . . . . **E**
SLEEP RHYMES AROUND THE WORLD./ 1994/ P-3 KD890 . **808.81**
Tam Lin./ 1990/ 3-4/4 KB384 . . . . **398.2**
Water music: poems for children./ 1995/ 2-6 KE051 . . . . . . **811**
Welcome to the green house./ 1993/ K-3/4 KC329 . . . . . **577.34**
Wings./ c1991, 1997/ 5-6/4 KA754 . . . . **292**
Wizard's Hall./ 1991/ 4-6/6 KH897 . . . . **FIC**
YORINKS, A/ Hey, Al./ 1986/ 1-3/3 KG781 . . . . **E**
Hey, Al (Braille)./ n.d./ 1-3/3 KG781 . . . . **E**
Louis the fish./ 1980/ K-3/4 KG782 . . . . **E**
Oh, brother./ 1989/ 1-4/5 KG783 . . . . **E**
YORKE, M/ Miss Butterpat goes wild!/ 1993/ 3-5/5 KH898 . . . **FIC**
YOSHI/ Farmer and the Poor God: a folktale from Japan./ 1996/
    2-4/3 KB785 . . . . **398.27**
Magical hands./ 1989/ 1-3/5 KF199 . . . . **E**
Who's hiding here?/ 1987/ K-3/2 KG784 . . . . **E**
YOUNG, E/ Cat and Rat: the legend of the Chinese zodiac./ 1995/
    K-6/4 KA608 . . . . **133.5**
CHINESE MOTHER GOOSE RHYMES./ c1968, 1989/
    P-3 KB794 . . . . **398.8**
Donkey trouble./ 1995/ 1-2/5 KB678 . . . . **398.24**
Double life of Pocahontas./ 1983/ 5-6/6 KE500 . . . **B POCAHONTAS**
Dreamcatcher./ 1992/ K-2/5 KG200 . . . . **E**
Emperor and the kite./ 1988/ 2-3/6 KB791 . . . . **398.27**
Eyes of the dragon./ 1987/ K-3/5 KF952 . . . . **E**
Foolish rabbit's big mistake./ 1985/ 3-4/4 KA760 . . . . **294.3**
I wish I were a butterfly./ 1987/ K-3/2 KF778 . . . . **E**
Iblis./ 1994/ 4-5/4 KA789 . . . . **297**
Little Plum./ 1994/ K-2/4 KB497 . . . . **398.22**
Lon Po Po: A Red-Riding Hood story from China./ 1989/
    3-4/4 KB679 . . . . **398.24**
Night visitors./ 1995/ 2-3/4 KB680 . . . . **398.24**
Sadako./ 1993/ 3-6/4 KA994 . . . . **CE 362.1**
Seven blind mice./ 1992/ K-3/2 KB681 . . . . **398.24**
Turkey girl: a Zuni Cinderella story./ 1996/ 2-4/6 KB764 . . . . **398.27**
Voices of the heart./ 1997/ A/7 KA675 . . . . **179**
White Wave: a Chinese tale. Rev. ed./ 1996/ 1-3/2 KB786 . . **398.27**
Yeh-Shen, a Cinderella story from China./ c1982, 1990/
    3-5/6 KB750 . . . . **398.27**

YOUNG, JD/ Head on the high road: ghost stories from the Southwest
    (Sound recording cassette)./ 1993/ 4-6 KB698 . . . . . . **SRC 398.25**
YOUNG, M/ Fortune branches out./ c1994, 1995/ 3-5/4 KH447 . . . **FIC**
Good Fortunes gang./ 1993/ 3-5/7 KH448 . . . . **FIC**
YOUNG, MO/ Fire at the Triangle Factory./ 1996/ 2-5/1 KF998 . . . **E**
YOUNG, N/ Finders keepers./ 1991/ 5-A/6 KH645 . . . . **FIC**
Toby./ 1994/ 1-3/3 KG718 . . . . **E**
YOUNG, R/ Chewing gum book./ 1989/ 5-6/6 KD322 . . . . . . **664**
Dolls./ 1992/ 5-6/6 KD353 . . . . **688.7**
Head on the high road: ghost stories from the Southwest (Sound
    recording cassette)./ 1993/ 4-6 KB698 . . . . **SRC 398.25**
Sneakers: the shoes we choose!/ 1991/ 5-6/6 KD344 . . . . . . **685**
Teddy bears./ 1992/ 5-6/6 KD354 . . . . **688.7**
YOUNG, RT/ Learning by heart./ 1993/ 6-A/6 KH899 . . . . . . **FIC**
Moving Mama to town./ 1997/ 6-A/4 KH900 . . . . **FIC**
YOUNG, S/ Scholastic rhyming dictionary./ 1994/ 5-A KB842 . . . **423.1**
YOUNKER, LQ/ What is a cat?/ 1991/ K-4/2 KD233 . . . . **636.8**
YOUNT, L/ Antoni van Leeuwenhoek: first to see microscopic life./ 1996/
    5-A/5 KE432 . . . . **B LEEUWENHOEK,A**
Cancer./ 1991/ A/9 KD034 . . . . **616.99**
Our endangered planet: air./ 1995/ 4-6/8 KB069 . . . . **363.73**
YOURS TILL BANANA SPLITS: 201 AUTOGRAPH RHYMES./ 1995/
    3-6 KD894 . . . . **808.88**
YUE, C/ Christopher Columbus: how he did it./ 1992/
    5-A/7 KE744 . . . . **970.01**
Igloo./ 1988/ 4-6/9 KE778 . . . . **970.3**
Pueblo./ 1986/ 5-6/8 KF065 . . . . **979**
Shoes: their history in words and pictures./ 1997/ 4-6/6 KB168 . **391.4**
YUE, D/ Christopher Columbus: how he did it./ 1992/
    5-A/7 KE744 . . . . **970.01**
Igloo./ 1988/ 4-6/9 KE778 . . . . **970.3**
Pueblo./ 1986/ 5-6/8 KF065 . . . . **979**
Shoes: their history in words and pictures./ 1997/ 4-6/6 KB168 . **391.4**
YUMOTO, K/ Friends./ 1996/ 6-A/7 KH901 . . . . **FIC**
ZALBEN, JB/ All in the woodland early: an ABC book./ c1979, 1991/
    K-1/3 KG776 . . . . **E**
Beni's family cookbook for the Jewish holidays./ 1996/
    4-6 KD283 . . . . **641.5**
Beni's first Chanukah./ 1988/ P/4 KG785 . . . . **E**
INNER CHIMES: POEMS ON POETRY./ 1992/ 2-6 KD885 . . **808.81**
Leo and Blossom's sukkah./ 1990/ P/4 KG785 . . . . **E**
ZALLINGER, JD/ Book of North American owls./ 1995/
    5-6/6 KC719 . . . . **598.9**
Earliest Americans./ 1993/ 5-A/8 KE743 . . . . **970.01**
ZAMORANO, A/ Let's eat!/ 1997/ P-2/1 KG786 . . . . **E**
ZARINS, JA/ Go-around dollar./ 1992/ 3-6/3 KA947 . . . . . . **332.4**
ZARNOWSKI, M/ Learning about biographies: a reading-and-writing
    approach for children./ 1990/ KA334 . . . . **PROF 808**
ZASLAVSKY, C/ Multicultural math classroom: bringing in the world./
    1996/ KA259 . . . . **PROF 372.7**
ZAWADZKI, M/ Ahaiyute and Cloud Eater./ 1996/
    3-4/5 KD708 . . . . **398.26**
Okino and the whales./ 1995/ 3-5/3 KH101 . . . . **FIC**
ZEINERT, K/ Across the plains in the Donner Party./ 1996/
    5-6/7 KF041 . . . . **978**
Amistad slave revolt and American abolition./ 1997/
    6-A/10 KA930 . . . . **326**
Memoirs of Andrew Sherburne: patriot and privateer of the American
    Revolution./ 1993/ 5-A/8 KE886 . . . . **973.3**
Those remarkable women of the American Revolution./ 1996/
    5-6/10 KE889 . . . . **973.3**
ZEITLIN, P/ Spin, spider, spin: songs for a greater appreciation of nature
    (Sound recording cassette)./ 1974/ P-1 KB916 . . . . . . **SRC 508**
ZELDIS, M/ Eve and her sisters: women of the Old Testament./ 1994/
    3-4/7 KA680 . . . . **221.9**
Honest Abe./ 1993/ 1-3/4 KE444 . . . . **B LINCOLN, A.**
Martin Luther King./ 1995/ 2-6/7 KE421 . . . . **B KING, M.L.**
SPRING: A HAIKU STORY./ 1996/ 1-6 KE137 . . . . **895.6**
ZELINSKY, PO/ Dear Mr. Henshaw./ 1983/ 4-A/4 KG993 . . . . . . **FIC**
Enano Saltarin./ 1992/ 1-4/7 KB385 . . . . **CE 398.2**
Enano Saltarin (Videocassette)./ 1992/ 1-4/7 KB385 . . . . . . **CE 398.2**
Enchanted castle./ 1992/ 5-A/6 KH542 . . . . **FIC**
Hansel and Gretel: a tale from the Brothers Grimm./ 1984/
    5/6 KB740 . . . . **CE 398.27**
History of Helpless Harry: to which is added a variety of amusing and
    entertaining adventures./ c1980, 1995/ 5-A/7 KG859 . . . . . **FIC**
Rumpelstiltskin./ 1986/ 1-4/7 KB385 . . . . **CE 398.2**
Rumpelstiltskin (Braille)./ n.d./ 1-4/7 KB385 . . . . **CE 398.2**
Rumpelstiltskin (Sound recording cassette)./ n.d./
    1-4/7 KB385 . . . . **CE 398.2**
Rumpelstiltskin (Videocassette)./ 1989/ 1-4/7 KB385 . . . . . **CE 398.2**
Strider./ 1991/ 5-A/4 KH008 . . . . **FIC**
Sun's asleep behind the hill./ 1982/ P-K/1 KF624 . . . . **E**
Swamp Angel./ 1994/ 2-5/6 KF810 . . . . **E**

ZELVER, P/ Wonderful Towers of Watts./ 1994/ 2-4/6 KD387 ... **725**
ZEMACH, H/ Duffy and the devil, a Cornish tale./ c1973/
    2-4/7 KB426 .... **CE 398.21**
  Duffy and the devil, a Cornish tale (Braille)./ n.d./
    2-4/7 KB426 .... **CE 398.21**
  Judge, an untrue tale./ c1969/ P-3/2 KG787 .... **CE E**
  Judge, an untrue tale (Braille)./ n.d./ P-3/2 KG787 ... **CE E**
  Mommy, buy me a china doll./ 1966/ P-1/1 KG788 ..... **E**
  Penny a look./ c1971/ K-2/2 KG789 .... **E**
ZEMACH, M/ Duffy and the devil, a Cornish tale./ c1973/
    2-4/7 KB426 .... **CE 398.21**
  Gallinita roja, un viejo cuento./ 1992/ P-K/2 KG790 ... **E**
  It could always be worse: a Yiddish folk tale./ 1976/
    2-4/4 KB792 .... **CE 398.27**
  Judge, an untrue tale./ c1969/ P-3/2 KG787 .... **CE E**
  Little red hen, an old story./ 1983/ P-K/2 KG790 ..... **E**
  Mazel and Shlimazel; or, The milk of a lioness./ 1967/
    4-6/6 KB779 .... **398.27**
  Mommy, buy me a china doll./ 1966/ P-1/1 KG788 ..... **E**
  Naftali the storyteller and his horse, Sus./ 1987/ 5-6/5 KH712 ... **FIC**
  Penny a look./ c1971/ K-2/2 KG789 .... **E**
  Siempre puede ser peor: un cuento folklorico Yiddish./ 1992/
    2-4/4 KB792 .... **CE 398.27**
  Sign in Mendel's window./ c1985, 1996/ 3-5/6 KH600 .... **FIC**
  Three little pigs./ 1988/ P-2/4 KB682 .... **398.24**
  Three wishes: an old story./ 1986/ 2-3/4 KB386 ..... **398.2**
  Tres deseos: un viejo cuento./ 1993/ 2-3/4 KB386 ... **398.2**
ZEMAN, A/ Everything you need to know about math homework./ 1994/
    4-10/7 KB934 .... **510**
ZEMAN, L/ Derniere quete de Gilgamesh./ 1995/ 4-6/4 KE131 ... **892.1**
  Gilgamesh the King./ 1992/ 4-6/4 KE130 .... **892.1**
  Last quest of Gilgamesh./ 1995/ 4-6/4 KE131 ..... **892.1**
  Revanche d'Ishtar./ 1993/ 4-6/4 KE132 .... **892.1**
  Revenge of Ishtar./ 1993/ 4-6/4 KE132 .... **892.1**
  Roi Gilgamesh./ 1992/ 4-6/4 KE130 .... **892.1**
ZHANG, A/ To the mountains by morning./ 1996/ 4-6/5 KH856 ... **FIC**
  Winter rescue./ 1995/ 3-5/4 KH819 .... **FIC**
ZHANG, SN/ Little tiger in the Chinese night: an autobiography in art./ /
    4-6/6 KE609 .... **B ZHANG, S.**
ZIA, H/ ASIAN AMERICAN BIOGRAPHY./ 1995/
    5-A KA399 .... **REF 305.8**
ZIEFERT, H/ Clown games./ 1993/ P-1/1 KG791 .... **E**
  Jason's bus ride./ c1987, 1993/ K-2/1 KG792 .... **E**
  Let's get a pet./ c1993, 1996/ K-3/2 KD193 .... **636.088**
  Little red hen./ 1995/ K-1/2 KG793 .... **E**
  Mike and Tony: best friends./ 1987/ K-2/1 KG794 ..... **E**
  Nicky upstairs and down./ c1987, 1994/ P-1/1 KG795 .... **E**
  Princess and the pea./ 1996/ K-2/1 KG796 .... **E**
  Three wishes./ c1993, 1996/ P-1/1 KG797 .... **E**
  Turnip./ 1996/ K-1/1 KB683 .... **398.24**
  What rhymes with eel?: a word-and-picture flap book./ 1996/
    P-1/2 KG798 .... **E**
  Who said moo?/ 1996/ P-1/2 KG799 .... **E**
ZIESLER, G/ Lion family book./ 1995/ 3-6/6 KC830 .... **599.757**
ZIMMER, D/ Great turtle drive./ 1996/ 2-6/4 KH676 .... **FIC**
  In a dark, dark room and other scary stories./ 1984/
    K-3/1 KB693 .... **398.25**
  Iron giant: a story in five nights./ 1988/ 3-6/3 KH289 .... **FIC**
  One Eye, Two Eyes, Three Eyes: a Hutzul tale./ 1996/
    2-4/7 KB401 .... **398.21**
  One that got away./ 1992/ K-2/2 KF540 .... **E**
ZINGHER, G/ At the Pirate Academy: adventures with language in the
    library media center./ 1990/ KA081 .... **PROF 027.8**
ZION, G/ Harry and the lady next door./ 1960/ P-2/2 KG800 ..... **CE E**
  Harry and the lady next door (Kit)./ 1996/ P-2/2 KG800 .... **CE E**
  Harry by the sea./ 1965/ P-2/2 KG800 .... **CE E**
  Harry el perrito sucio./ 1996/ P-2/2 KG800 .... **CE E**
  Harry, no quiere rosas!/ 1997/ P-2/2 KG800 .... **CE E**
  Harry the dirty dog./ c1956/ P-2/2 KG800 .... **CE E**
  Harry the dirty dog (Braille)./ n.d./ P-2/2 KG800 .... **CE E**
  No roses for Harry./ 1958/ P-2/2 KG800 .... **CE E**
ZOEHFELD, KW/ How mountains are made./ 1995/
    2-4/4 KC170 .... **551.43**
  What lives in a shell?/ 1994/ P-1/2 KC517 .... **594**
  What's alive?/ 1995/ 1-3/2 KC301 .... **577**
ZOLOTOW, C/ Hating book./ c1969, 1989/ K-2/2 KG801 .... **E**
  I know a lady./ 1984/ K-2/6 KG802 .... **E**
  I know a lady (Sound recording cassette)./ n.d./ K-2/6 KG802 .... **E**
  Moon was the best./ 1993/ K-2/5 KG803 .... **E**
  Mr. Rabbit and the lovely present./ c1962/ P-2/2 KG804 ..... **CE E**
  Mr. Rabbit and the lovely present (Braille)./ n.d./ P-2/2 KG804 . **CE E**
  Mr. Rabbit and the lovely present (Kit)./ 1987/ P-2/2 KG804 ... **CE E**
  My grandson Lew./ c1974/ K-2/2 KG805 .... **E**
  Old dog. Rev. and newly illustrated ed./ 1995/ K-2/2 KG806 ..... **E**
  Over and over./ c1957/ P-2/2 KG807 .... **E**
  Senor Conejo y el hermoso regalo./ 1995/ P-2/2 KG804 ...... **CE E**
  Sleepy book./ c1958, 1988/ P-1 KC481 .... **591.5**
  Tiger called Thomas./ c1963, 1988/ K-2/4 KG808 .... **E**
  Tiger called Thomas (Braille)./ n.d., K-2/4 KG808 .... **E**
  Tiger called Thomas (Sound recording cassette)./ n.d./
    K-2/4 KG808 .... **E**
  When the wind stops. Rev. and newly illustrated ed./ 1995/
    K-2/4 KG809 .... **E**
  William's doll./ c1972/ P-2/4 KG810 .... **E**
  William's doll (Braille)./ n.d./ P-2/4 KG810 .... **E**
ZOOFUL OF ANIMALS./ 1992/ K-4 KE090 .... **811.008**
ZUBIZARRETA-ADA, R/ Gathering the sun: an alphabet in Spanish and
    English./ 1997/ 1-3 KE122 .... **861**
  Woman who outshone the sun: the legend of Lucia Zenteno./La mujer que
    brillaba aun mas que el sol: la leyenda de Lucia Zenteno./ 1991/
    3-5/5 KB403 .... **398.21**
ZUBROWSKI, B/ Balloons: building and experimenting with inflatable toys./
    1990/ 4-A/7 KB888 .... **507**
  Bubbles./ 1979/ 4-6/8 KC085 .... **530.4**
  Making waves: finding out about rhythmic motion./ 1994/
    5-A/7 KC081 .... **530**
  Mirrors: finding out about the properties of light./ 1992/
    5-6/8 KC116 .... **535**
  Shadow play: making pictures with light and lenses./ 1995/
    4-8/7 KC117 .... **535**
  Wheels at work: building and experimenting with models of machines./
    1986/ 5-6/8 KD054 .... **621.8**
ZUDECK, DS/ Prairie songs./ 1985/ 5-A/7 KH023 .... **FIC**
ZWERGER, L/ Swineherd./ 1995/ 2-5/5 KG847 .... **FIC**
100 WORDS ABOUT ANIMALS./ 1987/ P-3 KC457 .... **CE 591**
100 WORDS ABOUT MY HOUSE./ 1988/ P-3 KD296 .... **645**

A is for Africa. /ONYEFULU, I/1993/2-4/5 KE178 . . . . **916**

A IS FOR AIDS (Videocassette). /1992/5-6/KD023 . . . . . . **VCR 616.97**

A is for aloha. /FEENEY, S/1980/K-3/KF546 . . . . **E**

A is for Asia. /CHIN-LEE, C/1997/K-3/8 KE700 . . . . **950**

A. NONNY MOUSE WRITES AGAIN!: POEMS. /1993/
K-2/KE052 . . . . **811.008**

A to Z beastly jamboree. /BENDER, R/1996/K-2/KB830 . . . . **421**

A to Z, the animals and me (Compact disc)./GALLINA, J/1993/
P-1/KD612 . . . . **SRC 789.3**

A to Z, the animals and me (Sound recording cassette). /GALLINA, J/
1993/P-1/KD612 . . . . **SRC 789.3**

A to zoo: subject access to children's picture books. 5th ed. /LIMA, CW/
1998//KA017 . . . . **PROF 011.62**

Aani and the tree huggers. /ATKINS, J/1995/3-5/3 KG853 . . . . **Fic**

Aardvarks, disembark! /JONAS, A/1990/2-A/4 KA963 . . . . **333.95**

Aaron Copland. /VENEZIA, M/1995/5-6/7 KE304 . . . . . **B COPLAND, A.**

AASL ELECTRONIC LIBRARY. 1997 ed. (CD-ROM). /1997/
/KA045 . . . . **CDR PROF 025**

Abacus contest: stories from Taiwan and China. /WU, P/1996/
3-5/4 KH884 . . . . **Fic**

ABC bunny. /GAG, W/c1933, 1997/P-K/KF591 . . . . **E**

ABC bunny (Talking book)./GAG, W/n.d./P-K/KF591 . . . . **E**

ABCDrive!: a car trip alphabet. /HOWLAND, N/1994/P-1/1 KF782 . . . **E**

ABC'S AND SUCH (Videocassette). /1993/P-2/KB099 . . . . . . **VCR 372.4**

ABC'S OF AIDS: THE COACH APPROACH (Videocassette). /1991/
5-6/KD024 . . . . **VCR 616.97**

ABC's of books and thinking skills. /POLETTE, N/1987/
/KA156 . . . . **PROF 153.4**

ABC'S OF NATURE: A FAMILY ANSWER BOOK. /1984/
P-A/KB900 . . . . **508**

Abe Lincoln goes to Washington 1837-1865. /HARNESS, C/1997/
2-4/7 KE443 . . . . **B LINCOLN, A.**

Abe Lincoln's hat. /BRENNER, M/1994/1-3/2 KE439 . . . **B LINCOLN, A.**

Abel's island. /STEIG, W/1976/4-6/6 KH749 . . . . **CE Fic**

Abel's island (Sound recording cassette)./STEIG, W/n.d./
4-6/6 KH749 . . . . **CE Fic**

Abel's island (Videocassette)./STEIG, W/1988/4-6/6 KH749 . . . . **CE Fic**

Abenaki Captive. /DUBOIS, ML/1994/6-A/6 KH085 . . . . **Fic**

Abiyoyo: based on a South African lullaby and folk story. /SEEGER, P/
1986/2-5/KD587 . . . . **789.2**

Abiyoyo: based on a South African lullaby and folk story (Braille)./
SEEGER, P/n.d./2-5/KD587 . . . . **789.2**

About birds: a guide for children. /SILL, C/1991/K-2/1 KC664 . . . . . **598**

ABOUT SHARKS (Videocassette). /1981/2-4/KC589 . . . . . . **VCR 597.3**

Abracadabra kid: a writer's life. /FLEISCHMAN, S/1996/
3-A/7 KE344 . . . . **B FLEISCHMAN, S**

Abracadabra to zigzag: an alphabet book. /LECOURT, N/1991/
K-3/KF954 . . . . **E**

Abraham Lincoln. /D'AULAIRE, I/c1957, 1993/
3-4/4 KE440 . . . . **CE B LINCOLN, A.**

Abraham Lincoln: a man for all the people: a ballad. /LIVINGSTON, MC/
1993/K-3/KD974 . . . . **811**

Abraham Lincoln (Braille)./D'AULAIRE, I/n.d./
3-4/4 KE440 . . . . **CE B LINCOLN, A.**

Abraham Lincoln (Sound recording cassette)./D'AULAIRE, I/n.d./
3-4/4 KE440 . . . . **CE B LINCOLN, A.**

ABRAHAM LINCOLN: THE GREAT EMANCIPATOR (Videocassette). /
1990/A/KE438 . . . . **VCR B LINCOLN, A.**

Abran paso a los patitos./MCCLOSKEY, R/1996/P-1/4 KG089 . . . **CE E**

Abridged Dewey decimal classification and relative index. Ed. 13. /DEWEY,
M/1997//KA058 . . . . **PROF 025.4**

ABRIDGED READERS' GUIDE TO PERIODICAL LITERATURE, AUTHOR
AND SUBJECT INDEX TO A SELECTED LIST OF PERIODICALS. /
1935-/3-6/KA496 . . . . **PER 050**

ABUBAKARI: THE EXPLORER KING OF MALI (Videocassette). /1992/
5-6/KE224 . . . . **VCR B ABUBAKARI**

Abuela. /DORROS, A/1991/P-2/2 KF488 . . . . **E**

Abuela (Spanish version)./DORROS, A/1995/P-2/2 KF488 . . . . **E**

Abuela (Videocassette). /DORROS, A/1994/P-2/KF489 . . . . **VCR E**

Abuelita de arriba y la Abueita de abajo./DE PAOLA, T/1991/
K-3/6 KF475 . . . . **E**

Abuelo y los tres osos./Abuelo and the three bears. /TELLO, J/1997/
K-2/2 KG598 . . . . **E**

ACADEMICALLY GIFTEDNESS (Videocassette)./1991/
/KA187 . . . . **VCR PROF 371.95**

Accidental witch. /MAZER, A/1995/3-5/4 KH463 . . . . **Fic**

Accidents may happen. /JONES, CF/1996/4-A/9 KC895 . . . . **609**

Ace: the very important pig./KING-SMITH, D/c1990, 1992/
2-5/5 KH346 . . . . **CE Fic**

Acorn tree and other folktales. /ROCKWELL, AF/1995/
P-2/2 KB362 . . . . **398.2**

Across America on an emigrant train. /MURPHY, J/1993/
6-A/8 KB140 . . . . **385**

Across five Aprils. /HUNT, I/1984/5-A/5 KH291 . . . . **CE Fic**

Across five Aprils (Braille). /HUNT, I/n.d./5-A/5 KH291 . . . . **CE Fic**

Across five Aprils (Sound recording cassette)./HUNT, I/n.d./
5-A/5 KH291 . . . . **CE Fic**

Across five Aprils (Talking book)./HUNT, I/1973/5-A/5 KH291 . . . **CE Fic**

Across five Aprils (Talking book)./HUNT, I/n.d./5-A/5 KH291 . . . **CE Fic**

Across the plains in the Donner Party. /MURPHY, VR/1996/
5-6/7 KF041 . . . . **978**

ACROSS THE SEA OF GRASS (Videocassette). /1991/
A/KF024 . . . . **VCR 978**

Across the stream. /GINSBURG, M/1982/P-K/2 KF621 . . . . **E**

Across the wide dark sea: the Mayflower journey. /VAN LEEUWEN, J/
1995/2-4/4 KG645 . . . . **E**

Action alphabet. /NEUMEIER, M/1985/1-3/KG171 . . . . **E**

Action alphabet. /ROTNER, S/1996/K-2/2 KB854 . . . . **428.2**

Activities handbook for teachers of young children. 5th ed. /CROFT, DJ/
1990//KA191 . . . . **PROF 372.1**

Adam of the road. /GRAY, EJ/c1942, 1970/5-6/6 KH194 . . . . . **CE Fic**

Adam of the road (Braille)./GRAY, EJ/n.d./5-6/6 KH194 . . . . . **CE Fic**

Adam of the road (Sound recording cassette)./GRAY, EJ/n.d./
5-6/6 KH194 . . . . **CE Fic**

Adam of the road (Talking book)./GRAY, EJ/1980/5-6/6 KH194 . **CE Fic**

Adam of the road (Talking book)./GRAY, EJ/n.d./5-6/6 KH194 . . **CE Fic**

Add it, dip it, fix it: a book of verbs. /SCHNEIDER, RM/1995/
K-2/2 KB855 . . . . **428.2**

Addie meets Max. /ROBINS, J/1985/K-2/1 KG338 . . . . **E**

Addie's bad day. /ROBINS, J/1993/K-1/2 KG339 . . . . **E**

Administering the school library media center. 3rd ed. /MORRIS, BJ/1992/
/KA077 . . . . **PROF 027.8**

Adopted by the eagles: a Plains Indian story of friendship and treachery. /
GOBLE, P/1994/2-5/4 KB706 . . . . **398.26**

Adventure in space: the flight to fix the Hubble. /SCOTT, E/1995/
A/7 KC006 . . . . **522**

ADVENTURE IN THE AMAZON. /1992/4-6/7 KE211 . . . . **918.1**
Adventures of Boone Barnaby. /COTTONWOOD, J/1992/
6-A/5 KH031 . . . . **Fic**
Adventures of Hershel of Ostropol. /KIMMEL, EA/1995/
2-4/7 KB459 . . . . **398.22**
Adventures of Hershel of Ostropol (Sound recording cassette)./KIMMEL,
EA/1997/2-4/7 KB459 . . . . **398.22**
Adventures of High John the Conqueror. /SANFIELD, S/1989/
3-6/5 KB480 . . . . **398.22**
Adventures of King Midas. /REID BANKS, L/1992/4-A/6 KH626 . . . . . **Fic**
Adventures of Odysseus. /PHILIP, N/1997/3-6/5 KE125 . . . . **883**
Adventures of Sherlock Holmes. /DOYLE, AC/1992/6-A/7 KH082 . . . . **Fic**
Adventures of Sparrowboy. /PINKNEY, JB/1997/K-2/3 KG242 . . . . . . **E**
Adventures of Spider: West African folktales. /ARKHURST, JC/c1964,
1992/2-3/5 KB524 . . . . **398.24**
Adventures of Sugar and Junior. /MEDEARIS, AS/1995/
2-3/2 KH494 . . . . **Fic**
Adventures of taxi dog. /BARRACCA, D/1990/P-2/2 KF200 . . . . . **CE E**
Adventures of Tom Sawyer. /TWAIN, M/1989/5-A/4 KH814 . . . . . . **Fic**
ADVENTURING WITH BOOKS: A BOOKLIST FOR PRE-K-GRADE 6. 1997
ed. /1997/KA009 . . . . **PROF 011.62**
Advice for a frog. /SCHERTLE, A/1995/3-5/KE019 . . . . **811**
AESOP'S FABLE: THE TORTOISE AND THE HARE (CD-ROM). /1993/
P-A/KB522 . . . . **CDR 398.24**
Aesop's fables. /PAXTON, T/1988/3-4/KB632 . . . . **398.24**
Aesop's fables (Sound recording cassette)./PAXTON, T/n.d./
3-4/KB632 . . . . **398.24**
Africa calling, nighttime falling. /ADLERMAN, D/1996/P-2/KF135 . . . . . **E**
AFRICA TRAIL (CD-ROM). /1995/4-A/KE723 . . . . **CDR 960**
AFRICA (Videocassette). /1991/4-A/KE724 . . . . **VCR 960**
AFRICAN AMERICAN ALMANAC. 7th ed. /1997/5-A/KA486 . . **REF 973**
AFRICAN AMERICAN ART: PAST AND PRESENT (Videocassette). /1992/
4-A/KD371 . . . . **VCR 704**
AFRICAN AMERICAN BIOGRAPHY. /1994/5-A/KA398 . . . . . **REF 305.8**
AFRICAN AMERICAN VOICES. /1996/5-A/KA487 . . . . **REF 973**
African animal tales. /BARBOSA, RA/1993/2-4/6 KB526 . . . . . . **398.24**
African elephants: giants of the land. /PATENT, DH/1991/
4-6/6 KC813 . . . . **599.67**
African journey. /CHIASSON, J/1987/A/11 KE725 . . . . **960**
African roots. /SILVERMAN, J/1994/5-A/KD590 . . . . **789.2**
African village folktales, vols 1-3 (Talking book). /KAULA, EM/n.d./
4-6/KB746 . . . . **TB 398.27**
African-American folk songs and rhythms (Sound recording cassette). /
JENKINS, E/c1960, 1992/K-6/KD572 . . . . **SRC 789.2**
African-American scientists. /MCKISSACK, P/1994/4-6/7 KB924 . . . . **509**
After the dancing days. /ROSTKOWSKI, MI/1996/6-A/4 KH656 . . . . **Fic**
After the flood. /GEISERT, A/1994/K-2/3 KF601 . . . . **E**
Afternoon of the elves. /LISLE, JT/1989/6-A/6 KH408 . . . . **Fic**
Agnes the sheep. /TAYLOR, W/1990/5-A/6 KH786 . . . . **Fic**
Agony of Alice. /NAYLOR, PR/1985/5-6/6 KH532 . . . . **Fic**
Agony of Alice (Sound recording cassette)./NAYLOR, PR/n.d./
5-6/6 KH532 . . . . **Fic**
Ahaiyute and Cloud Eater. /HULPACH, V/1996/3-4/5 KB708 . . . . **398.26**
Aida. /PRICE, L/1990/4-A/6 KD530 . . . . **782.1**
AIDS: how it works in the body. /GREENBERG, L/1992/
A/8 KD028 . . . . **616.97**
Air mail to the moon. /BIRDSEYE, T/1988/K-3/5 KF231 . . . . **E**
Aircraft: lift-the-flap book. /BROWNE, G/1992/3-6/5 KD106 . . **629.133**
Airplane book. /BELLVILLE, CW/1991/4-6/7 KD105 . . . . **629.133**
Airplanes. /BARTON, B/1986/P-1/2 KB155 . . . . **387.7**
AIT CATALOG OF EDUCATIONAL MATERIALS. /1962-/
/KA003 . . . . **PROF 011**
Ajeemah and his son. /BERRY, J/1992/6-A/7 KG899 . . . . **Fic**
Ajeemah and his son (Sound recording cassette)./BERRY, J/1994/
6-A/7 KG899 . . . . **Fic**
Al Gore, vice president. /STEFOFF, R/1994/4-5/6 KE374 . . **B GORE, A.**
ALA filing rules. /AMERICAN LIBRARY ASSOCIATION. FILING
COMMITTEE. /1980//KA055 . . . . **PROF 025.3**
Alabama. /BROWN, D/1994/4-6/7 KE996 . . . . **976.1**
ALABAMA TO WYOMING: FLAGS OF THE UNITED STATES
(Videocassette). /1994/4-6/KE612 . . . . **VCR 929.9**
ALABAMA TO WYOMING: STATE FACT CARDS. /1997/
4-6/KA488 . . . . **REF 973**
Aladdin and the magic lamp. /HAUTZIG, D/1993/1-2/2 KB314 . . . **398.2**
Aladdin and the magic lamp (Kit). /KUNSTLER, JH/1995/
3-5/KB333 . . . . **KIT 398.2**
Alamo! /SULLIVAN, G/1997/4-6/10 KF002 . . . . **976.4**
Alaska. /JOHNSTON, J/1994/4-6/7 KF099 . . . . **979.8**
Alaska. /HEINRICHS, A/1990/4-6/7 KF096 . . . . **979.8**
Alaska (Sound recording cassette)./HEINRICHS, A/1993/
4-6/7 KF096 . . . . **979.8**
ALASKA: THE MAGAZINE OF LIFE ON THE LAST FRONTIER. /1935-/
A/KA497 . . . . **PER 050**

Albatrosses of Midway Island. /JOHNSON, SA/1990/
5-6/7 KC681 . . . . **598.4**
Albert's alphabet. /TRYON, L/1991/P-1/KG620 . . . . **E**
Albert's ballgame./TRYON, L/1996/P-1/KG620. . . . . **E**
Albert's field trip./TRYON, L/1993/P-1/KG620 . . . . **E**
Albert's play./TRYON, L/1992/P-1/KG620 . . . . **E**
Albert's Thanksgiving. /TRYON, L/1994/K-2/2 KG621 . . . . **E**
ALBUM OF AMERICAN HISTORY. Rev. ed. /1981/5-6/KA489 . . **REF 973**
Alcohol--what it is, what it does. /SEIXAS, JS/c1977/
1-3/5 KD002 . . . . **613.81**
Alcott family Christmas. /WALLNER, A/1996/1-3/2 KG678 . . . . **E**
Aldo Applesauce. /HURWITZ, J/1979/4-6/6 KH296 . . . . **Fic**
Aldo Applesauce (Sound recording cassette)./HURWITZ, J/n.d./
4-6/6 KH296 . . . . **Fic**
Aldo Ice Cream./HURWITZ, J/1981/4-6/6 KH296 . . . . **Fic**
Aldo Ice Cream (Braille)./HURWITZ, J/n.d./4-6/6 KH296. . . . . **Fic**
Aldo Ice Cream (Sound recording cassette)./HURWITZ, J/n.d./
4-6/6 KH296 . . . . **Fic**
Aldo Peanut Butter./HURWITZ, J/1990/4-6/6 KH296 . . . . **Fic**
Alef-bet: a Hebrew alphabet book. /EDWARDS, M/1992/
1-3//KB864 . . . . **492.4**
Alegria de ser tu y yo. /NIKOLA-LISA, W/1996/P-2/KD996 . . . . . . **811**
Alejandro's gift. /ALBERT, RE/1994/1-3/6 KF144. . . . . **E**
Alexander and the terrible, horrible, no good, very bad day. /VIORST, J/
c1972/P-3/7 KG657 . . . . **CE E**
Alexander and the terrible, horrible, no good, very bad day and other
stories and poems (Talking book). /VIORST, J/1984/
P-3/KG658 . . . . **TB E**
Alexander and the terrible, horrible, no good, very bad day (Sound
recording cassette)./VIORST, J/n.d./P-3/7 KG657 . . . . . **CE E**
Alexander and the terrible, horrible, no good, very bad day (Talking
book)./VIORST, J/n.d./P-3/7 KG657 . . . . **CE E**
Alexander and the wind-up mouse. /LIONNI, L/1987/P-1/4 KF988 . . . . **E**
Alexander and the wind-up mouse (Braille)./LIONNI, L/n.d./
P-1/4 KF988 . . . . **E**
Alexander and the wind-up mouse (Talking book). /LIONNI, L/n.d./
P-1/4 KF988 . . . . **E**
Alexander and the wind-up mouse (Videocassette). /LIONNI, L/1985/
P-2/KF994 . . . . **VCR E**
Alexander, que de ninguna manera (le oyen? lo dice en serio!) se va a
mudar./VIORST, J/1995/1-3/2 KG660 . . . . **E**
Alexander, que era rico el domingo pasado./VIORST, J/1989/
P-3/5 KG659 . . . . **CE E**
Alexander, que era rico el domingo pasado (Kit)./VIORST, J/1991/
P-3/5 KG659 . . . . **CE E**
Alexander, who used to be rich last Sunday. /VIORST, J/c1978/
P-3/5 KG659 . . . . **CE E**
Alexander, who's not (Do you hear me? I mean it!) going to move. /
VIORST, J/1995/1-3/2 KG660 . . . . **E**
Alexander y el dia terrible, horrible, espantoso, horroroso./VIORST, J/
1989/P-3/7 KG657 . . . . **CE E**
Alexander y el dia terrible, horrible, espantoso, horroroso (Kit)./VIORST, J/
1991/P-3/7 KG657 . . . . **CE E**
Alfie gets in first. /HUGHES, S/1987/P-K/2 KF784 . . . . **E**
Alfie gets in first (Braille)./HUGHES, S/n.d./P-2/2 KF784 . . . . **E**
Alfonse, where are you? /WIKLER, L/1996/P-K/1 KG715 . . . . **E**
ALFRED HITCHCOCK'S SUPERNATURAL TALES OF TERROR AND
SUSPENSE. /c1973, 1983/A/6 KG842 . . . . **Fic**
Alfred Summer. /SLEPIAN, J/1980/4-6/4 KH718 . . . . **Fic**
Alfred Summer (Sound recording cassette)./SLEPIAN, J/n.d./
4-6/4 KH718 . . . . **Fic**
Algo especial para mi./WILLIAMS, VB/1994/P-3/2 KG738 . . . . **E**
Algonquians. /QUIRI, PR/1992/4-6/6 KE763 . . . . **970.3**
Ali, child of the desert. /LONDON, J/1997/K-3/3 KG019 . . . . **E**
Alice in April./NAYLOR, PR/1993/6-A/6 KH533 . . . . **Fic**
Alice in rapture, sort of. /NAYLOR, PR/1989/6-A/6 KH533 . . . . . . **Fic**
ALICE IN WONDERLAND IN DANCE (Videocassette). /1993/
3-6/KD691 . . . . **VCR 792.8**
Alice the brave./NAYLOR, PR/1995/6-A/6 KH533 . . . . **Fic**
Alice's adventures in Wonderland. /CARROLL, L/c1865, 1992/
5-A/7 KG980 . . . . **Fic**
Aliens ate my homework. /COVILLE, B/1993/4-6/5 KH035 . . . . . . **Fic**
Alison's zinnia. /LOBEL, A/1990/P-2/2 KF999 . . . . **E**
All aboard! /STEVENSON, J/1995/1-3/2 KG557 . . . . **E**
All aboard ABC. /MAGEE, D/1990/K-2/2 KD075 . . . . **625.1**
All aboard overnight: a book of compound words. /MAESTRO, B/1992/
P-3/3 KB848 . . . . **428.1**
All about asthma. /OSTROW, W/1989/5-6/7 KD015 . . . . **616.2**
All about football. /SULLIVAN, G/1987/4-6/6 KD787 . . . . . . **796.332**
All about owls. /ARNOSKY, J/1995/2-5/4 KC709 . . . . **598.9**
All about Sam. /LOWRY, L/1988/3-5/4 KH421 . . . . **Fic**
All about Sam (Sound recording cassette)./LOWRY, L/n.d./
3-5/4 KH421 . . . . **Fic**
All about Stacy. /GIFF, PR/1988/1-2/2 KF614 . . . . **CE E**

All about Stacy (Kit)./GIFF, PR/1994/1-2/2 KF614 . . . . **CE E**
All about where. /HOBAN, T/1991/P-1/KB853 . . . . **428.2**
All alone after school. /STANEK, M/1985/2-3/2 KG536. . . . . **E**
All but Alice./NAYLOR, PR/1992/6-A/6 KH533. . . . . **Fic**
All but Alice (Sound recording cassette)./NAYLOR, PR/1993/ 6-A/6 KH533 . . . . **Fic**
All in the woodland early: an ABC book. /YOLEN, J/c1979, 1991/ K-1/3 KG776 . . . . **E**
All Joseph wanted. /RADIN, RY/1991/3-5/4 KH617. . . . . **Fic**
All kinds of families. /SIMON, N/c1976/1-3/5 KA873 . . . . **306.85**
All new Jonah Twist. /HONEYCUTT, N/1987/3-5/4 KH277 . . . . **Fic**
ALL NIGHT, ALL DAY: A CHILD'S FIRST BOOK OF AFRICAN-AMERICAN SPIRITUALS. /1991/K-6/KD554. **789.2**
All the best contests for kids, 1996-1997. 5th ed. /BERGSTROM, JM/ 1996/3-6/7 KD677 . . . . **790.1**
All the colors of the earth. /HAMANAKA, S/1994/P-2/4 KF667. . . . . . **E**
All the colors of the race. /ADOFF, A/1982/4-6/KD907 . . . . **811**
All the colors of the race (Sound recording cassette)./ADOFF, A/n.d./ 4-6/KD907. . . . . **811**
All the places to love. /MACLACHLAN, P/1994/1-4/5 KG053 . . . . **E**
ALL TIME FAVORITE CHILDREN'S STORIES (Talking book). /1993/ K-2/KF150. . . . . **TB E**
All we needed to say: poems about school from Tanya and Sophie. / SINGER, M/1996/3-6/KE027 . . . . **811**
Allen Jay and the Underground Railroad. /BRILL, MT/1993/ 4-6/4 KE898 . . . . **973.7**
Allergies - what they are, what they do. /SEIXAS, JS/1991/ 3-5/6 KD033 . . . . **616.97**
Alligator arrived with apples, a potluck alphabet feast. / DRAGONWAGON, C/1987/K-2/5 KF494. . . . . **E**
ALLIGATOR PIE (Videocassette). /1993/P-2/KD912 . . . . **VCR 811**
Alligators all around: an alphabet. /SENDAK, M/c1962/ P-1/KG429 . . . . **CE E**
Alligators all around: an alphabet (Videocassette)./SENDAK, M/1976/ P-1/KG429 . . . . **CE E**
Allison. /SAY, A/1997/2-4/2 KH678. . . . . **Fic**
Allison's story: a book about homeschooling. /LURIE, J/1996/ 2-5/2 KD303 . . . . **649**
All-of-a-kind family. /TAYLOR, S/1951, 1988/4-6/5 KH782 . . . . **Fic**
All-of-a-kind family (Braille)./TAYLOR, S/n.d./4-6/5 KH782 . . . . **Fic**
All-of-a-kind family (Sound recording cassette)./TAYLOR, S/n.d./ 4-6/5 KH782 . . . . **Fic**
All-of-a-kind family (Talking book)./TAYLOR, S/n.d./4-6/5 KH782. . . . **Fic**
All-of-a-kind family uptown./TAYLOR, S/1958/4-6/5 KH782. . . . . **Fic**
All-of-a-kind family uptown (Braille)./TAYLOR, S/n.d./4-6/5 KH782 . . . **Fic**
All-of-a-kind family uptown (Talking book)./TAYLOR, S/n.d./ 4-6/5 KH782 . . . . **Fic**
ALL-TIME FAVORITE DANCES (Compact disc)./1991/ K-6/KD603 . . . . **SRC 789.3**
ALL-TIME FAVORITE DANCES (Sound recording cassette). /1991/ K-6/KD603 . . . . **SRC 789.3**
ALL-TIME FAVORITE DANCES (Vidoecassette)./1993/ K-6/KD603 . . . . **SRC 789.3**
Aloha, Salty! /RAND, G/1996/1-3/3 KG299 . . . . **E**
Along the Santa Fe Trail: Marion Russell's own story. /RUSSELL, M/1993/ 4-6/7 KE199 . . . . **917.8**
Alphabatics. /MACDONALD, S/1986/P-2/KG051 . . . . **E**
Alphabatics (Braille)./MACDONALD, S/n.d./P-2/KG051 . . . . **E**
Alphabet city. /JOHNSON, S/1995/K-A/KF838 . . . . **E**
Alphabet from Z to A: (with much confusion on the way). /VIORST, J/ 1994/2-5/KE036. . . . . **811**
Alphabet in action: consonants and vowels taught through song and motor activities (Sound recording cassette). /GALLINA, M/1978/ K-2/KB102. . . . . **SRC 372.4**
Alphabet of dinosaurs. /DODSON, P/1995/1-6/5 KC248 . . . . **567.9**
Alphabet parade. /CHWAST, S/1994/K-2/KF392 . . . . **E**
Alphabet tale. New ed., rev. and re-illustrated. /GARTEN, J/1994/ P-K/3 KF599 . . . . **E**
Alphabet times four: an international ABC: English, Spanish, French, German. /BROWN, R/1991/2-4/KB819 . . . . **411**
Alphabet tree. /LIONNI, L/c1968, 1990/1-2/3 KF989. . . . . **E**
ALPHABETTER ANSWER (Videocassette). /1989/5-A/KC992 . **VCR 613.8**
Altogether, one at a time. /KONIGSBURG, EL/c1971/A/6 KH372. . . . **Fic**
Alvin Ailey. /PINKNEY, AD/1993/2-4/5 KE231 . . . . **B AILEY, A.**
Always Prayer Shawl. /OBERMAN, S/1994/2-4/2 KG184 . . . . **E**
Always room for one more. /NIC LEODHAS, S/1965/ K-2/7 KB760 . . . . **398.27**
Always room for one more (Braille)./NIC LEODHAS, S/n.d./ K-2/7 KB760 . . . . **398.27**
Am I beautiful? /MINARIK, EH/1992/P-K/2 KG140 . . . . **E**
Amanda Pig and her big brother, Oliver./VAN LEEUWEN, J/1994/ K-2/1 KG648. . . . . **CE E**
Amanda Pig and her big brother, Oliver (Kit)./VAN LEEUWEN, J/1984/ K-2/1 KG648 . . . . **CE E**
Amanda Pig on her own./VAN LEEUWEN, J/1991/K-2/1 KG648 . . **CE E**
Amanda Pig, schoolgirl./VAN LEEUWEN, J/1997/K-2/1 KG648 . . . **CE E**
Amanecer./ACKERMAN, K/1994/K-2/5 KF129 . . . . **E**
Amazing American women: 40 fascinating 5-minute reads. /HAVEN, K/ 1995//KA166 . . . . **PROF 305.4**
AMAZING ANIMALS (CD-ROM). /1997/K-3/KC444 . . . . **CDR 591**
AMAZING ANIMALS (Videocassette). /1994/3-6/KD188 . **VCR 636.008**
Amazing apple book. /BOURGEOIS, P/1990/5-6/7 KD264. . . . . . **641.3**
Amazing armored animals. /SOWLER, S/1992/4-6/6 KC467 . . . . **591.47**
Amazing bikes. /LORD, T/1992/3-5/6 KD126. . . . . **629.227**
Amazing birds. /PARSONS, A/1990/3-6/5 KC658 . . . . **598**
Amazing boats. /LINCOLN, M/1992/3-5/5 KD064 . . . . **623.8**
Amazing bone. /STEIG, W/1976/1-3/5 KG539. . . . . **CE E**
Amazing bone (Kit)./STEIG, W/c1986, 1993/1-3/5 KG539. . . . . . **CE E**
Amazing bone (Sound recording cassette)./STEIG, W/n.d./ 1-3/5 KG539. . . . . **CE E**
Amazing bone (Videocassette)./STEIG, W/1986/1-3/5 KG539. . . . **CE E**
Amazing buildings. /WILKINSON, P/1993/4-A/9 KD385. . . . . **720**
Amazing Christmas extravaganza. /SHANNON, D/1995/2-5/6 KG475 . **E**
Amazing dirt book. /BOURGEOIS, P/1990/4-6/6 KD148 . . . . **631.4**
Amazing flying machines. /KERROD, R/1992/4-6/6 KD110 . . . . **629.133**
Amazing forwards. /DUPLACEY, J/1996/4-6/6 KD838 . . . . **796.962**
Amazing Grace. /HOFFMAN, M/1991/P-2/4 KF761 . . . . **CE E**
Amazing Grace (Videocassette)./HOFFMAN, M/1994/P-2/4 KF761 **CE E**
Amazing Grace (Videocassette)./HOFFMAN, M/1996/P-2/4 KF761 **CE E**
Amazing impossible Erie Canal. /HARNESS, C/1995/3-6/8 KB143 . . **386**
Amazing magic tricks. /BROWN, D/1995/4-6/KD744. . . . . **793.8**
Amazing mammals. /PARSONS, A/1990/2-6/6 KC726. . . . . **599**
Amazing paper book. /BOURGEOIS, P/1989/5-6/6 KD332. . . . . **676**
Amazing paper cuttings of Hans Christian Andersen. /BRUST, BW/1994/ 3-5/8 KE235 . . . . **B ANDERSEN, H.**
Amazing schemes within your genes. /BALKWILL, FR/1993/ 4-8/6 KC288 . . . . **576.5**
Amazing snakes. /PARSONS, A/1990/2-6/5 KC642 . . . . **597.96**
Amazing spiders. /PARSONS, A/1990/2-6/6 KC529 . . . . **595.4**
Amazing spiders. /SCHNIEPER, C/1989/4-6/6 KC531. . . . . **595.4**
Amazing world of ants. /SABIN, F/1982/2-4/2 KC579 . . . . . . **CE 595.79**
Amazing world of ants (Kit)./SABIN, F/1983/2-4/2 KC579 . . . **CE 595.79**
Amazing world of butterflies and moths. /SABIN, L/1982/ 2-4/4 KC566 . . . . **CE 595.78**
Amazing world of butterflies and moths (Kit)./SABIN, L/1983/ 2-4/4 KC566 . . . . **CE 595.78**
Amazingly easy puppet plays: 42 new scripts for one-person puppetry. / ANDERSON, D/1997//KA361 . . . . **PROF 812**
Amazon. /MURRAY, P/1994/3-6/7 KE212. . . . . **918.1**
Amazon ABC. /DARLING, K/1996/K-5/3 KC499. . . . . **591.981**
Amazon Basin: vanishing cultures. /REYNOLDS, J/1993/ 3-6/7 KF104 . . . . **981**
Amazon boy. /LEWIN, T/1993/K-2/5 KF974 . . . . **E**
Ambar en cuarto y sin su amigo./DANZIGER, P/1995/2-4/4 KH059 . . **Fic**
Amber Brown goes fourth. /DANZIGER, P/1995/2-4/4 KH059. . . . . . **Fic**
Amber Brown goes fourth (Sound recording cassette)./DANZIGER, P/ 1997/2-4/4 KH059 . . . . **Fic**
Amber Brown is not a crayon. /DANZIGER, P/1994/2-4/6 KH060 . . . **Fic**
Amber Brown wants extra credit. /DANZIGER, P/1996/2-4/4 KH061. . **Fic**
Amber cat. /MCKAY, H/1997/5-8/6 KH476 . . . . **Fic**
Amelia Bedelia goes camping./PARISH, P/1985/1-3/2 KG214 . . . . **CE E**
Amelia Bedelia's family album. /PARISH, P/1988/K-3/4 KG211 . . . . . . **E**
Amelia Earhart: courage in the sky. /KERBY, M/1990/ 3-4/5 KE327 . . . . **B EARHART, A.**
Amelia's road. /ALTMAN, LJ/1993/1-3/4 KF154. . . . . **E**
AMERICA: A NATION OF IMMIGRANTS (Picture). /1996/ 4-6/KA923 . . . . **PIC 325.73**
America in World War I. /DOLAN, EF/1996/5-A/7 KE651 . . . . . . **940.3**
America the beautiful. /BATES, KL/1993/K-3/KD558. . . . . **789.2**
AMERICAN ART AND ARCHITECTURE (Videocassette). /1991/ 4-A/KD381 . . . . **VCR 709.73**
American astronomers: searchers and wonderers. /CAMP, CA/1996/ A/10 KC000 . . . . **520**
American bison. /BERMAN, R/1992/5-6/7 KC790 . . . . **599.64**
AMERICAN BOOK OF DAYS. 3rd ed. /1978/4-6/KA412 . . . . **REF 394.2**
American dinosaur hunters. /AASENG, N/1996/A/9 KC232 . . . . . . **560**
AMERICAN FAIRY TALES: FROM RIP VAN WINKLE TO THE ROOTABAGA STORIES. /1996/4-6/7 KG843 . . . . **Fic**
American family farm. /ANDERSON, J/1989/5-6/8 KD145 . . . . **630.973**
American flag. /ARMBRUSTER, A/1991/4-6/8 KE613. . . . . **929.9**
AMERICAN GIRL. /1993-/3-5/KA498 . . . . **PER 050**
AMERICAN HERITAGE CHILDREN'S DICTIONARY. /1997/ 3-6/KA417 . . . . **REF 423**
AMERICAN HERITAGE FIRST DICTIONARY. /1997/1-3/KA418 . **REF 423**
American Heritage picture dictionary. /HILLERICH, RL/1994/ P-1/KA423. . . . . **REF 423**
AMERICAN HERITAGE STUDENT DICTIONARY. /1994/ 6-A/KA419 . . . . **REF 423**

AMERICAN HISTORY: GROWING PAINS (Picture). /c1974/
4-6/KE912. . . . . **PIC 973.8**
AMERICAN IN PARIS: GERSHWIN (Videocassette). /1993/
1-6/KD517. . . . . **VCR 780**
AMERICAN INDIAN ART MAGAZINE. /1975-/5-6/KA499 . . . . **PER 050**
American Indian children of the past. /SHERROW, V/1997/
3-6/7 KE764 . . . . **970.3**
American inventors of the 20th century. /JEFFREY, LS/1996/
4-6/12 KC894 . . . . **609**
AMERICAN MELODY SAMPLER (Compact disc). /1994/
K-6/KD555 . . . . **CD 789.2**
AMERICAN MELODY SAMPLER (Sound recording cassette)./1994/
K-6/KD555 . . . . **CD 789.2**
American revolution: how we fought the War of Independence. /DOLAN,
EF/1995/4-6/8 KE879 . . . . **973.3**
American revolutionaries: a history in their own words--1750-1800. /
MELTZER, M/1993/5-6/8 KE883 . . . . **973.3**
American too. /BARTONE, E/1996/1-3/3 KF210 . . . . **E**
America's deserts: guide to plants and animals. /WALLACE, MD/1996/
2-A/10 KC365 . . . . **578.754**
America's Paul Revere. /FORBES, E/c1946/A/7 KE509 . . . **B REVERE, P.**
America's Paul Revere (Braille)./FORBES, E/n.d./
A/7 KE509 . . . . **B REVERE, P.**
America's prairies. /STAUB, FJ/1994/4-6/7 KC332 . . . . . . **577.4**
America's religions: an educator's guide to beliefs and practices. /
HUBBARD, BJ/1997//KA160. . . . . **PROF 200**
AMERICA'S WESTERN NATIONAL PARKS (Videocassette). /1990/
4-6/KE200. . . . . **VCR 917.804**
Amigos de Osito./MINARIK, EH/n.d./P-1/2 KG141 . . . . **CE E**
Amish. /WILLIAMS, JK/1996/5-A/9 KA721 . . . . **289.7**
Amish Christmas. /AMMON, R/1996/3-5/4 KG844 . . . . **Fic**
Amish home. /BIAL, R/1993/5-A/8 KA719 . . . . **289.7**
AMISTAD REVOLT: "ALL WE WANT IS MAKE US FREE"
(Videocassette). /1996/6-A/KA926 . . . . **VCR 326**
Amistad slave revolt and American abolition. /ZEINERT, K/1997/
6-A/10 KA930 . . . . **326**
Among schoolchildren. /KIDDER, T/1989//KA192 . . . . . . **PROF 372.11**
Among schoolchildren (Sound recording cassette)./KIDDER, T/n.d./
/KA192. . . . . **PROF 372.11**
Amos and Boris. /STEIG, W/c1971/1-3/7 KG540 . . . . **CE E**
Amos Fortune, free man. /YATES, E/c1950/A/7 KE348. . **B FORTUNE, A.**
Amos Fortune, free man (Braille)./YATES, E/n.d./
A/7 KE348 . . . . **B FORTUNE, A.**
Amos Fortune, free man (Sound recording cassette)./YATES, E/n.d./
A/7 KE348 . . . . **B FORTUNE, A.**
Amos Fortune, free man (Talking book)./YATES, E/n.d./
A/7 KE348 . . . . **B FORTUNE, A.**
Amphibian. /CLARKE, B/1993/5-6/9 KC599 . . . . **597.8**
AMPHIBIANS AND REPTILES (Videocassette). /1996/
5-6/KC612. . . . . **VCR 597.9**
Amy Dunn quits school. /SHREVE, S/1993/5-A/7 KH706 . . . . . **Fic**
Anancy and Mr. Dry-Bone. /FRENCH, F/1991/K-2/2 KF583 . . . . **E**
Ananse's feast: an Ashanti tale. /MOLLEL, TM/1997/
K-2/3 KB622 . . . . **398.24**
Anansi and the moss-covered rock. /KIMMEL, EA/1988/
1-2/4 KB600 . . . . **CE 398.24**
Anansi and the moss-covered rock (Kit)./KIMMEL, EA/1991/
1-2/4 KB600 . . . . **CE 398.24**
Anansi and the talking melon. /KIMMEL, EA/1994/
2-3/2 KB601 . . . . **CE 398.24**
Anansi and the talking melon (Kit)./KIMMEL, EA/1995/
2-3/2 KB601 . . . . **CE 398.24**
Anansi and the talking melon (Videocassette)./KIMMEL, EA/1994/
2-3/2 KB601 . . . . **CE 398.24**
Anansi goes fishing. /KIMMEL, EA/1991, c1992/K-2/2 KB602 **CE 398.24**
Anansi goes fishing (Kit)./KIMMEL, EA/1993/K-2/2 KB602 . . . **CE 398.24**
Anansi goes fishing (Sound recording cassette)./KIMMEL, EA/1995/
K-2/2 KB602 . . . . **CE 398.24**
Anansi goes fishing (Videocassette)./KIMMEL, EA/1992/
K-2/2 KB602 . . . . **CE 398.24**
Anansi (Kit). /GLEESON, B/1992/3-5/KB572 . . . . **KIT 398.24**
Anansi the spider: a tale from the Ashanti. /MCDERMOTT, G/c1972/
1-3/2 KB616 . . . . **398.24**
Anansi the spider: a tale from the Ashanti (Braille)./MCDERMOTT, G/n.d./
1-3/2 KB616 . . . . **398.24**
Anansi the spider: a tale from the Ashanti (Sound recording cassette)./
MCDERMOTT, G/n.d./1-3/2 KB616 . . . . **398.24**
Anansi (Videocassette)./GLEESON, B/1991/3-5/KB572. . . . . **KIT 398.24**
Anastasia, absolutely. /LOWRY, L/1995/4-A/6 KH422 . . . . . . **Fic**
Anastasia again./LOWRY, L/1981/4-6/7 KH424 . . . . **Fic**
Anastasia again (Braille)./LOWRY, L/n.d./4-6/7 KH424. . . . . **Fic**
Anastasia again (Sound recording cassette)./LOWRY, L/n.d./
4-6/7 KH424 . . . . **Fic**
Anastasia ask your analyst./LOWRY, L/1984/4-6/7 KH424 . . . . **Fic**

Anastasia ask your analyst (Braille)./LOWRY, L/n.d./4-6/7 KH424 . . . . **Fic**
Anastasia ask your analyst (Sound recording cassette)./LOWRY, L/n.d./
4-6/7 KH424 . . . . **Fic**
Anastasia at this address./LOWRY, L/1991/4-6/6 KH425 . . . . **Fic**
Anastasia at your service./LOWRY, L/1982/4-6/7 KH424 . . . . **Fic**
Anastasia at your service (Braille)./LOWRY, L/n.d./4-6/7 KH424. . . . . **Fic**
Anastasia at your service (Sound recording cassette)./LOWRY, L/n.d./
4-6/7 KH424 . . . . **Fic**
Anastasia has the answers. /LOWRY, L/1986/4-6/7 KH423 . . . . . **Fic**
Anastasia has the answers (Sound recording cassette)./LOWRY, L/n.d./
4-6/7 KH423 . . . . **Fic**
Anastasia Krupnik. /LOWRY, L/1979/4-6/7 KH424 . . . . **Fic**
Anastasia Krupnik (Braille)./LOWRY, L/n.d./4-6/7 KH424 . . . . . **Fic**
Anastasia Krupnik (Sound recording cassette)./LOWRY, L/n.d./
4-6/7 KH424 . . . . **Fic**
Anastasia Krupnik (Spanish version)./LOWRY, L/1995/4-6/7 KH424 . . **Fic**
Anastasia Morningstar and the crystal butterfly. Rev. ed. /HUTCHINS, HJ/
1984/4-6/6 KH306 . . . . **Fic**
Anastasia on her own. /LOWRY, L/1985/4-6/6 KH425 . . . . . . **Fic**
Anastasia on her own (Braille)./LOWRY, L/n.d./4-6/6 KH425 . . . . **Fic**
Anastasia on her own (Sound recording cassette)./LOWRY, L/n.d./
4-6/6 KH425 . . . . **Fic**
Anastasia's album. /BREWSTER, H/1996/5-A/7 KE234 . . **B ANASTASIIA**
Anastasia's chosen career./LOWRY, L/1987/4-6/6 KH425 . . . . . **Fic**
Ancient China. /COTTERELL, A/1994/4-A/10 KE629 . . . . **931**
ANCIENT CIVILIZATIONS (Picture). /1991/4-6/KE620 . . . . **PIC 930**
Ancient cliff dwellers of Mesa Verde. /ARNOLD, C/1992/
5-6/8 KE790 . . . . **970.488**
Ancient cliff dwellers of Mesa Verde (Sound recording cassette)./ARNOLD,
C/1994/5-6/8 KE790 . . . . **970.488**
Ancient Egypt. /HART, G/1990/5-6/8 KE633 . . . . **932**
ANCIENT FORESTS (Videocassette). /1992/4-6/KC308 . . . . **VCR 577.3**
Ancient Olympics. /TAMES, R/1996/3-6/8 KD821 . . . . **796.48**
Ancient ones: the world of the old-growth Douglas fir. /BASH, B/1994/
3-6/7 KC435 . . . . **585**
Ancient Rome. /JAMES, S/1990/5-6/8 KE639 . . . . **937**
And I mean it, Stanley. /BONSALL, CN/1974/1-2/1 KF242 . . . . . . **E**
And now Miguel. /KRUMGOLD, J/1953/6-A/5 KH382 . . . . . . **CE Fic**
And now Miguel (Braille)./KRUMGOLD, J/n.d./6-A/5 KH382 . . . . **CE Fic**
And now Miguel (Sound recording cassette)./KRUMGOLD, J/n.d./
6-A/5 KH382 . . . . **CE Fic**
And now Miguel (Talking book)./KRUMGOLD, J/n.d./
6-A/5 KH382 . . . . **CE Fic**
And one and two and other songs for pre-school and primary children
(Compact disc). /JENKINS, E/1995/P-K/KD624 . . . . . **CD 789.3**
And one and two and other songs for pre-school and primary children
(Sound recording cassette)./JENKINS, E/1990/P-K/KD624 . **CD 789.3**
And Sunday makes seven. /BADEN, R/1990/2-3/2 KB388. . . . . **398.21**
And the Earth trembled: the creation of Adam and Eve. /OPPENHEIM, SL/
1996/5-6/3 KA788 . . . . **297**
And then there was one: the mysteries of extinction. /FACKLAM, M/1990/
5-6/7 KC488 . . . . **591.68**
And then what happened, Paul Revere? /FRITZ, J/c1973/
5-6/6 KE510 . . . . **CE B REVERE, P.**
And then what happened, Paul Revere? (Sound recording cassette)./FRITZ,
J/n.d./5-6/6 KE510. . . . . **CE B REVERE, P.**
And then what happened, Paul Revere? (Talking book)./FRITZ, J/1977/
5-6/6 KE510 . . . . **CE B REVERE, P.**
And to think that I saw it on Mulberry Street. /SEUSS, D/c1937, 1964/
K-2/2 KG445 . . . . **E**
And to think that I saw it on Mulberry Street (Talking book)./SEUSS, D/
n.d./K-2/2 KG445 . . . . **E**
AND YOU CAN'T COME: PREJUDICE HURTS (Videocassette). /1996/
5-6/KA803 . . . . **VCR 303.3**
Andre Agassi: reaching the top--again. /SAVAGE, J/1997/
4-5/7 KE229 . . . . **B AGASSI, A.**
Andrew Gold's Halloween howls (Compact disc). /GOLD, A/1996/
K-2/KB226. . . . . **CD 394.264**
Andrew Gold's Halloween howls (Sound recording cassette)./GOLD, A/
1996/K-2/KB226. . . . . **CD 394.264**
ANDREW JACKSON: THE PEOPLE'S PRESIDENT (Videocassette). /1990/
6-A/KE397. . . . . **VCR B JACKSON, A.**
Andrew Wyeth. /MERYMAN, R/1991/6-A/7 KE602. . . . . **B WYETH, A.**
Anfernee Hardaway: basketball's lucky penny. /TOWNSEND, B/1997/
3-5/6 KE384 . . . . **B HARDAWAY, A.**
Angel child, dragon child. /SURAT, MM/c1983, 1989/1-3/2 KG584 . . . **E**
Angel child, dragon child (Sound recording cassette)./SURAT, MM/1995/
1-3/2 KG584 . . . . **E**
Angelina and Alice./HOLABIRD, K/1987/P-2/5 KF764 . . . . . . **E**
Angelina and the princess. /HOLABIRD, K/1984/P-2/5 KF764. . . . . . **E**
Angelina Ballerina./HOLABIRD, K/1983/P-2/5 KF764 . . . . . . **E**
Angelina Ballerina and other stories (Talking book). /HOLABIRD, K/1986/
P-2/KF765 . . . . **TB E**
Angelina ice skates./HOLABIRD, K/1993/P-2/5 KF764 . . . . **E**

Angelina on stage./HOLABIRD, K/1986/P-2/5 KF764 . . . . **E**
Angelina's baby sister./HOLABIRD, K/1991/P-2/5 KF764 . . . . . . **E**
Angelina's birthday surprise./HOLABIRD, K/1989/P-2/5 KF764 . . . . . **E**
Angelina's Christmas./HOLABIRD, K/1985/P-2/5 KF764 . . . . **E**
Angelina's Christmas (Braille)./HOLABIRD, K/n.d./P-2/5 KF764 . . . . **E**
Angelina's Christmas (Sound recording cassette)./HOLABIRD, K/n.d./
    P-2/5 KF764 . . . . **E**
Angels in the dust. /RAVEN, M/1997/2-3/2 KG315. . . . . **E**
Angel's kite/La estrella de Angel. /BLANCO, A/1994/2-4/6 KG902 . . **Fic**
ANGLO-AMERICAN CATALOGUING RULES. 2ND ED., 1988 REVISION.
    /1988//KA056. . . . . **PROF 025.3**
ANGLO-AMERICAN CATALOGUING RULES. 2ND ED., 1988 REVISION.
    AMENDMENTS 1993./1993//KA056. . . . . **PROF 025.3**
ANGRY JOHN (Videocassette). /1994/4-6/KA622. . . . . . **VCR 152.4**
Ani y la anciana./MILES, M/1992/4-6/4 KH496 . . . . **Fic**
ANIMAL APPETITES (Videocassette). /1996/3-5/KC469 . . . . **VCR 591.5**
Animal crackers: a delectable collection of pictures, poems, and lullabies for
    the very young. /DYER, J/1996/P-1/6 KD882 . . . . **808.81**
Animal family. /JARRELL, R/1995/5-A/6 KH326 . . . . **Fic**
Animal family (Braille)./JARRELL, R/n.d./5-A/6 KH326 . . . . **Fic**
Animal family (Sound recording cassette)./JARRELL, R/n.d./
    5-A/6 KH326 . . . . **Fic**
Animal family (Talking book)./JARRELL, R/n.d./5-A/6 KH326 . . . . **Fic**
Animal fare: poems. /YOLEN, J/1994/K-3/KE047 . . . . **811**
Animal jokes. /WOODWORTH, V/1993/2-4/KD742. . . . . **793.735**
ANIMAL JOURNEYS (Videocassette). /1996/3-5/KC470. . . . **VCR 591.5**
ANIMAL PLANET (CD-ROM). /1996/4-A/KC439. . . . . **CDR 590**
Animal rights. /BLOYD, S/1990/5-A/8 KA672. . . . . **179**
Animal rights: yes or no? /OWEN, M/1993/6-A/9 KA674. . . . . **179**
ANIMAL TALES (Sound recording cassette). /1990/
    P-2/KB523. . . . . **SRC 398.24**
Animal tracks and traces. /KUDLINSKI, KV/1991/3-4/4 KC475 . . . . . **591.5**
ANIMAL WEAPONS (Videocassette). /1996/3-5/KC460. . . . . **VCR 591.4**
Animalia. /BASE, G/c1986, 1993/P-A/KF212 . . . . **E**
Animals. /MCHUGH, C/1993/4-A/7 KD373. . . . . **704.9**
Animals don't wear pajamas: a book about sleeping. /FELDMAN, EB/
    1992/P-2/6 KC473 . . . . **591.5**
Animals in winter. Rev. ed. /BANCROFT, H/1997/K-2/2 KC482 . . **591.56**
Animals observed: a look at animals in art. /MACCLINTOCK, D/1993/
    4-A/7 KD372. . . . . **704.9**
Animals: selected poems. /MADO, M/1992/2-6/KE135. . . . . **895.6**
Animals that ought to be: poems about imaginary pets. /MICHELSON, R/
    1996/K-3/KD985 . . . . **811**
ANIMATED ALMANAC (Videocassette). /1990/3-6/KA581 . . **VCR 025.5**
ANIMATED ATLAS (Videocassette). /1990/4-6/KA582 . . . . . **VCR 025.5**
ANIMATED DICTIONARY (Videocassette). /1992/
    3-5/KA588 . . . . **VCR 028.7**
ANIMATED ENCYCLOPEDIA (Videocassette). /1990/
    3-6/KA583 . . . . **VCR 025.5**
ANIMATION FOR KIDS: HOW TO MAKE YOUR CARTOON MOVE!
    (Videocassette). /1994/4-A/KD407. . . . . **VCR 741.5**
Animation magic: a behind-the-scenes look at how an animated film is
    made. /HAHN, D/1996/4-6/9 KD685. . . . . **791.43**
Anna is still here. /VOS, I/1993/5-A/4 KH834 . . . . **Fic**
Annabel Lee. /POE, EA/1987/3-6/KD997 . . . . **811**
Annabelle Swift, Kindergartner. /SCHWARTZ, A/1988/
    P-2/1 KG413. . . . . **CE E**
Annabelle Swift: Kindergartner (Kit)./SCHWARTZ, A/1996/
    P-2/1 KG413 . . . . **CE E**
Anne Frank, beyond the diary: a photographic remembrance. /VAN DER
    ROL, R/1993/6-A/7 KE353 . . . . **B FRANK, A.**
Anne of Avonlea./MONTGOMERY, LM/1976/4-A/6 KH503 . . . . . . **Fic**
Anne of Avonlea (Braille)./MONTGOMERY, LM/n.d./4-A/6 KH503 . . **Fic**
Anne of Avonlea (Sound recording cassette)./MONTGOMERY, LM/n.d./
    4-A/6 KH503 . . . . **Fic**
Anne of Green Gables. /MONTGOMERY, LM/c1908, 1983/
    4-A/6 KH503 . . . . **Fic**
Anne of Green Gables (Braille)./MONTGOMERY, LM/n.d./
    4-A/6 KH503 . . . . **Fic**
Anne of Green Gables cookbook. /MACDONALD, K/1986/
    5-6/7 KD274 . . . . **641.5**
Anne of Ingleside./MONTGOMERY, LM/1981/4-A/6 KH503 . . . . . . **Fic**
Anne of Ingleside (Sound recording cassette)./MONTGOMERY, LM/n.d./
    4-A/6 KH503 . . . . **Fic**
Anne of the island./MONTGOMERY, LM/1976/4-A/6 KH503 . . . . . . **Fic**
Anne of the island: an Anne of Green Gables story./MONTGOMERY, LM/
    1992/4-A/6 KH503 . . . . **Fic**
Anne of the island (Braille)./MONTGOMERY, LM/n.d./4-A/6 KH503. . **Fic**
Anne of the island (Sound recording cassette)./MONTGOMERY, LM/n.d./
    4-A/6 KH503 . . . . **Fic**
Anne of Windy Poplars./MONTGOMERY, LM/1981/4-A/6 KH503 . . . **Fic**
Anne of Windy Poplars (Braille)./MONTGOMERY, LM/n.d./
    4-A/6 KH503 . . . . **Fic**

Anne of Windy Poplars (Sound recording cassette)./MONTGOMERY, LM/
    n.d./4-A/6 KH503. . . . . **Fic**
Anne's house of dreams. /MONTGOMERY, LM/1981/4-A/6 KH503 . . **Fic**
Anne's house of dreams (Braille)./MONTGOMERY, LM/n.d./
    4-A/6 KH503 . . . . **Fic**
Anne's house of dreams (Sound recording cassette)./MONTGOMERY, LM/
    n.d./4-A/6 KH503 . . . . **Fic**
Annie and the old one. /MILES, M/c1971/4-6/4 KH496 . . . . **Fic**
Annie and the old one (Braille)./MILES, M/n.d./4-6/4 KH496 . . . . . **Fic**
Annie and the wild animals. /BRETT, J/1985/K-3/2 KF260 . . . . **E**
Annie flies the birthday bike. /DRAGONWAGON, C/1993/
    K-2/1 KF495 . . . . **E**
Annie Oakley. /WUKOVITS, JF/1997/5-6/8 KE480 . . . . **B OAKLEY, A.**
ANNIE OAKLEY (Videocassette). /1997/3-6/KE479 . **VCR B OAKLEY, A.**
Annie's promise./LEVITIN, S/5-A/5 KH398 . . . . **Fic**
Anno's counting book. /ANNO, M/1977/P-2/KB945 . . . . **513**
Anno's counting book (Big book)./ANNO, M/1992/P-2/KB945 . . . **513**
Anno's journey. /ANNO, M/1978/P-A/KF159. . . . . **E**
Anno's magic seeds. /ANNO, M/1995/P-4/3 KB987 . . . . **513.4**
Anno's magic seeds (Sound recording cassette). /ANNO, M/1997/
    P-4/3 KB987 . . . . **513.4**
Anno's mysterious multiplying jar. /ANNO, M/1983/P-A/2 KB944. . . **512**
Anpao: an American Indian odyssey. /HIGHWATER, J/c1977, 1992/
    5-6/5 KB743 . . . . **398.27**
Ant and the elephant. /PEET, B/c1972/K-3/5 KG223 . . . . **E**
Ant cities. /DORROS, A/1987/1-4/4 KC571 . . . . **595.79**
Ant plays Bear. /BYARS, BC/1997/K-1/1 KF324 . . . . **E**
Antarctic encounter: destination South Georgia. /PONCET, S/1995/
    4-6/6 KE217 . . . . **919.8**
Antarctica. /COWCHER, H/1990/1-3/4 KC500 . . . . **591.998**
Antarctica: the last unspoiled continent. /PRINGLE, LP/1992/
    4-6/6 KE218 . . . . **919.8**
ANTARCTICA (Videocassette). /1991/4-A/KF124. . . . . **VCR 998**
Antartida./COWCHER, H/1993/1-3/4 KC500 . . . . **591.998**
Antelope Woman: an Apache folktale. /LACAPA, M/1992/
    2-4/5 KB606 . . . . **398.24**
Anthony Reynoso: born to rope. /COOPER, M/1996/
    3-4/4 KA841 . . . . **305.8**
ANTics!: an alphabetical anthology. /HEPWORTH, C/1992/
    2-6/KB831 . . . . **421**
Antigua Roma./JAMES, S/n.d./5-6/8 KE639. . . . . **937**
Antiguo Egipto./HART, G/n.d./5-6/8 KE633 . . . . **932**
Antoni van Leeuwenhoek: first to see microscopic life. /YOUNT, L/1996/
    5-A/KE432 . . . . **B LEEUWENHOEK,A.**
Ants. /OVERBECK, C/1982/4-6/7 KC577 . . . . **595.79**
Ants (Compact disc). /SCRUGGS, J/1994/K-3/KD657 . . . . . . **CD 789.3**
Ants (Sound recording cassette)./SCRUGGS, J/1994/
    K-3/KD657 . . . . **CD 789.3**
Any bear can wear glasses: the spectacled bear and other curious creatures.
    /LONG, M/1995/4-6/6 KC451 . . . . **591**
Apache rodeo. /HOYT-GOLDSMITH, D/1995/4-6/7 KE798 . . . . **970.491**
Apaches. /SNEVE, V/1997/4-6/5 KE768 . . . . **970.3**
Appalachia: the voices of sleeping birds. /RYLANT, C/1991/
    3-6/6 KE925 . . . . **974**
Appaloosa horse. /STEWART, GB/1995/4-5/6 KD205 . . . . **636.1**
Appaloosa horses. /PATENT, DH/1988/4-6/7 KD203 . . . . **636.1**
Apple pie tree. /HALL, Z/1996/1-4/2 KC413 . . . . **582.16**
Apple tree Christmas. /NOBLE, TH/1984/K-3/6 KG175. . . . . **E**
Apple tree through the year. /SCHNIEPER, C/c1982, 1987/
    5-6/7 KD163 . . . . **634**
Apple trees. /JOHNSON, SA/1983/4-6/9 KD161 . . . . **634**
AppleBet; an ABC. /WATSON, C/1982/P-1/KG689. . . . . **E**
Apples from heaven: multicultural folk tales about stories and storytellers. /
    BALTUCK, N/1995//KA265 . . . . **PROF 398.2**
APPLES (Videocassette). /1996/3-5/KD156. . . . . **VCR 634**
APPRAISAL: SCIENCE BOOKS FOR YOUNG PEOPLE. /1967-/
    /KA095 . . . . **PER PROF 050**
APPRECIATING YOURSELF (Videocassette)./1990/4-6/KA655 . **VCR 158**
Apprenticeship of Lucas Whitaker. /DEFELICE, CC/1998/
    5-A/6 KH066 . . . . **CE Fic**
Apprenticeship of Lucas Whitaker (Talking book)./DEFELICE, CC/1997/
    5-A/6 KH066 . . . . **CE Fic**
April showers. /SHANNON, G/1995/P-1/2 KG477 . . . . **E**
Aquarium book. /ANCONA, G/1991/4-6/7 KD246 . . . . **639.3**
Aqui viene el ponchado (Braille)./KESSLER, L/n.d./1-2/2 KF898 . . . **CE E**
Aqui viene el que se poncha!/KESSLER, L/1995/1-2/2 KF898 . . . . . **CE E**
Arabian horse. /STEWART, GB/1995/4-6/5 KD206 . . . . **636.1**
Arabian nights. /PHILIP, N/1994/5-6/8 KB358 . . . . **398.2**
Arabian nights, or, Tales told by Sheherazade during a thousand nights and
    one night. /ALDERSON, B/1995/5-A/7 KB253 . . . . **398.2**
ARABIAN NIGHTS (Sound recording cassette). /1991/
    4-5/KB254 . . . . **SRC 398.2**
ARABIAN NIGHTS: THEIR BEST-KNOWN TALES. /c1909, 1994/
    5-A/9 KB255 . . . . **398.2**

Arabian nights: three tales. /LATTIMORE, DN/1995/3-5/6 KB334 . . **398.2**
Arbol./BURNIE, D/1995/K-6/7 KC409 . . . . **582.16**
Arbol es hermoso. /UDRY, JM/1995/K-2/2 KG633 . . . . **E**
Archaeologists dig for clues. /DUKE, K/1997/2-4/3 KE623 . . . . . . **930.1**
Archeology. /MCINTOSH, J/1994/4-A/11 KE627 . . . . **930.1**
Archer's goon. /JONES, DW/1984/A/6 KH329 . . . . **Fic**
Arctic and Antarctic. /TAYLOR, B/1995/3-6/7 KE220 . . . . **919.8**
ARCTIC AND ANTARCTIC (Videocassette). /1996/
4-6/KE213 . . . . **VCR 919.8**
Arctic animals. /KALMAN, B/1988/4-6/8 KC501 . . . . **591.998**
Arctic foxes. /MATTHEWS, D/1995/4-6/4 KC847 . . . . **599.776**
Arctic hunter. /HOYT-GOLDSMITH, D/1992/3-6/6 KF097 . . . . . **979.8**
Arctic memories. /EKOOMIAK, N/c1988, 1990/2-6/4 KF125 . . . . . **998**
Arctic National Wildlife Refuge. /SIY, A/1991/6-A/6 KC337 . . . . **577.5**
Arctic summer. /MATTHEWS, D/1993/5-6/3 KC732 . . . . **599.17**
Arctic whales and whaling. /KALMAN, B/1988/5-6/6 KC771 . . . . **599.5**
Are all the giants dead? /NORTON, M/c1975, 1997/4-A/5 KH552 . **Fic**
Are all the giants dead? (Braille)./NORTON, M/n.d./4-A/5 KH552 . . . **Fic**
Are those animals real?: how museums prepare wildlife exhibits. Rev. &
updated ed. /CUTCHINS, J/1995/3-A/7 KC443 . . . . **590.75**
Are you in the house alone? /PECK, R/1989/A/6 KH592 . . . . . . **Fic**
Are you in the house alone? (Sound recording cassette)./PECK, R/n.d./
A/6 KH592 . . . . **Fic**
Are you my mother? /EASTMAN, PD/c1960/P-1/1 KF504 . . . . . . **E**
Are you my mother? (Braille)./EASTMAN, PD/n.d./P-1/1 KF504 . . . . **E**
Are you my mother? plus two more P.D. Eastman classics (Videocassette). /
EASTMAN, PD/1991/P-1/KF505 . . . . **VCR E**
Are you my mother? (Sound recording cassette)./EASTMAN, PD/n.d./
P-1/1 KF504 . . . . **E**
Are you my mother? (Talking book)./EASTMAN, PD/n.d./P-1/1 KF504 . **E**
Are you there God? It's me, Margaret. /BLUME, J/c1970, 1982/
4-6/5 KG905 . . . . **CE Fic**
Are you there God? It's me, Margaret (Braille)./BLUME, J/n.d./
4-6/5 KG905 . . . . **CE Fic**
Are you there God? It's me, Margaret (Kit)./BLUME, J/1985/
4-6/5 KG905 . . . . **CE Fic**
Argentina: a wild west heritage. New ed. /PETERSON, M/1997/
5-6/8 KF107 . . . . **982**
Arizona. /FILBIN, D/1991/4-6/7 KF067 . . . . **979.1**
Arizona. /HEINRICHS, A/1991/4-6/7 KF070 . . . . **979.1**
ARIZONA HIGHWAYS. /1925-/P-A/KA500 . . . . **PER 050**
Arizona (Sound recording cassette)./HEINRICHS, A/1993/
4-6/7 KF070 . . . . **979.1**
Arkadians. /ALEXANDER, L/1995/5-A/5 KG832 . . . . **Fic**
Arkadians (Sound recording cassette)./ALEXANDER, L/1997/
5-A/5 KG832 . . . . **Fic**
Arkansas. /FRADIN, DB/1994/4-6/4 KF008 . . . . **976.7**
Arkansas. /DI PIAZZA, D/1994/4-6/7 KF007 . . . . **976.7**
Armadillo. /PEMBLETON, S/1992/5-6/7 KC740 . . . . **599.3**
Armadillo Ray. /BEIFUSS, J/1995/K-2/4 KF216 . . . . **E**
Armadillos. /PATTON, D/1996/4-6/9 KC739 . . . . **599.3**
Armas y armaduras./BYAM, M/n.d./A/10 KA986 . . . . **355.8**
Arms and armor. /BYAM, M/1988/A/10 KA986 . . . . **355.8**
Arnold Lobel book of Mother Goose. /LOBEL, A/1997/P-1/KB800 . **398.8**
Arnold Lobel video showcase (Videocassette). /LOBEL, A/1985/
1-3/KG000 . . . . **VCR E**
Around the pond: who's been here? /GEORGE, LB/1996/K-2/6 KF606 . **E**
AROUND THE WORLD: AN ATLAS OF MAPS AND PICTURES. /1994/
3-5/KE165 . . . . **912**
Around the world in 100 years: from Henry the Navigator to Magellan. /
FRITZ, J/1994/5-A/7 KE164 . . . . **910.92**
Around the world in 100 years: from Henry the Navigator to Magellan
(Sound recording cassette)./FRITZ, J/1996/5-A/7 KE164 . . . . **910.92**
Around town. /SOENTPIET, CK/1994/K-2/3 KA898 . . . . **307.76**
Arrow to the sun. /MCDERMOTT, G/1974/2-4/3 KB711 . . . . **CE 398.26**
ARROZ CON LECHE: POPULAR SONGS AND RHYMES FROM LATIN
AMERICA. /1989/P-3/KD556 . . . . **789.2**
Arruga en el tiempo./L'ENGLE, M/n.d./4-6/6 KH394 . . . . . . **CE Fic**
Art dog. /HURD, T/1996/1-3/2 KF792 . . . . **E**
Art lesson. /DE PAOLA, T/1989/K-2/4 KF464 . . . . **CE E**
Art lesson (Kit). /DE PAOLA, T/1991/K-2/4 KF464 . . . . . . **CE E**
Arthur and the sword. /SABUDA, R/1995/3-5/5 KB479 . . . . . **398.22**
Arthur Ashe and his match with history. /QUACKENBUSH, R/1994/
3-5/7 KE243 . . . . **B ASHE, A.**
Arthur babysits./BROWN, MT/1992/K-2/2 KF276 . . . . **CE E**
Arthur babysits (Kit). /BROWN, MT/1996/K-2/2 KF276 . . . . . **CE E**
Arthur babysits (Videocassette)/BROWN, MT/n.d./K-2/2 KF276 . . **CE E**
Arthur, for the very first time. /MACLACHLAN, P/1980/4-6/7 KH443 . **Fic**
Arthur, for the very first time (Sound recording cassette)./MACLACHLAN,
P/n.d./4-6/7 KH443 . . . . **Fic**
Arthur goes to camp. /BROWN, MT/1982/K-2/2 KF271 . . . . . **CE E**
Arthur meets the president./BROWN, MT/1991/K-2/2 KF276 . . . . **CE E**
Arthur meets the president (Kit)./BROWN, MT/1996/K-2/2 KF276 . . **CE E**
Arthur writes a story. /BROWN, MT/1996/K-2/2 KF272 . . . . . . **E**

Arthur's April fool. /BROWN, MT/1983/P-3/2 KF273 . . . . **E**
Arthur's April fool (Kit). /BROWN, MT/1995/P-3/2 KF273 . . . . . **E**
Arthur's baby. /BROWN, MT/1987/K-3/2 KF274 . . . . **E**
Arthur's baby (Braille)./BROWN, MT/n.d./K-3/2 KF274 . . . . . . **E**
Arthur's birthday./BROWN, MT/1989/K-3/4 KF277 . . . . . . **CE E**
Arthur's camp-out. /HOBAN, L/1993/1-3/2 KF733 . . . . . . **CE E**
Arthur's camp-out (Kit)./HOBAN, L/1996/1-3/2 KF734 . . . . . **CE E**
Arthur's chicken pox./BROWN, MT/1994/K-2/2 KF276 . . . . . **CE E**
Arthur's Christmas./BROWN, MT/1984/P-3/2 KF273 . . . . . . **E**
Arthur's Christmas cookies. /HOBAN, L/1972/1-3/2 KF734 . . . **CE E**
Arthur's eyes./BROWN, MT/1979/K-2/2 KF276 . . . . **CE E**
Arthur's eyes (Kit)./BROWN, MT/1993/K-2/2 KF276 . . . . . . **CE E**
Arthur's eyes (Sound recording cassette)./BROWN, MT/1997/
K-2/2 KF276 . . . . **CE E**
Arthur's family vacation./BROWN, MT/1993/K-2/2 KF271 . . . . **CE E**
Arthur's family vacation (Kit)./BROWN, MT/1996/K-2/2 KF271 . . . **CE E**
Arthur's first sleepover. /BROWN, MT/1994/K-2/2 KF275 . . . . **E**
Arthur's funny money. /HOBAN, L/1981/1-3/2 KF733 . . . . . **E**
Arthur's great big valentine./HOBAN, L/1989/1-3/2 KF734 . . . **CE E**
Arthur's Halloween./BROWN, MT/1982/P-3/2 KF273 . . . . . . **E**
Arthur's Halloween costume./HOBAN, L/1984/1-3/2 KF734 . . . **CE E**
Arthur's Halloween costume (Braille)./HOBAN, L/n.d./1-3/2 KF734 . **CE E**
Arthur's Halloween (Kit)./BROWN, MT/1996/P-3/2 KF273 . . . . **E**
Arthur's honey bear. /HOBAN, L/c1964/1-3/2 KF734 . . . . . **CE E**
Arthur's honey bear (Braille)./HOBAN, L/n.d./1-3/2 KF734 . . . **CE E**
Arthur's honey bear (Kit)./HOBAN, L/1986/1-3/2 KF734 . . . . **CE E**
Arthur's loose tooth./HOBAN, L/1985/1-3/2 KF734 . . . . . . **CE E**
Arthur's loose tooth (Braille)./HOBAN, L/n.d./1-3/2 KF734 . . . **CE E**
Arthur's new puppy./BROWN, MT/1993/K-2/2 KF271 . . . . . . **CE E**
Arthur's new puppy (Sound recording cassette)./BROWN, MT/1997/
K-2/2 KF271 . . . . **CE E**
Arthur's nose. /BROWN, MT/c1976/K-2/2 KF276 . . . . **CE E**
Arthur's pen pal. /HOBAN, L/c1976/1-3/2 KF735 . . . . **E**
Arthur's pen pal (Braille)./HOBAN, L/n.d./1-3/2 KF735 . . . . . **E**
Arthur's pet business./BROWN, MT/1990/K-2/2 KF276 . . . . . **CE E**
Arthur's pet business (Kit)./BROWN, MT/1995/K-2/2 KF276 . . . **CE E**
Arthur's prize reader./HOBAN, L/1978/1-3/2 KF734 . . . . . . **CE E**
Arthur's prize reader (Braille)./HOBAN, L/n.d./1-3/2 KF734. . . . **CE E**
Arthur's prize reader (Kit)./HOBAN, L/1985/1-3/2 KF734 . . . . **CE E**
Arthur's teacher trouble. /BROWN, MT/1986/K-3/4 KF277 . . . . **CE E**
ARTHUR'S TEACHER TROUBLE (CD-ROM). /1992/1-4/KF171 . . . **CDR E**
Arthur's teacher trouble (Microcomputer program). /BROWN, MT/1994/
2-6/KB109 . . . . **MCP 372.6**
Arthur's Thanksgiving./BROWN, MT/1983/P-3/2 KF273 . . . . . . **E**
Arthur's tooth. /BROWN, MT/1985/1-3/2 KF278 . . . . **CE E**
Arthur's tooth (Braille)./BROWN, MT/n.d./1-3/2 KF278 . . . . . **CE E**
Arthur's TV trouble. /BROWN, MT/1995/K-2/2 KF279 . . . . . . **E**
Arthur's Valentine./BROWN, MT/1980/P-3/2 KF273 . . . . **E**
Artist in overalls: the life of Grant Wood. /DUGGLEBY, J/1995/
5-A/6 KE599 . . . . **B WOOD, G.**
ARTISTICALLY GIFTED (Videocassette)./1991/
/KA187 . . . . **VCR PROF 371.95**
Artists who created great works. /CUSH, C/1995/4-A/8 KD377 . . **709.2**
ARTS AND ACTIVITIES: CREATIVE ACTIVITIES FOR THE CLASSROOM. /
1932-//KA096 . . . . **PER PROF 050**
Arturo y sus problemas con el profesor./BROWN, MT/1994/
K-3/4 KF277 . . . . **CE E**
Arturo's baton. /HOFF, S/1995/K-2/2 KF750 . . . . **E**
As long as the rivers flow: the stories of nine Native Americans. /ALLEN,
PG/1996/6-A/9 KE746 . . . . **970.1**
Ashanti to Zulu: African traditions. /MUSGROVE, M/c1976/
4-6/6 KE727 . . . . **960**
Ashpet: an American Cinderella (Videocassette)./DAVENPORT, T/1989/
5-A/KB281 . . . . **CE 398.2**
Ashpet: an Appalachian tale. /COMPTON, J/1994/2-3/4 KB727 . **398.2**
ASIA (Videocassette). /1991/4-A/KE699 . . . . **VCR 950**
ASIAN AMERICAN BIOGRAPHY. /1995/5-A/KA399 . . . . **REF 305.8**
Asian crafts. /CORWIN, JH/1992/4-A/7 KD426 . . . . **745.5**
Ask Mr. Bear. /FLACK, M/c1932/P-1/2 KF549 . . . . **CE E**
Ask Mr. Bear (Kit)./FLACK, M/1990/P-1/1 KF549 . . . . **CE E**
Aska's sea creatures. /ASKA, W/1994/3-5/KD914 . . . . **811**
ASKING FOR HELP (Videocassette)./1990/4-6/KA655 . . . . . **VCR 158**
Asleep, asleep. /GINSBURG, M/1992/P/1 KF622 . . . . **E**
Asombrosa Graciela./HOFFMAN, M/1996/P-2/4 KF761 . . . . . **CE E**
Asombrosos animales acorazados./SOWLER, S/1995/
4-6/6 KC467 . . . . **591.47**
Assassination of John F. Kennedy. /STEIN, RC/1992/
5-6/7 KE921 . . . . **973.922**
Astonishing armadillo. /STUART, D/1993/5-6/7 KC741 . . . . . **599.3**
Astronauts are sleeping. /STANDIFORD, N/1996/K-2/3 KG535 . . . . **E**
At home in the rain forest. /WILLOW, D/1991/K-A/6 KC328 . . . **577.34**
At the beach. /ROCKWELL, AF/1987/P-3/3 KG340 . . . . **E**
At the controls: women in aviation. /BRIGGS, CS/1991/
6-A/10 KD090 . . . . **629.13**

AT THE CRACK OF THE BAT: BASEBALL POEMS. /1992/
3-6/KE053. . . . . **811.008**
At the crossroads. /ISADORA, R/1991/K-2/1 KF811 . . . . **E**
At the crossroads (Videocassette). /ISADORA, R/1996/
K-2/KF812 . . . . **VCR E**
At the Pirate Academy: adventures with language in the library media
center. /ZINGHER, G/1990//KA081 . . . . **PROF 027.8**
At the plate with...Ken Griffey Jr. /CHRISTOPHER, M/1997/
3-6/6 KE380 . . . . **B GRIFFEY,K. JR**
At the supermarket. /HAUTZIG, D/1994/1-4/6 KB127 . . . . **381**
Atalanta's race: a Greek myth. /CLIMO, S/1995/3-6/4 KA735 . . . . **292**
Atariba and Niguayona: a story from the Taino people of Puerto Rico. /
ROHMER, H/c1976, 1988/4-5/5 KB769 . . . . **398.27**
Atariba and Niguayona: a story from the Taino people of Puerto Rico
(Braille)./ROHMER, H/n.d./4-5/5 KB769 . . . . **398.27**
Atariba and Niguayona: a story from the Taino people of Puerto Rico
(Sound recording cassette)./ROHMER, H/n.d./4-5/5 KB769. . . **398.27**
Athletes. /LINDOP, L/1996/4-6/7 KD763 . . . . **796**
Atlantic and Gulf coasts. /AMOS, WH/1985/A/KC345. . . . . . . **577.69**
Atlas of endangered animals. /POLLOCK, S/1993/5-6/7 KC491 . . **591.68**
Atlas of rain forests. /LEWINGTON, A/1997/3-6/7 KC321 . . . . . **577.34**
ATMOSPHERE: ON THE AIR (Videocassette). /1993/
5-6/KC186. . . . . **VCR 551.5**
Attaboy, Sam!/LOWRY, L/1992/3-5/4 KH421. . . . . **Fic**
Attaboy, Sam! (Sound recording cassette)./LOWRY, L/1993/
3-5/4 KH421. . . . . **Fic**
AUDUBON MAGAZINE: THE MAGAZINE OF THE NATIONAL AUDUBON
SOCIETY. /1899-/5-6/KA501 . . . . **PER 050**
Audubon Society field guide to North American birds--Eastern Region. /
BULL, J/1994/3-6/7 KC647 . . . . **598**
Audubon Society field guide to North American birds--Western Region. /
UDVARDY, MD/1977/3-6/7 KC668 . . . . **598**
AUDUBON SOCIETY FIELD GUIDE TO NORTH AMERICAN FISHES,
WHALES AND DOLPHINS. /1983/A/11 KC583 . . . . **597**
Audubon Society field guide to North American fossils. /THOMPSON, I/
1982/4-6/KC238 . . . . **560**
Audubon Society field guide to North American mammals. Rev. &
expanded. /WHITAKER, JO/1996/3-6/KC730 . . . . **599.097**
Audubon Society field guide to North American rocks and minerals. /
CHESTERMAN, CW/1978/3-6/KC225 . . . . **552**
Audubon Society field guide to North American seashells. /REHDER, HA/
1981/3-6/KC516 . . . . **594**
Audubon Society field guide to North American trees, Eastern Region. /
LITTLE, JR., EL/1980/3-6/KC417 . . . . **582.16**
Audubon Society field guide to North American trees, Western Region./
LITTLE, JR., EL/1980/3-6/KC417 . . . . **582.16**
Audubon Society field guide to North American wildflowers, Eastern
Region. /NIERING, WA/1979/3-6/KC407 . . . . **582.13**
Audubon Society field guide to North American wildflowers, Western
Region. /SPELLENBERG, R/1979/3-6/KC408 . . . . **582.13**
Auks, rocks and the odd dinosaur: inside stories from the Smithsonian's
Museum of Natural History. /THOMSON, P/1985/3-A/7 KB914 . **508**
Auks, rocks and the odd dinosaur: inside stories from the Smithsonian's
Museum of Natural History (Sound recording cassette)./THOMSON, P/
n.d./3-A/7 KB914 . . . . **508**
Aung San Suu Kyi: fearless voice of Burma. /STEWART, W/1997/
5-A/7 KE244 . . . . **B AUNG SAN SUU**
Aunt Chip and the great Triple Creek Dam affair. /POLACCO, P/1996/
2-4/2 KG248 . . . . **E**
Aunt Eater's mystery Christmas. /CUSHMAN, D/1995/1-2/2 KF440. . . . **E**
Aunt Eater's mystery vacation. /CUSHMAN, D/1992/1-3/2 KF441 . . . . **E**
Aunt Flossie's hats (and crab cakes later). /HOWARD, EF/1991/
1-3/2 KF772 . . . . **E**
Aunt Lulu. /PINKWATER, DM/1991/P-2/2 KG244 . . . . **E**
Aunt Maria. /JONES, DW/1991/6-A/6 KH330. . . . . **Fic**
Aunt Morbelia and the screaming skulls. /CARRIS, JD/1990/
4-6/5 KB978 . . . . **Fic**
Aunt Nancy and Old Man Trouble. /ROOT, P/1996/K-3/6 KG350 . . . . **E**
Auroras: light shows in the night sky. /SHEPHERD, DW/1995/
4-8/6 KC137 . . . . **538**
AUSTRALIA (Videocassette). /1991/4-A/KF114. . . . . **VCR 994**
Author a month (for dimes)./MCELMEEL, SL/1993/
/KA069. . . . . **PROF 027.62**
Author a month (for nickels)./MCELMEEL, SL/1990/
/KA069. . . . . **PROF 027.62**
Author a month (for pennies). /MCELMEEL, SL/1988/
/KA069. . . . . **PROF 027.62**
Author: a true story. /LESTER, H/1997/2-5/2 KE436 . . . . . **B LESTER, H.**
AUTHORS OF BOOKS FOR YOUNG PEOPLE. 3RD ED. /1990/
5-A/KA460 . . . . **REF 809**
Auto mechanic. /FLORIAN, D/1994/P-2/3 KD128 . . . . **629.28**
Autobus magico dentro de un huracan./COLE, J/1996/
2-4/4 KC197 . . . . **551.55**
Autobus magico en el cuerpo humano./COLE, J/1990/2-5/5 KC916 . **612**

Autobus magico en el fondo del mar./COLE, J/1994/
2-4/5 KC495 . . . . **591.77**
Autobus magico en el interior de la tierra./COLE, J/1993/
2-4/3 KC152 . . . . **551**
Autobus magico en el sistema solar./COLE, J/1992/2-6/4 KC008 . . **523.2**
Autobus magico en tiempos de los dinosaurios./COLE, J/1995/
2-4/3 KC245 . . . . **567.9**
Autobus magico viaja por el agua./COLE, J/1992/2-3/4 KD079 . . **628.1**
Automobile. /FORD, B/1987/5-6/8 KD114. . . . . **629.222**
Autumn across America. /SIMON, S/1993/4-6/7 KB918 . . . . . . **508.2**
Avalanche. /KRAMER, SP/1991/3-6/6 KC213. . . . . **551.57**
Aventuras de Maxi, el perro taxista./BARRACCA, D/1996/
P-2/2 KF200 . . . . **CE E**
Aztec, Inca and Maya. /BAQUEDANO, E/1993/4-6/9 KE829 . . . . . **972**
Aztecs. /SHEPHERD, DW/1992/4-6/7 KE838 . . . . **972**
Aztecs. /WOOD, T/1992/5-6/7 KE842 . . . . **972**
Aztecs and Spaniards: Cortes and the conquest of Mexico. /MARRIN, A/
1986/5-6/7 KE833 . . . . **972**
Aztecs and Spaniards: Cortes and the conquest of Mexico (Braille)./
MARRIN, A/n.d./5-6/7 KE833 . . . . **972**
B is for Bethlehem: a Christmas alphabet. /WILMER, I/1990/
K-3/KE043 . . . . **811**
"B" is for Betsy. /HAYWOOD, C/c1939/2-3/3 KH230 . . . . **Fic**
"B" is for Betsy (Braille)./HAYWOOD, C/n.d./2-3/3 KH230 . . . . **Fic**
"B" is for Betsy (Sound recording cassette)./HAYWOOD, C/n.d./
2-3/3 KH230 . . . . **Fic**
Baaa. /MACAULAY, D/1985/5-A/7 KH431 . . . . **Fic**
Baba Yaga: a Russian folktale. /ARNOLD, K/1993/2-3/3 KB387. . **398.21**
Baba Yaga and Vasilisa the Brave. /MAYER, M/1994/
3-5/5 KB466 . . . . **398.22**
Babar and his children./DE BRUNHOFF, J/c1938, 1989/P-2/3 KF453. . . **E**
Babcock. /COTTONWOOD, J/1996/6-A/3 KH032 . . . . **Fic**
Babe Didrikson Zaharias. /SANFORD, WR/1993/
4-5/4 KE608 . . . . **B ZAHARIAS, B.**
Babe: the gallant pig. /KING-SMITH, D/1994/2-5/5 KH346. . . . . **CE Fic**
Babe: the sheep-pig (Talking book)./KING-SMITH, D/c1986, 1996/
2-5/5 KH346. . . . . **CE Fic**
Babies. /SANDEMAN, A/1996/2-5/6 KC955 . . . . **612.6**
Baboushka and the three kings. /ROBBINS, R/c1960/
2-4/6 KB509 . . . . **398.23**
Baboushka and the three kings (Braille)./ROBBINS, R/n.d./
2-4/6 KB509 . . . . **398.23**
Baboushka and the three kings (Sound recording cassette)./ROBBINS, R/
n.d./2-4/6 KB509 . . . . **398.23**
Babushka Baba Yaga. /POLACCO, P/1993/1-3/5 KG249 . . . . **E**
Babushka's Mother Goose. /POLACCO, P/1995/P-2/3 KD878 . . . . **808.8**
Baby Duck and the bad eyeglasses. /HEST, A/1996/P-K/1 KF717 . . . **E**
Baby says. /STEPTOE, J/1988/P-K/KG551 . . . . **E**
Baby sister. /DE PAOLA, T/1996/K-2/2 KF465 . . . . **E**
Baby sister for Frances (Kit)./HOBAN, R/1977/P-1/2 KF739 . . . . . **CE E**
Baby sister for Frances. Newly ill. ed./HOBAN, R/1993/
P-1/2 KF739 . . . . **CE E**
Baby sister for Frances (Sound recording cassette)./HOBAN, R/1995/
P-1/2 KF739 . . . . **CE E**
Baby uggs are hatching. /PRELUTSKY, J/1982/1-3/KE000 . . . . . . **811**
Baby uggs are hatching (Braille)./PRELUTSKY, J/n.d./1-3/KE000 . . . . **811**
Baby whales drink milk. /ESBENSEN, BJ/1994/1-3/2 KC768 . . . . **599.5**
Back home. /PINKNEY, GJ/1992/1-3/4 KG240. . . . . **E**
Backbone of the king: the story of Paka'a and his son Ku. /BROWN, M/
1984/5-6/6 KB428 . . . . **398.22**
Backbone of the king: the story of Paka'a and his son Ku (Braille)./
BROWN, M/n.d./5-6/6 KB428 . . . . **398.22**
Backbone of the king: the story of Paka'a and his son Ku (Talking book)./
BROWN, M/n.d./5-6/6 KB428 . . . . **398.22**
Backfield package. /DYGARD, TJ/1992/6-A/7 KH090 . . . . **Fic**
Background notes of the countries of the world. /UNITED STATES.
BUREAU OF PUBLIC AFFAIRS, DEPT. OF STATE. /n.d./
4-6/KA404 . . . . **REF 310**
Backyard almanac. /WEBER, L/1996/3-A/7 KB915. . . . . **508**
Backyard birds of summer. /LERNER, C/1996/5-6/7 KC654 . . . . . **598**
Backyard dragon. /STERMAN, B/1993/4-6/6 KH753 . . . . **Fic**
Backyard safaris: 52 year-round science adventures. /BUSCH, PS/1995/
P-A/5 KB901 . . . . **508**
Backyard sunflower. /KING, E/1993/1-4/4 KD174 . . . . **635.9**
Bacteria. /FACKLAM, H/1994/5-A/9 KC378. . . . . **579.3**
Bad day at Riverbend. /VAN ALLSBURG, C/1995/1-3/3 KG637 . . . . . **E**
Bad girls. /VOIGT, C/1996/6-A/5 KH831 . . . . **Fic**
Bad Luck Boswell. /HEARN, DD/1995/1-3/5 KF690 . . . . **E**
Badger's parting gifts. /VARLEY, S/1984/1-3/7 KG650 . . . . **E**
BAILES FAVORITOS TODS LOS TIEMPOS (Sound recording cassette)./
1991/K-6/KD603 . . . . **SRC 789.3**
BAILEY'S BOOK HOUSE (CD-ROM). /1995/P-2/KB100 . . . . **CDR 372.4**
BAILEY'S BOOK HOUSE (Microcomputer program). /1993/
P-2/KB101. . . . . **MCP 372.4**

Baker's dozen: a Saint Nicholas tale. /SHEPARD, A/1995/
K-2/4 KB487 . . . . **398.22**
Bald eagle magic for kids. /GIECK, C/1991/5-6/6 KC714 . . . . **598.9**
Ball sports. /SANDELSON, R/1991/4-6/8 KD774 . . . . **796.3**
Ballad of Lucy Whipple. /CUSHMAN, K/1996/5-A/7 KH049 . . . . **CE Fic**
Ballad of Lucy Whipple (Talking book)./CUSHMAN, K/1997/
5-A/7 KH049 . . . . **CE Fic**
Ballena./BLUME, J/1983/4-6/3 KG906 . . . . **Fic**
Balloon science. /KANER, E/1989/2-6/6 KC079. . . . . **530**
Balloons: building and experimenting with inflatable toys. /ZUBROWSKI, B/
1990/4-A/7 KB888 . . . . **507**
Ballot box battle. /MCCULLY, EA/1996/1-3/2 KH473. . . . . . . **Fic**
Bambi: a life in the woods. /SALTEN, F/1992/5-A/6 KH673 . . . . . . **Fic**
Banner in the sky (Braille)./ULLMAN, JR/n.d./4-6/KH817. . . . . . **TB Fic**
Banner in the sky (Sound recording cassette)./ULLMAN, JR/n.d./
4-6/KH817. . . . . **TB Fic**
Banner in the sky (Talking book). /ULLMAN, JR/n.d./4-6/KH817. . **TB Fic**
Banshee train. /BODKIN, O/1995/1-3/4 KF240. . . . . **E**
Bar mitzvah: a Jewish boy's coming of age. /KIMMEL, EA/1995/
5-A/7 KA776 . . . . **296.4**
Barbara Frietchie. /WHITTIER, JG/1992/1-3/KE040 . . . . **811**
Barbara Jordan. /PATRICK-WEXLER, D/1996/
4-6/8 KE408 . . . . **B JORDAN, B.**
Barco de guerra del siglo XVIII./BIESTY, S/1995/4-6/7 KA988 . . . . **359.1**
Bard of Avon: the story of William Shakespeare. /STANLEY, D/1992/
4-6/7 KE538 . . . . **B SHAKESPEARE**
Barefoot: escape on the Underground Railroad. /EDWARDS, PD/1997/
1-3/4 KF510 . . . . **E**
Bargain for Frances. Newly ill. ed./HOBAN, R/1992/P-1/2 KF739. . **CE E**
Bargain for Frances (Sound recording cassette)./HOBAN, R/n.d./
P-1/2 KF739 . . . . **CE E**
Bargain for Frances (Talking book)./HOBAN, R/n.d./P-1/2 KF739. . **CE E**
Barkley. /HOFF, S/c1975/K-2/1 KF751 . . . . **E**
Barkley (Braille)./HOFF, S/n.d./K-2/1 KF751 . . . . **E**
Barmi: a Mediterranean city through the ages. /HERNANDEZ, X/1990/
A/11 KA895 . . . . **307.76**
Barn. /AVI /1994/5-A/3 KG856 . . . . **Fic**
Barn dance! /MARTIN, JR., B/1986/P-3/3 KG071 . . . . **E**
Barn owls. /EPPLE, W/1992/4-6/5 KC713 . . . . **598.9**
Barn (Sound recording cassette)./AVI /1997/5-A/3 KG856 . . . . . **Fic**
Barnacles eat with their feet: delicious facts about the tide pool food chain.
/SHAHAN, S/1996/3-6/5 KC348 . . . . **577.69**
Barnyard banter. /FLEMING, D/1994/P-1/3 KF553 . . . . **E**
Barry Bonds: Mr. Excitement. /SAVAGE, J/1997/
4-6/3 KE258 . . . . **B BONDS, B.**
Barry's scrapbook: a window into art (Videocassette). /POLISAR, BL/1994/
1-4/KD367. . . . . **VCR 701**
Bartholomew and the oobleck./SEUSS, D/c1949/P-3/6 KG446 . . . . . **E**
Bartholomew and the oobleck (Videocassette)./SEUSS, D/1985/
1-3/KG450 . . . . **VCR E**
Bartlett's familiar quotations: a collection of passages, phrases and proverbs
traced to sources in ancient and modern literature. 16th ed. /BARTLETT,
J/1992/A/KA458 . . . . **REF 803**
Baseball. /TEIRSTEIN, MA/1994/3-6/3 KD808 . . . . **796.357**
Baseball bats for Christmas. /KUSUGAK, M/1990/4-6/4 KH384 . . . . . **Fic**
Baseball birthday party. /PRAGER, A/1995/1-3/2 KG286. . . . . **E**
BASEBALL DIGEST. /1941-/4-6/KA502 . . . . **PER 050**
Baseball fever. /HURWITZ, J/1981/4-6/6 KH297 . . . . **Fic**
Baseball fever (Sound recording cassette)./HURWITZ, J/n.d./
4-6/KH297 . . . . **Fic**
Baseball in April and other stories. /SOTO, G/1990/6-A/6 KH738 . . . **Fic**
Baseball saved us. /MOCHIZUKI, K/1993/4-A/6 KH500 . . . . . . **Fic**
Basic cartooning with Mike Artell (Videocassette)./ARTELL, M/1995/
3-6/KD408. . . . . **VCR 741.5**
Basic skills for young children (Sound recording cassette). /JANIAK, W/
c1980, 1990/P-K/KD623 . . . . **SRC 789.3**
Basketball. /WITHERS, T/1994/3-6/4 KD781 . . . . **796.323**
Basketball player. /CARRIER, R/1996/4-6/3 KG975 . . . . **Fic**
Bat. /ARNOLD, C/1996/4-6/7 KC757 . . . . **599.4**
Bat in the boot. /CANNON, A/1996/1-3/2 KF333 . . . . **E**
Bat mitzvah: a Jewish girl's coming of age. /GOLDIN, BD/1995/
5-A/10 KA773 . . . . **296.4**
Batboy: an inside look at spring training. /ANDERSON, J/1996/
4-6/6 KD793 . . . . **796.357**
Batman: exploring the world of bats. /PRINGLE, LP/1991/
5-A/9 KC762 . . . . **599.4**
Bat-poet. /JARRELL, R/1996/4-A/6 KH327. . . . . **Fic**
Bats. /JOHNSON, SA/1985/4-6/9 KC760 . . . . **599.4**
Bats, bugs, and biodiversity: adventures in the Amazonian rain forest. /
GOODMAN, SE/1995/3-6/7 KC318 . . . . **577.34**
Bats: mysterious flyers of the night. /STUART, D/1994/
5-6/8 KC763 . . . . **599.4**
Bats: night fliers. /MAESTRO, B/1994/1-4/6 KC761 . . . . **599.4**
Bats: shadows in the night. /ACKERMAN, D/1997/5-6/7 KC756 . . **599.4**

Battle for the castle./WINTHROP, E/1993/4-6/5 KH869 . . . . **CE Fic**
Battle for the castle (Sound recording cassette)./WINTHROP, E/1995/
4-6/5 KH869 . . . . **CE Fic**
Battle for the castle (Talking book)./WINTHROP, E/1997/
4-6/5 KH869 . . . . **CE Fic**
Battle of Gettysburg. /CARTER, AR/1990/4-6/7 KE899 . . . . . . **973.7**
Battle of Lexington and Concord. /JOHNSON, N/1992/
4-6/7 KE881 . . . . **973.3**
Battle of the books: literary censorship in the public schools, 1950-1985. /
BURRESS, L/1989//KA051 . . . . **PROF 025.2**
Battle of the ironclads: the Monitor and the Merrimack. /CARTER, AR/
1993/4-6/8 KE900 . . . . **973.7**
Batty riddles. /HALL, K/1993/K-3/KD728 . . . . **793.735**
Batwings and the curtain of night. /DAVOL, MW/1997/1-3/2 KF449 . . . **E**
Bayou lullaby. /APPELT, K/1995/P-2/5 KF163 . . . . **E**
BE A FRIEND: CHILDREN WHO LIVE WITH HIV SPEAK. /1994/
2-6/2 KA993 . . . . **362.1**
Be a friend: the story of African American music in song, words and
pictures. /STANLEY, L/1994/K-3/KD670 . . . . **BA 789.4**
Be a friend to trees. /LAUBER, P/1994/P-2/3 KC416 . . . . **CE 582.16**
Be a friend to trees (Kit)./LAUBER, P/1996/P-2/3 KC416 . . . . . **CE 582.16**
Be an inventor. /TAYLOR, B/1987/5-6/7 KC888 . . . . **608**
Be nice to spiders. /GRAHAM, MB/c1967/P-2/3 KF633 . . . . **E**
Be nice to spiders (Talking book). /GRAHAM, MB/n.d./P-2/3 KF633 . . . **E**
Be ready at eight. /PARISH, P/1996/1-2/1 KG212 . . . . **E**
Be seated: a book about chairs. /GIBLIN, JC/1993/4-A/7 KD463 . . . **749**
Be seated: a book about chairs (Sound recording cassette)./GIBLIN, JC/
1996/4-A/7 KD463 . . . . **749**
Be well, Beware. /HAAS, J/1996/3-5/2 KH208 . . . . **Fic**
Be well, Beware (Sound recording cassette)./HAAS, J/1997/
3-5/2 KH208 . . . . **Fic**
Beach feet. /REISER, L/1996/P-3/2 KG318. . . . . **E**
Beacons of light: lighthouses. /GIBBONS, G/1990/3-6/6 KB149 . . . **387.1**
Beacons of light: lighthouses (Sound recording cassette)./GIBBONS, G/
1993/3-6/6 KB149 . . . . **387.1**
Bean and plant. /BACK, C/1986/K-2/2 KC426 . . . . **583**
Bear and Mrs. Duck. /WINTHROP, E/1988/P-1/1 KG744 . . . . **E**
Bear called Paddington. /BOND, M/c1958/2-4/5 KG916 . . . . . . **Fic**
Bear called Paddington (Braille)./BOND, M/n.d./2-4/5 KG916 . . . . **Fic**
Bear called Paddington (Large type)./BOND, M/n.d./2-4/5 KG916 . . . **Fic**
Bear called Paddington (Talking book)./BOND, M/n.d./2-4/5 KG916 . **Fic**
Bear for all seasons. /FUCHS, DM/1995/K-2/5 KF589 . . . . **E**
Bear nobody wanted. /AHLBERG, J/c1992, 1995/3-6/6 KG821 . . . . **Fic**
Bear shadow. /ASCH, F/1985/P-2/2 KF173 . . . . **E**
Bear that heard crying. /KINSEY-WARNOCK, N/1993/2-3/2 KF905 . . . . **E**
Bearhead: a Russian folktale. /KIMMEL, EA/1991/2-4/4 KB327 . . . **398.2**
Bearman: exploring the world of black bears. /PRINGLE, LP/1989/
5-6/7 KC852 . . . . **599.78**
Bears. /ROSENTHAL, M/1983/2-4/2 KC853 . . . . **599.78**
Bears. /STIRLING, I/1992/5-A/7 KC857 . . . . **599.78**
Bears and their forest cousins. /SCHMIDT, A/1991/5-6/7 KC854 . **599.78**
Bears at the beach: counting 10 to 20. /YEKTAI, N/1996/
P-1/KB985. . . . . **513.2**
Bear's bargain./ASCH, F/1989/P-1/2 KF174 . . . . **CE E**
Bear's bargain (Big book)./ASCH, F/1992/P-1/2 KF174 . . . . . . **CE E**
Bears, bears, and more bears. /MORRIS, J/1995/P/1 KC850. . . . **599.78**
Bear's bicycle. /MCLEOD, EW/c1975, 1986/P-2/2 KG109 . . . . . **CE E**
Bear's bicycle (Kit)./MCLEOD, EW/1977/P-2/2 KG109 . . . . . . **CE E**
Bear's Christmas surprise./WINTHROP, E/1991/P-1/1 KG744 . . . . . **E**
Bears on Hemlock Mountain. /DALGLIESH, A/c1952, 1990/
1-4/4 KH057 . . . . **Fic**
Bear's toothache. /MCPHAIL, D/c1972/K-2/2 KG116 . . . . **CE E**
Bear's toothache (Braille)./MCPHAIL, D/n.d./K-2/2 KG116 . . . . . **CE E**
Bear's toothache (Kit)./MCPHAIL, D/1980/K-2/2 KG116 . . . . . . **CE E**
Bearskin; or, The man who didn't wash for seven years (Videocassette)./
DAVENPORT, T/1983/5-A/KB281 . . . . **CE 398.2**
Beast feast. /FLORIAN, D/1994/K-3/KD935 . . . . **811**
Beasts of Bethlehem. /KENNEDY, XJ/1992/1-6/KD960 . . . . **811**
Beat the story-drum, pum-pum. /BRYAN, A/1980/4-6/4 KB542. . . **398.24**
Beat the turtle drum. /GREENE, CC/c1976, 1994/5-6/4 KH198 . . . . . **Fic**
Beat the turtle drum (Sound recording cassette)./GREENE, CC/n.d./
5-6/4 KH198 . . . . **Fic**
Beatrix Potter. /WALLNER, A/1995/3-5/4 KA369 . . . **PROF B POTTER,B**
Beauty: a retelling of the story of Beauty and the Beast. /MCKINLEY, R/
1978/6-A/6 KH485 . . . . **Fic**
Beauty: a retelling of the story of Beauty and the Beast (Braille)./
MCKINLEY, R/n.d./6-A/6 KH485 . . . . **Fic**
Beauty: a retelling of the story of Beauty and the Beast (Sound recording
cassette)./MCKINLEY, R/n.d./6-A/6 KH485 . . . . **Fic**
Beauty and the Beast. /DE BEAUMONT, ML/1990/4-5/6 KB282. . **398.2**
Beauty and the Beast. /BRETT, J/1989/4-5/6 KB268. . . . . **398.2**
Beauty and the Beast. /WILLARD, N/1992/4-A/6 KH862 . . . . **Fic**
BEAUTY AND THE BEAST (Videocassette). /c1989, 1996/
K-3/KB259 . . . . **VCR 398.2**

BEAVER: EXPLORING CANADA'S HISTORY. /1920-/A/KA503 . **PER 050**
Beavers. /LEPTHIEN, EU/1992/3-5/5 KC754. . . . . **599.37**
Becoming a nation of readers: the report of the Commission on Reading. / ANDERSON, RC/1985//KA205. . . . . **PROF 372.4**
Becoming myself: true stories about learning from life. /SIMMONS, CW/ 1994/5-A/6 KA664. . . . . **158**
Bed-knob and broomstick. /NORTON, M/c1957/4-6/5 KH553 . . . . . . **Fic**
Bed-knob and broomstick (Braille)./NORTON, M/n.d./4-6/5 KH553. . . **Fic**
Bedtime for Frances. Newly ill. ed. /HOBAN, R/1995/P-1/2 KF739 . **CE E**
Bee and the dream: a Japanese tale. /LONG, JF/1996/ 2-3/2 KB612 . . . . **398.24**
Bee tree. /POLACCO, P/1993/K-2/3 KG250 . . . . **E**
Beekeeper's year. /JOHNSON, SA/1994/5-6/6 KD240 . . . . **638**
Bee-man of Orn. /STOCKTON, FR/c1964, 1987/5-6/7 KH763 . . . . . . **Fic**
Bee-man of Orn (Braille)./STOCKTON, FR/n.d./5-6/7 KH763 . . . . **Fic**
Bee-man of Orn (Talking book)./STOCKTON, FR/n.d./5-6/7 KH763 . . **Fic**
Been to yesterdays: poems of a life. /HOPKINS, LB/1995/ 3-6/KD953. . . . . **811**
Beethoven lives upstairs. /NICHOL, B/1994/4-6/4 KH549 . . . . **Fic**
Beethoven lives upstairs (Talking book)./NICHOL, B/1991/ 4-6/KH550. . . . . **VCR Fic**
Beethoven lives upstairs (Talking book)./NICHOL, B/1991/ 4-6/KH550. . . . . **VCR Fic**
Beethoven lives upstairs (Videocassette). /NICHOL, B/1992/ 4-6/KH550. . . . . **VCR Fic**
Beethoven vive arriba./NICHOL, B/1996/4-6/4 KH549 . . . . **Fic**
Beetles, lightly toasted. /NAYLOR, PR/1987/5-6/6 KH534. . . . . **Fic**
Beezus and Ramona. /CLEARY, B/1955/2-5/3 KG992 . . . . **Fic**
Beezus and Ramona (Braille)./CLEARY, B/n.d./2-5/3 KG992 . . . . **Fic**
Before the sun dies: the story of evolution. /GALLANT, RA/1989/ A/11 KC292 . . . . **576.8**
Beggar King and other tales from around the world (Sound recording cassette). /BEN IZZY, J/1993/2-A/KB260 . . . . **SRC 398.2**
Beggar Queen./ALEXANDER, L/1984/5-6/6 KG841. . . . . **Fic**
Beggar Queen (Sound recording cassette)./ALEXANDER, L/n.d./ 5-6/6 KG841 . . . . **Fic**
BEGINNING AMERICAN SIGN LANGUAGE VIDEOCOURSE (Videocassette). /1991/3-A/KB822. . . . . **VCR 419**
Beginning of the armadillos. /KIPLING, R/1995/3-5/8 KH359 . . . . **Fic**
Beginning Spanish bilingual dictionary: a beginner's guide in words and pictures. 2nd rev. ed. /LIPTON, GC/1989/3-A/KB859 . . . . **463**
Behind the attic wall. /CASSEDY, S/1983/6-A/5 KG986. . . . . **Fic**
Behind the blue and gray: the soldier's life in the Civil War. /RAY, D/ 1991/5-A/7 KE911 . . . . **973.7**
Behind the couch. /GERSTEIN, M/1996/2-4/3 KH162. . . . . **Fic**
Behind the covers: interviews with authors and illustrators of books for children and young adults, Vol. I. /ROGINSKI, J/1985/ /KA335. . . . . **PROF 808.06**
Behind the covers: interviews with authors and illustrators of books for children and young adults, Vol. II./ROGINSKI, J/1989/ /KA335. . . . . **PROF 808.06**
BEHIND THE MASK. Rev. ed. (Videocassette). /1987/ 1-3/KA817 . . . . **VCR 305**
Behind the scenes at the ballet: rehearsing and performing "The Sleeping Beauty" /SPATT, LE/1995/4-6/9 KD697. . . . . **792.8**
Bein' with you this way. /NIKOLA-LISA, W/1994/P-2/KD996 . . . . . . **811**
BEING AN EXPLORER (Videocassette). /1996/K-3/KE161 . . . **VCR 910.9**
BEING FRIENDS (Videocassette)./1990/4-6/KA655 . . . . **VCR 158**
BEING RESPONSIBLE (Videocassette)./1990/4-6/KA655 . . . . . **VCR 158**
Beisbol en Abril y otras historias./SOTO, G/1995/6-A/6 KH738. . . . . **Fic**
Beisbol nos salvo./MOCHIZUKI, K/1995/4-A/6 KH500 . . . . **Fic**
Believers in America: poems about Americans of Asian and Pacific islander descent. /IZUKI, S/1994/3-6/KD955. . . . . **811**
Belle Prater's boy. /WHITE, R/1996/6-A/6 KH853 . . . . **Fic**
Belling the cat and other Aesop's fables./PAXTON, T/1990/ 3-4/KB632 . . . . **398.24**
Belling the cat and other Aesop's fables (Sound recording cassette)./ PAXTON, T/1993/3-4/KB632 . . . . **398.24**
Ben and me: a new and astonishing life of Benjamin Franklin, as written by his good mouse Amos; lately discovered. /LAWSON, R/c1939/ 3-5/5 KH388 . . . . **Fic**
Ben and me: a new and astonishing life of Benjamin Franklin, as written by his good mouse Amos; lately discovered (Talking book)./LAWSON, R/ n.d./3-5/5 KH388 . . . . **Fic**
Ben and me: a new and astonishing life of Benjamin Franklin, as written by his good mouse Amos; lately discovered (Braille)./LAWSON, R/n.d./ 3-5/5 KH388 . . . . **Fic**
Ben and the porcupine./CARRICK, C/1985/1-3/4 KF358 . . . . **E**
Ben Carson. /SIMMONS, A/1996/4-6/7 KE276 . . . . . . **B CARSON, B.**
BEN FRANKLIN BOOK OF EASY AND INCREDIBLE EXPERIMENTS. / 1995/A/8 KB889 . . . . **507.8**
Beneath a blue umbrella. /PRELUTSKY, J/1990/K-2/KE001. . . . . **811**
Beneath the waves: exploring the hidden world of the kelp forest. /WU, N/ 1992/3-6/7 KC353 . . . . **577.7**
Beni's family cookbook for the Jewish holidays. /ZALBEN, JB/1996/ 4-6/KD283. . . . . **641.5**
Beni's first Chanukah. /ZALBEN, JB/1988/P/4 KG785. . . . . **E**
Benjamin Bigfoot. /SERFOZO, M/1993/P-K/2 KG439. . . . . **E**
Benjamin Franklin. /D'AULAIRE, I/c1950/2-4/6 KE354. . **B FRANKLIN, B.**
Benny bakes a cake. /RICE, E/c1981, 1993/P-2/2 KG330. . . . . **E**
Ben's Christmas carol. /FORWARD, T/1996/2-3/4 KF567 . . . . **E**
Ben's trumpet. /ISADORA, R/c1979/1-3/3 KF813 . . . . **E**
Bently and egg. /JOYCE, W/1992/1-3/4 KF857 . . . . **E**
Bently and egg (Sound recording cassette)./JOYCE, W/1994/ 1-3/4 KF857 . . . . **E**
Berchick. /BLANC, ES/1989/3-5/5 KG901 . . . . **Fic**
Berenstain Bears and the sitter./BERENSTAIN, S/1981/K-2/4 KF226 . . . **E**
Berenstain Bears and the spooky old tree./BERENSTAIN, S/1978/ K-1/1 KF227 . . . . **E**
Berenstain Bears and too much birthday./BERENSTAIN, S/1986/ K-2/4 KF226 . . . . **E**
Berenstain Bears get in a fight./BERENSTAIN, S/1982/K-2/4 KF226 . . . **E**
BERENSTAIN BEARS GET IN A FIGHT. School ed. (CD-ROM). /1995/ K-3/KF223. . . . . **CDR E**
Berenstain Bears go to camp./BERENSTAIN, S/1982/K-2/4 KF226 . . . . **E**
BERENSTAIN BEARS IN THE DARK. School ed. (CD-ROM). /1996/ K-3/KF224. . . . . **CDR E**
Berenstain Bears learn about strangers. /BERENSTAIN, S/1985/ K-2/4 KF225 . . . . **CE E**
Berenstain Bears' moving day./BERENSTAIN, S/1981/K-2/4 KF226 . . . . **E**
Berenstain Bears: no girls allowed. /BERENSTAIN, S/1986/ K-2/4 KF226 . . . . **E**
Berenstain Bears visit the dentist./BERENSTAIN, S/1981/K-2/4 KF226 . . **E**
Berlioz the bear. /BRETT, J/1991/K-2/2 KF261 . . . . **E**
Berlioz the bear (Sound recording casssette)./BRETT, J/1994/ K-2/2 KF261 . . . . **E**
Bermuda triangle. /ABELS, H/1987/4-6/4 KA560. . . . . **001.94**
Bernal and Florinda: a Spanish tale. /KIMMEL, EA/1994/2-4/3 KF903 . . **E**
Bernie and the Bessledorf ghost./NAYLOR, PR/1990/4-6/5 KH535 . . . **Fic**
Best bad thing./UCHIDA, Y/1983/5-6/6 KH815. . . . . **Fic**
Best bad thing (Sound recording cassette)./UCHIDA, Y/n.d./ 5-6/6 KH815 . . . . **Fic**
Best books for children: preschool through grade 6. 5th ed. /GILLESPIE, JT/1994//KA084 . . . . **PROF 028.1**
Best bug parade. /MURPHY, SJ/1996/P-1/1 KG163 . . . . **E**
BEST CHILDREN'S BOOKS IN THE WORLD: A TREASURY OF ILLUSTRATED STORIES. /1996//KA336 . . . . **PROF 808.3**
Best Christmas pageant ever. /ROBINSON, B/c1972/4-6/7 KH640 . . . **Fic**
Best Christmas pageant ever (Braille)./ROBINSON, B/n.d./ 4-6/7 KH640 . . . . **Fic**
B-E-S-T friends./GIFF, PR/1988/1-2/2 KF614 . . . . **CE E**
Best friends. /KELLOGG, S/1986/K-3/2 KF888 . . . . **E**
Best friends book: true stories about real best friends... /ERLBACH, A/ 1995/5-A/4 KA656. . . . . **158**
Best friends for Frances. Newly ill. ed./HOBAN, R/1994/ P-1/2 KF739 . . . . **CE E**
Best friends for Frances (Talking book)./HOBAN, R/n.d./ P-1/2 KF739 . . . . **CE E**
B-E-S-T friends (Kit)./GIFF, PR/1994/1-2/2 KF614 . . . . **CE E**
Best friends (Sound recording cassette)./KELLOGG, S/n.d./ K-3/2 KF888 . . . . **E**
Best girl. /SMITH, DB/1993/5-A/6 KH720 . . . . **Fic**
Best in children's books: the University of Chicago guide to children's literature, 1985-1990. /SUTHERLAND, Z/1991/ /KA023. . . . . **PROF 011.62**
Best nest (Videocassette)./EASTMAN, PD/P-1/KF505 . . . . **VCR E**
BEST OF BOOKFINDER: A GUIDE TO CHILDREN'S LITERATURE ABOUT INTERESTS AND CONCERNS OF YOUTH AGED 2-18. /1992/ /KA083. . . . . **PROF 028.1**
Best school year ever. /ROBINSON, B/1994/3-A/5 KH641 . . . . **Fic**
Best school year ever (Sound recording cassette)./ROBINSON, B/1997/ 3-A/5 KH641 . . . . **Fic**
Best vacation ever. /MURPHY, SJ/1997/K-2/2 KG164 . . . . **E**
Best-laid plans of Jonah Twist./HONEYCUTT, N/1988/3-5/4 KH277 . . **Fic**
Bet you can!: science possibilities to fool you. /COBB, V/1990/ 4-A/7 KD745 . . . . **793.8**
Bet you can't: science impossibilities to fool you. /COBB, V/1980/ 5-6/6 KB880 . . . . **507**
Bet you can't: science impossibilities to fool you (Sound recording cassette)./COBB, V/n.d./5-6/6 KB880. . . . . **507**
Bethie's really silly songs about animals (Sound recording cassette). /BETHIE /1993/K-2/KD607. . . . . **SRC 789.3**
Betsy and Billy./HAYWOOD, C/c1941, 1988/2-3/3 KH230 . . . . **Fic**
Betsy and Billy (Braille)./HAYWOOD, C/n.d./2-3/3 KH230 . . . . **Fic**
Betsy and the boys./HAYWOOD, C/c1945/2-3/3 KH230 . . . . **Fic**
Betsy and the boys (Braille)./HAYWOOD, C/n.d./2-3/3 KH230 . . . . . **Fic**
Betsy and the boys (Sound recording cassette)./HAYWOOD, C/n.d./ 2-3/3 KH230 . . . . **Fic**

Betsy Ross. /WALLNER, A/1994/3-4/6 KE526 . . . . **B ROSS, B.**
Better not get wet, Jesse Bear./CARLSTROM, NW/1988/P-K/4 KF356. . **E**
Between earth and sky: legends of Native American sacred places. /
   BRUCHAC, J/1996/5-A/5 KB270 . . . . **398.2**
Beware the mare. /HAAS, J/1993/3-5/4 KH209 . . . . **Fic**
Beware the mare (Sound recording cassette)./HAAS, J/1997/
   3-5/4 KH209 . . . . **Fic**
Beware the ravens, Aunt Morbelia. /CARRIS, JD/1995/5-A/5 KG979 . **Fic**
Beyond picture books: a guide to first readers. 2nd ed. /BARSTOW, B/
   1995/KA011 . . . . **PROF 011.62**
Beyond storybooks: young children and the shared book experience. /
   SLAUGHTER, JP/1993//KA215 . . . . **PROF 372.4**
Beyond the bean seed: gardening activities for grades K-6. /JURENKA,
   NE/1996//KA202. . . . . **PROF 372.3**
Beyond the Mississippi: early westward expansion of the United States. /
   HERB, AM/1996/4-6/10 KF032 . . . . **978**
Beyond the ridge. /GOBLE, P/1989/2-4/4 KH177 . . . . **Fic**
Beyond the ridge (Sound recording cassette)./GOBLE, P/1993/
   2-4/4 KH177 . . . . **Fic**
Beyond the western sea: book one: the escape from home. /AVI /1996/
   6-A/5 KG857 . . . . **Fic**
Beyond the western sea: book two: Lord Kirkle's money. /AVI /1996/
   6-A/5 KG858 . . . . **Fic**
Beyond winning: sports and games all kids want to play. /ROWEN, L/
   1990//KA332 . . . . **PROF 796.1**
BIBBIDI BOBBODI BACH (Compact disc). /1996/4-6/KD674. . . **CD 789.8**
BIBBIDI BOBBODI BACH (Sound recording cassette)./1996/
   4-6/KD674. . . . . **CD 789.8**
Bicycle book. /GIBBONS, G/1995/2-5/3 KD124. . . . . **629.227**
Bicycle man. /SAY, A/1982/K-3/4 KG395 . . . . **E**
Bicycle race. /CREWS, D/1985/K-2/2 KF431 . . . . **E**
Bicycling. /FRANCIS, J/1996/3-6/6 KD827. . . . . **796.6**
BIG AIRCRAFT CARRIER (Videocassette). /1995/4-6/KA989 . **VCR 359.9**
Big Alfie and Annie Rose storybook. /HUGHES, S/1988/P-3/6 KF785 . . **E**
Big Alfie out of doors storybook./HUGHES, S/1992/P-3/6 KF785. . . . . **E**
Big and little alphabet. /ROSENBERG, L/1997/K-2/2 KG353 . . . . **E**
Big Anthony and the magic ring. /DE PAOLA, T/1979/1-3/5 KF466 . . . **E**
BIG ANTHONY'S MIXED-UP MAGIC (CD-ROM). /1996/
   K-2/KF229 . . . . **CDR E**
Big bad Bruce. /PEET, B/1977/K-3/3 KG224 . . . . **E**
Big Bazoohley. /CAREY, P/1995/3-6/5 KG973 . . . . **Fic**
Big Bear Cub Scout book. Rev. ed. /BOY SCOUTS OF AMERICA /1984/
   4-5/5 KB074 . . . . **369.43**
Big Bear Cub Scout book. Rev. ed. (Sound recording cassette)./BOY
   SCOUTS OF AMERICA /1997/4-5/5 KB074 . . . . **369.43**
Big bike race. /BLEDSOE, LJ/1995/3-6/2 KG903 . . . . **Fic**
Big blue whale. /DAVIES, N/1997/K-4/3 KC767 . . . . **599.5**
Big boy. /MOLLEL, TM/1995/K-2/3 KG150 . . . . **E**
Big cats. /SIMON, S/1991/4-6/6 KC826. . . . . **599.75**
Big cats. /KAPPELER, M/1991/5-6/7 KC822 . . . . **599.75**
Big cats. /LUMPKIN, S/1993/5-6/6 KC823. . . . . **599.75**
Big dipper and you. /KRUPP, EC/1989/1-6/4 KC050 . . . . **523.8**
BIG FAT HEN. /1994/P-1/1 KB793. . . . . **398.8**
Big green book. /GRAVES, R/c1962, 1990/3-6/4 KH192 . . . . **Fic**
Big green pocketbook. /RANSOM, CF/1993/P-1/2 KG303 . . . . **E**
Big idea. /SCHECTER, E/1996/3-5/2 KH679 . . . . **Fic**
BIG JOB (CD-ROM). /1995/K-3/KD120. . . . . **CDR 629.225**
Big little otter (Board book). /HOBAN, L/1997/P/1 KF736 . . . . . . **BB E**
Big machines (Board book). /BARTON, B/1995/P/KF204. . . . . . . **BB E**
Big men, big country: a collection of American tall tales. /WALKER, PR/
   1993/4-A/7 KB493 . . . . **398.22**
Big mile race./KESSLER, L/1983/K-3/2 KF901. . . . . **E**
Big pumpkin. /SILVERMAN, E/1992/P-2/2 KG504 . . . . **E**
Big pumpkin (Sound recording cassette)./SILVERMAN, E/1995/
   P-2/2 KG504 . . . . **E**
Big red barn. /BROWN, MW/c1956, 1989/P-1/3 KF283 . . . . **E**
Big Red: the story of a champion Irish setter and a trapper's son who grew
   up together, roaming the wilderness. New ed. /KJELGAARD, J/c1945,
   1956/6-A/7 KH365 . . . . **Fic**
Big Red: the story of a champion Irish setter and a trapper's son who grew
   up together, roaming the wilderness. New ed. (Braille)./KJELGAARD, J/
   n.d./6-A/7 KH365 . . . . **Fic**
Big Red: the story of a champion Irish setter and a trapper's son who grew
   up together, roaming the wilderness. New ed. (Sound recording
   cassette)./KJELGAARD, J/n.d./6-A/7 KH365 . . . . **Fic**
Big rigs. Rev. and updated ed. /MARSTON, HI/1993/
   K-5/4 KD119 . . . . **629.224**
Big rivers: the Missouri, the Mississipi, and the Ohio. /HISCOCK, B/1997/
   3-6/6 KC183 . . . . **551.48**
Big seed. /HOWARD, E/1993/1-3/2 KF775 . . . . **E**
Big Smith snatch. /CURRY, JL/1989/5-A/6 KH047 . . . . **Fic**
Big snow. /HADER, B/1948/K-2/5 KF658 . . . . **E**
Big snow (Braille)./HADER, B/n.d./K-2/5 KF658 . . . . **E**
Big storm. /HISCOCK, B/1993/4-6/6 KC198. . . . . **551.55**

Big tree. /HISCOCK, B/1991/1-5/6 KC414. . . . . **582.16**
BIG ZOO (Videocassette). /1995/2-5/KC440 . . . . **VCR 590.73**
Bigfoot. /BACH, JS/1995/3-6/7 KA562. . . . . **001.944**
Bigfoot and other legendary creatures. /WALKER, PR/1992/
   4-6/6 KA564 . . . . **001.944**
Biggest bear. /WARD, L/c1952/1-3/3 KG688. . . . . **CE E**
Biggest bear (Braille)./WARD, L/n.d./1-3/3 KG688 . . . . **CE E**
Biggest bear (Kit)./WARD, L/1993/1-3/3 KG688. . . . . **CE E**
Biggest bear (Talking book)./WARD, L/n.d./1-3/3 KG688 . . . . . . **CE E**
Biggest boy. /HENKES, K/1995/P/2 KF701 . . . . **E**
Biggest frog in Australia. /ROTH, SL/1996/2-3/2 KB643 . . . . . . **398.24**
Biggest nose. /CAPLE, K/1985/P-2/2 KF337 . . . . **E**
Biggest nose (Braille)./CAPLE, K/n.d./P-2/2 KF337 . . . . **E**
Biggest nose (Sound recording cassette)./CAPLE, K/n.d./P-2/2 KF337 . . **E**
Biggest, strongest, fastest. /JENKINS, S/1995/K-4/3 KC449 . . . . . . **591**
Bigmama's. /CREWS, D/1991/K-2/2 KE309 . . . . **CE B CREWS, D.**
Bigmama's (Videocassette)./CREWS, D/1993/
   K-2/2 KE309 . . . . **CE B CREWS, D.**
BILAL'S DREAM (Videocassette). /1990/5-6/KD004 . . . . . . **VCR 613.85**
BILINGUAL TIMELINER (Microcomputer program)./1994/
   K-A/KE142 . . . . **MCP 902**
BILINGUAL WRITING CENTER: SPANISH/ENGLISH (Microcomputer
   program)./1993/2-A/KD347 . . . . **MCP 686.2**
Bill Clinton: president of the 90s. Rev. ed. /CWIKLIK, R/1997/
   5-6/8 KE296 . . . . **B CLINTON, B.**
Bill Peet: an autobiography. /PEET, B/1989/6-A/8 KE494 . . . **B PEET, B.**
Bill Peet: an autobiography (Sound recording cassette)./PEET, B/n.d./
   6-A/8 KE494 . . . . **B PEET, B.**
Bill Pickett: rodeo-ridin' cowboy. /PINKNEY, AD/1996/
   2-5/7 KE496 . . . . **B PICKETT, B.**
Billion for Boris. /RODGERS, M/c1974/4-6/7 KH646 . . . . **CE Fic**
Billion for Boris (Braille)./RODGERS, M/n.d./4-6/7 KH646. . . . . . **CE Fic**
Billion for Boris (Kit)./RODGERS, M/1979/4-6/7 KH646 . . . . **CE Fic**
Billy Beg and his bull: an Irish tale. /GREENE, E/1994/
   2-4/5 KB304 . . . . **398.2**
Billy Lazroe and the King of the Sea: a tale of the Northwest. /KIMMEL,
   EA/1996/4-5/5 KB460 . . . . **398.22**
Bimmi finds a cat. /STEWART, EJ/1996/3-5/6 KH761. . . . . **Fic**
Bing bang boing. /FLORIAN, D/1994/3-6/KD936 . . . . **811**
Bingleman's Midway. /ACKERMAN, K/1995/2-4/5 KF128 . . . . **E**
Bingo Brown and the language of love. /BYARS, BC/1989/
   5-A/6 KG957. . . . . **Fic**
Bingo Brown's guide to romance./BYARS, BC/1992/5-A/5 KG957. . . . **Fic**
Bingo, the best dog in the world. /SIRACUSA, C/1991/K-1/1 KG510 . . **E**
Biodiversity. /PATENT, DH/1996/5-6/9 KA964 . . . . **333.95**
Biographical dictionary of Black Americans. /KRANZ, R/1992/
   /KA401 . . . . **REF 305.8**
BIOGRAPHY FOR BEGINNERS: SKETCHES FOR EARLY READERS. /
   1995-/3-5/KA476 . . . . **REF 920**
BIOGRAPHY TODAY ARTISTS SERIES: PROFILES OF INTEREST TO
   YOUNG READERS. /1996-/4-6/KA453. . . . . **REF 709.2**
BIOGRAPHY TODAY AUTHOR SERIES: PROFILES OF PEOPLE OF
   INTEREST TO YOUNG READERS. /1996-/4-6/KA461 . . . . . **REF 809**
BIOGRAPHY TODAY SCIENTISTS AND INVENTORS SERIES: PROFILES
   OF PEOPLE OF INTEREST TO YOUNG PEOPLE. /1996-/
   4-6/KA438 . . . . **REF 509**
BIOGRAPHY TODAY SPORTS SERIES: PROFILES OF PEOPLE OF
   INTEREST TO YOUNG READERS. /1996-/4-6/KA456 . . . . . **REF 796**
BIOGRAPHY TODAY WORLD LEADERS SERIES: PROFILES OF PEOPLE
   OF INTEREST TO YOUNG READERS. /1997-/4-6/KA407 . . **REF 350**
Biology for every kid: 101 easy experiments that really work. /
   VANCLEAVE, JP/1989/P-4/8 KC270 . . . . **570**
Bionic Bunny Show. /BROWN, MT/1984/K-3/5 KF280 . . . . **E**
Bird. /BURNIE, D/1988/A/9 KC648 . . . . **598**
Bird atlas. /TAYLOR, B/1993/4-6/9 KA449 . . . . **REF 598**
Birdie's lighthouse. /HOPKINSON, D/1997/3-5/3 KH282 . . . . **Fic**
Birding. /FORSHAW, J/c1994, 1995/5-6/8 KA448 . . . . **REF 598**
Birds. /KRULIK, NE/1993/2-4/4 KC652 . . . . **598**
Birds in the bushes: a story about Margaret Morse Nice. /DUNLAP, J/
   1996/3-5/9 KE477 . . . . **B NICE, M.**
BIRDS IN THE CITY: A FIRST FILM. 2ND ED. (Videocassette). /1992/
   2-6/KC646. . . . . **VCR 598**
Birds' nest. /WATTS, B/1986/2-5/2 KC706 . . . . **598.8**
Birds we know. /FRISKEY, M/1981/P-2/2 KC649. . . . . **598**
Birdwise: forty fun feats for finding out about our feathered friends. /
   HICKMAN, PM/1988/4-6/6 KC650 . . . . **598**
Birth of a foal. /ISENBART, H/1986/3-6/5 KD201 . . . . **636.1**
Birth of a koala. /BURT, D/1986/4-6/8 KC734 . . . . **599.2**
Birthday for Frances. /HOBAN, R/c1968, 1995/P-1/2 KF740 . . . . . . **E**
Birthday present./STOCK, C/P-K/2 KG574 . . . . **E**
Birthday presents. /RYLANT, C/1991/P-1/2 KG368 . . . . **E**
BIRTHDAY SURPRISES: TEN GREAT STORIES TO UNWRAP. /1995/
   5-A/6 KG900 . . . . **Fic**
Birthday swap. /LOPEZ, L/1997/K-2/2 KG032 . . . . **E**

Biscuit. /CAPUCILLI, A/1996/P-1/1 KF338 . . . . **E**

Biscuit finds a friend. /CAPUCILLI, A/1997/P-1/1 KF339 . . . . **E**

Bit by bit. /SANFIELD, S/1995/K-2/2 KB772 . . . . **398.27**

BITE OF THE BLACK WIDOW (Videocassette). /1994/
5-6/KC523. **VCR 595.4**

Biz kids' guide to success: money-making ideas for young entrepreneurs. /
THOMPSON, T/1992/5-6/6 KD307 . . . . **650.1**

Blabber mouth. /GLEITZMAN, M/1995/3-5/4 KH173 . . . . **Fic**

Blabber mouth (Sound recording cassette). /GLEITZMAN, M/1997/
3-5/4 KH173 . . . . **Fic**

Blabbermouths: adapted from a German folktale. /MANTINBAND, G/
1992/3-4/4 KB751 . . . . **398.27**

Black Americans: a history in their own words 1619-1983. /MELTZER, M/
1984/5-6/9 KE857 . . . . **973**

Black and blue magic. /SNYDER, ZK/c1966, 1994/4-6/7 KH729. . . . . **Fic**

Black and white. /MACAULAY, D/1990/3-A/5 KH432 . . . . **Fic**

Black artists in photography, 1840-1940. /SULLIVAN, G/1996/
5-6/12 KD510 . . . . **770**

Black bear magic for kids. /FAIR, J/1991/4-5/5 KC849. . . . . . . **599.78**

Black Beauty: the autobiography of a horse. /SEWELL, A/1997/
5-7/7 KH702 . . . . **Fic**

Black cauldron./ALEXANDER, L/1965/6-A/6 KG833 . . . . **Fic**

Black cauldron (Braille)./ALEXANDER, L/n.d./6-A/6 KG833 . . . . **Fic**

Black cauldron (Sound recording cassette)./ALEXANDER, L/n.d./
6-A/6 KG833 . . . . **Fic**

Black cauldron (Talking book)./ALEXANDER, L/n.d./6-A/6 KG833. . . . . **Fic**

Black diamond: the story of the Negro baseball leagues. /MCKISSACK, P/
1994/4-6/7 KD800 . . . . **796.357**

Black fighting men: a proud history. /REEF, C/1994/5-6/6 KA982 . . . **355**

Black frontiers: a history of African American heroes in the Old West. /
SCHLISSEL, L/1995/4-6/8 KF048 . . . . **978**

BLACK HERITAGE HOLIDAYS (Videocassette). /1992/
3-A/KB195. **VCR 394.26**

Black heroes of the American revolution. /DAVIS, B/1976/
5-6/10 KE877 . . . . **973.3**

BLACK HISTORY MONTH RESOURCE BOOK. /1993/
/KA370. . . . . **PROF 973**

BLACK INNOVATORS (Picture). /1994/4-6/KA837 . . . . **PIC 305.8**

Black is brown is tan. /ADOFF, A/1973/P-3/3 KF136 . . . . **E**

BLACK IS MY COLOR: THE AFRICAN AMERICAN EXPERIENCE
(Videocassette). /1992/4-6/KA838 . . . . **VCR 305.8**

Black pearl. /O'DELL, S/c1967/5-6/5 KH557 . . . . **CE Fic**

Black pearl (Braille)./O'DELL, S/n.d./5-6/5 KH557 . . . . **CE Fic**

Black pearl (Talking book)./O'DELL, S/n.d./5-6/5 KH557 . . . . . . **CE Fic**

Black ships before Troy: the story of the Iliad. /SUTCLIFF, R/1993/
5-A/8 KE127 . . . . **883**

Black Stallion. /FARLEY, W/c1941, 1994/4-6/5 KH105 . . . . **Fic**

Black Stallion and Flame./FARLEY, W/c1960, 1991/4-6/5 KH105 . . . . **Fic**

Black Stallion (Braille)./FARLEY, W/n.d./4-6/5 KH105 . . . . **Fic**

Black Stallion mystery./FARLEY, W/c1957, 1992/4-6/5 KH105 . . . . . **Fic**

Black Stallion's ghost./FARLEY, W/c1969, 1995/4-6/5 KH105 . . . . . **Fic**

Black stars in orbit: NASA'S African American astronauts. /BURNS, K/
1995/3-6/8 KD136 . . . . **629.45**

Black swan/white crow: haiku. /LEWIS, JP/1995/3-6/KD971 . . . . . . **811**

BLACK WEST (Videocassette). /1992/5-6/KF028 . . . . **VCR 978**

Black women of the Old West. /KATZ, WL/1995/5-6/9 KF036. . . . . **978**

Blair's nightmare (Sound recording cassette)./SNYDER, ZK/n.d./
4-6/7 KH733 . . . . **CE Fic**

Blast off!: a space counting book. /COLE, N/1994/P-3/6 KD131 . **629.43**

Blast off to Earth!: a look at geography. /LEEDY, L/1992/
1-4/4 KE151 . . . . **910**

Blizzards. /OTFINOSKI, S/1994/4-6/6 KB036. . . . . **363.34**

Blood and guts: a working guide to your own insides. /ALLISON, L/c1976/
4-6/4 KC912 . . . . **612**

Bloomers!. /BLUMBERG, R/1993/3-5/6 KA830 . . . . **305.42**

Blossom on the bough: a book of trees. /DOWDEN, AO/c1975, 1994/
5-8/9 KC411 . . . . **582.16**

Blossom promise./BYARS, BC/1990/4-A/4 KG962 . . . . **CE Fic**

Blossoms and the Green Phantom./BYARS, BC/c1987, 1988/
4-A/4 KG962 . . . . **CE Fic**

Blossoms meet the Vulture Lady./BYARS, BC/1986/4-A/4 KG962 . **CE Fic**

Blowing bubbles with the enemy. /JACKSON, A/1993/4-6/5 KH317 . . **Fic**

Blubber. /BLUME, J/1974/4-6/3 KG906 . . . . **Fic**

Blubber (Braille)./BLUME, J/n.d./4-6/3 KG906 . . . . **Fic**

Blubber (Sound recording cassette)./BLUME, J/n.d./4-6/3 KG906 . . . . **Fic**

Blue and the gray. /BUNTING, E/1996/3-5/3 KF297 . . . . **E**

Blue pages: resources for teachers from Invitations. Updated, expanded, and
rev. /ROUTMAN, R/1994/KA026 . . . . **PROF 016.372**

BLUE PLANET (Videocassette). /1993/5-A/KB058 . . . . . . **VCR 363.73**

Blue sword. /MCKINLEY, R/1982/A/7 KH486 . . . . **Fic**

Blue sword (Sound recording cassette)./MCKINLEY, R/n.d./
A/7 KH486 . . . . **Fic**

Blue whale. /KIM, M/1993/3-5/7 KC772 . . . . **599.5**

Blueberries for Sal. /MCCLOSKEY, R/c1948/P-2/7 KG087 . . . . . . **CE E**

Blueberries for Sal (Braille)./MCCLOSKEY, R/n.d./P-2/7 KG087 . . . **CE E**

Blueberries for Sal (Kit)./MCCLOSKEY, R/1993/P-2/7 KG087 . . . . **CE E**

Blueberries for Sal (Sound recording cassette)./MCCLOSKEY, R/n.d./
P-2/7 KG087 . . . . **CE E**

Blueberries for Sal (Videocassette)./MCCLOSKEY, R/n.d./
P-2/7 KG087 . . . . **CE E**

Blues. /SILVERMAN, J/1994/5-A/KD671 . . . . **789.43**

Blunder book: colossal errors, minor mistakes, and surprising slipups that
have changed the course of history. /GOLDBERG, MH/1984/
5-A/9 KA556 . . . . **001.9**

Blunder book: colossal errors, minor mistakes, and surprising slipups that
have changed the course of history (Braille). /GOLDBERG, MH/n.d./
5-A/9 KA556 . . . . **001.9**

Bo Jackson. /KRAMER, J/1996/4-5/6 KE398 . . . . **B JACKSON, B.**

Boat. /KENTLEY, E/1992/5-6/7 KD063 . . . . **623.8**

Boat book. /GIBBONS, G/1983/P-2/3 KB152 . . . . **387.2**

Boats. /BARTON, B/1986/P-1/2 KB151 . . . . **387.2**

Boats. /STEELE, P/1991/4-6/6 KD065 . . . . **623.8**

Bobby baseball. /SMITH, RK/1991/3-6/4 KH726. . . . . **Fic**

Boda: a Mexican wedding celebration. /VAN LAAN, N/1996/
1-3/2 KG641 . . . . **E**

Bodies in the Bessledorf Hotel. /NAYLOR, PR/1988/4-6/5 KH535 . . . . **Fic**

Body and how it works. /PARKER, S/1992/A/6 KC923 . . . . **612**

Body atlas. /PARKER, S/1993/A/7 KC905 . . . . **611**

Boggart. /COOPER, S/1993/6-A/7 KH026. . . . . **CE Fic**

Boggart and the monster. /COOPER, S/1997/5-A/6 KH027. . . . . . . **Fic**

Boggart (Sound recording cassette)./COOPER, S/1994/
6-A/7 KH026 . . . . **CE Fic**

Boggart (Talking book)./COOPER, S/1994/6-A/7 KH026 . . . . . . **CE Fic**

Bold carnivore: an alphabet of predators. /POWELL, C/1995/
P-5/5 KC454 . . . . **591**

Bolsillo para Corduroy./FREEMAN, D/1992/P-2/2 KF581 . . . . . . **CE E**

Bolsillo para Corduroy (Kit)./FREEMAN, D/1992/P-2/2 KF581 . . . . **CE E**

Bone from a dry sea. /DICKINSON, P/1993/6-A/7 KH075 . . . . **Fic**

Bones in the cliff. /STEVENSON, J/1995/4-6/6 KH755. . . . . **Fic**

Bones on Black Spruce Mountain. /BUDBILL, D/c1978, 1994/
4-A/5 KG935. . . . . **Fic**

Bonesy and Isabel. /ROSEN, MJ/1995/2-3/6 KG352 . . . . **E**

Bonicula./HOWE, D/1992/3-6/5 KH285. . . . . **Fic**

BONJOUR DE PARIS (French Version) (Videocassette)./1988/
5-A/KE683. . . . . **VCR 944**

BONJOUR DE PARIS (Videocassette). /1988/5-A/KE683. . . . **VCR 944**

Bonnie Blair: power on ice. /DALY, W/1996/4-6/6 KE255 . . **B BLAIR, B.**

Booby hatch. /LEWIN, B/1995/K-2/2 KF973 . . . . **E**

Boogie Bones. /LOREDO, E/1997/K-2/3 KG034 . . . . **E**

Book. /BROOKFIELD, K/1993/4-A/9 KA565. . . . . **002**

BOOK EXCHANGE (Microcomputer program). /1996/
3-6/KD862. . . . . **MCP 808**

BOOK LINKS: CONNECTING BOOKS, LIBRARIES AND CLASSROOMS. /
1991-//KA097 . . . . **PER PROF 050**

Book of changes: stories. /WYNNE-JONES, T/1995/6-A/3 KH885 . . . **Fic**

Book of changes: stories (Sound recording cassette)./WYNNE-JONES, T/
1997/6-A/3 KH885. . . . . **Fic**

Book of goddesses. /WALDHERR, K/1996/4-6/8 KA732 . . . . . . **291.2**

Book of little folk: faery stories and poems from around the world. /MILLS,
LA/1997/1-4/KD875 . . . . **808.8**

Book of myths: selections from Bulfinch's Age of fable. /BULFINCH, T/
c1942/A/9 KA734 . . . . **292**

Book of myths: selections from Bulfinch's Age of fable (Braille)./BULFINCH,
T/n.d./A/9 KA734 . . . . **292**

Book of North American owls. /SATTLER, HR/1995/5-6/6 KC719. . **598.9**

Book of tens. /PODWAL, M/1994/5-6/7 KA769 . . . . **296.1**

Book of three. /ALEXANDER, L/1964/6-A/6 KG833 . . . . **Fic**

Book of three (Braille). /ALEXANDER, L/n.d./6-A/6 KG833 . . . . . . **Fic**

Book of three (Sound recording cassette)./ALEXANDER, L/n.d./
6-A/6 KG833 . . . . **Fic**

Book of three (Talking book)./ALEXANDER, L/n.d./6-A/6 KG833 . . . . **Fic**

BOOK OF VIRTUES FOR YOUNG PEOPLE: A TREASURY OF GREAT
MORAL STORIES. /1997/KA343 . . . . **PROF 808.8**

Book of your own: keeping a diary or journal. /STEVENS, C/1993/
5-A/9 KD864 . . . . **808**

BOOK TALK AND BEYOND: CHILDREN AND TEACHERS RESPOND TO
LITERATURE. /1995/KA235. . . . . **PROF 372.64**

Book that Jack wrote. /SCIESZKA, J/1994/P-1/KE021 . . . . **811**

Booker T. Washington: educator and leader. /ROBERTS, JL/1995/
4-6/5 KE586 . . . . **B WASHINGTON, B**

BOOKER (Videocassette). /1983/3-6/KE585 . . **VCR B WASHINGTON, B**

BOOKLIST. /1905-//KA098 . . . . **PER PROF 050**

Bookmark book. /BRODIE, CS/1996//KA310 . . . . **PROF 741.6**

Books, children and men. 5th ed. /HAZARD, P/1983//KA351 . **PROF 809**

Books kids will sit still for: the complete read-aloud guide. 2nd ed. /
FREEMAN, J/1990//KA015 . . . . **PROF 011.62**

Books to help children cope with separation and loss: an annotated
bibliography. 4th ed. /RUDMAN, MK/1993//KA025 . **PROF 016.1559**

Bookshop dog. /RYLANT, C/1996/K-2/2 KG369 . . . . E
Bookstore cat. /WHEELER, C/1994/K-2/2 KG709 . . . . E
BOOKTALK! 2: BOOKTALKING FOR ALL AGES AND AUDIENCES. 2ND
   ED./1985//KA090 . . . . **PROF 028.5**
BOOKTALK! 3: MORE BOOKTALKS FOR ALL AGES AND AUDIENCES./
   1988//KA090 . . . . **PROF 028.5**
BOOKTALK! 4: SELECTIONS FROM THE BOOKTALKER FOR ALL AGES
   AND AUDIENCES. /1992//KA090 . . . . **PROF 028.5**
BOOKTALK! 5: MORE SELECTIONS FROM THE BOOKTALKER FOR ALL
   AGES AND AUDIENCES. /1993//KA090 . . . . . . **PROF 028.5**
Bookworks: making books by hand. /SWAIN, G/1995/
   3-6/5 KD437 . . . . **745.5**
Boomer's big day. /MCGEORGE, CW/1994/K-2/2 KG102 . . . . . E
Boots and his brothers: a Norwegian tale. /KIMMEL, EA/1992/
   2-4/2 KB400 . . . . **398.21**
Boots and his brothers: a Norwegian tale (Sound recording cassette)./
   KIMMEL, EA/1995/2-4/2 KB400 . . . . **398.21**
Born to trot. /HENRY, M/c1950, 1993/5-A/5 KH241 . . . . **Fic**
Borning room. /FLEISCHMAN, P/1991/6-A/5 KH115 . . . . **Fic**
Borning room (Sound recording cassette)./FLEISCHMAN, P/1994/
   6-A/1 KH115 . . . . **Fic**
Borreguita and the coyote: a tale from Ayutla, Mexico. /AARDEMA, V/
   1991/P-2/4 KB514 . . . . **398.24**
Borrowers. /NORTON, M/c1953, 1989/4-6/6 KH554 . . . . **CE Fic**
Borrowers afield. /NORTON, M/1970/4-6/6 KH554 . . . . . . **CE Fic**
Borrowers afield (Braille)./NORTON, M/n.d./4-6/6 KH554 . . . **CE Fic**
Borrowers afloat./NORTON, M/1955/4-6/6 KH554 . . . . . . **CE Fic**
Borrowers afloat (Sound recording cassette)./NORTON, M/1997/
   4-6/6 KH554 . . . . **CE Fic**
Borrowers aloft./NORTON, M/1961/4-6/6 KH554 . . . . **CE Fic**
Borrowers aloft (Braille)./NORTON, M/n.d./4-6/6 KH554 . . . . **CE Fic**
Borrowers aloft (Sound recording cassette)./NORTON, M/1997/
   4-6/6 KH554 . . . . **CE Fic**
Borrowers avenged./NORTON, M/1986/4-6/6 KH554 . . . . . **CE Fic**
Borrowers avenged (Braille)./NORTON, M/n.d./4-6/6 KH554 . . . **CE Fic**
Borrowers avenged (Sound recording cassette)./NORTON, M/n.d./
   4-6/6 KH554 . . . . **CE Fic**
Borrowers (Braille)./NORTON, M/n.d./4-6/6 KH554 . . . . . . **CE Fic**
Borrowers (Sound recording cassette)./NORTON, M/n.d./
   4-6/6 KH554 . . . . **CE Fic**
Bosque tropical./COWCHER, H/1992/2-4/4 KF428 . . . . E
Bossy gallito/el gallo de bodas: a traditional Cuban folktale. /GONZALEZ,
   LM/1994/K-2/4 KB577 . . . . **398.24**
Boston coffee party. /RAPPAPORT, D/1988/K-3/2 KG306 . . . . . E
Bouncing. /HUGHES, S/1995/P-2 KF786 . . . . E
Bound for Oregon. /VAN LEEUWEN, J/1994/5-A/5 KH828 . . . . . **Fic**
Bound for the promised land.: the great black migration. /COOPER, ML/
   1995/6-A/9 KE851 . . . . **973**
Boundless Grace. /HOFFMAN, M/1995/1-3/5 KF762 . . . . E
BOX AND TWO OTHER TITLES FOR FAMILY ENJOYMENT
   (Videocassette). /1992/1-4/KF253 . . . . **VCR E**
Box can be many things. /RAU, DM/1997/K-1/2 KG313 . . . . E
Box turtle at Long Pond. /GEORGE, WT/1989/1-3/3 KF608 . . . . . . E
Boxing champion. /CARRIER, R/1991/4-6/2 KG976 . . . . **Fic**
Boy, a dog and a frog. /MAYER, M/c1967/P-1/KG084 . . . . . . **CE E**
Boy, a dog and a frog (Videocassette)./MAYER, M/1981/
   P-1/KG084 . . . . **CE E**
Boy and his bear. /GRAHAM, H/1996/5-A/5 KH186 . . . . **Fic**
Boy and the ghost. /SAN SOUCI, RD/1989/2-3/6 KG392 . . . . . . E
Boy and the Samurai. /HAUGAARD, EC/1991/6-A/6 KH226 . . . **CE Fic**
Boy and the Samurai (Talking book)./HAUGAARD, EC/1993/
   6-A/6 KH226 . . . . **CE Fic**
Boy called Slow: the true story of Sitting Bull. /BRUCHAC, J/1994/
   3-4/4 KE541 . . . . **B SITTING BULL**
Boy of the three-year nap. /SNYDER, D/1988/K-3/6 KG525 . . . . . . E
Boy Scout handbook. 10th ed. /BIRKBY, RC/1990/4-6/6 KB073 . . **369.43**
Boy: tales of childhood. /DAHL, R/1984/5-6/6 KE312 . . . . . **B DAHL, R.**
Boy: tales of childhood (Large type)./DAHL, R/n.d./
   5-6/6 KE312 . . . . **B DAHL, R.**
BOY TO MAN. 3rd ed. (Videocassette). /1992/5-6/KC944 . . **VCR 612.6**
Boy who drew cats: a Japanese folktale. /LEVINE, AA/1993/
   2-4/4 KB609 . . . . **398.24**
Boy who lived with bears: and other Iroquois stories (Talking book)./
   BRUCHAC, J/c1990, 1996/2-4/4 KB537 . . . . . . **CE 398.24**
Boy who lived with the bears: and other Iroquois stories. /BRUCHAC, J/
   1995/2-4/4 KB537 . . . . **CE 398.24**
Boy who lived with the seals. /MARTIN, R/1993/2-4/6 KB614 . . **398.24**
Boy who wouldn't go to bed. /COOPER, H/1997/P-1/2 KF422 . . . . . E
Boys at work. /SOTO, G/1995/4-6/5 KH739 . . . . **Fic**
BOYS' LIFE. /1911-/2-A/KA504 . . . . **PER 050**
BOYS' LIFE (Braille). /n.d./2-A/KA504 . . . . **PER 050**
Boys' war: Confederate and Union soldiers talk about the Civil War. /
   MURPHY, J/1990/5-6/7 KE909 . . . . **973.7**

Boys' war: Confederate and Union soldiers talk about the Civil War (Sound
   recording cassette)./MURPHY, J/1993/5-6/7 KE909 . . . . **973.7**
Bracelet. /UCHIDA, Y/1993/2-5/3 KG631 . . . . E
Braided cord: memoirs of a school librarian. /GAVER, MV/1988/
   /KA368 . . . . **PROF B GAVER, M**
Brain. /MATHERS, D/1992/5-6/6 KC966 . . . . **612.8**
Brain: our nervous system. /SIMON, S/1997/5-6/6 KC980 . . . . **612.8**
Brain power through picture books: help children develop with books that
   stimulate specific parts of their minds. /POLETTE, N/1992/
   /KA227 . . . . **PROF 372.6**
Brain--what it is, what it does. /BRUUN, RD/1989/3-5/5 KC914 . . . . **612**
Brand is forever. /SCOTT, AH/1993/3-5/6 KH687 . . . . **Fic**
Brass. /SHIPTON, A/1994/4-A/7 KD553 . . . . **788.9**
Brats. /KENNEDY, XJ/1986/3-6/6 KD961 . . . . **811**
Brave as a mountain lion. /SCOTT, AH/1996/3-5/2 KH688 . . . . . **Fic**
Brave Eagle's account of the Fetterman Fight, 21 December 1866. /GOBLE,
   P/c1972, 1992/5-6/6 KE913 . . . . **973.8**
Brave Irene. /STEIG, W/1986/K-3/3 KG541 . . . . **CE E**
Brave Irene (Sound recording cassette)./STEIG, W/n.d./
   K-3/3 KG541 . . . . **CE E**
Brave Irene (Videocassette)./STEIG, W/1990/K-3/3 KG541 . . . . . **CE E**
Brave Martha and the dragon. /ROTH, SL/1996/2-4/4 KB476 . . . **398.22**
Brave Mary. /BRIMNER, LD/1996/K-1/2 KF266 . . . . E
Bravest dog ever: the true story of Balto. /STANDIFORD, N/1989/
   1-3/2 KD223 . . . . **636.7**
Bravest thing. /NAPOLI, DJ/1995/3-5/6 KH529 . . . . **Fic**
Braving the frozen frontier: women working in Antarctica. /JOHNSON, RL/
   1997/4-6/6 KE214 . . . . **919.8**
Bravo, Amelia Bedelia! /PARISH, H/1997/1-2/2 KG210 . . . . E
Brazilian rain forest. /SIY, A/1992/4-6/6 KC326 . . . . **577.34**
Bread and jam for Frances (Big book). /HOBAN, R/1993/
   P-1/2 KF739 . . . . **CE E**
Bread and jam for Frances (Braille)./HOBAN, R/n.d./P-1/2 KF739 . . **CE E**
Bread and jam for Frances. Newly ill. ed./HOBAN, R/1993/
   P-1/2 KF739 . . . . **CE E**
Bread, bread, bread. /MORRIS, A/1989/K-2/2 KD293 . . . . . . **641.8**
Bread is for eating. /GERSHATOR, D/1995/P-2/2 KF610 . . . . E
Breaker. /PEREZ, NA/1988/6-A/7 KH597 . . . . **Fic**
Breaking free. /GAEDDERT, L/1994/5-A/5 KH147 . . . . **Fic**
Breaking free (Sound recording cassette)./GAEDDERT, L/1997/
   5-A/5 KH147 . . . . **Fic**
Breaking into print: before and after the invention of the printing press. /
   KRENSKY, S/1996/3-5/5 KD346 . . . . **686.2**
Breaking the chains: African-American slave resistance. /KATZ, WL/1990/
   A/8 KE966 . . . . **975**
BREATH OF LIFE: OUR RESPIRATORY SYSTEM (Videocassette). /1992/
   5-6/KC938 . . . . **VCR 612.2**
Breathtaking noses. /MACHOTKA, H/1992/3-5/6 KC280 . . . . . . **573.2**
Bremen-Town musicians. /PLUME, I/1998/1-3/4 KB636 . . . . . . **398.24**
Brer Rabbit and Boss Lion (Kit). /KESSLER, B/1996/
   3-A/KB599 . . . . **KIT 398.24**
BRER RABBIT AND BOSS LION (Talking book). /1992/
   3-A/KB533 . . . . **TB 398.24**
Brer Rabbit stories (Sound recording cassette). /TORRENCE, J/1984/
   4-5/KB666 . . . . **SRC 398.24**
BREWER'S DICTIONARY OF PHRASE AND FABLE. 15th ed. /1995/
   5-6/KA459 . . . . **REF 803**
Brian Wildsmith's ABC. /WILDSMITH, B/1995/P-1/KG721 . . . . E
Bridge to Terabithia. /PATERSON, K/1977/5-A/6 KH573 . . . . . **Fic**
BRIDGE TO TERABITHIA: A MULTI-MEDIA STUDY (Microcomputer
   program). /1993/5-A/KB108 . . . . **MCP 372.6**
Bridges to change: how kids live on a South Carolina Sea Island. /KRULL,
   K/1995/4-6/7 KE987 . . . . **975.7**
BRIDGES (Videocassette). /1988/5-6/KD066 . . . . **VCR 624**
Brigham Young: pioneer and Mormon leader. /SANFORD, WR/1996/
   5-6/8 KE605 . . . . **B YOUNG, B.**
Brighter garden. /DICKINSON, E/1990/3-6/KD932 . . . . **811**
Brighty of the Grand Canyon. /HENRY, M/c1953, 1991/
   4-5/5 KH242 . . . . **CE Fic**
Brighty of the Grand Canyon (Braille)./HENRY, M/n.d./
   4-5/5 KH242 . . . . **CE Fic**
Brighty of the Grand Canyon (Talking book)./HENRY, M/n.d./
   4-5/5 KH242 . . . . **CE Fic**
Bringing out the best: a resource guide for parents of young gifted children.
   Rev. and updated. /SAUNDERS, J/1991//KA189 . . . . **PROF 371.95**
Bristle Face. /BALL, Z/1990/5-A/6 KG877 . . . . **Fic**
Bristlelip (Videocassette)./DAVENPORT, T/1982/5-A/KB281 . . . **CE 398.2**
British Columbia. /NANTON, I/1994/5-A/9 KE810 . . . . **971.1**
British Columbia. /BOWERS, V/1995/4-6/9 KE809 . . . . **971.1**
Broadway chicken. /FROMENTAL, J/1995/5-A/7 KH146 . . . . **Fic**
BROADWAY KIDS SING BROADWAY (Compact disc). /1994/
   2-6/KD528 . . . . **CD 782.1**
BROADWAY KIDS SING BROADWAY (Sound recording cassette)./1994/
   2-6/KD528 . . . . **CD 782.1**

Broken Arrow boy. /MOORE, A/1990/3-6/6 KA996 . . . . **362.1**
BROKEN PROMISES (Videocassette). /1991//KA298. **VCR PROF 613.81**
Broken tusk: stories of the Hindu god Ganesha. /KRISHNASWAMI, U/
 1996/3-4/4 KA764 . . . . **294.5**
Brooklyn Bridge. /MANN, E/1996/5-6/5 KD068 . . . . **624**
Brooklyn doesn't rhyme. /BLOS, JW/1994/4-6/6 KG904. . . . . **Fic**
Brother Francis and the friendly beasts. /HODGES, M/1991/
 3-5/5 KE349 . . . . **B FRANCIS, ST.**
BROTHER FUTURE (Videocassette). /c1991, 1997/6-A/KG930 . . **VCR Fic**
Brother to the wind. /WALTER, MP/1985/1-3/2 KG684 . . . . **E**
Brothers and sisters. /ROSENBERG, MB/1991/1-4/4 KA887 . . . **306.875**
Brown angels: an album of pictures and verse. /MYERS, WD/1993/
 K-6/KD992 . . . . **811**
Brown bear, brown bear, what do you see? /MARTIN, JR., B/1992/
 P-K/1 KG072 . . . . **E**
Brown cow, green grass, yellow mellow sun. /JACKSON, E/1995/
 P-1/2 KF818 . . . . **E**
Brown honey in broomwheat tea: poems. /THOMAS, JC/1993/
 K-6/KE031 . . . . **811**
Brown honey in broomwheat tea: poems (Sound recording cassette)./
 THOMAS, JC/1996/K-6/KE031 . . . . **811**
Brownie Scout handbook. /GIRL SCOUTS OF THE UNITED STATES OF
 AMERICA /1993/1-3/KB078. . . . . **369.463**
Bruno the baker. /KLINTING, L/1997/P-2/2 KF911 . . . . **E**
Bruno the carpenter. /KLINTING, L/1996/K-2/2 KF912 . . . . **E**
Bruno the tailor. /KLINTING, L/1996/K-2/2 KF913 . . . . **E**
Bub, or, The very best thing. /BABBITT, N/1994/P-2/2 KF182 . . . . . **E**
BUBBLEOLOGY I AND II (Videocassette). /1988/
 3-A/KA292 . . . . **VCR PROF 530.4**
Bubbles. /ZUBROWSKI, B/1979/4-6/8 KC085 . . . . **530.4**
Buddha. /DEMI /1996/2-6/6 KA758 . . . . **294.3**
Buddy: based on the true story of Gertrude Lintz. /JOYCE, W/1997/
 5-A/5 KH337 . . . . **Fic**
Buddy Love: now on video. /COOPER, I/1995/5-A/4 KH025 . . . . . **Fic**
Buddy: the first seeing eye dog. /MOORE, E/1996/1-3/5 KB006 . . **362.4**
Buen dia./HOGROGIAN, N/1997/P-2/5 KF763 . . . . **CE E**
Buenas acciones de Clifford./BRIDWELL, N/1978/P-2/1 KF264 . . . . **CE E**
Buenas noches, luna./BROWN, MW/1995/P-K/1 KF285 . . . . **CE E**
Buenas noches, luna (Kit)./BROWN, MW/1996/P-K/1 KF285 . . . . **CE E**
Buffalo. /LEPTHIEN, EU/1989/3-5/5 KC791 . . . . **599.64**
Buffalo Bill. /ROBISON, N/1991/5-6/6 KE267 . . . . . . **B BUFFALO BILL**
Buffalo Bill and the Pony Express. /COERR, E/1995/1-3/2 KF399 . . . **Fic**
Buffalo hunt. /FREEDMAN, R/1988/4-6/7 KE787 . . . . **970.48**
Buffalo Soldiers./MILLER, RH/1991/4-6/6 KF039 . . . . **978**
Buffalo: the American Bison today. /PATENT, DH/1986/
 5-6/8 KA965 . . . . **333.95**
Bugs. /PARKER, NW/1987/4-5/6 KC547 . . . . **595.7**
Bugwise: thirty incredible insect investigations and arachnid activities. /
 HICKMAN, PM/c1990, 1991/4-6/7 KC540 . . . . **595.7**
Building. /WILKINSON, P/1995/5-6/8 KD360 . . . . **690**
Building a house. /BARTON, B/1981/P-2/2 KD355 . . . . **690**
BUILDING PERSPECTIVE: STRATEGIES IN PROBLEM SOLVING
 (Microcomputer program). /1986/4-A/KA637 . . . . **MCP 153.7**
BUILDING THE FIRST TRANSCONTINENTAL RAILROAD (Picture). /n.d./
 5-6/KB138 . . . . **PIC 385**
Bull Run. /FLEISCHMAN, P/1993/5-A/5 KH116. . . . . **Fic**
Bull Run (Sound recording cassette)./FLEISCHMAN, P/1995/
 5-A/5 KH116 . . . . **Fic**
BULLETIN OF THE CENTER FOR CHILDREN'S BOOKS. /1947-/
 /KA099 . . . . **PER PROF 050**
Bully for you, Teddy Roosevelt! /FRITZ, J/1991/
 5-6/6 KE523 . . . . **B ROOSEVELT, T.**
Bully for you, Teddy Roosevelt (Sound recording cassette)./FRITZ, J/1993/
 5-6/6 KE523 . . . . **B ROOSEVELT, T.**
BULLY UP: FIGHTING FEELINGS (Videocassette). /c1990, 1991/
 K-3/KA807 . . . . **VCR 303.6**
Bunnicula: a rabbit-tale mystery. /HOWE, D/1979/3-6/5 KH285 . . . . **Fic**
Bunnicula: a rabbit-tale mystery (Braille)./HOWE, D/n.d./
 3-6/5 KH285 . . . . **Fic**
Bunnicula: a rabbit-tale mystery (Sound recording cassette). /HOWE, D/
 n.d./3-6/5 KH285 . . . . **Fic**
Bunny cakes. /WELLS, R/1997/P-1/2 KG696 . . . . **E**
Bunyans. /WOOD, A/1996/1-5/6 KG760 . . . . **E**
Buried treasures: a storyteller's journey (Compact disc)./BEN IZZY, J/1995/
 3-A/KB261 . . . . **SRC 398.2**
Buried treasures: a storyteller's journey (Sound recording cassette). /BEN
 IZZY, J/1995/3-A/KB261 . . . . **SRC 398.2**
Burning questions of Bingo Brown. /BYARS, BC/1990/5-A/5 KG958 . . **Fic**
Burnt stick. /HILL, A/1995/4-A/7 KH259 . . . . **Fic**
Burnt toast on Davenport Street. /EGAN, T/1997/1-3/2 KF514 . . . . . **E**
Burt Dow, deep-water man: a tale of the sea in the classic tradition. /
 MCCLOSKEY, R/c1963/P-A/6 KH468 . . . . **CE Fic**
Burt Dow, deep-water man: a tale of the sea in the classic tradition (Kit)./
 MCCLOSKEY, R/1990/P-A/6 KH468 . . . . **CE Fic**

Burt Dow, deep-water man: a tale of the sea in the classic tradition
 (Videocassette)./MCCLOSKEY, R/1990/P-A/6 KH468 . . . . . . **CE Fic**
Burton and Stanley. /O'ROURKE, F/1996/3-5/6 KH568 . . . . **Fic**
Burton and the giggle machine./HAAS, D/1992/4-6/5 KH207. . . . . . **Fic**
Burton's zoom zoom va-rooom machine. /HAAS, D/1996/
 4-6/5 KH207 . . . . **Fic**
Bus people. /ANDERSON, R/1995/6-A/6 KG850 . . . . **Fic**
Busy at day care head to toe. /DEMUTH, P/1996/P-K/2 KF460 . . . . . **E**
Busy Bea. /POYDAR, N/1994/P-1/2 KG285. . . . . **E**
Busy day at Mr. Kang's grocery store. /FLANAGAN, A/1996/
 1-3/2 KB126 . . . . **381**
Butter battle book. /SEUSS, D/1984/K-3/5 KG447 . . . . **E**
Butter battle book (Braille)./SEUSS, D/n.d./K-3/5 KG447 . . . . **E**
Butter battle book (Sound recording cassette)./SEUSS, D/n.d./
 K-3/5 KG447 . . . . **E**
Butterflies and moths. /PASCOE, E/1997/4-6/6 KC563 . . . . **595.78**
BUTTERFLIES (Videocassette). /1990/5-6/KC558 . . . . **VCR 595.78**
Butterfly alphabet. /SANDVED, KB/1996/3-6/6 KC567 . . . . . **595.78**
Butterfly and caterpillar. /WATTS, B/1985/2-4/4 KC568 . . . . . **595.78**
Butterfly and moth. /WHALLEY, P/1988/A/10 KC569 . . . . . . **595.78**
Butterfly jar. /MOSS, J/1989/2-6/KD991. . . . . **811**
Butterfly lion. /MORPURGO, M/1997/5-A/5 KH512 . . . . **Fic**
Buttons for General Washington. /ROOP, P/1986/4-6/4 KE885 . . . **973.3**
Buttons for General Washington (Braille)./ROOP, P/n.d./
 4-6/4 KE885 . . . . **973.3**
BUY ME THAT! A KID'S SURVIVAL GUIDE TO TV ADVERTISING
 (Videocassette). /1990/2-5/KD316 . . . . **VCR 659.14**
BUY ME THAT, TOO! (Videocassette)./1992/2-5/KD316 . . . **VCR 659.14**
BUY ME THAT 3!: A KID'S GUIDE TO FOOD ADVERTISING
 (Videocassette). /1993/2-5/KD316 . . . . **VCR 659.14**
Buzby. /HOBAN, J/1992/K-2/2 KF731 . . . . **CE E**
Buzby (Kit)./HOBAN, J/1996/K-2/2 KF731 . . . . **CE E**
Buzby to the rescue. /HOBAN, J/1995/K-2/2 KF732 . . . . **E**
By the dawn's early light. /ACKERMAN, K/1994/K-2/5 KF129 . . . . . . **E**
By the dawn's early light (Sound recording cassette)./ACKERMAN, K/
 1997/K-2/5 KF129 . . . . **E**
By the Great Horn Spoon! /FLEISCHMAN, S/c1963/4-6/4 KH119 . . . **Fic**
By the Great Horn Spoon! (Sound recording cassette)./FLEISCHMAN, S/
 n.d./4-6/4 KH119 . . . . **Fic**
By the light of the Halloween moon. /STUTSON, C/1993/
 1-3/3 KG582 . . . . **E**
By the shores of Silver Lake./WILDER, LI/1953/3-6/4 KH860 . . . . . . **Fic**
By the shores of Silver Lake (Braille)./WILDER, LI/n.d./3-6/4 KH860 . . . **Fic**
By the shores of Silver Lake (Sound recording cassette)./WILDER, LI/n.d./
 3-6/4 KH860 . . . . **Fic**
By the shores of Silver Lake (Talking book)./WILDER, LI/n.d./
 3-6/4 KH860 . . . . **Fic**
Caballo y su jinete./LEWIS, CS/1995/5-A/6 KH405 . . . . **CE Fic**
Caballos./CLUTTON-BROCK, J/1995/4-6/8 KD199 . . . . **636.1**
Cabbage and kings. /SEABROOK, E/1997/1-3/2 KG425 . . . . **E**
Cabin faced west. /FRITZ, J/c1958/4-6/6 KH143. . . . . **Fic**
Cabinetmakers. /FISHER, LE/1997/3-6/7 KD343 . . . . **684.1**
Cache of jewels and other collective nouns. /HELLER, R/c1987, 1989/
 P-3/KB846 . . . . **428.1**
Cactus. /LERNER, C/1992/5-6/7 KC429 . . . . **583**
Cada nino./Every child (Compact disc). /HINOJOSA, T/1996/
 2-6/KD568. . . . . **CD 789.2**
Cada nino./Every child (Sound recording cassette)./HINOJOSA, T/1995/
 2-6/KD568. . . . . **CD 789.2**
Caddie Woodlawn. New ed. /BRINK, CR/1973/4-6/6 KG922 . . . . **CE Fic**
Caddie Woodlawn (Talking book)./BRINK, CR/n.d./4-6/6 KG922 . **CE Fic**
Caitlin's Holiday. /GRIFFITH, HV/1990/4-6/4 KH204 . . . . **Fic**
Cake that Mack ate. /ROBART, R/1986/P-1/1 KG334 . . . . **E**
Cal Ripken, Jr. /CAMPBELL, J/1997/5-6/7 KE512 . . . . . . **B RIPKEN, C.**
Calamity Jane: her life and her legend. /FABER, D/1992/
 4-6/8 KE274 . . . . **B CALAMITY JANE**
CALCULATING CREW. School version. (CD-ROM). /1996/
 3-6/KB955 . . . . **CDR 513.2**
Calculator puzzles, tricks and games. /PALLAS, N/c1976, 1991/
 4-6/9 KB930 . . . . **510**
Calculator riddles. /ADLER, DA/1995/3-6/KD722 . . . . **793.735**
Calculators. /SMOOTHEY, M/1995/4-8/9 KB932 . . . . **510**
Caldecott and Co.: notes on books & pictures. /SENDAK, M/1988/
 /KA356 . . . . **PROF 809**
CALDECOTT VIDEO LIBRARY. VOL. I (Videocassette). /1992/
 P-3/KF328 . . . . **VCR E**
CALDECOTT VIDEO LIBRARY. VOL. II (Videocassette). /1992/
 P-3/KF329 . . . . **VCR E**
CALDECOTT VIDEO LIBRARY. VOL. III (Videocassette). /1992/
 P-3/KF330 . . . . **VCR E**
CALDECOTT VIDEO LIBRARY. VOL. IV (Videocassette). /1992/
 P-3/KB274 . . . . **VCR 398.2**
California. /PELTA, K/1994/4-6/7 KF085 . . . . **979.4**
California gold rush. /ITO, T/1997/5-6/11 KF080 . . . . **979.4**

CALIFORNIA GOLD RUSH (Picture). /n.d./5-6/KF078 . . . . . . **PIC 979.4**

CALIFORNIA GOLD RUSH: 1849 (Multimedia kit). /1991/
5-A/KF079. . . . . **MMK 979.4**

Call and response: rhythmic group singing (Sound recording cassette). /
JENKINS, E/1990/K-3/KD625. . . . . **SRC 789.3**

Call it courage. /SPERRY, A/c1940/5-6/6 KH743 . . . . **CE Fic**

Call it courage (Talking book). /SPERRY, A/n.d./5-6/6 KH743. . . . **CE Fic**

Call me Ahnighito. /CONRAD, P/1995/2-5/2 KF413 . . . . **E**

Call me Francis Tucket. /PAULSEN, G/1995/5-A/5 KH585 . . . . . . **Fic**

Call me Ruth. /SACHS, M/c1982, 1995/5-A/6 KH667 . . . . **Fic**

CALLIOPE: WORLD HISTORY FOR YOUNG PEOPLE. /1990-/
4-6/KA505 . . . . **PER 050**

Cam Jansen and the ghostly mystery. /ADLER, DA/1996/
2-4/2 KG815 . . . . **Fic**

Cam Jansen and the mystery at the haunted house. /ADLER, DA/1992/
2-4/3 KG817. . . . . **Fic**

Cam Jansen and the mystery at the monkey house. /ADLER, DA/1985/
2-4/3 KG817. . . . . **Fic**

Cam Jansen and the mystery of flight 54. /ADLER, DA/1989/
2-4/3 KG817. . . . . **Fic**

Cam Jansen and the mystery of the Babe Ruth baseball. /ADLER, DA/
1982/2-4/3 KG817 . . . . **Fic**

Cam Jansen and the mystery of the Babe Ruth baseball (Braille). /ADLER,
DA/n.d./2-4/3 KG817 . . . . **Fic**

Cam Jansen and the mystery of the carnival prize. /ADLER, DA/c1984,
1992/2-4/3 KG817 . . . . **Fic**

Cam Jansen and the mystery of the carnival prize (Braille). /ADLER, DA/
n.d./2-4/3 KG817 . . . . **Fic**

Cam Jansen and the mystery of the circus clown. /ADLER, DA/1983/
2-4/3 KG817. . . . . **Fic**

Cam Jansen and the mystery of the dinosaur bones. /ADLER, DA/1981/
2-4/4 KG816 . . . . **CE Fic**

Cam Jansen and the mystery of the dinosaur bones (Braille). /ADLER, DA/
n.d./2-4/4 KG816 . . . . **CE Fic**

Cam Jansen and the mystery of the dinosaur bones (Kit). /ADLER, DA/
1989/2-4/4 KG816 . . . . **CE Fic**

Cam Jansen and the mystery of the gold coins. /ADLER, DA/1982/
2-4/3 KG817. . . . . **Fic**

Cam Jansen and the mystery of the gold coins (Braille). /ADLER, DA/n.d./
2-4/3 KG817 . . . . **Fic**

Cam Jansen and the mystery of the monster movie. /ADLER, DA/1984/
2-4/3 KG817. . . . . **Fic**

Cam Jansen and the mystery of the monster movie (Braille). /ADLER, DA/
n.d./2-4/3 KG817 . . . . **Fic**

Cam Jansen and the mystery of the stolen diamonds. /ADLER, DA/1980/
2-4/3 KG817. . . . . **Fic**

Cam Jansen and the mystery of the stolen diamonds (Braille). /ADLER, DA/
n.d./2-4/3 KG817 . . . . **Fic**

Cam Jansen and the mystery of the television dog. /ADLER, DA/1981/
2-4/3 KG817. . . . . **Fic**

Cam Jansen and the mystery of the television dog (Braille). /ADLER, DA/
n.d./2-4/3 KG817 . . . . **Fic**

Cam Jansen and the mystery of the UFO. /ADLER, DA/1980/
2-4/3 KG817. . . . . **Fic**

Cam Jansen and the mystery of the UFO (Braille). /ADLER, DA/n.d./
2-4/3 KG817 . . . . **Fic**

Camel. /ARNOLD, C/1992/4-6/7 KC784 . . . . **599.63**

Camel caravan. /ROBERTS, B/1996/P-1/3 KG335 . . . . **E**

Camino de Amelia. /ALTMAN, LJ/1994/1-3/4 KF154 . . . . **E**

Camp Knock Knock. /DUFFEY, B/1996/1-3/2 KF500. . . . . **E**

Camping and survival. /EVANS, J/1992/4-A/6 KD825 . . . . **796.54**

Can a cherry pie wave goodbye? (Compact disc). /PALMER, H/1991/
P-K/KD641. . . . . **SRC 789.3**

Can a cherry pie wave goodbye?: songs for learning through music and
movement (Sound recording cassette). /PALMER, H/1991/
P-K/KD641. . . . . **SRC 789.3**

Can you dance, Dalila? /KROLL, VL/1996/K-2/5 KF932 . . . . **E**

Can you see me? /GREENWAY, S/1992/K-2/4 KC461 . . . . **591.4**

Canada. /SCHEMENAUER, E/1994/4-6/4 KE806 . . . . **971**

CANADA: PORTRAIT OF A NATION (Videocassette). /1991/
4-6/KE801. . . . . **VCR 971**

CANADA'S MAPLE TREE: THE STORY OF THE COUNTRY'S EMBLEM
(Videocassette). /1995/1-4/KE615 . . . . **VCR 929.9**

CANADIAN CHILDREN'S LITERATURE. /1975-//KA100 . **PER PROF 050**

Cancer. /YOUNT, L/1991/A/9 KD034 . . . . **616.99**

Cancion del coqui y otros cuentos de Puerto Rico. /MOHR, N/1995/
3-4/3 KB621. . . . . **398.24**

Candy witch. /KROLL, S/1979/K-1/6 KF927 . . . . **E**

Cannonball Simp. /BURNINGHAM, J/1994/K-2/4 KF314 . . . . **E**

Canopy crossing: a story of an Atlantic rainforest (Kit). /NAGDA, AW/
1997/2-A/4 KC873 . . . . **KIT 599.8**

Can't you make them behave, King George? /FRITZ, J/c1977/
5-6/7 KE365 . . . . **CE B GEORGE III**

Can't you make them behave, King George? (Talking book). /FRITZ, J/
1977/5-6/7 KE365 . . . . **CE B GEORGE III**

Can't you sleep, Little Bear? 2nd ed. /WADDELL, M/c1988, 1992/
P-K/3 KG674. . . . . **E**

Canto familiar. /SOTO, G/1995/4-6/KE028 . . . . **811**

Caps for sale: a tale of a peddler, some monkeys & their monkey business
(Big book). /SLOBODKINA, E/1996/P-2/1 KG519 . . . . **CE E**

Caps for sale: a tale of a peddler, some monkeys & their monkey business
(Kit). /SLOBODKINA, E/1987/P-2/1 KG519 . . . . **CE E**

Caps for sale: a tale of a peddler, some monkeys & their monkey business
(Videocassette). /SLOBODKINA, E/n.d./P-2/1 KG519 . . . . **CE E**

Caps for sale: a tale of a peddler, some monkeys and their monkey
business. /SLOBODKINA, E/c1947/P-2/1 KG519 . . . . **CE E**

Caps for sale: a tale of a peddler, some monkeys and their monkey
business (Kit). /SLOBODKINA, E/1995/P-2/1 KG519 . . . . **CE E**

Captain Abdul's pirate school. /MCNAUGHTON, C/1994/
1-3/3 KG113 . . . . **E**

Captain Cat: story and pictures. /HOFF, S/1993/K-2/2 KF752 . . . . **E**

CAPTAIN CONSERVATION: ALL ABOUT RECYCLING (Kit). /1992/
1-3/KB052. . . . . **KIT 363.72**

Captive. /O'DELL, S/1979/6-A/6 KH558 . . . . **Fic**

Captured by Indians: the life of Mary Jemison. /SEAVER, JE/1995/
5-A/8 KE405 . . . . **B JEMISON, M.**

Capyboppy. /PEET, B/c1966/1-3/8 KC746 . . . . **599.35**

Caravan. /MCKAY, JR., L/1995/3-5/6 KH480. . . . . **Fic**

Careers for computer buffs. /KAPLAN, A/1991/5-6/9 KA567. . . . . **004**

Careers for outdoor types. /KAPLAN, A/1991/4-A/8 KA952 . . . . . **333.7**

Careers for wordsmiths. /KAPLAN, A/1991/6-A/7 KA593 . . . . . . **070.4**

Careful what you wish for (Sound recording cassette). /BIRCH, C/1993/
2-6/KB264. . . . . **SRC 398.2**

Cargo machines and what they do. /RADFORD, D/1992/
P-2/4 KD089 . . . . **629.04**

Caribbean alphabet. /LESSAC, F/1994/1-3/KF962. . . . . **E**

Caribou. /HARRIS, L/1988/4-5/8 KC797 . . . . **599.65**

Carlos and the skunk. /Carlos y el zorrillo. /STEVENS, JR/1997/
1-3/3 KG554. . . . . **E**

CARNIVAL COUNTDOWN. School version (CD-ROM). /1996/
K-2/KB926. . . . . **CDR 510**

Carnivorous plants. /OVERBECK, C/1982/3-5/6 KC432. . . . . **583**

Carnivorous plants. /NIELSEN, NJ/1992/1-6/6 KC431 . . . . **583**

Carol for Christmas. /TOMPERT, A/1994/K-3/5 KG612 . . . . **E**

Carolina shout! /SCHROEDER, A/1995/1-5/3 KG411. . . . . **E**

CAROL'S MIRROR (Videocassette). /1991/4-6/KA854. . . . . . **VCR 305.8**

Carolyn's story: a book about an adopted girl. /SCHWARTZ, P/1996/
3-6/6 KB014 . . . . **362.73**

Carousel. /CREWS, D/1982/P-K/KF432 . . . . **E**

Carpentry for children. /WALKER, L/1985/4-6/8 KD342 . . . . **684**

Carrie's war. /BAWDEN, N/c1973/4-6/4 KG887 . . . . **Fic**

Carrot seed. /KRAUSS, R/c1945/P-2/2 KF920 . . . . **CE E**

Carrot seed (Big book). /KRAUSS, R/1978/P-2/2 KF920 . . . . . . **CE E**

Carrot seed (Kit). /KRAUSS, R/1990/P-2/2 KF920 . . . . **CE E**

Carry on, Mr. Bowditch. /LATHAM, JL/c1955/
5-A/3 KE260 . . . . **CE B BOWDITCH, N.**

Carry on, Mr. Bowditch (Talking book). /LATHAM, JL/1971/
5-A/3 KE260 . . . . **CE B BOWDITCH, N.**

Cars. /ROCKWELL, AF/1992/P/1 KD115 . . . . **629.222**

Cars. /ROYSTON, A/1991/P-2/2 KD116 . . . . **629.222**

Cars! cars! cars! /MACCARONE, G/1995/P-1/1 KG045 . . . . **E**

Cart and cwidder. /JONES, DW/c1977, 1995/6-A/6 KH331 . . . . . **Fic**

Carter G. Woodson: the father of black history. /MCKISSACK, P/1991/
3-6/2 KE601 . . . . **B WOODSON, C.**

Cartooning for kids. /LIGHTFOOT, M/1993/3-6/5 KD410 . . . . . . **741.5**

Cartoonist. /BYARS, BC/1978/4-6/3 KG959 . . . . **Fic**

Case of the cat's meow. /BONSALL, CN/1965/1-2/2 KF243 . . . . . **CE E**

Case of the double cross. /BONSALL, CN/1980/1-2/2 KF243 . . . . . **CE E**

Case of the dumb bells. /BONSALL, CN/1966/1-2/2 KF243 . . . . . **CE E**

Case of the hungry stranger. /BONSALL, CN/c1963/1-2/2 KF243. . **CE E**

Case of the hungry stranger (Kit). /BONSALL, CN/1985/
1-2/2 KF243 . . . . **CE E**

Case of the mummied pigs and other mysteries in nature. /QUINLAN, SE/
1995/4-A/7 KB911 . . . . **508**

Case of the scaredy cats. /BONSALL, CN/1971/1-2/2 KF243 . . . . . **CE E**

Case of the scaredy cats (Kit). /BONSALL, CN/1991/1-2/2 KF243. . **CE E**

Case of the two masked robbers. /HOBAN, L/1988/K-2/1 KF737 . . . . . **E**

Case of the weeping witch. /HILDICK, EW/1992/3-6/5 KH258 . . . . **Fic**

Case of the weeping witch (Sound recording cassette). /HILDICK, EW/
1997/3-6/5 KH258 . . . . **Fic**

Casey over there. /RABIN, S/1994/2-4/4 KG297 . . . . **E**

CASEY'S REVENGE: A STORY ABOUT FIGHTING AND
DISAGREEMENTS (Videocassette). /1991/3-5/KA808 . . . **VCR 303.6**

Caso del forastero hambriento. /BONSALL, CN/1996/1-2/2 KF243 . . **CE E**

Cassie's journey: going West in the 1860s. /HARVEY, B/1988/
1-3/5 KF677 . . . . **E**

Cassie's journey: going West in the 1860s (Sound recording cassette)./
HARVEY, B/n.d./1-3/5 KF677 . . . . E
Castle. /MACAULAY, D/1977/A/9 KD059 . . . . **CE 623**
Castle in the air. /JONES, DW/1991/6-A/7 KH332 . . . . **Fic**
Castle in the attic. /WINTHROP, E/1985/4-6/5 KH869 . . . . **CE Fic**
Castle in the attic (Talking book)./WINTHROP, E/1996/
4-6/5 KH869 . . . . **CE Fic**
Castle of Llyr./ALEXANDER, L/1989/6-A/6 KG833 . . . . **Fic**
Castle of Llyr (Sound recording cassette)./ALEXANDER, L/1993/
6-A/6 KG833. . . . . **Fic**
Castles. /STEELE, P/1995/4-6/7 KE650 . . . . **940.1**
Cat and Rat: the legend of the Chinese zodiac. /YOUNG, E/1995/
K-6/4 KA608 . . . . **133.5**
Cat and the cook and other fables of Krylov. /HEINS, E/1995/
3-5/6 KH234 . . . . **Fic**
Cat and the fiddle and more. /AYLESWORTH, J/1992/P-1/KD915 . . **811**
Cat came back: a traditional song. /SLAVIN, B/1992/
P-2/2 KD594 . . . . **789.2**
Cat in the hat. /SEUSS, D/c1957/P-2/1 KG448 . . . . **CE E**
CAT IN THE HAT BEGINNER BOOK DICTIONARY. /c1964, 1984/
1-2/KB833 . . . . **423**
Cat in the hat comes back./SEUSS, D/1958/P-2/1 KG448. . . . . . . **CE E**
Cat in the Hat gets grinched (Videocassette)./SEUSS, D/1982/
K-2/KG449 . . . . **VCR E**
Cat mummies. /TRUMBLE, K/1996/3-6/9 KE637 . . . . **932**
Cat of Artimus Pride. /HUTCHINS, HJ/1991/3-5/6 KH307. . . . . **Fic**
Cat running. /SNYDER, ZK/1994/5-A/7 KH730. . . . . **Fic**
Cat who went to heaven. New ed. /COATSWORTH, E/c1958/
A/6 KH010 . . . . **CE Fic**
Cat who went to heaven (Talking book)./COATSWORTH, E/n.d./
A/6 KH010 . . . . **CE Fic**
Cataloging nonbook resources: a how-to-do-it manual for librarians. /
FECKO, MB/1993//KA057 . . . . **PROF 025.3**
Cataloging of audiovisual materials and other special materials: a manual
based on AACR2. New 4th ed. /OLSON, NB/1998/
/KA060. . . . . **PROF 025.4**
Catalogue of color reproductions. /DETROIT INSTITUTE OF ARTS /n.d./
/KA307. . . . . **PROF 703**
Catalogue of color reproductions: books and catalogues, educational
materials. /NATIONAL GALLERY OF ART (U.S.) /n.d./
/KA308. . . . . **PROF 703**
Catch me if you can. /SOUZA, DM/1992/4-6/6 KC631 . . . . . . **597.95**
Catch the wind!: all about kites. /GIBBONS, G/1989/
1-3/4 KD108 . . . . **629.133**
Caterina, the clever farm girl: a tale from Italy. /PETERSON, J/1996/
2-4/3 KB357 . . . . **398.2**
Caterpillar and the polliwog. /KENT, J/1982/K-2/4 KF896. . . . . . **CE E**
Caterpillar and the polliwog (Videocassette). /KENT, J/n.d./
K-2/4 KF896. . . . . **CE E**
Cathedral: the story of its construction. /MACAULAY, D/c1973/
5-6/6 KD388 . . . . **726**
Cathedral (Videocassette). /MACAULAY, D/1986/6-A/KD389 . **VCR 726**
Catherine, called Birdy. /CUSHMAN, K/1994/6-A/6 KH050. . . . . **CE Fic**
Catherine, called Birdy (Sound recording cassette)./CUSHMAN, K/1997/
6-A/6 KH050 . . . . **CE Fic**
Catherine, called Birdy (Talking book)./CUSHMAN, K/1996/
6-A/6 KH050 . . . . **CE Fic**
Catkin. /BARBER, A/1996/4-6/6 KG878 . . . . **Fic**
Cats. /ROALF, P/1992/5-A/8 KD476 . . . . **758**
Cats. /GIBBONS, G/1996/K-3/3 KC821 . . . . **599.75**
Cat's body. /COLE, J/1982/4-6/6 KC818 . . . . **599.75**
Cats know best. /EISLER, C/1988/P-1/1 KD232 . . . . **636.8**
Cat's purr. /BRYAN, A/1985/K-3/2 KB543 . . . . **398.24**
Cats sleep anywhere. /FARJEON, E/1996/K-3/KE101 . . . . **821**
Causa: the migrant farmworkers' story. /DE RUIZ, DC/1993/
4-6/6 KA944 . . . . **331.88**
Cave. /KARR, K/1994/5-A/4 KH341 . . . . **Fic**
Caves: an underground wonderland. /WOOD, J/1991/
4-6/7 KC169 . . . . **551.4**
Caves and caverns. /GIBBONS, G/1993/K-6/6 KC166 . . . . **551.4**
Caves!: underground worlds. /BENDICK, J/1995/5-6/6 KC171 . . **551.44**
Cay. /TAYLOR, T/c1969/5-6/6 KH783 . . . . **Fic**
Cay (Braille). /TAYLOR, T/n.d./5-6/6 KH783 . . . . **Fic**
Cay (Sound recording cassette)./TAYLOR, T/1993/5-6/6 KH783. . . . **Fic**
Cay (Talking book)./TAYLOR, T/n.d./5-6/6 KH783. . . . . **Fic**
CBC FEATURES. /1945-//KA101 . . . . **PER PROF 050**
CDs, SUPER GLUE, AND SALSA: HOW EVERYDAY PRODUCTS ARE
MADE. /1995/5-A/KA452 . . . . **REF 670**
CDs, SUPER GULE, AND SALSA: HOW EVERYDAY PRODUCTS ARE
MADE. SERIES 2./1996/5-A/KA452 . . . . **REF 670**
Cecil's story. /LYON, GE/1991/K-3/2 KG042 . . . . E
CELEBRATE AMERICA IN POETRY AND ART. /1994/
3-6/KE054. . . . . **811.008**
Celebrate! in South Asia. /VIESTI, JF/1996/2-5/11 KB191 . . . . . . **394.2**

Celebrate! in Southeast Asia. /VIESTI, JF/1996/2-5/11 KB192 . . . . **394.2**
Celebrate the world: twenty tellable folktales for multicultural festivals. /
MACDONALD, MR/1994//KA270 . . . . **PROF 398.2**
Celebrating Hanukkah. /HOYT-GOLDSMITH, D/1996/
3-4/7 KA775 . . . . **296.4**
Celebrating Kwanzaa. /HOYT-GOLDSMITH, D/1993/
4-6/9 KB210 . . . . **394.261**
CELEBRATING WOMEN IN MATHEMATICS AND SCIENCE. /1996/
A/11 KA439 . . . . **REF 509**
Celebration! /THOMAS, JR/1997/1-3/3 KG604 . . . . E
Celebration: the story of American holidays. /PENNER, LR/1993/
4-6/7 KB201 . . . . **394.26**
Celebrations: read-aloud holiday and theme book programs. /BAUER, CF/
1985//KA342 . . . . **PROF 808.8**
Celery stalks at midnight./HOWE, D/1983/3-6/5 KH285 . . . . **Fic**
Celery stalks at midnight (Braille)./HOWE, D/n.d./3-6/5 KH285 . . . . **Fic**
Celery stalks at midnight (Sound recording cassette)./HOWE, D/n.d./
3-6/5 KH285 . . . . **Fic**
Celie and the harvest fiddler. /FLOURNOY, V/1995/2-4/6 KH130. . . . **Fic**
CELL DIVISION (Videocassette). /1995/5-6/KC274. . . . . . . **VCR 571.6**
Censorship and selection: issues and answers for schools. Rev. ed. /
REICHMAN, H/1993//KA053. . . . . **PROF 025.2**
Centerburg tales./MCCLOSKEY, R/1951/3-6/5 KH470 . . . . **CE Fic**
Centerburg tales (Braille). /MCCLOSKEY, R/n.d./3-6/5 KH470. . . . **CE Fic**
CENTRAL LOWLANDS (Videocassette)./1989/5-6/KE181 . . . . **VCR 917**
Cerdos a montones, cerdos a granel!/MCPHAIL, D/1996/P-2/2 KG122 . E
Cesar Chavez: labor leader. /CEDENO, ME/1993/
4-5/6 KE287 . . . . **B CHAVEZ, C.**
Chair for my mother. /WILLIAMS, VB/1982/P-3/3 KG734. . . . . E
Chair for my mother (Big book)./WILLIAMS, VB/1992/P-3/3 KG734. . . E
Chalk box kid. /BULLA, CR/1987/2-4/2 KG936. . . . . **Fic**
Chalk box kid (Sound recording cassette)./BULLA, CR/1993/
2-4/2 KG936 . . . . **Fic**
Chalk doll. /POMERANTZ, C/c1989, 1993/1-3/2 KG263 . . . . E
Challenge of technology: action strategies for the school library media
specialist. /WRIGHT, K/1993//KA080. . . . . **PROF 027.8**
CHALLENGE OF THE UNKNOWN (Videocassette). /1986/
5-A/KB935. . . . . **VCR 511**
Chameleons. /SCHNIEPER, C/1989/5-6/7 KC630. . . . . **597.95**
Chameleons (Sound recording cassette)./SCHNIEPER, C/1993/
5-6/7 KC630 . . . . **597.95**
Champion (French version)./CARRIER, R/1991/4-6/2 KG976 . . . . . **Fic**
Chance child. /PATON WALSH, J/c1978, 1991/6-A/7 KH582 . . . . . **Fic**
Chancy and the Grand Rascal. /FLEISCHMAN, S/c1966, 1997/
4-6/5 KH120 . . . . **Fic**
Chancy and the Grand Rascal (Sound recording cassette)./FLEISCHMAN,
S/n.d./4-6/5 KH120 . . . . **Fic**
CHANGE FOR THE BETTER: TEACHING CORRECT BEHAVIOR
(Videocassette). /1989//KA300. . . . . **VCR PROF 649**
Changes, changes. /HUTCHINS, P/c1971/P-1/KF795 . . . . **CE E**
Chang's paper pony. /COERR, E/1988/2-3/2 KF400 . . . . E
CHANUKAH AT HOME (Sound recording cassette). /1988/
K-6/KA771 . . . . **SRC 296.4**
Charles Darwin: naturalist. /ANDERSON, MJ/1994/
5-A/4 KE314 . . . . **B DARWIN, C.**
Charles Darwin: on the trail of evolution. /TWIST, C/1994/
5-8/8 KE315 . . . . **B DARWIN, C.**
Charles Dickens: the man who had great expectations. /STANLEY, D/
1993/5-6/7 KE321 . . . . **B DICKENS, C.**
Charlie needs a cloak. /DE PAOLA, T/1982/P-2/3 KD299 . . . . **CE 646.4**
Charlie needs a cloak (Braille). /DE PAOLA, T/n.d./
P-2/3 KD299 . . . . **CE 646.4**
Charlies needs a cloak (Videocassette)./DE PAOLA, T/n.d./
P-2/3 KD299 . . . . **CE 646.4**
Charlotte stories. /JAM, T/1994/2-3/2 KH321 . . . . **Fic**
Charlotte's web. /WHITE, EB/c1952/3-6/6 KH850 . . . . **Fic**
CHARLOTTE'S WEB: A WRITE ON! MULTI-MEDIA STUDY (Microcomputer
program). /1992/3-6/KB110 . . . . **MCP 372.6**
Charlotte's web (Braille)./WHITE, EB/n.d./3-6/6 KH850. . . . . **Fic**
Charlotte's web (Sound recording cassette)./WHITE, EB/n.d./
3-6/6 KH850 . . . . **Fic**
Charlotte's web (Talking book)./WHITE, EB/n.d./3-6/6 KH850 . . . . . **Fic**
Chase's calendar of annual events: special days, weeks and months. /
CHASE, WD/1958-//KA264 . . . . **PROF 394.2**
Chato y su cena./SOTO, G/1995/1-3/5 KG527 . . . . E
Chato's kitchen. /SOTO, G/c1995, 1997/1-3/5 KG527 . . . . E
Chato's kitchen (Sound recording cassette)./SOTO, G/1997/
1-3/5 KG527 . . . . E
Chattanooga sludge. /BANG, M/1996/4-6/7 KD081 . . . . **628.4**
Chatting. /HUGHES, S/1996/P-1/2 KF787 . . . . E
CHEATING, LYING AND STEALING (Videocassette). /1993/
5-6/KA669 . . . . **VCR 177**
Check it out!: the book about libraries. /GIBBONS, G/1985/
1-3/3 KA585 . . . . **CE 027**

Checking your grammar. /TERBAN, M/1993/5-A/KB856 . . . . **428.2**
Cheetah. /ARNOLD, C/1989/5-6/9 KC817. . . . . **599.75**
Cheetah: fast as lightning. /DUPONT, P/1992/1-4/5 KC819. . . . . **599.75**
Chef. /FLORIAN, D/1992/K-2/5 KD270. . . . . **641.5**
Chenille affamee./CARLE, E/1992/P-1/6 KF347 . . . . **E**
Cherokee summer. /HOYT-GOLDSMITH, D/1993/3-5/5 KE782. . **970.466**
Cherokees. /LANDAU, E/1992/4-6/7 KE760. . . . . **970.3**
Cherokees. /SNEVE, V/1996/4-6/5 KE769 . . . . **970.3**
Cherries and cherry pits. /WILLIAMS, VB/c1965, 1984/K-3/2 KG735 . . **E**
Cheshire cat and other eye-popping experiments on how we see the world. /DOHERTY, P/1995/4-A/5 KA612. . . . . **152.14**
Chess for children. /NOTTINGHAM, T/1993/4-A/8 KD756 . . . . . . **794.1**
Chester Cricket's new home. /SELDEN, G/1983/2-4/5 KH692 . . . . . . **Fic**
Chester Cricket's new home (Sound recording cassette)./SELDEN, G/n.d./ 2-4/5 KH692 . . . . **Fic**
Chester Cricket's pigeon ride. /SELDEN, G/1983/3-4/5 KH693. . . . . . **Fic**
Chester Cricket's pigeon ride (Sound recording cassette)./SELDEN, G/n.d./ 3-4/5 KH693 . . . . **Fic**
Chester's way. /HENKES, K/1988/K-2/5 KF702. . . . . **E**
Chester's way (Sound recording cassette)./HENKES, K/n.d./ K-2/5 KF702 . . . . **E**
Chewing gum book. /YOUNG, R/1989/5-6/6 KD322. . . . . **664**
CHEWING GUM (Videocassette). /1991/2-5/KD318 . . . . **VCR 664**
Cheyenne. /MYERS, A/1992/4-6/7 KE761 . . . . **970.3**
Cheyenne again. /BUNTING, E/1995/3-5/2 KG941 . . . . **Fic**
Cheyennes. /SNEVE, V/1996/4-6/6 KE770. . . . . **970.3**
Chick and the duckling. /SUTEEV, V/1972/P-1/1 KG585. . . . . **E**
CHICK EMBRYOLOGY (Videocassette). /c1974, 1986/ 5-A/KC693 . . . . **VCR 598.6**
Chick hatches. /COLE, J/1977/P-2/3 KC694. . . . . **598.6**
Chicka chicka boom boom. /MARTIN, JR., B/1989/P-1/2 KG073 . . . . . **E**
CHICKA CHICKA BOOM BOOM (CD-ROM). /1996/P-2/KF382 . . **CDR E**
Chicka chicka boom boom (Kit). /MARTIN, JR., B/1991/ P-1/KG074 . . . . **KIT E**
CHICKADEE: THE CANADIAN MAGAZINE FOR YOUNG CHILDREN. / 1979-/P-3/KA506 . . . . **PER 050**
Chicken and egg. /BACK, C/1986/K-3/2 KC692 . . . . **598.6**
Chicken Little. /KELLOGG, S/1985/K-3/5 KF889 . . . . **CE E**
Chicken Little. /HOBSON, S/1994/P-2/2 KF749 . . . . **E**
Chicken Little (Kit)./KELLOGG, S/1989/K-3/5 KF889 . . . . **CE E**
Chicken man. /EDWARDS, M/1991/K-2/2 KF509 . . . . **E**
Chicken soup, boots. /KALMAN, M/1993/P-K/3 KA941 . . . . **331.7**
Chicken soup with rice: a book of months. /SENDAK, M/c1962/ P-1/KG430 . . . . **CE E**
Chicken soup with rice: a book of months (Big book)./SENDAK, M/1992/ P-1/KG430 . . . . **CE E**
Chicken soup with rice: a book of months (Kit)./SENDAK, M/ P-1/KG430 . . . . **CE E**
Chicken soup with rice; a book of months (Videocassette)./SENDAK, M/ 1976/P-1/KG430 . . . . **CE E**
Chicken Sunday. /POLACCO, P/1992/1-3/2 KG251. . . . . **E**
Chickens aren't the only ones. /HELLER, R/1981/P-K/KC282. . . . . . **573.6**
Chico karateka./MORRIS, A/1996/2-4/5 KD832 . . . . **796.815**
Chi-hoon: a Korean girl. /MCMAHON, P/c1993, 1998/ 3-5/6 KE705 . . . . **951.95**
CHILD LIFE. /1921-/2-4/KA507 . . . . **PER 050**
Child of the owl. /YEP, L/c1977/A/6 KH891. . . . . **Fic**
Child of the owl (Sound recording cassette)./YEP, L/n.d./A/6 KH891 . . **Fic**
CHILDCRAFT: THE HOW AND WHY LIBRARY. /1964-/ P-2/KA378. . . . . **REF 031**
Children and books. 9th ed. /SUTHERLAND, Z/1997//KA358 . **PROF 809**
Children and painting. /TOPAL, CW/1992//KA217 . . . . . . **PROF 372.5**
Children and the AIDS virus: a book for children, parents, and teachers. / HAUSHERR, R/1989/2-4/7 KD029. . . . . **616.97**
Children as storytellers. /MALLAN, K/1992//KA341 . . . . . . **PROF 808.5**
Children from Australia to Zimbabwe: a photographic journey around the world. /AJMERA, M/1997/2-5/7 KA822 . . . . **305.23**
Children just like me. /KINDERSLEY, B/1995/2-6/8 KA825. . . . . . **305.23**
Children learning to read: a guide for parents and teachers. /ITZKOFF, SW/1996//KA209 . . . . **PROF 372.4**
Children of Bolivia. /HERMES, J/1996/4-6/10 KF108 . . . . **984**
Children of Christmas: stories for the season. /RYLANT, C/c1987, 1993/ 4-6/6 KH660 . . . . **Fic**
Children of clay: a family of Pueblo potters. /SWENTZELL, R/1992/ 4-6/6 KE795 . . . . **970.489**
Children of Cuba. /STAUB, FJ/1996/4-6/8 KE846 . . . . **972.91**
Children of Green Knowe. /BOSTON, LM/c1955, 1983/ 4-A/6 KG919. . . . . **Fic**
Children of Green Knowe (Braille)./BOSTON, LM/n.d./4-A/6 KG919. . **Fic**
Children of Green Knowe (Sound recording cassette)./BOSTON, LM/n.d./ 4-A/6 KG919. . . . . **Fic**
Children of India. /HERMES, J/1993/4-6/6 KE711. . . . . **954**
Children of Mauritania: days in the desert and by the river shore. / GOODSMITH, L/1993/4-6/6 KE733 . . . . **966.1**
Children of Micronesia. /HERMES, J/1994/4-6/9 KF122 . . . . **996.5**
Children of Morocco. /HERMES, J/1995/3-6/7 KE730 . . . . **964**
CHILDREN OF PROMISE: AFRICAN-AMERICAN LITERATURE AND ART FOR YOUNG PEOPLE. /1991/3-A/7 KD896 . . . . **810.8**
Children of the Dust Bowl: the true story of the school at Weedpatch Camp. /STANLEY, J/1992/5-A/7 KA835 . . . . **305.5**
Children of the Ecuadorean Highlands. /BEIRNE, B/1996/ 3-6/9 KF112 . . . . **986.6**
Children of the Morning Light: Wampanoag tales. /MEDICINE STORY / 1994/4-5/7 KB348 . . . . **398.2**
Children of the Philippines. /KINKADE, S/1996/3-6/8 KE722 . . . . . **959.9**
Children of the Sierra Madre. /STAUB, FJ/1996/4-6/8 KE839 . . . . . **972**
Children of the westward trail. /STEFOFF, R/1996/4-6/8 KF050 . . . . **978**
Children of the wild west. /FREEDMAN, R/1983/4-6/8 KA824 . . . **305.23**
Children of the wild west (Sound recording cassette)./FREEDMAN, R/n.d./ 4-6/8 KA824 . . . . **305.23**
Children of the wolf. /YOLEN, J/c1984, 1993/6-A/7 KH896 . . . . **Fic**
Children of Topaz: the story of a Japanese-American internment camp: based on a classroom diary. /TUNNELL, MO/1996/ 5-6/8 KE667 . . . . **940.53**
Children of Yucatan. /STAUB, FJ/1996/4-6/7 KE840 . . . . **972**
Children talking about books. /BORDERS, SG/1993/ /KA236. . . . . **PROF 372.64**
Children's all-time Mother Goose favorites (Sound recording cassette). / GLASS, H/1989//KA275 . . . . **SRC PROF 398.8**
Children's animal atlas: how animals have evolved, where they live today, why so many are in danger. /LAMBERT, D/1992/5-6/8 KC496 . **591.9**
Children's atlas of the human body: actual size bones, muscles, and organs in full color. /WALKER, R/1994/5-6/6 KC908 . . . . **611**
CHILDREN'S AUTHORS AND ILLUSTRATORS: AN INDEX TO BIOGRAPHICAL DICTIONARIES. /1976-//KA033 . . . . **PROF 016.809**
CHILDREN'S BOOK OF VIRTUES. /1995/K-3/KD871 . . . . **808.8**
CHILDREN'S BRITANNICA. 4th ed., (1995 revision). /1995/ 3-5/KA379 . . . . **REF 031**
CHILDREN'S CATALOG. 17th ed. /1996//KA012 . . . . . . **PROF 011.62**
Children's Homer: The Adventures of Odysseus and Tale of Troy. /COLUM, P/1982/A/6 KE123. . . . . **883**
Children's Homer: The Adventures of Odysseus and Tale of Troy (Braille)./ COLUM, P/n.d./A/6 KE123 . . . . **883**
Children's illustrated Bible. /HASTINGS, S/1994/4-6/5 KA676 . . . . . **220**
Children's jukebox: a subject guide to musical recordings and programming ideas for songsters ages one to twelve. /REID, R/1995/ /KA029. . . . . **PROF 016.7893**
Children's literature awards and winners: a directory of prizes, authors, and illustrators. 3rd ed. /JONES, DB/1994//KA354 . . . . **PROF 809**
CHILDREN'S LITERATURE IN THE CLASSROOM: WEAVING CHARLOTTE'S WEB. /1989//KA238 . . . . **PROF 372.64**
Children's machine: rethinking school in the age of the computer. /PAPERT, S/1993//KA180. . . . . **PROF 371.3**
CHILDREN'S MAGAZINE GUIDE: SUBJECT INDEX TO CHILDREN'S MAGAZINES. /1948-/3-A/KA508 . . . . **PER 050**
CHILDREN'S PLAYMATE. /1929-/1-3/KA509 . . . . **PER 050**
Children's songs. /SILVERMAN, J/1993/5-A/KD591. . . . . **789.2**
Children's songs around the world (Compact disc)./SLONECKI, C/1989/ K-3/KD595 . . . . **SRC 789.2**
Children's songs around the world (Sound recording cassette). /SLONECKI, C/1989/K-3/KD595. . . . . **SRC 789.2**
Children's traditional games: games from 137 countries and cultures. / SIERRA, J/1995//KA331 . . . . **PROF 796**
Children's zoo. /HOBAN, T/1985/P-K/KC448 . . . . **591**
Child's Alaska. /MURPHY, CR/1994/3-5/8 KF101 . . . . **979.8**
Child's book of art: great pictures, first words. /MICKLETHWAIT, L/1993/ P-1/KD366. . . . . **701**
Child's book of wildflowers. /KELLY, MA/1992/3-5/5 KC405 . . . . **582.13**
CHILD'S CELEBRATION OF SHOWTUNES (Compact disc)./1992/ P-3/KD529. . . . . **SRC 782.1**
CHILD'S CELEBRATION OF SHOWTUNES (Sound recording cassette). / 1992/P-3/KD529 . . . . **SRC 782.1**
CHILD'S CELEBRATION OF SONG (Compact disc)./1992/ P-3/KD608. . . . . **SRC 789.3**
CHILD'S CELEBRATION OF SONG (Sound recording cassette). /1992/ P-3/KD608. . . . . **SRC 789.3**
Child's Christmas in Wales. /THOMAS, D/1985/P-A/8 KE119 . . . . . **828**
Child's Christmas in Wales (Sound recording cassette)./THOMAS, D/n.d./ P-A/8 KE119 . . . . **828**
Child's garden of verses. /STEVENSON, RL/1905/P-2/KE110. . . . . . **821**
CHILD'S GARDEN OF VERSES AND A POTPOURRI OF POETRY: AN INTRODUCTION TO GREAT POETS (Sound recording cassette). /n.d./ 2-6/KE098 . . . . **SRC 821**
Child's garden of verses (Braille)./STEVENSON, RL/n.d./P-2/KE110. . **821**
Child's garden of verses (Talking book)./STEVENSON, RL/n.d./ P-2/KE110. . . . . **821**
Child's good night book. /BROWN, MW/c1943, 1992/P/2 KF284 . . . . **E**
CHILD'S SEASONAL TREASURY. /1996//KA193. . . . . . . **PROF 372.13**

Child's world of lullabies: multicultural songs for quiet times (Sound recording cassette). /PALMER, H/1993/P-2/KD642 . . . . . **SRC 789.3**
Child's world of lullabies: multicultural songs for quiet times (Compact disc)./PALMER, H/1993/P-2/KD642 . . . . **SRC 789.3**
Chile fever: a celebration of peppers. /KING, E/1995/ 5-6/6 KD267 . . . . **641.3**
Ch'i-lin purse: a collection of ancient Chinese stories. /FANG, L/1995/ 4-6/5 KB295 . . . . **398.2**
Chills run down my spine. /VIVELO, J/1994/5-A/4 KH830. . . . . **Fic**
Chimpanzee family book. /GOODALL, J/1997/4-6/6 KC878 . . . **599.885**
China homecoming. /FRITZ, J/1985/4-6/7 KE703. . . . . **951.05**
China homecoming (Sound recording cassette)./FRITZ, J/n.d./ 4-6/7 KE703 . . . . **951.05**
China's bravest girl: the legend of Hua Mu Lan = [Chin kuo ying hsiung Hua Mu-lan]. /CHIN, C/1993/3-5/4 KB430 . . . . **398.22**
China's long march: 6,000 miles of danger. /FRITZ, J/1988/ A/6 KE702 . . . . **951.04**
Chinatown. /LOW, W/1997/K-2/3 KG037 . . . . **E**
CHINESE MOTHER GOOSE RHYMES. /c1968, 1989/P-3/KB794 . . **398.8**
Chinese-American experience. /WU, DY/1993/5-6/8 KA864. . . . . . **305.8**
CHIPMUNK (Videocassette). /1988/3-6/KC750 . . . . **VCR 599.36**
Chita's Christmas tree. /HOWARD, EF/1989/2-4/5 KF773 . . . . **E**
Chitty Chitty Bang Bang: the magical car. /FLEMING, I/c1964, 1989/ 5-6/7 KH128 . . . . **Fic**
Chloe in the know./CASELEY, J/1993/3-5/4 KG985. . . . . **Fic**
Chocolate cow. /OBLIGADO, L/1993/K-2/2 KG185. . . . . **E**
CHOOSE TO REFUSE: SAYING NO AND KEEPING YOUR FRIENDS (Videocassette). /1993/3-5/KA654. . . . . **VCR 158**
Chop, simmer, season. /BRANDENBERG, A/1997/P-1/2 KF257 . . . . . . **E**
Chris Webber: star forward. /KNAPP, R/1997/ 5-6/7 KE590 . . . . **B WEBBER, C.**
Christina Katerina and the time she quit the family. /GAUCH, PL/1987/ K-2/6 KF600 . . . . **E**
Christmas around the world. /LANKFORD, MD/1995/ 3-6/7 KB237 . . . . **394.266**
Christmas Carol in prose, being a ghost story of Christmas. /DICKENS, C/ 1983/4-6/5 KH074 . . . . **CE Fic**
Christmas Carol in prose, being a ghost story of Christmas (Braille)./ DICKENS, C/n.d./4-6/5 KH074 . . . . **CE Fic**
Christmas carp. /TORNQVIST, R/1990/2-4/2 KH798 . . . . **Fic**
Christmas celebration: traditions and customs from around the world. / KENNEDY, P/1992/4-6/7 KB236 . . . . **394.266**
CHRISTMAS GIF': AN ANTHOLOGY OF CHRISTMAS POEMS, SONGS, AND STORIES WRITTEN BY AND ABOUT AFRICAN-AMERICANS. / 1993/4-6/KD897 . . . . **810.8**
CHRISTMAS IN CANADA. /1994/4-6/10 KB232. . . . . **394.266**
CHRISTMAS IN COLONIAL AND EARLY AMERICA. /c1996/ 4-6/8 KB233 . . . . **394.266**
Christmas in the barn. /BROWN, MW/c1952/P-K/KA700 . . . . . . **232.92**
Christmas in the barn (Sound recording cassette)./BROWN, MW/n.d./ P-K/KA700 . . . . **232.92**
Christmas in the big house, Christmas in the quarters. /MCKISSACK, P/ 1994/4-A/6 KE967 . . . . **975**
Christmas in the big house, Christmas in the quarters./MCKISSACK, P/ 1997/4-A/6 KE967 . . . . **975**
Christmas is a time of giving. /ANGLUND, JW/c1961/ P-2/KB230. . . . . **394.266**
Christmas kitten. /PACKARD, M/1994/K-1/1 KG204 . . . . **E**
Christmas Knight. /CURRY, JL/1993/2-5/3 KB435 . . . . **398.22**
Christmas memory. /CAPOTE, T/c1956, 1989/4-A/6 KG971 . . . . **CE Fic**
Christmas menorahs: how a town fought hate. /COHN, J/1995/ 3-6/5 KA818 . . . . **305**
Christmas miracle of Jonathan Toomey. /WOJCIECHOWSKI, S/1995/ 4-6/5 KH876 . . . . **Fic**
Christmas of the reddle moon. /LEWIS, JP/1994/1-3/4 KF975 . . . . **E**
Christmas songs. /SILVERMAN, J/1993/5-A/KD536 . . . . **782.28**
Christmas spirit: two stories. /WESTALL, R/1994/6-A/6 KH847. . . . . . **Fic**
CHRISTMAS STORY. /1996/2-3/4 KA701 . . . . **232.92**
Christmas surprise for Chabelita. /PALACIOS, A/1993/1-3/2 KG206 . . . **E**
Christmas time./STOCK, C/P-K/2 KG574 . . . . **E**
Christmas Witch: an Italian legend. /OPPENHEIM, J/1993/ 1-3/2 KB507 . . . . **398.23**
Christopher Columbus: great explorer. /ADLER, DA/1991/ 4-5/4 KE301 . . . . **B COLUMBUS, C.**
Christopher Columbus: how he did it. /YUE, C/1992/ 5-A/7 KE744 . . . . **970.01**
Christopher Columbus: navigator to the New World. /ASIMOV, I/1991/ 4-5/5 KE302 . . . . **B COLUMBUS, C.**
Christopher: the holy giant. /DE PAOLA, T/1994/2-3/4 KB438 . . . **398.22**
Chronicles of Narnia super-sound book (Talking book)./LEWIS, CS/1993/ 5-A/6 KH405 . . . . **CE Fic**
Chronology of African-American history: significant events and people from 1619 to the present. 2nd ed. /HORNSBY, JR., A/1997/ /KA490. . . . . **REF 973**
Chrysanthemum. /HENKES, K/1991/K-2/2 KF703. . . . . **E**
Chrysanthemum (Sound recording cassette)./HENKES, K/1995/ K-2/2 KF703 . . . . **E**
Chuck and Danielle. /DICKINSON, P/1996/4-6/7 KH076 . . . . **Fic**
CICADAS: THE 17-YEAR INVASION (Videocassette). /1993/ 4-6/KC535. . . . . **VCR 595.7**
Cinderella. /SAN JOSE, C/1994/2-4/6 KB364 . . . . **398.2**
Cinderella, or the little glass slipper. /PERRAULT, C/1954/ 1-3/7 KB762 . . . . **398.27**
Cinderella, or the little glass slipper (Braille)./PERRAULT, C/n.d./ 1-3/7 KB762 . . . . **398.27**
Cinnamon, mint, and mothballs: a visit to Grandmother's house. /TILLER, R/ 1993/K-3/KE033. . . . . **811**
Circles, triangles, and squares. /HOBAN, T/1974/P-1/KB990 . . . . . . **516**
Circus. /ROALF, P/1993/5-A/8 KD477 . . . . **758**
Circus baby. /PETERSHAM, M/c1950/P-2/3 KG235. . . . . **CE E**
Circus baby (Videocassette)./PETERSHAM, M/1965/P-2/3 KG235 . **CE E**
Circus of the wolves. /BUSHNELL, J/1994/4-6/5 KG952 . . . . **Fic**
Cities in the sand: the ancient civilizations of the Southwest. /WARREN, S/ 1992/5-6/8 KF064 . . . . **979**
City by the bay: a magical journey around San Francisco. /BROWN, T/ 1993/1-5/7 KE207 . . . . **917.94**
City green. /DISALVO-RYAN, D/1994/1-3/3 KF484. . . . . **E**
City of dragons. /YEP, L/1995/1-3/5 KG775 . . . . **E**
City of gold and lead./CHRISTOPHER, J/1989/4-6/6 KG991. . . . . . . **Fic**
City of gold and lead (Talking book)./CHRISTOPHER, J/n.d./ 4-6/6 KG991 . . . . **Fic**
City of light, city of dark: a comic-book novel. /AVI /1993/ 4-6/6 KD409 . . . . **741.5**
City of the gods: Mexico's ancient city of Teotihuacan. /ARNOLD, C/ 1994/5-6/7 KE828 . . . . **972**
City seen from A to Z. /ISADORA, R/1983/P-1/KF814. . . . . **E**
City street. /FLORIAN, D/1990/P-1/KA893 . . . . **307.3**
City trains: moving through America's cities by rail. /YEPSEN, R/1993/ 5-6/7 KB162 . . . . **388.4**
City under the sea: life in a coral reef. /WU, N/1996/ 4-6/8 KC354 . . . . **577.7**
City! Washington, D.C. /CLIMO, S/1991/4-6/7 KE193 . . . . **917.53**
Ciudades de hormigas./DORROS, A/1995/1-4/4 KC571 . . . . **595.79**
CIVIL WAR: THE FIERY TRIAL (Videocassette). /1988/ 5-A/KE901. . . . . **VCR 973.7**
Clambake: a Wampanoag tradition. /PETERS, RM/1992/ 4-6/5 KE780 . . . . **970.444**
Clap your hands. /CAULEY, LB/1992/P-K/2 KF373. . . . . **E**
Clara and the bookwagon. /LEVINSON, NS/1988/1-3/1 KF967. . . . . . **E**
Clara and the hoodoo man. /PARTRIDGE, E/1996/5-A/3 KH572 . . . . **Fic**
Clara Barton. /SONNEBORN, L/1992/4-6/6 KE250. . . . **B BARTON, C.**
Class clown. /HURWITZ, J/1987/2-4/4 KH298 . . . . **Fic**
Class president./HURWITZ, J/1990/2-4/4 KH298. . . . . **Fic**
Class president (Sound recording cassette)./HURWITZ, J/1994/ 2-4/4 KH298 . . . . **Fic**
Classic children's tales (Compact disc)./TORRENCE, J/1989/ P-1/KB667. . . . . **SRC 398.24**
Classic children's tales (Sound recording cassette). /TORRENCE, J/1989/ P-1/KB667. . . . . **SRC 398.24**
Classroom at the end of the hall. /EVANS, D/1996/3-5/4 KH104. . . . **Fic**
CLASSROOM CONNECT. /1994-//KA102. . . . . **PER PROF 050**
Classroom newspaper workshop (CD-ROM). /OWENS, P/1995/ 4-A/KA594 . . . . **CDR 070.4**
Classroom pet. /MACCARONE, G/1995/K-1/2 KG046. . . . . **E**
CLASSROOM STOREWORKS (Microcomputer program). /1997/ 2-5/KD313. . . . . **MCP 658**
Classroom success for the LD and ADHD child. /STEVENS, SH/1997/ /KA186. . . . . **PROF 371.92**
Claude Debussy. /THOMPSON, W/1993/6-A/9 KE316 . **B DEBUSSY, C.**
Claude Monet. /HARRISON, P/1996/4-6/7 KE466 . . . . . **B MONET, C.**
Clay. /DIXON, A/1990/K-5/4 KC230 . . . . **553.6**
Cleopatra. /STANLEY, D/1994/4-6/6 KE295 . . . . **B CLEOPATRA**
Click!: a book about cameras and taking pictures. /GIBBONS, G/1997/ 2-4/5 KD512 . . . . **771**
Clifford at the circus./BRIDWELL, N/1985/P-2/1 KF264. . . . . **CE E**
Clifford at the circus (Kit)./BRIDWELL, N/1987/P-2/1 KF264 . . . . . **CE E**
Clifford el grand perro colorado./BRIDWELL, N/1988/P-2/1 KF264. **CE E**
Clifford gets a job./BRIDWELL, N/1985/P-2/1 KF264. . . . . **CE E**
Clifford takes a trip./BRIDWELL, N/1985/P-2/1 KF264 . . . . **CE E**
Clifford the big red dog. /BRIDWELL, N/c1963, 1985/P-2/1 KF264. **CE E**
Clifford the small red puppy./BRIDWELL, N/1985/P-2/1 KF264. . . . **CE E**
Clifford va de viaje./BRIDWELL, N/1995/P-2/1 KF264 . . . . **CE E**
Clifford, we love you./BRIDWELL, N/1991/P-2/1 KF264 . . . . **CE E**
Clifford's good deeds./BRIDWELL, N/1985/P-2/1 KF264. . . . . **CE E**
Clifford's Halloween./BRIDWELL, N/1986/P-2/1 KF264. . . . . **CE E**
Clifford's sports day./BRIDWELL, N/1996/P-2/1 KF264. . . . . **CE E**
Cloak for the dreamer. /FRIEDMAN, A/1995/1-3/6 KF585 . . . . **E**
Cloudy with a chance of meatballs. /BARRETT, J/1978/P-2/7 KF203 . . . **E**

Clover County carrot contest./HIMMELMAN, J/1991/1-3/1 KF729 . . . . **E**
Clown games. /ZIEFERT, H/1993/P-1/1 KG791. . . . . **E**
Clown of God. /DE PAOLA, T/1978/K-3/6 KF467. . . . . **CE E**
Clown of God (Videocassette)./DE PAOLA, T/n.d./K-3/6 KF467. . . **CE E**
Coaching Ms. Parker. /HEYMSFELD, C/1992/2-4/4 KH255 . . . . **Fic**
Coast to coast with Alice. /HYATT, PR/1995/4-6/5 KH312 . . . . . . **Fic**
COBBLESTONE: THE HISTORY MAGAZINE FOR YOUNG PEOPLE. /
1978-/5-6/KA510 . . . . **PER 050**
Cobweb Christmas. /CLIMO, S/1982/K-2/5 KF397 . . . . **E**
Cobweb Christmas (Braille)./CLIMO, S/n.d./K-2/5 KF397 . . . . . . **E**
Cocina de noche./SENDAK, M/1997/K-3/3 KG432 . . . . . . **CE E**
Cocina de noche (Videocassette)./SENDAK, M/1993/K-3/3 KG432. . **CE E**
Cocodrilo enorme./DAHL, R/n.d./1-3/4 KF444 . . . . **E**
Code talkers: American Indians in World War II. /DAILY, R/1995/
4-6/9 KE669 . . . . **940.54**
Codes, ciphers and secret writing. /GARDNER, M/c1972, 1984/
5-6/8 KD308 . . . . **652**
Cold Shoulder Road. /AIKEN, J/1995/5-A/5 KG823 . . . . **Fic**
Cold Shoulder Road (Sound recording cassette)./AIKEN, J/1997/
5-A/5 KG823 . . . . **Fic**
Coldest winter. /LUTZEIER, E/1991/6-A/7 KH429 . . . . **Fic**
Colin Powell: straight to the top. Updated ed. /BLUE, R/1997/
3-6/7 KE502 . . . . **B POWELL, C.**
Collecting baseball cards. /OWENS, TS/1993/4-A/7 KD505 . . . . . **769**
Collection program in schools: concepts, practices, and information sources.
2nd ed. /VAN ORDEN, P/1995/KA054. . . . . **PROF 025.2**
Colombia: the gateway to South America. /MARKHAM, L/1997/
4-6/5 KF111 . . . . **986.1**
Colonial American craftspeople. /STEVENS, BS/1993/5-6/8 KD339. . **680**
Colonial crafts. /KALMAN, B/1992/4-5/6 KD338. . . . . **680**
COLONIZATION (Microcomputer program). /1986/
5-A/KA667 . . . . **MCP 172**
Color box. /DODDS, DA/1992/P-K/1 KF486 . . . . **E**
Color dance. /JONAS, A/1989/P-1/1 KF844 . . . . **E**
Color farm. /EHLERT, L/1990/P-K/KF515 . . . . **E**
COLOR: LIGHT FANTASTIC (Videocassette). /1988/
3-6/KC119. . . . . **VCR 535.6**
Color of his own. /LIONNI, L/c1975, 1997/K-2/5 KF990 . . . . **E**
Color sampler. /WESTRAY, K/1993/1-6/5 KC125 . . . . **535.6**
Color zoo. /EHLERT, L/1989/P-1/2 KF516 . . . . **E**
Colorado. /FRADIN, DB/1993/3-6/3 KF061 . . . . **978.8**
Colorado. /BLEDSOE, S/1993/4-6/7 KF060 . . . . **978.8**
Colors. /GOLDSEN, L/1991/K-3/2 KC121 . . . . **535.6**
Colors everywhere. /HOBAN, T/1995/P-1/KC122 . . . . **535.6**
Come a tide. /LYON, GE/1990/K-3/2 KG043. . . . . **E**
Come away from the water, Shirley. /BURNINGHAM, J/c1977/
P-2/2 KF315 . . . . **CE E**
Come back, Amelia Bedelia. Newly illustrated ed. /PARISH, P/1995/
K-2/1 KG213 . . . . **E**
Come back, salmon: how a group of dedicated kids adopted Pigeon Creek
and brought it back to life. /CONE, M/1992/4-6/6 KD248. . . . **639.3**
Come back, salmon: how a group of dedicated kids adopted Pigeon Creek
and brought it back to life (Sound recording cassette)./CONE, M/
1995/4-6/6 KD248. . . . . **639.3**
Come dance by the ocean (Compact disc)./JENKINS, E/1991/
P-2/KD626. . . . . **SRC 789.3**
Come dance by the ocean (Sound recording cassette). /JENKINS, E/1991/
P-2/KD626. . . . . **SRC 789.3**
Come look with me: discovering photographs with children. /TUCKER, JS/
1994/K-6/5 KD511 . . . . **770**
Come look with me: world of play. /BLIZZARD, GS/1993/
3-6/5 KD369 . . . . **701.1**
Come morning. /GUCCIONE, LD/1995/4-6/3 KH205 . . . . **Fic**
Come on everybody! Let's go to the fair (Kit). /TURNER, M/1991/
P/KB182 . . . . **KIT 394**
Come on out and play (Sound recording cassette)./HARLEY, B/1990/
1-3/KF671 . . . . **SRC E**
Come out and play, little mouse. /KRAUS, R/1986/P-1/1 KF919 . . **CE E**
Come out, muskrats. /ARNOSKY, J/1989/P-K/2 KC742 . . . . . **599.35**
Come sign with us: sign language activities for children. 2nd. ed. /HAFER,
JC/1996/KA279 . . . . **PROF 419**
Come sing, Jimmy Jo. /PATERSON, K/1985/5-A/4 KH574 . . . . . . **Fic**
Come sing, Jimmy Jo (Sound recording cassette)./PATERSON, K/n.d./
5-A/4 KH574 . . . . **Fic**
COME SIT BY ME: AIDS EDUCATION (Videocassette). /1992/
K-2/KD025 . . . . **VCR 616.97**
Come walk with me (Videocassette). /STOLTZ, WJ/1994/
P-3/KC309 . . . . **VCR 577.3**
Comeback!: four true stories. /O'CONNOR, J/1992/2-4/3 KD765 . . **796**
Comet in Moominland./JANSSON, T/c1946, 1992/3-6/7 KH325 . . . . **Fic**
Comet in Moominland (Sound recording cassette)./JANSSON, T/1997/
3-6/7 KH325 . . . . **Fic**
Comets, meteors, and asteroids. /SIMON, S/1994/4-6/7 KC043. . . **523.6**

Comic adventures of Old Mother Hubbard and her dog. /MARTIN, SC/
1981/P-2/KB802. . . . . **398.8**
Coming home: from the life of Langston Hughes. /COOPER, F/1994/
3-5/6 KE394 . . . . **B HUGHES, L.**
Coming to America: the story of immigration. /MAESTRO, B/1996/
1-3/8 KA921 . . . . **325**
Commodore Perry in the land of the Shogun. /BLUMBERG, R/1985/
5-A/7 KE706 . . . . **CE 952**
Commodore Perry in the land of the Shogun (Braille)./BLUMBERG, R/n.d./
5-A/7 KE706 . . . . **CE 952**
Commodore Perry in the land of the Shogun (Sound recording cassette)./
BLUMBERG, R/n.d./5-A/7 KE706 . . . . **CE 952**
Common cold and influenza. /STEDMAN, N/1986/A/10 KD016. . . **616.2**
COMMON GOAL: AN INTRODUCTION TO THE UN (Videocassette). /
1996/5-A/KA968 . . . . **VCR 341.23**
Commonsense copyright: a guide to the new technologies. /TALAB, RS/
1986/KA169 . . . . **PROF 346.73**
COMMUNICABLE DISEASES (Videocassette). /1992/
5-6/KD022. . . . . **VCR 616.9**
Communication. /ALIKI /1993/K-6/4 KA794 . . . . **302.2**
Communication. /GAN, G/1997/5-6/9 KA795 . . . . **302.2**
COMMUNICATIONS (Videocassette). /1992/2-4/KA799 . . . . . **VCR 302.2**
Como crece una semilla./JORDAN, HJ/1996/P-2/1 KC387 . . . . . . **580**
Como sabes que es otono?/FOWLER, A/1992/P-2/2 KB917 . . . . **508.2**
Como sabes que es otono? (Big book)./FOWLER, A/1992/
P-2/2 KB917 . . . . **508.2**
Como sabes que es primavera?/FOWLER, A/1994/P-2/2 KB917 . . **508.2**
Como sabes que es verano?/FOWLER, A/1992/P-2/2 KB917 . . . . **508.2**
Como sabes que es verano? (Big book)./FOWLER, A/1992/
P-2/2 KB917 . . . . **508.2**
Como se hace un libro./ALIKI /1989/K-3/3 KD345. . . . . **686**
Complete book of children's activities. /RICE, M/1993/
/KA194. . . . . **PROF 372.13**
Complete fairy tales of Charles Perrault. /PERRAULT, C/1993/
3-4/6 KB355 . . . . **398.2**
Complete guide to thematic units: creating the integrated curriculum. /
MEINBACH, AM/1995//KA195. . . . . **PROF 372.19**
Complete Just so stories. /KIPLING, R/1993/3-5/7 KH360 . . . . **Fic**
Complete karate. /QUEEN, JA/1993/4-6/6 KD834 . . . . **796.815**
Complete science fair handbook. /FREDERICKS, AD/1990/
/KA286. . . . . **PROF 507.8**
Compost critters. /LAVIES, B/1993/5-6/7 KC336 . . . . **577.5**
Compost!: growing gardens from your garbage. /GLASER, L/1996/
P-K/3 KD166 . . . . **635**
COMPTON'S ENCYCLOPEDIA AND FACT-INDEX. /1968-/
5-6/KA380 . . . . **REF 031**
COMPTON'S MULTIMEDIA ENCYCLOPEDIA (CD-ROM). /1994/
3-6/KA381 . . . . **CDR REF 031**
Computer dictionary for kids...and their parents. /BORMAN, JL/1995/
4-A/9 KA566 . . . . **004**
Conejito andarin./BROWN, MW/1995/P-K/2 KF287. . . . . **CE E**
Conejito andarin (Kit)./BROWN, MW/1995/P-K/2 KF287 . . . . . . **CE E**
Coney tale. /RATZ DE TAGYOS, P/1992/2-5/5 KH620 . . . . **Fic**
CONFRONTING THE WILDERNESS (Videocassette). /1991/
A/KE808 . . . . **VCR 971.01**
Congress of the United States. /KRONENWETTER, M/1996/
5-A/10 KA932 . . . . **328.73**
CONNECT: HANDS-ON SCIENCE AND MATH GUIDE FOR K-8
EDUCATORS. /1988-//KA103. . . . . **PER PROF 050**
Connecticut. /FRADIN, DB/1994/4-6/4 KE952. . . . . **974.6**
Connecting kids and the Internet: a handbook for librarians, teachers, and
parents. /BENSON, AC/1996/KA048 . . . . **PROF 025.06**
Connections: finding out about the environment (Sound recording cassette).
/SUZUKI, D/1990/P-2/KC297 . . . . **SRC 577**
CONQUERING THE SWAMPS (Videocassette). /1991/
A/KE990 . . . . **VCR 975.9**
Consider the lemming. /STEIG, J/1988/K-6/KE030 . . . . **811**
Consider the lemming (Sound recording cassette)./STEIG, J/n.d./
K-6/KE030 . . . . **811**
CONTEMPORARY NATIVE AMERICANS (Picture). /1995/
5-6/KE779 . . . . **PIC 970.4**
Contest. /HOGROGIAN, N/c1976/3-5/5 KB744 . . . . **398.27**
CONVERSATION WITH MAGIC (Videocassette). /1992/
4-6/KD026. . . . . **VCR 616.97**
Cookies. /JASPERSOHN, W/1993/3-5/8 KD320 . . . . **664**
Cooking the African way./CORONADA, R/1988/4-6/8 KD286. . . **641.59**
Cooking the Caribbean way./CORONADA, R/1988/
4-6/8 KD286 . . . . **641.59**
Cooking the French way./CORONADA, R/1982/4-6/8 KD286 . . . **641.59**
Cooking the German way./CORONADA, R/1988/4-6/8 KD286 . . . **641.59**
Cooking the Greek way./CORONADA, R/1984/4-6/8 KD286 . . . . **641.59**
Cooking the Hungarian way./CORONADA, R/1986/
4-6/8 KD286 . . . . **641.59**
Cooking the Indian way./CORONADA, R/1985/4-6/8 KD286 . . . . **641.59**

Cooking the Irish way./CORONADA, R/1996/4-6/8 KD286..... **641.59**
Cooking the Israeli way./CORONADA, R/1986/4-6/8 KD286. ... **641.59**
Cooking the Italian way./CORONADA, R/1982/4-6/8 KD286 . **641.59**
Cooking the Japanese way./CORONADA, R/1983/4-6/8 KD286. **641.59**
Cooking the Korean way./CORONADA, R/1988/4-6/8 KD286. ... **641.59**
Cooking the Lebanese way./CORONADA, R/1985/4-6/8 KD286. **641.59**
Cooking the Mexican way./CORONADA, R/1982/4-6/8 KD286 . **641.59**
Cooking the Polish way./CORONADA, R/1984/4-6/8 KD286 . **641.59**
Cooking the Russian way./CORONADA, R/1986/4-6/8 KD286. **641.59**
Cooking the Thai way./CORONADA, R/1986/4-6/8 KD286 . **641.59**
Cooking the Vietnamese way./CORONADA, R/1985/
    4-6/8 KD286 . . . . **641.59**
Cooking wizardry for kids. /KENDA, M/1990/5-6/KD273 . . . . . . **641.5**
Cool hot rod and other electrifying experiments on energy and matter. /
    DOHERTY, P/1996/4-A/5 KC093. . . . . **531**
COOPERATION (Videocassette). /1990/4-6/KA655 . . . . **VCR 158**
Cooperative learning activities in the library media center. /FARMER, LS/
    1991//KA073 . . . . **PROF 027.8**
Copier creations: using copy machines to make decals, silhouettes, flip
    books, films, and much more! /FLEISCHMAN, P/1993/
    3-6/7 KD503 . . . . **760**
Coraje de Sarah Noble. /DALGLIESH, A/n.d./3-5/3 KH058 . . . . **CE Fic**
Coral reef hideaway: the story of a clown anemonefish. /BOYLE, D/1995/
    K-2/7 KF255 . . . . **CE E**
Coral reef hideaway: the story of a clown anemonefish (Kit)./BOYLE, D/
    1995/K-2/7 KF255 . . . . **CE E**
Coral reefs: Earth's undersea treasures. /PRINGLE, LP/1995/
    5-6/7 KC351 . . . . **577.7**
Corduroy. /FREEMAN, D/c1968/P-2/2 KF578. . . . . **CE E**
Corduroy. /FREEMAN, D/1988/P-2/2 KF578. . . . . **CE E**
Corduroy (Kit)./FREEMAN, D/1982/P-2/2 KF578 . . . . **CE E**
Corduroy (Talking book)./FREEMAN, D/n.d./P-2/2 KF578 . . . **CE E**
Corduroy (Videocassette)./FREEMAN, D/n.d./P-2/2 KF578 . . . . . **CE E**
CORETTA SCOTT KING AWARDS BOOK: FROM VISION TO REALITY. /
    1994//KA008 . . . . **PROF 011.008**
Corn belt harvest. /BIAL, R/1991/4-5/7 KD150 . . . . **633.1**
Corn is maize: the gift of the Indians. /ALIKI /c1976/K-3/3 KD149 . **633.1**
Corn woman: audio stories and legends of the Hispanic Southwest/La mujer
    del maiz: cuentos y leyendas del sudoeste Hispano (Talking book)./
    VIGIL, A/1995/5-6/4 KB380. . . . . **CE 398.2**
Corn woman: stories and legends of the Hispanic Southwest/La mujer del
    maiz: cuentos y leyendas del sudoeste Hispano. /VIGIL, A/1994/
    5-6/4 KB380 . . . . **CE 398.2**
CORPUS ALMANAC AND CANADIAN SOURCEBOOK. /1964-/
    5-6/KA484 . . . . **REF 971**
Corre, perro, corre!/EASTMAN, PD/1992/P-1/1 KF506 . . . . **E**
Costume. /ROWLAND-WARNE, L/1992/4-6/8 KB165 . . . . **391**
Could be worse. /STEVENSON, J/c1977, 1987/K-3/4 KG558 . . . . **CE E**
Could we ever be friends?: poems for pals. /KATZ, B/1997/1-3/KD959 . . **811**
Could you ever build a time machine? /DARLING, DJ/1991/
    4-A/7 KC082 . . . . **530.1**
Could you ever meet an alien? /DARLING, DJ/1990/A/7 KC291 . **576.8**
COUNSELING (Videocassette)./1991//KA187 . . . . . . **VCR PROF 371.95**
Count! /FLEMING, D/1992/P-K/KF554 . . . . **E**
Count and see. /HOBAN, T/c1972/P/KF741 . . . . **E**
COUNT ON READING HANDBOOK: TIPS FOR PLANNING READING
    MOTIVATION PROGRAMS. /1997//KA206 . . . . **PROF 372.4**
Count Silvernose: a story from Italy. /KIMMEL, EA/1996/
    3-5/5 KB504 . . . . **398.23**
COUNTERPOINT AND BEYOND: A RESPONSE TO BECOMING A
    NATION OF READERS. /1988//KA207 . . . . **PROF 372.4**
Counting cranes. /OWENS, MB/1993/P-4/3 KB976 . . . . **513.2**
Counting games and rhythms for the little ones, vol. 1 (Sound recording
    cassette). /JENKINS, E/c1964, 1990/P-2/KB948 . . . . . **SRC 513**
Counting is for the birds. /MAZZOLA, F/1997/K-3/8 KB968 . . . . . **513.2**
Counting on Frank. /CLEMENT, R/1991/1-6/5 KB927 . . . . **510**
Country bunny and the little gold shoes, as told to Jenifer. /HEYWARD,
    DB/c1939/P-K/7 KF723 . . . . **E**
Country bunny and the little gold shoes, as told to Jenifer (Braille)./
    HEYWARD, DB/n.d./P-K/7 KF723 . . . . **E**
Country fair. /COOPER, E/1997/1-3/3 KF421. . . . . **E**
Country far away. /GRAY, N/1988/K-3/1 KF638 . . . . **E**
Courage of Sarah Noble. /DALGLIESH, A/c1954, 1987/
    3-5/3 KH058 . . . . **CE Fic**
Courage of Sarah Noble (Braille)./DALGLIESH, A/n.d./
    3-5/3 KH058 . . . . **CE Fic**
Courage of Sarah Noble (Sound recording cassette)./DALGLIESH, A/n.d./
    3-5/3 KH058 . . . . **CE Fic**
Courage of Sarah Noble (Talking book)./DALGLIESH, A/1978/
    3-5/3 KH058 . . . . **CE Fic**
Cousin Ruth's tooth. /MACDONALD, A/1996/K-2/2 KG048 . . . . **E**
Cousins. /HAMILTON, V/1990/6-A/5 KH213 . . . . **Fic**
Cousins in the castle. /WALLACE, BB/1996/5-A/7 KH837 . . . . **Fic**
Cow. /OLDER, J/1997/P-4/2 KD214. . . . . **636.2**

Cow, a bee, a cookie, and me. /HOOPER, M/1997/K-2/2 KF768 . . . . . **E**
Cowardly Clyde. /PEET, B/1979/K-2/6 KG225 . . . . **E**
Cowboy. /MURDOCH, DH/1993/4-A/8 KF040 . . . . **978**
Cowboy: an album. /GRANFIELD, L/1994/5-A/8 KF030 . . . . **978**
Cowboy and the black-eyed pea. /JOHNSTON, T/1992/K-2/5 KF839 . **E**
Cowboy Charlie: the story of Charles M. Russell. /WINTER, J/1995/
    2-5/5 KE528 . . . . **B RUSSELL, C.**
Cowboy country. /SCOTT, AH/1993/3-6/3 KF049. . . . . **978**
COWBOY SONGS (Compact disc)./1992/4-A/KD560 . . . . . **SRC 789.2**
COWBOY SONGS (Sound recording cassette). /1992/
    4-A/KD560 . . . . **SRC 789.2**
Cowboys. /ROUNDS, G/1991/P-K/6 KF047. . . . . **978**
Cowboys. /MILLER, RH/1991/4-6/6 KF039. . . . . **978**
Cowboys of the wild west. /FREEDMAN, R/1985/5-A/7 KF029 . . . . **978**
Cowboys: roundup on an American ranch. /ANDERSON, J/1996/
    3-5/6 KF025 . . . . **978**
Cowgirl dreams: a western childhood. /DEWEY, JO/1995/
    3-4/4 KE320 . . . . **B DEWEY, J.**
COWS! 2ND ED. (Videocassette). /1995/1-3/KD212 . . . . . . **VCR 636.2**
Cow-tail switch and other West African stories. /COURLANDER, H/c1947,
    1987/4-6/7 KB728 . . . . **398.27**
Coyote: a trickster tale from the American Southwest. /MCDERMOTT, G/
    1994/P-2/2 KB617 . . . . **398.24**
Coyote and the fire stick: a Pacific Northwest Indian tale. /GOLDIN, BD/
    1996/2-4/2 KB576 . . . . **398.24**
Coyote and the laughing butterflies. /TAYLOR, HP/1995/
    2-3/5 KB662 . . . . **398.24**
Coyote and the magic words. /ROOT, P/1993/P-2/2 KG351 . . . . **E**
Coyote steals the blanket: a Ute tale. /STEVENS, J/1993/
    2-4/2 KB657 . . . . **398.24**
Coyote steals the blanket: a Ute tale (Sound recording cassette)./STEVENS,
    J/1995/2-4/2 KB657 . . . . **398.24**
Coyotes in the crosswalk: true tales of animal life in the wilds...of the city! /
    SWANSON, D/1995/4-6/6 KC494 . . . . **591.75**
Crabs. /JOHNSON, SA/1982/4-6/7 KC520. . . . . **595.3**
Crafts for Christmas. /ROSS, K/1995/3-5/KD452 . . . . **745.594**
CRAFTS FOR DECORATION. /1993/3-6/7 KD451 . . . . **745.594**
Crafts for Easter. /ROSS, K/1995/3-6/7 KD453 . . . . **745.594**
Crafts for Halloween. /ROSS, K/1994/3-5 KD454 . . . . **745.594**
Crafts for Hanukkah. /ROSS, K/1996/3-6 KD455 . . . . **745.594**
Crafts for Kwanzaa. /ROSS, K/1994/3-6/6 KD456 . . . . **745.594**
CRAFTS FOR PLAY. /1993/3-6/7 KD445 . . . . **745.592**
Crafts for Thanksgiving. /ROSS, K/1995/3-5/KD457 . . . . **745.594**
Crafty chameleon. /HADITHI, M/c1987, 1995/P-2/7 KF659 . . . . **E**
Cranberries. /JASPERSOHN, W/1991/4-5/6 KD160 . . . . **634**
Cranberries: fruit of the bogs. /BURNS, DL/1994/5-6/7 KD157 . . . **634**
CRANBERRY BOUNCE (Videocassette). /1991/3-5/KD158 . . . . **VCR 634**
Crash. /SPINELLI, J/1996/5-A/3 KH744. . . . . **Fic**
Crawdads, doodlebugs and creasy greens: songs, stories and lore
    celebrating the natural world (Compact disc). /ELLIOTT, D/1996/
    3-5/KB291. . . . . **CD 398.2**
Crawdads, doodlebugs and creasy greens: songs, stories and lore
    celebrating the natural world (Sound recording cassette)./ELLIOTT, D/
    1995/3-5/KB291. . . . . **CD 398.2**
Crayon counting book. /RYAN, PM/1996/P-1/3 KB982. . . . . **513.2**
Crazy eights and other card games. /COLE, J/1994/3-6/5 KD758 . **795.4**
Crazy Horse. /ST. GEORGE, J/1994/A/9 KE308 . . . . **B CRAZY HORSE**
Creating and managing the literate classroom. /BARCHERS, SI/1990/
    /KA218. . . . . **PROF 372.6**
Creating the peaceable school: a comprehensive program for teaching
    conflict resolution: program guide. /BODINE, RJ/1994/
    /KA161. . . . . **PROF 303.6**
Creating the peaceable school: a comprehensive program for teaching
    conflict resolution: student manual./BODINE, RJ/1994/
    /KA161. . . . . **PROF 303.6**
Creation. /JOHNSON, JW/1994/K-3/KD956 . . . . **811**
Creation: a poem. /JOHNSON, JW/1993/1-6/KD957 . . . . **811**
CREATIVE DRAMA IN THE EARLY CHILDHOOD CLASSROOM
    (Videocassette). /1991//KA220 . . . . **VCR PROF 372.6**
CREATIVE DRAMA IN THE ELEMENTARY CLASSROOM (Videocassette)./
    1990//KA220 . . . . **VCR PROF 372.6**
Creative ideas for library media center facilities. /HART, TL/1990/
    /KA075. . . . . **PROF 027.8**
CREATIVE KIDS. /n.d./4-A/KA511 . . . . **PER 050**
Creative partnerships: librarians and teachers working together. /FARMER,
    LS/1993//KA074 . . . . **PROF 027.8**
CREATIVITY (Videocassette)./1991//KA187 . . . . . **VCR PROF 371.95**
Creature features. /GANERI, A/1997/3-6/6 KC447 . . . . **591**
Creepy, crawly caterpillars. /FACKLAM, M/1996/4-6/6 KC559. . . **595.78**
Creepy spooky science. /MARKLE, S/1996/3-6/8 KB894 . . . . . **507.8**
Creepy-crawly birthday./HOWE, J/1991/K-3/6 KF780 . . . . **E**
Cricket in Times Square. /SELDEN, G/c1960/4-6/6 KH694 . . . . **CE Fic**
Cricket in Times Square (Braille)./SELDEN, G/n.d./4-6/6 KH694 . . **CE Fic**

Cricket in Times Square (Talking book)./SELDEN, G/1971/
4-6/6 KH694 . . . . **CE Fic**

Cricket never does: a collection of haiku and tanka. /LIVINGSTON, MC/
1997/3-6/KD975 . . . . **811**

CRICKET: THE MAGAZINE FOR CHILDREN. /1973-/
3-6/KA512 . . . . **PER 050**

CRICKET, TIGLET AND FRIENDS (Videocassette). /1984/
4-6/KC712. . . . . **VCR 598.9**

Cricket warrior: a Chinese tale. /CHANG, M/1994/2-3/5 KB549 . **398.24**

Cricket's cage: a Chinese folktale. /CZERNECKI, S/1997/
K-3/7 KB553 . . . . **398.24**

Crictor. /UNGERER, T/c1958/K-2/KG634 . . . . **E**

Crime-fighting. /GRAHAM, I/1995/5-6/7 KB029 . . . . **363.2**

Crinkleroot's guide to knowing animal habitats. /ARNOSKY, J/1997/
2-5/4 KC471 . . . . **591.5**

Crinkleroot's guide to knowing butterflies and moths. /ARNOSKY, J/1996/
3-5/5 KC557 . . . . **595.78**

Crinkleroot's guide to knowing the birds. /ARNOSKY, J/1992/
2-5/6 KC644 . . . . **598**

Crinkleroot's 25 birds every child should know. /ARNOSKY, J/1993/
P-2/3 KC645 . . . . **598**

CRITTER JITTERS (Videocassette). /1986/P-2/KB016. . . . . **VCR 362.76**

Crocodile smile: 10 songs of the Earth as the animals see it. /WEEKS, S/
1994/P-2/KD665 . . . . **BA 789.3**

Cross-country cat. /CALHOUN, M/1979/K-2/4 KF331 . . . . . . **E**

Crow Boy. /YASHIMA, T/1955/1-3/3 KG772 . . . . **CE E**

Crow Boy (Braille)./YASHIMA, T/n.d./1-3/3 KG772. . . . . **CE E**

Crow Boy (Kit)./YASHIMA, T/1985/1-3/3 KG772. . . . . . **CE E**

Crow Boy (Talking book)./YASHIMA, T/n.d./1-3/3 KG772 . . **CE E**

Crow Chief: a Plains Indian story. /GOBLE, P/1992/3-4/4 KB573 . **398.24**

Crow Chief: a Plains Indian story (Sound recording cassette)./GOBLE, P/
1995/3-4/4 KB573 . . . . **398.24**

Crown of Dalemark./JONES, DW/1995/6-A/6 KH331 . . . . . . **Fic**

Cruise of the Arctic Star. /O'DELL, S/c1973/5-6/6 KE208 . . **917.94**

Cry of the wolf. /BURGESS, M/1994/5-A/7 KG948 . . . . **Fic**

CRYING RED GIANT: A JAPANESE FOLKTALE (Videocassette). /n.d./
K-2/KB391 . . . . **VCR 398.21**

Cuando tengo sueno./HOWARD, JR/1996/P-K/8 KF776 . . . . . **E**

Cub Scout fun book. /KENOWER, FT/c1956, 1986/2-4/6 KB077 . **369.43**

Cuckoo: a Mexican folktale./Cucu: un cuento folklorico mexicano. /EHLERT,
L/1997/P-2/3 KB561 . . . . **398.24**

Cuckoo child. /KING-SMITH, D/1993/4-6/6 KH347 . . . . **Fic**

Cuckoo child (Sound recording cassette)./KING-SMITH, D/1995/
4-6/6 KH347 . . . . **Fic**

Cuckoo's child. /FREEMAN, S/1996/5-A/5 KH142 . . . . **Fic**

Cuento de Ferdinando./LEAF, M/1988/P-1/3 KF953 . . . . . **CE E**

Cuento de Ferdinando (Kit)./LEAF, M/1990/P-1/3 KF953 . . . **CE E**

Cuento de Juanito Raton de la Ciudad./POTTER, B/1988/P-2/8 KG274 . **E**

Cuento de la Oca Carlota./POTTER, B/1988/P-2/6 KG273 . . . . . . **E**

CUENTO DE LOS DOS MALVADOS RATONES./POTTER, B/1988/
P-2/6 KG284 . . . . **E**

Cuento del Conejito Benjamin./POTTER, B/1988/P-2/8 KG272 . . . **E**

Cuento del Gato Tomas./POTTER, B/1988/P-2/7 KG283 . . . . . . **E**

Cuentos del cerdito Oliver./VAN LEEUWEN, J/1996/K-2/1 KG649 . **CE E**

Cuentos del pobre diablo./BABBITT, N/1994/3-5/4 KG869 . . . . **CE Fic**

Cupid and Psyche./CRAFT, MC/1996/4-5/6 KA737 . . . . **292**

Curious George. /REY, HA/c1941/P-2/2 KG322 . . . . **E**

Curious George and other stories about Curious George (Talking book). /
REY, HA/1973/P-2/KG323 . . . . **TB E**

Curious George (Big book)./REY, HA/1994/P-2/2 KG322 . . . . **E**

Curious George (Braille)./REY, HA/n.d./P-2/2 KG322 . . . . . **E**

Curious George flies a kite. /REY, M/c1958/P-2/1 KG328 . . . . **E**

Curious George flies a kite (Braille)./REY, M/n.d./P-2/1 KG328 . . . **E**

Curious George gets a medal./REY, HA/1957/P-2/2 KG324 . . . . . **E**

Curious George gets a medal (Braille)./REY, HA/n.d./P-2/2 KG324 . . **E**

Curious George goes to the hospital. /REY, M/c1966/P-2/2 KG329 . . . **E**

Curious George goes to the hospital (Braille)./REY, M/n.d./
P-2/2 KG329 . . . . **E**

Curious George learns the alphabet. /REY, HA/c1963/P-2/2 KG325 . . . **E**

Curious George learns the alphabet (Sound recording cassette)./REY, HA/
n.d./P-2/2 KG325 . . . . **E**

Curious George rides a bike. /REY, HA/c1952/P-2/1 KG326 . . . . . **CE E**

Curious George rides a bike (Kit)./REY, HA/1993/P-2/1 KG326 . . . **CE E**

Curious George rides a bike (Videocassette)./REY, HA/1985/
P-2/1 KG326 . . . . **CE E**

Curious George (Sound recording cassette)./REY, HA/n.d./
P-2/2 KG322 . . . . **E**

Curious George takes a job. /REY, HA/c1947/P-2/3 KG327 . . . . . . **E**

Curious George takes a job (Braille)./REY, HA/n.d./P-2/3 KG327 . . . **E**

Curious George (Talking book)./REY, HA/n.d./P-2/2 KG322 . . . . . **E**

CURRENT BIOGRAPHY YEARBOOK. /1967-/5-6/KA477 . . . . . . **REF 920**

CURRENT SCIENCE. /1927-/5-6/KA513 . . . . **PER 050**

CURRICULUM AND EVALUATION STANDARDS FOR SCHOOL
MATHEMATICS. /1989//KA252 . . . . **PROF 372.7**

Curriculum planning and teaching using the library media center. /URBANIK,
MK/1989//KA064 . . . . **PROF 025.5**

Cut from the same cloth: American women of myth, legend, and tall tale. /
SAN SOUCI, RD/1993/5-6/6 KB481 . . . . **398.22**

Cuts, breaks, bruises and burns: how your body heals. /COLE, J/1985/
4-6/6 KC932 . . . . **612.1**

Cutters, carvers and the cathedral. /ANCONA, G/1995/
5-6/7 KD392 . . . . **726.6**

Cybersurfer: the Owl Internet guide for kids. /AHMAD, N/1996/
3-A/8 KA575 . . . . **BC 025.04**

Cycling. /BAILEY, D/1990/2-4/2 KD826 . . . . **796.6**

Cyclops. /FISHER, LE/1991/1-6/4 KA739 . . . . **292**

Cynthia Gregory dances Swan Lake. /GREGORY, C/1990/
4-A/7 KD694 . . . . **792.8**

D- poems of Jeremy Bloom: a collection of poems about school, homework,
and life (sort of). /KORMAN, G/1992/4-A/KD966 . . . . **811**

Dad and me in the morning. /LAKIN, P/1994/1-3/2 KF942 . . . . . . **E**

Daddies. /GREENSPUN, AA/1991/1-3/4 KA878 . . . . **306.874**

Daddy, could I have an elephant? /WOLF, J/1996/K-2/2 KG755 . . . . . **E**

Daddy, Daddy, be there. /BOYD, CD/1995/1-3/2 KF254 . . . . . . **E**

DADDY DOESN'T LIVE WITH US (Videocassette). /1994/
P-1/KA889. . . . . **VCR 306.89**

Daddy's chair. /LANTON, S/1991/P-2/2 KF944 . . . . **E**

Dads are such fun. /WOOD, J/1992/P-K/1 KG769 . . . . **E**

Daffy down dillies: silly limericks. /LEAR, E/1992/K-A/KE103 . . . . **821**

Dahomey: the warrior kings. /KOSLOW, P/1997/6-A/9 KE736. . . **966.9**

Daily life in a Victorian house. /WILSON, L/1993/3-6/7 KE676 . **941.081**

DAIRY FARM (Videocassette). /1991/3-5/KD213. . . . . . **VCR 636.2**

Daisy. /POWELL, ES/1991/3-4/4 KH612 . . . . **Fic**

Daisy and the Girl Scouts: the story of Juliette Gordon Low. /BROWN,
FG/1996/3-6/7 KE448 . . . . **B LOW, J.**

Dakota dugout. /TURNER, A/1985/1-3/6 KG624 . . . . **E**

Dance. /MEDEARIS, AS/1997/4-6/11 KD704 . . . . **793.3**

Dance at Grandpa's. /WILDER, LI/1994/K-3/4 KG719 . . . . . . **E**

Dance in your pants: great songs for little kids to dance to (Sound
recording cassette)./JACK, D/1988/K-3/KD620 . . . . . **SRC 789.3**

Dance of the sacred circle: a Native American tale. /RODANAS, K/1994/
3-4/5 KB639 . . . . **398.24**

DANCE WITH US: A CREATIVE MOVEMENT VIDEO (Videocassette). /
1994/K-2/KD702 . . . . **VCR 793.3**

Dancers. /ROALF, P/1992/5-A/7 KD478 . . . . **758**

Dancing bear. /MORPURGO, M/1996/4-6/5 KH513 . . . . **Fic**

Dancing rainbows: a Pueblo boy's story. /MOTT, EC/1996/
2-4/2 KE794 . . . . **970.489**

Dancing skeleton. /DEFELICE, CC/1996/3-6/6 KB684 . . . . . **CE 398.25**

Dancing skeleton (Videocassette)./DEFELICE, CC/1991/
3-6/6 KB684 . . . . **CE 398.25**

Dandelion. /FREEMAN, D/c1964/K-1/2 KF579 . . . . **CE E**

Dandelion (Kit)./FREEMAN, D/1982/K-1/2 KF579 . . . . . . **CE E**

Dandelions. /BUNTING, E/1995/3-5/2 KG942 . . . . **Fic**

DANIEL BOONE'S FINAL FRONTIER (Videocassette). /1995/
4-5/KE259 . . . . **VCR B BOONE, D.**

Daniel "Chappie" James. /SUPER, N/1992/5-A/6 KE401. . **B JAMES, D.**

Daniel O'Rourke: an Irish tale. /MCDERMOTT, G/1986/
2/2 KB755. . . . . **398.27**

Daniel's duck. /BULLA, CR/1979/1-2/1 KF296. . . . . **E**

Danny ain't. /COTTONWOOD, J/1992/6-A/6 KH033 . . . . **Fic**

Danny and the dinosaur. /HOFF, S/c1958/K-2/2 KF753 . . . . **CE E**

Danny and the dinosaur (Braille)./HOFF, S/n.d./K-2/2 KF753 . . **CE E**

Danny and the dinosaur go to camp. /HOFF, S/1996/K-2/2 KF754 . . . **E**

Danny and the dinosaur (Kit)./HOFF, S/1985/K-2/2 KF753 . . **CE E**

Danny and the kings. /COOPER, S/1993/2-4/2 KF423 . . . . **E**

Danny, the champion of the world. /DAHL, R/c1975, 1988/
4-6/6 KH054 . . . . **Fic**

Dare to dream: Coretta Scott King and the civil rights movement. /
MEDEARIS, AS/1994/3-5/3 KE419 . . . . **B KING, C.S.**

Dare to dream: Coretta Scott King and the civil rights movement (Sound
recording cassette). /MEDEARIS, AS/1997/
3-5/3 KE419 . . . . **B KING, C.S.**

Dark secret of Weatherend. /BELLAIRS, J/c1984/6-A/6 KG895 . . . . **Fic**

Dark secret of Weatherend (Braille)./BELLAIRS, J/n.d./6-A/6 KG895 . . **Fic**

Dark secret of Weatherend (Sound recording cassette)./BELLAIRS, J/n.d./
6-A/6 KG895. . . . . **Fic**

Dark stairs. /BYARS, BC/1994/4-6/5 KG960 . . . . **CE Fic**

Dark stairs: a Herculeah Jones mystery (Talking book)./BYARS, BC/1995/
4-6/5 KG960 . . . . **CE Fic**

Dark stairs (Sound recording cassette)./BYARS, BC/1997/
4-6/5 KG960 . . . . **CE Fic**

Darkness and the butterfly. /GRIFALCONI, A/1987/K-2/4 KF645 . . . **E**

Dark-thirty: Southern tales of the supernatural. /MCKISSACK, P/1992/
5-A/6 KH491 . . . . **Fic**

Dark-thirty: Southern tales of the supernatural (Sound recording cassette)./
MCKISSACK, P/1994/5-A/6 KH491 . . . . **Fic**

Dashing through the snow: the story of the Jr. Iditarod. /SHAHAN, S/ 1997/4-6/7 KD860 . . . . 798.8
D'Aulaires' trolls. /D'AULAIRE, I/c1972, 1993/4-6/6 KB280. . . . . . 398.2
David and Goliath. /DE REGNIERS, BS/1996/1-4/6 KA683. . . . . **222**
David and Goliath (Kit)./METAXAS, E/1996/2-4/KA686. . . . . **VCR 222**
David and Goliath (Talking book). /METAXAS, E/1996/ 2-4/KA686 . . . . **VCR 222**
David and Goliath (Videocassette). /METAXAS, E/1992/ 2-4/KA686 . . . . **VCR 222**
David Balfour: being memoirs of the further adventures of David Balfour at home and abroad. /STEVENSON, RL/c1952, 1994/6-A/6 KH757 . **Fic**
David Jack... live!: Makin' music, makin' friends (Videocassette). /JACK, D/ 1991/P-2/KD621 . . . . **VCR 789.3**
Davy's dream. /LEWIS, PO/1988/1-3/3 KF977. . . . . **E**
Dawn. /BANG, M/1983/1-3/2 KF189. **E**
Dawn. /SHULEVITZ, U/1974/K-2/2 KG498 . . . . **E**
Day Gogo went to vote: South Africa, April 1994. /SISULU, E/1996/ 1-3/2 KG513 . . . . **E**
Day I had to play with my sister. /BONSALL, CN/c1972/1-2/1 KF244. . **E**
Day in the life of a beekeeper. /MICHELS, P/1990/4-5/6 KD242 . . . **638**
Day in the life of a carpenter. /MARTIN, JH/1985/4-6/7 KD362 . **CE 694**
Day in the life of a sports therapist. /PAIGE, D/1985/ 3-5/6 KC989 . . . . **613.7**
Day in the life of a zoo veterinarian. /PAIGE, D/1985/ 2-5/6 KD196 . . . . **CE 636.089**
Day Jimmy's boa ate the wash. /NOBLE, TH/1980/K-2/2 KG176 . . **CE E**
Day Jimmy's boa ate the wash (Braille). /NOBLE, TH/n.d./ K-2/2 KG176 . . . . **CE E**
Day Jimmy's boa ate the wash (Videocassette). /NOBLE, TH/1992/ K-2/2 KG176 . . . . **CE E**
Day of Ahmed's secret. /HEIDE, FP/1990/1-3/4 KF694. . . . . **E**
Day of delight: a Jewish Sabbath in Ethiopia. /SCHUR, MR/1994/ 1-3/4 KG412 . . . . **E**
Day of the Dead: a Mexican-American celebration. /HOYT-GOLDSMITH, D/1994/4-6/7 KB198 . . . . **394.26**
Day on the river. /MICHL, R/1986/1-3/4 KG133. . . . . **E**
Day Sun was stolen. /OLIVIERO, J/1995/K-2/5 KB712 . . . . . . **398.26**
Day that Elvis came to town. /MARINO, J/1993/6-A/6 KH456 . . . . . **Fic**
Day with Wilbur Robinson. /JOYCE, W/1990/1-3/4 KF858 . . . . **E**
Daydreamer. /MCEWAN, I/1994/4-6/6 KH474. . . . . **Fic**
Day-off machine. /HIMMELMAN, J/1990/1-3/1 KF729. . . . . **E**
Days of awe: stories for Rosh Hashanah and Yom Kippur. /KIMMEL, EA/ 1991/4-6/5 KA777. . . . . **296.4**
Days of the blackbird: a tale of northern Italy. /DE PAOLA, T/1997/ 1-3/6 KF468 . . . . **E**
Days of the Dead. /LASKY, K/1994/5-6/6 KB200 . . . . **394.26**
Days with Frog and Toad. /LOBEL, A/1979/K-2/1 KG001. . . . . **E**
Day's work. /BUNTING, E/1994/1-3/2 KF298 . . . . **E**
DE COLORES AND OTHER LATIN-AMERICAN FOLK SONGS FOR CHILDREN. /1994/K-3/KD561. . . . . **789.2**
De oro y esmeraldas: mitos, leyendas y cuentos populares de Latinoamerica./DELACRE, L/1996/4-5/6 KB283. . . . . **398.2**
Dead letter. /BYARS, BC/1996/4-6/5 KG960. . . . . **CE Fic**
Dead Sea Scrolls. /COOPER, I/1997/6-A/8 KA768 . . . . **296.1**
DEALING WITH DISAPPOINTMENT (Videocassette). /1990/ 4-6/KA655 . . . . **VCR 158**
DEALING WITH FEELINGS (Videocassette)./1990/4-6/KA655 . **VCR 158**
Dear Annie. /CASELEY, J/1991/K-2/2 KF363 . . . . **E**
Dear Benjamin Banneker. /PINKNEY, AD/1994/ 4-6/6 KE249 . . . . **B BANNEKER, B.**
Dear Benjamin Banneker (Sound recording cassette)./PINKNEY, AD/1997/ 4-6/6 KE249 . . . . **B BANNEKER, B.**
Dear Daddy. /SCHINDEL, J/1995/K-2/2 KG406 . . . . **E**
DEAR LAURA: LETTERS FROM CHILDREN TO LAURA INGALLS WILDER. /1996/3-6/KD893. . . . . **808.86**
Dear Levi: letters from the Overland Trail. /WOODRUFF, E/1994/ 4-6/6 KH880 . . . . **Fic**
Dear Mr. Henshaw. /CLEARY, B/1983/4-A/4 KG993 . . . . **Fic**
Dear Mr. Henshaw (Braille). /CLEARY, B/n.d./4-A/4 KG993 . . . . . **Fic**
Dear Mr. Henshaw (Sound recording cassette). /CLEARY, B/n.d./ 4-A/4 KG993 . . . . **Fic**
Dear Mrs. Parks: a dialogue with today's youth. /PARKS, R/1996/ 5-6/6 KA901 . . . . **323**
Dear old Donegal. /GRAHAM, S/1996/1-3/2 KD566. . . . . **789.2**
Dear Rebecca, winter is here. /GEORGE, JC/1993/1-3/3 KF605 . . . . . **E**
Death of the iron horse. /GOBLE, P/1987/K-3/2 KF626 . . . . **E**
Death's door. /BYARS, BC/1997/4-6/5 KG960 . . . . **CE Fic**
DECIDING HOW CLOSE TO MEASURE (Videocassette). /1982/ 3-5/KB996. . . . . **VCR 519**
Declaration of Independence. /STEIN, RC/1995/5-A/7 KE887 . . . . **973.3**
DECLARATION OF INDEPENDENCE (Videocassette). /1976/ 5-A/KE878. . . . . **VCR 973.3**
Deenie. /BLUME, J/1973/6/4 KG907 . . . . **Fic**
Deenie (Braille)./BLUME, J/n.d./6/4 KG907 . . . . **Fic**

Deenie (Sound recording cassette)./BLUME, J/1993/6/4 KG907 . . . . **Fic**
Deep-sea vents: living worlds without sun. /WATERS, JF/1994/ 4-6/7 KC179 . . . . **551.46**
Del interior de las cosas./BIESTY, S/1995/4-A/6 KC880 . . . . **600**
Delaware. /FRADIN, DB/1994/4-6/3 KE968 . . . . **975.1**
Dentro de la selva tropical./WILLOW, D/1993/K-4/6 KC328 . . . . **577.34**
Derniere quete de Gilgamesh./ZEMAN, L/1995/4-6/4 KE131 . . . . . **892.1**
Desert. /MACQUITTY, M/1994/4-6/7 KC364 . . . . **578.754**
Desert December. /HAARHOFF, D/1992/3-5/4 KH206 . . . . **Fic**
Desert fox family book. /LAUKEL, HG/1996/3-6/7 KC846. . . . . . **599.776**
Desert giant: the world of the saguaro cactus. /BASH, B/1989/ 2-6/6 KC427 . . . . **583**
Desert is my mother./El desierto es mi madre. /MORA, P/1994/ K-3/KD989 . . . . **811**
Desert is theirs. /BAYLOR, B/c1975/4-6/5 KC362 . . . . **578.754**
Desert scrapbook: dawn to dusk in the Sonoran Desert. /WRIGHT-FRIERSON, V/1996/3-5/7 KF072 . . . . **979.1**
Deserts. /SIMON, S/1990/1-5/7 KC167 . . . . **551.4**
Deserts. /MACMAHON, J/1985/A/KC338 . . . . **577.54**
Deserts. /GIBBONS, G/1996/K-3/4 KC363 . . . . **578.754**
DESTINATION: CASTLE. School version (CD-ROM)./1994/ 1-A/KB111. . . . . **CDR 372.6**
DESTINATION: NEIGHBORHOOD. School version (CD-ROM)./1994/ 1-A/KB111. . . . . **CDR 372.6**
DESTINATION: OCEAN. School version (CD-ROM). /1995/ 1-A/KB111. . . . . **CDR 372.6**
DESTINATION: PYRAMIDS. School version (CD-ROM)./1996/ 1-A/KB111. . . . . **CDR 372.6**
DESTINATION: RAIN FOREST. School version (CD-ROM)./1995/ 1-A/KB111. . . . . **CDR 372.6**
DESTINATION: TIME TRIP, USA. School version (CD-ROM)./1996/ 1-A/KB111. . . . . **CDR 372.6**
Detective dictionary: a handbook for aspiring sleuths. /BALLINGER, E/ 1994/4-6/7 KB028 . . . . **363.2**
Detective Dinosaur. /SKOFIELD, J/1996/1-3/2 KG514 . . . . **E**
Deux-Plumes et la solitude disparue./TAYLOR, CJ/1990/ 3-4/2 KB716 . . . . **398.26**
DEVELOPMENTAL EDUCATIONAL PROGRAMS (Videocassette)./1991/ /KA187. . . . . **VCR PROF 371.95**
Devil's other storybook. /BABBITT, N/1987/5-6/8 KG868 . . . . **Fic**
Devil's storybook. /BABBITT, N/1974/3-5/4 KG869 . . . . **CE Fic**
Dia de nieve./KEATS, EJ/1991/P-2/2 KF878. . . . . **CE E**
Dia de nieve (Kit)./KEATS, EJ/1991/P-2/2 KF878 . . . . **CE E**
Dia feliz./KRAUSS, R/1995/P-2/2 KF921 . . . . **E**
Dia que la boa de Jimmy se comio la ropa./NOBLE, TH/1997/ K-2/2 KG176 . . . . **CE E**
Diabetes. /TIGER, S/1987/A/9 KD018 . . . . **616.4**
Diablesse and the baby: a Caribbean folktale. /KEENS-DOUGLAS, R/ 1994/3-4/4 KB324 . . . . **398.2**
Diamond in the window. /LANGTON, J/c1962, 1973/4-6/5 KH385 . . **Fic**
Diamond in the window (Braille). /LANGTON, J/n.d./4-6/5 KH385 . . **Fic**
Diamond tree: Jewish tales from around the world. /SCHWARTZ, H/1991/ 3-4/6 KB368 . . . . **398.2**
Diamond tree: Jewish tales from around the world (Sound recording cassette)./SCHWARTZ, H/1994/3-4/6 KB368. . . . . **398.2**
DIANE GOODE BOOK OF AMERICAN FOLK TALES AND SONGS. / 1989/2-4/5 KB439 . . . . **398.22**
DIANE GOODE'S AMERICAN CHRISTMAS. /1997/K-A/KD898. . . **810.8**
DIANE GOODE'S BOOK OF SCARY STORIES AND SONGS. /1994/ 2-5/5 KB685 . . . . **398.25**
DIANE GOODE'S BOOK OF SILLY STORIES AND SONGS. /1992/ K-3/KD872 . . . . **808.8**
Diary of a young girl. /FRANK, A/c1967/4-6/6 KE352 . . . **B FRANK, A.**
Diary of a young girl (Braille)./FRANK, A/n.d./ 4-6/6 KE352 . . . . **B FRANK, A.**
Diary of a young girl (Sound recording cassette)./FRANK, A/n.d./ 4-6/6 KE352 . . . . **B FRANK, A.**
Diary of a young girl (Talking book)./FRANK, A/n.d./ 4-6/6 KE352 . . . . **B FRANK, A.**
Dias con Sapo y Sepo./LOBEL, A/1995/K-2/1 KG001 . . . . **E**
Dia's story cloth. /CHA, D/1996/2-6/6 KE716 . . . . **959.404**
Dicey's song. /VOIGT, C/1982/5-6/6 KH832 . . . . **Fic**
Dicey's song (Braille)./VOIGT, C/n.d./5-6/6 KH832 . . . . **Fic**
Dicey's song (Sound recording cassette)./VOIGT, C/n.d./ 5-6/6 KH832 . . . . **Fic**
Dick Rutan and Jeana Yeager: flying non-stop around the world. / ROZAKIS, L/1994/5-6/6 KD099 . . . . **629.13**
Dick Whittington and his cat. /BROWN, M/c1950, 1988/ 2-4/6 KB498 . . . . **398.23**
Dick Whittington and his cat (Braille). /BROWN, M/n.d./ 2-4/6 KB498 . . . . **398.23**
Dictionary of language games, puzzles, and amusements. /EISS, HE/1986/ 4-6/KA455 . . . . **REF 793.734**
Dictionary of nature. /BURNIE, D/1994/3-A/KA445 . . . . **REF 570**

Did you hear Wind sing your name?: an Oneida song of spring. /DE
   COTEAU ORIE, S/1995/K-2/3 KF454. . . . . **E**
Diego Rivera. /SHIRLEY, D/1995/5-6/7 KE513 . . . . **B RIVERA, D.**
Dig, drill, dump, fill. /HOBAN, T/1975/P-2/KD122. . . . . . . **629.225**
DIGESTIVE SYSTEM (Videocassette). /1994/5-6/KC939 . . . . **VCR 612.3**
Diggers and dump trucks. /ROYSTON, A/1991/P-2/4 KD123 . **629.225**
DIGGERS AND DUMPERS. /1994/K-2/5 KD121 . . . . **629.225**
Digging deeper: investigations into rocks, shocks, quakes, and other earthly
   matters. /MARKLE, S/1987/4-6/9 KC148 . . . . **550**
DIGGING DINOSAURS (Videocassette). /1986/3-A/KC247. . **VCR 567.9**
Dinner at Aunt Connie's house. /RINGGOLD, F/1993/2-4/5 KG332 . . . **E**
Dinosaur. /NORMAN, D/1989/3-A/7 KC258 . . . . **567.9**
Dinosaur and other prehistoric animal factfinder. /BENTON, M/1992/
   4-6/7 KC234 . . . . **560**
Dinosaur Bob and his adventures with the family Lazardo. /JOYCE, W/
   1988/K-3/5 KF859 . . . . **E**
Dinosaur day. /DONNELLY, L/1987/P-2/1 KF487 . . . . **E**
Dinosaur dinner (with a slice of alligator pie): favorite poems. /LEE, D/
   1997/K-3/KD970 . . . . **811**
Dinosaur dream. /NOLAN, D/1990/2-3/5 KG178 . . . . **E**
Dinosaur jokes. /BIXENMAN, J/1991/2-4/KD725 . . . . **793.735**
Dinosaur questions. /MOST, B/1995/K-4/7 KC257 . . . . **567.9**
Dinosaur tree. /HENDERSON, D/1994/3-6/5 KC235 . . . . **560**
Dinosaur Valley. /KUROKAWA, M/1992/2-6/6 KC250 . . . . . **567.9**
Dinosaur worlds: new dinosaurs, new discoveries. /LESSEM, D/1996/
   4-6/6 KC254 . . . . **567.9**
Dinosaurs. /GIBBONS, G/1987/P-2/4 KC249 . . . . **CE 567.9**
Dinosaurs. /ROYSTON, A/1991/K-2/4 KC259 . . . . **567.9**
DINOSAURS: A SUPPLEMENT TO CHILDCRAFT--THE HOW AND WHY
   LIBRARY. /1987/P-2/KA378. . . . . **REF 031**
Dinosaurs alive and well! a guide to good health. /BROWN, LK/1990/
   K-3/5 KC982 . . . . **613**
Dinosaurs all around: an artist's view of the prehistoric world. /ARNOLD,
   C/1993/3-6/8 KC243 . . . . **567.9**
Dinosaurs, beware: a safety guide. /BROWN, MT/1982/
   P-3/3 KB020 . . . . **363.1**
Dinosaurs (Board book). /BARTON, B/1995/P/KF205. . . . . **BB E**
Dinosaurs divorce: a guide for changing families. /BROWN, LK/1986/
   K-3/6 KA888 . . . . **CE 306.89**
Dinosaurs down under and other fossils from Australia. /ARNOLD, C/
   1990/3-6/8 KC240 . . . . **566**
Dinosaurs (Kit). /GIBBONS, G/1988/P-2/4 KC249 . . . . . . **CE 567.9**
Dinosaurs never say please and other stories (Sound recording cassette). /
   HARLEY, B/c1987, 1989/1-3/KF671 . . . . **SRC E**
Dinosaurs to the rescue!: a guide to protecting our planet. /BROWN, LK/
   1992/1-4/4 KB045 . . . . **CE 363.7**
Dinosaurs to the rescue!: a guide to protecting our planet (Sound recording
   cassette)./BROWN, LK/1995/1-4/4 KB045 . . . . **CE 363.7**
Dinosaurs! (Videocassette). /DEBECK, S/1989/2-5/KC246 . . . **VCR 567.9**
Dinosaurs walked here and other stories fossils tell. /LAUBER, P/1987/
   4-6/6 KC236 . . . . **560**
Dinosaurs walked here and other stories fossils tell (Braille). /LAUBER, P/
   n.d./4-6/6 KC236 . . . . **560**
Dirty, rotten, dead? /EMORY, J/1996/4-6/10 KC303 . . . . **577.1**
Discover: investigate the mysteries of history with 40 practical projects
   probing our past. /GRIER, K/1990/3-6/6 KA592 . . . . **069**
Discovering Christopher Columbus. /PELTA, K/1991/A/6 KE742 . . **970.01**
Discovering Christopher Columbus: how history is invented (Sound recording
   cassette)./PELTA, K/1993/A/6 KE742. . . . . **970.01**
Discovering dinosaur babies. /SCHLEIN, M/1991/3-6/5 KC262 . . **567.9**
Discovering seashells. /FLORIAN, D/1986/4-5/7 KC511 . . . . . . **594**
DISCOVERING THE CELL (Videocassette). /1992/5-6/KC275 . **VCR 571.6**
Discovering the Iceman: what was it like to find a 5,300-year-old mummy? /
   TANAKA, S/1997/3-5/4 KE642 . . . . **937**
Discovery of the Americas. /MAESTRO, B/1991/2-6/8 KE183 . . . **917.04**
Discovery of the Americas: activities book./MAESTRO, B/1992/
   2-6/8 KE183 . . . . **917.04**
Discovery of the Americas (Sound recording cassette). /MAESTRO, B/
   1994/2-6/8 KE183 . . . . **917.04**
Distant talking drum: poems from Nigeria. /OLALEYE, I/1995/
   K-2/KE139 . . . . **896**
Distant talking drum: poems from Nigeria (Sound recording cassette)./
   OLALEYE, I/1997/K-2/KE139 . . . . **896**
Dither Farm: a novel. /HITE, S/1992/5-A/7 KH265 . . . . **Fic**
Dither Farm: a novel (Sound recording cassette)./HITE, S/1996/
   5-A/7 KH265 . . . . **Fic**
Divers. /MCDONALD, K/1992/4-6/8 KD847 . . . . **797.2**
DK GEOGRAPHY OF THE WORLD. /1996/2-6/10 KE146. . . . **910**
DNA is here to stay. /BALKWILL, FR/1993/5-6/7 KC279. . . . . **572.8**
Do not disturb. /TAFURI, N/1987/P-2/KG587. . . . . **E**
Do not open. /TURKLE, B/1981/K-2/2 KG622 . . . . **E**
Do not open (Braille). /TURKLE, B/n.d./K-2/2 KG622 . . . . **E**

Do people grow on family trees?: genealogy for kids and other beginners:
   the official Ellis Island handbook. /WOLFMAN, I/1991/
   5-A/7 KE610 . . . . **929**
Do you know me. /FARMER, N/1993/4-A/5 KH107 . . . . **Fic**
Do you wanna bet?: your chance to find out about probability. /
   CUSHMAN, J/1991/4-6/4 KB997 . . . . **519.2**
Do you want to be my friend? /CARLE, E/1971/P-K/1 KF340 . . . **E**
Doctor Change. /COLE, J/1986/K-3/2 KF410 . . . . **E**
Doctor Change (Sound recording cassette)./COLE, J/n.d./K-3/2 KF410. . **E**
Doctor Coyote: a Native American Aesop's fables. /BIERHORST, J/1987/
   3/3 KB530. . . . . **398.24**
Doctor Coyote: a Native American Aesop's fables (Braille). /BIERHORST, J/
   n.d./3/3 KB530 . . . . **398.24**
Doctor De Soto. /STEIG, W/1982/P-3/4 KG542 . . . . **CE E**
Doctor De Soto (Braille). /STEIG, W/n.d./P-3/4 KG542. . . . . **CE E**
Doctor De Soto goes to Africa./STEIG, W/1992/P-3/4 KG542 . . . **CE E**
Doctor De Soto goes to Africa (Kit)./STEIG, W/1995/
   P-3/4 KG542 . . . . **CE E**
Doctor De Soto goes to Africa (Sound recording cassette)./STEIG, W/
   1995/P-3/4 KG542 . . . . **CE E**
Doctor De Soto (Kit)./STEIG, W/1993/P-3/4 KG542 . . . . . . **CE E**
Doctor De Soto (Spanish version)./STEIG, W/1991/P-3/4 KG542 . . **CE E**
Doctor De Soto (Spanish version) (Videocassette)./STEIG, W/1993/
   P-3/4 KG542 . . . . **CE E**
Doctor De Soto (Talking book)./STEIG, W/1993/P-3/4 KG542 . **CE E**
Doctor De Soto (Videocassette)./STEIG, W/1986/P-3/4 KG542 . . **CE E**
Doesn't Fall Off His Horse. /STROUD, VA/1994/2-3/4 KG580. . . . . **E**
Dog. /CLUTTON-BROCK, J/1991/A/8 KD217. . . . . **636.7**
Dog and Cat shake a leg. /SPOHN, K/1996/K-2/1 KG534 . . . . . **E**
Dog ate my homework: social skills for today (Compact disc)./SLONECKI,
   C/1995/1-3/KB242 . . . . **SRC 395**
Dog ate my homework: social skills for today (Sound recording cassette). /
   SLONECKI, C/1995/1-3/KB242 . . . . **SRC 395**
Dog breath: the horrible trouble with Hally Tosis. /PILKEY, D/1994/
   2-3/3 KG236 . . . . **E**
Dog came, too: a true story. /MANSON, A/1993/1-4/6 KE185. **917.104**
Dog days. /RODOWSKY, C/1993/4-5/6 KH649 . . . . **Fic**
Dog Friday. /MCKAY, H/1995/4-A/7 KH477 . . . . **Fic**
Dog in, cat out. /RUBINSTEIN, G/1993/P-1/1 KG359 . . . . **E**
Dog named Sam. /BOLAND, J/1996/K-2/2 KF241 . . . . **E**
Dog on Barkham Street. /STOLZ, M/c1960/4-6/4 KH765 . . . . . **Fic**
Dog on Barkham Street (Braille). /STOLZ, M/n.d./4-6/4 KH765 . . **Fic**
Dog people: native dog stories. /BRUCHAC, J/1995/4-6/5 KG934 . . **Fic**
DOG (Videocassette). /1994/3-6/KD219 . . . . **VCR 636.7**
Dog who cried woof. /COFFELT, N/1995/K-2/3 KF402 . . . . **E**
Dog who dared (Videocassette). /ARMSTRONG, T/1993/
   4-6/KC993 . . . . **VCR 613.8**
Dog who had kittens. /ROBERTUS, PM/1991/K-1/4 KG337 . . . . **CE E**
Dog who had kittens (Kit)./ROBERTUS, PM/1992/K-1/4 KG337 . . . **CE E**
Dog who had kittens (Videocassette)./ROBERTUS, PM/1992/
   K-1/4 KG337. . . . . **CE E**
Dog years. /WARNER, S/1995/4-6/3 KH840 . . . . **Fic**
Dogger. /HUGHES, S/c1978/P-2/3 KF788 . . . . **E**
Dogs: all about them. /SILVERSTEIN, A/1986/5-6/7 KD221 . . . **636.7**
Dogs don't tell jokes. /SACHAR, L/1992/5-A/5 KH665 . . . . . . **Fic**
Dogs don't tell jokes (Sound recording cassette)./SACHAR, L/1994/
   5-A/5 KH665 . . . . **Fic**
Dogs: wild and domestic. /KAPPELER, M/1991/5-6/6 KD220 . . **636.7**
Dogteam. /PAULSEN, G/1993/1-3/4 KG221 . . . . **E**
DOING THE RIGHT THING (Videocassette)./1990/4-6/KA655 . **VCR 158**
Doll who knew the future. /DEXTER, C/1994/4-6/6 KH072 . . . . **Fic**
Dollhouse murders. /WRIGHT, BR/1983/4-6/5 KH882 . . . . . . **Fic**
Dollhouse murders (Sound recording cassette)./WRIGHT, BR/n.d./
   4-6/5 KH882 . . . . **Fic**
Dolls. /YOUNG, R/1992/5-6/6 KD353 . . . . **688.7**
Dolphin. /MORRIS, RA/c1975/K-2/2 KC778. . . . . **599.53**
Dolphin (Braille). /MORRIS, RA/n.d./K-2/2 KC778 . . . . **599.53**
Dolphin man: exploring the world of dolphins. /PRINGLE, LP/1995/
   5-6/11 KC776 . . . . **599.5**
DOLPHINS. /1988/5-6/6 KD190 . . . . **636.088**
Dominic. /STEIG, W/c1972/4-6/7 KH750 . . . . **Fic**
Dominico./STEIG, W/1994/4-6/7 KH750 . . . . **Fic**
Domino addition. /LONG, L/1996/P-2/2 KB966 . . . . **513.2**
Donde esta mi osito?/ALBOROUGH, J/1995/P-1/2 KF145 . . . . . . **E**
Donde viven los monstruos./SENDAK, M/1996/P-3/2 KG438 . . . . **CE E**
Donde viven los monstruos (Videocassette)./SENDAK, M/1993/
   P-3/2 KG438. . . . . **CE E**
Done in the sun, solar projects for children. /HILLERMAN, A/1983/
   2-4/7 KD048 . . . . **621.47**
Donkey trouble. /YOUNG, E/1995/1-2/5 KB678 . . . . **398.24**
Don't be afraid, Amanda. /MOORE, L/1992/2-4/4 KH504 . . . . **Fic**
Don't be afraid, Amanda (Sound recording cassette)./MOORE, L/1994/
   2-4/4 KH504 . . . . **Fic**
Don't call me Beanhead! /WOJCIECHOWSKI, S/1994/2-3/5 KH877 . . **Fic**

Don't call me Slob-o. /ORGEL, D/1996/3-5/2 KH565. . . . . **Fic**
Don't eat too much turkey!/COHEN, M/1987/K-1/2 KF405 . . . . . . **CE E**
Don't fidget a feather! /SILVERMAN, E/1994/P-2/2 KG505 . . . . **E**
Don't fidget a feather! (Sound recording cassette)./SILVERMAN, E/1997/
   P-2/2 KG505 . . . . **E**
Don't forget the bacon! /HUTCHINS, P/c1976, 1987/P-2/3 KF796 . **CE E**
Don't forget the bacon! (Big book)./HUTCHINS, P/1994/
   P-2/3 KF796 . . . . **CE E**
Don't forget the bacon! (Kit)./HUTCHINS, P/1992/P-2/3 KF796 . . . **CE E**
Don't hurt Laurie! /ROBERTS, WD/1977/5-6/6 KH635 . . . . **Fic**
Don't open the door after the sun goes down: tales of the real and unreal.
   /CARUSONE, A/1994/4-6/4 KG982 . . . . **Fic**
Don't read this book, whatever you do!: more poems about school. /
   DAKOS, K/1993/4-6/KD928. . . . . **811**
Don't sing before breakfast, don't sleep in the moonlight: everyday
   superstitions and how they began. /PERL, L/1988/
   4-A/8 KA559 . . . . **001.9**
Don't sing before breakfast, don't sleep in the moonlight: everyday
   superstitions and how they began (Sound recording cassette)./PERL, L/
   n.d./4-A/8 KA559 . . . . **001.9**
Don't wake up Mama!/CHRISTELOW, E/1992/P-K/2 KF384 . . . . . . **E**
Don't wake up Mama! (Sound recording cassette)./CHRISTELOW, E/1995/
   P-K/2 KF384 . . . . **E**
Don't you know there's a war on? /STEVENSON, J/1992/
   K-3/2 KE552 . . . . **B STEVENSON, J.**
Don't you know there's a war on? (Sound recording cassette)./
   STEVENSON, J/1994/K-3/2 KE552 . . . . **B STEVENSON, J.**
Don't-give-up Kid and learning differences. 2nd ed. /GEHRET, J/1996/
   K-3/2 KB095 . . . . **371.92**
Doodle Dandy!: the complete book of Independence Day words. /
   GRAHAM-BARBER, L/1992/5-A/A KB220 . . . . **394.263**
Doodle Dandy!: the complete book of Independence Day words (Sound
   recording cassette)./GRAHAM-BARBER, L/1996/
   5-A/A KB220 . . . . **394.263**
Doodle flute. /PINKWATER, DM/1991/1-3/2 KG245 . . . . **E**
Doom of the haunted opera. /BELLAIRS, J/1995/4-6/6 KG896. . . . . . **Fic**
Door in the hedge. /MCKINLEY, R/1981/4-6/6 KH487 . . . . **Fic**
Door in the wall. /DE ANGELI, M/c1949, 1989/4-6/6 KH064 . . . . . **Fic**
Doorbell rang. /HUTCHINS, P/1986/P-2/2 KF797 . . . . **CE E**
Doorbell rang (Big book)./HUTCHINS, P/1994/P-2/2 KF797 . . . . . **CE E**
Doorbell rang (Braille)./HUTCHINS, P/n.d./P-2/2 KF797 . . . . . . **CE E**
Dorothea Lange. /TURNER, R/1994/5-A/7 KE427 . . . . **B LANGE, D.**
Dorothy's darkest days. /CASELEY, J/1997/3-5/4 KG983 . . . . **Fic**
Dots, spots, speckles, and stripes. /HOBAN, T/1987/P-A/KA613. . **152.14**
DOUBLE DUTCH--DOUBLE JEOPARDY (Videocassette). /1990/
   5-6/KD027. . . . . **VCR 616.97**
Double life of Pocahontas. /FRITZ, J/1983/
   5-6/6 KE500 . . . . **B POCAHONTAS**
Double life of Pocahontas (Sound recording cassette)./FRITZ, J/n.d./
   5-6/6 KE500 . . . . **B POCAHONTAS**
Doughnuts (Videocassette). /MCCLOSKEY, R/1984/2-6/KH469. . **VCR Fic**
Down at the bottom of the deep dark sea. /JONES, RC/1991/
   P-K/2 KF852 . . . . **E**
Down Buttermilk Lane. /MITCHELL, B/1993/1-3/2 KG144 . . . . **E**
Down in the sea: the jellyfish. /KITE, P/1993/3-5/4 KC509 . . . . . **593.5**
Down in the sea: the octopus. /KITE, P/1993/3-5/4 KC513 . . . . . . **594**
DOWN ON THE FARM: YESTERDAY AND TODAY (Videocassette). /
   1987/3-A/KD142 . . . . **VCR 630**
Down under, down under: diving adventures on the Great Barrier Reef. /
   MCGOVERN, A/1989/3-6/5 KF120 . . . . **994.3**
Down under: vanishing cultures. /REYNOLDS, J/1992/3-6/6 KF117 . . **994**
Dr. Dredd's wagon of wonders. /BRITTAIN, B/1987/3-6/5 KG923 . . . **Fic**
Dr. Seuss' Caldecotts (Videocassette). /SEUSS, D/1985/
   1-3/KG450 . . . . **VCR E**
Dr. Seuss's ABC. /SEUSS, D/c1963/P-2/2 KG451 . . . . **CE E**
DR. SEUSS'S ABC (CD-ROM). /1995/P-2/KF493 . . . . **CDR E**
Dr. Seuss's ABC (Talking book)./SEUSS, D/n.d./P-2/2 KG451 . . . . **CE E**
Drackenberg adventure./ALEXANDER, L/1988/5-A/5 KG837 . . . . . . **Fic**
Dragon feathers. /DUGIN, A/1993/4-5/7 KB289 . . . . **398.2**
DRAGON POEMS. /1991/K-A/KE055. . . . . **811.008**
Dragondrums./MCCAFFREY, A/1980/4-6 KH466 . . . . **Fic**
Dragondrums (Braille)./MCCAFFREY, A/n.d./6-A/6 KH466. . . . . . . **Fic**
Dragondrums (Sound recording cassette)./MCCAFFREY, A/n.d./
   6-A/6 KH466 . . . . **Fic**
Dragonfly. /BERNHARD, E/1993/2-4/4 KC534 . . . . **595.7**
Dragonfly's tale. /RODANAS, K/1992/2-3/4 KB767 . . . . **398.27**
Dragons and prehistoric monsters. /SANCHEZ SANCHEZ, I/1996/
   3-6/3 KD447 . . . . **745.592**
Dragons are singing tonight. /PRELUTSKY, J/1993/2-4/KE002 . . . . . **811**
Dragons are singing tonight (Sound recording cassette)./PRELUTSKY, J/
   1995/2-4/KE002. . . . . **811**
Dragons of Blueland./GANNETT, RS/1963/3-5/6 KH149 . . . . **Fic**
Dragonsinger./MCCAFFREY, A/1977/6-A/6 KH466 . . . . **Fic**
Dragonsinger (Braille)./MCCAFFREY, A/n.d./6-A/6 KH466. . . . . . . **Fic**

Dragonsinger (Sound recording cassette)./MCCAFFREY, A/n.d./
   6-A/6 KH466 . . . . **Fic**
Dragonsong. /MCCAFFREY, A/c1976, 1986/6-A/6 KH466 . . . . **Fic**
Dragonwings. /YEP, L/c1975/5-6/6 KH892. . . . . **Fic**
Dragonwings (Sound recording cassette)./YEP, L/n.d./5-6/6 KH892 . . **Fic**
Dragsters. /CONNOLLY, M/1992/4-A/4 KD829 . . . . **796.7**
Drat these brats! /KENNEDY, XJ/1993/3-6/KD962. . . . . **811**
Draw! /SOLGA, K/1991/2-6/4 KD405 . . . . **741.2**
Draw! cars. Rev. ed. /DUBOSQUE, D/1997/4-A/5 KD417. . . . . . . **743**
Draw 50 airplanes, aircraft and spacecraft./AMES, LJ/1987/
   4-6/KD416. . . . . **743**
Draw 50 animals./AMES, LJ/1974/4-6/KD416. . . . . **743**
Draw 50 beasties and yugglies and turnover uglies and things that go bump
   in the night./AMES, LJ/1990/4-6/KD416. . . . . **743**
Draw 50 boats, ships, trucks and trains./AMES, LJ/1987/4-6/KD416. **743**
Draw 50 cars, trucks, and motorcycles. /AMES, LJ/1986/4-6/KD415. **743**
Draw 50 dinosaurs. /AMES, LJ/1985/4-6/KD416 . . . . **743**
Draw 50 dogs./AMES, LJ/1986/4-6/KD416 . . . . **743**
Draw 50 horses. /AMES, LJ/1986/4-6/KD416 . . . . **743**
Drawing: a young artist's guide. /WELTON, J/1994/3-6/6 KD406 . **741.2**
Drawing dinosaurs. /SANCHEZ SANCHEZ, I/1996/5-A/3 KD418 . . **743**
Dreadful creatures./SANCHEZ SANCHEZ, I/1996/3-6/3 KD449 . . **745.592**
DREAM IS ALIVE: A WINDOW SEAT ON THE SPACE SHUTTLE
   (Videocassette). /1985/5-6/KD134. . . . . **VCR 629.44**
Dream jar. /PRYOR, B/1996/2-3/5 KG291. . . . . **E**
Dream keeper and other poems, including seven additional poems. /
   HUGHES, L/1994/4-6/KD954 . . . . **811**
Dream keeper (Videocassette). /POLACCO, P/1996/
   2-4/KE501 . . . . **VCR B POLACCO, P.**
Dream planes. /GUNNING, TG/1992/5-6/7 KD109. . . . . **629.133**
Dream quest. /COOPER, AJ/1987/5-A/4 KH024 . . . . **Fic**
Dream trains. /GUNNING, TG/1992/4-6/6 KD074 . . . . **625.1**
Dream wolf. /GOBLE, P/1990/K-3/4 KF627 . . . . **E**
Dream wolf (Sound recording cassette)./GOBLE, P/1994/K-3/4 KF627. . **E**
Dreamcatcher. /OSOFSKY, A/1992/K-2/5 KG200 . . . . **E**
Dreams. /SPIER, P/1986/P-2/KG531. . . . . **E**
Dreamtime: aboriginal stories. /OODGEROO /1994/
   4-5/6 KB506 . . . . **398.23**
Dress I'll wear to the party./NEITZEL, S/1992/P-2/2 KG168 . . . . . . **E**
Drinking gourd (Braille)./MONJO, FN/n.d./1-3/2 KG151 . . . . **E**
Drinking gourd. Newly illustrated ed. /MONJO, FN/1993/
   1-3/2 KG151 . . . . **E**
Drop dead. /COLE, B/1996/2-4/2 KF406. . . . . **E**
Drop of blood. Rev. ed. /SHOWERS, P/1989/K-2/2 KC936 . . . . . **612.1**
Drop of blood. Rev. ed. (Talking book)./SHOWERS, P/n.d./
   K-2/2 KC936 . . . . **612.1**
Drop of water: a book of science and wonder. /WICK, W/1997/
   K-6/6 KC142 . . . . **546**
Drowned Ammet./JONES, DW/c1978, 1995/6-A/6 KH331 . . . . **Fic**
DRUG DANGER: EASY TO START, HARD TO STOP (Videocassette). /
   1992/5-6/KC994 . . . . **VCR 613.8**
DRUG DANGER: IN THE BODY (Videocassette). /1992/
   5-6/KD019. . . . . **VCR 616.86**
Drugs and you. Rev. ed. /MADISON, A/1990/5-6/7 KC999 . . . . . **613.8**
DRUGS, YOUR FRIENDS, AND YOU: HANDLING PEER PRESSURE
   (Videocassette). /1988/6-A/KC995. . . . . **VCR 613.8**
Drumbeat...heartbeat: a celebration of the powwow. /BRAINE, S/1995/
   5-6/9 KB178 . . . . **394**
Dry or wet? /MCMILLAN, B/1988/P-1/KB844. . . . . **428**
Drylongso. /HAMILTON, V/1992/4-6/4 KH214. . . . . **Fic**
Dublin. /KENT, D/1997/3-5/8 KE678 . . . . **941.8**
Ducklings and pollywogs. /ROCKWELL, AF/1994/K-2/3 KG341 . . . . . **E**
Duffy and the devil, a Cornish tale. /ZEMACH, H/c1973/
   2-4/7 KB426 . . . . **CE 398.21**
Duffy and the devil, a Cornish tale (Braille)./ZEMACH, H/n.d./
   2-4/7 KB426 . . . . **CE 398.21**
Duke Ellington: giant of jazz. /OLD, WC/1996/
   5-A/9 KE338 . . . . **B ELLINGTON, D.**
Dumbstruck. /PENNYPACKER, S/1994/4-6/7 KH596 . . . . **Fic**
Dumpling soup. /RATTIGAN, JK/1993/1-3/2 KG312 . . . . **E**
Duplicate. /SLEATOR, W/1990/A/6 KH717 . . . . **Fic**
Dusk of Demons. /CHRISTOPHER, J/1994/5-A/4 KG990 . . . . **Fic**
DUST BOWL (Picture). /n.d./5-6/KE917 . . . . **PIC 973.917**
Dust for dinner. /TURNER, A/1995/2-5/2 KG625 . . . . **E**
DUSTY THE DRAGON TALKS TO DR. MARGIE HOGAN ABOUT
   TOBACCO (Videocassette). /1990/3-5/KD005 . . . . **VCR 613.85**
D.W. all wet./BROWN, MT/1988/P-2/1 KF281 . . . . **E**
D.W. flips. /BROWN, MT/1987/P-2/1 KF281 . . . . **E**
D.W. rides again!/BROWN, MT/1993/P-2/1 KF281 . . . . **E**
D.W. the picky eater./BROWN, MT/1995/P-2/1 KF281 . . . . **E**
D.W. the picky eater (Sound recording cassette)./BROWN, MT/1997/
   P-2/1 KF281 . . . . **E**
D.W. thinks big./BROWN, MT/1993/P-2/1 KF281 . . . . **E**

Dwarf, the giant, and the unicorn: a tale of King Arthur. /GIBLIN, JC/ 1996/3-5/4 KB443 . . . . 398.22

Dwight D. Eisenhower: a man called Ike. /DARBY, J/1989/ 5-6/6 KE335 . . . . **B EISENHOWER, D**

E I E I O: the story of Old MacDonald, who had a farm. /CLARKE, G/ 1993/K-1/KF393 . . . . **E**

E is for Elisa./HURWITZ, J/1991/2-4/4 KH303 . . . . . . **Fic**

E is for Elisa (Sound recording cassette)./HURWITZ, J/1994/ 2-4/4 KH303 . . . . **Fic**

Each orange had 8 slices: a counting book. /GIGANTI, JR., P/1992/ P-1/2 KB989 . . . . 513.5

Each orange had 8 slices: a counting book (Big book)./GIGANTI, JR., P/ 1994/P-1/2 KB989 . . . . 513.5

Each peach pear plum: an "I spy" story. /AHLBERG, J/1978/ P-1/3 KF141 . . . . **CE E**

Each peach pear plum: an "I spy" story (Videocassette)./AHLBERG, J/ 1992/P-1/3 KF141 . . . . **CE E**

Eagle and the rainbow: timeless tales from Mexico. /MADRIGAL, AH/ 1997/4-5/7 KB339 . . . . 398.2

Eagle and the river. /CRAIGHEAD, C/1994/5-6/7 KC339 . . . 577.6

EAGLE AND THE SNAKE (Videocassette). /1993/2-6/KC472. **VCR 591.5**

Eagle boy: a traditional Navajo legend. /HAUSMAN, G/1996/ 3-4/5 KB587 . . . . 398.24

Eagle drum: on the powwow trail with a young grass dancer. /CRUM, R/ 1994/5-A/5 KB197 . . . . 394.26

Eagles: lions of the sky. /BERNHARD, E/1994/3-6/6 KC710 . . . . . 598.9

Eagles of America. /PATENT, DH/1995/4-6/6 KC716 . . . . . . 598.9

Eagle's song: a tale from the Pacific Northwest. /RODANAS, K/1995/ 3-4/5 KB768 . . . . 398.27

Ear and hearing. Rev. ed. /PARKER, S/1989/5-6/8 KC971 . . . . . 612.8

Ear, the Eye and the Arm: a novel. /FARMER, N/1994/6-A/4 KH108 . **Fic**

Earliest Americans. /SATTLER, HR/1993/5-A/8 KE743 . . . . . 970.01

Earliest Americans (Sound recording cassette)./SATTLER, HR/1995/ 5-A/8 KE743 . . . . 970.01

Early American Christmas. /DE PAOLA, T/1987/K-3/5 KF469 . . . . . **E**

Early artisans. /KALMAN, B/1983/4-A/8 KD430 . . . . . . 745.5

Early childhood at risk: actions and advocacy for young children. / DIMIDJIAN, VJ/1989//KA190 . . . . **PROF 372**

Early loggers and the sawmill. /ADAMS, P/1981/4-6/6 KD164 . . . 634.9

Early morning in the barn. /TAFURI, N/1983/P/KG588 . . . . . . **E**

Early pleasures and pastimes. /KALMAN, B/1983/4-A/8 KD680 . . 790.1

Early thunder. /FRITZ, J/c1967, 1987/5-A/6 KH144 . . . . **Fic**

Early thunder (Talking book)./FRITZ, J/n.d./5-A/6 KH144 . . . . . **Fic**

Early violence prevention: tools for teachers of young children. /SLABY, RG/1995/KA162 . . . . **PROF 303.6**

Earrings! /VIORST, J/1990/1-3/2 KG661 . . . . **E**

Ears. /MATHERS, D/1992/5-6/6 KC967 . . . . 612.8

Earth. /FRADIN, DB/1989/4-5/4 KC058 525

Earth atlas. /VAN ROSE, S/1994/A/7 KA443 . . . . **REF 551**

Earth daughter: Alicia of Acoma Pueblo. /ANCONA, G/1995/ 2-4/6 KE791 . . . . 970.489

Earth, fire, water, air. /HOFFMAN, M/1995/2-6/7 KA814 . . . 304.2

EARTH IS PAINTED GREEN: A GARDEN OF POEMS ABOUT OUR PLANET. /1994/3-6/KD883 . . . . 808.81

Earth keepers. /ANDERSON, J/1993/A/9 KB044 . . . . . . 363.7

Earth mirth: the ecology riddle book. /THALER, M/1994/ 2-4/KD741 . . . . 793.735

Earth tunes (Compact disc)./WORLD PATROL KIDS /1995/ 3-6/KC300 . . . . **VCR 577**

Earth tunes for kids (Videocassette). /WORLD PATROL KIDS /1994/ 3-6/KC300 . . . . **VCR 577**

Earth tunes (Sound recording cassette)./WORLD PATROL KIDS /1995/ 3-6/KC300 . . . . **VCR 577**

Earth words: a dictionary of the environment. /SIMON, S/1995/ 3-6/9 KB067 . . . . 363.73

Earthkeepers: observers and protectors of nature. /KEENE, AT/1994/ 5-A/KA436 . . . . **REF 508**

Earthquake. /LAMPTON, C/1991/5-6/7 KC162 . . . . . . 551.22

Earthquake at dawn. /GREGORY, K/1992/5-A/6 KH202 . . . . **Fic**

Earthquakes. /BRANLEY, FM/1990/2-4/4 KC161 . . . . . 551.22

Earthquakes. /SIMON, S/1991/3-6/7 KC163 . . . . 551.22

Earthquakes. /SPIES, KB/1994/4-6/7 KB038 . . . . 363.34

EARTH'S SEASONS/CLIMATES (Videocassette). /1995/ 3-6/KB902 . . . . **VCR 508**

Earthshine: a novel. /NELSON, T/1994/6-A/6 KH540 . . . . **Fic**

Earthworms. /PASCOE, E/1997/4-6/4 KC506 592

EAST (Videocassette)./1989/5-6/KE181 . . . . **VCR 917**

Easter Bunny that overslept. /FRIEDRICH, P/1983/P-K/KF587 . . . . . . **E**

Easter story. /HEYER, C/1990/5-6/5 KA710 . . . . 232.96

Easter surprise./STOCK, C/P-K/2 KG574 . . . . **E**

Easy as pie: a guessing game of sayings. /FOLSOM, M/1985/ 1-3/3 KF564 . . . . **E**

Easy carpentry projects for children. /LEAVITT, J/c1959, 1986/ 5-6/4 KD340 684

Easy costumes you don't have to sew. /CHERNOFF, GT/c1975/ P-A/4 KD298 . . . . 646.4

Easy math puzzles. /ADLER, DA/1997/K-3/KD723 . . . . . 793.735

Easy-to-make spaceships that really fly. /BLOCKSMA, M/1983/ 3-5/3 KD140 . . . . 629.47

Eat up, Gemma. /HAYES, S/1988/P-2/2 KF685 . . . . **E**

Eating fractions. /MCMILLAN, B/1991/P-2/1 KB969 . . . . . . 513.2

Eating pretty. /KARLSBERG, E/1991/5-A/7 KC985 . . . . . 613.2

Eating the plates: a Pilgrim book of food and manners. /PENNER, LR/ 1991/3-6/4 KB186 . . . . 394.1

Eats. /ADOFF, A/c1979, 1992/P-A/KD908 811

Eats (Braille)./ADOFF, A/n.d./P-A/KD908 811

E.B. White: some writer! /GHERMAN, B/1992/ 6-A/8 KE593 . . . . **B WHITE, E.B.**

E.B. White: some writer! (Sound recording cassette)./GHERMAN, B/1995/ 6-A/8 KE593 . . . . **B WHITE, E.B.**

Echoes of World War II. /MARX, T/1994/A/7 KE660 . . . . 940.53

EcoArt!: earth-friendly art and craft experiences for 3-to 9-year olds. / CARLSON, L/1993/K-4/KD425 . . . . 745.5

Ecology A to Z. /FLEISHER, P/1994/6-A/KA410 . . . . . . **REF 363.7**

ECOLOGY WITH SEUSS (Microcomputer program). /1990/ 2-5/KB112 . . . . **MCP 372.6**

Eco-women: protectors of the earth. /SIRCH, WA/1996/ 4-6/7 KA953 . . . . 333.7

Edgar Allan: a novel. /NEUFELD, J/c1968/4-A/5 KH545 . . . . **Fic**

Edgar Allan: a novel (Braille)./NEUFELD, J/n.d./4-A/5 KH545 . . . **Fic**

Edgar Degas. /MEYER, SE/1994/6-A/9 KE318 . . . . . . **B DEGAS, E.**

Edge of the sea. /CARSON, R/c1955/A/10 KC367 . . . . . . 578.77

Edge of the sea (Braille)./CARSON, R/n.d./A/10 KC367 . . . . 578.77

Edge of the sea (Sound recording cassette)./CARSON, R/n.d./ A/10 KC367 . . . . 578.77

Eduardo cumpleanos en la piscina./WELLS, R/1996/P-K/2 KG697 . . . . . **E**

Eduardo: el primer dia de colegio./WELLS, R/1997/P-K/2 KG698 . . . . . **E**

EDUCATING ABLE LEARNERS (Videocassette). /1991/ /KA187 . . . . **VCR PROF 371.95**

EDUCATING PETER (Videocassette). /1993//KA185. . **VCR PROF 371.92**

EDUCATION DIGEST. /1935-//KA104 . . . . **PER PROF 050**

EDUCATION INDEX. /1929-//KA105 . . . . **PER PROF 050**

EDUCATION WEEK. /1981-//KA106. . . . . **PER PROF 050**

EDUCATIONAL SOFTWARE PREVIEW GUIDE. /1982-/ /KA107 . . . . **PER PROF 050**

EDUCATORS' ESSENTIAL INTERNET TRAINING SYSTEM (Multimedia kit). /1996//KA001 . . . . **MMK PROF 004.67**

Educator's Internet companion: CLASSROOM CONNECT's complete guide to educational resources on the Internet. 4th ed. /GIAGNOCAVO, G/ 1996//KA049 . . . . **BC PROF 025.06**

Edward and the pirates. /MCPHAIL, D/1997/K-2/3 KG117 . . . . **E**

Edward in deep water. /WELLS, R/1995/P-K/2 KG697 . . . . **E**

Edward unready for school. /WELLS, R/1995/P-K/2 KG698 . . . . . . **E**

Edward's overwhelming overnight. /WELLS, R/1995/P-1/2 KG699 . . . . **E**

Edwin and Emily. /WILLIAMS, S/1995/1-3/2 KG733 . . . . **E**

Eentsy, weentsy spider: fingerplays and action rhymes. /COLE, J/1991/ P-K/KD706 . . . . 793.4

Egg. /GOLDSEN, L/1992/P-3/2 KC281 . . . . 573.6

Egg to chick. Rev. ed. /SELSAM, ME/1970/P-2/2 KC698 . . . . . . 598.6

Egg tree. /MILHOUS, K/c1950, 1992/1-3/4 KG134 . . . . **E**

Eggs mark the spot. /AUCH, MJ/1996/K-2/3 KF176 . . . . . . **CE E**

Eggs mark the spot (Kit)./AUCH, MJ/1997/K-2/3 KF176 . . . . **CE E**

Eggs mark the spot (Videocassette)./AUCH, MJ/1997/K-2/3 KF176. **CE E**

Egypt: ancient traditions, modern hopes. /KING, DC/1997/ 4-6/7 KE634 932

Egypt game. /SNYDER, ZK/c1967/5-6/6 KH731 . . . . **Fic**

Egypt game (Braille)./SNYDER, ZK/n.d./5-6/6 KH731 . . . . **Fic**

Egypt game (Sound recording cassette)./SNYDER, ZK/1995/ 5-6/6 KH731 . . . . **Fic**

Egyptian tombs. /BENDICK, J/1989/4-6/7 KE632 932

El Chino. /SAY, A/1990/3-5/4 KE598 . . . . **B WONG, B.**

El Cuento de Pedro, el Conejo./POTTER, B/n.d./P-2/6 KG278 . . . . . **E**

El Dorado adventure. /ALEXANDER, L/1987/5-A/5 KG837 . . . . . . **Fic**

El gusto./PARRAMON, JM/1985/P-1/2 KC975 . . . . 612.8

El oido./PARRAMON, JM/1985/P-1/1 KC973 . . . . 612.8

El tacto./PARRAMON, JM/1985/P-1/2 KC976 . . . . 612.8

Eleanor. /COONEY, B/1996/4-5/7 KE520 . . . . . . **B ROOSEVELT, E.**

Eleanor Roosevelt: a life of discovery. /FREEDMAN, R/1993/ 6-A/7 KE521 . . . . **B ROOSEVELT, E.**

ELECTING A PRESIDENT: THE PROCESS (Videocassette). /1993/ 6-A/KA913 . . . . **VCR 324.973**

ELECTING A PRESIDENT (Videocassette). /1995/ 6-A/KA914 . . . . **VCR 324.973**

Electricity. /PARKER, S/1992/4-A/9 KC134 537

Electricity. /HOOPER, T/1994/5-6/11 KC131 537

ELEMENTARY SCHOOL LIBRARY COLLECTION: A GUIDE TO BOOKS AND OTHER MEDIA, PHASES 1-2-3. 21st ed. /1998/ /KA013 . . . . **PROF 011.62**

ELEMENTARY SCHOOL LIBRARY COLLECTION: A GUIDE TO BOOKS
AND OTHER MEDIA, PHASES 1-2-3. 21st ed. (CD-ROM). /1998/
/KA014 . . . . **CDR PROF 011.62**
Elephant. /REDMOND, I/1993/4-6/7 KC815 . . . . **599.67**
Elephant. /ARNOLD, C/1993/5-6/9 KC808 . . . . **599.67**
ELEPHANT DIARY (Videocassette). /1990/3-5/KC809 . . . . . **VCR 599.67**
Elephant seals. /JOHNSON, SA/1989/5-6/7 KC869 . . . . **599.79**
Elephants. /GRACE, ES/1993/5-6/8 KC810 . . . . **599.67**
Elephants: our last land giants. /MACMILLAN, D/1993/
5-6/8 KC811 . . . . **599.67**
Elephants swim. /RILEY, LC/1995/P-2/3 KC466 . . . . **591.47**
Elephant's wrestling match. /SIERRA, J/1992/P-2/4 KB652 . . . . . **398.24**
Eleven nature tales: a multicultural journey. /DESPAIN, P/1996/
3-5/7 KB286 . . . . **398.2**
Eleven turtle tales: adventure tales from around the world. /DESPAIN, P/
1994/2-3/4 KB559 . . . . **398.24**
Elfwyn's saga. /WISNIEWSKI, D/1990/4-6/6 KB422 . . . . . . **398.21**
Elijah's angel: a story for Chanukah and Christmas. /ROSEN, MJ/1992/
3-6/7 KH652 . . . . **Fic**
Elijah's angel: a story for Chanukah and Christmas (Sound recording
cassette)./ROSEN, MJ/1995/3-6/7 KH652 . . . . **Fic**
Elinda who danced in the sky: an Estonian folktale. /MORONEY, L/1990/
3-5/5 KB407 . . . . **398.21**
Elisa in the middle./HURWITZ, J/1995/2-4/4 KH303 . . . . **Fic**
Elk. /LEPTHIEN, EU/1994/4-6/5 KC798 . . . . **599.65**
Ella enchanted. /LEVINE, GC/1997/5-A/5 KH397 . . . . **Fic**
Ella Jenkins live!: at the Smithsonian (Videocassette). /JENKINS, E/1991/
P-K/KD627 . . . . **VCR 789.3**
Ella of all-of-a-kind family./TAYLOR, S/1978/4-6/5 KH782 . . . . . **Fic**
Ella of all-of-a-kind family (Sound recording cassette)./TAYLOR, S/n.d./
4-6/5 KH782 . . . . **Fic**
Ellen Tebbits. /CLEARY, B/1951/2-4/3 KG994 . . . . **Fic**
Ellen Tebbits (Braille)./CLEARY, B/n.d./2-4/3 KG994 . . . . **Fic**
Ellis Island: doorway to freedom. /KROLL, S/1995/2-4/10 KA920 . . . **325**
Ellis Island: new hope in a new land. /JACOBS, WJ/1990/
3-6/6 KA919 . . . . **325**
Ellis Island: new hope in a new land (Sound recording cassette)./JACOBS,
WJ/1993/3-6/6 KA919 . . . . **325**
Elmer and the dragon./GANNETT, RS/c1950, 1987/3-5/6 KH149 . . . **Fic**
Elmer and the dragon (Braille)./GANNETT, RS/n.d./3-5/6 KH149 . . . **Fic**
Elmer and the dragon (Talking book)./GANNETT, RS/n.d./
3-5/6 KH149 . . . . **Fic**
Elsa, star of the shelter! /WILSON, J/1996/4-6/5 KH868 . . . . **Fic**
E-mail. /BRIMNER, LD/1997/2-4/3 KB134 . . . . **384.3**
Emeka's gift: an African counting story. /ONYEFULU, I/1995/
1-4/5 KE728 . . . . **960**
Emerald City of Oz./BAUM, LF/1993/4-6/7 KG884 . . . . **Fic**
Emergency! /GIBBONS, G/1994/P-1/6 KB032 . . . . **363.3**
EMERGENCY LIBRARIAN. /1973-//KA108 . . . . **PER PROF 050**
EMERGENCY 911 (Videocassette). /1994/2-5/KB135 . . . . . **VCR 384.6**
Emily. /BEDARD, M/1992/2-5/2 KF215 . . . . **E**
Emily and Alice. /CHAMPION, J/1993/1-3/2 KF375 . . . . **E**
Emily and Alice again. /CHAMPION, J/1995/1-3/2 KF376 . . . . . . **E**
Emily and Alice (Sound recording cassette)./CHAMPION, J/1997/
1-3/2 KF375 . . . . **E**
Emily and the enchanted frog. /GRIFFITH, HV/1989/2-4/2 KF646 . . . . **E**
Emily Eyefinger. /BALL, D/1992/1-3/2 KG876 . . . . **Fic**
Emma Bean. /VAN LEEUWEN, J/1993/K-2/6 KC446 . . . . **E**
Emma's Christmas: an old song. /TRIVAS, I/1988/P-3/6 KG618 . . . . . **E**
Emma's eggs. /RUURS, M/1996/P-2/2 KG364 . . . . **E**
Emma's rug. /SAY, A/1996/1-3/3 KG396 . . . . **E**
Emmitt Smith: relentless rusher. /THORNLEY, S/1997/
4-6/7 KE543 . . . . **B SMITH, E.**
Emmy. /GREEN, CJ/1992/6-A/5 KH196 . . . . **Fic**
Emperor and the kite. /YOLEN, J/1988/2-3/6 KB791 . . . . **398.27**
Emperor and the kite (Braille)./YOLEN, J/n.d./2-3/6 KB791 . . . . **398.27**
Emperor's new clothes. /LEVINSON, R/1991/P-2/4 KF968 . . . . . **E**
Emperor's new clothes. /MENDELSON, ST/1992/1-3/7 KG128 . . . . . **E**
Emperor's panda. /DAY, D/c1986, 1987/4-A/8 KH063 . . . . . . **Fic**
Empress and the silkworm. /HONG, LT/1995/1-3/6 KF766 . . . . . **E**
Empress and the silkworm (Sound recording cassette)./HONG, LT/1997/
1-3/6 KF766 . . . . **E**
En el palacio del Rey del Oceano./SINGER, M/1995/2-3/5 KG509 . . . **E**
Enano Saltarin./ZELINSKY, PO/1992/1-4/7 KB385 . . . . **CE 398.2**
Enano Saltarin (Videocassette)./ZELINSKY, PO/1989/
1-4/7 KB385 . . . . **CE 398.2**
Enchanted castle. /NESBIT, E/c1907, 1985/5-6/7 KH541 . . . . . . **Fic**
Enchanted castle. /NESBIT, E/1992/5-A/6 KH542 . . . . **Fic**
Enchanted castle (Braille). /NESBIT, E/n.d./5-6/7 KH541 . . . . . . **Fic**
Enchanted castle (Sound recording cassette). /NESBIT, E/n.d./
5-6/7 KH541 . . . . **Fic**
Enchanted horse. /NABB, M/1993/4-6/7 KH525 . . . . **Fic**
Encore for Eleanor. /PEET, B/1981/K-2/7 KG226 . . . . **E**
Encounter at Easton./AVI /1980, 1994/5-A/6 KG860 . . . . **Fic**

Encyclopedia Brown and the case of Pablo's nose. /SOBOL, DJ/1996/
3-5/6 KH736 . . . . **Fic**
Encyclopedia Brown and the case of the dead eagles./SOBOL, DJ/1975/
3-5/6 KH737 . . . . **Fic**
Encyclopedia Brown and the case of the dead eagles (Braille). /SOBOL, DJ/
n.d./3-5/6 KH737 . . . . **Fic**
Encyclopedia Brown and the case of the dead eagles (Sound recording
cassette)./SOBOL, DJ/n.d./3-5/6 KH737 . . . . **Fic**
Encyclopedia Brown and the case of the midnight visitor./SOBOL, DJ/
1977/3-5/6 KH737 . . . . **Fic**
Encyclopedia Brown and the case of the midnight visitor (Sound recording
cassette)./SOBOL, DJ/n.d./3-5/6 KH737 . . . . **Fic**
Encyclopedia Brown and the case of the mysterious handprints./SOBOL,
DJ/1985/3-5/6 KH737 . . . . **Fic**
Encyclopedia Brown and the case of the secret pitch./SOBOL, DJ/1965/
3-5/6 KH737 . . . . **Fic**
Encyclopedia Brown and the case of the treasure hunt./SOBOL, DJ/1988/
3-5/6 KH737 . . . . **Fic**
Encyclopedia Brown, boy detective. /SOBOL, DJ/1963/3-5/6 KH737 . . **Fic**
Encyclopedia Brown: boy detective (Sound recording cassette)./SOBOL,
DJ/n.d./3-5/6 KH737 . . . . **Fic**
Encyclopedia Brown finds the clues./SOBOL, DJ/1966/3-5/6 KH737 . . **Fic**
Encyclopedia Brown gets his man./SOBOL, DJ/1967/3-5/6 KH737 . . . **Fic**
Encyclopedia Brown gets his man (Braille)./SOBOL, DJ/n.d./
3-5/6 KH737 . . . . **Fic**
Encyclopedia Brown gets his man (Sound recording cassette)./SOBOL, DJ/
n.d./3-5/6 KH737 . . . . **Fic**
Encyclopedia Brown keeps the peace./SOBOL, DJ/1969/
3-5/6 KH737 . . . . **Fic**
Encyclopedia Brown keeps the peace (Braille)./SOBOL, DJ/n.d./
3-5/6 KH737 . . . . **Fic**
Encyclopedia Brown lends a hand./SOBOL, DJ/1974/3-5/6 KH737 . . **Fic**
Encyclopedia Brown lends a hand (Braille)./SOBOL, DJ/n.d./
3-5/6 KH737 . . . . **Fic**
Encyclopedia Brown lends a hand (Sound recording cassette)./SOBOL, DJ/
n.d./3-5/6 KH737 . . . . **Fic**
Encyclopedia Brown saves the day./SOBOL, DJ/1972/3-5/6 KH737 . . **Fic**
Encyclopedia Brown sets the pace./SOBOL, DJ/1982/3-5/6 KH737 . . . **Fic**
Encyclopedia Brown shows the way (Sound recording cassette)./SOBOL,
DJ/n.d./3-5/6 KH737 . . . . **Fic**
Encyclopedia Brown solves them all./SOBOL, DJ/1968/3-5/6 KH737 . . **Fic**
Encyclopedia Brown solves them all (Braille)./SOBOL, DJ/n.d./
3-5/6 KH737 . . . . **Fic**
Encyclopedia Brown solves them all (Sound recording cassette)./SOBOL,
DJ/n.d./3-5/6 KH737 . . . . **Fic**
Encyclopedia Brown takes the case./SOBOL, DJ/1973/3-5/6 KH737 . . **Fic**
Encyclopedia Brown takes the case (Braille)./SOBOL, DJ/n.d./
3-5/6 KH737 . . . . **Fic**
Encyclopedia Brown tracks them down./SOBOL, DJ/1971/
3-5/6 KH737 . . . . **Fic**
ENCYCLOPEDIA OF AMERICAN HISTORY. 7th ed. /1992/
5-6/KA495 . . . . **REF 973.03**
Encyclopedia of Native America. /GRIFFIN-PIERCE, T/1995/
5-A/KA480 . . . . **REF 970.1**
Encyclopedia of Native American tribes. /WALDMAN, C/1988/
4-A/KA483 . . . . **REF 970.4**
ENDANGERED ANIMALS: SURVIVORS ON THE BRINK (Videocassette). /
1997/4-6/KC486 . . . . **VCR 591.68**
ENDANGERED SPECIES (Videocassette). /1991/4-6/KC487 **VCR 591.68**
ENDANGERED WILDLIFE OF THE WORLD. /1993/
5-A/KA446 . . . . **REF 578.68**
Endless steppe: growing up in Siberia. /HAUTZIG, E/c1968/
5-6/4 KE658 . . . . **940.53**
Endless steppe: growing up in Siberia (Sound recording cassette)./
HAUTZIG, E/n.d./5-6/4 KE658 . . . . **940.53**
Endless steppe: growing up in Siberia (Talking book)./HAUTZIG, E/n.d./
5-6/4 KE658 . . . . **940.53**
Enemy at Green Knowe./BOSTON, LM/1964/4-A/6 KG919 . . . . . . **Fic**
Enemy at Green Knowe (Sound recording cassette)./BOSTON, LM/n.d./
4-A/6 KG919 . . . . **Fic**
Enormous Crocodile. /DAHL, R/c1978, 1993/1-3/4 KF444 . . . . . . **E**
Enormous crocodile; and, The magic finger (Talking book). /DAHL, R/
1980/K-3/KF445 . . . . **TB E**
Enormous egg. /BUTTERWORTH, O/c1956/3-5/4 KG955 . . . . **Fic**
ENVIRONMENT (Microcomputer program). /1990/
5-A/KB059 . . . . **MCP 363.73**
Environmental experiments about air. /RYBOLT, TR/1993/
5-6/7 KD084 . . . . **628.5**
Environmental experiments about water. /RYBOLT, TR/1993/
5-6/7 KB066 . . . . **363.73**
Eric Carle's animals, animals. /CARLE, E/1989/P-3/KD880 . . . . . . **808.81**
Eric Carle's dragons dragons and other creatures that never were. /CARLE,
E/1991/K-3/KD881 . . . . **808.81**
Ernest and Celestine./VINCENT, G/1982/P-2/1 KG656 . . . . **E**

Ernest and Celestine at the circus. /VINCENT, G/1988/P-2/2 KG655. . . **E**
Ernest and Celestine's picnic. /VINCENT, G/1982/P-2/1 KG656 . . . . . . **E**
Escapada de Marvin el mono./BUEHNER, C/1997/P-2/3 KF294 . . . . . . **E**
Escape from slavery: five journeys to freedom. /RAPPAPORT, D/1991/ 4-6/4 KE863 . . . . **973**
Escape of Marvin the ape. /BUEHNER, C/1992/P-2/3 KF294. . . . . **E**
Escape to freedom: a play about young Frederick Douglass. /DAVIS, O/ c1976, 1990/A-6/KE091 . . . . **812**
Escoba de la viuda./VAN ALLSBURG, C/1993/4-A/5 KH824. . . . . . . **Fic**
Eskimo boy: life in an Inupiaq Eskimo village. /KENDALL, R/1992/ 3-6/6 KF100 . . . . **979.8**
Esta es mi casa./DORROS, A/1993/1-3/2 KD393 . . . . **728**
Estas ahi Dios? Soy yo, Margaret./BLUME, J/1983/4-6/5 KG905 . **CE Fic**
ESTEVANICO AND THE SEVEN CITIES OF GOLD (Videocassette). / 1992/5-6/KE341. . . . . **VCR B ESTEVANICO**
Esther's story. /WOLKSTEIN, D/1996/4-A/4 KA690. . . . . **222**
Esto es coraje./SPERRY, A/n.d./5-6/6 KH743 . . . . **CE Fic**
Estofado del lobo./KASZA, K/1991/P-2/2 KF870 . . . . **E**
Etcher's studio. /GEISERT, A/1997/2-5/2 KF602 . . . . **E**
ETs and UFOs: are they real? /KETTELKAMP, L/1996/ 4-6/8 KA558 . . . . **001.9**
Eugene Field: the children's poet. /GREENE, C/1994/ 2-4/4 KE343 . . . . **B FIELD, E.**
EUREKA! /1995/4-7/KA451. . . . . **REF 608**
EUROPE INSPIRER (CD-ROM). /1997/4-A/KE177 . . . . **CDR 914**
Evan's corner. /HILL, ES/c1967, 1991/K-2/2 KF727 . . . . **E**
Eve and her sisters: women of the Old Testament. /MCDONOUGH, YZ/ 1994/3-4/7 KA680 . . . . **221.9**
Even break. /HITE, S/1995/5-A/6 KH266 . . . . **Fic**
Even little kids get diabetes. /PIRNER, CW/1991/K-2/2 KD017. . . . **616.4**
EVEN MORE PRESCHOOL POWER (Videocassette)./1993/ P-K/KD263. . . . . **VCR 640.83**
Everett Anderson's Christmas coming. /CLIFTON, L/1991/P-1/KD925 . **811**
Everglades. /MURRAY, P/1993/3-6/6 KE195 . . . . **917.59**
Everglades. /GEORGE, JC/1995/2-5/7 KE991 . . . . **975.9**
Everglades: Buffalo Tiger and the river of grass. /LOURIE, P/c1994, 1998/ 4-6/6 KE992 . . . . **975.9**
Everglades (Sound recording cassette)./GEORGE, JC/1997/ 2-5/7 KE991 . . . . **975.9**
Every autumn comes the bear. /ARNOSKY, J/1993/P-2/2 KF168 . . . . . **E**
Every day is Earth Day: a craft book. /ROSS, K/1995/ K-3/5 KD442 . . . . **745.58**
Everybody sing and dance. /NELSON, EL/1989//KA321. **CE PROF 789.3**
Everybody sing and dance (Sound recording cassette)./NELSON, EL/1989/ /KA321. . . . . **CE PROF 789.3**
EVERYBODY'S DIFFERENT (Videocassette). /1994/ 3-6/KA639 . . . . **VCR 155.2**
Everyday children (Board book). /RYLANT, C/1993/P-K/2 KG370. . **BB E**
Everyday garden (Board book). /RYLANT, C/1993/P-K/2 KG371 . . **BB E**
Everyday house (Board book). /RYLANT, C/1993/P-K/2 KG372. . . **BB E**
Everyday pets (Board book). /RYLANT, C/1993/P-K/2 KG373. . . . **BB E**
Everyday science: fun and easy projects for making practical things./ LEVINE, S/1995/3-8/7 KB893. . . . . **507.8**
Everyday town (Board book). /RYLANT, C/1993/P-K/2 KG374 . . . **BB E**
Everything has a place. /LILLIE, P/1993/P-K/1 KF981 . . . . **E**
Everything you need to know about math homework. /ZEMAN, A/1994/ 4-10/7 KB934 . . . . **510**
Everything you need to know when a parent dies. /BRATMAN, F/1992/ 5-6/5 KA647 . . . . **155.9**
Evolution. /COLE, J/1987/3-4/5 KC290. . . . . **576.8**
Exactly the opposite. /HOBAN, T/1990/P-1/KB847 . . . . **428.1**
Exiles. /MCKAY, H/1992/6-A/7 KH478. . . . . **Fic**
Exiles at home. /MCKAY, H/1994/5-A/7 KH479 . . . . **Fic**
Exiles (Sound recording cassette)./MCKAY, H/1995/6-A/7 KH478. . . . **Fic**
EXPECTATIONS. /1948-/3-6/KD873 . . . . **808.8**
Experiment with water. /MURPHY, B/1991/K-3/4 KC101. . . . . **532**
Exploration and conquest: the Americas after Columbus: 1500 - 1620. / MAESTRO, B/1994/2-6/7 KE184 . . . . **917.04**
Explore the wild: a nature search-and-find book. /DUNCAN, BK/1996/ 2-6/7 KC358 . . . . **578.7**
Explorer. /MATTHEWS, R/1991/4-6/8 KE152. . . . . **910**
EXPLORERS AND DISCOVERERS: FROM ALEXANDER THE GREAT TO SALLY RIDE. /1995/5-A/KA470 . . . . **REF 910**
Exploring space: using Seymour Simon's astronomy books in the classroom. /BOURNE, B/1994//KA198 . . . . **PROF 372.3**
Exploring the Bismarck. /BALLARD, RD/1991/5-6/7 KE668 . . . . . **940.54**
EXPLORING THE GREAT LAKES STATES THROUGH LITERATURE. /1994/ /KA039. . . . . **PROF 016.977**
EXPLORING THE MOUNTAIN STATES THROUGH LITERATURE. /1994/ /KA040. . . . . **PROF 016.978**
EXPLORING THE NORTHEAST STATES THROUGH LITERATURE. /1994/ /KA036. . . . . **PROF 016.974**
EXPLORING THE OCEAN: A SUPPLEMENT TO CHILDCRAFT--THE HOW AND WHY LIBRARY./1996/P-2/KA378 . . . . **REF 031**
EXPLORING THE PACIFIC STATES THROUGH LITERATURE. /1994/ /KA042. . . . . **PROF 016.9795**
EXPLORING THE PLAINS STATES THROUGH LITERATURE. /1994/ /KA041. . . . . **PROF 016.978**
Exploring the sky by day: the equinox guide to weather and the atmosphere. /DICKINSON, T/1988/3-A/7 KC217 . . . . **551.6**
EXPLORING THE SOUTHEAST STATES THROUGH LITERATURE. /1994/ /KA037. . . . . **PROF 016.975**
EXPLORING THE SOUTHWEST STATES THROUGH LITERATURE. /1994/ /KA038. . . . . **PROF 016.976**
Exploring the Titanic. /BALLARD, RD/1988/4-6/8 KB025 . . . . **363.12**
EXPLORING THE WORLD OF REPTILES (Videocassette). /1992/ 2-4/KC614. . . . . **VCR 597.9**
Exploring time. /CHAPMAN, G/1995/3-6/6 KC069 . . . . **529**
Exploring with a magnifying glass. /RAINIS, KG/1991/ 6-A/7 KB897 . . . . **507.8**
Expreso polar./VAN ALLSBURG, C/1994/2-A/5 KH822 . . . . **CE Fic**
Extra! extra!: the who, what, where, when and why of newspapers. / GRANFIELD, L/1994/3-6/5 KA596 . . . . **071**
EXTRA INNINGS: BASEBALL POEMS. /1993/3-6/KE056 . . . . . **811.008**
Extraordinary American Indians. /AVERY, S/1992/5-6/7 KE747 . . . **970.1**
Extraordinary Asian Pacific Americans. /SINNOTT, S/1993/ 5-A/8 KA859 . . . . **305.8**
Extraordinary egg. /LIONNI, L/1994/1-3/2 KF991. . . . . **E**
Extraordinary Hispanic Americans. /SINNOTT, S/1991/ 5-A/7 KA860 . . . . **305.8**
Extraordinary Hispanic Americans (Sound recording cassette)./SINNOTT, S/1995/5-A/7 KA860 . . . . **305.8**
Extraordinary life: the story of a monarch butterfly. /PRINGLE, LP/1997/ 5-6/6 KC564 . . . . **595.78**
Extraordinary young people. /BRILL, MT/1996/4-A/7 KA823 . . . . **305.23**
Eye and seeing. Rev. ed. /PARKER, S/1989/A/8 KC972 . . . . **612.8**
Eye book. /LESIEG, T/c1968/1-2/1 KF958. . . . . **E**
Eye on the wild: a story about Ansel Adams. /DUNLAP, J/1995/ 3-6/7 KE225 . . . . **B ADAMS, A.**
Eye spy: a mysterious alphabet. /BOURKE, L/1991/1-4/KD720. . **793.734**
Eyeopeners II: children's books to answer children's questions about the world around them. /KOBRIN, B/1995//KA355 . . . . **PROF 809**
Eyes. /JEDROSZ, A/1992/5-6/6 KC965 . . . . **612.8**
EYES: BRIGHT AND SAFE. REV. ED. (Videocassette). /1997/ 3-5/KC964. . . . . **VCR 612.8**
Eyes of the dragon. /LEAF, M/1987/K-3/5 KF952. . . . . **E**
EYEWITNESS ENCYCLOPEDIA OF SPACE AND THE UNIVERSE (CD-ROM). /1996/5-A/KC003 . . . . **CDR 520**
Eyewitness handbook of rocks and minerals. /PELLANT, C/1992/ A/10 KC144 . . . . **549**
EYEWITNESS VIRTUAL REALITY: CAT (CD-ROM). /1995/ 3-A/KC820 . . . . **CDR 599.75**
Ezra Jack Keats Library (Videocassette). /KEATS, EJ/1992/ P-2/KF871 . . . . **VCR E**
Fables. /LOBEL, A/1980/3-A/5 KH416 . . . . **Fic**
FABRICA (Microcomputer program)./1983/2-4/KA635 . . . . . **MCP 153.4**
Fabulas./LOBEL, A/1980/3-A/5 KH416 . . . . **Fic**
Fabulous Firework Family. /FLORA, J/1994/1-3/4 KF559 . . . . **E**
FABULOUS FIVE: OUR SENSES (Videocassette). /1989/ P-2/KC917. . . . . **VCR 612**
Face in the Bessledorf Funeral Parlor./NAYLOR, PR/1993/ 4-6/5 KH535 . . . . **Fic**
Faces. /MCHUGH, C/1993/4-A/7 KD374 . . . . **704.9**
Faces. /ROTNER, S/1994/P-1/2 KC924. . . . . **612**
FACES: THE MAGAZINE ABOUT PEOPLE. /1984-/5-A/KA514 . **PER 050**
FACTORY: EXPLORATIONS IN PROBLEM SOLVING (Microcomputer program). /1983/2-4/KA635. . . . . **MCP 153.4**
Facts on File children's atlas. /WRIGHT, D/1997/4-6/KE176 . . . . . . **912**
FACTS ON FILE STUDENT'S THESAURUS. /1991/5-A/KA420 . . **REF 423**
Facts on File visual dictionary. /CORBEIL, J/1986/ 6-A/KA390 . . . . **REF 031.02**
Facts plus: an almanac of essential information. New 3rd ed. /ANTHONY, SC/1995/4-A/KA377 . . . . **REF 030**
Fair! /LEWIN, T/1997/1-3/6 KB180 . . . . **394**
Fairy tale jokes. /WOODWORTH, V/1993/2-4/KD743 . . . . **793.735**
Fairy tales, fables, legends and myths: using folk literature in your classroom. 2nd ed. /BOSMA, B/1992//KA177. . . . . . . **PROF 371.3**
FAIRY TALES FROM THE PICTURE BOOK PARADE (Talking book). / 1986/2-4/KB293. . . . . **TB 398.2**
FAIRYTALE FAVORITES IN STORY AND SONG (Sound recording cassette). /1993/K-3/KB294 . . . . **SRC 398.2**
FAITH AND BELIEF: FIVE MAJOR WORLD RELIGIONS (Videocassette). / 1992/5-A/KA722 . . . . **VCR 291**
Faith Ringgold. /TURNER, R/1993/4-A/7 KE511 . . . . . **B RINGGOLD, F.**
FAITH RINGGOLD PAINTS CROWN HEIGHTS (Videocassette). /1995/ 5-A/KD461 . . . . **VCR 746.46**
Faithful friend. /SAN SOUCI, RD/1995/4-6/5 KB411 . . . . **398.21**
Fakes and forgeries. /GRAHAM, I/1995/A/8 KA557 . . . . **001.9**

Falcon's egg. /GRAY, L/1995/5-A/6 KH195. . . . . **Fic**
Fall of Quebec and the French and Indian War. /OCHOA, G/1990/
5-6/7 KE873 . . . . **973.2**
Fall of the Soviet Union. /HARVEY, M/1995/5-A/7 KE689 . . . . **947**
Falling up: poems and drawings. /SILVERSTEIN, S/1996/P-A/KE024 . **811**
Falling up: poems and drawings (Sound recording cassette)./SILVERSTEIN,
S/1997/P-A/KE024. . . . . **811**
Families. /ROALF, P/1992/5-A/7 KD472 . . . . **757**
Families: a celebration of diversity, commitment, and love. /JENNESS, A/
1990/4-6/5 KA868 . . . . **306.85**
Families are different. /PELLEGRINI, N/1991/P-1/2 KG232 . . . . **E**
FAMILIES: POEMS CELEBRATING THE AFRICAN AMERICAN
EXPERIENCE. /1994/K-3/KE057 . . . . **811.008**
Family Christmas tree book. /DE PAOLA, T/c1980, 1984/
2-4/6 KB234 . . . . **394.266**
Family concert (Compact disc). /POLISAR, BL/1993/
1-6/KD648. . . . . **CD 789.3**
Family concert (Sound recording cassette). /POLISAR, BL/1993/
1-6/KD648. . . . . **CD 789.3**
FAMILY FOLK FESTIVAL: A MULTI-CULTURAL SING-ALONG (Sound
recording cassette). /1990/K-5/KD562 . . . . **SRC 789.2**
Family for Jamie: an adoption story. /BLOOM, S/1991/P-2/2 KF235. . . **E**
Family garden (Sound recording cassette). /MCCUTCHEON, J/1993/
P-3/KD581. . . . . **SRC 789.2**
FAMILY PC. /1994-/5-A/KA109 . . . . **PER PROF 050**
Family pictures: Cuadros de familia. /GARZA, CL/1990/
2-5/6 KA866 . . . . **306.85**
Family storytelling handbook. /PELLOWSKI, A/1987/
/KA070. . . . . **PROF 027.62**
Family treasury of Jewish holidays. /DRUCKER, M/1994/
2-6/6 KA772 . . . . **296.4**
Family under the bridge. /CARLSON, NS/c1958/3-5/4 KG974. . . . . **Fic**
Family under the bridge (Braille). /CARLSON, NS/n.d./3-5/4 KG974 . . **Fic**
Family under the bridge (Sound recording cassette). /CARLSON, NS/n.d./
3-5/4 KG974. . . . . **Fic**
Famous first facts. 5th ed. /KANE, JN/1997/4-6/KA382 . . . **REF 031**
Famous seaweed soup. /MARTIN, AT/1993/P-2/4 KG070. . . . . **E**
Famous Stanley kidnapping case./SNYDER, ZK/1985/
4-6/7 KH733 . . . . **CE Fic**
Fannie Farmer junior cookbook. New and rev. ed. /SCOBEY, J/1993/
A/KD280. . . . . **641.5**
Fanny's dream. /BUEHNER, C/1996/1-3/4 KF295 . . . . **E**
Fanny's dream (Sound recording cassette). /BUEHNER, C/1997/
1-3/4 KF295 . . . . **E**
Fantastic drawings of Danielle. /MCCLINTOCK, B/1996/3-5/4 KH467 . **Fic**
Fantasy literature for children and young adults: an annotated bibliography.
4th ed. /LYNN, RN/1994/KA032. . . . . **PROF 016.80883**
Far north: vanishing cultures. /REYNOLDS, J/1992/3-6/6 KE696. . **948.97**
Farewell, John Barleycorn: prohibition in the United States. /HINTZ, M/
1996/5-6/12 KB043 . . . . **363.4**
Farewell to Shady Glade. /PEET, B/c1966/K-2/KG227 . . . . **E**
FARM ANIMALS. /1991/P-2/2 KD180 . . . . **636**
Farm book. /SMITH, EB/c1910, 1982/2-4/6 KH723 . . . . **Fic**
Farm morning. /MCPHAIL, D/c1985, 1991/P-1/2 KG118 . . . . **E**
Farmer and the Poor God: a folktale from Japan. /WELLS, R/1996/
2-4/3 KB785 . . . . **398.27**
Farmer boy. /WILDER, LI/c1953/3-6/5 KH859 . . . . **Fic**
Farmer boy (Braille). /WILDER, LI/n.d./3-6/5 KH859 . . . . **Fic**
Farmer boy (Sound recording cassette). /WILDER, LI/n.d./
3-6/5 KH859. . . . . **Fic**
Farmer boy (Talking book). /WILDER, LI/n.d./3-6/5 KH859. . . . . . . **Fic**
Farmer duck. /WADDELL, M/1992/P-1/2 KG675 . . . . **E**
Farmer duck (Big book)./WADDELL, M/1996/P-1/2 KG675. . . . . . . **E**
Farmer Palmer's wagon ride. /STEIG, W/c1974, 1992/K-3/6 KG543. . . **E**
Farmers' market. /JOHNSON, PB/1997/P-1/2 KF837 . . . . **E**
Farming. /GIBBONS, G/1988/K-3/2 KD143 . . . . **630**
Farming the land, modern farmers and their machines. /BUSHEY, J/1987/
4-6/6 KD147 . . . . **631.3**
Farolitos of Christmas. /ANAYA, R/1995/3-6/2 KG845 . . . . **Fic**
Farthest shore. /LE GUIN, UK/1987/6-A/7 KH392 . . . . **Fic**
Fascinating world of frogs and toads. /JULIVERT, A/1993/
4-6/6 KC605 . . . . **597.8**
FASCINATING WORLD OF SNAKES (Videocassette). /1996/
5-6/KC635. . . . . **VCR 597.96**
Fast Freddie Frog and other tongue-twister rhymes. /REES, E/1993/
2-6/KB812. . . . . **398.8**
Fastback series. /PHI DELTA KAPPA EDUCATIONAL FOUNDATION /
1972/KA172 . . . . **PROF 370.11**
Fat Fanny, Beanpole Bertha, and the boys. /PORTE, BA/1991/
4-6/4 KH610 . . . . **Fic**
Fat man in a fur coat and other bear stories. /SCHWARTZ, A/1984/
5-6/5 KC855 . . . . **599.78**
Fat man in a fur coat and other bear stories (Sound recording cassette)./
SCHWARTZ, A/n.d./5-6/5 KC855 . . . . **599.78**

Fat men from space. /PINKWATER, DM/1977/5-A/7 KH602 . . . . . . **Fic**
Fat men from space (Sound recording cassette)./PINKWATER, DM/n.d./
5-A/7 KH602 . . . . **Fic**
Father Bear comes home./MINARIK, EH/1959/P-1/2 KG141 . . . . **CE E**
Father Bear comes home (Kit)./MINARIK, EH/1995/P-1/2 KG141 . . **CE E**
Father Bear comes home (Talking book)./MINARIK, EH/n.d./
P-1/2 KG141 . . . . **CE E**
Fathers and sons (Sound recording cassette). /HAVEN, K/1991/
1-4/KF679 . . . . **SRC E**
Fattest, tallest, biggest snowman ever. /LING, B/1997/K-2/2 KF987 . . . **E**
FAVORITE FOLKTALES FROM AROUND THE WORLD. /1986/
/KA267 . . . . **PROF 398.2**
FAVORITE FOLKTALES FROM AROUND THE WORLD (Sound recording
cassette)./n.d.//KA267. . . . . **PROF 398.2**
Favorite Norse myths. /OSBORNE, MP/1996/4-6/6 KA756. . . . . . . **293**
Favorite nursery tales. /DE PAOLA, T/1986/P-1/KB796. . . . . . . **398.8**
Favorite nursery tales (Sound recording cassette)./DE PAOLA, T/n.d./
P-1/KB796 . . . . **398.8**
Favorite poems, old and new, selected for boys and girls. /FERRIS, H/
c1957/5-6/KA467 . . . . **REF 811.008**
Faxing friends; a resource guide for forming international friendships among
students, age 5-9. /VANDERHEYDEN-TRESCONY, C/1992/
/KA173 . . . . **PROF 370.117**
Feather book. /O'CONNOR, K/1990/5-6/6 KC670 . . . . **598.147**
Feather merchants and other tales of the fools of Chelm. /SANFIELD, S/
1991/6-A/7 KB510 . . . . **398.23**
Feathers. /PATENT, DH/1992/5-6/6 KC671 . . . . **598.147**
Feathers for lunch. /EHLERT, L/1990/P-1/2 KF517 . . . . **E**
Feathers for lunch (Big book)./EHLERT, L/1993/P-1/2 KF517 . . . . . . **E**
Feel the wind. /DORROS, A/1989/P-2/2 KC190 . . . . **551.5**
Feelin' good (Sound recording cassette). /GALLINA, J/1981/
1-3/KC983. . . . . **SRC 613**
FEELINGS: INSIDE, OUTSIDE, UPSIDE DOWN (Videocassette). /1992/
6/KC946 . . . . **VCR 612.6**
Feet! /PARNALL, P/1988/P-2/1 KG219. . . . . **E**
Feliz nochebuena, feliz navidad: Christmas feasts of the Hispanic Caribbean.
/PRESILLA, ME/c1994, 1996/5-A/7 KB238 . . . . **394.266**
Fenwick's suit. /SMALL, D/1996/K-2/2 KG520 . . . . **E**
Ferrets. /JOHNSON, SA/1997/5-6/10 KD182 . . . . **636**
Ferryboat. /MAESTRO, B/1986/P-3/2 KB144 . . . . **386**
FESTIVAL IN MY HEART: POEMS BY JAPANESE CHILDREN. /1993/
3-A/KE134. . . . . **895.6**
Festivals. /LIVINGSTON, MC/1996/3-6/KD976. . . . . **811**
Field. /WARD, T/1996/3-6/8 KD812 . . . . **796.42**
Field beyond the outfield. /TEAGUE, M/1992/K-2/2 KG594 . . . . **E**
Field guide to animal tracks. 2nd ed. /MURIE, OJ/1974/
A/8 KC476 . . . . **591.5**
Field guide to the birds: a completely new guide to all birds of eastern and
central North America. 4th ed. /PETERSON, RT/1980/
4-6/7 KC659 . . . . **598**
Field guide to the insects of America north of Mexico. /BORROR, DJ/
1970/A/12 KA447 . . . . **REF 595.7**
Field guide to western birds. 3rd ed. /PETERSON, RT/1990/
4-6/7 KC660 . . . . **598**
FIELD TRIP INTO THE SEA (Microcomputer program). /1992/
3-A/KC368 . . . . **MCP 578.77**
FIELD TRIP TO THE RAINFOREST (Microcomputer program). /1991/
3-A/KC314 . . . . **MCP 577.34**
Fiery vision: the life and death of John Brown. /COX, C/1997/
5-A/8 KE264 . . . . **B BROWN, J.**
Fiesta! /GUY, GF/1996/P-1/1 KF655 . . . . **E**
Fiesta!: Mexico's greatest celebrations. /SILVERTHORNE, E/1992/
4-6/7 KB203 . . . . **394.26**
FIFTH BOOK OF JUNIOR AUTHORS AND ILLUSTRATORS./1983/
A/KA462. . . . . **REF 809**
Fig pudding. /FLETCHER, R/1995/5-A/4 KH129 . . . . **Fic**
Figgs and phantoms. /RASKIN, E/1974/4-6/6 KH618 . . . . **Fic**
Fighting fires. /KUKLIN, S/1993/K-3/5 KD087. . . . . **628.9**
Figment, your dog, speaking. /HAWKINS, L/1991/5-A/4 KH229. . . . . **Fic**
Figment, your dog, speaking (Sound recording cassette)./HAWKINS, L/
1995/5-A/4 KH229 . . . . **Fic**
Figure in the shadows./BELLAIRS, J/1993/4-6/5 KG897 . . . . **Fic**
Fill it up! All about service stations. /GIBBONS, G/1985/
K-3/4 KD129 . . . . **629.28**
Fin M'Coul: the giant of Knockmany Hill. /DE PAOLA, T/1981/
1-3/4 KB392 . . . . **398.21**
FIND IT ALL AT THE LIBRARY: AN INTRODUCTION TO THE LIBRARY
FOR CHILDREN (Videocassette). /1996/2-6/KA584 . . . . . . **VCR 027**
Find the constellations. Rev. ed. /REY, HA/1976/4-6/6 KC052 . . . **523.8**
Finders, keepers? /CRARY, E/1987/3-6/2 KA670 . . . . **177**
Finders keepers. /RODDA, E/1991/5-A/6 KH645 . . . . **Fic**
Finding a way: living with exceptional brothers and sisters. /ROSENBERG,
MB/1988/4-6/8 KB008 . . . . **362.4**
Finding Buck McHenry. /SLOTE, A/1991/4-A/4 KH719. . . . . **Fic**

TITLE INDEX

Finding Providence: the story of Roger Williams. /AVI /1997/
2-3/4 KE596 . . . . **B WILLIAMS, R.**
FINDING YOUR WAY: USING MAPS AND GLOBES (Videocassette). /
1990/3-6/KE168. . . . . **VCR 912**
Fine lines. /HELLER, R/1996/4-6/2 KE385 . . . . **B HELLER, R.**
Fine white dust. /RYLANT, C/1986/6-A/4 KH661. . . . . **Fic**
Fine white dust (Braille)./RYLANT, C/n.d./6-A/4 KH661. . . . . **Fic**
Fine white dust (Sound recording cassette)./RYLANT, C/1995/
6-A/4 KH661 . . . . **Fic**
Fingerplays and action chants: volume 1: animals. /WEIMER, TE/1995/
P-1/KD710. . . . . **BA 793.4**
Fingerplays and action chants: volume 1: animals (Sound recording
cassette)./WEIMER, TE/1986/P-1/KD710. . . . . **BA 793.4**
Fingerplays and action chants, volume 2: family and friends./WEIMER, TE/
1996/P-1/KD710. . . . . **BA 793.4**
Fingerplays and action chants, volume 2 (Sound recording cassette)./
WEIMER, TE/1986/P-1/KD710. . . . . **BA 793.4**
Fingerplays and footplays (Videocassette). /HALLUM, R/1997/
P-K/KD708. . . . . **VCR 793.4**
Finn Family Moomintroll. /JANSSON, T/c1948, 1990/3-6/7 KH325 . . **Fic**
Finn Family Moomintroll (Large type)./JANSSON, T/1989/
3-6/7 KH325 . . . . **Fic**
Finn McCoul (Kit)./GLEESON, B/1995/3-5/KB445 . . . . . . **VCR 398.22**
Finn McCoul (Videocassette). /GLEESON, B/1991/
3-5/KB445. . . . . **VCR 398.22**
Fir trees. /FISCHER-NAGEL, H/1989/3-6/7 KC436. . . . . **585**
Fire at the Triangle Factory. /LITTLEFIELD, H/1996/2-5/1 KF998. . . . . **E**
Fire cat. /AVERILL, E/c1960/K-2/2 KF177 . . . . **E**
Fire cat (Braille). /AVERILL, E/n.d./K-2/2 KF177 . . . . **E**
Fire cat (Talking book)./AVERILL, E/n.d./K-2/2 KF177. . . . . **E**
Fire engines. /ROCKWELL, AF/1986/P/3 KD088 . . . . **628.9**
Fire! Fire! /GIBBONS, G/1984/P-2/4 KD086 . . . . **628.9**
Fire! Fire! (Sound recording cassette)./GIBBONS, G/n.d./
P-2/4 KD086 . . . . **628.9**
Fire in the forest: a cycle of growth and renewal. /PRINGLE, LP/1995/
A/8 KC305 . . . . **577.2**
Fire in the wind. /LEVIN, B/1995/5-A/4 KH396. . . . . **Fic**
Fire on the mountain. /KURTZ, J/1994/2-4/6 KB747 . . . . **398.27**
Fire on the mountain and other stories from Ethiopia and Eritrea. /
COURLANDER, H/c1950, 1995/3-6/6 KB277 . . . . **398.2**
Fire race: a Karuk Coyote tale about how fire came to the people. /
LONDON, J/1993/3-4/4 KB611 . . . . **398.24**
FIRE STATION (Videocassette). /1990/2-4/KB031 . . . . **VCR 363.3**
Fire truck nuts and bolts. /BOUCHER, J/1993/4-5/6 KD085. . . . . **628.9**
Fireflies. /JOHNSON, SA/1986/A/10 KC553 . . . . **595.76**
Fireflies, fireflies, light my way. /LONDON, J/1996/P-2/2 KG020 . . . . . **E**
Fireflies in the night. Rev. ed./HAWES, J/c1991/P-2/4 KC552. . . . **595.76**
Fireflies, peach pies and lullabies. /KROLL, VL/1995/1-3/5 KF933 . . . . **E**
Fire-raiser. /GEE, M/1992/6-A/6 KH155 . . . . **Fic**
Fires. /WOOD, L/1994/4-6/7 KB042 . . . . **363.37**
Fireworks, picnics, and flags. /GIBLIN, JC/1983/3-5/8 KE880. . . . . **973.3**
Fireworks, picnics, and flags (Braille)./GIBLIN, JC/n.d./
3-5/8 KE880 . . . . **973.3**
Fireworks: the science, the art, and the magic. /KUKLIN, S/1996/
5-6/6 KD317 . . . . **662**
FIRST AND LAST FRONTIER (Videocassette). /1991/
A/KF095 . . . . **VCR 979.8**
First children: growing up in the White House. /LEINER, K/1996/
A/9 KE856 . . . . **973**
First Christmas. /DE PAOLA, T/1984/P-4/7 KA702 . . . . **232.92**
FIRST CHRISTMAS. /1992/6-A/5 KA704 . . . . **232.92**
First Christmas. /HOGROGIAN, N/1995/K-2/5 KA707 . . . . **232.92**
First facts about the presidents. /PASCOE, E/1996/3-6/8 KE860 . . . **973**
First four years./WILDER, LI/1953/3-6/4 KH860 . . . . **Fic**
First four years (Braille)./WILDER, LI/n.d./3-6/4 KH860. . . . . **Fic**
First four years (Sound recording cassette)./WILDER, LI/n.d./
3-6/4 KH860 . . . . **Fic**
First four years (Talking book)./WILDER, LI/n.d./3-6/4 KH860 . . . . . . **Fic**
First honest book about lies. /KINCHER, J/1992//KA159. . . . . **PROF 177**
First houses: Native American homes and sacred structures. /MONROE,
JG/1993/6-A/7 KB171 . . . . **392.3**
First Ladies: women who called the White House home. /GORMLEY, B/
1997/4-6/9 KE852 . . . . **973**
First look at animals with horns. /SELSAM, ME/1989/
1-3/2 KC792 . . . . **599.64**
First look at ducks, geese, and swans. /SELSAM, ME/1990/
1-3/2 KC683 . . . . **598.4**
First night. /HENNESSY, BG/1993/P-2/3 KA706 . . . . **232.92**
First snow, magic snow. /CECH, J/1992/2-4/6 KB390. . . . . **398.21**
First snowfall. /ROCKWELL, AF/1987/P-1/2 KG342 . . . . **E**
First strawberries: a Cherokee story. /BRUCHAC, J/1993/
1-3/4 KB538 . . . . **398.24**
First Thanksgiving. /HAYWARD, L/1990/1-4/2 KB227. . . . . . **CE 394.264**
First Thanksgiving. /GEORGE, JC/1993/4-6/6 KB223 . . . . **394.264**

First Thanksgiving feast. /ANDERSON, J/1984/2-4/7 KE935 . . . . . **974.4**
First thousand words in Russian. /AMERY, H/1983/4-6/KB863 . . . . **491.7**
Fish. /PARKER, S/1990/5-6/7 KC584 . . . . **597**
Fish eyes: a book you can count on. /EHLERT, L/1990/P-K/1 KF518 . . . **E**
Fish faces. /WU, N/c1993, 1997/1-6/3 KC588 . . . . **597**
Fish hatches. /COLE, J/c1978/P-A/3 KC596. . . . . **597.5**
Fish in his pocket. /CAZET, D/1987/P-2/2 KF374. . . . . **E**
Fish out of water. /PALMER, H/c1961/K-2/2 KG209 . . . . **E**
Fish out of water (Sound recording cassette)./PALMER, H/n.d./
K-2/2 KG209 . . . . **E**
FISH THAT'S A SONG: SONGS AND STORIES FOR CHILDREN (Sound
recording cassette). /1990/K-6/KD563 . . . . **SRC 789.2**
Fisher. /FLORIAN, D/1994/1-3/5 KD244. . . . . **639.2**
Fishermen of Nova Scotia. /JENSON, LB/1980/A/9 KD245. . . . . . **639.2**
Fishes. /WILDSMITH, B/1985/P/KC587 . . . . **597**
Fishing. /BAILEY, D/1990/K-2/2 KD861. . . . . **799.1**
FIVE LITTLE DUCKS: AN OLD RHYME. /1995/P-1/1 KB797. . . . . **398.8**
Five little monkeys sitting in a tree. /CHRISTELOW, E/1991/
P-K/2 KF384 . . . . **E**
Five little monkeys with nothing to do. /CHRISTELOW, E/1996/
P-2/2 KF385 . . . . **E**
Five little pumpkins. /VAN RYNBACH, I/1995/P-K/2 KB817. . . . . . **398.8**
Five notable inventors. /HUDSON, W/1995/3-5/4 KC892 . . . . **609**
FIVE OWLS. /1986-//KA110. . . . . **PER PROF 050**
Five sisters. /MAHY, M/1997/4-6/7 KH446 . . . . **Fic**
Five-dog night. /CHRISTELOW, E/1993/1-3/3 KF386 . . . . **E**
Flag. /CRAMPTON, WG/1989/5-A/8 KE616 . . . . **929.9**
FLAGS OF THE NATIONS (Videocassette). /1993/A/KE618 . **VCR 929.9**
Flame of peace, a tale of the Aztecs. /LATTIMORE, DN/1987/
2-3/2 KF948 . . . . **E**
Flamingos. /PATTON, D/1996/4-6/7 KC679. . . . . **598.3**
Flash, crash, rumble and roll. Rev. ed. /BRANLEY, FM/1985/
1-3/2 KC195 . . . . **CE 551.55**
Flash, crash, rumble and roll. Rev. ed. (Braille)./BRANLEY, FM/n.d./
1-3/2 KC195 . . . . **CE 551.55**
Flash, crash, rumble and roll. Rev. ed. (Kit)./BRANLEY, FM/1987/
1-3/2 KC195 . . . . **CE 551.55**
Flashy fantastic rain forest frogs. /PATENT, DH/1997/
4-6/4 KC607 . . . . **597.8**
Flat Stanley. /BROWN, J/c1964, 1989/2-4/5 KG931 . . . . **Fic**
Flecha al sol. /MCDERMOTT, G/1991/2-4/3 KB711 . . . . . . **CE 398.26**
Flight of the doves. /MACKEN, W/1992/5-A/3 KH442 . . . . **Fic**
Flight: the journey of Charles Lindbergh. /BURLEIGH, R/1991/
1-4/2 KD091 . . . . **629.13**
Flight: the journey of Charles Lindbergh. /BURLEIGH, R/1991/
4-6/3 KD092 . . . . **629.13**
Flight: the journey of Charles Lindbergh (Sound recording cassette)./
BURLEIGH, R/1994/1-4/2 KD091 . . . . **629.13**
Flightless birds. /BASKIN-SALZBERG, A/1993/5-6/7 KC691. . . . . . **598.5**
Flip-flap. /JENKINS, S/1995/P-K/2 KA619. . . . . **152.14**
Flip-flop girl. /PATERSON, K/1996/5-A/6 KH575 . . . . **Fic**
Flip-flop girl (Sound recording cassette)./PATERSON, K/1996/
5-A/6 KH575 . . . . **Fic**
Flood. /CALHOUN, M/1997/1-3/2 KF332 . . . . **E**
Flood: wrestling with the Mississippi. /LAUBER, P/1996/
4-6/4 KB035 . . . . **363.34**
Floods. /ROZENS, A/1994/4-6/7 KB037 . . . . **363.34**
Floppy teddy bear. /LILLIE, P/1995/P-1/2 KF982 . . . . **E**
Flora McDonnell's ABC. /MCDONNELL, F/1997/P-K/3 KG099 . . . . **E**
Florida. /SIRVAITIS, K/1994/4-6/7 KE993 . . . . **975.9**
Flossie and the fox. /MCKISSACK, P/1986/K-3/2 KG105 . . . . **CE E**
Flossie and the fox (Videocassette)./MCKISSACK, P/1992/
K-3/2 KG105 . . . . **CE E**
Flower garden. /BUNTING, E/1994/P-2/3 KF299 . . . . **E**
Flower of Sheba. /ORGEL, D/1994/1-2/2 KA687 . . . . **222**
FLOWER TO SEED (Videocassette). /1985/4-6/KC386 . . . . . **VCR 580**
Flowers. /ROALF, P/1993/5-A/8 KD479 . . . . **758**
Flunking of Joshua T. Bates. /SHREVE, S/c1984, 1993/4-6/6 KH707 . . **Fic**
Flush!: treating wastewater. /COOMBS, KM/1996/5-6/10 KD080 . . **628.3**
Flute player./La Flautista. /EVERSOLE, R/1995/K-2/2 KF541 . . . . **E**
Fly away home. /BUNTING, E/1991/K-3/2 KF300 . . . . **E**
Fly away home (Sound recording cassette)./BUNTING, E/1993/
K-3/2 KF300 . . . . **E**
Fly the hot ones. /LINDBLOM, S/1991/A/8 KD103 . . . . **629.132**
Flying. /CREWS, D/1986/P-1/KD093 . . . . **629.13**
Flying. /GIBBONS, G/1986/K-2/2 KD095 . . . . **629.13**
Flying Acorns. /STEVENSON, J/1993/1-3/3 KG559 . . . . **E**
Flying Dragon Room. /WOOD, A/1996/2-4/3 KG761 . . . . **E**
Flying in a hot air balloon. /BELLVILLE, CW/1993/4-6/7 KD852 . . **797.5**
Flying machines. /BARRETT, NS/1994/4-6/8 KD104 . . . . **629.133**
Flying ship. /LANG, A/1995/K-3/6 KB749 . . . . **398.27**
Flying squirrels. /MCDONALD, MA/1993/1-5/5 KC753 . . . . **599.36**
Flying tortoise: an Igbo tale. /MOLLEL, TM/1994/2-3/3 KB623 . . **398.24**

FOCUS ON COLLABORATIVE LEARNING: CLASSROOM PRACTICES IN TEACHING ENGLISH. /1988//KA221 . . . . **PROF 372.6**
FOLK ART COUNTING BOOK. /1992/P-3/1 KD420 . . . . **745**
Folk dance fun: simple folk songs and dances (Sound recording cassette). / STEWART, G/1984/2-6/KD705 . . . . **SRC 793.3**
FOLK DANCES FOR CHILDREN (Sound recording cassette). /1985/ 3-6/KD703 . . . . **SRC 793.3**
FOLKLORE OF WORLD HOLIDAYS. /1992/4-6/KA414 . . . . . **REF 394.26**
Folks call me Appleseed John. /GLASS, A/1995/3-5/6 KH172 . . . . **Fic**
Folks call me Appleseed John (Sound recording cassette)./GLASS, A/ 1997/3-5/6 KH172 . . . . **Fic**
FOLKTALES FROM THE PICTURE BOOK PARADE (Talking book). /1981/ 2-4/KB566 . . . . **TB 398.24**
Follow me! /TAFURI, N/1990/P-2/KG589 . . . . **E**
FOLLOW THE DRINKING GOURD. /1993/2-4/KF563 . . . . **BA E**
Follow the drinking gourd: a story of the Underground Railroad (Videocassette). /CONNELLY, B/1992/2-4/KF412 . . . . . . **VCR E**
Followers of the North Star: rhymes about African American heroes, heroines, and historical times. /ALTMAN, S/1993/3-A/KD913 . . . **811**
Food and digestion. Rev. ed. /PARKER, S/1990/5-6/8 KC940 . . . . **612.3**
Food and our history. /MACK-WILLIAMS, K/1995/5-6/7 KD287 . . . . **641.59**
FOOD FOR THOUGHT (Videocassette). /1991/4-6/KA851 . . . **VCR 305.8**
Fool of the world and the flying ship: a Russian tale. /RANSOME, A/ c1968/2-5/5 KB765 . . . . **398.27**
Fool of the world and the flying ship: a Russian tale (Braille)./RANSOME, A/n.d./2-5/5 KB765 . . . . **398.27**
Fool of the world and the flying ship: a Russian tale (Sound recording cassette)./RANSOME, A/n.d./2-5/5 KB765 . . . . **398.27**
Foolish rabbit's big mistake. /MARTIN, R/1985/3-4/4 KA760 . . . . . **294.3**
Fool's gold. /SNYDER, ZK/1993/6-A/7 KH732 . . . . **Fic**
Fool's gold (Sound recording cassette)./SNYDER, ZK/1995/ 6-A/7 KH732 . . . . **Fic**
Foot book. /SEUSS, D/c1968/P-1/1 KG452 . . . . **E**
Football. /RAFFO, D/1994/3-6/4 KD785 . . . . **796.332**
FOOTBALL DIGEST. /1971-/5-6/KA515 . . . . **PER 050**
Football that won... /SAMPSON, M/1996/K-2/2 KD786 . . . . . **796.332**
FOR LAUGHING OUT LOUD: POEMS TO TICKLE YOUR FUNNYBONE. / 1991/K-5/KE058 . . . . **811.008**
FOR LAUGHING OUT LOUD: POEMS TO TICKLE YOUR FUNNYBONE (Sound recording cassette)./1993/K-5/KE058 . . . . **811.008**
FOR LAUGHING OUT LOUDER: MORE POEMS TO TICKLE YOUR FUNNYBONE. /1995/K-5/KE059 . . . . **811.008**
Force and motion. /LAFFERTY, P/1992/4-A/7 KC095 . . . . **531**
Forest. /LISLE, JT/1993/5-A/7 KH409 . . . . **Fic**
Forest (Sound recording cassette)./LISLE, JT/1995/5-A/7 KH409 . . . . . **Fic**
Forestwife. /TOMLINSON, T/1995/6-A/5 KH797 . . . . **Fic**
Forever Amber Brown. /DANZIGER, P/1996/2-4/4 KH062 . . . . . **Fic**
Forever family. /BANISH, R/1992/2-4/3 KB011 . . . . **362.73**
Forgetful wishing well. /KENNEDY, XJ/1985/4-6/KD963 . . . . . . **811**
Formerly great Alexander family. /SHREVE, S/1995/3-5/6 KH708 . . . . **Fic**
Fortune branches out. /MAHY, M/c1994, 1995/3-5/4 KH447 . . . . **Fic**
Fortune-tellers. /ALEXANDER, L/1992/2-5/5 KG834 . . . . **Fic**
Forward pass. /DYGARD, TJ/1989/5-A/6 KH091 . . . . **Fic**
Fossil. /TAYLOR, PD/1990/4-A/9 KC237 . . . . **560**
Fossils tell of long ago. Rev. ed. /ALIKI /1990/1-3/2 KC233 . . . . . **560**
Fossils tell of long ago. Rev. ed. (Talking book). /ALIKI /n.d./ 1-3/2 KC233 . . . . **560**
Foundling. /CARRICK, C/1977/1-3/4 KF358 . . . . **E**
Foundling and other tales of Prydain. /ALEXANDER, L/c1973, 1982/ 4-A/5 KG835 . . . . **Fic**
Four ancestors: stories, songs, and poems from Native North America. / BRUCHAC, J/1996/2-6/3 KB271 . . . . **398.2**
Four famished foxes and Fosdyke. /EDWARDS, PD/1995/1-3/3 KF511 . . **E**
Four on the shore./MARSHALL, E/1985/K-3/1 KG066 . . . . . . **CE E**
Four-and-twenty watchbirds. /LEAF, M/c1939, 1990/P-3/6 KB240 . . . **395**
Four-legged ghosts. /HOFFMAN, M/1995/2-4/6 KH269 . . . . **Fic**
FOURTH BOOK OF JUNIOR AUTHORS AND ILLUSTRATORS./1978/ A/KA462 . . . . **REF 809**
Fourth of July on the plains. /VAN LEEUWEN, J/1997/2-5/2 KG647 . . **E**
Fourth-grade celebrity. /GIFF, PR/1981/4-6/6 KH164 . . . . **Fic**
Fox. /ARNOLD, C/1996/4-6/7 KC845 . . . . **599.776**
Fox all week./MARSHALL, E/c1984, 1992/K-2/1 KG064 . . . . . **CE E**
Fox and his friends. /MARSHALL, E/1994/K-2/1 KG064 . . . . . **CE E**
Fox and his friends (Kit)./MARSHALL, E/1985/K-2/1 KG064 . . . . **CE E**
Fox at school (Kit)./MARSHALL, E/1983/K-2/1 KG064 . . . . . **CE E**
Fox be nimble./MARSHALL, J/1990/K-3/2 KG067 . . . . **E**
Fox in love./MARSHALL, E/1994/K-2/1 KG064 . . . . **CE E**
Fox in love (Kit)./MARSHALL, E/1982/K-2/1 KG064 . . . . . . **CE E**
Fox in socks. /SEUSS, D/c1965/P-2/2 KG453 . . . . **E**
Fox on stage./MARSHALL, E/1993/K-2/1 KG064 . . . . **CE E**
Fox on the job. /MARSHALL, J/c1988, 1990/K-3/2 KG067 . . . . . . **E**
Fox on wheels (Kit)./MARSHALL, E/1983/K-2/1 KG064 . . . . . **CE E**
Fox outfoxed./MARSHALL, J/1992/K-3/2 KG067 . . . . **E**
Fox: playful prowler. /HAVARD, C/1995/3-5/4 KC842 . . . . . **599.775**

Fox tale. /ABOLAFIA, Y/1991/K-2/2 KF126 . . . . **E**
Fox's dream. /TEJIMA, K/1987/P-2/4 KG597 . . . . **E**
Fraction action. /LEEDY, L/1994/2-4/2 KB963 . . . . **513.2**
Fraction fun. /ADLER, DA/1996/3-6/2 KB952 . . . . **513.2**
Francisco Goya. /VENEZIA, M/1991/4-5/6 KE376 . . . . . **B GOYA, F.**
Frank and Ernest on the road. /DAY, A/1994/2-3/2 KF451 . . . . . . **E**
Frank and Ernest play ball. /DAY, A/1990/2-3/4 KF452 . . . . . . **E**
Frank Thomas: power hitter. /GUTMAN, B/1996/ 3-5/6 KE563 . . . . **B THOMAS, F.**
Frank Thompson: her Civil War story. /STEVENS, B/1992/ 6-A/7 KE332 . . . . **B EDMONDS, S.**
Frankenlouse. /JAMES, M/1994/6-A/6 KH322 . . . . **Fic**
Franklin Delano Roosevelt. /FREEDMAN, R/1990/ 6-A/7 KE522 . . . . **B ROOSEVELT, F.**
Frantic frogs and other frankly fractured folktales for readers theatre. / FREDERICKS, AD/1993//KA362 . . . . **PROF 812**
Freaky Friday. /RODGERS, M/c1972/5-6/5 KH647 . . . . **CE Fic**
Freaky Friday (Kit)./RODGERS, M/1978/5-6/5 KH647 . . . . . . **CE Fic**
Freckle juice. /BLUME, J/1971/2-4/3 KG908 . . . . **CE Fic**
Freckle juice (Braille)./BLUME, J/n.d./2-4/3 KG908 . . . . . . **CE Fic**
Freckle juice (Kit)./BLUME, J/1982/2-4/3 KG908 . . . . **CE Fic**
Freckle juice (Sound recording cassette)./BLUME, J/n.d./ 2-4/3 KG908 . . . . **CE Fic**
Fred Field. /BURGESS, BH/1994/6-A/6 KG947 . . . . **Fic**
Frederick. /LIONNI, L/c1967/P-2/2 KF992 . . . . **E**
Frederick (Braille)./LIONNI, L/n.d./P-2/2 KF992 . . . . **E**
FREDERICK DOUGLASS (Videocassette). /1992/ 4-A/KE325 . . . . **VCR B DOUGLASS, F.**
Frederick (Videocassette)./LIONNI, L/1985/P-2/2 KF994 . . . . . . **VCR E**
Frederick's fables: a Leo Lionni treasury of favorite stories. Rev. ed. / LIONNI, L/1997/P-2/4 KF993 . . . . **E**
Frederick's fables: a Leo Lionni treasury of favorite stories (Sound recording cassette)./LIONNI, L/n.d./P-2/4 KF993 . . . . **E**
FREE MATERIALS FOR SCHOOLS AND LIBRARIES. /1979-/ /KA111 . . . . **PER PROF 050**
Free spirits in the sky. /FINE, JC/1994/2-5/7 KD853 . . . . **797.5**
Free to dream: the making of a poet: Langston Hughes. /OSOFSKY, A/ 1996/6-A/7 KE395 . . . . **B HUGHES, L.**
Free to feel great: teaching children to excel at living. /ORLICK, T/1993/ /KA305 . . . . **PROF 649**
Freedom of assembly. /KING, DC/1997/4-6/7 KA972 . . . . . . **342.73**
Freedom of worship. /SHERROW, V/1997/4-6/12 KA908 . . . . . **323.44**
FREEDOM TRAIL (Videocassette). /1991/4-6/KE939 . . . **VCR 974.4**
Freedom's fruit. /HOOKS, WH/1996/4-6/3 KH279 . . . . **Fic**
Freight train. /CREWS, D/1978/P-K/KF433 . . . . **E**
Freight train (Board book)./CREWS, D/1996/P-K/KF433 . . . . . . **E**
Fresh brats. /KENNEDY, XJ/1990/3-6/KD964 . . . . **811**
FRESH WATER: RESOURCE AT RISK (Videocassette). /1993/ 6-A/KB060 . . . . **VCR 363.73**
Frida Maria: a story of the old Southwest. /LATTIMORE, DN/1994/ 1-3/2 KF949 . . . . **E**
Fried feathers for Thanksgiving. /STEVENSON, J/1986/P-2/2 KG560 . . **E**
Friedrich. /RICHTER, HP/c1970, 1987/5-A/5 KH633 . . . . **Fic**
FRIENDLY BEASTS: A TRADITIONAL CHRISTMAS CAROL. /1991/ K-2/KD533 . . . . **782.28**
Friends. /YUMOTO, K/1996/6-A/7 KH901 . . . . **Fic**
Friendship. /TAYLOR, MD/1987/4-6/5 KH776 . . . . **Fic**
Friendship (Braille)./TAYLOR, MD/n.d./4-6/5 KH776 . . . . **Fic**
Friendship's first Thanksgiving. /ACCORSI, W/1992/P-1/2 KF127 . . . . **E**
Frog and Toad all year. /LOBEL, A/c1976/K-2/1 KG002 . . . . . **CE E**
Frog and Toad all year (Braille)./LOBEL, A/n.d./K-2/1 KG002 . . . . **CE E**
Frog and Toad all year (Kit)./LOBEL, A/1985/K-2/1 KG002 . . . . **CE E**
Frog and Toad are friends. /LOBEL, A/c1972/K-2/2 KG003 . . . . **CE E**
Frog and Toad are friends (Kit)./LOBEL, A/1985/K-2/2 KG003 . . . . **CE E**
Frog and Toad together. /LOBEL, A/c1972/K-2/2 KG004 . . . . . **CE E**
Frog and Toad together (Kit)./LOBEL, A/1985/K-2/2 KG004 . . . . **CE E**
Frog and Toad together (Talking book)./LOBEL, A/n.d./ K-2/2 KG004 . . . . **CE E**
Frog goes to dinner./MAYER, M/1974/P-1/KG084 . . . . **CE E**
FROG INSIDE MY HAT: A FIRST BOOK OF POEMS. /1993/ P-1/KD884 . . . . **808.81**
Frog king; and, The making of the frog king (Videocassette)./DAVENPORT, T/1981/5-A/KB281 . . . . **CE 398.2**
Frog on his own./MAYER, M/1973/P-1/KG084 . . . . **CE E**
Frog prince. /BERENZY, A/1989/3-5/5 KG898 . . . . **Fic**
Frog prince. /TARCOV, EH/c1974, 1993/P-3/2 KB376 . . . . . . **398.2**
Frog Prince, continued. /SCIESZKA, J/1991/1-3/4 KG419 . . . . . . **E**
Frog Prince, continued (Sound recording cassette)./SCIESZKA, J/1993/ 1-3/4 KG419 . . . . **E**
Frog princess. /CECIL, L/1995/1-3/2 KB548 . . . . **398.24**
Frog Princess? /MANN, P/1995/1-3/2 KG058 . . . . **E**
Frog Princess of Pelham. /CONFORD, E/1997/4-A/3 KH019 . . . . . . **Fic**
Frog went a-courtin'. /LANGSTAFF, J/c1955/P-3/KD579 . . . . **CE 789.2**
Frog went a-courtin' (Kit)./LANGSTAFF, J/1965/P-3/KD579 . . **CE 789.2**

Frog went a-courtin' (Videocassette)./LANGSTAFF, J/1965/
P-3/KD579. **CE 789.2**
Frog where are you?/MAYER, M/1969/P-1/KG084 . . . . **CE E**
Froggy gets dressed. /LONDON, J/1992/P-K/2 KG021 . . . . **E**
Froggy gets dressed (Big book)./LONDON, J/1995/P-K/2 KG021 . . . . **E**
Froggy goes to school. /LONDON, J/1996/P-1/2 KG022 . . . . **E**
Froggy se viste./LONDON, J/1997/P-K/2 KG021 . . . . **E**
Frogs. /GIBBONS, G/1993/K-3/3 KC603 . . . . **597.8**
Frogs. /GERHOLDT, JE/1994/3-5/5 KC601 . . . . **597.8**
Frog's body. /COLE, J/1980/P-A/6 KC600 . . . . **597.8**
Frogs, toads, lizards and salamanders. /PARKER, NW/1990/
5-6/7 KC606 . . . . **597.8**
From caterpillar to butterfly. /HEILIGMAN, D/1996/K-2/2 KC561. **595.78**
From cover to cover: evaluating and reviewing children's books. /
HORNING, KT/1997//KA085 . . . . **PROF 028.1**
From egg to bird. /REIDEL, M/1981/P-2/2 KC661 . . . . **598**
From egg to butterfly. /REIDEL, M/1981/P-2/5 KC565 . . . . **595.78**
From hand to mouth, or how we invented knives, forks, spoons, and
chopsticks & the table manners to go with them. /GIBLIN, JC/1987/
5-6/8 KB185 . . . . **394.1**
From head to toe. /CARLE, E/1997/P-K/1 KF341 . . . . **E**
From head to toe: how a doll is made. /KUKLIN, S/1994/
4-6/6 KD350 . . . . **688.7**
From rice paddies and temple yards: traditional music of Vietnam. /
NGUYEN, PT/c1990, 1992//KA317 . . . . **BA PROF 789.2**
From rice paddies and temple yards: traditional music of Vietnam. /
NGUYEN, PT/1992//KA317 . . . . **BA PROF 789.2**
FROM SEA TO SHINING SEA: A TREASURY OF AMERICAN FOLKLORE
AND FOLK SONGS. /1993/K-6/KD899 . . . . **810.8**
From seed to plant. /GIBBONS, G/1991/K-3/4 KC398 . . . . . . **581.4**
From tadpole to frog. /PFEFFER, W/1994/K-2/2 KC608 . . . . . **CE 597.8**
From tadpole to frog (Kit)./PFEFFER, W/1996/K-2/2 KC608 . . **CE 597.8**
From the Brothers Grimm: a contemporary retelling of American folktales
and classic stories./DAVENPORT, T/1992/5-A/KB281 . . . . **CE 398.2**
From the mixed-up files of Mrs. Basil E. Frankweiler. /KONIGSBURG, EL/
c1967/4-6/7 KH373 . . . . **CE Fic**
From the mixed-up files of Mrs. Basil E. Frankweiler (Braille)./
KONIGSBURG, EL/n.d./4-6/7 KH373 . . . . **CE Fic**
From the mixed-up files of Mrs. Basil E. Frankweiler (Kit)./KONIGSBURG,
EL/1988/4-6/7 KH373 . . . . **CE Fic**
From the mixed-up files of Mrs. Basil E. Frankweiler (Sound recording
cassette)./KONIGSBURG, EL/n.d./4-6/7 KH373 . . . . . **CE Fic**
From the mixed-up files of Mrs. Basil E. Frankweiler (Talking book)./
KONIGSBURG, EL/n.d./4-6/7 KH373 . . . . **CE Fic**
From the mouth of the monster eel: stories from Micronesia. /FLOOD, NB/
1996/2-5/5 KB296 . . . . **398.2**
From tree to table. /MITGUTSCH, A/1981/P-2/2 KD329 . . . . . . **674**
Frontier home. /BIAL, R/1993/4-6/8 KF027 . . . . **978**
Frontier life. /RITCHIE, D/1996/5-6/9 KF045 . . . . **978**
Frontier living. /TUNIS, E/c1961/5-6/9 KE893. . . . . **973.4**
Frontier living (Talking book)./TUNIS, E/n.d./5-6/9 KE893. . . . **973.4**
Frontier surgeons: a story about the Mayo Brothers. /CROFFORD, E/1989/
5-6/6 KC899 . . . . **610.69**
Frozen land: vanishing cultures. /REYNOLDS, J/1993/3-6/6 KE827 . **971.9**
Frozen man. /GETZ, D/1994/4-6/7 KE638 . . . . **937**
Frozen waterfall. /HICYILMAZ, G/1994/6-A/6 KH257 . . . . **Fic**
Fruit. /GOLDSEN, L/1992/P-3/2 KD159 . . . . **634**
Fudge-a-mania. /BLUME, J/1990/4-6/3 KG909 . . . . **CE Fic**
Fudge-a-mania (Talking book)./BLUME, J/1992/4-6/3 KG909 . . . **CE Fic**
Full moon stories: thirteen Native American legends. /EAGLE WALKING
TURTLE /1997/3-5/7 KH096 . . . . **Fic**
Full speed ahead: stories and activities for children on transportation. /
IRVING, J/1988//KA223 . . . . **PROF 372.6**
Full steam ahead: the race to build a transcontinental railroad. /
BLUMBERG, R/1996/4-6/10 KB137 . . . . **385**
Fun magic with things around the house (Videocassette). /RAY, J/1995/
3-6/KD752. . . . . **VCR 793.8**
Fun no fun./STEVENSON, J/1994/3-4/4 KE551 . . . . . . **B STEVENSON, J.**
Fun with my friends. /KALMAN, B/1985/P-1/2 KA658 . . . . **158**
Fungi. /SILVERSTEIN, A/1996/4-8/8 KC380 . . . . **579.5**
Funny bones. /GANERI, A/1997/3-6/6 KC903 . . . . **611**
Funny, funny Lyle. /WABER, B/1987/P-2/3 KG667 . . . . **E**
Funnybones. /AHLBERG, J/c1980, 1981/P-3/2 KF142 . . . . **E**
Further tales of Uncle Remus: the misadventures of Brer Rabbit, Brer Fox,
Brer Wolf, the Doodang, and other creatures./LESTER, J/1990/
4-5/5 KB608 . . . . **398.24**
FUTURIST. /1967-//KA112 . . . . **PER PROF 050**
Gail Devers. /GUTMAN, B/1996/5-6/6 KE319 . . . . **B DEVERS, G.**
Galapagos: islands of change. /MYERS, LB/1995/4-A/8 KF113 . . **986.6**
Galapagos tortoise. /SCHAFER, S/1992/5-6/7 KC622 . . . . . **597.92**
Galimoto. /WILLIAMS, KL/1990/1-2/2 KG727 . . . . **CE E**
Galimoto (Kit)./WILLIAMS, KL/1993/1-2/2 KG727 . . . . . . **CE E**
Galimoto (Videocassette)./WILLIAMS, KL/1993/1-2/2 KG727 . . . **CE E**
Gallinita roja, un viejo cuento./ZEMACH, M/1992/P-K/2 KG790 . . . . **E**

Game plan. /DYGARD, TJ/1993/5-A/8 KH092 . . . . **Fic**
Gammage Cup. /KENDALL, C/c1959/5-6/7 KH344 . . . . **Fic**
Gammage Cup (Braille)./KENDALL, C/n.d./5-6/7 KH344 . . . . . . **Fic**
Gammage Cup (Talking book)./KENDALL, C/n.d./5-6/7 KH344 . . . . **Fic**
Gandhi. /FISHER, LE/1995/3-6/8 KE362 . . . . **B GANDHI, M.**
GANGS: DECISIONS AND OPTIONS (Videocassette). /1993/
A/KB070 . . . . **VCR 364.1**
Gaps in stone walls. /NEUFELD, J/1996/6-A/7 KH546 . . . . **Fic**
Garbage juice for breakfast./GIFF, PR/1989/2-3/2 KF615 . . . . **E**
GARBAGE STORY (Videocassette). /1996/5-A/KB054 . . . . **VCR 363.72**
Garden of Abdul Gasazi. /VAN ALLSBURG, C/1979/1-3/5 KG638 **CE E**
Garden of Abdul Gasazi (Sound recording cassette)./VAN ALLSBURG, C/
1993/1-3/5 KG638 . . . . **CE E**
Garden of Abdul Gasazi (Talking book)./VAN ALLSBURG, C/1983/
1-3/5 KG638 . . . . **CE E**
Garden of happiness. /TAMAR, E/1996/1-3/2 KG593 . . . . **E**
Gardener. /STEWART, S/1997/K-3/2 KG571 . . . . **E**
Garth Pig and the ice cream lady./RAYNER, M/1977/K-2/4 KG317 . . **E**
Garth Pig and the ice cream lady (Braille)./RAYNER, M/n.d./
K-2/4 KG317 . . . . **E**
Garth Pig and the ice cream lady (Sound recording cassette)./RAYNER, M/
n.d./K-2/4 KG317 . . . . **E**
Gathering: a northwoods counting book. /BOWEN, B/1995/
1-3/3 KB953 . . . . **513.2**
Gathering of garter snakes. /LAVIES, B/1993/4-6/7 KC638 . . . . **597.96**
Gathering of garter snakes (Sound recording cassette)./LAVIES, B/1995/
4-6/7 KC638 . . . . **597.96**
Gathering the sun: an alphabet in Spanish and English. /ADA, AF/1997/
1-3/KE122 . . . . **861**
Gato con botas./PERRAULT, C/1990/3-4/4 KB633 . . . . **398.24**
Gato ensombrerado (Kit)./SEUSS, D/1993/P-2/1 KG448 . . . . . . **CE E**
General Butterfingers. /GARDINER, JR/c1986, 1993/4-6/6 KH152 . . . **Fic**
General store. /FIELD, R/c1926, 1988/P-3/KF548 . . . . **E**
Genetics. /HOOPER, T/1994/5-6/9 KC289 . . . . **576.5**
Genghis Khan: a dog star is born. /SHARMAT, MW/1994/
2-5/2 KH703 . . . . **Fic**
Genghis Khan: dog-gone Hollywood. /SHARMAT, MW/1995/
2-5/2 KH704 . . . . **Fic**
Genie of Sutton Place. /SELDEN, G/c1973/4-6/7 KH695 . . . . . . **Fic**
Genie of Sutton Place (Sound recording cassette)./SELDEN, G/n.d./
4-6/7 KH695 . . . . **Fic**
Gentle Ben (Braille)./MOREY, W/n.d./5-A/6 KH508 . . . . **Fic**
Gentle Ben. Reissued. /MOREY, W/c1965, 1997/5-A/6 KH508 . . . . . **Fic**
Gentle Ben (Sound recording cassette)./MOREY, W/n.d./
5-A/6 KH508 . . . . **Fic**
Geoffrey Groundhog predicts the weather. /KOSCIELNIAK, B/1995/
K-2/2 KF915 . . . . **E**
GEOGRAPHY: FIVE THEMES FOR PLANET EARTH (Videocassette). /
1992/4-6/KE147 . . . . **VCR 910**
GEOGRAPHY FOR EVERYONE (Videocassette). /1992/
3-5/KE148 . . . . **VCR 910**
Geography from A to Z: a picture glossary. /KNOWLTON, J/1988/
3-6/KE150 . . . . **910**
GEOGRAPHY OF THE UNITED STATES (Videocassette). /1991/
4-6/KE188 . . . . **VCR 917.3**
GEOGRAPHY OF THE U.S.A. (Videocassette). /1991/
4-6/KE189 . . . . **VCR 917.3**
GEOMETRY AND MEASUREMENT: MEASURING ANGLES
(Videocassette). /1987/4-A/KB995 . . . . **VCR 516.2**
George and Martha. /MARSHALL, J/c1972/P-2/3 KG068 . . . . . . **CE E**
George and Martha back in town./MARSHALL, J/1984/
P-2/3 KG068 . . . . **CE E**
George and Martha encore./MARSHALL, J/1973/P-2/3 KG068 . . . **CE E**
George and Martha (Kit)./MARSHALL, J/1987/P-2/3 KG068 . . . **CE E**
George and Martha one fine day./MARSHALL, J/1978/
P-2/3 KG068 . . . . **CE E**
George and Martha rise and shine./MARSHALL, J/1976/
P-2/3 KG068 . . . . **CE E**
George and Martha 'round and 'round./MARSHALL, J/1988/
P-2/3 KG068 . . . . **CE E**
George Bush: forty-first president of the United States. /KENT, Z/1989/
5-6/8 KE272 . . . . **B BUSH, G.**
George Gershwin. /VENEZIA, M/1994/4-6/7 KE368 . . **B GERSHWIN, G.**
George shrinks. /JOYCE, W/1985/P-2/2 KF860 . . . . **E**
George, the drummer boy. /BENCHLEY, N/c1977/1-3/2 KF221 . . . . **E**
George, the drummer boy (Braille)./BENCHLEY, N/n.d./1-3/2 KF221 . . . **E**
GEORGE WASHINGTON CARVER: A MAN OF VISION (Videocassette).
/1990/5-A/KE281. . . . . **VCR B CARVER, G.**
George Washington Carver: a photo-illustrated biography. /MCLOONE,
M/1997/2-4/5 KE282 . . . . **B CARVER, G.**
George Washington: father of our country. /ADLER, DA/1988/
4-5/6 KE587 . . . . **B WASHINGTON, G**
GEORGE WASHINGTON: THE FIRST (Videocassette). /1990/
6-A/KE588. . . . . **VCR B WASHINGTON, G**

Georgia. /LADOUX, RC/1991/4-6/7 KE989 . . . . **975.8**
Georgia Colony. /FRADIN, DB/1989/5-6/7 KE988. . . . . **975.8**
Georgia O'Keeffe. /LOWERY, L/1996/2-3/2 KE482. . . . **B O'KEEFFE, G.**
Geraldine first. /KELLER, H/1996/K-2/2 KF881 . . . . **E**
Geraldine's big snow. /KELLER, H/1988/P-2/4 KF882. . . . . **E**
Germs make me sick! Rev. ed. /BERGER, M/1995/1-3/3 KD021 . . . **616.9**
Geronimo: Apache freedom fighter. /HERMANN, S/1997/
5-6/12 KE367 . . . . **B GERONIMO**
Gertie's green thumb. /DEXTER, C/1995/3-5/4 KH073 . . . . **Fic**
Gertrude, the bulldog detective. /CHRISTELOW, E/1992/K-2/3 KF387 . . **E**
Get it together: math problems for groups, grades 4-12. /ERICKSON, T/
1989//KA290 . . . . **PROF 510**
Get the message: telecommunications in your high-tech world. /
SKURZYNSKI, G/1993/A/8 KD044 . . . . **621.38**
GET TO KNOW BERNARD MOST (Videocassette). /1993/
2-3/KE471 . . . . **VCR B MOST, B.**
GET TO KNOW KEITH BAKER (Videocassette). /1994/
2-5/KE248 . . . . **VCR B BAKER, K.**
Get up and go!: the history of American road travel. /WHITMAN, S/
1996/4-A/10 KB160 . . . . **388.1**
Get your teddy ready (Videocassette). /LEWIS, S/1994/
P-2/KD681 . . . . **VCR 790.1**
Getting something on Maggie Marmelstein. /SHARMAT, MW/c1971/
4-6/4 KH705 . . . . **Fic**
Getting something on Maggie Marmelstein (Sound recording cassette)./
SHARMAT, MW/1997/4-6/4 KH705 . . . . **Fic**
Getting to know myself (Compact disc)./PALMER, H/1972/
P-1/KA641 . . . . **SRC 155.2**
Getting to know myself (Sound recording cassette)./PALMER, H/1972/
P-1/KA641 . . . . **SRC 155.2**
GETTING TO THE HEART OF IT (Videocassette). /1993/
5-A/KA809 . . . . **VCR 303.6**
Gettysburg Address. /LINCOLN, A/1995/4-6/6 KE906 . . . . **973.7**
GETTYSBURG (Videocassette). /1987/5-A/KE904 . . . . . **VCR 973.7**
Ghastlies, goops & pincushions. /KENNEDY, XJ/1989/4-A/KD965. . . **811**
Ghost and Lone Warrior: an Arapaho legend. /TAYLOR, CJ/1991/
2-5/4 KB696 . . . . **398.25**
Ghost canoe. /HOBBS, W/1997/5-A/6 KH267 . . . . **Fic**
Ghost eye. /BAUER, MD/1992/4-6/6 KG881 . . . . **Fic**
Ghost in the house. /WRIGHT, BR/1991/5-A/6 KH883 . . . . **Fic**
Ghost in the house. /COHEN, D/1993/5-6/5 KA598 . . . . **133.1**
Ghost in the mirror. /BELLAIRS, J/1993/4-6/5 KG897 . . . . **Fic**
Ghost in the noonday sun. /FLEISCHMAN, S/1965/5-A/7 KH121 . . . . **Fic**
Ghost of Nicholas Greebe. /JOHNSTON, T/1996/3-5/6 KH328 . . . . . **Fic**
Ghost of Thomas Kempe. /LIVELY, P/c1973/4-6/7 KH415 . . . . **Fic**
Ghost on Saturday night. /FLEISCHMAN, S/1997/3-5/4 KH122 . . . . . **Fic**
Ghost on Saturday night (Sound recording cassette)./FLEISCHMAN, S/
n.d./3-5/4 KH122 . . . . **Fic**
Ghost Train. /YEE, P/1996/4-6/5 KH889 . . . . **Fic**
Ghost-eye tree. /MARTIN, JR., B/1985/K-3/2 KG075 . . . . **E**
Ghostly tales of Japan (Sound recording cassette). /MARTIN, R/1989/
3-6/KB689 . . . . **SRC 398.25**
Ghostly warnings. /COHEN, D/1996/4-6/7 KA599 . . . . **133.1**
Ghosts!: ghostly tales from folklore. /SCHWARTZ, A/1991/
1-2/2 KB692 . . . . **CE 398.25**
Ghosts!: ghostly tales from folklore (Kit)./SCHWARTZ, A/1995/
1-2/2 KB692 . . . . **CE 398.25**
Ghost's hour, spook's hour. /BUNTING, E/1987/P-2/2 KF301 . . . . **E**
Ghost's hour, spook's hour (Braille). /BUNTING, E/n.d./P-2/2 KF301 . . . **E**
Ghosts of Austwick Manor. /MACDONALD, RE/c1983, 1991/
4-A/5 KH441 . . . . **Fic**
Ghosts of the deep. /COHEN, D/1993/4-6/7 KA600 . . . . **133.1**
Ghosts of War. /COHEN, D/1990/4-A/6 KA601 . . . . **133.1**
Giant and the rabbit: six bilingual folktales from Hispanic culture (Sound
recording cassette). /BARCHAS, S/1996/2-4/KB258 . . . . **SRC 398.2**
Giant baby. /AHLBERG, A/1994/3-5/7 KG820 . . . . **Fic**
Giant devil dingo (Videocassette). /ROUGHSEY, D/n.d./
1-3/KA791 . . . . **VCR 299**
GIANT ENCYCLOPEDIA OF CIRCLE TIME AND GROUP ACTIVITIES FOR
CHILDREN 3 TO 6: OVER 600 FAVORITE CIRCLE TIME ACTIVITES
CREATED BY TEACHERS FOR TEACHERS. /1996/
/KA197 . . . . **PROF 372.21**
Giants!: stories from around the world. /WALKER, PR/1995/
4-6/7 KB381 . . . . **398.2**
Giant's toe. /COLE, B/1986/P-2/2 KF407 . . . . **E**
Gift of Changing Woman. /SEYMOUR, TV/1993/6-A/7 KA792 . . . **299**
Gift of the girl who couldn't hear. /SHREVE, S/1991/4-6/6 KH709 . . **Fic**
Gift of the poinsettia./El regalo de la flor de nochebuena. /MORA, P/
1995/3-5/4 KH507 . . . . **Fic**
Gift of the tree. /TRESSELT, A/c1972, 1992/K-4/6 KC312 . . . . . . **577.3**
Gift of the tree (Sound recording cassette). /TRESSELT, A/1996/
K-4/6 KC312 . . . . **577.3**
GIFTED CHILD TODAY. /1978-//KA113 . . . . **PER PROF 050**
GIFTEDNESS (Videocassette)./1991//KA187 . . . . . **VCR PROF 371.95**

Gifts of Kwanzaa. /SAINT JAMES, S/1994/1-4/2 KB216 . . . . . **394.261**
Gifts of Wali Dad: a tale of India and Pakistan. /SHEPARD, A/1995/
2-3/2 KB488 . . . . **398.22**
Gila monsters meet you at the airport. /SHARMAT, MW/1980/
K-2/2 KG480 . . . . **E**
Gilberto and the wind. /ETS, MH/c1963/P-1/2 KF536 . . . . **CE E**
Gilberto and the wind (Kit)./ETS, MH/1996/P-1/2 KF536 . . . . . . **CE E**
Gilberto and the wind (Sound recording cassette)./ETS, MH/n.d./
P-1/2 KF536 . . . . **CE E**
Gilberto y el viento./ETS, MH/1995/P-1/2 KF536 . . . . **CE E**
Gilberto y el viento./ETS, MH/1996/P-1/2 KF536 . . . . **CE E**
Gilgamesh the King. /ZEMAN, L/1992/4-6/4 KE130 . . . . **892.1**
Gilly Martin the Fox. /HUNTER, M/1994/3-4/7 KB593 . . . . **398.24**
Gina. /WABER, B/1995/1-3/2 KG666 . . . . **E**
Ginger jumps. /ERNST, LC/1990/K-3/4 KF529 . . . . **E**
Gingerbread boy. /GALDONE, P/1975/P-2/4 KB736 . . . . . **CE 398.27**
Gingerbread days: poems. /THOMAS, JC/1995/K-4/KE032 . . . . . . **811**
Gingerbread doll. /TEWS, S/1993/1-3/5 KG602 . . . . **E**
Gingerbread Man: an old English folktale. /ROWE, JA/1996/
P-K/2 KB363 . . . . **398.2**
Giotto and medieval art: the lives and works of the medieval artists. /
CORRAIN, L/1995/4-A/9 KD494 . . . . **759.5**
Giraffes. /KALMAN, B/1997/3-5/7 KC788 . . . . **599.638**
Giraffes, the sentinels of the savannas. /SATTLER, HR/1989/
5-6/8 KC789 . . . . **599.638**
Girl from the snow country. /HIDAKA, M/1986/K-2/4 KF725 . . . . **E**
Girl from Yamhill. /CLEARY, B/1988/5-6/7 KE292 . . . . . . **B CLEARY, B.**
Girl named Disaster. /FARMER, N/1996/6-A/5 KH109 . . . . **Fic**
Girl named Helen Keller. /LUNDELL, M/1995/1-2/1 KE417 . **B KELLER, H.**
Girl who knew it all./GIFF, PR/1984/4-6/6 KH164 . . . . **Fic**
Girl who loved caterpillars: a twelfth-century tale from Japan. /MERRILL, J/
1992/2-4/5 KG132 . . . . **E**
Girl who loved wild horses. /GOBLE, P/1978/K-3/4 KF628 . . . . . . **CE E**
Girl who loved wild horses (Sound recording cassette). /GOBLE, P/1995/
K-3/4 KF628 . . . . **CE E**
Girl who loved wild horses (Videocassette)./GOBLE, P/1988/
K-3/4 KF628 . . . . **CE E**
Girl who wanted to hunt: a Siberian tale. /BERNHARD, E/1994/
3-5/3 KB720 . . . . **398.27**
Girl with the silver eyes. /ROBERTS, WD/1980/4-6/5 KH636 . . . . . . **Fic**
Girl with the silver eyes (Braille). /ROBERTS, WD/n.d./4-6/5 KH636 . . **Fic**
Girl with the silver eyes (Sound recording cassette). /ROBERTS, WD/n.d./
4-6/5 KH636 . . . . **Fic**
GIRLS' LIFE: THE NEW MAGAZINE FOR GIRLS. /1994-/
4-6/KA516 . . . . **PER 050**
Girls speak out: finding your true self. /JOHNSTON, A/1997/
A/6 KA646 . . . . **155.5**
Gittel's hands. /SILVERMAN, E/1996/K-2/2 KG506 . . . . **E**
GIVE A DOG A BONE: STORIES, POEMS, JOKES, AND RIDDLES
ABOUT DOGS. /1996/K-4/KD874 . . . . **808.8**
Giver. /LOWRY, L/1993/5-A/6 KH426 . . . . **Fic**
Giver (Sound recording cassette)./LOWRY, L/1995/5-A/6 KH426 . . . **Fic**
GIZMOS AND GADGETS! (Microcomputer program). /1993/
3-6/KB882 . . . . **MCP 507**
GLACIERS: ICE ON THE MOVE (Videocassette). /1994/
5-A/KC164 . . . . **VCR 551.3**
Glasses: who needs 'em?. /SMITH, L/1991/2-3/3 KG524 . . . . **E**
Glassmakers. /FISHER, LE/1997/3-6/7 KD323 . . . . **666**
Gloria Estefan. /RODRIGUEZ, J/1996/5-6/6 KE340 . . . . **B ESTEFAN, G.**
Glorious angels: a celebration of children. /MYERS, WD/1995/
K-6/KD993 . . . . **811**
Glorious flight: across the channel with Louis Bleriot. /PROVENSEN, A/
1983/K-2/4 KD098 . . . . **CE 629.13**
Glorious flight: across the channel with Louis Bleriot (Kit)./PROVENSEN, A/
n.d./K-2/4 KD098 . . . . **CE 629.13**
Glorious flight: across the channel with Louis Bleriot (Videocassette)./
PROVENSEN, A/n.d./K-2/4 KD098 . . . . **CE 629.13**
Glorious impossible. /L'ENGLE, M/1990/4-A/6 KA697 . . . . **232.9**
Glorious Mother Goose. /MOTHER GOOSE /1988/P-K/KB803 . . . **398.8**
Glory Field. /MYERS, WD/1994/6-A/6 KH522 . . . . **Fic**
Glory Field (Sound recording cassette)./MYERS, WD/1996/
6-A/6 KH522 . . . . **Fic**
Glovemen: twenty-seven of baseball's greatest. /SULLIVAN, G/1996/
4-6/8 KD804 . . . . **796.357**
Glues, brews, and goos: recipes and formulas for almost any classroom
project. /MARKS, DF/1996//KA216. . . . . **PROF 372.5**
Gluskabe and the four wishes. /BRUCHAC, J/1995/3-5/6 KB272 . . **398.2**
Gluskabe stories (Sound recording cassette). /BRUCHAC, J/1990/
4-5/KB273 . . . . **SRC 398.2**
Go away, big green monster! /EMBERLEY, E/1992/P-1/2 KF522 . . . . . **E**
Go away, dog. /NODSET, JL/c1963, 1993/P-1/1 KG177. . . . . **E**
Go, dog, go! /EASTMAN, PD/c1961/P-1/1 KF506 . . . . **E**
Go, dog, go! (Videocassette)./EASTMAN, PD/P-1/KF505 . . . . . . **VCR E**
Go fish. /STOLZ, M/1991/3-6/6 KH766 . . . . **Fic**

GO, GO, GOALS!: HOW TO GET THERE (Videocassette). /1993/
4-6/KA657 . . . . **VCR 158**
GO IN AND OUT THE WINDOW: AN ILLUSTRATED SONGBOOK FOR
YOUNG PEOPLE. /1987/2-A/KD564 . . . . **789.2**
Go jump in the pool!/KORMAN, G/1979/5-A/7 KH378 . . . . **Fic**
Go, team, go! /TUNIS, JR/c1954, 1991/5-A/6 KH808 . . . . **Fic**
Go-around dollar. /ADAMS, BJ/1992/3-6/3 KA947. . . . . **332.4**
Goat in the rug. /BLOOD, CL/1990/K-3/6 KF234 . . . . **E**
GODDESSES, HEROES, AND SHAMANS: THE YOUNG PEOPLE'S GUIDE
TO WORLD MYTHOLOY. /1994/4-6/KA393 . . . . **REF 291.1**
Gods and goddesses of Olympus. /ALIKI /1994/4-5/5 KA733 . . . . . **292**
God's mailbox: more stories about stories in the Bible. /GELLMAN, M/
1996/4-6/6 KA678 . . . . **221.9**
Goggles! /KEATS, EJ/c1969, 1971/K-2/2 KF872. . . . . **CE E**
Goggles! (Braille)./KEATS, EJ/n.d./K-2/2 KF872 . . . . **CE E**
Goggles! (Talking book)./KEATS, EJ/n.d./K-2/2 KF872 . . . . **CE E**
Goggles! (Videocassette)./KEATS, EJ/1974/K-2/2 KF872 . . . . . . **CE E**
Going home. /WILD, M/1993/1-3/3 KG716 . . . . **E**
Going home. /BUNTING, E/1996/1-3/2 KF302 . . . . **E**
Going solo./DAHL, R/1986/5-6/6 KE312 . . . . **B DAHL, R.**
Going solo (Sound recording cassette)./DAHL, R/n.d./
5-6/6 KE312 . . . . **B DAHL, R.**
Going to my gymnastics class. /KUKLIN, S/1991/3-5/4 KD816 . . **796.44**
Going to my nursery school. /KUKLIN, S/1990/P-3/2 KB098 . . . **372.21**
Going to school in 1776. /LOEPER, JJ/1973/4-6/8 KB123 . . . **372.973**
Going to school in 1876. /LOEPER, JJ/1984/3-6/7 KB124 . . . **372.973**
Going up! A color counting book. /SIS, P/1989/P-2/KG511 . . . . . . **E**
Gold and silver, silver and gold. /SCHWARTZ, A/1988/
4-6/6 KE628 . . . . **930.1**
Gold coin. /ADA, AF/1991/1-3/4 KF131 . . . . **E**
Gold dust letters. /LISLE, JT/1994/4-6/7 KH410 . . . . **Fic**
Gold dust letters (Sound recording cassette)./LISLE, JT/1996/
4-6/7 KH410 . . . . **Fic**
Gold rush. /KETCHUM, L/1996/4-6/6 KF081 . . . . **979.4**
Gold: the true story of why people search for it, mine it, trade it, steal it,
mint it, hoard it, shape it, wear it, fight and kill for it. /MELTZER, M/
1993/4-8/7 KC229 . . . . **553.4**
Golden Aquarians. /HUGHES, M/1995/5-A/6 KH287 . . . . **Fic**
Golden fleece and the heroes who lived before Achilles. /COLUM, P/
c1949/5-6/6 KA736 . . . . **292**
Golden fleece and the heroes who lived before Achilles (Sound recording
cassette)./COLUM, P/n.d./5-6/6 KA736 . . . . **292**
Golden flower: a Taino myth from Puerto Rico. /JAFFE, N/1996/
2-4/5 KB503 . . . . **398.23**
Golden Gate Bridge. /DOHERTY, CA/1995/5-6/8 KD067 . . . . . . **624**
Golden goose. /SHULEVITZ, U/1995/K-3/2 KB650 . . . . **398.24**
Golden goose book: a fairy tale picture book. /BROOKE, LL/1992/
P-3/6 KB269 . . . . **398.2**
Golden hoard: myths and legends of the world. /MCCAUGHREAN, G/
1996/2-5/7 KB344 . . . . **398.2**
Golden tales: myths, legends, and folktales from Latin America. /DELACRE,
L/1996/4-5/6 KB283 . . . . **398.2**
Goldie, the dollmaker. /GOFFSTEIN, MB/1969/3-6/6 KH180 . . . . . **Fic**
Golem. /WISNIEWSKI, D/1996/2-6/5 KB423 . . . . **398.21**
Golem: a giant made of mud. /PODWAL, M/1995/4-6/7 KB408 . **398.21**
Gollo and the lion. /OYONO, E/1995/2-4/4 KB628 . . . . **398.24**
Golly sisters go West. /BYARS, BC/1986/1-3/1 KF325 . . . . **CE E**
Golly sisters go West (Kit)./BYARS, BC/1995/1-3/1 KF325 . . . . . **CE E**
Golly sisters go West (Sound recording cassette)./BYARS, BC/1997/
1-3/1 KF325 . . . . **CE E**
Golly sisters ride again./BYARS, BC/1994/1-3/1 KF325 . . . . . . **CE E**
Golly sisters ride again (Sound recording cassette)./BYARS, BC/1997/
1-3/1 KF325 . . . . **CE E**
Gone fishing. /LONG, E/1984/P-1/1 KG030 . . . . **E**
Good bad cat. /ANTLE, N/1985/P-1/1 KF160 . . . . **E**
GOOD BOOKS, GOOD TIMES! /1990/K-3/KE060 . . . . **811.008**
Good Fortunes gang. /MAHY, M/1993/3-5/7 KH448 . . . . **Fic**
Good Fortunes gang. /MAHY, M/1995/3-5/7 KH448 . . . . **Fic**
Good grief, third grade. /MCKENNA, CO/1993/3-4/4 KH481 . . . . **Fic**
Good luck gold and other poems. /WONG, JS/1994/5-6/KE044 . . . **811**
Good morning exercises for kids (Sound recording cassette). /STEWART,
G/1987/P-3/KC991 . . . . **SRC 613.7**
Good morning, let's eat! /BADT, KL/1994/3-5/7 KB184 . . . . **394.1**
Good morning, Mr. President: a story about Carl Sandburg. /MITCHELL,
B/1988/4-6/6 KE531 . . . . **B SANDBURG, C.**
GOOD MORNING TO YOU, VALENTINE: POEMS FOR VALENTINE'S
DAY. /c1976, 1993/K-6/KE061 . . . . **811.008**
Good night, Gorilla. /RATHMANN, P/1994/K-2/1 KG309 . . . . **E**
Good night, Sigmund. /COFFELT, N/1992/P-1/2 KF403 . . . . **E**
Good Queen Bess: the story of Elizabeth I of England. /STANLEY, D/
1990/6-A/7 KE337 . . . . **B ELIZABETH I**
Good Queen Bess: the story of Elizabeth I of England (Sound recording
cassette)./STANLEY, D/1993/6-A/7 KE337 . . . . **B ELIZABETH I**
Good, the bad, and the goofy./SCIESZKA, J/1992/3-6/3 KH685 . . . . **Fic**

Good work, Amelia Bedelia. /PARISH, P/c1976/1-3/2 KG214 . . . . **CE E**
Good-bye book. /VIORST, J/1988/P-2/2 KG662 . . . . **E**
Good-bye, Curtis. /HENKES, K/1995/P-2/2 KF704. . . . . **E**
Goodnight moon. /BROWN, MW/c1947/P-K/1 KF285 . . . . **CE E**
Goodnight moon (Big book)./BROWN, MW/n.d./P-K/1 KF285. . . . **CE E**
Goodnight moon (Kit)./BROWN, MW/1984/P-K/1 KF285 . . . . **CE E**
Goodnight moon (Picture)./BROWN, MW/n.d./P-K/1 KF285 . . . **CE E**
Goodnight moon. 50th anniversary ed. (Kit)./BROWN, MW/1997/
P-K/1 KF285 . . . . **CE E**
Good-night owl. /HUTCHINS, P/c1972/P-2/3 KF798 . . . . **CE E**
Goody Hall. /BABBITT, N/c1971, 1992/5-6/6 KG870 . . . . **Fic**
Goody Hall (Talking book)./BABBITT, N/n.d./5-6/6 KG870 . . . . . . **Fic**
Goody O'Grumpity. /BRINK, CR/1994/K-3/3 KF268 . . . . **E**
GOOFY OVER DENTAL HEALTH (Videocassette). /1991/
1-3/KD036. . . . . **VCR 617.6**
Goose. /BANG, M/1996/P-2/2 KF190 . . . . **E**
Goose girl: a story from the Brothers Grimm. /KIMMEL, EA/1995/
3-5/5 KB328 . . . . **398.2**
Goose girl (Videocassette). /DAVENPORT, T/1984/5-A/KB281 . **CE 398.2**
Gooseberry Park. /RYLANT, C/1995/3-5/5 KH662 . . . . **Fic**
Gorillas. /BURGEL, PH/1993/5-6/7 KC874. . . . . **599.884**
Gotta hop (Sound recording cassette). /JACK, D/1990/
K-3/KD622 . . . . **SRC 789.3**
Grab hands and run. /TEMPLE, F/1993/6-A/6 KH788 . . . . **Fic**
Gracias a las vacas (Big book)./FOWLER, A/1992/K-2/2 KD238 . . . **637**
Gracias, the Thanksgiving turkey. /COWLEY, J/1996/K-2/1 KF430 . . . . **E**
Gran gilly Hopkins./PATERSON, K/n.d./5-A/5 KH576 . . . . **Fic**
Gran granero rojo. /BROWN, MW/1996/P-1/3 KF283 . . . . **E**
Gran negocio de Francisca./HOBAN, R/1996/P-1/2 KF739 . . . . . **CE E**
GRAND CANYON OF THE COLORADO (Videocassette). /1983/
5-A/KF069. . . . . **VCR 979.1**
Grand escape. /NAYLOR, PR/1993/3-6/7 KH536 . . . . **Fic**
Grand trees of America: our state and champion trees. /JORGENSON, L/
1992/3-6/6 KC415 . . . . **582.16**
Grandaddy and Janetta./GRIFFITH, HV/1993/1-4/1 KF647 . . . . **E**
Grandaddy and Janetta (Sound recording cassette)./GRIFFITH, HV/1995/
1-4/1 KF647 . . . . **E**
Grandaddy's place. /GRIFFITH, HV/1987/1-4/1 KF647. . . . . **E**
Grandaddy's place (Sound recording cassette)./GRIFFITH, HV/1997/
1-4/1 KF647 . . . . **E**
Grandaddy's stars. /GRIFFITH, HV/1995/1-4/2 KF648 . . . . **E**
Grandaddy's stars (Sound recording cassette)./GRIFFITH, HV/1997/
1-4/2 KF648 . . . . **E**
Grandchildren of the Incas. /PITKANEN, MA/1991/4-6/6 KF110 . . . . **985**
Grandchildren of the Vikings. /PITKANEN, MA/1996/4-6/8 KE694 . . **948**
Granddaddy's gift. /MITCHELL, MK/1997/1-3/2 KG146 . . . . **E**
Grandfather and I. /BUCKLEY, HE/1994/P-1/1 KF292 . . . . **E**
Grandfather Cherry-Blossom. /MCCARTHY, RF/1993/
2-3/3 KB753 . . . . **398.27**
Grandfather Symons' homestead book. /SYMONS, RD/1981/
3-5/6 KE815 . . . . **971.2**
Grandfather tales: American-English folk tales. /CHASE, R/c1948/
K-A/4 KB723 . . . . **398.27**
Grandfather tales: American-English folk tales (Talking book)./CHASE, R/
n.d./K-A/4 KB723 . . . . **398.27**
Grandfather Tang's story. /TOMPERT, A/1990/2-3/4 KG613 . . . . **E**
Grandfather's dream. /KELLER, H/1994/K-2/2 KF883 . . . . **E**
Grandfather's greatest hits (Compact disc)./HOLT, D/1991/
K-4/KD569 . . . . **SRC 789.2**
Grandfather's greatest hits (Sound recording cassette). /HOLT, D/1991/
K-4/KD569 . . . . **SRC 789.2**
Grandfather's journey. /SAY, A/1993/2-4/5 KG397 . . . . **E**
Grandma and grandpa. /OXENBURY, H/c1984, 1993/P-K/2 KG203 . . . **E**
Grandma Buffalo, May, and me. /STILZ, CC/1995/1-3/3 KG573 . . . . . **E**
Grandma drives a motor bed. /HAMM, DJ/1987/P-3/2 KF669 . . . . . . **E**
Grandma drives a motor bed (Sound recording cassette)./HAMM, DJ/n.d./
P-3/2 KF669 . . . . **E**
Grandma Essie's covered wagon. /WILLIAMS, D/1993/2-4/4 KG726 . . . **E**
Grandma Moses Night before Christmas. /MOORE, CC/1991/
P-A/KD987 . . . . **811**
Grandma went to market: a round-the-world counting rhyme. /
BLACKSTONE, S/1996/1-3/5 KF232 . . . . **E**
Grandma's house. /MOORE, E/1985/K-2/4 KG154 . . . . **E**
Grandma's promise./MOORE, E/1988/K-2/4 KG154 . . . . **E**
Grandmother and I. /BUCKLEY, HE/1994/P-1/2 KF293 . . . . **E**
Grandmother Bryant's pocket. /MARTIN, JB/1996/1-4/3 KG079 . . . . **E**
GRANDMOTHER'S NURSERY RHYMES: LULLABIES, TONGUE TWISTERS,
AND RIDDLES FROM SOUTH AMERICA/NANAS DE ABUELITA:
CANCIONES DE CUNA, TRABALENGUAS Y ADIVINANZAS DE
SURAMERICA. /1994/P-2/KB799 . . . . **398.8**
Grandpa Abe. /RUSSO, M/1996/K-2/2 KG360 . . . . **E**
Grandpa and Bo. /HENKES, K/1986/P-2/2 KF705. . . . . **E**
Grandpa is a flyer. /BAKER, SA/1995/1-3/5 KF188. . . . . **E**

Grandparents: a special kind of love. /LESHAN, E/1984/
  4-6/9 KA879 . . . . **306.874**
Grandpa's face. /GREENFIELD, E/1988/K-1/2 KF641 . . . . **E**
Grandpa's garden lunch. /CASELEY, J/1990/P-1/2 KF364 . . . . **E**
Grandpa's house. /STEVENSON, H/1994/P-1/2 KG556 . . . . **E**
Granny the Pag. /BAWDEN, N/1996/5-A/4 KG888 . . . . **Fic**
Grant Hill: basketball's high flier. /GUTMAN, B/1996/
  5-6/7 KE390 . . . . **B HILL, G.**
GRAPH ACTION (Microcomputer program). /1996/
  4-A/KB936. . . . . **MCP 511**
GRAPH ACTION PLUS (CD-ROM). /1996/4-A/KB937 . . . . . . **CDR 511**
Graph Club with Fizz and Martina (Microcomputer program). /STEARNS,
  PH/1993/K-4/KB942 . . . . **MCP 511**
Graphic alphabet. /PELLETIER, D/1996/2-4/2 KB832 . . . . **421**
Graphs. /SMOOTHEY, M/1995/4-A/7 KB941 . . . . **511**
Grass sandals: the travels of Basho. /SPIVAK, D/1997/
  1-4/5 KE136 . . . . **895.6**
Grasshopper on the road. /LOBEL, A/1978/K-2/2 KG005. . . . . . . **CE E**
Grasshopper on the road (Braille). /LOBEL, A/n.d./K-2/2 KG005 . . . **CE E**
Grasshopper on the road (Kit). /LOBEL, A/1991/K-2/2 KG005 . . . . **CE E**
Grasshoppers. /DALLINGER, J/c1981, 1990/K-2/3 KC537 . . . . . **595.7**
Grasslands. /BROWN, L/1985/A/KC330 . . . . **577.4**
GRAVEYARD TALES (Sound recording cassette). /1984/
  3-6/KH193 . . . . **SRC Fic**
Gray Fox. /LONDON, J/c1993, 1995/K-2/5 KG023 . . . . **E**
Gray wolf, red wolf. /PATENT, DH/1990/5-6/8 KC839 . . . . . . **599.773**
Great African Americans in music. /REDIGER, P/1996/3-6/8 KD524 . **780**
Great American businesswomen. /JEFFREY, LS/1996/5-6/7 KD315 . . **658.4**
Great American elephant chase. /CROSS, G/1993/6-A/6 KH043 . . . . **Fic**
Great Astrolabe Reef. /SIY, A/1992/4-6/7 KC352 . . . . **577.7**
Great Aunt Martha. /JONES, RC/1995/1-3/2 KF853 . . . . **E**
Great ball game: a Muskogee story. /BRUCHAC, J/1994/
  2-4/2 KB539 . . . . **398.24**
Great Barrier Reef. /GOUCK, M/1993/3-6/5 KF119 . . . . **994.3**
GREAT BLACK AMERICANS. Set I (Picture). /1996/
  4-6/KA846 . . . . **PIC 305.8**
GREAT BLACK AMERICANS. Set II (Picture). /1991/
  4-6/KA846 . . . . **PIC 305.8**
Great buffalo race: how the buffalo got its hump: a Seneca tale. /
  ESBENSEN, BJ/1994/3-4/6 KB564. . . . . **398.24**
Great buildings. /LYNCH, A/1996/4-6/12 KD386 . . . . **720.9**
GREAT DEPRESSION (Picture). /n.d./A/KA967. . . . . **PIC 338.5**
Great Depression. Rev. ed. /STEIN, RC/1993/4-6/7 KE918 . . . . **973.917**
Great dimpole oak. /LISLE, JT/1987/5-6/6 KH411. . . . . **Fic**
GREAT ENCOUNTER (Videocassette). /1991/A/KE868 . . . . . **VCR 973.1**
Great fire. /MURPHY, J/1995/A/7 KF015 . . . . **977.3**
Great getaway. /COSSI, O/1991/K-2/2 KF426 . . . . **E**
Great ghosts. /COHEN, D/1990/4-6/4 KA602 . . . . **133.1**
Great Gilly Hopkins. /PATERSON, K/c1978/5-A/5 KH576 . . . . . . **Fic**
Great Gilly Hopkins (Sound recording cassette). /PATERSON, K/n.d./
  5-A/5 KH576 . . . . **Fic**
Great goalies. /DUPLACEY, J/1996/4-6/6 KD839 . . . . **796.962**
Great kapok tree: a tale of the Amazon rain forest. /CHERRY, L/1990/
  2-3/4 KF380 . . . . **E**
Great kapok tree (Videocassette). /CHERRY, L/1996/2-3/KF381 . . **VCR E**
Great Lakes. /HENDERSON, K/1989/4-5/6 KC182 . . . . **551.48**
Great leaf blast-off. /HIMMELMAN, J/1990/1-3/1 KF729 . . . . . . **E**
Great little Madison. /FRITZ, J/1989/5-A/8 KE453 . . . . **B MADISON, J.**
Great lives: human rights. /JACOBS, WJ/1990/6-A/7 KA900 . . . . . **323**
Great lives: invention and technology. /LOMASK, M/1991/
  5-A/9 KC896 . . . . **609**
Great lives: nature and the environment. /FABER, D/1991/
  5-A/7 KB903 . . . . **508**
Great Midwest flood. /VOGEL, CG/1995/4-6/9 KB034 . . . . **363.3**
Great migration: an American story. /LAWRENCE, J/1993/
  K-5/7 KD488 . . . . **759.13**
Great miracle happened there: a Chanukah story. /KUSKIN, K/c1993,
  1995/3-4/4 KA778 . . . . **296.4**
Great new nonfiction reads. /MCELMEEL, SL/1995//KA086. **PROF 028.1**
Great Northern diver: the loon. /ESBENSEN, BJ/1990/
  3-5/6 KC680 . . . . **598.4**
Great Northern diver: the loon (Sound recording cassette). /ESBENSEN,
  BJ/1993/3-5/6 KC680 . . . . **598.4**
GREAT OCEAN RESCUE (CD-ROM). /1996/3-A/KC349. . . . **CDR 577.7**
GREAT OCEAN RESCUE (Videodisc). /1992/3-A/KC350 . . . . **VD 577.7**
Great pig escape. /CHRISTELOW, E/1994/1-3/2 KF388 . . . . **E**
Great piratical rumbustification and The librarian and the robbers. /MAHY,
  M/c1978, 1986/5-A/7 KH449. . . . . **Fic**
Great piratical rumbustification and The librarian and the robbers (Sound
  recording cassette). /MAHY, M/n.d./5-A/7 KH449 . . . . **Fic**
Great pumpkin switch. /MCDONALD, M/1992/K-3/5 KG098 . . . . . . **E**
Great Pyramid. /MANN, E/1996/4-6/6 KE635. . . . . **932**
Great Quillow. /THURBER, J/1994/2-3/6 KH791 . . . . **Fic**

Great race of the birds and animals. /GOBLE, P/1991/
  3-5/4 KB574 . . . . **398.24**
Great Smith house hustle. /CURRY, JL/1993/5-A/6 KH047 . . . . **Fic**
GREAT SOLAR SYSTEM RESCUE (CD-ROM). /1996/
  5-A/KC009 . . . . **CDR 523.2**
GREAT SOLAR SYSTEM RESCUE (Videodisc). /1992/
  5-A/KC010 . . . . **VD 523.2**
Great St. Lawrence Seaway. /GIBBONS, G/1992/2-5/6 KB142 . . . . **386**
Great St. Lawrence Seaway (Sound recording cassette). /GIBBONS, G/
  1995/2-5/6 KB142 . . . . **386**
Great turtle drive. /SANFIELD, S/1996/2-6/4 KH676 . . . . **Fic**
Great Voyager adventure: a guided tour through the solar system. /
  HARRIS, AW/1990/A/9 KC026. . . . . **523.4**
Great Wall of China. /FISHER, LE/1986/3-6/3 KE630 . . . . **931**
Great Wall of China (Sound recording cassette). /FISHER, LE/n.d./
  3-6/3 KE630 . . . . **931**
Great whales: the gentle giants. /LAUBER, P/1993/4-5/4 KC773 . **599.5**
Great white man-eating shark: a cautionary tale. /MAHY, M/1989/
  K-4/5 KG056 . . . . **CE E**
Great white man-eating shark: a cautionary tale (Kit). /MAHY, M/1992/
  K-4/5 KG056 . . . . **CE E**
Great white man-eating shark: a cautionary tale (Videocassette). /MAHY,
  M/1991/K-4/5 KG056 . . . . **CE E**
Greatest show off earth. /MAHY, M/1994/4-A/7 KH450 . . . . . **CE Fic**
Greatest show off earth (Sound recording cassette). /MAHY, M/1997/
  4-A/7 KH450 . . . . **CE Fic**
Greatest show off earth (Talking book). /MAHY, M/1995/
  4-A/7 KH450 . . . . **CE Fic**
GREEDY CAT (Videocassette). /1987/K-3/KB578 . . . . **VCR 398.24**
Greek myths. /MCCAUGHREAN, G/1993/4-6/6 KA748. . . . . **292**
GREEK MYTHS (Compact disc). /1989/5-6/KA743 . . . . **SRC 292**
Greek myths: gods, heroes and monsters, their sources, their stories and
  their meanings. /SWITZER, E/1988/6-A/KA395 . . . . **REF 292**
GREEK MYTHS (Sound recording cassette). /1989/5-6/KA743 . . **SRC 292**
Greek temple. /MACDONALD, F/1992/4-6/7 KE643 . . . . **938**
Green book. /PATON WALSH, J/1982/4-6/6 KH583. . . . . **Fic**
Green eggs and ham. /SEUSS, D/1960/P-2/1 KG454 . . . . **CE E**
GREEN EGGS AND HAM. School ed. (CD-ROM). /1996/
  K-2/KF639 . . . . **CDR E**
Green eggs and ham (Videocassette). /SEUSS, D/n.d./P-2/1 KG454 . **CE E**
Green frogs: a Korean folktale. /HEO, Y/1996/P-2/2 KB589 . . . **398.24**
Greening the city streets: the story of community gardens. /HUFF, BA/
  1990/5-6/7 KD168 . . . . **635**
Greenwitch. /COOPER, S/1974/A/5 KH028 . . . . **Fic**
Greenwitch (Braille). /COOPER, S/n.d./A/5 KH028 . . . . **Fic**
Greenwitch (Large type). /COOPER, S/1988/A/5 KH028 . . . . **Fic**
Greenwitch (Sound recording cassette). /COOPER, S/n.d./A/5 KH028 . **Fic**
Greetings! /BADT, KL/1994/3-5/6 KB245 . . . . **395.4**
Gregory, Maw, and the Mean One. /GIFALDI, D/1992/
  5-A/7 KH163 . . . . **Fic**
Gregory, the terrible eater. /SHARMAT, M/1980/K-2/4 KG488 . . . . . **E**
Griffin and the minor canon. /STOCKTON, FR/c1963, 1986/
  3-5/7 KH764 . . . . **Fic**
Griffin and the minor canon (Braille). /STOCKTON, FR/n.d./
  3-5/7 KH764 . . . . **Fic**
Griffin and the minor canon (Talking book). /STOCKTON, FR/n.d./
  3-5/7 KH764 . . . . **Fic**
Griffin's castle. /NIMMO, J/1997/6-A/5 KH551 . . . . **Fic**
Grizzlies. /STONE, LM/1993/5-6/6 KC861 . . . . **599.784**
Grizzly bear family book. /HOSHINO, M/1994/4-6/6 KC859 . . . **599.784**
Grizzwold. /HOFF, S/c1963/K-2/2 KF755 . . . . **E**
GROARK LEARNS ABOUT BULLYING (Videocassette). /1996/
  1-3/KA810 . . . . **VCR 303.6**
GROARK LEARNS ABOUT PREJUDICE (Videocassette). /1996/
  1-3/KA819 . . . . **VCR 305**
GROARK LEARNS TO WORK OUT CONFLICTS (Videocassette). /1996/
  1-3/KA811 . . . . **VCR 303.6**
Grouchy ladybug. New ed. /CARLE, E/1996/P-2/2 KF342. . . . . . . **E**
Growing colors. /MCMILLAN, B/1988/P-1/KC124 . . . . **535.6**
Growing rock: a Southwest Native American tale (Kit). /ROBBINS, S/
  1993/P-1/KB638. . . . . **KIT 398.24**
Growing up adopted. /ROSENBERG, MB/1989/5-6/7 KB013 . . . **362.73**
Growing up in America, 1830-1860. /TOYNTON, E/1995/
  A/7 KE896 . . . . **973.5**
Growing up in coal country. /BARTOLETTI, SC/1996/
  4-6/8 KA934 . . . . **331.3**
Growing up in colonial America. /BARRETT, T/1995/4-6/9 KE869. . **973.2**
Growing up with Ella Jenkins: rhythms songs and rhymes (Sound recording
  cassette). /JENKINS, E/1990/P-2/KD628 . . . . **SRC 789.3**
Growing-up feet. /CLEARY, B/1987/P-3/1 KF394 . . . . **E**
Growing-up feet (Sound recording cassette). /CLEARY, B/1993/
  P-3/1 KF394 . . . . **E**
Grownups are strange (Sound recording cassette). /HARLEY, B/1990/
  1-3/KF671 . . . . **SRC E**

Grunt!: the primitive cave boy. /BUSH, T/1995/K-2/2 KF323 . . . . **E**
GTV: A GEOGRAPHIC PERSPECTIVE ON AMERICAN HISTORY (Videodisc). /c1990/5-A/KE853. . . . . **VD 973**
Guerrier-Solitaire et le fantome. /TAYLOR, CJ/1991/2-5/4 KB696 . **398.25**
Guess what? /GARDNER, B/1985/K-3/KB904 . . . . **508**
Guests. /DORRIS, M/1994/5-A/7 KH079 . . . . **Fic**
Guide to homeschooling for librarians. /BROSTROM, DC/1995/ /KA065 . . . . **PROF 026.371**
Guide to math materials: resources to support the NCTM standards. / PERRY, PJ/1997//KA256 . . . . **PROF 372.7**
Guide to nature in winter, northeast and north central North America. / STOKES, DW/c1976, 1979/6-A/8 KB921 . . . . **508.2**
Guide to night sounds (Compact disc)./ELLIOTT, L/1992/ 3-6/KC484. . . . . **SRC 591.59**
Guide to night sounds (Sound recording cassette). /ELLIOTT, L/1992/ 3-6/KC484. . . . . **SRC 591.59**
Guide to reference books for school media centers. 4th ed. /WYNAR, CG/ 1992//KA007 . . . . **PROF 011**
GUIDE TO SUMMER CAMPS AND SUMMER SCHOOLS. 26th ed. / 1995/5-A/KA411 . . . . **REF 371.2**
Guidelines for children's services. /GAGNON, A/1989/ /KA068. . . . . **PROF 027.62**
Guillermo Jorge Manuel Jose./FOX, M/n.d./K-3/6 KF574 . . . . . **E**
Guinea pigs. /HANSEN, E/1992/4-6/6 KD181 . . . . **636**
Guinea pigs. /EVANS, M/1992/3-6/6 KD178 . . . . **636**
Guinea pigs don't read books. /BARE, CS/c1985, 1993/ P-2/3 KD177 . . . . **636**
GUINNESS BOOK OF WORLD RECORDS. /1955/-4-6/KA403 . **REF 310**
GUINNESS BOOK OF WORLD RECORDS (Braille)./n.d./ 4-6/KA403 . . . . **REF 310**
GUINNESS BOOK OF WORLD RECORDS (Sound recording cassette)./ n.d./4-6/KA403 . . . . **REF 310**
Gulls...gulls...gulls... /GIBBONS, G/1997/K-4/3 KC676 . . . . . . **598.3**
Gutenberg. /FISHER, LE/1993/5-A/8 KE382 . . . . **B GUTENBERG, J.**
Gwendolyn's gifts. /SHEEHAN, P/1991/1-3/5 KG491 . . . . **E**
Gymnastics. /NORMILE, D/1996/3-6/6 KD817 . . . . **796.44**
Gymnastics. /READHEAD, L/1996/3-6/8 KD818 . . . . **796.44**
Gypsy princess. /GILMAN, P/1997/K-2/3 KF619 . . . . **E**
Haiku: one breath poetry. /WAKAN, N/1993/5-A/KE138 . . . . . **895.6**
HAIR SCARE (Videocassette)./1991/A-6/KA851. . . . . **VCR 305.8**
Hair there and everywhere. /BADT, KL/1994/4-6/6 KB169. . . . **391.5**
Hakeem Olajuwon: superstar center. /GUTMAN, B/1995/ 4-5/6 KE483 . . . . **B OLAJUWON, H.**
Half magic. /EAGER, E/c1954, 1982/4-6/6 KH094 . . . . **Fic**
Half-a-Moon Inn. /FLEISCHMAN, P/c1980, 1991/6/7 KH117 . . . . **Fic**
Half-a-Moon Inn (Braille)./FLEISCHMAN, P/n.d./6/7 KH117. . . . . **Fic**
Halloween. /GIBBONS, G/1984/P-2/7 KB224. . . . . **CE 394.264**
Halloween A B C. /MERRIAM, E/1987/P-A/KD982 . . . . **811**
Halloween (Kit)./GIBBONS, G/1984/P-2/7 KB224. . . . . . **CE 394.264**
Halloween mask for Monster. /MUELLER, V/1986/P-1/1 KG162 . . . **E**
Halloween mice! /ROBERTS, B/1995/P-1/3 KG336 . . . . **E**
Halloween monster. /STOCK, C/1990/P-K/2 KG574. . . . . **E**
HALLOWEEN POEMS. /1989/K-4/KE062. . . . . **811.008**
Halloween tree. /BRADBURY, R/c1982/5-A/7 KG920 . . . . **Fic**
Halloween (Videocassette)./GIBBONS, G/1993/ P-2/7 KB224 . . . . **CE 394.264**
Hallo-wiener. /PILKEY, D/1995/K-2/2 KG237 . . . . **E**
Hallo-wiener (Sound recording cassette)./PILKEY, D/1997/ K-2/2 KG237 . . . . **E**
Hamster. /WATTS, B/1986/2-4/2 KC748 . . . . **599.35**
HAND IN HAND: AN AMERICAN HISTORY THROUGH POETRY. /1994/ 2-6/KE063 . . . . **811.008**
Hand of the necromancer. /STRICKLAND, B/1996/5-A/6 KH772. . . **Fic**
Handbook for the Newbery Medal and Honor Books, 1980-1989. / AMMON, BD/1991//KA347. . . . . **PROF 809**
Handful of thieves. /BAWDEN, N/c1967, 1991/5-A/5 KG889 . . . . . **Fic**
Handful of thieves (Sound recording cassette)./BAWDEN, N/1995/ 5-A/5 KG889 . . . . **Fic**
HANDGUNS: MADE FOR KILLING, NOT FOR KIDS (Videocassette). / 1996/6-A/KB033 . . . . **VCR 363.3**
Handmade alphabet. /RANKIN, L/1991/K-3/KB829 . . . . **419**
Hands around the world: 365 creative ways to build cultural awareness and global respect. /MILORD, S/1992//KA167 . . . . **PROF 306**
Hands on, thumbs up: secret handshakes, fingerprints, sign languages, and more handy ways to have fun with hands. /GRYSKI, C/1993/ 5-6/5 KC904 . . . . **611**
Handtalk: an ABC of finger spelling and sign language. /CHARLIP, R/ c1974, 1984/K-A/KB823 . . . . **419**
Handtalk birthday: a number and story book in sign language. /CHARLIP, R/1987/K-3/KB824 . . . . **419**
Handtalk school. /MILLER, MB/1991/K-A/KB827 . . . . **419**
Handtalk zoo. /ANCONA, G/1989/K-A/KB820 . . . . **419**
Hannah and Jack. /NETHERY, M/1996/K-2/2 KG170. . . . . **E**
Hannah in between. /RODOWSKY, C/1994/5-A/7 KH650 . . . . . . **Fic**

Hans Christian Andersen in Central Park (Sound recording cassette). / ANDERSEN, HC/1981/4-6/KG846. . . . . **SRC Fic**
Hansel and Gretel. /MARSHALL, J/1990/2-4/4 KB340 . . . . **398.2**
Hansel and Gretel: a tale from the Brothers Grimm. /GRIMM, J/1984/ 5/6 KB740 . . . . **CE 398.27**
Hansel and Gretel: a tale from the Brothers Grimm (Sound recording cassette)./GRIMM, J/n.d./5/6 KB740 . . . . **CE 398.27**
Hansel and Gretel: an Appalachian version (Videocassette)./DAVENPORT, T/1975/5-A/KB281 . . . . **CE 398.2**
Hanukkah! /SCHOTTER, R/1993/K-2/2 KA779 . . . . **296.4**
Hanukkah: eight lights around the world. /SUSSMAN, S/1988/ 3-5/5 KH774 . . . . **Fic**
HANUKKAH (Videocassette). /1994/2-5/KA774. . . . . **VCR 296.4**
Happiest ending./UCHIDA, Y/1985/5-6/6 KH815 . . . . **Fic**
Happiest ending (Sound recording cassette)./UCHIDA, Y/n.d./ 5-6/6 KH815 . . . . **Fic**
Happily-ever-after love stories...more or less (Sound recording cassette). / BIRCH, C/1987/2-6/KB265 . . . . **SRC 398.2**
Happy adoption day! /MCCUTCHEON, J/1996/2-4/3 KD637 . . . . **789.3**
Happy birth day! /HARRIS, RH/1996/P-2/3 KF676 . . . . **E**
Happy birthday, Danny and the dinosaur! /HOFF, S/1995/ K-1/2 KF756 . . . . **E**
Happy birthday, Jesse Bear! /CARLSTROM, NW/1994/P-K/4 KF356 . . **E**
Happy Birthday, Martin Luther King. /MARZOLLO, J/1993/ 1-5/5 KE422 . . . . **B KING, M.L.**
Happy birthday, moon. /ASCH, F/1982/P-1/2 KF174 . . . . **CE E**
Happy birthday, moon (Videocassette)./ASCH, F/n.d./P-1/2 KF174 . **CE E**
Happy birthday Rotten Ralph./GANTOS, J/1990/K-2/3 KF597 . . . . **E**
Happy Christmas Gemma. /HAYES, S/1986/P-1/2 KF686 . . . . . . **E**
Happy day. /KRAUSS, R/c1945, 1949/P-2/2 KF921 . . . . **E**
Happy Father's Day. /KROLL, S/1988/K-2/2 KF928 . . . . **E**
Happy New Year! /BERNHARD, E/1996/1-3/7 KB205 . . . . . . **394.261**
Happy Thanksgiving! /BARKIN, C/1987/3-6/6 KB221 . . . . . . **394.264**
Happy to be me (Sound recording cassette). /EPSTEIN-KRAVIS, A/1993/ P-1/KA638. . . . . **SRC 155.2**
Happy winter. /GUNDERSHEIMER, K/1982/P-1/3 KF653 . . . . . . **E**
Happy yellow car. /HORVATH, P/1994/4-6/6 KH283 . . . . **Fic**
Harbor. /CREWS, D/1982/P-1/KD062. . . . . **623.8**
HARCOURT BRACE STUDENT DICTIONARY. 2nd ed. /1994/ 4-6/KA421 . . . . **REF 423**
HARCOURT BRACE STUDENT THESAURUS. 2nd ed. /1994/ 4-6/KA422 . . . . **REF 423**
Hard to be six. /ADOFF, A/1991/1-2/KD909 . . . . **811**
Hare and the Tortoise. /JONES, C/1996/P-1/4 KB597 . . . . . . **398.24**
HARK! THE HERALD ANGELS SING. /1993/K-6/KD534 . . . . . **782.28**
Harlem: a poem. /MYERS, WD/1997/3-6/KD904 . . . . **811**
Harlem Globetrotters. /WILKER, J/1997/5-6/10 KD780. . . . . **796.323**
Harmony Arms. /KOERTGE, R/1994/A/5 KH371 . . . . **Fic**
Harold and the purple crayon. /JOHNSON, C/c1955, 1994/ P-2/2 KF835 . . . . **CE E**
Harold and the purple crayon (Talking book)./JOHNSON, C/n.d./ P-2/2 KF835 . . . . **CE E**
Harold and the purple crayon (Videocassette)./JOHNSON, C/1985/ P-2/2 KF835 . . . . **CE E**
Harold y el lapiz color morado./JOHNSON, C/1995/P-2/2 KF835 . **CE E**
Harold's ABC./JOHNSON, C/1963/P-2/2 KF835. . . . . **CE E**
Harold's fairy tale: further adventures with the purple crayon./JOHNSON, C/c1984, 1994/P-2/2 KF835 . . . . **CE E**
Harold's trip to the sky./JOHNSON, C/1957/P-2/2 KF835 . . . . . **CE E**
Harp seal pups. /MATTHEWS, D/1997/4-6/3 KC870 . . . . . . **599.79**
Harriet and the Promised Land. /LAWRENCE, J/1993/K-3/KD969 . . . **811**
Harriet Beecher Stowe and the Beecher preachers. /FRITZ, J/1994/ 6-A/7 KE556 . . . . **B STOWE, H.**
Harriet the spy. /FITZHUGH, L/c1964/3-5/4 KH114 . . . . **Fic**
Harriet the spy (Braille)./FITZHUGH, L/n.d./3-5/4 KH114. . . . . . **Fic**
Harriet the spy (Sound recording cassette)./FITZHUGH, L/n.d./ 3-5/4 KH114 . . . . **Fic**
Harriet the spy (Talking book)./FITZHUGH, L/n.d./3-5/4 KH114 . . . . **Fic**
Harriet Tubman and the Underground Railroad. /ELISH, D/1993/ 4-6/4 KE574 . . . . **B TUBMAN, H.**
Harriet Tubman: conductor on the Underground Railroad. /PETRY, A/ c1955, 1996/A/7 KE575 . . . . **B TUBMAN, H.**
Harris and me: a summer remembered. /PAULSEN, G/1993/ 6-A/7 KH586 . . . . **Fic**
Harry and Arney. /CASELEY, J/1994/3-5/6 KG984 . . . . **Fic**
Harry and the lady next door./ZION, G/1960/P-2/2 KG800 . . . . . **CE E**
Harry and the lady next door (Kit)./ZION, G/1996/P-2/2 KG800. . **CE E**
Harry and Tuck. /KELLER, H/1993/K-1/2 KF884 . . . . **E**
Harry and Willy and Carrothead. /CASELEY, J/1991/K-1/2 KF365 . . . **E**
Harry by the sea./ZION, G/1965/P-2/2 KG800 . . . . **CE E**
Harry el perrito sucio./ZION, G/1996/P-2/2 KG800 . . . . **CE E**
Harry gets an uncle./PORTE, BA/1991/1-3/2 KG267 . . . . **E**
Harry in trouble./PORTE, BA/1989/1-3/2 KG267 . . . . **E**
Harry Kitten and Tucker Mouse. /SELDEN, G/1986/2-4/4 KH696 . . . **Fic**

Harry, no quiere rosas!/ZION, G/1997/P-2/2 KG800 . . . . **CE E**
Harry S. Truman. /SCHUMAN, M/1997/5-A/9 KE571 . . **B TRUMAN, H.**
Harry the dirty dog. /ZION, G/c1956/P-2/2 KG800 . . . . **CE E**
Harry the dirty dog (Braille)./ZION, G/n.d./P-2/2 KG800 . . . . **CE E**
Harry's birthday./PORTE, BA/1994/1-3/2 KG267 . . . . **E**
Harry's dog. /PORTE, BA/1984/1-3/2 KG267 . . . . **E**
Harry's Mad. /KING-SMITH, D/c1984, 1997/5-A/7 KH348 . . . . **Fic**
Harry's pony./PORTE, BA/1997/1-3/2 KG267 . . . . **E**
Harvey Slumfenburger's Christmas present. /BURNINGHAM, J/1993/ K-2/2 KF316 . . . . **E**
Hat for Minerva Louise. /STOEKE, JM/1994/P-K/2 KG576 . . . . **E**
Hatchet. /PAULSEN, G/1987/5-A/6 KH587 . . . . **CE Fic**
Hatchet (Sound recording cassette)./PAULSEN, G/n.d./ 5-A/6 KH587 . . . . **CE Fic**
Hatchet (Talking book)./PAULSEN, G/1992/5-A/6 KH587 . . . . . . **CE Fic**
Hating book. /ZOLOTOW, C/c1969, 1989/K-2/2 KG801 . . . . **E**
Hats are for watering horses: why the cowboy dressed that way. / CHRISTIAN, MB/1993/4-6/4 KB163 . . . . **391**
Hats, hats, hats. /MORRIS, A/1989/1-4/1 KB167 . . . . **391.4**
Hattie and the fox. /FOX, M/1987/P-2/2 KF569 . . . . **E**
Hattie and the fox (Big book)./FOX, M/1988/P-2/2 KF569 . . . . **E**
Hattie and the wild waves. /COONEY, B/1990/1-3/5 KF418 . . . . **E**
Haunting. /MAHY, M/1982/5-A/6 KH451 . . . . **CE Fic**
Haunting (Braille)./MAHY, M/n.d./5-A/6 KH451 . . . . **CE Fic**
Haunting of Barney Palmer (Videocassette)./MAHY, M/c1986, 1997/ 5-A/6 KH451 . . . . **CE Fic**
Haunting of Cassie Palmer. /ALCOCK, V/1990/5-6/6 KG827 . . . . **Fic**
Haunting (Sound recording cassette)./MAHY, M/n.d./ 5-A/6 KH451 . . . . **CE Fic**
Haunting tales: live from the Culbertson Mansion State Historic Site (Sound recording cassette). /HAMILTON, M/1996/2-4/KB686 . . . **SRC 398.25**
Haunts: five hair-raising tales. /MEDEARIS, AS/1996/4-6/4 KH495 . . . **Fic**
Have a happy... a novel. /WALTER, MP/1989/4-6/4 KH838 . . . . **Fic**
Have you seen my cat? /CARLE, E/c1973, 1987/P-1/1 KF343 . . . . **E**
Have you seen my duckling? /TAFURI, N/1984/P-K/1 KG590. . . . . **E**
Have you seen my duckling? (Board book)./TAFURI, N/1996/ P-K/1 KG590 . . . . **E**
Have you seen trees? /OPPENHEIM, J/1995/P-2/3 KC420 . . . . . **582.16**
Hawaii is a rainbow. /FEENEY, S/1985/P-6/KF121 . . . . **996**
Hawai'i: the Pacific State. Rev. and updated edition. /RAYSON, A/1997/ 5-A/6 KF123 . . . . **996.9**
Hawaiian legends of tricksters and riddlers./THOMPSON, VL/c1969, 1991/4-5/4 KB491 . . . . **398.22**
Hawaiian tales of heroes and champions. /THOMPSON, VL/c1971, 1986/ 4-5/4 KB491 . . . . **398.22**
Hawk Hill. /GILBERT, S/1996/4-6/4 KH167 . . . . **Fic**
Haystack. /GEISERT, B/1995/K-3/5 KD153 . . . . **633.2**
Hazards at home. /GUTMAN, B/1996/5-6/7 KB022 . . . . **363.1**
HBJ STUDENT THESAURUS. /1994/3-5/KB841. . . . . **423.1**
He is risen: the Easter story. /WINTHROP, E/1985/5-6/7 KA711 . **232.96**
Head full of notions: a story about Robert Fulton. /BOWEN, AR/1997/ 4-5/8 KE359 . . . . **B FULTON, R.**
Head on the high road: ghost stories from the Southwest (Sound recording cassette). /YOUNG, R/1993/4-6/KB698 . . . . **SRC 398.25**
Headless cupid. /SNYDER, ZK/c1971/4-6/7 KH733 . . . . **CE Fic**
Headless cupid (Braille)./SNYDER, ZK/n.d./4-6/7 KH733 . . . . **CE Fic**
Headless cupid (Sound recording cassette)./SNYDER, ZK/n.d./ 4-6/7 KH733 . . . . **CE Fic**
Headless cupid (Talking book)./SNYDER, ZK/n.d./4-6/7 KH733 . . **CE Fic**
Headless haunt and other African-American ghost stories. /HASKINS, J/ 1994/4-5/4 KB687 . . . . **398.25**
Headless Horseman rides tonight: more poems to trouble your sleep. / PRELUTSKY, J/1980/2-4/KE003. . . . . **811**
Heads, I win./HERMES, P/1989/5-6/3 KH248. . . . . **Fic**
Heads or tails: stories from the sixth grade. /GANTOS, J/1994/ 5-A/4 KH150 . . . . **Fic**
Healing the land. /WILLIS, T/1994/4-6/7 KA954 . . . . **333.73**
Hearing. /PARRAMON, JM/1985/P-1/1 KC973 . . . . **612.8**
Heart and blood. Rev. ed. /PARKER, S/1989/5-6/8 KC933 . . . . . . **612.1**
Heart and lungs. /SAUNDERSON, J/1992/5-6/6 KC935. . . . . **612.1**
Heart: our circulatory system. /SIMON, S/1996/5-A/6 KC937 . . . . **612.1**
Hearts of gold: a celebration of Special Olympics and its heroes. /DINN, S/1996/4-6/9 KD760 . . . . **796**
HEAT, TEMPERATURE AND ENERGY (Videocassette). /1995/ 5-6/KC128. . . . . **VCR 536**
Heavenly zoo: legends and tales of the stars. /LURIE, A/c1979, 1996/ 5-6/8 KB710 . . . . **398.26**
Heckedy peg. /WOOD, A/1987/K-3/3 KG762 . . . . **E**
Hector Protector and As I went over the water: two nursery rhymes with pictures. /SENDAK, M/c1965, 1990/P-K/KB815 . . . . **398.8**
HECTOR'S BUNYIP (Videocassette). /c1986, 1997/4-6/KH231 . . **VCR Fic**
Heidi. /SPYRI, J/1996/5-A/6 KH746. . . . . **Fic**
HELEN KELLER (Videocassette). /1990/4-6/KE415 . . . **VCR B KELLER, H.**
Hello! Good-bye! /ALIKI /1996/P-1/2 KB244 . . . . **395.4**
Helpful alphabet of friendly objects: poems. /UPDIKE, J/1995/ P-1/KE035 . . . . **811**
HENDERSON AVENUE BUG PATROL (Videocassette). /1984/ 1-6/KB867 . . . . **VCR 500**
Henny Penny. /GALDONE, P/c1968/P-K/2 KF594 . . . . **CE E**
Henny Penny (Big book)./GALDONE, P/1992/P-K/2 KF594. . . . . . **CE E**
Henny Penny (Kit)./GALDONE, P/n.d./P-K/2 KF594 . . . . **CE E**
Henri de Toulouse-Lautrec. /VENEZIA, M/1995/ 4-6/8 KE568 . . . . **B TOULOUSE-LAUT**
Henry Aaron. /RENNERT, RS/1993/5-A/9 KE222 . . . . . . **B AARON, H.**
Henry and Beezus. /CLEARY, B/c1952/2-5/3 KG995 . . . . **CE Fic**
Henry and Beezus (Braille)./CLEARY, B/n.d./2-5/3 KG995 . . . . . . **CE Fic**
Henry and Beezus (Talking book)./CLEARY, B/n.d./2-5/3 KG995 . **CE Fic**
Henry and Beezus (Talking book)./CLEARY, B/1997/2-5/3 KG995 **CE Fic**
Henry and Mudge and the bedtime thumps./RYLANT, C/1991/ K-3/2 KG375 . . . . **CE E**
Henry and Mudge and the best day of all./RYLANT, C/1995/ K-3/2 KG375 . . . . **CE E**
Henry and Mudge and the careful cousin./RYLANT, C/1994/ K-3/2 KG375 . . . . **CE E**
Henry and Mudge and the careful cousin (Sound recording cassette)./ RYLANT, C/1997/K-3/2 KG375. . . . . **CE E**
Henry and Mudge and the forever sea./RYLANT, C/1989/ K-3/2 KG375 . . . . **CE E**
Henry and Mudge and the happy cat./RYLANT, C/1990/ K-3/2 KG375 . . . . **CE E**
Henry and Mudge and the long weekend./RYLANT, C/1992/ K-3/2 KG375 . . . . **CE E**
Henry and Mudge and the wild wind./RYLANT, C/1993/ K-3/2 KG375 . . . . **CE E**
Henry and Mudge get the cold shivers./RYLANT, C/1989/ K-3/2 KG375 . . . . **CE E**
Henry and Mudge in puddle trouble./RYLANT, C/1990/ K-3/2 KG375 . . . . **CE E**
Henry and Mudge in puddle trouble (Braille)./RYLANT, C/n.d./ K-3/2 KG375 . . . . **CE E**
Henry and Mudge in puddle trouble (Videocassette)./RYLANT, C/1987/ K-3/2 KG375 . . . . **CE E**
Henry and Mudge in the green time./RYLANT, C/1987/ K-3/2 KG375 . . . . **CE E**
Henry and Mudge in the green time (Braille)./RYLANT, C/n.d./ K-3/2 KG375 . . . . **CE E**
Henry and Mudge in the sparkle days./RYLANT, C/1988/ K-3/2 KG375 . . . . **CE E**
Henry and Mudge in the sparkle days (Videocassette)./RYLANT, C/1989/ K-3/2 KG375 . . . . **CE E**
Henry and Mudge take the big test./RYLANT, C/1991/ K-3/2 KG375 . . . . **CE E**
Henry and Mudge: the first book. /RYLANT, C/1987/K-3/2 KG375. **CE E**
Henry and Mudge: the first book (Braille)./RYLANT, C/n.d./ K-3/2 KG375 . . . . **CE E**
Henry and Mudge under the yellow moon./RYLANT, C/1997/ K-3/2 KG375 . . . . **CE E**
Henry and Mudge under the yellow moon (Braille)./RYLANT, C/n.d./ K-3/2 KG375 . . . . **CE E**
Henry and Mudge under the yellow moon (Sound recording cassette)./ RYLANT, C/n.d./K-3/2 KG375 . . . . **CE E**
Henry and Mudge under the yellow moon (Videocassette)./RYLANT, C/ 1989/K-3/2 KG375. . . . . **CE E**
Henry and Ribsy./CLEARY, B/1957/3-5/4 KG996 . . . . **Fic**
Henry and Ribsy (Braille)./CLEARY, B/n.d./3-5/4 KG996. . . . . **Fic**
Henry and Ribsy (Talking book)./CLEARY, B/n.d./3-5/4 KG996 . . . . . **Fic**
Henry and the paper route./CLEARY, B/1954/3-5/4 KG996. . . . . **Fic**
Henry and the paper route (Braille)./CLEARY, B/n.d./3-5/4 KG996 . . . **Fic**
Henry David Thoreau: in step with nature. /RING, E/1993/ 2-5/3 KE565 . . . . **B THOREAU, H.**
Henry Huggins. /CLEARY, B/1950/3-5/4 KG996 . . . . **Fic**
Henry Huggins (Braille)./CLEARY, B/n.d./3-5/4 KG996 . . . . **Fic**
Henry Huggins (Sound recording cassette)./CLEARY, B/1993/ 3-5/4 KG996 . . . . **Fic**
Henry Huggins (Spanish version)./CLEARY, B/1996/3-5/4 KG996 . . . . **Fic**
Henry Moore: from bones and stones to sketches and sculptures. / GARDNER, JM/1993/3-6/6 KD397 . . . . **730**
Henry O. Flipper. /PFEIFER, KB/1993/4-6/9 KE345 . . . . . **B FLIPPER, H.**
Henry Reed, Inc./ROBERTSON, K/1989/4-6/6 KH638 . . . . **Fic**
Henry Reed, Inc. (Braille)./ROBERTSON, K/n.d./4-6/6 KH638 . . . . . . **Fic**
Henry Reed, Inc. (Talking book). /ROBERTSON, K/1973/ 4-6/KH637. . . . . **TB Fic**
Henry Reed's baby-sitting service. /ROBERTSON, K/c1966/ 4-6/6 KH638 . . . . **Fic**
Henry Reed's baby-sitting service (Braille)./ROBERTSON, K/n.d./ 4-6/6 KH638 . . . . **Fic**
Henry Reed's baby-sitting service (Talking book)./ROBERTSON, K/n.d./ 4-6/6 KH638 . . . . **Fic**

Henry Reed's big show (Talking book)./ROBERTSON, K/n.d./
4-6/6 KH638 . . . . **Fic**
Henry Reed's journey (Braille)./ROBERTSON, K/n.d./4-6/6 KH638 . . . **Fic**
Henry Reed's journey (Sound recording cassette)./ROBERTSON, K/n.d./
4-6/6 KH638 . . . . **Fic**
Henry the sailor cat./CALHOUN, M/1994/K-2/4 KF331 . . . . **E**
Henry y Mudge con barro hasta el rabo./RYLANT, C/1996/
K-3/2 KG375 . . . . **CE E**
Henry y Mudge: el primer libro de sus aventuras./RYLANT, C/1996/
K-3/2 KG375 . . . . **CE E**
Henry y mudge y el mejor dia del ano./RYLANT, C/1997/
K-3/2 KG375 . . . . **CE E**
Her stories: African-American folktales, fairy tales, and true tales. /
HAMILTON, V/1995/4-6/3 KB312 . . . . **398.2**
Herbie Jones and Hamburger Head./KLINE, S/1989/3-4/2 KH367. . . . **Fic**
Herbie Jones and the birthday showdown. /KLINE, S/1995/
3-4/3 KH366 . . . . **Fic**
Herbie Jones and the class gift. /KLINE, S/1989/3-4/2 KH367 . . . . . **Fic**
Hercules: the man, the myth, the hero. /LASKY, K/1997/
5-6/4 KA747 . . . . **292**
Here are my hands. /MARTIN, JR., B/1987/P-1/2 KG076 . . . . **E**
Here come the babies. /ANHOLT, C/P-K/2 KA826 . . . . **305.232**
Here comes McBroom!: three more tall tales./FLEISCHMAN, S/1992/
3-6/4 KH124 . . . . **Fic**
Here comes the mail. /SKURZYNSKI, G/1992/1-4/4 KB133 . . . . . **383**
Here comes the snow. /MEDEARIS, AS/1996/K-1/2 KG126 . . . . . . **E**
Here comes the strikeout. /KESSLER, L/c1965/1-2/2 KF898 . . . . . **CE E**
Here comes the strikeout (Braille)./KESSLER, L/n.d./1-2/2 KF898 . . . **CE E**
Here comes the strikeout (Kit)./KESSLER, L/n.d./1-2/2 KF898 . . . . **CE E**
Here is the Arctic winter./DUNPHY, M/1993/K-4/2 KC731 . . . . . **599.17**
Here is the southwestern desert. /DUNPHY, M/1995/P-3/3 KF066. . **979.1**
HERE WE GO AGAIN! (Videocassette). /1986/1-4/KB157 . . . **VCR 388**
HERE WE GO. VOL. 1 (Videocassette). /1986/1-4/KB158. . . . **VCR 388**
HERE WE GO. VOL. 2 (Videocassette). /1986/1-4/KB158 . . . . **VCR 388**
Here's to you, Rachel Robinson. /BLUME, J/1993/6-A/6 KG910 . . . . . **Fic**
Hermit crabs. /JOHNSON, SA/1989/A/7 KC521 . . . . **595.3**
Hero and the crown./MCKINLEY, R/1984/5-A/7 KH488. . . . . . . **Fic**
Hero and the crown (Sound recording cassette)./MCKINLEY, R/n.d./
5-A/7 KH488 . . . . **Fic**
Hero of Bremen. /HODGES, M/1993/3-5/6 KB451 . . . . . . **398.22**
Heroes. /MOCHIZUKI, K/1995/3-5/4 KH501 . . . . **Fic**
Heroes: great men through the ages. /HAZELL, R/1997/
3-A/9 KA828 . . . . **305.3**
Heroine of the Titanic: a tale both true and otherwise of the life of Molly
Brown. /BLOS, JW/1991/5-6/6 KE265. . . . . **B BROWN, M.**
Heroines: great women through the ages. /HAZELL, R/1996/
4-A/10 KA829 . . . . **305.4**
Heron Street. /TURNER, A/1989/1-3/3 KG626 . . . . **E**
Herring gull. /O'CONNOR, K/1992/5-6/5 KC657 . . . . **598**
Hey, Al. /YORINKS, A/1986/1-3/3 KG781 . . . . **E**
Hey, Al (Braille)./YORINKS, A/n.d./1-3/3 KG781 . . . . **E**
Hey! I'm reading!: a how-to-read book for beginners. /MILES, B/1995/
P-1/2 KB103 . . . . **372.4**
HEY, KELLY (Videocassette)./1991/4-6/KA854. . . . . **VCR 305.8**
HEY! LISTEN TO THIS: STORIES TO READ ALOUD. /1992/
/KA338 . . . . **PROF 808.5**
Hey, Ludwig!: classical piano solos for playful times (Sound recording
cassette). /LOUCHARD, R/1993/P-3/KD675. . . . . **SRC 789.8**
Hey, Ludwig! (Compact disc)./LOUCHARD, R/1993/
P-3/KD675. . . . . **SRC 789.8**
HEY, WHAT ABOUT ME? (Videocassette). /1987/
P-3/KA884. . . . . **VCR 306.875**
Hey! What's that sound? /CHARLES, VM/1994/P-1/1 KF379 . . . . . **E**
Hi. /SCOTT, AH/1994/P-K/2 KG422 . . . . **E**
Hi, cat! /KEATS, EJ/c1970, 1988/P-2/2 KF873 . . . . **CE E**
Hi, cat! (Kit)./KEATS, EJ/1990/P-2/2 KF873 . . . . **CE E**
Hiawatha. /LONGFELLOW, HW/1983/P-A/KD979 . . . . . **CE 811**
Hiawatha (Braille)./LONGFELLOW, HW/n.d./P-A/KD979 . . . . . **CE 811**
Hiawatha: messenger of peace. /FRADIN, DB/1992/
5-6/7 KE389 . . . . **B HIAWATHA**
Hiawatha (Sound recording cassette)./LONGFELLOW, HW/n.d./
P-A/KD979 . . . . **CE 811**
Hiawatha (Spanish version)./LONGFELLOW, HW/1996/
P-A/KD979 . . . . **CE 811**
Hiawatha (Videocassette)./LONGFELLOW, HW/1995/
P-A/KD979 . . . . **CE 811**
Hidden children. /GREENFELD, H/1993/A/7 KE657 . . . . **940.53**
Hidden children (Sound recording cassette)./GREENFELD, H/1997/
A/7 KE657 . . . . **940.53**
Hidden in sand. /HODGES, M/1994/3-4/6 KA759 . . . . **294.3**
Hide and seek. /VOS, I/c1981, 1991/5-A/4 KH835 . . . . **Fic**
Hide and seek fog. /TRESSELT, A/c1965/K-2/KG615 . . . . **E**
Hide and shriek: riddles about ghosts and goblins. /GORDON, JR/1991/
2-5/KD727 . . . . **793.735**

Hide and snake. /BAKER, K/1991/P-1/2 KF186 . . . . **E**
Hiding. /HUGHES, S/1996/P-K/2 KF789 . . . . **E**
Hiding to survive: stories of Jewish children rescued from the Holocaust. /
ROSENBERG, MB/1994/A/6 KE665 . . . . **940.53**
Hieroglyphs, the writing of ancient Egypt. /KATAN, NJ/1981/
5-6/9 KB866 . . . . **493**
Higgle wiggle: happy rhymes. /MERRIAM, E/1994/P-1/KD983 . . . . **811**
Higglety pigglety pop, or, There must be more to life. /SENDAK, M/
c1967/1-3/6 KG431 . . . . **E**
Higglety pigglety pop, or, There must be more to life (Braille)./SENDAK,
M/n.d./1-3/6 KG431 . . . . **E**
High king (Braille)./ALEXANDER, L/n.d./6-A/6 KG833 . . . . **Fic**
High king (Talking book)./ALEXANDER, L/n.d./6-A/6 KG833 . . . . . **Fic**
Higher on the door. /STEVENSON, J/1987/
3-4/4 KE553 . . . . **B STEVENSON, J.**
HIGHLIGHTS FOR CHILDREN. /1946-/P-A/KA517 . . . . **PER 050**
Highpockets./TUNIS, JR/c1948/5-A/6 KH809 . . . . **Fic**
High-wire Henry./CALHOUN, M/1991/K-2/4 KF331 . . . . **E**
High-wire Henry (Sound recording cassette)./CALHOUN, M/1993/
K-2/4 KF331 . . . . **E**
Higo mas dulce./VAN ALLSBURG, C/1995/3-A/3 KH823 . . . . . . **Fic**
Hilde and Eli: children of the Holocaust. /ADLER, DA/1994/
4-6/5 KE655 . . . . **940.53**
Hildilid's night. /RYAN, CD/c1971, 1986/K-3/6 KG365 . . . . **E**
Hildilid's night (Talking book)./RYAN, CD/n.d./K-3/6 KG365 . . . . . **E**
Hill top tales./POTTER, B/c1907, 1987/P-2/2 KG268 . . . . **E**
Hillary Rodham Clinton, first lady. /LEVERT, S/1994/
4-6/9 KE297 . . . . **B CLINTON, H.**
Himalaya: vanishing cultures. /REYNOLDS, J/1991/4-6/7 KE714. . **954.96**
HIMALAYAN ADVENTURE (Videocassette). /1994/
K-6/KE712 . . . . **VCR 954.96**
Hippo. /ARNOLD, C/c1989, 1992/4-6/7 KC785 . . . . **599.63**
Hippopotamus hunt. /MOST, B/1994/1-3/2 KG160 . . . . **E**
Hired hand: an African-American folktale. /SAN SOUCI, RD/1997/
3-4/3 KB412 . . . . **398.21**
HIROSHIMA MAIDEN (Videocassette). /c1988, 1997/
5-A/KH264 . . . . **VCR Fic**
Hiroshima no pika. /MARUKI, T/1982/4-6/5 KE672 . . . . . **940.54**
HISPANIC AMERICAN BIOGRAPHY. /1995/5-A/KA400 . . . . **REF 305.8**
HISPANIC HERITAGE (Picture). /1997/4-6/KA848 . . . . **PIC 305.8**
Hispanic heritage, series II. /SCHON, I/1985/KA043 . . . . **PROF 016.98**
Hispanic heritage, series III./SCHON, I/1988//KA043 . . . . **PROF 016.98**
Hist whist. /CUMMINGS, EE/c1923, 1989/2-6/KD926 . . . . **811**
HISTORIA DE LA CREACION: SEGUN EL GENESIS./1993/
2-3/4 KA688 . . . . **222**
Historia de Ping./FLACK, M/1996/P-1/6 KF550. . . . . **CE E**
Historical album of Alabama. /WILLS, CA/1995/4-6/7 KE999 . . **976.1**
Historical album of California. /WILLS, CA/1994/4-6/7 KF088 . . . **979.4**
Historical album of Colorado. /WILLS, CA/1996/4-6/7 KF062 . . . **978.8**
Historical album of Connecticut. /WILLS, CA/1995/4-6/7 KE953 . . **974.6**
Historical album of Florida. /WILLS, CA/1994/4-6/7 KE994 . . . **975.9**
Historical album of Illinois. /WILLS, CA/1994/4-6/7 KF016 . . . **977.3**
Historical album of Kentucky. /SMITH, A/1995/4-6/7 KF011 . . . **976.9**
Historical album of Massachusetts. /AVAKIAN, M/1994/
5-6/7 KE936 . . . . **974.4**
Historical album of Michigan. /WILLS, CA/1996/4-6/7 KF018 . . . **977.4**
Historical album of Minnesota. /CARLSON, JD/1993/5-6/7 KF020 . **977.6**
Historical album of Nebraska. /WILLS, CA/1994/4-6/7 KF055 . . . **978.2**
Historical album of New Jersey. /TOPPER, F/1995/4-6/7 KE965. . . **974.9**
Historical album of New York. /AVAKIAN, M/1993/5-6/8 KE954. . **974.7**
Historical album of Ohio. /WILLS, CA/1996/4-6/7 KF013 . . . **977.1**
Historical album of Oregon. /WILLS, CA/1995/4-6/7 KF090 . . . **979.5**
Historical album of Pennsylvania. /WILLS, CA/1996/4-6/7 KE961 . **974.8**
Historical album of Texas. /WILLS, CA/1995/4-6/7 KF004 . . . **976.4**
Historical album of Virginia. /COCKE, W/1995/4-6/7 KE976 . . . **975.5**
Historical album of Washington. /COCKE, W/1995/4-6/7 KF092 . **979.7**
History of Helpless Harry: to which is added a variety of amusing and
entertaining adventures. /AVI /c1980, 1995/5-A/7 KG859 . . . . . . **Fic**
History of Western painting: a young person's guide. /HESLEWOOD, J/
1996/4-6/8 KD483 . . . . **759**
History of Western sculpture: a young person's guide. /HESLEWOOD, J/
1996/4-6/9 KD398 . . . . **730**
Ho Ho Ho!: the complete book of Christmas words. /GRAHAM-BARBER, L/
1993/2-6/8 KB235 . . . . **394.266**
Hoang Anh: a Vietnamese-American boy. /HOYT-GOLDSMITH, D/1992/
3-6/6 KA849 . . . . **305.8**
Hobbit; or, There and back again. /TOLKIEN, JR/n.d./4-6/5 KH796 . . **Fic**
Hobbit; or, There and back again (Braille)./TOLKIEN, JR/n.d/
4-6/5 KH796 . . . . **Fic**
Hobbit; or, There and back again (Sound recording cassette)./TOLKIEN,
JR/n.d./4-6/5 KH796. . . . . **Fic**
Hobbit; or, There and back again (Talking book)./TOLKIEN, JR/n.d./
4-6/5 KH796 . . . . **Fic**

Hobie Hanson, greatest hero of the mall./GILSON, J/1989/
3-5/6 KH168 . . . . **Fic**
Hobie Hanson, you're weird. /GILSON, J/1987/3-5/6 KH168 . . . . . **Fic**
Hoboken chicken emergency. /PINKWATER, DM/c1977/
5-A/6 KH603 . . . . **CE Fic**
Hoboken chicken emergency (Videocassette)./PINKWATER, DM/c1984,
1997/5-A/6 KH603 . . . . **CE Fic**
Hobyahs. /SAN SOUCI, RD/1996/3-4/6 KB647 . . . . **398.24**
Hockey. /HARRIS, L/1994/3-6/4 KD841 . . . . **796.962**
Hockey for kids: heroes, tips, and facts. /MCFARLANE, B/1996/
4-6/7 KD844 . . . . **796.962**
Hockey trick./CORBETT, S/1974/4-5/4 KH030 . . . . **Fic**
Hogaphone and other stories (Videocassette). /HOLT, D/1991/
2-6/KH275. . . . . **VCR Fic**
Hog-eye. /MEDDAUGH, S/1995/K-3/2 KG123 . . . . **E**
Hold your horses: a feedbag full of fact and fable. /MELTZER, M/1995/
5-6/7 KD202 . . . . **636.1**
Hole in the dike. /GREEN, NB/c1974, 1975/K-2/2 KF640 . . . **CE E**
Hole in the dike (Braille). /GREEN, NB/n.d./K-2/2 KF640 . . . . **CE E**
Hole is to dig: a first book of first definitions. /KRAUSS, R/c1952/
P-2/2 KF922 . . . . **CE E**
Hole is to dig: a first book of first definitions (Braille)./KRAUSS, R/n.d./
P-2/2 KF922 . . . . **CE E**
Hole is to dig: a first book of first definitions (Kit)./KRAUSS, R/1990/
P-2/2 KF922 . . . . **CE E**
Hole story. /MERRIAM, E/1995/P-1/2 KG131 . . . . **E**
Holes and peeks. /JONAS, A/1984/P-K/1 KF845 . . . . **E**
Holi. /KADODWALA, D/1997/4-6/7 KA763 . . . . **294.5**
Holiday folding stories: storytelling and origami together for holiday fun. /
KALLEVIG, CP/1992//KA309 . . . . **PROF 736**
Holiday handbook. /BARKIN, C/1994/5-A/7 KA413. . . . . . . **REF 394.26**
Holiday origami. /SMOLINSKI, J/1995/3-6/KD403 . . . . **736**
Holiday times (Compact disc). /JENKINS, E/1996/P-3/KB199. **CD 394.26**
Holiday times (Sound recording cassette)./JENKINS, E/1996/
P-3/KB199 . . . . **CD 394.26**
Holidays and festivals activities. /SMITH, D/1994/1-6/6 KD458 . **745.594**
Holly, reindeer and colored lights: the story of Christmas symbols. /BARTH,
E/c1971/5-6/7 KB231 . . . . **394.266**
Holly, reindeer and colored lights: the story of Christmas symbols (Sound
recording cassette)./BARTH, E/n.d./5-6/7 KB231 . . . . **394.266**
HOME. /1992/K-6/KD900 . . . . **810.8**
HOME ALONE: YOU'RE IN CHARGE (Videocassette). /1991/
2-4/KD259. . . . . **VCR 640**
HOME AT LAST (Videocassette). /c1988, 1997/5-A/KH276. . . . **VCR Fic**
Home crafts. /KALMAN, B/1990/3-6/6 KD431 . . . . **745.5**
Home is the North. /MOREY, W/c1967, 1990/5-A/5 KH509 . . . . . **Fic**
Home lovely. /PERKINS, LR/1995/K-3/6 KG233 . . . . **E**
Home on the bayou: a cowboy's story. /KARAS, GB/1996/
K-2/2 KF868 . . . . **E**
HOME ON YOUR OWN (Videocassette). /1994/4-6/KD260 . . **VCR 640**
Home schooling from scratch. /KENYON, MP/1996/
/KA175. . . . . **PROF 371.04**
Homecoming. /VOIGT, C/1981/6-A/4 KH833 . . . . **Fic**
Homecoming (Braille)./VOIGT, C/n.d./6-A/4 KH833 . . . . **Fic**
Homecoming (Sound recording cassette)./VOIGT, C/n.d./
6-A/4 KH833 . . . . **Fic**
Homeless. /WOLF, B/1995/4-6/4 KB010 . . . . **362.5**
Homeless students. /TOWER, CC/1989//KA183 . . . . **PROF 371.826**
Homeplace. /SHELBY, A/1995/1-3/3 KG493 . . . . **E**
Homer Price. /MCCLOSKEY, R/c1943/3-6/5 KH470 . . . . . . **CE Fic**
Homer Price (Kit). /MCCLOSKEY, R/1973/3-6/5 KH470 . . . . **CE Fic**
Homer Price (Sound recording cassette)./MCCLOSKEY, R/n.d./
3-6/5 KH470 . . . . **CE Fic**
Homer Price stories (Talking book). /MCCLOSKEY, R/n.d./
3-6/KH471. . . . . **TB Fic**
Homer Price (Talking book). /MCCLOSKEY, R/n.d./3-6/5 KH470 . . **CE Fic**
Homes in the wilderness: a pilgrim's journal of Plymouth Plantation in 1620.
/MOURT'S RELATION /c1939, 1988/5-A/8 KE941 . . . . . **974.4**
Homesick: my own story. /FRITZ, J/1982/4-A/4 KH145 . . . . . . **Fic**
Homesick: my own story (Sound recording cassette)./FRITZ, J/n.d./
4-A/4 KH145 . . . . **Fic**
HOMESPUN TALES (Sound recording cassette). /1986/
3-6/KH193. . . . . **SRC Fic**
HOMESTEADING: 70 YEARS ON THE GREAT PLAINS, 1862-1932
(Videocassette). /1992/4-6/KF034 . . . . **VCR 978**
Hominids: a look back at our ancestors. /SATTLER, HR/1988/
4-A/8 KC269 . . . . **569.9**
Honest Abe. /KUNHARDT, E/1993/1-3/4 KE444 . . . . **B LINCOLN, A.**
Honey makers. /GIBBONS, G/1997/3-5/6 KC573 . . . . **595.79**
Hooray! A pinata! /KLEVEN, E/1996/K-2/2 KF910. . . . . **E**
Hooray for the Golly sisters!/BYARS, BC/1990/1-3/1 KF325 . . . . . **CE E**
Hooray for the Golly sisters! (Sound recording cassette)./BYARS, BC/
1997/1-3/1 KF325 . . . . **CE E**
Hoover's bride. /SMALL, D/1995/1-3/5 KG521 . . . . **E**

Hop jump. /WALSH, ES/1993/P-K/2 KG679 . . . . **E**
Hop on pop. /SEUSS, D/c1963/P-1/1 KG455 . . . . **E**
Hop on pop (Braille)./SEUSS, D/n.d./P-1/1 KG455 . . . . **E**
Hope. /GAEDDERT, L/1995/5-A/6 KH148 . . . . **Fic**
Hopis. /SNEVE, V/1995/4-6/7 KE771 . . . . **970.3**
HOPSCOTCH: THE MAGAZINE FOR GIRLS. /1990-/
2-6/KA518 . . . . **PER 050**
Hora de acostarse de Francisca./HOBAN, R/1996/P-1/2 KF739 . . . **CE E**
HORN BOOK GUIDE TO CHILDREN'S AND YOUNG ADULT BOOKS. /
1990-//KA114 . . . . **PER PROF 050**
HORN BOOK MAGAZINE: ABOUT BOOKS FOR CHILDREN AND
YOUNG ADULTS. /1924-//KA115 . . . . **PER PROF 050**
Horrible Harry and the green slime. /KLINE, S/1989/2-4/2 KH368 . . **Fic**
Horrible Harry and the green slime (Sound recording cassette)./KLINE, S/
1995/2-4/2 KH368 . . . . **Fic**
Horrible Harry's secret./KLINE, S/1990/2-4/2 KH368 . . . . . . **Fic**
Horrible story and others (Talking book). /MAHY, M/1992/
3-A/KH452 . . . . **TB Fic**
Horse and his boy./LEWIS, CS/1994/5-A/6 KH405 . . . . . . **CE Fic**
Horse and his boy (Braille)./LEWIS, CS/n.d./5-A/6 KH405 . . . **CE Fic**
Horse and his boy (Sound recording cassette)./LEWIS, CS/n.d./
5-A/6 KH405 . . . . **CE Fic**
Horse and his boy (Talking book)./LEWIS, CS/n.d./5-A/6 KH405 . **CE Fic**
Horse in Harry's room. /HOFF, S/c1970/K-2/2 KF757 . . . . **E**
HORSE SENSE FOR KIDS AND OTHER PEOPLE (Compact disc)./1992/
2-4/KD668. . . . . **SRC 789.4**
HORSE SENSE FOR KIDS AND OTHER PEOPLE (Sound recording
cassette)./1992/2-4/KD668 . . . . **SRC 789.4**
Horseback riding. /EVANS, J/1992/4-A/6 KD855 . . . . **798.2**
Horses. /POSELL, E/1981/1-3/4 KD204. . . . . **636.1**
Horses. /CLUTTON-BROCK, J/1992/4-6/8 KD199 . . . . **636.1**
Horses. /ROALF, P/1992/5-A/8 KD480 . . . . **758**
Horses. /BUDD, J/1995/4-6/7 KD198 . . . . **636.1**
Horse's body. /COLE, J/1981/4-6/7 KC805 . . . . **599.665**
Horseshoe crab. /DAY, N/1992/5-6/7 KC524 . . . . **595.4**
Horton hatches the egg. /SEUSS, D/c1940/P-3/3 KG456 . . . . **CE E**
Horton hatches the egg (Braille)./SEUSS, D/n.d./P-3/3 KG456 . . **CE E**
Horton hatches the egg./If I ran the circus (Videocassette). /SEUSS, D/
1992/P-3/KG457 . . . . **VCR E**
Horton hears a Who./SEUSS, D/1954/P-3/3 KG456 . . . . . **CE E**
Horton hears a Who (Braille)./SEUSS, D/n.d./P-3/3 KG456 . . . . **CE E**
Horton hears a Who (Kit)./SEUSS, D/1990/P-3/3 KG456 . . . . . **CE E**
Horton hears a Who!/Thidwick the big-hearted moose (Videocassette). /
SEUSS, D/1992/P-3/KG458 . . . . **VCR E**
HOSPITAL (Videocassette). /1990/1-4/KA995 . . . . . . **VCR 362.1**
Hot fudge. /HOWE, J/1990/K-3/2 KF777 . . . . **E**
Hot Hippo. /HADITHI, M/1986/K-3/4 KF660 . . . . . . **CE E**
Hot Hippo (Braille). /HADITHI, M/n.d./K-3/4 KF660 . . . . . **CE E**
Hot Hippo (Videocassette)./HADITHI, M/n.d./K-3/4 KF660 . . **CE E**
HOT LINE: ALL ABOUT ELECTRICITY (Videocassette). /1987/
4-A/KD042 . . . . **VCR 621.31**
Hot-air Henry./CALHOUN, M/1981/K-2/4 KF331 . . . . **E**
House at Pooh Corner. /MILNE, AA/c1956/K-6/3 KH497 . . . . . **Fic**
House at Pooh Corner (Braille)./MILNE, AA/n.d./K-6/3 KH497 . . . **Fic**
House at Pooh Corner (Sound recording cassette)./MILNE, AA/n.d./
K-6/3 KH497 . . . . **Fic**
House at Pooh Corner (Talking book)./MILNE, AA/n.d./K-6/3 KH497 . **Fic**
House for Hermit Crab. /CARLE, E/1987/P-2/2 KF344 . . . . . . **E**
House Gobbaleen. /ALEXANDER, L/1995/3-5/4 KG836. . . . . . **Fic**
House of Dies Drear. /HAMILTON, V/c1968/4-6/5 KH215 . . . **CE Fic**
House of Dies Drear (Braille)./HAMILTON, V/n.d./4-6/5 KH215 . . **CE Fic**
House of Dies Drear (Talking book)./HAMILTON, V/n.d./
4-6/5 KH215 . . . . **CE Fic**
House of Dies Drear (Videocassette)./HAMILTON, V/c1984, 1997/
4-6/5 KH215 . . . . **CE Fic**
House of secrets. /BAWDEN, N/c1963, 1992/5-A/7 KG890 . . . . . . **Fic**
House on East 88th Street. /WABER, B/c1962/P-2/3 KG667 . . . . . **E**
House on Maple Street. /PRYOR, B/1987/K-3/4 KG292 . . . . . . **E**
House sparrows everywhere. /ARNOLD, C/1992/4-6/7 KC704. . . . **598.8**
House that Drac built. /SIERRA, J/1995/1-3/3 KG503 . . . . **E**
House with a clock in its walls. /BELLAIRS, J/c1973/4-6/5 KG897. . . **Fic**
Housefly. /FISCHER-NAGEL, H/1990/5-6/7 KC556 . . . . . . **595.77**
Houses and homes. /MORRIS, A/1992/2-4/6 KD394 . . . . . . **728**
Houses: structures, methods, and ways of living. /VENTURA, P/1993/
4-A/9 KD395 . . . . **728**
HOW A BILL BECOMES A LAW (Picture). /1989/5-6/KA931. . **PIC 328.3**
How a book is made. /ALIKI /1986/K-3/3 KD345 . . . . **686**
How a seed grows. Rev. ed. /JORDAN, HJ/1992/P-2/1 KC387 . . . . **580**
How a shirt grew in the field. /USHINSKY, K/1992/K-2/2 KG636. . . **E**
How an airport really works. /SULLIVAN, G/1993/5-6/8 KB156. . . **387.7**
How animals move (CD-ROM). /ALEXANDER, RM/1995/
4-A/KC464 . . . . **CDR 591.47**
HOW ANIMALS MOVE (Videocassette). /1989/5-6/KC283. . **VCR 573.7**
How big is a whale? /JOHNSON, J/1995/2-5/5 KC462 . . . . **591.4**

How Chipmunk got tiny feet: Native American animal origin stories. / HAUSMAN, G/1995/K-3/3 KB588 . . . . **398.24**
How come? /WOLLARD, K/1993/4-8/6 KB874 . . . . **500**
How did we find out about microwaves? /ASIMOV, I/1989/ A/9 KD045 . . . . **621.381**
How did we find out about microwaves? (Sound recording cassette)./ ASIMOV, I/n.d./A/9 KD045 . . . . **621.381**
How did we find out about photosynthesis? /ASIMOV, I/1989/ 6-A/9 KC277 . . . . **572**
How did we find out about photosynthesis? (Sound recording cassette)./ ASIMOV, I/1993/6-A/9 KC277. . . . . **572**
How did we find out about superconductivity? /ASIMOV, I/1988/ 5-A/7 KC135 . . . . **537.6**
How did we find out about superconductivity? (Sound recording cassette)./ ASIMOV, I/n.d./5-A/7 KC135. . . . . . **537.6**
How dinosaurs came to be. /LAUBER, P/1996/4-A/6 KC251 . . . . **567.9**
How do apples grow? /MAESTRO, B/1992/K-2/4 KC418 . . . . **582.16**
How do birds find their way? /GANS, R/1996/3-4/2 KC673 . . . **598.156**
HOW DO I FEEL? (Picture). /1974/1-3/3 KA625 . . . . . . **PIC 152.4**
How do you know it's fall? /FOWLER, A/1992/P-2/2 KB917 . . . . **508.2**
How do you know it's fall? (Big book)./FOWLER, A/1992/ P-2/2 KB917 . . . . **508.2**
How do you know it's spring?/FOWLER, A/1991/P-2/2 KB917 . . . . **508.2**
How do you know it's spring? (Big book)./FOWLER, A/1991/ P-2/2 KB917 . . . . **508.2**
How do you know it's summer?/FOWLER, A/1992/P-2/2 KB917 . . . **508.2**
How do you know it's summer? (Big book)./FOWLER, A/1992/ P-2/2 KB917 . . . . **508.2**
How do you know it's winter?/FOWLER, A/1991/P-2/2 KB917 . . . . **508.2**
How do you know it's winter? (Big book)./FOWLER, A/1991/ P-2/2 KB917 . . . . **508.2**
How do you say it today, Jesse Bear?/CARLSTROM, NW/1992/ P-K/4 KF356 . . . . **E**
How do you spell God?: answers to the big questions from the world. /GELLMAN, M/1995/5-A/4 KA724 . . . . **291**
How does the wind walk. /CARLSTROM, NW/1993/P-2/3 KF354 . . . . **E**
How dogs really work! /SNOW, A/1993/4-A/5 KH727 . . . . . . **Fic**
How Georgie Radbourn saved baseball. /SHANNON, D/1994/ 2-5/6 KG476 . . . . **E**
How glass is made. /PATERSON, AJ/1985/5-6/9 KD324 . . . . . . **666**
How humans make friends. /LEEDY, L/1996/K-3/3 KA660 . . . . . **158**
How I captured a dinosaur. /SCHWARTZ, H/c1989, 1993/ P-2/2 KG418 . . . . **E**
How I survived being a girl. /DRAANEN, WV/1997/4-A/KH084 . . . . . **Fic**
How I was adopted: Samantha's story. /COLE, J/1995/ 1-3/2 KB012 . . . . **362.73**
How leaves change. /JOHNSON, SA/1986/4-6/9 KC399 . . . . . **581.4**
How many spots does a leopard have? and other tales. /LESTER, J/c1989, 1994/5-6/6 KB335 . . . . **398.2**
How monkeys make chocolate: foods and medicines from the rainforest. / FORSYTH, A/1995/4-8/7 KC402 . . . . . . **581.6**
How mountains are made. /ZOEHFELD, KW/1995/2-4/4 KC170 . . . **551.43**
How much is a million? /SCHWARTZ, DM/1985/K-1/2 KB950 . . . . . **513**
How much is a million? (Big book)./SCHWARTZ, DM/1994/ K-1/2 KB950 . . . . **513**
HOW MUCH IS A MILLION? (Videocassette). /1997/ K-1/KB947 . . . . **VCR 513**
How my family lives in America. /KUKLIN, S/1992/1-3/5 KA850 . . **305.8**
How my library grew by Dinah. /ALEXANDER, M/1983/K-2/2 KF146 . . . **E**
How my parents learned to eat. /FRIEDMAN, IR/1984/1-3/2 KF586 . . . **E**
How my parents learned to eat (Sound recording cassette)./FRIEDMAN, IR/n.d./1-3/2 KF586 . . . . **E**
How now, brown cow? /SCHERTLE, A/1994/1-3/KE020 . . . . . . **811**
HOW PLANTS ARE USED (Videocassette). /1991/ 3-6/KC357 . . . . **VCR 578.6**
How proudly they wave: flags of the fifty states. /HABAN, RD/1989/ 5-6/8 KE619 . . . . **929.9**
How Rabbit tricked Otter and other Cherokee animal stories (Talking book)./ROSS, G/c1991, 1996/2-4/6 KB641 . . . . **CE 398.24**
How Rabbit tricked Otter and other Cherokee trickster stories. /ROSS, G/ 1994/2-4/6 KB641 . . . . **CE 398.24**
How seeds travel. /OVERBECK, C/1982/2-4/6 KC389 . . . . . . **580**
How skyscrapers are made. /MICHAEL, D/1987/A/10 KD358 . . . . **690**
How Snake got his hiss: an original tale. /DAVOL, MW/1996/ K-2/2 KF450 . . . . **E**
How Snowshoe Hare rescued the Sun: a tale from the Arctic. /BERNHARD, E/1993/1-2/4 KB529 . . . . **398.24**
How spider tricked snake. /BENITEZ, M/1989/K-1/1 KB528 . . . . . **398.24**
HOW SWEET THE SOUND: AFRICAN-AMERICAN SONGS FOR CHILDREN (Kit)./1995/K-6/KD571 . . . . **CE 789.2**
HOW SWEET THE SOUND: AFRICAN-AMERICAN SONGS FOR CHILDREN. /1995/K-6/KD571. . . . . **CE 789.2**
How teddy bears are made: a visit to the Vermont Teddy Bear factory. / MORRIS, A/1994/K-2/3 KD351 . . . . **688.7**

How the animals got their colors: animal myths from around the world. / ROSEN, M/1992/2-4/4 KB640 . . . . **398.24**
How the Grinch stole Christmas. /SEUSS, D/c1957/P-3/KG459 . . . . **E**
How the Grinch stole Christmas (Braille)./SEUSS, D/n.d./P-3/KG459 . . . **E**
How the Grinch stole Christmas (Sound recording cassette)./SEUSS, D/ n.d./P-3/KG459 . . . . **E**
How the Manx cat lost its tail. /STEVENS, J/1990/2-3/4 KB658. . **398.24**
How the ostrich got its long neck: a tale from the Akamba of Kenya. / AARDEMA, V/1995/P-2/6 KB515 . . . . **CE 398.24**
How the ostrich got its long neck (Talking book)./AARDEMA, V/1997/ P-2/6 KB515 . . . . **CE 398.24**
How the rhinoceros got his skin (Kit). /KIPLING, R/1988/ 3-5/KH362. . . . . **KIT Fic**
How the rhinoceros got his skin; and, How the camel got his hump (Videocassette). /KIPLING, R/1987/2-5/KH361. . . . . **VCR Fic**
How the west was one + three x four (Microcomputer program). /SEILER, B/c1987, 1989/4-A/KB951 . . . . **MCP 513**
HOW THINGS WORK. /1995/3-6/5 KC883 . . . . **603**
How to attract, house and feed birds. /SCHUTZ, WE/c1974/ 3-6/KC663 . . . . **598**
How to attract, house and feed birds (Sound recording cassette)./SCHUTZ, WE/n.d./3-6/KC663 . . . . **598**
How to be an ocean scientist in your own home. /SIMON, S/1988/ 5-A/5 KC176 . . . . **551.46**
How to be an ocean scientist in your own home (Sound recording cassette)./SIMON, S/n.d./5-A/5 KC176 . . . . **551.46**
HOW TO BUILD CHAMPION PINEWOOD CARS (Videocassette). /1995/ 2-6/KD349 . . . . **VCR 688.6**
How to dig a hole to the other side of the world. /MCNULTY, F/c1979, 1990/2-4/6 KC154 . . . . **CE 551.1**
How to dig a hole to the other side of the world (Kit)./MCNULTY, F/ 1991/2-4/6 KC154 . . . . **CE 551.1**
How to eat fried worms. /ROCKWELL, T/1973/4-6/5 KH643 . . . . . . **Fic**
How to find a ghost. /DEEM, JM/1988/4-A/7 KA604 . . . . . . **133.1**
HOW TO FOLD A PAPER CRANE (Videocassette). /1994/ 3-6/KD402. . . . . **VCR 736**
How to help your child with homework: every caring parent's guide to encouraging good study habits and ending the Homework Wars: for parents of children ages 6-13. Rev. and updated ed. /RADENCICH, MC/1997//KA181 . . . . **PROF 371.3**
How to hunt buried treasure. /DEEM, JM/1992/4-6/8 KD058 . . . . . **622**
HOW TO JUST SAY NO TO DRUGS (Sound filmstrip). /1987/ A/KC996. . . . . **VCR 613.8**
How to lose all your friends. /CARLSON, N/1994/K-2/2 KF350 . . . . . **E**
How to make a mummy talk. /DEEM, JM/1995/4-6/8 KB175. . . . . **393**
How to make an apple pie and see the world. /PRICEMAN, M/1994/ K-2/3 KG288 . . . . **E**
How to read and write poems. /RYAN, M/1991/4-6/7 KD869 . . . . **808.1**
HOW TO READ MUSIC. 2ND ED. (Videocassette). /1994/ 3-A/KD519 . . . . **VCR 780**
HOW TO STUDY (Videocassette). /1988/5-6/KB087 . . . . **VCR 371.302**
HOW TO SUCCEED IN MIDDLE SCHOOL (Videocassette). /1994/ 5-6/KB125. . . . . **VCR 373.2**
How to think like a scientist: answering questions by the scientific method. / KRAMER, SP/1987/4-6/6 KB883 . . . . **507**
How to use cooperative learning in the mathematics class. /ARTZT, AF/ 1990//KA250 . . . . **PROF 372.7**
HOW TO USE THE COMPOUND MICROSCOPE (Videocassette). /1991/ 6-A/KB876. . . . . **VCR 502.8**
How to write a great school report. /JAMES, E/1983/ 4-6/7 KB088 . . . . **371.302**
How to write, recite, and delight in all kinds of poetry. /HULME, JN/1996/ 3-6/KD867 . . . . **808.06**
How Turtle's back was cracked: a traditional Cherokee tale. /ROSS, G/ 1995/4-5/5 KB642 . . . . **398.24**
How Turtle's back was cracked: a traditional Cherokee tale (Sound recording cassette)./ROSS, G/1997/4-5/5 KB642 . . . . . . **398.24**
How Two-Feather was saved from loneliness: an Abenaki legend. /TAYLOR, CJ/1990/3-4/2 KB716. . . . . **398.26**
How we crossed the West: the adventures of Lewis and Clark. / SCHANZER, R/1997/3-6/7 KE205 . . . . **917.804**
How we learned the earth is round. /LAUBER, P/c1990, 1992/ K-3/2 KC060 . . . . **525**
How we saw the world: nine Native stories of the way things began. / TAYLOR, CJ/1993/4-5/4 KB377 . . . . **398.2**
How you were born. Rev. and expanded ed. /COLE, J/1993/ K-3/4 KC945 . . . . **612.6**
Howard Carter: searching for King Tut. /FORD, B/1995/ A/9 KE279 . . . . **B CARTER, H.**
Howie helps himself. /FASSLER, J/1974, c1975/K-2/4 KF544 . . . . . . **E**
Howie helps himself (Sound recording cassette)./FASSLER, J/n.d./ K-2/4 KF544 . . . . **E**
Howliday Inn./HOWE, D/1982/3-6/5 KH285 . . . . **Fic**
Howliday Inn (Braille)./HOWE, D/n.d./3-6/5 KH285 . . . . **Fic**

Howl's moving castle. /JONES, DW/1986/A/7 KH333 . . . . **Fic**
How's the weather?: a look at weather and how it changes. /BERGER, M/ 1993/K-5/2 KC187 . . . . **551.5**
Hudson River: an adventure from the mountains to the sea. /LOURIE, P/ 1992/4-6/6 KE192 . . . . **917.47**
Hueso prodigioso./STEIG, W/1993/1-3/5 KG539 . . . . **CE E**
Huevos hablantes./SAN SOUCI, RD/1996/3-5/5 KB415 . . . . . **CE 398.21**
Huevos verdes con jamon./SEUSS, D/1992/P-2/1 KG454 . . . . **CE E**
Hugger to the rescue. /PATENT, DH/1994/3-6/5 KD226. . . . . . . **636.73**
Hugh Glass, mountain man. /MCCLUNG, RM/1993/6-A/7 KH472 . . . **Fic**
Hugh Glass, mountain man (Sound recording cassette)./MCCLUNG, RM/ 1994/6-A/7 KH472. . . . . **Fic**
HUMAN AND ANIMAL BEGINNINGS. 3rd ed (Videocassette). /1990/ 2-5/KC950. . . . . **VCR 612.6**
Human body. /GABB, M/c1991, 1992/5-6/6 KC918 . . . . **612**
Human body: how we evolved. /COLE, J/1987/5-6/7 KC915. . . . . . **612**
Humbug. /BAWDEN, N/1992/5-A/5 KG891 . . . . **Fic**
Hummingbirds. /MURRAY, P/1993/3-5/6 KC700 . . . . **598.7**
Hummingbirds' gift. /CZERNECKI, S/1994/1-3/7 KF443 . . . . **E**
Hummingbirds: jewels in the sky. /TYRRELL, EQ/1992/ 5-6/5 KC703 . . . . **598.7**
HUMPTY DUMPTY'S MAGAZINE. /1952-/P-1/KA519 . . . . **PER 050**
Hunches in bunches. /SEUSS, D/1982/K-3/2 KG460 . . . . **E**
Hundred dresses. /ESTES, E/c1944/2-4/6 KH102. . . . . **Fic**
Hundred dresses (Braille)./ESTES, E/n.d./2-4/6 KH102 . . . . **Fic**
Hundred dresses (Sound recording cassette)./ESTES, E/1997/ 2-4/6 KH102 . . . . **Fic**
Hundred penny box. /MATHIS, SB/1975/4-6/4 KH461. . . . . **CE Fic**
Hundred penny box (Sound recording cassette)./MATHIS, SB/n.d./ 4-6/4 KH461 . . . . **CE Fic**
Hundred penny box (Talking book)./MATHIS, SB/1977/ 4-6/4 KH461 . . . . **CE Fic**
Hundred penny box (Videocassette)./MATHIS, SB/1979/ 4-6/4 KH461 . . . . **CE Fic**
Hundredth name. /OPPENHEIM, SL/c1995, 1997/2-3/2 KG194 . . . . . . **E**
Hungry giant of the tundra. /SLOAT, T/1993/K-3/5 KB419 . . . . . **398.21**
Hungry, hungry sharks. /COLE, J/1986/1-3/2 KC592 . . . . **597.3**
Hunter and the animals: a wordless picture book. /DE PAOLA, T/1981/ K-1/KF470. . . . . **E**
Hunter who was king and other African tales. /FORD, B/1994/ K-3/4 KB299 . . . . **398.2**
Hunterman and the crocodile: a West African folktale. /DIAKITE, BW/ 1997/2-3/5 KB560 . . . . **398.24**
Hunter's stew and hangtown fry: what pioneer America ate and why. / PERL, L/c1977/A/11 KD275 . . . . **641.5**
Hunting the white cow. /SEYMOUR, T/1993/1-3/2 KG474 . . . . **E**
Hurricane. /WIESNER, D/1990/K-2/2 KG712 . . . . **E**
Hurricane. /LAMPTON, C/1991/4-6/7 KC202. . . . . **551.55**
Hurricane City. /WEEKS, S/1993/K-2/2 KG691. . . . . **E**
Hurricane Harry. /CASELEY, J/1991/3-5/4 KG985. . . . . **Fic**
Hurricanes. /SOUZA, DM/1996/4-6/7 KC206. . . . . **551.55**
Hurricanes: Earth's mightiest storms. /LAUBER, P/1996/ 3-6/6 KC203 . . . . **551.55**
HURTFUL WORDS (Videocassette)./1993/5-6/KA666 . . . . **VCR 158**
Hush!: a Thai lullaby. /HO, M/1996/P-1/KD952 . . . . **811**
Hyena and the moon: stories to listen to from Kenya (Talking book). / MCNEIL, H/1995/5-6/KB346 . . . . **TB 398.2**
Hyena and the moon: stories to tell from Kenya. /MCNEIL, H/1994/ 5-6/7 KB347 . . . . **398.2**
Hyperactive child book. /KENNEDY, P/1994//KA303 . . . . **PROF 649**
HYPERSTUDIO (Microcomputer program). /1990/ 2-A/KA574 . . . . **MCP 006.7**
I am an American: a true story of Japanese internment. /STANLEY, J/ 1994/5-A/8 KE666 . . . . **940.53**
I am king! /PACKARD, M/1994/K-1/1 KG205 . . . . **E**
I am me! /BRANDENBERG, A/1996/P-K/1 KF258 . . . . **E**
I am not a crybaby. /SIMON, N/1989/P-4/2 KA644 . . . . **155.4**
I am not going to get up today! /SEUSS, D/1987/1-3/2 KG461 . . . . . **E**
I am not going to get up today! (Braille)./SEUSS, D/n.d./1-3/2 KG461 . **E**
I am not going to get up today! plus three more Dr. Seuss classics (Videocassette). /SEUSS, D/1991/1-3/KG462 . . . . **VCR E**
I am really a princess. /SHIELDS, CD/1993/1-3/3 KG494 . . . . **E**
I am Rosa Parks. /PARKS, R/1997/1-2/4 KE491 . . . . **B PARKS, R.**
I am the dog, I am the cat. /HALL, D/1994/K-3/3 KF661 . . . . **E**
I can read with my eyes shut. /SEUSS, D/1978/P-2/2 KG463 . . . . **E**
I dance in my red pajamas. /HURD, ET/1982/K-1/2 KF791 . . . . **E**
I don't want to go back to school. /RUSSO, M/1994/1-3/2 KG361 . . . **E**
I fly. /ROCKWELL, AF/1997/P-1/2 KG343. . . . . **E**
I GET SO MAD! (Videocassette). /1993/K-3/KA626. . . . . . . **VCR 152.4**
I got a bullfrog: folksongs for the fun of it (Compact disc)./HOLT, D/ 1994/2-4/KD570 . . . . **SRC 789.2**
I got a bullfrog: folksongs for the fun of it (Sound recording cassette). / HOLT, D/1994/2-4/KD570. **SRC 789.2**
I had a lot of wishes./STEVENSON, J/1995/ 3-4/4 KE551 . . . . **B STEVENSON, J.**
I have a friend. /NARAHASHI, K/1987/P-2/2 KG166. . . . . **CE E**
I have a sister--my sister is deaf. /PETERSON, JW/c1977/ 2-4/4 KB007 . . . . **362.4**
I know a lady. /ZOLOTOW, C/1984/K-2/6 KG802 . . . . **E**
I know a lady (Sound recording cassette)./ZOLOTOW, C/n.d./ K-2/6 KG802 . . . . **E**
I know an old lady who swallowed a fly. /WESTCOTT, NB/1980/ P-3/KE039 . . . . **CE 811**
I know an old lady who swallowed a fly. /ROUNDS, G/1990/ K-3/KD586 . . . . **789.2**
I like dessert (Sound recording cassette). /POLANSKY, DS/1987/ K-6/KD647 . . . . **SRC 789.3**
I LIKE YOU, IF YOU LIKE ME: POEMS OF FRIENDSHIP. /1987/ 3-A/KE065. . . . . **811.008**
I like you, if you like me: poems of friendship (Sound recording cassette)./ n.d./3-A/KE065 . . . . **811.008**
I love animals. /MCDONNELL, F/1994/P-1/2 KG100 . . . . **E**
I love animals (Big book)./MCDONNELL, F/1996/P-1/2 KG100 . . . . . . **E**
I love boats. /MCDONNELL, F/1995/P-1/3 KG101 . . . . **E**
I love guinea pigs. /KING-SMITH, D/1995/K-4/3 KD183. . . . . **636**
I love guinea pigs (Sound recording cassette)./KING-SMITH, D/1997/ K-4/3 KD183 . . . . **636**
I pledge allegiance. /SWANSON, J/1990/2-5/4 KA909 . . . . . **CE 323.6**
I pledge allegiance (Kit)./SWANSON, J/1991/2-5/4 KA909 . . **CE 323.6**
I read signs. /HOBAN, T/1983/P-1/KA800. . . . . **302.23**
I read symbols. /HOBAN, T/1983/P-1/KA797. . . . . **302.2**
I SAW ESAU: THE SCHOOLCHILD'S POCKET BOOK. /1992/ /KA276. . . . . **PROF 398.8**
I see animals hiding. /ARNOSKY, J/1995/2-4/6 KC465 . . . . **591.47**
I see, you saw. /KARLIN, N/1997/P-1/1 KF869 . . . . **E**
I slide into the white of winter. /AGELL, C/1994/K-2/3 KF137 . . . . **E**
I speak English for my mom. /STANEK, M/1989/2-4/2 KH747. . . . . **Fic**
I speak HyperCard. /FARMER, LS/1992/3-A/KA573 . . . . **005.265**
I spy a freight train: transportation in art. /MICKLETHWAIT, L/1996/ P-2/2 KD473 . . . . **758**
I spy a lion: animals in art. /MICKLETHWAIT, L/1994/P-2/2 KD474. . **758**
I spy: an alphabet in art. /MICKLETHWAIT, L/1992/P-2/2 KD484. . . **759**
I spy Christmas: a book of picture riddles. /WICK, W/1992/ P-2/KD715. . . . . **793.73**
I spy fantasy: a book of picture riddles. /WICK, W/1994/ K-3/3 KD716 . . . . **793.73**
I spy school days: a book of picture riddles. /WICK, W/1995/ K-3/3 KD717 . . . . **793.73**
I spy spooky night: a book of picture riddles. /WICK, W/1996/ P-3/5 KD718 . . . . **793.73**
I spy two eyes: numbers in art. /MICKLETHWAIT, L/1993/ P-A/KB970. . . . . **513.2**
I THOUGHT I'D TAKE MY RAT TO SCHOOL: POEMS FOR SEPTEMBER TO JUNE. /1993/2-5/KE066. . . . . **811.008**
I want a dog. /KHALSA, DK/1987/P-2/5 KF902 . . . . **E**
I want to be. /MOSS, T/1993/1-4/3 KG159 . . . . **E**
I want to be a puppeteer. /BULLOCH, I/1996/3-5/5 KD444. . . . **745.592**
I want to be... a veterinarian. /MAZE, S/1997/5-6/9 KD195 . . . **636.089**
I want to be an actor. /BULLOCH, I/1996/3-5/5 KD688 . . . . **792**
I want to be an astronaut. /BARTON, B/1988/P-2/2 KF206. . . . . **E**
I want to be... an astronaut. /MAZE, S/1997/5-6/9 KD137. . . . . **629.45**
I wanted to know all about God. /KROLL, VL/1994/K-2/2 KA694 . . **231**
I WAS DREAMING TO COME TO AMERICA: MEMORIES FROM THE ELLIS ISLAND ORAL HISTORY PROJECT. /1995/4-6/7 KA916 . . **325**
I was so mad. /SIMON, N/1974/P-2/2 KA630. . . . . **152.4**
I WAS WONDERING: A SUPPLEMENT TO CHILDCRAFT--THE HOW AND WHY LIBRARY./1991/P-2/KA378. . . . . **REF 031**
I wear long green hair in the summer. /AGELL, C/1994/K-2/2 KF138. . . **E**
I went walking. /WILLIAMS, S/1990/P-1/1 KG732 . . . . **CE E**
I went walking (Big book)./WILLIAMS, S/1991/P-1/1 KG732 . . . . **CE E**
I wish Daddy didn't drink so much. /VIGNA, J/1988/P-3/2 KG653. . . . **E**
I wish I were a butterfly. /HOWE, J/1987/K-3/2 KF778 . . . . **E**
Iblis. /OPPENHEIM, SL/1994/4-5/4 KA789 . . . . **297**
Ice hockey. /LITKE, R/1997/3-6/8 KD843. . . . . **796.962**
Ice horse. /CHRISTIANSEN, C/1993/2-3/6 KF391 . . . . **E**
Ice sports. /SANDELSON, R/1991/4-6/7 KD835. . . . . **796.9**
Icebergs and glaciers. /SIMON, S/1987/3-6/7 KC165 . . . . **551.3**
Iceman. /LESSEM, D/1994/4-6/6 KE640 . . . . **937**
Icky squishy science. /MARKLE, S/1996/4-8/6 KB895 . . . . **507.8**
Idaho. /KENT, Z/1990/4-6/9 KF091 . . . . **979.6**
Idaho (Sound recording cassette)./KENT, Z/1993/4-6/9 KF091. . . . **979.6**
Ideas and insights: language arts in the elementary school. /WATSON, DJ/ 1987//KA232 . . . . **PROF 372.6**
Id-ul-Fitr. /KERVEN, R/1997/3-5/7 KA787 . . . . **297**
If I ran the circus. /SEUSS, D/c1956/P-3/4 KG464 . . . . **E**
If I ran the circus (Braille)./SEUSS, D/n.d./P-3/4 KG464 . . . . **E**
If I ran the zoo. /SEUSS, D/1950/P-3/5 KG465 . . . . **E**

If I ran the zoo (Braille)./SEUSS, D/n.d./P-3/5 KG465 . . . . **E**
If I ran the zoo (Sound recording cassette)./SEUSS, D/1993/
  P-3/5 KG465 . . . . **E**
If I ran the zoo (Talking book)./SEUSS, D/n.d./P-3/5 KG465. . . . **E**
If I ran the zoo (Videocassette)./SEUSS, D/1985/1-3/KG450. . . . **VCR E**
If I were in charge of the world and other worries. /VIORST, J/1981/
  2-4/KE037 . . . . **811**
If pigs could fly. /LAWSON, J/1989/5-A/6 KH387 . . . . **Fic**
If the shoe fits...how to develop multiple intelligences in the classroom. /
  CHAPMAN, C/1993//KA157 . . . . **PROF 155.4**
...If you lived at the time of the Civil War. /MOORE, K/1994/
  3-5/6 KE908 . . . . **973.7**
If you made a million. /SCHWARTZ, DM/1989/2-5/5 KA946. . . **332.024**
If you were my bunny. /MCMULLAN, K/1996/P-K/3 KG112 . . . . . **E**
If you were there in 1776. /BRENNER, B/1994/5-6/6 KE875 . . . . . **973.3**
If you're not here, please raise your hand: poems about school. /DAKOS,
  K/1990/2-5/KD929 . . . . **811**
Igloo. /YUE, C/1988/4-6/9 KE778 . . . . **970.3**
Igor Stravinsky. /VENEZIA, M/1996/5-6/7 KE557 . . . **B STRAVINSKY, I**
Iguana Beach. /FRANKLIN, KL/1997/P-1/2 KF575 . . . . **E**
Iguanas. /PATTON, D/1996/4-6/7 KC627 . . . . **597.95**
I-know-not-what, I-know-not-where: a Russian tale. /KIMMEL, EA/1994/
  3-4/6 KB329 . . . . **398.2**
Iliad and the Odyssey. /WILLIAMS, M/1996/3-6/8 KE129 . . . . . . **883**
I'll meet you at the cucumbers. /MOORE, L/1988/2-4/5 KH505 . . . . **Fic**
I'll see you when the moon is full. /FOWLER, SG/1994/K-2/2 KF568. . . **E**
Illustrated book of myths: tales and legends of the world. /PHILIP, N/
  1995/5-A/KA394 . . . . **REF 291.1**
Illustrated rules of in-line hockey. /MAYO, T/1996/3-6/6 KD772 . **796.21**
Illustrated rules of softball. /SUBLETT, A/1996/3-6/6 KD803 . **796.357**
ILLUSTRATORS OF CHILDREN'S BOOKS, 1967-1976. /1978/
  /KA311 . . . . **PROF 741.6**
Illyrian adventure. /ALEXANDER, L/1986/5-A/5 KG837 . . . . **Fic**
Illyrian adventure (Sound recording cassette)./ALEXANDER, L/n.d./
  5-A/5 KG837. . . . . **Fic**
I'm a seed. /MARZOLLO, J/1996/K-2/1 KG081 . . . . **E**
I'M GONNA LET IT SHINE: A GATHERING OF VOICES FOR FREEDOM
  (Sound recording cassette). /1990/3-6/KD619 . . . . . . **SRC 789.3**
I'M GONNA LET IT SHINE: A GATHERING OF VOICES FOR FREEDOM
  (Compact disc)./n.d./3-6/KD619 . . . . . . **SRC 789.3**
I'm growing! /ALIKI /1992/P-1/2 KC943 . . . . **612.6**
I'm not moving, Mama! /CARLSTROM, NW/1990/P-1/1 KF355 . . . . . . **E**
I'm not scared. /HALL, K/1994/K-1/1 KF664. . . . . **E**
I'M SO FRUSTRATED! (Videocassette). /1994/1-3/KA627 . . . **VCR 152.4**
I'm terrific. /SHARMAT, MW/1977/P-1/3 KG481 . . . . **E**
I'm the best! /SHARMAT, MW/1991/K-2/1 KG482 . . . . **E**
I'm the big sister now. /EMMERT, N/1989/3-5/5 KD039 . . . . . **618.92**
I'm tyrannosaurus!: a book of dinosaur rhymes. /MARZOLLO, J/1993/
  K-2/3 KD981 . . . . **811**
IMAGINARY GARDENS: AMERICAN POETRY AND ART FOR YOUNG
  PEOPLE. /1989/4-A/KE067 . . . . **811.008**
Imani in the belly. /CHOCOLATE, DM/1994/2-3/5 KB431 . . . . . **398.22**
Immigrant girl: Becky of Eldridge Street. /HARVEY, B/1987/
  3-5/5 KH221 . . . . **Fic**
Immigrants. /SANDLER, MW/1995/5-A/7 KA922 . . . . **325**
IMMIGRATION (Microcomputer program). /1996/5-A/KA917 . **MCP 325**
IMMIGRATION (Picture). /n.d./5-6/KA918. . . . . **PIC 325**
IMMUNE SYSTEM: OUR INTERNAL DEFENDER (Videocassette). /1991/
  4-5/KD014. . . . . **VCR 616.07**
Imogene's antlers. /SMALL, D/1985/P-2/6 KG522 . . . . **CE E**
Imogene's antlers (Kit)./SMALL, D/1994/P-2/6 KG522 . . . . **CE E**
Impossible riddle. /JACKSON, E/1995/K-3/4 KF819 . . . . **E**
Impressionists: the origins of modern painting. /SALVI, F/1994/
  6-A/9 KD485 . . . . **759.05**
In a creepy, creepy place and other scary stories. /GOROG, J/1996/
  4-6/4 KH183 . . . . **Fic**
In a dark, dark room and other scary stories. /SCHWARTZ, A/1984/
  K-3/1 KB693 . . . . **398.25**
In a dark, dark wood. /CARTER, DA/1991/P-2/2 KF362. . . . . **E**
In a messy, messy room. /GOROG, J/1990/4-6/6 KH184 . . . . **Fic**
In days gone by: folklore and traditions of the Pennsylvania Dutch. /
  KIRCHNER, AB/1996//KA268 . . . . **PROF 398.2**
In Flanders Fields: the story of the poem by John McCrae. /GRANFIELD,
  L/1995/4-6/7 KD947 . . . . **811**
In for winter, out for spring. /ADOFF, A/1991/1-4/KD910 . . . . **811**
In I were in charge of the world and other worries (Sound recording
  cassette). /VIORST, J/n.d./2-4/KE037 . . . . **811**
In my family./En mi familia. /LOMAS GARZA, C/1996/
  2-5/6 KA870 . . . . **306.85**
In my mother's house. /CLARK, AN/c1941, 1991/1-4/KE759 . . . . **970.3**
In other words: a beginning thesaurus. /SCHILLER, A/1987/
  4-6/KA429 . . . . **REF 423**

IN PRAISE OF OUR FATHERS AND OUR MOTHERS: A BLACK FAMILY
  TREASURY BY OUTSTANDING AUTHORS AND ARTISTS. /1997/
  3-6/KA867 . . . . **306.85**
In search of the Grand Canyon. /FRASER, MA/1995/3-5/6 KF068 . **979.1**
In the beginning: creation stories from around the world. /HAMILTON, V/
  1988/5-6/4 KA731 . . . . **291.2**
IN THE COMPANY OF WHALES (CD-ROM). /1993/
  3-A/KC770 . . . . **CDR 599.5**
In the days of the Salem witchcraft trials. /ROACH, MK/1996/
  3-6/10 KE945 . . . . **974.4**
In the diner. /LOOMIS, C/1994/P-2/2 KG031 . . . . **E**
In the footsteps of the werewolf. /PIPE, J/1996/4-6/7 KB635. . . **398.24**
In the forest. /ETS, MH/c1944, 1976/P-1/2 KF537 . . . . **E**
In the forest (Braille)./ETS, MH/n.d./P-1/2 KF537 . . . . **E**
In the huddle with...Steve Young. /CHRISTOPHER, M/1996/
  3-5/8 KE606 . . . . **B YOUNG, S.**
In the land of the big red apple./MACBRIDE, RL/1995/4-6/6 KH436 . . **Fic**
In the land of the big red apple (Sound recording cassette)./MACBRIDE,
  RL/1997/4-6/6 KH436 . . . . **Fic**
In the month of Kislev: a story for Hanukkah. /JAFFE, N/1992/
  K-2/2 KF820 . . . . **CE E**
In the month of Kislev: a story for Hanukkah (Sound recording cassette)./
  JAFFE, N/1995/K-2/2 KF820 . . . . **CE E**
In the month of Kislev (Videocassette). /JAFFE, N/1993/
  K-2/2 KF820 . . . . **CE E**
In the night kitchen. /SENDAK, M/c1970/K-3/3 KG432 . . . . **CE E**
In the night kitchen (Picture). /SENDAK, M/n.d./K-3/3 KG432. . . . . **CE E**
In the night kitchen (Talking Book)./SENDAK, M/n.d./K-3/3 KG432. **CE E**
In the night kitchen (Videocassette)./SENDAK, M/n.d./
  K-3/3 KG432 . . . . **CE E**
In the palace of the Ocean King. /SINGER, M/1995/2-3/5 KG509 . . . . **E**
In the rain with Baby Duck. /HEST, A/1995/P-1/2 KF718 . . . . **E**
In the small, small pond. /FLEMING, D/1993/P-2/1 KF555 . . . . **E**
In the snow. /LEE, HV/1995/1-3/2 KF955 . . . . **E**
In the snow: who's been here? /GEORGE, LB/1995/1-3/2 KF607 . . . . **E**
In the spring. /BROWN, C/1994/P-1/2 KF269 . . . . **E**
In the swim: poems and paintings. /FLORIAN, D/1997/1-3/KD937 . . **811**
In the tall, tall grass. /FLEMING, D/1991/P-K/1 KF556 . . . . **E**
In the village of the elephants. /SCHMIDT, J/1994/4-6/6 KC816 . **599.67**
In two worlds: a Yup'ik Eskimo family. /JENNESS, A/1989/
  5-6/7 KF098 . . . . **979.8**
In-between days. /BUNTING, E/1994/4-6/4 KG943 . . . . **Fic**
In-between days (Sound recording cassette)./BUNTING, E/1997/
  4-6/4 KG943 . . . . **Fic**
Inca and Spaniard: Pizarro and the conquest of Peru. /MARRIN, A/1989/
  A/8 KF109 . . . . **985**
Incas. /NEWMAN, SP/1992/5-6/7 KF103 . . . . **980.3**
Inch-high samurai. /MCCARTHY, RF/1993/3-4/4 KB754 . . . . . **398.27**
Incident at Hawk's Hill. /ECKERT, AW/1971/6-A/7 KH097 . . . . . . **Fic**
Incident at Hawk's Hill (Braille)./ECKERT, AW/n.d./6-A/7 KH097 . . . . **Fic**
Incident at Hawk's Hill (Sound recording cassette)./ECKERT, AW/1996/
  6-A/7 KH097 . . . . **Fic**
Incredible plants. /DOW, L/1997/A/7 KC385 . . . . **580**
Incredible plants. /TAYLOR, B/1997/3-8/8 KC393 . . . . **580**
INDEPENDENCE: BIRTH OF A FREE NATION (Videocassette). /1976/
  A/KE890 . . . . **VCR 973.4**
INDEX TO CHILDREN'S POETRY./1942/5-6/KA374 . . . . . . **REF 016.811**
INDEX TO CHILDREN'S POETRY, FIRST SUPPLEMENT./1954/
  5-6/KA374 . . . . **REF 016.811**
INDEX TO CHILDREN'S POETRY, SECOND SUPPLEMENT./1965/
  5-6/KA374 . . . . **REF 016.811**
INDEX TO POETRY FOR CHILDREN AND YOUNG PEOPLE: 1964-1969./
  1972/5-6/KA374 . . . . **REF 016.811**
INDEX TO POETRY FOR CHILDREN AND YOUNG PEOPLE: 1970-1975./
  1978/5-6/KA374 . . . . **REF 016.811**
INDEX TO POETRY FOR CHILDREN AND YOUNG PEOPLE: 1976-1981./
  1984/5-6/KA374 . . . . **REF 016.811**
INDEX TO POETRY FOR CHILDREN AND YOUNG PEOPLE: 1982-1987./
  1988/5-6/KA374 . . . . **REF 016.811**
INDEX TO POETRY FOR CHILDREN AND YOUNG PEOPLE: 1988-1992. /
  1994/5-6/KA374 . . . . **REF 016.811**
Indian chiefs. /FREEDMAN, R/1987/5-6/8 KE749 . . . . **970.1**
Indian in the cupboard. /REID BANKS, L/1980/4-6/4 KH627 . . . . **CE Fic**
Indian in the cupboard (Braille)./REID BANKS, L/n.d./
  4-6/4 KH627 . . . . **CE Fic**
INDIAN IN THE CUPBOARD (Microcomputer program). /1991/
  4-6/KB113 . . . . **MCP 372.6**
Indian in the cupboard (Talking book)./REID BANKS, L/1992/
  4-6/4 KH627 . . . . **CE Fic**
Indian sign language. /HOFSINDE, R/c1956/2-4/4 KA798. . . . . . **302.2**
Indian terms of the Americas. /PATTERSON, L/1994/
  5-A/KA478 . . . . **REF 970.004**
Indian treaties. /GOLD, SD/1997/5-6/10 KA904 . . . . **323.1**

Indian way: learning to communicate with Mother Earth. /MCLAIN, G/ 1990/2-6/6 KE750 . . . . **970.1**

Indian winter. /FREEDMAN, R/1992/A/9 KE202 . . . . **917.804**

Indiana. /FRADIN, DB/1994/4-6/3 KF014 . . . . **977.2**

Indians of Canada. 7th ed. /JENNESS, D/1977/A/12 KA485 . . **REF 971**

Indians of the Great Plains: traditions, history, legends, and life. /SITA, L/ 1997/4-6/8 KE765 . . . . **970.3**

Indians of the Northeast: traditions, history, legends, and life. /SITA, L/ 1997/4-6/9 KE766 . . . . **970.3**

Indians of the Northwest: traditions, history, legends, and life. /PRESS, P/ 1997/4-6/9 KE762 . . . . **970.3**

INDIANS OF THE PLAINS (Picture). /n.d./5-6/KE788 . . . . . **PIC 970.48**

Indians of the Southwest: traditions, history, legends, and life. /SITA, L/ 1997/4-6/9 KE767 . . . . **970.3**

Indians. Rev. ed. /TUNIS, E/1979/4-6/7 KE754. . . . . **970.1**

Infield hit. /DYGARD, TJ/1995/5-A/7 KH093 . . . . **Fic**

INFORMATION PLEASE ALMANAC, ATLAS & YEARBOOK. /1947-/ 4-6/KA405 . . . . **REF 317.3**

Information problem-solving: the Big Six Skills approach to library and information skills instruction. /EISENBERG, MB/1990/ /KA063. . . . . **PROF 025.5**

Ingenious Mr. Peale: painter, patriot and man of science. /WILSON, J/ 1996/6-A/8 KE493 . . . . **B PEALE, C.**

Ingri and Edgar d'Aulaire's book of Greek myths (Sound recording cassette). /D'AULAIRE, I/n.d./2-6/7 KA738. . . . . **CE 292**

Ingri and Edgar Parin d'Aulaire's Book of Greek myths. /D'AULAIRE, I/ c1962/2-6/7 KA738 . . . . **CE 292**

Ininatig's gift of sugar: traditional native sugarmaking. /WITTSTOCK, LW/ c1993/3-6/3 KE786. . . . . **970.476**

Inktomi and the ducks and other Assiniboin trickster stories (Talking book). /EVANS, R/1994/3-5/KB441 . . . . **TB 398.22**

In-line skating: a complete guide for beginners. /SULLIVAN, G/1993/ 4-6/6 KD773 . . . . **796.21**

INNER CHIMES: POEMS ON POETRY. /1992/2-6/KD885 . . . . . **808.81**

Insect. /MOUND, L/1990/5-6/8 KC545 . . . . **595.7**

Insect metamorphosis from egg to adult. /GOOR, R/1990/ 4-6/6 KC539 . . . . **595.7**

Insects. /STEELE, P/1991/4-6/6 KC549 . . . . **595.7**

Insects are my life. /MCDONALD, M/1995/1-3/2 KG097 . . . . **E**

Insect's body. /COLE, J/1984/5-6/7 KC536 . . . . **595.7**

INSECTS (Videocassette). /c1979, 1986/2-6/KC541 . . . . . . **VCR 595.7**

Inside an egg. /JOHNSON, SA/1982/4-6/8 KC695 . . . . **598.6**

Inside, outside, upside down. /BERENSTAIN, S/c1968/K-1/1 KF227 . . . **E**

Inside the amazing Amazon. /LESSEM, D/1995/2-6/7 KC319 . . . **577.34**

Inside the body: a lift-the-flap book. /FORNARI, G/1996/ 5-6/7 KC902 . . . . **611**

Inside the museum: a children's guide to the Metropolitan Museum of Art. / RICHARDSON, J/1993/2-A/7 KD376. . . . . **708**

Inside-outside book of London. /MUNRO, R/c1989, 1996/ 2-A/KE681. . . . . **942.1**

Inside-outside book of Paris. /MUNRO, R/1992/2-6/8 KE684. . . . . **944**

Inspirations: stories about women artists. /SILLS, L/1989/ 5-A/7 KD486 . . . . **759.1**

Instead of three wishes. /TURNER, MW/1995/5-A/4 KH813 . . . . . **Fic**

INSTINCTS IN ANIMALS (Videocassette). /1996/4-6/KC474 . **VCR 591.5**

INSTRUCTOR: PRIMARY. /1891-//KA116 . . . . **PER PROF 050**

Integrating language arts through literature in elementary classrooms. / SPILLMAN, CV/1996//KA229 . . . . **PROF 372.6**

INTELLECTUAL FREEDOM MANUAL. 5th. ed. /1996/ /KA052. . . . . **PROF 025.2**

INTELLECTUAL GIFTEDNESS (Videocassette)./1991/ /KA187. . . . . **VCR PROF 371.95**

INTERNATIONAL INSPIRER (Microcomputer program). /1990/ 5-A/KE149. . . . . **MCP 910**

INTERNATIONAL WILDLIFE. /1971-/4-6/KA520 . . . . **PER 050**

Internet. /COCHRANE, K/1995/4-6/8 KA570 . . . . **004.67**

Internet and instruction: activities and ideas. /BARRON, AE/1996/ /KA047. . . . . **PROF 025.06**

Internet for kids. /KAZUNAS, C/1997/2-4/7 KA571. . . . . **004.67**

Internet resource directory for K-12 teachers and librarians. /MILLER, EB/ 1994-//KA179 . . . . **PROF 371.3**

INTERTIDAL ZONE (Videocassette). /c1985, 1986/ 5-A/KC346 . . . . **VCR 577.69**

INTERVENTION. /n.d.//KA117 . . . . **PER PROF 050**

Into the deep forest with Henry David Thoreau. /MURPHY, J/1995/ 5-A/7 KE929 . . . . **974.1**

Into the sea. /GUIBERSON, BZ/1996/1-3/3 KC618 . . . . **597.92**

INTO THE SHINING MOUNTAINS (Videocassette). /1991/ A/KF035. . . . . **VCR 978**

Intrepid birdmen: the fighter pilots of World War I (Sound recording cassette). /LIEBERMAN, S/1993/A/KE654. . . . . **SRC 940.4**

Introducing bookplots 3: a book talk guide for use with readers ages 8-12./ GILLESPIE, JT/1988//KA092. . . . . **PROF 028.5**

Introducing mammals to young naturalists: from Texas Parks & Wildlife Magazine. /HILLER, I/1990/A/7 KC721 . . . . **599**

Introducing more books: a guide for the middle grades./GILLESPIE, JT/ 1978//KA092 . . . . **PROF 028.5**

INTRODUCTION TO LETTERS AND NUMERALS (Videocassette). /1985/ P-1/KF809 . . . . **VCR E**

Inuits. /NEWMAN, SP/1993/4-6/7 KF102 . . . . **979.8**

INVENT IT! (Videocassette). /1988/3-A/KC886 . . . . **VCR 608**

Inventing, inventions, and inventors: a teaching resource book. /FLACK, JD/ 1989//KA297 . . . . **PROF 607**

Inventing kindergarten. /BROSTERMAN, N/1997/3/KA196 . **PROF 372.21**

INVENTION STUDIO (CD-ROM). /1996/5-A/KC887 . . . . **CDR 608**

INVENTORS AND INVENTIONS (Videocassette). /1995/ 5-6/KC893 . . . . **VCR 609**

Invertebrate zoology. /DORIS, E/1993/5-6/8 KC503 . . . . **592**

INVESTIGATING GLOBAL WARMING (Videocassette). /1997/ 5-A/KB063. . . . . **VCR 363.73**

Investigating the ozone hole. /JOHNSON, RL/1993/A/10 KC191 . . **551.5**

Invincible Louisa. /MEIGS, C/1933/5-6/8 KE232 . . . . . . **B ALCOTT, L.**

Invincible Louisa (Braille). /MEIGS, C/n.d./5-6/8 KE232 . . . **B ALCOTT, L.**

Invincible Louisa (Sound recording cassette)./MEIGS, C/n.d./ 5-6/8 KE232 . . . . **B ALCOTT, L.**

Invincible Louisa (Talking book)./MEIGS, C/n.d./ 5-6/8 KE232 . . . . **B ALCOTT, L.**

Invitation to the game. /HUGHES, M/1993/6-A/6 KH288 . . . . **Fic**

Invitation to the game (Sound recording cassette)./HUGHES, M/1996/ 6-A/6 KH288 . . . . **Fic**

Invitations: changing as teachers and learners K-12. Updated, expanded, and rev. resources and Blue pages. /ROUTMAN, R/c1991, 1994/ /KA214. . . . . **PROF 372.4**

Iowa. /KENT, D/1991/5-6/8 KF022 . . . . **977.7**

Iowa (Sound recording cassette)./KENT, D/1993/5-6/8 KF022 . . . **977.7**

Ira says goodbye./WABER, B/1988/K-2/2 KG668 . . . . **CE E**

Ira says goodbye (Kit)./WABER, B/1991/K-2/2 KG668. . . . . **CE E**

Ira says goodbye (Videocassette)./WABER, B/1989/K-2/2 KG668. . . **CE E**

Ira sleeps over. /WABER, B/c1972/K-2/2 KG668 . . . . **CE E**

Ira sleeps over (Kit)./WABER, B/1984/K-2/2 KG668 . . . . **CE E**

Ira sleeps over (Videocassette)./WABER, B/1992/K-2/2 KG668 . . . **CE E**

Irene, la valiente./STEIG, W/1991/K-3/3 KG541. . . . . **CE E**

Irish Cinderlad. /CLIMO, S/1996/2-4/3 KB275 . . . . **398.2**

Irish folk tales for children (Compact disc). /KENNEDY, S/1996/ 3-5/KB326 . . . . **CD 398.2**

Irish folk tales for children (Sound recording cassette)./KENNEDY, S/1996/ 3-5/KB326 . . . . **CD 398.2**

Irish piper. /LATIMER, J/1991/3-5/6 KB463 . . . . **398.22**

Irish-American experience. /CAVAN, S/1993/5-6/7 KA840 . . . . . **305.8**

Iroko-man: a Yoruba folktale. /GERSHATOR, P/1994/ 2-3/6 KB397 . . . . **398.21**

Iron dragon never sleeps. /KRENSKY, S/1995/3-5/2 KH381 . . . . . . **Fic**

Iron giant: a story in five nights. /HUGHES, T/1988/3-6/3 KH289. . . . **Fic**

Iron giant: a story in five nights (Sound recording cassette)./HUGHES, T/ n.d./3-6/3 KH289 . . . . **Fic**

Iron John. /KIMMEL, EA/1994/4-5/4 KB330. . . . . **398.2**

Iron ring. /ALEXANDER, L/1997/6-A/6 KG838 . . . . **Fic**

Iroquois. /SNEVE, V/1995/4-6/5 KE772 . . . . **970.3**

Is a blue whale the biggest thing there is? /WELLS, RE/1993/ K-2/2 KC087 . . . . **530.8**

Is it red? Is it yellow? Is it blue? An adventure in color. /HOBAN, T/1978/ P/KA614. . . . . **152.14**

Is it rough? Is it smooth? Is it shiny? /HOBAN, T/1984/P-1/KF742. . . . . **E**

Is there room on the feather bed? /GRAY, LM/1997/K-2/4 KF636 . . . . **E**

Is this a house for hermit crab? /MCDONALD, M/1990/ P-1/3 KC522 . . . . **595.3**

Is underground. /AIKEN, J/1993/5-A/7 KG824 . . . . **Fic**

Is underground (Sound recording cassette)./AIKEN, J/1996/ 5-A/7 KG824. . . . . **Fic**

Is your mama a llama? /GUARINO, D/1989/P-1/2 KF651 . . . . **E**

Is your mama a llama? (Big book)./GUARINO, D/1992/P-1/2 KF651 . . **E**

Isaac Newton: the greatest scientist of all time. /ANDERSON, MJ/1996/ 6-A/7 KE476 . . . . **B NEWTON, I.**

Isla. /DORROS, A/1995/K-2/KF490 . . . . **E**

Isla de Abel./STEIG, W/1992/4-6/6 KH749 . . . . **CE Fic**

Isla (Spanish version)./DORROS, A/1995/K-2/KF490. . . . . **E**

Island baby. /KELLER, H/1992/P-2/3 KF885 . . . . **E**

Island Christmas. /JOSEPH, L/1992/1-3/2 KF855. . . . . **E**

Island Christmas (Sound recording cassette)./JOSEPH, L/1994/ 1-3/2 KF855 . . . . **E**

Island keeper. /MAZER, H/1981/A/6 KH464 . . . . **Fic**

Island of the Blue Dolphins. /O'DELL, S/c1960/5-6/6 KH559 . . . . . **Fic**

Island of the Blue Dolphins. /O'DELL, S/c1960, 1990/5-6/6 KH560 . . **Fic**

Island of the Blue Dolphins (Braille)./O'DELL, S/n.d./5-6/6 KH559 . . . . **Fic**

Island of the Blue Dolphins (Sound recording cassette)./O'DELL, S/n.d./ 5-6/6 KH559 . . . . **Fic**

Island of the Blue Dolphins (Talking book)./O'DELL, S/n.d./
5-6/6 KH559 . . . . **Fic**
Island of the grass king./WILLARD, N/1979/3-5/6 KH863 . . . . **Fic**
Island of the skog. /KELLOGG, S/c1973/K-3/5 KF890 . . . . **CE E**
Island of the skog (Videocassette)./KELLOGG, S/1985/
K-3/5 KF890 . . . . **CE E**
Island on Bird Street. /ORLEV, U/1983/5-A/6 KH566 . . . . **Fic**
Island on Bird Street (Sound recording cassette)./ORLEV, U/n.d./
5-A/6 KH566 . . . . **Fic**
IT ALL ADDS UP (Videocassette)./1991/3-5/KB064 . . . . . . **VCR 363.73**
It could always be worse: a Yiddish folk tale. /ZEMACH, M/1976/
2-4/4 KB792 . . . . **CE 398.27**
It could still be water. /FOWLER, A/1992/P-2/2 KC231 . . . . **553.7**
It could still be water (Big book)./FOWLER, A/1992/P-2/2 KC231 . **553.7**
It figures!: fun figures of speech. /TERBAN, M/1993/5-A/8 KD865 . . **808**
It happened in America: true stories from the fifty states. /PERL, L/1992/
4-A/7 KE861 . . . . **973**
It takes a village. /COWEN-FLETCHER, J/1994/K-2/2 KF429 . . . . **E**
It was a dark and stormy night. /AHLBERG, J/1993/3-5/6 KG822 . . . **Fic**
ITALIAN FOLKTALES. /1980/5-6/KA415 . . . . **REF 398.23**
ITALIAN FOLKTALES (Braille)./n.d./5-6/KA415 . . . . **REF 398.23**
Itch book. /DRAGONWAGON, C/1990/K-3/KF496. . . . . **E**
It's a spoon, not a shovel. /BUEHNER, C/1995/2-6/2 KB248 . . . **395.5**
It's all in your head: a guide to understanding your brain and boosting your
brain power. Rev. ed. /BARRETT, SL/1992/A/8 KA633 . . . . **153**
IT'S GREAT TO BE ME! INCREASING YOUR CHILD'S SELF-ESTEEM
(Videocassette). /1989/KA302 . . . . **VCR PROF 649**
It's groundhog day! /KROLL, S/1987/K-2/4 KF929. . . . . **E**
It's Halloween. /PRELUTSKY, J/c1977/1-3/KE004 . . . . **811**
It's Halloween (Braille)./PRELUTSKY, J/n.d./1-3/KE004 . . . . **811**
It's Kwanzaa time! /GOSS, L/1995/2-6/6 KB208. . . . . **394.261**
It's Kwanzaa time! (Sound recording cassette)./GOSS, L/1997/
2-6/6 KB208 . . . . **394.261**
It's like this, Cat. /NEVILLE, EC/c1963/5-6/6 KH547. . . . . **CE Fic**
It's like this, Cat (Braille)./NEVILLE, EC/n.d./5-6/6 KH547 . . . . . **CE Fic**
It's like this, Cat (Sound recording cassette)./NEVILLE, EC/n.d./
5-6/6 KH547 . . . . **CE Fic**
It's like this, Cat (Talking book)./NEVILLE, EC/1970/5-6/6 KH547 . **CE Fic**
It's like this, Cat (Talking book)./NEVILLE, EC/n.d./5-6/6 KH547 . . **CE Fic**
IT'S NOT FAIR! (Videocassette). /1994/3-6/KA642 . . . . . . **VCR 155.4**
IT'S NOT MY FAULT: A PROGRAM ABOUT CONFLICT RESOLUTION
(Videocassette). /1981/4-6/KA628. . . . . **VCR 152.4**
It's not the end of the world. /BLUME, J/c1972/4-6/4 KG911 . . . . . **Fic**
It's not the end of the world (Braille)./BLUME, J/n.d./4-6/4 KG911 . . . **Fic**
It's not the end of the world (Sound recording cassette)./BLUME, J/n.d./
4-6/4 KG911 . . . . **Fic**
It's perfectly normal: a book about changing bodies, growing up, sex, and
sexual health. /HARRIS, RH/1994/5-6/6 KC949 . . . . **612.6**
It's pumpkin time! /HALL, Z/1994/P-2/3 KF666 . . . . **E**
It's snowing! It's snowing! /PRELUTSKY, J/1984/K-3/KE005 . . . . . . **811**
It's Thanksgiving. /PRELUTSKY, J/1982/1-3/KE006 . . . . **CE 811**
It's Thanksgiving (Braille)./PRELUTSKY, J/n.d./1-3/KE006. . . . . . **CE 811**
It's Thanksgiving (Sound recording cassette)./PRELUTSKY, J/n.d./
1-3/KE006 . . . . **CE 811**
It's the story that counts: more children's books for mathematical learning,
K-6. /WHITIN, DJ/1995//KA258. . . . . **PROF 372.7**
It's Valentine's Day. /PRELUTSKY, J/1983/K-2/KE007. . . . . **811**
Itse Selu: Cherokee harvest festival. /PENNINGTON, D/1994/
K-3/6 KB190 . . . . **394.2**
Itsy bitsy spider. /TRAPANI, I/1996/P-1/2 KD662 . . . . **789.3**
I've got chicken pox. /KELLEY, T/1994/K-3/2 KF887 . . . . **E**
Jabberwocky. /CARROLL, L/1992/K-2/3 KE097. . . . . **821**
JACK AND JILL: THE MAGAZINE FOR BOYS AND GIRLS. /1938-/
1-5/KA521 . . . . **PER 050**
JACK AND JILL: THE MAGAZINE FOR BOYS AND GIRLS (Braille)./n.d./
1-5/KA521. . . . . **PER 050**
JACK AND JILL: THE MAGAZINE FOR BOYS AND GIRLS (Sound
recording cassette)./n.d./1-5/KA521 . . . . **PER 050**
Jack and the animals: an Appalachian folktale. /DAVIS, D/1995/
2-4/5 KB555 . . . . **398.24**
Jack and the beanstalk. /KELLOGG, S/1991/2-3/4 KB325 . . . . . . **398.2**
Jack and the beanstalk./METAXAS, E/K-2/KB349. . . . . **VCR 398.2**
Jack and the beanstalk (Kit)./METAXAS, E/1997/K-2/KB349 . **VCR 398.2**
Jack and the beanstalk (Videocassette). /METAXAS, E/1991/
K-2/KB349 . . . . **VCR 398.2**
Jack and the dentist's daughter (Videocassette)./DAVENPORT, T/1984/
5-A/KB281. . . . . **CE 398.2**
Jack Horner: living with dinosaurs. /LESSEM, D/1994/
5-A/7 KE391 . . . . **B HORNER, J.**
Jack Horner: living with dinosaurs (Sound recording cassette)./LESSEM, D/
1996/5-A/8 KE391 . . . . **B HORNER, J.**
Jack tales. /CHASE, R/c1943/K-A/3 KB724 . . . . **398.27**
Jack tales (Braille)./CHASE, R/n.d./K-A/3 KB724 . . . . **398.27**

Jackal woman: exploring the world of jackals. /PRINGLE, LP/1993/
5-6/6 KC833 . . . . **599.77**
Jacket I wear in the snow. /NEITZEL, S/1989/P-2/2 KG168 . . . . **E**
Jacket I wear in the snow (Big book)./NEITZEL, S/1997/P-2/2 KG168. . **E**
Jackie Joyner-Kersee. /COHEN, N/1992/
4-6/6 KE412 . . . . **B JOYNER-KERSEE**
Jackie Kennedy Onassis: woman of courage. /ANDERSON, CC/1995/
A/7 KE484 . . . . **B ONASSIS, J.**
Jackie Robinson. /WEIDHORN, M/1993/6-A/7 KE518 . **B ROBINSON, J.**
Jackie Robinson. /RUDEEN, K/1996/5-6/6 KE516 . . . . **B ROBINSON, J.**
Jackie Robinson breaks the color line. /SANTELLA, A/1996/
4-6/6 KE517 . . . . **B ROBINSON, J.**
Jacks around the world. /LANKFORD, MD/1996/3-6/10 KD770. . . **796.2**
Jack's garden. /COLE, H/1995/K-3/3 KF409 . . . . **E**
Jack's new power: stories from a Caribbean year. /GANTOS, J/1995/
5-A/4 KH151 . . . . **Fic**
Jacob and the stranger. /DERBY, S/1994/3-5/4 KH071 . . . . **Fic**
JACOB LAWRENCE: THE GLORY OF EXPRESSION (Videocassette). /
1995/5-A/KD487 . . . . **VCR 759.13**
Jacques Cousteau: champion of the sea. /REEF, C/1992/
4-6/7 KE528 . . . . **B COUSTEAU, J.**
Jake: a Labrador puppy at work and play. /JONES, RF/1992/
2-5/5 KD228 . . . . **636.752**
Jakki Wood's animal hullabaloo: a wildlife noisy book. /WOOD, J/1995/
P-K/KC485. . . . . **591.59**
Jalapeno bagels. /WING, N/1996/1-3/2 KG742. . . . . **E**
Jamaica and Brianna. /HAVILL, J/1993/K-2/2 KF680 . . . . **E**
Jamaica Louise James. /HEST, A/1996/K-2/2 KF719 . . . . **E**
Jamaica's blue marker. /HAVILL, J/1995/K-1/2 KF681 . . . . **E**
Jamaica's find. /HAVILL, J/1986/K-2/2 KF682 . . . . **E**
Jamberry. /DEGEN, B/1983/P-2/KF456. . . . . **CE E**
Jamberry (Kit)./DEGEN, B/1996/P-2/KF456 . . . . **CE E**
Jambo and other call and response songs and chants (Sound recording
cassette)./JENKINS, E/1990/K-3/KD573 . . . . **SRC 789.2**
Jambo means hello: Swahili alphabet book. /FEELINGS, ML/1974/
1-3/7 KF545 . . . . **E**
James and the giant peach: the book and movie scrapbook. /DAHL, L/
1996/3-6/6 KD684 . . . . **791.43**
James and the rain. /KUSKIN, K/1995/K-2/5 KF938. . . . . **E**
JAMES DISCOVERS MATH. School ed. (CD-ROM). /1995/
1-3/KB962 . . . . **CDR 513.2**
James Madison and Dolley Madison and their times. /QUACKENBUSH, R/
1992/4-5/7 KE894 . . . . **973.5**
James McNeil Whistler. /BERMAN, A/1993/
5-A/7 KE592 . . . . **B WHISTLER, J.**
James Meredith and school desegregation. /ELISH, D/1994/
4-5/7 KE463 . . . . **B MEREDITH, J.**
James Printer: a novel of rebellion. /JACOBS, PS/1997/
5-A/6 KH319 . . . . **Fic**
Jamie O'Rourke and the big potato: an Irish folktale. /DE PAOLA, T/
1992/P-3/4 KB393 . . . . **398.21**
Jamie O'Rourke and the big potato: an Irish folktale (Sound recording
cassette)./DE PAOLA, T/1995/P-3/4 KB393 . . . . **398.21**
Jane Goodall: protector of chimpanzees. /MEACHUM, V/1997/
5-A/7 KE372 . . . . **B GOODALL, J.**
Jane Martin, dog detective. /BUNTING, E/1984/1-3/1 KF303 . . . . . . **E**
Jane Martin, dog detective (Braille)./BUNTING, E/n.d./1-3/1 KF303 . . . **E**
Jane Martin, dog detective (Sound recording cassette)./BUNTING, E/n.d./
1-3/1 KF303 . . . . **E**
JANE YOLEN'S MOTHER GOOSE SONGBOOK. /1992/
/KA277. . . . . **PROF 398.8**
Janet's thingamajigs./CLEARY, B/1987/P/2 KF396 . . . . **E**
Janet's thingamajigs (Braille)./CLEARY, B/n.d./P/2 KF396 . . . . **E**
JANEY JUNKFOOD'S FRESH ADVENTURE (Videocassette)./1992/
3-6/KC984 . . . . **VCR 613.2**
Janice VanCleave's guide to the best science fair projects. /VANCLEAVE,
JP/1997/3-6/KB899 . . . . **507.8**
Janice VanCleave's math for every kid: easy activities that make learning
math fun. /VANCLEAVE, JP/1991/4-6/6 KB933 . . . . **510**
Janice VanCleave's oceans for every kid: easy activities that make learning
science fun. /VANCLEAVE, JP/1996/3-6/8 KC178 . . . . **551.46**
Janice VanCleave's rocks and minerals: mind-boggling experiments you can
turn into science fair projects. /VANCLEAVE, JP/1996/
4-6/8 KC228 . . . . **552**
Janice VanCleave's the human body for every kid: easy activities that make
learning science fun. /VANCLEAVE, JP/1995/5-6/8 KC928 . . . . . **612**
Japan. /BORNOFF, N/1997/3-5/10 KE707 . . . . **952**
JAPAN: ASIA, VOLUME 2 (Videocassette). /1993/3-6/KE708 . **VCR 952**
JAPANESE FAIRY TALES. /1992/2-4/7 KB322 . . . . **398.2**
Jar of dreams. /UCHIDA, Y/1981/5-6/6 KH815 . . . . **Fic**
Jar of dreams (Sound recording cassette)./UCHIDA, Y/n.d./
5-6/6 KH815 . . . . **Fic**
Jasmine's parlour day. /JOSEPH, L/1994/1-3/3 KF856 . . . . **E**
Jason's bus ride. /ZIEFERT, H/c1987, 1993/K-2/1 KG792 . . . . **E**

Jazz, Pizzazz, and the silver threads. /QUATTLEBAUM, M/1996/
2-4/3 KH615 . . . . **Fic**
Jedera adventure. /ALEXANDER, L/1990/5-A/7 KG839 . . . . **Fic**
Jedera adventure (Sound recording cassette)./ALEXANDER, L/n.d./
5-A/7 KG839 . . . . **Fic**
Jeff Gordon. /BRINSTER, R/1997/5-6/7 KE373 . . . . . . **B GORDON, J.**
Jeffrey Strangeways. /MURPHY, J/1994/4-5/7 KH520 . . . . **Fic**
Jelly beans for sale. /MCMILLAN, B/1996/K-3/2 KA951 . . . . . . **332.4**
Jenius: the amazing guinea pig. /KING-SMITH, D/1996/2-4/5 KH349 . **Fic**
Jennifer and Josephine. /PEET, B/c1967/K-2/7 KG228 . . . . **E**
Jennifer, Hecate, Macbeth, William McKinley, and me, Elizabeth. /
KONIGSBURG, EL/c1967/3-6/4 KH374 . . . . **CE Fic**
Jennifer, Hecate, Macbeth, William McKinley, and me, Elizabeth (Talking
book)/KONIGSBURG, EL/n.d./3-6/4 KH374 . . . . **CE Fic**
Jenny's corner. /BELL, F/1995/5-A/7 KG894 . . . . **Fic**
Jeremiah and Mrs. Ming. /JENNINGS, S/1990/K-2/2 KF828 . . . . **E**
Jeremiah and Mrs. Ming (Big book)./JENNINGS, S/1990/
K-2/2 KF828 . . . . **E**
Jeremy Bean's St. Patrick's Day. /SCHERTLE, A/1987/K-2/4 KG404 . . . **E**
Jeremy Thatcher, dragon hatcher: a magic shop book. /COVILLE, B/1991/
4-A/4 KH036 . . . . **CE Fic**
Jeremy Thatcher, dragon hatcher (Talking book)./COVILLE, B/1995/
4-A/4 KH036 . . . . **CE Fic**
Jericho: a novel. /HICKMAN, J/1994/6-A/7 KH256 . . . . **Fic**
Jericho's journey. /WISLER, GC/1993/5-A/6 KH870 . . . . **Fic**
Jericho's journey (Sound recording cassette)./WISLER, GC/1995/
5-A/6 KH870 . . . . **Fic**
Jesse Bear, what will you wear? /CARLSTROM, NW/1986/
P-K/4 KF356 . . . . **E**
Jesse Bear, what will you wear? (Braille)./CARLSTROM, NW/n.d./
P-K/4 KF356 . . . . **E**
Jesse James. /WUKOVITS, JF/1997/4-6/10 KE402 . . . . . . **B JAMES, J.**
Jesse Owens: track and field legend. /JOSEPHSON, JP/1997/
5-A/8 KE487 . . . . **B OWENS, J.**
Jessica. /HENKES, K/1989/K-1/2 KF706 . . . . **E**
JESUS OF NAZARETH: A LIFE OF CHRIST THROUGH PICTURES. /1994/
4-A/5 KH508 . . . . **232.9**
Jethro and Joel were a troll. /PEET, B/1987/1-3/4 KG229 . . . . **E**
Jets. /JENSSEN, H/1996/4-6/8 KD061 . . . . **623.7**
Jewish kids catalog. /BURSTEIN, CM/1983/4-6/7 KB179 . . . . . . **394**
Jig, Fig, and Mrs. Pig. /HANSARD, P/1995/P-2/3 KB584 . . . . . . **398.24**
Jigsaw Jackson. /BIRCHMAN, DF/1996/1-3/3 KF230 . . . . **E**
Jim Abbott. /KRAMER, J/1996/4-5/6 KE223 . . . . **B ABBOTT, J.**
Jim Eisenreich. /GUTMAN, B/1996/3-5/6 KE336 . . . . **B EISENREICH, J.**
Jim Thorpe: 20th-century jock. /LIPSYTE, R/6-A/7 KE566 . . **B THORPE, J.**
Jim Ugly. /FLEISCHMAN, S/1992/4-A/6 KH123 . . . . **Fic**
Jim Ugly (Sound recording cassette)./FLEISCHMAN, S/1995/
4-A/6 KH123 . . . . **Fic**
Jimmy Carter: beyond the presidency. /CARRIGAN, M/1995/
5-6/7 KE280 . . . . **B CARTER, J.**
Jimmy, the pickpocket of the palace. /NAPOLI, DJ/1995/
3-A/3 KH530 . . . . **Fic**
Jimmy's boa and the big splash birthday bash./NOBLE, TH/1989/
K-2/2 KG176 . . . . **CE E**
Jimmy's boa bounces back./NOBLE, TH/1984/K-2/2 KG176 . . . . . **CE E**
Jimmy's boa bounces back (Braille)./NOBLE, TH/n.d./K-2/2 KG176 . **CE E**
Jip: his story. /PATERSON, K/1996/5-A/7 KH577 . . . . **Fic**
Jobs for kids: the guide to having fun and making money. /BARKIN, C/
1990/5-6/7 KD305 . . . . **650.1**
Jobs people do. /MAYNARD, C/1997/P-1/4 KA942 . . . . **331.7**
Joe Joe. /SERFOZO, M/1993/P-K/1 KG440 . . . . **E**
Joe Louis: a champ for all America. /LIPSYTE, R/1994/
4-6/6 KE447 . . . . **B LOUIS, J.**
Joey: the story of a baby kangaroo. /RYDEN, H/1994/
2-5/4 KC737 . . . . **599.2**
Johann Sebastian Bach: great man of music. /GREENE, C/1992/
2-4/2 KE246 . . . . **B BACH, J.**
John Brown and the fight against slavery. /COLLINS, JL/1991/
3-5/6 KE263 . . . . **B BROWN, J.**
John Burroughs, the sage of Slabsides. /WADSWORTH, G/1997/
A/7 KE271 . . . . **B BURROUGHS, J.**
John C. Fremont: soldier and pathfinder. /SANFORD, WR/1996/
5-6/4 KE357 . . . . **B FREMONT, J.**
John Henry. /LESTER, J/1994/2-5/4 KB464 . . . . **398.22**
John Lucas. /SIMMONS, A/1996/5-A/7 KE449 . . . . **B LUCAS, J.**
John Madden. /CHADWICK, B/1997/5-A/7 KE451 . . . . **B MADDEN, J.**
John McCutcheon's four seasons: wintersongs (Compact disc). /
MCCUTCHEON, J/1995/K-3/KD638. . . . . **CD 789.3**
John McCutcheon's four seasons: wintersongs (Sound recording cassette)./
MCCUTCHEON, J/1995/K-3/KD638. . . . . **CD 789.3**
John Muir: saving the wilderness. /NADEN, CJ/1992/
5-6/4 KE473 . . . . **B MUIR, J.**
John Philip Sousa: the march king. /GREENE, C/1992/
2-4/2 KE544 . . . . **B SOUSA, J.**

John Treegate's musket. /WIBBERLEY, L/c1959, 1986/5-6/7 KH855. . . **Fic**
Johnny Appleseed. /LINDBERGH, R/1990/K-3/KD973. . . . . **811**
Johnny Appleseed (Videocassette). /KUNSTLER, JH/1992/
2-5/KE239 . . . . **VCR B APPLESEED, J.**
Johnny Tremain: a novel for old and young. /FORBES, E/c1943, 1971/
4-6/6 KH131 . . . . **CE Fic**
Johnny Tremain: a novel for old and young (Braille)./FORBES, E/n.d./
4-6/6 KH131 . . . . **CE Fic**
Johnny Tremain: a novel for old and young (Sound recording cassette)./
FORBES, E/n.d./4-6/6 KH131 . . . . **CE Fic**
Johnny Tremain: a novel for old and young (Talking book)./FORBES, E/
1970/4-6/6 KH131 . . . . **CE Fic**
Johnny Tremain: a novel for old and young (Talking book)./FORBES, E/
n.d./4-6/6 KH131 . . . . **CE Fic**
Joining hands with other lands: multicultural songs and games (Sound
recording cassette). /WEISSMAN, J/1993/K-3/KD666. . . **SRC 789.3**
Joining hands with other lands: multicultural songs and games (Compact
disc)./WEISSMAN, J/1994/K-3/KD666. . . . . **SRC 789.3**
Jojofu. /WAITE, MP/1996/1-4/5 KB670 . . . . **398.24**
JoJo's flying side kick. /PINKNEY, JB/1995/K-3/2 KG243 . . . . **E**
JoJo's flying side kick (Sound recording cassette)./PINKNEY, JB/1997/
K-3/2 KG243 . . . . **E**
Jonah and the whale. /PATTERSON, G/1992/P-2/4 KA692 . . . . . **224**
Jonron mas largo./CARRIER, R/1993/2-4/4 KG977 . . . . **Fic**
Jorge el Curioso./REY, HA/n.d./P-2/2 KG322 . . . . **E**
Jo's boys./ALCOTT, LM/1984/5-A/7 KG829 . . . . **Fic**
Josefina. /WINTER, J/1996/1-3/6 KG743 . . . . **E**
Josefina story quilt. /COERR, E/1986/1-3/2 KF401 . . . . **CE E**
Josefina story quilt (Braille)./COERR, E/n.d./1-3/2 KF401 . . . . . . **CE E**
Josefina story quilt (Kit)./COERR, E/1995/1-3/2 KF401 . . . . . . **CE E**
Josefina y la colcha de retazos./COERR, E/1995/1-3/2 KF401 . . . . **CE E**
Joseph and his brothers (Videocassette). /GLEESON, B/1993/
5-6/KA685 . . . . **VCR 222**
Joseph and his magnificent coat of many colors. /WILLIAMS, M/1992/
2-4/5 KA689 . . . . **222**
Joshua and the big bad blue crabs. /CHILDRESS, M/1996/
3-4/5 KG988 . . . . **Fic**
Joshua by the sea (Board book). /JOHNSON, A/1994/P/2 KF829 . **BB E**
Joshua T. Bates takes charge. /SHREVE, S/c1993, 1995/
4-6/4 KH710 . . . . **Fic**
Joshua's night whispers (Board book). /JOHNSON, A/1994/
P/2 KF830 . . . . **BB E**
Joueur de basket-ball./CARRIER, R/1996/4-6/3 KG975. . . . . **Fic**
JOURNAL OF YOUTH SERVICES IN LIBRARIES. /1946-/
/KA118. . . . . **PER PROF 050**
Journey back./REISS, J/c1976, 1987/5-6/5 KE506 . . . . **B REISS, J.**
Journey cake, ho. /SAWYER, R/c1953, 1989/P-3/5 KB776 . . . . . **398.27**
Journey home. /HOLLAND, I/1993/6-A/6 KH270 . . . . **Fic**
Journey home (Sound recording cassette)./HOLLAND, I/1993/
6-A/6 KH270 . . . . **Fic**
Journey: Japanese Americans, racism, and renewal. /HAMANAKA, S/
1990/5-6/7 KE854 . . . . **973**
JOURNEY THROUGH THE SOLAR SYSTEM (Videocassette). /1991/
3-6/KC011. . . . . **VCR 523.2**
Journey to America. /LEVITIN, S/c1970, 1993/5-A/5 KH398 . . . **Fic**
Journey to America (Talking book)./LEVITIN, S/n.d./5-A/5 KH398 . . . **Fic**
Journey to the planets. 4th ed. /LAUBER, P/1993/4-6/6 KC028 . . . **523.4**
Journey to Topaz. /UCHIDA, Y/c1971, 1984/5-A/7 KH816 . . . . . **Fic**
Joy boys. /BYARS, BC/1996/2-3/1 KF326 . . . . **E**
Joyful noise: poems for two voices. /FLEISCHMAN, P/1988/
4-6/KD934 . . . . **811**
Joyful noise: poems for two voices (Sound recording cassette)./
FLEISCHMAN, P/n.d./4-6/KD934 . . . . **811**
J.R.R. Tolkien: master of fantasy. /COLLINS, DR/1992/
6-A/6 KE567 . . . . **B TOLKIEN, J.**
Juan Bobo and the pig: a Puerto Rican folktale. /PITRE, F/1993/
2-4/2 KB763 . . . . **398.27**
Juan Bobo: four folktales from Puerto Rico. /BERNIER-GRAND, CT/1994/
1-2/2 KB427 . . . . **398.22**
JUBA THIS AND JUBA THAT. /1995//KA366. . . . . **PROF 820.8**
JUBA THIS AND JUBA THAT (Talking book)./n.d.//KA366 . **PROF 820.8**
Judge, an untrue tale. /ZEMACH, H/c1969/P-3/2 KG787 . . . . . . **CE E**
Judge, an untrue tale (Braille)./ZEMACH, H/n.d./P-3/2 KG787 . . . . **CE E**
Judge Rabbit and the tree spirit: a folktale from Cambodia. /SPAGNOLI,
C/1991/3-4/4 KB655 . . . . **398.24**
Jugo de pecas./BLUME, J/n.d./2-4/3 KG908 . . . . **CE Fic**
Jules Verne: the man who invented tomorrow. /TEETERS, P/1992/
5-A/6 KE582 . . . . **B VERNE, J.**
Jules Verne: the man who invented tomorrow (Sound recording cassette)./
TEETERS, P/1995/5-A/6 KE582 . . . . **B VERNE, J.**
Julian, dream doctor./CAMERON, A/1990/3-4/4 KG970 . . . . . . **Fic**
Julian Messner illustrated dictionary of science. /STONE, J/1986/
4-6/9 KB878 . . . . **503**
Julian's glorious summer. /CAMERON, A/1987/2-4/2 KG967 . . . . . . **Fic**

Julian's glorious summer (Braille)./CAMERON, A/n.d./2-4/2 KG967 . . **Fic**
Julie. /GEORGE, JC/1994/5-A/3 KH156. . . . . **Fic**
Julie Krone. /GUTMAN, B/1996/5-6/5 KE425 . . . . **B KRONE, J.**
Julie of the wolves. /GEORGE, JC/c1972/6-A/6 KH157 . . . . **CE Fic**
Julie of the wolves (Braille)./GEORGE, JC/n.d./6-A/6 KH157. . . . **CE Fic**
Julie of the wolves (Talking book). /GEORGE, JC/1977/
    6-A/6 KH157. . . . . **CE Fic**
Julie of the wolves (Talking book). /GEORGE, JC/1993/
    6-A/KH158 . . . . **TB Fic**
Julie (Sound recording cassette)./GEORGE, JC/1996/5-A/3 KH156. . . **Fic**
Juliet Fisher and the foolproof plan./HONEYCUTT, N/1992/
    3-5/4 KH277 . . . . **Fic**
Julius. /HOFF, S/c1959/K-1/1 KF758 . . . . **E**
Julius. /JOHNSON, A/1993/P-2/2 KF831 . . . . **E**
Julius (Braille)./HOFF, S/n.d./K-1/1 KF758 . . . . **E**
Julius (Sound recording cassette)./JOHNSON, A/1995/P-2/2 KF831. . . **E**
Julius, the baby of the world. /HENKES, K/1990/K-3/2 KF707 . . . . **E**
July./STEVENSON, J/1990/3-4/4 KE551. . . . . **B STEVENSON, J.**
July is a mad mosquito. /LEWIS, JP/1994/P-3/KD972 . . . . **811**
Juma and the magic jinn. /ANDERSON, J/1986/2-3/4 KF156 . . . . . . **E**
Jumanji. /VAN ALLSBURG, C/1981/K-A/4 KH820 . . . . **Fic**
Jumanji (Braille)./VAN ALLSBURG, C/n.d./K-A/4 KH820. . . . . . . **Fic**
Jumanji (Kit). /VAN ALLSBURG, C/1995/K-A/KH821 . . . . **KIT Fic**
Jump, frog, jump! (Big book)./KALAN, R/1996/P-1/1 KF864 . . . . . **CE E**
Jump, frog, jump! New ed. /KALAN, R/c1981, 1995/P-1/1 KF864 . **CE E**
Jump ship to freedom. /COLLIER, JL/1981/5-6/5 KH015. . . . . . . **Fic**
Jump! The adventures of Brer Rabbit. /HARRIS, JC/1997/
    3-4/6 KB585 . . . . **398.24**
Jump! The adventures of Brer Rabbit (Sound recording cassette)./HARRIS,
    JC/n.d./3-4/6 KB585. . . . . **398.24**
Jumping the broom. /WRIGHT, CC/1994/K-3/5 KG771 . . . . **E**
June 29, 1999. /WIESNER, D/1992/1-5/4 KG713. . . . . **E**
Junebug. /MEAD, A/1995/5-A/5 KH493 . . . . **Fic**
Juneteenth jamboree. /WEATHERFORD, CB/1995/1-3/5 KG690. . . . . . **E**
Jungle animals. /ROYSTON, A/1991/P-2/4 KC493 . . . . **591.734**
Jungle book: the Mowgli stories. /KIPLING, R/1995/6-A/7 KH363 . . . **Fic**
JUNIOR AUTHOR SERIES. /1951-/A/KA462 . . . . **REF 809**
JUNIOR AUTHOR SERIES (Braille). /n.d./A/KA462 . . . . **REF 809**
JUNIOR BOOK OF AUTHORS. (2nd rev. ed.)/1971/A/KA462. . **REF 809**
JUNIOR DISCOVERING AUTHORS: BIOGRAPHIES AND PLOTLINES ON
    300 MOST-STUDIED AND POPULAR AUTHORS FOR YOUNG
    READERS (CD-ROM). /1994/5-A/KA463 . . . . **CDR REF 809**
JUNIOR ELECTRICIAN (Videocassette). /1991/3-6/KC132 . . . . **VCR 537**
Junior Girl Scout handbook. /GIRL SCOUTS OF THE UNITED STATES OF
    AMERICA /1994/4-6/KB079 . . . . **369.463**
Junior Girl Scout handbook (Braille)./GIRL SCOUTS OF THE UNITED
    STATES OF AMERICA /n.d./4-6/KB079 . . . . **369.463**
Junior Girl Scout handbook (Sound recording cassette)./GIRL SCOUTS OF
    THE UNITED STATES OF AMERICA /n.d./4-6/KB079 . . . . . **369.463**
JUNIOR JEWISH ENCYCLOPEDIA. 11th rev. ed. /1991/
    5-6/KA396 . . . . **REF 296**
JUNIOR SCHOLASTIC. /1937-/A/KA522. . . . . **PER 050**
Junior Seau: high-voltage linebacker. /MORGAN, T/1997/
    5-A/10 KE532 . . . . **B SEAU, J.**
Junior thunder lord. /YEP, L/1994/2-4/3 KB425. . . . . **398.21**
Juniorplots: a book talk manual for teachers and librarians./GILLESPIE, JT/
    1967//KA091 . . . . **PROF 028.5**
Juniorplots 3: a book talk guide for use with readers ages 12-16./
    GILLESPIE, JT/1987//KA091. . . . . **PROF 028.5**
Juniorplots 4: a book talk guide for use with readers ages 12-16. /
    GILLESPIE, JT/1993//KA091. . . . . **PROF 028.5**
JUNIPER TREE AND OTHER SONGS (Sound recording cassette). /1994/
    K-6/KD578 . . . . **SRC 789.2**
Juniper tree and other tales from Grimm. /GRIMM, J/c1973, 1992/
    5-A/7 KB306 . . . . **398.2**
Junk pile! /BORTON, L/1997/K-2/3 KF252. . . . . **E**
Jupiter. /SIMON, S/1985/3-6/7 KC038. . . . . **523.45**
JUST FOR ME (Videocassette). /1992/K-6/KC997 . . . . **VCR 613.8**
JUST GRANDMA AND ME (CD-ROM). /1992/P-2/KF863 . . . . . **CDR E**
Just look. /HOBAN, T/1996/P-2/KA615 . . . . **152.14**
Just rewards, or, Who is that man in the moon and what's he doing up
    there anyway? /SANFIELD, S/1996/K-2/4 KB713 . . . . . . **398.26**
Justin and the best biscuits in the world. /WALTER, MP/1986/
    4-6/6 KH839 . . . . **Fic**
Justin and the best biscuits in the world (Sound recording cassette)./
    WALTER, MP/n.d./4-6/6 KH839 . . . . **Fic**
Kancil and the crocodiles: a tale from Malaysia. /DAY, NY/1996/
    2-3/2 KB556 . . . . **398.24**
Kansas. /KENT, Z/1990/4-6/9 KF054 . . . . **978.1**
Kansas. /FREDEEN, C/1992/4-6/5 KF053 . . . . **978.1**
Kanu of Kathmandu: a journey in Nepal. /MARGOLIES, BA/1992/
    3-5/6 KE713 . . . . **954.96**
Karate and judo. /NARDI, TJ/1996/3-6/6 KD833 . . . . **796.815**
Karate boy. /MORRIS, A/1996/2-4/5 KD832 . . . . **796.815**

Kasper in the glitter. /RIDLEY, P/1997/5-A/4 KH634 . . . . **Fic**
Kate Shelley: bound for legend. /SAN SOUCI, RD/1995/
    3-5/5 KE539 . . . . **B SHELLEY, K.**
Katie Henio: Navajo sheepherder. /THOMSON, P/1995/
    5-6/6 KE796 . . . . **970.489**
Katie John. /CALHOUN, M/c1960/4-6/4 KG966 . . . . **Fic**
Katie's trunk. /TURNER, A/1992/3-5/3 KG627 . . . . **E**
Katy and the big snow. /BURTON, VL/c1943, 1973/P-1/4 KF319 . . . . **E**
Katy and the big snow (Braille)./BURTON, VL/n.d./P-1/4 KF319 . . . . **E**
Katya's book of mushrooms. /ARNOLD, K/1997/3-A/6 KC381. . . . **579.6**
Kavik, the wolf dog. /MOREY, W/c1968/4-6/6 KH510. . . . . **Fic**
Kayuktuk: an Arctic quest. /HEINZ, BJ/1996/4-A/3 KH235 . . . . . . **Fic**
K.C.'s first bus ride (Videocassette). /1994/P-1/KB023 . . . . . . **VCR 363.1**
Keep 'em laughing: jokes to amuse and annoy your friends. /PHILLIPS, L/
    1996/3-6/KD736 . . . . **793.735**
Keep looking. /SELSAM, ME/1989/P-3/2 KC728. . . . . **599**
Keep Ms. Sugarman in the fourth grade. /LEVY, E/1992/
    3-5/5 KH402 . . . . **Fic**
Keep Ms. Sugarman in the fourth grade (Sound recording cassette)./LEVY,
    E/1995/3-5-5 KH402 . . . . **Fic**
Keep on singing: a ballad of Marian Anderson. /LIVINGSTON, MC/1994/
    1-3/KD977 . . . . **811**
Keep the lights burning, Abbie. /ROOP, P/1985/
    1-3/1 KE270 . . . . **CE B BURGESS, A.**
Keep the lights burning, Abbie (Kit). /ROOP, P/1989/
    1-3/1 KE270 . . . . **CE B BURGESS, A.**
KEEP THE SPIRIT (Sound recording cassette). /1989/
    K-6/KD634 . . . . **SRC 789.3**
Keeping quilt. /POLACCO, P/1988/K-3/6 KG252 . . . . **CE E**
Keeping quilt (Videocassette)./POLACCO, P/1993/K-3/6 KG252. . . **CE E**
Keeping time: from the beginning and into the 21st century. /BRANLEY,
    FM/1993/4-6/6 KC067 . . . . **529**
Ken Griffey Junior: all-around all-star. /KRAMER, B/1996/
    4-5/4 KE381 . . . . **B GRIFFEY, K. JR**
Kentucky. /BROWN, D/1992/4-6/6 KF010 . . . . **976.9**
Kestrel (Sound recording cassette)./ALEXANDER, L/n.d./
    5-6/6 KG841 . . . . **Fic**
Kevin Corbett eats flies. /HERMES, P/1989/5-6/3 KH248 . . . . **Fic**
Khan's daughter: a Mongolian folktale. /YEP, L/1997/
    2-4/6 KB787 . . . . **398.27**
Ki con dau roi nhi./HILL, E/P-2/2 KF728 . . . . **E**
Kick, pass, and run. /KESSLER, L/c1966/1-2/2 KF899 . . . . **E**
Kick, pass, and run (Braille)./KESSLER, L/n.d./1-2/2 KF899 . . . . **E**
KID CAD (Microcomputer program). /1993/2-A/KD423. . . . . **MCP 745.4**
KID CITY. /1988-/2-4/KA523. **PER 050**
Kid comes back. /TUNIS, JR/c1946, 1990/5-A/7 KH810. . . . . **Fic**
Kid next door and other headaches./SMITH, JL/1984/2-4/4 KH725. . . **Fic**
Kid next door and other headaches (Braille)./SMITH, JL/n.d./
    2-4/4 KH725 . . . . **Fic**
KID PIX STUDIO (CD-ROM). /1994/P-A/KD468 . . . . **CDR 750.28**
Kid style nature crafts: 50 terrific things to make with nature's materials. /
    DIEHN, G/1995/4-8/6 KD428 . . . . **745.5**
KIDDESK (Microcomputer program). /1993/K-A/KA568 . . . . . **MCP 004**
KIDDESK. School version (CD-ROM). /1995/P-A/KA569 . . . . **CDR 004**
Kidnapped: being the memoirs of the adventures of David Balfour in the
    year 1751. /STEVENSON, RL/1982/5-6/6 KH758 . . . . **Fic**
Kidnapped: being the memoirs of the adventures of David Balfour in the
    year 1751 (Braille)./STEVENSON, RL/n.d./5-6/6 KH758 . . . . . . **Fic**
Kidnapped: being the memoirs of the adventures of David Balfour in the
    year 1751 (Sound recording cassette)./STEVENSON, RL/n.d/
    5-6/6 KH758 . . . . **Fic**
Kidnapped: being the memoirs of the adventures of David Balfour in the
    year 1751 (Talking book)./STEVENSON, RL/n.d./5-6/6 KH758 . . . **Fic**
Kids and the environment: taking responsibility for our surroundings
    (Microcomputer program). /HALPERN, NA/1994/
    1-5/KB046 . . . . **CDR 363.7**
Kids at work: Lewis Hine and the crusade against child labor. /FREEDMAN,
    R/1994/5-A/8 KA937 . . . . **331.3**
KID'S BOOK ABOUT DEATH AND DYING. /1985/4-6/6 KA650 . . . **155.9**
KID'S BOOK ABOUT DEATH AND DYING (Sound recording cassette)./
    n.d./4-6/6 KA650 . . . . **155.9**
KIDS BY THE BAY (Videocassette). /1997/3-6/KB047 . . . . . . **VCR 363.7**
Kids can save the animals!: 101 easy things to do. /NEWKIRK, I/1991/
    3-6/7 KA673 . . . . **179**
Kids can type too! /MOUNTFORD, C/c1985, 1987/4-6/KD311 . . . **652.3**
Kids' cat book. /DE PAOLA, T/1979/K-2/2 KD231 . . . . **636.8**
Kids' computer creations: using your computer for art and craft fun. /
    SABBETH, C/1995/3-5/KD434 . . . . **745.5**
Kid's cuisine. /RITCHIE, D/1988/4-6/KD278 . . . . **641.5**
KIDS EXPLORE ALASKA (Videocassette). /1990/3-6/KE209. . **VCR 917.98**
KIDS EXPLORE AMERICA'S NATIONAL PARKS (Videocassette). /1991/
    3-6/KE191 . . . . **VCR 917.304**
KIDS EXPLORE KENYA (Videocassette). /1990/3-5/KE179. **VCR 916.762**
KIDS EXPLORE MEXICO (Videocassette). /1990/3-6/KE186. . **VCR 917.2**

Kid's eye view of ecology (Videocassette). /MISH, M/1991/
3-6/KB049. . . . . **VCR 363.7**
Kid's eye view of the environment (Sound recording cassette) /MISH, M/
1989/P-2/KB050. . . . . **SRC 363.7**
Kids garden!: the anytime, anyplace guide to sowing and growing fun. /
HART, A/1996/3-5/6 KD167 635
KID'S GUIDE TO DRUG, ALCOHOL AND SMOKING AWARENESS
(Videocassette). /1985/K-4/KA997. . . . . **VCR 362.29**
Kid's guide to social action: how to solve the social problems you choose--
and turn creative thinking into positive action. /LEWIS, BA/1991/
3-6/6 KA991 . . . . 361.2
Kids in and out of trouble. /HYDE, MO/1995/A/8 KB072 . . . . 364.36
Kids' multicultural cookbook: food and fun around the world. /COOK, DF/
1995/3-5/KD285 . . . . 641.59
Kids' nature book: 365 indoor/outdoor activities and experiences. Rev. ed.
/MILORD, S/1996/4/6 KB910 508
Kids on-line: 150 ways for kids to surf the net for fun and information. /
SALZMAN, M/1995/3-6/6 KA572. . . . . 004.67
KIDS PICK THE FUNNIEST POEMS. /1991/3-6/KE068 . . . . . . 811.008
KIDS RULE THE NET: THE ONLY GUIDE TO THE INTERNET WRITTEN BY
KIDS. /1996/3-A/7 KA579. . . . . 025.04
Kids' science book: creative experiences for hands-on fun. /HIRSCHFELD,
R/1995/P-4/7 KB892. . . . . 507.8
Kids' summer handbook. /DRAKE, J/1994/3-6/6 KD678 . . . . . . 790.1
Killer asteroids. /POYNTER, M/1996/6-8/6 KC036. . . . . 523.44
Killer bees. Rev. ed. /PRINGLE, LP/1990/A/8 KC578 . . . . . . 595.79
Killer whale. /ARNOLD, C/1994/4-6/7 KC764 . . . . 599.5
Killer whales. /PATENT, DH/1993/4-6/6 KC775 . . . . 599.5
Kinaalda: a Navajo girl grows up. /ROESSEL, M/1993/
4-6/5 KE789 . . . . 970.48
Kinderdike. /FISHER, LE/1994/2-4/3 KB395 . . . . 398.21
Kindred spirit: a biography of L. M. Montgomery, creator of Anne of
Green Gables. /ANDRONIK, CM/1993/
5-A/6 KE469 . . . . **B MONTGOMERY, L.**
King and the tortoise. /MOLLEL, TM/1993/2-3/4 KB624 . . . . . . 398.24
KING ARTHUR AND HIS KNIGHTS (Compact disc)./1991/
5-6/KB462 . . . . **SRC 398.22**
KING ARTHUR AND HIS KNIGHTS (Sound recording cassette). /1991/
5-6/KB462 . . . . **SRC 398.22**
King Arthur and the Round Table. /TALBOTT, H/1995/
4-5/6 KB490 . . . . 398.22
King Arthur: the legends of Camelot. /PERHAM, M/1993/
5-A/7 KB471 . . . . 398.22
King Bidgood's in the bathtub. /WOOD, A/1985/P-2/1 KG763 . . . **CE E**
King Bidgood's in the bathtub (Big book)./WOOD, A/1993/
P-2/1 KG763 . . . . **CE E**
King Bidgood's in the bathtub (Sound recording cassette)./WOOD, A/n.d./
P-2/1 KG763 . . . . **CE E**
King Bidgood's in the bathtub (Videocassette)./WOOD, A/1988/
P-2/1 KG763 . . . . **CE E**
King Bobble. /BUSSER, M/1996/2-3/2 KG953 . . . . **Fic**
King Crow. /ARMSTRONG, J/1995/1-3/4 KF165 . . . . **E**
King Island Christmas. /ROGERS, J/1985/K-3/5 KG347 . . . . **E**
King of the cats. /JACOBS, J/1980/1-3/2 KB595 . . . . **CE 398.24**
King of the playground. /NAYLOR, PR/1991/K-3/2 KG167 . . . . . . **E**
King of the wind. /HENRY, M/c1948, 1990/4-6/6 KH243 . . . **CE Fic**
King of the wind (Braille). /HENRY, M/n.d./4-6/5 KH243 . . . . . **CE Fic**
King of the wind (Sound recording cassette)./HENRY, M/n.d./
4-6/5 KH243 . . . . **CE Fic**
King of the wind (Talking book). /HENRY, M/1971/4-6/5 KH243 . **CE Fic**
King Solomon and the bee. /RENBERG, DH/1994/2-3/4 KB475 . . **398.22**
King Stork. /PYLE, H/1973/3-5/6 KH614 . . . . **Fic**
King, the princess, and the tinker. /MCKENZIE, EK/1992/
3-5/4 KH483 . . . . **Fic**
King who tried to fry an egg on his head: based on a Russian tale. /
GINSBURG, M/1994/2-4/6 KB444 . . . . 398.22
Kingfisher book of the ancient world: from the Ice Age to the fall of Rome.
/MARTELL, H/1995/4-6/10 KE621 930
KINGFISHER CHILDREN'S ENCYCLOPEDIA. REV. ED. /1992/
/KA383. . . . . **REF 031**
KINGFISHER FIRST DICTIONARY. /1995/1-2/KA424 . . . . **REF 423**
King's equal. /PATERSON, K/1992/3-6/6 KH578 . . . . **Fic**
King's equal (Sound recording cassette)./PATERSON, K/1994/
3-6/6 KH578 . . . . **Fic**
King's fool: a book about medieval and renaissance fools. /FRADON, D/
1993/4-6/7 KE647 . . . . 940.1
Kirby Puckett's baseball games. /PUCKETT, K/1996/
3-6/3 KD801 . . . . 796.357
Kiss for Little Bear./MINARIK, EH/1968/P-1/2 KG141 . . . . . **CE E**
Kiss for Little Bear (Kit)./MINARIK, EH/1991/P-1/2 KG141 . . . **CE E**
Kit Carson: frontier scout. /SANFORD, WR/1996/
5-6/7 KE277 . . . . **B CARSON, K.**
Kitchen. /KALMAN, B/1990/4-5/5 KD295 643
Kitten who couldn't purr. /TITUS, E/1991/P-K/1 KG611 . . . . **E**

Klondike fever. /COOPER, ML/1989/5-6/6 KE823 . . . . **971.9**
KLONDIKE GOLD RUSH (Picture). /n.d./A/KE826 . . . . . **PIC 971.9**
Knee-Knock Rise. /BABBITT, N/c1970/4-6/6 KG871 . . . . . **CE Fic**
Knee-Knock Rise (Talking book)./BABBITT, N/n.d./4-6/6 KG871 . **CE Fic**
Knee-Knock Rise (Talking book)./BABBITT, N/1996/4-6/6 KG871 . **CE Fic**
Knight. /GRAVETT, C/1993/4-A/7 KE648 . . . . 940.1
Knight and the dragon. /DE PAOLA, T/1980/K-2/5 KF471 . . . . . . **E**
Knight with the lion: the story of Yvain. /HOWE, J/1996/
5-6/6 KB455 . . . . 398.22
Knights. /CORBIN, CL/1989/4-6/4 KE646 . . . . 940.1
Knight's castle./EAGER, E/c1956, 1984/4-6/6 KH094. . . . . **Fic**
Knight's castle (Sound recording cassette)./EAGER, E/n.d./
4-6/6 KH094 . . . . **Fic**
Knights: facts, things to make, activities. /WRIGHT, R/1991/
4-A/8 KD439 . . . . 745.5
Knights of the kitchen table. /SCIESZKA, J/1991/3-6/3 KH685 . . . . . . **Fic**
KNOCK AT THE DOOR. /1992/KA269 . . . . **PROF 398.2**
Knot in the grain and other stories. /MCKINLEY, R/1994/
6-A/7 KH489 . . . . **Fic**
Know about AIDS. 3rd ed. /HYDE, MO/1994/5-6/8 KD030 . . . . 616.97
Know it all: resource book for kids. /PETERSON, PR/1989/
4-A/6 KA591 . . . . 031.02
Know the score: video games in your high-tech world. /SKURZYNSKI, G/
1994/3-6/8 KD757 . . . . 794.8
KNOWLEDGE QUEST. /1997-//KA119 . . . . **PER PROF 050**
Know-Nothing birthday. /SPIRN, M/1997/1-2/1 KG533 . . . . **E**
Knoxville, Tennessee. /GIOVANNI, N/1994/P-1/2 KD945 811
Koala. /ARNOLD, C/c1987, 1992/4-6/8 KC733 . . . . 599.2
Koala is not a bear! /SOTZEK, H/1997/3-5/3 KC738 . . . . 599.2
KOALAS: THE BARE FACTS (Videocassette). /1993/
5-6/KC736. **VCR 599.2**
Kodomo: children of Japan. /KUKLIN, S/1995/3-5/6 KE710. . . . . 952.04
Kofi and his magic. /ANGELOU, M/1996/2-5/3 KE735 . . . . . . 966.7
Koi and the kola nuts (Kit). /GLEESON, B/1992/2-5/KB446. . **KIT 398.22**
Koko's kitten. /PATTERSON, F/1985/3-5/6 KC877 . . . . . . 599.884
Koko's kitten (Braille)./PATTERSON, F/n.d./3-5/6 KC877 . . . . 599.884
Komodo dragon. /SCHAFER, S/c1992, 1996/5-6/5 KC629 . . . . 597.95
Komodo dragon: on location. /DARLING, K/1997/4-6/7 KC625 . . 597.95
Kongi and Potgi: a Cinderella story from Korea. /HAN, OS/1996/
K-3/5 KB313 . . . . 398.2
Konnichiwa!: I am a Japanese-American girl. /BROWN, T/1995/
3-5/4 KA839 . . . . 305.8
Korean Cinderella. /CLIMO, S/1993/2-4/5 KB726 . . . . 398.27
Koya DeLaney and the good girl blues. /GREENFIELD, E/c1992, 1995/
4-6/6 KH199 . . . . **Fic**
Kristi Yamaguchi: pure gold. /SAVAGE, J/1993/
3-5/7 KE603 . . . . **B YAMAGUCHI, K.**
Kwanzaa karamu: cooking and crafts for a Kwanzaa feast. /BRADY, AA/
1995/5-6/5 KD284 . . . . 641.59
KWANZAA (Videocassette). /1994/3-6/KB212 . . . . . **VCR 394.261**
L. Frank Baum: royal historian of Oz. /CARPENTER, AS/1992/
4-6/4 KE251 . . . . **B BAUM, L.**
L. Frank Baum: royal historian of Oz (Sound recording cassette)./
CARPENTER, AS/1995/4-6/4 KE251 . . . . **B BAUM, L.**
Labor Day. /SCOTT, G/1982/2-3/2 KB228 . . . . 394.264
Lady and the spider. /MCNULTY, F/1986/1-3/2 KG114 . . . . **E**
Lady Daisy (Talking book). /KING-SMITH, D/1995/4-6/KH350 . . **TB Fic**
Lady in the box. /MCGOVERN, A/1997/1-3/2 KG103. . . . . **E**
Lady of Guadalupe. /DE PAOLA, T/1980/1-4/6 KA698 . . . . . 232.91
Lady with the alligator purse. /WESTCOTT, NB/1988/P-1/KB818 . . 398.8
Ladybug. /WATTS, B/1987/3-5/4 KC555. . . . . 595.76
Ladybug and other insects. /GOLDSEN, L/1991/K-3/4 KC538 . . . . 595.7
LADYBUG: THE MAGAZINE FOR YOUNG CHILDREN. /1990-/
P-2/KA524. **PER 050**
Ladybugs. /JOHNSON, SA/1983/A/11 KC554. . . . . 595.76
Land and people of Canada. /MALCOLM, AH/1991/A/10 KE805 . . 971
Land I lost: adventures of a boy in Vietnam. /HUYNH, QN/1982/
5-6/7 KE718 . . . . 959.7
Land I lost: adventures of a boy in Vietnam (Sound recording cassette)./
HUYNH, QN/n.d./5-6/7 KE718 . . . . 959.7
Landing of the Pilgrims. /DAUGHERTY, J/c1950/4-6/7 KE938 . . 974.4
LANDS AND PEOPLES. Rev. ed. /1997/5-6/KA469 . . . . . . **REF 909**
LANDS OF PLEASURE: ESSAYS ON LILLIAN H. SMITH AND THE
DEVELOPMENT OF CHILDREN'S LIBRARIES. /1990/
/KA044. . . . . **PROF 020**
Landscapes. /ROALF, P/1992/5-A/8 KD481 758
Laney's lost momma. /HAMM, DJ/1991/P-1/2 KF670. . . . . **E**
LANGUAGE ARTS. /1924-//KA120 . . . . **PER PROF 050**
Largest dinosaurs. /SIMON, S/1986/4-6/6 KC265. . . . . 567.9
LAROUSSE DICTIONARY OF SCIENTISTS. /1996/5-A/KA440. . **REF 509**
Las gallinas no son las unicas./HELLER, R/1992/P-K/KC282 . . . . . . 573.6
LAS NAVIDADES: POPULAR CHRISTMAS SONGS FROM LATIN
AMERICA. /1990/K-3/KD580 . . . . 789.2
Lassie come-home. /KNIGHT, E/1978/4-6/5 KH370 . . . . **Fic**

Lassie come-home (Sound recording cassette)./KNIGHT, E/n.d./
4-6/5 KH370 . . . . **Fic**
Lassie come-home (Talking book)./KNIGHT, E/n.d./4-6/5 KH370. . . . . **Fic**
Last battle./LEWIS, CS/1994/5-A/6 KH405 . . . . **CE Fic**
Last battle (Braille)./LEWIS, CS/n.d./5-A/6 KH405 . . . . . . **CE Fic**
Last battle (Sound recording cassette)./LEWIS, CS/n.d./
5-A/6 KH405 . . . . **CE Fic**
Last battle (Talking book)./LEWIS, CS/n.d./5-A/6 KH405 . . . . **CE Fic**
Last dragon. /NUNES, S/1995/2-3/3 KG183 . . . . **E**
Last mission. /MAZER, H/c1979, 1986/6-A/4 KH465 . . . . **Fic**
Last one in is a rotten egg. /KESSLER, L/c1969/1-2/1 KF900 . . . . **E**
Last one in is a rotten egg (Talking book)./KESSLER, L/n.d./
1-2/1 KF900 . . . . **E**
Last princess: the story of Princess Kaiulani of Hawaii. /STANLEY, F/1991/
5-6/7 KE413 . . . . **B KAIULANI**
Last quest of Gilgamesh. /ZEMAN, L/1995/4-6/4 KE131 . . . . . . **892.1**
Last stand at the Alamo. /CARTER, AR/1990/4-6/7 KF001 . . . . . **976.4**
Last tales of Uncle Remus./LESTER, J/1994/4-5/5 KB608. . . . . . **398.24**
LATCHKEY CHILDREN: WHEN YOU'RE IN CHARGE (Videocassette). /
1986/5-6/KD261 . . . . **VCR 640**
Latchkey dog. /AUCH, MJ/1994/3-5/4 KG855 . . . . **Fic**
LATE LAST NIGHT (Compact disc)./n.d./P-2/KD635 . . . . **SRC 789.3**
LATE LAST NIGHT (Sound recording cassette). /1984/
P-2/KD635. . . . . **SRC 789.3**
Later, Gator. /YEP, L/1995/4-6/4 KH893 . . . . **Fic**
Latest and greatest read-alouds. /MCELMEEL, SL/1994/
/KA239. . . . . **PROF 372.64**
Latin American and Caribbean crafts. /CORWIN, JH/1992/
4-A/5 KD427 . . . . **745.5**
Latino heritage, series V./SCHON, I/1995//KA043. . . . . . **PROF 016.98**
Latino rainbow: poems about Latino Americans. /CUMPIAN, C/1994/
3-6/KD927 . . . . **811**
LAUGHING TOGETHER: GIGGLES AND GRINS FROM AROUND THE
GLOBE. /c1977, 1992/3-A/KD731 . . . . **793.735**
Laura Ingalls Wilder: storyteller of the prairie. /WADSWORTH, G/1997/
4-A/5 KE595 . . . . **B WILDER, L.**
Laurie tells./LOWERY, L/1994/3-6/4 KH420 . . . . **Fic**
Lavender. /HESSE, K/1995/2-3/2 KH251 . . . . **Fic**
Lazy Jack. /FRENCH, V/1995/K-2/2 KB301 . . . . **398.2**
LEADERSHIP--MENTORING (Videocassette)./1991/
/KA187 . . . . **VCR PROF 371.95**
LEADERSHIP--MENTORING (Videocassette)./1991/
/KA187 . . . . **VCR PROF 371.95**
Leading kids to books through magic. /BAUER, CF/1996/
/KA066 . . . . **PROF 027.62**
Leaf Men and the brave good bugs. /JOYCE, W/1996/1-3/3 KF861. . . **E**
Leagues apart: the men and times of the Negro baseball leagues. /RITTER,
LS/1995/2-4/7 KD802. . . . . **796.357**
Learn to draw 3-D. /DUBOSQUE, D/1992/5-A/7 KD414 . . . . **742**
Learning about biographies: a reading-and-writing approach for children. /
ZARNOWSKI, M/1990//KA334 . . . . **PROF 808**
LEARNING AND LEADING WITH TECHNOLOGY. /1979-/
/KA121. . . . . **PER PROF 050**
Learning basic skills (Videocassette). /PALMER, H/1986/
P-1/KD700. . . . . **VCR 793**
Learning by heart. /YOUNG, RT/1993/6-A/6 KH899 . . . . **Fic**
LEARNING: SUCCESSFUL TEACHING TODAY. /1972-/
/KA122. . . . . **PER PROF 050**
Learning to say goodbye: when a parent dies. /LESHAN, E/c1976/
5-6/7 KA651 . . . . **155.9**
Learning to say goodbye: when a parent dies (Sound recording cassette)./
LESHAN, E/n.d./5-6/7 KA651 . . . . **155.9**
Leaving for America. /BRESNICK-PERRY, R/1992/1-4/6 KE688. . . . **947**
Lebek: a city of Northern Europe through the ages. /HERNANDEZ, X/
1991/A/10 KA896 . . . . **307.76**
Lee Trevino. /KRAMER, J/1996/5-6/6 KE570 . . . . **B TREVINO, L.**
Leeches, lampreys, and other cold-blooded bloodsuckers. /LABONTE, G/
1991/5-6/7 KC505 . . . . **592**
Left behind. /CARRICK, C/1988/1-3/2 KF359 . . . . **E**
Left-handed shortstop./GIFF, PR/1980/4-6/6 KH164 . . . . **Fic**
Legend of Slappy Hooper: an American tall tale. /SHEPARD, A/1993/
3-5/3 KB489 . . . . **398.22**
Legend of Sleepy Hollow. /IRVING, W/c1928, 1990/6-A/9 KH314. . . **Fic**
Legend of the Bluebonnet: an old tale of Texas. /DE PAOLA, T/1983/
2-4/4 KB558 . . . . **CE 398.24**
Legend of the Indian Paintbrush./DE PAOLA, T/1988/
2-4/4 KB558 . . . . **CE 398.24**
Legend of the Persian carpet. /DE PAOLA, T/1993/2-3/6 KB285 . . **398.2**
Legend of the Windigo: a tale from native North America. /ROSS, G/
1996/2-3/6 KB410 . . . . **398.21**
Lemon drop jar. /WIDMAN, C/1992/P-2/2 KG711 . . . . **E**
Lemonade trick. /CORBETT, S/1960/4-5/4 KH030 . . . . **Fic**
Lentil. /MCCLOSKEY, R/c1940/1-3/6 KG088 . . . . **CE E**
Lentil (Braille)./MCCLOSKEY, R/n.d./1-3/6 KG088 . . . . **CE E**

Lentil (Talking book)./MCCLOSKEY, R/n.d./1-3/6 KG088 . . . . . . **CE E**
Lentil (Videocassette)./MCCLOSKEY, R/1965/1-3/6 KG088 . . . . . **CE E**
Leo and Blossom's sukkah./ZALBEN, JB/1990/P/4 KG785 . . . . **E**
Leo Lionni's Caldecotts (Videocassette). /LIONNI, L/1985/
P-2/KF994 . . . . **VCR E**
Leo the late bloomer. /KRAUS, R/1971/P-2/2 KF918 . . . . **CE E**
Leon and Bob. /JAMES, S/1997/K-2/2 KF824 . . . . **E**
Leon, la bruja, y el armario./LEWIS, CS/n.d./5-A/6 KH405 . . . **CE Fic**
Leonard Bernstein: a passion for music. /HURWITZ, J/1993/
5-A/7 KE253 . . . . **B BERNSTEIN, L.**
Leonardo da Vinci. /PROVENSEN, A/1984/4-6/7 KE434 . **B LEONARDO**
Leonardo da Vinci. /MCLANATHAN, R/1990/6-A/6 KD495. . . . . **759.5**
Leonardo da Vinci. /STANLEY, D/1996/5-A/8 KE435 . . . **B LEONARDO**
Leopard's drum: an Asante tale from West Africa. /SOUHAMI, J/1995/
P-1/2 KB654 . . . . **398.24**
Leroy Potts meets the McCrooks. /SATHRE, V/1997/1-3/2 KH677 . . . **Fic**
Lessons from the animal people (Compact disc)./THOMASON, D/1996/
2-5/KB664. . . . . **SRC 398.24**
Lessons from the animal people (Sound recording cassette). /THOMASON,
D/1996/2-5/KB664. . . . . **SRC 398.24**
Lester's dog. /HESSE, K/1993/1-3/3 KF716 . . . . **E**
Lester's dog (Sound recording cassette)./HESSE, K/1995/1-3/3 KF716. . **E**
Let freedom ring: a ballad of Martin Luther King, Jr. /LIVINGSTON, MC/
1992/K-2/4 KD978 . . . . **811**
LET ME TELL YOU ALL ABOUT PLANES (Videocassette). /1994/
4-5/KD111. . . . . **VCR 629.133**
LET ME TELL YOU ALL ABOUT TRAINS (Videocassette). /1993/
3-4/KD076. . . . . **VCR 625.2**
Let the celebrations begin! /WILD, M/1991/4-A/4 KH858 . . . . . . **Fic**
Let the circle be unbroken. /TAYLOR, MD/1981/5-6/8 KH777 . . . . **Fic**
Let the circle be unbroken (Braille)./TAYLOR, MD/n.d./5-6/8 KH777 . . **Fic**
Let's be enemies. /UDRY, JM/c1961/P-1/2 KG632. . . . . **E**
Let's clean up our act: songs for the earth (Sound recording cassette). /
CALLINAN, T/1989/K-6/KD559 . . . . **SRC 789.2**
Let's count it out, Jesse Bear. /CARLSTROM, NW/1996/P-1/2 KF357 . . **E**
Let's eat! /ZAMORANO, A/1997/P-2/1 KG786 . . . . **E**
LET'S EXPLORE THE JUNGLE WITH BUZZY THE KNOWLEDGE BUG (CD-
ROM). /1995/K-3/KC320. . . . . **CDR 577.34**
Let's get a pet. /ZIEFERT, H/c1993, 1996/K-3/2 KD193 . . . . **636.088**
Let's go: a book in two languages./Vamos: un libro en dos lenguas. /
EMBERLEY, R/1993/K-2/2 KB857 . . . . **463**
Let's go, Froggy! /LONDON, J/1994/P-K/2 KG024 . . . . **E**
Let's go home, Little Bear. /WADDELL, M/1993/P-K/3 KG676 . . . . . **E**
LET'S GO TO THE FARM (Videocassette). /1994/1-6/KD144. . **VCR 630**
Let's go traveling. /KRUPP, RR/1992/3-5/4 KE155 . . . . **910.4**
Let's go traveling in Mexico. /KRUPP, RR/1996/2-4/6 KE187 . . . . **917.2**
Let's make magic. /DAY, J/1992/3-6/KD747 . . . . **793.8**
LET'S MOVE IT: NEWTON'S LAWS OF MOTION (Videocassette). /1987/
5-A/KC096 . . . . **VCR 531**
Let's play games (Videocassette). /LEWIS, S/1994/
P-2/KD709. . . . . **VCR 793.4**
Let's read together and other songs for sharing and caring (Sound
recording cassette). /HARTMANN, J/1991/P-2/KD616 . . **SRC 789.3**
Let's sing!: John Langstaff sings with children, ages 3-7. Teacher's guide./
LANGSTAFF, J/1997//KA314. . . . . **VCR PROF 780**
Let's sing!: John Langstaff sings with children, ages 3-7 (Videocassette). /
LANGSTAFF, J/1997//KA314. . . . . **VCR PROF 780**
LET'S TALK ABOUT AIDS! (Videocassette). /1992/
5-6/KD031. . . . . **VCR 616.97**
LET'S TALK ABOUT DRUGS (Videocassette). /1994/
1-3/KC998. . . . . **VCR 613.8**
Letter from an Apache: a true story (Videocassette). /WILK, B/1983/
4-6/KE777. . . . . **VCR 970.3**
Letter, the witch, and the ring./BELLAIRS, J/c1976, 1993/
4-6/5 KG897 . . . . **Fic**
Letter to Amy. /KEATS, EJ/c1968/P-2/2 KF874 . . . . **CE E**
Letter to Amy (Braille)./KEATS, EJ/n.d./P-2/2 KF874 . . . . . . **CE E**
Letter to Amy (Videocassette)./KEATS, EJ/1973/P-2/2 KF874 . . . **CE E**
Letters are lost! /ERNST, LC/1996/P-K/2 KF530 . . . . **E**
LETTERS FOR OUR CHILDREN: FIFTY AMERICANS SHARE LESSONS IN
LIVING. /1996//KA158. . . . . **PROF 170**
Letters from a slave girl: the story of Harriet Jacobs. /LYONS, ME/1992/
4-6/4 KH430 . . . . **Fic**
Letting off steam. /JACOBS, L/1989/4-A/7 KC156 . . . . **551.2**
Letting Swift River go. /YOLEN, J/1992/1-3/5 KG777 . . . . **E**
Letting Swift River go (Sound recording cassette)./YOLEN, J/1994/
1-3/5 KG777 . . . . **E**
Lewis and Clark. /STEFOFF, R/1992/5-6/5 KE206 . . . . **917.804**
LEWIS AND CLARK EXPEDITION (Videocassette). /1992/
5-6/KE204. . . . . **VCR 917.804**
Lewis and Clark: explorers of the American West. /KROLL, S/1994/
4-6/6 KE203 . . . . **917.804**
Leyenda de la Flor el Conejo: una antigua leyenda de Texas./DE PAOLA,
T/1993/2-4/4 KB558 . . . . **CE 398.24**

Leyenda del pincel Indio./DE PAOLA, T/1988/2-4/4 KB558 . . . **CE 398.24**

L'Histoire de Pierre Lapin./POTTER, B/n.d./P-2/6 KG278 . . . . **E**

Liar, liar, pants on fire!/COHEN, M/1985/K-1/2 KF405. . . . . **CE E**

Libby Bloom. /MASTERS, SR/1995/3-5/6 KH460 . . . . **Fic**

Librarian who measured the earth. /LASKY, K/1994/
4-A/6 KE339 . . . . **B ERATOSTHENES**

Library. /STEWART, S/1995/K-3/3 KG572 . . . . **CE E**

Library (Kit)./STEWART, S/1996/K-3/3 KG572 . . . . **CE E**

Library of Congress. /FOWLER, A/1996/3-6/11 KA587 . . . . . . **027.5**

LIBRARY TALK: THE MAGAZINE FOR ELEMENTARY SCHOOL
LIBRARIANS. /1988-//KA123 . . . . **PER PROF 050**

LIBRARY (Videocassette). /1991/1-4/KA586 . . . . **VCR 027.4**

Library (Vjdeocassette)./STEWART, S/1996/K-3/3 KG572 . . . . **CE E**

Libro de las arena movedizas. /DE PAOLA, T/1993/K-3/2 KC226 . . . **552**

Libro de las palomitas de maiz. /DE PAOLA, T/1993/2-4/6 KD290 . **641.6**

Libro illustrado sobre Cristobal Colon./ADLER, DA/1992/
2-3/4 KE300 . . . . **CE B COLUMBUS, C.**

Libro ilustrado sobre Martin Luther King, Hijo./ADLER, DA/1992/
3-4/4 KE420 . . . . **CE B KING, M.L.**

Libro ilustrado sobre Martin Luther King, Hijo (Kit)./ADLER, DA/1993/
3-4/4 KE420 . . . . **CE B KING, M.L.**

Lies, deception and truth. /WEISS, AE/1988/6-A/9 KA671 . . . . . . **177**

Life and death of Crazy Horse. /FREEDMAN, R/1996/
6-A/7 KE307 . . . . **B CRAZY HORSE**

Life and times of the apple. /MICUCCI, C/1992/3-5/5 KD162 . . . . . **634**

Life and times of the honeybee. /MICUCCI, C/1995/
4-6/6 KC576 . . . . **595.79**

Life and times of the peanut. /MICUCCI, C/1997/3-6/11 KD268. . . **641.3**

Life around the lake. /PRESILLA, ME/1996/2-6/8 KE837. . . . . . . **972**

LIFE CYCLE OF THE HONEYBEE (Videocassette). /c1976, 1986/
3-6/KC575. . . . . **VCR 595.79**

Life of the honeybee. /FISCHER-NAGEL, H/1986/4-6/7 KC572 . . **595.79**

Life of the ladybug. /FISCHER-NAGEL, H/1986/5-6/9 KC551 . . **595.76**

Life of the snail. /BUHOLZER, T/1987/4-6/7 KC510 . . . . **594**

Life's a funny proposition, Horatio. /POLIKOFF, BG/1992/
5-A/4 KH608 . . . . **Fic**

Lift every voice and sing. /JOHNSON, JW/1993/2-6/5 KD672 . **789.44**

Light. /BURNIE, D/1992/4-A/7 KC107. . . . . **535**

Light action!: amazing experiments with optics. /COBB, V/1993/
2-6/7 KC108 . . . . **535**

Light another candle: the story and meaning of Hanukkah. /CHAIKIN, M/
c1981, 1987/5-6/8 KA770 . . . . **296.4**

Light another candle: the story and meaning of Hanukkah (Sound recording
cassette)./CHAIKIN, M/n.d./5-6/8 KA770 . . . . **296.4**

LIGHT BULBS (Videocassette). /1991/1-3/KD043 . . . . . . **VCR 621.32**

Light in the attic. /SILVERSTEIN, S/1981/P-A/KE025 . . . . **811**

Light in the attic (Braille). /SILVERSTEIN, S/n.d./P-A/KE025 . . . . . **811**

Light in the attic (Sound recording cassette)./SILVERSTEIN, S/n.d./
P-A/KE025. . . . . **811**

Light in the forest. /RICHTER, C/1994/5-A/6 KH632. . . . . **Fic**

Light princess. /MACDONALD, G/1977/4-5/5 KH439 . . . . **Fic**

Light princess (Braille). /MACDONALD, G/n.d./4-5/5 KH439 . . . . . **Fic**

Light princess (Sound recording cassette). /MACDONALD, G/n.d./
4-5/5 KH439 . . . . **Fic**

Light princess (Talking book)./MACDONALD, G/n.d./4-5/5 KH439 . . . **Fic**

Lighthouses: watchers at sea. /GUIBERSON, BZ/1995/
5-6/8 KB150 . . . . **387.1**

LIGHTNING INSIDE YOU AND OTHER NATIVE AMERICAN RIDDLES. /
1992/3-6/KD733 . . . . **793.735**

Lights for Gita. /GILMORE, R/1994/1-3/5 KF620 . . . . **E**

Like Jake and me. /JUKES, M/1984/5-6/7 KH338 . . . . **Fic**

Like Jake and me (Sound recording cassette)./JUKES, M/n.d./
5-6/7 KH338 . . . . **Fic**

Likely place. /FOX, P/c1967, 1986/4-6/4 KH135. . . . . **Fic**

Lili at ballet. /ISADORA, R/1993/P-2/2 KF815 . . . . **E**

Lili backstage. /ISADORA, R/1997/K-2/3 KF816 . . . . **E**

Lilly's purple plastic purse. /HENKES, K/1996/K-2/2 KF708 . . . . **E**

Lily and the wooden bowl. /SCHROEDER, A/1994/3-5/7 KB366. . **398.2**

Lily's crossing. /GIFF, PR/1997/5-A/5 KH165 . . . . **Fic**

Lincoln, a photobiography. /FREEDMAN, R/1987/
A/11 KE441. . . . . **B LINCOLN, A.**

LINCOLN, IN HIS OWN WORDS. /1993/A/8 KE907. . . . . **973.7**

Line up book. /RUSSO, M/1986/P-1/1 KG362. . . . . **E**

Linnea's almanac. /BJORK, C/c1982, 1989/2-6/6 KB879 . . . . . . **507**

Linnea's windowsill garden. /BJORK, C/c1978, 1988/3-5/6 KD173 . **635.9**

Lion. /ARNOLD, C/1995/5-6/7 KC828 . . . . **599.757**

Lion and the mouse: an Aesop's fable. /WOOD, AJ/1995/
P-1/5 KB674 . . . . **398.24**

Lion and the ostrich chicks and other African folk tales. /BRYAN, A/1986/
4-6/3 KB544 . . . . **398.24**

Lion dancer: Ernie Wan's Chinese New Year. /WATERS, K/1990/
1-4/2 KB217 . . . . **394.261**

Lion family book. /HOFER, A/1995/3-6/6 KC830 . . . . **599.757**

Lion, the witch and the wardrobe. /LEWIS, CS/1994/
5-A/6 KH405 . . . . **CE Fic**

Lion, the witch and the wardrobe (Braille)./LEWIS, CS/n.d./
5-A/6 KH405 . . . . **CE Fic**

Lion, the witch and the wardrobe (Sound recording cassette)./LEWIS, CS/
n.d./5-A/6 KH405 . . . . **CE Fic**

Lion, the witch and the wardrobe (Talking book)./LEWIS, CS/n.d./
5-A/6 KH405 . . . . **CE Fic**

Lion, the witch and the wardrobe (Videocassette)./LEWIS, CS/1988/
5-A/6 KH405 . . . . **CE Fic**

Lion who had asthma. /LONDON, J/1992/P-2/2 KG025. . . . . **E**

Lionel and Louise./KRENSKY, S/1997/K-2/2 KF924 . . . . **E**

Lionel at large. /KRENSKY, S/1986/K-2/2 KF924 . . . . **E**

Lionel at large (Braille). /KRENSKY, S/n.d./K-2/2 KF924 . . . . **E**

Lionel in the winter./KRENSKY, S/1996/K-2/2 KF924 . . . . **E**

LION'S WHISKERS: AND OTHER ETHIOPIAN TALES. Rev. ed. /1997/
3-6/7 KB337 . . . . **398.2**

Listen Buddy. /LESTER, H/1995/K-2/2 KF964 . . . . **E**

Listen for the bus: David's story. /MCMAHON, P/1995/
1-3/3 KB004 . . . . **362.4**

Listen to the desert/Oye al desierto. /MORA, P/1994/P-1/KD990. . . **811**

Listen to the nightingale. /GODDEN, R/c1992, 1994/5-A/6 KH178 . . . **Fic**

Listen to the nightingale (Sound recording cassette)./GODDEN, R/1995/
5-A/6 KH178 . . . . **Fic**

Listen to the rain. /MARTIN, JR., B/1988/P-2/KG077 . . . . **E**

Listening to crickets: a story about Rachel Carson. /RANSOM, CF/1993/
5-6/6 KE278 . . . . **B CARSON, R.**

Listening walk. /SHOWERS, P/c1961, 1991/P-1/1 KG495. . . . . **E**

LITERARY LAURELS: KIDS' EDITION: A READER'S GUIDE TO AWARD-
WINNING CHILDREN'S BOOKS. /1996//KA034 . . . . **PROF 016.809**

Literature and the child. 3rd ed. /CULLINAN, BE/1993/
/KA348 . . . . **PROF 809**

LITERATURE TO ENJOY AND WRITE ABOUT, SERIES 1 (Videocassette). /
1989//KA344 . . . . **VCR PROF 808.8**

LITERATURE TO ENJOY AND WRITE ABOUT, SERIES 2 (Videocassette). /
1990//KA345 . . . . **VCR PROF 808.8**

Literature-based reading: children's books and activities to enrich the K-5
curriculum. /LAUGHLIN, MK/1990/KA210 . . . . **PROF 372.4**

Literature-based science: children's books and activities to enrich the K-5
curriculum. /HEFNER, CR/1990//KA200 . . . . **PROF 372.3**

Literature-based social studies: children's books and activities to enrich the
K-5 curriculum. /LAUGHLIN, MK/1991//KA261 . . . . . **PROF 372.83**

Little Bear. /MINARIK, EH/c1961/P-1/2 KG141. . . . . **CE E**

Little Bear (Braille). /MINARIK, EH/n.d./P-1/2 KG141 . . . . **CE E**

Little Bear (Kit)./MINARIK, EH/1986/P-1/2 KG141 . . . . **CE E**

Little Bear (Talking book)./MINARIK, EH/n.d./P-1/2 KG141 . . . . . **CE E**

Little Bear's friend. /MINARIK, EH/1960/P-1/2 KG141 . . . . **CE E**

Little Bear's friend (Braille). /MINARIK, EH/n.d./P-1/2 KG141 . . . . **CE E**

Little Bear's friend (Kit)./MINARIK, EH/1990/P-1/2 KG141 . . . . . **CE E**

Little Bear's visit./MINARIK, EH/1961/P-1/2 KG141 . . . . **CE E**

Little Bear's visit (Braille). /MINARIK, EH/n.d./P-1/2 KG141 . . . . . **CE E**

Little Bear's visit (Kit)./MINARIK, EH/1961/P-1/2 KG141. . . . . . **CE E**

Little Beaver and The Echo. /MACDONALD, A/1990/P-K/1 KG049. . . . **E**

Little big ears; the story of Ely. /MOSS, C/1997/K-4/6 KC812. . **599.67**

LITTLE BOOK OF LOVE. /1995/4-6/KD886 . . . . **808.81**

Little Donkey close your eyes. /BROWN, MW/1995/P-K/2 KF286 . . . **E**

Little Eight John. /WAHL, J/1992/2-3/2 KB783 . . . . **398.27**

Little elephant. /FORD, M/1994/P-K/1 KF565 . . . . **E**

Little engine that could. /PIPER, W/c1961/P-K/4 KG246 . . . . . . **CE E**

Little engine that could (Braille). /PIPER, W/n.d./P-K/4 KG246 . . . . **CE E**

Little engine that could (Kit)./PIPER, W/1985/P-K/4 KG246 . . . . . **CE E**

Little engine that could (Talking book)./PIPER, W/n.d./
P-K/4 KG246 . . . . **CE E**

Little farm in the Ozarks./MACBRIDE, RL/1994/4-6/6 KH436 . . . . **Fic**

Little fishes. /HAUGAARD, EC/c1967, 1987/A/6 KH227 . . . . . . **Fic**

Little fishes (Braille). /HAUGAARD, EC/n.d./A/6 KH227 . . . . . . **Fic**

Little fishes (Talking book)./HAUGAARD, EC/n.d./A/6 KH227 . . . . **Fic**

Little folk: stories from around the world. /WALKER, PR/1997/
2-4/6 KB494 . . . . **398.22**

Little green thumbs. /VAN HAGE, MA/1996/3-5/4 KD176 . . . . . **635.9**

Little Grunt and the big egg: a prehistoric fairy tale. /DE PAOLA, T/1990/
K-2/2 KF472 . . . . **E**

LITTLE HORSE THAT COULD: THE CONNEMARA STALLION: ERIN GO
BRAGH (Videocassette). /1996/2-6/KD857 . . . . **VCR 798.2**

Little house. /BURTON, VL/c1942, 1978/K-2/2 KF320 . . . . . . **CE E**

Little house (Braille)./BURTON, VL/n.d./K-2/2 KF320 . . . . **CE E**

Little House cookbook: frontier foods from Laura Ingalls Wilder's classic
stories. New ed. /WALKER, BM/1995/4-6/9 KD282 . . . . **641.5**

Little House cookbook: frontier foods from Laura Ingalls Wilder's classic
stories (Sound recording cassette)./WALKER, BM/n.d./
4-6/9 KD282 . . . . **641.5**

Little House guidebook. /ANDERSON, W/1996/3-5/10 KE196. . . **917.8**

Little house in Brookfield. /WILKES, MD/1996/4-6/5 KH861 . . . . **Fic**

Little house in the Big Woods. /WILDER, LI/c1953/3-6/4 KH860 . . . . **Fic**

Little house in the Big Woods (Braille)./WILDER, LI/n.d./3-6/4 KH860 . **Fic**
Little house in the Big Woods (Large type)./WILDER, LI/n.d./
3-6/4 KH860 . . . . **Fic**
Little house in the Big Woods (Sound recording cassette)./WILDER, LI/n.d./
3-6/4 KH860 . . . . **Fic**
Little house in the Big Woods (Talking book)./WILDER, LI/n.d./
3-6/4 KH860 . . . . **Fic**
Little house of your own. /DE REGNIERS, BS/c1954/K-1/4 KF483 . . . . **E**
Little house on Rocky Ridge. /MACBRIDE, RL/1993/4-6/6 KH436 . . . . **Fic**
Little house on the prairie./WILDER, LI/1954/3-6/4 KH860. . . . . **Fic**
Little house on the prairie (Braille)./WILDER, LI/n.d./3-6/4 KH860 . . . . **Fic**
Little house on the prairie (Talking book)./WILDER, LI/n.d./
3-6/4 KH860 . . . . **Fic**
Little Kit or, The Industrious Flea Circus girl. /MCCULLY, EA/1995/
2-4/4 KG092 . . . . **E**
Little Louis and the jazz band: the story of Louis "Satchmo" Armstrong. /
MEDEARIS, AS/1994/2-4/6 KE241 . . . . **B ARMSTRONG, L.**
Little men: life at Plumfield with Jo's boys. /ALCOTT, LM/c1947, 1982/
5-A/7 KG829 . . . . **Fic**
Little men: life at Plumfield with Jo's boys (Braille)./ALCOTT, LM/n.d./
5-A/7 KG829 . . . . **Fic**
Little men: life at Plumfield with Jo's boys (Sound recording cassette)./
ALCOTT, LM/n.d./5-A/7 KG829 . . . . **Fic**
Little men: life at Plumfield with Jo's boys (Talking book)./ALCOTT, LM/
n.d./5-A/7 KG829 . . . . **Fic**
Little old lady who was not afraid of anything. /WILLIAMS, L/1986/
P-2/4 KG730 . . . . **CE E**
Little old lady who was not afraid of anything (Kit). /WILLIAMS, L/1995/
P-2/4 KG730 . . . . **CE E**
Little Pink Pig. /HUTCHINS, P/1994/P-1/2 KF799 . . . . **E**
Little Plum. /YOUNG, E/1994/K-2/4 KB497 . . . . **398.22**
Little prince. /SAINT EXUPERY, AD/c1943/4-A/6 KH671 . . . . **Fic**
Little prince (Braille)./SAINT EXUPERY, AD/n.d./4-A/6 KH671 . . . . . **Fic**
Little prince (Sound recording cassette)./SAINT EXUPERY, AD/n.d./
4-A/6 KH671 . . . . **Fic**
Little princess. /BURNETT, FH/c1963/5-A/8 KG949 . . . . **Fic**
Little red ant and the great big crumb: a Mexican fable. /CLIMO, S/1995/
1-3/2 KF398 . . . . **E**
Little Red Cowboy Hat. /LOWELL, S/1997/1-3/3 KG038 . . . . **CE E**
Little red hen. /GALDONE, P/c1973/P-K/2 KF595 . . . . **CE E**
Little red hen. /ZIEFERT, H/1995/K-1/2 KG793 . . . . **E**
Little red hen, an old story. /ZEMACH, M/1983/P-K/2 KG790 . . . . . **CE E**
Little red hen (Braille)./GALDONE, P/n.d./P-K/2 KF595 . . . . **CE E**
Little red hen (Videocassette)./GALDONE, P/1991/P-K/2 KF595 . . . . **CE E**
Little Red Riding Hood. /GRIMM, J/1983/1-4/6 KB741 . . . . . **CE 398.27**
Little Red Riding Hood: a newfangled prairie tale. /ERNST, LC/1995/
K-2/4 KF531 . . . . **E**
Little Red Riding Hood (Braille)./GRIMM, J/n.d./1-4/6 KB741 . **CE 398.27**
Little seven-colored horse: a Spanish American folktale. /SAN SOUCI, RD/
1995/3-5/5 KB648 . . . . **398.24**
Little ships: the heroic rescue at Dunkirk in World War II. /BORDEN, L/
1997/3-5/3 KF251 . . . . **E**
Little Sister and the Month Brothers. /DE REGNIERS, BS/c1976, 1994/
2-3/2 KB501 . . . . **398.23**
Little swineherd and other tales. /FOX, P/1996/3-6/4 KH136 . . . . . **Fic**
Little tiger in the Chinese night: an autobiography in art. /ZHANG, SN/
4-6/6 KE609 . . . . **B ZHANG, S.**
Little Toot. /GRAMATKY, H/1981/P-1/4 KF634 . . . . **CE E**
Little Toot (Braille)./GRAMATKY, H/n.d./P-1/4 KF634 . . . . **CE E**
Little town at the crossroads./WILKES, MD/1997/4-6/5 KH861 . . . . . **Fic**
Little town in the Ozarks./MACBRIDE, RL/1996/4-6/6 KH436. . . . . . **Fic**
Little town on the prairie./WILDER, LI/1953/3-6/4 KH860 . . . . **Fic**
Little town on the prairie (Sound recording cassette)./WILDER, LI/n.d./
3-6/4 KH860 . . . . **Fic**
Little town on the prairie (Talking book)./WILDER, LI/n.d./
3-6/4 KH860 . . . . **Fic**
Little Vampire and the Midnight Bear. /KWITZ, MD/1995/1-3/2 KF941 . **E**
Little women (Talking book). /ALCOTT, LM/1975/5-A/KG830 . . . **TB Fic**
Lives and legends of the saints: with paintings from the great museums of
the world. /ARMSTRONG, C/1995/5-A/10 KA716. . . . . **270**
Lives of notable Asian Americans: business, politics, science. /RAGAZA, A/
1995/6-A/7 KA856. **305.8**
Lives of the musicians: good times, bad times (and what the neighbors
thought). /KRULL, K/1993/5-A/6 KD520 . . . . **780**
Lives of the musicians: good times, bad times (and what the neighbors
thought) (Sound recording cassette)./KRULL, K/1995/
5-A/6 KD520 . . . . **780**
Lives turned upside down: homeless children in their own words and
photographs. /HUBBARD, J/1996/3-6/4 KB009 . . . . **362.5**
Living clarinet. /TURNER, BC/1996/4-6/12 KD552 . . . . **BA 788.6**
Living flute. /TURNER, BC/1996/4-6/11 KD551. . . . . **BA 788.3**
Living fossils: animals that have withstood the test of time. /MARTIN, J/
1997/4-A/9 KC453 . . . . **591**
Living in space. /KETTELKAMP, L/1993/A/8 KD130 . . . . **629.4**

Living in space. /BERLINER, D/1993/5-6/9 KD139 . . . . **629.47**
LIVING ON THE EDGE (Videocassette). /1991/A/KF071 . . . **VCR 979.1**
Living piano. /TURNER, BC/1996/4-6/12 KD546 . . . . **BA 786.2**
Living violin. /TURNER, BC/1996/4-6/12 KD549 . . . . **BA 787.2**
Living with a parent who drinks too much. /SEIXAS, JS/1979/
4-6/7 KB000 . . . . **362.292**
Living with a single parent. /ROSENBERG, MB/1992/
4-6/6 KA872 . . . . **306.85**
Living with dinosaurs. /LAUBER, P/1991/3-6/5 KC252 . . . . **567.9**
Living with dinosaurs (Sound recording cassette)./LAUBER, P/1994/
3-6/5 KC252 . . . . **567.9**
LIVING WORLD. /1993/5-A/KA437 . . . . **REF 508**
Livingstone Mouse. /EDWARDS, PD/1996/K-2/2 KF512 . . . . **E**
Lizard in the jungle. /LINDLEY, M/1988/5-6/7 KC626. . . . . . . **597.95**
Lizard in the sun. /RYDER, J/1990/1-3/5 KC628 . . . . **597.95**
Llama. /ARNOLD, C/1988/5-6/7 KD210 . . . . **636.2**
Llaman a la puerta./HUTCHINS, P/1994/P-2/2 KF797 . . . . **CE E**
Llaman a la puerta (Kit)./HUTCHINS, P/1996/P-2/2 KF797 . . . . . . **CE E**
Loads of codes and secret ciphers. /JANECZKO, PB/1984/
A/7 KD309 . . . . **652**
Lobsters: gangsters of the sea. /CERULLO, MM/1994/
5-6/7 KC518 . . . . **595.3**
Local news. /SOTO, G/1993/6-A/6 KH740 . . . . **Fic**
Loch Ness Monster. /STEFFENS, B/1995/3-6/9 KA563. . . . . . **001.944**
Locks, crocs, and skeeters: the story of the Panama Canal. /PARKER, NW/
1996/3-5/7 KB147 . . . . **386**
LOCOMOTION (Videocassette). /1986/5-A/KC284 . . . . **VCR 573.7**
Log of Christopher Columbus' first voyage to America in the year 1492. /
COLUMBUS, C/c1938, 1989/4-6/7 KE741 . . . . **970.01**
LOGICAL JOURNEY OF THE ZOOMBINIS. School ed. (CD-ROM). /1996/
2-5/KB938 . . . . **CDR 511**
Lon Po Po: A Red-Riding Hood story from China. /YOUNG, E/1989/
3-4/4 KB679 . . . . **398.24**
London. /STEIN, RC/1996/3-5/8 KE682 . . . . **942.1**
Lonely lioness and the ostrich chicks: a Masai tale. /AARDEMA, V/1996/
K-2/3 KB516 . . . . **398.24**
Long journey home: stories from Black history. /LESTER, J/c1972, 1993/
6-A/4 KH395 . . . . **Fic**
Long road to Gettysburg. /MURPHY, J/1992/5-A/7 KE910 . . . . . **973.7**
Long secret./FITZHUGH, L/c1965, 1990/3-5/4 KH114 . . . . **Fic**
Long secret (Talking book)./FITZHUGH, L/n.d./3-5/4 KH114 . . . . . **Fic**
Long shots: they beat the odds. /JENNINGS, J/1990/5-6/6 KD762 . **796**
Long Spikes: a story. /ARNOSKY, J/1992/5-A/6 KG852 . . . . **Fic**
Long time to freedom (Sound recording cassette). /JENKINS, E/c1969,
1992/K-A/KD574 . . . . **SRC 789.2**
Long way to a new land. /SANDIN, J/1981/1-3/2 KG391 . . . . **E**
Long way westward./SANDIN, J/1989/1-3/2 KG391 . . . . **E**
Long winter./WILDER, LI/1953/3-6/4 KH860 . . . . **Fic**
Long winter (Braille)./WILDER, LI/n.d./3-6/4 KH860 . . . . **Fic**
Long winter (Sound recording cassette)./WILDER, LI/n.d./
3-6/4 KH860 . . . . **Fic**
Long winter (Talking book)./WILDER, LI/n.d./3-6/4 KH860 . . . . . . **Fic**
Longest home run. /CARRIER, R/1993/2-4/4 KG977 . . . . **Fic**
Long-haired girl: a Chinese legend. /RAPPAPORT, D/1995/
2-3/4 KB409 . . . . **398.21**
Long-haired girl: a Chinese legend (Sound recording cassette)./
RAPPAPORT, D/1997/2-3/4 KB409 . . . . **398.21**
Look at your eyes. Rev. ed. /SHOWERS, P/1992/P-1/2 KC978 . . . **612.8**
Look book. /HOBAN, T/1997/P-K/KD516 . . . . **779**
LOOK INTO SPACE: A SUPPLEMENT TO CHILDCRAFT--THE HOW AND
WHY LIBRARY./1994/P-2/KA378. . . . . **REF 031**
Look! look! look! /HOBAN, T/1988/P-3/KA616 . . . . **152.14**
Look out, it's April Fools' Day. /MODELL, F/1985/K-2/2 KG148 . . . . **E**
Look through the mouse hole. /FISCHER-NAGEL, H/1989/
4-6/6 KC743 . . . . **599.35**
Look up, look down. /HOBAN, T/1992/P-1/KF743 . . . . **E**
LOOK WHAT I GREW: WINDOWSILL GARDENS (Videocassette). /1993/
1-6/KD171. . . . . **VCR 635**
LOOK WHAT I MADE: PAPER, PLAYTHINGS AND GIFTS (Videocassette).
/1993/3-6/KD433. **VCR 745.5**
LOOK WHO'S GROWING UP (Videocassette). /1997/
5-6/KC920. . . . . **VCR 612**
LOOKING AT ART (Videocassette). /1992/4-A/KD365 . . . . . . **VCR 701**
Looking at bears. /PATENT, DH/1994/5-6/6 KC851 . . . . **599.78**
Looking at insects. /SUZUKI, D/1992/4-6/5 KC550 . . . . **595.7**
Looking at penguins. /PATENT, DH/1993/5-6/5 KC689 . . . . . . **598.47**
Looking at picture books. /STEWIG, JW/1995/KA312 . . . **PROF 741.6**
Looking down. /JENKINS, S/1995/K-3/KF827 . . . . **E**
Looking for Juliette. /LISLE, JT/1994/4-6/6 KH412. . . . . **Fic**
Looking for Juliette (Sound recording cassette)./LISLE, JT/1996/
4-6/6 KH412 . . . . **Fic**
Looking for Papito: family stories from Latin America (Sound recording
cassette). /SACRE, A/1996/1-6/KA857 . . . . **SRC 305.8**

LOOKING GOOD, FEELING GOOD (Videocassette). /1994/
5-6/KC951. . . . . **VCR 612.6**
Look-it-up book of presidents. Rev. ed. /BLASSINGAME, W/1996/
4-6/7 KE848 . . . . **973**
Loon magic for kids. /KLEIN, T/c1989, 1991/3-5-5 KC651 . . . . **598**
Loop the loop. /DUGAN, B/1992/1-3/4 KF501 . . . . **E**
Loop the loop (Sound recording cassette)./DUGAN, B/1997/
1-3/4 KF501 . . . . **E**
Lorax. /SEUSS, D/c1971/P-3/3 KG466 . . . . **CE E**
Lorax (Kit)./SEUSS, D/1992/P-3/3 KG466 . . . . **CE E**
Lorax (Sound recording cassette)./SEUSS, D/n.d./P-3/3 KG466 . . . **CE E**
Lorax (Spanish version)./SEUSS, D/1993/P-3/3 KG466 . . . . **CE E**
Lord of the animals: a Miwok Indian creation myth. /FRENCH, F/1997/
K-3/4 KB568 . . . . **398.24**
Los osos Berenstain y demasiada fiesta./BERENSTAIN, S/1993/
K-2/4 KF226 . . . . **E**
Losing Uncle Tim. /JORDAN, M/1989/3-5/4 KH336. . . . . **Fic**
Lost! /MCPHAIL, D/1990/P-1/2 KG119 . . . . **E**
Lost children: the boys who were neglected. /GOBLE, P/1993/
3-5/5 KB707 . . . . **398.26**
Lost cities. /GOLDENSTERN, J/1996/3-6/7 KE624 . . . . **930.1**
LOST CITY OF THE MAYA (Videocassette). /1990/
6-A/KE844. . . . . **VCR 972.81**
Lost garden. /YEP, L/1996/5-A/7 KE604 . . . . **B YEP, L.**
Lost in cyberspace. /PECK, R/1995/5-A/3 KH593 . . . . **Fic**
Lost in cyberspace (Sound recording cassette)./PECK, R/1997/
5-A/3 KH593 . . . . **Fic**
Lost in the barrens. /MOWAT, F/1962/5-6/6 KH518 . . . . **Fic**
Lost in the barrens (Braille)./MOWAT, F/n.d./5-6/6 KH518 . . . . . . **Fic**
Lost lake. /SAY, A/1989/1-3/2 KG398 . . . . **E**
Lost moose. /SLEPIAN, J/1995/K-2/2 KG517 . . . . **E**
Lostman's River. /DEFELICE, CC/1994/4-A/6 KH067. . . . . **Fic**
Lots of dads. /ROTNER, S/1997/P-1/2 KA881 . . . . **306.874**
LOTS OF LIMERICKS. /1991/3-6/KE069 . . . . **811.008**
Lots of moms. /ROTNER, S/1996/P-1/1 KA882 . . . . **306.874**
Lots of rot. /COBB, V/1981/K-3/3 KC302 . . . . **577.1**
Lotta's Christmas surprise. /LINDGREN, A/c1977, 1990/1-2/2 KF985 . . **E**
Lou Gehrig. /MACHT, NL/1993/5-A/7 KE364. . . . . **B GEHRIG, L.**
Louis the fish. /YORINKS, A/1980/K-3/4 KG782. . . . . **E**
Louisiana. /FRADIN, DB/1995/4-6/4 KF000 . . . . **976.3**
Lovable Lyle. /WABER, B/1977/P-2/3 KG672 . . . . **CE E**
Lovable Lyle (Braille)./WABER, B/n.d./P-2/2 KG672 . . . . **CE E**
Love flute. /GOBLE, P/1992/3-5/6 KB738 . . . . **CE 398.27**
Love flute (Kit)./GOBLE, P/1992/3-5/6 KB738 . . . . . . **CE 398.27**
Love flute (Videocassette)./GOBLE, P/1993/3-5/6 KB738 . . **CE 398.27**
Love letters. /ADOFF, A/1997/K-4/KD911 . . . . **811**
Loving. /MORRIS, A/1990/1-3/2 KA880 . . . . **306.874**
Lucie Babbidge's house. /CASSEDY, S/1993/6-A/7 KG987 . . . . . **Fic**
Luckiest kid on the planet. /ERNST, LC/1994/1-3/2 KF532 . . . . . . **E**
Lucky Christmas. /DUFFEY, B/1994/3-5/4 KH086. . . . . **Fic**
Lucky's 24-hour garage. /KIRK, D/1996/K-2/4 KF907 . . . . **E**
LUCY MAUD MONTGOMERY: THREADS FROM THE QUILT
(Videocassette). /1993/6-A/KE470. . . . **VCR B MONTGOMERY, L**
Lucy's Christmas. /HALL, D/1994/1-3/6 KF662 . . . . **E**
Lucy's picture. /MOON, N/1995/P-1/2 KG153 . . . . **E**
Luka's quilt. /GUBACK, G/1994/1-3/2 KF652 . . . . **E**
Lulu and the witch baby. /O'CONNOR, J/1986/K-3/2 KG188 . . . . . . **E**
Lumberjack. /KURELEK, W/1974/4-6/6 KD165 . . . . **634.9**
Lunch. /FLEMING, D/1992/P-K/2 KF557 . . . . **E**
Lunch bunnies. /LASKY, K/1996/K-2/2 KF946 . . . . **E**
Lunchroom tales: a natural history of the cafetorium (Compact disc)./
HARLEY, B/1996/2-4/KD615 . . . . **SRC 789.3**
Lunchroom tales: a natural history of the cafetorium (Sound recording
cassette). /HARLEY, B/1996/2-4/KD615 . . . . **SRC 789.3**
Lungs and breathing. Rev. ed. /PARKER, S/1989/5-6/8 KC934. . . . **612.1**
Lyddie. /PATERSON, K/1991/6-A/7 KH579 . . . . **Fic**
Lyle and the birthday party. /WABER, B/c1966/P-2/3 KG669 . . . . . . **E**
Lyle at the office. /WABER, B/1994/K-2/3 KG670 . . . . **E**
Lyle at the office (Sound recording cassette)./WABER, B/1997/
K-2/3 KG670 . . . . **E**
Lyle finds his mother. /WABER, B/1974/P-2/3 KG671 . . . . **E**
Lyle, Lyle, crocodile. /WABER, B/c1965/P-2/3 KG672 . . . . **CE E**
Lyle, Lyle, crocodile (Kit)./WABER, B/1987/P-2/3 KG672 . . . . . **CE E**
Lyndon B. Johnson, 36th president of the United states. /FALKOF, L/1989/
6-A/9 KE406 . . . . **B JOHNSON, L.**
LYRIC LANGUAGE: A BILINGUAL MUSIC PROGRAM: SPANISH/
ENGLISH (Videocassette). /1992/K-6/KD636 . . . . **VCR 789.3**
Lyrical life science (Multimedia kit). /HORTON, B/1995/
K-A/KA295 . . . . **MMK PROF 570**
Lyrical life science. Vol. 2: mammals, ecology and biomes (Multimedia kit)./
HORTON, B/1996/K-A/KA295 . . . . **MMK PROF 570**
Ma Dear's aprons. /MCKISSACK, P/1997/3-5/4 KH492 . . . . **Fic**
Mac and Marie and the train toss surprise. /HOWARD, EF/1993/
K-2/2 KF774 . . . . **E**

Machines. /ROCKWELL, AF/c1972/K-2/3 KD052 . . . . **621.8**
Machines at work. /BARTON, B/1987/P-K/2 KF207 . . . . **E**
Macmillan animal encyclopedia for children. /FEW, R/1991/
5-6/7 KC446 . . . . **591**
Macmillan book of baseball stories. /EGAN, T/1992/
4-A/5 KD796 . . . . **796.357**
MACMILLAN DICTIONARY FOR CHILDREN. 3rd. rev. ed. /1997/
2-4/KA425 . . . . **REF 423**
MACMILLAN FIRST DICTIONARY. /1990/K-2/KB834 . . . . **423**
Madam C.J. Walker: building a business empire. /COLMAN, P/1994/
4-6/7 KE583 . . . . **B WALKER, C.J.**
MADAM C.J. WALKER (Videocassette). /1992/
5-A/KE584. . . . . **VCR B WALKER, C.J.**
Made in China: ideas and inventions from Ancient China. /WILLIAMS, S/
1996/4-6-6 KE631 . . . . **931**
Madeline. /BEMELMANS, L/1962/P-2/4 KF218. . . . . **CE E**
Madeline and other Bemelmans (Talking book). /BEMELMANS, L/n.d./
P-2/KF219 . . . . **TB E**
Madeline (Big book)./BEMELMANS, L/1993/P-2/4 KF218. . . . . . . **CE E**
Madeline (Braille)./BEMELMANS, L/n.d./P-2/4 KF218 . . . . . . **CE E**
Madeline (Kit)./BEMELMANS, L/1975/P-2/4 KF218 . . . . **CE E**
Madeline (Spanish version)./BEMELMANS, L/1993/P-2/4 KF218 . . **CE E**
Madeline (Spanish version) (Kit)./BEMELMANS, L/1997/
P-2/4 KF218 . . . . **CE E**
Madeline (Videocassette)./BEMELMANS, L/1989/P-2/4 KF218. . . . **CE E**
Madeline's rescue./BEMELMANS, L/c1953/P-2/2 KF220 . . . . . . **CE E**
Madeline's rescue (Braille)./BEMELMANS, L/n.d./P-2/2 KF220 . . . . **CE E**
Madeline's rescue (Kit)./BEMELMANS, L/1978/P-2/2 KF220 . . . . . . **CE E**
Mag the magnificent. /GACKENBACH, D/1985/K-2/2 KF590 . . . . . . **E**
Magazines for children, a guide for parents, teachers, and librarians. /
RICHARDSON, SK/1983//KA022 . . . . **PROF 011.62**
MAGAZINES FOR KIDS AND TEENS: Rev. ed. /1997/
/KA018. . . . . **PROF 011.62**
Maggie and the pirate. /KEATS, EJ/1979/P-2/2 KF875 . . . . **E**
Maggie and the pirate (Braille)./KEATS, EJ/n.d./P-2/2 KF875 . . . . . **E**
Maggie Marmelstein for president./SHARMAT, MW/1975/
4-6/4 KH705 . . . . **Fic**
Magic bike (Sound recording cassette). /GREEN CHILI JAM BAND /1991/
P-3/KD613 . . . . **SRC 789.3**
Magic dreidels: a Hanukkah story. /KIMMEL, EA/1996/K-3/2 KF904 . . . **E**
MAGIC EYE: A NEW WAY OF LOOKING AT THE WORLD. /1993/
3-A/KA620 . . . . **152.14**
MAGIC EYE II: NOW YOU SEE IT..../1994/3-A/KA620 . . . . **152.14**
Magic finger. /DAHL, R/1995/3-5/3 KH055 . . . . **Fic**
Magic gold fish: a Russian folktale. /DEMI /1995/3-5/2 KB284 . . . **398.2**
Magic moonberry jump ropes. /HRU, D/1996/K-2/2 KF783 . . . . . **E**
Magic of Spider Woman. /DUNCAN, L/1996/4-5/6 KB733. . . . . **398.27**
Magic or not? /EAGER, E/c1959, 1985/4-6/6 KH094 . . . . **Fic**
Magic or not? (Sound recording cassette)./EAGER, E/n.d./
4-6/6 KH094 . . . . **Fic**
Magic pencil: teaching children creative writing: exercises and activities for
children, their parents, and their teachers. /SHELNUTT, E/1997/
/KA228 . . . . **PROF 372.6**
Magic porridge pot. /GALDONE, P/c1976/P-2/4 KF596 . . . . **E**
Magic porridge pot (Braille)./GALDONE, P/n.d./P-2/4 KF596 . . . . . . **E**
Magic purse. /UCHIDA, Y/1993/2-4/4 KB379. . . . . **398.2**
Magic School Bus at the waterworks. /COLE, J/1986/
2-3/4 KD079 . . . . **628.1**
Magic School Bus at the waterworks (Big book)./COLE, J/1986/
2-3/4 KD079 . . . . **628.1**
Magic School Bus in the time of the dinosaurs. /COLE, J/1994/
2-4/3 KC245 . . . . **567.9**
Magic School Bus inside a beehive. /COLE, J/1996/2-4/2 KC570 . **595.79**
Magic School Bus inside a hurricane. /COLE, J/1995/
2-4/4 KC197 . . . . **551.55**
Magic School Bus inside the earth. /COLE, J/1987/2-4/3 KC152 . . . **551**
Magic School Bus inside the human body. /COLE, J/1989/
2-5/5 KC916 . . . . **612**
Magic School Bus lost in the solar system. /COLE, J/1990/
2-6/4 KC008 . . . . **523.2**
Magic School Bus on the ocean floor. /COLE, J/1992/
2-4/5 KC495 . . . . **591.77**
Magic skateboard. /RICHEMONT, E/1992/3-5/3 KH631 . . . . . . **Fic**
Magic Squad and the dog of great potential. /QUATTLEBAUM, M/1997/
2-4/4 KH616 . . . . **Fic**
Magic wand and other bright experiments on light and color. /DOHERTY,
P/1995/4-A/5 KC110 . . . . **535**
Magic weaver of rugs: a tale of the Navajo. /OUGHTON, J/1994/
2-4/3 KB627 . . . . **398.24**
Magical hands. /BARKER, M/1989/1-3/5 KF199 . . . . **E**
Magical hands (Sound recording cassette)./BARKER, M/1994/
1-3/5 KF199 . . . . **E**
Magical melons./BRINK, CR/c1939/4-6/6 KG922 . . . . **CE Fic**
Magical melons (Talking book)./BRINK, CR/n.d./4-6/6 KG922 . . . **CE Fic**

MAGICAL MOTHER NATURE: THE FOUR SEASONS (Videocassette). /
1989/2-4/KC061 . . . . **VCR 525**
Magical starfruit tree: a Chinese folktale. /WANG, RC/1993/
2-3/6 KB784 . . . . 398.27
Magical tales from many lands. /MAYO, M/1993/4-5/6 KB343 . . . 398.2
Magician's nephew./LEWIS, CS/1994/5-A/6 KH405 . . . . . . **CE Fic**
Magician's nephew (Braille)./LEWIS, CS/n.d./5-A/6 KH405 . . . . . **CE Fic**
Magician's nephew (Sound recording cassette)./LEWIS, CS/n.d./
5-A/6 KH405 . . . . **CE Fic**
Magician's nephew (Talking book)./LEWIS, CS/n.d./5-A/6 KH405. **CE Fic**
Magician's visit: a Passover tale. /GOLDIN, BD/1993/K-3/5 KF629 . . . . **E**
Magid fasts for Ramadan. /MATTHEWS, M/1996/4-6/4 KH462 . . . . . **Fic**
Mago de Oz./BAUM, LF/1987/4-6/6 KG886 . . . . **CE Fic**
Magpies' nest. /FOSTER, J/1995/1-3/3 KB567 . . . . 398.24
Mahatma Gandhi. /LAZO, C/1993/4-6/7 KE363 . . . **B GANDHI, M.**
Maiden on the moor. /SINGER, M/1995/4-6/3 KB418 . . . . . . 398.21
Maine. /ENGFER, L/1991/4-6/7 KE927 . . . . 974.1
Maine. /FRADIN, DB/1994/4-6/4 KE928 . . . . 974.1
Maisie. /SCHERTLE, A/1995/1-3/4 KG405. . . . . **E**
MAJOR AUTHORS AND ILLUSTRATORS FOR CHILDREN AND YOUNG
ADULTS: A SELECTION OF SKETCHES FROM SOMETHING ABOUT
THE AUTHOR. /1993//KA464. . . . . **REF 809**
Make a friend, be a friend: songs for growing up and growing together
with friends (Sound recording cassette). /HARTMANN, J/1990/
K-5/KD617 . . . . **SRC 789.3**
MAKE A JOYFUL SOUND: POEMS FOR CHILDREN BY AFRICAN-
AMERICAN POETS. /1991/1-6/KE070 . . . . 811.008
Make cards! /SOLGA, K/1992/1-5/5 KD459 . . . . 745.594
Make costumes!: for creative play. /HERSHBERGER, P/1992/
4-6/2 KD300 . . . . 646.4
Make prints! /SOLGA, K/1991/P-6/4 KD504 760
Make room for Elisa./HURWITZ, J/1993/2-4/4 KH303 . . . . . **Fic**
Make way for ducklings. /MCCLOSKEY, R/c1941, 1963/
P-1/4 KG089 . . . . **CE E**
Make way for ducklings (Braille)./MCCLOSKEY, R/n.d./
P-1/4 KG089 . . . . **CE E**
Make way for ducklings (Kit)./MCCLOSKEY, R/1975/P-1/4 KG089. **CE E**
Make way for ducklings (Sound recording cassette)./MCCLOSKEY, R/
1997/P-1/4 KG089 . . . . **CE E**
Make way for ducklings (Talking book)./MCCLOSKEY, R/n.d./
P-1/4 KG089 . . . . **CE E**
Make way for ducklings (Videocassette)./MCCLOSKEY, R/1985/
P-1/4 KG089 . . . . **CE E**
Make way for Sam Houston. /FRITZ, J/1986/
6/7 KE392 . . . . **B HOUSTON, S.**
Make way for Sam Houston (Sound recording cassette)./FRITZ, J/n.d./
6/7 KE392 . . . . **B HOUSTON, S.**
Make your own animated movies and videotapes. /ANDERSEN, Y/1991/
5-A/6 KD515 . . . . 778.5
MAKING AND USING PUPPETS IN THE PRIMARY GRADES
(Videocassette). /1992/K-6/KD446 . . . . **VCR 745.592**
Making books. /CHAPMAN, G/1992/3-6/7 KD412 . . . . 741.6
Making friends with Frankenstein: a book of monstrous poems and pictures.
/MCNAUGHTON, C/1994/K-3/KE107 821
Making light work: the science of optics. /DARLING, DJ/1991/
6-A/8 KC109 535
Making music with children, ages 3-7 (Videocassette). /LANGSTAFF, J/
1995//KA315 . . . . **VCR PROF 780**
Making the team./CARLSON, N/1985/P-2/2 KF351 . . . . **CE E**
Making waves: finding out about rhythmic motion. /ZUBROWSKI, B/1994/
5-A/7 KC081 530
Mala: a women's folktale. /WOLF-SAMPATH, G/1996/
3-5/2 KB718 . . . . 398.26
Malcolm X and black pride. /CWIKLIK, R/1991/
5-6/6 KE455 . . . . **B MALCOLM X**
Malcolm X: by any means necessary: a biography. /MYERS, WD/1993/
6-A/8 KE456 . . . . **B MALCOLM X**
Mama, coming and going. /CASELEY, J/1994/1-3/4 KF366 . . . . . **E**
Mama, do you love me? /JOOSSE, BM/1991/P-1/2 KF854. . . . . . . **E**
Mama don't allow. /HURD, T/1984/K-3/2 KF793 . . . . **CE E**
Mama don't allow (Talking book)./HURD, T/1984/K-3/2 KF793 . . **CE E**
Mama don't allow (Videocassette)./HURD, T/1989/K-3/2 KF793 . . . **CE E**
Mama is a miner. /LYON, GE/1994/2-3/3 KG044. . . . . **E**
MAMA NO QUIERE (Videocassette)./HURD, T/1989/K-3/2 KF793 . **CE E**
Mama One, Mama Two. /MACLACHLAN, P/1982/2-3/1 KG054 . . . . . **E**
Mammal. /PARKER, S/1989/4-6/7 KC725 599
MAMMAL (Videocassette). /1996/5-6/KC723 . . . . **VCR 599**
MAMMALS: A MULTIMEDIA ENCYCLOPEDIA (CD-ROM). /1990/
2-A/KA450 . . . . **CDR REF 599**
Mammolina: a story about Maria Montessori. /O'CONNOR, B/1993/
4-6/6 KE467 . . . . **B MONTESSORI, M**
Man and mustang. /ANCONA, G/1992/5-6/6 KD197 . . . . 636.1
Man from the other side. /ORLEV, U/1991/5-A/6 KH567 . . . . **Fic**

Man from the other side (Sound recording cassette)./ORLEV, U/1995/
5-A/6 KH567 . . . . **Fic**
Man in the ceiling. /FEIFFER, J/1993/5-A/7 KH112 . . . . **Fic**
Man O'War. /FARLEY, W/c1962/5-6/6 KH106. . . . . **Fic**
Man who could call down owls. /BUNTING, E/1984/1-3/2 KF304 . . . . **E**
Man who could call down owls (Sound recording cassette)./BUNTING, E/
n.d./1-3/2 KF304 . . . . **E**
Man who kept his heart in a bucket. /LEVITIN, S/1991/K-2/3 KF970. . . **E**
Man who kept house. /ASBJORNSEN, PC/1992/2-4/6 KB719 . . . 398.27
Man who knew too much: a moral tale from the Baila of Zambia. /LESTER,
J/1994/4-5/3 KB607 . . . . 398.24
Man who loved machines (Videocassette). /GOLDSMITH, S/1983/
3-A/KC127 . . . . **VCR 536**
Man who tricked a ghost. /YEP, L/1993/1-3/4 KB697 . . . . . . 398.25
Manada de lobos: siguiendo las huellas de los lobos en su entorno natural./
JOHNSON, SA/1993/6/10 KC836 . . . . 599.773
Manatee: on location. /DARLING, K/1991/5-6/7 KC779 . . . . 599.55
Manatees. /LEPTHIEN, EU/1991/5-6/7 KC781 . . . . 599.55
MANATEES: RED ALERT (Videocassette). /1996/
5-6/KC782. . . . . **VCR 599.55**
Mandela: from the life of the South African statesman. /COOPER, F/1996/
3-6/7 KE457 . . . . **B MANDELA, N.**
Mandy. /BOOTH, BD/1991/K-2/5 KF250. . . . . **E**
Mangaboom. /POMERANTZ, C/1997/1-3/3 KG264 . . . . **E**
Mangrove wilderness: nature's nursery. /LAVIES, B/1994/
K-3/7 KC341 . . . . 577.68
Manitoba. /EMMOND, K/1992/5-A/8 KE816. . . . . 971.27
Manners. /ALIKI /1990/1-6/2 KB239. 395
Manners can be fun. Rev. ed. /LEAF, M/1985/1-3/4 KB249 . . . . . 395.5
Man-of-war. /BIESTY, S/1993/4-6/7 KA988. . . . . 359.1
Mansion in the mist./BELLAIRS, J/c1992, 1993/6-A/6 KG895 . . . . . . **Fic**
Many luscious lollipops: a book about adjectives. /HELLER, R/1989/
1-3/KB851 . . . . 428.2
Many moons. /THURBER, J/c1943, 1990/3-5/5 KH792. . . . . . **Fic**
Many moons. /THURBER, J/1990/3-5/5 KH793 . . . . **Fic**
Many moons (Sound recording cassette)./THURBER, J/1996/
3-5/5 KH792 . . . . **Fic**
MANY PEOPLE, MANY WAYS: UNDERSTANDING CULTURES AROUND
THE WORLD. /1995/4-A/KA402. . . . . **REF 306**
Many thousand gone: African Americans from slavery to freedom. /
HAMILTON, V/1993/4-6/7 KA927 326
MANY VOICES: TRUE TALES FROM AMERICA'S PAST. /1995/
/KA371. . . . . **PROF 973**
MANY VOICES (Videocassette). /1991/4-6/KA851 . . . . **VCR 305.8**
MAP OF THE UNIVERSE: THE NORTHERN HEMISPHERE (Picture). /1980/
3-A/KC051 . . . . **PIC 523.8**
Mapas y globos terraqueos./KNOWLTON, J/1996/2-5/7 KE169 . . . 912
MAPLES IN THE MIST: CHILDREN'S POEMS FROM THE TANG
DYNASTY. /1996/K-3/KE133 895
Mapmaker's daughter. /HELLDORFER, MC/1991/2-3/3 KF698 . . . . . . **E**
Mapping a changing world. /LA PIERRE, Y/1996/A/12 KC065 526
Maps and globes. /KNOWLTON, J/1985/2-5/7 KE169 912
Maps and mazes: a first guide to mapmaking. /CHAPMAN, G/1993/
K-6/6 KC064 526
Maps: getting from here to there. /WEISS, H/1991/3-6/6 KE173 . . . 912
MARC BROWN'S ARTHUR'S BIRTHDAY. School ed. (CD-ROM). /1994/
K-4/KG062 . . . . **CDR E**
Marc Chagall. /GREENFELD, H/1990/6-A/8 KE284 . . . **B CHAGALL, M.**
Margarete Steiff: toy maker. /GREENE, C/1993/
2-3/2 KE550 . . . . **B STEIFF, M.**
Maria Molina and the Days of the Dead. /KRULL, K/1994/
2-4/4 KF936 . . . . **E**
Maria Montessori: teacher of teachers. /SHEPHARD, MT/1996/
A/9 KE468 . . . . **B MONTESSORI, M**
Maria Montoya Martinez: master potter. /KREISCHER, EK/1995/
5-6/3 KE461 . . . . **B MARTINEZ, M.**
Marie Curie and her daughter Irene. /PFLAUM, R/1993/
6-A/8 KE139 . . . . 539.7
Marie Curie: discoverer of radium. /POYNTER, M/1994/
4-6/4 KE311 . . . . **B CURIE, M.**
Mario Lemieux: beating the odds. /HUGHES, ME/1996/
4-6/9 KE433 . . . . **B LEMIEUX, M.**
Mariquita malhumorada./CARLE, E/1996/P-2/2 KF342 . . . . **E**
Marjory Stoneman Douglas: voice of the Everglades. /BRYANT, J/1992/
4-5/6 KE324 . . . . **B DOUGLAS, M.**
Mark Messier: star center. /SULLIVAN, MJ/1997/
5-A/7 KE464 . . . . **B MESSIER, M.**
MARK SCHLICHTING'S HARRY AND THE HAUNTED HOUSE. School ed.
(CD-ROM). /1994/K-3/KG063 . . . . **CDR E**
Mark Twain: America's humorist, dreamer, prophet. /COX, C/1995/
6-A/8 KE579 . . . . **B TWAIN, M.**
Mark Twain? What kind of name is that?: a story of Samuel Langhorne
Clemens. /QUACKENBUSH, R/1984/6/8 KE580 . . . . . **B TWAIN, M.**
Market! /LEWIN, T/1996/1-3/6 KB128 381

Maroo of the winter caves. /TURNBULL, A/c1984, 1990/
5-6/6 KH811 .... **Fic**
Marriage of the rain goddess: a South African myth. /WOLFSON, M/
1996/4-5/5 KB424 .... **398.21**
Marrying Malcolm Murgatroyd. /FARRELL, M/1995/5-A/4 KH111 . . . **Fic**
Mars. /SIMON, S/1987/4-A/8 KC035 .... **523.43**
MARSH: NATURE'S NURSERY (Videocassette). /1988/
2-4/KC343. .... **VCR 577.68**
Martha blah blah. /MEDDAUGH, S/1996/K-2/2 KG124. .... **E**
Martin Luther King. /BRAY, RL/1995/2-6/7 KE421 .... **B KING, M.L.**
MARTIN LUTHER KING: I HAVE A DREAM (Videocassette). /1986/
4-A/KA907 .... **VCR 323.4**
Martin Manley's basketball heaven. /MANLEY, M/1987-/
4-A/KD778 .... **796.323**
Marushka and the Month Brothers: a folktale. /VOJTECH, A/1996/
1-3/4 KB513 .... **398.23**
Marvelous land of Oz (Talking book). /BAUM, LF/1993/
4-6/6 KG886 .... **CE Fic**
MARVELOUS MATH: A BOOK OF POEMS. /1997/1-4/KE071 . **811.008**
Mary Ann. /JAMES, B/1994/K-2/3 KF823 .... **E**
Mary Cassatt. /MEYER, SE/1990/6-A/8 KE283. ...... **B CASSATT, M.**
Mary Church Terrell: leader for equality. /MCKISSACK, P/1991/
3-6/2 KE562 .... **B TERRELL, M.**
Mary Marony hides out. /KLINE, S/1993/1-3/4 KH369. .... **Fic**
Mary McLeod Bethune. /MCKISSACK, P/1992/
4-6/5 KE254 .... **B BETHUNE, M.**
Mary of Mile 18. /BLADES, A/1971/1-3/3 KF233 .... **CE E**
Mary of Mile 18 (Sound recording cassette). /BLADES, A/n.d./
1-3/3 KF233 .... **CE E**
Mary Poppins comes back. /TRAVERS, PL/1987/4-6/6 KH800. ...... **Fic**
Mary Poppins in Cherry Tree Lane. /TRAVERS, PL/1982/4-6/6 KH800 . **Fic**
Mary Poppins in Cherry Tree Lane (Braille). /TRAVERS, PL/n.d./
4-6/6 KH800 .... **Fic**
Mary Poppins opens the door (Braille). /TRAVERS, PL/n.d./
4-6/6 KH800 .... **Fic**
Mary Poppins. Rev. ed. /TRAVERS, PL/c1962/4-6/6 KH800. ...... **Fic**
Mary Poppins. Rev. ed. (Braille). /TRAVERS, PL/n.d./4-6/6 KH800. ... **Fic**
Mary Poppins. Rev. ed. (Sound recording cassette). /TRAVERS, PL/n.d./
4-6/6 KH800 .... **Fic**
Mary Poppins (Talking book). /TRAVERS, PL/n.d./4-6/KH801 ... **TB Fic**
Mary: the mother of Jesus. /DE PAOLA, T/1995/3-6/5 KA699. . . **232.91**
Maryland. /FRADIN, DB/1994/4-6/3 KE969. .... **975.2**
Masai and I. /KROLL, VL/1992/K-2/4 KF934 .... **Fic**
Masks. /HATRICK, G/1996/6-A/3 KH225 .... **Fic**
Master puppeteer. /PATERSON, K/c1975/6-A/6 KH580. .... **Fic**
Master puppeteer (Sound recording cassette). /PATERSON, K/n.d./
6-A/6 KH580 .... **Fic**
Math curse. /SCIESZKA, J/1995/2-5/3 KG420 .... **E**
Math curse (Sound recording cassette). /SCIESZKA, J/1997/
2-5/3 KG420 .... **E**
Math for smarty pants. /BURNS, M/1982/4-6/5 KB946 .... **513**
MATH FOR THE VERY YOUNG: A HANDBOOK OF ACTIVITIES FOR
PARENTS AND TEACHERS. /1995/KA254. .... **PROF 372.7**
Math fun with a pocket calculator. /WYLER, R/1992/
4-A/4 KD713 .... **793.7**
Math fun with tricky lines and shapes. /WYLER, R/1992/
4-A/5 KD714 .... **793.7**
Math mini-mysteries. /MARKLE, S/1993/3-6/7 KB928 .... **510**
MATH, MONEY, AND YOU (Sound filmstrip). /1989/
K-2/KB967 .... **FSS 513.2**
Math readiness--vocabulary and concepts (Sound recording cassette). /
PALMER, H/1-3/KB931 .... **SRC 510**
MathArts: exploring math through art for 3 to 6 year olds. /KOHL, MA/
1996/KA253 .... **PROF 372.7**
Mathemagic. /BLUM, R/1997/5-A/KD711 .... **793.7**
Matilda. /DAHL, R/1988/5-A/7 KH056 .... **Fic**
Matilda (Sound recording cassette). /DAHL, R/n.d./5-A/7 KH056. .... **Fic**
Matilda (Spanish version). /DAHL, R/1995/5-A/7 KH056 .... **Fic**
Matter. /COOPER, C/1992/4-A/9 KC078 .... **530**
Matthew and the midnight pilot. /MORGAN, A/1997/1-2/3 KG156 . . . **E**
MATTHEW HENSON (Videocassette). /1994/
5-A/KE388. .... **VCR B HENSON, M.**
Matthew the cowboy. /HOOKER, R/1990/K-2/2 KF767 .... **E**
Matzah that Papa brought home. /MANUSHKIN, F/1995/
1-3/2 KG059 .... **E**
Maui and the Sun: a Maori tale. /BISHOP, G/1996/
3-4/3 KB700 .... **398.26**
Maurice Sendak Library (Videocassette). /SENDAK, M/1992/
P-2/KG433 .... **VCR E**
MAVIS BEACON TEACHES TYPING! (Microcomputer program). /1987/
4-A/KD310 .... **MCP 652.3**
Max and Maggie in autumn. /PALAZZO-CRAIG, J/1994/K-1/1 KG208 . **E**
Max and Maggie in spring. /PALAZZO-CRAIG, J/1995/K-1/1 KG208 . . **E**
Max and Maggie in summer. /PALAZZO-CRAIG, J/1994/K-1/1 KG208 . **E**

Max and Maggie in winter. /PALAZZO-CRAIG, J/1995/K-1/1 KG208 . . **E**
Max and Ruby's first Greek myth: Pandora's box. /WELLS, R/1993/
P-1/3 KG700 .... **E**
Max and Ruby's Midas: another Greek myth. /WELLS, R/1995/
P-1/3 KG701 .... **E**
MAXFIELD PARRISH: A TREASURY OF ART AND CHILDREN'S
LITERATURE. /1995/K-6/KD413. .... **741.6**
Maxi, the hero. /BARRACCA, D/1991/P-2/2 KF200 .... **CE E**
Maxi, the star. /BARRACCA, D/1993/P-2/2 KF201 .... **CE E**
Max's chocolate chicken. /WELLS, R/1989/P-2/2 KG702 .... **CE E**
Max's chocolate chicken (Videocassette). /WELLS, R/1991/
P-2/2 KG702 .... **CE E**
Max's Christmas. /WELLS, R/1986/P-1/2 KG703. .... **CE E**
Max's Christmas (Videocassette). /WELLS, R/n.d./P-1/2 KG703. .... **CE E**
Max's first word (Board book). /WELLS, R/1979/P/1 KG704 ..... **BB E**
Max's new suit. /WELLS, R/1979/P/1 KG704 .... **BB E**
Max's ride. /WELLS, R/1979/P/1 KG704 .... **BB E**
May Chinn: the best medicine. /BUTTS, ER/1995/
5-A/8 KE288 .... **B CHINN, M.**
Maya. /GREENE, JD/1992/4-6/7 KE843 .... **972.81**
Maya Angelou: journey of the heart. /PETTIT, J/1996/
4-6/8 KE237 .... **B ANGELOU, M.**
Maya Lin. /LING, B/1997/4-6/10 KE437. .... **B LIN, M.**
MAYAQUEST TRAIL (CD-ROM). /1996/5-A/KE845. .... **CDR 972.81**
Maybe I will do something. /UDE, W/1993/4-5/6 KB669 .... **398.24**
Maybelle the cable car. /BURTON, VL/1997/K-2/3 KF321 .... **E**
May'naise sandwiches and sunshine tea. /BELTON, S/1994/
1-3/3 KF217 .... **E**
Mazel and Shlimazel; or, The milk of a lioness. /SINGER, IB/1967/
4-6/6 KB779 .... **398.27**
M.C. Higgins, the great. /HAMILTON, V/1974/A/4 KH216 ...... **Fic**
M.C. Higgins, the great (Braille). /HAMILTON, V/n.d./A/4 KH216 .... **Fic**
M.C. Turtle and the Hip Hop Hare: a nursery rap. /VOZAR, D/1997/
2-3/2 KG665 .... **E**
McBroom's wonderful one-acre farm: three tall tales. /FLEISCHMAN, S/
1992/3-6/4 KH124 .... **Fic**
McDuff comes home. /WELLS, R/1997/K-2/2 KG705 .... **E**
McDuff moves in. /WELLS, R/1997/K-2/2 KG706 .... **E**
McElligot's pool. /SEUSS, D/c1947/P-3/KG467 .... **E**
McElligot's pool (Braille). /SEUSS, D/n.d./P-3/KG467 .... **E**
McElligot's pool (Videocassette). /SEUSS, D/1985/1-3/KG450 ... **VCR E**
McElmeel booknotes: literature across the curriculum. /MCELMEEL, SL/
1993/KA225 .... **PROF 372.6**
McMummy. /BYARS, BC/1993/5-A/5 KG961 .... **Fic**
Me and Neesie. /GREENFIELD, E/c1975/K-2/3 KF642 .... **E**
Me on the map. /SWEENEY, J/1996/K-1/1 KE172 .... **912**
Me two. /RYAN, MC/1993/5-A/6 KH658 .... **Fic**
Measuring up!: experiments, puzzles, and games exploring measurement. /
MARKLE, S/1995/5-6/6 KC086. .... **530.8**
Meat-eating plants. /AASENG, N/1996/5-8/6 KC425 .... **583**
MEDIA REVIEW DIGEST. /1970-/KA124 .... **PER PROF 050**
Medieval castle. /MACDONALD, F/1990/4-6/8 KE649. .... **940.1**
Medieval cathedral. /MACDONALD, F/1991/6-A/9 KD390 ...... **726**
Medieval feast. /ALIKI /1983/2-5/5 KB183. .... **CE 394.1**
Mediopollito/Half-Chicken. /ADA, AF/1995/K-2/2 KB521 ...... **398.24**
MEET ASHLEY BRYAN: STORYTELLER, ARTIST, WRITER (Videocassette). /
1992/4-6/KE266. .... **VCR B BRYAN, A.**
Meet Danitra Brown. /GRIMES, N/1994/2-4/KD949 .... **811**
MEET JACK PRELUTSKY (Videocassette). /1992/
3-6/KE503. .... **VCR B PRELUTSKY, J.**
Meet Posy Bates. /CRESSWELL, H/1992/3-5/5 KH038 .... **Fic**
MEET THE AUTHOR: HENRY WADSWORTH LONGFELLOW
(Videocassette). /1992/4-5/KE446. ...... **VCR B LONGFELLOW, H**
MEET THE AUTHOR: ROBERT LOUIS STEVENSON (Videocassette). /
1989/5-6/KE555. .... **VCR B STEVENSON, R.**
MEET THE NEWBERY AUTHOR: RUSSELL FREEDMAN (Videocassette). /
1991/5-A/KE356. .... **VCR B FREEDMAN, R.**
Meeting death. /HYDE, MO/1989/A/7 KA891 .... **306.9**
MEETING THE CHALLENGE: PARENTING CHILDREN WITH DISABILITIES
(Videocassette). /1992/KA306. .... **VCR PROF 649.8**
Melanie. /CARRICK, C/1996/1-3/2 KF360 .... **E**
MELA'S LUNCH (Videocassette). /1991/4-6/KA854. ...... **VCR 305.8**
Mel's Diner. /MOSS, M/1994/K-2/2 KG158 .... **E**
Mem Fox reads (Talking book). /FOX, M/1992/P-2/KF570 ..... **TB E**
Memoirs of Andrew Sherburne: patriot and privateer of the American
Revolution. /SHERBURNE, A/1993/5-A/8 KE886 .... **973.3**
Mennyms. /WAUGH, S/1994/5-A/7 KH843 .... **Fic**
Mennyms alone. /WAUGH, S/1996/5-A/5 KH844. .... **Fic**
Mennyms in the wilderness. /WAUGH, S/1995/5-A/5 KH845. .... **Fic**
Mennyms under siege. /WAUGH, S/1996/6-A/6 KH846. .... **Fic**
MENTAL COMPUTATION: USING MENTAL COMPUTATION FOR
MULTIPLICATION (Videocassette). /1987/4-5/KD949. .... **VCR 513**
MERCER MAYER'S LITTLE MONSTER AT SCHOOL. School ed. (CD-
ROM). /1994/K-3/KG130 .... **CDR E**

Mercury. /SIMON, S/1992/3-6/7 KC032. . . . . 523.41
MERMAID TALES FROM AROUND THE WORLD. /1993/ 3-5/5 KB405 . . . . 398.21
Mermaid's twin sister: more stories from Trinidad. /JOSEPH, L/1994/ 3-4/5 KB323 . . . . 398.2
Merry Christmas, Amelia Bedelia./PARISH, P/1987/1-3/2 KG214 . . CE E
Merry Christmas, Amelia Bedelia (Kit)./PARISH, P/1987/ 1-3/2 KG214 . . . . CE E
Merry Christmas, Old Armadillo. /BRIMNER, LD/1995/K-2/3 KF267 . . . E
Merry Christmas, Strega Nona. /DE PAOLA, T/1986/K-3/5 KF473 . . . . E
Merry Christmas, Strega Nona (Talking book). /DE PAOLA, T/1991/ K-3/KF474 . . . . TB E
Messages in the mailbox: how to write a letter. /LEEDY, L/1991/ 2-5/2 KB246 . . . . 395.4
Messipes: a microwave cookbook of deliciously messy masterpieces. / GORDON, L/1996/3-6/KD271 . . . . 641.5
METEORITES (Picture). /1991/4-A/KC042 . . . . PIC 523.5
METER (Videocassette). /1994/K-2/KD522 . . . . VCR 780
MEXICAN FOLK ART (Videocassette). /1992/5-A/KD421 . . . . VCR 745
Mexican Revolution. /FROST, MP/1997/5-A/11 KE830. 972
MEXICAN WAR OF INDEPENDENCE. /1997/5-A/11 KE835 972
MEXICO: A CHANGING LAND. 3rd ed. (Videocassette). /1996/ 6-A/KE836. . . . . VCR 972
Mexico and the United States: cooperation and conflict. /PASCOE, E/ 1996/6-A/11 KA805 . . . . 303.48
Mexico. Rev. ed. /IRIZARRY, C/1994/A/11 KE831 972
Mexico: rich in spirit and tradition. /KENT, D/1996/3-5/7 KE832 . . . 972
Mi casa es su casa/my house is your house: a bi-lingual musical journey through Latin America (Sound recording cassette). /VALERI, M/1991/ K-3/KD663 . . . . SRC 789.3
Mi libro de palabras Inglesas de todos los dias. /KAHN, M/1982/ 1-3/KB843. 428
Mi primer libro de palabras en Espanol./WILKES, A/1993/ P-2/KB839. 423
Mice squeak, we speak: a poem. /SHAPIRO, A/1997/P-1/3 KE022. . 811
Mice twice. /LOW, J/1980/P-2/2 KG036. E
Michael Dorris. /WEIL, A/1997/6-A/7 KE323 . . . . B DORRIS, M.
Michael Foreman's Mother Goose. /MOTHER GOOSE /1991/ P-1/KB804. . . . . 398.8
Michael Jordan: a life above the rim. /LIPSYTE, R/1994/ 4-6/7 KE411 . . . . B JORDAN, M.
Michael Jordan: basketball to baseball and back. Rev. ed. /GUTMAN, B/ 1995/4-6/8 KE410 . . . . B JORDAN, M.
Michael Rosen's ABC. /ROSEN, M/1996/2-4/KE109 821
Michelangelo. /DI CAGNO, G/1996/6-A/12 KD378 . . . . 709.2
Michigan. /SIRVAITIS, K/1994/4-6/7 KF017. . . . . 977.4
Mick Harte was here. /PARK, B/1995/4-6/4 KH570. . . . . Fic
MicroAliens: dazzling journeys with an electron microscope. /TOMB, H/ 1993/3-A/7 KC376. 579
MICROORGANISMS: THE INVISIBLE WORLD (Videocassette). /1995/ 4-8/KC373. . . . . VCR 579
MICROSOFT BOOKSHELF: MULTIMEDIA REFERENCE LIBRARY, 1998 ed. School ed. (CD-ROM). /1997/3-A/KA376. . . . . CDR REF 028.7
Microsoft composer collection (CD-ROM). /WINTER, R/1994/ 4-A/KD525 . . . . CDR 780
MICROSOFT CREATIVE WRITER 2. School ed. (CD-ROM). /1996/ 2-A/KB114. . . . . CDR 372.6
MICROSOFT DANGEROUS CREATURES: EXPLORE THE ENDANGERED WORLD OF WILDLIFE. Academic ed. (CD-ROM). /1994/ 4-A/KC490 . . . . CDR 591.68
MICROSOFT DINOSAURS: EXPLORE THE INCREDIBLE WORLD OF PREHISTORIC CREATURES. Academic ed. (CD-ROM). /1994/ 2-A/KC256 . . . . CDR 567.9
MICROSOFT ENCARTA 97 ENCYCLOPEDIA. Deluxe school ed. (CD-ROM). /1996/4-A/KA384 . . . . CDR REF 031
MICROSOFT ENCARTA 97 WORLD ATLAS (CD-ROM). /1996/ 3-A/KA472 . . . . CDR REF 912
MICROSOFT EXPLORAPEDIA: THE WORLD OF NATURE. Academic ed. (CD-ROM). /1995/1-4/KB909. CDR 508
MICROSOFT EXPLORAPEDIA: THE WORLD OF PEOPLE. Academic ed. (CD-ROM). /1994/1-4/KA892 . . . . CDR 307
Middle Ages. /CASELLI, G/1988/5-A/7 KE144 . . . . 909.07
MIDDLE AND JUNIOR HIGH SCHOOL LIBRARY CATALOG. 7th ed. / 1995//KA019 . . . . PROF 011.62
MIDDLE ATLANTIC REGION: NEW YORK, NEW JERSEY, DELAWARE, MARYLAND, PENNSYLVANIA, DISTRICT OF COLUMBIA (Videocassette). /1996/4-6/KE924 . . . . VCR 974
Middleplots 4: a book talk guide for use with readers ages 8-12. / GILLESPIE, JT/1994//KA092. PROF 028.5
Midnight horse. /FLEISCHMAN, S/1990/5-A/4 KH125 . . . . Fic
Midnight Rider. /RUEPP, K/1995/3-5/2 KH657 . . . . Fic
Midwife's apprentice. /CUSHMAN, K/1995/6-A/5 KH051 . . . . . . CE Fic
Midwife's apprentice (Talking book)./CUSHMAN, K/1996/ 6-A/5 KH051 . . . . CE Fic
Mighty Mountain and the three strong women. /HEDLUND, I/1990/ 3-5/5 KB316 . . . . 398.2
Mighty Movers. /LEVITT, S/1994/K-2/2 KF971 . . . . E
Migrant family. /BRIMNER, LD/1992/4-6/6 KA834 . . . . 305.5
Mike and Tony: best friends. /ZIEFERT, H/1987/K-2/1 KG794 . . . . E
Mike Fink. /KELLOGG, S/1992/3-4/5 KB456 . . . . 398.22
Mike Mulligan and his steam shovel. /BURTON, VL/c1939/ P-2/6 KF322 . . . . CE E
Mike Mulligan and his steam shovel (Braille)./BURTON, VL/n.d./ P-2/6 KF322 . . . . CE E
Mike Mulligan and his steam shovel (Sound recording cassette)./BURTON, VL/n.d./P-2/6 KF322. . . . . CE E
Mike Mulligan and his steam shovel (Talking book)./BURTON, VL/n.d./ P-2/6 KF322 . . . . CE E
Mike Mulligan and his steam shovel (Videocassette)./BURTON, VL/1985/ P-2/6 KF322 . . . . CE E
Mike Piazza: hard-hitting catcher. /SAVAGE, J/1997/ 4-6/7 KE495 . . . . B PIAZZA, M.
Milestones in science and technology: the ready reference guide to discoveries, inventions, and facts. 2nd ed. /MOUNT, E/1994/ 5-A/KA441 . . . . REF 509
Military badges and insignia. /LLOYD, M/1995/4-8/12 KA984. . . . 355.1
Milk. /CARRICK, D/1985/K-3/4 KD237 637
Milk from cow to carton. Rev. ed. /ALIKI /1992/1-3/2 KD236 637
Milk makers. /GIBBONS, G/1985/K-3/6 KD239 637
Milk makers (Braille)./GIBBONS, G/n.d./K-3/6 KD239 637
Mill. /MACAULAY, D/1983/A/9 KD336 677
Mill (Sound recording cassette)./MACAULAY, D/n.d./A/9 KD336 . . . 677
Millie Cooper and friends. /HERMAN, C/1995/3-4/7 KH247 . . . . Fic
MILLIE'S MATH HOUSE (CD-ROM). /1995/P-2/KB971. . . . . CDR 513.2
MILLIE'S MATH HOUSE (Microcomputer program). /1992/ P-2/KB972. . . . . MCP 513.2
Million fish...more or less. /MCKISSACK, P/c1992, 1996/1-3/4 KG106 . E
Million-Dollar Bear. /KOTZWINKLE, W/1995/2-3/2 KF916 . . . . E
Millions of cats. /GAG, W/c1928/P-1/6 KF592. . . . . CE E
Millions of cats (Braille)./GAG, W/n.d./P-1/6 KF592 . . . . CE E
Millions of cats (Videocassette)./GAG, W/1985/P-1/6 KF592 . . . . CE E
Milly and Tilly: the story of a town mouse and a country mouse. / SUMMERS, K/1997/K-2/2 KB661 . . . . 398.24
Milton, my father's dog. /COPELAND, E/1994/1-3/3 KF424 . . . . E
Mind your manners! /PARISH, P/1-3/KB250 . . . . 395.5
MINDING YOUR MANNERS AT SCHOOL (Videocassette). /1996/ 3-5/KB241. . . . . VCR 395
MIND'S EYE: JEAN LITTLE (Videocassette). /1996/ 5-6/KE445. . . . . VCR B LITTLE, J.
MINDS-ON SCIENCE: FOR PROFIT, FOR PLANET (Videodisc). /1995/ 5-A/KD348 . . . . VD 687
MINDS-ON SCIENCE: FOR THE SAKE OF THE NATION (Videodisc). / 1995/5-A/KA804 . . . . VD 303.48
MINDS-ON SCIENCE: THE IMPACT OF DISCOVERY (Videodisc). /1995/ 5-A/KB875. . . . . VD 502
Mine for keeps. /LITTLE, J/c1962, 1994/5-A/5 KH414 . . . . Fic
Mine will, said John. New ed. /GRIFFITH, HV/1992/P-2/2 KF649 . . . . . E
Miners, merchants, and maids. /HILTON, S/1995/4-6/8 KF033. 978
Minerva Louise at school. /STOEKE, JM/1996/P-1/2 KG577 . . . . E
Mine's the best. Newly illustrated ed. /BONSALL, CN/1996/ 1-2/1 KF245 . . . . E
Ming Lo moves the mountain. /LOBEL, A/1982/K-2/1 KG006. . . . . CE E
Ming Lo moves the mountain (Braille)./LOBEL, A/n.d./K-2/1 KG006. CE E
Ming Lo moves the mountain (Videocassette)./LOBEL, A/1993/ K-2/1 KG006 . . . . CE E
Minn of the Mississippi. /HOLLING, HC/c1951/5-6/6 KC619 . . . . 597.92
Minn of the Mississippi (Braille)./HOLLING, HC/n.d./ 5-6/6 KC619 . . . . 597.92
Minnesota. /FRADIN, DB/1994/4-6/3 KF021 . . . . 977.6
Minnie. /SCHMIDT, AM/1994/5-A/3 KH680 . . . . Fic
Minstrel and the dragon pup. /SUTCLIFF, R/c1993, 1996/ 3-6/7 KH775 . . . . Fic
Mira como salen las estrellas./LEVINSON, R/1992/K-2/2 KF969. . . . . . E
Miracle meals, eight nights of food 'n fun for Chanukah. /WIKLER, M/ 1987/4-5/KD288 . . . . 641.59
Miracles of Jesus. /DE PAOLA, T/1987/5-6/7 KA695. . . . . 232.9
Miraculous makeover of Lizard Flanagan. /GORMAN, C/c1994, 1996/ 5-A/3 KH182 . . . . Fic
Mirandy and Brother Wind. /MCKISSACK, P/1988/1-3/6 KG107 . . CE E
Mirette on the high wire. /MCCULLY, EA/1992/1-3/2 KG093 . . . . E
Mirette on the high wire (Sound recording cassette)./MCCULLY, EA/1994/ 1-3/2 KG093 . . . . E
Miro in the Kingdom of the Sun. /KURTZ, J/1996/3-4/5 KB505 . . 398.23
Mirror magic. /SIMON, S/1991/3-5/6 KC114 535
Mirrors: finding out about the properties of light. /ZUBROWSKI, B/1992/ 5-6/8 KC116 535
Mis cinco sentidos./MILLER, M/1995/P-1/2 KC969. . . . . 612.8
Mis cinco sentidos. Ed. rev./ALIKI /1995/K-2/2 KC962 . . . . 612.8

Misery guts. /GLEITZMAN, M/1993/5-A/7 KH174 . . . . **Fic**
Miss Bindergarten gets ready for kindergarten. /SLATE, J/1996/
P-K/2 KG515 . . . . **E**
Miss Butterpat goes wild! /YORKE, M/1993/3-5/5 KH898 . . . . **Fic**
Miss Hickory. /BAILEY, CS/c1946/4-6/4 KG875 . . . . **CE Fic**
Miss Hickory (Sound recording cassette)./BAILEY, CS/n.d./
4-6/4 KG875 . . . . **CE Fic**
Miss Hickory (Talking book)./BAILEY, CS/1972/4-6/4 KG875 . . . **CE Fic**
MISS MARY MACK AND OTHER CHILDREN'S STREET RHYMES. /1990/
2-5/KD766 . . . . **796.1**
Miss Nelson has a field day./ALLARD, H/1985/1-3/3 KF151 . . . . . **CE E**
Miss Nelson is back./ALLARD, H/1982/1-3/3 KF151 . . . . **CE E**
Miss Nelson is missing./ALLARD, H/1977/1-3/3 KF151 . . . . . **CE E**
Miss Nelson is missing (Braille)./ALLARD, H/n.d./1-3/3 KF151 . . . **CE E**
Miss Nelson is missing (Kit)./ALLARD, H/1987/1-3/3 KF151 . . . **CE E**
Miss Rumphius. /COONEY, B/1982/K-3/5 KF419 . . . . **E**
Miss Rumphius (Kit). /COONEY, B/1994/K-3/KF420 . . . . **KIT E**
Missing May. /RYLANT, C/1992/5-A/7 KH663 . . . . **Fic**
Missing May (Sound recording cassette)./RYLANT, C/1994/
5-A/7 KH663 . . . . **Fic**
Mission: addition. /LEEDY, L/1997/K-3/2 KB964 . . . . **513.2**
Mission: Earth: voyage to the home planet. /ENGLISH, JA/1996/
4-A/8 KC145 . . . . **550**
Mission to deep space: Voyagers' journey of discovery. /BURROWS, WE/
1993/4-8/11 KC024 . . . . **523.4**
Missions of the central coast. /BEHRENS, J/1996/4-6/9 KF076 . . . **979.4**
Missions of the inland valleys. /BROWER, P/1997/4-6/9 KF077 . . . **979.4**
Missions of the Los Angeles Area. /MACMILLAN, D/1996/
4-6/9 KF084 . . . . **979.4**
Missions of the Monterey Bay Area. /ABBINK, E/1996/
4-6/9 KF075 . . . . **979.4**
Missions of the San Francisco Bay Area. /WHITE, TN/1996/
4-6/9 KF087 . . . . **979.4**
Missions of the Southern Coast. /LEMKE, N/1996/4-6/9 KF083 . . . **979.4**
Mississippi bridge. /TAYLOR, MD/1990/5-A/4 KH778 . . . . **Fic**
Mississippi chariot. /ROBINET, HG/1994/5-A/5 KH639. . . . . **Fic**
Missouri. /FRADIN, DB/1994/4-6/4 KF023 . . . . **977.8**
Mist over the mountains: Appalachia and its people. /BIAL, R/1997/
4-6/9 KE923 . . . . **974**
Mister Fred. /PINKWATER, J/1994/5-A/4 KH606 . . . . **Fic**
Misty of Chincoteague. /HENRY, M/c1947/3-5/4 KH244 . . . . . **CE Fic**
Misty of Chincoteague (Braille)./HENRY, M/n.d./3-5/4 KH244 . . . **CE Fic**
Misty of Chincoteague (Sound recording cassette)./HENRY, M/n.d./
3-5/4 KH244 . . . . **CE Fic**
Misty of Chincoteague (Videocassette)./HENRY, M/1988/
3-5/4 KH244 . . . . **CE Fic**
Mitchell is moving. /SHARMAT, MW/1978/K-3/1 KG483 . . . . **E**
Mitten. /BRETT, J/1989/K-2/3 KB534 . . . . **398.24**
MODEL AIRPLANE NEWS. /1929-/4-A/KA525 . . . . **PER 050**
MODEL RAILROADER. /1934-/4-A/KA526 . . . . **PER 050**
Modeling dinosaurs. /SANCHEZ SANCHEZ, I/1996/
3-6/3 KD448 . . . . **745.592**
Modern Olympics. /TAMES, R/1996/3-6/8 KD822 . . . . **796.48**
Moffat museum. /ESTES, E/1983/3-5/3 KH103 . . . . **Fic**
Moffat museum (Braille)./ESTES, E/n.d./3-5/3 KH103 . . . . **Fic**
Moffat museum (Sound recording cassette)./ESTES, E/n.d./
3-5/3 KH103 . . . . **Fic**
Moffats. /ESTES, E/c1941/3-5/3 KH103 . . . . **Fic**
Moffats (Braille)./ESTES, E/n.d./3-5/3 KH103 . . . . **Fic**
Moffats (Sound recording cassette)./ESTES, E/n.d./3-5/3 KH103 . . . **Fic**
Moffats (Talking book)./ESTES, E/n.d./3-5/3 KH103 . . . . **Fic**
Mogul and me. /CUMMING, P/1989/5-A/7 KH046 . . . . **Fic**
Mola: Cuna life stories and art. /PRESILLA, ME/1996/
3-5/7 KA832 . . . . **305.48**
Moles and the Mireuk: a Korean folktale. /KWON, HH/1993/
K-2/4 KB605 . . . . **398.24**
Mole's hill: a woodland tale. /EHLERT, L/1994/K-2/3 KB562 . . . . **398.24**
Molly Limbo. /HODGES, M/1996/K-3/3 KB688 . . . . **398.25**
Molly Maguire: wide receiver. /SULLIVAN, A/1992/4-6/3 KH773 . . . **Fic**
Molly y los peregrinos./COHEN, B/1995/1-3/4 KH012 . . . . **CE Fic**
Molly's pilgrim. /COHEN, B/1983/1-3/4 KH012 . . . . **CE Fic**
Molly's pilgrim (Braille)./COHEN, B/n.d./1-3/4 KH012 . . . . . . **CE Fic**
Molly's pilgrim (Sound recording cassette)./COHEN, B/n.d./
1-3/4 KH012 . . . . **CE Fic**
Molly's pilgrim (Videocassette)./COHEN, B/1985/1-3/4 KH012. . . **CE Fic**
Mommy, buy me a china doll. /ZEMACH, H/1966/P-1/1 KG788 . . . . . **E**
Mommy's office. /HAZEN, BS/1992/P-2/2 KF688 . . . . **E**
Mom's best friend. /ALEXANDER, SH/1992/2-4/3 KB003 . . . . **362.4**
Mon premier livre de mots en Francais./WILKES, A/1993/P-2/KB839. **423**
Monarch butterflies: mysterious travelers. /LAVIES, B/1992/
5-6/7 KC562 . . . . **595.78**
Monarch butterfly. /GIBBONS, G/1989/K-2/4 KC560 . . . . **595.78**
Monday's troll: poems. /PRELUTSKY, J/1996/K-4/KE008 . . . . . . **CE 811**

Monday's troll: poems (Talking book)./PRELUTSKY, J/1996/
K-4/KE008 . . . . **CE 811**
Moneda de oro./ADA, AF/n.d./1-3/4 KF131 . . . . **E**
Monerans and protists. /SILVERSTEIN, A/1996/A/11 KC374 . . . . . **579**
Money. /CRIBB, J/1990/4-6/8 KA949 . . . . **332.4**
Money, money, money: the meaning of the art and symbols on United
States paper currency. /PARKER, NW/1995/3-6/11 KD506 . . . **769.5**
Mongolia: vanishing cultures. /REYNOLDS, J/1994/4-6/7 KE704. . . **951.7**
Monica Seles: returning champion. /FEHR, KS/1997/
4-6/10 KE533 . . . . **B SELES, M.**
Monkey and the crab. /KANI, S/1985/3/3 KB598 . . . . **398.24**
Monkey island. /FOX, P/1991/6-A/6 KH137 . . . . **Fic**
Monkey island (Sound recording cassette)./FOX, P/1993/
6-A/6 KH137 . . . . **Fic**
Monkey's haircut and other stories told by the Maya. /BIERHORST, J/
1986/3-4/4 KB531 . . . . **398.24**
Monster den: or look what happened at my house - and to it. /CIARDI, J/
c1966, 1991/3-6/KD922 . . . . **811**
Monster factory. /RAINEY, R/1993/3-6/8 KD895 . . . . **809.3**
Monster in the third dresser drawer and other stories about Adam Joshua.
/SMITH, JL/1981/2-4/4 KH725 . . . . **Fic**
Monster in the third dresser drawer and other stories about Adam Joshua
(Braille)./SMITH, JL/n.d./2-4/4 KH725 . . . . **Fic**
Monster in the third dresser drawer and other stories about Adam Joshua
(Sound recording cassette)./SMITH, JL/n.d./2-4/4 KH725 . . . . . . **Fic**
Monster mama. /ROSENBERG, L/1993/K-2/4 KG354 . . . . **E**
Monster mama (Videocassette). /ROSENBERG, L/1996/
K-2/KG355 . . . . **VCR E**
Monster money book. /LEEDY, L/1992/1-3/2 KF957 . . . . **E**
Monster Motel: poems and paintings. /FLORIAN, D/1993/
4-6/KD938 . . . . **811**
MONSTER SOUP AND OTHER SPOOKY POEMS. /1992/
K-3/KD986 . . . . **811**
Monsters and extraterrestrials. /SANCHEZ SANCHEZ, I/1996/
3-6/3 KD449 . . . . **745.592**
Monsters in the attic. /REGAN, DC/1995/4-6/6 KH625 . . . . **Fic**
Montana. /HEINRICHS, A/1991/5-6/8 KF058 . . . . **978.6**
Montana (Sound recording cassette)./HEINRICHS, A/1993/
5-6/8 KF058 . . . . **978.6**
Montgomery bus boycott. Rev. ed. /STEIN, RC/1993/
5-6/6 KE998 . . . . **976.1**
Monticello. /REEF, C/1991/3-5/6 KE892 . . . . **973.4**
Moominland midwinter./JANSSON, T/c1958, 1992/3-6/7 KH325 . . . **Fic**
Moominland midwinter (Sound recording cassette)./JANSSON, T/1997/
3-6/7 KH325 . . . . **Fic**
Moominpappa at sea./JANSSON, T/1993/3-6/7 KH325. . . . . **Fic**
Moominpappa at sea (Sound recording cassette)./JANSSON, T/1997/
3-6/7 KH325 . . . . **Fic**
Moominpappa's memoirs./JANSSON, T/1994/3-6/7 KH325 . . . . **Fic**
Moominpappa's memoirs (Sound recording cassette)./JANSSON, T/1997/
3-6/7 KH325 . . . . **Fic**
Moominsummer madness./JANSSON, T/c1954, 1991/3-6/7 KH325 . . **Fic**
Moon. /SIMON, S/1984/K-4/4 KC021 . . . . **523.3**
Moon and Otter and Frog. /SIMMS, L/1995/2-4/2 KB715 . . . . . **398.26**
Moon and you. /KRUPP, EC/1993/4-6/4 KC020 . . . . **523.3**
Moon book. /GIBBONS, G/1997/K-6/4 KC019 . . . . **523.3**
Moon for seasons. /TURNER, A/1994/3-6/KE034 . . . . **811**
Moon of the gray wolves. New ed. /GEORGE, JC/1991/
5-6/6 KC835 . . . . **599.773**
Moon princess. /MCCARTHY, RF/1993/3-4/4 KB404 . . . . **398.21**
Moon rope: a Peruvian folktale/Un lazo a la luna: una leyenda Peruana. /
EHLERT, L/1992/1-3/2 KB563 . . . . **398.24**
Moon was the best. /ZOLOTOW, C/1993/K-2/5 KG803 . . . . **E**
MOON/OUTER SPACE (Videocassette). /1994/3-6/KC007 . . . **VCR 523**
Moonbear's pet. /ASCH, F/1997/P-K/2 KF175 . . . . **E**
Moongame. /ASCH, F/1987/P-1/2 KF174. . . . . **CE E**
Moongame (Big book). /ASCH, F/1992/P-1/2 KF174 . . . . **CE E**
Moonlight. /ORMEROD, J/1982/P-1/KG195 . . . . **E**
Moonseed and mistletoe: a book of poisonous wild plants. /LERNER, C/
1988/4-A/8 KC403 . . . . **581.6**
Moony B. Finch, the fastest draw in the West. /MCPHAIL, D/1994/
1-3/4 KG120 . . . . **E**
Moorchild. /MCGRAW, EJ/1996/5-A/6 KH475. . . . . **Fic**
Moose. /PETERSEN, D/1994/3-6/6 KC580 . . . . **599.65**
Moose and friends. /LATIMER, J/1993/1-3/2 KF947 . . . . **E**
Moray eels. /ROTHAUS, D/1996/4-6/8 KC586 . . . . **597**
More all-of-a-kind family./TAYLOR, S/1954/4-6/5 KH782 . . . . . . **Fic**
More all-of-a-kind family (Braille)./TAYLOR, S/n.d./4-6/5 KH782 . . **Fic**
More all-of-a-kind family (Talking book)./TAYLOR, S/n.d./
4-6/5 KH782 . . . . **Fic**
More creative connections: literature and the reading program, grades 4-6.
/OLSEN, ML/1993//KA212 . . . . **PROF 372.4**
More errata: another book of historical errors. /ROLAND-ENTWISTLE, T/
1995/3-6/10 KE143 . . . . **909**

MORE JUNIOR AUTHORS./1972/A/KA462 . . . . **REF 809**

More juniorplots: a guide for teachers and librarians./GILLESPIE, JT/1977/ /KA091. . . . . **PROF 028.5**

More more more, said the baby. /WILLIAMS, VB/1990/P-K/2 KG736 . . **E**

More mudpies: 101 alternatives to television./BLAKEY, N/1994/ A/KD424. . . . . **745.5**

More perfect union: the story of our constitution. /MAESTRO, B/1987/ 4-6/8 KA974 . . . . **342.73**

MORE PRESCHOOL POWER! (Videocassette)./1991/ P-K/KD263. . . . . **VCR 640.83**

More scary stories to tell in the dark./SCHWARTZ, A/c1986/ 4-A/3 KB694 . . . . **CE 398.25**

More science experiments you can eat. /COBB, V/1979/ A/7 KB890 . . . . **507.8**

More stories Huey tells. /CAMERON, A/1997/2-4/2 KG968 . . . . **Fic**

More stories Julian tells./CAMERON, A/1989/3-4/4 KG970 . . . . **Fic**

More stories Julian tells (Braille)./CAMERON, A/n.d./-3-4/4 KG970 . . . **Fic**

More stories to solve: fifteen folktales from around the world./SHANNON, G/1991/5-6/6 KB714 . . . . **398.26**

More story stretchers: more activities to expand children's favorite books./ RAINES, SC/1991//KA240. **PROF 372.64**

More tales of Amanda Pig./VAN LEEUWEN, J/c1985, 1988/ K-2/1 KG648 . . . . **CE E**

More tales of Uncle Remus./LESTER, J/1987/4-5/5 KB608 . . . . . . **398.24**

More than anything else. /BRADBY, M/1995/1-3/3 KF256 . . . . **E**

More than just a flower garden. /KUHN, D/1990/4-5/6 KD175 . . . **635.9**

More than just a vegetable garden. /KUHN, D/1990/4-5/5 KD170 . . **635**

Morning Girl. /DORRIS, M/1992/6-A/7 KH080 . . . . **Fic**

Morning Girl (Sound recording cassette)./DORRIS, M/1995/ 6-A/7 KH080 . . . . **Fic**

Morning glories. /JOHNSON, SA/1985/4-6/7 KC428 . . . . **583**

Morning has broken. /FARJEON, E/1996/P-2/KD611 . . . . **789.3**

Morning, noon and nighttime tales (Sound recording cassette). /GORDH, B/1993/K-2/KD565. . . . . **SRC 789.2**

Morris and Boris. /WISEMAN, B/c1974, 1991/K-2/1 KG748. . . . . . . **E**

Morris and Boris at the circus./WISEMAN, B/1988/K-2/1 KG748 . . . . . **E**

Morris and Boris (Braille). /WISEMAN, B/n.d./K-2/1 KG748 . . . . . **E**

Morris goes to school. /WISEMAN, B/1970/K-2/2 KG749 . . . . **E**

Morris has a cold. /WISEMAN, B/c1978, 1997/K-2/1 KG748. . . . . . . **E**

Morris the Moose. /WISEMAN, B/1989/K-2/2 KG750 . . . . **CE E**

Morris the Moose (Kit)./WISEMAN, B/1996/K-2/2 KG750 . . . . . . **CE E**

Moses. /FISHER, LE/1995/3-4/3 KA677 . . . . **221.9**

Moses in the bulrushes./HUTTON, W/1986/P-2/6 KA679. . . . . . . **221.9**

Mosses. /JOHNSON, SA/1983/6/8 KC438 . . . . **588**

Most rugged all-terrain vehicles. /SMITH, JH/1995/5-6/6 KD830 . . **796.7**

Most wonderful movie in the world. /FORD, B/1996/6-A/4 KH132 . . . **Fic**

Mother and daughter tales. /EVETTS-SECKER, J/1996/ 3-4/6 KB292 . . . . **398.2**

Mother Jones and the march of the mill children. /COLMAN, P/1994/ 4-6/7 KA935 . . . . **331.3**

Mother Teresa: helping the poor. /JACOBS, WJ/1991/ 4-6/6 KE561 . . . . **B TERESA,MOTHER**

MOTHER TONGUE (Videocassette)./1991/4-6/KA851 . . . . . **VCR 305.8**

Mother's Day mice. /BUNTING, E/1986/P-2/2 KF305 . . . . **CE E**

Mother's Day mice (Braille)./BUNTING, E/n.d./P-2/2 KF305 . . . . . **CE E**

Mother's Day mice (Kit)./BUNTING, E/1989/P-2/2 KF305 . . . . . **CE E**

Motocross cycles. /CARSER, SX/1992/4-A/5 KD828 . . . . **796.7**

Mounds of earth and shell: the Southeast. /SHEMIE, B/1993/ 4-6/7 KB172 . . . . **392.3**

MOUNT VERNON: HOME OF GEORGE WASHINGTON (Videocassette). /1989/4-6/KE980. . . . . **VCR 975.5**

Mountain goats. /STAUB, FJ/1994/3-5/2 KC793 . . . . **599.64**

Mountain gorilla. /KIM, M/1993/4-5/8 KC875 . . . . **599.884**

MOUNTAIN GORILLAS: GENTLE GIANTS (Videocassette). /1993/ 4-6/KC876. . . . . **VCR 599.884**

Mountain Jack tales. /HALEY, GE/1992/4-6/6 KB449. . . . . **398.22**

Mountain light./YEP, L/c1985, 1997/6-A/6 KH894 . . . . **Fic**

Mountain lions. /GOUCK, M/1993/3-5/5 KC829 . . . . **599.757**

Mountains. /SIMON, S/1994/4-6/7 KC168 . . . . **551.4**

Mouse and the motorcycle. /CLEARY, B/1965/3-5/5 KG997 . . . . **CE Fic**

Mouse and the motorcycle (Braille)./CLEARY, B/n.d./ 3-5/5 KG997 . . . . **CE Fic**

Mouse and the motorcycle (Sound recording cassette)./CLEARY, B/n.d./ 3-5/5 KG997 . . . . **CE Fic**

Mouse and the motorcycle (Talking book)./CLEARY, B/1995/ 3-5/5 KG997 . . . . **CE Fic**

Mouse and the motorcycle (Talking book)./CLEARY, B/n.d./ 3-5/5 KG997 . . . . **CE Fic**

Mouse bride. /COWLEY, J/1995/P-2/2 KB552 . . . . **398.24**

Mouse called Wolf. /KING-SMITH, D/1997/3-5/3 KH351 . . . . **Fic**

Mouse chase. /SATHRE, V/1995/P-1/2 KG394 . . . . **E**

Mouse paint. /WALSH, ES/1989/P-1/2 KG680 . . . . **E**

Mouse soup. /LOBEL, A/c1977/K-2/1 KG007 . . . . **CE E**

Mouse soup (Braille)./LOBEL, A/n.d./K-2/1 KG007 . . . . **CE E**

Mouse soup (Kit)./LOBEL, A/1986/K-2/1 KG007 . . . . **CE E**

Mouse soup (Sound recording cassette)./LOBEL, A/n.d./ K-2/1 KG007 . . . . **CE E**

MOUSE SOUP (Videocassette). /1992/K-2/KG161 . . . . **VCR E**

Mouse tales. /LOBEL, A/c1972/K-2/2 KG008 . . . . **CE E**

Mouse tales (Kit)./LOBEL, A/1985/K-2/2 KG008 . . . . **CE E**

Mouse TV. /NOVAK, M/1994/K-2/3 KG180 . . . . **E**

Mouse views: what the class pet saw. /MCMILLAN, B/1993/ K-3/1 KG111 . . . . **E**

Mousehole cat. /BARBER, A/1990/4-6/6 KG879 . . . . **Fic**

Movie magic. /CROSS, R/1995/4-6/8 KD683 . . . . **791.43**

Moving day. /KALAN, R/1996/P-1/1 KF865 . . . . **E**

Moving heavy things. /ADKINS, J/1980/A/7 KC088 . . . . **531**

Moving Mama to town. /YOUNG, RT/1997/6-A/4 KH900 . . . . **Fic**

Moving within the circle: contemporary Native American music and dance. / BURTON, B/1993//KA316 . . . . **BA PROF 789.2**

Moving withing the circle: contemporary Native American music and dance./BURTON, B/1993//KA316 . . . . **BA PROF 789.2**

Mr. and Mrs. Pig's evening out. /RAYNER, M/c1976/K-2/4 KG317 . . . **E**

Mr. and Mrs. Pig's evening out (Braille)./RAYNER, M/n.d./ K-2/4 KG317 . . . . **E**

Mr. Carey's garden. /CUTLER, J/1996/K-2/3 KF442 . . . . **E**

Mr. Griggs' work. /RYLANT, C/c1989, 1993/P-2/6 KG376 . . . . **E**

Mr. Gumpy's motor car. /BURNINGHAM, J/c1973, 1976/ P-2/2 KF317 . . . . **CE E**

Mr. Gumpy's motor car (Braille)./BURNINGHAM, J/n.d./ P-2/2 KF317 . . . . **CE E**

Mr. Gumpy's outing. /BURNINGHAM, J/c1970/P-2/2 KF318. . . . . **CE E**

Mr. Gumpy's outing (Big book)./BURNINGHAM, J/1995/ P-2/2 KF318 . . . . **CE E**

Mr. Gumpy's outing (Talking book)./BURNINGHAM, J/n.d./ P-2/2 KF318 . . . . **CE E**

Mr. Lincoln's drummer. /WISLER, GC/1995/5-A/4 KH871 . . . . **Fic**

MR. MARFIL'S LAST WILL AND TESTAMENT (Videocassette). /1991/ 5-A/KB973. . . . . **VCR 513.2**

Mr. Mysterious and Company. /FLEISCHMAN, S/c1962, 1997/ 3-6/6 KH126 . . . . **Fic**

Mr. Pak buys a story. /FARLEY, CJ/1997/K-3/2 KB734 . . . . **398.27**

Mr. Popper's penguins /ATWATER, R/c1938/3-5/4 KG854 . . . . . **CE Fic**

Mr. Popper's penguins (Sound recording cassette)./ATWATER, R/n.d./ 3-5/4 KG854 . . . . **CE Fic**

Mr. Popper's penguins (Talking book)./ATWATER, R/1975/ 3-5/4 KG854 . . . . **CE Fic**

Mr. Popper's penguins (Talking book)./ATWATER, R/n.d./ 3-5/4 KG854 . . . . **CE Fic**

Mr. Potter's pet. /KING-SMITH, D/1996/3-5/2 KH352 . . . . **Fic**

Mr. Putter and Tabby bake the cake. /RYLANT, C/1994/1-3/2 KG377 . **E**

Mr. Putter and Tabby bake the cake (Sound recording cassette)./RYLANT, C/1997/1-3/2 KG377 . . . . **E**

Mr. Putter and Tabby fly the plane. /RYLANT, C/1997/K-2/2 KG378 . . **E**

Mr. Putter and Tabby pick the pears. /RYLANT, C/1995/1-3/2 KG379 . **E**

Mr. Putter and Tabby pour the tea. /RYLANT, C/1994/1-3/2 KG380 . . **E**

Mr. Putter and Tabby row the boat. /RYLANT, C/1997/K-2/2 KG381 . . **E**

Mr. Putter and Tabby walk the dog. /RYLANT, C/1994/1-3/2 KG382 . . **E**

Mr. Rabbit and the lovely present. /ZOLOTOW, C/c1962/ P-2/2 KG804 . . . . **CE E**

Mr. Rabbit and the lovely present (Braille)./ZOLOTOW, C/n.d./ P-2/2 KG804 . . . . **CE E**

Mr. Rabbit and the lovely present (Kit)./ZOLOTOW, C/1987/ P-2/2 KG804 . . . . **CE E**

Mr. Revere and I: being an account of certain episodes in the career of Paul Revere, Esq., as recently revealed by his horse, Scheherazada, late pride of His Royal Majesty's 14th Regiment of Foot. /LAWSON, R/ c1953/5-6/7 KH389 . . . . **Fic**

Mr. Revere and I: (Braille)./LAWSON, R/n.d./5-6/7 KH389 . . . . **Fic**

Mr. Revere and I: (Talking Book)./LAWSON, R/n.d./5-6/7 KH389 . . . **Fic**

Mr. Tucket. /PAULSEN, G/1994/5-A/5 KH588 . . . . **Fic**

Mrs. Brice's mice. /HOFF, S/1988/K-2/2 KF759 . . . . **E**

Mrs. Frisby and the rats of NIMH. /O'BRIEN, RC/c1971/ 4-A/6 KH556 . . . . **Fic**

Mrs. Frisby and the rats of NIMH (Braille)./O'BRIEN, RC/n.d./ 4-A/6 KH556 . . . . **Fic**

Mrs. Frisby and the rats of NIMH (Sound recording cassette)./O'BRIEN, RC/n.d./4-A/6 KH556 . . . . **Fic**

Mrs. Frisby and the rats of NIMH (Talking book)./O'BRIEN, RC/n.d./ 4-A/6 KH556 . . . . **Fic**

Mrs. Katz and Tush. /POLACCO, P/1992/1-3/2 KG253 . . . . **E**

Mrs. Katz and Tush (Sound recording cassette)./POLACCO, P/1994/ 1-3/2 KG253 . . . . **E**

Mrs. Pig's bulk buy./RAYNER, M/1981/K-2/4 KG317 . . . . **E**

Mrs. Rose's garden. /GREENSTEIN, E/1996/K-2/3 KF643 . . . . **E**

Much ado about Aldo./HURWITZ, J/c1978, 1989/4-6/6 KH296 . . . . **Fic**

Much bigger than Martin. /KELLOGG, S/c1976/K-2/2 KF891 . . . . **E**

Muchas palabras sobre animales./1987/P-3/KC457 . . . . **CE 591**

Muchas palabras sobre mi casa./1987/P-3/KD296 . . . . **645**
Mud. /RAY, ML/1996/P-2/2 KG316. . . . . **E**
Mud Flat mystery. /STEVENSON, J/1997/1-3/2 KG561 . . . . **E**
Mud Flat Olympics. /STEVENSON, J/1994/1-3/2 KG562 . . . . **E**
Mud Flat Olympics (Sound recording cassette)./STEVENSON, J/1997/ 1-3/2 KG562 . . . . **E**
Mud makes me dance in the spring. /AGELL, C/1994/K-2/2 KF139 . . . . **E**
Mudluscious: stories and activities featuring food for preschool children. / IRVING, J/1986//KA201 . . . . **PROF 372.3**
Mudpies activity book: recipes for invention. /BLAKEY, N/c1989, 1993/ A/KD424. . . . . **745.5**
Mufaro's beautiful daughters: an African tale. /STEPTOE, J/1987/ K-3/5 KG552 . . . . **CE E**
Mufaro's beautiful daughters: an African tale (Videocassette)./STEPTOE, J/ 1988/K-3/5 KG552. . . . . **CE E**
Muggie Maggie. /CLEARY, B/1990/3-5/5 KG998 . . . . **Fic**
Muhammad Ali. /MACHT, NL/1994/4-6/6 KE233 . . . . **B ALI, M.**
Multicultural children's songs (Compact disc). /JENKINS, E/1995/ K-2/KD629 . . . . **CD 789.3**
Multicultural children's songs (Sound recording cassette)./JENKINS, E/ 1995/K-2/KD629 . . . . **CD 789.3**
Multicultural cookbook for students. /ALBYN, CL/1993/ /KA299. . . . . **PROF 641.59**
Multicultural explorations: joyous journeys with books. /HELTSHE, MA/ 1991//KA262 . . . . **PROF 372.89**
Multicultural game book: more than 70 traditional games from 30 countries. /ORLANDO, L/1993//KA323 . . . . **PROF 790.1**
Multicultural math classroom: bringing in the world. /ZASLAVSKY, C/1996/ /KA259. . . . . **PROF 372.7**
MULTICULTURAL REVIEW: DEDICATED TO A BETTER UNDERSTANDING OF ETHNIC, RACIAL, AND RELIGIOUS DIVERSITY. /1992-/ /KA125. . . . . **PER PROF 050**
Multicultural rhythm stick fun (Compact disc)./STEWART, G/1992/ P-2/KD768. . . . . **SRC 796.1**
Multicultural rhythm stick fun (Sound recording cassette). /STEWART, G/ 1992/P-2/KD768 . . . . **SRC 796.1**
MULTIMEDIA, THE COMPLETE GUIDE. /1996/A/KA372 . . . . **REF 006.7**
MULTIMEDIA WORKSHOP BILINGUAL. Teacher ed. (CD-ROM)./1996/ 3-A/KB115. . . . . **CDR 372.6**
MULTIMEDIA WORKSHOP. Teacher ed. (CD-ROM). /1996/ 3-A/KB115. . . . . **CDR 372.6**
Mummies and their mysteries. /WILCOX, C/1993/5-6/6 KB177 . . . . . **393**
Mummies, dinosaurs, moon rocks: how we know how old things are. / JESPERSEN, J/1996/4-6/9 KE625 . . . . **930.1**
Mummies made in Egypt. /ALIKI /1979/4-6/6 KB173 . . . . **393**
Mummies, tombs, and treasure: secrets of ancient Egypt. /PERL, L/1987/ 5-A/8 KE636 . . . . **932**
Mummy. /PUTNAM, J/1993/4-6/8 KB176 . . . . **393**
Muscles and bones. /SAUNDERSON, J/1992/5-6/5 KC959. . . . . . . **612.7**
MUSE. /1997-/4-6/KA527 . . . . **PER 050**
Mush, a dog from space. /PINKWATER, DM/1995/3-6/4 KH604 . . . . **Fic**
Mushroom. /WATTS, B/1986/K-2/2 KC382 . . . . **579.6**
Mushroom in the rain. /GINSBURG, M/c1974, 1987/P-2/2 KF623 . . . . **E**
Mushy! the complete book of Valentine words. /GRAHAM-BARBER, L/ 1991/5-6/8 KB209 . . . . **394.261**
Music. /MEDEARIS, AS/1997/4-6/11 KD521 . . . . **780**
Music and song. /WOODYARD, S/1995/3-6/7 KD526. . . . . **780**
MUSIC EDUCATORS JOURNAL. /1934-//KA126 . . . . . **PER PROF 050**
Music, music for everyone. /WILLIAMS, VB/1984/P-3/4 KG737 . . . . . . **E**
Music, music for everyone (Sound recording cassette)./WILLIAMS, VB/n.d./ P-3/4 KG737 . . . . **E**
Music of dolphins. /HESSE, K/1996/5-A/3 KH252 . . . . **Fic**
Musica para todo el mundo!/WILLIAMS, VB/1995/P-3/4 KG737 . . . . . **E**
Mustang Flats. /WISLER, GC/1997/5-A/6 KH872 . . . . **Fic**
Mustang, wild spirit of the West. /HENRY, M/c1966, 1992/ 5-6/5 KH245 . . . . **Fic**
Mustang, wild spirit of the West (Braille)./HENRY, M/n.d./ 5-6/5 KH245 . . . . **Fic**
Mustang, wild spirit of the West (Sound recording cassette)./HENRY, M/ n.d./5-6/5 KH245 . . . . **Fic**
Mutzmag: an Appalachian folktale (Videocassette)/DAVENPORT, T/1993/ 5-A/KB281. . . . . **CE 398.2**
My bike. /JAKOB, D/1994/K-2/3 KF821 . . . . **E**
MY BODY. /1991/1-4/2 KC922 . . . . **612**
MY BODY BELONGS TO ME (Videocassette). /1992/ K-3/KA170 . . . . **VCR PROF 362.7**
MY BODY, MY BUDDY: HEALTHY FOOD (Videocassette). /1993/ 3-5/KC986. . . . . **VCR 613.2**
MY BODY, MY BUDDY: HEALTHY FUN (Videocassette). /1993/ 3-5/KC988. . . . . **VCR 613.7**
MY BODY, MY BUDDY: HEALTHY HABITS (Videocassette). /1993/ 2-4/KD301. . . . . **VCR 646.7**
My brother, Ant. /BYARS, BC/1996/K-2/1 KF327 . . . . **E**
My brother, my sister, and I. /WATKINS, YK/1994/A/4 KH841 . . . . . **Fic**
My brother, my sister, and I (Sound recording cassette)./WATKINS, YK/ 1996/A/4 KH841 . . . . **Fic**
My brother Sam is dead. /COLLIER, JL/1974/5-6/5 KH016 . . . . **Fic**
My Buddy. /OSOFSKY, A/1992/K-2/2 KG201 . . . . **E**
My cat Jack. /CASEY, P/1996/P-1/2 KF372. . . . . **E**
My cats Nick and Nora. /HARPER, I/1995/P-1/2 KF673 . . . . **E**
My dad. /DALY, N/1995/1-4/5 KF447 . . . . **E**
My dad takes care of me. /QUINLAN, P/1987/1-3/2 KG295 . . . . **E**
My dentist. /ROCKWELL, H/1975/P-1/2 KD037 . . . . **617.6**
My dentist (Braille)./ROCKWELL, H/n.d./P-1/2 KD037 . . . . **617.6**
My dog Rosie. /HARPER, I/1994/P-1/1 KF674 . . . . **E**
My dream of Martin Luther King. /RINGGOLD, F/1995/ 3-5/7 KE423 . . . . **B KING, M.L.**
My everyday Spanish word book. /KAHN, M/1982/1-3/KB861 . . . . **468**
MY FAMILY, YOUR FAMILY (Videocassette). /1994/ K-2/KA871 . . . . **VCR 306.85**
My father's dragon. /GANNETT, RS/c1948, 1986/3-5/6 KH149 . . . . **Fic**
My father's dragon (Braille)./GANNETT, RS/n.d./3-5/6 KH149 . . . . . **Fic**
My father's dragon (Sound recording cassette)./GANNETT, RS/n.d./ 3-5/6 KH149 . . . . **Fic**
My father's dragon (Talking book)./GANNETT, RS/n.d./ 3-5/6 KH149 . . . . **Fic**
My father's hands. /RYDER, J/1994/K-2/KG366 . . . . **E**
My feet. /ALIKI /1990/P-2/2 KC910. . . . . **612**
My fellow Americans: a family album. /PROVENSEN, A/1995/ 3-6/9 KE862 . . . . **973**
MY FIRST AMAZING WORDS AND PICTURES (CD-ROM). /1994/ K-3/KA426 . . . . **CDR REF 423**
MY FIRST AMAZING WORLD EXPLORER (CD-ROM). /1996/ 1-3/KE170. . . . . **CDR 912**
My first atlas. /BOYLE, B/1994/K-3/5 KE167 . . . . **912**
My first book of how things are made: crayons, jeans, peanut butter, guitars, and more. /JONES, G/1995/K-5/7 KD328 . . . . **670**
My first book of nature: how living things grow. /KUHN, D/1993/ P-2/4 KC276 . . . . **571.8**
My first book of sign. /BAKER, PJ/c1986, 1995/K-3/KB821. . . . . . . **419**
My first book of time. /LLEWELLYN, C/1992/K-3/2 KC072 . . . . **529**
My first Christmas activity book. /WILKES, A/1994/3-6/KD460 . **745.594**
My first dictionary. /ROOT, B/1993/P-2/KB835. . . . . **423**
My first Kwanzaa book. /CHOCOLATE, DM/1992/ 2-4/2 KB206 . . . . **394.261**
My first music book. /DREW, H/1993/2-4/2 KD543. . . . . **784.192**
My first paint book. /SIRETT, D/1994/3-6/7 KD436. . . . . **745.5**
My first photography book. /KING, D/1994/3-6/3 KD513 . . . . **771**
MY FIRST SENTENCES (Microcomputer program). /1987/ 1-3/KB116. . . . . **MCP 372.6**
My first word book. /WILKES, A/1991/P-2/KB839 . . . . **423**
My five senses. /MILLER, M/1994/P-1/2 KC969 . . . . **612.8**
My five senses. Rev. ed. /ALIKI /1989/K-2/2 KC962 . . . . **612.8**
My friend Harry. /LEWIS, K/1995/P-1/2 KF976 . . . . **E**
My grandmother's treasure (Sound recording cassette). /TORRENCE, J/ 1993/3-5/KH799 . . . . **SRC Fic**
My grandpa and the sea. /ORR, K/1990/K-2/2 KG198 . . . . **E**
My grandson Lew. /ZOLOTOW, C/c1974/K-2/2 KG805. . . . . **E**
My great-aunt Arizona. /HOUSTON, G/1992/ 3-5/4 KE393 . . . . **B HUGHES, A.**
My hands. Rev. ed. /ALIKI /1990/P-2/2 KC911. . . . . **612**
My hen is dancing. /WALLACE, K/c1994, 1996/K-2/2 KD215 . . . . **636.5**
My house: a book in two languages/Mi Casa: un libro en dos lenguas. / EMBERLEY, R/1990/K-2/KB858 . . . . **463**
My life among the aliens. /GAUTHIER, G/1996/4-6/5 KH154 . . . . . . **Fic**
My love for you. /ROTH, SL/1997/P-1/2 KG356 . . . . **E**
My mama needs me. /WALTER, MP/1983/P-2/1 KG685. . . . . **E**
My mama says there aren't any zombies, ghosts, vampires, creatures, demons, monsters, fiends, goblins, or things. /VIORST, J/1973/ P-3/4 KG663 . . . . **E**
My many colored days. /SEUSS, D/1996/K-2/2 KG468 . . . . **E**
My map book. /FANELLI, S/1995/K-2/KF543 . . . . **E**
My Mexico--Mexico mio. /JOHNSTON, T/1996/K-3/KD958 . . . . **811**
My mysterious world. /MAHY, M/1995/2-4/6 KE454. . . . **B MAHY, M.**
My name in books: a guide to character names in children's literature. / TUTEN-PUCKETT, KE/1993//KA360 . . . . **PROF 809**
My new kitten. /COLE, J/1995/P-1/2 KD230 . . . . **636.8**
My new sandbox. /JAKOB, D/1996/P-1/1 KF822 . . . . **E**
My New York. /JAKOBSEN, K/1993/2-5/3 KE957 . . . . **974.7**
My ol' man. /POLACCO, P/1995/1-3/3 KG254 . . . . **E**
My painted house, my friendly chicken, and me. /ANGELOU, M/1994/ 1-3/2 KE739 . . . . **968**
My parents think I'm sleeping. /PRELUTSKY, J/1985/2-5/KE009 . . . . **811**
My place. /WHEATLEY, N/1992/5-6/3 KF118 . . . . **994**
My prairie Christmas. /HARVEY, B/1990/2-4/4 KH222 . . . . **Fic**
My puppy is born. Rev. and expanded ed. /COLE, J/1991/ P-2/2 KD218 . . . . **636.7**

My rotten redheaded older brother. /POLACCO, P/1994/
1-3/3 KG255 . . . . **E**

My rotten redheaded older brother (Sound recording cassette)./POLACCO,
P/1997/1-3/3 KG255 . . . . **E**

My side of the mountain. /GEORGE, JC/c1959/5-6/6 KH159 . . . **Fic**

My side of the mountain (Braille). /GEORGE, JC/n.d./5-6/6 KH159 . . . **Fic**

My side of the mountain (Sound recording cassette). /GEORGE, JC/n.d./
5-6/6 KH159 . . . . **Fic**

MY SONG IS BEAUTIFUL: POEMS AND PICTURES IN MANY VOICES. /
1994/1-4/KD887 . . . . **808.81**

My stars, it's Mrs. Gaddy!: the three Mrs. Gaddy stories. /GAGE, W/
1991/1-3/2 KF593 . . . . **E**

My steps. /DERBY, S/1996/P-1/2 KF482 . . . . **E**

My two worlds. /GORDON, G/1993/3-6/4 KA844 . . . . **305.8**

MY VERY FIRST MOTHER GOOSE. /1996/P-K/2 KB808 . . . . **398.8**

My very own Halloween: a book of cooking and crafts. /WEST, R/1993/
3-6/5 KD701 . . . . **793.2**

My visit to the aquarium. /ALIKI /1993/2-4/5 KC582 . . . . . . **597**

My visit to the dinosaurs. Rev. ed. /ALIKI /c1969, 1985/
2-4/4 KC242 . . . . **CE 567.9**

My visit to the dinosaurs. Rev. ed. (Big book)./ALIKI /1994/
2-4/4 KC242 . . . . **CE 567.9**

My visit to the dinosaurs. Rev. ed. (Kit)./ALIKI /1985/
2-4/4 KC242 . . . . **CE 567.9**

My wartime summers. /CUTLER, J/1994/5-A/4 KH052 . . . . **Fic**

Mysterious mind powers. /GREEN, CR/1993/4-6/3 KA609 . . . . . **133.8**

Mysterious tales of Japan. /MARTIN, R/1996/3-5/3 KB690 . . . . . **398.25**

Mysterious valentine./CARLSON, N/1985/P-2/2 KF351 . . . . . . **CE E**

Mysterious valentine (Kit)./CARLSON, N/1987/P-2/2 KF351 . . . . **CE E**

Mysteriously yours, Maggie Marmelstein (Sound recording cassette)./
SHARMAT, MW/n.d./4-6/4 KH705 . . . . **Fic**

Mystery of Drear House./HAMILTON, V/1987/4-6/5 KH215 . . . . **CE Fic**

Mystery of the cupboard. /REID BANKS, L/1993/5-A/6 KH628 . . **CE Fic**

Mystery of the cupboard (Talking book)./REID BANKS, L/1993/
5-A/6 KH628 . . . . **CE Fic**

Mystery of the missing red mitten. /KELLOGG, S/1974/P-2/2 KF892 . . . **E**

Mystery of the several sevens. /BRITTAIN, B/1994/2-4/4 KG924 . . . . **Fic**

Mystery of the stolen blue paint. /KELLOGG, S/1982/P-1/2 KF893 . . . . **E**

Mystery of the Tooth Gremlin. /GRAVES, BB/1997/1-3/2 KH191 . . . . **Fic**

Mythology of Mexico and Central America./BIERHORST, J/1990/
5-A/KA392 . . . . **REF 291.1**

Mythology of North America. /BIERHORST, J/1985/
5-A/KA392 . . . . **REF 291.1**

Mythology of South America./BIERHORST, J/1988/
5-A/KA392 . . . . **REF 291.1**

Nabulela: a South Africa folk tale. /MOODIE, F/1997/
2-4/4 KB758 . . . . **398.27**

Naftali the storyteller and his horse, Sus. /SINGER, IB/1987/
5-6/5 KH712 . . . . **Fic**

Naked mole-rats. /JARROW, G/1996/4-6/7 KC744 . . . . **599.35**

Name that book! Questions and answers on outstanding children's books. /
GREESON, J/1996/KA350 . . . . **PROF 809**

Naming colors. /DEWEY, A/1995/4-8/8 KC120 . . . . **535.6**

Nana upstairs and Nana downstairs. /DE PAOLA, T/c1973, 1978/
K-3/6 KF475 . . . . **E**

Nana's birthday party. /HEST, A/1993/1-3/4 KF720 . . . . **E**

Napping house. /WOOD, A/1984/P-2/7 KG764 . . . . **CE E**

Napping house and other stories (Talking book). /WOOD, A/1987/
P-3/KG765 . . . . **TB E**

Napping house (Big book)./WOOD, A/1991/P-2/7 KG764 . . . . . . **CE E**

Napping house (Braille). /WOOD, A/n.d./P-2/7 KG764 . . . . **CE E**

Napping house (Videocassette)./WOOD, A/1986/P-2/7 KG764 . . . **CE E**

Nat Turner and the slave revolt. /BARRETT, T/c1993, 1995/
5-6/6 KE577 . . . . **B TURNER, N.**

Natalie Spitzer's turtles. /WILLNER-PARDO, G/1992/1-3/2 KG741 . . . . **E**

Nate the Great. /SHARMAT, MW/c1972/1-3/2 KG484 . . . . **CE E**

Nate the Great and the crunchy Christmas. /SHARMAT, MW/1996/
2-4/2 KG485 . . . . **E**

Nate the Great and the fishy prize (Braille). /SHARMAT, MW/n.d./
1-3/2 KG484 . . . . **CE E**

Nate the Great and the Halloween hunt./SHARMAT, MW/1990/
1-3/2 KG484 . . . . **CE E**

Nate the Great and the lost list. /SHARMAT, MW/1981/
1-3/2 KG484 . . . . **CE E**

Nate the Great and the lost list (Braille). /SHARMAT, MW/n.d./
1-3/2 KG484 . . . . **CE E**

Nate the Great and the missing key (Kit)./SHARMAT, MW/1989/
1-3/2 KG484 . . . . **CE E**

Nate the Great and the phony clue./SHARMAT, MW/1981/
1-3/2 KG484 . . . . **CE E**

Nate the Great and the pillowcase. /SHARMAT, MW/1993/
1-3/1 KG486 . . . . **E**

Nate the Great and the snowy trail (Braille). /SHARMAT, MW/n.d./
1-3/2 KG484 . . . . **CE E**

Nate the Great and the stolen base./SHARMAT, MW/1992/
1-3/2 KG484 . . . . **CE E**

Nate the Great and the tardy tortoise. /SHARMAT, MW/1995/
1-3/2 KG487 . . . . **E**

Nate the Great (Braille)./SHARMAT, MW/n.d./1-3/2 KG484. . . . . **CE E**

Nate the Great goes undercover./SHARMAT, MW/c1974, 1978/
1-3/2 KG484 . . . . **CE E**

Nate the Great goes undercover (Braille)./SHARMAT, MW/n.d./
1-3/2 KG484 . . . . **CE E**

Nate the Great goes undercover (Kit)./SHARMAT, MW/1995/
1-3/2 KG484 . . . . **CE E**

Nate the Great stalks stupidweed./SHARMAT, MW/1989/
1-3/2 KG484 . . . . **CE E**

Nathaniel talking. /GREENFIELD, E/1988/K-6/KD948 . . . . **811**

National Civil Rights Museum celebrates everyday people. /DUNCAN, AF/
1995/3-6/8 KA903 . . . . **323.1**

NATIONAL EDUCATION GOALS REPORT: BUILDING A NATION OF
LEARNERS. /1991-//KA171 . . . . **PROF 370**

NATIONAL EDUCATION GOALS REPORT: DATA VOLUMES./1994-/
/KA171 . . . . **PROF 370**

NATIONAL GEOGRAPHIC ATLAS OF THE WORLD. 6th ed., Rev. ed. /
1995/4-6/KA473 . . . . **REF 912**

NATIONAL GEOGRAPHIC INDEX, 1888-1988. /1989/
4-A/KA528 . . . . **PER 050**

NATIONAL GEOGRAPHIC MAGAZINE. /1888-/4-A/KA529 . . . **PER 050**

NATIONAL GEOGRAPHIC MAGAZINE (Sound recording cassette)./n.d./
4-A/KA529 . . . . **PER 050**

NATIONAL GEOGRAPHIC PICTURE ATLAS OF OUR FIFTY STATES. /
1994/4-A/KA475 . . . . **REF 912.73**

NATIONAL GEOGRAPHIC WORLD. /1975-/2-4/KA530 . . . . **PER 050**

NATIONAL GEOGRAPHIC WORLD (Sound recording cassette)./n.d./
2-4/KA530 . . . . **PER 050**

NATIONAL INSPIRER (Microcomputer program). /1997/
5-A/KE190 . . . . **MCP 917.3**

NATIONAL PARKS. /1919-/5-A/KA531 . . . . **PER 050**

NATIONAL SCIENCE EDUCATION STANDARDS: OBSERVE, INTERACT,
CHANGE, LEARN. /1996//KA284 . . . . **PROF 507**

National Velvet. /BAGNOLD, E/c1935, 1985/4-A/5 KG874 . . . . **Fic**

National Velvet (Braille). /BAGNOLD, E/n.d./4-A/5 KG874 . . . . . . **Fic**

National Velvet (Sound recording cassette)./BAGNOLD, E/n.d./
4-A/5 KG874. . . . . **Fic**

National Velvet (Talking book)./BAGNOLD, E/n.d./4-A/5 KG874. . . . **Fic**

NATIONAL WILDLIFE. /1962-/A/KA532 . . . . **PER 050**

National worm day. /STEVENSON, J/1990/K-2/1 KG563 . . . . **E**

Native American animal stories. /BRUCHAC, J/1992/
4-6/5 KB540 . . . . **398.24**

NATIVE AMERICAN CULTURES (Picture). /1992/4-6/KE752 . . **PIC 970.1**

Native American feast. /PENNER, LR/1994/4-6/6 KB187 . . . . . . **394.1**

NATIVE AMERICAN SERIES (Videocassette). /1993/
4-6/KE753 . . . . **VCR 970.1**

NATIVE AMERICANS: PEOPLE OF THE DESERT (Videocassette)./1993/
4-6/KE753 . . . . **VCR 970.1**

NATIVE AMERICANS: PEOPLE OF THE FOREST (Videocassette)./1993/
4-6/KE753 . . . . **VCR 970.1**

NATIVE AMERICANS: PEOPLE OF THE NORTHWEST COAST
(Videocassette)./1994/4-6/KE753. . . . . **VCR 970.1**

NATIVE AMERICANS: PEOPLE OF THE PLAINS (Videocassette)./1993/
4-6/KE753 . . . . **VCR 970.1**

NATIVE NORTH AMERICAN BIOGRAPHY. /1996/
6-A/KA481 . . . . **REF 970.1**

NATIVE NORTH AMERICAN VOICES. /1997/5-A/KA482. . . . **REF 970.1**

NATIVE WAYS: CALIFORNIA INDIAN STORIES AND MEMORIES. /
1995/5-A/6 KE800 . . . . **970.494**

NATIVITY. /1996/3-5/5 KA709 . . . . **232.92**

NATURAL HISTORY. /1900-/A/KA533 . . . . **PER 050**

NATURAL HISTORY (Sound recording cassette)./1994/
A/KA533. . . . . **PER 050**

Nature all year long. /LESLIE, CW/1991/1-5/6 KB908 . . . . **508**

Nature by design. /BROOKS, B/1991/A/9 KC483 . . . . **591.56**

Nature crafts for kids. /DIEHN, G/1992/4-6/6 KD429 . . . . **745.5**

Nature for the very young: a handbook of indoor and outdoor activities. /
BOWDEN, M/1989//KA199. . . . . **PROF 372.3**

Nature got there first. /GATES, P/1995/4-8/10 KB905 . . . . **508**

Nature puzzlers. /HILLMAN, LE/1989//KA289 . . . . **PROF 508**

Nature spy. /ROTNER, S/1992/P-1/4 KB912 . . . . **508**

Nature walk. /FLORIAN, D/1989/P-1/KB922 . . . . **508.3**

Nature's green umbrella: tropical rain forests. /GIBBONS, G/1994/
2-6/5 KC316 . . . . **577.34**

NATURE'S NEWBORN: BEAR, BIGHORN SHEEP, MOUNTAIN GOATS
(Videocassette). /1994/1-5/KC724 . . . . **VCR 599**

NATURE'S NEWBORN: ELK, MOOSE, DEER (Videocassette). /1994/
3-6/KC799. . . . . **VCR 599.65**

Navajo ABC: a Dine alphabet book. /TAPAHONSO, L/1995/
2-4/KE797 . . . . **970.49**

Navajos. /SNEVE, V/1993/4-6/6 KE773 . . . . 970.3
NBA basketball basics. /VANCIL, M/1995/5-6/6 KD779 . . . . . . 796.323
N.C. Wyeth's pilgrims. /SAN SOUCI, RD/1991/4-6/7 KE946 . . . . . 974.4
Nearer nature. /ARNOSKY, J/1996/A/6 KE933 . . . . 974.3
Neeny coming, Neeny going. /ENGLISH, K/1996/1-3/2 KF527 . . . . E
Negra perla./O'DELL, S/n.d./5-6/5 KH557 . . . . CE Fic
NEIGHBORHOOD MAPMACHINE (Microcomputer program). /1997/ 1-5/KC066 . . . . MCP 526
Neighborhood odes: poems. /SOTO, G/1992/3-A/KE029 811
Nekane, the lamina and the bear: a tale of the Basque Pyrenees. / ARAUJO, FP/1993/2-3/3 KB256 . . . . 398.2
Nekomah Creek. /CREW, L/1991/4-A/5 KH041 . . . . Fic
Nekomah Creek Christmas. /CREW, L/1994/4-6/4 KH042 . . . . Fic
Nellie Bly: reporter for the world. /KENDALL, ME/1992/ 4-6/5 KE256 . . . . B BLY, N.
Nellie Bly's monkey: his remarkable story in his own words. /BLOS, JW/ 1996/2-5/9 KF236 . . . . E
Neptune. /SIMON, S/1991/4-6/8 KC041 . . . . 523.48
NERVOUS SYSTEM (Videocassette). /1994/5-6/KC970 . . . . VCR 612.8
Nessa's fish. /LUENN, N/1990/K-2/2 KG041 . . . . CE E
Nessa's fish (Sound recording cassette)./LUENN, N/1993/ K-2/2 KG041 . . . . CE E
Nessa's fish (Videocassette)./LUENN, N/1993/K-2/2 KG041 . . . . . CE E
Nest full of eggs. /JENKINS, PB/1995/K-2/2 KC705 . . . . 598.8
Nettie Jo's friends. /MCKISSACK, P/1989/1-3/4 KG108 . . . . E
Nettie's trip south. /TURNER, A/1987/5-A/6 KH812 . . . . Fic
Nevada. /LILLEGARD, D/1990/4-6/9 KF074 . . . . 979.3
Nevada (Sound recording cassette)./LILLEGARD, D/1993/ 4-6/9 KF074 . . . . 979.3
Never grab a deer by the ear. /BARE, CS/1993/4-5/5 KC795 . . . 599.65
NEVER TAKE A PIG TO LUNCH AND OTHER POEMS ABOUT THE FUN OF EATING. /1994/1-4/KE073 . . . . 811.008
NEVER TAKE A PIG TO LUNCH AND OTHER POEMS ABOUT THE FUN OF EATING (Sound recording cassette)./1996/1-4/KE073 . . 811.008
Never to forget: the Jews of the Holocaust. /MELTZER, M/c1976/ A/7 KE674 . . . . 940.54
Never to forget: the Jews of the Holocaust (Sound recording cassette)./ MELTZER, M/n.d./A/7 KE674 . . . . 940.54
New adventures of Mother Goose: gentle rhymes for happy times. / LANSKY, B/1993/P-3/KD967 811
NEW ADVOCATE. /1988-//KA127 . . . . PER PROF 050
NEW AMERICAN DESK ENCYCLOPEDIA. 3RD REV. /1993/ 4-A/KA589 031
NEW BABY IN MY HOUSE (Videocassette). /1993/ P-1/KA886 . . . . VCR 306.875
New book of dinosaurs. /UNWIN, D/1997/K-6/9 KC266 . . . . 567.9
NEW BOOK OF KNOWLEDGE. /1997/4-6/KA385 . . . . REF 031
NEW BOOK OF POPULAR SCIENCE. Rev. ed. /1998/ 5-6/KA433 . . . . REF 503
New Brunswick. /GANN, M/1995/5-A/9 KE820 . . . . 971.5
New complete babysitter's handbook. /BARKIN, C/1995/ 5-6/6 KD302 649
New complete babysitter's handbook (Sound recording cassette)./BARKIN, C/1997/5-6/6 KD302 649
NEW DIRECTIONS FOR ELEMENTARY SCHOOL MATHEMATICS, 1989 YEARBOOK. /1989//KA255 . . . . PROF 372.7
New Hampshire. /BROWN, D/1993/4-6/7 KE930 . . . . 974.2
New Hampshire Colony. /FRADIN, DB/1988/5-6/9 KE931 . . . . 974.2
New Hope. /SORENSEN, H/1995/1-4/4 KG526 . . . . E
New illustrated dinosaur dictionary. Rev. ed. /SATTLER, HR/c1983, 1990/ 3-6/KA444 . . . . REF 567.9
NEW, IMPROVED ME: UNDERSTANDING BODY CHANGES (Videocassette). /1991/5-6/KC953 . . . . VCR 612.6
New Jersey. /FREDEEN, C/1993/4-6/5 KE964 . . . . 974.9
New Jersey Colony. /FRADIN, DB/1991/5-6/7 KE963 . . . . 974.9
New kid on the block. /PRELUTSKY, J/1984/2-6/KE010 . . . . . . CE 811
NEW KID ON THE BLOCK (CD-ROM). /1993/K-A/KD995 . . . CDR 811
New kid on the block (Sound recording cassette)./PRELUTSKY, J/n.d./ 2-6/KE010 . . . . CE 811
New kid on the block (Talking book)./PRELUTSKY, J/1986/ 2-6/KE010 . . . . CE 811
NEW KID PIX. School version (Microcomputer program). /1996/ P-A/KD469 . . . . MCP 750.28
New king. /RAPPAPORT, D/1995/4-A/3 KB473 . . . . 398.22
New king (Sound recording cassette)./RAPPAPORT, D/1997/ 4-A/3 KB473 . . . . 398.22
New moon. /SHEA, PD/1996/P-2/2 KG490 . . . . E
New neighbors for Nora. /HURWITZ, J/c1979, 1991/2-4/6 KH299 . . . Fic
New policy guidelines for reading: connecting research and practice. / HARSTE, JC/1989//KA208 . . . . PROF 372.4
New republic of childhood: a critical guide to Canadian children's literature in English. Rev. ed. /EGOFF, S/1990//KA349 . . . . PROF 809
New road! /GIBBONS, G/1983/1-3/4 KD078 . . . . 625.7
New shoes for Silvia. /HURWITZ, J/1993/K-2/2 KF794 . . . . E
New technologies for education: a beginner's guide. 3rd ed. /BARRON, AE/1997//KA176 . . . . PROF 371.3
New view almanac: the first all-visual resource of vital facts and statistics! Premiere edition. /TESAR, J/1996/4-A/KA391 . . . . REF 031.02
New world. /CROSS, G/1995/6-A/5 KH044 . . . . Fic
NEW YEAR'S DAY (Videocassette). /1994/1-4/KB213 . . . VCR 394.261
New York. /FRADIN, DB/1993/4-6/3 KE955 . . . . 974.7
New York City. /KENT, D/1996/3-5/8 KE958 . . . . 974.7
New York Colony. /FRADIN, DB/1988/5-6/8 KE956 . . . . 974.7
New York Public Library amazing space: a book of answers for kids. / CAMPBELL, A/1997/3-A/8 KC001 520
NEWBERY AND CALDECOTT AWARDS: A GUIDE TO THE MEDAL AND HONOR BOOKS. /n.d.//KA128 . . . . PER PROF 050
Newbery and Caldecott Medal and Honor books in other media. / SHARKEY, PB/1992//KA087 . . . . PROF 028.1
Newbery and Caldecott medal books, 1966-1975: with acceptance papers & related material chiefly from the Horn Book Magazine. /HORN BOOK MAGAZINE /1975//KA352 . . . . PROF 809
Newbery and Caldecott medal books, 1976-1985./HORN BOOK MAGAZINE /1986//KA352 . . . . PROF 809
NEWBERY AND CALDECOTT MEDALISTS AND HONOR BOOK WINNERS: BIBLIOGRAPHIES AND RESOURCE MATERIAL THROUGH 1991. 2nd ed. /1992//KA004 . . . . PROF 011
Newbery companion: booktalk and related materials for Newbery Medal and Honor Books. /GILLESPIE, JT/1996//KA035 . . . . PROF 016.813
NEWBERY HALLOWEEN: A DOZEN SCARY STORIES BY NEWBERY AWARD-WINNING AUTHORS. /1993/5-6/5 KH548 . . . . Fic
Newbery Medal books: 1922-1955: with their authors' acceptance papers, biographies, and related materials chiefly from the Horn Book Magazine. /HORN BOOK MAGAZINE /c1957//KA353 . . . PROF 809
Newfoundland and Labrador. /JACKSON, L/1995/4-6/8 KE822 . . . 971.8
News about dinosaurs. /LAUBER, P/1989/P-A/7 KC253 . . . . 567.9
News about dinosaurs (Sound recording cassette)./LAUBER, P/1993/ P-A/7 KC253 . . . . 567.9
Newspaper theatre: creative play production for low budgets and no budgets. /MORIN, A/1989//KA330 . . . . PROF 792
Newt. /NOVAK, M/1996/1-3/2 KG181 . . . . E
Next spring an oriole. /WHELAN, G/1987/2-4/5 KH848 . . . . Fic
Next year in Jerusalem: 3000 years of Jewish stories. /SCHWARTZ, H/ 1996/3-6/7 KA780 . . . . 296.4
Next year in Jerusalem: 3000 years of Jewish stories (Sound recording cassette)./SCHWARTZ, H/1997/3-6/7 KA780 . . . . 296.4
Nez Perce. /SNEVE, V/1994/4-6/7 KE774 . . . . 970.3
Nez Perce. /ANDERSON, MK/1994/4-6/7 KE757 . . . . 970.3
Nicholas Pipe. /SAN SOUCI, RD/1997/2-5/6 KB413 . . . . 398.21
Nickel buys a rhyme. /BENJAMIN, A/1993/P-2/KD916 811
Nicky upstairs and down. /ZIEFERT, H/c1987, 1994/P-1/1 KG795 . . . . E
Night after Christmas. /STEVENSON, J/1981/K-2/2 KG564 . . . . . CE E
Night becomes day. /MCGUIRE, R/1994/1-3/1 KG104 . . . . E
Night before Christmas: told in sign language: an adaptation of the original poem "A visit from St. Nicholas" by Clement C. Moore. /BORNSTEIN, H/1994/K-6/KD917 811
Night creatures. /WHAYNE, SS/1993/4-6/5 KC479 . . . . 591.5
Night crossing. /ACKERMAN, K/1994/3-4/8 KG812 . . . . Fic
Night gliders. /RYDER, J/1996/P-2/2 KG367 . . . . E
Night journeys. /AVI /c1979, 1994/5-A/6 KG860 . . . . Fic
Night letters. /LOMONACO, P/1996/K-3/3 KG018 . . . . E
Night ones. /GROSSMAN, P/1991/P-K/2 KF650 . . . . E
Night owl and the rooster: a Haitian legend. /REASONER, C/1995/ K-2/6 KB637 . . . . CE 398.24
Night owl and the rooster: a Haitian legend (Talking book)./REASONER, C/1996/K-2/6 KB637 . . . . CE 398.24
Night visitors. /YOUNG, E/1995/2-3/4 KB680 . . . . 398.24
Nightmares: poems to trouble your sleep. /PRELUTSKY, J/c1976/ 3-5/KE011 811
Nightmares: poems to trouble your sleep (Sound recording cassette)./ PRELUTSKY, J/n.d./3-5/KE011 811
Nightmares rising (Sound recording cassette). /BIRCH, C/1984/ 3-6/KB266 . . . . SRC 398.2
Nights of the pufflings. /MCMILLAN, B/1995/1-3/6 KC678 . . . . . . 598.3
NIGHTTIME ANIMALS (Videocassette). /1996/3-5/KC477. . . VCR 591.5
Nim and the war effort. /LEE, M/1997/2-4/5 KH391 . . . . Fic
Nina, Nina ballerina. /O'CONNOR, J/1993/P-1/1 KG189 . . . . E
Nine days to Christmas. /ETS, MH/c1959/1-3/2 KF538 . . . . E
Nine days to Christmas (Sound recording cassette)./ETS, MH/n.d./ 1-3/2 KF538 . . . . E
Nine-in-one, grr! grr! a folktale from the Hmong people of Laos. /XIONG, B/1989/P-3/4 KB677. . . . . 398.24
Nineteenth-century inventors. /NOONAN, J/1992/5-6/7 KC897 609
No good in art./COHEN, M/1980/K-1/2 KF405 . . . . CE E
No jumping on the bed! /ARNOLD, T/1987/P-3/5 KF167 . . . . E
No more animals! /MONFRIED, L/1995/1-3/2 KH502 . . . . Fic
No more dodos: how zoos help endangered wildlife. /NIRGIOTIS, N/ 1996/A/6 KD256 . . . . 639.9

No more monsters for me! /PARISH, P/1981/K-1/1 KG215 . . . . **E**
No more nice. /MACDONALD, A/1996/4-6/6 KH437 . . . . **Fic**
No more nice. /MACDONALD, A/1996/3-5/6 KH438 . . . . **Fic**
NO MORE TEASING! (Videocassette). /1995/3-4/KA661 . . . . **VCR 158**
No, no, Titus! /MASUREL, C/1997/P-1/2 KG083 . . . . **E**
NO ONE QUITE LIKE ME...OR YOU (Videocassette). /1992/
3-6/KA640 . . . . **VCR 155.2**
No room for Francie. /MACDONALD, M/1995/2-3/2 KH440 . . . . . **Fic**
No roses for Harry./ZION, G/1958/P-2/2 KG800 . . . . **CE E**
No turning back: a novel of South Africa. /NAIDOO, B/1997/
6-A/6 KH526 . . . . **Fic**
Noah. /GAUCH, PL/1994/K-2/4 KA684 . . . . **222**
NOAH'S ARK. /c1977/P-2/KA681 . . . . **221.9**
NOAH'S ARK (Videocassette). /c1989, 1996/P-2/KA682 . . . **VCR 221.9**
Noah's square dance. /WALTON, R/1995/K-2/3 KG687 . . . . **E**
Nobody owns the sky: the story of "Brave Bessie" Coleman. /
LINDBERGH, R/1996/1-3/2 KF983 . . . . **E**
Nobody's mother is in second grade. /PULVER, R/1992/K-2/2 KG293 . . **E**
NOEL'S LEMONADE STAND (UJAMAA) (Videocassette). /1982/
3-5/KD306 . . . . **VCR 650.1**
Noise lullaby. /OGBURN, JK/1995/P-2/2 KG190 . . . . **E**
Noisemakers. /CASELEY, J/1992/P-1/2 KF367 . . . . **E**
Noisy Nora. /WELLS, R/1997/K-1/4 KG707 . . . . **CE E**
Noisy Nora (Big book). /WELLS, R/1979/K-1/4 KG707 . . . . . . **CE E**
Noisy Nora (Kit)./WELLS, R/1993/K-1/4 KG707 . . . . **CE E**
Noisy Nora (Videocassette). /WELLS, R/1993/K-1/KG708 . . . . . **VCR E**
Nonfiction books for children: activities for thinking, learning and doing. /
DOLL, CA/1990//KA072 . . . . **PROF 027.8**
Nonsense songs. /LEAR, E/1997/K-3/KE104 . . . . **821**
Noonday friends. /STOLZ, M/c1965/4-6/6 KH767 . . . . **CE Fic**
Noonday friends (Braille)./STOLZ, M/n.d./4-6/6 KH767 . . . . **CE Fic**
Nora and Mrs. Mind-your-own business. /HURWITZ, J/c1977, 1991/
2-4/4 KH300 . . . . **Fic**
Nora la revoltosa./WELLS, R/1997/K-1/4 KG707 . . . . **CE E**
Norman the doorman. /FREEMAN, D/c1959/K-1/7 KF580 . . . . . **CE E**
Norman the doorman (Talking book)./FREEMAN, D/n.d./
K-1/7 KF580 . . . . **CE E**
Norman the doorman (Videocassette)./FREEMAN, D/n.d./
K-1/7 KF580 . . . . **CE E**
North American Indian. /MURDOCH, DH/1995/4-6/8 KE751 . . . . **970.1**
North American Indian ceremonies. /LIPTAK, K/1992/4-6/7 KA790 . . **299**
North American Indian sign language. /LIPTAK, K/1990/
4-A/5 KB826 . . . . **419**
North American Indians. /VIOLA, HJ/1996/4-6/10 KE755 . . . . . **970.1**
North Carolina. /SCHULZ, A/1993/4-6/7 KE983 . . . . **975.6**
North Carolina Colony. /FRADIN, DB/1991/5-6/7 KE982 . . . . . **975.6**
North Dakota. /FRADIN, DB/1994/4-6/3 KF057 . . . . **978.4**
North Star to freedom: the story of the Underground Railroad. /GORRELL,
GK/1997/5-6/8 KE905 . . . . **973.7**
Northern lights. /SOUZA, DM/1994/6-A/7 KC138 . . . . **538**
Northern lights: a Hanukkah story. /CONWAY, DC/1994/1-3/4 KF417 . **E**
Northern Nativity: Christmas dreams of a prairie boy. /KURELEK, W/
c1976/4-6/7 KA708 . . . . **CE 232.92**
NORTHLANDS (Videocassette)./1989/5-6/KE181 . . . . **VCR 917**
Northwest Territories. /HANCOCK, L/1993/5-6/8 KE824 . . . . **971.9**
Not a copper penny in me house: poems from the Caribbean. /GUNNING,
M/1993/P-3/KD950 . . . . **811**
Not in the house, Newton! /GILLILAND, JH/1995/P-2/2 KF618 . . . . . . **E**
Not so fast, Songololo. /DALY, N/1986/K-3/2 KF448 . . . . **CE E**
Not so fast, Songololo (Braille). /DALY, N/n.d./K-3/2 KF448 . . . **CE E**
Not so fast, Songololo (Videocassette)./DALY, N/1992/
K-3/2 KF448 . . . . **CE E**
Nothing but the truth: a documentary novel. /AVI /1991/
6-A/4 KG861 . . . . **Fic**
Nothing but the truth: a documentary novel (Sound recording cassette)./AVI
/1993/6-A/5 KG861 . . . . **Fic**
Nothing but trouble, trouble, trouble. /HERMES, P/1995/
4-6/6 KH249 . . . . **Fic**
Nothing but trouble, trouble, trouble (Sound recording cassette)./HERMES,
P/1997/4-6/6 KH249 . . . . **Fic**
Nothing ever happens on my block. /RASKIN, E/c1966/K-2/2 KG308 . . **E**
Nothing ever happens on 90th Street. /SCHOTTER, R/1997/
3-5/4 KH682 . . . . **Fic**
Nothing grows here. /THESMAN, J/1994/6-A/4 KH790 . . . . **Fic**
Nothing to be ashamed of: growing up with mental illness in your family. /
DINNER, SH/1989/5-6/9 KD020 . . . . **616.89**
Not-just-anybody family. /BYARS, BC/1986/4-A/4 KG962 . . . . . . **CE Fic**
Not-so-jolly Roger./SCIESZKA, J/1991/3-6/3 KH685 . . . . **Fic**
Not-so-normal Norman. /STOWE, C/1995/2-5/3 KH770 . . . . **Fic**
Not-so-normal Norman (Sound recording cassette)./STOWE, C/1997/
2-5/3 KH770 . . . . **Fic**
Nova Scotia. /LOTZ, J/1992/5-A/8 KE821 . . . . **971.6**
Now I'm big. /MILLER, M/1996/P/2 KG135 . . . . **E**

Now is your time!: the African-American struggle for freedom. /MYERS,
WD/1991/A/7 KE858 . . . . **973**
Now is your time!: the African-American struggle for freedom (Sound
recording cassette)./MYERS, WD/1993/A/7 KE858 . . . . **973**
Now one foot, now the other. /DE PAOLA, T/1981/K-3/5 KF476 . . . . . **E**
Nuestra Senora de Guadalupe./DE PAOLA, T/1980/
1-4/6 KA698 . . . . **232.91**
Nuestro planeta en peligro: la Antartida./WINCKLER, S/1993/
5-6/8 KE221 . . . . **919.8**
Nueva hermanita de Francisca./HOBAN, R/1997/P-1/2 KF739 . . . . **CE E**
Nueve dias para navidad./ETS, MH/1991/1-3/2 KF538 . . . . **E**
NUMBER HEROES. School version (CD-ROM). /1996/
3-6/KB929 . . . . **CDR 510**
Number of animals. /WORMELL, C/1993/P-2/3 KG770 . . . . **E**
Number the stars. /LOWRY, L/1989/5-6/5 KH427 . . . . **Fic**
Numbers. /REISS, JJ/c1971/P-1/KG321 . . . . **E**
Numbskulls. /TAYLOR, W/1995/4-A/7 KH787 . . . . **Fic**
Nunavut. /HANCOCK, L/1995/4-6/7 KE825 . . . . **971.9**
Nursery collection. /HUGHES, S/c1986, 1994/P/2 KF790 . . . . **E**
Nursery days (Compact disc). /GUTHRIE, W/1992/P-1/KD567 . . **CD 789.2**
NURSERY SONGS AND RHYMES (Videocassette). /1993/
P-2/KB104 . . . . **VCR 372.4**
NURSERY TALES AROUND THE WORLD. /1996/P-2/7 KB354 . . . . **398.2**
NUTRITION TO GROW ON (Videocassette). /1988/
5-6/KC987 . . . . **VCR 613.2**
Nutrition: what's in the food we eat. /PATENT, DH/1992/
4-6/6 KC941 . . . . **612.3**
Nuts to you! /EHLERT, L/1993/P-2/2 KF519 . . . . **E**
Nutshell library (Videocassette). /SENDAK, M/1987/P-2/KG434. . **VCR E**
NYSTROM DESK ATLAS. /1994/5-A/KA474 . . . . **REF 912**
O Canada. /HARRISON, T/1993/3-6/6 KE800 . . . . **971**
O Christmas tree. /RAHAMAN, V/1996/1-3/4 KG298 . . . . **E**
Occasional cow. /HORVATH, P/1989/5-6/8 KH284 . . . . **Fic**
Ocean. /MACQUITTY, M/1995/2-6/7 KC174 . . . . **551.46**
Ocean day. /ROTNER, S/1993/P-2/3 KG357 . . . . **E**
Ocean of story: fairy tales from India. /NESS, C/1996/
4-6/5 KB353 . . . . **398.2**
Oceans. /SIMON, S/1990/3-6/7 KC177 . . . . **551.46**
Oceans atlas. /GANERI, A/1994/4-A/6 KC173 . . . . **551.46**
Octopus is amazing. /LAUBER, P/1990/1-3/4 KC514 . . . . **594**
Odds and evens: a numbers book. /GOENNEL, H/1994/
P-1/2 KB957 . . . . **513.2**
Odin's family: myths of the Vikings. /PHILIP, N/1996/3-A/6 KA757 . . **293**
ODYSSEY. /1992-/3-5/KA534 . . . . **PER 050**
Odyssey of Ben O'Neal./TAYLOR, T/c1977, 1979/5-A/5 KH784 . . . . **Fic**
Odyssey of Homer. /PICARD, BL/c1952, 1992/5-A/7 KE126 . . . . . . **883**
Of bugs and beasts: fact, folklore, and activities. /LIVO, LJ/1995/
/KA296 . . . . **PROF 591**
Of colors and things. /HOBAN, T/1989/P-K/KC123 . . . . **535.6**
Of swords and sorcerers: the adventures of King Arthur and his knights. /
HODGES, M/1993/4-5/6 KB452. . . . . **398.22**
Off the map: the journals of Lewis and Clark. /CLARK, W/1993/
4-6/7 KE201 . . . . **917.804**
Officer Buckle and Gloria. /RATHMANN, P/1995/K-2/3 KG310 . . . . . . **E**
Official Boy Scout handbook (Sound recording cassette)./BIRKBY, RC/n.d./
4-6/6 KB073 . . . . **369.43**
OFFICIAL FAIR-USE GUIDELINES: COMPLETE TEXT OF FOUR OFFICIAL
DOCUMENTS ARRANGED FOR USE BY EDUCATORS. /1987/
/KA168 . . . . **PROF 346.73**
Ogbo: sharing life in an African village. /ONYEFULU, I/1996/
3-5/6 KE737 . . . . **966.9**
Oh, baby! /STEIN, S/1993/P-K/3 KA827 . . . . **305.232**
Oh, brother. /YORINKS, A/1989/1-4/5 KG783 . . . . **E**
Oh, cats! /BUCK, N/1997/P-1/1 KF290 . . . . **E**
Oh, cuan lejos llegaras!/SEUSS, D/1993/1-3/2 KG469 . . . . **E**
Oh, how waffle!: riddles you can eat. /MATHEWS, J/1993/
2-6/KD735 . . . . **793.735**
Oh, the places you'll go! /SEUSS, D/1990/1-3/2 KG469 . . . . **E**
Oh, the places you'll go! (Sound recording cassette)./SEUSS, D/n.d./
1-3/2 KG469 . . . . **E**
Oh, those Harper girls!; or Young and dangerous. /KARR, K/1992/
5-A/Y KH342 . . . . **Fic**
Oil spill! /BERGER, M/1994/1-4/4 KB057 . . . . **363.73**
Oil spills: damage, recovery, and prevention. /PRINGLE, LP/1993/
5-6/9 KB065 . . . . **363.73**
Okino and the whales. /ESTERL, A/1995/3-5/3 KH101 . . . . **E**
Oklahoma. /FRADIN, DB/1995/4-6/4 KF005 . . . . **976.6**
OKLAHOMA LAND RUSH (Multimedia kit). /1993/
5-A/KE997 . . . . **MMK 976.1**
Oksana: my own story. /BAIUL, O/1997/3-6/4 KE247 . . . . . **B BAIUL, O.**
Ol' Paul, the mighty logger: being a true account of the seemingly incredible
exploits and inventions of the great Paul Bunyon. /ROUNDS, G/1976/
4-6/7 KB477 . . . . **398.22**

Old bag of bones: a coyote tale. /STEVENS, J/1996/
1-3/2 KB659 . . . . **398.24**
Old Bet and the start of the American circus. /MCCLUNG, RM/1993/
4-6/6 KD682 . . . . **791.3**
Old black fly. /AYLESWORTH, J/1992/K-2/2 KF180 . . . . **E**
Old black fly (Big book). /AYLESWORTH, J/1995/K-2/2 KF180 . . . . . . **E**
Old dog. Rev. and newly illustrated ed. /ZOLOTOW, C/1995/
K-2/2 KG806 . . . . **E**
Old dogs, new tricks (Compact disc)./POLISAR, BL/
P-3/KD649 . . . . **SRC 789.3**
Old dogs, new tricks (Sound recording cassette). /POLISAR, BL/1993/
P-3/KD649 . . . . **SRC 789.3**
Old Henry. /BLOS, JW/1987/K-3/2 KF237 . . . . **CE E**
Old Henry (Sound recording cassette)./BLOS, JW/n.d./
K-3/2 KF237 . . . . **CE E**
Old man and his door. /SOTO, G/1996/K-2/2 KG528. . . . . . . **E**
Old meadow. /SELDEN, G/1987/3-5/5 KH697 . . . . **Fic**
OLD MOTHER HUBBARD AND HER WONDERFUL DOG. /1991/
P-K/KB809 . . . . **398.8**
Old Mother Hubbard's dog dresses up. /YEOMAN, J/c1989, 1990/
K-3/4 KG774 . . . . **E**
Old Mother Hubbard's dog learns to play./YEOMAN, J/1990/
K-3/4 KG774 . . . . **E**
Old Mother Hubbard's dog needs a doctor. /YEOMAN, J/1990/
K-3/4 KG774 . . . . **E**
Old Mother Hubbard's dog takes up sport./YEOMAN, J/1990/
K-3/4 KG774 . . . . **E**
Old Peter's Russian tales. /RANSOME, A/1975/5-6/6 KB766 . . . **398.27**
Old Peter's Russian tales (Sound recording cassette)./RANSOME, A/n.d./
5-6/6 KB766 . . . . **398.27**
Old possum's book of practical cats. /ELIOT, TS/1982/4-A/KE100 . . **821**
OLD STURBRIDGE VILLAGE (Videocassette). /1989/
4-6/KE942 . . . . **VCR 974.4**
Old synagogue. /ROSENBLUM, R/1989/3-6/7 KA783 . . . . **296.6**
Old synagogue (Sound recording cassette)./ROSENBLUM, R/n.d./
3-6/7 KA783 . . . . **296.6**
OLD TIME AMERICA (Picture). /n.d./5-6/KE859 . . . . **PIC 973**
Old Turtle. /WOOD, D/1992/3-5/3 KH879 . . . . **CE Fic**
Old Turtle (Talking book)./WOOD, D/1995/3-5/3 KH879 . . . . . **CE Fic**
Old Turtle's soccer team. /KESSLER, L/1988/K-3/2 KF901 . . . . . **E**
Old Turtle's 90 knock-knocks, jokes, and riddles. /KESSLER, L/1991/
2-4/KD730. . . . . **793.735**
Old woman and her pig. /KIMMEL, EA/1992/K-2/2 KB603 . . . **398.24**
Old woman who named things. /RYLANT, C/1996/1-3/2 KG383 . . . . . **E**
Old Yeller. /GIPSON, F/c1956/A/7 KH170 . . . . **CE Fic**
Old Yeller (Braille). /GIPSON, F/n.d./A/7 KH170 . . . . **CE Fic**
Old Yeller (Sound recording cassette)./GIPSON, F/n.d./
A/7 KH170 . . . . **CE Fic**
Old Yeller (Talking book)./GIPSON, F/1973/A/7 KH170 . . . . . **CE Fic**
Old Yeller (Talking book)./GIPSON, F/n.d./A/7 KH170 . . . . . **CE Fic**
Olde Mother Goose (Kit). /MOTHER GOOSE /1993/
P-K/KB805 . . . . **KIT 398.8**
Older brother, younger brother: a Korean folktale. /JAFFE, N/1995/
3-4/6 KB320 . . . . **398.2**
Oldest elf. /STEVENSON, J/1996/P-2/2 KG565 . . . . **E**
Oliver, Amanda, and Grandmother Pig./VAN LEEUWEN, J/c1987, 1990/
K-2/1 KG648 . . . . **CE E**
Oliver and Amanda and the big snow./VAN LEEUWEN, J/1995/
K-2/1 KG648 . . . . **CE E**
Oliver and Amanda's Christmas./VAN LEEUWEN, J/1989/
K-2/1 KG648 . . . . **CE E**
Oliver and Amanda's Halloween./VAN LEEUWEN, J/1992/
K-2/1 KG648 . . . . **CE E**
Oliver Button is a sissy. /DE PAOLA, T/1979/K-2/2 KF477 . . . . **E**
Oliver Pig at school. /VAN LEEUWEN, J/1994/K-2/1 KG648 . . . . **CE E**
Olympians: great gods and goddesses of Ancient Greece. /FISHER, LE/
1984/5-6/7 KA740 . . . . **292**
Olympics! /HENNESSY, BG/1996/P-2/4 KD820 . . . . **796.48**
Oma and Bobo. /SCHWARTZ, A/1987/K-3/2 KG414 . . . . **E**
On an island in the bay. /MILLS, P/1994/2-4/3 KE979 . . . . **975.5**
On being Sarah. /HELFMAN, E/1993/5-A/6 KH236. . . . . **Fic**
On beyond zebra. /SEUSS, D/1955/P-3/6 KG470 . . . . **E**
On board the Titanic. /TANAKA, S/1996/4-A/6 KB027 . . . . **363.12**
On Call Back Mountain. /BUNTING, E/1997/1-3/2 KF306. . . . . **E**
On Market Street. /LOBEL, A/1981/P-1/6 KG009 . . . . **E**
On Market Street (Big book)./LOBEL, A/1986/P-1/6 KG009 . . . . **E**
On Market Street (Videocassette)./1985/P-1/KF809 . . . . **VCR E**
On mother's lap. /SCOTT, AH/c1972, 1992/P-K/2 KG423 . . . . **E**
On mother's lap (Braille)./SCOTT, AH/n.d./P-K/2 KG423 . . . . **E**
On my honor. /BAUER, MD/1986/5-6/7 KG882 . . . . **CE Fic**
On my honor (Braille). /BAUER, MD/n.d./5-6/7 KG882 . . . . . . **CE Fic**
On my honor (Talking book). /BAUER, MD/1992/5-6/7 KG882 . . . **CE Fic**
On the banks of Plum Creek./WILDER, LI/1953/3-6/4 KH860. . . . . . **Fic**
On the banks of Plum Creek (Braille)./WILDER, LI/n.d./3-6/4 KH860 . . **Fic**

On the banks of Plum Creek (Sound recording cassette)./WILDER, LI/n.d./
3-6/4 KH860 . . . . **Fic**
On the banks of Plum Creek (Talking book)./WILDER, LI/n.d./
3-6/4 KH860 . . . . **Fic**
On the brink of extinction: the California condor. /ARNOLD, C/1993/
5-6/8 KD251 . . . . **639.9**
On the brink of extinction: the California condor (Sound recording
cassette)./ARNOLD, C/1995/5-6/8 KD251 . . . . **639.9**
On the court with...Michael Jordan. /CHRISTOPHER, M/1996/
4-6/8 KE409 . . . . **CE B JORDAN, M.**
On the court with...Michael Jordan (Talking book)./CHRISTOPHER, M/
1997/4-6/8 KE409 . . . . **CE B JORDAN, M.**
On the day you were born. /FRASIER, D/1991/P-3/5 KF577. . . . . . **E**
ON THE DAY YOU WERE BORN (Videocassette). /1996/
P-A/KG192 . . . . **VCR E**
On the ice with...Wayne Gretzky. /CHRISTOPHER, M/1997/
3-6/7 KE379 . . . . **B GRETZKY, W.**
On the long trail home. /STEWART, EJ/1994/4-6/4 KH762. . . . . . . **Fic**
On the long trail home (Sound recording cassette)./STEWART, EJ/1997/
4-6/4 KH762 . . . . **Fic**
On the mound with...Greg Maddux. /CHRISTOPHER, M/1997/
3-5/7 KE452 . . . . **B MADDUX, G.**
On the other side of the hill./MACBRIDE, RL/1995/4-6/6 KH436 . . . . **Fic**
On the pampas. /BRUSCA, MC/1991/3-6/6 KF106 . . . . **982**
ON THE PLAYGROUND (Microcomputer program). /1988/
1-6/KA662 . . . . **MCP 158**
ON THE ROAD AGAIN (Sound recording cassette). /1992/
K-4/KD640 . . . . **SRC 789.3**
On the road of stars: Native American night poems and sleep charms. /
BIERHORST, J/1994/2-6/KE141 . . . . **897.008**
On the road with Poppa Whopper. /BUSSER, M/1997/3-4/2 KG954 . . **Fic**
On the trail of the fox. /SCHNIEPER, C/1986/4-6/8 KC844. . . . . **599.775**
On the trail with Miss Pace. /DENSLOW, SP/1995/1-3/2 KF461 . . . . . **E**
On the wing: bird poems and paintings. /FLORIAN, D/1996/
1-4/KD939. . . . . **811**
On to Oregon. /MORROW, H/c1954/5-6/4 KH517 . . . . **Fic**
On to Oregon (Talking book)./MORROW, H/n.d./5-6/4 KH517 . . . . . **Fic**
Once a mouse. /BROWN, M/c1961/1-3/6 KB536 . . . . **CE 398.24**
Once a mouse (Braille)./BROWN, M/n.d./1-3/6 KB536. . . . . . **CE 398.24**
Once a mouse (Sound recording cassette)./BROWN, M/n.d./
1-3/6 KB536 . . . . **CE 398.24**
Once a mouse (Talking book)./BROWN, M/n.d./1-3/6 KB536 . . **CE 398.24**
Once upon a time. /BUNTING, E/1995/2-5/3 KE268 . . . . **B BUNTING, E.**
Once upon a time this morning. /ROCKWELL, AF/1997/P-K/2 KG344 . . **E**
Once we had a horse. /ROUNDS, G/1996/K-2/3 KG358 . . . . **E**
One April morning: children remember the Oklahoma City bombing. /LAMB,
N/1996/2-6/6 KF006 . . . . **976.6**
One day in the tropical rain forest. /GEORGE, JC/1990/
4-6/6 KC315 . . . . **577.34**
One day we had to run!: refugee children tell their stories in words and
paintings. /WILKES, S/1994/4-A/5 KB019 . . . . **362.87**
One duck, another duck. /POMERANTZ, C/1984/P-1/1 KG265 . . . . . . **E**
One Eye, Two Eyes, Three Eyes: a Hutzul tale. /KIMMEL, EA/1996/
2-4/7 KB401 . . . . **398.21**
One fine day. /HOGROGIAN, N/c1971/P-2/5 KF763 . . . . **CE E**
One fine day (Kit)./HOGROGIAN, N/1973/P-2/5 KF763 . . . . **CE E**
One fine day (Talking book)./HOGROGIAN, N/n.d./P-2/5 KF763 . **CE E**
One fish, two fish, red fish, blue fish. /SEUSS, D/c1960/P-1/1 KG471. . **E**
One fish, two fish, red fish, blue fish (Braille). /SEUSS, D/n.d./
P-1/1 KG471 . . . . **E**
One fish, two fish, red fish, blue fish (Sound recording cassette)./SEUSS,
D/n.d./P-1/1 KG471 . . . . **E**
One frog too many./MAYER, M/1975/P-1/KG084 . . . . **CE E**
One good horse: a cowpuncher's counting book. /SCOTT, AH/1990/
K-2/2 KG424 . . . . **E**
One grain of rice: a mathematical folktale. /DEMI /1997/
3-6/6 KB731 . . . . **398.27**
One happy classroom. /SIMON, C/1997/K-1/2 KG507 . . . . **E**
One hole in the road. /NIKOLA-LISA, W/1996/P-K/2 KG173 . . . . **E**
One hundred favorite folktales. /THOMPSON, S/c1968/
/KA274 . . . . **PROF 398.2**
One hundred words about animals (Kit)./1990/P-3/KC457 . . . . **CE 591**
One hunter. /HUTCHINS, P/1982/P-K/KF800 . . . . **E**
One in the middle is the green kangaroo. /BLUME, J/1981/
K-3/2 KF238 . . . . **CE E**
One in the middle is the green kangaroo (Kit)./BLUME, J/1983/
K-3/2 KF238 . . . . **CE E**
One little kitten. /HOBAN, T/1979/P-K/1 KF744 . . . . **E**
One more river to cross: the stories of twelve Black Americans. /HASKINS,
J/1992/5-A/7 KA847 . . . . **305.8**
One more river to cross: the stories of twelve Black Americans (Sound
recording cassette)./HASKINS, J/1995/5-A/7 KA847 . . . . **305.8**
One morning in Maine. /MCCLOSKEY, R/c1952, 1962/1-3/6 KG090 . . **E**
One morning in Maine (Braille). /MCCLOSKEY, R/n.d./1-3/6 KG090 . . . **E**

One nation, many tribes: how kids live in Milwaukee's Indian community. / KRULL, K/1995/4-6/7 KE783 . . . . **970.475**

One of three. /JOHNSON, A/1991/P-1/2 KF832 . . . . **E**

One on a web: counting animals at home. /WADSWORTH, G/1997/ P-2/3 KC456 . . . . **591**

One potato, two potato: the folklore of American children. /KNAPP, M/ 1978//KA278 . . . . **PROF 398.8**

One proud summer. /HEWITT, M/1981/A/7 KH254 . . . . **Fic**

One Saturday morning. /BAKER, B/1994/1-3/1 KF183 . . . . **E**

One Saturday morning (Sound recording cassette)./BAKER, B/1997/ 1-3/1 KF183 . . . . **E**

One smiling grandma: a Caribbean counting book. /LINDEN, AM/1995/ P-1/2 KF984 . . . . **E**

One sun rises: an African wildlife counting book. /HARTMANN, W/1994/ P-2/3 KB959 . . . . **513.2**

One that got away. /EVERETT, P/1992/K-2/2 KF540 . . . . **E**

One tough turkey: a Thanksgiving story. /KROLL, S/1982/K-2/2 KF930 . **E**

One voice for children (Videocassette). /HARTMANN, J/1993/ K-4/KD618 . . . . **VCR 789.3**

One was Johnny: a counting book. /SENDAK, M/c1962/ P-1/KG435 . . . . **CE E**

One was Johnny: a counting book (Videocassette)./SENDAK, M/1976/ P-1/KG435 . . . . **CE E**

One woolly wombat. /TRINCA, R/1985/P-2/4 KG617 . . . . **E**

One world, many religions: the ways we worship. /OSBORNE, MP/1996/ 4-A/7 KA726 . . . . **291**

One yellow daffodil: a Hanukkah story. /ADLER, DA/1995/ 3-5/4 KG818 . . . . **Fic**

One-eyed cat. /FOX, P/1984/A/7 KH138 . . . . **Fic**

One-eyed cat (Sound recording cassette)./FOX, P/n.d./A/7 KH138 . . . **Fic**

One-eyed giant and other monsters from the Greek myths. /ROCKWELL, AF/1996/2-5/6 KA750 . . . . **292**

One-Eyed Jake. /HUTCHINS, P/c1979, 1994/K-2/4 KF801 . . . . **E**

One-person puppet plays. /WRIGHT, DA/1990//KA365 . . . . . **PROF 812**

One-room school at Squabble Hollow. /HAUSHERR, R/1988/ 3-6/7 KB084 . . . . **371.19**

Onion sundaes. /ADLER, DA/1994/2-3/2 KG819 . . . . **Fic**

Online kids: a young surfer's guide to cyberspace. /GRALLA, P/1996/ 3-A/4 KA578 . . . . **025.04**

ONLINE--OFFLINE: THEMES AND RESOURCES K-8. /1996-/ /KA129. . . . . **PER PROF 050**

Only child. /HOOVER, HM/1992/5-A/5 KH280 . . . . **Fic**

Only the names remain: the Cherokees and the Trail of Tears. 2nd ed. / BEALER, AW/1996/5-6/8 KE758 . . . . **970.3**

Ontario. /MACKAY, K/1992/5-A/8 KE819. . . . . **971.3**

Ontario. /BARNES, M/1995/4-6/10 KE817 . . . . **971.3**

Ooh-la-la (Max in love). /KALMAN, M/1991/4-A/3 KH340 . . . . . . **Fic**

OPENING DAYS: SPORTS POEMS. /1996/3-6/KE074. . . . . . **811.008**

Operation grizzly bear. /CALABRO, M/1989/5-6/7 KC858 . . . . **599.784**

Optical illusion book. /SIMON, S/c1976, 1984/4-6/5 KC115. . . . . . **535**

Orchestra: an introduction to the world of classical music. /BLACKWOOD, A/1993/4-6/8 KD544 . . . . **784.2**

Ordinary genius: the story of Albert Einstein. /MCPHERSON, SS/1995/ 5-A/6 KE334 . . . . **B EINSTEIN, A.**

Oregon. /FRADIN, DB/1995/4-6/4 KF089 . . . . **979.5**

OREGON TRAIL II (CD-ROM). /1994/4-A/KE745 . . . . **CDR 970.04**

Origami for beginners: the creative world of paperfolding. /TEMKO, F/ 1991/4-6/4 KD404 . . . . **736**

Origami stories (Videocassette). /STOTTER, R/1993/ 1-3/KB122 . . . . **VCR 372.67**

Origin of life on Earth: an African creation myth. /ANDERSON, DA/1991/ 4-5/4 KA730 . . . . **291.2**

Orion, the Hunter. /APFEL, NH/1995/A/10 KC047 . . . . **523.8**

Orphan boy: a Maasai story. /MOLLEL, TM/1990/4-5/4 KB406 . . **398.21**

Orphan boy: a Maasai story (Sound recording cassette)./MOLLEL, TM/ 1994/4-5/4 KB406 . . . . **398.21**

Orphan of Ellis Island: a time-travel adventure. /WOODRUFF, E/1997/ 5-A/5 KH881 . . . . **Fic**

Orphan train rider: one boy's true story. /WARREN, A/1996/ 4-6/8 KB015 . . . . **362.73**

Osa menor: una historia del ferrocarril subterraneo./MONJO, FN/1997/ 1-3/2 KG151 . . . . **CE E**

Osito./MINARIK, EH/n.d./P-1/2 KG141 . . . . **CE E**

Osos Berenstain dia de mudanza./BERENSTAIN, S/1994/K-2/4 KF226. . **E**

Ospreys. /PATENT, DH/1993/A/7 KC717 . . . . **598.9**

Ostriches and other flightless birds. /ARNOLD, C/1990/ 5-6/7 KC690 . . . . **598.5**

OTHER THINGS THAT FLY (Videocassette). /1994/ 2-4/KD097 . . . . **VCR 629.13**

Other 1492: Jewish settlement in the new world. /FINKELSTEIN, NH/ 1992/5-6/8 KE687 . . . . **946**

Otherwise known as Sheila the Great. /BLUME, J/1972/ 4-6/4 KG912 . . . . **Fic**

Otis Spofford. /CLEARY, B/1953/3-5/6 KG999. . . . . **Fic**

Otis Spofford (Braille)./CLEARY, B/n.d./3-5/6 KG999. . . . . **Fic**

Ottawa: a kid's eye view. /EDWARDS, FB/1993/5-6/8 KE818. . . . **971.3**

Otter nonsense. /JUSTER, N/1994/3-6/KD721 . . . . **793.734**

Otters under water. /ARNOSKY, J/1992/K-2/2 KC832. . . . . . . **599.769**

OUR AMAZING BODIES: A SUPPLEMENT TO CHILDCRAFT--THE HOW AND WHY LIBRARY. /1995/P-2/KA378 . . . . **REF 031**

Our animal friends at Maple Hill Farm./PROVENSEN, A/1974/ K-2/4 KG290 . . . . **E**

Our beckoning borders: illegal immigration to America. /ASHABRANNER, B/1996/5-6/12 KA924 . . . . **325.73**

Our brother has Down's syndrome: an introduction for children. /CAIRO, S/1985/1-4/6 KB002 . . . . **362.3**

OUR CHANGING EARTH (Videocassette). /1991/3-5/KC153. . **VCR 551**

OUR CONSTITUTION: THE DOCUMENT THAT GAVE BIRTH TO A NATION (Videocassette). /1988/5-A/KA975 . . . . **VCR 342.73**

Our elections. /STEINS, R/1994/5-6/7 KA912 . . . . **324.6**

OUR ENDANGERED EARTH (Videocassette). /1990/ 3-6/KC307. . . . . **VCR 577.27**

Our endangered planet: air. /YOUNT, L/1995/4-6/8 KB069 . . . . **363.73**

Our endangered planet: Antarctica. /WINCKLER, S/1992/ 5-6/8 KE221 . . . . **919.8**

Our endangered planet: atmosphere. /HOFF, MK/1995/ 4-6/8 KB061 . . . . **363.73**

Our endangered planet: groundwater. /HOFF, MK/1991/ 5-6/8 KA959 . . . . **333.91**

Our endangered planet: life on land. /HOFF, MK/1992/ 5-6/8 KA962 . . . . **333.95**

Our endangered planet: oceans./HOFF, MK/1992/5-6/8 KA959 . . **333.91**

Our endangered planet: population growth. /WINCKLER, S/1990/ 5-6/9 KA816 . . . . **304.6**

Our endangered planet: rivers and lakes. /HOFF, MK/1991/ 5-6/8 KB062 . . . . **363.73**

Our family, our friends, our world: an annotated guide to significant multicultural books for children and teenagers. /MILLER-LACHMANN, L/ 1992//KA020 . . . . **PROF 011.62**

OUR FEDERAL GOVERNMENT: THE LEGISLATIVE BRANCH (Videocassette). /1993/5-A/KA933 . . . . **VCR 328.73**

OUR FEDERAL GOVERNMENT: THE PRESIDENCY (Videocassette). / 1993/5-A/KA980 . . . . **VCR 352.23**

OUR FEDERAL GOVERNMENT: THE SUPREME COURT (Videocassette). / 1993/A/KA979 . . . . **VCR 347.73**

Our granny. /WILD, M/1994/P-2/KG717. . . . . **E**

OUR HISPANIC HERITAGE (Videocassette). /1991/ 5-A/KA853 . . . . **VCR 305.8**

Our holidays in poetry. /CARNEGIE LIBRARY SCHOOL ASSOCIATION / 1965/5-6/KD598 . . . . **394.26**

Our house: the stories of Levittown. /CONRAD, P/1995/ 4-6/7 KH022 . . . . **Fic**

Our most dear friend: Bhagavad-gita for children. /VISHAKA /1996/ 2-5/5 KA767 . . . . **294.5**

Our national anthem. /ST. PIERRE, S/1992/4-A/6 KD598 . . . . . . **789.2**

Our national capital. /STEINS, R/1994/4-6/9 KE973 . . . . **975.3**

Our new puppy. /HARPER, I/1996/P-2/1 KF675 . . . . **E**

Our oceans: experiments and activities in marine science. /FLEISHER, P/ 1995/4-6/7 KC172 . . . . **551.46**

Our patchwork planet: the story of plate tectonics. /SATTLER, HR/1995/ A/7 KC155 . . . . **551.1**

Our people. /MEDEARIS, AS/1994/K-2/5 KA852 . . . . **305.8**

Our puppy's vacation. /BROWN, R/1987/P-1/1 KF288 . . . . **E**

Our solar system. /SIMON, S/1992/4-8/7 KC015 . . . . **523.2**

Our teacher's having a baby. /BUNTING, E/1992/P-1/2 KF307 . . . . . **E**

OUR WATERY WORLD (Videocassette). /1991/3-5/KB064 . **VCR 363.73**

OUR WONDERFUL WETLANDS (Videocassette). /1993/ 4-6/KC344. . . . . **VCR 577.68**

Our yard is full of birds. /ROCKWELL, AF/1992/K-2/4 KC662 . . . . . **598**

Out of darkness: the story of Louis Braille. /FREEDMAN, R/1997/ 3-5/6 KE262 . . . . **B BRAILLE, L.**

Out of sight! Out of mind! /LAPOINTE, C/1995/1-3/1 KF945 . . . . . . **E**

Out of the ark: stories from the world's religions. /GANERI, A/1996/ 3-6/5 KA729 . . . . **291.1**

Out of the gang. /GREENBERG, KE/1992/4-6/6 KB071 . . . . . . **364.1**

Outdoor adventure handbook. /MCMANNERS, H/1996/ 4-6/6 KD823 . . . . **796.5**

Outlaws of Sherwood. /MCKINLEY, R/1988/A/8 KH490 . . . . **Fic**

Outside and inside birds. /MARKLE, S/1994/4-6/5 KC655 . . . . . . **598**

Outside and inside sharks. /MARKLE, S/1996/4-6/5 KC594 . . . . **597.3**

Outside and inside snakes. /MARKLE, S/1995/4-6/4 KC641 . . . **597.96**

Outside and inside spiders. /MARKLE, S/1994/5-6/4 KC528 . . . . **595.4**

Outside and inside trees. /MARKLE, S/1993/3-6/6 KC419. . . . . **582.16**

Outside and inside you. /MARKLE, S/1991/4-6/4 KC921 . . . . . . **612**

Outside dog. /POMERANTZ, C/1993/P-2/2 KG266. . . . . **CE E**

Outside dog (Kit)./POMERANTZ, C/1996/P-2/2 KG266 . . . . **CE E**

Outside dog (Sound recording cassette)./POMERANTZ, C/1996/ P-2/2 KG266 . . . . **CE E**

Outward dreams: black inventors and their inventions. /HASKINS, J/1991/ A/10 KC890 .... **609**

Over and over. /ZOLOTOW, C/c1957/P-2/2 KG807 .... **E**

Over here it's different: Carolina's story. /DAWSON, ML/1993/ 5-6/7 KA842 .... **305.8**

Over sea, under stone. /COOPER, S/1966/A/5 KH028. .... **Fic**

Over sea, under stone (Large type)./COOPER, S/1988/A/5 KH028. .. **Fic**

Over sea, under stone (Sound recording cassette)./COOPER, S/n.d./ A/5 KH028. .... **Fic**

Over the green hills. /ISADORA, R/1992/1-3/2 KF817 .... **E**

Over the top of the world: explorer Will Steger's trek across the Arctic. / STEGER, W/1997/5-6/6 KE219 .... **919.8**

Over, under and through, and other spatial concepts. /HOBAN, T/1973/ P-K/KF745 .... **E**

OVERLAND TO CALIFORNIA IN 1859: A GUIDE FOR WAGON TRAIN TRAVELERS. /1983/A/12 KF042 .... **978**

Owen. /HENKES, K/1993/P-2/2 KF709 .... **E**

Owen (Videocassette). /HENKES, K/1995/P-2/KF710 .... **VCR E**

Owl and the Pussy-cat. /LEAR, E/1996/P-2/KE105. .... **821**

Owl and the Pussy-cat and other nonsense poems. /LEAR, E/1995/ 3-6/KE106 .... **821**

Owl and three pussycats. /PROVENSEN, A/1994/K-2/5 KG289 ..... **E**

Owl at home. /LOBEL, A/c1975/K-2/1 KG010 .... **E**

Owl at home (Sound recording cassette)./LOBEL, A/n.d./K-2/1 KG010 . **E**

Owl eyes. /GATES, F/1994/1-3/4 KB570 .... **398.24**

Owl moon. /YOLEN, J/1987/P-3/2 KG778 .... **CE E**

Owl moon (Videocassette)./YOLEN, J/1989/P-3/2 KF778. ...... **CE E**

OWL: THE DISCOVERY MAGAZINE FOR CHILDREN. /1976-/ 2-4/KA535 .... **PER 050**

Owl who became the moon. /LONDON, J/1993/P-2/3 KG026 ...... **E**

Owls. /BROWN, FG/1991/5-6/5 KC711 .... **598.9**

Owls. /KAPPELER, M/1991/5-6/6 KC715 .... **598.9**

Ox-cart man. /HALL, D/1979/K-3/7 KF663 .... **CE E**

Ox-cart man (Braille)./HALL, D/n.d./K-3/7 KF663. .... **CE E**

Ox-cart man (Kit)./HALL, D/1984/K-3/7 KF663. .... **CE E**

Ox-cart man (Sound recording cassette)./HALL, D/n.d./ K-3/7 KF663 .... **CE E**

Ox-cart man (Videocassette)./HALL, D/1992/K-3/7 KF663. ..... **CE E**

OXFORD BOOK OF SCARYTALES. /1992/6-A/7 KH569. .... **Fic**

OXFORD DICTIONARY OF NURSERY RHYMES. /1997/ 5-6/KA416 .... **REF 398.8**

Oxford picture dictionary of American English. English/Spanish ed. / PARNWELL, EC/c1978, 1988/4-6/KB860 .... **463**

Ozma of Oz./BAUM, LF/1989/4-6/7 KG884 .... **Fic**

Ozzie on his own. /HURWITZ, J/1995/3-5/4 KH301 .... **Fic**

Ozzie on his own (Sound recording cassette)./HURWITZ, J/1997/ 3-5/4 KH301 .... **Fic**

P. Bear's New Year's party!: a counting book. /LEWIS, PO/1989/ K-1/3 KF978 .... **E**

Pablo Picasso. /LORIA, S/1995/4-A/12 KD490 .... **759.4**

Pablo recuerda./ANCONA, G/1993/3-6/5 KB193 .... **394.26**

Pablo remembers: the Fiesta of the Day of the Dead. /ANCONA, G/ 1993/3-6/5 KB193 .... **394.26**

Pacific coast. /MCCONNAUGHEY, BH/1985/A/KC296. .... **577**

PACIFIC EDGE (Videocassette). /1989/5-6/KE181. .... **VCR 917**

Paddington audio collection (Talking book). /BOND, M/1978/ 2-4/KG917 .... **TB Fic**

Paddington on screen. /BOND, M/1982/2-4/5 KG916. .... **Fic**

Paddington takes the test./BOND, M/1980/2-4/5 KG916 .... **Fic**

Paddington's storybook. /BOND, M/1984/3-6/5 KG918 .... **Fic**

Paddington's storybook (Braille)./BOND, M/n.d./3-6/5 KG918. .... **Fic**

Paddle-to-the-sea. /HOLLING, HC/c1941/4-6/5 KH271 .... **Fic**

Pagoo. /HOLLING, HC/1957/5-6/4 KC519 .... **595.3**

Pagoo (Sound recording cassette)./HOLLING, HC/n.d./ 5-6/4 KC519 .... **595.3**

Pain and the great one. /BLUME, J/1984/K-3/4 KF239 .... **CE E**

Pain and the great one (Kit)./BLUME, J/1988/K-3/4 KF239 ..... **CE E**

Pain and the great one (Sound recording cassette)./BLUME, J/n.d./ K-3/4 KF239 .... **CE E**

Paint! /SOLGA, K/1991/2-6/4 KD370 .... **702.8**

PAINT (Videocassette). /1984/5-6/KD325 .... **VCR 667**

Painter. /FLORIAN, D/1993/1-2/4 KD464 .... **750**

Painting: a young artist's guide. /WATERS, E/1993/5-6/8 KD470 . **751.4**

Painting and coloring dinosaurs. /SANCHEZ SANCHEZ, I/1996/ 5-A/3 KD419 .... **743**

Pair of socks. /MURPHY, SJ/1996/P-1/2 KA634 .... **153.14**

Pal the pony. /HERMAN, RA/1996/K-1/2 KF714. .... **E**

Palace of stars. /LAKIN, P/1993/1-3/3 KF943 .... **E**

Palm trees. /COTE, N/1993/K-2/4 KF427 .... **E**

Pan y mermelada para Francisca./HOBAN, R/1995/P-1/2 KF739 .. **CE E**

Panama Canal. /MCNEESE, T/1997/5-6/11 KB145 .... **386**

PANAMA CANAL (Picture). /n.d./5-6/KB146 .... **PIC 386**

Pancakes for breakfast. /DE PAOLA, T/1978/1-2/KF478 ...... **E**

Pancho's pinata. /CZERNECKI, S/1992/2-4/7 KB703 .... **398.26**

Panda. /ARNOLD, C/1992/4-6/7 KC866 .... **599.789**

Pandilla en la orilla./MARSHALL, E/n.d./K-3/1 KG066 .... **CE E**

Papa Gatto: an Italian fairy tale. /SANDERSON, R/1995/ 3-4/6 KB646 .... **398.24**

Papa Oso vuelve a casa./MINARIK, EH/n.d./P-1/2 KG141 ...... **CE E**

Papagayo the mischief maker. /MCDERMOTT, G/1992/P-2/5 KG096 .. **E**

Paper. /DIXON, A/1991/3-5/6 KD333 .... **676**

Paper airplane book. /SIMON, S/c1971/3-5/6 KD113 .... **629.133**

Paper crane. /BANG, M/1985/K-3/4 KF191 .... **CE E**

Paper crane (Braille)./BANG, M/n.d./K-3/4 KF191 .... **CE E**

Paper crane (Sound recording cassette)./BANG, M/n.d./ K-3/4 KF191 .... **CE E**

PAPER (Videocassette). /1986/5-6/KD334 .... **VCR 676**

Paperboy. /PILKEY, D/1996/K-2/2 KG238 .... **E**

Paperboy. /KROEGER, MK/1996/1-3/2 KF926 .... **E**

Papercrafts around the world. /FIAROTTA, P/1996/2-6/6 KD440 . **745.54**

Parables of Jesus./DE PAOLA, T/1987/5-6/7 KA695 .... **232.9**

Parade. /CREWS, D/1983/P-2/4 KB188 .... **394.2**

PARENTS' CHOICE: A REVIEW OF CHILDREN'S MEDIA. /1978-/ /KA130 .... **PER PROF 050**

Parents in the pigpen, pigs in the tub. /EHRLICH, A/1993/K-2/6 KF521 . **E**

Paris. /STEIN, RC/1996/3-5/8 KE685 .... **944**

Parrots. /MURRAY, P/1993/3-5/7 KC701 .... **598.7**

Partners. /WAGGONER, K/1995/2-4/4 KH836. .... **Fic**

Paseo de Rosie./HUTCHINS, P/1997/P-1/1 KF802 .... **CE E**

Paseo por el bosque liuvio./A walk in the rainforest./PRATT, KJ/1993/ K-6/7 KC322 .... **577.34**

Pasito...y otro pasito./DE PAOLA, T/1986/K-3/5 KF476 .... **E**

PASS IT ON: AFRICAN-AMERICAN POETRY FOR CHILDREN. /1993/ 1-3/KE075 .... **811.008**

Pass the bread! /BADT, KL/1995/4-6/6 KD291 .... **641.8**

Passage to freedom: the Sugihara story. /MOCHIZUKI, K/1997/ 3-6/4 KE662 .... **940.53**

Passenger pigeon. /MORRISON, SD/1989/4-6/4 KC656. ...... **598**

Passover magic. /SCHOTTER, R/1995/K-2/2 KG410 .... **E**

Patakin: world tales of drums and drummers. /JAFFE, N/1994/ 5-6/6 KB321 .... **398.2**

Patchwork girl of Oz./BAUM, LF/1995/4-6/7 KG884. .... **Fic**

Patchwork quilt. /FLOURNOY, V/1985/K-3/5 KF561 .... **E**

Patchwork quilt (Braille)./FLOURNOY, V/n.d./K-3/5 KF561 ..... **E**

Path of the Quiet Elk: a Native American alphabet book. /STROUD, VA/ 1996/3-6/5 KA793 .... **299**

Patrick: patron saint of Ireland. /DE PAOLA, T/1992/ 2-4/KE492 .... **B PATRICK, ST.**

Patrick's dinosaurs. /CARRICK, C/1983/K-2/4 KF361 .... **CE E**

Patrick's dinosaurs (Kit)./CARRICK, C/1987/K-2/4 KF361 ...... **CE E**

PATRIOTIC SONGS AND MARCHES (Compact disc). /1991/ K-6/KD582 .... **SRC 789.2**

PATRIOTIC SONGS AND MARCHES (Sound recording cassette). /1991/ K-6/KD582 .... **SRC 789.2**

PATTERNS OF INFLUENCE ON GIFTED LEARNERS: THE HOME, SELF, AND THE SCHOOL. /1989//KA188. .... **PROF 371.95**

Pattysaurus and other tales (Sound recording cassette). /EDGECOMB, D/ 1995/P-3/KF508. .... **SRC E**

Paul Bunyan, a tall tale. /KELLOGG, S/1984/4-6/7 KB457 ..... **398.22**

Paul Bunyan, a tall tale (Big book)./KELLOGG, S/1993/ 4-6/7 KB457 .... **398.22**

Paul Bunyan swings his axe. /MCCORMICK, DJ/c1936, 1962/ 4-6/6 KB467 .... **398.22**

Paul Bunyan swings his axe (Braille)./MCCORMICK, DJ/n.d./ 4-6/6 KB467 .... **398.22**

Paul Bunyan: un cuento fantastico./KELLOGG, S/1994/ 4-6/7 KB457 .... **398.22**

Paul Bunyan (Videocassette). /GLEESON, B/1990/ 3-5/KB447 .... **VCR 398.22**

Paul Revere's ride. /LONGFELLOW, HW/1990/3-A/KD980 ..... **CE 811**

Paul Revere's ride (Videocassette)./LONGFELLOW, HW/1992/ 3-A/KD980 .... **CE 811**

Paul Robeson: a voice to remember. /MCKISSACK, P/1992/ 2-5/2 KE514 .... **B ROBESON, P.**

PAWS, CLAWS, FEATHERS AND FINS (Videocassette). /1993/ 3-5/KD191. .... **VCR 636.088**

Paws, wings, and hooves: mammals on the move. /YAMASHITA, K/1993/ 2-5/2 KC468 .... **591.47**

Peace and bread: the story of Jane Addams. /MCPHERSON, SS/1993/ 4-6/5 KE228 .... **B ADDAMS, J.**

Peace begins with you. /SCHOLES, K/1990/P-2/5 KA812 .... **303.6**

Peace crane. /HAMANAKA, S/1995/1-3/4 KF668 .... **E**

Peace tales: world folktales to talk about. /MACDONALD, MR/1992/ /KA271 .... **PROF 398.2**

Peachboy (Kit)./METAXAS, E/1995/2-5/KB469 .... **VCR 398.22**

Peachboy (Videocassette)./METAXAS, E/1991/2-5/KB469 . **VCR 398.22**

Peanut butter. /ERLBACH, A/1994/4-6/7 KD265 .... **641.3**

Pearl's first prize plant. /DELANEY, A/1997/K-2/1 KF459 .... **E**

Peas and honey: recipes for kids (with a pinch of poetry). /COLEN, K/ 1995/3-6/KD269 . . . . **641.5**

Peboan and Seegwun. /LARRY, C/1993/2-3/4 KB709. . . . . **398.26**

Peces./PARKER, S/1995/5-6/7 KC584. . . . . **597**

Peck slither and slide. /MACDONALD, S/1997/P-2/1 KC452 . . . . . **591**

Pecos Bill./KELLOGG, S/1986/4-6/7 KB457 . . . . **398.22**

Pecos Bill (Sound recording cassette)./KELLOGG, S/n.d./ 4-6/7 KB457 . . . . **398.22**

Pecos Bill: un cuento fantastico./KELLOGG, S/1995/4-6/7 KB457 . **398.22**

Peculiar zoo. /POLISAR, BL/1993/K-2/KD999 . . . . **811**

Pedal power: how a mountain bike is made. /HAUTZIG, D/1996/ 5-6/6 KD125 . . . . **629.227**

Peddler's dream. /SHEFELMAN, J/1992/1-3/2 KG492 . . . . **E**

Pedrito's Day. /GARAY, L/1997/1-3/2 KF598 . . . . **E**

Pedro and the monkey. /SAN SOUCI, RD/1996/3-4/2 KB649 . . . **398.24**

Pedro fools the gringo and other tales of a Latin American trickster. / BRUSCA, MC/1995/2-4/3 KB429 . . . . **398.22**

PEELING THE ONION: AN ANTHOLOGY OF POEMS. /1993/ A/KD888. . . . . **808.81**

Peep and the big wide world (Videocassette). /PINDAL, K/1991/ P-2/KG239 . . . . **VCR E**

Peeping and sleeping. /MANUSHKIN, F/1994/P-2/2 KG060 . . . . . **E**

PEGASUS (Videocassette). /1990/3-6/KA749 . . . . **VCR 292**

Pelican. /STONE, LM/1990/5-6/6 KC684 . . . . **598.4**

Pelicans. /PATENT, DH/1992/5-6/8 KC682 . . . . **598.4**

Penguin. /FLETCHER, N/1993/P-1/2 KC687 . . . . **598.47**

Penguin: a funny bird. /FONTANEL, B/1992/1-4/4 KC688. . . . . **598.47**

Penguins of the Antarctic (Picture). /CHESTER, J/1995/ 4-6/KC685. . . . . **PIC 598.47**

Penguins of the world (Picture). /CHESTER, J/1995/ 3-6/KC686. . . . . **PIC 598.47**

Pennsylvania. /SWAIN, G/1994/4-6/7 KE960. . . . . **974.8**

Pennsylvania Colony. /FRADIN, DB/1988/5-6/7 KE959 . . . . **974.8**

Penny a look. /ZEMACH, H/c1971/K-2/2 KG789 . . . . **E**

People apart. /KENNA, K/1995/4-6/7 KA720 . . . . **289.7**

People of corn: a Mayan story. /GERSON, M/1995/ 2-4/3 KB399 . . . . **398.21**

People of peace. /BLUE, R/1994/5-A/7 KA806 . . . . **303.6**

People of the breaking day. /SEWALL, M/1990/3-6/5 KA858 . . . . **305.8**

People of the breaking day (Sound recording cassette)./SEWALL, M/ 1993/3-6/5 KA858 . . . . **305.8**

People of the sacred arrows: the Southern Cheyenne today. /HOIG, S/ 1992/6-A/7 KE781 . . . . **970.466**

People of the short blue corn: tales and legends of the Hopi Indians. / COURLANDER, H/c1970, 1996/1-A/5 KB278 . . . . **398.2**

PEOPLE TO KNOW: A SUPPLEMENT TO CHILDCRAFT--THE HOW AND WHY LIBRARY./1989/P-2/KA378. . . . . **REF 031**

People with one heart (Talking book). /PINDER, M/1996/ P-1/KD876. . . . . **TB 808.8**

People with one heart (Talking book)./PINDER, M/1996/ P-1/KD876. . . . . **TB 808.8**

PEOPLES OF THE WORLD: NORTH AMERICANS. /1991/ 6-A/KA479 . . . . **REF 970.004**

Pepi and the secret names. /WALSH, JP/1995/2-3/6 KG683 . . . . **E**

Pepi and the secret names (Sound recording cassette)./WALSH, JP/1997/ 2-3/6 KG683 . . . . **E**

Peppe the lamplighter. /BARTONE, E/1993/1-3/2 KF211 . . . . . . **E**

Per and the Dala horse. /HICKOX, R/1995/1-3/6 KF724 . . . . . . **E**

Percussion. /SHIPTON, A/1994/4-6/7 KD547 . . . . **786.8**

Perfect family. /CARLSON, N/1985/P-2/2 KF351 . . . . **CE E**

Perfect family (Kit)./CARLSON, N/1987/P-2/2 KF351 . . . . **CE E**

Perilous gard. /POPE, EM/1974/5-6/6 KH609 . . . . **Fic**

Perilous gard (Sound recording cassette)./POPE, EM/n.d./ 5-6/6 KH609 . . . . **Fic**

Period: revised and updated with a parents' guide. /GARDNER-LOULAN, J/1991/5-6/7 KC947. . . . . **612.6**

Persephone. /HUTTON, W/1994/5-6/5 KA744 . . . . **292**

Persephone and the pomegranate: a myth from Greece. /WALDHERR, K/ 1993/4-6/6 KA753 . . . . **292**

Perseus. /HUTTON, W/1993/5-6/4 KA745. . . . . **292**

Persian Gulf War: "the mother of all battles." /KENT, Z/1994/ 6-A/6 KE715 . . . . **956.7044**

Persian Gulf War: "the mother of all battles" (Sound recording cassette)./ KENT, Z/1997/6-A/6 KE715 . . . . **956.7044**

Pesca de Nessa./LUENN, N/1994/K-2/2 KG041 . . . . **CE E**

Pet gerbils./WEXLER, J/1990/4-6/7 KD186. . . . . **636**

Pet hamsters./WEXLER, J/1992/4-6/7 KD187 . . . . **636**

Pet of the Met. /FREEMAN, L/c1953/1-2/7 KF582 . . . . **E**

Pet show. /KEATS, EJ/1987/P-2/2 KF876 . . . . **CE E**

Pet show (Kit)./KEATS, EJ/1992/P-2/2 KF876 . . . . **CE E**

Pet show (Talking book)./KEATS, EJ/n.d./P-2/2 KF876. . . . . **CE E**

Pet show (Videocassette)./KEATS, EJ/1992/P-2/2 KF876. . . . . . . **CE E**

Pete Seeger's family concert (Videocassette). /SEEGER, P/1992/ K-3/KD588 . . . . **VCR 789.2**

Peter and the wolf. /PROKOFIEV, S/1982/P-3/4 KD676 . . . . . **CE 789.8**

PETER COTTONTAIL: HOW HE GOT HIS HOP! (Videocasstte). /1993/ P-2/KD646. . . . . **VCR 789.3**

Peter, Paul and Mommy, too (Compact disc). /PETER, PAUL & MARY / 1993/P-3/KD583 . . . . **CD 789.2**

Peter Spier's circus! /SPIER, P/1992/P-2/4 KG532 . . . . **E**

Peter's chair. /KEATS, EJ/c1967/P-2/2 KF877. . . . . **CE E**

Peter's chair (Big book)./KEATS, EJ/1993/P-2/2 KF877. . . . . **CE E**

Peter's chair (Braille)./KEATS, EJ/n.d./P-2/2 KF877 . . . . **CE E**

Peter's chair (Kit)./KEATS, EJ/1995/P-2/2 KF877. . . . . **CE E**

Peter's chair (Videocassette)./KEATS, EJ/1969/P-2/2 KF877 . . . . . **CE E**

Peterson first guide to clouds and weather. /DAY, JA/1991/ 3-6/A KC211 . . . . **551.57**

Peterson first guide to insects of North America. /LEAHY, CW/1987/ 5-6/8 KC544 . . . . **595.7**

Peterson first guide to mammals of North America. /ALDEN, P/1987/ 4-6/6 KC720 . . . . **599**

Petey's bedtime story. /CLEARY, B/1993/2-3/3 KF395 . . . . **E**

Petrosinella: a Neapolitan Rapunzel. /STANLEY, D/1995/ 2-4/6 KB780 . . . . **398.27**

PETS AND OTHER ANIMALS: A SUPPLEMENT TO CHILDCRAFT--THE HOW AND WHY LIBRARY. /1992/P-2/KA378 . . . . **REF 031**

Pets without homes. /ARNOLD, C/1983/1-4/6 KD189 . . . . **636.08**

Petunia. /DUVOISIN, R/c1950/K-2/3 KF502 . . . . **CE E**

Petunia (Braille)./DUVOISIN, R/n.d./K-2/3 KF502 . . . . **CE E**

Petunia (Talking book)./DUVOISIN, R/n.d./K-2/3 KF502. . . . . . . **CE E**

Petunia (Videocassette)./DUVOISIN, R/1985/K-2/3 KF502. . . . . . **CE E**

Petunia's Christmas./DUVOISIN, R/c1952, 1980/K-2/3 KF502 . . . . **CE E**

PHANTOM OF THE BELL TOWER (Videocassette). /1991/ 5-A/KB978. . . . . **VCR 513.2**

Phantom tollbooth (Braille)./JUSTER, N/n.d./4-6/6 KH339 . . . . . . **CE Fic**

Phantom tollbooth (Sound recording cassette)./JUSTER, N/n.d./ 4-6/6 KH339 . . . . **CE Fic**

Phantom tollbooth. Special 35th anniversary ed. /JUSTER, N/1996/ 4-6/6 KH339 . . . . **CE Fic**

Phantom tollbooth (Talking book)./JUSTER, N/n.d./4-6/6 KH339 . **CE Fic**

PHI DELTA KAPPAN. /1915-//KA131 . . . . **PER PROF 050**

Philadelphia adventure. /ALEXANDER, L/1992/5-A/5 KG837 . . . . **Fic**

Philharmonic gets dressed. /KUSKIN, K/1982/K-3/5 KF939 . . . . **E**

Phillis Wheatley. /SHERROW, V/1992/4-6/7 KE591. . . . **B WHEATLEY, P.**

Phoebe's parade. /MILLS, C/1994/K-2/2 KG138 . . . . **E**

PHONE MANNERS (Videocassette). /1991/3-6/KB251 . . . . . **VCR 395.5**

PHOTOGRAPHY. /1994/5-A/7 KD514 . . . . **771**

Pickle song. /DECLEMENTS, B/1993/4-6/4 KH065. . . . . **Fic**

Picnic. /MCCULLY, EA/1984/P-2/KG094 . . . . **CE E**

Picnic (Videocassette)./MCCULLY, EA/1991/P-2/KG094 . . . . **CE E**

Picnic with Piggins./YOLEN, J/c1988, 1993/K-3/KG779 . . . . **E**

Picture book of Anne Frank. /ADLER, DA/1993/ 3-4/5 KE351 . . . . **CE B FRANK, A.**

Picture book of Anne Frank (Kit)./ADLER, DA/1995/ 3-4/5 KE351 . . . . **CE B FRANK, A.**

Picture book of Christopher Columbus. /ADLER, DA/1991/ 2-3/4 KE300 . . . . **CE B COLUMBUS, C.**

Picture book of Christopher Columbus (Kit)./ADLER, DA/1992/ 2-3/4 KE300 . . . . **CE B COLUMBUS, C.**

Picture book of Davy Crockett. /ADLER, DA/1996/ 2-3/7 KE310 . . . . **B CROCKETT, D.**

Picture book of Florence Nightingale. /ADLER, DA/1992/ 2-4/3 KE478 . . . . **B NIGHTINGALE**

Picture book of Jackie Robinson. /ADLER, DA/1994/ 2-4/6 KE515 . . . . **B ROBINSON, J.**

Picture book of Jesse Owens. /ADLER, DA/1992/ 3-4/6 KE486 . . . . **B OWENS, J.**

Picture book of Louis Braille. /ADLER, DA/1997/ 2-3/3 KE261 . . . . **B BRAILLE, L.**

Picture book of Martin Luther King, Jr. /ADLER, DA/1989/ 3-4/4 KE420 . . . . **CE B KING, M.L.**

Picture book of Martin Luther King, Jr. (Kit)./ADLER, DA/1990/ 3-4/4 KE420 . . . . **CE B KING, M.L.**

Picture book of Martin Luther King, Jr. (Videocassette)./ADLER, DA/1990/ 3-4/4 KE420 . . . . **CE B KING, M.L.**

Picture book of Paul Revere. /ADLER, DA/1995/ 2-4/5 KE508 . . . . **B REVERE, P.**

Picture book of Robert E. Lee. /ADLER, DA/1994/ 2-5/5 KE429 . . . . **B LEE, R.**

Picture book of Simon Bolivar. /ADLER, DA/1992/ 3-4/5 KE257 . . . . **B BOLIVAR, S.**

Picture book of Sitting Bull. /ADLER, DA/1993/ 3-4/5 KE540 . . . . **B SITTING BULL**

Picture book of Sojourner Truth. /ADLER, DA/1994/ 2-5/6 KE572 . . . . **B TRUTH, S.**

Picture book of Thomas Alva Edison. /ADLER, DA/1996/ 2-3/3 KE330 . . . . **B EDISON, T.**

Picture book of Thomas Jefferson. /ADLER, DA/1990/ 2-3/5 KE403 . . . . **B JEFFERSON, T.**
Picture books to enhance the curriculum. /HARMS, JM/1996/ /KA016. . . . . **PROF 011.62**
Picture for Harold's room./JOHNSON, C/1960/P-2/2 KF835 . . . . . **CE E**
Picture for Harold's room (Videocassette)./JOHNSON, C/n.d./ P-2/2 KF835 . . . . **CE E**
Picture puzzler. /WESTRAY, K/1994/1-6/7 KA621. . . . . **152.14**
Picture reference atlas. /PICKERING, M/1996/2-4/3 KE171 . . . . **912**
Pierre: a cautionary tale in five chapters and a prologue. /SENDAK, M/ c1962/P-1/KG436. . . . . **CE E**
Pierre: a cautionary tale in five chapters and a prologue (Videocassette)./ SENDAK, M/1976/P-1/KG436 . . . . **CE E**
Pig William. /DUBANEVICH, A/1985/P-2/1 KF498. . . . . **E**
Pigeons and doves. /NOFSINGER, R/1992/4-6/4 KC696 . . . . **598.6**
Piggie Pie! /PALATINI, M/1995/1-5/2 KG207. . . . . **E**
Piggies. /WOOD, D/1991/P-K/1 KG768 . . . . **E**
Piggins. /YOLEN, J/1987/K-3/4 KG779. . . . . **E**
Piggins and the royal wedding./YOLEN, J/1988/K-3/4 KG779 . . . . **E**
Piggle. /BONSALL, CN/1973/P-2/2 KF246. **E**
PIGGY BANKS TO MONEY MARKETS: A KID'S VIDEO GUIDE TO DOLLARS AND SENSE (Videocassette). /1993/ 4-6/KA945 . . . . **VCR 332.024**
Pigs ahoy! /MCPHAIL, D/1995/P-2/3 KG121 . . . . **E**
Pigs aplenty, pigs galore! /MCPHAIL, D/1993/P-2/2 KG122 . . . . **E**
Pigs aplenty, pigs galore! (Sound recording cassette)./MCPHAIL, D/1995/ P-2/2 KG122 . . . . **E**
Pigs from A to Z. /GEISERT, A/1986/1-3/3 KF603 . . . . **E**
Pigs from 1 to 10. /GEISERT, A/1992/1-3/3 KF604. . . . . **E**
Pigs in the mud in the middle of the rud. /PLOURDE, L/1997/ K-2/2 KG247 . . . . **E**
Pigs in the pantry: fun with math and cooking. /AXELROD, A/1997/ 1-3/3 KF178 . . . . **E**
Pigs on a blanket. /AXELROD, A/1996/2-3/2 KF179 . . . . **E**
Pigs' wedding. /HEINE, H/c1978, 1986/P-2/6 KF697 . . . . **CE E**
Pigsty. /TEAGUE, M/1994/K-2/2 KG595. . . . . **E**
PILGRIM VOICES: OUR FIRST YEAR IN THE NEW WORLD. /1995/ 3-6/7 KE944 . . . . **974.4**
Pilgrims at Plymouth. /PENNER, LR/1996/1-3/2 KE943 . . . . **974.4**
Pilgrims of Plimoth. /SEWALL, M/1986/4-6/7 KE947 . . . . **CE 974.4**
Pilgrims of Plimoth (Videocassette)./SEWALL, M/1990/ 4-6/7 KE947 . . . . **CE 974.4**
Pin the tail on the donkey and other party games. /COLE, J/1993/ K-2/3 KD698 . . . . **793**
Pinata!: bilingual songs for children (Compact disc)./BARCHAS, S/1991/ K-6/KD605 . . . . **SRC 789.3**
Pinata!: bilingual songs for children (Sound recording cassette). /BARCHAS, S/1991/K-6/KD605. . . . . **SRC 789.3**
Pinata maker./El Pinatero. /ANCONA, G/1994/3-6/6 KD450 . . **745.594**
Pinatas and paper flowers, holidays of the Americas in English and Spanish/ Pinatas y flores de papel, fiestas de las Americas en ingles y espanol. /PERL, L/1983/4-6/6 KB202 . . . . **394.26**
Pinballs. /BYARS, BC/c1977/5-6/3 KG963 . . . . **CE Fic**
Pinballs (Kit)./BYARS, BC/1988/5-6/3 KG963. . . . . **CE Fic**
Pinballs (Sound recording cassette)./BYARS, BC/n.d./ 5-6/3 KG963 . . . . **CE Fic**
Pink and Say. /POLACCO, P/1994/4-6/2 KH607 . . . . **Fic**
Pinkerton, behave. /KELLOGG, S/1979/P-2/2 KF894 . . . . **CE E**
Pioneer children of Appalachia. /ANDERSON, J/1986/ 4-6/6 KE974 . . . . **975.4**
Pioneer plowmaker: a story about John Deere. /COLLINS, DR/1990/ 5-6/6 KE317 . . . . **B DEERE, J.**
Pioneer projects. /KALMAN, B/1997/3-5/6 KD432. . . . . **745.5**
Pioneer sampler: the daily life of a pioneer family in 1840. / GREENWOOD, B/1995/4-6/6 KF031. . . . . **978**
Pioneering ocean depths. /MARKLE, S/1995/4-A/8 KC175 . . . . . **551.46**
Pioneers go west. /STEWART, GR/c1982, 1997/4-6/7 KF051 . . . . . **978**
PIP AND ZENA'S SCIENCE VOYAGE (Videodisc). /1996/ K-3/KB869. . . . . **VD 500**
Pippi goes on board./LINDGREN, A/1957/3-5/4 KH407. . . . . . . **CE Fic**
Pippi goes on board (Braille)./LINDGREN, A/n.d./3-5/4 KH407 . . **CE Fic**
Pippi goes on board (Talking book)./LINDGREN, A/n.d./ 3-5/4 KH407 . . . . **CE Fic**
Pippi in the South Seas./LINDGREN, A/c1959/3-5/4 KH407 . . . . **CE Fic**
Pippi in the South Seas (Talking book)./LINDGREN, A/n.d./ 3-5/4 KH407 . . . . **CE Fic**
Pippi Longstocking. /LINDGREN, A/c1950, 1978/3-5/4 KH407 . . **CE Fic**
Pippi Longstocking (Braille)./LINDGREN, A/n.d./3-5/4 KH407 . . . **CE Fic**
Pippi Longstocking (Large type)./LINDGREN, A/1987/ 3-5/4 KH407 . . . . **CE Fic**
Pippi Longstocking (Sound recording cassette)./LINDGREN, A/n.d./ 3-5/4 KH407 . . . . **CE Fic**
Pippi Longstocking (Talking book)./LINDGREN, A/1973/ 3-5/4 KH407 . . . . **CE Fic**
Pippi Longstocking (Talking book)./LINDGREN, A/n.d./ 3-5/4 KH407 . . . . **CE Fic**
Pirate. /PLATT, R/1994/4-A/7 KE157 . . . . **910.4**
Pirate queen. /MCCULLY, EA/1995/3-5/5 KE156. . . . . **910.4**
Pirate School. /DUBOWSKI, CE/1996/1-3/2 KF499 . . . . **E**
Pirates. /STEELE, P/1997/3-6/7 KE160 . . . . **910.4**
Pirate's promise. /BULLA, CR/c1986, 1994/2-4/2 KG937 . . . . **Fic**
Pirates: robbers of the high seas. /GIBBONS, G/1993/ 2-4/7 KE154 . . . . **910.4**
PITCH (Videocassette). /1994/K-2/KD523. . . . . **VCR 780**
Pitchers: twenty-seven of baseball's greatest. /SULLIVAN, G/1994/ 5-A/6 KD805 . . . . **796.357**
Pizza! /MARTINO, T/1989/3-4/2 KD292. . . . . **641.8**
Pizza for breakfast. /KOVALSKI, M/1991/K-2/2 KF917 . . . . **E**
Pizza party! /MACCARONE, G/1994/P-1/1 KG047 . . . . **E**
Pizza the size of the sun: poems. /PRELUTSKY, J/1996/K-A/KE012 . . **811**
P.J.'S READING ADVENTURES (CD-ROM). /1996/K-3/KB252. **CDR 398**
Place called Freedom. /SANDERS, SR/1997/1-3/3 KG390 . . . . **E**
Place called heartbreak: a story of Vietnam. /MYERS, WD/1993/ 5-6/6 KE721 . . . . **959.704**
Place for Ben. /TITHERINGTON, J/1987/P-2/2 KG608. . . . . **E**
PLACE MY WORDS ARE LOOKING FOR: WHAT POETS SAY ABOUT AND THROUGH THEIR WORK. /1990/3-A/KE076 . . . . **811.008**
Place to hide. /PETTIT, J/1993/5-A/7 KE663 . . . . **940.53**
Place where nobody stopped. /SEGAL, J/1994/5-A/7 KH690 . . . . . . **Fic**
Places of refuge: our national wildlife refuge system. /PATENT, DH/1992/ 4-6/7 KA966 . . . . **333.95**
Places of refuge: our national wildlife refuge system./PATENT, DH/1997/ 4-6/7 KA966 . . . . **333.95**
Plain City. /HAMILTON, V/1993/6-A/5 KH217 . . . . **Fic**
Plain City (Sound recording cassette)./HAMILTON, V/1995/ 6-A/5 KH217 . . . . **Fic**
Plane song. /SIEBERT, D/1993/3-6/KD112. . . . . **629.133**
Planes. /STEELE, P/1991/4-6/6 KD100 . . . . **629.13**
Planet Earth/inside out. /GIBBONS, G/1995/3-6/6 KC146 . . . . **550**
Planet of Junior Brown. /HAMILTON, V/c1971/A/6 KH218. . . . . **CE Fic**
Planet of Junior Brown (Talking book)./HAMILTON, V/1975/ A/6 KH218 . . . . **CE Fic**
PLANET OF THE GRAPES: SHOW BIZ JOKES AND RIDDLES. /1992/ 3-6/KD737. . . . . **793.735**
Planet with one mind: stories from around the world for the child within us all (Talking book). /PINDER, M/1995/1-4/KD877 . . . . **TB 808.8**
Planet with one mind: stories from around the world for the child within us all (Talking book)./PINDER, M/1995/1-4/KD877 . . . . **TB 808.8**
Planetary taxi (CD-ROM). /MOHL, R/1993/4-A/KC013 . . . . **CDR 523.2**
Planets. /GIBBONS, G/1993/2-4/4 KC025. . . . . **523.4**
Planets in our solar system. Rev. ed. /BRANLEY, FM/1987/ 2-4/4 KC023 . . . . **523.4**
PLANETS (Picture). /1990/3-6/KC029 . . . . **PIC 523.4**
Plant. /BURNIE, D/1989/3-A/7 KC383 . . . . **580**
Plant families. /LERNER, C/1989/A/7 KC388 . . . . **580**
Plant survival: adapting to a hostile world. /CAPON, B/1994/ A/9 KC397 . . . . **581.4**
Plant-and-grow project book. /DIETL, U/1993/P-4/5 KC384. . . . . . . **580**
Plants. /SILVERSTEIN, A/1996/5-A/7 KC392 . . . . **580**
PLANTS: ANGIOSPERMS (Videocassette). /1990/4-A/KC390 . **VCR 580**
Plants that make you sniffle and sneeze. /LERNER, C/1993/ 5-6/9 KC404 . . . . **581.6**
Plants up close. /RAHN, JE/1981/4-6/6 KC391. . . . . **580**
Plastics. /CASH, T/1990/3-5/5 KD327. . . . . **668.4**
Play ball, Amelia Bedelia. /PARISH, P/1996/1-3/2 KG216. . . . . **E**
Play, learn, and grow: an annotated guide to the best books and materials for very young children. /THOMAS, JL/1992//KA088 . . **PROF 028.1**
Play with me. /ETS, MH/c1955/P-1/2 KF539 . . . . **CE E**
Play with me (Braille)./ETS, MH/n.d./P-1/2 KF539. . . . . **CE E**
Play with me (Talking book)./ETS, MH/n.d./P-1/2 KF539 . . . . **CE E**
Play with paint. /LYNN, S/1993/K-2/3 KD465 . . . . **750**
Play with paper. /LYNN, S/1993/K-2/3 KD441. . . . . **745.54**
Playing Beatie Bow. /PARK, R/1982/5-A/6 KH571. . . . . **Fic**
PLAYING FAIR (Videocassette). /1991/4-6/KA854. . . . . **VCR 305.8**
Playing right field. /WELCH, W/1995/K-2/3 KG694. . . . . **E**
Playing smart: a parent's guide to enriching offbeat learning activities for ages 4-14. /PERRY, SK/1990//KA324 . . . . **PROF 790.1**
PLAYROOM (CD-ROM). /1990/P-2/KB085 . . . . **CDR 371.3**
Plays from African tales: one-act, royalty-free dramatizations for young people, from stories and folktales of Africa. /WINTHER, B/1992/ 4-A/KE093. . . . . **812**
PLAYS FROM FAVORITE FOLK TALES. /1987/3-6/KE094. . . . . **812.008**
PLAYS OF BLACK AMERICANS: THE BLACK EXPERIENCE IN AMERICA, DRAMATIZED FOR YOUN PEOPLE. New expanded ed. /1994/ 4-6/KE095. . . . . **812.008**
PLAYS: THE DRAMA MAGAZINE FOR YOUNG PEOPLE. /1941-/ 5-A/KA536 . . . . **PER 050**

Please do not touch: a collection of stories. /GOROG, J/c1993, 1995/
6-A/7 KH185 . . . . **Fic**
PLIGHT OF THE ASIAN ELEPHANT (Videocassette). /1993/
5-6/KC814 . . . . **VCR 599.67**
Plugging away (Sound recording cassette). /ALSOP, P/1990/
1-5/KD604 . . . . **SRC 789.3**
Plumas para almorzar./EHLERT, L/1996/P-1/2 KF517 . . . . **E**
Plus long circuit./CARRIER, R/1993/2-4/4 KG977 . . . . **Fic**
Pocket for Corduroy. /FREEMAN, D/1978/P-2/2 KF581 . . . . **CE E**
Pocket for Corduroy (Braille)./FREEMAN, D/n.d./P-2/2 KF581 . . . . **CE E**
Pocket full of seeds. /SACHS, M/c1973, 1994/4-A/5 KH668 . . . . **Fic**
Poem-making: ways to begin writing poetry. /LIVINGSTON, MC/1991/
5-6/7 KD868 . . . . **808.1**
POEMS FOR JEWISH HOLIDAYS. /1986/K-3/KE077 . . . . **811.008**
Poetry break: an annotated anthology with ideas for introducing children to
poetry. /BAUER, CF/1995//KA234 . . . . **PROF 372.64**
Poetry for young people. /FROST, R/1994/4-A/KD940. . . . . **811**
Poetry for young people. /DICKINSON, E/1994/4-A/KD933 . . . . . **811**
Poetry for young people. /SANDBURG, C/1995/4-A/KE018 . . . . . **811**
Poetry for young people. /POE, EA/1995/5-A/KD998 . . . . **811**
Poison! beware! be an ace poison spotter. /SKIDMORE, S/1991/
3-6/5 KD011 . . . . **615.9**
Polar bear family book. /LARSEN, T/1996/4-6/4 KC862. . . . **599.786**
Polar bear: master of the ice. /TRACQUI, V/1994/3-5/4 KC865. . **599.786**
Polar bear, polar bear, what do you hear?/MARTIN, JR., B/1991/
P-K/1 KG072 . . . . **E**
Polar bear, polar bear, what do you hear? (Big book)./MARTIN, JR., B/
1992/P-K/1 KG072 . . . . **E**
Polar bear son: an Inuit tale. /DABCOVICH, L/1997/
K-2/4 KB554 . . . . **398.24**
Polar bears. /LEPTHIEN, EU/1991/2-4/5 KC863 . . . . **599.786**
POLAR BEARS (Videocassette). /1986/4-A/KC864. . . . . **VCR 599.786**
Polar express. /VAN ALLSBURG, C/1985/2-A/5 KH822 . . . . . . **CE Fic**
Polar express (Braille)./VAN ALLSBURG, C/n.d./2-A/5 KH822 . . . **CE Fic**
Polar express (Sound recording cassette)./VAN ALLSBURG, C/n.d./
2-A/5 KH822 . . . . **CE Fic**
Polar, the Titanic bear. /SPEDDEN, DC/1994/4-6/7 KE158 . . . . . . **910.4**
Policymaking for school library media programs. /KARPISEK, ME/1989/
/KA050. . . . . **PROF 025.1**
Political leaders. /LINDOP, L/1996/6-A/12 KA899 . . . . **320**
Pollita Pequenita./KELLOGG, S/1991/K-3/5 KF889 . . . . **CE E**
POLLITOS DICEN: JUEGOS, RIMAS Y CANCIONES INFANTILES DE
PAISES DE HABLA HISPANA./THE BABY CHICKS SING:
TRADITIONAL GAMES, NURSERY RHYMES, AND SONGS FROM
SPANISH-SPEAKING COUNTRIES. /1994/P-1/2 KD584. . . . . . **789.2**
Pomegranate seeds: a classic Greek myth. /GERINGER, L/1995/
3-6/5 KA742 . . . . **292**
Pond and river. /PARKER, S/1988/1-6/7 KC340 . . . . **577.63**
Pond water zoo: an introduction to microscopic life. /LOEWER, HP/1996/
6-A/8 KC372 . . . . **579**
Pondlarker. /GWYNNE, F/1990/K-2/5 KF656 . . . . **E**
Pony Express! /KROLL, S/1996/4-6/6 KB130 . . . . **383**
Pool of fire./CHRISTOPHER, J/1968/4-6/6 KG991 . . . . **Fic**
Pool of fire (Braille)./CHRISTOPHER, J/n.d./4-6/6 KG991 . . . . . **Fic**
Pool of fire (Talking book)./CHRISTOPHER, J/n.d./4-6/6 KG991 . . . **Fic**
Pool party. /SOTO, G/c1993, 1995/4-6/5 KH741 . . . . **Fic**
Popcorn book. /DE PAOLA, T/c1978/2-4/6 KD290 . . . . **641.6**
Popcorn shop. /LOW, A/1993/P-2/2 KG035 . . . . **E**
Poppleton. /RYLANT, C/1997/K-2/2 KG384 . . . . **E**
Poppy. /AVI /1995/3-5/6 KG862 . . . . **Fic**
POPULAR SCIENCE: THE WHAT'S NEW MAGAZINE. /1872-/
5-A/KA537 . . . . **PER 050**
Por fin es Carnaval./DORROS, A/1991/1-3/4 KF492 . . . . **E**
Porcellus, the flying pig. /CORBALIS, J/1988/2-4/5 KH029 . . . . . **Fic**
Porcupine. /SHERROW, V/1991/5-6/6 KC747 . . . . **599.35**
Porcupines. /MURRAY, P/1994/1-4/6 KC745 . . . . **599.35**
POSITIVELY NATIVE (Videocassette)./1991/4-6/KA851. . . . . **VCR 305.8**
Possum come a-knockin'. /VAN LAAN, N/1990/K-2/2 KG642 . . . . . . **E**
Possum magic. /FOX, M/c1983, 1990/P-2/4 KF571 . . . . **E**
POST OFFICE (Videocassette). /1991/1-4/KB131 . . . . **VCR 383**
POSTAL STATION (Videocassette). /1991/K-4/KB132 . . . . . . **VCR 383**
Postcards from Pluto: a tour of the solar system. /LEEDY, L/1993/
1-6/3 KC012 . . . . **523.2**
Posy Bates, again! /CRESSWELL, H/1994/3-5/3 KH039 . . . . . **Fic**
Potato. /WATTS, B/1987/2-4/2 KD172 . . . . **635**
Potato: a tale from the Great Depression. /LIED, K/1997/K-3/2 KF980 . **E**
Potato man. /MCDONALD, M/1991/K-3/5 KG098 . . . . **E**
Potlatch: a Tsimshian celebration. /HOYT-GOLDSMITH, D/1997/
2-5/9 KB189 . . . . **394.2**
Pots and pans. /ROCKWELL, AF/1993/P/3 KD279 . . . . **641.5**
Powder puff puzzle. /GIFF, PR/1987/2-3/2 KF615 . . . . **E**
Power machines. /ROBBINS, K/c1993, 1997/K-4/6 KD051 . . . . **621.8**
Power of reading: insights from the research. /KRASHEN, S/1993/
/KA082. . . . . **PROF 028**

POWER UP?: ENERGY IN OUR ENVIRONMENT (Videocassette). /1992/
4-6/KA956 . . . . **VCR 333.79**
Power up: experiments, puzzles, and games exploring electricity. /MARKLE,
S/1989/3-6/7 KC133 . . . . **537**
POWER UP YOUR LIBRARY: CREATING THE NEW ELEMENTARY
SCHOOL LIBRARY PROGRAM. /1996//KA078 . . . . . . **PROF 027.8**
Powerful waves. /SOUZA, DM/1992/3-6/5 KC180 . . . . **551.47**
Powerhouse: inside a nuclear power plant. /WILCOX, C/1996/
5-A/11 KD049 . . . . **621.48**
Powwow. /ANCONA, G/1993/3-6/6 KB194 . . . . **394.26**
Powwow summer: a family celebrates the circle of life. /RENDON, MR/
1996/1-3/3 KB181 . . . . **394**
Prairie alphabet. /BANNATYNE-CUGNET, J/1992/2-6/6 KE811 . . . **971.2**
Prairie boy's summer. /KURELEK, W/1975/3-5/7 KE813 . . . . . . **971.2**
Prairie boy's winter. /KURELEK, W/c1973/3-6/7 KE814 . . . . **CE 971.2**
Prairie cabin: a Norwegian pioneer woman's story (Videocassette). /RILEY,
J/1991/A/KF012 . . . . **VCR 977**
Prairie dogs. /ARNOLD, C/1993/4-5/4 KC749 . . . . **599.36**
Prairie primer A to Z. /STUTSON, C/1996/1-3/3 KG583 . . . . **E**
Prairie songs. /CONRAD, P/1985/5-A/7 KH023 . . . . **Fic**
Prairie year. /BANNATYNE-CUGNET, J/1994/4-6/4 KE812. . . . . **971.2**
Prairies and grasslands. /ROWAN, JP/1983/3-6/4 KC331 . . . . . . **577.4**
Prayer for a child. /FIELD, R/1973/K-3/4 KA713 . . . . **242**
Precious gift: a Navaho creation myth. /JACKSON, E/1996/
2-3/2 KB594 . . . . **398.24**
Prehistoric animals. /GIBBONS, G/1988/P-3/5 KC241 . . . . **566**
Prehistoric Pinkerton. /KELLOGG, S/1987/P-3/5 KF895 . . . . **E**
PREJUDICE (Microcomputer program). /1992/5-A/KA820 . . . . . **MCP 305**
Pre-K hooray! (Sound recording cassette). /STEWART, G/1993/
P-K/KD659. . . . . **SRC 789.3**
PRESCHOOL ACTION TIME (Sound recording cassette). /1988/
P/KD650 . . . . **SRC 789.3**
Preschool favorites (Sound recording cassette). /STEWART, G/1990/
P-K/KD660. . . . . **SRC 789.3**
PRESCHOOL PLAYTIME BAND (Sound recording cassette). /1987/
P-K/KD651. . . . . **SRC 789.3**
PRESCHOOL POWER!: JACKET FLIPS AND OTHER TIPS (Videocassette). /
1991/P-K/KD263 . . . . **VCR 640.83**
PRESCHOOL POWER 3! (Videocassette)./1992/P-K/KD263. **VCR 640.83**
Presenting reader's theater: plays and poems to read aloud. /BAUER, CF/
1987//KA329 . . . . **PROF 792**
President has been shot!: true stories of the attacks on ten U.S. presidents.
/JONES, RC/1996/6-A/9 KE855 . . . . **973**
Presidential Medal of Freedom winners. /BREDESON, C/1996/
5-6/10 KE850 . . . . **973**
Presidents. /SANDLER, MW/1995/5-A/8 KE864 . . . . **973**
PRESIDENTS' DAY (Videocassette). /1994/2-5/KB215 . . . **VCR 394.261**
PRESIDENTS: IT ALL STARTED WITH GEORGE (CD-ROM). /1991/
2-A/KA491 . . . . **CDR REF 973**
Pretend soup and other real recipes: a cookbook for preschoolers and up. /
KATZEN, M/1994/P-3/KD272 . . . . **641.5**
Pretend you're a cat. /MARZOLLO, J/1990/P-1/KG082 . . . . **E**
PRIMARY VOICES K-6. /1993-//KA132 . . . . **PER PROF 050**
Primaryplots: a book talk guide for use with readers age 4-8./THOMAS,
RL/1989//KA093 . . . . **PROF 028.5**
Primaryplots 2: a book talk guide for use with readers ages 4-8. /
THOMAS, RL/1993//KA093 . . . . **PROF 028.5**
Primos./HAMILTON, V/1995/6-A/15 KH213 . . . . **Fic**
Prince and the Salmon People. /MURPHY, CR/1993/4-6/7 KB352 . **398.2**
Prince Caspian and the Voyage of the Dawn Treader (Videocassette)./
LEWIS, CS/1989/5-A/6 KH405 . . . . **CE Fic**
Prince Caspian (Braille)./LEWIS, CS/n.d./5-A/6 KH405 . . . . **CE Fic**
Prince Caspian (Sound recording cassette)./LEWIS, CS/n.d./
5-A/6 KH405 . . . . **CE Fic**
Prince Caspian (Talking book)./LEWIS, CS/n.d./5-A/6 KH405. . . . **CE Fic**
Prince Caspian: the return to Narnia./LEWIS, CS/1994/
5-A/6 KH405 . . . . **CE Fic**
Prince Henry the Navigator. /FISHER, LE/1990/
4-6/6 KE387 . . . . **B HENRY, PRINCE**
Prince of Tarn. /HUTCHINS, HJ/1997/4-6/5 KH308 . . . . **Fic**
Prince of the pond: otherwise known as De Fawg Pin. /NAPOLI, DJ/1992/
3-A/3 KH531 . . . . **Fic**
Prince William. /RAND, G/1992/2-3/4 KG300 . . . . **E**
Princess and the beggar: a Korean folktale. /O'BRIEN, AS/1993/
3-4/6 KB761 . . . . **398.27**
Princess and the pea. /STEVENS, J/1982/K-2/2 KG555 . . . . . . **CE E**
Princess and the pea. /ZIEFERT, H/1996/K-2/1 KG796 . . . . **E**
Princess and the pea (Kit)./STEVENS, J/1996/K-2/2 KG555 . . . . **CE E**
Princess Florecita and the iron shoes: a Spanish fairy tale. /STEWIG, JW/
1995/3-4/5 KB372 . . . . **398.2**
Princess Furball. /HUCK, CS/1989/3-4/6 KB745 . . . . **CE 398.27**
Princess Furball (Kit)./HUCK, CS/1993/3-4/6 KB745 . . . . . . **CE 398.27**
Princess Furball (Talking book)./HUCK, CS/1993/
3-4/6 KB745 . . . . **CE 398.27**

Princess Furball (Videocassette)./HUCK, CS/1993/
    3-4/6 KB745 . . . . **CE 398.27**
Princess Penelope's parrot. /LESTER, H/1996/K-2/2 KF965 . . . . **E**
Principe Caspio./LEWIS, CS/1995/5-A/6 KH405 . . . . **CE Fic**
PRINT SHOP DELUXE I (Microcomputer program). /1992/
    /KA002. **MCP PROF 006.6**
Priscilla twice. /CASELEY, J/1995/1-3/2 KF368 . . . . **E**
Prize in the snow. /EASTERLING, B/1994/2-3/4 KF503 . . . . **E**
PROBLEM SOLVING: RECOGNIZING NECESSARY INFORMATION
    (Videocassette). /1982/3-5/KB979 . . . . **VCR 513.2**
PROBLEM SOLVING: USING DIAGRAMS AND MODELS (Videocassette).
    /1985/5-6/KB943 . . . . **VCR 511.3**
PROBLEM SOLVING: USING GRAPHS (Videocassette). /1985/
    4-5/KB939 . . . . **VCR 511**
Professional collection for elementary educators. /WILSON, PP/1996/
    /KA079. . . . . **PROF 027.8**
PROFESSIONAL STANDARDS FOR TEACHING MATHEMATICS. /1991/
    /KA257. . . . . **PROF 372.7**
Professor Noah's spaceship. /WILDSMITH, B/1980/K-2/5 KG722 . . . . . **E**
Programming author visits. /WATKINS, J/1996//KA071 . . **PROF 027.62**
Promise is a promise. /MUNSCH, R/1988/3-5/2 KH519 . . . . **Fic**
PROTECT YOURSELF: HIV/AIDS EDUCATION PROGRAM (Videocassette).
    /1992/6-A/KD032 . . . . **VCR 616.97**
Protecting Marie. /HENKES, K/1995/5-A/6 KH238 . . . . **Fic**
Proud rooster and the fox. /THREADGALL, C/1992/P-1/4 KG607 . . . . **E**
Prudence Crandall: woman of courage. 2nd ed. /YATES, E/1996/
    6-A/6 KE306 . . . . **B CRANDALL, P.**
PSALM TWENTY-THREE. /1997/P-A/3 KA691 . . . . **223**
PUBLIC WORKS (Videocassette). /1992/2-4/KB055 . . . . . . **VCR 363.72**
Puddles. /LONDON, J/1997/P-1/3 KG027 . . . . **E**
Pueblo. /YUE, C/1986/5-6/8 KF065 . . . . **979**
Pueblo boy: growing up in two worlds. /KEEGAN, M/1991/
    4-6/5 KE793 . . . . **970.489**
Pueblo storyteller. /HOYT-GOLDSMITH, D/1991/3-6/6 KE792 . . **970.489**
Puerto Rico. /KENT, D/1992/5-6/6 KE847 . . . . **972.95**
Puerto Rico (Sound recording cassette)./KENT, D/1993/
    5-6/6 KE847 . . . . **972.95**
Puff...flash...bang!: a book about signals. /GIBBONS, G/1993/
    1-4/4 KA796 . . . . **302.2**
Puffins are back! /GIBBONS, G/1991/2-4/5 KC677 . . . . **598.3**
Pulling the lion's tail. /KURTZ, J/1995/1-3/6 KF937 . . . . **E**
PULL-OUT PROGRAMS (Videocassette)./1991/
    /KA187. . . . . **VCR PROF 371.95**
Pumpkin patch. /KING, E/1990/1-4/6 KD169 . . . . **635**
Pumpkin pumpkin. /TITHERINGTON, J/1986/P-2/1 KG609 . . . . **E**
Pumpkin pumpkin (Big book)./TITHERINGTON, J/1990/P-2/1 KG609 . . **E**
Punch with Judy. /AVI /1993/5-A/6 KG863 . . . . **Fic**
Punga, the goddess of ugly. /LATTIMORE, DN/1993/3-5/4 KF950 . . . . **E**
Punia and the King of Sharks: a Hawaiian folktale. /WARDLAW, L/1997/
    2-3/3 KB672 . . . . **398.24**
Puppet book: how to make and operate puppets and stage a puppet play.
    /BUCHWALD, C/1990//KA326 . . . . **PROF 791.5**
Puppetry in early childhood education. /HUNT, T/1982/
    /KA327. . . . . **PROF 791.5**
Puppetry, language, and the special child: discovering alternate languages.
    /RENFRO, N/1984//KA328 . . . . **PROF 791.5**
Puppies, dogs, and blue northers: reflections on being raised by a pack of
    sled dogs. /PAULSEN, G/1996/3-6/7 KD859. . . . . **798.8**
Puppy fat. /GLEITZMAN, M/1995/5-A/5 KH175. . . . . **Fic**
Puppy sister. /HINTON, SE/1995/3-5/4 KH263 . . . . **Fic**
Puppy who wanted a boy. /THAYER, J/c1958, 1986/1-3/2 KG603. . . . **E**
Puppy who wanted a boy (Sound recording cassette)./THAYER, J/n.d./
    1-3/2 KG603 . . . . **E**
Purely Rosie Pearl. /COCHRANE, PA/1996/4-6/6 KH011 . . . . **Fic**
Purple coat. /HEST, A/1986/K-3/4 KF721 . . . . **E**
PUSH AND PULL: SIMPLE MACHINES AT WORK (Videocassette). /1990/
    4-6/KC097. . . . . **VCR 531**
Push, pull, empty, full: a book of opposites. /HOBAN, T/c1972/
    P-K/KF746 . . . . **E**
Puss in boots. /PERRAULT, C/1990/3-4/4 KB633. . . . . **398.24**
Puss in boots. /KIRSTEIN, L/c1992, 1994/3-4/6 KB604. . . . . . . **398.24**
Puss in boots: a fairy tale. /PERRAULT, C/1996/K-3/5 KB634 . . . **398.24**
Puss in Boots (Kit). /METAXAS, E/1992/1-4/KB620 . . . . **KIT 398.24**
Put a fan in your hat!: inventions, contraptions, and gadgets kids can build.
    /CARROW, RS/1997/5-6/8 KC885 . . . . **608**
Put me in the zoo. /LOPSHIRE, R/c1960/K-1/1 KG033. . . . . **E**
Put me in the zoo (Braille)./LOPSHIRE, R/n.d./K-1/1 KG033 . . . . **E**
Put me in the zoo (Sound recording cassette)./LOPSHIRE, R/n.d./
    K-1/1 KG033 . . . . **E**
Putting on a play: the young playwright's guide to scripting, directing, and
    performing. /BENTLEY, N/1996/4-6/7 KD687 . . . . **792**
Putting on the brakes: young people's guide to understanding attention
    deficit hyperactivity disorder (ADHD). /QUINN, PO/1991/
    5-6/7 KD041 . . . . **618.92**

Putting the world in a nutshell: the art of the formula tale. /DAILEY, S/
    1994//KA337 . . . . **PROF 808.5**
Putting the world to sleep. /THOMAS, SM/1995/P-2/2 KG606 . . . . . . **E**
PUZZLE TANKS: A GAME OF NUMBERS AND LOGIC (Microcomputer
    program). /1984/3-A/KB940. . . . . **MCP 511**
Pyotr Ilyich Tchaikovsky. /THOMPSON, W/1993/
    6-A/8 KE558 . . . . **B TCHAIKOVSKY,P**
Pyramid. /MACAULAY, D/1975/A/10 KD357. . . . . **CE 690**
Pyramid. /PUTNAM, J/1994/4-A/7 KD359. . . . . **690**
Pyramid (Videocassette)./MACAULAY, D/1988/A/10 KD357 . . . . **CE 690**
Quake!: a novel. /COTTONWOOD, J/1995/5-A/5 KH034 . . . . **Fic**
Quarter horse. /STEWART, GB/1995/4-6/5 KD207 . . . . **636.1**
Queen Anne's lace. /WEXLER, J/1994/2-6/6 KC433 . . . . **583**
Queen of the air: the story of Katherine Stinson, 1891-1977. /POWELL,
    MC/1993/4-7/7 KH613 . . . . **CE Fic**
Queen of the air: the story of Katherine Stinson, 1891-1977
    (Videocassette)./POWELL, MC/1993/4-7/7 KH613 . . . . . . **CE Fic**
Queen of the cold-blooded tales. /BROWN, RS/1993/6-A/6 KG933 . . **Fic**
Querido Senor Henshaw./CLEARY, B/1986/4-A/4 KG993 . . . . **Fic**
Question of trust. /BAUER, MD/1994/5-A/6 KH883 . . . . **Fic**
Quetzal: sacred bird of the cloud forest. /PATENT, DH/1996/
    3-6/6 KC702 . . . . **598.7**
Quetzalcoatl tale of corn. /PARKE, M/1992/2-3/5 KB630 . . . . . **398.24**
Quick and easy cookbook. /SUPRANER, R/c1981, 1985/
    1-4/KD281. . . . . **641.5**
QUICK TO JUDGE (Videocassette)./1991/4-6/KA851. . . . . . **VCR 305.8**
Quickly, Quigley. /GRAVOIS, JM/1994/P-1/2 KF635. . . . . **E**
Quicksand book. /DE PAOLA, T/c1977/K-3/2 KC226. . . . . **552**
Quilt. /JONAS, A/1984/K-1/2 KF846 . . . . **E**
Quilt story. /JOHNSTON, T/1985/P-3/2 KF840 . . . . **E**
Quinceanera: a Latina's journey to womanhood. /LANKFORD, MD/1994/
    5-A/7 KA715 . . . . **265**
Quique duerme fuera de casa./WABER, B/1991/K-2/2 KG668 . . . . **CE E**
Quiza no lo haga./BLUME, J/1995/6-A/5 KG915 . . . . **Fic**
Rabbit. /EVANS, M/1992/3-6/4 KD179 . . . . **636**
Rabbit Hill. /LAWSON, R/c1944, 1962/4-6/7 KH390. . . . . **CE Fic**
Rabbit Hill (Braille)./LAWSON, R/n.d./4-6/7 KH390. . . . . **CE Fic**
Rabbit Hill (Kit)./LAWSON, R/1972/4-6/7 KH390 . . . . **CE Fic**
Rabbit Hill (Sound recording cassette)./LAWSON, R/n.d./
    4-6/7 KH390 . . . . **CE Fic**
Rabbit Hill (Talking book)./LAWSON, R/n.d./4-6/7 KH390 . . . . . **CE Fic**
Rabbit wishes. /SHUTE, L/1995/K-2/2 KB651 . . . . **398.24**
Rabbit-Cadabra! /HOWE, J/1993/K-3/3 KF779 . . . . **E**
Rabbits and raindrops. /ARNOSKY, J/1997/P-2/2 KF169 . . . . **E**
Rabbit's escape/Kusa ilsaenghan tookki. /HAN, SC/1995/
    P-2/3 KB583 . . . . **398.24**
Raccoon at Clear Creek Road. /OTTO, C/1995/K-2/3 KG202 . . . . **CE E**
Raccoon at Clear Creek Road (Kit)./OTTO, C/1995/K-2/3 KG202 . **CE E**
Raccoons and ripe corn. /ARNOSKY, J/c1987, 1991/
    P-2/3 KC831 . . . . **599.76**
RACE (Videocassette). /1993/A/KA855 . . . . **VCR 305.8**
Rachel and Obadiah./TURKLE, B/1978/K-3/5 KG623 . . . . **E**
Rachel and Obadiah (Braille)./TURKLE, B/n.d./K-3/5 KG623 . . . . **E**
Rachel Fister's blister. /MACDONALD, A/1990/K-2/2 KG050 . . . . **E**
Rachel Parker, kindergarten show-off. /MARTIN, AM/1992/
    K-2/1 KG069 . . . . **E**
Racing the Iditarod Trail. /CRISMAN, R/1993/5-6/7 KD858 . . . . . **798.8**
Racso and the rats of NIMH. /CONLY, JL/1986/5-6/6 KH020 . . . **Fic**
Racso and the rats of NIMH (Braille)./CONLY, JL/n.d./5-6/6 KH020 . . **Fic**
Racso and the rats of NIMH (Sound recording cassette)./CONLY, JL/n.d./
    5-6/6 KH020 . . . . **Fic**
Radio boy. /DENSLOW, SP/1995/1-3/7 KF462 . . . . **E**
Radio Man: a story in English and Spanish./Don Radio: un cuento en Ingles
    y Espanol. /DORROS, A/1993/2-5/2 KF491 . . . . **E**
Rafe Martin tells his children's books (Talking book). /MARTIN, R/1994/
    K-4/KB341. . . . . **TB 398.2**
Raffi's Christmas album (Sound recording cassette). /RAFFI /1983/
    P-3/KD535. . . . . **SRC 782.28**
Rag coat. /MILLS, LA/1991/2-3/4 KG139 . . . . **E**
Rag coat (Sound recording cassette)./MILLS, LA/1994/2-3/4 KG139. . . **E**
Raggin', a story about Scott Joplin. /MITCHELL, B/1987/
    A/8 KE407 . . . . **B JOPLIN, S.**
Railway children. /NESBIT, E/1994/4-5/7 KH543 . . . . **Fic**
Railway children (Large type). /NESBIT, E/1988/4-5/7 KH543 . . . . . **Fic**
Rain and hail. Rev. ed. /BRANLEY, FM/1983/K-3/2 KC188 . . . . . **551.5**
Rain: causes and effects. /STEELE, P/1991/3-6/7 KC215 . . . . . **551.57**
Rain feet (Board book). /JOHNSON, A/1994/P/2 KF833 . . . . **BB E**
Rain forest. /COWCHER, H/c1988, 1990/2-4/4 KF428 . . . . **E**
Rain makes applesauce. /SCHEER, J/c1964/P-A/2 KG403 . . . . **E**
Rain or shine activity book: fun things to make and do. /COLE, J/1997/
    3-6/KD699. . . . . **793**
Rain player. /WISNIEWSKI, D/1991/2-3/4 KG751 . . . . **CE E**
Rain player (Kit)./WISNIEWSKI, D/1996/2-3/4 KG751 . . . . **CE E**
Rain, rain rivers. /SHULEVITZ, U/c1969, 1998/P-2/2 KG499 . . . . . . **E**

Rain talk. /SERFOZO, M/1990/P-1/4 KG441 . . . . **E**

Rainbabies. /MELMED, LK/1992/2-3/5 KG127 . . . . **E**

Rainbow bridge: inspired by a Chumash tale. /WOOD, A/1995/
3-5/4 KB675 . . . . **398.24**

RAINBOW FAIRY BOOK. /1993/2-6/8 KB360 . . . . **398.2**

Rainbow people. /YEP, L/c1989, 1991/5-A/4 KB788 . . . . . . **398.27**

RAINBOW SIGN (Compact disc). /1992/P-A/KD585 . . . . **CD 789.2**

Rainbow Valley. /MONTGOMERY, LM/1985/4-A/6 KH503 . . . . **Fic**

RAINFOREST RESEARCHERS (CD-ROM). /1996/
5-A/KC323 . . . . **CDR 577.34**

RAINFOREST. /1993/5-A/KC324. . . . . **VCR 577.34**

RAINTREE STECK-VAUGHN ILLUSTRATED SCIENCE ENCYCLOPEDIA.
Newly revised. /1997/3-5/KA434 . . . . **REF 503**

Rainy day. /MARKLE, S/1993/P-2/6 KC214 . . . . **551.57**

RAINY DAY RHYMES. /1992/1-3/KE078 . . . . **811.008**

Rainy rainy Saturday. /PRELUTSKY, J/1980/1-3/KE013. . . . . **811**

Raising a reader: make your child a reader for life. /KROPP, P/c1993,
1996//KA182 . . . . **PROF 371.3028**

Ralph S. Mouse./CLEARY, B/1982/3-5/5 KG997 . . . . **CE Fic**

Ralph S. Mouse (Braille)./CLEARY, B/n.d./3-5/5 KG997 . . . . **CE Fic**

Ralph S. Mouse (Sound recording cassette)./CLEARY, B/n.d./
3-5/5 KG997 . . . . **CE Fic**

Ralph S. Mouse (Talking book)./CLEARY, B/n.d./3-5/5 KG997. . . **CE Fic**

Ralph S. Mouse (Talking book)./CLEARY, B/1995/3-5/5 KG997. . . **CE Fic**

Ralph S. Mouse (Videocassette). /CLEARY, B/1990/3-5/KH000 . **VCR Fic**

Ramadan. /GHAZI, SH/1996/3-5/7 KA785 . . . . **297**

Ramona and her father. /CLEARY, B/1977/3-5/7 KH001 . . . . **Fic**

Ramona and her father (Braille)./CLEARY, B/n.d./3-5/7 KH001 . . . . . **Fic**

Ramona and her father (Sound recording cassette)./CLEARY, B/n.d./
3-5/7 KH001 . . . . **Fic**

Ramona and her mother. /CLEARY, B/1979/3-5/6 KH002 . . . . . . **CE Fic**

Ramona and her mother (Sound recording cassette)./CLEARY, B/n.d./
3-5/6 KH002 . . . . **CE Fic**

Ramona Empieza el curso./CLEARY, B/1989/3-5/5 KH004. . . . . **Fic**

Ramona forever. /CLEARY, B/1984/3-5/6 KH003 . . . . **Fic**

Ramona forever (Braille)./CLEARY, B/n.d./3-5/6 KH003 . . . . **Fic**

Ramona forever (Sound recording cassette)./CLEARY, B/n.d./
3-5/6 KH003 . . . . **Fic**

Ramona la chinche./CLEARY, B/1984/3-5/5 KH006 . . . . **Fic**

Ramona Quimby, age 8. /CLEARY, B/1981/3-5/5 KH004 . . . . . **CE Fic**

Ramona Quimby, age 8 (Braille)./CLEARY, B/n.d./3-5/5 KH004 . . **CE Fic**

Ramona Quimby, age 8 (Talking book)./CLEARY, B/1981/
3-5/5 KH004 . . . . **CE Fic**

Ramona the brave. /CLEARY, B/1975/3-5/6 KH005 . . . . **Fic**

Ramona the brave (Braille)./CLEARY, B/n.d./3-5/6 KH005 . . . . **Fic**

Ramona the pest. /CLEARY, B/c1968/3-5/5 KH006 . . . . **Fic**

Ramona the pest (Braille)./CLEARY, B/n.d./3-5/5 KH006 . . . . **Fic**

Ramona the pest (Sound recording cassette)./CLEARY, B/n.d./
3-5/5 KH006 . . . . **Fic**

Ramona the pest (Talking book)./CLEARY, B/n.d./3-5/5 KH006 . . . . . **Fic**

Ramona y su madre./CLEARY, B/1989/3-5/5 KH002 . . . . **CE Fic**

Ramona y su padre./CLEARY, B/1987/3-5/7 KH001 . . . . **Fic**

Random House book of Mother Goose (Sound recording cassette)./LOBEL,
A/n.d./P-1/KB800 . . . . **398.8**

Random House book of stories from the ballet. /MCCAUGHREAN, G/
1994/3-6/6 KD696 . . . . **792.8**

RANDOM HOUSE WEBSTER'S COLLEGE DICTIONARY. 2nd ed. /1997/
6-A/KA428 . . . . **REF 423**

RANGER RICK. /1967/K-3/KA538 . . . . **PER 050**

Raptor rescue!: an eagle flies free. /JOHNSON, SA/1995/
5-6/7 KD254 . . . . **639.9**

Raptors, fossils, fins, and fangs: a prehistoric creature feature. /TROLL, R/
1996/3-6/6 KC239 . . . . **560**

Rapunzel. /GRIMM, J/1982/2-4/4 KB307 . . . . **398.2**

Rapunzel. /BERENZY, A/1995/2-4/4 KB263 . . . . **398.2**

Rapunzel, Rapunzel (Videocassette)./DAVENPORT, T/1978/
5-A/KB281 . . . . **CE 398.2**

Rat teeth. /GIFF, PR/c1984/3-5/3 KH166 . . . . **Fic**

Rata-pata-scata-fata: a Caribbean story. /GERSHATOR, P/1994/
K-2/2 KF611 . . . . **E**

RATIO/PROPORTION/PERCENT: THE MEANING OF PERCENT
(Videocassette). /1987/5-6/KB980 . . . . **VCR 513.2**

Rats on the range and other stories. /MARSHALL, J/1993/
1-4/2 KH458 . . . . **Fic**

Rats on the roof and other stories. /MARSHALL, J/1991/
1-4/2 KH459 . . . . **Fic**

Rats on the roof and other stories (Sound recording cassette)./MARSHALL,
J/1993/1-4/2 KH459 . . . . **Fic**

Rattlebang picnic. /MAHY, M/1994/K-2/5 KG057 . . . . **E**

Rattlebang picnic (Sound recording cassette)./MAHY, M/1997/
K-2/5 KG057 . . . . **E**

Rattlebone Rock. /ANDREWS, S/1995/1-3/3 KF158 . . . . **E**

Rattlesnake dance: true tales, mysteries, and rattlesnake ceremonies. /
DEWEY, JO/1997/4-6/4 KC634 . . . . **597.96**

Raven: a trickster tale from the Pacific Northwest. /MCDERMOTT, G/
1993/1-3/3 KB618 . . . . **398.24**

Raven and Snipe. /CAMERON, A/1991/3-4/6 KB546 . . . . **398.24**

Raven goes berrypicking. /CAMERON, A/1991/3-4/6 KB547. . . . **398.24**

RAW HEAD, BLOODY BONES: AFRICAN-AMERICAN TALES OF THE
SUPERNATURAL. /1991/4-6/4 KB361 . . . . **398.2**

Ray Charles: soul man. /TURK, R/1996/5-A/8 KE286 . . **B CHARLES, R.**

R.C. Gorman: Navajo artist. /HERMANN, S/1995/
3-5/3 KE375 . . . . **B GORMAN, R.C.**

Read for the fun of it: active programming with books for children. /
BAUER, CF/1992//KA067 . . . . **PROF 027.62**

Read to me: raising kids who love to read. /CULLINAN, BE/1992/
/KA301 . . . . **PROF 649**

READ, WRITE AND TYPE! (CD-ROM). /1996/K-2/KB105 . . . **CDR 372.4**

READABILITY ANALYSIS (Microcomputer program). /1994/
/KA213 . . . . **MCP PROF 372.4**

Read-aloud handbook. 4th ed. /TRELEASE, J/1995/
/KA242 . . . . **PROF 372.64**

READ-ALOUD RHYMES FOR THE VERY YOUNG. /c1986/
P-K/KE079 . . . . **811.008**

READ-ALOUD RHYMES FOR THE VERY YOUNG (Sound recording
cassette)./n.d./P-K/KE079 . . . . **811.008**

READER RABBIT 3 (Microcomputer program). /1993/
1-3/KB106 . . . . **MCP 372.4**

READER RABBIT'S READY FOR LETTERS (Microcomputer program). /
1994/P-1/KB107 . . . . **MCP 372.4**

Readers theatre for children: scripts and script development. /LAUGHLIN,
MK/1990//KA339 . . . . **PROF 808.5**

Reading crisis: why poor children fall behind. /CHALL, JS/1990/
/KA219 . . . . **PROF 372.6**

READING TEACHER. /1957-//KA133 . . . . **PER PROF 050**

READING THE NEWSPAPER INTELLIGENTLY (Videocassette). /1995/
5-6/KA801 . . . . **VCR 302.23**

READY...SET...READ!: THE BEGINNING READER'S TREASURY. /1990/
P-2/KD901 . . . . **810.8**

READY...SET...READ--AND LAUGH!: A FUNNY TREASURY FOR
BEGINNING READERS. /1995/K-2/KD902 . . . . **810.8**

READY-TO-TELL TALES: SURE-FIRE STORIES FROM AMERICA'S
FAVORITE STORYTELLERS. /1994//KA272 . . . . **PROF 398.2**

REAL COWBOYS (Picture). /n.d./5-6/KF044 . . . . **PIC 978**

Real hole. /CLEARY, B/c1960, 1986/P/2 KF396 . . . . **E**

Real hole (Braille)./CLEARY, B/n.d./P/2 KF396 . . . . **E**

Real hole (Sound recording cassette)./CLEARY, B/n.d./P/2 KF396 . . . . . **E**

Real Johnny Appleseed. /LAWLOR, L/1995/
5-6/8 KE240 . . . . **B APPLESEED, J.**

Real McCoy: the life of an African-American inventor. /TOWLE, W/c1993,
1995/4-6/7 KE462 . . . . **B MCCOY, E.**

Real Mother Goose. /MOTHER GOOSE /c1944, 1994/
P-2/KB806 . . . . **398.8**

REAL MOTHER GOOSE BOOK OF AMERICAN RHYMES. /1993/
P-2/KB811 . . . . **398.8**

Real Mother Goose (Braille)./MOTHER GOOSE /n.d./P-2/KB806 . . **398.8**

Real Mother Goose (Talking book)./MOTHER GOOSE /n.d./
P-2/KB806 . . . . **398.8**

Real mummies don't bleed: friendly tales for October nights. /WHITCHER,
S/1993/4-6/5 KH849 . . . . **Fic**

Real Plato Jones. /BAWDEN, N/1993/6-A/6 KG892 . . . . **Fic**

Real Plato Jones (Sound recording cassette)./BAWDEN, N/1995/
6-A/6 KG892. . . . . **Fic**

Real thief. /STEIG, W/c1973/4-6/6 KH751 . . . . **Fic**

REALMS OF LIFE (Picture). /1996/6-A/KC356 . . . . **PIC 578**

Real-skin rubber monster mask./COHEN, M/1990/K-1/2 KF404 . . . **CE E**

Real-skin rubber monster mask (Videocassette)./COHEN, M/1991/
K-1/2 KF404 . . . . **CE E**

Reasons for seasons. /GIBBONS, G/1995/P-4/5 KC059 . . . . **525**

Rebecca of Sunnybrook Farm. /WIGGIN, KD/1994/5-A/6 KH857. . . . **Fic**

Rebels against slavery: American slave revolts. /MCKISSACK, P/1996/
4-6/7 KA929 . . . . **326**

Rebuilding prairies and forests. /GOLDSTEIN, N/1994/
4-6/7 KA955 . . . . **333.74**

Recalling past lives. /GREEN, CR/1993/4-6/3 KA611. . . . . **133.9**

Rechenka's eggs. /POLACCO, P/1988/1-3/5 KG256 . . . . **CE E**

Rechenka's eggs (Videocassette)./POLACCO, P/1991/1-3/5 KG256 . . **CE E**

Recipes for art and craft material. Newly rev. /SATTLER, HR/c1973, 1994/
4-6/6 KD435 . . . . **745.5**

RECOMMENDED REFERENCE BOOKS FOR SMALL AND MEDIUM-SIZED
LIBRARIES AND MEDIA CENTERS. /1981-//KA005 . . . . . **PROF 011**

Record breakers of the air./MATTHEWS, R/1990/2-4/6 KA590 . . **031.02**

Record breakers of the land./MATTHEWS, R/1990/2-4/6 KA590 . **031.02**

Record breakers of the sea. /MATTHEWS, R/1990/2-4/6 KA590 . **031.02**

Recycling. /CHANDLER, G/1996/3-6/10 KB053 . . . . **363.72**

Recycling activities for the primary grades. /STANGL, J/1993/
/KA313 . . . . **PROF 745.5**

RECYCLING: IT'S EVERYBODY'S JOB (Videocassette). /1992/
5-6/KB056. . . . . **VCR 363.72**
RECYCLING: THE ENDLESS CIRCLE (Videocassette). /1992/
5-6/KD082. . . . . **VCR 628.4**
RECYCLING WITH WORMS (Videocassette). /1995/
3-6/KC507. . . . . **VCR 592**
Red Bird. /MITCHELL, B/1996/1-3/4 KG145. . . . . **E**
Red Cap. /WISLER, GC/1994/5-A/7 KH873. . . . . **Fic**
Red Cap (Sound recording cassette)./WISLER, GC/1994/
5-A/7 KH873. . . . . **Fic**
Red comb. /PICO, F/1994/3-5/7 KH601 . . . . **Fic**
Red Cross/Red Crescent: when help can't wait. /BURGER, L/1996/
4-6/8 KA992. . . . . **361.7**
Red dancing shoes. /PATRICK, DL/1993/P-1/2 KG220 . . . . **E**
Red Hawk's account of Custer's last battle; the Battle of the Little Bighorn,
25 June 1876. /GOBLE, P/c1969, 1992/5-6/6 KE914 . . . . . . **973.8**
Red heels. /SAN SOUCI, RD/1996/3-5/6 KG393 . . . . **E**
Red Hen and Sly Fox. /FRENCH, V/1995/P-2/2 KF584. . . . . . . **E**
Red leaf, yellow leaf. /EHLERT, L/1991/P-1/4 KC412 . . . . . . **582.16**
Red light, green light, Mama and me. /BEST, C/1995/K-2/2 KF228. . . . **E**
Red poppy. /LUCHT, I/1995/1-4/5 KC430 . . . . **583**
Red Riding Hood. /DE REGNIERS, BS/c1972, 1990/
P-2/KH732. . . . . **CE 398.27**
Red wolf country. /LONDON, J/1996/K-3/4 KG028 . . . . **E**
Red-eared ghosts. /ALCOCK, V/1997/5-A/4 KG828 . . . . **Fic**
REDUCING, REUSING AND RECYCLING: ENVIRONMENTAL CONCERNS
(Videocassette). /1992/4-6/KB051. . . . . **VCR 363.7**
Redwall. /JACQUES, B/1986/5-A/6 KH320 . . . . **Fic**
REFERENCE BOOKS BULLETIN, 1994-1995: A COMPILATION OF
EVALUATIONS APPEARING IN "REFERENCE BOOKS BULLETIN,"
SEPTEMBER 1, 1992 - AUGUST, 1993. /1995/KA006 . . . **PROF 011**
Reference books for children, 4th ed. /PETERSON, CS/1992/
/KA021. . . . . **PROF 011.62**
REGGAE FOR KIDS: A COLLECTION OF MUSIC FOR KIDS OF ALL
AGES! (Sound recording cassette). /1992/K-3/KD669 . . . **SRC 789.4**
REGGAE FOR KIDS: A COLLECTION OF MUSIC FOR KIDS OF ALL
AGES! (Compact disc)./1992/K-3/KD669 . . . . . . **SRC 789.4**
REGULAR CLASSROOM (Videocassette)./1991/
/KA187. . . . . **VCR PROF 371.95**
Rehema's journey: a visit in Tanzania. /MARGOLIES, BA/c1990/
3-6/4 KE180 . . . . **916.78**
Reindeer. /ARNOLD, C/1993/4-5/4 KD211 . . . . **636.2**
Reindeer. /BERNHARD, E/1994/4-5/7 KC796 . . . . **599.65**
Reindeer people. /LEWIN, T/1994/4-6/6 KE695 . . . . . . **948.97**
RELATING FRACTIONS AND DECIMALS (Videocassette). /1982/
3-5/KB981. . . . . **VCR 513.2**
Relatives came. /RYLANT, C/1985/K-3/8 KG385 . . . . **E**
Relatives came (Braille). /RYLANT, C/n.d./K-3/8 KG385 . . . . . . **E**
RELIGION (Videocassette). /1992/3-6/KA727 . . . . **VCR 291**
Religions explained: a beginner's guide to world faiths. /GANERI, A/1997/
3-5/9 KA723 . . . . **291**
Reluctant dragon. /GRAHAME, K/c1938/3-6/7 KH187 . . . . . . **CE Fic**
Reluctant dragon. /GRAHAME, K/1983/3-6/6 KH188. . . . . . **CE Fic**
Reluctant dragon (Braille). /GRAHAME, K/n.d./3-6/7 KH187. . . . **CE Fic**
Reluctant dragon (Sound recording cassette)./GRAHAME, K/n.d./
3-6/7 KH187 . . . . **CE Fic**
Reluctant dragon (Videocassette)./GRAHAME, K/1981/
3-6/7 KH187 . . . . **CE Fic**
Reluctantly Alice./NAYLOR, PR/1991/6-A/6 KH533 . . . . **Fic**
Reluctantly Alice (Sound recording cassette)./NAYLOR, PR/1993/
6-A/6 KH533 . . . . **Fic**
Remaking the earth: a creation story from the Great Plains of North
America. /GOBLE, P/1996/3-5/7 KB448 . . . . **398.22**
Remarkable Christmas of the cobbler's sons. /SAWYER, R/1994/
1-3/4 KB416 . . . . **398.21**
Remarkable journey of Prince Jen. /ALEXANDER, L/1991/
6-A/6 KG840 . . . . **Fic**
Remarkable voyages of Captain Cook. /BLUMBERG, R/1991/
5-6/7 KE163 . . . . **910.92**
Remarkable voyages of Captain Cook (Sound recording cassette)./
BLUMBERG, R/1995/5-6/7 KE163 . . . . **910.92**
Rembrandt. /SCHWARTZ, G/1992/6-A/7 KE507 . . . . . **B REMBRANDT**
Rembrandt and seventeenth-century Holland. /PESCIO, C/1995/
4-A/12 KD501 . . . . **759.9492**
Reptiles. /CREAGH, C/1996/3-6/8 KC613 . . . . **597.9**
Rescue: the story of how Gentiles saved Jews in the Holocaust. /MELTZER,
M/1988/5-A/7 KE661 . . . . **940.53**
Rescuing endangered species. /BLASHFIELD, JF/1994/
4-6/7 KA961 . . . . **333.95**
Research paper writer (Microcomputer program). /OWENS, P/c1990/
5-A/KB090. . . . . **MCP 371.302**
RESOLVING CONFLICTS (Videocassette). /1990/4-6/KA655 . . **VCR 158**

RESOURCE LINKS: CONNECTING CLASSROOMS, LIBRARIES AND
CANADIAN LEARNING RESOURCES. /1995-/
/KA134. . . . . **PER PROF 050**
RESOURCES FOR TEACHING ELEMENTARY SCHOOL SCIENCE. /1996/
/KA203. . . . . **PROF 372.3**
Return of the buffaloes: a Plains Indian story about famine and renewal of
the Earth. /GOBLE, P/1996/3-5/3 KB575 . . . . **398.24**
Return of the Indian. /REID BANKS, L/1986/5-A/6 KH629 . . . . . **Fic**
Return of the Indian (Braille)./REID BANKS, L/n.d./5-A/6 KH629 . . . **Fic**
Return to Bitter Creek. /SMITH, DB/1988/5-A/5 KH721 . . . . . . **Fic**
Return to Howliday Inn./HOWE, D/1992/3-6/5 KH285 . . . . . . **Fic**
Revanche d'Ishtar. /ZEMAN, L/1993/4-6/4 KE132 . . . . **892.1**
Revenge of Ishtar. /ZEMAN, L/1993/4-6/4 KE132 . . . . **892.1**
Revenge of the small Small. /LITTLE, J/1992/1-3/2 KF996 . . . . . . **E**
REVIEWS. /1993-//KA135 . . . . **PROF 050**
REVOLUTIONARY WARS: CHOOSING SIDES (Microcomputer program). /
1986/5-A/KA668 . . . . **MCP 172**
Rex and Lilly family time. /BROWN, LK/1995/K-1/1 KF270 . . . . . . **E**
Reynard the Fox. /HASTINGS, S/1991/2-3/6 KB586 . . . . **398.24**
Re-zoom. /BANYAI, I/1995/2-A/KF196 . . . . **E**
Rhino. /ARNOLD, C/1995/4-6/7 KC801 . . . . **599.66**
Rhino comes to America. /MAYNARD, T/1993/5-6/7 KC802 . . . . **599.66**
Rhinos. /WALKER, SM/1996/4-6/7 KC803 . . . . **599.66**
Rhinos for lunch and elephants for supper!: a Masai tale. /MOLLEL, TM/
1991/P-3/4 KB625 . . . . **398.24**
Rhode Island. /HEINRICHS, A/1990/4-6/9 KE932 . . . . **974.2**
Rhode Island Colony. /FRADIN, DB/1989/5-6/7 KE951 . . . . . . **974.5**
Rhode Island (Sound recording cassette)./HEINRICHS, A/1993/
4-6/9 KE932 . . . . **974.2**
Rhymes and verses: collected poems for children. /DE LA MARE, W/1947/
4-6/KE099 . . . . **821**
Rhymes for Annie Rose. /HUGHES, S/1995/P-2/KE102 . . . . **821**
Rhythm and game songs for the little ones (Sound recording cassette). /
JENKINS, E/1990/P-K/KD630 . . . . **SRC 789.3**
Rhythm of the rocks: a multicultural musical journey (Compact disc)./
SUNSERI, M/1996/K-2/KD599 . . . . **SRC 789.2**
Rhythm of the rocks: a multicultural musical journey (Sound recording
cassette). /SUNSERI, M/1993/K-2/KD599 . . . . **SRC 789.2**
Rhythm of the rocks songbook: a multicultural musical journey... /SUNSERI,
M/1994/K-2/KD600 . . . . **789.2**
Ribsy./CLEARY, B/1964/2-5/3 KG995 . . . . **CE Fic**
Ribsy (Braille)./CLEARY, B/n.d./2-5/3 KG995 . . . . **CE Fic**
Ribsy (Talking book)./CLEARY, B/n.d./2-5/3 KG995. . . . . . . **CE Fic**
Rice. /THOMSON, R/1990/3-5/4 KD152. . . . . **633.1**
Richard Chase tells three "Jack" tales from the Southern Appalachians
(Sound recording cassette). /CHASE, R/n.d./K-A/KB725. . **SRC 398.27**
Richard Orr's nature cross-sections. /ORR, R/1995/2-A/8 KC359 . . **578.7**
Riddle City, USA!: a book of geography riddles. /MAESTRO, M/1994/
2-6/KD734. . . . . **793.735**
Riddle of the Rosetta Stone: key to ancient Egypt. /GIBLIN, JC/1990/
5-A/7 KB865 . . . . **493**
Riddle of the Rosetta Stone: key to ancient Egypt (Sound recording
cassette)./GIBLIN, JC/1993/5-A/7 KB865 . . . . **493**
RIDDLE-ME RHYMES. /1994/3-5/KD738 . . . . **793.735**
Riddles to tell your cat. /LEVINE, CA/1992/2-5/KD732 . . . . . . **793.735**
Ride a purple pelican. /PRELUTSKY, J/1986/P-3/KE014 . . . . . . **811**
Ride a purple pelican (Braille)./PRELUTSKY, J/n.d./P-3/KE014 . . . . **811**
Ride on mother's back: a day of baby carrying around the world. /
BERNHARD, E/1996/1-2/7 KB170 . . . . **392.1**
Riding Silver Star. /COLE, J/1996/3-5/2 KD854 . . . . **798.2**
Right to speak out. /KING, DC/1997/4-6/7 KA973 . . . . . . **342.73**
Right to vote. /PASCOE, E/1997/4-6/12 KA910 . . . . **324.6**
Righteous revenge of Artemis Bonner. /MYERS, WD/1994/
5-A/7 KH523 . . . . **Fic**
Rikki-Tikki-Tavi and Wee Willie Winkie (Talking book). /KIPLING, R/n.d./
4-6/KH364. . . . . **TB Fic**
Rilla of Ingleside./MONTGOMERY, LM/1985/4-A/6 KH503 . . . . . . **Fic**
Rilla of Ingleside (Sound recording cassette)./MONTGOMERY, LM/1993/
4-A/6 KH503 . . . . **Fic**
Rimonah of the Flashing Sword: a North African tale. /KIMMEL, EA/1995/
3-4/4 KB331 . . . . **398.2**
Ring of Truth: an original Irish tale. /BATEMAN, T/1997/1-3/5 KF213 . . **E**
Ring o'roses: a nursery rhyme picture book. /MOTHER GOOSE /1992/
P-K/KB807 . . . . **398.8**
RING-A-RING O' ROSES AND A DING, DONG, BELL: A BOOK OF
NURSERY RHYMES. /1991/P-K/KB813 . . . . **398.8**
Rip Van Winkle. /IRVING, W/1987/4-A/9 KH315 . . . . **Fic**
Rip Van Winkle (Braille)./IRVING, W/n.d./4-A/9 KH315 . . . . . . **Fic**
Rip Van Winkle (Sound recording cassette)./IRVING, W/n.d./
4-A/9 KH315 . . . . **Fic**
Rip Van Winkle; and, The Legend of Sleepy Hollow (Talking book). /
IRVING, W/1986/5-6/KH316 . . . . **TB Fic**
Riptide. /WELLER, FW/1990/1-3/4 KG695 . . . . **E**

Rise and shine (Sound recording cassette). /RAFFI /c1982/
P-5/KD652. . . . . **SRC 789.3**
Rise of Islam. /CHILD, J/1995/5-A/6 KA784. . . . . **297**
RISING VOICES: WRITINGS OF YOUNG NATIVE AMERICANS. /1992/
5-A/7 KD903 . . . . **810.8**
RISING VOICES: WRITINGS OF YOUNG NATIVE AMERICANS (Sound
recording cassette)./1995/5-A/7 KD903 . . . . **810.8**
River. /GILLILAND, JH/1993/K-3/3 KC317. . . . . **577.34**
River at Green Knowe./BOSTON, LM/1989/4-A/6 KG919 . . . . . **Fic**
River dream. /SAY, A/1988/K-3/4 KG399 . . . . **E**
River ran wild: an environmental history. /CHERRY, L/1992/
4-6/6 KE937 . . . . **974.4**
Riverkeeper. /ANCONA, G/1990/4-6/7 KA958 . . . . **333.91**
Riverside Shakespeare. /SHAKESPEARE, W/1974/A/KA468 . . **REF 822.3**
Road from home: the story of an Armenian girl. /KHERDIAN, D/1979/
5-6/6 KE698 . . . . **949.6**
Road to Oz. /BAUM, LF/1991/4-6/7 KG884 . . . . **Fic**
Road to Oz (Sound recording cassette)./BAUM, LF/1993/
4-6/7 KG884 . . . . **Fic**
Roar and more. /KUSKIN, K/c1956, 1990/P-1/KF940. . . . . **E**
Robber baby: stories from the Greek myths. /ROCKWELL, AF/1994/
3-6/6 KA751 . . . . **292**
Robbery at the Diamond Dog Diner. /CHRISTELOW, E/1986/
K-3/4 KF389 . . . . **CE E**
Robbery at the Diamond Dog Diner (Kit)./CHRISTELOW, E/1989/
K-3/4 KF389 . . . . **CE E**
Robert E. Lee. /KAVANAGH, J/1995/4-5/6 KE430 . . . . **B LEE, R.**
ROBERT E. LEE (Videocassette). /1989/5-6/KE431 . . . . . **VCR B LEE, R.**
Robert Louis Stevenson: author of A CHILD'S GARDEN OF VERSES. /
GREENE, C/1994/2-4/4 KE554 . . . . **B STEVENSON, R.**
Robert the rose horse. /HEILBRONER, J/1962/K-2/1 KF696 . . . . **E**
Roberto Clemente. /MACHT, NL/1994/5-A/7 KE294 . . **B CLEMENTE, R.**
Roberto Clemente (Spanish version)./MACHT, NL/1995/
5-A/7 KE294 . . . . **B CLEMENTE, R.**
Robin at Hickory Street. /RAU, DM/1995/K-2/3 KG314 . . . . . **CE E**
Robin at Hickory Street (Kit)./RAU, DM/1995/K-2/3 KG314 . . . . . **CE E**
Robin Hood. /CRESWICK, P/1984/6/6 KB434 . . . . **398.22**
Robin Hood and his Merry Men. /CURRY, JL/1994/3-5/3 KB436 . **398.22**
Robin Hood and Little John. /COHEN, B/1995/2-4/4 KB433 . . . **398.22**
Robin Hood (Braille)./CRESWICK, P/n.d./6/6 KB434 . . . . . . **398.22**
Robin Hood in the greenwood. /CURRY, JL/1995/3-5/3 KB437 . **398.22**
Robin Hood (Sound recording cassette)./CRESWICK, P/n.d./
6/6 KB434. . . . . **398.22**
Robin Hood (Talking book)./CRESWICK, P/n.d./6/6 KB434 . . . **398.22**
Robin of Sherwood. /MORPURGO, M/1996/5-A/6 KH514 . . . . . **Fic**
Robins in your backyard. /WILLIS, NC/1996/K-3/5 KC707 . . . . **598.8**
Robinson Crusoe. /DEFOE, D/1983/5-A/7 KH068 . . . . **Fic**
Robots: your high-tech world. /SKURZYNSKI, G/1990/
5-6/8 KD141 . . . . **629.8**
ROCK 'N ROLL FITNESS FUN (Compact disc)./1987/
K-6/KC990. . . . . **SRC 613.7**
ROCK 'N ROLL FITNESS FUN (Sound recording cassette). /1989/
K-6/KC990. . . . . **SRC 613.7**
Rockabye crocodile. /ARUEGO, J/1988/P-K/2 KB525. . . . . . **398.24**
Rocket!: how a toy launched the space age. /MAURER, R/1995/
5-6/10 KD047 . . . . **621.43**
ROCKS AND MINERALS: THE HARD FACTS (Videocassette). /1987/
5-A/KC227 . . . . **VCR 552**
ROCKY MOUNTAIN REGION OF THE UNITED STATES (Videocassette). /
1993/4-6/KF046. . . . . **VCR 978**
ROCKY MOUNTAINS (Videocassette). /1989/5-6/KE181 . . . . **VCR 917**
Roi Gilgamesh./ZEMAN, L/1992/4-6/4 KE130 . . . . **892.1**
ROLL ALONG: POEMS ON WHEELS. /1993/4-A/KE080 . . . . . **811.008**
Roll of thunder, hear my cry. /TAYLOR, MD/c1976/5-6/6 KH779 . **CE Fic**
Roll of thunder, hear my cry (Braille). /TAYLOR, MD/n.d./
5-6/6 KH779 . . . . **CE Fic**
Roll of thunder, hear my cry (Sound recording cassette)./TAYLOR, MD/
n.d./5-6/6 KH779 . . . . **CE Fic**
Roll of thunder, hear my cry (Talking book)./TAYLOR, MD/1978/
5-6/6 KH779 . . . . **CE Fic**
Rolling Harvey down the hill. /PRELUTSKY, J/1980/1-4/KE015 . . **CE 811**
Rolling Harvey down the hill (Talking book)./PRELUTSKY, J/1993/
1-4/KE015 . . . . **CE 811**
Rolling Rose. /STEVENSON, J/1992/P-K/2 KG566 . . . . **E**
Rolling Rose (Sound recording cassette)./STEVENSON, J/1995/
P-K/2 KG566 . . . . **E**
Rollo and Tweedy and the ghost at Dougal Castle. /ALLEN, LJ/1992/
1-3/2 KF153 . . . . **CE E**
Rollo and Tweedy and the ghost at Dougal Castle (Kit)./ALLEN, LJ/1996/
1-3/2 KF153 . . . . **CE E**
Roman Empire and the Dark Ages. /CASELLI, G/1985/
5-A/9 KE644 . . . . **940.1**

Roman numerals I to MM./Numerabilia romana uno ad duo mila: liber de
difficillimo computando numerum. /GEISERT, A/1996/
K-4/6 KB988 . . . . **513.5**
Roman villa. /MORLEY, J/1992/4-6/7 KE641 . . . . **937**
Ronald Reagan. /JUDSON, K/1997/6-A/10 KE504 . . . . **B REAGAN, R.**
Rooftop astronomer: a story about Maria Mitchell. /MCPHERSON, SS/
1990/4-5/6 KE465 . . . . **B MITCHELL, M.**
Rooftop mystery. /LEXAU, JM/c1968/1-2/1 KF979 . . . . **E**
Rooftop mystery (Braille)./LEXAU, JM/n.d./1-2/1 KF979 . . . . . **E**
Rooster crows: a book of American rhymes and jingles. /PETERSHAM, M/
c1945/K-2/KB810 . . . . **398.8**
Rooster crows: a book of American rhymes and jingles (Braille)./
PETERSHAM, M/n.d./K-2/KB810 . . . . **398.8**
Rooster crows: a book of American rhymes and jingles (Sound recording
cassette)./PETERSHAM, M/n.d./K-2/KB810 . . . . **398.8**
Rooster's gift. /CONRAD, P/1996/K-2/3 KF414 . . . . **E**
Rooster's off to see the world. /CARLE, E/1972/P-2/2 KF345 . . . . **E**
Rootabaga stories. /SANDBURG, C/c1922, 1990/1-6/7 KH674 . . . **Fic**
Rootabaga stories: part two./SANDBURG, C/1990/1-6/7 KH674 . . . **Fic**
Roots and branches: a legacy of multicultural music for children. /
CAMPBELL, PS/1994/KA320 . . . . **BA PROF 789.3**
ROOTS OF AFRICAN CIVILIZATION (Videocassette). /1996/
6-A/KE729. . . . . **VCR 960**
Rosa Parks: my story. /PARKS, R/1992/6-A/5 KE490 . . . . **B PARKS, R.**
Rosata. /KELLER, H/1995/K-2/2 KF886 . . . . **E**
Rose for Abby. /GUTHRIE, D/1988/2-4/5 KF654 . . . . **E**
Rose for Pinkerton./KELLOGG, S/1984/P-2/2 KF894 . . . . . . **CE E**
Rose horse. /ROSE, DL/1995/3-5/6 KH651 . . . . **Fic**
Rose in bloom: a sequel to Eight cousins. Uniform ed. /ALCOTT, LM/
c1876, 1995/5-6/7 KG831 . . . . **Fic**
Rose in bloom (Braille)./ALCOTT, LM/n.d./5-6/7 KG831 . . . . . **Fic**
Rose in my garden. /LOBEL, A/1984/K-3/KG011. . . . . **E**
Rose in my garden (Sound recording cassette)./LOBEL, A/n.d./
K-3/KG011 . . . . **E**
Roses are pink, your feet really stink. /DE GROAT, D/1996/
K-2/2 KF457 . . . . **E**
Rosie, a visiting dog's story. /CALMENSON, S/1994/
3-6/2 KD216 . . . . **636.7**
Rosie the Riveter: women working on the home front in World War II. /
COLMAN, P/1995/5-A/7 KA938 . . . . **331.4**
Rosie's birthday rat. /GLASER, L/1996/1-3/2 KH171 . . . . **Fic**
Rosie's tiger. /MYERS, A/1994/4-A/4 KH521 . . . . **Fic**
Rosie's walk. /HUTCHINS, P/c1968/P-1/1 KF802 . . . . **CE E**
Rosie's walk (Big book)./HUTCHINS, P/1992/P-1/1 KF802 . . . . **CE E**
Rosie's Walk (Kit)./HUTCHINS, P/1992/P-1/1 KF802 . . . . . . **CE E**
Rosie's walk (Videocassette)./HUTCHINS, P/1986/P-1/1 KF802 . . **CE E**
Rosy Cole: she grows and graduates. /GREENWALD, S/1997/
3-5/4 KH200 . . . . **Fic**
Rosy Cole: she walks in beauty. /GREENWALD, S/1994/
3-6/3 KH201 . . . . **Fic**
Rotten Ralph. /GANTOS, J/1976/K-2/3 KF597. . . . . **E**
Rotten Ralph's show and tell./GANTOS, J/1989/K-2/3 KF597 . . . . **E**
Rough-face girl. /MARTIN, R/1992/3-5/4 KB752. . . . . **398.27**
Round and round again. /VAN LAAN, N/1994/P-2/3 KG643 . . . . . **E**
Round and round the money goes: what money is and how we use it. /
BERGER, M/1993/2-4/2 KA948 . . . . **332.4**
Round trip. /JONAS, A/1983/K-2/2 KF847 . . . . **CE E**
Round trip (Kit)./JONAS, A/1992/K-2/2 KF847 . . . . **CE E**
Roxaboxen. /MCLERRAN, A/1991/K-3/2 KG110 . . . . **CE E**
Roxaboxen (Videocassette)./MCLERRAN, A/1991/K-3/2 KG110. . . **CE E**
Roy Campanella: major-league champion. /GREENE, C/1994/
1-2/2 KE275 . . . . **B CAMPANELLA, R**
Royal kingdoms of Ghana, Mali, and Songhay: life in medieval Africa. /
MCKISSACK, P/c1994, 1995/A/8 KE734 . . . . **966.2**
Royal raven. /WILHELM, H/1996/K-2/2 KG723 . . . . **E**
Roz and Ozzie. /HURWITZ, J/1992/3-5/5 KH302 . . . . **Fic**
Roz and Ozzie (Sound recording cassette)./HURWITZ, J/1995/
3-5/5 KH302 . . . . **Fic**
Rubber. /COSNER, S/1986/5-6/9 KD337 . . . . **678**
Ruby. /EMBERLEY, M/1990/1-3/3 KF523 . . . . **E**
Ruby Mae has something to say. /SMALL, D/1992/1-3/4 KG523 . . . . **E**
Ruby the copycat. /RATHMANN, P/1991/K-2/2 KG311 . . . . **E**
Rudyard Kipling: author of the "Jungle books." /GREENE, C/1994/
3-6/2 KE424 . . . . **B KIPLING, R.**
Rumpelstiltskin. /ZELINSKY, PO/1986/1-4/7 KB385 . . . . . **CE 398.2**
Rumpelstiltskin. /GRIMM, J/1997/K-2/2 KB308 . . . . **398.2**
Rumpelstiltskin (Braille)./ZELINSKY, PO/n.d./1-4/7 KB385 . . . **CE 398.2**
Rumpelstiltskin (Sound recording cassette)./ZELINSKY, PO/n.d./
1-4/7 KB385 . . . . **CE 398.2**
Rumpelstiltskin (Videocassette)./ZELINSKY, PO/1989/
1-4/7 KB385 . . . . **CE 398.2**
Rumpelstiltskin's daughter. /STANLEY, D/1997/2-5/3 KG537 . . . . **E**
Runaway bunny. /BROWN, MW/c1972/P-K/2 KF287 . . . . **CE E**
Runaway bunny (Braille)./BROWN, MW/n.d./P-K/2 KF287 . . . . . **CE E**

Runaway bunny (Kit)./BROWN, MW/1985/P-K/2 KF287. . . . . CE E
Runaway bunny (Picture)./BROWN, MW/n.d./P-K/2 KF287 . . . . . . CE E
Runaway mittens. /ROGERS, J/1988/P-2/4 KG348 . . . . E
Runaway Ralph./CLEARY, B/1977/3-5/5 KG997 . . . . CE Fic
Runaway Ralph (Braille)./CLEARY, B/n.d./3-5/5 KG997. . . . . CE Fic
Runaway Ralph (Sound recording cassette)./CLEARY, B/n.d./ 3-5/5 KG997 . . . . CE Fic
Runaway Ralph (Talking book)./CLEARY, B/n.d./3-5/5 KG997 . . . CE Fic
Runaway Ralph (Talking book)./CLEARY, B/1995/3-5/5 KG997 . . CE Fic
Runaway (Videocassette)./HOLMAN, F/1989/6-A/7 KH274. . . . . CE Fic
Running out of time. /HADDIX, MP/1995/5-A/5 KH211 . . . . Fic
Running the road to ABC. /LAUTURE, D/1996/1-3/4 KF951 . . . . E
Russell and Elisa./HURWITZ, J/1989/2-4/4 KH303. . . . . Fic
Russell Sprouts. /HURWITZ, J/1987/2-4/4 KH303 . . . . Fic
Russian fairy tales (Talking book). /BUDBERG, M/n.d./ 4-6/KB722. . . . . TB 398.27
Russian girl: life in an old Russian town. /KENDALL, R/1994/ 3-6/5 KE690 947
Ruth Law thrills a nation. /BROWN, D/1993/2-3/4 KE428. . . B LAW, R.
Ryan White: my own story. /WHITE, R/1991/5-A/5 KE594 . B WHITE, R.
Sabbath lion: a Jewish folktale from Algeria. /SCHWARTZ, H/1992/ 4-6/6 KB511 . . . . 398.23
Sable. /HESSE, K/1994/3-5/4 KH253 . . . . Fic
SACAJAWEA (Videocassette). /1991/2-5/KE530. . VCR B SACAGAWEA
Sacred harvest: Ojibway wild rice gathering. /REGGUINTI, G/1992/ 4-6/6 KE785 . . . . 970.476
Sacred places. /YOLEN, J/1996/3-6/KE048 811
Sacred river. /LEWIN, T/1995/4-6/6 KA765. . . . . 294.5
Sad Night: the story of an Aztec victory and a Spanish loss. /MATHEWS, SS/1994/4-6/6 KE834. 972
Sad underwear and other complications: more poems for children and their parents. /VIORST, J/1995/2-4/KE038 811
Sadako. /COERR, E/1993/3-6/4 KA994 . . . . CE 362.1
Sadako and the thousand paper cranes (Videocassette)./COERR, E/1990/ 3-6/4 KA994 . . . . CE 362.1
Safari beneath the sea: the wonder world of the North Pacific coast. / SWANSON, D/1994/4-6/7 KC370 . . . . 578.77
Safe horse, safe rider: a young rider's guide to responsible horsekeeping. / HAAS, J/1994/5-6/6 KD200 . . . . 636.1
SAFETY ON WHEELS (Videocassette). /1994/P-1/KB024 . . . VCR 363.1
Sahara. /MURRAY, P/1994/3-6/6 KE731. 966
Sahara: vanishing cultures. /REYNOLDS, J/1991/4-6/6 KE732 966
Sail away. /CREWS, D/1995/P-2/2 KF434. . . . . E
Sailing to Cythera, and other Anatole stories. /WILLARD, N/1974/ 3-5/6 KH863 . . . . Fic
Saint Francis. /WILDSMITH, B/1996/2-4/2 KE350 . . . . . B FRANCIS, ST.
Saint George and the dragon: a golden legend. /HODGES, M/1984/ 5/7 KB453. . . . . CE 398.22
Saint George and the dragon: a golden legend (Sound recording cassette)./HODGES, M/n.d./5/7 KB453 . . . . CE 398.22
Saint Patrick and the peddler. /HODGES, M/1993/3-4/5 KB454 . 398.22
Saint Valentine. /SABUDA, R/1992/4-6/4 KE581. . . . . B VALENTINE,ST.
Saint Valentine (Sound recording cassette)./SABUDA, R/1995/ 4-6/4 KE581 . . . . B VALENTINE,ST.
Salamanders. /WINNER, C/1993/A/7 KC611 . . . . 597.8
Salamanders. /BERNHARD, E/1995/2-5/6 KC598 . . . . 597.8
SALAMANDERS (Videocassette). /1985/5-6/KC609. . . . . . . VCR 597.8
Salem witch trials. /WILSON, LL/1997/A/7 KA607 . . . . 133.4
Sali de paseo./WILLIAMS, S/1995/P-1/1 KG732 . . . . CE E
Sali de paseo (Kit)./WILLIAMS, S/1996/P-1/1 KG732 . . . . CE E
Sally Ann Thunder Ann Whirlwind Crockett: a tall tale. /KELLOGG, S/ 1995/2-5/5 KB458 . . . . 398.22
Salta, ranita, salta!/KALAN, R/1994/P-1/1 KF864 . . . . CE E
Salta, ranita, salta! (Kit)./KALAN, R/1996/P-1/1 KF864 . . . . CE E
Salty dog. /RAND, G/1991/2-3/5 KG301 . . . . E
Salvador Dali. /VENEZIA, M/1993/4-6/7 KE313. . . . . B DALI, S.
Sam and the firefly. /EASTMAN, PD/c1958/P-1/1 KF507 . . . . E
Sam and the lucky money. /CHINN, K/1995/1-3/4 KF383 . . . . E
Sam and the tigers: a new telling of LITTLE BLACK SAMBO. /LESTER, J/ 1996/K-3/2 KF966 . . . . E
Sam goes trucking. /HORENSTEIN, H/1989/2-3/3 KD118. . . . . 629.224
Sam the minuteman. /BENCHLEY, N/c1969/1-3/2 KF222. . . . . E
Sam the minuteman (Talking book)./BENCHLEY, N/n.d./1-3/2 KF222. . . E
Sam the sea cow. /JACOBS, F/1991/1-3/2 KC780 . . . . 599.55
Samantha. /WALSH, ES/1996/K-2/2 KG681 . . . . E
Sambalena show-off. /GERSHATOR, P/1995/1-3/2 KF612 . . . . E
Sami and the time of the troubles. /HEIDE, FP/1992/2-4/4 KF695. . . . . E
Sammy and other songs from "Getting to know myself" (Videocassette). / PALMER, H/1993/P-1/KD643 . . . . VCR 789.3
SAMMY'S SCIENCE HOUSE (CD-ROM). /1994/K-3/KB870 . . CDR 500
Sam's sneaker search. /O'BRIEN, C/1997/P-2/3 KG186 . . . . E
Sam's Wild West Show. /ANTLE, N/1995/1-3/2 KF161 . . . . E
Samuel Eaton's day: a day in the life of a Pilgrim boy. /WATERS, K/ 1993/3-5/6 KE948 . . . . 974.4
Samurai's daughter: a Japanese legend. /SAN SOUCI, RD/1992/ 3-4/6 KB365 . . . . 398.2
Samurai's tale. /HAUGAARD, EC/1984/6-A/5 KH228 . . . . Fic
Samurai's tale (Sound recording cassette)./HAUGAARD, EC/n.d./ 6-A/5 KH228 . . . . Fic
San Rafael: a Central American city through the ages. /HERNANDEZ, X/ 1992/A/8 KA897 . . . . 307.76
Sancocho del sabado./TORRES, L/1995/K-2/5 KG614 . . . . E
Sand and fog: adventures in Southern Africa. /BRANDENBURG, J/1994/ 5-6/6 KE740 . . . . 968.81
Sand tiger shark. /CARRICK, C/c1977/4-6/7 KC591. . . . . 597.3
Sandra Day O'Connor. /MACHT, NL/1992/ 4-5/8 KE481 . . . . B O'CONNOR, S.
Santa calls. /JOYCE, W/1993/2-4/4 KF862 . . . . E
Santa Fe Trail. /LAVENDER, DS/1995/A/6 KF037. 978
Sapo y Sepo inseparables./LOBEL, A/n.d./K-2/2 KG004. . . . . CE E
Sapo y Sepo son amigos./LOBEL, A/n.d./K-2/2 KG003 . . . . CE E
Sapo y Sepo un ano entero./LOBEL, A/n.d./K-2/1 KG002. . . . . . . CE E
Sara Crewe. /BURNETT, FH/1986/4-6/7 KG950 . . . . Fic
Sarah, also known as Hannah. /ROSS, LH/1994/4-6/4 KH655 . . . . . . Fic
Sarah and the people of Sand River. /VALGARDSON, WD/1996/ 4-6/2 KH818 . . . . Fic
Sarah Bishop. /O'DELL, S/1980/5-6/5 KH561. . . . . Fic
Sarah Bishop (Braille)./O'DELL, S/n.d./5-6/5 KH561. . . . . Fic
Sarah Bishop (Sound recording cassette)./O'DELL, S/n.d./ 5-6/5 KH561 . . . . Fic
Sarah Morton's day: a day in the life of a Pilgrim girl. /WATERS, K/1989/ 3-5/3 KE949 . . . . 974.4
Sarah, plain and tall. /MACLACHLAN, P/1985/3-5/4 KH444. . . . . CE Fic
Sarah, plain and tall (Sound recording cassette)./MACLACHLAN, P/n.d./ 3-5/4 KH444 . . . . CE Fic
Sarah, plain and tall (Talking book)./MACLACHLAN, P/1986/ 3-5/4 KH444 . . . . CE Fic
Sarah, sencilla y alta./MACLACHLAN, P/n.d./3-5/4 KH444 . . . . . CE Fic
SARI TALE (Videocassette)./1991/4-6/KA851 . . . . VCR 305.8
Satchel Paige: the best arm in baseball. /MCKISSACK, P/1992/ 3-5/2 KE489 . . . . B PAIGE, S.
Saturday at The New You. /BARBER, BE/1994/K-3/3 KF198 . . . . E
Saturday sancocho. /TORRES, L/1995/K-2/5 KG614 . . . . E
Saturdays. /ENRIGHT, E/c1941, 1988/4-6/5 KH099 . . . . Fic
Saturdays (Braille)./ENRIGHT, E/n.d./4-6/5 KH099 . . . . Fic
Saturn. /SIMON, S/1985/3-6/6 KC039. . . . . 523.46
Save Halloween! /TOLAN, SS/1993/5-A/7 KH794. . . . . Fic
Save the animals, save the earth: songs about endangered animals and the earth (Sound recording cassette). /SKIERA-ZUCEK, L/1991/ K-4/KD658 . . . . SRC 789.3
Saving endangered mammals: a field guide to some of the earth's rarest animals. /MAYNARD, T/1992/5-6/8 KC489 . . . . 591.68
Saving endangered mammals: a field guide to some of the earth's rarest animals (Sound recording cassette)./MAYNARD, T/1995/ 5-6/8 KC489 . . . . 591.68
Saving our wetlands and their wildlife. /LIPTAK, K/1991/ 4-6/8 KA960 . . . . 333.91
Saving Shiloh. /NAYLOR, PR/1997/4-A/4 KH537 . . . . Fic
Saving Sweetness. /STANLEY, D/1996/1-3/4 KG538. . . . . E
SAVING THE MANATEE (Videocassette). /1993/ 2-6/KC783. . . . . VCR 599.55
Saving the peregrine falcon. /ARNOLD, C/1990/4-6/7 KC708 . . . . 598.9
Savior is born (Kit). /GLEESON, B/1992/3-5/KA705 . . . . . . KIT 232.92
Savior is born (Kit)./GLEESON, B/1992/3-5/KA705. . . . . . . KIT 232.92
Savitri: a tale of ancient India. /SHEPARD, A/1992/3-4/4 KA766. . 294.5
Say hola to Spanish. /ELYA, SM/1996/K-2/3 KB862 . . . . 468.1
Say it with music: a story about Irving Berlin. /STREISSGUTH, T/1994/ 4-5/5 KE252 . . . . B BERLIN, I.
Say no and know why: kids learn about drugs. /WAX, W/1992/ 5-6/5 KA999 . . . . 362.29
SAY NO AND MEAN IT (Videocassette). /1991/3-5/KA663 . . VCR 158
Say woof!: the day of a country veterinarian. /GIBBONS, G/1992/ P-2/2 KD194 . . . . 636.089
SAYING GOOD-BYE (Videocassette). /1993/2-4/KA652. . . . VCR 155.9
SAYING NO (Videocassette)./1990/4-6/KA655 . . . . VCR 158
Sayonara, Mrs. Kackleman. /KALMAN, M/1989/1-3/3 KF867 . . . . . . E
Scaly babies: reptiles growing up. /JOHNSTON, G/1988/ 5-6/6 KC615 . . . . 597.9
Scaly things. /LAMPRELL, K/1996/4-6/5 KC616 . . . . 597.9
SCANDINAVIAN FOLK & FAIRY TALES. /1984//KA273. . . PROF 398.2
Scarebird. /FLEISCHMAN, S/1987/1-3/5 KF552 . . . . E
Scarecrow of Oz. /BAUM, LF/1997/4-6/7 KG885 . . . . Fic
SCARED SILLY! A BOOK FOR THE BRAVE. /1994/K-3/KD904. . . . 810.8
Scared silly: a Halloween treat. /HOWE, J/1989/K-3/3 KF780 . . . . . . E
SCARY BOOK. /1991/2-4/2 KB691 . . . . 398.25
Scary, scary Halloween. /BUNTING, E/1986/P-K/4 KF308. . . . . E
Scary, scary Halloween (Braille)./BUNTING, E/n.d./P-K/4 KF308. . . . . . E

Scary stories to tell in the dark. /SCHWARTZ, A/1981/
4-A/3 KB694 . . . . **CE 398.25**
Scary stories to tell in the dark (Braille). /SCHWARTZ, A/n.d./
4-A/3 KB694 . . . . **CE 398.25**
Scary stories to tell in the dark (Sound recording cassette). /SCHWARTZ,
A/n.d./4-A/3 KB694 . . . . **CE 398.25**
Scary stories to tell in the dark (Talking book). /SCHWARTZ, A/1986/
4-A/3 KB694 . . . . **CE 398.25**
Scary stories 3: more tales to chill your bones./SCHWARTZ, A/1991/
4-A/3 KB694 . . . . **CE 398.25**
SCHOLASTIC CHILDREN'S DICTIONARY. Rev. ed. /1996/
4-6/KA430 . . . . **REF 423**
Scholastic dictionary of idioms. /TERBAN, M/1996/4-6/KA431 . . **REF 423**
Scholastic encyclopedia of the presidents and their times. Updated ed. /
RUBEL, D/1997/4-A/KA492 . . . . **REF 973**
Scholastic rhyming dictionary. /YOUNG, S/1994/5-A/KB842 . . . . . **423.1**
SCHOLASTIC'S MAGIC SCHOOL BUS EXPLORES IN THE AGE OF
DINOSAURS. School ed. (CD-ROM). /1996/1-4/KC263. . . . **CDR 567.9**
SCHOLASTIC'S THE MAGIC SCHOOL BUS EXPLORES INSIDE THE
EARTH. School ed. (CD-ROM). /1996/4-A/KC149 . . . . . . **CDR 550**
SCHOLASTIC'S THE MAGIC SCHOOL BUS EXPLORES THE HUMAN
BODY. School ed. (CD-ROM). /1995/2-A/KC925 . . . . **CDR 612**
SCHOLASTIC'S THE MAGIC SCHOOL BUS EXPLORES THE OCEAN.
Teacher ed. (CD-ROM). /1995/2-A/KC369 . . . . **CDR 578.77**
SCHOLASTIC'S THE MAGIC SCHOOL BUS EXPLORES THE RAINFOREST.
School ed. (CD-ROM). /1997/6-A/KC325 . . . . **CDR 577.34**
SCHOLASTIC'S THE MAGIC SCHOOL BUS EXPLORES THE SOLAR
SYSTEM. Academic ed. (CD-ROM). /1994/2-5/KC014. . . **CDR 523.2**
School. /MCCULLY, EA/1987/P-K/KG095 . . . . **E**
SCHOOL ARTS MAGAZINE. /1901-//KA136 . . . . . . **PER PROF 050**
School bus. /CREWS, D/1984/P-2/1 KF435 . . . . **E**
School days. /HENNESSY, BG/1990/P-1/3 KF713 . . . . **E**
School for Pompey Walker. /ROSEN, MJ/1995/4-8/6 KH653 . . . . . **Fic**
School for Pompey Walker (Sound recording cassette)./ROSEN, MJ/1997/
4-8/6 KH653 . . . . **Fic**
SCHOOL LIBRARIAN'S WORKSHOP. /1980-//KA137 . . **PER PROF 050**
SCHOOL LIBRARIES IN CANADA. /1974-//KA138 . . . . **PER PROF 050**
SCHOOL LIBRARY JOURNAL: FOR CHILDREN'S, YOUNG ADULT, AND
SCHOOL LIBRARIES. /1954-//KA139 . . . . **PER PROF 050**
SCHOOL LIBRARY MEDIA ACTIVITIES MONTHLY. /1984-/
/KA140. . . . . **PER PROF 050**
SCHOOL LIBRARY MEDIA ANNUAL. /1983-//KA141. . . **PER PROF 050**
SCHOOL LIBRARY MEDIA QUARTERLY. /1972-//KA142 **PER PROF 050**
School mouse. /KING-SMITH, D/1995/3-5/7 KH353 . . . . **Fic**
SCHOOL RAP (Sound recording cassette). /1990/2-6/KD656. **SRC 789.3**
SCHOOL SCIENCE AND MATHEMATICS. /1901-/
/KA143. . . . . **PER PROF 050**
School spirit./HURWITZ, J/1994/2-4/4 KH298 . . . . **Fic**
School survival guide for kids with LD (Learning differences). /CUMMINGS,
RW/1991/4-6/4 KB093 . . . . **371.92**
Schoolmasters. /FISHER, LE/1997/3-6/7 KB083. . . . . **371.1**
School's out./HURWITZ, J/1991/2-4/4 KH298 . . . . **Fic**
Science. /RUBEL, D/1995/4-6/7 KB877 . . . . **503**
SCIENCE ACTIVITIES FOR YOUNG PEOPLE. /1983/5-A/9 KB884 . . **507**
SCIENCE AND CHILDREN. /1963-//KA144 . . . . . . **PER PROF 050**
SCIENCE BLASTER JR. Teacher ed. (CD-ROM). /1997/
K-3/KB871 . . . . **CDR 500**
Science book. /STEIN, S/1979/2-A/5 KB873 . . . . **500**
Science book of air. /ARDLEY, N/1991/4-6/4 KC102. . . . . **533**
Science book of color. /ARDLEY, N/1991/4-6/4 KC118 . . . . **535.6**
Science book of electricity. /ARDLEY, N/1991/2-5/3 KC129 . . . . . **537**
Science book of gravity. /ARDLEY, N/1992/K-3/2 KC089 . . . . . . **531**
Science book of hot and cold. /ARDLEY, N/1992/K-3/2 KC126 . . . . **536**
Science book of light. /ARDLEY, N/1991/K-3/6 KC105. . . . . **535**
Science book of machines. /ARDLEY, N/1992/4-6/4 KD050. . . . . **621.8**
Science book of magnets. /ARDLEY, N/1991/2-5/2 KC136 . . . . . **538**
Science book of motion. /ARDLEY, N/1992/K-3/2 KC090 . . . . . . **531**
Science book of numbers. /CHALLONER, J/1992/K-3/2 KB956. . . **513.2**
Science book of sound. /ARDLEY, N/1991/2-5/3 KC076. . . . . . . **530**
Science book of things that grow. /ARDLEY, N/1991/
K-3/3 KC273 . . . . **571.2**
Science book of water. /ARDLEY, N/1991/2-4/4 KC091. . . . . . . **531**
Science book of weather. /ARDLEY, N/1992/K-3/3 KC185 . . . . . **551.5**
SCIENCE BOOKS AND FILMS. /1975-//KA145 . . . . **PER PROF 050**
SCIENCE BOOKS AND FILMS' BEST BOOKS FOR CHILDREN, 1992-1995.
/1996//KA028. **PROF 016.5**
Science dictionary of the human body. /RICHARDSON, J/1992/
4-6/7 KC906 . . . . **611**
Science experiences with everyday things. /MUNSON, HR/1988/
/KA283. . . . . **PROF 507**
Science experiments you can eat. Rev. and updated. /COBB, V/1994/
3-5/7 KB891 . . . . **507.8**
SCIENCE FAIR PROJECTS (Videocassette). /1995/
5-A/KB898. . . . . **VCR 507.8**

Science fun with mud and dirt. /WYLER, R/1986/K-4/2 KB887 . . . . . **507**
Science in your backyard. /GARDNER, R/1987/A/6 KB881. . . . . . . **507**
SCIENCE IN YOUR EAR (CD-ROM). /1996/4-A/KC104 . . . . . **CDR 534**
Science is...2nd ed. /BOSAK, SV/1991//KA285 . . . . **PROF 507.8**
Science magic with air. /OXLADE, C/1994/4-A/6 KD748 . . . . . **793.8**
Science magic with light. /OXLADE, C/1994/3-6/5 KD749 . . . . . **793.8**
Science magic with magnets. /OXLADE, C/1995/3-6/6 KD750 . . . **793.8**
Science magic with shapes and materials. /OXLADE, C/1995/
3-6/5 KD751 . . . . **793.8**
SCIENCE NEWS. /1921-/4-6/KA539. . . . . **PER 050**
SCIENCE OF EXPLORATION (Videocassette). /1996/
4-6/KE162 . . . . **VCR 910.9**
Science on the ice: an Antarctic journal. /JOHNSON, RL/1995/
5-A/7 KE215 . . . . **919.8**
SCIENCE, SCIENCE EVERYWHERE: A SUPPLEMENT TO CHILDCRAFT--THE
HOW AND WHY LIBRARY./1997/P-2/KA378 . . . . **REF 031**
SCIENCE SLEUTHS. VOL. 1: THE MYSTERIES OF THE BLOB AND THE
EXPLODING LAWNMOWERS (CD-ROM). /1995/
4-A/KB885. . . . . **CDR 507**
SCIENCE SLEUTHS. VOL. 2: THE MYSTERIES OF THE BIOGENE PICNIC
AND THE TRAFFIC ACCIDENT (CD-ROM)./1995/
4-A/KB885. . . . . **CDR 507**
Science to the rescue. /MARKLE, S/1994/6-A/8 KB896. . . . . . . **507.8**
SCIENCE YEAR: THE WORLD ANNUAL SCIENCE SUPPLEMENT. /1965-/
A/KA435. . . . . **REF 505**
Scientific explorers: travels in search of knowledge. /STEFOFF, R/1992/
6-A/9 KB925 . . . . **509**
SCIENTIFIC METHOD (Videocassette). /1993/5-6/KB886 . . . . **VCR 507**
SCIENTISTS: THE LIVES AND WORKS OF 150 SCIENTISTS. /1996/
5-A/KA442 . . . . **REF 509**
Scooter. /WILLIAMS, VB/1993/4-A/4 KH865 . . . . **Fic**
Scooter (Sound recording cassette)./WILLIAMS, VB/1996/
4-A/4 KH865 . . . . **Fic**
Scorpion man: exploring the world of scorpions. /PRINGLE, LP/1994/
5-6/8 KC530 . . . . **595.4**
SCOTT FORESMAN BEGINNING DICTIONARY. /c1983, 1994/
2-4/KB836 . . . . **423**
Scottie Pippen: reluctant superstar. /SCHNAKENBERG, R/1997/
4-6/6 KE498 . . . . **B PIPPEN, S.**
Screen of frogs: an old tale. /HAMANAKA, S/1993/
2-4/4 KB581 . . . . **398.24**
Scrub dog of Alaska. /MOREY, W/c1971, 1989/5-A/6 KH511 . . . **Fic**
Scruffy. /PARISH, P/1988/K-3/1 KG217 . . . . **E**
SEA ANIMALS ASHORE (Videocassette). /1996/
3-6/KC872. . . . . **VCR 599.79**
Sea lion. /ARNOLD, C/1994/4-6/6 KC867 . . . . **599.79**
Sea shapes. /MACDONALD, S/1994/P-2/KB993. . . . . **516**
Sea squares. /HULME, JN/1991/K-3/3 KB960 . . . . **513.2**
Sea sums. /HULME, JN/1996/P-2/3 KB961 . . . . **513.2**
Sea turtle journey: the story of a loggerhead turtle. /JAY, LA/1995/
K-2/5 KF826 . . . . **CE E**
Sea turtle journey: the story of a loggerhead turtle (Kit)./JAY, LA/1995/
K-2/5 KF826 . . . . **CE E**
Sea turtles. /GIBBONS, G/1995/2-4/6 KC617 . . . . **597.92**
Sea View Hotel. /STEVENSON, J/c1978, 1994/K-3/3 KG567 . . . . . **E**
Sea watch: a book of poetry. /YOLEN, J/1996/4-6/KE049 . . . . . . **811**
Seabird. /HOLLING, HC/c1948/5-6/5 KH272 . . . . **Fic**
Seabird (Braille)./HOLLING, HC/n.d./5-6/5 KH272 . . . . **Fic**
Seabird (Sound recording cassette)./HOLLING, HC/n.d./5-6/5 KH272 . **Fic**
Seal oil lamp. /DEARMOND, D/1988/5-6/6 KB499 . . . . **398.23**
Search for delicious. /BABBITT, N/c1969/4-6/5 KG872. . . . . . . **CE Fic**
Search for delicious (Talking book)./BABBITT, N/n.d./
4-6/5 KG872 . . . . **CE Fic**
Search for delicious (Talking book)./BABBITT, N/1995/
4-6/5 KG872 . . . . **CE Fic**
Search for the killer asteroid. /VOGT, G/1994/A/8 KC037 . . . . . **523.44**
Searching for Laura Ingalls: a reader's journey. /LASKY, K/1993/
3-6/6 KE198 . . . . **917.8**
SEARCHING FOR PARADISE (Videocassette). /1991/
A/KF086 . . . . **VCR 979.4**
SEARS LIST OF SUBJECT HEADINGS: CANADIAN COMPANION. 5th ed.
Revised by Lynne Lighthall./1995/KA061 . . . . **PROF 025.4**
SEARS LIST OF SUBJECT HEADINGS. 16th ed. /1997/
/KA061. . . . . **PROF 025.4**
Seascapes. /ROALF, P/1992/5-A/7 KD482 . . . . **758**
Seashore. /PLUCKROSE, H/1994/P-2/4 KC347 . . . . **577.69**
Seashore. /COHAT, E/1995/1-4/4 KC366 . . . . **578.769**
Seashore book. /SMITH, EB/1985/3-6/9 KH724 . . . . **Fic**
Seasons and Someone. /KROLL, VL/1994/K-3/5 KF935 . . . . **E**
SEASONS. Rev. ed. (Sound filmstrip). /c1975, 1993/
K-2/KC063. . . . . **FSS 525**
Seasons sewn: a year in patchwork. /PAUL, AW/1996/
3-6/7 KD462 . . . . **746.46**

Sea-Star: orphan of Chincoteague./HENRY, M/1970/
3-5/4 KH244 . . . . **CE Fic**
SEAT BELTS ARE FOR KIDS TOO (Videocassette). /1987/
K-6/KD127 . . . . **VCR 629.27**
Secret elephant of Harlan Kooter. /HARVEY, D/1992/4-A/6 KH223 . . **Fic**
Secret elephant of Harlan Kooter (Sound recording cassette)./HARVEY, D/
1995/4-A/6 KH223 . . . . **Fic**
Secret garden. /BURNETT, FH/c1911, 1987/3-6/5 KG951 . . . **CE Fic**
Secret garden (Talking book)./BURNETT, FH/1997/3-6/5 KG951 . **CE Fic**
Secret of the Indian./REID BANKS, L/1989/5-A/6 KH629 . . . . **Fic**
Secret of the Indian (Sound recording cassette)./REID BANKS, L/1994/
5-A/6 KH629 . . . . **Fic**
Secret shortcut. /TEAGUE, M/1996/1-3/2 KG596 . . . . **E**
Secret signs: along the Underground Railroad. /RIGGIO, A/1997/
2-3/2 KG331 . . . . **E**
Secret super powers of Marco. /WILLIS, MS/1994/4-A/4 KH866 . . . . **Fic**
Secret super powers of Marco (Sound recording cassette)./WILLIS, MS/
1996/4-A/4 KH866 . . . . **Fic**
Secrets. /SENISI, EB/1995/K-2/2 KA643 . . . . **155.4**
Secrets of a wildlife watcher. /ARNOSKY, J/c1983, 1991/
5-6/7 KC580 . . . . **596**
See how you grow. /PEARSE, P/1988/K-3/5 KC954 . . . . . . **612.6**
See you around, Sam! /LOWRY, L/1996/3-6/6 KH428 . . . . . . **Fic**
See you in second grade! /COHEN, M/1989/K-1/2 KF404 . . . . **CE E**
See you in the second grade (Videocassette)./COHEN, M/1991/
K-1/2 KF404 . . . . **CE E**
Seedfolks. /FLEISCHMAN, P/1997/5-A/5 KH118. . . . . **Fic**
Seeds. /SHANNON, G/1994/K-2/2 KG478 . . . . **E**
Seeing is believing. /SHUB, E/1979/K-2/2 KG496 . . . . **E**
Seeing the unseen. /GREEN, CR/1993/4-6/5 KA610 . . . . **133.8**
SEEING THINGS (Videocassette). /1987/4-A/KB913 . . . . . **VCR 508**
Sees Behind Trees. /DORRIS, M/1996/5-A/4 KH081 . . . . **Fic**
Seiji Ozawa: symphony conductor. /SIMON, C/1992/
4-5/6 KE488 . . . . **B OZAWA, S.**
Selkie girl. /COOPER, S/1986/3-4/6 KB551 . . . . **CE 398.24**
Selkie girl (Sound recording cassette)./COOPER, S/n.d./
3-4/6 KB551 . . . . **CE 398.24**
Selkie girl (Videocassette)./COOPER, S/1991/3-4/6 KB551 . . . **CE 398.24**
Selma, Lord, Selma: girlhood memories of the civil-rights days. /WEBB, S/
c1980, 1997/A/7 KA906 . . . . **323.1**
Seminoles. /SNEVE, V/1994/4-6/7 KE775 . . . . **970.3**
SENDAK (Videocassette). /1993/4-A/KE534 . . . . . . **VCR B SENDAK, M.**
Seneca. /BAKER, KL/1997/K-2/2 KF185 . . . . **E**
Senor Cat's romance and other favorite stories from Latin America. /
GONZALEZ, LM/1997/K-2/3 KB303 . . . . **398.2**
Senor Conejo y el hermoso regalo./ZOLOTOW, C/1995/
P-2/2 KG804 . . . . **CE E**
Senora a Frisby y las ratas de nimh./O'BRIEN, RC/1985/
4-A/6 KH556 . . . . **Fic**
Senorita Emilia./COONEY, B/n.d./K-3/5 KF419 . . . . **E**
Sense suspense: a guessing game for the five senses. /MCMILLAN, B/
1994/P-2/KC968 . . . . **612.8**
Senses: a lift-the-flap body book. /ROYSTON, A/1993/
1-3/4 KC977 . . . . **612.8**
Sequiremos siendo amigos./DANZIGER, P/1994/2-4/6 KH060 . . . **Fic**
Sequoyah's gift: a portrait of the Cherokee leader. /KLAUSNER, J/1993/
5-6/7 KE535 . . . . **B SEQUOYAH**
Serengeti. /PETERS, LW/1989/4-6/6 KE738 . . . . **967.8**
Serengeti migration: Africa's animals on the move. /LINDBLAD, L/1994/
5-6/10 KC497 . . . . **591.96**
Serious science: an Adam Joshua story./SMITH, JL/1993/
2-4/4 KH725 . . . . **Fic**
Serpent's children. /YEP, L/c1984, 1996/6-A/6 KH894 . . . . **Fic**
SESAME STREET MAGAZINE. /1971-/P/KA540 . . . . **PER 050**
Seth and Samona. /HYPPOLITE, J/1995/4-6/6 KH313 . . . . **Fic**
Seven blind mice. /YOUNG, E/1992/K-3/2 KB681 . . . . **398.24**
Seven brave women. /HEARNE, B/1997/1-3/2 KF691 . . . . **E**
Seven candles for Kwanzaa. /PINKNEY, AD/1993/2-6/7 KB214 . **394.261**
Seven little rabbits. /BECKER, J/1973/P-2/3 KF214 . . . . **E**
Seven loaves of bread. /WOLFF, F/1993/1-3/2 KG758 . . . . **E**
Seven pathways of learning: teaching students and parents about multiple
intelligences. /LAZEAR, DG/1994//KA174 . . . . . . **PROF 370.15**
Seven ravens. /GERINGER, L/1994/2-3/6 KB302 . . . . **398.2**
Seven ravens: a fairy tale. /GRIMM, J/1995/3-5/7 KB309 . . . . . . **398.2**
Seven-day magic. /EAGER, E/c1962/4-6/6 KH095 . . . . **Fic**
Seven-day magic (Braille)./EAGER, E/n.d./4-6/6 KH095 . . . . **Fic**
Seven-day magic (Sound recording cassette)./EAGER, E/n.d./
4-6/6 KH095 . . . . **Fic**
SEVENTH BOOK OF JUNIOR AUTHORS AND ILLUSTRATORS. /1996/
A/KA462. . . . . **REF 809**
Sewing by hand. /HOFFMAN, C/1994/3-5/3 KD297 . . . . **646.2**
Sewing quilts. /TURNER, A/1994/1-3/6 KG628 . . . . **E**
SEXUALITY (Videocassette). /1995/6/KC956 . . . . **VCR 612.6**
Shabanu, daughter of the wind. /STAPLES, SF/1989/6-A/6 KH748 . . . **Fic**

Shadow. /CENDRARS, B/1982/3-5/KE120 . . . . **CE 841**
Shadow children. /SCHNUR, S/1994/4-A/7 KH681 . . . . **Fic**
Shadow of a bull. /WOJCIECHOWSKA, M/1964/5-6/6 KH875 . . **CE Fic**
Shadow of a bull (Sound recording cassette)./WOJCIECHOWSKA, M/
n.d./5-6/6 KH875 . . . . **CE Fic**
Shadow of a bull (Talking book)./WOJCIECHOWSKA, M/n.d./
5-6/6 KH875 . . . . **CE Fic**
Shadow play: making pictures with light and lenses. /ZUBROWSKI, B/
1995/4-8/7 KC117 . . . . **535**
Shadowgraphs anyone can make. /WEBB, PH/1991/K-6/KD753 . . . **793.9**
Shadows. /HASELEY, D/1991/4-6/5 KH224 . . . . **Fic**
Shadows and reflections. /HOBAN, T/1990/P-6/KC112 . . . . **535**
Shadows: here, there, and everywhere. /GOOR, R/1981/
1-3/5 KC111 . . . . **535**
Shadows of night: the hidden world of the Little Brown Bat. /BASH, B/
1993/1-3/5 KC758 . . . . **599.4**
Shadrach. /DEJONG, M/c1953/2-3/5 KH069 . . . . **Fic**
Shadrach (Talking book)./DEJONG, M/n.d./2-3/5 KH069 . . . . . **Fic**
Shaka, king of the Zulus. /STANLEY, D/1988/
4-6/6 KE537 . . . . **B SHAKA, KING**
SHAKE IT TO THE ONE THAT YOU LOVE THE BEST./1989/
K-4/KD767 . . . . **BA 796.1**
SHAKE IT TO THE ONE THAT YOU LOVE THE BEST: PLAY SONGS AND
LULLABIES FROM BLACK MUSICAL TRADITIONS. /1989/
K-4/KD767 . . . . **BA 796.1**
Shake, rattle, and strum. /CORBETT, S/1995/3-6/6 KD542 . . . **784.19**
Shaker home. /BIAL, R/1994/4-6/8 KA717 . . . . **289**
Shaker villages. /BOLICK, NO/1993/5-6/8 KA718 . . . . **289**
Shakespeare and Macbeth: the story behind the play. /ROSS, S/1994/
5-A/7 KE116 . . . . **822.3**
SHAKESPEARE FOR CHILDREN (Compact disc)./1995/
4-6/KE117 . . . . **SRC 822.3**
SHAKESPEARE FOR CHILDREN (Sound recording cassette). /1995/
4-6/KE117 . . . . **SRC 822.3**
Shakespeare's theater. /MORLEY, J/1994/4-A/7 KD689 . . . . **792**
Shamrocks, harps, and shillelaghs: the story of the St. Patrick's Day
symbols. /BARTH, E/c1977/5-6/7 KB218 . . . . **394.262**
Shannon: an Ojibway dancer. /KING, S/1993/4-6/4 KE784 . . . **970.476**
Shapes. /REISS, JJ/c1974/P-1/KB994 . . . . **516**
Shapes and things. /HOBAN, T/c1970/P-1/KA617 . . . . **152.14**
Shapes, shapes, shapes. /HOBAN, T/1986/2-6/KB991 . . . . **516**
Shaquille O'Neal: star center. /MACNOW, G/1996/
4-5/6 KE485 . . . . **B O'NEAL, S.**
Sharks. /GIBBONS, G/1992/P-3/3 KC593 . . . . **597.3**
Sharks. /SIMON, S/1995/5-6/7 KC595 . . . . **597.3**
SHE AND HE: ADVENTURES IN MYTHOLOGY (Sound recording cassette).
/1991/5-6/KA752 . . . . **SRC 292**
SHEENA AZAK OF CANADA (Videocassette). /1995/
4-6/KE807 . . . . **VCR 971**
Sheep dog. /ANCONA, G/1985/A/8 KD227 . . . . **636.737**
Sheep in a jeep. /SHAW, N/1986/K-3/2 KG489 . . . . **E**
Sheep in a shop. /SHAW, N/1991/K-3/2 KG489 . . . . **E**
Sheep in a shop (Sound recording cassette)./SHAW, N/1994/
K-3/2 KG489 . . . . **E**
Sheep on a ship. /SHAW, N/1989/K-3/2 KG489 . . . . **E**
Sheep out to eat. /SHAW, N/1992/K-3/2 KG489 . . . . **E**
Sheep out to eat (Sound recording cassette)./SHAW, N/1994/
K-3/2 KG489 . . . . **E**
Sheila la magnifica./BLUME, J/1991/4-6/4 KG912 . . . . **Fic**
Sheila Rae, the brave. /HENKES, K/1987/P-2/4 KF711 . . . . **E**
Shell woman and the king: a Chinese folktale. /YEP, L/1993/
3-5/5 KB496 . . . . **398.22**
She's wearing a dead bird on her head! /LASKY, K/1995/
3-5/5 KH386 . . . . **Fic**
Shh! We're writing the Constitution. /FRITZ, J/1987/
3-6/6 KA971 . . . . **CE 342.73**
Shiloh. /NAYLOR, PR/1991/4-6/6 KH538 . . . . **CE Fic**
Shiloh season. /NAYLOR, PR/1996/4-A/4 KH539 . . . . **CE Fic**
Shiloh (Sound recording cassette)./NAYLOR, PR/1993/
4-6/6 KH538 . . . . **CE Fic**
Shiloh (Talking book)./NAYLOR, PR/1992/4-6/6 KH538 . . . . **CE Fic**
Shimmershine Queens. /YARBROUGH, C/1989/5-6/6 KH887 . . . . . . **Fic**
Shiniest rock of all. /PATTERSON, NR/1991/4-6/4 KH584 . . . . . . **Fic**
Shin's tricycle. /KODAMA, T/1995/4-6/4 KE670 . . . . **940.54**
Ship. /MACAULAY, D/1993/5-6/8 KH433 . . . . **Fic**
Ships of the air. /CURLEE, L/1996/5-6/8 KD107 . . . . **629.133**
Shirley Chisholm. /POLLACK, JS/1994/5-6/10 KE289 . . **B CHISHOLM, S.**
Shock waves through Los Angeles: the Northridge earthquake. /VOGEL,
CG/1996/3-6/10 KB039 . . . . **363.34**
Shoebag. /JAMES, M/1992/6-A/6 KH323 . . . . **Fic**
Shoebag returns. /JAMES, M/1996/6-A/6 KH324 . . . . **Fic**
Shoemaker and the elves. /PLUME, I/1991/2-4/6 KB359 . . . . . . **398.2**
Shoes. /WINTHROP, E/1986/P-K/4 KG745 . . . . **CE E**
Shoes (Big book)./WINTHROP, E/1993/P-K/4 KG745 . . . . **CE E**

Shoes (Kit)./WINTHROP, E/1996/P-K/4 KG745 . . . . **CE E**

Shoes (Sound recording cassette)./WINTHROP, E/n.d./
P-K/4 KG745 . . . . **CE E**

Shoes: their history in words and pictures. /YUE, C/1997/
4-6/6 KB168 . . . . **391.4**

Shoeshine girl. /BULLA, CR/1975/3-5/2 KG938 . . . . **Fic**

Shoeshine girl (Braille)./BULLA, CR/n.d./3-5/2 KG938 . . . . . . **Fic**

Shooting star summer. /RANSOM, CF/1992/K-2/2 KG304 . . . . **E**

Short walk around the Pyramids and through the world of art. /
ISAACSON, P/1993/5-A/6 KD363 . . . . **700**

Shortcut. /CREWS, D/1992/K-2/2 KF436 . . . . **E**

Shortcut. /MACAULAY, D/1995/3-A/3 KH434 . . . . **Fic**

Show and tell day. /ROCKWELL, AF/1997/P-K/2 KG345 . . . . **E**

Show and tell war./SMITH, JL/c1988, 1995/2-4/4 KH725 . . . . **Fic**

Show and tell war (Sound recording cassette)./SMITH, JL/n.d./
2-4/4 KH725 . . . . **Fic**

SHOW TIME (Videocassette). /1994/K-2/KD690 . . . . . **VCR 792**

Show-and-tell. /SALTZBERG, B/1994/K-2/2 KG388 . . . . **E**

Showdown at Lonesome Pellet. /RATZ DE TAGYOS, P/1994/
1-4/5 KH621 . . . . **Fic**

Shrinking mouse. /HUTCHINS, P/1997/P-K/1 KF803 . . . . **E**

Shrinking of Treehorn. /HEIDE, FP/c1971/3-A/6 KH232 . . . . . **CE Fic**

Shrinking of Treehorn (Kit)./HEIDE, FP/1983/3-A/6 KH232 . . . **CE Fic**

Shrinking of Treehorn (Sound recording cassette)./HEIDE, FP/1997/
3-A/6 KH232 . . . . **CE Fic**

Sibling rivalry: brothers and sisters at odds. /LANDAU, E/1994/
5-A/6 KA885 . . . . **306.875**

Sid and Sam. /BUCK, N/1996/P-1/1 KF291 . . . . **E**

Sidewalk games around the world. /ERLBACH, A/1997/
2-5/6 KD769 . . . . **796.2**

Sideways arithmetic from Wayside School. /SACHAR, L/1989/
3-6/6 KD712 . . . . **793.7**

Sideways stories from Wayside School./SACHAR, L/c1978, 1996/
3-5/4 KH666 . . . . **CE Fic**

Sideways stories from Wayside School (Kit)./SACHAR, L/1993/
3-5/4 KH666 . . . . **CE Fic**

Siempre puede ser peor: un cuento folklorico Yiddish./ZEMACH, M/1992/
2-4/4 KB792 . . . . **CE 398.27**

Sierra. /SIEBERT, D/1991/2-6/6 KE023 . . . . **811**

Sierra Club book of great mammals. /KNIGHT, L/1992/
5-6/7 KC722 . . . . **599**

SIERRA CLUB BOOK OF SMALL MAMMALS. /1993/5-6/6 KC729 . . **599**

Sierra Club kid's guide to planet care and repair. /MCVEY, V/1993/
4-6/7 KB048 . . . . **363.7**

Siesta de tres anos./SNYDER, D/1995/K-3/6 KG525 . . . . **E**

Sight. /PARRAMON, JM/1985/P-1/1 KC974 . . . . **612.8**

Sign for friends (Videocassette). /PARKER, D/1991/3-5/KB828 . . **VCR 419**

Sign in Mendel's window. /PHILLIPS, M/c1985, 1996/3-5/6 KH600 . . **E**

Sign in Mendel's window (Sound recording cassette)./PHILLIPS, M/n.d./
3-5/6 KH600 . . . . **Fic**

Sign language talk. /GREENE, L/1989/5-A/9 KB825 . . . . **419**

Sign of the chrysanthemum. /PATERSON, K/c1973, 1991/
5-A/6 KH581 . . . . **Fic**

Silba por Willie./KEATS, EJ/1992/P-2/3 KF880 . . . . **CE E**

Silent Lotus. /LEE, JM/1991/P-2/4 KF956 . . . . **E**

Silent temples, songful hearts: traditional music of Cambodia. /SAM, S/
1991//KA318 . . . . **BA PROF 789.2**

Silent temples, songful hearts: traditional music of Cambodia./SAM, S/
1991//KA318 . . . . **BA PROF 789.2**

Silk Route: 7,000 miles of history. /MAJOR, JS/c1995, 1996/
4-6/6 KE701 . . . . **950**

Silkworms. /JOHNSON, SA/1982/4-6/8 KD241 . . . . **638**

Silla de Pedro./KEATS, EJ/1996/P-2/2 KF877 . . . . **CE E**

Silliest joke book ever. /HARTMAN, V/1993/2-4/5 KD729 . . . . **793.735**

Sillon de plata./LEWIS, CS/n.d./5-A/6 KH405 . . . . **CE Fic**

Sillon para mi mama./WILLIAMS, VB/1994/P-3/3 KG734 . . . . . **E**

Sillon para mi mama (Kit)./WILLIAMS, VB/1994/P-3/3 KG734 . . . . . . **E**

Silly Billy!/HUTCHINS, P/1992/P-2/2 KF806 . . . . **CE E**

Silly Sally. /WOOD, A/1992/P-K/2 KG766 . . . . **E**

Silly science: strange and startling projects to amaze your family and
friends. /LEVINE, S/1995/3-8/7 KB893 . . . . **507.8**

Silly Tilly and the Easter Bunny./HOBAN, L/K-2/2 KF738 . . . . **E**

Silly Tilly's Thanksgiving dinner. /HOBAN, L/1990/K-2/2 KF738 . . . . . . **E**

Silly Willy workout (Compact disc)./COLGATE, B/1996/
P-1/KD609. . . . . **SRC 789.3**

Silly Willy workout (Sound recording cassette). /COLGATE, B/1994/
P-1/KD609. . . . . **SRC 789.3**

Silver chair./LEWIS, CS/1994/5-A/6 KH405 . . . . **CE Fic**

Silver chair (Braille). /LEWIS, CS/n.d./5-A/6 KH405 . . . . **CE Fic**

Silver chair (Sound recording cassette)./LEWIS, CS/n.d./
5-A/6 KH405 . . . . **CE Fic**

Silver chair (Talking book)./LEWIS, CS/n.d./5-A/6 KH405 . . . . . . **CE Fic**

Silver chair (Videocassette)./LEWIS, CS/1990/5-A/6 KH405 . . . . **CE Fic**

Silver days./LEVITIN, S/1992/5-A/5 KH398 . . . . **Fic**

Silver on the tree./COOPER, S/1977/A/5 KH028 . . . . **Fic**

Silver on the tree (Large type)./COOPER, S/n.d./A/5 KH028 . . . . . . **Fic**

Silver on the tree (Sound recording cassette)./COOPER, S/n.d./
A/5 KH028 . . . . **Fic**

Silver packages: an Appalachian Christmas story. /RYLANT, C/1997/
1-3/2 KG386 . . . . **E**

Silver sword. /SERRAILLIER, I/c1959/5-6/6 KH699 . . . . **Fic**

Silver treasure: myths and legends of the world. /MCCAUGHREAN, G/
1996/K-6/6 KB345 . . . . **398.2**

Silvestre y la piedrecita magica./STEIG, W/1990/K-2/6 KG544 . . . **CE E**

Silvestre y la piedrecita magica (Kit)./STEIG, W/1992/
K-2/6 KG544 . . . . **CE E**

Simon and Schuster children's guide to insects and spiders. /JOHNSON, J/
1996/5-6/7 KC542 . . . . **595.7**

Simon's book. /DRESCHER, H/1983/K-2/6 KF497 . . . . **CE E**

SIMPLE MACHINE (Videocassette). /1993/5-6/KC098 . . . . . . **VCR 531**

SIMPLE MACHINES: USING MECHANICAL ADVANTAGE (Videocassette).
/1992/5-6/KC099. . . . . **VCR 531**

Simple pictures are best. /WILLARD, N/c1977/K-3/6 KG724 . . . . **E**

Simple puppets from everyday materials. /BUETTER, BM/1997/
2-5/3 KD443 . . . . **745.592**

SIMPLE THINGS YOU CAN DO TO SAVE ENERGY IN YOUR SCHOOL
(Videocassette). /1995/4-6/KA957 . . . . **VCR 333.791**

Sincerely yours: how to write great letters. /JAMES, E/1993/
3-6/7 KD870 . . . . **808.6**

Sing down the moon. /O'DELL, S/c1970/5-6/3 KH562 . . . . . . **CE Fic**

Sing down the moon (Sound recording cassette)./O'DELL, S/n.d./
5-6/3 KH562 . . . . **CE Fic**

Sing down the moon (Talking book)./O'DELL, S/1973/
5-6/3 KH562 . . . . **CE Fic**

Sing down the moon (Talking book)./O'DELL, S/n.d./
5-6/3 KH562 . . . . **CE Fic**

Sing down the moon (Videocassette)./O'DELL, S/1986/
5-6/3 KH562 . . . . **CE Fic**

Singing. /SHIPTON, A/1994/4-6/7 KD527 . . . . **782**

Singing calendar (Sound recording cassette). /JAMES, DL/1984/
P-1/KC071. . . . . **SRC 529**

Singing green: new and selected poems for all seasons. /MERRIAM, E/
1992/3-A/KD984 . . . . **811**

Singing man: adapted from a West African folktale. /MEDEARIS, AS/
1994/4-5/6 KB757 . . . . **398.27**

Singing multiplication tables (Sound recording cassette). /PALMER, H/
1971/2-4/KB977 . . . . **SRC 513.2**

Sioux. /SNEVE, V/1993/4-6/5 KE776 . . . . **970.3**

Sip of Aesop. /YOLEN, J/1995/K-3/KE050 . . . . **811**

Sir Gawain and the green knight. /HASTINGS, S/1981/
6/6 KB450. . . . . **398.22**

Sit still! /CARLSON, N/1996/K-2/2 KF352 . . . . **E**

Sitti and the cats: a tale of friendship. /BAHOUS, S/1993/
3-4/7 KB257 . . . . **398.2**

Sitting down to eat. /HARLEY, B/1996/P-2/2 KF672 . . . . **E**

Six sick sheep: 101 tongue twisters. /COLE, J/3-5/KB795 . . . . **398.8**

SIXTH BOOK OF JUNIOR AUTHORS AND ILLUSTRATORS./1987/
A/KA462. . . . . **REF 809**

Ska-tat! /KNUTSON, K/1993/P-2/3 KF914. . . . . **E**

Skeleton. /PARKER, S/1988/5-6/8 KC285 . . . . **573.7**

Skeleton and movement. Rev. ed. /PARKER, S/1989/5-6/7 KC958 . **612.7**

Skiing. /EVANS, J/1992/5-A/7 KD837 . . . . **796.93**

Skit book: 101 skits from kids. /MACDONALD, MR/1990/
3-6/KE092. . . . . **812**

Sky dancers: the amazing world of North American birds. /SWANSON,
D/1995/4-5/5 KC667 . . . . **598**

Sky dogs. /YOLEN, J/1990/2-3/6 KG780 . . . . **E**

Sky dogs (Sound recording cassette)./YOLEN, J/1993/2-3/6 KG780. . . . **E**

Sky is falling. /PEARSON, K/1995/5-A/6 KH591 . . . . **Fic**

Sky legends of Vietnam. /VUONG, LD/1993/3-5/7 KB717 . . . . **398.26**

Sky pioneer: a photobiography of Amelia Earhart. /SZABO, C/1997/
4-6/12 KE329 . . . . **B EARHART, A.**

Sky tree portfolio guide: an interdisciplinary environmental curriculum. /
WOODS, ML/1995/2-6/KC424. . . . . **582.16**

Sky tree portfolio: science and art (Picture). /CHRISTIANSEN, C/1995/
2-6/KC410. . . . . **PIC 582.16**

Sky tree: seeing science through art./CHRISTIANSEN, C/1995/
2-6/KC410. . . . . **PIC 582.16**

Skylark. /MACLACHLAN, P/1994/3-5/3 KH445 . . . . **Fic**

Skyscrapers. /DUNN, A/1993/3-6/7 KD383 . . . . **720**

SKYTRIP AMERICA: AN INCREDIBLE RIDE THROUGH U.S. HISTORY.
Teacher ed. (CD-ROM). /1996/3-A/KE865 . . . . **CDR 973**

Slake's limbo. /HOLMAN, F/1974/6-A/7 KH274 . . . . **CE Fic**

SLAM DUNK: BASKETBALL POEMS. /1995/4-6/KE081 . . . . . . **811.008**

Slave dancer: a novel. /FOX, P/c1973/5-6/6 KH139 . . . . **CE Fic**

Slave dancer: a novel (Braille)./FOX, P/n.d./5-6/6 KH139 . . . . . **CE Fic**

Slave dancer: a novel (Sound recording cassette)./FOX, P/n.d./
5-6/6 KH139 . . . . **CE Fic**

Slave dancer: a novel (Talking book)./FOX, P/1996/5-6/6 KH139. **CE Fic**
Slave songs. /SILVERMAN, J/1994/5-A/KD592 . . . . **789.2**
Sledding. /WINTHROP, E/1989/P-K/2 KG746 . . . . **E**
SLEEP, BABY, SLEEP: LULLABIES AND NIGHT POEMS. /1994/ P-K/KD889. . . . . **808.81**
Sleep is for everyone (Braille)./SHOWERS, P/n.d./K-2/3 KC979 . . . **612.8**
Sleep is for everyone. Newly illustrated ed. /SHOWERS, P/1997/ K-2/3 KC979 . . . . **612.8**
Sleep is for everyone (Sound recording cassette)./SHOWERS, P/n.d./ K-2/3 KC979 . . . . **612.8**
SLEEP RHYMES AROUND THE WORLD. /1994/P-3/KD890. . . . . **808.81**
Sleep, sleep, sleep: a lullaby for little ones around the world. /VAN LAAN, N/1995/P-2/3 KG644. . . . . **E**
SLEEPING BEARS (Videocassette). /1986/4-A/KC856. . . . . **VCR 599.78**
Sleeping Beauty. /EARLY, M/1993/2-5/5 KB290 . . . . **398.2**
Sleeping Beauty: the ballet story. /HOROSKO, M/1994/ 1-5/7 KD695 . . . . **792.8**
Sleepless Beauty. /MINTERS, F/1996/2-3/3 KG142 . . . . **E**
Sleepy book. /ZOLOTOW, C/c1958, 1988/P-1/KC481. . . . . **591.5**
SLIGHTLY SCARY STORIES (Videocassette). /1987/P-2/KG518 . . **VCR E**
Sluggers: twenty-seven of baseball's greatest. /SULLIVAN, G/1991/ 5-A/6 KD806 . . . . **796.357**
Slumber party! /CASELEY, J/1996/2-3/2 KF369 . . . . **E**
Slumps, grunts, and snickerdoodles: what Colonial America ate and why. / PERL, L/1975/A/9 KD276 . . . . **641.5**
Slumps, grunts, and snickerdoodles: what Colonial America ate and why (Braille)./PERL, L/n.d./A/9 KD276 . . . . **641.5**
SMACKERS: ELEMENTARY ENTREPRENEURS (Videocassette). /1991/ 3-6/KD314. . . . . **VCR 658**
Small cats. /LUMPKIN, S/1993/5-6/8 KC824 . . . . **599.75**
Small Green Snake. /GRAY, LM/1994/P-2/6 KF637 . . . . **E**
Small pig. /LOBEL, A/c1969/K-2/2 KG012. . . . . **E**
Small pig (Braille)./LOBEL, A/n.d./K-2/2 KG012 . . . . **E**
Small steps: the year I got polio. /KEHRET, P/1996/ 2-5/5 KE414 . . . . **B KEHRET, P.**
SMALLER THAN THE EYE CAN SEE (Videocassette). /1989/ 5-6/KC379. . . . . **VCR 579.4**
Smart spending: a young consumer's guide. /SCHMITT, L/1989/ 5-6/8 KD262 . . . . **640**
Smarten up! how to increase your brain power. /YEPSEN, R/1990/ 6-A/7 KA645 . . . . **155.42**
Smilin' island of song (Compact disc)./BOOKER, CM/1993/ K-4/KD667 . . . . **SRC 789.4**
Smilin' island of song (Sound recording cassette). /BOOKER, CM/1994/ K-4/KD667 . . . . **SRC 789.4**
Smiling at yourself: educating young children about stress and self-esteem. / MENDLER, AN/1990//KA304. **PROF 649**
SMITHSONIAN. /1970-/A/KA541 . . . . **PER 050**
SMITHSONIAN BOOK OF THE FIRST LADIES: THEIR LIVES, TIMES, AND ISSUES. /1996/6-A/9 KE866 . . . . **973**
Smoke and ashes: the story of the Holocaust. /ROGASKY, B/1988/ A/8 KE664 . . . . **940.53**
SMOKE SIGNALS (Videocassette). /1995/5-6/KD006 . . . . **VCR 613.85**
Smoking: a risky business. /PRINGLE, LP/1996/4-6/9 KA998 . . . . **362.29**
Smoky Mountain Rose: an Appalachian Cinderella. /SCHROEDER, A/ 1997/2-3/4 KB367 . . . . **398.2**
Smoky night. /BUNTING, E/1994/2-5/2 KF309. . . . . **E**
Smugglers' Island. /AVI /1994/4-6/5 KG864 . . . . **Fic**
Snail. /OLESEN, J/1986/2-4/2 KC515 . . . . **594**
Snails. /JOHNSON, SA/1982/4-6/7 KC512. . . . . **594**
Snake. /ARNOLD, C/1991/5-6/7 KC632 . . . . **597.96**
Snake book. /LING, M/1997/2-6/6 KC639 . . . . **597.96**
Snake in the house. /MCNULTY, F/1994/1-3/2 KG115. . . . . **E**
Snakes. /BROEKEL, R/1982/2-4/2 KC633 . . . . **597.96**
Snakes. /SIMON, S/1992/4-6/6 KC643 . . . . **597.96**
Snakes are hunters. /LAUBER, P/1988/2-4/3 KC637. . . . . **597.96**
Snakes: giant snakes and non-venomous snakes in the terrarium. /GRIEHL, K/1984/A/9 KD249 . . . . **639.3**
Snakes. Rev. ed. /GROSS, RB/1990/4-6/4 KC636. . . . . **597.96**
Snap! /VAUGHAN, MK/1996/K-2/2 KG651 . . . . **E**
SNAPDRAGON (Microcomputer program). /1992/ P-1/KA636. . . . . **MCP 153.4**
Snapshot: America discovers the camera. /CZECH, KP/1996/ 5-6/10 KD509 . . . . **770**
Snapshots from the wedding. /SOTO, G/1997/K-2/2 KG529. . . . . **E**
Sneakers: the shoes we choose! /YOUNG, R/1991/5-6/6 KD344 . . . **685**
Snow: causes and effects. /STEELE, P/1991/3-6/7 KC216 . . . . . . **551.57**
Snow is falling. Rev. ed. /BRANLEY, FM/1986/K-1/2 KC210 . . . . **551.57**
Snow is falling. Rev. ed. (Sound recording disc)./BRANLEY, FM/n.d./ K-1/2 KC210 . . . . **551.57**
Snow: learning for the fun of it. /BIANCHI, J/1992/ 5-A/9 KC208 . . . . **551.57**
Snow on snow on snow. /CHAPMAN, C/1994/K-3/3 KF377 . . . . **E**
SNOW TOWARD EVENING: A YEAR IN A RIVER VALLEY: NATURE POEMS. /1995/2-6/KE082. . . . . **811.008**
Snow wife. /SAN SOUCI, RD/1993/3-9/5 KB414 . . . . **398.21**
Snowballs. /EHLERT, L/1995/P-2/2 KF520 . . . . **E**
Snowbear Whittington: an Appalachian Beauty and the Beast. /HOOKS, WH/1994/2-3/4 KB318 . . . . **398.2**
Snowbound: the tragic story of the Donner Party. /LAVENDER, DS/1996/ 5-6/6 KF038 . . . . **978**
Snowflakes, sugar, and salt: crystals up close. /MAKI, C/1993/ P-2/5 KC143 . . . . **548**
Snowman. /BRIGGS, R/1978/P-1/KF265 . . . . **CE E**
Snowman on Sycamore Street. /CHRISTIANSEN, CB/1996/ 2-3/2 KG989 . . . . **Fic**
Snowman (Videocassette)./BRIGGS, R/n.d./P-1/KF265 . . . . **CE E**
Snowshoe Thompson. /LEVINSON, NS/1992/ K-3/2 KE564 . . . . **B THOMPSON, S.**
Snow-White and the seven dwarfs. /GRIMM, J/1972/ 3-4/6 KB310 . . . . **398.2**
Snowy day. /KEATS, EJ/c1962, 1963/P-2/2 KF878 . . . . **CE E**
Snowy day (Braille)./KEATS, EJ/n.d./P-2/2 KF878 . . . . **CE E**
Snowy day (Kit)./KEATS, EJ/1974/P-2/2 KF878 . . . . **CE E**
Snowy day (Videocassette)./KEATS, EJ/P-2/2 KF878 . . . . **CE E**
SNUFFLES AND SNOUTS: POEMS. /1995/P-2/KE083. . . . . . . **811.008**
So big: activity songs for little ones (Compact disc). /PALMER, H/1994/ P-2/KD644. . . . . **CD 789.3**
So far from the bamboo grove. /WATKINS, YK/c1986, 1994/ 5-A/5 KH842 . . . . **Fic**
So many dynamos!: and other palindromes. /AGEE, J/1994/ 3-6/KD719. . . . . **793.734**
SO YOU WANT TO BE?: JUDGE (Videocassette). /1994/ 5-6/KA977 . . . . **VCR 347**
SO YOU WANT TO BE?: NEWSPAPER ARTIST (Videocassette). /1994/ 5-6/KA595 . . . . **VCR 070.4**
Soap! soap! don't forget the soap!: an Appalachian folktale. /BIRDSEYE, T/1993/K-2/3 KB267. . . . . **398.2**
SOAP (Videocassette). /1984/5-6/KD326. . . . . **VCR 668**
Soccer. /WILNER, B/1994/3-6/4 KD789 . . . . **796.334**
Soccer circus. /GILSON, J/1993/3-5/5 KH169 . . . . **Fic**
Soccer circus (Sound recording cassette)./GILSON, J/1996/ 3-5/5 KH169 . . . . **Fic**
Soccer stars. /HOWARD, DE/1994/3-6/6 KD788 . . . . **796.334**
SOCIAL EDUCATION. /1937-//KA146 . . . . **PER PROF 050**
Social smarts: manners for today's kids. /JAMES, E/1996/ 4-6/6 KB243 . . . . **395.3**
SOCIAL STUDIES AND THE YOUNG LEARNER: A QUARTERLY FOR CREATIVE TEACHING IN GRADES K-6. /1988-/ /KA147. . . . . **PER PROF 050**
Social studies readers theatre for children: scripts and script development. / LAUGHLIN, MK/1991//KA224 . . . . **PROF 372.6**
Social studies through children's literature: an integrated approach. / FREDERICKS, AD/1991//KA260 . . . . **PROF 372.83**
Socks. /CLEARY, B/c1973/3-4/6 KH007 . . . . **Fic**
Socks (Sound recording cassette)./CLEARY, B/n.d./3-4/6 KH007. . . . . **Fic**
Sod houses on the Great Plains. /ROUNDS, G/1995/2-6/7 KD361. . **693**
Sod houses on the Great Plains (Sound recording cassette)./ROUNDS, G/ 1997/2-6/7 KD361 . . . . **693**
Sody sallyratus. /COMPTON, J/K-3/3 KB550 . . . . **398.24**
Sody sallyratus. /SLOAT, T/1997/1-3/5 KB653. . . . . **398.24**
Sofie's role. /HEATH, A/1992/P-2/2 KF692 . . . . **E**
Sojourner Truth: ain't I a woman? /MCKISSACK, P/1992/ 6-A/7 KE573 . . . . **B TRUTH, S.**
SOLAR SYSTEM (Picture). /1990/4-A/KC016 . . . . **PIC 523.2**
Soldier Jack; or, The man who caught Death in a sack (Videocassette)/ DAVENPORT, T/1988/5-A/KB281 . . . . **CE 398.2**
SOLID, LIQUID, GAS (Videocassette). /1986/3-6/KC083 . . . **VCR 530.4**
SOLIDS, LIQUIDS AND GASES (Videocassette). /1994/ 4-6/KC084. . . . . **VCR 530.4**
SOLO PARA MI (Videocassette)./1992/K-6/KC997 . . . . **VCR 613.8**
Some birthday! /POLACCO, P/1991/K-2/4 KG257 . . . . **E**
Some days, other days. /PETERSEN, PJ/1994/K-2/2 KG234 . . . . **E**
SOME DOG AND OTHER KENTUCKY WONDERS (Sound recording cassette). /1992/3-4/KB370 . . . . **SRC 398.2**
Some of the kinder planets. /WYNNE-JONES, T/1995/5-A/5 KH886 . **Fic**
Some of the kinder planets (Sound recording cassette)./WYNNE-JONES, T/1997/5-A/5 KH886 . . . . **Fic**
Some smug slug. /EDWARDS, PD/1996/P-2/3 KF513. . . . . **E**
Somebody catch my homework. /HARRISON, DL/1993/2-6/KD951. . **811**
Somebody's new pajamas. /JACKSON, I/1996/3-5/4 KH318. . . . . . . **Fic**
Somebody's new pajamas (Sound recording cassette)./JACKSON, I/1997/ 3-5/4 KH318 . . . . **Fic**
Someone special, just like you. /BROWN, T/1984/P-2/6 KA623 . . . **152.4**
Someone to count on: a novel. /HERMES, P/1993/6-A/7 KH250 . . . . **Fic**
Someone to count on: a novel (Sound recording cassette)./HERMES, P/ 1996/6-A/7 KH250. . . . . **Fic**

SOMETHING ABOUT THE AUTHOR. /1971-/5-6/KA465 . . . . . **REF 809**
SOMETHING ABOUT THE AUTHOR AUTOBIOGRAPHY SERIES. /1986-/ 4-6/KA466 . . . . . **REF 809**
Something big has been here (Talking book). /PRELUTSKY, J/1991/ K-4/KE016 . . . . . **TB 811**
Something fishy at Macdonald Hall./KORMAN, G/1995/ 5-A/7 KH378 . . . . . **Fic**
Something from nothing: adapted from a Jewish folktale. /GILMAN, P/ 1993/1-3/3 KB737 . . . . . **398.27**
Something nasty in the cabbages. /WALLIS, D/1991/ 2-4/3 KB671 . . . . . **398.24**
Something queer at the haunted school./LEVY, E/1982/ 1-3/3 KF972 . . . . . **CE E**
Something queer at the haunted school (Kit)./LEVY, E/n.d./ 1-3/3 KF972 . . . . . **CE E**
Something queer at the lemonade stand./LEVY, E/1982/ 1-3/3 KF972 . . . . . **CE E**
Something queer at the scary movie. /LEVY, E/1995/3-5/3 KH403 . . . **Fic**
Something queer in outer space./LEVY, E/1993/1-3/3 KF972 . . . . . **CE E**
Something queer is going on (a mystery). /LEVY, E/C1973/ 1-3/3 KF972 . . . . . **CE E**
Something queer is going on (a mystery) (Kit)./LEVY, E/1983/ 1-3/3 KF972 . . . . . **CE E**
SOMETHING RICH AND STRANGE: A TREASURY OF SHAKESPEARE'S VERSE. /1995/6-A/KE118 . . . . . **822.3**
Something special for me. /WILLIAMS, VB/1983/P-3/2 KG738 . . . . . . **E**
SOMETHING WRONG AT HOME: THE ALCOHOLIC FAMILY (Videocassette). /1994/3-5/KB001 . . . . . **VCR 362.292**
Somewhere in Africa. /MENNEN, I/1992/K-2/4 KG129 . . . . . **E**
Song and dance man./ACKERMAN, K/1988/K-2/6 KF130. . . . . **E**
Song and play time (Sound recording cassette). /SEEGER, P/1990/ K-3/KD589 . . . . . **SRC 789.2**
Song of el coqui and other tales of Puerto Rico. /MOHR, N/1995/ 3-4/3 KB621 . . . . . **398.24**
Song of the swallows. /POLITI, L/c1949, 1987/K-3/6 KG262. . . . . **CE E**
Song of the swallows (Braille)./POLITI, L/n.d./K-3/6 KG262. . . . . . **CE E**
Song of the trees. /TAYLOR, MD/1975/4-6/4 KH780. . . . . **Fic**
Song of the trees (Sound recording cassette)./TAYLOR, MD/1996/ 4-6/4 KH780 . . . . . **Fic**
Songs about insects, bugs and squiggly things (Compact disc)./MURPHY, J/ 1993/P-2/KC546 . . . . . **SRC 595.7**
Songs about insects, bugs and squiggly things (Sound recording cassette). / MURPHY, J/1993/P-2/KC546 . . . . . **SRC 595.7**
Songs and rhythms from near and far (Compact disc)./JENKINS, E/1997/ K-2/KD575 . . . . . **SRC 789.2**
Songs and rhythms from near and far (Sound recording cassette). / JENKINS, E/c1964, 1992/K-2/KD575. . . . . **SRC 789.2**
Songs and stories from Uganda. /SERWADDA, WM/c1974, 1987/ /KA319. . . . . **BA PROF 789.2**
Songs and stories from Uganda./SERWADDA, WM/1987/ /KA319. . . . . **BA PROF 789.2**
SONGS ARE THOUGHTS: POEMS OF THE INUIT. /1995/ 4-6/KE140 . . . . . **897**
Songs children love to sing (Compact disc). /JENKINS, E/1996/ K-3/KD631 . . . . . **CD 789.3**
Songs children love to sing (Sound recording cassette)./JENKINS, E/1996/ K-3/KD631 . . . . . **CD 789.3**
SONGS FOR SURVIVAL: SONGS AND CHANTS FROM TRIBAL PEOPLES AROUND THE WORLD. /1996/1-6/KD596 . . . . . **789.2**
Songs for you and me: kids learn about feelings and emotions (Sound recording cassette). /MURPHY, J/n.d./K-1/KA629 . . . . . . **SRC 152.4**
Songs from the loom: a Navajo girl learns to weave. /ROESSEL, M/1995/ 4-6/6 KE799 . . . . . **970.491**
Songs of nature and environment (Sound recording cassette). /AXELROD, G/1978/1-3/KC293 . . . . . **SRC 577**
Songs of protest and civil rights. /SILVERMAN, J/1992/ 5-A/KD593 . . . . . **789.2**
SONGS OF THE WILD WEST. /1991/2-A/KD597 . . . . . **789.2**
Songspinner: folktales and fables sung and told (Sound recording cassette). /FOREST, H/1982/2-4/KB735. . . . . **SRC 398.27**
Sonidos a mi alrededor./SHOWERS, P/1996/P-1/1 KG495 . . . . . **E**
Sootface: an Ojibwa Cinderella story. /SAN SOUCI, RD/1994/ 1-3/6 KB774 . . . . . **398.27**
Sopa de piedras./BROWN, M/1991/K-3/2 KB721 . . . . . **CE 398.27**
Sopa de piedras (Kit)./BROWN, M/1992/K-3/2 KB721 . . . . . **CE 398.27**
Sophie and Sammy's library sleepover. /CASELEY, J/1993/ P-1/4 KF370 . . . . . **E**
Sophie hits six. /KING-SMITH, D/1993/2-4/6 KH354 . . . . . **Fic**
Sophie in the saddle. /KING-SMITH, D/1996/3-5/6 KH355 . . . . . **Fic**
Sophie's Lucky. /KING-SMITH, D/1996/3-4/8 KH356. . . . . **Fic**
Sophie's Tom. /KING-SMITH, D/c1991, 1994/3-5/5 KH357 . . . . . **Fic**
S.O.R. losers. /AVI /1984/5-A/6 KG865 . . . . . **Fic**
S.O.R. losers (Braille)./AVI /n.d./5-A/6 KG865 . . . . . **Fic**
S.O.R. losers (Sound recording cassette)./AVI /n.d./5-A/6 KG865 . . . **Fic**
Sorcerer's apprentice. /WILLARD, N/1993/2-5/KE041 . . . . . **811**
Sorpresa de Navidad para Chabelita./PALACIOS, A/1994/ 1-3/2 KG206 . . . . . **E**
Sorrow's kitchen: the life and folklore of Zora Neale Hurston. /LYONS, ME/1990/6-A/6 KE396 . . . . . **B HURSTON, Z.**
SOUL LOOKS BACK IN WONDER. /1993/4-A/KE084 . . . . . **811.008**
Sound of music. Selections. 2nd ed. (Sound recording cassette). / RODGERS, R/1965/K-A/KD531 . . . . . **SRC 782.1**
Sound the jubilee. /FORRESTER, S/1995/5-A/6 KH133. . . . . **Fic**
Sound the jubilee (Sound recording cassette)./FORRESTER, S/1997/ 5-A/6 KH133 . . . . . **Fic**
Sound the Shofar./CHAIKIN, M/1986/5-6/8 KA770. . . . . **296.4**
SOUND/LIGHT AND COLOR (Videocassette). /1994/ 3-6/KC080. . . . . **VCR 530**
Sounder. /ARMSTRONG, WH/c1969/4-A/4 KG851 . . . . . **CE Fic**
Sounder (Braille)./ARMSTRONG, WH/n.d./4-A/4 KG851 . . . . . **CE Fic**
Sounder (Sound recording cassette)./ARMSTRONG, WH/n.d./ 4-A/4 KG851. . . . . **CE Fic**
Sounder (Talking book)./ARMSTRONG, WH/n.d./4-A/4 KG851 . **CE Fic**
Sounder (Talking book)./ARMSTRONG, WH/1992/4-A/4 KG851 **CE Fic**
Sounds interesting: the science of acoustics. /DARLING, DJ/1991/ 6-A/8 KC103 . . . . . **534**
Soup. /PECK, RN/1974/4-6/6 KH594 . . . . . **Fic**
Soup bone. /JOHNSTON, T/1990/K-2/2 KF841 . . . . . **E**
Soup in the saddle (Sound recording cassette)./PECK, RN/n.d./ 4-6/6 KH594 . . . . . **Fic**
Soup should be seen, not heard!: the kids' etiquette book. /BRAINARD, B/ c1988, 1990/2-6/5 KB247 . . . . . **395.5**
Soup (Sound recording disc)./PECK, RN/n.d./4-6/6 KH594 . . . . . **Fic**
SOUP (Videocassette). /1991/2-4/KD321. . . . . **VCR 664**
Soup's goat (Sound recording cassette)./PECK, RN/n.d./4-6/6 KH594 . **Fic**
SOURCE OF LIFE?: WATER IN OUR ENVIRONMENT (Videocassette). / 1992/4-6/KB068. . . . . **VCR 363.73**
South Carolina. /FRADIN, DB/1992/4-6/5 KE984 . . . . . **975.7**
South Carolina. /FREDEEN, C/1991/4-6/6 KE986 . . . . . **975.7**
South Carolina Colony. /FRADIN, DB/1992/A/7 KE985 . . . . . **975.7**
SOUTH CENTRAL REGION: TEXAS, NEW MEXICO, OKLAHOMA (Videocassette). /1995/3-5/KE995 . . . . . **VCR 976**
South Dakota. /FRADIN, DB/1995/4-6/7 KF056 . . . . . **978.3**
Sovietrek: a journey by bicycle across Russia. /BUETTNER, D/1994/ 4-6/8 KE692 . . . . . **947.086**
Sovietrek: a journey by bicycle across Russia (Sound recording cassette)./ BUETTNER, D/1997/4-6/8 KE692 . . . . . **947.086**
Space atlas. /COUPER, H/1992/3-6/6 KC002. . . . . **520**
Space camp. /ALSTON, E/1990/4-5/7 KD135 . . . . . **629.45**
Space case. /MARSHALL, E/1980/P-2/4 KG065 . . . . . **E**
Space probes to the planets. /ROBINSON, F/1993/2-5/5 KC031 . . **523.4**
Spaceman. /CUTLER, J/1997/4-A/2 KH053 . . . . . **Fic**
Spaghetti factory. /COREY, M/1990/3-4/7 KD319 . . . . . **664**
Spain: bridge between continents. /CHICOINE, S/1997/ 4-6/7 KE686 . . . . . **946**
Spanish-American War. /MARRIN, A/1991/A/7 KE915 . . . . . **973.8**
Spare parts for people. /FACKLAM, M/1987/A/9 KD035. . . . . **617**
Speaking of animals: a dictionary of animal metaphors. /PALMATIER, RA/ 1995/6-A/KA427 . . . . . **REF 423**
Special Olympics. /BROWN, FG/1992/4-A/7 KD759 . . . . . **796**
Special trade. /WITTMAN, S/1978/P-3/4 KG754 . . . . . **E**
Spellcoats./JONES, DW/c1979, 1995/6-A/6 KH331 . . . . . **Fic**
Spider spider. /BANKS, K/1996/P-1/2 KF194. . . . . **E**
SPIDER SPINS A STORY: FOURTEEN LEGENDS FROM NATIVE AMERICA. /1997/2-5/6 KB371 . . . . . **398.2**
SPIDER SURVIVAL (Videocassette). /1991/4-6/KC532 . . . . . **VCR 595.4**
SPIDER: THE MAGAZINE FOR CHILDREN. /1993-/1-3/KA542. . **PER 050**
Spiders. /GIBBONS, G/1993/1-3/4 KC525 . . . . . **595.4**
Spin a soft black song. Rev. ed. /GIOVANNI, N/c1971, 1985/ 1-4/KD946. . . . . **811**
Spin, spider, spin: songs for a greater appreciation of nature (Sound recording cassette). /ZEITLIN, P/1974/P-1/KB916 . . . . . **SRC 508**
Spinky sulks. /STEIG, W/1988/1-A/5 KH752 . . . . . **Fic**
Spinning blackboard and other dynamic experiments on force and motion. / DOHERTY, P/1996/4-A/5 KC094. . . . . **531**
Spirals, curves, fanshapes and lines. /HOBAN, T/1992/P-2/KB992. . . **516**
Spirit of Tio Fernando: a Day of the Dead story./El espiritu de tio Fernando: una historia del Dia de los Muertos. /LEVY, J/1995/ 1-3/5 KH404 . . . . . **Fic**
Spirit walker: poems. /WOOD, N/1993/6-A/KE046. . . . . **811**
Splash! /JONAS, A/1995/P-2/1 KF848. . . . . **E**
Sponges are skeletons. /ESBENSEN, BJ/1993/1-3/2 KC508. . . . . **593.4**
Spooky Halloween party. /PRAGER, A/1981/1-3/2 KG287. . . . . **E**
SPOOKY STORIES FOR A DARK AND STORMY NIGHT. /1994/ 2-4/4 KB695 . . . . . **398.25**
SPOOKY STORIES OF THE SUPERNATURAL. /1985/6-A/KH745 . . . . **Fic**
Spoon for every bite. /HAYES, J/1996/2-4/4 KF684 . . . . . **E**
SPORT. /1946-/4-6/KA543 . . . . . **PER 050**

Sports. /HAMMOND, T/1988/4-A/8 KD761 796
SPORTS ILLUSTRATED. /1954-/5-A/KA544 . . . . PER 050
SPORTS ILLUSTRATED FOR KIDS. /1989-/2-4/KA545 . . . . . . PER 050
Sports stars. /PARE, MA/1994/5-A/KA457 . . . . REF 796
Sports stars. Series 2./PARE, MA/1996/5-A/KA457 . . . . REF 796
Spot a cat. /MICKLETHWAIT, L/1995/K-2/2 KD466 750
Spot a dog. /MICKLETHWAIT, L/1995/K-2/1 KD467 750
Spots, feathers, and curly tails. /TAFURI, N/1988/P-K/1 KD185 636
SPRING: A HAIKU STORY. /1996/1-6/KE137 . . . . 895.6
Spring across America. /SIMON, S/1996/5-8/7 KB919 . . . . . . 508.2
SPRING (Videocassette). /1994/2-5/KC666 . . . . VCR 598
Spying on Miss Muller. /BUNTING, E/1995/6-A/6 KG944 . . . . Fic
Squanto and the first Thanksgiving (Kit). /METAXAS, E/1996/
   2-6/KC548. . . . . KIT B SQUANTO
Squanto: friend of the Pilgrims. /BULLA, CR/c1954, 1982/
   3/3 KE547. . . . . B SQUANTO
Squiggle. /SCHAEFER, CL/1996/P-2/3 KG402 . . . . E
Squirrel Park. /ERNST, LC/1993/K-2/5 KF533. . . . . E
Squirrels. /LEPTHIEN, EU/1992/4-6/4 KC751 . . . . 599.36
Squish!: a wetland walk. /LUENN, N/1994/P-2/3 KC342 . . . . 577.68
St. Lawrence Seaway. /ARMBRUSTER, A/1996/2-4/6 KB141 386
St. Patrick's Day. /GIBBONS, G/1994/2-5/2 KB219 . . . . 394.262
St. Patrick's Day in the morning. /BUNTING, E/1980/K-2/2 KF310 . . . . E
St. Patrick's Day shamrock mystery. /MARKHAM, MM/1995/
   2-4/3 KH457 . . . . Fic
Stacy says good-bye. /GIFF, PR/1989/1-2/2 KF614 . . . . CE E
Stacy says good-bye (Kit). /GIFF, PR/1994/1-2/2 KF614 . . . . . CE E
Stamp collecting. /GRANGER, N/1994/4-6/8 KD508 . . . . . . 769.56
Stamps. /ANSARY, MT/1997/1-3/2 KD507 . . . . 769.56
Stan Musial. /GRABOWSKI, J/1993/5-A/7 KE474 . . . . . B MUSIAL, S.
Stan the hot dog man. /KESSLER, E/1990/1-2/1 KF897 . . . . E
Stand back, said the elephant, I'm going to sneeze! /THOMAS, P/c1971,
   1990/K-3/2 KG605. . . . . E
Stanley and the magic lamp. /BROWN, J/1996/2-4/3 KG932 . . . . . Fic
STANLEY'S STICKER STORIES. School version (CD-ROM). /1996/
   P-2/KB117. . . . . CDR 372.6
Star fisher. /YEP, L/1991/6-A/6 KH895. . . . . Fic
Star of fear, star of hope. /HOESTLANDT, J/1995/3-5/5 KH268 . . . . Fic
STAR WALK. /1995/4-8/KE085 . . . . 811.008
Starfishing (Compact disc)./GREEN CHILI JAM BAND /1993/
   P-2/KD614. . . . . SRC 789.3
Starfishing (Sound recording cassette). /GREEN CHILI JAM BAND /1993/
   P-2/KD614. . . . . SRC 789.3
Stargazers. /GIBBONS, G/1992/K-2/4 KC049 . . . . 523.8
Stargone John. /MCKENZIE, EK/1990/3-5/5 KH484 . . . . Fic
Starlight and candles: the joys of the Sabbath. /MANUSHKIN, F/1995/
   1-3/2 KG061. . . . . E
Starlit somersault downhill. /WILLARD, N/1993/K-2/3 KG725 . . . . E
Starry messenger: a book depicting the life of a famous scientist,
   mathematician, astronomer, philosopher, physicist: Galileo Galilei. /SIS,
   P/1996/3-6/6 KE360. . . . . CE B GALILEO
Starry messenger: a book depicting the life of a famous scientist,
   mathematician, astronomer, philosopher, physicist Galileo Galilei (Talking
   book)./SIS, P/1997/3-6/6 KE360 . . . . CE B GALILEO
Starry sky. /WYLER, R/1989/P-2/2 KC056 . . . . 523.8
Stars. /SIMON, S/1986/4-6/6 KC054. . . . . 523.8
Stars: a new way to see them. /REY, HA/c1967/4-6/8 KC053 . . . 523.8
STARS AND CONSTELLATIONS (Videocassette). /1993/
   3-6/KC055. . . . . VCR 523.8
Stars and Stripes: our national flag. /FISHER, LE/1993/
   3-6/7 KE617 . . . . 929.9
Starting home: the story of Horace Pippin, painter. /LYONS, ME/1993/
   5-A/5 KE499 . . . . B PIPPIN, H.
State birds: including the Commonwealth of Puerto Rico. /LANDAU, E/
   1992/4-6/8 KC653 598
State flags: including the Commonwealth of Puerto Rico. /BRANDT, SR/
   1992/4-6/7 KE614 . . . . 929.9
State flowers: including the Commonwealth of Puerto Rico. /LANDAU, E/
   1992/3-6/8 KC406 . . . . 582.13
State names, seals, flags, and symbols: a historical guide. Rev. and
   expanded ed. /SHEARER, BF/1994/4-A/KA493 . . . . REF 973
STATISTICS: UNDERSTANDING MEAN, MEDIAN, AND MODE
   (Videocassette). /1987/4-A/KB999 . . . . VCR 519.5
Statue of Liberty. /FISHER, LE/1985/5-6/7 KD400 735
Stay in line. /SLATER, T/1996/K-2/2 KG516 . . . . E
Staying cool. /ANTLE, N/1997/1-3/2 KF162 . . . . E
Staying with Grandmother. /BAKER, B/1994/1-3/1 KF184 . . . . . . E
STEAL AWAY: THE HARRIET TUBMAN STORY (Videocassette). /1997/
   4-A/KE576. . . . . VCR B TUBMAN, H.
Stealing home. /STOLZ, M/1992/3-5/6 KH768 . . . . Fic
Stegosaurs: the solar-powered dinosaurs. /SATTLER, HR/1992/
   3-6/8 KC260 . . . . 567.9
Stelaluna (Spanish version)./CANNON, J/1993/K-2/3 KF334 . . . . . . E
Stella and Roy. /WOLFF, A/1993/P-1/3 KG756 . . . . E

Stellaluna. /CANNON, J/1993/K-2/3 KF334 . . . . E
STELLALUNA (CD-ROM). /1996/K-3/KG550 . . . . CDR E
Stellaluna (Talking book). /CANNON, J/1996/K-2/KF335 . . . . . . TB E
Stellaluna (Talking book)./CANNON, J/1996/K-2/KF335 . . . . . . TB E
Stephen Biesty's incredible cross-sections. /BIESTY, S/1992/
   4-A/6 KC880 600
Stephen Biesty's incredible explosions. /BIESTY, S/1996/
   5-6/7 KD411 . . . . 741.6
Stepping out with Hap Palmer (Videocassette). /PALMER, H/1994/
   P-2/KD645. . . . . VCR 789.3
Steve Young: NFL passing wizard. /GUTMAN, B/1996/
   4-6/7 KE607 . . . . B YOUNG, S.
Steven Caney's invention book. /CANEY, S/1985/A/10 KC884 608
Steven Caney's Kids' America. /CANEY, S/1978/4-6/7 KE920 . . . 973.92
Steven Jobs and Stephen Wozniak: creating the Apple computer. /
   GREENBERG, KE/1994/4-6/7 KD046. . . . . 621.39
Steven Spielberg: Hollywood filmmaker. /MEACHUM, V/1996/
   4-6/8 KE545 . . . . B SPIELBERG, S.
Steven Spielberg: master storyteller. /POWERS, T/1997/
   5-A/7 KE546 . . . . B SPIELBERG, S.
Stevie. /STEPTOE, J/c1969/K-3/3 KG553 . . . . E
Stevie (Spanish version)./STEPTOE, J/1996/K-3/3 KG553 . . . . . . E
Stevie (Talking book)./STEPTOE, J/n.d./K-3/3 KG553 . . . . E
Stick up for yourself!: every kid's guide to personal power and positive
   self-esteem. /KAUFMAN, G/1990/6-A/6 KA659 158
Sticks. /BAUER, J/1996/6-A/4 KG880 . . . . Fic
Sticks and stones and skeleton bones./GILSON, J/1991/
   3-5/6 KH168 . . . . Fic
Sticky Beak. /GLEITZMAN, M/1995/3-5/4 KH176 . . . . Fic
Sticky Beak (Sound recording cassette)./GLEITZMAN, M/1997/
   3-5/4 KH176 . . . . Fic
Still more stories to solve: fourteen folktales from around the world./
   SHANNON, G/1994/5-6/6 KB714 . . . . 398.26
Stinker from space. /SERVICE, PF/1988/3-5/5 KH700 . . . . Fic
Stinker from space (Sound recording cassette)./SERVICE, PF/1993/
   3-5/5 KH700 . . . . Fic
Stinker's return./SERVICE, PF/1993/3-5/5 KH700 . . . . Fic
Stinker's return (Sound recording cassette)./SERVICE, PF/1994/
   3-5/5 KH700 . . . . Fic
Stinky Cheese Man and other fairly stupid tales. /SCIESZKA, J/1992/
   4-6/4 KH686 . . . . Fic
Stinky Cheese Man and other fairly stupid tales (Sound recording
   cassette)./SCIESZKA, J/1995/4-6/4 KH686 . . . . Fic
Stolen thunder: a Norse myth. /CLIMO, S/1994/4-5/5 KA755 293
Stone Age farmers beside the sea: Scotland's prehistoric village of Skara
   Brae. /ARNOLD, C/1997/3-6/8 KE677 . . . . 941.1
Stone men. /WEISS, N/1993/K-2/2 KG693 . . . . E
STONE SOUP: A MAGAZINE BY CHILDREN. /1973-/
   2-A/KA546 . . . . PER 050
Stone soup: an old tale. /BROWN, M/c1947/K-3/2 KB721 . . . CE 398.27
Stone soup (Braille)./BROWN, M/n.d./K-3/2 KB721 . . . . . . CE 398.27
Stonecutter (Videocassette)./MCDERMOTT, G/1976/
   2-4/KB756 . . . . VCR 398.27
Stone-faced boy. /FOX, P/1987/4-6/3 KH140 . . . . Fic
Stone-faced boy (Braille)./FOX, P/n.d./4-6/3 KH140 . . . . Fic
Stonewall. /FRITZ, J/1979/5-A/8 KE399 . . . . B JACKSON, T.
STONEWALL JACKSON (Videocassette). /1989/
   6-A/KE400. . . . . VCR B JACKSON, T.
Stonewall (Sound recording cassette)./FRITZ, J/n.d./
   5-A/8 KE399 . . . . B JACKSON, T.
Stop that ball. /MCCLINTOCK, M/c1959, 1987/K-2/1 KG086 . . . . . E
Stop, thief! /KALAN, R/1993/K-2/1 KF866 . . . . E
Stopping by the woods on a snowy evening. /FROST, R/1978/
   P-A/KD941 811
Stopping for a spell: three fantasies. /JONES, DW/1993/
   5-A/6 KH334 . . . . Fic
STORIES AND READERS: NEW PERSPECTIVES ON LITERATURE IN THE
   ELEMENTARY CLASSROOM. /1992//KA241 . . . . . . PROF 372.64
Stories for children. /SINGER, IB/1984/5-A/6 KH713 . . . . Fic
Stories for children (Sound recording cassette)./SINGER, IB/n.d./
   5-A/6 KH713 . . . . Fic
Stories for the road (Sound recording cassette). /FOLKTELLERS /1992/
   5-A/KB297. . . . . SRC 398.2
STORIES FROM ASIA TODAY: COLLECTION FOR YOUNG READERS,
   BOOKS ONE AND TWO. /1979/4-6/6 KH769 . . . . Fic
Stories from far away (Sound recording cassette). /BEN IZZY, J/1991/
   3-A/KB262. . . . . SRC 398.2
STORIES FROM MANY LANDS FROM THE PICTURE BOOK PARADE
   (Talking book). /1986/3-4/KB373 . . . . TB 398.2
Stories from the sea. /RIORDAN, J/1996/K-3/3 KB508 . . . . . . 398.23
Stories Huey tells. /CAMERON, A/1995/2-4/2 KG969 . . . . Fic
Stories Julian tells. /CAMERON, A/1981/3-4/4 KG970 . . . . Fic
Stories Julian tells (Braille)./CAMERON, A/n.d./3-4/4 KG970 . . . . . . Fic

Stories Julian tells (Sound recording cassette)./CAMERON, A/n.d./
3-4/4 KG970 . . . . **Fic**
STORIES OF INVENTION AND INGENUITY. VOL. 1 (Videocassette). /
1995/3-5/KC898 . . . . **VCR 609**
STORIES OF INVENTION AND INGENUITY. VOL. 2 (Videocassette)./
1995/3-5/KC898 . . . . **VCR 609**
STORIES ON STAGE: SCRIPTS FOR READER'S THEATER. /1993/
/KA363 . . . . **PROF 812**
Stories to solve. /SHANNON, G/1985/5-6/6 KB714 . . . . **398.26**
Stories to solve (Sound recording cassette)./SHANNON, G/n.d./
5-6/6 KB714 . . . . **398.26**
Storm. /NIKOLA-LISA, W/1993/P-1/2 KG174 . . . . **E**
Storm boy. /LEWIS, PO/1995/2-4/3 KB610 . . . . **398.24**
Storm in the night. /STOLZ, M/1988/K-3/4 KG578 . . . . **E**
Storm warning: tornadoes and hurricanes. /KAHL, JD/1993/
4-7/8 KC200 . . . . **551.55**
Stormalong (Kit). /METAXAS, E/1995/2-5/KB470 . . . . . . **KIT 398.22**
Stormalong (Videocassette)./METAXAS, E/1992/2-5/KB470. . **KIT 398.22**
Storms. /SIMON, S/1989/2-6/7 KC205 . . . . **551.55**
Stormy, Misty's foal. /HENRY, M/1963/3-5/4 KH244 . . . . **CE Fic**
Stormy, Misty's foal (Braille). /HENRY, M/n.d./3-5/4 KH244 . . . . . **CE Fic**
Stormy, Misty's foal (Sound recording cassette)./HENRY, M/n.d./
3-5/4 KH244 . . . . **CE Fic**
Stormy, Misty's foal (Talking book)./HENRY, M/n.d./
3-5/4 KH244 . . . . **CE Fic**
Story, a story: an African tale. /HALEY, GE/c1970/
3-5/5 KB580 . . . . **CE 398.24**
Story, a story: an African tale (Braille). /HALEY, GE/n.d./
3-5/5 KB580 . . . . **CE 398.24**
Story, a story: an African tale (Sound recording cassette)./HALEY, GE/
1997/3-5/5 KB580 . . . . **CE 398.24**
Story, a story: an African tale (Talking book)./HALEY, GE/n.d./
3-5/5 KB580 . . . . **CE 398.24**
Story, a story: an African tale (Talking book)./HALEY, GE/1993/
3-5/5 KB580 . . . . **CE 398.24**
Story, a story: an African tale (Videocassette)./HALEY, GE/n.d./
3-5/5 KB580 . . . . **CE 398.24**
Story about Ping. /FLACK, M/c1933/P-1/6 KF550 . . . . **CE E**
Story about Ping (Braille)./FLACK, M/n.d./P-1/6 KF550 . . . . . . **CE E**
Story about Ping (Kit). /FLACK, M/1993/P-1/6 KF550 . . . . **CE E**
Story about Ping (Talking book)./FLACK, M/n.d./P-1/6 KF550 . . . **CE E**
Story about Ping (Videocassette)./FLACK, M/1956/P-1/6 KF550. . . **CE E**
Story in a picture: animals in art. /RICHMOND, R/1993/
4-A/7 KD475 . . . . **758**
Story in a picture: children in art. /RICHMOND, R/1992/
3-6/7 KD471 . . . . **757**
Story lady (Sound recording cassette). /TORRENCE, J/1982/
4-6/KB781 . . . . **SRC 398.27**
Story of a castle. /GOODALL, JS/1986/2-6/KE680 . . . . **942**
Story of a dolphin. /ORR, K/1993/1-3/6 KG199 . . . . **E**
Story of a main street. /GOODALL, JS/1987/K-3/KF631 . . . . **E**
STORY OF A PATRIOT (Videocassette). /1957/4-6/KE888 . . **VCR 973.3**
Story of Babar, the little elephant. /DE BRUNHOFF, J/c1937, 1960/
P-2/3 KF453 . . . . **E**
Story of Babar, the little elephant (Braille)./DE BRUNHOFF, J/n.d./
P-2/3 KF453 . . . . **E**
Story of Babar, the little elephant (Sound recording cassette)./DE
BRUNHOFF, J/n.d./P-2/3 KF453 . . . . **E**
Story of Canada. /LUNN, J/1992/5-A/7 KE804 . . . . **971**
Story of Easter. /FISHER, AL/1997/2-3/2 KA714 . . . . **263**
Story of Ferdinand. /LEAF, M/c1936/P-1/3 KF953 . . . . **CE E**
Story of Ferdinand (Braille). /LEAF, M/n.d./P-1/3 KF953 . . . . . **CE E**
Story of Ferdinand (Kit). /LEAF, M/1978/P-1/3 KF953 . . . . . . **CE E**
Story of Ferdinand (Sound recording cassette). /LEAF, M/n.d./
P-1/3 KF953 . . . . **CE E**
Story of Ferdinand (Talking book)./LEAF, M/n.d./P-1/3 KF953. . . . **CE E**
Story of football. /ANDERSON, D/1985/4-A/7 KD782 . . . . . . **796.332**
Story of football (Braille)./ANDERSON, D/4-A/7 KD782 . . . . . **796.332**
Story of Frederick Douglass: voice of freedom. /WEINER, E/1996/
3-5/3 KE326 . . . . **B DOUGLASS, F.**
Story of Holly and Ivy. /GODDEN, R/1985/3-5/4 KH179 . . . . . . **Fic**
Story of Holly and Ivy (Braille). /GODDEN, R/n.d./3-5/4 KH179 . . . . . **Fic**
Story of Holly and Ivy (Sound recording cassette). /GODDEN, R/n.d./
3-5/4 KH179 . . . . **Fic**
Story of jazz (Sound recording cassette). /HUGHES, L/1954/
5-6/KD673. . . . . **SRC 789.5**
Story of Jumping Mouse: a Native American legend. /STEPTOE, J/1984/
4-5/5 KB656 . . . . **CE 398.24**
Story of Jumping Mouse: a native American legend (Sound recording
cassette)./STEPTOE, J/n.d./4-5/5 KB656 . . . . **CE 398.24**
Story of Junipero Serra: brave adventurer. /WHITE, FM/1996/
4-6/9 KE536 . . . . **B SERRA, J.**
Story of King Arthur. /LISTER, R/1997/4/7 KB465 . . . . **398.22**

Story of King Arthur and his knights. /PYLE, H/c1933, 1984/
A/9 KB472 . . . . **398.22**
Story of King Arthur and his knights (Braille)./PYLE, H/n.d./
A/9 KB472 . . . . **398.22**
Story of King Arthur and his knights (Talking book)./PYLE, H/n.d./
A/9 KB472 . . . . **398.22**
Story of lightning and thunder. /BRYAN, A/1993/K-2/2 KB702. . . **398.26**
Story of Little Babaji. /BANNERMAN, H/1996/K-2/2 KF195 . . . . **E**
Story of Miss Moppet. /POTTER, B/1987/K-2/4 KG269 . . . . **E**
Story of Miss Moppet (Sound recording cassette)./POTTER, B/n.d./
K-2/4 KG269 . . . . **E**
Story of money. /MAESTRO, B/1993/3-6/5 KA950. . . . . **332.4**
Story of my life. /KELLER, H/c1988, 1990/6-A/8 KE416 . . . **B KELLER, H.**
Story of Passover. /SIMON, N/1997/2-4/3 KA781 . . . . **296.4**
Story of religion. /MAESTRO, B/1996/3-4/9 KA725 . . . . **291**
Story of rosy dock. /BAKER, J/1995/K-4/6 KF115 . . . . **994**
Story of Ruby Bridges. /COLES, R/1995/2-5/4 KA902. . . . . . **323.1**
Story of Ruby Bridges (Sound recording cassette). /COLES, R/1997/
2-5/4 KA902 . . . . **323.1**
Story of Sacajawea: guide to Lewis and Clark. /ROWLAND, D/1995/
5-6/6 KE529 . . . . **B SACAGAWEA**
Story of sculpture. /ROMEI, F/1995/4-A/9 KD399. . . . . **730**
Story of Sir Launcelot and his champions./PYLE, H/c1984, 1991/
A/9 KB472 . . . . **398.22**
Story of Sleeping Beauty (Sound recording cassette). /PERRAULT, C/1980/
4-6/KB356 . . . . **SRC 398.2**
Story of space exploration (Picture). /KERROD, R/1994/
4-6/KC027 . . . . **PIC 523.4**
Story of the Champions of the Round Table./PYLE, H/1984/
A/9 KB472 . . . . **398.22**
STORY OF THE CREATION: WORDS FROM GENESIS. /1993/
2-3/4 KA688 . . . . **222**
Story of the Grail and the passing of Arthur./PYLE, H/1984/
A/9 KB472 . . . . **398.22**
Story of the Milky Way: a Cherokee tale. /BRUCHAC, J/1995/
2-3/3 KB701 . . . . **398.26**
Story of the Olympics. /ANDERSON, D/1996/4-6/11 KD819 . . . **796.48**
Story of the Statue of Liberty. /MAESTRO, B/1986/P-3/6 KD401. . . **735**
Story of the three kingdoms. /MYERS, WD/1995/1-3/3 KG165 . . . . . . **E**
Story of the three kingdoms (Sound recording cassette)./MYERS, WD/
1997/1-3/3 KG165 . . . . **E**
Story of the treasure seekers. /NESBIT, E/1986/5-6/7 KH544 . . . . . **Fic**
Story of time and clocks. /GANERI, A/1996/4-6/8 KC070 . . . . . **529**
Story of two American generals: Benjamin O. Davis, Jr.; Colin L. Powell. /
APPLEGATE, K/1995/5-6/5 KA981 . . . . **355**
STORY PACK FOR STORYBOOK WEAVER DELUXE FEATURING
DINKYTOWN DAY CARE KIDS (Microcomputer program)./1995/
1-5/KB118 . . . . **CDR 372.6**
STORY PACK FOR STORYBOOK WEAVER DELUXE FEATURING
HOLLYWOOD HOUNDS (Microcomputer program)./1995/
1-5/KB118 . . . . **CDR 372.6**
STORY STARTERS. Vol. 1 (Videocassette). /1995/
/KA231. . . . . **VCR PROF 372.6**
Story stretchers for the primary grades: activities to expand children's
favorite books. /RAINES, SC/1992/KA240. . . . . **PROF 372.64**
Story vine: a source book of unusual and easy-to-tell stories from around
the world. /PELLOWSKI, A/1984/KA248 . . . . **PROF 372.67**
STORYBOOK WEAVER DELUXE (CD-ROM). /1995/
1-5/KB118 . . . . **CDR 372.6**
Storyteller's sourcebook: a subject, title, and motif index to folklore
collections for children. /MACDONALD, MR/1982/
4-6/KA027 . . . . **PROF 016.3982**
Storytelling activities. /LIVO, NJ/1987//KA247 . . . . **PROF 372.67**
Storytelling, art and technique. 3rd ed. /BAKER, G/1995/
/KA244. . . . . **PROF 372.67**
Storytelling folklore sourcebook. /LIVO, NJ/1991//KA340. . **PROF 808.5**
Storytelling handbook: a young people's collection of unusual tales and
helpful hints on how to tell them. /PELLOWSKI, A/1995/
/KA249. . . . . **PROF 372.67**
Storytelling: learning and sharing (Videocassette). /JENKINS, S/1995/
/KA246. . . . . **VCR PROF 372.67**
Storytelling: tales and techniques (Videocassette). /FOLKTELLERS /1994/
/KA245. . . . . **VCR PROF 372.67**
STORYTELLING TIME IS HERE (Sound recording cassette). /1992/
2-4/KB374. . . . . **SRC 398.2**
Straight talk about child abuse. /MUFSON, S/1991/A/10 KB017 . **362.76**
Stranded at Plimoth Plantation, 1626. /BOWEN, G/1994/
5-6/7 KE870 . . . . **973.2**
Strange and distant shore: Indians of the Great Plains in exile. /
ASHABRANNER, B/1996/4-6/7 KF026 . . . . **978**
Strange and wonderful aircraft. /WEISS, H/1995/4-6/6 KD102 . . **629.13**
Strange mysteries from around the world. Rev. ed. /SIMON, S/1997/
4-6/7 KA561 . . . . **001.94**

Stranger at Green Knowe./BOSTON, LM/c1961, 1983/
4-A/6 KG919 . . . . **Fic**
Stranger at Green Knowe (Sound recording cassette)./BOSTON, LM/n.d./
4-A/6 KG919 . . . . **Fic**
Stranger came ashore. /HUNTER, M/c1975/A/7 KH293 . . . . **Fic**
STRATEGY CHALLENGES COLLECTION 1: AROUND THE WORLD. School
version (CD-ROM). /1995/3-A/KD754 . . . . **CDR 794**
STRATEGY CHALLENGES COLLECTION 2: IN THE WILD. School version
(CD-ROM). /1996/4-A/KD755 . . . . **CDR 794**
Street child. /DOHERTY, B/1994/5-A/6 KH078 . . . . **Fic**
Streets are free. Rev. ed. /KURUSA/1995/3-4/5 KH383 . . . . **Fic**
Strega Nona: an old tale. /DE PAOLA, T/1975/1-4/6 KB394. . **CE 398.21**
Strega Nona: an old tale (Videocassette)./DE PAOLA, T/1978/
1-4/6 KB394 . . . . **CE 398.21**
Strega Nona (Big book)./DE PAOLA, T/1992/1-4/6 KB394. . . **CE 398.21**
Strega Nona meets her match. /DE PAOLA, T/1993/1-3/2 KF479. . . . **E**
Strega Nonna (Kit)./DE PAOLA, T/1993/1-4/6 KB394 . . . . **CE 398.21**
STRESSBUSTERS (Videocassette). /1994/3-6/KA653 . . . . . . **VCR 155.9**
Strider. /CLEARY, B/1991/5-A/4 KH008 . . . . **Fic**
Strider (Sound recording cassette)./CLEARY, B/1995/5-A/4 KH008 . . . . **Fic**
Striking it rich: the story of the California gold rush. /KRENSKY, S/1996/
2-4/5 KF082 . . . . **979.4**
Stringbean's trip to the shining sea. /WILLIAMS, VB/1988/
K-A/2 KG739 . . . . **E**
Strings. /SHIPTON, A/1994/4-6/7 KD548 . . . . **787**
Strongheart Jack and the beanstalk. /DESPAIN, P/1995/
2-5/3 KB287 . . . . **398.2**
Structures that changed the way the world looked. /SINGER, D/1995/
4-A/9 KD384 . . . . **720**
Strudel, strudel, strudel. /SANFIELD, S/1995/2-3/4 KB773 . . . . . **398.27**
Struggle for a continent: the French and Indian wars 1690-1760. /MARRIN,
A/1987/5-6/8 KE872 . . . . **973.2**
Stuart Little. /WHITE, EB/c1945/3-6/5 KH851 . . . . **Fic**
Stuart Little (Braille)./WHITE, EB/n.d./3-6/5 KH851 . . . . . . **Fic**
Stuart Little (Spanish version)./WHITE, EB/n.d./3-6/5 KH851 . . . . . . **Fic**
Stuart Little (Talking book)./WHITE, EB/n.d./3-6/5 KH851 . . . . . **Fic**
STUDENT WORKSHOP: CONFLICT RESOLUTION SKILLS (Videocassette)./
1994/2-6/KA164 . . . . **VCR PROF 303.6**
STUDENT WORKSHOP: MEDIATION SKILLS (Videocassette). /1996/
/KA163 . . . . **VCR PROF 303.6**
STUDENT WORKSHOP: SOLVING CONFLICTS (Videocassette). /1994/
2-6/KA164 . . . . **VCR PROF 303.6**
STUDENT WRITING AND RESEARCH CENTER WITH COMPTON'S
CONCISE ENCYCLOPEDIA (CD-ROM). /1995/
4-A/KB091 . . . . **CDR 371.302**
STUDENT WRITING CENTER FOR WINDOWS (Microcomputer program)./
1993/2-A/KD347 . . . . **MCP 686.2**
STUDY SKILLS PLUS ATTITUDE: THE WINNING COMBINATION
(Videocassette). /1989/5-A/KB092 . . . . . . **VCR 371.302**
Stupids die./ALLARD, H/1981/K-2/5 KF152 . . . . **E**
Stupids have a ball./ALLARD, H/1978/K-2/5 KF152 . . . . . . **E**
Stupids step out. /ALLARD, H/1974/K-2/5 KF152 . . . . **E**
Stupids take off./ALLARD, H/1989/K-2/5 KF152 . . . . **E**
STV: HUMAN BODY: CIRCULATORY, RESPIRATORY, AND DIGESTIVE
SYSTEMS. VOL. 1 (Videodisc)./1992/4-A/KC926 . . . . **VD 612**
STV: HUMAN BODY: IMMUNE AND REPRODUCTIVE SYSTEMS. VOL. 3
(Videodisc)./1992/4-A/KC926 . . . . **VD 612**
STV: HUMAN BODY: MUSCULAR, SKELETAL, AND NERVOUS SYSTEMS.
VOL. 2 (Videodisc)./1992/4-A/KC926 . . . . **VD 612**
STV: HUMAN BODY (Videodisc). /1992/4-A/KC926 . . . . . . **VD 612**
STV: RAIN FOREST (Videodisc). /1991/4-A/KC327 . . . . . . **VD 577.34**
STV: RESTLESS EARTH (Videodisc). /1992/4-A/KC150. . . . . **VD 550**
SUBJECT HEADINGS FOR CHILDREN: A LIST OF SUBJECT HEADINGS
USED BY THE LIBRARY OF CONGRESS WITH DEWEY NUMBERS
ADDED. 2nd ed. /1998//KA062 . . . . **PROF 025.4**
Subject headings for school and public libraries: an LCSH/Sears companion.
2nd ed. /FOUNTAIN, JF/1996//KA059 . . . . . **PROF 025.4**
Subject index for children & young people to Canadian poetry in English.
2nd ed. /SNOW, K/1986/A/KA375 . . . . **REF 016.811**
SUBSTANCE ABUSE (Microcomputer program). /1992/
4-A/KD000 . . . . **MCP 613.8**
SUBSTANCE ABUSE (Videocassette). /1995/4-6/KD001 . . . . **VCR 613.8**
Successful field trips. /LANKFORD, MD/1992//KA178 . . . . **PROF 371.3**
SUEMI'S STORY: MY MODERN MAYAN HOME (Videocassette). /c1991/
5-A/KE841. . . . . **VCR 972**
Sueno del Zorro./TEJIMA, K/1989/P-2/4 KG597. . . . . **E**
Sugaring. /HAAS, J/1996/K-2/2 KF657 . . . . **E**
Sugaring season: making maple syrup. /BURNS, DL/1990/
5-6/7 KD154 . . . . **633.6**
Sugaring season: making maple syrup (Sound recording cassette)./BURNS,
DL/1993/5-6/7 KD154 . . . . **633.6**
Sugaring time. /LASKY, K/1983/4-6/9 KD155 . . . . **CE 633.6**
Sugaring time (Videocassette)./LASKY, K/1989/4-6/9 KD155 . . . . **CE 633.6**

Suho and the white horse: a legend of Mongolia (Videocassette). /
OTSUKA, Y/1981/3-4/KB626 . . . . **VCR 398.24**
Suitcase of seaweed and other poems. /WONG, JS/1996/
5-A/KE045. . . . . **811**
Sukey and the mermaid. /SAN SOUCI, RD/1992/3-4/6 KB775. . . **398.27**
Sukey and the mermaid (Sound recording cassette)./SAN SOUCI, RD/
1997/3-4/6 KB775 . . . . **398.27**
Sumemos con el domino./LONG, L/1997/P-2/2 KB966 . . . . . **513.2**
Summer day./FLORIAN, D/1988/P-1/1 KF560 . . . . **E**
Summer ice: life along the Antarctic Peninsula. /MCMILLAN, B/1995/
A/8 KE216 . . . . **919.8**
Summer of my German soldier. /GREENE, B/c1973, 1993/
A/8 KH197 . . . . **Fic**
Summer of the monkeys. /RAWLS, W/1976/4-6/6 KH623 . . . . **Fic**
Summer of the monkeys (Sound recording cassette)./RAWLS, W/n.d./
4-6/6 KH623 . . . . **Fic**
Summer of the swans. /BYARS, BC/c1970/5-6/6 KG964. . . . . **CE Fic**
Summer of the swans (Sound recording cassette)./BYARS, BC/n.d./
5-6/6 KG964 . . . . **CE Fic**
Summer of the swans (Talking book)./BYARS, BC/1972/
5-6/6 KG964 . . . . **CE Fic**
Summer switch. /RODGERS, M/1982/5-6/7 KH648 . . . . **Fic**
Summer switch (Sound recording cassette)./RODGERS, M/n.d./
5-6/7 KH648 . . . . **Fic**
Summer tunes: a Martha's Vineyard vacation. /MCMAHON, P/1996/
2-5/7 KB005 . . . . **362.4**
Summit up: riddles about mountains. /SWANSON, J/1994/
3-6/KD739. . . . . **793.735**
Sun. /SIMON, S/1986/P-A/7 KC046 . . . . **523.7**
Sun and spoon. /HENKES, K/1997/5-A/6 KH239 . . . . **Fic**
SUN, EARTH, MOON (Videocassette). /1995/4-6/KC017 . . . **VCR 523.2**
Sun: our very own star. /BENDICK, J/1991/1-3/5 KC044 . . . . **523.7**
Sun up, sun down. /GIBBONS, G/1983/P-2/2 KC045 . . . . . . **523.7**
Sun up, sun down (Braille)./GIBBONS, G/n.d./P-2/2 KC045 . . . . . **523.7**
Sun up, sun down (Sound recording cassette)./GIBBONS, G/n.d./
P-2/2 KC045 . . . . **523.7**
Sunday outing. /PINKNEY, GJ/1994/1-3/2 KG241 . . . . **E**
Sundiata: Lion King of Mali. /WISNIEWSKI, D/1992/
3-5/4 KB495 . . . . **398.22**
SUNFLAKES: POEMS FOR CHILDREN. /1992/P-2/KE086 . . . . **811.008**
Sunflower. /FORD, M/1995/P-1/1 KF566 . . . . **E**
Sunflower family. /WINNER, C/1996/3-6/7 KC434 . . . . **583**
Sunflower house. /BUNTING, E/1996/P-2/2 KF311 . . . . **E**
Sunita experiment. /PERKINS, J/1993/5-A/6 KH598 . . . . . . **Fic**
Sunken treasure. /GIBBONS, G/1988/4-6/6 KE194 . . . . . . **917.59**
Sun's asleep behind the hill. /GINSBURG, M/1982/P-K/1 KF624 . . . . **E**
Sunshine. /ORMEROD, J/1981/P-1/KG196 . . . . **E**
Sunshine makes the season (Braille)./BRANLEY, FM/n.d./
K-2/3 KC057 . . . . **525**
Sunshine makes the season. Rev. ed. /BRANLEY, FM/1985/
K-2/3 KC057 . . . . **525**
Super book of baseball. /BERLER, R/1991/4-A/7 KD794 . . . . . **796.357**
Super camper caper./HIMMELMAN, J/1991/1-3/1 KF729 . . . . **E**
Super kids publishing company. /ROBERTSON, D/1990/
/KA333 . . . . **PROF 808**
SUPER SITTERS: A TRAINING COURSE (Videocassette). /1988/
5-A/KD304 . . . . **VCR 649**
Superduper Teddy. /HURWITZ, J/c1980, 1990/2-4/4 KH304 . . . . **Fic**
Superdupers! really funny real words. /TERBAN, M/1989/
3-6/6 KB850 . . . . **428.1**
Superfudge. /BLUME, J/1980/2-4/2 KG913 . . . . **CE Fic**
Superfudge (Braille)./BLUME, J/n.d./2-4/2 KG913 . . . . **CE Fic**
Superfudge (Kit)./BLUME, J/1994/2-4/2 KG913 . . . . **CE Fic**
Superfudge (Spanish version)./BLUME, J/1996/2-4/2 KG913 . . . . **CE Fic**
Supergrandpa. /SCHWARTZ, DM/1991/K-3/5 KG416 . . . . **E**
Superstars of women's basketball. /KELLY, J/1997/
4-6/7 KD775 . . . . **796.323**
Superstars of women's figure skating. /SMITH, P/1997/
4-6/7 KD836 . . . . **796.91**
Superstars of women's golf. /WILNER, B/1997/4-6/7 KD792 . . . **796.352**
Superstars of women's gymnastics. /COHEN, JH/1997/
4-6/7 KD815 . . . . **796.44**
Superstars of women's tennis. /SCHWABACHER, M/1997/
4-6/7 KD791 . . . . **796.342**
Superstars of women's track and field. /WICKHAM, M/1997/
4-6/7 KD814 . . . . **796.42**
Supreme Court of the United States. /KRONENWETTER, M/1996/
5-A/10 KA978 . . . . **347.73**
Surprise! /NOLL, S/1997/P-K/2 KG179 . . . . **E**
Surprise family. /REISER, L/1994/P-2/2 KG319 . . . . **E**
Surtsey: the newest place on earth. /LASKY, K/1992/A/7 KE697 . **949.12**
Survival guide for kids with LD (Learning differences). /FISHER, GL/1990/
4-6/4 KB094 . . . . **371.92**
Swamp Angel. /ISAACS, A/1994/2-5/6 KF810. . . . . **E**

Swan Lake. /FONTEYN, M/1989/4-6/7 KD693. . . . . **CE 792.8**
Swan Lake (Kit)./FONTEYN, M/1991/4-6/7 KD693 . . . . **CE 792.8**
Swan Maiden. /PYLE, H/1994/2-4/6 KG294 . . . . **E**
Sweet Clara and the freedom quilt. /HOPKINSON, D/1993/
  1-3/4 KF770 . . . . **E**
Sweet Creek Holler. /WHITE, R/1988/6/7 KH854 . . . . **Fic**
SWEET HONEY IN THE ROCK: ALL FOR FREEDOM (Compact disc)./n.d./
  3-6/KD601. . . . . **SRC 789.2**
SWEET HONEY IN THE ROCK: ALL FOR FREEDOM (Sound recording
  cassette). /1989/3-6/KD601 . . . . **SRC 789.2**
Sweet, sweet fig banana. /GERSHATOR, P/1996/K-2/2 KF613 . . . . . . **E**
Sweet words so brave: the story of African American literature. /CURRY,
  BK/1996/K-6/7 KD906 . . . . **810.9**
Sweetest fig. /VAN ALLSBURG, C/1993/3-A/3 KH823. . . . . . . **Fic**
Sweetgrass. /HUDSON, J/1989/6-A/5 KH286 . . . . **Fic**
Swimming. /BAILEY, D/1990/2-4/2 KD846 . . . . **797.2**
Swimming. /WILNER, R/1996/3-6/6 KD850 . . . . **797.2**
Swimming and diving. /VERRIER, J/1996/3-6/8 KD849 . . . . . . **797.2**
Swimmy. /LIONNI, L/c1968/K-2/6 KF995 . . . . **E**
Swimmy (Videocassette)./LIONNI, L/1985/P-2/4 KF994 . . . . . **VCR E**
Swineherd. /ANDERSEN, HC/1995/2-5/5 KG847 . . . . **E**
Swinger of birches: poems of Robert Frost for young people. /FROST, R/
  1982/3-6/KD942 . . . . **811**
Switch on, switch off. /BERGER, M/1989/K-3/5 KC130 . . . . **537**
Sword in the tree. /BULLA, CR/c1956/3-5/2 KG939 . . . . **Fic**
Sword in the tree (Braille)./BULLA, CR/n.d./3-5/2 KG939 . . . . . **Fic**
Sybil rides for independence. /BROWN, DP/1985/3-6/4 KE876 . . . **973.3**
Sylvester and the magic pebble. /STEIG, W/c1969, 1988/
  K-2/6 KG544 . . . . **CE E**
Sylvester and the magic pebble (Videocassette). /STEIG, W/1992/
  K-2/KG545 . . . . **VCR E**
Tabby: a story in pictures. /ALIKI /1995/P-1/KF148 . . . . **E**
TADPOLES AND FROGS (Videocassette). /c1979, 1986/
  3-6/KC610. . . . . **VCR 597.8**
Tailor of Gloucester. /POTTER, B/c1931, 1987/P-3/7 KG270. . . . . . **E**
Tailor of Gloucester (Sound recording cassette)./POTTER, B/n.d./
  P-3/7 KG270 . . . . **E**
Tailor of Gloucester (Talking book)./POTTER, B/1988/
  1-3/KG271 . . . . **VCR E**
Tailor of Gloucester (Videocassette). /POTTER, B/1988/
  1-3/KG271 . . . . **VCR E**
Tails and childhood (Sound recording cassette). /PARENT, M/1985/
  K-3/KB629. . . . . **SRC 398.24**
Tailypo! /WAHL, J/1991/4-5/4 KB421 . . . . **398.24**
Tainos./DORRIS, M/1995/6-A/7 KH080 . . . . **Fic**
Take a look: an introduction to the experience of art. /DAVIDSON, R/
  1994/5-6/7 KD364 . . . . **701**
Take a look at snakes. /MAESTRO, B/1992/3-5/6 KC640. . . . . **597.96**
Take another look. /HOBAN, T/1981/P-A/KA618 . . . . **152.14**
Take it easy. /HILL, D/1997/6-A/4 KH260 . . . . **Fic**
Take me out to the ballgame. /NORWORTH, J/1992/K-2/KD639 . . **789.3**
TAKE ME TO YOUR LITER: SCIENCE AND MATH JOKES. /1991/
  3-6/KD740. . . . . **793.735**
Taking a walk/Caminando./EMBERLEY, R/c1990, 1994/K-2/KB858 . . **463**
Taking care of your gerbils. /PIERS, H/1993/3-5/6 KD184 . . . . . **636**
Taking flight: my story. /VAN METER, V/1995/3-6/6 KD101 . . . . **629.13**
Taking flight: my story (Sound recording cassette)./VAN METER, V/1997/
  3-6/6 KD101 . . . . **629.13**
Taking my cat to the vet. /KUKLIN, S/1988/P-K/4 KD234 . . . . . **636.8**
TAKING RESPONSIBILITY (Microcomputer program). /1988/
  1-6/KA665 . . . . **MCP 158**
Taking time out: recreation and play. /MILLER, TR/1996/
  5-A/7 KA865 . . . . **306.4**
Tale of Ali Baba and the forty thieves: a story from the Arabian Nights. /
  KIMMEL, EA/1996/3-4/6 KB332 . . . . **398.2**
Tale of Benjamin Bunny. /POTTER, B/c1932, 1987/P-2/8 KG272 . . . . . **E**
Tale of Jemima Puddle-Duck. /POTTER, B/c1936, 1987/P-2/6 KG273 . . **E**
Tale of Jemima Puddle-Duck (Braille)./POTTER, B/n.d./P-2/6 KG273 . . . **E**
Tale of Jemima Puddle-Duck (Large type)./POTTER, B/1996/
  P-2/6 KG273 . . . . **E**
Tale of Jemima Puddle-Duck (Sound recording cassette)./POTTER, B/n.d./
  P-2/6 KG273 . . . . **E**
Tale of Johnny Town-Mouse. /POTTER, B/c1946, 1987/P-2/8 KG274 . . **E**
Tale of Mr. Jeremy Fisher. /POTTER, B/1989/K-2/7 KG275. . . . . **E**
Tale of Mrs. Tiggy-Winkle. /POTTER, B/c1905, 1987/P-2/7 KG276. . . . **E**
Tale of Mrs. Tittlemouse. /POTTER, B/c1938, 1987/P-2/7 KG277 . . . . . **E**
Tale of Mrs. Tittlemouse (Sound recording cassette)./POTTER, B/n.d./
  P-2/7 KG277 . . . . **E**
Tale of Peter Rabbit. /POTTER, B/n.d., 1987/P-2/6 KG278 . . . . **E**
Tale of Peter Rabbit, and four other stories (Talking book). /POTTER, B/
  1984/P-2/KG279 . . . . **TB E**
Tale of Peter Rabbit (Big book)./POTTER, B/c1902, 1993/
  P-2/6 KG278 . . . . **E**
Tale of Peter Rabbit (Braille)./POTTER, B/n.d./P-2/6 KG278 . . . . **E**

Tale of Peter Rabbit (Sound recording cassette)./POTTER, B/n.d./
  P-2/6 KG278 . . . . **E**
Tale of Peter Rabbit (Talking book)./POTTER, B/n.d./P-2/6 KG278 . . . . **E**
Tale of Rabbit and Coyote. /JOHNSTON, T/1994/2-3/2 KB596. . . **398.24**
Tale of Squirrel Nutkin. /POTTER, B/c1931, 1987/P-2/7 KG280 . . . . . **E**
Tale of Squirrel Nutkin (Sound recording cassette)./POTTER, B/n.d./
  P-2/7 KG280 . . . . **E**
Tale of the Flopsy Bunnies. /POTTER, B/c1937, 1987/P-2/7 KG281 . . . **E**
Tale of the Flopsy Bunnies (Sound recording cassette)./POTTER, B/n.d./
  P-2/7 KG281 . . . . **E**
Tale of the mandarin ducks. /PATERSON, K/1990/2-3/6 KB631 . . **398.24**
Tale of the pie and the patty-pan. /POTTER, B/c1933, 1987/
  K-2/5 KG282 . . . . **E**
Tale of Thomas Mead. /HUTCHINS, P/1980/1-2/2 KF804 . . . . . **CE E**
Tale of Tobias. /MARK, J/1996/1-3/2 KA693. . . . . **229**
Tale of Tom Kitten. /POTTER, B/c1935/P-2/7 KG283 . . . . **E**
Tale of two bad mice. /POTTER, B/c1932, 1987/P-2/6 KG284 . . . . . . **E**
Talent show./CARLSON, N/1985/P-2/2 KF351 . . . . **CE E**
Tales for the perfect child. /HEIDE, FP/1985/2-5/2 KH233. . . . . . **Fic**
Tales for the perfect child (Braille)./HEIDE, FP/n.d./2-5/2 KH233. . . . **Fic**
TALES FROM CULTURES FAR AND NEAR (Sound recording cassette). /
  1990/3-4/KB375 . . . . **SRC 398.2**
Tales from Gold Mountain: stories of the Chinese in the New World. /YEE,
  P/1989/5-A/7 KH890 . . . . **Fic**
Tales from Gold Mountain: stories of the Chinese in the New World (Sound
  recording cassette)./YEE, P/1993/5-A/7 KH890 . . . . **Fic**
Tales from Moominvalley./JANSSON, T/c1964, 1995/3-6/7 KH325 . . **Fic**
Tales from Shakespeare. /LAMB, C/1979/A/9 KE115. . . . . **822.3**
Tales from Shakespeare (Braille)./LAMB, C/n.d./A/9 KE115 . . . . **822.3**
Tales from Shakespeare (Sound recording cassette)./LAMB, C/n.d./
  A/9 KE115 . . . . **822.3**
Tales from the Brothers Grimm and the Sisters Weird. /VANDE VELDE, V/
  1995/5-A/6 KH827 . . . . **Fic**
Tales from the homeplace: adventures of a Texas farm girl. /BURANDT, H/
  1997/5-A/4 KG946 . . . . **Fic**
Tales from the Southwest (Sound recording cassette). /HAYES, J/1984/
  4-5/KB502 . . . . **SRC 398.23**
Tales mummies tell. /LAUBER, P/1985/4-6/8 KE626 . . . . **930.1**
Tales of a fourth grade nothing. /BLUME, J/1972/2-4/3 KG914. . **CE Fic**
Tales of a fourth grade nothing (Braille)./BLUME, J/n.d./
  2-4/3 KG914 . . . . **CE Fic**
Tales of a fourth grade nothing (Sound recording cassette)./BLUME, J/
  1996/2-4/3 KG914 . . . . **CE Fic**
Tales of a fourth grade nothing (Talking book)./BLUME, J/1996/
  2-4/3 KG914 . . . . **CE Fic**
Tales of a gambling grandma. /KHALSA, DK/1986/3-5/6 KH345 . . . . **Fic**
Tales of Amanda Pig./VAN LEEUWEN, J/1994/K-2/1 KG648 . . . . **CE E**
Tales of Amanda Pig (Braille)./VAN LEEUWEN, J/n.d./
  K-2/1 KG648 . . . . **CE E**
Tales of an October moon: haunting stories from New England (Sound
  recording cassette). /LEVITT, MJ/1992/4-6/KH399 . . . . **SRC Fic**
Tales of Oliver Pig. /VAN LEEUWEN, J/1979/K-2/1 KG649 . . . . . **CE E**
Tales of Oliver Pig (Kit)./VAN LEEUWEN, J/1983/K-2/1 KG649 . . . **CE E**
Tales of the early world. /HUGHES, T/1991/4-A/5 KH290 . . . . **Fic**
Tales of the early world (Sound recording cassette)./HUGHES, T/1994/
  4-A/5 KH290 . . . . **Fic**
Tales of the wicked witch. /KRAAN, H/1995/3-5/3 KH379 . . . . . . **Fic**
Tales of Uncle Remus: the adventures of Brer Rabbit. /LESTER, J/1987/
  4-5/5 KB608 . . . . **398.24**
Tales of Uncle Remus: the adventures of Brer Rabbit (Sound recording
  cassette)./LESTER, J/n.d./4-5/5 KB608 . . . . **398.24**
Tales of womenfolk (Sound recording cassette)./FOREST, H/1985/
  2-4/KB735 . . . . **SRC 398.27**
Tales to grow on (Sound recording cassette). /FOLKTELLERS /c1981/
  K-3/KB298 . . . . **SRC 398.2**
Tales to tell from around the world. Vol. 1 (Sound recording cassette). /
  DESPAIN, P/1995/K-2/KB288 . . . . **SRC 398.2**
Tales to tell from around the world. Vol. 2 (Sound recording cassette)./
  DESPAIN, P/1995/K-2/KB288 . . . . **SRC 398.2**
TALK WITH AVI (Videocassette). /1995/5-6/KE245 . . . . . . **VCR B AVI**
TALK WITH BETSY BYARS (Videocassette). /1995/
  4-6/KE249 . . . . **VCR B BYARS, B.**
TALK WITH JEAN FRITZ (Videocassette). /1993/
  5-6/KE358 . . . . **VCR B FRITZ, J.**
TALK WITH LYNNE REID BANKS (Videocassette). /1995/
  4-6/KE505 . . . . **VCR B REID BANKS, L**
TALKING ABOUT SEA TURTLES (Videocassette). /1992/
  4-6/KC623 . . . . **VCR 597.92**
Talking eggs. /SAN SOUCI, RD/1989/3-5/5 KB415 . . . . **CE 398.21**
Talking eggs (Videocassette)./SAN SOUCI, RD/1991/
  3-5/5 KB415 . . . . **CE 398.21**
TALKING EGGS (Videocassette). /1993/2-5/KB420 . . . . . . **VCR 398.21**
TALKING LIKE THE RAIN: A FIRST BOOK OF POEMS. /1992/
  P-2/KE112 . . . . **821.008**

Talking to Faith Ringgold. /RINGGOLD, F/1996/4-6/6 KD379 . . . . 709.2
Talking to fireflies, shrinking the moon: nature activities for all ages. / DUENSING, E/1997//KA288 . . . . PROF 508
TALKING TO THE SUN: AN ILLUSTRATED ANTHOLOGY OF POEMS FOR YOUNG PEOPLE. /1985/6-A/KE087 . . . . 811.008
TALL GRASS PRAIRIE: AN AMERICAN STORY (Videocassette). /1997/ 3-A/KC333 . . . . VCR 577.4
Tall story and other tales. /MAHY, M/1992/4-6/4 KH453 . . . . Fic
Tall timber tales: more Paul Bunyan stories. /MCCORMICK, DJ/c1939/ 4-6/6 KB468 . . . . 398.22
Tallyho, Pinkerton./KELLOGG, S/1982/P-2/2 KF894. . . . . CE E
Tam Lin. /YOLEN, J/1990/3-4/4 KB384. . . . . 398.2
Tam Lin. /COOPER, S/1991/3-4/4 KB276 . . . . 398.2
Tamika and the wisdom rings. /YARBROUGH, C/1994/3-4/2 KH888 . . Fic
Tanks. /CHASEMORE, R/1996/4-6/8 KD060 . . . . 623.7
Tanners. /FISHER, LE/c1966, 1986/5-6/7 KD331. 675
Tanya and the Tobo Man/Tanya y el Hombre Tobo: a story in English and Spanish for children entering therapy /KOPLOW, L/1991/ K-2/2 KD040 . . . . 618.92
Tanya's reunion. /FLOURNOY, V/1995/K-3/3 KF562 . . . . E
Tapenum's day: a Wampanoag Indian boy in pilgrim times. /WATERS, K/ 1996/3-5/2 KE950 . . . . 974.4
Tap-tap. /WILLIAMS, KL/1994/K-2/2 KG728 . . . . CE E
Tap-tap (Kit)./WILLIAMS, KL/1996/K-2/2 KG728 . . . . CE E
Tar beach. /RINGGOLD, F/1991/2-3/4 KG333 . . . . E
Taran wanderer./ALEXANDER, L/c1967/6-A/6 KG833 . . . . Fic
Taran wanderer (Braille)./ALEXANDER, L/n.d./6-A/6 KG833 . . . . Fic
Taran wanderer (Talking book)./ALEXANDER, L/n.d./6-A/6 KG833. . . Fic
Tarantula. /LABONTE, G/1991/5-6/7 KC527 . . . . 595.4
Tarantula in my purse and 172 other wild pets. /GEORGE, JC/1996/ 4-6/4 KE366 . . . . B GEORGE, J.
Tarot says beware./BYARS, BC/1995/4-6/5 KG960 . . . . CE Fic
Tarot says beware (Talking book)./BYARS, BC/1996/ 4-6/5 KG960 . . . . CE Fic
Tasmanian devil: on location. /DARLING, K/1992/5-6/6 KC735 . . . 599.2
Taste. /PARRAMON, JM/1985/P-1/2 KC975 . . . . 612.8
Taste of blackberries. /SMITH, DB/c1973/4-6/4 KH722 . . . . Fic
Tatterhood and the hobgoblins: a Norwegian folktale. /MILLS, LA/1993/ 3-4/6 KB350 . . . . 398.2
Taxi Dog Christmas. /BARRACCA, D/1994/P-2/3 KF202 . . . . E
Taxonomies of the school library media program. /LOERTSCHER, DV/ 1988//KA076 . . . . PROF 027.8
T-backs, T-shirts, COAT, and suit. /KONIGSBURG, EL/1993/ 6-A/7 KH375 . . . . Fic
T-backs, T-shirts, COAT, and suit (Sound recording cassette)./ KONIGSBURG, EL/1995/6-A/7 KH375 . . . . Fic
Teach us, Amelia Bedelia./PARISH, P/1977/1-3/2 KG214 . . . . CE E
Teacher's pet. /HURWITZ, J/1988/3-5/4 KH305 . . . . Fic
TEACHING CHILDREN MATHEMATICS. /1954-//KA148. PER PROF 050
TEACHING ELEMENTARY PHYSICAL EDUCATION. /1990-/ /KA149. . . . . PER PROF 050
TEACHING EXCEPTIONAL CHILDREN. /1968-//KA150. . PER PROF 050
TEACHING K-8. /1971-//KA151 . . . . PER PROF 050
Teaching physics with toys: activities for grades K-9. /TAYLOR, BA/1995/ /KA204. . . . . PROF 372.3
Teaching thinking skills: English/language arts. /JONES, BF/1987/ /KA280. . . . . PROF 428
Teaching vocabulary to improve reading comprehension. /NAGY, WE/ 1988//KA211 . . . . PROF 372.4
Teammates. /GOLENBOCK, P/1990/3-6/6 KD798 . . . . 796.357
Teatro!: Hispanic plays for young people. /VIGIL, A/1996/ /KA364. . . . . PROF 812
TECH GIRL'S INTERNET ADVENTURE. /1997/4-A/KA580. . . BC 025.04
TECHNOLOGY AND LEARNING. /1980-//KA152 . . . . . PER PROF 050
TECHTRENDS: FOR LEADERS IN EDUCATION AND TRAINING. /1956-/ /KA153. . . . . PER PROF 050
Teddy bears. /YOUNG, R/1992/5-6/6 KD354 . . . . 688.7
Teeny tiny baby. /SCHWARTZ, A/1994/P-2/2 KG415 . . . . E
Teetoncey. /TAYLOR, T/c1975/5-A/5 KH784 . . . . Fic
Teetoncey and Ben O'Neal./TAYLOR, T/c1975/5-A/5 KH784. . . . . . . Fic
Tehanu: the last book of Earthsea./LE GUIN, UK/1990/6-A/7 KH392 . Fic
Tela Charlottae./WHITE, EB/1991/3-6/6 KH850 . . . . Fic
Tell me a Mitzi. /SEGAL, L/c1970/K-3/6 KG426. . . . . E
Tell me a Mitzi (Braille)./SEGAL, L/n.d./K-3/6 KG426 . . . . E
Tell me a season. /SIDDALS, MM/1997/P-1/1 KG500 . . . . E
Tell me a Trudy. /SEGAL, L/c1977, 1981/K-3/4 KG427 . . . . E
Tell me some more. /BONSALL, CN/c1961/K-2/2 KF247. . . . . E
Teller of tales. /BROOKE, WJ/1994/5-A/5 KG927 . . . . Fic
Telling of the tales: five stories. /BROOKE, WJ/1994/5-A/7 KG928 . . Fic
TELLING THE WEATHER (Videocassette). /1996/4-6/KC194 . VCR 551.5
Temperate forests. /STONE, LM/1989/4-6/9 KC310 . . . . 577.3
Ten apples up on top! /LESIEG, T/c1961/1-2/1 KF959 . . . . E
Ten black dots. Rev. and redesigned ed. /CREWS, D/c1968, 1986/ P-2/2 KF437 . . . . E
Ten flashing fireflies. /STURGES, P/1995/K-2/2 KG581 . . . . E
Ten mile day and the building of the transcontinental railroad. /FRASER, MA/c1993, 1996/5-6/7 KB139 385
Ten, nine, eight. /BANG, M/1983/P-K/KF192 . . . . E
Ten, nine, eight (Big book)./BANG, M/1993/P-K/KF192 . . . . E
Ten, nine, eight (Board book)./BANG, M/1996/P-K/KF192 . . . . E
Ten, nine, eight (Videocassette)./1985/P-1/KF809. . . . . VCR E
Ten out of bed. /DALE, P/1994/P-1/2 KF446 . . . . E
Ten small tales. /LOTTRIDGE, CB/1994/P-1/2 KB338 . . . . 398.2
TENDER TALE OF CINDERELLA PENGUIN (Videocassette). /1990/ 1-3/KG600 . . . . VCR E
Tennessee. /FRADIN, DB/1992/4-6/2 KF009. . . . . 976.8
TEN-SECOND RAINSHOWERS: POEMS BY YOUNG PEOPLE. /1996/ 3-6/KE088. . . . . 811.008
Tenth good thing about Barney. /VIORST, J/c1971/K-3/2 KG664. . . . . E
Terrible, wonderful tellin' at Hog Hammock. /SIEGELSON, KL/1996/ 4-6/6 KH711 . . . . Fic
Terrific tails. /MACHOTKA, H/1994/3-5/7 KC272 . . . . 571.1
Tesoro./SHULEVITZ, U/1992/2-4/4 KB778 . . . . 398.27
Tess. /HUTCHINS, HJ/1995/3-5/4 KH309 . . . . Fic
Test your luck. /WYLER, R/1992/5-6/4 KB998 . . . . 519.2
Texas traditions: the culture of the Lone Star State. /TURNER, R/1996/ 4-6/10 KF003. . . . . 976.4
Thank you, Amelia Bedelia (Kit)./PARISH, P/1995/1-3/2 KG218. . . CE E
Thank you, Amelia Bedelia. Rev. ed. /PARISH, P/1993/ 1-3/2 KG218. . . . . CE E
Thank you, Jackie Robinson /COHEN, B/1997/4-A/4 KH013 . . . . Fic
Thanks be to God: prayers from around the world. /BAYNES, P/1990/ 3-6/KA712 242
Thanks to cows. /FOWLER, A/1992/K-2/2 KD238 637
Thanks to cows (Big book)./FOWLER, A/1992/K-2/2 KD238 637
Thanksgiving Day. /GIBBONS, G/1983/P-2/4 KB225 . . . . . . CE 394.264
Thanksgiving Day (Kit)./GIBBONS, G/1984/P-2/4 KB225 . . . CE 394.264
Thanksgiving Day (Videocassette)./GIBBONS, G/1993/ P-2/4 KB225 . . . . CE 394.264
THANKSGIVING DAY (Videocassette). /1994/3-6/KB229 . VCR 394.264
THANKSGIVING POEMS. /1985/K-6/KE089 . . . . 811.008
Thanksgiving poems (Sound recording cassette)./n.d./K-6/KE089 . 811.008
Thanksgiving story. /DALGLIESH, A/c1954/3-6/4 KB222. . . . . . 394.264
Thanksgiving story (Braille)./DALGLIESH, A/n.d./3-6/4 KB222 . . 394.264
Thanksgiving treat./STOCK, C/P-K/2 KG574. . . . . E
Thanksgiving visitor. /CAPOTE, T/1996/5-A/8 KG972 . . . . Fic
That horse Whiskey! /ADLER, CS/1994/4-6/5 KG814. . . . . Fic
That Kookoory! /FROEHLICH, MW/1995/K-2/3 KF588 . . . . E
That terrible baby. /ARMSTRONG, J/1994/K-2/3 KF166 . . . . E
That terrible Halloween night./STEVENSON, J/1988/K-3/4 KG558 . CE E
That's fresh!: seasonal recipes for young cooks. /REX-JOHNSON, B/1995/ 5-6/KD277. . . . . 641.5
THAT'S WHAT FRIENDS ARE FOR (Videocassette). /1994/ 5-6/KA666 . . . . VCR 158
Themba. /SACKS, M/1994/3-5/5 KH670. . . . . Fic
Then again, maybe I won't. /BLUME, J/1971/6-A/5 KG915. . . . . Fic
Then again, maybe I won't (Braille)./BLUME, J/n.d./6-A/5 KG915. . . . Fic
THEN ONE YEAR. 2ND ED. (Videocassette). /1992/ 5-6/KC957. . . . . VCR 612.6
Theodore Roosevelt takes charge. /WHITELAW, N/1992/ 5-A/7 KE525 . . . . B ROOSEVELT, T.
Theodore Roosevelt takes charge (Sound recording cassette)./WHITELAW, N/1995/5-A/7 KE525 . . . . B ROOSEVELT, T.
THEODORE ROOSEVELT: THE COWBOY PRESIDENT (Videocassette). / 1990/6-A/KE524 . . . . VCR B ROOSEVELT, T.
Theodoric's rainbow. /KRAMER, SP/1995/3-6/4 KH380 . . . . Fic
There will be wolves. /BRADFORD, K/1992/6-A/5 KG921. . . . . Fic
There's a monster under my bed. /HOWE, J/1986/P-2/2 KF781 . . . . . . E
There's a monster under my bed (Braille)./HOWE, J/n.d./P-2/2 KF781 . . E
There's a square: a book about shapes. /SERFOZO, M/1996/ P-1/1 KG442 . . . . E
There's an alligator under my bed. /MAYER, M/1987/P-2/2 KG085 . . . E
These happy golden years./WILDER, LI/1953/3-6/4 KH860 . . . . Fic
These lands are ours: Tecumseh's fight for the Old Northwest. /CONNELL, K/1993/5-6/7 KE559 . . . . B TECUMSEH
Theseus and the Minotaur. /FISHER, LE/1988/5-6/6 KA741 292
Theseus and the Minotaur. /HUTTON, W/1989/5-6/6 KA746 292
They came from DNA. /ARONSON, B/1993/5-A/6 KC278 . . . . . . 572.8
They thought they saw him. /STRETE, CK/1996/K-2/2 KG579 . . . . E
They were strong and good. /LAWSON, R/c1940/4-6/KE891 . . . . 973.4
They're off!: the story of the Pony Express. /HARNESS, C/1996/ 2-5/8 KB129 383
Thimble summer. /ENRIGHT, E/1966/4-6/6 KH100. . . . . CE Fic
Thimble summer (Sound recording cassette)./ENRIGHT, E/n.d./ 4-6/6 KH100 . . . . CE Fic
Thimble summer (Talking book)./ENRIGHT, E/n.d./4-6/6 KH100 . . CE Fic
Thimble summer (Talking book)./ENRIGHT, E/1966/4-6/6 KH100 . . CE Fic
Things people do. /CIVARDI, A/1986/2-6/6 KA940 . . . . 331.7

Things that go bump in the night. /JONES, LC/c1959, 1983/ A/9 KA605 . . . . **133.1**
Things with wings. /CREAGH, C/1996/4-6/5 KC445. . . . . **591**
Think of a beaver. /WALLACE, K/1993/K-2/4 KC755. . . . . **599.37**
THINKIN' THINGS COLLECTION 1 (Microcomputer program). /1993/ K-3/KB080. . . . . **MCP 370.15**
THINKIN' THINGS COLLECTION 2. School version (CD-ROM). /1995/ 1-6/KB081. . . . . **CDR 370.15**
THINKIN' THINGS COLLECTION 3. School version (CD-ROM). /1995/ 3-A/KB082. . . . . **CDR 370.15**
THIRD BOOK OF JUNIOR AUTHORS./1972/A/KA462 . . . . **REF 809**
Third eye. /DUNCAN, L/1984/A/5 KH089 . . . . **Fic**
Third eye. /HUNTER, M/1991/A/7 KH294 . . . . **Fic**
Third eye (Sound recording cassette)./HUNTER, M/n.d./A/7 KH294 . . **Fic**
Third planet: exploring the earth from space. /RIDE, S/1994/ 2-8/7 KC062 . . . . **525**
Thirteen moons on turtle's back: a Native American year of moons. / BRUCHAC, J/1992/2-6/KD919 . . . . **811**
This and that. /SYKES, J/1996/P-1/2 KG586 . . . . **E**
This book is about time. /BURNS, M/1978/4-6/6 KC068. . . . . **529**
This can't be happening at Macdonald Hall!/KORMAN, G/1978/ 5-A/7 KH378 . . . . **Fic**
This for that: a Tonga tale. /AARDEMA, V/1997/K-2/2 KB517. . . **398.24**
This is baseball. /BLACKSTONE, M/c1993, 1997/P-1/2 KD795 . **796.357**
This is my house. /DORROS, A/1992/1-3/2 KD393 . . . . **728**
This is rhythm (Compact disc). /JENKINS, E/1994/K-2/KD632 . **CD 789.3**
This is rhythm (Sound recording cassette)./JENKINS, E/1994/ K-2/KD632 . . . . **CD 789.3**
This is the farmer. /TAFURI, N/1994/P-1/1 KG591 . . . . **E**
This is the star. /DUNBAR, J/1996/2-3/2 KA703 . . . . **232.92**
This land is my land. /LITTLECHILD, G/1993/2-A/4 KE803. . . . . **971**
This little piggy. /HELLER, N/1997/P-1/2 KF699 . . . . **E**
THIS OLD MAN. /1990/P-1/KD602 . . . . **789.2**
This old man/Este viejito (Sound recording cassette). /BARCHAS, S/1997/ K-2/KD606 . . . . **SRC 789.3**
This place is lonely. /COBB, V/1991/3-6/7 KF116 . . . . **994**
This place is wet. /COBB, V/1989/3-6/6 KC287 . . . . **574.5**
This time, Tempe Wick? /GAUCH, PL/c1974, 1992/3-5/7 KH153 . . . . **Fic**
This time, Tempe Wick? (Sound recording cassette)./GAUCH, PL/n.d./ 3-5/7 KH153 . . . . **Fic**
This way to books. /BAUER, CF/1983//KA089 . . . . **PROF 028.5**
Thomas Jefferson: a picture book biography. /GIBLIN, JC/1994/ 3-5/5 KE404 . . . . **B JEFFERSON, T.**
Thoroughbred horse: born to run. /STEWART, GB/1995/ 4-6/5 KD208 . . . . **636.1**
Those amazing eels. /HALTON, CM/1990/5-6/7 KC597 . . . . **597.5**
Those amazing leeches. /HALTON, CM/1989/5-6/9 KC504 . . . . **592**
Those happy golden years (Braille)./WILDER, LI/n.d./3-6/4 KH860 . . . **Fic**
Those happy golden years (Sound recording cassette)./WILDER, LI/n.d./ 3-6/4 KH860 . . . . **Fic**
Those happy golden years (Talking book)./WILDER, LI/n.d./ 3-6/4 KH860 . . . . **Fic**
Those remarkable women of the American Revolution. /ZEINERT, K/1996/ 5-6/10 KE889 . . . . **973.3**
Those summers. /ALIKI /1996/K-2/4 KF149 . . . . **E**
Thoughts, pictures, and words. /KUSKIN, K/1995/ 2-5/6 KE426 . . . . **B KUSKIN, K.**
Three and many wishes of Jason Reid. /HUTCHINS, HJ/1988/ 4-6/6 KH310 . . . . **Fic**
Three and many wishes of Jason Reid (Sound recording cassette)./ HUTCHINS, HJ/1993/4-6/6 KH310 . . . . **Fic**
Three bears. /BARTON, B/1991/P-K/1 KB527. . . . . **398.24**
Three billy goats Gruff. /ROUNDS, G/1993/P-1/2 KB644. . . . . . . **398.24**
THREE BILLY GOATS GRUFF; AND, THE THREE LITTLE PIGS (Videocassette). /1989/P-K/KB665 . . . . **VCR 398.24**
Three blind mice mystery. /KRENSKY, S/1995/1-3/2 KF925 . . . . **E**
Three by the sea. /MARSHALL, E/1981/K-3/1 KG066 . . . . **CE E**
Three by the sea (Braille)./MARSHALL, E/n.d./K-3/1 KG066 . . . . . **CE E**
Three by the sea (Kit)./MARSHALL, E/1984/K-3/1 KG066 . . . . **CE E**
Three by the sea (Sound recording cassette)./MARSHALL, E/n.d./ K-3/1 KG066 . . . . **CE E**
Three cool kids. /EMBERLEY, R/1995/P-1/3 KF525 . . . . **E**
Three cool kids (Sound recording cassette)./EMBERLEY, R/1997/ P-1/3 KF525 . . . . **E**
Three days on a river in a red canoe. /WILLIAMS, VB/1981/ K-3/5 KG740 . . . . **E**
Three friends: a counting book./Tres amigos: un cuento para contar. / BRUSCA, MC/1995/P-2/1 KB954 . . . . **513.2**
Three golden keys. /SIS, P/1994/5-A/4 KH714. . . . . **Fic**
Three hat day. /GERINGER, L/1985/P-3/2 KF609 . . . . **E**
Three hat day (Sound recording cassette)./GERINGER, L/n.d./ P-3/2 KF609 . . . . **E**
Three little javelinas. /LOWELL, S/1992/K-2/4 KG039 . . . . **E**
Three little kittens. /GALDONE, P/1986/P-1/5 KB798. . . . . **398.8**
Three little kittens (Braille)./GALDONE, P/n.d./P-1/5 KB798. . . . . . **398.8**
Three little pigs. /ZEMACH, M/1988/P-2/4 KB682. . . . . **398.24**
Three little pigs. /MARSHALL, J/1989/K-2/2 KB613 . . . . **CE 398.24**
Three little pigs and the big bad wolf. /ROUNDS, G/1992/ K-3/4 KB645 . . . . **398.24**
Three little pigs and the fox. /HOOKS, WH/1989/2-4/5 KB592 . . **398.24**
Three little pigs (Videocassette)./MARSHALL, J/1992/ K-2/2 KB613 . . . . **CE 398.24**
Three little wolves and the big bad pig. /TRIVIZAS, E/1993/ P-3/4 KG619 . . . . **E**
Three Names. /MACLACHLAN, P/1991/2-3/5 KG055 . . . . **E**
Three Names (Sound recording cassette)./MACLACHLAN, P/1994/ 2-3/5 KG055 . . . . **E**
Three princes: a tale from the Middle East. /KIMMEL, EA/1994/ 2-3/4 KB461 . . . . **398.22**
Three River Junction: a story of an Alaskan bald eagle preserve (Kit). / BURNHAM, SD/1997/2-4/KF313. . . . . **KIT E**
Three stories you can read to your cat. /MILLER, SS/1997/ K-2/2 KG137 . . . . **E**
Three terrible trins. /KING-SMITH, D/1994/3-5/6 KH358 . . . . . . **CE Fic**
Three terrible trins (Talking book)./KING-SMITH, D/1996/ 3-5/6 KH358 . . . . **CE Fic**
Three up a tree./MARSHALL, E/1986/K-3/1 KG066. . . . . **CE E**
Three wishes. /CRAIG, MJ/c1968, 1986/2/2 KB730 . . . . **398.27**
Three wishes. /ZIEFERT, H/c1993, 1996/P-1/1 KG797 . . . . **E**
Three wishes: an old story. /ZEMACH, M/1986/2-3/4 KB386. . . . . **398.2**
Through moon and stars and night skies. /TURNER, A/1990/ P-2/1 KG629 . . . . **CE E**
Through moon and stars and night skies (Kit)./TURNER, A/1995/ P-2/1 KG629 . . . . **CE E**
Through the looking-glass and what Alice found there. /CARROLL, L/ c1872, 1993/5-A/7 KG981 . . . . **Fic**
Throwing shadows. /KONIGSBURG, EL/1979/5-6/6 KH376. . . . . **Fic**
Throwing shadows (Braille)./KONIGSBURG, EL/n.d./5-6/6 KH376. . . . **Fic**
Throwing shadows (Sound recording cassette)./KONIGSBURG, EL/n.d./ 5-6/6 KH376 . . . . **Fic**
Thumbs up, Rico! /TESTA, M/1994/1-3/2 KG601 . . . . **E**
Thunder at Gettysburg. /GAUCH, PL/c1975, 1990/4-6/4 KE903. . . **973.7**
Thunder cake. /POLACCO, P/1990/1-3/4 KG258 . . . . **CE E**
Thunder cake (Videocassette)./POLACCO, P/1990/1-3/4 KG258 . . **CE E**
Thunder from the clear sky. /SEWALL, M/1995/4-6/7 KE874. . . . . **973.2**
Thunder rolling in the mountains. /O'DELL, S/1992/5-A/5 KH563 . . . . **Fic**
Thunder rolling in the mountains (Sound recording cassette)./O'DELL, S/ 1996/5-A/5 KH563. . . . . **Fic**
Thunderbolt: learning about lightning. /KAHL, JD/1993/ 4-6/9 KC207 . . . . **551.56**
Thy friend, Obadiah. /TURKLE, B/c1969/K-3/5 KG623 . . . . **E**
Thy friend, Obadiah (Braille)./TURKLE, B/n.d./K-3/5 KG623. . . . . **E**
TICK TOCK: ALL ABOUT THE CLOCK (Videocassette). /1992/ 2-3/KC074. . . . . **VCR 529**
Ticket to Canada. /LOTTRIDGE, CB/1996/4-A/5 KH418 . . . . **Fic**
Tickle Day: poems from Father Goose. /GHIGNA, C/1994/ P-1/KD944. . . . . **811**
Tidy Titch./HUTCHINS, P/1991/P-2/2 KF808 . . . . **E**
Tie man's miracle: a Chanukah tale. /SCHNUR, S/1995/2-3/4 KG409 . . **E**
Tiger called Thomas. /ZOLOTOW, C/c1963, 1988/K-2/4 KG808 . . . . . **E**
Tiger called Thomas (Braille)./ZOLOTOW, C/n.d./K-2/4 KG808 . . . . . . **E**
Tiger called Thomas (Sound recording cassette)./ZOLOTOW, C/n.d./ K-2/4 KG808 . . . . **E**
Tiger soup: an Anansi story from Jamaica. /TEMPLE, F/1994/ 2-3/2 KB663 . . . . **398.24**
Tiger soup: an Anansi story from Jamaica (Sound recording cassette)./ TEMPLE, F/1996/2-3/2 KB663 . . . . **398.24**
Tiger Woman. /YEP, L/1995/1-3/6 KB789 . . . . **398.27**
Tiger Woods: golfing to greatness. /KRAMER, S/1997/ 2-6/6 KE600 . . . . **B WOODS, T.**
Tiger's whisker and other tales from Asia and the Pacific. /COURLANDER, H/c1959, 1995/3-5/7 KB279 . . . . **398.2**
Tight times. /HAZEN, BS/1983/K-2/1 KF689. . . . . **E**
Tigresa./COWCHER, H/1993/1-3/6 KC827 . . . . **599.756**
Tigress. /COWCHER, H/1991/1-3/6 KC827 . . . . **599.756**
Tikki Tikki Tembo. /MOSEL, A/1967/P-2/5 KB759. . . . . **398.27**
Tikki Tikki Tembo (Big book)./MOSEL, A/1992/P-2/5 KB759 . . . . **398.27**
Tikki Tikki Tembo (Talking book)./MOSEL, A/n.d./P-2/5 KB759 . . **398.27**
Tik-Tok of Oz./BAUM, LF/1996/4-6/7 KG884 . . . . **Fic**
Tikvah means hope. /POLACCO, P/1994/1-3/2 KG259 . . . . **E**
Tim O'Toole and the weefolk./MCDERMOTT, G/1992/ 2/2 KB755. . . . . **398.27**
Time and the clockmice etcetera. /DICKINSON, P/1994/ 3-A/8 KH077 . . . . **Fic**
Time flies. /ROHMANN, E/1994/1-3/KG349 . . . . **E**
Time for bed. /FOX, M/1993/P-1/2 KF572 . . . . **E**
Time for bed (Big book)./FOX, M/1996/P-1/2 KF572. . . . . **E**

Time for bed, the babysitter said. /ANDERSON, PP/1987/ P-2/1 KF157 . . . . E
TIME FOR KIDS. /1995/3-6/KA547 . . . . **PER 050**
Time garden./EAGER, E/c1958/4-6/6 KH094 . . . . **Fic**
Time of wonder. /MCCLOSKEY, R/c1957, 1962/P-A/6 KG091. . . . **CE E**
Time of wonder (Braille)./MCCLOSKEY, R/n.d./P-A/6 KG091. . . . **CE E**
Time of wonder (Videocassette)./MCCLOSKEY, R/n.d./P-A/6 KG091. **CE E**
TIME: THE WEEKLY NEWSMAGAZINE. /1923-/4-A/KA548 . . . **PER 050**
Time to keep: the Tasha Tudor book of holidays. /TUDOR, T/1996/ P-A/4 KB204 . . . . **394.26**
Time to sleep. /FLEMING, D/1997/P-1/2 KF558 . . . . E
Time train. /FLEISCHMAN, P/1994/1-3/2 KF551 . . . . E
Time windows. /REISS, K/1991/6-A/7 KH630 . . . . **Fic**
TIMELINER: HISTORY IN PERSPECTIVE (Microcomputer program). /1986/ K-A/KE142 . . . . **MCP 902**
Timothy of the cay. /TAYLOR, T/1993/5-A/5 KH785 . . . . **Fic**
Timothy of the cay (Sound recording cassette)./TAYLOR, T/1995/ 5-A/5 KH785 . . . . **Fic**
Tinderbox. Newly illustrated ed. /ANDERSEN, HC/1988/K-3/5 KF155 . . E
Tingleberries, tuckertubs and telephones: a tale of love and ice-cream. / MAHY, M/1996/3-6/5 KH454 . . . . **Fic**
Titanic. /KENT, D/1993/4-6/7 KB026 . . . . **363.12**
Titch and Daisy. /HUTCHINS, P/1996/P-K/2 KF805 . . . . E
Tituba of Salem Village. /PETRY, A/1991/5-6/4 KH599 . . . . **Fic**
Tituba of Salem Village (Braille). /PETRY, A/n.d./5-6/4 KH599 . . . . **Fic**
TNT: two hundred and ninety-two activites for literature and language arts! /GEIGER, E/1989//KA222 . . . . **PROF 372.6**
To be a slave. /LESTER, J/c1968/A/7 KA928 . . . . **326**
To be a slave (Braille). /LESTER, J/n.d./A/7 KA928 . . . . **326**
To hold this ground: a desperate battle at Gettysburg. /BELLER, SP/1995/ A/9 KE897 . . . . **973.7**
TO JEW IS NOT A VERB (Videocassette)./1991/4-6/KA851 . **VCR 305.8**
To see with the heart: the life of Sitting Bull. /ST. GEORGE, J/1996/ 5-A/6 KE542 . . . . **B SITTING BULL**
To seek a better world: the Haitian minority in America. /ASHABRANNER, B/1997/5-6/8 KA836 . . . . **305.8**
To space and back. /RIDE, S/1986/4-6/6 KD138 . . . . **629.45**
To spoil the sun. /ROCKWOOD, J/c1976, 1994/6-A/6 KH644. . . . . . **Fic**
To the mountains by morning. /WIELER, DJ/1996/4-6/5 KH856 . . . . **Fic**
To the top of the world: adventures with arctic wolves. /BRANDENBURG, J/1993/5-6/7 KC834. . . . . **599.773**
Toad. /BROWN, R/1997/K-2/3 KF289 . . . . E
Toad for Tuesday. /ERICKSON, RE/1974/1-3/3 KF528 . . . . **CE E**
Toad for Tuesday (Braille). /ERICKSON, RE/n.d./1-3/3 KF528 . . . . **CE E**
Toad for Tuesday (Kit)./ERICKSON, RE/1981/1-3/3 KF528 . . . . . **CE E**
Toad for Tuesday (Sound recording cassette). /ERICKSON, RE/n.d./ 1-3/3 KF528 . . . . **CE E**
Toad or frog, swamp or bog?: a big book of nature's confusables. / GRAHAM-BARBER, L/1994/K-4/4 KB906 . . . . **508**
Toads and diamonds. /HUCK, CS/1996/2-3/3 KB319 . . . . **398.2**
Toady and Dr. Miracle. /CHRISTIAN, MB/1997/1-3/2 KF390 . . . . . . E
TOBACCO ACTION CURRICULUM: THE YOUNG AND THE BREATHLESS (Videocassette). /1991/5-6/KD007 . . . . **VCR 613.85**
TOBACCO FREE YOU AND ME (Videocassette). /1994/ 4-6/KD008. . . . . **VCR 613.85**
Toby. /WILD, M/1994/1-3/3 KG718 . . . . E
Toby lived here. /WOLITZER, H/c1978, 1986/4-6/6 KH878. . . . . . **Fic**
Toby the tabby kitten. /BARE, CS/1995/K-3/2 KD229 . . . . **636.8**
Toby, where are you? /STEIG, W/1997/P-1/2 KG546 . . . . E
TODAY IS MONDAY. /1993/P-1/KD661 . . . . **789.3**
Today was a terrible day. /GIFF, PR/1980/1-2/2 KF616. . . . . . . **CE E**
Today was a terrible day (Kit). /GIFF, PR/1993/1-2/KF617 . . . . **KIT E**
Today was a terrible day (Videocassette)/GIFF, PR/1988/ 1-2/2 KF616 . . . . **CE E**
Toilets, bathtubs, sinks, and sewers: a history of the bathroom. /COLMAN, P/1994/5-6/5 KD294 . . . . **643**
Tokyo. /KENT, D/1996/3-5/8 KE709 . . . . **952**
Toll-bridge troll. /WOLFF, PR/1995/1-3/2 KG759 . . . . E
Tom. /DE PAOLA, T/1993/K-2/2 KF480 . . . . E
Tom, Babette, and Simon: three tales of transformation. /AVI /1995/ 3-6/4 KG866 . . . . **Fic**
TOM TIT TOT: AN ENGLISH FOLK TALE. /c1965, 1997/ P-3/6 KB378 . . . . **398.2**
Tombs of the ancient Americas. /BENDICK, J/1993/3-5/8 KB174 . . **393**
Tomi Ungerer Library (Videocassette). /UNGERER, T/1993/ K-2/KG635 . . . . **VCR E**
TOMIE DE PAOLA'S BOOK OF POEMS. /1988/K-3/KD891 . . . . **808.81**
Tomie De Paola's Mother Goose. /DE PAOLA, T/1985/P-1/KB796 . **398.8**
Tomie de paola's Mother Goose (Braille). /DE PAOLA, T/n.d./ P-1/KB796 . . . . **398.8**
Tomorrow's alphabet. /SHANNON, G/1996/K-2/2 KG479 . . . . E
Tom's midnight garden. /PEARCE, AP/c1958, 1991/5-6/5 KH589 . . **Fic**
Tomten. /LINDGREN, A/c1965, 1997/K-2/3 KF986 . . . . **CE E**
Tomten and the fox./LINDGREN, A/1965/K-2/3 KF986 . . . . **CE E**

Tomten (Videocassette)./LINDGREN, A/1982/K-2/3 KF986 . . . . . . **CE E**
Tonight, by sea: a novel. /TEMPLE, F/1995/6-A/5 KH789 . . . . **Fic**
Tonight, by sea: a novel (Sound recording cassette)./TEMPLE, F/1997/ 6-A/5 KH789 . . . . **Fic**
Tonight is Carnaval. /DORROS, A/1991/1-3/4 KF492 . . . . E
Tontimundo y el barco volador./RANSOME, A/1991/ 2-5/5 KB765 . . . . **398.27**
Tony's bread. /DE PAOLA, T/1989/K-3/5 KB500 . . . . **398.23**
Tony's bread (Sound recording cassette)./DE PAOLA, T/1993/ K-3/5 KB500 . . . . **398.23**
Too far away to touch. /NEWMAN, L/1995/1-3/6 KG172 . . . . E
Too many Babas. /CROLL, C/c1979, 1994/K-2/2 KF439 . . . . E
Too many kangaroo things to do! /MURPHY, SJ/1996/ P-3/2 KB974 . . . . **513.2**
Too many people? /BLASHFIELD, JF/1992/A/7 KA815 . . . . **304.6**
Too many rabbits and other fingerplays about animals, nature, weather, and the universe. /COOPER, K/1995/P-1/KD707 . . . . **793.4**
Too many tamales. /SOTO, G/1993/K-3/3 KG530 . . . . E
Tool book. /GIBBONS, G/1982/P-K/2 KD055 . . . . **621.9**
Toolbox. /ROCKWELL, AF/1990/P-K/3 KD057 . . . . **621.9**
Toolbox (Braille)./ROCKWELL, AF/n.d./P-K/3 KD057 . . . . **621.9**
Tools. /MORRIS, A/1992/P-2/2 KD056 . . . . **621.9**
Tools (Board book). /BARTON, B/1995/P/KF208 . . . . **BB E**
Tooth book. /LESIEG, T/1981/K-2/2 KF960 . . . . E
Tooth fairy. /HALL, K/1994/K-1/1 KF665 . . . . E
Top rookies. /DUPLACEY, J/1996/4-6/6 KD840 . . . . **796.962**
Top 10 baseball pitchers. /SULLIVAN, MJ/1994/3-6/4 KD807 . . **796.357**
Top 10 basketball centers. /KNAPP, R/1994/3-6/4 KD776 . . . . **796.323**
Top 10 basketball scorers. /KNAPP, R/1994/3-6/4 KD777 . . . . **796.323**
Top 10 football quarterbacks. /LACE, WW/1994/3-6/4 KD783 . **796.332**
Top 10 football rushers. /LACE, WW/1994/3-6/4 KD784 . . . . **796.332**
Top 10 hockey scorers. /KNAPP, R/1994/4-6/5 KD842 . . . . . **796.962**
Top 10 women tennis players. /HARRINGTON, DJ/1995/ 3-6/7 KD790 . . . . **796.342**
Tops and bottoms. /STEVENS, J/1995/K-2/2 KB660 . . . . **398.24**
Torah is written. /COWAN, P/1986/5-6/7 KA782 . . . . **296.6**
Tornado. /KRAMER, SP/1992/3-6/6 KC201 . . . . **551.55**
Tornado. /BYARS, BC/1996/2-5/3 KG965 . . . . **Fic**
Tornado alert. /BRANLEY, FM/1988/P-4/3 KC196. . . . . **551.55**
TORTILLITAS PARA MAMA AND OTHER SPANISH NURSERY RHYMES. / 1981/1-3/KB816. . . . . **398.8**
Tortoise and the jackrabbit. /LOWELL, S/1994/K-2/3 KG040. . . . . . . E
Tortoise's flying lesson. /MAYO, M/1995/P-2/3 KB615. . . . . . . **398.24**
Tot's tunes (Sound recording cassette). /EPSTEIN-KRAVIS, A/c1987, 1990/P-1/KD610 . . . . **SRC 789.3**
Touch. /PARRAMON, JM/1985/P-1/2 KC976. . . . . **612.8**
Touching all the bases: baseball for kids of all ages. /MACKAY, C/c1994, 1996/4-6/7 KD799 . . . . **796.357**
TOUCHSTONES: REFLECTIONS ON THE BEST IN CHILDREN'S LITERATURE, VOL. 1. /1985//KA359 . . . . **PROF 809**
TOUCHSTONES: REFLECTIONS ON THE BEST IN CHILDREN'S LITERATURE, VOL. 2: FAIRY TALES, FABLES, MYTHS, LEGENDS, AND POETRY./1987//KA359 . . . . **PROF 809**
TOUCHSTONES: REFLECTIONS ON THE BEST IN CHILDREN'S LITERATURE, VOL. 3: PICTURE BOOKS./1989//KA359 . . . **PROF 809**
Tough Boris. /FOX, M/1994/K-2/2 KF573 . . . . E
Toughboy and sister. /HILL, K/1990/4-6/6 KH261 . . . . **Fic**
Toussaint L'Ouverture: the fight for Haiti's freedom. /LAWRENCE, J/1996/ 4-A/8 KE569 . . . . **B TOUSSAINT**
Tower of London. /FISHER, LE/1987/3-6/7 KE679. . . . . **942**
Town Mouse, Country Mouse. /BRETT, J/1994/K-3/3 KB535 . . . . **398.24**
Toy brother. /STEIG, W/1996/2-5/6 KG547 . . . . E
TOYS. /1991/K-2/2 KD352. . . . . **688.7**
Toys in space: exploring science with the astronauts. /SUMNERS, C/1997/ /KA282. . . . . **PROF 500.5**
Track. /WARD, T/1996/3-6/8 KD813 . . . . **796.42**
Track and field. /BAILEY, D/1991/1-3/4 KD809 . . . . **796.42**
Track and field. /ROSENTHAL, B/1994/3-6/4 KD810 . . . . **796.42**
Track athletics. /SANDELSON, R/1991/4-6/7 KD811 . . . . . . **796.42**
Tracking the facts: how to develop research skills. /MCINERNEY, C/1990/ 5-A/6 KB089 . . . . **371.302**
Tractor. /BROWN, C/1995/K-2/2 KD146. . . . . **631.3**
Traditional crafts from Africa. /TEMKO, F/1996/4-6/7 KD422 . . . . . **745**
Traditional crafts from Mexico and Central America. /TEMKO, F/1996/ 3-6/5 KD438 . . . . **745.5**
Traditions: a potpourri of tales (Sound recording cassette). /TORRENCE, J/ 1994/3-6/KB668. . . . . **SRC 398.24**
Trail fever: the life of a Texas cowboy. /LIGHTFOOT, DJ/1992/ 4-6/5 KH406 . . . . **Fic**
Trail fever: the life of a Texas cowboy (Sound recording cassette)./ LIGHTFOOT, DJ/1995/4-6/5 KH406 . . . . **Fic**
Train. /COILEY, J/1992/5-6/8 KD072 . . . . **625.1**
Train. /TEMPLE, C/1996/K-3/2 KG599 . . . . E
Train song. /SIEBERT, D/1990/P-3/KG501. . . . . E

Train to Somewhere. /BUNTING, E/1996/3-5/4 KG945 . . . . **Fic**
Train to Somewhere (Sound recording cassette)./BUNTING, E/1997/
  3-5/4 KG945 . . . . **Fic**
Trains. /GIBBONS, G/1987/1-3/3 KD073 . . . . **625.1**
TRAINS (Videocassette). /1995/2-4/KD077 . . . . **VCR 625.2**
TRANSPORTATION (Videocassette). /1992/2-4/KB159 . . . . . . **VCR 388**
Trash trucks. /KIRK, D/1997/K-2/3 KF908 . . . . **E**
Traveling backward. /FORWARD, T/1994/4-6/4 KH134 . . . . **E**
Travellin' with Ella Jenkins: a bilingual journey (Compact disc). /JENKINS,
  E/1989/K-2/KD576 . . . . **CD 789.2**
Travellin' with Ella Jenkins: a bilingual journey (Sound recording cassette)./
  JENKINS, E/1989/K-2/KD576 . . . . **CD 789.2**
Treasure. /SHULEVITZ, U/1978/2-4/4 KB778 . . . . **398.27**
Treasure Island. /STEVENSON, RL/c1911, 1981/5-A/6 KH759 . . . . . **Fic**
Treasure Island (Braille)./STEVENSON, RL/n.d./5-A/6 KH759 . . . . . **Fic**
Treasure Island (Sound recording cassette)./STEVENSON, RL/n.d./
  5-A/6 KH759 . . . . **Fic**
Treasure Island (Talking book)./STEVENSON, RL/n.d./5-A/6 KH759 . . **Fic**
Treasure Island (Talking book). /STEVENSON, RL/1993/
  5-A/KH760 . . . . **TB Fic**
Treasure nap. /HAVILL, J/1992/P-1/2 KF683 . . . . **E**
Treasure of Alpheus Winterborn./BELLAIRS, J/1997/6-A/6 KG895 . . . **Fic**
Treasure of Alpheus Winterborn (Braille)./BELLAIRS, J/n.d./
  6-A/6 KG895 . . . . **Fic**
Treasure of Alpheus Winterborn (Sound recording cassette)./BELLAIRS, J/
  n.d./6-A/6 KG895 . . . . **Fic**
Treasure of Green Knowe (Braille)./BOSTON, LM/n.d./4-A/6 KG919 . **Fic**
Treasure of Green Knowe (Sound recording cassette)./BOSTON, LM/n.d./
  4-A/6 KG919 . . . . **Fic**
TREASURY OF ANIMAL STORIES. /1992/3-6/6 KH802 . . . . **Fic**
TREASURY OF CHILDREN'S LITERATURE. /1992/P-3/KD879 . . . . . **808.8**
TREASURY OF GIANT AND MONSTER STORIES. /1992/
  3-5/6 KH803 . . . . **Fic**
Treasury of princesses: princess tales from around the world. /CLIMO, S/
  1996/3-5/6 KB432 . . . . **398.22**
TREASURY OF SPOOKY STORIES. /1992/4-A/6 KH804 . . . . **Fic**
TREASURY OF STORIES FOR FIVE YEAR OLDS. /1992/
  2-4/5 KH805 . . . . **Fic**
TREASURY OF STORIES FOR SEVEN YEAR OLDS. /1992/
  3-5/6 KH806 . . . . **Fic**
TREASURY OF STORIES FOR SIX YEAR OLDS. /1992/2-4/5 KH807. . **Fic**
TREASURY OF TURKISH FOLKTALES FOR CHILDREN. /1988/
  4-5/7 KB512 . . . . **398.23**
Tree. /BURNIE, D/1988/K-6/7 KC409 . . . . **582.16**
TREE: A LIVING COMMUNITY (Videocassette). /1988/
  4-6/KC355 . . . . **VCR 577.8**
Tree almanac: a year-round activity guide. /RUSSO, M/1993/
  3-6/6 KC423 . . . . **582.16**
Tree frogs. /JOHNSON, SA/1986/5-6/7 KC604 . . . . **597.8**
Tree frogs. /GERHOLDT, JE/1994/3-5/5 KC602 . . . . **597.8**
Tree in a forest. /THORNHILL, J/1992/3-5/6 KC311 . . . . **577.3**
Tree in the ancient forest. /REED-JONES, C/1995/K-3/3 KC437 . . . . **585**
Tree in the trail. /HOLLING, HC/c1942/5-6/5 KH273 . . . . **Fic**
Tree in the trail (Braille)./HOLLING, HC/n.d./5-6/5 KH273 . . . . . . **Fic**
Tree in the trail (Sound recording cassette)./HOLLING, HC/n.d./
  5-6/5 KH273 . . . . **Fic**
Tree in the wood: an old nursery song. /MANSON, C/1993/
  P-1/2 KB801 . . . . **398.8**
Tree is nice. /UDRY, JM/c1956/K-2/2 KG633 . . . . **E**
Tree is nice (Braille)./UDRY, JM/n.d./K-2/2 KG633 . . . . **E**
TREE IS OLDER THAN YOU ARE: A BILINGUAL GATHERING OF POEMS
  AND STORIES FROM MEXICO WITH PAINTINGS BY MEXICAN
  ARTISTS. /1995/5-A/KE121 . . . . **860.9**
Tree of cranes. /SAY, A/1991/1-3/4 KG400 . . . . **E**
Tree of dreams: ten tales from the garden of night. /YEP, L/1995/
  4-6/3 KB790 . . . . **398.27**
Tree that rains: the flood myth of the Huichol Indians of Mexico. /
  BERNHARD, E/1994/3-4/5 KB699 . . . . **398.26**
Treeful of pigs. /LOBEL, A/1979/P-2/4 KG013 . . . . **E**
TREEHOUSE (CD-ROM). /1991/K-4/KB086 . . . . **CDR 371.3**
Trees. /PLUCKROSE, H/1994/P-2/4 KC422 . . . . **582.16**
Trees. /PINE, J/1995/3-6/3 KC421 . . . . **582.16**
Trees of the dancing goats. /POLACCO, P/1996/1-3/3 KG260 . . . . . **E**
Trek. /JONAS, A/1985/P-2/4 KF849 . . . . **E**
Tres deseos: un viejo cuento./ZEMACH, M/1993/2-3/4 KB386 . . . . **398.2**
Tres en un arbol./MARSHALL, E/n.d./K-3/1 KG066 . . . . **CE E**
Tres lobitos y el cochino feroz./TRIVIZAS, E/1995/P-3/4 KG619. . . . . **E**
Tres pequenos jabalies./The three little javelinas./LOWELL, S/1996/
  K-2/4 KG039 . . . . **E**
Trespassers. /SNYDER, ZK/1995/5-A/6 KH734 . . . . **Fic**
Trip. /KEATS, EJ/c1978/K-2/2 KF879 . . . . **CE E**
Trip (Videocassette)./KEATS, EJ/1979/K-2/2 KF879 . . . . **CE E**
Trojan horse. /HUTTON, W/1992/2-5/5 KE124 . . . . **883**

Trojan horse (Sound recording cassette)./HUTTON, W/1995/
  2-5/5 KE124 . . . . **883**
Tropical fish: a complete pet owner's manual. /BRAEMER, H/1983/
  5-6/9 KD247 . . . . **639.3**
Trouble. /KURTZ, J/1997/K-2/3 KB748 . . . . **398.27**
Trouble for Lucy. /STEVENS, C/1979/3-5/6 KH754 . . . . **Fic**
Trouble with perfect. /RYAN, ME/1995/6-A/3 KH659 . . . . **Fic**
Trouble with school: a family story about learning disabilities. /DUNN, KB/
  1993//KA184 . . . . **PROF 371.9**
TROUBLE WITH TOBACCO (Videocassette). /1996/
  5-6/KD009 . . . . **VCR 613.85**
Trouble with trolls. /BRETT, J/1992/P-1/3 KF262 . . . . **E**
Trout summer. /CONLY, JL/1995/6-A/5 KH021 . . . . **Fic**
Trout summer (Sound recording cassette)./CONLY, JL/1997/
  6-A/5 KH021 . . . . **Fic**
Troy Aikman: quick-draw quarterback. /DIPPOLD, J/1994/
  4-6/6 KE230 . . . . **B AIKMAN, T.**
Truck. /CREWS, D/1980/P-K/KF438 . . . . **CE E**
Truck (Big book)./CREWS, D/1992/P-K/KF438 . . . . **CE E**
Truck song. /SIEBERT, D/1984/P-1/KG502 . . . . **CE E**
Truck song (Braille)./SIEBERT, D/n.d./P-1/KG502 . . . . **CE E**
Truck song (Kit)./SIEBERT, D/n.d./P-1/KG502 . . . . **CE E**
Truck song (Videocassette)./SIEBERT, D/1992/P-1/KG502 . . . . . **CE E**
Trucks. /BARTON, B/1986/P-1/2 KB161 . . . . **388.3**
Trucks. /GIBBONS, G/1981/P-1/1 KD117 . . . . **629.224**
Trucks (Board book). /SEIDEN, A/1983/P/KG428 . . . . **BB E**
TRUDY'S TIME AND PLACE HOUSE. School version (CD-ROM). /1995/
  P-3/KC075 . . . . **CDR 529**
True adventure of Daniel Hall. /STANLEY, D/1995/2-5/7 KE159 . . . **910.4**
True Blue. /ELSTE, J/1996/2-4/2 KH098 . . . . **Fic**
True confessions of Charlotte Doyle. /AVI /1990/5-A/6 KG867 . . . . . **Fic**
True confessions of Charlotte Doyle (Talking book). /AVI /1992/
  5-A/6 KG867 . . . . **Fic**
True Francine. /BROWN, MT/1987/1-2/1 KF282 . . . . **E**
True story of the 3 little pigs. /SCIESZKA, J/1989/K-3/2 KG421 . . **CE E**
True tale of Johnny Appleseed. /HODGES, M/1997/
  2-4/6 KE238 . . . . **B APPLESEED, J.**
Trueno./ARMSTRONG, WH/1996/4-A/4 KG851 . . . . **CE Fic**
Trumpet of the swan. /WHITE, EB/c1970/3-6/6 KH852 . . . . **Fic**
Trumpet of the swan (Braille)./WHITE, EB/n.d./3-6/6 KH852 . . . . . . **Fic**
Trumpet of the swan (Sound recording cassette)./WHITE, EB/n.d./
  3-6/6 KH852 . . . . **Fic**
Trumpet of the swan (Talking book)./WHITE, EB/n.d./3-6/6 KH852 . . **Fic**
Trumpeter of Krakow. New ed. /KELLY, EP/c1966, 1973//7 KH343. . . **Fic**
Trumpeter of Krakow. New ed. (Sound recording cassette)./KELLY, EP/
  n.d.//7 KH343 . . . . **Fic**
Trumpeter of Krakow. New ed. (Talking book)./KELLY, EP/n.d./
  /7 KH343 . . . . **Fic**
Truth about castles. /CLEMENTS, G/c1988, 1990/3-6/6 KE645 . . . **940.1**
Truth about cats. /SNOW, A/1996/4-A/7 KH728 . . . . **Fic**
Truth about Mary Rose /SACHS, M/1995/5-A/6 KH669 . . . . **Fic**
Truth about unicorns. /GIBLIN, JC/c1991, 1996/5-A/7 KB571 . . . **398.24**
Truth about unicorns (Sound recording cassette)./GIBLIN, JC/1993/
  5-A/7 KB571 . . . . **398.24**
Tsubu the little snail. /WILLIAMS, CA/1995/3-5/4 KB673 . . . . . . **398.24**
Tu mama es una llama?/GUARINO, D/1993/P-1/2 KF651 . . . . **E**
Tub Grandfather. /CONRAD, P/1993/1-3/4 KF415 . . . . **E**
Tub people. /CONRAD, P/1989/1-3/4 KF416 . . . . **CE E**
Tub people (Kit)./CONRAD, P/1996/1-3/4 KF416 . . . . **CE E**
Tuck everlasting. /BABBITT, N/c1975/4-6/4 KG873 . . . . **CE Fic**
Tuck everlasting (Kit)./BABBITT, N/1988/4-6/4 KG873 . . . . **CE Fic**
TUCK EVERLASTING (Microcomputer program). /1989/
  4-6/KB119 . . . . **MCP 372.6**
Tuck everlasting (Sound recording cassette)./BABBITT, N/n.d./
  4-6/4 KG873 . . . . **CE Fic**
Tuck para siempre./BABBITT, N/1991/4-6/4 KG873 . . . . **CE Fic**
Tuck para siempre (Sound recording cassette)./BABBITT, N/1993/
  4-6/4 KG873 . . . . **CE Fic**
Tucker Pfeffercorn: an old story retold. /MOSER, B/1994/
  2-3/4 KB351 . . . . **398.2**
Tucker's countryside. /SELDEN, G/c1969, 1989/4-6/5 KH698 . . . . . **Fic**
Tucker's countryside (Braille)./SELDEN, G/n.d./4-6/5 KH698 . . . . . **Fic**
Tucking mommy in. /LOH, M/1987/P-2/2 KG017 . . . . **E**
Tuesday. /WIESNER, D/1991/P-3/KG714 . . . . **E**
TUGBOATS: MASTERS OF OUR HARBORS (Videocassette). /1996/
  2-4/KB153 . . . . **VCR 387.2**
Tukama Tootles the flute: a tale from the Antilles. /GERSHATOR, P/1994/
  K-2/6 KB398 . . . . **398.21**
Tule elk. /ARNOLD, C/1989/5-6/8 KC794 . . . . **599.65**
Tumbleweed Christmas. /FERGUSON, A/1996/1-3/3 KF547 . . . . **E**
Tundra, the Arctic land. /HISCOCK, B/1986/4-A/7 KC335 . . . . . . **577.5**
Tunnels. /GIBBONS, G/c1984, 1987/K-2/2 KD069 . . . . **624.1**
TUNNELS (Videocassette). /1987/5-6/KD071 . . . . **VCR 624.1**

TUN-TA-CA-TUN: MORE STORIES AND POEMS IN ENGLISH AND SPANISH FOR CHILDREN. /1986/K-6/KD905 . . . . **810.8**
Turandot. /MAYER, M/1995/3-5/5 KB342 . . . . **398.2**
Turkey drive and other tales. /PORTE, BA/1993/1-3/2 KH611 . . . . . . **Fic**
Turkey for Thanksgiving. /BUNTING, E/1991/P-2/2 KF312 . . . . **E**
Turkey girl: a Zuni Cinderella story. /POLLOCK, P/1996/ 2-4/6 KB764 . . . . **398.27**
TURKEYS IN THE WILD (Videocassette). /1991/4-6/6 KC699 . . **VCR 598.6**
Turkey's side of it: Adam Joshua's Thanksgiving. /SMITH, JL/1990/ 2-4/4 KH725 . . . . **Fic**
Turnip. /DE LA MARE, W/1992/3-5/6 KB557 . . . . **398.24**
Turnip. /ZIEFERT, H/1996/K-1/1 KB683 . . . . **398.24**
Turtle knows your name. /BRYAN, A/1989/K-3/6 KB545 . . . . . . **398.24**
Turtles. /PALAZZO-CRAIG, J/1982/P-K/1 KC621 . . . . **597.92**
Turtle's day. /KUHN, D/1994/P-2/4 KC620 . . . . **597.92**
Turtles: everything about purchase, care, nutrition and diseases. /WILKE, H/ 1983/5-6/9 KD250 . . . . **639.3**
Tut, tut./SCIESZKA, J/1996/3-6/3 KH685 . . . . **Fic**
Tutankhamen's gift. /SABUDA, R/1994/ 2-4/3 KE578 . . . . **B TUTANKHAMEN**
TV's forgotten hero: the story of Philo Farnsworth. /MCPHERSON, SS/ 1996/5-A/9 KE342 . . . . **B FARNSWORTH, P**
Twas the night before Christmas: a visit from St. Nicholas. /MOORE, CC/ c1912, 1992/P-A/KD988 . . . . **811**
Twelve dancing princesses: a fairy tale. /GRIMM, J/1995/ 3-4/6 KB311 . . . . **398.2**
TWELVE DAYS OF CHRISTMAS. /1986/P-A/KD537 . . . . **782.28**
TWELVE DAYS OF CHRISTMAS. /1993/P-A/KD538 . . . . **782.28**
TWELVE DAYS OF CHRISTMAS. /1995/K-3/KD539. . . . . . . **782.28**
TWELVE DAYS OF CHRISTMAS (Videocassette). /1990/ P-A/KD540 . . . . **VCR 782.28**
Twelve snails to one lizard: a tale of mischief and measurement. / HIGHTOWER, S/1997/1-3/2 KF726 . . . . **E**
Twelve tales. /ANDERSEN, HC/1994/3-6/5 KG848 . . . . **Fic**
Twentieth-century inventors. /AASENG, N/1991/A/9 KC889 . . . . . **609**
Twenty-one balloons. /PENE DU BOIS, W/c1947/4-6/7 KH595 . . **CE Fic**
Twenty-one balloons (Braille). /PENE DU BOIS, W/n.d./ 4-6/7 KH595 . . . . **CE Fic**
Twenty-one balloons (Sound recording cassette)./PENE DU BOIS, W/n.d./ 4-6/7 KH595 . . . . **CE Fic**
Twenty-one balloons (Talking book). /PENE DU BOIS, W/n.d./ 4-6/7 KH595 . . . . **CE Fic**
Twenty-one balloons (Talking book). /PENE DU BOIS, W/1972/ 4-6/7 KH595 . . . . **CE Fic**
Twilight in Grace Falls. /HONEYCUTT, N/1997/6-A/6 KH278 . . . . . **Fic**
Twilight struggle: the life of John Fitzgerald Kennedy. /HARRISON, B/ 1992/6-A/8 KE418 . . . . **B KENNEDY, J.**
Twinkle, twinkle, little star. /TAYLOR, J/1992/P-K/KE111. . . . . . . **821**
Twisters! /PENNER, LR/1996/2-4/3 KC204 . . . . **551.55**
Two bad ants. /VAN ALLSBURG, C/1988/1-3/4 KG639 . . . . **E**
Two bad boys: a very old Cherokee tale. /HALEY, GE/1996/ 2-5/5 KB742 . . . . **398.27**
Two dog biscuits./CLEARY, B/c1961, 1986/P/2 KF396 . . . . **E**
Two dog biscuits (Braille)./CLEARY, B/n.d./P/2 KF396 . . . . **E**
Two lands, one heart: an American boy's journey to his mother's Vietnam. / SCHMIDT, J/1995/1-3/7 KE719 . . . . **959.7**
Two mice in three fables. /REISER, L/1995/P-2/3 KG320 . . . . **E**
Two of everything. /HONG, LT/1993/2-3/4 KB317 . . . . **398.2**
Two orphan cubs. /BRENNER, B/1989/K-2/2 KC848 . . . . **599.78**
Two short and one long. /AAMUNDSEN, NR/1990/4-6/5 KG811 . . . **Fic**
Two terrible frights. /AYLESWORTH, J/1987/P-1/3 KF181 . . . . **E**
Two very little sisters. /CARRICK, C/1993/2-4/5 KC879 . . . . . . **599.9**
Two's company. /GREENWAY, S/1997/K-2/3 KB845 . . . . **428.1**
Ty Cobb: bad boy of baseball. /KRAMER, SA/1995/ 2-4/4 KE298 . . . . **B COBB, T.**
Tye May and the magic brush. /BANG, M/c1981, 1992/1-3/2 KF193. . **E**
Tyger. /BLAKE, W/1993/1-4/KE096 . . . . **821**
TYPE TO LEARN: A NEW APPROACH TO KEYBOARDING (Microcomputer program). /1986/2-A/KD312 . . . . **MCP 652.3**
Tyrannosaurus. /LINDSAY, W/1992/5-6/9 KC255 . . . . **567.9**
Tyrannosaurus game. /KROLL, S/c1976/K-2/6 KF931 . . . . **CE E**
Tyrannosaurus game (Kit)./KROLL, S/1986/K-2/6 KF931 . . . . **CE E**
Tyrannosaurus rex and its kin: the Mesozoic monsters. /SATTLER, HR/ 1989/3-6/8 KC261 . . . . **567.9**
Tyrannosaurus was a beast: dinosaur poems. /PRELUTSKY, J/c1988, 1992/ 1-5/KE017 . . . . **CE 811**
Tyrannosaurus was a beast: dinosaur poems (Big book)./PRELUTSKY, J/ 1992/1-5/KE017. . . . . **CE 811**
Tyrannosaurus was a beast: dinosaur poems (Kit)./PRELUTSKY, J/1988/ 1-5/KE017. **CE 811**
Ty's one-man band. /WALTER, MP/c1980, 1987/1-3/2 KG686 . . . . . . **E**
UFO diary. /KITAMURA, S/1989/K-2/2 KF909 . . . . **E**
Ugly Duckling. /MITCHELL, A/1994/P-A/4 KG143 . . . . **E**

Ugly duckling (Videocassette). /ANDERSEN, HC/1977/ 2-5/KG849 . . . . **VCR Fic**
Ultima batalla./LEWIS, CS/n.d./5-A/6 KH405 . . . . **CE Fic**
ULTIMATE HUMAN BODY (CD-ROM). /1996/4-A/KC927. . . . . **CDR 612**
ULTIMATE WRITING AND CREATIVITY CENTER. School ed. (CD-ROM). / 1996/K-5/KB120. . . . . **CDR 372.6**
Ultimo en tirarse es un miedoso./KESSLER, L/1995/1-2/1 KF900. . . . . **E**
Ulysses S. Grant and the strategy of victory. /RICKARBY, LA/1991/ 6-A/6 KE377. . . . . **B GRANT, U.**
ULYSSES S. GRANT (Videocassette). /1989/ 6-A/KE378. . . . . **VCR B GRANT, U.**
Umbrella. /YASHIMA, T/c1958/P-K/6 KG773 . . . . **CE E**
Umbrella (Kit)./YASHIMA, T/1985/P-K/2 KG773 . . . . **CE E**
Umbrella (Talking book). /YASHIMA, T/n.d./P-K/2 KG773 . . . . . **CE E**
Unbeatable bread. /HOOPES, LL/1996/K-2/3 KF769 . . . . **E**
Uncegila's seventh spot: a Lakota legend. /RUBALCABA, J/1995/ 3-5/3 KB478 . . . . **398.22**
Uncle Bouqui of Haiti (Talking book). /COURLANDER, H/1959/ K-A/6 KB729 . . . . **TB 398.27**
Uncle Daney's way. /HAAS, J/1994/4-6/4 KH210 . . . . **Fic**
Uncle Elephant. /LOBEL, A/1981/K-1/1 KG014 . . . . **E**
Uncle Jed's barbershop. /MITCHELL, MK/1993/1-3/4 KG147. . . . . . **E**
Uncle Nacho's hat: a folktale from Nicaragua/El sombrero de Tio Nacho: un cuento de Nicaragua. /ROHMER, H/1989/2-4/2 KB770. . . **398.27**
Uncle Ronald. /DOYLE, B/1997/5-A/5 KH083. . . . . **Fic**
Uncle Sam wants you!: military men and women of World War II. / WHITMAN, S/1993/A/8 KE675 . . . . **940.54**
Uncle Vova's tree. /POLACCO, P/1989/1-3/6 KG261 . . . . **E**
Uncle Willie and the soup kitchen. /DISALVO-RYAN, D/1991/ 1-3/2 KF485 . . . . **E**
Under my nose. /EHLERT, L/1996/3-6/2 KE333 . . . . **B EHLERT, L.**
Under the blood-red sun. /SALISBURY, G/1994/6-A/4 KH672 . . . . . **Fic**
Under the cherry blossom tree: an old Japanese tale. /SAY, A/1997/ P-1/5 KB777 . . . . **398.27**
Under the ground. /PLUCKROSE, H/1994/P-2/4 KC360 . . . . . . **578.75**
Under the mermaid angel. /MOORE, M/1995/6-A/5 KH506 . . . . . . **Fic**
Under the sun and the moon and other poems. /BROWN, MW/1993/ P-2/KD918. . . . . **811**
Under the table. /RUSSO, M/1997/P-K/2 KG363 . . . . **E**
Underground. /MACAULAY, D/1976/A/10 KD070. . . . . **624.1**
UNDER-REPRESENTED GIFTED (Videocassette)./1991/ /KA187. . . . . **VCR PROF 371.95**
Underrunners. /MAHY, M/1992/6-A/6 KH455 . . . . **Fic**
Understanding American history through children's literature: instructional units and activities for grades K-8. /PEREZ-STABLE, MA/1994/ /KA263. . . . . **PROF 372.89**
Understanding man's best friend: why dogs look and act the way they do. / SQUIRE, A/1991/5-6/7 KD222 . . . . **636.7**
UNFORGETTABLE PEN PAL: A STORY ABOUT PREJUDICE AND DISCRIMINATION (Videocassette). /1991/3-5/KA821 . . . . **VCR 305**
United Nations. Rev. ed. /STEIN, RC/1994/4-6/7 KA969 . . . . . **341.23**
UNITED STATES GOVERNMENT MANUAL. /1935-/A/KA409. . **REF 353**
United States in the 19th century. /RUBEL, D/1996/4-A/8 KE895 . . **973.5**
United States in the 20th century. /RUBEL, D/1995/4-A/8 KE916 . . **973.9**
United States of America. /STEIN, RC/1994/4-A/9 KE867. . . . . . . **973**
Uno, dos, tres: one, two, three. /MORA, P/1996/P-1/3 KG155 . . . . . **E**
Unraveling fibers. /KEELER, PA/1995/4-6/6 KD335 . . . . **677**
Unreluctant years: a critical approach to children's literature. /SMITH, L/ c1953, 1991/KA357 . . . . **PROF 809**
Untold tales. /BROOKE, WJ/1992/6-A/7 KG929. . . . . **Fic**
Up a road slowly. /HUNT, I/1993/A/7 KH292 . . . . **Fic**
Up goes the skyscraper! /GIBBONS, G/1986/K-3/6 KD356 . . . . **690**
Up in the air: the story of Bessie Coleman. /HART, PS/1996/ 4-6/8 KE299 . . . . **B COLEMAN, B.**
Up the chimney down and other stories. /AIKEN, J/1987/ 4-6/6 KG825 . . . . **Fic**
Up the chimney down and other stories (Braille)./AIKEN, J/n.d./ 4-6/6 KG825 . . . . **Fic**
Up to the plate: the All American Girls Professional Baseball League. / GALT, MF/1995/4-6/6 KD797 . . . . **796.357**
Up, up and away: a book about adverbs. /HELLER, R/1991/ 1-3/KB852 . . . . **428.2**
Upon the head of the goat: a childhood in Hungary 1939-1944. /SIEGAL, A/1981/4-6/8 KE691 . . . . **CE 947.084**
Upstairs room. /REISS, J/c1972/5-6/5 KE506 . . . . **B REISS, J.**
Uranus. /SIMON, S/1987/4-6/6 KC040 . . . . **523.47**
Urban roosts: where birds nest in the city. /BASH, B/1990/ 3-6/7 KC672 . . . . **598.156**
U.S. CONSTITUTION: A DOCUMENT FOR DEMOCRACY (Videocassette). /1986/5-A/KA976 . . . . **VCR 342.73**
U*S* KIDS: A WEEKLY READER MAGAZINE. /1987-/ 2-4/KA549 . . . . **PER 050**
U.S. Marine Corps. /WARNER, JF/1991/5-6/7 KA990 . . . . **359.9**

U.S. Marine Corps (Sound recording cassette)./WARNER, JF/1995/
5-6/7 KA990 . . . . 359.9
USING FRACTIONS (Videocassette). /1982/3-4/KB983 . . . . **VCR 513.2**
USING LITERATURE IN THE ELEMENTARY CLASSROOM. Rev. ed. /
1989//KA243 . . . . **PROF 372.64**
Using poetry across the curriculum: a whole language approach. /
CHATTON, B/1993//KA237 . . . . **PROF 372.64**
USING 911: PROTECT YOURSELF (Videocassette). /1995/
2-6/KB136 . . . . **VCR 384.6**
Utah. /SIRVAITIS, K/1991/4-6/6 KF073 . . . . 979.2
Utterly yours, Booker Jones. /DUFFEY, B/1995/4-6/5 KH087 . . . . . . **Fic**
V is for victory: America remembers World War II. /KRULL, K/1995/
A/7 KE659 . . . . 940.53
V is for victory: the American home front during World War II. /
WHITMAN, S/1993/5-6/8 KE919 . . . . 973.917
Valentine's Day. /GIBBONS, G/1986/1-6/5 KB207 . . . . . . **CE 394.261**
Valentine's Day can be murder. /MCKENNA, CO/1996/3-5/4 KH482 . . **Fic**
Valentine's Day (Kit)./GIBBONS, G/1986/1-6/5 KB207 . . . . . **CE 394.261**
Vamos a cazar un oso./ROSEN, M/n.d./P-2/2 KB814 . . . . 398.8
Van Gogh. /HUGHES, A/1994/6-A/9 KE370 . . . . **B GOGH, V.**
Van Gogh. /CRISPINO, E/1996/6-A/12 KD499 . . . . 759.9492
Van Gogh Cafe. /RYLANT, C/1995/5-A/7 KH664 . . . . **Fic**
Vanished!: the mysterious disappearance of Amelia Earhart. /KULLING, M/
1996/2-4/7 KE328 . . . . **B EARHART, A.**
VARIATIONS IN LIFE SCIENCE INVESTIGATIONS (CD-ROM). /1996/
6-A/KC298 . . . . **CDR 577**
Vegetable show. /BROWN, LK/1995/P-2/2 KD289 . . . . 641.6
Vejigante masquerader. /DELACRE, L/1993/1-3/4 KF458 . . . . **E**
Velveteen Rabbit; or, How toys become real. /WILLIAMS, M/1988/
3-5/6 KH864 . . . . **CE Fic**
Velveteen Rabbit; or, How toys become real (Braille)./WILLIAMS, M/n.d./
3-5/6 KH864 . . . . **CE Fic**
Velveteen Rabbit; or, How toys become real (Sound recording cassette)./
WILLIAMS, M/n.d./3-5/6 KH864 . . . . **CE Fic**
Velveteen Rabbit; or, How toys become real (Talking book)./WILLIAMS,
M/c1975/3-5/6 KH864 . . . . **CE Fic**
Velveteen Rabbit; or, How toys become real (Talking book)./WILLIAMS,
M/n.d./3-5/6 KH864 . . . . **CE Fic**
Venden gorras: la historia de un vendedor ambulante, unos monos y sus
travesuras./SLOBODKINA, E/1995/P-2/1 KG519 . . . . **CE E**
Venden gorras: la historia de un vendedor ambulante, unos monos y sus
travesuras (Kit)./SLOBODKINA, E/1995/P-2/1 KG519 . . . . . **CE E**
VENTURE INTO CULTURES: A RESOURCE BOOK OF MULTICULTURAL
MATERIALS AND PROGRAMS. /1992//KA024 . . . . . **PROF 011.62**
Venus. /SCHLOSS, M/1991/4-6/8 KC033 . . . . 523.42
Venus. /SIMON, S/1992/3-6/8 KC034 . . . . 523.42
Verdadera historia de los tres cerditos!/SCIESZKA, J/1991/
K-3/2 KG421 . . . . **CE E**
Verdadera historia de los tres cerditos (Kit)./SCIESZKA, J/1997/
K-3/2 KG421 . . . . **CE E**
Verdi. /CANNON, J/1997/K-2/3 KF336 . . . . **E**
Vermont. /FRADIN, DB/1993/4-6/4 KE934. . . . . 974.3
Veronica the show-off. /ROBINSON, NK/c1982/3-6/4 KH642 . . . . . **Fic**
Vertebrates. /SILVERSTEIN, A/1996/A/9 KC581. 596
Very busy spider. /CARLE, E/1985/P-2/2 KF346 . . . . **E**
Very busy spider (Braille)./CARLE, E/n.d./P-2/2 KF346 . . . . **E**
Very hungry caterpillar. /CARLE, E/1981/P-1/6 KF347 . . . . **E**
Very important day. /HEROLD, MR/1995/K-3/2 KF715 . . . . **E**
Very important day (Sound recording cassette)./HEROLD, MR/1997/
K-3/2 KF715 . . . . **E**
Very lonely firefly. /CARLE, E/1995/P-2/2 KF348 . . . . **E**
Very noisy girl. /WINTHROP, E/1991/K-2/2 KG747. . . . . **E**
Very scary. /JOHNSTON, T/1995/P-2/3 KF842 . . . . **E**
Very special house. /KRAUSS, R/c1953/P-1/1 KF923 . . . . **E**
Very worst monster. /HUTCHINS, P/1985/P-2/2 KF806 . . . . **CE E**
Very worst monster (Kit)./HUTCHINS, P/1988/P-2/2 KF806 . . . . . **CE E**
Viaje del Amanecer./LEWIS, CS/n.d./5-A/6 KH405 . . . . **CE Fic**
Vico y boa./FIENBERG, A/1992/5-6/7 KH113 . . . . **Fic**
Victory in the Pacific. /MARRIN, A/1983/4-6/7 KE671 . . . . . . 940.54
VIDEO SOURCE BOOK. /1979-//KA030 . . . . **PROF 016.791**
Viejecita que no le tenia miedo a nada./WILLIAMS, L/1996/
P-2/4 KG730 . . . . **CE E**
Viernes embrujado./RODGERS, M/1987/5-6/5 KH647 . . . . **CE Fic**
Vietnam: rebuilding a nation. /GARLAND, S/1990/5-6/7 KE717 . . . 959.7
Vietnam Women's Memorial. /KENT, D/1995/4-6/7 KE720 . . . 959.704
View from Saturday. /KONIGSBURG, EL/1996/5-A/7 KH377 . . . . **Fic**
VIEW FROM THE REAR TERRACE (Videocassette). /1991/
A/KB984 . . . . **VCR 513.2**
Viking. /MARGESON, SM/1994/4-6/7 KE693 948
Viking and the Mars landing. /VOGT, G/1991/A/10 KD132 . . . . 629.43
Village basket weaver. /LONDON, J/1996/2-3/6 KG029 . . . . **E**
Village full of valentines. /STEVENSON, J/1995/1-3/2 KG568 . . . . . . **E**
Village of blue stone. /TRIMBLE, S/1990/4-6/6 KF063 979

Village of round and square houses. /GRIFALCONI, A/1986/
3-4/6 KB739 . . . . **CE 398.27**
Village of round and square houses (Videocassette)./GRIFALCONI, A/
1989/3-4/6 KB739 . . . . **CE 398.27**
VILLAGE STEW (Videocassette). /1987/K-3/KB782 . . . . . . **VCR 398.27**
Vincent van Gogh. /HARRISON, P/1996/4-6/7 KE369 . . . . **B GOGH, V.**
VIOLENCE IN THE MEDIA (Microcomputer program). /1994/
5-A/KA802 . . . . **MCP 302.23**
Virginia. /SIRVAITIS, K/1991/4-6/6 KE981. . . . . 975.5
Virginia Colony. /FRADIN, DB/1986/A/10 KE977 . . . . 975.5
Virtual Cody. /DUFFEY, B/1997/1-4/2 KH088 . . . . **Fic**
Virtual war. /SKURZYNSKI, G/1997/5-A/4 KH716 . . . . **Fic**
Virus invaders. /NOURSE, AE/1992/A/10 KD012 616
VIRUS! (Videocassette). /1994/A/KD013 . . . . **VCR 616**
Viruses. /FACKLAM, H/1994/5-A/8 KC377 . . . . 579.2
Visions: stories about women artists. /SILLS, L/1993/4-A/6 KD380 . 709.2
Visit to Grandma's. /CARLSON, N/1991/P-2/2 KF353 . . . . **E**
Visit to the big house. /BUTTERWORTH, O/1993/3-5/5 KG956 . . . . . **Fic**
Visit to William Blake's inn: poems for innocent and experienced travelers. /
WILLARD, N/1981/5-A/KE042 . . . . **CE 811**
Visit to William Blake's inn: poems for innocent and experienced travelers
(Braille)./WILLARD, N/n.d./5-A/KE042 . . . . **CE 811**
Visit to William Blake's inn: poems for innocent and experienced travelers
(Sound recording cassette)./WILLARD, N/n.d./5-A/KE042 . . . . **CE 811**
VISIT WITH BILL MARTIN, JR. (Videocassette). /1996/
3-4/KE460 . . . . **VCR B MARTIN, B.**
VISIT WITH EVE BUNTING (Videocassette). /1991/
4-6/KE269 . . . . **VCR B BUNTING, E.**
VISIT WITH MARVIN TERBAN (Videocassette). /c1991, 1992/
5-A/KE560. . . . . **VCR B TERBAN, M.**
Visita de Osito./MINARIK, EH/1994/P-1/2 KG141. . . . . **CE E**
Vista./PARRAMON, JM/1985/P-1/1 KC974. . . . . 612.8
VISUAL DICTIONARY OF ANCIENT CIVILIZATIONS. /1994/
4-6/8 KE622 930
VISUAL DICTIONARY OF DINOSAURS. /1993/3-A/8 KC267 . . . . 567.9
VISUAL DICTIONARY OF MILITARY UNIFORMS. /1992/
4-A/8 KA985 . . . . 355.1
VISUAL DICTIONARY OF PLANTS. /1992/P-A/A KC394 580
VISUAL DICTIONARY OF SHIPS AND SAILING. /1991/
4-A/6 KB154 . . . . 387.2
VISUAL DICTIONARY OF SPECIAL MILITARY FORCES. /1993/
4-A/8 KA987 356
VISUAL DICTIONARY OF THE EARTH. /1993/1-A/9 KC151 550
VISUAL DICTIONARY OF THE HORSE. /1994/5-A/7 KD209 . . . 636.1
VISUAL DICTIONARY OF THE HUMAN BODY. /1991/4-6/8 KC907 . 611
VISUAL DICTIONARY OF THE SKELETON. /1995/4-A/8 KC286. . . 573.7
VISUAL DICTIONARY OF THE UNIVERSE. /1993/3-A/11 KC004 . . . 520
Viva! Una pinata!/KLEVEN, E/1996/K-2/2 KF910 . . . . **E**
Voice for the people: the life and work of Harold Courlander. /JAFFE, N/
1997//KA367 . . . . **PROF B COURLAND**
Voice of the people: American democracy in action. /MAESTRO, B/1996/
4-6/8 KA915 . . . . 324.973
Voices from the fields: children of migrant farmworkers tell their stories. /
ATKIN, SB/1993/A/6 KA833 . . . . 305.5
Voices of the heart. /YOUNG, E/1997/A/7 KA675 179
Voices of the river: adventures on the Delaware. /CHERIPKO, J/1996/
5-A/5 KE962 . . . . 974.9
Voices of the winds: Native American legends. /EDMONDS, M/1989/
/KA266 . . . . **PROF 398.2**
Volcano. /LAMPTON, C/1991/4-6/7 KC157 . . . . 551.21
Volcano and earthquake. /VAN ROSE, S/1992/3-6/7 KC160 . . . 551.21
Volcano: the eruption and healing of Mount St. Helens. /LAUBER, P/1986/
P-A/6 KC158 . . . . **CE 551.21**
Volcanoes. /SIMON, S/1988/3-6/6 KC159 . . . . 551.21
Voyage of the Dawn Treader./LEWIS, CS/1994/5-A/6 KH405 . . . **CE Fic**
Voyage of the Dawn Treader (Braille)./LEWIS, CS/n.d./
5-A/6 KH405 . . . . **CE Fic**
Voyage of the Dawn Treader (Sound recording cassette)./LEWIS, CS/n.d./
5-A/6 KH405 . . . . **CE Fic**
Voyage of the Dawn Treader (Talking book)./LEWIS, CS/n.d./
5-A/6 KH405 . . . . **CE Fic**
VOYAGE OF THE LOGGERHEAD (Videocassette). /1995/
3-6/KC624 . . . . **VCR 597.92**
Voyager: an adventure to the edge of the solar system. /RIDE, S/1992/
3-6/7 KC030 . . . . 523.4
Voyager: an adventure to the edge of the solar system (Sound recording
cassette)./RIDE, S/1996/3-6/7 KC030 . . . . 523.4
Voyager to the planets. /APFEL, NH/1991/3-6/7 KC022 . . . . . . 523.4
Vulpes, the red fox. /GEORGE, JC/c1948, 1996/5-A/5 KH160 . . . . **Fic**
Wackiest nature riddles on earth. /ARTELL, M/1992/3-6/KD724. 793.735
Wacky Wednesday. /LESIEG, T/c1974/1-2/1 KF961 . . . . **E**
WAGGING TAILS: THE DOG AND PUPPY MUSIC VIDEO (Videocassette).
/1994/P-6/KD225. . . . . **VCR 636.7**
Wagon. /JOHNSTON, T/1996/2-5/2 KF843 . . . . **E**

Wagon train: a family goes West in 1865. /WRIGHT, CC/1995/
4-6/3 KF052 . . . . **978**
Wagon wheels. /BRENNER, B/1978/1-3/1 KF259 . . . . **CE E**
Wagon wheels (Braille)./BRENNER, B/n.d./1-3/1 KF259 . . . . **CE E**
Wagon wheels (Kit)./BRENNER, B/1995/1-3/1 KF259 . . . . . . **CE E**
Wagonload of fish. /BODNAR, JZ/1996/K-2/5 KB532 . . . . . . **398.24**
Wah Ming Chang: artist and master of special effects. /RILEY, GB/1995/
5-6/6 KE285 . . . . **B CHANG, W.**
Wainscott weasel. /SEIDLER, T/1993/4-6/5 KH691 . . . . **Fic**
Waiting for Anya. /MORPURGO, M/1991/5-A/7 KH515 . . . . . . **Fic**
Waiting for baby Joe. /COLLINS, PL/1990/K-3/2 KD038 . . . . . . **618.92**
Wake up, city! /TRESSELT, A/c1957, 1990/1-3/5 KG616 . . . . . **E**
Wake up, city! (Sound recording cassette)./TRESSELT, A/1993/
1-3/5 KG616 . . . . **E**
Waking upside down. /HECKMAN, P/1996/1-3/6 KF693 . . . . **E**
Walk in the rainforest. /PRATT, KJ/1992/K-6/7 KC322 . . . . . . **577.34**
Walk two moons. /CREECH, S/1994/5-A/5 KH037 . . . . **Fic**
WALKER. /1991/4-6/KA854 . . . . **VCR 305.8**
Walking stones. /HUNTER, M/1996/6-A/8 KH295 . . . . **Fic**
WALKING THE BRIDGE OF YOUR NOSE. /1995/2-4/KE113. . . **821.008**
Wallpaper from space. /PINKWATER, DM/1996/2-5/3 KH605 . . . . . **Fic**
Walrus: on location. /DARLING, K/1991/5-6/6 KC868 . . . . . . **599.79**
Walruses. /ROTTER, C/1993/3-5/5 KC871 . . . . **599.79**
Walt Disney: creator of Mickey Mouse. /COLE, MD/1996/
4-6/8 KE322 . . . . **B DISNEY, W.**
Walter Dean Myers. /PATRICK-WEXLER, D/1996/
5-6/6 KE475 . . . . **B MYERS, W.**
Walter's tail. /ERNST, LC/1992/P-2/3 KF534 . . . . **E**
Wanderings of Odysseus: the story of the Odyssey. /SUTCLIFF, R/1996/
5-A/7 KE128 . . . . **883**
Wanna bet?: science challenges to fool you. /COBB, V/1993/
4-6/6 KD746 . . . . **793.8**
Wanted: best friend. /MONSON, AM/1997/K-2/2 KG152 . . . . **E**
Wanted...Mud Blossom./BYARS, BC/1991/4-A/4 KG962 . . . . . . **CE Fic**
Wanted...Mud Blossom (Sound recording cassette)./BYARS, BC/1995/
4-A/4 KG962 . . . . **CE Fic**
Wanted...Mud Blossom (Talking book)./BYARS, BC/1995/
4-A/4 KG962 . . . . **CE Fic**
War between the Vowels and the Consonants. /TURNER, P/1996/
1-3/3 KG630 . . . . **E**
War boy: a country childhood. /FOREMAN, M/1990/
4-A/6 KE347 . . . . **B FOREMAN, M.**
War comes to Willy Freeman. /COLLIER, JL/1983/5-6/6 KH017 . . . **Fic**
War for independence: the story of the American Revolution. /MARRIN, A/
1988/5-6/9 KE882 . . . . **973.3**
Warm as wool. /SANDERS, SR/1992/3-5/5 KH675 . . . . **Fic**
Warm Place. /FARMER, N/1995/4-A/3 KH110 . . . . **Fic**
Warrior and the wise man. /WISNIEWSKI, D/1989/1-3/5 KG752 . . . . . **E**
Warrior maiden: a Hopi legend. /SCHECTER, E/1992/
1-2/2 KB485 . . . . **398.22**
Warriors, warthogs, and wisdom: growing up in Africa. /WATSON, L/
1997/4-6/7 KE589 . . . . **B WATSON, L.**
Warthogs. /ROTHAUS, D/1995/4-6/8 KC787 . . . . **599.63**
Washington. /POWELL, ES/1993/4-6/6 KF094 . . . . **979.7**
Washington. /FRADIN, DB/1994/4-6/6 KF093 . . . . **979.7**
Washington, D.C. /JOHNSTON, J/1993/4-6/7 KE971 . . . . **975.3**
Wasps. /JOHNSON, SA/1984/5-6/8 KC574 . . . . **595.79**
Watch out for clever women!/Cuidado con las mujeres astutas!: Hispanic
folktales. /HAYES, J/1994/2-5/4 KB315 . . . . **398.2**
Watch out for sharks! /ARNOLD, C/1991/4-6/7 KC590 . . . . . **597.3**
Watch out for the chicken feet in your soup. /DE PAOLA, T/1974/
K-2/2 KF481 . . . . **E**
Watch the stars come out. /LEVINSON, R/c1985, 1995/K-2/2 KF969 . . **E**
Watchers: a mystery at Alton Towers. /CRESSWELL, H/1994/
5-A/3 KH040 . . . . **Fic**
Watching desert wildlife. /ARNOLD, C/1994/4-6/7 KC361 . . . . **578.754**
Watching foxes. /ARNOSKY, J/1985/P-K/1 KF170 . . . . **E**
Watching water birds. /ARNOSKY, J/1997/4-6/6 KC674 . . . . . **598.176**
Water. /WALPOLE, B/1990/K-2/5 KC141 . . . . **546**
Water. /MCHUGH, C/1993/4-A/7 KD375 . . . . **704.9**
Water insects. /JOHNSON, SA/1989/4-A/7 KC543 . . . . **595.7**
Water music: poems for children. /YOLEN, J/1995/2-6/KE051 . . . **811**
WATER ROCKETS I (Videocassette). /1994/5-A/KA291 . **VCR PROF 530**
WATER ROCKETS II (Videocassette)./1994/5-A/KA291 . **VCR PROF 530**
Water up, water down: the hydrologic cycle. /WALKER, SM/1992/
4-6/7 KC184 . . . . **551.48**
Watermelon Day. /APPELT, K/1996/K-2/2 KF164 . . . . **E**
Water's journey. /SCHMID, E/1989/2-4/7 KG408 . . . . **E**
Watership Down. /ADAMS, R/c1972, 1974/6-A/5 KG813 . . . . . . **Fic**
Watership Down (Braille)./ADAMS, R/n.d./6-A/5 KG813 . . . . . . **Fic**
Waterskiing and kneeboarding. /WALKER, C/1992/4-A/7 KD851 . . **797.3**
Watsons go to Birmingham--1963: a novel./CURTIS, CP/1995/
6-A/7 KH048 . . . . **CE Fic**

Watsons go to Birmingham--1963: a novel (Sound recording cassette)./
CURTIS, CP/1997/6-A/7 KH048 . . . . **CE Fic**
Watsons go to Birmingham--1963 (Talking book)./CURTIS, CP/1996/
6-A/7 KH048 . . . . **CE Fic**
Wave of the Sea-Wolf. /WISNIEWSKI, D/1994/1-3/6 KG753 . . . . . . **E**
Waving: a counting book. /SIS, P/1988/P-2/KG512. . . . . **E**
Way I feel--sometimes. /DE REGNIERS, BS/1988/1-4/KD931 . . . . . **811**
Way of our people. /GRIESE, AA/1997/5-6/5 KH203 . . . . **Fic**
Way of the ferret: finding and using educational resources on the Internet.
2nd. ed. /HARRIS, J/1995/KA046 . . . . **PROF 025.04**
Way of the grizzly. /PATENT, DH/1987/5-6/8 KC860 . . . . . . **599.784**
Way things work. /MACAULAY, D/1988/A/11 KC881 . . . . **600**
Way things work (CD-ROM). /MACAULAY, D/1996/
3-A/KC882 . . . . **CDR 600**
Way west: journal of a pioneer woman. /KNIGHT, AS/1993/
5-6/5 KE197 . . . . **917.8**
Way west: journal of a pioneer woman (Sound recording cassette)./
KNIGHT, AS/1996/5-6/5 KE197 . . . . **917.8**
Wayside School is falling down. /SACHAR, L/1989/3-5/4 KH666 . **CE Fic**
Wayside School is falling down (Talking book)./SACHAR, L/1994/
3-5/4 KH666 . . . . **CE Fic**
We are America's children (Compact disc). /JENKINS, E/1989/
1-6/KD577. . . . . **CD 789.2**
We are America's children (Sound recording cassette)./JENKINS, E/1989/
1-6/KD577. . . . . **CD 789.2**
We came from Vietnam. /STANEK, M/1985/4-6/7 KA861 . . . . . . **305.8**
WE CAN WORK IT OUT!: CONFLICT RESOLUTION (Videocassette). /
1994/K-2/KA165 . . . . **VCR PROF 303.6**
We hate rain! /STEVENSON, J/1988/P-3/2 KG569 . . . . **E**
We have a baby. /FALWELL, C/1993/P-K/1 KF542 . . . . **E**
We have marched together: the working children's crusade. /CURRIE, S/
1997/5-6/8 KA936 . . . . **331.3**
We hide, you seek. /ARUEGO, J/1979/P-K/1 KF172 . . . . **E**
We recycle and other songs for Earth keepers (Sound recording cassette). /
VAN MANENS /1990/K-4/KD664 . . . . **SRC 789.3**
We remember the holocaust. /ADLER, DA/c1989, 1995/
5-6/8 KE656 . . . . **940.53**
We remember the holocaust (Sound recording cassette)./ADLER, DA/
1993/5-6/8 KE656 . . . . **940.53**
We shall not be moved: the women's factory strike of 1909. /DASH, J/
1996/6-A/8 KA939 . . . . **331.4**
Weapons and warfare: from the stone age to the space age. /MELTZER,
M/1996/4-6/8 KA983 . . . . **355.02**
Weather. /SIMON, S/1993/3-6/7 KC193 . . . . **551.5**
Weather. /PLUCKROSE, H/1994/P-2/4 KC192 . . . . **551.5**
Weather companion. /LOCKHART, G/1988//KA293 . . . . . . **PROF 551.5**
Weather everywhere. /CASEY, D/1995/P-2/6 KC189 . . . . **551.5**
Weather forecasting. /GIBBONS, G/1987/2-4/7 KC224 . . . . . . **551.63**
Weather: poems. /HOPKINS, LB/1994/K-3/KE064 . . . . **811.008**
Weather sky. /MCMILLAN, B/1991/5-A/7 KC220 . . . . **551.6**
Weather watch. /WYATT, V/1990/3-6/6 KC222 . . . . **551.6**
Weather words and what they mean. /GIBBONS, G/1990/
K-4/4 KC218 . . . . **551.6**
Weatherwise: learning about the weather. /KAHL, JD/1992/
4-6/6 KC219 . . . . **551.6**
WEAVE AND SPIN (Videocassette). /1986/6-A/KC533. . . . . **VCR 595.4**
Web weavers and other spiders. /KALMAN, B/1997/3-5/5 KC526 . **595.4**
Webelos Scout book. Rev. ed. /BOY SCOUTS OF AMERICA /1987/
4-6/3 KB075 . . . . **369.43**
WEBSTER'S GEOGRAPHICAL DICTIONARY. 3rd. ed. /1997/
5-6/KA471 . . . . **REF 910.3**
WEBSTER'S INTERMEDIATE DICTIONARY: A NEW SCHOOL
DICTIONARY. /c1977, 1994/4-6/KB837 . . . . **423**
WEBSTER'S NEW WORLD CHILDREN'S DICTIONARY. New ed. /1997/
3-5/KB838 . . . . **423**
Week of raccoons. /WHELAN, G/1988/K-2/5 KG710 . . . . **E**
Weekend with Wendell. /HENKES, K/1986/P-2/2 KF712 . . . . **E**
WEEKLY READER. /1947-/K-6/KA550 . . . . **PER 050**
WEEKLY READER--EDITION 1./K-6/KA550 . . . . **PER 050**
WEEKLY READER-EDITION 2./K-6/KA550 . . . . **PER 050**
WEEKLY READER-EDITION 3./K-6/KA550 . . . . **PER 050**
WEEKLY READER-EDITION 4./K-6/KA550 . . . . **PER 050**
WEEKLY READER-EDITION 5./K-6/KA550 . . . . **PER 050**
WEEKLY READER-SENIOR EDITION./K-6/KA550 . . . . **PER 050**
Weird parents. /WOOD, A/1990/K-2/4 KG767 . . . . **E**
Weirdos of the universe, unite! /SERVICE, PF/1992/6-A/6 KH701 . . . **Fic**
Welcome back, Sun. /EMBERLEY, M/1993/1-3/3 KF524 . . . . **E**
Welcome home! /WHITE, S/1995/4-6/6 KD396 . . . . **728**
Welcome to the green house. /YOLEN, J/1993/K-3/4 KC329 . . . . **577.34**
Welcoming babies. /KNIGHT, MB/1994/P-1/2 KA875 . . . . **306.87**
Well: David's story. /TAYLOR, MD/1995/4-A/4 KH781 . . . . **Fic**
We'll never forget you, Roberto Clemente. /ENGEL, T/1997/
2-4/2 KE293 . . . . **B CLEMENTE, R.**

We'll race you, Henry: a story about Henry Ford. /MITCHELL, B/1986/ 4-5/3 KE346 . . . . **B FORD, H.**

Well wishers (Sound recording cassette)./EAGER, E/n.d./ 4-6/6 KH094 . . . . **Fic**

WE'RE A FAMILY (Videocassette). /1992/3-5/KA874 . . . . . **VCR 306.85**

We're going on a bear hunt. /ROSEN, M/1989/P-2/2 KB814 . . . . **398.8**

We're going on a bear hunt (Sound recording cassette)./ROSEN, M/ 1993/P-2/2 KB814 . . . . **398.8**

We're making breakfast for Mother. /NEITZEL, S/1997/P-1/2 KG169 . . **E**

West by covered wagon: retracing the pioneer trails. /PATENT, DH/1995/ 2-4/8 KF043 . . . . **978**

West Virginia. /FRADIN, DB/1994/4-6/7 KE975 . . . . **975.4**

WESTERN DRY LANDS (Videocassette)./1989/5-6/KE181 . . . . **VCR 917**

Western forests. /WHITNEY, S/1985/A/KC313 . . . . **577.3**

Western wind: a novel. /FOX, P/1993/5-A/5 KH141 . . . . **Fic**

Western wind: a novel (Sound recording cassette)./FOX, P/1995/ 5-A/5 KH141 . . . . **Fic**

Westing game. /RASKIN, E/c1978/5-6/5 KH619 . . . . **Fic**

Westing game (Braille)./RASKIN, E/n.d./5-6/5 KH619 . . . . **Fic**

Westing game (Sound recording cassette)./RASKIN, E/n.d./ 5-6/5 KH619 . . . . **Fic**

Westmark. /ALEXANDER, L/1982/5-6/6 KG841 . . . . **Fic**

Westmark (Braille)./ALEXANDER, L/n.d./5-6/6 KG841 . . . . **Fic**

Westmark (Sound recording cassette)./ALEXANDER, L/n.d./ 5-6/6 KG841 . . . . **Fic**

Wet weather: rain showers and snowfall. /KAHL, JD/1992/ 4-6/7 KC212 . . . . **551.57**

Wet world. /SIMON, N/1995/P-1/3 KG508 . . . . **E**

We've all got stories: songs from the Dream Project (Compact disc). / SAPP, J/1996/K-6/KD655 . . . . **CD 789.3**

We've all got stories: songs from the Dream Project (Sound recording cassette)./SAPP, J/1996/K-6/KD655 . . . . **CD 789.3**

Whales. /SIMON, S/1989/5-6/6 KC777 . . . . **599.51**

Whales. /GIBBONS, G/1991/K-4/3 KC769 . . . . **599.5**

Whales of the world. /BEHRENS, J/1987/3-5/4 KC765 . . . . **599.5**

Whales: the gentle giants. /MILTON, J/1989/1-3/2 KC774 . . . . . **599.5**

Whalewatch. /BEHRENS, J/1978/2-4/4 KC766 . . . . **599.5**

Whaling days. /CARRICK, C/1993/4-5/6 KD243 . . . . **639.2**

Whaling days (Sound recording cassette)./CARRICK, C/1995/ 4-5/6 KD243 . . . . **639.2**

WHAT A MORNING! THE CHRISTMAS STORY IN BLACK SPIRITUALS. / 1987/K-6/KD532 . . . . **782.25**

What a wonderful day to be a cow. /LESSER, C/1995/K-2/3 KF963 . . . **E**

What a wonderful world. /WEISS, GD/1995/P-2/2 KG692 . . . . **E**

What about my goldfish? /GREENWOOD, PD/1993/1-3/2 KF644 . . . . **E**

What am I?: looking through shapes at apples and grapes. /CHARLES, NN/1994/P-2/2 KF378 . . . . **E**

WHAT ARE ECOSYSTEMS? (Videocassette). /1975/ 4-6/KC299 . . . . **VCR 577**

What can one little person do? (Compact disc)./ROGERS, S/1992/ P-2/KD654 . . . . **SRC 789.3**

What can one little person do? (Sound recording cassette). /ROGERS, S/ 1992/P-2/KD654 . . . . **SRC 789.3**

What do authors do? /CHRISTELOW, E/1995/2-4/2 KD866 . . . . **808.06**

What do children read next?: a reader's guide to fiction for children. / COLBORN, C/1997/KA031 . . . . **PROF 016.80883**

What do we know about Hinduism? /GANERI, A/1995/ 5-A/9 KA762 . . . . **294.5**

What do we know about Islam? /HUSAIN, S/1996/4-6/9 KA786 . . . **297**

What do you see and how do you see it?: exploring light, color, and vision. /LAUBER, P/1994/1-6/4 KC113 . . . . **535**

What food is this? /HAUSHERR, R/1994/K-2/2 KD266 . . . . **641.3**

What happened to Patrick's dinosaurs?/CARRICK, C/1986/ K-2/4 KF361 . . . . **CE E**

What happened to Patrick's dinosaurs? (Braille)./CARRICK, C/n.d./ K-2/4 KF361 . . . . **CE E**

What happened to Patrick's dinosaurs? (Kit)./CARRICK, C/1988/ K-2/4 KF361 . . . . **CE E**

What happened to Patrick's dinosaurs? (Sound recording cassette)./ CARRICK, C/n.d./K-2/4 KF361 . . . . **CE E**

What happened to the dinosaurs? /BRANLEY, FM/1989/ 2-4/5 KC244 . . . . **567.9**

What happens to a hamburger? Rev. ed. /SHOWERS, P/1985/ K-2/3 KC942 . . . . **612.3**

What his father did. /GREENE, JD/1992/2-4/5 KB305 . . . . **398.2**

What I had was singing: the story of Marian Anderson. /FERRIS, J/1994/ 5-A/6 KE236 . . . . **B ANDERSON, M.**

WHAT IS A BELLYBUTTON?: FIRST QUESTIONS AND ANSWERS ABOUT THE HUMAN BODY. /1993/P-K/2 KC929 . . . . **612**

WHAT IS A BELLYBUTTON?: FUN AND INTERACTIVE QUESTIONS AND ANSWERS ABOUT THE HUMAN BODY (CD-ROM). /1994/ 2-6/KC930. . . . . **CDR 612**

What is a bird? /SNEDDEN, R/1993/4-6/6 KC665 . . . . **598**

What is a cat? /HIRSCHI, R/1991/K-4/2 KD233 . . . . **636.8**

WHAT IS A LEAF? (Videocassette). /1991/K-3/KC401 . . . . . **VCR 581.4**

WHAT IS A PLANT? (Videocassette). /1991/3-6/KC395 . . . . . **VCR 580**

What is an insect? /SNEDDEN, R/1993/4-6/6 KC548. . . . . **595.7**

What Jamie saw. /COMAN, C/1995/5-A/6 KH018 . . . . **Fic**

What Joe saw. /HINES, AG/1994/K-2/3 KF730 . . . . **E**

What lives in a shell? /ZOEHFELD, KW/1994/P-1/2 KC517 . . . . . . **594**

What makes a Bruegel a Bruegel? /MUHLBERGER, R/1993/ 5-A/8 KD502 . . . . **759.9493**

What makes a Cassatt a Cassatt? /MUHLBERGER, R/1994/ 5-A/7 KD489 . . . . **759.13**

What makes a Degas a Degas? /MUHLBERGER, R/1993/ 5-A/7 KD491 . . . . **759.4**

What makes a Goya a Goya? /MUHLBERGER, R/1994/ 5-A/7 KD498 . . . . **759.6**

What makes a Leonardo a Leonardo? /MUHLBERGER, R/1994/ 5-A/7 KD496 . . . . **759.5**

What makes a Monet a Monet? /MUHLBERGER, R/1993/ 5-A/7 KD492 . . . . **759.4**

What makes a Picasso a Picasso? /MUHLBERGER, R/1994/ 5-A/7 KD493 . . . . **759.4**

What makes a Raphael a Raphael? /MUHLBERGER, R/1993/ 5-A/7 KD497 . . . . **759.5**

What makes a Rembrandt a Rembrandt? /MUHLBERGER, R/1993/ 5-A/7 KD500 . . . . **759.9492**

What makes a shadow? Rev. ed. /BULLA, CR/1994/ K-2/2 KC106 . . . . **CE 535**

What makes a shadow? Rev. ed. (Kit)./BULLA, CR/1996/ K-2/2 KC106 . . . . **CE 535**

What makes it rain? The story of a raindrop. /BRANDT, K/1982/ P-K/2 KC209 . . . . **551.57**

What makes popcorn pop?: and other questions about the world around us. /MYERS, J/c1991, 1994/3-6/7 KB868 . . . . **500**

What, me worry?: how to hang in when your problems stress you out. / FLEMING, A/1992/4-6/8 KA624 . . . . **152.4**

What rhymes with eel?: a word-and-picture flap book. /ZIEFERT, H/1996/ P-1/2 KG798 . . . . **E**

What rot!: nature's mighty recycler. /RING, E/1996/1-3/3 KC304 . . **577.1**

What time is it? /SMITH, AG/1992/4-A/8 KC073 . . . . **529**

What was it like before television? /HANKIN, R/1995/ 1-3/2 KD679 . . . . **790.1**

WHAT WE LEARN ABOUT EARTH FROM SPACE (Videocassette). /1995/ 5-8/KD133 . . . . **VCR 629.43**

What we like. /ROCKWELL, AF/1992/P/KB849 . . . . **428.1**

What will Mommy do when I'm at school? /JOHNSON, D/1990/ K-1/2 KF836 . . . . **E**

What will the weather be like today? /ROGERS, P/1990/ P-1/2 KC221 . . . . **551.6**

What would Mama do? /ENDERLE, JR/1995/K-2/2 KF526 . . . . . . **E**

WHAT'S A GOOD BOOK? (Videocassette). /1993/ /KA094 . . . . **VCR PROF 028.5**

What's alive? /ZOEHFELD, KW/1995/1-3/2 KC301 . . . . **577**

What's for lunch? /SCHINDEL, J/1994/P-1/2 KG407 . . . . **E**

What's happening to my body? Book for girls. Rev. ed. /MADARAS, L/ 1983/5-6/9 KC952 . . . . **612.6**

WHAT'S IN A NAME (Videocassette)./1991/4-6/KA851 . . . . **VCR 305.8**

What's inside us? /GANERI, A/1995/5-6/8 KC919 . . . . **612**

What's it like to be a fish? /PFEFFER, W/1996/K-3/3 KC585 . . . . . **597**

WHAT'S OUT THERE?: OUR SOLAR SYSTEM AND BEYOND (Videocassette). /1997/5-A/KC018. . . . . **VCR 523.2**

What's smaller than a pygmy shrew? /WELLS, RE/1995/ 3-6/5 KC140 . . . . **539.7**

What's the big idea, Ben Franklin? /FRITZ, J/c1976/ 5-6/7 KE355 . . . . **CE B FRANKLIN, B.**

What's the big idea, Ben Franklin? (Kit)./FRITZ, J/1977/ 5-6/7 KE355 . . . . **CE B FRANKLIN, B.**

What's the big idea, Ben Franklin? (Sound recording cassette)./FRITZ, J/ n.d./5-6/7 KE355 . . . . **CE B FRANKLIN, B.**

What's the big idea, Ben Franklin? (Talking book)./FRITZ, J/1977/ 5-6/7 KE355 . . . . **CE B FRANKLIN, B.**

What's the big idea, Ben Franklin? (Videocassette)./FRITZ, J/1993/ 5-6/7 KE355 . . . . **CE B FRANKLIN, B.**

What's the difference?: a guide to some familiar animal look-alikes. / LACEY, EA/1993/5-6/8 KC450 . . . . **591**

What's the difference between apes and monkeys and other living things? / SOUCIE, G/1995/4-6/7 KC271 . . . . **571**

What's the difference between lenses and prisms and other scientific things? /SOUCIE, G/1995/4-6/7 KB872 . . . . **500**

What's under my bed? /STEVENSON, J/1983/K-3/4 KG558 . . . . . **CE E**

What's under my bed (Videocassette)./STEVENSON, J/n.d./ K-3/4 KG558 . . . . **CE E**

What's what?: a guessing game. /SERFOZO, M/1996/P-1/2 KG443 . . . **E**

WHAT'S WRONG WITH BEER? (Videocassette). /1992/ 5-6/KD003 . . . . **VCR 613.81**

What's your name?: from Ariel to Zoe. /SANDERS, M/1995/
K-3/2 KE611 . . . . **929.4**

Wheat. /JOHNSON, SA/1990/5-6/7 KD151 . . . . **633.1**

Wheel on the school. /DEJONG, M/c1954/4-6/3 KH070 . . . . **Fic**

Wheel on the school (Braille). /DEJONG, M/n.d./4-6/3 KH070 . . . . . . **Fic**

Wheel on the school (Sound recording cassette). /DEJONG, M/n.d./
4-6/3 KH070 . . . . **Fic**

Wheels around. /ROTNER, S/1995/P-2/3 KD053 . . . . **621.8**

Wheels at work: building and experimenting with models of machines. /
ZUBROWSKI, B/1986/5-6/8 KD054 . . . . **621.8**

Wheels on the bus. /RAFFI /c1988, 1990/P-2/KD653 . . . . **789.3**

When Africa was home. /WILLIAMS, KL/1991/K-3/2 KG729 . . . . . . **E**

When Artie was little. /SCHWARTZ, HB/1996/1-3/2 KG417 . . . . **E**

When birds could talk and bats could sing: the adventures of Bruh Sparrow,
Sis Wren, and their friends. /HAMILTON, V/1996/
2-5/2 KB582 . . . . **398.24**

When clay sings. /BAYLOR, B/c1972, 1987/3-5/6 KE748 . . . . **970.1**

When dinosaurs die: a guide to understanding death. /BROWN, LK/1996/
K-4/5 KA648 . . . . **155.9**

When Eric's mom fought cancer. /VIGNA, J/1993/1-3/3 KG654 . . . . **E**

When I am old with you. /JOHNSON, A/1990/P-2/6 KF834 . . . . **E**

WHEN I GET MAD (Videocassette). /1994/5-6/KA631 . . . . **VCR 152.4**

When I left my village. /SCHUR, MR/1996/4-A/5 KH683 . . . . **Fic**

When I see my doctor. /KUKLIN, S/1988/P-K/4 KC901 . . . . . . **610.69**

When I was nine. /STEVENSON, J/1986/
3-4/4 KE551 . . . . **B STEVENSON, J.**

When I was young in the mountains. /RYLANT, C/1982/
K-3/6 KG387 . . . . **CE E**

When I was young in the mountains (Talking book). /RYLANT, C/1983/
K-3/6 KG387 . . . . **CE E**

When I'm alone. /OCHS, CP/1993/P-2/4 KG187 . . . . **E**

When I'm sleepy. /HOWARD, JR/1996/P-K/8 KF776 . . . . **E**

When jaguars ate the moon: and other stories about animals and plants of
the Americas. /BRUSCA, MC/1995/2-3/5 KB541 . . . . . **398.24**

When Jane-Marie told my secret. /WILLNER-PARDO, G/1995/
2-3/2 KH867 . . . . **Fic**

When learning is tough: kids talk about their learning disabilities. /ROBY,
C/1994/4-6/6 KB096 . . . . **371.92**

WHEN MOM AND DAD DIVORCE (Videocassette). /1994/
4-6/KA890 . . . . **VCR 306.89**

When plague strikes: the Black Death, smallpox, AIDS. /GIBLIN, JC/1995/
A/11 KD010 . . . . **614.4**

WHEN SHOULD YOU TELL?: DEALING WITH ABUSE (Videocassette). /
1995/5-6/KB018. . . . . **VCR 362.76**

When someone dies. /GREENLEE, S/1992/K-3/4 KA649 . . . . **155.9**

When spring comes. /KINSEY-WARNOCK, N/1993/P-2/3 KF906 . . . . . **E**

When the tide is low. /COLE, S/1985/P-2/3 KF411 . . . . **E**

When the whippoorwill calls. /RANSOM, CF/1995/1-3/2 KG305 . . . . . **E**

When the wind stops. Rev. and newly illustrated ed. /ZOLOTOW, C/1995/
K-2/4 KG809 . . . . **E**

WHEN THERE'S TROUBLE AT HOME (Videocassette). /1991/
A/KA883. . . . . **VCR 306.874**

WHEN THEY DON'T ALL SPEAK ENGLISH: INTEGRATING THE ESL
STUDENT INTO THE REGULAR CLASSROOM. /1989/
/KA281. . . . . **PROF 428**

When this cruel war is over: the Civil War home front. /DAMON, D/1996/
5-6/10 KE902 . . . . **973.7**

When we went to the zoo. /ORMEROD, J/1991/P-2/3 KC442. . . **590.73**

When will I read?/COHEN, M/1977/K-1/2 KF405 . . . . **CE E**

When Willard met Babe Ruth. /HALL, D/1996/4-6/6 KH212 . . . . . . **Fic**

When you go to kindergarten. Rev. and updated ed. /HOWE, J/1994/
P-K/2 KB097 . . . . **372.21**

When you were a baby. /JONAS, A/1982/P-K/2 KF850 . . . . **E**

WHEN YOU'RE MAD, MAD, MAD!: DEALING WITH ANGER
(Videocassette). /1993/4-6/KA632 . . . . **VCR 152.4**

Where are the stars during the day?: a book about stars. /BERGER, M/
1993/1-4/2 KC048 . . . . **523.8**

Where are you, Ernest and Celestine?/VINCENT, G/1986/
P-2/1 KG656 . . . . **E**

Where are you going, Emma? /TITHERINGTON, J/1988/P-K/3 KG610 . **E**

Where are you going little mouse?/KRAUS, R/1986/P-1/1 KF919 . . **CE E**

Where are you going Manyoni? /STOCK, C/1993/K-3/3 KG575 . . . . . **E**

Where did your family come from?: a book about immigrants. /BERGER,
M/1993/2-4/2 KA925 . . . . **325.73**

WHERE DO ANIMALS GO IN WINTER? (Videocassette). /1995/
3-6/KC463. . . . . **VCR 591.4**

Where do you think you're going, Christopher Columbus? /FRITZ, J/1980/
4-6/6 KE303 . . . . **CE B COLUMBUS, C.**

Where do you think you're going, Christopher Columbus? (Sound recording
cassette)./FRITZ, J/n.d./4-6/6 KE303 . . . . . . **CE B COLUMBUS, C.**

Where do you think you're going, Christopher Columbus? (Talking book)./
FRITZ, J/1982/4-6/6 KE303 . . . . **CE B COLUMBUS, C.**

Where do you think you're going, Christopher Columbus? (Videocassette)./
FRITZ, J/1991/4-6/6 KE303 . . . . **CE B COLUMBUS, C.**

Where does it go? /MILLER, M/1992/P-K/1 KG136 . . . . **E**

Where does the garbage go? Rev. ed. /SHOWERS, P/1994/
2-3/3 KD083 . . . . **628.4**

Where does the trail lead? /ALBERT, B/1991/K-2/3 KF143 . . . . **E**

WHERE IN SPACE IS CARMEN SANDIEGO? (Microcomputer program). /
1993/4-A/KC005 . . . . **MCP 520**

WHERE IN THE U.S.A. IS CARMEN SANDIEGO? New ed. (CD-ROM). /
1996/3-A/KE182 . . . . **CDR 917**

Where in the world are you? a guide to looking at the world. /COOPER,
K/1990/4-6/7 KE145 . . . . **910**

WHERE IN THE WORLD IS CARMEN SANDIEGO? JUNIOR DETECTIVE
EDITION (CD-ROM). /1994/3-6/KE174 . . . . **CDR 912**

WHERE IN THE WORLD IS CARMEN SANDIEGO? New ed. (CD-ROM). /
1996/3-A/KE175 . . . . **CDR 912**

Where is it? /HOBAN, T/c1972/P-K/1 KF747 . . . . **E**

Where on earth: a geografunny guide to the globe. /ROSENTHAL, P/
1992/4-6/6 KE153 . . . . **910**

Where once there was a wood. /FLEMING, D/1996/1-4/3 KD253 . **639.9**

Where the bald eagles gather. /PATENT, DH/1984/5-6/7 KC718 . **598.9**

Where the lilies bloom. /CLEAVER, V/c1969/5-6/6 KH009 . . . . **Fic**

Where the lilies bloom (Sound recording cassette). /CLEAVER, V/n.d./
5-6/6 KH009 . . . . **Fic**

Where the red fern grows: the story of two dogs and a boy. /RAWLS, W/
c1961, 1988/A/4 KH624 . . . . **Fic**

Where the red fern grows: the story of two dogs and a boy (Braille)./
RAWLS, W/n.d./A/4 KH624 . . . . **Fic**

Where the red fern grows: the story of two dogs and a boy (Talking
book)./RAWLS, W/n.d./A/4 KH624 . . . . **Fic**

Where the river begins. /LOCKER, T/1984/K-3/5 KG016 . . . . **E**

Where the river runs: a portrait of a refugee family. /GRAFF, NP/1993/
4-6/7 KA845 . . . . **305.8**

Where the sidewalk ends: the poems and drawings of Shel Silverstein. /
SILVERSTEIN, S/c1974/P-A/KE026 . . . . **811**

Where the sidewalk ends: the poems and drawings of Shel Silverstein
(Braille). /SILVERSTEIN, S/n.d./P-A/KE026 . . . . **811**

Where the sidewalk ends: the poems and drawings of Shel Silverstein
(Sound recording cassette). /SILVERSTEIN, S/1993/P-A/KE026. . . **811**

Where the wild horses roam. /PATENT, DH/1989/5-6/7 KD257 . . . **639.9**

Where the wild things are and other stories (Talking book). /SENDAK, M/
1977/P-2/KG437 . . . . **TB E**

Where the wild things are (Braille). /SENDAK, M/n.d./P-3/2 KG438 **CE E**

Where the wild things are (Picture). /SENDAK, M/n.d./
P-3/2 KG438 . . . . **CE E**

Where the wild things are (Sound recording cassette)./SENDAK, M/n.d./
P-3/2 KG438 . . . . **CE E**

Where the wild things are (Talking book)./SENDAK, M/n.d./
P-3/2 KG438 . . . . **CE E**

Where the wild things are (Videocassette)./SENDAK, M/1985/
P-3/2 KG438 . . . . **CE E**

Where the wild things are. 25th anniv. ed. /SENDAK, M/c1963, 1988/
P-3/2 KG438 . . . . **CE E**

Where was Patrick Henry on the 29th of May? /FRITZ, J/c1975, 1982/
5-6/7 KE386 . . . . **CE B HENRY, P.**

Where was Patrick Henry on the 29th of May? (Sound recording
cassette)./FRITZ, J/n.d./5-6/7 KE386 . . . . **CE B HENRY, P.**

Where was Patrick Henry on the 29th of May? (Talking book)./FRITZ, J/
1977/5-6/7 KE386 . . . . **CE B HENRY, P.**

Where's Chimpy? /RABE, B/1988/P-2/2 KG296 . . . . **E**

Where's my teddy? /ALBOROUGH, J/1992/P-1/2 KF145 . . . . **E**

Where's our mama? /GOODE, D/1991/P-2/2 KF632 . . . . **E**

Where's Spot? Sign language edition. /HILL, E/1987/P-2/2 KF728 . . . . **E**

Where's the baby?/HUTCHINS, P/1988/P-2/2 KF806 . . . . **CE E**

Which witch is which? /HUTCHINS, P/1989/P-1/2 KF807 . . . . **E**

Whistle for Willie. /KEATS, EJ/c1964, 1977/P-2/3 KF880 . . . . **CE E**

Whistle for Willie (Kit)./KEATS, EJ/1975/P-2/3 KF880 . . . . **CE E**

Whistle for Willie (Talking book)./KEATS, EJ/n.d./P-2/3 KF880 . . . **CE E**

Whistle for Willie (Videocassette)./KEATS, EJ/1965/P-2/3 KF880 . . **CE E**

White bird. /BULLA, CR/c1966, 1990/1-6/2 KG940 . . . . **Fic**

WHITE CAT (Talking book). /1997/K-2/KB382 . . . . **VCR 398.2**

WHITE CAT (Videocassette). /1997/K-2/KB382 . . . . **VCR 398.2**

White Dynamite and Curly Kidd. /MARTIN, JR, B/c1986, 1989/
K-3/2 KG078 . . . . **E**

White Fang. /LONDON, J/c1905, 1985/6-A/6 KH417 . . . . **Fic**

White Fang (Braille). /LONDON, J/n.d./6-A/6 KH417 . . . . **Fic**

White Fang (Sound recording cassette). /LONDON, J/n.d./
6-A/6 KH417 . . . . **Fic**

White Fang (Talking book). /LONDON, J/n.d./6-A/6 KH417 . . . . . . **Fic**

White House. /FISHER, LE/1989/5-6/8 KE970 . . . . **975.3**

White House. /QUIRI, PR/1996/4-6/10 KE972 . . . . **975.3**

White House kids. /BLUE, R/1995/5-6/7 KE849 . . . . **973**

White House kids (Sound recording cassette). /BLUE, R/1997/
5-6/7 KE849 . . . . **973**

White House (Sound recording cassette). /FISHER, LE/n.d./
5-6/8 KE970 . . . . **975.3**

White Mountains. /CHRISTOPHER, J/1967/4-6/6 KG991 . . . . **Fic**
White Mountains (Braille)./CHRISTOPHER, J/n.d./4-6/6 KG991 . . . . . . **Fic**
White Mountains (Sound recording cassette)./CHRISTOPHER, J/n.d./ 4-6/6 KG991 . . . . **Fic**
White Mountains (Talking book)./CHRISTOPHER, J/n.d./ 4-6/6 KG991 . . . . **Fic**
White socks only. /COLEMAN, E/1996/3-4/4 KH014. . . . . **Fic**
White stag. /SEREDY, K/c1937/5-6/7 KB486 . . . . **398.22**
White stag (Braille)./SEREDY, K/n.d./5-6/7 KB486 . . . . **398.22**
White stag (Sound recording cassette)./SEREDY, K/n.d./ 5-6/7 KB486 . . . . **398.22**
White stag (Talking book)./SEREDY, K/n.d./5-6/7 KB486 . . . . . . **398.22**
White stallion. /SHUB, E/1982/1-3/2 KG497 . . . . **E**
White stallion (Braille)./SHUB, E/n.d./1-3/2 KG497 . . . . **E**
White stallion of Lipizza. /HENRY, M/c1964, 1994/4-6/6 KH246 . . . . **Fic**
White stallion (Sound recording cassette)./SHUB, E/n.d./1-3/2 KG497 . . **E**
White stone in the castle wall. /OBERMAN, S/1995/4-6/2 KH555 . . . **Fic**
White Wave: a Chinese tale. Rev. ed. /WOLKSTEIN, D/1996/ 1-3/2 KB786 . . . . **398.27**
WHITEWASH (Videocassette) /1994/3-6/KA862 . . . . **VCR 305.8**
Whitewater kayaking. /EVANS, J/1992/4-A/7 KD845 . . . . **797.1**
Who eats what?: food chains and food webs. /LAUBER, P/1995/ K-3/2 KC295 . . . . **577**
Who hid it? /GOMI, T/1991/P-K/2 KF630. **E**
Who is a stranger and what should I do? /GIRARD, LW/1985/ 1-3/6 KB021 . . . . **363.1**
Who is tapping at my window? /DEMING, AG/c1988, 1994/ P-K/KD930. . . . . **811**
Who is tapping at my window? (Big book)./DEMING, AG/c1988, 1994/ P-K/KD930. . . . . **811**
Who is the beast? /BAKER, K/1990/P-K/1 KF187 . . . . **E**
Who is the beast? (Big book)./BAKER, K/1991/P-K/1 KF187 . . . . **E**
Who killed Cock Robin? /O'MALLEY, K/1993/1-3/2 KG191 . . . . **E**
Who really killed Cock Robin?: an ecological mystery. /GEORGE, JC/ c1971, 1991/5-A/7 KH161. . . . . **Fic**
Who said boo?: Halloween poems for the very young. /CARLSTROM, NW/1995/P-1/KD920 . . . . **811**
Who said moo? /ZIEFERT, H/1996/P-1/2 KG799 . . . . **E**
Who said red? /SERFOZO, M/1988/P-K/2 KG444 . . . . **E**
Who said that?: famous Americans speak. /BURLEIGH, R/1997/ 4-A/7 KA597 . . . . **080**
Who stole the cookies? /MOFFATT, J/1996/P-1/1 KG149 . . . . **E**
Who uses this? /MILLER, M/1990/P-K/KA943. . . . . **331.7**
Who will be my friends? /HOFF, S/c1960/K-1/1 KF760 . . . . **E**
Whoever you are. /FOX, M/1997/P-1/1 KA843 . . . . **305.8**
WHOLE LANGUAGE: BELIEFS AND PRACTICES, K-8. /1989/ /KA233. . . . . **PROF 372.6**
Whole language: literature, learning, and literacy: a workshop in print. / STANEK, LW/1993//KA230 . . . . **PROF 372.6**
Whole world in your hands: looking at maps. /BERGER, M/1993/ 1-3/2 KE166 . . . . **912**
Whoopi Goldberg: from street to stardom. /ADAMS, MA/1993/ 4-6/7 KE371 . . . . **B GOLDBERG, W.**
Whooping crane: a comeback story. /PATENT, DH/1988/ A/9 KD258 . . . . **639.9**
Whooping crane (Sound recording cassette)./PATENT, DH/n.d./ A/9 KD258 . . . . **639.9**
Who's a pest? /BONSALL, CN/c1962/P-2/2 KF248 . . . . **E**
Who's afraid? and other strange stories. /PEARCE, AP/1987/ 5-6/6 KH590 . . . . **Fic**
Who's afraid of the dark? /BONSALL, CN/1980/P-1/1 KF249 . . . . **E**
Who's counting? /TAFURI, N/1986/P-K/KG592. . . . . **E**
Who's hiding here? /YOSHI /1987/K-3/2 KG784 . . . . **E**
Who's in Rabbit's house? (Videocassette). /AARDEMA, V/1995/ K-3/KB518. . . . . **VCR 398.24**
Who's that stepping on Plymouth Rock? /FRITZ, J/c1975/ 3-5/5 KE940 . . . . **CE 974.4**
Who's that stepping on Plymouth Rock? (Talking book)./FRITZ, J/1982/ 3-5/5 KE940 . . . . **CE 974.4**
Who's there? /TOLAN, SS/1994/5-A/5 KH795. . . . . **Fic**
Who's who in my family. /LEEDY, L/1995/K-2/2 KA869 . . . . **306.85**
Whose baby am I? /GREENWAY, S/1992/K-2/4 KC458. . . . . **591.3**
Whose hat? /MILLER, M/1988/P-K/KB166 . . . . **391.4**
Whose mouse are you? /KRAUS, R/c1970/P-1/1 KF919 . . . . **CE E**
Whose shoe?/MILLER, M/1991/P-K/KB166. . . . . **391.4**
Why a disguise? /NUMEROFF, LJ/1996/K-2/2 KG182 . . . . **E**
Why do leaves change color? /MAESTRO, B/1994/ P-4/2 KC400 . . . . **CE 581.4**
Why do leaves change color? (Kit)./MAESTRO, B/1996/ P-4/2 KC400 . . . . **CE 581.4**
Why doesn't the earth fall up? /COBB, V/1988/4-6/5 KC092. . . . . . **531**
Why don't you get a horse, Sam Adams? /FRITZ, J/c1974/ 3-5/7 KE227 . . . . **CE B ADAMS, S.**
Why I cough, sneeze, shiver, hiccup, and yawn. /BERGER, M/1983/ 1-3/2 KC963 . . . . **612.8**
Why I cough, sneeze, shiver, hiccup, and yawn (Sound recording cassette)./ BERGER, M/n.d./1-3/2 KC963 . . . . **612.8**
Why mammals have fur. /PATENT, DH/1995/4-6/6 KC727 . . . . **599**
Why mosquitoes buzz in people's ears: a West African tale. /AARDEMA, V/1975/1-3/5 KB519 . . . . **CE 398.24**
Why mosquitoes buzz in people's ears: a West African tale (Braille)./ AARDEMA, V/n.d./1-3/5 KB519 . . . . **CE 398.24**
Why mosquitoes buzz in people's ears: a West African tale (Sound recording cassette)./AARDEMA, V/n.d./1-3/5 KB519. . . . . **CE 398.24**
Why mosquitoes buzz in people's ears: a West African tale (Videocassette)./AARDEMA, V/n.d./1-3/5 KB519 . . . . . . **CE 398.24**
Why mosquitoes buzz in people's ears (Big book)./AARDEMA, V/1993/ 1-3/5 KB519 . . . . **CE 398.24**
Why mosquitoes buzz in people's ears (Talking book). /AARDEMA, V/ 1978/2-4/KB520. . . . . **TB 398.24**
Why ostriches don't fly and other tales from the African bush. /LEWIS, IM/ 1997/4-6/6 KB336 . . . . **398.2**
Why the chicken crossed the road. /MACAULAY, D/1987/ 4-A/7 KH435 . . . . **Fic**
Why the dog chases the cat: great animal stories (Sound recording cassette). /HOLT, D/1994/1-3/KB591. . . . . **SRC 398.24**
Why the sky is far away: a Nigerian folktale. /GERSON, M/1992/ 2-4/5 KB705 . . . . **398.26**
Why the sun and the moon live in the sky: an African folktale. /DAYRELL, E/c1968/K-3/6 KB704 . . . . **CE 398.26**
Why the sun and the moon live in the sky (Videocassette)./DAYRELL, E/ n.d./K-3/6 KB704 . . . . **CE 398.26**
Wicked witch is at it again./KRAAN, H/1997/3-5/3 KH379 . . . . **Fic**
Widow's broom. /VAN ALLSBURG, C/1992/4-A/5 KH824 . . . . **Fic**
Wiggy and Boa. /FIENBERG, A/c1988, 1990/5-6/7 KH113. . . . . **Fic**
Wilbur and Orville and the flying machine. /MARQUARDT, M/1989/ 1-3/1 KD096 . . . . **629.13**
Wild and woolly mammoths. Rev. ed. /ALIKI /1996/1-3/4 KC268 . . . **569**
Wild and woolly mammoths (Sound recording cassette)./ALIKI /n.d./ 1-3/4 KC268 . . . . **569**
Wild babies. /SIMON, S/1997/3-5/6 KC459 . . . . **591.3**
Wild boars. /NICHOLSON, D/1987/5-6/9 KC786 . . . . **599.63**
Wild Christmas reindeer. /BRETT, J/1990/K-2/2 KF263 . . . . **E**
Wild fox: a true story. /MASON, C/1993/4-5/5 KC843 . . . . . . **599.775**
Wild horse winter. /HONDA, T/1992/K-3/4 KC806 . . . . **599.665**
Wild in the city. /THORNHILL, J/1996/P-2/5 KC478. . . . . **591.5**
Wild turkey, tame turkey. /PATENT, DH/1989/5-6/7 KC697 . . . . . **598.6**
Wild turkey, tame turkey (Sound recording cassette)./PATENT, DH/1993/ 5-6/7 KC697 . . . . **598.6**
Wild weather. Tornadoes! /HOPPING, LJ/1994/2-6/3 KC199 . . . **551.55**
WILD, WONDERFUL ANIMALS IN THE WOODS (Videocassette). /1996/ 1-4/KC492. . . . . **VCR 591.73**
Wild woods. /JAMES, S/1996/P-2/2 KF825. . . . . **E**
Wildfire. /CONE, P/1997/4-A/6 KB040. . . . . **363.37**
Wildfires. /SIMON, S/1996/3-6/7 KB041 . . . . **363.37**
Wildlife A-B-C: a nature alphabet book. /THORNHILL, J/1990/ P-2/3 KC498 . . . . **591.97**
WILDLIFE CONSERVATION. /1897-/K-A/KA551 . . . . **PER 050**
Wildlife rescue: the work of Dr. Kathleen Ramsay. /DEWEY, JO/1994/ 4-6/7 KD252 . . . . **639.9**
Wildlife 1 2 3: a nature counting book. /THORNHILL, J/1989/ P-2/KC455. . . . . **591**
Wiley and the Hairy Man. /SIERRA, J/1996/K-3/4 KB417. . . . . . **398.21**
Wiley and the Hairy Man./BANG, M/n.d./1-3/2 KB389 . . . . **398.21**
Wiley and the Hairy Man: adapted from an American folk tale. /BANG, M/c1976, 1987/1-3/2 KB389 . . . . **398.21**
Wilfrid Gordon McDonald Partridge. /FOX, M/1985/K-3/6 KF574 . . . . **E**
Wilfrid Gordon McDonald Partridge (Big book)./FOX, M/1995/ K-3/6 KF574 . . . . **E**
Will I have a friend? /COHEN, M/c1967/K-1/2 KF405 . . . . **CE E**
Will Rogers. /SCHOTT, JA/1996/1-3/2 KE519 . . . . **B ROGERS, W.**
Will there be a lap for me? /COREY, D/1992/P-1/2 KF425 . . . . **E**
Will you sign here, John Hancock? /FRITZ, J/c1976, 1997/ 5-6/7 KE383 . . . . **CE B HANCOCK, J.**
Will you sign here, John Hancock? (Sound recording cassette)./FRITZ, J/ n.d./5-6/7 KE383 . . . . **CE B HANCOCK, J.**
Will you sign here, John Hancock? (Talking book)./FRITZ, J/1977/ 5-6/7 KE383 . . . . **CE B HANCOCK, J.**
William Parker: rebel without rights: a novel based on fact. /ROSENBURG, JM/1996/6-A/7 KH654 . . . . **Fic**
William Shakespeare's A midsummer night's dream. /COVILLE, B/1996/ 4-6/4 KE114 . . . . **822.3**
William Steig library (Videocassette). /STEIG, W/1995/ 1-3/KG548 . . . . **VCR E**
William Tell. /EARLY, M/1991/4-6/6 KB440 . . . . **398.22**
William Tell. /FISHER, LE/1996/3-5/4 KB442 . . . . **398.22**

William Tell (Sound recording cassette)./EARLY, M/1994/
4-6/6 KB440 . . . . **398.22**
William's doll. /ZOLOTOW, C/c1972/P-2/4 KG810 . . . . **E**
William's doll (Braille)./ZOLOTOW, C/n.d./-P-2/4 KG810 . . . . **E**
Williamsburg. /KENT, Z/1992/4-6/5 KE871 . . . . **973.2**
Williamsburg: cradle of the revolution. /GOOR, R/1994/
5-A/7 KE978 . . . . **975.5**
Willie Bea and the time the Martians landed. /HAMILTON, V/1983/
5-6/3 KH219 . . . . **Fic**
Willie Bea and the time the Martians landed (Sound recording cassette)./
HAMILTON, V/n.d./5-6/3 KH219 . . . . **Fic**
Willie takes a hike. /RAND, G/1996/K-2/3 KG302 . . . . **E**
Will's mammoth. /MARTIN, R/1989/1-3/2 KG080 . . . . **CE E**
Will's mammoth (Videocassette)./MARTIN, R/1991/1-3/2 KG080 . . **CE E**
Willy and May. /SCHACHNER, JB/1995/1-3/5 KG401. . . . . **E**
Willy's silly grandma. /DEFELICE, CC/1997/1-3/2 KF455. . . . . **E**
Wilma Mankiller. /LOWERY, L/1996/2-3/4 KE458 . . . **B MANKILLER, W.**
Wilma unlimited: how Wilma Rudolph became the world's fastest woman. /
KRULL, K/1996/3-5/7 KE527 . . . . **B RUDOLPH, W.**
Wind in the door. /L'ENGLE, M/c1973/5-6/7 KH393 . . . . **Fic**
Wind in the door (Sound recording cassette)./L'ENGLE, M/1997/
5-6/7 KH393 . . . . **Fic**
WIND IN THE LONG GRASS: A COLLECTION OF HAIKU. /1991/
2-5/KD892. . . . . **808.81**
Wind in the willows. /GRAHAME, K/1980/5-6/8 KH189 . . . . **Fic**
Wind in the willows (Braille)./GRAHAME, K/n.d./5-6/8 KH190 . . . . . **Fic**
Wind in the willows (Sound recording cassette)./GRAHAME, K/n.d./
5-6/8 KH190 . . . . **Fic**
Wind in the willows (Talking book)./GRAHAME, K/n.d./5-6/8 KH190 . **Fic**
Wind in the willows. 75th anniversary edition. /GRAHAME, K/1983/
5-6/8 KH190 . . . . **Fic**
Wind spins me around in the fall. /AGELL, C/1994/K-2/3 KF140 . . . . **E**
Wind warrior: the training of a Karate champion. /GOEDECKE, CJ/1992/
4-6/5 KD831 . . . . **796.815**
Winds of Mars. /HOOVER, HM/1995/6-A/4 KH281 . . . . **Fic**
Wings. /YOLEN, J/c1991, 1997/5-6/4 KA754 . . . . **292**
Wings along the waterway. /BROWN, MB/1992/5-6/6 KC675. . . **598.176**
Wings along the waterway (Sound recording cassette)./BROWN, MB/
1995/5-6/6 KC675 . . . . **598.176**
Wings to fly. /LOTTRIDGE, CB/1997/5-A/5 KH419 . . . . **Fic**
Winnie-the-Pooh. /MILNE, AA/1974/K-6/3 KH498 . . . . **Fic**
Winnie-the-Pooh (Braille)./MILNE, AA/n.d./K-6/3 KH498 . . . . **Fic**
Winnie-the-Pooh (Sound recording cassette)./MILNE, AA/n.d./
K-6/3 KH498 . . . . **Fic**
Winnie-the-Pooh (Talking book)./MILNE, AA/n.d./K-6/3 KH498 . . . . **Fic**
Winning ways: a photohistory of American women in sports. /MACY, S/
1996/4-6/12 KD764 . . . . **796**
Winston Churchill: an unbreakable spirit. /DRIEMEN, JE/1990/
5-6/7 KE290 . . . . **B CHURCHILL, W.**
Winston Churchill: soldier, statesman, artist. /SEVERANCE, JB/1996/
6-A/10 KE291 . . . . **B CHURCHILL, W.**
Winter across America. /SIMON, S/1994/4-6/6 KB920 . . . . **508.2**
Winter camp. /HILL, K/1993/5-A/6 KH262 . . . . **Fic**
Winter camp (Sound recording cassette)./HILL, K/1996/5-A/6 KH262 . **Fic**
Winter day. /FLORIAN, D/1987/P-1/1 KF560. . . . . **E**
Winter days in the Big Woods. /WILDER, LI/1994/K-3/4 KG720 . . . . **E**
Winter magic. /HASLER, E/1989/K-3/4 KF678 . . . . **E**
Winter rescue. /VALGARDSON, WD/1995/3-5/4 KH819 . . . . **Fic**
Winter solstice. /JACKSON, E/1994/3-5/6 KB211 . . . . **394.261**
WINTER (Videocassette). /1994/2-5/KC669 . . . . **VCR 598**
Winter worm business./GIFF, PR/1981/4-6/6 KH164 . . . . **Fic**
Winter wren. /COLE, B/1984/K-3/2 KF408. . . . . **E**
Wisconsin. /BRATVOLD, G/1991/4-6/7 KF019 . . . . **977.5**
Wise old woman. /UCHIDA, Y/1994/2-4/5 KB492 . . . . **398.22**
Wise washerman: a folktale from Burma. /FROESE, DL/1996/
K-2/7 KB569 . . . . **398.24**
Wish giver. /BRITTAIN, B/1983/3-6/7 KG925 . . . . **Fic**
Wish giver (Sound recording cassette)./BRITTAIN, B/n.d./
3-6/7 KG925 . . . . **Fic**
Wish me luck. /HENEGHAN, J/1997/6-A/5 KH237 . . . . **Fic**
Wishbones: a folk tale from China. /WILSON, BK/1993/
2-3/6 KB383 . . . . **398.2**
Wishes, lies, and dreams: teaching children to write poetry. /KOCH, K/
c1970, 1980//KA346 . . . . **PROF 808.81**
Witch hunt: it happened in Salem Village. /KRENSKY, S/1989/
3-5/4 KA606 . . . . **133.4**
Witch lady./CARLSON, N/1985/P-2/2 KF351. . . . . **CE E**
Witch Mama. /CASELEY, J/1996/K-2/3 KF371 . . . . **E**
Witch of Blackbird Pond. /SPEARE, EG/c1958/5-6/5 KH742 . . . **CE Fic**
Witch of Blackbird Pond (Braille)./SPEARE, EG/n.d./5-6/5 KH742. . **CE Fic**
Witch of Blackbird Pond (Sound recording cassette)./SPEARE, EG/n.d./
5-6/5 KH742 . . . . **CE Fic**
Witch of Blackbird Pond (Talking book)./SPEARE, EG/n.d./
5-6/5 KH742 . . . . **CE Fic**

Witch of Fourth Street, and other stories. /LEVOY, M/c1972/
4-6/7 KH400 . . . . **Fic**
Witch of Fourth Street and other stories (Kit). /LEVOY, M/1978/
4-6/KH401 . . . . **KIT Fic**
Witch week. New ed. /JONES, DW/c1982, 1993/6-A/6 KH335 . . . . **Fic**
Witches of Worm. /SNYDER, ZK/c1965/4-6/7 KH735 . . . . **Fic**
Witches' supermarket. /MEDDAUGH, S/1991/1-3/2 KG125 . . . . **E**
Witch's daughter. /BAWDEN, N/c1966, 1991/5-A/6 KG893 . . . . . . **Fic**
Witch's face: a Mexican tale. /KIMMEL, EA/1993/3-5/2 KB402 . . **398.21**
With my brother/Con mi hermano. /ROE, E/1991/P-2/2 KG346 . . . . . **E**
WITH OPEN EYES: IMAGES FROM THE ART INSTITUTE OF CHICAGO
(CD-ROM). /1995/2-A/KD368 . . . . **CDR 701**
Within a painted past. /HUTCHINS, HJ/1994/5-A/4 KH311. . . . . . . **Fic**
WITHIN REACH: TEN STORIES. /1993/5-A/6 KH874. . . . . **Fic**
Witnesses to freedom: young people who fought for civil rights. /
ROCHELLE, B/1993/5-6/7 KA905 . . . . **323.1**
Wizard next door. /GLASSMAN, P/1993/K-2/2 KF625 . . . . **E**
Wizard of Earthsea. /LE GUIN, UK/c1968, 1991/6-A/7 KH392 . . . . . **Fic**
Wizard of Earthsea (Sound recording cassette)./LE GUIN, UK/n.d./
6-A/7 KH392 . . . . **Fic**
Wizard of Earthsea (Talking book)./LE GUIN, UK/n.d./6-A/7 KH392. . **Fic**
Wizard of sound: a story about Thomas Edison. /MITCHELL, B/1991/
4-6/6 KE331 . . . . **B EDISON, T.**
Wizards and the monster. /BRITTAIN, B/1994/2-4/4 KG926 . . . . . . **Fic**
Wizard's Hall. /YOLEN, J/1991/4-6/6 KH897. . . . . **Fic**
Wolf. /CROSS, G/1991/A/6 KH045. **Fic**
Wolf and the seven little kids: a fairy tale. /GRIMM, J/1995/
1-2/4 KB579 . . . . **398.24**
Wolf Cub Scout book. Rev. ed. /BOY SCOUTS OF AMERICA /1986/
3-4/4 KB076 . . . . **369.43**
Wolf Cub Scout book. Rev. ed. (Sound recording cassette)./BOY SCOUTS
OF AMERICA /1997/3-4/4 KB076. . . . . **369.43**
Wolf Island. /GODKIN, C/1993/3-5/4 KC334 . . . . **577.5**
Wolf magic for kids. /WOLPERT, T/c1990, 1991/5-6/5 KC841 . . **599.773**
Wolf pack: tracking wolves in the wild. /JOHNSON, SA/1985/
6/10 KC836 . . . . **599.773**
Wolfhound. /FRANKLIN, KL/1996/1-3/3 KF576. . . . . **E**
Wolf's chicken stew. /KASZA, K/1987/P-2/2 KF870. . . . . **E**
Wolves. /LAWRENCE, RD/1990/5-6/7 KC837 . . . . **599.773**
Wolves. /LEPTHIEN, EU/1991/2-4/5 KC838 . . . . **599.773**
Wolves. /SIMON, S/1993/4-6/7 KC840 . . . . **599.773**
Wolves of Willoughby Chase. /AIKEN, J/c1962, 1987/
5-A/7 KG826 . . . . **CE Fic**
Woman in the moon: a story from Hawaii. /RATTIGAN, JK/1996/
K-2/6 KB474 . . . . **398.22**
Woman who flummoxed the fairies: an old tale from Scotland. /FOREST,
H/1990/3-4/5 KB396 . . . . **398.21**
Woman who outshone the sun: the legend of Lucia Zenteno./La mujer que
brillaba aun mas que el sol: la leyenda de Lucia Zenteno. /MARTINEZ,
AC/1991/3-5/5 KB403 . . . . **398.21**
Wombat stew. /VAUGHAN, MK/c1984/P-2/4 KG652 . . . . **E**
WOMEN IN POLICING (Videocassette). /1994/5-6/KB030 . . . . **VCR 363.2**
WOMEN OF HOPE: AFRICAN AMERICANS WHO MADE A DIFFERENCE
(Picture). /1994/4-6/KA863 . . . . **PIC 305.8**
WOMEN OF RURAL AMERICA (Videocassette). /1995/
5-A/KA831 . . . . **VCR 305.42**
Women of the lights. /FLEMING, C/1996/4-6/6 KB148 . . . . **387.1**
Women win the vote. /SMITH, BC/1989/5-6/9 KA911 . . . . **324.6**
WOMEN'S ALMANAC. /1997/5-A/KA397 . . . . **REF 305.4**
Wonder child and other Jewish fairy tales. /SCHWARTZ, H/1996/
2-4/5 KB369 . . . . **398.2**
Wonder tales from around the world. /FOREST, H/1995/
3-5/6 KB300 . . . . **398.2**
Wonder thing. /HATHORN, L/1996/P-2/KC181. . . . . **551.48**
Wonderful Towers of Watts. /ZELVER, P/1994/2-4/6 KD387 . . . . . **725**
Wonderful Wizard of Oz. /BAUM, LF/1987/4-6/6 KG886 . . . . . **CE Fic**
Wonderful Wizard of Oz (Braille)./BAUM, LF/n.d./4-6/6 KG886 . . **CE Fic**
Wonderful Wizard of Oz (Talking book)./BAUM, LF/n.d./
4-6/6 KG886 . . . . **CE Fic**
WONDERS OF GROWING PLANTS. 3rd ed. (Videocassette). /1992/
K-3/KC396 . . . . **VCR 580**
WONDERS OF GROWING PLANTS. 3rd ed. (Videodisc)./1992/
K-3/KC396 . . . . **VCR 580**
Wonders of the world. /CASELLI, G/1992/4-A/8 KD382 . . . . **720**
WONDERSCIENCE: FUN PHYSICAL SCIENCE ACTIVITIES FOR CHILDREN
AND ADULTS TO DO TOGETHER. /1987-//KA154 . **PER PROF 050**
WOOD (Videocassette). /1985/5-6/KD330. . . . . **VCR 674**
Woodchucks. /LEPTHIEN, EU/1992/3-4/4 KC752. . . . . **599.36**
Woodland Christmas: twelve days of Christmas in the North Woods. /
TYRRELL, F/1996/K-2/KD541 . . . . **782.28**
Woodrow Wilson: twenty-eighth President of the United States. /OSINSKI,
A/1989/5-A/8 KE597 . . . . **B WILSON, W.**
Woodsong. /PAULSEN, G/1990/5-A/6 KD824 . . . . **796.5**

Woodsong (Sound recording cassette)./PAULSEN, G/1993/
5-A/6 KD824 . . . . **796.5**
Woodwinds. /SHIPTON, A/1994/4-6/7 KD550 . . . . **788.2**
Woodworking for kids: 40 fabulous, fun and useful things for kids to make.
/MCGUIRE, K/1993/5-A/KD341 . . . . **684**
WOPILA--A GIVEAWAY: LAKOTA STORIES (Sound recording cassette). /
1993/3-5/KB676 . . . . **SRC 398.24**
Wordful child. /LYON, GE/1996/4-5/4 KE450 . . . . **B LYON, G. E.**
Words by heart. /SEBESTYEN, O/1997/5-A/7 KH689 . . . . **CE Fic**
Words by heart (Sound recording cassette)./SEBESTYEN, O/n.d./
5-A/7 KH689 . . . . **CE Fic**
Words by heart (Videocassette)./SEBESTYEN, O/1984/
5-A/7 KH689 . . . . **CE Fic**
Words in our hands. /LITCHFIELD, AB/1980/4-6/5 KH413 . . . . **Fic**
Words of stone. /HENKES, K/1992/5-A/6 KH240 . . . . **Fic**
Working cotton. /WILLIAMS, SA/1992/1-3/2 KG731 . . . . **E**
WORKING IT OUT: CONFLICT RESOLUTION (Videocassette). /1993/
5-6/KA813 . . . . **VCR 303.6**
Worksong. /PAULSEN, G/1997/K-2/2 KG222 . . . . **E**
WORLD ALIVE (Videocassette). /1990/4-6/KC480 . . . . . **VCR 591.5**
WORLD ALMANAC AND BOOK OF FACTS. /1868-/
4-6/KA406 . . . . **REF 317.3**
WORLD AT MY DOOR (Videocassette)./1991/4-6/KA851. . . **VCR 305.8**
WORLD BOOK DICTIONARY. /1996/5-6/KA432 . . . . . . **REF 423**
WORLD BOOK ENCYCLOPEDIA. /1931-/5-A/KA386. . . . **REF 031**
WORLD BOOK ENCYCLOPEDIA OF PEOPLE AND PLACES. /1997/
/KA387 . . . . **REF 031**
WORLD BOOK STUDENT DICTIONARY. REV. ED. /1995/
3-5/KB840 . . . . **423**
WORLD BOOK 1997 MULTIMEDIA ENCYCLOPEDIA. Deluxe ed. (CD-
ROM). /1997/3-A/KA388 . . . . **CDR REF 031**
World desk: a student handbook to the Internet. Rev. ed. /BOE, T/1996/
A/10 KA576 . . . . **025.04**
World from my window. /SAMTON, SW/c1985, 1991/P-2/3 KG389 . . **E**
World in Grandfather's hands. /STRETE, CK/1995/5-A/4 KH771 . . . . **Fic**
WORLD IN OUR HANDS: IN HONOR OF THE FIFTIETH ANNIVERSARY
OF THE UNITED NATIONS. /1995/5-A/8 KA970 . . . . **341.23**
WORLD LEADERS: PEOPLE WHO SHAPED THE WORLD. /1994/
5-A/KA408 . . . . **REF 350**
WORLD NEWSMAP OF THE WEEK: HEADLINE FOCUS. /1938-/
/KA155 . . . . **PER PROF 050**
WORLD OF CHILDREN'S SONGS. /1993/KA322 . . . . . **PROF 789.3**
World of Christopher Robin: the complete When we were very young and
Now we are six. /MILNE, AA/c1958/P-2/KE108 . . . . **821**
World of Christopher Robin: the complete When we were very young and
Now we are six (Braille)./MILNE, AA/n.d./P-2/KE108 . . . . **821**
World of Christopher Robin: the complete When we were very young and
Now we are six (Sound recording cassette)./MILNE, AA/n.d./
P-2/KE108 . . . . **821**
World of Christopher Robin: the complete When we were very young and
Now we are six (Talking book)./MILNE, AA/n.d./P-2/KE108. . . . **821**
World of knowing: a story about Thomas Hopkins Gallaudet. /BOWEN,
AR/1995/3-5/6 KE361 . . . . **B GALLAUDET, T.**
World of Pooh: the complete "Winnie-the-Pooh" and "The House at Pooh
Corner." /MILNE, AA/c1957/K-6/3 KH499 . . . . **Fic**
World of Pooh: the complete "Winnie-the-Pooh" and "The House at Pooh
Corner" (Sound recording cassette)./MILNE, AA/n.d./
K-6/3 KH499 . . . . **Fic**
World of Pooh: the complete "Winnie-the-Pooh" and "The House at Pooh
Corner" (Talking book)./MILNE, AA/n.d./K-6/3 KH499 . . . . . . **Fic**
World of wonders: a trip through numbers. /OCKENGA, S/1988/
3-A/3 KB975 . . . . **513.2**
World War I. /MCGOWEN, T/1993/4-6/8 KE653 . . . . . . **940.3**
World War II. /MCGOWEN, T/1993/4-6/8 KE673 . . . . . **940.54**
World water watch. /KOCH, M/1993/K-2/4 KD255 . . . . . . **639.9**
World Wide Web. /BRIMNER, LD/1997/2-6/6 KA577 . . . . . . **025.04**
WORLDMARK ENCYCLOPEDIA OF THE NATIONS. 9th ed. /1997/
A/KA389 . . . . **REF 031**
WORLDMARK ENCYCLOPEDIA OF THE STATES. 3rd ed. /1995/
A/KA494 . . . . **REF 973**
WORLDS BELOW (Videocassette). /1988/4-6/KC371 . . . . . **VCR 578.77**
World's birthday: a Rosh Hashanah story. /GOLDIN, BD/1990/
2-3/2 KH181 . . . . **Fic**
Worlds of belief: religion and spirituality. /SITA, L/1995/
4-A/10 KA728 . . . . **291**
World's regions and weather: linking fiction to nonfiction. /PERRY, PJ/
1996//KA294 . . . . **PROF 551.6**
Worms eat my garbage. /APPELHOF, M/1982/A/12 KC502 . . . . **592**
Worm's eye view: make your own wildlife refuge. /JOHNSON, K/1991/
2-4/5 KC294 . . . . **577**
Worry warts./GLEITZMAN, M/1993/5-A/7 KH174 . . . . . **Fic**
Worse than the worst./STEVENSON, J/1994/K-3/4 KG570 . . . . **E**
Worst goes South./STEVENSON, J/1995/K-3/4 KG570 . . . . **E**
Worst person in the world. /STEVENSON, J/c1978/K-3/4 KG570 . . . . **E**

Worth a thousand words: an annotated guide to picture books for older
readers. /AMMON, BD/1996//KA010 . . . . **PROF 011.62**
Would they love a lion? /DENTON, KM/1995/P-1/1 KF463 . . . . **E**
Wouldbegoods./NESBIT, E/1985/5-6/7 KH544 . . . . **Fic**
Wreck of the Zanzibar. /MORPURGO, M/1995/4-6/3 KH516 . . . . . . **Fic**
Wreck of the Zephyr. /VAN ALLSBURG, C/1983/1-5/3 KH825 . . **CE Fic**
Wreck of the Zephyr (Picture)./VAN ALLSBURG, C/n.d./
1-5/3 KH825 . . . . **CE Fic**
Wrecker. /SKINNER, D/1995/6-A/4 KH715 . . . . **Fic**
Wretched stone. /VAN ALLSBURG, C/1991/4-A/4 KH826 . . . . **Fic**
Wright brothers: how they invented the airplane. /FREEDMAN, R/1991/
A/7 KD094 . . . . **629.13**
Wright brothers: how they invented the airplane (Sound recording
cassette)./FREEDMAN, R/1993/A/7 KD094 . . . . . . **629.13**
Wrinkle in time. /L'ENGLE, M/c1962/4-6/6 KH394 . . . . . . **CE Fic**
Wrinkle in time (Braille)./L'ENGLE, M/n.d./4-6/6 KH394 . . . . **CE Fic**
Wrinkle in time (Sound recording cassette)./L'ENGLE, M/n.d./
4-6/6 KH394 . . . . **CE Fic**
WRITING ALONG THE OREGON TRAIL (Microcomputer program). /
1994/4-A/KB121 . . . . **MCP 372.6**
WRITING CENTER (Microcomputer program). /1991/
2-A/KD347 . . . . **MCP 686.2**
Written & illustrated by... a revolutionary two-brain approach for teaching
students how to write and illustrate amazing books. /MELTON, D/
1985//KA226 . . . . **PROF 372.6**
Wump World. /PEET, B/c1970/1-3/7 KG230 . . . . **E**
Wynton Marsalis. /ELLIS, VF/1997/5-A/10 KE459 . . . . **B MARSALIS, W.**
Wyoming. /FRISCH, C/1994/4-6/7 KF059 . . . . **978.7**
X-ray picture book of dinosaurs and other prehistoric creatures. /SENIOR,
K/1995/4-8/7 KC264 . . . . **567.9**
Y aun podria ser agua./FOWLER, A/1993/P-2/2 KC231 . . . . . **553.7**
Y domingo, siete./BADEN, R/1990/2-3/2 KB388 . . . . . **398.21**
Yang the third and her impossible family. /NAMIOKA, L/1995/
3-6/5 KH527 . . . . **Fic**
Yang the youngest and his terrible ear. /NAMIOKA, L/1994/
5-A/5 KH528 . . . . **Fic**
Yankee Doodle. 2nd ed. /BANGS, E/c1976, 1996/P-2/KD557 . . . . **789.2**
Yanks are coming: the United States in the First World War. /MARRIN, A/
1986/A/7 KE652 . . . . **940.3**
Yanomami: people of the Amazon. /SCHWARTZ, DM/1995/
4-6/7 KF105 . . . . **981**
Yard sale. /STEVENSON, J/1996/2-3/2 KH756 . . . . **Fic**
Year at Maple Hill Farm. /PROVENSEN, A/1978/K-2/4 KG290 . . . . . . **E**
Year in the city. /HENDERSON, K/1996/K-2/2 KF700 . . . . **E**
Year of beasts. /WOLFF, A/1986/P-K/1 KG757 . . . . **E**
Year of the perfect Christmas tree. /HOUSTON, G/1988/K-3/6 KF771 . **E**
Year on Monhegan Island. /DEAN, J/1995/4-6/8 KE926 . . . . **974.1**
Year on Monhegan Island (Sound recording cassette)./DEAN, J/1997/
4-6/8 KE926 . . . . **974.1**
Year you were born, 1981./MARTINET, J/1994/4-6/7 KE922 . . **973.927**
Year you were born, 1982./MARTINET, J/1994/4-6/7 KE922 . . **973.927**
Year you were born, 1983. /MARTINET, J/1992/4-6/7 KE922 . . **973.927**
Year you were born, 1984./MARTINET, J/1992/4-6/7 KE922 . . **973.927**
Year you were born, 1985./MARTINET, J/1992/4-6/7 KE922 . . **973.927**
Year you were born, 1986./MARTINET, J/1993/4-6/7 KE922 . . **973.927**
Year you were born, 1987./MARTINET, J/1993/4-6/7 KE922 . . **973.927**
Year you were born, 1988./MARTINET, J/1995/4-6/7 KE922 . . **973.927**
Year you were born, 1989./MARTINET, J/1996/4-6/7 KE922 . . **973.927**
Yearling. /RAWLINGS, MK/c1938, 1967/5-A/5 KH622 . . . . . . **Fic**
Yearling (Braille)./RAWLINGS, MK/n.d./5-A/5 KH622 . . . . . . **Fic**
Yearling (Talking book)./RAWLINGS, MK/n.d./5-A/5 KH622 . . . . **Fic**
Yeh-Shen, a Cinderella story from China. /LOUIE, A/c1982, 1990/
3-5/6 KB750 . . . . **398.27**
Yellowstone's cycle of fire. /STAUB, FJ/1993/4-6/8 KC306 . . . . **577.2**
Yertle the turtle, and other stories. /SEUSS, D/c1958/P-3/3 KG472 . . **CE E**
Yertle the turtle, and other stories (Sound recording cassette)./SEUSS, D/
1993/P-3/3 KG472 . . . . **CE E**
Yertle the turtle, and other stories (Videocassette)./SEUSS, D/1992/
P-3/3 KG472 . . . . **CE E**
YES MAG: CANADA'S SCIENCE MAGAZINE FOR KIDS. /1996-/
4-6/KA552 . . . . **050**
Yettele's feathers./ROTHENBERG, J/1995/2-4/3 KB771 . . . . . . **398.27**
Yo! Yes?./RASCHKA, C/1993/P-3/1 KG307 . . . . **E**
Yorubaland: the flowering of genius. /KOSLOW, P/1996/
6-A/12 KE726 . . . . **960**
Yoshiko and the foreigner. /LITTLE, MO/1996/3-5/2 KF997 . . . . **E**
Yossel Zissel and the wisdom of Chelm. /SCHWARTZ, A/1986/
2-4/2 KH684 . . . . **Fic**
You and me, Little Bear. /WADDELL, M/1996/P-K/1 KG677 . . . . **E**
You and me: poems of friendship. /MAVOR, S/1997/
K-2/KE072 . . . . **811.008**
You and your cat. /TAYLOR, D/1986/5-A/KD235 . . . . **636.8**
You and your dad. /ALPERT, L/1992/P-1/2 KA876 . . . . **306.874**
You and your dog. /TAYLOR, D/1986/5-A/KD224 . . . . **636.7**

You animal! /BOOTH, J/1996/4-6/5 KC913 612
You can't catch me! /OPPENHEIM, J/1986/P-1/KG193. . . . . E
You can't catch me! (Sound recording cassette)./OPPENHEIM, J/n.d./ P-1/KG193 . . . . E
You come too: favorite poems for young readers. /FROST, R/c1959, 1987/5-6/KD943 811
You come too: favorite poems for young readers (Braille)./FROST, R/n.d./ 5-6/KD943. 811
You know who. /CIARDI, J/c1964, 1991/3-5/KD923 811
You know who, John J. Plenty and Fiddler Dan, and other poems (Kit). / CIARDI, J/n.d./3-5/KD924 . . . . Kit 811
You know who, John J. Plenty and Fiddler Dan, and other poems (Talking book)./CIARDI, J/n.d./3-5/KD924 . . . . Kit 811
You look ridiculous said the rhinoceros to the hippopotamus. /WABER, B/ c1966/1-2/2 KG673 . . . . E
You silly goose. /WALSH, ES/1992/P-K/2 KG682 . . . . E
You want women to vote, Lizzie Stanton? /FRITZ, J/1995/ 3-6/5 KE549 . . . . B STANTON, E.
You were born on your very first birthday. /GIRARD, LW/1982/ P-2 KC948 . . . . 612.6
You'll sing a song and I'll sing a song (Compact disc). /JENKINS, E/1989/ P-2/KD633 . . . . SRC 789.3
You'll sing a song and I'll sing a song (Sound recording cassette). / JENKINS, E/c1966, 1989/P-2/KD633 . . . . SRC 789.3
You'll soon grow into them, Titch. /HUTCHINS, P/1983/P-2/2 KF808 . . . E
Young Abe Lincoln: the frontier days, 1809-1837. /HARNESS, C/1996/ 2-4/5 KE442 . . . . B LINCOLN, A.
Young Arthur Ashe: brave champion. /DEXTER, R/1996/ 2-3/6 KE242 . . . . CE B ASHE, A.
Young Arthur Ashe: brave champion (Talking book)./DEXTER, R/1996/ 2-3/6 KE242 . . . . CE B ASHE, A.
Young author's do-it-yourself book: how to write, illustrate, and produce your own book. /GUTHRIE, D/1994/2-6/4 KD863 808
Young Black Stallion./FARLEY, W/1991/4-6/5 KH105. . . . . Fic
Young Cam Jansen and the dinosaur game. /ADLER, DA/1996/ 1-2/2 KF132 . . . . E
Young Cam Jansen and the lost tooth. /ADLER, DA/1997/1-2/2 KF133 . E
Young Cam Jansen and the missing cookie. /ADLER, DA/1996/ 1-2/2 KF134 . . . . E
Young dancer. /BUSSELL, D/1994/3-6/8 KD692 . . . . 792.8
Young ghosts. Rev ed. /COHEN, D/c1978, 1994/4-A/9 KA603 . . . . . 133.1
Young Guinevere. /SAN SOUCI, RD/1993/3-4/6 KB482. . . . . . 398.22
Young inline skater. /EDWARDS, C/1996/3-6/6 KD771 . . . . . . 796.21
Young John Quincy. /HARNESS, C/1994/3-5/6 KE226 . . . B ADAMS, J.Q.
Young Lancelot. /SAN SOUCI, RD/1996/4-5/6 KB483 . . . . 398.22
Young landlords. /MYERS, WD/c1979/5-6/6 KH524 . . . . Fic
Young landlords (Sound recording cassette)./MYERS, WD/n.d./ 5-6/6 KH524 . . . . Fic
Young Merlin. /SAN SOUCI, RD/c1990, 1996/4-5/6 KB484 . . . . . 398.22
Young Mouse and Elephant: an East African folktale. /FARRIS, PJ/1996/ K-2/4 KB565 . . . . 398.24
Young Mozart. /ISADORA, R/1997/2-3/6 KE472 . . . . . . B MOZART, W.
Young naturalist, from Texas Parks and Wildlife Magazine. /HILLER, I/ 1983/3-A/9 KB907 508
Young patriot: the American Revolution as experienced by one boy. / MURPHY, J/1996/5-A/9 KE884 . . . . 973.3
Young person's guide to music. /ARDLEY, N/1995/ 5-A/8 KD518 . . . . BA 780
Young person's guide to the orchestra: Benjamin Britten's composition on CD. /GANERI, A/1996/4-6/10 KD545 . . . . BA 784.2
Young producer's video book: how to write, direct, and shoot your own video. /BENTLEY, N/1995/3-6/4 KD686 . . . . 791.45
Young rider. /GREEN, L/1993/3-8/8 KD856 . . . . 798.2
Young swimmer. /ROUSE, J/1997/3-6/6 KD848 . . . . 797.2
YOUR BODY: CIRCULATORY AND RESPIRATORY SYSTEMS (Videocassette). /1988/5-6/KC931 . . . . VCR 612
YOUR BODY: MUSCULAR AND SKELETAL SYSTEMS (Videocassette). / 1994/5-6/KC961 . . . . VCR 612.7
Your cat's wild cousins. /RYDEN, H/1991/4-6/5 KC825 . . . . . . 599.75
Your mother was a Neanderthal./SCIESZKA, J/1995/3-6/3 KH685 . . . Fic
Your mother was a neanderthal (Sound recording cassette)./SCIESZKA, J/ 1997/3-6/3 KH685 . . . . Fic
YOUR READING: AN ANNOTATED BOOKLIST FOR MIDDLE SCHOOL AND JUNIOR HIGH. 1995-96 ed. /1996/5-A/KA373 . . . REF 011.62
Your skin and mine. Rev. ed. /SHOWERS, P/1991/K-2/2 KC960 . . 612.7
YOUR TEETH (Kit). /1987/1-3/KC909 . . . . KIT 611
Your two brains. /STAFFORD, P/1986/5-6/8 KC981 . . . . 612.8
You're a genius, Blackboard Bear. /ALEXANDER, M/1995/ K-2/2 KF147 . . . . E
You're aboard spaceship Earth. /LAUBER, P/1996/1-3/3 KC147 550
You're invited to Bruce Lansky's poetry party! /LANSKY, B/1996/ 3-6/KD968. 811
You're the boss, Baby Duck! /HEST, A/1997/P-1/2 KF722 . . . . E

YOURS TILL BANANA SPLITS: 201 AUTOGRAPH RHYMES. /1995/ 3-6/KD894. . . . . 808.88
Yuck!: a big book of little horrors. /SNEDDEN, R/1996/ 3-8/7 KC375 579
Yukon River: an adventure to the gold fields of the Klondike. /LOURIE, P/ 1992/4-6/6 KE210 . . . . 917.98
Z was zapped. /VAN ALLSBURG, C/1987/2-A/KG640 . . . . E
Zack's story: growing up with same-sex parents. /GREENBERG, KE/1996/ 4-6/4 KA877 . . . . 306.874
Zany knock knocks. /COLE, RM/1993/3-6/KD726 . . . . 793.735
Zebra. /ARNOLD, C/1987/5-6/8 KC804 . . . . 599.665
Zebras. /LEPTHIEN, EU/1994/3-5/4 KC807 . . . . 599.665
Zebulon Pike: explorer of the Southwest. /SANFORD, WR/1996/ 5-6/8 KE497 . . . . B PIKE, Z.
Zeely. /HAMILTON, V/c1967/4-A/4 KH220 . . . . Fic
Zeely (Braille)./HAMILTON, V/n.d./4-A/4 KH220. . . . . Fic
Zeely (Talking book)./HAMILTON, V/n.d./4-A/4 KH220 . . . . Fic
Zeke Pippin. /STEIG, W/1994/1-3/6 KG549 . . . . E
Zella, Zack and Zodiac. /PEET, B/1986/K-3/4 KG231. . . . . E
Zella, Zack and Zodiac (Sound recording cassette)./PEET, B/n.d./ K-3/4 KG231. . . . . E
Zero gravity. /SKURZYNSKI, G/1994/3-6/5 KC100 531
Zero Street (Videocassette). /BERGIN, DP/1995/ 4-6/KA894 . . . . VCR 307.76
Zia. /O'DELL, S/1976/6-A/7 KH564 . . . . CE Fic
Zia (Talking book)./O'DELL, S/1993/6-A/7 KH564 . . . . CE Fic
ZILLIONS. /1980-/3-5/KA553 . . . . PER 050
Zin! zin! zin! a violin. /MOSS, L/1995/K-3/5 KG157 . . . . E
Zinnia and Dot. /ERNST, LC/1992/P-1/2 KF535 . . . . E
Zinnia and Dot (Sound recording cassette)./ERNST, LC/1994/ P-1/2 KF535 . . . . E
Zipping, zapping, zooming bats. /EARLE, A/1995/1-3/4 KC759 . . . 599.4
Zomo the rabbit: a trickster tale from West Africa. /MCDERMOTT, G/ 1992/K-2/1 KB619 . . . . 398.24
Zomo the Rabbit: a trickster tale from West Africa. (Big book)./ MCDERMOTT, G/1996/K-2/1 KB619 . . . . 398.24
Zoo. /GIBBONS, G/1991/K-2/4 KC441 . . . . CE 590.73
Zoo animals (Board book). /BARTON, B/1995/P/KF209 . . . . BB E
Zoo dreams. /HAZELAAR, C/1997/P-1/3 KF687 . . . . E
Zoo for Mister Muster. /LOBEL, A/c1962/P-1/5 KG015 . . . . E
Zoo (Kit)./GIBBONS, G/n.d./K-2/4 KC441 . . . . CE 590.73
ZOO ZILLIONS. School version (CD-ROM). /1966/ K-2/KB986. . . . . CDR 513.2
ZOOFUL OF ANIMALS. /1992/K-4/KE090. . . . . 811.008
Zoolutions: a mathematical expedition with topics for grades 4 through 8. / BURGUNDER, A/c1993, 1996//KA251 . . . . PROF 372.7
Zoom. /BANYAI, I/1995/P-A/KF197 . . . . E
Zoomrimes: poems about things that go. /CASSEDY, S/1993/ 3-6/KD921 811
ZOONOOZ. /1926-/4-6/KA554. . . . . PER 050
Zorro and Quwi: tales of a trickster guinea pig. /HICKOX, R/1997/ 1-3/3 KB590 . . . . 398.24
Zorro y sus amigos./MARSHALL, E/1996/K-2/1 KG064 . . . . CE E
Zucchini warriors. /KORMAN, G/1991/5-A/7 KH378 . . . . Fic
1, 2, 3 to the zoo. /CARLE, E/c1968/P-K/KF349 . . . . E
10 bears in my bed: a goodnight countdown. /MACK, S/1974/ P-1/1 KG052 . . . . E
100 amazing make-it-yourself science fair projects. /VECCHIONE, G/1995/ /KA287. . . . . PROF 507.8
100 great operas and their stories. Rev. ed. /SIMON, HW/c1957, 1989/ 4-A/KA454 . . . . REF 792.5
100 WORDS ABOUT ANIMALS. /1987/P-3/KC457 . . . . CE 591
100 WORDS ABOUT MY HOUSE. /1988/P-3/KD296 645
101 physics tricks: fun experiments with everyday materials. /CASH, T/ 1993/4-8/7 KC077 530
101 questions and answers about pets and people. /SQUIRE, A/1988/ 5-6/7 KD192 . . . . 636.088
101 things to do with a baby. /ORMEROD, J/1984/P-K/KG197 . . . . . E
11 African-American doctors. Rev. and expanded ed. /HAYDEN, RC/ 1992/5-6/8 KC900 . . . . 610.69
13th clue. /JONAS, A/1992/1-2/1 KF851 . . . . E
13th floor: a ghost story. /FLEISCHMAN, S/1995/5-A/6 KH127 . . CE Fic
13th floor: a ghost story (Talking book)./FLEISCHMAN, S/1995/ 5-A/6 KH127 . . . . CE Fic
14th Dalai Lama: spiritual leader of Tibet. /STEWART, W/1996/ 5-A/10 KA761 . . . . 294.3
16th century mosque. /MACDONALD, F/1994/4-A/10 KD391 726
18th century clothing. /KALMAN, B/1993/4-6/6 KB164 391
19th century clothing./KALMAN, B/1993/4-6/6 KB164 391
2 x 2 = boo!: a set of spooky multiplication stories. /LEEDY, L/1995/ 1-3/2 KB965 . . . . 513.2
20,000 leagues under the sea. /VERNE, J/1980/5-6/6 KH829 . . . . . . Fic
20,000 leagues under the sea (Braille)./VERNE, J/n.d./5-6/6 KH829 . . Fic

20,000 leagues under the sea (Sound recording cassette)./VERNE, J/n.d./
   5-6/6 KH829 . . . . **Fic**
20,000 leagues under the sea (Talking book)./VERNE, J/n.d./
   5-6/6 KH829 . . . . **Fic**
26 letters and 99 cents. /HOBAN, T/1987/P-2/KF748 . . . . **E**
3 pandas planting. /HALSEY, M/1994/P-1/2 KB958. . . . . **513.2**
3-2-1 CONTACT. /1979-/3-5/KA555. . . . . **PER 050**
3-2-1 CONTACT: EXPLORING WEATHER, CLIMATE AND SEASONS
   (Videocassette). /1988/2-A/KC223. . . . . **VCR 551.6**
450 more story stretchers for the primary grades: activities to expand
   children's favorite books./RAINES, SC/1994//KA240. . **PROF 372.64**
500 five minute games: quick and easy activities for 3-6 year olds. /
   SILBERG, J/1995//KA325 . . . . **PROF 790.1**
500 hats of Bartholomew Cubbins. /SEUSS, D/c1938, 1989/
   P-A/6 KG473. . . . . **E**
500 hats of Bartholomew Cubbins (Braille)./SEUSS, D/n.d./
   P-A/6 KG473. . . . . **E**
500 hats of Bartholomew Cubbins (Talking book)./SEUSS, D/n.d./
   P-A/6 KG473. . . . . **E**
500 NATIONS: STORIES OF THE NORTH AMERICAN INDIAN
   EXPERIENCE Academic ed. (CD-ROM). /1995/
   4-A/KE756. . . . . **CDR 970.1**
7 African-American scientists. Rev. and expanded ed. /HAYDEN, RC/1992/
   6-A/6 KB923 . . . . **509**
9 African-American inventors. Rev. and expanded ed. /HAYDEN, RC/
   1992/6-A/7 KC891. . . . . **609**

Aardvark--Fiction.
BROWN, MT/Arthur goes to camp. /1982/K-2/2 KF271 . . . **CE E**
Arthur writes a story. /1996/K-2/2 KF272 . . . . **E**
Arthur's baby. /1987/K-3/2 KF274 . . . . **E**
Arthur's first sleepover. /1994/K-2/2 KF275 . . . . **E**
Arthur's nose. /c1976/K-2/2 KF276. . . . . **CE E**
Arthur's teacher trouble. /1986/K-3/4 KF277 . . . . . . **CE E**
Arthur's tooth. /1985/1-3/2 KF278 . . . . **CE E**
Arthur's TV trouble. /1995/K-2/2 KF279 . . . . **E**
D.W. flips. /1987/P-2/1 KF281 . . . . **E**
Aaron, Henry.
RENNERT, RS/Henry Aaron. /1993/5-A/9 KE222 . **B AARON, H.**
Abandoned children.
WARREN, A/Orphan train rider: one boy's true story. /1996/
4-6/8 KB015 . . . . **362.73**
Abbott, Jim.
JENNINGS, J/Long shots: they beat the odds. /1990/
5-6/6 KD762 . . . . **796**
KRAMER, J/Jim Abbott. /1996/4-5/6 KE223 . . . . **B ABBOTT, J.**
Abby Aldrich Rockefeller Folk Art Center.
FOLK ART COUNTING BOOK. /1992/P-3/1 KD420. . . . . . **745**
ABC books SEE Alphabet.
Abenaki Indians--Captivities--Fiction.
DUBOIS, ML/Abenaki Captive. /1994/6-A/6 KH085. . . . . . . **Fic**
Abenaki Indians--Fiction.
BRUCHAC, J/Dog people: native dog stories. /1995/
4-6/5 KG934. . . . . **Fic**
Abenaki Indians--Folklore.
BRUCHAC, J/Gluskabe and the four wishes. /1995/
3-5/6 KB272 . . . . **398.2**
Gluskabe stories (Sound recording cassette). /1990/
4-5/KB273. . . . . **SRC 398.2**
TAYLOR, CJ/How Two-Feather was saved from loneliness: an
Abenaki legend. /1990/3-4/2 KB716 . . . . **398.26**
Abolitionists.
ADLER, DA/Picture book of Sojourner Truth. /1994/
2-5/6 KE572 . . . . **B TRUTH, S.**
COLLINS, JL/John Brown and the fight against slavery. /1991/
3-5/6 KE263 . . . . **B BROWN, J.**
COX, C/Fiery vision: the life and death of John Brown. /1997/
5-A/8 KE264 . . . . **B BROWN, J.**
FREDERICK DOUGLASS (VIDEOCASSETTE). /1992/
4-A/KE325. . . . . **VCR B DOUGLASS, F.**
FRITZ, J/Harriet Beecher Stowe and the Beecher preachers. /1994/
6-A/7 KE556 . . . . **B STOWE, H.**
MCKISSACK, P/Sojourner Truth: ain't I a woman? /1992/
6-A/7 KE573 . . . . **B TRUTH, S.**
WEINER, E/Story of Frederick Douglass: voice of freedom. /1996/
3-5/3 KE326 . . . . **B DOUGLASS, F.**
YATES, E/Prudence Crandall: woman of courage. 2nd ed. /1996/
6-A/6 KE306 . . . . **B CRANDALL, P.**
Abolitionists--Fiction.
ROSEN, MJ/School for Pompey Walker. /1995/4-8/6 KH653 . **Fic**
Aborigines SEE Ethnology; and names of Aboriginal races e.g. Australian
aborigines; Indians of North America.
Abubakari.
ABUBAKARI: THE EXPLORER KING OF MALI (VIDEOCASSETTE). /
1992/5-6/KE224. . . . . **VCR B ABUBAKARI**

Academic achievement.
DIMIDJIAN, VJ/Early childhood at risk: actions and advocacy for
young children. /1989//KA190 . . . . **PROF 372**
Academy Awards (Motion pictures)--Fiction.
SHARMAT, MW/Genghis Khan: dog-gone Hollywood. /1995/
2-5/2 KH704 . . . . **Fic**
Accidents SEE ALSO Disasters; Fires; First aid; Shipwrecks.
Accidents--Fiction.
BAUER, MD/On my honor. /1986/5-6/7 KG882 . . . . . . **CE Fic**
Accidents--Prevention SEE ALSO Safety.
Accidents--Prevention.
GUTMAN, B/Hazards at home. /1996/5-6/7 KB022. . . . . . **363.1**
K.C.'S FIRST BUS RIDE (VIDEOCASSETTE). /1994/
P-1/KB023 . . . . **VCR 363.1**
SAFETY ON WHEELS (VIDEOCASSETTE). /1994/
P-1/KB024 . . . . **VCR 363.1**
Acid rain--Experiments.
RYBOLT, TR/Environmental experiments about water. /1993/
5-6/7 KB066 . . . . **363.73**
Acoma Indians--Social life and customs.
ANCONA, G/Earth daughter: Alicia of Acoma Pueblo. /1995/
2-4/6 KE791 . . . . **970.489**
Acoma Pueblo (N.M.).
ANCONA, G/Earth daughter: Alicia of Acoma Pueblo. /1995/
2-4/6 KE791 . . . . **970.489**
Acoustics--Experiments.
DARLING, DJ/Sounds interesting: the science of acoustics. /1991/
6-A/8 KC103 . . . . **534**
Acrobats--Fiction.
STEVENSON, J/Flying Acorns. /1993/1-3/3 KG559. . . . . **E**
Acting SEE ALSO Drama in education; Plays; Puppet plays.
Acting.
BULLOCH, I/I want to be an actor. /1996/3-5/5 KD688 . . . . **792**
Acting--Costume SEE Costume.
Acting--Makeup SEE Makeup, Theatrical.
Activity programs in education.
BARCHERS, SI/Creating and managing the literate classroom. /
1990/ /KA218 . . . . **PROF 372.6**
BAUER, CF/Celebrations: read-aloud holiday and theme book
programs. /1985//KA342. . . . . **PROF 808.8**
CREATIVE DRAMA IN THE EARLY CHILDHOOD CLASSROOM
(VIDEOCASSETTE). /1991//KA220 . . . . **VCR PROF 372.6**
LAUGHLIN, MK/Literature-based reading: /1990/
/KA210. . . . . **PROF 372.4**
Literature-based social studies: /1991//KA261 . . . **PROF 372.83**
LAZEAR, DG/Seven pathways of learning: teaching students and
parents about multiple /1994//KA174. . . . . **PROF 370.15**
MCELMEEL, SL/McElmeel booknotes: literature across the
curriculum. /1993//KA225 . . . . **PROF 372.6**
Activity programs in education--Handbooks, manuals, etc.
MARKS, DF/Glues, brews, and goos: recipes and formulas for
almost any classroom project. /1996//KA216 . . . . . **PROF 372.5**
Actors and actresses.
ADAMS, MA/Whoopi Goldberg: from street to stardom. /1993/
4-6/7 KE371 . . . . **B GOLDBERG, W.**
JUDSON, K/Ronald Reagan. /1997/
6-A/10 KE504 . . . . **B REAGAN, R.**

MCKISSACK, P/Paul Robeson: a voice to remember. /1992/
2-5/2 KE514 . . . . **B ROBESON, P.**

Actors and actresses--Fiction.
GREENFIELD, E/Grandpa's face. /1988/K-1/2 KF641 . . . . **E**

Adam (Biblical figure).
OPPENHEIM, SL/And the Earth trembled: the creation of Adam and
Eve. /1996/5-6/3 KA788 . . . . **297**
Iblis. /1994/4-5/4 KA789 . . . . **297**

Adams, Ansel.
DUNLAP, J/Eye on the wild: a story about Ansel Adams. /1995/
3-6/7 KE225 . . . . **B ADAMS, A.**

Adams, John Quincy--Childhood and youth.
HARNESS, C/Young John Quincy. /1994/
3-5/6 KE226 . . . . **B ADAMS, J.Q.**

Adams, Lucy.
CARRICK, C/Two very little sisters. /1993/2-4/5 KC879 . . . **599.9**

Adams, Sam.
FRITZ, J/Why don't you get a horse, Sam Adams? /c1974/
3-5/7 KE227 . . . . **CE B ADAMS, S.**

Adams, Sarah.
CARRICK, C/Two very little sisters. /1993/2-4/5 KC879 . . . **599.9**
Adaptation (Biology) SEE ALSO Man--Influence on environment.

Adaptation (Biology).
CAPON, B/Plant survival: adapting to a hostile world. /1994/
A/9 KC397 . . . . **581.4**
WHERE DO ANIMALS GO IN WINTER? (VIDEOCASSETTE). /
1995/3-6/KC463 . . . . **VCR 591.4**
3-2-1 CONTACT: EXPLORING WEATHER, CLIMATE AND
SEASONS (VIDEOCASSETTE). /1988/2-A/KC223 . . **VCR 551.6**

Addams, Jane.
MCPHERSON, SS/Peace and bread: the story of Jane Addams. /
1993/4-6/5 KE228 . . . . **B ADDAMS, J.**

Addition.
GIGANTI, JR., P/Each orange had 8 slices: a counting book. /
1992/P-1/2 KB989 . . . . **513.5**
HULME, JN/Sea sums. /1996/P-2/3 KB961 . . . . **513.2**
LEEDY, L/Mission: addition. /1997/K-3/2 KB964 . . . . . **513.2**
LONG, L/Domino addition. /1996/P-2/2 KB966 . . . . . . **513.2**
MCMILLAN, B/Jelly beans for sale. /1996/K-3/2 KA951 . . . **332.4**
MURPHY, SJ/Too many kangaroo things to do! /1996/
P-3/2 KB974 . . . . **513.2**

Adolescence.
JOHNSTON, A/Girls speak out: finding your true self. /1997/
A/6 KA646 . . . . **155.5**
SIMMONS, CW/Becoming myself: true stories about learning from
life. /1994/5-A/6 KA664 . . . . **158**

Adolescence--Fiction.
BLUME, J/Are you there God? It's me, Margaret. /c1970, 1982/
4-6/5 KG905 . . . . **CE Fic**
Deenie. /1973/6/4 KG907 . . . . **Fic**
Otherwise known as Sheila the Great. /1972/4-6/4 KG912 . . **Fic**
Then again, maybe I won't. /1971/6-A/5 KG915 . . . . **Fic**
BYARS, BC/Bingo Brown and the language of love. /1989/
5-A/5 KG957 . . . . **Fic**
Burning questions of Bingo Brown. /1990/5-A/5 KG958 . . . . **Fic**
Summer of the swans. /c1970/5-6/6 KG964 . . . . . **CE Fic**
HUNT, I/Up a road slowly. /1993/A/7 KH292 . . . . **Fic**
NAYLOR, PR/Alice in rapture, sort of. /1989/6-A/6 KH533 . . . Fic
Adoption SEE ALSO Foster home care.

Adoption.
BANISH, R/Forever family. /1992/2-4/3 KB011 . . . . **362.73**
COLE, J/How I was adopted: Samantha's story. /1995/
1-3/2 KB012 . . . . **362.73**
ROSENBERG, MB/Growing up adopted. /1989/
5-6/7 KB013 . . . . **362.73**
SCHWARTZ, P/Carolyn's story: a book about an adopted girl. /
1996/3-6/6 KB014 . . . . **362.73**

Adoption--Fiction.
BLOOM, S/Family for Jamie: an adoption story. /1991/
P-2/2 KF235 . . . . **E**
HOME AT LAST (VIDEOCASSETTE). /c1988, 1997/
5-A/KH276 . . . . **VCR Fic**
NEUFELD, J/Edgar Allan: a novel. /c1968/4-A/5 KH545 . . . **Fic**
PELLEGRINI, N/Families are different. /1991/P-1/2 KG232 . . . . **E**
ROSEN, MJ/Bonesy and Isabel. /1995/2-3/6 KG352 . . . . **E**
SAY, A/Allison. /1997/2-4/2 KH678 . . . . **Fic**
TURNER, A/Through moon and stars and night skies. /1990/
P-2/1 KG629 . . . . **CE E**

Adoption--Songs and music.
MCCUTCHEON, J/Happy adoption day! /1996/
2-4/3 KD637 . . . . **789.3**

Adventure and adventurers SEE ALSO Discoveries (in geography);
Explorers; Frontier and pioneer life; Shipwrecks; Survival.

Adventure and adventurers.
STANLEY, D/True adventure of Daniel Hall. /1995/
2-5/7 KE159 . . . . **910.4**

Adventure and adventurers--Fiction.
AIKEN, J/Cold Shoulder Road. /1995/5-A/5 KG823 . . . . **Fic**
Is underground. /1993/5-A/7 KG824 . . . . **Fic**
ALEXANDER, L/Illyrian adventure. /1986/5-A/5 KG837 . . . . **Fic**
Jedera adventure. /1990/5-A/7 KG839 . . . . **Fic**
Remarkable journey of Prince Jen. /1991/6-A/6 KG840 . . . . **Fic**
Westmark. /1982/5-6/6 KG841 . . . . **Fic**
AVI /Beyond the western sea: book one: the escape from home. /
1996/6-A/5 KG857 . . . . **Fic**
Beyond the western sea: book two: Lord Kirkle's money. /1996/
6-A/5 KG858 . . . . **Fic**
FARMER, N/Girl named Disaster. /1996/6-A/5 KH109 . . . . **Fic**
FLEISCHMAN, S/Chancy and the Grand Rascal. /c1966, 1997/
4-6/5 KH120 . . . . **Fic**
Midnight horse. /1990/5-A/4 KH125 . . . . **Fic**
HOBBS, W/Ghost canoe. /1997/5-A/6 KH267 . . . . **Fic**
NAYLOR, PR/Grand escape. /1993/3-6/7 KH536 . . . . . . **Fic**
PINKWATER, DM/Wallpaper from space. /1996/
2-5/3 KH605 . . . . **Fic**
RIDLEY, P/Kasper in the glitter. /1997/5-A/4 KH634 . . . . . **Fic**
STEVENSON, J/All aboard! /1995/1-3/2 KG557 . . . . **E**
STEVENSON, RL/David Balfour: being memoirs of the further
adventures of David Balfour at home and abroad. /c1952, 1994/
6-A/6 KH757 . . . . **Fic**
Kidnapped: being the memoirs of the adventures of David Balfour
in the year 1751. /1982/5-6/6 KH758 . . . . **Fic**
Treasure Island. /c1911, 1981/5-A/6 KH759 . . . . **Fic**
Treasure Island (Talking book). /1993/5-A/KH760 . . . **TB Fic**
TEAGUE, M/Secret shortcut. /1996/1-3/2 KG596 . . . . **E**
VERNE, J/20,000 leagues under the sea. /1980/5-6/6 KH829 . **Fic**
WALLACE, BB/Cousins in the castle. /1996/5-A/7 KH837 . . . . **Fic**
YORKE, M/Miss Butterpat goes wild! /1993/3-5/5 KH898 . . . . **Fic**

Advertising--Fiction.
BROWN, MT/Arthur's TV trouble. /1995/K-2/2 KF279 . . . . . . **E**

Advertising--Television.
BUY ME THAT! A KID'S SURVIVAL GUIDE TO TV ADVERTISING
(VIDEOCASSETTE). /1990/2-5/KD316 . . . . **VCR 659.14**

Advertising, Truth in.
BUY ME THAT! A KID'S SURVIVAL GUIDE TO TV ADVERTISING
(VIDEOCASSETTE). /1990/2-5/KD316 . . . . **VCR 659.14**

Aerobics.
ROCK 'N ROLL FITNESS FUN (SOUND RECORDING CASSETTE).
/1989/K-6/KC990 . . . . **SRC 613.7**

Aeronautics SEE ALSO Air pilots; Airplanes; Airports; Astronautics;
Balloons; Flight; Gliders (Aeronautics); Helicopters; Kites; Rockets
(Aeronautics); Unidentified flying objects.

Aeronautics.
GUNNING, TG/Dream planes. /1992/5-6/7 KD109 . . . . **629.133**

Aeronautics--Biography.
FREEDMAN, R/Wright brothers: how they invented the airplane. /
1991/A/7 KD094 . . . . **629.13**
MARQUARDT, M/Wilbur and Orville and the flying machine. /
1989/1-3/1 KD096 . . . . **629.13**
Aeronautics--Flights SEE ALSO Space flight.

Aeronautics--History.
GIBBONS, G/Flying. /1986/K-2/2 KD095 . . . . **629.13**

Aeronautics, Military--History.
LIEBERMAN, S/Intrepid birdmen: the fighter pilots of World War I
(Sound recording cassette). /1993/A/KE654. . . . . . **SRC 940.4**

Afghanistan--Fiction.
MCKAY, JR., L/Caravan. /1995/3-5/6 KH480 . . . . **Fic**

Africa.
ONYEFULU, I/A is for Africa. /1993/2-4/5 KE178 . . . . . . **916**
ROOTS OF AFRICAN CIVILIZATION (VIDEOCASSETTE). /1996/
6-A/KE729. . . . . **VCR 960**

Africa--Description and travel.
BRANDENBURG, J/Sand and fog: adventures in Southern Africa. /
1994/5-6/6 KE740 . . . . **968.81**
CHIASSON, J/African journey. /1987/A/11 KE725 . . . . **960**

Africa--Drama.
WINTHER, B/Plays from African tales: one-act, royalty-free
dramatizations for young people, /1992/4-A/KE093 . . . . . . **812**

Africa--Fiction.
ADLERMAN, D/Africa calling, nighttime falling. /1996/
P-2/KF135 . . . . **E**
DAVOL, MW/How Snake got his hiss: an original tale. /1996/
K-2/2 KF450 . . . . **E**
GRIFALCONI, A/Darkness and the butterfly. /1987/
K-2/4 KF645 . . . . **E**

HOFFMAN, M/Boundless Grace. /1995/1-3/5 KF762 . . . . **E**
MENNEN, I/Somewhere in Africa. /1992/K-2/4 KG129 . . . . . **E**
MOLLEL, TM/Big boy. /1995/K-2/3 KG150 . . . . **E**
STEPTOE, J/Mufaro's beautiful daughters: an African tale. /1987/
K-3/5 KG552 . . . . **CE E**
WALTER, MP/Brother to the wind. /1985/1-3/3 KG684 . . . . . **E**
WILLIAMS, KL/Galimoto. /1990/1-2/2 KG727 . . . . **CE E**
When Africa was home. /1991/K-3/2 KG729 . . . . **E**

Africa--Folklore.
AARDEMA, V/Lonely lioness and the ostrich chicks: a Masai tale. /
1996/K-2/5 KB516 . . . . **398.24**
This for that: a Tonga tale. /1997/K-2/2 KB517. . . . . . **398.24**
Who's in Rabbit's house? (Videocassette). /1995/
K-3/KB518 . . . . **VCR 398.24**
ANDERSON, DA/Origin of life on Earth: an African creation myth.
/1991/4-5/4 KA730 . . . . **291.2**
BARBOSA, RA/African animal tales. /1993/2-4/6 KB526. . **398.24**
BRYAN, A/Lion and the ostrich chicks and other African folk tales. /
1986/4-6/3 KB544 . . . . **398.24**
CALDECOTT VIDEO LIBRARY. VOL. IV (VIDEOCASSETTE). /1992/
P-3/KB274. . . . . **VCR 398.2**
CHOCOLATE, DM/Imani in the belly. /1994/2-3/5 KB431 . **398.22**
COURLANDER, H/Fire on the mountain and other stories from
Ethiopia and Eritrea. /c1950, 1995/3-6/6 KB277. . . . . . **398.2**
FARRIS, PJ/Young Mouse and Elephant: an East African folktale. /
1996/K-2/4 KB565 . . . . **398.24**
FORD, B/Hunter who was king and other African tales. /1994/
K-3/4 KB299 . . . . **398.2**
GLEESON, B/Koi and the kola nuts (Kit). /1992/
2-5/KB446 . . . . **KIT 398.22**
GRIFALCONI, A/Village of round and square houses. /1986/
3-4/6 KB739 . . . . **CE 398.27**
HALEY, GE/Story, a story: an African tale. /c1970/
3-5/5 KB580 . . . . **CE 398.24**
JAFFE, N/Voice for the people: the life and work of Harold
Courlander. /1997/KA367. . . . . **PROF B COURLAND**
KAULA, EM/African village folktales, vols 1-3 (Talking book). /n.d./
4-6/KB746 . . . . **TB 398.27**
KIMMEL, EA/Anansi and the talking melon. /1994/
2-3/2 KB601 . . . . **CE 398.24**
Anansi goes fishing. /1991, c1992/K-2/2 KB602 . . . . **CE 398.24**
KURTZ, J/Trouble. /1997/K-2/3 KB748 . . . . **398.27**
LESTER, J/How many spots does a leopard have? and other tales. /
c1989, 1994/5-6/6 KB335 . . . . **398.2**
LEWIS, IM/Why ostriches don't fly and other tales from the African
bush. /1997/4-6/6 KB336 . . . . **398.2**
MCNEIL, H/Hyena and the moon: stories to listen to from Kenya
(Talking book). /1995/5-6/KB346 . . . . **TB 398.2**
Hyena and the moon: stories to tell from Kenya. /1994/
5-6/7 KB347 . . . . **398.2**
MOLLEL, TM/Orphan boy: a Maasai story. /1990/
4-5/4 KB406 . . . . **398.21**
RAPPAPORT, D/New king. /1995/4-A/3 KB473 . . . . **398.22**
SIERRA, J/Elephant's wrestling match. /1992/
P-2/4 KB652 . . . . **398.24**

Africa--Folklore--Drama.
WINTHER, B/Plays from African tales: one-act, royalty-free
dramatizations for young people, /1992/4-A/KE093 . . . . . . **812**

Africa--Folklore--Software.
P.J.'S READING ADVENTURES (CD-ROM). /1996/
K-3/KB252. . . . . **CDR 398**

Africa--Geography.
AFRICA (VIDEOCASSETTE). /1991/4-A/KE724 . . . . . . **VCR 960**

Africa--History.
KOSLOW, P/Dahomey: the warrior kings. /1997/
6-A/9 KE736 . . . . **966.9**
Yorubaland: the flowering of genius. /1996/6-A/12 KE726 . **960**
MCKISSACK, P/Royal kingdoms of Ghana, Mali, and Songhay: life
in medieval Africa. /c1994, 1995/A/8 KE734 . . . . **966.2**
ROOTS OF AFRICAN CIVILIZATION (VIDEOCASSETTE). /1996/
6-A/KE729. . . . . **VCR 960**

Africa--Poetry.
OLALEYE, I/Distant talking drum: poems from Nigeria. /1995/
K-2/KE139 . . . . **896**

Africa--Social life and customs.
CHIASSON, J/African journey. /1987/A/11 KE725 . . . . . . **960**
KAULA, EM/African village folktales, vols 1-3 (Talking book). /n.d./
4-6/KB746 . . . . **TB 398.27**
MUSGROVE, M/Ashanti to Zulu: African traditions. /c1976/
4-6/6 KE727 . . . . **960**
ONYEFULU, I/Emeka's gift: an African counting story. /1995/
1-4/5 KE728 . . . . **960**

Africa--Software.
AFRICA TRAIL (CD-ROM). /1995/4-A/KE723 . . . . . . **CDR 960**

Africa, East--Social life and customs.
FEELINGS, ML/Jambo means hello: Swahili alphabet book. /1974/
1-3/7 KF545 . . . . **E**

Africa, West--Folklore.
AARDEMA, V/Why mosquitoes buzz in people's ears: a West
African tale. /1975/1-3/5 KB519 . . . . **CE 398.24**
Why mosquitoes buzz in people's ears (Talking book). /1978/
2-4/KB520 . . . . **TB 398.24**
ARKHURST, JC/Adventures of Spider: West African folktales. /
c1964, 1992/2-3/5 KB524 . . . . **398.24**
BRYAN, A/Story of lightning and thunder. /1993/
K-2/2 KB702 . . . . **398.26**
COURLANDER, H/Cow-tail switch and other West African stories. /
c1947, 1987/4-6/7 KB728 . . . . **398.27**
DIAKITE, BW/Hunterman and the crocodile: a West African folktale.
/1997/2-3/5 KB560 . . . . **398.24**
KIMMEL, EA/Anansi and the moss-covered rock. /1988/
1-2/4 KB600 . . . . **CE 398.24**
MCDERMOTT, G/Anansi the spider: a tale from the Ashanti. /
c1972/1-3/2 KB616. . . . . **398.24**
Zomo the rabbit: a trickster tale from West Africa. /1992/
K-2/1 KB619 . . . . **398.24**
MEDEARIS, AS/Singing man: adapted from a West African folktale.
/1994/4-5/6 KB757 . . . . **398.27**
SOUHAMI, J/Leopard's drum: an Asante tale from West Africa. /
1995/P-1/2 KB654 . . . . **398.24**

Africa, West--Social life and customs.
ANGELOU, M/Kofi and his magic. /1996/2-5/3 KE735. . . . **966.7**
African Americans SEE Afro-Americans; and subjects beginning with Afro-
American.

African elephant.
MOSS, C/Little big ears; the story of Ely. /1997/
K-4/6 KC812 . . . . **599.67**
PATENT, DH/African elephants: giants of the land. /1991/
4-6/6 KC813 . . . . **599.67**

Africanized honeybee.
PRINGLE, LP/Killer bees. Rev. ed. /1990/A/8 KC578 . . . . **595.79**

Afro-American air pilots.
MYERS, WD/Place called heartbreak: a story of Vietnam. /1993/
5-6/6 KE721 . . . . **959.704**

Afro-American art.
AFRICAN AMERICAN ART: PAST AND PRESENT
(VIDEOCASSETTE). /1992/4-A/KD371. . . . . **VCR 704**

Afro-American artists.
AFRICAN AMERICAN ART: PAST AND PRESENT
(VIDEOCASSETTE). /1992/4-A/KD371. . . . . **VCR 704**
FAITH RINGGOLD PAINTS CROWN HEIGHTS (VIDEOCASSETTE).
/1995/5-A/KD461 . . . . **VCR 746.46**
IN PRAISE OF OUR FATHERS AND OUR MOTHERS: A BLACK
FAMILY TREASURY BY OUTSTANDING /1997/
3-6/KA867 . . . . **306.85**
JACOB LAWRENCE: THE GLORY OF EXPRESSION
(VIDEOCASSETTE). /1995/5-A/KD487 . . . . **VCR 759.13**

Afro-American artists--Bio-bibliography.
CORETTA SCOTT KING AWARDS BOOK: FROM VISION TO
REALITY. /1994/KA008 . . . . **PROF 011.008**

Afro-American authors.
IN PRAISE OF OUR FATHERS AND OUR MOTHERS: A BLACK
FAMILY TREASURY BY OUTSTANDING /1997/
3-6/KA867 . . . . **306.85**
LYONS, ME/Sorrow's kitchen: the life and folklore of Zora Neale
Hurston. /1990/6-A/6 KE396 . . . . **B HURSTON, Z.**

Afro-American authors--Bio-bibliography.
CORETTA SCOTT KING AWARDS BOOK: FROM VISION TO
REALITY. /1994/KA008 . . . . **PROF 011.008**

Afro-American cookery.
BRADY, AA/Kwanzaa karamu: cooking and crafts for a Kwanzaa
feast. /1995/5-6/5 KD284 . . . . **641.59**

Afro-American cookery--History.
MACK-WILLIAMS, K/Food and our history. /1995/
5-6/7 KD287 . . . . **641.59**

Afro-American dance--History.
MEDEARIS, AS/Dance. /1997/4-6/11 KD704 . . . . **793.3**

Afro-American families.
IN PRAISE OF OUR FATHERS AND OUR MOTHERS: A BLACK
FAMILY TREASURY BY OUTSTANDING AUTHORS AND
ARTISTS. /1997/3-6/KA867 . . . . **306.85**

Afro-American soldiers.
SCHLISSEL, L/Black frontiers: a history of African American heroes
in the Old West. /1995/4-6/8 KF048 . . . . **978**

Afro-American women--Biography.
WOMEN OF HOPE: AFRICAN AMERICANS WHO MADE A
DIFFERENCE (PICTURE). /1994/4-6/KA863 . . . . **PIC 305.8**

Afro-Americans.
AFRICAN AMERICAN ALMANAC. 7TH ED. /1997/
5-A/KA486 . . . . **REF 973**

Afro-Americans--Biography.
ADAMS, MA/Whoopi Goldberg: from street to stardom. /1993/
4-6/7 KE371 . . . . **B GOLDBERG, W.**
ADLER, DA/Picture book of Jackie Robinson. /1994/
2-4/6 KE515 . . . . **B ROBINSON, J.**
Picture book of Jesse Owens. /1992/
3-4/6 KE486 . . . . **B OWENS, J.**
Picture book of Martin Luther King, Jr. /1989/
3-4/4 KE420 . . . . **CE B KING, M.L.**
Picture book of Sojourner Truth. /1994/
2-5/6 KE572 . . . . **B TRUTH, S.**
AFRICAN AMERICAN ALMANAC. 7TH ED. /1997/
5-A/KA486 . . . . **REF 973**
AFRICAN AMERICAN BIOGRAPHY. /1994/
5-A/KA398 . . . . **REF 305.8**
AFRICAN AMERICAN VOICES. /1996/5-A/KA487 . . . . **REF 973**
APPLEGATE, K/Story of two American generals: Benjamin O. Davis,
Jr.; Colin L. Powell. /1995/5-6/6 KA981 355
BARRETT, T/Nat Turner and the slave revolt. /c1993, 1995/
5-6/6 KE577 . . . . **B TURNER, N.**
BLACK INNOVATORS (PICTURE). /1994/4-6/KA837 . . **PIC 305.8**
BLACK WEST (VIDEOCASSETTE). /1992/5-6/KF028 . . **VCR 978**
BLUE, R/Colin Powell: straight to the top. Updated ed. /1997/
3-6/7 KE502 . . . . **B POWELL, C.**
BOOKER (VIDEOCASSETTE). /1983/
3-6/KE585 . . . . **VCR B WASHINGTON, B**
BRAY, RL/Martin Luther King. /1995/2-6/7 KE421 . **B KING, M.L.**
BURNS, K/Black stars in orbit: NASA'S African American
astronauts. /1995/3-6/8 KD136 . . . . **629.45**
BUTTS, ER/May Chinn: the best medicine. /1995/
5-A/8 KE288 . . . . **B CHINN, M.**
CHRISTOPHER, M/At the plate with...Ken Griffey Jr. /1997/
3-6/6 KE380 . . . . **B GRIFFEY,K. JR**
On the court with...Michael Jordan. /1996/
4-6/8 KE409 . . . . **CE B JORDAN, M.**
COHEN, N/Jackie Joyner-Kersee. /1992/
4-6/6 KE412 . . . . **B JOYNER-KERSEE**
COLES, R/Story of Ruby Bridges. /1995/2-5/4 KA902 . . . . **323.1**
COLMAN, P/Madam C.J. Walker: building a business empire. /
1994/4-6/7 KE583 . . . . **B WALKER, C.J.**
COOPER, F/Coming home: from the life of Langston Hughes. /
1994/3-5/6 KE394 . . . . **B HUGHES, L.**
CREWS, D/Bigmama's. /1991/K-2/2 KE309 . . . **CE B CREWS, D.**
CWIKLIK, R/Malcolm X and black pride. /1991/
5-6/6 KE455 . . . . **B MALCOLM X**
DAVIS, B/Black heroes of the American revolution. /1976/
5-6/10 KE877 . . . . **973.3**
DEXTER, R/Young Arthur Ashe: brave champion. /1996/
2-3/6 KE242 . . . . **CE B ASHE, A.**
ELISH, D/Harriet Tubman and the Underground Railroad. /1993/
4-6/4 KE574 . . . . **B TUBMAN, H.**
James Meredith and school desegregation. /1994/
4-5/7 KE463 . . . . **B MEREDITH, J.**
ELLIS, VF/Wynton Marsalis. /1997/
5-A/10 KE459 . . . . **B MARSALIS, W.**
FAITH RINGGOLD PAINTS CROWN HEIGHTS (VIDEOCASSETTE).
/1995/5-A/KE461 . . . . **VCR 746.46**
FERRIS, J/What I had was singing: the story of Marian Anderson. /
1994/5-A/6 KE236 . . . . **B ANDERSON, M.**
FREDERICK DOUGLASS (VIDEOCASSETTE). /1992/
4-A/KE325. . . . . **VCR B DOUGLASS, F.**
GEORGE WASHINGTON CARVER: A MAN OF VISION
(VIDEOCASSETTE). /1990/5-A/KE281 . . . . **VCR B CARVER, G.**
GOLENBOCK, P/Teammates. /1990/3-6/6 KD798 . . . . . **796.357**
GREAT BLACK AMERICANS. SET I (PICTURE). /1996/
4-6/KA846 . . . . **PIC 305.8**
GREENE, C/Roy Campanella: major-league champion. /1994/
1-2/2 KE275 . . . . **B CAMPANELLA, R**
GUTMAN, B/Frank Thomas: power hitter. /1996/
3-5/6 KE563 . . . . **B THOMAS, F.**
Gail Devers. /1996/5-6/6 KE319 . . . . **B DEVERS, G.**
Grant Hill: basketball's high flier. /1996/
5-6/7 KE390 . . . . **B HILL, G.**
Michael Jordan: basketball to baseball and back. Rev. ed. /1995/
4-6/8 KE410 . . . . **B JORDAN, M.**
HART, PS/Up in the air: the story of Bessie Coleman. /
4-6/8 KE299 . . . . **B COLEMAN, B.**
HASKINS, J/One more river to cross: the stories of twelve Black
Americans. /1992/5-A/7 KA847 . . . . **305.8**
Outward dreams: black inventors and their inventions. /1991/
A/10 KC890 . . . . **609**

HAYDEN, RC/11 African-American doctors. Rev. and expanded ed.
/1992/5-6/8 KC900 . . . . **610.69**
7 African-American scientists. Rev. and expanded ed. /1992/
6-A/6 KB923 . . . . **509**
9 African-American inventors. Rev. and expanded ed. /1992/
6-A/7 KC891 . . . . **609**
HUDSON, W/Five notable inventors. /1995/3-5/4 KC892 . . . **609**
JACOB LAWRENCE: THE GLORY OF EXPRESSION
(VIDEOCASSETTE). /1995/5-A/KD487 . . . . **VCR 759.13**
JOSEPHSON, JP/Jesse Owens: track and field legend. /1997/
5-A/8 KE487 . . . . **B OWENS, J.**
KNAPP, R/Chris Webber: star forward. /1997/
5-6/7 KE590 . . . . **B WEBBER, C.**
KRAMER, B/Ken Griffey Junior: all-around all-star. /1996/
4-5/4 KE381 . . . . **B GRIFFEY,K. JR**
KRAMER, J/Bo Jackson. /1996/4-5-6 KE398 . . **B JACKSON, B.**
KRANZ, R/Biographical dictionary of Black Americans. /1992/
/KA401 . . . . **REF 305.8**
KRULL, K/Wilma unlimited: how Wilma Rudolph became the world's
fastest woman. /1996/3-5/7 KE527 . . . . . **B RUDOLPH, W.**
LIPSYTE, R/Joe Louis: a champ for all America. /1994/
4-6/6 KE447 . . . . **B LOUIS, J.**
Michael Jordan: a life above the rim. /1994/
4-6/7 KE411 . . . . **B JORDAN, M.**
LYONS, ME/Sorrow's kitchen: the life and folklore of Zora Neale
Hurston. /1990/6-A/6 KE396 . . . . **B HURSTON, Z.**
Starting home: the story of Horace Pippin, painter. /1993/
5-A/5 KE499 . . . . **B PIPPIN, H.**
MACHT, NL/Muhammad Ali. /1994/4-6/6 KE233 . . . . **B ALI, M.**
MACNOW, G/Shaquille O'Neal: star center. /1996/
4-5/6 KE485 . . . . **B O'NEAL, S.**
MADAM C.J. WALKER (VIDEOCASSETTE). /1992/
5-A/KE584 . . . . **VCR B WALKER, C.J.**
MARZOLLO, J/Happy Birthday, Martin Luther King. /1993/
1-5/5 KE422 . . . . **B KING, M.L.**
MATTHEW HENSON (VIDEOCASSETTE). /1994/
5-A/KE388 . . . . **VCR B HENSON, M.**
MCKISSACK, P/African-American scientists. /1994/
4-6/7 KB924 . . . . **509**
Black diamond: the story of the Negro baseball leagues. /1994/
4-6/7 KD800 . . . . **796.357**
Carter G. Woodson: the father of black history. /1991/
3-6/2 KE601 . . . . **B WOODSON, C.**
Mary Church Terrell: leader for equality. /1991/
3-6/2 KE562 . . . . **B TERRELL, M.**
Mary McLeod Bethune. /1992/4-6/5 KE254 . . . **B BETHUNE, M.**
Paul Robeson: a voice to remember. /1992/
2-5/2 KE514 . . . . **B ROBESON, P.**
Satchel Paige: the best arm in baseball. /1992/
3-5/2 KE489 . . . . **B PAIGE, S.**
Sojourner Truth: ain't I a woman? /1992/
6-A/7 KE573 . . . . **B TRUTH, S.**
MCLOONE, M/George Washington Carver: a photo-illustrated
biography. /1997/2-4/5 KE282 . . . . **B CARVER, G.**
MEDEARIS, AS/Dare to dream: Coretta Scott King and the civil
rights movement. /1994/3-5/3 KE419 . . . . **B KING, C.S.**
Little Louis and the jazz band: the story of Louis "Satchmo"
Armstrong. /1994/2-4/6 KE241 . . . . **B ARMSTRONG, L.**
MILLER, RH/Cowboys. /1991/4-6/6 KF039 . . . . **978**
MITCHELL, B/Raggin', a story about Scott Joplin. /1987/
A/8 KE407 . . . . **B JOPLIN, S.**
MYERS, WD/Malcolm X: by any means necessary: a biography. /
1993/6-A/8 KE456 . . . . **B MALCOLM X**
OLD, WC/Duke Ellington: giant of jazz. /1996/
5-A/9 KE338 . . . . **B ELLINGTON, D.**
OSOFSKY, A/Free to dream: the making of a poet: Langston
Hughes. /1996/6-A/7 KE395 . . . . **B HUGHES, L.**
PARKS, R/I am Rosa Parks. /1997/1-2/4 KE491 . . . **B PARKS, R.**
Rosa Parks: my story. /1992/6-A/5 KE490 . . . . . **B PARKS, R.**
PATRICK-WEXLER, D/Barbara Jordan. /1996/
4-6/8 KE408 . . . . **B JORDAN, B.**
Walter Dean Myers. /1996/5-6/6 KE475 . . . . . . **B MYERS, W.**
PETRY, A/Harriet Tubman: conductor on the Underground Railroad.
/c1955, 1996/A/7 KE575 . . . . **B TUBMAN, H.**
PETTIT, J/Maya Angelou: journey of the heart. /1996/
4-6/8 KE237 . . . . **B ANGELOU, M.**
PFEIFER, KB/Henry O. Flipper. /1993/
4-6/9 KE345 . . . . **B FLIPPER, H.**
PINKNEY, AD/Alvin Ailey. /1993/2-4/5 KE231 . . . . **B AILEY, A.**
Bill Pickett: rodeo-ridin' cowboy. /1996/
2-5/7 KE496 . . . . **B PICKETT, B.**
Dear Benjamin Banneker. /1994/4-6/6 KE249 . **B BANNEKER, B.**
POLLACK, JS/Shirley Chisholm. /1994/
5-6/10 KE289 . . . . **B CHISHOLM, S.**

QUACKENBUSH, R/Arthur Ashe and his match with history. /1994/
3-5/7 KE243 . . . . **B ASHE, A.**
REDIGER, P/Great African Americans in music. /1996/
3-6/8 KD524 . . . . **780**
REEF, C/Black fighting men: a proud history. /1994/
5-6/6 KA982 . . . . **355**
RENNERT, RS/Henry Aaron. /1993/5-A/9 KE222 . **B AARON, H.**
RINGGOLD, F/My dream of Martin Luther King. /1995/
3-5/7 KE423 . . . . **B KING, M.L.**
Talking to Faith Ringgold. /1996/4-6/6 KD379 . . . . **709.2**
ROBERTS, JL/Booker T. Washington: educator and leader. /1995/
4-6/5 KE586 . . . . **B WASHINGTON, B**
RUDEEN, K/Jackie Robinson. /1996/
5-6/6 KE516 . . . . **B ROBINSON, J.**
SANTELLA, A/Jackie Robinson breaks the color line. /1996/
4-6/6 KE517 . . . . **B ROBINSON, J.**
SAVAGE, J/Barry Bonds: Mr. Excitement. /1997/
4-6/3 KE258 . . . . **B BONDS, B.**
SCHLISSEL, L/Black frontiers: a history of African American heroes
in the Old West. /1995/4-6/8 KF048 . . . . **978**
SCHNAKENBERG, R/Scottie Pippen: reluctant superstar. /1997/
4-6/6 KE498 . . . . **B PIPPEN, S.**
SHERROW, V/Phillis Wheatley. /1992/
4-6/7 KE591 . . . . **B WHEATLEY, P.**
SIMMONS, A/Ben Carson. /1996/4-6/7 KE276 . **B CARSON, B.**
John Lucas. /1996/5-A/7 KE449. . . . . **B LUCAS, J.**
STEAL AWAY: THE HARRIET TUBMAN STORY (VIDEOCASSETTE).
/1997/4-A/KE576. . . . . **VCR B TUBMAN, H.**
SULLIVAN, G/Black artists in photography, 1840-1940. /1996/
5-6/12 KD510 . . . . **770**
SUPER, N/Daniel "Chappie" James. /1992/
5-A/6 KE401 . . . . **B JAMES, D.**
THORNLEY, S/Emmitt Smith: relentless rusher. /1997/
4-6/7 KE543 . . . . **B SMITH, E.**
TOWLE, W/Real McCoy: the life of an African-American inventor. /
c1993, 1995/4-6/7 KE462 . . . . **B MCCOY, E.**
TOWNSEND, B/Anfernee Hardaway: basketball's lucky penny. /
1997/3-5/6 KE384 . . . . **B HARDAWAY, A.**
TURK, R/Ray Charles: soul man. /1996/
5-A/8 KE286 . . . . **B CHARLES, R.**
TURNER, R/Faith Ringgold. /1993/
4-A/7 KE511 . . . . **B RINGGOLD, F.**
WEIDHORN, M/Jackie Robinson. /1993/
6-A/7 KE518 . . . . **B ROBINSON, J.**
WEINER, E/Story of Frederick Douglass: voice of freedom. /1996/
3-5/3 KE326 . . . . **B DOUGLASS, F.**
WILKER, J/Harlem Globetrotters. /1997/5-6/10 KD780 . **796.323**
WOMEN OF HOPE: AFRICAN AMERICANS WHO MADE A
DIFFERENCE (PICTURE). /1994/4-6/KA863 . . . . . . **PIC 305.8**
YATES, E/Amos Fortune, free man. /c1950/
A/7 KE348 . . . . **B FORTUNE, A.**

Afro-Americans--Civil rights SEE ALSO Civil rights; Civil rights workers.
Afro-Americans--Civil rights.
BLACK IS MY COLOR: THE AFRICAN AMERICAN EXPERIENCE
(VIDEOCASSETTE). /1992/4-6/KA838 . . . . **VCR 305.8**
DUNCAN, AF/National Civil Rights Museum celebrates everyday
people. /1995/3-6/8 KA903 . . . . **323.1**
PARKS, R/Rosa Parks: my story. /1992/
6-A/5 KE490 . . . . **B PARKS, R.**
ROCHELLE, B/Witnesses to freedom: young people who fought for
civil rights. /1993/5-6/7 KA905 . . . . **323.1**
STEIN, RC/Montgomery bus boycott. Rev. ed. /1993/
5-6/6 KE998 . . . . **976.1**
WEBB, S/Selma, Lord, Selma: girlhood memories of the civil-rights
days. /c1980, 1997/A/7 KA906 . . . . **323.1**
Afro-Americans--Civil rights--Songs and music.
SILVERMAN, J/Songs of protest and civil rights. /1992/
5-A/KD593 . . . . **789.2**
Afro-Americans--Drama.
DAVIS, O/Escape to freedom: a play about young Frederick
Douglass. /c1976, 1990/A-6/KE091. . . . . **812**
PLAYS OF BLACK AMERICANS: THE BLACK EXPERIENCE IN
AMERICA, DRAMATIZED FOR YOUN PEOPLE. NEW EXPANDED
ED. /1994/4-6/KE095. . . . . **812.008**
Afro-Americans--Education.
ELISH, D/James Meredith and school desegregation. /1994/
4-5/7 KE463 . . . . **B MEREDITH, J.**
Afro-Americans--Education--Connecticut.
YATES, E/Prudence Crandall: woman of courage. 2nd ed. /1996/
6-A/6 KE306 . . . . **B CRANDALL, P.**
Afro-Americans--Fiction.
ACKERMAN, K/By the dawn's early light. /1994/K-2/5 KF129 . . **E**
ALBERT, B/Where does the trail lead? /1991/K-2/3 KF143 . . . . **E**
ANTLE, N/Staying cool. /1997/1-3/2 KF162 . . . . **E**

ARMSTRONG, WH/Sounder. /c1969/4-A/4 KG851 . . . . **CE Fic**
BARBER, BE/Saturday at The New You. /1994/K-3/3 KF198 . . . **E**
BELTON, S/May'naise sandwiches and sunshine tea. /1994/
1-3/3 KF217 . . . . **E**
BEST, C/Red light, green light, Mama and me. /1995/
K-2/2 KF228 . . . . **E**
BLEDSOE, LJ/Big bike race. /1995/3-6/2 KG903. . . . . **Fic**
BRADBY, M/More than anything else. /1995/1-3/3 KF256 . . . . **E**
BRENNER, B/Wagon wheels. /1978/1-3/1 KF259 . . . . . . **CE E**
BUCKLEY, HE/Grandfather and I. /1994/P-1/1 KF292. . . . . . **E**
Grandmother and I. /1994/P-1/2 KF293 . . . . **E**
BUNTING, E/Blue and the gray. /1996/3-5/3 KF297 . . . . **E**
BURGESS, BH/Fred Field. /1994/6-A/6 KG947. . . . . **Fic**
CAMERON, A/More stories Huey tells. /1997/2-4/2 KG968 . . **Fic**
Stories Huey tells. /1995/2-4/2 KG969 . . . . **Fic**
Stories Julian tells. /1981/3-4/4 KG970. . . . . **Fic**
CHAPMAN, C/Snow on snow on snow. /1994/K-3/3 KF377 . . . **E**
COLEMAN, E/White socks only. /1996/3-4/4 KH014. . . . . . **Fic**
COLLIER, JL/Jump ship to freedom. /1981/5-6/5 KH015. . . . **Fic**
War comes to Willy Freeman. /1983/5-6/6 KH017. . . . . . **Fic**
COSSI, O/Great getaway. /1991/K-2/2 KF426. . . . . **E**
COTE, N/Palm trees. /1993/K-2/4 KF427. . . . . **E**
COTTONWOOD, J/Babcock. /1996/6-A/3 KH032. . . . . . . **Fic**
CREWS, D/Shortcut. /1992/K-2/2 KF436. . . . . **E**
CURTIS, CP/Watsons go to Birmingham--1963: a novel. /1995/
6-A/7 KH048 . . . . **CE Fic**
DERBY, S/My steps. /1996/P-1/2 KF482 . . . . **E**
EDWARDS, PD/Barefoot: escape on the Underground Railroad. /
1997/1-3/3 KF510 . . . . **E**
ENGLISH, K/Neeny coming, Neeny going. /1996/1-3/2 KF527. . **E**
FLOURNOY, V/Celie and the harvest fiddler. /1995/
2-4/6 KH130 . . . . **Fic**
Patchwork quilt. /1985/K-3/5 KF561. . . . . **E**
Tanya's reunion. /1995/K-3/3 KF562 . . . . **E**
GREENFIELD, E/Koya DeLaney and the good girl blues. /c1992,
1995/4-6/6 KH199 . . . . **Fic**
GUCCIONE, LD/Come morning. /1995/4-6/3 KH205 . . . . . **Fic**
HAMANAKA, S/Peace crane. /1995/1-3/4 KF668 . . . . **E**
HAMILTON, V/Drylongso. /1992/4-6/4 KH214 . . . . **Fic**
House of Dies Drear. /c1968/4-6/5 KH215. . . . . **CE Fic**
M.C. Higgins, the great. /1974/A/4 KH216 . . . . **Fic**
Plain City. /1993/6-A/5 KH217 . . . . **Fic**
Planet of Junior Brown. /c1971/A/6 KH218 . . . . **CE Fic**
Willie Bea and the time the Martians landed. /1983/
5-6/3 KH219 . . . . **Fic**
Zeely. /c1967/4-A/4 KH220 . . . . **Fic**
HAVILL, J/Jamaica and Brianna. /1993/K-2/2 KF680 . . . . . . **E**
Jamaica's blue marker. /1995/K-1/2 KF681 . . . . **E**
Jamaica's find. /1986/K-2/2 KF682 . . . . **E**
HAYES, S/Eat up, Gemma. /1988/P-2/2 KF685 . . . . **E**
Happy Christmas Gemma. /1986/P-1/2 KF686 . . . . **E**
HEATH, A/Sofie's role. /1992/P-2/2 KF692 . . . . **E**
HEST, A/Jamaica Louise James. /1996/K-2/2 KF719. . . . . . . **E**
HILL, ES/Evan's corner. /c1967, 1991/K-2/2 KF727 . . . . **E**
HOFFMAN, M/Amazing Grace. /1991/P-2/4 KF761 . . . . . **CE E**
Boundless Grace. /1995/1-3/5 KF762 . . . . **E**
HOOKS, WH/Freedom's fruit. /1996/4-6/3 KH279. . . . . . . **Fic**
HOWARD, EF/Mac and Marie and the train toss surprise. /1993/
K-2/2 KF774 . . . . **E**
HRU, D/Magic moonberry jump ropes. /1996/K-2/2 KF783 . . . **E**
HYPPOLITE, J/Seth and Samona. /1995/4-6/6 KH313 . . . . . **Fic**
ISADORA, R/Ben's trumpet. /c1979/1-3/3 KF813 . . . . **E**
JACKSON, I/Somebody's new pajamas. /1996/3-5/4 KH318 . . **Fic**
JOHNSON, A/Joshua by the sea (Board book). /1994/
P/2 KF829 . . . . **BB E**
Joshua's night whispers (Board book). /1994/P/2 KF830 . . **BB E**
Rain feet (Board book). /1994/P/2 KF833 . . . . **BB E**
JOHNSTON, T/Wagon. /1996/2-5/2 KF843 . . . . **E**
KEATS, EJ/Ezra Jack Keats Library (Videocassette). /1992/
P-2/KF871 . . . . **VCR E**
Peter's chair. /c1967/P-2/2 KF877 . . . . **CE E**
Snowy day. /c1962, 1963/P-2/2 KF878. . . . . **CE E**
Whistle for Willie. /c1964, 1977/P-2/3 KF880 . . . . . . **CE E**
KROLL, VL/Can you dance, Dalila? /1996/K-2/5 KF932. . . . . . **E**
Masai and I. /1992/K-2/4 KF934 . . . . **E**
LESTER, J/Long journey home: stories from Black history. /c1972,
1993/6-A/6 KH395. . . . . **Fic**
LINDBERGH, R/Nobody owns the sky: the story of "Brave Bessie"
Coleman. /1996/1-3/2 KF983 . . . . **E**
LYONS, ME/Letters from a slave girl: the story of Harriet Jacobs. /
1992/4-6/4 KH430 . . . . **Fic**
MARINO, J/Day that Elvis came to town. /1993/
6-A/6 KH456 . . . . **Fic**

MCKISSACK, P/Dark-thirty: Southern tales of the supernatural. /
1992/5-A/6 KH491 . . . . **Fic**
Flossie and the fox. /1986/K-3/2 KG105 . . . . **CE E**
Million fish...more or less. /c1992, 1996/1-3/4 KG106 . . . . . . **E**
Mirandy and Brother Wind. /1988/1-3/6 KG107 . . . . **CE E**
MEAD, A/Junebug. /1995/5-A/5 KH493 . . . . **Fic**
MEDEARIS, AS/Adventures of Sugar and Junior. /1995/
2-3/2 KH494 . . . . **Fic**
Here comes the snow. /1996/K-1/2 KG126 . . . . **E**
MITCHELL, MK/Uncle Jed's barbershop. /1993/1-3/4 KG147 . . . **E**
MOSS, M/Mel's Diner. /1994/K-2/2 KG158 . . . . **E**
MOSS, T/I want to be. /1993/1-4/3 KG159 . . . . **E**
MYERS, WD/Glory Field. /1994/6-A/6 KH522 . . . . **Fic**
Righteous revenge of Artemis Bonner. /1994/5-A/7 KH523 . **Fic**
NETHERY, M/Hannah and Jack. /1996/K-2/2 KG170 . . . . . . **E**
NEUFELD, J/Edgar Allan: a novel. /c1968/4-A/5 KH545 . . . . . **Fic**
PARTRIDGE, E/Clara and the hoodoo man. /1996/
5-A/3 KH572 . . . . **Fic**
PATERSON, K/Jip: his story. /1996/5-A/7 KH577 . . . . **Fic**
PATRICK, DL/Red dancing shoes. /1993/P-1/2 KG220 . . . . . . **E**
PETRY, A/Tituba of Salem Village. /1991/5-6/4 KH599. . . . . **Fic**
PILKEY, D/Paperboy. /1996/K-2/2 KG238 . . . . **E**
PINKNEY, GJ/Back home. /1992/1-3/4 KG240 . . . . **E**
Sunday outing. /1994/1-3/2 KG241 . . . . **E**
PINKNEY, JB/JoJo's flying side kick. /1995/K-3/2 KG243 . . . . **E**
POLACCO, P/Mrs. Katz and Tush. /1992/1-3/2 KG253 . . . . . **E**
POYDAR, N/Busy Bea. /1994/P-1/2 KG285 . . . . **E**
RASCHKA, C/Yo! Yes?. /1993/P-3/1 KG307 . . . . **E**
RINGGOLD, F/Dinner at Aunt Connie's house. /1993/
2-4/5 KG332 . . . . **E**
Tar beach. /1991/2-3/4 KG333 . . . . **E**
ROBINET, HG/Mississippi chariot. /1994/5-A/5 KH639 . . . . . **Fic**
ROSENBURG, JM/William Parker: rebel without rights: a novel
based on fact. /1996/6-A/7 KH654 . . . . **Fic**
ROSEN, MJ/Elijah's angel: a story for Chanukah and Christmas. /
1992/3-6/7 KH652 . . . . **Fic**
School for Pompey Walker. /1995/4-8/6 KH653 . . . . . . **Fic**
SCHROEDER, A/Carolina shout! /1995/1-5/3 KG411 . . . . . . **E**
SEBESTYEN, O/Words by heart. /1997/5-A/7 KH689 . . . . **CE Fic**
SERFOZO, M/What's what?: a guessing game. /1996/
P-1/2 KG443 . . . . **E**
SIEGELSON, KL/Terrible, wonderful tellin' at Hog Hammock. /
1996/4-6/6 KH711 . . . . **Fic**
SLOTE, A/Finding Buck McHenry. /1991/4-A/4 KH719 . . . . **Fic**
STEPTOE, J/Baby says. /1988/P-K/KG551 . . . . **E**
Stevie. /c1969/K-3/3 KG553 . . . . **E**
STOLZ, M/Go fish. /1991/3-6/6 KH766 . . . . **Fic**
Stealing home. /1992/3-5/6 KH768 . . . . **Fic**
TAYLOR, MD/Friendship. /1987/4-6/5 KH776. . . . . **Fic**
Let the circle be unbroken. /1981/5-6/8 KH777. . . . . . **Fic**
Mississippi bridge. /1990/5-A/4 KH778 . . . . **Fic**
Roll of thunder, hear my cry. /c1976/5-6/6 KH779. . . . . **CE Fic**
Song of the trees. /1975/4-6/4 KH780 . . . . **Fic**
Well: David's story. /1995/5-A/4 KH781 . . . . **Fic**
TEMPLE, C/Train. /1996/K-3/2 KG599 . . . . **E**
THOMAS, JR/Celebration! /1997/1-3/3 KG604 . . . . **E**
WALTER, MP/Have a happy... a novel. /1989/4-6/4 KH838 . . **Fic**
Justin and the best biscuits in the world. /1986/
4-6/6 KH839 . . . . **Fic**
Ty's one-man band. /c1980, 1987/1-3/2 KG686 . . . . . . **E**
WEATHERFORD, CB/Juneteenth jamboree. /1995/
1-3/5 KG690 . . . . **E**
WILLIAMS, SA/Working cotton. /1992/1-3/2 KG731 . . . . . . **E**
WRIGHT, CC/Jumping the broom. /1994/K-3/5 KG771 . . . . **E**
YARBROUGH, C/Shimmershine Queens. /1989/5-6/6 KH887 . . **Fic**
Tamika and the wisdom rings. /1994/3-4/2 KH888. . . . . **Fic**
YOUNG, RT/Learning by heart. /1993/6-A/6 KH899 . . . . . **Fic**
ZOLOTOW, C/Old dog. Rev. and newly illustrated ed. /1995/
K-2/2 KG806 . . . . **E**

Afro-Americans--Folklore.
BRER RABBIT AND BOSS LION (TALKING BOOK). /1992/
3-A/KB533. . . . . **TB 398.24**
HAMILTON, V/Her stories: African-American folktales, fairy tales,
and true tales. /1995/4-6/3 KB312 . . . . **398.2**
When birds could talk and bats could sing: the adventures of Bruh
Sparrow, Sis Wren, and their friends. /1996/
2-5/2 KB582 . . . . **398.24**
HARRIS, JC/Jump! The adventures of Brer Rabbit. /1997/
3-4/6 KB585 . . . . **398.24**
HASKINS, J/Headless haunt and other African-American ghost
stories. /1994/4-5/4 KB687 . . . . **398.25**
JAFFE, N/Voice for the people: the life and work of Harold
Courlander. /1997//KA367 . . . . **PROF B COURLAND**

KESSLER, B/Brer Rabbit and Boss Lion (Kit). /1996/
3-A/KB599. . . . . **KIT 398.24**
LESTER, J/John Henry. /1994/2-5/4 KB464 . . . . **398.22**
Tales of Uncle Remus: the adventures of Brer Rabbit. /1987/
4-5/5 KB608 . . . . **398.24**
RAW HEAD, BLOODY BONES: AFRICAN-AMERICAN TALES OF
THE SUPERNATURAL. /1991/4-6/4 KB361 . . . . **398.2**
SAN SOUCI, RD/Hired hand: an African-American folktale. /1997/
3-4/3 KB412 . . . . **398.21**
Sukey and the mermaid. /1992/3-4/6 KB775 . . . . **398.27**
SANFIELD, S/Adventures of High John the Conqueror. /1989/
3-6/5 KB480 . . . . **398.22**
SIERRA, J/Wiley and the Hairy Man. /1996/K-3/4 KB417 . . . **398.21**
STEVENS, J/Tops and bottoms. /1995/K-2/2 KB660 . . . . . **398.24**
TORRENCE, J/Traditions: a potpourri of tales (Sound recording
cassette). /1994/2-3/KB668 . . . . **SRC 398.24**
WAHL, J/Little Eight John. /1992/2-3/2 KB783 . . . . **398.27**

Afro-Americans--History.
AFRICAN AMERICAN ALMANAC. 7TH ED. /1997/
5-A/KA486 . . . . **REF 973**
BLACK IS MY COLOR: THE AFRICAN AMERICAN EXPERIENCE
(VIDEOCASSETTE). /1992/4-6/KA838 . . . . **VCR 305.8**
LAWRENCE, J/Great migration: an American story. /1993/
K-5/7 KD488 . . . . **759.13**
MACK-WILLIAMS, K/Food and our history. /1995/
5-6/7 KD287 . . . . **641.59**
MEDEARIS, AS/Our people. /1994/K-2/5 KA852 . . . . . . **305.8**
MYERS, WD/Now is your time!: the African-American struggle for
freedom. /1991/A/7 KE858 . . . . **973**

Afro-Americans--History--Chronology.
HORNSBY, JR., A/Chronology of African-American history:
significant events and people from 1619 to the present. 2nd ed. /
1997//KA490 . . . . **REF 973**

Afro-Americans--History--Sources.
AFRICAN AMERICAN VOICES. /1996/5-A/KA487 . . . . **REF 973**
MELTZER, M/Black Americans: a history in their own words 1619-
1983. /1984/5-6/9 KE857 . . . . **973**

Afro-Americans--History--1815-1861--Fiction.
SANDERS, SR/Place called Freedom. /1997/1-3/3 KG390 . . . . **E**

Afro-Americans--History--1863-1877.
WRIGHT, CC/Wagon train: a family goes West in 1865. /1995/
4-6/3 KF052 . . . . **978**

Afro-Americans--History--1877-1964.
COOPER, ML/Bound for the promised land.: the great black
migration. /1995/6-A/9 KE851 . . . . **973**

Afro-Americans--Literary collections.
CHILDREN OF PROMISE: AFRICAN-AMERICAN LITERATURE AND
ART FOR YOUNG PEOPLE. /1991/3-A/7 KD896 . . . . . . **810.8**
CHRISTMAS GIF': AN ANTHOLOGY OF CHRISTMAS POEMS,
SONGS, AND STORIES WRITTEN BY /1993/4-6/KD897. . **810.8**
IN PRAISE OF OUR FATHERS AND OUR MOTHERS: A BLACK
FAMILY TREASURY BY OUTSTANDING /1997/
3-6/KA867 . . . . **306.85**

Afro-Americans--Mississippi--Fiction.
MITCHELL, MK/Granddaddy's gift. /1997/1-3/2 KG146 . . . . . . **E**

Afro-Americans--Music--History and criticism.
MEDEARIS, AS/Music. /1997/4-6/11 KD521 . . . . **780**
STANLEY, L/Be a friend: the story of African American music in
song, words and pictures. /1994/K-3/KD670 . . . . . **BA 789.4**
WOODYARD, S/Music and song. /1995/3-6/7 KD526 . . . . . **780**

Afro-Americans--Poetry.
ALTMAN, S/Followers of the North Star: rhymes about African
American heroes, heroines, and historical times. /1993/
3-A/KD913 . . . . **811**
CLIFTON, L/Everett Anderson's Christmas coming. /1991/
P-1/KD925. . . . . **811**
GIOVANNI, N/Knoxville, Tennessee. /1994/P-1/2 KD945 . . . **811**
Spin a soft black song. Rev. ed. /c1971, 1985/1-4/KD946 . **811**
GRIMES, N/Meet Danitra Brown. /1994/2-4/KD949 . . . . . . **811**
HUGHES, L/Dream keeper and other poems, including seven
additional poems. /1994/4-6/KD954 . . . . **811**
LAWRENCE, J/Harriet and the Promised Land. /1993/
K-3/KD969 . . . . **811**
LIVINGSTON, MC/Keep on singing: a ballad of Marian Anderson.
/1994/1-3/KD977 . . . . **811**
Let freedom ring: a ballad of Martin Luther King, Jr. /1992/
K-2/4 KD978 . . . . **811**
MYERS, WD/Brown angels: an album of pictures and verse. /1993/
K-6/KD992 . . . . **811**
Harlem: a poem. /1997/3-6/KD994. . . . . **811**
THOMAS, JC/Brown honey in broomwheat tea: poems. /1993/
K-6/KE031 . . . . **811**
Gingerbread days: poems. /1995/K-4/KE032 . . . . **811**

Afro-Americans--Poetry--Collections.
FAMILIES: POEMS CELEBRATING THE AFRICAN AMERICAN
EXPERIENCE. /1994/K-3/KE057 . . . . **811.008**
MAKE A JOYFUL SOUND: POEMS FOR CHILDREN BY AFRICAN-
AMERICAN POETS. /1991/1-6/KE070 . . . . **811.008**
PASS IT ON: AFRICAN-AMERICAN POETRY FOR CHILDREN. /
1993/1-3/KE075. . . . . **811.008**
SOUL LOOKS BACK IN WONDER. /1993/4-A/KE084 . . **811.008**
Afro-Americans--Social conditions.
BERGIN, DP/Zero Street (Videocassette). /1995/
4-6/KA894 . . . . **VCR 307.76**
WHITEWASH (VIDEOCASSETTE) /1994/3-6/KA862 . **VCR 305.8**
Afro-Americans--Social life and customs.
BLACK HERITAGE HOLIDAYS (VIDEOCASSETTE). /1992/
3-A/KB195. . . . . **VCR 394.26**
CHOCOLATE, DM/My first Kwanzaa book. /1992/
2-4/2 KB206 . . . . **394.261**
GOSS, L/It's Kwanzaa time! /1995/2-6/6 KB208 . . . . . . **394.261**
HOYT-GOLDSMITH, D/Celebrating Kwanzaa. /1993/
4-6/7 KB210 . . . . **394.261**
KRULL, K/Bridges to change: how kids live on a South Carolina Sea
Island. /1995/4-6/7 KE987 . . . . **975.7**
KUKLIN, S/How my family lives in America. /1992/
1-3/5 KA850 . . . . **305.8**
KWANZAA (VIDEOCASSETTE). /1994/3-6/KB212. **VCR 394.261**
PINKNEY, AD/Seven candles for Kwanzaa. /1993/
2-6/7 KB214 . . . . **394.261**
SAINT JAMES, S/Gifts of Kwanzaa. /1994/
1-4/2 KB216 . . . . **394.261**
Afro-Americans--Songs and music.
ALL NIGHT, ALL DAY: A CHILD'S FIRST BOOK OF AFRICAN-
AMERICAN SPIRITUALS. /1991/K-6/KD554 . . . . **789.2**
HOW SWEET THE SOUND: AFRICAN-AMERICAN SONGS FOR
CHILDREN. /1995/K-6/KD571. . . . . **CE 789.2**
I'M GONNA LET IT SHINE: A GATHERING OF VOICES FOR
FREEDOM /1990/3-6/KD619 . . . . **SRC 789.3**
JENKINS, E/African-American folk songs and rhythms (Sound
recording cassette). /c1960, 1992/K-6/KD572 . . . . . **SRC 789.2**
Long time to freedom (Sound recording cassette). /c1969, 1992/
K-A/KD574 . . . . **SRC 789.2**
JOHNSON, JW/Lift every voice and sing. /1993/
2-6/5 KD672 . . . . **789.44**
SHAKE IT TO THE ONE THAT YOU LOVE THE BEST: PLAY
SONGS AND LULLABIES FROM BLACK /1989/
K-4/KD767 . . . . **BA 796.1**
SILVERMAN, J/Blues. /1994/5-A/KD671 . . . . **789.43**
Children's songs. /1993/5-A/KD591 . . . . **789.2**
Christmas songs. /1993/5-A/KD536 . . . . **782.28**
Slave songs. /1994/5-A/KD592 . . . . **789.2**
SWEET HONEY IN THE ROCK: ALL FOR FREEDOM (SOUND
RECORDING CASSETTE). /1989/3-6/KD601 . . . . . . **SRC 789.2**
Afro-Americans--Study and teaching--Activity programs.
BLACK HISTORY MONTH RESOURCE BOOK. /1993/
/KA370. . . . . **PROF 973**
Afro-Americans--West (U.S.).
BLACK WEST (VIDEOCASSETTE). /1992/5-6/KF028 . . **VCR 978**
KATZ, WL/Black women of the Old West. /1995/
5-6/9 KF036 . . . . **978**
Afro-Americans in art.
JACOB LAWRENCE: THE GLORY OF EXPRESSION
(VIDEOCASSETTE). /1995/5-A/KD487 . . . . **VCR 759.13**
LAWRENCE, J/Great migration: an American story. /1993/
K-5/7 KD488 . . . . **759.13**
Agassi, Andre.
SAVAGE, J/Andre Agassi: reaching the top--again. /1997/
4-5/7 KE229 . . . . **B AGASSI, A.**
Aged SEE ALSO Old age.
Aged--Fiction.
CARRIS, JD/Aunt Morbelia and the screaming skulls. /1990/
4-6/5 KG978 . . . . **Fic**
Agribusiness.
DOWN ON THE FARM: YESTERDAY AND TODAY
(VIDEOCASSETTE). /1987/3-A/KD142 . . . . **VCR 630**
Agricultural laborers SEE ALSO Migrant labor.
Agricultural laborers.
ATKIN, SB/Voices from the fields: children of migrant farmworkers
tell their stories. /1993/A/6 KA833 . . . . **305.5**
BRIMNER, LD/Migrant family. /1992/4-6/6 KA834 . . . . . . **305.5**
STANLEY, J/Children of the Dust Bowl: the true story of the school
at Weedpatch Camp. /1992/5-A/7 KA835 . . . . **305.5**
Agricultural laborers--Poetry.
ADA, AF/Gathering the sun: an alphabet in Spanish and English. /
1997/1-3/KE122. . . . . **861**

Agricultural machinery.
BUSHEY, J/Farming the land, modern farmers and their machines. /
1987/4-6/6 KD147 . . . . **631.3**
Agricultural machinery industry--History.
COLLINS, DR/Pioneer plowmaker: a story about John Deere. /
1990/5-6/6 KE317 . . . . **B DEERE, J.**
Agriculture SEE ALSO Botany, Economic; Dairying; Farms; Gardening;
Livestock; Soils.
Agriculture.
ANDERSON, J/American family farm. /1989/
5-6/8 KD145 . . . . **630.973**
BUSHEY, J/Farming the land, modern farmers and their machines. /
1987/4-6/6 KD147 . . . . **631.3**
LET'S GO TO THE FARM (VIDEOCASSETTE). /1994/
1-6/KD144. . . . . **VCR 630**
Agriculture--Exhibitions.
LEWIN, T/Fair! /1997/1-3/6 KB180 . . . . **394**
Agriculture--Vocational guidance.
KAPLAN, A/Careers for outdoor types. /1991/
4-A/8 KA952 . . . . **333.7**
Agriculturists.
GEORGE WASHINGTON CARVER: A MAN OF VISION
(VIDEOCASSETTE). /1990/5-A/KE281 . . . . **VCR B CARVER, G.**
MCLOONE, M/George Washington Carver: a photo-illustrated
biography. /1997/2-4/5 KE282 . . . . **B CARVER, G.**
Aida (Opera).
PRICE, L/Aida. /1990/4-A/6 KD530 . . . . **782.1**
AIDS (Disease).
A IS FOR AIDS (VIDEOCASSETTE). /1992/
5-6/KD023. . . . . **VCR 616.97**
ABC'S OF AIDS: THE COACH APPROACH (VIDEOCASSETTE). /
1991/5-6/KD024 . . . . **VCR 616.97**
COME SIT BY ME: AIDS EDUCATION (VIDEOCASSETTE). /1992/
K-2/KD025 . . . . **VCR 616.97**
CONVERSATION WITH MAGIC (VIDEOCASSETTE). /1992/
4-6/KD026. . . . . **VCR 616.97**
DOUBLE DUTCH--DOUBLE JEOPARDY (VIDEOCASSETTE). /1990/
5-6/KD027. . . . . **VCR 616.97**
GREENBERG, L/AIDS: how it works in the body. /1992/
A/8 KD028 . . . . **616.97**
HAUSHERR, R/Children and the AIDS virus: a book for children,
parents, and teachers. /1989/2-4/7 KD029 . . . . **616.97**
HYDE, MO/Know about AIDS. 3rd ed. /1994/
5-6/8 KD030 . . . . **616.97**
LET'S TALK ABOUT AIDS! (VIDEOCASSETTE). /1992/
5-6/KD031. . . . . **VCR 616.97**
PROTECT YOURSELF: HIV/AIDS EDUCATION PROGRAM
(VIDEOCASSETTE). /1992/6-A/KD032 . . . . **VCR 616.97**
AIDS (Disease)--Fiction.
JORDAN, M/Losing Uncle Tim. /1989/3-5/4 KH336 . . . . . . **Fic**
NELSON, T/Earthshine: a novel. /1994/6-A/6 KH540 . . . . . **Fic**
NEWMAN, L/Too far away to touch. /1995/1-3/6 KG172 . . . . **E**
AIDS (Disease)--History.
GIBLIN, JC/When plague strikes: the Black Death, smallpox, AIDS.
/1995/A/11 KD010 . . . . **614.4**
AIDS (Disease)--Patients.
BE A FRIEND: CHILDREN WHO LIVE WITH HIV SPEAK. /1994/
2-6/2 KA993 . . . . **362.1**
WHITE, R/Ryan White: my own story. /1991/
5-A/5 KE594 . . . . **B WHITE, R.**
Aikman, Troy.
DIPPOLD, J/Troy Aikman: quick-draw quarterback. /1994/
4-6/6 KE230 . . . . **B AIKMAN, T.**
Ailey, Alvin.
PINKNEY, AD/Alvin Ailey. /1993/2-4/5 KE231 . . . . **B AILEY, A.**
Air SEE ALSO Atmosphere.
Air.
HOFFMAN, M/Earth, fire, water, air. /1995/2-6/7 KA814 . **304.2**
Air--Experiments.
ARDLEY, N/Science book of air. /1991/4-6/4 KC102 . . . . . **533**
OXLADE, C/Science magic with air. /1994/4-A/6 KD748. . . **793.8**
RYBOLT, TR/Environmental experiments about air. /1993/
5-6/7 KD084 . . . . **628.5**
Air--Pollution.
YOUNT, L/Our endangered planet: air. /1995/
4-6/8 KB069 . . . . **363.73**
Air--Pollution--Experiments.
RYBOLT, TR/Environmental experiments about air. /1993/
5-6/7 KD084 . . . . **628.5**
Air pilots.
BRIGGS, CS/At the controls: women in aviation. /1991/
6-A/10 KD090 . . . . **629.13**
BROWN, D/Ruth Law thrills a nation. /1993/
2-3/4 KE428 . . . . **B LAW, R.**

BURLEIGH, R/Flight: the journey of Charles Lindbergh. /1991/
1-4/2 KD091 . . . . **629.13**
Flight: the journey of Charles Lindbergh. /1991/
4-6/3 KD092 . . . . **629.13**
HART, PS/Up in the air: the story of Bessie Coleman. /1996/
4-6/8 KE299 . . . . **B COLEMAN, B.**
KERBY, M/Amelia Earhart: courage in the sky. /1990/
3-4/5 KE327 . . . . **B EARHART, A.**
KULLING, M/Vanished!: the mysterious disappearance of Amelia
Earhart. /1996/2-4/7 KE328 . . . . **B EARHART, A.**
PROVENSEN, A/Glorious flight: across the channel with Louis
Bleriot. /1983/K-2/4 KD098 . . . . **CE 629.13**
SZABO, C/Sky pioneer: a photobiography of Amelia Earhart. /
1997/4-6/12 KE329 . . . . **B EARHART, A.**
VAN METER, V/Taking flight: my story. /1995/
3-6/6 KD101 . . . . **629.13**

Air pilots--Fiction.
LINDBERGH, R/Nobody owns the sky: the story of "Brave Bessie"
Coleman. /1996/1-3/2 KF983 . . . . **E**
POWELL, MC/Queen of the air: the story of Katherine Stinson,
1891-1977. /1993/4-7/7 KH613 . . . . **CE Fic**

Aircraft carriers.
BIG AIRCRAFT CARRIER (VIDEOCASSETTE). /1995/
4-6/KA989 . . . . **VCR 359.9**

Airplanes.
BARRETT, NS/Flying machines. /1994/4-6/8 KD104 . . . . **629.133**
BARTON, B/Airplanes. /1986/P-1/2 KB155 . . . . **387.7**
BELLVILLE, CW/Airplane book. /1991/4-6/7 KD105 . . . **629.133**
BROWNE, G/Aircraft: lift-the-flap book. /1992/
3-6/5 KD106 . . . . **629.133**
CREWS, D/Flying. /1986/P-1/KD093. . . . . **629.13**
GUNNING, TG/Dream planes. /1992/5-6/7 KD109 . . . . **629.133**
LET ME TELL YOU ALL ABOUT PLANES (VIDEOCASSETTE). /
1994/4-5/KD111 . . . . **VCR 629.133**
SIEBERT, D/Plane song. /1993/3-6/KD112 . . . . **629.133**
STEELE, P/Planes. /1991/4-6/6 KD100 . . . . **629.13**

Airplanes--Design and construction.
PROVENSEN, A/Glorious flight: across the channel with Louis
Bleriot. /1983/K-2/4 KD098 . . . . **CE 629.13**

Airplanes--Fiction.
MORGAN, A/Matthew and the midnight pilot. /1997/
1-2/3 KG156 . . . . **E**
ROCKWELL, AF/I fly. /1997/P-1/2 KG343 . . . . **E**
YEP, L/Dragonwings. /c1975/5-6/6 KH892 . . . . **Fic**

Airplanes--History.
KERROD, R/Amazing flying machines. /1992/
4-6/6 KD110 . . . . **629.133**
LET ME TELL YOU ALL ABOUT PLANES (VIDEOCASSETTE). /
1994/4-5/KD111 . . . . **VCR 629.133**
WEISS, H/Strange and wonderful aircraft. /1995/
4-6/6 KD102 . . . . **629.13**
Airplanes--Models SEE ALSO Paper airplanes.

Airplanes--Models.
SIMON, S/Paper airplane book. /c1971/3-5/6 KD113 . . **629.133**

Airplanes--Models--Periodicals.
MODEL AIRPLANE NEWS. /1929-/4-A/KA525 . . . . **PER 050**

Airplanes--Piloting.
LINDBLOM, S/Fly the hot ones. /1991/A/8 KD103 . . . . **629.132**

Airplanes, Military.
JENSSEN, H/Jets. /1996/4-6/8 KD061 . . . . **623.7**

Airports.
SULLIVAN, G/How an airport really works. /1993/
5-6/8 KB156 . . . . **387.7**

Airports--Fiction.
BUNTING, E/Fly away home. /1991/K-3/2 KF300 . . . . **E**
Airships SEE ALSO Aeronautics; Balloons; Hot-air balloons.

Airships--History.
CURLEE, L/Ships of the air. /1996/5-6/8 KD107 . . . . . . **629.133**

Akamba (African people)--Folklore.
AARDEMA, V/How the ostrich got its long neck: a tale from the
Akamba of Kenya. /1995/P-2/6 KB515 . . . . **CE 398.24**

Alabama.
BROWN, D/Alabama. /1994/4-6/7 KE996 . . . . **976.1**

Alabama--Fiction.
CAPOTE, T/Thanksgiving visitor. /1996/5-A/8 KG972 . . . . . . **Fic**

Alabama--History.
WILLS, CA/Historical album of Alabama. /1995/
4-6/7 KE999 . . . . **976.1**

Alamo (San Antonio, Tex.)--Siege, 1836.
CARTER, AR/Last stand at the Alamo. /1990/4-6/7 KF001 . **976.4**
SULLIVAN, G/Alamo! /1997/4-6/10 KF002 . . . . **976.4**

Alaska SEE ALSO Yukon Valley; Yukon Territory; Klondike gold fields;
Klondike River Valley; also names of specific cities e.g. Anchorage.
Alaska.
HEINRICHS, A/Alaska. /1990/4-6/7 KF096 . . . . **979.8**
JOHNSTON, J/Alaska. /1994/4-6/7 KF099 . . . . **979.8**
MURPHY, CR/Child's Alaska. /1994/3-5/8 KF101 . . . . . . **979.8**

Alaska--Bibliography.
EXPLORING THE PACIFIC STATES THROUGH LITERATURE. /
1994//KA042 . . . . **PROF 016.9795**

Alaska--Description and travel.
KIDS EXPLORE ALASKA (VIDEOCASSETTE). /1990/
3-6/KE209 . . . . **VCR 917.98**

Alaska--Fiction.
BURNHAM, SD/Three River Junction: a story of an Alaskan bald
eagle preserve (Kit). /1997/2-4/KF313 . . . . **KIT E**
GRIESE, AA/Way of our people. /1997/5-6/5 KH203 . . . . . . **Fic**
HILL, K/Winter camp. /1993/5-A/6 KH262 . . . . **Fic**
MOREY, W/Gentle Ben. Reissued. /c1965, 1997/
5-A/6 KH508 . . . . **Fic**
Home is the North. /c1967, 1990/5-A/5 KH509 . . . . **Fic**
Kavik, the wolf dog. /c1968/4-6/6 KH510 . . . . **Fic**
Scrub dog of Alaska. /c1971, 1989/5-A/6 KH511 . . . . **Fic**
PINKWATER, DM/Aunt Lulu. /1991/P-2/2 KG244 . . . . **E**
RAND, G/Prince William. /1992/2-3/4 KG300 . . . . **E**

Alaska--History.
FIRST AND LAST FRONTIER (VIDEOCASSETTE). /1991/
A/KF095 . . . . **VCR 979.8**
STANDIFORD, N/Bravest dog ever: the true story of Balto. /1989/
1-3/2 KD223 . . . . **636.7**

Alaska--Periodicals.
ALASKA: THE MAGAZINE OF LIFE ON THE LAST FRONTIER. /
1935-/A/KA497 . . . . **PER 050**

Alaska--Social life and customs.
KIDS EXPLORE ALASKA (VIDEOCASSETTE). /1990/
3-6/KE209 . . . . **VCR 917.98**

Albatrosses.
JOHNSON, SA/Albatrosses of Midway Island. /1990/
5-6/7 KC681 . . . . **598.4**

Alcohol.
ARMSTRONG, T/Dog who dared (Videocassette). /1993/
4-6/KC993 . . . . **VCR 613.8**
KID'S GUIDE TO DRUG, ALCOHOL AND SMOKING
AWARENESS (VIDEOCASSETTE). /1985/
K-4/KA997 . . . . **VCR 362.29**
LET'S TALK ABOUT DRUGS (VIDEOCASSETTE). /1994/
1-3/KC998. . . . . **VCR 613.8**
SEIXAS, JS/Alcohol--what it is, what it does. /c1977/
1-3/5 KD002 . . . . **613.81**
WHAT'S WRONG WITH BEER? (VIDEOCASSETTE). /1992/
5-6/KD003. . . . . **VCR 613.81**

Alcohol abuse--Prevention.
ARMSTRONG, T/Dog who dared (Videocassette). /1993/
4-6/KC993 . . . . **VCR 613.8**
JUST FOR ME (VIDEOCASSETTE). /1992/
K-6/KC997 . . . . **VCR 613.8**

Alcoholic beverages--Law and legislation.
HINTZ, M/Farewell, John Barleycorn: prohibition in the United
States. /1996/5-6/12 KB043. . . . . **363.4**

Alcoholics.
SEIXAS, JS/Living with a parent who drinks too much. /1979/
4-6/7 KB000 . . . . **362.292**
SOMETHING WRONG AT HOME: THE ALCOHOLIC FAMILY
(VIDEOCASSETTE). /1994/3-5/KB001 . . . . **VCR 362.292**

Alcoholism.
BROKEN PROMISES (VIDEOCASSETTE). /1991/
/KA298. . . . . **VCR PROF 613.81**
DRUG DANGER: EASY TO START, HARD TO STOP
(VIDEOCASSETTE). /1992/5-6/KC994 . . . . **VCR 613.8**
DRUG DANGER: IN THE BODY (VIDEOCASSETTE). /1992/
5-6/KD019. . . . . **VCR 616.86**
SEIXAS, JS/Alcohol--what it is, what it does. /c1977/
1-3/5 KD002 . . . . **613.81**
Living with a parent who drinks too much. /1979/
4-6/7 KB000 . . . . **362.292**
SOMETHING WRONG AT HOME: THE ALCOHOLIC FAMILY
(VIDEOCASSETTE). /1994/3-5/KB001 . . . . **VCR 362.292**

Alcoholism--Fiction.
DALY, N/My dad. /1995/1-4/5 KF447 . . . . **E**
MARINO, J/Day that Elvis came to town. /1993/
6-A/6 KH456 . . . . **Fic**
RODOWSKY, C/Hannah in between. /1994/5-A/7 KH650 . . . **Fic**
RYAN, ME/Trouble with perfect. /1995/6-A/3 KH659 . . . . **Fic**
VIGNA, J/I wish Daddy didn't drink so much. /1988/
P-3/2 KG653 . . . . **E**

Alcott, Louisa May.
MEIGS, C/Invincible Louisa. /1933/5-6/8 KE232 . . **B ALCOTT, L.**
Alcott, Louisa May--Fiction.
WALLNER, A/Alcott family Christmas. /1996/1-3/2 KG678 . . . . **E**
Alexander Doll Company.
KUKLIN, S/From head to toe: how a doll is made. /1994/
4-6/6 KD350 . . . . **688.7**
Algeria--Folklore.
SCHWARTZ, H/Sabbath lion: a Jewish folktale from Algeria. /
1992/4-6/6 KB511 . . . . **398.23**
Algonquin Indians SEE ALSO Abnaki Indians; Cheyenne Indians; Chippewa
Indians; Delaware Indians.
Algonquin Indians.
QUIRI, PR/Algonquians. /1992/4-6/6 KE763 . . . . **970.3**
Algonquin Indians--Fiction.
DORRIS, M/Guests. /1994/5-A/7 KH079 . . . . **Fic**
Algonquin Indians--Folklore.
GOBLE, P/Remaking the earth: a creation story from the Great
Plains of North America. /1996/3-5/7 KB448 . . . . **398.22**
MARTIN, R/Rough-face girl. /1992/3-5/4 KB752 . . . . **398.27**
ROSS, G/Legend of the Windigo: a tale from native North
America. /1996/2-3/6 KB410 . . . . **398.21**
Ali, Muhammad.
MACHT, NL/Muhammad Ali. /1994/4-6/6 KE233 . . . . **B ALI, M.**
Alien beings SEE Extraterrestrial beings.
Aliens, Illegal--Fiction.
TEMPLE, F/Grab hands and run. /1993/6-A/6 KH788 . . . . . . **Fic**
All Saints' Day--Mexico.
LASKY, K/Days of the Dead. /1994/5-6/6 KB200 . . . . . **394.26**
All Souls' Day.
HOYT-GOLDSMITH, D/Day of the Dead: a Mexican-American
celebration. /1994/4-6/7 KB198 . . . . **394.26**
All Souls' Day--Mexico.
ANCONA, G/Pablo remembers: the Fiesta of the Day of the Dead.
/1993/3-6/5 KB193 . . . . **394.26**
LASKY, K/Days of the Dead. /1994/5-6/6 KB200 . . . . . **394.26**
All Souls' Day--Mexico--Fiction.
CZERNECKI, S/Hummingbirds' gift. /1994/1-3/7 KF443 . . . . . . **E**
KRULL, K/Maria Molina and the Days of the Dead. /1994/
2-4/4 KF936 . . . . **E**
LEVY, J/Spirit of Tio Fernando: a Day of the Dead story./El espiritu
de tio Fernando: una historia del Dia de los Muertos. /1995/
1-3/5 KH404 . . . . **Fic**
All terrain vehicle racing.
SMITH, JH/Most rugged all-terrain vehicles. /1995/
5-6/6 KD830 . . . . **796.7**
All-American Girls Professional Baseball League--History.
GALT, MF/Up to the plate: the All American Girls Professional
Baseball League. /1995/4-6/6 KD797 . . . . **796.357**
Allegories.
MACAULAY, D/Baaa. /1985/5-A/7 KH431 . . . . **Fic**
Alleman, Tillie Pierce.
GAUCH, PL/Thunder at Gettysburg. /c1975, 1990/
4-6/4 KE903 . . . . **973.7**
Allergy SEE ALSO Asthma.
Allergy.
LERNER, C/Plants that make you sniffle and sneeze. /1993/
5-6/9 KC404 . . . . **581.6**
SEIXAS, JS/Allergies - what they are, what they do. /1991/
3-5/6 KD033 . . . . **616.97**
Allergy--Fiction.
HEILBRONER, J/Robert the rose horse. /1962/K-2/1 KF696 . . . . **E**
PORTE, BA/Harry's dog. /1984/1-3/2 KG267 . . . . **E**
Alligators--Fiction.
HURD, T/Mama don't allow. /1984/K-3/2 KF793 . . . . . . **CE E**
LIONNI, L/Extraordinary egg. /1994/1-3/2 KF991 . . . . **E**
MAYER, M/There's an alligator under my bed. /1987/
P-2/2 KG085 . . . . **E**
YEP, L/Later, Gator. /1995/4-6/4 KH893 . . . . **Fic**
Alliteration.
EDWARDS, PD/Four famished foxes and Fosdyke. /1995/
1-3/3 KF511 . . . . **E**
Some smug slug. /1996/P-2/3 KF513 . . . . **E**
Alliteration--Software.
DR. SEUSS'S ABC (CD-ROM). /1995/P-2/KF493 . . . . . . **CDR E**
Allosaurus.
SATTLER, HR/Tyrannosaurus rex and its kin: the Mesozoic monsters.
/1989/3-6/8 KC261 . . . . **567.9**
Almanacs.
AFRICAN AMERICAN ALMANAC. 7TH ED. /1997/
5-A/KA486 . . . . **REF 973**
ANIMATED ALMANAC (VIDEOCASSETTE). /1990/
3-6/KA581 . . . . **VCR 025.5**

ANTHONY, SC/Facts plus: an almanac of essential information.
New 3rd ed. /1995/4-A/KA377 . . . . **REF 030**
CHASE, WD/Chase's calendar of annual events: special days, weeks
and months. /1958-//KA264 . . . . **PROF 394.2**
CORPUS ALMANAC AND CANADIAN SOURCEBOOK. /1964-/
5-6/KA484 . . . . **REF 971**
INFORMATION PLEASE ALMANAC, ATLAS & YEARBOOK. /
1947-/4-6/KA405 . . . . **REF 317.3**
TESAR, J/New view almanac: the first all-visual resource of vital
facts and statistics! Premiere edition. /1996/
4-A/KA391 . . . . **REF 031.02**
WEBER, L/Backyard almanac. /1996/3-A/7 KB915 . . . . . . **508**
WOMEN'S ALMANAC. /1997/5-A/KA397 . . . . **REF 305.4**
WORLD ALMANAC AND BOOK OF FACTS. /1868-/
4-6/KA406 . . . . **REF 317.3**
Almanacs--History.
PINKNEY, AD/Dear Benjamin Banneker. /1994/
4-6/6 KE249 . . . . **B BANNEKER, B.**
Alphabet.
ABC'S AND SUCH (VIDEOCASSETTE). /1993/
P-2/KB099 . . . . **VCR 372.4**
ADA, AF/Gathering the sun: an alphabet in Spanish and English. /
1997/1-3/KE122 . . . . **861**
AJMERA, M/Children from Australia to Zimbabwe: a photographic
journey around the world. /1997/2-5/7 KA822 . . . . . . **305.23**
AYLESWORTH, J/Old black fly. /1992/K-2/2 KF180 . . . . **E**
BANNATYNE-CUGNET, J/Prairie alphabet. /1992/
2-6/6 KE811 . . . . **971.2**
BASE, G/Animalia. /c1986, 1993/P-A/KF212 . . . . **E**
BENDER, R/A to Z beastly jamboree. /1996/K-2/KB830 . . . . **421**
BOURKE, L/Eye spy: a mysterious alphabet. /1991/
1-4/KD720. . . . . **793.734**
BROWN, R/Alphabet times four: an international ABC: English,
Spanish, French, German. /1991/2-4/KB819. . . . . **411**
BRUSCA, MC/When jaguars ate the moon: and other stories about
animals and plants of the /1995/2-3/5 KB541 . . . . **398.24**
CHARLIP, R/Handtalk: an ABC of finger spelling and sign language.
/c1974, 1984/K-A/KB823. . . . . **419**
CHIN-LEE, C/A is for Asia. /1997/K-3/8 KE700. . . . . **950**
CHWAST, S/Alphabet parade. /1994/K-2/KF392. . . . . **E**
DARLING, K/Amazon ABC. /1996/K-5/3 KC499 . . . . . . **591.981**
DRAGONWAGON, C/Alligator arrived with apples, a potluck
alphabet feast. /1987/K-2/5 KF494 . . . . **E**
EDWARDS, M/Alef-bet: a Hebrew alphabet book. /1992/
1-3/KB864. . . . . **492.4**
ERNST, LC/Letters are lost! /1996/P-K/2 KF530. . . . . **E**
FEELINGS, ML/Jambo means hello: Swahili alphabet book. /1974/
1-3/7 KF545 . . . . **E**
FEENEY, S/A is for aloha. /1980/K-3/KF546 . . . . **E**
FOLSOM, M/Easy as pie: a guessing game of sayings. /1985/
1-3/3 KF564 . . . . **E**
GAG, W/ABC bunny. /c1933, 1997/P-K/KF591 . . . . **E**
GARTEN, J/Alphabet tale. New ed., rev. and re-illustrated. /1994/
P-K/3 KF599 . . . . **E**
GEISERT, A/Pigs from A to Z. /1986/1-3/3 KF603 . . . . **E**
HEPWORTH, C/ANTics!: an alphabetical anthology. /1992/
2-6/KB831 . . . . **421**
HOBAN, T/26 letters and 99 cents. /1987/P-2/KF748. . . . . . . **E**
HOWLAND, N/ABCDrive!: a car trip alphabet. /1994/
P-1/1 KF782 . . . . **E**
INTRODUCTION TO LETTERS AND NUMERALS
(VIDEOCASSETTE). /1985/P-1/KF809 . . . . **VCR E**
ISADORA, R/City seen from A to Z. /1983/P-1/KF814. . . . . . . **E**
JOHNSON, S/Alphabet city. /1995/K-A/KF838 . . . . **E**
JONAS, A/Aardvarks, disembark! /1990/2-A/4 KA963. . . **333.95**
LECOURT, N/Abracadabra to zigzag: an alphabet book. /1991/
K-3/KF954. . . . . **E**
LESSAC, F/Caribbean alphabet. /1994/1-3/KF962. . . . . **E**
LIONNI, L/Alphabet tree. /c1968, 1990/1-2/3 KF989. . . . . . **E**
LOBEL, A/Alison's zinnia. /1990/P-2/2 KF999 . . . . **E**
On Market Street. /1981/P-1/6 KG009. . . . . **E**
MACDONALD, S/Alphabatics. /1986/P-2/KG051 . . . . **E**
MAGEE, D/All aboard ABC. /1990/K-2/2 KD075 . . . . . . **625.1**
MARTIN, JR., B/Chicka chicka boom boom. /1989/
P-1/2 KG073 . . . . **E**
Chicka chicka boom boom (Kit). /1991/P-1/KG074 . . . . . **KIT E**
MCDONNELL, F/Flora McDonnell's ABC. /1997/P-K/3 KG099 . . **E**
MERRIAM, E/Halloween A B C. /1987/P-A/KD982 . . . . **811**
MICKLETHWAIT, L/I spy: an alphabet in art. /1992/
P-2/2 KD484 . . . . **759**
MUSGROVE, M/Ashanti to Zulu: African traditions. /c1976/
4-6/6 KE727 . . . . **960**
NEUMEIER, M/Action alphabet. /1985/1-3/KG171 . . . . **E**
ONYEFULU, I/A is for Africa. /1993/2-4/5 KE178 . . . . **916**

PALMER, H/Learning basic skills (Videocassette). /1986/
P-1/KD700. . . . . **VCR 793**
PELLETIER, D/Graphic alphabet. /1996/2-4/2 KB832 . . . . . . **421**
POWELL, C/Bold carnivore: an alphabet of predators. /1995/
P-5/5 KC454 . . . . **591**
PRATT, KJ/Walk in the rainforest. /1992/K-6/7 KC322 . . . **577.34**
RANKIN, L/Handmade alphabet. /1991/K-3/3 KB829 . . . . **419**
REY, HA/Curious George learns the alphabet. /c1963/
P-2/2 KG325 . . . . **E**
ROSENBERG, L/Big and little alphabet. /1997/K-2/2 KG353 . . . **E**
ROSEN, M/Michael Rosen's ABC. /1996/2-4/KE109 . . . . . . **821**
ROTNER, S/Action alphabet. /1996/K-2/2 KB854 . . . . **428.2**
SANDERS, M/What's your name?: from Ariel to Zoe. /1995/
K-3/2 KE611 . . . . **929.4**
SANDVED, KB/Butterfly alphabet. /1996/3-6/6 KC567 . . . **595.78**
SCHNEIDER, RM/Add it, dip it, fix it: a book of verbs. /1995/
K-2/2 KB855 . . . . **428.2**
SENDAK, M/Alligators all around: an alphabet. /c1962/
P-1/KG429 . . . . **CE E**
SEUSS, D/Dr. Seuss's ABC. /c1963/P-2/2 KG451 . . . . **CE E**
On beyond zebra. /1955/P-3/6 KG470 . . . . **E**
SHANNON, G/Tomorrow's alphabet. /1996/K-2/2 KG479 . . . . . **E**
SLATE, J/Miss Bindergarten gets ready for kindergarten. /1996/
P-K/2 KG515 . . . . **E**
STROUD, VA/Path of the Quiet Elk: a Native American alphabet
book. /1996/3-6/5 KA793 . . . . **299**
STUTSON, C/Prairie primer A to Z. /1996/1-3/3 KG583 . . . . . **E**
TAPAHONSO, L/Navajo ABC: a Dine alphabet book. /1995/
2-4/KE797 . . . . **970.49**
THORNHILL, J/Wildlife A-B-C: a nature alphabet book. /1990/
P-2/3 KC498 . . . . **591.97**
TRYON, L/Albert's alphabet. /1991/P-1/KG620 . . . . **E**
TURNER, P/War between the Vowels and the Consonants. /1996/
1-3/3 KG630 . . . . **E**
UPDIKE, J/Helpful alphabet of friendly objects: poems. /1995/
P-1/KE035. . . . . **811**
VAN ALLSBURG, C/Z was zapped. /1987/2-A/KG640. . . . . . . **E**
VIORST, J/Alphabet from Z to A: (with much confusion on the
way). /1994/2-5/KE036. . . . . **811**
WALDHERR, K/Book of goddesses. /1995/4-6/8 KA732 . . . **291.2**
WATSON, C/AppleBet; an ABC. /1982/P-1/KG689. . . . . **E**
WEEKS, S/Hurricane City. /1993/K-2/2 KG691 . . . . **E**
WILDSMITH, B/Brian Wildsmith's ABC. /1995/P-1/KG721 . . . . . **E**
WILMER, I/B is for Bethlehem: a Christmas alphabet. /1990/
K-3/KE043. . . . . **811**
YOLEN, J/All in the woodland early: an ABC book. /c1979, 1991/
K-1/3 KG776 . . . . **E**

Alphabet--Software.
CHICKA CHICKA BOOM BOOM (CD-ROM). /1996/
P-2/KF382. . . . . **CDR E**
DR. SEUSS'S ABC (CD-ROM). /1995/P-2/KF493. . . . . . . **CDR E**
Alphabet--Songs and music.
GALLINA, J/A to Z, the animals and me (Sound recording
cassette). /1993/P-1/KD612 . . . . **SRC 789.3**
Alphabetizing.
AMERICAN LIBRARY ASSOCIATION. FILING COMMITTEE. /ALA
filing rules. /1980//KA055 . . . . **PROF 025.3**
Alzheimer's disease--Fiction.
KROLL, VL/Fireflies, peach pies and lullabies. /1995/
1-3/5 KF933 . . . . **E**
Amateur motion pictures.
ANDERSEN, Y/Make your own animated movies and videotapes. /
1991/5-A/6 KD515. . . . . **778.5**
Amateur theatricals SEE ALSO Drama in education; Plays; Puppet plays;
Shadow pantomines and plays.
Amazon River.
GILLILAND, JH/River. /1993/K-3/3 KC317 . . . . **577.34**
MURRAY, P/Amazon. /1994/3-6/7 KE212 . . . . **918.1**
Amazon River Region--Description and travel.
ADVENTURE IN THE AMAZON. /1992/4-6/7 KE211 . . . . . **918.1**
COBB, V/This place is wet. /1989/3-6/6 KC287 . . . . **574.5**
Amazon River Region--Fiction.
LEWIN, T/Amazon boy. /1993/K-2/5 KF974. . . . . **E**
Amazon River Region--Social life and customs.
REYNOLDS, J/Amazon Basin: vanishing cultures. /1993/
3-6/7 KF104 . . . . **981**
America SEE ALSO Central America; Latin America; North America; South
America.
America--Antiquities.
SATTLER, HR/Earliest Americans. /1993/5-A/8 KE743. . . . **970.01**
America--Discovery and exploration SEE ALSO Explorers; Oregon Trail.
America--Discovery and exploration.
COLUMBUS, C/Log of Christopher Columbus' first voyage to
America in the year 1492. /c1938, 1989/4-6/7 KE741. . . **970.01**

MAESTRO, B/Discovery of the Americas. /1991/
2-6/8 KE183 . . . . **917.04**
Exploration and conquest: the Americas after Columbus: 1500 -
1620. /1994/2-6/7 KE184 . . . . **917.04**
America--Discovery and exploration--English.
GREAT ENCOUNTER (VIDEOCASSETTE). /1991/
A/KE868. . . . . **VCR 973.1**
America--Discovery and exploration--English--Fiction.
DORRIS, M/Guests. /1994/5-A/7 KH079. . . . . **Fic**
America--Discovery and exploration--Fiction.
ROCKWOOD, J/To spoil the sun. /c1976, 1994/
6-A/6 KH644 . . . . **Fic**
America--Discovery and exploration--Spanish.
ADLER, DA/Christopher Columbus: great explorer. /1991/
4-5/4 KE301 . . . . **B COLUMBUS, C.**
ASIMOV, I/Christopher Columbus: navigator to the New World. /
1991/4-5/5 KE302 . . . . **B COLUMBUS, C.**
CONQUERING THE SWAMPS (VIDEOCASSETTE). /1991/
A/KE990. . . . . **VCR 975.9**
ESTEVANICO AND THE SEVEN CITIES OF GOLD
(VIDEOCASSETTE). /1992/5-6/6 KE341 . . . **VCR B ESTEVANICO**
FRITZ, J/Where do you think you're going, Christopher Columbus? /
1980/4-6/6 KE303 . . . . **CE B COLUMBUS, C.**
MARRIN, A/Aztecs and Spaniards: Cortes and the conquest of
Mexico. /1986/5-6/7 KE833. . . . . **972**
YUE, C/Christopher Columbus: how he did it. /1992/
5-A/7 KE744 . . . . **970.01**
America--Discovery and exploration--Spanish--Fiction.
DORRIS, M/Morning Girl. /1992/6-A/7 KH080. . . . . **Fic**
America--Discovery and exploration--Spanish--Historiography.
PELTA, K/Discovering Christopher Columbus. /1991/
A/6 KE742 . . . . **970.01**
America--Folklore.
BRUSCA, MC/When jaguars ate the moon: and other stories about
animals and plants of the /1995/2-3/5 KB541 . . . . **398.24**
America--History--To 1810.
MAESTRO, B/Exploration and conquest: the Americas after
Columbus: 1500 - 1620. /1994/2-6/7 KE184 . . . . **917.04**
American Association of School Librarians.
AASL ELECTRONIC LIBRARY. 1997 ED. (CD-ROM). /1997/
/KA045. . . . . **CDR PROF 025**
American Indians SEE Indians of North America; Indians of South America;
names of tribes e.g. Abnaki Indians.
American literature--Afro-American authors--Bibliography.
CORETTA SCOTT KING AWARDS BOOK: FROM VISION TO
REALITY. /1994//KA008 . . . . **PROF 011.008**
American literature--Afro-American authors--Collections.
CHILDREN OF PROMISE: AFRICAN-AMERICAN LITERATURE AND
ART FOR YOUNG PEOPLE. /1991/3-A/7 KD896. . . . . . . **810.8**
American literature--Afro-American authors--History and criticism.
CURRY, BK/Sweet words so brave: the story of African American
literature. /1996/K-6/7 KD906 . . . . **810.9**
American literature--Collections.
TUN-TA-CA-TUN: MORE STORIES AND POEMS IN ENGLISH
AND SPANISH FOR CHILDREN. /1986/K-6/KD905. . . . . **810.8**
American literature--Indian authors--Collections.
RISING VOICES: WRITINGS OF YOUNG NATIVE AMERICANS. /
1992/5-A/7 KD903 . . . . **810.8**
American loyalists--Fiction.
O'DELL, S/Sarah Bishop. /1980/5-6/5 KH561 . . . . **Fic**
American National Red Cross.
SONNEBORN, L/Clara Barton. /1992/
4-6/6 KE250 . . . . **B BARTON, C.**
American poetry SEE ALSO Afro-Americans--Poetry.
American poetry.
ADOFF, A/All the colors of the race. /1982/4-6/KD907 . . . . **811**
Eats. /c1979, 1992/P-A/KD908 . . . . **811**
In for winter, out for spring. /1991/1-4/KD910 . . . . **811**
Love letters. /1997/K-4/KD911. . . . . **811**
ALTMAN, S/Followers of the North Star: rhymes about African
American heroes, heroines, and /1993/3-A/KD913 . . . . **811**
AYLESWORTH, J/Cat and the fiddle and more. /1992/
P-1/KD915 . . . . **811**
BENJAMIN, A/Nickel buys a rhyme. /1993/P-2/KD916. . . . . **811**
BORNSTEIN, H/Night before Christmas: told in sign language: an
adaptation of the original /1994/K-6/KD917 . . . . **811**
BROWN, MW/Under the sun and the moon and other poems. /
1993/P-2/KD918 . . . . **811**
BRUCHAC, J/Thirteen moons on turtle's back: a Native American
year of poems. /1992/2-6/KD919 . . . . **811**
CARLSTROM, NW/Who said boo?: Halloween poems for the very
young. /1995/P-1/KD920 . . . . **811**
CASSEDY, S/Zoomrimes: poems about things that go. /1993/
3-6/KD921. . . . . **811**

CIARDI, J/Monster den: or look what happened at my house - and to it. /c1966, 1991/3-6/KD922 . . . . **811**
You know who. /c1964, 1991/3-5/KD923 . . . . **811**
You know who, John J. Plenty and Fiddler Dan, and other poems (Kit). /n.d./3-5/KD924 . . . . **Kit 811**
CUMMINGS, EE/Hist whist. /c1923, 1989/2-6/KD926 . . . . . **811**
CUMPIAN, C/Latino rainbow: poems about Latino Americans. / 1994/3-6/KD927 . . . . **811**
DAKOS, K/Don't read this book, whatever you do!: more poems about school. /1993/4-6/KD928 . . . . **811**
If you're not here, please raise your hand: poems about school. / 1990/2-5/KD929 . . . . **811**
DE REGNIERS, BS/Way I feel--sometimes. /1988/1-4/KD931 . **811**
DEMING, AG/Who is tapping at my window? /c1988, 1994/ P-K/KD930 . . . . **811**
DICKINSON, E/Brighter garden. /1990/3-6/KD932 . . . . **811**
Poetry for young people. /1994/4-A/KD933 . . . . **811**
FLEISCHMAN, P/Joyful noise: poems for two voices. /1988/ 4-6/KD934 . . . . **811**
FLORIAN, D/Beast feast. /1994/K-3/KD935 . . . . **811**
Bing bang boing. /1994/3-6/KD936 . . . . **811**
In the swim: poems and paintings. /1997/1-3/KD937 . . . . **811**
Monster Motel: poems and paintings. /1993/4-6/KD938 . . . **811**
On the wing: bird poems and paintings. /1996/1-4/KD939 . **811**
FROST, R/Poetry for young people. /1994/4-A/KD940 . . . . . **811**
Stopping by the woods on a snowy evening. /1978/ P-A/KD941 . . . . **811**
Swinger of birches: poems of Robert Frost for young people. / 1982/3-6/KD942 . . . . **811**
You come too: favorite poems for young readers. /c1959, 1987/ 5-6/KD943 . . . . **811**
GHIGNA, C/Tickle Day: poems from Father Goose. /1994/ P-1/KD944 . . . . **811**
GRIMES, N/Meet Danitra Brown. /1994/2-4/KD949 . . . . . **811**
HARRISON, DL/Somebody catch my homework. /1993/ 2-6/KD951 . . . . **811**
HO, M/Hush!: a Thai lullaby. /1996/P-1/KD952 . . . . **811**
IZUKI, S/Believers in America: poems about Americans of Asian and Pacific islander /1994/3-6/KD955 . . . . **811**
KATZ, B/Could we be friends?: poems for pals. /1997/ 1-3/KD959 . . . . **811**
KENNEDY, XJ/Beasts of Bethlehem. /1992/1-6/KD960 . . . . . **811**
Brats. /1986/3-6/KD961 . . . . **811**
Drat these brats! /1993/3-6/KD962 . . . . **811**
Forgetful wishing well. /1985/4-6/KD963 . . . . **811**
Fresh brats. /1990/3-6/KD964 . . . . **811**
Ghastlies, goops & pincushions. /1989/4-A/KD965 . . . **811**
LANSKY, B/New adventures of Mother Goose: gentle rhymes for happy times. /1993/P-3/KD967 . . . . **811**
You're invited to Bruce Lansky's poetry party! /1996/ 3-6/KD968 . . . . **811**
LEWIS, JP/Black swan/white crow: haiku. /1995/3-6/KD971 . **811**
July is a mad mosquito. /1994/P-3/KD972 . . . . **811**
LINDBERGH, R/Johnny Appleseed. /1990/K-3/KD973 . . . . . **811**
LIVINGSTON, MC/Abraham Lincoln: a man for all the people: a ballad. /1993/K-3/KD974 . . . . **811**
Cricket never does: a collection of haiku and tanka. /1997/ 3-6/KD975. . . . . **811**
Festivals. /1996/3-6/KD976 . . . . **811**
Keep on singing: a ballad of Marian Anderson. /1994/ 1-3/KD977 . . . . **811**
Let freedom ring: a ballad of Martin Luther King, Jr. /1992/ K-2/4 KD978 . . . . **811**
LONGFELLOW, HW/Hiawatha. /1983/P-A/KD979 . . . . . . **CE 811**
Paul Revere's ride. /1990/3-A/KD980 . . . . . **CE 811**
MARZOLLO, J/I'm tyrannosaurus!: a book of dinosaur rhymes. / 1993/K-2/3 KD981 . . . . **811**
MERRIAM, E/Higgle wiggle: happy rhymes. /1994/ P-1/KD983 . . . . **811**
Singing green: new and selected poems for all seasons. /1992/ 3-A/KD984 . . . . **811**
MICHELSON, R/Animals that ought to be: poems about imaginary pets. /1996/K-3/KD985 . . . . **811**
MONSTER SOUP AND OTHER SPOOKY POEMS. /1992/ K-3/KD986 . . . . **811**
MOORE, CC/Grandma Moses Night before Christmas. /1991/ P-A/KD987 . . . . **811**
Twas the night before Christmas: a visit from St. Nicholas. /c1912, 1992/P-A/KD988 . . . . **811**
MORA, P/Desert is my mother./El desierto es mi madre. /1994/ K-3/KD989 . . . . **811**
Listen to the desert/Oye al desierto. /1994/P-1/KD990 . . . . **811**
MOSS, J/Butterfly jar. /1989/2-6/KD991 . . . . **811**

MYERS, WD/Brown angels: an album of pictures and verse. /1993/ K-6/KD992 . . . . **811**
Glorious angels: a celebration of children. /1995/ K-6/KD993 . . . . **811**
Harlem: a poem. /1997/3-6/KD994 . . . . **811**
NIKOLA-LISA, W/Bein' with you this way. /1994/P-2/KD996 . **811**
POE, EA/Annabel Lee. /1987/3-6/KD997 . . . . **811**
Poetry for young people. /1995/5-A/KD998 . . . . **811**
POLACCO, P/Babushka's Mother Goose. /1995/ P-2/3 KD878 . . . . **808.8**
PRELUTSKY, J/Baby uggs are hatching. /1982/1-3/KE000 . . . **811**
Beneath a blue umbrella. /1990/K-2/KE001. . . . . **811**
Dragons are singing tonight. /1993/2-4/KE002 . . . . **811**
Headless Horseman rides tonight: more poems to trouble your sleep. /1980/2-4/KE003 . . . . **811**
It's Halloween. /c1977/1-3/KE004 . . . . **811**
It's snowing! It's snowing! /1984/K-3/KE005 . . . . **811**
It's Thanksgiving. /1982/1-3/KE006 . . . . **CE 811**
It's Valentine's Day. /1983/K-2/KE007 . . . . **811**
Monday's troll: poems. /1996/K-4/KE008 . . . . **CE 811**
My parents think I'm sleeping. /1985/2-5/KE009 . . . . **811**
New kid on the block. /1984/2-6/KE010 . . . . **CE 811**
Nightmares: poems to trouble your sleep. /c1976/ 3-5/KE011 . . . . **811**
Pizza the size of the sun: poems. /1996/K-A/KE012 . . . . **811**
Rainy rainy Saturday. /1980/1-3/KE013 . . . . **811**
Ride a purple pelican. /1986/P-3/KE014 . . . . **811**
Rolling Harvey down the hill. /1980/1-4/KE015 . . . . . **CE 811**
Something big has been here (Talking book). /1991/ K-4/KE016. . . . . **TB 811**
Tyrannosaurus was a beast: dinosaur poems. /c1988, 1992/ 1-5/KE017. . . . . **CE 811**
SANDBURG, C/Poetry for young people. /1995/4-6/KE018. . **811**
SCHERTLE, A/Advice for a frog. /1995/3-5/KE019 . . . . **811**
How now, brown cow? /1994/1-3/KE020 . . . . **811**
SHAPIRO, A/Mice squeak, we speak: a poem. /1997/ P-1/3 KE022 . . . . **811**
SILVERSTEIN, S/Falling up: poems and drawings. /1996/ P-A/KE024. . . . . **811**
Light in the attic. /1981/P-A/KE025 . . . . **811**
Where the sidewalk ends: the poems and drawings of Shel Silverstein. /c1974/P-A/KE026 . . . . **811**
SINGER, M/All we needed to say: poems about school from Tanya and Sophie. /1996/3-6/KE027 . . . . **811**
SOTO, G/Canto familiar. /1995/4-6/KE028 . . . . **811**
Neighborhood odes: poems. /1992/3-A/KE029 . . . . **811**
STAR WALK. /1995/4-8/KE085 . . . . **811.008**
STEIG, J/Consider the lemming. /1988/K-6/KE030 . . . . **811**
THOMAS, JC/Brown honey in broomwheat tea: poems. /1993/ K-6/KE031. . . . . **811**
Gingerbread days: poems. /1995/K-4/KE032 . . . . **811**
TILLER, R/Cinnamon, mint, and mothballs: a visit to Grandmother's house. /1993/K-3/KE033 . . . . **811**
TURNER, A/Moon for seasons. /1994/3-6/KE034 . . . . **811**
UPDIKE, J/Helpful alphabet of friendly objects: poems. /1995/ P-1/KE035 . . . . **811**
VIORST, J/Alphabet from Z to A: (with much confusion on the way). /1994/2-5/KE036 . . . . **811**
If I were in charge of the world and other worries. /1981/ 2-4/KE037 . . . . **811**
Sad underwear and other complications: more poems for children and their /1995/2-4/KE038 . . . . **811**
WHITTIER, JG/Barbara Frietchie. /1992/1-3/KE040 . . . . . . **811**
WILLARD, N/Visit to William Blake's inn: poems for innocent and experienced travelers. /1981/5-A/KE042 . . . . **CE 811**
WILMER, I/B is for Bethlehem: a Christmas alphabet. /1990/ K-3/KE043 . . . . **811**
WONG, JS/Suitcase of seaweed and other poems. /1996/ 5-A/KE045. . . . . **811**
WOOD, N/Spirit walker: poems. /1993/6-A/KE046 . . . . **811**
YOLEN, J/Animal fare: poems. /1994/K-3/KE047. . . . . **811**
Sacred places. /1996/3-6/KE048 . . . . **811**
Sea watch: a book of poetry. /1996/4-6/KE049 . . . . **811**

American poetry--Afro-American authors.
GIOVANNI, N/Knoxville, Tennessee. /1994/P-1/2 KD945 . . . **811**
Spin a soft black song. Rev. ed. /c1971, 1985/1-4/KD946 . **811**
GREENFIELD, E/Nathaniel talking. /1988/K-6/KD948 . . . . . **811**
HUGHES, L/Dream keeper and other poems, including seven additional poems. /1994/4-6/KD954. . . . . **811**
JOHNSON, JW/Creation. /1994/K-3/KD956 . . . . **811**
Creation: a poem. /1993/1-6/KD957 . . . . **811**
SOUL LOOKS BACK IN WONDER. /1993/4-A/KE084 . . **811.008**

American poetry--Afro-American authors--Collections.
    MAKE A JOYFUL SOUND: POEMS FOR CHILDREN BY AFRICAN-
    AMERICAN POETS. /1991/1-6/KE070 . . . . **811.008**
    PASS IT ON: AFRICAN-AMERICAN POETRY FOR CHILDREN. /
    1993/1-3/KE075. . . . . **811.008**
American poetry--Asian American authors.
    WONG, JS/Good luck gold and other poems. /1994/
    5-6/KE044. . . . . **811**
        Suitcase of seaweed and other poems. /1996/5-A/KE045 . . **811**
American poetry--Collections.
    A. NONNY MOUSE WRITES AGAIN!: POEMS. /1993/
    K-2/KE052. . . . . **811.008**
    AT THE CRACK OF THE BAT: BASEBALL POEMS. /1992/
    3-6/KE053. . . . . **811.008**
    CELEBRATE AMERICA IN POETRY AND ART. /1994/
    3-6/KE054. . . . . **811.008**
    DRAGON POEMS. /1991/K-A/KE055. . . . . **811.008**
    EXTRA INNINGS: BASEBALL POEMS. /1993/
    3-6/KE056. . . . . **811.008**
    FAMILIES: POEMS CELEBRATING THE AFRICAN AMERICAN
    EXPERIENCE. /1994/K-3/KE057 . . . . **811.008**
    FOR LAUGHING OUT LOUD: POEMS TO TICKLE YOUR
    FUNNYBONE. /1991/K-5/KE058. . . . . **811.008**
    FOR LAUGHING OUT LOUDER: MORE POEMS TO TICKLE YOUR
    FUNNYBONE. /1995/K-5/KE059 . . . . **811.008**
    GOOD BOOKS, GOOD TIMES! /1990/K-3/KE060 . . . . **811.008**
    HALLOWEEN POEMS. /1989/K-4/KE062 . . . . **811.008**
    HAND IN HAND: AN AMERICAN HISTORY THROUGH POETRY. /
    1994/2-6/KE063. . . . . **811.008**
    HOPKINS, LB/Weather: poems. /1994/K-3/KE064 . . . . . **811.008**
    I LIKE YOU, IF YOU LIKE ME: POEMS OF FRIENDSHIP. /1987/
    3-A/KE065. . . . . **811.008**
    I THOUGHT I'D TAKE MY RAT TO SCHOOL: POEMS FOR
    SEPTEMBER TO JUNE. /1993/2-5/KE066 . . . . **811.008**
    IMAGINARY GARDENS: AMERICAN POETRY AND ART FOR
    YOUNG PEOPLE. /1989/4-A/KE067 . . . . **811.008**
    KIDS PICK THE FUNNIEST POEMS. /1991/3-6/KE068 . . **811.008**
    LOTS OF LIMERICKS. /1991/3-6/KE069 . . . . **811.008**
    MAKE A JOYFUL SOUND: POEMS FOR CHILDREN BY AFRICAN-
    AMERICAN POETS. /1991/1-6/KE070 . . . . **811.008**
    MARVELOUS MATH: A BOOK OF POEMS. /1997/
    1-4/KE071. . . . . **811.008**
    MAVOR, S/You and me: poems of friendship. /1997/
    K-2/KE072. . . . . **811.008**
    NEVER TAKE A PIG TO LUNCH AND OTHER POEMS ABOUT THE
    FUN OF EATING. /1994/1-4/KE073 . . . . **811.008**
    OPENING DAYS: SPORTS POEMS. /1996/3-6/KE074 . . **811.008**
    PLACE MY WORDS ARE LOOKING FOR: WHAT POETS SAY
    ABOUT AND THROUGH THEIR WORK. /1990/
    3-A/KE076. . . . . **811.008**
    POEMS FOR JEWISH HOLIDAYS. /1986/K-3/KE077 . . . **811.008**
    RAINY DAY RHYMES. /1992/1-3/KE078 . . . . **811.008**
    READ-ALOUD RHYMES FOR THE VERY YOUNG. /c1986/
    P-K/KE079. . . . . **811.008**
    ROLL ALONG: POEMS ON WHEELS. /1993/
    4-A/KE080. . . . . **811.008**
    SLAM DUNK: BASKETBALL POEMS. /1995/4-6/KE081. . **811.008**
    SNOW TOWARD EVENING: A YEAR IN A RIVER VALLEY:
    NATURE POEMS. /1995/2-6/KE082 . . . . **811.008**
    SNUFFLES AND SNOUTS: POEMS. /1995/P-2/KE083 . . **811.008**
    SUNFLAKES: POEMS FOR CHILDREN. /1992/
    P-2/KE086. . . . . **811.008**
    TEN-SECOND RAINSHOWERS: POEMS BY YOUNG PEOPLE. /
    1996/3-6/KE088. . . . . **811.008**
    YOURS TILL BANANA SPLITS: 201 AUTOGRAPH RHYMES. /
    1995/3-6/KD894 . . . . **808.88**
    ZOOFUL OF ANIMALS. /1992/K-4/KE090. . . . . **811.008**
American poetry--Software.
    NEW KID ON THE BLOCK (CD-ROM). /1993/
    K-A/KD995 . . . . **CDR 811**
Americanization SEE United States--Emigration and immigration.
Americans--Barbados--Fiction.
    GANTOS, J/Jack's new power: stories from a Caribbean year. /
    1995/5-A/4 KH151. . . . . **Fic**
Amish.
    BIAL, R/Amish home. /1993/5-A/8 KA719 . . . . **289.7**
    WILLIAMS, JK/Amish. /1996/5-A/9 KA721 . . . . **289.7**
Amish--Fiction.
    AMMON, R/Amish Christmas. /1996/3-5/4 KG844 . . . . . . **Fic**
    MITCHELL, B/Down Buttermilk Lane. /1993/1-3/2 KG144 . . . . . **E**
Amistad (Schooner).
    AMISTAD REVOLT: "ALL WE WANT IS MAKE US FREE"
    (VIDEOCASSETTE). /1996/6-A/KA926 . . . . **VCR 326**

    ZEINERT, K/Amistad slave revolt and American abolition. /1997/
    6-A/10 KA930 326
Amphibians SEE ALSO names of Amphibians e.g. Frogs; Salamanders.
Amphibians.
    AMPHIBIANS AND REPTILES (VIDEOCASSETTE). /1996/
    5-6/KC612. . . . . **VCR 597.9**
    CLARKE, B/Amphibian. /1993/5-6/9 KC599 . . . . **597.8**
Amusement parks--Fiction.
    CRESSWELL, H/Watchers: a mystery at Alton Towers. /1994/
    5-A/3 KH040 . . . . **Fic**
Amusements SEE ALSO Circus; Dancing; Games; Handicraft; Hobbies;
    Jokes; Magic; Mathematical recreations; Motion pictures; Plays; Puzzles;
    Recreation; Riddles; Scientific recreations; Sports; Television.
Amusements.
    CANEY, S/Steven Caney's Kids' America. /1978/
    4-6/7 KE920 . . . . **973.92**
    COLE, J/Rain or shine activity book: fun things to make and do. /
    1997/3-6/KD699 . . . . **793**
    GRYSKI, C/Hands on, thumbs up: secret handshakes, fingerprints,
    sign languages, and more /1993/5-6/5 KC904 . . . . **611**
    RICE, M/Complete book of children's activities. /1993/
    /KA194. . . . . **PROF 372.13**
Amusements--History.
    HANKIN, R/What was it like before television? /1995/
    1-3/2 KD679 . . . . **790.1**
    KALMAN, B/Early pleasures and pastimes. /1983/
    4-A/8 KD680 . . . . **790.1**
Amyotrophic lateral sclerosis.
    MACHT, NL/Lou Gehrig. /1993/5-A/7 KE364. . . . **B GEHRIG, L.**
Anansi (Legendary character).
    ARKHURST, JC/Adventures of Spider: West African folktales. /
    c1964, 1992/2-3/5 KB524 . . . . **398.24**
    GLEESON, B/Anansi (Kit). /1992/3-5/KB572 . . . . . . **KIT 398.24**
    KIMMEL, EA/Anansi and the moss-covered rock. /1988/
    1-2/4 KB600 . . . . **CE 398.24**
        Anansi and the talking melon. /1994/2-3/2 KB601 . . . **CE 398.24**
        Anansi goes fishing. /1991, c1992/K-2/2 KB602 . . . . **CE 398.24**
    MCDERMOTT, G/Anansi the spider: a tale from the Ashanti. /
    c1972/1-3/2 KB616. . . . . **398.24**
    MOLLEL, TM/Ananse's feast: an Ashanti tale. /1997/
    K-2/3 KB622 . . . . **398.24**
    TEMPLE, F/Tiger soup: an Anansi story from Jamaica. /1994/
    2-3/2 KB663 . . . . **398.24**
Anansi (Legendary character)--Fiction.
    FRENCH, F/Anancy and Mr. Dry-Bone. /1991/K-2/2 KF583 . . . . **E**
Anasazi Indians SEE Cliff dwellings--Southwest, New; Indians of North
    America--Southwest, New--Social life and customs; Mesa Verde National
    Park (Colo.); Pueblo Indians--Social life and customs.
**Anastasiia Nikolaevna, Grand Duchess, daughter of Nicholas II,
Emperor of Russia.**
    BREWSTER, H/Anastasia's album. /1996/
    5-A/7 KE234 . . . . **B ANASTASIIA**
Anatomy, Comparative.
    PARKER, S/Skeleton. /1988/5-6/8 KC285 . . . . **573.7**
    VISUAL DICTIONARY OF THE SKELETON. /1995/
    4-A/8 KC286 . . . . **573.7**
Anatomy, Human SEE Human anatomy.
Ancestry SEE Genealogy.
Andersen, Hans Christian.
    BRUST, BW/Amazing paper cuttings of Hans Christian Andersen. /
    1994/3-5/8 KE235 . . . . **B ANDERSEN, H.**
Anderson, Marian.
    FERRIS, J/What I had was singing: the story of Marian Anderson. /
    1994/5-A/6 KE236 . . . . **B ANDERSON, M.**
Anderson, Marian--Poetry.
    LIVINGSTON, MC/Keep on singing: a ballad of Marian Anderson.
    /1994/1-3/KD977 . . . . **811**
Andersonville Prison--Fiction.
    WISLER, GC/Red Cap. /1994/5-A/7 KH873 . . . . **Fic**
Androids SEE Robots.
Angelou, Maya.
    PETTIT, J/Maya Angelou: journey of the heart. /1996/
    4-6/8 KE237 . . . . **B ANGELOU, M.**
Anger.
    ANGRY JOHN (VIDEOCASSETTE). /1994/
    4-6/KA622 . . . . **VCR 152.4**
    I GET SO MAD! (VIDEOCASSETTE). /1993/
    K-3/KA626 . . . . **VCR 152.4**
    IT'S NOT MY FAULT: A PROGRAM ABOUT CONFLICT
    RESOLUTION (VIDEOCASSETTE). /1981/
    4-6/KA628 . . . . **VCR 152.4**
    WHEN I GET MAD (VIDEOCASSETTE). /1994/
    5-6/KA631 . . . . **VCR 152.4**

WHEN YOU'RE MAD, MAD, MAD!: DEALING WITH ANGER
(VIDEOCASSETTE). /1993/4-6/KA632 . . . . **VCR 152.4**
Anger--Fiction.
    GREENFIELD, E/Koya DeLaney and the good girl blues. /c1992,
    1995/4-6/6 KH199 . . . . **Fic**
Angles (Geometry).
    GEOMETRY AND MEASUREMENT: MEASURING ANGLES
    (VIDEOCASSETTE). /1987/4-A/KB995 . . . . **VCR 516.2**
Animal communication SEE ALSO Animal sounds.
Animal defenses.
    SOWLER, S/Amazing armored animals. /1992/
    4-6/6 KC467 . . . . **591.47**
    ZOEHFELD, KW/What lives in a shell? /1994/P-1/2 KC517 . . **594**
Animal distribution SEE Animals--Migration; Freshwater animals; Marine
animals.
Animal ecology--Arctic regions.
    BRANDENBURG, J/To the top of the world: adventures with arctic
    wolves. /1993/5-6/7 KC834 . . . . **599.773**
    KALMAN, B/Arctic animals. /1988/4-6/8 KC501 . . . . . **591.998**
Animal flight.
    CREAGH, C/Things with wings. /1996/4-6/5 KC445 . . . . . . **591**
Animal ghosts--Fiction.
    BAUER, MD/Ghost eye. /1992/4-6/6 KG881 . . . . **Fic**
    HOFFMAN, M/Four-legged ghosts. /1995/2-4/6 KH269 . . . . . **Fic**
Animal intelligence SEE ALSO Animals--Habits and behavior.
Animal locomotion.
    ANIMAL JOURNEYS (VIDEOCASSETTE). /1996/
    3-5/KC470. . . . . **VCR 591.5**
    HOW ANIMALS MOVE (VIDEOCASSETTE). /1989/
    5-6/KC283. . . . . **VCR 573.7**
    LOCOMOTION (VIDEOCASSETTE). /1986/
    5-A/KC284 . . . . **VCR 573.7**
    WORLD ALIVE (VIDEOCASSETTE). /1990/
    4-6/KC480. . . . . **VCR 591.5**
    YAMASHITA, K/Paws, wings, and hooves: mammals on the move. /
    1993/2-5/2 KC468 . . . . **591.47**
Animal locomotion--Software.
    ALEXANDER, RM/How animals move (CD-ROM). /1995/
    4-A/KC464 . . . . **CDR 591.47**
Animal painting and illustration SEE ALSO Animals--Pictorial works; Animals
in art.
Animal rights.
    BLOYD, S/Animal rights. /1990/5-A/8 KA672 . . . . **179**
    NEWKIRK, I/Kids can save the animals!: 101 easy things to do. /
    1991/3-6/7 KA673 . . . . **179**
    OWEN, M/Animal rights: yes or no? /1993/6-A/9 KA674 . . . **179**
Animal sounds SEE ALSO Animal communication.
Animal sounds.
    ELLIOTT, L/Guide to night sounds (Sound recording cassette). /
    1992/3-6/KC484 . . . . **SRC 591.59**
    TURNER, M/Come on everybody! Let's go to the fair (Kit). /1991/
    P/KB182 . . . . **KIT 394**
    WOOD, J/Jakki Wood's animal hullabaloo: a wildlife noisy book. /
    1995/KC485. . . . . **591.59**
Animal sounds--Fiction.
    FLEMING, D/Barnyard banter. /1994/P-1/3 KF553 . . . . **E**
    HUTCHINS, P/Little Pink Pig. /1994/P-1/2 KF799 . . . . **E**
    KUSKIN, K/Roar and more. /c1956, 1990/P-1/KF940 . . . . . **E**
    TITUS, E/Kitten who couldn't purr. /1991/P-K/1 KG611 . . . . . **E**
    ZIEFERT, H/Who said moo? /1996/P-1/2 KG799 . . . . **E**
Animal sounds--Poetry.
    MORA, P/Listen to the desert/Oye al desierto. /1994/
    P-1/KD990. . . . . **811**
    SHAPIRO, A/Mice squeak, we speak: a poem. /1997/
    P-1/3 KE022 . . . . **811**
Animal swimming.
    RILEY, LC/Elephants swim. /1995/P-2/3 KC466 . . . . **591.47**
Animal tracks.
    KUDLINSKI, KV/Animal tracks and traces. /1991/
    3-4/4 KC475 . . . . **591.5**
Animal tracks--Fiction.
    GEORGE, LB/In the snow: who's been here? /1995/
    1-3/2 KF607 . . . . **E**
Animal weapons.
    ANIMAL WEAPONS (VIDEOCASSETTE). /1996/
    3-5/KC460. . . . . **VCR 591.4**
Animals SEE ALSO Domestic animals; Invertebrates; Marine animals; Pets;
Rare and endangered species; Rare animals; Rare birds; Vertebrates; Zoo
animals; names of animal groups e.g. Amphibians; names of specific
animals e.g. Anteaters.
Animals.
    BENDER, R/A to Z beastly jamboree. /1996/K-2/KB830 . . . . **421**
    COOPER, K/Too many rabbits and other fingerplays about animals,
    nature, weather, and the /1995/P-1/KD707 . . . . **793.4**

CREAGH, C/Things with wings. /1996/4-6/5 KC445 . . . . . . **591**
GRAHAM-BARBER, L/Toad or frog, swamp or bog?: a big book of
    nature's confusables. /1994/K-4/4 KB906 . . . . **508**
GREENWAY, S/Two's company. /1997/K-2/3 KB845 . . . . . **428.1**
HOBAN, T/Children's zoo. /1985/P-K/KC448 . . . . **591**
JOHNSON, J/How big is a whale? /1995/2-5/5 KC462 . . . **591.4**
JOHNSON, K/Worm's eye view: make your own wildlife refuge. /
    1991/2-4/5 KC294 . . . . **577**
LACEY, EA/What's the difference?: a guide to some familiar animal
    look-alikes. /1993/5-6/8 KC450. . . . . **591**
LIVING WORLD. /1993/5-A/KA437 . . . . **REF 508**
LIVO, LJ/Of bugs and beasts: fact, folklore, and activities. /1995/
    /KA296. . . . . **PROF 591**
POWELL, C/Bold carnivore: an alphabet of predators. /1995/
    P-5/5 KC454 . . . . **591**
REALMS OF LIFE (PICTURE). /1996/6-A/KC356 . . . . . . **PIC 578**
SEEING THINGS (VIDEOCASSETTE). /1987/
    K-3/KB913. . . . . **VCR 508**
THORNHILL, J/Wildlife A-B-C: a nature alphabet book. /1990/
    P-2/3 KC498 . . . . **591.97**
    Wildlife 1 2 3: a nature counting book. /1989/P-2/KC455 . . **591**
WADSWORTH, G/One on a web: counting animals at home. /
    1997/P-2/3 KC456 . . . . **591**
WEBER, L/Backyard almanac. /1996/3-A/7 KB915 . . . . **508**
WILD, WONDERFUL ANIMALS IN THE WOODS
    (VIDEOCASSETTE). /1996/1-4/KC492 . . . . **VCR 591.73**
Animals--Antarctica.
    COWCHER, H/Antarctica. /1990/1-3/4 KC500 . . . . **591.998**
Animals--Encyclopedias.
    FEW, R/Macmillan animal encyclopedia for children. /1991/
    5-6/7 KC446 . . . . **591**
Animals--Fiction SEE ALSO Animals--Habits and behavior--Fiction; Fables;
also names of animals with the subdivision Fiction e.g. Anteaters--Fiction.
Animals--Fiction.
    ABOLAFIA, Y/Fox tale. /1991/K-2/2 KF126 . . . . **E**
    ADLERMAN, D/Africa calling, nighttime falling. /1996/
    P-2/KF135. . . . . **E**
    BASE, G/Animalia. /c1986, 1993/P-A/KF212 . . . . **E**
    BONSALL, CN/Piggle. /1973/P-2/2 KF246 . . . . **E**
    Who's a pest? /c1962/P-2/2 KF248 . . . . **E**
    BRETT, J/Annie and the wild animals. /1985/K-3/2 KF260 . . . . **E**
    Berlioz the bear. /1991/K-2/2 KF261 . . . . **E**
    BROWN, MT/Arthur writes a story. /1996/K-2/2 KF272 . . . . **E**
    Arthur's first sleepover. /1994/K-2/2 KF275 . . . . **E**
    Arthur's nose. /c1976/K-2/2 KF276. . . . . **CE E**
    Arthur's teacher trouble. /1986/K-3/4 KF277 . . . . **CE E**
    Little Donkey close your eyes. /1995/P-K/2 KF286 . . . . . . **E**
    BURNINGHAM, J/Mr. Gumpy's motor car. /c1973, 1976/
    P-2/2 KF317 . . . . **CE E**
    Mr. Gumpy's outing. /c1970/P-2/2 KF318 . . . . **CE E**
    CAPLE, K/Biggest nose. /1985/P-2/2 KF337 . . . . **E**
    CARLE, E/Rooster's off to see the world. /1972/P-2/2 KF345 . . **E**
    CHRISTELOW, E/Robbery at the Diamond Dog Diner. /1986/
    K-3/4 KF389 . . . . **CE E**
    CLIMO, S/Little red ant and the great big crumb: a Mexican fable.
    /1995/1-3/2 KF398 . . . . **E**
    DALE, P/Ten out of bed. /1994/P-1/2 KF446 . . . . **E**
    DAVOL, MW/Batwings and the curtain of night. /1997/
    1-3/2 KF449 . . . . **E**
    How Snake got his hiss: an original tale. /1996/K-2/2 KF450 . . **E**
    DENTON, KM/Would they love a lion? /1995/P-1/1 KF463 . . . . **E**
    DRAGONWAGON, C/Alligator arrived with apples, a potluck
    alphabet feast. /1987/K-2/5 KF494 . . . . **E**
    EDWARDS, PD/Barefoot: escape on the Underground Railroad. /
    1997/1-3/3 KF510 . . . . **E**
    Some smug slug. /1996/P-2/3 KF513 . . . . **E**
    ETS, MH/In the forest. /c1944, 1976/P-1/2 KF537 . . . . **E**
    Play with me. /c1955/P-1/2 KF539 . . . . **CE E**
    FARMER, N/Warm Place. /1995/4-A/3 KH110 . . . . **Fic**
    FLACK, M/Ask Mr. Bear. /c1932/P-1/2 KF549 . . . . **CE E**
    FLEMING, D/Count! /1992/P-K/KF554 . . . . **E**
    In the tall, tall grass. /1991/P-K/1 KF556 . . . . **E**
    Time to sleep. /1997/P-1/2 KF558 . . . . **E**
    FOX, M/Mem Fox reads (Talking book). /1992/P-2/KF570 . . **TB E**
    Time for bed. /1993/P-1/2 KF572 . . . . **E**
    FOX, P/Little swineherd and other tales. /1996/3-6/4 KH136 . . **Fic**
    GALDONE, P/Henny Penny. /c1968/P-K/2 KF594 . . . . . . **CE E**
    Little red hen. /c1973/P-K/2 KF595 . . . . **CE E**
    GANNETT, RS/My father's dragon. /c1948, 1986/
    3-5/6 KH149 . . . . **Fic**
    GARTEN, J/Alphabet tale. New ed., rev. and re-illustrated. /1994/
    P-K/3 KF599 . . . . **E**
    GINSBURG, M/Mushroom in the rain. /c1974, 1987/
    P-2/2 KF623 . . . . **E**

GRAHAME, K/Wind in the willows. /1980/5-6/8 KH189 . . . . . **Fic**
 Wind in the willows. 75th anniversary edition. /1983/
 5-6/8 KH190 . . . . **Fic**
GUARINO, D/Is your mama a llama? /1989/P-1/2 KF651 . . . . . **E**
HARLEY, B/Sitting down to eat. /1996/P-2/2 KF672 . . . . **E**
HOBAN, L/Case of the two masked robbers. /1988/
 K-2/1 KF737 . . . . **E**
 Silly Tilly's Thanksgiving dinner. /1990/K-2/2 KF738 . . . . . **E**
HOBSON, S/Chicken Little. /1994/P-2/2 KF749 . . . . **E**
HUGHES, T/Tales of the early world. /1991/4-A/5 KH290 . . . **Fic**
HUTCHINS, P/One hunter. /1982/P-K/KF800 . . . . **E**
 Shrinking mouse. /1997/P-K/1 KF803 . . . . **E**
JARRELL, R/Bat-poet. /1996/4-A/6 KH327 . . . . **Fic**
JONAS, A/Splash! /1995/P-2/1 KF848 . . . . **E**
KALAN, R/Stop, thief! /1993/K-2/1 KF866 . . . . **E**
KELLOGG, S/Chicken Little. /1985/K-3/5 KF889 . . . . **CE E**
KESSLER, L/Kick, pass, and run. /c1966/1-2/2 KF899 . . . . **E**
 Old Turtle's soccer team. /1988/K-3/2 KF901 . . . . **E**
KIPLING, R/Beginning of the armadillos. /1995/3-5/8 KH359 . . **Fic**
 Complete Just so stories. /1993/3-5/7 KH360 . . . . **Fic**
 How the rhinoceros got his skin; and, How the camel got his hump
 /1987/2-5/KH361 . . . . **VCR Fic**
 Jungle book: the Mowgli stories. /1995/6-A/7 KH363 . . . . . **Fic**
 Rikki-Tikki-Tavi and Wee Willie Winkie (Talking book). /n.d./
 4-6/KH364 . . . . **TB Fic**
KRAUSS, R/Happy day. /c1945, 1949/P-2/2 KF921 . . . . **E**
KROLL, S/It's groundhog day! /1987/K-2/4 KF929 . . . . **E**
KUSKIN, K/James and the rain. /1995/K-2/5 KF938 . . . . **E**
 Roar and more. /c1956, 1990/P-1/KF940 . . . . **E**
LAPOINTE, C/Out of sight! Out of mind! /1995/1-3/1 KF945 . . . **E**
LATIMER, J/Moose and friends. /1993/1-3/2 KF947 . . . . **E**
LAWSON, R/Rabbit Hill. /c1944, 1962/4-6/7 KH390 . . . . **CE Fic**
LESIEG, T/Ten apples up on top! /c1961/1-2/1 KF959 . . . . . . **E**
LIONNI, L/Frederick's fables: a Leo Lionni treasury of favorite
 stories. Rev. ed. /1997/P-2/4 KF993 . . . . **E**
 Leo Lionni's Caldecotts (Videocassette). /1985/
 P-2/KF994 . . . . **VCR E**
LOBEL, A/Arnold Lobel video showcase (Videocassette). /1985/
 1-3/KG000 . . . . **VCR E**
 Fables. /1980/3-A/5 KH416 . . . . **Fic**
 Grasshopper on the road. /1978/K-2/2 KG005 . . . . **CE E**
 Zoo for Mister Muster. /c1962/P-1/5 KG015 . . . . **E**
LONDON, J/Fireflies, fireflies, light my way. /1996/
 P-2/2 KG020 . . . . **E**
 Owl who became the moon. /1993/P-2/3 KG026 . . . . **E**
LOPSHIRE, R/Put me in the zoo. /c1960/K-1/1 KG033 . . . . . . **E**
LOW, J/Mice twice. /1980/P-2/2 KG036 . . . . **E**
MACDONALD, A/Little Beaver and The Echo. /1990/
 P-K/1 KG049 . . . . **E**
MARSHALL, J/Rats on the range and other stories. /1993/
 1-4/2 KH458 . . . . **Fic**
 Rats on the roof and other stories. /1991/1-4/2 KH459 . . . . **Fic**
MARTIN, JR., B/Brown bear, brown bear, what do you see? /
 1992/P-K/1 KG072 . . . . **E**
MARZOLLO, J/Pretend you're a cat. /1990/P-1/4 KG082 . . . . . **E**
MCKISSACK, P/Nettie Jo's friends. /1989/1-3/4 KG108 . . . . . . **E**
MINARIK, EH/Am I beautiful? /1992/P-K/2 KG140 . . . . **E**
MOFFATT, J/Who stole the cookies? /1996/P-1/1 KG149 . . . . . **E**
MYERS, WD/Story of the three kingdoms. /1995/1-3/3 KG165 . **E**
OCHS, CP/When I'm alone. /1993/P-2/4 KG187 . . . . **E**
OPPENHEIM, J/You can't catch me! /1986/P-1/KG193 . . . . . . **E**
PARNALL, P/Feet! /1988/P-2/1 KG219 . . . . **E**
PEET, B/Ant and the elephant. /c1972/K-3/5 KG223 . . . . **E**
 Farewell to Shady Glade. /c1966/K-2/KG227 . . . . **E**
POTTER, B/Hill top tales. /c1907, 1987/P-2/2 KG268 . . . . . . **E**
 Tale of Peter Rabbit, and four other stories (Talking book). /
 1984/P-2/KG279 . . . . **TB E**
REISER, L/Beach feet. /1996/P-3/2 KG318 . . . . **E**
 Two mice in three fables. /1995/P-2/3 KG320 . . . . **E**
ROSENBERG, L/Big and little alphabet. /1997/K-2/2 KG353 . . . **E**
RYLANT, C/Everyday pets (Board book). /1993/
 P-K/2 KG373 . . . . **BB E**
 Gooseberry Park. /1995/3-5/5 KH662 . . . . **Fic**
SCHINDEL, J/What's for lunch? /1994/P-1/2 KG407 . . . . **E**
SEIDLER, T/Wainscott weasel. /1993/4-6/5 KH691 . . . . **Fic**
SELDEN, G/Old meadow. /1987/3-5/5 KH697 . . . . **Fic**
 Tucker's countryside. /c1969, 1989/4-6/5 KH698 . . . . **Fic**
SENDAK, M/Higglety pigglety pop, or, There must be more to life.
 /c1967/1-3/6 KG431 . . . . **E**
 Where the wild things are and other stories (Talking book). /
 1977/P-2/KG437 . . . . **TB E**
SEUSS, D/If I ran the zoo. /1950/P-3/5 KG465 . . . . **E**
 Yertle the turtle, and other stories. /c1958/P-3/3 KG472 . . **CE E**
SHARMAT, MW/I'm terrific. /1977/P-1/3 KG481 . . . . **E**

SLATE, J/Miss Bindergarten gets ready for kindergarten. /1996/
 P-K/2 KG515 . . . . **E**
STEIG, W/Toby, where are you? /1997/P-1/2 KG546 . . . . **E**
STEVENSON, J/Mud Flat Olympics. /1994/1-3/2 KG562 . . . . . **E**
 National worm day. /1990/K-2/1 KG563 . . . . **E**
 Sea View Hotel. /c1978, 1994/K-3/3 KG567 . . . . **E**
STOCK, C/Where are you going Manyoni? /1993/
 K-3/3 KG575 . . . . **E**
TAFURI, N/Do not disturb. /1987/P-2/KG587 . . . . **E**
THOMAS, P/Stand back, said the elephant, I'm going to sneeze! /
 c1971, 1990/K-3/2 KG605 . . . . **E**
TREASURY OF ANIMAL STORIES. /1992/3-6/6 KH802 . . . . . **Fic**
TRYON, L/Albert's Thanksgiving. /1994/K-2/2 KG621 . . . . . . **E**
VAN LAAN, N/Sleep, sleep, sleep: a lullaby for little ones around
 the world. /1995/P-2/3 KG644 . . . . **E**
VARLEY, S/Badger's parting gifts. /1984/1-3/7 KG650 . . . . . . **E**
VAUGHAN, MK/Snap! /1996/K-2/2 KG651 . . . . **E**
 Wombat stew. /c1984/P-2/4 KG652 . . . . **E**
WABER, B/You look ridiculous said the rhinoceros to the
 hippopotamus. /c1966/1-2/2 KG673 . . . . **E**
WALSH, JP/Pepi and the secret names. /1995/2-3/6 KG683 . . . **E**
WALTON, R/Noah's square dance. /1995/K-2/3 KG687 . . . . . **E**
WHITE, EB/Charlotte's web. /c1952/3-6/6 KH850 . . . . **Fic**
WILLIAMS, S/I went walking. /1990/P-1/1 KG732 . . . . **CE E**
WISEMAN, B/Morris the Moose. /1989/K-2/2 KG750 . . . . . **CE E**
WOLFF, A/Year of beasts. /1986/P-K/1 KG757 . . . . **E**
WOLF, J/Daddy, could I have an elephant? /1996/
 K-2/2 KG755 . . . . **E**
WOOD, J/Dads are such fun. /1992/P-K/1 KG769 . . . . **E**
YOLEN, J/All in the woodland early: an ABC book. /c1979, 1991/
 K-1/3 KG776 . . . . **E**
YOSHI /Who's hiding here? /1987/K-3/2 KG784 . . . . **E**
ZEMACH, M/Little red hen, an old story. /1983/P-K/2 KG790 . **E**
ZIEFERT, H/Little red hen. /1995/K-1/2 KG793 . . . . **E**

Animals--Fiction--Software.
 ARTHUR'S TEACHER TROUBLE (CD-ROM). /1992/
 1-4/KF171 . . . . **CDR E**
 MARK SCHLICHTING'S HARRY AND THE HAUNTED HOUSE.
 SCHOOL ED. (CD-ROM). /1994/K-3/KG063 . . . . **CDR E**

Animals--Folklore.
 AARDEMA, V/Borreguita and the coyote: a tale from Ayutla,
 Mexico. /1991/P-2/4 KB514 . . . . **398.24**
 This for that: a Tonga tale. /1997/K-2/2 KB517 . . . . . . **398.24**
 Who's in Rabbit's house? (Videocassette). /1995/
 K-3/KB518 . . . . **VCR 398.24**
 Why mosquitoes buzz in people's ears: a West African tale. /
 1975/1-3/5 KB519 . . . . **CE 398.24**
 Why mosquitoes buzz in people's ears (Talking book). /1978/
 2-4/KB520 . . . . **TB 398.24**
 ANIMAL TALES (SOUND RECORDING CASSETTE). /1990/
 P-2/KB523 . . . . **SRC 398.24**
 BARBOSA, RA/African animal tales. /1993/2-4/6 KB526 . . **398.24**
 BRER RABBIT AND BOSS LION (TALKING BOOK). /1992/
 3-A/KB533 . . . . **TB 398.24**
 BRETT, J/Mitten. /1989/K-2/3 KB534 . . . . **398.24**
 BROWN, M/Once a mouse. /c1961/1-3/6 KB536 . . . . **CE 398.24**
 BRUCHAC, J/Boy who lived with the bears: and other Iroquois
 stories. /1995/2-4/4 KB537 . . . . **CE 398.24**
 Great ball game: a Muskogee story. /1994/
 2-4/2 KB539 . . . . **398.24**
 Native American animal stories. /1992/2-4/4 KB540 . . . **398.24**
 BRUSCA, MC/When jaguars ate the moon: and other stories about
 animals and plants of the /1995/2-3/5 KB541 . . . . **398.24**
 BRYAN, A/Beat the story-drum, pum-pum. /1980/
 4-6/4 KB542 . . . . **398.24**
 Lion and the ostrich chicks and other African folk tales. /1986/
 4-6/3 KB544 . . . . **398.24**
 CHOCOLATE, DM/Imani in the belly. /1994/2-3/5 KB431 . **398.22**
 DAY, NY/Kancil and the crocodiles: a tale from Malaysia. /1996/
 2-3/5 KB556 . . . . **398.24**
 GALDONE, P/Gingerbread boy. /1975/P-2/4 KB736 . . **CE 398.27**
 HARRIS, JC/Jump! The adventures of Brer Rabbit. /1997/
 3-4/6 KB585 . . . . **398.24**
 HAUSMAN, G/How Chipmunk got tiny feet: Native American
 animal origin stories. /1995/K-3/3 KB588 . . . . **398.24**
 HOLT, D/Why the dog chases the cat: great animal stories (Sound
 recording cassette). /1994/1-3/KB591 . . . . **SRC 398.24**
 JOHNSTON, T/Tale of Rabbit and Coyote. /1994/
 2-3/2 KB596 . . . . **398.24**
 KESSLER, B/Brer Rabbit and Boss Lion (Kit). /1996/
 3-A/KB599. . . . . **KIT 398.24**
 LESTER, J/Tales of Uncle Remus: the adventures of Brer Rabbit. /
 1987/4-5/5 KB608 . . . . **398.24**

LIVO, LJ/Of bugs and beasts: fact, folklore, and activities. /1995/
/KA296. . . . . **PROF 591**
MAYO, M/Tortoise's flying lesson. /1995/P-2/3 KB615. . . **398.24**
MOHR, N/Song of el coqui and other tales of Puerto Rico. /1995/
3-4/3 KB621. . . . . **398.24**
MOLLEL, TM/King and the tortoise. /1993/2-3/4 KB624 . . **398.24**
Rhinos for lunch and elephants for supper!: a Masai tale. /1991/
P-3/4 KB625. . . . . **398.24**
OLIVIERO, J/Day Sun was stolen. /1995/K-2/5 KB712 . . . **398.26**
PLUME, I/Bremen-Town musicians. /1998/1-3/4 KB636 . . . **398.24**
PROKOFIEV, S/Peter and the wolf. /1982/
P-3/4 KD676. . . . . **CE 789.8**
ROSEN, M/How the animals got their colors: animal myths from
around the world. /1992/2-4/4 KB640 . . . . **398.24**
SIERRA, J/Elephant's wrestling match. /1992/
P-2/4 KB652. . . . . **398.24**
SOUHAMI, J/Leopard's drum: an Asante tale from West Africa. /
1995/P-1/2 KB654 . . . . **398.24**
THOMASON, D/Lessons from the animal people (Sound recording
cassette). /1996/2-5/KB664 . . . . **SRC 398.24**
THREE BILLY GOATS GRUFF; AND, THE THREE LITTLE PIGS
(VIDEOCASSETTE). /1989/P-K/KB665 . . . . **VCR 398.24**
TREASURY OF ANIMAL STORIES. /1992/3-6/6 KH802 . . . . . **Fic**
WOOD, AJ/Lion and the mouse: an Aesop's fable. /1995/
P-1/5 KB674 . . . . **398.24**
WOPILA--A GIVEAWAY: LAKOTA STORIES (SOUND
RECORDING CASSETTE). /1993/3-5/KB676 . . . . . . **SRC 398.24**
YOUNG, E/Donkey trouble. /1995/1-2/5 KB678 . . . . **398.24**

Animals--Folklore--Dictionaries.
PALMATIER, RA/Speaking of animals: a dictionary of animal
metaphors. /1995/6-A/KA427. . . . . **REF 423**
Animals--Food habits.
ANIMAL APPETITES (VIDEOCASSETTE). /1996/
3-5/KC469. . . . . **VCR 591.5**
Animals--Habitations.
BROOKS, B/Nature by design. /1991/A/9 KC483 . . . . . **591.56**
THORNHILL, J/Wild in the city. /1996/P-2/5 KC478. . . . . **591.5**
WILD, WONDERFUL ANIMALS IN THE WOODS
(VIDEOCASSETTE). /1996/1-4/KC492 . . . . **VCR 591.73**
Animals--Habitations--Fiction.
ARUEGO, J/We hide, you seek. /1979/P-K/1 KF172 . . . . **E**
Animals--Habitations--Folklore.
FOSTER, J/Magpies' nest. /1995/1-3/3 KB567 . . . . **398.24**
Animals--Habitats and behavior--Software.
MICROSOFT DANGEROUS CREATURES: EXPLORE THE
ENDANGERED WORLD OF WILDLIFE. /1994/
4-A/KC490 . . . . **CDR 591.68**
Animals--Habits and behavior SEE ALSO Animal defenses; Animal
intelligence; Animals--Fiction; Animals--Habitations; Animals--Infancy;
Animals--Migration; Animals--Hibernation.
Animals--Habits and behavior.
ANIMAL JOURNEYS (VIDEOCASSETTE). /1996/
3-5/KC470. . . . . **VCR 591.5**
ANIMAL WEAPONS (VIDEOCASSETTE). /1996/
3-5/KC460. . . . . **VCR 591.4**
BANCROFT, H/Animals in winter. Rev. ed. /1997/
K-2/2 KC482 . . . . **591.56**
CHIPMUNK (VIDEOCASSETTE). /1988/3-6/KC750 . **VCR 599.36**
EAGLE AND THE SNAKE (VIDEOCASSETTE). /1993/
2-6/KC472. . . . . **VCR 591.5**
FELDMAN, EB/Animals don't wear pajamas: a book about sleeping.
/1992/P-2/6 KC473 . . . . **591.5**
INSTINCTS IN ANIMALS (VIDEOCASSETTE). /1996/
4-6/KC474. . . . . **VCR 591.5**
KUDLINSKI, KV/Animal tracks and traces. /1991/
3-4/4 KC475 . . . . **591.5**
MACHOTKA, H/Terrific tails. /1994/3-5/7 KC272 . . . . . . **571.1**
MURIE, OJ/Field guide to animal tracks. 2nd ed. /1974/
A/8 KC476 . . . . **591.5**
NIGHTTIME ANIMALS (VIDEOCASSETTE). /1996/
3-5/KC477. . . . . **VCR 591.5**
RILEY, LC/Elephants swim. /1995/P-2/3 KC466 . . . . . . **591.47**
SEA ANIMALS ASHORE (VIDEOCASSETTE). /1996/
3-6/KC872. . . . . **VCR 599.79**
SEASONS. REV. ED. (SOUND FILMSTRIP). /c1975, 1993/
K-2/KC063. . . . . **FSS 525**
SELSAM, ME/Keep looking. /1989/P-3/2 KC728. . . . . **599**
SWANSON, D/Coyotes in the crosswalk: true tales of animal life in
the wilds...of the city! /1995/4-6/6 KC494. . . . . . . **591.75**
TAYLOR, B/Arctic and Antarctic. /1995/3-6/7 KE220 . . . . **919.8**
WHERE DO ANIMALS GO IN WINTER? (VIDEOCASSETTE). /
1995/3-6/KC463. . . . . **VCR 591.4**
WORLD ALIVE (VIDEOCASSETTE). /1990/
4-6/KC480. . . . . **VCR 591.5**

ZOLOTOW, C/Sleepy book. /c1958, 1988/P-1/KC481. . . . **591.5**
3-2-1 CONTACT: EXPLORING WEATHER, CLIMATE AND
SEASONS (VIDEOCASSETTE). /1988/2-A/KC223 . . **VCR 551.6**
Animals--Habits and behavior--Fiction.
GEORGE, LB/Around the pond: who's been here? /1996/
K-2/2 KF606 . . . . **E**
HADER, B/Big snow. /1948/K-2/5 KF658. . . . . **E**
Animals--Habits and behavior--Periodicals.
WILDLIFE CONSERVATION. /1897-/K-A/KA551 . . . . . **PER 050**
Animals--Homes SEE Animals--Habitations.
Animals--Infancy.
BARE, CS/Toby the tabby kitten. /1995/K-3/2 KD229 . . . . **636.8**
COLE, J/My new kitten. /1995/P-1/2 KD230 . . . . **636.8**
My puppy is born. Rev. and expanded ed. /1991/
P-2/2 KD218 . . . . **636.7**
FLETCHER, N/Penguin. /1993/P-1/2 KC687 . . . . **598.47**
GREENWAY, S/Whose baby am I? /1992/K-2/4 KC458. . . **591.3**
ISENBART, H/Birth of a foal. /1986/3-6/5 KD201 . . . . . . **636.1**
NATURE'S NEWBORN: BEAR, BIGHORN SHEEP, MOUNTAIN
GOATS (VIDEOCASSETTE). /1994/1-5/KC724 . . . . . **VCR 599**
NATURE'S NEWBORN: ELK, MOOSE, DEER (VIDEOCASSETTE). /
1994/3-6/KC799 . . . . **VCR 599.65**
PFEFFER, W/From tadpole to frog. /1994/
K-2/2 KC608 . . . . **CE 597.8**
RYDEN, H/Joey: the story of a baby kangaroo. /1994/
2-5/4 KC737 . . . . **599.2**
SCHLEIN, M/Discovering dinosaur babies. /1991/
3-6/5 KC262 . . . . **567.9**
SIMON, S/Wild babies. /1997/3-5/6 KC459 . . . . **591.3**
Animals--Infancy--Fiction.
MCMULLAN, K/If you were my bunny. /1996/P-K/3 KG112 . . . **E**
Animals--Migration.
LINDBLAD, L/Serengeti migration: Africa's animals on the move. /
1994/5-6/10 KC497 . . . . **591.96**
Animals--Migration--Maps.
LAMBERT, D/Children's animal atlas: how animals have evolved,
where they live today, why so many are in danger. /1992/
5-6/8 KC496 . . . . **591.9**
Animals--Miscellanea.
GANERI, A/Creature features. /1997/3-6/6 KC447 . . . . **591**
GREENWAY, S/Whose baby am I? /1992/K-2/4 KC458. . . **591.3**
JENKINS, S/Biggest, strongest, fastest. /1995/K-4/3 KC449. . **591**
MACDONALD, S/Peck slither and slide. /1997/P-2/1 KC452 . **591**
MACHOTKA, H/Breathtaking noses. /1992/3-5/6 KC280. . . **573.2**
SOUCIE, G/What's the difference between apes and monkeys and
other living things? /1995/4-6/7 KC271. . . . . **571**
Animals--Periodicals.
ZOONOOZ. /1926-/4-6/KA554 . . . . **PER 050**
Animals--Physiology.
BOOTH, J/You animal! /1996/4-6/5 KC913 . . . . **612**
GANERI, A/Creature features. /1997/3-6/6 KC447 . . . . **591**
HOW ANIMALS MOVE (VIDEOCASSETTE). /1989/
5-6/KC283. . . . . **VCR 573.7**
MACHOTKA, H/Breathtaking noses. /1992/3-5/6 KC280. . . **573.2**
Animals--Physiology--Software.
ALEXANDER, RM/How animals move (CD-ROM). /1995/
4-A/KC464 . . . . **CDR 591.47**
Animals--Pictorial works.
GARDNER, B/Guess what? /1985/K-3/KB904 . . . . **508**
100 WORDS ABOUT ANIMALS. /1987/P-3/KC457 . . . . . **CE 591**
Animals--Poetry.
CARLE, E/Eric Carle's animals, animals. /1989/P-3/KD880 . **808.81**
FLORIAN, D/Beast feast. /1994/K-3/KD935 . . . . **811**
KENNEDY, XJ/Beasts of Bethlehem. /1992/1-6/KD960 . . . . . **811**
LEAR, E/Owl and the Pussy-cat. /1996/P-2/KE105 . . . . **821**
MADO, M/Animals: selected poems. /1992/2-6/KE135 . . . . **895.6**
MICHELSON, R/Animals that ought to be: poems about imaginary
pets. /1996/K-3/KD985 . . . . **811**
POLISAR, BL/Peculiar zoo. /1993/K-2/KD999 . . . . **811**
SCHERTLE, A/Advice for a frog. /1995/3-5/KE019 . . . . **811**
STEIG, J/Consider the lemming. /1988/K-6/KE030 . . . . **811**
ZOOFUL OF ANIMALS. /1992/K-4/KE090 . . . . **811.008**
Animals--Sleep behavior.
FELDMAN, EB/Animals don't wear pajamas: a book about sleeping.
/1992/P-2/6 KC473 . . . . **591.5**
Animals--Software.
AMAZING ANIMALS (CD-ROM). /1997/K-3/KC444 . . **CDR 591**
ANIMAL PLANET (CD-ROM). /1996/4-A/KC439. . . . **CDR 590**
MAMMALS: A MULTIMEDIA ENCYCLOPEDIA (CD-ROM). /1990/
2-A/KA450 . . . . **CDR REF 599**
MICROSOFT EXPLORAPEDIA: THE WORLD OF NATURE.
ACADEMIC ED. (CD-ROM). /1995/1-4/KB909. . . . . . **CDR 508**

Animals--Songs and music.
BETHIE /Bethie's really silly songs about animals (Sound recording cassette). /1993/K-2/KD607 . . . . **SRC 789.3**
GALLINA, J/A to Z, the animals and me (Sound recording cassette). /1993/P-1/KD612 . . . . **SRC 789.3**
LANGSTAFF, J/Frog went a-courtin'. /c1955/ P-3/KD579 . . . . **CE 789.2**
WEEKS, S/Crocodile smile: 10 songs of the Earth as the animals see it. /1994/P-2/KD665 . . . . **BA 789.3**

Animals--Study and teaching--Activity programs.
LIVO, LJ/Of bugs and beasts: fact, folklore, and activities. /1995/ /KA296 . . . . **PROF 591**

Animals--Treatment.
ARNOLD, C/Pets without homes. /1983/1-4/6 KD189 . . . . **636.08**
BLOYD, S/Animal rights. /1990/5-A/8 KA672 . . . . **179**
NEWKIRK, I/Kids can save the animals!: 101 easy things to do. / 1991/3-6/7 KA673 . . . . **179**
OWEN, M/Animal rights: yes or no? /1993/6-A/9 KA674 . . . **179**

Animals--Treatment--Fiction.
JOYCE, W/Buddy: based on the true story of Gertrude Lintz. / 1997/5-A/5 KH337 . . . . **Fic**
NAYLOR, PR/Shiloh. /1991/4-6/6 KH538. . . . . **CE Fic**
QUATTLEBAUM, M/Magic Squad and the dog of great potential. / 1997/2-4/4 KH616 . . . . **Fic**

Animals--Wit and humor.
JUSTER, N/Otter nonsense. /1994/3-6/KD721 . . . . **793.734**
KESSLER, L/Old Turtle's 90 knock-knocks, jokes, and riddles. / 1991/2-4/KD730 . . . . **793.735**
WOODWORTH, V/Animal jokes. /1993/2-4/KD742 . . . . **793.735**

Animals, Mythical--Poetry.
CARLE, E/Eric Carle's dragons dragons and other creatures that never were. /1991/K-3/KD881 . . . . **808.81**
YOLEN, J/Animal fare: poems. /1994/K-3/KE047 . . . . **811**

Animals, Prehistoric SEE Prehistoric animals.
Animals in art SEE ALSO names of specific animals e.g. Horses in art.

Animals in art.
MACCLINTOCK, D/Animals observed: a look at animals in art. / 1993/4-A/7 KD372 . . . . **704.9**
MCHUGH, C/Animals. /1993/4-A/7 KD373 . . . . **704.9**
MICKLETHWAIT, L/I spy a lion: animals in art. /1994/ P-2/2 KD474 . . . . **758**
RICHMOND, R/Story in a picture: animals in art. /1993/ 4-A/7 KD475 . . . . **758**

Animals in literature SEE ALSO Animals--Fiction; Animals--Poetry; Animals--Folklore.

Animated films.
HAHN, D/Animation magic: a behind-the-scenes look at how an animated film is made. /1996/4-6/9 KD685 . . . . **791.43**

Animation (Cinematography).
ANDERSEN, Y/Make your own animated movies and videotapes. / 1991/5-A/6 KD515 . . . . **778.5**
ANIMATION FOR KIDS: HOW TO MAKE YOUR CARTOON MOVE! (VIDEOCASSETTE). /1994/4-A/KD407 . . . . **VCR 741.5**

Anonymous writings.
A. NONNY MOUSE WRITES AGAIN!: POEMS. /1993/ K-2/KE052 . . . . **811.008**

Antarctic regions.
PRINGLE, LP/Antarctica: the last unspoiled continent. /1992/ 4-6/6 KE218 . . . . **919.8**
WINCKLER, S/Our endangered planet: Antarctica. /1992/ 5-6/8 KE221 . . . . **919.8**

Antarctica.
JOHNSON, RL/Science on the ice: an Antarctic journal. /1995/ 5-A/7 KE215 . . . . **919.8**
MCMILLAN, B/Summer ice: life along the Antarctic Peninsula. / 1995/A/8 KE216 . . . . **919.8**

Antarctica--Discovery and exploration.
JOHNSON, RL/Braving the frozen frontier: women working in Antarctica. /1997/4-6/6 KE214 . . . . **919.8**

Antarctica--Geography.
ANTARCTICA (VIDEOCASSETTE). /1991/4-A/KF124 . . **VCR 998**

Anteaters--Fiction.
CUSHMAN, D/Aunt Eater's mystery Christmas. /1995/ 1-2/2 KF440 . . . . **E**
Aunt Eater's mystery vacation. /1992/1-3/2 KF441 . . . . **E**

Antelopes--Folklore.
LACAPA, M/Antelope Woman: an Apache folktale. /1992/ 2-4/5 KB606 . . . . **398.24**

Anthropology SEE ALSO Archaeology; Biculturalism; Civilization; Ethnology.

Anthropology--Periodicals.
FACES: THE MAGAZINE ABOUT PEOPLE. /1984-/ 5-A/KA514 . . . . **PER 050**

Antiquities.
MARTELL, H/Kingfisher book of the ancient world: from the Ice Age to the fall of Rome. /1995/4-6/10 KE621 . . . . **930**
WILCOX, C/Mummies and their mysteries. /1993/ 5-6/6 KB177 . . . . **393**

Antisemitism.
COHN, J/Christmas menorahs: how a town fought hate. /1995/ 3-6/5 KA818 . . . . **305**

Antislavery movements.
AMISTAD REVOLT: "ALL WE WANT IS MAKE US FREE" (VIDEOCASSETTE). /1996/6-A/KA926 . . . . **VCR 326**
KATZ, WL/Breaking the chains: African-American slave resistance. / 1990/A/8 KE966 . . . . **975**
ZEINERT, K/Amistad slave revolt and American abolition. /1997/ 6-A/10 KA930 . . . . **326**

Ants.
OVERBECK, C/Ants. /1982/4-6/7 KC577 . . . . **595.79**
SABIN, F/Amazing world of ants. /1982/ 2-4/2 KC579 . . . . **CE 595.79**

Ants--Fiction.
CLIMO, S/Little red ant and the great big crumb: a Mexican fable. /1995/1-3/2 KF398 . . . . **E**
VAN ALLSBURG, C/Two bad ants. /1988/1-3/4 KG639 . . . . . **E**

Ants--Habits and behavior.
DORROS, A/Ant cities. /1987/1-4/4 KC571 . . . . **595.79**

Apache Indians.
SNEVE, V/Apaches. /1997/4-6/5 KE768 . . . . **970.3**
WILK, B/Letter from an Apache: a true story (Videocassette). / 1983/4-6/KE777 . . . . **VCR 970.3**

Apache Indians--Biography.
HERMANN, S/Geronimo: Apache freedom fighter. /1997/ 5-6/12 KE367 . . . . **B GERONIMO**

Apache Indians--Folklore.
LACAPA, M/Antelope Woman: an Apache folktale. /1992/ 2-4/5 KB606 . . . . **398.24**
SEYMOUR, TV/Gift of Changing Woman. /1993/ 6-A/7 KA792 . . . . **299**

Apache Indians--Rites and ceremonies.
HOYT-GOLDSMITH, D/Apache rodeo. /1995/ 4-6/7 KE798 . . . . **970.491**
SEYMOUR, TV/Gift of Changing Woman. /1993/ 6-A/7 KA792 . . . . **299**

Apache Indians--Social life and customs.
HOYT-GOLDSMITH, D/Apache rodeo. /1995/ 4-6/7 KE798 . . . . **970.491**

Apartment houses SEE ALSO Dwellings.

Apartment houses--Fiction.
ARNOLD, T/No jumping on the bed! /1987/P-3/5 KF167 . . . . . **E**
HILL, ES/Evan's corner. /c1967, 1991/K-2/2 KF727 . . . . **E**
HURWITZ, J/New neighbors for Nora. /c1979, 1991/ 2-4/6 KH299 . . . . **Fic**
Nora and Mrs. Mind-your-own business. /c1977, 1991/ 2-4/4 KH300 . . . . **Fic**
Superduper Teddy. /c1980, 1990/2-4/4 KH304 . . . . **Fic**
PRAGER, A/Spooky Halloween party. /1981/1-3/2 KG287 . . . . **E**
SIS, P/Going up! A color counting book. /1989/P-2/KG511 . . . **E**
THESMAN, J/Nothing grows here. /1994/6-A/4 KH790 . . . . . **Fic**

Apartment houses--Poetry.
CLIFTON, L/Everett Anderson's Christmas coming. /1991/ P-1/KD925 . . . . **811**

Apes--Fiction.
BUEHNER, C/Escape of Marvin the ape. /1992/P-2/3 KF294 . . . **E**

Appalachian Mountains--Fiction.
CLEAVER, V/Where the lilies bloom. /c1969/5-6/6 KH009 . . . . **Fic**
RYLANT, C/When I was young in the mountains. /1982/ K-3/6 KG387 . . . . **CE E**

Appalachian Region SEE ALSO names of particular states e.g. North Carolina.

Appalachian Region.
BIAL, R/Mist over the mountains: Appalachia and its people. / 1997/4-6/9 KE923 . . . . **974**

Appalachian Region--Fiction.
BORTON, L/Junk pile! /1997/K-2/3 KF252 . . . . **E**
HOUSTON, G/Year of the perfect Christmas tree. /1988/ K-3/6 KF771 . . . . **E**
MILLS, LA/Rag coat. /1991/2-3/4 KG139 . . . . **E**
RYLANT, C/Silver packages: an Appalachian Christmas story. / 1997/1-3/3 KG386 . . . . **E**
SMITH, DB/Return to Bitter Creek. /1988/5-A/5 KH721 . . . . . **Fic**

Appalachian Region--Folklore.
BIRDSEYE, T/Soap! soap! don't forget the soap!: an Appalachian folktale. /1993/K-2/3 KB267 . . . . **398.2**
COMPTON, J/Ashpet: an Appalachian tale. /1994/ 2-3/4 KB727 . . . . **398.27**

DAVIS, D/Jack and the animals: an Appalachian folktale. /1995/
2-4/5 KB555 . . . . **398.24**
FOLKTELLERS /Tales to grow on (Sound recording cassette). /
c1981/K-3/KB298 . . . . **SRC 398.2**
HOOKS, WH/Snowbear Whittington: an Appalachian Beauty and
the Beast. /1994/2-3/4 KB318 . . . . **398.2**
Three little pigs and the fox. /1989/2-4/5 KB592 . . . . . **398.24**
SCHROEDER, A/Smoky Mountain Rose: an Appalachian Cinderella.
/1997/2-3/4 KB367 . . . . **398.2**
SLOAT, T/Sody sallyratus. /1997/1-3/5 KB653 . . . . **398.24**
SOME DOG AND OTHER KENTUCKY WONDERS (SOUND
RECORDING CASSETTE). /1992/3-4/KB370 . . . . . . **SRC 398.2**

Appalachian Region--Social life and customs.
ANDERSON, J/Pioneer children of Appalachia. /1986/
4-6/6 KE974 . . . . **975.4**

Appalachian Region, Southern--Description and travel.
RYLANT, C/Appalachia: the voices of sleeping birds. /1991/
3-6/6 KE925 . . . . **974**

Appalachian Region, Southern--Social life and customs.
RYLANT, C/Appalachia: the voices of sleeping birds. /1991/
3-6/6 KE925 . . . . **974**

Appaloosa horse.
PATENT, DH/Appaloosa horses. /1988/4-6/7 KD203 . . . . . **636.1**
STEWART, GB/Appaloosa horse. /1995/4-5/6 KD205 . . . . **636.1**
Apparitions SEE Ghosts.

Apple Computer, Inc.
GREENBERG, KE/Steven Jobs and Stephen Wozniak: creating the
Apple computer. /1994/4-6/7 KD046 . . . . **621.39**

Apple growers.
HODGES, M/True tale of Johnny Appleseed. /1997/
2-4/6 KE238 . . . . **B APPLESEED, J.**
KUNSTLER, JH/Johnny Appleseed (Videocassette). /1992/
2-5/KE239 . . . . **VCR B APPLESEED, J.**
LAWLOR, L/Real Johnny Appleseed. /1995/
5-6/8 KE240 . . . . **B APPLESEED, J.**

Apples.
APPLES (VIDEOCASSETTE). /1996/3-5/KD156 . . . . . . **VCR 634**
BOURGEOIS, P/Amazing apple book. /1990/5-6/7 KD264 . **641.3**
HALL, Z/Apple pie tree. /1996/1-4/2 KC413 . . . . **582.16**
JOHNSON, SA/Apple trees. /1983/4-6/9 KD161 . . . . **634**
MAESTRO, B/How do apples grow? /1992/K-2/4 KC418 . **582.16**
MICUCCI, C/Life and times of the apple. /1992/
3-5/5 KD162 . . . . **634**
SCHNIEPER, C/Apple tree through the year. /c1982, 1987/
5-6/7 KD163 . . . . **634**

Apples--Ecology.
SCHNIEPER, C/Apple tree through the year. /c1982, 1987/
5-6/7 KD163 . . . . **634**

Apples--Fiction.
LESIEG, T/Ten apples up on top! /c1961/1-2/1 KF959 . . . . **E**

Appleseed, Johnny.
HODGES, M/True tale of Johnny Appleseed. /1997/
2-4/6 KE238 . . . . **B APPLESEED, J.**
KUNSTLER, JH/Johnny Appleseed (Videocassette). /1992/
2-5/KE239 . . . . **VCR B APPLESEED, J.**
LAWLOR, L/Real Johnny Appleseed. /1995/
5-6/8 KE240 . . . . **B APPLESEED, J.**

Appleseed, Johnny--Fiction.
GLASS, A/Folks call me Appleseed John. /1995/
3-5/6 KH172 . . . . **Fic**

Appleseed, Johnny--Poetry.
LINDBERGH, R/Johnny Appleseed. /1990/K-3/KD973 . . . . . . **811**

Apprentices--Fiction.
DEFELICE, CC/Apprenticeship of Lucas Whitaker. /1998/
5-A/6 KH066 . . . . **CE Fic**

April Fools' Day--Fiction.
BROWN, MT/Arthur's April fool. /1983/P-3/2 KF273 . . . . **E**
MODELL, F/Look out, it's April Fools' Day. /1985/
K-2/2 KG148 . . . . **E**

Aprons--Fiction.
MCKISSACK, P/Ma Dear's aprons. /1997/3-5/4 KH492 . . . . . **Fic**

Aquarium fishes.
BRAEMER, H/Tropical fish: a complete pet owner's manual. /1983/
5-6/9 KD247 . . . . **639.3**
Aquariums SEE ALSO names of specific fish e.g. Sharks.

Aquariums.
BRAEMER, H/Tropical fish: a complete pet owner's manual. /1983/
5-6/9 KD247 . . . . **639.3**

Aquariums, Public.
ALIKI /My visit to the aquarium. /1993/2-4/5 KC582 . . . . . . **597**
ANCONA, G/Aquarium book. /1991/4-6/7 KD246 . . . . . **639.3**
Aquatic animals SEE Marine animals.

Aquatic biology.
ALIKI /My visit to the aquarium. /1993/2-4/5 KC582 . . . . . . **597**

Arab countries SEE ALSO Middle East.
Arab countries--Folklore.
ALDERSON, B/Arabian nights, or, Tales told by Sheherezade during
a thousand nights and one /1995/5-A/7 KB253 . . . . . **398.2**
ARABIAN NIGHTS: THEIR BEST-KNOWN TALES. /c1909, 1994/
5-A/9 KB255 . . . . **398.2**
ARABIAN NIGHTS (SOUND RECORDING CASSETTE). /1991/
4-5/KB254 . . . . **SRC 398.2**
HAUTZIG, D/Aladdin and the magic lamp. /1993/
1-2/2 KB314 . . . . **398.2**
KIMMEL, EA/Tale of Ali Baba and the forty thieves: a story from
the Arabian Nights. /1996/3-4/6 KB332 . . . . **398.2**
Three princes: a tale from the Middle East. /1994/
2-3/4 KB461 . . . . **398.22**
KUNSTLER, JH/Aladdin and the magic lamp (Kit). /1995/
3-5/KB333 . . . . **KIT 398.2**
LATTIMORE, DN/Arabian nights: three tales. /1995/
3-5/6 KB334 . . . . **398.2**
MAYER, M/Turandot. /1995/3-5/5 KB342 . . . . **398.2**
PHILIP, N/Arabian nights. /1994/5-6/6 KB358. . . . . . **398.2**

Arabian horse.
STEWART, GB/Arabian horse. /1995/4-6/5 KD206 . . . . . **636.1**

Arabian horse--Fiction.
HENRY, M/King of the wind. /c1948, 1990/4-6/5 KH243 . . **CE Fic**

Arabs--Folklore.
KIMMEL, EA/Tale of Ali Baba and the forty thieves: a story from
the Arabian Nights. /1996/3-4/6 KB332 . . . . **398.2**

Arapaho Indians--Fiction.
EAGLE WALKING TURTLE /Full moon stories: thirteen Native
American legends. /1997/3-5/7 KH096. . . . . **Fic**

Arapaho Indians--Folklore.
TAYLOR, CJ/Ghost and Lone Warrior: an Arapaho legend. /1991/
2-5/4 KB696 . . . . **398.25**

Arawak Indians--Fiction.
DORRIS, M/Morning Girl. /1992/6-A/7 KH080. . . . . **Fic**

Archaeological dating.
JESPERSEN, J/Mummies, dinosaurs, moon rocks: how we know how
old things are. /1996/4-6/9 KE625 . . . . **930.1**

Archaeologists.
FORD, B/Howard Carter: searching for King Tut. /1995/
A/9 KE279 . . . . **B CARTER, H.**
Archaeology SEE ALSO Art, Primitive; Cities and towns, Ancient; Cliff
dwellings; Excavations (Archaeology); Indians of North America--
Antiquities; Man, Prehistoric; Mummies; Pyramids; Stone Age; Underwater
archaeology; subdivision Antiquities under names of regions, countries.

Archaeology.
BENDICK, J/Tombs of the ancient Americas. /1993/
3-5/8 KB174 . . . . **393**
DUKE, K/Archaeologists dig for clues. /1997/2-4/3 KE623. . **930.1**
MCINTOSH, J/Archeology. /1994/4-A/11 KE627 . . . . **930.1**
WARREN, S/Cities in the sand: the ancient civilizations of the
Southwest. /1992/5-6/8 KF064 . . . . **979**

Archaeology--Experiments.
GRIER, K/Discover: /1990/3-6/6 KA592 . . . . **069**

Archaeology--History.
GOLDENSTERN, J/Lost cities. /1996/3-6/7 KE624. . . . . . . **930.1**

Architects.
LING, B/Maya Lin. /1997/4-6/10 KE437 . . . . **B LIN, M.**
Architecture SEE ALSO Building; Castles; Cathedrals; Dwellings; Housing;
Skyscrapers.

Architecture.
BIESTY, S/Stephen Biesty's incredible cross-sections. /1992/
4-A/6 KC880 . . . . **600**
CASELLI, G/Wonders of the world. /1992/4-A/8 KD382. . . . **720**
DORROS, A/This is my house. /1992/1-3/2 KD393 . . . . . . **728**
SINGER, D/Structures that changed the way the world looked. /
1995/4-A/9 KD384 . . . . **720**

Architecture--History.
AMERICAN ART AND ARCHITECTURE (VIDEOCASSETTE). /1991/
4-A/KD381 . . . . **VCR 709.73**
LYNCH, A/Great buildings. /1996/4-6/12 KD386 . . . . **720.9**

Architecture, Domestic--History.
VENTURA, P/Houses: structures, methods, and ways of living. /
1993/4-A/9 KD395 . . . . **728**

Architecture, Gothic.
MACAULAY, D/Cathedral: the story of its construction. /c1973/
5-6/6 KD388 . . . . **726**

Architecture, Modern--20th century.
BROSTERMAN, N/Inventing kindergarten. /1997/
/KA196. **PROF 372.21**

Arctic fox.
MATTHEWS, D/Arctic foxes. /1995/4-6/4 KC847 . . . . . **599.776**

Arctic National Wildlife Refuge (Alaska).
SIY, A/Arctic National Wildlife Refuge. /1991/
6-A/6 KC337 .... **577.5**

Arctic regions--Discovery and exploration.
STEGER, W/Over the top of the world: explorer Will Steger's trek
across the Arctic. /1997/5-6/6 KE219. .... **919.8**

Arctic regions--Fiction.
HEINZ, BJ/Kayuktuk: an Arctic quest. /1996/4-A/3 KH235. .... **Fic**
JOOSSE, BM/Mama, do you love me? /1991/P-1/2 KF854. .... **E**
KUSUGAK, M/Baseball bats for Christmas. /1990/
4-6/4 KH384 .... **Fic**

Arctic regions--Folklore.
DABCOVICH, L/Polar bear son: an Inuit tale. /1997/
K-2/4 KB554 .... **398.24**

Arctic tundra--Fiction.
LUENN, N/Nessa's fish. /1990/K-2/2 KG041 .... **CE E**

Argentina.
PETERSON, M/Argentina: a wild west heritage. New ed. /1997/
5-6/8 KF107 .... **982**

Argentina--Social life and customs.
BRUSCA, MC/On the pampas. /1991/3-6/6 KF106 .... **982**
Arithmetic SEE ALSO Addition; Division; Multiplication; Subtraction.

Arithmetic.
ANNO, M/Anno's magic seeds. /1995/P-4/3 KB987 ..... **513.4**
DECIDING HOW CLOSE TO MEASURE (VIDEOCASSETTE). /
1982/3-5/KB996. .... **VCR 519**
LEEDY, L/Fraction action. /1994/2-4/2 KB963 ...... **513.2**
MATH, MONEY, AND YOU (SOUND FILMSTRIP). /1989/
K-2/KB967. .... **FSS 513.2**
PROBLEM SOLVING: RECOGNIZING NECESSARY
INFORMATION (VIDEOCASSETTE). /1982/
3-5/KB979. .... **VCR 513.2**
RELATING FRACTIONS AND DECIMALS (VIDEOCASSETTE). /
1982/3-5/KB981. .... **VCR 513.2**
STATISTICS: UNDERSTANDING MEAN, MEDIAN, AND MODE
(VIDEOCASSETTE). /1987/4-A/KB999 .... **VCR 519.5**
USING FRACTIONS (VIDEOCASSETTE). /1982/
3-4/KB983. .... **VCR 513.2**

Arithmetic--Fiction.
SENDAK, M/One was Johnny: a counting book. /c1962/
P-1/KG435 .... **CE E**
SLATER, T/Stay in line. /1996/K-2/2 KG516. .... **E**

Arithmetic--Software.
CALCULATING CREW. SCHOOL VERSION. (CD-ROM). /1996/
3-6/KB955. .... **CDR 513.2**
CARNIVAL COUNTDOWN. SCHOOL VERSION (CD-ROM). /
1996/K-2/KB926. .... **CDR 510**
JAMES DISCOVERS MATH. SCHOOL ED. (CD-ROM). /1995/
1-3/KB962. .... **CDR 513.2**
MILLIE'S MATH HOUSE (CD-ROM). /1995/
P-2/KB971. .... **CDR 513.2**
MILLIE'S MATH HOUSE (MICROCOMPUTER PROGRAM). /1992/
P-2/KB972. .... **MCP 513.2**
PUZZLE TANKS: A GAME OF NUMBERS AND LOGIC
(MICROCOMPUTER PROGRAM). /1984/3-A/KB940. . **MCP 511**
SEILER, B/How the west was one + three x four (Microcomputer
program). /c1987, 1989/4-A/KB951. .... **MCP 513**
ZOO ZILLIONS. SCHOOL VERSION (CD-ROM). /1966/
K-2/KB986. .... **CDR 513.2**

Arithmetic--Study and teaching--Periodicals.
TEACHING CHILDREN MATHEMATICS. /1954-/
/KA148. .... **PER PROF 050**

Arizona.
FILBIN, D/Arizona. /1991/4-6/7 KF067 .... **979.1**
HEINRICHS, A/Arizona. /1991/4-6/7 KF070. .... **979.1**

Arizona--Description and travel--Periodicals.
ARIZONA HIGHWAYS. /1925-/P-A/KA500 .... **PER 050**

Arizona--Folklore.
COURLANDER, H/People of the short blue corn: tales and legends
of the Hopi Indians. /c1970, 1996/1-A/5 KB278. .... **398.2**
ROESSEL, M/Songs from the loom: a Navajo girl learns to weave.
/1995/4-6/6 KE799 .... **970.491**

Arizona--History.
LIVING ON THE EDGE (VIDEOCASSETTE). /1991/
A/KF071. .... **VCR 979.1**

Arkansas.
DI PIAZZA, D/Arkansas. /1994/4-6/7 KF007 .... **976.7**
FRADIN, DB/Arkansas. /1994/4-6/4 KF008 .... **976.7**

Armadillos.
PATTON, D/Armadillos. /1996/4-6/9 KC739 .... **599.3**
PEMBLETON, S/Armadillo. /1992/5-6/7 KC740 .... **599.3**
STUART, D/Astonishing armadillo. /1993/5-6/7 KC741 .... **599.3**

Armadillos--Fiction.
BEIFUSS, J/Armadillo Ray. /1995/K-2/4 KF216 .... **E**

KIPLING, R/Beginning of the armadillos. /1995/3-5/8 KH359 . . **Fic**

Armed Forces--History.
LLOYD, M/Military badges and insignia. /1995/
4-8/12 KA984 .... **355.1**

Armenia--Folklore.
HOGROGIAN, N/Contest. /c1976/3-5/5 KB744 .... **398.27**

Armenian massacres--1915-1923.
KHERDIAN, D/Road from home: the story of an Armenian girl. /
1979/5-6/6 KE698 .... **949.6**

Armenians--Turkey--Biography.
KHERDIAN, D/Road from home: the story of an Armenian girl. /
1979/5-6/6 KE698 .... **949.6**

Armored animals.
SOWLER, S/Amazing armored animals. /1992/
4-6/6 KC467 .... **591.47**

Arms and armor.
BYAM, M/Arms and armor. /1988/A/10 KA986 .... **355.8**

Armstrong, Louis.
MEDEARIS, AS/Little Louis and the jazz band: the story of Louis
"Satchmo" Armstrong. /1994/
2-4/6 KE241 .... **B ARMSTRONG, L.**

Arnosky, Jim.
ARNOSKY, J/Nearer nature. /1996/A/6 KE933 .... **974.3**

Arpilleras (Handicraft).
DORROS, A/Tonight is Carnaval. /1991/1-3/4 KF492 .... **E**

Arson--Fiction.
GEE, M/Fire-raiser. /1992/6-A/6 KH155 .... **Fic**

Art.
DAVIDSON, R/Take a look: an introduction to the experience of
art. /1994/5-6/7 KD364 .... **701**
FLORIAN, D/Painter. /1993/1-2/4 KD464 .... **750**
ISAACSON, P/Short walk around the Pyramids and through the
world of art. /1993/5-A/6 KD363 .... **700**
POLISAR, BL/Barry's scrapbook: a window into art (Videocassette).
/1994/1-4/KD367. .... **VCR 701**
TALKING TO THE SUN: AN ILLUSTRATED ANTHOLOGY OF
POEMS FOR YOUNG PEOPLE. /1985/6-A/KE087 .... **811.008**

Art--Catalogs.
DETROIT INSTITUTE OF ARTS /Catalogue of color reproductions. /
n.d.//KA307 .... **PROF 703**
NATIONAL GALLERY OF ART (U.S.) /Catalogue of color
reproductions: books and catalogues, educational materials. /n.d./
/KA308. .... **PROF 703**

Art--Fiction.
MOON, N/Lucy's picture. /1995/P-1/2 KG153 .... **E**

Art--Periodicals.
MUSE. /1997-/4-6/KA527. .... **PER 050**

Art--Software.
KID PIX STUDIO (CD-ROM). /1994/P-A/KD468 ... **CDR 750.28**
NEW KID PIX. SCHOOL VERSION (MICROCOMPUTER
PROGRAM). /1996/P-A/KD469 .... **MCP 750.28**

Art--Study and teaching.
LOOKING AT ART (VIDEOCASSETTE). /1992/
4-A/KD365 .... **VCR 701**

Art--Study and teaching--Periodicals.
ARTS AND ACTIVITIES: CREATIVE ACTIVITIES FOR THE
CLASSROOM. /1932-//KA096 .... **PER PROF 050**
SCHOOL ARTS MAGAZINE. /1901-//KA136 ... **PER PROF 050**

Art--Study and teaching--Software.
WITH OPEN EYES: IMAGES FROM THE ART INSTITUTE OF
CHICAGO (CD-ROM). /1995/2-A/KD368 .... **CDR 701**

Art--Technique.
DAVIDSON, R/Take a look: an introduction to the experience of
art. /1994/5-6/7 KD364 .... **701**

Art, Abstract--History--20th century.
BROSTERMAN, N/Inventing kindergarten. /1997/
/KA196. .... **PROF 372.21**

Art, African.
AFRICAN AMERICAN ART: PAST AND PRESENT
(VIDEOCASSETTE). /1992/4-A/KD371. .... **VCR 704**
ANGELOU, M/My painted house, my friendly chicken, and me. /
1994/1-3/2 KE739 .... **968**
KOSLOW, P/Yorubaland: the flowering of genius. /1996/
6-A/12 KE726 .... **960**

Art, American--History.
AMERICAN ART AND ARCHITECTURE (VIDEOCASSETTE). /1991/
4-A/KD381 .... **VCR 709.73**

Art, Medieval.
CORRAIN, L/Giotto and medieval art: the lives and works of the
medieval artists. /1995/4-A/9 KD494 .... **759.5**

Art, Mexican.
MEXICAN FOLK ART (VIDEOCASSETTE). /1992/
5-A/KD421 .... **VCR 745**

Art, Modern--19th century.
SALVI, F/Impressionists: the origins of modern painting. /1994/
6-A/9 KD485 . . . . **759.05**
Art, Modern--20th century.
SALVI, F/Impressionists: the origins of modern painting. /1994/
6-A/9 KD485 . . . . **759.05**
Art, Ndebele.
ANGELOU, M/My painted house, my friendly chicken, and me. /
1994/1-3/2 KE739 . . . . **968**
Art, Primitive SEE ALSO Cave drawings; Indians of North America--Art.
Art, Renaissance.
DI CAGNO, G/Michelangelo. /1996/6-A/12 KD378 . . . . . **709.2**
Art and science.
CHRISTIANSEN, C/Sky tree portfolio: science and art (Picture). /
1995/2-6/KC410 . . . . **PIC 582.16**
WOODS, ML/Sky tree portfolio guide: an interdisciplinary
environmental curriculum. /1995/2-6/KC424 . . . . **582.16**
Art appreciation.
AMERICAN ART AND ARCHITECTURE (VIDEOCASSETTE). /1991/
4-A/KD381 . . . . **VCR 709.73**
ARMSTRONG, C/Lives and legends of the saints: with paintings
from the great museums of the /1995/5-A/10 KA716 . . . . . **270**
BLIZZARD, GS/Come look with me: world of play. /1993/
3-6/5 KD369 . . . . **701.1**
CHILDREN OF PROMISE: AFRICAN-AMERICAN LITERATURE AND
ART FOR YOUNG PEOPLE. /1991/3-A/7 KD896 . . . . . . **810.8**
CHRISTIANSEN, C/Sky tree portfolio: science and art (Picture). /
1995/2-6/KC410 . . . . **PIC 582.16**
CORRAIN, L/Giotto and medieval art: the lives and works of the
medieval artists. /1995/4-A/9 KD494 . . . . **759.5**
CRISPINO, E/Van Gogh. /1996/6-A/12 KD499. . . . . **759.9492**
CUSH, C/Artists who created great works. /1995/
4-A/8 KD377 . . . . **709.2**
DAVIDSON, R/Take a look: an introduction to the experience of
art. /1994/5-6/7 KD364 . . . . **701**
DI CAGNO, G/Michelangelo. /1996/6-A/12 KD378 . . . . . **709.2**
GREENFELD, H/Marc Chagall. /1990/
6-A/8 KE284 . . . . **B CHAGALL, M.**
HARRISON, P/Claude Monet. /1996/4-6/7 KE466 . **B MONET, C.**
Vincent van Gogh. /1996/4-6/7 KE369 . . . . . . **B GOGH, V.**
HUGHES, A/Van Gogh. /1994/6-A/9 KE370 . . . . . **B GOGH, V.**
IMAGINARY GARDENS: AMERICAN POETRY AND ART FOR
YOUNG PEOPLE. /1989/4-A/KE067 . . . . **811.008**
JACOB LAWRENCE: THE GLORY OF EXPRESSION
(VIDEOCASSETTE). /1995/5-A/KD487 . . . . **VCR 759.13**
LOOKING AT ART (VIDEOCASSETTE). /1992/
4-A/KD365 . . . . **VCR 701**
LORIA, S/Pablo Picasso. /1995/4-A/12 KD490 . . . . . . **759.4**
LYONS, ME/Starting home: the story of Horace Pippin, painter. /
1993/4-A/5 KE499 . . . . **B PIPPIN, H.**
MACCLINTOCK, D/Animals observed: a look at animals in art. /
1993/4-A/7 KD372 . . . . **704.9**
MCHUGH, C/Animals. /1993/4-A/7 KD373 . . . . **704.9**
Faces. /1993/4-A/7 KD374 . . . . **704.9**
Water. /1993/4-A/7 KD375 . . . . **704.9**
MCLANATHAN, R/Leonardo da Vinci. /1990/
6-A/6 KD495 . . . . **759.5**
MERYMAN, R/Andrew Wyeth. /1991/
6-A/7 KE602 . . . . **B WYETH, A.**
MEYER, SE/Mary Cassatt. /1990/4-A/8 KE283 . **B CASSATT, M.**
MICKLETHWAIT, L/Child's book of art: great pictures, first words. /
1993/P-1/KD366 . . . . **701**
I spy: an alphabet in art. /1992/P-2/2 KD484 . . . . **759**
I spy a freight train: transportation in art. /1996/
P-2/2 KD473 . . . . **758**
I spy a lion: animals in art. /1994/P-2/2 KD474. . . . . . . **758**
I spy two eyes: numbers in art. /1993/P-A/KB970 . . . . . **513.2**
Spot a cat. /1995/K-2/2 KD466 . . . . **750**
Spot a dog. /1995/K-2/1 KD467 . . . . **750**
MUHLBERGER, R/What makes a Bruegel a Bruegel? /1993/
5-A/8 KD502 . . . . **759.9493**
What makes a Cassatt a Cassatt? /1994/5-A/7 KD489. . **759.13**
What makes a Degas a Degas? /1993/5-A/7 KD491 . . **759.4**
What makes a Goya a Goya? /1994/5-A/7 KD498 . . . . **759.6**
What makes a Leonardo a Leonardo? /1994/
5-A/7 KD496 . . . . **759.5**
What makes a Monet a Monet? /1993/5-A/7 KD492 . . **759.4**
What makes a Picasso a Picasso? /1994/5-A/7 KD493 . . **759.4**
What makes a Raphael a Raphael? /1993/5-A/7 KD497 . **759.5**
What makes a Rembrandt a Rembrandt? /1993/
5-A/7 KD500 . . . . **759.9492**
PESCIO, C/Rembrandt and seventeenth-century Holland. /1995/
4-A/12 KD501 . . . . **759.9492**

POLISAR, BL/Barry's scrapbook: a window into art (Videocassette).
/1994/1-4/KD367 . . . . **VCR 701**
RICHMOND, R/Story in a picture: animals in art. /1993/
4-A/7 KD475 . . . . **758**
Story in a picture: children in art. /1992/3-6/7 KD471 . . . . **757**
RINGGOLD, F/Talking to Faith Ringgold. /1996/
4-6/6 KD379 . . . . **709.2**
ROALF, P/Cats. /1992/5-A/8 KD476 . . . . **758**
Circus. /1993/5-A/8 KD477. . . . . **758**
Dancers. /1992/5-A/7 KD478 . . . . **758**
Families. /1992/5-A/7 KD472 . . . . **757**
Flowers. /1993/5-A/8 KD479 . . . . **758**
Horses. /1992/5-A/8 KD480 . . . . **758**
Landscapes. /1992/5-A/8 KD481 . . . . **758**
Seascapes. /1992/5-A/7 KD482. . . . . **758**
ROMEI, F/Story of sculpture. /1995/4-A/9 KD399 . . . . . **730**
SALVI, F/Impressionists: the origins of modern painting. /1994/
6-A/9 KD485 . . . . **759.05**
STANLEY, D/Leonardo da Vinci. /1996/
5-A/8 KE435 . . . . **B LEONARDO**
TUCKER, JS/Come look with me: discovering photographs with
children. /1994/K-6/5 KD511 . . . . **770**
TURNER, R/Faith Ringgold. /1993/
4-A/7 KE511 . . . . **B RINGGOLD, F.**
VENEZIA, M/Francisco Goya. /1991/4-5/6 KE376. . **B GOYA, F.**
Henri de Toulouse-Lautrec. /1995/
4-6/8 KE568 . . . . **B TOULOUSE-LAUT**
Salvador Dali. /1993/4-6/7 KE313 . . . . **B DALI, S.**
WOODS, ML/Sky tree portfolio guide: an interdisciplinary
environmental curriculum. /1995/2-6/KC424 . . . . **582.16**
Art appreciation--Software.
WITH OPEN EYES: IMAGES FROM THE ART INSTITUTE OF
CHICAGO (CD-ROM). /1995/2-A/KD368 . . . . **CDR 701**
Art in mathematics education.
KOHL, MA/MathArts: exploring math through art for 3 to 6 year
olds. /1996//KA253 . . . . **PROF 372.7**
Arthur, King.
GIBLIN, JC/Dwarf, the giant, and the unicorn: a tale of King Arthur.
/1996/3-5/4 KB443 . . . . **398.22**
HODGES, M/Of swords and sorcerers: the adventures of King
Arthur and his knights. /1993/4-5/6 KB452 . . . . **398.22**
HOWE, J/Knight with the lion: the story of Yvain. /1996/
5-6/6 KB455 . . . . **398.22**
KING ARTHUR AND HIS KNIGHTS (SOUND RECORDING
CASSETTE). /1991/5-6/KB462 . . . . **SRC 398.22**
LISTER, R/Story of King Arthur. /1997/4/7 KB465 . . . . . **398.22**
PERHAM, M/King Arthur: the legends of Camelot. /1993/
5-A/7 KB471 . . . . **398.22**
PYLE, H/Story of King Arthur and his knights. /c1933, 1984/
A/9 KB472 . . . . **398.22**
SABUDA, R/Arthur and the sword. /1995/3-5/5 KB479 . . **398.22**
SAN SOUCI, RD/Young Guinevere. /1993/3-4/6 KB482 . . **398.22**
TALBOTT, H/King Arthur and the Round Table. /1995/
4-5/6 KB490 . . . . **398.22**
Arthur, King--Fiction.
BULLA, CR/Sword in the tree. /c1956/3-5/2 KG939 . . . . **Fic**
HASTINGS, S/Sir Gawain and the green knight. /1981/
6/6 KB450. . . . . **398.22**
Artificial limbs SEE Prosthesis.
Artificial organs.
FACKLAM, M/Spare parts for people. /1987/A/9 KD035 . . . **617**
Artificial satellites SEE ALSO Space stations.
Artificial satellites.
WHAT WE LEARN ABOUT EARTH FROM SPACE
(VIDEOCASSETTE). /1995/5-8/KD133 . . . . **VCR 629.43**
Artisans--History.
KALMAN, B/Colonial crafts. /1992/4-5/6 KD338 . . . . . . **680**
STEVENS, BS/Colonial American craftspeople. /1993/
5-6/8 KD339 . . . . **680**
Artists SEE ALSO Actors and actresses; Afro-American artists; Architects;
Authors; Ballet dancers; Dancers; Musicians; Painters; Women artists.
Artists.
BERMAN, A/James McNeil Whistler. /1993/
5-A/7 KE592 . . . . **B WHISTLER, J.**
BIOGRAPHY TODAY ARTISTS SERIES: PROFILES OF INTEREST
TO YOUNG READERS. /1996/-4-6/KA453 . . . . **REF 709.2**
CORRAIN, L/Giotto and medieval art: the lives and works of the
medieval artists. /1995/4-A/9 KD494 . . . . **759.5**
CRISPINO, E/Van Gogh. /1996/6-A/12 KD499. . . . . . **759.9492**
CUSH, C/Artists who created great works. /1995/
4-A/8 KD377 . . . . **709.2**
DI CAGNO, G/Michelangelo. /1996/6-A/12 KD378 . . . . . **709.2**
DUGGLEBY, J/Artist in overalls: the life of Grant Wood. /1995/
5-A/6 KE599 . . . . **B WOOD, G.**

FLORIAN, D/Painter. /1993/1-2/4 KD464 . . . . **750**
HARRISON, P/Claude Monet. /1996/4-6/7 KE466. **B MONET, C.**
  Vincent van Gogh. /1996/4-6/7 KE369 . . . . **B GOGH, V.**
HERMANN, S/R.C. Gorman: Navajo artist. /1995/
  3-5/3 KE375 . . . . **B GORMAN, R.C.**
HUGHES, A/Van Gogh. /1994/6-A/9 KE370 . . . . . **B GOGH, V.**
JACOB LAWRENCE: THE GLORY OF EXPRESSION
  (VIDEOCASSETTE). /1995/5-A/KD487 . . . . **VCR 759.13**
LING, B/Maya Lin. /1997/4-6/10 KE437 . . . . **B LIN, M.**
LORIA, S/Pablo Picasso. /1995/4-A/12 KD490 . . . . **759.4**
LOWERY, L/Georgia O'Keeffe. /1996/
  2-3/2 KE482 . . . . **B O'KEEFFE, G.**
LYONS, ME/Starting home: the story of Horace Pippin, painter. /
  1993/5-A/5 KE499 . . . . **B PIPPIN, H.**
MAXFIELD PARRISH: A TREASURY OF ART AND CHILDREN'S
  LITERATURE. /1995/K-6/KD413. . . . . **741.6**
MCLANATHAN, R/Leonardo da Vinci. /1990/
  6-A/6 KD495 . . . . **759.5**
MERYMAN, R/Andrew Wyeth. /1991/
  6-A/6 KE602 . . . . **B WYETH, A.**
MEYER, SE/Edgar Degas. /1994/6-A/9 KE318 . . . . **B DEGAS, E.**
  Mary Cassatt. /1990/6-A/8 KE283 . . . . **B CASSATT, M.**
MUHLBERGER, R/What makes a Bruegel a Bruegel? /1993/
  5-A/8 KD502 . . . . **759.9493**
  What makes a Degas a Degas? /1993/5-A/7 KD491 . . . . **759.4**
  What makes a Goya a Goya? /1994/5-A/7 KD498 . . . . . **759.6**
  What makes a Leonardo a Leonardo? /1994/
  5-A/7 KD496 . . . . **759.5**
  What makes a Monet a Monet? /1993/5-A/7 KD492 . . . . **759.4**
  What makes a Picasso a Picasso? /1994/5-A/7 KD493 . . . **759.4**
  What makes a Raphael a Raphael? /1993/5-A/7 KD497 . . **759.5**
  What makes a Rembrandt a Rembrandt? /1993/
  5-A/7 KD500 . . . . **759.9492**
PESCIO, C/Rembrandt and seventeenth-century Holland. /1995/
  4-A/12 KD501 . . . . **759.9492**
PROVENSEN, A/Leonardo da Vinci. /1984/
  4-6/7 KE434 . . . . **B LEONARDO**
RILEY, GB/Wah Ming Chang: artist and master of special effects. /
  1995/5-6/6 KE285 . . . . **B CHANG, W.**
RINGGOLD, F/Talking to Faith Ringgold. /1996/
  4-6/6 KD379 . . . . **709.2**
SALVI, F/Impressionists: the origins of modern painting. /1994/
  6-A/9 KD485 . . . . **759.05**
SCHWARTZ, G/Rembrandt. /1992/
  6-A/7 KE507 . . . . **B REMBRANDT**
SHIRLEY, D/Diego Rivera. /1995/5-6/7 KE513 . . . **B RIVERA, D.**
SILLS, L/Inspirations: stories about women artists. /1989/
  5-A/7 KD486 . . . . **759.1**
  Visions: stories about women artists. /1993/4-A/6 KD380 . **709.2**
STANLEY, D/Leonardo da Vinci. /1996/
  5-A/8 KE435 . . . . **B LEONARDO**
TURNER, R/Faith Ringgold. /1993/
  4-A/7 KE511 . . . . **B RINGGOLD, F.**
VENEZIA, M/Francisco Goya. /1991/4-5/6 KE376. . **B GOYA, F.**
  Henri de Toulouse-Lautrec. /1995/
  4-6/8 KE568 . . . . **B TOULOUSE-LAUT**
  Salvador Dali. /1993/4-6/7 KE313 . . . . **B DALI, S.**
WALLNER, A/Beatrix Potter. /1995/
  3-5/4 KA369 . . . . **PROF B POTTER,B**
WILSON, J/Ingenious Mr. Peale: painter, patriot and man of
  science. /1996/6-A/8 KE493 . . . . **B PEALE, C.**
WINTER, J/Cowboy Charlie: the story of Charles M. Russell. /
  1995/2-5/5 KE528 . . . . **B RUSSELL, C.**
ZHANG, SN/Little tiger in the Chinese night: an autobiography in
  art. /4-6/6 KE609 . . . . **B ZHANG, S.**
Artists--Fiction.
BULLA, CR/Chalk box kid. /1987/2-4/2 KG936. . . . . **Fic**
COONEY, B/Hattie and the wild waves. /1990/1-3/5 KF418 . . . **E**
DE PAOLA, T/Art lesson. /1989/K-2/4 KF464. . . . . **CE E**
GEISERT, A/Etcher's studio. /1997/2-5/2 KF602 . . . . **E**
HEST, A/Nana's birthday party. /1993/1-3/4 KF720 . . . . **E**
HURD, T/Art dog. /1996/1-3/2 KF792 . . . . **E**
LEAF, M/Eyes of the dragon. /1987/K-3/5 KF952 . . . . **E**
MCCLINTOCK, B/Fantastic drawings of Danielle. /1996/
  3-5/4 KH467 . . . . **Fic**
PEET, B/Encore for Eleanor. /1981/K-2/7 KG226. . . . . **E**
SHEEHAN, P/Gwendolyn's gifts. /1991/1-3/5 KG491. . . . . **E**
WALTER, MP/Have a happy... a novel. /1989/4-6/4 KH838 . . **Fic**
WINTER, J/Josefina. /1996/1-3/6 KG743 . . . . **E**
Artists--Soviet Union.
GREENFELD, H/Marc Chagall. /1990/
  6-A/8 KE284 . . . . **B CHAGALL, M.**

Artists' materials.
SATTLER, HR/Recipes for art and craft material. Newly rev. /
  c1973, 1994/4-6/6 KD435 . . . . **745.5**
Arts and crafts SEE ALSO Handicrafts; Pottery.
Arts and crafts--Periodicals.
ARTS AND ACTIVITIES: CREATIVE ACTIVITIES FOR THE
  CLASSROOM. /1932-//KA096 . . . . **PER PROF 050**
HIGHLIGHTS FOR CHILDREN. /1946-/P-A/KA517 . . . . . **PER 050**
Ashanti (African People)--Folklore.
MOLLEL, TM/Ananse's feast: an Ashanti tale. /1997/
  K-2/3 KB622 . . . . **398.24**
Ashanti (African poeple).
ANGELOU, M/Kofi and his magic. /1996/2-5/3 KE735. . . . **966.7**
Ashe, Arthur.
DEXTER, R/Young Arthur Ashe: brave champion. /1996/
  2-3/6 KE242 . . . . **CE B ASHE, A.**
QUACKENBUSH, R/Arthur Ashe and his match with history. /1994/
  3-5/7 KE243 . . . . **B ASHE, A.**
Asia.
CHIN-LEE, C/A is for Asia. /1997/K-3/8 KE700. . . . . **950**
Asia--Fiction.
STORIES FROM ASIA TODAY: COLLECTION FOR YOUNG
  READERS, BOOKS ONE AND TWO. /1979/4-6/6 KH769 . . . **Fic**
Asia--Geography.
ASIA (VIDEOCASSETTE). /1991/4-A/KE699. . . . . . . **VCR 950**
Asia--Social life and customs.
CORWIN, JH/Asian crafts. /1992/4-A/7 KD426 . . . . **745.5**
Asia, Southeastern--Folklore.
COURLANDER, H/Tiger's whisker and other tales from Asia and the
  Pacific. /c1959, 1995/3-5/7 KB279 . . . . **398.2**
Asia, Southeastern--Social life and customs.
VIESTI, JF/Celebrate! in Southeast Asia. /1996/
  2-5/11 KB192 . . . . **394.2**
Asian Americans.
RAGAZA, A/Lives of notable Asian Americans: business, politics,
  science. /1995/6-A/7 KA856 . . . . **305.8**
SINNOTT, S/Extraordinary Asian Pacific Americans. /1993/
  5-A/8 KA859 . . . . **305.8**
Asian Americans--Biography.
ASIAN AMERICAN BIOGRAPHY. /1995/5-A/KA399 . . **REF 305.8**
RILEY, GB/Wah Ming Chang: artist and master of special effects. /
  1995/5-6/6 KE285 . . . . **B CHANG, W.**
Asian Americans--Fiction.
CHINN, K/Sam and the lucky money. /1995/1-3/4 KF383 . . . . . **E**
HAVILL, J/Jamaica and Brianna. /1993/K-2/2 KF680 . . . . **E**
LEE, HV/In the snow. /1995/1-3/2 KF955 . . . . **E**
MYERS, A/Rosie's tiger. /1994/4-A/4 KH521 . . . . **Fic**
NAMIOKA, L/Yang the third and her impossible family. /1995/
  3-6/5 KH527 . . . . **Fic**
NUNES, S/Last dragon. /1995/2-3/3 KG183 . . . . **E**
YEP, L/Later, Gator. /1995/4-6/4 KH893 . . . . **Fic**
Asian Americans--Poetry.
IZUKI, S/Believers in America: poems about Americans of Asian and
  Pacific islander descent. /1994/3-6/KD955 . . . . **811**
WONG, JS/Suitcase of seaweed and other poems. /1996/
  5-A/KE045. . . . . **811**
Asian Americans--Social life and customs.
BROWN, T/Konnichiwa!: I am a Japanese-American girl. /1995/
  3-5/4 KA839 . . . . **305.8**
KUKLIN, S/How my family lives in America. /1992/
  1-3/5 KA850 . . . . **305.8**
Asiatic elephant.
PLIGHT OF THE ASIAN ELEPHANT (VIDEOCASSETTE). /1993/
  5-6/KC814. . . . . **VCR 599.67**
Asparagus--Fiction.
SEABROOK, E/Cabbage and kings. /1997/1-3/2 KG425 . . . . . **E**
Assateague Island (Md. and Va.)--Fiction.
HENRY, M/Misty of Chincoteague. /c1947/3-5/4 KH244. . **CE Fic**
Assembly, Right of.
KING, DC/Freedom of assembly. /1997/4-6/7 KA972 . . . **342.73**
Assertiveness (Psychology).
CHOOSE TO REFUSE: SAYING NO AND KEEPING YOUR
  FRIENDS (VIDEOCASSETTE). /1993/3-5/KA654 . . . . **VCR 158**
DRUGS, YOUR FRIENDS, AND YOU: HANDLING PEER PRESSURE
  (VIDEOCASSETTE). /1988/6-A/KC995 . . . . **VCR 613.8**
KAUFMAN, G/Stick up for yourself!: every kid's guide to personal
  power and positive self-esteem. /1990/6-A/6 KA659 . . . . . . **158**
NO MORE TEASING! (VIDEOCASSETTE). /1995/
  3-4/KA661 . . . . **VCR 158**
SAY NO AND MEAN IT (VIDEOCASSETTE). /1991/
  3-5/KA663 . . . . **VCR 158**

Asses and mules SEE ALSO Donkeys.

Assiniboine Indians--Folklore.
EVANS, R/Inktomi and the ducks and other Assiniboin trickster stories /1994/3-5/KB441 . . . . **TB 398.22**

Asteroids.
POYNTER, M/Killer asteroids. /1996/6-8/6 KC036 . . . . . **523.44**
SIMON, S/Comets, meteors, and asteroids. /1994/4-6/7 KC043 . . . . **523.6**
VOGT, G/Search for the killer asteroid. /1994/A/8 KC037 . . . . **523.44**

Asthma.
OSTROW, W/All about asthma. /1989/5-6/7 KD015 . . . . . **616.2**

Asthma--Fiction.
HOFFMAN, M/Four-legged ghosts. /1995/2-4/6 KH269 . . . . . **Fic**
LONDON, J/Lion who had asthma. /1992/P-2/2 KG025 . . . . . . **E**

Astrology SEE ALSO Occult sciences.

Astrology, Chinese.
YOUNG, E/Cat and Rat: the legend of the Chinese zodiac. /1995/K-6/4 KA608 . . . . **133.5**

Astronautics.
ALSTON, E/Space camp. /1990/4-5/7 KD135 . . . . **629.45**
RIDE, S/Third planet: exploring the earth from space. /1994/2-8/7 KC062 . . . . **525**
SKURZYNSKI, G/Zero gravity. /1994/3-6/5 KC100 . . . . **531**

Astronautics--Fiction.
BARTON, B/I want to be an astronaut. /1988/P-2/2 KF206 . . . . **E**

Astronautics--Vocational guidance.
MAZE, S/I want to be... an astronaut. /1997/5-6/9 KD137 . . . . **629.45**

Astronautics in earth sciences.
ENGLISH, JA/Mission: Earth: voyage to the home planet. /1996/4-A/8 KC145 . . . . **550**

Astronauts.
BURNS, K/Black stars in orbit: NASA'S African American astronauts. /1995/3-6/8 KD136 . . . . **629.45**
DREAM IS ALIVE: A WINDOW SEAT ON THE SPACE SHUTTLE (VIDEOCASSETTE). /1985/5-6/KD134 . . . . **VCR 629.44**
MAZE, S/I want to be... an astronaut. /1997/5-6/9 KD137 . . . . **629.45**

Astronauts--Fiction.
BARTON, B/I want to be an astronaut. /1988/P-2/2 KF206 . . . . **E**
STANDIFORD, N/Astronauts are sleeping. /1996/K-2/3 KG535 . **E**

Astronomers.
CAMP, CA/American astronomers: searchers and wonderers. /1996/A/10 KC000 . . . . **520**
MCPHERSON, SS/Rooftop astronomer: a story about Maria Mitchell. /1990/4-5/6 KE465 . . . . **B MITCHELL, M.**
PINKNEY, AD/Dear Benjamin Banneker. /1994/4-6/6 KE249 . . . . **B BANNEKER, B.**

Astronomy SEE ALSO Almanacs; Astrology; Calendars; Comets; Earth; Eclipses, Solar; Life on other planets; Meteors; Milky Way; Moon; Planets; Seasons; Solar system; Sun; Tides.

Astronomy.
BERGER, M/Where are the stars during the day?: a book about stars. /1993/1-4/2 KC048 . . . . **523.8**
COLE, J/Magic School Bus lost in the solar system. /1990/2-6/4 KC008 . . . . **523.2**
COOPER, K/Too many rabbits and other fingerplays about animals, nature, weather, and the /1995/P-1/KD707 . . . . **793.4**
COUPER, H/Space atlas. /1992/3-6/6 KC002 . . . . **520**
GIBBONS, G/Stargazers. /1992/K-2/4 KC049 . . . . **523.8**
MAP OF THE UNIVERSE: THE NORTHERN HEMISPHERE (PICTURE). /1980/3-A/KC051 . . . . **PIC 523.8**
MOON/OUTER SPACE (VIDEOCASSETTE). /1994/3-6/KC007 . . . . **VCR 523**
RIDE, S/Third planet: exploring the earth from space. /1994/2-8/7 KC062 . . . . **525**
STARS AND CONSTELLATIONS (VIDEOCASSETTE). /1993/3-6/KC055 . . . . **VCR 523.8**
VISUAL DICTIONARY OF THE UNIVERSE. /1993/3-A/11 KC004 . . . . **520**
WHAT'S OUT THERE?: OUR SOLAR SYSTEM AND BEYOND (VIDEOCASSETTE). /1997/5-A/KC018 . . . . **VCR 523.2**
WYLER, R/Starry sky. /1989/P-2/2 KC056 . . . . **523.8**

Astronomy--Miscellanea.
CAMPBELL, A/New York Public Library amazing space: a book of answers for kids. /1997/3-A/8 KC001 . . . . **520**

Astronomy--Periodicals.
ODYSSEY. /1992-/3-5/KA534 . . . . **PER 050**

Astronomy--Software.
EYEWITNESS ENCYCLOPEDIA OF SPACE AND THE UNIVERSE (CD-ROM). /1996/5-A/KC003 . . . . **CDR 520**
MOHL, R/Planetary taxi (CD-ROM). /1993/4-A/KC013 . . . . **CDR 523.2**

WHERE IN SPACE IS CARMEN SANDIEGO? (MICROCOMPUTER PROGRAM). /1993/4-A/KC005 . . . . **MCP 520**

Astronomy--Study and teaching--Activity programs.
BOURNE, B/Exploring space: using Seymour Simon's astronomy books in the classroom. /1994//KA198 . . . . **PROF 372.3**

Atalanta (Greek mythology).
CLIMO, S/Atalanta's race: a Greek myth. /1995/3-6/4 KA735 . . . . **292**

Athabascan Indians--Fiction.
HILL, K/Winter camp. /1993/5-A/6 KH262 . . . . **Fic**

Athens (Greece)--Antiquities.
MACDONALD, F/Greek temple. /1992/4-6/7 KE643 . . . . . **938**

Athletes SEE ALSO Afro-American athletes; Women athletes; and specific sports e.g. Baseball players; and names of individual athletes e.g. Abbott, Jim.

Athletes.
BIOGRAPHY TODAY SPORTS SERIES: PROFILES OF PEOPLE OF INTEREST TO YOUNG READERS. /1996-/4-6/KA456 . . **REF 796**
DINN, S/Hearts of gold: a celebration of Special Olympics and its heroes. /1996/4-6/9 KD760 . . . . **796**
JENNINGS, J/Long shots: they beat the odds. /1990/5-6/6 KD762 . . . . **796**
LINDOP, L/Athletes. /1996/4-6/7 KD763 . . . . **796**
LIPSYTE, R/Jim Thorpe: 20th-century jock. /6-A/7 KE566 . . . . **B THORPE, J.**
PARE, MA/Sports stars. /1994/5-A/KA457 . . . . **REF 796**
SANFORD, WR/Babe Didrikson Zaharias. /1993/4-5/4 KE608 . . . . **B ZAHARIAS, B.**
SAVAGE, J/Kristi Yamaguchi: pure gold. /1993/3-5/7 KE603 . . . . **B YAMAGUCHI, K.**

Athletes--Wounds and injuries.
O'CONNOR, J/Comeback!: four true stories. /1992/2-4/3 KD765 . . . . **796**

Athletics SEE ALSO Physical education and training; Sports; Physical fitness; names of particular sports e.g. Baseball.

Atlases.
ANIMATED ATLAS (VIDEOCASSETTE). /1990/4-6/KA582 . . . . **VCR 025.5**
AROUND THE WORLD: AN ATLAS OF MAPS AND PICTURES. /1994/3-5/KE165 . . . . **912**
BOYLE, B/My first atlas. /1994/K-3/5 KE167 . . . . **912**
INFORMATION PLEASE ALMANAC, ATLAS & YEARBOOK. /1947-/4-6/KA405 . . . . **REF 317.3**
LEWINGTON, A/Atlas of rain forests. /1997/3-6/7 KC321 . . . . **577.34**
NATIONAL GEOGRAPHIC ATLAS OF THE WORLD. 6TH ED., REV. ED. /1995/4-6/KA473 . . . . **REF 912**
NATIONAL GEOGRAPHIC PICTURE ATLAS OF OUR FIFTY STATES. /1994/4-A/KA475 . . . . **REF 912.73**
NEW AMERICAN DESK ENCYCLOPEDIA. 3RD REV. /1993/4-A/KA589 . . . . **031**
NYSTROM DESK ATLAS. /1994/5-A/KA474 . . . . **REF 912**
PICKERING, M/Picture reference atlas. /1996/2-4/3 KE171 . . **912**
VAN ROSE, S/Earth atlas. /1994/A/7 KA443 . . . . **REF 551**
WRIGHT, D/Facts on File children's atlas. /1997/4-6/KE176 . . **912**

Atlases--Software.
MICROSOFT BOOKSHELF: MULTIMEDIA REFERENCE LIBRARY, 1998 ED. SCHOOL ED. (CD-ROM). /1997/3-A/KA376 . . . . **CDR REF 028.7**
MICROSOFT ENCARTA 97 WORLD ATLAS (CD-ROM). /1996/3-A/KA472 . . . . **CDR REF 912**

Atmosphere SEE ALSO Air; Meteorology.

Atmosphere.
ATMOSPHERE: ON THE AIR (VIDEOCASSETTE). /1993/5-6/KC186 . . . . **VCR 551.5**
HOFF, MK/Our endangered planet: atmosphere. /1995/4-6/8 KB061 . . . . **363.73**

Atomic bomb.
KODAMA, T/Shin's tricycle. /1995/4-6/4 KE670 . . . . **940.54**
MARUKI, T/Hiroshima no pika. /1982/4-6/5 KE672 . . . . . **940.54**

Atomic bomb--Physiological effect.
COERR, E/Sadako. /1993/3-6/4 KA994 . . . . **CE 362.1**

Atoms.
COOPER, C/Matter. /1992/4-A/9 KC078 . . . . **530**
WELLS, RE/What's smaller than a pygmy shrew? /1995/3-6/5 KC140 . . . . **539.7**

Attention deficit disorders.
KENNEDY, P/Hyperactive child book. /1994//KA303 . . **PROF 649**
QUINN, PO/Putting on the brakes: young people's guide to understanding attention deficit hyperactivity disorder (ADHD). /1991/5-6/7 KD041 . . . . **618.92**

Attention-deficit-disordered children--Education--United States.
STEVENS, SH/Classroom success for the LD and ADHD child. /1997//KA186 . . . . **PROF 371.92**

Audio-visual education SEE ALSO Television in education.
Audio-visual education--Periodicals.
　　TECHTRENDS: FOR LEADERS IN EDUCATION AND TRAINING. /
　　1956-//KA153 . . . . **PER PROF 050**
Audio-visual library service--Handbooks, manuals, etc.
　　FECKO, MB/Cataloging nonbook resources: a how-to-do-it manual
　　for librarians. /1993//KA057 . . . . **PROF 025.3**
　　OLSON, NB/Cataloging of audiovisual materials and other special
　　materials: a manual based /1998//KA060 . . . . . . **PROF 025.4**
Audio-visual library service--Periodicals.
　　SCHOOL LIBRARY MEDIA ANNUAL. /1983-/
　　/KA141 . . . . **PER PROF 050**
Audio-visual materials SEE ALSO Instructional materials center.
Audio-visual materials--Catalogs.
　　ELEMENTARY SCHOOL LIBRARY COLLECTION: A GUIDE TO
　　BOOKS AND OTHER MEDIA, /1998//KA013 . . . **PROF 011.62**
　　THOMAS, JL/Play, learn, and grow: an annotated guide to the best
　　books and materials for /1992//KA088 . . . . . **PROF 028.1**
　　VIDEO SOURCE BOOK. /1979//KA030 . . . . **PROF 016.791**
Audio-visual materials--Catalogs--Software.
　　ELEMENTARY SCHOOL LIBRARY COLLECTION: A GUIDE TO
　　BOOKS AND OTHER MEDIA, /1998/
　　/KA014 . . . . **CDR PROF 011.62**
Audio-visual materials--Reviews.
　　PARENTS' CHOICE: A REVIEW OF CHILDREN'S MEDIA. /1978-/
　　/KA130 . . . . **PER PROF 050**
　　SCIENCE BOOKS AND FILMS. /1975//KA145 . . **PER PROF 050**
Audio-visual materials--Reviews--Indexes.
　　MEDIA REVIEW DIGEST. /1970//KA124 . . . . . **PER PROF 050**
Audio-visual materials--Reviews--Periodicals.
　　REVIEWS. /1993//KA135 . . . . **PROF 050**
Aung San Suu Kyi.
　　STEWART, W/Aung San Suu Kyi: fearless voice of Burma. /1997/
　　5-A/7 KE244 . . . . **B AUNG SAN SUU**
Aunts--Fiction.
　　CAPOTE, T/Christmas memory. /c1956, 1989/
　　4-A/6 KG971 . . . . **CE Fic**
　　CARRIS, JD/Beware the ravens, Aunt Morbelia. /1995/
　　5-A/5 KG979 . . . . **Fic**
　　COONEY, B/Miss Rumphius. /1982/K-3/5 KF419 . . . . **E**
　　Miss Rumphius (Kit). /1994/K-3/KF420 . . . . **KIT E**
　　DOYLE, B/Uncle Ronald. /1997/5-A/5 KH083 . . . . **Fic**
　　GREENFIELD, E/Me and Neesie. /c1975/K-2/3 KF642 . . . . **E**
　　HESSE, K/Lavender. /1995/2-3/2 KH251 . . . . **Fic**
　　HUNT, I/Up a road slowly. /1993/A/7 KH292 . . . . **Fic**
　　KONIGSBURG, EL/T-backs, T-shirts, COAT, and suit. /1993/
　　6-A/7 KH375 . . . . **Fic**
　　MATHIS, SB/Hundred penny box. /1975/4-6/4 KH461 . . . **CE Fic**
　　PINKWATER, DM/Aunt Lulu. /1991/P-2/2 KG244 . . . . **E**
　　RYLANT, C/Missing May. /1992/5-A/7 KH663 . . . . **Fic**
　　SACHS, M/Truth about Mary Rose /1995/3-A/6 KH669 . . . . . **Fic**
　　WIGGIN, KD/Rebecca of Sunnybrook Farm. /1994/
　　5-A/6 KH857 . . . . **Fic**
Auroras.
　　SHEPHERD, DW/Auroras: light shows in the night sky. /1995/
　　4-8/6 KC137 . . . . **538**
　　SOUZA, DM/Northern lights. /1994/6-A/7 KC138 . . . . **538**
Australia--Description and travel.
　　COBB, V/This place is lonely. /1991/3-6/7 KF116 . . . . **994**
Australia--Fiction.
　　FIENBERG, A/Wiggy and Boa. /c1988, 1990/5-6/7 KH113 . . . **Fic**
　　FOX, M/Possum magic. /c1983, 1990/P-2/4 KF571 . . . . **E**
　　GLEITZMAN, M/Blabber mouth. /1995/3-5/4 KH173 . . . . . . **Fic**
　　Misery guts. /1993/5-A/7 KH174 . . . . **Fic**
　　Sticky Beak. /1995/3-5/4 KH176 . . . . **Fic**
　　HECTOR'S BUNYIP (VIDEOCASSETTE). /c1986, 1997/
　　4-6/KH231 . . . . **VCR Fic**
　　HILL, A/Burnt stick. /1995/4-A/7 KH259 . . . . **Fic**
　　PARK, R/Playing Beatie Bow. /1982/5-A/6 KH571 . . . . **Fic**
　　TRINCA, R/One woolly wombat. /1985/P-2/4 KG617 . . . . **E**
　　VAUGHAN, MK/Snap! /1996/K-2/2 KG651 . . . . **E**
　　Wombat stew. /c1984/P-2/4 KG652 . . . . **E**
Australia--Folklore.
　　OODGEROO /Dreamtime: aboriginal stories. /1994/
　　4-5/6 KB506 . . . . **398.23**
　　ROTH, SL/Biggest frog in Australia. /1996/2-3/2 KB643 . . **398.24**
Australia--Geography.
　　AUSTRALIA (VIDEOCASSETTE). /1991/4-A/KF114 . . . **VCR 994**
Australia--Social life and customs.
　　WHEATLEY, N/My place. /1992/5-6/3 KF118 . . . . **994**
Australian aborigines.
　　REYNOLDS, J/Down under: vanishing cultures. /1992/
　　3-6/6 KF117 . . . . **994**

Australian aborigines--Fiction.
　　HILL, A/Burnt stick. /1995/4-A/7 KH259 . . . . **Fic**
Australian aborigines--Folklore.
　　OODGEROO /Dreamtime: aboriginal stories. /1994/
　　4-5/6 KB506 . . . . **398.23**
　　ROUGHSEY, D/Giant devil dingo (Videocassette). /n.d./
　　1-3/KA791 . . . . **VCR 299**
Austria--Fiction.
　　ACKERMAN, K/Night crossing. /1994/3-4/8 KG812 . . . . **Fic**
Austria--Folklore.
　　DUGIN, A/Dragon feathers. /1993/4-5/7 KB289 . . . . **398.2**
　　SAWYER, R/Remarkable Christmas of the cobbler's sons. /1994/
　　1-3/4 KB416 . . . . **398.21**
Authors SEE ALSO Afro-American authors; Children as authors; names of
　specific authors e.g. Cleary, Beverly.
Authors.
　　BIOGRAPHY TODAY AUTHOR SERIES: PROFILES OF PEOPLE OF
　　INTEREST TO YOUNG READERS. /1996/-4-6/KA461 . . **REF 809**
　　CBC FEATURES. /1945-//KA101 . . . . **PER PROF 050**
　　CHRISTELOW, E/What do authors do? /1995/
　　2-4/2 KD866 . . . . **808.06**
　　MAJOR AUTHORS AND ILLUSTRATORS FOR CHILDREN AND
　　YOUNG ADULTS: A SELECTION OF /1993//KA464 . . . **REF 809**
　　RAINEY, R/Monster factory. /1993/3-6/8 KD895 . . . . **809.3**
　　SOMETHING ABOUT THE AUTHOR. /1971-/
　　5-6/KA465 . . . . **REF 809**
　　SOMETHING ABOUT THE AUTHOR AUTOBIOGRAPHY SERIES. /
　　1986-/4-6/KA466 . . . . **REF 809**
Authors--Biography--Indexes.
　　CHILDREN'S AUTHORS AND ILLUSTRATORS: AN INDEX TO
　　BIOGRAPHICAL DICTIONARIES. /1976//KA033 . **PROF 016.809**
Authors--Dictionaries.
　　AUTHORS OF BOOKS FOR YOUNG PEOPLE. 3RD ED. /1990/
　　5-A/KA460 . . . . **REF 809**
　　JUNIOR AUTHOR SERIES. /1951-/A/KA462. . . . . . . **REF 809**
Authors--Fiction.
　　FITZHUGH, L/Harriet the spy. /c1964/3-5/4 KH114 . . . . **Fic**
　　HEST, A/Nana's birthday party. /1993/1-3/4 KF720 . . . . . **E**
　　KLINE, S/Mary Marony hides out. /1993/1-3/4 KH369 . . . . . . **Fic**
Authors--Software.
　　JUNIOR DISCOVERING AUTHORS: BIOGRAPHIES AND
　　PLOTLINES ON 300 MOST-STUDIED AND POPULAR AUTHORS
　　FOR YOUNG READERS (CD-ROM). /1994/
　　5-A/KA463 . . . . **CDR REF 809**
Authors, American.
　　BUNTING, E/Once upon a time. /1995/
　　2-5/3 KE268 . . . . **B BUNTING, E.**
　　CARPENTER, AS/L. Frank Baum: royal historian of Oz. /1992/
　　4-6/4 KE251 . . . . **B BAUM, L.**
　　CLEARY, B/Girl from Yamhill. /1988/5-6/7 KE292 . **B CLEARY, B.**
　　COX, C/Mark Twain: America's humorist, dreamer, prophet. /1995/
　　6-A/8 KE579 . . . . **B TWAIN, M.**
　　CREWS, D/Bigmama's. /1991/K-2/2 KE309 . . . **CE B CREWS, D.**
　　DEWEY, JO/Cowgirl dreams: a western childhood. /1995/
　　3-4/4 KE320 . . . . **B DEWEY, J.**
　　EHLERT, L/Under my nose. /1996/3-6/2 KE333 . . . . **B EHLERT, L.**
　　FLEISCHMAN, S/Abracadabra kid: a writer's life. /1996/
　　3-A/7 KE344 . . . . **B FLEISCHMAN, S**
　　FRITZ, J/Harriet Beecher Stowe and the Beecher preachers. /1994/
　　6-A/7 KE556 . . . . **B STOWE, H.**
　　GET TO KNOW BERNARD MOST (VIDEOCASSETTE). /1993/
　　2-3/KE471 . . . . **VCR B MOST, B.**
　　GET TO KNOW KEITH BAKER (VIDEOCASSETTE). /1994/
　　2-5/KE248 . . . . **VCR B BAKER, K.**
　　GHERMAN, B/E.B. White: some writer! /1992/
　　6-A/8 KE593 . . . . **B WHITE, E.B.**
　　KEHRET, P/Small steps: the year I got polio. /1996/
　　2-5/5 KE414 . . . . **B KEHRET, P.**
　　KUSKIN, K/Thoughts, pictures, and words. /1995/
　　2-5/6 KE426 . . . . **B KUSKIN, K.**
　　LASKY, K/Searching for Laura Ingalls: a reader's journey. /1993/
　　3-6/6 KE198 . . . . **917.8**
　　LESTER, H/Author: a true story. /1997/
　　2-5/2 KE436 . . . . **B LESTER, H.**
　　LYON, GE/Wordful child. /1996/4-5/4 KE450 . . . **B LYON, G. E.**
　　LYONS, ME/Sorrow's kitchen: the life and folklore of Zora Neale
　　Hurston. /1990/6-A/6 KE396 . . . . **B HURSTON, Z.**
　　MEET ASHLEY BRYAN: STORYTELLER, ARTIST, WRITER
　　(VIDEOCASSETTE). /1992/4-6/KE266 . . . . . **VCR B BRYAN, A.**
　　MEET THE NEWBERY AUTHOR: RUSSELL FREEDMAN
　　(VIDEOCASSETTE). /1991/5-A/KE356 . . **VCR B FREEDMAN, R.**
　　MEIGS, C/Invincible Louisa. /1933/5-6/8 KE232 . **B ALCOTT, L.**
　　PATRICK-WEXLER, D/Walter Dean Myers. /1996/
　　5-6/6 KE475 . . . . **B MYERS, W.**

PEET, B/Bill Peet: an autobiography. /1989/
6-A/8 KE494 . . . . **B PEET, B.**
PETTIT, J/Maya Angelou: journey of the heart. /1996/
4-6/8 KE237 . . . . **B ANGELOU, M.**
QUACKENBUSH, R/Mark Twain? What kind of name is that?: a
story of Samuel Langhorne Clemens. /1984/
6/8 KE580 . . . . **B TWAIN, M.**
RING, E/Henry David Thoreau: in step with nature. /1993/
2-5/3 KE565 . . . . **B THOREAU, H.**
SENDAK (VIDEOCASSETTE). /1993/
4-A/KE534 . . . . **VCR B SENDAK, M.**
STEVENSON, J/Don't you know there's a war on? /1992/
K-3/2 KE552 . . . . **B STEVENSON, J.**
Higher on the door. /1987/3-4/4 KE553 . . . **B STEVENSON, J.**
When I was nine. /1986/3-4/4 KE551 . . . . . **B STEVENSON, J.**
TALK WITH AVI (VIDEOCASSETTE). /1995/
5-6/KE245 . . . . **VCR B AVI**
TALK WITH BETSY BYARS (VIDEOCASSETTE). /1995/
4-6/KE273 . . . . **VCR B BYARS, B.**
TALK WITH JEAN FRITZ (VIDEOCASSETTE). /1993/
5-6/KE358 . . . . **VCR B FRITZ, J.**
VISIT WITH BILL MARTIN, JR. (VIDEOCASSETTE). /1996/
3-4/KE460 . . . . **VCR B MARTIN, B.**
VISIT WITH EVE BUNTING (VIDEOCASSETTE). /1991/
4-6/KE269 . . . . **VCR B BUNTING, E.**
VISIT WITH MARVIN TERBAN (VIDEOCASSETTE). /c1991, 1992/
5-A/KE560 . . . . **VCR B TERBAN, M.**
WADSWORTH, G/Laura Ingalls Wilder: storyteller of the prairie. /
1997/4-A/5 KE595 . . . . **B WILDER, L.**
WEIL, A/Michael Dorris. /1997/6-A/7 KE323 . . . . **B DORRIS, M.**
YEP, L/Lost garden. /1996/5-A/7 KE604 . . . . **B YEP, L.**

Authors, American--Homes and haunts.
ANDERSON, W/Little House guidebook. /1996/
3-5/10 KE196 . . . . **917.8**

Authors, American--20th century--Interviews.
ROGINSKI, J/Behind the covers: /1985//KA335 . . **PROF 808.06**

Authors, Australian.
OODGEROO /Dreamtime: aboriginal stories. /1994/
4-5/6 KB506 . . . . **398.23**
Authors, Black SEE Afro-American authors.

Authors, Canadian.
ANDRONIK, CM/Kindred spirit: a biography of L. M. Montgomery,
creator of Anne of Green /1993/
5-A/6 KE469 . . . . **B MONTGOMERY, L**
LUCY MAUD MONTGOMERY: THREADS FROM THE QUILT
(VIDEOCASSETTE). /1993/
6-A/KE470. . . . . **VCR B MONTGOMERY, L**
MIND'S EYE: JEAN LITTLE (VIDEOCASSETTE). /1996/
5-6/KE445 . . . . **VCR B LITTLE, J.**

Authors, Danish.
BRUST, BW/Amazing paper cuttings of Hans Christian Andersen. /
1994/3-5/8 KE235 . . . . **B ANDERSEN, H.**

Authors, English.
COLLINS, DR/J.R.R. Tolkien: master of fantasy. /1992/
6-A/6 KE567 . . . . **B TOLKIEN, J.**
DAHL, L/James and the giant peach: the book and movie
scrapbook. /1996/3-6/6 KD684. . . . . **791.43**
DAHL, R/Boy: tales of childhood. /1984/
5-6/6 KE312 . . . . **B DAHL, R.**
GREENE, C/Rudyard Kipling: author of the "Jungle books." /
1994/3-6/2 KE424 . . . . **B KIPLING, R.**
ROSS, S/Shakespeare and Macbeth: the story behind the play. /
1994/5-A/7 KE116 . . . . **822.3**
STANLEY, D/Charles Dickens: the man who had great expectations.
/1993/5-6/7 KE321 . . . . **B DICKENS, C.**
TALK WITH LYNNE REID BANKS (VIDEOCASSETTE). /1995/
4-6/KE505. . . . . **VCR B REID BANKS, L**
WALLNER, A/Beatrix Potter. /1995/
3-5/4 KA369 . . . . **PROF B POTTER,B**

Authors, French.
TEETERS, P/Jules Verne: the man who invented tomorrow. /1992/
5-A/6 KE582 . . . . **B VERNE, J.**

Authors, New Zealand.
MAHY, M/My mysterious world. /1995/
2-4/6 KE454 . . . . **B MAHY, M.**

Authors, Scottish.
GREENE, C/Robert Louis Stevenson: author of A CHILD'S GARDEN
OF VERSES. /1994/2-4/4 KE554. . . . . **B STEVENSON, R.**
MEET THE AUTHOR: ROBERT LOUIS STEVENSON
(VIDEOCASSETTE). /1989/5-6/KE555 . . **VCR B STEVENSON, R.**
Authorship SEE ALSO Creative writing.

Authorship.
BUNTING, E/Once upon a time. /1995/
2-5/3 KE268 . . . . **B BUNTING, E.**

CHRISTELOW, E/What do authors do? /1995/
2-4/2 KD866 . . . . **808.06**
FLEISCHMAN, S/Abracadabra kid: a writer's life. /1996/
3-A/7 KE344 . . . . **B FLEISCHMAN, S**
GUTHRIE, D/Young author's do-it-yourself book: how to write,
illustrate, and produce your own book. /1994/2-6/4 KD863 . **808**
KUSKIN, K/Thoughts, pictures, and words. /1995/
2-5/6 KE426 . . . . **B KUSKIN, K.**
LESTER, H/Author: a true story. /1997/
2-5/2 KE436 . . . . **B LESTER, H.**
MAHY, M/My mysterious world. /1995/
2-4/6 KE454 . . . . **B MAHY, M.**
SENDAK, M/Caldecott and Co.: notes on books & pictures. /1988/
/KA356. **PROF 809**

Authorship--Fiction.
BROWN, MT/Arthur writes a story. /1996/K-2/2 KF272 . . . . . . **E**
DUFFEY, B/Utterly yours, Booker Jones. /1995/4-6/5 KH087 . . **Fic**
SCHOTTER, R/Nothing ever happens on 90th Street. /1997/
3-5/4 KH682 . . . . **Fic**

Autograph verses.
YOURS TILL BANANA SPLITS: 201 AUTOGRAPH RHYMES. /
1995/3-6/KD894 . . . . **808.88**
Automata SEE ALSO Robotics; Robots.

Automobile driving--Fiction.
PLOURDE, L/Pigs in the mud in the middle of the rud. /1997/
K-2/2 KG247 . . . . **E**

Automobile industry and trade--Biography.
MITCHELL, B/We'll race you, Henry: a story about Henry Ford. /
1986/4-5/3 KE346 . . . . **B FORD, H.**

Automobile mechanics.
FLORIAN, D/Auto mechanic. /1994/P-2/3 KD128 . . . . . . **629.28**

Automobile racing drivers.
BRINSTER, R/Jeff Gordon. /1997/5-6/7 KE373 . . **B GORDON, J.**

Automobile travel--Fiction.
HYATT, PR/Coast to coast with Alice. /1995/4-6/5 KH312 . . . **Fic**

Automobile travel--Songs and music.
ON THE ROAD AGAIN (SOUND RECORDING CASSETTE). /
1992/K-4/KD640 . . . . **SRC 789.3**
Automobiles SEE ALSO Buses; Motor vehicles; Sports cars; Trucks.

Automobiles.
FORD, B/Automobile. /1987/5-6/8 KD114 . . . . **629.222**
ROCKWELL, AF/Cars. /1992/P/1 KD115 . . . . **629.222**
ROYSTON, A/Cars. /1991/P-2/2 KD116 . . . . **629.222**

Automobiles--Fiction.
BURNINGHAM, J/Mr. Gumpy's motor car. /c1973, 1976/
P-2/2 KF317 . . . . **CE E**
FLEMING, I/Chitty Chitty Bang Bang: the magical car. /c1964,
1989/5-6/7 KH128 . . . . **Fic**
HOWLAND, N/ABCDrive!: a car trip alphabet. /1994/
P-1/1 KF782 . . . . **E**
MACCARONE, G/Cars! cars! cars! /1995/P-1/1 KG045 . . . . . **E**
MAHY, M/Rattlebang picnic. /1994/K-2/5 KG057 . . . . **E**
PEET, B/Jennifer and Josephine. /c1967/K-2/7 KG228 . . . . . **E**

Automobiles--Safety measures.
SAFETY ON WHEELS (VIDEOCASSETTE). /1994/
P-1/KB024 . . . . **VCR 363.1**

Automobiles--Service stations.
GIBBONS, G/Fill it up! All about service stations. /1985/
K-3/4 KD129 . . . . **629.28**

Automobiles, Racing.
CONNOLLY, M/Dragsters. /1992/4-A/4 KD829 . . . . **796.7**

Automobiles in art.
DUBOSQUE, D/Draw! cars. Rev. ed. /1997/4-A/5 KD417 . . . **743**

Autumn.
FOWLER, A/How do you know it's fall? /1992/
P-2/2 KB917 . . . . **508.2**
MAGICAL MOTHER NATURE: THE FOUR SEASONS
(VIDEOCASSETTE). /1989/C-A/KC061 . . . . **VCR 525**
SEASONS. REV. ED. (SOUND FILMSTRIP). /c1975, 1993/
K-2/KC063. **FSS 525**
SIMON, S/Autumn across America. /1993/4-6/7 KB918 . . . **508.2**

Autumn--Fiction.
AGELL, C/Wind spins me around in the fall. /1994/
K-2/3 KF140 . . . . **E**
KNUTSON, K/Ska-tat! /1993/P-2/3 KF914 . . . . **E**

Avalanches.
KRAMER, SP/Avalanche. /1991/3-6/6 KC213 . . . . **551.57**

Average.
STATISTICS: UNDERSTANDING MEAN, MEDIAN, AND MODE
(VIDEOCASSETTE). /1987/4-A/KB999 . . . . **VCR 519.5**

Avi.
TALK WITH AVI (VIDEOCASSETTE). /1995/
5-6/KE245. . . . . **VCR B AVI**

Aviation SEE ALSO Aeronautics; Airplanes; Ballooning; Space flight.

Aztecs.
BAQUEDANO, E/Aztec, Inca and Maya. /1993/
4-6/9 KE829 . . . . **972**
SHEPHERD, DW/Aztecs. /1992/4-6/7 KE838 . . . . **972**
WOOD, T/Aztecs. /1992/5-6/7 KE842 . . . . **972**

Aztecs--Fiction.
LATTIMORE, DN/Flame of peace, a tale of the Aztecs. /1987/
2-3/2 KF948 . . . . **E**

Aztecs--Folklore.
BIERHORST, J/Doctor Coyote: a Native American Aesop's fables. /
1987/3/3 KB530 . . . . **398.24**

Aztecs--History.
MARRIN, A/Aztecs and Spaniards: Cortes and the conquest of
Mexico. /1986/5-6/7 KE833 . . . . **972**
MATHEWS, SS/Sad Night: the story of an Aztec victory and a
Spanish loss. /1994/4-6/6 KE834. . . . . **972**

Baba Yaga (Legendary character).
ARNOLD, K/Baba Yaga: a Russian folktale. /1993/
2-3/3 KB387 . . . . **398.21**
MAYER, M/Baba Yaga and Vasilisa the Brave. /1994/
3-5/5 KB466 . . . . **398.22**

Baba Yaga (Legendary character)--Fiction.
POLACCO, P/Babushka Baba Yaga. /1993/1-3/5 KG249 . . . . . **E**
SERVICE, PF/Weirdos of the universe, unite! /1992/
6-A/6 KH701 . . . . **Fic**

Babies SEE ALSO Brothers and sisters.

Babies.
ANHOLT, C/Here come the babies. /P-K/2 KA826 . . . . . **305.232**
BERNHARD, E/Ride on mother's back: a day of baby carrying
around the world. /1996/1-2/7 KB170 . . . . **392.1**
COLE, J/How you were born. Rev. and expanded ed. /1993/
K-3/4 KC945 . . . . **612.6**
COLLINS, PL/Waiting for baby Joe. /1990/K-3/2 KD038 . **618.92**
GIRARD, LW/You were born on your very first birthday. /1982/
P/2 KC948 . . . . **612.6**
HEY, WHAT ABOUT ME? (VIDEOCASSETTE). /1987/
P-3/KA884. . . . . **VCR 306.875**
KNIGHT, MB/Welcoming babies. /1994/P-1/2 KA875 . . . **306.87**
NEW BABY IN MY HOUSE (VIDEOCASSETTE). /1993/
P-1/KA886. . . . . **VCR 306.875**
SANDEMAN, A/Babies. /1996/2-5/6 KC955 . . . . **612.6**
STEIN, S/Oh, baby! /1993/P-K/3 KA827 . . . . **305.232**

Babies--Fiction.
AHLBERG, A/Giant baby. /1994/3-5/7 KG820 . . . . **Fic**
ARMSTRONG, J/That terrible baby. /1994/K-2/3 KF166 . . . . . **E**
BROWN, C/In the spring. /1994/P-1/2 KF269 . . . . **E**
BROWN, MT/Arthur's baby. /1987/K-3/2 KF274 . . . . **E**
BUNTING, E/Our teacher's having a baby. /1992/P-1/2 KF307 . **E**
CASELEY, J/Harry and Arney. /1994/3-5/6 KG984 . . . . **Fic**
Mama, coming and going. /1994/1-3/4 KF366 . . . . **E**
COREY, D/Will there be a lap for me? /1992/P-1/2 KF425 . . . . **E**
DE PAOLA, T/Baby sister. /1996/K-2/2 KF465 . . . . **E**
FALWELL, C/We have a baby. /1993/P-K/1 KF542 . . . . **E**
HAARHOFF, D/Desert December. /1992/3-5/4 KH206 . . . . . . **Fic**
HARRIS, RH/Happy birth day! /1996/P-2/3 KF676. . . . . **E**
HAYES, S/Eat up, Gemma. /1988/P-2/2 KF685 . . . . **E**
HENKES, K/Julius, the baby of the world. /1990/K-3/2 KF707 . . **E**
HESSE, K/Lavender. /1995/2-3/2 KH251 . . . . **Fic**
HEST, A/You're the boss, Baby Duck! /1997/P-1/2 KF722 . . . . **E**
JONAS, A/When you were a baby. /1982/P-K/2 KF850. . . . . . **E**
MCMULLAN, K/If you were my bunny. /1996/P-K/3 KG112 . . . **E**
MILLER, M/Now I'm big. /1996/P/2 KG135. . . . . **E**
ORMEROD, J/101 things to do with a baby. /1984/
P-K/KG197 . . . . **E**
OSOFSKY, A/Dreamcatcher. /1992/K-2/5 KG200 . . . . **E**
ROSE, DL/Rose horse. /1995/3-5/6 KH651 . . . . **Fic**
SCHWARTZ, A/Teeny tiny baby. /1994/P-2/2 KG415 . . . . . . **E**
STEPTOE, J/Baby says. /1988/P-K/KG551 . . . . **E**
STEVENSON, J/Rolling Rose. /1992/P-K/2 KG566 . . . . **E**
TITHERINGTON, J/Place for Ben. /1987/P-2/2 KG608 . . . . . . **E**
WALTER, MP/My mama needs me. /1983/P-2/1 KG685 . . . . . **E**
WILLIAMS, VB/More more more, said the baby. /1990/
P-K/2 KG736 . . . . **E**

Babouska (Legendary character).
ROBBINS, R/Baboushka and the three kings. /c1960/
2-4/6 KB509 . . . . **398.23**

Baby animals SEE Animals--Infancy.

Babysitters--Fiction.
ANDERSON, PP/Time for bed, the babysitter said. /1987/
P-2/1 KF157 . . . . **E**
FOX, P/Likely place. /c1967, 1986/4-6/4 KH135 . . . . **Fic**
RAYNER, M/Mr. and Mrs. Pig's evening out. /c1976/
K-2/4 KG317 . . . . **E**

ROBERTSON, K/Henry Reed's baby-sitting service. /c1966/
4-6/6 KH638 . . . . **Fic**
WINTHROP, E/Bear and Mrs. Duck. /1988/P-1/1 KG744 . . . . . **E**

Babysitters--Handbooks, manuals, etc.
BARKIN, C/New complete babysitter's handbook. /1995/
5-6/6 KD302 . . . . **649**
SUPER SITTERS: A TRAINING COURSE (VIDEOCASSETTE).
1988/5-A/KD304 . . . . **VCR 649**

Bach, Johann Sebastian.
GREENE, C/Johann Sebastian Bach: great man of music. /1992/
2-4/2 KE246 . . . . **B BACH, J.**

Backpacking--Fiction.
BUDBILL, D/Bones on Black Spruce Mountain. /c1978, 1994/
4-A/5 KG935. . . . . **Fic**

Bacteria.
BERGER, M/Germs make me sick! Rev. ed. /1995/
1-3/5 KD021 . . . . **616.9**
FACKLAM, H/Bacteria. /1994/5-A/9 KC378 . . . . **579.3**
IMMUNE SYSTEM: OUR INTERNAL DEFENDER
(VIDEOCASSETTE). /1991/4-5/KD014 . . . . **VCR 616.07**

Bad breath--Fiction.
PILKEY, D/Dog breath: the horrible trouble with Hally Tosis. /1994/
2-3/3 KG236 . . . . **E**

Badgers--Fiction.
ECKERT, AW/Incident at Hawk's Hill. /1971/6-A/7 KH097. . . . **Fic**
HOBAN, R/Bedtime for Frances. Newly ill. ed. /1995/
P-1/2 KF739 . . . . **CE E**
Birthday for Frances. /c1968, 1995/P-1/2 KF740 . . . . **E**
VARLEY, S/Badger's parting gifts. /1984/1-3/7 KG650. . . . . . **E**

Bagels--Fiction.
WING, N/Jalapeno bagels. /1996/1-3/2 KG742 . . . . **E**

Bagus (Rhinoceros).
MAYNARD, T/Rhino comes to America. /1993/
5-6/7 KC802 . . . . **599.66**

Baiul, Oksana.
BAIUL, O/Oksana: my own story. /1997/
3-6/4 KE247 . . . . **B BAIUL, O.**

Baja California--Fiction.
O'DELL, S/Black pearl. /c1967/5-6/5 KH557 . . . . **CE Fic**

Baker, Keith.
GET TO KNOW KEITH BAKER (VIDEOCASSETTE). /1994/
2-5/KE248. . . . . **VCR B BAKER, K.**

Bakers and bakeries--Fiction.
HEATH, A/Sofie's role. /1992/P-2/2 KF692 . . . . **E**
WING, N/Jalapeno bagels. /1996/1-3/2 KG742 . . . . **E**

Bakers and bakeries--Folklore.
SHEPARD, A/Baker's dozen: a Saint Nicholas tale. /1995/
K-2/4 KB487 . . . . **398.22**

Baking SEE ALSO Bread; Cookery.

Baking--Fiction.
BRINK, CR/Goody O'Grumpity. /1994/K-3/3 KF268 . . . . **E**
HOOPER, M/Cow, a bee, a cookie, and me. /1997/
K-2/2 KF768 . . . . **E**
KLINTING, L/Bruno the baker. /1997/P-2/2 KF911. . . . . **E**
WELLS, R/Bunny cakes. /1997/P-1/2 KG696 . . . . **E**
WOLFF, F/Seven loaves of bread. /1993/1-3/2 KG758 . . . . . . **E**

Bald eagle.
GIECK, C/Bald eagle magic for kids. /1991/5-6/6 KC714 . . **598.9**
PATENT, DH/Eagles of America. /1995/4-6/6 KC716 . . . . . **598.9**
Where the bald eagles gather. /1984/5-6/7 KC718 . . . . . **598.9**

Bald eagle--Fiction.
BURNHAM, SD/Three River Junction: a story of an Alaskan bald
eagle preserve (Kit). /1997/2-4/KF313 . . . . **KIT E**

Bald eagle--Snake River (Wyo.-Wash.).
CRAIGHEAD, C/Eagle and the river. /1994/5-6/7 KC339 . . **577.6**

Bald eagle--Wounds and injuries--Treatment.
JOHNSON, SA/Raptor rescue!: an eagle flies free. /1995/
5-6/7 KD254 . . . . **639.9**

Ball games.
SANDELSON, R/Ball sports. /1991/4-6/8 KD774 . . . . **796.3**

Ballads SEE ALSO Folk songs.

Ballads, English.
SINGER, M/Maiden on the moor. /1995/4-6/3 KB418 . . . **398.21**

Ballet.
ALICE IN WONDERLAND IN DANCE (VIDEOCASSETTE). /1993/
3-6/KD691. . . . . **VCR 792.8**

Ballet companies--Fiction.
ISADORA, R/Lili backstage. /1997/K-2/3 KF816 . . . . **E**

Ballet dancers.
GREGORY, C/Cynthia Gregory dances Swan Lake. /1990/
4-A/7 KD694 . . . . **792.8**
SPATT, LE/Behind the scenes at the ballet: rehearsing and
performing "The Sleeping /1995/4-6/9 KD697. . . . . **792.8**

Ballet dancing.
ALICE IN WONDERLAND IN DANCE (VIDEOCASSETTE). /1993/
3-6/KD691. . . . . **VCR 792.8**
BUSSELL, D/Young dancer. /1994/3-6/8 KD692 . . . . **792.8**
SPATT, LE/Behind the scenes at the ballet: rehearsing and
performing "The Sleeping Beauty" /1995/4-6/9 KD697. . . **792.8**

Ballet dancing--Fiction.
GODDEN, R/Listen to the nightingale. /c1992, 1994/
5-A/6 KH178 . . . . **Fic**
HOLABIRD, K/Angelina and the princess. /1984/P-2/5 KF764. . . **E**
ISADORA, R/Lili at ballet. /1993/P-2/2 KF815 . . . . **E**
O'CONNOR, J/Nina, Nina ballerina. /1993/P-1/1 KG189. . . . . **E**

Ballets--Stories, plots, etc.
FONTEYN, M/Swan Lake. /1989/4-6/7 KD693 . . . . . . **CE 792.8**
HOROSKO, M/Sleeping Beauty: the ballet story. /1994/
1-5/7 KD695 . . . . **792.8**
MCCAUGHREAN, G/Random House book of stories from the
ballet. /1994/3-6/6 KD696 . . . . **792.8**

Ballooning.
BELLVILLE, CW/Flying in a hot air balloon. /1993/
4-6/7 KD852 . . . . **797.5**
FINE, JC/Free spirits in the sky. /1994/2-5/7 KD853 . . . . . **797.5**

Balloons--Experiments.
KANER, E/Balloon science. /1989/2-6/6 KC079 . . . . **530**
ZUBROWSKI, B/Balloons: building and experimenting with inflatable
toys. /1990/4-A/7 KB888. . . . . **507**

Balloons--Fiction.
BONSALL, CN/Mine's the best. Newly illustrated ed. /1996/
1-2/1 KF245 . . . . **E**
PENE DU BOIS, W/Twenty-one balloons. /c1947/
4-6/7 KH595 . . . . **CE Fic**

Baltimore (Md.)--Fiction.
HOWARD, EF/Aunt Flossie's hats (and crab cakes later). /1991/
1-3/4 KF772 . . . . **E**
Chita's Christmas tree. /1989/2-4/5 KF773 . . . . **E**

Balto (Dog).
STANDIFORD, N/Bravest dog ever: the true story of Balto. /1989/
1-3/2 KD223 . . . . **636.7**

Banana--Fiction.
GERSHATOR, P/Sweet, sweet fig banana. /1996/K-2/2 KF613 . **E**

Bands (Music)--Fiction.
HURD, T/Mama don't allow. /1984/K-3/2 KF793 . . . . . . **CE E**
WILLIAMS, VB/Music, music for everyone. /1984/P-3/4 KG737 . **E**

Banneker, Benjamin.
PINKNEY, AD/Dear Benjamin Banneker. /1994/
4-6/6 KE249 . . . . **B BANNEKER, B.**

Bar mitzvah.
KIMMEL, EA/Bar mitzvah: a Jewish boy's coming of age. /1995/
5-A/7 KA776 . . . . **296.4**

Barbados--Fiction.
GANTOS, J/Jack's new power: stories from a Caribbean year. /
1995/5-A/4 KH151 . . . . **Fic**

Barbers--Fiction.
MITCHELL, MK/Uncle Jed's barbershop. /1993/1-3/4 KG147. . . **E**

Barking--Fiction.
COFFELT, N/Dog who cried woof. /1995/K-2/3 KF402 . . . . . . **E**

Barn owl.
EPPLE, W/Barn owls. /1992/4-6/5 KC713 . . . . **598.9**

Barter--Fiction.
MCKAY, JR., L/Caravan. /1995/3-5/6 KH480 . . . . **Fic**
TORRES, L/Saturday sancocho. /1995/K-2/5 KG614 . . . . . . **E**

Barton, Clara.
SONNEBORN, L/Clara Barton. /1992/
4-6/6 KE250 . . . . **B BARTON, C.**
Baseball SEE ALSO Little league baseball; Softball; teams e.g. Boston Red
Sox (Baseball team).

Baseball.
ANDERSON, J/Batboy: an inside look at spring training. /1996/
4-6/6 KD793 . . . . **796.357**
BLACKSTONE, M/This is baseball. /c1993, 1997/
P-1/2 KD795 . . . . **796.357**
PUCKETT, K/Kirby Puckett's baseball games. /1996/
3-6/3 KD801 . . . . **796.357**
TEIRSTEIN, MA/Baseball. /1994/3-6/3 KD808 . . . . **796.357**

Baseball--Fiction.
CARRIER, R/Longest home run. /1993/2-4/4 KG977 . . . . **Fic**
COHEN, B/Thank you, Jackie Robinson. /1997/4-A/4 KH013 . . **Fic**
DAY, A/Frank and Ernest play ball. /1990/2-3/4 KF452 . . . . . . **E**
DYGARD, TJ/Infield hit. /1995/5-A/7 KH093 . . . . **Fic**
HALL, D/When Willard met Babe Ruth. /1996/4-6/6 KH212. . . **Fic**
HEYMSFELD, C/Coaching Ms. Parker. /1992/2-4/4 KH255 . . . **Fic**
HURWITZ, J/Baseball fever. /1981/4-6/6 KH297 . . . . **Fic**
KESSLER, L/Here comes the strikeout. /c1965/1-2/1 KF898 . **CE E**

KUSUGAK, M/Baseball bats for Christmas. /1990/
4-6/4 KH384 . . . . **Fic**
MOCHIZUKI, K/Baseball saved us. /1993/4-A/6 KH500 . . . . . **Fic**
PARISH, P/Play ball, Amelia Bedelia. /1996/1-3/2 KG216. . . . **E**
PRAGER, A/Baseball birthday party. /1995/1-3/2 KG286 . . . . **E**
SHANNON, D/How Georgie Radbourn saved baseball. /1994/
2-5/6 KG476 . . . . **E**
SLOTE, A/Finding Buck McHenry. /1991/4-A/4 KH719 . . . . . **Fic**
SMITH, RK/Bobby baseball. /1991/3-6/4 KH726 . . . . **Fic**
STOLZ, M/Stealing home. /1992/3-5/6 KH768 . . . . **Fic**
TEAGUE, M/Field beyond the outfield. /1992/K-2/2 KG594 . . . **E**
TUNIS, JR/Highpockets. /c1948/5-A/6 KH809 . . . . **Fic**
Kid comes back. /c1946, 1990/5-A/7 KH810 . . . . **Fic**
WELCH, W/Playing right field. /1995/K-2/3 KG694 . . . . **E**

Baseball--History.
BERLER, R/Super book of baseball. /1991/4-A/7 KD794. **796.357**
GALT, MF/Up to the plate: the All American Girls Professional
Baseball League. /1995/4-6/6 KD797 . . . . **796.357**
MCKISSACK, P/Black diamond: the story of the Negro baseball
leagues. /1994/4-6/7 KD800 . . . . **796.357**
RITTER, LS/Leagues apart: the men and times of the Negro baseball
leagues. /1995/2-4/7 KD802 . . . . **796.357**

Baseball--Miscellanea.
EGAN, T/Macmillan book of baseball stories. /1992/
4-A/5 KD796 . . . . **796.357**
MACKAY, C/Touching all the bases: baseball for kids of all ages. /
c1994, 1996/4-6/7 KD799 . . . . **796.357**

Baseball--Periodicals.
BASEBALL DIGEST. /1941-/4-6/KA502 . . . . **PER 050**

Baseball--Poetry.
AT THE CRACK OF THE BAT: BASEBALL POEMS. /1992/
3-6/KE053. . . . . **811.008**
EXTRA INNINGS: BASEBALL POEMS. /1993/
3-6/KE056. . . . . **811.008**

Baseball--Songs and music.
NORWORTH, J/Take me out to the ballgame. /1992/
K-2/KD639 . . . . **789.3**

Baseball cards--Collectors and collecting.
OWENS, TS/Collecting baseball cards. /1993/4-A/7 KD505 . **769**

Baseball players.
ADLER, DA/Picture book of Jackie Robinson. /1994/
2-4/6 KE515 . . . . **B ROBINSON, J.**
CAMPBELL, J/Cal Ripken, Jr. /1997/5-6/7 KE512 . **B RIPKEN, C.**
CHRISTOPHER, M/At the plate with...Ken Griffey Jr. /1997/
3-6/6 KE380 . . . . **B GRIFFEY,K. JR**
On the mound with...Greg Maddux. /1997/
3-5/7 KE452 . . . . **B MADDUX, G.**
ENGEL, T/We'll never forget you, Roberto Clemente. /1997/
2-4/2 KE293 . . . . **B CLEMENTE, R.**
GOLENBOCK, P/Teammates. /1990/3-6/6 KD798 . . . . . **796.357**
GRABOWSKI, J/Stan Musial. /1993/5-A/7 KE474. **B MUSIAL, S.**
GREENE, C/Roy Campanella: major-league champion. /1994/
1-2/2 KE275 . . . . **B CAMPANELLA, R**
GUTMAN, B/Frank Thomas: power hitter. /1996/
3-5/6 KE563 . . . . **B THOMAS, F.**
Jim Eisenreich. /1996/3-5/6 KE336 . . . . **B EISENREICH, J**
KRAMER, B/Ken Griffey Junior: all-around all-star. /1996/
4-5/4 KE381 . . . . **B GRIFFEY,K. JR**
KRAMER, J/Bo Jackson. /1996/4-5/6 KE398 . . . **B JACKSON, B.**
Jim Abbott. /1996/4-5/6 KE223. . . . . **B ABBOTT, J.**
KRAMER, SA/Ty Cobb: bad boy of baseball. /1995/
2-4/4 KE298 . . . . **B COBB, T.**
MACHT, NL/Lou Gehrig. /1993/5-A/7 KE364. . . . **B GEHRIG, L.**
Roberto Clemente. /1994/5-A/7 KE294 . . . . . **B CLEMENTE, R.**
MCKISSACK, P/Satchel Paige: the best arm in baseball. /1992/
3-5/2 KE489 . . . . **B PAIGE, S.**
RENNERT, RS/Henry Aaron. /1993/5-A/9 KE222 . **B AARON, H.**
RUDEEN, K/Jackie Robinson. /1996/
5-6/6 KE516 . . . . **B ROBINSON, J.**
SANTELLA, A/Jackie Robinson breaks the color line. /1996/
4-6/6 KE517 . . . . **B ROBINSON, J.**
SAVAGE, J/Barry Bonds: Mr. Excitement. /1997/
4-6/3 KE258 . . . . **B BONDS, B.**
Mike Piazza: hard-hitting catcher. /1997/
4-6/7 KE495 . . . . **B PIAZZA, M.**
SULLIVAN, G/Glovemen: twenty-seven of baseball's greatest. /
1996/4-6/8 KD804 . . . . **796.357**
Pitchers: twenty-seven of baseball's greatest. /1994/
5-A/6 KD805 . . . . **796.357**
Sluggers: twenty-seven of baseball's greatest. /1991/
5-A/6 KD806 . . . . **796.357**
SULLIVAN, MJ/Top 10 baseball pitchers. /1994/
3-6/4 KD807 . . . . **796.357**

WEIDHORN, M/Jackie Robinson. /1993/
6-A/7 KE518 . . . . **B ROBINSON, J.**
Basketball.
MANLEY, M/Martin Manley's basketball heaven. /1987-/
4-A/KD778 . . . . **796.323**
VANCIL, M/NBA basketball basics. /1995/5-6/6 KD779 . **796.323**
WITHERS, T/Basketball. /1994/3-6/4 KD781 . . . . . . **796.323**
Basketball--Fiction.
CARRIER, R/Basketball player. /1996/4-6/3 KG975 . . . . **Fic**
JACKSON, A/Blowing bubbles with the enemy. /1993/
4-6/5 KH317 . . . . **Fic**
TUNIS, JR/Go, team, go! /c1954, 1991/5-A/6 KH808 . . . . . . **Fic**
Basketball--Poetry.
SLAM DUNK: BASKETBALL POEMS. /1995/4-6/KE081. . **811.008**
Basketball players.
CHRISTOPHER, M/On the court with...Michael Jordan. /1996/
4-6/8 KE409 . . . . **CE B JORDAN, M.**
GUTMAN, B/Grant Hill: basketball's high flier. /1996/
5-6/7 KE390 . . . . **B HILL, G.**
Hakeem Olajuwon: superstar center. /1995/
4-5/6 KE483 . . . . **B OLAJUWON, H.**
Michael Jordan: basketball to baseball and back. Rev. ed. /1995/
4-6/8 KE410 . . . . **B JORDAN, M.**
KELLY, J/Superstars of women's basketball. /1997/
4-6/7 KD775 . . . . **796.323**
KNAPP, R/Chris Webber: star forward. /1997/
5-6/7 KE590 . . . . **B WEBBER, C.**
Top 10 basketball centers. /1994/3-6/4 KD776 . . . . . **796.323**
Top 10 basketball scorers. /1994/3-6/4 KD777 . . . . . **796.323**
LIPSYTE, R/Michael Jordan: a life above the rim. /1994/
4-6/7 KE411 . . . . **B JORDAN, M.**
MACNOW, G/Shaquille O'Neal: star center. /1996/
4-5/6 KE485 . . . . **B O'NEAL, S.**
SCHNAKENBERG, R/Scottie Pippen: reluctant superstar. /1997/
4-6/6 KE498 . . . . **B PIPPEN, S.**
SIMMONS, A/John Lucas. /1996/5-A/7 KE449 . . . **B LUCAS, J.**
TOWNSEND, B/Anfernee Hardaway: basketball's lucky penny. /
1997/3-5/6 KE384 . . . . **B HARDAWAY, A.**
WILKER, J/Harlem Globetrotters. /1997/5-6/10 KD780 . . **796.323**
Basques--Folklore.
ARAUJO, FP/Nekane, the lamina and the bear: a tale of the
Basque Pyrenees. /1993/2-3/3 KB256 . . . . **398.2**
Bat mitzvah.
GOLDIN, BD/Bat mitzvah: a Jewish girl's coming of age. /1995/
5-A/10 KA773 . . . . **296.4**
Bathrooms--History.
COLMAN, P/Toilets, bathtubs, sinks, and sewers: a history of the
bathroom. /1994/5-6/5 KD294 . . . . **643**
Baths SEE ALSO Cleanliness.
Baths--Fiction.
CONRAD, P/Tub people. /1989/1-3/4 KF416 . . . . **CE E**
MCDONNELL, F/I love boats. /1995/P-1/3 KG101 . . . . **E**
WOOD, A/King Bidgood's in the bathtub. /1985/
P-2/1 KG763 . . . . **CE E**
Bathtubs--History.
COLMAN, P/Toilets, bathtubs, sinks, and sewers: a history of the
bathroom. /1994/5-6/5 KD294 . . . . **643**
Bats.
ACKERMAN, D/Bats: shadows in the night. /1997/
5-6/7 KC756 . . . . **599.4**
ARNOLD, C/Bat. /1996/4-6/7 KC757 . . . . **599.4**
BASH, B/Shadows of night: the hidden world of the Little Brown
Bat. /1993/1-3/5 KC758 . . . . **599.4**
EARLE, A/Zipping, zapping, zooming bats. /1995/
1-3/4 KC759 . . . . **599.4**
JOHNSON, SA/Bats. /1985/4-6/9 KC760 . . . . **599.4**
MAESTRO, B/Bats: night fliers. /1994/1-4/6 KC761 . . . . . . **599.4**
PRINGLE, LP/Batman: exploring the world of bats. /1991/
5-A/9 KC762 . . . . **599.4**
STUART, D/Bats: mysterious flyers of the night. /1994/
5-6/8 KC763 . . . . **599.4**
Bats--Fiction.
CANNON, A/Bat in the boot. /1996/1-3/2 KF333 . . . . **E**
CANNON, J/Stellaluna. /1993/K-2/3 KF334 . . . . **E**
Stellaluna (Talking book). /1996/K-2/KF335 . . . . **TB E**
JARRELL, R/Bat-poet. /1996/4-A/6 KH327 . . . . **Fic**
Bats--Fiction--Software.
STELLALUNA (CD-ROM). /1996/K-3/KG550 . . . . **CDR E**
Bats--Wit and humor.
HALL, K/Batty riddles. /1993/K-3/KD728 . . . . **793.735**
Battles SEE names of individual battles e.g. Concord, Battle of, 1775.
Baum, L. Frank.
CARPENTER, AS/L. Frank Baum: royal historian of Oz. /1992/
4-6/4 KE251 . . . . **B BAUM, L.**

Bayous--Fiction.
APPELT, K/Bayou lullaby. /1995/P-2/5 KF163 . . . . **E**
KARAS, GB/Home on the bayou: a cowboy's story. /1996/
K-2/2 KF868 . . . . **E**
Beaches--Fiction.
AGELL, C/I wear long green hair in the summer. /1994/
K-2/2 KF138 . . . . **E**
ALIKI /Those summers. /1996/K-2/4 KF149. . . . . **E**
AXELROD, A/Pigs on a blanket. /1996/2-3/2 KF179 . . . . **E**
COLE, S/When the tide is low. /1985/P-2/3 KF411 . . . . **E**
COONEY, B/Hattie and the wild waves. /1990/1-3/5 KF418 . . . **E**
GIFF, PR/Lily's crossing. /1997/5-A/5 KH165 . . . . **Fic**
JONES, RC/Down at the bottom of the deep dark sea. /1991/
P-K/2 KF852 . . . . **E**
REISER, L/Beach feet. /1996/P-3/2 KG318. . . . . **E**
ROCKWELL, AF/At the beach. /1987/P-3/3 KG340 . . . . **E**
Beaches--Fiction--Software.
JUST GRANDMA AND ME (CD-ROM). /1992/
P-2/KF863 . . . . **CDR E**
Beagle Expedition (1831-1836).
TWIST, C/Charles Darwin: on the trail of evolution. /1994/
5-8/8 KE315 . . . . **B DARWIN, C.**
Beans--Development.
BACK, C/Bean and plant. /1986/K-2/2 KC426 . . . . **583**
Bears SEE ALSO names of specific species e.g. Grizzly bears.
Bears.
BRENNER, B/Two orphan cubs. /1989/K-2/2 KC848 . . . . **599.78**
CALABRO, M/Operation grizzly bear. /1989/
5-6/7 KC858 . . . . **599.784**
FAIR, J/Black bear magic for kids. /1991/4-5/5 KC849 . . . **599.78**
HOSHINO, M/Grizzly bear family book. /1994/
4-6/6 KC859 . . . . **599.784**
LARSEN, T/Polar bear family book. /1996/4-6/4 KC862. **599.786**
LEPTHIEN, EU/Polar bears. /1991/2-4/5 KC863 . . . . . . **599.786**
MORRIS, J/Bears, bears, and more bears. /1995/
P/1 KC850 . . . . **599.78**
NATURE'S NEWBORN: BEAR, BIGHORN SHEEP, MOUNTAIN
GOATS (VIDEOCASSETTE). /1994/1-5/KC724 . . . . . **VCR 599**
PATENT, DH/Looking at bears. /1994/5-6/6 KC851 . . . . **599.78**
Way of the grizzly. /1987/5-6/8 KC860 . . . . **599.784**
POLAR BEARS (VIDEOCASSETTE). /1986/
4-A/KC864 . . . . **VCR 599.786**
PRINGLE, LP/Bearman: exploring the world of black bears. /1989/
5-6/7 KC852 . . . . **599.78**
ROSENTHAL, M/Bears. /1983/2-4/2 KC853. . . . . **599.78**
SCHMIDT, A/Bears and their forest cousins. /1991/
5-6/7 KC854 . . . . **599.78**
SCHWARTZ, A/Fat man in a fur coat and other bear stories. /
1984/5-6/5 KC855 . . . . **599.78**
SLEEPING BEARS (VIDEOCASSETTE). /1986/
4-A/KC856 . . . . **VCR 599.78**
STIRLING, I/Bears. /1992/5-A/7 KC857. . . . . **599.78**
STONE, LM/Grizzlies. /1993/5-6/6 KC861 . . . . **599.784**
TRACQUI, V/Polar bear: master of the ice. /1994/
3-5/4 KC865 . . . . **599.786**
Bears--Fiction.
ALBOROUGH, J/Where's my teddy? /1992/P-1/2 KF145 . . . . . **E**
ALEXANDER, M/You're a genius, Blackboard Bear. /1995/
K-2/2 KF147 . . . . **E**
ARNOSKY, J/Every autumn comes the bear. /1993/
P-2/2 KF168 . . . . **E**
ASCH, F/Bear shadow. /1985/P-2/2 KF173 . . . . **E**
Happy birthday, moon. /1982/P-1/2 KF174 . . . . **CE E**
Moonbear's pet. /1997/P-K/2 KF175 . . . . **E**
BAKER, B/One Saturday morning. /1994/1-3/1 KF183 . . . . . . **E**
BERENSTAIN, S/Berenstain Bears: no girls allowed. /1986/
K-2/4 KF226 . . . . **E**
Berenstain Bears learn about strangers. /1985/
K-2/4 KF225 . . . . **CE E**
BOND, M/Bear called Paddington. /c1958/2-4/5 KG916 . . . . **Fic**
Paddington audio collection (Talking book). /1978/
2-4/KG917 . . . . **TB Fic**
Paddington's storybook. /1984/3-6/5 KG918 . . . . **Fic**
BRETT, J/Berlioz the bear. /1991/K-2/2 KF261 . . . . **E**
CARLSTROM, NW/Jesse Bear, what will you wear? /1986/
P-K/4 KF356 . . . . **E**
Let's count it out, Jesse Bear. /1996/P-1/2 KF357 . . . . . . **E**
DALGLIESH, A/Bears on Hemlock Mountain. /c1952, 1990/
1-4/4 KH057 . . . . **Fic**
DAY, A/Frank and Ernest on the road. /1994/2-3/2 KF451 . . . . **E**
Frank and Ernest play ball. /1990/2-3/4 KF452 . . . . **E**
FUCHS, DM/Bear for all seasons. /1995/K-2/2 KF589 . . . . **E**
GRAHAM, H/Boy and his bear. /1996/5-A/5 KH186 . . . . . . **Fic**
HOFF, S/Grizzwold. /c1963/K-2/2 KF755 . . . . **E**

KINSEY-WARNOCK, N/Bear that heard crying. /1993/
2-3/2 KF905 . . . . E
KWITZ, MD/Little Vampire and the Midnight Bear. /1995/
1-3/2 KF941 . . . . E
LEWIS, PO/P. Bear's New Year's party!: a counting book. /1989/
K-1/3 KF978 . . . . E
MACK, S/10 bears in my bed: a goodnight countdown. /1974/
P-1/1 KG052 . . . . E
MCCLOSKEY, R/Blueberries for Sal. /c1948/P-2/7 KG087 . . **CE E**
MCLEOD, EW/Bear's bicycle. /c1975, 1986/P-2/2 KG109 . . **CE E**
MCPHAIL, D/Bear's toothache. /c1972/K-2/2 KG116 . . . . . **CE E**
Lost! /1990/P-1/2 KG119 . . . . **CE E**
MINARIK, EH/Little Bear. /c1961/P-1/2 KG141 . . . . **CE E**
MOREY, W/Gentle Ben. Reissued. /c1965, 1997/
5-A/6 KH508 . . . . **Fic**
MORPURGO, M/Dancing bear. /1996/4-6/5 KH513 . . . . **Fic**
PEET, B/Big bad Bruce. /1977/K-3/3 KG224 . . . . E
TELLO, J/Abuelo y los tres osos./Abuelo and the three bears. /
1997/K-2/2 KG598 . . . . E
VINCENT, G/Ernest and Celestine at the circus. /1988/
P-2/2 KG655 . . . . E
Ernest and Celestine's picnic. /1982/P-2/1 KG656 . . . . E
WADDELL, M/Can't you sleep, Little Bear? 2nd ed. /c1988, 1992/
P-K/3 KG674 . . . . E
Let's go home, Little Bear. /1993/P-K/3 KG676 . . . . E
You and me, Little Bear. /1996/P-K/1 KG677 . . . . E
WARD, L/Biggest bear. /c1952/1-3/3 KG688 . . . . **CE E**
WELLS, R/Edward in deep water. /1995/P-K/2 KG697 . . . . . . E
Edward unready for school. /1995/P-K/2 KG698 . . . . E
Edward's overwhelming overnight. /1995/P-1/2 KG699 . . . . . E
WILLARD, N/Starlit somersault downhill. /1993/K-2/3 KG725 . . E
WINTHROP, E/Bear and Mrs. Duck. /1988/P-1/1 KG744 . . . . E
WISEMAN, B/Morris and Boris. /c1974, 1991/K-2/1 KG748 . . . E
ZALBEN, JB/Beni's first Chanukah. /1988/P/4 KG785 . . . . . . E

Bears--Fiction--Software.
BERENSTAIN BEARS GET IN A FIGHT. SCHOOL ED. (CD-ROM).
/1995/K-3/KF223 . . . . **CDR E**
BERENSTAIN BEARS IN THE DARK. SCHOOL ED. (CD-ROM). /
1996/K-3/KF224 . . . . **CDR E**

Bears--Folklore.
BARTON, B/Three bears. /1991/P-K/1 KB527 . . . . **398.24**
SLOAT, T/Sody sallyratus. /1997/1-3/5 KB653 . . . . **398.24**
STEVENS, J/Tops and bottoms. /1995/K-2/2 KB660 . . . . **398.24**

Beauty, Personal SEE ALSO Costume; Hair; Skin; Teeth.

Beauty, Personal--Fiction.
GLEITZMAN, M/Puppy fat. /1995/5-A/5 KH175 . . . . **Fic**
GREENWALD, S/Rosy Cole: she walks in beauty. /1994/
3-6/3 KH201 . . . . **Fic**
ROBINS, J/Addie's bad day. /1993/K-1/2 KG339 . . . . E

Beauty shops--Fiction.
BARBER, BE/Saturday at The New You. /1994/K-3/3 KF198 . . . E

Beavers.
LEPTHIEN, EU/Beavers. /1992/3-5/5 KC754 . . . . **599.37**
WALLACE, K/Think of a beaver. /1993/K-2/4 KC755 . . . . **599.37**

Beavers--Fiction.
HIGHTOWER, S/Twelve snails to one lizard: a tale of mischief and
measurement. /1997/1-3/2 KF726 . . . . E
HIMMELMAN, J/Day-off machine. /1990/1-3/1 KF729 . . . . . . E
KLINTING, L/Bruno the baker. /1997/P-2/2 KF911 . . . . E
Bruno the carpenter. /1996/K-2/2 KF912 . . . . E
Bruno the tailor. /1996/K-2/2 KF913 . . . . E
MACDONALD, A/Little Beaver and The Echo. /1990/
P-K/1 KG049 . . . . E

Bedrooms--Fiction.
HECKMAN, P/Waking upside down. /1996/1-3/6 KF693 . . . . . E

Beds--Fiction.
SEUSS, D/I am not going to get up today! /1987/
1-3/2 KG461 . . . . E
I am not going to get up today! plus three more Dr. Seuss classics
/1991/1-3/KG462 . . . . **VCR E**

Bedtime SEE ALSO Night; Sleep.

Bedtime--Fiction.
ANDERSON, PP/Time for bed, the babysitter said. /1987/
P-2/1 KF157 . . . . E
APPELT, K/Bayou lullaby. /1995/P-2/5 KF163 . . . . E
AYLESWORTH, J/Two terrible frights. /1987/P-1/3 KF181 . . . . . E
BROWN, MW/Little Donkey close your eyes. /1995/
P-K/2 KF286 . . . . E
CAPUCILLI, A/Biscuit. /1996/P-1/1 KF338 . . . . E
CLEARY, B/Petey's bedtime story. /1993/2-3/3 KF395 . . . . E
COOPER, H/Boy who wouldn't go to bed. /1997/P-1/2 KF422 . E
DALE, P/Ten out of bed. /1994/P-1/2 KF446 . . . . E
EMBERLEY, E/Go away, big green monster! /1992/
P-1/2 KF522 . . . . E

FOX, M/Time for bed. /1993/P-1/2 KF572 . . . . E
GINSBURG, M/Sun's asleep behind the hill. /1982/
P-K/1 KF624 . . . . E
HECKMAN, P/Waking upside down. /1996/1-3/6 KF693 . . . . . E
HELLER, N/This little piggy. /1997/P-1/2 KF699 . . . . E
HOBAN, R/Bedtime for Frances. Newly ill. ed. /1995/
P-1/2 KF739 . . . . **CE E**
HUTCHINS, P/Little Pink Pig. /1994/P-1/2 KF799 . . . . E
JENNINGS, S/Jeremiah and Mrs. Ming. /1990/K-2/2 KF828 . . . E
JONAS, A/Quilt. /1984/K-1/2 KF846 . . . . E
LOH, M/Tucking mommy in. /1987/P-2/2 KG017 . . . . E
MAYER, M/There's an alligator under my bed. /1987/
P-2/2 KG085 . . . . E
MCMULLAN, K/If you were my bunny. /1996/P-K/3 KG112 . . . E
OGBURN, JK/Noise lullaby. /1995/P-2/2 KG190 . . . . E
ORMEROD, J/Moonlight. /1982/P-1/KG195 . . . . E
SIDDALS, MM/Tell me a season. /1997/P-1/1 KG500 . . . . E
THOMAS, SM/Putting the world to sleep. /1995/P-2/2 KG606 . E
WADDELL, M/Can't you sleep, Little Bear? 2nd ed. /c1988, 1992/
P-K/3 KG674 . . . . E
WOOD, D/Piggies. /1991/P-K/1 KG768 . . . . E

Bedtime--Poetry.
SLEEP, BABY, SLEEP: LULLABIES AND NIGHT POEMS. /1994/
P-K/KD889 . . . . **808.81**
SLEEP RHYMES AROUND THE WORLD. /1994/
P-3/KD890 . . . . **808.81**
TILLER, R/Cinnamon, mint, and mothballs: a visit to Grandmother's
house. /1993/K-3/KE033 . . . . **811**

Bee culture.
GIBBONS, G/Honey makers. /1997/3-5/6 KC573 . . . . . **595.79**
JOHNSON, SA/Beekeeper's year. /1994/5-6/6 KD240 . . . . . **638**
MICHELS, P/Day in the life of a beekeeper. /1990/
4-5/6 KD242 . . . . **638**
MICUCCI, C/Life and times of the honeybee. /1995/
4-6/6 KC576 . . . . **595.79**

Beecher family.
FRITZ, J/Harriet Beecher Stowe and the Beecher preachers. /1994/
6-A/7 KE556 . . . . **B STOWE, H.**

Beehives.
COLE, J/Magic School Bus inside a beehive. /1996/
2-4/2 KC570 . . . . **595.79**

Beekeepers.
MICHELS, P/Day in the life of a beekeeper. /1990/
4-5/6 KD242 . . . . **638**

Bees SEE ALSO Honeybee.

Bees.
COLE, J/Magic School Bus inside a beehive. /1996/
2-4/2 KC570 . . . . **595.79**
FISCHER-NAGEL, H/Life of the honeybee. /1986/
4-6/7 KC572 . . . . **595.79**
GIBBONS, G/Honey makers. /1997/3-5/6 KC573 . . . . . **595.79**
INSECTS (VIDEOCASSETTE). /c1979, 1986/
2-6/KC541 . . . . **VCR 595.7**
PRINGLE, LP/Killer bees. Rev. ed. /1990/A/8 KC578 . . . . **595.79**

Bees--Fiction.
LOBEL, A/Rose in my garden. /1984/K-3/KG011 . . . . E
POLACCO, P/Bee tree. /1993/K-2/3 KG250 . . . . E

Beethoven, Ludwig van--Fiction.
NICHOL, B/Beethoven lives upstairs. /1994/4-6/4 KH549 . . . . . **Fic**
Beethoven lives upstairs (Videocassette). /1992/
4-6/KH550 . . . . **VCR Fic**

Beethoven, Ludwig van--Software.
WINTER, R/Microsoft composer collection (CD-ROM). /1994/
4-A/KD525 . . . . **CDR 780**

Beetles.
JOHNSON, SA/Ladybugs. /1983/A/11 KC554 . . . . **595.76**

Befana (Legendary character).
OPPENHEIM, J/Christmas Witch: an Italian legend. /1993/
1-3/2 KB507 . . . . **398.23**

Behavior SEE ALSO Conduct of life; Courage; Ethics; Etiquette; Family life;
Self control.

Behavior.
ANGRY JOHN (VIDEOCASSETTE). /1994/
4-6/KA622 . . . . **VCR 152.4**
CHANGE FOR THE BETTER: TEACHING CORRECT BEHAVIOR
(VIDEOCASSETTE). /1989//KA300 . . . . **VCR PROF 649**
I GET SO MAD! (VIDEOCASSETTE). /1993/
K-3/KA626 . . . . **VCR 152.4**
I'M SO FRUSTRATED! (VIDEOCASSETTE). /1994/
1-3/KA627 . . . . **VCR 152.4**
IT'S GREAT TO BE ME! INCREASING YOUR CHILD'S SELF-
ESTEEM (VIDEOCASSETTE). /1989//KA302 . . . **VCR PROF 649**

IT'S NOT MY FAULT: A PROGRAM ABOUT CONFLICT RESOLUTION (VIDEOCASSETTE). /1981/ 4-6/KA628 . . . . **VCR 152.4**
LEAF, M/Manners can be fun. Rev. ed. /1985/ 1-3/4 KB249 . . . . **395.5**
MINDING YOUR MANNERS AT SCHOOL (VIDEOCASSETTE). /1996/3-5/KB241 . . . . **VCR 395**
MURPHY, J/Songs for you and me: kids learn about feelings and emotions /n.d./K-1/KA629 . . . . **SRC 152.4**
SLONECKI, C/Dog ate my homework: social skills for today (Sound recording cassette). /1995/1-3/KB242. . . . . **SRC 395**
WHEN I GET MAD (VIDEOCASSETTE). /1994/ 5-6/KA631 . . . . **VCR 152.4**
WHEN YOU'RE MAD, MAD, MAD!: DEALING WITH ANGER (VIDEOCASSETTE). /1993/4-6/KA632 . . . . **VCR 152.4**
WORKING IT OUT: CONFLICT RESOLUTION (VIDEOCASSETTE). /1993/5-6/KA813 . . . . **VCR 303.6**

Behavior--Fiction.
ALLARD, H/Miss Nelson is missing. /1977/1-3/3 KF151 . . **CE E**
ARMSTRONG, J/That terrible baby. /1994/K-2/3 KF166 . . . . **E**
CARLE, E/Grouchy ladybug. New ed. /1996/P-2/2 KF342 . . . . . **E**
CARLSON, N/How to lose all your friends. /1994/K-2/2 KF350 . **E**
Sit still! /1996/K-2/2 KF352. . . . . **E**
EVANS, D/Classroom at the end of the hall. /1996/ 3-5/4 KH104 . . . . **Fic**
GANTOS, J/Rotten Ralph. /1976/K-2/3 KF597 . . . . **E**
GIFALDI, D/Gregory, Maw, and the Mean One. /1992/ 5-A/7 KH163 . . . . **Fic**
GIFF, PR/Today was a terrible day. /1980/1-2/2 KF616 . . . **CE E**
Today was a terrible day (Kit). /1993/1-2/KF617 . . . . . . **KIT E**
GLEITZMAN, M/Misery guts. /1993/5-A/7 KH174. . . . . **Fic**
GRAVOIS, JM/Quickly, Quigley. /1994/P-1/2 KF635 . . . . **E**
HERMES, P/Nothing but trouble, trouble, trouble. /1995/ 4-6/6 KH249 . . . . **Fic**
HOBAN, R/Birthday for Frances. /c1968, 1995/P-1/2 KF740 . . . **E**
HURWITZ, J/Class clown. /1987/2-4/4 KH298 . . . . **Fic**
KELLER, H/Geraldine first. /1996/K-2/2 KF881 . . . . **E**
LESTER, H/Princess Penelope's parrot. /1996/K-2/2 KF965. . . . . **E**
MACDONALD, A/No more nice. /1996/4-6/6 KH437 . . . . . . **Fic**
No more nice. /1996/3-5/6 KH438. . . . . **Fic**
NESBIT, E/Story of the treasure seekers. /1986/5-A/7 KH544. . . **Fic**
RATHMANN, P/Ruby the copycat. /1991/K-2/2 KG311 . . . . . . **E**
ROBINSON, NK/Veronica the show-off. /c1982/3-6/4 KH642 . **Fic**
ROCKWELL, AF/Once upon a time this morning. /1997/ P-K/2 KG344 . . . . **E**
SENDAK, M/Pierre: a cautionary tale in five chapters and a prologue. /c1962/P-1/KG436 . . . . **CE E**
SERVICE, PF/Weirdos of the universe, unite! /1992/ 6-A/6 KH701 . . . . **Fic**
VIORST, J/Alexander and the terrible, horrible, no good, very bad day. /c1972/P-3/7 KG657 . . . . **CE E**
VOIGT, C/Bad girls. /1996/6-A/5 KH831 . . . . **Fic**
WELLS, R/Noisy Nora. /1997/K-1/4 KG707 . . . . **CE E**
Noisy Nora (Videocassette). /1993/K-1/KG708. . . . . . . **VCR E**
ZOLOTOW, C/William's doll. /c1972/P-2/4 KG810 . . . . **E**

Behavior--Fiction--Software.
BERENSTAIN BEARS GET IN A FIGHT. SCHOOL ED. (CD-ROM). /1995/K-3/KF223 . . . . **CDR E**

Behavior--Folklore.
ARUEGO, J/Rockabye crocodile. /1988/P-K/2 KB525 . . . . **398.24**

Behavior--Poetry.
KENNEDY, XJ/Brats. /1986/3-6/6 KD961 . . . . **811**
Drat these brats! /1993/3-6/6 KD962. . . . . **811**
Fresh brats. /1990/3-6/6 KD964. . . . . **811**
Behavior problems (Children) SEE Problem children.

Belize--Fiction.
LONDON, J/Village basket weaver. /1996/2-3/6 KG029 . . . . . **E**

Bell, Alexander Graham.
NOONAN, J/Nineteenth-century inventors. /1992/ 5-6/7 KC897 . . . . **609**

Bells--Fiction.
BLANCO, A/Angel's kite/La estrella de Angel. /1994/ 2-4/6 KG902 . . . . **Fic**

Benin--Fiction.
COWEN-FLETCHER, J/It takes a village. /1994/K-2/2 KF429 . . . **E**

Benin--History--To 1894.
KOSLOW, P/Dahomey: the warrior kings. /1997/ 6-A/9 KE736 . . . . **966.9**
Bereavement SEE ALSO Death; Grief.

Bereavement--Psychological aspects--Bibliography.
RUDMAN, MK/Books to help children cope with separation and loss: an annotated bibliography. /1993//KA025 . **PROF 016.1559**

Berlin, Irving.
STREISSGUTH, T/Say it with music: a story about Irving Berlin. / 1994/4-5/5 KE252 . . . . **B BERLIN, I.**

Bermuda Triangle.
ABELS, H/Bermuda triangle. /1987/4-6/4 KA560 . . . . . . **001.94**

Bernstein, Leonard.
HURWITZ, J/Leonard Bernstein: a passion for music. /1993/ 5-A/7 KE253 . . . . **B BERNSTEIN, L.**
Best books SEE Bibliography--Best books; Books and reading--Best books.

Best books--Children's literature--Bibliography.
GILLESPIE, JT/Newbery companion: booktalk and related materials for Newbery Medal and Honor /1996//KA035. . . **PROF 016.813**
SCIENCE BOOKS AND FILMS' BEST BOOKS FOR CHILDREN, 1992-1995. /1996//KA028 . . . . **PROF 016.5**

Bethune, Mary McLeod.
MCKISSACK, P/Mary McLeod Bethune. /1992/ 4-6/5 KE254 . . . . **B BETHUNE, M.**

Bhagavadgita.
VISHAKA /Our most dear friend: Bhagavad-gita for children. / 1996/2-5/5 KA767 . . . . **294.5**
Bible SEE ALSO names of Biblical characters e.g. Abraham (Biblical patriarch).

Bible--Folklore.
ORGEL, D/Flower of Sheba. /1994/1-2/2 KA687 . . . . **222**
PODWAL, M/Book of tens. /1994/5-6/7 KA769 . . . . **296.1**

Bible--History.
COOPER, I/Dead Sea Scrolls. /1997/6-A/8 KA768 . . . . . . **296.1**

Bible. N.T. Luke.
FIRST CHRISTMAS. /1992/6-A/5 KA704 . . . . **232.92**

Bible. O.T.--Wit and humor.
GELLMAN, M/God's mailbox: more stories about stories in the Bible. /1996/4-6/6 KA678 . . . . **221.9**

Bible. O.T. Psalms XXIII.
PSALM TWENTY-THREE. /1997/P-A/3 KA691 . . . . **223**

Bible stories--N.T.
CHRISTMAS STORY. /1996/2-3/4 KA701 . . . . **232.92**
DE PAOLA, T/Mary: the mother of Jesus. /1995/ 3-6/5 KA699 . . . . **232.91**
Miracles of Jesus. /1987/5-6/7 KA695 . . . . **232.9**
GLEESON, B/Savior is born (Kit). /1992/3-5/KA705 . **KIT 232.92**
HASTINGS, S/Children's illustrated Bible. /1994/ 4-6/5 KA676 . . . . **220**
HEYER, C/Easter story. /1990/5-6/5 KA710 . . . . **232.96**
HOGROGIAN, N/First Christmas. /1995/K-2/5 KA707 . . **232.92**
NATIVITY. /1996/3-5/5 KA709 . . . . **232.92**
WINTHROP, E/He is risen: the Easter story. /1985/ 5-6/7 KA711 . . . . **232.96**

Bible stories--O.T.
DE REGNIERS, BS/David and Goliath. /1996/1-4/6 KA683. . **222**
FISHER, LE/Moses. /1995/3-4/3 KA677. . . . . **221.9**
GAUCH, PL/Noah. /1994/K-2/4 KA684. . . . . **222**
GLEESON, B/Joseph and his brothers (Videocassette). /1993/ 5-6/KA685 . . . . **VCR 222**
HASTINGS, S/Children's illustrated Bible. /1994/ 4-6/5 KA676 . . . . **220**
HUTTON, W/Moses in the bulrushes. /1986/P-2/6 KA679. . **221.9**
JOHNSON, JW/Creation. /1994/K-3/KD956 . . . . **811**
Creation: a poem. /1993/1-6/KD957 . . . . **811**
JONAS, A/Aardvarks, disembark! /1990/2-A/4 KA963. . **333.95**
MARK, J/Tale of Tobias. /1996/1-3/2 KA693 . . . . **229**
MCDONOUGH, YZ/Eve and her sisters: women of the Old Testament. /1994/3-4/7 KA680. . . . . **221.9**
METAXAS, E/David and Goliath (Videocassette). /1992/ 2-4/KA686 . . . . **VCR 222**
NOAH'S ARK. /c1977/P-2/KA681 . . . . **221.9**
NOAH'S ARK (VIDEOCASSETTE). /c1989, 1996/ P-2/KA682. . . . . **VCR 221.9**
PATTERSON, G/Jonah and the whale. /1992/P-2/4 KA692. . **224**
WILLIAMS, M/Joseph and his magnificent coat of many colors. / 1992/2-4/5 KA689 . . . . **222**
WOLKSTEIN, D/Esther's story. /1996/4-A/4 KA690. . . . . . **222**

Bible stories--O.T.--Genesis.
STORY OF THE CREATION: WORDS FROM GENESIS. /1993/ 2-3/4 KA688 . . . . **222**

Bibliography--Best books--Children's literature.
ADVENTURING WITH BOOKS: A BOOKLIST FOR PRE-K-GRADE 6. 1997 ED. /1997//KA009 . . . . . . **PROF 011.62**
FREEMAN, J/Books kids will sit still for: the complete read-aloud guide. 2nd ed. /1990//KA015. . . . . **PROF 011.62**
GILLESPIE, JT/Best books for children: preschool through grade 6. 5th ed. /1994//KA084 . . . . **PROF 028.1**
NEWBERY AND CALDECOTT MEDALISTS AND HONOR BOOK WINNERS: BIBLIOGRAPHIES AND /1992//KA004 . . . **PROF 011**

SUTHERLAND, Z/Best in children's books: the University of Chicago guide to children's literature, 1985-1990. /1991/ /KA023. . . . . **PROF 011.62**
THOMAS, JL/Play, learn, and grow: an annotated guide to the best books and materials for very young children. /1992/ /KA088. . . . . **PROF 028.1**
WYNAR, CG/Guide to reference books for school media centers. 4th ed. /1992//KA007 . . . . **PROF 011**

Bibliography--Best books--Children's literature--Periodicals.
NEWBERY AND CALDECOTT AWARDS: A GUIDE TO THE MEDAL AND HONOR BOOKS. /n.d.//KA128 . . **PER PROF 050**

Bicycle racing--Fiction.
BLEDSOE, LJ/Big bike race. /1995/3-6/2 KG903. . . . . **Fic**
CREWS, D/Bicycle race. /1985/K-2/2 KF431. . . . . **E**
SCHWARTZ, DM/Supergrandpa. /1991/K-3/5 KG416 . . . . . . **E**

Bicycles and bicycling.
BAILEY, D/Cycling. /1990/2-4/2 KD826. . . . . **796.6**
FRANCIS, J/Bicycling. /1996/3-6/6 KD827. . . . . . . **796.6**
GIBBONS, G/Bicycle book. /1995/2-5/3 KD124. . . . **629.227**
HAUTZIG, D/Pedal power: how a mountain bike is made. /1996/ 5-6/6 KD125 . . . . **629.227**

Bicycles and bicycling--Fiction.
BLEDSOE, LJ/Big bike race. /1995/3-6/2 KG903. . . . . **Fic**
CAMERON, A/Julian's glorious summer. /1987/2-4/2 KG967. . **Fic**
DRAGONWAGON, C/Annie flies the birthday bike. /1993/ K-2/2 KF495 . . . . **E**
JAKOB, D/My bike. /1994/K-2/3 KF821 . . . . **E**
REY, HA/Curious George rides a bike. /c1952/ P-2/1 KG326 . . . . **CE E**
SAY, A/Bicycle man. /1982/K-3/4 KG395 . . . . **E**
WOLFF, A/Stella and Roy. /1993/P-1/3 KG756 . . . . **E**

Bicycles and bicycling--History.
LORD, T/Amazing bikes. /1992/3-5/6 KD126 . . . . **629.227**

Bicycles and bicycling--Safety measures.
GIBBONS, G/Bicycle book. /1995/2-5/3 KD124. . . . **629.227**
SAFETY ON WHEELS (VIDEOCASSETTE). /1994/ P-1/KB024. **VCR 363.1**

Bicycles and bicycling--Safety measures--Fiction.
MCLEOD, EW/Bear's bicycle. /c1975, 1986/P-2/2 KG109. . **CE E**
PARK, B/Mick Harte was here. /1995/4-6/4 KH570 . . . . **Fic**
Bigfoot SEE Sasquatch.

Bighorn sheep.
NATURE'S NEWBORN: BEAR, BIGHORN SHEEP, MOUNTAIN GOATS (VIDEOCASSETTE). /1994/1-5/KC724 . . . . . **VCR 599**

Bilingual materials.
JENKINS, E/Travellin' with Ella Jenkins: a bilingual journey (Compact disc). /1989/K-2/KD576. . . . . **CD 789.2**
SLEEP RHYMES AROUND THE WORLD. /1994/ P-3/KD890. . . . . **808.81**

Bilingual materials--Chinese.
CHIN, C/China's bravest girl: the legend of Hua Mu Lan = [Chin kuo ying hsiung Hua /1993/3-5/4 KB430. . . . . **398.22**
CHINESE MOTHER GOOSE RHYMES. /c1968, 1989/ P-3/KB794. . . . . **398.8**
MAPLES IN THE MIST: CHILDREN'S POEMS FROM THE TANG DYNASTY. /1996/K-3/KE133 . . . . **895**

Bilingual materials--Eskimo.
EKOOMIAK, N/Arctic memories. /c1988, 1990/2-6/4 KF125 . **998**

Bilingual materials--Japanese.
MADO, M/Animals: selected poems. /1992/2-6/KE135. . . . **895.6**

Bilingual materials--Japanese--Software.
JUST GRANDMA AND ME (CD-ROM). /1992/ P-2/KF863. . . . . **CDR E**

Bilingual materials--Khmer.
SPAGNOLI, C/Judge Rabbit and the tree spirit: a folktale from Cambodia. /1991/3-4/4 KB655. . . . . **398.24**

Bilingual materials--Korean.
HAN, SC/Rabbit's escape/Kusa ilsaenghan tookki. /1995/ P-2/3 KB583. . . . . **398.24**

Bilingual materials--Russian.
AMERY, H/First thousand words in Russian. /1983/ 4-6/KB863. . . . . **491.7**

Bilingual materials--Spanish.
ADA, AF/Gathering the sun: an alphabet in Spanish and English. / 1997/1-3/KE122. **861**
Mediopollito/Half-Chicken. /1995/K-2/2 KB521 . . . . **398.24**
ANCONA, G/Pinata maker./El Pinatero. /1994/ 3-6/6 KD450. . . . . **745.594**
ARROZ CON LECHE: POPULAR SONGS AND RHYMES FROM LATIN AMERICA. /1989/P-3/KD556 . . . . **789.2**
BARCHAS, S/Giant and the rabbit: six bilingual folktales from Hispanic culture (Sound /1996/2-4/KB258 . . . . . **SRC 398.2**
Pinata!: bilingual songs for children (Sound recording cassette). / 1991/K-6/KD605 . . . . **SRC 789.3**

This old man/Este viejito (Sound recording cassette). /1997/ K-2/KD606 . . . . **SRC 789.3**
BERNIER-GRAND, CT/Juan Bobo: four folktales from Puerto Rico. / 1994/1-2/2 KB427 . . . . **398.22**
BLANCO, A/Angel's kite/La estrella de Angel. /1994/ 2-4/6 KG902 . . . . **Fic**
BRUSCA, MC/Three friends: a counting book./Tres amigos: un cuento para contar. /1995/P-2/1 KB954 . . . . **513.2**
DE COLORES AND OTHER LATIN-AMERICAN FOLK SONGS FOR CHILDREN. /1994/K-3/KD561. . . . . **789.2**
DELACRE, L/Vejigante masquerader. /1993/1-3/4 KF458. . . . . . **E**
DORROS, A/Radio Man: a story in English and Spanish./Don Radio: un cuento en Ingles y /1993/2-5/2 KF491 . . . . **E**
EHLERT, L/Cuckoo: a Mexican folktale./Cucu: un cuento folklorico mexicano. /1997/P-2/3 KB561 . . . . **398.24**
Moon rope: a Peruvian folktale/Un lazo a la luna: una leyenda Peruana. /1992/1-3/2 KB563. . . . . **398.24**
ELYA, SM/Say hola to Spanish. /1996/K-2/3 KB862 . . . . . **468.1**
EMBERLEY, R/Let's go: a book in two languages./Vamos: un libro en dos lenguas. /1993/K-2/2 KB857. . . . . **463**
My house: a book in two languages/Mi Casa: un libro en dos lenguas. /1990/K-2/KB858 . . . . **463**
EVERSOLE, R/Flute player./La Flautista. /1995/K-2/2 KF541 . . . **E**
GARZA, CL/Family pictures: Cuadros de familia. /1990/ 2-5/6 KA866 . . . . **306.85**
GONZALEZ, LM/Bossy gallito el gallo de bodas: a traditional Cuban folktale. /1994/K-2/4 KB577 . . . . **398.24**
GRANDMOTHER'S NURSERY RHYMES: LULLABIES, TONGUE TWISTERS, AND RIDDLES FROM /1994/P-2/KB799 . . . . . **398.8**
GUY, GF/Fiesta! /1996/P-1/1 KF655 . . . . **E**
HAFER, JC/Come sign with us: sign language activities for children. 2nd. ed. /1996/KA279. . . . . **PROF 419**
HAYES, J/Watch out for clever women!/Cuidado con las mujeres astutas!: Hispanic /1994/2-5/4 KB315. . . . . **398.2**
HINOJOSA, T/Cada nino./Every child (Compact disc). /1996/ 2-6/KD568. . . . . **CD 789.2**
JOHNSTON, T/My Mexico--Mexico mio. /1996/K-3/KD958. . **811**
Tale of Rabbit and Coyote. /1994/2-3/2 KB596 . . . . . **398.24**
KAHN, M/Mi libro de palabras Inglesas de todos los dias. /1982/ 1-3/KB843 . . . . **428**
My everyday Spanish word book. /1982/1-3/KB861 . . . . . **468**
KOPLOW, L/Tanya and the Tobo Man/Tanya y el Hombre Tobo: / 1991/K-2/2 KD040 . . . . **618.92**
LAS NAVIDADES: POPULAR CHRISTMAS SONGS FROM LATIN AMERICA. /1990/K-3/KD580. . . . . **789.2**
LEVY, J/Spirit of Tio Fernando./El espiritu de tio Fernando. /1995/1-3/5 KH404 . . . . **Fic**
LOMAS GARZA, C/In my family./En mi familia. /1996/ 2-5/6 KA870 . . . . **306.85**
LOWELL, S/Three little javelinas. /1992/K-2/4 KG039. . . . . . . **E**
LYRIC LANGUAGE: A BILINGUAL MUSIC PROGRAM: SPANISH/ ENGLISH (VIDEOCASSETTE). /1992/K-6/KD636 . . . **VCR 789.3**
MARTINEZ, AC/Woman who outshone the sun: the legend of Lucia Zenteno./La mujer que brillaba /1991/3-5/5 KB403 . . . . **398.21**
MCMILLAN, B/Sense suspense: a guessing game for the five senses. /1994/P-2/KC968. **612.8**
MORA, P/Desert is my mother./El desierto es mi madre. /1994/ K-3/KD989 . . . . **811**
Gift of the poinsettia./El regalo de la flor de nochebuena. /1995/ 3-5/4 KH507 . . . . **Fic**
Listen to the desert/Oye al desierto. /1994/P-1/KD990. . . . **811**
Uno, dos, tres: one, two, three. /1996/P-1/3 KG155 . . . . . . **E**
PARNWELL, EC/Oxford picture dictionary of American English. English/Spanish ed. /c1978, 1988/4-6/KB860. . . . . **463**
PERL, L/Pinatas and paper flowers, holidays of the Americas in English and Spanish /1983/4-6/6 KB202 . . . . **394.26**
POLLITOS DICEN: JUEGOS, RIMAS Y CANCIONES INFANTILES DE PAISES DE HABLA /1994/P-1/2 KD584. . . . . **789.2**
PRATT, KJ/Walk in the rainforest. /1992/K-6/7 KC322 . . . **577.34**
ROE, E/With my brother/Con mi hermano. /1991/ P-2/2 KG346 . . . . **E**
ROHMER, H/Atariba and Niguayona: a story from the Taino people of Puerto Rico. /c1976, 1988/4-5/5 KB769 . . . . **398.27**
Uncle Nacho's hat: a folktale from Nicaragua/El sombrero de Tio Nacho: /1989/2-4/2 KB770. . . . . **398.27**
SACRE, A/Looking for Papito: family stories from Latin America (Sound recording /1996/1-6/KA857. . . . . **SRC 305.8**
SESAME STREET MAGAZINE. /1971-/P/KA540 . . . . . . **PER 050**
STEVENS, JR/Carlos and the skunk./Carlos y el zorrillo. /1997/ 1-3/3 KG554 . . . . **E**
TORTILLITAS PARA MAMA AND OTHER SPANISH NURSERY RHYMES. /1981/1-3/KB816 . . . . **398.8**
TREE IS OLDER THAN YOU ARE: A BILINGUAL GATHERING OF POEMS AND STORIES FROM /1995/5-A/KE121. . . . . . . **860.9**

TUN-TA-CA-TUN: MORE STORIES AND POEMS IN ENGLISH
AND SPANISH FOR CHILDREN. /1986/K-6/KD905...... **810.8**
VALERI, M/Mi casa es su casa/my house is your house: a bi-lingual
musical journey through /1991/K-3/KD663........ **SRC 789.3**
VIGIL, A/Corn woman: stories and legends of the Hispanic
Southwest/La mujer del maiz: /1994/5-6/4 KB380. .... **CE 398.2**

Bilingual materials--Spanish--Software.
AESOP'S FABLE: THE TORTOISE AND THE HARE (CD-ROM). /
1993/P-A/KB522 .... **CDR 398.24**
ARTHUR'S TEACHER TROUBLE (CD-ROM). /1992/
1-4/KF171............................. **CDR E**
BERENSTAIN BEARS GET IN A FIGHT. SCHOOL ED. (CD-ROM).
/1995/K-3/KF223....................... **CDR E**
BROWN, MT/Arthur's teacher trouble (Microcomputer program). /
1994/2-6/KB109..................... **MCP 372.6**
JUST GRANDMA AND ME (CD-ROM). /1992/
P-2/KF863 .... **CDR E**
KID PIX STUDIO (CD-ROM). /1994/P-A/KD468 ... **CDR 750.28**
MARC BROWN'S ARTHUR'S BIRTHDAY. SCHOOL ED. (CD-ROM).
/1994/K-4/KG062 .... **CDR E**
MARK SCHLICHTING'S HARRY AND THE HAUNTED HOUSE.
SCHOOL ED. /1994/K-3/KG063......... **CDR E**
MERCER MAYER'S LITTLE MONSTER AT SCHOOL. SCHOOL ED.
(CD-ROM). /1994/K-3/KG130........ **CDR E**
MULTIMEDIA WORKSHOP. TEACHER ED. (CD-ROM). /1996/
3-A/KB115.......................... **CDR 372.6**
NEW KID PIX. SCHOOL VERSION (MICROCOMPUTER
PROGRAM). /1996/P-A/KD469 .... **MCP 750.28**
STORYBOOK WEAVER DELUXE (CD-ROM). /1995/
1-5/KB118......................... **CDR 372.6**

Bill of Rights SEE United States. Constitution.
Billion (The number).
HOW MUCH IS A MILLION? (VIDEOCASSETTE). /1997/
K-1/KB947........................... **VCR 513**
SCHWARTZ, DM/How much is a million? /1985/
K-1/2 KB950 .... **513**

Biodegradation.
COBB, V/Lots of rot. /1981/K-3/3 KC302 .... **577.1**
EMORY, J/Dirty, rotten, dead? /1996/4-6/10 KC303 ..... **577.1**
RING, E/What rot!: nature's mighty recycler. /1996/
1-3/3 KC304 .... **577.1**

Biogeochemical cycles.
EMORY, J/Dirty, rotten, dead? /1996/4-6/10 KC303 ..... **577.1**

Biography--Dictionaries.
BIOGRAPHY FOR BEGINNERS: SKETCHES FOR EARLY READERS.
/1995/-/3-5/KA476 .... **REF 920**
CURRENT BIOGRAPHY YEARBOOK. /1967-/5-6/KA477 . **REF 920**
EXPLORERS AND DISCOVERERS: FROM ALEXANDER THE GREAT
TO SALLY RIDE. /1995/5-A/KA470 ...... **REF 910**
HISPANIC AMERICAN BIOGRAPHY. /1995/
5-A/KA400 .... **REF 305.8**
NATIVE NORTH AMERICAN BIOGRAPHY. /1996/
6-A/KA481 .... **REF 970.1**
PARE, MA/Sports stars. /1994/5-A/KA457 .... **REF 796**
WORLD LEADERS: PEOPLE WHO SHAPED THE WORLD. /1994/
5-A/KA408 .... **REF 350**

Biography (as a literary form)--Study and teaching (Elementary).
ZARNOWSKI, M/Learning about biographies: a reading-and-writing
approach for children. /1990//KA334............. **PROF 808**

Biological diversity.
PATENT, DH/Biodiversity. /1996/5-6/9 KA964 .... **333.95**

Biological diversity conservation.
PATENT, DH/Biodiversity. /1996/5-6/9 KA964 .... **333.95**

Biologists.
PRINGLE, LP/Scorpion man: exploring the world of scorpions. /
1994/5-6/8 KC530 .... **595.4**
RANSOM, CF/Listening to crickets: a story about Rachel Carson. /
1993/5-6/6 KE278 .... **B CARSON, R.**
YOUNT, L/Antoni van Leeuwenhoek: first to see microscopic life. /
1996/5-A/5 KE432 .... **B LEEUWENHOEK,A**

Biology SEE ALSO Adaptation (Biology); Anatomy; Botany; Cells; Evolution;
Freshwater biology; Genetics; Heredity; Marine biology; Microbiology;
Natural history; Physiology; Reproduction; Seashore biology; Zoology.

Biology.
STEIN, S/Science book. /1979/2-A/5 KB873 .... **500**
ZOEHFELD, KW/What's alive? /1995/1-3/2 KC301 .... **577**

Biology--Classification.
REALMS OF LIFE (PICTURE). /1996/6-A/KC356 ...... **PIC 578**

Biology--Dictionaries.
BURNIE, D/Dictionary of nature. /1994/3-A/KA445 .... **REF 570**

Biology--Encyclopedias.
BURNIE, D/Dictionary of nature. /1994/3-A/KA445 .... **REF 570**

Biology--Experiments.
VANCLEAVE, JP/Biology for every kid: 101 easy experiments that
really work. /1989/P-4/8 KC270 .... **570**

Biology--Software.
VARIATIONS IN LIFE SCIENCE INVESTIGATIONS (CD-ROM). /
1996/6-A/KC298 .... **CDR 577**

Biomechanics--Software.
ALEXANDER, RM/How animals move (CD-ROM). /1995/
4-A/KC464 .... **CDR 591.47**

Bird houses.
SCHUTZ, WE/How to attract, house and feed birds. /c1974/
3-6/KC663 .... **598**

Bird watching.
FORSHAW, J/Birding. /c1994, 1995/5-6/8 KA448 .... **REF 598**
Birds SEE ALSO names of specific species e.g. Robins.

Birds.
ARNOSKY, J/Crinkleroot's guide to knowing the birds. /1992/
2-5/6 KC644 .... **598**
Crinkleroot's 25 birds every child should know. /1993/
P-2/3 KC645 .... **598**
Watching water birds. /1997/4-6/6 KC674. ...... **598.176**
BASKIN-SALZBERG, A/Flightless birds. /1993/
5-6/7 KC691 .... **598.5**
BIRDS IN THE CITY: A FIRST FILM. 2ND ED. (VIDEOCASSETTE). /
1992/2-6/KC646 .... **VCR 598**
BROWN, MB/Wings along the waterway. /1992/
5-6/6 KC675 .... **598.176**
BURNIE, D/Bird. /1988/A/9 KC648 .... **598**
EHLERT, L/Feathers for lunch. /1990/P-1/2 KF517 .... **E**
FORSHAW, J/Birding. /c1994, 1995/5-6/8 KA448 .... **REF 598**
FRISKEY, M/Birds we know. /1981/P-2/2 KC649 .... **598**
HENDERSON AVENUE BUG PATROL (VIDEOCASSETTE). /1984/
1-6/KB867 .... **VCR 500**
HICKMAN, PM/Birdwise: forty fun feats for finding out about our
feathered friends. /1988/4-6/6 KC650 .... **598**
JENKINS, PB/Nest full of eggs. /1995/K-2/2 KC705 ..... **598.8**
KRULIK, NE/Birds. /1993/2-4/4 KC652 .... **598**
LANDAU, E/State birds: including the Commonwealth of Puerto
Rico. /1992/4-6/8 KC653. .... **598**
MARKLE, S/Outside and inside birds. /1994/4-6/5 KC655... **598**
MAZZOLA, F/Counting is for the birds. /1997/
K-3/3 KB968 .... **513.2**
O'CONNOR, K/Feather book. /1990/5-6/6 KC670 .... **598.147**
PARSONS, A/Amazing birds. /1990/3-6/5 KC658........ **598**
PATENT, DH/Feathers. /1992/5-6/6 KC671 .... **598.147**
ROCKWELL, AF/Our yard is full of birds. /1992/
K-2/4 KC662 .... **598**
SELSAM, ME/Egg to chick. Rev. ed. /1970/P-2/2 KC698 .. **598.6**
SILL, C/About birds: a guide for children. /1991/
K-2/1 KC664 .... **598**
SNEDDEN, R/What is a bird? /1993/4-6/6 KC665 .... **598**
TAYLOR, B/Bird atlas. /1993/4-6/9 KA449. .... **REF 598**
WATTS, B/Birds' nest. /1986/2-5/2 KC706. .... **598.8**

Birds--Attracting.
FORSHAW, J/Birding. /c1994, 1995/5-6/8 KA448 .... **REF 598**
LERNER, C/Backyard birds of summer. /1996/5-6/7 KC654 .. **598**
SCHUTZ, WE/How to attract, house and feed birds. /c1974/
3-6/KC663. .... **598**

Birds--Development.
REIDEL, M/From egg to bird. /1981/P-2/2 KC661 ..... **598**

Birds--Eggs and nests.
BASH, B/Urban roosts: where birds nest in the city. /1990/
3-6/7 KC672 .... **598.156**

Birds--Fiction.
ASCH, F/Moonbear's pet. /1997/P-K/2 KF175 .... **E**
BUNTING, E/Fly away home. /1991/K-3/2 KF300 .... **E**
CANNON, J/Stellaluna. /1993/K-2/3 KF334. .... **E**
Stellaluna (Talking book). /1996/K-2/KF335 .... **TB E**
EASTMAN, PD/Are you my mother? /c1960/P-1/1 KF504..... **E**
Are you my mother? plus two more P.D. Eastman classics
(Videocassette). /1991/P-1/KF505 .... **VCR E**
EHLERT, L/Feathers for lunch. /1990/P-1/2 KF517 .... **E**
KELLER, H/Island baby. /1992/P-2/3 KF885 .... **E**
LEWIN, B/Booby hatch. /1995/K-2/2 KF973 .... **E**
O'MALLEY, K/Who killed Cock Robin? /1993/1-3/2 KG191... **E**
PINDAL, K/Peep and the big wide world (Videocassette). /1991/
P-2/KG239 .... **VCR E**
POMERANTZ, C/One duck, another duck. /1984/P-1/1 KG265 .. **E**
RAU, DM/Robin at Hickory Street. /1995/K-2/3 KG314 ... **CE E**
ROHMANN, E/Time flies. /1994/1-3/KG349 .... **E**
WIKLER, L/Alfonse, where are you? /1996/P-K/1 KG715....... **E**
WILHELM, H/Royal raven. /1996/K-2/2 KG723. .... **E**

Birds--Fiction--Software.
STELLALUNA (CD-ROM). /1996/K-3/KG550. .... **CDR E**

Birds--Folklore.
BRUCHAC, J/Great ball game: a Muskogee story. /1994/
2-4/2 KB539 . . . . **398.24**
HAMILTON, V/When birds could talk and bats could sing: the
adventures of Bruh Sparrow, Sis /1996/2-5/2 KB582 . . . . **398.24**

Birds--Habits and behavior.
FRISKEY, M/Birds we know. /1981/P-2/2 KC649 . . . . **598**
JENKINS, PB/Nest full of eggs. /1995/K-2/2 KC705 . . . . . **598.8**
LERNER, C/Backyard birds of summer. /1996/5-6/7 KC654 . . **598**
SPRING (VIDEOCASSETTE). /1994/2-5/KC666 . . . . **VCR 598**
WILLIS, NC/Robins in your backyard. /1996/K-3/5 KC707 . . **598.8**
WINTER (VIDEOCASSETTE). /1994/2-5/KC669 . . . . . . **VCR 598**

Birds--Migration.
GANS, R/How do birds find their way? /1996/
3-4/2 KC673 . . . . **598.156**

Birds--Nests--Folklore.
FOSTER, J/Magpies' nest. /1995/1-3/3 KB567 . . . . **398.24**

Birds--North America.
BULL, J/Audubon Society field guide to North American birds--
Eastern Region. /1994/3-6/7 KC647 . . . . **598**
LERNER, C/Backyard birds of summer. /1996/5-6/7 KC654 . . **598**
PETERSON, RT/Field guide to the birds: a completely new guide to
all birds of eastern and central North America. 4th ed. /1980/
4-6/7 KC659 . . . . **598**
Field guide to western birds. 3rd ed. /1990/4-6/7 KC660 . . **598**
SPRING (VIDEOCASSETTE). /1994/2-5/KC666 . . . . **VCR 598**
SWANSON, D/Sky dancers: the amazing world of North American
birds. /1995/4-5/5 KC667 . . . . **598**
UDVARDY, MD/Audubon Society field guide to North American
birds--Western Region. /1977/3-6/7 KC668 . . . . **598**
WINTER (VIDEOCASSETTE). /1994/2-5/KC669 . . . . . . **VCR 598**

Birds--Periodicals.
AUDUBON MAGAZINE: THE MAGAZINE OF THE NATIONAL
AUDUBON SOCIETY. /1899-/5-6/KA501 . . . . **PER 050**

Birds--Poetry.
FLORIAN, D/On the wing: bird poems and paintings. /1996/
1-4/KD939 . . . . **811**

Birds--Protection.
ARNOLD, C/Saving the peregrine falcon. /1990/
4-6/7 KC708 . . . . **598.9**
AUDUBON MAGAZINE: THE MAGAZINE OF THE NATIONAL
AUDUBON SOCIETY. /1899-/5-6/KA501 . . . . **PER 050**
PATENT, DH/Whooping crane: a comeback story. /1988/
A/9 KD258 . . . . **639.9**

Birds--Protection--Fiction.
LASKY, K/She's wearing a dead bird on her head! /1995/
3-5/5 KH386 . . . . **Fic**
Birds, Extinct SEE Extinct birds.
Birds of prey SEE ALSO names of specific species e.g. Eagles.

Birds of prey--Wounds and injuries--Treatment.
JOHNSON, SA/Raptor rescue!: an eagle flies free. /1995/
5-6/7 KD254 . . . . **639.9**
Birds' nests SEE Birds-Eggs and nests.
Birth SEE ALSO Childbirth.

Birth--Fiction.
BROWN, C/In the spring. /1994/P-1/2 KF269 . . . . **E**
FRASIER, D/On the day you were born. /1991/P-3/5 KF577 . . . **E**
ON THE DAY YOU WERE BORN (VIDEOCASSETTE). /1996/
P-A/KG192 . . . . **VCR E**

Birth customs.
KNIGHT, MB/Welcoming babies. /1994/P-1/2 KA875 . . . **306.87**

Birthday cakes--Fiction.
KLINTING, L/Bruno the baker. /1997/P-2/2 KF911 . . . . **E**

Birthdays.
CHARLIP, R/Handtalk birthday: a number and story book in sign
language. /1987/K-3/KB824 . . . . **419**

Birthdays--Fiction.
ADLER, DA/Young Cam Jansen and the dinosaur game. /1996/
1-2/2 KF132 . . . . **E**
ASCH, F/Happy birthday, moon. /1982/P-1/2 KF174 . . . . . **CE E**
BARKER, M/Magical hands. /1989/1-3/5 KF199 . . . . **E**
BIRTHDAY SURPRISES: TEN GREAT STORIES TO UNWRAP. /
1995/5-A/6 KG900 . . . . **Fic**
BUNTING, E/Flower garden. /1994/P-2/3 KF299 . . . . **E**
CASELEY, J/Slumber party! /1996/2-3/2 KF369 . . . . **E**
DRAGONWAGON, C/Annie flies the birthday bike. /1993/
K-2/2 KF495 . . . . **E**
FLACK, M/Ask Mr. Bear. /c1932/P-1/2 KF549 . . . . **CE E**
HEST, A/Jamaica Louise James. /1996/K-2/2 KF719 . . . . **E**
Nana's birthday party. /1993/1-3/4 KF720 . . . . **E**
HOBAN, R/Birthday for Frances. /c1968, 1995/P-1/2 KF740 . . . **E**
HOFF, S/Happy birthday, Danny and the dinosaur! /1995/
K-1/2 KF756 . . . . **E**
JONAS, A/13th clue. /1992/1-2/1 KF851 . . . . **E**

KLEVEN, E/Hooray! A pinata! /1996/K-2/2 KF910 . . . . **E**
KLINE, S/Herbie Jones and the birthday showdown. /1995/
3-4/3 KH366 . . . . **Fic**
LOPEZ, L/Birthday swap. /1997/K-2/2 KG032 . . . . **E**
MORA, P/Uno, dos, tres: one, two, three. /1996/P-1/3 KG155 . **E**
NOLL, S/Surprise! /1997/P-K/2 KG179 . . . . **E**
PARISH, P/Be ready at eight. /1996/1-2/1 KG212 . . . . **E**
Scruffy. /1988/K-3/1 KG217 . . . . **E**
POLACCO, P/Some birthday! /1991/K-2/4 KG257 . . . . **E**
PRAGER, A/Baseball birthday party. /1995/1-3/2 KG286 . . . . **E**
RICE, E/Benny bakes a cake. /c1981, 1993/P-2/2 KG330 . . . . . **E**
RYLANT, C/Birthday presents. /1991/P-1/2 KG368 . . . . **E**
SIS, P/Going up! A color counting book. /1989/P-2/KG511 . . . **E**
SPIRN, M/Know-Nothing birthday. /1997/1-2/1 KG533 . . . . . **E**
WABER, B/Lyle and the birthday party. /c1966/P-2/3 KG669 . . **E**
WALTER, MP/Have a happy... a novel. /1989/4-6/4 KH838 . . . **Fic**
WELLS, R/Edward in deep water. /1995/P-K/2 KG697 . . . . . . **E**
YEP, L/Later, Gator. /1995/4-6/4 KH893 . . . . **Fic**
ZOLOTOW, C/Mr. Rabbit and the lovely present. /c1962/
P-2/2 KG804 . . . . **CE E**

Birthdays--Fiction--Software.
MARC BROWN'S ARTHUR'S BIRTHDAY. SCHOOL ED. (CD-ROM).
/1994/K-4/KG062 . . . . **CDR E**

Bismarck (Battleship).
BALLARD, RD/Exploring the Bismarck. /1991/
5-6/7 KE668 . . . . **940.54**
Bison SEE ALSO Buffaloes.

Bison.
BERMAN, R/American bison. /1992/5-6/7 KC790 . . . . . . **599.64**
LEPTHIEN, EU/Buffalo. /1989/3-5/5 KC791 . . . . **599.64**
PATENT, DH/Buffalo: the American Bison today. /1986/
5-6/8 KA965 . . . . **333.95**

Bison--Fiction.
STILZ, CC/Grandma Buffalo, May, and me. /1995/
1-3/3 KG573 . . . . **E**

Bison--Folklore.
ESBENSEN, BJ/Great buffalo race: how the buffalo got its hump: a
Seneca tale. /1994/3-4/6 KB564 . . . . **398.24**
Black art SEE Afro-American artists.
Black athletes SEE Afro-American athletes.
Black authors SEE Afro-American authors.

Black bear.
BRENNER, B/Two orphan cubs. /1989/K-2/2 KC848 . . . . . **599.78**
FAIR, J/Black bear magic for kids. /1991/4-5/5 KC849 . . . **599.78**
PRINGLE, LP/Bearman: exploring the world of black bears. /1989/
5-6/7 KC852 . . . . **599.78**

Black Carib Indians--Fiction.
LONDON, J/Village basket weaver. /1996/2-3/6 KG029 . . . . . **E**
Black poetry SEE Afro-Americans--Poetry.
Black soldiers SEE Afro-American soldiers.

Black widow spider.
BITE OF THE BLACK WIDOW (VIDEOCASSETTE). /1994/
5-6/KC523 . . . . **VCR 595.4**

Blackbirds--Fiction.
DE PAOLA, T/Days of the blackbird: a tale of northern Italy. /
1997/1-3/6 KF468 . . . . **E**

Blacks--Africa--Music.
SILVERMAN, J/African roots. /1994/5-A/KD590 . . . . **789.2**

Blacks--Biography.
COOPER, F/Mandela: from the life of the South African statesman.
/1996/3-6/7 KE457 . . . . **B MANDELA, N.**

Blacks--Caribbean Area--Fiction.
TAYLOR, T/Timothy of the cay. /1993/5-A/5 KH785 . . . . **Fic**

Blacks--England--Fiction.
JAMES, S/Leon and Bob. /1997/K-2/2 KF824 . . . . **E**
RICHEMONT, E/Magic skateboard. /1992/3-5/3 KH631 . . . . . **Fic**

Blacks--Fiction.
ALEXANDER, L/Fortune-tellers. /1992/2-5/5 KG834 . . . . . . **Fic**
HAARHOFF, D/Desert December. /1992/3-5/4 KH206 . . . . . **Fic**
TAYLOR, T/Cay. /c1969/5-6/6 KH783 . . . . **Fic**

Blacks--Folklore.
RAW HEAD, BLOODY BONES: AFRICAN-AMERICAN TALES OF
THE SUPERNATURAL. /1991/4-6/4 KB361 . . . . **398.2**
SHUTE, L/Rabbit wishes. /1995/K-2/2 KB651 . . . . **398.24**

Blacks--Haiti--Biography.
LAWRENCE, J/Toussaint L'Ouverture: the fight for Haiti's freedom.
/1996/4-A/8 KE569 . . . . **B TOUSSAINT**

Blacks--Haiti--Fiction.
LAUTURE, D/Running the road to ABC. /1996/1-3/4 KF951 . . . . **E**
TEMPLE, F/Tonight, by sea: a novel. /1995/6-A/5 KH789 . . . . **Fic**

Blacks--Nigeria--Biography.
GUTMAN, B/Hakeem Olajuwon: superstar center. /1995/
4-5/6 KE483 . . . . **B OLAJUWON, H.**

Blacks--Puerto Rico--Fiction.
PICO, F/Red comb. /1994/3-5/7 KH601 . . . . **Fic**

Blacks--South Africa--Fiction.
ISADORA, R/Over the green hills. /1992/1-3/2 KF817 . . . . **E**
NAIDOO, B/No turning back: a novel of South Africa. /1997/
6-A/6 KH526 . . . . **Fic**
SACKS, M/Themba. /1994/3-5/5 KH670 . . . . **Fic**
SISULU, E/Day Gogo went to vote: South Africa, April 1994. /
1996/1-3/2 KG513 . . . . **E**

Blacks--Zimbabwe--Fiction.
FARMER, N/Ear, the Eye and the Arm: a novel. /1994/
6-A/4 KH108 . . . . **Fic**

Blair, Bonnie.
DALY, W/Bonnie Blair: power on ice. /1996/
4-6/6 KE255 . . . . **B BLAIR, B.**

Blankets--Fiction.
HENKES, K/Owen. /1993/P-2/2 KF709 . . . . **E**
Owen (Videocassette). /1995/P-2/KF710 . . . . **VCR E**

Bleriot, Louis.
PROVENSEN, A/Glorious flight: across the channel with Louis
Bleriot. /1983/K-2/4 KD098 . . . . **CE 629.13**

Blind.
MCMAHON, P/Listen for the bus: David's story. /1995/
1-3/3 KB004 . . . . **362.4**
MOORE, E/Buddy: the first seeing eye dog. /1996/
1-3/3 KB006 . . . . **362.4**

Blind--Biography.
ADLER, DA/Picture book of Louis Braille. /1997/
2-3/3 KE261 . . . . **B BRAILLE, L.**
FREEDMAN, R/Out of darkness: the story of Louis Braille. /1997/
3-5/6 KE262 . . . . **B BRAILLE, L.**
HELEN KELLER (VIDEOCASSETTE). /1990/
4-6/KE415 . . . . **VCR B KELLER, H.**
KELLER, H/Story of my life. /c1988, 1990/
6-A/8 KE416 . . . . **B KELLER, H.**
LUNDELL, M/Girl named Helen Keller. /1995/
1-2/1 KE417 . . . . **B KELLER, H.**
MIND'S EYE: JEAN LITTLE (VIDEOCASSETTE). /1996/
5-6/KE445 . . . . **VCR B LITTLE, J.**
TURK, R/Ray Charles: soul man. /1996/
5-A/8 KE286 . . . . **B CHARLES, R.**

Blind--Books and reading.
EXPECTATIONS. /1948/-3-6/KD873 . . . . **808.8**

Blind--Fiction.
BAWDEN, N/Witch's daughter. /c1966, 1991/5-A/6 KG893 . . **Fic**
CARRICK, C/Melanie. /1996/1-3/2 KF360 . . . . **E**
DORRIS, M/Sees Behind Trees. /1996/5-A/4 KH081 . . . . . . **Fic**
MCKENZIE, EK/Stargone John. /1990/3-5/5 KH484 . . . . **Fic**
MOON, N/Lucy's picture. /1995/P-1/2 KG153 . . . . **E**
TAYLOR, T/Cay. /c1969/5-6/6 KH783 . . . . **Fic**
Timothy of the cay. /1993/5-A/5 KH785 . . . . **Fic**
WILDER, LI/Little house in the Big Woods. /c1953/
3-6/4 KH860 . . . . **Fic**

Blind--Folklore.
DEARMOND, D/Seal oil lamp. /1988/5-6/6 KB499 . . . . . **398.23**

Blizzards.
OTFINOSKI, S/Blizzards. /1994/4-6/7 KB036 . . . . **363.34**

Blizzards--Fiction.
NOBLE, TH/Apple tree Christmas. /1984/K-3/6 KG175 . . . . . . **E**

Blood.
PARKER, S/Heart and blood. Rev. ed. /1989/5-6/8 KC933 . **612.1**
SHOWERS, P/Drop of blood. Rev. ed. /1989/
K-2/2 KC936 . . . . **612.1**

Blood--Circulation.
PARKER, S/Heart and blood. Rev. ed. /1989/5-6/8 KC933 . **612.1**
SIMON, S/Heart: our circulatory system. /1996/
5-A/6 KC937 . . . . **612.1**
YOUR BODY: CIRCULATORY AND RESPIRATORY SYSTEMS
(VIDEOCASSETTE). /1988/5-6/KC931 . . . . **VCR 612**

Blood cells.
COLE, J/Cuts, breaks, bruises and burns: how your body heals. /
1985/4-6/6 KC932 . . . . **612.1**

Bloodsucking animals.
LABONTE, G/Leeches, lampreys, and other cold-blooded
bloodsuckers. /1991/5-6/7 KC505 . . . . **592**

Blue Ridge Mountains--Fiction.
RANSOM, CF/When the whippoorwill calls. /1995/
1-3/2 KG305 . . . . **E**

Blue tit.
WATTS, B/Birds' nest. /1986/2-5/2 KC706. . . . . **598.8**

Blue whale.
DAVIES, N/Big blue whale. /1997/K-4/3 KC767 . . . . **599.5**
KIM, M/Blue whale. /1993/3-5/7 KC772 . . . . **599.5**

Blue-footed booby--Fiction.
LEWIN, B/Booby hatch. /1995/K-2/2 KF973 . . . . **E**

Bluegrass music--United States.
HOLT, D/Grandfather's greatest hits (Sound recording cassette). /
1991/K-4/KD569 . . . . **SRC 789.2**

Blues (Music).
SILVERMAN, J/Blues. /1994/5-A/KD671 . . . . **789.43**

Bly, Nellie.
KENDALL, ME/Nellie Bly: reporter for the world. /1992/
4-6/5 KE256 . . . . **B BLY, N.**

Bly, Nellie--Fiction.
BLOS, JW/Nellie Bly's monkey: his remarkable story in his own
words. /1996/2-5/9 KF236. **E**

Boa constrictors--Fiction.
NOBLE, TH/Day Jimmy's boa ate the wash. /1980/
K-2/2 KG176 . . . . **CE E**
Boarding houses SEE Lodging houses.

Boarding schools--Fiction.
BUNTING, E/Cheyenne again. /1995/3-5/2 KG941 . . . . **Fic**
Spying on Miss Muller. /1995/6-A/6 KG944 . . . . **Fic**
BURNETT, FH/Little princess. /c1963/5-A/8 KG949 . . . . . . **Fic**
Sara Crewe. /1986/4-6/7 KG950 . . . . **Fic**
CARRIER, R/Basketball player. /1996/4-6/3 KG975 . . . . . . **Fic**
JONES, DW/Witch week. New ed. /c1982, 1993/
6-A/6 KH335 . . . . **Fic**
KORMAN, G/Zucchini warriors. /1991/5-A/7 KH378 . . . . . . **Fic**
Boats and boating SEE ALSO Boatbuilding; Sailboat racing; Sailing;
Steamboats.

Boats and boating.
BARTON, B/Boats. /1986/P-1/2 KB151 . . . . **387.2**
CREWS, D/Harbor. /1982/P-1/KD062 . . . . **623.8**
GIBBONS, G/Boat book. /1983/P-2/3 KB152 . . . . **387.2**
STEELE, P/Boats. /1991/4-6/6 KD065 . . . . **623.8**
TUGBOATS: MASTERS OF OUR HARBORS (VIDEOCASSETTE). /
1996/2-4/KB153 . . . . **VCR 387.2**

Boats and boating--Fiction.
BURNINGHAM, J/Mr. Gumpy's outing. /c1970/
P-2/2 KF318 . . . . **CE E**
CREWS, D/Sail away. /1995/P-2/2 KF434 . . . . **E**
MCDONNELL, F/I love boats. /1995/P-1/3 KG101 . . . . **E**
RAND, G/Salty dog. /1991/2-3/5 KG301 . . . . **E**

Boats and boating--History.
KENTLEY, E/Boat. /1992/5-6/7 KD063 . . . . **623.8**
LINCOLN, M/Amazing boats. /1992/3-5/5 KD064 . . . . **623.8**

Bodmer, Karl--Journeys--Missouri River Valley.
FREEDMAN, R/Indian winter. /1992/A/9 KE202 . . . . . . **917.804**
Body, Human SEE ALSO Anatomy; Physiology.

Body, Human.
BOOTH, J/You animal! /1996/4-6/5 KC913 . . . . **612**
COLE, J/Magic School Bus inside the human body. /1989/
2-5/5 KC916 . . . . **612**
FORNARI, G/Inside the body: a lift-the-flap book. /1996/
5-6/7 KC902 . . . . **611**
GABB, M/Human body. /c1991, 1992/5-6/6 KC918 . . . . . . **612**
GANERI, A/Funny bones. /1997/3-6/6 KC903 . . . . **611**
What's inside us? /1995/5-6/8 KC919 . . . . **612**
LIVING WORLD. /1993/5-A/KA437 . . . . **REF 508**
LOOK WHO'S GROWING UP (VIDEOCASSETTE). /1997/
5-6/KC920. . . . . **VCR 612**
MARKLE, S/Outside and inside you. /1991/4-6/4 KC921 . . . **612**
MY BODY. /1991/1-4/2 KC922 . . . . **612**
PARKER, S/Body and how it works. /1992/A/6 KC923. . . . . **612**
Body atlas. /1993/A/7 KC905 . . . . **611**
VISUAL DICTIONARY OF THE HUMAN BODY. /1991/
4-6/8 KC907 . . . . **611**
WALKER, R/Children's atlas of the human body: actual size bones,
muscles, and organs in /1994/5-6/6 KC908 . . . . **611**
WHAT IS A BELLYBUTTON?: FIRST QUESTIONS AND ANSWERS
ABOUT THE HUMAN BODY. /1993/P-K/2 KC929 . . . . . . **612**

Body, Human--Dictionaries.
RICHARDSON, J/Science dictionary of the human body. /1992/
4-6/7 KC906 . . . . **611**

Body, Human--Experiments.
VANCLEAVE, JP/Janice VanCleave's the human body for every kid:
easy activities that make /1995/5-6/8 KC928 . . . . **612**

Body, Human--Fiction.
MARTIN, JR., B/Here are my hands. /1987/P-1/2 KG076 . . . . . **E**

Body, Human--Software.
SCHOLASTIC'S THE MAGIC SCHOOL BUS EXPLORES THE
HUMAN BODY. SCHOOL ED. (CD-ROM). /1995/
2-A/KC925 . . . . **CDR 612**
STV: HUMAN BODY (VIDEODISC). /1992/4-A/KC926 . . **VD 612**
ULTIMATE HUMAN BODY (CD-ROM). /1996/
4-A/KC927 . . . . **CDR 612**

WHAT IS A BELLYBUTTON?: FUN AND INTERACTIVE
QUESTIONS AND ANSWERS ABOUT THE HUMAN BODY (CD-
ROM). /1994/2-6/KC930. . . . . **CDR 612**

Body covering (Anatomy).
LAMPRELL, K/Scaly things. /1996/4-6/5 KC616. . . . . 597.9
ZOEHFELD, KW/What lives in a shell? /1994/P-1/2 KC517 . . 594

Bolivar, Simon.
ADLER, DA/Picture book of Simon Bolivar. /1992/
3-4/5 KE257 . . . . **B BOLIVAR, S.**

Bolivia--Social life and customs.
HERMES, J/Children of Bolivia. /1996/4-6/10 KF108 984

Bonds, Barry.
SAVAGE, J/Barry Bonds: Mr. Excitement. /1997/
4-6/3 KE258 . . . . **B BONDS, B.**
Bones SEE ALSO Skeleton.

Bones.
PARKER, S/Skeleton. /1988/5-6/8 KC285 . . . . 573.7
SAUNDERSON, J/Muscles and bones. /1992/
5-6/6 KC959 . . . . 612.7
VISUAL DICTIONARY OF THE SKELETON. /1995/
4-A/8 KC286 . . . . 573.7
YOUR BODY: MUSCULAR AND SKELETAL SYSTEMS
(VIDEOCASSETTE). /1994/5-6/KC961 . . . . **VCR 612.7**

Bones--Fiction.
JOHNSTON, T/Ghost of Nicholas Greebe. /1996/
3-5/6 KH328 . . . . Fic

Book design.
SWAIN, G/Bookworks: making books by hand. /1995/
3-6/5 KD437 . . . . 745.5
Book illustration SEE Illustration of books.

Book industries and trade.
ALIKI /How a book is made. /1986/K-3/3 KD345 686

Book reviewing.
HORNING, KT/From cover to cover: evaluating and reviewing
children's books. /1997/KA085 . . . . **PROF 028.1**

Book selection.
WHAT'S A GOOD BOOK? (VIDEOCASSETTE). /1993/
/KA094. **VCR PROF 028.5**

Book talks.
BAUER, CF/Leading kids to books through magic. /1996/
/KA066. . . . . **PROF 027.62**
BOOKTALK! 5: MORE SELECTIONS FROM THE BOOKTALKER
FOR ALL AGES AND AUDIENCES. /1993/KA090. **PROF 028.5**
GILLESPIE, JT/Juniorplots 4: a book talk guide for use with readers
ages 12-16. /1993/KA091 . . . . **PROF 028.5**
Middleplots 4: a book talk guide for use with readers ages 8-12.
/1994/KA092 . . . . **PROF 028.5**
THOMAS, RL/Primaryplots 2: a book talk guide for use with
readers ages 4-8. /1993/KA093. . . . . **PROF 028.5**

Bookbinding.
CHAPMAN, G/Making books. /1992/3-6/7 KD412 . . . . . 741.6

Bookmarks.
BRODIE, CS/Bookmark book. /1996/KA310 . . . . . **PROF 741.6**
Books SEE ALSO Authors; Children's literature; Illustration of books;
Libraries; Literature; Paperback books; Printing; Publishers and publishing.

Books.
ALIKI /How a book is made. /1986/K-3/3 KD345 686
CHAPMAN, G/Making books. /1992/3-6/7 KD412 . . . . . 741.6
GUTHRIE, D/Young author's do-it-yourself book: how to write,
illustrate, and produce your /1994/2-6/4 KD863 808
SWAIN, G/Bookworks: making books by hand. /1995/
3-6/5 KD437 . . . . 745.5

Books--History.
BROOKFIELD, K/Book. /1993/4-A/9 KA565 002

Books--Reviews.
BOOK LINKS: CONNECTING BOOKS, LIBRARIES AND
CLASSROOMS. /1991-//KA097 . . . . **PER PROF 050**
BOOKLIST. /1905-//KA098 . . . . **PER PROF 050**
CANADIAN CHILDREN'S LITERATURE. /1975-/
/KA100. . . . . **PER PROF 050**
SCIENCE BOOKS AND FILMS. /1975-//KA145. . **PER PROF 050**
Books and reading SEE ALSO Books--Reviews; Children's literature;
Libraries; Literature; Reference books.

Books and reading.
BAUER, CF/This way to books. /1983//KA089 . . . . **PROF 028.5**
BOOKTALK! 5: MORE SELECTIONS FROM THE BOOKTALKER
FOR ALL AGES AND AUDIENCES. /1993//KA090. **PROF 028.5**
CULLINAN, BE/Literature and the child. 3rd ed. /1993/
/KA348. . . . . **PROF 809**
DEAR LAURA: LETTERS FROM CHILDREN TO LAURA INGALLS
WILDER. /1996/3-6/KD893 . . . . 808.86
HAZARD, P/Books, children and men. 5th ed. /1983/
/KA351. . . . . **PROF 809**

KRASHEN, S/Power of reading: insights from the research. /1993/
/KA082. . . . . **PROF 028**
POLETTE, N/ABC's of books and thinking skills. /1987/
/KA156. . . . . **PROF 153.4**

Books and reading--Best books.
AMMON, BD/Handbook for the Newbery Medal and Honor Books,
1980-1989. /1991//KA347 . . . . **PROF 809**
BOOK LINKS: CONNECTING BOOKS, LIBRARIES AND
CLASSROOMS. /1991-//KA097 . . . . **PER PROF 050**
BOOKLIST. /1905-//KA098 . . . . **PER PROF 050**

Books and reading--Fiction.
BRADBY, M/More than anything else. /1995/1-3/3 KF256. . . . . E
CASELEY, J/Sophie and Sammy's library sleepover. /1993/
P-1/4 KF370 . . . . E
LEVINSON, NS/Clara and the bookwagon. /1988/
1-3/1 KF967 . . . . E
MCPHAIL, D/Edward and the pirates. /1997/K-2/3 KG117 . . . . E
POLACCO, P/Aunt Chip and the great Triple Creek Dam affair. /
1996/2-4/2 KG248. . . . . E
Bee tree. /1993/K-2/3 KG250. . . . . E
RYLANT, C/Poppleton. /1997/K-2/2 KG384 . . . . E
STEWART, S/Library. /1995/K-3/3 KG572. . . . . **CE E**

Books and reading--History.
KRENSKY, S/Breaking into print: before and after the invention of
the printing press. /1996/3-5/5 KD346 . . . . 686.2

Books and reading--Poetry.
GOOD BOOKS, GOOD TIMES! /1990/K-3/KE060 . . . . 811.008

Books and reading--Software.
READABILITY ANALYSIS (MICROCOMPUTER PROGRAM). /1994/
/KA213. . . . . **MCP PROF 372.4**
Books for children SEE Books and reading; Children's literature.
Books for the blind SEE Blind--Books and reading.

Bookstores--Fiction.
WHEELER, C/Bookstore cat. /1994/K-2/2 KG709 . . . . E

Boone, Daniel.
DANIEL BOONE'S FINAL FRONTIER (VIDEOCASSETTE). /1995/
4-5/KE259. . . . . **VCR B BOONE, D.**
Boots SEE Shoes.

Boots--Fiction.
CLEARY, B/Growing-up feet. /1987/P-3/1 KF394. . . . . E
HAVILL, J/Jamaica and Brianna. /1993/K-2/2 KF680 . . . . . . E

Boston (Mass.)--Description.
FREEDOM TRAIL (VIDEOCASSETTE). /1991/
4-6/KE939. **VCR 974.4**

Boston (Mass.)--Fiction.
FORBES, E/Johnny Tremain: a novel for old and young. /c1943,
1971/4-6/6 KH131 . . . . **CE Fic**
MCCLOSKEY, R/Make way for ducklings. /c1941, 1963/
P-1/4 KG089 . . . . **CE E**
RAPPAPORT, D/Boston coffee party. /1988/K-3/2 KG306. . . . . E

Boston (Mass.)--History.
ADLER, DA/Picture book of Paul Revere. /1995/
2-4/5 KE508 . . . . **B REVERE, P.**
FORBES, E/America's Paul Revere. /c1946/
A/7 KE509 . . . . **B REVERE, P.**
FREEDOM TRAIL (VIDEOCASSETTE). /1991/
4-6/KE939. **VCR 974.4**
FRITZ, J/And then what happened, Paul Revere? /c1973/
5-6/6 KE510 . . . . **CE B REVERE, P.**
Botanists SEE ALSO Agriculturists; names of specific botanists e.g. Burbank,
Luther.
Botany SEE ALSO Flowers; Fruit; Leaves; Plants; Seeds; Trees; Vegetables;
and names of specific plants e.g. Giant Sequoya.

Botany.
COOPER, K/Too many rabbits and other fingerplays about animals,
nature, weather, and the /1995/P-1/KD707 . . . . 793.4
FLOWER TO SEED (VIDEOCASSETTE). /1985/
4-6/KC386. . . . . **VCR 580**
HOW PLANTS ARE USED (VIDEOCASSETTE). /1991/
3-6/KC357. **VCR 578.6**
LERNER, C/Plant families. /1989/A/7 KC388. 580
PLANTS: ANGIOSPERMS (VIDEOCASSETTE). /1990/
4-A/KC390 . . . . **VCR 580**
RAHN, JE/Plants up close. /1981/4-6/6 KC391. 580
SILVERSTEIN, A/Plants. /1996/5-A/7 KC392. 580
TAYLOR, B/Incredible plants. /1997/3-8/8 KC393. 580
WHAT IS A PLANT? (VIDEOCASSETTE). /1991/
3-6/KC395. . . . . **VCR 580**
WONDERS OF GROWING PLANTS. 3RD ED. (VIDEOCASSETTE).
/1992/K-3/KC396. . . . . **VCR 580**

Botany--Anatomy.
VISUAL DICTIONARY OF PLANTS. /1992/P-A/A KC394. . . . 580

Botany--Experiments.
DIETL, U/Plant-and-grow project book. /1993/P-4/5 KC384 . . 580

Botany--Study and teaching-

JURENKA, NE/Beyond the bean seed: gardening activities for grades K-6. /1996//KA202. . . . . **PROF 372.3**

Botany--Study and teaching--Activity programs.

JURENKA, NE/Beyond the bean seed: gardening activities for grades K-6. /1996//KA202. . . . . **PROF 372.3**

Botany projects.

DIETL, U/Plant-and-grow project book. /1993/P-4/5 KC384 . . **580**

Bovidae.

SELSAM, ME/First look at animals with horns. /1989/ 1-3/2 KC792 . . . . **599.64**

Bowditch, Nathaniel.

LATHAM, JL/Carry on, Mr. Bowditch. /c1955/ 5-A/3 KE260 . . . . **CE B BOWDITCH, N.**

Box turtle.

KUHN, D/Turtle's day. /1994/P-2/4 KC620 . . . . **597.92**

Box turtle--Fiction.

GEORGE, WT/Box turtle at Long Pond. /1989/1-3/3 KF608 . . . **E**

Boxers (Sports).

LIPSYTE, R/Joe Louis: a champ for all America. /1994/ 4-6/6 KE447 . . . . **B LOUIS, J.**

MACHT, NL/Muhammad Ali. /1994/4-6/6 KE233 . . . . **B ALI, M.**

Boxes--Fiction.

RAU, DM/Box can be many things. /1997/K-1/2 KG313 . . . . . . **E**

STEVENSON, J/Mud Flat mystery. /1997/1-3/2 KG561 . . . . . . **E**

Boxing--Fiction.

ANTLE, N/Staying cool. /1997/1-3/2 KF162 . . . . **E**

CARRIER, R/Boxing champion. /1991/4-6/2 KG976 . . . . **Fic**

KROEGER, MK/Paperboy. /1996/1-3/2 KF926 . . . . **E**

Boy Scouts SEE ALSO Cub Scouts.

Boy Scouts.

KENOWER, FT/Cub Scout fun book. /c1956, 1986/ 2-4/6 KB077 . . . . **369.43**

Boy Scouts--Handbooks, manuals, etc.

BIRKBY, RC/Boy Scout handbook. 10th ed. /1990/ 4-6/6 KB073 . . . . **369.43**

BOY SCOUTS OF AMERICA /Big Bear Cub Scout book. Rev. ed. / 1984/4-5/5 KB074 . . . . **369.43**

Webelos Scout book. Rev. ed. /1987/4-6/3 KB075 . . . . **369.43**

Wolf Cub Scout book. Rev. ed. /1986/3-4/4 KB076. . . **369.43**

Boy Scouts--Periodicals.

BOYS' LIFE. /1911-/2-A/KA504 . . . . **PER 050**

Boys.

NEW, IMPROVED ME: UNDERSTANDING BODY CHANGES (VIDEOCASSETTE). /1991/5-6/KC953 . . . . **VCR 612.6**

Boys--Fiction.

ALCOTT, LM/Little men: life at Plumfield with Jo's boys. /c1947, 1982/5-A/7 KG829 . . . . **Fic**

GRAY, N/Country far away. /1988/K-3/1 KF638. . . . . **E**

PAULSEN, G/Harris and me: a summer remembered. /1993/ 6-A/7 KH586 . . . . **Fic**

WILDER, LI/Farmer boy. /c1953/3-6/5 KH859. . . . . **Fic**

Braces SEE Orthodontics.

Bradford, William.

MOURT'S RELATION /Homes in the wilderness: a pilgrim's journal of Plymouth Plantation in 1620. /c1939, 1988/ 5-A/8 KE941 . . . . **974.4**

Braille.

ADLER, DA/Picture book of Louis Braille. /1997/ 2-3/3 KE261 . . . . **B BRAILLE, L.**

FREEDMAN, R/Out of darkness: the story of Louis Braille. /1997/ 3-5/6 KE262 . . . . **B BRAILLE, L.**

Braille, Louis.

ADLER, DA/Picture book of Louis Braille. /1997/ 2-3/3 KE261 . . . . **B BRAILLE, L.**

FREEDMAN, R/Out of darkness: the story of Louis Braille. /1997/ 3-5/6 KE262 . . . . **B BRAILLE, L.**

Brain SEE ALSO Dreams; Psychology; Sleep.

Brain.

BARRETT, SL/It's all in your head: a guide to understanding your brain and boosting your brain power. Rev. ed. /1992/ A/8 KA633 . . . . **153**

BRUUN, RD/Brain--what it is, what it does. /1989/ 3-5/5 KC914 . . . . **612**

MATHERS, D/Brain. /1992/5-6/6 KC966 . . . . **612.8**

NERVOUS SYSTEM (VIDEOCASSETTE). /1994/ 5-6/KC970. . . . . **VCR 612.8**

SIMON, S/Brain: our nervous system. /1997/5-6/6 KC980 . **612.8**

YEPSEN, R/Smarten up! how to increase your brain power. /1990/ 6-A/7 KA645 . . . . **155.42**

Brain--Localization of function.

STAFFORD, P/Your two brains. /1986/5-6/8 KC981 . . . . . **612.8**

Brain--Wounds and injuries--Patients.

MOORE, A/Broken Arrow boy. /1990/3-6/6 KA996 . . . . **362.1**

Brass instruments.

SHIPTON, A/Brass. /1994/4-A/7 KD553 . . . . **788.9**

Bravery SEE Courage.

Brazil--Description and travel.

COBB, V/This place is wet. /1989/3-6/6 KC287 . . . . **574.5**

Brazil--Fiction.

LEWIN, T/Amazon boy. /1993/K-2/5 KF974. . . . . **E**

Bread SEE ALSO Baking; Cookery.

Bread.

BADT, KL/Pass the bread! /1995/4-6/6 KD291 . . . . **641.8**

MORRIS, A/Bread, bread, bread. /1989/K-2/2 KD293 . . . . **641.8**

Bread--Fiction.

GERSHATOR, D/Bread is for eating. /1995/P-2/2 KF610 . . . . . **E**

HOOPES, LL/Unbeatable bread. /1996/K-2/3 KF769 . . . . **E**

WOLFF, F/Seven loaves of bread. /1993/1-3/2 KG758 . . . . . . **E**

Bread--Folklore.

DE PAOLA, T/Tony's bread. /1989/K-3/5 KB500. . . . . . . **398.23**

Breakfast.

BADT, KL/Good morning, let's eat! /1994/3-5/7 KB184 . . . **394.1**

Breakfasts--Fiction.

NEITZEL, S/We're making breakfast for Mother. /1997/ P-1/2 KG169 . . . . **E**

Breathing SEE Respiration.

Breeding SEE Livestock.

Bresnick-Perry, Roslyn.

BRESNICK-PERRY, R/Leaving for America. /1992/ 1-4/6 KE688 . . . . **947**

Bride, Harold.

TANAKA, S/On board the Titanic. /1996/4-A/6 KB027 . . **363.12**

Bridges.

BRIDGES (VIDEOCASSETTE). /1988/5-6/KD066 . . . . . **VCR 624**

DOHERTY, CA/Golden Gate Bridge. /1995/5-6/8 KD067 . . . **624**

MANN, E/Brooklyn Bridge. /1996/5-6/5 KD068 . . . . **624**

Bridges, Ruby.

COLES, R/Story of Ruby Bridges. /1995/2-5/4 KA902 . . . . **323.1**

British Columbia (Canada).

BOWERS, V/British Columbia. /1995/4-6/9 KE809. . . . . . **971.1**

NANTON, I/British Columbia. /1994/5-A/9 KE810 . . . . . **971.1**

British Columbia (Canada)--Fiction.

BLADES, A/Mary of Mile 18. /1971/1-3/3 KF233 . . . . **CE E**

British Columbia (Canada)--Pacific Coast--Folklore.

CAMERON, A/Raven and Snipe. /1991/3-4/6 KB546. . . . **398.24**

Raven goes berrypicking. /1991/3-4/6 KB547 . . . . **398.24**

Brontosaurus SEE Apatosaurus.

Brooklyn (New York, N.Y.)--Fiction.

BLOS, JW/Brooklyn doesn't rhyme. /1994/4-6/6 KG904 . . . . . **Fic**

Brooklyn (New York, N.Y.)--Folklore.

FAITH RINGGOLD PAINTS CROWN HEIGHTS (VIDEOCASSETTE). /1995/5-A/KD461 . . . . **VCR 746.46**

Brooklyn Bridge (New York, N.Y.)--History.

MANN, E/Brooklyn Bridge. /1996/5-6/5 KD068 . . . . **624**

Brooklyn Dodgers (Baseball team)--Fiction.

COHEN, B/Thank you, Jackie Robinson /1997/4-A/4 KH013 . . **Fic**

TUNIS, JR/Highpockets. /c1948/5-A/6 KH809. . . . . **Fic**

Kid comes back. /c1946, 1990/5-A/7 KH810 . . . . **Fic**

Brooms and brushes--Fiction.

VAN ALLSBURG, C/Widow's broom. /1992/4-A/5 KH824 . . . **Fic**

Brotherliness--Fiction.

HAMANAKA, S/All the colors of the earth. /1994/ P-2/4 KF667 . . . . **E**

Brotherliness--Poetry.

NIKOLA-LISA, W/Bein' with you this way. /1994/P-2/KD996 . **811**

Brothers SEE ALSO Brothers and sisters.

Brothers--Fiction.

BLUME, J/Fudge-a-mania. /1990/4-6/3 KG909 . . . . **CE Fic**

Tales of a fourth grade nothing. /1972/2-4/3 KG914 . . . **CE Fic**

BYARS, BC/Ant plays Bear. /1997/K-1/1 KF324 . . . . **E**

Joy boys. /1996/2-3/1 KF326 . . . . **E**

My brother, Ant. /1996/K-2/1 KF327 . . . . **E**

CAMERON, A/More stories Huey tells. /1997/2-4/2 KG968 . . **Fic**

Stories Huey tells. /1995/2-4/2 KG969 . . . . **Fic**

Stories Julian tells. /1981/3-4/4 KG970 . . . . **Fic**

COLLIER, JL/My brother Sam is dead. /1974/5-6/5 KH016 . . . **Fic**

COOPER, S/Danny and the kings. /1993/2-4/2 KF423 . . . . . . **E**

GAUTHIER, G/My life among the aliens. /1996/4-6/5 KH154 . **Fic**

HATRICK, G/Masks. /1996/6-A/3 KH225 . . . . **Fic**

HICKOX, R/Per and the Dala horse. /1995/1-3/6 KF724 . . . . . **E**

KELLOGG, S/Much bigger than Martin. /c1976/K-2/2 KF891. . . **E**

KRUMGOLD, J/And now Miguel. /1953/6-A/5 KH382 . . . **CE Fic**

POLACCO, P/My rotten redheaded older brother. /1994/ 1-3/3 KG255 . . . . **E**

RABIN, S/Casey over there. /1994/2-4/4 KG297 . . . . **E**

ROE, E/With my brother/Con mi hermano. /1991/ P-2/2 KG346 . . . . **E**

SEIDLER, T/Wainscott weasel. /1993/4-6/5 KH691 . . . . **Fic**
STEIG, W/Toy brother. /1996/2-5/6 KG547 . . . . **E**
STEPTOE, J/Baby says. /1988/P-K/KG551 . . . . **E**
TITHERINGTON, J/Place for Ben. /1987/P-2/2 KG608 . . . . . . **E**
WIESNER, D/Hurricane. /1990/K-2/2 KG712 . . . . **E**
YEP, L/Later, Gator. /1995/4-6/4 KH893 . . . . **Fic**
ZEMACH, H/Penny a look. /c1971/K-2/2 KG789 . . . . **E**

Brothers and sisters SEE ALSO Babies; Brothers; Sisters.

Brothers and sisters.
ANHOLT, C/Here come the babies. /P-K/2 KA826 . . . . . **305.232**
COLLINS, PL/Waiting for baby Joe. /1990/K-3/2 KD038 . **618.92**
HEY, WHAT ABOUT ME? (VIDEOCASSETTE). /1987/
P-3/KA884. . . . . **VCR 306.875**
LANDAU, E/Sibling rivalry: brothers and sisters at odds. /1994/
5-A/6 KA885 . . . . **306.875**
NEW BABY IN MY HOUSE (VIDEOCASSETTE). /1993/
P-1/KA886. . . . . **VCR 306.875**
PETERSON, JW/I have a sister--my sister is deaf. /c1977/
2-4/4 KB007 . . . . **362.4**
ROSENBERG, MB/Brothers and sisters. /1991/
1-4/4 KA887 . . . . **306.875**
Finding a way: living with exceptional brothers and sisters. /1988/
4-6/8 KB008 . . . . **362.4**

Brothers and sisters--Fiction.
ARMSTRONG, J/That terrible baby. /1994/K-2/3 KF166 . . . . . **E**
BARTONE, E/Peppe the lamplighter. /1993/1-3/2 KF211 . . . . . **E**
BERENSTAIN, S/Berenstain Bears: no girls allowed. /1986/
K-2/4 KF226 . . . . **E**
BLUME, J/Here's to you, Rachel Robinson. /1993/
6-A/6 KG910. . . . . **Fic**
One in the middle is the green kangaroo. /1981/
K-3/2 KF238 . . . . **CE E**
Pain and the great one. /1984/K-3/4 KF239 . . . . **CE E**
Superfudge. /1980/2-4/2 KG913 . . . . **CE Fic**
BONSALL, CN/Day I had to play with my sister. /c1972/
1-2/1 KF244 . . . . **E**
Piggle. /1973/P-2/2 KF246 . . . . **E**
BROWN, LK/Rex and Lilly family time. /1995/K-1/1 KF270 . . . **E**
BROWN, MT/Arthur's baby. /1987/K-3/2 KF274. . . . . **E**
Arthur's TV trouble. /1995/K-2/2 KF279 . . . . **E**
BYARS, BC/Not-just-anybody family. /1986/4-A/4 KG962. **CE Fic**
CARLSON, N/Perfect family. /1985/P-2/2 KF351 . . . . . . **CE E**
CASELEY, J/Dorothy's darkest days. /1997/3-5/4 KG983 . . . . **Fic**
Harry and Arney. /1994/3-5/6 KG984 . . . . **Fic**
Sophie and Sammy's library sleepover. /1993/P-1/4 KF370 . . . **E**
Witch Mama. /1996/K-2/3 KF371 . . . . **E**
COLE, B/Winter wren. /1984/K-3/2 KF408 . . . . **E**
CONLY, JL/Trout summer. /1995/6-A/5 KH021 . . . . **Fic**
COTTONWOOD, J/Quake!: a novel. /1995/5-A/5 KH034 . . . **Fic**
COWEN-FLETCHER, J/It takes a village. /1994/K-2/2 KF429 . . . **E**
CURRY, JL/Big Smith snatch. /1989/5-A/6 KH047 . . . . . . **Fic**
CURTIS, CP/Watsons go to Birmingham--1963: a novel. /1995/
6-A/7 KH048 . . . . **CE Fic**
DE PAOLA, T/Baby sister. /1996/K-2/2 KF465 . . . . **E**
DORRIS, M/Morning Girl. /1992/6-A/7 KH080 . . . . **Fic**
DRAANEN, WV/How I survived being a girl. /1997/
4-A/KH084 . . . . **Fic**
FLEISCHMAN, S/13th floor: a ghost story. /1995/
5-A/6 KH127 . . . . **CE Fic**
FOX, P/Western wind: a novel. /1993/5-A/5 KH141 . . . . . . **Fic**
GREENE, CC/Beat the turtle drum. /c1976, 1994/
5-6/4 KH198 . . . . **Fic**
HAARHOFF, D/Desert December. /1992/3-5/4 KH206 . . . . . **Fic**
HECKMAN, P/Waking upside down. /1996/1-3/6 KF693 . . . . . **E**
HENKES, K/Julius, the baby of the world. /1990/K-3/2 KF707 . . **E**
HILL, K/Toughboy and sister. /1990/4-6/6 KH261 . . . . . . **Fic**
HINTON, SE/Puppy sister. /1995/3-5/4 KH263 . . . . **Fic**
HOBAN, L/Arthur's funny money. /1981/1-3/2 KF733 . . . . . . **E**
Arthur's honey bear. /c1964/1-3/2 KF734 . . . . **CE E**
Arthur's pen pal. /c1976/1-3/2 KF735 . . . . **E**
HOWARD, EF/Mac and Marie and the train toss surprise. /1993/
K-2/2 KF774 . . . . **E**
HUGHES, S/Big Alfie and Annie Rose storybook. /1988/
P-3/6 KF785 . . . . **E**
Dogger. /c1978/P-2/3 KF788 . . . . **E**
HURWITZ, J/New neighbors for Nora. /c1979, 1991/
2-4/6 KH299 . . . . **Fic**
Nora and Mrs. Mind-your-own business. /c1977, 1991/
2-4/4 KH300 . . . . **Fic**
Superduper Teddy. /c1980, 1990/2-4/4 KH304. . . . . **Fic**
HUTCHINS, P/Very worst monster. /1985/P-2/4 KF806 . . . . **CE E**
You'll soon grow into them, Titch. /1983/P-2/2 KF808 . . . . . **E**
JOYCE, W/Santa calls. /1993/2-4/4 KF862 . . . . **E**
KELLER, H/Geraldine first. /1996/K-2/2 KF881 . . . . **E**

LEVIN, B/Fire in the wind. /1995/5-A/4 KH396 . . . . **Fic**
LITTLE, J/Revenge of the small Small. /1992/1-3/2 KF996 . . . . . **E**
MACDONALD, M/No room for Francie. /1995/2-3/2 KH440. . **Fic**
MACKEN, W/Flight of the doves. /1992/5-A/8 KH442 . . . . . **Fic**
MARSHALL, E/Fox and his friends. /1994/K-2/1 KG064 . . . **CE E**
MARTIN, JR., B/Ghost-eye tree. /1985/K-3/2 KG075. . . . . . . **E**
MEAD, A/Junebug. /1995/5-A/5 KH493 . . . . **Fic**
MILLS, C/Phoebe's parade. /1994/K-2/2 KG138 . . . . **E**
MOORE, M/Under the mermaid angel. /1995/6-A/5 KH506 . . **Fic**
MORROW, H/On to Oregon. /c1954/5-6/4 KH517 . . . . . . **Fic**
MYERS, A/Rosie's tiger. /1994/4-A/4 KH521 . . . . **Fic**
NESBIT, E/Railway children. /1994/4-5/7 KH543 . . . . **Fic**
Story of the treasure seekers. /1986/5-6/7 KH544 . . . . . . **Fic**
ORMEROD, J/101 things to do with a baby. /1984/
P-K/KG197 . . . . **E**
PARK, B/Mick Harte was here. /1995/4-6/4 KH570 . . . . . . **Fic**
PATERSON, K/Flip-flop girl. /1996/5-A/6 KH575 . . . . **Fic**
PEARSON, K/Sky is falling. /1995/5-A/6 KH591 . . . . **Fic**
PECK, R/Lost in cyberspace. /1995/5-A/3 KH593 . . . . **Fic**
ROBINSON, B/Best Christmas pageant ever. /c1972/
4-6/7 KH640 . . . . **Fic**
RODGERS, M/Billion for Boris. /c1974/4-6/7 KH646 . . . . **CE Fic**
RUSSO, M/I don't want to go back to school. /1994/
1-3/2 KG361 . . . . **E**
SHEA, PD/New moon. /1996/P-2/2 KG490 . . . . **E**
SHREVE, S/Formerly great Alexander family. /1995/
3-5/6 KH708 . . . . **Fic**
SIRACUSA, C/Bingo, the best dog in the world. /1991/
K-1/1 KG510 . . . . **E**
TESTA, M/Thumbs up, Rico! /1994/1-3/2 KG601 . . . . **E**
TOLAN, SS/Who's there? /1994/5-A/5 KH795 . . . . **Fic**
VOIGT, C/Dicey's song. /1982/5-6/6 KH832 . . . . **Fic**
WAGGONER, K/Partners. /1995/2-4/4 KH836 . . . . **Fic**
WALSH, ES/Samantha. /1996/K-2/2 KG681 . . . . **E**
WELLS, R/Bunny cakes. /1997/P-1/2 KG696 . . . . **E**
Max and Ruby's first Greek myth: Pandora's box. /1993/
P-1/3 KG700 . . . . **E**
Max and Ruby's Midas: another Greek myth. /1995/
P-1/3 KG701 . . . . **E**
Max's first word (Board book). /1979/P/1 KG704. . . . . . **BB E**
WILLIAMS, S/Edwin and Emily. /1995/1-3/2 KG733 . . . . **E**
WISLER, GC/Jericho's journey. /1993/5-A/6 KH870. . . . . . . **Fic**

Brothers and sisters--Folklore.
KURTZ, J/Fire on the mountain. /1994/2-4/6 KB747 . . . . . **398.27**
OYONO, E/Gollo and the lion. /1995/2-4/4 KB628 . . . . . **398.24**
TALKING EGGS (VIDEOCASSETTE). /1993/
2-5/KB420. . . . . **VCR 398.21**

Brown, John.
COLLINS, JL/John Brown and the fight against slavery. /1991/
3-5/6 KE263 . . . . **B BROWN, J.**
COX, C/Fiery vision: the life and death of John Brown. /1997/
5-A/8 KE264 . . . . **B BROWN, J.**

Brown, Margaret Tobin.
BLOS, JW/Heroine of the Titanic: a tale both true and otherwise of
the life of Molly Brown. /1991/5-6/6 KE265 . . . **B BROWN, M.**

Brown bear.
STONE, LM/Grizzlies. /1993/5-6/6 KC861 . . . . **599.784**

Brownie Scouts.
GIRL SCOUTS OF THE UNITED STATES OF AMERICA /Brownie
Scout handbook. /1993/1-3/KB078 . . . . **369.463**

Bruegel, Pieter.
MUHLBERGER, R/What makes a Bruegel a Bruegel? /1993/
5-A/8 KD502 . . . . **759.9493**

Bryan, Ashley.
MEET ASHLEY BRYAN: STORYTELLER, ARTIST, WRITER
(VIDEOCASSETTE). /1992/4-6/KE266 . . . . . **VCR B BRYAN, A.**

Bubbles.
BUBBLEOLOGY I AND II (VIDEOCASSETTE). /1988/
3-A/KA292 . . . . **VCR PROF 530.4**
ZUBROWSKI, B/Bubbles. /1979/4-6/8 KC085 . . . . **530.4**

Buccaneers SEE ALSO Pirates.

Buddha.
DEMI /Buddha. /1996/2-6/6 KA758 . . . . **294.3**

Buddhism.
FAITH AND BELIEF: FIVE MAJOR WORLD RELIGIONS
(VIDEOCASSETTE). /1992/5-A/KA722 . . . . **VCR 291**

Buddhism--Biography.
DEMI /Buddha. /1996/2-6/6 KA758 . . . . **294.3**
STEWART, W/14th Dalai Lama: spiritual leader of Tibet. /1996/
5-A/10 KA761 . . . . **294.3**

Buddhist stories SEE Jataka stories.

Buddy (dog).
MOORE, E/Buddy: the first seeing eye dog. /1996/
1-3/3 KB006 . . . . **362.4**

Budget, Household SEE Finance, Personal.
Budgets, Personal SEE Finance, Personal.
Buffalo Bill.
    ROBISON, N/Buffalo Bill. /1991/5-6/6 KE267 . **B BUFFALO BILL**
Buffalo Bill--Fiction.
    COERR, E/Buffalo Bill and the Pony Express. /1995/
    1-3/2 KF399 . . . . **E**
Buffaloes SEE ALSO Bison.
Buffaloes.
    TALL GRASS PRAIRIE: AN AMERICAN STORY (VIDEOCASSETTE).
    /1997/3-A/KC333 . . . . **VCR 577.4**
Buffaloes--Folklore.
    GOBLE, P/Return of the buffaloes: a Plains Indian story about
    famine and renewal of the /1996/3-5/3 KB575. . . . . . . **398.24**
Building SEE ALSO Architecture; Carpentry; Engineering; House construction.
Building.
    GIBBONS, G/Tool book. /1982/P-K/2 KD055 . . . . . . **621.9**
    Up goes the skyscraper! /1986/K-3/6 KD356 . . . . **690**
    MACAULAY, D/Pyramid. /1975/A/10 KD357 . . . . **CE 690**
    PUTNAM, J/Pyramid. /1994/4-A/7 KD359 . . . . **690**
Building--Fiction.
    AVI /Barn. /1994/5-A/3 KG856. . . . . **Fic**
    BARTON, B/Machines at work. /1987/P-K/2 KF207 . . . . **E**
    TRYON, L/Albert's alphabet. /1991/P-1/KG620 . . . . **E**
Building materials.
    WILKINSON, P/Building. /1995/5-6/7 KD360 . . . . **690**
Buildings SEE ALSO Apartment houses; Dwellings; Farm buildings; Housing;
Skyscrapers.
Buildings.
    WILKINSON, P/Amazing buildings. /1993/4-A/9 KD385 . . . . **720**
Bull Run, 1st Battle of, Va., 1861--Fiction.
    FLEISCHMAN, P/Bull Run. /1993/5-A/5 KH116 . . . . **Fic**
Bulldozers SEE Construction equipment.
Bullfighters.
    SAY, A/El Chino. /1990/3-5/4 KE598 . . . . **B WONG, B.**
Bullfights--Fiction.
    LEAF, M/Story of Ferdinand. /c1936/P-1/3 KF953 . . . . **CE E**
    WOJCIECHOWSKA, M/Shadow of a bull. /1964/
    5-6/6 KH875 . . . . **CE Fic**
Bullies.
    BULLY UP: FIGHTING FEELINGS (VIDEOCASSETTE). /c1990,
    1991/K-3/KA807 . . . . **VCR 303.6**
    GROARK LEARNS ABOUT BULLYING (VIDEOCASSETTE). /1996/
    1-3/KA810 . . . . **VCR 303.6**
    NO MORE TEASING! (VIDEOCASSETTE). /1995/
    3-4/KA661 . . . . **VCR 158**
Bullies--Fiction.
    BROWN, MT/Arthur's April fool. /1983/P-3/2 KF273 . . . . **E**
    CAPOTE, T/Thanksgiving visitor. /1996/5-A/8 KG972 . . . . . . **Fic**
    NAYLOR, PR/King of the playground. /1991/K-3/2 KG167 . . . . **E**
    ROSENBERG, L/Monster mama. /1993/K-2/4 KG354. . . . . **E**
    Monster mama (Videocassette). /1996/K-2/KG355. . . . . **VCR E**
    SHREVE, S/Joshua T. Bates takes charge. /c1993, 1995/
    4-6/4 KH710 . . . . **Fic**
    SKINNER, D/Wrecker. /1995/6-A/4 KH715 . . . . **Fic**
Bulls--Fiction.
    LEAF, M/Story of Ferdinand. /c1936/P-1/3 KF953 . . . . **CE E**
Bunting, Eve.
    BUNTING, E/Once upon a time. /1995/
    2-5/3 KE268 . . . . **B BUNTING, E.**
    VISIT WITH EVE BUNTING (VIDEOCASSETTE). /1991/
    4-6/KE269 . . . . **VCR B BUNTING, E.**
Bunyan, Paul (Legendary character).
    GLEESON, B/Paul Bunyan (Videocassette). /1990/
    3-5/KB447 . . . . **VCR 398.22**
    KELLOGG, S/Paul Bunyan, a tall tale. /1984/
    4-6/7 KB457 . . . . **398.22**
    MCCORMICK, DJ/Paul Bunyan swings his axe. /c1936, 1962/
    4-6/6 KB467 . . . . **398.22**
    Tall timber tales: more Paul Bunyan stories. /c1939/
    4-6/6 KB468 . . . . **398.22**
    ROUNDS, G/Ol' Paul, the mighty logger: being a true account of
    the seemingly incredible exploits and inventions of the great Paul
    Bunyon. /1976/4-6/7 KB477. . . . . **398.22**
Bunyan, Paul (Legendary character)--Fiction.
    WOOD, A/Bunyans. /1996/1-5/6 KG760 . . . . **E**
Bunyan, Paul (Legendary character)--Software.
    P.J.'S READING ADVENTURES (CD-ROM). /1996/
    K-3/KB252. . . . . **CDR 398**
Burgess, Abbie.
    ROOP, P/Keep the lights burning, Abbie. /1985/
    1-3/1 KE270 . . . . **CE B BURGESS, A.**

Buried treasure SEE ALSO Treasure trove.
Buried treasure.
    DEEM, JM/How to hunt buried treasure. /1992/
    4-6/8 KD058 . . . . **622**
    GIBBONS, G/Sunken treasure. /1988/4-6/6 KE194 . . . . . **917.59**
    SCHWARTZ, A/Gold and silver, silver and gold. /1988/
    4-6/6 KE628 . . . . **930.1**
Buried treasure--Fiction.
    FLEISCHMAN, S/Ghost in the noonday sun. /1965/
    5-A/7 KH121 . . . . **Fic**
    HOBBS, W/Ghost canoe. /1997/5-A/6 KH267 . . . . **Fic**
    MOWAT, F/Lost in the barrens. /1962/5-6/6 KH518 . . . . . . **Fic**
    MYERS, WD/Righteous revenge of Artemis Bonner. /1994/
    5-A/7 KH523 . . . . **Fic**
    STEVENSON, RL/Treasure Island. /c1911, 1981/
    5-A/6 KH759 . . . . **Fic**
    Treasure Island (Talking book). /1993/5-A/KH760 . . . . . **TB Fic**
Burma--Folklore.
    FROESE, DL/Wise washerman: a folktale from Burma. /1996/
    K-2/7 KB569 . . . . **398.24**
Burma--Politics and government--1948-.
    STEWART, W/Aung San Suu Kyi: fearless voice of Burma. /1997/
    5-A/7 KE244 . . . . **B AUNG SAN SUU**
Burma--Politics and government--1988-.
    STEWART, W/Aung San Suu Kyi: fearless voice of Burma. /1997/
    5-A/7 KE244 . . . . **B AUNG SAN SUU**
Burroughs, John.
    WADSWORTH, G/John Burroughs, the sage of Slabsides. /1997/
    A/7 KE271 . . . . **B BURROUGHS, J.**
Buses--Fiction.
    CREWS, D/School bus. /1984/P-2/1 KF435 . . . . **E**
Buses--Safety measures.
    K.C.'S FIRST BUS RIDE (VIDEOCASSETTE). /1994/
    P-1/KB023 . . . . **VCR 363.1**
Buses--Songs and music.
    RAFFI /Wheels on the bus. /c1988, 1990/P-2/KD653 . . . . . **789.3**
Bush, George Herbert.
    KENT, Z/George Bush: forty-first president of the United States. /
    1989/5-6/8 KE272 . . . . **B BUSH, G.**
Business enterprises SEE ALSO names of specific business enterprises e.g.
Agribusiness.
Business enterprises.
    BARKIN, C/Jobs for kids: the guide to having fun and making
    money. /1990/5-6/7 KD305 . . . . **650.1**
    NOEL'S LEMONADE STAND (UJAMAA) (VIDEOCASSETTE). /
    1982/3-5/KD306 . . . . **VCR 650.1**
    SMACKERS: ELEMENTARY ENTREPRENEURS (VIDEOCASSETTE).
    /1991/3-6/KD314 . . . . **VCR 658**
    THOMPSON, T/Biz kids' guide to success: money-making ideas for
    young entrepreneurs. /1992/5-6/6 KD307 . . . . **650.1**
Business enterprises--Software.
    CLASSROOM STOREWORKS (MICROCOMPUTER PROGRAM). /
    1997/2-5/KD313 . . . . **MCP 658**
Businesswomen.
    COLMAN, P/Madam C.J. Walker: building a business empire. /
    1994/4-6/7 KE583 . . . . **B WALKER, C.J.**
    GREENE, C/Margarete Steiff: toy maker. /1993/
    2-3/2 KE550 . . . . **B STEIFF, M.**
    JEFFREY, LS/Great American businesswomen. /1996/
    5-6/7 KD315 . . . . **658.4**
    MADAM C.J. WALKER (VIDEOCASSETTE). /1992/
    5-A/KE584. . . . . **VCR B WALKER, C.J.**
Butchers--Fiction.
    PHILLIPS, M/Sign in Mendel's window. /c1985, 1996/
    3-5/6 KH600 . . . . **Fic**
Butterflies.
    ARNOSKY, J/Crinkleroot's guide to knowing butterflies and moths.
    /1996/3-5/5 KC557 . . . . **595.78**
    BUTTERFLIES (VIDEOCASSETTE). /1990/5-6/KC558. **VCR 595.78**
    GIBBONS, G/Monarch butterfly. /1989/K-2/4 KC560. . . . **595.78**
    INSECTS (VIDEOCASSETTE). /c1979, 1986/
    2-6/KC541. . . . . **VCR 595.7**
    LAVIES, B/Monarch butterflies: mysterious travelers. /1992/
    5-6/7 KC562 . . . . **595.78**
    PASCOE, E/Butterflies and moths. /1997/4-6/6 KC563 . . . **595.78**
    PRINGLE, LP/Extraordinary life: the story of a monarch butterfly. /
    1997/5-6/6 KC564 . . . . **595.78**
    SABIN, L/Amazing world of butterflies and moths. /1982/
    2-4/4 KC566 . . . . **CE 595.78**
    SANDVED, KB/Butterfly alphabet. /1996/3-6/6 KC567 . . . **595.78**
    WATTS, B/Butterfly and caterpillar. /1985/2-4/4 KC568 . . **595.78**
    WHALLEY, P/Butterfly and moth. /1988/A/10 KC569 . . . **595.78**
Butterflies--Experiments.
    PASCOE, E/Butterflies and moths. /1997/4-6/6 KC563 . . . **595.78**

Butterflies--Metamorphosis.
HEILIGMAN, D/From caterpillar to butterfly. /1996/
K-2/2 KC561 . . . . **595.78**
REIDEL, M/From egg to butterfly. /1981/P-2/5 KC565 . . . **595.78**
Byars, Betsy Cromer.
TALK WITH BETSY BYARS (VIDEOCASSETTE). /1995/
4-6/KE273 . . . . **VCR B BYARS, B.**
Cabbage--Fiction.
SEABROOK, E/Cabbage and kings. /1997/1-3/2 KG425 . . . . . **E**
Cabinetmakers.
FISHER, LE/Cabinetmakers. /1997/3-6/7 KD343 . . . . **684.1**
Cabinetwork.
FISHER, LE/Cabinetmakers. /1997/3-6/7 KD343 . . . . **684.1**
Cable cars (Streetcars)--Fiction.
BURTON, VL/Maybelle the cable car. /1997/K-2/3 KF321 . . . . . **E**
Cactus.
BASH, B/Desert giant: the world of the saguaro cactus. /1989/
2-6/6 KC427 . . . . **583**
LERNER, C/Cactus. /1992/5-6/7 KC429 . . . . **583**
Cairo (Egypt)--Fiction.
HEIDE, FP/Day of Ahmed's secret. /1990/1-3/4 KF694 . . . . . . **E**
MATTHEWS, M/Magid fasts for Ramadan. /1996/
4-6/4 KH462 . . . . **Fic**
Cajuns--Fiction.
APPELT, K/Bayou lullaby. /1995/P-2/5 KF163 . . . . **E**
Cake--Fiction.
KLINTING, L/Bruno the baker. /1997/P-2/2 KF911 . . . . **E**
RICE, E/Benny bakes a cake. /c1981, 1993/P-2/2 KG330 . . . . . **E**
ROBART, R/Cake that Mack ate. /1986/P-1/1 KG334 . . . . . . **E**
RYLANT, C/Mr. Putter and Tabby bake the cake. /1994/
1-3/2 KG377 . . . . **E**
WELLS, R/Bunny cakes. /1997/P-1/2 KG696 . . . . **E**
Cake--Folklore.
FOREST, H/Woman who flummoxed the fairies: an old tale from
Scotland. /1990/3-4/5 KB396 . . . . **398.21**
Calamity Jane.
FABER, D/Calamity Jane: her life and her legend. /1992/
4-6/8 KE274 . . . . **B CALAMITY JANE**
Calculating machines SEE ALSO Computers; Microcomputers.
Calculators.
ADLER, DA/Calculator riddles. /1995/3-6/KD722 . . . . . **793.735**
WYLER, R/Math fun with a pocket calculator. /1992/
4-A/4 KD713 . . . . **793.7**
Calculators--Problems, exercises, etc.
PALLAS, N/Calculator puzzles, tricks and games. /c1976, 1991/
4-6/9 KB930 . . . . **510**
SMOOTHEY, M/Calculators. /1995/4-8/9 KB932 . . . . **510**
Calcutta (India)--Biography.
JACOBS, WJ/Mother Teresa: helping the poor. /1991/
4-6/6 KE561 . . . . **B TERESA,MOTHER**
Caldecott Medal books.
CALDECOTT VIDEO LIBRARY. VOL. I (VIDEOCASSETTE). /1992/
P-3/KF328 . . . . **VCR E**
CALDECOTT VIDEO LIBRARY. VOL. II (VIDEOCASSETTE). /1992/
P-3/KF329 . . . . **VCR E**
CALDECOTT VIDEO LIBRARY. VOL. III (VIDEOCASSETTE). /1992/
P-3/KF330 . . . . **VCR E**
CALDECOTT VIDEO LIBRARY. VOL. IV (VIDEOCASSETTE). /1992/
P-3/KB274 . . . . **VCR 398.2**
HORN BOOK MAGAZINE /Newbery and Caldecott medal books,
1966-1975: /1975//KA352 . . . . **PROF 809**
NEWBERY AND CALDECOTT MEDALISTS AND HONOR BOOK
WINNERS: BIBLIOGRAPHIES AND /1992//KA004 . . . **PROF 011**
Caldecott Medal books--Audio-visual aids.
SHARKEY, PB/Newbery and Caldecott Medal and Honor books in
other media. /1992//KA087 . . . . **PROF 028.1**
Caldecott Medal books--Periodicals.
NEWBERY AND CALDECOTT AWARDS: A GUIDE TO THE
MEDAL AND HONOR BOOKS. /n.d.//KA128 . . **PER PROF 050**
Calendars SEE ALSO Almanacs.
Calendars.
BRANLEY, FM/Keeping time: from the beginning and into the 21st
century. /1993/4-6/6 KC067 . . . . **529**
CHASE, WD/Chase's calendar of annual events: special days, weeks
and months. /1958//KA264 . . . . **PROF 394.2**
GANERI, A/Story of time and clocks. /1996/4-6/8 KC070. . . **529**
MARTINET, J/Year you were born, 1983. /1992/
4-6/7 KE922 . . . . **973.927**
SMITH, AG/What time is it? /1992/4-A/8 KC073 . . . . **529**
Calendars--Songs and music.
JAMES, DL/Singing calendar (Sound recording cassette). /1984/
P-1/KC071 . . . . **SRC 529**
California.
PELTA, K/California. /1994/4-6/7 KF085 . . . . **979.4**

California--Description and travel.
O'DELL, S/Cruise of the Arctic Star. /c1973/5-6/6 KE208 . **917.94**
California--Fiction.
COCHRANE, PA/Purely Rosie Pearl. /1996/4-6/6 KH011 . . . . **Fic**
COTTONWOOD, J/Adventures of Boone Barnaby. /1992/
6-A/5 KH031 . . . . **Fic**
Quake!: a novel. /1995/5-A/5 KH034 . . . . **Fic**
KRENSKY, S/Iron dragon never sleeps. /1995/3-5/2 KH381. . . **Fic**
POLITI, L/Song of the swallows. /c1949, 1987/
K-3/6 KG262 . . . . **CE E**
SNYDER, ZK/Cat running. /1994/5-A/7 KH730 . . . . **Fic**
SOTO, G/Pool party. /c1993, 1995/4-6/5 KH741 . . . . **Fic**
California--Gold discoveries.
CALIFORNIA GOLD RUSH: 1849 (MULTIMEDIA KIT). /1991/
5-A/KF079. . . . . **MMK 979.4**
CALIFORNIA GOLD RUSH (PICTURE). /n.d./
5-6/KF078 . . . . **PIC 979.4**
ITO, T/California gold rush. /1997/5-6/11 KF080 . . . . **979.4**
KETCHUM, L/Gold rush. /1996/4-6/6 KF081 . . . . **979.4**
KRENSKY, S/Striking it rich: the story of the California gold rush. /
1996/2-4/5 KF082 . . . . **979.4**
California--Gold discoveries--Fiction.
CUSHMAN, K/Ballad of Lucy Whipple. /1996/
5-A/7 KH049 . . . . **CE Fic**
FLEISCHMAN, S/By the Great Horn Spoon! /c1963/
4-6/4 KH119 . . . . **Fic**
California--History.
ABBINK, E/Missions of the Monterey Bay Area. /1996/
4-6/9 KF075 . . . . **979.4**
BEHRENS, J/Missions of the central coast. /1996/
4-6/9 KF076 . . . . **979.4**
BROWER, P/Missions of the inland valleys. /1997/
4-6/9 KF077 . . . . **979.4**
LEMKE, N/Missions of the Southern Coast. /1996/
4-6/9 KF083 . . . . **979.4**
MACMILLAN, D/Missions of the Los Angeles Area. /1996/
4-6/9 KF084 . . . . **979.4**
OVERLAND TO CALIFORNIA IN 1859: A GUIDE FOR WAGON
TRAIN TRAVELERS. /1983/A/12 KF042 . . . . **978**
SEARCHING FOR PARADISE (VIDEOCASSETTE). /1991/
A/KF086 . . . . **VCR 979.4**
WHITE, TN/Missions of the San Francisco Bay Area. /1996/
4-6/9 KF087 . . . . **979.4**
WILLS, CA/Historical album of California. /1994/
4-6/7 KF088 . . . . **979.4**
California--History--To 1846.
WHITE, FM/Story of Junipero Serra: brave adventurer. /1996/
4-6/7 KE536 . . . . **B SERRA, J.**
California--History--1846-1850.
KRENSKY, S/Striking it rich: the story of the California gold rush. /
1996/2-4/5 KF082 . . . . **979.4**
California condor.
ARNOLD, C/On the brink of extinction: the California condor. /
1993/5-6/8 KD251 . . . . **639.9**
California sea lion.
ARNOLD, C/Sea lion. /1994/4-6/6 KC867 . . . . **599.79**
Calypso (Songs).
BOOKER, CM/Smilin' island of song (Sound recording cassette). /
1994/K-4/KD667 . . . . **SRC 789.4**
Cambodia--Fiction.
LEE, JM/Silent Lotus. /1991/P-2/4 KF956. . . . . **E**
Cambodia--Folklore.
SPAGNOLI, C/Judge Rabbit and the tree spirit: a folktale from
Cambodia. /1991/3-4/4 KB655 . . . . **398.24**
Cambodian Americans.
GRAFF, NP/Where the river runs: a portrait of a refugee family. /
1993/4-6/7 KA845 . . . . **305.8**
Camels.
ARNOLD, C/Camel. /1992/4-6/7 KC784 . . . . **599.63**
Camels--Fiction.
KIPLING, R/How the rhinoceros got his skin; and, How the camel
got his hump /1987/2-5/KH361. . . . . **VCR Fic**
OPPENHEIM, SL/Hundredth name. /c1995, 1997/2-3/2 KG194 . **E**
ROBERTS, B/Camel caravan. /1996/P-1/3 KG335 . . . . **E**
Cameras.
GIBBONS, G/Click!: a book about cameras and taking pictures. /
1997/2-4/5 KD512 . . . . **771**
Cameroon--Folklore.
GRIFALCONI, A/Village of round and square houses. /1986/
3-4/6 KB739 . . . . **CE 398.27**
MOLLEL, TM/King and the tortoise. /1993/2-3/4 KB624 . . **398.24**
OYONO, E/Gollo and the lion. /1995/2-4/4 KB628 . . . . . **398.24**
Camouflage (Biology).
ARNOSKY, J/I see animals hiding. /1995/2-4/6 KC465. . . **591.47**

GREENWAY, S/Can you see me? /1992/K-2/4 KC461 .... **591.4**

Camouflage (Biology)--Fiction.
ARUEGO, J/We hide, you seek. /1979/P-K/1 KF172 .... **E**
HUTCHINS, P/One hunter. /1982/P-K/KF800 .... **E**
STRETE, CK/They thought they saw him. /1996/K-2/2 KG579 .. **E**
YOSHI /Who's hiding here? /1987/K-3/2 KG784. .... **E**

Campanella, Roy.
GREENE, C/Roy Campanella: major-league champion. /1994/
1-2/2 KE275 .... **B CAMPANELLA, R**
Camping SEE ALSO Backpacking; Outdoor life.

Camping.
EVANS, J/Camping and survival. /1992/4-A/6 KD825 ... **796.54**

Camping--Fiction.
BROWN, MT/Arthur goes to camp. /1982/K-2/2 KF271 ... **CE E**
LOCKER, T/Where the river begins. /1984/K-3/5 KG016. ...... **E**
SAY, A/Lost lake. /1989/1-3/2 KG398 .... **E**
TAFURI, N/Do not disturb. /1987/P-2/KG587 .... **E**
WILLIAMS, VB/Three days on a river in a red canoe. /1981/
K-3/5 KG740. .... **E**

Camping--Handbooks, manuals, etc.
MCMANNERS, H/Outdoor adventure handbook. /1996/
4-6/6 KD823 .... **796.5**

Camps--Fiction.
DUFFEY, B/Camp Knock Knock. /1996/1-3/2 KF500. .... **E**
HOFF, S/Danny and the dinosaur go to camp. /1996/
K-2/2 KF754 .... **E**

Camps--Handbooks.
GUIDE TO SUMMER CAMPS AND SUMMER SCHOOLS. 26TH
ED. /1995/5-A/KA411 .... **REF 371.2**
Canada SEE ALSO specific cities and provinces.

Canada.
CANADA: PORTRAIT OF A NATION (VIDEOCASSETTE). /1991/
4-6/KE801. .... **VCR 971**
LUNN, J/Story of Canada. /1992/5-A/7 KE804 .... **971**
MALCOLM, AH/Land and people of Canada. /1991/
A/10 KE805. .... **971**
SCHEMENAUER, E/Canada. /1994/4-6/4 KE806. .... **971**

Canada--Description and travel.
HARRISON, T/O Canada. /1993/3-6/6 KE802 .... **971**

Canada--Description and travel--Periodicals.
BEAVER: EXPLORING CANADA'S HISTORY. /1920-/
A/KA503. .... **PER 050**

Canada--Directories.
CORPUS ALMANAC AND CANADIAN SOURCEBOOK. /1964-/
5-6/KA484 .... **REF 971**

Canada--Fiction.
COOPER, S/Boggart. /1993/6-A/7 KH026. .... **CE Fic**
DOYLE, B/Uncle Ronald. /1997/5-A/5 KH083. ...... **Fic**
DUBOIS, ML/Abenaki Captive. /1994/6-A/6 KH085. ...... **Fic**
HUTCHINS, HJ/Within a painted past. /1994/5-A/4 KH311 ... **Fic**
LONDON, J/White Fang. /c1905, 1985/6-A/6 KH417 ...... **Fic**
LOTTRIDGE, CB/Ticket to Canada. /1996/4-A/5 KH418 ..... **Fic**
Wings to fly. /1997/5-A/5 KH419 .... **Fic**
MONTGOMERY, LM/Anne of Green Gables. /c1908, 1983/
4-A/6 KH503 .... **Fic**
PEARSON, K/Sky is falling. /1995/5-A/6 KH591 .... **Fic**
VALGARDSON, WD/Sarah and the people of Sand River. /1996/
4-6/2 KH818 .... **Fic**

Canada--History.
CANADA'S MAPLE TREE: THE STORY OF THE COUNTRY'S
EMBLEM (VIDEOCASSETTE). /1995/1-4/KE615. .... **VCR 929.9**
LUNN, J/Story of Canada. /1992/5-A/7 KE804 .... **971**

Canada--History--Fiction.
OBERMAN, S/White stone in the castle wall. /1995/
4-6/2 KH555 .... **Fic**

Canada--History--To 1763.
CONFRONTING THE WILDERNESS (VIDEOCASSETTE). /1991/
A/KE808. .... **VCR 971.01**

Canada--Social life and customs.
CHRISTMAS IN CANADA. /1994/4-6/10 KB232 ...... **394.266**
KURELEK, W/Lumberjack. /1974/4-6/6 KD165 .... **634.9**
SHEENA AZAK OF CANADA (VIDEOCASSETTE). /1995/
4-6/KE807. .... **VCR 971**
Canadian goose SEE Canada goose.
Canadian literature SEE ALSO French Canadian literature.

Canadian literature--History and criticism.
EGOFF, S/New republic of childhood: a critical guide to Canadian
children's literature in English. Rev. ed. /1990/
/KA349. .... **PROF 809**

Canadian literature--Periodicals.
CANADIAN CHILDREN'S LITERATURE. /1975-/
/KA100. .... **PER PROF 050**
RESOURCE LINKS: CONNECTING CLASSROOMS, LIBRARIES
AND CANADIAN LEARNING /1995-//KA134 .. **PER PROF 050**

Canadian poetry.
ALLIGATOR PIE (VIDEOCASSETTE). /1993/P-2/KD912 **VCR 811**
ASKA, W/Aska's sea creatures. /1994/3-5/KD914. .... **811**
KORMAN, G/D- poems of Jeremy Bloom: a collection of poems
about school, homework, and life /1992/4-A/KD966 ...... **811**
LEE, D/Dinosaur dinner (with a slice of alligator pie): favorite
poems. /1997/K-3/KD970 .... **811**

Canadian poetry (English)--Indexes.
SNOW, K/Subject index for children & young people to Canadian
poetry in English. 2nd ed. /1986/A/KA375 ...... **REF 016.811**
Canals SEE ALSO names of specific canals e.g. Erie Canal; Panama Canal,
etc.

Canaries--Fiction.
SCHACHNER, JB/Willy and May. /1995/1-3/5 KG401. ...... **E**

Cancer.
YOUNT, L/Cancer. /1991/A/9 KD034. .... **616.99**

Cancer--Fiction.
VIGNA, J/When Eric's mom fought cancer. /1993/
1-3/3 KG654. .... **E**
Candy SEE Confectionery.
Canoes and canoeing SEE ALSO Kayaks and kayaking.

Canoes and canoeing.
EVANS, J/Whitewater kayaking. /1992/4-A/7 KD845 .... **797.1**
LOURIE, P/Hudson River: an adventure from the mountains to the
sea. /1992/4-6/6 KE192 .... **917.47**
Yukon River: an adventure to the gold fields of the Klondike. /
1992/4-6/6 KE210 .... **917.98**

Canoes and canoeing--Delaware River (N.Y.-Del. and N.J.).
CHERIPKO, J/Voices of the river: adventures on the Delaware. /
1996/5-A/5 KE962 .... **974.9**

Canoes and canoeing--Fiction.
CONLY, JL/Trout summer. /1995/6-A/5 KH021 ...... **Fic**
WILLIAMS, VB/Three days on a river in a red canoe. /1981/
K-3/5 KG740. .... **E**

Canterbury (Conn.)--History.
YATES, E/Prudence Crandall: woman of courage. 2nd ed. /1996/
6-A/6 KE306 .... **B CRANDALL, P.**

Cape Cod (Mass.)--Fiction.
TRESSELT, A/Hide and seek fog. /c1965/K-2/KG615 .... **E**
WELLER, FW/Riptide. /1990/1-3/4 KG695. .... **E**

Captive wild animals.
ARNOLD, C/Killer whale. /1994/4-6/7 KC764. .... **599.5**

Capybaras.
PEET, B/Capyboppy. /c1966/1-3/8 KC746 .... **599.35**

Caravans--Fiction.
MCKAY, JR., L/Caravan. /1995/3-5/6 KH480 .... **Fic**

Caravels--Fiction.
MACAULAY, D/Ship. /1993/5-6/8 KH433 .... **Fic**

Card games.
COLE, J/Crazy eights and other card games. /1994/
3-6/3 KD758 .... **795.4**
Card tricks SEE ALSO Magic tricks.

Cardiopulmonary system.
SAUNDERSON, J/Heart and lungs. /1992/5-6/6 KC935 ... **612.1**

Cargo handling--Equipment.
RADFORD, D/Cargo machines and what they do. /1992/
P-2/4 KD089 .... **629.04**

Caribbean Area.
LESSAC, F/Caribbean alphabet. /1994/1-3/KF962 .... **E**

Caribbean Area--Fiction.
DORROS, A/Isla. /1995/K-2/2 KF490 .... **E**
GERSHATOR, P/Rata-pata-scata-fata: a Caribbean story. /1994/
K-2/2 KF611 .... **E**
Sambalena show-off. /1995/1-3/2 KF612 .... **E**
Sweet, sweet fig banana. /1996/K-2/2 KF613 .... **E**
KELLER, H/Island baby. /1992/P-2/3 KF885 .... **E**
LINDEN, AM/One smiling grandma: a Caribbean counting book. /
1995/P-1/2 KF984 .... **E**
ORR, K/Story of a dolphin. /1993/1-3/6 KG199 .... **E**
RAHAMAN, V/O Christmas tree. /1996/1-3/4 KG298 ...... **E**
TAYLOR, T/Cay. /c1969/5-6/6 KH783. .... **Fic**
Timothy of the cay. /1993/5-A/5 KH785 .... **Fic**

Caribbean Area--Folklore.
JAFFE, N/Voice for the people: the life and work of Harold
Courlander. /1997//KA367. .... **PROF B COURLAND**
KEENS-DOUGLAS, R/Diablesse and the baby: a Caribbean folktale.
/1994/3-4/4 KB324 .... **398.2**
SAN SOUCI, RD/Faithful friend. /1995/4-6/5 KB411 .... **398.21**

Caribbean Area--Poetry.
GUNNING, M/Not a copper penny in me house: poems from the
Caribbean. /1993/P-3/KD950 .... **811**

Caribbean poetry (English).
GUNNING, M/Not a copper penny in me house: poems from the
Caribbean. /1993/P-3/KD950 .... **811**

Caribbean Sea--Antiquities--Fiction.
MACAULAY, D/Ship. /1993/5-6/8 KH433 . . . . **Fic**
Caribou.
HARRIS, L/Caribou. /1988/4-5/8 KC797 . . . . **599.65**
Carnival--Fiction.
DELACRE, L/Vejigante masquerader. /1993/1-3/4 KF458 . . . . . **E**
Carnival--South America--Fiction.
DORROS, A/Tonight is Carnaval. /1991/1-3/4 KF492 . . . . **E**
Carnivals--Fiction.
ACKERMAN, K/Bingleman's Midway. /1995/2-4/5 KF128 . . . . . **E**
Carnivorous plants SEE Insectivorous plants.
Carnivorous plants.
AASENG, N/Meat-eating plants. /1996/5-8/6 KC425 . . . . . **583**
NIELSEN, NJ/Carnivorous plants. /1992/1-6/6 KC431 . . . . . **583**
OVERBECK, C/Carnivorous plants. /1982/3-5/6 KC432 . . . . . **583**
Carols.
DE PAOLA, T/Merry Christmas, Strega Nona (Talking book). /
1991/K-3/KF474 . . . . **TB E**
HARK! THE HERALD ANGELS SING. /1993/K-6/KD534 . . **782.28**
SILVERMAN, J/Christmas songs. /1993/5-A/KD536 . . . . **782.28**
TWELVE DAYS OF CHRISTMAS (VIDEOCASSETTE). /1990/
P-A/KD540 . . . . **VCR 782.28**
Carols--Fiction.
TOMPERT, A/Carol for Christmas. /1994/K-3/5 KG612 . . . . . . **E**
Carols, English.
FRIENDLY BEASTS: A TRADITIONAL CHRISTMAS CAROL. /1991/
K-2/KD533 . . . . **782.28**
Carpenters--Fiction.
KLINTING, L/Bruno the carpenter. /1996/K-2/2 KF912 . . . . . . **E**
Carpentry SEE ALSO Building; Woodwork.
Carpentry.
LEAVITT, J/Easy carpentry projects for children. /c1959, 1986/
5-6/4 KD340 . . . . **684**
MARTIN, JH/Day in the life of a carpenter. /1985/
4-6/7 KD362 . . . . **CE 694**
WALKER, L/Carpentry for children. /1985/4-6/8 KD342 . . . . **684**
Carpentry--Fiction.
HESSE, K/Sable. /1994/3-5/4 KH253 . . . . **Fic**
Carpets--Folklore.
DE PAOLA, T/Legend of the Persian carpet. /1993/
2-3/6 KB285 . . . . **398.2**
Carrots--Fiction.
RATZ DE TAGYOS, P/Coney tale. /1992/2-5/5 KH620 . . . . . **Fic**
Cars SEE Automobiles; Motor vehicles.
Carson, Ben.
SIMMONS, A/Ben Carson. /1996/4-6/7 KE276 . . **B CARSON, B.**
Carson, Kit.
SANFORD, WR/Kit Carson: frontier scout. /1996/
5-6/7 KE277 . . . . **B CARSON, K.**
Carson, Rachel.
RANSOM, CF/Listening to crickets: a story about Rachel Carson. /
1993/5-6/6 KE278 . . . . **B CARSON, R.**
Carter, Howard.
FORD, B/Howard Carter: searching for King Tut. /1995/
A/9 KE279 . . . . **B CARTER, H.**
Carter, Jimmy.
CARRIGAN, M/Jimmy Carter: beyond the presidency. /1995/
5-6/7 KE280 . . . . **B CARTER, J.**
Cartography.
LA PIERRE, Y/Mapping a changing world. /1996/
A/12 KC065 . . . . **526**
Cartooning.
ANIMATION FOR KIDS: HOW TO MAKE YOUR CARTOON
MOVE! (VIDEOCASSETTE). /1994/4-A/KD407 . . . . **VCR 741.5**
ARTELL, M/Basic cartooning with Mike Artell (Videocassette). /
1995/3-6/KD408 . . . . **VCR 741.5**
LIGHTFOOT, M/Cartooning for kids. /1993/3-6/5 KD410 . . **741.5**
Cartooning--Fiction.
FEIFFER, J/Man in the ceiling. /1993/5-A/7 KH112 . . . . **Fic**
Cartoons and comics.
AVI /City of light, city of dark: a comic-book novel. /1993/
4-6/6 KD409 . . . . **741.5**
DUBANEVICH, A/Pig William. /1985/P-2/1 KF498 . . . . **E**
STEVENSON, J/Sea View Hotel. /c1978, 1994/K-3/3 KG567 . . **E**
WILLIAMS, M/Iliad and the Odyssey. /1996/3-6/8 KE129 . . . **883**
Cartoons and comics--Fiction.
JAMES, M/Frankenlouse. /1994/6-A/6 KH322 . . . . **Fic**
PINKNEY, JB/Adventures of Sparrowboy. /1997/K-2/3 KG242 . . **E**
Carver, George Washington.
GEORGE WASHINGTON CARVER: A MAN OF VISION
(VIDEOCASSETTE). /1990/5-A/KE281 . . . . **VCR B CARVER, G.**
MCLOONE, M/George Washington Carver: a photo-illustrated
biography. /1997/2-4/5 KE282 . . . . **B CARVER, G.**

Casa Loma (Toronto, Ont.)--Fiction.
OBERMAN, S/White stone in the castle wall. /1995/
4-6/2 KH555 . . . . **Fic**
Cassatt, Mary.
MEYER, SE/Mary Cassatt. /1990/6-A/8 KE283 . . **B CASSATT, M.**
MUHLBERGER, R/What makes a Cassatt a Cassatt? /1994/
5-A/7 KD489 . . . . **759.13**
Cassowaries.
ARNOLD, C/Ostriches and other flightless birds. /1990/
5-6/7 KC690 . . . . **598.5**
Castillo de San Marcos National Monument (Saint Augustine, Fla.)--
History.
ASHABRANNER, B/Strange and distant shore: Indians of the Great
Plains in exile. /1996/4-6/7 KF026 . . . . **978**
Castles.
CLEMENTS, G/Truth about castles. /c1988, 1990/
3-6/6 KE645 . . . . **940.1**
MACAULAY, D/Castle. /1977/A/9 KD059 . . . . **CE 623**
MACDONALD, F/Medieval castle. /1990/4-6/8 KE649 . . . . **940.1**
STEELE, P/Castles. /1995/4-6/7 KE650 . . . . **940.1**
Castles--Fiction.
ALLEN, LJ/Rollo and Tweedy and the ghost at Dougal Castle. /
1992/1-3/2 KF153 . . . . **CE E**
WINTHROP, E/Castle in the attic. /1985/4-6/5 KH869 . . . **CE Fic**
Castles--History.
GOODALL, JS/Story of a castle. /1986/2-6/KE680 . . . . **942**
Cataloging.
ANGLO-AMERICAN CATALOGUING RULES. 2ND ED., 1988
REVISION. /1988//KA056 . . . . **PROF 025.3**
Cataloging of audio-visual materials--Handbooks, manuals, etc.
FECKO, MB/Cataloging nonbook resources: a how-to-do-it manual
for librarians. /1993//KA057 . . . . **PROF 025.3**
OLSON, NB/Cataloging of audiovisual materials and other special
materials: a manual based on AACR2. New 4th ed. /1998/
/KA060 . . . . **PROF 025.4**
Cataloging of children's literature--Specimens.
CHILDREN'S CATALOG. 17TH ED. /1996//KA012. **PROF 011.62**
Cataloging of nonbook materials--Handbooks, manuals, etc.
FECKO, MB/Cataloging nonbook resources: a how-to-do-it manual
for librarians. /1993//KA057 . . . . **PROF 025.3**
OLSON, NB/Cataloging of audiovisual materials and other special
materials: a manual based /1998//KA060 . . . . **PROF 025.4**
Catastrophes (Geology).
POYNTER, M/Killer asteroids. /1996/6-8/6 KC036 . . . . . . **523.44**
VOGT, G/Search for the killer asteroid. /1994/
A/8 KC037 . . . . **523.44**
Caterpillars.
FACKLAM, M/Creepy, crawly caterpillars. /1996/
4-6/6 KC559 . . . . **595.78**
HEILIGMAN, D/From caterpillar to butterfly. /1996/
K-2/2 KC561 . . . . **595.78**
WATTS, B/Butterfly and caterpillar. /1985/2-4/4 KC568 . . **595.78**
Caterpillars--Fiction.
CARLE, E/Very hungry caterpillar. /1981/P-1/6 KF347 . . . . **E**
KENT, J/Caterpillar and the polliwog. /1982/K-2/4 KF896 . . **CE E**
Cathedral of St. John the Divine (New York, N.Y.).
ANCONA, G/Cutters, carvers and the cathedral. /1995/
5-6/7 KD392 . . . . **726.6**
Cathedrals.
ANCONA, G/Cutters, carvers and the cathedral. /1995/
5-6/7 KD392 . . . . **726.6**
MACAULAY, D/Cathedral: the story of its construction. /c1973/
5-6/6 KD388 . . . . **726**
Cathedral (Videocassette). /1986/6-A/KD389 . . . . . **VCR 726**
MACDONALD, F/Medieval cathedral. /1991/6-A/9 KD390 . . **726**
Catholics--Fiction.
FORD, B/Most wonderful movie in the world. /1996/
6-A/4 KH132 . . . . **Fic**
Cats.
BARE, CS/Toby the tabby kitten. /1995/K-3/2 KD229 . . . . **636.8**
COLE, J/Cat's body. /1982/2-4/6 KC818 . . . . **599.75**
My new kitten. /1995/P-1/2 KD230 . . . . **636.8**
DE PAOLA, T/Kids' cat book. /1979/K-2/2 KD231 . . . . . . **636.8**
EISLER, C/Cats know best. /1988/P-1/1 KD232 . . . . **636.8**
GIBBONS, G/Cats. /1996/K-3/3 KC821 . . . . **599.75**
HIRSCHI, R/What is a cat? /1991/K-4/2 KD233 . . . . **636.8**
KAPPELER, M/Big cats. /1991/5-6/7 KC822 . . . . **599.75**
LUMPKIN, S/Big cats. /1993/5-6/6 KC823 . . . . **599.75**
Small cats. /1993/5-6/8 KC824 . . . . **599.75**
RYDEN, H/Your cat's wild cousins. /1991/4-6/5 KC825 . . . **599.75**
SIMON, S/Big cats. /1991/4-6/6 KC826 . . . . **599.75**
TAYLOR, D/You and your cat. /1986/5-A/KD235 . . . . **636.8**
Cats--Diseases.
KUKLIN, S/Taking my cat to the vet. /1988/P-K/4 KD234 . . **636.8**

Cats--Fiction.
ALEXANDER, L/House Gobbaleen. /1995/3-5/4 KG836 . . . . . **Fic**
ALIKI /Tabby: a story in pictures. /1995/P-1/KF148 . . . . **E**
ANTLE, N/Good bad cat. /1985/P-1/1 KF160 . . . . **E**
AVERILL, E/Fire cat. /c1960/K-2/2 KF177 . . . . **E**
BARBER, A/Catkin. /1996/4-6/6 KG878 . . . . **Fic**
    Mousehole cat. /1990/4-6/6 KG879 . . . . **Fic**
BAUER, MD/Ghost eye. /1992/4-6/6 KG881 . . . . **Fic**
    Question of trust. /1994/5-A/6 KG883 . . . . **Fic**
BRETT, J/Annie and the wild animals. /1985/K-3/2 KF260 . . . . . **E**
BUCK, N/Oh, cats! /1997/P-1/1 KF290 . . . . **E**
BUNTING, E/Scary, scary Halloween. /1986/P-K/4 KF308 . . . . . **E**
CALHOUN, M/Cross-country cat. /1979/K-2/4 KF331 . . . . **E**
CARLE, E/Have you seen my cat? /c1973, 1987/P-1/1 KF343 . . **E**
CASEY, P/My cat Jack. /1996/P-1/2 KF372 . . . . **E**
CLEARY, B/Socks. /c1973/3-4/6 KH007 . . . . **Fic**
COATSWORTH, E/Cat who went to heaven. New ed. /c1958/
    A/6 KH010 . . . . **CE Fic**
COFFELT, N/Dog who cried woof. /1995/K-2/3 KF402 . . . . **E**
    Good night, Sigmund. /1992/P-1/2 KF403 . . . . **E**
DERBY, S/Jacob and the stranger. /1994/3-5/4 KH071 . . . . . . **Fic**
EHLERT, L/Feathers for lunch. /1990/P-1/2 KF517 . . . . **E**
EMBERLEY, M/Ruby. /1990/1-3/3 KF523 . . . . **E**
FOX, P/One-eyed cat. /1984/A/7 KH138 . . . . **Fic**
FREEMAN, L/Pet of the Met. /c1953/1-2/7 KF582 . . . . **E**
GAG, W/Millions of cats. /c1928/P-1/6 KF592 . . . . **CE E**
GANTOS, J/Rotten Ralph. /1976/K-2/3 KF597 . . . . **E**
GIFF, PR/Powder puff puzzle. /1987/2-3/2 KF615 . . . . **E**
HALL, D/I am the dog, I am the cat. /1994/K-3/3 KF661 . . . . . **E**
HARPER, I/My cats Nick and Nora. /1995/P-1/2 KF673 . . . . . . **E**
HASLER, E/Winter magic. /1989/K-3/4 KF678 . . . . **E**
HEARN, DD/Bad Luck Boswell. /1995/1-3/5 KF690 . . . . **E**
HOBAN, J/Buzby. /1992/K-2/2 KF731 . . . . **CE E**
    Buzby to the rescue. /1995/K-2/2 KF732 . . . . **E**
HOBAN, T/One little kitten. /1979/P-K/1 KF744 . . . . **E**
HOFF, S/Captain Cat: story and pictures. /1993/K-2/2 KF752 . . **E**
HOWE, J/Hot fudge. /1990/K-3/2 KF777 . . . . **E**
    Rabbit-Cadabra! /1993/K-3/3 KF779 . . . . **E**
    Scared silly: a Halloween treat. /1989/K-3/3 KF780 . . . . . . **E**
HUTCHINS, HJ/Cat of Artimus Pride. /1991/3-5/6 KH307 . . . . **Fic**
KARLIN, N/I see, you saw. /1997/P-1/1 KF869 . . . . **E**
KEATS, EJ/Hi, cat! /c1970, 1988/P-2/2 KF873 . . . . **CE E**
KING-SMITH, D/Sophie's Tom. /c1991, 1994/3-5/5 KH357 . . . **Fic**
    Three terrible trins. /1994/3-5/6 KH358 . . . . **CE Fic**
LISLE, JT/Looking for Juliette. /1994/4-6/6 KH412 . . . . **Fic**
MILLER, SS/Three stories you can read to your cat. /1997/
    K-2/2 KG137 . . . . **E**
MONSON, AM/Wanted: best friend. /1997/K-2/2 KG152 . . . . **E**
NAMIOKA, L/Yang the third and her impossible family. /1995/
    3-6/5 KH527 . . . . **Fic**
NAYLOR, PR/Grand escape. /1993/3-6/7 KH536 . . . . **Fic**
NETHERY, M/Hannah and Jack. /1996/K-2/2 KG170 . . . . **E**
NEVILLE, EC/It's like this, Cat. /c1963/5-6/6 KH547 . . . . . **CE Fic**
NOLL, S/Surprise! /1997/P-K/2 KG179 . . . . **E**
PACKARD, M/Christmas kitten. /1994/K-1/1 KG204 . . . . **E**
PARISH, P/Scruffy. /1988/K-3/1 KG217 . . . . **E**
PEET, B/Jennifer and Josephine. /c1967/K-2/7 KG228 . . . . . . **E**
POLACCO, P/Mrs. Katz and Tush. /1992/1-3/2 KG253 . . . . . . **E**
    Tikvah means hope. /1994/1-3/2 KG259 . . . . **E**
POTTER, B/Story of Miss Moppet. /1987/K-2/4 KG269 . . . . . . **E**
    Tale of the pie and the patty-pan. /c1933, 1987/
    K-2/5 KG282 . . . . **E**
    Tale of Tom Kitten. /c1935/P-2/7 KG283 . . . . **E**
PROVENSEN, A/Owl and three pussycats. /1994/
    K-2/5 KG289 . . . . **E**
ROBERTS, B/Halloween mice! /1995/P-1/3 KG336 . . . . **E**
ROBERTUS, PM/Dog who had kittens. /1991/K-1/4 KG337 . . **CE E**
RUBINSTEIN, G/Dog in, cat out. /1993/P-1/1 KG359 . . . . **E**
RYLANT, C/Mr. Putter and Tabby fly the plane. /1997/
    K-2/2 KG378 . . . . **E**
    Mr. Putter and Tabby pick the pears. /1995/1-3/2 KG379 . . . **E**
    Mr. Putter and Tabby pour the tea. /1994/1-3/2 KG380 . . . . **E**
    Mr. Putter and Tabby walk the dog. /1994/1-3/2 KG382 . . . . **E**
SATHRE, V/Mouse chase. /1995/P-1/2 KG394 . . . . **E**
SAY, A/Allison. /1997/2-4/2 KH678 . . . . **Fic**
SCHMIDT, AM/Minnie. /1994/5-A/3 KH680 . . . . **Fic**
SELDEN, G/Harry Kitten and Tucker Mouse. /1986/
    2-4/4 KH696 . . . . **Fic**
SEUSS, D/Cat in the hat. /c1957/P-2/1 KG448 . . . . **CE E**
    Cat in the Hat gets grinched (Videocassette). /1982/
    K-2/KG449 . . . . **VCR E**
SNOW, A/Truth about cats. /1996/4-A/7 KH728 . . . . **Fic**
SNYDER, ZK/Witches of Worm. /c1965/4-6/7 KH735 . . . . . . **Fic**
SOTO, G/Chato's kitchen. /c1995, 1997/1-3/5 KG527 . . . . . . **E**

SPOHN, K/Dog and Cat shake a leg. /1996/K-2/1 KG534 . . . . **E**
STEWART, EJ/Bimmi finds a cat. /1996/3-5/6 KH761 . . . . **Fic**
SYKES, J/This and that. /1996/P-1/2 KG586 . . . . **E**
TITUS, E/Kitten who couldn't purr. /1991/P-K/1 KG611 . . . . . . **E**
TURKLE, B/Do not open. /1981/K-2/2 KG622 . . . . **E**
VIORST, J/Tenth good thing about Barney. /c1971/
    K-3/2 KG664 . . . . **E**
WALSH, JP/Pepi and the secret names. /1995/2-3/6 KG683 . . . **E**
WHEELER, C/Bookstore cat. /1994/K-2/2 KG709 . . . . **E**

Cats--Folklore.
BROWN, M/Dick Whittington and his cat. /c1950, 1988/
    2-4/6 KB498 . . . . **398.23**
BRYAN, A/Cat's purr. /1985/K-3/2 KB543 . . . . **398.24**
GALDONE, P/Three little kittens. /1986/P-1/5 KB798 . . . . . **398.8**
GREEDY CAT (VIDEOCASSETTE). /1987/
    K-3/KB578 . . . . **VCR 398.24**
JACOBS, J/King of the cats. /1980/1-3/2 KB595 . . . **CE 398.24**
KIRSTEIN, L/Puss in boots. /c1992, 1994/3-4/6 KB604 . . . **398.24**
LEVINE, AA/Boy who drew cats: a Japanese folktale. /1993/
    2-4/4 KB609 . . . . **398.24**
METAXAS, E/Puss in Boots (Kit). /1992/1-4/KB620 . . **KIT 398.24**
PERRAULT, C/Puss in boots. /1990/3-4/4 KB633 . . . . . . **398.24**
    Puss in boots: a fairy tale. /1996/K-3/5 KB634 . . . . . **398.24**
SANDERSON, R/Papa Gatto: an Italian fairy tale. /1995/
    3-4/6 KB646 . . . . **398.24**
STEVENS, J/How the Manx cat lost its tail. /1990/
    2-3/4 KB658 . . . . **398.24**
WHITE CAT (VIDEOCASSETTE). /1997/K-2/KB382 . . **VCR 398.2**

Cats--Poetry.
ELIOT, TS/Old possum's book of practical cats. /1982/
    4-A/KE100. . . . . **821**
FARJEON, E/Cats sleep anywhere. /1996/K-3/KE101 . . . . . **821**

Cats--Religious aspects.
TRUMBLE, K/Cat mummies. /1996/3-6/9 KE637 . . . . **932**

Cats--Software.
EYEWITNESS VIRTUAL REALITY: CAT (CD-ROM). /1995/
    3-A/KC820 . . . . **CDR 599.75**

Cats--Songs and music.
SLAVIN, B/Cat came back: a traditional song. /1992/
    P-2/2 KD594 . . . . **789.2**

Cats--Wit and humor.
LEVINE, CA/Riddles to tell your cat. /1992/2-5/KD732 . . **793.735**

Cats in art.
MICKLETHWAIT, L/Spot a cat. /1995/K-2/2 KD466 . . . . **750**
ROALF, P/Cats. /1992/5-A/8 KD476 . . . . **758**

Catskill Mountains Region (N.Y.)--Fiction.
GEORGE, JC/My side of the mountain. /c1959/5-6/6 KH159 . **Fic**
Cattle SEE ALSO Dairy cattle.

Cattle--Marking--Fiction.
SCOTT, AH/Brand is forever. /1993/3-5/6 KH687 . . . . **Fic**

Cattle brands--Fiction.
SCOTT, AH/Brand is forever. /1993/3-5/6 KH687 . . . . **Fic**

Cave dwellers--Fiction.
BUSH, T/Grunt!: the primitive cave boy. /1995/K-2/2 KF323 . . . **E**
DE PAOLA, T/Little Grunt and the big egg: a prehistoric fairy tale.
    /1990/K-2/2 KF472 . . . . **E**

Cave paintings--Fiction.
BUSH, T/Grunt!: the primitive cave boy. /1995/K-2/2 KF323 . . . **E**

Caves.
BENDICK, J/Caves!: underground worlds. /1995/
    5-6/6 KC171 . . . . **551.44**
GIBBONS, G/Caves and caverns. /1993/K-6/6 KC166 . . . . **551.4**
WOOD, J/Caves: an underground wonderland. /1991/
    4-6/7 KC169 . . . . **551.4**

Caves--Fiction.
KARR, K/Cave. /1994/5-A/4 KH341 . . . . **Fic**

Celebrities.
BURLEIGH, R/Who said that?: famous Americans speak. /1997/
    4-A/7 KA597 . . . . **080**

Cells.
CELL DIVISION (VIDEOCASSETTE). /1995/
    5-6/KC274. . . . . **VCR 571.6**
DISCOVERING THE CELL (VIDEOCASSETTE). /1992/
    5-6/KC275. . . . . **VCR 571.6**

Censorship.
BURRESS, L/Battle of the books: literary censorship in the public
    schools, 1950-1985. /1989//KA051 . . . . **PROF 025.2**
REICHMAN, H/Censorship and selection: issues and answers for
    schools. Rev. ed. /1993//KA053 . . . . **PROF 025.2**

Censorship--Handbooks, manuals, etc.
INTELLECTUAL FREEDOM MANUAL. 5TH. ED. /1996/
    /KA052. . . . . **PROF 025.2**

Central America--Fiction.
ALEXANDER, L/Illyrian adventure. /1986/5-A/5 KG837 . . . . . **Fic**

Central America--Folklore.
PARKE, M/Quetzalcoatl tale of corn. /1992/2-3/5 KB630 . **398.24**
Central Highlands (Vietnam)--Social life and customs.
HUYNH, QN/Land I lost: adventures of a boy in Vietnam. /1982/
5-6/7 KE718 . . . . **959.7**
Central Pacific Railroad Company--History.
BLUMBERG, R/Full steam ahead: the race to build a transcontinental
railroad. /1996/4-6/10 KB137. . . . . **385**
Central Utah Relocation Center.
TUNNELL, MO/Children of Topaz: the story of a Japanese-
American internment camp: based on a /1996/
5-6/8 KE667 . . . . **940.53**
Cerebral palsy.
EMMERT, M/I'm the big sister now. /1989/3-5/5 KD039 . **618.92**
MCMAHON, P/Summer tunes: a Martha's Vineyard vacation. /
1996/2-5/7 KB005 . . . . **362.4**
Cerebral palsy--Fiction.
FASSLER, J/Howie helps himself. /1974, c1975/K-2/4 KF544 . . . **E**
HELFMAN, E/On being Sarah. /1993/5-A/6 KH236. . . . . . . **Fic**
LITTLE, J/Mine for keeps. /c1962, 1994/5-A/5 KH414 . . . . . **Fic**
Cervidae.
SELSAM, ME/First look at animals with horns. /1989/
1-3/2 KC792 . . . . **599.64**
Ceylon SEE Sri Lanka.
Chagall, Marc.
GREENFELD, H/Marc Chagall. /1990/
6-A/8 KE284 . . . . **B CHAGALL, M.**
Chairs.
GIBLIN, JC/Be seated: a book about chairs. /1993/
4-A/7 KD463 . . . . **749**
Chairs--Fiction.
WILLIAMS, VB/Chair for my mother. /1982/P-3/3 KG734 . . . . . **E**
Chaka, Zulu Chief.
STANLEY, D/Shaka, king of the Zulus. /1988/
4-6/6 KE537 . . . . **B SHAKA, KING**
Chameleons.
RYDER, J/Lizard in the sun. /1990/1-3/5 KC628 . . . . . . **597.95**
SCHNIEPER, C/Chameleons. /1989/5-6/7 KC630 . . . . . . **597.95**
Chameleons--Fiction.
HADITHI, M/Crafty chameleon. /c1987, 1995/P-2/7 KF659 . . . . **E**
LIONNI, L/Color of his own. /c1975, 1997/K-2/5 KF990 . . . . . . **E**
STRETE, CK/They thought they saw him. /1996/K-2/2 KG579 . . **E**
Chang, Wah.
RILEY, GB/Wah Ming Chang: artist and master of special effects. /
1995/5-6/6 KE285 . . . . **B CHANG, W.**
Change--Fiction.
PRYOR, B/House on Maple Street. /1987/K-3/4 KG292 . . . . . . **E**
YOLEN, J/Letting Swift River go. /1992/1-3/5 KG777 . . . . **E**
Chanukah SEE Hanukkah.
Characters and characteristics in literature--Dictionaries.
TUTEN-PUCKETT, KE/My name in books: a guide to character
names in children's literature. /1993/KA360 . . . . . . **PROF 809**
Characters and characteristics in literature--Fiction.
BRITTAIN, B/Mystery of the several sevens. /1994/
2-4/4 KG924 . . . . **Fic**
Charles, Ray.
TURK, R/Ray Charles: soul man. /1996/
5-A/8 KE286 . . . . **B CHARLES, R.**
Charleston (S.C.)--Fiction.
BROTHER FUTURE (VIDEOCASSETTE). /c1991, 1997/
6-A/KG930 . . . . **VCR Fic**
Charleston (S.C.)--Social life and customs--Fiction.
SCHROEDER, A/Carolina shout! /1995/1-5/3 KG411 . . . . **E**
Chavez, Cesar.
CEDENO, ME/Cesar Chavez: labor leader. /1993/
4-5/6 KE287 . . . . **B CHAVEZ, C.**
DE RUIZ, DC/Causa: the migrant farmworkers' story. /1993/
4-6/6 KA944 . . . . **331.88**
Cheerfulness--Fiction.
GLEITZMAN, M/Misery guts. /1993/5-A/7 KH174. . . . . **Fic**
Cheetahs.
ARNOLD, C/Cheetah. /1989/5-6/9 KC817 . . . . **599.75**
DUPONT, P/Cheetah: fast as lightning. /1992/
1-4/5 KC819 . . . . **599.75**
Chelm (Chelm, Poland)--Folklore.
SANFIELD, S/Feather merchants and other tales of the fools of
Chelm. /1991/6-A/7 KB510 . . . . **398.23**
Strudel, strudel, strudel. /1995/2-3/4 KB773 . . . . . . **398.27**
Chemistry SEE ALSO Color; Poisons.
Chemists.
PFLAUM, R/Marie Curie and her daughter Irene. /1993/
6-A/8 KC139 . . . . **539.7**
POYNTER, M/Marie Curie: discoverer of radium. /1994/
4-6/4 KE311 . . . . **B CURIE, M.**

Cherokee Indians.
HOYT-GOLDSMITH, D/Cherokee summer. /1993/
3-5/5 KE782 . . . . **970.466**
LANDAU, E/Cherokees. /1992/4-6/7 KE760 . . . . **970.3**
PENNINGTON, D/Itse Selu: Cherokee harvest festival. /1994/
K-3/6 KB190 . . . . **394.2**
SNEVE, V/Cherokees. /1996/4-6/5 KE769 . . . . **970.3**
Cherokee Indians--Biography.
KLAUSNER, J/Sequoyah's gift: a portrait of the Cherokee leader. /
1993/5-6/7 KE535 . . . . **B SEQUOYAH**
LOWERY, L/Wilma Mankiller. /1996/
2-3/4 KE458 . . . . **B MANKILLER, W.**
Cherokee Indians--Fiction.
ROCKWOOD, J/To spoil the sun. /c1976, 1994/
6-A/6 KH644 . . . . **Fic**
STEWART, EJ/On the long trail home. /1994/4-6/4 KH762 . . . **Fic**
Cherokee Indians--Folklore.
BRUCHAC, J/First strawberries: a Cherokee story. /1993/
1-3/4 KB538 . . . . **398.24**
Story of the Milky Way: a Cherokee tale. /1995/
2-3/3 KB701 . . . . **398.26**
HALEY, GE/Two bad boys: a very old Cherokee tale. /1996/
2-5/5 KB742 . . . . **398.27**
ROSS, G/How Rabbit tricked Otter and other Cherokee trickster
stories. /1994/2-4/6 KB641 . . . . **CE 398.24**
How Turtle's back was cracked: a traditional Cherokee tale. /
1995/4-5/5 KB642 . . . . **398.24**
Cherokee Indians--History.
BEALER, AW/Only the names remain: the Cherokees and the Trail
of Tears. 2nd ed. /1996/5-6/8 KE758 . . . . **970.3**
Cherry, Fred V.
MYERS, WD/Place called heartbreak: a story of Vietnam. /1993/
5-6/6 KE721 . . . . **959.704**
Chesapeake Bay (Md. and Va.).
MILLS, P/On an island in the bay. /1994/2-4/3 KE979 . . . . **975.5**
Chess.
NOTTINGHAM, T/Chess for children. /1993/4-A/8 KD756 . **794.1**
Chewing gum.
CHEWING GUM (VIDEOCASSETTE). /1991/
2-5/KD318. . . . . **VCR 664**
YOUNG, R/Chewing gum book. /1989/5-6/6 KD322 . . . . . . **664**
Cheyenne Indians.
GOBLE, P/Red Hawk's account of Custer's last battle; the Battle of
the Little Bighorn. /c1969, 1992/5-6/6 KE914. . . . . . . **973.8**
HOIG, S/People of the sacred arrows: the Southern Cheyenne
today. /1992/6-A/7 KE781 . . . . **970.466**
MYERS, A/Cheyenne. /1992/4-6/7 KE771 . . . . **970.3**
SNEVE, V/Cheyennes. /1996/4-6/6 KE770 . . . . **970.3**
Cheyenne Indians--Ethnic identity--Fiction.
BUNTING, E/Cheyenne again. /1995/3-5/2 KG941 . . . . **Fic**
Cheyenne Indians--Folklore.
GOBLE, P/Great race of the birds and animals. /1991/
3-5/4 KB574 . . . . **398.24**
Cheyenne Indians--History--Fiction.
GOBLE, P/Death of the iron horse. /1987/K-3/2 KF626 . . . . . . **E**
Chicago (Ill.)--History--To 1875.
MURPHY, J/Great fire. /1995/A/7 KF015 . . . . **977.3**
Chicanos SEE Mexican Americans.
Chick embryo.
BACK, C/Chicken and egg. /1986/K-3/2 KC692 . . . . . . **598.6**
JOHNSON, SA/Inside an egg. /1982/4-6/8 KC695 . . . . . **598.6**
Chicken pox--Fiction.
KELLEY, T/I've got chicken pox. /1994/K-3/2 KF887. . . . . **E**
Chickens.
CHICK EMBRYOLOGY (VIDEOCASSETTE). /c1974, 1986/
5-A/KC693 . . . . **VCR 598.6**
COLE, J/Chick hatches. /1977/P-2/3 KC694 . . . . **598.6**
WALLACE, K/My hen is dancing. /c1994, 1996/
K-2/2 KD215 . . . . **636.5**
Chickens--Fiction.
AUCH, MJ/Eggs mark the spot. /1996/K-2/3 KF176 . . . . . . **CE E**
COERR, E/Josefina story quilt. /1986/1-3/2 KF401 . . . . . . **CE E**
CONRAD, P/Rooster's gift. /1996/K-2/3 KF414 . . . . **E**
EDWARDS, M/Chicken man. /1991/K-2/2 KF509 . . . . **E**
ERNST, LC/Zinnia and Dot. /1992/P-1/2 KF535 . . . . **E**
FOX, M/Hattie and the fox. /1987/P-2/2 KF569 . . . . **E**
FRENCH, V/Red Hen and Sly Fox. /1995/P-2/2 KF584. . . . . . . **E**
FROMENTAL, J/Broadway chicken. /1995/5-A/7 KH146. . . . **Fic**
GALDONE, P/Little red hen. /c1973/P-K/2 KF595 . . . . . . **CE E**
GINSBURG, M/Across the stream. /1982/P-K/2 KF621. . . . . . . **E**
KASZA, K/Wolf's chicken stew. /1987/P-2/2 KF870 . . . . **E**
PINKWATER, DM/Hoboken chicken emergency. /c1977/
5-A/6 KH603 . . . . **CE Fic**
REISER, L/Surprise family. /1994/P-2/2 KG319 . . . . **E**

RUURS, M/Emma's eggs. /1996/P-2/2 KG364 . . . . E
STOEKE, JM/Hat for Minerva Louise. /1994/P-K/2 KG576 . . . . E
Minerva Louise at school. /1996/P-1/2 KG577 . . . . E
ZEMACH, M/Little red hen, an old story. /1983/P-K/2 KG790 . . E
ZIEFERT, H/Little red hen. /1995/K-1/2 KG793 . . . . E

Child abuse.
CRITTER JITTERS (VIDEOCASSETTE). /1986/
P-2/KB016. . . . . **VCR 362.76**
MUFSON, S/Straight talk about child abuse. /1991/
A/10 KB017. . . . . **362.76**

Child abuse--Fiction.
COMAN, C/What Jamie saw. /1995/5-A/6 KH018 . . . . Fic
POWELL, ES/Daisy. /1991/3-4/4 KH612 . . . . Fic
ROBERTS, WD/Don't hurt Laurie! /1977/5-6/6 KH635 . . . . . . Fic

Child development.
HUMAN AND ANIMAL BEGINNINGS. 3RD ED
(VIDEOCASSETTE). /1990/2-5/KC950 . . . . **VCR 612.6**
PEARSE, P/See how you grow. /1988/K-3/5 KC954 . . . . . 612.6
STEIN, S/Oh, baby! /1993/P-K/3 KA827 . . . . 305.232

Child labor--Great Britain--Fiction.
PATON WALSH, J/Chance child. /c1978, 1991/6-A/7 KH582 . Fic

Child rearing.
ORLICK, T/Free to feel great: teaching children to excel at living. /
1993//KA305 . . . . **PROF 649**

Child sexual abuse.
CRITTER JITTERS (VIDEOCASSETTE). /1986/
P-2/KB016. . . **VCR 362.76**
WHEN SHOULD YOU TELL?: DEALING WITH ABUSE
(VIDEOCASSETTE). /1995/5-6/KB018 . . . . **VCR 362.76**

Child sexual abuse--Fiction.
LOWERY, L/Laurie tells. /1994/3-6/4 KH420. . . . . Fic

Child sexual abuse--Prevention.
MY BODY BELONGS TO ME (VIDEOCASSETTE). /1992/
K-3/KA170 . . . . **VCR PROF 362.7**
Child welfare SEE ALSO Child abuse; Children--Care and hygiene.

Childbirth.
COLE, J/How you were born. Rev. and expanded ed. /1993/
K-3/4 KC945 . . . . 612.6
HUMAN AND ANIMAL BEGINNINGS. 3RD ED
(VIDEOCASSETTE). /1990/2-5/KC950 . . . . **VCR 612.6**

Childbirth--Fiction.
HARRIS, RH/Happy birth day! /1996/P-2/3 KF676. . . . . E

Children--Books and reading.
AMMON, BD/Worth a thousand words: an annotated guide to
picture books for older readers. /1996//KA010 . . **PROF 011.62**
BARSTOW, B/Beyond picture books: a guide to first readers. 2nd
ed. /1995//KA011 . . . . **PROF 011.62**
BAUER, CF/Celebrations: read-aloud holiday and theme book
programs. /1985//KA342 . . . . **PROF 808.8**
Read for the fun of it: active programming with books for children.
/1992//KA067 . . . . **PROF 027.62**
BEST OF BOOKFINDER: A GUIDE TO CHILDREN'S LITERATURE
ABOUT INTERESTS /1992//KA083 . . . . . . **PROF 028.1**
BOOK TALK AND BEYOND: CHILDREN AND TEACHERS
RESPOND TO LITERATURE. /1995//KA235. . . . . **PROF 372.64**
BORDERS, SG/Children talking about books. /1993/
/KA236. . . . . **PROF 372.64**
CULLINAN, BE/Read to me: raising kids who love to read. /1992/
/KA301 . . . . **PROF 649**
DOLL, CA/Nonfiction books for children: activities for thinking,
learning and doing. /1990//KA072 . . . . **PROF 027.8**
GILLESPIE, JT/Middleplots 4: a book talk guide for use with readers
ages 8-12. /1994//KA092 . . . . **PROF 028.5**
HEFNER, CR/Literature-based science: children's books and activities
to enrich the K-5 /1995//KA200 . . . . **PROF 372.3**
IRVING, J/Full speed ahead: stories and activities for children on
transportation. /1988//KA223 . . . . **PROF 372.6**
KROPP, P/Raising a reader: make your child a reader for life. /
c1993, 1996//KA182 . . . . **PROF 371.3028**
LANDS OF PLEASURE: /1990//KA044 . . . . **PROF 020**
LAUGHLIN, MK/Literature-based reading: /1990/
/KA210. . . . . **PROF 372.4**
LYNN, RN/Fantasy literature for children and young adults: an
annotated bibliography. 4th ed. /1994/
/KA032. . . . . **PROF 016.80883**
MCELMEEL, SL/Author a month (for pennies). /1988/
/KA069. . . . . **PROF 027.62**
Great new nonfiction reads. /1995//KA086 . . . . . **PROF 028.1**
Latest and greatest read-alouds. /1994//KA239. . **PROF 372.64**
OLSEN, ML/More creative connections: literature and the reading
program, grades 4-6. /1993//KA212 . . . . **PROF 372.4**
POLETTE, N/Brain power through picture books: /1992/
/KA227. . . . . **PROF 372.6**

ROGINSKI, J/Behind the covers: interviews with authors and
illustrators of books for children and young adults, Vol. I. /1985/
/KA335. **PROF 808.06**
ROUTMAN, R/Invitations: changing as teachers and learners K-12.
Updated, expanded, and /c1991, 1994//KA214 . . . **PROF 372.4**
SLAUGHTER, JP/Beyond storybooks: young children and the shared
book experience. /1993//KA215 . . . . **PROF 372.4**
SUTHERLAND, Z/Children and books. 9th ed. /1997/
/KA358. . . . . **PROF 809**
THOMAS, RL/Primaryplots 2: a book talk guide for use with
readers ages 4-8. /1993//KA093 . . . . **PROF 028.5**
TRELEASE, J/Read-aloud handbook. 4th ed. /1995/
/KA242. . . . . **PROF 372.64**
WATKINS, J/Programming author visits. /1996/
/KA071. . . . . **PROF 027.62**

Children--Books and reading--Bibliography.
COLBORN, C/What do children read next?: a reader's guide to
fiction for children. /1997//KA031 . . . . **PROF 016.80883**

Children--Books and reading--Handbooks, manuals, etc.
RAINES, SC/Story stretchers for the primary grades: activities to
expand children's /1992//KA240 . . . . **PROF 372.64**

Children--Books and reading--Periodicals.
REVIEWS. /1993-//KA135. . . . . **PROF 050**

Children--Care and hygiene.
BROWN, LK/Dinosaurs alive and well! a guide to good health. /
1990/K-3/5 KC982 613

Children--Conduct of life.
LETTERS FOR OUR CHILDREN: FIFTY AMERICANS SHARE
LESSONS IN LIVING. /1996//KA158. . . . . **PROF 170**
ORLICK, T/Free to feel great: teaching children to excel at living. /
1993//KA305 . . . . **PROF 649**

Children--Employment--Fiction.
DOHERTY, B/Street child. /1994/5-A/6 KH078 . . . . Fic

Children--Employment--History.
BARTOLETTI, SC/Growing up in coal country. /1996/
4-6/8 KA934 . . . . 331.3
COLMAN, P/Mother Jones and the march of the mill children. /
1994/4-6/7 KA935 . . . . 331.3
CURRIE, S/We have marched together: the working children's
crusade. /1997/5-6/8 KA936 . . . . 331.3
FREEDMAN, R/Kids at work: Lewis Hine and the crusade against
child labor. /1994/5-A/8 KA937 . . . . 331.3

Children--Fiction.
RYLANT, C/Everyday children (Board book). /1993/
P-K/2 KG370 . . . . BB E

Children--Foreign countries.
KINDERSLEY, B/Children just like me. /1995/
2-6/8 KA825 . . . . 305.23

Children--Growth--Fiction.
KEATS, EJ/Peter's chair. /c1967/P-2/2 KF877 . . . . CE E

Children--Pictorial works.
KINDERSLEY, B/Children just like me. /1995/
2-6/8 KA825 . . . . 305.23

Children--Poetry.
HUGHES, S/Rhymes for Annie Rose. /1995/P-2/KE102. 821
MYERS, WD/Glorious angels: a celebration of children. /1995/
K-6/KD993 811

Children--United States--History--17th century.
BARRETT, T/Growing up in colonial America. /1995/
4-6/9 KE869 . . . . 973.2

Children--United States--History--18th century.
BARRETT, T/Growing up in colonial America. /1995/
4-6/9 KE869 . . . . 973.2

Children and folklore.
SIERRA, J/Children's traditional games: games from 137 countries
and cultures. /1995//KA331 . . . . **PROF 796**

Children as artists.
TOPAL, CW/Children and painting. /1992//KA217. . **PROF 372.5**

Children as authors.
MELTON, D/Written & illustrated by... a revolutionary two-brain
approach for teaching /1985//KA226 . . . . **PROF 372.6**

Children as authors--Periodicals.
CREATIVE KIDS. /n.d./4-A/KA511 . . . . **PER 050**
STONE SOUP: A MAGAZINE BY CHILDREN. /1973-/
2-A/KA546 . . . . **PER 050**

Children in art.
RICHMOND, R/Story in a picture: children in art. /1992/
3-6/7 KD471 757

Children of presidents.
BLUE, R/White House kids. /1995/5-6/7 KE849 973
LEINER, K/First children: growing up in the White House. /1996/
A/9 KE856 973

Children of working parents.
HOME ALONE: YOU'RE IN CHARGE (VIDEOCASSETTE). /1991/
2-4/KD259. . . . . **VCR 640**
HOME ON YOUR OWN (VIDEOCASSETTE). /1994/
4-6/KD260. . . . . **VCR 640**
LATCHKEY CHILDREN: WHEN YOU'RE IN CHARGE
(VIDEOCASSETTE). /1986/5-6/KD261 . . . . **VCR 640**

Children-s libraries--Activity programs.
WATKINS, J/Programming author visits. /1996/
/KA071. . . . . **PROF 027.62**

Children's art.
BE A FRIEND: CHILDREN WHO LIVE WITH HIV SPEAK. /1994/
2-6/2 KA993 . . . . **362.1**
WILKES, S/One day we had to run!: refugee children tell their
stories in words and /1994/4-A/5 KB019 . . . . **362.87**

Children's books, Illustrated--Audio-visual aids.
SHARKEY, PB/Newbery and Caldecott Medal and Honor books in
other media. /1992/KA087 . . . . **PROF 028.1**

Children's gardens.
JURENKA, NE/Beyond the bean seed: gardening activities for
grades K-6. /1996/KA202. . . . . **PROF 372.3**

Children's libraries--Activity programs.
REID, R/Children's jukebox: a subject guide to musical recordings
and programming ideas /1995//KA029 . . . . . . **PROF 016.7893**
Children's literature SEE ALSO Children's periodicals; Children's poetry;
Children's reference books; Libraries, Children's; Storytelling.

Children's literature.
AASL ELECTRONIC LIBRARY. 1997 ED. (CD-ROM). /1997/
/KA045. . . . . **CDR PROF 025**
CHILDREN'S BOOK OF VIRTUES. /1995/K-3/KD871 . . . . . **808.8**
CULLINAN, BE/Literature and the child. 3rd ed. /1993/
/KA348. . . . . **PROF 809**
FREDERICKS, AD/Social studies through children's literature: an
integrated approach. /1991/KA260. . . . . **PROF 372.83**
HEY! LISTEN TO THIS: STORIES TO READ ALOUD. /1992/
/KA338. . . . . **PROF 808.5**
JONES, DB/Children's literature awards and winners: a directory of
prizes, authors, and illustrators. 3rd ed. /1994/
/KA354. . . . . **PROF 809**
POLETTE, N/ABC's of books and thinking skills. /1987/
/KA156. . . . . **PROF 153.4**
SENDAK, M/Caldecott and Co.: notes on books & pictures. /1988/
/KA356. . . . . **PROF 809**
SHARKEY, PB/Newbery and Caldecott Medal and Honor books in
other media. /1992/KA087 . . . . **PROF 028.1**
WHAT'S A GOOD BOOK? (VIDEOCASSETTE). /1993/
/KA094. . . . . **VCR PROF 028.5**

Children's literature--Abstracting and indexing.
FOUNTAIN, JF/Subject headings for school and public libraries: an
LCSH/Sears companion. 2nd /1996/KA059 . . . . . **PROF 025.4**

Children's literature--Appreciation--Problems, exercises, etc.
BAUER, CF/Read for the fun of it: active programming with books
for children. /1992/KA067 . . . . **PROF 027.62**

Children's literature--Authorship.
LANDS OF PLEASURE: /1990//KA044 . . . . **PROF 020**
ROGINSKI, J/Behind the covers: /1985//KA335 . . **PROF 808.06**

Children's literature--Bibliography.
ADVENTURING WITH BOOKS: A BOOKLIST FOR PRE-K-GRADE
6. 1997 ED. /1997//KA009 . . . . **PROF 011.62**
AMMON, BD/Handbook for the Newbery Medal and Honor Books,
1980-1989. /1991//KA347 . . . . **PROF 809**
BARSTOW, B/Beyond picture books: a guide to first readers. 2nd
ed. /1995//KA011 . . . . **PROF 011.62**
BAUER, CF/Leading kids to books through magic. /1996/
/KA066. . . . . **PROF 027.62**
CHILDREN'S CATALOG. 17TH ED. /1996//KA012. **PROF 011.62**
DOLL, CA/Nonfiction books for children: activities for thinking,
learning and doing. /1990//KA072 . . . . **PROF 027.8**
EGOFF, S/New republic of childhood: /1990//KA349. . **PROF 809**
ELEMENTARY SCHOOL LIBRARY COLLECTION: A GUIDE TO
BOOKS AND OTHER MEDIA, PHASES 1-2-3. 21ST ED. /1998/
/KA013. . . . . **PROF 011.62**
EXPLORING THE GREAT LAKES STATES THROUGH LITERATURE.
/1994//KA039. **PROF 016.977**
EXPLORING THE MOUNTAIN STATES THROUGH LITERATURE. /
1994//KA040 . . . . **PROF 016.978**
EXPLORING THE NORTHEAST STATES THROUGH LITERATURE. /
1994//KA036 . . . . **PROF 016.974**
EXPLORING THE PACIFIC STATES THROUGH LITERATURE. /
1994//KA042 . . . . **PROF 016.9795**
EXPLORING THE PLAINS STATES THROUGH LITERATURE. /1994/
/KA041. . . . . **PROF 016.978**
EXPLORING THE SOUTHEAST STATES THROUGH LITERATURE. /
1994//KA037 . . . . **PROF 016.975**

EXPLORING THE SOUTHWEST STATES THROUGH LITERATURE. /
1994//KA038 . . . . **PROF 016.976**
FREEMAN, J/Books kids will sit still for: the complete read-aloud
guide. 2nd ed. /1990//KA015. . . . . **PROF 011.62**
GILLESPIE, JT/Best books for children: preschool through grade 6.
5th ed. /1994//KA084 . . . . **PROF 028.1**
Middleplots 4: a book talk guide for use with readers ages 8-12.
/1994//KA092 . . . . **PROF 028.5**
HARMS, JM/Picture books to enhance the curriculum. /1996/
/KA016. . . . . **PROF 011.62**
LIMA, CW/A to zoo: subject access to children's picture books. 5th
ed. /1998//KA017 . . . . **PROF 011.62**
LITERARY LAURELS: KIDS' EDITION: A READER'S GUIDE TO
AWARD-WINNING CHILDREN'S /1996//KA034 . **PROF 016.809**
LYNN, RN/Fantasy literature for children and young adults: an
annotated bibliography. /1994//KA032. . . . . . **PROF 016.80883**
MILLER-LACHMANN, L/Our family, our friends, our world: an
annotated guide to significant multicultural books for children and
teenagers. /1992//KA020 . . . . **PROF 011.62**
SUTHERLAND, Z/Best in children's books: /1991/
/KA023. . . . . **PROF 011.62**
THOMAS, JL/Play, learn, and grow: an annotated guide to the best
books and materials for /1992//KA088. . . . . **PROF 028.1**
VENTURE INTO CULTURES: A RESOURCE BOOK OF
MULTICULTURAL MATERIALS AND PROGRAMS. /1992/
/KA024. . . . . **PROF 011.62**

Children's literature--Bibliography--Periodicals.
BOOK LINKS: CONNECTING BOOKS, LIBRARIES AND
CLASSROOMS. /1991-//KA097 . . . . **PER PROF 050**
BULLETIN OF THE CENTER FOR CHILDREN'S BOOKS. /1947-/
/KA099. . . . . **PER PROF 050**
CANADIAN CHILDREN'S LITERATURE. /1975-/
/KA100. . . . . **PER PROF 050**
HORN BOOK GUIDE TO CHILDREN'S AND YOUNG ADULT
BOOKS. /1990-/KA114 . . . . **PER PROF 050**
HORN BOOK MAGAZINE: ABOUT BOOKS FOR CHILDREN AND
YOUNG ADULTS. /1924-/KA115 . . . . **PER PROF 050**
NEWBERY AND CALDECOTT AWARDS: A GUIDE TO THE
MEDAL AND HONOR BOOKS. /n.d.//KA128 . . **PER PROF 050**
RESOURCE LINKS: CONNECTING CLASSROOMS, LIBRARIES
AND CANADIAN LEARNING RESOURCES. /1995-/
/KA134. . . . . **PER PROF 050**
SCHOOL LIBRARY JOURNAL: FOR CHILDREN'S, YOUNG ADULT,
AND SCHOOL LIBRARIES. /1954-/KA139 . . . . **PER PROF 050**

Children's literature--Bibliography--Software.
ELEMENTARY SCHOOL LIBRARY COLLECTION: A GUIDE TO
BOOKS AND OTHER MEDIA, PHASES 1-2-3. 21ST ED. (CD-
ROM). /1998//KA014. . . . . **CDR PROF 011.62**

Children's literature--Bio-bibliography.
AUTHORS OF BOOKS FOR YOUNG PEOPLE. 3RD ED. /1990/
5-A/KA460 . . . . **REF 809**
BIOGRAPHY TODAY AUTHOR SERIES: PROFILES OF PEOPLE OF
INTEREST TO YOUNG READERS. /1996-/4-6/KA461 . . **REF 809**
MAJOR AUTHORS AND ILLUSTRATORS FOR CHILDREN AND
YOUNG ADULTS: A SELECTION OF SKETCHES FROM
SOMETHING ABOUT THE AUTHOR. /1993//KA464. . . **REF 809**
SOMETHING ABOUT THE AUTHOR. /1971-/
5-6/KA465 . . . . **REF 809**

Children's literature--Book lists.
CHILDREN'S CATALOG. 17TH ED. /1996//KA012. **PROF 011.62**

Children's literature--Book reviews.
BEST OF BOOKFINDER: A GUIDE TO CHILDREN'S LITERATURE
ABOUT INTERESTS AND CONCERNS OF YOUTH AGED 2-18. /
1992//KA083 . . . . **PROF 028.1**
SUTHERLAND, Z/Best in children's books: /1991/
/KA023. . . . . **PROF 011.62**
THOMAS, RL/Primaryplots 2: a book talk guide for use with
readers ages 4-8. /1993//KA093. . . . . **PROF 028.5**

Children's literature--Censorship.
BURRESS, L/Battle of the books: literary censorship in the public
schools, 1950-1985. /1989//KA051 . . . . **PROF 025.2**
REICHMAN, H/Censorship and selection: issues and answers for
schools. Rev. ed. /1993//KA053 . . . . **PROF 025.2**

Children's literature--Collections.
CHILDCRAFT: THE HOW AND WHY LIBRARY. /1964-/
P-2/KA378. . . . . **REF 031**

Children's literature--Criticism.
TOUCHSTONES: REFLECTIONS ON THE BEST IN CHILDREN'S
LITERATURE, VOL. 1. /1985//KA359 . . . . **PROF 809**

Children's literature--History and criticism.
HAZARD, P/Books, children and men. 5th ed. /1983/
/KA351. . . . . **PROF 809**

HORN BOOK MAGAZINE /Newbery Medal books: 1922-1955: with their authors' acceptance papers, /c1957/ /KA353. . . . . **PROF 809**
HORNING, KT/From cover to cover: evaluating and reviewing children's books. /1997//KA085 . . . . **PROF 028.1**
ILLUSTRATORS OF CHILDREN'S BOOKS, 1967-1976. /1978/ /KA311. . . . . **PROF 741.6**
KOBRIN, B/Eyeopeners II: children's books to answer children's questions about the world around them. /1995/ /KA355. . . . . **PROF 809**
SUTHERLAND, Z/Children and books. 9th ed. /1997/ /KA358. . . . . **PROF 809**

Children's literature--History and criticism--Dictionaries.
TUTEN-PUCKETT, KE/My name in books: a guide to character names in children's literature. /1993//KA360 . . . . . . **PROF 809**

Children's literature--Illustrators.
SOMETHING ABOUT THE AUTHOR. /1971-/ 5-6/KA465 . . . . **REF 809**

Children's literature--Indexes.
CHILDREN'S AUTHORS AND ILLUSTRATORS: AN INDEX TO BIOGRAPHICAL DICTIONARIES. /1976//KA033 . **PROF 016.809**

Children's literature--Miscellanea.
GREESON, J/Name that book! Questions and answers on outstanding children's books. /1996//KA350 . . . . . . **PROF 809**

Children's literature--Periodicals.
CANADIAN CHILDREN'S LITERATURE. /1975-/ /KA100. . . . . **PER PROF 050**
CBC FEATURES. /1945-//KA101 . . . . **PER PROF 050**
CRICKET: THE MAGAZINE FOR CHILDREN. /1973-/ 3-6/KA512 . . . . **PER 050**
FIVE OWLS. /1986-//KA110 . . . . **PER PROF 050**
JOURNAL OF YOUTH SERVICES IN LIBRARIES. /1946-/ /KA118. . . . . **PER PROF 050**
LADYBUG: THE MAGAZINE FOR YOUNG CHILDREN. /1990-/ P-2/KA524. . . . . **PER 050**
NEW ADVOCATE. /1988-//KA127 . . . . **PER PROF 050**
RESOURCE LINKS: CONNECTING CLASSROOMS, LIBRARIES AND CANADIAN LEARNING /1995-//KA134 . . **PER PROF 050**
SPIDER: THE MAGAZINE FOR CHILDREN. /1993-/ 1-3/KA542 . . . . **PER 050**

Children's literature--Reviews.
AMMON, BD/Handbook for the Newbery Medal and Honor Books, 1980-1989. /1991//KA347 . . . . **PROF 809**
PARENTS' CHOICE: A REVIEW OF CHILDREN'S MEDIA. /1978-/ /KA130. . . . . **PER PROF 050**

Children's literature--Reviews--Periodicals.
RESOURCE LINKS: CONNECTING CLASSROOMS, LIBRARIES AND CANADIAN LEARNING /1995-//KA134 . . **PER PROF 050**
REVIEWS. /1993-//KA135. . . . . **PROF 050**

Children's literature--Software.
JUNIOR DISCOVERING AUTHORS: BIOGRAPHIES AND PLOTLINES ON 300 MOST-STUDIED AND /1994/ 5-A/KA463 . . . . **CDR REF 809**

Children's literature--Stories, plots, etc.
GILLESPIE, JT/Middleplots 4: a book talk guide for use with readers ages 8-12. /1994//KA092 . . . . **PROF 028.5**
THOMAS, RL/Primaryplots 2: a book talk guide for use with readers ages 4-8. /1993//KA093 . . . . **PROF 028.5**

Children's literature--Study and teaching.
CHILDREN'S LITERATURE IN THE CLASSROOM: WEAVING CHARLOTTE'S WEB. /1989//KA238 . . . . **PROF 372.64**
HEFNER, CR/Literature-based science: children's books and activities to enrich the K-5 /1995//KA200 . . . . **PROF 372.3**
IRVING, J/Full speed ahead: stories and activities for children on transportation. /1988//KA223 . . . . **PROF 372.6**
MCELMEEL, SL/Author a month (for pennies). /1988/ /KA069. . . . . **PROF 027.62**
RAINES, SC/Story stretchers for the primary grades: activities to expand children's favorite books. /1992//KA240 . . **PROF 372.64**
TOUCHSTONES: REFLECTIONS ON THE BEST IN CHILDREN'S LITERATURE, VOL. 1. /1985//KA359 . . . . **PROF 809**
USING LITERATURE IN THE ELEMENTARY CLASSROOM. REV. ED. /1989//KA243 . . . . **PROF 372.64**

Children's literature--Study and teaching (Elementary).
PEREZ-STABLE, MA/Understanding American history through children's literature: instructional /1994//KA263 . . . **PROF 372.89**
SPILLMAN, CV/Integrating language arts through literature in elementary classrooms. /1996//KA229 . . . . **PROF 372.6**

Children's literature, American--Awards.
NEWBERY AND CALDECOTT MEDALISTS AND HONOR BOOK WINNERS: BIBLIOGRAPHIES AND RESOURCE MATERIAL THROUGH 1991. 2ND ED. /1992//KA004 . . . . **PROF 011**

Children's literature, American--Bibliography.
GILLESPIE, JT/Newbery companion: booktalk and related materials for Newbery Medal and Honor /1996//KA035. . . **PROF 016.813**

Children's literature, American--Illustrators--Awards.
NEWBERY AND CALDECOTT MEDALISTS AND HONOR BOOK WINNERS: BIBLIOGRAPHIES AND /1992//KA004 . . . **PROF 011**

Children's literature in mathematics education.
WHITIN, DJ/It's the story that counts: more children's books for mathematical learning, /1995//KA258 . . . . **PROF 372.7**

Children's periodicals.
AMERICAN GIRL. /1993-/3-5/KA498 . . . . **PER 050**
CALLIOPE: WORLD HISTORY FOR YOUNG PEOPLE. /1990-/ 4-6/KA505 . . . . **PER 050**
CHILD LIFE. /1921-/2-4/KA507 . . . . **PER 050**
CHILDREN'S PLAYMATE. /1929-/1-3/KA509 . . . . **PER 050**
CREATIVE KIDS. /n.d./4-A/KA511 . . . . **PER 050**
GIRLS' LIFE: THE NEW MAGAZINE FOR GIRLS. /1994-/ 4-6/KA516 . . . . **PER 050**
HIGHLIGHTS FOR CHILDREN. /1946-/P-A/KA517 . . . . . **PER 050**
HOPSCOTCH: THE MAGAZINE FOR GIRLS. /1990-/ 2-6/KA518 . . . . **PER 050**
HUMPTY DUMPTY'S MAGAZINE. /1952-/P-1/KA519. . . **PER 050**
JACK AND JILL: THE MAGAZINE FOR BOYS AND GIRLS. /1938-/1-5/KA521. . . . . **PER 050**
KID CITY. /1988-/2-4/KA523 . . . . **PER 050**
LADYBUG: THE MAGAZINE FOR YOUNG CHILDREN. /1990-/ P-2/KA524. . . . . **PER 050**
MUSE. /1997-/4-6/KA527. . . . . **PER 050**
NATIONAL GEOGRAPHIC WORLD. /1975-/2-4/KA530 . **PER 050**
SESAME STREET MAGAZINE. /1971-/P/KA540 . . . . . **PER 050**
SPIDER: THE MAGAZINE FOR CHILDREN. /1993-/ 1-3/KA542 . . . . **PER 050**
STONE SOUP: A MAGAZINE BY CHILDREN. /1973-/ 2-A/KA546 . . . . **PER 050**
TIME FOR KIDS. /1995-/3-6/KA547 . . . . **PER 050**
U*S* KIDS: A WEEKLY READER MAGAZINE. /1987-/ 2-4/KA549 . . . . **PER 050**
3-2-1 CONTACT. /1979-/3-5/KA555 . . . . **PER 050**

Children's periodicals--Bibliography.
MAGAZINES FOR KIDS AND TEENS: REV. ED. /1997/ /KA018. . . . . **PROF 011.62**

Children's periodicals--Indexes.
CHILDREN'S MAGAZINE GUIDE: SUBJECT INDEX TO CHILDREN'S MAGAZINES. /1948-/3-A/KA508 . . . . . . **PER 050**

Children's plays.
LAUGHLIN, MK/Social studies readers theatre for children: scripts and script development. /1991//KA224 . . . . **PROF 372.6**

Children's poetry SEE ALSO Children's songs; Lullabies; Nursery rhymes.

Children's poetry.
CHILD'S SEASONAL TREASURY. /1996//KA193 . . **PROF 372.13**

Children's poetry--Indexes.
INDEX TO POETRY FOR CHILDREN AND YOUNG PEOPLE: 1988-1992. /1994/5-6/KA374 . . . . **REF 016.811**

Children's poetry--Study and teaching.
BAUER, CF/Poetry break: an annotated anthology with ideas for introducing children to poetry. /1995//KA234. . . . **PROF 372.64**

Children's poetry, Canadian (English)--Indexes.
SNOW, K/Subject index for children & young people to Canadian poetry in English. /1986/A/KA375 . . . . **REF 016.811**

Children's reference books--Bibliography.
PETERSON, CS/Reference books for children, 4th ed. /1992/ /KA021. . . . . **PROF 011.62**
WYNAR, CG/Guide to reference books for school media centers. 4th ed. /1992//KA007 . . . . **PROF 011**

Children's songs SEE Folk songs; Lullabies; Nursery rhymes; Singing games; Songs.

Children's songs.
CAMPBELL, PS/Roots and branches: a legacy of multicultural music for children. /1994//KA320 . . . . **BA PROF 789.3**
CHILD'S SEASONAL TREASURY. /1996//KA193 . . **PROF 372.13**
WORLD OF CHILDREN'S SONGS. /1993//KA322 . **PROF 789.3**

Children's songs--Discography--Indexes.
REID, R/Children's jukebox: a subject guide to musical recordings and programming ideas for songsters ages one to twelve. /1995/ /KA029. . . . . **PROF 016.7893**

Children's songs--Reviews.
REID, R/Children's jukebox: a subject guide to musical recordings and programming ideas /1995//KA029 . . . . . . **PROF 016.7893**

Children's stories.
BEST CHILDREN'S BOOKS IN THE WORLD: A TREASURY OF ILLUSTRATED STORIES. /1996//KA336 . . . . **PROF 808.3**

Children's stories--Bibliography.
COLBORN, C/What do children read next?: a reader's guide to fiction for children. /1997//KA031 . . . . **PROF 016.80883**

Children's stories--History and criticism.
STEWIG, JW/Looking at picture books. /1995/
/KA312 . . . . **PROF 741.6**
Children's writings SEE ALSO Children as authors.
Children's writings
ATKIN, SB/Voices from the fields: children of migrant farmworkers
tell their stories. /1993/A/6 KA833 . . . . **305.5**
BANISH, R/Forever family. /1992/2-4/3 KB011 . . . . **362.73**
BE A FRIEND: CHILDREN WHO LIVE WITH HIV SPEAK. /1994/
2-6/2 KA993 . . . . **362.1**
DEAR LAURA: LETTERS FROM CHILDREN TO LAURA INGALLS
WILDER. /1996/3-6/KD893 . . . . **808.86**
FESTIVAL IN MY HEART: POEMS BY JAPANESE CHILDREN. /
1993/3-A/KE134 . . . . **895.6**
I SAW ESAU: THE SCHOOLCHILD'S POCKET BOOK. /1992/
/KA276 . . . . **PROF 398.8**
KID'S BOOK ABOUT DEATH AND DYING. /1985/
4-6/6 KA650 . . . . **155.9**
KOCH, K/Wishes, lies, and dreams: teaching children to write
poetry. /c1970, 1980//KA346 . . . . **PROF 808.81**
LIED, K/Potato: a tale from the Great Depression. /1997/
K-3/2 KF980 . . . . **E**
MACDONALD, MR/Skit book: 101 skits from kids. /1990/
3-6/KE092 . . . . **812**
MOORE, A/Broken Arrow boy. /1990/3-6/6 KA996 . . . . . **362.1**
OSTROW, W/All about asthma. /1989/5-6/7 KD015 . . . . . **616.2**
RISING VOICES: WRITINGS OF YOUNG NATIVE AMERICANS. /
1992/5-A/7 KD903 . . . . **810.8**
TEN-SECOND RAINSHOWERS: POEMS BY YOUNG PEOPLE. /
1996/3-6/KE088 . . . . **811.008**
VAN METER, V/Taking flight: my story. /1995/
3-6/6 KD101 . . . . **629.13**
WILKES, S/One day we had to run!: refugee children tell their
stories in words and /1994/4-A/5 KB019 . . . . **362.87**
Childrens' literature--History and criticism.
SMITH, L/Unreluctant years: a critical approach to children's
literature. /c1953, 1991//KA357 . . . . **PROF 809**
Chimpanzees.
GOODALL, J/Chimpanzee family book. /1997/
4-6/6 KC878 . . . . **599.885**
MEACHUM, V/Jane Goodall: protector of chimpanzees. /1997/
5-A/7 KE372 . . . . **B GOODALL, J.**
Chimpanzees--Fiction.
HOBAN, L/Arthur's funny money. /1981/1-3/2 KF733 . . . . . . **E**
Arthur's honey bear. /c1964/1-3/2 KF734 . . . . **CE E**
Arthur's pen pal. /c1976/1-3/2 KF735 . . . . **E**
China--Civilization.
COTTERELL, A/Ancient China. /1994/4-A/10 KE629 . . . . . . **931**
WILLIAMS, S/Made in China: ideas and inventions from Ancient
China. /1996/4-6/6 KE631 . . . . **931**
China--Description and travel.
FRITZ, J/China homecoming. /1985/4-6/7 KE703 . . . . . . **951.05**
China--Fiction.
DAY, D/Emperor's panda. /c1986, 1987/4-A/8 KH063 . . . . . **Fic**
FLACK, M/Story about Ping. /c1933/P-1/6 KF550 . . . . . . **CE E**
FRITZ, J/Homesick: my own story. /1982/4-A/4 KH145 . . . . **Fic**
HONG, LT/Empress and the silkworm. /1995/1-3/6 KF766 . . . **E**
LEAF, M/Eyes of the dragon. /1987/K-3/5 KF952 . . . . **E**
YEP, L/City of dragons. /1995/1-3/5 KG775 . . . . **E**
China--Folklore.
CHANG, M/Cricket warrior: a Chinese tale. /1994/
2-3/5 KB549 . . . . **398.24**
CHIN, C/China's bravest girl: the legend of Hua Mu Lan = [Chin
kuo ying hsiung Hua /1993/3-5/4 KB430 . . . . **398.22**
CZERNECKI, S/Cricket's cage: a Chinese folktale. /1997/
K-3/7 KB553 . . . . **398.24**
FANG, L/Ch'i-lin purse: a collection of ancient Chinese stories. /
1995/4-6/5 KB295 . . . . **398.2**
HONG, LT/Two of everything. /1993/2-3/4 KB317 . . . . . . **398.2**
LOUIE, A/Yeh-Shen, a Cinderella story from China. /c1982, 1990/
3-5/6 KB750 . . . . **398.27**
MOSEL, A/Tikki Tikki Tembo. /1967/P-2/5 KB759 . . . . . **398.27**
RAPPAPORT, D/Long-haired girl: a Chinese legend. /1995/
2-3/4 KB409 . . . . **398.21**
SANFIELD, S/Just rewards, or, Who is that man in the moon and
what's he doing up there anyway? /1996/K-2/4 KB713 . . **398.26**
WANG, RC/Magical starfruit tree: a Chinese folktale. /1993/
2-3/6 KB784 . . . . **398.27**
WILSON, BK/Wishbones: a folk tale from China. /1993/
2-3/6 KB383 . . . . **398.2**
WOLKSTEIN, D/White Wave: a Chinese tale. Rev. ed. /1996/
1-3/2 KB786 . . . . **398.27**
YEP, L/Junior thunder lord. /1994/2-4/3 KB425 . . . . **398.21**
Man who tricked a ghost. /1993/1-3/4 KB697 . . . . . . **398.25**

Rainbow people. /c1989, 1991/5-A/4 KB788 . . . . **398.27**
Shell woman and the king: a Chinese folktale. /1993/
3-5/5 KB496 . . . . **398.22**
Tiger Woman. /1995/1-3/6 KB789 . . . . **398.27**
YOLEN, J/Emperor and the kite. /1988/2-3/6 KB791 . . . . . **398.27**
YOUNG, E/Cat and Rat: the legend of the Chinese zodiac. /1995/
K-6/4 KA608 . . . . **133.5**
Little Plum. /1994/K-2/4 KB497 . . . . **398.22**
Lon Po Po: A Red-Riding Hood story from China. /1989/
3-4/4 KB679 . . . . **398.24**
Night visitors. /1995/2-3/4 KB680 . . . . **398.24**
China--History--Long March, 1934-1935.
FRITZ, J/China's long march: 6,000 miles of danger. /1988/
A/6 KE702 . . . . **951.04**
China--History--To 221 B.C.
FISHER, LE/Great Wall of China. /1986/3-6/3 KE630 . . . . . **931**
China--History--19th century--Fiction.
YEP, L/Serpent's children. /c1984, 1996/6-A/6 KH894 . . . . . **Fic**
China--History--1949-.
ZHANG, SN/Little tiger in the Chinese night: an autobiography in
art. /4-6/6 KE609 . . . . **B ZHANG, S.**
Chinatown (New York, N.Y.)--Fiction.
LOW, W/Chinatown. /1997/K-2/3 KG037 . . . . **E**
Chincoteague Island (Va.)--Fiction.
HENRY, M/Misty of Chincoteague. /c1947/3-5/4 KH244 . . **CE Fic**
Chinese--San Francisco (Calif.)--Fiction.
YEP, L/Dragonwings. /c1975/5-6/6 KH892 . . . . **Fic**
Chinese--United States--Fiction.
COERR, E/Chang's paper pony. /1988/2-3/2 KF400 . . . . **E**
YEE, P/Ghost Train. /1996/4-6/5 KH889 . . . . **Fic**
YEP, L/Child of the owl. /c1977/A/6 KH891 . . . . **Fic**
Chinese Americans--Biography.
LING, B/Maya Lin. /1997/4-6/10 KE437 . . . . **B LIN, M.**
RILEY, GB/Wah Ming Chang: artist and master of special effects. /
1995/5-6/6 KE285 . . . . **B CHANG, W.**
YEP, L/Lost garden. /1996/5-A/7 KE604 . . . . **B YEP, L.**
Chinese Americans--Fiction.
CHINN, K/Sam and the lucky money. /1995/1-3/4 KF383 . . . . . **E**
KRENSKY, S/Iron dragon never sleeps. /1995/3-5/2 KH381 . . . **Fic**
LEE, HV/In the snow. /1995/1-3/2 KF955 . . . . **E**
LEE, M/Nim and the war effort. /1997/2-4/5 KH391 . . . . . **Fic**
LOW, W/Chinatown. /1997/K-2/3 KG037 . . . . **E**
NAMIOKA, L/Yang the third and her impossible family. /1995/
3-6/5 KH527 . . . . **Fic**
Yang the youngest and his terrible ear. /1994/5-A/5 KH528 . **Fic**
NUNES, S/Last dragon. /1995/2-3/3 KG183 . . . . **E**
YEE, P/Tales from Gold Mountain: stories of the Chinese in the New
World. /1989/5-A/7 KH890 . . . . **Fic**
YEP, L/Later, Gator. /1995/4-6/4 KH893 . . . . **Fic**
Star fisher. /1991/6-A/6 KH895 . . . . **Fic**
Chinese Americans--History.
WU, DY/Chinese-American experience. /1993/
5-6/8 KA864 . . . . **305.8**
Chinese language--Vocabulary.
LEE, HV/In the snow. /1995/1-3/2 KF955 . . . . **E**
YOUNG, E/Voices of the heart. /1997/A/7 KA675 . . . . **179**
Chinese language materials.
CHIN, C/China's bravest girl: the legend of Hua Mu Lan = [Chin
kuo ying hsiung Hua /1993/3-5/4 KB430 . . . . **398.22**
CHINESE MOTHER GOOSE RHYMES. /c1968, 1989/
P-3/KB794 . . . . **398.8**
MAPLES IN THE MIST: CHILDREN'S POEMS FROM THE TANG
DYNASTY. /1996/K-3/KE133 . . . . **895**
Chinese New Year.
WATERS, K/Lion dancer: Ernie Wan's Chinese New Year. /1990/
1-4/2 KB217 . . . . **394.261**
Chinese New Year--Fiction.
CHINN, K/Sam and the lucky money. /1995/1-3/4 KF383 . . . . . **E**
LOW, W/Chinatown. /1997/K-2/3 KG037 . . . . **E**
Chinese poetry--T'ang dynasty, 618-907.
MAPLES IN THE MIST: CHILDREN'S POEMS FROM THE TANG
DYNASTY. /1996/K-3/KE133 . . . . **895**
Chinn, May Edward.
BUTTS, ER/May Chinn: the best medicine. /1995/
5-A/8 KE288 . . . . **B CHINN, M.**
Chinook Indians--Folklore.
MARTIN, R/Boy who lived with the seals. /1993/
2-4/6 KB614 . . . . **398.24**
Chipmunks.
CHIPMUNK (VIDEOCASSETTE). /1988/3-6/KC750 . **VCR 599.36**
Chisholm, Shirley.
POLLACK, JS/Shirley Chisholm. /1994/
5-6/10 KE289 . . . . **B CHISHOLM, S.**

Chivalry SEE ALSO Arthur, King; Civilization, Medieval; Knights and knighthood; Middle Ages.

Chocolate--Fiction.
  HOWE, J/Hot fudge. /1990/K-3/2 KF777 . . . . **E**

Chocolate chip cookies.
  JASPERSOHN, W/Cookies. /1993/3-5/8 KD320 . . . . **664**

Cholistan Desert (Pakistan)--Fiction.
  STAPLES, SF/Shabanu, daughter of the wind. /1989/
  6-A/6 KH748 . . . . **Fic**

Choreography.
  PINKNEY, AD/Alvin Ailey. /1993/2-4/5 KE231 . . . . **B AILEY, A.**

Christian life--Fiction.
  TOLAN, SS/Save Halloween! /1993/5-A/7 KH794 . . . . **Fic**

Christiana (Pa.)--Fiction.
  ROSENBURG, JM/William Parker: rebel without rights: a novel based on fact. /1996/6-A/7 KH654 . . . . **Fic**

Christianity SEE ALSO Jesus Christ--Nativity.

Christianity.
  FAITH AND BELIEF: FIVE MAJOR WORLD RELIGIONS (VIDEOCASSETTE). /1992/5-A/KA722. . . . . **VCR 291**

Christmas SEE ALSO Jesus Christ--Nativity.

Christmas.
  ANGLUND, JW/Christmas is a time of giving. /c1961/
  P-2/KB230. . . . . **394.266**
  BARTH, E/Holly, reindeer and colored lights: the story of Christmas symbols. /c1971/5-6/7 KB231 . . . . **394.266**
  BROWN, MW/Christmas in the barn. /c1952/P-K/KA700 . **232.92**
  DE PAOLA, T/Family Christmas tree book. /c1980, 1984/
  2-4/6 KB234 . . . . **394.266**
  First Christmas. /1984/P-4/7 KA702 . . . . **232.92**
  DUNBAR, J/This is the star. /1996/2-3/2 KA703 . . . . . . **232.92**
  GRAHAM-BARBER, L/Ho Ho Ho!: the complete book of Christmas words. /1993/2-6/8 KB235 . . . . **394.266**
  KENNEDY, P/Christmas celebration: traditions and customs from around the world. /1992/4-6/7 KB236 . . . . **394.266**
  LANKFORD, MD/Christmas around the world. /1995/
  3-6/7 KB237 . . . . **394.266**

Christmas--Canada.
  CHRISTMAS IN CANADA. /1994/4-6/10 KB232 . . . . . . **394.266**

Christmas--Caribbean Area.
  PRESILLA, ME/Feliz nochebuena, feliz navidad: Christmas feasts of the Hispanic Caribbean. /c1994, 1996/5-A/7 KB238 . . . **394.266**

Christmas--Fiction.
  AMMON, R/Amish Christmas. /1996/3-5/4 KG844 . . . . **Fic**
  ANAYA, R/Farolitos of Christmas. /1995/3-6/2 KG845. . . . . **Fic**
  BARRACCA, D/Taxi Dog Christmas. /1994/P-2/3 KF202 . . . . . **E**
  BOND, M/Paddington audio collection (Talking book). /1978/
  2-4/KG917 . . . . **TB Fic**
  BRETT, J/Wild Christmas reindeer. /1990/K-2/2 KF263 . . . . . . **E**
  BRIMNER, LD/Merry Christmas, Old Armadillo. /1995/
  K-2/3 KF267 . . . . **E**
  BROWN, MT/Arthur's April fool. /1983/P-3/2 KF273 . . . . **E**
  BUNTING, E/Going home. /1996/1-3/2 KF302 . . . . **E**
  BURNINGHAM, J/Harvey Slumfenburger's Christmas present. /1993/K-2/2 KF316 . . . . **E**
  CAPOTE, T/Christmas memory. /c1956, 1989/
  4-A/6 KG971 . . . . **CE Fic**
  CARLSON, NS/Family under the bridge. /c1958/
  3-5/4 KG974 . . . . **Fic**
  CLIMO, S/Cobweb Christmas. /1982/K-2/5 KF397 . . . . **E**
  COOPER, S/Danny and the kings. /1993/2-4/2 KF423 . . . . **E**
  CREW, L/Nekomah Creek Christmas. /1994/4-6/4 KH042 . . . . **Fic**
  CUSHMAN, D/Aunt Eater's mystery Christmas. /1995/
  1-2/2 KF440 . . . . **E**
  DE PAOLA, T/Clown of God. /1978/K-3/6 KF467 . . . . . . **CE E**
  Early American Christmas. /1987/K-3/5 KF469 . . . . **E**
  Merry Christmas, Strega Nona. /1986/K-3/5 KF473 . . . . **E**
  Merry Christmas, Strega Nona (Talking book). /1991/
  K-3/KF474 . . . . **TB E**
  DICKENS, C/Christmas Carol in prose, being a ghost story of Christmas. /1983/4-6/5 KH074 . . . . **CE Fic**
  DUFFEY, B/Lucky Christmas. /1994/3-5/4 KH086 . . . . **Fic**
  ETS, MH/Nine days to Christmas. /c1959/1-3/2 KF538 . . . . . . **E**
  FERGUSON, A/Tumbleweed Christmas. /1996/1-3/3 KF547. . . . **E**
  FORWARD, T/Ben's Christmas carol. /1996/2-3/4 KF567 . . . . **E**
  GODDEN, R/Story of Holly and Ivy. /1985/3-5/4 KH179 . . . . **Fic**
  HAARHOFF, D/Desert December. /1992/3-5/4 KH206 . . . . . **Fic**
  HALL, D/Lucy's Christmas. /1994/1-3/6 KF662 . . . . **E**
  HARVEY, B/My prairie Christmas. /1990/2-4/4 KH222 . . . . . **Fic**
  HAYES, S/Happy Christmas Gemma. /1986/P-1/2 KF686 . . . . . **E**
  HEATH, A/Sofie's role. /1992/P-2/2 KF692 . . . . **E**
  HOUSTON, G/Year of the perfect Christmas tree. /1988/
  K-3/6 KF771 . . . . **E**
  HOWARD, EF/Chita's Christmas tree. /1989/2-4/5 KF773 . . . . . **E**

JOSEPH, L/Island Christmas. /1992/1-3/2 KF855 . . . . **E**
JOYCE, W/Santa calls. /1993/2-4/4 KF862 . . . . **E**
LEWIS, JP/Christmas of the reddle moon. /1994/1-3/4 KF975 . . **E**
LINDGREN, A/Lotta's Christmas surprise. /c1977, 1990/
  1-2/2 KF985 . . . . **E**
MORA, P/Gift of the poinsettia./El regalo de la flor de nochebuena. /1995/3-5/4 KH507 . . . . **Fic**
NOBLE, TH/Apple tree Christmas. /1984/K-3/6 KG175 . . . . . . **E**
PACKARD, M/Christmas kitten. /1994/K-1/1 KG204 . . . . **E**
PALACIOS, A/Christmas surprise for Chabelita. /1993/
  1-3/2 KG206 . . . . **E**
POLACCO, P/Trees of the dancing goats. /1996/1-3/3 KG260. . **E**
  Uncle Vova's tree. /1989/1-3/6 KG261 . . . . **E**
POTTER, B/Tailor of Gloucester. /c1931, 1987/P-3/7 KG270 . . . **E**
  Tailor of Gloucester (Videocassette). /1988/1-3/KG271 . **VCR E**
RAHAMAN, V/O Christmas tree. /1996/1-3/4 KG298 . . . . . . **E**
ROBINSON, B/Best Christmas pageant ever. /c1972/
  4-6/7 KH640 . . . . **Fic**
ROGERS, J/King Island Christmas. /1985/K-3/5 KG347 . . . . . **E**
ROSEN, MJ/Elijah's angel: a story for Chanukah and Christmas. /1992/3-6/7 KH652 . . . . **Fic**
RYLANT, C/Children of Christmas: stories for the season. /c1987, 1993/4-6/6 KH660 . . . . **Fic**
  Mr. Putter and Tabby bake the cake. /1994/1-3/2 KG377 . . . **E**
  Silver packages: an Appalachian Christmas story. /1997/
  1-3/2 KG386 . . . . **E**
SAY, A/Tree of cranes. /1991/1-3/4 KG400 . . . . **E**
SCHACHNER, JB/Willy and May. /1995/1-3/5 KG401 . . . . **E**
SEUSS, D/How the Grinch stole Christmas. /c1957/P-3/KG459. . **E**
SHANNON, D/Amazing Christmas extravaganza. /1995/
  2-5/6 KG475 . . . . **E**
SHARMAT, MW/Nate the Great and the crunchy Christmas. /1996/2-4/2 KG485 . . . . **E**
SOTO, G/Too many tamales. /1993/K-3/3 KG530 . . . . **E**
STEVENSON, J/Oldest elf. /1996/P-2/2 KG565 . . . . **E**
TEWS, S/Gingerbread doll. /1993/1-3/5 KG602 . . . . **E**
THAYER, J/Puppy who wanted a boy. /c1958, 1986/
  1-3/2 KG603 . . . . **E**
TOMPERT, A/Carol for Christmas. /1994/K-3/5 KG612 . . . . . . **E**
TORNQVIST, R/Christmas carp. /1990/2-4/2 KH798 . . . . **Fic**
TRIVAS, I/Emma's old song. /1988/P-3/6 KG618 . . . . **E**
VAN ALLSBURG, C/Polar express. /1985/2-A/5 KH822 . . **CE Fic**
WALLNER, A/Alcott family Christmas. /1996/1-3/2 KG678 . . . . **E**
WALTER, MP/Have a happy... a novel. /1989/4-6/4 KH838 . . **Fic**
WELLS, R/Max's Christmas. /1986/P-1/2 KG703 . . . . **CE E**
WESTALL, R/Christmas spirit: two stories. /1994/
  6-A/6 KH847 . . . . **Fic**
WOJCIECHOWSKI, S/Christmas miracle of Jonathan Toomey. /1995/4-6/5 KH876 . . . . **Fic**

Christmas--Folklore.
  CURRY, JL/Christmas Knight. /1993/2-5/3 KB435. . . . . . **398.22**
  CZERNECKI, S/Pancho's pinata. /1992/2-4/7 KB703 . . . . **398.26**
  OPPENHEIM, J/Christmas Witch: an Italian legend. /1993/
  1-3/2 KB507 . . . . **398.23**
  ROBBINS, R/Baboushka and the three kings. /c1960/
  2-4/6 KB509 . . . . **398.23**
  SAWYER, R/Remarkable Christmas of the cobbler's sons. /1994/
  1-3/4 KB416 . . . . **398.21**

Christmas--Literary collections.
  CHRISTMAS GIF': AN ANTHOLOGY OF CHRISTMAS POEMS, SONGS, AND STORIES WRITTEN BY AND ABOUT AFRICAN-AMERICANS. /1993/4-6/KD897 . . . . **810.8**
  DIANE GOODE'S AMERICAN CHRISTMAS. /1997/
  K-A/KD898 . . . . **810.8**

Christmas--Miscellanea.
  WICK, W/I spy Christmas: a book of picture riddles. /1992/
  P-2/KD715. . . . . **793.73**

Christmas--Poetry.
  BORNSTEIN, H/Night before Christmas: told in sign language: an adaptation of the original /1994/K-6/KD917 . . . . **811**
  CLIFTON, L/Everett Anderson's Christmas coming. /1991/
  P-1/KD925. . . . . **811**
  DIANE GOODE'S AMERICAN CHRISTMAS. /1997/
  K-A/KD898 . . . . **810.8**
  KENNEDY, XJ/Beasts of Bethlehem. /1992/1-6/KD960 . . . . . **811**
  MOORE, CC/Grandma Moses Night before Christmas. /1991/
  P-A/KD987 . . . . **811**
  Twas the night before Christmas: a visit from St. Nicholas. /c1912, 1992/P-A/KD988 . . . . **811**
  WILMER, I/B is for Bethlehem: a Christmas alphabet. /1990/
  K-3/KE043 . . . . **811**

Christmas--Songs SEE ALSO Carols.
Christmas--Southern States--History--19th century.
MCKISSACK, P/Christmas in the big house, Christmas in the quarters. /1994/4-A/6 KE967 . . . . **975**
Christmas--United States.
CHRISTMAS IN COLONIAL AND EARLY AMERICA. /c1996/ 4-6/8 KB233 . . . . **394.266**
Christmas--Wales.
THOMAS, D/Child's Christmas in Wales. /1985/ P-A/8 KE119 . . . . **828**
Christmas carols SEE Carols.
Christmas cookery.
WILKES, A/My first Christmas activity book. /1994/ 3-6/KD460. . . . . **745.594**
Christmas cookery--Caribbean Area.
PRESILLA, ME/Feliz nochebuena, feliz navidad: Christmas feasts of the Hispanic Caribbean. /c1994, 1996/5-A/7 KB238 . . . **394.266**
Christmas decorations.
LANKFORD, MD/Christmas around the world. /1995/ 3-6/7 KB237 . . . . **394.266**
ROSS, K/Crafts for Christmas. /1995/3-5/KD452 . . . . . **745.594**
WILKES, A/My first Christmas activity book. /1994/ 3-6/KD460. . . . . **745.594**
Christmas decorations--Fiction.
SHANNON, D/Amazing Christmas extravaganza. /1995/ 2-5/6 KG475 . . . . **E**
Christmas music SEE ALSO Carols.
Christmas music.
DIANE GOODE'S AMERICAN CHRISTMAS. /1997/ K-A/KD898 . . . . **810.8**
FRIENDLY BEASTS: A TRADITIONAL CHRISTMAS CAROL. /1991/ K-2/KD533 . . . . **782.28**
HARK! THE HERALD ANGELS SING. /1993/K-6/KD534 . . **782.28**
KEEP THE SPIRIT (SOUND RECORDING CASSETTE). /1989/ K-6/KD634 . . . . **SRC 789.3**
LAS NAVIDADES: POPULAR CHRISTMAS SONGS FROM LATIN AMERICA. /1990/K-3/KD580 . . . . **789.2**
RAFFI /Raffi's Christmas album (Sound recording cassette). /1983/ P-3/KD535. . . . . **SRC 782.28**
SILVERMAN, J/Christmas songs. /1993/5-A/KD536 . . . . . **782.28**
TWELVE DAYS OF CHRISTMAS. /1986/P-A/KD537. . . . . **782.28**
TWELVE DAYS OF CHRISTMAS. /1993/P-A/KD538. . . . . **782.28**
TWELVE DAYS OF CHRISTMAS. /1995/K-3/KD539. . . . . **782.28**
TWELVE DAYS OF CHRISTMAS (VIDEOCASSETTE). /1990/ P-A/KD540 . . . . **VCR 782.28**
TYRRELL, F/Woodland Christmas: twelve days of Christmas in the North Woods. /1996/K-2/KD541. . . . . **782.28**
WHAT A MORNING! THE CHRISTMAS STORY IN BLACK SPIRITUALS. /1987/K-6/KD532. . . . . **782.25**
Christmas trees.
DE PAOLA, T/Family Christmas tree book. /c1980, 1984/ 2-4/6 KB234 . . . . **394.266**
Christmas trees--Fiction.
COOPER, S/Danny and the kings. /1993/2-4/2 KF423 . . . . . **E**
HOUSTON, G/Year of the perfect Christmas tree. /1988/ K-3/6 KF771 . . . . **E**
HOWARD, EF/Chita's Christmas tree. /1989/2-4/5 KF773 . . . . . **E**
KUSUGAK, M/Baseball bats for Christmas. /1990/ 4-6/4 KH384 . . . . **Fic**
RAHAMAN, V/O Christmas tree. /1996/1-3/4 KG298 . . . . . . **E**
Christopher, Saint.
DE PAOLA, T/Christopher: the holy giant. /1994/ 2-3/4 KB438 . . . . **398.22**
Chronology--Software.
TIMELINER: HISTORY IN PERSPECTIVE (MICROCOMPUTER PROGRAM). /1986/K-A/KE142 . . . . **MCP 902**
Chronology, Historical.
ENCYCLOPEDIA OF AMERICAN HISTORY. 7TH ED. /1992/ 5-6/KA495 . . . . **REF 973.03**
Chumash Indians--Folklore.
WOOD, A/Rainbow bridge: inspired by a Chumash tale. /1995/ 3-5/4 KB675 . . . . **398.24**
Chumash Indians--Missions--California.
BEHRENS, J/Missions of the central coast. /1996/ 4-6/9 KF076 . . . . **979.4**
BROWER, P/Missions of the inland valleys. /1997/ 4-6/9 KF077 . . . . **979.4**
MACMILLAN, D/Missions of the Los Angeles Area. /1996/ 4-6/9 KF084 . . . . **979.4**
Church music SEE ALSO Hymns.
Church of Jesus Christ of Latter-Day Saints--Presidents.
SANFORD, WR/Brigham Young: pioneer and Mormon leader. / 1996/5-6/8 KE605 . . . . **B YOUNG, B.**

Churches--Fiction.
GUTHRIE, D/Rose for Abby. /1988/2-4/5 KF654. . . . . **E**
Churchill, Winston, Sir.
DRIEMEN, JE/Winston Churchill: an unbreakable spirit. /1990/ 5-6/7 KE290 . . . . **B CHURCHILL, W.**
SEVERANCE, JB/Winston Churchill: soldier, statesman, artist. / 1996/6-A/10 KE291 . . . . **B CHURCHILL, W.**
Cicada.
CICADAS: THE 17-YEAR INVASION (VIDEOCASSETTE). /1993/ 4-6/KC535. . . . . **VCR 595.7**
Cinematography.
ANDERSEN, Y/Make your own animated movies and videotapes. / 1991/5-A/6 KD515. . . . . **778.5**
Ciphers SEE ALSO Cryptography; Writing.
Ciphers.
GARDNER, M/Codes, ciphers and secret writing. /c1972, 1984/ 5-6/8 KD308 . . . . **652**
JANECZKO, PB/Loads of codes and secret ciphers. /1984/ A/7 KD309 . . . . **652**
Circle.
HOBAN, T/Circles, triangles, and squares. /1974/P-1/KB990 . **516**
Shapes, shapes, shapes. /1986/2-6/KB991 . . . . . . **516**
Circulatory system.
SIMON, S/Heart: our circulatory system. /1996/ 5-A/6 KC937 . . . . **612.1**
YOUR BODY: CIRCULATORY AND RESPIRATORY SYSTEMS (VIDEOCASSETTE). /1988/5-6/KC931 . . . . **VCR 612**
Circus--Fiction.
BURNINGHAM, J/Cannonball Simp. /1994/K-2/4 KF314. . . . . **E**
BUSHNELL, J/Circus of the wolves. /1994/4-6/5 KG952 . . . . . **Fic**
ERNST, LC/Ginger jumps. /1990/K-3/4 KF529 . . . . **E**
GANTOS, J/Rotten Ralph. /1976/K-2/3 KF597 . . . . **E**
HOFF, S/Barkley. /c1975/K-2/1 KF751 . . . . **E**
Julius. /c1959/K-1/1 KF758 . . . . **E**
MAHY, M/Greatest show off earth. /1994/A/7 KH450 . . **CE Fic**
PETERSHAM, M/Circus baby. /c1950/P-2/3 KG235. . . . . **CE E**
SEUSS, D/Horton hatches the egg./If I ran the circus (Videocassette). /1992/P-3/KG457. . . . . **VCR E**
If I ran the circus. /c1956/P-3/4 KG464. . . . . **E**
SPIER, P/Peter Spier's circus! /1992/P-2/4 KG532 . . . . **E**
VINCENT, G/Ernest and Celestine at the circus. /1988/ P-2/2 KG655 . . . . **E**
Circus--History.
MCCLUNG, RM/Old Bet and the start of the American circus. / 1993/4-6/6 KD682 . . . . **791.3**
Circus animals.
MCCLUNG, RM/Old Bet and the start of the American circus. / 1993/4-6/6 KD682 . . . . **791.3**
Circus in art.
ROALF, P/Circus. /1993/5-A/8 KD477. . . . . **758**
Cities and towns.
MACAULAY, D/Underground. /1976/A/10 KD070. . . . . . **624.1**
SOENTPIET, CK/Around town. /1994/K-2/3 KA898 . . . . . **307.76**
WHAT ARE ECOSYSTEMS? (VIDEOCASSETTE). /1975/ 4-6/KC299. **VCR 577**
Cities and towns--Central America--History.
HERNANDEZ, X/San Rafael: a Central American city through the ages. /1992/A/8 KA897 . . . . **307.76**
Cities and towns--Europe, Northern--History.
HERNANDEZ, X/Lebek: a city of Northern Europe through the ages. /1991/A/10 KA896 . . . . **307.76**
Cities and towns--Fiction.
BURTON, VL/Little house. /c1942, 1978/K-2/2 KF320. . . . **CE E**
GOODALL, JS/Story of a main street. /1987/K-3/KF631 . . . . . . **E**
HURWITZ, J/New neighbors for Nora. /c1979, 1991/ 2-4/6 KH299 . . . . **Fic**
Nora and Mrs. Mind-your-own business. /c1977, 1991/ 2-4/4 KH300 . . . . **Fic**
JONAS, A/Round trip. /1983/K-2/2 KF847 . . . . **CE E**
RASKIN, E/Nothing ever happens on my block. /c1966/ K-2/4 KG308 . . . . **E**
Cities and towns--History.
HERNANDEZ, X/Barmi: a Mediterranean city through the ages. / 1990/A/11 KA895 . . . . **307.76**
ROSENBLUM, R/1989/3-6/7 KA783 . . . . **296.6**
Cities and towns, Ancient SEE ALSO Excavations (Archaeology).
Cities and towns, Ancient.
GOLDENSTERN, J/Lost cities. /1996/3-6/7 KE624. . . . . . **930.1**
Citizen band radio--Slang--Fiction.
DAY, A/Frank and Ernest on the road. /1994/2-3/2 KF451 . . . . **E**
City and town life.
SOENTPIET, CK/Around town. /1994/K-2/3 KA898 . . . . . **307.76**
THORNHILL, J/Wild in the city. /1996/P-2/5 KC478. . . . . . **591.5**

YEPSEN, R/City trains: moving through America's cities by rail. /
1993/5-6/7 KB162 . . . . **388.4**

City and town life--Fiction.
BARRACCA, D/Adventures of taxi dog. /1990/P-2/2 KF200 **CE E**
BEST, C/Red light, green light, Mama and me. /1995/
K-2/2 KF228 . . . . **E**
BUEHNER, C/Escape of Marvin the ape. /1992/P-2/3 KF294 . . . **E**
DISALVO-RYAN, D/City green. /1994/1-3/3 KF484 . . . . **E**
FLEISCHMAN, P/Seedfolks. /1997/5-A/5 KH118 . . . . **Fic**
GRIFFITH, HV/Grandaddy's stars. /1995/1-4/2 KF648 . . . . **E**
GUTHRIE, D/Rose for Abby. /1988/2-4/5 KF654 . . . . **E**
HENDERSON, K/Year in the city. /1996/K-2/2 KF700 . . . . **E**
HITE, S/Even break. /1995/5-A/6 KH266 . . . . **Fic**
HURWITZ, J/Superduper Teddy. /c1980, 1990/2-4/4 KH304 . . **Fic**
KURUSA /Streets are free. Rev. ed. /1995/3-4/5 KH383 . . . . **Fic**
MENNEN, I/Somewhere in Africa. /1992/K-2/4 KG129 . . . . . . **E**
ORGEL, D/Don't call me Slob-o. /1996/3-5/2 KH565 . . . . . . **Fic**
PHILLIPS, M/Sign in Mendel's window. /c1985, 1996/
3-5/6 KH600 . . . . **Fic**
RANSOM, CF/Big green pocketbook. /1993/P-1/2 KG303 . . . . **E**
RYLANT, C/Everyday town (Board book). /1993/
P-K/2 KG374 . . . . **BB E**
SCHWARTZ, A/Teeny tiny baby. /1994/P-2/2 KG415 . . . . **E**
TAMAR, E/Garden of happiness. /1996/1-3/2 KG593 . . . . **E**
TRESSELT, A/Wake up, city! /c1957, 1990/1-3/5 KG616 . . . . . **E**
WILLIS, MS/Secret super powers of Marco. /1994/
4-A/4 KH866 . . . . **Fic**

City and town life--New England.
OLD STURBRIDGE VILLAGE (VIDEOCASSETTE). /1989/
4-6/KE942 . . . . **VCR 974.4**

City and town life--New York (N.Y.)--Fiction.
SCHECTER, E/Big idea. /1996/3-5/2 KH679 . . . . **Fic**

City and town life--Pictorial works.
FLORIAN, D/City street. /1990/P-1/KA893 . . . . **307.3**
ISADORA, R/City seen from A to Z. /1983/P-1/KF814 . . . . **E**

City and town life--Poetry.
GRIMES, N/Meet Danitra Brown. /1994/2-4/KD949 . . . . . . **811**

City of Benares (Ship)--Fiction.
HENEGHAN, J/Wish me luck. /1997/6-A/5 KH237 . . . . **Fic**
City planning SEE ALSO Housing.

City sounds--Fiction.
SCHROEDER, A/Carolina shout! /1995/1-5/3 KG411 . . . . **E**
Civil rights SEE ALSO Afro-Americans--Civil rights; Human rights.

Civil rights.
AFRICAN AMERICAN ALMANAC. 7TH ED. /1997/
5-A/KA486 . . . . **REF 973**

Civil rights--Songs and music.
I'M GONNA LET IT SHINE: A GATHERING OF VOICES FOR
FREEDOM /1990/3-6/KD619 . . . . **SRC 789.3**
JENKINS, E/Long time to freedom (Sound recording cassette). /
c1969, 1992/K-A/KD574 . . . . **SRC 789.2**

Civil rights movements--History.
BRAY, RL/Martin Luther King. /1995/2-6/7 KE421 . **B KING, M.L.**
DUNCAN, AF/National Civil Rights Museum celebrates everyday
people. /1995/3-6/8 KA903 . . . . **323.1**
MEDEARIS, AS/Dare to dream: Coretta Scott King and the civil
rights movement. /1994/3-5/3 KE419 . . . . **B KING, C.S.**
ROCHELLE, B/Witnesses to freedom: young people who fought for
civil rights. /1993/5-6/7 KA905 . . . . **323.1**

Civil rights movements--Songs and music.
SILVERMAN, J/Songs of protest and civil rights. /1992/
5-A/KD593 . . . . **789.2**

Civil rights workers.
ADLER, DA/Picture book of Martin Luther King, Jr. /1989/
3-4/4 KE420 . . . . **CE B KING, M.L.**
BRAY, RL/Martin Luther King. /1995/2-6/7 KE421 . **B KING, M.L.**
COOPER, F/Mandela: from the life of the South African statesman.
/1996/3-6/7 KE457 . . . . **B MANDELA, N.**
CWIKLIK, R/Malcolm X and black pride. /1991/
5-6/6 KE455 . . . . **B MALCOLM X**
MARTIN LUTHER KING: I HAVE A DREAM (VIDEOCASSETTE). /
1986/4-A/KA907 . . . . **VCR 323.4**
MARZOLLO, J/Happy Birthday, Martin Luther King. /1993/
1-5/5 KE422 . . . . **B KING, M.L.**
MCKISSACK, P/Mary Church Terrell: leader for equality. /1991/
3-6/2 KE562 . . . . **B TERRELL, M.**
MEDEARIS, AS/Dare to dream: Coretta Scott King and the civil
rights movement. /1994/3-5/3 KE419 . . . . **B KING, C.S.**
MYERS, WD/Malcolm X: by any means necessary: a biography. /
1993/6-A/8 KE456 . . . . **B MALCOLM X**
PARKS, R/I am Rosa Parks. /1997/1-2/4 KE491 . . . **B PARKS, R.**
Rosa Parks: my story. /1992/6-A/5 KE490 . . . . . **B PARKS, R.**
RINGGOLD, F/My dream of Martin Luther King. /1995/
3-5/7 KE423 . . . . **B KING, M.L.**

Civilization--Fiction.
MACAULAY, D/Baaa. /1985/5-A/7 KH431 . . . . **Fic**

Civilization--History.
ROLAND-ENTWISTLE, T/More errata: another book of historical
errors. /1995/3-6/10 KE143 . . . . **909**

Civilization, African.
ROOTS OF AFRICAN CIVILIZATION (VIDEOCASSETTE). /1996/
6-A/KE729 . . . . **VCR 960**

Civilization, Ancient.
ANCIENT CIVILIZATIONS (PICTURE). /1991/4-6-KE620 . **PIC 930**
CASELLI, G/Roman Empire and the Dark Ages. /1985/
5-A/9 KE644 . . . . **940.1**
GOLDENSTERN, J/Lost cities. /1996/3-6/7 KE624. . . . . . **930.1**
KRUPP, RR/Let's go traveling. /1992/3-5/4 KE155 . . . . . **910.4**
MARTELL, H/Kingfisher book of the ancient world: from the Ice Age
to the fall of Rome. /1995/4-6/10 KE621 . . . . **930**
VISUAL DICTIONARY OF ANCIENT CIVILIZATIONS. /1994/
4-6/8 KE622 . . . . **930**

Civilization, Islamic.
CHILD, J/Rise of Islam. /1995/5-A/6 KA784 . . . . **297**

Civilization, Medieval.
ALIKI /Medieval feast. /1983/2-5/5 KB183 . . . . **CE 394.1**
CASELLI, G/Middle Ages. /1988/5-A/7 KE144 . . . . . . **909.07**
Roman Empire and the Dark Ages. /1985/5-A/9 KE644 . . **940.1**
CLEMENTS, G/Truth about castles. /c1988, 1990/
3-6/6 KE645 . . . . **940.1**
CORBIN, CL/Knights. /1989/4-6/4 KE646. . . . . **940.1**
FRADON, D/King's fool: a book about medieval and renaissance
fools. /1993/4-6/7 KE647 . . . . **940.1**
GRAVETT, C/Knight. /1993/4-A/7 KE648 . . . . **940.1**
MACDONALD, F/Medieval castle. /1990/4-6/8 KE649. . . . **940.1**
Medieval cathedral. /1991/6-A/9 KD390 . . . . **726**
STEELE, P/Castles. /1995/4-6/7 KE650 . . . . **940.1**

Civilization, Renaissance.
FRADON, D/King's fool: a book about medieval and renaissance
fools. /1993/4-6/7 KE647 . . . . **940.1**
Clairvoyance SEE ALSO Etrasensory perception.

Clairvoyance.
GREEN, CR/Seeing the unseen. /1993/4-6/5 KA610 . . . . . **133.8**

Clairvoyance--Fiction.
ALCOCK, V/Haunting of Cassie Palmer. /1990/5-6/6 KG827 . . **Fic**

Clambakes.
PETERS, RM/Clambake: a Wampanoag tradition. /1992/
4-6/5 KE780 . . . . **970.444**

Clarinet.
TURNER, BC/Living clarinet. /1996/4-6/12 KD552 . . . . **BA 788.6**

Clark, William.
CLARK, W/Off the map: the journals of Lewis and Clark. /1993/
4-6/7 KE201 . . . . **917.804**
KROLL, S/Lewis and Clark: explorers of the American West. /1994/
4-6/6 KE203 . . . . **917.804**
LEWIS AND CLARK EXPEDITION (VIDEOCASSETTE). /1992/
5-6/KE204 . . . . **VCR 917.804**
SCHANZER, R/How we crossed the West: the adventures of Lewis
and Clark. /1997/3-6/7 KE205 . . . . **917.804**
STEFOFF, R/Lewis and Clark. /1992/5-6/5 KE206 . . . . . **917.804**

Clark, William--Diaries.
CLARK, W/Off the map: the journals of Lewis and Clark. /1993/
4-6/7 KE201 . . . . **917.804**

Classification--Books--Children's literature.
SUBJECT HEADINGS FOR CHILDREN: A LIST OF SUBJECT
HEADINGS USED BY THE LIBRARY /1998//KA062. **PROF 025.4**

Classification, Dewey Decimal.
DEWEY, M/Abridged Dewey decimal classification and relative
index. Ed. 13. /1997//KA058 . . . . **PROF 025.4**
SUBJECT HEADINGS FOR CHILDREN: A LIST OF SUBJECT
HEADINGS USED BY THE LIBRARY /1998//KA062. **PROF 025.4**

Classroom environment.
BODINE, RJ/Creating the peaceable school: a comprehensive
program for teaching conflict /1994//KA161 . . . . **PROF 303.6**

Classroom management.
BARCHERS, SI/Creating and managing the literate classroom. /
1990//KA218 . . . . **PROF 372.6**
Clay SEE ALSO Modeling; Pottery.

Clay.
DIXON, A/Clay. /1990/K-5/4 KC230 . . . . **553.6**
Cleanliness SEE ALSO Baths; Grooming.

Cleanliness.
PRESCHOOL POWER!: JACKET FLIPS AND OTHER TIPS
(VIDEOCASSETTE). /1991/P-K/KD263 . . . . **VCR 640.83**

Cleanliness--Fiction.
OCHS, CP/When I'm alone. /1993/P-2/4 KG187 . . . . **E**
TEAGUE, M/Pigsty. /1994/K-2/2 KG595 . . . . **E**

Cleary, Beverly.
  CLEARY, B/Girl from Yamhill. /1988/5-6/7 KE292 . **B CLEARY, B.**
Clemens, Samuel Langhorne See Twain, Mark.
Clemente, Roberto.
  ENGEL, T/We'll never forget you, Roberto Clemente. /1997/
  2-4/2 KE293 . . . . **B CLEMENTE, R.**
  MACHT, NL/Roberto Clemente. /1994/
  5-A/7 KE294 . . . . **B CLEMENTE, R.**
Cleopatra, Queen of Egypt.
  STANLEY, D/Cleopatra. /1994/4-6/6 KE295. . . . **B CLEOPATRA**
Clergy.
  ADLER, DA/Picture book of Martin Luther King, Jr. /1989/
  3-4/4 KE420 . . . . **CE B KING, M.L.**
  BRAY, RL/Martin Luther King. /1995/2-6/7 KE421 . **B KING, M.L.**
  RINGGOLD, F/My dream of Martin Luther King. /1995/
  3-5/7 KE423 . . . . **B KING, M.L.**
Cliff dwellings--Colorado.
  TRIMBLE, S/Village of blue stone. /1990/4-6/6 KF063 . . . . . **979**
Cliff dwellings--Southwest, New.
  ARNOLD, C/Ancient cliff dwellers of Mesa Verde. /1992/
  5-6/8 KE790 . . . . **970.488**
Climate SEE ALSO Rain and rainfall; Meteorology; Seasons; Weather.
Climate.
  EARTH'S SEASONS/CLIMATES (VIDEOCASSETTE). /1995/
  3-6/KB902. . . . . **VCR 508**
  3-2-1 CONTACT: EXPLORING WEATHER, CLIMATE AND
  SEASONS (VIDEOCASSETTE). /1988/2-A/KC223 . . **VCR 551.6**
Clinton, Bill.
  CWIKLIK, R/Bill Clinton: president of the 90s. Rev. ed. /1997/
  5-6/8 KE296 . . . . **B CLINTON, B.**
Clinton, Hillary Rodham.
  LEVERT, S/Hillary Rodham Clinton, first lady. /1994/
  4-6/9 KE297 . . . . **B CLINTON, H.**
Clocks and watches.
  BRANLEY, FM/Keeping time: from the beginning and into the 21st
  century. /1993/4-6/6 KC067. . . . . **529**
  GANERI, A/Story of time and clocks. /1996/4-6/8 KC070. . **529**
  LLEWELLYN, C/My first book of time. /1992/K-3/2 KC072 . . **529**
  SMITH, AG/What time is it? /1992/4-A/8 KC073 . . . . . . **529**
  TICK TOCK: ALL ABOUT THE CLOCK (VIDEOCASSETTE). /1992/
  2-3/KC074. . . . . **VCR 529**
Clocks and watches--Fiction.
  DICKINSON, P/Time and the clockmice etcetera. /1994/
  3-A/8 KH077 . . . . **Fic**
Cloning--Fiction.
  RYAN, MC/Me two. /1993/5-A/6 KH658 . . . . **Fic**
Clothing and dress SEE ALSO Clothing trade; Costume; Hats; Shoes.
Clothing and dress.
  DE PAOLA, T/Charlie needs a cloak. /1982/
  P-2/3 KD299 . . . . **CE 646.4**
Clothing and dress--Fiction.
  HUTCHINS, P/You'll soon grow into them, Titch. /1983/
  P-2/2 KF808 . . . . **E**
  KUSKIN, K/Philharmonic gets dressed. /1982/K-3/5 KF939. . . . . **E**
  LONDON, J/Froggy gets dressed. /1992/P-K/2 KG021 . . . . . . **E**
  MILLER, M/Where does it go? /1992/P-K/1 KG136 . . . . **E**
  NEITZEL, S/Jacket I wear in the snow. /1989/P-2/2 KG168. . . . **E**
  SMALL, D/Fenwick's suit. /1996/K-2/2 KG520 . . . . **E**
  USHINSKY, K/How a shirt grew in the field. /1992/
  K-2/2 KG636. . . . . **E**
Clothing and dress--Folklore.
  SANFIELD, S/Bit by bit. /1995/K-2/2 KB772. . . . . **398.27**
Clothing trade.
  KEELER, PA/Unraveling fibers. /1995/4-6/4 KD335 . . . . **677**
  MINDS-ON SCIENCE: FOR PROFIT, FOR PLANET (VIDEODISC). /
  1995/5-A/KD348 . . . . **VD 687**
Clouds.
  DAY, JA/Peterson first guide to clouds and weather. /1991/
  3-6/A KC211 . . . . **551.57**
  MCMILLAN, B/Weather sky. /1991/5-A/7 KC220 . . . . . . **551.6**
Clouds--Fiction.
  SPIER, P/Dreams. /1986/P-2/KG531 . . . . **E**
Clown anemonefish--Fiction.
  BOYLE, D/Coral reef hideaway: the story of a clown anemonefish. /
  1995/K-2/7 KF255 . . . . **CE E**
Clowns--Fiction.
  VINCENT, G/Ernest and Celestine at the circus. /1988/
  P-2/2 KG655 . . . . **E**
  ZIEFERT, H/Clown games. /1993/P-1/1 KG791 . . . . **E**
Clubs SEE ALSO names of organizations e.g. Boy Scouts, Girl Scouts, etc.
Clubs--Fiction.
  LEEDY, L/Monster money book. /1992/1-3/2 KF957. . . . . . . **E**
  MACDONALD, M/No room for Francie. /1995/2-3/2 KH440. . **Fic**

Coal miners.
  BARTOLETTI, SC/Growing up in coal country. /1996/
  4-6/8 KA934 . . . . **331.3**
Coal mines and mining.
  BARTOLETTI, SC/Growing up in coal country. /1996/
  4-6/8 KA934 . . . . **331.3**
Coal mines and mining--Fiction.
  AIKEN, J/Is underground. /1993/5-A/7 KG824 . . . . **Fic**
  GREEN, CJ/Emmy. /1992/6-A/5 KH196 . . . . **Fic**
  PEREZ, NA/Breaker. /1988/6-A/7 KH597. . . . . **Fic**
  WHITE, R/Sweet Creek Holler. /1988/6/7 KH854 . . . . **Fic**
Coast changes SEE ALSO Seashore ecology.
Coaster cars.
  HOW TO BUILD CHAMPION PINEWOOD CARS
  (VIDEOCASSETTE). /1995/2-6/KD349 . . . . **VCR 688.6**
Coats--Fiction.
  HEST, A/Purple coat. /1986/K-3/4 KF721 . . . . **E**
  MILLS, LA/Rag coat. /1991/2-3/4 KG139 . . . . **E**
Cobb, Ty.
  KRAMER, SA/Ty Cobb: bad boy of baseball. /1995/
  2-4/4 KE298 . . . . **B COBB, T.**
Cochiti Indians.
  HOYT-GOLDSMITH, D/Pueblo storyteller. /1991/
  3-6/6 KE792 . . . . **970.489**
Cochiti Pueblo (N.M.)--Social life and customs.
  HOYT-GOLDSMITH, D/Pueblo storyteller. /1991/
  3-6/6 KE792 . . . . **970.489**
Cockroaches--Fiction.
  JAMES, M/Shoebag. /1992/6-A/6 KH323 . . . . **Fic**
  Shoebag returns. /1996/6-A/6 KH324. . . . . **Fic**
Codes SEE Ciphers; Cryptography.
Cognition in children.
  CHAPMAN, C/If the shoe fits...how to develop multiple intelligences
  in the classroom. /1993//KA157 . . . . **PROF 155.4**
  POLETTE, N/Brain power through picture books: /1992/
  /KA227 . . . . **PROF 372.6**
Cognitive learning.
  CHAPMAN, C/If the shoe fits...how to develop multiple intelligences
  in the classroom. /1993//KA157 . . . . **PROF 155.4**
Cognitive styles.
  LAZEAR, DG/Seven pathways of learning: teaching students and
  parents about multiple /1994//KA174. . . . . **PROF 370.15**
Coinage SEE ALSO Mints; Money.
Coins.
  HOBAN, T/26 letters and 99 cents. /1987/P-2/KF748. . . . . . . **E**
  MCMILLAN, B/Jelly beans for sale. /1996/K-3/2 KA951 . . . **332.4**
Coins--Fiction.
  MATHIS, SB/Hundred penny box. /1975/4-6/4 KH461 . . . **CE Fic**
Cold--Experiments.
  ARDLEY, N/Science book of hot and cold. /1992/
  K-3/2 KC126 . . . . **536**
Cold (Disease).
  STEDMAN, N/Common cold and influenza. /1986/
  A/10 KD016 . . . . **616.2**
Coleman, Bessie.
  HART, PS/Up in the air: the story of Bessie Coleman. /1996/
  4-6/8 KE299 . . . . **B COLEMAN, B.**
Coleman, Bessie--Fiction.
  LINDBERGH, R/Nobody owns the sky: the story of "Brave Bessie"
  Coleman. /1996/1-3/2 KF983 . . . . **E**
Collectors and collecting--Fiction.
  STEVENSON, J/Yard sale. /1996/2-3/2 KH756 . . . . **Fic**
Colleges SEE Universities and colleges.
Colombia.
  MARKHAM, L/Colombia: the gateway to South America. /1997/
  4-6/7 KF111 . . . . **986.1**
Colonization SEE ALSO Emigration and immigration.
Colonization--Software.
  COLONIZATION (MICROCOMPUTER PROGRAM). /1986/
  5-A/KA667 . . . . **MCP 172**
Color.
  COLOR: LIGHT FANTASTIC (VIDEOCASSETTE). /1988/
  3-6/KC119. . . . . **VCR 535.6**
  CREWS, D/Freight train. /1978/P-K/KF433. . . . . **E**
  DEWEY, A/Naming colors. /1995/4-8/8 KC120. . . . . **535.6**
  GOLDSEN, L/Colors. /1991/K-3/2 KC121 . . . . **535.6**
  GOMI, T/Who hid it? /1991/P-K/2 KF630 . . . . **E**
  HOBAN, T/Is it red? Is it yellow? Is it blue? An adventure in color.
  /1978/P/KA614 . . . . **152.14**
  Of colors and things. /1989/P-K/KC123. . . . . **535.6**
  LAUBER, P/What do you see and how do you see it?: exploring
  light, color, and vision. /1994/1-6/4 KC113 . . . . **535**
  MCMILLAN, B/Growing colors. /1988/P-1/KC124 . . . . . . **535.6**

PALMER, H/Learning basic skills (Videocassette). /1986/
P-1/KD700. . . . . **VCR 793**
RYAN, PM/Crayon counting book. /1996/P-1/3 KB982. . . . **513.2**
SOUND/LIGHT AND COLOR (VIDEOCASSETTE). /1994/
3-6/KC080. . . . . **VCR 530**
WESTRAY, K/Color sampler. /1993/1-6/5 KC125 . . . . . **535.6**

Color--Experiments.
ARDLEY, N/Science book of color. /1991/4-6/4 KC118 . . . **535.6**
DOHERTY, P/Magic wand and other bright experiments on light and
color. /1995/4-A/5 KC110. . . . . **535**

Color--Fiction.
CHARLES, NN/What am I?: looking through shapes at apples and
grapes. /1994/P-2/2 KF378 . . . . **E**
DODDS, DA/Color box. /1992/P-K/1 KF486 . . . . **E**
EHLERT, L/Color farm. /1990/P-K/KF515 . . . . **E**
Color zoo. /1989/P-1/2 KF516 . . . . **E**
FLEMING, D/Lunch. /1992/P-K/2 KF557 . . . . **E**
JACKSON, E/Brown cow, green grass, yellow mellow sun. /1995/
P-1/2 KF818 . . . . **E**
JONAS, A/Color dance. /1989/P-1/1 KF844 . . . . **E**
MARTIN, JR., B/Brown bear, brown bear, what do you see? /
1992/P-K/1 KG072. **E**
SERFOZO, M/Who said red? /1988/P-K/2 KG444 . . . . . . **E**
SEUSS, D/My many colored days. /1996/K-2/2 KG468 . . . **E**
SIDDALS, MM/Tell me a season. /1997/P-1/1 KG500 . . . . . **E**
WALSH, ES/Mouse paint. /1989/P-1/2 KG680 . . . . **E**
WILLIAMS, S/I went walking. /1990/P-1/1 KG732 . . . . . **CE E**
ZOLOTOW, C/Mr. Rabbit and the lovely present. /c1962/
P-2/2 KG804. . . . . **CE E**

Color--Pictorial works.
HOBAN, T/Colors everywhere. /1995/P-1/KC122 . . . . . . **535.6**

Color of man.
RACE (VIDEOCASSETTE). /1993/A/KA855 . . . . **VCR 305.8**

Color of man--Fiction.
ADOFF, A/Black is brown is tan. /1973/P-3/3 KF136. . . . . . **E**

Colorado.
BLEDSOE, S/Colorado. /1993/4-6/7 KF060 . . . . **978.8**
FRADIN, DB/Colorado. /1993/3-6/3 KF061 . . . . **978.8**

Colorado--Description and travel.
GRAND CANYON OF THE COLORADO (VIDEOCASSETTE). /
1983/5-A/KF069 . . . . **VCR 979.1**

Colorado--History.
WILLS, CA/Historical album of Colorado. /1996/
4-6/7 KF062 . . . . **978.8**

Colorado River (Colo.-Mexico)--Discovery and exploration.
FRASER, MA/In search of the Grand Canyon. /1995/
3-5/6 KF068 . . . . **979.1**

Colored pencil drawing--Technique.
SANCHEZ SANCHEZ, I/Drawing dinosaurs. /1996/
5-A/3 KD418 . . . . **743**

Coloring books--Fiction.
VAN ALLSBURG, C/Bad day at Riverbend. /1995/
1-3/3 KG637. . . . . **E**

Columbus, Christopher.
ADLER, DA/Christopher Columbus: great explorer. /1991/
4-5/4 KE301 . . . . **B COLUMBUS, C.**
Picture book of Christopher Columbus. /1991/
2-3/4 KE300 . . . . **CE B COLUMBUS, C.**
ASIMOV, I/Christopher Columbus: navigator to the New World. /
1991/4-5/5 KE302 . . . . **B COLUMBUS, C.**
COLUMBUS, C/Log of Christopher Columbus' first voyage to
America in the year 1492. /c1938, 1989/4-6/7 KE741. . . **970.01**
FRITZ, J/Where do you think you're going, Christopher Columbus? /
1980/4-6/6 KE303 . . . . **CE B COLUMBUS, C.**
PELTA, K/Discovering Christopher Columbus. /1991/
A/6 KE742 . . . . **970.01**
YUE, C/Christopher Columbus: how he did it. /1992/
5-A/7 KE744 . . . . **970.01**

Comanche Indians--Folklore.
DE PAOLA, T/Legend of the Bluebonnet: an old tale of Texas. /
1983/2-4/4 KB558 . . . . **CE 398.24**

Comets.
SIMON, S/Comets, meteors, and asteroids. /1994/
4-6/7 KC043 . . . . **523.6**

Comic books, strips, etc SEE Cartoons and comics.
Commerce SEE ALSO Business enterprises; Trademarks; Transportation.

Commercials--Television.
BUY ME THAT! A KID'S SURVIVAL GUIDE TO TV ADVERTISING
(VIDEOCASSETTE). /1990/2-5/KD316 . . . . **VCR 659.14**

Communal living--Fiction.
CROSS, G/Wolf. /1991/A/6 KH045 . . . . **Fic**

Communicable diseases.
COMMUNICABLE DISEASES (VIDEOCASSETTE). /1992/
5-6/KD022. . . . . **VCR 616.9**

Communication SEE ALSO Books and reading; Language arts; Mass media;
Newspapers; Postal service; Television; Writing.

Communication.
ALIKI /Communication. /1993/K-6/4 KA794 . . . . **302.2**
GAN, G/Communication. /1997/5-6/9 KA795. . . . . **302.2**
SKURZYNSKI, G/Get the message: telecommunications in your
high-tech world. /1993/A/8 KD044 . . . . **621.38**

Community gardens--Fiction.
DISALVO-RYAN, D/City green. /1994/1-3/3 KF484 . . . . **E**
SCHECTER, E/Big idea. /1996/3-5/2 KH679 . . . . **Fic**
TAMAR, E/Garden of happiness. /1996/1-3/2 KG593 . . . . **E**

Community gardens--New York (N.Y.).
HUFF, BA/Greening the city streets: the story of community gardens.
/1990/5-6/7 KD168 . . . . **635**

Community life SEE ALSO Cities and towns; Community service.

Community service.
PUBLIC WORKS (VIDEOCASSETTE). /1992/
2-4/KB055. . . . . **VCR 363.72**

Competition (Psychology)--Fiction.
LEE, M/Nim and the war effort. /1997/2-4/5 KH391 . . . . . . **Fic**
SILVERMAN, E/Don't fidget a feather! /1994/P-2/2 KG505. . . . **E**

Composers.
AMERICAN IN PARIS: GERSHWIN (VIDEOCASSETTE). /1993/
1-6/KD517. . . . . **VCR 780**
GREENE, C/Johann Sebastian Bach: great man of music. /1992/
2-4/2 KE246 . . . . **B BACH, J.**
John Philip Sousa: the march king. /1992/
2-4/2 KE544 . . . . **B SOUSA, J.**
HURWITZ, J/Leonard Bernstein: a passion for music. /1993/
5-A/7 KE253 . . . . **B BERNSTEIN, L.**
ISADORA, R/Young Mozart. /1997/
2-3/6 KE472 . . . . **B MOZART, W.**
MITCHELL, B/Raggin', a story about Scott Joplin. /1987/
A/8 KE407 . . . . **B JOPLIN, S.**
OLD, WC/Duke Ellington: giant of jazz. /1996/
5-A/9 KE338 . . . . **B ELLINGTON, D.**
STREISSGUTH, T/Say it with music: a story about Irving Berlin. /
1994/4-5/5 KE252 . . . . **B BERLIN, I.**
THOMPSON, W/Claude Debussy. /1993/
6-A/9 KE316 . . . . **B DEBUSSY, C.**
Pyotr Ilyich Tchaikovsky. /1993/
6-A/8 KE558 . . . . **B TCHAIKOVSKY, P**
VENEZIA, M/Aaron Copland. /1995/
5-6/7 KE304 . . . . **B COPLAND, A.**
George Gershwin. /1994/4-6/7 KE368 . . . . . **B GERSHWIN, G.**
Igor Stravinsky. /1996/5-6/7 KE557 . . . . . **B STRAVINSKY, I**

Composers--Software.
WINTER, R/Microsoft composer collection (CD-ROM). /1994/
4-A/KD525 . . . . **CDR 780**

Composites (Plants).
WINNER, C/Sunflower family. /1996/3-6/7 KC434 . . . . **583**

Compost.
GLASER, L/Compost!: growing gardens from your garbage. /1996/
P-K/3 KD166 . . . . **635**
LAVIES, B/Compost critters. /1993/5-6/7 KC336 . . . . . . **577.5**
RECYCLING WITH WORMS (VIDEOCASSETTE). /1995/
3-6/KC507. . . . . **VCR 592**

Computer art.
SABBETH, C/Kids' computer creations: using your computer for art
and craft fun. /1995/3-5/KD434 . . . . **745.5**

Computer engineers.
GREENBERG, KE/Steven Jobs and Stephen Wozniak: creating the
Apple computer. /1994/4-6/7 KD046 . . . . **621.39**

Computer games--Fiction.
CROSS, G/New world. /1995/6-A/5 KH044 . . . . **Fic**

Computer managed instruction.
BARRON, AE/Internet and instruction: activities and ideas. /1996/
/KA047. . . . . **PROF 025.06**
WRIGHT, K/Challenge of technology: action strategies for the
school library media /1993//KA080 . . . . **PROF 027.8**

Computer programs--Software.
KIDDESK. SCHOOL VERSION (CD-ROM). /1995/
P-A/KA569 . . . . **CDR 004**
KIDDESK (MICROCOMPUTER PROGRAM). /1993/
K-A/KA568 . . . . **MCP 004**

Computer software--Catalogs.
EDUCATIONAL SOFTWARE PREVIEW GUIDE. /1982-/
/KA107. . . . . **PER PROF 050**

Computer-assisted instruction.
PAPERT, S/Children's machine: rethinking school in the age of the
computer. /1993//KA180. . . . . **PROF 371.3**
WRIGHT, K/Challenge of technology: action strategies for the
school library media /1993//KA080 . . . . **PROF 027.8**

Computer-assisted instruction--Catalogs.
EDUCATIONAL SOFTWARE PREVIEW GUIDE. /1982-/
/KA107 . . . . **PER PROF 050**
Computers.
COCHRANE, K/Internet. /1995/4-6/8 KA570 . . . . **004.67**
COMMUNICATIONS (VIDEOCASSETTE). /1992/
2-4/KA799 . . . . **VCR 302.23**
KAZUNAS, C/Internet for kids. /1997/2-4/7 KA571 . . . . . **004.67**
MULTIMEDIA, THE COMPLETE GUIDE. /1996/
A/KA372 . . . . **REF 006.7**
Computers--Dictionaries.
BORMAN, JL/Computer dictionary for kids...and their parents. /
1995/4-A/9 KA566 . . . . **004**
Computers--Fiction.
SERVICE, PF/Weirdos of the universe, unite! /1992/
6-A/6 KH701 . . . . **Fic**
Computers--Periodicals.
FAMILY PC. /1994-/5-A/KA109 . . . . **PER PROF 050**
LEARNING AND LEADING WITH TECHNOLOGY. /1979-/
/KA121 . . . . **PER PROF 050**
Computers--Vocational guidance.
KAPLAN, A/Careers for computer buffs. /1991/5-6/9 KA567 . **004**
Concentration camps--Fiction.
WILD, M/Let the celebrations begin! /1991/4-A/4 KH858 . . . . **Fic**
Concepts.
HOBAN, T/Over, under and through, and other spatial concepts. /
1973/P-K/KF745 . . . . **E**
Push, pull, empty, full: a book of opposites. /c1972/
P-K/KF746 . . . . **E**
HUGHES, S/Nursery collection. /c1986, 1994/P/2 KF790 . . . . . **E**
JENKINS, S/Flip-flap. /1995/P-K/2 KA619 . . . . **152.14**
Concerts--Fiction.
PARISH, H/Bravo, Amelia Bedelia! /1997/1-2/2 KG210 . . . . . . **E**
Concord, Battle of, 1775.
JOHNSON, N/Battle of Lexington and Concord. /1992/
4-6/7 KE881 . . . . **973.3**
Concord, Battle of, 1775--Fiction.
BENCHLEY, N/George, the drummer boy. /c1977/1-3/2 KF221 . **E**
Condors.
ARNOLD, C/On the brink of extinction: the California condor. /
1993/5-6/8 KD251 . . . . **639.9**
Conduct of life SEE ALSO Behavior.
Conduct of life.
BODINE, RJ/Creating the peaceable school: a comprehensive
program for teaching conflict /1994//KA161 . . . . . **PROF 303.6**
CASEY'S REVENGE: A STORY ABOUT FIGHTING AND
DISAGREEMENTS (VIDEOCASSETTE). /1991/
3-5/KA808 . . . . **VCR 303.6**
FLEMING, A/What, me worry?: how to hang in when your
problems stress you out. /1992/4-6/8 KA624 . . . . **152.4**
GETTING TO THE HEART OF IT (VIDEOCASSETTE). /1993/
5-A/KA809 . . . . **VCR 303.6**
GROARK LEARNS ABOUT BULLYING (VIDEOCASSETTE). /1996/
1-3/KA810 . . . . **VCR 303.6**
GROARK LEARNS TO WORK OUT CONFLICTS
(VIDEOCASSETTE). /1996/1-3/KA811 . . . . . . **VCR 303.6**
IT'S NOT FAIR! (VIDEOCASSETTE). /1994/
3-6/KA642 . . . . **VCR 155.4**
JAMES, E/Social smarts: manners for today's kids. /1996/
4-6/6 KB243 . . . . **395.3**
JUST FOR ME (VIDEOCASSETTE). /1992/
K-6/KC997 . . . . **VCR 613.8**
LEAF, M/Four-and-twenty watchbirds. /c1939, 1990/
P-3/6 KB240 . . . . **395**
MINDING YOUR MANNERS AT SCHOOL (VIDEOCASSETTE). /
1996/3-5/KB241 . . . . **VCR 395**
PARKS, R/Dear Mrs. Parks: a dialogue with today's youth. /1996/
5-6/6 KA901 . . . . **323**
SLABY, RG/Early violence prevention: tools for teachers of young
children. /1995//KA162 . . . . **PROF 303.6**
SLONECKI, C/Dog ate my homework: social skills for today
(Sound recording cassette). /1995/1-3/KB242 . . . . **SRC 395**
STUDENT WORKSHOP: MEDIATION SKILLS (VIDEOCASSETTE). /
1996//KA163 . . . . **VCR PROF 303.6**
STUDENT WORKSHOP: SOLVING CONFLICTS
(VIDEOCASSETTE). /1994/2-6/KA164 . . . . . . **VCR PROF 303.6**
WE CAN WORK IT OUT!: CONFLICT RESOLUTION
(VIDEOCASSETTE). /1994/K-2/KA165 . . . . . . **VCR PROF 303.6**
YOUNG, E/Voices of the heart. /1997/A/7 KA675 . . . . **179**
Conduct of life--Case studies.
LETTERS FOR OUR CHILDREN: FIFTY AMERICANS SHARE
LESSONS IN LIVING. /1996//KA158 . . . . **PROF 170**
Conduct of life--Fiction.
ADA, AF/Gold coin. /1991/1-3/4 KF131 . . . . **E**

CHRISTIAN, MB/Toady and Dr. Miracle. /1997/1-3/2 KF390 . . . **E**
COONEY, B/Miss Rumphius. /1982/K-3/5 KF419 . . . . **E**
Miss Rumphius (Kit). /1994/K-3/KF420 . . . . **KIT E**
DEFELICE, CC/Lostman's River. /1994/4-A/6 KH067 . . . . **Fic**
HEIDE, FP/Tales for the perfect child. /1985/2-5/2 KH233 . . . . **Fic**
MERRILL, J/Girl who loved caterpillars: a twelfth-century tale from
Japan. /1992/2-4/5 KG132 . . . . **E**
SPINELLI, J/Crash. /1996/5-A/3 KH744 . . . . **Fic**
WOJCIECHOWSKI, S/Don't call me Beanhead! /1994/
2-3/5 KH877 . . . . **Fic**
Conduct of life--Literary collections.
BOOK OF VIRTUES FOR YOUNG PEOPLE: A TREASURY OF
GREAT MORAL STORIES. /1997//KA343 . . . . . **PROF 808.8**
CHILDREN'S BOOK OF VIRTUES. /1995/K-3/KD871 . . . . . **808.8**
Conducting--Fiction.
HOFF, S/Arturo's baton. /1995/K-2/2 KF750 . . . . **E**
Conductors (Music).
HURWITZ, J/Leonard Bernstein: a passion for music. /1993/
5-A/7 KE253 . . . . **B BERNSTEIN, L.**
SIMON, C/Seiji Ozawa: symphony conductor. /1992/
4-5/6 KE488 . . . . **B OZAWA, S.**
Coney Island (New York, N.Y.)--Fiction.
ROSE, DL/Rose horse. /1995/3-5/6 KH651 . . . . **Fic**
Confectionery SEE ALSO Cake; Cookies; Ice cream, ices, etc.
Confectionery--Fiction.
KROLL, S/Candy witch. /1979/K-1/6 KF927 . . . . **E**
Confederate States of America. Army--History.
RAY, D/Behind the blue and gray: the soldier's life in the Civil War.
/1991/5-A/7 KE911 . . . . **973.7**
Conflict management.
BODINE, RJ/Creating the peaceable school: a comprehensive
program for teaching conflict resolution: program guide. /1994/
/KA161 . . . . **PROF 303.6**
BULLY UP: FIGHTING FEELINGS (VIDEOCASSETTE). /c1990,
1991/K-3/KA807 . . . . **VCR 303.6**
CASEY'S REVENGE: A STORY ABOUT FIGHTING AND
DISAGREEMENTS (VIDEOCASSETTE). /1991/
3-5/KA808 . . . . **VCR 303.6**
GETTING TO THE HEART OF IT (VIDEOCASSETTE). /1993/
5-A/KA809 . . . . **VCR 303.6**
GROARK LEARNS ABOUT BULLYING (VIDEOCASSETTE). /1996/
1-3/KA810 . . . . **VCR 303.6**
GROARK LEARNS TO WORK OUT CONFLICTS
(VIDEOCASSETTE). /1996/1-3/KA811 . . . . . **VCR 303.6**
NO MORE TEASING! (VIDEOCASSETTE). /1995/
3-4/KA661 . . . . **VCR 158**
SLABY, RG/Early violence prevention: tools for teachers of young
children. /1995//KA162 . . . . **PROF 303.6**
STUDENT WORKSHOP: MEDIATION SKILLS (VIDEOCASSETTE). /
1996//KA163 . . . . **VCR PROF 303.6**
STUDENT WORKSHOP: SOLVING CONFLICTS
(VIDEOCASSETTE). /1994/2-6/KA164 . . . . . . **VCR PROF 303.6**
WE CAN WORK IT OUT!: CONFLICT RESOLUTION
(VIDEOCASSETTE). /1994/K-2/KA165 . . . . . . **VCR PROF 303.6**
WORKING IT OUT: CONFLICT RESOLUTION (VIDEOCASSETTE).
/1993/5-6/KA813 . . . . **VCR 303.6**
Conflict of generations.
LESHAN, E/Grandparents: a special kind of love. /1984/
4-6/9 KA879 . . . . **306.874**
Conjuring SEE Magic tricks.
Conjuring.
BAUER, CF/Leading kids to books through magic. /1996/
/KA066 . . . . **PROF 027.62**
Connecticut.
FRADIN, DB/Connecticut. /1994/4-6/4 KE952 . . . . **974.6**
Connecticut--Fiction.
SPEARE, EG/Witch of Blackbird Pond. /c1958/
5-6/5 KH742 . . . . **CE Fic**
Connecticut--History.
WILLS, CA/Historical album of Connecticut. /1995/
4-6/7 KE953 . . . . **974.6**
Connecticut--Revolution, 1775-1783--Campaigns.
MURPHY, J/Young patriot: the American Revolution as experienced
by one boy. /1996/5-A/9 KE884 . . . . **973.3**
Conquistadors SEE America--Discovery and exploration--Spanish.
Conscience--Fiction.
FORD, B/Most wonderful movie in the world. /1996/
6-A/4 KH132 . . . . **Fic**
Conservation of natural resources SEE ALSO Energy conservation; Wildlife
conservation.
Conservation of natural resources.
ANCONA, G/Riverkeeper. /1990/4-6/7 KA958 . . . . **333.91**
LIPTAK, K/Saving our wetlands and their wildlife. /1991/
4-6/8 KA960 . . . . **333.91**

OUR ENDANGERED EARTH (VIDEOCASSETTE). /1990/
3-6/KC307. . . . . **VCR 577.27**
REDUCING, REUSING AND RECYCLING: ENVIRONMENTAL
CONCERNS (VIDEOCASSETTE). /1992/4-6/KB051. . **VCR 363.7**

Conservation of natural resources--Fiction.
ATKINS, J/Aani and the tree huggers. /1995/3-5-3 KG853 . . . **Fic**
CHERRY, L/Great kapok tree: a tale of the Amazon rain forest. /
1990/2-3/4 KF380 . . . . **E**
    Great kapok tree (Videocassette). /1996/2-3/KF381. . . . **VCR E**
ERNST, LC/Squirrel Park. /1993/K-2/5 KF533 . . . . **E**

Conservation of natural resources--San Francisco Bay Area (Calif.).
KIDS BY THE BAY (VIDEOCASSETTE). /1997/
3-6/KB047. . . . . **VCR 363.7**

Conservationists.
BRYANT, J/Marjory Stoneman Douglas: voice of the Everglades. /
1992/4-5/6 KE324 . . . . **B DOUGLAS, M.**
FABER, D/Great lives: nature and the environment. /1991/
5-A/7 KB903 . . . . **508**
NADEN, CJ/John Muir: saving the wilderness. /1992/
5-6/4 KE473 . . . . **B MUIR, J.**

Conservationists--Biography.
KEENE, AT/Earthkeepers: observers and protectors of nature. /
1994/5-A/KA436 . . . . **REF 508**

Constellations.
GIBBONS, G/Stargazers. /1992/K-2/4 KC049 . . . . **523.8**
KRUPP, EC/Big dipper and you. /1989/1-6/4 KC050 . . . . . **523.8**
LURIE, A/Heavenly zoo: legends and tales of the stars. /c1979,
1996/5-6/8 KB710 . . . . **398.26**
MAP OF THE UNIVERSE: THE NORTHERN HEMISPHERE
(PICTURE). /1980/3-A/KC051. . . . . **PIC 523.8**
REY, HA/Find the constellations. Rev. ed. /1976/
4-6/6 KC052 . . . . **523.8**
STARS AND CONSTELLATIONS (VIDEOCASSETTE). /1993/
3-6/KC055. . . . . **VCR 523.8**

Constitution, U.S SEE United States. Constitution; United States.
Constitutional Convention (1787).

Construction equipment.
DIGGERS AND DUMPERS. /1994/K-2/5 KD121 . . . . . . **629.225**

Construction equipment--Fiction.
BARTON, B/Machines at work. /1987/P-K/2 KF207 . . . . **E**

Construction equipment--Pictorial works.
HOBAN, T/Dig, drill, dump, fill. /1975/P-2/KD122 . . . . . . **629.225**

Construction equipment--Software.
BIG JOB (CD-ROM). /1995/K-3/KD120. . . . . . . **CDR 629.225**

Consumer education SEE ALSO Consumer protection; Shopping.

Consumer education.
BUY ME THAT! A KID'S SURVIVAL GUIDE TO TV ADVERTISING
(VIDEOCASSETTE). /1990/2-5/KD316 . . . . **VCR 659.14**
SCHMITT, L/Smart spending: a young consumer's guide. /1989/
5-6/8 KD262 . . . . **640**

Consumer education--Periodicals.
ZILLIONS. /1980-/3-5/KA553 . . . . **PER 050**

Consumer protection--Periodicals.
ZILLIONS. /1980-/3-5/KA553 . . . . **PER 050**

Contests.
BERGSTROM, JM/All the best contests for kids, 1996-1997. 5th
ed. /1996/3-6/7 KD677. **790.1**

Contests--Fiction.
BATEMAN, T/Ring of Truth: an original Irish tale. /1997/
1-3/5 KF213 . . . . **E**
CAREY, P/Big Bazoohley. /1995/3-6/5 KG973 . . . . **Fic**
DUFFEY, B/Camp Knock Knock. /1996/1-3/2 KF500. . . . . **E**
GREENSTEIN, E/Mrs. Rose's garden. /1996/K-2/3 KF643 . . . . **E**
KONIGSBURG, EL/View from Saturday. /1996/5-A/7 KH377 . **Fic**
LOREDO, E/Boogie Bones. /1997/K-2/3 KG034 . . . . **E**
NAYLOR, PR/Beetles, lightly toasted. /1987/5-6/6 KH534 . . . . **Fic**

Continental drift.
SATTLER, HR/Our patchwork planet: the story of plate tectonics. /
1995/A/7 KC155 . . . . **551.1**

Continents.
LEEDY, L/Blast off to Earth!: a look at geography. /1992/
1-4/4 KE151 . . . . **910**

Conversation--Fiction.
HUGHES, S/Chatting. /1996/P-1/2 KF787 . . . . **E**

Cook, James.
BLUMBERG, R/Remarkable voyages of Captain Cook. /1991/
5-6/7 KE163 . . . . **910.92**

Cookery SEE ALSO Baking; Bread; Cake; Confectionery; Food; Soup.

Cookery.
BRADY, AA/Kwanzaa karamu: cooking and crafts for a Kwanzaa
feast. /1995/5-6/5 KD284 . . . . **641.59**
COBB, V/More science experiments you can eat. /1979/
A/7 KB890 . . . . **507.8**

Science experiments you can eat. Rev. and updated. /1994/
3-5/7 KB891 . . . . **507.8**
COLEN, K/Peas and honey: recipes for kids (with a pinch of
poetry). /1995/3-6/KD269 . . . . **641.5**
CORWIN, JH/Asian crafts. /1992/4-A/7 KD426 . . . . **745.5**
FLORIAN, D/Chef. /1992/K-2/5 KD270. . . . . **641.5**
GORDON, L/Messipes: a microwave cookbook of deliciously messy
masterpieces. /1996/3-6/KD271 . . . . **641.5**
KALMAN, B/Kitchen. /1990/4-5/5 KD295 . . . . **643**
KATZEN, M/Pretend soup and other real recipes: a cookbook for
preschoolers and up. /1994/P-3/KD272. . . . . **641.5**
KENDA, M/Cooking wizardry for kids. /1990/5-6/KD273 . **641.5**
MACDONALD, K/Anne of Green Gables cookbook. /1986/
5-6/7 KD274 . . . . **641.5**
PERL, L/Hunter's stew and hangtown fry: what pioneer America ate
and why. /c1977/A/11 KD275 . . . . **641.5**
    Slumps, grunts, and snickerdoodles: what Colonial America ate and
why. /1975/A/9 KD276 . . . . **641.5**
RITCHIE, D/Kid's cuisine. /1988/4-6/KD278 . . . . **641.5**
SCOBEY, J/Fannie Farmer junior cookbook. New and rev. ed. /
1993/A/KD280 . . . . **641.5**
SUPRANER, R/Quick and easy cookbook. /c1981, 1985/
1-4/KD281. . . . . **641.5**
WEST, R/My very own Halloween: a book of cooking and crafts. /
1993/3-6/KD701 . . . . **793.2**

Cookery--Apples.
HALL, Z/Apple pie tree. /1996/1-4/2 KC413 . . . . **582.16**

Cookery--Fiction.
AXELROD, A/Pigs in the pantry: fun with math and cooking. /
1997/1-3/3 KF178 . . . . **E**
BRANDENBERG, A/Chop, simmer, season. /1997/P-1/2 KF257 . **E**
CROLL, C/Too many Babas. /c1979, 1994/K-2/2 KF439 . . . . . **E**
PARISH, P/Good work, Amelia Bedelia. /c1976/
1-3/2 KG214 . . . . **CE E**
RATTIGAN, JK/Dumpling soup. /1993/1-3/2 KG312 . . . . **E**
TORRES, L/Saturday sancocho. /1995/K-2/5 KG614 . . . . **E**

Cookery--Rice.
THOMSON, R/Rice. /1990/3-5/4 KD152 . . . . **633.1**

Cookery, American.
MACK-WILLIAMS, K/Food and our history. /1995/
5-6/7 KD287 . . . . **641.59**
PENNER, LR/Eating the plates: a Pilgrim book of food and manners.
/1991/3-6/4 KB186 . . . . **394.1**
REX-JOHNSON, B/That's fresh!: seasonal recipes for young cooks.
/1995/5-6/KD277 . . . . **641.5**

Cookery, American--History.
WALKER, BM/Little House cookbook: frontier foods from Laura
Ingalls Wilder's classic stories. New ed. /1995/
4-6/9 KD282 . . . . **641.5**

Cookery, Caribbean.
CORWIN, JH/Latin American and Caribbean crafts. /1992/
4-A/5 KD427 . . . . **745.5**

Cookery, Indian.
PENNER, LR/Native American feast. /1994/4-6/6 KB187. . . **394.1**

Cookery, International.
ALBYN, CL/Multicultural cookbook for students. /1993/
/KA299. . . . . **PROF 641.59**
COOK, DF/Kids' multicultural cookbook: food and fun around the
world. /1995/3-5/KD285 . . . . **641.59**
CORONADA, R/Cooking the Mexican way. /1982/
4-6/8 KD286 . . . . **641.59**

Cookery, Jewish.
ZALBEN, JB/Beni's family cookbook for the Jewish holidays. /1996/
4-6/KD283 . . . . **641.5**

Cookery, Jewish--Fiction.
WING, N/Jalapeno bagels. /1996/1-3/2 KG742. . . . . **E**

Cookery, Latin American.
CORWIN, JH/Latin American and Caribbean crafts. /1992/
4-A/5 KD427 . . . . **745.5**

Cookery, Mexican American--Fiction.
WING, N/Jalapeno bagels. /1996/1-3/2 KG742. . . . . **E**

Cookie industry.
JASPERSOHN, W/Cookies. /1993/3-5/8 KD320 . . . . **664**

Cookies--Fiction.
ADLER, DA/Young Cam Jansen and the missing cookie. /1996/
1-2/2 KF134 . . . . **E**
HOOPER, M/Cow, a bee, a cookie, and me. /1997/
K-2/2 KF768 . . . . **E**
HUTCHINS, P/Doorbell rang. /1986/P-2/2 KF797 . . . . **CE E**
MOFFATT, J/Who stole the cookies? /1996/P-1/1 KG149. . . . . **E**

Cooks.
FLORIAN, D/Chef. /1992/K-2/5 KD270 . . . . **641.5**

Cooperation.
COOPERATION (VIDEOCASSETTE). /1990/4-6/KA655 **VCR 158**

Cooperativeness--Fiction.
SILVERMAN, E/Big pumpkin. /1992/P-2/2 KG504 . . . . **E**

Copland, Aaron.
VENEZIA, M/Aaron Copland. /1995/
5-6/7 KE304 . . . . **B COPLAND, A.**

Copper Age.
GETZ, D/Frozen man. /1994/4-6/7 KE638 . . . . **937**
LESSEM, D/Iceman. /1994/4-6/6 KE640 . . . . **937**
TANAKA, S/Discovering the Iceman: what was it like to find a
5,300-year-old mummy? /1997/3-5/4 KE642 . . . . **937**

Copy art.
FLEISCHMAN, P/Copier creations: using copy machines to make
decals, silhouettes, flip books, films, and much more! /1993/
3-6/7 KD503 . . . . **760**

Copyright.
OFFICIAL FAIR-USE GUIDELINES: COMPLETE TEXT OF FOUR
OFFICIAL DOCUMENTS ARRANGED FOR USE BY EDUCATORS.
/1987//KA168 . . . . **PROF 346.73**
TALAB, RS/Commonsense copyright: a guide to the new
technologies. /1986//KA169 . . . . **PROF 346.73**

Coral reef animals--Australia--Great Barrier Reef (Qld.).
GOUCK, M/Great Barrier Reef. /1993/3-6/5 KF119 . . . . . . **994.3**
MCGOVERN, A/Down under, down under: diving adventures on
the Great Barrier Reef. /1989/3-6/5 KF120 . . . . **994.3**

Coral reef animals--Fiction.
BOYLE, D/Coral reef hideaway: the story of a clown anemonefish. /
1995/K-2/7 KF255 . . . . **CE E**

Coral reef biology.
SIY, A/Great Astrolabe Reef. /1992/4-6/7 KC352 . . . . . . **577.7**

Coral reef ecology.
PRINGLE, LP/Coral reefs: Earth's undersea treasures. /1995/
5-6/7 KC351 . . . . **577.7**
SIY, A/Great Astrolabe Reef. /1992/4-6/7 KC352 . . . . . . **577.7**
WU, N/City under the sea: life in a coral reef. /1996/
4-6/8 KC354 . . . . **577.7**

Coral reefs and islands.
WU, N/City under the sea: life in a coral reef. /1996/
4-6/8 KC354 . . . . **577.7**

Corals.
SIY, A/Great Astrolabe Reef. /1992/4-6/7 KC352 . . . . . . **577.7**

Coretta Scott King Award--Bibliography.
CORETTA SCOTT KING AWARDS BOOK: FROM VISION TO
REALITY. /1994//KA008 . . . . **PROF 011.008**

Corn.
ALIKI /Corn is maize: the gift of the Indians. /c1976/
K-3/3 KD149 . . . . **633.1**
BIAL, R/Corn belt harvest. /1991/4-5/7 KD150 . . . . **633.1**
BROWN, C/Tractor. /1995/K-2/2 KD146 . . . . **631.3**

Corn--Folklore.
GERSON, M/People of corn: a Mayan story. /1995/
2-4/3 KB399 . . . . **398.21**
PARKE, M/Quetzalcoatl tale of corn. /1992/2-3/5 KB630 . **398.24**

Cornwall (England)--Folklore.
BARBER, A/Mousehole cat. /1990/4-6/6 KG879 . . . . **Fic**
ZEMACH, H/Duffy and the devil, a Cornish tale. /c1973/
2-4/7 KB426 . . . . **CE 398.21**

Cortes, Hernando.
MARRIN, A/Aztecs and Spaniards: Cortes and the conquest of
Mexico. /1986/5-6/7 KE833 . . . . **972**

Cosmetics industry--History.
COLMAN, P/Madam C.J. Walker: building a business empire. /
1994/4-6/7 KE583 . . . . **B WALKER, C.J.**

Costa Rica--Folklore.
BADEN, R/And Sunday makes seven. /1990/
2-3/2 KB388 . . . . **398.21**

Costanoan Indians--Missions--California.
ABBINK, E/Missions of the Monterey Bay Area. /1996/
4-6/9 KF075 . . . . **979.4**
WHITE, TN/Missions of the San Francisco Bay Area. /1996/
4-6/9 KF087 . . . . **979.4**

Costume SEE ALSO Arms and armor; Clothing and dress; Hats; Jewelry.

Costume.
CHERNOFF, GT/Easy costumes you don't have to sew. /c1975/
P-A/4 KD298 . . . . **646.4**
HERSHBERGER, P/Make costumes!: for creative play. /1992/
4-6/2 KD300 . . . . **646.4**
MORIN, A/Newspaper theatre: creative play production for low
budgets and no budgets. /1989//KA330 . . . . **PROF 792**
SHOW TIME (VIDEOCASSETTE). /1994/K-2/KD690 . . **VCR 792**

Costume--History.
BLUMBERG, R/Bloomers!. /1993/3-5/6 KA830 . . . . **305.42**
KALMAN, B/18th century clothing. /1993/4-6/6 KB164 . . . . . **391**
ROWLAND-WARNE, L/Costume. /1992/4-6/8 KB165 . . . . . . **391**

Costume--West(U.S.)--History.
CHRISTIAN, MB/Hats are for watering horses: why the cowboy
dressed that way. /1993/4-6/4 KB163 . . . . **391**

Cotton picking--Fiction.
WILLIAMS, SA/Working cotton. /1992/1-3/2 KG731 . . . . **E**

Counting SEE ALSO Number games.

Counting.
ANNO, M/Anno's counting book. /1977/P-2/KB945 . . . . . **513**
BANG, M/Ten, nine, eight. /1983/P-K/KF192 . . . . **E**
BECKER, J/Seven little rabbits. /1973/P-2/3 KF214 . . . . **E**
BIG FAT HEN. /1994/P-1/1 KB793 . . . . **398.8**
BLACKSTONE, S/Grandma went to market: a round-the-world
counting rhyme. /1996/1-3/5 KF232 . . . . **E**
BOWEN, B/Gathering: a northwoods counting book. /1995/
1-3/3 KB953 . . . . **513.2**
BRUSCA, MC/Three friends: a counting book./Tres amigos: un
cuento para contar. /1995/P-2/1 KB954 . . . . **513.2**
CARLE, E/Rooster's off to see the world. /1972/P-2/2 KF345 . . . **E**
1, 2, 3 to the zoo. /c1968/P-K/KF349. . . . . **E**
CARLSTROM, NW/Let's count it out, Jesse Bear. /1996/
P-1/2 KF357 . . . . **E**
CHALLONER, J/Science book of numbers. /1992/
K-3/2 KB956 . . . . **513.2**
CHRISTELOW, E/Five little monkeys sitting in a tree. /1991/
P-K/2 KF384 . . . . **E**
COLE, N/Blast off!: a space counting book. /1994/
P-3/6 KD131 . . . . **629.43**
CREWS, D/Ten black dots. Rev. and redesigned ed. /c1968, 1986/
P-2/2 KF437 . . . . **E**
DALE, P/Ten out of bed. /1994/P-1/2 KF446 . . . . **E**
EHLERT, L/Fish eyes: a book you can count on. /1990/
P-K/1 KF518 . . . . **E**
FIVE LITTLE DUCKS: AN OLD RHYME. /1995/
P-1/1 KB797 . . . . **398.8**
FOLK ART COUNTING BOOK. /1992/P-3/1 KD420. . . . . . **745**
GEISERT, A/Pigs from 1 to 10. /1992/1-3/3 KF604 . . . . **E**
Roman numerals I to MM./Numerabilia romana uno ad duo mila:
liber de /1996/K-4/6 KB988 . . . . **513.5**
GIGANTI, JR., P/Each orange had 8 slices: a counting book. /
1992/P-1/2 KB989 . . . . **513.5**
GOENNEL, H/Odds and evens: a numbers book. /1994/
P-1/2 KB957 . . . . **513.2**
GUY, GF/Fiesta! /1996/P-1/1 KF655 . . . . **E**
HALSEY, M/3 pandas planting. /1994/P-1/2 KB958 . . . . . **513.2**
HARLEY, B/Sitting down to eat. /1996/P-2/2 KF672 . . . . **E**
HARTMANN, W/One sun rises: an African wildlife counting book. /
1994/P-2/3 KB959 . . . . **513.2**
HOBAN, T/Count and see. /c1972/P/KF741 . . . . **E**
26 letters and 99 cents. /1987/P-2/KF748 . . . . **E**
HULME, JN/Sea squares. /1991/K-3/3 KB960. . . . . **513.2**
HUTCHINS, P/One hunter. /1982/P-K/KF800 . . . . **E**
INTRODUCTION TO LETTERS AND NUMERALS
(VIDEOCASSETTE). /1985/P-1/KF809 . . . . **VCR E**
JENKINS, E/Counting games and rhythms for the little ones, vol. 1
(Sound recording cassette). /c1964, 1990/P-2/KB948 . . **SRC 513**
LESIEG, T/Ten apples up on top! /c1961/1-2/1 KF959 . . . . . . **E**
Wacky Wednesday. /c1974/1-2/1 KF961 . . . . **E**
LEWIS, PO/P. Bear's New Year's party!: a counting book. /1989/
K-1/3 KF978 . . . . **E**
LINDEN, AM/One smiling grandma: a Caribbean counting book. /
1995/P-1/2 KF984 . . . . **E**
MACK, S/10 bears in my bed: a goodnight countdown. /1974/
P-1/1 KG052 . . . . **E**
MATH, MONEY, AND YOU (SOUND FILMSTRIP). /1989/
K-2/KB967 . . . . **FSS 513.2**
MAZZOLA, F/Counting is for the birds. /1997/
K-3/3 KB968 . . . . **513.2**
MICKLETHWAIT, L/I spy two eyes: numbers in art. /1993/
P-A/KB970 . . . . **513.2**
MORA, P/Uno, dos, tres: one, two, three. /1996/P-1/3 KG155 . **E**
MOSS, L/Zin! zin! zin! a violin. /1995/K-3/3 KG157 . . . . **E**
NIKOLA-LISA, W/One hole in the road. /1996/P-K/2 KG173 . . . **E**
NOLL, S/Surprise! /1997/P-K/2 KG179 . . . . **E**
OCHS, CP/When I'm alone. /1993/P-2/4 KG187 . . . . **E**
OCKENGA, S/World of wonders: a trip through numbers. /1988/
3-A/3 KB975 . . . . **513.2**
ONYEFULU, I/Emeka's gift: an African counting story. /1995/
1-4/5 KE728 . . . . **960**
OWENS, MB/Counting cranes. /1993/P-4/3 KB976 . . . . . **513.2**
REISS, JJ/Numbers. /c1971/P-1/KG321 . . . . **E**
ROTH, SL/My love for you. /1997/P-1/2 KG356 . . . . **E**
RYAN, PM/Crayon counting book. /1996/P-1/3 KB982 . . . . **513.2**
SAMTON, SW/World from my window. /c1985, 1991/
P-K/2 KG389 . . . . **E**

SCOTT, AH/One good horse: a cowpuncher's counting book. /
1990/K-2/2 KG424. . . . . E
SENDAK, M/One was Johnny: a counting book. /c1962/
P-1/KG435 . . . . **CE E**
SIMON, C/One happy classroom. /1997/K-1/2 KG507 . . . . . E
SIS, P/Going up! A color counting book. /1989/P-2/KG511 . . E
Waving: a counting book. /1988/P-2/KG512 . . . . E
STURGES, P/Ten flashing fireflies. /1995/K-2/2 KG581. . . . . . . E
TAFURI, N/Who's counting? /1986/P-K/KG592 . . . . E
THIS OLD MAN. /1990/P-1/KD602 . . . . **789.2**
THORNHILL, J/Wildlife 1 2 3: a nature counting book. /1989/
P-2/KC455. . . . . **591**
TRINCA, R/One woolly wombat. /1985/P-2/4 KG617 . . . . . E
WADSWORTH, G/One on a web: counting animals at home. /
1997/P-2/3 KC456 . . . . **591**
WEIMER, TE/Fingerplays and action chants: volume 1: animals. /
1995/P-1/KD710 . . . . **BA 793.4**
WINTER, J/Josefina. /1996/1-3/6 KG743 . . . . E
YEKTAI, N/Bears at the beach: counting 10 to 20. /1996/
P-1/KB985. . . . . **513.2**

Counting--Fiction.
FLEMING, D/Count! /1992/P-K/KF554 . . . . E
JONAS, A/Splash! /1995/P-2/1 KF848 . . . . E
KUSKIN, K/James and the rain. /1995/K-2/5 KF938 . . . . . E
POMERANTZ, C/One duck, another duck. /1984/P-1/1 KG265 . E
WORMELL, C/Number of animals. /1993/P-2/3 KG770 . . . . . E

Counting rhymes.
MISS MARY MACK AND OTHER CHILDREN'S STREET RHYMES. /
1990/2-5/KD766 . . . . **796.1**

Country life.
CREWS, D/Bigmama's. /1991/K-2/2 KE309 . . . **CE B CREWS, D.**

Country life--Fiction.
GREEN, CJ/Emmy. /1992/6-A/5 KH196 . . . . Fic
HAAS, J/Uncle Daney's way. /1994/4-6/4 KH210 . . . . . Fic
HITE, S/Dither Farm: a novel. /1992/5-A/7 KH265. . . . . . Fic
JONAS, A/Round trip. /1983/K-2/2 KF847 . . . . **CE E**
LYON, GE/Come a tide. /1990/K-3/2 KG043. . . . . E
MACLACHLAN, P/All the places to love. /1994/1-4/5 KG053 . . E
MARTIN, JR., B/Barn dance! /1986/P-3/3 KG071 . . . . E
MOORE, E/Grandma's house. /1985/K-2/4 KG154 . . . . . . E
MOORE, L/Don't be afraid, Amanda. /1992/2-4/4 KH504 . . . Fic
WILDER, LI/Farmer boy. /c1953/3-6/5 KH859. . . . . Fic
WOLFF, A/Year of beasts. /1986/P-K/1 KG757 . . . . E
YOLEN, J/Letting Swift River go. /1992/1-3/5 KG777 . . . . . . E

Country life--Minnesota.
BOWEN, B/Gathering: a northwoods counting book. /1995/
1-3/3 KB953 . . . . **513.2**

Country life--Rome.
MORLEY, J/Roman villa. /1992/4-6/7 KE641 . . . . **937**

Country music--Fiction.
PATERSON, K/Come sing, Jimmy Jo. /1985/5-A/4 KH574 . . . Fic

Courage--Fiction.
BRIMNER, LD/Brave Mary. /1996/K-1/2 KF266. . . . . E
GEORGE, JC/Julie of the wolves. /c1972/6-A/6 KH157 . . **CE Fic**
Julie of the wolves (Talking book). /1993/6-A/KH158. . . **TB Fic**
HALL, K/I'm not scared. /1994/K-1/1 KF664. . . . . E
HEARNE, B/Seven brave women. /1997/1-3/2 KF691. . . . . . E
HENKES, K/Sheila Rae, the brave. /1987/P-2/4 KF711 . . . . . E
KNIGHT, E/Lassie come-home. /1978/4-6/5 KH370 . . . . . Fic
NAYLOR, PR/King of the playground. /1991/K-3/2 KG167 . . . . E
O'BRIEN, RC/Mrs. Frisby and the rats of NIMH. /c1971/
4-A/6 KH556. . . . . Fic
PEET, B/Cowardly Clyde. /1979/K-2/6 KG225 . . . . E
PINKNEY, JB/JoJo's flying side kick. /1995/K-3/2 KG243 . . . . . E
SCOTT, AH/Brave as a mountain lion. /1996/3-5/2 KH688 . . . Fic
SLEPIAN, J/Alfred Summer. /1980/4-6/4 KH718 . . . . Fic
SPERRY, A/Call it courage. /c1940/5-6/6 KH743. . . . . . **CE Fic**
STEIG, W/Brave Irene. /1986/K-3/3 KG541. . . . . **CE E**

Courlander, Harold.
JAFFE, N/Voice for the people: the life and work of Harold
Courlander. /1997//KA367. . . . . **PROF B COURLAND**

Courtesy SEE Etiquette.

Courts and courtiers.
ALIKI /Medieval feast. /1983/2-5/5 KB183. . . . . **CE 394.1**

Courtship SEE ALSO Dating (Social customs).

Cousins--Fiction.
ALCOTT, LM/Rose in bloom: a sequel to Eight cousins. Uniform ed.
/c1876, 1995/5-6/7 KG831 . . . . Fic
ENGLISH, K/Neeny coming, Neeny going. /1996/1-3/2 KF527. . E
HAMILTON, V/Cousins. /1990/6-A/5 KH213 . . . . Fic
HESSE, K/Lavender. /1995/2-3/2 KH251 . . . . Fic
HEST, A/Nana's birthday party. /1993/1-3/4 KF720 . . . . E
HORVATH, P/Occasional cow. /1989/5-6/8 KH284 . . . . . . Fic
LEVIN, B/Fire in the wind. /1995/5-A/4 KH396 . . . . Fic

MAHY, M/Fortune branches out. /c1994, 1995/3-5/4 KH447 . . **Fic**
Good Fortunes gang. /1993/3-5/7 KH448 . . . . **Fic**
NAYLOR, PR/Beetles, lightly toasted. /1987/5-6/6 KH534 . . . . **Fic**
PAULSEN, G/Harris and me: a summer remembered. /1993/
6-A/7 KH586. . . . . **Fic**
WHITE, R/Belle Prater's boy. /1996/6-A/6 KH853 . . . . **Fic**

Cousteau, Jacques Yves.
ADVENTURE IN THE AMAZON. /1992/4-6/7 KE211 . . . . . **918.1**
REEF, C/Jacques Cousteau: champion of the sea. /1992/
4-6/7 KE305 . . . . **B COUSTEAU, J.**

Cowboys.
ANDERSON, J/Cowboys: roundup on an American ranch. /1996/
3-5/6 KF025 . . . . **978**
GRANFIELD, L/Cowboy: an album. /1994/5-A/8 KF030 . . . . **978**
MILLER, RH/Cowboys. /1991/4-6/6 KF039. . . . . **978**
MURDOCH, DH/Cowboy. /1993/4-A/8 KF040 . . . . **978**
PINKNEY, AD/Bill Pickett: rodeo-ridin' cowboy. /1996/
2-5/7 KE496 . . . . **B PICKETT, B.**
REAL COWBOYS (PICTURE). /n.d./5-6/KF044. . . . . . . **PIC 978**
ROUNDS, G/Cowboys. /1991/P-K/6 KF047 . . . . **978**
SCHLISSEL, L/Black frontiers: a history of African American heroes
in the Old West. /1995/4-6/8 KF048 . . . . **978**
SCOTT, AH/Cowboy country. /1993/3-6/3 KF049 . . . . **978**

Cowboys--Costume.
CHRISTIAN, MB/Hats are for watering horses: why the cowboy
dressed that way. /1993/4-6/4 KB163 . . . . **391**

Cowboys--Fiction.
ANTLE, N/Sam's Wild West Show. /1995/1-3/2 KF161 . . . . . . E
DENSLOW, SP/On the trail with Miss Pace. /1995/
1-3/2 KF461 . . . . E
EVERETT, P/One that got away. /1992/K-2/2 KF540 . . . . E
HOOKER, R/Matthew the cowboy. /1990/K-2/2 KF767 . . . . . . E
JOHNSTON, T/Cowboy and the black-eyed pea. /1992/
K-2/5 KF839 . . . . E
KARAS, GB/Home on the bayou: a cowboy's story. /1996/
K-2/2 KF868 . . . . E
LIGHTFOOT, DJ/Trail fever: the life of a Texas cowboy. /1992/
4-6/5 KH406 . . . . Fic
SANFIELD, S/Great turtle drive. /1996/2-6/4 KH676 . . . . . . Fic
SCOTT, AH/One good horse: a cowpuncher's counting book. /
1990/K-2/2 KG424. . . . . E
VAN ALLSBURG, C/Bad day at Riverbend. /1995/
1-3/3 KG637. . . . . E

Cowboys--Songs and music.
COWBOY SONGS (SOUND RECORDING CASSETTE). /1992/
4-A/KD560 . . . . **SRC 789.2**
HORSE SENSE FOR KIDS AND OTHER PEOPLE (SOUND
RECORDING CASSETTE). /1992/2-4/KD668 . . . . . . **SRC 789.4**
SONGS OF THE WILD WEST. /1991/2-A/KD597 . . . . **789.2**

Cowboys--West (U.S.).
BRUSCA, MC/Three friends: a counting book./Tres amigos: un
cuento para contar. /1995/P-2/1 KB954 . . . . **513.2**
FREEDMAN, R/Cowboys of the wild west. /1985/
5-A/7 KF029 . . . . **978**
GRANFIELD, L/Cowboy: an album. /1994/5-A/8 KF030 . . . . . **978**
MURDOCH, DH/Cowboy. /1993/4-A/8 KF040 . . . . **978**

Cowgirls.
FABER, D/Calamity Jane: her life and her legend. /1992/
4-6/8 KE274 . . . . **B CALAMITY JANE**
GRANFIELD, L/Cowboy: an album. /1994/5-A/8 KF030 . . . . **978**
MURDOCH, DH/Cowboy. /1993/4-A/8 KF040 . . . . **978**

Cowgirls--Fiction.
ANTLE, N/Sam's Wild West Show. /1995/1-3/2 KF161 . . . . . E

Cows.
ALIKI /Milk from cow to carton. Rev. ed. /1992/
1-3/2 KD236. . . . . **637**
COWS! 2ND ED. (VIDEOCASSETTE). /1995/
1-3/KD212. . . . . **VCR 636.2**
FOWLER, A/Thanks to cows. /1992/K-2/2 KD238 . . . . **637**
GIBBONS, G/Milk makers. /1985/K-3/6 KD239 . . . . **637**
OLDER, J/Cow. /1997/P-4/2 KD214. . . . . **636.2**

Cows--Fiction.
OBLIGADO, L/Chocolate cow. /1993/K-2/2 KG185 . . . . E
SEYMOUR, T/Hunting the white cow. /1993/1-3/2 KG474 . . . . E

Cows--Poetry.
SCHERTLE, A/How now, brown cow? /1994/1-3/KE020 . . . . **811**

Coyote (Legendary character).
BIERHORST, J/Doctor Coyote: a Native American Aesop's fables. /
1987/3/3 KB530 . . . . **398.24**
FRENCH, F/Lord of the animals: a Miwok Indian creation myth. /
1997/K-3/4 KB568 . . . . **398.24**
GOLDIN, BD/Coyote and the fire stick: a Pacific Northwest Indian
tale. /1996/2-4/2 KB576 . . . . **398.24**

HAUSMAN, G/Eagle boy: a traditional Navajo legend. /1996/
3-4/5 KB587 . . . . **398.24**
JOHNSTON, T/Tale of Rabbit and Coyote. /1994/
2-3/2 KB596 . . . . **398.24**
LONDON, J/Fire race: a Karuk Coyote tale about how fire came to
the people. /1993/3-4/4 KB611. . . . . **398.24**
MCDERMOTT, G/Coyote: a trickster tale from the American
Southwest. /1994/P-2/2 KB617. . . . . **398.24**
STEVENS, J/Coyote steals the blanket: a Ute tale. /1993/
2-4/2 KB657 . . . . **398.24**
Old bag of bones: a coyote tale. /1996/1-3/2 KB659 . . **398.24**
TAYLOR, HP/Coyote and the laughing butterflies. /1995/
2-3/5 KB662 . . . . **398.24**
UDE, W/Maybe I will do something. /1993/4-5/6 KB669 . **398.24**
Coyote (Legendary character)--Fiction.
ROOT, P/Coyote and the magic words. /1993/P-2/2 KG351 . . . **E**
Coyotes--Fiction.
LOWELL, S/Three little javelinas. /1992/K-2/4 KG039. . . . . . . **E**
Crabs.
HOLLING, HC/Pagoo. /1957/5-6/4 KC519. . . . . **595.3**
JOHNSON, SA/Crabs. /1982/4-6/7 KC520. . . . . **595.3**
Crabs--Fiction.
CARLE, E/House for Hermit Crab. /1987/P-2/2 KF344 . . . . . . **E**
CHILDRESS, M/Joshua and the big bad blue crabs. /1996/
3-4/5 KG988 . . . . **Fic**
GRIFFITH, HV/Emily and the enchanted frog. /1989/
2-4/2 KF646 . . . . **E**
KALAN, R/Moving day. /1996/P-1/1 KF865 . . . . **E**
MACCARONE, G/Classroom pet. /1995/K-1/2 KG046. . . . . **E**
TAFURI, N/Follow me! /1990/P-2/KG589. . . . . **E**
Crabs--Folklore.
KANI, S/Monkey and the crab. /1985/3/3 KB598 . . . . . **398.24**
Craighead, Frank C.
CALABRO, M/Operation grizzly bear. /1989/
5-6/7 KC858 . . . . **599.784**
Craighead, John J.
CALABRO, M/Operation grizzly bear. /1989/
5-6/7 KC858 . . . . **599.784**
Cranberries.
BURNS, DL/Cranberries: fruit of the bogs. /1994/
5-6/7 KD157 . . . . **634**
CRANBERRY BOUNCE (VIDEOCASSETTE). /1991/
3-5/KD158. . . . . **VCR 634**
JASPERSOHN, W/Cranberries. /1991/4-5/6 KD160. . . . . . **634**
Crandall, Prudence.
YATES, E/Prudence Crandall: woman of courage. 2nd ed. /1996/
6-A/6 KE306 . . . . **B CRANDALL, P.**
Cranes (Birds).
OWENS, MB/Counting cranes. /1993/P-4/3 KB976 . . . . . . **513.2**
Cranes (Birds)--Fiction.
BANG, M/Paper crane. /1985/K-3/4 KF191. . . . . **CE E**
KELLER, H/Grandfather's dream. /1994/K-2/2 KF883 . . . . **E**
Crayon drawing--Fiction.
JOHNSON, C/Harold and the purple crayon. /c1955, 1994/
P-2/2 KF835 . . . . **CE E**
Crayons.
RYAN, PM/Crayon counting book. /1996/P-1/3 KB982. . . **513.2**
Crayons--Fiction.
GILLILAND, JH/Not in the house, Newton! /1995/P-2/2 KF618 . **E**
VAN ALLSBURG, C/Bad day at Riverbend. /1995/
1-3/3 KG637. . . . . **E**
Crazy Horse.
FREEDMAN, R/Life and death of Crazy Horse. /1996/
6-A/7 KE307 . . . . **B CRAZY HORSE**
ST. GEORGE, J/Crazy Horse. /1994/
A/9 KE308 . . . . **B CRAZY HORSE**
Creation SEE ALSO Bible stories--O.T.--Genesis; Earth; Evolution; Geology;
Indians of North America--Legends; Mythology; Universe.
Creation.
HAMILTON, V/In the beginning: creation stories from around the
world. /1988/5-6/4 KA731 . . . . **291.2**
STORY OF THE CREATION: WORDS FROM GENESIS. /1993/
2-3/4 KA688 . . . . **222**
Creation--Fiction.
DAVOL, MW/Batwings and the curtain of night. /1997/
1-3/2 KF449 . . . . **E**
HUGHES, T/Tales of the early world. /1991/4-A/5 KH290 . . . **Fic**
ROOT, P/Coyote and the magic words. /1993/P-2/2 KG351 . . . **E**
Creation--Folklore.
ANDERSON, DA/Origin of life on Earth: an African creation myth.
/1991/4-5/4 KA730 . . . . **291.2**
FRENCH, F/Lord of the animals: a Miwok Indian creation myth. /
1997/K-3/4 KB568 . . . . **398.24**

GERSON, M/People of corn: a Mayan story. /1995/
2-4/3 KB399 . . . . **398.21**
GOBLE, P/Remaking the earth: a creation story from the Great
Plains of North America. /1996/3-5/7 KB448 . . . . **398.22**
JACKSON, E/Precious gift: a Navaho creation myth. /1996/
2-3/2 KB594 . . . . **398.24**
JAFFE, N/Golden flower: a Taino myth from Puerto Rico. /1996/
2-4/5 KB503 . . . . **398.23**
MEDICINE STORY /Children of the Morning Light: Wampanoag
tales. /1994/4-5/7 KB348 . . . . **398.2**
MONROE, JG/First houses: Native American homes and sacred
structures. /1993/6-A/7 KB171 . . . . **392.3**
TAYLOR, CJ/How we saw the world: nine Native stories of the way
things began. /1993/4-5/4 KB377 . . . . **398.2**
Creation--Poetry.
JOHNSON, JW/Creation. /1994/K-3/KD956 . . . . **811**
Creation: a poem. /1993/1-6/KD957. . . . . **811**
Creative ability--Fiction.
SEUSS, D/On beyond zebra. /1955/P-3/6 KG470. . . . . **E**
Creative ability--Software.
THINKIN' THINGS COLLECTION 2. SCHOOL VERSION (CD-
ROM). /1995/1-6/KB081. . . . . **CDR 370.15**
Creative activities and seatwork.
CHILD'S SEASONAL TREASURY. /1996//KA193. . **PROF 372.13**
CROFT, DJ/Activities handbook for teachers of young children. 5th
ed. /1990//KA191 . . . . **PROF 372.1**
GIANT ENCYCLOPEDIA OF CIRCLE TIME AND GROUP
ACTIVITIES FOR CHILDREN 3 TO 6: /1996/
/KA197. . . . . **PROF 372.21**
RICE, M/Complete book of children's activities. /1993/
/KA194. . . . . **PROF 372.13**
STANGL, J/Recycling activities for the primary grades. /1993/
/KA313. . . . . **PROF 745.5**
Creative thinking (Education).
PERRY, SK/Playing smart: /1990//KA324. . . . . . . **PROF 790.1**
Creative writing.
GUTHRIE, D/Young author's do-it-yourself book: how to write,
illustrate, and produce your /1994/2-6/4 KD863. . . . . . . **808**
LIVINGSTON, MC/Poem-making: ways to begin writing poetry. /
1991/5-6/7 KD868 . . . . **808.1**
MELTON, D/Written & illustrated by... a revolutionary two-brain
approach for teaching students how to write and illustrate amazing
books. /1985//KA226. . . . . **PROF 372.6**
RYAN, M/How to read and write poems. /1991/
4-6/7 KD869 . . . . **808.1**
WAKAN, N/Haiku: one breath poetry. /1993/5-A/KE138 . . **895.6**
Creative writing--Fiction.
JARRELL, R/Bat-poet. /1996/4-A/6 KH327 . . . . **Fic**
Creative writing--Software.
STANLEY'S STICKER STORIES. SCHOOL VERSION (CD-ROM). /
1996/P-2/KB117. . . . . **CDR 372.6**
WRITING ALONG THE OREGON TRAIL (MICROCOMPUTER
PROGRAM). /1994/4-A/KB121 . . . . **MCP 372.6**
Creative writing--Study and teaching.
STORY STARTERS. VOL. 1 (VIDEOCASSETTE). /1995/
/KA231. . . . . **VCR PROF 372.6**
Creative writing (Elementary education).
SHELNUTT, E/Magic pencil: teaching children creative writing:
exercises and activities for children, their parents, and their
teachers. /1994//KA228 . . . . **PROF 372.6**
Creativity--Fiction.
SAY, A/Emma's rug. /1996/1-3/3 KG396 . . . . **E**
Cree Indians--Biography.
LITTLECHILD, G/This land is my land. /1993/2-A/4 KE803. . . **971**
Creek Indians--Folklore.
BRUCHAC, J/Great ball game: a Muskogee story. /1994/
2-4/2 KB539 . . . . **398.24**
Creoles--Fiction.
STEWART, EJ/Bimmi finds a cat. /1996/3-5/6 KH761 . . . . . . **Fic**
Crews, Donald.
CREWS, D/Bigmama's. /1991/K-2/2 KE309 . . . **CE B CREWS, D.**
Crickets.
COLE, J/Insect's body. /1984/5-6/7 KC536 . . . . **595.7**
Crickets--Fiction.
HOWE, J/I wish I were a butterfly. /1987/K-3/2 KF778 . . . . . . **E**
SELDEN, G/Chester Cricket's new home. /1983/2-4/5 KH692 . **Fic**
Chester Cricket's pigeon ride. /1983/3-4/5 KH693 . . . . **Fic**
Cricket in Times Square. /c1960/4-6/6 KH694. . . . . **CE Fic**
Crickets--Folklore.
CZERNECKI, S/Cricket's cage: a Chinese folktale. /1997/
K-3/7 KB553 . . . . **398.24**
Crime--Dictionaries.
BALLINGER, E/Detective dictionary: a handbook for aspiring sleuths.
/1994/4-6/7 KB028 . . . . **363.2**

Crime and criminals SEE ALSO Arson; Detectives; Pirates; Police; Robbers and outlaws; Smuggling.

Criminal investigation SEE ALSO Detectives; Police.

Criminal investigation.
GRAHAM, I/Crime-fighting. /1995/5-6/7 KB029 . . . . 363.2

Criminal investigation--Dictionaries.
BALLINGER, E/Detective dictionary: a handbook for aspiring sleuths. /1994/4-6/7 KB028 . . . . 363.2

Criminals--Fiction.
STEVENSON, J/Bones in the cliff. /1995/4-6/6 KH755 . . . . . . Fic

Croatian Americans--Fiction.
ORGEL, D/Don't call me Slob-o. /1996/3-5/2 KH565 . . . . . . Fic

Crockett, Davy.
ADLER, DA/Picture book of Davy Crockett. /1996/ 2-3/7 KE310 . . . . B CROCKETT, D.

Crockett, Davy--Legends.
KELLOGG, S/Sally Ann Thunder Ann Whirlwind Crockett: a tall tale. /1995/2-5/5 KB458 . . . . 398.22

Crockett, Sally Ann Thunder Ann Whirlwind--Legends.
KELLOGG, S/Sally Ann Thunder Ann Whirlwind Crockett: a tall tale. /1995/2-5/5 KB458 . . . . 398.22

Crocodiles--Fiction.
CHRISTELOW, E/Five little monkeys sitting in a tree. /1991/ P-K/2 KF384 . . . . E
DAHL, R/Enormous Crocodile. /c1978, 1993/1-3/4 KF444 . . . . E
WABER, B/House on East 88th Street. /c1962/P-2/3 KG667 . . . E
Lyle, Lyle, crocodile. /c1965/P-2/3 KG672 . . . . . . CE E
Lyle and the birthday party. /c1966/P-2/3 KG669 . . . . E
Lyle at the office. /1994/K-2/3 KG670 . . . . E
Lyle finds his mother. /1974/P-2/3 KG671 . . . . E

Crocodiles--Folklore.
DIAKITE, BW/Hunterman and the crocodile: a West African folktale. /1997/2-3/5 KB560 . . . . 398.24

Cross-country flying.
BROWN, D/Ruth Law thrills a nation. /1993/ 2-3/4 KE428 . . . . B LAW, R.

Cross-country skiing--Fiction.
CALHOUN, M/Cross-country cat. /1979/K-2/4 KF331 . . . . E

Cross-cultural studies.
BERNHARD, E/Ride on mother's back: a day of baby carrying around the world. /1996/1-2/7 KB170 . . . . 392.1

Crows--Fiction.
ARMSTRONG, J/King Crow. /1995/1-3/4 KF165 . . . . E

Cruise ships--Fiction.
MCPHAIL, D/Pigs ahoy! /1995/P-2/3 KG121 . . . . E

Crusades--Fiction.
BRADFORD, K/There will be wolves. /1992/6-A/5 KG921 . . . . Fic

Crying.
SIMON, N/I am not a crybaby. /1989/P-4/2 KA644 . . . . . 155.4

Cryptography SEE ALSO Ciphers.

Cryptography.
DAILY, R/Code talkers: American Indians in World War II. /1995/ 4-6/9 KE669 . . . . 940.54
GARDNER, M/Codes, ciphers and secret writing. /c1972, 1984/ 5-6/8 KD308 652
JANECZKO, PB/Loads of codes and secret ciphers. /1984/ A/7 KD309 652

Crystallography SEE Mineralogy.

Crystals.
MAKI, C/Snowflakes, sugar, and salt: crystals up close. /1993/ P-2/5 KC143 548

Cub Scouts SEE ALSO Boy Scouts.

Cub Scouts.
KENOWER, FT/Cub Scout fun book. /c1956, 1986/ 2-4/6 KB077 . . . . 369.43

Cuba--Folklore.
GONZALEZ, LM/Bossy gallito/el gallo de bodas: a traditional Cuban folktale. /1994/K-2/4 KB577 . . . . 398.24
SHUTE, L/Rabbit wishes. /1995/K-2/2 KB651 . . . . 398.24

Cuba--Social life and customs.
STAUB, FJ/Children of Cuba. /1996/4-6/8 KE846 . . . . . . 972.91

Cuban Americans.
SACRE, A/Looking for Papito: family stories from Latin America (Sound recording cassette). /1996/1-6/KA857 . . . . . SRC 305.8

Cuban Americans--Biography.
RODRIGUEZ, J/Gloria Estefan. /1996/ 5-6/6 KE340 . . . . B ESTEFAN, G.

Culture.
LEWIN, T/Market! /1996/1-3/6 KB128 381
MANY PEOPLE, MANY WAYS: UNDERSTANDING CULTURES AROUND THE WORLD. /1995/4-A/KA402 . . . . REF 306
MILORD, S/Hands around the world: 365 creative ways to build cultural awareness and global respect. /1992//KA167 . PROF 306

Culture--Software.
MICROSOFT EXPLORAPEDIA: THE WORLD OF PEOPLE. ACADEMIC ED. (CD-ROM). /1994/1-4/KA892 . . . . . CDR 307

Culture--Songs and music.
FAMILY FOLK FESTIVAL: A MULTI-CULTURAL SING-ALONG (SOUND RECORDING CASSETTE). /1990/ K-5/KD562 . . . . SRC 789.2
GORDH, B/Morning, noon and nighttime tales (Sound recording cassette). /1993/K-2/KD565 . . . . SRC 789.2
JENKINS, E/Call and response: rhythmic group singing (Sound recording cassette). /1990/K-3/KD625 . . . . SRC 789.3
Come dance by the ocean (Sound recording cassette). /1991/ P-2/KD626 . . . . SRC 789.3
Jambo and other call and response songs and chants (Sound recording cassette). /1990/K-3/KD573 . . . . SRC 789.2
Multicultural children's songs (Compact disc). /1995/ K-2/KD629 . . . . CD 789.3
Songs and rhythms from near and far (Sound recording cassette). /c1964, 1992/K-2/KD575 . . . . SRC 789.2
Travellin' with Ella Jenkins: a bilingual journey (Compact disc). / 1989/K-2/KD576 . . . . CD 789.2
PALMER, H/Child's world of lullabies: multicultural songs for quiet times /1993/P-2/KD642 . . . . SRC 789.3
PETER, PAUL & MARY /Peter, Paul and Mommy, too (Compact disc). /1993/P-A/KD583 . . . . CD 789.2
RAINBOW SIGN (COMPACT DISC). /1992/ P-A/KD585 . . . . CD 789.2
SLONECKI, C/Children's songs around the world (Sound recording cassette). /1989/K-3/KD595 . . . . SRC 789.2
SONGS FOR SURVIVAL: SONGS AND CHANTS FROM TRIBAL PEOPLES AROUND THE WORLD. /1996/1-6/KD596 . . . . 789.2
SUNSERI, M/Rhythm of the rocks: a multicultural musical journey (Sound recording cassette). /1993/K-2/KD599 . . . . SRC 789.2
Rhythm of the rocks songbook: a multicultural musical journey... / 1994/K-2/KD600 . . . . 789.2
WEISSMAN, J/Joining hands with other lands: multicultural songs and games /1993/K-3/KD666 . . . . SRC 789.3

Cuna Indians--Social life and customs.
PRESILLA, ME/Mola: Cuna life stories and art. /1996/ 3-5/7 KA832 . . . . 305.48

Cuna women--Industries.
PRESILLA, ME/Mola: Cuna life stories and art. /1996/ 3-5/7 KA832 . . . . 305.48

Cupid (Roman deity).
CRAFT, MC/Cupid and Psyche. /1996/4-5/6 KA737 292

Curie, Marie.
PFLAUM, R/Marie Curie and her daughter Irene. /1993/ 6-A/8 KC139 . . . . 539.7
POYNTER, M/Marie Curie: discoverer of radium. /1994/ 4-6/4 KE311 . . . . B CURIE, M.

Curiosities and wonders.
GUINNESS BOOK OF WORLD RECORDS. /1955-/ 4-6/KA403 . . . . REF 310
MATTHEWS, R/Record breakers of the sea. /1990/ 2-4/6 KA590 . . . . 031.02
SIMON, S/Strange mysteries from around the world. Rev. ed. / 1997/4-6/7 KA561 . . . . 001.94

Curiosity--Fiction.
STEVENSON, J/Mud Flat mystery. /1997/1-3/2 KG561 . . . . . . E
WELLS, R/Max and Ruby's first Greek myth: Pandora's box. / 1993/P-1/3 KG700 . . . . E

Current events.
READING THE NEWSPAPER INTELLIGENTLY (VIDEOCASSETTE). / 1995/5-6/KA801 . . . . VCR 302.23

Current events--Periodicals.
JUNIOR SCHOLASTIC. /1937-/A/KA522 . . . . PER 050
SCIENCE NEWS. /1921-/4-6/KA539 . . . . PER 050
TIME FOR KIDS. /1995-/3-6/KA547 . . . . PER 050
WEEKLY READER. /1947-/K-6/KA550 . . . . PER 050
WORLD NEWSMAP OF THE WEEK: HEADLINE FOCUS. /1938-/ /KA155 . . . . PER PROF 050

Current events--Songs and music.
ALSOP, P/Plugging away (Sound recording cassette). /1990/ 1-5/KD604 . . . . SRC 789.3

Curriculum planning.
URBANIK, MK/Curriculum planning and teaching using the library media center. /1989//KA064 . . . . PROF 025.5

Custer, George Armstrong.
GOBLE, P/Red Hawk's account of Custer's last battle; the Battle of the Little Bighorn, /c1969, 1992/5-6/6 KE914. . . . . 973.8

Cycling SEE Bicycles and bicycling.

Cyclops (Greek mythology).
FISHER, LE/Cyclops. /1991/1-6/4 KA739 292

Czech Republic--Folklore.
WISNIEWSKI, D/Golem. /1996/2-6/5 KB423 . . . . **398.21**

Czechoslovakia--Fiction.
TORNQVIST, R/Christmas carp. /1990/2-4/2 KH798 . . . . **Fic**
Da Vinci, Leonardo SEE Leonardo da Vinci.

Dachshunds--Fiction.
PILKEY, D/Hallo-wiener. /1995/K-2/2 KG237 . . . . **E**

Daedalus (Greek mythology).
YOLEN, J/Wings. /c1991, 1997/5-6/4 KA754 . . . . **292**

Dahl, Roald.
DAHL, L/James and the giant peach: the book and movie
scrapbook. /1996/3-6/6 KD684. . . . . **791.43**
DAHL, R/Boy: tales of childhood. /1984/
5-6/6 KE312 . . . . **B DAHL, R.**

Dairy cattle.
DAIRY FARM (VIDEOCASSETTE). /1991/3-5/KD213 . **VCR 636.2**
GIBBONS, G/Milk makers. /1985/K-3/6 KD239 . . . . **637**
OLDER, J/Cow. /1997/P-4/2 KD214. . . . . **636.2**
Dairy products SEE ALSO Milk.

Dairy products--Fiction.
JACKSON, E/Brown cow, green grass, yellow mellow sun. /1995/
P-1/2 KF818 . . . . **E**

Dairying.
ALIKI /Milk from cow to carton. Rev. ed. /1992/
1-3/2 KD236 . . . . **637**
CARRICK, D/Milk. /1985/K-3/4 KD237 . . . . **637**
COWS! 2ND ED. (VIDEOCASSETTE). /1995/
1-3/KD212. **VCR 636.2**
DAIRY FARM (VIDEOCASSETTE). /1991/3-5/KD213 . **VCR 636.2**
FOWLER, A/Thanks to cows. /1992/K-2/2 KD238 . . . . **637**
GIBBONS, G/Milk makers. /1985/K-3/6 KD239 . . . . **637**

Dakota Indians.
SNEVE, V/Sioux. /1993/4-6/5 KE776 . . . . **970.3**

Dakota Indians--Biography.
ADLER, DA/Picture book of Sitting Bull. /1993/
3-4/5 KE540 . . . . **B SITTING BULL**
BRUCHAC, J/Boy called Slow: the true story of Sitting Bull. /1994/
3-4/6 KE541 . . . . **B SITTING BULL**
ST. GEORGE, J/To see with the heart: the life of Sitting Bull. /
1996/5-A/6 KE542 . . . . **B SITTING BULL**

Dakota Indians--Folklore.
EVANS, R/Inktomi and the ducks and other Assiniboin trickster
stories /1994/3-5/KB441 . . . . **TB 398.22**
GOBLE, P/Adopted by the eagles: a Plains Indian story of
friendship and treachery. /1994/2-5/4 KB706. . . . . . . **398.26**
Crow Chief: a Plains Indian story. /1992/3-4/4 KB573 . . **398.24**
Great race of the birds and animals. /1991/
3-5/4 KB574 . . . . **398.24**
RUBALCABA, J/Uncegila's seventh spot: a Lakota legend. /1995/
3-5/3 KB478 . . . . **398.22**
WOPILA--A GIVEAWAY: LAKOTA STORIES (SOUND
RECORDING CASSETTE). /1993/3-5/KB676 . . . . . . **SRC 398.24**

Dalai lamas.
STEWART, W/14th Dalai Lama: spiritual leader of Tibet. /1996/
5-A/10 KA761 . . . . **294.3**

Dali, Salvador.
VENEZIA, M/Salvador Dali. /1993/4-6/7 KE313 . . . . **B DALI, S.**

Danbury (Conn.)--Burning by the British, 1775--Biography.
BROWN, DP/Sybil rides for independence. /1985/
3-6/4 KE876 . . . . **973.3**

Dance--History.
MEDEARIS, AS/Dance. /1997/4-6/11 KD704 . . . . **793.3**
Dance music SEE ALSO Ballet dance music; Jazz music.

Dance music.
ALL-TIME FAVORITE DANCES (SOUND RECORDING CASSETTE).
/1991/K-6/KD603. . . . . **SRC 789.3**
JACK, D/Dance in your pants: great songs for little kids to dance to
(Sound recording /1988/K-3/KD620. . . . . **SRC 789.3**
David Jack... live!: Makin' music, makin' friends (Videocassette). /
1991/P-2/KD621 . . . . **VCR 789.3**
Gotta hop (Sound recording cassette). /1990/
K-3/KD622 . . . . **SRC 789.3**
JENKINS, E/Growing up with Ella Jenkins: rhythms songs and
rhymes /1990/P-2/KD628. . . . . **SRC 789.3**
NELSON, EL/Everybody sing and dance. /1989/
/KA321. **CE PROF 789.3**

Dancers.
PINKNEY, AD/Alvin Ailey. /1993/2-4/5 KE231 . . . . **B AILEY, A.**

Dancers--Fiction.
HOLABIRD, K/Angelina and the princess. /1984/P-2/5 KF764. . . **E**

Dancers in art.
ROALF, P/Dancers. /1992/5-A/7 KD478 . . . . **758**

Dancing SEE ALSO Ballet dancing; Folk dancing.

Dancing.
ALL-TIME FAVORITE DANCES (SOUND RECORDING CASSETTE).
/1991/K-6/KD603. . . . . **SRC 789.3**
DANCE WITH US: A CREATIVE MOVEMENT VIDEO
(VIDEOCASSETTE). /1994/K-2/KD702 . . . . **VCR 793.3**

Dancing--Fiction.
DE PAOLA, T/Oliver Button is a sissy. /1979/K-2/2 KF477 . . . . **E**
JONAS, A/Color dance. /1989/P-1/1 KF844 . . . . **E**
KROLL, VL/Can you dance, Dalila? /1996/K-2/5 KF932. . . . . . **E**
LEE, JM/Silent Lotus. /1991/P-2/4 KF956. . . . . **E**
LOREDO, E/Boogie Bones. /1997/K-2/3 KG034 . . . . **E**
MARTIN, JR., B/Barn dance! /1986/P-3/3 KG071 . . . . **E**
MCKISSACK, P/Mirandy and Brother Wind. /1988/
1-3/6 KG107 . . . . **CE E**
PATRICK, DL/Red dancing shoes. /1993/P-1/2 KG220 . . . . . . **E**
SHANNON, G/April showers. /1995/P-1/2 KG477 . . . . **E**
WALSH, ES/Hop jump. /1993/P-K/2 KG679. . . . . **E**

Dancing in art.
ROALF, P/Dancers. /1992/5-A/7 KD478 . . . . **758**

Darragh, John.
ROOP, P/Buttons for General Washington. /1986/
4-6/4 KE885 . . . . **973.3**

Darwin, Charles.
ANDERSON, MJ/Charles Darwin: naturalist. /1994/
5-A/4 KE314 . . . . **B DARWIN, C.**
TWIST, C/Charles Darwin: on the trail of evolution. /1994/
5-8/8 KE315 . . . . **B DARWIN, C.**
Data processing SEE ALSO Word processing.

Data processing--Keyboarding.
MOUNTFORD, C/Kids can type too! /c1985, 1987/
4-6/KD311. . . . . **652.3**

Data processing--Vocational guidance.
KAPLAN, A/Careers for computer buffs. /1991/5-6/9 KA567 . **004**

Databases--Directories.
MILLER, EB/Internet resource directory for K-12 teachers and
librarians. /1994-//KA179 . . . . **PROF 371.3**

David, King of Israel.
DE REGNIERS, BS/David and Goliath. /1996/1-4/6 KA683. . **222**
METAXAS, E/David and Goliath (Videocassette). /1992/
2-4/KA686 . . . . **VCR 222**

Davis, Benjamin O. (Benjamin Oliver).
APPLEGATE, K/Story of two American generals: Benjamin O. Davis,
Jr.; Colin L. Powell. /1995/5-6/5 KA981 . . . . **355**

Day.
BRANLEY, FM/Sunshine makes the season. Rev. ed. /1985/
K-2/3 KC057 . . . . **525**

Day--Fiction.
MCGUIRE, R/Night becomes day. /1994/1-3/1 KG104. . . . . . **E**
SEUSS, D/My many colored days. /1996/K-2/2 KG468 . . . . . **E**
TRESSELT, A/Wake up, city! /c1957, 1990/1-3/5 KG616 . . . . . **E**

Day care centers--Fiction.
DEMUTH, P/Busy at day care head to toe. /1996/P-K/2 KF460 . **E**
Days SEE ALSO Birthdays; Fasts and feasts; Festivals; Holidays and names
of special days e.g. Christmas, Mother's Day, etc.

Dead Sea scrolls.
COOPER, I/Dead Sea Scrolls. /1997/6-A/8 KA768 . . . . . . **296.1**
Deaf SEE ALSO Hearing aids; Sign language.

Deaf.
ANCONA, G/Handtalk zoo. /1989/K-A/KB820. . . . . **419**
CHARLIP, R/Handtalk birthday: a number and story book in sign
language. /1987/K-3/KB824 . . . . **419**
GREENE, L/Sign language talk. /1989/5-A/9 KB825 . . . . . . **419**
MILLER, MB/Handtalk school. /1991/K-A/KB827 . . . . **419**
PETERSON, JW/I have a sister--my sister is deaf. /c1977/
2-4/4 KB007 . . . . **362.4**
RANKIN, L/Handmade alphabet. /1991/K-3/KB829 . . . . . . **419**

Deaf--Biography.
BROWN, FG/Daisy and the Girl Scouts: the story of Juliette
Gordon Low. /1996/3-6/7 KE448 . . . . **B LOW, J.**
HELEN KELLER (VIDEOCASSETTE). /1990/
4-6/KE415 . . . . **VCR B KELLER, H.**
KELLER, H/Story of my life. /c1988, 1990/
6-A/8 KE416 . . . . **B KELLER, H.**
LUNDELL, M/Girl named Helen Keller. /1995/
1-2/1 KE417 . . . . **B KELLER, H.**

Deaf--Education.
BOWEN, AR/World of knowing: a story about Thomas Hopkins
Gallaudet. /1995/3-5/6 KE361 . . . . **B GALLAUDET, T.**

Deaf--Fiction.
LAKIN, P/Dad and me in the morning. /1994/1-3/2 KF942 . . . . **E**
LEE, JM/Silent Lotus. /1991/P-2/4 KF956. . . . . **E**
LITCHFIELD, AB/Words in our hands. /1980/4-6/5 KH413 . . . . **Fic**
NEUFELD, J/Gaps in stone walls. /1996/6-A/7 KH546 . . . . . . **Fic**

RIGGIO, A/Secret signs: along the Underground Railroad. /1997/
2-3/2 KG331 . . . . **E**
SHREVE, S/Gift of the girl who couldn't hear. /1991/
4-6/6 KH709 . . . . **Fic**

Deaf--Means of communication.
BEGINNING AMERICAN SIGN LANGUAGE VIDEOCOURSE
(VIDEOCASSETTE). /1991/3-A/KB822 . . . . **VCR 419**
HAFER, JC/Come sign with us: sign language activities for children.
2nd. ed. /1996/KA279 . . . . **PROF 419**
Death SEE ALSO Funeral rites and ceremonies.

Death.
BRATMAN, F/Everything you need to know when a parent dies. /
1992/5-6/5 KA647 . . . . **155.9**
BROWN, LK/When dinosaurs die: a guide to understanding death. /
1996/K-4/5 KA648 . . . . **155.9**
COERR, E/Sadako. /1993/3-6/4 KA994 . . . . **CE 362.1**
EMORY, J/Dirty, rotten, dead? /1996/4-6/10 KC303 . . . **577.1**
GREENLEE, S/When someone dies. /1992/K-3/4 KA649 . . . **155.9**
HYDE, MO/Meeting death. /1989/A/7 KA891 . . . . **306.9**
KID'S BOOK ABOUT DEATH AND DYING. /1985/
4-6/6 KA650 . . . . **155.9**
LESHAN, E/Learning to say goodbye: when a parent dies. /c1976/
5-6/7 KA651 . . . . **155.9**
SAYING GOOD-BYE (VIDEOCASSETTE). /1993/
2-4/KA652 . . . . **VCR 155.9**

Death--Fiction.
BUNTING, E/On Call Back Mountain. /1997/1-3/2 KF306 . . . . . **E**
CASELEY, J/Dorothy's darkest days. /1997/3-5/4 KG983 . . . . **Fic**
COLE, B/Drop dead. /1996/2-4/2 KF406 . . . . **E**
CREECH, S/Walk two moons. /1994/5-A/5 KH037 . . . . **Fic**
DE PAOLA, T/Nana upstairs and Nana downstairs. /c1973, 1978/
K-3/6 KF475 . . . . **E**
FLETCHER, R/Fig pudding. /1995/5-A/4 KH129 . . . . **Fic**
FORWARD, T/Traveling backward. /1994/4-6/4 KH134 . . . . . **Fic**
GOBLE, P/Beyond the ridge. /1989/2-4/4 KH177 . . . . **Fic**
GREENE, CC/Beat the turtle drum. /c1976, 1994/
5-6/4 KH198 . . . . **Fic**
HAMILTON, V/Cousins. /1990/6-A/5 KH213 . . . . **Fic**
HENKES, K/Sun and spoon. /1997/5-A/6 KH239. . . . . **Fic**
HONEYCUTT, N/Twilight in Grace Falls. /1997/6-A/6 KH278. . **Fic**
HURWITZ, J/Ozzie on his own. /1995/3-5/4 KH301 . . . . **Fic**
JORDAN, M/Losing Uncle Tim. /1989/3-5/4 KH336. . . . . **Fic**
KROLL, VL/Fireflies, peach pies and lullabies. /1995/
1-3/5 KF933 . . . . **E**
LANTON, S/Daddy's chair. /1991/P-2/2 KF944 . . . . **E**
MILES, M/Annie and the old one. /c1971/4-6/4 KH496 . . . . . **Fic**
NAPOLI, DJ/Bravest thing. /1995/3-5/6 KH529. . . . . **Fic**
NEWMAN, L/Too far away to touch. /1995/1-3/6 KG172 . . . . **E**
PARK, B/Mick Harte was here. /1995/4-6/4 KH570 . . . . **Fic**
PATERSON, K/Bridge to Terabithia. /1977/5-A/6 KH573 . . . . **Fic**
Flip-flop girl. /1996/5-A/6 KH575 . . . . **Fic**
POLIKOFF, BG/Life's a funny proposition, Horatio. /1992/
5-A/4 KH608 . . . . **Fic**
ROSEN, MJ/Bonesy and Isabel. /1995/2-3/6 KG352 . . . . **E**
RUSSO, M/Grandpa Abe. /1996/K-2/2 KG360 . . . . **E**
RYLANT, C/Missing May. /1992/5-A/7 KH663 . . . . **Fic**
SMITH, DB/Taste of blackberries. /c1973/4-6/4 KH722. . . . . **Fic**
STEWART, EJ/Bimmi finds a cat. /1996/3-5/6 KH761 . . . . . . **Fic**
STRETE, CK/World in Grandfather's hands. /1995/
5-A/4 KH771 . . . . **Fic**
THESMAN, J/Nothing grows here. /1994/6-A/4 KH790 . . . . . **Fic**
VARLEY, S/Badger's parting gifts. /1984/1-3/7 KG650 . . . . . . **E**
VIORST, J/Tenth good thing about Barney. /c1971/
K-3/2 KG664 . . . . **E**
WILD, M/Toby. /1994/1-3/3 KG718 . . . . **E**
YUMOTO, K/Friends. /1996/6-A/7 KH901 . . . . **Fic**
ZOLOTOW, C/My grandson Lew. /c1974/K-2/2 KG805 . . . . . . **E**
Old dog. Rev. and newly illustrated ed. /1995/K-2/2 KG806 . . **E**

Death--Folklore.
RAPPAPORT, D/New king. /1995/4-A/3 KB473 . . . . . . **398.22**

Debussy, Claude.
THOMPSON, W/Claude Debussy. /1993/
6-A/9 KE316 . . . . **B DEBUSSY, C.**

Decimals.
RELATING FRACTIONS AND DECIMALS (VIDEOCASSETTE). /
1982/3-5/KB981 . . . . **VCR 513.2**

Decision making.
CHOOSE TO REFUSE: SAYING NO AND KEEPING YOUR
FRIENDS (VIDEOCASSETTE). /1993/3-5/KA654 . . . . **VCR 158**
DRUGS, YOUR FRIENDS, AND YOU: HANDLING PEER PRESSURE
(VIDEOCASSETTE). /1988/6-A/KC995. . . . . **VCR 613.8**
JUST FOR ME (VIDEOCASSETTE). /1992/
K-6/KC997. . . . . **VCR 613.8**

SAY NO AND MEAN IT (VIDEOCASSETTE). /1991/
3-5/KA663 . . . . **VCR 158**

Decision making--Fiction.
SEUSS, D/Hunches in bunches. /1982/K-3/2 KG460. . . . . . . **E**

Decision making--Software.
HALPERN, NA/Kids and the environment: taking responsibility for
our surroundings /1994/1-5/KB046. . . . . **CDR 363.7**
TAKING RESPONSIBILITY (MICROCOMPUTER PROGRAM). /
1988/1-6/KA665 . . . . **MCP 158**

Decoration and ornament.
CRAFTS FOR DECORATION. /1993/3-6/7 KD451 . . . . . **745.594**

Decorations of honor.
LLOYD, M/Military badges and insignia. /1995/
4-8/12 KA984 . . . . **355.1**

Deer.
BARE, CS/Never grab a deer by the ear. /1993/
4-5/5 KC795 . . . . **599.65**
NATURE'S NEWBORN: ELK, MOOSE, DEER (VIDEOCASSETTE). /
1994/3-6/KC799 . . . . **VCR 599.65**

Deer--Fiction.
ARNOSKY, J/Long Spikes: a story. /1992/5-A/6 KG852. . . . . **Fic**
RAWLINGS, MK/Yearling. /c1938, 1967/5-A/5 KH622 . . . . . **Fic**
SALTEN, F/Bambi: a life in the woods. /1992/5-A/6 KH673. . . **Fic**

Deere, John.
COLLINS, DR/Pioneer plowmaker: a story about John Deere. /
1990/5-6/6 KE317 . . . . **B DEERE, J.**

Degas, Edgar.
MEYER, SE/Edgar Degas. /1994/6-A/9 KE318 . . . . **B DEGAS, E.**
MUHLBERGER, R/What makes a Degas a Degas? /1993/
5-A/7 KD491 . . . . **759.4**

Delaware.
FRADIN, DB/Delaware. /1994/4-6/3 KE968 . . . . **975.1**
MIDDLE ATLANTIC REGION: NEW YORK, NEW JERSEY,
DELAWARE, MARYLAND, PENNSYLVANIA, /1996/
4-6/KE924 . . . . **VCR 974**

Delaware Indians--Fiction.
RICHTER, C/Light in the forest. /1994/5-A/5 KH632. . . . . . . **Fic**

Delaware River (N.Y.-Del. and N.J.)--Description and travel.
CHERIPKO, J/Voices of the river: adventures on the Delaware. /
1996/5-A/5 KE962 . . . . **974.9**

Deluge--Folklore.
BERNHARD, E/Tree that rains: the flood myth of the Huichol Indians
of Mexico. /1994/3-4/5 KB699 . . . . **398.26**

Denmark--Fiction.
LOWRY, L/Number the stars. /1989/5-6/5 KH427 . . . . **Fic**

Dental care.
GOOFY OVER DENTAL HEALTH (VIDEOCASSETTE). /1991/
1-3/KD036. . . . . **VCR 617.6**

Dentists.
GOOFY OVER DENTAL HEALTH (VIDEOCASSETTE). /1991/
1-3/KD036. . . . . **VCR 617.6**
ROCKWELL, H/My dentist. /1975/P-1/2 KD037. . . . . . . **617.6**

Dentists--Fiction.
STEIG, W/Doctor De Soto. /1982/P-3/4 KG542 . . . . **CE E**

Department stores--Fiction.
HAMM, DJ/Laney's lost momma. /1991/P-1/2 KF670. . . . . . . **E**

Depressions--1929.
STANLEY, J/Children of the Dust Bowl: the true story of the school
at Weedpatch Camp. /1992/5-A/7 KA835 . . . . **305.5**
STEIN, RC/Great Depression. Rev. ed. /1993/
4-6/7 KE918 . . . . **973.917**

Depressions--1929--Fiction.
COCHRANE, PA/Purely Rosie Pearl. /1996/4-6/6 KH011 . . . . **Fic**
HORVATH, P/Happy yellow car. /1994/4-6/6 KH283 . . . . . . **Fic**
KARR, K/Cave. /1994/5-A/4 KH341 . . . . **Fic**
LIED, K/Potato: a tale from the Great Depression. /1997/
K-3/2 KF980 . . . . **E**
SNYDER, ZK/Cat running. /1994/5-A/7 KH730 . . . . **Fic**
TAYLOR, MD/Roll of thunder, hear my cry. /c1976/
5-6/6 KH779 . . . . **CE Fic**
Song of the trees. /1975/4-6/4 KH780 . . . . **Fic**
TURNER, A/Dust for dinner. /1995/2-5/2 KG625 . . . . **E**

Depressions--1929--Pictorial works.
GREAT DEPRESSION (PICTURE). /n.d./A/KA967. . . . . **PIC 338.5**

Desert animals.
WALLACE, MD/America's deserts: guide to plants and animals. /
1996/2-A/10 KC365 . . . . **578.754**
WRIGHT-FRIERSON, V/Desert scrapbook: dawn to dusk in the
Sonoran Desert. /1996/3-5/7 KF072 . . . . **979.1**

Desert animals--Fiction.
ALBERT, RE/Alejandro's gift. /1994/1-3/6 KF144 . . . . **E**
BEIFUSS, J/Armadillo Ray. /1995/K-2/4 KF216 . . . . **E**

Desert biology.
ARNOLD, C/Watching desert wildlife. /1994/
4-6/7 KC361 . . . . **578.754**
Desert ecology.
BASH, B/Desert giant: the world of the saguaro cactus. /1989/
2-6/6 KC427 . . . . **583**
Desert ecology--Guides.
MACMAHON, J/Deserts. /1985/A/KC338 . . . . **577.54**
Desert ecology--Sonoran Desert.
DUNPHY, M/Here is the southwestern desert. /1995/
P-3/3 KF066 . . . . **979.1**
Desert plants.
WALLACE, MD/America's deserts: guide to plants and animals. /
1996/2-A/10 KC365 . . . . **578.754**
WRIGHT-FRIERSON, V/Desert scrapbook: dawn to dusk in the
Sonoran Desert. /1996/3-5/7 KF072 . . . . **979.1**
Deserts.
ARNOLD, C/Watching desert wildlife. /1994/
4-6/7 KC361 . . . . **578.754**
BAYLOR, B/Desert is theirs. /c1975/4-6/5 KC362 . . . . . . **578.754**
GIBBONS, G/Deserts. /1996/K-3/4 KC363 . . . . . . **578.754**
MACQUITTY, M/Desert. /1994/4-6/7 KC364 . . . . . . **578.754**
MURRAY, P/Sahara. /1994/3-6/6 KE731 . . . . **966**
SIMON, S/Deserts. /1990/1-5/7 KC167 . . . . **551.4**
WALLACE, MD/America's deserts: guide to plants and animals. /
1996/2-A/10 KC365 . . . . **578.754**
Deserts--Fiction.
FERGUSON, A/Tumbleweed Christmas. /1996/1-3/3 KF547 . . . . **E**
HAARHOFF, D/Desert December. /1992/3-5/4 KH206 . . . . **Fic**
JONAS, A/Trek. /1985/P-2/4 KF849 . . . . **E**
LONDON, J/Ali, child of the desert. /1997/K-3/3 KG019 . . . . . **E**
LOWELL, S/Tortoise and the jackrabbit. /1994/K-2/3 KG040 . . . **E**
ROBERTS, B/Camel caravan. /1996/P-1/3 KG335 . . . . **E**
Deserts--Poetry.
MORA, P/Desert is my mother./El desierto es mi madre. /1994/
K-3/KD989 . . . . **811**
Listen to the desert/Oye al desierto. /1994/P-1/KD990 . . . . **811**
Design--Software.
KID CAD (MICROCOMPUTER PROGRAM). /1993/
2-A/KD423 . . . . **MCP 745.4**
MULTIMEDIA WORKSHOP. TEACHER ED. (CD-ROM). /1996/
3-A/KB115 . . . . **CDR 372.6**
Desktop publishing--Software.
MICROSOFT CREATIVE WRITER 2. SCHOOL ED. (CD-ROM). /
1996/2-A/KB114 . . . . **CDR 372.6**
MULTIMEDIA WORKSHOP. TEACHER ED. (CD-ROM). /1996/
3-A/KB115 . . . . **CDR 372.6**
STANLEY'S STICKER STORIES. SCHOOL VERSION (CD-ROM). /
1996/P-2/KB117 . . . . **CDR 372.6**
STUDENT WRITING AND RESEARCH CENTER WITH COMPTON'S
CONCISE ENCYCLOPEDIA /1995/4-A/KB091 . . . **CDR 371.302**
ULTIMATE WRITING AND CREATIVITY CENTER. SCHOOL ED.
(CD-ROM). /1996/K-5/KB120 . . . . **CDR 372.6**
WRITING CENTER (MICROCOMPUTER PROGRAM). /1991/
2-A/KD347 . . . . **MCP 686.2**
Detectives--Dictionaries.
BALLINGER, E/Detective dictionary: a handbook for aspiring sleuths.
/1994/4-6/7 KB028 . . . . **363.2**
Detectives--Fiction SEE ALSO Mystery and detective stories.
Detectives--Fiction.
SHARMAT, MW/Nate the Great. /c1972/1-3/2 KG484 . . . **CE E**
Detroit (Mich.)--Fiction.
BURGESS, BH/Fred Field. /1994/6-A/6 KG947 . . . . **Fic**
Devers, Gail.
GUTMAN, B/Gail Devers. /1996/5-6/6 KE319 . . . **B DEVERS, G.**
Devil--Fiction.
BABBITT, N/Devil's other storybook. /1987/5-6/8 KG868 . . . . **Fic**
Devil's storybook. /1974/3-5/4 KG869 . . . . **CE Fic**
BRITTAIN, B/Dr. Dredd's wagon of wonders. /1987/
3-6/5 KG923 . . . . **Fic**
Devil--Folklore.
ZEMACH, H/Duffy and the devil, a Cornish tale. /c1973/
2-4/7 KB426 . . . . **CE 398.21**
Dewey, Jennifer Owings.
DEWEY, JO/Cowgirl dreams: a western childhood. /1995/
3-4/4 KE320 . . . . **B DEWEY, J.**
Rattlesnake dance: true tales, mysteries, and rattlesnake
ceremonies. /1997/4-6/4 KC634 . . . . **597.96**
Diabetes.
PIRNER, CW/Even little kids get diabetes. /1991/
K-2/2 KD017 . . . . **616.4**
TIGER, S/Diabetes. /1987/A/9 KD018 . . . . **616.4**

Diaries.
BOWEN, G/Stranded at Plimoth Plantation, 1626. /1994/
5-6/7 KE870 . . . . **973.2**
CLARK, W/Off the map: the journals of Lewis and Clark. /1993/
4-6/7 KE201 . . . . **917.804**
COLUMBUS, C/Log of Christopher Columbus' first voyage to
America in the year 1492. /c1938, 1989/4-6/7 KE741 . . . **970.01**
KNIGHT, AS/Way west: journal of a pioneer woman. /1993/
5-6/5 KE197 . . . . **917.8**
MORPURGO, M/Wreck of the Zanzibar. /1995/4-6/3 KH516 . **Fic**
MOURT'S RELATION /Homes in the wilderness: a pilgrim's journal
of Plymouth Plantation in 1620. /c1939, 1988/
5-A/8 KE941 . . . . **974.4**
PILGRIM VOICES: OUR FIRST YEAR IN THE NEW WORLD. /
1995/3-6/7 KE944 . . . . **974.4**
RILEY, J/Prairie cabin: a Norwegian pioneer woman's story
(Videocassette). /1991/A/KF012 . . . . **VCR 977**
STEGER, W/Over the top of the world: explorer Will Steger's trek
across the Arctic. /1997/5-6/6 KE219 . . . . **919.8**
STEVENS, C/Book of your own: keeping a diary or journal. /1993/
5-A/9 KD864 . . . . **808**
TUNNELL, MO/Children of Topaz: the story of a Japanese-
American internment camp: based on a /1996/
5-6/8 KE667 . . . . **940.53**
Diaries--Fiction.
CLEARY, B/Strider. /1991/5-A/4 KH008 . . . . **Fic**
CUSHMAN, K/Catherine, called Birdy. /1994/
6-A/6 KH050 . . . . **CE Fic**
HESSE, K/Music of dolphins. /1996/5-A/3 KH252 . . . . . . **Fic**
HOPKINSON, D/Birdie's lighthouse. /1997/3-5/3 KH282 . . . . **Fic**
HYATT, PR/Coast to coast with Alice. /1995/4-6/5 KH312 . . . **Fic**
LOMONACO, P/Night letters. /1996/K-3/3 KG018 . . . . **E**
MACAULAY, D/Ship. /1993/5-6/8 KH433 . . . . **Fic**
Dickens, Charles.
STANLEY, D/Charles Dickens: the man who had great expectations.
/1993/5-6/7 KE321 . . . . **B DICKENS, C.**
Dickinson, Emily--Fiction.
BEDARD, M/Emily. /1992/2-5/2 KF215 . . . . **E**
Dictionaries SEE ALSO Encyclopedias and dictionaries; English language--
Dictionaries; Spanish language--Dictionaries.
Diego, Juana.
DE PAOLA, T/Lady of Guadalupe. /1980/1-4/6 KA698 . . **232.91**
Diet.
JANEY JUNKFOOD'S FRESH ADVENTURE (VIDEOCASSETTE). /
1992/3-6/KC984 . . . . **VCR 613.2**
KARLSBERG, E/Eating pretty. /1991/5-A/7 KC985 . . . . . . **613.2**
Diet--Fiction.
SHARMAT, M/Gregory, the terrible eater. /1980/
K-2/4 KG488 . . . . **E**
Digestion SEE ALSO Food; Nutrition.
Digestion.
SHOWERS, P/What happens to a hamburger? Rev. ed. /1985/
K-2/3 KC942 . . . . **612.3**
Digestive system.
DIGESTIVE SYSTEM (VIDEOCASSETTE). /1994/
5-6/KC939 . . . . **VCR 612.3**
PARKER, S/Food and digestion. Rev. ed. /1990/
5-6/8 KC940 . . . . **612.3**
Diners (Restaurants)--Fiction.
MOSS, M/Mel's Diner. /1994/K-2/2 KG158 . . . . **E**
Dinners and dining--Fiction.
RINGGOLD, F/Dinner at Aunt Connie's house. /1993/
2-4/5 KG332 . . . . **E**
ZAMORANO, A/Let's eat! /1997/P-2/1 KG786 . . . . **E**
Dinners and dining--History.
GIBLIN, JC/From hand to mouth, or how we invented knives, forks,
/1987/5-6/8 KB185 . . . . **394.1**
Dinosaurs SEE ALSO names of specific dinosaurs e.g. Allosaurus.
Dinosaurs.
ALIKI /My visit to the dinosaurs. Rev. ed. /c1969, 1985/
2-4/4 KC242 . . . . **CE 567.9**
ARNOLD, C/Dinosaurs all around: an artist's view of the prehistoric
world. /1993/3-6/8 KC243. . . . . **567.9**
BARTON, B/Dinosaurs (Board book). /1995/P/KF205 . . . . . **BB E**
BRANLEY, FM/What happened to the dinosaurs? /1989/
2-4/5 KC244 . . . . **567.9**
COLE, J/Magic School Bus in the time of the dinosaurs. /1994/
2-4/3 KC245 . . . . **567.9**
DEBECK, S/Dinosaurs! (Videocassette). /1989/
2-5/KC246. . . . . **VCR 567.9**
DIGGING DINOSAURS (VIDEOCASSETTE). /1986/
3-A/KC247 . . . . **VCR 567.9**
DODSON, P/Alphabet of dinosaurs. /1995/1-6/5 KC248 . . **567.9**
GIBBONS, G/Dinosaurs. /1987/P-2/4 KC249 . . . . **CE 567.9**

HENDERSON, D/Dinosaur tree. /1994/3-6/5 KC235 . . . . . . **560**
KUROKAWA, M/Dinosaur Valley. /1992/2-6/6 KC250 . . . . **567.9**
LAUBER, P/How dinosaurs came to be. /1996/
   4-A/6 KC251 . . . . **567.9**
   Living with dinosaurs. /1991/3-6/5 KC252 . . . . **567.9**
   News about dinosaurs. /1989/P-A/7 KC253 . . . . **567.9**
LESSEM, D/Dinosaur worlds: new dinosaurs, new discoveries. /
   1996/4-6/6 KC254 . . . . **567.9**
LINDSAY, W/Tyrannosaurus. /1992/5-6/9 KC255 . . . . **567.9**
MOST, B/Dinosaur questions. /1995/K-4/7 KC257 . . . . . . **567.9**
NORMAN, D/Dinosaur. /1989/3-A/7 KC258 . . . . **567.9**
ROYSTON, A/Dinosaurs. /1991/K-2/4 KC259 . . . . **567.9**
SANCHEZ SANCHEZ, I/Drawing dinosaurs. /1996/
   5-A/3 KD418 . . . . **743**
   Painting and coloring dinosaurs. /1996/5-A/3 KD419 . . . . . **743**
SATTLER, HR/Stegosaurs: the solar-powered dinosaurs. /1992/
   3-6/8 KC260 . . . . **567.9**
   Tyrannosaurus rex and its kin: the Mesozoic monsters. /1989/
   3-6/8 KC261 . . . . **567.9**
SCHLEIN, M/Discovering dinosaur babies. /1991/
   3-6/5 KC262 . . . . **567.9**
SIMON, S/Largest dinosaurs. /1986/4-6/6 KC265 . . . . **567.9**
UNWIN, D/New book of dinosaurs. /1997/K-6/9 KC266 . . **567.9**
VISUAL DICTIONARY OF DINOSAURS. /1993/
   3-A/8 KC267 . . . . **567.9**

Dinosaurs--Anatomy.
SENIOR, K/X-ray picture book of dinosaurs and other prehistoric
   creatures. /1995/4-8/7 KC264 . . . . **567.9**

Dinosaurs--Australia.
ARNOLD, C/Dinosaurs down under and other fossils from Australia.
   /1990/3-6/8 KC240 . . . . **566**

Dinosaurs--Dictionaries.
BENTON, M/Dinosaur and other prehistoric animal factfinder. /
   1992/4-6/7 KC234 . . . . **560**
SATTLER, HR/New illustrated dinosaur dictionary. Rev. ed. /c1983,
   1990/3-6/KA444 . . . . **REF 567.9**

Dinosaurs--Fiction.
BROWN, LK/Rex and Lilly family time. /1995/K-1/1 KF270 . . . . **E**
BUTTERWORTH, O/Enormous egg. /c1956/3-5/4 KG955 . . . . **Fic**
CARRICK, C/Patrick's dinosaurs. /1983/K-2/4 KF361 . . . . . **CE E**
DE PAOLA, T/Little Grunt and the big egg: a prehistoric fairy tale.
   /1990/K-2/2 KF472 . . . . **E**
DONNELLY, L/Dinosaur day. /1987/P-2/1 KF487 . . . . **E**
FLEISCHMAN, P/Time train. /1994/1-3/2 KF551 . . . . **E**
HARLEY, B/Dinosaurs never say please and other stories (Sound
   recording cassette). /c1987, 1989/1-3/KF671 . . . . **SRC E**
HOFF, S/Danny and the dinosaur. /c1958/K-2/2 KF753 . . . **CE E**
   Danny and the dinosaur go to camp. /1996/K-2/2 KF754 . . . **E**
   Happy birthday, Danny and the dinosaur! /1995/K-1/2 KF756 . **E**
JOYCE, W/Dinosaur Bob and his adventures with the family
   Lazardo. /1988/K-3/5 KF859 . . . . **E**
KROLL, S/Tyrannosaurus game. /c1976/K-2/6 KF931 . . . . . **CE E**
NOLAN, D/Dinosaur dream. /1990/2-3/5 KG178 . . . . **E**
ROHMANN, E/Time flies. /1994/1-3/KG349 . . . . **E**
SCHWARTZ, H/How I captured a dinosaur. /c1989, 1993/
   P-2/2 KG418 . . . . **E**
SHARMAT, MW/Mitchell is moving. /1978/K-3/1 KG483 . . . . . **E**
SKOFIELD, J/Detective Dinosaur. /1996/1-3/2 KG514 . . . . . . **E**

Dinosaurs--Models--Design and construction.
ARNOLD, C/Dinosaurs all around: an artist's view of the prehistoric
   world. /1993/3-6/8 KC243. . . . . **567.9**

Dinosaurs--Poetry.
MARZOLLO, J/I'm tyrannosaurus!: a book of dinosaur rhymes. /
   1993/K-2/3 KD981 . . . . **811**
PRELUTSKY, J/Tyrannosaurus was a beast: dinosaur poems. /c1988,
   1992/1-5/KE017. . . . . **CE 811**

Dinosaurs--Software.
MICROSOFT DINOSAURS: EXPLORE THE INCREDIBLE WORLD OF
   PREHISTORIC CREATURES. ACADEMIC ED. (CD-ROM). /1994/
   2-A/KC256 . . . . **CDR 567.9**
SCHOLASTIC'S MAGIC SCHOOL BUS EXPLORES IN THE AGE OF
   DINOSAURS. SCHOOL ED. (CD-ROM). /1996/
   1-4/KC263. . . . . **CDR 567.9**

Dinosaurs--Wit and humor.
BIXENMAN, J/Dinosaur jokes. /1991/2-4/KD725. . . . . . **793.735**

Dinosaurs in art.
SANCHEZ SANCHEZ, I/Drawing dinosaurs. /1996/
   5-A/3 KD418 . . . . **743**
   Modeling dinosaurs. /1996/3-6/3 KD448 . . . . **745.592**
   Painting and coloring dinosaurs. /1996/5-A/3 KD419 . . . . . **743**

Diphtheria--Alaska--Nome.
STANDIFORD, N/Bravest dog ever: the true story of Balto. /1989/
   1-3/2 KD223 . . . . **636.7**

Diphtheria--Fiction.
HADDIX, MP/Running out of time. /1995/5-A/5 KH211 . . . . . **Fic**

Diplomats--Japan--Biography.
MOCHIZUKI, K/Passage to freedom: the Sugihara story. /1997/
   3-6/4 KE662 . . . . **940.53**

Dirigibles SEE Airships.
Dirtiness SEE Cleanliness.
Disarmament SEE ALSO Nuclear armament.
Disasters SEE ALSO Communicable diseases; Earthquakes; Epidemics; Fires;
   Floods; Natural disasters; Shipwrecks; Storms; also names of diseases.
Discoveries in geography SEE ALSO America--Discovery and exploration;
   Antarctic regions; Arctic regions; Explorers; Northwest Passage; Voyages
   and travel.

Discoveries in geography.
EXPLORERS AND DISCOVERERS: FROM ALEXANDER THE GREAT
   TO SALLY RIDE. /1995/5-A/KA470 . . . . **REF 910**
FRITZ, J/Around the world in 100 years: from Henry the Navigator
   to Magellan. /1994/5-A/7 KE164 . . . . **910.92**
MATTHEWS, R/Explorer. /1991/4-6/8 KE152 . . . . **910**

Discoveries in science.
EUREKA! /1995/4-7/KA451 . . . . **REF 608**
JONES, CF/Accidents may happen. /1996/4-A/9 KC895 . . . . **609**

Discrimination.
AND YOU CAN'T COME: PREJUDICE HURTS (VIDEOCASSETTE).
   /1996/5-6/KA803. . . . . **VCR 303.3**
UNFORGETTABLE PEN PAL: A STORY ABOUT PREJUDICE AND
   DISCRIMINATION /1991/3-5/KA821 . . . . **VCR 305**

Discrimination in sports.
SANTELLA, A/Jackie Robinson breaks the color line. /1996/
   4-6/6 KE517 . . . . **B ROBINSON, J.**

Diseases.
COMMUNICABLE DISEASES (VIDEOCASSETTE). /1992/
   5-6/KD022. . . . . **VCR 616.9**
FACKLAM, H/Viruses. /1994/5-A/8 KC377. . . . . **579.2**

Diseases--History.
GIBLIN, JC/When plague strikes: the Black Death, smallpox, AIDS.
   /1995/A/11 KD010 . . . . **614.4**

Disguise--Fiction.
NUMEROFF, LJ/Why a disguise? /1996/K-2/2 KG182 . . . . **E**

Disney, Walt.
COLE, MD/Walt Disney: creator of Mickey Mouse. /1996/
   4-6/8 KE322 . . . . **B DISNEY, W.**

Divali--Fiction.
GILMORE, R/Lights for Gita. /1994/1-3/5 KF620 . . . . **E**

Divers.
MCDONALD, K/Divers. /1992/4-6/8 KD847. . . . . **797.2**

Diving.
VERRIER, J/Swimming and diving. /1996/3-6/8 KD849 . . . **797.2**

Diving, Submarine.
MCDONALD, K/Divers. /1992/4-6/8 KD847. . . . . **797.2**

Division--Fiction.
HUTCHINS, P/Doorbell rang. /1986/P-2/2 KF797 . . . . **CE E**

Divorce.
BROWN, LK/Dinosaurs divorce: a guide for changing families. /
   1986/K-3/6 KA888 . . . . **CE 306.89**
DADDY DOESN'T LIVE WITH US (VIDEOCASSETTE). /1994/
   P-1/KA889. . . . . **VCR 306.89**
WHEN MOM AND DAD DIVORCE (VIDEOCASSETTE). /1994/
   4-6/KA890 . . . . **VCR 306.89**

Divorce--Fiction.
BLUME, J/It's not the end of the world. /c1972/4-6/4 KG911 . **Fic**
CASELEY, J/Priscilla twice. /1995/1-3/2 KF368 . . . . **E**
CLEARY, B/Dear Mr. Henshaw. /1983/4-A/4 KG993 . . . . . . **Fic**
   Strider. /1991/5-A/4 KH008 . . . . **Fic**
DANZIGER, P/Amber Brown goes fourth. /1995/
   2-4/4 KH059 . . . . **Fic**
   Amber Brown wants extra credit. /1996/2-4/4 KH061. . . . . **Fic**
GIFF, PR/Rat teeth. /c1984/3-5/3 KH166. . . . . **Fic**
GLEITZMAN, M/Puppy fat. /1995/5-A/5 KH175 . . . . **Fic**
LISLE, JT/Gold dust letters. /1994/4-6/7 KH410 . . . . **Fic**
PAULSEN, G/Hatchet. /1987/5-A/6 KH587 . . . . **CE Fic**
SCHINDEL, J/Dear Daddy. /1995/K-2/2 KG406 . . . . **E**
SHREVE, S/Formerly great Alexander family. /1995/
   3-5/6 KH708 . . . . **Fic**
WILLIAMS, VB/Scooter. /1993/4-A/4 KH865 . . . . **Fic**

DNA.
ARONSON, B/They came from DNA. /1993/5-A/6 KC278 . **572.8**
BALKWILL, FR/DNA is here to stay. /1993/5-6/7 KC279 . . . **572.8**

Doctors SEE Physicians.

Dog breeds.
CLUTTON-BROCK, J/Dog. /1991/A/8 KD217 . . . . **636.7**
KAPPELER, M/Dogs: wild and domestic. /1991/
   5-6/6 KD220 . . . . **636.7**

SQUIRE, A/Understanding man's best friend: why dogs look and act the way they do. /1991/5-6/7 KD222 . . . . **636.7**

Dog shows--Fiction.

SIRACUSA, C/Bingo, the best dog in the world. /1991/ K-1/1 KG510 . . . . **E**

Dogs SEE ALSO Guide dogs; Police dogs; Working dogs; and names of specific breeds of dogs e.g. Poodles; Dalmatian dog; Greyhound.

Dogs.

ANCONA, G/Sheep dog. /1985/A/8 KD227 . . . . **636.737**

CLUTTON-BROCK, J/Dog. /1991/A/8 KD217 . . . . **636.7**

COLE, J/My puppy is born. Rev. and expanded ed. /1991/ P-2/2 KD218 . . . . **636.7**

DOG (VIDEOCASSETTE). /1994/3-6/KD219 . . . . . . **VCR 636.7**

KAPPELER, M/Dogs: wild and domestic. /1991/ 5-6/6 KD220 . . . . **636.7**

MANSON, A/Dog came, too: a true story. /1993/ 1-4/6 KE185 . . . . **917.104**

MOORE, E/Buddy: the first seeing eye dog. /1996/ 1-3/3 KB006 . . . . **362.4**

SILVERSTEIN, A/Dogs: all about them. /1986/ 5-6/7 KD221 . . . . **636.7**

STANDIFORD, N/Bravest dog ever: the true story of Balto. /1989/ 1-3/2 KD223 . . . . **636.7**

TAYLOR, D/You and your dog. /1986/5-A/7 KD224 . . . . . . **636.7**

WAGGING TAILS: THE DOG AND PUPPY MUSIC VIDEO (VIDEOCASSETTE). /1994/P-6/KD225 . . . . **VCR 636.7**

Dogs--Fiction.

ACCORSI, W/Friendship's first Thanksgiving. /1992/ P-1/2 KF127 . . . . **E**

ARMSTRONG, WH/Sounder. /c1969/4-A/4 KG851 . . . . **CE Fic**

AUCH, MJ/Latchkey dog. /1994/3-5/4 KG855 . . . . **Fic**

BALL, Z/Bristle Face. /1990/5-A/6 KG877 . . . . **Fic**

BARRACCA, D/Adventures of taxi dog. /1990/P-2/2 KF200 **CE E**

Maxi, the star. /1993/P-2/2 KF201 . . . . **E**

Taxi Dog Christmas. /1994/P-2/3 KF202 . . . . **E**

BEMELMANS, L/Madeline's rescue. /c1953/P-2/2 KF220. . . **CE E**

BOLAND, J/Dog named Sam. /1996/K-2/2 KF241 . . . . . . **E**

BONSALL, CN/And I mean it, Stanley. /1974/1-2/1 KF242 . . . . **E**

BRIDWELL, N/Clifford the big red dog. /c1963, 1985/ P-2/1 KF264 . . . . **CE E**

BROWN, R/Our puppy's vacation. /1987/P-1/1 KF288 . . . . . . **E**

BRUCHAC, J/Dog people: native dog stories. /1995/ 4-6/5 KG934 . . . . **Fic**

BUNTING, E/Ghost's hour, spook's hour. /1987/P-2/2 KF301 . . **E**

Jane Martin, dog detective. /1984/1-3/1 KF303 . . . . **E**

BURNINGHAM, J/Cannonball Simp. /1994/K-2/4 KF314. . . **E**

BYARS, BC/Joy boys. /1996/2-3/1 KF326 . . . . **E**

Tornado. /1996/2-5/3 KG965 . . . . **Fic**

CAPUCILLI, A/Biscuit. /1996/P-1/1 KF338 . . . . **E**

Biscuit finds a friend. /1997/P-1/1 KF339 . . . . **E**

CARRICK, C/Foundling. /1977/1-3/4 KF358 . . . . **E**

CHAPMAN, C/Snow on snow on snow. /1994/K-3/3 KF377 . . . **E**

CHRISTELOW, E/Five-dog night. /1993/1-3/3 KF386 . . . . . **E**

Gertrude, the bulldog detective. /1992/K-2/3 KF387 . . . . **E**

Robbery at the Diamond Dog Diner. /1986/K-3/4 KF389. . **CE E**

CLEARY, B/Henry and Beezus. /c1952/2-5/3 KG995 . . . . **CE Fic**

Henry Huggins. /1950/3-5/4 KG996 . . . . **Fic**

Strider. /1991/5-A/4 KH008 . . . . **Fic**

COFFELT, N/Dog who cried woof. /1995/K-2/3 KF402. . . . . **E**

COPELAND, E/Milton, my father's dog. /1994/1-3/3 KF424 . . . **E**

CRESSWELL, H/Posy Bates, again! /1994/3-5/3 KH039 . . . **Fic**

DICKINSON, P/Chuck and Danielle. /1996/4-6/7 KH076. . . . **Fic**

DUFFEY, B/Lucky Christmas. /1994/3-5/4 KH086 . . . . . . **Fic**

EASTMAN, PD/Are you my mother? plus two more P.D. Eastman classics (Videocassette). /1991/P-1/KF505 . . . . . . **VCR E**

Go, dog, go! /c1961/P-1/1 KF506 . . . . **E**

EGAN, T/Burnt toast on Davenport Street. /1997/1-3/2 KF514 . **E**

ELSTE, J/True Blue. /1996/2-4/2 KH098 . . . . **Fic**

ERNST, LC/Ginger jumps. /1990/K-3/4 KF529 . . . . **E**

Walter's tail. /1992/P-2/3 KF534 . . . . **E**

FLEISCHMAN, S/Jim Ugly. /1992/4-A/6 KH123 . . . . **Fic**

FRANKLIN, KL/Wolfhound. /1996/1-3/3 KF576. . . . . **E**

GIPSON, F/Old Yeller. /c1956/A/7 KH170 . . . . **CE Fic**

GODDEN, R/Listen to the nightingale. /c1992, 1994/ 5-A/6 KH178 . . . . **Fic**

GRAY, EJ/Adam of the road. /c1942, 1970/5-6/6 KH194. **CE Fic**

HALL, D/I am the dog, I am the cat. /1994/K-3/3 KF661 . . . . **E**

HARPER, I/My dog Rosie. /1994/P-1/1 KF674 . . . . **E**

Our new puppy. /1996/P-2/1 KF675. . . . . **E**

HAWKINS, L/Figment, your dog, speaking. /1991/ 5-A/4 KH229 . . . . **Fic**

HENKES, K/Protecting Marie. /1995/5-A/6 KH238 . . . . . . **Fic**

HESSE, K/Lester's dog. /1993/1-3/3 KF716 . . . . **E**

Sable. /1994/3-5/4 KH253 . . . . **Fic**

HINTON, SE/Puppy sister. /1995/3-5/4 KH263 . . . . **Fic**

HOFF, S/Barkley. /c1975/K-2/1 KF751 . . . . **E**

HOWE, J/Hot fudge. /1990/K-3/2 KF777 . . . . **E**

Rabbit-Cadabra! /1993/K-3/3 KF779. . . . . **E**

Scared silly: a Halloween treat. /1989/K-3/3 KF780 . . . . **E**

HURD, T/Art dog. /1996/1-3/2 KF792 . . . . **E**

JOHNSTON, T/Ghost of Nicholas Greebe. /1996/ 3-5/6 KH328 . . . . **Fic**

KALMAN, M/Ooh-la-la (Max in love). /1991/4-A/3 KH340. . . **Fic**

KEATS, EJ/Whistle for Willie. /c1964, 1977/P-2/3 KF880 . . **CE E**

KELLOGG, S/Pinkerton, behave. /1979/P-2/2 KF894 . . . . . **E**

Prehistoric Pinkerton. /1987/P-3/5 KF895. . . . . **E**

KHALSA, DK/I want a dog. /1987/P-2/5 KF902 . . . . **E**

KJELGAARD, J/Big Red: the story of a champion Irish setter and a trapper's son who grew up together, roaming the wilderness. New ed. /c1945, 1956/6-A/7 KH365 . . . . **Fic**

KLEVEN, E/Hooray! A pinata! /1996/K-2/2 KF910 . . . . . . **E**

KNIGHT, E/Lassie come-home. /1978/4-6/5 KH370 . . . . . **Fic**

LEVY, E/Something queer is going on (a mystery). /C1973/ 1-3/3 KF972 . . . . **CE E**

LITTLE, J/Mine for keeps. /c1962, 1994/5-A/5 KH414 . . . **Fic**

LOWRY, L/Anastasia, absolutely. /1995/4-A/6 KH422 . . . . **Fic**

MACLACHLAN, P/Three Names. /1991/2-3/5 KG055 . . . . **E**

MASUREL, C/No, no, Titus! /1997/P-1/2 KG083 . . . . **E**

MAYER, M/Boy, a dog and a frog. /c1967/P-1/KG084 . . . **CE E**

MCGEORGE, CW/Boomer's big day. /1994/K-2/2 KG102 . . . . **E**

MCKAY, H/Dog Friday. /1995/4-A/7 KH477 . . . . **Fic**

MEDDAUGH, S/Martha blah blah. /1996/K-2/2 KG124 . . . . **E**

Witches' supermarket. /1991/1-3/2 KG125. . . . . **E**

MOREY, W/Home is the North. /c1967, 1990/5-A/5 KH509 . . **Fic**

Kavik, the wolf dog. /c1968/4-6/6 KH510 . . . . **Fic**

Scrub dog of Alaska. /c1971, 1989/5-A/6 KH511 . . . . . **Fic**

NAYLOR, PR/Saving Shiloh. /1997/4-A/4 KH537 . . . . . . **Fic**

Shiloh. /1991/4-6/6 KH538. . . . . **CE Fic**

Shiloh season. /1996/4-A/4 KH539. . . . . **Fic**

NODSET, JL/Go away, dog. /c1963, 1993/P-1/1 KG177 . . . . **E**

OSOFSKY, A/My Buddy. /1992/K-2/2 KG201 . . . . **E**

PILKEY, D/Dog breath: the horrible trouble with Hally Tosis. /1994/ 2-3/3 KG236 . . . . **E**

Hallo-wiener. /1995/K-2/2 KG237 . . . . **E**

PINKWATER, DM/Mush, a dog from space. /1995/ 3-6/4 KH604 . . . . **Fic**

POMERANTZ, C/Outside dog. /1993/P-2/2 KG266 . . . . . . **CE E**

PORTE, BA/Harry's dog. /1984/1-3/2 KG267 . . . . **E**

POTTER, B/Tale of the pie and the patty-pan. /c1933, 1987/ K-2/5 KG282 . . . . **E**

QUATTLEBAUM, M/Magic Squad and the dog of great potential. /1997/2-4/4 KH616 . . . . **Fic**

RAND, G/Aloha, Salty! /1996/1-3/3 KG299 . . . . **E**

Salty dog. /1991/2-3/5 KG301 . . . . **E**

RAWLS, W/Where the red fern grows: the story of two dogs and a boy. /c1961, 1988/A/4 KH624 . . . . **Fic**

ROBERTUS, PM/Dog who had kittens. /1991/K-1/4 KG337. **CE E**

RODOWSKY, C/Dog days. /1993/4-5/6 KH649 . . . . **Fic**

ROSEN, MJ/Bonesy and Isabel. /1995/2-3/6 KG352 . . . . . . **E**

RUBINSTEIN, G/Dog in, cat out. /1993/P-1/1 KG359 . . . . . **E**

RYLANT, C/Bookshop dog. /1996/K-2/2 KG369 . . . . **E**

Henry and Mudge: the first book. /1987/K-3/2 KG375 . . **CE E**

Mr. Putter and Tabby walk the dog. /1994/1-3/2 KG382 . . . . **E**

Old woman who named things. /1996/1-3/2 KG383 . . . . . **E**

SCHWARTZ, A/Oma and Bobo. /1987/K-3/2 KG414. . . . . . **E**

SENDAK, M/Higglety pigglety pop, or, There must be more to life. /c1967/1-3/6 KG431 . . . . **E**

SERFOZO, M/What's what?: a guessing game. /1996/ P-1/2 KG443 . . . . **E**

SHARMAT, MW/Genghis Khan: a dog star is born. /1994/ 2-5/2 KH703 . . . . **Fic**

Genghis Khan: dog-gone Hollywood. /1995/2-5/2 KH704 . . . **Fic**

I'm the best! /1991/K-2/1 KG482 . . . . **E**

Nate the Great and the crunchy Christmas. /1996/ 2-4/2 KG485 . . . . **E**

SIRACUSA, C/Bingo, the best dog in the world. /1991/ K-1/1 KG510 . . . . **E**

SNOW, A/How dogs really work! /1993/4-A/5 KH727 . . . . . **Fic**

SPOHN, K/Dog and Cat shake a leg. /1996/K-2/1 KG534 . . . . **E**

STEIG, W/Dominic. /c1972/4-6/7 KH750 . . . . **Fic**

STEVENS, C/Trouble for Lucy. /1979/3-5/6 KH754 . . . . . . **Fic**

STOLZ, M/Dog on Barkham Street. /c1960/4-6/4 KH765 . . . . **Fic**

THAYER, J/Puppy who wanted a boy. /c1958, 1986/ 1-3/2 KG603 . . . . **E**

VAN ALLSBURG, C/Garden of Abdul Gasazi. /1979/ 1-3/5 KG638 . . . . **CE E**

Sweetest fig. /1993/3-A/3 KH823 . . . . **Fic**

WELLER, FW/Riptide. /1990/1-3/4 KG695 . . . . **E**

WELLS, R/McDuff comes home. /1997/K-2/2 KG705 . . . . **E**
   McDuff moves in. /1997/K-2/2 KG706 . . . . **E**
WILD, M/Toby. /1994/1-3/3 KG718. . . . . **E**
YEOMAN, J/Old Mother Hubbard's dog dresses up. /c1989,
   1990/K-3/4 KG774. . . . . **E**
ZIEFERT, H/Jason's bus ride. /c1987, 1993/K-2/1 KG792 . . . . . **E**
ZION, G/Harry the dirty dog. /c1956/P-2/2 KG800. . . . . . **CE E**
ZOLOTOW, C/Old dog. Rev. and newly illustrated ed. /1995/
   K-2/2 KG806 . . . . **E**

Dogs--Folklore.
WAITE, MP/Jojofu. /1996/1-4/5 KB670 . . . . **398.24**

Dogs--Habits and behavior.
SQUIRE, A/Understanding man's best friend: why dogs look and act
   the way they do. /1991/5-6/7 KD222 . . . . **636.7**

Dogs--History.
SQUIRE, A/Understanding man's best friend: why dogs look and act
   the way they do. /1991/5-6/7 KD222 . . . . **636.7**

Dogs--Literary collections.
GIVE A DOG A BONE: STORIES, POEMS, JOKES, AND RIDDLES
   ABOUT DOGS. /1996/K-4/KD874. . . . . **808.8**

Dogs--Training.
CALMENSON, S/Rosie, a visiting dog's story. /1994/
   3-6/2 KD216 . . . . **636.7**
JONES, RF/Jake: a Labrador puppy at work and play. /1992/
   2-5/5 KD228 . . . . **636.752**

Dogs--Training--Fiction.
KELLOGG, S/Pinkerton, behave. /1979/P-2/2 KF894 . . . . . **CE E**

Dogs in art.
MICKLETHWAIT, L/Spot a dog. /1995/K-2/1 KD467 . . . . **750**

Dogsledding--Fiction.
PAULSEN, G/Dogteam. /1993/1-3/4 KG221 . . . . **E**

Dollar, American.
ADAMS, BJ/Go-around dollar. /1992/3-6/3 KA947 . . . . . **332.4**

Dollhouses--Fiction.
REISS, K/Time windows. /1991/6-A/7 KH630 . . . . **Fic**
WRIGHT, BR/Dollhouse murders. /1983/4-6/5 KH882 . . . . . . **Fic**

Dollmaking.
KUKLIN, S/From head to toe: how a doll is made. /1994/
   4-6/6 KD350 . . . . **688.7**

Dolls.
YOUNG, R/Dolls. /1992/5-6/6 KD353 . . . . **688.7**

Dolls--Fiction.
BAILEY, CS/Miss Hickory. /c1946/4-6/4 KG875 . . . . **CE Fic**
CASSEDY, S/Lucie Babbidge's house. /1993/6-A/7 KG987 . . . **Fic**
DEXTER, C/Doll who knew the future. /1994/4-6/6 KH072 . . . **Fic**
GODDEN, R/Story of Holly and Ivy. /1985/3-5/4 KH179 . . . . **Fic**
GOFFSTEIN, MB/Goldie, the dollmaker. /1969/3-6/6 KH180 . . **Fic**
GRIFFITH, HV/Caitlin's Holiday. /1990/4-6/4 KH204 . . . . . . **Fic**
HUTCHINS, P/Changes, changes. /c1971/P-1/KF795 . . . . . **CE E**
KING-SMITH, D/Lady Daisy (Talking book). /1995/
   4-6/KH350. . . . . **TB Fic**
LEXAU, JM/Rooftop mystery. /c1968/1-2/1 KF979 . . . . **E**
MCKISSACK, P/Nettie Jo's friends. /1989/1-3/4 KG108 . . . . . . **E**
POMERANTZ, C/Chalk doll. /c1989, 1993/1-3/2 KG263 . . . . . **E**
SAY, A/Allison. /1997/2-4/2 KH678 . . . . **Fic**
STEVENSON, J/Night after Christmas. /1981/K-2/2 KG564 . **CE E**
TEWS, S/Gingerbread doll. /1993/1-3/5 KG602 . . . . **E**
WAUGH, S/Mennyms. /1994/5-A/7 KH843 . . . . **Fic**
   Mennyms alone. /1996/5-A/5 KH844 . . . . **Fic**
   Mennyms in the wilderness. /1995/5-A/5 KH845 . . . . **Fic**
   Mennyms under siege. /1996/6-A/6 KH846 . . . . **Fic**
WRIGHT, BR/Dollhouse murders. /1983/4-6/5 KH882 . . . . . . **Fic**
ZOLOTOW, C/William's doll. /c1972/P-2/4 KG810 . . . . **E**

Dolphins.
AUDUBON SOCIETY FIELD GUIDE TO NORTH AMERICAN
   FISHES, WHALES AND DOLPHINS. /1983/A/11 KC583 . . . **597**
MORRIS, RA/Dolphin. /c1975/K-2/2 KC778 . . . . **599.53**
PRINGLE, LP/Dolphin man: exploring the world of dolphins. /1995/
   5-6/11 KC776 . . . . **599.5**

Dolphins--Fiction.
HESSE, K/Music of dolphins. /1996/5-A/3 KH252 . . . . **Fic**
ORR, K/Story of a dolphin. /1993/1-3/6 KG199 . . . . **E**

Dolphins--Folklore.
WOOD, A/Rainbow bridge: inspired by a Chumash tale. /1995/
   3-5/4 KB675 . . . . **398.24**

Dolphins--Training.
DOLPHINS. /1988/5-6/6 KD190. . . . . **636.088**
Domestic animals SEE ALSO Animals--Treatment; names of specific domestic
   animals e.g. Cats.

Domestic animals.
FARM ANIMALS. /1991/P-2/2 KD180 . . . . **636**
TAFURI, N/Spots, feathers, and curly tails. /1988/
   P-K/1 KD185 . . . . **636**

Domestic animals--Fiction.
BIRCHMAN, DF/Jigsaw Jackson. /1996/1-3/3 KF230 . . . . **E**
BROWN, MW/Big red barn. /c1956, 1989/P-1/3 KF283 . . . . . **E**
CARLE, E/Very busy spider. /1985/P-2/2 KF346 . . . . **E**
EHLERT, L/Color farm. /1990/P-K/KF515 . . . . **E**
EHRLICH, A/Parents in the pigpen, pigs in the tub. /1993/
   K-2/6 KF521 . . . . **E**
FLEMING, D/Barnyard banter. /1994/P-1/3 KF553 . . . . **E**
FOX, M/Hattie and the fox. /1987/P-2/2 KF569 . . . . **E**
GRAY, LM/Is there room on the feather bed? /1997/
   K-2/4 KF636 . . . . **E**
HUTCHINS, P/Little Pink Pig. /1994/P-1/2 KF799 . . . . **E**
KING-SMITH, D/Babe: the gallant pig. /1994/
   2-5/5 KH346 . . . . **CE Fic**
LESSER, C/What a wonderful day to be a cow. /1995/
   K-2/3 KF963 . . . . **E**
MCDONNELL, F/I love animals. /1994/P-1/2 KG100 . . . . **E**
MCPHAIL, D/Farm morning. /c1985, 1991/P-1/2 KG118 . . . . . **E**
PALATINI, M/Piggie Pie! /1995/1-5/2 KG207 . . . . **E**
PLOURDE, L/Pigs in the mud in the middle of the rud. /1997/
   K-2/2 KG247 . . . . **E**
SYKES, J/This and that. /1996/P-1/2 KG586 . . . . **E**
WADDELL, M/Farmer duck. /1992/P-1/2 KG675 . . . . **E**
WORMELL, C/Number of animals. /1993/P-2/3 KG770 . . . . . . **E**
ZIEFERT, H/Who said moo? /1996/P-1/2 KG799 . . . . **E**

Domestic animals--Infancy--Fiction.
BROWN, C/In the spring. /1994/P-1/2 KF269 . . . . **E**

Domestic animals--Pictorial works.
TAFURI, N/Early morning in the barn. /1983/P/KG588 . . . . **E**
Domestic relations SEE ALSO Divorce; Family life; Parent and child.

Domestic relations.
MY FAMILY, YOUR FAMILY (VIDEOCASSETTE). /1994/
   K-2/KA871 . . . . **VCR 306.85**
SIMON, N/All kinds of families. /c1976/1-3/5 KA873 . . . **306.85**
WE'RE A FAMILY (VIDEOCASSETTE). /1992/
   3-5/KA874 . . . . **VCR 306.85**

Domestic relations--Fiction.
CLEARY, B/Ramona and her father. /1977/3-5/7 KH001 . . . . . **Fic**

Dominican Americans.
GORDON, G/My two worlds. /1993/3-6/4 KA844 . . . . . . **305.8**

Dominican Americans--New York (N.Y.).
DAWSON, ML/Over here it's different: Carolina's story. /1993/
   5-6/7 KA842 . . . . **305.8**

Dominican Americans--Social life and customs.
DAWSON, ML/Over here it's different: Carolina's story. /1993/
   5-6/7 KA842 . . . . **305.8**

Dominican Republic--Social life and customs.
GORDON, G/My two worlds. /1993/3-6/4 KA844 . . . . . . **305.8**

Dominion Textile Company Strike, 1946--Fiction.
HEWITT, M/One proud summer. /1981/A/7 KH254 . . . . **Fic**

Dominoes.
LONG, L/Domino addition. /1996/P-2/2 KB966. . . . . **513.2**

Donkeys--Fiction.
HENRY, M/Brighty of the Grand Canyon. /c1953, 1991/
   4-5/5 KH242 . . . . **CE Fic**
STEIG, W/Farmer Palmer's wagon ride. /c1974, 1992/
   K-3/6 KG543 . . . . **E**
   Sylvester and the magic pebble. /c1969, 1988/
   K-2/6 KG544 . . . . **CE E**
   Sylvester and the magic pebble (Videocassette). /1992/
   K-2/KG545 . . . . **VCR E**

Donkeys--Folklore.
YOUNG, E/Donkey trouble. /1995/1-2/5 KB678 . . . . **398.24**

Donner Party.
LAVENDER, DS/Snowbound: the tragic story of the Donner Party. /
   1996/5-6/6 KF038 . . . . **978**
MURPHY, VR/Across the plains in the Donner Party. /1996/
   5-6/7 KF041 . . . . **978**

Doors--Fiction.
SOTO, G/Old man and his door. /1996/K-2/2 KG528 . . . . **E**

Dorris, Michael.
WEIL, A/Michael Dorris. /1997/6-A/7 KE323 . . . . **B DORRIS, M.**

Dos Pilas Site (Guatemala).
LOST CITY OF THE MAYA (VIDEOCASSETTE). /1990/
   6-A/KE844. . . . . **VCR 972.81**

Douglas, Marjory Stoneman
BRYANT, J/Marjory Stoneman Douglas: voice of the Everglades. /
   1992/4-5/6 KE324 . . . . **B DOUGLAS, M.**

Douglas fir.
BASH, B/Ancient ones: the world of the old-growth Douglas fir. /
   1994/3-6/7 KC435 . . . . **585**
REED-JONES, C/Tree in the ancient forest. /1995/
   K-3/3 KC437 . . . . **585**

Douglass, Frederick.
FREDERICK DOUGLASS (VIDEOCASSETTE). /1992/
4-A/KE325 . . . . **VCR B DOUGLASS, F.**
WEINER, E/Story of Frederick Douglass: voice of freedom. /1996/
3-5/3 KE326 . . . . **B DOUGLASS, F.**

Douglass, Frederick--Drama.
DAVIS, O/Escape to freedom: a play about young Frederick
Douglass. /c1976, 1990/A-6/KE091 . . . . **812**

Down's syndrome.
CAIRO, S/Our brother has Down's syndrome: an introduction for
children. /1985/1-4/6 KB002 . . . . **362.3**
EDUCATING PETER (VIDEOCASSETTE). /1993/
/KA185 . . . . **VCR PROF 371.92**

Down's syndrome--Fiction.
RABE, B/Where's Chimpy? /1988/P-2/2 KG296 . . . . **E**
TESTA, M/Thumbs up, Rico! /1994/1-3/2 KG601 . . . . **E**

Drag racing.
CONNOLLY, M/Dragsters. /1992/4-A/4 KD829 . . . . . . **796.7**

Dragonflies.
BERNHARD, E/Dragonfly. /1993/2-4/4 KC534 . . . . . . **595.7**

Dragons--Fiction.
COVILLE, B/Jeremy Thatcher, dragon hatcher: a magic shop book. /
1991/4-A/4 KH036 . . . . **CE Fic**
DE PAOLA, T/Knight and the dragon. /1980/K-2/5 KF471 . . . . . **E**
GANNETT, RS/My father's dragon. /c1948, 1986/
3-5/6 KH149 . . . . **Fic**
GRAHAME, K/Reluctant dragon. /c1938/3-6/7 KH187 . . . **CE Fic**
Reluctant dragon. /1983/3-6/6 KH188 . . . . **Fic**
GRAY, L/Falcon's egg. /1995/5-A/6 KH195 . . . . **Fic**
LEAF, M/Eyes of the dragon. /1987/K-3/5 KF952 . . . . **E**
MCCAFFREY, A/Dragonsong. /c1976, 1986/6-A/6 KH466 . . . **Fic**
NUNES, S/Last dragon. /1995/2-3/3 KG183 . . . . **E**
STERMAN, B/Backyard dragon. /1993/4-6/6 KH753 . . . . . . **Fic**
SUTCLIFF, R/Minstrel and the dragon pup. /c1993, 1996/
3-6/7 KH775 . . . . **Fic**
YEP, L/City of dragons. /1995/1-3/5 KG775 . . . . **E**

Dragons--Folklore.
HODGES, M/Saint George and the dragon: a golden legend. /
1984/5/7 KB453 . . . . **CE 398.22**
ROTH, SL/Brave Martha and the dragon. /1996/
2-4/4 KB476 . . . . **398.22**

Dragons--Poetry.
DRAGON POEMS. /1991/K-A/KE055 . . . . **811.008**
PRELUTSKY, J/Dragons are singing tonight. /1993/
2-4/KE002 . . . . **811**

Dragons in art.
SANCHEZ SANCHEZ, I/Dragons and prehistoric monsters. /1996/
3-6/3 KD447 . . . . **745.592**
Drama SEE ALSO types of drama e.g. Readers Theater.
Drama--Collections SEE Plays--Collections.

Drama--Periodicals.
PLAYS: THE DRAMA MAGAZINE FOR YOUNG PEOPLE. /1941-/
5-A/KA536 . . . . **PER 050**

Drama in education.
BAUER, CF/Presenting reader's theater: plays and poems to read
aloud. /1987//KA329 . . . . **PROF 792**
CREATIVE DRAMA IN THE EARLY CHILDHOOD CLASSROOM
(VIDEOCASSETTE). /1991//KA220 . . . . **VCR PROF 372.6**
LAUGHLIN, MK/Social studies readers theatre for children: scripts
and script development. /1991//KA224 . . . . **PROF 372.6**

Dramatists, English.
STANLEY, D/Bard of Avon: the story of William Shakespeare. /
1992/4-6/7 KE538 . . . . **B SHAKESPEARE**
Drawing SEE ALSO Illustrations of books; Painting; Perspective.

Drawing.
BIESTY, S/Stephen Biesty's incredible explosions. /1996/
5-6/7 KD411 . . . . **741.6**

Drawing--Fiction.
COVILLE, B/Jeremy Thatcher, dragon hatcher: a magic shop book. /
1991/4-A/4 KH036 . . . . **CE Fic**
DRESCHER, H/Simon's book. /1983/K-2/6 KF497 . . . . . . **CE E**
GACKENBACH, D/Mag the magnificent. /1985/K-2/2 KF590 . . . **E**
GILLILAND, JH/Not in the house, Newton! /1995/P-2/2 KF618 . **E**
MCPHAIL, D/Moony B. Finch, the fastest draw in the West. /1994/
1-3/4 KG120 . . . . **E**
RUSSO, M/Under the table. /1997/P-K/2 KG363 . . . . **E**
SAY, A/Emma's rug. /1996/1-3/3 KG396 . . . . **E**
WILLIAMS, VB/Cherries and cherry pits. /c1965, 1984/
K-3/2 KG735 . . . . **E**

Drawing--Technique.
AMES, LJ/Draw 50 cars, trucks, and motorcycles. /1986/
4-6/KD415 . . . . **743**
Draw 50 horses. /1986/4-6/KD416 . . . . **743**

ANIMATION FOR KIDS: HOW TO MAKE YOUR CARTOON
MOVE! (VIDEOCASSETTE). /1994/4-A/KD407 . . . . **VCR 741.5**
ARTELL, M/Basic cartooning with Mike Artell (Videocassette). /
1995/3-6-KD408 . . . . **VCR 741.5**
DUBOSQUE, D/Draw! cars. Rev. ed. /1997/4-A/5 KD417 . . . **743**
Learn to draw 3-D. /1992/5-A/7 KD414 . . . . **742**
LIGHTFOOT, M/Cartooning for kids. /1993/3-6/5 KD410 . . **741.5**
SANCHEZ SANCHEZ, I/Drawing dinosaurs. /1996/
5-A/3 KD418 . . . . **743**
Painting and coloring dinosaurs. /1996/5-A/3 KD419 . . . . **743**
SOLGA, K/Draw! /1991/2-6/4 KD405 . . . . **741.2**
WELTON, J/Drawing: a young artist's guide. /1994/
3-6/6 KD406 . . . . **741.2**

Drawing--Technique--Software.
KID CAD (MICROCOMPUTER PROGRAM). /1993/
2-A/KD423 . . . . **MCP 745.4**

Drawing books.
AMES, LJ/Draw 50 cars, trucks, and motorcycles. /1986/
4-6/KD415 . . . . **743**
Draw 50 horses. /1986/4-6/KD416 . . . . **743**
Dreams SEE ALSO Brain; Psychology; Sleep.

Dreams--Fiction.
BRIGGS, R/Snowman. /1978/P-1/KF265 . . . . **CE E**
GINSBURG, M/Across the stream. /1982/P-K/2 KF621 . . . . . . **E**
HATRICK, G/Masks. /1996/6-A/3 KH225 . . . . **Fic**
LEWIS, PO/Davy's dream. /1988/1-3/3 KF977 . . . . **E**
NOLAN, D/Dinosaur dream. /1990/2-3/5 KG178 . . . . **E**
OSOFSKY, A/Dreamcatcher. /1992/K-2/5 KG200 . . . . **E**
RINGGOLD, F/Tar beach. /1991/2-3/4 KG333 . . . . **E**
STANDIFORD, N/Astronauts are sleeping. /1996/K-2/3 KG535 . **E**
STEVENSON, J/Could be worse. /c1977, 1987/
K-3/4 KG558 . . . . **CE E**
VAN ALLSBURG, C/Sweetest fig. /1993/3-A/3 KH823 . . . . . . **Fic**
WILD, M/Going home. /1993/1-3/3 KG716 . . . . **E**

Dreams--Folklore.
SHULEVITZ, U/Treasure. /1978/2-4/4 KB778 . . . . . . **398.27**
YEP, L/Tree of dreams: ten tales from the garden of night. /1995/
4-6/3 KB790 . . . . **398.27**
YOUNG, E/Night visitors. /1995/2-3/4 KB680 . . . . . . **398.24**

Dreidel (Game)--Fiction.
KIMMEL, EA/Magic dreidels: a Hanukkah story. /1996/
K-3/2 KF904 . . . . **E**
Driving, Motor vehicle SEE Motor vehicle driving.

Droughts--Fiction.
HAMILTON, V/Drylongso. /1992/4-6/4 KH214 . . . . **Fic**
KARR, K/Cave. /1994/5-A/4 KH341 . . . . **Fic**
MACLACHLAN, P/Skylark. /1994/3-5/3 KH445 . . . . **Fic**
PATERSON, K/Master puppeteer. /c1975/6-A/6 KH580 . . . . **Fic**
TAYLOR, MD/Well: David's story. /1995/5-A/4 KH781 . . . **Fic**

Droughts--Great Plains--Fiction.
RAVEN, M/Angels in the dust. /1997/2-3/2 KG315 . . . . **E**

Drug abuse.
DRUG DANGER: EASY TO START, HARD TO STOP
(VIDEOCASSETTE). /1992/5-6/KC994 . . . . **VCR 613.8**
DRUG DANGER: IN THE BODY (VIDEOCASSETTE). /1992/
5-6/KD019 . . . . **VCR 616.86**
HOW TO JUST SAY NO TO DRUGS (SOUND FILMSTRIP). /
1987/A/KC996 . . . . **VCR 613.8**
LET'S TALK ABOUT DRUGS (VIDEOCASSETTE). /1994/
1-3/KC998 . . . . **VCR 613.8**
MADISON, A/Drugs and you. Rev. ed. /1990/
5-6/7 KC999 . . . . **613.8**
WAX, W/Say no and know why: kids learn about drugs. /1992/
5-6/5 KA999 . . . . **362.29**
WHAT'S WRONG WITH BEER? (VIDEOCASSETTE). /1992/
5-6/KD003 . . . . **VCR 613.81**

Drug abuse--Prevention.
ALPHABETTER ANSWER (VIDEOCASSETTE). /1989/
5-A/KC992 . . . . **VCR 613.8**
ARMSTRONG, T/Dog who dared (Videocassette). /1993/
4-6/KC993 . . . . **VCR 613.8**
DRUGS, YOUR FRIENDS, AND YOU: HANDLING PEER PRESSURE
(VIDEOCASSETTE). /1988/6-A/KC995 . . . . **VCR 613.8**
JUST FOR ME (VIDEOCASSETTE). /1992/
K-6/KC997 . . . . **VCR 613.8**
SUBSTANCE ABUSE (VIDEOCASSETTE). /1995/
4-6/KD001 . . . . **VCR 613.8**

Drug abuse--Software.
SUBSTANCE ABUSE (MICROCOMPUTER PROGRAM). /1992/
4-A/KD000 . . . . **MCP 613.8**

Drug smuggling SEE Narcotics, Control of.
Drugs SEE ALSO Alcohol; Narcotics, Control of; Poisons.
Drugs.
    ARMSTRONG, T/Dog who dared (Videocassette). /1993/
    4-6/KC993 . . . . **VCR 613.8**
    DRUG DANGER: EASY TO START, HARD TO STOP
    (VIDEOCASSETTE). /1992/5-6/KC994 . . . . . . **VCR 613.8**
    DRUG DANGER: IN THE BODY (VIDEOCASSETTE). /1992/
    5-6/KD019 . . . . **VCR 616.86**
    HOW TO JUST SAY NO TO DRUGS (SOUND FILMSTRIP). /
    1987/A/KC996 . . . . **VCR 613.8**
    KID'S GUIDE TO DRUG, ALCOHOL AND SMOKING
    AWARENESS (VIDEOCASSETTE). /1985/
    K-4/KA997 . . . . **VCR 362.29**
    LET'S TALK ABOUT DRUGS (VIDEOCASSETTE). /1994/
    1-3/KC998 . . . . **VCR 613.8**
    MADISON, A/Drugs and you. Rev. ed. /1990/
    5-6/7 KC999 . . . . **613.8**
    SUBSTANCE ABUSE (VIDEOCASSETTE). /1995/
    4-6/KD001 . . . . **VCR 613.8**
Drugs--Software.
    SUBSTANCE ABUSE (MICROCOMPUTER PROGRAM). /1992/
    4-A/KD000 . . . . **MCP 613.8**
Drum--Folklore.
    JAFFE, N/Patakin: world tales of drums and drummers. /1994/
    5-6/6 KB321 . . . . **398.2**
    SOUHAMI, J/Leopard's drum: an Asante tale from West Africa. /
    1995/P-1/2 KB654 . . . . **398.24**
Drum majorettes--Fiction.
    MILLS, C/Phoebe's parade. /1994/K-2/2 KG138 . . . . **E**
Dublin (Ireland).
    KENT, D/Dublin. /1997/3-5/8 KE678 . . . . **941.8**
Ducks.
    SELSAM, ME/First look at ducks, geese, and swans. /1990/
    1-3/2 KC683 . . . . **598.4**
Ducks--Fiction.
    CAPUCILLI, A/Biscuit finds a friend. /1997/P-1/1 KF339 . . . . . . **E**
    FLACK, M/Story about Ping. /c1933/P-1/6 KF550 . . . . . . **CE E**
    GINSBURG, M/Across the stream. /1982/P-K/2 KF621 . . . . **E**
    HEST, A/Baby Duck and the bad eyeglasses. /1996/
    P-K/1 KF717 . . . . **E**
    In the rain with Baby Duck. /1995/P-1/2 KF718 . . . . **E**
    You're the boss, Baby Duck! /1997/P-1/2 KF722 . . . . **E**
    JOYCE, W/Bently and egg. /1992/1-3/4 KF857 . . . . **E**
    MCCLOSKEY, R/Make way for ducklings. /c1941, 1963/
    P-1/4 KG089 . . . . **CE E**
    POTTER, B/Tale of Jemima Puddle-Duck. /c1936, 1987/
    P-2/6 KG273 . . . . **E**
    REISER, L/Surprise family. /1994/P-2/2 KG319 . . . . **E**
    ROCKWELL, AF/Ducklings and pollywogs. /1994/K-2/3 KG341 . . **E**
    SILVERMAN, E/Don't fidget a feather! /1994/P-2/2 KG505 . . . **E**
    TAFURI, N/Have you seen my duckling? /1984/P-K/1 KG590 . . . **E**
    TRYON, L/Albert's alphabet. /1991/P-1/KG620 . . . . **E**
    Albert's Thanksgiving. /1994/K-2/2 KG621 . . . . **E**
    WINTHROP, E/Bear and Mrs. Duck. /1988/P-1/1 KG744 . . . . . **E**
Ducks--Folklore.
    PATERSON, K/Tale of the mandarin ducks. /1990/
    2-3/6 KB631 . . . . **398.24**
Ducks--Poetry.
    FIVE LITTLE DUCKS: AN OLD RHYME. /1995/
    P-1/1 KB797 . . . . **398.8**
Dunkerque (France), Battle of, 1940--Fiction.
    BORDEN, L/Little ships: the heroic rescue at Dunkirk in World War
    II. /1997/3-5/3 KF251 . . . . **E**
Dust storms--Fiction.
    HAMILTON, V/Drylongso. /1992/4-6/4 KH214 . . . . **Fic**
Dust storms--Great Plains--Fiction.
    RAVEN, M/Angels in the dust. /1997/2-3/2 KG315 . . . . **E**
Dwarfs--Folklore.
    GIBLIN, JC/Dwarf, the giant, and the unicorn: a tale of King Arthur.
    /1996/3-5/4 KB443 . . . . **398.22**
    WALKER, PR/Little folk: stories from around the world. /1997/
    2-4/6 KB494 . . . . **398.22**
Dwellings SEE ALSO Apartment houses; Houses; Housing.
Dwellings.
    DORROS, A/This is my house. /1992/1-3/2 KD393 . . . . **728**
    EMBERLEY, R/My house: a book in two languages/Mi Casa: un
    libro en dos lenguas. /1990/K-2/KB858 . . . . **463**
    MORRIS, A/Houses and homes. /1992/2-4/6 KD394 . . . . **728**
    WHITE, S/Welcome home! /1995/4-6/6 KD396 . . . . **728**
Dwellings--Fiction.
    BUNTING, E/Blue and the gray. /1996/3-5/3 KF297 . . . . **E**
    CALHOUN, M/Katie John. /c1960/4-6/4 KG966 . . . . **Fic**
    CARLE, E/House for Hermit Crab. /1987/P-2/2 KF344 . . . . **E**

    EDWARDS, PD/Livingstone Mouse. /1996/K-2/2 KF512 . . . . . . **E**
    KALAN, R/Moving day. /1996/P-1/1 KF865 . . . . **E**
    LOBEL, A/Ming Lo moves the mountain. /1982/
    K-2/1 KG006 . . . . **CE E**
    RYLANT, C/Everyday house (Board book). /1993/
    P-K/2 KG372 . . . . **BB E**
Dwellings--Great Britain.
    WILSON, L/Daily life in a Victorian house. /1993/
    3-6/7 KE676 . . . . **941.081**
Dwellings--History.
    VENTURA, P/Houses: structures, methods, and ways of living. /
    1993/4-A/9 KD395 . . . . **728**
Dyslexia--Fiction.
    CARRIS, JD/Aunt Morbelia and the screaming skulls. /1990/
    4-6/5 KG978 . . . . **Fic**
Eagles SEE ALSO Birds of prey; names of specific types e.g. Bald eagles.
Eagles.
    BERNHARD, E/Eagles: lions of the sky. /1994/
    3-6/6 KC710 . . . . **598.9**
    GIECK, C/Bald eagle magic for kids. /1991/5-6/6 KC714 . . **598.9**
    PATENT, DH/Eagles of America. /1995/4-6/6 KC716 . . . . . **598.9**
    Where the bald eagles gather. /1984/5-6/7 KC718 . . . . . **598.9**
Eagles--Fiction.
    BURNHAM, SD/Three River Junction: a story of an Alaskan bald
    eagle preserve (Kit). /1997/2-4/KF313 . . . . **KIT E**
Ear SEE ALSO Hearing.
Ear.
    MATHERS, D/Ears. /1992/5-6/6 KC967 . . . . **612.8**
    PARKER, S/Ear and hearing. Rev. ed. /1989/5-6/8 KC971 . **612.8**
    PARRAMON, JM/Hearing. /1985/P-1/1 KC973 . . . . **612.8**
Earhart, Amelia.
    KERBY, M/Amelia Earhart: courage in the sky. /1990/
    3-4/5 KE327 . . . . **B EARHART, A.**
    KULLING, M/Vanished!: the mysterious disappearance of Amelia
    Earhart. /1996/2-4/7 KE328 . . . . **B EARHART, A.**
    SZABO, C/Sky pioneer: a photobiography of Amelia Earhart. /
    1997/4-6/12 KE329 . . . . **B EARHART, A.**
Early childhood education.
    DIMIDJIAN, VJ/Early childhood at risk: actions and advocacy for
    young children. /1989/KA190 . . . . **PROF 372**
Early childhood education--Activity programs.
    CHILD'S SEASONAL TREASURY. /1996//KA193 . . **PROF 372.13**
    GIANT ENCYCLOPEDIA OF CIRCLE TIME AND GROUP
    ACTIVITIES FOR CHILDREN 3 TO 6: OVER 600 FAVORITE
    CIRCLE TIME ACTIVITES CREATED BY TEACHERS FOR
    TEACHERS. /1996//KA197 . . . . **PROF 372.21**
    SILBERG, J/500 five minute games: quick and easy activities for 3-6
    year olds. /1995//KA325 . . . . **PROF 790.1**
Early childhood education--Case studies.
    DIMIDJIAN, VJ/Early childhood at risk: actions and advocacy for
    young children. /1989/KA190 . . . . **PROF 372**
Earrings--Fiction.
    VIORST, J/Earrings! /1990/1-3/2 KG661 . . . . **E**
Earth SEE ALSO Antarctic regions; Atmosphere; Creation; Earthquake;
Geography; Geology; Geophysics; Glacial epoch; Meteorology; Ocean;
Oceanography; Physical geography; Universe.
Earth.
    BLUE PLANET (VIDEOCASSETTE). /1993/
    5-A/KB058 . . . . **VCR 363.73**
    FRADIN, DB/Earth. /1989/4-5/4 KC058 . . . . **525**
    GIBBONS, G/Planet Earth/inside out. /1995/3-6/6 KC146 . . **550**
    HOFFMAN, M/Earth, fire, water, air. /1995/2-6/7 KA814 . **304.2**
    LASKY, K/Librarian who measured the earth. /1994/
    4-A/6 KE339 . . . . **B ERATOSTHENES**
    LAUBER, P/How we learned the earth is round. /c1990, 1992/
    K-3/2 KC060 . . . . **525**
    You're aboard spaceship Earth. /1996/1-3/3 KC147 . . . . . . **550**
    RIDE, S/Third planet: exploring the earth from space. /1994/
    2-8/7 KC062 . . . . **525**
    SUN, EARTH, MOON (VIDEOCASSETTE). /1995/
    4-6/KC017 . . . . **VCR 523.2**
    WYLER, R/Science fun with mud and dirt. /1986/
    K-4/2 KB887 . . . . **507**
Earth--Crust.
    LAMPTON, C/Volcano. /1991/4-6/7 KC157 . . . . **551.21**
Earth--Fiction.
    FRASIER, D/On the day you were born. /1991/P-3/5 KF577 . . . **E**
    ON THE DAY YOU WERE BORN (VIDEOCASSETTE). /1996/
    P-A/KG192 . . . . **VCR E**
Earth--Internal structure.
    COLE, J/Magic School Bus inside the earth. /1987/
    2-4/3 KC152 . . . . **551**
    MCNULTY, F/How to dig a hole to the other side of the world. /
    c1979, 1990/2-4/6 KC154 . . . . **CE 551.1**

Earth--Poetry.
EARTH IS PAINTED GREEN: A GARDEN OF POEMS ABOUT OUR
PLANET. /1994/3-6/KD883 . . . . **808.81**

Earth Day.
ROSS, K/Every day is Earth Day: a craft book. /1995/
K-3/5 KD442 . . . . **745.58**

Earth sciences.
OUR CHANGING EARTH (VIDEOCASSETTE). /1991/
3-5/KC153. . . . . **VCR 551**
STV: RESTLESS EARTH (VIDEODISC). /1992/
4-A/KC150 . . . . **VD 550**
VISUAL DICTIONARY OF THE EARTH. /1993/1-A/9 KC151 . **550**

Earth sciences--Remote sensing.
ENGLISH, JA/Mission: Earth: voyage to the home planet. /1996/
4-A/8 KC145 . . . . **550**

Earth sciences--Software.
SCHOLASTIC'S THE MAGIC SCHOOL BUS EXPLORES INSIDE THE
EARTH. SCHOOL ED. /1996/4-A/KC149 . . . . **CDR 550**

Earthmoving machinery.
DIGGERS AND DUMPERS. /1994/K-2/5 KD121 . . . . . . **629.225**
ROYSTON, A/Diggers and dump trucks. /1991/
P-2/4 KD123 . . . . **629.225**

Earthmoving machinery--Pictorial works.
HOBAN, T/Dig, drill, dump, fill. /1975/P-2/KD122 . . . . **629.225**
Earthquakes SEE ALSO Volcanoes.

Earthquakes.
BRANLEY, FM/Earthquakes. /1990/2-4/4 KC161 . . . . . . **551.22**
LAMPTON, C/Earthquake. /1991/5-6/7 KC162 . . . . . . **551.22**
SIMON, S/Earthquakes. /1991/3-6/7 KC163 . . . . **551.22**
SPIES, KB/Earthquakes. /1994/4-6/7 KB038 . . . . **363.34**
STV: RESTLESS EARTH (VIDEODISC). /1992/
4-A/KC150 . . . . **VD 550**
VAN ROSE, S/Volcano and earthquake. /1992/
3-6/7 KC160 . . . . **551.21**

Earthquakes--California--Fiction.
COTTONWOOD, J/Quake!: a novel. /1995/5-A/5 KH034 . . . **Fic**

Earthquakes--California--Northridge (Los Angeles).
VOGEL, CG/Shock waves through Los Angeles: the Northridge
earthquake. /1996/3-6/10 KB039 . . . . **363.34**

Earthquakes--California--San Francisco--Fiction.
GREGORY, K/Earthquake at dawn. /1992/5-A/6 KH202 . . . . . **Fic**

Earthworms.
APPELHOF, M/Worms eat my garbage. /1982/A/12 KC502 . **592**
PASCOE, E/Earthworms. /1997/4-6/4 KC506 . . . . **592**
RECYCLING WITH WORMS (VIDEOCASSETTE). /1995/
3-6/KC507. . . . . **VCR 592**

Earthworms--Experiments.
PASCOE, E/Earthworms. /1997/4-6/4 KC506 . . . . **592**

East Indian Americans--Fiction.
GILMORE, R/Lights for Gita. /1994/1-3/5 KF620 . . . . **E**
PERKINS, M/Sunita experiment. /1993/5-A/6 KH598 . . . . . . **Fic**

Easter.
FISHER, AL/Story of Easter. /1997/2-3/2 KA714 . . . . **263**
HEYER, W/Easter story. /1990/5-6/5 KA710 . . . . . . **232.96**
WINTHROP, E/He is risen: the Easter story. /1985/
5-6/7 KA711 . . . . **232.96**

Easter--Fiction.
FRIEDRICH, P/Easter Bunny that overslept. /1983/P-K/KF587 . . . **E**
HEYWARD, DB/Country bunny and the little gold shoes, as told to
Jenifer. /c1939/P-K/7 KF723. . . . . **E**
HOBAN, T/Where is it? /c1972/P-K/1 KF747 . . . . **E**
MILHOUS, K/Egg tree. /c1950, 1992/1-3/4 KG134 . . . . **E**
POLACCO, P/Chicken Sunday. /1992/1-3/2 KG251. . . . . **E**
WELLS, R/Max's chocolate chicken. /1989/P-2/2 KG702. . . **CE E**

Easter decorations.
ROSS, K/Crafts for Easter. /1995/3-5/KD453 . . . . **745.594**

Easter eggs--Fiction.
MILHOUS, K/Egg tree. /c1950, 1992/1-3/4 KG134 . . . . **E**
POLACCO, P/Rechenka's eggs. /1988/1-3/5 KG256 . . . . . **CE E**
WELLS, R/Max's chocolate chicken. /1989/P-2/2 KG702. . . **CE E**

Eating customs--History.
GIBLIN, JC/From hand to mouth, or how we invented knives, forks,
/1987/5-6/8 KB185 . . . . **394.1**

Eating customs--Wit and humor.
MATHEWS, J/Oh, how waffle!: riddles you can eat. /1993/
2-6/KD735. . . . . **793.735**

Eby family.
ANDERSON, J/Cowboys: roundup on an American ranch. /1996/
3-5/6 KF025 . . . . **978**

Echoes--Fiction.
MACDONALD, A/Little Beaver and The Echo. /1990/
P-K/1 KG049 . . . . **E**

Ecology SEE ALSO Adaption (Biology); Botany--Ecology; Desert ecology;
Forest ecology; Marine ecology; Seashore ecology; etc.

Ecology.
BASH, B/Desert giant: the world of the saguaro cactus. /1989/
2-6/6 KC427 . . . . **583**
CAPON, B/Plant survival: adapting to a hostile world. /1994/
A/9 KC397 . . . . **581.4**
DUNCAN, BK/Explore the wild: a nature search-and-find book. /
1996/2-6/7 KC358 . . . . **578.7**
FISCHER-NAGEL, H/Fir trees. /1989/3-6/7 KC436 . . . . **585**
GEORGE, JC/One day in the tropical rain forest. /1990/
4-6/6 KC315 . . . . **577.34**
GIBBONS, G/Nature's green umbrella: tropical rain forests. /1994/
2-6/5 KC316 . . . . **577.34**
GODKIN, C/Wolf Island. /1993/3-5/4 KC334. . . . . **577.5**
GOLDSTEIN, N/Rebuilding prairies and forests. /1994/
4-6/7 KA955 . . . . **333.74**
HISCOCK, B/Tundra, the Arctic land. /1986/4-A/7 KC335. . **577.5**
HOFF, MK/Our endangered planet: life on land. /1992/
5-6/8 KA962 . . . . **333.95**
JOHNSON, K/Worm's eye view: make your own wildlife refuge. /
1991/2-4/5 KC294 . . . . **577**
KUHN, D/More than just a flower garden. /1990/
4-5/6 KD175 . . . . **635.9**
More than just a vegetable garden. /1990/4-5/5 KD170 . **635**
LAUBER, P/Who eats what?: food chains and food webs. /1995/
K-3/2 KC295 . . . . **577**
LAVIES, B/Compost critters. /1993/5-6/7 KC336 . . . . . **577.5**
Mangrove wilderness: nature's nursery. /1994/
K-3/7 KC341 . . . . **577.68**
LESSEM, D/Inside the amazing Amazon. /1995/
2-6/7 KC319 . . . . **577.34**
LIPTAK, K/Saving our wetlands and their wildlife. /1991/
4-6/8 KA960 . . . . **333.91**
LOEWER, HP/Pond water zoo: an introduction to microscopic life. /
1996/6-A/8 KC372. . . . . **579**
LUENN, N/Squish!: a wetland walk. /1994/P-2/3 KC342. **577.68**
MCLAIN, G/Indian way: learning to communicate with Mother
Earth. /1990/2-6/6 KE750 . . . . **970.1**
MISH, M/Kid's eye view of ecology (Videocassette). /1991/
3-6/KB049 . . . . **VCR 363.7**
ORR, R/Richard Orr's nature cross-sections. /1995/
2-A/8 KC359 . . . . **578.7**
OUR WONDERFUL WETLANDS (VIDEOCASSETTE). /1993/
4-6/KC344. . . . . **VCR 577.68**
PRATT, KJ/Walk in the rainforest. /1992/K-6/7 KC322 . . . **577.34**
PRINGLE, LP/Coral reefs: Earth's undersea treasures. /1995/
5-6/7 KC351 . . . . **577.7**
Fire in the forest: a cycle of growth and renewal. /1995/
A/8 KC305 . . . . **577.2**
RAINFOREST (VIDEOCASSETTE). /1993/
5-A/KC324 . . . . **VCR 577.34**
RING, E/What rot!: nature's mighty recycler. /1996/
1-3/3 KC304 . . . . **577.1**
ROWAN, JP/Prairies and grasslands. /1983/3-6/4 KC331 . . **577.4**
SCHNIEPER, C/Apple tree through the year. /c1982, 1987/
5-6/7 KD163 . . . . **634**
SHAHAN, S/Barnacles eat with their feet: delicious facts about the
tide pool food chain. /1996/3-6/5 KC348 . . . . **577.69**
SIMON, S/Wildfires. /1996/3-6/7 KB041 . . . . **363.37**
SIY, A/Arctic National Wildlife Refuge. /1991/
6-A/6 KC337 . . . . **577.5**
Brazilian rain forest. /1992/4-6/6 KC326 . . . . **577.34**
Great Astrolabe Reef. /1992/4-6/7 KC352. . . . . **577.7**
STAUB, FJ/Yellowstone's cycle of fire. /1993/4-6/8 KC306 . **577.2**
STONE, LM/Temperate forests. /1989/4-6/9 KC310. . . . . . **577.3**
THORNHILL, J/Tree in a forest. /1992/3-5/6 KC311. . . . . . **577.3**
TREE: A LIVING COMMUNITY (VIDEOCASSETTE). /1988/
4-6/KC355. . . . . **VCR 577.8**
TRESSELT, A/Gift of the tree. /c1972, 1992/K-4/6 KC312 . **577.3**
WHAT ARE ECOSYSTEMS? (VIDEOCASSETTE). /1975/
4-6/KC299. . . . . **VCR 577**
WILLOW, D/At home in the rain forest. /1991/
K-4/6 KC328 . . . . **577.34**
WORLD PATROL KIDS /Earth tunes for kids (Videocassette). /
1994/3-6/KC300 . . . . **VCR 577**
YOLEN, J/Welcome to the green house. /1993/
K-3/4 KC329 . . . . **577.34**

Ecology--Amazon River Region.
GOODMAN, SE/Bats, bugs, and biodiversity: adventures in the
Amazonian rain forest. /1995/3-6/7 KC318 . . . . **577.34**

Ecology--Dictionaries.
SIMON, S/Earth words: a dictionary of the environment. /1995/
3-6/9 KB067 . . . . **363.73**

Ecology--Fiction.
    CHERRY, L/Great kapok tree: a tale of the Amazon rain forest. /
        1990/2-3/4 KF380 . . . . **E**
            Great kapok tree (Videocassette). /1996/2-3/KF381. . . . **VCR E**
    GEORGE, JC/Who really killed Cock Robin?: an ecological mystery.
        /c1971, 1991/5-A/7 KH161 . . . . **Fic**
    KELLER, H/Grandfather's dream. /1994/K-2/2 KF883 . . . . **E**
    KELLOGG, S/Island of the skog. /c1973/K-3/5 KF890 . . . . **CE E**
    SELDEN, G/Tucker's countryside. /c1969, 1989/4-6/5 KH698 . **Fic**
    SEUSS, D/Lorax. /c1971/P-3/3 KG466 . . . . **CE E**
    WILDSMITH, B/Professor Noah's spaceship. /1980/
        K-2/5 KG722 . . . . **E**

Ecology--Folklore.
    DESPAIN, P/Eleven nature tales: a multicultural journey. /1996/
        3-5/7 KB286 . . . . **398.2**

Ecology--Iceland--Surtsey.
    LASKY, K/Surtsey: the newest place on earth. /1992/
        A/7 KE697 . . . . **949.12**

Ecology--Software.
    ECOLOGY WITH SEUSS (MICROCOMPUTER PROGRAM). /1990/
        2-5/KB112. . . . . **MCP 372.6**

Ecology--Songs and music.
    AXELROD, G/Songs of nature and environment (Sound recording
        cassette). /1978/1-3/KC293 . . . . **SRC 577**
    CALLINAN, T/Let's clean up our act: songs for the earth (Sound
        recording cassette). /1989/K-6/KD559 . . . . **SRC 789.2**
    STOLTZ, WJ/Come walk with me (Videocassette). /1994/
        P-3/KC309. . . . . **VCR 577.3**
    SUZUKI, D/Connections: finding out about the environment (Sound
        recording cassette). /1990/P-2/KC297. . . . . **SRC 577**

Ecology--Sonoran Desert.
    DUNPHY, M/Here is the southwestern desert. /1995/
        P-3/3 KF066 . . . . **979.1**

Ecology--Wit and humor.
    ARTELL, M/Wackiest nature riddles on earth. /1992/
        3-6/KD724. . . . . **793.735**
    THALER, M/Earth mirth: the ecology riddle book. /1994/
        2-4/KD741. . . . . **793.735**

Ecology, Human SEE Human ecology.
Economics SEE ALSO Depressions-1929; Labor and laboring classes; Land;
    Money; Population; Supply and demand.

Economics--Periodicals.
    ZILLIONS. /1980-/3-5/KA553 . . . . **PER 050**

Ecuador--Social life and customs.
    BEIRNE, B/Children of the Ecuadorean Highlands. /1996/
        3-6/9 KF112 . . . . **986.6**

Edison, Thomas Alva.
    ADLER, DA/Picture book of Thomas Alva Edison. /1996/
        2-3/3 KE330 . . . . **B EDISON, T.**
    MITCHELL, B/Wizard of sound: a story about Thomas Edison. /
        1991/4-6/6 KE331 . . . . **B EDISON, T.**
    NOONAN, J/Nineteenth-century inventors. /1992/
        5-6/7 KC897 . . . . **609**

Edmonds, S. Emma E.
    STEVENS, B/Frank Thompson: her Civil War story. /1992/
        6-A/7 KE332 . . . . **B EDMONDS, S.**

Education SEE ALSO Audio visual education; books and reading; Child
    development; Instructional materials centers; Libraries; Physical education
    and training; Schools; Teachers.

Education.
    PHI DELTA KAPPA EDUCATIONAL FOUNDATION /Fastback series.
        /1972/KA172. . . . . **PROF 370.11**

Education--Aims and objectives--Statistics--Periodicals.
    NATIONAL EDUCATION GOALS REPORT: BUILDING A NATION
        OF LEARNERS. /1991-/KA171 . . . . **PROF 370**

Education--Bibliography.
    EDUCATION INDEX. /1929-/KA105 . . . . **PER PROF 050**

Education--Computer network resources.
    BARRON, AE/Internet and instruction: activities and ideas. /1996/
        /KA047. . . . . **PROF 025.06**
    BENSON, AC/Connecting kids and the Internet: a handbook for
        librarians, teachers, and /1996/KA048. . . . . . **PROF 025.06**

Education--Computer network resources--Directories.
    GIAGNOCAVO, G/Educator's Internet companion: CLASSROOM
        CONNECT's complete guide to educational resources on the
        Internet. 4th ed. /1996/KA049. . . . . **BC PROF 025.06**
    HARRIS, J/Way of the ferret: finding and using educational
        resources on the Internet. 2nd ed. /1995//KA046. **PROF 025.04**

Education--Curricula.
    MEINBACH, AM/Complete guide to thematic units: creating the
        integrated curriculum. /1995//KA195 . . . . **PROF 372.19**

Education--Curricula--Censorship.
    REICHMAN, H/Censorship and selection: issues and answers for
        schools. Rev. ed. /1993//KA053 . . . . **PROF 025.2**

Education--Data processing.
    PAPERT, S/Children's machine: rethinking school in the age of the
        computer. /1993//KA180. . . . . **PROF 371.3**

Education--History.
    FISHER, LE/Schoolmasters. /1997/3-6/7 KB083 . . . . **371.1**

Education--Parent participation.
    KENYON, MP/Home schooling from scratch. /1996/
        /KA175. . . . . **PROF 371.04**
    RADENCICH, MC/How to help your child with homework: every
        caring parent's guide to encouraging /1997/
        /KA181. . . . . **PROF 371.3**

Education--Periodicals.
    EDUCATION DIGEST. /1935-//KA104. . . . . . . **PER PROF 050**
    EDUCATION WEEK. /1981-//KA106. . . . . **PER PROF 050**
    INSTRUCTOR: PRIMARY. /1891-//KA116. . . . . **PER PROF 050**
    LEARNING: SUCCESSFUL TEACHING TODAY. /1972-/
        /KA122. . . . . **PER PROF 050**
    ONLINE--OFFLINE: THEMES AND RESOURCES K-8. /1996-/
        /KA129. . . . . **PER PROF 050**
    PHI DELTA KAPPAN. /1915-//KA131 . . . . **PER PROF 050**

Education--Periodicals--Indexes.
    EDUCATION INDEX. /1929-//KA105 . . . . **PER PROF 050**

Education--Statistics--Periodicals.
    NATIONAL EDUCATION GOALS REPORT: BUILDING A NATION
        OF LEARNERS. /1991-//KA171 . . . . **PROF 370**

Education--United States--History--Colonial period, ca. 1600-1775.
    LOEPER, JJ/Going to school in 1776. /1973/
        4-6/8 KB123 . . . . **372.973**

Education, Elementary SEE ALSO Kindergarten; Montessori method of
    education; Piaget, Jean.

Education, Elementary.
    LANKFORD, MD/Successful field trips. /1992/
        /KA178. . . . . **PROF 371.3**

Education, Elementary--Activity programs.
    HEFNER, CR/Literature-based science: children's books and activities
        to enrich the K-5 /1995//KA200 . . . . **PROF 372.3**

Education, Elementary--Curricula.
    CHILDREN'S LITERATURE IN THE CLASSROOM: WEAVING
        CHARLOTTE'S WEB. /1989//KA238 . . . . **PROF 372.64**
    STORIES AND READERS: NEW PERSPECTIVES ON LITERATURE
        IN THE ELEMENTARY CLASSROOM. /1992/
        /KA241. . . . . **PROF 372.64**
    USING LITERATURE IN THE ELEMENTARY CLASSROOM. REV.
        ED. /1989//KA243. . . . . **PROF 372.64**

Education, Elementary--Information services--Directories.
    MILLER, EB/Internet resource directory for K-12 teachers and
        librarians. /1994-//KA179 . . . . **PROF 371.3**

Education, Elementary--Periodicals.
    TEACHING K-8. /1971-//KA151. . . . . **PER PROF 050**

Education, Preschool.
    BOWDEN, M/Nature for the very young: a handbook of indoor
        and outdoor activities. /1989//KA199. . . . . **PROF 372.3**

Education, Preschool--Periodicals.
    SESAME STREET MAGAZINE. /1971-/P/KA540 . . . . . . **PER 050**

Education, Primary.
    VANDERHEYDEN-TRESCONY, C/Faxing friends; a resource guide
        for forming international friendships among /1992/
        /KA173. . . . . **PROF 370.117**

Education, Primary--Activity programs.
    STORY STARTERS. VOL. 1 (VIDEOCASSETTE). /1995/
        /KA231. . . . . **VCR PROF 372.6**

Education, Primary--Activity programs--Handbooks, manuals, etc.
    RAINES, SC/Story stretchers for the primary grades: activities to
        expand children's /1992//KA240 . . . . **PROF 372.64**

Education, Primary--Case studies.
    DUNN, KB/Trouble with school: a family story about learning
        disabilities. /1993//KA184 . . . . **PROF 371.9**

Education, Secondary--Information services--Directories.
    MILLER, EB/Internet resource directory for K-12 teachers and
        librarians. /1994-//KA179 . . . . **PROF 371.3**

Education libraries.
    WILSON, PP/Professional collection for elementary educators. /
        1996//KA079 . . . . **PROF 027.8**

Educational change--United States.
    STEVENS, SH/Classroom success for the LD and ADHD child. /
        1997//KA186 . . . . **PROF 371.92**

Educational evaluation--States--Statistics--Periodicals.
    NATIONAL EDUCATION GOALS REPORT: BUILDING A NATION
        OF LEARNERS. /1991-//KA171 . . . . **PROF 370**

Educational games.
    GREESON, J/Name that book! Questions and answers on
        outstanding children's books. /1996//KA350 . . . . . . **PROF 809**
    HILLMAN, LE/Nature puzzlers. /1989//KA289 . . . . . . **PROF 508**

ORLANDO, L/Multicultural game book: more than 70 traditional games from 30 countries. /1993//KA323. . . . . . . **PROF 790.1**
RICE, M/Complete book of children's activities. /1993/ /KA194. . . . . **PROF 372.13**
SILBERG, J/500 five minute games: quick and easy activities for 3-6 year olds. /1995//KA325. . . . . **PROF 790.1**

Educational games--Software.
GIZMOS AND GADGETS! (MICROCOMPUTER PROGRAM). /1993/3-6/KB882. . . . . **MCP 507**
NATIONAL INSPIRER (MICROCOMPUTER PROGRAM). /1997/5-A/KE190. . . . . **MCP 917.3**
PLAYROOM (CD-ROM). /1990/P-2/KB085. . . . . . . **CDR 371.3**
PUZZLE TANKS: A GAME OF NUMBERS AND LOGIC (MICROCOMPUTER PROGRAM). /1984/3-A/KB940. . **MCP 511**
SNAPDRAGON (MICROCOMPUTER PROGRAM). /1992/P-1/KA636. . . . . **MCP 153.4**
STRATEGY CHALLENGES COLLECTION 1: AROUND THE WORLD. SCHOOL VERSION (CD-ROM). /1995/3-A/KD754. . . **CDR 794**
STRATEGY CHALLENGES COLLECTION 2: IN THE WILD. SCHOOL VERSION (CD-ROM). /1996/4-A/KD755 . . . . . **CDR 794**
TREEHOUSE (CD-ROM). /1991/K-4/KB086 . . . . **CDR 371.3**
Educational psychology SEE ALSO Child development; Child study; Imagination; Memory; Perception; Thought and thinking.

Educational technology.
BARRON, AE/New technologies for education: a beginner's guide. 3rd ed. /1997//KA176 . . . . **PROF 371.3**
Educators SEE ALSO Teachers.

Educators.
GEORGE WASHINGTON CARVER: A MAN OF VISION (VIDEOCASSETTE). /1990/5-A/KE281 . . . . **VCR B CARVER, G.**
MCKISSACK, P/Carter G. Woodson: the father of black history. /1991/3-6/2 KE601 . . . . **B WOODSON, C.**
Mary McLeod Bethune. /1992/4-6/5 KE254 . . . **B BETHUNE, M.**
O'CONNOR, B/Mammolina: a story about Maria Montessori. /1993/4-6/6 KE467 . . . . **B MONTESSORI, M**
SHEPHARD, MT/Maria Montessori: teacher of teachers. /1996/A/9 KE468 . . . . **B MONTESSORI, M**
VISIT WITH MARVIN TERBAN (VIDEOCASSETTE). /c1991, 1992/5-A/KE560. . . . . **VCR B TERBAN, M.**

Eels.
HALTON, CM/Those amazing eels. /1990/5-6/7 KC597 . . . **597.5**

Egg decoration--Fiction.
POLACCO, P/Chicken Sunday. /1992/1-3/2 KG251. . . . . **E**
Eggs SEE ALSO Birds--Eggs and nests.

Eggs.
BACK, C/Chicken and egg. /1986/K-3/2 KC692 . . . . **598.6**
CHICK EMBRYOLOGY (VIDEOCASSETTE). /c1974, 1986/5-A/KC693 . . . . **VCR 598.6**
COLE, J/Chick hatches. /1977/P-2/3 KC694 . . . . **598.6**
GOLDSEN, L/Egg. /1992/P-3/2 KC281. . . . . **573.6**
JENKINS, PB/Nest full of eggs. /1995/K-2/2 KC705 . . . . **598.8**
JOHNSON, SA/Inside an egg. /1982/4-6/8 KC695. . . . . . **598.6**

Eggs--Fiction.
ERNST, LC/Zinnia and Dot. /1992/P-1/2 KF535 . . . . **E**
JOYCE, W/Bently and egg. /1992/1-3/4 KF857 . . . . **E**
POLACCO, P/Rechenka's eggs. /1988/1-3/5 KG256 . . . . . **CE E**
RUURS, M/Emma's eggs. /1996/P-2/2 KG364 . . . . **E**

Egypt.
KING, DC/Egypt: ancient traditions, modern hopes. /1997/4-6/7 KE634 . . . . **932**

Egypt--Antiquities.
ALIKI /Mummies made in Egypt. /1979/4-6/6 KB173 . . . . . . **393**
BENDICK, J/Egyptian tombs. /1989/4-6/7 KE632 . . . . . . **932**
MANN, E/Great Pyramid. /1996/4-6/6 KE635 . . . . **932**
PERL, L/Mummies, tombs, and treasure: secrets of ancient Egypt. /1987/5-A/8 KE636 . . . . **932**
TRUMBLE, K/Cat mummies. /1996/3-6/9 KE637 . . . . **932**

Egypt--Antiquities--Biography.
FORD, B/Howard Carter: searching for King Tut. /1995/A/9 KE279 . . . . **B CARTER, H.**

Egypt--Antiquities--Fiction.
SNYDER, ZK/Egypt game. /c1967/5-6/6 KH731 . . . . **Fic**

Egypt--Civilization.
MACAULAY, D/Pyramid. /1975/A/10 KD357 . . . . **CE 690**

Egypt--Civilization--To 332 B.C.
HART, G/Ancient Egypt. /1990/5-6/8 KE633 . . . . **932**
MANN, E/Great Pyramid. /1996/4-6/6 KE635 . . . . **932**

Egypt--Fiction.
OPPENHEIM, SL/Hundredth name. /c1995, 1997/2-3/2 KG194 . **E**
WALSH, JP/Pepi and the secret names. /1995/2-3/6 KG683 . . . **E**

Egypt--Folklore.
KIMMEL, EA/Rimonah of the Flashing Sword: a North African tale. /1995/3-4/4 KB331 . . . . **398.2**

Egyptian language--Writing, Hieroglyphic.
GIBLIN, JC/Riddle of the Rosetta Stone: key to ancient Egypt. /1990/5-A/7 KB865 . . . . **493**
KATAN, NJ/Hieroglyphs, the writing of ancient Egypt. /1981/5-6/9 KB866 . . . . **493**

Ehlert, Lois.
EHLERT, L/Under my nose. /1996/3-6/2 KE333 . . . . **B EHLERT, L.**

Einstein, Albert.
MCPHERSON, SS/Ordinary genius: the story of Albert Einstein. /1995/5-A/6 KE334 . . . . **B EINSTEIN, A.**

Eisenhower, Dwight D.
DARBY, J/Dwight D. Eisenhower: a man called Ike. /1989/5-6/6 KE335 . . . . **B EISENHOWER, D**

Eisenreich, Jim.
GUTMAN, B/Jim Eisenreich. /1996/3-5/6 KE336 . . . . **B EISENREICH, J**

El Chino (Bong Way Wong).
SAY, A/El Chino. /1990/3-5/4 KE598 . . . . **B WONG, B.**
Elderly SEE ALSO Aged; Old Age.
Elections SEE ALSO Women--Suffrage.

Elections.
MAESTRO, B/Voice of the people: American democracy in action. /1996/4-6/8 KA915 . . . . **324.973**

Elections--United States.
ELECTING A PRESIDENT: THE PROCESS (VIDEOCASSETTE). /1993/6-A/KA913 . . . . **VCR 324.973**
ELECTING A PRESIDENT (VIDEOCASSETTE). /1995/6-A/KA914 . . . . **VCR 324.973**
STEINS, R/Our elections. /1994/5-6/7 KA912. . . . . **324.6**

Electric circuits.
HOT LINE: ALL ABOUT ELECTRICITY (VIDEOCASSETTE). /1987/4-A/KD042 . . . . **VCR 621.31**

Electric currents.
JUNIOR ELECTRICIAN (VIDEOCASSETTE). /1991/3-6/KC132. . . . . **VCR 537**

Electric engineering.
JUNIOR ELECTRICIAN (VIDEOCASSETTE). /1991/3-6/KC132. . . . . **VCR 537**

Electric lamps.
LIGHT BULBS (VIDEOCASSETTE). /1991/1-3/KD043. **VCR 621.32**

Electric lighting.
LIGHT BULBS (VIDEOCASSETTE). /1991/1-3/KD043. **VCR 621.32**

Electric power.
PARKER, S/Electricity. /1992/4-A/9 KC134. . . . . **537**

Electricity.
BERGER, M/Switch on, switch off. /1989/K-3/5 KC130. . . . **537**
HOOPER, T/Electricity. /1994/5-6/11 KC131. . . . . **537**
HOT LINE: ALL ABOUT ELECTRICITY (VIDEOCASSETTE). /1987/4-A/KD042 . . . . **VCR 621.31**
JUNIOR ELECTRICIAN (VIDEOCASSETTE). /1991/3-6/KC132. . . . . **VCR 537**
PARKER, S/Electricity. /1992/4-A/9 KC134. . . . . **537**

Electricity--Experiments.
ARDLEY, N/Science book of electricity. /1991/2-5/3 KC129. . **537**
HOT LINE: ALL ABOUT ELECTRICITY (VIDEOCASSETTE). /1987/4-A/KD042 . . . . **VCR 621.31**
MARKLE, S/Power up: experiments, puzzles, and games exploring electricity. /1989/3-6/7 KC133 . . . . **537**

Electronic mail systems.
BRIMNER, LD/E-mail. /1997/2-4/3 KB134 . . . . **384.3**

Elementary school libraries.
POWER UP YOUR LIBRARY: CREATING THE NEW ELEMENTARY SCHOOL LIBRARY PROGRAM. /1996//KA078 . . . **PROF 027.8**

Elementary school libraries--Book lists.
ADVENTURING WITH BOOKS: A BOOKLIST FOR PRE-K-GRADE 6. 1997 ED. /1997//KA009 . . . . **PROF 011.62**
ELEMENTARY SCHOOL LIBRARY COLLECTION: A GUIDE TO BOOKS AND OTHER MEDIA, /1998//KA013 . . . **PROF 011.62**

Elementary school libraries--Book lists--Software.
ELEMENTARY SCHOOL LIBRARY COLLECTION: A GUIDE TO BOOKS AND OTHER MEDIA, /1998/ /KA014. . . . . **CDR PROF 011.62**

Elementary school teaching--United States.
MEINBACH, AM/Complete guide to thematic units: creating the integrated curriculum. /1995//KA195 . . . . **PROF 372.19**

Elementary school teaching--United States--Case studies.
KIDDER, T/Among schoolchildren. /1989//KA192 . . . . **PROF 372.11**

Elephants.
ARNOLD, C/Elephant. /1993/5-6/9 KC808. . . . . **599.67**
ELEPHANT DIARY (VIDEOCASSETTE). /1990/3-5/KC809. **VCR 599.67**
GRACE, ES/Elephants. /1993/5-6/8 KC810 . . . . **599.67**

MACMILLAN, D/Elephants: our last land giants. /1993/
5-6/8 KC811 . . . . **599.67**
MCCLUNG, RM/Old Bet and the start of the American circus. /
1993/4-6/6 KD682 . . . . **791.3**
MOSS, C/Little big ears; the story of Ely. /1997/
K-4/6 KC812 . . . . **599.67**
PATENT, DH/African elephants: giants of the land. /1991/
4-6/6 KC813 . . . . **599.67**
PLIGHT OF THE ASIAN ELEPHANT (VIDEOCASSETTE). /1993/
5-6/KC814. . . . . **VCR 599.67**
REDMOND, I/Elephant. /1993/4-6/7 KC815 . . . . **599.67**
SCHMIDT, J/In the village of the elephants. /1994/
4-6/6 KC816 . . . . **599.67**

Elephants--Fiction.
CAPLE, K/Biggest nose. /1985/P-2/2 KF337 . . . . **E**
CROSS, G/Great American elephant chase. /1993/
6-A/6 KH043 . . . . **Fic**
CUMMING, P/Mogul and me. /1989/5-A/7 KH046 . . . . **Fic**
DAY, A/Frank and Ernest on the road. /1994/2-3/2 KF451 . . . . **E**
    Frank and Ernest play ball. /1990/2-3/4 KF452 . . . . . . **E**
DE BRUNHOFF, J/Story of Babar, the little elephant. /c1937,
1960/P-2/3 KF453 . . . . **E**
FORD, M/Little elephant. /1994/P-K/1 KF565 . . . . **E**
HARVEY, D/Secret elephant of Harlan Kooter. /1992/
4-A/6 KH223 . . . . **Fic**
LEWIS, K/My friend Harry. /1995/P-1/2 KF976 . . . . **E**
LOBEL, A/Uncle Elephant. /1981/K-1/1 KG014 . . . . **E**
PEET, B/Encore for Eleanor. /1981/K-2/7 KG226. . . . . **E**
PETERSHAM, M/Circus baby. /c1950/P-2/3 KG235. . . . . . **CE E**
SEUSS, D/Horton hatches the egg. /c1940/P-3/3 KG456 . . **CE E**
    Horton hatches the egg./If I ran the circus (Videocassette). /
1992/P-3/KG457 . . . . **VCR E**
    Horton hears a Who!/Thidwick the big-hearted moose
(Videocassette). /1992/P-3/KG458 . . . . **VCR E**

Elephants--Folklore.
FARRIS, PJ/Young Mouse and Elephant: an East African folktale. /
1996/K-2/4 KB565 . . . . **398.24**
FROESE, DL/Wise washerman: a folktale from Burma. /1996/
K-2/7 KB569 . . . . **398.24**
YOUNG, E/Seven blind mice. /1992/K-3/2 KB681 . . . . . . **398.24**

Elevators--Fiction.
SIS, P/Going up! A color counting book. /1989/P-2/KG511 . . . **E**

Elijah (Biblical prophet)--Fiction.
SILVERMAN, E/Gittel's hands. /1996/K-2/2 KG506 . . . . **E**

Elizabeth I, Queen of England.
STANLEY, D/Good Queen Bess: the story of Elizabeth I of England.
/1990/6-A/7 KE337 . . . . **B ELIZABETH I**

Elk.
ARNOLD, C/Tule elk. /1989/5-6/8 KC794 . . . . **599.65**
LEPTHIEN, EU/Elk. /1994/4-6/5 KC798 . . . . **599.65**
NATURE'S NEWBORN: ELK, MOOSE, DEER (VIDEOCASSETTE). /
1994/3-6/KC799 . . . . **VCR 599.65**

Ellington, Duke.
OLD, WC/Duke Ellington: giant of jazz. /1996/
5-A/9 KE338 . . . . **B ELLINGTON, D.**

Ellis Island Immigration Station (New York, N.Y.)--Fiction.
WOODRUFF, E/Orphan of Ellis Island: a time-travel adventure. /
1997/5-A/5 KH881 . . . . **Fic**

Ellis Island Immigration Station (New York, N.Y.)--History.
I WAS DREAMING TO COME TO AMERICA: MEMORIES FROM
THE ELLIS ISLAND ORAL HISTORY PROJECT. /1995/
4-6/7 KA916 . . . . **325**
JACOBS, WJ/Ellis Island: new hope in a new land. /1990/
3-6/6 KA919 . . . . **325**
KROLL, S/Ellis Island: doorway to freedom. /1995/
2-4/10 KA920 . . . . **325**
MAESTRO, B/Coming to America: the story of immigration. /1996/
1-3/8 KA921 . . . . **325**

Elves--Fiction.
STEVENSON, J/Oldest elf. /1996/P-2/2 KG565 . . . . **E**

Emblems, National--Canada.
CANADA'S MAPLE TREE: THE STORY OF THE COUNTRY'S
EMBLEM (VIDEOCASSETTE). /1995/1-4/KE615. . . . **VCR 929.9**

Emblems, State.
ALABAMA TO WYOMING: FLAGS OF THE UNITED STATES
(VIDEOCASSETTE). /1994/4-6/KE612 . . . . **VCR 929.9**
LANDAU, E/State birds: including the Commonwealth of Puerto
Rico. /1992/4-6/8 KC653. . . . . **598**
    State flowers: including the Commonwealth of Puerto Rico. /1992/
3-6/8 KC406 . . . . **582.13**
SHEARER, BF/State names, seals, flags, and symbols: a historical
guide. Rev. and expanded /1994/4-A/KA493. . . . . . . **REF 973**

Embroidery--Panama.
PRESILLA, ME/Mola: Cuna life stories and art. /1996/
3-5/7 KA832 . . . . **305.48**

Embroidery, Hmong.
CHA, D/Dia's story cloth. /1996/2-6/6 KE716 . . . . **959.404**

Embroidery, Mexican.
PRESILLA, ME/Life around the lake. /1996/2-6/8 KE837 . . . . **972**
Embryology SEE ALSO Cells; Reproduction.

Embryology.
CHICK EMBRYOLOGY (VIDEOCASSETTE). /c1974, 1986/
5-A/KC693 . . . . **VCR 598.6**
COLE, J/Chick hatches. /1977/P-2/3 KC694 . . . . **598.6**
SELSAM, ME/Egg to chick. Rev. ed. /1970/P-2/2 KC698 . . **598.6**
Emergencies SEE Disasters; First aid; Floods; Hurricanes; Natural disasters.

Emergency medical services.
EMERGENCY 911 (VIDEOCASSETTE). /1994/
2-5/KB135. . . . . **VCR 384.6**
USING 911: PROTECT YOURSELF (VIDEOCASSETTE). /1995/
2-6/KB136 . . . . **VCR 384.6**

Emergency vehicles.
GIBBONS, G/Emergency! /1994/P-1/6 KB032 . . . . **363.3**

Emigration and immigration--Fiction.
AVI /Beyond the western sea: book one: the escape from home. /
1996/6-A/5 KG857 . . . . **Fic**
    Beyond the western sea: book two: Lord Kirkle's money. /1996/
6-A/5 KG858. . . . . **Fic**
BARTONE, E/American too. /1996/1-3/3 KF210 . . . . **E**
COHEN, B/Molly's pilgrim. /1983/1-3/4 KH012 . . . . . . **CE Fic**
GILMORE, R/Lights for Gita. /1994/1-3/5 KF620 . . . . **E**
HARVEY, B/Immigrant girl: Becky of Eldridge Street. /1987/
3-5/5 KH221 . . . . **Fic**
HEROLD, MR/Very important day. /1995/K-3/2 KF715 . . . . . . **E**
POLACCO, P/Keeping quilt. /1988/K-3/6 KG252 . . . . **CE E**
PRYOR, B/Dream jar. /1996/2-3/5 KG291 . . . . **E**
ROSS, LH/Sarah, also known as Hannah. /1994/
4-6/4 KH655 . . . . **Fic**
SACHS, M/Call me Ruth. /c1982, 1995/5-A/6 KH667 . . . . . . **Fic**
SAY, A/Grandfather's journey. /1993/2-4/5 KG397. . . . . **E**
SCHUR, MR/When I left my village. /1996/4-A/5 KH683 . . . . **Fic**
STANEK, M/I speak English for my mom. /1989/
2-4/2 KH747 . . . . **Fic**
WOODRUFF, E/Orphan of Ellis Island: a time-travel adventure. /
1997/5-A/5 KH881 . . . . **Fic**

Emigration and immigration--Software.
IMMIGRATION (MICROCOMPUTER PROGRAM). /1996/
5-A/KA917 . . . . **MCP 325**

Emotional problems--Fiction.
CASSEDY, S/Lucie Babbidge's house. /1993/6-A/7 KG987 . . . **Fic**
CUTLER, J/Spaceman. /1997/4-A/2 KH053 . . . . **Fic**
MCKENZIE, EK/Stargone John. /1990/3-5/5 KH484. . . . . . **Fic**
SNYDER, ZK/Trespassers. /1995/5-A/6 KH734 . . . . **Fic**
Emotions SEE ALSO Fear; Happiness; Joy and sorrow; Love; Prejudices.

Emotions.
ANGRY JOHN (VIDEOCASSETTE). /1994/
4-6/KA622 . . . . **VCR 152.4**
DADDY DOESN'T LIVE WITH US (VIDEOCASSETTE). /1994/
P-1/KA889. . . . . **VCR 306.89**
I'M SO FRUSTRATED! (VIDEOCASSETTE). /1994/
1-3/KA627 . . . . **VCR 152.4**
MURPHY, J/Songs for you and me: kids learn about feelings and
emotions (Sound recording cassette). /n.d./
K-1/KA629 . . . . **SRC 152.4**
SIMON, N/I was so mad. /1974/P-2/2 KA630 . . . . **152.4**
WHEN I GET MAD (VIDEOCASSETTE). /1994/
5-6/KA631 . . . . **VCR 152.4**
WHEN MOM AND DAD DIVORCE (VIDEOCASSETTE). /1994/
4-6/KA890 . . . . **VCR 306.89**
WHEN THERE'S TROUBLE AT HOME (VIDEOCASSETTE). /1991/
A/KA883 . . . . **VCR 306.874**
YOUNG, E/Voices of the heart. /1997/A/7 KA675 . . . . **179**

Emotions--Fiction.
SEUSS, D/My many colored days. /1996/K-2/2 KG468 . . . . . . **E**
STEIG, W/Spinky sulks. /1988/1-A/5 KH752 . . . . **Fic**

Emotions--Pictorial works.
HOW DO I FEEL? (PICTURE). /1974/1-3/KA625 . . . . . **PIC 152.4**

Emotions--Poetry.
DE REGNIERS, BS/Way I feel--sometimes. /1988/1-4/KD931 . . **811**

Emotions--Songs and music.
HARTMANN, J/Let's read together and other songs for sharing and
caring /1991/P-2/KD616 . . . . **SRC 789.3**

Emotions and social attitudes--Software.
PREJUDICE (MICROCOMPUTER PROGRAM). /1992/
5-A/KA820 . . . . **MCP 305**

Emperors SEE Kings, queens, rulers, etc.
Employment of Women SEE Women--Employment; Women artists, etc.

Emus.
> ARNOLD, C/Ostriches and other flightless birds. /1990/
> 5-6/7 KC690 . . . . **598.5**

Encyclopedias and dictionaries SEE ALSO English language--Dictionaries;
Spanish language--Dictionaries, etc.

Encyclopedias and dictionaries.
> ANIMATED DICTIONARY (VIDEOCASSETTE). /1992/
> 3-5/KA588 . . . . **VCR 028.7**
> ANIMATED ENCYCLOPEDIA (VIDEOCASSETTE). /1990/
> 3-6/KA583 . . . . **VCR 025.5**
> CHILDCRAFT: THE HOW AND WHY LIBRARY. /1964-/
> P-2/KA378. . . . . **REF 031**
> CHILDREN'S BRITANNICA. 4TH ED., (1995 REVISION). /1995/
> 3-5/KA379 . . . . **REF 031**
> COMPTON'S ENCYCLOPEDIA AND FACT-INDEX. /1968-/
> 5-6/KA380 . . . . **REF 031**
> GUINNESS BOOK OF WORLD RECORDS. /1955-/
> 4-6/KA403 . . . . **REF 310**
> KANE, JN/Famous first facts. 5th ed. /1997/4-6/KA382 . **REF 031**
> KINGFISHER CHILDREN'S ENCYCLOPEDIA. REV. ED. /1992/
> /KA383 . . . . **REF 031**
> NEW AMERICAN DESK ENCYCLOPEDIA. 3RD REV. /1993/
> 4-A/KA589 . . . . **031**
> NEW BOOK OF KNOWLEDGE. /1997/4-6/KA385 . . . **REF 031**
> PETERSON, PR/Know it all: resource book for kids. /1989/
> 4-A/6 KA591 . . . . **031.02**
> RAINTREE STECK-VAUGHN ILLUSTRATED SCIENCE
> ENCYCLOPEDIA. NEWLY REVISED. /1997/3-5/KA434 . **REF 503**
> WORLD BOOK ENCYCLOPEDIA. /1931-/5-A/KA386 . . . **REF 031**
> WORLD BOOK ENCYCLOPEDIA OF PEOPLE AND PLACES. /
> 1997//KA387 . . . . **REF 031**
> WORLDMARK ENCYCLOPEDIA OF THE NATIONS. 9TH ED. /
> 1997/A/KA389 . . . . **REF 031**

Encyclopedias and dictionaries--Software.
> COMPTON'S MULTIMEDIA ENCYCLOPEDIA (CD-ROM). /1994/
> 3-6/KA381 . . . . **CDR REF 031**
> MICROSOFT BOOKSHELF: MULTIMEDIA REFERENCE LIBRARY,
> 1998 ED. SCHOOL ED. (CD-ROM). /1997/
> 3-A/KA376 . . . . **CDR REF 028.7**
> MICROSOFT ENCARTA 97 ENCYCLOPEDIA. DELUXE SCHOOL
> ED. (CD-ROM). /1996/4-A/KA384 . . . . **CDR REF 031**
> PRESIDENTS: IT ALL STARTED WITH GEORGE (CD-ROM). /
> 1991/2-A/KA491 . . . . **CDR REF 973**
> STUDENT WRITING AND RESEARCH CENTER WITH COMPTON'S
> CONCISE ENCYCLOPEDIA /1995/4-A/KB091 . . . **CDR 371.302**
> WORLD BOOK 1997 MULTIMEDIA ENCYCLOPEDIA. DELUXE ED.
> (CD-ROM). /1997/3-A/KA388 . . . . **CDR REF 031**

Endangered species SEE ALSO Rare and endangered species; Rare animals;
Rare birds.

Endangered species.
> BLASHFIELD, JF/Rescuing endangered species. /1994/
> 4-6/7 KA961 . . . . **333.95**
> ENDANGERED ANIMALS: SURVIVORS ON THE BRINK
> (VIDEOCASSETTE). /1997/4-6/KC486 . . . . **VCR 591.68**
> ENDANGERED SPECIES (VIDEOCASSETTE). /1991/
> 4-6/KC487. . . . . **VCR 591.68**
> KIM, M/Mountain gorilla. /1993/4-5/8 KC875 . . . . . . **599.884**
> LONG, M/Any bear can wear glasses: the spectacled bear and
> other curious creatures. /1995/4-6/6 KC451. . . . . **591**
> MANATEES: RED ALERT (VIDEOCASSETTE). /1996/
> 5-6/KC782. . . . . **VCR 599.55**
> NIRGIOTIS, N/No more dodos: how zoos help endangered wildlife.
> /1996/A/6 KD256 . . . . **639.9**
> SAVING THE MANATEE (VIDEOCASSETTE). /1993/
> 2-6/KC783. . . . . **VCR 599.55**

Endangered species--Songs and music.
> WEEKS, S/Crocodile smile: 10 songs of the Earth as the animals see
> it. /1994/P-2/KD665 . . . . **BA 789.3**

Energy SEE ALSO Force and energy; Power resources.

Energy--Software.
> COLONIZATION (MICROCOMPUTER PROGRAM). /1986/
> 5-A/KA667 . . . . **MCP 172**

Energy conservation.
> GOLDSMITH, S/Man who loved machines (Videocassette). /1983/
> 3-A/KC127 . . . . **VCR 536**
> POWER UP?: ENERGY IN OUR ENVIRONMENT
> (VIDEOCASSETTE). /1992/4-6/KA956 . . . . **VCR 333.79**
> SIMPLE THINGS YOU CAN DO TO SAVE ENERGY IN YOUR
> SCHOOL (VIDEOCASSETTE). /1995/4-6/KA957 . **VCR 333.791**

Energy resources.
> SIMPLE THINGS YOU CAN DO TO SAVE ENERGY IN YOUR
> SCHOOL (VIDEOCASSETTE). /1995/4-6/KA957 . **VCR 333.791**

Engineering SEE ALSO Aeronautics; Airplanes--Design and construction; Civil
engineering; Mechanics.

Engineering.
> TUNNELS (VIDEOCASSETTE). /1987/5-6/KD071. . . . **VCR 624.1**

Engineering--Experiments.
> BEN FRANKLIN BOOK OF EASY AND INCREDIBLE EXPERIMENTS.
> /1995/A/8 KB889 . . . . **507.8**

Engineers.
> MANN, E/Brooklyn Bridge. /1996/5-6/5 KD068 . . . . **624**

Engines SEE ALSO Fire engines; Locomotives; Steam engines.
England SEE ALSO Great Britain.

England--Fiction.
> AIKEN, J/Cold Shoulder Road. /1995/5-A/5 KG823 . . . . . **Fic**
> Is underground. /1993/5-A/7 KG824 . . . . **Fic**
> Wolves of Willoughby Chase. /c1962, 1987/
> 5-A/7 KG826 . . . . **CE Fic**
> ANDERSON, R/Bus people. /1995/6-A/6 KG850 . . . . . . **Fic**
> AVI /Beyond the western sea: book one: the escape from home. /
> 1996/6-A/5 KG857 . . . . **Fic**
> BAWDEN, N/House of secrets. /c1963, 1992/5-A/7 KG890 . . **Fic**
> BURNETT, FH/Little princess. /c1963/5-A/8 KG949 . . . . . **Fic**
> Sara Crewe. /1986/4-6/7 KG950. . . . . **Fic**
> CUSHMAN, K/Catherine, called Birdy. /1994/
> 6-A/6 KH050 . . . . **CE Fic**
> DICKENS, C/Christmas Carol in prose, being a ghost story of
> Christmas. /1983/4-6/5 KH074 . . . . **CE Fic**
> DICKINSON, P/Chuck and Danielle. /1996/4-6/7 KH076. . . . **Fic**
> GLEITZMAN, M/Misery guts. /1993/5-A/7 KH174. . . . . . . **Fic**
> GODDEN, R/Listen to the nightingale. /c1992, 1994/
> 5-A/6 KH178 . . . . **Fic**
> GRAHAM, H/Boy and his bear. /1996/5-A/5 KH186 . . . . . **Fic**
> JAMES, S/Leon and Bob. /1997/K-2/2 KF824 . . . . **E**
> JONES, DW/Witch week. New ed. /c1982, 1993/
> 6-A/6 KH335 . . . . **Fic**
> KING-SMITH, D/Lady Daisy (Talking book). /1995/
> 4-6/KH350 . . . . **TB Fic**
> Sophie's Tom. /c1991, 1994/3-5/5 KH357 . . . . **Fic**
> LEWIS, JP/Christmas of the reddle moon. /1994/1-3/4 KF975 . . **E**
> MCCULLY, EA/Little Kit or, The Industrious Flea Circus girl. /1995/
> 2-4/4 KG092 . . . . **E**
> MCKAY, H/Amber cat. /1997/5-8/6 KH476 . . . . **Fic**
> Dog Friday. /1995/4-A/7 KH477 . . . . **Fic**
> Exiles at home. /1994/5-A/7 KH479 . . . . **Fic**
> MORPURGO, M/Butterfly lion. /1997/5-A/5 KH512 . . . . . . **Fic**
> NESBIT, E/Enchanted castle. /1992/5-A/6 KH542 . . . . . . **Fic**
> TRAVERS, PL/Mary Poppins. Rev. ed. /c1962/4-6/6 KH800. . . **Fic**
> WAUGH, S/Mennyms. /1994/5-A/7 KH843 . . . . **Fic**
> Mennyms alone. /1996/5-A/5 KH844 . . . . **Fic**
> Mennyms in the wilderness. /1995/5-A/5 KH845 . . . . . **Fic**
> Mennyms under siege. /1996/6-A/6 KH846 . . . . **Fic**

England--Folklore.
> COHEN, B/Robin Hood and Little John. /1995/
> 2-4/4 KB433 . . . . **398.22**
> CURRY, JL/Christmas Knight. /1993/2-5/3 KB435. . . . . . **398.22**
> Robin Hood and his Merry Men. /1994/3-5/3 KB436 . . **398.22**
> Robin Hood in the greenwood. /1995/3-5/3 KB437 . . . **398.22**
> DESPAIN, P/Strongheart Jack and the beanstalk. /1995/
> 2-5/3 KB287 . . . . **398.2**
> FOSTER, J/Magpies' nest. /1995/1-3/3 KB567 . . . . **398.24**
> FRENCH, V/Lazy Jack. /1995/K-2/2 KB301 . . . . **398.2**
> GIBLIN, JC/Dwarf, the giant, and the unicorn: a tale of King Arthur.
> /1996/3-5/4 KB443 . . . . **398.22**
> HODGES, M/Molly Limbo. /1996/K-3/3 KB688. . . . . . . **398.25**
> Of swords and sorcerers: the adventures of King Arthur and his
> knights. /1993/4-5/6 KB452 . . . . **398.22**
> Saint George and the dragon: a golden legend. /1984/
> 5/7 KB453. . . . . **CE 398.22**
> HOWE, J/Knight with the lion: the story of Yvain. /1996/
> 5-6/6 KB455 . . . . **398.22**
> HUCK, CS/Princess Furball. /1989/3-4/6 KB465 . . . . **CE 398.27**
> KELLOGG, S/Jack and the beanstalk. /1991/2-3/4 KB325. . **398.2**
> KIMMEL, EA/Old woman and her pig. /1992/
> K-2/2 KB603 . . . . **398.24**
> LISTER, R/Story of King Arthur. /1997/4/7 KB465. . . . . . **398.22**
> METAXAS, E/Jack and the beanstalk (Videocassette). /1991/
> K-2/KB349. . . . . **VCR 398.2**
> PERHAM, M/King Arthur: the legends of Camelot. /1993/
> 5-A/7 KB471 . . . . **398.22**
> ROWE, JA/Gingerbread Man: an old English folktale. /1996/
> P-K/2 KB363 . . . . **398.2**
> SABUDA, R/Arthur and the sword. /1995/3-5/5 KB479 . . **398.22**
> SAN SOUCI, RD/Hobyahs. /1996/3-4/6 KB647. . . . . . . **398.24**
> Young Guinevere. /1993/3-4/6 KB482. . . . . **398.22**
> Young Lancelot. /1996/4-5/6 KB483 . . . . **398.22**

Young Merlin. /c1990, 1996/4-5/6 KB484 . . . . **398.22**
SINGER, M/Maiden on the moor. /1995/4-6/3 KB418 . . . **398.21**
TALBOTT, H/King Arthur and the Round Table. /1995/
4-5/6 KB490 . . . . **398.22**
English authors SEE Authors, English.

English language--Adjectives.
HELLER, R/Many luscious lollipops: a book about adjectives. /1989/
1-3/KB851 . . . . **428.2**

English language--Adverb.
HELLER, R/Up, up and away: a book about adverbs. /1991/
1-3/KB852 . . . . **428.2**

English language--Collective nouns.
GREENWAY, S/Two's company. /1997/K-2/3 KB845 . . . . . **428.1**
HELLER, R/Cache of jewels and other collective nouns. /c1987,
1989/P-3/KB846 . . . . **428.1**

English language--Composition and exercises.
BOSMA, B/Fairy tales, fables, legends and myths: using folk
literature in your classroom. /1992//KA177 . . . . . . **PROF 371.3**
JAMES, E/How to write a great school report. /1983/
4-6/7 KB088 . . . . **371.302**
MELTON, D/Written & illustrated by... a revolutionary two-brain
approach for teaching /1985//KA226 . . . . **PROF 372.6**

English language--Composition and exercises--Software.
BRIDGE TO TERABITHIA: A MULTI-MEDIA STUDY
(MICROCOMPUTER PROGRAM). /1993/
5-A/KB108 . . . . **MCP 372.6**
CHARLOTTE'S WEB: A WRITE ON! MULTI-MEDIA STUDY
(MICROCOMPUTER PROGRAM). /1992/3-6/KB110 . **MCP 372.6**
DESTINATION: OCEAN. SCHOOL VERSION (CD-ROM). /1995/
1-A/KB111 . . . . **CDR 372.6**
MICROSOFT CREATIVE WRITER 2. SCHOOL ED. (CD-ROM). /
1996/2-A/KB114 . . . . : **CDR 372.6**
STORYBOOK WEAVER DELUXE (CD-ROM). /1995/
1-5/KB118 . . . . **CDR 372.6**
WRITING ALONG THE OREGON TRAIL (MICROCOMPUTER
PROGRAM). /1994/4-A/KB121 . . . . **MCP 372.6**

English language--Composition and exercises--Study and teaching.
LANKFORD, MD/Successful field trips. /1992/
/KA178 . . . . **PROF 371.3**
ROBERTSON, D/Super kids publishing company. /1990/
/KA333 . . . . **PROF 808**
SHELNUTT, E/Magic pencil: teaching children creative writing:
exercises and activities for /1994//KA228 . . . . **PROF 372.6**
STORY STARTERS. VOL. 1 (VIDEOCASSETTE). /1995/
/KA231 . . . . **VCR PROF 372.6**

**English language--Composition and exercises--Study and teaching
(Primary).**
SLAUGHTER, JP/Beyond storybooks: young children and the shared
book experience. /1993//KA215 . . . . **PROF 372.4**

English language--Compound words.
MAESTRO, B/All aboard overnight: a book of compound words. /
1992/P-3/3 KB848 . . . . **428.1**

English language--Consonants--Fiction.
TURNER, P/War between the Vowels and the Consonants. /1996/
1-3/3 KG630 . . . . **E**

English language--Dictionaries.
AMERICAN HERITAGE CHILDREN'S DICTIONARY. /1997/
3-6/KA417 . . . . **REF 423**
AMERICAN HERITAGE FIRST DICTIONARY. /1997/
1-3/KA418 . . . . **REF 423**
AMERICAN HERITAGE STUDENT DICTIONARY. /1994/
6-A/KA419 . . . . **REF 423**
CAT IN THE HAT BEGINNER BOOK DICTIONARY. /c1964, 1984/
1-2/KB833 . . . . **423**
HARCOURT BRACE STUDENT DICTIONARY. 2ND ED. /1994/
4-6/KA421 . . . . **REF 423**
KINGFISHER FIRST DICTIONARY. /1995/1-2/KA424 . . . **REF 423**
MACMILLAN DICTIONARY FOR CHILDREN. 3RD. REV. ED. /
1997/2-4/KA425 . . . . **REF 423**
MACMILLAN FIRST DICTIONARY. /1990/K-2/KB834 . . . . **423**
RANDOM HOUSE WEBSTER'S COLLEGE DICTIONARY. 2ND ED.
/1997/6-A/KA428 . . . . **REF 423**
ROOT, B/My first dictionary. /1993/P-2/KB835 . . . . **423**
SCHOLASTIC CHILDREN'S DICTIONARY. REV. ED. /1996/
4-6/KA430 . . . . **REF 423**
SCOTT FORESMAN BEGINNING DICTIONARY. /c1983, 1994/
2-4/KB836 . . . . **423**
WEBSTER'S INTERMEDIATE DICTIONARY: A NEW SCHOOL
DICTIONARY. /c1977, 1994/4-6/KB837 . . . . **423**
WEBSTER'S NEW WORLD CHILDREN'S DICTIONARY. NEW ED. /
1997/3-5/KB838 . . . . **423**
WORLD BOOK DICTIONARY. /1996/5-6/KA432 . . . . . . **REF 423**
WORLD BOOK STUDENT DICTIONARY. REV. ED. /1995/
3-5/KB840 . . . . **423**

English language--Dictionaries--Software.
MY FIRST AMAZING WORDS AND PICTURES (CD-ROM). /
1994/K-3/KA426 . . . . **CDR REF 423**

English language--Dictionaries--Spanish.
LIPTON, GC/Beginning Spanish bilingual dictionary: a beginner's
guide in words and /1989/3-A/KB859 . . . . **463**

English language--Etymology.
BREWER'S DICTIONARY OF PHRASE AND FABLE. 15TH ED. /
1995/5-6/KA459 . . . . **REF 803**
DEWEY, A/Naming colors. /1995/4-8/8 KC120. . . . . **535.6**
GRAHAM-BARBER, L/Doodle Dandy!: the complete book of
Independence Day words. /1992/5-A/A KB220. . . . . . **394.263**
Ho Ho Ho!: the complete book of Christmas words. /1993/
2-6/8 KB235 . . . . **394.266**
Mushy! the complete book of Valentine words. /1991/
5-6/8 KB209 . . . . **394.261**
PALMATIER, RA/Speaking of animals: a dictionary of animal
metaphors. /1995/6-A/KA427. . . . . **REF 423**
TERBAN, M/Superdupers! really funny real words. /1989/
3-6/6 KB850 . . . . **428.1**

English language--Grammar.
TERBAN, M/Checking your grammar. /1993/5-A/KB856 . . . **428.2**

English language--Grammar--Software.
DR. SEUSS'S ABC (CD-ROM). /1995/P-2/KF493. . . . . . . **CDR E**
MY FIRST SENTENCES (MICROCOMPUTER PROGRAM). /1987/
1-3/KB116 . . . . **MCP 372.6**

English language--Idioms--Dictionaries.
TERBAN, M/Scholastic dictionary of idioms. /1996/
4-6/KA431 . . . . **REF 423**

English language--Poetry.
VIORST, J/Alphabet from Z to A: (with much confusion on the
way). /1994/2-5/KE036. . . . . **811**

English language--Prepositions.
HOBAN, T/All about where. /1991/P-1/KB853 . . . . **428.2**

English language--Rhyme--Dictionaries.
YOUNG, S/Scholastic rhyming dictionary. /1994/
5-A/KB842. . . . . **423.1**

English language--Spelling--Fiction.
MOST, B/Hippopotamus hunt. /1994/1-3/2 KG160 . . . . **E**
TAYLOR, W/Numbskulls. /1995/4-A/7 KH787. . . . . **Fic**
ZIEFERT, H/What rhymes with eel?: a word-and-picture flap book. /
1996/P-1/2 KG798. . . . . **E**

English language--Study and teaching.
JONES, BF/Teaching thinking skills: English/language arts. /1987/
/KA280. . . . . **PROF 428**

English language--Study and teaching--Foreign speakers.
WHEN THEY DON'T ALL SPEAK ENGLISH: INTEGRATING THE
ESL STUDENT INTO THE REGULAR CLASSROOM. /1989/
/KA281. . . . . **PROF 428**

English language--Study and teaching--Periodicals.
LANGUAGE ARTS. /1924-//KA120 . . . . **PER PROF 050**
PRIMARY VOICES K-6. /1993-//KA132 . . . . **PER PROF 050**

English language--Style.
TERBAN, M/It figures!: fun figures of speech. /1993/
5-A/8 KD865 . . . . **808**

English language--Synonyms and antonyms.
FACTS ON FILE STUDENT'S THESAURUS. /1991/
5-A/KA420 . . . . **REF 423**
HARCOURT BRACE STUDENT THESAURUS. 2ND ED. /1994/
4-6/KA422 . . . . **REF 423**
HBJ STUDENT THESAURUS. /1994/3-5/KB841 . . . . **423.1**
HOBAN, T/Exactly the opposite. /1990/P-1/KB847 . . . . . **428.1**
Push, pull, empty, full: a book of opposites. /c1972/
P-K/KF746 . . . . **E**
SCHILLER, A/In other words: a beginning thesaurus. /1987/
4-6/KA429 . . . . **REF 423**

English language--Synonyms and antonyms--Fiction.
KALAN, R/Moving day. /1996/P-1/1 KF865 . . . . **E**
MACCARONE, G/Cars! cars! cars! /1995/P-1/1 KG045 . . . . . **E**
RUBINSTEIN, G/Dog in, cat out. /1993/P-1/1 KG359 . . . . . . **E**
SERFOZO, M/What's what?: a guessing game. /1996/
P-1/2 KG443 . . . . **E**
ZIEFERT, H/Nicky upstairs and down. /c1987, 1994/
P-1/1 KG795 . . . . **E**

English language--Synonyms and antonyms--Pictorial works.
MCMILLAN, B/Dry or wet? /1988/P-1/KB844. . . . . **428**

English language--Terms and phrases.
CORBEIL, J/Facts on File visual dictionary. /1986/
6-A/KA390 . . . . **REF 031.02**
DAY, A/Frank and Ernest play ball. /1990/2-3/4 KF452 . . . . . **E**
GREENWAY, S/Two's company. /1997/K-2/3 KB845 . . . . . **428.1**
PALMATIER, RA/Speaking of animals: a dictionary of animal
metaphors. /1995/6-A/KA427. . . . . **REF 423**

English language--Usage.
TERBAN, M/Checking your grammar. /1993/5-A/KB856 . . . **428.2**
English language--Verb.
BENDER, R/A to Z beastly jamboree. /1996/K-2/KB830 . . . . **421**
MACDONALD, S/Peck slither and slide. /1997/P-2/1 KC452 . **591**
ROTNER, S/Action alphabet. /1996/K-2/2 KB854 . . . . . . **428.2**
SCHNEIDER, RM/Add it, dip it, fix it: a book of verbs. /1995/
K-2/2 KB855 . . . . **428.2**
English language--Vocabulary.
KAHN, M/Mi libro de palabras Inglesas de todos los dias. /1982/
1-3/KB843 . . . . **428**
PARNWELL, EC/Oxford picture dictionary of American English.
English/Spanish ed. /c1978, 1988/4-6/KB860. . . . . **463**
English language--Vowels--Fiction.
TURNER, P/War between the Vowels and the Consonants. /1996/
1-3/3 KG630 . . . . **E**
English literature SEE ALSO Authors, English; English poetry; Short stories.
English literature.
COVILLE, B/William Shakespeare's A midsummer night's dream. /
1996/4-6/4 KE114 . . . . **822.3**
LAMB, C/Tales from Shakespeare. /1979/A/9 KE115 . . . . . **822.3**
SHAKESPEARE FOR CHILDREN (SOUND RECORDING
CASSETTE). /1995/4-6/KE117 . . . . **SRC 822.3**
English literature--History.
ROSS, S/Shakespeare and Macbeth: the story behind the play. /
1994/5-A/7 KE116 . . . . **822.3**
English literature--Study and teaching--Periodicals.
LANGUAGE ARTS. /1924-//KA120 . . . . **PER PROF 050**
English poetry.
BLAKE, W/Tyger. /1993/1-4/KE096 . . . . **821**
CARROLL, L/Jabberwocky. /1992/K-2/3 KE097 . . . . **821**
DE LA MARE, W/Rhymes and verses: collected poems for children.
/1947/4-6/KE099 . . . . **821**
ELIOT, TS/Old possum's book of practical cats. /1982/
4-A/KE100. . . . . **821**
FARJEON, E/Cats sleep anywhere. /1996/K-3/KE101 . . . . . **821**
HUGHES, S/Rhymes for Annie Rose. /1995/P-2/KE102 . . . . **821**
LEAR, E/Daffy down dillies: silly limericks. /1992/K-A/KE103 . **821**
Nonsense songs. /1997/K-3/KE104 . . . . **821**
Owl and the Pussy-cat. /1996/P-2/KE105 . . . . **821**
Owl and the Pussy-cat and other nonsense poems. /1995/
3-6/KE106 . . . . **821**
MCNAUGHTON, C/Making friends with Frankenstein: a book of
monstrous poems and pictures. /1994/K-3/KE107 . . . . . . **821**
MILNE, AA/World of Christopher Robin: the complete When we
were very young and Now we are six. /c1958/P-2/KE108 . . **821**
ROSEN, M/Michael Rosen's ABC. /1996/2-4/KE109 . . . . . **821**
STAR WALK. /1995/4-8/KE085 . . . . **811.008**
STEVENSON, RL/Child's garden of verses. /1905/P-2/KE110. **821**
TAYLOR, J/Twinkle, twinkle, little star. /1992/P-K/KE111 . . . **821**
English poetry--Collections.
HOPKINS, LB/Weather: poems. /1994/K-3/KE064 . . . . . **811.008**
I SAW ESAU: THE SCHOOLCHILD'S POCKET BOOK. /1992/
/KA276 . . . . **PROF 398.8**
LOTS OF LIMERICKS. /1991/3-6/KE069 . . . . **811.008**
NEVER TAKE A PIG TO LUNCH AND OTHER POEMS ABOUT THE
FUN OF EATING. /1994/1-4/KE073 . . . . **811.008**
READ-ALOUD RHYMES FOR THE VERY YOUNG. /c1986/
P-K/KE079. . . . . **811.008**
SNOW TOWARD EVENING: A YEAR IN A RIVER VALLEY:
NATURE POEMS. /1995/2-6/KE082 . . . . **811.008**
SNUFFLES AND SNOUTS: POEMS. /1995/P-2/KE083 . . **811.008**
WALKING THE BRIDGE OF YOUR NOSE. /1995/
2-4/KE113. . . . . **821.008**
ZOOFUL OF ANIMALS. /1992/K-4/KE090 . . . . **811.008**
English sparrow.
ARNOLD, C/House sparrows everywhere. /1992/
4-6/7 KC704 . . . . **598.8**
Entertainers.
ADAMS, MA/Whoopi Goldberg: from street to stardom. /1993/
4-6/7 KE371 . . . . **B GOLDBERG, W.**
SCHOTT, JA/Will Rogers. /1996/1-3/2 KE519 . . **B ROGERS, W.**
WUKOVITS, JF/Annie Oakley. /1997/
5-6/8 KE480 . . . . **B OAKLEY, A.**
Entertainers--Fiction.
ACKERMAN, K/Song and dance man. /1988/K-2/6 KF130 . . . . **E**
BYARS, BC/Golly sisters go West. /1986/1-3/1 KF325 . . . . **CE E**
FROMENTAL, J/Broadway chicken. /1995/5-A/7 KH146 . . . . **Fic**
Entertaining SEE ALSO Parties.
Entrepreneurship.
NOEL'S LEMONADE STAND (UJAMAA) (VIDEOCASSETTE). /
1982/3-5/KD306 . . . . **VCR 650.1**
SMACKERS: ELEMENTARY ENTREPRENEURS (VIDEOCASSETTE).
/1991/3-6/KD314. . . . . **VCR 658**

THOMPSON, T/Biz kids' guide to success: money-making ideas for
young entrepreneurs. /1992/5-6/6 KD307 . . . . **650.1**
Entrepreneurship--Software.
CLASSROOM STOREWORKS (MICROCOMPUTER PROGRAM). /
1997/2-5/KD313 . . . . **MCP 658**
Entropy.
GOLDSMITH, S/Man who loved machines (Videocassette). /1983/
3-A/KC127 . . . . **VCR 536**
Environment SEE ALSO Adaptation (Biology); Ecology; Human ecology;
Man--Influence of environment; Man--Influence on nature; Rain forest
ecology; Seashore ecology.
Environment--Songs and music.
SUZUKI, D/Connections: finding out about the environment (Sound
recording cassette). /1990/P-2/KC297. . . . . **SRC 577**
Environmental degradation.
WILLIS, T/Healing the land. /1994/4-6/7 KA954 . . . . **333.73**
Environmental policy SEE Conservation of natural resources; Energy
conservation; Human ecology; Man--Influence on nature; Natural
resources; Pollution; Wildlife conservation.
Environmental policy.
WILLIS, T/Healing the land. /1994/4-6/7 KA954 . . . . **333.73**
WINCKLER, S/Our endangered planet: population growth. /1990/
5-6/9 KA816 . . . . **304.6**
Environmental pollution SEE Pollution.
Environmental protection.
ANDERSON, J/Earth keepers. /1993/A/9 KB044 . . . . **363.7**
BANG, M/Chattanooga sludge. /1996/4-6/7 KD081 . . . . . **628.4**
BROWN, LK/Dinosaurs to the rescue!: a guide to protecting our
planet. /1992/1-4/4 KB045 . . . . **CE 363.7**
CONE, M/Come back, salmon: how a group of dedicated kids
adopted Pigeon Creek. /1992/4-6/6 KD248 . . . . **639.3**
GREAT OCEAN RESCUE (VIDEODISC). /1992/
3-A/KC350 . . . . **VD 577.7**
HALSEY, M/3 pandas planting. /1994/P-1/2 KB958 . . . . . **513.2**
KIDS BY THE BAY (VIDEOCASSETTE). /1997/
3-6/KB047 . . . . **VCR 363.7**
MCVEY, V/Sierra Club kid's guide to planet care and repair. /
1993/4-6/7 KB048 . . . . **363.7**
MISH, M/Kid's eye view of ecology (Videocassette). /1991/
3-6/KB049 . . . . **VCR 363.7**
OUR WONDERFUL WETLANDS (VIDEOCASSETTE). /1993/
4-6/KC344. . . . . **VCR 577.68**
PRINGLE, LP/Oil spills: damage, recovery, and prevention. /1993/
5-6/9 KB065 . . . . **363.73**
RECYCLING: IT'S EVERYBODY'S JOB (VIDEOCASSETTE). /1992/
5-6/KB056 . . . . **VCR 363.72**
WORLD PATROL KIDS /Earth tunes for kids (Videocassette). /
1994/3-6/KC300 . . . . **VCR 577**
Environmental protection--Fiction.
DEFELICE, CC/Lostman's River. /1994/4-A/6 KH067 . . . . **Fic**
GEORGE, JC/Who really killed Cock Robin?: an ecological mystery.
/c1971, 1991/5-A/7 KH161 . . . . **Fic**
HUGHES, M/Golden Aquarians. /1995/5-A/6 KH287. . . . . . . **Fic**
LEWIN, T/Amazon boy. /1993/K-2/5 KF974. . . . . **E**
Environmental protection--Periodicals.
NATIONAL PARKS. /1919-/5-A/KA531 . . . . **PER 050**
Environmental protection--Software.
ENVIRONMENT (MICROCOMPUTER PROGRAM). /1990/
5-A/KB059. . . . . **MCP 363.73**
GREAT OCEAN RESCUE (CD-ROM). /1996/
3-A/KC349 . . . . **CDR 577.7**
HALPERN, NA/Kids and the environment: taking responsibility for
our surroundings (Microcomputer program). /1994/
1-5/KB046 . . . . **CDR 363.7**
Environmental protection--Songs and music.
JENKINS, E/Come dance by the ocean (Sound recording cassette).
/1991/P-2/KD626. . . . . **SRC 789.3**
MISH, M/Kid's eye view of the environment (Sound recording
cassette) /1989/P-2/KB050. . . . . **SRC 363.7**
SEEGER, P/Pete Seeger's family concert (Videocassette). /1992/
K-3/KD588 . . . . **VCR 789.2**
SKIERA-ZUCEK, L/Save the animals, save the earth: /1991/
K-4/KD658 . . . . **SRC 789.3**
Environmental sciences--Encyclopedias.
FLEISHER, P/Ecology A to Z. /1994/6-A/KA410 . . . . . **REF 363.7**
Environmentalists.
DUNLAP, J/Eye on the wild: a story about Ansel Adams. /1995/
3-6/7 KE225 . . . . **B ADAMS, A.**
FABER, D/Great lives: nature and the environment. /1991/
5-A/7 KB903 . . . . **508**
RANSOM, CF/Listening to crickets: a story about Rachel Carson. /
1993/5-6/6 KE278 . . . . **B CARSON, R.**
SIRCH, WA/Eco-women: protectors of the earth. /1996/
4-6/7 KA953 . . . . **333.7**

Epic poetry.
    PICARD, BL/Odyssey of Homer. /c1952, 1992/5-A/7 KE126 . **883**
    SUTCLIFF, R/Wanderings of Odysseus: the story of the Odyssey. /
        1996/5-A/7 KE128 . . . . **883**
    ZEMAN, L/Gilgamesh the King. /1992/4-6/4 KE130 . . . . . . **892.1**
        Last quest of Gilgamesh. /1995/4-6/4 KE131 . . . . **892.1**
        Revenge of Ishtar. /1993/4-6/4 KE132 . . . . **892.1**
Epic poetry--Paraphrases, tales, etc.
    COLUM, P/Children's Homer: The Adventures of Odysseus and Tale
        of Troy. /1982/A/6 KE123 . . . . **883**
Epidemics--History.
    GIBLIN, JC/When plague strikes: the Black Death, smallpox, AIDS.
        /1995/A/11 KD010 . . . . **614.4**
Eratosthenes.
    LASKY, K/Librarian who measured the earth. /1994/
        4-A/6 KE339 . . . . **B ERATOSTHENES**
Erie Canal (N.Y.)--History.
    HARNESS, C/Amazing impossible Erie Canal. /1995/
        3-6/8 KB143 . . . . **386**
Eritrea--Folklore.
    COURLANDER, H/Fire on the mountain and other stories from
        Ethiopia and Eritrea. /c1950, 1995/3-6/6 KB277. . . . . . . **398.2**
    KURTZ, J/Trouble. /1997/K-2/3 KB748 . . . . **398.27**
Errors, Popular.
    GOLDBERG, MH/Blunder book: colossal errors, minor mistakes, and
        surprising slipups that have changed the course of history. /1984/
        5-A/9 KA556 . . . . **001.9**
Eskimo language materials--Bilingual.
    EKOOMIAK, N/Arctic memories. /c1988, 1990/2-6/4 KF125 . **998**
Eskimos.
    EKOOMIAK, N/Arctic memories. /c1988, 1990/2-6/4 KF125 . **998**
    HANCOCK, L/Nunavut. /1995/4-6/7 KE825 . . . . **971.9**
    HOYT-GOLDSMITH, D/Arctic hunter. /1992/3-6/6 KF097 . . **979.8**
    NEWMAN, SP/Inuits. /1993/4-6/7 KF102 . . . . **979.8**
Eskimos--Alaska.
    KENDALL, R/Eskimo boy: life in an Inupiaq Eskimo village. /1992/
        3-6/6 KF100 . . . . **979.8**
Eskimos--Alaska--Fiction.
    CONWAY, DC/Northern lights: a Hanukkah story. /1994/
        1-3/4 KF417 . . . . **E**
Eskimos--Alaska--Social life and customs.
    HOYT-GOLDSMITH, D/Arctic hunter. /1992/3-6/6 KF097 . . **979.8**
    JENNESS, A/In two worlds: a Yup'ik Eskimo family. /1989/
        5-6/7 KF098 . . . . **979.8**
Eskimos--Dwellings.
    YUE, C/Igloo. /1988/4-6/9 KE778 . . . . **970.3**
Eskimos--Fiction.
    GEORGE, JC/Julie. /1994/5-A/3 KH156 . . . . **Fic**
        Julie of the wolves. /c1972/6-A/6 KH157. . . . . **CE Fic**
        Julie of the wolves (Talking book). /1993/6-A/KH158. . . **TB Fic**
    GRIESE, AA/Way of our people. /1997/5-6/5 KH203 . . . . . . **Fic**
    HEINZ, BJ/Kayuktuk: an Arctic quest. /1996/4-A/3 KH235. . . . **Fic**
    HILL, K/Winter camp. /1993/5-A/6 KH262 . . . . **Fic**
    JOOSSE, BM/Mama, do you love me? /1991/P-1/2 KF854. . . . **E**
    KROLL, VL/Seasons and Someone. /1994/K-3/5 KF935. . . . . . **E**
    KUSUGAK, M/Baseball bats for Christmas. /1990/
        4-6/4 KH384 . . . . **Fic**
    LUENN, N/Nessa's fish. /1990/K-2/2 KG041 . . . . **CE E**
    MUNSCH, R/Promise is a promise. /1988/3-5/2 KH519 . . . . . **Fic**
    ROGERS, J/King Island Christmas. /1985/K-3/5 KG347 . . . . . . **E**
        Runaway mittens. /1988/P-2/4 KG348. . . . . **E**
    SCOTT, AH/On mother's lap. /c1972, 1992/P-K/2 KG423 . . . . **E**
Eskimos--Folklore.
    DABCOVICH, L/Polar bear son: an Inuit tale. /1997/
        K-2/4 KB554 . . . . **398.24**
    DEARMOND, D/Seal oil lamp. /1988/5-6/6 KB499 . . . . . **398.23**
    SLOAT, T/Hungry giant of the tundra. /1993/
        K-3/5 KB419 . . . . **398.21**
Eskimos--Northwest Territories.
    REYNOLDS, J/Frozen land: vanishing cultures. /1993/
        3-6/6 KE827 . . . . **971.9**
Eskimos--Poetry.
    SONGS ARE THOUGHTS: POEMS OF THE INUIT. /1995/
        4-6/KE140. . . . . **897**
Eskimos--Russia--Folklore.
    BERNHARD, E/How Snowshoe Hare rescued the Sun: a tale from
        the Arctic. /1993/1-2/4 KB529 . . . . **398.24**
ESP SEE Extrasensory perception.
Espionage SEE Spies.
Estefan, Gloria.
    RODRIGUEZ, J/Gloria Estefan. /1996/
        5-6/6 KE340 . . . . **B ESTEFAN, G.**

Estevanico.
    ESTEVANICO AND THE SEVEN CITIES OF GOLD
        (VIDEOCASSETTE). /1992/5-6/KE341 . . . **VCR B ESTEVANICO**
Esther, Queen of Persia.
    WOLKSTEIN, D/Esther's story. /1996/4-A/4 KA690. . . . . . . **222**
Estonia--Folklore.
    MORONEY, L/Elinda who danced in the sky: an Estonian folktale. /
        1990/3-5/5 KB407 . . . . **398.21**
Etching--Fiction.
    GEISERT, A/Etcher's studio. /1997/2-5/2 KF602 . . . . **E**
Ethics SEE ALSO Behavior; Conduct of life; Honesty; Social ethics; Values.
Ethics--Software.
    COLONIZATION (MICROCOMPUTER PROGRAM). /1986/
        5-A/KA667 . . . . **MCP 172**
    REVOLUTIONARY WARS: CHOOSING SIDES (MICROCOMPUTER
        PROGRAM). /1986/5-A/KA668 . . . . **MCP 172**
Ethiopia--Fiction.
    KURTZ, J/Pulling the lion's tail. /1995/1-3/6 KF937 . . . . **E**
Ethiopia--Folklore.
    COURLANDER, H/Fire on the mountain and other stories from
        Ethiopia and Eritrea. /c1950, 1995/3-6/6 KB277. . . . . . . **398.2**
    KURTZ, J/Fire on the mountain. /1994/2-4/6 KB747. . . . . . **398.27**
    LION'S WHISKERS: AND OTHER ETHIOPIAN TALES. REV. ED. /
        1997/3-6/7 KB337 . . . . **398.2**
Ethiopia--Social life and customs--Fiction.
    SCHUR, MR/Day of delight: a Jewish Sabbath in Ethiopia. /1994/
        1-3/4 KG412 . . . . **E**
Ethnic attitudes.
    MANY VOICES (VIDEOCASSETTE). /1991/
        4-6/KA851 . . . . **VCR 305.8**
Ethnic groups.
    MANY VOICES (VIDEOCASSETTE). /1991/
        4-6/KA851 . . . . **VCR 305.8**
Ethnic groups--Music.
    STEWART, G/Multicultural rhythm stick fun (Sound recording
        cassette). /1992/P-2/KD768 . . . . **SRC 796.1**
Ethnic groups--Poetry.
    NIKOLA-LISA, W/Bein' with you this way. /1994/P-2/KD996 . **811**
Ethnic groups in literature--Bibliography.
    MILLER-LACHMANN, L/Our family, our friends, our world: /1992/
        /KA020. . . . . **PROF 011.62**
    VENTURE INTO CULTURES: A RESOURCE BOOK OF
        MULTICULTURAL MATERIALS AND PROGRAMS. /1992/
        /KA024. . . . . **PROF 011.62**
Ethnicity.
    FOX, M/Whoever you are. /1997/P-1/1 KA843 . . . . **305.8**
Ethnicity--Periodicals.
    MULTICULTURAL REVIEW: DEDICATED TO A BETTER
        UNDERSTANDING OF ETHNIC, RACIAL, /1992-/
        /KA125. . . . . **PER PROF 050**
Ethnology SEE ALSO Archaeology; Biculturism; Civilization; Costume;
    Folklore; Man, Prehistoric; Man, Primitive; Manners and customs; Race
    relations.
Ethnology.
    MANY PEOPLE, MANY WAYS: UNDERSTANDING CULTURES
        AROUND THE WORLD. /1995/4-A/KA402. . . . . **REF 306**
Ethnology--Africa.
    CHIASSON, J/African journey. /1987/A/11 KE725 . . . . **960**
    MUSGROVE, M/Ashanti to Zulu: African traditions. /c1976/
        4-6/6 KE727 . . . . **960**
Ethnology--North America.
    PEOPLES OF THE WORLD: NORTH AMERICANS. /1991/
        6-A/KA479 . . . . **REF 970.004**
Etiquette SEE ALSO Behavior; Manners and customs.
Etiquette.
    ALIKI /Manners. /1990/1-6/2 KB239 . . . . **395**
    BRAINARD, B/Soup should be seen, not heard!: the kids' etiquette
        book. /c1988, 1990/2-6/5 KB247 . . . . **395.5**
    JAMES, E/Social smarts: manners for today's kids. /1996/
        4-6/6 KB243 . . . . **395.3**
    LEAF, M/Four-and-twenty watchbirds. /c1939, 1990/
        P-3/6 KB240 . . . . **395**
        Manners can be fun. Rev. ed. /1985/1-3/4 KB249 . . . . . . **395.5**
    MINDING YOUR MANNERS AT SCHOOL (VIDEOCASSETTE). /
        1996/3-5/KB241 . . . . **VCR 395**
    PARISH, P/Mind your manners! /1-3/KB250 . . . . **395.5**
    PHONE MANNERS (VIDEOCASSETTE). /1991/
        3-6/KB251 . . . . **VCR 395.5**
    SLONECKI, C/Dog ate my homework: social skills for today (Sound
        recording cassette). /1995/1-3/KB242. . . . . **SRC 395**
Etiquette--Wit and humor.
    BUEHNER, C/It's a spoon, not a shovel. /1995/
        2-6/2 KB248 . . . . **395.5**

Europe--Geography--Software.
EUROPE INSPIRER (CD-ROM). /1997/4-A/KE177 .... **CDR 914**
Europe--Pictorial works.
ANNO, M/Anno's journey. /1978/P-A/KF159. . . . . **E**
Europe, Eastern--Folklore.
ROTHENBERG, J/Yettele's feathers. /1995/2-4/3 KB771 . . **398.27**
SANFIELD, S/Feather merchants and other tales of the fools of
Chelm. /1991/6-A/7 KB510 . . . . **398.23**
Strudel, strudel, strudel. /1995/2-3/4 KB773 . . . . **398.27**
Eve (Biblical figure).
OPPENHEIM, SL/And the Earth trembled: the creation of Adam and
Eve. /1996/5-6/3 KA788 . . . . **297**
Iblis. /1994/4-5/4 KA789 . . . . **297**
Everglades (Fla.).
BRYANT, J/Marjory Stoneman Douglas: voice of the Everglades. /
1992/4-5/6 KE324 . . . . **B DOUGLAS, M.**
GEORGE, JC/Everglades. /1995/2-5/7 KE991 . . . . **975.9**
LOURIE, P/Everglades: Buffalo Tiger and the river of grass. /c1994,
1998/4-6/6 KE992 . . . . **975.9**
MURRAY, P/Everglades. /1993/3-6/6 KE195 . . . . **917.59**
Everglades (Fla.)--Fiction.
DEFELICE, CC/Lostman's River. /1994/4-A/6 KH067. . . . . . . **Fic**
Evolution.
COLE, J/Evolution. /1987/3-4/5 KC290 . . . . **576.8**
Human body: how we evolved. /1987/5-6/7 KC915. . . . . . **612**
GALLANT, RA/Before the sun dies: the story of evolution. /1989/
A/11 KC292 . . . . **576.8**
LAUBER, P/How dinosaurs came to be. /1996/
4-A/6 KC251 . . . . **567.9**
SALAMANDERS (VIDEOCASSETTE). /1985/
5-6/KC609. . . . . **VCR 597.8**
TWIST, C/Charles Darwin: on the trail of evolution. /1994/
5-8/8 KE315 . . . . **B DARWIN, C.**
Excavations (Archaeology) SEE ALSO Underwater archaeology.
Excavations (Archaeology).
GETZ, D/Frozen man. /1994/4-6/7 KE638 . . . . **937**
LESSEM, D/Iceman. /1994/4-6/6 KE640 . . . . **937**
Executive power--United States.
OUR FEDERAL GOVERNMENT: THE PRESIDENCY
(VIDEOCASSETTE). /1993/5-A/KA980. . . . . **VCR 352.23**
Exercise SEE ALSO Aerobics; Gymnastics; Physical education and training;
Physical fitness.
Exercise.
CARLE, E/From head to toe. /1997/P-K/1 KF341. . . . . **E**
DANCE WITH US: A CREATIVE MOVEMENT VIDEO
(VIDEOCASSETTE). /1994/K-2/KD702 . . . . **VCR 793.3**
MY BODY, MY BUDDY: HEALTHY FUN (VIDEOCASSETTE). /
1993/3-5/KC988 . . . . **VCR 613.7**
Expeditions SEE names of expeditions e.g. Lewis and Clark expedition.
Experiments SEE ALSO Science--Experiments; and branches of science with
the subdivision Experiments e.g. Biology--Experiments.
Experiments.
ARDLEY, N/Science book of air. /1991/4-6/4 KC102 . . . . . . **533**
Science book of color. /1991/4-6/4 KC118 . . . . **535.6**
Science book of electricity. /1991/2-5/3 KC129. . . . . **537**
Science book of gravity. /1992/K-3/2 KC089 . . . . **531**
Science book of hot and cold. /1992/K-3/2 KC126 . . . . . . **536**
Science book of light. /1991/K-3/6 KC105 . . . . **535**
Science book of machines. /1992/4-6/4 KD050 . . . . **621.8**
Science book of magnets. /1991/2-5/2 KC136 . . . . **538**
Science book of motion. /1992/K-3/2 KC090 . . . . **531**
Science book of sound. /1991/2-5/3 KC076. . . . . **530**
Science book of things that grow. /1991/K-3/3 KC273 . . **571.2**
Science book of water. /1991/2-4/4 KC091 . . . . **531**
Science book of weather. /1992/K-3/3 KC185 . . . . **551.5**
BEN FRANKLIN BOOK OF EASY AND INCREDIBLE EXPERIMENTS.
/1995/A/8 KB889 . . . . **507.8**
BLAKEY, N/Mudpies activity book: recipes for invention. /c1989,
1993/A/KD424 . . . . **745.5**
BOSAK, SV/Science is...2nd ed. /1991//KA285. . . . **PROF 507.8**
BUBBLEOLOGY I AND II (VIDEOCASSETTE). /1988/
3-A/KA292 . . . . **VCR PROF 530.4**
CASH, T/Plastics. /1990/3-5/5 KD327 . . . . **668.4**
101 physics tricks: fun experiments with everyday materials. /
1993/4-8/7 KC077 . . . . **530**
COBB, V/Bet you can!: science possibilities to fool you. /1990/
4-A/7 KD745 . . . . **793.8**
Bet you can't: science impossibilities to fool you. /1980/
5-6/6 KB880 . . . . **507**
More science experiments you can eat. /1979/A/7 KB890. **507.8**
Science experiments you can eat. Rev. and updated. /1994/
3-5/7 KB891 . . . . **507.8**
DARLING, DJ/Making light work: the science of optics. /1991/
6-A/8 KC109 . . . . **535**

Sounds interesting: the science of acoustics. /1991/
6-A/8 KC103 . . . . **534**
DIETL, U/Plant-and-grow project book. /1993/P-4/5 KC384 . . **580**
DOHERTY, P/Cheshire cat and other eye-popping experiments on
how we see the world. /1995/4-A/5 KA612 . . . . **152.14**
Cool hot rod and other electrifying experiments on energy and
matter. /1996/4-A/5 KC093 . . . . **531**
Magic wand and other bright experiments on light and color. /
1995/4-A/5 KC110. . . . . **535**
Spinning blackboard and other dynamic experiments on force and
motion. /1996/4-A/5 KC094 . . . . **531**
EARTH'S SEASONS/CLIMATES (VIDEOCASSETTE). /1995/
3-6/KB902. . . . . **VCR 508**
FLEISHER, P/Our oceans: experiments and activities in marine
science. /1995/4-6/7 KC172 . . . . **551.46**
GRIER, K/Discover. /1990/3-6/6 KA592 . . . . **069**
HILLERMAN, A/Done in the sun, solar projects for children. /1983/
2-4/7 KD048 . . . . **621.47**
HIRSCHFELD, R/Kids' science book: creative experiences for hands-
on fun. /1995/P-4/7 KB892 . . . . **507.8**
JOHNSON, SA/Morning glories. /1985/4-6/7 KC428 . . . . . **583**
KANER, E/Balloon science. /1989/2-6/6 KC079. . . . . **530**
KENDA, M/Cooking wizardry for kids. /1990/5-6/KD273 . . **641.5**
KRAMER, SP/How to think like a scientist: answering questions by
the scientific method. /1987/4-6/6 KB883 . . . . **507**
LEVINE, S/Silly science: strange and startling projects to amaze your
family and friends. /1995/3-8/7 KB893. . . . . **507.8**
LOOK WHAT I GREW: WINDOWSILL GARDENS
(VIDEOCASSETTE). /1993/1-6/KD171 . . . . **VCR 635**
MARKLE, S/Creepy spooky science. /1996/3-6/8 KB894 . . . **507.8**
Icky squishy science. /1996/4-8/6 KB895 . . . . **507.8**
Measuring up!: experiments, puzzles, and games exploring
measurement. /1995/5-6/6 KC086 . . . . **530.8**
Power up: experiments, puzzles, and games exploring electricity. /
1989/3-6/7 KC133 . . . . **537**
MOON/OUTER SPACE (VIDEOCASSETTE). /1994/
3-6/KC007. . . . . **VCR 523**
MUNSON, HR/Science experiences with everyday things. /1988/
/KA283. . . . . **PROF 507**
MURPHY, B/Experiment with water. /1991/K-3/4 KC101 . . . . **532**
PASCOE, E/Butterflies and moths. /1997/4-6/6 KC563 . . . **595.78**
Earthworms. /1997/4-6/4 KC506 . . . . **592**
RAINIS, KG/Exploring with a magnifying glass. /1991/
6-A/7 KB897 . . . . **507.8**
RYBOLT, TR/Environmental experiments about air. /1993/
5-6/7 KD084 . . . . **628.5**
Environmental experiments about water. /1993/
5-6/7 KB066 . . . . **363.73**
SCIENCE ACTIVITIES FOR YOUNG PEOPLE. /1983/
5-A/9 KB884 . . . . **507**
SCIENCE FAIR PROJECTS (VIDEOCASSETTE). /1995/
5-A/KB898. . . . . **VCR 507.8**
SCIENTIFIC METHOD (VIDEOCASSETTE). /1993/
5-6/KB886. . . . . **VCR 507**
SIMON, S/How to be an ocean scientist in your own home. /
1988/5-A/5 KC176. **551.46**
Optical illusion book. /c1976, 1984/4-6/5 KC115 . . . . **535**
SOUND/LIGHT AND COLOR (VIDEOCASSETTE). /1994/
3-6/KC080. . . . . **VCR 530**
STEIN, S/Science book. /1979/2-A/5 KB873 . . . . **500**
VANCLEAVE, JP/Biology for every kid: 101 easy experiments that
really work. /1989/P-4/8 KC270 . . . . **570**
Janice VanCleave's oceans for every kid: easy activities that make
learning /1996/3-6/8 KC178 . . . . **551.46**
Janice VanCleave's rocks and minerals: mind-boggling experiments
you can turn /1996/4-6/8 KC228 . . . . **552**
Janice VanCleave's the human body for every kid: easy activities
that make /1995/5-6/8 KC928 . . . . **612**
VECCHIONE, G/100 amazing make-it-yourself science fair projects.
/1995//KA287. . . . . **PROF 507.8**
WALPOLE, B/Water. /1990/K-2/5 KC141 . . . . **546**
WICK, W/Drop of water: a book of science and wonder. /1997/
K-6/6 KC142 . . . . **546**
WYLER, R/Science fun with mud and dirt. /1986/
K-4/2 KB887 . . . . **507**
ZUBROWSKI, B/Balloons: building and experimenting with inflatable
toys. /1990/4-A/7 KB888. . . . . **507**
Bubbles. /1979/4-6/8 KC085. . . . . **530.4**
Making waves: finding out about rhythmic motion. /1994/
5-A/7 KC081 . . . . **530**
Mirrors: finding out about the properties of light. /1992/
5-6/8 KC116 . . . . **535**
Shadow play: making pictures with light and lenses. /1995/
4-8/7 KC117 . . . . **535**

Wheels at work: building and experimenting with models of machines. /1986/5-6/8 KD054 . . . . **621.8**
Experiments, Scientific SEE Science--Experiments; and branches of science with the subdivision Experiments e.g. Biology--Experiments.

Exploration.

BEING AN EXPLORER (VIDEOCASSETTE). /1996/ K-3/KE161 . . . . **VCR 910.9**
SCIENCE OF EXPLORATION (VIDEOCASSETTE). /1996/ 4-6/KE162 . . . . **VCR 910.9**
Explorations SEE America--Discovery and exploration; Discoveries (in geography); Explorers.

Explorers.

ABUBAKARI: THE EXPLORER KING OF MALI (VIDEOCASSETTE). / 1992/5-6/KE224. . . . . **VCR B ABUBAKARI**
ADLER, DA/Christopher Columbus: great explorer. /1991/ 4-5/4 KE301 . . . . **B COLUMBUS, C.**
Picture book of Christopher Columbus. /1991/ 2-3/4 KE300 . . . . **CE B COLUMBUS, C.**
ASIMOV, I/Christopher Columbus: navigator to the New World. / 1991/4-5/5 KE302 . . . . **B COLUMBUS, C.**
BEING AN EXPLORER (VIDEOCASSETTE). /1996/ K-3/KE161 . . . . **VCR 910.9**
BLUMBERG, R/Remarkable voyages of Captain Cook. /1991/ 5-6/7 KE163 . . . . **910.92**
COLUMBUS, C/Log of Christopher Columbus' first voyage to America in the year 1492. /c1938, 1989/4-6/7 KE741 . . . **970.01**
ESTEVANICO AND THE SEVEN CITIES OF GOLD (VIDEOCASSETTE). /1992/5-6/KE341 . . . **VCR B ESTEVANICO**
EXPLORERS AND DISCOVERERS: FROM ALEXANDER THE GREAT TO SALLY RIDE. /1995/5-A/KA470 . . . . **REF 910**
FISHER, LE/Prince Henry the Navigator. /1990/ 4-6/6 KE387 . . . . **B HENRY, PRINCE**
FRITZ, J/Around the world in 100 years: from Henry the Navigator to Magellan. /1994/5-A/7 KE164 . . . . **910.92**
Where do you think you're going, Christopher Columbus? /1980/ 4-6/6 KE303 . . . . **CE B COLUMBUS, C.**
JOHNSON, RL/Braving the frozen frontier: women working in Antarctica. /1997/4-6/6 KE214 . . . . **919.8**
KROLL, S/Lewis and Clark: explorers of the American West. /1994/ 4-6/6 KE203 . . . . **917.804**
LEWIS AND CLARK EXPEDITION (VIDEOCASSETTE). /1992/ 5-6/KE204. **VCR 917.804**
MANSON, A/Dog came, too: a true story. /1993/ 1-4/6 KE185 . . . . **917.104**
MATTHEW HENSON (VIDEOCASSETTE). /1994/ 5-A/KE388. . . . . **VCR B HENSON, M.**
MATTHEWS, R/Explorer. /1991/4-6/8 KE152 . . . . **910**
PELTA, K/Discovering Christopher Columbus. /1991/ A/6 KE742 . . . . **970.01**
SANFORD, WR/John C. Fremont: soldier and pathfinder. /1996/ 5-6/4 KE357 . . . . **B FREMONT, J.**
Zebulon Pike: explorer of the Southwest. /1996/ 5-6/8 KE497 . . . . **B PIKE, Z.**
SCIENCE OF EXPLORATION (VIDEOCASSETTE). /1996/ 4-6/KE162 . . . . **VCR 910.9**
STEFOFF, R/Lewis and Clark. /1992/5-6/5 KE206 . . . . . **917.804**
Scientific explorers: travels in search of knowledge. /1992/ 6-A/9 KB925 . . . . **509**
STEGER, W/Over the top of the world: explorer Will Steger's trek across the Arctic. /1997/5-6/6 KE219 . . . . **919.8**
WHITE, FM/Story of Junipero Serra: brave adventurer. /1996/ 4-6/7 KE536 . . . . **B SERRA, J.**

Explorers--Diaries.

CLARK, W/Off the map: the journals of Lewis and Clark. /1993/ 4-6/7 KE201 . . . . **917.804**

Extinct animals.

FACKLAM, M/And then there was one: the mysteries of extinction. /1990/5-6/7 KC488 . . . . **591.68**

Extinct animals--Dictionaries.

SATTLER, HR/New illustrated dinosaur dictionary. Rev. ed. /c1983, 1990/3-6/KA444 . . . . **REF 567.9**

Extinct birds.

MORRISON, SD/Passenger pigeon. /1989/4-6/4 KC656 . . . . **598**

Extinction (Biology).

BRANLEY, FM/What happened to the dinosaurs? /1989/ 2-4/5 KC244 . . . . **567.9**
HOFF, MK/Our endangered planet: life on land. /1992/ 5-6/8 KA962 . . . . **333.95**
Extrasensory perception SEE ALSO Clairvoyance.

Extrasensory perception.

GREEN, CR/Seeing the unseen. /1993/4-6/5 KA610 . . . . . **133.8**

Extrasensory perception--Fiction.

AIKEN, J/Cold Shoulder Road. /1995/5-A/5 KG823 . . . . **Fic**
DUNCAN, L/Third eye. /1984/A/5 KH089 . . . . **Fic**

HUNTER, M/Third eye. /1991/A/7 KH294 . . . . **Fic**
MAHY, M/Haunting. /1982/5-A/6 KH451 . . . . **CE Fic**
PINKWATER, J/Mister Fred. /1994/5-A/4 KH606 . . . . **Fic**
ROBERTS, WD/Girl with the silver eyes. /1980/4-6/5 KH636 . . **Fic**
RODGERS, M/Billion for Boris. /c1974/4-6/7 KH646 . . . . . **CE Fic**
SNYDER, ZK/Headless cupid. /c1971/4-6/7 KH733 . . . . . **CE Fic**
Extraterrestrial beings SEE ALSO Life on other planets.

Extraterrestrial beings.

DARLING, DJ/Could you ever meet an alien? /1990/ A/7 KC291 . . . . **576.8**
KETTELKAMP, L/ETs and UFOs: are they real? /1996/ 4-6/8 KA558 . . . . **001.9**

Extraterrestrial beings--Fiction.

COVILLE, B/Aliens ate my homework. /1993/4-6/5 KH035. . . . **Fic**
GAUTHIER, G/My life among the aliens. /1996/4-6/5 KH154 . **Fic**
HAMILTON, V/Willie Bea and the time the Martians landed. / 1983/5-6/3 KH219 . . . . **Fic**
HOOVER, HM/Only child. /1992/5-A/5 KH280 . . . . **Fic**
HUGHES, M/Golden Aquarians. /1995/5-A/6 KH287 . . . . **Fic**
PINKWATER, J/Mister Fred. /1994/5-A/4 KH606 . . . . **Fic**
SERVICE, PF/Stinker from space. /1988/3-5/5 KH700 . . . . . . **Fic**
Eye SEE ALSO Vision.

Eye.

EYES: BRIGHT AND SAFE. REV. ED. (VIDEOCASSETTE). /1997/ 3-5/KC964 . . . . **VCR 612.8**
JEDROSZ, A/Eyes. /1992/5-6/6 KC965 . . . . **612.8**
PARKER, S/Eye and seeing. Rev. ed. /1989/A/8 KC972 . . . **612.8**
PARRAMON, JM/Sight. /1985/P-1/1 KC974 . . . . **612.8**
SHOWERS, P/Look at your eyes. Rev. ed. /1992/ P-1/2 KC978 . . . . **612.8**
SIMON, S/Optical illusion book. /c1976, 1984/4-6/5 KC115. **535**

Eye--Fiction.

BALL, D/Emily Eyefinger. /1992/1-3/2 KG876. . . . . **Fic**
LESIEG, T/Eye book. /c1968/1-2/1 KF958 . . . . **E**

Eyeglasses--Fiction.

HEST, A/Baby Duck and the bad eyeglasses. /1996/ P-K/1 KF717 . . . . **E**
KEATS, EJ/Goggles! /c1969, 1971/K-2/2 KF872 . . . . **CE E**
SMITH, L/Glasses: who needs 'em?. /1991/2-3/3 KG524 . . . . **E**
Fables SEE ALSO Animals--Fiction; Folklore; Parables.

Fables.

BIERHORST, J/Doctor Coyote: a Native American Aesop's fables. / 1987/3/3 KB530 . . . . **398.24**
BRETT, J/Town Mouse, Country Mouse. /1994/ K-3/3 KB535 . . . . **398.24**
FOREST, H/Songspinner: folktales and fables sung and told (Sound recording cassette). /1982/2-4/KB735 . . . . **SRC 398.27**
FOX, P/Little swineherd and other tales. /1996/3-6/4 KH136 . . **Fic**
HASTINGS, S/Reynard the Fox. /1991/2-3/6 KB586 . . . . **398.24**
HEINS, E/Cat and the cook and other fables of Krylov. /1995/ 3-5/6 KH234 . . . . **Fic**
JONES, C/Hare and the Tortoise. /1996/P-1/4 KB597 . . . **398.24**
LOBEL, A/Fables. /1980/3-A/5 KH416 . . . . **Fic**
PAXTON, T/Aesop's fables. /1988/3-4/KB632 . . . . **398.24**
REISER, L/Two mice in three fables. /1995/P-2/3 KG320. . . . . **E**
SUMMERS, K/Milly and Tilly: the story of a town mouse and a country mouse. /1997/K-2/2 KB661 . . . . **398.24**
WALLIS, D/Something nasty in the cabbages. /1991/ 2-4/3 KB671 . . . . **398.24**
WOOD, AJ/Lion and the mouse: an Aesop's fable. /1995/ P-1/5 KB674 . . . . **398.24**
WOOD, D/Old Turtle. /1992/3-5/3 KH879 . . . . **CE Fic**
YOLEN, J/Sip of Aesop. /1995/K-3/KE050 . . . . **811**
YOUNG, E/Donkey trouble. /1995/1-2/5 KB678 . . . . . . **398.24**
Seven blind mice. /1992/K-3/2 KB681 . . . . **398.24**

Fables--Parodies, imitations, etc.

VOZAR, D/M.C. Turtle and the Hip Hop Hare: a nursery rap. / 1997/2-3/2 KG665 . . . . **E**

Fables--Software.

AESOP'S FABLE: THE TORTOISE AND THE HARE (CD-ROM). / 1993/P-A/KB522 . . . . **CDR 398.24**

Face.

ROTNER, S/Faces. /1994/P-1/2 KC924 . . . . **612**

Face in art.

MCHUGH, C/Faces. /1993/4-A/7 KD374. . . . . **704.9**

Facsimile transmission.

VANDERHEYDEN-TRESCONY, C/Faxing friends; a resource guide for forming international friendships among /1992/ /KA173. . . . . **PROF 370.117**

Factorials.

ANNO, M/Anno's mysterious multiplying jar. /1983/ P-A/2 KB944 . . . . **512**

Factories SEE ALSO Manufactures.
Factories--Fiction.
    PATERSON, K/Lyddie. /1991/6-A/7 KH579 . . . . Fic
Fair use (Copyright).
    TALAB, RS/Commonsense copyright: a guide to the new
      technologies. /1986//KA169 . . . . **PROF 346.73**
Fairies SEE ALSO names of specific kinds of fairies e.g. Leprechauns.
Fairies--Fiction.
    MCGRAW, EJ/Moorchild. /1996/5-A/6 KH475 . . . . Fic
    TOMPERT, A/Grandfather Tang's story. /1990/2-3/4 KG613. . . E
    WALSH, ES/Samantha. /1996/K-2/2 KG681 . . . . E
Fairies--Folklore.
    WALKER, PR/Little folk: stories from around the world. /1997/
      2-4/6 KB494 . . . . **398.22**
Fairies--Literary collections.
    MILLS, LA/Book of little folk: faery stories and poems from around
      the world. /1997/1-4/KD875 . . . . **808.8**
Fairness.
    IT'S NOT FAIR! (VIDEOCASSETTE). /1994/
      3-6/KA642 . . . . **VCR 155.4**
Fairs.
    COOPER, E/Country fair. /1997/1-3/3 KF421 . . . . E
    LEWIN, T/Fair! /1997/1-3/6 KB180 394
    TURNER, M/Come on everybody! Let's go to the fair (Kit). /1991/
      P/KB182 . . . . **KIT 394**
Fairs--Fiction.
    FROEHLICH, MW/That Kookoory! /1995/K-2/3 KF588 . . . . E
    GREENSTEIN, E/Mrs. Rose's garden. /1996/K-2/3 KF643 . . . . . E
Fairy tales SEE ALSO Folklore.
Fairy tales.
    ALDERSON, B/Arabian nights, or, Tales told by Sheherezade during
      a thousand nights and one night. /1995/5-A/7 KB253 . . . . 398.2
    AMERICAN FAIRY TALES: FROM RIP VAN WINKLE TO THE
      ROOTABAGA STORIES. /1996/4-6/7 KG843 . . . . Fic
    ANDERSEN, HC/Hans Christian Andersen in Central Park (Sound
      recording cassette). /1981/4-6/KG846 . . . . **SRC Fic**
      Swineherd. /1995/2-5/5 KG847. . . . . Fic
      Tinderbox. Newly illustrated ed. /1988/K-3/5 KF155. . . . . . E
      Twelve tales. /1994/3-6/5 KG848 . . . . Fic
      Ugly duckling (Videocassette). /1977/2-5/KG849. . . . . **VCR Fic**
    ARABIAN NIGHTS: THEIR BEST-KNOWN TALES. /c1909, 1994/
      5-A/9 KB255 . . . . 398.2
    ARABIAN NIGHTS (SOUND RECORDING CASSETTE). /1991/
      4-5/KB254 . . . . **SRC 398.2**
    ARNOLD, K/Baba Yaga: a Russian folktale. /1993/
      2-3/3 KB387 . . . . 398.21
    AVI /Tom, Babette, and Simon: three tales of transformation. /
      1995/3-6/4 KG866 . . . . Fic
    BABBITT, N/Search for delicious. /c1969/4-6/5 KG872. . . CE Fic
    BAHOUS, S/Sitti and the cats: a tale of friendship. /1993/
      3-4/7 KB257 . . . . 398.2
    BANG, M/Dawn. /1983/1-3/2 KF189 . . . . E
    BARBER, A/Catkin. /1996/4-6/6 KG878 . . . . Fic
    BATEMAN, T/Ring of Truth: an original Irish tale. /1997/
      1-3/5 KF213 . . . . E
    BEAUTY AND THE BEAST (VIDEOCASSETTE). /c1989, 1996/
      K-3/KB259. . . . . **VCR 398.2**
    BERENZY, A/Frog prince. /1989/3-5/5 KG898 . . . . Fic
      Rapunzel. /1995/2-4/4 KB263 . . . . 398.2
    BOSTON, LM/Children of Green Knowe. /c1955, 1983/
      4-A/6 KG919. . . . . Fic
    BOX AND TWO OTHER TITLES FOR FAMILY ENJOYMENT
      (VIDEOCASSETTE). /1992/1-4/KF253 . . . . **VCR E**
    BRETT, J/Beauty and the Beast. /1989/4-5/6 KB268 . . . . . 398.2
    BROOKE, LL/Golden goose book: a fairy tale picture book. /1992/
      P-3/6 KB269 . . . . 398.2
    BROOKE, WJ/Teller of tales. /1994/5-A/5 KG927. . . . . . . Fic
      Telling of the tales: five stories. /1994/5-A/7 KG928 . . . . . Fic
      Untold tales. /1992/6-A/7 KG929 . . . . Fic
    CECIL, L/Frog princess. /1995/1-3/2 KB548 . . . . 398.24
    CLIMO, S/Irish Cinderlad. /1996/2-4/3 KB275 . . . . 398.2
      Korean Cinderella. /1993/2-4/5 KB726 . . . . 398.27
      Treasury of princesses: princess tales from around the world. /
      1996/3-5/6 KB432 . . . . 398.22
    COATSWORTH, E/Cat who went to heaven. New ed. /c1958/
      A/6 KH010 . . . . **CE Fic**
    COMPTON, J/Ashpet: an Appalachian tale. /1994/
      2-3/4 KB727 . . . . 398.27
    COOPER, S/Tam Lin. /1991/3-4/4 KB276 . . . . 398.2
    DAVENPORT, T/From the Brothers Grimm: a contemporary retelling
      of American folktales and classic stories. /1992/
      5-A/KB281 . . . . **CE 398.2**
    DE BEAUMONT, ML/Beauty and the Beast. /1990/
      4-5/6 KB282 . . . . 398.2

    DE LA MARE, W/Turnip. /1992/3-5/6 KB557 . . . . 398.24
    DE REGNIERS, BS/Little Sister and the Month Brothers. /c1976,
      1994/2-3/2 KB501 . . . . 398.23
    DEMI /Magic gold fish: a Russian folktale. /1995/
      3-5/2 KB284 . . . . 398.2
    DESPAIN, P/Strongheart Jack and the beanstalk. /1995/
      2-5/3 KB287 . . . . 398.2
    DUGIN, A/Dragon feathers. /1993/4-5/7 KB289 . . . . 398.2
    EARLY, M/Sleeping Beauty. /1993/2-5/5 KB290 . . . . 398.2
    FAIRY TALES FROM THE PICTURE BOOK PARADE (TALKING
      BOOK). /1986/2-4/KB293 . . . . **TB 398.2**
    FAIRYTALE FAVORITES IN STORY AND SONG (SOUND
      RECORDING CASSETTE). /1993/K-3/KB294 . . . . . . **SRC 398.2**
    FONTEYN, M/Swan Lake. /1989/4-6/7 KD693 . . . . . **CE 792.8**
    FRENCH, V/Lazy Jack. /1995/K-2/2 KB301 . . . . 398.2
    GANNETT, RS/My father's dragon. /c1948, 1986/
      3-5/6 KH149 . . . . Fic
    GERINGER, L/Seven ravens. /1994/2-3/6 KB302 . . . . 398.2
    GREENE, E/Billy Beg and his bull: an Irish tale. /1994/
      2-4/5 KB304 . . . . 398.2
    GRIMM, J/Juniper tree and other tales from Grimm. /c1973,
      1992/5-A/7 KB306 . . . . 398.2
      Rapunzel. /1982/2-4/4 KB307 . . . . 398.2
      Rumpelstiltskin. /1997/K-2/2 KB308. . . . . 398.2
      Seven ravens: a fairy tale. /1995/3-5/7 KB309 . . . . 398.2
      Snow-White and the seven dwarfs. /1972/3-4/6 KB310 . . 398.2
      Twelve dancing princesses: a fairy tale. /1995/
      3-4/6 KB311 . . . . 398.2
      Wolf and the seven little kids: a fairy tale. /1995/
      1-2/4 KB579 . . . . 398.24
    HAN, OS/Kongi and Potgi: a Cinderella story from Korea. /1996/
      K-3/5 KB313 . . . . 398.2
    HANSARD, P/Jig, Fig, and Mrs. Pig. /1995/P-2/3 KB584 . 398.24
    HAUTZIG, D/Aladdin and the magic lamp. /1993/
      1-2/2 KB314 . . . . 398.2
    HEDLUND, I/Mighty Mountain and the three strong women. /1990/
      3-5/5 KB316 . . . . 398.2
    HELLDORFER, MC/Mapmaker's daughter. /1991/2-3/3 KF698 . . E
    HICKOX, R/Per and the Dala horse. /1995/1-3/6 KF724 . . . . . . E
    HONG, LT/Two of everything. /1993/2-3/4 KB317 . . . . . . 398.2
    HOOKS, WH/Snowbear Whittington: an Appalachian Beauty and
      the Beast. /1994/2-3/4 KB318 . . . . 398.2
    HUCK, CS/Toads and diamonds. /1996/2-3/3 KB319 . . . . 398.2
    HUNTER, M/Gilly Martin the Fox. /1994/3-4/7 KB593 . . 398.24
    JAPANESE FAIRY TALES. /1992/2-4/7 KB322 . . . . 398.2
    KELLOGG, S/Jack and the beanstalk. /1991/2-3/4 KB325. . 398.2
    KIMMEL, EA/Bearhead: a Russian folktale. /1991/
      2-4/4 KB327 . . . . 398.2
      Bernal and Florinda: a Spanish tale. /1994/2-4/3 KF903 . . . . . E
      Goose girl: a story from the Brothers Grimm. /1995/
      3-5/5 KB328 . . . . 398.2
      I-know-not-what, I-know-not-where: a Russian tale. /1994/
      3-4/6 KB329 . . . . 398.2
      Iron John. /1994/4-5/5 KB330. . . . . 398.2
      Magic dreidels: a Hanukkah story. /1996/K-3/2 KF904 . . . . . . E
      Rimonah of the Flashing Sword: a North African tale. /1995/
      3-4/4 KB331 . . . . 398.2
      Tale of Ali Baba and the forty thieves: a story from the Arabian
      Nights. /1996/3-4/6 KB332 . . . . 398.2
      Three princes: a tale from the Middle East. /1994/
      2-3/4 KB461 . . . . 398.22
    KIRSTEIN, L/Puss in boots. /c1992, 1994/3-4/6 KB604 . . . 398.24
    KNOCK AT THE DOOR. /1992//KA269. . . . . **PROF 398.2**
    KUNSTLER, JH/Aladdin and the magic lamp (Kit). /1995/
      3-5/KB333 . . . . **KIT 398.2**
    LATTIMORE, DN/Arabian nights: three tales. /1995/
      3-5/6 KB334 . . . . 398.2
    LEVINSON, R/Emperor's new clothes. /1991/P-2/4 KF968. . . . . E
    LINDGREN, A/Tomten. /c1965, 1997/K-2/3 KF986 . . . . . . **CE E**
    MACDONALD, G/Light princess. /1977/4-5/5 KH439. . . . . Fic
    MAHY, M/Tall story and other tales. /1992/4-6/4 KH453 . . . . Fic
    MARSHALL, J/Hansel and Gretel. /1990/2-4/4 KB340 . . . . 398.2
    MARTIN, R/Mysterious tales of Japan. /1996/
      3-5/3 KB690 . . . . 398.25
    MAYER, M/Baba Yaga and Vasilisa the Brave. /1994/
      3-5/5 KB466 . . . . 398.22
      Turandot. /1995/3-5/5 KB342 . . . . 398.2
    MAYO, M/Magical tales from many lands. /1993/
      4-5/6 KB343 . . . . 398.2
    MCCARTHY, RF/Grandfather Cherry-Blossom. /1993/
      2-3/3 KB753 . . . . 398.27
      Inch-high samurai. /1993/3-4/4 KB754 . . . . 398.27
    MCKINLEY, R/Beauty: a retelling of the story of Beauty and the
      Beast. /1978/6-A/6 KH485. . . . . Fic

Door in the hedge. /1981/4-6/6 KH487 . . . . **Fic**
MELMED, LK/Rainbabies. /1992/2-3/5 KG127 . . . . **E**
MENDELSON, ST/Emperor's new clothes. /1992/1-3/7 KG128 . **E**
METAXAS, E/Jack and the beanstalk (Videocassette). /1991/
K-2/KB349 . . . . **VCR 398.2**
MILLS, LA/Tatterhood and the hobgoblins: a Norwegian folktale. /
1993/3-4/6 KB350 . . . . **398.2**
MITCHELL, A/Ugly Duckling. /1994/P-A/4 KG143 . . . . **E**
MOSER, B/Tucker Pfeffercorn: an old story retold. /1994/
2-3/5 KB351 . . . . **398.2**
NESS, C/Ocean of story: fairy tales from India. /1996/
4-6/5 KB353 . . . . **398.2**
NORTON, M/Are all the giants dead? /c1975, 1997/
4-A/5 KH552 . . . . **Fic**
Bed-knob and broomstick. /c1957/4-6/5 KH553 . . . . **Fic**
PATERSON, K/King's equal. /1992/3-6/6 KH578. . . . . **Fic**
Tale of the mandarin ducks. /1990/2-3/6 KB631 . . . . . **398.24**
PERRAULT, C/Cinderella, or the little glass slipper. /1954/
1-3/7 KB762 . . . . **398.27**
Complete fairy tales of Charles Perrault. /1993/
3-4/6 KB355 . . . . **398.2**
Puss in boots: a fairy tale. /1996/K-3/5 KB634 . . . . . . **398.24**
PETERSON, J/Caterina, the clever farm girl: a tale from Italy. /
1996/2-4/3 KB357 . . . . **398.2**
PHILIP, N/Arabian nights. /1994/6-6/6 KB358. . . . . **398.2**
PLUME, I/Shoemaker and the elves. /1991/2-4/4 KB359 . . . **398.2**
PYLE, H/King Stork. /1973/3-5/6 KH614 . . . . **Fic**
Swan Maiden. /1994/2-4/6 KG294 . . . . **E**
RAINBOW FAIRY BOOK. /1993/2-6/8 KB360. . . . . **398.2**
ROUNDS, G/Three billy goats Gruff. /1993/P-1/2 KB644. **398.24**
ROWE, JA/Gingerbread Man: an old English folktale. /1996/
P-K/2 KB363 . . . . **398.2**
SAINT EXUPERY, AD/Little prince. /c1943/4-A/6 KH671 . . . . . **Fic**
SAN JOSE, C/Cinderella. /1994/2-4/6 KB364 . . . . **398.2**
SAN SOUCI, RD/Hobyahs. /1996/3-4/6 KB647 . . . . **398.24**
SANDERSON, R/Papa Gatto: an Italian fairy tale. /1995/
3-4/6 KB646 . . . . **398.24**
SCHROEDER, A/Lily and the wooden bowl. /1994/
3-5/7 KB366 . . . . **398.2**
Smoky Mountain Rose: an Appalachian Cinderella. /1997/
2-3/4 KB367 . . . . **398.2**
SCHWARTZ, H/Wonder child and other Jewish fairy tales. /1996/
2-4/5 KB369 . . . . **398.2**
SHEPARD, A/Gifts of Wali Dad: a tale of India and Pakistan. /
1995/2-3/2 KB488 . . . . **398.22**
SHULEVITZ, U/Golden goose. /1995/K-3/2 KB650 . . . . . . **398.24**
SINGER, M/In the palace of the Ocean King. /1995/
2-3/5 KG509 . . . . **E**
SIS, P/Three golden keys. /1994/5-A/4 KH714 . . . . **Fic**
STANLEY, D/Petrosinella: a Neapolitan Rapunzel. /1995/
2-4/6 KB780 . . . . **398.27**
STEWIG, JW/Princess Florecita and the iron shoes: a Spanish fairy
tale. /1995/3-4/5 KB372 . . . . **398.2**
STOCKTON, FR/Bee-man of Orn. /c1964, 1987/
5-6/7 KH763 . . . . **Fic**
TARCOV, EH/Frog prince. /c1974, 1993/P-3/2 KB376 . . . . **398.2**
TENDER TALE OF CINDERELLA PENGUIN (VIDEOCASSETTE). /
1990/1-3/KG600 . . . . **VCR E**
THOMPSON, S/One hundred favorite folktales. /c1968/
/KA274. . . . . **PROF 398.2**
THURBER, J/Great Quillow. /1994/2-3/6 KH791 . . . . **Fic**
Many moons. /c1943, 1990/3-5/5 KH792 . . . . **Fic**
Many moons. /1990/3-5/5 KH793 . . . . **Fic**
TOM TIT TOT: AN ENGLISH FOLK TALE. /c1965, 1997/
P-3/6 KB378 . . . . **398.2**
UCHIDA, Y/Magic purse. /1993/2-4/4 KB379 . . . . **398.2**
VOJTECH, A/Marushka and the Month Brothers: a folktale. /1996/
1-3/4 KB513 . . . . **398.23**
VUONG, LD/Sky legends of Vietnam. /1993/
3-5/7 KB717 . . . . **398.26**
WHITE CAT (VIDEOCASSETTE). /1997/K-2/KB382 . . **VCR 398.2**
WILLARD, N/Beauty and the Beast. /1992/4-A/6 KH862. . . . . **Fic**
WILLIAMS, M/Velveteen Rabbit; or, How toys become real. /1988/
3-5/6 KH864 . . . . **CE Fic**
WILSON, BK/Wishbones: a folk tale from China. /1993/
2-3/6 KB383 . . . . **398.2**
WISNIEWSKI, D/Elfwyn's saga. /1990/4-6/6 KB422 . . . . **398.21**
Wave of the Sea-Wolf. /1994/1-3/6 KG753 . . . . **E**
YEP, L/Shell woman and the king: a Chinese folktale. /1993/
3-5/5 KB496 . . . . **398.22**
YOLEN, J/Tam Lin. /1990/3-4/4 KB384 . . . . **398.2**
ZELINSKY, PO/Rumpelstiltskin. /1986/1-4/7 KB385 . . **CE 398.2**
ZEMACH, H/Penny a look. /c1971/K-2/2 KG789 . . . . **E**

ZEMACH, M/Three wishes: an old story. /1986/
2-3/4 KB386 . . . . **398.2**
ZIEFERT, H/Princess and the pea. /1996/K-2/1 KG796 . . . . . . **E**
Fairy tales--Parodies, imitations, etc.
EMBERLEY, R/Three cool kids. /1995/P-1/3 KF525 . . . . **E**
ERNST, LC/Little Red Riding Hood: a newfangled prairie tale. /
1995/K-2/4 KF531 . . . . **E**
FREDERICKS, AD/Frantic frogs and other frankly fractured folktales
for readers theatre. /1993//KA362 . . . . **PROF 812**
GWYNNE, F/Pondlarker. /1990/K-2/5 KF656 . . . . **E**
JOHNSTON, T/Cowboy and the black-eyed pea. /1992/
K-2/5 KF839 . . . . **E**
LOWELL, S/Little Red Cowboy Hat. /1997/1-3/3 KG038. . . . . . **E**
MANN, P/Frog Princess? /1995/1-3/2 KG058 . . . . **E**
MINTERS, F/Sleepless Beauty. /1996/2-3/3 KG142 . . . . **E**
SCIESZKA, J/Frog Prince, continued. /1991/1-3/4 KG419 . . . . . **E**
Stinky Cheese Man and other fairly stupid tales. /1992/
4-6/4 KH686 . . . . **Fic**
True story of the 3 little pigs. /1989/K-3/2 KG421. . . . . . . **CE E**
STANLEY, D/Rumpelstiltskin's daughter. /1997/2-5/3 KG537 . . **E**
STEVENS, J/Princess and the pea. /1982/K-2/2 KG555 . . . **CE E**
TELLO, J/Abuelo y los tres osos./Abuelo and the three bears. /
1997/K-2/2 KG598 . . . . **E**
TRIVIZAS, E/Three little wolves and the big bad pig. /1993/
P-3/4 KG619 . . . . **E**
VANDE VELDE, V/Tales from the Brothers Grimm and the Sisters
Weird. /1995/5-A/6 KH827 . . . . **Fic**
Fairy tales--Wit and humor.
WOODWORTH, V/Fairy tale jokes. /1993/2-4/KD743 . . **793.735**
Falcons SEE ALSO Birds of prey; names of specific species e.g. Peregrine
falcon.
Falcons.
ARNOLD, C/Saving the peregrine falcon. /1990/
4-6/7 KC708 . . . . **598.9**
Fall foliage.
JOHNSON, SA/How leaves change. /1986/4-6/9 KC399 . . **581.4**
MAESTRO, B/Why do leaves change color? /1994/
P-4/2 KC400 . . . . **CE 581.4**
Family.
GORDON, G/My two worlds. /1993/3-6/4 KA844 . . . . . . **305.8**
GREENBERG, KE/Zack's story: growing up with same-sex parents. /
1996/4-6/4 KA877 . . . . **306.874**
LEEDY, L/Who's who in my family. /1995/K-2/2 KA869 . . **306.85**
MORRIS, A/Loving. /1990/1-3/2 KA880 . . . . **306.874**
MY FAMILY, YOUR FAMILY (VIDEOCASSETTE). /1994/
K-2/KA871 . . . . **VCR 306.85**
SIMON, N/All kinds of families. /c1976/1-3/5 KA873 . . . **306.85**
WE'RE A FAMILY (VIDEOCASSETTE). /1992/
3-5/KA874 . . . . **VCR 306.85**
Family--Fiction.
ADOFF, A/Black is brown is tan. /1973/P-3/3 KF136 . . . . **E**
ALIKI /Those summers. /1996/K-2/4 KF149. . . . . **E**
BABBITT, N/Bub, or, The very best thing. /1994/P-2/2 KF182 . . **E**
BELTON, S/May'naise sandwiches and sunshine tea. /1994/
1-3/3 KF217 . . . . **E**
CALHOUN, M/Flood. /1997/1-3/2 KF332 . . . . **E**
CLEAVER, V/Where the lilies bloom. /c1969/5-6/6 KH009. . . . **Fic**
DE PAOLA, T/Baby sister. /1996/K-2/2 KF465 . . . . **E**
HASELEY, D/Shadows. /1991/4-6/5 KH224 . . . . **Fic**
HAVILL, J/Treasure nap. /1992/P-1/2 KF683 . . . . **E**
MYERS, WD/Glory Field. /1994/6-A/6 KH522 . . . . **Fic**
PARISH, P/Amelia Bedelia's family album. /1988/K-3/4 KG211.. **E**
PELLEGRINI, N/Families are different. /1991/P-1/2 KG232 . . . . **E**
REISER, L/Surprise family. /1994/P-2/2 KG319 . . . . **E**
STILZ, CC/Grandma Buffalo, May, and me. /1995/
1-3/3 KG573 . . . . **E**
Family--Great Britain.
WILSON, L/Daily life in a Victorian house. /1993/
3-6/7 KE676 . . . . **941.081**
Family--Poetry.
ADOFF, A/All the colors of the race. /1982/4-6/KD907 . . . . **811**
THOMAS, JC/Gingerbread days: poems. /1995/K-4/KE032.. **811**
Family--Religious life--Fiction.
OBERMAN, S/Always Prayer Shawl. /1994/2-4/2 KG184. . . . . **E**
Family in art.
ROALF, P/Families. /1992/5-A/7 KD472 . . . . **757**
Family life.
BANISH, R/Forever family. /1992/2-4/3 KB011 . . . . **362.73**
BROKEN PROMISES (VIDEOCASSETTE). /1991/
/KA298. . . . . **VCR PROF 613.81**
CREWS, D/Bigmama's. /1991/K-2/2 KE309 . . . **CE B CREWS, D.**
GORDON, G/My two worlds. /1993/3-6/4 KA844 . . . . . . **305.8**
JENNESS, A/Families: a celebration of diversity, commitment, and
love. /1990/4-6/5 KA868 . . . . **306.85**

MY FAMILY, YOUR FAMILY (VIDEOCASSETTE). /1994/
  K-2/KA871 . . . . **VCR 306.85**
SOMETHING WRONG AT HOME: THE ALCOHOLIC FAMILY
  (VIDEOCASSETTE). /1994/3-5/KB001 . . . . **VCR 362.292**
WE'RE A FAMILY (VIDEOCASSETTE). /1992/
  3-5/KA874 . . . . **VCR 306.85**
Family life--Bolivia.
  HERMES, J/Children of Bolivia. /1996/4-6/10 KF108 . . . . . . **984**
Family life--Brooklyn (New York, N.Y.)--Fiction.
  BLOS, JW/Brooklyn doesn't rhyme. /1994/4-6/6 KG904 . . . . . **Fic**
Family life--California--Fiction.
  COTTONWOOD, J/Quake!: a novel. /1995/5-A/5 KH034 . . . **Fic**
  CUSHMAN, K/Ballad of Lucy Whipple. /1996/
  5-A/7 KH049 . . . . **CE Fic**
Family life--China--Fiction.
  YEP, L/Serpent's children. /c1984, 1996/6-A/6 KH894 . . . . . . **Fic**
Family life--Cuba.
  STAUB, FJ/Children of Cuba. /1996/4-6/8 KE846 . . . . . **972.91**
Family life--Ecuador.
  BEIRNE, B/Children of the Ecuadorean Highlands. /1996/
  3-6/9 KF112 . . . . **986.6**
Family life--England--Fiction.
  WAUGH, S/Mennyms. /1994/5-A/7 KH843 . . . . **Fic**
  Mennyms alone. /1996/5-A/5 KH844 . . . . **Fic**
  Mennyms in the wilderness. /1995/5-A/5 KH845 . . . . . . **Fic**
  Mennyms under siege. /1996/6-A/6 KH846 . . . . **Fic**
Family life--Fiction.
  AGELL, C/I slide into the white of winter. /1994/K-2/3 KF137 . . **E**
  Mud makes me dance in the spring. /1994/K-2/2 KF139 . . . **E**
  Wind spins me around in the fall. /1994/K-2/3 KF140. . . . . . **E**
  AHLBERG, J/Bear nobody wanted. /c1992, 1995/
  3-6/6 KG821 . . . . **Fic**
  ALCOTT, LM/Little women (Talking book). /1975/
  5-A/KG830 . . . . **TB Fic**
  ALLARD, H/Stupids step out. /1974/K-2/5 KF152 . . . . **E**
  BAKER, B/One Saturday morning. /1994/1-3/1 KF183 . . . . . . **E**
  BAWDEN, N/Carrie's war. /c1973/4-6/6 KG887 . . . . **Fic**
  BLANC, ES/Berchick. /1989/3-5/5 KG901 . . . . **Fic**
  BLUME, J/Fudge-a-mania. /1990/4-6/3 KG909 . . . . . . **CE Fic**
  One in the middle is the green kangaroo. /1981/
  K-3/2 KF238 . . . . **CE E**
  Superfudge. /1980/2-4/2 KG913 . . . . **CE Fic**
  BROWN, LK/Rex and Lilly family time. /1995/K-1/1 KF270 . . . . **E**
  BYARS, BC/Cartoonist. /1978/4-6/3 KG959 . . . . **Fic**
  My brother, Ant. /1996/K-2/1 KF327 . . . . **E**
  CALHOUN, M/Katie John. /c1960/4-6/4 KG966 . . . . **Fic**
  CAMERON, A/More stories Huey tells. /1997/2-4/2 KG968 . . **Fic**
  Stories Huey tells. /1995/2-4/2 KG969 . . . . **Fic**
  CARLSON, NS/Family under the bridge. /c1958/
  3-5/4 KG974 . . . . **Fic**
  Perfect family. /1985/P-2/2 KF351 . . . . **CE E**
  CASELEY, J/Dorothy's darkest days. /1997/3-5/4 KG983 . . . . **Fic**
  Harry and Arney. /1994/3-5/6 KG984 . . . . **Fic**
  Hurricane Harry. /1991/3-5/4 KG985 . . . . **Fic**
  CLEARY, B/Ramona and her father. /1977/3-5/7 KH001 . . . . **Fic**
  Ramona and her mother. /1979/3-5/6 KH002 . . . . **CE Fic**
  Ramona forever. /1984/3-5/6 KH003 . . . . **Fic**
  Ramona Quimby, age 8. /1981/3-5/5 KH004 . . . . **CE Fic**
  Real hole. /c1960, 1986/P/2 KF396 . . . . **E**
  CONRAD, P/Prairie songs. /1985/5-A/7 KH023 . . . . **Fic**
  COOPER, I/Buddy Love: now on video. /1995/5-A/4 KH025 . . **Fic**
  COPELAND, E/Milton, my father's dog. /1994/1-3/3 KF424 . . . **E**
  CREECH, S/Walk two moons. /1994/5-A/5 KH037 . . . . **Fic**
  CRESSWELL, H/Posy Bates, again! /1994/3-5/3 KH039 . . . . . **Fic**
  CREW, L/Nekomah Creek. /1991/4-A/5 KH041. . . . . **Fic**
  Nekomah Creek Christmas. /1994/4-6/6 KH042. . . . . **Fic**
  CURTIS, CP/Watsons go to Birmingham--1963: a novel. /1995/
  6-A/7 KH048 . . . . **CE Fic**
  CUTLER, J/My wartime summers. /1994/5-A/4 KH052 . . . . . . **Fic**
  DANZIGER, P/Forever Amber Brown. /1996/2-4/4 KH062 . . . **Fic**
  DRAANEN, WV/How I survived being a girl. /1997/
  4-A/KH084 . . . . **Fic**
  DUFFEY, B/Utterly yours, Booker Jones. /1995/4-6/5 KH087 . . **Fic**
  ENRIGHT, E/Saturdays. /c1941, 1988/4-6/5 KH099 . . . . **Fic**
  ESTES, E/Moffats. /c1941/3-5/5 KH103 . . . . **Fic**
  FARMER, N/Do you know me. /1993/4-A/5 KH107 . . . . **Fic**
  FEIFFER, J/Man in the ceiling. /1993/5-A/7 KH112 . . . . **Fic**
  FLETCHER, R/Fig pudding. /1995/5-A/4 KH129. . . . . **Fic**
  FLOURNOY, V/Patchwork quilt. /1985/K-3/5 KF561. . . . . **E**
  FREEMAN, S/Cuckoo's child. /1996/5-A/5 KH142 . . . . **Fic**
  GANTOS, J/Heads or tails: stories from the sixth grade. /1994/
  5-A/4 KH150 . . . . **Fic**
  Jack's new power: stories from a Caribbean year. /1995/
  5-A/4 KH151 . . . . **Fic**

  GAUCH, PL/Christina Katerina and the time she quit the family. /
  1987/K-2/6 KF600 . . . . **E**
  GREEN, CJ/Emmy. /1992/6-A/5 KH196 . . . . **Fic**
  HAMILTON, V/M.C. Higgins, the great. /1974/A/4 KH216 . . . **Fic**
  HEATH, A/Sofie's role. /1992/P-2/2 KF692 . . . . **E**
  HECKMAN, P/Waking upside down. /1996/1-3/6 KF693 . . . . **E**
  HEIDE, FP/Sami and the time of the troubles. /1992/
  2-4/4 KF695 . . . . **E**
  HELFMAN, E/On being Sarah. /1993/5-A/6 KH236. . . . . . **Fic**
  HICKMAN, J/Jericho: a novel. /1994/6-A/7 KH256 . . . . . . **Fic**
  HILL, ES/Evan's corner. /c1967, 1991/K-2/2 KF727 . . . . **E**
  HIMMELMAN, J/Day-off machine. /1990/1-3/1 KF729 . . . . . . **E**
  HINTON, SE/Puppy sister. /1995/3-5/4 KH263 . . . . **Fic**
  HIROSHIMA MAIDEN (VIDEOCASSETTE). /c1988, 1997/
  5-A/KH264 . . . . **VCR Fic**
  HITE, S/Dither Farm: a novel. /1992/5-A/7 KH265. . . . . . . **Fic**
  HOME AT LAST (VIDEOCASSETTE). /c1988, 1997/
  5-A/KH276 . . . . **VCR Fic**
  HONEYCUTT, N/Twilight in Grace Falls. /1997/6-A/6 KH278. . **Fic**
  HUGHES, S/Alfie gets in first. /1987/P-K/2 KF784 . . . . **E**
  HURWITZ, J/Ozzie on his own. /1995/3-5/4 KH301 . . . . . . **Fic**
  Roz and Ozzie. /1992/3-5/5 KH302. . . . . **Fic**
  HYPPOLITE, J/Seth and Samona. /1995/4-6/6 KH313 . . **Fic**
  JACKSON, I/Somebody's new pajamas. /1996/3-5/4 KH318 . . **Fic**
  JOHNSON, A/One of three. /1991/P-1/2 KF832 . . . . **E**
  JONES, RC/Great Aunt Martha. /1995/1-3/2 KF853 . . . . **E**
  JOYCE, W/Dinosaur Bob and his adventures with the family
  Lazardo. /1988/K-3/5 KF859 . . . . **E**
  KELLER, H/Geraldine first. /1996/K-2/2 KF881 . . . . **E**
  KHALSA, DK/Tales of a gambling grandma. /1986/
  3-5/6 KH345 . . . . **Fic**
  KING-SMITH, D/School mouse. /1995/3-5/7 KH353 . . . . . **Fic**
  KINSEY-WARNOCK, N/When spring comes. /1993/
  P-2/3 KF906 . . . . **E**
  KRENSKY, S/Lionel at large. /1986/K-2/2 KF924. . . . . **E**
  KWITZ, MD/Little Vampire and the Midnight Bear. /1995/
  1-3/2 KF941 . . . . **E**
  LAKIN, P/Palace of stars. /1993/1-3/3 KF943 . . . . **E**
  LITTLE, J/Revenge of the small Small. /1992/1-3/2 KF996 . . . . **E**
  LOWRY, L/All about Sam. /1988/3-5/4 KH421 . . . . **Fic**
  Anastasia has the answers. /1986/4-6/7 KH423 . . . . **Fic**
  Anastasia Krupnik. /1979/4-6/7 KH424 . . . . **Fic**
  Anastasia on her own. /1985/4-6/6 KH425 . . . . **Fic**
  MACDONALD, M/No room for Francie. /1995/2-3/2 KH440. . **Fic**
  MACLACHLAN, P/Sarah, plain and tall. /1985/
  3-5/4 KH444 . . . . **CE Fic**
  MATHIS, SB/Hundred penny box. /1975/4-6/4 KH461 . . . **CE Fic**
  MAZER, H/Island keeper. /1981/A/6 KH464 . . . . **Fic**
  MCCLOSKEY, R/One morning in Maine. /c1952, 1962/
  1-3/6 KG090 . . . . **E**
  MCDONALD, M/Insects are my life. /1995/1-3/2 KG097 . . . . **E**
  MCEWAN, I/Daydreamer. /1994/4-6/6 KH474 . . . . **Fic**
  MCKAY, H/Exiles at home. /1994/5-A/7 KH479 . . . . **Fic**
  NAMIOKA, L/Yang the third and her impossible family. /1995/
  3-6/5 KH527 . . . . **Fic**
  NEUFELD, J/Edgar Allan: a novel. /c1968/4-A/5 KH545 . . . . **Fic**
  NOVAK, M/Mouse TV. /1994/K-2/3 KG180 . . . . **E**
  ORMEROD, J/Sunshine. /1981/P-1/KG196 . . . . **E**
  OSOFSKY, A/Dreamcatcher. /1992/K-2/5 KG200 . . . . **E**
  PARK, R/Playing Beatie Bow. /1982/5-A/6 KH571 . . . . . . **Fic**
  PATERSON, K/Come sing, Jimmy Jo. /1985/5-A/4 KH574 . . . **Fic**
  PERKINS, M/Sunita experiment. /1993/5-A/6 KH598 . . . . . **Fic**
  PETERSEN, PJ/Some days, some days. /1994/K-2/2 KG234 . . **Fic**
  PORTE, BA/Turkey drive and other tales. /1993/1-3/2 KH611 . **Fic**
  PRYOR, B/Dream jar. /1996/2-3/5 KG291 . . . . **E**
  RASKIN, E/Figgs and phantoms. /1974/4-6/6 KH618 . . . . . **Fic**
  RATTIGAN, JK/Dumpling soup. /1993/1-3/2 KG312 . . . . **E**
  RAVEN, M/Angels in the dust. /1997/2-3/2 KG315. . . . . **E**
  REID BANKS, L/Mystery of the cupboard. /1993/
  5-A/6 KH628 . . . . **CE Fic**
  RODGERS, M/Freaky Friday. /c1972/5-6/5 KH647 . . . . . **CE Fic**
  RYLANT, C/Relatives came. /1985/K-3/8 KG385 . . . . **E**
  SANDERS, SR/Place called Freedom. /1997/1-3/3 KG390 . . . . **E**
  SCHERTLE, A/Maisie. /1995/1-3/4 KG405 . . . . **E**
  SCHWARTZ, HB/When Artie was little. /1996/1-3/2 KG417 . . . **E**
  SCOTT, AH/On mother's lap. /c1972, 1992/P-K/2 KG423 . . . . **E**
  SEGAL, L/Tell me a Mitzi. /c1970/K-3/6 KG426 . . . . **E**
  Tell me a Trudy. /c1977, 1981/K-3/4 KG427 . . . . **E**
  SHELBY, A/Homeplace. /1995/1-3/3 KG493. . . . . **E**
  SMITH, DB/Return to Bitter Creek. /1988/5-A/5 KH721 . . . . . **Fic**
  SMITH, JL/Monster in the third dresser drawer and other stories
  about Adam Joshua. /1981/2-4/4 KH725 . . . . **Fic**
  SNYDER, ZK/Cat running. /1994/5-A/7 KH730 . . . . **Fic**
  SORENSEN, H/New Hope. /1995/1-4/4 KG526 . . . . **E**

SOTO, G/Pool party. /c1993, 1995/4-6/5 KH741 . . . . **Fic**
SPINELLI, J/Crash. /1996/5-A/3 KH744 . . . . **Fic**
STOLZ, M/Noonday friends. /c1965/4-6/6 KH767 . . . . . . **CE Fic**
STOWE, C/Not-so-normal Norman. /1995/2-5/3 KH770 . . . . . **Fic**
TAYLOR, S/All-of-a-kind family. /1951, 1988/4-6/5 KH782 . . . **Fic**
TAYLOR, W/Numbskulls. /1995/4-A/7 KH787 . . . . **Fic**
THOMAS, JR/Celebration! /1997/1-3/3 KG604 . . . . **E**
TURNER, A/Dust for dinner. /1995/2-5/2 KG625 . . . . **E**
UCHIDA, Y/Jar of dreams. /1981/5-6/6 KH815 . . . . **Fic**
VAN LAAN, N/Possum come a-knockin'. /1990/K-2/2 KG642 . . **E**
VAN LEEUWEN, J/Tales of Oliver Pig. /1979/K-2/1 KG649 **CE E**
VIORST, J/Alexander and the terrible, horrible, no good, very bad
    day. /c1972/P-3/7 KG657 . . . . **CE E**
    Alexander and the terrible, horrible, no good, very bad day and
    other stories and poems (Talking book). /1984/
    P-3/KG658 . . . . **TB E**
VOIGT, C/Dicey's song. /1982/5-6/6 KH832 . . . . **Fic**
    Homecoming. /1981/6-A/4 KH833 . . . . **Fic**
WABER, B/Ira sleeps over. /c1972/K-2/2 KG668 . . . . **CE E**
WALLNER, A/Alcott family Christmas. /1996/1-3/2 KG678 . . . . **E**
WALTER, MP/Have a happy... a novel. /1989/4-6/4 KH838 . . **Fic**
    Justin and the best biscuits in the world. /1986/
    4-6/6 KH839 . . . . **Fic**
WEATHERFORD, CB/Juneteenth jamboree. /1995/
    1-3/5 KG690 . . . . **E**
WELLS, R/Noisy Nora. /1997/K-1/4 KG707 . . . . **CE E**
    Noisy Nora (Videocassette). /1993/K-1/KG708 . . . . . . **VCR E**
WHITE, R/Sweet Creek Holler. /1988/6/7 KH854 . . . . **Fic**
WILDER, LI/Dance at Grandpa's. /1994/K-3/4 KG719 . . . . **E**
    Little house in the Big Woods. /c1953/3-6/4 KH860 . . . . . . **Fic**
    Winter days in the Big Woods. /1994/K-3/4 KG720 . . . . **E**
WILLIAMS, SA/Working cotton. /1992/1-3/2 KG731 . . . . **E**
WILLIAMS, VB/Chair for my mother. /1982/P-3/3 KG734 . . . . **E**
    Music, music for everyone. /1984/P-3/4 KG737 . . . . **E**
    Something special for me. /1983/P-3/2 KG738 . . . . **E**
WILSON, J/Elsa, star of the shelter! /1996/4-6/5 KH868 . . . . **Fic**
WISLER, GC/Mustang Flats. /1997/5-A/6 KH872 . . . . **Fic**
WOJCIECHOWSKI, S/Don't call me Beanhead! /1994/
    2-3/5 KH877 . . . . **Fic**
YOUNG, RT/Learning by heart. /1993/6-A/6 KH899 . . . . **Fic**
ZAMORANO, A/Let's eat! /1997/P-2/1 KG786 . . . . **E**
ZOLOTOW, C/My grandson Lew. /c1974/K-2/2 KG805 . . . . . . **E**

Family life--Georgia--Fiction.
YOUNG, RT/Moving Mama to town. /1997/6-A/4 KH900 . . . **Fic**

Family life--Iceland.
PITKANEN, MA/Grandchildren of the Vikings. /1996/
    4-6/8 KE694 . . . . **948**

Family life--India.
HERMES, J/Children of India. /1993/4-6/6 KE711 . . . . **954**

Family life--Maine--Fiction.
LEVIN, B/Fire in the wind. /1995/5-A/4 KH396 . . . . **Fic**

Family life--Mauritania.
GOODSMITH, L/Children of Mauritania: days in the desert and by
    the river shore. /1993/4-6/6 KE733 . . . . **966.1**

Family life--Mexico.
STAUB, FJ/Children of Yucatan. /1996/4-6/7 KE840 . . . . . . **972**

Family life--Micronesia.
HERMES, J/Children of Micronesia. /1994/4-6/9 KF122 . . . **996.5**

Family life--Missouri--Fiction.
HORVATH, P/Happy yellow car. /1994/4-6/6 KH283 . . . . **Fic**

Family life--Morocco.
HERMES, J/Children of Morocco. /1995/3-6/7 KE730 . . . . . **964**

Family life--Nebraska--Fiction.
BUNTING, E/Dandelions. /1995/3-5/2 KG942 . . . . **Fic**

Family life--New York (N.Y.).
WOLF, B/Homeless. /1995/4-6/4 KB010 . . . . **362.5**

Family life--Nigeria.
ONYEFULU, I/Ogbo: sharing life in an African village. /1996/
    3-5/6 KE737 . . . . **966.9**

Family life--Philippines.
KINKADE, S/Children of the Philippines. /1996/
    3-6/8 KE722 . . . . **959.9**

Family life--Poetry.
ADOFF, A/Hard to be six. /1991/1-2/KD909 . . . . **811**
    In for winter, out for spring. /1991/1-4/KD910 . . . . **811**
FAMILIES: POEMS CELEBRATING THE AFRICAN AMERICAN
    EXPERIENCE. /1994/K-3/KE057 . . . . **811.008**
GIOVANNI, N/Knoxville, Tennessee. /1994/P-1/2 KD945 . . . **811**
GREENFIELD, E/Nathaniel talking. /1988/K-6/KD948 . . . . . **811**
HUGHES, S/Rhymes for Annie Rose. /1995/P-2/KE102 . . . . **821**
WONG, JS/Suitcase of seaweed and other poems. /1996/
    5-A/KE045 . . . . **811**

Family life--Songs and music.
MCCUTCHEON, J/Happy adoption day! /1996/
    2-4/3 KD637 . . . . **789.3**

Family life--Taiwan--Fiction.
WU, P/Abacus contest: stories from Taiwan and China. /1996/
    3-5/4 KH884 . . . . **Fic**

Family life--Texas--Fiction.
BURANDT, H/Tales from the homeplace: adventures of a Texas
    farm girl. /1997/5-A/4 KG946 . . . . **Fic**

Family life--West Virginia--Fiction.
NAYLOR, PR/Saving Shiloh. /1997/4-A/4 KH537 . . . . **Fic**

Family life--Wisconsin--Fiction.
WILKES, MD/Little house in Brookfield. /1996/4-6/5 KH861. . . **Fic**

Family problems.
BROKEN PROMISES (VIDEOCASSETTE). /1991/
    /KA298 . . . . **VCR PROF 613.81**
SOMETHING WRONG AT HOME: THE ALCOHOLIC FAMILY
    (VIDEOCASSETTE). /1994/3-5/KB001 . . . . **VCR 362.292**
WHEN THERE'S TROUBLE AT HOME (VIDEOCASSETTE). /1991/
    A/KA883 . . . . **VCR 306.874**

Family problems--Fiction.
BLUME, J/Here's to you, Rachel Robinson. /1993/
    6-A/6 KG910 . . . . **Fic**
BYARS, BC/Not-just-anybody family. /1986/4-A/4 KG962. **CE Fic**
COMAN, C/What Jamie saw. /1995/5-A/6 KH018 . . . . **Fic**
COTTONWOOD, J/Danny ain't. /1992/6-A/6 KH033 . . . . **Fic**
HAZEN, BS/Tight times. /1983/K-2/1 KF689 . . . . **E**
QUINLAN, P/My dad takes care of me. /1987/1-3/2 KG295 . . . **E**
RODOWSKY, C/Hannah in between. /1994/5-A/7 KH650 . . . . **Fic**
SMITH, DB/Best girl. /1993/5-A/6 KH720 . . . . **Fic**
STEVENSON, J/Bones in the cliff. /1995/4-6/6 KH755 . . . . . **Fic**
YARBROUGH, C/Tamika and the wisdom rings. /1994/
    3-4/2 KH888 . . . . **Fic**

Family recreation.
PELLOWSKI, A/Family storytelling handbook. /1987/
    /KA070 . . . . **PROF 027.62**
PERRY, SK/Playing smart: a parent's guide to enriching offbeat
    learning activities for ages 4-14. /1990//KA324 . . . **PROF 790.1**

Family reunions--Fiction.
FLOURNOY, V/Tanya's reunion. /1995/K-3/3 KF562 . . . . **E**

Famous Amos Chocolate Chip Cookie Corporation.
JASPERSOHN, W/Cookies. /1993/3-5/8 KD320 . . . . **664**

Fantastic literature--Bibliography.
LYNN, RN/Fantasy literature for children and young adults: an
    annotated bibliography. /1994//KA032 . . . . . . **PROF 016.80883**

Fantasy.
ADAMS, R/Watership Down. /c1972, 1974/6-A/5 KG813 . . . **Fic**
ALEXANDER, L/Arkadians. /1995/5-A/5 KG832 . . . . **Fic**
    Book of three. /1964/6-A/6 KG833 . . . . **Fic**
    Foundling and other tales of Prydain. /c1973, 1982/
    4-A/5 KG835 . . . . **Fic**
    Illyrian adventure. /1986/5-A/5 KG837 . . . . **Fic**
    Iron ring. /1997/6-A/6 KG838 . . . . **Fic**
    Remarkable journey of Prince Jen. /1991/6-A/6 KG840 . . . . **Fic**
AVI /City of light, city of dark: a comic-book novel. /1993/
    4-6/6 KD409 . . . . **741.5**
BABBITT, N/Search for delicious. /c1969/4-6/5 KG872 . . . **CE Fic**
    Tuck everlasting. /c1975/4-6/4 KG873 . . . . **CE Fic**
BAUM, LF/Road to Oz. /1991/4-6/7 KG884 . . . . **Fic**
    Scarecrow of Oz. /1997/4-6/7 KG885 . . . . **Fic**
    Wonderful Wizard of Oz. /1987/4-6/6 KG886 . . . . **CE Fic**
BRADBURY, R/Halloween tree. /c1982/5-A/7 KG920 . . . . . . **Fic**
BUTTERWORTH, O/Enormous egg. /c1956/3-5/4 KG955 . . . . **Fic**
CARROLL, L/Alice's adventures in Wonderland. /c1865, 1992/
    5-A/7 KG980 . . . . **Fic**
    Through the looking-glass and what Alice found there. /c1872,
    1993/5-A/7 KG981 . . . . **Fic**
CASSEDY, S/Behind the attic wall. /1983/6-A/5 KG986 . . . . . **Fic**
CLEARY, B/Mouse and the motorcycle. /1965/
    3-5/5 KG997 . . . . **CE Fic**
    Ralph S. Mouse (Videocassette). /1990/3-5/KH000 . . . **VCR Fic**
COOPER, S/Over sea, under stone. /1966/A/5 KH028 . . . . . . **Fic**
DAHL, R/Enormous crocodile; and, The magic finger (Talking book).
    /1980/K-3/KF445 . . . . **TB E**
GRAHAME, K/Reluctant dragon. /c1938/3-6/7 KH187 . . . **CE Fic**
    Reluctant dragon. /1983/3-6/6 KH188 . . . . **CE Fic**
    Wind in the willows. /1980/5-6/8 KH189 . . . . **Fic**
    Wind in the willows. 75th anniversary edition. /1983/
    5-6/8 KH190 . . . . **Fic**
GRAVES, R/Big green book. /c1962, 1990/3-6/4 KH192 . . . . **Fic**
HASLER, E/Winter magic. /1989/K-3/4 KF678 . . . . **E**
HUGHES, T/Iron giant: a story in five nights. /1988/
    3-6/3 KH289 . . . . **Fic**
HUNTER, M/Stranger came ashore. /c1975/A/7 KH293 . . . . . **Fic**

HUTCHINS, HJ/Anastasia Morningstar and the crystal butterfly. Rev. ed. /1984/4-6/6 KH306 . . . . **Fic**
Prince of Tarn. /1997/4-6/5 KH308 . . . . **Fic**
Within a painted past. /1994/5-A/4 KH311 . . . . **Fic**
JACQUES, B/Redwall. /1986/5-A/6 KH320 . . . . **Fic**
JAMES, M/Shoebag. /1992/6-A/6 KH323 . . . . **Fic**
JANSSON, T/Finn Family Moomintroll. /c1948, 1990/ 3-6/7 KH325 . . . . **Fic**
JARRELL, R/Animal family. /1995/5-A/6 KH326. . . . . **Fic**
JONES, DW/Archer's goon. /1984/A/6 KH329. . . . . **Fic**
Cart and cwidder. /c1977, 1995/6-A/6 KH331 . . . . **Fic**
Castle in the air. /1991/6-A/7 KH332 . . . . **Fic**
Howl's moving castle. /1986/A/7 KH333 . . . . **Fic**
JOYCE, W/Leaf Men and the brave good bugs. /1996/ 1-3/3 KF861 . . . . **E**
JUSTER, N/Phantom tollbooth. Special 35th anniversary ed. /1996/ 4-6/6 KH339 . . . . **CE Fic**
KEATS, EJ/Ezra Jack Keats Library (Videocassette). /1992/ P-2/KF871 . . . . **VCR E**
Trip. /c1978/K-2/2 KF879 . . . . **CE E**
KENDALL, C/Gammage Cup. /c1959/5-6/7 KH344 . . . . **Fic**
L'ENGLE, M/Wind in the door. /1973/5-6/7 KH393 . . . . **Fic**
LANGTON, J/Diamond in the window. /c1962, 1973/ 4-6/5 KH385 . . . . **Fic**
LE GUIN, UK/Wizard of Earthsea. /c1968, 1991/ 6-A/7 KH392 . . . . **Fic**
LEVINE, GC/Ella enchanted. /1997/5-A/5 KH397 . . . . **Fic**
LEWIS, CS/Lion, the witch and the wardrobe. /1994/ 5-A/6 KH405 . . . . **CE Fic**
LISLE, JT/Forest. /1993/5-A/7 KH409 . . . . **Fic**
MACDONALD, G/Light princess. /1977/4-5/5 KH439. . . . . . . **Fic**
MAHY, M/Five sisters. /1997/4-6/7 KH446 . . . . **Fic**
MCCAFFREY, A/Dragonsong. /c1976, 1986/6-A/6 KH466 . . . **Fic**
MCGRAW, EJ/Moorchild. /1996/5-A/6 KH475 . . . . **Fic**
MCKINLEY, R/Blue sword. /1982/A/7 KH486 . . . . **Fic**
Hero and the crown. /1984/5-A/7 KH488 . . . . **Fic**
MORGAN, A/Matthew and the midnight pilot. /1997/ 1-2/3 KG156 . . . . **E**
NAPOLI, DJ/Jimmy, the pickpocket of the palace. /1995/ 3-A/3 KH530 . . . . **Fic**
NESBIT, E/Enchanted castle. /c1907, 1985/5-6/7 KH541. . . . . **Fic**
Enchanted castle. /1992/5-A/6 KH542 . . . . **Fic**
NORTON, M/Are all the giants dead? /c1975, 1997/ 4-A/5 KH552 . . . . **Fic**
Borrowers. /c1953, 1989/4-6/6 KH554 . . . . **CE Fic**
PEARCE, AP/Tom's midnight garden. /c1958, 1991/ 5-6/5 KH589 . . . . **Fic**
POPE, EM/Perilous gard. /1974/5-6/6 KH609. . . . . **Fic**
RASKIN, E/Figgs and phantoms. /1974/4-6/6 KH618 . . . . **Fic**
SANDBURG, C/Rootabaga stories. /c1922, 1990/ 1-6/7 KH674 . . . . **Fic**
SEIDLER, T/Wainscott weasel. /1993/4-6/5 KH691 . . . . **Fic**
SELDEN, G/Old meadow. /1987/3-5/5 KH697 . . . . **Fic**
Tucker's countryside. /c1969, 1989/4-6/5 KH698. . . . . . . **Fic**
SENDAK, M/Higglety pigglety pop, or, There must be more to life. /c1967/1-3/6 KG431 . . . . **E**
In the night kitchen. /c1970/K-3/2 KG432 . . . . **CE E**
Maurice Sendak Library (Videocassette). /1992/ P-2/KG433 . . . . **VCR E**
Where the wild things are. 25th anniv. ed. /c1963, 1988/ P-3/2 KG438 . . . . **CE E**
Where the wild things are and other stories (Talking book). / 1977/P-2/KG437 . . . . **TB E**
SERVICE, PF/Weirdos of the universe, unite! /1992/ 6-A/6 KH701 . . . . **Fic**
SEUSS, D/Bartholomew and the oobleck. /c1949/P-3/6 KG446 . **E**
SNYDER, ZK/Black and blue magic. /c1966, 1994/ 4-6/7 KH729 . . . . **Fic**
STOCKTON, FR/Griffin and the minor canon. /c1963, 1986/ 3-5/7 KH764 . . . . **Fic**
TOLKIEN, JR/Hobbit; or, There and back again. /n.d./ 4-6/5 KH796 . . . . **Fic**
TRAVERS, PL/Mary Poppins. Rev. ed. /c1962/4-6/6 KH800 . . . **Fic**
Mary Poppins (Talking book). /n.d./4-6/KH801 . . . . . . **TB Fic**
TURNER, MW/Instead of three wishes. /1995/5-A/4 KH813 . . **Fic**
VAN ALLSBURG, C/Jumanji. /1981/K-A/4 KH820 . . . . **Fic**
Jumanji (Kit). /1995/K-A/KH821 . . . . **KIT Fic**
Wreck of the Zephyr. /1983/1-5/3 KH825 . . . . **CE E**
WHITE, EB/Charlotte's web. /c1952/3-6/6 KH850 . . . . **Fic**
WILLARD, N/Sailing to Cythera, and other Anatole stories. /1974/ 3-5/6 KH863 . . . . **Fic**
WINTHROP, E/Castle in the attic. /1985/4-6/6 KH869 . . . **CE Fic**
YOLEN, J/Wizard's Hall. /1991/4-6/6 KH897 . . . . **Fic**
YORINKS, A/Hey, Al. /1986/1-3/3 KG781 . . . . **E**

Louis the fish. /1980/K-3/4 KG782 . . . . **E**
Farm life SEE ALSO Country life; Ranch life.
Farm life.
ANDERSON, J/American family farm. /1989/ 5-6/8 KD145 . . . . **630.973**
BROWN, C/Tractor. /1995/K-2/2 KD146. . . . . **631.3**
DAIRY FARM (VIDEOCASSETTE). /1991/3-5/KD213 . **VCR 636.2**
GEISERT, B/Haystack. /1995/K-3/5 KD153. . . . . **633.2**
GIBBONS, G/Farming. /1988/K-3/2 KD143 . . . . **630**
Farm life--Canada.
BANNATYNE-CUGNET, J/Prairie alphabet. /1992/ 2-6/6 KE811 . . . . **971.2**
Prairie year. /1994/4-6/4 KE812 . . . . **971.2**
KURELEK, W/Prairie boy's summer. /1975/3-5/7 KE813 . . . **971.2**
Prairie boy's winter. /c1973/3-6/7 KE814. . . . . **CE 971.2**
Farm life--Canada--Fiction.
LOTTRIDGE, CB/Ticket to Canada. /1996/4-A/5 KH418 . . . . **Fic**
Wings to fly. /1997/5-A/5 KH419 . . . . **Fic**
Farm life--Fiction.
AVI /Barn. /1994/5-A/3 KG856. . . . . **Fic**
BIRCHMAN, DF/Jigsaw Jackson. /1996/1-3/3 KF230 . . . . . . **E**
BROWN, MW/Big red barn. /c1956, 1989/P-1/3 KF283. . . . . **E**
BUEHNER, C/Fanny's dream. /1996/1-3/4 KF295 . . . . **E**
BYARS, BC/Joy boys. /1996/2-3/1 KF326. . . . . **E**
EHRLICH, A/Parents in the pigpen, pigs in the tub. /1993/ K-2/6 KF521 . . . . **E**
ENRIGHT, E/Thimble summer. /1966/4-6/6 KH100 . . . . . **CE Fic**
FLEISCHMAN, S/Scarebird. /1987/1-3/5 KF552 . . . . **E**
FLEMING, D/Barnyard banter. /1994/P-1/3 KF553 . . . . **E**
GAEDDERT, L/Breaking free. /1994/5-A/5 KH147 . . . . **Fic**
GAGE, W/My stars, it's Mrs. Gaddy!: the three Mrs. Gaddy stories. /1991/1-3/2 KF593 . . . . **E**
GRIFFITH, HV/Grandaddy's place. /1987/1-4/1 KF647 . . . . . **E**
HALL, D/Ox-cart man. /1979/K-3/7 KF663. . . . . **CE E**
HAMILTON, V/Drylongso. /1992/4-6/4 KH214 . . . . **Fic**
Willie Bea and the time the Martians landed. /1983/ 5-6/3 KH219 . . . . **Fic**
Zeely. /c1967/4-A/4 KH220 . . . . **Fic**
HUTCHINS, P/Little Pink Pig. /1994/P-1/2 KF799. . . . . **E**
JACKSON, E/Brown cow, green grass, yellow mellow sun. /1995/ P-1/2 KF818 . . . . **E**
KING-SMITH, D/Cuckoo child. /1993/4-6/6 KH347 . . . . **Fic**
KINSEY-WARNOCK, N/When spring comes. /1993/ P-2/3 KF906 . . . . **E**
LEVINSON, NS/Clara and the bookwagon. /1988/ 1-3/1 KF967 . . . . **E**
MASUREL, C/No, no, Titus! /1997/P-1/2 KG083. . . . . **E**
MCDONNELL, F/I love animals. /1994/P-1/2 KG100 . . . . **E**
MCPHAIL, D/Farm morning. /c1985, 1991/P-1/2 KG118. . . . . **E**
NABB, M/Enchanted horse. /1993/4-6/7 KH525 . . . . **Fic**
NOBLE, TH/Apple tree Christmas. /1984/K-3/6 KG175. . . . . . **E**
PAULSEN, G/Harris and me: a summer remembered. /1993/ 6-A/7 KH586 . . . . **Fic**
PINKNEY, GJ/Back home. /1992/1-3/4 KG240. . . . . **E**
PROVENSEN, A/Owl and three pussycats. /1994/ K-2/5 KG289 . . . . **E**
Year at Maple Hill Farm. /1978/K-2/4 KG290. . . . . **E**
RAWLS, W/Summer of the monkeys. /1976/4-6/6 KH623 . . . . **Fic**
SCHERTLE, A/Maisie. /1995/1-3/4 KG405. . . . . **E**
SMITH, EB/Farm book. /c1910, 1982/2-4/6 KH723 . . . . **Fic**
TAFURI, N/This is the farmer. /1994/P-1/1 KG591. . . . . **E**
TURNER, A/Dust for dinner. /1995/2-5/5 KG625 . . . . **E**
WADDELL, M/Farmer duck. /1992/P-1/2 KG675. . . . . **E**
WOLFF, F/Seven loaves of bread. /1993/1-3/2 KG758 . . . . . **E**
Farm life--Florida--Fiction.
RAWLINGS, MK/Yearling. /c1938, 1967/5-A/5 KH622 . . . . . **Fic**
Farm life--France--Fiction.
SCHNUR, S/Shadow children. /1994/4-A/7 KH681 . . . . **Fic**
Farm life--Missouri--Fiction.
MACBRIDE, RL/Little house on Rocky Ridge. /1993/ 4-6/6 KH436 . . . . **Fic**
Farm life--Nebraska--Fiction.
HOME AT LAST (VIDEOCASSETTE). /c1988, 1997/ 5-A/KH276 . . . . **VCR Fic**
Farm life--New Mexico--Fiction.
STEVENS, JR/Carlos and the skunk./Carlos y el zorrillo. /1997/ 1-3/3 KG554 . . . . **E**
Farm life--Oklahoma--Fiction.
RAVEN, M/Angels in the dust. /1997/2-3/2 KG315. . . . . **E**
Farm life--South Dakota--Fiction.
KARR, K/Cave. /1994/5-A/4 KH341 . . . . **Fic**
Farm life--Texas--Fiction.
BURANDT, H/Tales from the homeplace: adventures of a Texas farm girl. /1997/5-A/4 KG946 . . . . **Fic**

Farm life--Vermont.
ARNOSKY, J/Nearer nature. /1996/A/6 KE933 . . . . **974.3**
LET'S GO TO THE FARM (VIDEOCASSETTE). /1994/
1-6/KD144. . . . . **VCR 630**

Farm life--Virginia--Fiction.
FLOURNOY, V/Tanya's reunion. /1995/K-3/3 KF562 . . . . . . **E**

Farmers.
ANDERSON, J/American family farm. /1989/
5-6/8 KD145 . . . . **630.973**

Farmers' markets--Fiction.
JOHNSON, PB/Farmers' market. /1997/P-1/2 KF837 . . . . . . **E**
Farming SEE ALSO Agriculture; Dairying; Gardening; Livestock.

Farming--Vocational guidance.
ANDERSON, J/American family farm. /1989/
5-6/8 KD145 . . . . **630.973**

Farms.
DOWN ON THE FARM: YESTERDAY AND TODAY
(VIDEOCASSETTE). /1987/3-A/KD142. . . . . **VCR 630**
GIBBONS, G/Farming. /1988/K-3/2 KD143 . . . . **630**
LET'S GO TO THE FARM (VIDEOCASSETTE). /1994/
1-6/KD144. . . . . **VCR 630**

Farms--Fiction.
FLEISCHMAN, S/McBroom's wonderful one-acre farm: three tall
tales. /1992/3-6/4 KH124 . . . . **Fic**
MACLACHLAN, P/All the places to love. /1994/1-4/5 KG053 . . **E**
NOBLE, TH/Day Jimmy's boa ate the wash. /1980/
K-2/2 KG176 . . . . **CE E**
SYKES, J/This and that. /1996/P-1/2 KG586 . . . . **E**

Farnsworth, Philo Taylor.
MCPHERSON, SS/TV's forgotten hero: the story of Philo
Farnsworth. /1996/5-A/9 KE342 . . . . **B FARNSWORTH, P**

Fashion--History.
ROWLAND-WARNE, L/Costume. /1992/4-6/8 KB165. . . . . . **391**
Fasts and feasts SEE ALSO Christmas; Easter; Festivals; Holidays;
Thanksgiving.

Fasts and feasts--Hinduism.
KADODWALA, D/Holi. /1997/4-6/7 KA763 . . . . **294.5**

Fasts and feasts--Hinduism--Fiction.
GILMORE, R/Lights for Gita. /1994/1-3/5 KF620 . . . . **E**

Fasts and feasts--Islam.
GHAZI, SH/Ramadan. /1996/3-5/7 KA785 . . . . **297**
KERVEN, R/Id-ul-Fitr. /1997/3-5/7 KA787 . . . . **297**

Fasts and feasts--Islam--Fiction.
MATTHEWS, M/Magid fasts for Ramadan. /1996/
4-6/4 KH462 . . . . **Fic**
Fasts and feasts--Judaism SEE ALSO names of specific holidays e.g.
Hanukkah.

Fasts and feasts--Judaism.
DRUCKER, M/Family treasury of Jewish holidays. /1994/
2-6/6 KA772 . . . . **296.4**
ZALBEN, JB/Beni's family cookbook for the Jewish holidays. /1996/
4-6/KD283. . . . . **641.5**

Fasts and feasts--Judaism--Poetry.
POEMS FOR JEWISH HOLIDAYS. /1986/K-3/KE077 . . . **811.008**

Fasts and feasts--Mexico.
HOYT-GOLDSMITH, D/Day of the Dead: a Mexican-American
celebration. /1994/4-6/7 KB198 . . . . **394.26**

Fasts and feasts--United States.
AMERICAN BOOK OF DAYS. 3RD ED. /1978/
4-6/KA412 . . . . **REF 394.2**

Father and child.
ALPERT, L/You and your dad. /1992/P-1/2 KA876 . . . . **306.874**
GREENSPUN, AA/Daddies. /1991/1-3/4 KA878 . . . . . . **306.874**
ROTNER, S/Lots of dads. /1997/P-1/2 KA881 . . . . **306.874**

Father and child--Fiction.
AVI /Barn. /1994/5-A/3 KG856. . . . . **Fic**
BOYD, CD/Daddy, Daddy, be there. /1995/1-3/2 KF254 . . . . . **E**
MCKENZIE, EK/King, the princess, and the tinker. /1992/
3-5/4 KH483 . . . . **Fic**
WOOD, J/Dads are such fun. /1992/P-K/1 KG769 . . . . **E**

Father's Day--Fiction.
KROLL, S/Happy Father's Day. /1988/K-2/2 KF928 . . . . **E**

Fathers.
GREENSPUN, AA/Daddies. /1991/1-3/4 KA878 . . . . . . **306.874**
ROTNER, S/Lots of dads. /1997/P-1/2 KA881 . . . . **306.874**

Fathers--Fiction.
BUTTERWORTH, O/Visit to the big house. /1993/
3-5/5 KG956 . . . . **Fic**
DALY, N/My dad. /1995/1-4/5 KF447 . . . . **E**
ISADORA, R/At the crossroads. /1991/K-2/1 KF811 . . . . **E**
At the crossroads (Videocassette). /1996/K-2/KF812 . . . **VCR E**
POLACCO, P/My ol' man. /1995/1-3/3 KG254 . . . . **E**
Some birthday! /1991/K-2/4 KG257 . . . . **E**

VIGNA, J/I wish Daddy didn't drink so much. /1988/
P-3/2 KG653 . . . . **E**

Fathers and daughters.
DAHL, L/James and the giant peach: the book and movie
scrapbook. /1996/3-6/6 KD684. . . . . **791.43**

Fathers and daughters--Fiction.
AGELL, C/I wear long green hair in the summer. /1994/
K-2/2 KF138 . . . . **E**
BANG, M/Ten, nine, eight. /1983/P-K/KF192 . . . . **E**
BORDEN, L/Little ships: the heroic rescue at Dunkirk in World War
II. /1997/3-5/3 KF251. . . . . **E**
BUNTING, E/Spying on Miss Muller. /1995/6-A/6 KG944 . . . **Fic**
BUSSER, M/On the road with Poppa Whopper. /1997/
3-4/2 KG954 . . . . **Fic**
CLEARY, B/Ramona and her father. /1977/3-5/7 KH001 . . . . . **Fic**
DE PAOLA, T/Days of the blackbird: a tale of northern Italy. /
1997/1-3/6 KF468 . . . . **E**
GLEITZMAN, M/Blabber mouth. /1995/3-5/4 KH173 . . . . . . **Fic**
Sticky Beak. /1995/3-5/4 KH176 . . . . **Fic**
HAMILTON, V/Plain City. /1993/6-A/5 KH217 . . . . **Fic**
HENKES, K/Protecting Marie. /1995/5-A/6 KH238 . . . . **Fic**
HESSE, K/Sable. /1994/3-5/4 KH253 . . . . **Fic**
LISLE, JT/Gold dust letters. /1994/4-6/7 KH410 . . . . **Fic**
LOWERY, L/Laurie tells. /1994/3-6/4 KH420. . . . . **Fic**
MARTIN, JR., B/White Dynamite and Curly Kidd. /c1986, 1989/
K-3/2 KG078 . . . . **E**
MCCLINTOCK, B/Fantastic drawings of Danielle. /1996/
3-5/4 KH467 . . . . **Fic**
MCPHAIL, D/Farm morning. /c1985, 1991/P-1/2 KG118. . . . . **E**
NELSON, T/Earthshine: a novel. /1994/6-A/6 KH540 . . . . . . **Fic**
ROCKWELL, AF/Ducklings and pollywogs. /1994/K-2/3 KG341 . **E**
RYDER, J/My father's hands. /1994/K-2/KG366 . . . . **E**
SEBESTYEN, O/Words by heart. /1997/5-A/7 KH689 . . . **CE Fic**
SHOWERS, P/Listening walk. /c1961, 1991/P-1/1 KG495. . . . . **E**
SILVERMAN, E/Gittel's hands. /1996/K-2/2 KG506. . . . . . . **E**
YOLEN, J/Owl moon. /1987/P-3/2 KG778. . . . . **CE E**

Fathers and daughters--Folklore.
YOLEN, J/Emperor and the kite. /1988/2-3/6 KB791 . . . . **398.27**

Fathers and sons--Fiction.
ACKERMAN, K/Bingleman's Midway. /1995/2-4/5 KF128 . . . . . **E**
BARTONE, E/Peppe the lamplighter. /1993/1-3/2 KF211. . . . . **E**
BAUER, J/Sticks. /1996/6-A/4 KG880. . . . . **Fic**
BERRY, J/Ajeemah and his son. /1992/6-A/7 KG899 . . . . . . **Fic**
COTTONWOOD, J/Danny ain't. /1992/6-A/6 KH033 . . . . . . **Fic**
DAHL, R/Danny, the champion of the world. /c1975, 1988/
4-6/6 KH054 . . . . **Fic**
ERNST, LC/Squirrel Park. /1993/K-2/5 KF533. . . . . **E**
FOWLER, SG/I'll see you when the moon is full. /1994/
K-2/2 KF568 . . . . **E**
FRIEDMAN, A/Cloak for the dreamer. /1995/1-3/6 KF585 . . . . **E**
HAVEN, K/Fathers and sons (Sound recording cassette). /1991/
1-4/KF679 . . . . **SRC E**
HERMES, P/Kevin Corbett eats flies. /1989/5-6/3 KH248 . . . . **Fic**
HILL, D/Take it easy. /1997/6-A/4 KH260 . . . . **Fic**
HUGHES, M/Golden Aquarians. /1995/5-A/6 KH287 . . . . . . **Fic**
HURWITZ, J/Baseball fever. /1981/4-6/6 KH297 . . . . **Fic**
Ozzie on his own. /1995/3-5/4 KH301 . . . . **Fic**
JAMES, M/Frankenlouse. /1994/6-A/6 KH322 . . . . **Fic**
JOHNSON, A/Joshua's night whispers (Board book). /1994/
P/2 KF830 . . . . **BB E**
KOERTGE, R/Harmony Arms. /1994/A/5 KH371 . . . . **Fic**
LAKIN, P/Dad and me in the morning. /1994/1-3/2 KF942 . . . . **E**
LONDON, J/Let's go, Froggy! /1994/P-K/2 KG024 . . . . **E**
LONG, E/Gone fishing. /1984/P-1/1 KG030 . . . . **E**
MANUSHKIN, F/Peeping and sleeping. /1994/P-2/2 KG060 . . . **E**
MCKAY, JR., L/Caravan. /1995/3-5/6 KH480 . . . . **Fic**
QUINLAN, P/My dad takes care of me. /1987/1-3/2 KG295. . . **E**
RODGERS, M/Summer switch. /1982/5-6/7 KH648 . . . . **Fic**
RYAN, ME/Trouble with perfect. /1995/6-A/3 KH659. . . . . . **Fic**
SACKS, M/Themba. /1994/3-5/5 KH670. . . . . **Fic**
SAY, A/Lost lake. /1989/1-3/2 KG398 . . . . **E**
SCHINDEL, J/Dear Daddy. /1995/K-2/2 KG406 . . . . **E**
SHREVE, S/Formerly great Alexander family. /1995/
3-5/6 KH708 . . . . **Fic**
SMITH, RK/Bobby baseball. /1991/3-6/4 KH726 . . . . **Fic**
STEVENSON, J/Bones in the cliff. /1995/4-6/6 KH755 . . . . . **Fic**
WISLER, GC/Mustang Flats. /1997/5-A/6 KH872 . . . . **Fic**
YEP, L/Dragonwings. /c1975/5-6/6 KH892. . . . . **Fic**
YOUNG, RT/Moving Mama to town. /1997/6-A/4 KH900 . . . **Fic**

Fear.
KOPLOW, L/Tanya and the Tobo Man/Tanya y el Hombre Tobo: /
1991/K-2/2 KD040 . . . . **618.92**
MURPHY, J/Songs for you and me: kids learn about feelings and
emotions /n.d./K-1/KA629 . . . . **SRC 152.4**

Fear--Fiction.
BUNTING, E/Ghost's hour, spook's hour. /1987/P-2/2 KF301 . . **E**
CAMERON, A/Julian's glorious summer. /1987/2-4/2 KG967. . **Fic**
CROSS, G/New world. /1995/6-A/5 KH044 . . . . **Fic**
DICKINSON, P/Chuck and Danielle. /1996/4-6/7 KH076. . . . . **Fic**
EMBERLEY, E/Go away, big green monster! /1992/
P-1/2 KF522 . . . . **E**
GRIESE, AA/Way of our people. /1997/5-6/5 KH203 . . . . . . **Fic**
GRIFALCONI, A/Darkness and the butterfly. /1987/
K-2/4 KF645 . . . . **E**
HALL, K/I'm not scared. /1994/K-1/1 KF664 . . . . **E**
HENKES, K/Words of stone. /1992/5-A/6 KH240 . . . . **Fic**
HESSE, K/Lester's dog. /1993/1-3/3 KF716 . . . . **E**
HOLMAN, F/Slake's limbo. /1974/6-A/7 KH274 . . . . **CE Fic**
HOWE, J/There's a monster under my bed. /1986/
P-2/2 KF781 . . . . **E**
MARTIN, JR., B/Ghost-eye tree. /1985/K-3/2 KG075 . . . . . . **E**
MARTIN, JB/Grandmother Bryant's pocket. /1996/
1-4/3 KG079 . . . . **E**
POLACCO, P/Thunder cake. /1990/1-3/4 KG258 . . . . **CE E**
STOLZ, M/Storm in the night. /1988/K-3/4 KG578 . . . . **E**
TEAGUE, M/Field beyond the outfield. /1992/K-2/2 KG594 . . . **E**
WADDELL, M/Let's go home, Little Bear. /1993/P-K/3 KG676 . . **E**
WELLS, R/Edward in deep water. /1995/P-K/2 KG697 . . . . . **E**
WILLIAMS, L/Little old lady who was not afraid of anything. /
1986/P-2/4 KG730 . . . . **CE E**
Fear--Fiction--Software.
BERENSTAIN BEARS IN THE DARK. SCHOOL ED. (CD-ROM). /
1996/K-3/KF224 . . . . **CDR E**
Fear of the dark--Fiction.
HOBAN, R/Bedtime for Frances. Newly ill. ed. /1995/
P-1/2 KF739 . . . . **CE E**
WADDELL, M/Can't you sleep, Little Bear? 2nd ed. /c1988, 1992/
P-K/3 KG674 . . . . **E**
Feathers.
O'CONNOR, K/Feather book. /1990/5-6/6 KC670 . . . . **598.147**
PATENT, DH/Feathers. /1992/5-6/6 KC671 . . . . **598.147**
Feelings SEE Emotions.
Felidae SEE ALSO Cats.
Felidae.
GIBBONS, G/Cats. /1996/K-3/3 KC821 . . . . **599.75**
LUMPKIN, S/Big cats. /1993/5-6/6 KC823 . . . . **599.75**
Small cats. /1993/5-6/8 KC824 . . . . **599.75**
RYDEN, H/Your cat's wild cousins. /1991/4-6/5 KC825. . . **599.75**
SIMON, S/Big cats. /1991/4-6/6 KC826 . . . . **599.75**
Felidae--Software.
EYEWITNESS VIRTUAL REALITY: CAT (CD-ROM). /1995/
3-A/KC820 . . . . **CDR 599.75**
Feminism SEE ALSO Sex role.
Feminists.
FRITZ, J/You want women to vote, Lizzie Stanton? /1995/
3-6/5 KE549 . . . . **B STANTON, E.**
Feminists--Fiction.
MCCULLY, EA/Ballot box battle. /1996/1-3/2 KH473 . . . . . . **Fic**
Fennec.
LAUKEL, HG/Desert fox family book. /1996/
3-6/7 KC846 . . . . **599.776**
Feral children--Fiction.
HESSE, K/Music of dolphins. /1996/5-A/3 KH252 . . . . **Fic**
YOLEN, J/Children of the wolf. /c1984, 1993/6-A/7 KH896 . . **Fic**
Ferret.
JOHNSON, SA/Ferrets. /1997/5-6/10 KD182 . . . . **636**
Ferrets as pets.
JOHNSON, SA/Ferrets. /1997/5-6/10 KD182 . . . . **636**
Ferries.
MAESTRO, B/Ferryboat. /1986/P-3/2 KB144 . . . . **386**
Festivals.
BERNHARD, E/Happy New Year! /1996/1-3/7 KB205 . . **394.261**
CHASE, WD/Chase's calendar of annual events: special days, weeks
and months. /1958-//KA264 . . . . **PROF 394.2**
FOLKLORE OF WORLD HOLIDAYS. /1992/
4-6/KA414 . . . . **REF 394.26**
MACDONALD, MR/Celebrate the world: twenty tellable folktales
for multicultural festivals. /1994//KA270 . . . . **PROF 398.2**
SMITH, D/Holidays and festivals activities. /1994/
1-6/6 KD458 . . . . **745.594**
Festivals--Asia, Southeastern.
VIESTI, JF/Celebrate! in Southeast Asia. /1996/
2-5/11 KB192 . . . . **394.2**
Festivals--Fiction.
BARTONE, E/American too. /1996/1-3/3 KF210 . . . . **E**
Festivals--Mexico.
SILVERTHORNE, E/Fiesta!: Mexico's greatest celebrations. /1992/
4-6/7 KB203 . . . . **394.26**

Festivals--Mexico--Fiction.
FLORA, J/Fabulous Firework Family. /1994/1-3/4 KF559 . . . . . **E**
Festivals--Poetry.
LIVINGSTON, MC/Festivals. /1996/3-6/KD976 . . . . **811**
Festivals--South Asia.
VIESTI, JF/Celebrate! in South Asia. /1996/2-5/11 KB191 . . **394.2**
Festivals--United States.
AMERICAN BOOK OF DAYS. 3RD ED. /1978/
4-6/KA412 . . . . **REF 394.2**
Fetterman Fight, Wyo., 1866.
FREEDMAN, R/Life and death of Crazy Horse. /1996/
6-A/7 KE307 . . . . **B CRAZY HORSE**
GOBLE, P/Brave Eagle's account of the Fetterman Fight, 21
December 1866. /c1972, 1992/5-6/6 KE913 . . . . **973.8**
Fibers.
KEELER, PA/Unraveling fibers. /1995/4-6/4 KD335 . . . . **677**
Fiction SEE ALSO Animals--Fiction; Fables; Fairy tales; Fantasy; Folklore;
Ghosts--Fiction; Legends; Mystery and detective stories; Science fiction;
Sea stories; Short stories; etc.
Field, Eugene.
GREENE, C/Eugene Field: the children's poet. /1994/
2-4/4 KE343 . . . . **B FIELD, E.**
Fielding (Baseball).
SULLIVAN, G/Glovemen: twenty-seven of baseball's greatest. /
1996/4-6/8 KD804 . . . . **796.357**
Fifth grade (Education)--United States--Case studies.
KIDDER, T/Among schoolchildren. /1989//KA192. . **PROF 372.11**
Fighting SEE Boxing.
Figures of speech.
TERBAN, M/It figures!: fun figures of speech. /1993/
5-A/8 KD865 . . . . **808**
Figures of speech--Dictionaries.
TERBAN, M/Scholastic dictionary of idioms. /1996/
4-6/KA431 . . . . **REF 423**
Finance, Personal.
BARKIN, C/Jobs for kids: the guide to having fun and making
money. /1990/5-6/7 KD305 . . . . **650.1**
PIGGY BANKS TO MONEY MARKETS: A KID'S VIDEO GUIDE TO
DOLLARS AND SENSE (VIDEOCASSETTE). /1993/
4-6/KA945 . . . . **VCR 332.024**
SCHWARTZ, DM/If you made a million. /1989/
2-5/5 KA946 . . . . **332.024**
Finance, Personal--Fiction.
VIORST, J/Alexander, who used to be rich last Sunday. /c1978/
P-3/5 KG659 . . . . **CE E**
Fine arts SEE Art; Drawing; Painting; Sculpture.
Finger play.
COLE, J/Eentsy, weentsy spider: fingerplays and action rhymes. /
1991/P-K/KD706 . . . . **793.4**
COOPER, K/Too many rabbits and other fingerplays about animals,
nature, weather, and the universe. /1995/P-1/KD707 . . . . . **793.4**
HALLUM, R/Fingerplays and footplays (Videocassette). /1997/
P-K/KD708 . . . . **VCR 793.4**
HELLER, N/This little piggy. /1997/P-1/2 KF699 . . . . **E**
JUBA THIS AND JUBA THAT. /1995/KA366 . . . . . **PROF 820.8**
LEWIS, S/Let's play games (Videocassette). /1994/
P-2/KD709 . . . . **VCR 793.4**
NELSON, EL/Everybody sing and dance. /1989/
/KA321 . . . . **CE PROF 789.3**
PETERSHAM, M/Rooster crows: a book of American rhymes and
jingles. /c1945/K-2/KB810 . . . . **398.8**
PRESCHOOL ACTION TIME (SOUND RECORDING CASSETTE). /
1988/P/KD650 . . . . **SRC 789.3**
VAN RYNBACH, I/Five little pumpkins. /1995/P-K/2 KB817 . **398.8**
WEIMER, TE/Fingerplays and action chants: volume 1: animals. /
1995/P-1/KD710 . . . . **BA 793.4**
WOOD, D/Piggies. /1991/P-K/1 KG768 . . . . **E**
Fink, Mike SEE Mike Fink (Legendary character).
Fink, Mike--Legends.
KELLOGG, S/Mike Fink. /1992/3-4/5 KB456 . . . . **398.22**
Sally Ann Thunder Ann Whirlwind Crockett: a tall tale. /1995/
2-5/5 KB458 . . . . **398.22**
Finmark (Norway)--Social life and customs.
REYNOLDS, J/Far north: vanishing cultures. /1992/
3-6/6 KE696 . . . . **948.97**
Finn MacCool.
DE PAOLA, T/Fin M'Coul: the giant of Knockmany Hill. /1981/
1-3/4 KB392 . . . . **398.21**
GLEESON, B/Finn McCoul (Videocassette). /1991/
3-5/KB445 . . . . **VCR 398.22**
Fir.
FISCHER-NAGEL, H/Fir trees. /1989/3-6/7 KC436 . . . . **585**
Fire.
HOFFMAN, M/Earth, fire, water, air. /1995/2-6/7 KA814 . **304.2**

Fire--Folklore.
LONDON, J/Fire race: a Karuk Coyote tale about how fire came to the people. /1993/3-4/4 KB611 . . . . **398.24**

Fire departments.
FIRE STATION (VIDEOCASSETTE). /1990/
2-4/KB031 . . . . **VCR 363.3**

Fire departments--Fiction.
AVERILL, E/Fire cat. /c1960/K-2/2 KF177 . . . . **E**

Fire ecology.
CONE, P/Wildfire. /1997/4-A/6 KB040 . . . . **363.37**
PRINGLE, LP/Fire in the forest: a cycle of growth and renewal. /
1995/A/8 KC305 . . . . **577.2**
SIMON, S/Wildfires. /1996/3-6/7 KB041 . . . . **363.37**
STAUB, FJ/Yellowstone's cycle of fire. /1993/4-6/8 KC306 . **577.2**

Fire engines.
ROCKWELL, AF/Fire engines. /1986/P/3 KD088 . . . . **628.9**

Fire engines--Design and construction.
BOUCHER, J/Fire truck nuts and bolts. /1993/
4-5/6 KD085 . . . . **628.9**

Fire extinction.
GIBBONS, G/Fire! Fire! /1984/P-2/4 KD086 . . . . **628.9**
KUKLIN, S/Fighting fires. /1993/K-3/5 KD087 . . . . **628.9**

Fire fighters.
FIRE STATION (VIDEOCASSETTE). /1990/
2-4/KB031 . . . . **VCR 363.3**
GIBBONS, G/Fire! Fire! /1984/P-2/4 KD086 . . . . **628.9**
KUKLIN, S/Fighting fires. /1993/K-3/5 KD087 . . . . **628.9**
ROCKWELL, AF/Fire engines. /1986/P/3 KD088 . . . . **628.9**

Fire lookout stations--Fiction.
BUNTING, E/On Call Back Mountain. /1997/1-3/2 KF306 . . . . . **E**

Firearms--Fiction.
FOX, P/One-eyed cat. /1984/A/7 KH138 . . . . **Fic**

Firearms--Safety measures.
HANDGUNS: MADE FOR KILLING, NOT FOR KIDS
(VIDEOCASSETTE). /1996/6-A/KB033 . . . . **VCR 363.3**

Fireflies.
HAWES, J/Fireflies in the night. Rev. ed. /c1991/
P-2/4 KC552 . . . . **595.76**
JOHNSON, SA/Fireflies. /1986/A/10 KC553 . . . . . . **595.76**

Fireflies--Fiction.
CARLE, E/Very lonely firefly. /1995/P-2/2 KF348 . . . . **E**
EASTMAN, PD/Sam and the firefly. /c1958/P-1/1 KF507 . . . . . **E**
LONDON, J/Fireflies, fireflies, light my way. /1996/
P-2/2 KG020 . . . . **E**
STURGES, P/Ten flashing fireflies. /1995/K-2/2 KG581 . . . . . . **E**

Firemen SEE Fire fighters.
Fires SEE ALSO Arson; Forest fires.

Fires.
CONE, P/Wildfire. /1997/4-A/6 KB040 . . . . **363.37**
SIMON, S/Wildfires. /1996/3-6/7 KB041 . . . . **363.37**
WOOD, L/Fires. /1994/4-6/7 KB042 . . . . **363.37**

Fires--California--Oakland--Fiction.
POLACCO, P/Tikvah means hope. /1994/1-3/2 KG259 . . . . . . **E**

Fires--Fiction.
LEVIN, B/Fire in the wind. /1995/5-A/4 KH396 . . . . **Fic**

Fires--Illinois--Chicago--History--19th century.
MURPHY, J/Great fire. /1995/A/7 KF015 . . . . **977.3**

Fireworks.
KUKLIN, S/Fireworks: the science, the art, and the magic. /1996/
5-6/6 KD317 . . . . **662**

Fireworks--Fiction.
FLORA, J/Fabulous Firework Family. /1994/1-3/4 KF559 . . . . . . **E**

First day of school--Fiction.
COHEN, M/Will I have a friend? /c1967/K-1/2 KF405 . . . . **CE E**
LASKY, K/Lunch bunnies. /1996/K-2/2 KF946 . . . . **E**
LONDON, J/Froggy goes to school. /1996/P-1/2 KG022 . . . . . **E**
SLATE, J/Miss Bindergarten gets ready for kindergarten. /1996/
P-K/2 KF515 . . . . **E**
STOEKE, JM/Minerva Louise at school. /1996/P-1/2 KG577 . . . **E**
VAN LEEUWEN, J/Oliver Pig at school. /1994/
K-2/1 KG648 . . . . **CE E**

First ladies SEE ALSO names of specific First ladies e.g. Roosevelt, Eleanor.

First ladies.
ANDERSON, CC/Jackie Kennedy Onassis: woman of courage. /
1995/A/7 KE484 . . . . **B ONASSIS, J.**
COONEY, B/Eleanor. /1996/4-5/7 KE520 . . . **B ROOSEVELT, E.**
FREEDMAN, R/Eleanor Roosevelt: a life of discovery. /1993/
6-A/7 KE521 . . . . **B ROOSEVELT, E.**
GORMLEY, B/First Ladies: women who called the White House
home. /1997/4-6/9 KE852 . . . . **973**
LEVERT, S/Hillary Rodham Clinton, first lady. /1994/
4-6/9 KE297 . . . . **B CLINTON, H.**
QUACKENBUSH, R/James Madison and Dolley Madison and their
times. /1992/4-5/7 KE894 . . . . **973.5**

SMITHSONIAN BOOK OF THE FIRST LADIES: THEIR LIVES,
TIMES, AND ISSUES. /1996/6-A/9 KE866 . . . . **973**

Fish habitat improvement.
CONE, M/Come back, salmon: how a group of dedicated kids
adopted Pigeon Creek and brought it back to life. /1992/
4-6/6 KD248 . . . . **639.3**

Fisheries SEE ALSO Fishes; Whaling.

Fisheries.
BAILEY, D/Fishing. /1990/K-2/2 KD861 . . . . **799.1**
JENSON, LB/Fishermen of Nova Scotia. /1980/
A/9 KD245 . . . . **639.2**

Fishers.
FLORIAN, D/Fisher. /1994/1-3/5 KD244 . . . . **639.2**

Fishers--Fiction.
ORR, K/My grandpa and the sea. /1990/K-2/2 KG198 . . . . . **E**

Fishes SEE ALSO Aquariums; Fisheries; Fishing; Tropical fish; also names of fish e.g. Sharks, etc.

Fishes.
AUDUBON SOCIETY FIELD GUIDE TO NORTH AMERICAN
FISHES, WHALES AND DOLPHINS. /1983/A/11 KC583 . . . **597**
COLE, J/Fish hatches. /c1978/P-A/3 KC596 . . . . **597.5**
PARKER, S/Fish. /1990/5-6/7 KC584 . . . . **597**
PFEFFER, W/What's it like to be a fish? /1996/K-3/3 KC585 . **597**
WILDSMITH, B/Fishes. /1985/P/KC587 . . . . **597**
WU, N/Fish faces. /c1993, 1997/1-6/3 KC588 . . . . **597**

Fishes--Fiction.
BOYLE, D/Coral reef hideaway: the story of a clown anemonefish. /
1995/K-2/7 KF255 . . . . **CE E**
CAZET, D/Fish in his pocket. /1987/P-2/2 KF374 . . . . **E**
EHLERT, L/Fish eyes: a book you can count on. /1990/
P-K/1 KF518 . . . . **E**
JONAS, A/Splash! /1995/P-2/1 KF848 . . . . **E**
LIONNI, L/Swimmy. /c1968/K-2/6 KF995 . . . . **E**
PALMER, H/Fish out of water. /c1961/K-2/2 KG209 . . . . **E**
SEUSS, D/McElligot's pool. /c1947/P-3/KG467 . . . . **E**
TORNQVIST, R/Christmas carp. /1990/2-4/2 KH798 . . . . . . **Fic**

Fishing SEE ALSO Fly fishing.

Fishing.
BAILEY, D/Fishing. /1990/K-2/2 KD861 . . . . **799.1**
FLORIAN, D/Fisher. /1994/1-3/5 KD244 . . . . **639.2**

Fishing--Fiction.
LONG, E/Gone fishing. /1984/P-1/1 KG030 . . . . **E**
MCKISSACK, P/Million fish...more or less. /c1992, 1996/
1-3/4 KG106 . . . . **E**
SAY, A/River dream. /1988/K-3/4 KG399 . . . . **E**
STOLZ, M/Go fish. /1991/3-6/6 KH766 . . . . **Fic**
VALGARDSON, WD/Winter rescue. /1995/3-5/4 KH819 . . . . **Fic**

Flags.
CRAMPTON, WG/Flag. /1989/5-A/8 KE616 . . . . **929.9**
FLAGS OF THE NATIONS (VIDEOCASSETTE). /1993/
A/KE618 . . . . **VCR 929.9**

Flags--United States.
WALLNER, A/Betsy Ross. /1994/3-4/6 KE526 . . . . . **B ROSS, B.**

Flags--United States--History.
ARMBRUSTER, A/American flag. /1991/4-6/8 KE613 . . . . **929.9**
FISHER, LE/Stars and Stripes: our national flag. /1993/
3-6/7 KE617 . . . . **929.9**

Flags--United States--States--History.
ALABAMA TO WYOMING: FLAGS OF THE UNITED STATES
(VIDEOCASSETTE). /1994/4-6/KE612 . . . . **VCR 929.9**
BRANDT, SR/State flags: including the Commonwealth of Puerto
Rico. /1992/4-6/7 KE614 . . . . **929.9**
HABAN, RD/How proudly they wave: flags of the fifty states. /
1989/5-6/8 KE619 . . . . **929.9**
SHEARER, BF/State names, seals, flags, and symbols: a historical
guide. Rev. and expanded /1994/4-A/KA493 . . . . **REF 973**

Flamingos.
PATTON, D/Flamingos. /1996/4-6/7 KC679 . . . . **598.3**

Flanders--Fiction.
RATZ DE TAGYOS, P/Coney tale. /1992/2-5/5 KH620 . . . . . . **Fic**

Flatware--History.
GIBLIN, JC/From hand to mouth, or how we invented knives, forks,
spoons, and chopsticks & the table manners to go with them. /
1987/5-6/8 KB185 . . . . **394.1**

Fleas--Fiction.
MCCULLY, EA/Little Kit or, The Industrious Flea Circus girl. /1995/
2-4/4 KG092 . . . . **E**
WOOD, A/Napping house. /1984/P-2/7 KG764 . . . . **CE E**

Fleischman, Sid.
FLEISCHMAN, S/Abracadabra kid: a writer's life. /1996/
3-A/7 KE344 . . . . **B FLEISCHMAN, S**

Flies.
FISCHER-NAGEL, H/Housefly. /1990/5-6/7 KC556 . . . . . **595.77**

Flies--Fiction.
AYLESWORTH, J/Old black fly. /1992/K-2/2 KF180 . . . . **E**
Flight SEE ALSO Aeronautics, Space flight.
Flight.
BARRETT, NS/Flying machines. /1994/4-6/8 KD104 . . . . **629.133**
CREWS, D/Flying. /1986/P-1/KD093. . . . . **629.13**
OTHER THINGS THAT FLY (VIDEOCASSETTE). /1994/
2-4/KD097. . . . . **VCR 629.13**
Flight--Experiments.
ARDLEY, N/Science book of air. /1991/4-6/4 KC102 . . . . . . **533**
Flight--Fiction.
BAKER, SA/Grandpa is a flyer. /1995/1-3/5 KF188. . . . . **E**
DORROS, A/Abuela. /1991/P-2/2 KF488 . . . . **E**
Abuela (Videocassette). /1994/P-2/KF489 . . . . **VCR E**
KWITZ, MD/Little Vampire and the Midnight Bear. /1995/
1-3/2 KF491 . . . . **E**
PINKNEY, JB/Adventures of Sparrowboy. /1997/K-2/3 KG242. . **E**
RINGGOLD, F/Tar beach. /1991/2-3/4 KG333. . . . . **E**
ROCKWELL, AF/I fly. /1997/P-1/2 KG343 . . . . **E**
SCHWARTZ, HB/When Artie was little. /1996/1-3/2 KG417 . . . **E**
SNYDER, ZK/Black and blue magic. /c1966, 1994/
4-6/7 KH729 . . . . **Fic**
Flight--History.
GIBBONS, G/Flying. /1986/K-2/2 KD095 . . . . **629.13**
KERROD, R/Amazing flying machines. /1992/
4-6/6 KD110 . . . . **629.133**
LET ME TELL YOU ALL ABOUT PLANES (VIDEOCASSETTE). /
1994/4-5/KD111 . . . . **VCR 629.133**
WEISS, H/Strange and wonderful aircraft. /1995/
4-6/6 KD102 . . . . **629.13**
Flightless birds.
BASKIN-SALZBERG, A/Flightless birds. /1993/
5-6/7 KC691 . . . . **598.5**
Flights around the world.
ROZAKIS, L/Dick Rutan and Jeana Yeager: flying non-stop around
the world. /1994/5-6/6 KD099 . . . . **629.13**
Flint (Mich.)--Fiction.
CURTIS, CP/Watsons go to Birmingham--1963: a novel. /1995/
6-A/7 KH048 . . . . **CE Fic**
Flipper, Henry Ossian.
PFEIFER, KB/Henry O. Flipper. /1993/
4-6/9 KE345 . . . . **B FLIPPER, H.**
Floods.
ROZENS, A/Floods. /1994/4-6/7 KB037 . . . . **363.34**
Floods--Fiction.
GREEN, NB/Hole in the dike. /c1974, 1975/K-2/2 KF640 . . **CE E**
LYON, GE/Come a tide. /1990/K-3/2 KG043. . . . . **E**
Floods--Middle West.
VOGEL, CG/Great Midwest flood. /1995/4-6/9 KB034 . . . **363.3**
Floods--Mississippi River.
LAUBER, P/Flood: wrestling with the Mississippi. /1996/
4-6/4 KB035 . . . . **363.34**
Floods--Mississippi River--Fiction.
CALHOUN, M/Flood. /1997/1-3/2 KF332 . . . . **E**
Floods--Mississippi River Valley.
HISCOCK, B/Big rivers: the Missouri, the Mississipi, and the Ohio. /
1997/3-6/6 KC183 . . . . **551.48**
Florida.
SIRVAITIS, K/Florida. /1994/4-6/7 KE993 . . . . **975.9**
Florida--Fiction.
HARVEY, D/Secret elephant of Harlan Kooter. /1992/
4-A/6 KH223 . . . . **Fic**
KONIGSBURG, EL/T-backs, T-shirts, COAT, and suit. /1993/
6-A/7 KH375 . . . . **Fic**
RAWLINGS, MK/Yearling. /c1938, 1967/5-A/5 KH622 . . . . . **Fic**
STOLZ, M/Stealing home. /1992/3-5/6 KH768 . . . . **Fic**
Florida--History.
CONQUERING THE SWAMPS (VIDEOCASSETTE). /1991/
A/KE990 . . . . **VCR 975.9**
WILLS, CA/Historical album of Florida. /1994/
4-6/7 KE994 . . . . **975.9**
Florists--Fiction.
ADLER, DA/One yellow daffodil: a Hanukkah story. /1995/
3-5/4 KG818 . . . . **Fic**
Flower gardening.
KUHN, D/More than just a flower garden. /1990/
4-5/6 KD175 . . . . **635.9**
Flowers SEE ALSO Plants; Wildflowers.
Flowers.
KUHN, D/More than just a flower garden. /1990/
4-5/6 KD175 . . . . **635.9**
LANDAU, E/State flowers: including the Commonwealth of Puerto
Rico. /1992/3-6/8 KC406 . . . . **582.13**
WEXLER, J/Queen Anne's lace. /1994/2-6/6 KC433. . . . . . . **583**

Flowers--Fiction.
FORD, M/Sunflower. /1995/P-1/1 KF566. . . . . **E**
LOBEL, A/Alison's zinnia. /1990/P-2/2 KF999 . . . . **E**
MARZOLLO, J/I'm a seed. /1996/K-2/1 KG081 . . . . **E**
Flowers in art.
ROALF, P/Flowers. /1993/5-A/8 KD479 . . . . **758**
Flute.
TURNER, BC/Living flute. /1996/4-6/11 KD551 . . . . . . **BA 788.3**
Flute--Fiction.
EVERSOLE, R/Flute player./La Flautista. /1995/K-2/2 KF541 . . . **E**
PINKWATER, DM/Doodle flute. /1991/1-3/2 KG245 . . . . **E**
Fly (Insect).
INSECTS (VIDEOCASSETTE). /c1979, 1986/
2-6/KC541. . . . . **VCR 595.7**
Fly (Insect)--Fiction.
OPPENHEIM, J/You can't catch me! /1986/P-1/KG193. . . . . . . **E**
Flying--Fiction.
WALTER, MP/Brother to the wind. /1985/1-3/2 KG684 . . . . . **E**
Flying saucers SEE Unidentified flying objects.
Flying squirrels.
MCDONALD, MA/Flying squirrels. /1993/1-5/5 KC753. . . **599.36**
Flying squirrels--Fiction.
RYDER, J/Night gliders. /1996/P-2/2 KG367 . . . . **E**
Fog--Fiction.
FLEISCHMAN, S/Ghost on Saturday night. /1997/
3-5/4 KH122 . . . . **Fic**
TRESSELT, A/Hide and seek fog. /c1965/K-2/KG615 . . . . **E**
Folk art SEE ALSO Art, Primitive; Art industries and trade; Arts and crafts;
Handicraft.
Folk art.
FOLK ART COUNTING BOOK. /1992/P-3/1 KD420. . . . . . **745**
Folk art, Mexican.
MEXICAN FOLK ART (VIDEOCASSETTE). /1992/
5-A/KD421 . . . . **VCR 745**
Folk dancing SEE ALSO Indians of North America--Dances.
Folk dancing.
FOLK DANCES FOR CHILDREN (SOUND RECORDING
CASSETTE). /1985/3-6/KD703 . . . . **SRC 793.3**
STEWART, G/Folk dance fun: simple folk songs and dances (Sound
recording cassette). /1984/2-6/KD705 . . . . **SRC 793.3**
Folk dancing--United States.
BURTON, B/Moving within the circle: contemporary Native American
music and dance. /1993//KA316 . . . . **BA PROF 789.2**
Folk literature--Study and teaching (Elementary).
BOSMA, B/Fairy tales, fables, legends and myths: using folk
literature in your classroom. 2nd ed. /1992//KA177. **PROF 371.3**
Folk music--Africa.
SILVERMAN, J/African roots. /1994/5-A/KD590 . . . . **789.2**
Folk music--Cambodia.
SAM, S/Silent temples, songful hearts: traditional music of
Cambodia. /1991//KA318 . . . . **BA PROF 789.2**
Folk music--Uganda.
SERWADDA, WM/Songs and stories from Uganda. /c1974, 1987/
/KA319. . . . . **BA PROF 789.2**
Folk music--United States.
BURTON, B/Moving within the circle: contemporary Native American
music and dance. /1993//KA316 . . . . **BA PROF 789.2**
Folk music--Vietnam.
NGUYEN, PT/From rice paddies and temple yards: traditional music
of Vietnam. /c1990, 1992//KA317. . . . . **BA PROF 789.2**
Folk music--West (U.S.).
SONGS OF THE WILD WEST. /1991/2-A/KD597 . . . . **789.2**
Folk songs SEE ALSO Ballads; Carols; Folklore.
Folk songs.
CAMPBELL, PS/Roots and branches: a legacy of multicultural music
for children. /1994//KA320 . . . . **BA PROF 789.3**
DIANE GOODE BOOK OF AMERICAN FOLK TALES AND
SONGS. /1989/2-4/5 KB439 . . . . **398.22**
FAMILY FOLK FESTIVAL: A MULTI-CULTURAL SING-ALONG
(SOUND RECORDING CASSETTE). /1990/
K-5/KD562 . . . . **SRC 789.2**
FISH THAT'S A SONG: SONGS AND STORIES FOR CHILDREN
(SOUND RECORDING CASSETTE). /1990/
K-6/KD563 . . . . **SRC 789.2**
GUTHRIE, W/Nursery days (Compact disc). /1992/
P-1/KD567. . . . . **CD 789.2**
JENKINS, E/Call and response: rhythmic group singing (Sound
recording cassette). /1990/K-3/KD625 . . . . **SRC 789.3**
Multicultural children's songs (Compact disc). /1995/
K-2/KD629 . . . . **CD 789.3**
Songs and rhythms from near and far (Sound recording cassette).
/c1964, 1992/K-2/KD575 . . . . **SRC 789.2**
Travellin' with Ella Jenkins: a bilingual journey (Compact disc). /
1989/K-2/KD576 . . . . **CD 789.2**

JUNIPER TREE AND OTHER SONGS (SOUND RECORDING
   CASSETTE). /1994/K-6/KD578 . . . .   **SRC 789.2**
MANSON, C/Tree in the wood: an old nursery song. /1993/
   P-1/2 KB801 . . . .   **398.8**
NGUYEN, PT/From rice paddies and temple yards: traditional music
   of Vietnam. /c1990, 1992//KA317 . . . .   **BA PROF 789.2**
PETER, PAUL & MARY /Peter, Paul and Mommy, too (Compact
   disc). /1993/P-3/KD583 . . . .   **CD 789.2**
RAINBOW SIGN (COMPACT DISC). /1992/
   P-A/KD585 . . . .   **CD 789.2**
SEEGER, P/Pete Seeger's family concert (Videocassette). /1992/
   K-3/KD588 . . . .   **VCR 789.2**
   Song and play time (Sound recording cassette). /1990/
   K-3/KD589 . . . .   **SRC 789.2**
SHAKE IT TO THE ONE THAT YOU LOVE THE BEST: PLAY
   SONGS AND LULLABIES FROM BLACK /1989/
   K-4/KD767 . . . .   **BA 796.1**
SLAVIN, B/Cat came back: a traditional song. /1992/
   P-2/2 KD594 . . . .   **789.2**
SLONECKI, C/Children's songs around the world (Sound recording
   cassette). /1989/K-3/KD595 . . . .   **SRC 789.2**
SONGS FOR SURVIVAL: SONGS AND CHANTS FROM TRIBAL
   PEOPLES AROUND THE WORLD. /1996/1-6/KD596 . . . .   **789.2**
WORLD OF CHILDREN'S SONGS. /1993//KA322   **PROF 789.3**

Folk songs--Africa.
JENKINS, E/Jambo and other call and response songs and chants
   (Sound recording cassette). /1990/K-3/KD573 . . . . .   **SRC 789.2**
SWEET HONEY IN THE ROCK: ALL FOR FREEDOM (SOUND
   RECORDING CASSETTE). /1989/3-6/KD601 . . . . . .   **SRC 789.2**

Folk songs--Cambodia.
SAM, S/Silent temples, songful hearts: traditional music of
   Cambodia. /1991//KA318 . . . .   **BA PROF 789.2**

Folk songs--England.
TWELVE DAYS OF CHRISTMAS. /1986/P-A/KD537 . . . . .   **782.28**
TWELVE DAYS OF CHRISTMAS. /1993/P-A/KD538 . . . . .   **782.28**
TWELVE DAYS OF CHRISTMAS. /1995/K-3/KD539 . . . . .   **782.28**
TWELVE DAYS OF CHRISTMAS (VIDEOCASSETTE). /1990/
   P-A/KD540 . . . .   **VCR 782.28**
TYRRELL, F/Woodland Christmas: twelve days of Christmas in the
   North Woods. /1996/K-2/KD541 . . . .   **782.28**

Folk songs--Great Britain.
FRIENDLY BEASTS: A TRADITIONAL CHRISTMAS CAROL. /1991/
   K-2/KD533 . . . .   **782.28**

Folk songs--Latin America.
ARROZ CON LECHE: POPULAR SONGS AND RHYMES FROM
   LATIN AMERICA. /1989/P-3/KD556 . . . .   **789.2**

Folk songs--Scotland.
NIC LEODHAS, S/Always room for one more. /1965/
   K-2/7 KB760 . . . .   **398.27**

Folk songs--South Africa.
SEEGER, P/Abiyoyo: based on a South African lullaby and folk
   story. /1986/2-5/KD587 . . . .   **789.2**

Folk songs--Southern States.
ZEMACH, H/Mommy, buy me a china doll. /1966/
   P-1/1 KG788 . . . .   **E**

Folk songs--Uganda.
SERWADDA, WM/Songs and stories from Uganda. /c1974, 1987/
   /KA319 . . . .   **BA PROF 789.2**

Folk songs--United States.
AMERICAN MELODY SAMPLER (COMPACT DISC). /1994/
   K-6/KD555 . . . .   **CD 789.2**
CLARKE, G/E I E I O: the story of Old MacDonald, who had a
   farm. /1993/K-1/KF393 . . . .   **E**
COWBOY SONGS (SOUND RECORDING CASSETTE). /1992/
   4-A/KD560 . . . .   **SRC 789.2**
FROM SEA TO SHINING SEA: A TREASURY OF AMERICAN
   FOLKLORE AND FOLK SONGS. /1993/K-6/KD899 . . . . .   **810.8**
HOLT, D/Grandfather's greatest hits (Sound recording cassette). /
   1991/K-4/KD569 . . . .   **SRC 789.2**
   I got a bullfrog: folksongs for the fun of it (Sound recording
   cassette). /1994/2-4/KD570 . . . .   **SRC 789.2**
HORSE SENSE FOR KIDS AND OTHER PEOPLE (SOUND
   RECORDING CASSETTE). /1992/2-4/KD668 . . . . . .   **SRC 789.4**
JENKINS, E/African-American folk songs and rhythms (Sound
   recording cassette). /c1960, 1992/K-6/KD572 . . . . .   **SRC 789.2**
   Long time to freedom (Sound recording cassette). /c1969, 1992/
   K-A/KD574 . . . .   **SRC 789.2**
   We are America's children (Compact disc). /1989/
   1-6/KD577 . . . .   **CD 789.2**
SILVERMAN, J/Slave songs. /1994/5-A/KD592 . . . .   **789.2**

Folk songs, English--Africa.
SILVERMAN, J/African roots. /1994/5-A/KD590 . . . .   **789.2**

Folk songs, English--West (U.S.).
SONGS OF THE WILD WEST. /1991/2-A/KD597 . . . . . .   **789.2**

Folk songs, Spanish--Latin America.
DE COLORES AND OTHER LATIN-AMERICAN FOLK SONGS FOR
   CHILDREN. /1994/K-3/KD561 . . . .   **789.2**
LAS NAVIDADES: POPULAR CHRISTMAS SONGS FROM LATIN
   AMERICA. /1990/K-3/KD580 . . . .   **789.2**

Folklore SEE ALSO Devil; Fables; Fairy tales; Folk songs; Ghosts;
   Halloween; Legends; Mythology; Nursery rhymes; Proverbs; Superstition;
   Witchcraft.

Folklore.
BALTUCK, N/Apples from heaven: multicultural folk tales about
   stories and storytellers. /1995//KA265 . . . .   **PROF 398.2**
BARCHAS, S/Giant and the rabbit: six bilingual folktales from
   Hispanic culture (Sound recording cassette). /1996/
   2-4/KB258 . . . .   **SRC 398.2**
BARTON, B/Three bears. /1991/P-K/1 KB527 . . . .   **398.24**
BEN IZZY, J/Beggar King and other tales from around the world
   (Sound recording cassette). /1993/2-A/KB260 . . . . .   **SRC 398.2**
   Buried treasures: a storyteller's journey (Sound recording cassette).
   /1995/3-A/KB261 . . . .   **SRC 398.2**
   Stories from far away (Sound recording cassette). /1991/
   3-A/KB262 . . . .   **SRC 398.2**
BIRCH, C/Careful what you wish for (Sound recording cassette). /
   1993/2-6/KB264 . . . .   **SRC 398.2**
   Happily-ever-after love stories...more or less (Sound recording
   cassette). /1987/2-6/KB265 . . . .   **SRC 398.2**
   Nightmares rising (Sound recording cassette). /1984/
   3-6/KB266 . . . .   **SRC 398.2**
BROOKE, LL/Golden goose book: a fairy tale picture book. /1992/
   P-3/6 KB269 . . . .   **398.2**
CLIMO, S/Treasury of princesses: princess tales from around the
   world. /1996/3-5/6 KB432 . . . .   **398.22**
CRAIG, MJ/Three wishes. /c1968, 1986/2/2 KB730 . . . . .   **398.27**
DEMI /Magic gold fish: a Russian folktale. /1995/
   3-5/2 KB284 . . . .   **398.2**
DESPAIN, P/Eleven nature tales: a multicultural journey. /1996/
   3-5/7 KB286 . . . .   **398.2**
   Eleven turtle tales: adventure tales from around the world. /1994/
   2-3/4 KB559 . . . .   **398.24**
   Tales to tell from around the world. Vol. 1 (Sound recording
   cassette). /1995/K-2/KB288. . . . .   **SRC 398.2**
DIANE GOODE'S BOOK OF SCARY STORIES AND SONGS. /
   1994/2-5/5 KB685 . . . .   **398.25**
DIANE GOODE'S BOOK OF SILLY STORIES AND SONGS. /
   1992/K-3/KD872 . . . .   **808.8**
EDGECOMB, D/Pattysaurus and other tales (Sound recording
   cassette). /1995/P-3/KF508 . . . .   **SRC E**
ELLIOTT, D/Crawdads, doodlebugs and creasy greens: songs, stories
   and lore celebrating the natural world (Compact disc). /1996/
   3-5/KB291 . . . .   **CD 398.2**
EVETTS-SECKER, J/Mother and daughter tales. /1996/
   3-4/6 KB292 . . . .   **398.2**
FAIRY TALES FROM THE PICTURE BOOK PARADE (TALKING
   BOOK). /1986/2-4/KB293 . . . .   **TB 398.2**
FAIRYTALE FAVORITES IN STORY AND SONG (SOUND
   RECORDING CASSETTE). /1993/K-3/KB294 . . . . . .   **SRC 398.2**
FAVORITE FOLKTALES FROM AROUND THE WORLD. /1986/
   /KA267 . . . .   **PROF 398.2**
FOLKLORE OF WORLD HOLIDAYS. /1992/
   4-6/KA414 . . . .   **REF 394.26**
FOLKTALES FROM THE PICTURE BOOK PARADE (TALKING
   BOOK). /1981/2-4/KB566 . . . .   **TB 398.24**
FOREST, H/Songspinner: folktales and fables sung and told (Sound
   recording cassette). /1982/2-4/KB735 . . . .   **SRC 398.27**
   Wonder tales from around the world. /1995/
   3-5/6 KB300 . . . .   **398.2**
GALDONE, P/Gingerbread boy. /1975/P-2/4 KB736 . .   **CE 398.27**
GODDESSES, HEROES, AND SHAMANS: THE YOUNG PEOPLE'S
   GUIDE TO WORLD MYTHOLOY. /1994/4-6/KA393 . .   **REF 291.1**
HAMILTON, V/In the beginning: creation stories from around the
   world. /1988/5-6/4 KA731 . . . .   **291.2**
HOFFMAN, M/Earth, fire, water, air. /1995/2-6/7 KA814 .   **304.2**
JAFFE, N/Patakin: world tales of drums and drummers. /1994/
   5-6/6 KB321 . . . .   **398.2**
KIMMEL, EA/Adventures of Hershel of Ostropol. /1995/
   2-4/7 KB459 . . . .   **398.22**
KNOCK AT THE DOOR. /1992//KA269 . . . .   **PROF 398.2**
LIVO, NJ/Storytelling folklore sourcebook. /1991/
   /KA340. . . . .   **PROF 808.5**
LOTTRIDGE, CB/Ten small tales. /1994/P-1/2 KB338 . . . . .   **398.2**
MACDONALD, MR/Celebrate the world: twenty tellable folktales
   for multicultural festivals. /1994//KA270 . . . .   **PROF 398.2**
   Peace tales: world folktales to talk about. /1992/
   /KA271. . . . .   **PROF 398.2**

MANTINBAND, G/Blabbermouths: adapted from a German folktale. /1992/3-4/4 KB751. . . . . **398.27**

MARSHALL, J/Three little pigs. /1989/K-2/2 KB613 . . **CE 398.24**

MARTIN, R/Rafe Martin tells his children's books (Talking book). /1994/K-4/KB341. . . . . **TB 398.2**

MAYO, M/Magical tales from many lands. /1993/ 4-5/6 KB343 . . . . **398.2**

Tortoise's flying lesson. /1995/P-2/3 KB615 . . . . **398.24**

MCCAUGHREAN, G/Golden hoard: myths and legends of the world. /1996/2-5/7 KB344 . . . . **398.2**

Silver treasure: myths and legends of the world. /1996/ K-6/6 KB345 . . . . **398.2**

MERMAID TALES FROM AROUND THE WORLD. /1993/ 3-5/5 KB405 . . . . **398.21**

NURSERY TALES AROUND THE WORLD. /1996/ P-2/7 KB354 . . . . **398.2**

PELLOWSKI, A/Story vine: /1984//KA248 . . . . . . **PROF 372.67**

Storytelling handbook: a young people's collection of unusual tales and helpful /1995//KA249 . . . . **PROF 372.67**

PINDER, M/People with one heart (Talking book). /1996/ P-1/KD876. . . . . **TB 808.8**

Planet with one mind: stories from around the world for the child within us all /1995/1-4/KD877 . . . . **TB 808.8**

PODWAL, M/Golem: a giant made of mud. /1995/ 4-6/7 KB408 . . . . **398.21**

RAINBOW FAIRY BOOK. /1993/2-6/8 KB360. . . . . **398.2**

READY-TO-TELL TALES: SURE-FIRE STORIES FROM AMERICA'S FAVORITE STORYTELLERS. /1994//KA272 . . . . **PROF 398.2**

ROCKWELL, AF/Acorn tree and other folktales. /1995/ P-2/4 KB362 . . . . **398.2**

ROSEN, M/How the animals got their colors: animal myths from around the world. /1992/2-4/4 KB640 . . . . **398.24**

ROUNDS, G/Three little pigs and the big bad wolf. /1992/ K-3/4 KB645 . . . . **398.24**

SAN SOUCI, RD/Nicholas Pipe. /1997/2-5/6 KB413 . . . . **398.21**

SCARY BOOK. /1991/2-4/2 KB691 . . . . **398.25**

SCHWARTZ, A/Ghosts!: ghostly tales from folklore. /1991/ 1-2/2 KB692 . . . . **CE 398.25**

In a dark, dark room and other scary stories. /1984/ K-3/1 KB693 . . . . **398.25**

SCHWARTZ, H/Next year in Jerusalem: 3000 years of Jewish stories. /1996/3-6/7 KA780 . . . . **296.4**

Wonder child and other Jewish fairy tales. /1996/ 2-4/5 KB369 . . . . **398.2**

SHANNON, G/Stories to solve. /1985/5-6/6 KB714 . . . . **398.26**

SPOOKY STORIES FOR A DARK AND STORMY NIGHT. /1994/ 2-4/4 KB695 . . . . **398.25**

STEVENS, J/How the Manx cat lost its tail. /1990/ 2-3/4 KB658 . . . . **398.24**

STORIES FROM MANY LANDS FROM THE PICTURE BOOK PARADE (TALKING BOOK). /1986/3-4/KB373. . . . . . **TB 398.2**

STORYTELLING TIME IS HERE (SOUND RECORDING CASSETTE). /1992/2-4/KB374. . . . . **SRC 398.2**

TALES FROM CULTURES FAR AND NEAR (SOUND RECORDING CASSETTE). /1990/3-4/KB375 . . . . **SRC 398.2**

THOMPSON, S/One hundred favorite folktales. /c1968/ /KA274. . . . . **PROF 398.2**

TORRENCE, J/Classic children's tales (Sound recording cassette). / 1989/P-1/KB667. . . . . **SRC 398.24**

TREASURY OF ANIMAL STORIES. /1992/3-6/6 KH802 . . . . . **Fic**

TREASURY OF GIANT AND MONSTER STORIES. /1992/ 3-5/6 KH803 . . . . **Fic**

TREASURY OF SPOOKY STORIES. /1992/4-A/6 KH804 . . . . . **Fic**

TREASURY OF STORIES FOR FIVE YEAR OLDS. /1992/ 2-4/5 KH805 . . . . **Fic**

TREASURY OF STORIES FOR SEVEN YEAR OLDS. /1992/ 3-5/6 KH806 . . . . **Fic**

TREASURY OF STORIES FOR SIX YEAR OLDS. /1992/ 2-4/5 KH807 . . . . **Fic**

WALDHERR, K/Book of goddesses. /1995/4-6/8 KA732 . . **291.2**

WALKER, PR/Giants!: stories from around the world. /1995/ 4-6/7 KB381 . . . . **398.2**

Little folk: stories from around the world. /1997/ 2-4/6 KB494 . . . . **398.22**

YEP, L/Tree of dreams: ten tales from the garden of night. /1995/ 4-6/3 KB790 . . . . **398.27**

Folklore--Africa.

AARDEMA, V/Lonely lioness and the ostrich chicks: a Masai tale. / 1996/K-2/3 KB516 . . . . **398.24**

This for that: a Tonga tale. /1997/K-2/2 KB517. . . . . . **398.24**

Who's in Rabbit's house? (Videocassette). /1995/ K-3/KB518. **VCR 398.24**

ANDERSON, DA/Origin of life on Earth: an African creation myth. /1991/4-5/4 KA730 . . . . **291.2**

BARBOSA, RA/African animal tales. /1993/2-4/6 KB526. . **398.24**

BRYAN, A/Lion and the ostrich chicks and other African folk tales. / 1986/4-6/3 KB544 . . . . **398.24**

CALDECOTT VIDEO LIBRARY. VOL. IV (VIDEOCASSETTE). /1992/ P-3/KB274. **VCR 398.2**

CENDRARS, B/Shadow. /1982/3-5/KE120 . . . . **CE 841**

CHOCOLATE, DM/Imani in the belly. /1994/2-3/5 KB431 . **398.22**

COURLANDER, H/Fire on the mountain and other stories from Ethiopia and Eritrea. /c1950, 1995/3-6/6 KB277. . . . . **398.2**

FARRIS, PJ/Young Mouse and Elephant: an East African folktale. / 1996/K-2/4 KB565 . . . . **398.24**

FORD, B/Hunter who was king and other African tales. /1994/ K-3/4 KB299 . . . . **398.2**

GLEESON, B/Koi and the kola nuts (Kit). /1992/ 2-5/KB446. **KIT 398.22**

GRIFALCONI, A/Village of round and square houses. /1986/ 3-4/6 KB739 . . . . **CE 398.27**

HALEY, GE/Story, a story: an African tale. /c1970/ 3-5/5 KB580 . . . . **CE 398.24**

JAFFE, N/Voice for the people: the life and work of Harold Courlander. /1997//KA367. . . . . **PROF B COURLAND**

KAULA, EM/African village folktales, vols 1-3 (Talking book). /n.d./ 4-6/KB746. **TB 398.27**

KIMMEL, EA/Anansi and the talking melon. /1994/ 2-3/2 KB601 . . . . **CE 398.24**

Anansi goes fishing. /1991, c1992/K-2/2 KB602 . . . . **CE 398.24**

KURTZ, J/Trouble. /1997/K-2/3 KB748 . . . . **398.27**

LESTER, J/How many spots does a leopard have? and other tales. / c1989, 1994/5-6/6 KB335 . . . . **398.2**

LEWIS, IM/Why ostriches don't fly and other tales from the African bush. /1997/4-6/6 KB336 . . . . **398.2**

MCNEIL, H/Hyena and the moon: stories to listen to from Kenya (Talking book). /1995/5-6/KB346 . . . . **TB 398.2**

Hyena and the moon: stories to tell from Kenya. /1994/ 5-6/7 KB347 . . . . **398.2**

MOLLEL, TM/Orphan boy: a Maasai story. /1990/ 4-5/4 KB406 . . . . **398.21**

RAPPAPORT, D/New king. /1995/4-A/3 KB473 . . . . . **398.22**

SIERRA, J/Elephant's wrestling match. /1992/ P-2/4 KB652 . . . . **398.24**

Folklore--Africa--Drama.

WINTHER, B/Plays from African tales: one-act, royalty-free dramatizations for young people, from stories and folktales of Africa. /1992/4-A/KE093 . . . . **812**

Folklore--Africa--Software.

P.J.'S READING ADVENTURES (CD-ROM). /1996/ K-3/KB252. . . . . **CDR 398**

Folklore--Africa, West.

AARDEMA, V/Why mosquitoes buzz in people's ears: a West African tale. /1975/1-3/5 KB519 . . . . **CE 398.24**

Why mosquitoes buzz in people's ears (Talking book). /1978/ 2-4/KB520. **TB 398.24**

ARKHURST, JC/Adventures of Spider: West African folktales. / c1964, 1992/2-3/5 KB524 . . . . **398.2**

BRYAN, A/Story of lightning and thunder. /1993/ K-2/2 KB702 . . . . **398.26**

COURLANDER, H/Cow-tail switch and other West African stories. / c1947, 1987/4-6/7 KB728 . . . . **398.27**

DIAKITE, BW/Hunterman and the crocodile: a West African folktale. /1997/2-3/5 KB560 . . . . **398.24**

KIMMEL, EA/Anansi and the moss-covered rock. /1988/ 1-2/4 KB600 . . . . **CE 398.24**

MCDERMOTT, G/Anansi the spider: a tale from the Ashanti. / c1972/1-3/2 KB616. . . . . **398.24**

Zomo the rabbit: a trickster tale from West Africa. /1992/ K-2/1 KB619 . . . . **398.24**

MEDEARIS, AS/Singing man: adapted from a West African folktale. /1994/4-5/6 KB757 . . . . **398.27**

SOUHAMI, J/Leopard's drum: an Asante tale from West Africa. / 1995/P-1/2 KB654 . . . . **398.24**

Folklore--Algeria.

SCHWARTZ, H/Sabbath lion: a Jewish folktale from Algeria. / 1992/4-6/6 KB511 . . . . **398.23**

Folklore--America.

BRUSCA, MC/When jaguars ate the moon: and other stories about animals and plants of the /1995/2-3/5 KB541 . . . . **398.24**

Folklore--Appalachian Region.

BIRDSEYE, T/Soap! soap! don't forget the soap!: an Appalachian folktale. /1993/K-2/3 KB267. . . . . **398.2**

COMPTON, J/Ashpet: an Appalachian tale. /1994/ 2-3/4 KB727 . . . . **398.27**

DAVIS, D/Jack and the animals: an Appalachian folktale. /1995/ 2-4/5 KB555 . . . . **398.24**

FOLKTELLERS /Tales to grow on (Sound recording cassette). /
c1981/K-3/KB298 . . . . **SRC 398.2**
HOOKS, WH/Snowbear Whittington: an Appalachian Beauty and
the Beast. /1994/2-3/4 KB318 . . . . **398.2**
Three little pigs and the fox. /1989/2-4/5 KB592 . . . . . **398.24**
SCHROEDER, A/Smoky Mountain Rose: an Appalachian Cinderella.
/1997/2-3/4 KB367 . . . . **398.2**
SLOAT, T/Sody sallyratus. /1997/1-3/5 KB653 . . . . **398.24**
SOME DOG AND OTHER KENTUCKY WONDERS (SOUND
RECORDING CASSETTE). /1992/3-4/KB370 . . . . . . **SRC 398.2**

Folklore--Arab countries.
ALDERSON, B/Arabian nights, or, Tales told by Sheherezade during
a thousand nights and one /1995/5-A/7 KB253 . . . . **398.2**
ARABIAN NIGHTS: THEIR BEST-KNOWN TALES. /c1909, 1994/
5-A/9 KB255 . . . . **398.2**
ARABIAN NIGHTS (SOUND RECORDING CASSETTE). /1991/
4-5/KB254 . . . . **SRC 398.2**
HAUTZIG, D/Aladdin and the magic lamp. /1993/
1-2/2 KB314 . . . . **398.2**
KIMMEL, EA/Tale of Ali Baba and the forty thieves: a story from
the Arabian Nights. /1996/3-4/6 KB332 . . . . **398.2**
Three princes: a tale from the Middle East. /1994/
2-3/4 KB461 . . . . **398.22**
KUNSTLER, JH/Aladdin and the magic lamp (Kit). /1995/
3-5/KB333 . . . . **KIT 398.2**
LATTIMORE, DN/Arabian nights: three tales. /1995/
3-5/6 KB334 . . . . **398.2**
MAYER, M/Turandot. /1995/3-5/5 KB342 . . . . **398.2**
PHILIP, N/Arabian nights. /1994/5-6/6 KB358 . . . . **398.2**

Folklore--Arctic regions.
DABCOVICH, L/Polar bear son: an Inuit tale. /1997/
K-2/4 KB554 . . . . **398.24**

Folklore--Arizona.
COURLANDER, H/People of the short blue corn: tales and legends
of the Hopi Indians. /c1970, 1996/1-A/5 KB278 . . . . **398.2**
ROESSEL, M/Songs from the loom: a Navajo girl learns to weave.
/1995/4-6/6 KE799 . . . . **970.491**

Folklore--Armenia.
HOGROGIAN, N/Contest. /c1976/3-5/5 KB744 . . . . . . **398.27**

Folklore--Asia, Southeastern.
COURLANDER, H/Tiger's whisker and other tales from Asia and the
Pacific. /c1959, 1995/3-5/7 KB279 . . . . **398.2**

Folklore--Australia.
OODGEROO /Dreamtime: aboriginal stories. /1994/
4-5/6 KB506 . . . . **398.23**
ROTH, SL/Biggest frog in Australia. /1996/2-3/2 KB643 . . **398.24**

Folklore--Austria.
DUGIN, A/Dragon feathers. /1993/4-5/7 KB289 . . . . . . **398.2**
SAWYER, R/Remarkable Christmas of the cobbler's sons. /1994/
1-3/4 KB416 . . . . **398.21**

Folklore--British Columbia (Canada)--Pacific Coast.
CAMERON, A/Raven and Snipe. /1991/3-4/6 KB546 . . . . **398.24**
Raven goes berrypicking. /1991/3-4/6 KB547 . . . . . **398.24**

Folklore--Burma.
FROESE, DL/Wise washerman: a folktale from Burma. /1996/
K-2/7 KB569 . . . . **398.24**

Folklore--Cambodia.
SPAGNOLI, C/Judge Rabbit and the tree spirit: a folktale from
Cambodia. /1991/3-4/4 KB655 . . . . **398.24**

Folklore--Cameroon.
GRIFALCONI, A/Village of round and square houses. /1986/
3-4/6 KB739 . . . . **CE 398.27**
MOLLEL, TM/King and the tortoise. /1993/2-3/4 KB624 . . **398.24**
OYONO, E/Gollo and the lion. /1995/2-4/4 KB628 . . . . . **398.24**

Folklore--Caribbean Area.
JAFFE, N/Voice for the people: the life and work of Harold
Courlander. /1997//KA367 . . . . **PROF B COURLAND**
KEENS-DOUGLAS, R/Diablesse and the baby: a Caribbean folktale.
/1994/3-4/4 KB324 . . . . **398.2**
SAN SOUCI, RD/Faithful friend. /1995/4-6/5 KB411 . . . . **398.21**

Folklore--Central America.
PARKE, M/Quetzalcoatl tale of corn. /1992/2-3/5 KB630 . **398.24**

Folklore--Chelm (Chelm, Poland).
SANFIELD, S/Feather merchants and other tales of the fools of
Chelm. /1991/6-A/7 KB510 . . . . **398.23**
Strudel, strudel, strudel. /1995/2-3/4 KB773 . . . . . . **398.27**

Folklore--China.
CHANG, M/Cricket warrior: a Chinese tale. /1994/
2-3/5 KB549 . . . . **398.24**
CHIN, C/China's bravest girl: the legend of Hua Mu Lan = [Chin
kuo ying hsiung Hua /1993/3-5/4 KB430 . . . . **398.22**
CZERNECKI, S/Cricket's cage: a Chinese folktale. /1997/
K-3/7 KB553 . . . . **398.24**

FANG, L/Ch'i-lin purse: a collection of ancient Chinese stories. /
1995/4-6/5 KB295 . . . . **398.2**
HONG, LT/Two of everything. /1993/2-3/4 KB317 . . . . . **398.2**
LOUIE, A/Yeh-Shen, a Cinderella story from China. /c1982, 1990/
3-5/6 KB750 . . . . **398.27**
MOSEL, A/Tikki Tikki Tembo. /1967/P-2/5 KB759 . . . . . **398.27**
RAPPAPORT, D/Long-haired girl: a Chinese legend. /1995/
2-3/4 KB409 . . . . **398.21**
SANFIELD, S/Just rewards, or, Who is that man in the moon and
what's he doing up there /1996/K-2/4 KB713 . . . . . . **398.26**
WANG, RC/Magical starfruit tree: a Chinese folktale. /1993/
2-3/6 KB784 . . . . **398.27**
WILSON, BK/Wishbones: a folk tale from China. /1993/
2-3/6 KB383 . . . . **398.2**
WOLKSTEIN, D/White Wave: a Chinese tale. Rev. ed. /1996/
1-3/2 KB786 . . . . **398.27**
YEP, L/Junior thunder lord. /1994/2-4/3 KB425 . . . . . . **398.21**
Man who tricked a ghost. /1993/1-3/4 KB697 . . . . . **398.25**
Rainbow people. /c1989, 1991/5-A/4 KB788 . . . . . . **398.2**
Shell woman and the king: a Chinese folktale. /1993/
3-5/5 KB496 . . . . **398.22**
Tiger Woman. /1995/1-3/6 KB789 . . . . **398.27**
YOLEN, J/Emperor and the kite. /1988/2-3/6 KB791 . . . . **398.27**
YOUNG, E/Cat and Rat: the legend of the Chinese zodiac. /1995/
K-6/4 KA608 . . . . **133.5**
Little Plum. /1994/K-2/4 KB497 . . . . **398.22**
Lon Po Po: A Red-Riding Hood story from China. /1989/
3-4/4 KB679 . . . . **398.24**
Night visitors. /1995/2-3/4 KB680 . . . . **398.24**

Folklore--Classification.
MACDONALD, MR/Storyteller's sourcebook: a subject, title, and
motif index to folklore collections for children. /1982/
4-6/KA027 . . . . **PROF 016.3982**

Folklore--Cornwall (England).
BARBER, A/Mousehole cat. /1990/4-6/6 KG879 . . . . . . **Fic**
ZEMACH, H/Duffy and the devil, a Cornish tale. /c1973/
2-4/7 KB426 . . . . **CE 398.21**

Folklore--Costa Rica.
BADEN, R/And Sunday makes seven. /1990/
2-3/2 KB388 . . . . **398.21**

Folklore--Cuba.
GONZALEZ, LM/Bossy gallito/el gallo de bodas: a traditional
Cuban folktale. /1994/K-2/4 KB577 . . . . **398.24**
SHUTE, L/Rabbit wishes. /1995/K-2/2 KB651 . . . . **398.24**

Folklore--Czech Republic.
WISNIEWSKI, D/Golem. /1996/2-6/5 KB423 . . . . **398.21**

Folklore--Dictionaries.
BREWER'S DICTIONARY OF PHRASE AND FABLE. 15TH ED. /
1995/5-6/KA459 . . . . **REF 803**

Folklore--Drama.
PLAYS FROM FAVORITE FOLK TALES. /1987/
3-6/KE094 . . . . **812.008**

Folklore--Egypt.
KIMMEL, EA/Rimonah of the Flashing Sword: a North African tale.
/1995/3-4/4 KB331 . . . . **398.2**

Folklore--England.
COHEN, B/Robin Hood and Little John. /1995/
2-4/4 KB433 . . . . **398.22**
CURRY, JL/Christmas Knight. /1993/2-5/3 KB435 . . . . . . **398.22**
Robin Hood and his Merry Men. /1994/3-5/3 KB436 . . . **398.22**
Robin Hood in the greenwood. /1995/3-5/3 KB437 . . . . **398.22**
DESPAIN, P/Strongheart Jack and the beanstalk. /1995/
2-5/3 KB287 . . . . **398.2**
FOSTER, J/Magpies' nest. /1995/1-3/3 KB567 . . . . **398.24**
FRENCH, V/Lazy Jack. /1995/K-2/2 KB301 . . . . **398.2**
GIBLIN, JC/Dwarf, the giant, and the unicorn: a tale of King Arthur.
/1996/3-5/4 KB443 . . . . **398.22**
HODGES, M/Molly Limbo. /1996/K-3/3 KB688 . . . . **398.25**
Of swords and sorcerers: the adventures of King Arthur and his
knights. /1993/4-5/6 KB452 . . . . **398.22**
Saint George and the dragon: a golden legend. /1984/
5/7 KB453 . . . . **CE 398.22**
HOWE, J/Knight with the lion: the story of Yvain. /1996/
5-6/6 KB455 . . . . **398.22**
HUCK, CS/Princess Furball. /1989/3-4/6 KB745 . . . . . . **CE 398.27**
KELLOGG, S/Jack and the beanstalk. /1991/2-3/4 KB325 . . **398.2**
KIMMEL, EA/Old woman and her pig. /1992/
K-2/2 KB603 . . . . **398.24**
LISTER, R/Story of King Arthur. /1997/4/7 KB465 . . . . . **398.22**
METAXAS, E/Jack and the beanstalk (Videocassette). /1991/
K-2/KB349 . . . . **VCR 398.2**
PERHAM, M/King Arthur: the legends of Camelot. /1993/
5-A/7 KB471 . . . . **398.22**

ROWE, JA/Gingerbread Man: an old English folktale. /1996/
P-K/2 KB363 . . . . **398.2**
SABUDA, R/Arthur and the sword. /1995/3-5/5 KB479 . . **398.22**
SAN SOUCI, RD/Hobyahs. /1996/3-4/6 KB647 . . . . **398.24**
  Young Guinevere. /1993/3-4/6 KB482 . . . . **398.22**
  Young Lancelot. /1996/4-5/6 KB483 . . . . **398.22**
  Young Merlin. /c1990, 1996/4-5/6 KB484 . . . . **398.22**
SINGER, M/Maiden on the moor. /1995/4-6/3 KB418 . . . **398.21**
TALBOTT, H/King Arthur and the Round Table. /1995/
4-5/6 KB490 . . . . **398.22**

Folklore--Eritrea.
COURLANDER, H/Fire on the mountain and other stories from
  Ethiopia and Eritrea. /c1950, 1995/3-6/6 KB277. . . . . . . **398.2**
KURTZ, J/Trouble. /1997/K-2/3 KB748 . . . . **398.27**

Folklore--Estonia.
MORONEY, L/Elinda who danced in the sky: an Estonian folktale. /
1990/3-5/5 KB407 . . . . **398.21**

Folklore--Ethiopia.
COURLANDER, H/Fire on the mountain and other stories from
  Ethiopia and Eritrea. /c1950, 1995/3-6/6 KB277. . . . . . . **398.2**
KURTZ, J/Fire on the mountain. /1994/2-4/6 KB747 . . . . . **398.27**
LION'S WHISKERS: AND OTHER ETHIOPIAN TALES. REV. ED. /
1997/3-6/7 KB337 . . . . **398.2**

Folklore--Europe, Eastern.
ROTHENBERG, J/Yettele's feathers. /1995/2-4/3 KB771 . . **398.27**
SANFIELD, S/Feather merchants and other tales of the fools of
  Chelm. /1991/6-A/7 KB510 . . . . **398.23**
  Strudel, strudel, strudel. /1995/2-3/4 KB773 . . . . **398.27**

Folklore--France.
ARAUJO, FP/Nekane, the lamina and the bear: a tale of the
  Basque Pyrenees. /1993/2-3/3 KB256. . . . . **398.2**
BEAUTY AND THE BEAST (VIDEOCASSETTE). /c1989, 1996/
K-3/KB259 . . . . **VCR 398.2**
BRETT, J/Beauty and the Beast. /1989/4-5/6 KB268. . . . . **398.2**
BROWN, M/Stone soup: an old tale. /c1947/
K-3/2 KB721 . . . . **CE 398.27**
DE BEAUMONT, ML/Beauty and the Beast. /1990/
4-5/6 KB282 . . . . **398.2**
EARLY, M/Sleeping Beauty. /1993/2-5/5 KB290 . . . . **398.2**
HANSARD, P/Jig, Fig, and Mrs. Pig. /1995/P-2/3 KB584 . **398.24**
HUCK, CS/Toads and diamonds. /1996/2-3/3 KB319 . . . . **398.2**
KIRSTEIN, L/Puss in boots. /c1992, 1994/3-4/6 KB604 . . . **398.24**
METAXAS, E/Puss in Boots (Kit). /1992/1-4/KB620 . . . **KIT 398.24**
PERRAULT, C/Cinderella, or the little glass slipper. /1954/
1-3/7 KB762 . . . . **398.27**
  Complete fairy tales of Charles Perrault. /1993/
  3-4/6 KB355 . . . . **398.2**
  Puss in boots. /1990/3-4/4 KB633 . . . . **398.24**
  Puss in boots: a fairy tale. /1996/K-3/5 KB634 . . . . . **398.24**
  Story of Sleeping Beauty (Sound recording cassette). /1980/
  4-6/KB356 . . . . **SRC 398.2**
ROTH, SL/Brave Martha and the dragon. /1996/
2-4/4 KB476 . . . . **398.22**
SAN JOSE, C/Cinderella. /1994/2-4/6 KB364 . . . . **398.2**
SCHROEDER, A/Smoky Mountain Rose: an Appalachian Cinderella.
/1997/2-3/4 KB367 . . . . **398.2**
WHITE CAT (VIDEOCASSETTE). /1997/K-2/KB382 . . **VCR 398.2**
ZEMACH, M/Three wishes: an old story. /1986/
2-3/4 KB386 . . . . **398.2**

Folklore--Germany.
BERENZY, A/Rapunzel. /1995/2-4/4 KB263 . . . . **398.2**
DAVENPORT, T/From the Brothers Grimm: a contemporary retelling
  of American folktales and /1992/5-A/KB281 . . . . . . **CE 398.2**
DE LA MARE, W/Turnip. /1992/3-5/6 KB557 . . . . **398.24**
DE REGNIERS, BS/Red Riding Hood. /c1972, 1990/
P-2/KB732 . . . . **CE 398.27**
GERINGER, L/Seven ravens. /1994/2-3/6 KB302. . . . . . . **398.2**
GRIMM, J/Hansel and Gretel: a tale from the Brothers Grimm. /
1984/5/6 KB740 . . . . **CE 398.27**
  Juniper tree and other tales from Grimm. /c1973, 1992/
  5-A/7 KB306 . . . . **398.2**
  Little Red Riding Hood. /1983/1-4/6 KB741 . . . . . . **CE 398.27**
  Rapunzel. /1982/2-4/4 KB307 . . . . **398.2**
  Rumpelstiltskin. /1997/K-2/2 KB308. . . . . **398.2**
  Seven ravens: a fairy tale. /1995/3-5/7 KB309 . . . . . . **398.2**
  Snow-White and the seven dwarfs. /1972/3-4/6 KB310 . . **398.2**
  Twelve dancing princesses: a fairy tale. /1995/
  3-4/6 KB311 . . . . **398.2**
  Wolf and the seven little kids: a fairy tale. /1995/
  1-2/4 KB579 . . . . **398.24**
KIMMEL, EA/Goose girl: a story from the Brothers Grimm. /1995/
3-5/5 KB328 . . . . **398.2**
  Iron John. /1994/4-5/4 KB330. . . . . **398.2**
MARSHALL, J/Hansel and Gretel. /1990/2-4/4 KB340 . . . . **398.2**

MOSER, B/Tucker Pfeffercorn: an old story retold. /1994/
2-3/5 KB351 . . . . **398.2**
PLUME, I/Bremen-Town musicians. /1998/1-3/4 KB636 . . . **398.24**
  Shoemaker and the elves. /1991/2-4/4 KB359 . . . . **398.2**
SHULEVITZ, U/Golden goose. /1995/K-3/2 KB650. . . . . . **398.24**
TARCOV, EH/Frog prince. /c1974, 1993/P-3/2 KB376 . . . . **398.2**
ZELINSKY, PO/Rumpelstiltskin. /1986/1-4/7 KB385 . . . **CE 398.2**

Folklore--Germany--Bremen.
HODGES, M/Hero of Bremen. /1993/3-5/6 KB451 . . . . . **398.22**

Folklore--Germany--Hamelin.
LATIMER, J/Irish piper. /1991/3-5/6 KB463 . . . . **398.22**

Folklore--Ghana.
MOLLEL, TM/Ananse's feast: an Ashanti tale. /1997/
K-2/3 KB622 . . . . **398.24**

Folklore--Great Britain.
BROWN, M/Dick Whittington and his cat. /c1950, 1988/
2-4/6 KB498 . . . . **398.23**
COOPER, S/Selkie girl. /1986/3-4/6 KB551 . . . . **CE 398.24**
CRESWICK, P/Robin Hood. /1984/6/6 KB434. . . . . **398.22**
JACOBS, J/King of the cats. /1980/1-3/2 KB595. . . . . **CE 398.24**
KING ARTHUR AND HIS KNIGHTS (SOUND RECORDING
  CASSETTE). /1991/5-6/KB462 . . . . **SRC 398.22**
PYLE, H/Story of King Arthur and his knights. /c1933, 1984/
A/9 KB472 . . . . **398.22**
TOM TIT TOT: AN ENGLISH FOLK TALE. /c1965, 1997/
P-3/6 KB378 . . . . **398.2**

Folklore--Great Plains.
GOBLE, P/Remaking the earth: a creation story from the Great
  Plains of North America. /1996/3-5/7 KB448 . . . . **398.22**
  Return of the buffaloes: a Plains Indian story about famine and
  renewal of the /1996/3-5/3 KB575 . . . . **398.24**

Folklore--Guatemala.
GERSON, M/People of corn: a Mayan story. /1995/
2-4/3 KB399 . . . . **398.21**

Folklore--Haiti.
COURLANDER, H/Uncle Bouqui of Haiti (Talking book). /1959/
K-A/KB729 . . . . **TB 398.27**
REASONER, C/Night owl and the rooster: a Haitian legend. /
1995/K-2/6 KB637 . . . . **CE 398.24**

Folklore--Hawaii.
BROWN, M/Backbone of the king: the story of Paka'a and his son
  Ku. /1984/5-6/6 KB428. . . . . **398.22**
RATTIGAN, JK/Woman in the moon: a story from Hawaii. /1996/
K-2/6 KB474 . . . . **398.22**
THOMPSON, VL/Hawaiian tales of heroes and champions. /c1971,
1986/4-5/4 KB491 . . . . **398.2**
WARDLAW, L/Punia and the King of Sharks: a Hawaiian folktale. /
1997/2-3/3 KB672 . . . . **398.24**

Folklore--Hungary.
BODNAR, JZ/Wagonload of fish. /1996/K-2/5 KB532 . . . **398.24**
SEREDY, K/White stag. /c1937/5-6/7 KB486 . . . . **398.22**

Folklore--Iceland.
WISNIEWSKI, D/Elfwyn's saga. /1990/4-6/6 KB422 . . . . **398.21**

Folklore--Indexes.
MACDONALD, MR/Storyteller's sourcebook: a subject, title, and
  motif index to folklore /1982/4-6/KA027. . . . . . **PROF 016.3982**

Folklore--India.
BROWN, M/Once a mouse. /c1961/1-3/6 KB536 . . . . **CE 398.24**
DEMI /One grain of rice: a mathematical folktale. /1997/
3-6/6 KB731 . . . . **398.27**
NESS, C/Ocean of story: fairy tales from India. /1996/
4-6/5 KB353 . . . . **398.2**
SHEPARD, A/Gifts of Wali Dad: a tale of India and Pakistan. /
1995/2-3/2 KB488 . . . . **398.22**
WOLF-SAMPATH, G/Mala: a women's folktale. /1996/
3-5/2 KB718 . . . . **398.26**
YOUNG, E/Seven blind mice. /1992/K-3/2 KB681 . . . . . . **398.24**

Folklore--Iran.
DE PAOLA, T/Legend of the Persian carpet. /1993/
2-3/6 KB285 . . . . **398.2**

Folklore--Ireland.
CLIMO, S/Irish Cinderlad. /1996/2-4/3 KB275 . . . . **398.2**
DE PAOLA, T/Fin M'Coul: the giant of Knockmany Hill. /1981/
1-3/4 KB392 . . . . **398.21**
  Jamie O'Rourke and the big potato: an Irish folktale. /1992/
  P-3/4 KB393 . . . . **398.21**
GLEESON, B/Finn McCoul (Videocassette). /1991/
3-5/KB445 . . . . **VCR 398.22**
GREENE, E/Billy Beg and his bull: an Irish tale. /1994/
2-4/5 KB304 . . . . **398.2**
HODGES, M/Saint Patrick and the peddler. /1993/
3-4/5 KB454 . . . . **398.22**
KENNEDY, S/Irish folk tales for children (Compact disc). /1996/
3-5/KB326. . . . . **CD 398.2**

MCDERMOTT, G/Daniel O'Rourke: an Irish tale. /1986/
2/2 KB755. . . . . **398.27**

Folklore--Italy.
DE PAOLA, T/Strega Nona: an old tale. /1975/
1-4/6 KB394 . . . . **CE 398.21**
Tony's bread. /1989/K-3/5 KB500 . . . . **398.23**
ITALIAN FOLKTALES. /1980/5-6/KA415 . . . . **REF 398.23**
KIMMEL, EA/Count Silvernose: a story from Italy. /1996/
3-5/5 KB504 . . . . **398.23**
OPPENHEIM, J/Christmas Witch: an Italian legend. /1993/
1-3/2 KB507 . . . . **398.23**
PETERSON, J/Caterina, the clever farm girl: a tale from Italy. /
1996/2-4/3 KB357 . . . . **398.2**
SANDERSON, R/Papa Gatto: an Italian fairy tale. /1995/
3-4/6 KB646 . . . . **398.24**
STANLEY, D/Petrosinella: a Neapolitan Rapunzel. /1995/
2-4/6 KB780 . . . . **398.27**

Folklore--Jamaica.
BENITEZ, M/How spider tricked snake. /1989/
K-1/1 KB528 . . . . **398.24**
GLEESON, B/Anansi (Kit). /1992/3-5/KB572 . . . . . **KIT 398.24**
TEMPLE, F/Tiger soup: an Anansi story from Jamaica. /1994/
2-3/2 KB663 . . . . **398.24**

Folklore--Japan.
COWLEY, J/Mouse bride. /1995/P-2/2 KB552 . . . . . **398.24**
CRYING RED GIANT: A JAPANESE FOLKTALE (VIDEOCASSETTE).
/n.d./K-2/KB391 . . . . **VCR 398.21**
HAMANAKA, S/Screen of frogs: an old tale. /1993/
2-4/4 KB581 . . . . **398.24**
HEDLUND, I/Mighty Mountain and the three strong women. /1990/
3-5/5 KB316 . . . . **398.2**
JAPANESE FAIRY TALES. /1992/2-4/7 KB322 . . . . **398.2**
KANI, S/Monkey and the crab. /1985/3/3 KB598 . . . . . . **398.24**
LEVINE, AA/Boy who drew cats: a Japanese folktale. /1993/
2-4/4 KB609 . . . . **398.24**
LONG, JF/Bee and the dream: a Japanese tale. /1996/
2-3/2 KB612 . . . . **398.24**
MARTIN, R/Ghostly tales of Japan (Sound recording cassette). /
1989/3-6/KB689 . . . . **SRC 398.25**
Mysterious tales of Japan. /1996/3-5/3 KB690 . . . . . . **398.25**
MCCARTHY, RF/Grandfather Cherry-Blossom. /1993/
2-3/3 KB753 . . . . **398.27**
Inch-high samurai. /1993/3-4/4 KB754 . . . . **398.27**
Moon princess. /1993/3-4/4 KB404 . . . . **398.21**
MCDERMOTT, G/Stonecutter (Videocassette). /1976/
2-4/KB756 . . . . **VCR 398.27**
METAXAS, E/Peachboy (Videocassette). /1991/
2-5/KB469 . . . . **VCR 398.22**
PATERSON, K/Tale of the mandarin ducks. /1990/
2-3/6 KB631 . . . . **398.24**
SAN SOUCI, RD/Samurai's daughter: a Japanese legend. /1992/
3-4/6 KB365 . . . . **398.2**
Snow wife. /1993/3-9/5 KB414 . . . . **398.21**
SAY, A/Under the cherry blossom tree: an old Japanese tale. /
1997/P-1/5 KB777 . . . . **398.27**
SCHROEDER, A/Lily and the wooden bowl. /1994/
3-5/7 KB366 . . . . **398.2**
UCHIDA, Y/Magic purse. /1993/2-4/4 KB379 . . . . **398.2**
Wise old woman. /1994/2-4/5 KB492 . . . . **398.22**
WAITE, MP/Jojofu. /1996/1-4/5 KB670 . . . . **398.24**
WELLS, R/Farmer and the Poor God: a folktale from Japan. /
1996/2-4/3 KB785 . . . . **398.27**
WILLIAMS, CA/Tsubu the little snail. /1995/3-5/4 KB673 . **398.24**

Folklore--Jerusalem.
SCHWARTZ, H/Next year in Jerusalem: 3000 years of Jewish
stories. /1996/3-6/7 KA780 . . . . **296.4**

Folklore--Kentucky.
SOME DOG AND OTHER KENTUCKY WONDERS (SOUND
RECORDING CASSETTE). /1992/3-4/KB370 . . . . . . **SRC 398.2**

Folklore--Kenya.
AARDEMA, V/How the ostrich got its long neck: a tale from the
Akamba of Kenya. /1995/P-2/6 KB515. . . . . **CE 398.24**
MCNEIL, H/Hyena and the moon: stories to listen to from Kenya
(Talking book). /1995/5-6/KB346 . . . . **TB 398.2**
Hyena and the moon: stories to tell from Kenya. /1994/
5-6/7 KB347 . . . . **398.2**

Folklore--Korea.
CLIMO, S/Korean Cinderella. /1993/2-4/5 KB726 . . . . . **398.27**
FARLEY, CJ/Mr. Pak buys a story. /1997/K-3/2 KB734. . . **398.27**
HAN, OS/Kongi and Potgi: a Cinderella story from Korea. /1996/
K-3/5 KB313 . . . . **398.2**
HAN, SC/Rabbit's escape/Kusa ilsaenghan tookki. /1995/
P-2/3 KB583 . . . . **398.24**

HEO, Y/Green frogs: a Korean folktale. /1996/
P-2/2 KB589 . . . . **398.24**
JAFFE, N/Older brother, younger brother: a Korean folktale. /
1995/3-4/6 KB320 . . . . **398.2**
KWON, HH/Moles and the Mireuk: a Korean folktale. /1993/
K-2/4 KB605 . . . . **398.24**
O'BRIEN, AS/Princess and the beggar: a Korean folktale. /1993/
3-4/6 KB761 . . . . **398.27**

Folklore--Laos.
XIONG, B/Nine-in-one, grr! grr! a folktale from the Hmong people
of Laos. /1989/P-3/4 KB677. . . . . **398.24**

Folklore--Latin America.
BRUSCA, MC/Pedro fools the gringo and other tales of a Latin
American trickster. /1995/2-4/3 KB429 . . . . **398.22**
DELACRE, L/Golden tales: myths, legends, and folktales from Latin
America. /1996/4-5/6 KB283 . . . . **398.2**
GONZALEZ, LM/Senor Cat's romance and other favorite stories
from Latin America. /1997/K-2/3 KB303 . . . . **398.2**
SAN SOUCI, RD/Little seven-colored horse: a Spanish American
folktale. /1995/3-5/5 KB648. . . . . **398.24**

Folklore--Madagascar.
RAPPAPORT, D/New king. /1995/4-A/3 KB473 . . . . . . **398.22**

Folklore--Malaysia.
DAY, NY/Kancil and the crocodiles: a tale from Malaysia. /1996/
2-3/2 KB556 . . . . **398.24**

Folklore--Mali.
WISNIEWSKI, D/Sundiata: Lion King of Mali. /1992/
3-5/4 KB495 . . . . **398.22**

Folklore--Martinique.
SAN SOUCI, RD/Faithful friend. /1995/4-6/5 KB411 . . . . **398.21**

Folklore--Mexico.
AARDEMA, V/Borreguita and the coyote: a tale from Ayutla,
Mexico. /1991/P-2/4 KB514. . . . . **398.24**
ADA, AF/Mediopollito/Half-Chicken. /1995/K-2/2 KB521 . **398.24**
CZERNECKI, S/Pancho's pinata. /1992/2-4/7 KB703 . . . **398.26**
EHLERT, L/Cuckoo: a Mexican folktale./Cucu: un cuento folklorico
mexicano. /1997/P-2/3 KB561 . . . . **398.24**
KIMMEL, EA/Witch's face: a Mexican tale. /1993/
3-5/2 KB402 . . . . **398.21**
MADRIGAL, AH/Eagle and the rainbow: timeless tales from Mexico.
/1997/4-5/7 KB339 . . . . **398.2**
PARKE, M/Quetzalcoatl tale of corn. /1992/2-3/5 KB630 . **398.24**

Folklore--Micronesia.
FLOOD, NB/From the mouth of the monster eel: stories from
Micronesia. /1996/2-5/5 KB296 . . . . **398.2**

Folklore--Middle East.
COURLANDER, H/Tiger's whisker and other tales from Asia and the
Pacific. /c1959, 1995/3-5/7 KB279 . . . . **398.2**

Folklore--Mongolia.
OTSUKA, Y/Suho and the white horse: a legend of Mongolia
(Videocassette). /1981/3-4/KB626 . . . . **VCR 398.24**
YEP, L/Khan's daughter: a Mongolian folktale. /1997/
2-4/6 KB787 . . . . **398.27**

Folklore--Netherlands.
FISHER, LE/Kinderdike. /1994/2-4/3 KB395 . . . . **398.21**

Folklore--New Mexico.
HAYES, J/Watch out for clever women!/Cuidado con las mujeres
astutas!: Hispanic /1994/2-5/4 KB315 . . . . **398.2**
HULPACH, V/Ahaiyute and Cloud Eater. /1996/
3-4/5 KB708 . . . . **398.26**

Folklore--New Zealand.
BISHOP, G/Maui and the Sun: a Maori tale. /1996/
3-4/3 KB700 . . . . **398.26**

Folklore--Nicaragua.
ROHMER, H/Uncle Nacho's hat: a folktale from Nicaragua/El
sombrero de Tio Nacho: un cuento de Nicaragua. /1989/
2-4/2 KB770 . . . . **398.27**

Folklore--Nigeria.
BRYAN, A/Beat the story-drum, pum-pum. /1980/
4-6/4 KB542 . . . . **398.24**
DAYRELL, E/Why the sun and the moon live in the sky: an African
folktale. /c1968/K-3/6 KB704 . . . . **CE 398.26**
GERSHATOR, P/Iroko-man: a Yoruba folktale. /1994/
2-3/6 KB397 . . . . **398.21**
GERSON, M/Why the sky is far away: a Nigerian folktale. /1992/
2-4/5 KB705 . . . . **398.26**
MOLLEL, TM/Flying tortoise: an Igbo tale. /1994/
2-3/3 KB623 . . . . **398.24**

Folklore--North America.
BRUCHAC, J/Between earth and sky: legends of Native American
sacred places. /1996/5-A/5 KB270 . . . . **398.2**
Boy who lived with the bears: and other Iroquois stories. /1995/
2-4/4 KB537 . . . . **CE 398.24**

Four ancestors: stories, songs, and poems from Native North
America. /1996/2-6/3 KB271................ **398.2**
RODANAS, K/Eagle's song: a tale from the Pacific Northwest. /
1995/3-4/5 KB768 .... **398.27**
SPIDER SPINS A STORY: FOURTEEN LEGENDS FROM NATIVE
AMERICA. /1997/2-5/6 KB371................ **398.2**
TAYLOR, HP/Coyote and the laughing butterflies. /1995/
2-3/5 KB662 .... **398.24**

Folklore--North Carolina.
WAHL, J/Little Eight John. /1992/2-3/2 KB783 ...... **398.27**

Folklore--Northwest, Pacific.
LEWIS, PO/Storm boy. /1995/2-4/3 KB610 .... **398.24**

Folklore--Norway.
ASBJORNSEN, PC/Man who kept house. /1992/
2-4/6 KB719 .... **398.27**
D'AULAIRE, I/D'Aulaires' trolls. /c1972, 1993/
4-6/6 KB280 .... **398.2**
KIMMEL, EA/Boots and his brothers: a Norwegian tale. /1992/
2-4/2 KB400 .... **398.21**
MILLS, LA/Tatterhood and the hobgoblins: a Norwegian folktale. /
1993/3-4/6 KB350 .... **398.2**
ROUNDS, G/Three billy goats Gruff. /1993/P-1/2 KB644. **398.24**

Folklore--Oceania.
COURLANDER, H/Tiger's whisker and other tales from Asia and the
Pacific. /c1959, 1995/3-5/7 KB279 .... **398.2**

Folklore--Oregon.
KIMMEL, EA/Billy Lazroe and the King of the Sea: a tale of the
Northwest. /1996/4-5/5 KB460. .... **398.22**

Folklore--Pakistan.
SHEPARD, A/Gifts of Wali Dad: a tale of India and Pakistan. /
1995/2-3/2 KB488 .... **398.22**

Folklore--Palestine.
BAHOUS, S/Sitti and the cats: a tale of friendship. /1993/
3-4/7 KB257 .... **398.2**

Folklore--Parodies, imitations, etc.
ERNST, LC/Little Red Riding Hood: a newfangled prairie tale. /
1995/K-2/4 KF531 .... **E**
LOWELL, S/Little Red Cowboy Hat. /1997/1-3/3 KG038...... **E**
MINTERS, F/Sleeping Beauty. /1996/2-3/3 KG142 ..... **E**
VANDE VELDE, V/Tales from the Brothers Grimm and the Sisters
Weird. /1995/5-A/6 KH827 .... **Fic**

Folklore--Pennsylvania.
KIRCHNER, AB/In days gone by: folklore and traditions of the
Pennsylvania Dutch. /1996//KA268 .... **PROF 398.2**

Folklore--Peru.
EHLERT, L/Moon rope: a Peruvian folktale/Un lazo a la luna: una
leyenda Peruana. /1992/1-3/2 KB563........... **398.24**
HICKOX, R/Zorro and Quwi: tales of a trickster guinea pig. /1997/
1-3/3 KB590 .... **398.24**
KURTZ, J/Miro in the Kingdom of the Sun. /1996/
3-4/5 KB505 .... **398.23**

Folklore--Philippines.
ARUEGO, J/Rockabye crocodile. /1988/P-K/2 KB525.... **398.24**
SAN SOUCI, RD/Pedro and the monkey. /1996/
3-4/2 KB649 .... **398.24**

Folklore--Puerto Rico.
BERNIER-GRAND, CT/Juan Bobo: four folktales from Puerto Rico. /
1994/1-2/2 KB427 .... **398.22**
JAFFE, N/Golden flower: a Taino myth from Puerto Rico. /1996/
2-4/5 KB503 .... **398.23**
MOHR, N/Song of el coqui and other tales of Puerto Rico. /1995/
3-4/3 KB621 .... **398.24**
PITRE, F/Juan Bobo and the pig: a Puerto Rican folktale. /1993/
2-4/2 KB763 .... **398.27**

Folklore--Russia.
ARNOLD, K/Baba Yaga: a Russian folktale. /1993/
2-3/3 KB387 .... **398.21**
CECIL, L/Frog princess. /1995/1-3/2 KB548 .... **398.24**
KIMMEL, EA/I-know-not-what, I-know-not-where: a Russian tale. /
1994/3-4/6 KB329 .... **398.2**
MAYER, M/Baba Yaga and Vasilisa the Brave. /1994/
3-5/5 KB466 .... **398.22**
ZIEFERT, H/Turnip. /1996/K-1/1 KB683 .... **398.24**

Folklore--Russia (Federation)--Siberia.
BERNHARD, E/Girl who wanted to hunt: a Siberian tale. /1994/
3-5/3 KB720 .... **398.27**

Folklore--Scandinavia.
SCANDINAVIAN FOLK & FAIRY TALES. /1984/
/KA273................................. **PROF 398.2**

Folklore--Scotland.
COOPER, S/Tam Lin. /1991/3-4/4 KB276 .... **398.2**
FOREST, H/Woman who flummoxed the fairies: an old tale from
Scotland. /1990/3-4/5 KB396.............. **398.21**
HUNTER, M/Gilly Martin the Fox. /1994/3-4/7 KB593 ... **398.24**

NIC LEODHAS, S/Always room for one more. /1965/
K-2/7 KB760 .... **398.27**
VILLAGE STEW (VIDEOCASSETTE). /1987/
K-3/KB782. .... **VCR 398.27**
YOLEN, J/Tam Lin. /1990/3-4/4 KB384 .... **398.2**

Folklore--Slavic Countries.
DE REGNIERS, BS/Little Sister and the Month Brothers. /c1976,
1994/2-3/2 KB501 .... **398.23**
VOJTECH, A/Marushka and the Month Brothers: a folktale. /1996/
1-3/4 KB513 .... **398.23**

Folklore--South Africa.
MOODIE, F/Nabulela: a South Africa folk tale. /1997/
2-4/4 KB758 .... **398.27**
WOLFSON, M/Marriage of the rain goddess: a South African
myth. /1996/4-5/5 KB424 .... **398.21**

Folklore--Southern States.
HAMILTON, V/When birds could talk and bats could sing: the
adventures of Bruh Sparrow, Sis /1996/2-5/2 KB582.... **398.24**

Folklore--Southwest, New.
DUNCAN, L/Magic of Spider Woman. /1996/
4-5/6 KB733 .... **398.27**
HAYES, J/Watch out for clever women!/Cuidado con las mujeres
astutas!: Hispanic /1994/2-5/4 KB315. .... **398.2**
JACKSON, E/Precious gift: a Navaho creation myth. /1996/
2-3/2 KB594 .... **398.24**
SAN SOUCI, RD/Little seven-colored horse: a Spanish American
folktale. /1995/3-5/5 KB648. .... **398.24**
YOUNG, R/Head on the high road: ghost stories from the
Southwest /1993/4-6/KB698.............. **SRC 398.25**

Folklore--Soviet Union.
BUDBERG, M/Russian fairy tales (Talking book). /n.d./
4-6/KB722. .... **TB 398.27**
CECH, J/First snow, magic snow. /1992/2-4/6 KB390.... **398.21**
GINSBURG, M/King who tried to fry an egg on his head: based on
a Russian tale. /1994/2-4/6 KB444 .... **398.22**
KIMMEL, EA/Bearhead: a Russian folktale. /1991/
2-4/4 KB327 .... **398.2**
LANG, A/Flying ship. /1995/K-3/6 KB749 .... **398.27**
PROKOFIEV, S/Peter and the wolf. /1982/
P-3/4 KD676 .... **CE 789.8**
RANSOME, A/Fool of the world and the flying ship: a Russian tale.
/c1968/2-5/5 KB765. .... **398.27**
Old Peter's Russian tales. /1975/5-6/6 KB766 ..... **398.27**
ROBBINS, R/Baboushka and the three kings. /c1960/
2-4/6 KB509 .... **398.23**

Folklore--Spain.
ARAUJO, FP/Nekane, the lamina and the bear: a tale of the
Basque Pyrenees. /1993/2-3/3 KB256........... **398.2**
HAYES, J/Tales from the Southwest (Sound recording cassette). /
1984/4-5/KB502. .... **SRC 398.23**
STEWIG, JW/Princess Florecita and the iron shoes: a Spanish fairy
tale. /1995/3-4/5 KB372 .... **398.2**

Folklore--Switzerland.
EARLY, M/William Tell. /1991/4-6/6 KB440 .... **398.22**
FISHER, LE/William Tell. /1996/3-5/4 KB442......... **398.22**

Folklore--Trinidad and Tobago.
JOSEPH, L/Mermaid's twin sister: more stories from Trinidad. /
1994/3-4/5 KB323 .... **398.2**

Folklore--Turkey.
TREASURY OF TURKISH FOLKTALES FOR CHILDREN. /1988/
4-5/7 KB512 .... **398.23**

Folklore--Uganda.
SERWADDA, WM/Songs and stories from Uganda. /c1974, 1987/
/KA319................................. **BA PROF 789.2**

Folklore--Ukraine.
BRETT, J/Mitten. /1989/K-2/3 KB534 .... **398.24**
KIMMEL, EA/One Eye, Two Eyes, Three Eyes: a Hutzul tale. /
1996/2-4/7 KB401 .... **398.21**

Folklore--United States.
BANG, M/Wiley and the Hairy Man: adapted from an American
folk tale. /c1976, 1987/1-3/2 KB389 .... **398.21**
BRER RABBIT AND BOSS LION (TALKING BOOK). /1992/
3-A/KB533. .... **TB 398.24**
CHASE, R/Grandfather tales: American-English folk tales. /c1948/
K-A/4 KB723 .... **398.27**
Jack tales. /c1943/K-A/3 KB724. .... **398.27**
Richard Chase tells three "Jack" tales from the Southern
Appalachians (Sound recording cassette). /n.d./
K-A/KB725 .... **SRC 398.27**
COMPTON, J/Ashpet: an Appalachian tale. /1994/
2-3/4 KB727 .... **398.27**
Sody sallyratus. /K-3/3 KB550 .... **398.24**
DEFELICE, CC/Dancing skeleton. /1996/3-6/6 KB684 .. **CE 398.25**

DIANE GOODE BOOK OF AMERICAN FOLK TALES AND SONGS. /1989/2-4/5 KB439 . . . . **398.22**

FOLKTELLERS /Stories for the road (Sound recording cassette). / 1992/5-A/KB297 . . . . **SRC 398.2**

Tales to grow on (Sound recording cassette). /c1981/ K-3/KB298 . . . . **SRC 398.2**

GLEESON, B/Paul Bunyan (Videocassette). /1990/ 3-5/KB447 . . . . **VCR 398.22**

GONZALEZ, LM/Senor Cat's romance and other favorite stories from Latin America. /1997/K-2/3 KB303 . . . . . . **398.2**

HALEY, GE/Mountain Jack tales. /1992/4-6/6 KB449 . . . . **398.22**

Two bad boys: a very old Cherokee tale. /1996/ 2-5/5 KB742 . . . . **398.27**

HAMILTON, M/Haunting tales: live from the Culbertson Mansion State Historic Site (Sound /1996/2-4/KB686 . . . . . . **SRC 398.25**

HASKINS, J/Headless haunt and other African-American ghost stories. /1994/4-5/4 KB687 . . . . **398.25**

HAYES, J/Tales from the Southwest (Sound recording cassette). / 1984/4-5/KB502 . . . . **SRC 398.23**

HOOKS, WH/Snowbear Whittington: an Appalachian Beauty and the Beast. /1994/2-3/4 KB318 . . . . **398.2**

Three little pigs and the fox. /1989/2-4/5 KB592 . . . . **398.24**

IRVING, W/Legend of Sleepy Hollow. /c1928, 1990/ 6-A/9 KH314 . . . . **Fic**

Rip Van Winkle. /1987/4-A/9 KH315 . . . . **Fic**

Rip Van Winkle; and, The Legend of Sleepy Hollow (Talking book). /1986/5-6/KH316 . . . . **TB Fic**

JONES, LC/Things that go bump in the night. /c1959, 1983/ A/9 KA605 . . . . **133.1**

KELLOGG, S/Mike Fink. /1992/3-4/5 KB456 . . . . **398.22**

Paul Bunyan, a tall tale. /1984/4-6/7 KB457 . . . . **398.22**

Sally Ann Thunder Ann Whirlwind Crockett: a tall tale. /1995/ 2-5/5 KB458 . . . . **398.22**

KESSLER, B/Brer Rabbit and Boss Lion (Kit). /1996/ 3-A/KB599 . . . . **KIT 398.24**

KNAPP, M/One potato, two potato: the folklore of American children. /1978//KA278 . . . . **PROF 398.8**

LESTER, J/John Henry. /1994/2-5/4 KB464 . . . . **398.22**

MCCORMICK, DJ/Paul Bunyan swings his axe. /c1936, 1962/ 4-6/6 KB467 . . . . **398.22**

Tall timber tales: more Paul Bunyan stories. /c1939/ 4-6/6 KB468 . . . . **398.22**

METAXAS, E/Stormalong (Kit). /1995/2-5/KB470 . . . **KIT 398.22**

PETERSHAM, M/Rooster crows: a book of American rhymes and jingles. /c1945/K-2/KB810 . . . . **398.8**

ROUNDS, G/Ol' Paul, the mighty logger: /1976/ 4-6/7 KB477 . . . . **398.22**

SAN SOUCI, RD/Cut from the same cloth: American women of myth, legend, and tall tale. /1993/5-6/6 KB481 . . . . **398.22**

Hired hand: an African-American folktale. /1997/ 3-4/3 KB412 . . . . **398.21**

Talking eggs. /1989/3-5/5 KB415 . . . . **CE 398.21**

SANFIELD, S/Adventures of High John the Conqueror. /1989/ 3-6/6 KB480 . . . . **398.22**

SAWYER, R/Journey cake, ho. /c1953, 1989/ P-3/5 KB776 . . . . **398.27**

SCHWARTZ, A/Scary stories to tell in the dark. /1981/ 4-A/3 KB694 . . . . **CE 398.25**

SHEPARD, A/Baker's dozen: a Saint Nicholas tale. /1995/ K-2/4 KB487 . . . . **398.22**

Legend of Slappy Hooper: an American tall tale. /1993/ 3-5/3 KB489 . . . . **398.22**

SIERRA, J/Wiley and the Hairy Man. /1996/K-3/4 KB417 . **398.21**

SLOAT, T/Sody sallyratus. /1997/1-3/5 KB653 . . . . **398.24**

TALKING EGGS (VIDEOCASSETTE). /1993/ 2-5/KB420 . . . . **VCR 398.21**

TORRENCE, J/Brer Rabbit stories (Sound recording cassette). / 1984/4-5/KB666 . . . . **SRC 398.24**

Story lady (Sound recording cassette). /1982/ 4-6/KB781 . . . . **SRC 398.27**

Traditions: a potpourri of tales (Sound recording cassette). /1994/ 2-3/KB668 . . . . **SRC 398.24**

WAHL, J/Tailypo! /1991/4-5/4 KB421 . . . . **398.21**

WALKER, PR/Big men, big country: a collection of American tall tales. /1993/4-A/7 KB493 . . . . **398.22**

YOUNG, R/Head on the high road: ghost stories from the Southwest /1993/4-6/KB698 . . . . **SRC 398.25**

Folklore--United States--Collections.

FROM SEA TO SHINING SEA: A TREASURY OF AMERICAN FOLKLORE AND FOLK SONGS. /1993/K-6/KD899 . . . . . **810.8**

Folklore--United States--Software.

P.J.'S READING ADVENTURES (CD-ROM). /1996/ K-3/KB252 . . . . **CDR 398**

Folklore--Vietnam.

VUONG, LD/Sky legends of Vietnam. /1993/ 3-5/7 KB717 . . . . **398.26**

Folklore--Virgin Islands of the United States.

GERSHATOR, P/Tukama Tootles the flute: a tale from the Antilles. /1994/K-2/5 KB398 . . . . **398.21**

Folklore--West Indies.

BRYAN, A/Turtle knows your name. /1989/K-3/6 KB545 . . **398.24**

Folklore--Zambia.

LESTER, J/Man who knew too much: a moral tale from the Baila of Zambia. /1994/4-5/3 KB607 . . . . **398.24**

Folklore, Afro-American SEE Afro-Americans--Folklore.

Folklore, Ila.

LESTER, J/Man who knew too much: a moral tale from the Baila of Zambia. /1994/4-5/3 KB607 . . . . **398.24**

Folklore, Jewish SEE Jews--Folklore.

Folklorists--Biography.

JAFFE, N/Voice for the people: the life and work of Harold Courlander. /1997//KA367 . . . . **PROF B COURLAND**

Food SEE ALSO Cookery; Diet; Farm produce; Fruit; Markets; Nutrition; Peanuts; Poultry; Vegetables; Vitamins; Weight control.

Food.

HAUSHERR, R/What food is this? /1994/K-2/2 KD266 . . . . **641.3**

MY BODY, MY BUDDY: HEALTHY FOOD (VIDEOCASSETTE). / 1993/3-5/KC986 . . . . **VCR 613.2**

Food--Fiction.

BARRETT, J/Cloudy with a chance of meatballs. /1978/ P-2/7 KF203 . . . . **E**

DE PAOLA, T/Pancakes for breakfast. /1978/1-2/KF478 . . . . . **E**

HOOPER, M/Cow, a bee, a cookie, and me. /1997/ K-2/2 KF768 . . . . **E**

PINKWATER, DM/Fat men from space. /1977/5-A/7 KH602 . . **Fic**

PRICEMAN, M/How to make an apple pie and see the world. / 1994/K-2/3 KG288 . . . . **E**

ROCKWELL, T/How to eat fried worms. /1973/4-6/5 KH643 . . **Fic**

SCHINDEL, J/What's for lunch? /1994/P-1/2 KG407 . . . . **E**

SEUSS, D/Green eggs and ham. /1960/P-2/1 KG454 . . . . **CE E**

Food--Fiction--Software.

GREEN EGGS AND HAM. SCHOOL ED. (CD-ROM). /1996/ K-2/KF639 . . . . **CDR E**

Food--Poetry.

ADOFF, A/Eats. /c1979, 1992/P-A/KD908 . . . . **811**

COLEN, K/Peas and honey: recipes for kids (with a pinch of poetry). /1995/3-6/KD269 . . . . **641.5**

NEVER TAKE A PIG TO LUNCH AND OTHER POEMS ABOUT THE FUN OF EATING. /1994/1-4/KE073 . . . . **811.008**

Food--Songs and music.

TODAY IS MONDAY. /1993/P-1/KD661 . . . . **789.3**

Food--Study and teaching (Elementary).

IRVING, J/Mudluscious: stories and activities featuring food for preschool children. /1986//KA201 . . . . **PROF 372.3**

Food--Wit and humor.

MATHEWS, J/Oh, how waffle!: riddles you can eat. /1993/ 2-6/KD735 . . . . **793.735**

Food chains (Ecology).

GODKIN, C/Wolf Island. /1993/3-5/4 KC334 . . . . **577.5**

LAUBER, P/Who eats what?: food chains and food webs. /1995/ K-3/2 KC295 . . . . **577**

SHAHAN, S/Barnacles eat with their feet: delicious facts about the tide pool food chain. /1996/3-6/5 KC348 . . . . **577.69**

Food chains (Ecology)--Software.

FIELD TRIP TO THE RAINFOREST (MICROCOMPUTER PROGRAM). /1991/3-A/KC314 . . . . **MCP 577.34**

Food crops.

ALBYN, CL/Multicultural cookbook for students. /1993/ /KA299 . . . . **PROF 641.59**

Food habits.

ALBYN, CL/Multicultural cookbook for students. /1993/ /KA299 . . . . **PROF 641.59**

BADT, KL/Good morning, let's eat! /1994/3-5/7 KB184 . . . **394.1**

Food habits--Fiction.

FLEMING, D/Lunch. /1992/P-K/2 KF557 . . . . **E**

HAYES, S/Eat up, Gemma. /1988/P-2/2 KF685 . . . . **E**

WELLS, R/Max and Ruby's Midas: another Greek myth. /1995/ P-1/3 KG701 . . . . **E**

Food habits--United States.

PENNER, LR/Eating the plates: a Pilgrim book of food and manners. /1991/3-6/4 KB186 . . . . **394.1**

Food industry and trade.

SOUP (VIDEOCASSETTE). /1991/2-4/KD321 . . . . **VCR 664**

Food supply--History.

PERL, L/Hunter's stew and hangtown fry: what pioneer America ate and why. /c1977/A/11 KD275 . . . . **641.5**

Fools and jesters.
  FRADON, D/King's fool: a book about medieval and renaissance
    fools. /1993/4-6/7 KE647 . . . . **940.1**
Foot.
  ALIKI /My feet. /1990/P-2/2 KC910 . . . . **612**
Foot--Fiction.
  PARNALL, P/Feet! /1988/P-2/1 KG219 . . . . **E**
  REISER, L/Beach feet. /1996/P-3/2 KG318 . . . . **E**
  SEUSS, D/Foot book. /c1968/P-1/1 KG452 . . . . **E**
  WINTHROP, E/Shoes. /1986/P-K/4 KG745 . . . . **CE E**
Football SEE ALSO Soccer.
Football.
  RAFFO, D/Football. /1994/3-6/4 KD785 . . . . **796.332**
  SAMPSON, M/Football that won... /1996/K-2/2 KD786. **796.332**
  SULLIVAN, G/All about football. /1987/4-6/6 KD787 . . **796.332**
Football--Fiction.
  DYGARD, TJ/Backfield package. /1992/6-A/7 KH090 . . . . . . **Fic**
    Forward pass. /1989/5-A/6 KH091 . . . . **Fic**
    Game plan. /1993/5-A/8 KH092 . . . . **Fic**
  KESSLER, L/Kick, pass, and run. /c1966/1-2/2 KF899 . . . . **E**
  KORMAN, G/Zucchini warriors. /1991/5-A/7 KH378 . . . . **Fic**
  SULLIVAN, A/Molly Maguire: wide receiver. /1992/
    4-6/3 KH773 . . . . **Fic**
Football--History.
  ANDERSON, D/Story of football. /1985/4-A/7 KD782. . **796.332**
Football--Periodicals.
  FOOTBALL DIGEST. /1971/-5-6/KA515 . . . . **PER 050**
Football coaches.
  CHADWICK, B/John Madden. /1997/
    5-A/7 KE451 . . . . **B MADDEN, J.**
Football players.
  CHRISTOPHER, M/In the huddle with...Steve Young. /1996/
    3-5/8 KE606 . . . . **B YOUNG, S.**
  DIPPOLD, J/Troy Aikman: quick-draw quarterback. /1994/
    4-6/6 KE230 . . . . **B AIKMAN, T.**
  GUTMAN, B/Steve Young: NFL passing wizard. /1996/
    4-6/7 KE607 . . . . **B YOUNG, S.**
  KRAMER, J/Bo Jackson. /1996/4-5/6 KE398 . . . **B JACKSON, B.**
  LACE, WW/Top 10 football quarterbacks. /1994/
    3-6/4 KD783 . . . . **796.332**
    Top 10 football rushers. /1994/3-6/4 KD784 . . . . **796.332**
  MORGAN, T/Junior Seau: high-voltage linebacker. /1997/
    5-A/10 KE532 . . . . **B SEAU, J.**
  THORNLEY, S/Emmitt Smith: relentless rusher. /1997/
    4-6/7 KE543 . . . . **B SMITH, E.**
Force and energy SEE ALSO Dynamics; Mechanics; Motion.
Force and energy.
  ADKINS, J/Moving heavy things. /1980/A/7 KC088. . . . . . **531**
  COBB, V/Why doesn't the earth fall up? /1988/
    4-6/5 KC092 . . . . **531**
  HEAT, TEMPERATURE AND ENERGY (VIDEOCASSETTE). /1995/
    5-6/KC128. . . . . **VCR 536**
  LAFFERTY, P/Force and motion. /1992/4-A/7 KC095 . . . . . . **531**
  LET'S MOVE IT: NEWTON'S LAWS OF MOTION
    (VIDEOCASSETTE). /1987/5-A/KC096 . . . . **VCR 531**
  PUSH AND PULL: SIMPLE MACHINES AT WORK
    (VIDEOCASSETTE). /1990/4-6/KC097 . . . . **VCR 531**
  SIMPLE MACHINE (VIDEOCASSETTE). /1993/
    5-6/KC098. . . . . **VCR 531**
  SIMPLE MACHINES: USING MECHANICAL ADVANTAGE
    (VIDEOCASSETTE). /1992/5-6/KC099 . . . . **VCR 531**
Force and energy--Experiments.
  DOHERTY, P/Cool hot rod and other electrifying experiments on
    energy and matter. /1996/4-A/5 KC093 . . . . **531**
Ford, Henry.
  MITCHELL, B/We'll race you, Henry: a story about Henry Ford. /
    1986/4-5/3 KE346 . . . . **B FORD, H.**
Foreign language SEE Specific language e.g. Chinese language.
Foreman, Michael.
  FOREMAN, M/War boy: a country childhood. /1990/
    4-A/6 KE347 . . . . **B FOREMAN, M.**
Forest animals.
  WILD, WONDERFUL ANIMALS IN THE WOODS
    (VIDEOCASSETTE). /1996/1-4/KC492 . . . . **VCR 591.73**
Forest animals--Fiction.
  DE PAOLA, T/Hunter and the animals: a wordless picture book. /
    1981/K-1/KF470. . . . . **E**
  KRAAN, H/Tales of the wicked witch. /1995/3-5/3 KH379 . . . **Fic**
Forest animals--Songs and music.
  STOLTZ, WJ/Come walk with me (Videocassette). /1994/
    P-3/KC309. . . . . **VCR 577.3**
Forest conservation.
  GOLDSTEIN, N/Rebuilding prairies and forests. /1994/
    4-6/7 KA955 . . . . **333.74**

Forest ecology.
  ANCIENT FORESTS (VIDEOCASSETTE). /1992/
    4-6/KC308. . . . . **VCR 577.3**
  BASH, B/Ancient ones: the world of the old-growth Douglas fir. /
    1994/3-6/7 KC435. . . . . **585**
  FISCHER-NAGEL, H/Fir trees. /1989/3-6/7 KC436. . . . . . **585**
  PRINGLE, LP/Fire in the forest: a cycle of growth and renewal. /
    1995/A/8 KC305 . . . . **577.2**
  REED-JONES, C/Tree in the ancient forest. /1995/
    K-3/3 KC437 . . . . **585**
  STONE, LM/Temperate forests. /1989/4-6/9 KC310. . . . . **577.3**
  THORNHILL, J/Tree in a forest. /1992/3-5/6 KC311. . . . . **577.3**
  TRESSELT, A/Gift of the tree. /c1972, 1992/K-4/6 KC312 . **577.3**
  WHAT ARE ECOSYSTEMS? (VIDEOCASSETTE). /1975/
    4-6/KC299. . . . . **VCR 577**
Forest ecology--Guides.
  WHITNEY, S/Western forests. /1985/A/KC313 . . . . **577.3**
Forest ecology--Songs and music.
  STOLTZ, WJ/Come walk with me (Videocassette). /1994/
    P-3/KC309. . . . . **VCR 577.3**
Forest fires.
  CONE, P/Wildfire. /1997/4-A/6 KB040 . . . . **363.37**
  PRINGLE, LP/Fire in the forest: a cycle of growth and renewal. /
    1995/A/8 KC305 . . . . **577.2**
  SIMON, S/Wildfires. /1996/3-6/7 KB041 . . . . **363.37**
Forest fires--Yellowstone National Park.
  STAUB, FJ/Yellowstone's cycle of fire. /1993/4-6/8 KC306 . **577.2**
Forests and forestry SEE ALSO Lumber and lumbering; Trees.
Forests and forestry.
  ANCIENT FORESTS (VIDEOCASSETTE). /1992/
    4-6/KC308. . . . . **VCR 577.3**
  DOWDEN, AO/Blossom on the bough: a book of trees. /c1975,
    1994/5-8/9 KC411 . . . . **582.16**
  STONE, LM/Temperate forests. /1989/4-6/9 KC310. . . . . **577.3**
Form perception.
  HOBAN, T/Dots, spots, speckles, and stripes. /1987/
    P-A/KA613 . . . . **152.14**
  OXLADE, C/Science magic with shapes and materials. /1995/
    3-6/5 KD751 . . . . **793.8**
Former Soviet republics--History.
  HARVEY, M/Fall of the Soviet Union. /1995/5-A/7 KE689. . . **947**
Fortification.
  MACAULAY, D/Castle. /1977/A/9 KD059 . . . . **CE 623**
  STEELE, P/Castles. /1995/4-6/7 KE650 . . . . **940.1**
Fortune, Amos.
  YATES, E/Amos Fortune, free man. /c1950/
    A/7 KE348 . . . . **B FORTUNE, A.**
Fortune telling--Fiction.
  ALEXANDER, L/Fortune-tellers. /1992/2-5/5 KG834 . . . . . . **Fic**
Fossil man.
  SATTLER, HR/Hominids: a look back at our ancestors. /1988/
    4-A/8 KC269 . . . . **569.9**
Fossils SEE ALSO Extinct animals; Mammals, Fossil; Paleontology; Retiles,
  Fossil.
Fossils.
  ALIKI /Fossils tell of long ago. Rev. ed. /1990/1-3/2 KC233 . **560**
    My visit to the dinosaurs. Rev. ed. /c1969, 1985/
    2-4/4 KC242 . . . . **CE 567.9**
  COLE, J/Evolution. /1987/3-4/5 KC290. . . . . **576.8**
  DEBECK, S/Dinosaurs! (Videocassette). /1989/
    2-5/KC246. . . . . **VCR 567.9**
  DIGGING DINOSAURS (VIDEOCASSETTE). /1986/
    3-A/KC247. . . . . **VCR 567.9**
  LAUBER, P/Dinosaurs walked here and other stories fossils tell. /
    1987/4-6/6 KC236 . . . . **560**
  LINDSAY, W/Tyrannosaurus. /1992/5-6/9 KC255 . . . . . **567.9**
  SCHLEIN, M/Discovering dinosaur babies. /1991/
    3-6/5 KC262 . . . . **567.9**
  TAYLOR, PD/Fossil. /1990/4-A/9 KC237 . . . . **560**
  THOMPSON, I/Audubon Society field guide to North American
    fossils. /1982/4-6/KC238 . . . . **560**
  TROLL, R/Raptors, fossils, fins, and fangs: a prehistoric creature
    feature. /1996/3-6/6 KC239. . . . . **560**
Fossils--Experiments.
  GRIER, K/Discover: /1990/3-6/6 KA592 . . . . **069**
Fossils--Fiction.
  DICKINSON, P/Bone from a dry sea. /1993/6-A/7 KH075 . . . **Fic**
  KELLOGG, S/Prehistoric Pinkerton. /1987/P-3/5 KF895. . . . . . **E**
Fossils--Handbooks, manuals, etc.
  THOMPSON, I/Audubon Society field guide to North American
    fossils. /1982/4-6/KC238 . . . . **560**
Foster home care SEE ALSO Adoption.
Foster home care.
  BANISH, R/Forever family. /1992/2-4/3 KB011 . . . . **362.73**

Foster home care--Fiction.
   BYARS, BC/Pinballs. /c1977/5-6/3 KG963 . . . . **CE Fic**
   HECTOR'S BUNYIP (VIDEOCASSETTE). /c1986, 1997/
   4-6/KH231. . . . . **VCR Fic**
   MACLACHLAN, P/Mama One, Mama Two. /1982/
   2-3/1 KG054 . . . . **E**
   PATERSON, K/Great Gilly Hopkins. /c1978/5-A/5 KH576. . . . **Fic**
   WOLITZER, H/Toby lived here. /c1978, 1986/4-6/6 KH878 . . . **Fic**
   WOODRUFF, E/Orphan of Ellis Island: a time-travel adventure. /
   1997/5-A/5 KH881 . . . . **Fic**
Four elements (Philosophy).
   HOFFMAN, M/Earth, fire, water, air. /1995/2-6/7 KA814 . **304.2**
Fourth of July.
   GIBLIN, JC/Fireworks, picnics, and flags. /1983/
   3-5/8 KE880 . . . . **973.3**
   GRAHAM-BARBER, L/Doodle Dandy!: the complete book of
   Independence Day words. /1992/5-A/A KB220. . . . . . . **394.263**
Fourth of July--Fiction.
   THOMAS, JR/Celebration! /1997/1-3/3 KG604 . . . . **E**
   VAN LEEUWEN, J/Fourth of July on the plains. /1997/
   2-5/2 KG647 . . . . **E**
Fox hunting--Fiction.
   BALL, Z/Bristle Face. /1990/5-A/6 KG877 . . . . **Fic**
Foxes.
   ARNOLD, C/Fox. /1996/4-6/7 KC845. . . . . **599.776**
   HAVARD, C/Fox: playful prowler. /1995/3-5/4 KC842 . . **599.775**
   LAUKEL, HG/Desert fox family book. /1996/
   3-6/7 KC846 . . . . **599.776**
   MASON, C/Wild fox: a true story. /1993/4-5/5 KC843 . **599.775**
   MATTHEWS, D/Arctic foxes. /1995/4-6/4 KC847 . . . . . **599.776**
   SCHNIEPER, C/On the trail of the fox. /1986/
   4-6/8 KC844 . . . . **599.775**
Foxes--Fiction.
   ABOLAFIA, Y/Fox tale. /1991/K-2/2 KF126 . . . . **E**
   ARNOSKY, J/Watching foxes. /1985/P-K/1 KF170 . . . . **E**
   EDWARDS, PD/Four famished foxes and Fosdyke. /1995/
   1-3/3 KF511 . . . . **E**
   ENDERLE, JR/What would Mama do? /1995/K-2/2 KF526 . . . . **E**
   FOX, M/Hattie and the fox. /1987/P-2/2 KF569 . . . . **E**
   FRENCH, V/Red Hen and Sly Fox. /1995/P-2/2 KF584 . . . . . . **E**
   FUCHS, DM/Bear for all seasons. /1995/K-2/2 KF589 . . . . . . **E**
   GEORGE, JC/Vulpes, the red fox. /c1948, 1996/
   5-A/5 KH160 . . . . **Fic**
   HOBSON, S/Chicken Little. /1994/P-2/2 KF749 . . . . **E**
   HOGROGIAN, N/One fine day. /c1971/P-2/5 KF763 . . . . **CE E**
   HUTCHINS, P/Rosie's walk. /c1968/P-1/1 KF802. . . . . **CE E**
   KELLOGG, S/Chicken Little. /1985/K-3/5 KF889 . . . . **CE E**
   LONDON, J/Gray Fox. /c1993, 1995/K-2/5 KG023 . . . . . . **CE E**
   MARSHALL, E/Fox and his friends. /1994/K-2/1 KG064 . . . **CE E**
   MARSHALL, J/Fox on the job. /c1988, 1990/K-3/2 KG067 . . . . **E**
   MCKISSACK, P/Flossie and the fox. /1986/K-3/2 KG105 . . **CE E**
   TEJIMA, K/Fox's dream. /1987/P-2/4 KG597 . . . . **E**
   THREADGALL, C/Proud rooster and the fox. /1992/
   P-1/4 KG607 . . . . **E**
   TOMPERT, A/Grandfather Tang's story. /1990/2-3/4 KG613. . . **E**
   WALSH, ES/You silly goose. /1992/P-K/2 KG682 . . . . **E**
Foxes--Folklore.
   BODNAR, JZ/Wagonload of fish. /1996/K-2/5 KB532 . . . **398.24**
   HASTINGS, S/Reynard the Fox. /1991/2-3/6 KB586 . . . . **398.24**
   HOOKS, WH/Three little pigs and the fox. /1989/
   2-4/5 KB592 . . . . **398.24**
   WALLIS, D/Something nasty in the cabbages. /1991/
   2-4/3 KB671 . . . . **398.24**
Fractions.
   ADLER, DA/Fraction fun. /1996/3-6/2 KB952 . . . . **513.2**
   LEEDY, L/Fraction action. /1994/2-4/2 KB963 . . . . **513.2**
   MCMILLAN, B/Eating fractions. /1991/P-2/1 KB969 . . . . . . **513.2**
   RELATING FRACTIONS AND DECIMALS (VIDEOCASSETTE). /
   1982/3-5/KB981. . . . . **VCR 513.2**
   USING FRACTIONS (VIDEOCASSETTE). /1982/
   3-4/KB983. . . . . **VCR 513.2**
France--Fiction.
   SCHNUR, S/Shadow children. /1994/4-A/7 KH681 . . . . **Fic**
   UNGERER, T/Crictor. /c1958/K-2/KG634. . . . . **E**
France--Folklore.
   ARAUJO, FP/Nekane, the lamina and the bear: a tale of the
   Basque Pyrenees. /1993/2-3/3 KB256. . . . . **398.2**
   BEAUTY AND THE BEAST (VIDEOCASSETTE). /c1989, 1996/
   K-3/KB259. . . . . **VCR 398.2**
   BRETT, J/Beauty and the Beast. /1989/4-5/6 KB268. . . . . . **398.2**
   BROWN, M/Stone soup: an old tale. /c1947/
   K-3/2 KB721 . . . . **CE 398.27**
   DE BEAUMONT, ML/Beauty and the Beast. /1990/
   4-5/6 KB282 . . . . **398.2**

EARLY, M/Sleeping Beauty. /1993/2-5/5 KB290 . . . . **398.2**
HANSARD, P/Jig, Fig, and Mrs. Pig. /1995/P-2/3 KB584 . **398.24**
HUCK, CS/Toads and diamonds. /1996/2-3/3 KB319 . . . . **398.2**
KIRSTEIN, L/Puss in boots. /c1992, 1994/3-4/6 KB604 . . . **398.24**
METAXAS, E/Puss in Boots (Kit). /1992/1-4/KB620 . . **KIT 398.24**
PERRAULT, C/Cinderella, or the little glass slipper. /1954/
   1-3/7 KB762 . . . . **398.27**
   Complete fairy tales of Charles Perrault. /1993/
   3-4/6 KB355 . . . . **398.2**
   Puss in boots. /1990/3-4/4 KB633 . . . . **398.24**
   Puss in boots: a fairy tale. /1996/K-3/5 KB634 . . . . **398.24**
   Story of Sleeping Beauty (Sound recording cassette). /1980/
   4-6/KB356. . . . . **SRC 398.2**
ROTH, SL/Brave Martha and the dragon. /1996/
   2-4/4 KB476 . . . . **398.22**
SAN JOSE, C/Cinderella. /1994/2-4/6 KB364 . . . . **398.2**
SCHROEDER, A/Smoky Mountain Rose: an Appalachian Cinderella.
   /1997/2-3/4 KB367 . . . . **398.2**
WHITE CAT (VIDEOCASSETTE). /1997/K-2/KB382 . . **VCR 398.2**
ZEMACH, M/Three wishes: an old story. /1986/
   2-3/4 KB386 . . . . **398.2**
France--History--German Occupation, 1940-1945--Fiction.
   SACHS, M/Pocket full of seeds. /c1973, 1994/4-A/5 KH668 . . **Fic**
Francis of Assisi, Saint.
   HODGES, M/Brother Francis and the friendly beasts. /1991/
   3-5/5 KE349 . . . . **B FRANCIS, ST.**
   WILDSMITH, B/Saint Francis. /1996/
   2-4/2 KE350 . . . . **B FRANCIS, ST.**
Frank, Anne.
   ADLER, DA/Picture book of Anne Frank. /1993/
   3-4/5 KE351 . . . . **CE B FRANK, A.**
   FRANK, A/Diary of a young girl. /c1967/
   4-6/6 KE352 . . . . **B FRANK, A.**
   VAN DER ROL, R/Anne Frank, beyond the diary: a photographic
   remembrance. /1993/6-A/7 KE353. . . . . **B FRANK, A.**
Frankfurters--Fiction.
   KESSLER, E/Stan the hot dog man. /1990/1-2/1 KF897 . . . . . . **E**
Franklin, Benjamin.
   BEN FRANKLIN BOOK OF EASY AND INCREDIBLE EXPERIMENTS.
   /1995/A/8 KB889 . . . . **507.8**
   D'AULAIRE, I/Benjamin Franklin. /c1950/
   2-4/6 KE354 . . . . **B FRANKLIN, B.**
   FRITZ, J/What's the big idea, Ben Franklin? /c1976/
   5-6/7 KE355 . . . . **CE B FRANKLIN, B.**
Franklin, Benjamin--Fiction.
   LAWSON, R/Ben and me: a new and astonishing life of Benjamin
   Franklin, as written by his good mouse Amos; lately discovered. /
   c1939/3-5/5 KH388 . . . . **Fic**
Fraud in science.
   GRAHAM, I/Fakes and forgeries. /1995/A/8 KA557 . . . . . **001.9**
Free material.
   FREE MATERIALS FOR SCHOOLS AND LIBRARIES. /1979-/
   /KA111. . . . . **PER PROF 050**
Freedman, Russell.
   MEET THE NEWBERY AUTHOR: RUSSELL FREEDMAN
   (VIDEOCASSETTE). /1991/5-A/KE356 . . **VCR B FREEDMAN, R.**
Freedom--Fiction.
   WIELER, DJ/To the mountains by morning. /1996/
   4-6/5 KH856 . . . . **Fic**
Freedom of Information--Handbooks, manuals, etc.
   INTELLECTUAL FREEDOM MANUAL. 5TH. ED. /1996/
   /KA052. . . . . **PROF 025.2**
Freedom of religion.
   SHERROW, V/Freedom of worship. /1997/4-6/12 KA908 . **323.44**
Freedom of speech.
   KING, DC/Freedom of assembly. /1997/4-6/7 KA972 . . . **342.73**
   Right to speak out. /1997/4-6/7 KA973. . . . . **342.73**
Freedom of the press.
   KING, DC/Right to speak out. /1997/4-6/7 KA973 . . . . . **342.73**
Fremont, John Charles.
   SANFORD, WR/John C. Fremont: soldier and pathfinder. /1996/
   5-6/4 KE357 . . . . **B FREMONT, J.**
French language materials SEE ALSO Bilingual materials--French.
French language materials.
   BONJOUR DE PARIS (VIDEOCASSETTE). /1988/
   5-A/KE683. . . . . **VCR 944**
   BROWN, R/Alphabet times four: an international ABC: English,
   Spanish, French, German. /1991/2-4/KB819. . . . . **411**
   CARRIER, R/Basketball player. /1996/4-6/3 KG975 . . . . **Fic**
   Boxing champion. /1991/4-6/2 KG976 . . . . **Fic**
   JENNINGS, S/Jeremiah and Mrs. Ming. /1990/K-2/2 KF828 . . . **E**
   LIONNI, L/Frederick. /c1967/P-2/2 KF992 . . . . **E**
   POE, EA/Annabel Lee. /1987/3-6/KD997 . . . . **811**
   POTTER, B/Tailor of Gloucester. /c1931, 1987/P-3/7 KG270 . . . **E**

Tale of Peter Rabbit. /n.d., 1987/P-2/6 KG278 . . . . **E**
TAYLOR, CJ/Ghost and Lone Warrior: an Arapaho legend. /1991/
2-5/4 KB696 . . . . **398.25**
How Two-Feather was saved from loneliness: an Abenaki legend. /
1990/3-4/2 KB716 . . . . **398.26**
ZEMAN, L/Gilgamesh the King. /1992/4-6/4 KE130 . . . . . **892.1**
Last quest of Gilgamesh. /1995/4-6/4 KE131 . . . . **892.1**
Revenge of Ishtar. /1993/4-6/4 KE132 . . . . **892.1**
Freshwater animals SEE ALSO Aquariums; also names of specific animals
e.g. Salamanders.
Freshwater animals.
ALIKI /My visit to the aquarium. /1993/2-4/5 KC582 . . . . . . **597**
Freshwater biology SEE ALSO Aquariums.
Freshwater biology.
LOEWER, HP/Pond water zoo: an introduction to microscopic life. /
1996/6-A/8 KC372 . . . . **579**
Friars--Fiction.
KRAMER, SP/Theodoric's rainbow. /1995/3-6/4 KH380 . . . . . **Fic**
Friends, Society of See Quakers.
Friendship.
ERLBACH, A/Best friends book: true stories about real best friends...
/1995/5-A/4 KA656 . . . . **158**
KALMAN, B/Fun with my friends. /1985/P-1/2 KA658 . . . . . **158**
LEEDY, L/How humans make friends. /1996/K-3/3 KA660 . . **158**
MORRIS, A/Loving. /1990/1-3/2 KA880 . . . . **306.874**
THAT'S WHAT FRIENDS ARE FOR (VIDEOCASSETTE). /1994/
5-6/KA666 . . . . **VCR 158**
Friendship--Fiction.
AAMUNDSEN, NR/Two short and one long. /1990/
4-6/5 KG811 . . . . **Fic**
ASCH, F/Moonbear's pet. /1997/P-K/2 KF175 . . . . **E**
BARKER, M/Magical hands. /1989/1-3/5 KF199 . . . . **E**
BAUER, J/Sticks. /1996/6-A/4 KG880 . . . . **Fic**
BAWDEN, N/Witch's daughter. /c1966, 1991/5-A/6 KG893 . . **Fic**
BLUME, J/Here's to you, Rachel Robinson. /1993/
6-A/4 KG910 . . . . **Fic**
Otherwise known as Sheila the Great. /1972/4-6/4 KG912 . . **Fic**
BONSALL, CN/Mine's the best. Newly illustrated ed. /1996/
1-2/1 KF245 . . . . **E**
BORTON, L/Junk pile! /1997/K-2/3 KF252 . . . . **E**
BRIMNER, LD/Merry Christmas, Old Armadillo. /1995/
K-2/3 KF267 . . . . **E**
BROWN, MT/True Francine. /1987/1-2/1 KF282 . . . . . . **E**
BUCK, N/Sid and Sam. /1996/P-1/1 KF291 . . . . **E**
BULLA, CR/Shoeshine girl. /1975/3-5/2 KG938 . . . . . . **Fic**
BUNTING, E/Blue and the gray. /1996/3-5/3 KF297 . . . . . **E**
On Call Back Mountain. /1997/1-3/2 KF306 . . . . **E**
BYARS, BC/Pinballs. /c1977/5-6/3 KG963 . . . . . . **CE Fic**
CAPOTE, T/Christmas memory. /c1956, 1989/
4-A/6 KG971 . . . . **CE Fic**
Thanksgiving visitor. /1996/5-A/8 KG972 . . . . **Fic**
CARLE, E/Do you want to be my friend? /1971/P-K/1 KF340 . . . **E**
CARLSON, N/How to lose all your friends. /1994/K-2/2 KF350 . **E**
CASELEY, J/Harry and Willy and Carrothead. /1991/
K-1/2 KF365 . . . . **E**
CHAMPION, J/Emily and Alice. /1993/1-3/2 KF375 . . . . **E**
Emily and Alice again. /1995/1-3/2 KF376 . . . . **E**
CHRISTIANSEN, CB/Snowman on Sycamore Street. /1996/
2-3/2 KG989 . . . . **Fic**
CLEARY, B/Henry and Beezus. /c1952/2-5/3 KG995 . . . . **CE Fic**
COHEN, B/Thank you, Jackie Robinson /1997/4-A/4 KH013 . . **Fic**
COTE, N/Palm trees. /1993/K-2/4 KF427 . . . . **E**
COTTONWOOD, J/Adventures of Boone Barnaby. /1992/
6-A/5 KH031 . . . . **Fic**
Babcock. /1996/6-A/3 KH032 . . . . **Fic**
COVILLE, B/Jeremy Thatcher, dragon hatcher: a magic shop book. /
1991/4-A/4 KH036 . . . . **CE Fic**
CREECH, S/Walk two moons. /1994/5-A/5 KH037 . . . . . . **Fic**
CRESSWELL, H/Watchers: a mystery at Alton Towers. /1994/
5-A/3 KH040 . . . . **Fic**
CUMMING, P/Mogul and me. /1989/5-A/7 KH046 . . . . . . **Fic**
DANZIGER, P/Amber Brown goes fourth. /1995/
2-4/4 KH059 . . . . **Fic**
Amber Brown is not a crayon. /1994/2-4/6 KH060 . . . . . **Fic**
Forever Amber Brown. /1996/2-4/4 KH062 . . . . **Fic**
DECLEMENTS, B/Pickle song. /1993/4-6/4 KH065 . . . . **Fic**
DUGAN, B/Loop the loop. /1992/1-3/4 KF501 . . . . **E**
DYGARD, TJ/Backfield package. /1992/6-A/7 KH090 . . . . . **Fic**
Infield hit. /1995/5-A/7 KH093 . . . . **Fic**
ELSTE, J/True Blue. /1996/2-4/2 KH098 . . . . **Fic**
ERICKSON, RE/Toad for Tuesday. /1974/1-3/3 KF528 . . . . **CE E**
FIENBERG, A/Wiggy and Boa. /c1988, 1990/5-6/7 KH113 . . . **Fic**
FLEISCHMAN, S/Scarebird. /1987/1-3/5 KF552 . . . . **E**
FREEMAN, D/Dandelion. /c1964/K-1/2 KF579 . . . . **CE E**

FUCHS, DM/Bear for all seasons. /1995/K-2/2 KF589 . . . . . . **E**
GIFF, PR/Lily's crossing. /1997/5-A/5 KH165 . . . . **Fic**
GILBERT, S/Hawk Hill. /1996/4-6/4 KH167 . . . . **Fic**
GORMAN, C/Miraculous makeover of Lizard Flanagan. /c1994,
1996/5-A/3 KH182 . . . . **Fic**
GRAHAME, K/Wind in the willows. /1980/5-6/8 KH189 . . . . . **Fic**
Wind in the willows. 75th anniversary edition. /1983/
5-6/8 KH190 . . . . **Fic**
GRAHAM, H/Boy and his bear. /1996/5-A/5 KH186 . . . . **Fic**
GREENWALD, S/Rosy Cole: she grows and graduates. /1997/
3-5/4 KH200 . . . . **Fic**
HAMILTON, V/Zeely. /c1967/4-A/4 KH220 . . . . **Fic**
HARVEY, D/Secret elephant of Harlan Kooter. /1992/
4-A/6 KH223 . . . . **Fic**
HAVILL, J/Jamaica and Brianna. /1993/K-2/2 KF680 . . . . . **E**
HELFMAN, E/On being Sarah. /1993/5-A/6 KH236 . . . . . . **Fic**
HENKES, K/Chester's way. /1988/K-2/5 KF702 . . . . **E**
Words of stone. /1992/5-A/6 KH240 . . . . **Fic**
HERMAN, C/Millie Cooper and friends. /1995/3-4/7 KH247 . **Fic**
HERMES, P/Kevin Corbett eats flies. /1989/5-6/3 KH248 . . . . **Fic**
HOESTLANDT, J/Star of fear, star of hope. /1995/
3-5/5 KH268 . . . . **Fic**
HOFF, S/Who will be my friends? /c1960/K-1/1 KF760 . . . . **E**
HONEYCUTT, N/All new Jonah Twist. /1987/3-5/4 KH277 . . . **Fic**
HOWE, J/I wish I were a butterfly. /1987/K-3/2 KF778 . . . . . **E**
HUNTER, M/Walking stones. /1996/6-A/8 KH295 . . . . **Fic**
HURWITZ, J/New neighbors for Nora. /c1979, 1991/
2-4/6 KH299 . . . . **Fic**
Nora and Mrs. Mind-your-own business. /c1977, 1991/
2-4/4 KH300 . . . . **Fic**
Teacher's pet. /1988/3-5/4 KH305 . . . . **Fic**
HUTCHINS, P/Titch and Daisy. /1996/P-K/2 KF805 . . . . . . **E**
HYPPOLITE, J/Seth and Samona. /1995/4-6/6 KH313 . . . . . **Fic**
JACKSON, I/Somebody's new pajamas. /1996/3-5/4 KH318 . . **E**
JAMES, B/Mary Ann. /1994/K-2/3 KF823 . . . . **E**
JAMES, S/Leon and Bob. /1997/K-2/2 KF824 . . . . **E**
JAM, T/Charlotte stories. /1994/2-3/2 KH321 . . . . **Fic**
JOHNSTON, T/Soup bone. /1990/K-2/2 KF841 . . . . **E**
KEATS, EJ/Maggie and the pirate. /1979/P-2/2 KF875 . . . . **E**
KELLER, H/Rosata. /1995/K-2/2 KF886 . . . . **E**
KELLOGG, S/Best friends. /1986/K-3/2 KF888 . . . . **E**
KING-SMITH, D/Mr. Potter's pet. /1996/3-5/2 KH352 . . . . . **Fic**
KLINE, S/Herbie Jones and the birthday showdown. /1995/
3-4/3 KH366 . . . . **Fic**
Horrible Harry and the green slime. /1989/2-4/2 KH368 . . . . **Fic**
KONIGSBURG, EL/Jennifer, Hecate, Macbeth, William McKinley,
and me, Elizabeth. /c1967/3-6/4 KH374 . . . . **CE Fic**
View from Saturday. /1996/5-A/7 KH377 . . . . **Fic**
LIONNI, L/Color of his own. /c1975, 1997/K-2/5 KF990 . . . . **E**
Extraordinary egg. /1994/1-3/2 KF991 . . . . **E**
LISLE, JT/Afternoon of the elves. /1989/6-A/6 KH408 . . . . . **Fic**
Gold dust letters. /1994/4-6/7 KH410 . . . . **Fic**
Looking for Juliette. /1994/4-6/6 KH412 . . . . **Fic**
LITTLEFIELD, H/Fire at the Triangle Factory. /1996/
2-5/1 KF998 . . . . **E**
LOBEL, A/Days with Frog and Toad. /1979/K-2/1 KG001 . . . . **E**
Frog and Toad all year. /c1976/K-2/1 KG002 . . . . . . **CE E**
Frog and Toad are friends. /c1972/K-2/2 KG003 . . . . . **CE E**
Frog and Toad together. /c1972/K-2/2 KG004 . . . . . . **CE E**
LOTTRIDGE, CB/Wings to fly. /1997/5-A/5 KH419 . . . . . . **Fic**
LOWRY, L/Anastasia, absolutely. /1995/4-A/6 KH422 . . . . . **Fic**
Number the stars. /1989/5-6/5 KH427 . . . . **Fic**
MACDONALD, A/Little Beaver and The Echo. /1990/
P-K/1 KG049 . . . . **E**
MARSHALL, J/George and Martha. /c1972/P-2/3 KG068 . . **CE E**
MARTIN, AM/Rachel Parker, kindergarten show-off. /1992/
K-2/1 KG069 . . . . **E**
MCKAY, H/Amber cat. /1997/5-6/5 KH476 . . . . **Fic**
MCKENNA, CO/Valentine's Day can be murder. /1996/
3-5/4 KH482 . . . . **Fic**
MEDEARIS, AS/Adventures of Sugar and Junior. /1995/
2-3/2 KH494 . . . . **Fic**
MONSON, AM/Wanted: best friend. /1997/K-2/2 KG152 . . **E**
MONTGOMERY, LM/Anne of Green Gables. /c1908, 1983/
4-A/6 KH503 . . . . **Fic**
MOORE, L/Don't be afraid, Amanda. /1992/2-4/4 KH504 . . . **Fic**
I'll meet you at the cucumbers. /1988/2-4/5 KH505 . . . . . **Fic**
MOORE, M/Under the mermaid angel. /1995/6-A/5 KH506 . . **Fic**
MORPURGO, M/Dancing bear. /1996/4-6/5 KH513 . . . . . . **Fic**
MYERS, A/Rosie's tiger. /1994/4-A/4 KH521 . . . . **Fic**
MYERS, WD/Young landlords. /c1979/5-6/6 KH524 . . . . . . **Fic**
NAMIOKA, L/Yang the third and her impossible family. /1995/
3-6/5 KH527 . . . . **Fic**
NAYLOR, PR/King of the playground. /1991/K-3/2 KG167 . . . . **E**

NOVAK, M/Newt. /1996/1-3/2 KG181. . . . . E
ORGEL, D/Don't call me Slob-o. /1996/3-5/2 KH565. . . . . . **Fic**
PALAZZO-CRAIG, J/Max and Maggie in spring. /1995/
   K-1/1 KG208. . . . . E
PATERSON, K/Bridge to Terabithia. /1977/5-A/6 KH573. . . **Fic**
   Flip-flop girl. /1996/5-A/6 KH575. . . . . **Fic**
PECK, RN/Soup. /1974/4-6/6 KH594. . . . . **Fic**
PEET, B/Zella, Zack and Zodiac. /1986/K-3/4 KG231. . . . . E
PERKINS, LR/Home lovely. /1995/K-2/5 KG233. . . . . E
PERKINS, M/Sunita experiment. /1993/5-A/6 KH598. . . . . **Fic**
PINKWATER, DM/Doodle flute. /1991/1-3/2 KG245. . . . . . E
POLACCO, P/Chicken Sunday. /1992/1-3/2 KG251. . . . . . . E
   Mrs. Katz and Tush. /1992/1-3/2 KG253. . . . . E
   Pink and Say. /1994/4-6/2 KH607. . . . . **Fic**
RANSOM, CF/Shooting star summer. /1992/K-2/2 KG304. . . . E
RASCHKA, C/Yo! Yes?. /1993/P-3/1 KG307. . . . . E
RICHTER, HP/Friedrich. /c1970, 1987/5-A/5 KH633. . . . . **Fic**
ROBINS, J/Addie meets Max. /1985/K-2/1 KG338. . . . . . . E
   Addie's bad day. /1993/K-1/2 KG339. . . . . E
RODOWSKY, C/Dog days. /1993/4-5/6 KH649. . . . . **Fic**
RUEPP, K/Midnight Rider. /1995/3-5/2 KH657. . . . . **Fic**
RYLANT, C/Fine white dust. /1986/6-A/4 KH661. . . . . . . **Fic**
   Poppleton. /1997/K-2/2 KG384. . . . . E
SHANNON, G/Seeds. /1994/K-2/2 KG478. . . . . E
SHARMAT, MW/Mitchell is moving. /1978/K-3/1 KG483. . . . . E
SHREVE, S/Gift of the girl who couldn't hear. /1991/
   4-6/6 KH709. . . . . **Fic**
SLEPIAN, J/Alfred Summer. /1980/4-6/4 KH718. . . . . . . **Fic**
SMITH, DB/Taste of blackberries. /c1973/4-6/4 KH722. . . . **Fic**
SNYDER, ZK/Fool's gold. /1993/6-A/7 KH732. . . . . **Fic**
SOTO, G/Boys at work. /1995/4-6/5 KH739. . . . . **Fic**
SPINELLI, J/Crash. /1996/5-A/3 KH744. . . . . **Fic**
SPIRN, M/Know-Nothing birthday. /1997/1-2/1 KG533. . . . . E
SPOHN, K/Dog and Cat shake a leg. /1996/K-2/1 KG534. . . . E
STEIG, W/Amos and Boris. /c1971/1-3/7 KG540. . . . . . **CE E**
STEPTOE, J/Stevie. /c1969/K-3/3 KG553. . . . . E
STEVENSON, J/Bones in the cliff. /1995/4-6/6 KH755. . . . **Fic**
   Worst person in the world. /c1978/K-3/4 KG570. . . . . . . E
UCHIDA, Y/Bracelet. /1993/2-5/3 KG631. . . . . E
UDRY, JM/Let's be enemies. /c1961/P-1/2 KG632. . . . . . . E
VINCENT, G/Ernest and Celestine at the circus. /1988/
   P-2/2 KG655. . . . . E
   Ernest and Celestine's picnic. /1982/P-2/1 KG656. . . . . . E
VOIGT, C/Bad girls. /1996/6-A/5 KH831. . . . . **Fic**
WABER, B/Gina. /1995/1-3/2 KG666. . . . . E
   Ira sleeps over. /c1972/K-2/2 KG668. . . . . **CE E**
WALLACE, BB/Cousins in the castle. /1996/5-A/7 KH837. . . . **Fic**
WARNER, S/Dog years. /1995/4-6/3 KH840. . . . . **Fic**
WILLIAMS, VB/Scooter. /1993/4-A/4 KH865. . . . . **Fic**
WILLIS, MS/Secret super powers of Marco. /1994/
   4-A/4 KH866. . . . . **Fic**
WILLNER-PARDO, G/Natalie Spitzer's turtles. /1992/
   1-3/2 KG741. . . . . E
   When Jane-Marie told my secret. /1995/2-3/2 KH867. . . **Fic**
WITTMAN, S/Special trade. /1978/P-3/4 KG754. . . . . E
WOJCIECHOWSKI, S/Christmas miracle of Jonathan Toomey. /
   1995/4-6/5 KH876. . . . . **Fic**
YUMOTO, K/Friends. /1996/6-A/7 KH901. . . . . **Fic**
ZIEFERT, H/Mike and Tony: best friends. /1987/K-2/1 KG794. . E
ZOLOTOW, C/Hating book. /c1969, 1989/K-2/2 KG801. . . . . E
   Tiger called Thomas. /c1963, 1988/K-2/4 KG808. . . . . . . E

Friendship--Fiction--Software.
BERENSTAIN BEARS GET IN A FIGHT. SCHOOL ED. (CD-ROM).
   /1995/K-3/KF223. . . . . **CDR E**
MARC BROWN'S ARTHUR'S BIRTHDAY. SCHOOL ED. (CD-ROM).
   /1994/K-4/KG062. . . . . **CDR E**

Friendship--Folklore.
CRYING RED GIANT: A JAPANESE FOLKTALE (VIDEOCASSETTE).
   /n.d./K-2/KB391. **VCR 398.21**
TALKING EGGS (VIDEOCASSETTE). /1993/
   2-5/KB420. . . . . **VCR 398.21**

Friendship--Poetry.
GRIMES, N/Meet Danitra Brown. /1994/2-4/KD949. 811
I LIKE YOU, IF YOU LIKE ME: POEMS OF FRIENDSHIP. /1987/
   3-A/KE065. . . . . 811.008
KATZ, B/Could we be friends?: poems for pals. /1997/
   1-3/KD959. 811
MAVOR, S/You and me: poems of friendship. /1997/
   K-2/KE072. . . . . 811.008
PRELUTSKY, J/Rolling Harvey down the hill. /1980/
   1-4/KE015. . . . . **CE 811**

Friendship--Songs and music.
EPSTEIN-KRAVIS, A/Tot's tunes (Sound recording cassette). /
   c1987, 1990/P-1/KD610. . . . . **SRC 789.3**

HARTMANN, J/Make a friend, be a friend: songs for growing up
   and growing together with friends (Sound recording cassette). /
   1990/K-5/KD617. . . . . **SRC 789.3**
Fritchie, Barbara--Poetry.
WHITTIER, JG/Barbara Frietchie. /1992/1-3/KE040. 811
Fritz, Jean.
FRITZ, J/China homecoming. /1985/4-6/7 KE703. . . . . . . 951.05
TALK WITH JEAN FRITZ (VIDEOCASSETTE). /1993/
   5-6/KE358. **VCR B FRITZ, J.**
Fritz, Jean--Fiction.
FRITZ, J/Homesick: my own story. /1982/4-A/4 KH145. . . . . **Fic**
Frobel, Friedrich.
BROSTERMAN, N/Inventing kindergarten. /1997/
   /KA196. . . . . **PROF 372.21**
Frogs.
GERHOLDT, JE/Frogs. /1994/3-5/5 KC601. . . . . 597.8
   Tree frogs. /1994/3-5/5 KC602. . . . . 597.8
GIBBONS, G/Frogs. /1993/K-3/3 KC603. . . . . 597.8
JOHNSON, SA/Tree frogs. /1986/5-6/7 KC604. . . . . 597.8
JULIVERT, A/Fascinating world of frogs and toads. /1993/
   4-6/6 KC605. . . . . 597.8
PARKER, NW/Frogs, toads, lizards and salamanders. /1990/
   5-6/7 KC606. . . . . 597.8
PATENT, DH/Flashy fantastic rain forest frogs. /1997/
   4-6/4 KC607. . . . . 597.8
PFEFFER, W/From tadpole to frog. /1994/
   K-2/2 KC608. . . . . **CE 597.8**
TADPOLES AND FROGS (VIDEOCASSETTE). /c1979, 1986/
   3-6/KC610. . . . . **VCR 597.8**
Frogs--Anatomy.
COLE, J/Frog's body. /1980/P-A/6 KC600. . . . . 597.8
Frogs--Fiction.
ANDERSON, PP/Time for bed, the babysitter said. /1987/
   P-2/1 KF157. . . . . E
BERENZY, A/Frog prince. /1989/3-5/5 KG898. . . . . **Fic**
CONFORD, E/Frog Princess of Pelham. /1997/4-A/3 KH019. . . **Fic**
ERICKSON, RE/Toad for Tuesday. /1974/1-3/3 KF528. . . . **CE E**
GRIFFITH, HV/Emily and the enchanted frog. /1989/
   2-4/2 KF646. . . . . E
GWYNNE, F/Pondlarker. /1990/K-2/5 KF656. . . . . E
HIGHTOWER, S/Twelve snails to one lizard: a tale of mischief and
   measurement. /1997/1-3/2 KF726. . . . . E
JOYCE, W/Bently and egg. /1992/1-3/4 KF857. . . . . E
KALAN, R/Jump, frog, jump! New ed. /c1981, 1995/
   P-1/1 KF864. . . . . **CE E**
LIONNI, L/Extraordinary egg. /1994/1-3/2 KF991. . . . . . . E
LOBEL, A/Days with Frog and Toad. /1979/K-2/1 KG001. . . . E
   Frog and Toad all year. /c1976/K-2/1 KG002. . . . . . . **CE E**
   Frog and Toad are friends. /c1972/K-2/2 KG003. . . . . **CE E**
   Frog and Toad together. /c1972/K-2/2 KG004. . . . . . **CE E**
LONDON, J/Froggy gets dressed. /1992/P-K/2 KG021. . . . . E
   Froggy goes to school. /1996/P-1/2 KG022. . . . . E
   Let's go, Froggy! /1994/P-K/2 KG024. . . . . E
MANN, P/Frog Princess? /1995/1-3/2 KG058. . . . . E
MANUSHKIN, F/Peeping and sleeping. /1994/P-2/2 KG060. . . . E
MAYER, M/Boy, a dog and a frog. /c1967/P-1/KG084. . . . **CE E**
NAPOLI, DJ/Jimmy, the pickpocket of the palace. /1995/
   3-A/3 KH530. . . . . **Fic**
   Prince of the pond: otherwise known as De Fawg Pin. /1992/
   3-A/3 KH531. . . . . **Fic**
NORTON, M/Are all the giants dead? /c1975, 1997/
   4-A/5 KH552. . . . . **Fic**
POTTER, B/Tale of Mr. Jeremy Fisher. /1989/K-2/7 KG275. . . . E
SCIESZKA, J/Frog Prince, continued. /1991/1-3/4 KG419. . . . E
SHANNON, G/April showers. /1995/P-1/2 KG477. . . . . E
WALSH, ES/Hop jump. /1993/P-K/2 KG679. . . . . E
WIESNER, D/Tuesday. /1991/P-3/KG714. . . . . E
Frogs--Folklore.
HAMANAKA, S/Screen of frogs: an old tale. /1993/
   2-4/4 KB581. . . . . 398.24
HEO, Y/Green frogs: a Korean folktale. /1996/
   P-2/2 KB589. . . . . 398.24
ROTH, SL/Biggest frog in Australia. /1996/2-3/2 KB643. . 398.24
TARCOV, EH/Frog prince. /c1974, 1993/P-3/2 KB376. . . . 398.2
Frontier and pioneer life SEE ALSO Cowboys; Indians of North America--
   Captivities; Overland journeys to the Pacific; Ranch life.
Frontier and pioneer life.
BIAL, R/Frontier home. /1993/4-6/8 KF027. 978
HODGES, M/True tale of Johnny Appleseed. /1997/
   2-4/6 KE238. . . . . **B APPLESEED, J.**
KALMAN, B/Colonial crafts. /1992/4-5/6 KD338. 680
   Home crafts. /1990/3-6/6 KD431. . . . . 745.5
   Kitchen. /1990/4-5/5 KD295. 643
   Pioneer projects. /1997/3-5/6 KD432. . . . . 745.5

KNIGHT, AS/Way west: journal of a pioneer woman. /1993/
5-6/5 KE197 . . . . **917.8**
LASKY, K/Searching for Laura Ingalls: a reader's journey. /1993/
3-6/6 KE198 . . . . **917.8**
PAUL, AW/Seasons sewn: a year in patchwork. /1996/
3-6/7 KD462 . . . . **746.46**
PERL, L/Hunter's stew and hangtown fry: what pioneer America ate
and why. /c1977/A/11 KD275 . . . . **641.5**
SCHLISSEL, L/Black frontiers: a history of African American heroes
in the Old West. /1995/4-6/8 KF048 . . . . **978**
STEWART, GR/Pioneers go west. /c1982, 1997/
4-6/7 KF051 . . . . **978**
TUNIS, E/Frontier living. /c1961/5-6/9 KE893 . . . . . . **973.4**
WADSWORTH, G/Laura Ingalls Wilder: storyteller of the prairie. /
1997/4-A/5 KE595 . . . . **B WILDER, L.**
WALKER, BM/Little House cookbook: frontier foods from Laura
Ingalls Wilder's classic /1995/4-6/9 KD282 . . . . . . **641.5**
WRIGHT, CC/Wagon train: a family goes West in 1865. /1995/
4-6/3 KF052 . . . . **978**

Frontier and pioneer life--Appalachian region.
ANDERSON, J/Pioneer children of Appalachia. /1986/
4-6/6 KE974 . . . . **975.4**

Frontier and pioneer life--Biography.
DANIEL BOONE'S FINAL FRONTIER (VIDEOCASSETTE). /1995/
4-5/KE259 . . . . **VCR B BOONE, D.**
KUNSTLER, JH/Johnny Appleseed (Videocassette). /1992/
2-5/KE239 . . . . **VCR B APPLESEED, J.**
LAWLOR, L/Real Johnny Appleseed. /1995/
5-6/8 KE240 . . . . **B APPLESEED, J.**
LAWSON, R/They were strong and good. /c1940/
4-6/KE891 . . . . **973.4**

Frontier and pioneer life--California--Fiction.
CUSHMAN, K/Ballad of Lucy Whipple. /1996/
5-A/7 KH049 . . . . **CE Fic**
KRENSKY, S/Iron dragon never sleeps. /1995/3-5/2 KH381 . . . **Fic**

Frontier and pioneer life--Canada.
SYMONS, RD/Grandfather Symons' homestead book. /1981/
3-5/6 KE815 . . . . **971.2**

Frontier and pioneer life--Canada--Fiction.
HUTCHINS, HJ/Cat of Artimus Pride. /1991/3-5/6 KH307 . . . . **Fic**
Tess. /1995/3-5/4 KH309 . . . . **Fic**
LOTTRIDGE, CB/Ticket to Canada. /1996/4-A/5 KH418 . . . . . **Fic**
VALGARDSON, WD/Sarah and the people of Sand River. /1996/
4-6/2 KH818 . . . . **Fic**

Frontier and pioneer life--Connecticut--Fiction.
DALGLIESH, A/Courage of Sarah Noble. /c1954, 1987/
3-5/3 KH058 . . . . **CE Fic**

Frontier and pioneer life--Fiction.
BLANC, ES/Berchick. /1989/3-5/5 KG901 . . . . **Fic**
BRENNER, B/Wagon wheels. /1978/1-3/1 KF259 . . . . **CE E**
BRINK, CR/Caddie Woodlawn. New ed. /1973/
4-6/6 KG922 . . . . **CE Fic**
BYARS, BC/Golly sisters go West. /1986/1-3/1 KF325 . . . . **CE E**
CONRAD, P/Prairie songs. /1985/5-A/7 KH023 . . . . **Fic**
FLEISCHMAN, P/Borning room. /1991/6-A/5 KH115 . . . . **Fic**
FRITZ, J/Cabin faced west. /c1958/4-6/6 KH143 . . . . **Fic**
GIPSON, F/Old Yeller. /c1956/A/7 KH170 . . . . **CE Fic**
GLASS, A/Folks call me Appleseed John. /1995/
3-5/6 KH172 . . . . **Fic**
HARVEY, B/Cassie's journey: going West in the 1860s. /1988/
1-3/5 KF677 . . . . **E**
My prairie Christmas. /1990/2-4/4 KH222 . . . . **Fic**
MACLACHLAN, P/Sarah, plain and tall. /1985/
3-5/4 KH444 . . . . **CE Fic**
Skylark. /1994/3-5/3 KH445 . . . . **Fic**
MCCLUNG, RM/Hugh Glass, mountain man. /1993/
6-A/7 KH472 . . . . **Fic**
MORROW, H/On to Oregon. /c1954/5-6/4 KH517 . . . . **Fic**
SANDERS, SR/Warm as wool. /1992/3-5/5 KH675 . . . . **Fic**
SORENSEN, H/New Hope. /1995/1-4/4 KG526 . . . . **E**
STEVENS, C/Trouble for Lucy. /1979/3-5/6 KH754 . . . . **Fic**
STUTSON, C/Prairie primer A to Z. /1996/1-3/3 KG583 . . . . . **E**
TURNER, A/Dakota dugout. /1985/1-3/6 KG624 . . . . **E**
Sewing quilts. /1994/1-3/6 KG628 . . . . **E**
VAN LEEUWEN, J/Fourth of July on the plains. /1997/
2-5/2 KG647 . . . . **E**
WILDER, LI/Dance at Grandpa's. /1994/K-3/4 KG719 . . . . . . **E**
Little house in the Big Woods. /c1953/3-6/4 KH860 . . . . **Fic**
Winter days in the Big Woods. /1994/K-3/4 KG720. . . . . . **E**
WILLIAMS, D/Grandma Essie's covered wagon. /1993/
2-4/4 KG726 . . . . **E**
WISLER, GC/Jericho's journey. /1993/5-A/6 KH870 . . . . . . **Fic**
WOODRUFF, E/Dear Levi: letters from the Overland Trail. /1994/
4-6/6 KH880 . . . . **Fic**

Frontier and pioneer life--Great Plains.
ROUNDS, G/Sod houses on the Great Plains. /1995/
2-6/7 KD361 . . . . **693**
Frontier and pioneer life--Indiana--Fiction.
SANDERS, SR/Place called Freedom. /1997/1-3/3 KG390 . . . . **E**
Frontier and pioneer life--Kansas--Fiction.
FLEISCHMAN, S/Chancy and the Grand Rascal. /c1966, 1997/
4-6/5 KH120 . . . . **Fic**
Frontier and pioneer life--Michigan--Fiction.
WHELAN, G/Next spring an oriole. /1987/2-4/5 KH848. . . . . **Fic**
Frontier and pioneer life--Middle West.
RILEY, J/Prairie cabin: a Norwegian pioneer woman's story
(Videocassette). /1991/A/KF012 . . . . **VCR 977**
Frontier and pioneer life--Missouri--Fiction.
MACBRIDE, RL/Little house on Rocky Ridge. /1993/
4-6/6 KH436 . . . . **Fic**
Frontier and pioneer life--Nebraska--Fiction.
BUNTING, E/Dandelions. /1995/3-5/2 KG942 . . . . **Fic**
Frontier and pioneer life--Pictorial works.
AMERICAN HISTORY: GROWING PAINS (PICTURE). /c1974/
4-6/KE912 . . . . **PIC 973.8**
Frontier and pioneer life--Software.
OREGON TRAIL II (CD-ROM). /1994/4-A/KE745 . . **CDR 970.04**
Frontier and pioneer life--Southwest, New.
LAVENDER, DS/Santa Fe Trail. /1995/A/6 KF037 . . . . **978**
RUSSELL, M/Along the Santa Fe Trail: Marion Russell's own story.
/1993/4-6/7 KE199 . . . . **917.8**
Frontier and pioneer life--Tennessee--Fiction.
ISAACS, A/Swamp Angel. /1994/2-5/6 KF810. . . . . **E**
Frontier and pioneer life--Texas--Fiction.
KARR, K/Oh, those Harper girls!; or Young and dangerous. /1992/
5-A/Y KH342 . . . . **Fic**
LIGHTFOOT, DJ/Trail fever: the life of a Texas cowboy. /1992/
4-6/5 KH406 . . . . **Fic**
Frontier and pioneer life--United States.
ANDERSON, W/Little House guidebook. /1996/
3-5/10 KE196 . . . . **917.8**
LOEPER, JJ/Going to school in 1776. /1973/
4-6/8 KB123 . . . . **372.973**
Frontier and pioneer life--West (U.S.).
BLACK WEST (VIDEOCASSETTE). /1992/5-6/KF028 . . **VCR 978**
FREEDMAN, R/Cowboys of the wild west. /1985/
5-A/7 KF029 . . . . **978**
GREENWOOD, B/Pioneer sampler: the daily life of a pioneer family
in 1840. /1995/4-6/6 KF031 . . . . **978**
HOMESTEADING: 70 YEARS ON THE GREAT PLAINS, 1862-1932
(VIDEOCASSETTE). /1992/4-6/KF034 . . . . **VCR 978**
KATZ, WL/Black women of the Old West. /1995/
5-6/9 KF036 . . . . **978**
LEVINSON, NS/Snowshoe Thompson. /1992/
K-3/2 KE564 . . . . **B THOMPSON, S.**
RITCHIE, D/Frontier life. /1996/5-6/9 KF045. . . . . **978**
STEFOFF, R/Children of the westward trail. /1996/
4-6/8 KF050 . . . . **978**
WUKOVITS, JF/Annie Oakley. /1997/
5-6/8 KE480 . . . . **B OAKLEY, A.**
Jesse James. /1997/4-6/10 KE402 . . . . **B JAMES, J.**
Frontier and pioneer life--West (U.S.)--Fiction.
PAULSEN, G/Call me Francis Tucket. /1995/5-A/5 KH585. . . . **Fic**
Mr. Tucket. /1994/5-A/5 KH588 . . . . **Fic**
Frontier and pioneer life--Wisconsin--Fiction.
WILKES, MD/Little house in Brookfield. /1996/4-6/5 KH861. . . **Fic**
Fruit.
GOLDSEN, L/Fruit. /1992/P-3/2 KD159 . . . . **634**
JOHNSON, SA/Apple trees. /1983/4-6/9 KD161 . . . . **634**
MCMILLAN, B/Growing colors. /1988/P-1/KC124 . . . . **535.6**
Fruit--Fiction.
CHARLES, NN/What am I?: looking through shapes at apples and
grapes. /1994/P-2/2 KF378 . . . . **E**
RYLANT, C/Mr. Putter and Tabby pick the pears. /1995/
1-3/2 KG379 . . . . **E**
Fruit trees.
HALL, Z/Apple pie tree. /1996/1-4/2 KC413 . . . . **582.16**
JOHNSON, SA/Apple trees. /1983/4-6/9 KD161 . . . . **634**
Frustration.
I'M SO FRUSTRATED! (VIDEOCASSETTE). /1994/
1-3/KA627 . . . . **VCR 152.4**
Fudge--Fiction.
HOWE, J/Hot fudge. /1990/K-3/2 KF777 . . . . **E**
Fuel SEE ALSO Coal; Gas; Oil; Petroleum industry and trade; Power
resources.
Fugitive slaves.
BRILL, MT/Allen Jay and the Underground Railroad. /1993/
4-6/4 KE898 . . . . **973.7**

GORRELL, GK/North Star to freedom: the story of the
Underground Railroad. /1997/5-6/8 KE905 . . . . **973.7**
HAMILTON, V/Many thousand gone: African Americans from
slavery to freedom. /1993/4-6/7 KA927 . . . . **326**
RAPPAPORT, D/Escape from slavery: five journeys to freedom. /
1991/4-6/4 KE863 . . . . **973**

Fugitive slaves--Fiction.
EDWARDS, PD/Barefoot: escape on the Underground Railroad. /
1997/1-3/3 KF510 . . . . **E**
PATERSON, K/Jip: his story. /1996/5-A/7 KH577 . . . . **Fic**
PICO, F/Red comb. /1994/3-5/7 KH601 . . . . **Fic**
ROSENBURG, JM/William Parker: rebel without rights: a novel
based on fact. /1996/6-A/7 KH654 . . . . **Fic**
ROSEN, MJ/School for Pompey Walker. /1995/4-8/6 KH653 . **Fic**

Fulton, Robert.
BOWEN, AR/Head full of notions: a story about Robert Fulton. /
1997/4-5/8 KE359 . . . . **B FULTON, R.**
NOONAN, J/Nineteenth-century inventors. /1992/
5-6/7 KC897 . . . . **609**

Fund raising.
SMACKERS: ELEMENTARY ENTREPRENEURS (VIDEOCASSETTE).
/1991/3-6/KD314. . . . . **VCR 658**

Fund raising--Fiction.
MAHY, M/Fortune branches out. /c1994, 1995/3-5/4 KH447 . . **Fic**

Funeral rites and ceremonies.
ALIKI /Mummies made in Egypt. /1979/4-6/6 KB173 . . . . . . **393**
Fungi SEE ALSO Mushrooms.

Fungi.
SILVERSTEIN, A/Fungi. /1996/4-8/8 KC380 . . . . **579.5**

Fur.
PATENT, DH/Why mammals have fur. /1995/4-6/6 KC727 . . **599**

Furniture--United States.
FISHER, LE/Cabinetmakers. /1997/3-6/7 KD343 . . . . **684.1**

Furniture making.
MITGUTSCH, A/From tree to table. /1981/P-2/2 KD329. . . . **674**

Future--Fiction.
CHRISTOPHER, J/White Mountains. /1967/4-6/6 KG991 . . . . **Fic**
HOOVER, HM/Only child. /1992/5-A/5 KH280. . . . . **Fic**

Future--Periodicals.
FUTURIST. /1967-//KA112 . . . . **PER PROF 050**

Gabrielino Indians--Missions--California.
MACMILLAN, D/Missions of the Los Angeles Area. /1996/
4-6/9 KF084 . . . . **979.4**

Galapagos Islands.
MYERS, LB/Galapagos: islands of change. /1995/
4-A/8 KF113 . . . . **986.6**

Galapagos Islands--Fiction.
LEWIN, B/Booby hatch. /1995/K-2/2 KF973 . . . . **E**

Galapagos tortoise.
SCHAFER, S/Galapagos tortoise. /1992/5-6/7 KC622 . . . **597.92**

Galileo.
SIS, P/Starry messenger: a book depicting the life of a famous
scientist, mathematician, astronomer, philosopher, physicist: Galileo
Galilei. /1996/3-6/6 KE360 . . . . **CE B GALILEO**

Gallaudet, T. H. (Thomas Hopkins).
BOWEN, AR/World of knowing: a story about Thomas Hopkins
Gallaudet. /1995/3-5/6 KE361 . . . . **B GALLAUDET, T.**

Galveston Island (Tex.)--Fiction.
STEWART, EJ/Bimmi finds a cat. /1996/3-5/6 KH761 . . . . . . **Fic**

Game shows--Fiction.
RODDA, E/Finders keepers. /1991/5-A/6 KH645 . . . . **Fic**
Games SEE ALSO Amusements; Educational games; Indoor games; Play;
Sports; also names of specific games e.g. Chess.

Games.
COLE, J/Crazy eights and other card games. /1994/
3-6/3 KD758 . . . . **795.4**
Pin the tail on the donkey and other party games. /1993/
K-2/3 KD698 . . . . **793**
Rain or shine activity book: fun things to make and do. /1997/
3-6/KD699. . . . . **793**
ERLBACH, A/Sidewalk games around the world. /1997/
2-5/6 KD769 . . . . **796.2**
LANKFORD, MD/Jacks around the world. /1996/
3-6/10 KD770 . . . . **796.2**
LEWIS, S/Let's play games (Videocassette). /1994/
P-2/KD709. . . . . **VCR 793.4**
MILORD, S/Hands around the world: 365 creative ways to build
cultural awareness and global /1992//KA167 . . . . . . **PROF 306**
MISS MARY MACK AND OTHER CHILDREN'S STREET RHYMES. /
1990/2-5/KD766 . . . . **796.1**
ROWEN, L/Beyond winning: sports and games all kids want to play.
/1990//KA332 . . . . **PROF 796.1**
SKURZYNSKI, G/Know the score: video games in your high-tech
world. /1994/3-6/8 KD757. **794.8**

Games--Cross-cultural studies.
SIERRA, J/Children's traditional games: games from 137 countries
and cultures. /1995//KA331 . . . . **PROF 796**

Games--Fiction.
KROLL, S/Tyrannosaurus game. /c1976/K-2/6 KF931 . . . . **CE E**
STEVENSON, J/Mud Flat Olympics. /1994/1-3/2 KG562 . . . . . **E**
VAUGHAN, MK/Snap! /1996/K-2/2 KG651. . . . . **E**
WISNIEWSKI, D/Rain player. /1991/2-3/4 KG751. . . . . . . **CE E**

Games--History.
HANKIN, R/What was it like before television? /1995/
1-3/2 KD679 . . . . **790.1**

Games--Periodicals.
HIGHLIGHTS FOR CHILDREN. /1946-/P-A/KA517 . . . . . **PER 050**

Games--Social aspects.
MILLER, TR/Taking time out: recreation and play. /1996/
5-A/7 KA865 . . . . **306.4**

Games--Study and teaching.
SIERRA, J/Children's traditional games: games from 137 countries
and cultures. /1995//KA331 . . . . **PROF 796**

Games in art.
BLIZZARD, GS/Come look with me: world of play. /1993/
3-6/5 KD369 . . . . **701.1**

Gandhi, Mahatma.
FISHER, LE/Gandhi. /1995/3-6/8 KE362 . . . . . . **B GANDHI, M.**
LAZO, C/Mahatma Gandhi. /1993/4-6/7 KE363 . **B GANDHI, M.**

Ganesha (Hindu deity).
KRISHNASWAMI, U/Broken tusk: stories of the Hindu god
Ganesha. /1996/3-4/4 KA764 . . . . **294.5**

Ganges River (India and Bangladesh)--Description and travel.
LEWIN, T/Sacred river. /1995/4-6/6 KA765 . . . . **294.5**

Gangs.
GANGS: DECISIONS AND OPTIONS (VIDEOCASSETTE). /1993/
A//KB070 . . . . **VCR 364.1**
GREENBERG, KE/Out of the gang. /1992/4-6/6 KB071 . . . **364.1**

Garage sales--Fiction.
STEVENSON, J/Yard sale. /1996/2-3/2 KH756 . . . . **Fic**
Garbage SEE Refuse and refuse disposal.

Garden ecology.
KUHN, D/More than just a flower garden. /1990/
4-5/6 KD175 . . . . **635.9**
More than just a vegetable garden. /1990/4-5/5 KD170 . . . **635**
Gardening SEE ALSO Gardens; Indoor gardening; Insects, Injurious and
beneficial; Plants; Vegetable gardening.

Gardening.
GLASER, L/Compost!: growing gardens from your garbage. /1996/
P-K/3 KD166 . . . . **635**
HART, A/Kids garden!: the anytime, anyplace guide to sowing and
growing fun. /1996/3-5/6 KD167 . . . . **635**
HUFF, BA/Greening the city streets: the story of community gardens.
/1990/5-6/7 KD168 . . . . **635**
KUHN, D/More than just a vegetable garden. /1990/
4-5/5 KD170 . . . . **635**
LOOK WHAT I GREW: WINDOWSILL GARDENS
(VIDEOCASSETTE). /1993/1-6/KD171 . . . . **VCR 635**

Gardening--Experiments.
JURENKA, NE/Beyond the bean seed: gardening activities for
grades K-6. /1996//KA202. . . . . **PROF 372.3**

Gardening--Fiction.
BUNTING, E/Flower garden. /1994/P-2/3 KF299. . . . . **E**
CASELEY, J/Grandpa's garden lunch. /1990/P-1/2 KF364 . . . . **E**
COLE, H/Jack's garden. /1995/K-3/3 KF409. . . . . **E**
DELANEY, A/Pearl's first prize plant. /1997/K-2/1 KF459 . . . . **E**
GREENSTEIN, E/Mrs. Rose's garden. /1996/K-2/3 KF643 . . . . **E**
HALL, Z/It's pumpkin time! /1994/P-2/3 KF666 . . . . **E**
KRAUSS, R/Carrot seed. /c1945/P-2/2 KF920. . . . . **CE E**
PERKINS, LR/Home lovely. /1995/K-2/5 KG233 . . . . **E**
RYDER, J/My father's hands. /1994/K-2/KG366 . . . . **E**
STEWART, S/Gardener. /1997/K-3/2 KG571 . . . . **E**
TITHERINGTON, J/Pumpkin pumpkin. /1986/P-2/1 KG609 . . . **E**

Gardens--Fiction.
BULLA, CR/Chalk box kid. /1987/2-4/2 KG936. . . . . **Fic**
BURNETT, FH/Secret garden. /c1911, 1987/3-6/5 KG951. . **CE Fic**
CUTLER, J/Mr. Carey's garden. /1996/K-2/3 KF442. . . . . **E**
DISALVO-RYAN, D/City green. /1994/1-3/3 KF484. . . . . **E**
FLEISCHMAN, P/Seedfolks. /1997/5-A/5 KH118. . . . . **Fic**
JOYCE, W/Leaf Men and the brave good bugs. /1996/
1-3/3 KF861 . . . . **E**
RYLANT, C/Everyday garden (Board book). /1993/
P-K/2 KG371. . . . . **BB E**
SCHECTER, E/Big idea. /1996/3-5/2 KH679 . . . . **Fic**
SEABROOK, E/Cabbage and kings. /1997/1-3/2 KG425 . . . . . **E**
SHANNON, G/Seeds. /1994/K-2/2 KG478 . . . . **E**
TAMAR, E/Garden of happiness. /1996/1-3/2 KG593 . . . . . . **E**
THESMAN, J/Nothing grows here. /1994/6-A/4 KH790 . . . . . **Fic**

Garter snakes.
LAVIES, B/Gathering of garter snakes. /1993/
4-6/7 KC638 . . . . **597.96**

Gauchos.
BRUSCA, MC/On the pampas. /1991/3-6/6 KF106 . . . . **982**

Gaver, Mary Virginia.
GAVER, MV/Braided cord: memoirs of a school librarian. /1988/
/KA368. . . . . **PROF B GAVER, M**

Gawain (Legendary character).
HASTINGS, S/Sir Gawain and the green knight. /1981/
6/6 KB450. . . . . **398.22**

Gay parents.
GREENBERG, KE/Zack's story: growing up with same-sex parents. /
1996/4-6/4 KA877 . . . . **306.874**

Geese SEE ALSO names of specific species e.g. Canada Goose.

Geese.
SELSAM, ME/First look at ducks, geese, and swans. /1990/
1-3/2 KC683 . . . . **598.4**

Geese--Fiction.
BANG, M/Goose. /1996/P-2/2 KF190 . . . . **E**
DUVOISIN, R/Petunia. /c1950/K-2/3 KF502 . . . . **CE E**
ENDERLE, JR/What would Mama do? /1995/K-2/2 KF526 . . . . **E**
KING-SMITH, D/Cuckoo child. /1993/4-6/6 KH347 . . . . **Fic**
POLACCO, P/Rechenka's eggs. /1988/1-3/5 KG256 . . . . . . **CE E**
SILVERMAN, E/Don't fidget a feather! /1994/P-2/2 KG505. . . . **E**
STEIG, W/Real thief. /c1973/4-6/6 KH751 . . . . **Fic**
WALSH, ES/You silly goose. /1992/P-K/2 KG682 . . . . **E**
WIKLER, L/Alfonse, where are you? /1996/P-K/1 KG715. . . . . **E**

Gehrig, Lou.
MACHT, NL/Lou Gehrig. /1993/5-A/7 KE364. . . . **B GEHRIG, L.**

Genealogy.
CANEY, S/Steven Caney's Kids' America. /1978/
4-6/7 KE920 . . . . **973.92**
LEEDY, L/Who's who in my family. /1995/K-2/2 KA869 . . **306.85**
WOLFMAN, I/Do people grow on family trees?: genealogy for kids
and other beginners: the official Ellis Island handbook. /1991/
5-A/7 KE610 . . . . **929**

Genealogy--Fiction.
HEARNE, B/Seven brave women. /1997/1-3/2 KF691 . . . . **E**
SHELBY, A/Homeplace. /1995/1-3/3 KG493. . . . . **E**

General stores--Fiction.
FIELD, R/General store. /c1926, 1988/P-3/KF548 . . . . **E**

Generals.
ADLER, DA/Picture book of Robert E. Lee. /1994/
2-5/5 KE429 . . . . **B LEE, R.**
BLUE, R/Colin Powell: straight to the top. Updated ed. /1997/
3-6/7 KE502 . . . . **B POWELL, C.**
FRITZ, J/Stonewall. /1979/5-A/8 KE399 . . . . . **B JACKSON, T.**
KAVANAGH, J/Robert E. Lee. /1995/4-5/6 KE430 . . . **B LEE, R.**
LAWRENCE, J/Toussaint L'Ouverture: the fight for Haiti's freedom.
/1996/4-A/8 KE569 . . . . **B TOUSSAINT**
RICKARBY, LA/Ulysses S. Grant and the strategy of victory. /1991/
6-A/6 KE377 . . . . **B GRANT, U.**
ROBERT E. LEE (VIDEOCASSETTE). /1989/
5-6/KE431. . . . . **VCR B LEE, R.**
SANFORD, WR/John C. Fremont: soldier and pathfinder. /1996/
5-6/4 KE357 . . . . **B FREMONT, J.**
STONEWALL JACKSON (VIDEOCASSETTE). /1989/
6-A/KE400. . . . . **VCR B JACKSON, T.**
SUPER, N/Daniel "Chappie" James. /1992/
5-A/6 KE401 . . . . **B JAMES, D.**
ULYSSES S. GRANT (VIDEOCASSETTE). /1989/
6-A/KE378. . . . . **VCR B GRANT, U.**

Genetic engineering SEE ALSO Cloning.

Genetics SEE ALSO Adaptation (Biology); Cloning; Evolution; Heredity; Life
(Biology); Natural selection; Reproduction; Variation (Biology).

Genetics.
ARONSON, B/They came from DNA. /1993/5-A/6 KC278 . **572.8**
BALKWILL, FR/Amazing schemes within your genes. /1993/
4-8/6 KC288 . . . . **576.5**
CELL DIVISION (VIDEOCASSETTE). /1995/
5-6/KC274. . . . . **VCR 571.6**
HOOPER, T/Genetics. /1994/5-6/9 KC289 . . . . **576.5**

Genius--Fiction.
SKINNER, D/Wrecker. /1995/6-A/4 KH715 . . . . **Fic**

Geographers.
LASKY, K/Librarian who measured the earth. /1994/
4-A/6 KE339 . . . . **B ERATOSTHENES**

Geography SEE ALSO Atlases; Discoveries (in geography); Globes; Maps;
Physical geography; Voyages and travels.

Geography.
COOPER, K/Where in the world are you? a guide to looking at the
world. /1990/4-6/7 KE145. . . . . **910**
DK GEOGRAPHY OF THE WORLD. /1996/2-6/10 KE146 . . . **910**

FLAGS OF THE NATIONS (VIDEOCASSETTE). /1993/
A/KE618. . . . . **VCR 929.9**
GEOGRAPHY: FIVE THEMES FOR PLANET EARTH
(VIDEOCASSETTE). /1992/4-6/KE147 . . . . **VCR 910**
GEOGRAPHY FOR EVERYONE (VIDEOCASSETTE). /1992/
3-5/KE148. . . . . **VCR 910**
GEOGRAPHY OF THE U.S.A. (VIDEOCASSETTE). /1991/
4-6/KE189. . . . . **VCR 917.3**
GEOGRAPHY OF THE UNITED STATES (VIDEOCASSETTE). /
1991/4-6/KE188. **VCR 917.3**
KINDERSLEY, B/Children just like me. /1995/
2-6/8 KA825 . . . . **305.23**
LEEDY, L/Blast off to Earth!: a look at geography. /1992/
1-4/4 KE151 . . . . **910**
NYSTROM DESK ATLAS. /1994/5-A/KA474 . . . . **REF 912**
PICKERING, M/Picture reference atlas. /1996/2-4/3 KE171 . . **912**
ROSENTHAL, P/Where on earth: a geografunny guide to the globe.
/1992/4-6/6 KE153 . . . . **910**
WORLDMARK ENCYCLOPEDIA OF THE NATIONS. 9TH ED. /
1997/A/KA389 . . . . **REF 031**

Geography--Dictionaries.
KNOWLTON, J/Geography from A to Z: a picture glossary. /
1988/3-6/KE150. . . . . **910**
WEBSTER'S GEOGRAPHICAL DICTIONARY. 3RD. ED. /1997/
5-6/KA471 . . . . **REF 910.3**

Geography--Fiction.
BLACKSTONE, S/Grandma went to market: a round-the-world
counting rhyme. /1996/1-3/5 KF232 . . . . **E**

Geography--Periodicals.
NATIONAL GEOGRAPHIC MAGAZINE. /1888-/
4-A/KA529 . . . . **PER 050**

Geography--Periodicals--Indexes.
NATIONAL GEOGRAPHIC INDEX, 1888-1988. /1989/
4-A/KA528 . . . . **PER 050**

Geography--Pictorial works.
LANDS AND PEOPLES. REV. ED. /1997/5-6/KA469 . . . **REF 909**

Geography--Software.
GTV: A GEOGRAPHIC PERSPECTIVE ON AMERICAN HISTORY
(VIDEODISC). /c1990/5-A/KE853 . . . . **VD 973**
INTERNATIONAL INSPIRER (MICROCOMPUTER PROGRAM). /
1990/5-A/KE149 . . . . **MCP 910**
MICROSOFT ENCARTA 97 WORLD ATLAS (CD-ROM). /1996/
3-A/KA472 . . . . **CDR REF 912**
MY FIRST AMAZING WORLD EXPLORER (CD-ROM). /1996/
1-3/KE170. . . . . **CDR 912**
NATIONAL INSPIRER (MICROCOMPUTER PROGRAM). /1997/
5-A/KE190. . . . . **MCP 917.3**
TRUDY'S TIME AND PLACE HOUSE. SCHOOL VERSION (CD-
ROM). /1995/P-3/KC075. . . . . **CDR 529**
WHERE IN THE U.S.A. IS CARMEN SANDIEGO? NEW ED. (CD-
ROM). /1996/3-A/KE182 . . . . **CDR 917**
WHERE IN THE WORLD IS CARMEN SANDIEGO? JUNIOR
DETECTIVE EDITION (CD-ROM). /1994/3-6/KE174 . . **CDR 912**
WHERE IN THE WORLD IS CARMEN SANDIEGO? NEW ED.
(CD-ROM). /1996/3-A/KE175 . . . . **CDR 912**

Geography--Study and teaching (Elementary).
HELTSHE, MA/Multicultural explorations: joyous journeys with
books. /1991/KA262. . . . . **PROF 372.89**

Geology SEE ALSO Coral reefs and islands; Creation; Earth; Earthquakes;
Glaciers; Mineralogy; Mountains; Oceanography; Petrology; Plate
tectonics; Volcanoes.

Geology.
COLE, J/Magic School Bus inside the earth. /1987/
2-4/3 KC152 . . . . **551**
LAMPTON, C/Volcano. /1991/4-6/7 KC157 . . . . **551.21**
LAUBER, P/Dinosaurs walked here and other stories fossils tell. /
1987/4-6/6 KC236 . . . . **560**
MARKLE, S/Digging deeper: investigations into rocks, shocks,
quakes, and other earthly matters. /1987/4-6/9 KC148 . . **550**
OUR CHANGING EARTH (VIDEOCASSETTE). /1991/
3-5/KC153. . . . . **VCR 551**
SATTLER, HR/Our patchwork planet: the story of plate tectonics. /
1995/A/7 KC155 . . . . **551.1**
STV: RESTLESS EARTH (VIDEODISC). /1992/
4-A/KC150 . . . . **VD 550**
VISUAL DICTIONARY OF THE EARTH. /1993/1-A/9 KC151 . **550**
ZOEHFELD, KW/How mountains are made. /1995/
2-4/4 KC170 . . . . **551.43**

Geology--Maps.
VAN ROSE, S/Earth atlas. /1994/A/7 KA443. . . . . . . **REF 551**

Geology--Software.
SCHOLASTIC'S THE MAGIC SCHOOL BUS EXPLORES INSIDE THE
EARTH. SCHOOL ED. (CD-ROM). /1996/4-A/KC149 . **CDR 550**

Geometry.
GEOMETRY AND MEASUREMENT: MEASURING ANGLES
(VIDEOCASSETTE). /1987/4-A/KB995 . . . . **VCR 516.2**
REISS, JJ/Shapes. /c1974/P-1/KB994 . . . . **516**
WYLER, R/Math fun with tricky lines and shapes. /1992/
4-A/5 KD714 . . . . **793.7**

Geometry--Software.
CARNIVAL COUNTDOWN. SCHOOL VERSION (CD-ROM). /
1996/K-2/KB926. . . . . **CDR 510**
NUMBER HEROES. SCHOOL VERSION (CD-ROM). /1996/
3-6/KB929. . . . . **CDR 510**
Geophysics SEE ALSO Meteorology; Oceanography.

George, Jean Craighead.
GEORGE, JC/Tarantula in my purse and 172 other wild pets. /
1996/4-6/4 KE366 . . . . **B GEORGE, J.**

George, Saint.
HODGES, M/Saint George and the dragon: a golden legend. /
1984/5/7 KB453 . . . . **CE 398.22**

George III, King of Great Britain.
FRITZ, J/Can't you make them behave, King George? /c1977/
5-6/7 KE365 . . . . **CE B GEORGE III**

Georgia.
LADOUX, RC/Georgia. /1991/4-6/7 KE989 . . . . **975.8**

Georgia--Fiction.
YOUNG, RT/Moving Mama to town. /1997/6-A/4 KH900 . . . **Fic**

Georgia--History--Colonial period, ca. 1600-1775.
FRADIN, DB/Georgia Colony. /1989/5-6/7 KE988. . . . . . . **975.8**

Geothermal engineering.
JACOBS, L/Letting off steam. /1989/4-A/7 KC156. . . . . . **551.2**

Gerbils as pets.
PIERS, H/Taking care of your gerbils. /1993/3-5/6 KD184. . . **636**
WEXLER, J/Pet gerbils. /1990/4-6/7 KD186 . . . . **636**

German language materials.
BROWN, R/Alphabet times four: an international ABC: English,
Spanish, French, German. /1991/2-4/KB819. . . . . **411**
ZELINSKY, PO/Rumpelstiltskin. /1986/1-4/7 KB385 . . . **CE 398.2**

Germany--Bremen--Folklore.
HODGES, M/Hero of Bremen. /1993/3-5/6 KB451 . . . . . **398.22**

Germany--Folklore.
BERENZY, A/Rapunzel. /1995/2-4/4 KB263 . . . . **398.2**
DAVENPORT, T/From the Brothers Grimm: a contemporary retelling
of American folktales and /1992/5-A/KB281 . . . . **CE 398.2**
DE LA MARE, W/Turnip. /1992/3-5/6 KB557 . . . . **398.24**
DE REGNIERS, BS/Red Riding Hood. /c1972, 1990/
P-2/KB732 . . . . **CE 398.27**
GERINGER, L/Seven ravens. /1994/2-3/6 KB302 . . . . **398.2**
GRIMM, J/Hansel and Gretel: a tale from the Brothers Grimm. /
1984/5/6 KB740 . . . . **CE 398.27**
Juniper tree and other tales from Grimm. /c1973, 1992/
5-A/7 KB306 . . . . **398.2**
Little Red Riding Hood. /1983/1-4/6 KB741 . . . **CE 398.27**
Rapunzel. /1982/2-4/4 KB307 . . . . **398.2**
Rumpelstiltskin. /1997/K-2/2 KB308 . . . . **398.2**
Seven ravens: a fairy tale. /1995/3-5/7 KB309 . . . . . . **398.2**
Snow-White and the seven dwarfs. /1972/3-4/6 KB310 . . **398.2**
Twelve dancing princesses: a fairy tale. /1995/
3-4/6 KB311 . . . . **398.2**
Wolf and the seven little kids: a fairy tale. /1995/
1-2/4 KB579 . . . . **398.24**
KIMMEL, EA/Goose girl: a story from the Brothers Grimm. /1995/
3-5/5 KB328 . . . . **398.2**
Iron John. /1994/4-5/4 KB330 . . . . **398.2**
MARSHALL, J/Hansel and Gretel. /1990/2-4/4 KB340 . . . . **398.2**
MOSER, B/Tucker Pfeffercorn: an old story retold. /1994/
2-3/5 KB351 . . . . **398.2**
PLUME, I/Bremen-Town musicians. /1998/1-3/4 KB636 . . . **398.24**
Shoemaker and the elves. /1991/2-4/4 KB359 . . . . . . **398.2**
SHULEVITZ, U/Golden goose. /1995/K-3/2 KB650. . . . . **398.24**
TARCOV, EH/Frog prince. /c1974, 1993/P-3/2 KB376 . . . **398.2**
ZELINSKY, PO/Rumpelstiltskin. /1986/1-4/7 KB385 . . . **CE 398.2**

Germany--Hamelin--Folklore.
LATIMER, J/Irish piper. /1991/3-5/6 KB463 . . . . **398.22**

Germany--Politics and government--1933-1945.
MELTZER, M/Never to forget: the Jews of the Holocaust. /c1976/
A/7 KE674 . . . . **940.54**

Germination.
GIBBONS, G/From seed to plant. /1991/K-3/4 KC398 . . . . **581.4**

Geronimo, Apache Chief.
HERMANN, S/Geronimo: Apache freedom fighter. /1997/
5-6/12 KE367 . . . . **B GERONIMO**

Gershwin, George.
AMERICAN IN PARIS: GERSHWIN (VIDEOCASSETTE). /1993/
1-6/KD517. . . . . **VCR 780**

VENEZIA, M/George Gershwin. /1994/
4-6/7 KE368 . . . . **B GERSHWIN, G.**

Gettysburg, Battle of, 1863.
BELLER, SP/To hold this ground: a desperate battle at Gettysburg.
/1995/A/9 KE897 . . . . **973.7**
CARTER, AR/Battle of Gettysburg. /1990/4-6/7 KE899. . . . **973.7**
GAUCH, PL/Thunder at Gettysburg. /c1975, 1990/
4-6/4 KE903 . . . . **973.7**
GETTYSBURG (VIDEOCASSETTE). /1987/5-A/KE904. **VCR 973.7**
MURPHY, J/Long road to Gettysburg. /1992/5-A/7 KE910 . **973.7**

Ghana--Folklore.
MOLLEL, TM/Ananse's feast: an Ashanti tale. /1997/
K-2/3 KB622 . . . . **398.24**

Ghana--Social life and customs.
ANGELOU, M/Kofi and his magic. /1996/2-5/3 KE735. . . . **966.7**

Ghana Empire--History.
MCKISSACK, P/Royal kingdoms of Ghana, Mali, and Songhay: life
in medieval Africa. /c1994, 1995/A/8 KE734 . . . . **966.2**
Ghosts SEE ALSO Psychical research; Superstition.

Ghosts.
COHEN, D/Ghost in the house. /1993/5-6/5 KA598 . . . . . **133.1**
Ghostly warnings. /1996/4-6/7 KA599 . . . . **133.1**
Ghosts of the deep. /1993/4-6/7 KA600 . . . . **133.1**
Ghosts of War. /1990/4-A/6 KA601 . . . . **133.1**
Great ghosts. /1990/4-6/4 KA602 . . . . **133.1**
Young ghosts. Rev ed. /c1978, 1994/4-A/9 KA603 . . . . **133.1**
DEEM, JM/How to find a ghost. /1988/4-A/7 KA604 . . . . **133.1**
JONES, LC/Things that go bump in the night. /c1959, 1983/
A/9 KA605 . . . . **133.1**

Ghosts--Fiction.
ADLER, DA/Cam Jansen and the ghostly mystery. /1996/
2-4/2 KG815 . . . . **Fic**
AIKEN, J/Up the chimney down and other stories. /1987/
4-6/6 KG825 . . . . **Fic**
ALCOCK, V/Haunting of Cassie Palmer. /1990/5-6/6 KG827 . . **Fic**
ALLEN, LJ/Rollo and Tweedy and the ghost at Dougal Castle. /
1992/1-3/2 KF153 . . . . **CE E**
BAUER, MD/Ghost eye. /1992/4-6/6 KG881 . . . . **Fic**
BODKIN, O/Banshee train. /1995/1-3/4 KF240 . . . . **E**
CARTER, DA/In a dark, dark wood. /1991/P-2/2 KF362 . . . . . **E**
CASSEDY, S/Behind the attic wall. /1983/6-A/5 KG986 . . . . **Fic**
DICKENS, C/Christmas Carol in prose, being a ghost story of
Christmas. /1983/4-6/5 KH074 . . . . **CE Fic**
FLEISCHMAN, S/Ghost on Saturday night. /1997/
3-5/4 KH122 . . . . **Fic**
Midnight horse. /1990/5-A/4 KH125 . . . . **Fic**
HAMILTON, M/Haunting tales: live from the Culbertson Mansion
State Historic Site (Sound recording cassette). /1996/
2-4/KB686 . . . . **SRC 398.25**
HAMILTON, V/House of Dies Drear. /c1968/4-6/5 KH215 **CE Fic**
HOFFMAN, M/Four-legged ghosts. /1995/2-4/6 KH269 . . . . **Fic**
JOHNSTON, T/Ghost of Nicholas Greebe. /1996/
3-5/6 KH328 . . . . **Fic**
LEVITT, MJ/Tales of an October moon: haunting stories from New
England (Sound recording cassette). /1992/4-6/KH399. **SRC Fic**
LEVITT, S/Mighty Movers. /1994/K-2/2 KF971 . . . . **E**
LIVELY, P/Ghost of Thomas Kempe. /c1973/4-6/7 KH415 . . . **Fic**
MARTIN, JR., B/Ghost-eye tree. /1985/K-3/2 KG075. . . . . . . **E**
MARTIN, R/Ghostly tales of Japan (Sound recording cassette). /
1989/3-6/KB689. . . . . **SRC 398.25**
MCKAY, H/Amber cat. /1997/5-8/6 KH476 . . . . **Fic**
MCKISSACK, P/Dark-thirty: Southern tales of the supernatural. /
1992/5-A/6 KH491 . . . . **Fic**
MEDEARIS, AS/Haunts: five hair-raising tales. /1996/
4-6/4 KH495 . . . . **Fic**
OXFORD BOOK OF SCARYTALES. /1992/6-A/7 KH569 . . . . . **Fic**
PEARCE, AP/Who's afraid? and other strange stories. /1987/
5-6/6 KH590 . . . . **Fic**
SAN SOUCI, RD/Boy and the ghost. /1989/2-3/6 KG392 . . . . . **E**
SCHNUR, S/Shadow children. /1994/4-A/7 KH681 . . . . **Fic**
SLIGHTLY SCARY STORIES (VIDEOCASSETTE). /1987/
P-2/KG518 . . . . **VCR E**
SNYDER, ZK/Trespassers. /1995/5-A/6 KH734 . . . . **Fic**
SPOOKY STORIES FOR A DARK AND STORMY NIGHT. /1994/
2-4/4 KB695 . . . . **398.25**
SPOOKY STORIES OF THE SUPERNATURAL. /1985/
6-A/KH745 . . . . **Fic**
TOLAN, SS/Who's there? /1994/5-A/5 KH795 . . . . **Fic**
TREASURY OF SPOOKY STORIES. /1992/4-A/6 KH804 . . . . . **Fic**
WRIGHT, BR/Ghost in the house. /1991/5-A/6 KH883 . . . . . **Fic**

Ghosts--Folklore.
HASKINS, J/Headless haunt and other African-American ghost
stories. /1994/4-5/4 KB687 . . . . **398.25**
HODGES, M/Molly Limbo. /1996/K-3/3 KB688. . . . . . . **398.25**

MARTIN, R/Ghostly tales of Japan (Sound recording cassette). /
1989/3-6/KB689. **SRC 398.25**
Mysterious tales of Japan. /1996/3-5/3 KB690. . . . . . . 398.25
SCARY BOOK. /1991/2-4/2 KB691 . . . . 398.25
SCHWARTZ, A/Ghosts!: ghostly tales from folklore. /1991/
1-2/2 KB692 . . . . **CE 398.25**
In a dark, dark room and other scary stories. /1984/
K-3/1 KB693 . . . . 398.25
Scary stories to tell in the dark. /1981/4-A/3 KB694 . **CE 398.25**
TAYLOR, CJ/Ghost and Lone Warrior: an Arapaho legend. /1991/
2-5/4 KB696 . . . . 398.25
TREASURY OF SPOOKY STORIES. /1992/4-A/6 KH804 . . . . **Fic**
YEP, L/Man who tricked a ghost. /1993/1-3/4 KB697. . . . 398.25
YOUNG, R/Head on the high road: ghost stories from the
Southwest (Sound recording cassette). /1993/
4-6/KB698 . . . . **SRC 398.25**

Ghosts--Literary collections.
DIANE GOODE'S BOOK OF SCARY STORIES AND SONGS. /
1994/2-5/5 KB685 . . . . 398.25
SCARED SILLY! A BOOK FOR THE BRAVE. /1994/
K-3/KD904 . . . . 810.8

Ghosts--Wit and humor.
GORDON, JR/Hide and shriek: riddles about ghosts and goblins. /
1991/2-5/KD727 . . . . 793.735

Giant panda.
ARNOLD, C/Panda. /1992/4-6/7 KC866 . . . . 599.789

Giants--Fiction.
COLE, B/Giant's toe. /1986/P-2/2 KF407. . . . . **E**
NORTON, M/Are all the giants dead? /c1975, 1997/
4-A/5 KH552 . . . . **Fic**
POMERANTZ, C/Mangaboom. /1997/1-3/3 KG264. . . . . **E**
THURBER, J/Great Quillow. /1994/2-3/6 KH791 . . . . . **Fic**
TREASURY OF GIANT AND MONSTER STORIES. /1992/
3-5/6 KH803 . . . . **Fic**
YEP, L/City of dragons. /1995/1-3/5 KG775 . . . . **E**

Giants--Folklore.
CRYING RED GIANT: A JAPANESE FOLKTALE (VIDEOCASSETTE).
/n.d./K-2/KB391. . . . . **VCR 398.21**
DE PAOLA, T/Fin M'Coul: the giant of Knockmany Hill. /1981/
1-3/4 KB392 . . . . 398.21
DESPAIN, P/Strongheart Jack and the beanstalk. /1995/
2-5/3 KB287 . . . . 398.2
GERSHATOR, P/Tukama Tootles the flute: a tale from the Antilles.
/1994/K-2/5 KB398 . . . . 398.21
GIBLIN, JC/Dwarf, the giant, and the unicorn: a tale of King Arthur.
/1996/3-5/4 KB443 . . . . 398.22
GLEESON, B/Finn McCoul (Videocassette). /1991/
3-5/KB445. . . . . **VCR 398.22**
KELLOGG, S/Jack and the beanstalk. /1991/2-3/4 KB325. . 398.2
METAXAS, E/Jack and the beanstalk (Videocassette). /1991/
K-2/KB349. . . . . **VCR 398.2**
SEEGER, P/Abiyoyo: based on a South African lullaby and folk
story. /1986/2-5/KD587 . . . . 789.2
SLOAT, T/Hungry giant of the tundra. /1993/
K-3/5 KB419 . . . . 398.21
TREASURY OF GIANT AND MONSTER STORIES. /1992/
3-5/6 KH803 . . . . **Fic**
WALKER, PR/Giants!: stories from around the world. /1995/
4-6/7 KB381 . . . . 398.2

Gifted children.
BRILL, MT/Extraordinary young people. /1996/
4-A/7 KA823 . . . . 305.23

Gifted children--Education.
EDUCATING ABLE LEARNERS (VIDEOCASSETTE). /1991/
/KA187. . . . . **VCR PROF 371.95**
FLACK, JD/Inventing, inventions, and inventors: a teaching resource
book. /1989//KA297 . . . . **PROF 607**
GIFTED CHILD TODAY. /1978-//KA113. . . . . . . **PER PROF 050**
PATTERNS OF INFLUENCE ON GIFTED LEARNERS: THE HOME,
SELF, AND THE SCHOOL. /1989//KA188. . . . . . **PROF 371.95**

Gifted children--Education (Preschool).
SAUNDERS, J/Bringing out the best: a resource guide for parents
of young gifted children. Rev. and updated. /1991/
/KA189. . . . . **PROF 371.95**

Gifted children--Family relationships.
PATTERNS OF INFLUENCE ON GIFTED LEARNERS: THE HOME,
SELF, AND THE SCHOOL. /1989//KA188. . . . . . **PROF 371.95**

Gifted children--Fiction.
BLUME, J/Here's to you, Rachel Robinson. /1993/
6-A/6 KG910 . . . . **Fic**

Gifted children--Psychology.
PATTERNS OF INFLUENCE ON GIFTED LEARNERS: THE HOME,
SELF, AND THE SCHOOL. /1989//KA188. . . . . . **PROF 371.95**

Gifts--Fiction.
BUNTING, E/Mother's Day mice. /1986/P-2/2 KF305. . . . . **CE E**
GERSHATOR, P/Sweet, sweet fig banana. /1996/K-2/2 KF613 . **E**
HALL, D/Lucy's Christmas. /1994/1-3/6 KF662 . . . . **E**
KLINE, S/Herbie Jones and the class gift. /1989/3-4/2 KH367 . **Fic**
RYLANT, C/Mr. Putter and Tabby bake the cake. /1994/
1-3/2 KG377 . . . . **E**
WILLIAMS, VB/Something special for me. /1983/P-3/2 KG738. . **E**

Gilgamesh.
ZEMAN, L/Gilgamesh the King. /1992/4-6/4 KE130. . . . . 892.1
Last quest of Gilgamesh. /1995/4-6/4 KE131 . . . . . . 892.1
Revenge of Ishtar. /1993/4-6/4 KE132 . . . . 892.1

Giotto.
CORRAIN, L/Giotto and medieval art: the lives and works of the
medieval artists. /1995/4-A/9 KD494 . . . . 759.5

Giraffes.
KALMAN, B/Giraffes. /1997/3-5/7 KC788 . . . . 599.638
SATTLER, HR/Giraffes, the sentinels of the savannas. /1989/
5-6/8 KC789 . . . . 599.638

Giraffes--Fiction.
FARMER, N/Warm Place. /1995/4-A/3 KH110 . . . . **Fic**
Girl Scouts SEE ALSO Brownie Scouts.

Girl Scouts.
GIRL SCOUTS OF THE UNITED STATES OF AMERICA /Brownie
Scout handbook. /1993/1-3/KB078 . . . . 369.463
Junior Girl Scout handbook. /1994/4-6/KB079 . . . . . . 369.463

Girl Scouts of The United States of America--Biography.
BROWN, FG/Daisy and the Girl Scouts: the story of Juliette
Gordon Low. /1996/3-6/7 KE448 . . . . **B LOW, J.**
Girls SEE ALSO Children; Women; Youth.

Girls.
NEW, IMPROVED ME: UNDERSTANDING BODY CHANGES
(VIDEOCASSETTE). /1991/5-6/KC953 . . . . **VCR 612.6**

Girls--Fiction.
ALCOTT, LM/Little women (Talking book). /1975/
5-A/KG830 . . . . **TB Fic**
BRINK, CR/Caddie Woodlawn. New ed. /1973/
4-6/6 KG922 . . . . **CE Fic**
CALHOUN, M/Katie John. /c1960/4-6/4 KG966 . . . . . **Fic**
HAYWOOD, C/"B" is for Betsy. /c1939/2-3/3 KH230 . . . **Fic**
KARR, K/Oh, those Harper girls!; or Young and dangerous. /1992/
5-A/Y KH342 . . . . **Fic**
KONIGSBURG, EL/Jennifer, Hecate, Macbeth, William McKinley,
and me, Elizabeth. /c1967/3-6/4 KH374 . . . . **CE Fic**
MONTGOMERY, LM/Anne of Green Gables. /c1908, 1983/
4-A/6 KH503 . . . . **Fic**
SNYDER, ZK/Egypt game. /c1967/5-6/6 KH731 . . . . . **Fic**
TAYLOR, S/All-of-a-kind family. /1951, 1988/4-6/5 KH782 . . . **Fic**
WIGGIN, KD/Rebecca of Sunnybrook Farm. /1994/
5-A/6 KH857 . . . . **Fic**
WILDER, LI/Little house in the Big Woods. /c1953/
3-6/4 KH860 . . . . **Fic**

Girls--Periodicals.
AMERICAN GIRL. /1993/-/3-5/KA498 . . . . **PER 050**
GIRLS' LIFE: THE NEW MAGAZINE FOR GIRLS. /1994-/
4-6/KA516 . . . . **PER 050**

Glacier National Park (Mont.).
PATENT, DH/Where the bald eagles gather. /1984/
5-6/7 KC718 . . . . 598.9

Glaciers.
GLACIERS: ICE ON THE MOVE (VIDEOCASSETTE). /1994/
5-A/KC164 . . . . **VCR 551.3**
SIMON, S/Icebergs and glaciers. /1987/3-6/7 KC165 . . . . 551.3

Glass, Hugh--Fiction.
MCCLUNG, RM/Hugh Glass, mountain man. /1993/
6-A/7 KH472 . . . . **Fic**

Glass manufacture.
FISHER, LE/Glassmakers. /1997/3-6/7 KD323 666
PATERSON, AJ/How glass is made. /1985/5-6/9 KD324 . . . 666

Global warming.
HOFF, MK/Our endangered planet: atmosphere. /1995/
4-6/8 KB061 . . . . 363.73
INVESTIGATING GLOBAL WARMING (VIDEOCASSETTE). /1997/
5-A/KB063. . . . . **VCR 363.73**

Globe Theatre (Southwark, London, England).
MORLEY, J/Shakespeare's theater. /1994/4-A/7 KD689 792

Globes.
FINDING YOUR WAY: USING MAPS AND GLOBES
(VIDEOCASSETTE). /1990/3-6/KE168 . . . . **VCR 912**
KNOWLTON, J/Maps and globes. /1985/2-5/7 KE169 912

Gloves--Fiction.
KELLOGG, S/Mystery of the missing red mitten. /1974/
P-2/2 KF892 . . . . **E**

Gnus--Migration.
LINDBLAD, L/Serengeti migration: Africa's animals on the move. / 1994/5-6/10 KC497 . . . . **591.96**

Goats--Fiction.
BLOOD, CL/Goat in the rug. /1990/K-3/6 KF234 . . . . **E**
EMBERLEY, R/Three cool kids. /1995/P-1/3 KF525. . . . . **E**
SHARMAT, M/Gregory, the terrible eater. /1980/
K-2/4 KG488 . . . . **E**

Goats--Folklore.
THREE BILLY GOATS GRUFF; AND, THE THREE LITTLE PIGS (VIDEOCASSETTE). /1989/P-K/6/KB665 . . . . **VCR 398.24**
God SEE ALSO Creation; Jesus Christ; Islam; Mythology; Religion.

God.
KROLL, VL/I wanted to know all about God. /1994/
K-2/2 KA694 . . . . **231**

God--Fiction.
WOOD, D/Old Turtle. /1992/3-5/3 KH879 . . . . **CE Fic**

Goddard, Robert Hutchings.
MAURER, R/Rocket!: how a toy launched the space age. /1995/
5-6/10 KD047 . . . . **621.43**

Goddesses.
WALDHERR, K/Book of goddesses. /1995/4-6/8 KA732 . . . **291.2**

Gogh, Vincent van.
CRISPINO, E/Van Gogh. /1996/6-A/12 KD499. . . . . . **759.9492**
HARRISON, P/Vincent van Gogh. /1996/
4-6/7 KE369 . . . . **B GOGH, V.**
HUGHES, A/Van Gogh. /1994/6-A/9 KE370 . . . . . **B GOGH, V.**

Gold.
MELTZER, M/Gold: the true story of why people search for it, mine it, trade it, steal it, mint it, hoard it, shape it, wear it, fight and kill for it. /1993/4-8/7 KC229 . . . . **553.4**
Gold mines and mining SEE ALSO Prospecting.

Gold mines and mining--California--History--19th century.
CALIFORNIA GOLD RUSH: 1849 (MULTIMEDIA KIT). /1991/
5-A//KF079. . . . . **MMK 979.4**
CALIFORNIA GOLD RUSH (PICTURE). /n.d./
5-6/KF078 . . . . **PIC 979.4**
ITO, T/California gold rush. /1997/5-6/11 KF080 . . . . **979.4**
KETCHUM, L/Gold rush. /1996/4-6/6 KF081 . . . . **979.4**

Gold mines and mining--Fiction.
COERR, E/Chang's paper pony. /1988/2-3/2 KF400 . . . . **E**
SNYDER, ZK/Fool's gold. /1993/6-A/7 KH732 . . . . **Fic**

Gold mines and mining--History.
KRENSKY, S/Striking it rich: the story of the California gold rush. /
1996/2-4/5 KF082 . . . . **979.4**

Gold mines and mining--Klondike River Valley (Yukon)--History.
COOPER, ML/Klondike fever. /1989/5-6/6 KE823 . . . . **971.9**
KLONDIKE GOLD RUSH (PICTURE). /n.d./A/KE826 . . . **PIC 971.9**

Goldberg, Whoopi.
ADAMS, MA/Whoopi Goldberg: from street to stardom. /1993/
4-6/7 KE371 . . . . **B GOLDBERG, W.**

Golden eagle.
PATENT, DH/Eagles of America. /1995/4-6/6 KC716 . . . . . **598.9**

Golden Gate Bridge (San Francisco, Calif.).
DOHERTY, CA/Golden Gate Bridge. /1995/5-6/8 KD067 . . . **624**

Golem.
PODWAL, M/Golem: a giant made of mud. /1995/
4-6/7 KB408 . . . . **398.21**
WISNIEWSKI, D/Golem. /1996/2-6/5 KB423 . . . . **398.21**

Golfers.
KRAMER, J/Lee Trevino. /1996/5-6/6 KE570 . . . **B TREVINO, L.**
KRAMER, S/Tiger Woods: golfing to greatness. /1997/
2-6/6 KE600 . . . . **B WOODS, T.**
WILNER, B/Superstars of women's golf. /1997/
4-6/7 KD792 . . . . **796.352**

Goliath (Biblical giant).
DE REGNIERS, BS/David and Goliath. /1996/1-4/6 KA683 . . **222**
METAXAS, E/David and Goliath (Videocassette). /1992/
2-4/KA686 . . . . **VCR 222**

Gombe National Park (Tanzania).
GOODALL, J/Chimpanzee family book. /1997/
4-6/6 KC878 . . . . **599.885**

Gone with the wind (Motion picture)--Fiction.
FORD, B/Most wonderful movie in the world. /1996/
6-A/4 KH132 . . . . **Fic**

Good and evil--Fiction.
COOPER, S/Over sea, under stone. /1966/A/5 KH028 . . . . . . **Fic**
HUNTER, M/Stranger came ashore. /c1975/A/7 KH293 . . . . **Fic**
JACQUES, B/Redwall. /1986/5-A/6 KH320 . . . . **Fic**
LEWIS, CS/Lion, the witch and the wardrobe. /1994/
5-A/6 KH405 . . . . **CE Fic**
REISS, K/Time windows. /1991/6-A/7 KH630 . . . . **Fic**

Good and evil--Folklore.
SINGER, IB/Mazel and Shlimazel; or, The milk of a lioness. /1967/
4-6/6 KB779 . . . . **398.27**

Goodall, Jane.
GOODALL, J/Chimpanzee family book. /1997/
4-6/6 KC878 . . . . **599.885**
MEACHUM, V/Jane Goodall: protector of chimpanzees. /1997/
5-A/7 KE372 . . . . **B GOODALL, J.**

Goodyear, Charles.
NOONAN, J/Nineteenth-century inventors. /1992/
5-6/7 KC897 . . . . **609**

Gordon, Jeff.
BRINSTER, R/Jeff Gordon. /1997/5-6/7 KE373 . . **B GORDON, J.**

Gore, Albert.
STEFOFF, R/Al Gore, vice president. /1994/
4-5/6 KE374 . . . . **B GORE, A.**

Gorilla.
BURGEL, PH/Gorillas. /1993/5-6/7 KC874 . . . . **599.884**
KIM, M/Mountain gorilla. /1993/4-5/8 KC875 . . . . **599.884**
MOUNTAIN GORILLAS: GENTLE GIANTS (VIDEOCASSETTE). /
1993/4-6/KC876 . . . . **VCR 599.884**
PATTERSON, F/Koko's kitten. /1985/3-5/6 KC877. . . . . **599.884**

Gorilla--Fiction.
HOFF, S/Julius. /c1959/K-1/1 KF758 . . . . **E**
JOYCE, W/Buddy: based on the true story of Gertrude Lintz. /
1997/5-A/5 KH337 . . . . **Fic**
RATHMANN, P/Good night, Gorilla. /1994/K-2/1 KG309 . . . . . **E**

Gorman, R. C.
HERMANN, S/R.C. Gorman: Navajo artist. /1995/
3-5/3 KE375 . . . . **B GORMAN, R.C.**

Gossip--Fiction.
WHITE, R/Sweet Creek Holler. /1988/6/7 KH854 . . . . **Fic**

Gossip--Folklore.
MANTINBAND, G/Blabbermouths: adapted from a German folktale. /1992/3-4/4 KB751 . . . . **398.27**

Governors.
FRITZ, J/Make way for Sam Houston. /1986/
6/7 KE392 . . . . **B HOUSTON, S.**

Goya, Francisco.
MUHLBERGER, R/What makes a Goya a Goya? /1994/
5-A/7 KD498 . . . . **759.6**
VENEZIA, M/Francisco Goya. /1991/4-5/6 KE376. . **B GOYA, F.**
Grain SEE ALSO names of cereal plants e.g. Corn, etc.
Grammar SEE names of language with the subdivision Grammar e.g. English language--Grammar.

Grand Canyon (Ariz.)--Discovery and exploration.
FRASER, MA/In search of the Grand Canyon. /1995/
3-5/6 KF068 . . . . **979.1**

Grand Canyon National Park (Ariz.).
GRAND CANYON OF THE COLORADO (VIDEOCASSETTE). /
1983/5-A/KF069 . . . . **VCR 979.1**

Grand Canyon National Park (Ariz.)--Fiction.
HENRY, M/Brighty of the Grand Canyon. /c1953, 1991/
4-5/5 KH242 . . . . **CE Fic**

Grandfathers--Fiction.
ACKERMAN, K/Song and dance man. /1988/K-2/6 KF130 . . . . **E**
ANAYA, R/Farolitos of Christmas. /1995/3-6/2 KG845 . . . . . . **Fic**
ANTLE, N/Staying cool. /1997/1-3/2 KF162. . . . . **E**
BAKER, SA/Grandpa is a flyer. /1995/1-3/5 KF188 . . . . **E**
BAWDEN, N/Real Plato Jones. /1993/6-A/6 KG892 . . . . . . **Fic**
BUCKLEY, HE/Grandfather and I. /1994/P-1/1 KF292 . . . . . . **E**
BUNTING, E/Day's work. /1994/1-3/2 KF298. . . . . **E**
CARRICK, C/Melanie. /1996/1-3/2 KF360 . . . . **E**
CASELEY, J/Dear Annie. /1991/K-2/2 KF363 . . . . **E**
CONRAD, P/Tub Grandfather. /1993/1-3/4 KF415 . . . . **E**
DE PAOLA, T/Now one foot, now the other. /1981/
K-3/5 KF476 . . . . **E**
Tom. /1993/K-2/2 KF480 . . . . **E**
DUFFEY, B/Utterly yours, Booker Jones. /1995/4-6/5 KH087 . . **Fic**
ERNST, LC/Luckiest kid on the planet. /1994/1-3/2 KF532. . . . **E**
FORWARD, T/Traveling backward. /1994/4-6/4 KH134 . . . . **Fic**
GEISERT, A/Etcher's studio. /1997/2-5/2 KF602 . . . . **E**
GREENFIELD, E/Grandpa's face. /1988/K-1/2 KF641 . . . . **E**
GRIFFITH, HV/Grandaddy's place. /1987/1-4/1 KF647. . . . . . **E**
Grandaddy's stars. /1995/1-4/2 KF648 . . . . **E**
HAAS, J/Beware the mare. /1993/3-5/4 KH209 . . . . **Fic**
Sugaring. /1996/K-2/2 KF657 . . . . **E**
HASELEY, D/Shadows. /1991/4-6/5 KH224 . . . . **Fic**
HENKES, K/Grandpa and Bo. /1986/P-2/2 KF705 . . . . **E**
Sun and spoon. /1997/5-A/6 KH239 . . . . **Fic**
HERMES, P/Someone to count on: a novel. /1993/
6-A/7 KH250 . . . . **Fic**
HEST, A/Baby Duck and the bad eyeglasses. /1996/
P-K/1 KF717 . . . . **E**

In the rain with Baby Duck. /1995/P-1/2 KF718 . . . . E
Purple coat. /1986/K-3/4 KF721 . . . . E
You're the boss, Baby Duck! /1997/P-1/2 KF722 . . . . E
ISADORA, R/Lili backstage. /1997/K-2/3 KF816 . . . . E
JAMES, S/Wild woods. /1996/P-2/2 KF825 . . . . E
JOHNSON, A/When I am old with you. /1990/P-2/6 KF834 . . . E
KELLER, H/Grandfather's dream. /1994/K-2/2 KF883 . . . . . . E
KURTZ, J/Pulling the lion's tail. /1995/1-3/6 KF937 . . . . . . E
LEE, M/Nim and the war effort. /1997/2-4/5 KH391 . . . . **Fic**
LOCKER, T/Where the river begins. /1984/K-3/5 KG016 . . . . . E
LONDON, J/Village basket weaver. /1996/2-3/6 KG029 . . . . E
MACLACHLAN, P/Three Names. /1991/2-3/5 KG055 . . . . . . E
MITCHELL, MK/Granddaddy's gift. /1997/1-3/2 KG146 . . . . E
MOON, N/Lucy's picture. /1995/P-1/2 KG153 . . . . E
OBERMAN, S/Always Prayer Shawl. /1994/2-4/2 KG184 . . . . E
ORR, K/My grandpa and the sea. /1990/K-2/2 KG198 . . . . E
POLIKOFF, BG/Life's funny proposition, Horatio. /1992/
    5-A/4 KH608 . . . . **Fic**
POMERANTZ, C/Outside dog. /1993/P-2/2 KG266 . . . . . **CE E**
RUSSO, M/Grandpa Abe. /1996/K-2/2 KG360 . . . . E
SAY, A/Grandfather's journey. /1993/2-4/5 KG397 . . . . . . E
SCHNUR, S/Shadow children. /1994/4-A/7 KH681 . . . . **Fic**
SCHWARTZ, DM/Supergrandpa. /1991/K-3/5 KG416 . . . . . E
SIEGELSON, KL/Terrible, wonderful tellin' at Hog Hammock. /
    1996/4-6/6 KH711 . . . . **Fic**
SPYRI, J/Heidi. /1996/5-A/6 KH746 . . . . **Fic**
STEVENSON, H/Grandpa's house. /1994/P-1/2 KG556 . . . . . E
STEVENSON, J/Could be worse. /c1977, 1987/
    K-3/4 KG558 . . . . **CE E**
    We hate rain! /1988/P-3/2 KG569 . . . . E
STOLZ, M/Go fish. /1991/3-6/6 KH766 . . . . **Fic**
    Stealing home. /1992/3-5/6 KH768 . . . . **Fic**
    Storm in the night. /1988/K-3/4 KG578 . . . . E
STRETE, CK/World in Grandfather's hands. /1995/
    5-A/4 KH771 . . . . **Fic**
STROUD, VA/Doesn't Fall Off His Horse. /1994/2-3/4 KG580 . . E
TITHERINGTON, J/Where are you going, Emma? /1988/
    P-K/3 KG610 . . . . E
VALGARDSON, WD/Winter rescue. /1995/3-5/4 KH819 . . . . **Fic**
WALTER, MP/Justin and the best biscuits in the world. /1986/
    4-6/6 KH839 . . . . **Fic**
ZOLOTOW, C/My grandson Lew. /c1974/K-2/2 KG805 . . . . . E

Grandmothers--Fiction.
ACKERMAN, K/By the dawn's early light. /1994/K-2/5 KF129 . . E
BAKER, B/Staying with Grandmother. /1994/1-3/1 KF184 . . . . E
BAUER, J/Sticks. /1996/6-A/4 KG880 . . . . **Fic**
BAWDEN, N/Granny the Pag. /1996/5-A/4 KG888 . . . . . **Fic**
BELTON, S/May'naise sandwiches and sunshine tea. /1994/
    1-3/3 KF217 . . . . E
BLEDSOE, LJ/Big bike race. /1995/3-6/2 KG903 . . . . . **Fic**
BOOTH, BD/Mandy. /1991/K-2/5 KF250 . . . . E
BUCKLEY, HE/Grandmother and I. /1994/P-1/2 KF293 . . . . . E
CARLSON, N/Visit to Grandma's. /1991/P-2/2 KF353 . . . . . E
DALY, N/Not so fast, Songololo. /1986/K-3/2 KF448 . . . . **CE E**
DEFELICE, CC/Willy's silly grandma. /1997/1-3/2 KF455 . . . . E
DORROS, A/Abuela. /1991/P-2/2 KF488 . . . . E
    Abuela (Videocassette). /1994/P-2/KF489 . . . . **VCR E**
    Isla. /1995/K-2/2 KF490 . . . . E
FLOURNOY, V/Patchwork quilt. /1985/K-3/5 KF561 . . . . . . E
    Tanya's reunion. /1995/K-3/3 KF562 . . . . E
FOX, P/Western wind: a novel. /1993/5-A/5 KH141 . . . . **Fic**
GEORGE, JC/Dear Rebecca, winter is here. /1993/
    1-3/3 KF605 . . . . E
GERSHATOR, P/Sambalena show-off. /1995/1-3/2 KF612 . . . . E
GUBACK, G/Luka's quilt. /1994/1-3/2 KF652 . . . . E
HAMILTON, V/Cousins. /1990/6-A/5 KH213 . . . . **Fic**
HAMM, DJ/Grandma drives a motor bed. /1987/P-3/2 KF669 . . E
HELLER, N/This little piggy. /1997/P-1/2 KF699 . . . . E
HENKES, K/Sun and spoon. /1997/5-A/6 KH239 . . . . **Fic**
HEST, A/Nana's birthday party. /1993/1-3/4 KF720 . . . . . . E
HOOPER, M/Cow, a bee, a cookie, and me. /1997/
    K-2/2 KF768 . . . . E
KHALSA, DK/Tales of a gambling grandma. /1986/
    3-5/6 KH345 . . . . **Fic**
LEVINSON, R/Watch the stars come out. /c1985, 1995/
    K-2/2 KF969 . . . . E
LOWELL, S/Little Red Cowboy Hat. /1997/1-3/3 KG038 . . . . . E
LOW, W/Chinatown. /1997/K-2/3 KG037 . . . . E
LUENN, N/Nessa's fish. /1990/K-2/2 KG041 . . . . **CE E**
MCKAY, H/Exiles. /1992/6-A/7 KH478 . . . . **Fic**
    Exiles at home. /1994/5-A/7 KH479 . . . . **Fic**
MILES, M/Annie and the old one. /c1971/4-6/4 KH496 . . . . **Fic**
MOORE, E/Grandma's house. /1985/K-2/4 KG154 . . . . E
NETHERY, M/Hannah and Jack. /1996/K-2/2 KG170 . . . . . . E

PLOURDE, L/Pigs in the mud in the middle of the rud. /1997/
    K-2/2 KG247 . . . . E
POLACCO, P/Babushka Baba Yaga. /1993/1-3/5 KG249 . . . . E
    Thunder cake. /1990/1-3/4 KG258 . . . . **CE E**
POYDAR, N/Busy Bea. /1994/P-1/2 KG285 . . . . E
SCHWARTZ, A/Oma and Bobo. /1987/K-3/2 KG414 . . . . . . E
TORRES, L/Saturday sancocho. /1995/K-2/5 KG614 . . . . . . E
WEISS, N/Stone men. /1993/K-2/2 KG693 . . . . E
WILD, M/Our granny. /1994/P-2/KG717 . . . . E
WILLIAMS, VB/Music, music for everyone. /1984/P-3/4 KG737 . E
YEP, L/Child of the owl. /c1977/A/6 KH891 . . . . **Fic**

Grandmothers--Folklore.
BRYAN, A/Turtle knows your name. /1989/K-3/6 KB545 . . **398.24**

Grandmothers--Poetry.
TILLER, R/Cinnamon, mint, and mothballs: a visit to Grandmother's
    house. /1993/K-3/KE033 . . . . **811**

Grandparents.
LESHAN, E/Grandparents: a special kind of love. /1984/
    4-6/9 KA879 . . . . **306.874**

Grandparents--Fiction.
CASELEY, J/Grandpa's garden lunch. /1990/P-1/2 KF364 . . . . E
COLE, B/Drop dead. /1996/2-4/2 KF406 . . . . E
CREECH, S/Walk two moons. /1994/5-A/5 KH037 . . . . **Fic**
DE PAOLA, T/Nana upstairs and Nana downstairs. /c1973, 1978/
    K-3/6 KF475 . . . . E
    Watch out for the chicken feet in your soup. /1974/
    K-2/2 KF481 . . . . E
HURD, ET/I dance in my red pajamas. /1982/K-1/2 KF791 . . . E
MARTIN, JB/Grandmother Bryant's pocket. /1996/
    1-4/3 KG079 . . . . E
OXENBURY, H/Grandma and grandpa. /c1984, 1993/
    P-K/2 KG203 . . . . E
PALACIOS, A/Christmas surprise for Chabelita. /1993/
    1-3/2 KG206 . . . . E
PERKINS, M/Sunita experiment. /1993/5-A/6 KH598 . . . . **Fic**
POLACCO, P/Trees of the dancing goats. /1996/1-3/3 KG260 . . E
SHULEVITZ, U/Dawn. /1974/K-2/2 KG498 . . . . E

Grant, Ulysses S.
RICKARBY, LA/Ulysses S. Grant and the strategy of victory. /1991/
    6-A/6 KE377 . . . . **B GRANT, U.**
ULYSSES S. GRANT (VIDEOCASSETTE). /1989/
    6-A/KE378 . . . . **VCR B GRANT, U.**

Graphic arts.
BIESTY, S/Stephen Biesty's incredible explosions. /1996/
    5-6/7 KD411 . . . . **741.6**
PELLETIER, D/Graphic alphabet. /1996/2-4/2 KB832 . . . . . . **421**

Graphic arts--Vocational guidance.
SO YOU WANT TO BE?: NEWSPAPER ARTIST
    (VIDEOCASSETTE). /1994/5-6/KA595 . . . . **VCR 070.4**

Graphic methods.
SMOOTHEY, M/Graphs. /1995/A/7 KB941 . . . . **511**

Graphics--Software.
PRINT SHOP DELUXE I (MICROCOMPUTER PROGRAM). /1992/
    /KA002 . . . . **MCP PROF 006.6**

Graphs.
PROBLEM SOLVING: USING GRAPHS (VIDEOCASSETTE). /
    1985/4-5/KB939 . . . . **VCR 511**

Grasshoppers.
DALLINGER, J/Grasshoppers. /c1981, 1990/K-2/3 KC537 . . **595.7**

Grassland ecology.
ROWAN, JP/Prairies and grasslands. /1983/3-6/4 KC331 . . **577.4**
TALL GRASS PRAIRIE: AN AMERICAN STORY (VIDEOCASSETTE).
    /1997/3-A/KC333 . . . . **VCR 577.4**

Grassland ecology--Guides.
BROWN, L/Grasslands. /1985/A/KC330 . . . . **577.4**

Graves' disease.
GUTMAN, B/Gail Devers. /1996/5-6/6 KE319 . . . **B DEVERS, G.**
Graveyards SEE Cemeteries.

Gravity.
COBB, V/Why doesn't the earth fall up? /1988/
    4-6/5 KC092 . . . . **531**
SKURZYNSKI, G/Zero gravity. /1994/3-6/5 KC100 . . . . . . **531**

Gravity--Experiments.
ARDLEY, N/Science book of gravity. /1992/K-3/2 KC089 . . . **531**

Gravity--Fiction.
HECKMAN, P/Waking upside down. /1996/1-3/6 KF693 . . . . . E

Great Astrolabe Reef (Fiji).
SIY, A/Great Astrolabe Reef. /1992/4-6/7 KC352 . . . . . **577.7**

Great Barrier Reef (Qld.).
GOUCK, M/Great Barrier Reef. /1993/3-6/5 KF119 . . . . . **994.3**
MCGOVERN, A/Down under, down under: diving adventures on
    the Great Barrier Reef. /1989/3-6/5 KF120 . . . . **994.3**

Great Britain SEE ALSO England.

Great Britain--Fiction.
  BOSTON, LM/Children of Green Knowe. /c1955, 1983/
    4-A/6 KG919. . . . . **Fic**
  COOPER, S/Over sea, under stone. /1966/A/5 KH028. . . . . . **Fic**
  GOODALL, JS/Story of a main street. /1987/K-3/KF631 . . . . . **E**
  NESBIT, E/Enchanted castle. /c1907, 1985/5-6/7 KH541. . . . . **Fic**
    Story of the treasure seekers. /1986/5-6/7 KH544. . . . . . . **Fic**

Great Britain--Folklore.
  BROWN, M/Dick Whittington and his cat. /c1950, 1988/
    2-4/6 KB498. . . . . **398.23**
  COOPER, S/Selkie girl. /1986/3-4/6 KB551. . . . . **CE 398.24**
  CRESWICK, P/Robin Hood. /1984/6/6 KB434. . . . . **398.22**
  JACOBS, J/King of the cats. /1980/1-3/2 KB595. . . . . **CE 398.24**
  KING ARTHUR AND HIS KNIGHTS (SOUND RECORDING
    CASSETTE). /1991/5-6/KB462 . . . . **SRC 398.22**
  PYLE, H/Story of King Arthur and his knights. /c1933, 1984/
    A/9 KB472. . . . . **398.22**
  TOM TIT TOT: AN ENGLISH FOLK TALE. /c1965, 1997/
    P-3/6 KB378 . . . . **398.2**

Great Britain--History.
  GOODALL, JS/Story of a castle. /1986/2-6/KE680. . . . . . . **942**

Great Britain--History-- Plantagenets, 1154-1399--Fiction.
  GRAY, EJ/Adam of the road. /c1942, 1970/5-6/6 KH194. **CE Fic**

Great Britain--History--Edward III, 1327-1377--Fiction.
  DE ANGELI, M/Door in the wall. /c1949, 1989/4-6/6 KH064. **Fic**

Great Britain--History--Richard I, 1189-1199--Fiction.
  MORPURGO, M/Robin of Sherwood. /1996/5-A/6 KH514. . . **Fic**
  TOMLINSON, T/Forestwife. /1995/6-A/5 KH797. . . . . **Fic**

Great Britain--History--Tudors, 1485-1603--Fiction.
  POPE, EM/Perilous gard. /1974/5-6/6 KH609. . . . . **Fic**

Great Britain--History--Victoria, 1837-1901.
  WILSON, L/Daily life in a Victorian house. /1993/
    3-6/7 KE676. . . . . **941.081**

Great Britain--History--1066-1687.
  FISHER, LE/Tower of London. /1987/3-6/7 KE679. . . . . . . **942**

Great Britain--History--1714-1837--Biography.
  FRITZ, J/Can't you make them behave, King George? /c1977/
    5-6/7 KE365 . . . . **CE B GEORGE III**

Great Britain--History--19th century--Fiction.
  PATON WALSH, J/Chance child. /c1978, 1991/6-A/7 KH582. **Fic**
  SEWELL, A/Black Beauty: the autobiography of a horse. /1997/
    5-7/7 KH702. . . . . **Fic**

Great Britain--History--20th Century.
  SEVERANCE, JB/Winston Churchill: soldier, statesman, artist. /
    1996/6-A/10 KE291 . . . . **B CHURCHILL, W.**

Great Britain--Kings and rulers.
  FRITZ, J/Can't you make them behave, King George? /c1977/
    5-6/7 KE365 . . . . **CE B GEORGE III**

Great Britain--Politics and government--20th Century.
  DRIEMEN, JE/Winston Churchill: an unbreakable spirit. /1990/
    5-6/7 KE290 . . . . **B CHURCHILL, W.**

Great Britain--Social life and customs--19th century.
  WILSON, L/Daily life in a Victorian house. /1993/
    3-6/7 KE676. . . . . **941.081**

Great Britain, Royal Navy--Sea life.
  BIESTY, S/Man-of-war. /1993/4-6/7 KA988. . . . . **359.1**

Great Lakes.
  HENDERSON, K/Great Lakes. /1989/4-5/6 KC182 . . . . . **551.48**

Great Lakes--Fiction.
  HOLLING, HC/Paddle-to-the-sea. /c1941/4-6/5 KH271. . . . . . **Fic**

Great Plains--Bibliography.
  EXPLORING THE PLAINS STATES THROUGH LITERATURE. /1994/
    /KA041. **PROF 016.978**

Great Plains--Fiction.
  TURNER, A/Dakota dugout. /1985/1-3/6 KG624 . . . . **E**

Great Pyramid (Egypt).
  MANN, E/Great Pyramid. /1996/4-6/6 KE635 . . . . **932**

Great Wall of China (China)--History.
  FISHER, LE/Great Wall of China. /1986/3-6/3 KE630. . . . . . **931**

Great-aunts--Fiction.
  DUFFEY, B/Lucky Christmas. /1994/3-5/4 KH086 . . . . **Fic**
  HOWARD, EF/Aunt Flossie's hats (and crab cakes later). /1991/
    1-3/2 KF772. . . . . **E**
  JONES, DW/Aunt Maria. /1991/6-A/6 KH330. . . . . **Fic**
  JONES, RC/Great Aunt Martha. /1995/1-3/2 KF853. . . . . **E**
  KING-SMITH, D/Sophie's Lucky. /1996/3-4/8 KH356. . . . . . . **Fic**
  MACDONALD, A/No more nice. /1996/4-6/6 KH437. . . . . . . **Fic**
    No more nice. /1996/3-5/6 KH438. . . . . **Fic**
  NUNES, S/Last dragon. /1995/2-3/3 KG183 . . . . **E**
  SCHACHNER, JB/Willy and May. /1995/1-3/5 KG401. . . . . . . **E**
  STOLZ, M/Stealing home. /1992/3-5/6 KH768 . . . . **Fic**
  WIDMAN, C/Lemon drop jar. /1992/P-2/2 KG711 . . . . **E**
  WRIGHT, BR/Ghost in the house. /1991/5-A/6 KH883 . . . . . . **Fic**

Great-grandmothers--Fiction.
  HICKMAN, J/Jericho: a novel. /1994/6-A/7 KH256 . . . . **Fic**
  SISULU, E/Day Gogo went to vote: South Africa, April 1994. /
    1996/1-3/2 KG513. . . . . **E**
  STILZ, CC/Grandma Buffalo, May, and me. /1995/
    1-3/3 KG573 . . . . **E**

Great-uncles--Fiction.
  HAAS, J/Uncle Daney's way. /1994/4-6/4 KH210 . . . . **Fic**
  LAKIN, P/Palace of stars. /1993/1-3/3 KF943. . . . . **E**

Greece--Fiction.
  BAWDEN, N/Real Plato Jones. /1993/6-A/6 KG892 . . . . . . **Fic**

Greed--Fiction.
  KOTZWINKLE, W/Million-Dollar Bear. /1995/2-3/2 KF916. . . . **E**
  MAHY, M/Great white man-eating shark: a cautionary tale. /1989/
    K-4/5 KG056. . . . . **CE E**
  STANLEY, D/Rumpelstiltskin's daughter. /1997/2-5/3 KG537 . . . **E**

Greed--Folklore.
  YEP, L/Tiger Woman. /1995/1-3/6 KB789 . . . . **398.27**

Greenhouse effect, Atmospheric.
  HOFF, MK/Our endangered planet: atmosphere. /1995/
    4-6/8 KB061. . . . . **363.73**
  INVESTIGATING GLOBAL WARMING (VIDEOCASSETTE). /1997/
    5-A/KB063. . . . . **VCR 363.73**

Greenhouse effect, Atmospheric--Experiments.
  RYBOLT, TR/Environmental experiments about air. /1993/
    5-6/7 KD084 . . . . **628.5**

Greenland--Fiction.
  CONRAD, P/Call me Ahnighito. /1995/2-5/2 KF413. . . . . **E**

Greeting cards.
  SOLGA, K/Make cards! /1992/1-5/5 KD459 . . . . **745.594**

Gregory, Cynthia.
  GREGORY, C/Cynthia Gregory dances Swan Lake. /1990/
    4-A/7 KD694. . . . . **792.8**

Gretzky, Wayne.
  CHRISTOPHER, M/On the ice with...Wayne Gretzky. /1997/
    3-6/7 KE379 . . . . **B GRETZKY, W.**

Grief SEE ALSO Bereavement.

Grief.
  BROWN, LK/When dinosaurs die: a guide to understanding death. /
    1996/K-4/5 KA648 . . . . **155.9**
  GREENLEE, S/When someone dies. /1992/K-3/4 KA649. . . **155.9**
  HYDE, MO/Meeting death. /1989/A/7 KA891 . . . . **306.9**
  SAYING GOOD-BYE (VIDEOCASSETTE). /1993/
    2-4/KA652 . . . . **VCR 155.9**

Grief--Fiction.
  HENKES, K/Sun and spoon. /1997/5-A/6 KH239. . . . . **Fic**
  HONEYCUTT, N/Twilight in Grace Falls. /1997/6-A/6 KH278. . **Fic**
  PATERSON, K/Flip-flop girl. /1996/5-A/6 KH575 . . . . **Fic**
  RYLANT, C/Missing May. /1992/5-A/7 KH663 . . . . **Fic**
  STEWART, EJ/Bimmi finds a cat. /1996/3-5/6 KH761 . . . . . . **Fic**
  TOLAN, SS/Who's there? /1994/5-A/5 KH795 . . . . **Fic**
  ZOLOTOW, C/Old dog. Rev. and newly illustrated ed. /1995/
    K-2/2 KG806 . . . . **E**

Griffey, Ken, Jr.
  CHRISTOPHER, M/At the plate with...Ken Griffey Jr. /1997/
    3-6/6 KE380 . . . . **B GRIFFEY,K. JR**
  KRAMER, B/Ken Griffey Junior: all-around all-star. /1996/
    4-5/4 KE381 . . . . **B GRIFFEY,K. JR**

Griffins--Fiction.
  STOCKTON, FR/Griffin and the minor canon. /c1963, 1986/
    3-5/7 KH764 . . . . **Fic**

Grizzly bear.
  CALABRO, M/Operation grizzly bear. /1989/
    5-6/7 KC858 . . . . **599.784**
  HOSHINO, M/Grizzly bear family book. /1994/
    4-6/6 KC859 . . . . **599.784**
  PATENT, DH/Way of the grizzly. /1987/5-6/8 KC860 . . **599.784**
  STONE, LM/Grizzlies. /1993/5-6/6 KC861 . . . . **599.784**

Grocery trade SEE ALSO Supermarkets.

Grocery trade.
  FLANAGAN, A/Busy day at Mr. Kang's grocery store. /1996/
    1-3/2 KB126 . . . . **381**

Grooming SEE ALSO Cleanliness.

Grooming.
  MY BODY, MY BUDDY: HEALTHY HABITS (VIDEOCASSETTE). /
    1993/2-4/KD301 . . . . **VCR 646.7**

Groundhog Day--Fiction.
  KOSCIELNIAK, B/Geoffrey Groundhog predicts the weather. /
    1995/K-2/2 KF915. . . . . **E**
  KROLL, S/It's groundhog day! /1987/K-2/4 KF929. . . . . **E**

Groundhogs SEE Woodchucks.

Group work in education.
  ERICKSON, T/Get it together: math problems for groups, grades
    4-12. /1989//KA290. **PROF 510**

GIANT ENCYCLOPEDIA OF CIRCLE TIME AND GROUP
ACTIVITIES FOR CHILDREN 3 TO 6: /1996/
/KA197 . . . . **PROF 372.21**
MEINBACH, AM/Complete guide to thematic units: creating the
integrated curriculum. /1995//KA195 . . . . **PROF 372.19**
Growth SEE ALSO Children--Growth.
Growth.
ALIKI /I'm growing! /1992/P-1/2 KC943 . . . . **612.6**
HARRIS, RH/It's perfectly normal: a book about changing bodies,
growing up, sex, and /1994/5-6/6 KC949 . . . . **612.6**
KUHN, D/My first book of nature: how living things grow. /1993/
P-2/4 KC276 . . . . **571.8**
LOOK WHO'S GROWING UP (VIDEOCASSETTE). /1997/
5-6/KC920 . . . . **VCR 612**
NEW, IMPROVED ME: UNDERSTANDING BODY CHANGES
(VIDEOCASSETTE). /1991/5-6/KC953 . . . . . . **VCR 612.6**
NUTRITION TO GROW ON (VIDEOCASSETTE). /1988/
5-6/KC987 . . . . **VCR 613.2**
SANDEMAN, A/Babies. /1996/2-5/6 KC955 . . . . **612.6**
THEN ONE YEAR. 2ND ED. (VIDEOCASSETTE). /1992/
5-6/KC957 . . . . **VCR 612.6**
Growth--Fiction.
HENKES, K/Biggest boy. /1995/P/2 KF701 . . . . **E**
HERMES, P/Nothing but trouble, trouble, trouble. /1995/
4-6/6 KH249 . . . . **Fic**
HURWITZ, J/Russell Sprouts. /1987/2-4/4 KH303 . . . . **Fic**
MILLER, M/Now I'm big. /1996/P/2 KG135 . . . . **E**
MOLLEL, TM/Big boy. /1995/K-2/3 KG150 . . . . **E**
MOSS, T/I want to be. /1993/1-4/3 KG159 . . . . **E**
VAN LEEUWEN, J/Emma Bean. /1993/K-2/2 KG646 . . . . **E**
WELLS, R/Edward's overwhelming overnight. /1995/
P-1/2 KG699 . . . . **E**
Growth--Poetry.
ADOFF, A/Hard to be six. /1991/1-2/KD909 . . . . **811**
Growth (Plants)--Experiments.
ARDLEY, N/Science book of things that grow. /1991/
K-3/3 KC273 . . . . **571.2**
Grucci family.
KUKLIN, S/Fireworks: the science, the art, and the magic. /1996/
5-6/6 KD317 . . . . **662**
Guadalupe, Nuestra Senora de.
DE PAOLA, T/Lady of Guadalupe. /1980/1-4/6 KA698 . . **232.91**
Guatemala--Fiction.
FRANKLIN, KL/Iguana Beach. /1997/P-1/2 KF575 . . . . **E**
Guatemala--Folklore.
GERSON, M/People of corn: a Mayan story. /1995/
2-4/3 KB399 . . . . **398.21**
Guide dogs SEE ALSO Working dogs.
Guide dogs.
ALEXANDER, SH/Mom's best friend. /1992/2-4/3 KB003 . . **362.4**
Guide dogs--Training.
MOORE, E/Buddy: the first seeing eye dog. /1996/
1-3/3 KB006 . . . . **362.4**
Guillain-Barre syndrome--Fiction.
HATRICK, G/Masks. /1996/6-A/3 KH225 . . . . **Fic**
Guinea pigs.
BARE, CS/Guinea pigs don't read books. /c1985, 1993/
P-2/3 KD177 . . . . **636**
EVANS, M/Guinea pigs. /1992/3-6/6 KD178 . . . . **636**
HANSEN, E/Guinea pigs. /1992/4-6/6 KD181 . . . . **636**
KING-SMITH, D/I love guinea pigs. /1995/K-4/3 KD183 . . . . **636**
Guinea pigs--Fiction.
KING-SMITH, D/Jenius: the amazing guinea pig. /1996/
2-4/5 KH349 . . . . **Fic**
Guinea pigs--Folklore.
HICKOX, R/Zorro and Quwi: tales of a trickster guinea pig. /1997/
1-3/3 KB590 . . . . **398.24**
Guinevere, Queen (Legendary character).
SAN SOUCI, RD/Young Guinevere. /1993/3-4/6 KB482 . . **398.22**
Gullahs.
KRULL, K/Bridges to change: how kids live on a South Carolina Sea
Island. /1995/4-6/7 KE987 . . . . **975.7**
Gullahs--Fiction.
SIEGELSON, KL/Terrible, wonderful tellin' at Hog Hammock. /
1996/4-6/6 KH711 . . . . **Fic**
Gulls.
GIBBONS, G/Gulls...gulls...gulls... /1997/K-4/3 KC676 . . . . **598.3**
O'CONNOR, K/Herring gull. /1992/5-6/5 KC657 . . . . **598**
Gulls--Fiction.
TURKLE, B/Thy friend, Obadiah. /c1969/K-3/5 KG623 . . . . **E**
Gun control.
HANDGUNS: MADE FOR KILLING, NOT FOR KIDS
(VIDEOCASSETTE). /1996/6-A/KB033 . . . . . . **VCR 363.3**

Gutenberg, Johann.
FISHER, LE/Gutenberg. /1993/5-A/8 KE382 . . **B GUTENBERG, J.**
Gymnastics SEE ALSO Physical education and training.
Gymnastics.
COHEN, JH/Superstars of women's gymnastics. /1997/
4-6/7 KD815 . . . . **796.44**
KUKLIN, S/Going to my gymnastics class. /1991/
3-5/4 KD816 . . . . **796.44**
NORMILE, D/Gymnastics. /1996/3-6/6 KD817 . . . . **796.44**
READHEAD, L/Gymnastics. /1996/3-6/8 KD818 . . . . **796.44**
Gymnastics--Fiction.
BROWN, MT/D.W. flips. /1987/P-2/1 KF281 . . . . **E**
Gymnasts.
COHEN, JH/Superstars of women's gymnastics. /1997/
4-6/7 KD815 . . . . **796.44**
Gypsies--Fiction.
CARLSON, NS/Family under the bridge. /c1958/
3-5/4 KG974 . . . . **Fic**
GILMAN, P/Gypsy princess. /1997/K-2/3 KF619 . . . . **E**
Habitat (Ecology).
ARNOSKY, J/Crinkleroot's guide to knowing animal habitats. /
1997/2-5/4 KC471 . . . . **591.5**
DUNCAN, BK/Explore the wild: a nature search-and-find book. /
1996/2-6/7 KC358 . . . . **578.7**
ORR, R/Richard Orr's nature cross-sections. /1995/
2-A/8 KC359 . . . . **578.7**
Habitats SEE Animals--Habitations.
Haida Indians--Folklore.
LEWIS, PO/Storm boy. /1995/2-4/3 KB610 . . . . **398.24**
OLIVIERO, J/Day Sun was stolen. /1995/K-2/5 KB712 . . . **398.26**
Haiku.
LEWIS, JP/Black swan/white crow: haiku. /1995/3-6/KD971 . **811**
LIVINGSTON, MC/Cricket never does: a collection of haiku and
tanka. /1997/3-6/KD890 . . . . **811**
SPIVAK, D/Grass sandals: the travels of Basho. /1997/
1-4/5 KE136 . . . . **895.6**
SPRING: A HAIKU STORY. /1996/1-6/KE137 . . . . **895.6**
TILLER, R/Cinnamon, mint, and mothballs: a visit to Grandmother's
house. /1993/K-3/KE033 . . . . **811**
WAKAN, N/Haiku: one breath poetry. /1993/5-A/KE138 . . **895.6**
WIND IN THE LONG GRASS: A COLLECTION OF HAIKU. /1991/
2-5/KD892 . . . . **808.81**
Hail.
BRANLEY, FM/Rain and hail. Rev. ed. /1983/K-3/2 KC188 . **551.5**
Hair.
BADT, KL/Hair there and everywhere. /1994/4-6/6 KB169 . . **391.5**
PATENT, DH/Why mammals have fur. /1995/4-6/6 KC727 . . **599**
Hair--Fiction.
COTE, N/Palm trees. /1993/K-2/4 KF427 . . . . **E**
Haircutting--Fiction.
ROBINS, J/Addie's bad day. /1993/K-1/2 KG339 . . . . **E**
Hairstyles.
BADT, KL/Hair there and everywhere. /1994/4-6/6 KB169 . . **391.5**
Haiti--Fiction.
LAUTURE, D/Running the road to ABC. /1996/1-3/4 KF951 . . . . **E**
WILLIAMS, KL/Tap-tap. /1994/K-2/2 KG728 . . . . **CE E**
Haiti--Folklore.
COURLANDER, H/Uncle Bouqui of Haiti (Talking book). /1959/
K-A/KB729 . . . . **TB 398.27**
REASONER, C/Night owl and the rooster: a Haitian legend. /
1995/K-2/6 KB637 . . . . **CE 398.24**
Haiti--History--Revolution, 1791-1804.
LAWRENCE, J/Toussaint L'Ouverture: the fight for Haiti's freedom.
/1996/4-A/8 KE569 . . . . **B TOUSSAINT**
Haiti--History--1986- --Fiction.
TEMPLE, F/Tonight, by sea: a novel. /1995/6-A/5 KH789 . . . . **Fic**
Haitian Americans.
ASHABRANNER, B/To seek a better world: the Haitian minority in
America. /1997/5-6/8 KA836 . . . . **305.8**
Haitian Americans--Fiction.
HYPPOLITE, J/Seth and Samona. /1995/4-6/6 KH313 . . . . . . **Fic**
Hall, Daniel Weston.
STANLEY, D/True adventure of Daniel Hall. /1995/
2-5/7 KE159 . . . . **910.4**
Hall, Minna--Fiction.
LASKY, K/She's wearing a dead bird on her head! /1995/
3-5/5 KH386 . . . . **Fic**
Halloween.
GIBBONS, G/Halloween. /1984/P-2/7 KB224 . . . . . . **CE 394.264**
LEEDY, L/2 x 2 = boo!: a set of spooky multiplication stories. /
1995/1-3/2 KB965 . . . . **513.2**
WEST, R/My very own Halloween: a book of cooking and crafts. /
1993/3-6/5 KD701 . . . . **793.2**

Halloween--Fiction.
ANDREWS, S/Rattlebone Rock. /1995/1-3/3 KF158 . . . . **E**
BRADBURY, R/Halloween tree. /c1982/5-A/7 KG920 . . . . **Fic**
BROWN, MT/Arthur's April fool. /1983/P-3/2 KF273 . . . . **E**
BUNTING, E/Scary, scary Halloween. /1986/P-K/4 KF308 . . . . . **E**
CASELEY, J/Witch Mama. /1996/K-2/3 KF371 . . . . **E**
FLOURNOY, V/Celie and the harvest fiddler. /1995/
2-4/6 KH130 . . . . **Fic**
HALL, Z/It's pumpkin time! /1994/P-2/3 KF666 . . . . **E**
HAMILTON, V/Willie Bea and the time the Martians landed. /
1983/5-6/3 KH219 . . . . **Fic**
HOWE, J/Scared silly: a Halloween treat. /1989/K-3/3 KF780 . . **E**
JOHNSTON, T/Soup bone. /1990/K-2/2 KF841 . . . . **E**
Very scary. /1995/P-2/3 KF842 . . . . **E**
KEATS, EJ/Trip. /c1978/K-2/2 KF879 . . . . **CE E**
KROLL, S/Candy witch. /1979/K-1/6 KF927 . . . . **E**
LEVITT, MJ/Tales of an October moon: haunting stories from New
England /1992/4-6/KH399 . . . . **SRC Fic**
MARSHALL, E/Space case. /1980/P-2/4 KG065 . . . . **E**
MEDDAUGH, S/Witches' supermarket. /1991/1-3/2 KG125 . . . **E**
MUELLER, V/Halloween mask for Monster. /1986/
P-1/1 KG162 . . . . **E**
NEWBERY HALLOWEEN: A DOZEN SCARY STORIES BY
NEWBERY AWARD-WINNING AUTHORS. /1993/
5-6/5 KH548 . . . . **Fic**
PILKEY, D/Hallo-wiener. /1995/K-2/2 KG237 . . . . **E**
PRAGER, A/Spooky Halloween party. /1981/1-3/2 KG287 . . . . **E**
ROBERTS, B/Halloween mice! /1995/P-1/3 KG336 . . . . **E**
SIERRA, J/House that Drac built. /1995/1-3/3 KG503 . . . . **E**
SILVERMAN, E/Big pumpkin. /1992/P-2/2 KG504 . . . . **E**
STOCK, C/Halloween monster. /1990/P-K/2 KG574 . . . . **E**
STUTSON, C/By the light of the Halloween moon. /1993/
1-3/3 KG582 . . . . **E**
TOLAN, SS/Save Halloween! /1993/5-A/7 KH794 . . . . **Fic**

Halloween--Poetry.
CARLSTROM, NW/Who said boo?: Halloween poems for the very
young. /1995/P-1/KD920 . . . . **811**
CUMMINGS, EE/Hist whist. /c1923, 1989/2-6/KD926 . . . . . **811**
HALLOWEEN POEMS. /1989/K-4/KE062 . . . . **811.008**
MERRIAM, E/Halloween A B C. /1987/P-A/KD982 . . . . **811**
PRELUTSKY, J/It's Halloween. /c1977/1-3/KE004. . . . . **811**
VAN RYNBACH, I/Five little pumpkins. /1995/P-K/2 KB817 . **398.8**

Halloween--Songs and music.
GOLD, A/Andrew Gold's Halloween howls (Compact disc). /1996/
K-2/KB226. . . . . **CD 394.264**

Halloween decorations.
ROSS, K/Crafts for Halloween. /1994/3-5/KD454 . . . . . **745.594**

Hambletonian 10 (Horse)--Fiction.
HENRY, M/Born to trot. /c1950, 1993/5-A/5 KH241 . . . . . . **Fic**

Hampton Roads (Va.), Battle of, 1862.
CARTER, AR/Battle of the ironclads: the Monitor and the
Merrimack. /1993/4-6/8 KE900. . . . . **973.7**

Hamsters.
WATTS, B/Hamster. /1986/2-4/2 KC748 . . . . **599.35**
WEXLER, J/Pet hamsters. /1992/4-6/7 KD187. . . . . **636**

Hamsters--Fiction.
QUATTLEBAUM, M/Jazz, Pizzazz, and the silver threads. /1996/
2-4/3 KH615 . . . . **Fic**

Hancock, John.
FRITZ, J/Will you sign here, John Hancock? /c1976, 1997/
5-6/7 KE383 . . . . **CE B HANCOCK, J.**

Hand.
ALIKI /My hands. Rev. ed. /1990/P-2/2 KC911 . . . . **612**
GRYSKI, C/Hands on, thumbs up: secret handshakes, fingerprints,
sign languages, and more handy ways to have fun with hands. /
1993/5-6/5 KC904 . . . . **611**

Hand weaving.
ROESSEL, M/Songs from the loom: a Navajo girl learns to weave.
/1995/4-6/6 KE799 . . . . **970.491**

Handbags--Fiction.
RANSOM, CF/Big green pocketbook. /1993/P-1/2 KG303 . . . . **E**
Handbooks, manuals, etc SEE general subjects with the subdivision.
Handicapped SEE ALSO Mentally handicapped; Physically handicapped;
also specific handicaps e.g. Blind.

Handicapped.
BROWN, T/Someone special, just like you. /1984/
P-2/6 KA623 . . . . **152.4**
DINN, S/Hearts of gold: a celebration of Special Olympics and its
heroes. /1996/4-6/9 KD760 . . . . **796**
RENFRO, N/Puppetry, language, and the special child: discovering
alternate languages. /1984//KA328 . . . . **PROF 791.5**

Handicapped--Education.
TEACHING EXCEPTIONAL CHILDREN. /1968-/
/KA150. . . . . **PER PROF 050**

Handicapped--Education--Periodicals.
INTERVENTION. /n.d.//KA117. . . . . **PER PROF 050**

Handicapped--Fiction.
ANDERSON, R/Bus people. /1995/6-A/6 KG850 . . . . **Fic**
HAAS, J/Uncle Daney's way. /1994/4-6/4 KH210 . . . . **Fic**

Handicapped children--Care.
MEETING THE CHALLENGE: PARENTING CHILDREN WITH
DISABILITIES (VIDEOCASSETTE). /1992/
/KA306. . . . . **VCR PROF 649.8**
Handicraft SEE ALSO Arts and crafts; Hobbies; also names of crafts e.g.
Pottery.

Handicraft.
BLAKEY, N/Mudpies activity book: recipes for invention. /c1989,
1993/A/KD424 . . . . **745.5**
BRADY, AA/Kwanzaa karamu: cooking and crafts for a Kwanzaa
feast. /1995/5-6/5 KD284 . . . . **641.59**
BUETTER, BM/Simple puppets from everyday materials. /1997/
2-5/3 KD443 . . . . **745.592**
BULLOCH, I/I want to be a puppeteer. /1996/
3-5/5 KD444 . . . . **745.592**
CANEY, S/Steven Caney's Kids' America. /1978/
4-6/7 KE920 . . . . **973.92**
CARLSON, L/EcoArt!: earth-friendly art and craft experiences for
3-to 9-year olds. /1993/K-4/KD425 . . . . **745.5**
COLE, J/Rain or shine activity book: fun things to make and do. /
1997/3-6/KD699 . . . . **793**
CRAFTS FOR DECORATION. /1993/3-6/7 KD451 . . . . **745.594**
CRAFTS FOR PLAY. /1993/3-6/7 KD445 . . . . **745.592**
DIEHN, G/Kid style nature crafts: 50 terrific things to make with
nature's materials. /1995/4-8/6 KD428 . . . . **745.5**
Nature crafts for kids. /1992/4-6/6 KD429. . . . . **745.5**
DRAKE, J/Kids' summer handbook. /1994/3-6/6 KD678 . . . **790.1**
FIAROTTA, P/Papercrafts around the world. /1996/
2-6/6 KD440 . . . . **745.54**
GRANFIELD, L/Extra! extra!: the who, what, where, when and why
of newspapers. /1994/3-6/5 KA596. . . . . **071**
GREEN CHILI JAM BAND /Magic bike (Sound recording cassette).
/1991/P-3/KD613. . . . . **SRC 789.3**
HERSHBERGER, P/Make costumes!: for creative play. /1992/
4-6/2 KD300 . . . . **646.4**
HILLERMAN, A/Done in the sun, solar projects for children. /1983/
2-4/7 KD048 . . . . **621.47**
HOFFMAN, C/Sewing by hand. /1994/3-5/3 KD297 . . . . . **646.2**
HOW TO FOLD A PAPER CRANE (VIDEOCASSETTE). /1994/
3-6/KD402. . . . . **VCR 736**
KALLEVIG, CP/Holiday folding stories: storytelling and origami
together for holiday fun. /1992//KA309 . . . . **PROF 736**
KALMAN, B/Home crafts. /1990/3-6/6 KD431 . . . . **745.5**
Pioneer projects. /1997/3-5/6 KD432 . . . . **745.5**
KENOWER, FT/Cub Scout fun book. /c1956, 1986/
2-4/6 KB077 . . . . **369.43**
KING, D/My first photography book. /1994/3-6/5 KD513. . . **771**
LANKFORD, MD/Christmas around the world. /1995/
3-6/7 KB237 . . . . **394.266**
LEWIS, S/Get your teddy ready (Videocassette). /1994/
P-2/KD681. . . . . **VCR 790.1**
LOOK WHAT I MADE: PAPER, PLAYTHINGS AND GIFTS
(VIDEOCASSETTE). /1993/3-6/KD433 . . . . **VCR 745.5**
LYNN, S/Play with paper. /1993/K-2/3 KD441 . . . . **745.54**
MAKING AND USING PUPPETS IN THE PRIMARY GRADES
(VIDEOCASSETTE). /1992/K-6/KD446 . . . . **VCR 745.592**
MCGUIRE, K/Woodworking for kids: 40 fabulous, fun and useful
things for kids to make. /1993/5-A/KD341 . . . . **684**
RICE, M/Complete book of children's activities. /1993/
/KA194. . . . . **PROF 372.13**
ROSS, K/Crafts for Christmas. /1995/3-5/KD452. . . . . . **745.594**
Crafts for Easter. /1995/3-5/KD453 . . . . **745.594**
Crafts for Halloween. /1994/3-5/KD454. . . . . **745.594**
Crafts for Hanukkah. /1996/3-6/KD455 . . . . **745.594**
Crafts for Kwanzaa. /1994/3-6/KD456 . . . . **745.594**
Crafts for Thanksgiving. /1995/3-5/KD457 . . . . **745.594**
Every day is Earth Day: a craft book. /1995/
K-3/5 KD442 . . . . **745.58**
RUSSO, M/Tree almanac: a year-round activity guide. /1993/
3-6/6 KC423 . . . . **582.16**
SABBETH, C/Kids' computer creations: using your computer for art
and craft fun. /1995/3-5/KD434 . . . . **745.5**
SANCHEZ SANCHEZ, I/Dragons and prehistoric monsters. /1996/
3-6/3 KD447 . . . . **745.592**
Modeling dinosaurs. /1996/3-6/3 KD448 . . . . **745.592**
Monsters and extraterrestrials. /1996/3-6/3 KD449 . . **745.592**
SIRETT, D/My first paint book. /1994/3-6/7 KD436 . . . . . . **745.5**
SMITH, D/Holidays and festivals activities. /1994/
1-6/6 KD458 . . . . **745.594**

SMOLINSKI, J/Holiday origami. /1995/3-6/KD403. . . . . . . **736**
SOLGA, K/Make cards! /1992/1-5/5 KD459 . . . . **745.594**
STANGL, J/Recycling activities for the primary grades. /1993/
/KA313. . . . . **PROF 745.5**
SWAIN, G/Bookworks: making books by hand. /1995/
3-6/5 KD437. . . . . **745.5**
VAN HAGE, MA/Little green thumbs. /1996/3-5/4 KD176 . **635.9**
WILKES, A/My first Christmas activity book. /1994/
3-6/KD460. . . . . **745.594**
WRIGHT, R/Knights: facts, things to make, activities. /1991/
4-A/8 KD439. . . . . **745.5**
Handicraft--Africa.
TEMKO, F/Traditional crafts from Africa. /1996/
4-6/7 KD422 . . . . **745**
Handicraft--Asia.
CORWIN, JH/Asian crafts. /1992/4-A/7 KD426 . . . . **745.5**
Handicraft--Caribbean Area.
CORWIN, JH/Latin American and Caribbean crafts. /1992/
4-A/5 KD427 . . . . **745.5**
Handicraft--Central America.
TEMKO, F/Traditional crafts from Mexico and Central America. /
1996/3-6/5 KD438. . . . . **745.5**
Handicraft--Equipment and supplies.
SATTLER, HR/Recipes for art and craft material. Newly rev. /
c1973, 1994/4-6/6 KD435 . . . . **745.5**
Handicraft--Fiction.
GOFFSTEIN, MB/Goldie, the dollmaker. /1969/3-6/6 KH180. . **Fic**
Handicraft--History.
STEVENS, BS/Colonial American craftspeople. /1993/
5-6/8 KD339 . . . . **680**
Handicraft--History--18th century.
KALMAN, B/Early artisans. /1983/4-A/8 KD430 . . . . **745.5**
Handicraft--History--19th century.
KALMAN, B/Early artisans. /1983/4-A/8 KD430 . . . . **745.5**
Handicraft--Latin America.
CORWIN, JH/Latin American and Caribbean crafts. /1992/
4-A/5 KD427 . . . . **745.5**
Handicraft--Mexico.
TEMKO, F/Traditional crafts from Mexico and Central America. /
1996/3-6/5 KD438 . . . . **745.5**
Handicraft--South America.
DORROS, A/Tonight is Carnaval. /1991/1-3/4 KF492 . . . . . . **E**
Hanukkah.
CHAIKIN, M/Light another candle: the story and meaning of
Hanukkah. /c1981, 1987/5-6/8 KA770. . . . . **296.4**
COHN, J/Christmas menorahs: how a town fought hate. /1995/
3-6/5 KA818 . . . . **305**
HANUKKAH (VIDEOCASSETTE). /1994/2-5/KA774 . . **VCR 296.4**
HOYT-GOLDSMITH, D/Celebrating Hanukkah. /1996/
3-4/7 KA775 . . . . **296.4**
KUSKIN, K/Great miracle happened there: a Chanukah story. /
c1993, 1995/3-4/4 KA778 . . . . **296.4**
SCHOTTER, R/Hanukkah! /1993/K-2/2 KA779 . . . . **296.4**
WIKLER, M/Miracle meals, eight nights of food 'n fun for
Chanukah. /1987/4-5/KD288 . . . . **641.59**
Hanukkah--Fiction.
ADLER, DA/One yellow daffodil: a Hanukkah story. /1995/
3-5/4 KG818 . . . . **Fic**
CONWAY, DC/Northern lights: a Hanukkah story. /1994/
1-3/4 KF417 . . . . **E**
JAFFE, N/In the month of Kislev: a story for Hanukkah. /1992/
K-2/2 KF820 . . . . **CE E**
KIMMEL, EA/Magic dreidels: a Hanukkah story. /1996/
K-3/2 KF904 . . . . **E**
POLACCO, P/Trees of the dancing goats. /1996/1-3/3 KG260. . **E**
ROSEN, MJ/Elijah's angel: a story for Chanukah and Christmas. /
1992/3-6/7 KH652 . . . . **Fic**
SCHNUR, S/Tie man's miracle: a Chanukah tale. /1995/
2-3/4 KG409 . . . . **E**
SUSSMAN, S/Hanukkah: eight lights around the world. /1988/
3-5/5 KH774 . . . . **Fic**
ZALBEN, JB/Beni's first Chanukah. /1988/P/4 KG785 . . . . **E**
Hanukkah--Songs and music.
CHANUKAH AT HOME (SOUND RECORDING CASSETTE). /
1988/K-6/KA771 . . . . **SRC 296.4**
Hanukkah cookery.
WIKLER, M/Miracle meals, eight nights of food 'n fun for
Chanukah. /1987/4-5/KD288 . . . . **641.59**
Hanukkah decorations.
ROSS, K/Crafts for Hanukkah. /1996/3-6/KD455 . . . . . **745.594**
Happiness SEE ALSO Joy and sorrow.
Harbors.
CREWS, D/Harbor. /1982/P-1/KD062. . . . . **623.8**

Hardaway, Anfernee.
TOWNSEND, B/Anfernee Hardaway: basketball's lucky penny. /
1997/3-5/6 KE384 . . . . **B HARDAWAY, A.**
Hares--Fiction.
VOZAR, D/M.C. Turtle and the Hip Hop Hare: a nursery rap. /
1997/2-3/2 KG665. **E**
Hares--Folklore.
STEVENS, J/Tops and bottoms. /1995/K-2/2 KB660 . . . . **398.24**
Harlem (New York, N.Y.)--Fiction.
MYERS, WD/Young landlords. /c1979/5-6/6 KH524 . . . . **Fic**
RINGGOLD, F/Tar beach. /1991/2-3/4 KG333. . . . . **E**
Harlem (New York, N.Y.)--Poetry.
MYERS, WD/Harlem: a poem. /1997/3-6/KD994. . . . . **811**
Harlem Globetrotters.
WILKER, J/Harlem Globetrotters. /1997/5-6/10 KD780. . **796.323**
Harlem Renaissance.
COOPER, ML/Bound for the promised land.: the great black
migration. /1995/6-A/9 KE851 . . . . **973**
Harmonica--Fiction.
STEIG, W/Zeke Pippin. /1994/1-3/6 KG549. . . . . **E**
Harness racing--Fiction.
HENRY, M/Born to trot. /c1950, 1993/5-A/5 KH241 . . . . . **Fic**
Harp seal.
MATTHEWS, D/Harp seal pups. /1997/4-6/3 KC870 . . . . **599.79**
Harvest festivals.
PENNINGTON, D/Itse Selu: Cherokee harvest festival. /1994/
K-3/6 KB190 . . . . **394.2**
Hatch (N.M.)--Social life and customs.
KING, E/Chile fever: a celebration of peppers. /1995/
5-6/6 KD267 . . . . **641.3**
Hatch Chile Festival, Hatch, N.M.
KING, E/Chile fever: a celebration of peppers. /1995/
5-6/6 KD267 . . . . **641.3**
Hate crimes.
COHN, J/Christmas menorahs: how a town fought hate. /1995/
3-6/5 KA818 . . . . **305**
Hats.
MILLER, M/Whose hat? /1988/P-K/KB166 . . . . **391.4**
MORRIS, A/Hats, hats, hats. /1989/1-4/1 KB167 . . . . **391.4**
Hats--Fiction.
GERINGER, L/Three hat day. /1985/P-3/2 KF609 . . . . **E**
HOWARD, EF/Aunt Flossie's hats (and crab cakes later). /1991/
1-3/2 KF772 . . . . **E**
KELLER, H/Rosata. /1995/K-2/2 KF886 . . . . **E**
SEUSS, D/500 hats of Bartholomew Cubbins. /c1938, 1989/
P-A/6 KG473. . . . . **E**
SLOBODKINA, E/Caps for sale: a tale of a peddler, some monkeys
and their monkey business. /c1947/P-2/1 KG519 . . . . **CE E**
STOEKE, JM/Hat for Minerva Louise. /1994/P-K/2 KG576 . . . . **E**
UNGERER, T/Tomi Ungerer Library (Videocassette). /1993/
K-2/KG635 . . . . **VCR E**
Hats--Folklore.
ROHMER, H/Uncle Nacho's hat: a folktale from Nicaragua/El
sombrero de Tio Nacho: /1989/2-4/2 KB770 . . . . **398.27**
Haunted houses.
COHEN, D/Ghost in the house. /1993/5-6/5 KA598 . . . . . **133.1**
Haunted houses--Fiction.
SAN SOUCI, RD/Boy and the ghost. /1989/2-3/6 KG392. . . . . **E**
SIERRA, J/House that Drac built. /1995/1-3/3 KG503 . . . . . . **E**
Haunted houses--Fiction--Software.
MARK SCHLICHTING'S HARRY AND THE HAUNTED HOUSE.
SCHOOL ED. (CD-ROM). /1994/K-3/KG063. . . . . **CDR E**
Hawaii.
FEENEY, S/Hawaii is a rainbow. /1985/P-6/KF121. . . . . . **996**
RAYSON, A/Hawai'i: the Pacific State. Rev. and updated edition. /
1997/5-A/6 KF123 . . . . **996.9**
Hawaii--Bibliography.
EXPLORING THE PACIFIC STATES THROUGH LITERATURE. /
1994//KA042 . . . . **PROF 016.9795**
Hawaii--Fiction.
FEENEY, S/A is for aloha. /1980/K-3/KF546 . . . . **E**
GUBACK, G/Luka's quilt. /1994/1-3/2 KF652 . . . . **E**
RAND, G/Aloha, Salty! /1996/1-3/3 KG299 . . . . **E**
RATTIGAN, JK/Dumpling soup. /1993/1-3/2 KG312 . . . . . . **E**
SALISBURY, G/Under the blood-red sun. /1994/6-A/4 KH672 . **Fic**
Hawaii--Folklore.
BROWN, M/Backbone of the king: the story of Paka'a and his son
Ku. /1984/5-6/6 KB428. . . . . **398.22**
RATTIGAN, JK/Woman in the moon: a story from Hawaii. /1996/
K-2/6 KB474 . . . . **398.22**
THOMPSON, VL/Hawaiian tales of heroes and champions. /c1971,
1986/4-5/4 KB491 . . . . **398.22**
WARDLAW, L/Punia and the King of Sharks: a Hawaiian folktale. /
1997/2-3/3 KB672 . . . . **398.24**

SUBJECT INDEX

Hawaii--History.
STANLEY, F/Last princess: the story of Princess Kaiulani of Hawaii.
/1991/5-6/7 KE413 . . . . **B KAIULANI**
Hawks SEE ALSO Birds of prey.
Hawks--Fiction.
GILBERT, S/Hawk Hill. /1996/4-6/4 KH167 . . . . **Fic**
Hay.
GEISERT, B/Haystack. /1995/K-3/5 KD153. . . . . **633.2**
Hay fever.
LERNER, C/Plants that make you sniffle and sneeze. /1993/
5-6/9 KC404 . . . . **581.6**
Hay-fever plants.
LERNER, C/Plants that make you sniffle and sneeze. /1993/
5-6/9 KC404 . . . . **581.6**
Heads of state.
ADLER, DA/Picture book of Simon Bolivar. /1992/
3-4/5 KE257 . . . . **B BOLIVAR, S.**
BIOGRAPHY TODAY WORLD LEADERS SERIES: PROFILES OF
PEOPLE OF INTEREST TO YOUNG READERS. /1997/
4-6/KA407 . . . . **REF 350**
WORLD LEADERS: PEOPLE WHO SHAPED THE WORLD. /1994/
5-A/KA408 . . . . **REF 350**
Health SEE ALSO Immunology.
Health.
DUSTY THE DRAGON TALKS TO DR. MARGIE HOGAN ABOUT
TOBACCO (VIDEOCASSETTE). /1990/3-5/KD005 . **VCR 613.85**
LOOKING GOOD, FEELING GOOD (VIDEOCASSETTE). /1994/
5-6/KC951. . . . . **VCR 612.6**
MY BODY, MY BUDDY: HEALTHY FOOD (VIDEOCASSETTE). /
1993/3-5/KC986 . . . . **VCR 613.2**
MY BODY, MY BUDDY: HEALTHY HABITS (VIDEOCASSETTE). /
1993/2-4/KD301 . . . . **VCR 646.7**
Hearing.
FABULOUS FIVE: OUR SENSES (VIDEOCASSETTE). /1989/
P-2/KC917. . . . . **VCR 612**
MATHERS, D/Ears. /1992/5-6/6 KC967 . . . . **612.8**
PARKER, S/Ear and hearing. Rev. ed. /1989/5-6/8 KC971 . **612.8**
PARRAMON, JM/Hearing. /1985/P-1/1 KC973 . . . . **612.8**
Hearing--Software.
SCIENCE IN YOUR EAR (CD-ROM). /1996/4-A/KC104 **CDR 534**
Hearing disorders SEE ALSO Deaf.
Hearing disorders--Fiction.
BOOTH, BD/Mandy. /1991/K-2/5 KF250. . . . . **E**
Heart SEE ALSO Blood--Circulation.
Heart.
PARKER, S/Heart and blood. Rev. ed. /1989/5-6/8 KC933 . **612.1**
SAUNDERSON, J/Heart and lungs. /1992/5-6/6 KC935 . . . **612.1**
SIMON, S/Heart: our circulatory system. /1996/
5-A/6 KC937 . . . . **612.1**
YOUR BODY: CIRCULATORY AND RESPIRATORY SYSTEMS
(VIDEOCASSETTE). /1988/5-6/KC931 . . . . **VCR 612**
Heat.
HEAT, TEMPERATURE AND ENERGY (VIDEOCASSETTE). /1995/
5-6/KC128. . . . . **VCR 536**
Heat--Experiments.
ARDLEY, N/Science book of hot and cold. /1992/
K-3/2 KC126 . . . . **536**
Heat--Fiction.
DRAGONWAGON, C/Itch book. /1990/K-3/KF496. . . . . **E**
RYLANT, C/Mr. Putter and Tabby row the boat. /1997/
K-2/2 KG381. . . . . **E**
Hebrew language--Alphabet.
EDWARDS, M/Alef-bet: a Hebrew alphabet book. /1992/
1-3/KB864. . . . . **492.4**
Hedgehogs--Fiction.
POTTER, B/Tale of Mrs. Tiggy-Winkle. /c1905, 1987/
P-2/7 KG276. . . . . **E**
Heller, Ruth.
HELLER, R/Fine lines. /1996/4-6/2 KE385. . . . . **B HELLER, R.**
Helpfulness--Fiction.
MCGOVERN, A/Lady in the box. /1997/1-3/2 KG103. . . . . . . **E**
WADDELL, M/You and me, Little Bear. /1996/P-K/1 KG677 . . . **E**
Hemenway, Harriet--Fiction.
LASKY, K/She's wearing a dead bird on her head! /1995/
3-5/5 KH386 . . . . **Fic**
Henio, Katie.
THOMSON, P/Katie Henio: Navajo sheepherder. /1995/
5-6/6 KE796 . . . . **970.489**
Henry, John SEE John Henry (Legendary character).
Henry, Patrick.
FRITZ, J/Where was Patrick Henry on the 29th of May? /c1975,
1982/5-6/7 KE386 . . . . **CE B HENRY, P.**

Henry the Navigator.
FISHER, LE/Prince Henry the Navigator. /1990/
4-6/6 KE387 . . . . **B HENRY, PRINCE**
Henson, Matthew Alexander.
MATTHEW HENSON (VIDEOCASSETTE). /1994/
5-A/KE388. . . . . **VCR B HENSON, M.**
Heracles (Greek mythology) SEE ALSO Hercules (Roman mythology).
Heracles (Greek mythology).
LASKY, K/Hercules: the man, the myth, the hero. /1997/
5-6/4 KA747 . . . . **292**
Hercules (Roman mythology) SEE ALSO Heracles (Greek mythology).
Heredity SEE ALSO Evolution; Genetics; Natural selection; Variation
(Biology).
Hermit crabs.
JOHNSON, SA/Hermit crabs. /1989/A/7 KC521. . . . . . . **595.3**
MCDONALD, M/Is this a house for hermit crab? /1990/
P-1/3 KC522 . . . . **595.3**
Hermit crabs--Fiction.
CARLE, E/House for Hermit Crab. /1987/P-2/2 KF344 . . . . **E**
KALAN, R/Moving day. /1996/P-1/1 KF865. . . . . **E**
MACCARONE, G/Classroom pet. /1995/K-1/2 KG046. . . . . . . **E**
Hermits--Fiction.
BULLA, CR/White bird. /c1966, 1990/1-6/2 KG940 . . . . . . **Fic**
Heroes.
HAZELL, R/Heroes: great men through the ages. /1997/
3-A/9 KA828 . . . . **305.3**
Heroes--Biography--Methodology.
ZARNOWSKI, M/Learning about biographies: a reading-and-writing
approach for children. /1990/KA334. . . . . **PROF 808**
Heroes--Fiction.
ROSTKOWSKI, MI/After the dancing days. /1986/
6-A/4 KH656 . . . . **Fic**
SACHS, M/Truth about Mary Rose /1995/5-A/6 KH669 . . . . . **Fic**
VALGARDSON, WD/Winter rescue. /1995/3-5/4 KH819 . . . . **Fic**
Heroines.
HAZELL, R/Heroines: great women through the ages. /1996/
4-A/10 KA829 . . . . **305.4**
SAN SOUCI, RD/Kate Shelley: bound for legend. /1995/
3-5/5 KE539 . . . . **B SHELLEY, K.**
Herons SEE ALSO names of specific species e.g. Great blue heron.
Herring gulls.
O'CONNOR, K/Herring gull. /1992/5-6/5 KC657 . . . . **598**
Hiawatha.
FRADIN, DB/Hiawatha: messenger of peace. /1992/
5-6/7 KE389 . . . . **B HIAWATHA**
Hibernation SEE ALSO Animals--Hibernation.
Hibernation--Fiction.
ARNOSKY, J/Every autumn comes the bear. /1993/
P-2/2 KF168 . . . . **E**
FLEMING, D/Time to sleep. /1997/P-1/2 KF558 . . . . **E**
WILLARD, N/Starlit somersault downhill. /1993/K-2/3 KG725 . . **E**
Hide-and-seek--Fiction.
ARUEGO, J/We hide, you seek. /1979/P-K/1 KF172 . . . . **E**
HILL, E/Where's Spot? Sign language edition. /1987/
P-2/2 KF728 . . . . **E**
HUGHES, S/Hiding. /1996/P-K/2 KF789 . . . . **E**
STEIG, W/Toby, where are you? /1997/P-1/2 KG546 . . . . **E**
WIKLER, L/Alfonse, where are you? /1996/P-K/1 KG715. . . . . . **E**
Hieroglyphics.
KATAN, NJ/Hieroglyphs, the writing of ancient Egypt. /1981/
5-6/9 KB866 . . . . **493**
High schools--Fiction.
AVI/Nothing but the truth: a documentary novel. /1991/
6-A/5 KG861. . . . . **Fic**
CLEARY, B/Strider. /1991/5-A/4 KH008 . . . . **Fic**
DYGARD, TJ/Backfield package. /1992/6-A/7 KH090 . . . . . . **Fic**
Forward pass. /1989/5-A/6 KH091. . . . . **Fic**
Game plan. /1993/5-A/8 KH092 . . . . **Fic**
TUNIS, JR/Go, team, go! /c1954, 1991/5-A/6 KH808 . . . . . . **Fic**
High technology SEE ALSO Technology.
High technology.
MULTIMEDIA, THE COMPLETE GUIDE. /1996/
A/KA372. . . . . **REF 006.7**
Hiking SEE ALSO Backpacking.
Hiking--Fiction.
HILL, D/Take it easy. /1997/6-A/4 KH260 . . . . **Fic**
RAND, G/Willie takes a hike. /1996/K-2/3 KG302 . . . . **E**
Hill, Grant.
GUTMAN, B/Grant Hill: basketball's high flier. /1996/
5-6/7 KE390 . . . . **B HILL, G.**
Himalaya Mountains.
HIMALAYAN ADVENTURE (VIDEOCASSETTE). /1994/
K-6/KE712. . . . . **VCR 954.96**

Himalaya Mountains Region--Social life and customs.
REYNOLDS, J/Himalaya: vanishing cultures. /1991/
4-6/7 KE714 . . . . **954.96**

Hinduism.
FAITH AND BELIEF: FIVE MAJOR WORLD RELIGIONS
(VIDEOCASSETTE). /1992/5-A/KA722. . . . . **VCR 291**
GANERI, A/What do we know about Hinduism? /1995/
5-A/9 KA762 . . . . **294.5**
KADODWALA, D/Holi. /1997/4-6/7 KA763 . . . . **294.5**
VISHAKA /Our most dear friend: Bhagavad-gita for children. /
1996/2-5/5 KA767 . . . . **294.5**

Hinduism--Customs and practices.
LEWIN, T/Sacred river. /1995/4-6/6 KA765 . . . . **294.5**

Hine, Lewis Wickes.
FREEDMAN, R/Kids at work: Lewis Hine and the crusade against
child labor. /1994/5-A/8 KA937 . . . . **331.3**

Hippopotamus.
ARNOLD, C/Hippo. /c1989, 1992/4-6/7 KC785 . . . . **599.63**

Hippopotamus--Fiction.
HADITHI, M/Hot Hippo. /1986/K-3/4 KF660 . . . . **CE E**
MARSHALL, J/George and Martha. /c1972/P-2/3 KG068. . **CE E**
MINARIK, EH/Am I beautiful? /1992/P-K/2 KG140 . . . . **E**
MOST, B/Hippopotamus hunt. /1994/1-3/2 KG160 . . . . **E**
WABER, B/You look ridiculous said the rhinoceros to the
hippopotamus. /c1966/1-2/2 KG673 . . . . **E**

Hiroshima-shi (Japan)--Bombardment, 1945.
KODAMA, T/Shin's tricycle. /1995/4-6/4 KE670 . . . . . . **940.54**
MARUKI, T/Hiroshima no pika. /1982/4-6/5 KE672 . . . . **940.54**

Hiroshima-shi (Japan)--History--Bombardment, 1945.
COERR, E/Sadako. /1993/3-6/4 KA994 . . . . **CE 362.1**

Hispanic American poetry (Spanish).
ADA, AF/Gathering the sun: an alphabet in Spanish and English. /
1997/1-3/KE122 . . . . **861**

Hispanic Americans.
OUR HISPANIC HERITAGE (VIDEOCASSETTE). /1991/
5-A/KA853 . . . . **VCR 305.8**
PERL, L/Pinatas and paper flowers, holidays of the Americas in
English and Spanish/ /1983/4-6/6 KB202 . . . . **394.26**
SACRE, A/Looking for Papito: family stories from Latin America
(Sound recording /1996/1-6/KA857 . . . . **SRC 305.8**

Hispanic Americans--Biography.
HISPANIC AMERICAN BIOGRAPHY. /1995/
5-A/KA400 . . . . **REF 305.8**
HISPANIC HERITAGE (PICTURE). /1997/4-6/6 KA848. . . **PIC 305.8**
SINNOTT, S/Extraordinary Hispanic Americans. /1991/
5-A/7 KA860 . . . . **305.8**

Hispanic Americans--Drama.
VIGIL, A/Teatro!: Hispanic plays for young people. /1996/
/KA364 . . . . **PROF 812**

Hispanic Americans--Fiction.
ALTMAN, LJ/Amelia's road. /1993/1-3/4 KF154 . . . . **E**
ANAYA, R/Farolitos of Christmas. /1995/3-6/2 KG845 . . . . . . **Fic**
BUNTING, E/Day's work. /1994/1-3/2 KF298 . . . . **E**
DORROS, A/Abuela. /1991/P-2/2 KF488 . . . . **E**
Abuela (Videocassette). /1994/P-2/KF489 . . . . . . **VCR E**
Isla. /1995/K-2/2 KF490 . . . . **E**
GERSHATOR, D/Bread is for eating. /1995/P-2/2 KF610 . . . . . **E**
KLEVEN, E/Hooray! A pinata! /1996/K-2/2 KF910 . . . . **E**
MEDEARIS, AS/Adventures of Sugar and Junior. /1995/
2-3/2 KH494 . . . . **Fic**
SCHECTER, E/Big idea. /1996/3-5/2 KH679 . . . . **Fic**

Hispanic Americans--Folklore.
VIGIL, A/Corn woman: stories and legends of the Hispanic
Southwest/La mujer del maiz: cuentos y leyendas del sudoeste
Hispano. /1994/5-6/4 KB380 . . . . **CE 398.2**

Hispanic Americans--Poetry.
CUMPIAN, C/Latino rainbow: poems about Latino Americans. /
1994/3-6/KD927 . . . . **811**
SOTO, G/Canto familiar. /1995/4-6/KE028 . . . . **811**
Neighborhood odes: poems. /1992/3-A/KE029 . . . . **811**

Hispanic Americans--Rites and ceremonies.
LANKFORD, MD/Quinceanera: a Latina's journey to womanhood. /
1994/5-6/7 KA715 . . . . **265**

Hispanic Americans--Social life and customs.
COOPER, M/Anthony Reynoso: born to rope. /1996/
3-4/4 KA841 . . . . **305.8**
KUKLIN, S/How my family lives in America. /1992/
1-3/5 KA850 . . . . **305.8**
LOMAS GARZA, C/In my family./En mi familia. /1996/
2-5/6 KA870 . . . . **306.85**

Histia, Alicia.
ANCONA, G/Earth daughter: Alicia of Acoma Pueblo. /1995/
2-4/6 KE791 . . . . **970.489**

Historians.
MCKISSACK, P/Carter G. Woodson: the father of black history. /
1991/3-6/2 KE601 . . . . **B WOODSON, C.**

Historic buildings.
LYNCH, A/Great buildings. /1996/4-6/12 KD386 . . . . . . **720.9**

History SEE ALSO Archaeology; Biography; Civilization; Discoveries (in
geography); Ethnology; Kings, queens, rulers, etc.; Middle Ages; Political
science.

History.
WORLDMARK ENCYCLOPEDIA OF THE NATIONS. 9TH ED. /
1997/A/KA389 . . . . **REF 031**

History--Periodicals.
CALLIOPE: WORLD HISTORY FOR YOUNG PEOPLE. /1990-/
4-6/KA505 . . . . **PER 050**
MUSE. /1997-/4-6/KA527 . . . . **PER 050**
SMITHSONIAN. /1970-/A/KA541 . . . . **PER 050**
TIME: THE WEEKLY NEWSMAGAZINE. /1923-/
4-A/KA548 . . . . **PER 050**

History, Modern--Miscellanea.
JONES, CF/Accidents may happen. /1996/4-A/9 KC895. . . . **609**

HIV infections.
COME SIT BY ME: AIDS EDUCATION (VIDEOCASSETTE). /1992/
K-2/KD025 . . . . **VCR 616.97**
CONVERSATION WITH MAGIC (VIDEOCASSETTE). /1992/
4-6/KD026. . . . . **VCR 616.97**
GREENBERG, L/AIDS: how it works in the body. /1992/
A/8 KD028 . . . . **616.97**
PROTECT YOURSELF: HIV/AIDS EDUCATION PROGRAM
(VIDEOCASSETTE). /1992/6-A/KD032 . . . . **VCR 616.97**

Hmong (Asian people).
CHA, D/Dia's story cloth. /1996/2-6/6 KE716 . . . . **959.404**

Hmong Americans.
CHA, D/Dia's story cloth. /1996/2-6/6 KE716 . . . . **959.404**

Hoang, Anh Chau.
HOYT-GOLDSMITH, D/Hoang Anh: a Vietnamese-American boy. /
1992/3-6/6 KA849 . . . . **305.8**

Hobbies SEE ALSO Arts and crafts; Collectors and collecting; Handicraft;
also names of hobbies e.g. Coins.

Hobbies.
BERGSTROM, JM/All the best contests for kids, 1996-1997. 5th
ed. /1996/3-6/7 KD677. **790.1**

Hobbies--History.
HANKIN, R/What was it like before television? /1995/
1-3/2 KD679 . . . . **790.1**

Hockey.
HARRIS, L/Hockey. /1994/3-6/4 KD841 . . . . **796.962**
LITKE, R/Ice hockey. /1997/3-6/8 KD843 . . . . **796.962**
MAYO, T/Illustrated rules of in-line hockey. /1996/
3-6/6 KD772 . . . . **796.21**
MCFARLANE, B/Hockey for kids: heroes, tips, and facts. /1996/
4-6/7 KD844 . . . . **796.962**

Hockey--Records.
KNAPP, R/Top 10 hockey scorers. /1994/4-6/5 KD842. . **796.962**

Hockey players.
DUPLACEY, J/Amazing forwards. /1996/4-6/6 KD838 . . **796.962**
Great goalies. /1996/4-6/6 KD839 . . . . **796.962**
Top rookies. /1996/4-6/6 KD840 . . . . **796.962**
HUGHES, ME/Mario Lemieux: beating the odds. /1996/
4-6/9 KE433 . . . . **B LEMIEUX, M.**
KNAPP, R/Top 10 hockey scorers. /1994/4-6/5 KD842. . **796.962**
SULLIVAN, MJ/Mark Messier: star center. /1997/
5-A/7 KE464 . . . . **B MESSIER, M.**

Hockey players--Canada--Biography.
CHRISTOPHER, M/On the ice with...Wayne Gretzky. /1997/
3-6/7 KE379 . . . . **B GRETZKY, W.**

Hohokam culture.
WARREN, S/Cities in the sand: the ancient civilizations of the
Southwest. /1992/5-6/8 KF064 . . . . **979**

Holes--Fiction.
MERRIAM, E/Hole story. /1995/P-1/2 KG131 . . . . **E**

Holi (Hindu festival).
KADODWALA, D/Holi. /1997/4-6/7 KA763 . . . . **294.5**

Holiday decorations.
SMOLINSKI, J/Holiday origami. /1995/3-6/KD403. . . . . . . **736**

Holidays SEE ALSO Fasts and feasts; Festivals; also names of holidays e.g.
Memorial Day.

Holidays.
BARKIN, C/Holiday handbook. /1994/5-A/7 KA413. . **REF 394.26**
BAUER, CF/Celebrations: read-aloud holiday and theme book
programs. /1985/KA342. . . . . **PROF 808.8**
CHASE, WD/Chase's calendar of annual events: special days, weeks
and months. /1958-//KA264. . . . . **PROF 394.2**
FOLKLORE OF WORLD HOLIDAYS. /1992/
4-6/KA414 . . . . **REF 394.26**

KALLEVIG, CP/Holiday folding stories: storytelling and origami together for holiday fun. /1992//KA309 . . . . **PROF 736**
PENNER, LR/Celebration: the story of American holidays. /1993/ 4-6/7 KB201 . . . . **394.26**
PERL, L/Pinatas and paper flowers, holidays of the Americas in English and Spanish/ Pinatas y flores de papel, fiestas de las Americas en ingles y espanol. /1983/4-6/6 KB202. . . . . . **394.26**
SCOTT, G/Labor Day. /1982/2-3/2 KB228 . . . . **394.264**
SMITH, D/Holidays and festivals activities. /1994/ 1-6/6 KD458 . . . . **745.594**
TUDOR, T/Time to keep: the Tasha Tudor book of holidays. /1996/ P-A/4 KB204 . . . . **394.26**

Holidays--Asia, Southeastern.
VIESTI, JF/Celebrate! in Southeast Asia. /1996/ 2-5/11 KB192 . . . . **394.2**

Holidays--Fiction.
STOCK, C/Halloween monster. /1990/P-K/2 KG574. . . . . . . **E**
ZOLOTOW, C/Over and over. /c1957/P-2/2 KG807 . . . . **E**

Holidays--Poetry.
CARNEGIE LIBRARY SCHOOL ASSOCIATION /Our holidays in poetry. /1965/5-6/KB196. . . . . **394.26**

Holidays--Songs.
JENKINS, E/Holiday times (Compact disc). /1996/ P-3/KB199 . . . . **CD 394.26**
KEEP THE SPIRIT (SOUND RECORDING CASSETTE). /1989/ K-6/KD634 . . . . **SRC 789.3**

Holidays--South Asia.
VIESTI, JF/Celebrate! in South Asia. /1996/2-5/11 KB191 . . **394.2**

Holidays--United States.
AMERICAN BOOK OF DAYS. 3RD ED. /1978/ 4-6/KA412 . . . . **REF 394.2**
Holland SEE Netherlands.

Hollerith, Herman.
NOONAN, J/Nineteenth-century inventors. /1992/ 5-6/7 KC897 . . . . **609**

Holocaust, Jewish (1939-1945).
ADLER, DA/We remember the holocaust. /c1989, 1995/ 5-6/8 KE656 . . . . **940.53**
GREENFELD, H/Hidden children. /1993/A/7 KE657 . . **940.53**
MELTZER, M/Never to forget: the Jews of the Holocaust. /c1976/ A/7 KE674 . . . . **940.54**
Rescue: the story of how Gentiles saved Jews in the Holocaust. / 1988/5-A/7 KE661 . . . . **940.53**
ROGASKY, B/Smoke and ashes: the story of the Holocaust. /1988/ A/8 KE664 . . . . **940.53**

Holocaust, Jewish (1939-1945)--Biography.
ADLER, DA/Hilde and Eli: children of the Holocaust. /1994/ 4-6/5 KE655 . . . . **940.53**

Holocaust, Jewish (1939-1945)--Fiction.
ACKERMAN, K/Night crossing. /1994/3-4/8 KG812 . . . . . . **Fic**
ORLEV, U/Island on Bird Street. /1983/5-A/6 KH566 . . . . . . **Fic**
RICHTER, HP/Friedrich. /c1970, 1987/5-A/5 KH633 . . . . **Fic**
SCHNUR, S/Shadow children. /1994/4-A/7 KH681 . . . . **Fic**

Holocaust, Jewish (1939-1945)--France--Paris--Fiction.
HOESTLANDT, J/Star of fear, star of hope. /1995/ 3-5/5 KH268 . . . . **Fic**

Holocaust, Jewish (1939-1945)--Netherlands--Amsterdam.
ADLER, DA/Picture book of Anne Frank. /1993/ 3-4/5 KE351 . . . . **CE B FRANK, A.**
VAN DER ROL, R/Anne Frank, beyond the diary: a photographic remembrance. /1993/6-A/7 KE353. . . . . **B FRANK, A.**

Holocaust, Jewish (1939-1945)--Netherlands--Amsterdam--Personal narratives.
FRANK, A/Diary of a young girl. /c1967/ 4-6/6 KE352 . . . . **B FRANK, A.**

Holocaust, Jewish (1939-1945)--Personal narratives.
ADLER, DA/We remember the holocaust. /c1989, 1995/ 5-6/8 KE656 . . . . **940.53**
GREENFELD, H/Hidden children. /1993/A/7 KE657 . . . . . **940.53**
PETTIT, J/Place to hide. /1993/5-A/7 KE663 . . . . **940.53**
ROSENBERG, MB/Hiding to survive: stories of Jewish children rescued from the Holocaust. /1994/A/6 KE665 . . . . **940.53**
SIEGAL, A/Upon the head of the goat: a childhood in Hungary 1939-1944. /1981/4-6/8 KE691 . . . . **CE 947.084**

Holocaust, Jewish (1939-1945)--Poland.
MOCHIZUKI, K/Passage to freedom: the Sugihara story. /1997/ 3-6/4 KE662 . . . . **940.53**

Holocaust, Jewish (1939-1945)--Poland--Fiction.
ORLEV, U/Man from the other side. /1991/5-A/6 KH567 . . . . **Fic**

Holocaust survivors.
GREENFELD, H/Hidden children. /1993/A/7 KE657 . . . . . **940.53**
ROSENBERG, MB/Hiding to survive: stories of Jewish children rescued from the Holocaust. /1994/A/6 KE665 . . . . **940.53**

Holocaust survivors--Fiction.
ADLER, DA/One yellow daffodil: a Hanukkah story. /1995/ 3-5/4 KG818 . . . . **Fic**
VOS, I/Anna is still here. /1993/5-A/4 KH834 . . . . **Fic**
Home SEE ALSO Apartment houses; Dwellings; Houses; Housing.

Home--Fiction.
BUNTING, E/Going home. /1996/1-3/2 KF302 . . . . **E**
FARMER, N/Warm Place. /1995/4-A/3 KH110 . . . . **Fic**
HAMILTON, V/M.C. Higgins, the great. /1974/A/4 KH216 . . . **Fic**
Home economics SEE ALSO Consumer education; Cookery; Finance, Personal; Food; Furniture; Nutrition; Sewing; Shopping.

Home schooling.
BROSTROM, DC/Guide to homeschooling for librarians. /1995/ /KA065. . . . . **PROF 026.371**
KENYON, MP/Home schooling from scratch. /1996/ /KA175. . . . . **PROF 371.04**
LURIE, J/Allison's story: a book about homeschooling. /1996/ 2-5/2 KD303 . . . . **649**

Homeless persons.
HUBBARD, J/Lives turned upside down: homeless children in their own words and photographs. /1996/3-6/4 KB009. . . . . . . **362.5**
WOLF, B/Homeless. /1995/4-6/4 KB010 . . . . **362.5**

Homeless persons--Fiction.
BUNTING, E/Fly away home. /1991/K-3/2 KF300 . . . . **E**
DOHERTY, B/Street child. /1994/5-A/6 KH078 . . . . **Fic**
FOX, P/Monkey island. /1991/6-A/6 KH137 . . . . **Fic**
GUTHRIE, D/Rose for Abby. /1988/2-4/5 KF654. . . . . **E**
MCGOVERN, A/Lady in the box. /1997/1-3/2 KG103 . . . . . . **E**
WILSON, J/Elsa, star of the shelter! /1996/4-6/5 KH868 . . . . **Fic**

Homeless persons--Literary collections.
HOME. /1992/K-6/KD900. . . . . **810.8**

Homeless students.
TOWER, CC/Homeless students. /1989//KA183. . . **PROF 371.826**

Homeless students--Education.
TOWER, CC/Homeless students. /1989//KA183. . . **PROF 371.826**

Homesickness--Fiction.
BAKER, B/Staying with Grandmother. /1994/1-3/1 KF184 . . . . . **E**
SAY, A/Grandfather's journey. /1993/2-4/5 KG397 . . . . **E**

Homework.
JAMES, E/How to write a great school report. /1983/ 4-6/7 KB088 . . . . **371.302**
RADENCICH, MC/How to help your child with homework: every caring parent's guide to encouraging good study habits and ending the Homework Wars: for parents of children ages 6-13. Rev. and updated ed. /1997//KA181 . . . . **PROF 371.3**
ZEMAN, A/Everything you need to know about math homework. / 1994/4-10/7 KB934 . . . . **510**

Homing pigeons.
NOFSINGER, R/Pigeons and doves. /1992/4-6/4 KC696 . . **598.6**
Homonyms--English language SEE English language--Homonyms.

Homosexuality.
GREENBERG, KE/Zack's story: growing up with same-sex parents. / 1996/4-6/4 KA877 . . . . **306.874**

Honduran Americans.
SCHWARTZ, P/Carolyn's story: a book about an adopted girl. / 1996/3-6/6 KB014 . . . . **362.73**

Honesty.
CHEATING, LYING AND STEALING (VIDEOCASSETTE). /1993/ 5-6/KA669 . . . . **VCR 177**
CRARY, E/Finders, keepers? /1987/3-6/2 KA670 . . . . **177**
KINCHER, J/First honest book about lies. /1992/ /KA159 . . . . **PROF 177**
WEISS, AE/Lies, deception and truth. /1988/6-A/9 KA671 . . **177**

Honesty--Fiction.
BATEMAN, T/Ring of Truth: an original Irish tale. /1997/ 1-3/5 KF213 . . . . **E**
BAWDEN, N/Humbug. /1992/5-A/5 KG891. . . . . **Fic**
BROWN, MT/True Francine. /1987/1-2/1 KF282 . . . . **E**
BUNTING, E/Day's work. /1994/1-3/2 KF298 . . . . **E**
HAVILL, J/Jamaica's find. /1986/K-2/2 KF682. . . . . **E**
HAWKINS, L/Figment, your dog, speaking. /1991/ 5-A/4 KH229 . . . . **Fic**
RYAN, ME/Trouble with perfect. /1995/6-A/3 KH659. . . . . . . **Fic**
WARNER, S/Dog years. /1995/4-6/3 KH840 . . . . **Fic**

Honey.
COLE, J/Magic School Bus inside a beehive. /1996/ 2-4/2 KC570 . . . . **595.79**
GIBBONS, G/Honey makers. /1997/3-5/6 KC573 . . . . . . **595.79**
MICUCCI, C/Life and times of the honeybee. /1995/ 4-6/6 KC576 . . . . **595.79**
Honeybee SEE ALSO Bees; Brazilian honeybee.

Honeybee.
COLE, J/Magic School Bus inside a beehive. /1996/ 2-4/2 KC570 . . . . **595.79**

FISCHER-NAGEL, H/Life of the honeybee. /1986/
4-6/7 KC572 . . . . **595.79**
GIBBONS, G/Honey makers. /1997/3-5/6 KC573 . . **595.79**
JOHNSON, SA/Beekeeper's year. /1994/5-6/6 KD240. . . **638**
LIFE CYCLE OF THE HONEYBEE (VIDEOCASSETTE). /c1976,
1986/3-6/KC575 . . . . **VCR 595.79**
MICUCCI, C/Life and times of the honeybee. /1995/
4-6/6 KC576 . . . . **595.79**
Hopi Indians.
SNEVE, V/Hopis. /1995/4-6/7 KE771 . . . . **970.3**
Hopi Indians--Folklore.
COURLANDER, H/People of the short blue corn: tales and legends
of the Hopi Indians. /c1970, 1996/1-A/5 KB278. . . . . . . **398.2**
SCHECTER, E/Warrior maiden: a Hopi legend. /1992/
1-2/2 KB485 . . . . **398.22**
Hopi Indians--Social life and customs.
DEWEY, JO/Rattlesnake dance: true tales, mysteries, and rattlesnake
ceremonies. /1997/4-6/4 KC634 . . . . **597.96**
Hopkins, Lee Bennett.
HOPKINS, LB/Been to yesterdays: poems of a life. /1995/
3-6/KD953 . . . . **811**
Horner, John R.
LESSEM, D/Jack Horner: living with dinosaurs. /1994/
5-A/8 KE391 . . . . **B HORNER, J.**
Horns.
SELSAM, ME/First look at animals with horns. /1989/
1-3/2 KC792 . . . . **599.64**
Horror--Folklore.
SCHWARTZ, A/In a dark, dark room and other scary stories. /
1984/K-3/1 KB693 . . . . **398.25**
Horror stories.
ALFRED HITCHCOCK'S SUPERNATURAL TALES OF TERROR AND
SUSPENSE. /c1973, 1983/A/6 KG842. . . . . **Fic**
BROWN, RS/Queen of the cold-blooded tales. /1993/
6-A/6 KG933 . . . . **Fic**
CARUSONE, A/Don't open the door after the sun goes down: tales
of the real and unreal. /1994/4-6/4 KG982 . . . . **Fic**
GOROG, J/In a creepy, creepy place and other scary stories. /
1996/4-6/4 KH183 . . . . **Fic**
In a messy, messy room. /1990/4-6/6 KH184 . . . . **Fic**
Please do not touch: a collection of stories. /c1993, 1995/
6-A/7 KH185 . . . . **Fic**
GRAVEYARD TALES (SOUND RECORDING CASSETTE). /1984/
3-6/KH193. . . . . **SRC Fic**
MAHY, M/Horrible story and others (Talking book). /1992/
3-A/KH452 . . . . **TB Fic**
MCKISSACK, P/Dark-thirty: Southern tales of the supernatural. /
1992/5-A/6 KH491 . . . . **Fic**
OXFORD BOOK OF SCARYTALES. /1992/6-A/7 KH569 . . . . . **Fic**
SPOOKY STORIES FOR A DARK AND STORMY NIGHT. /1994/
2-4/4 KB695 . . . . **398.25**
TREASURY OF SPOOKY STORIES. /1992/4-A/6 KH804 . . . . . **Fic**
WHITCHER, S/Real mummies don't bleed: friendly tales for October
nights. /1993/4-6/5 KH849 . . . . **Fic**
YOUNG, R/Head on the high road: ghost stories from the
Southwest /1993/4-6/KB698. . . . . **SRC 398.25**
Horror stories--History and criticism.
RAINEY, R/Monster factory. /1993/3-6/8 KD895. . . . . **809.3**
Horse breeds.
CLUTTON-BROCK, J/Horses. /1992/4-6/8 KD199 . . . . . . **636.1**
Horse racing--Fiction.
FARLEY, W/Black Stallion. /c1941, 1994/4-6/5 KH105 . . . . . **Fic**
Man O'War. /c1962/5-6/6 KH106 . . . . **Fic**
HENRY, M/Born to trot. /c1950, 1993/5-A/5 KH241 . . . . . . **Fic**
Horsemanship.
COLE, J/Riding Silver Star. /1996/3-5/2 KD854 . . . . **798.2**
EVANS, J/Horseback riding. /1992/4-A/6 KD855 . . . . **798.2**
GREEN, L/Young rider. /1993/3-8/8 KD856 . . . . **798.2**
HAAS, J/Safe horse, safe rider: a young rider's guide to
responsible horsekeeping. /1994/5-6/6 KD200 . . . . **636.1**
LITTLE HORSE THAT COULD: THE CONNEMARA STALLION: ERIN
GO BRAGH (VIDEOCASSETTE). /1996/2-6/KD857 . . **VCR 798.2**
Horsemanship--Fiction.
HENRY, M/White stallion of Lipizza. /c1964, 1994/
4-6/6 KH246 . . . . **Fic**
Horses SEE ALSO Ponies; names of specific breeds of horses e.g. Arabian
horse.
Horses.
BUDD, J/Horses. /1995/4-6/7 KD198 . . . . **636.1**
CLUTTON-BROCK, J/Horses. /1992/4-6/8 KD199 . . . . . . **636.1**
COLE, J/Horse's body. /1981/4-6/7 KC805 . . . . **599.665**
Riding Silver Star. /1996/3-5/2 KD854 . . . . **798.2**
EVANS, J/Horseback riding. /1992/4-A/6 KD855 . . . . **798.2**

HAAS, J/Safe horse, safe rider: a young rider's guide to
responsible horsekeeping. /1994/5-6/6 KD200 . . . . **636.1**
HONDA, T/Wild horse winter. /1992/K-3/4 KC806 . . . . **599.665**
ISENBART, H/Birth of a foal. /1986/3-6/5 KD201 . . . . **636.1**
LITTLE HORSE THAT COULD: THE CONNEMARA STALLION: ERIN
GO BRAGH (VIDEOCASSETTE). /1996/2-6/KD857 . . **VCR 798.2**
MELTZER, M/Hold your horses: a feedbag full of fact and fable. /
1995/5-6/7 KD202 . . . . **636.1**
PATENT, DH/Appaloosa horses. /1988/4-6/7 KD203 . . . . **636.1**
Where the wild horses roam. /1989/5-6/7 KD257 . . . . . . **639.9**
POSELL, E/Horses. /1981/1-3/4 KD204 . . . . **636.1**
STEWART, GB/Appaloosa horse. /1995/4-5/6 KD205 . . . . **636.1**
Arabian horse. /1995/4-6/5 KD206 . . . . **636.1**
Quarter horse. /1995/4-6/5 KD207 . . . . **636.1**
Thoroughbred horse: born to run. /1995/4-6/5 KD208 . . . **636.1**
VISUAL DICTIONARY OF THE HORSE. /1994/
5-A/7 KD209 . . . . **636.1**
Horses--Anatomy.
VISUAL DICTIONARY OF THE HORSE. /1994/
5-A/7 KD209 . . . . **636.1**
Horses--Fiction.
ADLER, CS/That horse Whiskey! /1994/4-6/5 KG814. . . . . . **Fic**
BAGNOLD, E/National Velvet. /c1935, 1985/4-A/5 KG874 . . **Fic**
BAKER, KL/Seneca. /1997/K-2/1 KF185 . . . . **E**
BLANC, ES/Berchick. /1989/3-5-5 KG901 . . . . **E**
CHRISTIANSEN, C/Ice horse. /1993/2-3/6 KF391 . . . . **E**
FARLEY, W/Black Stallion. /c1941, 1994/4-6/5 KH105 . . . . . **Fic**
GOBLE, P/Girl who loved wild horses. /1978/K-3/4 KF628 . **CE E**
GREENE, CC/Beat the turtle drum. /c1976, 1994/
5-6/4 KH198 . . . . **Fic**
HAAS, J/Be well, Beware. /1996/3-5/2 KH208 . . . . **Fic**
Beware the mare. /1993/3-5/4 KH209 . . . . **Fic**
Sugaring. /1996/K-2/2 KF657 . . . . **E**
Uncle Daney's way. /1994/4-6/4 KH210 . . . . **Fic**
HEILBRONER, J/Robert the rose horse. /1962/K-2/1 KF696 . . . **E**
HENRY, M/Born to trot. /c1950, 1993/5-A/5 KH241 . . . . . . **Fic**
King of the wind. /c1948, 1990/4-6/5 KH243 . . . . **CE Fic**
Mustang, wild spirit of the West. /c1966, 1992/
5-6/5 KH245 . . . . **Fic**
HICKOX, R/Per and the Dala horse. /1995/1-3/6 KF724 . . . . . **E**
HOFF, S/Horse in Harry's room. /c1970/K-2/2 KF757 . . . . . . **E**
LAWSON, R/Mr. Revere and I: being an account of certain
episodes in the career of Paul Revere, Esq., as recently revealed by
his horse, Scheherazada, late pride of His Royal Majesty's 14th
Regiment of Foot. /c1953/5-6/7 KH389 . . . . **Fic**
NABB, M/Enchanted horse. /1993/4-6/7 KH525 . . . . **Fic**
PEET, B/Cowardly Clyde. /1979/K-2/6 KG225 . . . . **E**
ROUNDS, G/Once we had a horse. /1996/K-2/3 KG358 . . . . . **E**
RUEPP, K/Midnight Rider. /1995/3-5/2 KH657 . . . . **Fic**
SEWELL, A/Black Beauty: the autobiography of a horse. /1997/
5-7/7 KH702 . . . . **Fic**
SHUB, E/White stallion. /1982/1-3/2 KG497 . . . . **E**
WIELER, DJ/To the mountains by morning. /1996/
4-6/5 KH856 . . . . **Fic**
YOLEN, J/Sky dogs. /1990/2-3/6 KG780 . . . . **E**
Horses--Folklore.
OTSUKA, Y/Suho and the white horse: a legend of Mongolia
(Videocassette). /1981/3-4/KB626 . . . . **VCR 398.24**
RODANAS, K/Dance of the sacred circle: a Native American tale. /
1994/3-4/5 KB639 . . . . **398.24**
Horses in art.
ROALF, P/Horses. /1992/5-A/8 KD480 . . . . **758**
Horseshoe crabs.
DAY, N/Horseshoe crab. /1992/5-6/7 KC524 . . . . **595.4**
Hospitals SEE ALSO Nurses; Physicians.
Hospitals.
HOSPITAL (VIDEOCASSETTE). /1990/1-4/KA995 . . . **VCR 362.1**
Hospitals--Fiction.
REY, M/Curious George goes to the hospital. /c1966/
P-2/2 KG329 . . . . **E**
WABER, B/Lyle and the birthday party. /c1966/P-2/3 KG669 . . **E**
WILD, M/Going home. /1993/1-3/3 KG716 . . . . **E**
Hot air balloons.
BELLVILLE, CW/Flying in a hot air balloon. /1993/
4-6/7 KD852 . . . . **797.5**
FINE, JC/Free spirits in the sky. /1994/2-5/7 KD853 . . . . . **797.5**
Hot air balloons--History.
CURLEE, L/Ships of the air. /1996/5-6/8 KD107 . . . . . . **629.133**
Hot peppers.
KING, E/Chile fever: a celebration of peppers. /1995/
5-6/6 KD267 . . . . **641.3**
Hotels, motels, etc.--Fiction.
CUSHMAN, D/Aunt Eater's mystery vacation. /1992/
1-3/2 KF441 . . . . **E**

FLEISCHMAN, P/Half-a-Moon Inn. /c1980, 1991/6/7 KH117 . . **Fic**
GILSON, J/Soccer circus. /1993/3-5/5 KH169 . . . . **Fic**
HOBAN, J/Buzby. /1992/K-2/2 KF731 . . . . **CE E**
   Buzby to the rescue. /1995/K-2/2 KF732 . . . . **E**

House cleaning--Fiction.
CHRISTELOW, E/Five little monkeys with nothing to do. /1996/
P-2/2 KF385 . . . . **E**

House construction.
BARTON, B/Building a house. /1981/P-2/2 KD355 . . . . **690**
WILKINSON, P/Building. /1995/5-6/7 KD360 . . . . **690**

House furnishings--Pictorial works.
100 WORDS ABOUT MY HOUSE. /1988/P-3/KD296 . . . . . **645**
House plants SEE ALSO Indoor gardening.

Housefly.
FISCHER-NAGEL, H/Housefly. /1990/5-6/7 KC556 . . . . . **595.77**

Household employees--Fiction.
PARISH, P/Thank you, Amelia Bedelia. Rev. ed. /1993/
1-3/2 KG218 . . . . **CE E**

Houses--Fiction.
BURTON, VL/Little house. /c1942, 1978/K-2/2 KF320. . . . . **CE E**

Houston, Sam.
FRITZ, J/Make way for Sam Houston. /1986/
6/7 KE392. . . . . **B HOUSTON, S.**

Hua, Mu-lan (Legendary character).
CHIN, C/China's bravest girl: the legend of Hua Mu Lan = [Chin
kuo ying hsiung Hua Mu-lan]. /1993/3-5/4 KB430. . . . . **398.22**

Hubble Space Telescope.
SCOTT, E/Adventure in space: the flight to fix the Hubble. /1995/
A/7 KC006 . . . . **522**

Hudson River (N.Y. and N.J.).
ANCONA, G/Riverkeeper. /1990/4-6/7 KA958 . . . . **333.91**

Hudson River (N.Y. and N.J.)--Description and travel.
LOURIE, P/Hudson River: an adventure from the mountains to the
sea. /1992/4-6/6 KE192 . . . . **917.47**

Huerta, Dolores.
DE RUIZ, DC/Causa: the migrant farmworkers' story. /1993/
4-6/6 KA944 . . . . **331.88**

Hughes, Arizona Houston.
HOUSTON, G/My great-aunt Arizona. /1992/
3-5/4 KE393 . . . . **B HUGHES, A.**

Hughes, Langston.
OSOFSKY, A/Free to dream: the making of a poet: Langston
Hughes. /1996/6-A/7 KE395 . . . . **B HUGHES, L.**

Hughes, Langston--Childhood and youth.
COOPER, F/Coming home: from the life of Langston Hughes. /
1994/3-5/6 KE394 . . . . **B HUGHES, L.**

Huichol Indians--Folklore.
BERNHARD, E/Tree that rains: the flood myth of the Huichol Indians
of Mexico. /1994/3-4/5 KB699. . . . . **398.26**

Hull House (Chicago, Ill.)--History.
MCPHERSON, SS/Peace and bread: the story of Jane Addams. /
1993/4-6/5 KE228 . . . . **B ADDAMS, J.**

Human anatomy.
ALLISON, L/Blood and guts: a working guide to your own insides. /
c1976/4-6/4 KC912 . . . . **612**
FEELINGS: INSIDE, OUTSIDE, UPSIDE DOWN (VIDEOCASSETTE).
/1992/6/KC946 . . . . **VCR 612.6**
FORNARI, G/Inside the body: a lift-the-flap book. /1996/
5-6/7 KC902 . . . . **611**
HARRIS, RH/It's perfectly normal: a book about changing bodies,
growing up, sex, and /1994/5-6/6 KC949 . . . . **612.6**
LOOK WHO'S GROWING UP (VIDEOCASSETTE). /1997/
5-6/KC920. . . . . **VCR 612**
MARKLE, S/Outside and inside you. /1991/4-6/4 KC921 . . . **612**
MY BODY. /1991/1-4/2 KC922 . . . . **612**
NEW, IMPROVED ME: UNDERSTANDING BODY CHANGES
(VIDEOCASSETTE). /1991/5-6/KC953 . . . . **VCR 612.6**
PARKER, S/Body atlas. /1993/A/7 KC905 . . . . **611**
THEN ONE YEAR. 2ND ED. (VIDEOCASSETTE). /1992/
5-6/KC957. . . . . **VCR 612.6**
VISUAL DICTIONARY OF THE HUMAN BODY. /1991/
4-6/8 KC907 . . . . **611**
WALKER, R/Children's atlas of the human body: actual size bones,
muscles, and organs in full color. /1994/5-6/6 KC908 . . . . . **611**
YOUR BODY: CIRCULATORY AND RESPIRATORY SYSTEMS
(VIDEOCASSETTE). /1988/5-6/KC931 . . . . **VCR 612**
YOUR BODY: MUSCULAR AND SKELETAL SYSTEMS
(VIDEOCASSETTE). /1994/5-6/KC961 . . . . **VCR 612.7**

Human anatomy--Dictionaries.
RICHARDSON, J/Science dictionary of the human body. /1992/
4-6/7 KC906 . . . . **611**

Human anatomy--Software.
STV: HUMAN BODY (VIDEODISC). /1992/4-A/KC926. . **VD 612**

ULTIMATE HUMAN BODY (CD-ROM). /1996/
4-A/KC927 . . . . **CDR 612**

Human ecology.
MCLAIN, G/Indian way: learning to communicate with Mother
Earth. /1990/2-6/6 KE750 . . . . **970.1**
WHAT ARE ECOSYSTEMS? (VIDEOCASSETTE). /1975/
4-6/KC299 . . . . **VCR 577**

Human geography.
AJMERA, M/Children from Australia to Zimbabwe: a photographic
journey around the world. /1997/2-5/7 KA822 . . . . **305.23**

Human physiology.
GABB, M/Human body. /c1991, 1992/5-6/6 KC918 . . . . . . **612**
GANERI, A/Funny bones. /1997/3-6/6 KC903 . . . . **611**
   What's inside us? /1995/5-6/8 KC919 . . . . **612**
MY BODY. /1991/1-4/2 KC922 . . . . **612**
PARKER, S/Body and how it works. /1992/A/6 KC923 . . . . . **612**
WHAT IS A BELLYBUTTON?: FIRST QUESTIONS AND ANSWERS
ABOUT THE HUMAN BODY. /1993/P-K/2 KC929 . . **612**

Human physiology--Experiments.
VANCLEAVE, JP/Janice VanCleave's the human body for every kid:
easy activities that make learning science fun. /1995/
5-6/8 KC928 . . . . **612**

Human physiology--Software.
STV: HUMAN BODY (VIDEODISC). /1992/4-A/KC926. . **VD 612**
ULTIMATE HUMAN BODY (CD-ROM). /1996/
4-A/KC927 . . . . **CDR 612**
WHAT IS A BELLYBUTTON?: FUN AND INTERACTIVE
QUESTIONS AND ANSWERS ABOUT THE /1994/
2-6/KC930. . . . . **CDR 612**

Human relations--Fiction.
MATHIS, SB/Hundred penny box. /1975/4-6/4 KH461 . . . **CE Fic**

Human rights.
JACOBS, WJ/Great lives: human rights. /1990/
6-A/7 KA900 . . . . **323**

Human rights--Songs and music.
ROGERS, S/What can one little person do? (Sound recording
cassette). /1992/P-2/KD654 . . . . **SRC 789.3**

Human-alien encounters.
KETTELKAMP, L/ETs and UFOs: are they real? /1996/
4-6/8 KA558 . . . . **001.9**

Human-animal communication.
PATTERSON, F/Koko's kitten. /1985/3-5/6 KC877. . . . . **599.884**

Human-animal communications--Fiction.
O'ROURKE, F/Burton and Stanley. /1996/3-5/6 KH568 . . . . . **Fic**

Human-animal relationships.
CALMENSON, S/Rosie, a visiting dog's story. /1994/
3-6/2 KD216 . . . . **636.7**

Human-animal relationships--Fiction.
MYERS, WD/Story of the three kingdoms. /1995/1-3/3 KG165 . **E**

Hummingbirds.
MURRAY, P/Hummingbirds. /1993/3-5/6 KC700 . . . . **598.7**
TYRRELL, EQ/Hummingbirds: jewels in the sky. /1992/
5-6/5 KC703 . . . . **598.7**

Hummingbirds--Fiction.
CZERNECKI, S/Hummingbirds' gift. /1994/1-3/7 KF443 . . . . **E**

Humorists.
COX, C/Mark Twain: America's humorist, dreamer, prophet. /1995/
6-A/8 KE579 . . . . **B TWAIN, M.**
QUACKENBUSH, R/Mark Twain? What kind of name is that?: a
story of Samuel Langhorne Clemens. /1984/
6/8 KE580 . . . . **B TWAIN, M.**
SCHOTT, JA/Will Rogers. /1996/1-3/2 KE519 . . **B ROGERS, W.**

Humorous poetry.
CIARDI, J/Monster den: or look what happened at my house - and
to it. /c1966, 1991/3-6/KD922 . . . . **811**
   You know who. /c1964, 1991/3-5/KD923 . . . . **811**
FLORIAN, D/Beast feast. /1994/K-3/KD935 . . . . **811**
   In the swim: poems and paintings. /1997/1-3/KD937 . . . . . **811**
FOR LAUGHING OUT LOUD: POEMS TO TICKLE YOUR
FUNNYBONE. /1991/K-5/KE058 . . . . **811.008**
FOR LAUGHING OUT LOUDER: MORE POEMS TO TICKLE YOUR
FUNNYBONE. /1995/K-5/KE059 . . . . **811.008**
KENNEDY, XJ/Brats. /1986/3-6/KD961 . . . . **811**
   Drat these brats! /1993/3-6/KD962. . . . . **811**
   Fresh brats. /1990/3-6/KD964 . . . . **811**
   Ghastlies, goops & pincushions. /1989/4-A/KD965 . . . . . **811**
KORMAN, G/D- poems of Jeremy Bloom: a collection of poems
about school, homework, and life /1992/4-A/KD966 . . . . . . **811**
LANSKY, B/You're invited to Bruce Lansky's poetry party! /1996/
3-6/KD968. . . . . **811**
LEAR, E/Daffy down dillies: silly limericks. /1992/K-A/KE103 . **821**
   Owl and the Pussy-cat and other nonsense poems. /1995/
3-6/KE106. . . . . **821**

LEE, D/Dinosaur dinner (with a slice of alligator pie): favorite
  poems. /1997/K-3/KD970 811
PRELUTSKY, J/Baby uggs are hatching. /1982/1-3/KE000 . . . 811
  Beneath a blue umbrella. /1990/K-2/KE001. 811
  New kid on the block. /1984/2-6/KE010 . . . . CE 811
  Pizza the size of the sun: poems. /1996/K-A/KE012. 811
  Rainy rainy Saturday. /1980/1-3/KE013. 811
  Rolling Harvey down the hill. /1980/1-4/KE015 . . . . CE 811
  Something big has been here (Talking book). /1991/
  K-4/KE016. . . . . TB 811
READY...SET...READ--AND LAUGH!: A FUNNY TREASURY FOR
  BEGINNING READERS. /1995/K-2/KD902 . . . . 810.8
SILVERSTEIN, S/Falling up: poems and drawings. /1996/
  P-A/KE024. 811
  Light in the attic. /1981/P-A/KE025. 811
  Where the sidewalk ends: the poems and drawings of Shel
  Silverstein. /c1974/P-A/KE026. 811
VIORST, J/If I were in charge of the world and other worries. /
  1981/2-4/KE037. 811
  Sad underwear and other complications: more poems for children
  and their parents. /1995/2-4/KE038 811
WALKING THE BRIDGE OF YOUR NOSE. /1995/
  2-4/KE113. . . . . 821.008

Humorous poetry--Collections.
KIDS PICK THE FUNNIEST POEMS. /1991/3-6/KE068 . . 811.008
YOURS TILL BANANA SPLITS: 201 AUTOGRAPH RHYMES. /
  1995/3-6/KD894 . . . . 808.88

Humorous poetry--Software.
NEW KID ON THE BLOCK (CD-ROM). /1993/
  K-A/KD995 . . . . CDR 811

Humorous songs.
BETHIE /Bethie's really silly songs about animals (Sound recording
  cassette). /1993/K-2/KD607 . . . . SRC 789.3
HARLEY, B/Lunchroom tales: a natural history of the cafetorium
  (Sound recording cassette). /1996/2-4/KD615 . . . . . . SRC 789.3
JACK, D/Dance in your pants: great songs for little kids to dance to
  (Sound recording /1988/K-3/KD620. . . . . SRC 789.3
  David Jack... live!: Makin' music, makin' friends (Videocassette). /
  1991/P-2/KD621 . . . . VCR 789.3
  Gotta hop (Sound recording cassette). /1990/
  K-3/KD622 . . . . SRC 789.3
LATE LAST NIGHT (SOUND RECORDING CASSETTE). /1984/
  P-2/KD635. . . . . SRC 789.3
ON THE ROAD AGAIN (SOUND RECORDING CASSETTE). /
  1992/K-4/KD640 . . . . SRC 789.3
POLISAR, BL/Family concert (Compact disc). /1993/
  1-6/KD648. . . . . CD 789.3
  Old dogs, new tricks (Sound recording cassette). /1993/
  P-3/KD649. . . . . SRC 789.3

Humorous stories.
AHLBERG, A/Giant baby. /1994/3-5/7 KG820 . . . . Fic
ALEXANDER, L/Fortune-tellers. /1992/2-5/5 KG834 . . . . Fic
ALLARD, H/Miss Nelson is missing. /1977/1-3/3 KF151 . . . CE E
  Stupids step out. /1974/K-2/5 KF152 . . . . E
ANDERSON, PP/Time for bed, the babysitter said. /1987/
  P-2/1 KF157 . . . . E
ARNOLD, T/No jumping on the bed! /1987/P-3/5 KF167 . . . . E
ATWATER, R/Mr. Popper's penguins. /c1938/
  3-5/4 KG854 . . . . CE Fic
AVI /History of Helpless Harry: to which is added a variety of
  amusing, 1995/5-A/7 KG859 . . . . Fic
BALL, D/Emily Eyefinger. /1992/1-3/2 KG876 . . . . Fic
BANNERMAN, H/Story of Little Babaji. /1996/K-2/2 KF195 . . . E
BLUME, J/Fudge-a-mania. /1990/4-6/3 KG909 . . . . CE Fic
  Otherwise known as Sheila the Great. /1972/4-6/4 KG912 . . Fic
  Superfudge. /1980/2-4/2 KG913 . . . . CE Fic
  Tales of a fourth grade nothing. /1972/2-4/3 KG914 . . . CE Fic
BRIDWELL, N/Clifford the big red dog. /c1963, 1985/
  P-2/1 KF264 . . . . CE E
BROWN, J/Flat Stanley. /c1964, 1989/2-4/5 KG931 . . . . . Fic
BROWN, MT/Arthur's nose. /c1976/K-2/2 KF276 . . . . . . CE E
BUSSER, M/King Bobble. /1996/2-3/2 KG953 . . . . Fic
BUTTERWORTH, O/Enormous egg. /c1956/3-5/4 KG955 . . . . Fic
BYARS, BC/Bingo Brown and the language of love. /1989/
  5-A/5 KG957 . . . . Fic
CHARLES, VM/Hey! What's that sound? /1994/P-1/1 KF379 . . . E
COLE, J/Giant's toe. /1986/P-2/1 KF407. . . . . E
CONFORD, E/Frog Princess of Pelham. /1997/4-A/3 KH019 . . Fic
CORBALIS, J/Porcellus, the flying pig. /1988/2-4/5 KH029 . . . Fic
CORBETT, S/Lemonade trick. /1960/4-5/4 KH030 . . . . Fic
DAHL, R/Matilda. /1988/5-A/7 KH056. . . . . Fic
DE PAOLA, T/Tom. /1993/K-2/2 KF480 . . . . E
DEXTER, C/Gertie's green thumb. /1995/3-5/4 KH073 . . . . . Fic
DICKINSON, P/Chuck and Danielle. /1996/4-6/7 KH076. . . . . Fic

DUFFEY, B/Virtual Cody. /1997/1-4/2 KH088 . . . . Fic
EGAN, T/Burnt toast on Davenport Street. /1997/1-3/2 KF514 . E
EHRLICH, A/Parents in the pigpen, pigs in the tub. /1993/
  K-2/6 KF521 . . . . E
ENDERLE, JR/What would Mama do? /1995/K-2/2 KF526 . . . . E
FIENBERG, A/Wiggy and Boa. /c1988, 1990/5-6/7 KH113. . . Fic
FLEISCHMAN, S/By the Great Horn Spoon! /c1963/
  4-6/4 KH119 . . . . Fic
  Chancy and the Grand Rascal. /c1966, 1997/4-6/5 KH120 . . Fic
  McBroom's wonderful one-acre farm: three tall tales. /1992/
  3-6/4 KH124 . . . . Fic
  Mr. Mysterious and Company. /c1962, 1997/3-6/6 KH126 . . Fic
FLEMING, I/Chitty Chitty Bang Bang: the magical car. /c1964,
  1989/5-6/7 KH128 . . . . Fic
GANNETT, RS/My father's dragon. /c1948, 1986/
  3-5/6 KH149 . . . . Fic
GANTOS, J/Heads or tails: stories from the sixth grade. /1994/
  5-A/4 KH150 . . . . Fic
GAUTHIER, G/My life among the aliens. /1996/4-6/5 KH154 . Fic
GELLMAN, M/God's mailbox: more stories about stories in the
  Bible. /1996/4-6/6 KA678 . . . . 221.9
GERINGER, L/Three hat day. /1985/P-3/2 KF609 . . . . E
GIFALDI, D/Gregory, Maw, and the Mean One. /1992/
  5-A/7 KH163 . . . . Fic
GILSON, J/Hobie Hanson, you're weird. /1987/3-5/6 KH168. . Fic
GLEITZMAN, M/Misery guts. /1993/5-A/7 KH174. . . . . Fic
GRAHAME, K/Reluctant dragon. /c1938/3-6/7 KH187 . . . CE Fic
  Reluctant dragon. /1983/3-6/6 KH188. . . . . CE Fic
GRAVES, R/Big green book. /c1962, 1990/3-6/4 KH192 . . . . Fic
GREENE, JD/What his father did. /1992/2-4/5 KB305 . . . . 398.2
HEINE, H/Pigs' wedding. /c1978, 1986/P-2/6 KF697 . . . . CE E
HINTON, SE/Puppy sister. /1995/3-5/4 KH263 . . . . Fic
HOFF, S/Mrs. Brice's mice. /1988/K-2/2 KF759. . . . . E
HOLT, D/Hogaphone and other stories (Videocassette). /1991/
  2-6/KH275. . . . . VCR Fic
HURWITZ, J/Aldo Applesauce. /1979/4-6/6 KH296 . . . . Fic
HUTCHINS, HJ/Three and many wishes of Jason Reid. /1988/
  4-6/6 KH310 . . . . Fic
HUTCHINS, P/Don't forget the bacon! /c1976, 1987/
  P-2/3 KF796 . . . . CE E
  Good-night owl. /c1972/P-2/3 KF798 . . . . CE E
JAMES, M/Shoebag. /1992/6-A/6 KH323 . . . . Fic
JAM, T/Charlotte stories. /1994/2-3/2 KH321. . . . . Fic
JENNINGS, S/Jeremiah and Mrs. Ming. /1990/K-2/2 KF828 . . E
JONES, DW/Stopping for a spell: three fantasies. /1993/
  5-A/6 KH334 . . . . Fic
JOYCE, W/Day with Wilbur Robinson. /1990/1-3/4 KF858 . . . E
KARLIN, N/I see, you saw. /1997/P-1/1 KF869 . . . . E
KASZA, K/Wolf's chicken stew. /1987/P-2/2 KF870 . . . . E
KELLOGG, S/Pinkerton, behave. /1979/P-2/2 KF894 . . . . CE E
KLINE, S/Herbie Jones and the class gift. /1989/3-4/2 KH367 . Fic
KORMAN, G/Zucchini warriors. /1991/5-A/7 KH378 . . . . . . Fic
KRAUSS, R/Hole is to dig: a first book of first definitions. /c1952/
  P-2/2 KF922 . . . . CE E
LAWSON, J/If pigs could fly. /1989/5-A/6 KH387 . . . . Fic
LESIEG, T/Wacky Wednesday. /c1974/1-2/1 KF961 . . . . E
LESTER, J/Sam and the tigers: a new telling of LITTLE BLACK
  SAMBO. /1996/K-3/2 KF966 . . . . E
LINDGREN, A/Pippi Longstocking. /c1950, 1978/
  3-5/4 KH407 . . . . CE Fic
LOWRY, L/Anastasia, absolutely. /1995/4-A/6 KH422 . . . . . Fic
  Anastasia has the answers. /1986/4-6/7 KH423. . . . . . . Fic
  See you around, Sam! /1996/3-6/6 KH428 . . . . Fic
MACAULAY, D/Why the chicken crossed the road. /1987/
  4-A/7 KH435 . . . . Fic
MACDONALD, A/No more nice. /1996/4-6/6 KH437 . . . . . . Fic
MACLACHLAN, P/Arthur, for the very first time. /1980/
  4-6/7 KH443 . . . . Fic
MAHY, M/Great piratical rumbustification and The librarian and the
  robbers. /c1978, 1986/5-A/7 KH449 . . . . Fic
  Horrible story and others (Talking book). /1992/
  3-A/KH452 . . . . TB Fic
  Tingleberries, tuckertubs and telephones: a tale of love and ice-
  cream. /1996/3-6/5 KH454 . . . . Fic
MARSHALL, E/Fox and his friends. /1994/K-2/1 KG064 . . . CE E
MARSHALL, J/Fox on the job. /c1988, 1990/K-3/2 KG067 . . . E
MAYER, M/There's an alligator under my bed. /1987/
  P-2/2 KG085. . . . . E
MCCLINTOCK, M/Stop that ball. /c1959, 1987/K-2/1 KG086 . . E
MCCLOSKEY, R/Burt Dow, deep-water man: a tale of the sea in the
  classic tradition. /c1963/P-A/6 KH468. . . . . CE Fic
  Doughnuts (Videocassette). /1984/2-6/KH469 . . . . VCR Fic
  Homer Price. /c1943/3-6/5 KH470 . . . . CE Fic
  Homer Price stories (Talking book). /n.d./3-6/KH471 . . . TB Fic

MCKAY, H/Exiles. /1992/6-A/7 KH478 . . . . **Fic**
    Exiles at home. /1994/5-A/7 KH479 . . . . **Fic**
NAYLOR, PR/Alice in rapture, sort of. /1989/6-A/6 KH533 . . . **Fic**
    Bodies in the Bessledorf Hotel. /1988/4-6/5 KH535 . . . . **Fic**
PALATINI, M/Piggie Pie! /1995/1-5/2 KG207 . . . . **E**
PARISH, H/Bravo, Amelia Bedelia! /1997/1-2/2 KG210 . . . . . . **E**
PARISH, P/Amelia Bedelia's family album. /1988/K-3/4 KG211. . **E**
    Come back, Amelia Bedelia. Newly illustrated ed. /1995/
    K-2/2 KG213 . . . . **E**
    Good work, Amelia Bedelia. /c1976/1-3/2 KG214. . . . . . **CE E**
    Play ball, Amelia Bedelia. /1996/1-3/2 KG216 . . . . **E**
    Thank you, Amelia Bedelia. Rev. ed. /1993/1-3/2 KG218 . **CE E**
PEET, B/Jethro and Joel were a troll. /1987/1-3/4 KG229 . . . **E**
PENNYPACKER, S/Dumbstruck. /1994/4-6/7 KH596 . . . . **Fic**
PILKEY, D/Dog breath: the horrible trouble with Hally Tosis. /1994/
    2-3/3 KG236 . . . . **E**
PINKWATER, DM/Aunt Lulu. /1991/P-2/2 KG244 . . . . **E**
    Fat men from space. /1977/5-A/7 KH602 . . . . **Fic**
    Hoboken chicken emergency. /c1977/5-A/6 KH603 . . . . **CE Fic**
    Mush, a dog from space. /1995/3-6/4 KH604 . . . . **Fic**
    Wallpaper from space. /1996/2-5/3 KH605 . . . . **Fic**
PINKWATER, J/Mister Fred. /1994/5-A/4 KH606 . . . . **Fic**
PORTE, BA/Fat Fanny, Beanpole Bertha, and the boys. /1991/
    4-6/4 KH610 . . . . **Fic**
PRICEMAN, M/How to make an apple pie and see the world. /
    1994/K-2/3 KG288 . . . . **E**
READY...SET...READ--AND LAUGH!: A FUNNY TREASURY FOR
    BEGINNING READERS. /1995/K-2/5 KD902 . . . . **810.8**
RIDLEY, P/Kasper in the glitter. /1997/5-A/4 KH634. . . . . . . **Fic**
ROBERTSON, K/Henry Reed, Inc. (Talking book). /1973/
    4-6/KH637. . . . . **TB Fic**
    Henry Reed's baby-sitting service. /c1966/4-6/6 KH638. . . . **Fic**
ROBINSON, B/Best school year ever. /1994/3-A/5 KH641 . . . **Fic**
ROCKWELL, T/How to eat fried worms. /1973/4-6/5 KH643 . . **Fic**
RODGERS, M/Summer switch. /1982/5-6/7 KH648 . . . . **Fic**
SACHAR, L/Wayside School is falling down. /1989/
    3-5/4 KH666 . . . . **CE Fic**
SANFIELD, S/Great turtle drive. /1996/2-6/4 KH676 . . . . **Fic**
SCHWARTZ, A/Yossel Zissel and the wisdom of Chelm. /1986/
    2-4/2 KH684 . . . . **Fic**
SEGAL, L/Tell me a Mitzi. /c1970/K-3/6 KG426 . . . . **E**
    Tell me a Trudy. /c1977, 1981/K-3/4 KG427 . . . . **E**
SELDEN, G/Chester Cricket's new home. /1983/2-4/5 KH692 . **Fic**
SEUSS, D/Dr. Seuss' Caldecotts (Videocassette). /1985/
    1-3/KG450 . . . . **VCR E**
    I am not going to get up today! /1987/1-3/2 KG461 . . . . . . **E**
    I am not going to get up today! plus three more Dr. Seuss classics
    /1991/1-3/KG462 . . . . **VCR E**
    500 hats of Bartholomew Cubbins. /c1938, 1989/
    P-A/6 KG473. . . . . **E**
SMALL, D/Hoover's bride. /1995/1-3/5 KG521 . . . . **E**
    Imogene's antlers. /1985/P-2/6 KG522 . . . . **CE E**
SNOW, A/How dogs really work! /1993/4-A/5 KH727 . . . . . **Fic**
    Truth about cats. /1996/4-A/7 KH728 . . . . **Fic**
SPIRN, M/Know-Nothing birthday. /1997/1-2/1 KG533 . . . . . **E**
STANLEY, D/Saving Sweetness. /1996/1-3/4 KG538 . . . . **E**
STEIG, W/Farmer Palmer's wagon ride. /c1974, 1992/
    K-3/6 KG543 . . . . **E**
    William Steig library (Videocassette). /1995/1-3/KG548 . **VCR E**
STEVENSON, J/Could be worse. /c1977, 1987/
    K-3/4 KG558 . . . . **CE E**
    National worm day. /1990/K-2/1 KG563 . . . . **E**
    Yard sale. /1996/2-3/2 KH756 . . . . **Fic**
TRIVAS, I/Emma's Christmas: an old song. /1988/P-3/6 KG618 . **E**
TWAIN, M/Adventures of Tom Sawyer. /1989/5-A/4 KH814. . **Fic**
VANDE VELDE, V/Tales from the Brothers Grimm and the Sisters
    Weird. /1995/5-A/6 KH827 . . . . **Fic**
VAUGHAN, MK/Wombat stew. /c1984/P-2/4 KG652 . . . . **E**
VIORST, J/Alexander and the terrible, horrible, no good, very bad
    day and other stories /1984/P-3/KG658 . . . . **TB E**
WELLS, R/Max's first word (Board book). /1979/
    P/1 KG704 . . . . **BB E**
WILLARD, N/Simple pictures are best. /c1977/K-3/6 KG724 . . . **E**
WISEMAN, B/Morris and Boris. /c1974, 1991/K-2/1 KG748 . . . **E**
    Morris the Moose. /1989/K-2/2 KG750 . . . . **CE E**
WOOD, A/Napping house and other stories (Talking book). /
    1987/P-3/KG765 . . . . **TB E**
    Silly Sally. /1992/P-K/2 KG766 . . . . **E**
YOLEN, J/Piggins. /1987/K-3/4 KG779 . . . . **E**
YORKE, M/Miss Butterpat goes wild! /1993/3-5/5 KH898 . . . **Fic**
ZEMACH, H/Penny a look. /c1971/K-2/2 KG789 . . . . **E**
Humpback whale.
ESBENSEN, BJ/Baby whales drink milk. /1994/
    1-3/2 KC768 . . . . **599.5**

Hungary--Folklore.
BODNAR, JZ/Wagonload of fish. /1996/K-2/5 KB532 . . . **398.24**
SEREDY, K/White stag. /c1937/5-6/7 KB486 . . . . **398.22**
Hunger--Fiction.
DISALVO-RYAN, D/Uncle Willie and the soup kitchen. /1991/
    1-3/2 KF485 . . . . **E**
Hunkpapa Indians--Biography.
ST. GEORGE, J/To see with the heart: the life of Sitting Bull. /
    1996/5-A/6 KE542 . . . . **B SITTING BULL**
Hunting SEE ALSO Game and game birds; Tracking and trailing.
Hunting--Fiction.
BELL, F/Jenny's corner. /1995/5-A/7 KG894. . . . . **Fic**
BUSH, T/Grunt!: the primitive cave boy. /1995/K-2/2 KF323 . . . **E**
DAHL, R/Magic finger. /1995/3-5/3 KH055 . . . . **Fic**
DE PAOLA, T/Hunter and the animals: a wordless picture book. /
    1981/K-1/KF470. . . . . **E**
EASTERLING, B/Prize in the snow. /1994/2-3/4 KF503. . . . . . **E**
ELSTE, J/True Blue. /1996/2-4/2 KH098 . . . . **Fic**
Hurricanes.
COLE, J/Magic School Bus inside a hurricane. /1995/
    2-4/4 KC197 . . . . **551.55**
KAHL, JD/Storm warning: tornadoes and hurricanes. /1993/
    4-7/8 KC200 . . . . **551.55**
LAMPTON, C/Hurricane. /1991/4-6/7 KC202 . . . . **551.55**
LAUBER, P/Hurricanes: Earth's mightiest storms. /1996/
    3-6/6 KC203 . . . . **551.55**
PENNER, LR/Twisters! /1996/2-4/3 KC204 . . . . **551.55**
SOUZA, DM/Hurricanes. /1996/4-6/7 KC206 . . . . **551.55**
Hurricanes--Fiction.
MCCLOSKEY, R/Time of wonder. /c1957, 1962/
    P-A/6 KG091. . . . . **CE E**
WEEKS, S/Hurricane City. /1993/K-2/2 KG691 . . . . **E**
WIESNER, D/Hurricane. /1990/K-2/2 KG712 . . . . **E**
Hurston, Zora Neale.
LYONS, ME/Sorrow's kitchen: the life and folklore of Zora Neale
    Hurston. /1990/6-A/6 KE396 . . . . **B HURSTON, Z.**
Hutsuls--Folklore.
KIMMEL, EA/One Eye, Two Eyes, Three Eyes: a Hutzul tale. /
    1996/2-4/7 KB401 . . . . **398.21**
Huynh, Quang Nhuong.
HUYNH, QN/Land I lost: adventures of a boy in Vietnam. /1982/
    5-6/7 KE718 . . . . **959.7**
Hydrologic cycle.
BRANDT, K/What makes it rain? The story of a raindrop. /1982/
    P-K/2 KC209 . . . . **551.57**
WALKER, SM/Water up, water down: the hydrologic cycle. /1992/
    4-6/7 KC184 . . . . **551.48**
Hydrothermal vents.
WATERS, JF/Deep-sea vents: living worlds without sun. /1994/
    4-6/7 KC179 . . . . **551.46**
Hygiene SEE Cleanliness; Health.
Hymns SEE ALSO Carols; Church music.
Hyperactive child syndrome.
KENNEDY, P/Hyperactive child book. /1994/KA303 . . **PROF 649**
QUINN, PO/Putting on the brakes: /1991/5-6/7 KD041 . . **618.92**
HyperCard (Computer program).
FARMER, LS/I speak HyperCard. /1992/3-A/KA573. . . . **005.265**
Hypermedia--Software.
HYPERSTUDIO (MICROCOMPUTER PROGRAM). /1990/
    2-A/KA574 . . . . **MCP 006.7**
Ice Age SEE Glacial epoch.
Ice fishing--Fiction.
VALGARDSON, WD/Winter rescue. /1995/3-5/4 KH819 . . . . **Fic**
Ice industry--Fiction.
CHRISTIANSEN, C/Ice horse. /1993/2-3/6 KF391 . . . . **E**
Ice skaters.
BAIUL, O/Oksana: my own story. /1997/
    3-6/4 KE247 . . . . **B BAIUL, O.**
DALY, W/Bonnie Blair: power on ice. /1996/
    4-6/6 KE255 . . . . **B BLAIR, B.**
SAVAGE, J/Kristi Yamaguchi: pure gold. /1993/
    3-5/7 KE603 . . . . **B YAMAGUCHI, K.**
SMITH, P/Superstars of women's figure skating. /1997/
    4-6/7 KD836 . . . . **796.91**
Icebergs.
SIMON, S/Icebergs and glaciers. /1987/3-6/7 KC165 . . . **551.3**
Iceland--Description and travel.
PITKANEN, MA/Grandchildren of the Vikings. /1996/
    4-6/8 KE694 . . . . **948**
Iceland--Folklore.
WISNIEWSKI, D/Elfwyn's saga. /1990/4-6/6 KB422 . . . . **398.21**
Idaho.
KENT, Z/Idaho. /1990/4-6/9 KF091 . . . . **979.6**

Identity--Fiction.
BANG, M/Goose. /1996/P-2/2 KF190 . . . . E
BAWDEN, N/Real Plato Jones. /1993/6-A/6 KG892 . . . . Fic
HAMILTON, V/Plain City. /1993/6-A/5 KH217 . . . . Fic
HOFFMAN, M/Amazing Grace. /1991/P-2/4 KF761 . . . . . CE E
HUTCHINS, P/Which witch is which? /1989/P-1/2 KF807 . . . . . E
LIONNI, L/Extraordinary egg. /1994/1-3/2 KF991 . . . . E
MCGRAW, EJ/Moorchild. /1996/5-A/6 KH475 . . . . Fic
NAMIOKA, L/Yang the youngest and his terrible ear. /1994/
5-A/5 KH528 . . . . Fic
NUMEROFF, LJ/Why a disguise? /1996/K-2/2 KG182 . . . . . . E
PATERSON, K/Jip: his story. /1996/5-A/7 KH577 . . . . Fic
WHITE, R/Belle Prater's boy. /1996/6-A/6 KH853 . . . . Fic
Idioms--English language SEE English language--Idioms.
Iditarod Trail Sled Dog Race, Alaska.
CRISMAN, R/Racing the Iditarod Trail. /1993/
5-6/7 KD858 . . . . **798.8**
Igbo (African people)--Folklore.
MOLLEL, TM/Flying tortoise: an Igbo tale. /1994/
2-3/3 KB623 . . . . **398.24**
Igbo (African people)--Social conditions.
ONYEFULU, I/Ogbo: sharing life in an African village. /1996/
3-5/6 KE737 . . . . **966.9**
Igloos.
YUE, C/Igloo. /1988/4-6/9 KE778 . . . . **970.3**
Iguanas.
PATTON, D/Iguanas. /1996/4-6/7 KC627 . . . . **597.95**
Illegal aliens.
ASHABRANNER, B/Our beckoning borders: illegal immigration to
America. /1996/5-6/12 KA924 . . . . **325.73**
Illinois--Fiction.
HUNT, I/Across five Aprils. /1984/5-A/5 KH291 . . . . . . CE Fic
Illinois--History.
WILLS, CA/Historical album of Illinois. /1994/4-6/7 KF016. . **977.3**
Illness SEE: Sick.
Illustrated books, Children's--Bibliography.
AMMON, BD/Worth a thousand words: an annotated guide to
picture books for older readers. /1996//KA010 . . **PROF 011.62**
NEWBERY AND CALDECOTT MEDALISTS AND HONOR BOOK
WINNERS: BIBLIOGRAPHIES AND /1992//KA004 . . . **PROF 011**
Illustrated books, Children's--Bibliography--Periodicals.
NEWBERY AND CALDECOTT AWARDS: A GUIDE TO THE
MEDAL AND HONOR BOOKS. /n.d.//KA128 . . **PER PROF 050**
Illustration of books.
HELLER, R/Fine lines. /1996/4-6/2 KE385 . . . . **B HELLER, R.**
ILLUSTRATORS OF CHILDREN'S BOOKS, 1967-1976. /1978/
/KA311. . . . . **PROF 741.6**
STEWIG, JW/Looking at picture books. /1995/
/KA312. . . . . **PROF 741.6**
Illustrators.
CHRISTELOW, E/What do authors do? /1995/
2-4/2 KD866 . . . . **808.06**
CREWS, D/Bigmama's. /1991/K-2/2 KE309 . . . **CE B CREWS, D.**
DEWEY, JO/Cowgirl dreams: a western childhood. /1995/
3-4/4 KE320 . . . . **B DEWEY, J.**
EHLERT, L/Under my nose. /1996/3-6/2 KE333 . . . . **B EHLERT, L.**
GET TO KNOW BERNARD MOST (VIDEOCASSETTE). /1993/
2-3/KE471 . . . . **VCR B MOST, B.**
GET TO KNOW KEITH BAKER (VIDEOCASSETTE). /1994/
2-5/KE248 . . . . **VCR B BAKER, K.**
HELLER, R/Fine lines. /1996/4-6/2 KE385 . . . . **B HELLER, R.**
ILLUSTRATORS OF CHILDREN'S BOOKS, 1967-1976. /1978/
/KA311. . . . . **PROF 741.6**
MAJOR AUTHORS AND ILLUSTRATORS FOR CHILDREN AND
YOUNG ADULTS: A SELECTION OF /1993//KA464. . . **REF 809**
MAXFIELD PARRISH: A TREASURY OF ART AND CHILDREN'S
LITERATURE. /1995/K-6/KD413. . . . . **741.6**
MEET ASHLEY BRYAN: STORYTELLER, ARTIST, WRITER
(VIDEOCASSETTE). /1992/4-6/KE266 . . . . . **VCR B BRYAN, A.**
PEET, B/Bill Peet: an autobiography. /1989/
6-A/8 KE494 . . . . **B PEET, B.**
SENDAK (VIDEOCASSETTE). /1993/
4-A/KE534. . . . . **VCR B SENDAK, M.**
STEVENSON, J/Don't you know there's a war on? /1992/
K-3/2 KE552 . . . . **B STEVENSON, J.**
Higher on the door. /1987/3-4/4 KE553 . . . **B STEVENSON, J.**
When I was nine. /1986/3-4/4 KE551 . . . . . **B STEVENSON, J.**
Illustrators--Biography--Indexes.
CHILDREN'S AUTHORS AND ILLUSTRATORS: AN INDEX TO
BIOGRAPHICAL DICTIONARIES. /1976-//KA033 . **PROF 016.809**
Illustrators--Dictionaries.
AUTHORS OF BOOKS FOR YOUNG PEOPLE. 3RD ED. /1990/
5-A/KA460 . . . . **REF 809**
JUNIOR AUTHOR SERIES. /1951-/A/KA462. . . . . **REF 809**

Illustrators, American--20th century--Interviews.
ROGINSKI, J/Behind the covers: /1985//KA335 . . **PROF 808.06**
Imaginary playmates--Fiction.
HENKES, K/Jessica. /1989/K-1/2 KF706 . . . . E
JAMES, S/Leon and Bob. /1997/K-2/2 KF824 . . . . E
Imagination--Fiction.
ADLERMAN, D/Africa calling, nighttime falling. /1996/
P-2/KF135 . . . . E
AGELL, C/Mud makes me dance in the spring. /1994/
K-2/2 KF139 . . . . E
BANKS, K/Spider spider. /1996/P-1/2 KF194 . . . . E
BORTON, L/Junk pile! /1997/K-2/3 KF252 . . . . E
BULLA, CR/Chalk box kid. /1987/2-4/2 KG936 . . . . Fic
BURNINGHAM, J/Come away from the water, Shirley. /c1977/
P-2/2 KF315 . . . . CE E
COOPER, H/Boy who wouldn't go to bed. /1997/P-1/2 KF422 . . . E
DENTON, KM/Would they love a lion? /1995/P-1/1 KF463. . . . E
DORROS, A/Abuela. /1991/P-2/2 KF488 . . . . E
Abuela (Videocassette). /1994/P-2/KF489 . . . . . . **VCR E**
GEISERT, A/Etcher's studio. /1997/2-5/2 KF602 . . . . E
GERSTEIN, M/Behind the couch. /1996/2-4/3 KH162 . . . . . . Fic
GLASSMAN, P/Wizard next door. /1993/K-2/2 KF625 . . . . . . E
GREENFIELD, E/Me and Neesie. /c1975/K-2/3 KF642 . . . . . E
HECTOR'S BUNYIP (VIDEOCASSETTE). /c1986, 1997/
4-6/KH231. . . . . **VCR Fic**
HOFF, S/Horse in Harry's room. /c1970/K-2/2 KF757. . . . . . E
HOOKER, R/Matthew the cowboy. /1990/K-2/2 KF767 . . . . . E
JOHNSON, C/Harold and the purple crayon. /c1955, 1994/
P-2/2 KF835 . . . . CE E
JONAS, A/Trek. /1985/P-2/4 KF849 . . . . E
KHALSA, DK/I want a dog. /1987/P-2/5 KF902 . . . . E
KRAUSS, R/Very special house. /c1953/P-1/1 KF923 . . . . . . E
LISLE, JT/Afternoon of the elves. /1989/6-A/6 KH408 . . . . . Fic
LONDON, J/Lion who had asthma. /1992/P-2/2 KG025. . . . . . E
MCEWAN, I/Daydreamer. /1994/4-6/6 KH474 . . . . Fic
MCLERRAN, A/Roxaboxen. /1991/K-3/2 KG110. . . . . CE E
MCPHAIL, D/Edward and the pirates. /1997/K-2/3 KG117 . . . E
MENNEN, I/Somewhere in Africa. /1992/K-2/4 KG129 . . . . . E
OCHS, CP/When I'm alone. /1993/P-2/4 KG187. . . . . E
PACKARD, M/I am king! /1994/K-1/1 KG205. . . . . E
RAU, DM/Box can be many things. /1997/K-1/2 KG313. . . . . E
RODOWSKY, C/Dog days. /1993/4-5/6 KH649 . . . . Fic
SCHAEFER, CL/Squiggle. /1996/P-2/3 KG402 . . . . E
SEUSS, D/And to think that I saw it on Mulberry Street. /c1937,
1964/K-2/2 KG445. . . . . E
SPIER, P/Dreams. /1986/P-2/KG531. . . . . E
TEAGUE, M/Secret shortcut. /1996/1-3/2 KG596. . . . . E
WIESNER, D/Hurricane. /1990/K-2/2 KG712 . . . . E
WILLIAMS, VB/Cherries and cherry pits. /c1965, 1984/
K-3/2 KG735 . . . . E
WINTHROP, E/Very noisy girl. /1991/K-2/2 KG747. . . . . . . E
WOOD, A/Flying Dragon Room. /1996/2-4/3 KG761 . . . . . . E
Imagination--Poetry.
ALLIGATOR PIE (VIDEOCASSETTE). /1993/P-2/KD912 **VCR 811**
MICHELSON, R/Animals that ought to be: poems about imaginary
pets. /1996/K-3/KD985 . . . . **811**
Immigrants.
BERGER, M/Where did your family come from?: a book about
immigrants. /1993/2-4/2 KA925 . . . . **325.73**
Immigrants--Fiction.
HICYILMAZ, G/Frozen waterfall. /1994/6-A/6 KH257 . . . . . . Fic
Immigrants--United States--History.
AMERICA: A NATION OF IMMIGRANTS (PICTURE). /1996/
4-6/KA923 . . . . **PIC 325.73**
MAESTRO, B/Coming to America: the story of immigration. /1996/
1-3/8 KA921 . . . . **325**
SANDLER, MW/Immigrants. /1995/5-A/7 KA922 . . . . **325**
Immigrants--United States--Pictorial works.
SANDLER, MW/Immigrants. /1995/5-A/7 KA922 . . . . **325**
Immigration and emigration SEE Emigration and immigration; United States-
-Emigration and immigration.
Immunity.
IMMUNE SYSTEM: OUR INTERNAL DEFENDER
(VIDEOCASSETTE). /1991/4-5/KD014 . . . . **VCR 616.07**
Immunology.
IMMUNE SYSTEM: OUR INTERNAL DEFENDER
(VIDEOCASSETTE). /1991/4-5/KD014 . . . . **VCR 616.07**
Implants, Artificial.
FACKLAM, M/Spare parts for people. /1987/A/9 KD035 . . . **617**
Implements, utensils, etc.
MORRIS, A/Tools. /1992/P-2/2 KD056 . . . . **621.9**
Impostors and imposture.
GRAHAM, I/Fakes and forgeries. /1995/A/8 KA557 . . . . . **001.9**

Impressionism (Art).
    SALVI, F/Impressionists: the origins of modern painting. /1994/
    6-A/9 KD485 . . . . **759.05**

In-line skating.
    EDWARDS, C/Young inline skater. /1996/3-6/6 KD771. . . **796.21**
    SULLIVAN, G/In-line skating: a complete guide for beginners. /
    1993/4-6/5 KD773 . . . . **796.21**

Incas.
    BAQUEDANO, E/Aztec, Inca and Maya. /1993/
    4-6/9 KE829 . . . . **972**
    MARRIN, A/Inca and Spaniard: Pizarro and the conquest of Peru. /
    1989/A/8 KF109 . . . . **985**
    NEWMAN, SP/Incas. /1992/5-6/7 KF103 . . . . **980.3**
    PITKANEN, MA/Grandchildren of the Incas. /1991/
    4-6/6 KF110 . . . . **985**

Incas--Folklore.
    KURTZ, J/Miro in the Kingdom of the Sun. /1996/
    3-4/5 KB505 . . . . **398.23**

Incest--Fiction.
    LOWERY, L/Laurie tells. /1994/3-6/4 KH420. . . . . **Fic**

Indentured servants--Fiction.
    AVI /Night journeys. /c1979, 1994/5-A/6 KG860 . . . . **Fic**

India--Fiction.
    ATKINS, J/Aani and the tree huggers. /1995/3-5/3 KG853 . . . **Fic**
    BANNERMAN, H/Story of Little Babaji. /1996/K-2/2 KF195 . . . **E**
    KIPLING, R/Jungle book: the Mowgli stories. /1995/
    6-A/7 KH363 . . . . **Fic**
    Rikki-Tikki-Tavi and Wee Willie Winkie (Talking book). /n.d./
    4-6/KH364. . . . . **TB Fic**
    YOLEN, J/Children of the wolf. /c1984, 1993/6-A/7 KH896 . . **Fic**

India--Folklore.
    BROWN, M/Once a mouse. /c1961/1-3/6 KB536 . . . . **CE 398.24**
    DEMI /One grain of rice: a mathematical folktale. /1997/
    3-6/6 KB731 . . . . **398.27**
    NESS, C/Ocean of story: fairy tales from India. /1996/
    4-6/5 KB353 . . . . **398.2**
    SHEPARD, A/Gifts of Wali Dad: a tale of India and Pakistan. /
    1995/2-3/2 KB488 . . . . **398.22**
    WOLF-SAMPATH, G/Mala: a women's folktale. /1996/
    3-5/2 KB718 . . . . **398.26**
    YOUNG, E/Seven blind mice. /1992/K-3/2 KB681 . . . . . **398.24**

India--Social life and customs.
    HERMES, J/Children of India. /1993/4-6/6 KE711 . . . . **954**
    SCHMIDT, J/In the village of the elephants. /1994/
    4-6/6 KC816 . . . . **599.67**

Indian art--Florida.
    ASHABRANNER, B/Strange and distant shore: Indians of the Great
    Plains in exile. /1996/4-6/7 KF026 . . . . **978**

Indian authors.
    WEIL, A/Michael Dorris. /1997/6-A/7 KE323 . . . . **B DORRIS, M.**

Indian philosophy--North America.
    STROUD, VA/Path of the Quiet Elk: a Native American alphabet
    book. /1996/3-6/5 KA793 . . . . **299**

Indian poetry--Collections.
    BIERHORST, J/On the road of stars: Native American night poems
    and sleep charms. /1994/2-6/KE141. . . . . **897.008**

Indiana.
    FRADIN, DB/Indiana. /1994/4-6/3 KF014 . . . . **977.2**

Indiana--Fiction.
    HADDIX, MP/Running out of time. /1995/5-A/5 KH211 . . . . . **Fic**
    SANDERS, SR/Place called Freedom. /1997/1-3/3 KG390 . . . . **E**

Indians--Dictionaries.
    PATTERSON, L/Indian terms of the Americas. /1994/
    5-A/KA478 . . . . **REF 970.004**

Indians--Folklore.
    BRUSCA, MC/When jaguars ate the moon: and other stories about
    animals and plants of the Americas. /1995/2-3/5 KB541. . **398.24**
    DELACRE, L/Golden tales: myths, legends, and folktales from Latin
    America. /1996/4-5/6 KB283 . . . . **398.2**
    LIGHTNING INSIDE YOU AND OTHER NATIVE AMERICAN
    RIDDLES. /1992/3-6/KD733 . . . . **793.735**

Indians--Funeral customs and rites.
    BENDICK, J/Tombs of the ancient Americas. /1993/
    3-5/8 KB174 . . . . **393**

Indians--Humor.
    LIGHTNING INSIDE YOU AND OTHER NATIVE AMERICAN
    RIDDLES. /1992/3-6/KD733 . . . . **793.735**

Indians--Origin.
    SATTLER, HR/Earliest Americans. /1993/5-A/8 KE743. . . . **970.01**

Indians--Terminology.
    PATTERSON, L/Indian terms of the Americas. /1994/
    5-A/KA478 . . . . **REF 970.004**

Indians of Central America.
    BAQUEDANO, E/Aztec, Inca and Maya. /1993/
    4-6/9 KE829 . . . . **972**
    GREENE, JD/Maya. /1992/4-6/7 KE843 . . . . **972.81**
    LOST CITY OF THE MAYA (VIDEOCASSETTE). /1990/
    6-A/KE844. . . . . **VCR 972.81**

Indians of Central America--Fiction.
    LONDON, J/Village basket weaver. /1996/2-3/6 KG029 . . . . . **E**
    WISNIEWSKI, D/Rain player. /1991/2-3/4 KG751. . . . . . . **CE E**

Indians of Central America--Folklore.
    BIERHORST, J/Monkey's haircut and other stories told by the
    Maya. /1986/3-4/4 KB531. . . . . **398.24**
    GERSON, M/People of corn: a Mayan story. /1995/
    2-4/3 KB399 . . . . **398.21**

Indians of Central America--History.
    PATENT, DH/Quetzal: sacred bird of the cloud forest. /1996/
    3-6/6 KC702 . . . . **598.7**

Indians of Central America--Panama--Social life and customs.
    PRESILLA, ME/Mola: Cuna life stories and art. /1996/
    3-5/7 KA832 . . . . **305.48**

Indians of Central America--Software.
    MAYAQUEST TRAIL (CD-ROM). /1996/5-A/KE845 . **CDR 972.81**

Indians of Mexico.
    BAQUEDANO, E/Aztec, Inca and Maya. /1993/
    4-6/9 KE829 . . . . **972**
    SHEPHERD, DW/Aztecs. /1992/4-6/7 KE838 . . . . **972**

Indians of Mexico--Antiquities.
    ARNOLD, C/City of the gods: Mexico's ancient city of Teotihuacan.
    /1994/5-6/7 KE828 . . . . **972**

Indians of Mexico--Fiction.
    LATTIMORE, DN/Flame of peace, a tale of the Aztecs. /1987/
    2-3/2 KF948 . . . . **E**
    O'DELL, S/Captive. /1979/6-A/6 KH558 . . . . **Fic**

Indians of Mexico--Folklore.
    BERNHARD, E/Tree that rains: the flood myth of the Huichol Indians
    of Mexico. /1994/3-4/5 KB699. . . . . **398.26**
    BIERHORST, J/Doctor Coyote: a Native American Aesop's fables. /
    1987/3/3 KB530 . . . . **398.24**
    EHLERT, L/Cuckoo: a Mexican folktale./Cucu: un cuento folklorico
    mexicano. /1997/P-2/3 KB561 . . . . **398.24**
    JOHNSTON, T/Tale of Rabbit and Coyote. /1994/
    2-3/2 KB596 . . . . **398.24**
    MADRIGAL, AH/Eagle and the rainbow: timeless tales from Mexico.
    /1997/4-5/7 KB339 . . . . **398.2**
    MARTINEZ, AC/Woman who outshone the sun: the legend of Lucia
    Zenteno./La mujer que brillaba /1991/3-5/5 KB403. . . . **398.21**

Indians of Mexico--History.
    MARRIN, A/Aztecs and Spaniards: Cortes and the conquest of
    Mexico. /1986/5-6/7 KE833 . . . . **972**
    MATHEWS, SS/Sad Night: the story of an Aztec victory and a
    Spanish loss. /1994/4-6/6 KE834. . . . . **972**
    PATENT, DH/Quetzal: sacred bird of the cloud forest. /1996/
    3-6/6 KC702 . . . . **598.7**

Indians of Mexico--Sierra Madre Occidental Region.
    STAUB, FJ/Children of the Sierra Madre. /1996/
    4-6/8 KE839 . . . . **972**

Indians of Mexico--Social life and customs.
    PRESILLA, ME/Life around the lake. /1996/2-6/8 KE837 . . . . **972**
    STAUB, FJ/Children of Yucatan. /1996/4-6/7 KE840 . . . . . . **972**
    SUEMI'S STORY: MY MODERN MAYAN HOME
    (VIDEOCASSETTE). /c1991/5-A/KE841. . . . . **VCR 972**

Indians of Mexico--Social life and customs--Fiction.
    VAN LAAN, N/Boda: a Mexican wedding celebration. /1996/
    1-3/2 KG641 . . . . **E**

Indians of North America SEE ALSO names of tribes and linguistic families
    e.g. Abenaki Indians, etc.

Indians of North America.
    ANDERSON, MK/Nez Perce. /1994/4-6/7 KE757 . . . . **970.3**
    CLARK, AN/In my mother's house. /c1941, 1991/
    1-4/KE759 . . . . **970.3**
    DAILY, R/Code talkers: American Indians in World War II. /1995/
    4-6/9 KE669 . . . . **940.54**
    HOYT-GOLDSMITH, D/Arctic hunter. /1992/3-6/6 KF097 . . **979.8**
    JENNESS, A/In two worlds: a Yup'ik Eskimo family. /1989/
    5-6/7 KF098 . . . . **979.8**
    LANDAU, E/Cherokees. /1992/4-6/7 KE760. . . . . **970.3**
    MURDOCH, DH/North American Indian. /1995/
    4-6/8 KE751 . . . . **970.1**
    MYERS, A/Cheyenne. /1992/4-6/7 KE761. . . . . **970.3**
    NEWMAN, SP/Inuits. /1993/4-6/7 KF102 . . . . **979.8**
    PENNINGTON, D/Itse Selu: Cherokee harvest festival. /1994/
    K-3/6 KB190 . . . . **394.2**
    QUIRI, PR/Algonquians. /1992/4-6/6 KE763 . . . . **970.3**

SEWALL, M/People of the breaking day. /1990/
3-6/5 KA858 . . . . **305.8**
SHERROW, V/American Indian children of the past. /1997/
3-6/7 KE764 . . . . **970.3**
SNEVE, V/Cherokees. /1996/4-6/5 KE769 . . . . . **970.3**
  Cheyennes. /1996/4-6/6 KE770 . . . . **970.3**
  Hopis. /1995/4-6/7 KE771 . . . . **970.3**
  Iroquois. /1995/4-6/5 KE772. . . . . **970.3**
  Nez Perce. /1994/4-6/7 KE774 . . . . **970.3**
  Seminoles. /1994/4-6/7 KE775 . . . . **970.3**
TUNIS, E/Indians. Rev. ed. /1979/4-6/7 KE754 . . . **970.1**
WATERS, K/Tapenum's day: a Wampanoag Indian boy in pilgrim
times. /1996/3-5/2 KE950 . . . . **974.4**

Indians of North America--Alaska.
KENDALL, R/Eskimo boy: life in an Inupiaq Eskimo village. /1992/
3-6/6 KF100 . . . . **979.8**

Indians of North America--Alaska--Fiction.
GEORGE, JC/Julie. /1994/5-A/3 KH156 . . . . **Fic**
HEINZ, BJ/Kayuktuk: an Arctic quest. /1996/4-A/3 KH235. . . . **Fic**

Indians of North America--Alaska--History.
FIRST AND LAST FRONTIER (VIDEOCASSETTE). /1991/
A/KF095 . . . . **VCR 979.8**

Indians of North America--Antiquities.
BAYLOR, B/When clay sings. /c1972, 1987/3-5/6 KE748 . . **970.1**

Indians of North America--Arizona.
LIVING ON THE EDGE (VIDEOCASSETTE). /1991/
A/KF071 . . . . **VCR 979.1**

Indians of North America--Arizona--Folklore.
COURLANDER, H/People of the short blue corn: tales and legends
of the Hopi Indians. /c1970, 1996/1-A/5 KB278. . . . . . . **398.2**
ROESSEL, M/Songs from the loom: a Navajo girl learns to weave.
/1995/4-6/6 KE799 . . . . **970.491**

Indians of North America--Art--Periodicals.
AMERICAN INDIAN ART MAGAZINE. /1975-/
5-6/KA499 . . . . **PER 050**

Indians of North America--Biography.
ALLEN, PG/As long as the rivers flow: the stories of nine Native
Americans. /1996/6-A/9 KE746. /. **970.1**
AVERY, S/Extraordinary American Indians. /1992/
5-6/7 KE747 . . . . **970.1**
BRUCHAC, J/Boy called Slow: the true story of Sitting Bull. /1994/
3-4/6 KE541 . . . . **B SITTING BULL**
CONNELL, K/These lands are ours: Tecumseh's fight for the Old
Northwest. /1993/5-6/7 KE559 . . . . **B TECUMSEH**
CONTEMPORARY NATIVE AMERICANS (PICTURE). /1995/
5-6/KE779 . . . . **PIC 970.4**
FREEDMAN, R/Indian chiefs. /1987/5-6/8 KE749 . . . . **970.1**
  Life and death of Crazy Horse. /1996/
6-A/7 KE307 . . . . **B CRAZY HORSE**
FRITZ, J/Double life of Pocahontas. /1983/
5-6/6 KE500 . . . . **B POCAHONTAS**
HERMANN, S/Geronimo: Apache freedom fighter. /1997/
5-6/12 KE367 . . . . **B GERONIMO**
  R.C. Gorman: Navajo artist. /1995/
3-5/3 KE375 . . . . **B GORMAN, R.C.**
KLAUSNER, J/Sequoyah's gift: a portrait of the Cherokee leader. /
1993/5-6/7 KE535 . . . . **B SEQUOYAH**
LIPSYTE, R/Jim Thorpe: 20th-century jock. /
6-A/7 KE566 . . . . **B THORPE, J.**
LOWERY, L/Wilma Mankiller. /1996/
2-3/4 KE458 . . . . **B MANKILLER, W.**
NATIVE NORTH AMERICAN BIOGRAPHY. /1996/
6-A/KA481 . . . . **REF 970.1**
NATIVE NORTH AMERICAN VOICES. /1997/
5-A/KA482 . . . . **REF 970.1**
ROWLAND, D/Story of Sacajawea: guide to Lewis and Clark. /
1995/5-6/6 KE529 . . . . **B SACAJAWEA**
SACAJAWEA (VIDEOCASSETTE). /1991/
2-5/KE530. . . . . **VCR B SACAJAWEA**
ST. GEORGE, J/Crazy Horse. /1994/
A/9 KE308 . . . . **B CRAZY HORSE**
  To see with the heart: the life of Sitting Bull. /1996/
5-A/6 KE542 . . . . **B SITTING BULL**
THOMSON, P/Katie Henio: Navajo sheepherder. /1995/
5-6/6 KE796 . . . . **970.489**
WEIL, A/Michael Dorris. /1997/6-A/7 KE323 . . . . **B DORRIS, M.**

Indians of North America--California.
NATIVE WAYS: CALIFORNIA INDIAN STORIES AND MEMORIES.
/1995/5-A/6 KE800 . . . . **970.494**

Indians of North America--California--Fiction.
O'DELL, S/Zia. /1976/6-A/7 KH564 . . . . **CE Fic**

Indians of North America--California--Folklore.
FRENCH, F/Lord of the animals: a Miwok Indian creation myth. /
1997/K-3/4 KB568 . . . . **398.24**

LONDON, J/Fire race: a Karuk Coyote tale about how fire came to
the people. /1993/3-4/4 KB611. . . . . **398.24**

Indians of North America--California--History.
NATIVE WAYS: CALIFORNIA INDIAN STORIES AND MEMORIES.
/1995/5-A/6 KE800 . . . . **970.494**
SEARCHING FOR PARADISE (VIDEOCASSETTE). /1991/
A/KF086 . . . . **VCR 979.4**

Indians of North America--Canada.
CONFRONTING THE WILDERNESS (VIDEOCASSETTE). /1991/
A/KE808. . . . . **VCR 971.01**
JENNESS, D/Indians of Canada. 7th ed. /1977/
A/12 KA485 . . . . **REF 971**
LITTLECHILD, G/This land is my land. /1993/2-A/4 KE803. . . **971**

Indians of North America--Canada--Fiction.
COOPER, AJ/Dream quest. /1987/5-A/4 KH024 . . . . **Fic**
HUDSON, J/Sweetgrass. /1989/6-A/5 KH286 . . . . **Fic**
VALGARDSON, WD/Sarah and the people of Sand River. /1996/
4-6/2 KH818 . . . . **Fic**

Indians of North America--Canada--Folklore.
CAMERON, A/Raven and Snipe. /1991/3-4/6 KB546. . . . **398.24**
  Raven goes berrypicking. /1991/3-4/6 KB547 . . . . . **398.24**
TAYLOR, CJ/How Two-Feather was saved from loneliness: an
Abenaki legend. /1990/3-4/2 KB716 . . . . **398.26**

Indians of North America--Canada--Social life and customs.
SHEENA AZAK OF CANADA (VIDEOCASSETTE). /1995/
4-6/KE807 . . . . **VCR 971**

Indians of North America--Captivities.
SEAVER, JE/Captured by Indians: the life of Mary Jemison. /1995/
5-A/8 KE405 . . . . **B JEMISON, M.**
WILK, B/Letter from an Apache: a true story (Videocassette). /
1983/4-6/KE777. **VCR 970.3**

Indians of North America--Captivities--Fiction.
RICHTER, C/Light in the forest. /1994/5-A/5 KH632 . . . . **Fic**

Indians of North America--Dances.
BURTON, B/Moving within the circle: contemporary Native American
music and dance. /1993//KA316 . . . . **BA PROF 789.2**
CRUM, R/Eagle drum: on the powwow trail with a young grass
dancer. /1994/5-A/5 KB197 . . . . **394.26**
MOTT, EC/Dancing rainbows: a Pueblo boy's story. /1996/
2-4/2 KE794 . . . . **970.489**

Indians of North America--Dictionaries.
WALDMAN, C/Encyclopedia of Native American tribes. /1988/
4-A/KA483 . . . . **REF 970.4**

Indians of North America--Dwellings.
MONROE, JG/First houses: Native American homes and sacred
structures. /1993/6-A/7 KB171 . . . . **392.3**
SHEMIE, B/Mounds of earth and shell: the Southeast. /1993/
4-6/7 KB172 . . . . **392.3**
YUE, C/Igloo. /1988/4-6/9 KE778 . . . . **970.3**

Indians of North America--Ethnic identity--Fiction.
BUNTING, E/Cheyenne again. /1995/3-5/2 KG941 . . . . **Fic**

Indians of North America--Fiction.
BRUCHAC, J/Dog people: native dog stories. /1995/
4-6/5 KG934 . . . . **Fic**
CONWAY, DC/Northern lights: a Hanukkah story. /1994/
1-3/4 KF417 . . . . **E**
DALGLIESH, A/Courage of Sarah Noble. /c1954, 1987/
3-5/3 KH058 . . . . **CE Fic**
DE COTEAU ORIE, S/Did you hear Wind sing your name?: an
Oneida song of spring. /1995/K-2/3 KF454 . . . . **E**
DORRIS, M/Guests. /1994/5-A/7 KH079. . . . . **Fic**
  Sees Behind Trees. /1996/5-A/4 KH081. . . . . **Fic**
GOBLE, P/Dream wolf. /1990/K-3/4 KF627 . . . . **E**
GRIESE, AA/Way of our people. /1997/5-6/5 KH203 . . . . . . **Fic**
HILL, K/Winter camp. /1993/5-A/6 KH262 . . . . **Fic**
KROLL, VL/Seasons and Someone. /1994/K-3/5 KF935. . . . . . **E**
LUENN, N/Nessa's fish. /1990/K-2/2 KG041 . . . . **CE E**
MILES, M/Annie and the old one. /c1971/4-6/4 KH496 . . . . . **Fic**
MITCHELL, B/Red Bird. /1996/1-3/4 KG145 . . . . **E**
MOWAT, F/Lost in the barrens. /1962/5-6/6 KH518 . . . . . . **Fic**
O'DELL, S/Island of the Blue Dolphins. /c1960/6-6/6 KH559 . . **Fic**
  Island of the Blue Dolphins. /c1960, 1990/5-6/6 KH560 . . . . **Fic**
  Thunder rolling in the mountains. /1992/5-A/5 KH563. . . . . **Fic**
OSOFSKY, A/Dreamcatcher. /1992/K-2/5 KG200 . . . . **E**
REID BANKS, L/Indian in the cupboard. /1980/
4-6/4 KH627 . . . . **CE Fic**
  Return of the Indian. /1986/5-A/6 KH629 . . . . **Fic**
ROCKWOOD, J/To spoil the sun. /c1976, 1994/
6-A/6 KH644 . . . . **Fic**
ROGERS, J/Runaway mittens. /1988/P-2/4 KG348 . . . . **E**
SCOTT, AH/Brave as a mountain lion. /1996/3-5/2 KH688 . . . **Fic**
  On mother's lap. /c1972, 1992/P-K/2 KG423 . . . . **E**
STEWART, EJ/On the long trail home. /1994/4-6/4 KH762 . . . **Fic**
STROUD, VA/Doesn't Fall Off His Horse. /1994/2-3/4 KG580. . **E**

WHELAN, G/Next spring an oriole. /1987/2-4/5 KH848 . . . . . **Fic**
YOLEN, J/Sky dogs. /1990/2-3/6 KG780 . . . . **E**

Indians of North America--Florida.
CONQUERING THE SWAMPS (VIDEOCASSETTE). /1991/
A/KE990 . . . . **VCR 975.9**
LOURIE, P/Everglades: Buffalo Tiger and the river of grass. /c1994,
1998/4-6/6 KE992 . . . . **975.9**

Indians of North America--Folklore.
BRUCHAC, J/Boy who lived with the bears: and other Iroquois
stories. /1995/2-4/4 KB537 . . . . **CE 398.24**
First strawberries: a Cherokee story. /1993/
1-3/4 KB538 . . . . **398.24**
Four ancestors: stories, songs, and poems from Native North
America. /1996/2-6/3 KB271 . . . . **398.2**
Gluskabe and the four wishes. /1995/3-5/6 KB272 . . . . . **398.2**
Gluskabe stories (Sound recording cassette). /1990/
4-5/KB273 . . . . **SRC 398.2**
Great ball game: a Muskogee story. /1994/
2-4/2 KB539 . . . . **398.24**
Native American animal stories. /1992/4-6/5 KB540 . . . . **398.24**
Story of the Milky Way: a Cherokee tale. /1995/
2-3/3 KB701 . . . . **398.26**
Thirteen moons on turtle's back: a Native American year of moons.
/1992/2-6/KD919 . . . . **811**
DEARMOND, D/Seal oil lamp. /1988/5-6/6 KB499 . . . . . **398.23**
DUNCAN, L/Magic of Spider Woman. /1996/
4-5/6 KB733 . . . . **398.27**
EDMONDS, M/Voices of the winds: Native American legends. /
1989//KA266 . . . . **PROF 398.2**
EHLERT, L/Mole's hill: a woodland tale. /1994/
K-2/3 KB562 . . . . **398.24**
ESBENSEN, BJ/Great buffalo race: how the buffalo got its hump: a
Seneca tale. /1994/3-4/6 KB564 . . . . **398.24**
EVANS, R/Inktomi and the ducks and other Assiniboin trickster
stories (Talking book). /1994/3-5/KB441 . . . . **TB 398.22**
GATES, R/Owl eyes. /1994/1-3/4 KB570 . . . . **398.24**
GOBLE, P/Adopted by the eagles: a Plains Indian story of
friendship and treachery. /1994/2-5/4 KB706 . . . . **398.26**
Great race of the birds and animals. /1991/
3-5/4 KB574 . . . . **398.24**
Lost children: the boys who were neglected. /1993/
3-5/5 KB707 . . . . **398.26**
HALEY, GE/Two bad boys: a very old Cherokee tale. /1996/
2-5/5 KB742 . . . . **398.27**
HAUSMAN, G/Eagle boy: a traditional Navajo legend. /1996/
3-4/5 KB587 . . . . **398.24**
How Chipmunk got tiny feet: Native American animal origin
stories. /1995/K-3/5 KB588 . . . . **398.24**
HAYES, J/Tales from the Southwest (Sound recording cassette). /
1984/4-5/KB502 . . . . **SRC 398.23**
HIGHWATER, J/Anpao: an American Indian odyssey. /c1977,
1992/5-6/5 KB743 . . . . **398.27**
JACKSON, E/Precious gift: a Navaho creation myth. /1996/
2-3/2 KB594 . . . . **398.24**
LACAPA, M/Antelope Woman: an Apache folktale. /1992/
2-4/5 KB606 . . . . **398.24**
LARRY, C/Peboan and Seegwun. /1993/2-3/4 KB709 . . . . **398.26**
LEWIS, PO/Storm boy. /1995/2-4/3 KB610 . . . . **398.24**
MARTIN, R/Boy who lived with the seals. /1993/
2-4/6 KB614 . . . . **398.24**
Rafe Martin tells his children's books (Talking book). /1994/
K-4/KB341 . . . . **TB 398.2**
Rough-face girl. /1992/3-5/4 KB752 . . . . **398.27**
MCDERMOTT, G/Arrow to the sun. /1974/
2-4/3 KB711 . . . . **CE 398.26**
MONROE, JG/First houses: Native American homes and sacred
structures. /1993/6-A/7 KB171 . . . . **392.3**
MURPHY, CR/Prince and the Salmon People. /1993/
4-6/7 KB352 . . . . **398.2**
OLIVIERO, J/Day Sun was stolen. /1995/K-2/5 KB712 . . . . **398.26**
OUGHTON, J/Magic weaver of rugs: a tale of the Navajo. /1994/
2-4/3 KB627 . . . . **398.24**
RODANAS, K/Dance of the sacred circle: a Native American tale. /
1994/3-4/5 KB639 . . . . **398.24**
ROSS, G/How Rabbit tricked Otter and other Cherokee trickster
stories. /1994/2-4/6 KB641 . . . . **CE 398.24**
How Turtle's back was cracked: a traditional Cherokee tale. /
1995/4-5/5 KB642 . . . . **398.24**
Legend of the Windigo: a tale from native North America. /1996/
2-3/6 KB410 . . . . **398.21**
RUBALCABA, J/Uncegila's seventh spot: a Lakota legend. /1995/
3-5/3 KB478 . . . . **398.22**
SAN SOUCI, RD/Sootface: an Ojibwa Cinderella story. /1994/
1-3/6 KB774 . . . . **398.27**

SCHECTER, E/Warrior maiden: a Hopi legend. /1992/
1-2/2 KB485 . . . . **398.22**
SIMMS, L/Moon and Otter and Frog. /1995/
2-4/2 KB715 . . . . **398.26**
SLOAT, T/Hungry giant of the tundra. /1993/
K-3/5 KB419 . . . . **398.21**
STEVENS, J/Coyote steals the blanket: a Ute tale. /1993/
2-4/2 KB657 . . . . **398.24**
Old bag of bones: a coyote tale. /1996/1-3/2 KB659 . . **398.24**
TAYLOR, CJ/Ghost and Lone Warrior: an Arapaho legend. /1991/
2-5/4 KB696 . . . . **398.25**
How we saw the world: nine Native stories of the way things
began. /1993/4-5/4 KB377 . . . . **398.2**
TAYLOR, HP/Coyote and the laughing butterflies. /1995/
2-3/5 KB662 . . . . **398.24**
THOMASON, D/Lessons from the animal people (Sound recording
cassette). /1996/2-5/KB664 . . . . **SRC 398.24**
UDE, W/Maybe I will do something. /1993/4-5/6 KB669 . **398.24**
WOOD, A/Rainbow bridge: inspired by a Chumash tale. /1995/
3-5/4 KB675 . . . . **398.24**

Indians of North America--Food.
ALIKI /Corn is maize: the gift of the Indians. /c1976/
K-3/3 KD149 . . . . **633.1**
PENNER, LR/Native American feast. /1994/4-6/6 KB187. . . **394.1**

Indians of North America--Government relations.
BEALER, AW/Only the names remain: the Cherokees and the Trail
of Tears. 2nd ed. /1996/5-6/8 KE758 . . . . **970.3**
GOLD, SD/Indian treaties. /1997/5-6/10 KA904 . . . . **323.1**

Indians of North America--Great Plains.
FREEDMAN, R/Buffalo hunt. /1988/4-6/7 KE787 . . . . . . **970.48**
INDIANS OF THE PLAINS (PICTURE). /n.d./
5-6/KE788 . . . . **PIC 970.48**
SNEVE, V/Sioux. /1993/4-6/5 KE776 . . . . **970.3**

Indians of North America--Great Plains--Biography.
ADLER, DA/Picture book of Sitting Bull. /1993/
3-4/5 KE540 . . . . **B SITTING BULL**

Indians of North America--Great Plains--Fiction.
EAGLE WALKING TURTLE /Full moon stories: thirteen Native
American legends. /1997/3-5/7 KH096 . . . . **Fic**
GOBLE, P/Beyond the ridge. /1989/2-4/4 KH177 . . . . **Fic**
Girl who loved wild horses. /1978/K-3/4 KF628 . . . . **CE E**
PAULSEN, G/Mr. Tucket. /1994/5-A/5 KH588 . . . . **Fic**

Indians of North America--Great Plains--Folklore.
GOBLE, P/Crow Chief: a Plains Indian story. /1992/
3-4/4 KB573 . . . . **398.24**
Love flute. /1992/3-5/6 KB738 . . . . **CE 398.27**
Remaking the earth: a creation story from the Great Plains of
North America. /1996/3-5/7 KB448 . . . . **398.22**
Return of the buffaloes: a Plains Indian story about famine and
renewal of the /1996/3-5/3 KB575 . . . . **398.24**
STEPTOE, J/Story of Jumping Mouse: a Native American legend. /
1984/4-5/5 KB656 . . . . **CE 398.24**
WOPILA--A GIVEAWAY: LAKOTA STORIES (SOUND
RECORDING CASSETTE). /1993/3-5/KB676 . . . . . . **SRC 398.24**

Indians of North America--Great Plains--History.
ASHABRANNER, B/Strange and distant shore: Indians of the Great
Plains in exile. /1996/4-6/7 KF026 . . . . **978**
SITA, L/Indians of the Great Plains: traditions, history, legends, and
life. /1997/4-6/8 KE765 . . . . **970.3**

Indians of North America--Great Plains--Hunting bison.
FREEDMAN, R/Buffalo hunt. /1988/4-6/7 KE787 . . . . . . **970.48**

Indians of North America--Great Plains--Social life and customs.
SITA, L/Indians of the Great Plains: traditions, history, legends, and
life. /1997/4-6/8 KE765 . . . . **970.3**

Indians of North America--History.
AVERY, S/Extraordinary American Indians. /1992/
5-6/7 KE747 . . . . **970.1**
GREAT ENCOUNTER (VIDEOCASSETTE). /1991/
A/KE868 . . . . **VCR 973.1**
GRIFFIN-PIERCE, T/Encyclopedia of Native America. /1995/
5-A/KA480 . . . . **REF 970.1**
KRULL, K/One nation, many tribes: how kids live in Milwaukee's
Indian community. /1995/4-6/7 KE783 . . . . **970.475**
NATIVE AMERICAN CULTURES (PICTURE). /1992/
4-6/KE752 . . . . **PIC 970.1**
NATIVE AMERICAN SERIES (VIDEOCASSETTE). /1993/
4-6/KE753 . . . . **VCR 970.1**
NATIVE NORTH AMERICAN VOICES. /1997/
5-A/KA482 . . . . **REF 970.1**
VIOLA, HJ/North American Indians. /1996/4-6/10 KE755 . **970.1**

Indians of North America--History--Fiction.
GOBLE, P/Death of the iron horse. /1987/K-3/2 KF626 . . . . . . **E**

Indians of North America--Legends.
BRUCHAC, J/Between earth and sky: legends of Native American
sacred places. /1996/5-A/5 KB270 . . . . **398.2**
SPIDER SPINS A STORY: FOURTEEN LEGENDS FROM NATIVE
AMERICA. /1997/2-5/6 KB371 . . . . **398.2**

Indians of North America--Literary collections.
RISING VOICES: WRITINGS OF YOUNG NATIVE AMERICANS. /
1992/5-A/7 KD903 . . . . **810.8**

Indians of North America--Magic.
BIERHORST, J/On the road of stars: Native American night poems
and sleep charms. /1994/2-6/KE141 . . . . **897.008**

Indians of North America--Massachusetts--Biography.
BULLA, CR/Squanto: friend of the Pilgrims. /c1954, 1982/
3/3 KE547 . . . . **B SQUANTO**
METAXAS, E/Squanto and the first Thanksgiving (Kit). /1996/
2-6/KE548 . . . . **KIT B SQUANTO**

Indians of North America--Massachusetts--Fiction.
JACOBS, PS/James Printer: a novel of rebellion. /1997/
5-A/6 KH319 . . . . **Fic**

Indians of North America--Massachusetts--Folklore.
MEDICINE STORY /Children of the Morning Light: Wampanoag
tales. /1994/4-5/7 KB348 . . . . **398.2**

Indians of North America--Massachusetts--History.
SEWALL, M/Thunder from the clear sky. /1995/
4-6/7 KE874 . . . . **973.2**

Indians of North America--Massachusetts--Religion and mythology.
MEDICINE STORY /Children of the Morning Light: Wampanoag
tales. /1994/4-5/7 KB348 . . . . **398.2**

Indians of North America--Massachusetts--Rites and ceremonies.
PETERS, RM/Clambake: a Wampanoag tradition. /1992/
4-6/5 KE780 . . . . **970.444**

Indians of North America--Minnesota--Costume and adornment.
KING, S/Shannon: an Ojibway dancer. /1993/
4-6/4 KE784 . . . . **970.476**

Indians of North America--Minnesota--Dances.
KING, S/Shannon: an Ojibway dancer. /1993/
4-6/4 KE784 . . . . **970.476**

Indians of North America--Minnesota--Social life and customs.
WITTSTOCK, LW/Ininatig's gift of sugar: traditional native
sugarmaking. /c1993/3-6/3 KE786 . . . . **970.476**

Indians of North America--Missions--California.
ABBINK, E/Missions of the Monterey Bay Area. /1996/
4-6/9 KF075 . . . . **979.4**
BEHRENS, J/Missions of the central coast. /1996/
4-6/9 KF076 . . . . **979.4**
BROWER, P/Missions of the inland valleys. /1997/
4-6/9 KF077 . . . . **979.4**
LEMKE, N/Missions of the Southern Coast. /1996/
4-6/9 KF083 . . . . **979.4**
MACMILLAN, D/Missions of the Los Angeles Area. /1996/
4-6/9 KF084 . . . . **979.4**
WHITE, FM/Story of Junipero Serra: brave adventurer. /1996/
4-6/7 KE536 . . . . **B SERRA, J.**
WHITE, TN/Missions of the San Francisco Bay Area. /1996/
4-6/9 KF087 . . . . **979.4**

Indians of North America--Missions--Fiction.
O'DELL, S/Zia. /1976/6-A/7 KH564 . . . . **CE Fic**

Indians of North America--Missouri River Valley.
FREEDMAN, R/Indian winter. /1992/A/9 KE202 . . . . . . **917.804**

Indians of North America--Music.
BURTON, B/Moving within the circle: contemporary Native American
music and dance. /1993/KA316 . . . . **BA PROF 789.2**

Indians of North America--New Mexico.
SNEVE, V/Apaches. /1997/4-6/5 KE768 . . . . **970.3**

Indians of North America--New Mexico--Biography.
KEEGAN, M/Pueblo boy: growing up in two worlds. /1991/
4-6/5 KE793 . . . . **970.489**
KREISCHER, EK/Maria Montoya Martinez: master potter. /1995/
5-6/3 KE461 . . . . **B MARTINEZ, M.**

Indians of North America--New Mexico--Folklore.
HULPACH, V/Ahaiyute and Cloud Eater. /1996/
3-4/5 KB708 . . . . **398.26**
POLLOCK, P/Turkey girl: a Zuni Cinderella story. /1996/
2-4/6 KB764 . . . . **398.27**
RODANAS, K/Dragonfly's tale. /1992/2-3/4 KB767 . . . . . **398.27**

Indians of North America--New Mexico--Social life and customs.
KEEGAN, M/Pueblo boy: growing up in two worlds. /1991/
4-6/5 KE793 . . . . **970.489**

Indians of North America--Northeastern States--History.
SITA, L/Indians of the Northeast: traditions, history, legends, and
life. /1997/4-6/9 KE766 . . . . **970.3**

Indians of North America--Northeastern States--Social life and customs.
SITA, L/Indians of the Northeast: traditions, history, legends, and
life. /1997/4-6/9 KE766 . . . . **970.3**

Indians of North America--Northwest, Pacific--Fiction.
HOBBS, W/Ghost canoe. /1997/5-A/6 KH267 . . . . **Fic**
WISNIEWSKI, D/Wave of the Sea-Wolf. /1994/1-3/6 KG753 . . **E**

Indians of North America--Northwest, Pacific--Folklore.
GOLDIN, BD/Coyote and the fire stick: a Pacific Northwest Indian
tale. /1996/2-4/2 KB576 . . . . **398.24**
MCDERMOTT, G/Raven: a trickster tale from the Pacific Northwest.
/1993/1-3/3 KB618 . . . . **398.24**
RODANAS, K/Eagle's song: a tale from the Pacific Northwest. /
1995/3-4/5 KB768 . . . . **398.27**

Indians of North America--Northwest, Pacific--History.
PRESS, P/Indians of the Northwest: traditions, history, legends, and
life. /1997/4-6/9 KE762 . . . . **970.3**

Indians of North America--Northwest, Pacific--Social life and customs.
HOYT-GOLDSMITH, D/Potlatch: a Tsimshian celebration. /1997/
2-5/9 KB189 . . . . **394.2**
PRESS, P/Indians of the Northwest: traditions, history, legends, and
life. /1997/4-6/9 KE762 . . . . **970.3**

Indians of North America--Poetry.
BRUCHAC, J/Thirteen moons on turtle's back: a Native American
year of moons. /1992/2-6/KD919 . . . . **811**
LONGFELLOW, HW/Hiawatha. /1983/P-A/KD979 . . . . . **CE 811**
SONGS ARE THOUGHTS: POEMS OF THE INUIT. /1995/
4-6/KE140 . . . . **897**
WOOD, N/Spirit walker: poems. /1993/6-A/KE046 . . . . . . **811**

Indians of North America--Religion and mythology.
BIERHORST, J/Mythology of North America. /1985/
5-A/KA392 . . . . **REF 291.1**
BRUCHAC, J/Between earth and sky: legends of Native American
sacred places. /1996/5-A/5 KB270 . . . . **398.2**
HIGHWATER, J/Anpao: an American Indian odyssey. /c1977,
1992/5-6/5 KB743 . . . . **398.27**
STROUD, VA/Path of the Quiet Elk: a Native American alphabet
book. /1996/3-6/5 KA793 . . . . **299**

Indians of North America--Rites and ceremonies.
ANCONA, G/Powwow. /1993/3-6/6 KB194 . . . . **394.26**
BRAINE, S/Drumbeat...heartbeat: a celebration of the powwow. /
1995/5-6/9 KB178 . . . . **394**
LIPTAK, K/North American Indian ceremonies. /1992/
4-6/7 KA790 . . . . **299**
MONROE, JG/First houses: Native American homes and sacred
structures. /1993/6-A/7 KB171 . . . . **392.3**
SEYMOUR, TV/Gift of Changing Woman. /1993/
6-A/7 KA792 . . . . **299**

Indians of North America--Rites and ceremonies--Fiction.
MITCHELL, B/Red Bird. /1996/1-3/4 KG145 . . . . **E**

Indians of North America--Sign language.
HOFSINDE, R/Indian sign language. /c1956/2-4/4 KA798 . . **302.2**
LIPTAK, K/North American Indian sign language. /1990/
4-A/5 KB826 . . . . **419**

Indians of North America--Social life and customs.
ANCONA, G/Earth daughter: Alicia of Acoma Pueblo. /1995/
2-4/6 KE791 . . . . **970.489**
BRAINE, S/Drumbeat...heartbeat: a celebration of the powwow. /
1995/5-6/9 KB178 . . . . **394**
DEWEY, JO/Rattlesnake dance: true tales, mysteries, and rattlesnake
ceremonies. /1997/4-6/4 KC634 . . . . **597.96**
GRIFFIN-PIERCE, T/Encyclopedia of Native America. /1995/
5-A/KA480 . . . . **REF 970.1**
HOIG, S/People of the sacred arrows: the Southern Cheyenne
today. /1992/6-A/7 KE781 . . . . **970.466**
HOYT-GOLDSMITH, D/Cherokee summer. /1993/
3-5/5 KE782 . . . . **970.466**
KING, S/Shannon: an Ojibway dancer. /1993/
4-6/4 KE784 . . . . **970.476**
LIPTAK, K/North American Indian ceremonies. /1992/
4-6/7 KA790 . . . . **299**
North American Indian sign language. /1990/4-A/5 KB826 . **419**
MCLAIN, G/Indian way: learning to communicate with Mother
Earth. /1990/2-6/6 KE750 . . . . **970.1**
MOTT, EC/Dancing rainbows: a Pueblo boy's story. /1996/
2-4/2 KE794 . . . . **970.489**
NATIVE AMERICAN CULTURES (PICTURE). /1992/
4-6/KE752 . . . . **PIC 970.1**
NATIVE AMERICAN SERIES (VIDEOCASSETTE). /1993/
4-6/KE753 . . . . **VCR 970.1**
NATIVE WAYS: CALIFORNIA INDIAN STORIES AND MEMORIES.
/1995/5-A/6 KE800 . . . . **970.494**
PENNER, LR/Native American feast. /1994/4-6/6 KB187 . . . **394.1**

REGGUINTI, G/Sacred harvest: Ojibway wild rice gathering. /
1992/4-6/6 KE785 . . . . **970.476**
RENDON, MR/Powwow summer: a family celebrates the circle of
life. /1996/1-3/3 KB181 . . . . **394**
SWENTZELL, R/Children of clay: a family of Pueblo potters. /1992/
4-6/6 KE795 . . . . **970.489**
THOMSON, P/Katie Henio: Navajo sheepherder. /1995/
5-6/6 KE796 . . . . **970.489**
VIOLA, HJ/North American Indians. /1996/4-6/10 KE755 . . **970.1**

Indians of North America--Software.
500 NATIONS: STORIES OF THE NORTH AMERICAN INDIAN
EXPERIENCE ACADEMIC ED. (CD-ROM). /1995/
4-A/KE756. . . . . **CDR 970.1**

Indians of North America--Southern states.
SHEMIE, B/Mounds of earth and shell: the Southeast. /1993/
4-6/7 KB172 . . . . **392.3**

Indians of North America--Southwest, New.
SNEVE, V/Navajos. /1993/4-6/6 KE773 . . . . **970.3**
YUE, C/Pueblo. /1986/5-6/8 KF065 . . . . **979**

Indians of North America--Southwest, New--Antiquities.
WARREN, S/Cities in the sand: the ancient civilizations of the
Southwest. /1992/5-6/8 KF064 . . . . **979**

Indians of North America--Southwest, New--Fiction.
STRETE, CK/World in Grandfather's hands. /1995/
5-A/4 KH771 . . . . **Fic**

Indians of North America--Southwest, New--Folklore.
JAFFE, N/Voice for the people: the life and work of Harold
Courlander. /1997//KA367 . . . . **PROF B COURLAND**
MCDERMOTT, G/Coyote: a trickster tale from the American
Southwest. /1994/P-2/2 KB617 . . . . **398.24**
ROBBINS, S/Growing rock: a Southwest Native American tale (Kit).
/1993/P-1/KB638 . . . . **KIT 398.24**
VIGIL, A/Corn woman: stories and legends of the Hispanic
Southwest/La mujer del maiz: /1994/5-6/4 KB380. . . . **CE 398.2**

Indians of North America--Southwest, New--History.
SITA, L/Indians of the Southwest: traditions, history, legends, and
life. /1997/4-6/9 KE767 . . . . **970.3**

Indians of North America--Southwest, New--Rites and ceremonies.
HOYT-GOLDSMITH, D/Apache rodeo. /1995/
4-6/7 KE798 . . . . **970.491**
ROESSEL, M/Kinaalda: a Navajo girl grows up. /1993/
4-6/5 KE789 . . . . **970.48**

Indians of North America--Southwest, New--Social life and customs.
ARNOLD, C/Ancient cliff dwellers of Mesa Verde. /1992/
5-6/8 KE790 . . . . **970.488**
HOYT-GOLDSMITH, D/Apache rodeo. /1995/
4-6/7 KE798 . . . . **970.491**
Pueblo storyteller. /1991/3-6/6 KE792. . . . . **970.489**
SITA, L/Indians of the Southwest: traditions, history, legends, and
life. /1997/4-6/9 KE767 . . . . **970.3**
TRIMBLE, S/Village of blue stone. /1990/4-6/6 KF063 . . . . . **979**

Indians of North America--Texas--Folklore.
DE PAOLA, T/Legend of the Bluebonnet: an old tale of Texas. /
1983/2-4/4 KB558 . . . . **CE 398.24**

Indians of North America--Treaties.
GOLD, SD/Indian treaties. /1997/5-6/10 KA904 . . . . **323.1**

Indians of North America--West (U.S.).
ACROSS THE SEA OF GRASS (VIDEOCASSETTE). /1991/
A/KF024. . . . . **VCR 978**
INTO THE SHINING MOUNTAINS (VIDEOCASSETTE). /1991/
A/KF035. . . . . **VCR 978**

Indians of North America--Wisconsin--Social life and customs.
KRULL, K/One nation, many tribes: how kids live in Milwaukee's
Indian community. /1995/4-6/7 KE783 . . . . **970.475**

Indians of North America--Women.
ALLEN, PG/As long as the rivers flow: the stories of nine Native
Americans. /1996/6-A/9 KE746. . . . . **970.1**
CONTEMPORARY NATIVE AMERICANS (PICTURE). /1995/
5-6/KE779. . . . . **PIC 970.4**
FRITZ, J/Double life of Pocahontas. /1983/
5-6/6 KE500 . . . . **B POCAHONTAS**
KREISCHER, EK/Maria Montoya Martinez: master potter. /1995/
5-6/3 KE461 . . . . **B MARTINEZ, M.**
LOWERY, L/Wilma Mankiller. /1996/
2-3/4 KE458 . . . . **B MANKILLER, W.**
ROWLAND, D/Story of Sacajawea: guide to Lewis and Clark. /
1995/5-6/6 KE529 . . . . **B SACAGAWEA**
SACAJAWEA (VIDEOCASSETTE). /1991/
2-5/KE530. **VCR B SACAGAWEA**
THOMSON, P/Katie Henio: Navajo sheepherder. /1995/
5-6/6 KE796 . . . . **970.489**

Indians of South America SEE ALSO names of specific groups e.g. Incas.
Indians of South America.
BAQUEDANO, E/Aztec, Inca and Maya. /1993/
4-6/9 KE829 . . . . **972**
MARRIN, A/Inca and Spaniard: Pizarro and the conquest of Peru. /
1989/A/8 KF109 . . . . **985**
NEWMAN, SP/Incas. /1992/5-6/7 KF103 . . . . **980.3**
REYNOLDS, J/Amazon Basin: vanishing cultures. /1993/
3-6/7 KF104 . . . . **981**

Indians of South America--Amazon River Region.
ADVENTURE IN THE AMAZON. /1992/4-6/7 KE211 . . . . . **918.1**
SCHWARTZ, DM/Yanomami: people of the Amazon. /1995/
4-6/7 KF105 . . . . **981**

Indians of South America--Folklore.
KURTZ, J/Miro in the Kingdom of the Sun. /1996/
3-4/5 KB505 . . . . **398.23**

Indians of South America--Peru.
PITKANEN, MA/Grandchildren of the Incas. /1991/
4-6/6 KF110 . . . . **985**

Indians of the West Indies--Fiction.
DORRIS, M/Morning Girl. /1992/6-A/7 KH080. . . . . **Fic**

Indians of the West Indies--Puerto Rico--Folklore.
JAFFE, N/Golden flower: a Taino myth from Puerto Rico. /1996/
2-4/5 KB503 . . . . **398.23**
ROHMER, M/Atariba and Niguayona: a story from the Taino people
of Puerto Rico. /c1976, 1988/4-5/5 KB769 . . . . **398.27**

Individuality SEE ALSO Personality; Self.
Individuality.
AVI /S.O.R. losers. /1984/5-A/6 KG865 . . . . **Fic**
BEHIND THE MASK. REV. ED. (VIDEOCASSETTE). /1987/
1-3/KA817 . . . . **VCR 305**
EPSTEIN-KRAVIS, A/Happy to be me (Sound recording cassette). /
1993/P-1/KA818 . . . . **SRC 155.2**
EVERYBODY'S DIFFERENT (VIDEOCASSETTE). /1994/
3-6/KA639 . . . . **VCR 155.2**
FOX, M/Whoever you are. /1997/P-1/1 KA843 . . . . **305.8**
GROARK LEARNS ABOUT PREJUDICE (VIDEOCASSETTE). /1996/
1-3/KA819 . . . . **VCR 305**
NO ONE QUITE LIKE ME...OR YOU (VIDEOCASSETTE). /1992/
3-6/KA640 . . . . **VCR 155.2**
PALMER, H/Getting to know myself (Sound recording cassette). /
1972/P-1/KA641 . . . . **SRC 155.2**
ROTNER, S/Faces. /1994/P-1/2 KC924 . . . . **612**

Individuality--Fiction.
DE PAOLA, T/Art lesson. /1989/K-2/4 KF464 . . . . **CE E**
FRIEDMAN, A/Cloak for the dreamer. /1995/1-3/6 KF585 . . . . **E**
HENKES, K/Chester's way. /1988/K-2/5 KF702 . . . . **E**
KELLER, H/Harry and Tuck. /1993/K-1/2 KF884. . . . . **E**
MACDONALD, A/No more nice. /1996/4-6/6 KH437 . . . . . **Fic**
No more nice. /1996/3-5/6 KH438 . . . . **Fic**
MACLACHLAN, P/Sarah, plain and tall. /1985/
3-5/4 KH444 . . . . **CE Fic**
MCDONALD, M/Insects are my life. /1995/1-3/2 KG097 . . . . . **E**
YASHIMA, T/Crow Boy. /1955/1-3/3 KG772 . . . . **CE E**

Individuality--Software.
ON THE PLAYGROUND (MICROCOMPUTER PROGRAM). /1988/
1-6/KA662 . . . . **MCP 158**

Indoor gardening.
BJORK, C/Linnea's windowsill garden. /c1978, 1988/
3-5/6 KD173 . . . . **635.9**
HART, A/Kids garden!: the anytime, anyplace guide to sowing and
growing fun. /1996/3-5/6 KD167 . . . . **635**
VAN HAGE, MA/Little green thumbs. /1996/3-5/4 KD176 . **635.9**

Industrialists.
COLLINS, DR/Pioneer plowmaker: a story about John Deere. /
1990/5-6/6 KE317 . . . . **B DEERE, J.**

Industry SEE ALSO Manufactures.
Infant carriers.
BERNHARD, E/Ride on mother's back: a day of baby carrying
around the world. /1996/1-2/7 KB170 . . . . **392.1**

Infants SEE Animals--Infancy; Babies.
Influenza.
STEDMAN, N/Common cold and influenza. /1986/
A/10 KD016 . . . . **616.2**

Information retrieval--Study and teaching.
EISENBERG, MB/Information problem-solving: the Big Six Skills
approach to library and /1990//KA063. . . . . **PROF 025.5**

Information science literature.
AASL ELECTRONIC LIBRARY. 1997 ED. (CD-ROM). /1997/
/KA045. . . . . **CDR PROF 025**

Information services--User education.
EISENBERG, MB/Information problem-solving: the Big Six Skills
approach to library and /1990//KA063. . . . . **PROF 025.5**

Information superhighway.
 BRIMNER, LD/E-mail. /1997/2-4/3 KB134 . . . . **384.3**
Ingalls, Caroline Lake Quiner--Fiction.
 WILKES, MD/Little house in Brookfield. /1996/4-6/5 KH861. . . **Fic**
Inheritance and succession--Fiction.
 KING-SMITH, D/Harry's Mad. /c1984, 1997/5-A/7 KH348 . . . **Fic**
 RASKIN, E/Westing game. /c1978/5-6/5 KH619 . . . . **Fic**
Inner cities.
 BERGIN, DP/Zero Street (Videocassette). /1995/
 4-6/KA894 . . . . **VCR 307.76**
Inner cities--Fiction.
 MEAD, A/Junebug. /1995/5-A/5 KH493 . . . . **Fic**
Insect societies.
 JOHNSON, SA/Wasps. /1984/5-6/8 KC574 . . . . **595.79**
Insectivorous plants SEE ALSO names of specific insectivorous plants e.g.
 Pitcher plants.
Insects SEE ALSO names of insects e.g. Bees, etc.
Insects.
 BORROR, DJ/Field guide to the insects of America north of Mexico.
 /1970/A/12 KA447 . . . . **REF 595.7**
 CICADAS: THE 17-YEAR INVASION (VIDEOCASSETTE). /1993/
 4-6/KC535. . . . . **VCR 595.7**
 GOLDSEN, L/Ladybug and other insects. /1991/
 K-3/4 KC538 . . . . **595.7**
 HENDERSON AVENUE BUG PATROL (VIDEOCASSETTE). /1984/
 1-6/KB867. . . . . **VCR 500**
 HICKMAN, PM/Bugwise: thirty incredible insect investigations and
 arachnid activities. /c1990, 1991/4-6/7 KC540 . . . . **595.7**
 INSECTS (VIDEOCASSETTE). /c1979, 1986/
 2-6/KC541. . . . . **VCR 595.7**
 JOHNSON, J/Simon and Schuster children's guide to insects and
 spiders. /1996/5-6/7 KC542 . . . . **595.7**
 MOUND, L/Insect. /1990/5-6/8 KC545 . . . . **595.7**
 PARKER, NW/Bugs. /1987/4-5/6 KC547 . . . . **595.7**
 SNEDDEN, R/What is an insect? /1993/4-6/6 KC548 . . . . . **595.7**
 SUZUKI, D/Looking at insects. /1992/4-6/5 KC550. . . . . . **595.7**
Insects--Fiction.
 JOYCE, W/Leaf Men and the brave good bugs. /1996/
 1-3/3 KF861 . . . . **E**
 MCDONALD, M/Insects are my life. /1995/1-3/2 KG097 . . . . . **E**
 MURPHY, SJ/Best bug parade. /1996/P-1/1 KG163 . . . . **E**
 RYDER, J/My father's hands. /1994/K-2/KG366 . . . . **E**
Insects--Identification.
 LEAHY, CW/Peterson first guide to insects of North America. /
 1987/5-6/8 KC544 . . . . **595.7**
Insects--Metamorphosis.
 GOOR, R/Insect metamorphosis from egg to adult. /1990/
 4-6/6 KC539 . . . . **595.7**
 REIDEL, M/From egg to butterfly. /1981/P-2/5 KC565 . . . **595.78**
Insects--Miscellanea.
 STEELE, P/Insects. /1991/4-6/6 KC549 . . . . **595.7**
Insects--Poetry.
 FLEISCHMAN, P/Joyful noise: poems for two voices. /1988/
 4-6/KD934. . . . . **811**
Insects--Songs and music.
 MURPHY, J/Songs about insects, bugs and squiggly things (Sound
 recording cassette). /1993/P-2/KC546. . . . . **SRC 595.7**
Insects, Aquatic.
 JOHNSON, SA/Water insects. /1989/A/7 KC543 . . . . **595.7**
Insects as food--Fiction.
 NAYLOR, PR/Beetles, lightly toasted. /1987/5-6/6 KH534 . . . . **Fic**
Insects as pets--Fiction.
 CRESSWELL, H/Meet Posy Bates. /1992/3-5/5 KH038 . . . . . . **Fic**
Instinct.
 INSTINCTS IN ANIMALS (VIDEOCASSETTE). /1996/
 4-6/KC474. . . . . **VCR 591.5**
Instructional materials centers.
 WYNAR, CG/Guide to reference books for school media centers.
 4th ed. /1992//KA007 . . . . **PROF 011**
Instructional materials centers--Periodicals.
 SCHOOL LIBRARY MEDIA ANNUAL. /1983-/
 /KA141. **PER PROF 050**
Instructional music SEE Bands (Music); Dance music; Musical instruments;
 Orchestral music.
Insults SEE Invectives.
Insurance SEE ALSO Saving and investment; Investments.
Intellect SEE ALSO Cleverness.
Intellect.
 BARRETT, SL/It's all in your head: a guide to understanding your
 brain and boosting your /1992/A/8 KA633 . . . . **153**
 CHAPMAN, C/If the shoe fits...how to develop multiple intelligences
 in the classroom. /1993//KA157 . . . . **PROF 155.4**
 LAZEAR, DG/Seven pathways of learning: teaching students and
 parents about multiple /1994//KA174. . . . . **PROF 370.15**

 STAFFORD, P/Your two brains. /1986/5-6/8 KC981 . . . . . **612.8**
 YEPSEN, R/Smarten up! how to increase your brain power. /1990/
 6-A/7 KA645 . . . . **155.42**
Interactive media.
 AESOP'S FABLE: THE TORTOISE AND THE HARE (CD-ROM). /
 1993/P-A/KB522 . . . . **CDR 398.24**
 AFRICA TRAIL (CD-ROM). /1995/4-A/KE723 . . . . **CDR 960**
 ALEXANDER, RM/How animals move (CD-ROM). /1995/
 4-A/KC464 . . . . **CDR 591.47**
 AMAZING ANIMALS (CD-ROM). /1997/K-3/KC444 . . **CDR 591**
 ANIMAL PLANET (CD-ROM). /1996/4-A/KC439 . . . . . **CDR 590**
 ARTHUR'S TEACHER TROUBLE (CD-ROM). /1992/
 1-4/KF171 . . . . **CDR E**
 BAILEY'S BOOK HOUSE (CD-ROM). /1995/
 P-2/KB100 . . . . **CDR 372.4**
 BERENSTAIN BEARS GET IN A FIGHT. SCHOOL ED. (CD-ROM).
 /1995/K-3/KF223 . . . . **CDR E**
 BERENSTAIN BEARS IN THE DARK. SCHOOL ED. (CD-ROM). /
 1996/K-3/KF224. **CDR E**
 BIG ANTHONY'S MIXED-UP MAGIC (CD-ROM). /1996/
 K-2/KF229. . . . . **CDR E**
 BIG JOB (CD-ROM). /1995/K-3/KD120. . . . . . . **CDR 629.225**
 BOOK EXCHANGE (MICROCOMPUTER PROGRAM). /1996/
 3-6/KD862. . . . . **MCP 808**
 CALCULATING CREW. SCHOOL VERSION. (CD-ROM). /1996/
 3-6/KB955. **CDR 513.2**
 CARNIVAL COUNTDOWN. SCHOOL VERSION (CD-ROM). /
 1996/K-2/KB926. . . . . **CDR 510**
 CHICKA CHICKA BOOM BOOM (CD-ROM). /1996/
 P-2/KF382 . . . . **CDR E**
 CLASSROOM STOREWORKS (MICROCOMPUTER PROGRAM). /
 1997/2-5/KD313 . . . . **MCP 658**
 DESTINATION: OCEAN. SCHOOL VERSION (CD-ROM). /1995/
 1-A/KB111. **CDR 372.6**
 DR. SEUSS'S ABC (CD-ROM). /1995/P-2/KF493. . . . . . **CDR E**
 EYEWITNESS ENCYCLOPEDIA OF SPACE AND THE UNIVERSE
 (CD-ROM). /1996/5-A/KC003 . . . . **CDR 520**
 EYEWITNESS VIRTUAL REALITY: CAT (CD-ROM). /1995/
 3-A/KC820 . . . . **CDR 599.75**
 GREAT OCEAN RESCUE (CD-ROM). /1996/
 3-A/KC349 . . . . **CDR 577.7**
 GREAT OCEAN RESCUE (VIDEODISC). /1992/
 3-A/KC350 . . . . **VD 577.7**
 GREAT SOLAR SYSTEM RESCUE (CD-ROM). /1996/
 5-A/KC009 . . . . **CDR 523.2**
 GREAT SOLAR SYSTEM RESCUE (VIDEODISC). /1992/
 5-A/KC010 . . . . **VD 523.2**
 GREEN EGGS AND HAM. SCHOOL ED. (CD-ROM). /1996/
 K-2/KF639 . . . . **CDR E**
 IN THE COMPANY OF WHALES (CD-ROM). /1993/
 3-A/KC770 . . . . **CDR 599.5**
 INVENTION STUDIO (CD-ROM). /1996/5-A/KC887 . . **CDR 608**
 JAMES DISCOVERS MATH. SCHOOL ED. (CD-ROM). /1995/
 1-3/KB962. **CDR 513.2**
 JUST GRANDMA AND ME (CD-ROM). /1992/
 P-2/KF863 . . . . **CDR E**
 KID PIX STUDIO (CD-ROM). /1994/P-A/KD468 . . . **CDR 750.28**
 KIDDESK. SCHOOL VERSION (CD-ROM). /1995/
 P-A/KA569 . . . . **CDR 004**
 LET'S EXPLORE THE JUNGLE WITH BUZZY THE KNOWLEDGE
 BUG (CD-ROM). /1995/K-3/KC320. . . . . **CDR 577.34**
 LOGICAL JOURNEY OF THE ZOOMBINIS. SCHOOL ED. (CD-
 ROM). /1996/2-5/KB938. . . . . **CDR 511**
 MACAULAY, D/Way things work (CD-ROM). /1996/
 3-A/KC882 . . . . **CDR 600**
 MARC BROWN'S ARTHUR'S BIRTHDAY. SCHOOL ED. (CD-ROM).
 /1994/K-4/KG062 . . . . **CDR E**
 MARK SCHLICHTING'S HARRY AND THE HAUNTED HOUSE.
 SCHOOL ED. (CD-ROM). /1994/K-3/KG063. . . . . . . **CDR E**
 MAYAQUEST TRAIL (CD-ROM). /1996/5-A/KE845 . **CDR 972.81**
 MERCER MAYER'S LITTLE MONSTER AT SCHOOL. SCHOOL ED.
 (CD-ROM). /1994/K-3/KG130 . . . . **CDR E**
 MICROSOFT CREATIVE WRITER 2. SCHOOL ED. (CD-ROM). /
 1996/2-A/KB114 . . . . **CDR 372.6**
 MICROSOFT DANGEROUS CREATURES: EXPLORE THE
 ENDANGERED WORLD OF WILDLIFE. /1994/
 4-A/KC490 . . . . **CDR 591.68**
 MICROSOFT DINOSAURS: EXPLORE THE INCREDIBLE WORLD OF
 PREHISTORIC CREATURES. /1994/2-A/KC256. . . . . **CDR 567.9**
 MICROSOFT ENCARTA 97 ENCYCLOPEDIA. DELUXE SCHOOL
 ED. (CD-ROM). /1996/4-A/KA384 . . . . **CDR REF 031**
 MICROSOFT ENCARTA 97 WORLD ATLAS (CD-ROM). /1996/
 3-A/KA472 . . . . **CDR REF 912**

MICROSOFT EXPLORAPEDIA: THE WORLD OF NATURE. ACADEMIC ED. (CD-ROM). /1995/1-4/KB909 . . . . . . **CDR 508**
MICROSOFT EXPLORAPEDIA: THE WORLD OF PEOPLE. ACADEMIC ED. (CD-ROM). /1994/1-4/KA892 . . . . . **CDR 307**
MILLIE'S MATH HOUSE (CD-ROM). /1995/ P-2/KB971 . . . . **CDR 513.2**
MINDS-ON SCIENCE: FOR PROFIT, FOR PLANET (VIDEODISC). /1995/5-A/KD348 . . . . **VD 687**
MINDS-ON SCIENCE: FOR THE SAKE OF THE NATION (VIDEODISC). /1995/5-A/KA804 . . . . **VD 303.48**
MINDS-ON SCIENCE: THE IMPACT OF DISCOVERY (VIDEODISC). /1995/5-A/KB875 . . . . **VD 502**
MOHL, R/Planetary taxi (CD-ROM). /1993/ 4-A/KC013 . . . . **CDR 523.2**
MULTIMEDIA WORKSHOP. TEACHER ED. (CD-ROM). /1996/ 3-A/KB115. **CDR 372.6**
MY FIRST AMAZING WORDS AND PICTURES (CD-ROM). / 1994/K-3/KA426 . . . . **CDR REF 423**
MY FIRST AMAZING WORLD EXPLORER (CD-ROM). /1996/ 1-3/KE170 . . . . **CDR 912**
NEIGHBORHOOD MAPMACHINE (MICROCOMPUTER PROGRAM). /1997/1-5/KC066. . . . . **MCP 526**
NEW KID ON THE BLOCK (CD-ROM). /1993/ K-A/KB995 . . . . **CDR 811**
NEW KID PIX. SCHOOL VERSION (MICROCOMPUTER PROGRAM). /1996/P-A/KD469 . . . . **MCP 750.28**
NUMBER HEROES. SCHOOL VERSION (CD-ROM). /1996/ 3-6/KB929. **CDR 510**
OREGON TRAIL II (CD-ROM). /1994/4-A/KE745 . . **CDR 970.04**
OWENS, P/Classroom newspaper workshop (CD-ROM). /1995/ 4-A/KA594 . . . . **CDR 070.4**
P.J.'S READING ADVENTURES (CD-ROM). /1996/ K-3/KB252. . . . . **CDR 398**
RAINFOREST RESEARCHERS (CD-ROM). /1996/ 5-A/KC323 . . . . **CDR 577.34**
READ, WRITE AND TYPE! (CD-ROM). /1996/ K-2/KB105. . . . . **CDR 372.4**
SCHOLASTIC'S MAGIC SCHOOL BUS EXPLORES IN THE AGE OF DINOSAURS. SCHOOL ED. /1996/1-4/KC263. . . . . **CDR 567.9**
SCHOLASTIC'S THE MAGIC SCHOOL BUS EXPLORES INSIDE THE EARTH. SCHOOL ED. /1996/4-A/KC149 . . . . . . **CDR 550**
SCHOLASTIC'S THE MAGIC SCHOOL BUS EXPLORES THE HUMAN BODY. SCHOOL ED. (CD-ROM). /1995/ 2-A/KC925 . . . . **CDR 612**
SCHOLASTIC'S THE MAGIC SCHOOL BUS EXPLORES THE OCEAN. TEACHER ED. (CD-ROM). /1995/ 2-A/KC369 . . . . **CDR 578.77**
SCHOLASTIC'S THE MAGIC SCHOOL BUS EXPLORES THE RAINFOREST. SCHOOL ED. (CD-ROM). /1997/ 6-A/KC325 . . . . **CDR 577.34**
SCHOLASTIC'S THE MAGIC SCHOOL BUS EXPLORES THE SOLAR SYSTEM. ACADEMIC ED. /1994/2-5/KC014 . . . . . . **CDR 523.2**
SCIENCE BLASTER JR. TEACHER ED. (CD-ROM). /1997/ K-3/KB871 . . . . **CDR 500**
SCIENCE IN YOUR EAR (CD-ROM). /1996/4-A/KC104 **CDR 534**
SKYTRIP AMERICA: AN INCREDIBLE RIDE THROUGH U.S. HISTORY. TEACHER ED. (CD-ROM). /1996/ 3-A/KE865. **CDR 973**
STANLEY'S STICKER STORIES. SCHOOL VERSION (CD-ROM). / 1996/P-2/KB117. . . . . **CDR 372.6**
STELLALUNA (CD-ROM). /1996/K-3/KG550. . . . . **CDR E**
STORYBOOK WEAVER DELUXE (CD-ROM). /1995/ 1-5/KB118. **CDR 372.6**
STRATEGY CHALLENGES COLLECTION 1: AROUND THE WORLD. SCHOOL VERSION (CD-ROM). /1995/3-A/KD754. . . **CDR 794**
STRATEGY CHALLENGES COLLECTION 2: IN THE WILD. SCHOOL VERSION (CD-ROM). /1996/4-A/KD755 . . . . **CDR 794**
STUDENT WRITING AND RESEARCH CENTER WITH COMPTON'S CONCISE ENCYCLOPEDIA /1995/4-A/KB091 . . . **CDR 371.302**
STV: HUMAN BODY (VIDEODISC). /1992/4-A/KC926. . **VD 612**
STV: RAIN FOREST (VIDEODISC). /1991/ 4-A/KC327 . . . . **VD 577.34**
THINKIN' THINGS COLLECTION 1 (MICROCOMPUTER PROGRAM). /1993/K-3/KB080. . . . . **MCP 370.15**
THINKIN' THINGS COLLECTION 2. SCHOOL VERSION (CD-ROM). /1995/1-6/KB081. . . . . **CDR 370.15**
THINKIN' THINGS COLLECTION 3. SCHOOL VERSION (CD-ROM). /1995/3-A/KB082 . . . . **CDR 370.15**
TRUDY'S TIME AND PLACE HOUSE. SCHOOL VERSION (CD-ROM). /1995/P-3/KC075. . . . . **CDR 529**
ULTIMATE HUMAN BODY (CD-ROM). /1996/ 4-A/KC927 . . . . **CDR 612**
ULTIMATE WRITING AND CREATIVITY CENTER. SCHOOL ED. (CD-ROM). /1996/K-5/KB120. . . . . **CDR 372.6**

WINTER, R/Microsoft composer collection (CD-ROM). /1994/ 4-A/KD525 . . . . **CDR 780**
WITH OPEN EYES: IMAGES FROM THE ART INSTITUTE OF CHICAGO (CD-ROM). /1995/2-A/KD368. . . . . . . **CDR 701**
ZOO ZILLIONS. SCHOOL VERSION (CD-ROM). /1966/ K-2/KB986. **CDR 513.2**
500 NATIONS: STORIES OF THE NORTH AMERICAN INDIAN EXPERIENCE ACADEMIC ED. /1995/4-A/KE756. . . . **CDR 970.1**
Interactive multimedia.
MULTIMEDIA, THE COMPLETE GUIDE. /1996/ A/KA372. **REF 006.7**
Intercountry adoption.
SCHWARTZ, P/Carolyn's story: a book about an adopted girl. / 1996/3-6/6 KB014 . . . . **362.73**
Intercultural education.
HELTSHE, MA/Multicultural explorations: joyous journeys with books. /1991/KA262. . . . . **PROF 372.89**
VANDERHEYDEN-TRESCONY, C/Faxing friends; a resource guide for forming international friendships among students, age 5-9. / 1992/KA173 . . . . **PROF 370.117**
Interdisciplinary approach in education.
CHATTON, B/Using poetry across the curriculum: a whole language approach. /1993//KA237. . . . . **PROF 372.64**
MCELMEEL, SL/McElmeel booknotes: literature across the curriculum. /1993//KA225 . . . . **PROF 372.6**
MEINBACH, AM/Complete guide to thematic units: creating the integrated curriculum. /1995//KA195 . . . . **PROF 372.19**
PERRY, PJ/World's regions and weather: linking fiction to nonfiction. /1996//KA294. . . . . **PROF 551.6**
SPILLMAN, CV/Integrating language arts through literature in elementary classrooms. /1996//KA229 . . . . **PROF 372.6**
Interdisciplinary approach in education--Periodicals.
ONLINE--OFFLINE: THEMES AND RESOURCES K-8. /1996-/ /KA129 . . . . **PER PROF 050**
Interior architecture.
BIESTY, S/Stephen Biesty's incredible cross-sections. /1992/ 4-A/6 KC880 . . . . **600**
Internet (Computer network).
AHMAD, N/Cybersurfer: the Owl Internet guide for kids. /1996/ 3-A/8 KA575 . . . . **BC 025.04**
BARRON, AE/Internet and instruction: activities and ideas. /1996/ /KA047. . . . . **PROF 025.06**
BOE, T/World desk: a student handbook to the Internet. Rev. ed. / 1996/A/10 KA576 . . . . **025.04**
BRIMNER, LD/E-mail. /1997/2-4/3 KB134 . . . . **384.3**
COCHRANE, K/Internet. /1995/4-6/8 KA570 . . . . **004.67**
GRALLA, P/Online kids: a young surfer's guide to cyberspace. / 1996/3-A/4 KA578. . . . . **025.04**
KAZUNAS, C/Internet for kids. /1997/2-4/7 KA571 . . . . . **004.67**
KIDS RULE THE NET: THE ONLY GUIDE TO THE INTERNET WRITTEN BY KIDS. /1996/3-A/7 KA579. . . . . . . **025.04**
SALZMAN, M/Kids on-line: 150 ways for kids to surf the net for fun and information. /1995/3-6/6 KA572 . . . . **004.67**
Internet (Computer network)--Directories.
GIAGNOCAVO, G/Educator's Internet companion: CLASSROOM CONNECT's complete guide to educational /1996/ /KA049. . . . . **BC PROF 025.06**
HARRIS, J/Way of the ferret: finding and using educational resources on the Internet. /1995//KA046. . . . . . . **PROF 025.04**
MILLER, EB/Internet resource directory for K-12 teachers and librarians. /1994-//KA179 . . . . **PROF 371.3**
TECH GIRL'S INTERNET ADVENTURE. /1997/ 4-A/KA580 . . . . **BC 025.04**
Internet (Computer network)--Directories--Software.
MICROSOFT BOOKSHELF: MULTIMEDIA REFERENCE LIBRARY, 1998 ED. SCHOOL ED. (CD-ROM). /1997/ 3-A/KA376. . . . . **CDR REF 028.7**
Internet (Computer network)--Handbooks, manuals, etc.
EDUCATORS' ESSENTIAL INTERNET TRAINING SYSTEM (MULTIMEDIA KIT). /1996//KA001 . . . . . . **MMK PROF 004.67**
Internet (Computer network)--Periodicals.
CLASSROOM CONNECT. /1994-//KA102 . . . . . **PER PROF 050**
Internet (Computer network)--Study and teaching--Handbooks, manuals, etc.
BENSON, AC/Connecting kids and the Internet: a handbook for librarians, teachers, and /1996//KA048. . . . . . . **PROF 025.06**
Internet (Computer network) in education--Handbooks, manuals, etc.
BENSON, AC/Connecting kids and the Internet: a handbook for librarians, teachers, and parents. /1996//KA048 . . **PROF 025.06**
Interpersonal communication.
ALIKI /Hello! Good-bye! /1996/P-1/2 KB244 . . . . **395.4**
Interpersonal relations.
BODINE, RJ/Creating the peaceable school: a comprehensive program for teaching conflict /1994//KA161 . . . . . **PROF 303.6**

CASEY'S REVENGE: A STORY ABOUT FIGHTING AND DISAGREEMENTS (VIDEOCASSETTE). /1991/ 3-5/KA808 . . . . **VCR 303.6**
CHOOSE TO REFUSE: SAYING NO AND KEEPING YOUR FRIENDS (VIDEOCASSETTE). /1993/3-5/KA654 . . . . **VCR 158**
COOPERATION (VIDEOCASSETTE). /1990/4-6/KA655 **VCR 158**
GETTING TO THE HEART OF IT (VIDEOCASSETTE). /1993/ 5-A/KA809 . . . . **VCR 303.6**
GROARK LEARNS TO WORK OUT CONFLICTS (VIDEOCASSETTE). /1996/1-3/KA811 . . . . . . **VCR 303.6**
NO MORE TEASING! (VIDEOCASSETTE). /1995/ 3-4/KA661 . . . . **VCR 158**
NOEL'S LEMONADE STAND (UJAMAA) (VIDEOCASSETTE). / 1982/3-5/KD306 . . . . **VCR 650.1**
SLABY, RG/Early violence prevention: tools for teachers of young children. /1995//KA162. . . . . **PROF 303.6**
STUDENT WORKSHOP: MEDIATION SKILLS (VIDEOCASSETTE). / 1996//KA163 . . . . **VCR PROF 303.6**
STUDENT WORKSHOP: SOLVING CONFLICTS (VIDEOCASSETTE). /1994/2-6/KA164 . . . . . . **VCR PROF 303.6**
THAT'S WHAT FRIENDS ARE FOR (VIDEOCASSETTE). /1994/ 5-6/KA666 . . . . **VCR 158**
UNFORGETTABLE PEN PAL: A STORY ABOUT PREJUDICE AND DISCRIMINATION /1991/3-5/KA821 . . . . **VCR 305**
WE CAN WORK IT OUT!: CONFLICT RESOLUTION (VIDEOCASSETTE). /1994/K-2/KA165 . . . . . . **VCR PROF 303.6**

Interpersonal relations--Fiction.
BUNTING, E/Smoky night. /1994/2-5/2 KF309 . . . . **E**
COOPER, I/Buddy Love: now on video. /1995/5-A/4 KH025 . . **Fic**
DECLEMENTS, B/Pickle song. /1993/4-6/4 KH065 . . . . **Fic**
FARRELL, M/Marrying Malcolm Murgatroyd. /1995/ 5-A/4 KH111 . . . . **Fic**
MCKENNA, CO/Good grief, third grade. /1993/ 3-4/4 KH481 . . . . **Fic**
RYLANT, C/Fine white dust. /1986/6-A/4 KH661 . . . . **Fic**
SACHS, M/Truth about Mary Rose /1995/5-A/6 KH669 . . . . . **Fic**
SCOTT, AH/Hi. /1994/P-K/2 KG422 . . . . **E**

Interpersonal relations--Software.
ON THE PLAYGROUND (MICROCOMPUTER PROGRAM). /1988/ 1-6/KA662 . . . . **MCP 158**
Interplanetary visitors SEE Extraterrestrial beings.

Interplanetary voyages--Fiction.
SAINT EXUPERY, AD/Little prince. /c1943/4-A/6 KH671 . . . . **Fic**

Interracial marriage--Fiction.
LITTLE, MO/Yoshiko and the foreigner. /1996/3-5/2 KF997 . . . . **E**
Inuit SEE ALSO Eskimos.

Inuit.
HANCOCK, L/Nunavut. /1995/4-6/7 KE825 . . . . **971.9**

Inuit--Folklore.
DABCOVICH, L/Polar bear son: an Inuit tale. /1997/ K-2/4 KB554 . . . . **398.24**

Inventions.
CANEY, S/Steven Caney's invention book. /1985/ A/10 KC884 . . . . **608**
CARROW, RS/Put a fan in your hat!: inventions, contraptions, and gadgets kids can build. /1997/5-6/8 KC885. . . . . **608**
EUREKA! /1995/4-7/KA451. . . . . **REF 608**
FLACK, JD/Inventing, inventions, and inventors: a teaching resource book. /1989//KA297 . . . . **PROF 607**
INVENT IT! (VIDEOCASSETTE). /1988/3-A/KC886 . . . **VCR 608**
INVENTORS AND INVENTIONS (VIDEOCASSETTE). /1995/ 5-6/KC893 . . . . **VCR 609**
JONES, CF/Accidents may happen. /1996/4-A/9 KC895. . . . **609**
LOMASK, M/Great lives: invention and technology. /1991/ 5-A/9 KC896 . . . . **609**
NOONAN, J/Nineteenth-century inventors. /1992/ 5-6/7 KC897 . . . . **609**
STORIES OF INVENTION AND INGENUITY. VOL. 1 (VIDEOCASSETTE). /1995/3-5/KC898 . . . . **VCR 609**
TAYLOR, B/Be an inventor. /1987/5-6/7 KC888 . . . . **608**

Inventions--China--History.
WILLIAMS, S/Made in China: ideas and inventions from Ancient China. /1996/4-6/6 KE631. **931**

Inventions--Dictionaries.
MOUNT, E/Milestones in science and technology: /1994/ 5-A/ KA441 . . . . **REF 509**

Inventions--Fiction.
SKINNER, D/Wrecker. /1995/6-A/4 KH715 . . . . **Fic**
SMALL, D/Ruby Mae has something to say. /1992/ 1-3/4 KG523 . . . . **E**

Inventions--History--20th century.
JEFFREY, LS/American inventors of the 20th century. /1996/ 4-6/12 KC894 . . . . **609**

Inventions--Miscellanea.
GATES, P/Nature got there first. /1995/4-8/10 KB905 . . . . . **508**

Inventions--Software.
INVENTION STUDIO (CD-ROM). /1996/5-A/KC887 . . **CDR 608**

Inventors.
AASENG, N/Twentieth-century inventors. /1991/A/9 KC889 . **609**
ADLER, DA/Picture book of Thomas Alva Edison. /1996/ 2-3/3 KE330 . . . . **B EDISON, T.**
BIOGRAPHY TODAY SCIENTISTS AND INVENTORS SERIES: PROFILES OF PEOPLE OF INTEREST /1996-/ 4-6/KA438 . . . . **REF 509**
BOWEN, AR/Head full of notions: a story about Robert Fulton. / 1997/4-5/8 KE359 . . . . **B FULTON, R.**
COLLINS, DR/Pioneer plowmaker: a story about John Deere. / 1990/5-6/6 KE317 . . . . **B DEERE, J.**
D'AULAIRE, I/Benjamin Franklin. /c1950/ 2-4/6 KE354 . . . . **B FRANKLIN, B.**
EUREKA! /1995/4-7/KA451. . . . . **REF 608**
FRITZ, J/What's the big idea, Ben Franklin? /c1976/ 5-6/7 KE355 . . . . **CE B FRANKLIN, B.**
HASKINS, J/Outward dreams: black inventors and their inventions. /1991/A/10 KC890 . . . . **609**
HAYDEN, RC/9 African-American inventors. Rev. and expanded ed. /1992/6-A/7 KC891 . . . . **609**
HUDSON, W/Five notable inventors. /1995/3-5/4 KC892 . . . **609**
INVENTORS AND INVENTIONS (VIDEOCASSETTE). /1995/ 5-6/KC893 . . . . **VCR 609**
JEFFREY, LS/American inventors of the 20th century. /1996/ 4-6/12 KC894 . . . . **609**
LOMASK, M/Great lives: invention and technology. /1991/ 5-A/9 KC896 . . . . **609**
MCPHERSON, SS/TV's forgotten hero: the story of Philo Farnsworth. /1996/5-A/9 KE342 . . . . **B FARNSWORTH, P**
MITCHELL, B/We'll race you, Henry: a story about Henry Ford. / 1986/4-5/3 KE346 . . . . **B FORD, H.**
Wizard of sound: a story about Thomas Edison. /1991/ 4-6/6 KE331 . . . . **B EDISON, T.**
NOONAN, J/Nineteenth-century inventors. /1992/ 5-6/7 KC897 . . . . **609**
PROVENSEN, A/Leonardo da Vinci. /1984/ 4-6/7 KE434 . . . . **B LEONARDO**
STANLEY, D/Leonardo da Vinci. /1996/ 5-A/8 KE435 . . . . **B LEONARDO**
TOWLE, W/Real McCoy: the life of an African-American inventor. / c1993, 1995/4-6/7 KE462 . . . . **B MCCOY, E.**

Inventors--Fiction.
DENSLOW, SP/Radio boy. /1995/1-3/7 KF462 . . . . **E**
HAAS, D/Burton's zoom zoom va-rooom machine. /1996/ 4-6/5 KH207 . . . . **Fic**
HIMMELMAN, J/Day-off machine. /1990/1-3/1 KF729 . . . . . . **E**
Invertebrates SEE ALSO Corals; Insects.

Invertebrates.
DORIS, E/Invertebrate zoology. /1993/5-6/8 KC503 . . . . . **592**

Iowa.
KENT, D/Iowa. /1991/5-6/8 KF022 . . . . **977.7**

Iowa--Fiction.
HORVATH, P/Occasional cow. /1989/5-6/8 KH284 . . . . **Fic**

Iran--Folklore.
DE PAOLA, T/Legend of the Persian carpet. /1993/ 2-3/6 KB285 . . . . **398.2**

Ireland--Fiction.
BUNTING, E/Spying on Miss Muller. /1995/6-A/6 KG944 . . . **Fic**
LUTZEIER, E/Coldest winter. /1991/6-A/7 KH429. . . . . . . **Fic**
MACKEN, W/Flight of the doves. /1992/5-A/3 KH442 . . . . . **Fic**
MCDERMOTT, G/Daniel O'Rourke: an Irish tale. /1986/ 2/2 KB755. . . . . **398.27**

Ireland--Folklore.
CLIMO, S/Irish Cinderlad. /1996/2-4/3 KB275 . . . . **398.2**
DE PAOLA, T/Fin M'Coul: the giant of Knockmany Hill. /1981/ 1-3/4 KB392 . . . . **398.21**
Jamie O'Rourke and the big potato: an Irish folktale. /1992/ P-3/4 KB393 . . . . **398.21**
GLEESON, B/Finn McCoul (Videocassette). /1991/ 3-5/KB445 . . . . **VCR 398.22**
GREENE, E/Billy Beg and his bull: an Irish tale. /1994/ 2-4/5 KB304 . . . . **398.2**
HODGES, M/Saint Patrick and the peddler. /1993/ 3-4/5 KB454 . . . . **398.22**
KENNEDY, S/Irish folk tales for children (Compact disc). /1996/ 3-5/KB326. . . . . **CD 398.2**

Ireland--History--1558-1603.
MCCULLY, EA/Pirate queen. /1995/3-5/5 KE156 . . . . . . **910.4**

Ireland--Songs and music.
GRAHAM, S/Dear old Donegal. /1996/1-3/2 KD566 . . . . . **789.2**

Irish--United States--Fiction.
    STOLZ, M/Noonday friends. /c1965/4-6/6 KH767 . . . . . . **CE Fic**
Irish Americans--History.
    CAVAN, S/Irish-American experience. /1993/5-6/7 KA840 . **305.8**
Iroquois Indians.
    SNEVE, V/Iroquois. /1995/4-6/5 KE772 . . . . **970.3**
Iroquois Indians--Biography.
    FRADIN, DB/Hiawatha: messenger of peace. /1992/
    5-6/7 KE389 . . . . **B HIAWATHA**
Iroquois Indians--Folklore.
    BRUCHAC, J/Boy who lived with the bears: and other Iroquois
    stories. /1995/2-4/4 KB537 . . . . **CE 398.24**
    GATES, F/Owl eyes. /1994/1-3/4 KB570. . . . . **398.24**
Iroquois Indians--Tribal government.
    FRADIN, DB/Hiawatha: messenger of peace. /1992/
    5-6/7 KE389 . . . . **B HIAWATHA**
Irvine, Edith--Fiction.
    GREGORY, K/Earthquake at dawn. /1992/5-A/6 KH202 . . . . . **Fic**
Ishtar.
    ZEMAN, L/Revenge of Ishtar. /1993/4-6/4 KE132 . . . . . . **892.1**
Islam.
    FAITH AND BELIEF: FIVE MAJOR WORLD RELIGIONS
    (VIDEOCASSETTE). /1992/5-A/KA722 . . . . **VCR 291**
    HUSAIN, S/What do we know about Islam? /1996/
    4-6/9 KA786 . . . . **297**
    MACDONALD, F/16th century mosque. /1994/
    4-A/10 KD391 . . . . **726**
Islam--Customs and practices.
    GHAZI, SH/Ramadan. /1996/3-5/7 KA785 . . . . **297**
    KERVEN, R/Id-ul-Fitr. /1997/3-5/7 KA787 . . . . **297**
Islam--History.
    CHILD, J/Rise of Islam. /1995/5-A/6 KA784. . . . . **297**
Islamic Empire--Biography.
    CHILD, J/Rise of Islam. /1995/5-A/6 KA784. . . . . **297**
Islamic Empire--History.
    CHILD, J/Rise of Islam. /1995/5-A/6 KA784. . . . . **297**
Islamic stories.
    OPPENHEIM, SL/Iblis. /1994/4-5/4 KA789 . . . . **297**
Island ecology.
    GODKIN, C/Wolf Island. /1993/3-5/4 KC334. . . . . **577.5**
Island ecology--Iceland--Surtsey.
    LASKY, K/Surtsey: the newest place on earth. /1992/
    A/7 KE697 . . . . **949.12**
Islands SEE ALSO Coral reefs and islands; also names of islands and
   groups of islands e.g. Islands of the Pacific, etc.
Islands.
    MILLS, P/On an island in the bay. /1994/2-4/3 KE979 . . . . **975.5**
Islands--Fiction.
    AVI /Smugglers' Island. /1994/4-6/5 KG864 . . . . **Fic**
    BUNTING, E/In-between days. /1994/4-6/4 KG943 . . . . **Fic**
    DORROS, A/Isla. /1995/K-2/2 KF490 . . . . **E**
    ENGLISH, K/Neeny coming, Neeny going. /1996/1-3/2 KF527. . **E**
    FOX, P/Western wind: a novel. /1993/5-A/5 KH141 . . . . **Fic**
    GANTOS, J/Jack's new power: stories from a Caribbean year. /
    1995/5-A/4 KH151 . . . . **Fic**
    KELLER, H/Island baby. /1992/P-2/3 KF885 . . . . **E**
    KELLOGG, S/Island of the skog. /c1973/K-3/5 KF890 . . . . **CE E**
    MAZER, H/Island keeper. /1981/A/6 KH464 . . . . **Fic**
    MORPURGO, M/Wreck of the Zanzibar. /1995/4-6/3 KH516 . **Fic**
    O'DELL, S/Island of the Blue Dolphins. /c1960/5-6/6 KH559 . . **Fic**
    Island of the Blue Dolphins. /c1960, 1990/5-6/6 KH560 . . . . **Fic**
    STEIG, W/Abel's island. /1976/4-6/6 KH749 . . . . **CE Fic**
    STEVENSON, J/Bones in the cliff. /1995/4-6/6 KH755 . . . . . . **Fic**
Islands--Scandinavia--Description and travel.
    PITKANEN, MA/Grandchildren of the Vikings. /1996/
    4-6/8 KE694 . . . . **948**
Israel--Fiction.
    EDWARDS, M/Chicken man. /1991/K-2/2 KF509 . . . . **E**
Italian Americans--Fiction.
    BARTONE, E/American too. /1996/1-3/3 KF210 . . . . **E**
    Peppe the lamplighter. /1993/1-3/2 KF211. . . . . **E**
    LITTLEFIELD, H/Fire at the Triangle Factory. /1996/
    2-5/1 KF998 . . . . **E**
    WOODRUFF, E/Orphan of Ellis Island: a time-travel adventure. /
    1997/5-A/5 KH881. . . . . **Fic**
Italian language materials.
    BURTON, VL/Mike Mulligan and his steam shovel. /c1939/
    P-2/6 KF322 . . . . **CE E**
    FLACK, M/Story about Ping. /c1933/P-1/6 KF550 . . . . **CE E**
    GAG, W/Millions of cats. /c1928/P-1/6 KF592 . . . . **CE E**
Italians--United States--Fiction.
    DE PAOLA, T/Watch out for the chicken feet in your soup. /1974/
    K-2/2 KF481 . . . . **E**

Italy--Fiction.
    DE PAOLA, T/Clown of God. /1978/K-3/6 KF467 . . . . **CE E**
    Days of the blackbird: a tale of northern Italy. /1997/
    1-3/6 KF468 . . . . **E**
Italy--Folklore.
    DE PAOLA, T/Strega Nona: an old tale. /1975/
    1-4/6 KB394 . . . . **CE 398.21**
    Tony's bread. /1989/K-3/5 KB500 . . . . **398.23**
    ITALIAN FOLKTALES. /1980/5-6/KA415 . . . . **REF 398.23**
    KIMMEL, EA/Count Silvernose: a story from Italy. /1996/
    3-5/5 KB504 . . . . **398.23**
    OPPENHEIM, J/Christmas Witch: an Italian legend. /1993/
    1-3/2 KB507 . . . . **398.23**
    PETERSON, J/Caterina, the clever farm girl: a tale from Italy. /
    1996/2-4/3 KB357 . . . . **398.2**
    SANDERSON, R/Papa Gatto: an Italian fairy tale. /1995/
    3-4/6 KB646 . . . . **398.24**
    STANLEY, D/Petrosinella: a Neapolitan Rapunzel. /1995/
    2-4/6 KB780 . . . . **398.27**
Italy--History--1914-1946--Fiction.
    HAUGAARD, EC/Little fishes. /c1967, 1987/A/6 KH227 . . . . . **Fic**
Jack-o-lanterns--Fiction.
    HALL, Z/It's pumpkin time! /1994/P-2/3 KF666 . . . . **E**
    JOHNSTON, T/Very scary. /1995/P-2/3 KF842 . . . . **E**
Jackals.
    PRINGLE, LP/Jackal woman: exploring the world of jackals. /1993/
    5-6/6 KC833 . . . . **599.77**
Jacks (Game).
    LANKFORD, MD/Jacks around the world. /1996/
    3-6/10 KD770 . . . . **796.2**
Jackson, Andrew.
    ANDREW JACKSON: THE PEOPLE'S PRESIDENT
    (VIDEOCASSETTE). /1990/6-A/KE397 . . . **VCR B JACKSON, A.**
Jackson, Bo.
    KRAMER, J/Bo Jackson. /1996/4-5/6 KE398 . . . **B JACKSON, B.**
Jackson, Glen.
    REGGUINTI, G/Sacred harvest: Ojibway wild rice gathering. /
    1992/4-6/6 KE785 . . . . **970.476**
Jackson, Thomas Jonathan.
    FRITZ, J/Stonewall. /1979/5-A/8 KE399 . . . . . . **B JACKSON, T.**
    STONEWALL JACKSON (VIDEOCASSETTE). /1989/
    6-A/KE400. . . . . **VCR B JACKSON, T.**
Jackson Elementary School (Everett, Wash.)
    CONE, M/Come back, salmon: how a group of dedicated kids
    adopted Pigeon Creek and /1992/4-6/6 KD248 . . . . **639.3**
Jacobs, Harriet A. (Harriet Ann)--Fiction.
    LYONS, ME/Letters from a slave girl: the story of Harriet Jacobs. /
    1992/4-6/4 KH430 . . . . **Fic**
Jahns, Hermine--Fiction.
    HYATT, PR/Coast to coast with Alice. /1995/4-6/5 KH312 . . . **Fic**
Jamaica--Fiction.
    BERRY, J/Ajeemah and his son. /1992/6-A/7 KG899 . . . . **Fic**
Jamaica--Folklore.
    BENITEZ, M/How spider tricked snake. /1989/
    K-1/1 KB528 . . . . **398.24**
    GLEESON, B/Anansi (Kit). /1992/3-5/KB572 . . . . . . **KIT 398.24**
    TEMPLE, F/Tiger soup: an Anansi story from Jamaica. /1994/
    2-3/2 KB663 . . . . **398.24**
Jamaica--Songs and music.
    BOOKER, CM/Smilin' island of song (Sound recording cassette). /
    1994/K-4/KD667 . . . . **SRC 789.4**
James, Daniel.
    SUPER, N/Daniel "Chappie" James. /1992/
    5-A/6 KE401 . . . . **B JAMES, D.**
James, Jesse.
    WUKOVITS, JF/Jesse James. /1997/4-6/10 KE402 . **B JAMES, J.**
Jamestown (Va.)--History.
    FRITZ, J/Double life of Pocahontas. /1983/
    5-6/6 KE500 . . . . **B POCAHONTAS**
Japan.
    BORNOFF, N/Japan. /1997/3-5/10 KE707 . . . . **952**
    JAPAN: ASIA, VOLUME 2 (VIDEOCASSETTE). /1993/
    3-6/KE708. . . . . **VCR 952**
    KUKLIN, S/Kodomo: children of Japan. /1995/
    3-5/6 KE710 . . . . **952.04**
Japan--Description and travel.
    SPIVAK, D/Grass sandals: the travels of Basho. /1997/
    1-4/5 KE136 . . . . **895.6**
Japan--Fiction.
    COATSWORTH, E/Cat who went to heaven. New ed. /c1958/
    A/6 KH010 . . . . **CE Fic**
    ESTERL, A/Okino and the whales. /1995/3-5/3 KH101 . . . . . . **Fic**
    FRIEDMAN, IR/How my parents learned to eat. /1984/
    1-3/2 KF586 . . . . **E**

HIDAKA, M/Girl from the snow country. /1986/K-2/4 KF725 . . .   E
KALMAN, M/Sayonara, Mrs. Kackleman. /1989/1-3/3 KF867 . .   E
LITTLE, MO/Yoshiko and the foreigner. /1996/3-5/2 KF997 . . . .   E
MERRILL, J/Girl who loved caterpillars: a twelfth-century tale from
    Japan. /1992/2-4/5 KG132 . . . .   E
SAY, A/Bicycle man. /1982/K-3/4 KG395 . . . .   E
    Grandfather's journey. /1993/2-4/5 KG397 . . . .   E
    Tree of cranes. /1991/1-3/4 KG400 . . . .   E
SNYDER, D/Boy of the three-year nap. /1988/K-3/6 KG525 . . .   E
WATKINS, YK/My brother, my sister, and I. /1994/
    A/4 KH841 . . . .   Fic
    So far from the bamboo grove. /c1986, 1994/5-A/5 KH842 .   Fic
WISNIEWSKI, D/Warrior and the wise man. /1989/
    1-3/5 KG752 . . . .   E
YASHIMA, T/Crow Boy. /1955/1-3/3 KG772 . . . .   CE E
YUMOTO, K/Friends. /1996/6-A/7 KH901 . . . .   Fic

Japan--Folklore.
COWLEY, J/Mouse bride. /1995/P-2/2 KB552 . . . .   398.24
CRYING RED GIANT: A JAPANESE FOLKTALE (VIDEOCASSETTE).
    /n.d./K-2/KB391 . . . .   VCR 398.21
HAMANAKA, S/Screen of frogs: an old tale. /1993/
    2-4/4 KB581 . . . .   398.24
HEDLUND, I/Mighty Mountain and the three strong women. /1990/
    3-5/5 KB316 . . . .   398.2
JAPANESE FAIRY TALES. /1992/2-4/7 KB322 . . . .   398.2
KANI, S/Monkey and the crab. /1985/3/3 KB598 . . . . . .   398.24
LEVINE, AA/Boy who drew cats: a Japanese folktale. /1993/
    2-4/4 KB609 . . . .   398.24
LONG, JF/Bee and the dream: a Japanese tale. /1996/
    2-3/2 KB612 . . . .   398.24
MARTIN, R/Ghostly tales of Japan (Sound recording cassette). /
    1989/3-6/KB689 . . . .   SRC 398.25
    Mysterious tales of Japan. /1996/3-5/3 KB690 . . . . .   398.25
MCCARTHY, RF/Grandfather Cherry-Blossom. /1993/
    2-3/3 KB753 . . . .   398.27
    Inch-high samurai. /1993/3-4/4 KB754 . . . .   398.27
    Moon princess. /1993/3-4/4 KB404 . . . .   398.21
MCDERMOTT, G/Stonecutter (Videocassette). /1976/
    2-4/KB756 . . . .   VCR 398.27
METAXAS, E/Peachboy (Videocassette). /1991/
    2-5/KB469 . . . .   VCR 398.22
PATERSON, K/Tale of the mandarin ducks. /1990/
    2-3/6 KB631 . . . .   398.24
SAN SOUCI, RD/Samurai's daughter: a Japanese legend. /1992/
    3-4/6 KB365 . . . .   398.2
    Snow wife. /1993/3-9/5 KB414 . . . .   398.21
SAY, A/Under the cherry blossom tree: an old Japanese tale. /
    1997/P-1/5 KB777 . . . .   398.27
SCHROEDER, A/Lily and the wooden bowl. /1994/
    3-5/7 KB366 . . . .   398.2
UCHIDA, Y/Magic purse. /1993/2-4/4 KB379 . . . .   398.2
    Wise old woman. /1994/2-4/5 KB492 . . . .   398.22
WAITE, MP/Jojofu. /1996/1-4/5 KB670 . . . .   398.24
WELLS, R/Farmer and the Poor God: a folktale from Japan. /
    1996/2-4/3 KB785 . . . .   398.27
WILLIAMS, CA/Tsubu the little snail. /1995/3-5/4 KB673 .   398.24

Japan--Foreign relations--United States.
BLUMBERG, R/Commodore Perry in the land of the Shogun. /
    1985/5-A/7 KE706 . . . .   CE 952

Japan--History--Fiction.
PATERSON, K/Master puppeteer. /c1975/6-A/6 KH580 . . . . .   Fic
    Sign of the chrysanthemum. /c1973, 1991/5-A/6 KH581 . . . .   Fic

Japan--History--Period of civil wars, 1480-1603--Fiction.
HAUGAARD, EC/Boy and the Samurai. /1991/
    6-A/6 KH226 . . . .   CE Fic
    Samurai's tale. /1984/6-A/5 KH228 . . . .   Fic

Japan--Social life and customs.
JAPAN: ASIA, VOLUME 2 (VIDEOCASSETTE). /1993/
    3-6/KE708 . . . .   VCR 952
KUKLIN, S/Kodomo: children of Japan. /1995/
    3-5/6 KE710 . . . .   952.04

Japan--Social life and customs--Fiction.
KALMAN, M/Sayonara, Mrs. Kackleman. /1989/1-3/3 KF867 . .   E

Japanese--United States--Fiction.
HIROSHIMA MAIDEN (VIDEOCASSETTE). /c1988, 1997/
    5-A/KH264 . . . .   VCR Fic
UCHIDA, Y/Jar of dreams. /1981/5-6/6 KH815 . . . .   Fic

Japanese--United States--History.
HAMANAKA, S/Journey: Japanese Americans, racism, and renewal.
    /1990/5-6/7 KE854   973

Japanese Americans--Biography.
SAVAGE, J/Kristi Yamaguchi: pure gold. /1993/
    3-5/7 KE603 . . . .   B YAMAGUCHI, K.

Japanese Americans--California--San Francisco--Social life and customs.
BROWN, T/Konnichiwa!: I am a Japanese-American girl. /1995/
    3-5/4 KA839 . . . .   305.8

Japanese Americans--Evacuation and relocation, 1942-1945.
STANLEY, J/I am an American: a true story of Japanese internment.
    /1994/5-A/8 KE666 . . . .   940.53
TUNNELL, MO/Children of Topaz: the story of a Japanese-
    American internment camp: based on a classroom diary. /1996/
    5-6/8 KE667 . . . .   940.53

Japanese Americans--Evacuation and relocation, 1942-1945--Fiction.
MOCHIZUKI, K/Baseball saved us. /1993/4-A/6 KH500 . . . . .   Fic
UCHIDA, Y/Bracelet. /1993/2-5/3 KG631 . . . .   E
    Journey to Topaz. /c1971, 1984/5-A/7 KH816 . . . .   Fic

Japanese Americans--Fiction.
MOCHIZUKI, K/Heroes. /1995/3-5/4 KH501 . . . .   Fic
SALISBURY, G/Under the blood-red sun. /1994/6-A/4 KH672 .   Fic
SAY, A/Grandfather's journey. /1993/2-4/5 KG397 . . . .   E

Japanese Americans--History.
HAMANAKA, S/Journey: Japanese Americans, racism, and renewal.
    /1990/5-6/7 KE854   973

Japanese Americans--Social life and customs.
BROWN, T/Konnichiwa!: I am a Japanese-American girl. /1995/
    3-5/4 KA839 . . . .   305.8

Japanese language materials.
MADO, M/Animals: selected poems. /1992/2-6/KE135 . . . .   895.6

Japanese language materials--Software.
JUST GRANDMA AND ME (CD-ROM). /1992/
    P-2/KF863 . . . .   CDR E

Japanese poetry SEE ALSO Haiku.
Japanese poetry.
MADO, M/Animals: selected poems. /1992/2-6/KE135 . . . .   895.6

Japanese poetry--Collections.
FESTIVAL IN MY HEART: POEMS BY JAPANESE CHILDREN. /
    1993/3-A/KE134 . . . .   895.6
SPRING: A HAIKU STORY. /1996/1-6/KE137 . . . .   895.6

Jason (Greek mythology).
COLUM, P/Golden fleece and the heroes who lived before Achilles.
    /c1949/5-6/6 KA736   292
FISHER, LE/Theseus and the Minotaur. /1988/5-6/6 KA741 . .   292

Jataka stories.
HODGES, M/Hidden in sand. /1994/3-4/6 KA759. . . . . . .   294.3
MARTIN, R/Foolish rabbit's big mistake. /1985/
    3-4/4 KA760 . . . .   294.3

Jay, Allen.
BRILL, MT/Allen Jay and the Underground Railroad. /1993/
    4-6/4 KE898 . . . .   973.7

Jazz.
MEDEARIS, AS/Little Louis and the jazz band: the story of Louis
    "Satchmo" Armstrong. /1994/
    2-4/6 KE241 . . . .   B ARMSTRONG, L.
WEISS, GD/What a wonderful world. /1995/P-2/2 KG692 . . . .   E

Jazz--History.
HUGHES, L/Story of jazz (Sound recording cassette). /1954/
    5-6/KD673. . . . .   SRC 789.5

Jazz musicians.
ELLIS, VF/Wynton Marsalis. /1997/
    5-A/10 KE459 . . . .   B MARSALIS, W.

Jealousy--Fiction.
CLEARY, B/Socks. /c1973/3-4/6 KH007. . . . .   Fic
HAVILL, J/Jamaica and Brianna. /1993/K-2/2 KF680 . . . .   E
O'CONNOR, J/Lulu and the witch baby. /1986/K-3/2 KG188 . .   E

Jealousy--Folklore.
GRIMM, J/Snow-White and the seven dwarfs. /1972/
    3-4/6 KB310 . . . .   398.2

Jefferson, Thomas.
ADLER, DA/Picture book of Thomas Jefferson. /1990/
    2-3/5 KE403 . . . .   B JEFFERSON, T.
GIBLIN, JC/Thomas Jefferson: a picture book biography. /1994/
    3-5/5 KE404 . . . .   B JEFFERSON, T.
REEF, C/Monticello. /1991/3-5/6 KE892 . . . .   973.4

Jelly beans.
MCMILLAN, B/Jelly beans for sale. /1996/K-3/2 KA951 . . .   332.4

Jellyfishes.
KITE, P/Down in the sea: the jellyfish. /1993/3-5/4 KC509. .   593.5

Jemison, Mary.
SEAVER, JE/Captured by Indians: the life of Mary Jemison. /1995/
    5-A/8 KE405 . . . .   B JEMISON, M.

Jerusalem--Folklore.
SCHWARTZ, H/Next year in Jerusalem: 3000 years of Jewish
    stories. /1996/3-6/7 KA780 . . . .   296.4

Jesus Christ--Art.
JESUS OF NAZARETH: A LIFE OF CHRIST THROUGH PICTURES.
    /1994/4-A/5 KA696 . . . .   232.9

L'ENGLE, M/Glorious impossible. /1990/4-A/6 KA697 .... **232.9**

Jesus Christ--Biography.
JESUS OF NAZARETH: A LIFE OF CHRIST THROUGH PICTURES.
/1994/4-A/5 KA696 . . . . **232.9**
L'ENGLE, M/Glorious impossible. /1990/4-A/6 KA697 .... **232.9**

Jesus Christ--Crucifixion.
WINTHROP, E/He is risen: the Easter story. /1985/
5-6/7 KA711 . . . . **232.96**

Jesus Christ--Miracles.
DE PAOLA, T/Miracles of Jesus. /1987/5-6/7 KA695 . . . . . **232.9**

Jesus Christ--Nativity.
BROWN, MW/Christmas in the barn. /c1952/P-K/KA700 . **232.92**
CHRISTMAS STORY. /1996/2-3/4 KA701 . . . . **232.92**
DUNBAR, J/This is the star. /1996/2-3/2 KA703 . . . . . . **232.92**
FIRST CHRISTMAS. /1992/6-A/5 KA704 . . . . **232.92**
GLEESON, B/Savior is born (Kit). /1992/3-5/KA705 . **KIT 232.92**
HENNESSY, BG/First night. /1993/P-2/3 KA706 . . . . . **232.92**
HOGROGIAN, N/First Christmas. /1995/K-2/5 KA707 . . . **232.92**
KURELEK, W/Northern Nativity: Christmas dreams of a prairie boy.
/c1976/4-6/7 KA708 . . . . **CE 232.92**
NATIVITY. /1996/3-5/5 KA709 . . . . **232.92**

Jesus Christ--Nativity--Poetry.
KENNEDY, XJ/Beasts of Bethlehem. /1992/1-6/6 KD960 . . . . . **811**
WILMER, I/B is for Bethlehem: a Christmas alphabet. /1990/
K-3/KE043 . . . . **811**

Jesus Christ--Nativity--Songs and music.
WHAT A MORNING! THE CHRISTMAS STORY IN BLACK
SPIRITUALS. /1987/K-6/KD532 . . . . **782.25**

Jesus Christ--Parables.
DE PAOLA, T/Miracles of Jesus. /1987/5-6/7 KA695 . . . . **232.9**

Jesus Christ--Passion.
HEYER, C/Easter story. /1990/5-6/5 KA710 . . . . **232.96**

Jesus Christ--Resurrection.
FISHER, AL/Story of Easter. /1997/2-3/2 KA714. . . . . . . **263**
WINTHROP, E/He is risen: the Easter story. /1985/
5-6/7 KA711 . . . . **232.96**

Jet planes, Military.
BIG AIRCRAFT CARRIER (VIDEOCASSETTE). /1995/
4-6/KA989 . . . . **VCR 359.9**
JENSSEN, H/Jets. /1996/4-6/8 KD061 . . . . **623.7**
Jet propulsion SEE Rockets (Aeronautics).
Jewelry SEE ALSO Silversmithing.
Jewish religion SEE Judaism.

Jews--Austria--Fiction.
ACKERMAN, K/Night crossing. /1994/3-4/8 KG812 . . . . . . **Fic**

Jews--Billings (Mont.).
COHN, J/Christmas menorahs: how a town fought hate. /1995/
3-6/5 KA818 . . . . **305**

Jews--Biography.
ADLER, DA/Hilde and Eli: children of the Holocaust. /1994/
4-6/5 KE655 . . . . **940.53**
Picture book of Anne Frank. /1993/
3-4/5 KE351 . . . . **CE B FRANK, A.**
REISS, J/Upstairs room. /c1972/5-6/5 KE506 . . . . . **B REISS, J.**
ROSENBERG, MB/Hiding to survive: stories of Jewish children
rescued from the Holocaust. /1994/A/6 KE665 . . . . . . **940.53**
STREISSGUTH, T/Say it with music: a story about Irving Berlin. /
1994/4-5/5 KE252 . . . . **B BERLIN, I.**
VAN DER ROL, R/Anne Frank, beyond the diary: a photographic
remembrance. /1993/6-A/7 KE353 . . . . **B FRANK, A.**

Jews--Czech Republic--Folklore.
WISNIEWSKI, D/Golem. /1996/2-6/5 KB423 . . . . **398.21**

Jews--Dictionaries.
JUNIOR JEWISH ENCYCLOPEDIA. 11TH REV. ED. /1991/
5-6/KA396 . . . . **REF 296**

Jews--Ethiopia--Fiction.
SCHUR, MR/Day of delight: a Jewish Sabbath in Ethiopia. /1994/
1-3/4 KG412 . . . . **E**
When I left my village. /1996/4-A/5 KH683 . . . . **Fic**

Jews--Europe--Fiction.
SILVERMAN, E/Gittel's hands. /1996/K-2/2 KG506 . . . . **E**

Jews--Fiction.
GOLDIN, BD/Magician's visit: a Passover tale. /1993/
K-3/5 KF629 . . . . **E**
LANTON, S/Daddy's chair. /1991/P-2/2 KF944 . . . . **E**
LITTLEFIELD, H/Fire at the Triangle Factory. /1996/
2-5/1 KF998 . . . . **E**
MANUSHKIN, F/Starlight and candles: the joys of the Sabbath. /
1995/1-3/2 KG061 . . . . **E**
POLACCO, P/Keeping quilt. /1988/K-3/6 KG252 . . . . **CE E**
Mrs. Katz and Tush. /1992/1-3/2 KG253 . . . . **E**
Trees of the dancing goats. /1996/1-3/3 KG260 . . . . **Fic**
ROSE, DL/Rose horse. /1995/3-5/6 KH651 . . . . **Fic**
SACHS, M/Call me Ruth. /c1982, 1995/5-A/6 KH667 . . . . . . **Fic**

SCHNUR, S/Tie man's miracle: a Chanukah tale. /1995/
2-3/4 KG409 . . . . **E**
SCHOTTER, R/Passover magic. /1995/K-2/2 KG410. . . . . **E**
WEISS, N/Stone men. /1993/K-2/2 KG693 . . . . **E**
WILD, M/Let the celebrations begin! /1991/4-A/4 KH858 . . . . **Fic**

Jews--Folklore.
GILMAN, P/Something from nothing: adapted from a Jewish
folktale. /1993/1-3/3 KB737 . . . . **398.27**
GREENE, JD/What his father did. /1992/2-4/5 KB305 . . . . **398.2**
KIMMEL, EA/Adventures of Hershel of Ostropol. /1995/
2-4/7 KB459 . . . . **398.22**
Days of awe: stories for Rosh Hashanah and Yom Kippur. /1991/
4-6/5 KA777 . . . . **296.4**
LESTER, J/How many spots does a leopard have? and other tales. /
c1989, 1994/5-6/6 KB335 . . . . **398.2**
ORGEL, D/Flower of Sheba. /1994/1-2/2 KA687 . . . . **222**
PODWAL, M/Book of tens. /1994/5-6/7 KA769 . . . . **296.1**
Golem: a giant made of mud. /1995/4-6/7 KB408 . . . . **398.21**
RENBERG, DH/King Solomon and the bee. /1994/
2-3/4 KB475 . . . . **398.22**
ROTHENBERG, J/Yettele's feathers. /1995/2-4/3 KB771 . . **398.27**
SANFIELD, S/Bit by bit. /1995/K-2/2 KB772. . . . . **398.27**
Feather merchants and other tales of the fools of Chelm. /1991/
6-A/7 KB510 . . . . **398.23**
Strudel, strudel, strudel. /1995/2-3/4 KB773 . . . . . . **398.27**
SCHWARTZ, H/Diamond tree: Jewish tales from around the world.
/1991/3-4/6 KB368 . . . . **398.2**
Next year in Jerusalem: 3000 years of Jewish stories. /1996/
3-6/7 KA780 . . . . **296.4**
Sabbath lion: a Jewish folktale from Algeria. /1992/
4-6/6 KB511 . . . . **398.23**
Wonder child and other Jewish fairy tales. /1996/
2-4/5 KB369 . . . . **398.2**
SHULEVITZ, U/Treasure. /1978/2-4/4 KB778 . . . . **398.27**
SINGER, IB/Mazel and Shlimazel; or, The milk of a lioness. /1967/
4-6/6 KB779 . . . . **398.27**
Naftali the storyteller and his horse, Sus. /1987/
5-6/5 KH712 . . . . **Fic**
ZEMACH, M/It could always be worse: a Yiddish folk tale. /1976/
2-4/4 KB792 . . . . **CE 398.27**

Jews--France--Fiction.
SACHS, M/Pocket full of seeds. /c1973, 1994/4-A/5 KH668 . . **Fic**

Jews--France--Paris--Fiction.
HOESTLANDT, J/Star of fear, star of hope. /1995/
3-5/5 KH268 . . . . **Fic**

Jews--Germany--1933-1945--Fiction.
LEVITIN, S/Journey to America. /c1970, 1993/5-A/5 KH398 . . **Fic**

Jews--Israel--Fiction.
EDWARDS, M/Chicken man. /1991/K-2/2 KF509 . . . . **E**

Jews--Miscellanea.
BURSTEIN, CM/Jewish kids catalog. /1983/4-6/7 KB179. . . . **394**

Jews--Netherlands.
REISS, J/Upstairs room. /c1972/5-6/5 KE506 . . . . . . **B REISS, J.**

Jews--Netherlands--Fiction.
VOS, I/Anna is still here. /1993/5-A/4 KH834 . . . . **Fic**
Hide and seek. /c1981, 1991/5-A/4 KH835 . . . . **Fic**

Jews--New York (N.Y.)--Fiction.
HARVEY, B/Immigrant girl: Becky of Eldridge Street. /1987/
3-5/5 KH221 . . . . **Fic**

Jews--Persecutions.
FRANK, A/Diary of a young girl. /c1967/
4-6/6 KE352 . . . . **B FRANK, A.**
MELTZER, M/Never to forget: the Jews of the Holocaust. /c1976/
A/7 KE674 . . . . **940.54**

Jews--Persecutions--Fiction.
SCHUR, MR/When I left my village. /1996/4-A/5 KH683 . . . . **Fic**

Jews--Poland--Fiction.
ORLEV, U/Island on Bird Street. /1983/5-A/6 KH566 . . . . . **Fic**
Man from the other side. /1991/5-A/6 KH567 . . . . **Fic**
SINGER, IB/Naftali the storyteller and his horse, Sus. /1987/
5-6/5 KH712 . . . . **Fic**

Jews--Rites and ceremonies.
GOLDIN, BD/Bat mitzvah: a Jewish girl's coming of age. /1995/
5-A/10 KA773 . . . . **296.4**
KIMMEL, EA/Bar mitzvah: a Jewish boy's coming of age. /1995/
5-A/7 KA776 . . . . **296.4**

Jews--Social life and customs--Fiction.
OBERMAN, S/Always Prayer Shawl. /1994/2-4/2 KG184. . . . . **E**

Jews--Soviet Union.
BRESNICK-PERRY, R/Leaving for America. /1992/
1-4/6 KE688 . . . . **947**

Jews--Soviet Union--Fiction.
SEGAL, J/Place where nobody stopped. /1994/5-A/7 KH690 . **Fic**

Jews--Spain--History.
FINKELSTEIN, NH/Other 1492: Jewish settlement in the new world. /1992/5-6/8 KE687 . . . . **946**

Jews--United States--Fiction.
ADLER, DA/One yellow daffodil: a Hanukkah story. /1995/ 3-5/4 KG818 . . . . **Fic**
BLANC, ES/Berchick. /1989/3-5/5 KG901 . . . . **Fic**
BLOS, JW/Brooklyn doesn't rhyme. /1994/4-6/6 KG904 . . . . . **Fic**
COHEN, B/Molly's pilgrim. /1983/1-3/4 KH012 . . . . **CE Fic**
KIMMEL, EA/Magic dreidels: a Hanukkah story. /1996/ K-3/2 KF904 . . . . **E**
MAZER, H/Last mission. /c1979, 1986/6-A/4 KH465 . . . . . . **Fic**
TAYLOR, S/All-of-a-kind family. /1951, 1988/4-6/5 KH782 . . . **Fic**

Jigsaw puzzles--Fiction.
BIRCHMAN, DF/Jigsaw Jackson. /1996/1-3/3 KF230 . . . . **E**
Jiujitsu SEE Judo.
Jobs SEE Occupations; Vocational guidance.

Jobs, Steven.
GREENBERG, KE/Steven Jobs and Stephen Wozniak: creating the Apple computer. /1994/4-6/7 KD046 . . . . **621.39**

Jockeys.
GUTMAN, B/Julie Krone. /1996/5-6/5 KE425 . . . . . **B KRONE, J.**
Jogging SEE Running.

John Henry (Legendary character).
LESTER, J/John Henry. /1994/2-5/4 KB464 . . . . **398.22**

Johnson, Lyndon B.
FALKOF, L/Lyndon B. Johnson, 36th president of the United states. /1989/6-A/9 KE406 . . . . **B JOHNSON, L.**

Johnston, Annie Bronn--Fiction.
HENRY, M/Mustang, wild spirit of the West. /c1966, 1992/ 5-6/5 KH245 . . . . **Fic**

Johnston, William J.--Fiction.
WISLER, GC/Mr. Lincoln's drummer. /1995/5-A/4 KH871 . . . . **Fic**
Jokes SEE ALSO Knock-knock jokes; Wit and humor.

Jokes.
BIXENMAN, J/Dinosaur jokes. /1991/2-4/KD725 . . . . . . **793.735**
COLE, RM/Zany knock knocks. /1993/3-6/KD726 . . . . . **793.735**
HARTMAN, V/Silliest joke book ever. /1993/ 2-4/5 KD729 . . . . **793.735**
KESSLER, L/Old Turtle's 90 knock-knocks, jokes, and riddles. / 1991/2-4/KD730 . . . . **793.735**
LAUGHING TOGETHER: GIGGLES AND GRINS FROM AROUND THE GLOBE. /c1977, 1992/3-A/KD731 . . . . **793.735**
LEVINE, CA/Riddles to tell your cat. /1992/2-5/KD732 . . **793.735**
MATHEWS, J/Oh, how waffle!: riddles you can eat. /1993/ 2-6/KD735 . . . . **793.735**
PHILLIPS, L/Keep 'em laughing: jokes to amuse and annoy your friends. /1996/3-6/KD736 . . . . **793.735**
PLANET OF THE GRAPES: SHOW BIZ JOKES AND RIDDLES. / 1992/3-6/KD737 . . . . **793.735**
SWANSON, J/Summit up: riddles about mountains. /1994/ 3-6/KD739 . . . . **793.735**
TAKE ME TO YOUR LITER: SCIENCE AND MATH JOKES. /1991/ 3-6/KD740. . . . . **793.735**
THALER, M/Earth mirth: the ecology riddle book. /1994/ 2-4/KD741. . . . . **793.735**
WOODWORTH, V/Animal jokes. /1993/2-4/KD742 . . . . **793.735**
Fairy tale jokes. /1993/2-4/KD743 . . . . **793.735**

Jokes--Fiction.
DUFFEY, B/Camp Knock Knock. /1996/1-3/2 KF500 . . . . **E**
MODELL, F/Look out, it's April Fools' Day. /1985/ K-2/2 KG148 . . . . **E**

Joliot-Curie, Irene.
PFLAUM, R/Marie Curie and her daughter Irene. /1993/ 6-A/8 KC139 . . . . **539.7**

Jonah (Biblical prophet).
PATTERSON, G/Jonah and the whale. /1992/P-2/4 KA692. . **224**

Jones, Mother.
COLMAN, P/Mother Jones and the march of the mill children. / 1994/4-6/7 KA935. . . . . **331.3**
CURRIE, S/We have marched together: the working children's crusade. /1997/5-6/8 KA936 . . . . **331.3**

Joplin, Scott.
MITCHELL, B/Raggin', a story about Scott Joplin. /1987/ A/8 KE407 . . . . **B JOPLIN, S.**

Jordan, Barbara.
PATRICK-WEXLER, D/Barbara Jordan. /1996/ 4-6/8 KE408 . . . . **B JORDAN, B.**

Jordan, Michael.
CHRISTOPHER, M/On the court with...Michael Jordan. /1996/ 4-6/8 KE409 . . . . **CE B JORDAN, M.**
GUTMAN, B/Michael Jordan: basketball to baseball and back. Rev. ed. /1995/4-6/8 KE410 . . . . **B JORDAN, M.**

LIPSYTE, R/Michael Jordan: a life above the rim. /1994/ 4-6/7 KE411 . . . . **B JORDAN, M.**

Jordan-Wong, Jennifer.
BANISH, R/Forever family. /1992/2-4/3 KB011 . . . . **362.73**

Joseph, Nez Perce Chief.
FREEDMAN, R/Indian chiefs. /1987/5-6/8 KE749 . . . . . . **970.1**

Joseph (Son of Jacob).
GLEESON, B/Joseph and his brothers (Videocassette). /1993/ 5-6/KA685 . . . . **VCR 222**
WILLIAMS, M/Joseph and his magnificent coat of many colors. / 1992/2-4/5 KA689 . . . . **222**
Journalism SEE ALSO Newspapers; Reporters and reporting; Television broadcasting of the news.

Journalism--Software.
OWENS, P/Classroom newspaper workshop (CD-ROM). /1995/ 4-A/KA594 . . . . **CDR 070.4**

Journalism--Vocational guidance.
KAPLAN, A/Careers for wordsmiths. /1991/6-A/7 KA593 . . **070.4**
SO YOU WANT TO BE?: NEWSPAPER ARTIST (VIDEOCASSETTE). /1994/5-6/KA595 . . . . **VCR 070.4**

Journalists.
KENDALL, ME/Nellie Bly: reporter for the world. /1992/ 4-6/5 KE256 . . . . **B BLY, N.**

Journalists--Fiction.
BLOS, JW/Nellie Bly's monkey: his remarkable story in his own words. /1996/2-5/9 KF236. . . . . **E**

Joy and sorrow--Fiction.
SMITH, DB/Taste of blackberries. /c1973/4-6/4 KH722 . . . . . **Fic**

Joyner-Kersee, Jacqueline.
COHEN, N/Jackie Joyner-Kersee. /1992/ 4-6/6 KE412 . . . . **B JOYNER-KERSEE**

Juan Bobo (Legendary character).
BERNIER-GRAND, CT/Juan Bobo: four folktales from Puerto Rico. / 1994/1-2/2 KB427 . . . . **398.22**
PITRE, F/Juan Bobo and the pig: a Puerto Rican folktale. /1993/ 2-4/2 KB763 . . . . **398.27**
Judaism SEE ALSO Bible. O.T; Hanukkah; Jews; Passover; Purim; Synagogues.

Judaism.
FAITH AND BELIEF: FIVE MAJOR WORLD RELIGIONS (VIDEOCASSETTE). /1992/5-A/KA722. . . . . **VCR 291**

Judaism--Customs and practices.
DRUCKER, M/Family treasury of Jewish holidays. /1994/ 2-6/6 KA772 . . . . **296.4**
GOLDIN, BD/Bat mitzvah: a Jewish girl's coming of age. /1995/ 5-A/10 KA773 . . . . **296.4**
KIMMEL, EA/Bar mitzvah: a Jewish boy's coming of age. /1995/ 5-A/7 KA776 . . . . **296.4**

Judaism--Customs and practices--Fiction.
POLACCO, P/Tikvah means hope. /1994/1-3/2 KG259. . . . . . **E**

Judaism--Feasts and holidays.
CHAIKIN, M/Light another candle: the story and meaning of Hanukkah. /c1981, 1987/5-6/8 KA770 . . . . **296.4**
HANUKKAH (VIDEOCASSETTE). /1994/2-5/KA774 . . **VCR 296.4**
HOYT-GOLDSMITH, D/Celebrating Hanukkah. /1996/ 3-4/7 KA775 . . . . **296.4**

Judaism--Miscellanea.
BURSTEIN, CM/Jewish kids catalog. /1983/4-6/7 KB179. . . . **394**
Judges SEE ALSO Jurys; Lawyers.

Judges.
MACHT, NL/Sandra Day O'Connor. /1992/ 4-5/8 KE481 . . . . **B O'CONNOR, S.**
SO YOU WANT TO BE?: JUDGE (VIDEOCASSETTE). /1994/ 5-6/KA977 . . . . **VCR 347**

Judges--Fiction.
ZEMACH, H/Judge, an untrue tale. /c1969/P-3/2 KG787 . . **CE E**
Judo SEE ALSO Karate; Martial arts.

Judo.
NARDI, TJ/Karate and judo. /1996/3-6/6 KD833 . . . . . **796.815**

Jugglers and juggling--Fiction.
DE PAOLA, T/Clown of God. /1978/K-3/6 KF467 . . . . **CE E**
Jump rope SEE Rope skipping.

Jump rope rhymes.
MISS MARY MACK AND OTHER CHILDREN'S STREET RHYMES. / 1990/2-5/KD766 . . . . **796.1**
WESTCOTT, NB/Lady with the alligator purse. /1988/ P-1/KB818 . . . . **398.8**

Jumping.
WARD, T/Field. /1996/3-6/8 KD812 . . . . **796.42**

Juneteenth (Holiday).
BLACK HERITAGE HOLIDAYS (VIDEOCASSETTE). /1992/ 3-A/KB195 . . . . **VCR 394.26**

Jungle animals.
ROYSTON, A/Jungle animals. /1991/P-2/4 KC493 . . . . . **591.734**

Jungle animals--Fiction.
BAKER, K/Who is the beast? /1990/P-K/1 KF187 . . . . **E**
Jungle ecology.
GEORGE, JC/One day in the tropical rain forest. /1990/
4-6/6 KC315 . . . . **577.34**
Jungles--Fiction.
JONAS, A/Trek. /1985/P-2/4 KF849 . . . . **E**
KIPLING, R/Beginning of the armadillos. /1995/3-5/8 KH359 . . **Fic**
Jungle book: the Mowgli stories. /1995/6-A/7 KH363 . . . . . **Fic**
Jungles--Software.
LET'S EXPLORE THE JUNGLE WITH BUZZY THE KNOWLEDGE
BUG (CD-ROM). /1995/K-3/KC320 . . . . **CDR 577.34**
Junior high school libraries--Book lists.
MIDDLE AND JUNIOR HIGH SCHOOL LIBRARY CATALOG. 7TH
ED. /1995//KA019 . . . . **PROF 011.62**
YOUR READING: AN ANNOTATED BOOKLIST FOR MIDDLE
SCHOOL AND JUNIOR HIGH. /1996/5-A/KA373 . . **REF 011.62**
Junior Iditarod Trail Sled Dog Race, Alaska.
SHAHAN, S/Dashing through the snow: the story of the Jr.
Iditarod. /1997/4-6/7 KD860 . . . . **798.8**
Junk--Fiction.
BORTON, L/Junk pile! /1997/K-2/3 KF252 . . . . **E**
Jupiter (Planet).
SIMON, S/Jupiter. /1985/3-6/7 KC038 . . . . **523.45**
Justice, Administration of.
HYDE, MO/Kids in and out of trouble. /1995/A/8 KB072 . **364.36**
Juvenile delinquents.
HYDE, MO/Kids in and out of trouble. /1995/A/8 KB072 . **364.36**
Kaiulani, Princess of Hawaii.
STANLEY, F/Last princess: the story of Princess Kaiulani of Hawaii.
/1991/5-6/7 KE413 . . . . **B KAIULANI**
Kalahari Desert--Social life and customs.
LEWIS, IM/Why ostriches don't fly and other tales from the African
bush. /1997/4-6/6 KB336 . . . . **398.2**
Kalispel Indians.
CRUM, R/Eagle drum: on the powwow trail with a young grass
dancer. /1994/5-A/5 KB197 . . . . **394.26**
Kamiya, Lauren Seiko.
BROWN, T/Konnichiwa!: I am a Japanese-American girl. /1995/
3-5/4 KA839 . . . . **305.8**
Kampuchea SEE Cambodia.
Kangaroos.
RYDEN, H/Joey: the story of a baby kangaroo. /1994/
2-5/4 KC737 . . . . **599.2**
Kangaroos--Fiction.
VAUGHAN, MK/Snap! /1996/K-2/2 KG651 . . . . **E**
Kansas.
FREDEEN, C/Kansas. /1992/4-6/5 KF053 . . . . **978.1**
KENT, Z/Kansas. /1990/4-6/9 KF054 . . . . **978.1**
Kapok (Tree)--Fiction.
CHERRY, L/Great kapok tree: a tale of the Amazon rain forest. /
1990/2-3/4 KF380 . . . . **E**
Great kapok tree (Videocassette). /1996/2-3/KF381 . . . . **VCR E**
Karate SEE ALSO Judo; Martial arts.
Karate.
GOEDECKE, CJ/Wind warrior: the training of a Karate champion. /
1992/4-6/5 KD831 . . . . **796.815**
MORRIS, A/Karate boy. /1996/2-4/5 KD832 . . . . **796.815**
NARDI, TJ/Karate and judo. /1996/3-6/6 KD833 . . . . . **796.815**
QUEEN, JA/Complete karate. /1993/4-6/6 KD834 . . . . . **796.815**
Karuk Indians--Folklore.
LONDON, J/Fire race: a Karuk Coyote tale about how fire came to
the people. /1993/3-4/4 KB611 . . . . **398.24**
Katahdin, Mount, Region (Me.)--Description and travel.
MURPHY, J/Into the deep forest with Henry David Thoreau. /1995/
5-A/7 KE929 . . . . **974.1**
Kayaks and kayaking.
EVANS, J/Whitewater kayaking. /1992/4-A/7 KD845 . . . . **797.1**
Kehret, Peg.
KEHRET, P/Small steps: the year I got polio. /1996/
2-5/5 KE414 . . . . **B KEHRET, P.**
Keita, Soundiata.
WISNIEWSKI, D/Sundiata: Lion King of Mali. /1992/
3-5/4 KB495 . . . . **398.22**
Keller, Helen.
HELEN KELLER (VIDEOCASSETTE). /1990/
4-6/KE415 . . . . **VCR B KELLER, H.**
KELLER, H/Story of my life. /c1988, 1990/
6-A/8 KE416 . . . . **B KELLER, H.**
LUNDELL, M/Girl named Helen Keller. /1995/
1-2/1 KE417 . . . . **B KELLER, H.**
Kelp bed ecology.
WU, N/Beneath the waves: exploring the hidden world of the kelp
forest. /1992/3-6/7 KC353 . . . . **577.7**

Kennedy, John Fitzgerald.
ANDERSON, CC/Jackie Kennedy Onassis: woman of courage. /
1995/A/7 KE484 . . . . **B ONASSIS, J.**
HARRISON, B/Twilight struggle: the life of John Fitzgerald Kennedy.
/1992/6-A/8 KE418 . . . . **B KENNEDY, J.**
Kennedy, John Fitzgerald--Assassination.
STEIN, RC/Assassination of John F. Kennedy. /1992/
5-6/7 KE921 . . . . **973.922**
Kentucky.
BROWN, D/Kentucky. /1992/4-6/6 KF010 . . . . **976.9**
Kentucky--Folklore.
SOME DOG AND OTHER KENTUCKY WONDERS (SOUND
RECORDING CASSETTE). /1992/3-4/KB370 . . . . . **SRC 398.2**
Kentucky--History.
SMITH, A/Historical album of Kentucky. /1995/
4-6/7 KF011 . . . . **976.9**
Kenya--Description and travel.
KIDS EXPLORE KENYA (VIDEOCASSETTE). /1990/
3-5/KE179 . . . . **VCR 916.762**
Kenya--Folklore.
AARDEMA, V/How the ostrich got its long neck: a tale from the
Akamba of Kenya. /1995/P-2/6 KB515 . . . . **CE 398.24**
MCNEIL, H/Hyena and the moon: stories to listen to from Kenya
(Talking book). /1995/5-6/KB346 . . . . **TB 398.2**
Hyena and the moon: stories to tell from Kenya. /1994/
5-6/7 KB347 . . . . **398.2**
Kenya--Social life and customs.
KIDS EXPLORE KENYA (VIDEOCASSETTE). /1990/
3-5/KE179 . . . . **VCR 916.762**
Keyboard instruments.
TURNER, BC/Living piano. /1996/4-6/12 KD546 . . . . . **BA 786.2**
Keyboarding--Software.
MAVIS BEACON TEACHES TYPING! (MICROCOMPUTER
PROGRAM). /1987/4-A/KD310 . . . . **MCP 652.3**
Kherdian, Veron.
KHERDIAN, D/Road from home: the story of an Armenian girl. /
1979/5-6/6 KE698 . . . . **949.6**
Khmer language materials.
SPAGNOLI, C/Judge Rabbit and the tree spirit: a folktale from
Cambodia. /1991/3-4/4 KB655 . . . . **398.24**
Kibbutzim--Fiction.
EDWARDS, M/Chicken man. /1991/K-2/2 KF509 . . . . **E**
Kidnapping--Fiction.
AHLBERG, A/Giant baby. /1994/3-5/7 KG820 . . . . **Fic**
BABBITT, N/Tuck everlasting. /c1975/4-6/4 KG873 . . . . . **CE Fic**
CURRY, JL/Big Smith snatch. /1989/5-A/6 KH047 . . . . **Fic**
DUNCAN, L/Third eye. /1984/A/5 KH089 . . . . **Fic**
FLEISCHMAN, P/Half-a-Moon Inn. /c1980, 1991/6/7 KH117 . . **Fic**
FOX, P/Slave dancer: a novel. /c1973/5-6/6 KH139. . . . . **CE Fic**
SHARMAT, MW/Genghis Khan: a dog star is born. /1994/
2-5/2 KH703 . . . . **Fic**
Killer whale.
ARNOLD, C/Killer whale. /1994/4-6/7 KC764. . . . . **599.5**
PATENT, DH/Killer whales. /1993/4-6/6 KC775. . . . . **599.5**
Killer whale--Training.
ARNOLD, C/Killer whale. /1994/4-6/7 KC764. . . . . **599.5**
Killer whales--Folklore.
LEWIS, PO/Storm boy. /1995/2-4/3 KB610 . . . . **398.24**
Kinaalda (Navajo rite).
ROESSEL, M/Kinaalda: a Navajo girl grows up. /1993/
4-6/5 KE789 . . . . **970.48**
Kindergarten SEE ALSO Montessori method of education; Nursery schools.
Kindergarten.
HOWE, J/When you go to kindergarten. Rev. and updated ed. /
1994/P-K/2 KB097 . . . . **372.21**
MCMAHON, P/Listen for the bus: David's story. /1995/
1-3/3 KB004 . . . . **362.4**
Kindergarten--Fiction.
CLEARY, B/Ramona the pest. /c1968/3-5/5 KH006 . . . . **Fic**
KELLER, H/Harry and Tuck. /1993/K-1/2 KF884. . . . . **E**
MARTIN, AM/Rachel Parker, kindergarten show-off. /1992/
K-2/1 KG069 . . . . **E**
SCHWARTZ, A/Annabelle Swift, Kindergartner. /1988/
P-2/1 KG413 . . . . **CE E**
SERFOZO, M/Benjamin Bigfoot. /1993/P-K/2 KG439 . . . . **E**
SIMON, C/One happy classroom. /1997/K-1/2 KG507 . . . . . . **E**
SLATE, J/Miss Bindergarten gets ready for kindergarten. /1996/
P-K/2 KG515 . . . . **E**
Kindergarten--History--19th century.
BROSTERMAN, N/Inventing kindergarten. /1997/
/KA196 . . . . **PROF 372.21**
Kindergarten--History--20th century.
BROSTERMAN, N/Inventing kindergarten. /1997/
/KA196 . . . . **PROF 372.21**

Kindergarten--Methods and manuals.
BROSTERMAN, N/Inventing kindergarten. /1997/
/KA196. . . . . **PROF 372.21**
Kindness--Fiction.
NAYLOR, PR/Shiloh season. /1996/4-A/4 KH539 . . . . **Fic**
PEET, B/Ant and the elephant. /c1972/K-3/5 KG223 . . . . **E**
King, Coretta Scott.
MEDEARIS, AS/Dare to dream: Coretta Scott King and the civil
rights movement. /1994/3-5/3 KE419 . . . . **B KING, C.S.**
King, Martin Luther, Jr.
ADLER, DA/Picture book of Martin Luther King, Jr. /1989/
3-4/4 KE420 . . . . **CE B KING, M.L.**
BRAY, RL/Martin Luther King. /1995/2-6/7 KE421 . **B KING, M.L.**
MARTIN LUTHER KING: I HAVE A DREAM (VIDEOCASSETTE). /
1986/4-A/KA907 . . . . **VCR 323.4**
MARZOLLO, J/Happy Birthday, Martin Luther King. /1993/
1-5/5 KE422 . . . . **B KING, M.L.**
RINGGOLD, F/My dream of Martin Luther King. /1995/
3-5/7 KE423 . . . . **B KING, M.L.**
King, Martin Luther, Jr.--Poetry.
LIVINGSTON, MC/Let freedom ring: a ballad of Martin Luther
King, Jr. /1992/K-2/4 KD978 . . . . **811**
King Arthur, King SEE Arthur, King.
King Philip's War, 1675-1676.
SEWALL, M/Thunder from the clear sky. /1995/
4-6/7 KE874 . . . . **973.2**
King Philip's War, 1675-1676--Fiction.
JACOBS, PS/James Printer: a novel of rebellion. /1997/
5-A/6 KH319 . . . . **Fic**
Kings, queens, rulers, etc.
ABUBAKARI: THE EXPLORER KING OF MALI (VIDEOCASSETTE). /
1992/5-6/KE224 . . . . **VCR B ABUBAKARI**
BIOGRAPHY TODAY WORLD LEADERS SERIES: PROFILES OF
PEOPLE OF INTEREST TO YOUNG /1997-/4-6/KA407 . **REF 350**
SABUDA, R/Tutankhamen's gift. /1994/
2-4/3 KE578 . . . . **B TUTANKHAMEN**
STANLEY, D/Cleopatra. /1994/4-6/6 KE295. . . . **B CLEOPATRA**
Good Queen Bess: the story of Elizabeth I of England. /1990/
6-A/7 KE337 . . . . **B ELIZABETH I**
WORLD LEADERS: PEOPLE WHO SHAPED THE WORLD. /1994/
5-A/KA408 . . . . **REF 350**
Kings, queens, rulers, etc.--Fiction.
ARMSTRONG, J/King Crow. /1995/1-3/4 KF165 . . . . **E**
BABBITT, N/Bub, or, The very best thing. /1994/P-2/2 KF182 . . **E**
BUSSER, M/King Bobble. /1996/2-3/2 KG953 . . . . **Fic**
JACKSON, E/Impossible riddle. /1995/K-3/4 KF819 . . . . . . **E**
MCKENZIE, EK/King, the princess, and the tinker. /1992/
3-5/4 KH483 . . . . **Fic**
PACKARD, M/I am king! /1994/K-1/1 KG205. . . . . **E**
REID BANKS, L/Adventures of King Midas. /1992/
4-A/6 KH626 . . . . **Fic**
SHEEHAN, P/Gwendolyn's gifts. /1991/1-3/5 KG491. . . . . . **E**
STEIG, W/Real thief. /c1973/4-6/6 KH751. . . . . **Fic**
WOOD, A/King Bidgood's in the bathtub. /1985/
P-2/1 KG763 . . . . **CE E**
Kings, queens, rulers, etc.--Folklore.
WISNIEWSKI, D/Sundiata: Lion King of Mali. /1992/
3-5/4 KB495 . . . . **398.22**
Kiowa Indians--Fiction.
STROUD, VA/Doesn't Fall Off His Horse. /1994/2-3/4 KG580. . **E**
Kipling, Rudyard.
GREENE, C/Rudyard Kipling: author of the "Jungle books." /
1994/3-6/2 KE424 . . . . **B KIPLING, R.**
Kitchen utensils.
KALMAN, B/Kitchen. /1990/4-5/5 KD295 . . . . **643**
ROCKWELL, AF/Pots and pans. /1993/P/3 KD279. . . . . . **641.5**
Kites.
GIBBONS, G/Catch the wind!: all about kites. /1989/
1-3/4 KD108 . . . . **629.133**
Kites--Fiction.
BLANCO, A/Angel's kite/La estrella de Angel. /1994/
2-4/6 KG902 . . . . **Fic**
Kites--Folklore.
YOLEN, J/Emperor and the kite. /1988/2-3/6 KB791 . . . . **398.27**
Kites (Bird) SEE ALSO Birds of Prey.
Kittens SEE Cats.
Kiwis.
ARNOLD, C/Ostriches and other flightless birds. /1990/
5-6/7 KC690 . . . . **598.5**
Klondike River Valley (Yukon)--Gold discoveries.
COOPER, ML/Klondike fever. /1989/5-6/6 KE823 . . . . . . **971.9**
KLONDIKE GOLD RUSH (PICTURE). /n.d./A/KE826 . . . **PIC 971.9**
LOURIE, P/Yukon River: an adventure to the gold fields of the
Klondike. /1992/4-6/6 KE210 . . . . **917.98**

Kneeboarding.
WALKER, C/Waterskiing and kneeboarding. /1992/
4-A/7 KD851 . . . . **797.3**
Knight, Amelia Stewart.
KNIGHT, AS/Way west: journal of a pioneer woman. /1993/
5-6/5 KE197 . . . . **917.8**
Knights and knighthood.
CORBIN, CL/Knights. /1989/4-6/4 KE646. . . . . **940.1**
GRAVETT, C/Knight. /1993/4-A/7 KE648 . . . . **940.1**
WRIGHT, R/Knights: facts, things to make, activities. /1991/
4-A/8 KD439 . . . . **745.5**
Knights and knighthood--Fiction.
BULLA, CR/Sword in the tree. /c1956/3-5/2 KG939. . . . . . **Fic**
DE PAOLA, T/Knight and the dragon. /1980/K-2/5 KF471. . . . **E**
MURPHY, J/Jeffrey Strangeways. /1994/4-5/7 KH520 . . . . . . **Fic**
WINTHROP, E/Castle in the attic. /1985/4-6/5 KH869 . . . **CE Fic**
Knights and knighthood--Folklore.
CURRY, JL/Christmas Knight. /1993/2-5/3 KB435. . . . . . **398.22**
GIBLIN, JC/Dwarf, the giant, and the unicorn: a tale of King Arthur.
/1996/3-5/4 KB443 . . . . **398.22**
HASTINGS, S/Sir Gawain and the green knight. /1981/
6/6 KB450. . . . . **398.22**
HODGES, M/Of swords and sorcerers: the adventures of King
Arthur and his knights. /1993/4-5/6 KB452 . . . . . . **398.22**
Saint George and the dragon: a golden legend. /1984/
5/7 KB453. . . . . **CE 398.22**
HOWE, J/Knight with the lion: the story of Yvain. /1996/
5-6/6 KB455 . . . . **398.22**
KING ARTHUR AND HIS KNIGHTS (SOUND RECORDING
CASSETTE). /1991/5-6/KB462 . . . . **SRC 398.22**
LISTER, R/Story of King Arthur. /1997/4/7 KB465 . . . . . **398.22**
PERHAM, M/King Arthur: the legends of Camelot. /1993/
5-A/7 KB471 . . . . **398.22**
PYLE, H/Story of King Arthur and his knights. /c1933, 1984/
A/9 KB472 . . . . **398.22**
SABUDA, R/Arthur and the sword. /1995/3-5/5 KB479 . . **398.22**
SAN SOUCI, RD/Young Lancelot. /1996/4-5/6 KB483 . . . **398.22**
TALBOTT, H/King Arthur and the Round Table. /1995/
4-5/6 KB490 . . . . **398.22**
Knights of the Round Table SEE Arthur, King.
Knock-knock jokes.
COLE, RM/Zany knock knocks. /1993/3-6/5 KD726 . . . . . **793.735**
KESSLER, L/Old Turtle's 90 knock-knocks, jokes, and riddles. /
1991/2-4/KD730 . . . . **793.735**
Knoxville (Tenn.)--Poetry.
GIOVANNI, N/Knoxville, Tennessee. /1994/P-1/2 KD945 . . . **811**
Koala.
ARNOLD, C/Koala. /c1987, 1992/4-6/8 KC733 . . . . **599.2**
BURT, D/Birth of a koala. /1986/4-6/8 KC734 . . . . **599.2**
KOALAS: THE BARE FACTS (VIDEOCASSETTE). /1993/
5-6/KC736. . . . . **VCR 599.2**
SOTZEK, H/Koala is not a bear! /1997/3-5/3 KC738 . . . . . **599.2**
Koko (Gorilla).
PATTERSON, F/Koko's kitten. /1985/3-5/6 KC877. . . . . **599.884**
Komodo dragon.
DARLING, K/Komodo dragon: on location. /1997/
4-6/7 KC625 . . . . **597.95**
SCHAFER, S/Komodo dragon. /c1992, 1996/
5-6/5 KC629 . . . . **597.95**
Koran stories.
OPPENHEIM, SL/And the Earth trembled: the creation of Adam and
Eve. /1996/5-6/3 KA788 . . . . **297**
Korea--Fiction.
WATKINS, YK/So far from the bamboo grove. /c1986, 1994/
5-A/5 KH842 . . . . **Fic**
Korea--Folklore.
CLIMO, S/Korean Cinderella. /1993/2-4/5 KB726 . . . . . **398.27**
FARLEY, CJ/Mr. Pak buys a story. /1997/K-3/2 KB734. . . **398.27**
HAN, OS/Kongi and Potgi: a Cinderella story from Korea. /1996/
K-3/5 KB313 . . . . **398.2**
HAN, SC/Rabbit's escape/Kusa ilsaenghan tookki. /1995/
P-2/3 KB583 . . . . **398.24**
HEO, Y/Green frogs: a Korean folktale. /1996/
P-2/2 KB589 . . . . **398.24**
JAFFE, N/Older brother, younger brother: a Korean folktale. /
1995/3-4/6 KB320 . . . . **398.2**
KWON, HH/Moles and the Mireuk: a Korean folktale. /1993/
K-2/4 KB605 . . . . **398.24**
O'BRIEN, AS/Princess and the beggar: a Korean folktale. /1993/
3-4/6 KB761 . . . . **398.27**
Korea (South).
MCMAHON, P/Chi-hoon: a Korean girl. /c1993, 1998/
3-5/6 KE705 . . . . **951.95**

Korean Americans--Fiction.
MYERS, A/Rosie's tiger. /1994/4-A/4 KH521 . . . . **Fic**
PELLEGRINI, N/Families are different. /1991/P-1/2 KG232 . . . . **E**
Korean language materials.
HAN, SC/Rabbit's escape/Kusa ilsaenghan tookki. /1995/
P-2/3 KB583 . . . . **398.24**
Krone, Julie.
GUTMAN, B/Julie Krone. /1996/5-6/5 KE425 . . . . . **B KRONE, J.**
Kurelek, William.
KURELEK, W/Lumberjack. /1974/4-6/6 KD165 . . . . **634.9**
Kuskin, Karla.
KUSKIN, K/Thoughts, pictures, and words. /1995/
2-5/6 KE426 . . . . **B KUSKIN, K.**
Kwanzaa.
BLACK HERITAGE HOLIDAYS (VIDEOCASSETTE). /1992/
3-A/KB195. . . . . **VCR 394.26**
BRADY, AA/Kwanzaa karamu: cooking and crafts for a Kwanzaa
feast. /1995/5-6/5 KD284 . . . . **641.59**
CHOCOLATE, DM/My first Kwanzaa book. /1992/
2-4/2 KB206 . . . . **394.261**
GOSS, L/It's Kwanzaa time! /1995/2-6/6 KB208 . . . . . . **394.261**
HOYT-GOLDSMITH, D/Celebrating Kwanzaa. /1993/
4-6/7 KB210 . . . . **394.261**
KWANZAA (VIDEOCASSETTE). /1994/3-6/KB212. **VCR 394.261**
PINKNEY, AD/Seven candles for Kwanzaa. /1993/
2-6/7 KB214 . . . . **394.261**
ROSS, K/Crafts for Kwanzaa. /1994/3-6/KD456 . . . . . . **745.594**
SAINT JAMES, S/Gifts of Kwanzaa. /1994/
1-4/2 KB216 . . . . **394.261**
Kwanzaa--Fiction.
WALTER, MP/Have a happy... a novel. /1989/4-6/4 KH838 . . **Fic**
Kwanzaa decorations.
BRADY, AA/Kwanzaa karamu: cooking and crafts for a Kwanzaa
feast. /1995/5-6/5 KD284 . . . . **641.59**
ROSS, K/Crafts for Kwanzaa. /1994/3-6/KD456 . . . . . . **745.594**
Labor and laboring classes SEE ALSO Labor unions; Migrant labor;
Occupations; Slavery; Unemployed.
Labor and laboring classes--Fiction.
PEREZ, NA/Breaker. /1988/6-A/7 KH597 . . . . **Fic**
Labor Day.
SCOTT, G/Labor Day. /1982/2-3/2 KB228 . . . . **394.264**
Labor leaders.
CEDENO, ME/Cesar Chavez: labor leader. /1993/
4-5/6 KE287 . . . . **B CHAVEZ, C.**
DE RUIZ, DC/Causa: the migrant farmworkers' story. /1993/
4-6/6 KA944 . . . . **331.88**
Labor unions--Clothing workers--History.
DASH, J/We shall not be moved: the women's factory strike of
1909. /1996/6-A/8 KA939. . . . . **331.4**
Labor unions--Fiction.
SACHS, M/Call me Ruth. /c1982, 1995/5-A/6 KH667 . . . . . . **Fic**
Labrador retriever.
JONES, RF/Jake: a Labrador puppy at work and play. /1992/
2-5/5 KD228 . . . . **636.752**
Ladybugs.
FISCHER-NAGEL, H/Life of the ladybug. /1986/
5-6/9 KC551 . . . . **595.76**
GOLDSEN, L/Ladybug and other insects. /1991/
K-3/4 KC538 . . . . **595.7**
JOHNSON, SA/Ladybugs. /1983/A/11 KC554 . . . . **595.76**
WATTS, B/Ladybug. /1987/3-5/4 KC555 . . . . **595.76**
Ladybugs--Fiction.
CARLE, E/Grouchy ladybug. New ed. /1996/P-2/2 KF342 . . . . . **E**
Lake States--Bibliography.
EXPLORING THE GREAT LAKES STATES THROUGH LITERATURE.
/1994//KA039. **PROF 016.977**
Lamu (Island)--Fiction.
ANDERSON, J/Juma and the magic jinn. /1986/2-3/4 KF156 . . **E**
Lancelot (Legendary character).
SAN SOUCI, RD/Young Lancelot. /1996/4-5/6 KB483 . . . **398.22**
Land SEE ALSO Agriculture; Farms.
Landlord and tenant--Fiction.
MYERS, WD/Young landlords. /c1979/5-6/6 KH524 . . . . **Fic**
Landscape in art.
ROALF, P/Landscapes. /1992/5-A/8 KD481 . . . . **758**
Lange, Dorothea.
TURNER, R/Dorothea Lange. /1994/5-A/7 KE427 . . **B LANGE, D.**
Language arts SEE ALSO Creative writing; English language; Literature;
Reading; Speech; Writing.
Language arts.
BAUER, CF/Presenting reader's theater: plays and poems to read
aloud. /1987//KA329 . . . . **PROF 792**
JONES, BF/Teaching thinking skills: English/language arts. /1987/
/KA280. . . . . **PROF 428**

MALLAN, K/Children as storytellers. /1992//KA341 . **PROF 808.5**
MCELMEEL, SL/McElmeel booknotes: literature across the
curriculum. /1993//KA225 . . . . **PROF 372.6**
Language arts--Bibliography.
ROUTMAN, R/Blue pages: resources for teachers from Invitations.
Updated, expanded, and rev. /1994//KA026 . . . . **PROF 016.372**
Language arts (Elementary)
BARCHERS, SI/Creating and managing the literate classroom. /
1990//KA218 . . . . **PROF 372.6**
CHALL, JS/Reading crisis: why poor children fall behind. /1990/
/KA219. . . . . **PROF 372.6**
GEIGER, E/TNT: two hundred and ninety-two activites for literature
and language arts! /1989//KA222 . . . . **PROF 372.6**
SPILLMAN, CV/Integrating language arts through literature in
elementary classrooms. /1996//KA229 . . . . **PROF 372.6**
WATSON, DJ/Ideas and insights: language arts in the elementary
school. /1987//KA232. . . . . **PROF 372.6**
WHOLE LANGUAGE: BELIEFS AND PRACTICES, K-8. /1989/
/KA233. . . . . **PROF 372.6**
Language arts (Elementary)--Periodicals.
PRIMARY VOICES K-6. /1993-//KA132 . . . . **PER PROF 050**
Language experience approach in education.
CHATTON, B/Using poetry across the curriculum: a whole language
approach. /1993//KA237. . . . . **PROF 372.64**
FREDERICKS, AD/Social studies through children's literature: an
integrated approach. /1991//KA260. . . . . **PROF 372.83**
LANKFORD, MD/Successful field trips. /1992/
/KA178. . . . . **PROF 371.3**
STANEK, LW/Whole language: literature, learning, and literacy: a
workshop in print. /1993//KA230 . . . . **PROF 372.6**
WHOLE LANGUAGE: BELIEFS AND PRACTICES, K-8. /1989/
/KA233. . . . . **PROF 372.6**
Language experience approach in education--Bibliography.
ROUTMAN, R/Blue pages: resources for teachers from Invitations.
Updated, expanded, and rev. /1994//KA026 . . . . **PROF 016.372**
Languages, Modern SEE ALSO names of specific languages e.g. English
language.
Laos--Folklore.
XIONG, B/Nine-in-one, grr! grr! a folktale from the Hmong people
of Laos. /1989/P-3/4 KB677 . . . . **398.24**
Lapland.
LEWIN, T/Reindeer people. /1994/4-6/6 KE695 . . . . . . **948.97**
REYNOLDS, J/Far north: vanishing cultures. /1992/
3-6/6 KE696 . . . . **948.97**
Latchkey children SEE ALSO Children of working parents.
Latchkey children.
HOME ALONE: YOU'RE IN CHARGE (VIDEOCASSETTE). /1991/
2-4/KD259. . . . . **VCR 640**
HOME ON YOUR OWN (VIDEOCASSETTE). /1994/
4-6/KD260. . . . . **VCR 640**
LATCHKEY CHILDREN: WHEN YOU'RE IN CHARGE
(VIDEOCASSETTE). /1986/5-6/KD261 . . . . **VCR 640**
Latchkey children--Fiction.
AUCH, MJ/Latchkey dog. /1994/3-5/4 KG855 . . . . **Fic**
Latin America SEE ALSO Central America; South America; also names of
individual countries.
Latin America--Bibliography.
SCHON, I/Hispanic heritage, series II. /1985/
/KA043. . . . . **PROF 016.98**
Latin America--Fiction.
HURWITZ, J/New shoes for Silvia. /1993/K-2/2 KF794 . . . . . . **E**
Latin America--Folklore.
BRUSCA, MC/Pedro fools the gringo and other tales of a Latin
American trickster. /1995/2-4/3 KB429 . . . . **398.22**
DELACRE, L/Golden tales: myths, legends, and folktales from Latin
America. /1996/4-5/6 KB283 . . . . **398.2**
GONZALEZ, LM/Senor Cat's romance and other favorite stories
from Latin America. /1997/K-2/3 KB303 . . . . **398.2**
SAN SOUCI, RD/Little seven-colored horse: a Spanish American
folktale. /1995/3-5/5 KB648. . . . . **398.24**
Latin Americans--Songs and music.
VALERI, M/Mi casa es su casa/my house is your house: a bi-lingual
musical journey through /1991/K-3/KD663. . . . . **SRC 789.3**
Latin Americans--Fiction.
GARAY, L/Pedrito's Day. /1997/1-3/2 KF598 . . . . **E**
Latin language materials.
WHITE, EB/Charlotte's web. /c1952/3-6/6 KH850 . . . . **Fic**
Law SEE ALSO Judges; Lawyers; Police.
Law.
HOW A BILL BECOMES A LAW (PICTURE). /1989/
5-6/KA931 . . . . **PIC 328.3**
Law--Vocational guidance.
SO YOU WANT TO BE?: JUDGE (VIDEOCASSETTE). /1994/
5-6/KA977 . . . . **VCR 347**

Law, Ruth.
BROWN, D/Ruth Law thrills a nation. /1993/
2-3/4 KE428 . . . . **B LAW, R.**

Lawrence, Jacob.
JACOB LAWRENCE: THE GLORY OF EXPRESSION
(VIDEOCASSETTE). /1995/5-A/KD487 . . . . **VCR 759.13**

Lawson family.
LAWSON, R/They were strong and good. /c1940/
4-6/KE891 . . . . **973.4**

Lax, Eli.
ADLER, DA/Hilde and Eli: children of the Holocaust. /1994/
4-6/5 KE655 . . . . **940.53**

Laysan albatross.
JOHNSON, SA/Albatrosses of Midway Island. /1990/
5-6/7 KC681 . . . . **598.4**

Laziness--Fiction.
GALDONE, P/Little red hen. /c1973/P-K/2 KF595 . . . . . . **CE E**
LOBEL, A/Treeful of pigs. /1979/P-2/4 KG013 . . . . **E**
SNYDER, D/Boy of the three-year nap. /1988/K-3/6 KG525 . . . **E**
ZEMACH, M/Little red hen, an old story. /1983/P-K/2 KG790 . . **E**
ZIEFERT, H/Little red hen. /1995/K-1/2 KG793 . . . . **E**

Learning.
FOCUS ON COLLABORATIVE LEARNING: CLASSROOM
PRACTICES IN TEACHING ENGLISH. /1988/
/KA221 . . . . **PROF 372.6**
LAZEAR, DG/Seven pathways of learning: teaching students and
parents about multiple intelligences. /1994/
/KA174 . . . . **PROF 370.15**
POLETTE, N/Brain power through picture books: /1992/
/KA227 . . . . **PROF 372.6**

Learning, Art of SEE Study, Method of.
Learning centers SEE Instructional materials centers.
Learning disabilities SEE ALSO names of specific disabilities e.g. Dyslexia.

Learning disabilities.
CUMMINGS, RW/School survival guide for kids with LD (Learning
differences). /1991/4-6/4 KB093 . . . . **371.92**
FISHER, GL/Survival guide for kids with LD (Learning differences). /
1990/4-6/4 KB094 . . . . **371.92**
GEHRET, J/Don't-give-up Kid and learning differences. 2nd ed. /
1996/K-3/2 KB095 . . . . **371.92**
ROBY, C/When learning is tough: kids talk about their learning
disabilities. /1994/4-6/6 KB096 . . . . **371.92**

Learning disabilities--Biography.
POLACCO, P/Dream keeper (Videocassette). /1996/
2-4/KE501 . . . . **VCR B POLACCO, P.**

Learning disabilities--Case studies.
DUNN, KB/Trouble with school: a family story about learning
disabilities. /1993//KA184 . . . . **PROF 371.9**

Learning disabilities--Fiction.
CUTLER, J/Spaceman. /1997/4-A/2 KH053 . . . . **Fic**
WILLIS, MS/Secret super powers of Marco. /1994/
4-A/4 KH866 . . . . **Fic**

Learning disabled children--Education--United States--Case studies.
STEVENS, SH/Classroom success for the LD and ADHD child. /
1997//KA186 . . . . **PROF 371.92**

Leather--History.
FISHER, LE/Tanners. /c1966, 1986/5-6/7 KD331 . . . . **675**

Leaves.
JOHNSON, SA/How leaves change. /1986/4-6/9 KC399 . . **581.4**
MAESTRO, B/Why do leaves change color? /1994/
P-4/2 KC400 . . . . **CE 581.4**
WHAT IS A LEAF? (VIDEOCASSETTE). /1991/
K-3/KC401 . . . . **VCR 581.4**

Leaves--Fiction.
KNUTSON, K/Ska-tat! /1993/P-2/3 KF914 . . . . **E**

Lebanese Americans--Fiction.
SHEFELMAN, J/Peddler's dream. /1992/1-3/2 KG492 . . . . . . **E**

Lebanon--History--Civil War--Fiction.
HEIDE, FP/Sami and the time of the troubles. /1992/
2-4/4 KF695 . . . . **E**

Lectures and lecturing--Planning.
WATKINS, J/Programming author visits. /1996/
/KA071 . . . . **PROF 027.62**

Lee, Robert E.
ADLER, DA/Picture book of Robert E. Lee. /1994/
2-5/5 KE429 . . . . **B LEE, R.**
KAVANAGH, J/Robert E. Lee. /1995/4-5/6 KE430 . . . **B LEE, R.**
ROBERT E. LEE (VIDEOCASSETTE). /1989/
5-6/KE431 . . . . **VCR B LEE, R.**

Leeches.
HALTON, CM/Those amazing leeches. /1989/5-6/9 KC504 . . **592**

Leeuwenhoek, Antoni van.
YOUNT, L/Antoni van Leeuwenhoek: first to see microscopic life. /
1996/5-A/5 KE432 . . . . **B LEEUWENHOEK, A**

Legendary characters SEE names of specific lengendary characters e.g. John
Henry (Legendary character).
Legends SEE ALSO Fables; Fairy tales; Folklore; Mythology and names of
specific social groups with subheadings Legends e.g. Aztecs--Legends.

Legends.
MCCAUGHREAN, G/Golden hoard: myths and legends of the
world. /1996/2-5/7 KB344 . . . . **398.2**
Silver treasure: myths and legends of the world. /1996/
K-6/6 KB345 . . . . **398.2**

Legends, Indian SEE Indians of North America--Legends; Indians of South
America--Legends; etc.

Legislation.
HOW A BILL BECOMES A LAW (PICTURE). /1989/
5-6/KA931 . . . . **PIC 328.3**

Legislative bodies.
OUR FEDERAL GOVERNMENT: THE LEGISLATIVE BRANCH
(VIDEOCASSETTE). /1993/5-A/KA933 . . . . **VCR 328.73**

Legislators.
ADLER, DA/Picture book of Davy Crockett. /1996/
2-3/7 KE310 . . . . **B CROCKETT, D.**
FRITZ, J/Make way for Sam Houston. /1986/
6/7 KE392 . . . . **B HOUSTON, S.**
PATRICK-WEXLER, D/Barbara Jordan. /1996/
4-6/8 KE408 . . . . **B JORDAN, B.**
POLLACK, JS/Shirley Chisholm. /1994/
5-6/10 KE289 . . . . **B CHISHOLM, S.**

Leisure SEE Hobbies; Recreation.

Leisure--Social aspects.
MILLER, TR/Taking time out: recreation and play. /1996/
5-A/7 KA865 . . . . **306.4**

Lemieux, Mario.
HUGHES, ME/Mario Lemieux: beating the odds. /1996/
4-6/9 KE433 . . . . **B LEMIEUX, M.**

Leonardo, da Vinci.
MCLANATHAN, R/Leonardo da Vinci. /1990/
6-A/6 KD495 . . . . **759.5**
MUHLBERGER, R/What makes a Leonardo a Leonardo? /1994/
5-A/7 KD496 . . . . **759.5**
PROVENSEN, A/Leonardo da Vinci. /1984/
4-6/7 KE434 . . . . **B LEONARDO**
STANLEY, D/Leonardo da Vinci. /1996/
5-A/8 KE435 . . . . **B LEONARDO**

Leopard--Fiction--Software.
P.J.'S READING ADVENTURES (CD-ROM). /1996/
K-3/KB252 . . . . **CDR 398**

Leopards--Folklore.
HALEY, GE/Story, a story: an African tale. /c1970/
3-5/5 KB580 . . . . **CE 398.24**

Leprechauns--Fiction.
BATEMAN, T/Ring of Truth: an original Irish tale. /1997/
1-3/5 KF213 . . . . **E**
SHUB, E/Seeing is believing. /1979/K-2/2 KG496 . . . . **E**

Leprechauns--Folklore.
WALKER, PR/Little folk: stories from around the world. /1997/
2-4/6 KB494 . . . . **398.22**

Lesbians.
GREENBERG, KE/Zack's story: growing up with same-sex parents. /
1996/4-6/4 KA877 . . . . **306.874**

Lester, Helen.
LESTER, H/Author: a true story. /1997/
2-5/2 KE436 . . . . **B LESTER, H.**

Letter writing.
JAMES, E/Sincerely yours: how to write great letters. /1993/
3-6/7 KD870 . . . . **808.6**
LEEDY, L/Messages in the mailbox: how to write a letter. /1991/
2-5/2 KB246 . . . . **395.4**
POSTAL STATION (VIDEOCASSETTE). /1991/
K-4/KB132 . . . . **VCR 383**

Letter writing--Fiction.
KEATS, EJ/Letter to Amy. /c1968/P-2/2 KF874 . . . . **CE E**

Letters.
JAKOBSEN, K/My New York. /1993/2-5/3 KE957 . . . . . **974.7**
PARKS, R/Dear Mrs. Parks: a dialogue with today's youth. /1996/
5-6/6 KA901 . . . . **323**

Letters--Fiction.
CASELEY, J/Dear Annie. /1991/K-2/2 KF363 . . . . **E**
LYONS, ME/Letters from a slave girl: the story of Harriet Jacobs. /
1992/4-6/4 KH430 . . . . **Fic**
NICHOL, B/Beethoven lives upstairs. /1994/4-6/4 KH549 . . . . . **Fic**
Beethoven lives upstairs (Videocassette). /1992/
4-6/KH550 . . . . **VCR Fic**
SCHINDEL, J/Dear Daddy. /1995/K-2/2 KG406 . . . . **E**
STEWART, S/Gardener. /1997/K-3/2 KG571 . . . . **E**
TRYON, L/Albert's Thanksgiving. /1994/K-2/2 KG621 . . . . **E**

WOODRUFF, E/Dear Levi: letters from the Overland Trail. /1994/
4-6/6 KH880 . . . . **Fic**

Leukemia.
COERR, E/Sadako. /1993/3-6/4 KA994 . . . . **CE 362.1**

Levittown (N.Y.)--Fiction.
CONRAD, P/Our house: the stories of Levittown. /1995/
4-6/7 KH022 . . . . **Fic**

Lewis, Meriwether.
CLARK, W/Off the map: the journals of Lewis and Clark. /1993/
4-6/7 KE201 . . . . **917.804**
KROLL, S/Lewis and Clark: explorers of the American West. /1994/
4-6/6 KE203 . . . . **917.804**
LEWIS AND CLARK EXPEDITION (VIDEOCASSETTE). /1992/
5-6/KE204 . . . . **VCR 917.804**
SCHANZER, R/How we crossed the West: the adventures of Lewis
and Clark. /1997/3-6/7 KE205 . . . . **917.804**
STEFOFF, R/Lewis and Clark. /1992/5-6/5 KE206 . . . . . **917.804**

Lewis, Meriwether--Diaries.
CLARK, W/Off the map: the journals of Lewis and Clark. /1993/
4-6/7 KE201 . . . . **917.804**

Lewis and Clark Expedition (1804-1806).
CLARK, W/Off the map: the journals of Lewis and Clark. /1993/
4-6/7 KE201 . . . . **917.804**
KROLL, S/Lewis and Clark: explorers of the American West. /1994/
4-6/6 KE203 . . . . **917.804**
LEWIS AND CLARK EXPEDITION (VIDEOCASSETTE). /1992/
5-6/KE204 . . . . **VCR 917.804**
ROWLAND, D/Story of Sacajawea: guide to Lewis and Clark. /
1995/5-6/6 KE529 . . . . **B SACAGAWEA**
SACAJAWEA (VIDEOCASSETTE). /1991/
2-5/KE530. . . . . **VCR B SACAGAWEA**
SCHANZER, R/How we crossed the West: the adventures of Lewis
and Clark. /1997/3-6/7 KE205 . . . . **917.804**
STEFOFF, R/Lewis and Clark. /1992/5-6/5 KE206 . . . . . **917.804**

Lexington, Battle of, 1775.
JOHNSON, N/Battle of Lexington and Concord. /1992/
4-6/7 KE881 . . . . **973.3**

Lexington, Battle of, 1775--Fiction.
BENCHLEY, N/George, the drummer boy. /c1977/1-3/2 KF221 . **E**
Sam the minuteman. /c1969/1-3/2 KF222. . . . . **E**

Lexington, Battle of, 1775--Poetry.
LONGFELLOW, HW/Paul Revere's ride. /1990/
3-A/KD980 . . . . **CE 811**
Liberty SEE ALSO Civil rights; Slavery.

Librarians--Biography.
GAVER, MV/Braided cord: memoirs of a school librarian. /1988/
/KA368. **PROF B GAVER, M**
LANDS OF PLEASURE: /1990//KA044 . . . . **PROF 020**

Librarians--Fiction.
BELLAIRS, J/Dark secret of Weatherend. /c1984/
6-A/6 KG895. . . . . **Fic**
MAHY, M/Great piratical rumbustification and The librarian and the
robbers. /c1978, 1986/5-A/7 KH449 . . . . **Fic**
MANN, P/Frog Princess? /1995/1-3/2 KG058 . . . . **E**
PINKWATER, DM/Aunt Lulu. /1991/P-2/2 KG244 . . . . **E**
Libraries SEE ALSO Instructional materials centers; School libraries.

Libraries.
ANIMATED DICTIONARY (VIDEOCASSETTE). /1992/
3-5/KA588 . . . . **VCR 028.7**
FIND IT ALL AT THE LIBRARY: AN INTRODUCTION TO THE
LIBRARY FOR CHILDREN (VIDEOCASSETTE). /1996/
2-6/KA584 . . . . **VCR 027**
FOWLER, A/Library of Congress. /1996/3-6/11 KA587 . . . **027.5**
GIBBONS, G/Check it out!: the book about libraries. /1985/
1-3/3 KA585 . . . . **CE 027**

Libraries--Censorship--Handbooks, manuals, etc.
INTELLECTUAL FREEDOM MANUAL. 5TH. ED. /1996/
/KA052. . . . . **PROF 025.2**

Libraries--Fiction.
ALEXANDER, M/How my library grew by Dinah. /1983/
K-2/2 KF146 . . . . **E**
BEST, C/Red light, green light, Mama and me. /1995/
K-2/2 KF228 . . . . **E**
BONSALL, CN/Tell me some more. /c1961/K-2/2 KF247. . . . . . **E**

Libraries--Special collections--Databases.
WRIGHT, K/Challenge of technology: action strategies for the
school library media /1993//KA080 . . . . **PROF 027.8**

Libraries--Special collections--Software.
WRIGHT, K/Challenge of technology: action strategies for the
school library media /1993//KA080 . . . . **PROF 027.8**

Libraries, Children's.
GAGNON, A/Guidelines for children's services. /1989/
/KA068. . . . . **PROF 027.62**
LANDS OF PLEASURE: /1990//KA044 . . . . **PROF 020**

Libraries, Children's--Acitivity programs.
BAUER, CF/Leading kids to books through magic. /1996/
/KA066. . . . . **PROF 027.62**

Libraries, Children's--Activity programs.
BAUER, CF/Celebrations: read-aloud holiday and theme book
programs. /1985//KA342. . . . . **PROF 808.8**
Read for the fun of it: active programming with books for children.
/1992//KA067 . . . . **PROF 027.62**
THOMAS, RL/Primaryplots 2: a book talk guide for use with
readers ages 4-8. /1993//KA093. . . . . **PROF 028.5**

Libraries, Children's--Book lists.
BARSTOW, B/Beyond picture books: a guide to first readers. 2nd
ed. /1995//KA011 . . . . **PROF 011.62**
GILLESPIE, JT/Best books for children: preschool through grade 6.
5th ed. /1994//KA084 . . . . **PROF 028.1**
PETERSON, CS/Reference books for children, 4th ed. /1992/
/KA021. . . . . **PROF 011.62**

Libraries, Children's--Book selection.
SMITH, L/Unreluctant years: a critical approach to children's
literature. /c1953, 1991//KA357 . . . . **PROF 809**

Libraries, Children's--Periodicals.
EMERGENCY LIBRARIAN. /1973-//KA108 . . . . . **PER PROF 050**
JOURNAL OF YOUTH SERVICES IN LIBRARIES. /1946-/
/KA118. . . . . **PER PROF 050**

Libraries, Public.
LIBRARY (VIDEOCASSETTE). /1991/1-4/KA586 . . . . **VCR 027.4**

Libraries, Traveling--Fiction.
LEVINSON, NS/Clara and the bookwagon. /1988/
1-3/1 KF967 . . . . **E**

Libraries and education.
BROSTROM, DC/Guide to homeschooling for librarians. /1995/
/KA065. . . . . **PROF 026.371**
FARMER, LS/Cooperative learning activities in the library media
center. /1991//KA073. . . . . **PROF 027.8**
URBANIK, MK/Curriculum planning and teaching using the library
media center. /1989//KA064 . . . . **PROF 025.5**

Libraries and readers.
BOOKTALK! 5: MORE SELECTIONS FROM THE BOOKTALKER
FOR ALL AGES AND AUDIENCES. /1993//KA090. **PROF 028.5**

Library of Congress.
FOWLER, A/Library of Congress. /1996/3-6/11 KA587 . . . **027.5**

Library orientation.
EISENBERG, MB/Information problem-solving: the Big Six Skills
approach to library and information skills instruction. /1990/
/KA063. . . . . **PROF 025.5**

Library science.
GAGNON, A/Guidelines for children's services. /1989/
/KA068. . . . . **PROF 027.62**

Library science literature.
AASL ELECTRONIC LIBRARY. 1997 ED. (CD-ROM). /1997/
/KA045. . . . . **CDR PROF 025**

Life--Fiction.
BABBITT, N/Tuck everlasting. /c1975/4-6/4 KG873 . . . . . **CE Fic**
Life (Biology) SEE ALSO Biology; Genetics; Reproduction.

Life (Biology).
LAUBER, P/You're aboard spaceship Earth. /1996/
1-3/3 KC147 . . . . **550**
ZOEHFELD, KW/What's alive? /1995/1-3/2 KC301 . . . . **577**

Life (Biology)--Software.
VARIATIONS IN LIFE SCIENCE INVESTIGATIONS (CD-ROM). /
1996/6-A/KC298 . . . . **CDR 577**
Life on other planets SEE ALSO Extraterrestrial beings.

Life on other planets.
DARLING, DJ/Could you ever meet an alien? /1990/
A/7 KC291 . . . . **576.8**

Life sciences--Songs and music.
HORTON, B/Lyrical life science (Multimedia kit). /1995/
K-A/KA295 . . . . **MMK PROF 570**

Life skills.
HOME ALONE: YOU'RE IN CHARGE (VIDEOCASSETTE). /1991/
2-4/KD259. . . . . **VCR 640**
HOME ON YOUR OWN (VIDEOCASSETTE). /1994/
4-6/KD260. . . . . **VCR 640**
LATCHKEY CHILDREN: WHEN YOU'RE IN CHARGE
(VIDEOCASSETTE). /1986/5-6/KD261 . . . . **VCR 640**
PRESCHOOL POWER!: JACKET FLIPS AND OTHER TIPS
(VIDEOCASSETTE). /1991/P-K/KD263 . . . . **VCR 640.83**
Light SEE ALSO Color; Lasers.

Light.
BURNIE, D/Light. /1992/4-A/7 KC107 . . . . **535**
COBB, V/Light action!: amazing experiments with optics. /1993/
2-6/7 KC108 . . . . **535**
COLOR: LIGHT FANTASTIC (VIDEOCASSETTE). /1988/
3-6/KC119. . . . . **VCR 535.6**

LAUBER, P/What do you see and how do you see it?: exploring
    light, color, and vision. /1994/1-6/4 KC113 . . . . **535**
OXLADE, C/Science magic with light. /1994/3-6/5 KD749 . **793.8**
SOUND/LIGHT AND COLOR (VIDEOCASSETTE). /1994/
    3-6/KC080. . . . . **VCR 530**

Light--Experiments.
    ARDLEY, N/Science book of light. /1991/K-3/6 KC105 . . . . . **535**
    DARLING, DJ/Making light work: the science of optics. /1991/
        6-A/8 KC109 . . . . **535**
    DOHERTY, P/Magic wand and other bright experiments on light and
        color. /1995/4-A/5 KC110 . . . . **535**
    ZUBROWSKI, B/Mirrors: finding out about the properties of light. /
        1992/5-6/8 KC116 . . . . **535**

Lighthouse keepers.
    FLEMING, C/Women of the lights. /1996/4-6/6 KB148. . . . **387.1**
    ROOP, P/Keep the lights burning, Abbie. /1985/
        1-3/1 KE270 . . . . **CE B BURGESS, A.**

Lighthouses.
    FLEMING, C/Women of the lights. /1996/4-6/6 KB148. . . . **387.1**
    GIBBONS, G/Beacons of light: lighthouses. /1990/
        3-6/6 KB149 . . . . **387.1**
    GUIBERSON, BZ/Lighthouses: watchers at sea. /1995/
        5-6/8 KB150 . . . . **387.1**

Lighthouses--Fiction.
    HOPKINSON, D/Birdie's lighthouse. /1997/3-5/3 KH282 . . . . . **Fic**

Lighting.
    LIGHT BULBS (VIDEOCASSETTE). /1991/
        1-3/KD043. . . . . **VCR 621.32**

Lightning.
    BRANLEY, FM/Flash, crash, rumble and roll. Rev. ed. /1985/
        1-3/2 KC195 . . . . **CE 551.55**
    KAHL, JD/Thunderbolt: learning about lightning. /1993/
        4-6/9 KC207 . . . . **551.56**

Lightning--Folklore.
    BRYAN, A/Story of lightning and thunder. /1993/
        K-2/2 KB702 . . . . **398.26**

Limbs, Artificial SEE Prosthesis.

Limericks.
    LEAR, E/Daffy down dillies: silly limericks. /1992/K-A/KE103 . **821**
        Owl and the Pussy-cat and other nonsense poems. /1995/
        3-6/KE106 . . . . **821**
    LOTS OF LIMERICKS. /1991/3-6/KE069 . . . . **811.008**

Lin, Maya Ying.
    LING, B/Maya Lin. /1997/4-6/10 KE437 . . . . **B LIN, M.**

Lincoln, Abraham.
    ABRAHAM LINCOLN: THE GREAT EMANCIPATOR
        (VIDEOCASSETTE). /1990/A/KE438 . . . . **VCR B LINCOLN, A.**
    BRENNER, M/Abe Lincoln's hat. /1994/
        1-3/2 KE439 . . . . **B LINCOLN, A.**
    D'AULAIRE, I/Abraham Lincoln. /c1957, 1993/
        3-4/4 KE440 . . . . **CE B LINCOLN, A.**
    FREEDMAN, R/Lincoln, a photobiography. /1987/
        A/11 KE441 . . . . **B LINCOLN, A.**
    HARNESS, C/Abe Lincoln goes to Washington 1837-1865. /1997/
        2-4/7 KE443 . . . . **B LINCOLN, A.**
    KUNHARDT, E/Honest Abe. /1993/1-3/4 KE444 . **B LINCOLN, A.**
    LINCOLN, IN HIS OWN WORDS. /1993/A/8 KE907 . . . . . **973.7**
    LINCOLN, A/Gettysburg Address. /1995/4-6/6 KE906 . . . . **973.7**

Lincoln, Abraham--Childhood and youth.
    HARNESS, C/Young Abe Lincoln: the frontier days, 1809-1837. /
        1996/2-4/5 KE442 . . . . **B LINCOLN, A.**

Lincoln, Abraham--Poetry.
    LIVINGSTON, MC/Abraham Lincoln: a man for all the people: a
        ballad. /1993/K-3/KD974. **811**

Lincoln, Abraham. Gettysburg address.
    LINCOLN, A/Gettysburg Address. /1995/4-6/6 KE906 . . . **973.7**
    MURPHY, J/Long road to Gettysburg. /1992/5-A/7 KE910 . **973.7**

Lindbergh, Charles A.
    BURLEIGH, R/Flight: the journey of Charles Lindbergh. /1991/
        1-4/2 KD091 . . . . **629.13**
        Flight: the journey of Charles Lindbergh. /1991/
        4-6/3 KD092 . . . . **629.13**

Lintz, Gertrude--Fiction.
    JOYCE, W/Buddy: based on the true story of Gertrude Lintz. /
        1997/5-A/5 KH337 . . . . **Fic**

Lions.
    ARNOLD, C/Lion. /1995/5-6/7 KC828 . . . . **599.757**
    HOFER, A/Lion family book. /1995/3-6/6 KC830. . . . . . **599.757**

Lions--Fiction.
    FREEMAN, D/Dandelion. /c1964/K-1/2 KF579 . . . . **CE E**
    MORPURGO, M/Butterfly lion. /1997/5-A/5 KH512 . . . . **Fic**

Lipizzaner horse--Fiction.
    HENRY, M/White stallion of Lipizza. /c1964, 1994/
        4-6/6 KH246 . . . . **Fic**

Listening--Fiction.
    LESTER, H/Listen Buddy. /1995/K-2/2 KF964 . . . . **E**

Literacy.
    CHALL, JS/Reading crisis: why poor children fall behind. /1990/
        /KA219. . . . . **PROF 372.6**
    COUNTERPOINT AND BEYOND: A RESPONSE TO BECOMING A
        NATION OF READERS. /1988//KA207 . . . . **PROF 372.4**

Literacy--Fiction.
    GAEDDERT, L/Breaking free. /1994/5-A/5 KH147 . . . . **Fic**
    POLACCO, P/Aunt Chip and the great Triple Creek Dam affair. /
        1996/2-4/2 KG248. . . . . **E**
    RADIN, RY/All Joseph wanted. /1991/3-5/4 KH617 . . . . **Fic**

Literary cookbooks.
    ZALBEN, JB/Beni's family cookbook for the Jewish holidays. /1996/
        4-6/KD283. . . . . **641.5**

Literary prizes SEE ALSO names of awards e.g. Newbery Medal books.

Literary prizes.
    CBC FEATURES. /1945-//KA101 . . . . **PER PROF 050**
    HORN BOOK MAGAZINE /Newbery Medal books: 1922-1955:
        with their authors' acceptance papers, /c1957/
        /KA353. . . . . **PROF 809**
    JONES, DB/Children's literature awards and winners: a directory of
        prizes, authors, and /1994/KA354 . . . . **PROF 809**
    NEWBERY AND CALDECOTT MEDALISTS AND HONOR BOOK
        WINNERS: BIBLIOGRAPHIES AND /1992//KA004 . . . **PROF 011**

Literary prizes--Bibliography.
    LITERARY LAURELS: KIDS' EDITION: A READER'S GUIDE TO
        AWARD-WINNING CHILDREN'S BOOKS. /1996/
        /KA034. . . . . **PROF 016.809**

Literary prizes--Periodicals.
    NEWBERY AND CALDECOTT AWARDS: A GUIDE TO THE
        MEDAL AND HONOR BOOKS. /n.d.//KA128 . . **PER PROF 050**

Literary recreations.
    GREESON, J/Name that book! Questions and answers on
        outstanding children's books. /1996//KA350 . . . . . . **PROF 809**
    MACAULAY, D/Black and white. /1990/3-A/5 KH432 . . . . . . **Fic**
        Shortcut. /1995/3-A/3 KH434 . . . . **Fic**
    SHANNON, G/Stories to solve. /1985/5-6/6 KB714 . . . . **398.26**

Literary recreations--Dictionaries.
    EISS, HE/Dictionary of language games, puzzles, and amusements.
        /1986/4-6/KA455. . . . . **REF 793.734**

Literature SEE ALSO Authorship; Children's literature; and other literary
    forms e.g. Biography.

Literature--Collections SEE ALSO Quotations; Short stories; American
    poetry--Collections; English literature--Collections; Poetry--Collections, etc.

Literature--Collections.
    EXPECTATIONS. /1948-/3-6/KD873 . . . . **808.8**
    HOME. /1992/K-6/KD900. **810.8**
    JUBA THIS AND JUBA THAT. /1995//KA366 . . . . . **PROF 820.8**
    MAXFIELD PARRISH: A TREASURY OF ART AND CHILDREN'S
        LITERATURE. /1995/K-6/KD413. . . . . **741.6**
    PINDER, M/People with one heart (Talking book). /1996/
        P-1/KD876. . . . . **TB 808.8**
        Planet with one mind: stories from around the world for the child
        within us all (Talking book). /1995/1-4/KD877 . . . . . **TB 808.8**
    READY...SET...READ!: THE BEGINNING READER'S TREASURY. /
        1990/P-2/KD901 . . . . **810.8**
    READY...SET...READ--AND LAUGH!: A FUNNY TREASURY FOR
        BEGINNING READERS. /1995/K-2/KD902 . . . . **810.8**
    SCARED SILLY! A BOOK FOR THE BRAVE. /1994/
        K-3/KD904 . . . . **810.8**
    TREASURY OF CHILDREN'S LITERATURE. /1992/
        P-3/KD879. . . . . **808.8**

Literature--Criticism and interpretation--Software.
    BOOK EXCHANGE (MICROCOMPUTER PROGRAM). /1996/
        3-6/KD862. . . . . **MCP 808**

Literature--Dictionaries.
    BREWER'S DICTIONARY OF PHRASE AND FABLE. 15TH ED. /
        1995/5-6/KA459 . . . . **REF 803**

Literature--Study and teaching.
    GEIGER, E/TNT: two hundred and ninety-two activites for literature
        and language arts! /1989//KA222 . . . . **PROF 372.6**
    MCELMEEL, SL/McElmeel booknotes: literature across the
        curriculum. /1993//KA225 . . . . **PROF 372.6**
    WATKINS, J/Programming author visits. /1996/
        /KA071. . . . . **PROF 027.62**

Literature--Study and teaching (Elementary).
    BOOK TALK AND BEYOND: CHILDREN AND TEACHERS
        RESPOND TO LITERATURE. /1995//KA235. . . . . **PROF 372.64**
    BORDERS, SG/Children talking about books. /1993/
        /KA236. . . . . **PROF 372.64**
    LITERATURE TO ENJOY AND WRITE ABOUT, SERIES 1
        (VIDEOCASSETTE). /1989//KA344 . . . . **VCR PROF 808.8**

LITERATURE TO ENJOY AND WRITE ABOUT, SERIES 2
(VIDEOCASSETTE). /1990//KA345 . . . . **VCR PROF 808.8**
STORIES AND READERS: NEW PERSPECTIVES ON LITERATURE
IN THE ELEMENTARY CLASSROOM. /1992/
/KA241. **PROF 372.64**

Little, Jean.
MIND'S EYE: JEAN LITTLE (VIDEOCASSETTE). /1996/
5-6/KE445. . . . . **VCR B LITTLE, J.**

Little Big Horn, Battle of the, 1876.
FREEDMAN, R/Life and death of Crazy Horse. /1996/
6-A/7 KE307 . . . . **B CRAZY HORSE**
GOBLE, P/Red Hawk's account of Custer's last battle; the Battle of
the Little Bighorn, 25 June 1876. /c1969, 1992/
5-6/6 KE914 . . . . **973.8**

Little brown bat.
BASH, B/Shadows of night: the hidden world of the Little Brown
Bat. /1993/1-3/5 KC758 . . . . **599.4**

Littlechild, George.
LITTLECHILD, G/This land is my land. /1993/2-A/4 KE803 . . . **971**
Livestock SEE ALSO Bulls; Cattle; Cows; Dairying; Domestic animals; Goats;
Horses; Pigs; Sheep; Veterinary medicine.

Living fossils.
MARTIN, J/Living fossils: animals that have withstood the test of
time. /1997/4-A/9 KC453 . . . . **591**
Lizards SEE ALSO names of specific species e.g. Chameleons.

Lizards.
DARLING, K/Komodo dragon: on location. /1997/
4-6/7 KC625 . . . . **597.95**
LINDLEY, M/Lizard in the jungle. /1988/5-6/7 KC626. . . . **597.95**
PARKER, NW/Frogs, toads, lizards and salamanders. /1990/
5-6/7 KC606 . . . . **597.8**
RYDER, J/Lizard in the sun. /1990/1-3/5 KC628 . . . . . . **597.95**
SCHNIEPER, C/Chameleons. /1989/5-6/7 KC630. . . . . . **597.95**
SOUZA, DM/Catch me if you can. /1992/4-6/6 KC631 . . **597.95**

Llamas.
ARNOLD, C/Llama. /1988/5-6/7 KD210 . . . . **636.2**

Llamas--Fiction.
GUARINO, D/Is your mama a llama? /1989/P-1/2 KF651 . . . . . **E**

Lobel, Arnold.
LOBEL, A/Arnold Lobel video showcase (Videocassette). /1985/
1-3/KG000 . . . . **VCR E**

Lobsters.
CERULLO, MM/Lobsters: gangsters of the sea. /1994/
5-6/7 KC518 . . . . **595.3**
Local government SEE ALSO Cities and towns; Villages.

Loch Ness monster.
STEFFENS, B/Loch Ness Monster. /1995/3-6/9 KA563 . . **001.944**

Loch Ness monster--Fiction.
COOPER, S/Boggart and the monster. /1997/5-A/6 KH027 . . . **Fic**

Locomotives--Fiction.
PIPER, W/Little engine that could. /c1961/P-K/4 KG246 . . . **CE E**

Loggerhead turtle.
TALKING ABOUT SEA TURTLES (VIDEOCASSETTE). /1992/
4-6/KC623. . . . . **VCR 597.92**
VOYAGE OF THE LOGGERHEAD (VIDEOCASSETTE). /1995/
3-6/KC624. . . . . **VCR 597.92**

Loggerhead turtle--Fiction.
JAY, LA/Sea turtle journey: the story of a loggerhead turtle. /
1995/K-2/5 KF826 . . . . **CE E**

Logging--Fiction.
HONEYCUTT, N/Twilight in Grace Falls. /1997/6-A/6 KH278. . **Fic**

Logging--History.
ADAMS, P/Early loggers and the sawmill. /1981/
4-6/6 KD164 . . . . **634.9**

Logic--Folklore.
SHANNON, G/Stories to solve. /1985/5-6/6 KB714 . . . . **398.26**

Logic--Software.
FACTORY: EXPLORATIONS IN PROBLEM SOLVING
(MICROCOMPUTER PROGRAM). /1983/
2-4/KA635 . . . . **MCP 153.4**
LOGICAL JOURNEY OF THE ZOOMBINIS. SCHOOL ED. (CD-
ROM). /1996/2-5/KB938. . . . . **CDR 511**

London (England).
STEIN, RC/London. /1996/3-5/8 KE682. . . . . **942.1**

London (England)--Buildings, structures, etc.
FISHER, LE/Tower of London. /1987/3-6/7 KE679 . . . . **942**

London (England)--Fiction.
CARRIS, JD/Beware the ravens, Aunt Morbelia. /1995/
5-A/5 KG979. . . . . **Fic**
DOHERTY, B/Street child. /1994/5-A/6 KH078 . . . . **Fic**
GLEITZMAN, M/Puppy fat. /1995/5-A/5 KH175. . . . . **Fic**
RICHEMONT, E/Magic skateboard. /1992/3-5/3 KH631 . . . . . **Fic**

London (England)--Pictorial works.
MUNRO, R/Inside-outside book of London. /c1989, 1996/
2-A/KE681. . . . . **942.1**

Longfellow, Henry Wadsworth.
MEET THE AUTHOR: HENRY WADSWORTH LONGFELLOW
(VIDEOCASSETTE). /1992/
5-A/KE446. . . . . **VCR B LONGFELLOW, H**

Loons.
ESBENSEN, BJ/Great Northern diver: the loon. /1990/
3-5/6 KC680 . . . . **598.4**
KLEIN, T/Loon magic for kids. /c1989, 1991/3-5/5 KC651. . . **598**

Los Angeles (Calif.)--Buildings, structures, etc.
ZELVER, P/Wonderful Towers of Watts. /1994/2-4/6 KD387 . **725**

Los Angeles (Calif.)--Fiction.
KOERTGE, R/Harmony Arms. /1994/A/5 KH371 . . . . **Fic**
SOTO, G/Chato's kitchen. /c1995, 1997/1-3/5 KG527 . . . . . . **E**
Losing and winning SEE Winning and losing.

Loss (Psychology)--Fiction.
WHITE, R/Belle Prater's boy. /1996/6-A/6 KH853 . . . . **Fic**

Lost and found possessions--Fiction.
ERNST, LC/Letters are lost! /1996/P-K/2 KF530. . . . . **E**
GERSTEIN, M/Behind the couch. /1996/2-4/3 KH162. . . . . . **Fic**
HAVILL, J/Jamaica's find. /1986/K-2/2 KF682. . . . . **E**
LONDON, J/Let's go, Froggy! /1994/P-K/2 KG024 . . . . **E**
O'BRIEN, C/Sam's sneaker search. /1997/P-2/3 KG186 . . . . . . **E**
POYDAR, N/Busy Bea. /1994/P-1/2 KG285 . . . . **E**
RABE, B/Where's Chimpy? /1988/P-2/2 KG296 . . . . **E**
RODDA, E/Finders keepers. /1991/5-A/6 KH645 . . . . **Fic**
STEWART, EJ/Bimmi finds a cat. /1996/3-5/6 KH761 . . . . . . **Fic**

Lost children--Fiction.
CARRICK, C/Left behind. /1988/1-3/2 KF359 . . . . **E**
HAMM, DJ/Laney's lost momma. /1991/P-1/2 KF670 . . . . **E**
KINSEY-WARNOCK, N/Bear that heard crying. /1993/
2-3/2 KF905 . . . . **E**
LONDON, J/Ali, child of the desert. /1997/K-3/3 KG019 . . . . . **E**
MCPHAIL, D/Lost! /1990/P-1/2 KG119 . . . . **E**
RAND, G/Willie takes a hike. /1996/K-2/3 KG302 . . . . **E**
TAFURI, N/Have you seen my duckling? /1984/P-K/1 KG590. . . **E**

Louis, Joe.
LIPSYTE, R/Joe Louis: a champ for all America. /1994/
4-6/6 KE447 . . . . **B LOUIS, J.**

Louisiana.
FRADIN, DB/Louisiana. /1995/4-6/4 KF000 . . . . **976.3**

Love.
MORRIS, A/Loving. /1990/1-3/2 KA880 . . . . **306.874**

Love--Fiction.
BABBITT, N/Bub, or, The very best thing. /1994/P-2/2 KF182 . . **E**
COTTONWOOD, J/Babcock. /1996/6-A/3 KH032 . . . . **Fic**
JOOSSE, BM/Mama, do you love me? /1991/P-1/2 KF854. . . . **E**
LEVITIN, S/Man who kept his heart in a bucket. /1991/
K-2/3 KF970 . . . . **E**
MCKINLEY, R/Beauty: a retelling of the story of Beauty and the
Beast. /1978/6-A/6 KH485. . . . . **Fic**
PATERSON, K/Great Gilly Hopkins. /c1978/5-A/5 KH576. . . . **Fic**
ROTH, SL/My love for you. /1997/P-1/2 KG356. . . . . **E**

Love--Poetry.
ADOFF, A/Love letters. /1997/K-4/KD911 . . . . **811**
LITTLE BOOK OF LOVE. /1995/4-6/KD886 . . . . **808.81**

Low, Juliette Gordon.
BROWN, FG/Daisy and the Girl Scouts: the story of Juliette
Gordon Low. /1996/3-6/7 KE448 . . . . **B LOW, J.**

Loyalty--Fiction.
KROEGER, MK/Paperboy. /1996/1-3/2 KF926 . . . . **E**

Lucas, John (John H.).
SIMMONS, A/John Lucas. /1996/5-A/7 KE449 . . . **B LUCAS, J.**

Luck--Fiction.
ALEXANDER, L/House Gobbaleen. /1995/3-5/4 KG836 . . . . . **Fic**
CAREY, P/Big Bazoohley. /1995/3-6/5 KG973 . . . . **Fic**
ERNST, LC/Luckiest kid on the planet. /1994/1-3/2 KF532. . . . **E**
HEARN, DD/Bad Luck Boswell. /1995/1-3/5 KF690 . . . . **E**

Ludington, Sybil.
BROWN, DP/Sybil rides for independence. /1985/
3-6/4 KE876 . . . . **973.3**
Luggage SEE Trunks (Luggage).

Lullabies.
APPELT, K/Bayou lullaby. /1995/P-2/5 KF163 . . . . **E**
BANG, M/Ten, nine, eight. /1983/P-K/KF192 . . . . **E**
DYER, J/Animal crackers: a delectable collection of pictures, poems,
and lullabies for /1996/P-1/KD882. . . . . **808.81**
HO, M/Hush!: a Thai lullaby. /1996/P-1/KD952. . . . . **811**
MCMULLAN, K/If you were my bunny. /1996/P-K/3 KG112 . . . **E**
PALMER, H/Child's world of lullabies: multicultural songs for quiet
times (Sound recording cassette). /1993/P-2/KD642 . **SRC 789.3**

SHAKE IT TO THE ONE THAT YOU LOVE THE BEST: PLAY
SONGS AND LULLABIES FROM BLACK /1989/
K-4/KD767 . . . . **BA 796.1**
SLEEP, BABY, SLEEP: LULLABIES AND NIGHT POEMS. /1994/
P-K/KD889. . . . . **808.81**
VAN LAAN, N/Sleep, sleep, sleep: a lullaby for little ones around
the world. /1995/P-2/3 KG644 . . . . **E**

Lumber and lumbering--Canada.
KURELEK, W/Lumberjack. /1974/4-6/6 KD165 . . . . **634.9**

Lumber and lumbering--Fiction.
HONEYCUTT, N/Twilight in Grace Falls. /1997/6-A/6 KH278. . **Fic**

Lumber and lumbering--Folklore.
MCCORMICK, DJ/Paul Bunyan swings his axe. /c1936, 1962/
4-6/6 KB467 . . . . **398.22**
Tall timber tales: more Paul Bunyan stories. /c1939/
4-6/6 KB468 . . . . **398.22**
ROUNDS, G/Ol' Paul, the mighty logger: /1976/
4-6/7 KB477 . . . . **398.22**

Lumber and lumbering--History.
ADAMS, P/Early loggers and the sawmill. /1981/
4-6/6 KD164 . . . . **634.9**

Lumber camps.
KURELEK, W/Lumberjack. /1974/4-6/6 KD165 . . . . **634.9**

Lumbermen--Fiction.
HONEYCUTT, N/Twilight in Grace Falls. /1997/6-A/6 KH278. . **Fic**

Lungs.
SAUNDERSON, J/Heart and lungs. /1992/5-6/6 KC935 . . . **612.1**
YOUR BODY: CIRCULATORY AND RESPIRATORY SYSTEMS
(VIDEOCASSETTE). /1988/5-6/KC931 . . . . **VCR 612**

Lyon, George Ella.
LYON, GE/Wordful child. /1996/4-5/4 KE450 . . . **B LYON, G. E.**

Machinery.
BARTON, B/Big machines (Board book). /1995/P/KF204 . . . **BB E**
PUSH AND PULL: SIMPLE MACHINES AT WORK
(VIDEOCASSETTE). /1990/4-6/KC097 . . . . **VCR 531**
RADFORD, D/Cargo machines and what they do. /1992/
P-2/4 KD089 . . . . **629.04**
ROBBINS, K/Power machines. /c1993, 1997/K-4/6 KD051. . **621.8**
ROCKWELL, AF/Machines. /c1972/K-2/3 KD052 . . . . **621.8**
SIMPLE MACHINE (VIDEOCASSETTE). /1993/
5-6/KC098. . . . . **VCR 531**
SIMPLE MACHINES: USING MECHANICAL ADVANTAGE
(VIDEOCASSETTE). /1992/5-6/KC099 . . . . **VCR 531**

Machinery--Experiments.
ARDLEY, N/Science book of machines. /1992/
4-6/4 KD050 . . . . **621.8**
ZUBROWSKI, B/Wheels at work: building and experimenting with
models of machines. /1986/5-6/8 KD054. . . . . **621.8**

Machinery--Fiction.
BARTON, B/Machines at work. /1987/P-K/2 KF207 . . . . **E**

Machinery--Models.
ZUBROWSKI, B/Wheels at work: building and experimenting with
models of machines. /1986/5-6/8 KD054. . . . . **621.8**

Machinery--Pictorial works.
HOBAN, T/Dig, drill, dump, fill. /1975/P-2/KD122 . . . . . **629.225**

Macintosh (Computer)--Programming.
FARMER, LS/I speak HyperCard. /1992/3-A/KA573. . . . **005.265**

Mackenzie, Alexander, Sir.
MANSON, A/Dog came, too: a true story. /1993/
1-4/6 KE185 . . . . **917.104**

Madagascar--Folklore.
RAPPAPORT, D/New king. /1995/4-A/3 KB473 . . . . **398.22**

Madden, John.
CHADWICK, B/John Madden. /1997/
5-A/7 KE451 . . . . **B MADDEN, J.**

Maddux, Greg.
CHRISTOPHER, M/On the mound with...Greg Maddux. /1997/
3-5/7 KE452 . . . . **B MADDUX, G.**

Madison, Dolley.
QUACKENBUSH, R/James Madison and Dolley Madison and their
times. /1992/4-5/7 KE894 . . . . **973.5**

Madison, James.
FRITZ, J/Great little Madison. /1989/
5-A/8 KE453 . . . . **B MADISON, J.**
QUACKENBUSH, R/James Madison and Dolley Madison and their
times. /1992/4-5/7 KE894 . . . . **973.5**

Magic SEE ALSO Occult sciences; Tricks.

Magic--Fiction.
ANDERSON, J/Juma and the magic jinn. /1986/2-3/4 KF156 . . **E**
BANG, M/Tye May and the magic brush. /c1981, 1992/
1-3/2 KF193 . . . . **E**
BELLAIRS, J/Dark secret of Weatherend. /c1984/
6-A/6 KG895. . . . . **Fic**
Doom of the haunted opera. /1995/4-6/6 KG896 . . . . . . **Fic**

BRITTAIN, B/Dr. Dredd's wagon of wonders. /1987/
3-6/5 KG923 . . . . **Fic**
Mystery of the several sevens. /1994/2-4/4 KG924 . . . . . . **Fic**
Wish giver. /1983/3-6/7 KG925 . . . . **Fic**
Wizards and the monster. /1994/2-4/4 KG926 . . . . **Fic**
BROWN, J/Stanley and the magic lamp. /1996/2-4/3 KG932 . **Fic**
CORBETT, S/Lemonade trick. /1960/4-5/4 KH030 . . . . **Fic**
CRESSWELL, H/Watchers: a mystery at Alton Towers. /1994/
5-A/3 KH040 . . . . **Fic**
DAHL, R/Magic finger. /1995/3-5/3 KH055 . . . . **Fic**
Matilda. /1988/5-A/7 KH056 . . . . **Fic**
DAY, D/Emperor's panda. /c1986, 1987/4-A/8 KH063 . . . . . **Fic**
DE PAOLA, T/Big Anthony and the magic ring. /1979/
1-3/5 KF466 . . . . **E**
DERBY, S/Jacob and the stranger. /1994/3-5/4 KH071. . . . . **Fic**
EAGER, E/Magic or not? /c1959, 1985/4-6/6 KH094. . . . . . **Fic**
Seven-day magic. /c1962/4-6/6 KH095 . . . . **Fic**
FIENBERG, A/Wiggy and Boa. /c1988, 1990/5-6/7 KH113 . . . **Fic**
FLEISCHMAN, S/Mr. Mysterious and Company. /c1962, 1997/
3-6/6 KH126 . . . . **Fic**
FLEMING, I/Chitty Chitty Bang Bang: the magical car. /c1964,
1989/5-6/7 KH128 . . . . **Fic**
FORWARD, T/Traveling backward. /1994/4-6/4 KH134 . . . . . **Fic**
FOX, M/Possum magic. /c1983, 1990/P-2/4 KF571 . . . . **E**
GACKENBACH, D/Mag the magnificent. /1985/K-2/2 KF590 . . **E**
GALDONE, P/Magic porridge pot. /c1976/P-2/4 KF596 . . . . . **E**
GILLILAND, JH/Not in the house, Newton! /1995/P-2/2 KF618 . **E**
GLASSMAN, P/Wizard next door. /1993/K-2/2 KF625 . . . . . . **E**
HOFFMAN, M/Four-legged ghosts. /1995/2-4/6 KH269 . . . . **Fic**
HOOKS, WH/Freedom's fruit. /1996/4-6/3 KH279. . . . . . . **Fic**
HUTCHINS, HJ/Anastasia Morningstar and the crystal butterfly. Rev.
ed. /1984/4-6/6 KH306. . . . . **Fic**
JONES, DW/Aunt Maria. /1991/6-A/6 KH330 . . . . **Fic**
Stopping for a spell: three fantasies. /1993/5-A/6 KH334 . . . **Fic**
LEWIS, JP/Christmas of the reddle moon. /1994/1-3/4 KF975 . **E**
MAZER, A/Accidental witch. /1995/3-5/4 KH463 . . . . **Fic**
MCPHAIL, D/Moony B. Finch, the fastest draw in the West. /1994/
1-3/4 KG120 . . . . **E**
NABB, M/Enchanted horse. /1993/4-6/7 KH525 . . . . **Fic**
POLACCO, P/My ol' man. /1995/1-3/3 KG254 . . . . **E**
REID BANKS, L/Adventures of King Midas. /1992/
4-A/6 KH626 . . . . **Fic**
Indian in the cupboard. /1980/4-6/4 KH627 . . . . **CE Fic**
Mystery of the cupboard. /1993/5-A/6 KH628 . . . . . . **CE Fic**
Return of the Indian. /1986/5-A/6 KH629 . . . . **Fic**
RICHEMONT, E/Magic skateboard. /1992/3-5/3 KH631 . . . . . **Fic**
RYLANT, C/Van Gogh Cafe. /1995/5-A/7 KH664 . . . . **Fic**
SELDEN, G/Genie of Sutton Place. /c1973/4-6/7 KH695 . . . . **Fic**
SNYDER, ZK/Black and blue magic. /c1966, 1994/
4-6/7 KH729 . . . . **Fic**
Witches of Worm. /c1965/4-6/7 KH735 . . . . **Fic**
STEIG, W/Sylvester and the magic pebble. /c1969, 1988/
K-2/6 KG544 . . . . **CE E**
Sylvester and the magic pebble (Videocassette). /1992/
K-2/KG545 . . . . **VCR E**
Toy brother. /1996/2-5/6 KG547 . . . . **E**
STERMAN, B/Backyard dragon. /1993/4-6/6 KH753 . . . . . . **Fic**
STOCKTON, FR/Bee-man of Orn. /c1964, 1987/
5-6/7 KH763 . . . . **Fic**
STRICKLAND, B/Hand of the necromancer. /1996/
5-A/6 KH772 . . . . **Fic**
TRAVERS, PL/Mary Poppins. Rev. ed. /c1962/4-6/6 KH800. . . **Fic**
TURKLE, B/Do not open. /1981/K-2/2 KG622 . . . . **E**
VAN ALLSBURG, C/Sweetest fig. /1993/3-A/3 KH823 . . . . . **Fic**
Widow's broom. /1992/4-A/5 KH824 . . . . **Fic**
WOOD, A/Flying Dragon Room. /1996/2-4/3 KG761 . . . . . . **E**
YOLEN, J/Wizard's Hall. /1991/4-6/6 KH897 . . . . **Fic**

Magic--Poetry.
WILLARD, N/Sorcerer's apprentice. /1993/2-5/KE041. . . . . . **811**

Magic tricks.
BROWN, D/Amazing magic tricks. /1995/4-6/KD744 . . . . . **793.8**
COBB, V/Wanna bet?: science challenges to fool you. /1993/
4-6/6 KD746 . . . . **793.8**
DAY, J/Let's make magic. /1992/3-6/KD747 . . . . **793.8**
OXLADE, C/Science magic with air. /1994/4-A/6 KD748. . . **793.8**
Science magic with light. /1994/3-6/5 KD749 . . . . **793.8**
Science magic with magnets. /1995/3-6/6 KD750 . . . . . **793.8**
Science magic with shapes and materials. /1995/
3-6/5 KD751 . . . . **793.8**
RAY, J/Fun magic with things around the house (Videocassette). /
1995/3-6/KD752 . . . . **VCR 793.8**

Magic tricks--Fiction.
ADLER, DA/Onion sundaes. /1994/2-3/2 KG819 . . . . **Fic**
BROWN, MT/Arthur's April fool. /1983/P-3/2 KF273 . . . . **E**

Magic tricks--Software.
 BIG ANTHONY'S MIXED-UP MAGIC (CD-ROM). /1996/
  K-2/KF229 . . . . **CDR E**
Magicians--Fiction.
 FLEISCHMAN, S/Midnight horse. /1990/5-A/4 KH125 . . . . . . **Fic**
 HOWE, J/Rabbit-Cadabra! /1993/K-3/3 KF779 . . . . **E**
 JONES, DW/Archer's goon. /1984/A/6 KH329. . . . . **Fic**
 QUATTLEBAUM, M/Jazz, Pizzazz, and the silver threads. /1996/
  2-4/3 KH615 . . . . **Fic**
 VAN ALLSBURG, C/Garden of Abdul Gasazi. /1979/
  1-3/5 KG638 . . . . **CE E**
Magicians--Folklore.
 SEEGER, P/Abiyoyo: based on a South African lullaby and folk
  story. /1986/2-5/KD587 . . . . **789.2**
Magicians--Poetry.
 WILLARD, N/Sorcerer's apprentice. /1993/2-5/KE041 . . . . . . **811**
Magnetism.
 JUNIOR ELECTRICIAN (VIDEOCASSETTE). /1991/
  3-6/KC132. . . . . **VCR 537**
Magnets.
 OXLADE, C/Science magic with magnets. /1995/
  3-6/6 KD750 . . . . **793.8**
Magnets--Experiments.
 ARDLEY, N/Science book of magnets. /1991/2-5/2 KC136 . . **538**
Magnifying glasses--Experiments.
 RAINIS, KG/Exploring with a magnifying glass. /1991/
  6-A/7 KB897 . . . . **507.8**
Mahabharata.
 SHEPARD, A/Savitri: a tale of ancient India. /1992/
  3-4/4 KA766 . . . . **294.5**
Mahy, Margaret.
 MAHY, M/My mysterious world. /1995/
  2-4/6 KE454 . . . . **B MAHY, M.**
Maid Marian (Legendary character)--Fiction.
 TOMLINSON, T/Forestwife. /1995/6-A/5 KH797 . . . . **Fic**
Maine.
 ENGFER, L/Maine. /1991/4-6/7 KE927 . . . . **974.1**
 FRADIN, DB/Maine. /1994/4-6/4 KE928 . . . . **974.1**
Maine--Fiction.
 HOPKINSON, D/Birdie's lighthouse. /1997/3-5/3 KH282. . . . . **Fic**
 LEVIN, B/Fire in the wind. /1995/5-A/4 KH396 . . . . **Fic**
 MARTIN, JB/Grandmother Bryant's pocket. /1996/
  1-4/3 KG079 . . . . **E**
 MCCLOSKEY, R/Blueberries for Sal. /c1948/P-2/7 KG087. . . **CE E**
  One morning in Maine. /c1952, 1962/1-3/6 KG090. . . . . . . **E**
  Time of wonder. /c1957, 1962/P-A/6 KG091 . . . . . . **CE E**
Mainstreaming in education.
 EDUCATING PETER (VIDEOCASSETTE). /1993/
  /KA185. . . . . **VCR PROF 371.92**
 TEACHING EXCEPTIONAL CHILDREN. /1968-/
  /KA150. **PER PROF 050**
Makah Indians--Fiction.
 HOBBS, W/Ghost canoe. /1997/5-A/6 KH267 . . . . **Fic**
Malaysia--Folklore.
 DAY, NY/Kancil and the crocodiles: a tale from Malaysia. /1996/
  2-3/2 KB556 . . . . **398.24**
Malcolm X.
 CWIKLIK, R/Malcolm X and black pride. /1991/
  5-6/6 KE455 . . . . **B MALCOLM X**
 MYERS, WD/Malcolm X: by any means necessary: a biography. /
  1993/6-A/8 KE456 . . . . **B MALCOLM X**
Mali--Folklore.
 WISNIEWSKI, D/Sundiata: Lion King of Mali. /1992/
  3-5/4 KB495 . . . . **398.22**
Mali Empire--History.
 MCKISSACK, P/Royal kingdoms of Ghana, Mali, and Songhay: life
  in medieval Africa. /c1994, 1995/A/8 KE734 . . . . **966.2**
Mammals.
 ESBENSEN, BJ/Baby whales drink milk. /1994/
  1-3/2 KC768 . . . . **599.5**
 HILLER, I/Introducing mammals to young naturalists: from Texas
  Parks & Wildlife Magazine. /1990/4-7/7 KC721 . . . . **599**
 KNIGHT, L/Sierra Club book of great mammals. /1992/
  5-6/7 KC722 . . . . **599**
 MAMMAL (VIDEOCASSETTE). /1996/5-6/KC723 . . . . **VCR 599**
 MAYNARD, T/Saving endangered mammals: a field guide to some
  of the earth's rarest animals. /1992/5-6/8 KC489 . . . . . . **591.68**
 PARKER, S/Mammal. /1989/4-6/7 KC725 . . . . **599**
 PARSONS, A/Amazing mammals. /1990/2-6/6 KC726 . . . . . **599**
 PATENT, DH/Why mammals have fur. /1995/4-6/6 KC727 . . **599**
 SIERRA CLUB BOOK OF SMALL MAMMALS. /1993/
  5-6/6 KC729 . . . . **599**

Mammals--Identification.
 ALDEN, P/Peterson first guide to mammals of North America. /
  1987/4-6/6 KC720 . . . . **599**
Mammals--North America.
 WHITAKER, JO/Audubon Society field guide to North American
  mammals. Rev. & expanded. /1996/3-6/KC730. . . . . . **599.097**
Mammals--Software.
 MAMMALS: A MULTIMEDIA ENCYCLOPEDIA (CD-ROM). /1990/
  2-A/KA450 . . . . **CDR REF 599**
Mammoths.
 ALIKI /Wild and woolly mammoths. Rev. ed. /1996/
  1-3/4 KC268 . . . . **569**
Mammoths--Fiction.
 MARTIN, R/Will's mammoth. /1989/1-3/2 KG080 . . . . . . **CE E**
Man--Influence of environment.
 MACQUITTY, M/Desert. /1994/4-6/7 KC364 . . . . **578.754**
Man--Influence of environment--Africa.
 CHIASSON, J/African journey. /1987/A/11 KE725 . . . . **960**
Man--Influence on nature.
 BAKER, J/Story of rosy dock. /1995/K-4/6 KF115 . . . . **994**
 BANG, M/Chattanooga sludge. /1996/4-6/7 KD081 . . . . . **628.4**
 BLASHFIELD, JF/Rescuing endangered species. /1994/
  4-6/7 KA961 . . . . **333.95**
 CHERRY, L/River ran wild: an environmental history. /1992/
  4-6/6 KE937 . . . . **974.4**
 DEFELICE, CC/Lostman's River. /1994/4-A/6 KH067 . . . . . . **Fic**
 ENDANGERED ANIMALS: SURVIVORS ON THE BRINK
  (VIDEOCASSETTE). /1997/4-6/KC486 . . . . **VCR 591.68**
 FACKLAM, M/And then there was one: the mysteries of extinction.
  /1990/5-6/7 KC488 . . . . **591.68**
 FLEMING, D/Where once there was a wood. /1996/
  1-4/3 KD253 . . . . **639.9**
 GEORGE, JC/Everglades. /1995/2-5/7 KE991 . . . . **975.9**
 GOLDSTEIN, N/Rebuilding prairies and forests. /1994/
  4-6/7 KA955 . . . . **333.74**
 HOFF, MK/Our endangered planet: atmosphere. /1995/
  4-6/8 KB061 . . . . **363.73**
  Our endangered planet: life on land. /1992/
  5-6/8 KA962 . . . . **333.95**
 JOHNSON, RL/Investigating the ozone hole. /1993/
  A/10 KC191 . . . . **551.5**
 KOCH, M/World water watch. /1993/K-2/4 KD255 . . . . . . **639.9**
 LOURIE, P/Everglades: Buffalo Tiger and the river of grass. /c1994,
  1998/4-6/6 KE992 . . . . **975.9**
 MCVEY, V/Sierra Club kid's guide to planet care and repair. /
  1993/4-6/7 KB048 . . . . **363.7**
 MINDS-ON SCIENCE: FOR PROFIT, FOR PLANET (VIDEODISC). /
  1995/5-A/KD348 . . . . **VD 687**
 MINDS-ON SCIENCE: FOR THE SAKE OF THE NATION
  (VIDEODISC). /1995/5-A/KA804 . . . . **VD 303.48**
 RAINFOREST (VIDEOCASSETTE). /1993/
  5-A/KC324 . . . . **VCR 577.34**
 SALAMANDERS (VIDEOCASSETTE). /1985/
  5-6/KC609. . . . . **VCR 597.8**
 STAUB, FJ/America's prairies. /1994/4-6/7 KC332. . . . . . . **577.4**
 TALKING ABOUT SEA TURTLES (VIDEOCASSETTE). /1992/
  4-6/KC623. . . . . **VCR 597.92**
 TALL GRASS PRAIRIE: AN AMERICAN STORY (VIDEOCASSETTE).
  /1997/3-A/KC333 . . . . **VCR 577.4**
 VOYAGE OF THE LOGGERHEAD (VIDEOCASSETTE). /1995/
  3-6/KC624. . . . . **VCR 597.92**
 WILLIS, T/Healing the land. /1994/4-6/7 KA954 . . . . **333.73**
 YOUNT, L/Our endangered planet: air. /1995/
  4-6/8 KB069 . . . . **363.73**
Man--Influence on nature--Fiction.
 TURNER, A/Heron Street. /1989/1-3/3 KG626 . . . . **E**
 WOOD, D/Old Turtle. /1992/3-5/3 KH879 . . . . **CE Fic**
Man O'War (Racehorse).
 FARLEY, W/Man O'War. /c1962/5-6/6 KH106 . . . . **Fic**
Man--Origin and antiquity SEE ALSO Evolution; Man, Prehistoric.
Manatees.
 DARLING, K/Manatee: on location. /1991/5-6/7 KC779 . . **599.55**
 JACOBS, F/Sam the sea cow. /1991/1-3/2 KC780 . . . . . **599.55**
 LEPTHIEN, EU/Manatees. /1991/5-6/7 KC781 . . . . **599.55**
 MANATEES: RED ALERT (VIDEOCASSETTE). /1996/
  5-6/KC782. . . . . **VCR 599.55**
 SAVING THE MANATEE (VIDEOCASSETTE). /1993/
  2-6/KC783. . . . . **VCR 599.55**
Mandela, Nelson.
 COOPER, F/Mandela: from the life of the South African statesman.
  /1996/3-6/7 KE457 . . . . **B MANDELA, N.**
Mandingo (African people)--Folklore.
 WISNIEWSKI, D/Sundiata: Lion King of Mali. /1992/
  3-5/4 KB495 . . . . **398.22**

Manitoba (Canada).
EMMOND, K/Manitoba. /1992/5-A/8 KE816 . . . . **971.27**
Mankiller, Wilma Pearl.
LOWERY, L/Wilma Mankiller. /1996/
2-3/4 KE458 . . . . **B MANKILLER, W.**
Manned space flight SEE ALSO Astronauts; Outer space--Exploration;
Space flight; also names of projects e.g. Apollo project.
Manned space flight.
BERLINER, D/Living in space. /1993/5-6/9 KD139 . . . . . **629.47**
Manners and customs.
ALIKI /Hello! Good-bye! /1996/P-1/2 KB244 . . . . **395.4**
BADT, KL/Greetings! /1994/3-5/6 KB245 . . . . **395.4**
BERNHARD, E/Ride on mother's back: a day of baby carrying
around the world. /1996/1-2/7 KB170 . . . . **392.1**
COOK, DF/Kids' multicultural cookbook: food and fun around the
world. /1995/3-5/KD285 . . . . **641.59**
SITA, L/Worlds of belief: religion and spirituality. /1995/
4-A/10 KA728 . . . . **291**
Manners and customs--Fiction.
FRIEDMAN, IR/How my parents learned to eat. /1984/
1-3/2 KF586 . . . . **E**
GRAY, N/Country far away. /1988/K-3/1 KF638 . . . . **E**
Manufactures SEE ALSO Industry; specific types of manufacturing e.g.
Bicycles and bicycling--Design and construction.
Manufactures.
CDS, SUPER GLUE, AND SALSA: HOW EVERYDAY PRODUCTS
ARE MADE. /1995/5-A/KA452 . . . . **REF 670**
COREY, M/Spaghetti factory. /1990/3-4/7 KD319 . . . . **664**
JONES, G/My first book of how things are made: crayons, jeans,
peanut butter, guitars, and more. /1995/K-5/7 KD328 . . . . . **670**
MINDS-ON SCIENCE: FOR PROFIT, FOR PLANET (VIDEODISC). /
1995/5-A/KD348 . . . . **VD 687**
PAINT (VIDEOCASSETTE). /1984/5-6/KD325 . . . . . . **VCR 667**
PAPER (VIDEOCASSETTE). /1986/5-6/KD334 . . . . . . **VCR 676**
SOAP (VIDEOCASSETTE). /1984/5-6/KD326 . . . . . . **VCR 668**
WOOD (VIDEOCASSETTE). /1985/5-6/KD330 . . . . . . **VCR 674**
Manufacturing processes--Environmental aspects.
MINDS-ON SCIENCE: FOR PROFIT, FOR PLANET (VIDEODISC). /
1995/5-A/KD348 . . . . **VD 687**
Manuscripts--History.
COOPER, I/Dead Sea Scrolls. /1997/6-A/8 KA768 . . . . . **296.1**
Manx cat.
BARE, CS/Toby the tabby kitten. /1995/K-3/2 KD229 . . . . **636.8**
Maori (New Zealand people)--Fiction.
LATTIMORE, DN/Punga, the goddess of ugly. /1993/
3-5/4 KF950 . . . . **E**
Maori (New Zealand people)--Folklore.
BISHOP, G/Maui and the Sun: a Maori tale. /1996/
3-4/3 KB700 . . . . **398.26**
Map drawing.
CHAPMAN, G/Maps and mazes: a first guide to mapmaking. /
1993/K-6/6 KC064 . . . . **526**
Map drawing--Software.
NEIGHBORHOOD MAPMACHINE (MICROCOMPUTER
PROGRAM). /1997/1-5/KC066. . . . . **MCP 526**
Maple.
THORNHILL, J/Tree in a forest. /1992/3-5/6 KC311 . . . . . . **577.3**
Maple--Canada.
CANADA'S MAPLE TREE: THE STORY OF THE COUNTRY'S
EMBLEM (VIDEOCASSETTE). /1995/1-4/KE615 . . . . **VCR 929.9**
Maple sugar.
LASKY, K/Sugaring time. /1983/4-6/9 KD155 . . . . . . **CE 633.6**
WITTSTOCK, LW/Ininatig's gift of sugar: traditional native
sugarmaking. /c1993/3-6/3 KE786 . . . . **970.476**
Maple syrup.
BURNS, DL/Sugaring season: making maple syrup. /1990/
5-6/7 KD154 . . . . **633.6**
LASKY, K/Sugaring time. /1983/4-6/9 KD155 . . . . . . **CE 633.6**
WITTSTOCK, LW/Ininatig's gift of sugar: traditional native
sugarmaking. /c1993/3-6/3 KE786 . . . . **970.476**
Maple syrup--Fiction.
HAAS, J/Sugaring. /1996/K-2/2 KF657 . . . . **E**
Maps SEE ALSO Atlases; Globes; and names of countries with the
subdivision Maps e.g. United States--Maps.
Maps.
BERGER, M/Whole world in your hands: looking at maps. /1993/
1-3/2 KE166 . . . . **912**
FINDING YOUR WAY: USING MAPS AND GLOBES
(VIDEOCASSETTE). /1990/3-6/KE168 . . . . **VCR 912**
KNOWLTON, J/Maps and globes. /1985/2-5/7 KE169 . . . . **912**
LA PIERRE, Y/Mapping a changing world. /1996/
A/12 KC065 . . . . **526**
SWEENEY, J/Me on the map. /1996/K-1/1 KE172 . . . . **912**

WEISS, H/Maps: getting from here to there. /1991/
3-6/6 KE173 . . . . **912**
Maps--Fiction.
FANELLI, S/My map book. /1995/K-2/KF543 . . . . **E**
Maps--Software.
EUROPE INSPIRER (CD-ROM). /1997/4-A/KE177 . . . . **CDR 914**
INTERNATIONAL INSPIRER (MICROCOMPUTER PROGRAM). /
1990/5-A/KE149 . . . . **MCP 910**
MICROSOFT ENCARTA 97 WORLD ATLAS (CD-ROM). /1996/
3-A/KA472 . . . . **CDR REF 912**
MY FIRST AMAZING WORLD EXPLORER (CD-ROM). /1996/
1-3/KE170. . . . . **CDR 912**
NEIGHBORHOOD MAPMACHINE (MICROCOMPUTER
PROGRAM). /1997/1-5/KC066 . . . . **MCP 526**
TRUDY'S TIME AND PLACE HOUSE. SCHOOL VERSION (CD-
ROM). /1995/P-3/KC075. . . . . **CDR 529**
Marches.
PATRIOTIC SONGS AND MARCHES (SOUND RECORDING
CASSETTE). /1991/K-6/KD582 . . . . **SRC 789.2**
Marco Polo SEE Polo, Marco.
Marine animals SEE ALSO Corals; Fishes, etc.
Marine animals.
ALIKI /My visit to the aquarium. /1993/2-4/5 KC582 . . . . . **597**
COLE, J/Magic School Bus on the ocean floor. /1992/
2-4/5 KC495 . . . . **591.77**
HOLLING, HC/Pagoo. /1957/5-6/4 KC519. . . . . **595.3**
HULME, JN/Sea squares. /1991/K-3/3 KB960 . . . . **513.2**
MACDONALD, S/Sea shapes. /1994/P-2/KB993 . . . . **516**
SWANSON, D/Safari beneath the sea: the wonder world of the
North Pacific coast. /1994/4-6/7 KC370 . . . . **578.77**
WORLDS BELOW (VIDEOCASSETTE). /1988/
4-6/KC371. . . . . **VCR 578.77**
WU, N/Beneath the waves: exploring the hidden world of the kelp
forest. /1992/3-6/7 KC353. **577.7**
Marine animals--Fiction.
CARLE, E/House for Hermit Crab. /1987/P-2/2 KF344 . . . . **E**
Marine animals--Poetry.
ASKA, W/Aska's sea creatures. /1994/3-5/KD914 . . . . **811**
FLORIAN, D/In the swim: poems and paintings. /1997/
1-3/KD937. . . . . **811**
YOLEN, J/Sea watch: a book of poetry. /1996/4-6/KE049 . . **811**
Marine animals--Software.
SCHOLASTIC'S THE MAGIC SCHOOL BUS EXPLORES THE
OCEAN. TEACHER ED. (CD-ROM). /1995/
2-A/KC369 . . . . **CDR 578.77**
Marine biology SEE ALSO Seashore biology.
Marine biology.
CARSON, R/Edge of the sea. /c1955/A/10 KC367 . . . . . **578.77**
MACQUITTY, M/Ocean. /1995/2-6/7 KC174 . . . . **551.46**
WATERS, JF/Deep-sea vents: living worlds without sun. /1994/
4-6/7 KC299 . . . . **551.46**
WU, N/Fish faces. /c1993, 1997/1-6/3 KC588 . . . . **597**
Marine biology--Northwest, Pacific.
SWANSON, D/Safari beneath the sea: the wonder world of the
North Pacific coast. /1994/4-6/7 KC370 . . . . **578.77**
Marine biology--Software.
FIELD TRIP INTO THE SEA (MICROCOMPUTER PROGRAM). /
1992/3-A/KC368 . . . . **MCP 578.77**
Marine ecology.
GREAT OCEAN RESCUE (VIDEODISC). /1992/
3-A/KC350 . . . . **VD 577.7**
VOYAGE OF THE LOGGERHEAD (VIDEOCASSETTE). /1995/
3-6/KC624. . . . . **VCR 597.92**
WHAT ARE ECOSYSTEMS? (VIDEOCASSETTE). /1975/
4-6/KC299 . . . . **VCR 577**
Marine ecology--Fiction.
ORR, K/My grandpa and the sea. /1990/K-2/2 KG198 . . . . . . **E**
Marine ecology--Software.
FIELD TRIP INTO THE SEA (MICROCOMPUTER PROGRAM). /
1992/3-A/KC368 . . . . **MCP 578.77**
GREAT OCEAN RESCUE (CD-ROM). /1996/
3-A/KC349 . . . . **CDR 577.7**
Marine painting.
ROALF, P/Seascapes. /1992/5-A/7 KD482. . . . . **758**
Marine plants SEE ALSO Algae.
Marine plants.
SWANSON, D/Safari beneath the sea: the wonder world of the
North Pacific coast. /1994/4-6/7 KC370 . . . . **578.77**
WORLDS BELOW (VIDEOCASSETTE). /1988/
4-6/KC371. . . . . **VCR 578.77**
Marine resources.
GANERI, A/Oceans atlas. /1994/4-A/6 KC173 . . . . **551.46**

Marionettes SEE Puppets.
Markets.
   LEWIN, T/Market! /1996/1-3/6 KB128 . . . . **381**
Markets--Fiction.
   WILLIAMS, KL/Tap-tap. /1994/K-2/2 KG728 . . . . **CE E**
Markets--Trinidad and Tobago--Fiction.
   JOSEPH, L/Jasmine's parlour day. /1994/1-3/3 KF856 . . . . **E**
Marmots.
   LEPTHIEN, EU/Woodchucks. /1992/3-4/4 KC752 . . . . . . **599.36**
Marriage--Fiction.
   BUEHNER, C/Fanny's dream. /1996/1-3/4 KF295 . . . . **E**
   SMALL, D/Hoover's bride. /1995/1-3/5 KG521. . . . . **E**
Marriage--Folklore.
   COWLEY, J/Mouse bride. /1995/P-2/2 KB552 . . . . . . **398.24**
Marriage, Mixed--Fiction.
   ADOFF, A/Black is brown is tan. /1973/P-3/3 KF136 . . . . **E**
Mars (Planet).
   SIMON, S/Mars. /1987/4-A/8 KC035 . . . . **523.43**
   VOGT, G/Viking and the Mars landing. /1991/
   A/10 KD132 . . . . **629.43**
Marsalis, Wynton.
   ELLIS, VF/Wynton Marsalis. /1997/
   5-A/10 KE459 . . . . **B MARSALIS, W.**
Marshes.
   MARSH: NATURE'S NURSERY (VIDEOCASSETTE). /1988/
   2-4/KC343. . . . . **VCR 577.68**
   WHAT ARE ECOSYSTEMS? (VIDEOCASSETTE). /1975/
   4-6/KC299. . . . . **VCR 577**
Martha, Saint--Legends.
   ROTH, SL/Brave Martha and the dragon. /1996/
   2-4/4 KB476 . . . . **398.22**
Martha's Vineyard (Mass.)--Biography.
   MCMAHON, P/Summer tunes: a Martha's Vineyard vacation. /
   1996/2-5/7 KB005 . . . . **362.4**
Martial arts--Fiction.
   PINKNEY, JB/JoJo's flying side kick. /1995/K-3/2 KG243 . . . . . **E**
Martin, Bill, Jr.
   VISIT WITH BILL MARTIN, JR. (VIDEOCASSETTE). /1996/
   3-4/KE460. **VCR B MARTIN, B.**
Martin, Joseph Plumb.
   MURPHY, J/Young patriot: the American Revolution as experienced
   by one boy. /1996/5-A/9 KE884. . . . . **973.3**
Martinez, Maria Montoya.
   KREISCHER, EK/Maria Montoya Martinez: master potter. /1995/
   5-6/3 KE461 . . . . **B MARTINEZ, M.**
Martinique--Folklore.
   SAN SOUCI, RD/Faithful friend. /1995/4-6/5 KB411 . . . . **398.21**
Mary, Blessed Virgin, Saint.
   DE PAOLA, T/Mary: the mother of Jesus. /1995/
   3-6/5 KA699 . . . . **232.91**
Maryland.
   FRADIN, DB/Maryland. /1994/4-6/3 KE969 . . . . **975.2**
   MIDDLE ATLANTIC REGION: NEW YORK, NEW JERSEY,
   DELAWARE, MARYLAND, PENNSYLVANIA, /1996/
   4-6/KE924. . . . . **VCR 974**
Masai (African people)--Fiction.
   KROLL, VL/Masai and I. /1992/K-2/4 KF934 . . . . **E**
Masai (African people)--Folklore.
   AARDEMA, V/Lonely lioness and the ostrich chicks: a Masai tale. /
   1996/K-2/3 KB516 . . . . **398.24**
   Who's in Rabbit's house? (Videocassette). /1995/
   K-3/KB518. . . . . **VCR 398.24**
   MOLLEL, TM/Orphan boy: a Maasai story. /1990/
   4-5/4 KB406 . . . . **398.21**
   Rhinos for lunch and elephants for supper!: a Masai tale. /1991/
   P-3/4 KB625 . . . . **398.24**
Masks--Fiction.
   FLOURNOY, V/Celie and the harvest fiddler. /1995/
   2-4/6 KH130 . . . . **Fic**
Mass media SEE ALSO Motion pictures; Newspapers; Radio; Television.
Mass media.
   COMMUNICATIONS (VIDEOCASSETTE). /1992/
   2-4/KA799. . . . . **VCR 302.23**
   READING THE NEWSPAPER INTELLIGENTLY (VIDEOCASSETTE). /
   1995/5-6/KA801 . . . . **VCR 302.23**
Mass media--Influence.
   SEXUALITY (VIDEOCASSETTE). /1995/6/KC956 . . . . **VCR 612.6**
   SUBSTANCE ABUSE (VIDEOCASSETTE). /1995/
   4-6/KD001. . . . . **VCR 613.8**
Mass media--Influence--Software.
   VIOLENCE IN THE MEDIA (MICROCOMPUTER PROGRAM). /
   1994/5-A/KA802 . . . . **MCP 302.23**

Mass media--Moral and ethical aspects--Software.
   VIOLENCE IN THE MEDIA (MICROCOMPUTER PROGRAM). /
   1994/5-A/KA802 . . . . **MCP 302.23**
Massachusetts--Fiction.
   YOLEN, J/Letting Swift River go. /1992/1-3/5 KG777 . . . . . . **E**
Massachusetts--History.
   AVAKIAN, M/Historical album of Massachusetts. /1994/
   5-6/7 KE936 . . . . **974.4**
   DAUGHERTY, J/Landing of the Pilgrims. /c1950/
   4-6/7 KE938 . . . . **974.4**
Massachusetts--History--Colonial period, ca. 1600-1775--Fiction.
   JACOBS, PS/James Printer: a novel of rebellion. /1997/
   5-A/6 KH319 . . . . **Fic**
Massachusetts--History--New Plymouth, 1620-1691.
   ANDERSON, J/First Thanksgiving feast. /1984/
   2-4/4 KE935 . . . . **974.4**
   BOWEN, G/Stranded at Plimoth Plantation, 1626. /1994/
   5-6/7 KE870 . . . . **973.2**
   GEORGE, JC/First Thanksgiving. /1993/4-6/6 KB223 . . . **394.264**
   HAYWARD, L/First Thanksgiving. /1990/
   1-4/2 KB227 . . . . **CE 394.264**
   MOURT'S RELATION /Homes in the wilderness: a pilgrim's journal
   of Plymouth Plantation in 1620. /c1939, 1988/
   5-A/8 KE941 . . . . **974.4**
   PENNER, LR/Pilgrims at Plymouth. /1996/1-3/2 KE943 . . . . **974.4**
   PILGRIM VOICES: OUR FIRST YEAR IN THE NEW WORLD. /
   1995/3-6/7 KE944 . . . . **974.4**
   SAN SOUCI, RD/N.C. Wyeth's pilgrims. /1991/
   4-6/7 KE946 . . . . **974.4**
Massachusetts--History--New Plymouth, 1620-1691--Fiction.
   VAN LEEUWEN, J/Across the wide dark sea: the Mayflower
   journey. /1995/2-4/4 KG645 . . . . **E**
Massachusetts--Social life and customs.
   OLD STURBRIDGE VILLAGE (VIDEOCASSETTE). /1989/
   4-6/KE942. . . . . **VCR 974.4**
**Massachusetts--Social life and customs--Colonial period, ca. 1600-
1775.**
   SEWALL, M/Pilgrims of Plimoth. /1986/4-6/7 KE947 . . **CE 974.4**
   WATERS, K/Samuel Eaton's day: a day in the life of a Pilgrim boy.
   /1993/3-5/6 KE948 . . . . **974.4**
   Sarah Morton's day: a day in the life of a Pilgrim girl. /1989/
   3-5/3 KE949 . . . . **974.4**
Massachusetts--Social life and customs--To 1775.
   BOWEN, G/Stranded at Plimoth Plantation, 1626. /1994/
   5-6/7 KE870 . . . . **973.2**
   WATERS, K/Tapenum's day: a Wampanoag Indian boy in pilgrim
   times. /1996/3-5/2 KE950 . . . . **974.4**
Massachusetts Audubon Society--Fiction.
   LASKY, K/She's wearing a dead bird on her head! /1995/
   3-5/5 KH386 . . . . **Fic**
Math anxiety--Fiction.
   SCIESZKA, J/Math curse. /1995/2-5/3 KG420 . . . . **E**
Mathematical recreations.
   ADLER, DA/Calculator riddles. /1995/3-6/KD722 . . . . . **793.735**
   Easy math puzzles. /1997/K-3/KD723 . . . . **793.735**
   ANNO, M/Anno's magic seeds. /1995/P-4/3 KB987 . . . . . **513.4**
   BLUM, R/Mathemagic. /1997/5-A/KD711. . . . . **793.7**
   CHALLONER, J/Science book of numbers. /1992/
   K-3/2 KB956 . . . . **513.2**
   MARKLE, S/Math mini-mysteries. /1993/3-6/7 KB928 . . . . **510**
   PALLAS, N/Calculator puzzles, tricks and games. /c1976, 1991/
   4-6/9 KB930 . . . . **510**
   SACHAR, L/Sideways arithmetic from Wayside School. /1989/
   3-6/6 KD712 . . . . **793.7**
   SMOOTHEY, M/Calculators. /1995/4-8/9 KB932 . . . . **510**
   WYLER, R/Math fun with a pocket calculator. /1992/
   4-A/4 KD713 . . . . **793.7**
   Math fun with tricky lines and shapes. /1992/
   4-A/5 KD714 . . . . **793.7**
   Test your luck. /1992/5-6/4 KB998 . . . . **519.2**
Mathematical recreations--Software.
   JAMES DISCOVERS MATH. SCHOOL ED. (CD-ROM). /1995/
   1-3/KB962. . . . . **CDR 513.2**
   MILLIE'S MATH HOUSE (CD-ROM). /1995/
   P-2/KB971. . . . . **CDR 513.2**
   MILLIE'S MATH HOUSE (MICROCOMPUTER PROGRAM). /1992/
   P-2/KB972. . . . . **MCP 513.2**
   PUZZLE TANKS: A GAME OF NUMBERS AND LOGIC
   (MICROCOMPUTER PROGRAM). /1984/3-A/KB940. . **MCP 511**
Mathematics SEE ALSO Arithmetic; Binary system; Factorials; Geometry;
  Logic, Symbolic and mathematical; Measurements; Numbers, Theory of.
Mathematics.
   ANNO, M/Anno's mysterious multiplying jar. /1983/
   P-A/2 KB944 . . . . **512**

BURNS, M/Math for smarty pants. /1982/4-6/5 KB946 .... **513**
CHALLENGE OF THE UNKNOWN (VIDEOCASSETTE). /1986/
5-A/KB935. **VCR 511**
CLEMENT, R/Counting on Frank. /1991/1-6/5 KB927...... **510**
MARKLE, S/Math mini-mysteries. /1993/3-6/7 KB928...... **510**
MR. MARFIL'S LAST WILL AND TESTAMENT (VIDEOCASSETTE).
/1991/5-A/KB973. **VCR 513.2**
PALMER, H/Math readiness--vocabulary and concepts (Sound
recording cassette). /n.d./1-3/KB931. **SRC 510**
PHANTOM OF THE BELL TOWER (VIDEOCASSETTE). /1991/
5-A/KB978. **VCR 513.2**
PROBLEM SOLVING: USING DIAGRAMS AND MODELS
(VIDEOCASSETTE). /1985/5-6/KB943 .... **VCR 511.3**
VANCLEAVE, JP/Janice VanCleave's math for every kid: easy
activities that make learning math fun. /1991/4-6/6 KB933 .. **510**
VIEW FROM THE REAR TERRACE (VIDEOCASSETTE). /1991/
A/KB984. .... **VCR 513.2**
ZEMAN, A/Everything you need to know about math homework. /
1994/4-10/7 KB934 .... **510**

Mathematics--Fiction.
BAUER, J/Sticks. /1996/6-A/4 KG880. .... **Fic**
SCIESZKA, J/Math curse. /1995/2-5/3 KG420 .... **E**
STURGES, P/Ten flashing fireflies. /1995/K-2/2 KG581....... **E**

Mathematics--Folklore.
DEMI /One grain of rice: a mathematical folktale. /1997/
3-6/6 KB731 . **398.27**

Mathematics--Graphic methods--Software.
GRAPH ACTION (MICROCOMPUTER PROGRAM). /1996/
4-A/KB936. **MCP 511**
GRAPH ACTION PLUS (CD-ROM). /1996/4-A/KB937 . **CDR 511**
STEARNS, PH/Graph Club with Fizz and Martina (Microcomputer
program). /1993/K-4/KB942. **MCP 511**

Mathematics--Periodicals.
CONNECT: HANDS-ON SCIENCE AND MATH GUIDE FOR K-8
EDUCATORS. /1988-//KA103. **PER PROF 050**
YES MAG: CANADA'S SCIENCE MAGAZINE FOR KIDS. /1996-/
4-6/KA552. **050**

Mathematics--Poetry.
MARVELOUS MATH: A BOOK OF POEMS. /1997/
1-4/KE071. **811.008**

Mathematics--Software.
CARNIVAL COUNTDOWN. SCHOOL VERSION (CD-ROM). /
1996/K-2/KB926. **CDR 510**
JAMES DISCOVERS MATH. SCHOOL ED. (CD-ROM). /1995/
1-3/KB962. **CDR 513.2**
LOGICAL JOURNEY OF THE ZOOMBINIS. SCHOOL ED. (CD-
ROM). /1996/2-5/KB938. **CDR 511**
NUMBER HEROES. SCHOOL VERSION (CD-ROM). /1996/
3-6/KB929. **CDR 510**

Mathematics--Study and teaching.
ARTZT, AF/How to use cooperative learning in the mathematics
class. /1990//KA250. **PROF 372.7**
CONNECT: HANDS-ON SCIENCE AND MATH GUIDE FOR K-8
EDUCATORS. /1988-//KA103. **PER PROF 050**
CURRICULUM AND EVALUATION STANDARDS FOR SCHOOL
MATHEMATICS. /1989//KA252. **PROF 372.7**
ERICKSON, T/Get it together: math problems for groups, grades
4-12. /1989//KA290. **PROF 510**

Mathematics--Study and teaching--Audio-visual aids--Catalogs.
PERRY, PJ/Guide to math materials: resources to support the NCTM
standards. /1997//KA256 .... **PROF 372.7**

Mathematics--Study and teaching--Periodicals.
SCHOOL SCIENCE AND MATHEMATICS. /1901-/
/KA143. **PER PROF 050**

Mathematics--Study and teaching--Standards.
PROFESSIONAL STANDARDS FOR TEACHING MATHEMATICS. /
1991//KA257. **PROF 372.7**

Mathematics--Study and teaching (Early childhood).
KOHL, MA/MathArts: exploring math through art for 3 to 6 year
olds. /1996//KA253. **PROF 372.7**

Mathematics--Study and teaching (Elementary).
BURGUNDER, A/Zoolutions: a mathematical expedition with topics
for grades 4 through 8. /c1993, 1996//KA251.... **PROF 372.7**
NEW DIRECTIONS FOR ELEMENTARY SCHOOL MATHEMATICS,
1989 YEARBOOK. /1989//KA255. **PROF 372.7**
PERRY, PJ/Guide to math materials: resources to support the NCTM
standards. /1997//KA256. **PROF 372.7**
WHITIN, DJ/It's the story that counts: more children's books for
mathematical learning, K-6. /1995//KA258. **PROF 372.7**
ZASLAVSKY, C/Multicultural math classroom: bringing in the world.
/1996//KA259. **PROF 372.7**

Mathematics--Study and teaching (Primary).
MATH FOR THE VERY YOUNG: A HANDBOOK OF ACTIVITIES
FOR PARENTS AND TEACHERS. /1995//KA254 .. **PROF 372.7**

Mathematics--Wit and humor.
TAKE ME TO YOUR LITER: SCIENCE AND MATH JOKES. /1991/
3-6/KD740. **793.735**

Matsuo, Basho.
SPIVAK, D/Grass sandals: the travels of Basho. /1997/
1-4/5 KE136. **895.6**

Matter.
COOPER, C/Matter. /1992/4-A/9 KC078 . **530**
SOLIDS, LIQUIDS AND GASES (VIDEOCASSETTE). /1994/
4-6/KC084. **VCR 530.4**

Matter--Properties.
SOLID, LIQUID, GAS (VIDEOCASSETTE). /1986/
3-6/KC083. **VCR 530.4**

Matterhorn--Fiction.
ULLMAN, JR/Banner in the sky (Talking book). /n.d./
4-6/KH817. **TB Fic**

Maturity--Fiction.
KRUMGOLD, J/And now Miguel. /1953/6-A/5 KH382 ... **CE Fic**

Mauritania--Social life and customs.
GOODSMITH, L/Children of Mauritania: days in the desert and by
the river shore. /1993/4-6/6 KE733 ...... **966.1**

Mayas.
BAQUEDANO, E/Aztec, Inca and Maya. /1993/
4-6/9 KE829. **972**
GREENE, JD/Maya. /1992/4-6/7 KE843. **972.81**
LOST CITY OF THE MAYA (VIDEOCASSETTE). /1990/
6-A/KE844. **VCR 972.81**

Mayas--Fiction.
O'DELL, S/Captive. /1979/6-A/6 KH558 . **Fic**
WISNIEWSKI, D/Rain player. /1991/2-3/4 KG751. **CE E**

Mayas--Folklore.
BIERHORST, J/Monkey's haircut and other stories told by the
Maya. /1986/3-4/4 KB531. **398.24**
EHLERT, L/Cuckoo: a Mexican folktale./Cucu: un cuento folklorico
mexicano. /1997/P-2/3 KB561. **398.24**
GERSON, M/People of corn: a Mayan story. /1995/
2-4/3 KB399. **398.21**

Mayas--Social life and customs.
STAUB, FJ/Children of Yucatan. /1996/4-6/7 KE840 ...... **972**
SUEMI'S STORY: MY MODERN MAYAN HOME
(VIDEOCASSETTE). /c1991/5-A/KE841. **VCR 972**

Mayas--Software.
MAYAQUEST TRAIL (CD-ROM). /1996/5-A/KE845 . **CDR 972.81**

Mayflower (Ship)--Fiction.
VAN LEEUWEN, J/Across the wide dark sea: the Mayflower
journey. /1995/2-4/4 KG645. **E**

Mayo, Charles Horace.
CROFFORD, E/Frontier surgeons: a story about the Mayo Brothers.
/1989/5-6/6 KC899. **610.69**

Mayo, William James.
CROFFORD, E/Frontier surgeons: a story about the Mayo Brothers.
/1989/5-6/6 KC899. **610.69**

Mayors SEE ALSO names of specific mayors e.g. Cisneros, Henry.

McCormick, Cyrus.
NOONAN, J/Nineteenth-century inventors. /1992/
5-6/7 KC897. **609**

McCoy, Elijah.
TOWLE, W/Real McCoy: the life of an African-American inventor. /
c1993, 1995/4-6/7 KE462. **B MCCOY, E.**

McCrae, John. In Flanders fields.
GRANFIELD, L/In Flanders Fields: the story of the poem by John
McCrae. /1995/4-6/7 KD947. **811**

Measurement.
DECIDING HOW CLOSE TO MEASURE (VIDEOCASSETTE). /
1982/3-5/KB996. **VCR 519**

Measurement--Fiction.
AXELROD, A/Pigs in the pantry: fun with math and cooking. /
1997/1-3/3 KF178. **E**
HIGHTOWER, S/Twelve snails to one lizard: a tale of mischief and
measurement. /1997/1-3/2 KF726. **E**
LING, B/Fattest, tallest, biggest snowman ever. /1997/
K-2/2 KF987. **E**

Mechanics SEE ALSO Engineering; Force and energy; Inclined planes;
Machinery; Motion; Power (Mechanics); Pulleys; Statics; Steam engines.

Mechanics.
ADKINS, J/Moving heavy things. /1980/A/7 KC088....... **531**
PUSH AND PULL: SIMPLE MACHINES AT WORK
(VIDEOCASSETTE). /1990/4-6/KC097. **VCR 531**
SIMPLE MACHINE (VIDEOCASSETTE). /1993/
5-6/KC098. **VCR 531**
SIMPLE MACHINES: USING MECHANICAL ADVANTAGE
(VIDEOCASSETTE). /1992/5-6/KC099. **VCR 531**

Mechanics--Experiments.
DOHERTY, P/Spinning blackboard and other dynamic experiments on force and motion. /1996/4-A/5 KC094 . . . . **531**

Media SEE Mass media.

Media centers (Education) SEE ALSO Instructional materials centers.

Media programs (Education) SEE ALSO Instructional materials centers.

Media programs (Education).
FARMER, LS/Cooperative learning activities in the library media center. /1991//KA073 . . . . **PROF 027.8**
Creative partnerships: librarians and teachers working together. / 1993//KA074 . . . . **PROF 027.8**
HART, TL/Creative ideas for library media center facilities. /1990/ /KA075 . . . . **PROF 027.8**
LOERTSCHER, DV/Taxonomies of the school library media program. /1988//KA076 . . . . **PROF 027.8**
MORRIS, BJ/Administering the school library media center. 3rd ed. /1992//KA077 . . . . **PROF 027.8**
URBANIK, MK/Curriculum planning and teaching using the library media center. /1989//KA064 . . . . **PROF 025.5**
WILSON, PP/Professional collection for elementary educators. / 1996//KA079 . . . . **PROF 027.8**
ZINGHER, G/At the Pirate Academy: adventures with language in the library media center. /1990//KA081 . . . . **PROF 027.8**

Media programs (Education)--Management--Decision making.
KARPISEK, ME/Policymaking for school library media programs. / 1989//KA050 . . . . **PROF 025.1**

Media programs (Education)--Periodicals.
KNOWLEDGE QUEST. /1997-//KA119 . . . . **PER PROF 050**
SCHOOL LIBRARY MEDIA ACTIVITIES MONTHLY. /1984-/ /KA140 . . . . **PER PROF 050**
SCHOOL LIBRARY MEDIA ANNUAL. /1983-/ /KA141 . . . . **PER PROF 050**

Medical care.
KUKLIN, S/When I see my doctor. /1988/P-K/4 KC901 . . . **610.69**

Medicinal plants.
FORSYTH, A/How monkeys make chocolate: foods and medicines from the rainforest. /1995/4-8/7 KC402 . . . . **581.6**

Medicine--History--Fiction.
DEFELICE, CC/Apprenticeship of Lucas Whitaker. /1998/ 5-A/6 KH066 . . . . **CE Fic**

Medicine shows--Fiction.
AVI /Punch with Judy. /1993/5-A/6 KG863 . . . . **Fic**
CHRISTIAN, MB/Toady and Dr. Miracle. /1997/1-3/2 KF390. . . **E**

Medina, Juan.
BRIMNER, LD/Migrant family. /1992/4-6/6 KA834 . . . . . . **305.5**

Medusa (Greek mythology).
HUTTON, W/Perseus. /1993/5-6/4 KA745. . . . . **292**

Memory--Fiction.
CASELEY, J/Mama, coming and going. /1994/1-3/4 KF366. . . . **E**
FOX, M/Wilfrid Gordon McDonald Partridge. /1985/ K-3/6 KF574 . . . . **E**
HUTCHINS, P/Don't forget the bacon! /c1976, 1987/ P-2/3 KF796 . . . . **CE E**
KROLL, VL/Fireflies, peach pies and lullabies. /1995/ 1-3/5 KF933 . . . . **E**
PARISH, P/Be ready at eight. /1996/1-2/1 KG212. . . . . **E**

Mennonites.
KENNA, K/People apart. /1995/4-6/7 KA720. . . . . **289.7**

Mennonites--Fiction.
BLADES, A/Mary of Mile 18. /1971/1-3/3 KF233 . . . . **CE E**

Menstruation.
GARDNER-LOULAN, J/Period: revised and updated with a parents' guide. /1991/5-6/7 KC947 . . . . **612.6**
MADARAS, L/What's happening to my body? Book for girls. Rev. ed. /1983/5-6/9 KC952 . . . . **612.6**

Mensuration SEE Measurement.

Mental illness.
DINNER, SH/Nothing to be ashamed of: growing up with mental illness in your family. /1989/5-6/9 KD020 . . . . **616.89**

Mentally handicapped SEE ALSO Down's syndrome; Learning disabilities; Problem children; Slow learning children.

Mentally handicapped.
BROWN, T/Someone special, just like you. /1984/ P-2/6 KA623 . . . . **152.4**
CAIRO, S/Our brother has Down's syndrome: an introduction for children. /1985/1-4/6 KB002 . . . . **362.3**
RENFRO, N/Puppetry, language, and the special child: discovering alternate languages. /1984//KA328 . . . . . . **PROF 791.5**

Mentally handicapped--Fiction.
BYARS, BC/Summer of the swans. /c1970/5-6/6 KG964 . . **CE Fic**
RABE, B/Where's Chimpy? /1988/P-2/2 KG296. . . . . **E**
SLEPIAN, J/Alfred Summer. /1980/4-6/4 KH718 . . . . **Fic**
TESTA, M/Thumbs up, Rico! /1994/1-3/2 KG601 . . . . **E**

Mentally ill--Family relationships.
DINNER, SH/Nothing to be ashamed of: growing up with mental illness in your family. /1989/5-6/9 KD020 . . . . **616.89**

Mentally ill--Fiction.
LISLE, JT/Afternoon of the elves. /1989/6-A/6 KH408 . . . . . . **Fic**
MACLACHLAN, P/Mama One, Mama Two. /1982/ 2-3/1 KG054 . . . . **E**

Merchants--West (U.S.)--History--19th century.
HILTON, S/Miners, merchants, and maids. /1995/ 4-6/8 KF033 . . . . **978**

Mercury (Planet).
SIMON, S/Mercury. /1992/3-6/7 KC032 . . . . **523.41**

Meredith, James.
ELISH, D/James Meredith and school desegregation. /1994/ 4-5/7 KE463 . . . . **B MEREDITH, J.**

Merlin (Legendary character).
SAN SOUCI, RD/Young Merlin. /c1990, 1996/ 4-5/6 KB484 . . . . **398.22**

Mermaids.
MERMAID TALES FROM AROUND THE WORLD. /1993/ 3-5/5 KB405 . . . . **398.21**
SAN SOUCI, RD/Sukey and the mermaid. /1992/ 3-4/6 KB775 . . . . **398.27**

Mermen--Folklore.
SAN SOUCI, RD/Nicholas Pipe. /1997/2-5/6 KB413 . . . . **398.21**

Merrimack (Frigate).
CARTER, AR/Battle of the ironclads: the Monitor and the Merrimack. /1993/4-6/8 KE900. . . . . **973.7**

Merry-go-round--Fiction.
CREWS, D/Carousel. /1982/P-K/KF432 . . . . **E**
ROSE, DL/Rose horse. /1995/3-5/6 KH651 . . . . **Fic**

Mesa Verde National Park (Colo.).
ARNOLD, C/Ancient cliff dwellers of Mesa Verde. /1992/ 5-6/8 KE790 . . . . **970.488**
TRIMBLE, S/Village of blue stone. /1990/4-6/6 KF063 . . . . . **979**

Messier, Mark.
SULLIVAN, MJ/Mark Messier: star center. /1997/ 5-A/7 KE464 . . . . **B MESSIER, M.**

Metallurgy SEE ALSO Chemistry.

Metals SEE ALSO Mineralogy.

Metalwork SEE Silversmithing.

Metamorphosis SEE ALSO names of specific animals with this subheading e.g. Butterflies--Metamorphosis.

Metamorphosis.
FACKLAM, M/Creepy, crawly caterpillars. /1996/ 4-6/6 KC559 . . . . **595.78**
HEILIGMAN, D/From caterpillar to butterfly. /1996/ K-2/2 KC561 . . . . **595.78**
TADPOLES AND FROGS (VIDEOCASSETTE). /c1979, 1986/ 3-6/KC610. . . . . **VCR 597.8**
WATTS, B/Butterfly and caterpillar. /1985/2-4/4 KC568 . . **595.78**

Metamorphosis--Fiction.
CARLE, E/Very hungry caterpillar. /1981/P-1/6 KF347 . . . . **E**
KENT, J/Caterpillar and the polliwog. /1982/K-2/4 KF896. . **CE E**

Metaphor--Dictionaries.
PALMATIER, RA/Speaking of animals: a dictionary of animal metaphors. /1995/6-A/KA427. . . . . **REF 423**

Meteorites.
METEORITES (PICTURE). /1991/4-A/KC042 . . . . **PIC 523.5**

Meteorites--Fiction.
CONRAD, P/Call me Ahnighito. /1995/2-5/2 KF413. . . . . **E**

Meteorological stations.
GIBBONS, G/Weather forecasting. /1987/2-4/7 KC224 . . **551.63**

Meteorology SEE ALSO Air; Atmosphere; Climate; Clouds; Hurricanes; Storms; Weather; Winds.

Meteorology.
ATMOSPHERE: ON THE AIR (VIDEOCASSETTE). /1993/ 5-6/KC186. . . . . **VCR 551.5**
BERGER, M/How's the weather?: a look at weather and how it changes. /1993/K-5/2 KC187 . . . . **551.5**
COLE, J/Magic School Bus inside a hurricane. /1995/ 2-4/4 KC197 . . . . **551.55**
LAMPTON, C/Hurricane. /1991/4-6/7 KC202 . . . . **551.55**
LAUBER, P/Hurricanes: Earth's mightiest storms. /1996/ 3-6/6 KC203 . . . . **551.55**
PLUCKROSE, H/Weather. /1994/P-2/4 KC192 . . . . **551.5**
SIMON, S/Weather. /1993/3-6/7 KC193 . . . . **551.5**
SOUZA, DM/Hurricanes. /1996/4-6/7 KC206 . . . . **551.55**
TELLING THE WEATHER (VIDEOCASSETTE). /1996/ 4-6/KC194. . . . . **VCR 551.5**

Meteorology--Bibliography.
PERRY, PJ/World's regions and weather: linking fiction to nonfiction. /1996//KA294 . . . . **PROF 551.6**

Meteorology--Miscellanea.
  LOCKHART, G/Weather companion. /1988//KA293 . **PROF 551.5**
Meteorology--Study and teaching.
  PERRY, PJ/World's regions and weather: linking fiction to nonfiction.
  /1996//KA294. **PROF 551.6**
Meteorology--Terminology.
  GIBBONS, G/Weather words and what they mean. /1990/
  K-4/4 KC218 . . . . 551.6
Meteors.
  SIMON, S/Comets, meteors, and asteroids. /1994/
  4-6/7 KC043 . . . . 523.6
Metropolitan Museum of Art (New York, N.Y.)
  RICHARDSON, J/Inside the museum: a children's guide to the
  Metropolitan Museum of Art. /1993/2-A/7 KD376 708
Metropolitan Opera House, New York (N.Y.)--Fiction.
  FREEMAN, L/Pet of the Met. /c1953/1-2/7 KF582 . . . . E
Mexican Americans.
  ATKIN, SB/Voices from the fields: children of migrant farmworkers
  tell their stories. /1993/A/6 KA833 . . . . 305.5
  BRIMNER, LD/Migrant family. /1992/4-6/6 KA834 . . . . . 305.5
  GARZA, CL/Family pictures: Cuadros de familia. /1990/
  2-5/6 KA866 . . . . 306.85
Mexican Americans--Biography.
  CEDENO, ME/Cesar Chavez: labor leader. /1993/
  4-5/6 KE287 . . . . **B CHAVEZ, C.**
  DE RUIZ, DC/Causa: the migrant farmworkers' story. /1993/
  4-6/6 KA944 . . . . 331.88
  KRAMER, J/Lee Trevino. /1996/5-6/6 KE570 . . . **B TREVINO, L.**
Mexican Americans--California--Fiction.
  SOTO, G/Baseball in April and other stories. /1990/
  6-A/6 KH738 . . . . Fic
  Boys at work. /1995/4-6/5 KH739 . . . . Fic
  Local news. /1993/6-A/6 KH740 . . . . Fic
Mexican Americans--Fiction.
  ANAYA, R/Farolitos of Christmas. /1995/3-6/2 KG845. . . . . Fic
  BUNTING, E/Day's work. /1994/1-3/2 KF298. . . . . E
  DORROS, A/Radio Man: a story in English and Spanish./Don
  Radio: un cuento en Ingles y /1993/2-5/2 KF491 . . . . E
  HAVILL, J/Treasure nap. /1992/P-1/2 KF683 . . . . E
  KRUMGOLD, J/And now Miguel. /1953/6-A/5 KH382 . . . **CE Fic**
  LOPEZ, L/Birthday swap. /1997/K-2/2 KG032. . . . . E
  SOTO, G/Pool party. /c1993, 1995/4-6/5 KH741. . . . . Fic
  Snapshots from the wedding. /1997/K-2/2 KG529. . . . . . . E
  Too many tamales. /1993/K-3/3 KG530 . . . . E
  STANEK, M/I speak English for my mom. /1989/
  2-4/2 KH747 . . . . Fic
Mexican Americans--Poetry.
  SOTO, G/Canto familiar. /1995/4-6/KE028 811
Mexican Americans--Social life and customs.
  COOPER, M/Anthony Reynoso: born to rope. /1996/
  3-4/4 KA841 . . . . 305.8
  HOYT-GOLDSMITH, D/Day of the Dead: a Mexican-American
  celebration. /1994/4-6/7 KB198 . . . . 394.26
Mexican literature--Collections.
  TREE IS OLDER THAN YOU ARE: A BILINGUAL GATHERING OF
  POEMS AND STORIES FROM MEXICO WITH PAINTINGS BY
  MEXICAN ARTISTS. /1995/5-A/KE121. . . . . 860.9
Mexican poetry--Collections.
  TREE IS OLDER THAN YOU ARE: A BILINGUAL GATHERING OF
  POEMS AND STORIES FROM /1995/5-A/KE121. . . . . . 860.9
Mexicans--United States--Fiction.
  BUNTING, E/Going home. /1996/1-3/2 KF302 . . . . E
Mexico.
  IRIZARRY, C/Mexico. Rev. ed. /1994/A/11 KE831 972
  KENT, D/Mexico: rich in spirit and tradition. /1996/
  3-5/7 KE832 972
  MEXICO: A CHANGING LAND. 3RD ED. (VIDEOCASSETTE). /
  1996/6-A/KE836 . . . . **VCR 972**
Mexico--Antiquities.
  ARNOLD, C/City of the gods: Mexico's ancient city of Teotihuacan.
  /1994/5-6/7 KE828 972
Mexico--Civilization.
  WOOD, T/Aztecs. /1992/5-6/7 KE842 972
Mexico--Description and travel.
  KIDS EXPLORE MEXICO (VIDEOCASSETTE). /1990/
  3-6/KE186 . . . . **VCR 917.2**
  KRUPP, RR/Let's go traveling in Mexico. /1996/
  2-4/6 KE187 . . . . 917.2
Mexico--Fiction.
  CZERNECKI, S/Hummingbirds' gift. /1994/1-3/7 KF443 . . . . . . E
  ETS, MH/Gilberto and the wind. /c1963/P-1/2 KF536 . . . . **CE E**
  Nine days to Christmas. /c1959/1-3/2 KF538 . . . . E
  FLORA, J/Fabulous Firework Family. /1994/1-3/4 KF559. . . . . E

  KRULL, K/Maria Molina and the Days of the Dead. /1994/
  2-4/4 KF936 . . . . E
  LEVY, J/Spirit of Tio Fernando: a Day of the Dead story./El espiritu
  de tio Fernando /1995/1-3/5 KH404 . . . . Fic
  MORA, P/Gift of the poinsettia./El regalo de la flor de
  nochebuena. /1995/3-5/4 KH507 . . . . Fic
  WINTER, J/Josefina. /1996/1-3/6 KG743 . . . . E
Mexico--Folklore.
  AARDEMA, V/Borreguita and the coyote: a tale from Ayutla,
  Mexico. /1991/P-2/4 KB514. . . . . 398.24
  ADA, AF/Mediopollito/Half-Chicken. /1995/K-2/2 KB521 . 398.24
  CZERNECKI, S/Pancho's pinata. /1992/2-4/7 KB703 . . . . 398.26
  EHLERT, L/Cuckoo: a Mexican folktale./Cucu: un cuento folklorico
  mexicano. /1997/P-2/3 KB561 . . . . 398.24
  KIMMEL, EA/Witch's face: a Mexican tale. /1993/
  3-5/2 KB402 . . . . 398.21
  MADRIGAL, AH/Eagle and the rainbow: timeless tales from Mexico.
  /1997/4-5/7 KB339 . . . . 398.2
  PARKE, M/Quetzalcoatl tale of corn. /1992/2-3/5 KB630 . 398.24
Mexico--History.
  KRUPP, RR/Let's go traveling in Mexico. /1996/
  2-4/6 KE187 . . . . 917.2
Mexico--History--Conquest, 1519-1540.
  MARRIN, A/Aztecs and Spaniards: Cortes and the conquest of
  Mexico. /1986/5-6/7 KE833 972
  MATHEWS, SS/Sad Night: the story of an Aztec victory and a
  Spanish loss. /1994/4-6/6 KE834. 972
Mexico--History--Conquest, 1519-1540--Fiction.
  O'DELL, S/Captive. /1979/6-A/6 KH558 . . . . Fic
Mexico--History--Revolution, 1910-1920.
  FROST, MP/Mexican Revolution. /1997/5-A/11 KE830 972
Mexico--History--Wars of Independence, 1810-1821.
  MEXICAN WAR OF INDEPENDENCE. /1997/5-A/11 KE835 . 972
Mexico--Poetry.
  JOHNSTON, T/My Mexico--Mexico mio. /1996/K-3/KD958. . 811
Mexico--Relations--United States.
  PASCOE, E/Mexico and the United States: cooperation and conflict.
  /1996/6-A/11 KA805 . . . . 303.48
Mexico--Social life and customs.
  ANCONA, G/Pablo remembers: the Fiesta of the Day of the Dead.
  /1993/3-6/5 KB193 . . . . 394.26
  KIDS EXPLORE MEXICO (VIDEOCASSETTE). /1990/
  3-6/KE186 . . . . **VCR 917.2**
  KRUPP, RR/Let's go traveling in Mexico. /1996/
  2-4/6 KE187 . . . . 917.2
  LASKY, K/Days of the Dead. /1994/5-6/6 KB200 . . . . . 394.26
  SILVERTHORNE, E/Fiesta!: Mexico's greatest celebrations. /1992/
  4-6/7 KB203 . . . . 394.26
Mexico, Gulf of--Fiction.
  STOLZ, M/Go fish. /1991/3-6/6 KH766 . . . . Fic
Mice.
  FISCHER-NAGEL, H/Look through the mouse hole. /1989/
  4-6/6 KC743 . . . . 599.35
Mice--Fiction.
  AVI /Poppy. /1995/3-5/6 KG862. . . . . Fic
  AYLESWORTH, J/Two terrible frights. /1987/P-1/3 KF181. . . . E
  BUNTING, E/Mother's Day mice. /1986/P-2/2 KF305 . . . **CE E**
  CARLE, E/Do you want to be my friend? /1971/P-K/1 KF340. . E
  CLEARY, B/Mouse and the motorcycle. /1965/
  3-5/5 KG997 . . . . **CE Fic**
  Ralph S. Mouse (Videocassette). /1990/3-5/KH000 . . . **VCR Fic**
  CONLY, JL/Racso and the rats of NIMH. /1986/5-6/6 KH020 . Fic
  DICKINSON, P/Time and the clockmice etcetera. /1994/
  3-A/8 KH077 . . . . Fic
  EDWARDS, PD/Livingstone Mouse. /1996/K-2/2 KF512 . . . . . E
  EMBERLEY, M/Ruby. /1990/1-3/3 KF523 . . . . E
  FLEMING, D/Lunch. /1992/P-K/2 KF557 . . . . E
  FORWARD, T/Ben's Christmas carol. /1996/2-3/4 KF567 . . . . E
  FREEMAN, D/Norman the doorman. /c1959/K-1/7 KF580. . **CE E**
  FREEMAN, L/Pet of the Met. /c1953/1-2/7 KF582 . . . . E
  HOFFMAN, M/Four-legged ghosts. /1995/2-4/6 KH269 . . . . Fic
  HOFF, S/Mrs. Brice's mice. /1988/K-2/2 KF759 . . . . E
  HOLABIRD, K/Angelina and the princess. /1984/P-2/5 KF764. . . E
  Angelina Ballerina and other stories (Talking book). /1986/
  P-2/KF765 . . . . **TB E**
  JACQUES, B/Redwall. /1986/5-A/6 KH320 . . . . Fic
  KELLOGG, S/Island of the skog. /c1973/K-3/5 KF890 . . . **CE E**
  KING-SMITH, D/Mouse called Wolf. /1997/3-5/3 KH351 . . . . Fic
  School mouse. /1995/3-5/7 KH353. . . . . Fic
  Three terrible trins. /1994/3-5/6 KH358 . . . . **CE Fic**
  KRAUS, R/Whose mouse are you? /c1970/P-1/1 KF919 . . **CE E**
  KRENSKY, S/Three blind mice mystery. /1995/1-3/2 KF925 . . . E
  LAWSON, R/Ben and me: /c1939/3-5/5 KH388 . . . . Fic

LIONNI, L/Alexander and the wind-up mouse. /1987/
P-1/4 KF988 . . . . E
Frederick. /c1967/P-2/2 KF992 . . . . E
LOBEL, A/Mouse soup. /c1977/K-2/1 KG007 . . . . . . **CE E**
Mouse tales. /c1972/K-2/2 KG008 . . . . **CE E**
MCCULLY, EA/Picnic. /1984/P-2/KG094 . . . . **CE E**
School. /1987/P-K/KG095 . . . . E
MCMILLAN, B/Mouse views: what the class pet saw. /1993/
K-3/1 KG111 . . . . E
MONSON, AM/Wanted: best friend. /1997/K-2/2 KG152 . . . . E
MOORE, L/Don't be afraid, Amanda. /1992/2-4/4 KH504 . . . **Fic**
I'll meet you at the cucumbers. /1988/2-4/5 KH505 . . . . . . **Fic**
MOUSE SOUP (VIDEOCASSETTE). /1992/K-2/KG161 . . . **VCR E**
NOVAK, M/Mouse TV. /1994/K-2/3 KG180 . . . . E
O'BRIEN, RC/Mrs. Frisby and the rats of NIMH. /c1971/
4-A/6 KH556 . . . . **Fic**
PALAZZO-CRAIG, J/Max and Maggie in spring. /1995/
K-1/1 KG208 . . . . E
POTTER, B/Tailor of Gloucester. /c1931, 1987/P-3/7 KG270 . . . E
Tailor of Gloucester (Videocassette). /1988/1-3/KG271 . **VCR E**
Tale of Johnny Town-Mouse. /c1946, 1987/P-2/8 KG274 . . . . E
Tale of Mrs. Tittlemouse. /c1938, 1987/P-2/7 KG277 . . . . . . E
Tale of two bad mice. /c1932, 1987/P-2/6 KG284 . . . . E
RAND, G/Willie takes a hike. /1996/K-2/3 KG302 . . . . E
REISER, L/Two mice in three fables. /1995/P-2/3 KG320 . . . . . E
ROBERTS, B/Halloween mice! /1995/P-1/3 KG336 . . . . E
ROTH, SL/My love for you. /1997/P-1/2 KG356 . . . . E
SATHRE, V/Mouse chase. /1995/P-1/2 KG394 . . . . E
SCHINDEL, J/What's for lunch? /1994/P-1/2 KG407 . . . . . . E
SELDEN, G/Harry Kitten and Tucker Mouse. /1986/
2-4/4 KH696 . . . . **Fic**
SOTO, G/Chato's kitchen. /c1995, 1997/1-3/5 KG527 . . . . . . E
STEIG, W/Abel's island. /1976/4-6/6 KH749 . . . . **CE Fic**
Amos and Boris. /c1971/1-3/7 KG540 . . . . **CE E**
Doctor De Soto. /1982/P-3/4 KG542 . . . . **CE E**
STEVENSON, J/All aboard! /1995/1-3/2 KG557 . . . . E
TOMPERT, A/Carol for Christmas. /1994/K-3/5 KG612 . . . . . E
VINCENT, G/Ernest and Celestine at the circus. /1988/
P-2/2 KG655 . . . . E
Ernest and Celestine's picnic. /1982/P-2/1 KG656 . . . . E
WAGGONER, K/Partners. /1995/2-4/4 KH836 . . . . **Fic**
WALSH, ES/Mouse paint. /1989/P-1/2 KG680 . . . . E
Samantha. /1996/K-2/2 KG681 . . . . E
WELLS, R/Noisy Nora. /1997/K-1/4 KG707 . . . . **CE E**
Noisy Nora (Videocassette). /1993/K-1/KG708 . . . . . **VCR E**
WHITE, EB/Stuart Little. /c1945/3-6/5 KH851 . . . . **Fic**

Mice--Folklore.
BRETT, J/Town Mouse, Country Mouse. /1994/
K-3/3 KB535 . . . . **398.24**
COWLEY, J/Mouse bride. /1995/P-2/2 KB552 . . . . **398.24**
FARRIS, PJ/Young Mouse and Elephant: an East African folktale. /
1996/K-2/4 KB565 . . . . **398.24**
STEPTOE, J/Story of Jumping Mouse: a Native American legend. /
1984/4-5/5 KB656 . . . . **CE 398.24**
SUMMERS, K/Milly and Tilly: the story of a town mouse and a
country mouse. /1997/K-2/2 KB661 . . . . **398.24**

Michelangelo Buonarroti.
DI CAGNO, G/Michelangelo. /1996/6-A/12 KD378 . . . . . **709.2**

Michigan.
SIRVAITIS, K/Michigan. /1994/4-6/7 KF017 . . . . **977.4**

Michigan--Fiction.
WHELAN, G/Next spring an oriole. /1987/2-4/5 KH848 . . . . . **Fic**

Michigan--History.
WILLS, CA/Historical album of Michigan. /1996/
4-6/7 KF018 . . . . **977.4**

Microbiology.
COBB, V/Lots of rot. /1981/K-3/3 KC302 . . . . **577.1**
FACKLAM, H/Bacteria. /1994/5-A/9 KC378 . . . . **579.3**
SILVERSTEIN, A/Monerans and protists. /1996/A/11 KC374 . **579**
Microcomputer programs SEE ALSO Word processing--Software; Utility
programs--Software; Subject heading--Software.

Microcomputers--Periodicals.
FAMILY PC. /1994-/5-A/KA109 . . . . **PER PROF 050**
LEARNING AND LEADING WITH TECHNOLOGY. /1979-/
/KA121 . . . . **PER PROF 050**
TECHNOLOGY AND LEARNING. /1980-/
/KA152 . . . . **PER PROF 050**

Micronesia--Folklore.
FLOOD, NB/From the mouth of the monster eel: stories from
Micronesia. /1996/2-5/5 KB296 . . . . **398.2**

Micronesia--Social life and customs.
HERMES, J/Children of Micronesia. /1994/4-6/9 KF122 . . . **996.5**

Microorganisms.
LOEWER, HP/Pond water zoo: an introduction to microscopic life. /
1996/6-A/8 KC372 . . . . **579**
MICROORGANISMS: THE INVISIBLE WORLD (VIDEOCASSETTE).
/1995/4-8/KC373 . . . . **VCR 579**
REALMS OF LIFE (PICTURE). /1996/6-A/KC356 . . . . . **PIC 578**
SILVERSTEIN, A/Monerans and protists. /1996/A/11 KC374 . **579**
SMALLER THAN THE EYE CAN SEE (VIDEOCASSETTE). /1989/
5-6/KC379 . . . . **VCR 579.4**
Microscope and microscopy SEE ALSO Microbiology; names of specific
types of microscopes e.g. Scanning electron microscope.

Microscope and microscopy.
DISCOVERING THE CELL (VIDEOCASSETTE). /1992/
5-6/KC275 . . . . **VCR 571.6**
MICROORGANISMS: THE INVISIBLE WORLD (VIDEOCASSETTE).
/1995/4-8/KC373 . . . . **VCR 579**
SMALLER THAN THE EYE CAN SEE (VIDEOCASSETTE). /1989/
5-6/KC379 . . . . **VCR 579.4**
SNEDDEN, R/Yuck!: a big book of little horrors. /1996/
3-8/7 KC375 . . . . **579**
TOMB, H/MicroAliens: dazzling journeys with an electron
microscope. /1993/3-A/7 KC376 . . . . **579**
YOUNT, L/Antoni van Leeuwenhoek: first to see microscopic life. /
1996/5-A/5 KE432 . . . . **B LEEUWENHOEK,A**

Microscopes.
HOW TO USE THE COMPOUND MICROSCOPE
(VIDEOCASSETTE). /1991/6-A/KB876 . . . . **VCR 502.8**
YOUNT, L/Antoni van Leeuwenhoek: first to see microscopic life. /
1996/5-A/5 KE432 . . . . **B LEEUWENHOEK,A**

Microwave cookery.
GORDON, L/Messipes: a microwave cookbook of deliciously messy
masterpieces. /1996/3-6/KD271 . . . . **641.5**

Microwaves.
ASIMOV, I/How did we find out about microwaves? /1989/
A/9 KD045 . . . . **621.381**

Midas (Legendary character)--Fiction.
REID BANKS, L/Adventures of King Midas. /1992/
4-A/6 KH626 . . . . **Fic**

Middle Ages.
MACAULAY, D/Cathedral (Videocassette). /1986/
6-A/KD389 . . . . **VCR 726**

Middle Ages--Fiction.
BRITTAIN, B/Wizards and the monster. /1994/2-4/4 KG926 . . **Fic**
CUSHMAN, K/Catherine, called Birdy. /1994/
6-A/6 KH050 . . . . **CE Fic**
Midwife's apprentice. /1995/6-A/5 KH051 . . . . **CE Fic**
DE ANGELI, M/Door in the wall. /c1949, 1989/4-6/6 KH064 . **Fic**
GRAY, EJ/Adam of the road. /c1942, 1970/5-6/6 KH194 . **CE Fic**
KELLY, EP/Trumpeter of Krakow. New ed. /c1966, 1973/
/7 KH343 . . . . **Fic**

Middle Atlantic States.
MIDDLE ATLANTIC REGION: NEW YORK, NEW JERSEY,
DELAWARE, MARYLAND, PENNSYLVANIA, DISTRICT OF
COLUMBIA (VIDEOCASSETTE). /1996/4-6/KE924 . . . **VCR 974**
Middle East SEE ALSO Arab countries; also names of individual countries
e.g. Egypt.

Middle East--Fiction.
ALEXANDER, L/Jedera adventure. /1990/5-A/7 KG839 . . . . . **Fic**

Middle East--Folklore.
COURLANDER, H/Tiger's whisker and other tales from Asia and the
Pacific. /c1959, 1995/3-5/7 KB279 . . . . **398.2**

Middle school libraries--Book lists.
YOUR READING: AN ANNOTATED BOOKLIST FOR MIDDLE
SCHOOL AND JUNIOR HIGH. /1996/5-A/KA373 . . **REF 011.62**

Middle schools.
HOW TO SUCCEED IN MIDDLE SCHOOL (VIDEOCASSETTE). /
1994/5-6/KB125 . . . . **VCR 373.2**

Middle schools--Fiction.
DUFFEY, B/Utterly yours, Booker Jones. /1995/4-6/5 KH087 . . **Fic**

Middle West--Fiction.
WILLIAMS, D/Grandma Essie's covered wagon. /1993/
2-4/4 KG726 . . . . E

Middle West--History.
RILEY, J/Prairie cabin: a Norwegian pioneer woman's story
(Videocassette). /1991/A/KF012 . . . . **VCR 977**

Midgets.
CARRICK, C/Two very little sisters. /1993/2-4/5 KC879 . . . **599.9**

Midrash--Legends.
PODWAL, M/Book of tens. /1994/5-6/7 KA769 . . . . **296.1**

Midwives--Fiction.
CUSHMAN, K/Midwife's apprentice. /1995/6-A/5 KH051 . **CE Fic**

Migrant labor.
ATKIN, SB/Voices from the fields: children of migrant farmworkers
tell their stories. /1993/A/6 KA833 . . . . **305.5**

BRIMNER, LD/Migrant family. /1992/4-6/6 KA834 . . . . . . **305.5**
CEDENO, ME/Cesar Chavez: labor leader. /1993/
    4-5/6 KE287 . . . . **B CHAVEZ, C.**
DE RUIZ, DC/Causa: the migrant farmworkers' story. /1993/
    4-6/6 KA944 . . . . **331.88**
STANLEY, J/Children of the Dust Bowl: the true story of the school
    at Weedpatch Camp. /1992/5-A/7 KA835 . . . . **305.5**

Migrant labor--Fiction.
ALTMAN, LJ/Amelia's road. /1993/1-3/4 KF154 . . . . **E**
BUNTING, E/Going home. /1996/1-3/2 KF302 . . . . **E**
COCHRANE, PA/Purely Rosie Pearl. /1996/4-6/6 KH011 . . . . **Fic**
DORROS, A/Radio Man: a story in English and Spanish./Don
    Radio: un cuento en Ingles y Espanol. /1993/2-5/2 KF491 . . . . **E**
WILLIAMS, SA/Working cotton. /1992/1-3/2 KG731 . . . . **E**
YEE, P/Ghost Train. /1996/4-6/5 KH889 . . . . **Fic**

Military art and science.
MELTZER, M/Weapons and warfare: from the stone age to the
    space age. /1996/4-6/8 KA983. . . . . **355.02**

Military decorations.
LLOYD, M/Military badges and insignia. /1995/
    4-8/12 KA984 . . . . **355.1**

Military uniforms.
VISUAL DICTIONARY OF MILITARY UNIFORMS. /1992/
    4-A/8 KA985 . . . . **355.1**

Military weapons.
CHASEMORE, R/Tanks. /1996/4-6/8 KD060 . . . . **623.7**
MELTZER, M/Weapons and warfare: from the stone age to the
    space age. /1996/4-6/8 KA983. . . . . **355.02**

Milk SEE ALSO Cheese; Dairy products.

Milk.
ALIKI /Milk from cow to carton. Rev. ed. /1992/
    1-3/2 KD236 . . . . **637**
CARRICK, D/Milk. /1985/K-3/4 KD237 . . . . **637**
COWS! 2ND ED. (VIDEOCASSETTE). /1995/
    1-3/KD212. . . . . **VCR 636.2**
DAIRY FARM (VIDEOCASSETTE). /1991/3-5/KD213 . **VCR 636.2**
FOWLER, A/Thanks to cows. /1992/K-2/2 KD238 . . . . **637**
GIBBONS, G/Milk makers. /1985/K-3/6 KD239 . . . . **637**

Milky Way--Folklore.
BRUCHAC, J/Story of the Milky Way: a Cherokee tale. /1995/
    2-3/3 KB701 . . . . **398.26**

Million (The number).
HOW MUCH IS A MILLION? (VIDEOCASSETTE). /1997/
    K-1/KB947. . . . . **VCR 513**
SCHWARTZ, DM/How much is a million? /1985/
    K-1/2 KB950 . . . . **513**

Mimicry (Biology) SEE Camouflage (Biology).

Mineralogy SEE ALSO Petrology.

Mineralogy--Handbooks, manuals, etc.
CHESTERMAN, CW/Audubon Society field guide to North
    American rocks and minerals. /1978/3-6/KC225 . . . . **552**
PELLANT, C/Eyewitness handbook of rocks and minerals. /1992/
    A/10 KC144 . . . . **549**

Minerals.
CHESTERMAN, CW/Audubon Society field guide to North
    American rocks and minerals. /1978/3-6/KC225 . . . . **552**
PELLANT, C/Eyewitness handbook of rocks and minerals. /1992/
    A/10 KC144 . . . . **549**
ROCKS AND MINERALS: THE HARD FACTS (VIDEOCASSETTE). /
    1987/5-A/KC227 . . . . **VCR 552**

Minerals--Experiments.
VANCLEAVE, JP/Janice VanCleave's rocks and minerals: mind-
    boggling experiments you can turn /1996/4-6/8 KC228 . . . . **552**

Miners--Fiction.
LYON, GE/Mama is a miner. /1994/2-3/3 KG044 . . . . **E**

Mines and mineral resources--West (U.S.)--History--19th century.
HILTON, S/Miners, merchants, and maids. /1995/
    4-6/8 KF033 . . . . **978**

Ministers SEE Clergy.

Minnesota.
FRADIN, DB/Minnesota. /1994/4-6/3 KF021 . . . . **977.6**

Minnesota--Fiction.
BELLAIRS, J/Dark secret of Weatherend. /c1984/
    6-A/6 KG895. . . . . **Fic**

Minnesota--History.
CARLSON, JD/Historical album of Minnesota. /1993/
    5-6/7 KF020 . . . . **977.6**

Minorities.
PLAYING FAIR (VIDEOCASSETTE). /1991/
    4-6/KA854 . . . . **VCR 305.8**

Minorities--United States--Bibliography.
VENTURE INTO CULTURES: A RESOURCE BOOK OF
    MULTICULTURAL MATERIALS AND PROGRAMS. /1992/
    /KA024. . . . . **PROF 011.62**

Minorities in literature--Bibliography.
MILLER-LACHMANN, L/Our family, our friends, our world: /1992/
    /KA020. . . . . **PROF 011.62**
VENTURE INTO CULTURES: A RESOURCE BOOK OF
    MULTICULTURAL MATERIALS AND PROGRAMS. /1992/
    /KA024. . . . . **PROF 011.62**

Minotaur (Greek mythology).
FISHER, LE/Theseus and the Minotaur. /1988/5-6/6 KA741 . . **292**
HUTTON, W/Theseus and the Minotaur. /1989/
    5-6/6 KA746 . . . . **292**

Minstrels--Fiction.
GRAY, EJ/Adam of the road. /c1942, 1970/5-6/6 KH194. **CE Fic**
SUTCLIFF, R/Minstrel and the dragon pup. /c1993, 1996/
    3-6/7 KH775 . . . . **Fic**

Mirrors.
SIMON, S/Mirror magic. /1991/3-5/6 KC114. . . . . **535**

Mirrors--Experiments.
ZUBROWSKI, B/Mirrors: finding out about the properties of light. /
    1992/5-6/8 KC116 . . . . **535**

Miscellanea.
ANTHONY, SC/Facts plus: an almanac of essential information.
    New 3rd ed. /1995/4-A/KA377 . . . . **REF 030**
PETERSON, PR/Know it all: resource book for kids. /1989/
    4-A/6 KA591 . . . . **031.02**

Misers--Fiction.
DICKENS, C/Christmas Carol in prose, being a ghost story of
    Christmas. /1983/4-6/5 KH074 . . . . **CE Fic**

Missionaries.
JACOBS, WJ/Mother Teresa: helping the poor. /1991/
    4-6/6 KE561 . . . . **B TERESA,MOTHER**
WHITE, FM/Story of Junipero Serra: brave adventurer. /1996/
    4-6/7 KE536 . . . . **B SERRA, J.**

Missionaries of Charity.
JACOBS, WJ/Mother Teresa: helping the poor. /1991/
    4-6/6 KE561 . . . . **B TERESA,MOTHER**

Missions--Australia--Fiction.
HILL, A/Burnt stick. /1995/4-A/7 KH259 . . . . **Fic**

Missions--California.
ABBINK, E/Missions of the Monterey Bay Area. /1996/
    4-6/9 KF075 . . . . **979.4**
BEHRENS, J/Missions of the central coast. /1996/
    4-6/9 KF076 . . . . **979.4**
BROWER, P/Missions of the inland valleys. /1997/
    4-6/9 KF077 . . . . **979.4**
LEMKE, N/Missions of the Southern Coast. /1996/
    4-6/9 KF083 . . . . **979.4**
MACMILLAN, D/Missions of the Los Angeles Area. /1996/
    4-6/9 KF084 . . . . **979.4**
WHITE, TN/Missions of the San Francisco Bay Area. /1996/
    4-6/9 KF087 . . . . **979.4**

Missions--Fiction.
POLITI, L/Song of the swallows. /c1949, 1987/
    K-3/6 KG262 . . . . **CE E**

Mississippi--Fiction.
BALL, Z/Bristle Face. /1990/5-A/6 KG877 . . . . **Fic**
COLEMAN, E/White socks only. /1996/3-4/4 KH014 . . . . . . **Fic**
MITCHELL, MK/Granddaddy's gift. /1997/1-3/2 KG146 . . . . . **E**
ROBINET, HG/Mississippi chariot. /1994/5-A/5 KH639 . . . . . **Fic**
TAYLOR, MD/Let the circle be unbroken. /1981/5-6/8 KH777 . **Fic**
    Roll of thunder, hear my cry. /c1976/5-6/6 KH779. . . . . **CE Fic**
    Song of the trees. /1975/4-6/4 KH780 . . . . **Fic**

Mississippi--Race relations.
ELISH, D/James Meredith and school desegregation. /1994/
    4-5/7 KE463 . . . . **B MEREDITH, J.**

Mississippi River.
HOLLING, HC/Minn of the Mississippi. /c1951/
    5-6/6 KC619 . . . . **597.92**
LAUBER, P/Flood: wrestling with the Mississippi. /1996/
    4-6/4 KB035 . . . . **363.34**

Mississippi River--Fiction.
TWAIN, M/Adventures of Tom Sawyer. /1989/5-A/4 KH814. . **Fic**

Missouri.
FRADIN, DB/Missouri. /1994/4-6/4 KF023 . . . . **977.8**

Missouri--Fiction.
HORVATH, P/Happy yellow car. /1994/4-6/6 KH283 . . . . . . **Fic**
MACBRIDE, RL/Little house on Rocky Ridge. /1993/
    4-6/6 KH436 . . . . **Fic**
TWAIN, M/Adventures of Tom Sawyer. /1989/5-A/4 KH814. . **Fic**

Missouri River Valley--Description and travel.
FREEDMAN, R/Indian winter. /1992/A/9 KE202 . . . . . . **917.804**

Mitchell, Maria.
MCPHERSON, SS/Rooftop astronomer: a story about Maria
    Mitchell. /1990/4-5/6 KE465 . . . . **B MITCHELL, M.**

Mittens--Fiction.
ROGERS, J/Runaway mittens. /1988/P-2/4 KG348 . . . . **E**

Mittens--Folklore.
BRETT, J/Mitten. /1989/K-2/3 KB534 . . . . **398.24**

Miwok Indians--Folklore.
FRENCH, F/Lord of the animals: a Miwok Indian creation myth. /
1997/K-3/4 KB568 . . . . **398.24**

Miwok Indians--Missions--California.
WHITE, TN/Missions of the San Francisco Bay Area. /1996/
4-6/9 KF087 . . . . **979.4**

Model airplanes; Model cars, etc SEE Airplanes--Models; Automobiles--
Models, etc.

Modeling SEE ALSO Clay.

Modeling.
SANCHEZ SANCHEZ, I/Modeling dinosaurs. /1996/
3-6/3 KD448 . . . . **745.592**
Monsters and extraterrestrials. /1996/3-6/3 KD449 . . . **745.592**

Models and modelmaking.
ZUBROWSKI, B/Wheels at work: building and experimenting with
models of machines. /1986/5-6/8 KD054. . . . . **621.8**

Modoc Indians--Biography.
WEIL, A/Michael Dorris. /1997/6-A/7 KE323 . . . . **B DORRIS, M.**

Modoc Indians--Folklore.
SIMMS, L/Moon and Otter and Frog. /1995/
2-4/2 KB715 . . . . **398.26**

Moehlman, Patricia Des Roses.
PRINGLE, LP/Jackal woman: exploring the world of jackals. /1993/
5-6/6 KC833 . . . . **599.77**

Mogollon culture.
WARREN, S/Cities in the sand: the ancient civilizations of the
Southwest. /1992/5-6/8 KF064 . . . . **979**

Mohawk Indians--Folklore.
GATES, F/Owl eyes. /1994/1-3/4 KB570. . . . . **398.24**

Molecules.
COOPER, C/Matter. /1992/4-A/9 KC078 . . . . **530**

Moles (Animals)--Fiction.
HOBAN, L/Silly Tilly's Thanksgiving dinner. /1990/K-2/2 KF738 . **E**

Moles (Animals)--Folklore.
EHLERT, L/Mole's hill: a woodland tale. /1994/
K-2/3 KB562 . . . . **398.24**
KWON, HH/Moles and the Mireuk: a Korean folktale. /1993/
K-2/4 KB605 . . . . **398.24**

Monarch butterfly.
GIBBONS, G/Monarch butterfly. /1989/K-2/4 KC560. . . . **595.78**
INSECTS (VIDEOCASSETTE). /c1979, 1986/
2-6/KC541. . . . . **VCR 595.7**
LAVIES, B/Monarch butterflies: mysterious travelers. /1992/
5-6/7 KC562 . . . . **595.78**
PRINGLE, LP/Extraordinary life: the story of a monarch butterfly. /
1997/5-6/6 KC564 . . . . **595.78**

Monarchs SEE Kings, queens, rulers, etc.

Monet, Claude.
HARRISON, P/Claude Monet. /1996/4-6/7 KE466. **B MONET, C.**
MUHLBERGER, R/What makes a Monet a Monet? /1993/
5-A/7 KD492 . . . . **759.4**

Money SEE ALSO Coins; Finance, Personal.

Money.
ADAMS, BJ/Go-around dollar. /1992/3-6/3 KA947 . . . . . **332.4**
BERGER, M/Round and round the money goes: what money is and
how we use it. /1993/2-4/2 KA948 . . . . **332.4**
CRIBB, J/Money. /1990/4-6/8 KA949 . . . . **332.4**
MATH, MONEY, AND YOU (SOUND FILMSTRIP). /1989/
K-2/KB967 . . . . **FSS 513.2**
MCMILLAN, B/Jelly beans for sale. /1996/K-3/2 KA951 . . **332.4**
PIGGY BANKS TO MONEY MARKETS: A KID'S VIDEO GUIDE TO
DOLLARS AND SENSE /1993/4-6/KA945. . . . . . **VCR 332.024**
SCHWARTZ, DM/If you made a million. /1989/
2-5/5 KA946 . . . . **332.024**

Money--Fiction.
LEEDY, L/Monster money book. /1992/1-3/2 KF957. . . . . . . **E**

Money--History.
MAESTRO, B/Story of money. /1993/3-6/5 KA950 . . . . . **332.4**
PARKER, NW/Money, money, money: the meaning of the art and
symbols on United States paper /1995/3-6/11 KD506 . . . . **769.5**

Moneymaking projects SEE ALSO Business enterprises.

Moneymaking projects.
BARKIN, C/Jobs for kids: the guide to having fun and making
money. /1990/5-6/7 KD305 . . . . **650.1**
SMACKERS: ELEMENTARY ENTREPRENEURS (VIDEOCASSETTE).
/1991/3-6/KD314. . . . . **VCR 658**
THOMPSON, T/Biz kids' guide to success: money-making ideas for
young entrepreneurs. /1992/5-6/6 KD307 . . . . **650.1**

Moneymaking projects--Fiction.
BROWN, MT/Arthur's TV trouble. /1995/K-2/2 KF279 . . . . . . **E**

BYARS, BC/McMummy. /1993/5-A/5 KG961 . . . . **Fic**
HOBAN, L/Arthur's funny money. /1981/1-3/2 KF733 . . . . . . **E**
MAHY, M/Fortune branches out. /c1994, 1995/3-5/4 KH447. . . **Fic**
MCKAY, H/Exiles at home. /1994/5-A/7 KH479 . . . . **Fic**
SOTO, G/Boys at work. /1995/4-6/5 KH739 . . . . **Fic**
STOWE, C/Not-so-normal Norman. /1995/2-5/3 KH770 . . . . **Fic**
WAGGONER, K/Partners. /1995/2-4/4 KH836. . . . . **Fic**

Mongolia--Folklore.
OTSUKA, Y/Suho and the white horse: a legend of Mongolia
(Videocassette). /1981/3-4/KB626 . . . . **VCR 398.24**
YEP, L/Khan's daughter: a Mongolian folktale. /1997/
2-4/6 KB787 . . . . **398.27**

Mongols--Social life and customs.
REYNOLDS, J/Mongolia: vanishing cultures. /1994/
4-6/7 KE704 . . . . **951.7**

Monhegan Island (Me.)--Social life and customs.
DEAN, J/Year on Monhegan Island. /1995/4-6/8 KE926. . . **974.1**

Monitor (Ironclad).
CARTER, AR/Battle of the ironclads: the Monitor and the
Merrimack. /1993/4-6/8 KE900. . . . . **973.7**

Monkeys.
NAGDA, AW/Canopy crossing: a story of an Atlantic rainforest
(Kit). /1997/2-4/KC873 . . . . **KIT 599.8**

Monkeys--Fiction.
BLOS, JW/Nellie Bly's monkey: his remarkable story in his own
words. /1996/2-5/9 KF236. . . . . **E**
CHRISTELOW, E/Five little monkeys sitting in a tree. /1991/
P-K/2 KF384 . . . . **E**
Five little monkeys with nothing to do. /1996/P-2/2 KF385. . . . **E**
DODDS, DA/Color box. /1992/P-K/1 KF486 . . . . **E**
RAWLS, W/Summer of the monkeys. /1976/4-6/6 KH623 . . . . **Fic**
REY, HA/Curious George. /c1941/P-2/2 KG322 . . . . **E**
Curious George and other stories about Curious George (Talking
book). /1973/P-2/KG323. . . . . **TB**
Curious George gets a medal. /1957/P-2/2 KG324 . . . . . **E**
Curious George learns the alphabet. /1963/P-2/2 KG325. . . . **E**
Curious George rides a bike. /c1952/P-2/1 KG326 . . . . **CE E**
Curious George takes a job. /c1947/P-2/3 KG327. . . . . . **E**
REY, M/Curious George flies a kite. /c1958/P-2/1 KG328 . . . **E**
Curious George goes to the hospital. /c1966/P-2/2 KG329 . . **E**
SLOBODKINA, E/Caps for sale: a tale of a peddler, some monkeys
and their monkey business. /c1947/P-2/1 KG519 . . . . **CE E**

Monkeys--Folklore.
KANI, S/Monkey and the crab. /1985/3/3 KB598 . . . . . **398.24**
SAN SOUCI, RD/Pedro and the monkey. /1996/
3-4/2 KB649 . . . . **398.24**

Monsters SEE ALSO Giants; Loch Ness monster; Sasquatch; Vampires;
Werewolves.

Monsters.
BANG, M/Wiley and the Hairy Man: adapted from an American
folk tale. /c1976, 1987/1-3/2 KB389 . . . . **398.21**
STEFFENS, B/Loch Ness Monster. /1995/3-6/9 KA563 . . **001.944**
WALKER, PR/Bigfoot and other legendary creatures. /1992/
4-6/6 KA564 . . . . **001.944**

Monsters--Fiction.
BROWN, R/Toad. /1997/K-2/3 KF289 . . . . **E**
DRESCHER, H/Simon's book. /1983/K-2/6 KF497 . . . . . **CE E**
EMBERLEY, E/Go away, big green monster! /1992/
P-1/2 KF522 . . . . **E**
GACKENBACH, D/Mag the magnificent. /1985/K-2/2 KF590 . . . **E**
HOWE, J/There's a monster under my bed. /1986/
P-2/2 KF781 . . . . **E**
HUTCHINS, P/Very worst monster. /1985/P-2/2 KF806. . . . **CE E**
LEEDY, L/Monster money book. /1992/1-3/2 KF957. . . . . . . **E**
MUELLER, V/Halloween mask for Monster. /1986/
P-1/1 KG162 . . . . **E**
OXFORD BOOK OF SCARYTALES. /1992/6-A/7 KH569. . . . . **Fic**
PARISH, P/No more monsters for me! /1981/K-1/1 KG215 . . . . **E**
REGAN, DC/Monsters in the attic. /1995/4-6/6 KH625. . . . . **Fic**
SILVERMAN, E/Big pumpkin. /1992/P-2/2 KG504 . . . . **E**
TREASURY OF GIANT AND MONSTER STORIES. /1992/
3-5/6 KH803 . . . . **Fic**
TURKLE, B/Do not open. /1981/K-2/2 KG622 . . . . **E**
UNGERER, T/Tomi Ungerer Library (Videocassette). /1993/
K-2/KG635 . . . . **VCR E**
VIORST, J/My mama says there aren't any zombies, ghosts,
vampires, creatures, demons, /1973/P-3/4 KG663 . . . . **E**

Monsters--Fiction--Software.
MERCER MAYER'S LITTLE MONSTER AT SCHOOL. SCHOOL ED.
(CD-ROM). /1994/K-3/KG130 . . . . **CDR E**

Monsters--Folklore.
TREASURY OF GIANT AND MONSTER STORIES. /1992/
3-5/6 KH803 . . . . **Fic**

Monsters--Literary collections.
SCARED SILLY! A BOOK FOR THE BRAVE. /1994/
K-3/KD904 . . . . **810.8**
Monsters--Poetry.
FLORIAN, D/Monster Motel: poems and paintings. /1993/
4-6/KD938. . . . . **811**
MCNAUGHTON, C/Making friends with Frankenstein: a book of
monstrous poems and pictures. /1994/K-3/KE107 . . . . **821**
MONSTER SOUP AND OTHER SPOOKY POEMS. /1992/
K-3/KD986 . . . . **811**
PRELUTSKY, J/Headless Horseman rides tonight: more poems to
trouble your sleep. /1980/2-4/KE003 . . . . **811**
Nightmares: poems to trouble your sleep. /c1976/
3-5/KE011. . . . . **811**
Monsters in art.
SANCHEZ SANCHEZ, I/Dragons and prehistoric monsters. /1996/
3-6/3 KD447 . . . . **745.592**
Monsters and extraterrestrials. /1996/3-6/3 KD449 . . . **745.592**
Monsters in literature.
RAINEY, R/Monster factory. /1993/3-6/8 KD895. . . . . . . **809.3**
Montana.
HEINRICHS, A/Montana. /1991/5-6/8 KF058 . . . . **978.6**
Montessori, Maria.
O'CONNOR, B/Mammolina: a story about Maria Montessori. /
1993/4-6/6 KE467 . . . . **B MONTESSORI, M**
SHEPHARD, MT/Maria Montessori: teacher of teachers. /1996/
A/9 KE468 . . . . **B MONTESSORI, M**
Montessori method of education.
O'CONNOR, B/Mammolina: a story about Maria Montessori. /
1993/4-6/6 KE467 . . . . **B MONTESSORI, M**
SHEPHARD, MT/Maria Montessori: teacher of teachers. /1996/
A/9 KE468 . . . . **B MONTESSORI, M**
Montgomery, Lucy M.
ANDRONIK, CM/Kindred spirit: a biography of L. M. Montgomery,
creator of Anne of Green Gables. /1993/
5-A/6 KE469 . . . . **B MONTGOMERY, L**
LUCY MAUD MONTGOMERY: THREADS FROM THE QUILT
(VIDEOCASSETTE). /1993/
6-A/KE470. . . . . **VCR B MONTGOMERY, L**
Montgomery (Ala.)--Race relations.
STEIN, RC/Montgomery bus boycott. Rev. ed. /1993/
5-6/6 KE998 . . . . **976.1**
Months.
LESLIE, CW/Nature all year long. /1991/1-5/6 KB908 . . . . . **508**
Months--Fiction.
HENDERSON, K/Year in the city. /1996/K-2/2 KF700 . . . . . . **E**
LESSER, C/What a wonderful day to be a cow. /1995/
K-2/3 KF963 . . . . **E**
Months--Poetry.
LEWIS, JP/July is a mad mosquito. /1994/P-3/KD972. . . . . **811**
SNOW TOWARD EVENING: A YEAR IN A RIVER VALLEY:
NATURE POEMS. /1995/2-6/KE082 . . . . **811.008**
THOMAS, JC/Gingerbread days: poems. /1995/K-4/KE032. . **811**
Monticello (Va.).
REEF, C/Monticello. /1991/3-5/6 KE892 . . . . **973.4**
Monuments.
SINGER, D/Structures that changed the way the world looked. /
1995/4-A/9 KD384. . . . . **720**
Moon SEE ALSO Tides.
Moon.
GIBBONS, G/Moon book. /1997/K-6/4 KC019 . . . . **523.3**
KRUPP, EC/Moon and you. /1993/4-6/4 KC020 . . . . . . **523.3**
MOON/OUTER SPACE (VIDEOCASSETTE). /1994/
3-6/KC007. . . . . **VCR 523**
SIMON, S/Moon. /1984/K-4/4 KC021 . . . . **523.3**
SUN, EARTH, MOON (VIDEOCASSETTE). /1995/
4-6/KC017. . . . . **VCR 523.2**
Moon--Fiction.
ASCH, F/Happy birthday, moon. /1982/P-1/2 KF174 . . . . . **CE E**
BEIFUSS, J/Armadillo Ray. /1995/K-2/4 KF216 . . . . **E**
FOWLER, SG/I'll see you when the moon is full. /1994/
K-2/2 KF568 . . . . **E**
MCDERMOTT, G/Papagayo the mischief maker. /1992/
P-2/5 KG096. . . . . **E**
SHEA, PD/New moon. /1996/P-2/2 KG490 . . . . **E**
THURBER, J/Many moons. /c1943, 1990/3-5/5 KH792 . . . . . **Fic**
Many moons. /1990/3-5/5 KH793 . . . . **Fic**
UNGERER, T/Tomi Ungerer Library (Videocassette). /1993/
K-2/KG635 . . . . **VCR E**
Moon--Folklore.
DAYRELL, E/Why the sun and the moon live in the sky: an African
folktale. /c1968/K-3/6 KB704 . . . . **CE 398.26**
EHLERT, L/Moon rope: a Peruvian folktale/Un lazo a la luna: una
leyenda Peruana. /1992/1-3/2 KB563 . . . . **398.24**

RATTIGAN, JK/Woman in the moon: a story from Hawaii. /1996/
K-2/6 KB474 . . . . **398.22**
SANFIELD, S/Just rewards, or, Who is that man in the moon and
what's he doing up there /1996/K-2/4 KB713 . . . . . . **398.26**
SIMMS, L/Moon and Otter and Frog. /1995/
2-4/2 KB715 . . . . **398.26**
Moore, Adam.
MOORE, A/Broken Arrow boy. /1990/3-6/6 KA996 . . . . . **362.1**
Moore, Henry.
GARDNER, JM/Henry Moore: from bones and stones to sketches
and sculptures. /1993/3-6/6 KD397 . . . . **730**
Moose.
NATURE'S NEWBORN: ELK, MOOSE, DEER (VIDEOCASSETTE). /
1994/3-6/KC799 . . . . **VCR 599.65**
PETERSEN, D/Moose. /1994/3-6/6 KC800. . . . . **599.65**
Moose--Fiction.
BUNTING, E/Turkey for Thanksgiving. /1991/P-2/2 KF312. . . . . **E**
LATIMER, J/Moose and friends. /1993/1-3/2 KF947 . . . . **E**
SEUSS, D/Horton hears a Who!/Thidwick the big-hearted moose
(Videocassette). /1992/P-3/KG458. . . . . **VCR E**
SLEPIAN, J/Lost moose. /1995/K-2/2 KG517 . . . . **E**
WISEMAN, B/Morris and Boris. /c1974, 1991/K-2/1 KG748 . . . **E**
Morris goes to school. /1970/K-2/2 KG749. . . . . **E**
Morris the Moose. /1989/K-2/2 KG750. . . . . **CE E**
Morays.
ROTHAUS, D/Moray eels. /1996/4-6/8 KC586 . . . . **597**
Mormon Church--Presidents.
SANFORD, WR/Brigham Young: pioneer and Mormon leader. /
1996/5-6/8 KE605 . . . . **B YOUNG, B.**
Morning--Fiction.
LAKIN, P/Dad and me in the morning. /1994/1-3/2 KF942 . . . . **E**
PILKEY, D/Paperboy. /1996/K-2/2 KG238 . . . . **E**
Morning--Songs and music.
FARJEON, E/Morning has broken. /1996/P-2/KD611 . . . . . **789.3**
Morning glories.
JOHNSON, SA/Morning glories. /1985/4-6/7 KC428 . . . . . **583**
Morocco--Social life and customs.
HERMES, J/Children of Morocco. /1995/3-6/7 KE730 . . . . . **964**
Morse, Samuel.
NOONAN, J/Nineteenth-century inventors. /1992/
5-6/7 KC897 . . . . **609**
Moses (Biblical leader).
FISHER, LE/Moses. /1995/3-4/3 KA677. . . . . **221.9**
HUTTON, W/Moses in the bulrushes. /1986/P-2/6 KA679. . **221.9**
Mosques.
MACDONALD, F/16th century mosque. /1994/
4-A/10 KD391 . . . . **726**
Mosses.
JOHNSON, SA/Mosses. /1983/6/8 KC438 . . . . **588**
Most, Bernard.
GET TO KNOW BERNARD MOST (VIDEOCASSETTE). /1993/
2-3/KE471. **VCR B MOST, B.**
Motels SEE Hotels, motels, etc.
Mother and child.
ROTNER, S/Lots of moms. /1996/P-1/1 KA882. . . . . . . **306.874**
Mother and child--Fiction.
CARLSTROM, NW/I'm not moving, Mama! /1990/P-1/1 KF355 . **E**
CASELEY, J/Mama, coming and going. /1994/1-3/4 KF366. . . . **E**
ESTERL, A/Okino and the whales. /1995/3-5/3 KH101 . . . . . . **Fic**
HENKES, K/Words of stone. /1992/5-A/6 KH240 . . . . **Fic**
JOOSSE, BM/Mama, do you love me? /1991/P-1/2 KF854 . . . . **E**
MCMULLAN, K/If you were my bunny. /1996/P-K/3 KG112 . . . **E**
VAN LAAN, N/Sleep, sleep, sleep: a lullaby for little ones around
the world. /1995/P-2/3 KG644 . . . . **E**
WHITE, R/Belle Prater's boy. /1996/6-A/6 KH853 . . . . **Fic**
Mother Teresa SEE Teresa, Mother.
Mother's Day--Fiction.
BUNTING, E/Mother's Day mice. /1986/P-2/2 KF305 . . . . . **CE E**
Mothers.
ROTNER, S/Lots of moms. /1996/P-1/1 KA882. . . . . . . **306.874**
Mothers--Employment--Fiction.
ACKERMAN, K/By the dawn's early light. /1994/K-2/5 KF129 . . **E**
STANEK, M/All alone after school. /1985/2-3/2 KG536 . . . . . . **E**
Mothers--Fiction.
GOODE, D/Where's our mama? /1991/P-2/2 KF632 . . . . **E**
JOHNSON, D/What will Mommy do when I'm at school? /1990/
K-1/2 KF836 . . . . **E**
LYON, GE/Mama is a miner. /1994/2-3/3 KG044. . . . . **E**
MINARIK, EH/Little Bear. /c1961/P-1/2 KG141 . . . . **CE E**
SAY, A/Tree of cranes. /1991/1-3/4 KG400 . . . . **E**
VIORST, J/My mama says there aren't any zombies, ghosts,
vampires, creatures, demons, monsters, fiends, goblins, or things. /
1973/P-3/4 KG663 . . . . **E**
WABER, B/Lyle finds his mother. /1974/P-2/3 KG671. . . . . . . **E**

Mothers and daughters--Fiction.

BARBER, BE/Saturday at The New You. /1994/K-3/3 KF198 . . . **E**
BEST, C/Red light, green light, Mama and me. /1995/
K-2/2 KF228 . . . . **E**
CASELEY, J/Witch Mama. /1996/K-2/3 KF371 . . . . **E**
CLEARY, B/Ramona and her mother. /1979/3-5/6 KH002 . **CE Fic**
GALDONE, P/Magic porridge pot. /c1976/P-2/4 KF596 . . . . . **E**
GLASER, L/Rosie's birthday rat. /1996/1-3/2 KH171 . . . . . . **Fic**
GRAY, L/Falcon's egg. /1995/5-A/6 KH195 . . . . **Fic**
HAZEN, BS/Mommy's office. /1992/P-2/2 KF688 . . . . . . **E**
HERMES, P/Someone to count on: a novel. /1993/
6-A/7 KH250 . . . . **Fic**
JOSEPH, L/Jasmine's parlour day. /1994/1-3/3 KF856 . . . . **E**
LOH, M/Tucking mommy in. /1987/P-2/2 KG017. . . . . **E**
MACLACHLAN, P/Mama One, Mama Two. /1982/
2-3/1 KG054 . . . . **E**
NIMMO, J/Griffin's castle. /1997/6-A/7 KH551 . . . . . . **Fic**
PALACIOS, A/Christmas surprise for Chabelita. /1993/
1-3/2 KG206 . . . . **E**
PERKINS, LR/Home lovely. /1995/K-2/5 KG233 . . . . **E**
POMERANTZ, C/Chalk doll. /c1989, 1993/1-3/2 KG263 . . . . . **E**
PULVER, R/Nobody's mother is in second grade. /1992/
K-2/2 KG293 . . . . **E**
RANSOM, CF/Big green pocketbook. /1993/P-1/2 KG303 . . . . **E**
RODGERS, M/Freaky Friday. /c1972/5-6/5 KH647 . . . . . **CE Fic**
RODOWSKY, C/Hannah in between. /1994/5-A/7 KH650. . . . **Fic**
SACHS, M/Call me Ruth. /c1982, 1995/5-A/6 KH667 . . . . **Fic**
SHREVE, S/Amy Dunn quits school. /1993/5-A/7 KH706 . . . . **Fic**
SMITH, DB/Best girl. /1993/5-A/6 KH720 . . . . **Fic**
Return to Bitter Creek. /1988/5-A/5 KH721 . . . . **Fic**
STANEK, M/I speak English for my mom. /1989/
2-4/2 KH747 . . . . **Fic**
STEIG, W/Brave Irene. /1986/K-3/3 KG541 . . . . **CE E**
WILLIAMS, KL/Tap-tap. /1994/K-2/2 KG728 . . . . **CE E**
WILLIAMS, VB/Scooter. /1993/4-A/4 KH865 . . . . **Fic**
WINTHROP, E/Very noisy girl. /1991/K-2/2 KG747. . . . . . . **E**
ZOLOTOW, C/Moon was the best. /1993/K-2/5 KG803. . . . . **E**

Mothers and daughters--Folklore.

EVETTS-SECKER, J/Mother and daughter tales. /1996/
3-4/6 KB292 . . . . **398.2**

Mothers and sons.

GREENBERG, KE/Zack's story: growing up with same-sex parents. /
1996/4-6/4 KA877 . . . . **306.874**

Mothers and sons--Fiction.

BANKS, K/Spider spider. /1996/P-1/2 KF194 . . . . **E**
BAUER, J/Sticks. /1996/6-A/4 KG880. . . . . **Fic**
BAUER, MD/Question of trust. /1994/5-A/6 KG883. . . . . **Fic**
COREY, D/Will there be a lap for me? /1992/P-1/2 KF425 . . . . **E**
GAUTHIER, G/My life among the aliens. /1996/4-6/5 KH154 . **Fic**
HILL, A/Burnt stick. /1995/4-A/7 KH259 . . . . **Fic**
LEE, HV/In the snow. /1995/1-3/2 KF955 . . . . **E**
MCKISSACK, P/Ma Dear's aprons. /1997/3-5/4 KH492 . . . . **Fic**
RADIN, RY/All Joseph wanted. /1991/3-5/4 KH617 . . . . . . **Fic**
RODGERS, M/Billion for Boris. /c1974/4-6/7 KH646 . . . . **CE Fic**
ROSENBERG, L/Monster mama. /1993/K-2/4 KG354. . . . . **Fic**
Monster mama (Videocassette). /1996/K-2/KG355. . . . . **VCR E**
SCOTT, AH/On mother's lap. /c1972, 1992/P-K/2 KG423 . . . . **E**

Mothers and sons--Folklore.

BANG, M/Wiley and the Hairy Man: adapted from an American
folk tale. /c1976, 1987/1-3/2 KB389 . . . . **398.21**
SIERRA, J/Wiley and the Hairy Man. /1996/K-3/4 KB417. **398.21**
WAHL, J/Little Eight John. /1992/2-3/2 KB783 . . . . **398.27**

Moths.

ARNOSKY, J/Crinkleroot's guide to knowing butterflies and moths.
/1996/3-5/5 KC557 . . . . **595.78**
JOHNSON, SA/Silkworms. /1982/4-6/8 KD241 . . . . **638**
PASCOE, E/Butterflies and moths. /1997/4-6/6 KC563 . . . **595.78**
SABIN, L/Amazing world of butterflies and moths. /1982/
2-4/4 KC566 . . . . **CE 595.78**
SANDVED, KB/Butterfly alphabet. /1996/3-6/6 KC567 . . . . **595.78**
WHALLEY, P/Butterfly and moth. /1988/A/10 KC569 . . . . **595.78**

Moths--Experiments.

PASCOE, E/Butterflies and moths. /1997/4-6/6 KC563 . . . **595.78**
Motion SEE ALSO Force and energy; Mechanics.

Motion.

ADKINS, J/Moving heavy things. /1980/A/7 KC088. . . . . . **531**
COBB, V/Why doesn't the earth fall up? /1988/
4-6/5 KC092 . . . . **531**
LET'S MOVE IT: NEWTON'S LAWS OF MOTION
(VIDEOCASSETTE). /1987/5-A/KC096 . . . . **VCR 531**

Motion--Experiments.

ARDLEY, N/Science book of motion. /1992/K-3/2 KC090 . . . **531**

Motion picture producers and directors.

MEACHUM, V/Steven Spielberg: Hollywood filmmaker. /1996/
4-6/8 KE545 . . . . **B SPIELBERG, S.**
POWERS, T/Steven Spielberg: master storyteller. /1997/
5-A/7 KE546 . . . . **B SPIELBERG, S.**
Motion picture stars SEE Actors and actresses.
Motion pictures SEE ALSO Animation (Cinematography); Cartoons and
comics.

Motion pictures--Biography.

COLE, MD/Walt Disney: creator of Mickey Mouse. /1996/
4-6/8 KE322 . . . . **B DISNEY, W.**

Motion pictures--Catalogs.

AIT CATALOG OF EDUCATIONAL MATERIALS. /1962-/
/KA003. . . . . **PROF 011**

Motion pictures--Fiction.

LAKIN, P/Palace of stars. /1993/1-3/3 KF943 . . . . **E**

Motion pictures--Production and direction.

CROSS, R/Movie magic. /1995/4-6/8 KD683 . . . . **791.43**
DAHL, L/James and the giant peach: the book and movie
scrapbook. /1996/3-6/6 KD684. . . . . **791.43**

Motion pictures--Production and direction--Fiction.

LEVY, E/Something queer at the scary movie. /1995/
3-5/3 KH403 . . . . **Fic**
SHARMAT, MW/Genghis Khan: a dog star is born. /1994/
2-5/2 KH703 . . . . **Fic**
Genghis Khan: dog-gone Hollywood. /1995/2-5/2 KH704 . . . **Fic**

Motivation (Psychology).

GO, GO, GOALS!: HOW TO GET THERE (VIDEOCASSETTE). /
1993/4-6/KA657 . . . . **VCR 158**

Motivation in education.

COUNT ON READING HANDBOOK: TIPS FOR PLANNING
READING MOTIVATION PROGRAMS. /1997/
/KA206. . . . . **PROF 372.4**

Motocross.

CARSER, SX/Motocross cycles. /1992/4-A/5 KD828 . . . . . **796.7**

Motor ability.

DANCE WITH US: A CREATIVE MOVEMENT VIDEO
(VIDEOCASSETTE). /1994/K-2/KD702 . . . . **VCR 793.3**
SILBERG, J/500 five minute games: quick and easy activities for 3-6
year olds. /1995//KA325. . . . . **PROF 790.1**
Motor vehicle driving SEE ALSO Traffic signs and signals.
Motor vehicles SEE ALSO Automobiles.

Motor vehicles in art.

AMES, LJ/Draw 50 cars, trucks, and motorcycles. /1986/
4-6/KD415. . . . . **743**
Motorcycles SEE ALSO names of specific types e.g. Harley Davidson
motorcycle.

Motorcycles--History.

LORD, T/Amazing bikes. /1992/3-5/6 KD126 . . . . **629.227**
Mounds SEE ALSO Excavations (Archaeology).

Mount Vernon (Va.).

MOUNT VERNON: HOME OF GEORGE WASHINGTON
(VIDEOCASSETTE). /1989/4-6/KE980 . . . . **VCR 975.5**

Mountain life--Appalachian Region.

BIAL, R/Mist over the mountains: Appalachia and its people. /
1997/4-6/9 KE923 . . . . **974**

Mountain life--Fiction.

BULLA, CR/White bird. /c1966, 1990/1-6/2 KG940. . . . . . . **Fic**
DRAGONWAGON, C/Itch book. /1990/K-3/KF496. . . . . **E**
MORPURGO, M/Dancing bear. /1996/4-6/5 KH513 . . . . . . **Fic**
RYLANT, C/When I was young in the mountains. /1982/
K-3/6 KG387 . . . . **CE E**

Mountain life--Switzerland--Fiction.

SPYRI, J/Heidi. /1996/5-A/6 KH746 . . . . **Fic**

Mountain life--Tennessee--Fiction.

PARTRIDGE, E/Clara and the hoodoo man. /1996/
5-A/3 KH572 . . . . **Fic**

Mountain life--Virginia--Fiction.

RANSOM, CF/When the whippoorwill calls. /1995/
1-3/2 KG305 . . . . **E**

Mountaineering--Fiction.

ULLMAN, JR/Banner in the sky (Talking book). /n.d./
4-6/KH817. . . . . **TB Fic**
Mountains SEE ALSO Volcanoes; also names of mountains e.g. Appalachian
Mountain region.

Mountains.

LAMPTON, C/Volcano. /1991/4-6/7 KC157 . . . . **551.21**
SIMON, S/Mountains. /1994/4-6/7 KC168 . . . . **551.4**
ZOEHFELD, KW/How mountains are made. /1995/
2-4/4 KC170 . . . . **551.43**

Mountains--Fiction.

BABBITT, N/Knee-Knock Rise. /c1970/4-6/6 KG871 . . . . **CE Fic**
LOBEL, A/Ming Lo moves the mountain. /1982/
K-2/1 KG006 . . . . **CE E**

Mountains--Wit and humor.
SWANSON, J/Summit up: riddles about mountains. /1994/
3-6/KD739. . . . . **793.735**
Mouth-organ--Fiction.
MCCLOSKEY, R/Lentil. /c1940/1-3/6 KG088 . . . . **CE E**
Movement education SEE ALSO Motor ability; Movement, Psychology of;
Physical education and training.
Movies SEE Motion pictures.
Moving, Household--Fiction.
BLUME, J/Then again, maybe I won't. /1971/6-A/5 KG915. . . **Fic**
CARLSTROM, NW/I'm not moving, Mama! /1990/P-1/1 KF355 . **E**
CASELEY, J/Hurricane Harry. /1991/3-5/4 KG985. . . . . **Fic**
DANZIGER, P/Amber Brown is not a crayon. /1994/
2-4/6 KH060 . . . . **Fic**
DYGARD, TJ/Infield hit. /1995/5-A/7 KH093 . . . . **Fic**
GILBERT, S/Hawk Hill. /1996/4-6/4 KH167 . . . . **Fic**
GREENWOOD, PD/What about my goldfish? /1993/
1-3/2 KF644 . . . . **E**
HAVILL, J/Jamaica's blue marker. /1995/K-1/2 KF681 . . . . . **E**
HERMES, P/Kevin Corbett eats flies. /1989/5-6/3 KH248 . . . . **Fic**
JOHNSTON, T/Quilt story. /1985/P-3/2 KF840 . . . . **E**
KARAS, GB/Home on the bayou: a cowboy's story. /1996/
K-2/2 KF868 . . . . **E**
MAHY, M/Good Fortunes gang. /1993/3-5/7 KH448 . . . . . **Fic**
MCGEORGE, CW/Boomer's big day. /1994/K-2/2 KG102 . . . **E**
NAMIOKA, L/Yang the youngest and his terrible ear. /1994/
5-A/5 KH528 . . . . **Fic**
PATERSON, K/Flip-flop girl. /1996/5-A/6 KH575 . . . . **Fic**
PINKWATER, DM/Mush, a dog from space. /1995/
3-6/4 KH604 . . . . **Fic**
RANSOM, CF/When the whippoorwill calls. /1995/
1-3/2 KG305 . . . . **E**
REID BANKS, L/Mystery of the cupboard. /1993/
5-A/6 KH628 . . . . **CE Fic**
REISS, K/Time windows. /1991/6-A/7 KH630 . . . . **Fic**
SHANNON, G/Seeds. /1994/K-2/2 KG478 . . . . **E**
SHARMAT, MW/Mitchell is moving. /1978/K-3/1 KG483 . . . . **E**
THESMAN, J/Nothing grows here. /1994/6-A/4 KH790 . . . **Fic**
VIORST, J/Alexander, who's not (Do you hear me? I mean it!)
going to move. /1995/1-3/2 KG660 . . . . **E**
WABER, B/Gina. /1995/1-3/2 KG666 . . . . **E**
WILLIAMS, VB/Scooter. /1993/4-A/4 KH865 . . . . **Fic**
YEP, L/Star fisher. /1991/6-A/6 KH895 . . . . **Fic**
ZOLOTOW, C/Tiger called Thomas. /c1963, 1988/
K-2/4 KG808 . . . . **E**
Mozart, Wolfgang Amadeus.
ISADORA, R/Young Mozart. /1997/
2-3/6 KE472 . . . . **B MOZART, W.**
Mozart, Wolfgang Amadeus--Software.
WINTER, R/Microsoft composer collection (CD-ROM). /1994/
4-A/KD525 . . . . **CDR 780**
Mud--Fiction.
RAY, ML/Mud. /1996/P-2/2 KG316 . . . . **E**
Mud dauber wasps SEE Potter wasps.
Muir, John.
NADEN, CJ/John Muir: saving the wilderness. /1992/
5-6/4 KE473 . . . . **B MUIR, J.**
Muldowney, Shirley.
JENNINGS, J/Long shots: they beat the odds. /1990/
5-6/6 KD762 . . . . **796**
Mule deer.
BARE, CS/Never grab a deer by the ear. /1993/
4-5/5 KC795 . . . . **599.65**
Mules--Fiction.
PAULSEN, G/Call me Francis Tucket. /1995/5-A/5 KH585. . . . **Fic**
Multicultural education.
ORLANDO, L/Multicultural game book: more than 70 traditional
games from 30 countries. /1993//KA323. . . . . **PROF 790.1**
ZASLAVSKY, C/Multicultural math classroom: bringing in the world.
/1996//KA259. **PROF 372.7**
Multicultural education--Periodicals.
MULTICULTURAL REVIEW: DEDICATED TO A BETTER
UNDERSTANDING OF ETHNIC, RACIAL, AND RELIGIOUS
DIVERSITY. /1992-//KA125 . . . . **PER PROF 050**
Multiculturalism.
FOX, M/Whoever you are. /1997/P-1/1 KA843 . . . . **305.8**
MANY PEOPLE, MANY WAYS: UNDERSTANDING CULTURES
AROUND THE WORLD. /1995/4-A/KA402. . . . . **REF 306**
Multimedia--Software.
HYPERSTUDIO (MICROCOMPUTER PROGRAM). /1990/
2-A/KA574 . . . . **MCP 006.7**
Multiplication.
HULME, JN/Sea squares. /1991/K-3/3 KB960. . . . . **513.2**

LEEDY, L/2 x 2 = boo!: a set of spooky multiplication stories. /
1995/1-3/2 KB965 . . . . **513.2**
MENTAL COMPUTATION: USING MENTAL COMPUTATION FOR
MULTIPLICATION (VIDEOCASSETTE). /1987/
4-5/KB949. . . . . **VCR 513**
MURPHY, SJ/Too many kangaroo things to do! /1996/
P-3/2 KB974 . . . . **513.2**
PALMER, H/Singing multiplication tables (Sound recording cassette).
/1971/2-4/KB977. **SRC 513.2**
Mummies.
DEEM, JM/How to make a mummy talk. /1995/
4-6/8 KB175 . . . . **393**
LAUBER, P/Tales mummies tell. /1985/4-6/8 KE626 . . . . . . **930.1**
PUTNAM, J/Mummy. /1993/4-6/8 KB176 . . . . **393**
TRUMBLE, K/Cat mummies. /1996/3-6/9 KE637 . . . . **932**
WILCOX, C/Mummies and their mysteries. /1993/
5-6/6 KB177 . . . . **393**
Mummies--Egypt.
ALIKI /Mummies made in Egypt. /1979/4-6/6 KB173 . . . . . . **393**
PERL, L/Mummies, tombs, and treasure: secrets of ancient Egypt. /
1987/5-A/8 KE636 . . . . **932**
Murder--Fiction.
BABBITT, N/Tuck everlasting. /c1975/4-6/4 KG873 . . . . . **CE Fic**
NEUFELD, J/Gaps in stone walls. /1996/6-A/7 KH546 . . . . . . **Fic**
Murphy, Virginia Reed.
MURPHY, VR/Across the plains in the Donner Party. /1996/
5-6/7 KF041 . . . . **978**
Muscles.
PARKER, S/Skeleton and movement. Rev. ed. /1989/
5-6/7 KC958 . . . . **612.7**
SAUNDERSON, J/Muscles and bones. /1992/
5-6/5 KC959 . . . . **612.7**
YOUR BODY: MUSCULAR AND SKELETAL SYSTEMS
(VIDEOCASSETTE). /1994/5-6/KC961 . . . . **VCR 612.7**
Muscular dystrophy--Fiction.
FARRELL, M/Marrying Malcolm Murgatroyd. /1995/
5-A/4 KH111 . . . . **Fic**
OSOFSKY, A/My Buddy. /1992/K-2/2 KG201 . . . . **E**
Museum techniques.
ARNOLD, C/Dinosaurs down under and other fossils from Australia.
/1990/3-6/8 KC240 . . . . **566**
CUTCHINS, J/Are those animals real?: how museums prepare
wildlife exhibits. Rev. & updated /1995/3-A/7 KC443 . . . **590.75**
Museums.
RICHARDSON, J/Inside the museum: a children's guide to the
Metropolitan Museum of Art. /1993/2-A/7 KD376 . . . . . . **708**
THOMSON, P/Auks, rocks and the odd dinosaur: inside stories
from the Smithsonian's Museum /1985/3-A/7 KB914 . . . . . **508**
Museums--Fiction.
FREEMAN, D/Norman the doorman. /c1959/K-1/7 KF580. . **CE E**
KELLOGG, S/Prehistoric Pinkerton. /1987/P-3/5 KF895. . . . . . **E**
KONIGSBURG, EL/From the mixed-up files of Mrs. Basil E.
Frankweiler. /c1967/4-6/7 KH373 . . . . **CE Fic**
ROHMANN, E/Time flies. /1994/1-3/KG349 . . . . **E**
Mushers.
PAULSEN, G/Puppies, dogs, and blue northers: reflections on being
raised by a pack of sled /1996/3-6/7 KD859. . . . . **798.8**
Mushrooms.
ARNOLD, K/Katya's book of mushrooms. /1997/
3-A/6 KC381 . . . . **579.6**
WATTS, B/Mushroom. /1986/K-2/2 KC382 . . . . **579.6**
Mushrooms--Fiction.
GINSBURG, M/Mushroom in the rain. /c1974, 1987/
P-2/2 KF623 . . . . **E**
Musial, Stan.
GRABOWSKI, J/Stan Musial. /1993/5-A/7 KE474. **B MUSIAL, S.**
Music SEE ALSO Ballet dance music; Church music; Dance music; Jazz
music; Rock music.
Music--Acoustics and physics.
ARDLEY, N/Science book of sound. /1991/2-5/3 KC076. . . . **530**
PITCH (VIDEOCASSETTE). /1994/K-2/KD523 . . . . **VCR 780**
Music--Acoustics and physics--Software.
SCIENCE IN YOUR EAR (CD-ROM). /1996/4-A/KC104 **CDR 534**
Music--Fiction.
EVERSOLE, R/Flute player./La Flautista. /1995/K-2/2 KF541 . . . **E**
KING-SMITH, D/Mouse called Wolf. /1997/3-5/3 KH351 . . . . **Fic**
MOSS, L/Zin! zin! zin! a violin. /1995/K-3/3 KG157 . . . . **E**
WALTER, MP/Ty's one-man band. /c1980, 1987/1-3/2 KG686 . **E**
Music--Folklore.
MEDEARIS, AS/Singing man: adapted from a West African folktale.
/1994/4-5/6 KB757 . . . . **398.27**
Music--History and criticism.
ARDLEY, N/Young person's guide to music. /1995/
5-A/8 KD518 . . . . **BA 780**

STANLEY, L/Be a friend: the story of African American music in song, words and pictures. /1994/K-3/KD670 . . . . **BA 789.4**
WOODYARD, S/Music and song. /1995/3-6/7 KD526 . . . . **780**

Music--Periodicals.
MUSIC EDUCATORS JOURNAL. /1934-//KA126. **PER PROF 050**

Music--Software.
PLAYROOM (CD-ROM). /1990/P-2/KB085 . . . . **CDR 371.3**
TREEHOUSE (CD-ROM). /1991/K-4/KB086 . . . . **CDR 371.3**

Music--Study and teaching.
ARDLEY, N/Young person's guide to music. /1995/
5-A/8 KD518 . . . . **BA 780**
HOW TO READ MUSIC. 2ND ED. (VIDEOCASSETTE). /1994/
3-A/KD519 . . . . **VCR 780**
LANGSTAFF, J/Let's sing!: John Langstaff sings with children, ages
3-7 (Videocassette). /1997//KA314 . . . . **VCR PROF 780**
Making music with children, ages 3-7 (Videocassette). /1995/
/KA315 . . . . **VCR PROF 780**
METER (VIDEOCASSETTE). /1994/K-2/KD522 . . . . . . **VCR 780**
MUSIC EDUCATORS JOURNAL. /1934-//KA126. **PER PROF 050**
PITCH (VIDEOCASSETTE). /1994/K-2/KD523 . . . . **VCR 780**

Music--Theory--Software.
WINTER, R/Microsoft composer collection (CD-ROM). /1994/
4-A/KD525 . . . . **CDR 780**

Music appreciation.
BIBBIDI BOBBODI BACH (COMPACT DISC). /1996/
4-6/KD674 . . . . **CD 789.8**
GANERI, A/Young person's guide to the orchestra: Benjamin
Britten's composition on CD. /1996/4-6/10 KD545 . . . **BA 784.2**
LOUCHARD, R/Hey, Ludwig!: classical piano solos for playful times
/1993/P-3/KD675 . . . . **SRC 789.8**
NICHOL, B/Beethoven lives upstairs (Videocassette). /1992/
4-6/KH550 . . . . **VCR Fic**
ON THE DAY YOU WERE BORN (VIDEOCASSETTE). /1996/
P-A/KG192 . . . . **VCR E**
TURNER, BC/Living clarinet. /1996/4-6/12 KD552 . . . . **BA 788.6**
Living flute. /1996/4-6/11 KD551 . . . . **BA 788.3**
Living piano. /1996/4-6/12 KD546 . . . . **BA 786.2**
Living violin. /1996/4-6/12 KD549 . . . . **BA 787.2**

Music appreciation--Software.
WINTER, R/Microsoft composer collection (CD-ROM). /1994/
4-A/KD525 . . . . **CDR 780**

Musical instruments.
BLACKWOOD, A/Orchestra: an introduction to the world of
classical music. /1993/4-6/8 KD544 . . . . **784.2**
CORBETT, S/Shake, rattle, and strum. /1995/
3-6/6 KD542 . . . . **784.19**
GANERI, A/Young person's guide to the orchestra: Benjamin
Britten's composition on CD. /1996/4-6/10 KD545 . . . **BA 784.2**

Musical instruments--Construction.
DREW, H/My first music book. /1993/2-4/2 KD543 . . . . **784.192**

Musical instruments--Fiction.
MOSS, L/Zin! zin! zin! a violin. /1995/K-3/3 KG157 . . . . **E**

Musical meter and rhythm.
HOW TO READ MUSIC. 2ND ED. (VIDEOCASSETTE). /1994/
3-A/KD519 . . . . **VCR 780**
METER (VIDEOCASSETTE). /1994/K-2/KD522 . . . . . . **VCR 780**

Musical revues, comedies, etc.
RODGERS, R/Sound of music. Selections. 2nd ed. (Sound recording
cassette). /1965/K-A/KD531 . . . . **SRC 782.1**

Musicals.
BROADWAY KIDS SING BROADWAY (COMPACT DISC). /1994/
2-6/KD528 . . . . **CD 782.1**
CHILD'S CELEBRATION OF SHOWTUNES (SOUND RECORDING
CASSETTE). /1992/P-3/KD529 . . . . **SRC 782.1**

Musicians SEE ALSO Afro-American musicians; Composers; Women artists;
also names of specific musicians e.g. Ellington, Duke; types of musicians
e.g. Pianists.

Musicians.
ELLIS, VF/Wynton Marsalis. /1997/
5-A/10 KE459 . . . . **B MARSALIS, W.**
GREENE, C/John Philip Sousa: the march king. /1992/
2-4/2 KE544 . . . . **B SOUSA, J.**
HURWITZ, J/Leonard Bernstein: a passion for music. /1993/
5-A/7 KE253 . . . . **B BERNSTEIN, L.**
KRULL, K/Lives of the musicians: good times, bad times (and what
the neighbors thought). /1993/5-A/6 KD520 . . . . **780**
MEDEARIS, AS/Little Louis and the jazz band: the story of Louis
"Satchmo" Armstrong. /1994/
2-4/6 KE241 . . . . **B ARMSTRONG, L.**
OLD, WC/Duke Ellington: giant of jazz. /1996/
5-A/9 KE338 . . . . **B ELLINGTON, D.**
REDIGER, P/Great African Americans in music. /1996/
3-6/8 KD524 . . . . **780**

Musicians--Fiction.
BRETT, J/Berlioz the bear. /1991/K-2/2 KF261 . . . . **E**
HURD, T/Mama don't allow. /1984/K-3/2 KF793 . . . . **CE E**
ISADORA, R/Ben's trumpet. /c1979/1-3/3 KF813 . . . . **E**
MCCAFFREY, A/Dragonsong. /c1976, 1986/6-A/6 KH466 . . . **Fic**
PATERSON, K/Come sing, Jimmy Jo. /1985/5-A/4 KH574 . . . **Fic**

Muskrats.
ARNOSKY, J/Come out, muskrats. /1989/P-K/2 KC742 . . . **599.35**

Mustang.
ANCONA, G/Man and mustang. /1992/5-6/6 KD197 . . . . **636.1**

Mustang--Fiction.
HENRY, M/Mustang, wild spirit of the West. /c1966, 1992/
5-6/5 KH245 . . . . **Fic**

Mutiny--Fiction.
GAUCH, PL/This time, Tempe Wick? /c1974, 1992/
3-5/7 KH153 . . . . **Fic**

Mutism SEE ALSO Sign language.

Mutism--Fiction.
FLEISCHMAN, P/Half-a-Moon Inn. /c1980, 1991/6/7 KH117 . . **Fic**
GLEITZMAN, M/Blabber mouth. /1995/3-5/4 KH173 . . . . **Fic**
Sticky Beak. /1995/3-5/4 KH176 . . . . **Fic**
HENRY, M/King of the wind. /c1948, 1990/4-6/5 KH243 . **CE Fic**
LEE, JM/Silent Lotus. /1991/P-2/4 KF956 . . . . **E**

Mutism, Elective--Fiction.
PATERSON, K/Flip-flop girl. /1996/5-A/6 KH575 . . . . **Fic**
TOLAN, SS/Who's there? /1994/5-A/5 KH795 . . . . **Fic**

Myers, Walter Dean.
PATRICK-WEXLER, D/Walter Dean Myers. /1996/
5-6/6 KE475 . . . . **B MYERS, W.**

Mynahs--Fiction.
KING-SMITH, D/Mr. Potter's pet. /1996/3-5/2 KH352 . . . . . **Fic**

Mystery and detective stories.
ADLER, DA/Cam Jansen and the ghostly mystery. /1996/
2-4/2 KG815 . . . . **Fic**
Cam Jansen and the mystery of the dinosaur bones. /1981/
2-4/4 KG816 . . . . **CE Fic**
Cam Jansen and the mystery of the stolen diamonds. /1980/
2-4/3 KG817 . . . . **Fic**
Onion sundaes. /1994/2-3/2 KG819 . . . . **Fic**
Young Cam Jansen and the dinosaur game. /1996/
1-2/2 KF132 . . . . **E**
Young Cam Jansen and the lost tooth. /1997/1-2/2 KF133 . . . **E**
Young Cam Jansen and the missing cookie. /1996/
1-2/2 KF134 . . . . **E**
AIKEN, J/Is underground. /1993/5-A/7 KG824 . . . . **Fic**
Wolves of Willoughby Chase. /c1962, 1987/
5-A/7 KG826 . . . . **CE Fic**
ALLEN, LJ/Rollo and Tweedy and the ghost at Dougal Castle. /
1992/1-3/2 KF153 . . . . **CE E**
BABBITT, N/Goody Hall. /c1971, 1992/5-6/6 KG870 . . . . **Fic**
Knee-Knock Rise. /c1970/4-6/6 KG871 . . . . **CE Fic**
BAWDEN, N/Handful of thieves. /c1967, 1991/5-A/5 KG889 . **Fic**
House of secrets. /c1963, 1992/5-A/7 KG890 . . . . . **Fic**
Witch's daughter. /c1966, 1991/5-A/6 KG893 . . . . . **Fic**
BELLAIRS, J/Dark secret of Weatherend. /c1984/
6-A/6 KG895 . . . . **Fic**
BOND, M/Paddington audio collection (Talking book). /1978/
2-4/KG917 . . . . **TB Fic**
BONSALL, CN/Case of the hungry stranger. /c1963/
1-2/2 KF243 . . . . **CE E**
BUNTING, E/Jane Martin, dog detective. /1984/1-3/1 KF303 . . **E**
BURGESS, BH/Fred Field. /1994/6-A/6 KG947 . . . . **Fic**
BYARS, BC/Dark stairs. /1994/4-6/5 KG960 . . . . **CE Fic**
CARRIS, JD/Beware the ravens, Aunt Morbelia. /1995/
5-A/5 KG979 . . . . **Fic**
CHRISTELOW, E/Gertrude, the bulldog detective. /1992/
K-2/3 KF387 . . . . **E**
CUSHMAN, D/Aunt Eater's mystery Christmas. /1995/
1-2/2 KF440 . . . . **E**
Aunt Eater's mystery vacation. /1992/1-3/2 KF441 . . . . **E**
DOYLE, AC/Adventures of Sherlock Holmes. /1992/
6-A/7 KH082 . . . . **Fic**
DUNCAN, L/Third eye. /1984/A/5 KH089 . . . . **Fic**
FLEISCHMAN, S/Jim Ugly. /1992/4-A/6 KH123 . . . . **Fic**
GEE, M/Fire-raiser. /1992/6-A/6 KH155 . . . . **Fic**
GIFF, PR/Powder puff puzzle. /1987/2-3/2 KF615 . . . . . . **E**
GILSON, J/Soccer circus. /1993/3-5/5 KH169 . . . . **Fic**
GRAVES, BB/Mystery of the Tooth Gremlin. /1997/
1-3/2 KH191 . . . . **Fic**
HADDIX, MP/Running out of time. /1995/5-A/5 KH211 . . . **Fic**
HAMILTON, V/House of Dies Drear. /c1968/4-6/5 KH215 **CE Fic**
HOBAN, J/Buzby to the rescue. /1995/K-2/2 KF732 . . . . **E**
HOBAN, L/Case of the two masked robbers. /1988/
K-2/1 KF737 . . . . **E**

HOWE, D/Bunnicula: a rabbit-tale mystery. /1979/
  3-6/5 KH285 . . . . **Fic**
KEATS, EJ/Maggie and the pirate. /1979/P-2/2 KF875. . . . . . . **E**
KELLOGG, S/Mystery of the stolen blue paint. /1982/
  P-1/2 KF893 . . . . **E**
KRENSKY, S/Three blind mice mystery. /1995/1-3/2 KF925 . . . . **E**
LANGTON, J/Diamond in the window. /c1962, 1973/
  4-6/5 KH385 . . . . **Fic**
LEVY, E/Something queer at the scary movie. /1995/
  3-5/3 KH403 . . . . **Fic**
  Something queer is going on (a mystery). /C1973/
  1-3/3 KF972 . . . . **CE E**
LEXAU, JM/Rooftop mystery. /c1968/1-2/1 KF979 . . . . **E**
MACDONALD, RE/Ghosts of Austwick Manor. /c1983, 1991/
  4-A/1 KH441 . . . . **Fic**
MAHY, M/Underrunners. /1992/6-A/6 KH455. . . . . **Fic**
MARKHAM, MM/St. Patrick's Day shamrock mystery. /1995/
  2-4/3 KH457 . . . . **Fic**
NAYLOR, PR/Bodies in the Bessledorf Hotel. /1988/
  4-6/5 KH535 . . . . **Fic**
O'MALLEY, K/Who killed Cock Robin? /1993/1-3/2 KG191. . . . **E**
RASKIN, E/Westing game. /c1978/5-6/5 KH619 . . . . **Fic**
SHARMAT, MW/Nate the Great. /c1972/1-3/2 KG484 . . . **CE E**
  Nate the Great and the crunchy Christmas. /1996/
  2-4/2 KG485 . . . . **E**
  Nate the Great and the pillowcase. /1993/.1-3/1 KG486 . . . . **E**
  Nate the Great and the tardy tortoise. /1995/1-3/2 KG487. . . **E**
SKOFIELD, J/Detective Dinosaur. /1996/1-3/2 KG514 . . . . **E**
SOBOL, DJ/Encyclopedia Brown, boy detective. /1963/
  3-5/6 KH737 . . . . **Fic**
  Encyclopedia Brown and the case of Pablo's nose. /1996/
  3-5/6 KH736 . . . . **Fic**
STRICKLAND, B/Hand of the necromancer. /1996/
  5-A/6 KH772 . . . . **Fic**
WRIGHT, BR/Dollhouse murders. /1983/4-6/5 KH882. . . . . . . **Fic**
YOLEN, J/Piggins. /1987/K-3/4 KG779 . . . . **E**
Mythology SEE ALSO Animals, Mythical; Folklore; Heroes; Indians of North
  America--Religion and mythology.
Mythology.
BIERHORST, J/Mythology of North America. /1985/
  5-A/KA392 . . . . **REF 291.1**
GANERI, A/Out of the ark: stories from the world's religions. /
  1996/3-6/5 KA729 . . . . **291.1**
GODDESSES, HEROES, AND SHAMANS: THE YOUNG PEOPLE'S
  GUIDE TO WORLD MYTHOLOY. /1994/4-6/KA393 . . **REF 291.1**
HAMILTON, V/In the beginning: creation stories from around the
  world. /1988/5-6/4 KA731 . . . . **291.2**
MCCAUGHREAN, G/Golden hoard: myths and legends of the
  world. /1996/2-5/7 KB344 . . . . **398.2**
  Silver treasure: myths and legends of the world. /1996/
  K-6/6 KB345 . . . . **398.2**
PHILIP, N/Illustrated book of myths: tales and legends of the world.
  /1995/5-A/KA394 . . . . **REF 291.1**
WALDHERR, K/Book of goddesses. /1995/4-6/8 KA732 . . . **291.2**
Mythology--Fiction.
ALEXANDER, L/Arkadians. /1995/5-A/5 KG832 . . . . **Fic**
Mythology, Greek.
ALIKI /Gods and goddesses of Olympus. /1994/
  4-5/5 KA733 . . . . **292**
BULFINCH, T/Book of myths: selections from Bulfinch's Age of fable.
  /c1942/A/9 KA734. . . . . **292**
CLIMO, S/Atalanta's race: a Greek myth. /1995/
  3-6/4 KA735 . . . . **292**
COLUM, P/Golden fleece and the heroes who lived before Achilles.
  /c1949/5-6/6 KA736 . . . . **292**
CRAFT, MC/Cupid and Psyche. /1996/4-5/6 KA737. . . . . . . **292**
D'AULAIRE, I/Ingri and Edgar Parin d'Aulaire's Book of Greek
  myths. /c1962/2-6/7 KA738 . . . . **CE 292**
FISHER, LE/Cyclops. /1991/1-6/4 KA739 . . . . **292**
  Olympians: great gods and goddesses of Ancient Greece. /1984/
  5-6/7 KA740 . . . . **292**
  Theseus and the Minotaur. /1988/5-6/6 KA741 . . . . **292**
GERINGER, L/Pomegranate seeds: a classic Greek myth. /1995/
  3-6/5 KA742 . . . . **292**
GREEK MYTHS (SOUND RECORDING CASSETTE). /1989/
  5-/KA743 . . . . **SRC 292**
HUTTON, W/Persephone. /1994/5-6/5 KA744 . . . . **292**
  Perseus. /1993/5-6/4 KA745 . . . . **292**
  Theseus and the Minotaur. /1989/5-6/6 KA746. . . . . **292**
  Trojan horse. /1992/2-5/5 KE124 . . . . **883**
LASKY, K/Hercules: the man, the myth, the hero. /1997/
  5-6/4 KA747 . . . . **292**
MCCAUGHREAN, G/Greek myths. /1993/4-6/6 KA748 . . . . **292**
PEGASUS (VIDEOCASSETTE). /1990/3-6/KA749 . . . . **VCR 292**

PHILIP, N/Adventures of Odysseus. /1997/3-6/5 KE125 . . . . **883**
ROCKWELL, AF/One-eyed giant and other monsters from the Greek
  myths. /1996/2-5-6 KA750 . . . . **292**
  Robber baby: stories from the Greek myths. /1994/
  3-6/6 KA751 . . . . **292**
SHE AND HE: ADVENTURES IN MYTHOLOGY (SOUND
  RECORDING CASSETTE). /1991/5-6/KA752. . . . . . . **SRC 292**
SUTCLIFF, R/Black ships before Troy: the story of the Iliad. /1993/
  5-A/8 KE127 . . . . **883**
  Wanderings of Odysseus: the story of the Odyssey. /1996/
  5-A/7 KE128 . . . . **883**
SWITZER, E/Greek myths: gods, heroes and monsters, their sources,
  their stories and their meanings. /1988/6-A/KA395 . . . . **REF 292**
WALDHERR, K/Persephone and the pomegranate: a myth from
  Greece. /1993/4-6/6 KA753 . . . . **292**
YOLEN, J/Wings. /c1991, 1997/5-6/4 KA754 . . . . **292**
Mythology, Greek--Cartoons and comics.
WILLIAMS, M/Iliad and the Odyssey. /1996/3-6/8 KE129. . . **883**
Mythology, Greek--Fiction.
DEXTER, C/Doll who knew the future. /1994/4-6/6 KH072 . . . **Fic**
WELLS, R/Max and Ruby's first Greek myth: Pandora's box. /
  1993/P-1/3 KG700 . . . . **E**
  Max and Ruby's Midas: another Greek myth. /1995/
  P-1/3 KG701 . . . . **E**
Mythology, Hindu.
KRISHNASWAMI, U/Broken tusk: stories of the Hindu god
  Ganesha. /1996/3-4/4 KA764 . . . . **294.5**
SHEPARD, A/Savitri: a tale of ancient India. /1992/
  3-4/4 KA766 . . . . **294.5**
Mythology, Norse.
CLIMO, S/Stolen thunder: a Norse myth. /1994/
  4-5/5 KA755 . . . . **293**
OSBORNE, MP/Favorite Norse myths. /1996/4-6/6 KA756 . . **293**
PHILIP, N/Odin's family: myths of the Vikings. /1996/
  3-A/6 KA757 . . . . **293**
Nailling, Lee.
WARREN, A/Orphan train rider: one boy's true story. /1996/
  4-6/8 KB015 . . . . **362.73**
Naked mole rat.
JARROW, G/Naked mole-rats. /1996/4-6/7 KC744 . . . . . **599.35**
Names, Geographical--States.
SHEARER, BF/State names, seals, flags, and symbols: a historical
  guide. Rev. and expanded ed. /1994/4-A/KA493 . . . . . **REF 973**
Names, Personal.
SANDERS, M/What's your name?: from Ariel to Zoe. /1995/
  K-3/2 KE611 . . . . **929.4**
Names, Personal--Fiction.
DUFFEY, B/Virtual Cody. /1997/1-4/2 KH088 . . . . **Fic**
HENKES, K/Chrysanthemum. /1991/K-2/2 KF703 . . . . **E**
Names, Personal--Folklore.
BRYAN, A/Turtle knows your name. /1989/K-3/6 KB545. . **398.24**
MOSEL, A/Tikki Tikki Tembo. /1967/P-2/5 KB759 . . . . . . **398.27**
Names, Personal, in literature--Dictionaries.
TUTEN-PUCKETT, KE/My name in books: a guide to character
  names in children's literature. /1993//KA360 . . . . **PROF 809**
Namibia--Description and travel.
BRANDENBURG, J/Sand and fog: adventures in Southern Africa. /
  1994/5-6/6 KE740 . . . . **968.81**
Nanticoke Indians--Fiction.
MITCHELL, B/Red Bird. /1996/1-3/4 KG145 . . . . **E**
Nantucket (Mass.)--Fiction.
TURKLE, B/Thy friend, Obadiah. /c1969/K-3/5 KG623 . . . . . . **E**
Narcotics, Control of.
WAX, W/Say no and know why: kids learn about drugs. /1992/
  5-6/5 KA999 . . . . **362.29**
Narrative poetry.
BORNSTEIN, H/Night before Christmas: told in sign language: an
  adaptation of the original /1994/K-6/KD917 . . . . **811**
LIVINGSTON, MC/Abraham Lincoln: a man for all the people: a
  ballad. /1993/K-3/KD974 . . . . **811**
  Keep on singing: a ballad of Marian Anderson. /1994/
  1-3/KD977 . . . . **811**
LONGFELLOW, HW/Hiawatha. /1983/P-A/KD979 . . . . . . **CE 811**
  Paul Revere's ride. /1990/3-A/KD980 . . . . **CE 811**
MOORE, CC/Grandma Moses Night before Christmas. /1991/
  P-A/KD987 . . . . **811**
  Twas the night before Christmas: a visit from St. Nicholas. /c1912,
  1992/P-A/KD988 . . . . **811**
POE, EA/Annabel Lee. /1987/3-6/KD997 . . . . **811**
WHITTIER, JG/Barbara Frietchie. /1992/1-3/KE040 . . . . . . **811**
Nashua River (Mass. and N.H.)--History.
CHERRY, L/River ran wild: an environmental history. /1992/
  4-6/6 KE937 . . . . **974.4**

National Civil Rights Museum.
DUNCAN, AF/National Civil Rights Museum celebrates everyday people. /1995/3-6/8 KA903 . . . . 323.1
National Football League.
LACE, WW/Top 10 football quarterbacks. /1994/ 3-6/4 KD783 . . . . 796.332
Top 10 football rushers. /1994/3-6/4 KD784 . . . . 796.332
National Hockey League.
DUPLACEY, J/Amazing forwards. /1996/4-6/6 KD838 . . 796.962
Great goalies. /1996/4-6/6 KD839 . . . . 796.962
Top rookies. /1996/4-6/6 KD840 . . . . 796.962
National monuments SEE ALSO names of specific monuments e.g. Vietnam Veterans Memorial (Washington, D.C.).
National monuments.
FISHER, LE/Statue of Liberty. /1985/5-6/7 KD400 735
MAESTRO, B/Story of the Statue of Liberty. /1986/ P-3/6 KD401 735
National monuments--Guides.
AMERICA'S WESTERN NATIONAL PARKS (VIDEOCASSETTE). / 1990/4-6/KE200. VCR 917.804
National Museum of Natural History.
THOMSON, P/Auks, rocks and the odd dinosaur: inside stories from the Smithsonian's Museum of Natural History. /1985/ 3-A/7 KB914 508
National parks and reserves SEE ALSO names of national parks e.g. Yellowstone National Park.
National parks and reserves.
GRAND CANYON OF THE COLORADO (VIDEOCASSETTE). / 1983/5-A/KF069 . . . . VCR 979.1
KIDS EXPLORE AMERICA'S NATIONAL PARKS (VIDEOCASSETTE). /1991/3-6/KE191 . . . . VCR 917.304
PATENT, DH/Places of refuge: our national wildlife refuge system. / 1992/4-6/7 KA966 . . . . 333.95
STAUB, FJ/Yellowstone's cycle of fire. /1993/4-6/8 KC306 . 577.2
National parks and reserves--Fiction.
WOOD, A/Bunyans. /1996/1-5/6 KG760 . . . . E
National parks and reserves--Guides.
AMERICA'S WESTERN NATIONAL PARKS (VIDEOCASSETTE). / 1990/4-6/KE200. VCR 917.804
National parks and reserves--Periodicals.
NATIONAL PARKS. /1919-/5-A/KA531 . . . . PER 050
National parks and reserves--Tanzania.
LINDBLAD, L/Serengeti migration: Africa's animals on the move. / 1994/5-6/10 KC497 . . . . 591.96
PETERS, LW/Serengeti. /1989/4-6/6 KE738 . . . . 967.8
National songs.
PATRIOTIC SONGS AND MARCHES (SOUND RECORDING CASSETTE). /1991/K-6/KD582 . . . . SRC 789.2
National songs--Canada.
HARRISON, T/O Canada. /1993/3-6/6 KE802 971
National songs--United States.
BATES, KL/America the beautiful. /1993/K-3/KD558 . . . . . 789.2
ST. PIERRE, S/Our national anthem. /1992/4-A/6 KD598 . . 789.2
Native Americans SEE Indians of North America; and names of individual Indian tribes.
Natural disasters.
OTFINOSKI, S/Blizzards. /1994/4-6/7 KB036 . . . . 363.34
ROZENS, A/Floods. /1994/4-6/7 KB037 . . . . 363.34
SPIES, KB/Earthquakes. /1994/4-6/7 KB038 . . . . 363.34
VOGEL, CG/Great Midwest flood. /1995/4-6/9 KB034 . . . 363.3
Shock waves through Los Angeles: the Northridge earthquake. / 1996/3-6/10 KB039 . . . . 363.34
WOOD, L/Fires. /1994/4-6/7 KB042. . . . . 363.37
Natural disasters--Fiction.
CALHOUN, M/Flood. /1997/1-3/2 KF332 . . . . E
Natural history SEE ALSO Aquariums; Biology; Botany; Fossils; Freshwater biology; Geology; Marine biology; Mineralogy; Smithsonian Institution; Zoology.
Natural history.
DUNCAN, BK/Explore the wild: a nature search-and-find book. / 1996/2-6/7 KC358 . . . . 578.7
GRAHAM-BARBER, L/Toad or frog, swamp or bog?: a big book of nature's confusables. /1994/K-4/4 KB906 508
HILLER, I/Young naturalist, from Texas Parks and Wildlife Magazine. /1983/3-A/9 KB907 508
LIVING WORLD. /1993/5-A/KA437 . . . . REF 508
NEW BOOK OF POPULAR SCIENCE. REV. ED. /1998/ 5-8/KA433 . . . . REF 503
STOKES, DW/Guide to nature in winter, northeast and north central North America. /c1976, 1979/6-A/8 KB921. . . . . 508.2
Natural history--Alaska.
HOSHINO, M/Grizzly bear family book. /1994/ 4-6/6 KC859 . . . . 599.784

SIY, A/Arctic National Wildlife Refuge. /1991/ 6-A/6 KC337 . . . . 577.5
Natural history--Amazon River Region.
ADVENTURE IN THE AMAZON. /1992/4-6/7 KE211 . . . 918.1
GILLILAND, JH/River. /1993/K-3/3 KC317 . . . . 577.34
MURRAY, P/Amazon. /1994/3-6/7 KE212 . . . . 918.1
Natural history--Antarctica.
MCMILLAN, B/Summer ice: life along the Antarctic Peninsula. / 1995/A/8 KE216 . . . . 919.8
Natural history--Australia.
BAKER, J/Story of rosy dock. /1995/K-4/6 KF115 994
Natural history--Chesapeake Bay (Md. and Va.).
MILLS, P/On an island in the bay. /1994/2-4/3 KE979 . . . . 975.5
Natural history--Florida--Everglades.
GEORGE, JC/Everglades. /1995/2-5/7 KE991 . . . . 975.9
MURRAY, P/Everglades. /1993/3-6/6 KE195 . . . . 917.59
Natural history--Galapagos Islands.
MYERS, LB/Galapagos: islands of change. /1995/ 4-A/8 KF113 . . . . 986.6
Natural history--Guides.
AMOS, WH/Atlantic and Gulf coasts. /1985/A/KC345. . . 577.69
BROWN, L/Grasslands. /1985/A/KC330 . . . . 577.4
MACMAHON, J/Deserts. /1985/A/KC338 . . . . 577.54
MCCONNAUGHEY, BH/Pacific coast. /1985/A/KC296 577
WHITNEY, S/Western forests. /1985/A/KC313 . . . . 577.3
Natural history--Maine.
MURPHY, J/Into the deep forest with Henry David Thoreau. /1995/ 5-A/7 KE929 . . . . 974.1
Natural history--Minnesota.
BOWEN, B/Gathering: a northwoods counting book. /1995/ 1-3/3 KB953 . . . . 513.2
Natural history--Miscellanea.
ABC'S OF NATURE: A FAMILY ANSWER BOOK. /1984/ P-A/KB900 508
WEBER, L/Backyard almanac. /1996/3-A/7 KB915 508
Natural history--Namibia.
BRANDENBURG, J/Sand and fog: adventures in Southern Africa. / 1994/5-6/6 KE740 . . . . 968.81
Natural history--Nepal.
HIMALAYAN ADVENTURE (VIDEOCASSETTE). /1994/ K-6/KE712 . . . . VCR 954.96
Natural history--Outdoor books.
DUENSING, E/Talking to fireflies, shrinking the moon: nature activities for all ages. /1997//KA288 . . . . PROF 508
MILORD, S/Kids' nature book: 365 indoor/outdoor activities and experiences. Rev. ed. /1996/4/6 KB910 508
Natural history--Periodicals.
NATURAL HISTORY. /1900-/A/KA533 . . . . PER 050
Natural history--Polar regions.
ARCTIC AND ANTARCTIC (VIDEOCASSETTE). /1996/ 4-6/KE213 . . . . VCR 919.8
Natural history--Study and teaching.
HILLMAN, LE/Nature puzzlers. /1989//KA289 . . . . . . PROF 508
Natural history--Vermont.
ARNOSKY, J/Nearer nature. /1996/A/6 KE933 . . . . 974.3
Natural monuments--Fiction.
WOOD, A/Bunyans. /1996/1-5/6 KG760 . . . . E
Natural resources SEE ALSO Conservation of natural resources; Fisheries; Forests and forestry; Marine resources; Mines and mineral resources; Power resources; Water resources development; Water supply.
Natural resources.
BLASHFIELD, JF/Too many people? /1992/A/7 KA815 . . . . 304.6
Natural resources--Periodicals.
NATIONAL WILDLIFE. /1962-/A/KA532 . . . . PER 050
Natural selection SEE ALSO Evolution; Heredity.
Naturalists.
ANDERSON, MJ/Charles Darwin: naturalist. /1994/ 5-A/4 KE314 . . . . B DARWIN, C.
FABER, D/Great lives: nature and the environment. /1991/ 5-A/7 KB903 508
GEORGE, JC/Tarantula in my purse and 172 other wild pets. / 1996/4-6/4 KE366 . . . . B GEORGE, J.
NADEN, CJ/John Muir: saving the wilderness. /1992/ 5-6/4 KE473 . . . . B MUIR, J.
RING, E/Henry David Thoreau: in step with nature. /1993/ 2-5/3 KE565 . . . . B THOREAU, H.
TWIST, C/Charles Darwin: on the trail of evolution. /1994/ 5-8/8 KE315 . . . . B DARWIN, C.
WADSWORTH, G/John Burroughs, the sage of Slabsides. /1997/ A/7 KE271 . . . . B BURROUGHS, J.
Naturalists--Biography.
KEENE, AT/Earthkeepers: observers and protectors of nature. / 1994/5-A/KA436 . . . . REF 508

Naturalization--Fiction.

HEROLD, MR/Very important day. /1995/K-3/2 KF715. . . . . . . **E**

Nature.

FLORIAN, D/Nature walk. /1989/P-1/KB922 . . . . **508.3**

QUINLAN, SE/Case of the mummified pigs and other mysteries in nature. /1995/4-A/7 KB911 . . . . **508**

ROTNER, S/Nature spy. /1992/P-1/4 KB912 . . . . **508**

Nature--Fiction.

DE COTEAU ORIE, S/Did you hear Wind sing your name?: an Oneida song of spring. /1995/K-2/3 KF454. . . . . **E**

DEXTER, C/Gertie's green thumb. /1995/3-5/4 KH073 . . . . . . **Fic**

GEORGE, JC/Dear Rebecca, winter is here. /1993/ 1-3/3 KF605 . . . . **E**

HINES, AG/What Joe saw. /1994/K-2/3 KF730 . . . . **E**

LAPOINTE, C/Out of sight! Out of mind! /1995/1-3/1 KF945. . . **E**

LOMONACO, P/Night letters. /1996/K-3/3 KG018 . . . . **E**

LONDON, J/Fireflies, fireflies, light my way. /1996/ P-2/2 KG020 . . . . **E**

Gray Fox. /c1993, 1995/K-2/5 KG023 . . . . **E**

SHULEVITZ, U/Dawn. /1974/K-2/2 KG498. . . . . **E**

WOLFF, A/Stella and Roy. /1993/P-1/3 KG756 . . . . **E**

WOOD, D/Old Turtle. /1992/3-5/3 KH879 . . . . **CE Fic**

ZOLOTOW, C/When the wind stops. Rev. and newly illustrated ed. /1995/K-2/4 KG809 . . . . **E**

Nature--Miscellanea.

GATES, P/Nature got there first. /1995/4-8/10 KB905 . . . . . **508**

Nature--Poetry.

EARTH IS PAINTED GREEN: A GARDEN OF POEMS ABOUT OUR PLANET. /1994/3-6/KD883 . . . . **808.81**

FROST, R/You come too: favorite poems for young readers. / c1959, 1987/5-6/KD943 . . . . **811**

GHIGNA, C/Tickle Day: poems from Father Goose. /1994/ P-1/KD944. . . . . **811**

LEWIS, JP/Black swan/white crow: haiku. /1995/3-6/KD971 . **811**

July is a mad mosquito. /1994/P-3/KD972 . . . . **811**

SNOW TOWARD EVENING: A YEAR IN A RIVER VALLEY: NATURE POEMS. /1995/2-6/KE082 . . . . **811.008**

TURNER, A/Moon for seasons. /1994/3-6/KE034 . . . . **811**

Nature--Songs and music.

ELLIOTT, D/Crawdads, doodlebugs and creasy greens: songs, stories and lore celebrating the /1996/3-5/KB291. . . . . **CD 398.2**

ZEITLIN, P/Spin, spider, spin: songs for a greater appreciation of nature (Sound recording cassette). /1974/P-1/KB916 . . . **SRC 508**

Nature conservation SEE ALSO Conservation of natural resources.

Nature conservation.

KEENE, AT/Earthkeepers: observers and protectors of nature. / 1994/5-A/KA436 . . . . **REF 508**

Nature craft.

CARLSON, L/EcoArt!: earth-friendly art and craft experiences for 3-to 9-year olds. /1993/K-4/KD425 . . . . **745.5**

DIEHN, G/Kid style nature crafts: 50 terrific things to make with nature's materials. /1995/4-8/6 KD428 . . . . **745.5**

Nature crafts for kids. /1992/4-6/6 KD429. . . . . **745.5**

DRAKE, J/Kids' summer handbook. /1994/3-6/6 KD678 . . . **790.1**

Nature photography.

HOBAN, T/Look book. /1997/P-K/KD516 . . . . **779**

Nature study.

ARNOSKY, J/Secrets of a wildlife watcher. /c1983, 1991/ 5-6/7 KC580 . . . . **596**

BJORK, C/Linnea's almanac. /c1982, 1989/2-6/6 KB879 . . . **507**

BOWDEN, M/Nature for the very young: a handbook of indoor and outdoor activities. /1989//KA199. . . . . **PROF 372.3**

BRANLEY, FM/Snow is falling. Rev. ed. /1986/ K-1/2 KC210 . . . . **551.57**

BUSCH, PS/Backyard safaris: 52 year-round science adventures. / 1995/P-A/5 KB901 . . . . **508**

EARTH'S SEASONS/CLIMATES (VIDEOCASSETTE). /1995/ 3-6/KB902. . . . . **VCR 508**

LESLIE, CW/Nature all year long. /1991/1-5/6 KB908 . . . . . **508**

MARSH: NATURE'S NURSERY (VIDEOCASSETTE). /1988/ 2-4/KC343. . . . . **VCR 577.68**

MILORD, S/Kids' nature book: 365 indoor/outdoor activities and experiences. Rev. ed. /1996/K-A/KB910 . . . . **508**

SEEING THINGS (VIDEOCASSETTE). /1987/ K-3/KB913. . . . . **VCR 508**

STOKES, DW/Guide to nature in winter, northeast and north central North America. /c1976, 1979/6-A/8 KB921. . . . . **508.2**

Nature study--Activity programs.

DUENSING, E/Talking to fireflies, shrinking the moon: nature activities for all ages. /1997//KA288 . . . . **PROF 508**

Nature study--Fiction.

GEORGE, JC/My side of the mountain. /c1959/5-6/6 KH159 . **Fic**

Nature study--Periodicals.

CHICKADEE: THE CANADIAN MAGAZINE FOR YOUNG CHILDREN. /1979-/P-3/KA506 . . . . **PER 050**

OWL: THE DISCOVERY MAGAZINE FOR CHILDREN. /1976-/ 2-4/KA535 . . . . **PER 050**

RANGER RICK. /1967/K-3/KA538 . . . . **PER 050**

WILDLIFE CONSERVATION. /1897-/K-A/KA551 . . . . . . **PER 050**

Nature study--Software.

MICROSOFT EXPLORAPEDIA: THE WORLD OF NATURE. ACADEMIC ED. (CD-ROM). /1995/1-4/KB909. . . . . . . **CDR 508**

Nature study--Songs and music.

AXELROD, G/Songs of nature and environment (Sound recording cassette). /1978/1-3/KC293 . . . . **SRC 577**

Navaho Indians See Navajo Indians.

Navajo Indians.

DAILY, R/Code talkers: American Indians in World War II. /1995/ 4-6/9 KE669 . . . . **940.54**

SNEVE, V/Navajos. /1993/4-6/6 KE773 . . . . **970.3**

TAPAHONSO, L/Navajo ABC: a Dine alphabet book. /1995/ 2-4/KE797 . . . . **970.49**

Navajo Indians--Biography.

HERMANN, S/R.C. Gorman: Navajo artist. /1995/ 3-5/3 KE375 . . . . **B GORMAN, R.C.**

THOMSON, P/Katie Henio: Navajo sheepherder. /1995/ 5-6/6 KE796 . . . . **970.489**

Navajo Indians--Fiction.

O'DELL, S/Sing down the moon. /c1970/5-6/3 KH562 . . . **CE Fic**

Navajo Indians--Folklore.

DUNCAN, L/Magic of Spider Woman. /1996/ 4-5/6 KB733 . . . . **398.27**

HAUSMAN, G/Eagle boy: a traditional Navajo legend. /1996/ 3-4/5 KB587 . . . . **398.24**

JACKSON, E/Precious gift: a Navaho creation myth. /1996/ 2-3/2 KB594 . . . . **398.24**

OUGHTON, J/Magic weaver of rugs: a tale of the Navajo. /1994/ 2-4/3 KB627 . . . . **398.24**

ROESSEL, M/Songs from the loom: a Navajo girl learns to weave. /1995/4-6/6 KE799 . . . . **970.491**

Navajo Indians--Industries--Fiction.

BLOOD, CL/Goat in the rug. /1990/K-3/6 KF234 . . . . **E**

Navajo Indians--Rites and ceremonies.

ROESSEL, M/Kinaalda: a Navajo girl grows up. /1993/ 4-6/5 KE789 . . . . **970.48**

Navajo Indians--Social life and customs.

ROESSEL, M/Songs from the loom: a Navajo girl learns to weave. /1995/4-6/6 KE799 . . . . **970.491**

THOMSON, P/Katie Henio: Navajo sheepherder. /1995/ 5-6/6 KE796 . . . . **970.489**

Navajo language--Glossaries, vocabularies, etc.

TAPAHONSO, L/Navajo ABC: a Dine alphabet book. /1995/ 2-4/KE797 . . . . **970.49**

Navajo textile fabrics.

ROESSEL, M/Songs from the loom: a Navajo girl learns to weave. /1995/4-6/6 KE799 . . . . **970.491**

Navigation--History.

LATHAM, JL/Carry on, Mr. Bowditch. /c1955/ 5-A/3 KE260 . . . . **CE B BOWDITCH, N.**

NCTM Standards.

PERRY, PJ/Guide to math materials: resources to support the NCTM standards. /1997//KA256 . . . . **PROF 372.7**

Near East SEE Middle East.

Neatness SEE Cleanliness.

Nebraska--Fiction.

BUNTING, E/Dandelions. /1995/3-5/2 KG942 . . . . **Fic**

CONRAD, P/Prairie songs. /1985/5-A/7 KH023 . . . . **Fic**

CROSS, G/Great American elephant chase. /1993/ 6-A/6 KH043 . . . . **Fic**

Nebraska--History.

WILLS, CA/Historical album of Nebraska. /1994/ 4-6/7 KF055 . . . . **978.2**

Needlework SEE Sewing.

Negro leagues--History.

MCKISSACK, P/Black diamond: the story of the Negro baseball leagues. /1994/4-6/7 KD800 . . . . **796.357**

RITTER, LS/Leagues apart: the men and times of the Negro baseball leagues. /1995/2-4/7 KD802 . . . . **796.357**

Negroes SEE Afro-Americans.

Neighborhood--Fiction.

FLEISCHMAN, P/Seedfolks. /1997/5-A/5 KH118. . . . . **Fic**

LOWRY, L/See you around, Sam! /1996/3-6/6 KH428 . . . . . . **Fic**

MCGOVERN, A/Lady in the box. /1997/1-3/2 KG103 . . . . **E**

Neighborhood--Poetry.

SOTO, G/Neighborhood odes: poems. /1992/3-A/KE029 . . . **811**

Neighborliness--Fiction.
BEDARD, M/Emily. /1992/2-5/2 KF215 . . . . **E**
BLOS, JW/Old Henry. /1987/K-3/2 KF237 . . . . **CE E**
BUNTING, E/Smoky night. /1994/2-5/2 KF309 . . . . **E**
CHRISTELOW, E/Five-dog night. /1993/1-3/3 KF386 . . . . **E**
RYLANT, C/Bookshop dog. /1996/K-2/2 KG369 . . . . . . **E**
   Mr. Putter and Tabby walk the dog. /1994/1-3/2 KG382 . . . . **E**
SCHOTTER, R/Nothing ever happens on 90th Street. /1997/
   3-5/4 KH682 . . . . **Fic**

Nelson, Rachel West.
WEBB, S/Selma, Lord, Selma: girlhood memories of the civil-rights
   days. /c1980, 1997/A/7 KA906 . . . . **323.1**

Nepal--Social life and customs.
MARGOLIES, BA/Kanu of Kathmandu: a journey in Nepal. /1992/
   3-5/6 KE713 . . . . **954.96**

Neptune (Planet).
SIMON, S/Neptune. /1991/4-6/8 KC041 . . . . **523.48**

Nervous system.
MATHERS, D/Brain. /1992/5-6/6 KC966 . . . . **612.8**
NERVOUS SYSTEM (VIDEOCASSETTE). /1994/
   5-6/KC970. . . . . **VCR 612.8**
SIMON, S/Brain: our nervous system. /1997/5-6/6 KC980 . **612.8**
Ness, Loch (Monster) SEE Loch Ness monster.

Nest building--Folklore.
FOSTER, J/Magpies' nest. /1995/1-3/3 KB567 . . . . **398.24**

Netherlands--Civilization--17th Century.
PESCIO, C/Rembrandt and seventeenth-century Holland. /1995/
   4-A/12 KD501 . . . . **759.9492**

Netherlands--Fiction.
DEJONG, M/Wheel on the school. /c1954/4-6/3 KH070 . . . . **Fic**
GREEN, NB/Hole in the dike. /c1974, 1975/K-2/2 KF640 . . **CE E**
VOS, I/Anna is still here. /1993/5-A/4 KH834 . . . . **Fic**

Netherlands--Folklore.
FISHER, LE/Kinderdike. /1994/2-4/3 KB395 . . . . **398.21**

Netherlands--History--German occupation, 1940-1945.
FRANK, A/Diary of a young girl. /c1967/
   4-6/6 KE352 . . . . **B FRANK, A.**

Netherlands--History--German Occupation, 1940-1945--Fiction.
VOS, I/Hide and seek. /c1981, 1991/5-A/4 KH835 . . . . . . **Fic**

Neurosurgeons.
SIMMONS, A/Ben Carson. /1996/4-6/7 KE276 . **B CARSON, B.**

Nevada.
LILLEGARD, D/Nevada. /1990/4-6/9 KF074 . . . . **979.3**

New Brunswick (Canada).
GANN, M/New Brunswick. /1995/5-A/9 KE820 . . . . **971.5**

New England--Fiction.
ALCOTT, LM/Little women (Talking book). /1975/
   5-A/KG830 . . . . **TB Fic**
FOX, P/Stone-faced boy. /1987/4-6/3 KH140. . . . . **Fic**
HALL, D/Ox-cart man. /1979/K-3/7 KF663. . . . . **CE E**
LEVITT, MJ/Tales of an October moon: haunting stories from New
   England /1992/4-6/KH399 . . . . **SRC Fic**
MONJO, FN/Drinking gourd. Newly illustrated ed. /1993/
   1-3/2 KG151 . . . . **E**
WIGGIN, KD/Rebecca of Sunnybrook Farm. /1994/
   5-A/6 KH857 . . . . **Fic**

New England--Social life and customs.
OLD STURBRIDGE VILLAGE (VIDEOCASSETTE). /1989/
   4-6/KE942. . . . . **VCR 974.4**
TUDOR, T/Time to keep: the Tasha Tudor book of holidays. /1996/
   P-A/4 KB204 . . . . **394.26**

New Hampshire.
BROWN, D/New Hampshire. /1993/4-6/7 KE930 . . . . . **974.2**

New Hampshire--Fiction.
BAILEY, CS/Miss Hickory. /c1946/4-6/4 KG875 . . . . **CE Fic**

New Hampshire--History--Colonial period, ca. 1600-1775.
FRADIN, DB/New Hampshire Colony. /1988/5-6/9 KE931 . . **974.2**

New Jersey.
FREDEEN, C/New Jersey. /1993/4-6/5 KE964 . . . . **974.9**
MIDDLE ATLANTIC REGION: NEW YORK, NEW JERSEY,
   DELAWARE, MARYLAND, PENNSYLVANIA, /1996/
   4-6/KE924. . . . . **VCR 974**

New Jersey--Fiction.
BLUME, J/Are you there God? It's me, Margaret. /c1970, 1982/
   4-6/5 KG905 . . . . **CE Fic**
ROBERTSON, K/Henry Reed, Inc. (Talking book). /1973/
   4-6/KH637. . . . . **TB Fic**
   Henry Reed's baby-sitting service. /c1966/4-6/6 KH638. . . . . **Fic**

New Jersey--History.
TOPPER, F/Historical album of New Jersey. /1995/
   4-6/7 KE965 . . . . **974.9**

New Jersey--History--Colonial period, ca. 1600-1775.
FRADIN, DB/New Jersey Colony. /1991/5-6/7 KE963 . . . . **974.9**

New Jersey--History--Colonial period, ca. 1600-1775--Biography.
FRADIN, DB/New Jersey Colony. /1991/5-6/7 KE963 . . . . **974.9**

New Jersey--History--Revolution, 1775-1783.
FRADIN, DB/New Jersey Colony. /1991/5-6/7 KE963 . . . . **974.9**

New Jersey--History--Revolution, 1775-1783--Biography.
FRADIN, DB/New Jersey Colony. /1991/5-6/7 KE963 . . . . **974.9**

New Jersey--History--Revolution, 1775-1783--Fiction.
GAUCH, PL/This time, Tempe Wick? /c1974, 1992/
   3-5/7 KH153 . . . . **Fic**

New Mexico.
SOUTH CENTRAL REGION: TEXAS, NEW MEXICO, OKLAHOMA
   (VIDEOCASSETTE). /1995/3-5/KE995 . . . . **VCR 976**

New Mexico--Biography.
DEWEY, JO/Cowgirl dreams: a western childhood. /1995/
   3-4/4 KE320 . . . . **B DEWEY, J.**

New Mexico--Fiction.
ANAYA, R/Farolitos of Christmas. /1995/3-6/2 KG845 . . . . . . **Fic**
KRUMGOLD, J/And now Miguel. /1953/6-A/5 KH382 . . . **CE Fic**
STEVENS, JR/Carlos and the skunk./Carlos y el zorrillo. /1997/
   1-3/3 KG554 . . . . **E**

New Mexico--Folklore.
HAYES, J/Watch out for clever women!/Cuidado con las mujeres
   astutas!: Hispanic folktales. /1994/2-5/4 KB315 . . . . **398.2**
HULPACH, V/Ahaiyute and Cloud Eater. /1996/
   3-4/5 KB708 . . . . **398.26**

New Mexico--Social life and customs.
ANDERSON, J/Cowboys: roundup on an American ranch. /1996/
   3-5/6 KF025 . . . . **978**

New Orleans (La.)--Race relations.
COLES, R/Story of Ruby Bridges. /1995/2-5/4 KA902 . . . . **323.1**

New Year.
BERNHARD, E/Happy New Year! /1996/1-3/7 KB205 . . **394.261**
NEW YEAR'S DAY (VIDEOCASSETTE). /1994/
   1-4/KB213. . . . . **VCR 394.261**

New Year--Fiction.
LEWIS, PO/P. Bear's New Year's party!: a counting book. /1989/
   K-1/3 KF978 . . . . **E**

New York (N.Y.).
JAKOBSEN, K/My New York. /1993/2-5/3 KE957 . . . . . . **974.7**
KENT, D/New York City. /1996/3-5/8 KE958 . . . . **974.7**

New York (N.Y.)--Fiction.
BARRACCA, D/Adventures of taxi dog. /1990/P-2/2 KF200 **CE E**
BARTONE, E/American too. /1996/1-3/3 KF210 . . . . **E**
   Peppe the lamplighter. /1993/1-3/2 KF211 . . . . **E**
COWLEY, J/Gracias, the Thanksgiving turkey. /1996/
   K-2/1 KF430 . . . . **E**
DORROS, A/Abuela. /1991/P-2/2 KF488 . . . . **E**
   Abuela (Videocassette). /1994/P-2/KF489 . . . . . . **VCR E**
ENRIGHT, E/Saturdays. /c1941, 1988/4-6/5 KH099 . . . . **Fic**
FOX, P/Monkey island. /1991/6-A/6 KH137. . . . . **Fic**
GRAY, L/Falcon's egg. /1995/5-A/6 KH195 . . . . **Fic**
HARVEY, B/Immigrant girl: Becky of Eldridge Street. /1987/
   3-5/5 KH221 . . . . **Fic**
HEROLD, MR/Very important day. /1995/K-3/2 KF715 . . . . . . **E**
HOLMAN, F/Slake's limbo. /1974/6-A/7 KH274 . . . . . . **CE Fic**
KONIGSBURG, EL/Jennifer, Hecate, Macbeth, William McKinley,
   and me, Elizabeth. /c1967/3-6/4 KH374 . . . . **CE Fic**
LEVOY, M/Witch of Fourth Street, and other stories. /c1972/
   4-6/7 KH400 . . . . **Fic**
   Witch of Fourth Street and other stories (Kit). /1978/
   4-6/KH401. . . . . **KIT Fic**
NEVILLE, EC/It's like this, Cat. /c1963/5-6/6 KH547 . . . . . **CE Fic**
SACHS, M/Call me Ruth. /c1982, 1995/5-A/6 KH667 . . . . . . **Fic**
   Truth about Mary Rose /1995/5-A/6 KH669 . . . . **Fic**
SCHECTER, E/Big idea. /1996/3-5/2 KH679 . . . . **Fic**
SELDEN, G/Chester Cricket's pigeon ride. /1983/
   3-4/5 KH693 . . . . **Fic**
   Cricket in Times Square. /c1960/4-6/6 KH694. . . . . . **CE Fic**
   Genie of Sutton Place. /c1973/4-6/7 KH695. . . . . **Fic**
   Harry Kitten and Tucker Mouse. /1986/2-4/4 KH696 . . . . **Fic**
SHREVE, S/Amy Dunn quits school. /1993/5-A/7 KH706 . . . **Fic**
STOLZ, M/Noonday friends. /c1965/4-6/6 KH767 . . . . . **CE Fic**
TAYLOR, S/All-of-a-kind family. /1951, 1988/4-6/5 KH782 . . . **Fic**
WABER, B/Lyle, Lyle, crocodile. /c1965/P-2/3 KG672 . . . . . **CE E**
WHITE, EB/Stuart Little. /c1945/3-6/5 KH851 . . . . **Fic**
WILLARD, N/Beauty and the Beast. /1992/4-A/6 KH862 . . . **Fic**

New York (N.Y.) Metropolitan Museum of Art--Fiction.
KONIGSBURG, EL/From the mixed-up files of Mrs. Basil E.
   Frankweiler. /c1967/4-6/7 KH373 . . . . **CE Fic**

New York (State).
FRADIN, DB/New York. /1993/4-6/3 KE955. . . . . **974.7**
MIDDLE ATLANTIC REGION: NEW YORK, NEW JERSEY,
   DELAWARE, MARYLAND, PENNSYLVANIA, /1996/
   4-6/KE924. . . . . **VCR 974**

New York (State)--Biography.
FRADIN, DB/New York Colony. /1988/5-6/8 KE956 . . . . . **974.7**
New York (State)--Fiction.
IRVING, W/Legend of Sleepy Hollow. /c1928, 1990/
6-A/9 KH314 . . . . **Fic**
   Rip Van Winkle. /1987/4-A/9 KH315 . . . . **Fic**
   Rip Van Winkle and, The Legend of Sleepy Hollow (Talking
   book). /1986/5-6/KH316 . . . . **TB Fic**
WILDER, LI/Farmer boy. /c1953/3-6/5 KH859. . . . . . **Fic**
New York (State)--History.
AVAKIAN, M/Historical album of New York. /1993/
5-6/8 KE954 . . . . **974.7**
New York (State)--History--Colonial period, ca. 1600-1775.
FRADIN, DB/New York Colony. /1988/5-6/8 KE956 . . . . . **974.7**
New York (State)--History--Revolution, 1775-1783.
FRADIN, DB/New York Colony. /1988/5-6/8 KE956 . . . . . **974.7**
New York Mets (Baseball team).
JENNINGS, J/Long shots: they beat the odds. /1990/
5-6/6 KD762 . . . . **796**
New Zealand--Fiction.
GEE, M/Fire-raiser. /1992/6-A/6 KH155 . . . . **Fic**
HILL, D/Take it easy. /1997/6-A/4 KH260 . . . . **Fic**
LATTIMORE, DN/Punga, the goddess of ugly. /1993/
3-5/4 KF950 . . . . **E**
MAHY, M/Fortune branches out. /c1994, 1995/3-5/4 KH447. . **Fic**
   Good Fortunes gang. /1993/3-5/7 KH448 . . . . **Fic**
New Zealand--Folklore.
BISHOP, G/Maui and the Sun: a Maori tale. /1996/
3-4/3 KB700 . . . . **398.26**
Newbery Medal--Bibliography.
GILLESPIE, JT/Newbery companion: booktalk and related materials
for Newbery Medal and Honor Books. /1996/
/KA035. . . . . **PROF 016.813**
Newbery Medal books.
AMMON, BD/Handbook for the Newbery Medal and Honor Books,
1980-1989. /1991//KA347 . . . . **PROF 809**
HORN BOOK MAGAZINE /Newbery and Caldecott medal books,
1966-1975: with acceptance papers & related material chiefly from
the Horn Book Magazine. /1975//KA352 . . . . **PROF 809**
   Newbery Medal books: 1922-1955: with their authors' acceptance
   papers, biographies, and related materials chiefly from the Horn
   Book Magazine. /c1957//KA353 . . . . **PROF 809**
NEWBERY AND CALDECOTT MEDALISTS AND HONOR BOOK
WINNERS: BIBLIOGRAPHIES AND /1992//KA004 . . . **PROF 011**
TALK WITH AVI (VIDEOCASSETTE). /1995/
5-6/KE245 . . . . **VCR B AVI**
TALK WITH BETSY BYARS (VIDEOCASSETTE). /1995/
4-6/KE273 . . . . **VCR B BYARS, B.**
Newbery Medal books--Audio-visual aids.
SHARKEY, PB/Newbery and Caldecott Medal and Honor books in
other media. /1992//KA087 . . . . **PROF 028.1**
Newbery Medal books--Periodicals.
NEWBERY AND CALDECOTT AWARDS: A GUIDE TO THE
MEDAL AND HONOR BOOKS. /n.d.//KA128 . . **PER PROF 050**
Newfoundland.
JACKSON, L/Newfoundland and Labrador. /1995/
4-6/8 KE822 . . . . **971.8**
Newfoundland dog.
PATENT, DH/Hugger to the rescue. /1994/3-6/5 KD226 . . **636.73**
Newspaper carriers--Fiction.
KROEGER, MK/Paperboy. /1996/1-3/2 KF926 . . . . **E**
PILKEY, D/Paperboy. /1996/K-2/2 KG238 . . . . **E**
PINKNEY, JB/Adventures of Sparrowboy. /1997/K-2/3 KG242. . **E**
Newspapers SEE ALSO Journalism; Mass media; Periodicals; Reporters and
reporting.
Newspapers.
COMMUNICATIONS (VIDEOCASSETTE). /1992/
2-4/KA799 . . . . **VCR 302.23**
GRANFIELD, L/Extra! extra: the who, what, where, when and why
of newspapers. /1994/3-6/5 KA596 . . . . **071**
READING THE NEWSPAPER INTELLIGENTLY (VIDEOCASSETTE). /
1995/5-6/KA801 . . . . **VCR 302.23**
Newspapers--Software.
OWENS, P/Classroom newspaper workshop (CD-ROM). /1995/
4-A/KA594 . . . . **CDR 070.4**
READER RABBIT 3 (MICROCOMPUTER PROGRAM). /1993/
1-3/KB106 . . . . **MCP 372.4**
Newton, Isaac, Sir.
ANDERSON, MJ/Isaac Newton: the greatest scientist of all time. /
1996/6-A/7 KE476 . . . . **B NEWTON, I.**
Newts--Fiction.
NOVAK, M/Newt. /1996/1-3/2 KG181 . . . . **E**
Nez Perce Indians.
ANDERSON, MK/Nez Perce. /1994/4-6/7 KE757 . . . . . . **970.3**

SNEVE, V/Nez Perce. /1994/4-6/7 KE774 . . . . **970.3**
Nez Perce Indians--Fiction.
O'DELL, S/Thunder rolling in the mountains. /1992/
5-A/5 KH563 . . . . **Fic**
Nguni (African people)--Folklore.
MOODIE, F/Nabulela: a South Africa folk tale. /1997/
2-4/4 KB758 . . . . **398.27**
Nicaragua--Folklore.
ROHMER, H/Uncle Nacho's hat: a folktale from Nicaragua/El
sombrero de Tio Nacho: /1989/2-4/2 KB770 . . . . **398.27**
Nice, Margaret Morse.
DUNLAP, J/Birds in the bushes: a story about Margaret Morse
Nice. /1996/3-5/9 KE477 . . . . **B NICE, M.**
Nicholas, Saint, Bp. of Myra--Legends.
SHEPARD, A/Baker's dozen: a Saint Nicholas tale. /1995/
K-2/4 KB487 . . . . **398.22**
Nigeria--Folklore.
BRYAN, A/Beat the story-drum, pum-pum. /1980/
4-6/4 KB542 . . . . **398.24**
DAYRELL, E/Why the sun and the moon live in the sky: an African
folktale. /c1968/K-3/6 KB704 . . . . **CE 398.26**
GERSHATOR, P/Iroko-man: a Yoruba folktale. /1994/
2-3/6 KB397 . . . . **398.21**
GERSON, M/Why the sky is far away: a Nigerian folktale. /1992/
2-4/5 KB705 . . . . **398.26**
MOLLEL, TM/Flying tortoise: an Igbo tale. /1994/
2-3/3 KB623 . . . . **398.24**
Nigeria--History.
KOSLOW, P/Yorubaland: the flowering of genius. /1996/
6-A/12 KE726 . . . . **960**
Nigeria--Poetry.
OLALEYE, I/Distant talking drum: poems from Nigeria. /1995/
K-2/KE139 . . . . **896**
Nigeria--Social life and customs.
ONYEFULU, I/Emeka's gift: an African counting story. /1995/
1-4/5 KE728 . . . . **960**
Nigeria, Eastern--Social conditions.
ONYEFULU, I/Ogbo: sharing life in an African village. /1996/
3-5/6 KE737 . . . . **966.9**
Nigerian poetry (English).
OLALEYE, I/Distant talking drum: poems from Nigeria. /1995/
K-2/KE139 . . . . **896**
Night SEE ALSO Bedtime.
Night--Fiction.
APPELT, K/Bayou lullaby. /1995/P-2/5 KF163 . . . . **E**
BANG, M/Ten, nine, eight. /1983/P-K/KF192 . . . . **E**
BONSALL, CN/Who's afraid of the dark? /1980/P-1/1 KF249 . . **E**
BROWN, MW/Child's good night book. /c1943, 1992/
P/2 KF284 . . . . **E**
   Goodnight moon. /c1947/P-K/1 KF285 . . . . **CE E**
BUNTING, E/Ghost's hour, spook's hour. /1987/P-2/2 KF301 . . **E**
DAVOL, MW/Batwings and the curtain of night. /1997/
1-3/2 KF449 . . . . **E**
GINSBURG, M/Sun's asleep behind the hill. /1982/
P-K/1 KF624 . . . . **E**
GRIFALCONI, A/Darkness and the butterfly. /1987/
K-2/4 KF645 . . . . **E**
HOWE, J/There's a monster under my bed. /1986/
P-2/2 KF781 . . . . **E**
JOHNSON, A/Joshua's night whispers (Board book). /1994/
P/2 KF830 . . . . **BB E**
LOBEL, A/Owl at home. /c1975/K-2/1 KG010 . . . . **E**
LOMONACO, P/Night letters. /1996/K-3/3 KG018 . . . . **E**
LONDON, J/Owl who became the moon. /1993/P-2/3 KG026. . **E**
MANUSHKIN, F/Peeping and sleeping. /1994/P-2/2 KG060 . . . **E**
RYAN, CD/Hildilid's night. /c1971, 1986/K-3/6 KG365. . . . . . **E**
SAMTON, SW/World from my window. /c1985, 1991/
P-K/2 KG389. . . . . **E**
STURGES, P/Ten flashing fireflies. /1995/K-2/2 KG581. . . . . . **E**
THOMAS, SM/Putting the world to sleep. /1995/P-2/2 KG606 . **E**
Night--Fiction--Software.
BERENSTAIN BEARS IN THE DARK. SCHOOL ED. (CD-ROM). /
1996/K-3/KF224 . . . . **CDR E**
Night--Poetry.
BIERHORST, J/On the road of stars: Native American night poems
and sleep charms. /1994/2-6/KE141. . . . . **897.008**
SLEEP, BABY, SLEEP: LULLABIES AND NIGHT POEMS. /1994/
P-K/KD889. . . . . **808.81**
Night work--Fiction.
GROSSMAN, P/Night ones. /1991/P-K/2 KF650 . . . . **E**
Nightingale, Florence.
ADLER, DA/Picture book of Florence Nightingale. /1992/
2-4/3 KE478 . . . . **B NIGHTINGALE**

Nightmares--Fiction.
  CROSS, G/New world. /1995/6-A/5 KH044 . . . . **Fic**
  MARTIN, JB/Grandmother Bryant's pocket. /1996/
  1-4/3 KG079 . . . . **E**
NIMH--Fiction.
  CONLY, JL/Racso and the rats of NIMH. /1986/5-6/6 KH020 . **Fic**
Nimitz (Aircraft carrier).
  BIG AIRCRAFT CARRIER (VIDEOCASSETTE). /1995/
  4-6/KA989 . . . . **VCR 359.9**
Noah (Biblical figure).
  GAUCH, PL/Noah. /1994/K-2/4 KA684. . . . . **222**
Noah (Biblical figure)--Fiction.
  GEISERT, A/After the flood. /1994/K-2/3 KF601 . . . . **E**
Noah's ark.
  JONAS, A/Aardvarks, disembark! /1990/2-A/4 KA963. . . **333.95**
  NOAH'S ARK. /c1977/P-2/KA681. . . . . **221.9**
  NOAH'S ARK (VIDEOCASSETTE). /c1989, 1996/
  P-2/KA682. . . . . **VCR 221.9**
Noah's ark--Fiction.
  WALTON, R/Noah's square dance. /1995/K-2/3 KG687. . . . . **E**
Noah's ark--Folklore.
  STEVENS, J/How the Manx cat lost its tail. /1990/
  2-3/4 KB658 . . . . **398.24**
Nocturnal animals.
  ELLIOTT, L/Guide to night sounds (Sound recording cassette). /
  1992/3-6/KC484 . . . . **SRC 591.59**
  NIGHTTIME ANIMALS (VIDEOCASSETTE). /1996/
  3-5/KC477. . . . . **VCR 591.5**
  WHAYNE, SS/Night creatures. /1993/4-6/5 KC479 . . . . . **591.5**
Noise--Fiction.
  CASELEY, J/Noisemakers. /1992/P-1/2 KF367 . . . . **E**
  COFFELT, N/Dog who cried woof. /1995/K-2/3 KF402. . . . . . **E**
  WADDELL, M/Let's go home, Little Bear. /1993/P-K/3 KG676 . . **E**
  WINTHROP, E/Very noisy girl. /1991/K-2/2 KG747 . . . . **E**
Nonbook materials.
  SHARKEY, PB/Newbery and Caldecott Medal and Honor books in
  other media. /1992//KA087 . . . . **PROF 028.1**
Nonsense verses.
  ALLIGATOR PIE (VIDEOCASSETTE). /1993/P-2/KD912   **VCR 811**
  BERENSTAIN, S/Inside, outside, upside down. /c1968/
  K-1/1 KF227 . . . . **E**
  CARROLL, L/Jabberwocky. /1992/K-2/3 KE097 . . . . **821**
  CIARDI, J/You know who, John J. Plenty and Fiddler Dan, and
  other poems (Kit). /n.d./3-5/KD924 . . . . **Kit 811**
  FLORIAN, D/Bing bang boing. /1994/3-6/KD936 . . . . **811**
  LEAR, E/Daffy down dillies: silly limericks. /1992/K-A/KE103 . **821**
  Nonsense songs. /1997/K-3/KE104 . . . . **821**
  Owl and the Pussy-cat. /1996/P-2/KE105. . . . . **821**
  Owl and the Pussy-cat and other nonsense poems. /1995/
  3-6/KE106. . . . . **821**
  PRELUTSKY, J/Ride a purple pelican. /1986/P-3/KE014. . . . . **811**
  ROSEN, M/Michael Rosen's ABC. /1996/2-4/KE109 . . . . **821**
  ROUNDS, G/I know an old lady who swallowed a fly. /1990/
  K-3/KD586 . . . . **789.2**
  SCHEER, J/Rain makes applesauce. /c1964/P-A/2 KG403 . . . . . **E**
  SENDAK, M/Pierre: a cautionary tale in five chapters and a
  prologue. /c1962/P-1/KG436 . . . . **CE E**
  SEUSS, D/And to think that I saw it on Mulberry Street. /c1937,
  1964/K-2/2 KG445. . . . . **E**
  Cat in the hat. /c1957/P-2/1 KG448. . . . . **CE E**
  Cat in the Hat gets grinched (Videocassette). /1982/
  K-2/KG449 . . . . **VCR E**
  Dr. Seuss's ABC. /c1963/P-2/2 KG451 . . . . **CE E**
  Fox in socks. /c1965/P-2/2 KG453 . . . . **E**
  Hop on pop. /c1963/P-1/1 KG455 . . . . **E**
  Horton hatches the egg. /c1940/P-3/3 KG456 . . . . **CE E**
  Horton hatches the egg./If I ran the circus (Videocassette). /
  1992/P-3/KG457 . . . . **VCR E**
  Horton hears a Who!/Thidwick the big-hearted moose
  (Videocassette). /1992/P-3/KG458 . . . . **VCR E**
  How the Grinch stole Christmas. /c1957/P-3/KG459. . . . . . . **E**
  If I ran the circus. /c1956/P-3/4 KG464 . . . . **E**
  If I ran the zoo. /1950/P-3/5 KG465 . . . . **E**
  McElligot's pool. /c1947/P-3/KG467. . . . . **E**
  One fish, two fish, red fish, blue fish. /c1960/P-1/1 KG471 . . . **E**
  WALKING THE BRIDGE OF YOUR NOSE. /1995/
  2-4/KE113. . . . . **821.008**
  WESTCOTT, NB/I know an old lady who swallowed a fly. /1980/
  P-3/KE039. . . . . **CE 811**
  Lady with the alligator purse. /1988/P-1/KB818. . . . . . . **398.8**
  YOLEN, J/Animal fare: poems. /1994/K-3/KE047. . . . . **811**
North America--Climate.
  SIMON, S/Autumn across America. /1993/4-6/7 KB918 . . . **508.2**
  Spring across America. /1996/5-8/7 KB919 . . . . **508.2**

  Winter across America. /1994/4-6/6 KB920 . . . . **508.2**
North America--Folklore.
  BRUCHAC, J/Between earth and sky: legends of Native American
  sacred places. /1996/5-A/5 KB270 . . . . **398.2**
  Boy who lived with the bears: and other Iroquois stories. /1995/
  2-4/4 KB537 . . . . **CE 398.24**
  Four ancestors: stories, songs, and poems from Native North
  America. /1996/2-6/3 KB271 . . . . **398.2**
  RODANAS, K/Eagle's song: a tale from the Pacific Northwest. /
  1995/3-4/5 KB768 . . . . **398.27**
  SPIDER SPINS A STORY: FOURTEEN LEGENDS FROM NATIVE
  AMERICA. /1997/2-5/6 KB371 . . . . **398.2**
  TAYLOR, HP/Coyote and the laughing butterflies. /1995/
  2-3/5 KB662 . . . . **398.24**
North America--Social life and customs.
  PEOPLES OF THE WORLD: NORTH AMERICANS. /1991/
  6-A/KA479 . . . . **REF 970.004**
North American porcupine.
  SHERROW, V/Porcupine. /1991/5-6/6 KC747. . . . . **599.35**
North Carolina.
  SCHULZ, A/North Carolina. /1993/4-6/7 KE983 . . . . **975.6**
North Carolina--Fiction.
  PINKNEY, GJ/Back home. /1992/1-3/4 KG240 . . . . **E**
  TAYLOR, T/Teetoncey. /c1975/5-A/5 KH784 . . . . **Fic**
  TORRENCE, J/My grandmother's treasure (Sound recording
  cassette). /1993/3-5/KH799 . . . . **SRC Fic**
North Carolina--Folklore.
  WAHL, J/Little Eight John. /1992/2-3/2 KB783 . . . . **398.27**
North Carolina--History--Colonial period. ca. 1600-1775.
  FRADIN, DB/North Carolina Colony. /1991/5-6/7 KE982 . . **975.6**
North Dakota.
  FRADIN, DB/North Dakota. /1994/4-6/3 KF057 . . . . **978.4**
North Pole--Discovery and exploration.
  STEGER, W/Over the top of the world: explorer Will Steger's trek
  across the Arctic. /1997/5-6/6 KE219. . . . . **919.8**
North Pole--Fiction.
  VAN ALLSBURG, C/Polar express. /1985/2-A/5 KH822 . . **CE Fic**
Northeastern States--Bibliography.
  EXPLORING THE NORTHEAST STATES THROUGH LITERATURE. /
  1994//KA036 . . . . **PROF 016.974**
Northern elephant seal.
  JOHNSON, SA/Elephant seals. /1989/5-6/7 KC869. . . . . **599.79**
Northwest, Canadian--Fiction.
  MOWAT, F/Lost in the barrens. /1962/5-6/6 KH518 . . . . . **Fic**
Northwest, Pacific--Fiction.
  HOBBS, W/Ghost canoe. /1997/5-A/6 KH267 . . . . **Fic**
Northwest, Pacific--Folklore.
  LEWIS, PO/Storm boy. /1995/2-4/3 KB610 . . . . **398.24**
Northwest Territories.
  HANCOCK, L/Northwest Territories. /1993/5-6/8 KE824. . . **971.9**
  REYNOLDS, J/Frozen land: vanishing cultures. /1993/
  3-6/6 KE827 . . . . **971.9**
Norway--Fiction.
  AAMUNDSEN, NR/Two short and one long. /1990/
  4-6/5 KG811 . . . . **Fic**
  EMBERLEY, M/Welcome back, Sun. /1993/1-3/3 KF524 . . . . . **E**
Norway--Folklore.
  ASBJORNSEN, PC/Man who kept house. /1992/
  2-4/6 KB719 . . . . **398.27**
  D'AULAIRE, I/D'Aulaires' trolls. /c1972, 1993/
  4-6/6 KB280 . . . . **398.2**
  KIMMEL, EA/Boots and his brothers: a Norwegian tale. /1992/
  2-4/2 KB400 . . . . **398.21**
  MILLS, LA/Tatterhood and the hobgoblins: a Norwegian folktale. /
  1993/3-4/6 KB350 . . . . **398.2**
  ROUNDS, G/Three billy goats Gruff. /1993/P-1/2 KB644 . **398.24**
Norwegian Americans.
  RILEY, J/Prairie cabin: a Norwegian pioneer woman's story
  (Videocassette). /1991/A/KF012 . . . . **VCR 977**
Nose.
  MACHOTKA, H/Breathtaking noses. /1992/3-5/6 KC280. . . **573.2**
Nose--Fiction.
  BROWN, MT/Arthur's nose. /c1976/K-2/2 KF276 . . . . . . **CE E**
  CAPLE, K/Biggest nose. /1985/P-2/2 KF337 . . . . **E**
Nova Scotia (Canada).
  JENSON, LB/Fishermen of Nova Scotia. /1980/
  A/9 KD245 . . . . **639.2**
  LOTZ, J/Nova Scotia. /1992/5-A/8 KE821. . . . . **971.6**
Nuclear armament SEE ALSO Atomic bomb.
Nuclear energy SEE ALSO Atomic energy; Atomic power.
Nuclear power plants.
  WILCOX, C/Powerhouse: inside a nuclear power plant. /1996/
  5-A/11 KD049 . . . . **621.48**

Nuestra Senora de Atocha (Ship).
   GIBBONS, G/Sunken treasure. /1988/4-6/6 KE194 . . . . . **917.59**
Number concept.
   HOW MUCH IS A MILLION? (VIDEOCASSETTE). /1997/
   K-1/KB947 . . . . **VCR 513**
   SCHWARTZ, DM/How much is a million? /1985/
   K-1/2 KB950 . . . . **513**
   WELLS, RE/Is a blue whale the biggest thing there is? /1993/
   K-2/2 KC087 . . . . **530.8**
Number games SEE ALSO Mathematical recreations.
Number games.
   MATH, MONEY, AND YOU (SOUND FILMSTRIP). /1989/
   K-2/KB967 . . . . **FSS 513.2**
Number systems.
   CHALLONER, J/Science book of numbers. /1992/
   K-3/2 KB956 . . . . **513.2**
   PALMER, H/Learning basic skills (Videocassette). /1986/
   P-1/KD700 . . . . **VCR 793**
Numbers.
   CARLE, E/Rooster's off to see the world. /1972/P-2/2 KF345. . . **E**
Numerals SEE ALSO Roman numerals.
Numeration SEE Number systems; Numerals.
Numismatics SEE Coins.
Nunavut (N.W.T.).
   HANCOCK, L/Nunavut. /1995/4-6/7 KE825 . . . . **971.9**
Nuns.
   JACOBS, WJ/Mother Teresa: helping the poor. /1991/
   4-6/6 KE561 . . . . **B TERESA,MOTHER**
Nursery rhymes.
   BIG FAT HEN. /1994/P-1/1 KB793 . . . . **398.8**
   CHINESE MOTHER GOOSE RHYMES. /c1968, 1989/
   P-3/KB794 . . . . **398.8**
   DE PAOLA, T/Tomie De Paola's Mother Goose. /1985/
   P-1/KB796 . . . . **398.8**
   DYER, J/Animal crackers: a delectable collection of pictures, poems,
   and lullabies for /1996/P-1/KD882 . . . . **808.81**
   FIVE LITTLE DUCKS: AN OLD RHYME. /1995/
   P-1/1 KB797 . . . . **398.8**
   GALDONE, P/Three little kittens. /1986/P-1/5 KB798 . . . . . **398.8**
   GLASS, H/Children's all-time Mother Goose favorites (Sound
   recording cassette). /1989//KA275 . . . . **SRC PROF 398.8**
   I SAW ESAU: THE SCHOOLCHILD'S POCKET BOOK. /1992/
   /KA276. . . . . **PROF 398.8**
   JANE YOLEN'S MOTHER GOOSE SONGBOOK. /1992/
   /KA277 . . . . **PROF 398.8**
   KNAPP, M/One potato, two potato: the folklore of American
   children. /1978//KA278 . . . . **PROF 398.8**
   LOBEL, A/Arnold Lobel book of Mother Goose. /1997/
   P-1/KB800 . . . . **398.8**
   MACK, S/10 bears in my bed: a goodnight countdown. /1974/
   P-1/1 KG052 . . . . **E**
   MANSON, C/Tree in the wood: an old nursery song. /1993/
   P-1/2 KB801 . . . . **398.8**
   MARTIN, SC/Comic adventures of Old Mother Hubbard and her
   dog. /1981/P-2/KB802 . . . . **398.8**
   MISS MARY MACK AND OTHER CHILDREN'S STREET RHYMES. /
   1990/2-5/KD766 . . . . **796.1**
   MOTHER GOOSE /Glorious Mother Goose. /1988/
   P-K/KB803 . . . . **398.8**
      Michael Foreman's Mother Goose. /1991/P-1/KB804 . . **398.8**
      Olde Mother Goose (Kit). /1993/P-K/KB805 . . . . **KIT 398.8**
      Real Mother Goose. /c1944, 1994/P-2/KB806 . . . . **398.8**
      Ring o'roses: a nursery rhyme picture book. /1992/
      P-K/KB807 . . . . **398.8**
   MY VERY FIRST MOTHER GOOSE. /1996/P-K/2 KB808. . . **398.8**
   NURSERY SONGS AND RHYMES (VIDEOCASSETTE). /1993/
   P-2/KB104 . . . . **VCR 372.4**
   O'MALLEY, K/Who killed Cock Robin? /1993/1-3/2 KG191. . . **E**
   OLD MOTHER HUBBARD AND HER WONDERFUL DOG. /1991/
   P-K/KB809 . . . . **398.8**
   OXFORD DICTIONARY OF NURSERY RHYMES. /1997/
   5-6/KA416 . . . . **REF 398.8**
   PETERSHAM, M/Rooster crows: a book of American rhymes and
   jingles. /c1945/K-2/KB810 . . . . **398.8**
   POLLITOS DICEN: JUEGOS, RIMAS Y CANCIONES INFANTILES
   DE PAISES DE HABLA /1994/P-1/1/2 KD584. . . . . **789.2**
   REAL MOTHER GOOSE BOOK OF AMERICAN RHYMES. /1993/
   P-2/KB811 . . . . **398.8**
   RING-A-RING O' ROSES AND A DING, DONG, BELL: A BOOK
   OF NURSERY RHYMES. /1991/P-K/2 KB813 . . . . **398.8**
   ROSEN, M/We're going on a bear hunt. /1989/
   P-2/2 KB814 . . . . **398.8**
   SENDAK, M/Hector Protector and As I went over the water: two
   nursery rhymes with pictures. /c1965, 1990/P-K/KB815. . . **398.8**

VAN RYNBACH, I/Five little pumpkins. /1995/P-K/2 KB817 . **398.8**
WEIMER, TE/Fingerplays and action chants: volume 1: animals. /
   1995/P-1/KD710 . . . . **BA 793.4**
Nursery rhymes--Adaptations.
   AYLESWORTH, J/Cat and the fiddle and more. /1992/
   P-1/KD915. . . . . **811**
   LANSKY, B/New adventures of Mother Goose: gentle rhymes for
   happy times. /1993/P-3/KD967 . . . . **811**
   POLACCO, P/Babushka's Mother Goose. /1995/
   P-2/3 KD878 . . . . **808.8**
   PRELUTSKY, J/Ride a purple pelican. /1986/P-3/KE014. . . . . **811**
   SCIESZKA, J/Book that Jack wrote. /1994/P-1/KE021 . . . . . **811**
   SIERRA, J/House that Drac built. /1995/1-3/3 KG503 . . . . **E**
Nursery rhymes, Spanish American.
   GRANDMOTHER'S NURSERY RHYMES: LULLABIES, TONGUE
   TWISTERS, AND RIDDLES FROM SOUTH AMERICA/NANAS DE
   ABUELITA: CANCIONES DE CUNA, TRABALENGUAS Y
   ADIVINANZAS DE SURAMERICA. /1994/P-2/KB799 . . . . **398.8**
   TORTILLITAS PARA MAMA AND OTHER SPANISH NURSERY
   RHYMES. /1981/1-3/KB816 . . . . **398.8**
Nursery schools SEE ALSO Day care centers; Kindergarten.
Nursery schools.
   CROFT, DJ/Activities handbook for teachers of young children. 5th
   ed. /1990//KA191 . . . . **PROF 372.1**
   KUKLIN, S/Going to my nursery school. /1990/
   P-3/2 KB098 . . . . **372.21**
Nursery schools--Periodicals.
   TEACHING K-8. /1971-//KA151. . . . . **PER PROF 050**
Nurses.
   ADLER, DA/Picture book of Florence Nightingale. /1992/
   2-4/3 KE478 . . . . **B NIGHTINGALE**
   SONNEBORN, L/Clara Barton. /1992/
   4-6/6 KE250 . . . . **B BARTON, C.**
Nutrition.
   BROWN, LK/Vegetable show. /1995/P-2/2 KD289. . . . . . **641.6**
   COBB, V/More science experiments you can eat. /1979/
   A/7 KB890 . . . . **507.8**
   DIGESTIVE SYSTEM (VIDEOCASSETTE). /1994/
   5-6/KC939. . . . . **VCR 612.3**
   JANEY JUNKFOOD'S FRESH ADVENTURE (VIDEOCASSETTE). /
   1992/3-6/KC984 . . . . **VCR 613.2**
   KARLSBERG, E/Eating pretty. /1991/5-A/7 KC985. . . . . . **613.2**
   LOOKING GOOD, FEELING GOOD (VIDEOCASSETTE). /1994/
   5-6/KC951 . . . . **VCR 612.6**
   MY BODY, MY BUDDY: HEALTHY FOOD (VIDEOCASSETTE). /
   1993/3-5/KC986 . . . . **VCR 613.2**
   NUTRITION TO GROW ON (VIDEOCASSETTE). /1988/
   5-6/KC987. . . . . **VCR 613.2**
   PARKER, S/Food and digestion. Rev. ed. /1990/
   5-6/8 KC940 . . . . **612.3**
   PATENT, DH/Nutrition: what's in the food we eat. /1992/
   4-6/6 KC941 . . . . **612.3**
Nutrition--Study and teaching (Elementary).
   IRVING, J/Mudluscious: stories and activities featuring food for
   preschool children. /1986//KA201 . . . . **PROF 372.3**
O'Connor, Sandra Day.
   MACHT, NL/Sandra Day O'Connor. /1992/
   4-5/8 KE481 . . . . **B O'CONNOR, S.**
O'Keeffe, Georgia.
   LOWERY, L/Georgia O'Keeffe. /1996/
   2-3/2 KE482 . . . . **B O'KEEFFE, G.**
O'Malley, Grace.
   MCCULLY, EA/Pirate queen. /1995/3-5/5 KE156. . . . . . . **910.4**
O'Neal, Shaquille.
   MACNOW, G/Shaquille O'Neal: star center. /1996/
   4-5/6 KE485 . . . . **B O'NEAL, S.**
Oak.
   TRESSELT, A/Gift of the tree. /c1972, 1992/K-4/6 KC312 . **577.3**
Oakley, Annie.
   ANNIE OAKLEY (VIDEOCASSETTE). /1997/
   3-6/KE479 . . . . **VCR B OAKLEY, A.**
   WUKOVITS, JF/Annie Oakley. /1997/
   5-6/8 KE480 . . . . **B OAKLEY, A.**
Obedience--Fiction.
   BAUER, MD/On my honor. /1986/5-6/7 KG882 . . . . **CE Fic**
Obesity SEE Weight control.
Occult sciences SEE ALSO Astrology; Fortune telling; Magic; Superstition;
   Witchcraft.
Occult sciences--Fiction.
   SNYDER, ZK/Headless cupid. /c1971/4-6/7 KH733 . . . . . **CE Fic**
Occupations.
   CIVARDI, A/Things people do. /1986/2-6/6 KA940 . . . . . **331.7**
   FLANAGAN, A/Busy day at Mr. Kang's grocery store. /1996/
   1-3/2 KB126 . . . . **381**

FLORIAN, D/Auto mechanic. /1994/P-2/3 KD128 . . . . . . **629.28**
Chef. /1992/K-2/5 KD270. . . . . **641.5**
Fisher. /1994/1-3/5 KD244 . . . . **639.2**
Painter. /1993/1-2/4 KD464 . . . . **750**
GIBBONS, G/Say woof!: the day of a country veterinarian. /1992/
P-2/2 KD194 . . . . **636.089**
KALMAN, M/Chicken soup, boots. /1993/P-K/3 KA941 . . **331.7**
MARTIN, JH/Day in the life of a carpenter. /1985/
4-6/7 KD362 . . . . **CE 694**
MAYNARD, C/Jobs people do. /1997/P-1/4 KA942 . . . . . **331.7**
MAZE, S/I want to be... a veterinarian. /1997/
5-6/9 KD195 . . . . **636.089**
I want to be... an astronaut. /1997/5-6/9 KD137. . . . . . **629.45**
MICHELS, P/Day in the life of a beekeeper. /1990/
4-5/6 KD242 . . . . **638**
MILLER, M/Who uses this? /1990/P-K/KA943 . . . . **331.7**
PAIGE, D/Day in the life of a sports therapist. /1985/
3-5/6 KC989 . . . . **613.7**
Day in the life of a zoo veterinarian. /1985/
2-5/6 KD196 . . . . **CE 636.089**
SO YOU WANT TO BE?: JUDGE (VIDEOCASSETTE). /1994/
5-6/KA977 . . . . **VCR 347**
SO YOU WANT TO BE?: NEWSPAPER ARTIST
(VIDEOCASSETTE). /1994/5-6/KA595 . . . . **VCR 070.4**
WOMEN IN POLICING (VIDEOCASSETTE). /1994/
5-6/KB030 . . . . **VCR 363.2**

Occupations--Fiction.
BRANDENBERG, A/I am me! /1996/P-K/1 KF258 . . . . **E**
BUSSER, M/On the road with Poppa Whopper. /1997/
3-4/2 KG954 . . . . **Fic**
EDWARDS, M/Chicken man. /1991/K-2/2 KF509 . . . . **E**
GROSSMAN, P/Night ones. /1991/P-K/2 KF650. . . . . **E**
HENKES, K/Good-bye, Curtis. /1995/P-2/2 KF704. . . . . **E**
KESSLER, E/Stan the hot dog man. /1990/1-2/1 KF897 . . . . . **E**
PAULSEN, G/Worksong. /1997/K-2/2 KG222 . . . . **E**
RYLANT, C/Mr. Griggs' work. /c1989, 1993/P-2/6 KG376 . . . . **E**

Occupations--History.
STEVENS, BS/Colonial American craftspeople. /1993/
5-6/8 KD339 . . . . **680**

Occupations--Software.
MICROSOFT EXPLORAPEDIA: THE WORLD OF PEOPLE.
ACADEMIC ED. (CD-ROM). /1994/1-4/KA892 . . . . . **CDR 307**
Ocean SEE ALSO Icebergs; Seashore; Storms; Tides.

Ocean.
COLE, J/Magic School Bus on the ocean floor. /1992/
2-4/5 KC495 . . . . **591.77**
GANERI, A/Oceans atlas. /1994/4-A/6 KC173. . . . . **551.46**
GREAT OCEAN RESCUE (VIDEODISC). /1992/
3-A/KC350 . . . . **VD 577.7**
MACQUITTY, M/Ocean. /1995/2-6/7 KC174 . . . . **551.46**
PIP AND ZENA'S SCIENCE VOYAGE (VIDEODISC). /1996/
K-3/KB869 . . . . **VD 500**
SIMON, S/Oceans. /1990/3-6/7 KC177 . . . . **551.46**

Ocean--Folklore.
RIORDAN, J/Stories from the sea. /1996/K-3/3 KB508 . . . **398.23**

Ocean--Software.
GREAT OCEAN RESCUE (CD-ROM). /1996/
3-A/KC349 . . . . **CDR 577.7**
SCHOLASTIC'S THE MAGIC SCHOOL BUS EXPLORES THE
OCEAN. TEACHER ED. (CD-ROM). /1995/
2-A/KC369 . . . . **CDR 578.77**

Ocean waves.
SOUZA, DM/Powerful waves. /1992/3-6/5 KC180 . . . . . **551.47**

Oceania--Folklore.
COURLANDER, H/Tiger's whisker and other tales from Asia and the
Pacific. /c1959, 1995/3-5/7 KB279 . . . . **398.2**

Oceanographers.
REEF, C/Jacques Cousteau: champion of the sea. /1992/
4-6/7 KE305 . . . . **B COUSTEAU, J.**
Oceanography SEE ALSO Marine biology; Marine resources; Navigation;
Underwater exploration.

Oceanography.
GANERI, A/Oceans atlas. /1994/4-A/6 KC173 . . . . **551.46**
MARKLE, S/Pioneering ocean depths. /1995/
4-A/8 KC175 . . . . **551.46**
WATERS, JF/Deep-sea vents: living worlds without sun. /1994/
4-6/7 KC179 . . . . **551.46**

Oceanography--Experiments.
FLEISHER, P/Our oceans: experiments and activities in marine
science. /1995/4-6/7 KC172 . . . . **551.46**
SIMON, S/How to be an ocean scientist in your own home. /
1988/5-A/5 KC176 . . . . **551.46**

VANCLEAVE, JP/Janice VanCleave's oceans for every kid: easy
activities that make learning science fun. /1996/
3-6/8 KC178 . . . . **551.46**

Octopus.
KITE, P/Down in the sea: the octopus. /1993/3-5/4 KC513 . . **594**
LAUBER, P/Octopus is amazing. /1990/1-3/4 KC514 . . . . . **594**

Odysseus (Greek mythology).
COLUM, P/Children's Homer: The Adventures of Odysseus and Tale
of Troy. /1982/A/6 KE123. . . . . **883**
FISHER, LE/Cyclops. /1991/1-6/4 KA739 . . . . **292**
PHILIP, N/Adventures of Odysseus. /1997/3-6/5 KE125 . . . **883**
PICARD, BL/Odyssey of Homer. /c1952, 1992/5-A/7 KE126 . **883**
SUTCLIFF, R/Wanderings of Odysseus: the story of the Odyssey. /
1996/5-A/7 KE128 . . . . **883**
WILLIAMS, M/Iliad and the Odyssey. /1996/3-6/8 KE129. . . **883**

Oglala Indians--Biography.
FREEDMAN, R/Life and death of Crazy Horse. /1996/
6-A/7 KE307 . . . . **B CRAZY HORSE**
ST. GEORGE, J/Crazy Horse. /1994/
A/9 KE308 . . . . **B CRAZY HORSE**

Ohio--Fiction.
FLEISCHMAN, P/Borning room. /1991/6-A/5 KH115 . . . . . **Fic**
HAMILTON, V/M.C. Higgins, the great. /1974/A/4 KH216 . . . **Fic**
MCCLOSKEY, R/Lentil. /c1940/1-3/6 KG088 . . . . **CE E**
SANDERS, SR/Warm as wool. /1992/3-5/5 KH675 . . . . **Fic**

Ohio--History.
WILLS, CA/Historical album of Ohio. /1996/4-6/7 KF013 . . **977.1**
Oil SEE ALSO Petroleum.

Oil spills.
BERGER, M/Oil spill! /1994/1-4/4 KB057 . . . . **363.73**
PRINGLE, LP/Oil spills: damage, recovery, and prevention. /1993/
5-6/9 KB065 . . . . **363.73**

Oil spills--Fiction.
RAND, G/Prince William. /1992/2-3/4 KG300 . . . . **E**

Ojibwa Indians--Costume and adornment.
KING, S/Shannon: an Ojibway dancer. /1993/
4-6/4 KE784 . . . . **970.476**

Ojibwa Indians--Dances.
KING, S/Shannon: an Ojibway dancer. /1993/
4-6/4 KE784 . . . . **970.476**

Ojibwa Indians--Fiction.
COOPER, AJ/Dream quest. /1987/5-A/4 KH024 . . . . **Fic**
OSOFSKY, A/Dreamcatcher. /1992/K-2/5 KG200 . . . . **E**

Ojibwa Indians--Folklore.
LARRY, C/Peboan and Seegwun. /1993/2-3/4 KB709 . . . . **398.26**
SAN SOUCI, RD/Sootface: an Ojibwa Cinderella story. /1994/
1-3/6 KB774 . . . . **398.27**

Ojibwa Indians--Social life and customs.
REGGUINTI, G/Sacred harvest: Ojibway wild rice gathering. /
1992/4-6/6 KE785 . . . . **970.476**
RENDON, MR/Powwow summer: a family celebrates the circle of
life. /1996/1-3/3 KB181 . . . . **394**
WITTSTOCK, LW/Ininatig's gift of sugar: traditional native
sugarmaking. /c1993/3-6/3 KE786. . . . . **970.476**

Oklahoma.
FRADIN, DB/Oklahoma. /1995/4-6/4 KF005. . . . . **976.6**
SOUTH CENTRAL REGION: TEXAS, NEW MEXICO, OKLAHOMA
(VIDEOCASSETTE). /1995/3-5/KE995 . . . . **VCR 976**

Oklahoma--Fiction.
MYERS, A/Rosie's tiger. /1994/4-A/4 KH521 . . . . **Fic**
RAWLS, W/Summer of the monkeys. /1976/4-6/6 KH623 . . . . **Fic**

Oklahoma--History.
OKLAHOMA LAND RUSH (MULTIMEDIA KIT). /1993/
5-A/KE997. . . . . **MMK 976.1**

**Oklahoma City Federal Building Bombing, Oklahoma City, Okla.,
1995.**
LAMB, N/One April morning: children remember the Oklahoma City
bombing. /1996/2-6/6 KF006 . . . . **976.6**

Olajuwon, Hakeem.
GUTMAN, B/Hakeem Olajuwon: superstar center. /1995/
4-5/6 KE483 . . . . **B OLAJUWON, H.**

Old age--Fiction.
BAWDEN, N/Humbug. /1992/5-A/5 KG891 . . . . **Fic**
CANNON, J/Verdi. /1997/K-2/3 KF336 . . . . **E**
CONLY, JL/Trout summer. /1995/6-A/5 KH021 . . . . **Fic**
DUGAN, B/Loop the loop. /1992/1-3/4 KF501 . . . . **E**
FOX, M/Wilfrid Gordon McDonald Partridge. /1985/
K-3/6 KF574 . . . . **E**
GARDINER, JR/General Butterfingers. /c1986, 1993/
4-6/6 KH152 . . . . **Fic**
JOHNSON, A/When I am old with you. /1990/P-2/6 KF834 . . . **E**
JONES, RC/Great Aunt Martha. /1995/1-3/2 KF853 . . . . **E**
JOYCE, W/Leaf Men and the brave good bugs. /1996/
1-3/3 KF861 . . . . **E**

LISLE, JT/Looking for Juliette. /1994/4-6/6 KH412 . . . . **Fic**
RYLANT, C/Mr. Putter and Tabby fly the plane. /1997/
 K-2/2 KG378 . . . . **E**
  Mr. Putter and Tabby pick the pears. /1995/1-3/2 KG379 . . . . **E**
  Mr. Putter and Tabby pour the tea. /1994/1-3/2 KG380 . . . . **E**
  Old woman who named things. /1996/1-3/2 KG383 . . . . **E**
SCHWARTZ, HB/When Artie was little. /1996/1-3/2 KG417 . . . . **E**
STOLZ, M/Stealing home. /1992/3-5/6 KH768 . . . . **Fic**
WITTMAN, S/Special trade. /1978/P-3/4 KG754 . . . . **E**
YUMOTO, K/Friends. /1996/6-A/7 KH901 . . . . **Fic**
ZOLOTOW, C/I know a lady. /1984/K-2/6 KG802 . . . . **E**
Old age--Folklore.
 UCHIDA, Y/Wise old woman. /1994/2-4/5 KB492 . . . . . . **398.22**
Old Bet (Elephant).
 MCCLUNG, RM/Old Bet and the start of the American circus. /
 1993/4-6/6 KD682 . . . . **791.3**
Old growth forests.
 BASH, B/Ancient ones: the world of the old-growth Douglas fir. /
 1994/3-6/7 KC435 . . . . **585**
 REED-JONES, C/Tree in the ancient forest. /1995/
 K-3/3 KC437 . . . . **585**
Old Order Mennonites.
 KENNA, K/People apart. /1995/4-6/7 KA720 . . . . **289.7**
Old Sturbridge Village (Mass.).
 OLD STURBRIDGE VILLAGE (VIDEOCASSETTE). /1989/
 4-6/KE942 . . . . **VCR 974.4**
Olympic games (Ancient).
 TAMES, R/Ancient Olympics. /1996/3-6/8 KD821 . . . . . **796.48**
Olympics.
 HENNESSY, BG/Olympics! /1996/P-2/4 KD820 . . . . . . **796.48**
 READHEAD, L/Gymnastics. /1996/3-6/8 KD818 . . . . . . **796.44**
 SANDELSON, R/Ball sports. /1991/4-6/8 KD774 . . . . . . **796.3**
  Ice sports. /1991/4-6/7 KD835 . . . . **796.9**
  Track athletics. /1991/4-6/7 KD811 . . . . **796.42**
 VERRIER, J/Swimming and diving. /1996/3-6/8 KD849 . . . **797.2**
 WARD, T/Field. /1996/3-6/8 KD812 . . . . **796.42**
  Track. /1996/3-6/8 KD813 . . . . **796.42**
Olympics--History.
 ANDERSON, D/Story of the Olympics. /1996/
 4-6/11 KD819 . . . . **796.48**
 TAMES, R/Modern Olympics. /1996/3-6/8 KD822 . . . . . . **796.48**
Onassis, Jacqueline Kennedy.
 ANDERSON, CC/Jackie Kennedy Onassis: woman of courage. /
 1995/A/7 KE484 . . . . **B ONASSIS, J.**
One (The number)--Fiction.
 EVERETT, P/One that got away. /1992/K-2/2 KF540 . . . . **E**
One act plays SEE Plays.
Oneida Indians--Fiction.
 DE COTEAU ORIE, S/Did you hear Wind sing your name?: an
 Oneida song of spring. /1995/K-2/3 KF454 . . . . **E**
Online bibliographic searching.
 FIND IT ALL AT THE LIBRARY: AN INTRODUCTION TO THE
 LIBRARY FOR CHILDREN /1996/2-6/KA584. . . . . . . **VCR 027**
Online information services.
 BOE, T/World desk: a student handbook to the Internet. Rev. ed. /
 1996/A/10 KA576 . . . . **025.04**
 GRALLA, P/Online kids: a young surfer's guide to cyberspace. /
 1996/3-A/4 KA578 . . . . **025.04**
Online information services--Directories.
 GIAGNOCAVO, G/Educator's Internet companion: CLASSROOM
 CONNECT's complete guide to educational /1996/
 /KA049. **BC PROF 025.06**
 HARRIS, J/Way of the ferret: finding and using educational
 resources on the Internet. /1995//KA046. . . . . . . **PROF 025.04**
Online information services--Periodicals.
 CLASSROOM CONNECT. /1994-//KA102 . . . . . **PER PROF 050**
Ontario.
 BARNES, M/Ontario. /1995/4-6/10 KE817 . . . . **971.3**
 MACKAY, K/Ontario. /1992/5-A/8 KE819 . . . . **971.3**
Opera--Fiction.
 FREEMAN, L/Pet of the Met. /c1953/1-2/7 KF582 . . . . **E**
Operas--Stories, plots, etc.
 PRICE, L/Aida. /1990/4-A/6 KD530 . . . . **782.1**
 SIMON, HW/100 great operas and their stories. Rev. ed. /c1957,
 1989/4-A/KA454 . . . . **REF 792.5**
Opossums--Fiction.
 FOX, M/Possum magic. /c1983, 1990/P-2/4 KF571 . . . . **E**
 VAN LAAN, N/Possum come a-knockin'. /1990/K-2/2 KG642 . . **E**
Opposites SEE English language--Synonyms and antonyms.
Optical illusions.
 MAGIC EYE: A NEW WAY OF LOOKING AT THE WORLD. /
 1993/3-A/KA620 . . . . **152.14**
 SIMON, S/Optical illusion book. /c1976, 1984/4-6/5 KC115 . **535**
 WESTRAY, K/Picture puzzler. /1994/1-6/7 KA621 . . . . . . **152.14**

Optics.
 COBB, V/Light action!: amazing experiments with optics. /1993/
 2-6/7 KC108 . . . . **535**
Optics--Experiments.
 DARLING, DJ/Making light work: the science of optics. /1991/
 6-A/8 KC109 . . . . **535**
Oracles--Fiction.
 DEXTER, C/Doll who knew the future. /1994/4-6/6 KH072 . . . **Fic**
Oral interpretation of poetry.
 BAUER, CF/Poetry break: an annotated anthology with ideas for
 introducing children to /1995//KA234. . . . . **PROF 372.64**
Oral reading.
 FREEMAN, J/Books kids will sit still for: the complete read-aloud
 guide. 2nd ed. /1990//KA015. . . . . **PROF 011.62**
 MCELMEEL, SL/Great new nonfiction reads. /1995/
 /KA086. . . . . **PROF 028.1**
  Latest and greatest read-alouds. /1994//KA239. . **PROF 372.64**
 TRELEASE, J/Read-aloud handbook. 4th ed. /1995/
 /KA242. . . . . **PROF 372.64**
Oral-formulaic analysis.
 DAILEY, S/Putting the world in a nutshell: the art of the formula
 tale. /1994//KA337 . . . . **PROF 808.5**
Orchards.
 SCHNIEPER, C/Apple tree through the year. /c1982, 1987/
 5-6/7 KD163 . . . . **634**
Orchestra.
 ARDLEY, N/Young person's guide to music. /1995/
 5-A/8 KD518 . . . . **BA 780**
 BLACKWOOD, A/Orchestra: an introduction to the world of
 classical music. /1993/4-6/8 KD544 . . . . **784.2**
 GANERI, A/Young person's guide to the orchestra: Benjamin
 Britten's composition on CD. /1996/4-6/10 KD545 . . . **BA 784.2**
Orchestra--Fiction.
 KUSKIN, K/Philharmonic gets dressed. /1982/K-3/5 KF939 . . . **E**
Orchestral music.
 BIBBIDI BOBBODI BACH (COMPACT DISC). /1996/
 4-6/KD674. . . . . **CD 789.8**
Orderliness--Fiction.
 TEAGUE, M/Pigsty. /1994/K-2/2 KG595 . . . . **E**
Oregon.
 FRADIN, DB/Oregon. /1995/4-6/4 KF089 . . . . **979.5**
Oregon--Fiction.
 CREW, L/Nekomah Creek Christmas. /1994/4-6/4 KH042 . . . . **Fic**
Oregon--Folklore.
 KIMMEL, EA/Billy Lazroe and the King of the Sea: a tale of the
 Northwest. /1996/4-5/5 KB460 . . . . **398.22**
Oregon--History.
 WILLS, CA/Historical album of Oregon. /1995/
 4-6/7 KF090 . . . . **979.5**
Oregon Trail--Fiction.
 MORROW, H/On to Oregon. /c1954/5-6/4 KH517 . . . . **Fic**
 STEVENS, C/Trouble for Lucy. /1979/3-5/6 KH754 . . . . **Fic**
 VAN LEEUWEN, J/Bound for Oregon. /1994/5-A/5 KH828 . . . **Fic**
Oregon Trail--Software.
 OREGON TRAIL II (CD-ROM). /1994/4-A/KE745 . . **CDR 970.04**
 WRITING ALONG THE OREGON TRAIL (MICROCOMPUTER
 PROGRAM). /1994/4-A/KB121 . . . . **MCP 372.6**
Organizations SEE Clubs; names of specific clubs e.g. Boy Scouts.
Origami.
 HOW TO FOLD A PAPER CRANE (VIDEOCASSETTE). /1994/
 3-6/KD402. . . . . **VCR 736**
 KALLEVIG, CP/Holiday folding stories: storytelling and origami
 together for holiday fun. /1992//KA309 . . . . **PROF 736**
 SMOLINSKI, J/Holiday origami. /1995/3-6/KD403. . . . . . . **736**
 STOTTER, R/Origami stories (Videocassette). /1993/
 1-3/KB122 . . . . **VCR 372.67**
 TEMKO, F/Origami for beginners: the creative world of
 paperfolding. /1991/4-6/4 KD404 . . . . **736**
Orion (Constellation).
 APFEL, NH/Orion, the Hunter. /1995/A/10 KC047. . . . . . **523.8**
Ornithologists.
 DUNLAP, J/Birds in the bushes: a story about Margaret Morse
 Nice. /1996/3-5/9 KE477 . . . . **B NICE, M.**
Orphan trains.
 WARREN, A/Orphan train rider: one boy's true story. /1996/
 4-6/8 KB015 . . . . **362.73**
Orphan trains--Fiction.
 BUNTING, E/Train to Somewhere. /1996/3-5/4 KG945 . . . . . **Fic**
Orphans.
 WARREN, A/Orphan train rider: one boy's true story. /1996/
 4-6/8 KB015 . . . . **362.73**
Orphans--Fiction.
 AVI /Punch with Judy. /1993/5-A/6 KG863 . . . . **Fic**

BANG, M/Tye May and the magic brush. /c1981, 1992/
1-3/2 KF193 . . . . **E**
BUDBILL, D/Bones on Black Spruce Mountain. /c1978, 1994/
4-A/5 KG935 . . . . **Fic**
BULLA, CR/White bird. /c1966, 1990/1-6/2 KG940 . . . . **Fic**
BUNTING, E/Train to Somewhere. /1996/3-5/4 KG945 . . . . . **Fic**
BURNETT, FH/Little princess. /c1963/5-A/8 KG949 . . . . . . **Fic**
Sara Crewe. /1986/4-6/7 KG950. . . . . **Fic**
Secret garden. /c1911, 1987/3-6/5 KG951 . . . . . **CE Fic**
CASSEDY, S/Behind the attic wall. /1983/6-A/5 KG986 . . . . . **Fic**
Lucie Babbidge's house. /1993/6-A/7 KG987 . . . . . **Fic**
CLEAVER, V/Where the lilies bloom. /c1969/5-6/6 KH009 . . . **Fic**
CONFORD, E/Frog Princess of Pelham. /1997/4-A/3 KH019 . . **Fic**
DEFELICE, CC/Apprenticeship of Lucas Whitaker. /1998/
5-A/6 KH066 . . . . **CE Fic**
DOHERTY, B/Street child. /1994/5-A/6 KH078 . . . . **Fic**
FLEISCHMAN, S/By the Great Horn Spoon! /c1963/
4-6/4 KH119 . . . . **Fic**
Midnight horse. /1990/5-A/4 KH125. . . . . **Fic**
GAEDDERT, L/Hope. /1995/5-A/6 KH148 . . . . **Fic**
GODDEN, R/Listen to the nightingale. /c1992, 1994/
5-A/6 KH178 . . . . **Fic**
HECTOR'S BUNYIP (VIDEOCASSETTE). /c1986, 1997/
4-6/KH231 . . . . **VCR Fic**
HOLLAND, I/Journey home. /1993/6-A/6 KH270. . . . . . . **Fic**
HOME AT LAST (VIDEOCASSETTE). /c1988, 1997/
5-A/KH276 . . . . **VCR Fic**
MACKEN, W/Flight of the doves. /1992/5-A/3 KH442 . . . . . **Fic**
MCCULLY, EA/Little Kit or, The Industrious Flea Circus girl. /1995/
2-4/4 KG092 . . . . **E**
PENNYPACKER, S/Dumbstruck. /1994/4-6/7 KH596 . . . . . . **Fic**
SPYRI, J/Heidi. /1996/5-A/6 KH746 . . . . **Fic**
STANLEY, D/Saving Sweetness. /1996/1-3/4 KG538 . . . . . **E**
WALLACE, BB/Cousins in the castle. /1996/5-A/7 KH837 . . . **Fic**
YORINKS, A/Oh, brother. /1989/1-4/5 KG783. . . . . **E**

Ospreys.
PATENT, DH/Ospreys. /1993/A/7 KC717 . . . . **598.9**

Ostriches.
ARNOLD, C/Ostriches and other flightless birds. /1990/
5-6/7 KC690 . . . . **598.5**

Ostriches--Fiction.
KING-SMITH, D/Cuckoo child. /1993/4-6/6 KH347 . . . . . . **Fic**
PEET, B/Zella, Zack and Zodiac. /1986/K-3/4 KG231 . . . . **E**

Ostropoler, Hershele, 18th cent.--Legends.
KIMMEL, EA/Adventures of Hershel of Ostropol. /1995/
2-4/7 KB459 . . . . **398.22**

Ottawa (Ont.).
EDWARDS, FB/Ottawa: a kid's eye view. /1993/
5-6/8 KE818 . . . . **971.3**

Otters.
ARNOSKY, J/Otters under water. /1992/K-2/2 KC832 . . **599.769**

Otters--Fiction.
HOBAN, L/Big little otter (Board book). /1997/P/1 KF736. . **BB E**
Outdoor life SEE ALSO Backpacking; Camping; Country life; Hiking;
Mountaineering; Nature study; Sports; Wilderness survival.

Outdoor life--Fiction.
GEORGE, JC/My side of the mountain. /c1959/5-6/6 KH159 . **Fic**
KJELGAARD, J/Big Red: the story of a champion Irish setter and a
trapper's son who grew up /c1945, 1956/6-A/7 KH365 . . . . . **Fic**

Outdoor life--Handbooks, manuals, etc.
MCMANNERS, H/Outdoor adventure handbook. /1996/
4-6/6 KD823 . . . . **796.5**

Outdoor life--Minnesota.
PAULSEN, G/Puppies, dogs, and blue northers: reflections on being
raised by a pack of sled /1996/3-6/7 KD859. . . . . **798.8**
Woodsong. /1990/5-A/6 KD824 . . . . **796.5**

Outdoor life--Periodicals.
CHICKADEE: THE CANADIAN MAGAZINE FOR YOUNG
CHILDREN. /1979/-P-3/KA506 . . . . **PER 050**
OWL: THE DISCOVERY MAGAZINE FOR CHILDREN. /1976-/
2-4/KA535 . . . . **PER 050**

Outdoor recreation.
DRAKE, J/Kids' summer handbook. /1994/3-6/6 KD678 . . . **790.1**

Outdoor recreation--Handbooks, manuals, etc.
MCMANNERS, H/Outdoor adventure handbook. /1996/
4-6/6 KD823 . . . . **796.5**

Outdoor recreation--Vocational guidance.
KAPLAN, A/Careers for outdoor types. /1991/
4-A/8 KA952 . . . . **333.7**
Outer space SEE ALSO headings beginning with the word Space.

Outer space.
COUPER, H/Space atlas. /1992/3-6/6 KC002 . . . . **520**

Outer space--Exploration.
APFEL, NH/Voyager to the planets. /1991/3-6/7 KC022 . . . **523.4**

BURROWS, WE/Mission to deep space: Voyagers' journey of
discovery. /1993/4-8/11 KC024 . . . . **523.4**
COLE, N/Blast off!: a space counting book. /1994/
P-3/6 KD131 . . . . **629.43**
HARRIS, AW/Great Voyager adventure: a guided tour through the
solar system. /1990/A/9 KC026 . . . . **523.4**
KERROD, R/Story of space exploration (Picture). /1994/
4-6/KC027. . . . . **PIC 523.4**
KETTELKAMP, L/Living in space. /1993/A/8 KD130 . . . . . . **629.4**
RIDE, S/Voyager: an adventure to the edge of the solar system. /
1992/3-6/7 KC030 . . . . **523.4**
SCOTT, E/Adventure in space: the flight to fix the Hubble. /1995/
A/7 KC006 . . . . **522**
WHAT WE LEARN ABOUT EARTH FROM SPACE
(VIDEOCASSETTE). /1995/5-8/KD133 . . . . **VCR 629.43**

Outer space--Fiction.
PINKWATER, DM/Wallpaper from space. /1996/
2-5/3 KH605 . . . . **Fic**

Outer space--Miscellanea.
CAMPBELL, A/New York Public Library amazing space: a book of
answers for kids. /1997/3-A/8 KC001 . . . . **520**

Outer space--Periodicals.
ODYSSEY. /1992-/3-5/KA534 . . . . **PER 050**

Outer space--Poetry.
STAR WALK. /1995/4-8/KE085 . . . . **811.008**

Outer space--Study and teaching.
BOURNE, B/Exploring space: using Seymour Simon's astronomy
books in the classroom. /1994//KA198 . . . . **PROF 372.3**
Outlaws SEE Robbers and outlaws.
Overland journeys to the Pacific SEE ALSO Oregon Trail.

Overland journeys to the Pacific.
KNIGHT, AS/Way west: journal of a pioneer woman. /1993/
5-6/5 KE197 . . . . **917.8**
LAVENDER, DS/Santa Fe Trail. /1995/A/6 KF037 . . . . **978**
Snowbound: the tragic story of the Donner Party. /1996/
5-6/6 KF038 . . . . **978**
MANSON, A/Dog came, too: a true story. /1993/
1-4/6 KE185 . . . . **917.104**
MURPHY, VR/Across the plains in the Donner Party. /1996/
5-6/7 KF041 . . . . **978**
PATENT, DH/West by covered wagon: retracing the pioneer trails.
/1995/2-4/8 KF043 . . . . **978**
RUSSELL, M/Along the Santa Fe Trail: Marion Russell's own story.
/1993/4-6/7 KE199 . . . . **917.8**
STEFOFF, R/Children of the westward trail. /1996/
4-6/8 KF050 . . . . **978**
STEWART, GR/Pioneers go west. /c1982, 1997/
4-6/7 KF051 . . . . **978**
WRIGHT, CC/Wagon train: a family goes West in 1865. /1995/
4-6/3 KF052 . . . . **978**

Overland journeys to the Pacific--Fiction.
COERR, E/Josefina story quilt. /1986/1-3/2 KF401 . . . . . . **CE E**
FLEISCHMAN, S/Mr. Mysterious and Company. /c1962, 1997/
3-6/6 KH126 . . . . **Fic**
HARVEY, B/Cassie's journey: going West in the 1860s. /1988/
1-3/5 KF677 . . . . **E**
MORROW, H/On to Oregon. /c1954/5-6/4 KH517 . . . . . **Fic**
PAULSEN, G/Mr. Tucket. /1994/5-A/6 KH588 . . . . **Fic**
VAN LEEUWEN, J/Bound for Oregon. /1994/5-A/5 KH828. . . **Fic**
Fourth of July on the plains. /1997/2-5/2 KG647 . . . . . **E**
WOODRUFF, E/Dear Levi: letters from the Overland Trail. /1994/
4-6/6 KH880 . . . . **Fic**

Overland journeys to the Pacific--Handbooks, manuals, etc.
OVERLAND TO CALIFORNIA IN 1859: A GUIDE FOR WAGON
TRAIN TRAVELERS. /1983/A/12 KF042 . . . . **978**

Overland journeys to the Pacific--Software.
OREGON TRAIL II (CD-ROM). /1994/4-A/KE745 . . **CDR 970.04**
WRITING ALONG THE OREGON TRAIL (MICROCOMPUTER
PROGRAM). /1994/4-A/KB121 . . . . **MCP 372.6**

Owens, Jesse.
ADLER, DA/Picture book of Jesse Owens. /1992/
3-4/6 KE486 . . . . **B OWENS, J.**
JOSEPHSON, JP/Jesse Owens: track and field legend. /1997/
5-A/8 KE487 . . . . **B OWENS, J.**
Owls SEE ALSO Birds of prey; names of specific species e.g. Snowy owl.

Owls.
ARNOSKY, J/All about owls. /1995/2-5/4 KC709 . . . . . . **598.9**
BROWN, FG/Owls. /1991/5-6/5 KC711 . . . . **598.9**
CRICKET, TIGLET AND FRIENDS (VIDEOCASSETTE). /1984/
4-6/KC712. . . . . **VCR 598.9**
EPPLE, W/Barn owls. /1992/4-6/5 KC713 . . . . **598.9**
KAPPELER, M/Owls. /1991/5-6/6 KC715. . . . . **598.9**
SATTLER, HR/Book of North American owls. /1995/
5-6/6 KC719 . . . . **598.9**

Owls--Fiction.
AVI /Poppy. /1995/3-5/6 KG862. . . . . **Fic**
BUNTING, E/Man who could call down owls. /1984/
1-3/2 KF304. . . . . **E**
EASTMAN, PD/Sam and the firefly. /c1958/P-1/1 KF507 . . . . . **E**
ERICKSON, RE/Toad for Tuesday. /1974/1-3/3 KF528. . . . **CE E**
HUTCHINS, P/Good-night owl. /c1972/P-2/3 KF798 . . . . . **CE E**
LOBEL, A/Owl at home. /c1975/K-2/1 KG010 . . . . **E**
PROVENSEN, A/Owl and three pussycats. /1994/
K-2/5 KG289. . . . . **E**
YOLEN, J/Owl moon. /1987/P-3/2 KG778. . . . . **CE E**

Owls--Folklore.
GATES, F/Owl eyes. /1994/1-3/4 KB570. . . . . **398.24**

Ozark Mountains--Fiction.
RAWLS, W/Where the red fern grows: the story of two dogs and a
boy. /c1961, 1988/A/4 KH624. . . . . **Fic**

Ozawa, Seiji.
SIMON, C/Seiji Ozawa: symphony conductor. /1992/
4-5/6 KE488 . . . . **B OZAWA, S.**

Ozone layer.
HOFF, MK/Our endangered planet: atmosphere. /1995/
4-6/8 KB061 . . . . **363.73**
JOHNSON, RL/Investigating the ozone hole. /1993/
A/10 KC191 . . . . **551.5**

Ozone layer depletion.
JOHNSON, RL/Investigating the ozone hole. /1993/
A/10 KC191 . . . . **551.5**

Pacific Islander Americans.
SINNOTT, S/Extraordinary Asian Pacific Americans. /1993/
5-A/8 KA859. . . . . **305.8**

Pacific Islander Americans--Biography.
ASIAN AMERICAN BIOGRAPHY. /1995/5-A/KA399 . . **REF 305.8**

Pacific Islander Americans--Poetry.
IZUKI, S/Believers in America: poems about Americans of Asian and
Pacific islander /1994/3-6/KD955 . . . . **811**

Pacific States--Bibliography.
EXPLORING THE PACIFIC STATES THROUGH LITERATURE. /
1994//KA042 . . . . **PROF 016.9795**

Pacifists.
BLUE, R/People of peace. /1994/5-A/7 KA806 . . . . **303.6**

Paige, Leroy.
MCKISSACK, P/Satchel Paige: the best arm in baseball. /1992/
3-5/2 KE489 . . . . **B PAIGE, S.**
Pain SEE ALSO Analgesia.

Paint.
LYNN, S/Play with paint. /1993/K-2/3 KD465. . . . . **750**
PAINT (VIDEOCASSETTE). /1984/5-6/KD325 . . . . **VCR 667**
Painters SEE ALSO Color; Perspective; Stencil work.

Painting.
MICKLETHWAIT, L/Spot a cat. /1995/K-2/2 KD466. . . . . . **750**
Spot a dog. /1995/K-2/1 KD467 . . . . **750**
RICHMOND, R/Story in a picture: animals in art. /1993/
4-A/7 KD475. . . . . **758**

Painting--Fiction.
AUCH, MJ/Eggs mark the spot. /1996/K-2/3 KF176 . . . . . **CE E**
BANG, M/Tye May and the magic brush. /c1981, 1992/
1-3/2 KF193 . . . . **E**
HEST, A/Jamaica Louise James. /1996/K-2/2 KF719. . . . . . . **E**
YEE, P/Ghost Train. /1996/4-6/5 KH889 . . . . **Fic**

Painting--History.
HESLEWOOD, J/History of Western painting: a young person's
guide. /1996/4-6/8 KD483. . . . . **759**
RICHMOND, R/Story in a picture: children in art. /1992/
3-6/7 KD471 . . . . **757**
ROALF, P/Cats. /1992/5-A/8 KD476 . . . . **758**
Circus. /1993/5-A/8 KD477. . . . . **758**
Dancers. /1992/5-A/7 KD478 . . . . **758**
Families. /1992/5-A/7 KD472 . . . . **757**
Flowers. /1993/5-A/8 KD479 . . . . **758**
Horses. /1992/5-A/8 KD480 . . . . **758**
Landscapes. /1992/5-A/8 KD481 . . . . **758**
Seascapes. /1992/5-A/7 KD482 . . . . **758**

Painting--Study and teaching.
TOPAL, CW/Children and painting. /1992//KA217. . **PROF 372.5**

Painting--Technique.
SANCHEZ SANCHEZ, I/Painting and coloring dinosaurs. /1996/
5-A/3 KD419. . . . . **743**
SIRETT, D/My first paint book. /1994/3-6/7 KD436. . . . . **745.5**
SOLGA, K/Paint! /1991/2-6/4 KD370. . . . . **702.8**
WATERS, E/Painting: a young artist's guide. /1993/
5-6/8 KD470 . . . . **751.4**

Painting--Technique--Software.
KID PIX STUDIO (CD-ROM). /1994/P-A/KD468 . . . **CDR 750.28**

NEW KID PIX. SCHOOL VERSION (MICROCOMPUTER
PROGRAM). /1996/P-A/KD469 . . . . **MCP 750.28**

Painting, American.
AMERICAN HISTORY: GROWING PAINS (PICTURE). /c1974/
4-6/KE912. . . . . **PIC 973.8**
BERMAN, A/James McNeil Whistler. /1993/
5-A/7 KE592 . . . . **B WHISTLER, J.**
JACOB LAWRENCE: THE GLORY OF EXPRESSION
(VIDEOCASSETTE). /1995/5-A/KD487 . . . . **VCR 759.13**
LAWRENCE, J/Great migration: an American story. /1993/
K-5/7 KD488 . . . . **759.13**
LOWERY, L/Georgia O'Keeffe. /1996/
2-3/2 KE482 . . . . **B O'KEEFFE, G.**
LYONS, ME/Starting home: the story of Horace Pippin, painter. /
1993/5-A/5 KE499. . . . . **B PIPPIN, H.**
MERYMAN, R/Andrew Wyeth. /1991/
6-A/7 KE602 . . . . **B WYETH, A.**
MEYER, SE/Mary Cassatt. /1990/6-A/8 KE283 . . **B CASSATT, M.**
MUHLBERGER, R/What makes a Cassatt a Cassatt? /1994/
5-A/7 KD489 . . . . **759.13**

Painting, Dutch.
CRISPINO, E/Van Gogh. /1996/6-A/12 KD499. . . . . **759.9492**
HARRISON, P/Vincent van Gogh. /1996/
4-6/7 KE369 . . . . **B GOGH, V.**
HUGHES, A/Van Gogh. /1994/6-A/9 KE370 . . . **B GOGH, V.**
MUHLBERGER, R/What makes a Rembrandt a Rembrandt? /1993/
5-A/7 KD500. . . . . **759.9492**
PESCIO, C/Rembrandt and seventeenth-century Holland. /1995/
4-A/12 KD501 . . . . **759.9492**
SCHWARTZ, G/Rembrandt. /1992/
6-A/7 KE507 . . . . **B REMBRANDT**

Painting, Flemish.
MUHLBERGER, R/What makes a Bruegel a Bruegel? /1993/
5-A/8 KD502. . . . . **759.9493**

Painting, French.
HARRISON, P/Claude Monet. /1996/4-6/7 KE466. **B MONET, C.**
LORIA, S/Pablo Picasso. /1995/4-A/12 KD490. . . . . **759.4**
MEYER, SE/Edgar Degas. /1994/6-A/9 KE318 . . . **B DEGAS, E.**
MUHLBERGER, R/What makes a Degas a Degas? /1993/
5-A/7 KD491. . . . . **759.4**
What makes a Monet a Monet? /1993/5-A/7 KD492. . . . . **759.4**
What makes a Picasso a Picasso? /1994/5-A/7 KD493 . . . **759.4**
VENEZIA, M/Henri de Toulouse-Lautrec. /1995/
4-6/8 KE568 . . . . **B TOULOUSE-LAUT**

Painting, Italian.
MCLANATHAN, R/Leonardo da Vinci. /1990/
6-A/6 KD495. . . . . **759.5**
MUHLBERGER, R/What makes a Leonardo a Leonardo? /1994/
5-A/7 KD496. . . . . **759.5**
What makes a Raphael a Raphael? /1993/5-A/7 KD497. . **759.5**

Painting, Modern--Spain.
VENEZIA, M/Salvador Dali. /1993/4-6/7 KE313 . . . . **B DALI, S.**

Painting, Modern--19th century--Netherlands.
CRISPINO, E/Van Gogh. /1996/6-A/12 KD499. . . . . **759.9492**
HARRISON, P/Vincent van Gogh. /1996/
4-6/7 KE369 . . . . **B GOGH, V.**
HUGHES, A/Van Gogh. /1994/6-A/9 KE370 . . . . . **B GOGH, V.**

Painting, Modern--20th century.
LYONS, ME/Starting home: the story of Horace Pippin, painter. /
1993/5-A/5 KE499. . . . . **B PIPPIN, H.**
MERYMAN, R/Andrew Wyeth. /1991/
6-A/7 KE602 . . . . **B WYETH, A.**

Painting, Modern--20th century--France.
MUHLBERGER, R/What makes a Picasso a Picasso? /1994/
5-A/7 KD493. . . . . **759.4**

Painting, Russian.
GREENFELD, H/Marc Chagall. /1990/
6-A/8 KE284 . . . . **B CHAGALL, M.**

Painting, Spanish.
MUHLBERGER, R/What makes a Goya a Goya? /1994/
5-A/7 KD498. . . . . **759.6**
VENEZIA, M/Francisco Goya. /1991/4-5/6 KE376. . **B GOYA, F.**
Salvador Dali. /1993/4-6/7 KE313 . . . . **B DALI, S.**

Paintings.
HOW DO I FEEL? (PICTURE). /1974/1-3/KA625 . . . . . **PIC 152.4**

Pajamas--Fiction.
JACKSON, I/Somebody's new pajamas. /1996/3-5/4 KH318. . **Fic**

Pakistan--Fiction.
STAPLES, SF/Shabanu, daughter of the wind. /1989/
6-A/6 KH748 . . . . **Fic**

Pakistan--Folklore.
SHEPARD, A/Gifts of Wali Dad: a tale of India and Pakistan. /
1995/2-3/2 KB488 . . . . **398.22**

Paleontologists.
AASENG, N/American dinosaur hunters. /1996/A/9 KC232 . . **560**
LESSEM, D/Jack Horner: living with dinosaurs. /1994/
5-A/8 KE391 . . . . **B HORNER, J.**

Paleontology.
ALIKI /Wild and woolly mammoths. Rev. ed. /1996/
1-3/4 KC268 . . . . **569**
DEBECK, S/Dinosaurs! (Videocassette). /1989/
2-5/KC246 . . . . **VCR 567.9**
DIGGING DINOSAURS (VIDEOCASSETTE). /1986/
3-A/KC247 . . . . **VCR 567.9**
LAUBER, P/Dinosaurs walked here and other stories fossils tell. /
1987/4-6/6 KC236 . . . . **560**
LESSEM, D/Dinosaur worlds: new dinosaurs, new discoveries. /
1996/4-6/6 KC254 . . . . **567.9**
LINDSAY, W/Tyrannosaurus. /1992/5-6/9 KC255 . . . **567.9**
TAYLOR, PD/Fossil. /1990/4-A/9 KC237 . . . . **560**

Paleontology--Australia.
ARNOLD, C/Dinosaurs down under and other fossils from Australia.
/1990/3-6/8 KC240 . . . . **566**

Paleontology--Fiction.
DICKINSON, P/Bone from a dry sea. /1993/6-A/7 KH075 . . . **Fic**

Palestine--Folklore.
BAHOUS, S/Sitti and the cats: a tale of friendship. /1993/
3-4/7 KB257 . . . . **398.2**

Palindromes.
AGEE, J/So many dynamos!: and other palindromes. /1994/
3-6/KD719 . . . . **793.734**

Pampas (Argentina)--Description and travel.
BRUSCA, MC/On the pampas. /1991/3-6/6 KF106 . . . . . . **982**

Panama--Fiction.
PALACIOS, A/Christmas surprise for Chabelita. /1993/
1-3/2 KG206 . . . . **E**

Panama--History.
PARKER, NW/Locks, crocs, and skeeters: the story of the Panama
Canal. /1996/3-5/7 KB147 . . . . **386**

Panama Canal (Panama)--History.
MCNEESE, T/Panama Canal. /1997/5-6/11 KB145 . . . . . . **386**
PANAMA CANAL (PICTURE). /n.d./5-6/KB146 . . . . . **PIC 386**
PARKER, NW/Locks, crocs, and skeeters: the story of the Panama
Canal. /1996/3-5/7 KB147 . . . . **386**

Pandas SEE ALSO Giant panda.

Pandas.
ARNOLD, C/Panda. /1992/4-6/7 KC866 . . . . **599.789**
SCHMIDT, A/Bears and their forest cousins. /1991/
5-6/7 KC854 . . . . **599.78**

Pandas--Fiction.
DAY, D/Emperor's panda. /c1986, 1987/4-A/8 KH063 . . . . . **Fic**

Panthera.
KAPPELER, M/Big cats. /1991/5-6/7 KC822 . . . . **599.75**

Paper SEE ALSO Papermaking. SEE ALSO Papermaking and trade.

Paper.
BOURGEOIS, P/Amazing paper book. /1989/5-6/6 KD332 . . **676**
DIXON, A/Paper. /1991/3-5/6 KD333 . . . . **676**
PAPER (VIDEOCASSETTE). /1986/5-6/KD334 . . . . . . **VCR 676**

Paper crafts SEE Paper work.

Paper dolls--Fiction.
MAHY, M/Five sisters. /1997/4-6/7 KH446 . . . . **Fic**

Paper money--History.
PARKER, NW/Money, money, money: the meaning of the art and
symbols on United States paper currency. /1995/
3-6/11 KD506 . . . . **769.5**

Paper work SEE ALSO Origami.

Paper work.
ANCONA, G/Pinata maker./El Pinatero. /1994/
3-6/6 KD450 . . . . **745.594**
CHERNOFF, GT/Easy costumes you don't have to sew. /c1975/
P-A/4 KD298 . . . . **646.4**
FIAROTTA, P/Papercrafts around the world. /1996/
2-6/6 KD440 . . . . **745.54**
HOW TO FOLD A PAPER CRANE (VIDEOCASSETTE). /1994/
3-6/KD402 . . . . **VCR 736**
LOOK WHAT I MADE: PAPER, PLAYTHINGS AND GIFTS
(VIDEOCASSETTE). /1995/3-6/KD433 . . . . **VCR 745.5**
LYNN, S/Play with paper. /1993/K-2/3 KD441 . . . . . . **745.54**
SIMON, S/Paper airplane book. /c1971/3-5/6 KD113 . . **629.133**
SMOLINSKI, J/Holiday origami. /1995/3-6/KD403 . . . . **736**

Papermaking.
BOURGEOIS, P/Amazing paper book. /1989/5-6/6 KD332 . . **676**
PAPER (VIDEOCASSETTE). /1986/5-6/KD334 . . . . . . **VCR 676**

Parades--Fiction.
BUNTING, E/St. Patrick's Day in the morning. /1980/
K-2/2 KF310 . . . . **E**
MILLS, C/Phoebe's parade. /1994/K-2/2 KG138 . . . . **E**

MURPHY, SJ/Best bug parade. /1996/P-1/1 KG163 . . . . **E**

Parades--Pictorial works.
CREWS, D/Parade. /1983/P-2/4 KB188 . . . . **394.2**

Parapsychology.
COHEN, D/Ghostly warnings. /1996/4-6/7 KA599 . . . . . **133.1**

Parent and child SEE ALSO Child rearing; Fathers; Mothers; Parenting.

Parent and child.
BRATMAN, F/Everything you need to know when a parent dies. /
1992/5-6/5 KA647 . . . . **155.9**
DADDY DOESN'T LIVE WITH US (VIDEOCASSETTE). /1994/
P-1/KA889 . . . . **VCR 306.89**
LESHAN, E/Learning to say goodbye: when a parent dies. /c1976/
5-6/7 KA651 . . . . **155.9**
MORRIS, A/Loving. /1990/1-3/2 KA880 . . . . **306.874**
SAUNDERS, J/Bringing out the best: a resource guide for parents
of young gifted children. /1991//KA189 . . . . **PROF 371.95**
WHEN THERE'S TROUBLE AT HOME (VIDEOCASSETTE). /1991/
A/KA883. . . . . **VCR 306.874**

Parent and child--Fiction.
BAWDEN, N/Granny the Pag. /1996/5-A/4 KG888 . . . . . . **Fic**
Humbug. /1992/5-A/5 KG891 . . . . **Fic**
BUNTING, E/Flower garden. /1994/P-2/3 KF299. . . . . **E**
CAREY, P/Big Bazoohley. /1995/3-6/5 KG973 . . . . **Fic**
CASELEY, J/Priscilla twice. /1995/1-3/2 KF368 . . . . **E**
CLEARY, B/Dear Mr. Henshaw. /1983/4-A/4 KG993 . . . . . **Fic**
Petey's bedtime story. /1993/2-3/3 KF395. . . . . **E**
FREEMAN, S/Cuckoo's child. /1996/5-A/5 KH142 . . . . . . **Fic**
GLEITZMAN, M/Misery guts. /1993/5-A/7 KH174. . . . . . **Fic**
HENKES, K/Owen. /1993/P-2/2 KF709 . . . . **E**
Owen (Videocassette). /1995/P-2/KF710 . . . . **VCR E**
RAWLINGS, MK/Yearling. /c1938, 1967/5-A/5 KH622 . . . . . **Fic**
RUSSO, M/Under the table. /1997/P-K/2 KG363 . . . . **E**
RYLANT, C/Birthday presents. /1991/P-1/2 KG368 . . . . **E**
SALTZBERG, B/Show-and-tell. /1994/K-2/2 KG388 . . . . . . **E**
SHIELDS, CD/I am really a princess. /1993/1-3/3 KG494 . . . . . **E**
TURNER, A/Through moon and stars and night skies. /1990/
P-2/1 KG629 . . . . **CE E**
VIGNA, J/When Eric's mom fought cancer. /1993/
1-3/3 KG654 . . . . **E**
VIORST, J/Good-bye book. /1988/P-2/2 KG662. . . . . **E**
WILLIAMS, VB/More more more, said the baby. /1990/
P-K/2 KG736 . . . . **E**
WOOD, A/Weird parents. /1990/K-2/4 KG767 . . . . **E**

Parental behavior in animals.
SIMON, S/Wild babies. /1997/3-5/6 KC459 . . . . **591.3**

Parenting.
CHANGE FOR THE BETTER: TEACHING CORRECT BEHAVIOR
(VIDEOCASSETTE). /1989//KA300 . . . . **VCR PROF 649**
IT'S GREAT TO BE ME! INCREASING YOUR CHILD'S SELF-
ESTEEM (VIDEOCASSETTE). /1989//KA302 . . . **VCR PROF 649**
MEETING THE CHALLENGE: PARENTING CHILDREN WITH
DISABILITIES (VIDEOCASSETTE). /1992/
/KA306 . . . . **VCR PROF 649.8**

Paris (France).
STEIN, RC/Paris. /1996/3-5/8 KE685 . . . . **944**

Paris (France)--Description.
AMERICAN IN PARIS: GERSHWIN (VIDEOCASSETTE). /1993/
1-6/KD517. . . . . **VCR 780**
BONJOUR DE PARIS (VIDEOCASSETTE). /1988/
5-A/KE683. . . . . **VCR 944**

Paris (France)--Fiction.
BEMELMANS, L/Madeline. /1962/P-2/4 KF218. . . . . **CE E**
Madeline and other Bemelmans (Talking book). /n.d./
P-2/KF219 . . . . **TB E**
Madeline's rescue. /c1953/P-2/2 KF220. . . . . **CE E**
CARLSON, NS/Family under the bridge. /c1958/
3-5/4 KG974. . . . . **Fic**
GOODE, D/Where's our mama? /1991/P-2/2 KF632. . . . . . . **E**
KALMAN, M/Ooh-la-la (Max in love). /1991/4-A/3 KH340. . . **Fic**
MCCULLY, EA/Mirette on the high wire. /1992/1-3/2 KG093. . . **E**
ZOLOTOW, C/Moon was the best. /1993/K-2/5 KG803. . . . . . **E**

Paris (France)--History--1940-1944--Fiction.
HOESTLANDT, J/Star of fear, star of hope. /1995/
3-5/5 KH268 . . . . **Fic**

Paris (France)--Pictorial works.
MUNRO, R/Inside-outside book of Paris. /1992/
2-6/8 KE684 . . . . **944**

Parker, Williams--Fiction.
ROSENBURG, JM/William Parker: rebel without rights: a novel
based on fact. /1996/6-A/7 KH654 . . . . **Fic**

Parks--Fiction.
ERNST, LC/Squirrel Park. /1993/K-2/5 KF533 . . . . **E**
WOLFF, A/Stella and Roy. /1993/P-1/3 KG756 . . . . **E**

Parks, Rosa.
    PARKS, R/I am Rosa Parks. /1997/1-2/4 KE491 . . . **B PARKS, R.**
    Rosa Parks: my story. /1992/6-A/5 KE490 . . . . . **B PARKS, R.**
Parks, Rosa--Correspondence.
    PARKS, R/Dear Mrs. Parks: a dialogue with today's youth. /1996/
    5-6/6 KA901 . . . . **323**
Parrish, Maxfield.
    MAXFIELD PARRISH: A TREASURY OF ART AND CHILDREN'S
    LITERATURE. /1995/K-6/KD413 . . . . **741.6**
Parrots.
    MURRAY, P/Parrots. /1993/3-5/7 KC701 . . . . **598.7**
Parrots--Fiction.
    KING-SMITH, D/Harry's Mad. /c1984, 1997/5-A/7 KH348 . . . **Fic**
    LESTER, H/Princess Penelope's parrot. /1996/K-2/2 KF965 . . . . . **E**
    MCDERMOTT, G/Papagayo the mischief maker. /1992/
    P-2/5 KG096 . . . . **E**
Parthenon (Athens, Greece).
    MACDONALD, F/Greek temple. /1992/4-6/7 KE643 . . . . . . **938**
Parties.
    COLE, J/Pin the tail on the donkey and other party games. /1993/
    K-2/3 KD698 . . . . **793**
    WEST, R/My very own Halloween: a book of cooking and crafts. /
    1993/3-6/5 KD701 . . . . **793.2**
Parties--Fiction.
    ADLER, DA/Young Cam Jansen and the dinosaur game. /1996/
    1-2/2 KF132 . . . . **E**
    GUY, GF/Fiesta! /1996/P-1/1 KF655 . . . . **E**
    HUTCHINS, P/Titch and Daisy. /1996/P-K/2 KF805 . . . . **E**
    Which witch is which? /1989/P-1/2 KF807 . . . . **E**
    JONAS, A/13th clue. /1992/1-2/1 KF851 . . . . **E**
    KLEVEN, E/Hooray! A pinata! /1996/K-2/2 KF910 . . . . . . **E**
    KLINE, S/Herbie Jones and the birthday showdown. /1995/
    3-4/3 KH366 . . . . **Fic**
    PRAGER, A/Baseball birthday party. /1995/1-3/2 KG286 . . . . . **E**
    Spooky Halloween party. /1981/1-3/2 KG287 . . . . . . **E**
    SOTO, G/Old man and his door. /1996/K-2/2 KG528 . . . . . . **E**
    WILDER, LI/Dance at Grandpa's. /1994/K-3/4 KG719 . . . . . . **E**
Parties--Fiction--Software.
    MARC BROWN'S ARTHUR'S BIRTHDAY. SCHOOL ED. (CD-ROM).
    /1994/K-4/KG062 . . . . **CDR E**
Passenger pigeons.
    MORRISON, SD/Passenger pigeon. /1989/4-6/4 KC656 . . . . **598**
Passover.
    CHAIKIN, M/Light another candle: the story and meaning of
    Hanukkah. /c1981, 1987/5-6/8 KA770 . . . . **296.4**
    SIMON, N/Story of Passover. /1997/2-4/3 KA781 . . . . . . **296.4**
Passover--Fiction.
    GOLDIN, BD/Magician's visit: a Passover tale. /1993/
    K-3/5 KF629 . . . . **E**
    MANUSHKIN, F/Matzah that Papa brought home. /1995/
    1-3/2 KG059 . . . . **E**
    SCHOTTER, R/Passover magic. /1995/K-2/2 KG410 . . . . . . **E**
    SILVERMAN, E/Gittel's hands. /1996/K-2/2 KG506 . . . . **E**
Pasta products.
    COREY, M/Spaghetti factory. /1990/3-4/7 KD319 . . . . **664**
Patchwork.
    PAUL, AW/Seasons sewn: a year in patchwork. /1996/
    3-6/7 KD462 . . . . **746.46**
Patience--Fiction.
    KURTZ, J/Pulling the lion's tail. /1995/1-3/6 KF937 . . . . **E**
Patrick, Saint.
    DE PAOLA, T/Patrick: patron saint of Ireland. /1992/
    2-4/4 KE492 . . . . **B PATRICK, ST.**
    HODGES, M/Saint Patrick and the peddler. /1993/
    3-4/5 KB454 . . . . **398.22**
Pattern perception.
    MURPHY, SJ/Pair of socks. /1996/P-1/2 KA634 . . . . . . **153.14**
Paulsen, Gary.
    PAULSEN, G/Puppies, dogs, and blue northers: reflections on being
    raised by a pack of sled dogs. /1996/3-6/7 KD859 . . . . . **798.8**
    Woodsong. /1990/5-A/6 KD824 . . . . **796.5**
Pawnee Indians--Fiction.
    PAULSEN, G/Mr. Tucket. /1994/5-A/5 KH588 . . . . **Fic**
Peace.
    BLUE, R/People of peace. /1994/5-A/7 KA806 . . . . **303.6**
    SCHOLES, K/Peace begins with you. /1990/P-2/5 KA812 . . . **303.6**
Peace--Fiction.
    HAMANAKA, S/Peace crane. /1995/1-3/4 KF668 . . . . **E**
    WOOD, D/Old Turtle. /1992/3-5/3 KH879 . . . . **CE Fic**
Peace--Folklore.
    MACDONALD, MR/Peace tales: world folktales to talk about. /
    1992//KA271 . . . . **PROF 398.2**

Peace--Songs and music.
    ROGERS, S/What can one little person do? (Sound recording
    cassette). /1992/P-2/KD654 . . . . **SRC 789.3**
Peale, Charles Willson.
    WILSON, J/Ingenious Mr. Peale: painter, patriot and man of
    science. /1996/6-A/8 KE493 . . . . **B PEALE, C.**
Peanut butter.
    ERLBACH, A/Peanut butter. /1994/4-6/7 KD265 . . . . **641.3**
Peanuts.
    ERLBACH, A/Peanut butter. /1994/4-6/7 KD265 . . . . **641.3**
    MICUCCI, C/Life and times of the peanut. /1997/
    3-6/11 KD268 . . . . **641.3**
Pearl fisheries--Fiction.
    O'DELL, S/Black pearl. /c1967/5-6/5 KH557 . . . . **CE Fic**
Pearl Harbor (Hawaii), Attack on, 1941--Fiction.
    SALISBURY, G/Under the blood-red sun. /1994/6-A/4 KH672 . **Fic**
Peary, Robert E. (Robert Edwin)--Fiction.
    CONRAD, P/Call me Ahnighito. /1995/2-5/2 KF413 . . . . **E**
Peddlers and peddling--Fiction.
    MCDONALD, M/Potato man. /1991/K-3/5 KG098 . . . . **E**
    SCHROEDER, A/Carolina shout! /1995/1-5/3 KG411 . . . . . . **E**
    SLOBODKINA, E/Caps for sale: a tale of a peddler, some monkeys
    and their monkey business. /c1947/P-2/1 KG519 . . . . . . **CE E**
    WEISS, N/Stone men. /1993/K-2/2 KG693 . . . . **E**
Peet, Bill.
    PEET, B/Bill Peet: an autobiography. /1989/
    6-A/8 KE494 . . . . **B PEET, B.**
Pegasus (Greek mythology).
    PEGASUS (VIDEOCASSETTE). /1990/3-6/KA749 . . . . **VCR 292**
Pelicans.
    PATENT, DH/Pelicans. /1992/5-6/8 KC682 . . . . **598.4**
    STONE, LM/Pelican. /1990/5-6/6 KC684 . . . . **598.4**
Pellatt, Henry Mill, Sir--Fiction.
    OBERMAN, S/White stone in the castle wall. /1995/
    4-6/2 KH555 . . . . **Fic**
Pen pals.
    VANDERHEYDEN-TRESCONY, C/Faxing friends; a resource guide
    for forming international friendships among /1992/
    /KA173 . . . . **PROF 370.117**
Pen pals--Fiction.
    HOBAN, L/Arthur's pen pal. /c1976/1-3/2 KF735 . . . . **E**
Penguins.
    CHESTER, J/Penguins of the Antarctic (Picture). /1995/
    4-6/KC685 . . . . **PIC 598.47**
    Penguins of the world (Picture). /1995/3-6/KC686 . . **PIC 598.47**
    FLETCHER, N/Penguin. /1993/P-1/2 KC687 . . . . . . **598.47**
    FONTANEL, B/Penguin: a funny bird. /1992/
    1-4/4 KC688 . . . . **598.47**
    PATENT, DH/Looking at penguins. /1993/5-6/5 KC689 . . . **598.47**
Penguins--Fiction.
    ATWATER, R/Mr. Popper's penguins. /c1938/
    3-5/4 KG854 . . . . **CE Fic**
    GRAVOIS, JM/Quickly, Quigley. /1994/P-1/2 KF635 . . . . **E**
Penmanship SEE ALSO Calligraphy.
Penmanship--Fiction.
    CLEARY, B/Muggie Maggie. /1990/3-5/5 KG998 . . . . **Fic**
Pennsylvania.
    MIDDLE ATLANTIC REGION: NEW YORK, NEW JERSEY,
    DELAWARE, MARYLAND, PENNSYLVANIA, /1996/
    4-6/KE924 . . . . **VCR 974**
    SWAIN, G/Pennsylvania. /1994/4-6/7 KE960 . . . . **974.8**
Pennsylvania--Fiction.
    AVI /Night journeys. /c1979, 1994/5-A/6 KG860 . . . . **Fic**
    FRITZ, J/Cabin faced west. /c1958/4-6/6 KH143 . . . . **Fic**
    RICHTER, C/Light in the forest. /1994/5-A/5 KH632 . . . . **Fic**
Pennsylvania--Folklore.
    KIRCHNER, AB/In days gone by: folklore and traditions of the
    Pennsylvania Dutch. /1996//KA268 . . . . **PROF 398.2**
Pennsylvania--History.
    BARTOLETTI, SC/Growing up in coal country. /1996/
    4-6/8 KA934 . . . . **331.3**
    WILLS, CA/Historical album of Pennsylvania. /1996/
    4-6/7 KE961 . . . . **974.8**
Pennsylvania--History--Colonial period, ca. 1600-1775.
    FRADIN, DB/Pennsylvania Colony. /1988/5-6/7 KE959 . . . . **974.8**
Pennsylvania--History--Fiction.
    BELL, F/Jenny's corner. /1995/5-A/7 KG894 . . . . **Fic**
Pennsylvania--History--Revolution, 1775-1783.
    FRADIN, DB/Pennsylvania Colony. /1988/5-6/7 KE959 . . . . **974.8**
Pennsylvania--History--1865--Fiction.
    PEREZ, NA/Breaker. /1988/6-A/7 KH597 . . . . **Fic**
Pennsylvania Dutch.
    KIRCHNER, AB/In days gone by: folklore and traditions of the
    Pennsylvania Dutch. /1996//KA268 . . . . **PROF 398.2**

Pennsylvania Dutch--Fiction.
MILHOUS, K/Egg tree. /c1950, 1992/1-3/4 KG134 . . . . **E**

Pennsylvania Dutch--Folklore.
KIRCHNER, AB/In days gone by: folklore and traditions of the Pennsylvania Dutch. /1996//KA268 . . . . **PROF 398.2**

Percentage.
RATIO/PROPORTION/PERCENT: THE MEANING OF PERCENT (VIDEOCASSETTE). /1987/5-6/KB980 . . . . **VCR 513.2**

Perception SEE ALSO Space perception; Visual perception.

Perception--Fiction.
LILLIE, P/Everything has a place. /1993/P-K/1 KF981 . . . . **E**
SHARMAT, MW/Gila monsters meet you at the airport. /1980/ K-2/1 KG480 . . . . **E**

Percussion instruments.
SHIPTON, A/Percussion. /1994/4-6/7 KD547 . . . . **786.8**

Peregrine falcon.
ARNOLD, C/Saving the peregrine falcon. /1990/ 4-6/7 KC708 . . . . **598.9**

Performance in children.
DIMIDJIAN, VJ/Early childhood at risk: actions and advocacy for young children. /1989//KA190 . . . . **PROF 372**

Performing arts SEE ALSO Actors and actresses; Afro-American musicians; Ballet; Circus; Musicians; Opera; Orchestra.

Performing arts--Wit and humor.
PLANET OF THE GRAPES: SHOW BIZ JOKES AND RIDDLES. / 1992/3-6/KD737 . . . . **793.735**

Periodicals.
RICHARDSON, SK/Magazines for children, a guide for parents, teachers, and librarians. /1983//KA022 . . . . **PROF 011.62**

Periodicals--Bibliography.
MAGAZINES FOR KIDS AND TEENS: REV. ED. /1997/ /KA018 . . . . **PROF 011.62**

Periodicals--Indexes.
ABRIDGED READERS' GUIDE TO PERIODICAL LITERATURE, AUTHOR AND SUBJECT INDEX TO A SELECTED LIST OF PERIODICALS. /1935-/3-6/KA496 . . . . **PER 050**

Perry, Matthew Calbraith.
BLUMBERG, R/Commodore Perry in the land of the Shogun. / 1985/5-A/7 KE706 . . . . **CE 952**

Persephone (Greek deity).
GERINGER, L/Pomegranate seeds: a classic Greek myth. /1995/ 3-6/5 KA742 . . . . **292**
HUTTON, W/Persephone. /1994/5-6/5 KA744 . . . . **292**
WALDHERR, K/Persephone and the pomegranate: a myth from Greece. /1993/4-6/6 KA753 . . . . **292**

Perseus (Greek mythology).
HUTTON, W/Perseus. /1993/5-6/4 KA745 . . . . **292**

Perseverance (Ethics)--Fiction.
PIPER, W/Little engine that could. /c1961/P-K/4 KG246 . . . **CE E**
YOLEN, J/Wizard's Hall. /1991/4-6/6 KH897 . . . . **Fic**

Persian Gulf War, 1991.
KENT, Z/Persian Gulf War: "the mother of all battles." /1994/ 6-A/6 KE715 . . . . **956.7044**

Personality SEE ALSO Individuality; Self.
Perspective SEE ALSO Drawing.

Perspective.
DUBOSQUE, D/Learn to draw 3-D. /1992/5-A/7 KD414. . . . **742**

Peru--Folklore.
EHLERT, L/Moon rope: a Peruvian folktale/Un lazo a la luna: una leyenda Peruana. /1992/1-3/2 KB563 . . . . **398.24**
HICKOX, R/Zorro and Quwi: tales of a trickster guinea pig. /1997/ 1-3/3 KB590 . . . . **398.24**
KURTZ, J/Miro in the Kingdom of the Sun. /1996/ 3-4/5 KB505 . . . . **398.23**

Peru--History--Conquest, 1522-1548.
MARRIN, A/Inca and Spaniard: Pizarro and the conquest of Peru. / 1989/A/8 KF109 . . . . **985**

Peters, Steven.
PETERS, RM/Clambake: a Wampanoag tradition. /1992/ 4-6/5 KE780 . . . . **970.444**

Petroleum.
PRINGLE, LP/Oil spills: damage, recovery, and prevention. /1993/ 5-6/9 KB065 . . . . **363.73**

Petrology SEE ALSO Geology; Mineralogy; Rocks.
Pets SEE ALSO Domestic animals.

Pets.
ARNOLD, C/Pets without homes. /1983/1-4/6 KD189. . . . **636.08**
BARE, CS/Guinea pigs don't read books. /c1985, 1993/ P-2/3 KD177 . . . . **636**
Toby the tabby kitten. /1995/K-3/2 KD229. . . . . **636.8**
COLE, J/My new kitten. /1995/P-1/2 KD230. . . . . **636.8**
EVANS, M/Guinea pigs. /1992/3-6/6 KD178 . . . . **636**
Rabbit. /1992/3-6/4 KD179 . . . . **636**
GIBBONS, G/Cats. /1996/K-3/3 KC821 . . . . **599.75**

GRIEHL, K/Snakes: giant snakes and non-venomous snakes in the terrarium. /1984/A/9 KD249 . . . . **639.3**
HANSEN, E/Guinea pigs. /1992/4-6/6 KD181 . . . . **636**
JOHNSON, SA/Ferrets. /1997/5-6/10 KD182 . . . . **636**
KING-SMITH, D/I love guinea pigs. /1995/K-4/3 KD183 . . . . **636**
PAWS, CLAWS, FEATHERS AND FINS (VIDEOCASSETTE). / 1993/3-5/KD191 . . . . **VCR 636.088**
PFEFFER, W/What's it like to be a fish? /1996/K-3/3 KC585 . **597**
PIERS, H/Taking care of your gerbils. /1993/3-5/6 KD184. . . **636**
TAYLOR, D/You and your dog. /1986/5-A/KD224. . . . . . **636.7**
WEXLER, J/Pet gerbils. /1990/4-6/7 KD186 . . . . **636**
Pet hamsters. /1992/4-6/7 KD187 . . . . **636**
WILKE, H/Turtles: everything about purchase, care, nutrition and diseases. /1983/5-6/9 KD250 . . . . **639.3**
ZIEFERT, H/Let's get a pet. /c1993, 1996/K-3/2 KD193 . **636.088**

Pets--Fiction.
BAKER, KL/Seneca. /1997/K-2/2 KF185. . . . . **E**
BRETT, J/Annie and the wild animals. /1985/K-3/2 KF260 . . . . **E**
COVILLE, B/Jeremy Thatcher, dragon hatcher: a magic shop book. / 1991/4-A/4 KH036. . . . . **CE Fic**
CRESSWELL, H/Meet Posy Bates. /1992/3-5/5 KH038 . . . . . . **Fic**
DE PAOLA, T/Little Grunt and the big egg: a prehistoric fairy tale. /1990/K-2/2 KF472 . . . . **E**
DEJONG, M/Shadrach. /c1953/2-3/5 KH069. . . . . **Fic**
GLASER, L/Rosie's birthday rat. /1996/1-3/2 KH171 . . . . . **Fic**
GREENWOOD, PD/What about my goldfish? /1993/ 1-3/2 KF644 . . . . **E**
GRIFFITH, HV/Mine will, said John. New ed. /1992/ P-2/2 KF649 . . . . **E**
HOFFMAN, M/Four-legged ghosts. /1995/2-4/6 KH269 . . . . . **Fic**
KEATS, EJ/Ezra Jack Keats Library (Videocassette). /1992/ P-2/KF871 . . . . **VCR E**
Maggie and the pirate. /1979/P-2/2 KF875 . . . . **E**
Pet show. /1987/P-2/2 KF876 . . . . **CE E**
KING-SMITH, D/Mr. Potter's pet. /1996/3-5/2 KH352 . . . . . **Fic**
Sophie hits six. /1993/2-4/6 KH354 . . . . **Fic**
Sophie in the saddle. /1996/3-5/6 KH355 . . . . **Fic**
MONFRIED, L/No more animals! /1995/1-3/2 KH502. . . . . **Fic**
NAPOLI, DJ/Bravest thing. /1995/3-5/6 KH529 . . . . **Fic**
PARISH, P/No more monsters for me! /1981/K-1/1 KG215 . . . **E**
QUATTLEBAUM, M/Jazz, Pizzazz, and the silver threads. /1996/ 2-4/3 KH615 . . . . **Fic**
Magic Squad and the dog of great potential. /1997/ 2-4/4 KH616 . . . . **Fic**
RYLANT, C/Everyday pets (Board book). /1993/ P-K/2 KF373 . . . . **BB E**
Mr. Putter and Tabby row the boat. /1997/K-2/2 KG381 . . . . **E**
WAGGONER, K/Partners. /1995/2-4/4 KH836. . . . . **Fic**
WOLF, J/Daddy, could I have an elephant? /1996/ K-2/2 KF755 . . . . **E**
ZOLOTOW, C/Old dog. Rev. and newly illustrated ed. /1995/ K-2/2 KG806 . . . . **E**

Pets--Miscellanea.
SQUIRE, A/101 questions and answers about pets and people. / 1988/5-6/7 KD192 . . . . **636.088**

Pharaohs SEE Kings, queens, rulers, etc.; names of specific individuals e.g. Tutankhamun.

Philadelphia (Pa.)--History.
INDEPENDENCE: BIRTH OF A FREE NATION (VIDEOCASSETTE). /1976/A/KE890 . . . . **VCR 973.4**

Philippines--Folklore.
ARUEGO, J/Rockabye crocodile. /1988/P-K/2 KB525. . . . **398.24**
SAN SOUCI, RD/Pedro and the monkey. /1996/ 3-4/2 KB649 . . . . **398.24**

Philippines--Social life and customs.
KINKADE, S/Children of the Philippines. /1996/ 3-6/8 KE722 . . . . **959.9**

Phobias--Fiction.
SNYDER, ZK/Fool's gold. /1993/6-A/7 KH732 . . . . **Fic**

Phonograph record SEE Sound recording.
Photographers SEE ALSO names of specific photographers e.g. Brady, Matthew.

Photographers.
DUNLAP, J/Eye on the wild: a story about Ansel Adams. /1995/ 3-6/7 KE225 . . . . **B ADAMS, A.**
FREEDMAN, R/Kids at work: Lewis Hine and the crusade against child labor. /1994/5-A/8 KA937 . . . . **331.3**
SULLIVAN, G/Black artists in photography, 1840-1940. /1996/ 5-6/12 KD510 . . . . **770**
TURNER, R/Dorothea Lange. /1994/5-A/7 KE427 . . **B LANGE, D.**

Photography SEE ALSO Animation (Cinematography); Cameras; Motion picture photography; Nature Photography.

Photography.
GIBBONS, G/Click!: a book about cameras and taking pictures. / 1997/2-4/5 KD512 . . . . **771**
HOBAN, T/Look book. /1997/P-K/KD516 . . . . **779**
KING, D/My first photography book. /1994/3-6/3 KD513. . . **771**
PHOTOGRAPHY. /1994/5-A/7 KD514. . . . . **771**

Photography--Fiction.
GREGORY, K/Earthquake at dawn. /1992/5-A/6 KH202. . . . . **Fic**
WILLARD, N/Simple pictures are best. /c1977/K-3/6 KG724 . . . **E**

Photography--History.
CZECH, KP/Snapshot: America discovers the camera. /1996/ 5-6/10 KD509 . . . . **770**
SULLIVAN, G/Black artists in photography, 1840-1940. /1996/ 5-6/12 KD510 . . . . **770**

Photography--Lighting--Experiments.
ZUBROWSKI, B/Shadow play: making pictures with light and lenses. /1995/4-8/7 KC117 . . . . **535**

Photography, artistic.
TUCKER, JS/Come look with me: discovering photographs with children. /1994/K-6/5 KD511 . . . . **770**

Photosynthesis.
ASIMOV, I/How did we find out about photosynthesis? /1989/ 6-A/9 KC277 . . . . **572**
WHAT IS A LEAF? (VIDEOCASSETTE). /1991/ K-3/KC401. . . . . **VCR 581.4**
WHAT IS A PLANT? (VIDEOCASSETTE). /1991/ 3-6/KC395. . . . . **VCR 580**

Physical education and training SEE ALSO Aerobics; Exercise; Games; Gymnastics; Physical fitness; Sports.

Physical education and training--Periodicals.
TEACHING ELEMENTARY PHYSICAL EDUCATION. /1990-/ /KA149. . . . . **PER PROF 050**

Physical education and training--Study and teaching.
TEACHING ELEMENTARY PHYSICAL EDUCATION. /1990-/ /KA149. . . . . **PER PROF 050**

Physical fitness.
CARLE, E/From head to toe. /1997/P-K/1 KF341 . . . . **E**
COLGATE, B/Silly Willy workout (Sound recording cassette). / 1994/P-1/KD609 . . . . **SRC 789.3**
GALLINA, J/Feelin' good (Sound recording cassette). /1981/ 1-3/KC983. . . . . **SRC 613**
LOOKING GOOD, FEELING GOOD (VIDEOCASSETTE). /1994/ 5-6/KC951. . . . . **VCR 612.6**
MY BODY, MY BUDDY: HEALTHY FUN (VIDEOCASSETTE). / 1993/3-5/KC988 . . . . **VCR 613.7**
MY BODY, MY BUDDY: HEALTHY HABITS (VIDEOCASSETTE). / 1993/2-4/KD301 . . . . **VCR 646.7**
PAIGE, D/Day in the life of a sports therapist. /1985/ 3-5/6 KC989 . . . . **613.7**
PALMER, H/Sammy and other songs from "Getting to know myself" (Videocassette). /1993/P-1/KD643 . . . . **VCR 789.3**
ROCK 'N ROLL FITNESS FUN (SOUND RECORDING CASSETTE). /1989/K-6/KC990. . . . . **SRC 613.7**
STEWART, G/Good morning exercises for kids (Sound recording cassette). /1987/P-3/KC991 . . . . **SRC 613.7**

Physical geography SEE ALSO Climate; Earth; Earthquakes; Geophysics; Glaciers; Icebergs; Lakes; Meteorology; Ocean; Rivers; Tides; Volcanoes; Winds.

Physical geography--Africa.
AFRICA (VIDEOCASSETTE). /1991/4-A/KE724 . . . . . . **VCR 960**

Physical geography--Antarctica.
ANTARCTICA (VIDEOCASSETTE). /1991/4-A/KF124 . . **VCR 998**

Physical geography--Asia.
ASIA (VIDEOCASSETTE). /1991/4-A/KE699. . . . . . . **VCR 950**

Physical geography--Australia.
AUSTRALIA (VIDEOCASSETTE). /1991/4-A/KF114 . . . **VCR 994**

Physical geography--Hawaii.
RAYSON, A/Hawai'i: the Pacific State. Rev. and updated edition. / 1997/5-A/6 KF123 . . . . **996.9**

Physical geography--North America.
ROCKY MOUNTAINS (VIDEOCASSETTE). /1989/ 5-6/KE181. . . . . **VCR 917**

Physical measurements--Experiments.
MARKLE, S/Measuring up!: experiments, puzzles, and games exploring measurement. /1995/5-6/6 KC086 . . . . **530.8**

Physically handicapped SEE ALSO Blind; Deaf; Mutism; etc.

Physically handicapped.
ADLER, DA/Picture book of Louis Braille. /1997/ 2-3/3 KE261 . . . . **B BRAILLE, L.**
BROWN, T/Someone special, just like you. /1984/ P-2/6 KA262 . . . . **152.4**
EMMERT, M/I'm the big sister now. /1989/3-5/5 KD039 . **618.92**

FREEDMAN, R/Out of darkness: the story of Louis Braille. /1997/ 3-5/6 KE262 . . . . **B BRAILLE, L.**
GREENE, L/Sign language talk. /1989/5-A/9 KB825 . . . . . **419**
KRAMER, J/Jim Abbott. /1996/4-5/6 KE223 . . . . **B ABBOTT, J.**
MCMAHON, P/Listen for the bus: David's story. /1995/ 1-3/3 KB004 . . . . **362.4**
  Summer tunes: a Martha's Vineyard vacation. /1996/ 2-5/7 KB005 . . . . **362.4**
MOORE, E/Buddy: the first seeing eye dog. /1996/ 1-3/3 KB006 . . . . **362.4**
RENFRO, N/Puppetry, language, and the special child: discovering alternate languages. /1984//KA328 . . . . **PROF 791.5**
ROSENBERG, MB/Finding a way: living with exceptional brothers and sisters. /1988/4-6/8 KB008. . . . . **362.4**

Physically handicapped--Biography.
GREENE, C/Margarete Steiff: toy maker. /1993/ 2-3/2 KE550 . . . . **B STEIFF, M.**
HELEN KELLER (VIDEOCASSETTE). /1990/ 4-6/KE415. **VCR B KELLER, H.**
KELLER, H/Story of my life. /c1988, 1990/ 6-A/8 KE416 . . . . **B KELLER, H.**
LUNDELL, M/Girl named Helen Keller. /1995/ 1-2/1 KE417 . . . . **B KELLER, H.**

Physically handicapped--Fiction.
BLUME, J/Deenie. /1973/6/4 KG907 . . . . **Fic**
BOOTH, BD/Mandy. /1991/K-2/5 KF250. . . . . **E**
BURNETT, FH/Secret garden. /c1911, 1987/3-6/5 KG951. . **CE Fic**
CARRICK, C/Melanie. /1996/1-3/2 KF360 . . . . **E**
CASELEY, J/Harry and Willy and Carrothead. /1991/ K-1/2 KF365 . . . . **E**
DE ANGELI, M/Door in the wall. /c1949, 1989/4-6/6 KH064 . **Fic**
DE PAOLA, T/Now one foot, now the other. /1981/ K-3/5 KF476 . . . . **E**
DORRIS, M/Sees Behind Trees. /1996/5-A/4 KH081 . . . . **Fic**
FARRELL, M/Marrying Malcolm Murgatroyd. /1995/ 5-A/4 KH111 . . . . **Fic**
FASSLER, J/Howie helps himself. /1974, c1975/K-2/4 KF544 . . . **E**
FLEISCHMAN, P/Half-a-Moon Inn. /c1980, 1991/6/7 KH117 . . **Fic**
GLEITZMAN, M/Blabber mouth. /1995/3-5/4 KH173 . . . . . . **Fic**
  Sticky Beak. /1995/3-5/4 KH176 . . . . **Fic**
HAMM, DJ/Grandma drives a motor bed. /1987/P-3/2 KF669. . **E**
HATRICK, G/Masks. /1996/6-A/3 KH225 . . . . **Fic**
HELFMAN, E/On being Sarah. /1993/5-A/6 KH236. . . . . . . **Fic**
HIROSHIMA MAIDEN (VIDEOCASSETTE). /c1988, 1997/ 5-A/KH264 . . . . **VCR Fic**
KONIGSBURG, EL/View from Saturday. /1996/5-A/7 KH377 . . **Fic**
LAKIN, P/Dad and me in the morning. /1994/1-3/2 KF942 . . . . **E**
LEE, JM/Silent Lotus. /1991/P-2/4 KF956. . . . . **E**
LITCHFIELD, AB/Words in our hands. /1980/4-6/5 KH413 . . . **Fic**
LITTLE, J/Mine for keeps. /c1962, 1994/5-A/5 KH414 . . . . . **Fic**
MCKENZIE, EK/Stargone John. /1990/3-5/5 KH484 . . . . **Fic**
MOON, N/Lucy's picture. /1995/P-1/2 KG153 . . . . **E**
NEUFELD, J/Gaps in stone walls. /1996/6-A/7 KH546 . . . . . **Fic**
ROSTKOWSKI, MI/After the dancing days. /1986/ 6-A/4 KH656 . . . . **Fic**
SLEPIAN, J/Alfred Summer. /1980/4-6/4 KH718 . . . . **Fic**
TAYLOR, T/Timothy of the cay. /1993/5-A/5 KH785 . . . . . . **Fic**

Physicians SEE ALSO Medicine--Vocational guidance; Women physicians.

Physicians.
BUTTS, ER/May Chinn: the best medicine. /1995/ 5-A/8 KE288 . . . . **B CHINN, M.**
CROFFORD, E/Frontier surgeons: a story about the Mayo Brothers. /1989/5-6/6 KC899 . . . . **610.69**
HAYDEN, RC/11 African-American doctors. Rev. and expanded ed. /1992/5-6/8 KC900 . . . . **610.69**
SIMMONS, A/Ben Carson. /1996/4-6/7 KE276 . **B CARSON, B.**

Physicians--Fiction.
DEFELICE, CC/Apprenticeship of Lucas Whitaker. /1998/ 5-A/6 KH066 . . . . **CE Fic**

Physicists.
MCPHERSON, SS/Ordinary genius: the story of Albert Einstein. / 1995/5-A/6 KE334 . . . . **B EINSTEIN, A.**
PFLAUM, R/Marie Curie and her daughter Irene. /1993/ 6-A/8 KC139 . . . . **539.7**

Physics SEE ALSO Dynamics; Electronics; Geophysics; Gravity; Light; Magnetism; Matter; Mechanics; Sound; Statics.

Physics.
CASH, T/101 physics tricks: fun experiments with everyday materials. /1993/4-8/7 KC077. . . . . **530**
LET'S MOVE IT: NEWTON'S LAWS OF MOTION (VIDEOCASSETTE). /1987/5-A/KC096 . . . . **VCR 531**
SOLID, LIQUID, GAS (VIDEOCASSETTE). /1986/ 3-6/KC083. . . . . **VCR 530.4**

SOLIDS, LIQUIDS AND GASES (VIDEOCASSETTE). /1994/
4-6/KC084. . . . . **VCR 530.4**

Physics--Experiments.
BUBBLEOLOGY I AND II (VIDEOCASSETTE). /1988/
3-A/KA292. . . . . **VCR PROF 530.4**
CASH, T/101 physics tricks: fun experiments with everyday
materials. /1993/4-8/7 KC077. . . . . **530**
SIMON, S/Optical illusion book. /c1976, 1984/4-6/5 KC115. **535**
WATER ROCKETS I (VIDEOCASSETTE). /1994/
5-A/KA291 . . . . **VCR PROF 530**
ZUBROWSKI, B/Bubbles. /1979/4-6/8 KC085 . . . . **530.4**

Physics--Study and teaching (Elementary)--Activity programs.
TAYLOR, BA/Teaching physics with toys: activities for grades K-9. /
1995//KA204 . . . . **PROF 372.3**

Physiology SEE ALSO Anatomy; Blood; Bones; Cells; Digestion; Growth;
Muscles; Nervous system; Nutrition; Old age; Reproduction; Respiration;
Senses and sensation.

Physiology.
ALLISON, L/Blood and guts: a working guide to your own insides. /
c1976/4-6/4 KC912 . . . . **612**
NERVOUS SYSTEM (VIDEOCASSETTE). /1994/
5-6/KC970. . . . . **VCR 612.8**
PARKER, S/Eye and seeing. Rev. ed. /1989/A/8 KC972 . . . **612.8**

Piano.
TURNER, BC/Living piano. /1996/4-6/12 KD546 . . . . . **BA 786.2**

Piano music.
LOUCHARD, R/Hey, Ludwig!: classical piano solos for playful times
(Sound recording cassette). /1993/P-3/KD675 . . . . . **SRC 789.8**

Piazza, Mike.
SAVAGE, J/Mike Piazza: hard-hitting catcher. /1997/
4-6/7 KE495 . . . . **B PIAZZA, M.**

Picasso, Pablo.
LORIA, S/Pablo Picasso. /1995/4-A/12 KD490 . . . . . . **759.4**
MUHLBERGER, R/What makes a Picasso a Picasso? /1994/
5-A/7 KD493 . . . . **759.4**

Pickett, Bill.
PINKNEY, AD/Bill Pickett: rodeo-ridin' cowboy. /1996/
2-5/7 KE496 . . . . **B PICKETT, B.**

Picnicking--Fiction.
COHEN, M/See you in second grade! /1989/K-1/2 KF404 . **CE E**
DUBANEVICH, A/Pig William. /1985/P-2/1 KF498. . . . . **E**
MAHY, M/Rattlebang picnic. /1994/K-2/5 KG057 . . . . **E**
MCCULLY, EA/Picnic. /1984/P-2/KG094 . . . . **CE E**
RYLANT, C/Mr. Putter and Tabby row the boat. /1997/
K-2/2 KG381 . . . . **E**
THOMAS, JR/Celebration! /1997/1-3/3 KG604 . . . . **E**

Picture books for children--Authorship.
STEWIG, JW/Looking at picture books. /1995/
/KA312 . . . . **PROF 741.6**

Picture books for children--Bibliography.
AMMON, BD/Worth a thousand words: an annotated guide to
picture books for older readers. /1996//KA010 . . **PROF 011.62**
LIMA, CW/A to zoo: subject access to children's picture books. 5th
ed. /1998//KA017 . . . . **PROF 011.62**

Picture books for children--Educational aspects--Bibliography.
HARMS, JM/Picture books to enhance the curriculum. /1996/
/KA016 . . . . **PROF 011.62**

Picture books for children--Educational aspects--Indexes.
HARMS, JM/Picture books to enhance the curriculum. /1996/
/KA016 . . . . **PROF 011.62**

Picture dictionaries.
BAKER, PJ/My first book of sign. /c1986, 1995/K-3/KB821 . . **419**
CORBEIL, J/Facts on File visual dictionary. /1986/
6-A/KA390 . . . . **REF 031.02**
HILLERICH, RL/American Heritage picture dictionary. /1994/
P-1/KA423. . . . . **REF 423**

Picture puzzles.
BAKER, K/Hide and snake. /1991/P-1/2 KF186 . . . . **E**
GARDNER, B/Guess what? /1985/A-3/KB904 . . . . **508**
GEISERT, A/Pigs from 1 to 10. /1992/1-3/3 KF604 . . . . **E**
MACAULAY, D/Shortcut. /1995/3-A/3 KH434 . . . . **Fic**
MACDONALD, S/Peck slither and slide. /1997/P-2/1 KC452 . **591**
ROLAND-ENTWISTLE, T/More errata: another book of historical
errors. /1995/3-6/10 KE143 . . . . **909**
ROSEN, M/Michael Rosen's ABC. /1996/2-4/KE109 . . . . . . **821**
WICK, W/I spy Christmas: a book of picture riddles. /1992/
P-2/KD715. . . . . **793.73**
I spy fantasy: a book of picture riddles. /1994/
K-3/3 KD716 . . . . **793.73**
I spy school days: a book of picture riddles. /1995/
K-3/3 KD717 . . . . **793.73**
I spy spooky night: a book of picture riddles. /1996/
P-3/5 KD718 . . . . **793.73**

Pied Piper of Hamelin (Legendary character).
LATIMER, J/Irish piper. /1991/3-5/6 KB463 . . . . **398.22**

Pierce, Elijah--Fiction.
ROSEN, MJ/Elijah's angel: a story for Chanukah and Christmas. /
1992/3-6/7 KH652 . . . . **Fic**

Pierre, Louis.
CRUM, R/Eagle drum: on the powwow trail with a young grass
dancer. /1994/5-A/5 KB197 . . . . **394.26**

Pies--Fiction.
PRICEMAN, M/How to make an apple pie and see the world. /
1994/K-2/3 KG288 . . . . **E**

Pigeons.
NOFSINGER, R/Pigeons and doves. /1992/4-6/4 KC696 . . **598.6**

Pigeons--Fiction.
SELDEN, G/Chester Cricket's pigeon ride. /1983/
3-4/5 KH693 . . . . **Fic**

Pigs.
NICHOLSON, D/Wild boars. /1987/5-6/9 KC786 . . . . . . **599.63**

Pigs--Fiction.
AXELROD, A/Pigs in the pantry: fun with math and cooking. /
1997/1-3/3 KF178 . . . . **E**
Pigs on a blanket. /1996/2-3/2 KF179. . . . . **E**
CHRISTELOW, E/Great pig escape. /1994/1-3/2 KF388 . . . . . **E**
CORBALIS, J/Porcellus, the flying pig. /1988/2-4/5 KH029 . . . **Fic**
DUBANEVICH, A/Pig William. /1985/P-2/1 KF498. . . . . **E**
GEISERT, A/Pigs from A to Z. /1986/1-3/3 KF603 . . . . **E**
Pigs from 1 to 10. /1992/1-3/3 KF604 . . . . **E**
HEINE, H/Pigs' wedding. /c1978, 1986/P-2/6 KF697 . . . . **CE E**
HELLER, N/This little piggy. /1997/P-1/2 KF699. . . . . **E**
HUTCHINS, P/Little Pink Pig. /1994/P-1/2 KF799 . . . . **E**
JOHNSON, A/Julius. /1993/P-2/2 KF831 . . . . **E**
KELLER, H/Geraldine first. /1996/K-2/2 KF881 . . . . **E**
KING-SMITH, D/Babe: the gallant pig. /1994/
2-5/5 KH346 . . . . **CE Fic**
LOBEL, A/Small pig. /c1969/K-2/2 KG012 . . . . **E**
LOWELL, S/Three little javelinas. /1992/K-2/4 KG039. . . . . . **E**
MCPHAIL, D/Pigs ahoy! /1995/P-2/3 KG121 . . . . **E**
Pigs aplenty, pigs galore! /1993/P-2/2 KG122 . . . . **E**
MEDDAUGH, S/Hog-eye. /1995/K-3/2 KG123 . . . . **E**
RAYNER, M/Mr. and Mrs. Pig's evening out. /c1976/
K-2/4 KG317 . . . . **E**
RYLANT, C/Poppleton. /1997/K-2/2 KG384 . . . . **E**
SCIESZKA, J/True story of the 3 little pigs. /1989/
K-3/2 KG421 . . . . **CE E**
STEIG, W/Amazing bone. /1976/1-3/5 KG539 . . . . . . **CE E**
Farmer Palmer's wagon ride. /c1974, 1992/K-3/6 KG543 . . . **E**
Zeke Pippin. /1994/1-3/6 KG549 . . . . **E**
TEAGUE, M/Pigsty. /1994/K-2/2 KG595 . . . . **E**
TRIVIZAS, E/Three little wolves and the big bad pig. /1993/
P-3/4 KG619 . . . . **E**
VAN LEEUWEN, J/Oliver Pig at school. /1994/
K-2/1 KG648 . . . . **CE E**
Tales of Oliver Pig. /1979/K-2/1 KG649 . . . . **CE E**
WHITE, EB/Charlotte's web. /c1952/3-6/6 KH850 . . . . **Fic**
WOOD, D/Piggies. /1991/P-K/1 KG768 . . . . **E**
YOLEN, J/Piggins. /1987/K-3/4 KG779 . . . . **E**

Pigs--Folklore.
ARUEGO, J/Rockabye crocodile. /1988/P-K/2 KB525 . . . **398.24**
HOOKS, WH/Three little pigs and the fox. /1989/
2-4/5 KB592 . . . . **398.24**
MARSHALL, J/Three little pigs. /1989/K-2/2 KB613 . . . **CE 398.24**
ROUNDS, G/Three little pigs and the big bad wolf. /1992/
K-3/4 KB645 . . . . **398.24**
THREE BILLY GOATS GRUFF; AND, THE THREE LITTLE PIGS
(VIDEOCASSETTE). /1989/P-K/KB665 . . . . **VCR 398.24**
ZEMACH, M/Three little pigs. /1988/P-2/4 KB682 . . . . . **398.24**

Pigs--Poetry.
SNUFFLES AND SNOUTS: POEMS. /1995/P-2/KE083 . . **811.008**

Pike, Zebulon Montgomery.
SANFORD, WR/Zebulon Pike: explorer of the Southwest. /1996/
5-6/8 KE497 . . . . **B PIKE, Z.**

Pilgrims (New Plymouth Colony).
ANDERSON, J/First Thanksgiving feast. /1984/
2-4/7 KE935 . . . . **974.4**
BOWEN, G/Stranded at Plimoth Plantation, 1626. /1994/
5-6/7 KE870 . . . . **973.2**
BULLA, CR/Squanto: friend of the Pilgrims. /c1954, 1982/
3/3 KE547. . . . . **B SQUANTO**
DALGLIESH, A/Thanksgiving story. /c1954/3-6/4 KB222 . **394.264**
DAUGHERTY, J/Landing of the Pilgrims. /c1950/
4-6/7 KE938 . . . . **974.4**
FRITZ, J/Who's that stepping on Plymouth Rock? /c1975/
3-5/5 KE940 . . . . **CE 974.4**
GEORGE, JC/First Thanksgiving. /1993/4-6/6 KB223 . . . **394.264**

HAYWARD, L/First Thanksgiving. /1990/
1-4/2 KB227 . . . . **CE 394.264**
METAXAS, E/Squanto and the first Thanksgiving (Kit). /1996/
2-6/KE548 . . . . **KIT B SQUANTO**
MOURT'S RELATION /Homes in the wilderness: a pilgrim's journal
of Plymouth Plantation in 1620. /c1939, 1988/
5-A/8 KE941 . . . . **974.4**
PENNER, LR/Pilgrims at Plymouth. /1996/1-3/2 KE943 . . . **974.4**
PILGRIM VOICES: OUR FIRST YEAR IN THE NEW WORLD. /
1995/3-6/7 KE944 . . . . **974.4**
SAN SOUCI, RD/N.C. Wyeth's pilgrims. /1991/
4-6/7 KE946 . . . . **974.4**
SEWALL, M/Pilgrims of Plimoth. /1986/4-6/7 KE947 . . **CE 974.4**
WATERS, K/Samuel Eaton's day: a day in the life of a Pilgrim boy.
/1993/3-5/6 KE948 . . . . **974.4**
Sarah Morton's day: a day in the life of a Pilgrim girl. /1989/
3-5/3 KE949 . . . . **974.4**
Tapenum's day: a Wampanoag Indian boy in pilgrim times. /
1996/3-5/2 KE950 . . . . **974.4**
Pilgrims (New Plymouth Colony)--Fiction.
ACCORSI, W/Friendship's first Thanksgiving. /1992/
P-1/2 KF127 . . . . **E**
BRINK, CR/Goody O'Grumpity. /1994/K-3/3 KF268 . . . . **E**
VAN LEEUWEN, J/Across the wide dark sea: the Mayflower
journey. /1995/2-4/4 KG645 . . . . **E**
Pilgrims (New Plymouth Colony)--Social life and customs.
PENNER, LR/Eating the plates: a Pilgrim book of food and manners.
/1991/3-6/4 KB186 . . . . **394.1**
Pilgrims (New Plymouth Colony) in art.
SAN SOUCI, RD/N.C. Wyeth's pilgrims. /1991/
4-6/7 KE946 . . . . **974.4**
Pilots, Airplane SEE Air pilots.
Pinatas.
ANCONA, G/Pinata maker./El Pinatero. /1994/
3-6/6 KD450 . . . . **745.594**
Pinatas--Fiction.
KLEVEN, E/Hooray! A pinata! /1996/K-2/2 KF910 . . . . **E**
Pioneer life SEE Frontier and pioneer life.
Pioneers.
ADLER, DA/Picture book of Davy Crockett. /1996/
2-3/7 KE310 . . . . **B CROCKETT, D.**
DANIEL BOONE'S FINAL FRONTIER (VIDEOCASSETTE). /1995/
4-5/KE259. . . . . **VCR B BOONE, D.**
KNIGHT, AS/Way west: journal of a pioneer woman. /1993/
5-6/5 KE197 . . . . **917.8**
LEVINSON, NS/Snowshoe Thompson. /1992/
K-3/2 KE564 . . . . **B THOMPSON, S.**
SANFORD, WR/Kit Carson: frontier scout. /1996/
5-6/7 KE277 . . . . **B CARSON, K.**
SEAVER, JE/Captured by Indians: the life of Mary Jemison. /1995/
5-A/8 KE405 . . . . **B JEMISON, M.**
STEFOFF, R/Children of the westward trail. /1996/
4-6/8 KF050 . . . . **978**
Pippen, Scottie.
SCHNAKENBERG, R/Scottie Pippen: reluctant superstar. /1997/
4-6/6 KE498 . . . . **B PIPPEN, S.**
Pippin, Horace.
LYONS, ME/Starting home: the story of Horace Pippin, painter. /
1993/5-A/5 KE499 . . . . **B PIPPIN, H.**
Pirates.
GIBBONS, G/Pirates: robbers of the high seas. /1993/
2-4/7 KE154 . . . . **910.4**
MCCULLY, EA/Pirate queen. /1995/3-5/5 KE156 . . . . **910.4**
PLATT, R/Pirate. /1994/4-A/7 KE157 . . . . **910.4**
STEELE, P/Pirates. /1997/3-6/7 KE160 . . . . **910.4**
Pirates--Fiction.
AHLBERG, J/It was a dark and stormy night. /1993/
3-5/6 KG822 . . . . **Fic**
BULLA, CR/Pirate's promise. /c1986, 1994/2-4/2 KG937. . . . . **Fic**
DUBOWSKI, CE/Pirate School. /1996/1-3/2 KF499 . . . . **E**
FIENBERG, A/Wiggy and Boa. /c1988, 1990/5-6/7 KH113 . . . **Fic**
FLEISCHMAN, S/Ghost in the noonday sun. /1965/
5-A/7 KH121 . . . . **Fic**
13th floor: a ghost story. /1995/5-A/6 KH127 . . . . **CE Fic**
FOX, M/Tough Boris. /1994/K-2/2 KF573 . . . . **E**
HUTCHINS, P/One-Eyed Jake. /c1979, 1994/K-2/4 KF801 . . . . **E**
MAHY, M/Great piratical rumbustification and The librarian and the
robbers. /c1978, 1986/5-A/7 KH449 . . . . **Fic**
Tingleberries, tuckertubs and telephones: a tale of love and ice-
cream. /1996/3-6/5 KH454 . . . . **Fic**
MCNAUGHTON, C/Captain Abdul's pirate school. /1994/
1-3/3 KG113 . . . . **E**
MCPHAIL, D/Edward and the pirates. /1997/K-2/3 KG117 . . . . **E**

STEVENSON, RL/Treasure Island. /c1911, 1981/
5-A/6 KH759 . . . . **Fic**
Treasure Island (Talking book). /1993/5-A/KH760 . . . . . **TB Fic**
Pizarro, Francisco.
MARRIN, A/Inca and Spaniard: Pizarro and the conquest of Peru. /
1989/A/8 KF109 . . . . **985**
Pizza.
MARTINO, T/Pizza! /1989/3-4/2 KD292 . . . . **641.8**
Pizza--Fiction.
MACCARONE, G/Pizza party! /1994/P-1/1 KG047 . . . . **E**
Plague--History.
GIBLIN, JC/When plague strikes: the Black Death, smallpox, AIDS.
/1995/A/11 KD010 . . . . **614.4**
Planets SEE ALSO Life on other planets; Solar system; Stars; also names of
planets e.g. Mars (Planet).
Planets.
BRANLEY, FM/Planets in our solar system. Rev. ed. /1987/
2-4/4 KC023 . . . . **523.4**
COLE, J/Magic School Bus lost in the solar system. /1990/
2-6/4 KC008 . . . . **523.2**
GIBBONS, G/Planets. /1993/2-4/4 KC025 . . . . **523.4**
GREAT SOLAR SYSTEM RESCUE (VIDEODISC). /1992/
5-A/KC010 . . . . **VD 523.2**
LAUBER, P/Journey to the planets. 4th ed. /1993/
4-6/6 KC028 . . . . **523.4**
LEEDY, L/Postcards from Pluto: a tour of the solar system. /1993/
1-6/3 KC012 . . . . **523.2**
PLANETS (PICTURE). /1990/3-6/KC029 . . . . **PIC 523.4**
ROBINSON, F/Space probes to the planets. /1993/
2-5/5 KC031 . . . . **523.4**
SIMON, S/Jupiter. /1985/3-6/7 KC038 . . . . **523.45**
Mars. /1987/4-A/8 KC035 . . . . **523.43**
Our solar system. /1992/4-8/7 KC015. . . . . **523.2**
Saturn. /1985/3-6/6 KC039 . . . . **523.46**
Uranus. /1987/4-6/6 KC040 . . . . **523.47**
SOLAR SYSTEM (PICTURE). /1990/4-A/KC016. . . . . . . **PIC 523.2**
Planets--Exploration.
APFEL, NH/Voyager to the planets. /1991/3-6/7 KC022 . . . **523.4**
BURROWS, WE/Mission to deep space: Voyagers' journey of
discovery. /1993/4-8/11 KC024 . . . . **523.4**
HARRIS, AW/Great Voyager adventure: a guided tour through the
solar system. /1990/A/9 KC026 . . . . **523.4**
KERROD, R/Story of space exploration (Picture). /1994/
4-6/KC027 . . . . **PIC 523.4**
RIDE, S/Voyager: an adventure to the edge of the solar system. /
1992/3-6/7 KC030 . . . . **523.4**
Planets--Software.
GREAT SOLAR SYSTEM RESCUE (CD-ROM). /1996/
5-A/KC009 . . . . **CDR 523.2**
SCHOLASTIC'S THE MAGIC SCHOOL BUS EXPLORES THE SOLAR
SYSTEM. ACADEMIC ED. /1994/2-5/KC014 . . . . . . **CDR 523.2**
Plant introduction--Australia.
BAKER, J/Story of rosy dock. /1995/K-4/6 KF115 . . . . **994**
Plantation life--Southern States--History--19th century.
MCKISSACK, P/Christmas in the big house, Christmas in the
quarters. /1994/4-A/6 KE967 . . . . **975**
Plants SEE ALSO Desert plants; Flowers; Gardening; Marine plants; also
names of plants e.g. Cactus.
Plants.
BURNIE, D/Plant. /1989/3-A/7 KC383 . . . . **580**
CAPON, B/Plant survival: adapting to a hostile world. /1994/
A/9 KC397 . . . . **581.4**
DOW, L/Incredible plants. /1997/A/7 KC385 . . . . **580**
GIBBONS, G/From seed to plant. /1991/K-3/4 KC398 . . . . **581.4**
HOW PLANTS ARE USED (VIDEOCASSETTE). /1991/
3-6/KC357. . . . . **VCR 578.6**
LIVING WORLD. /1993/5-A/KA437 . . . . **REF 508**
OVERBECK, C/Carnivorous plants. /1982/3-5/6 KC432. . . . . **583**
PLANTS: ANGIOSPERMS (VIDEOCASSETTE). /1990/
4-A/KC390 . . . . **VCR 580**
RAHN, JE/Plants up close. /1981/4-6/6 KC391 . . . . **580**
REALMS OF LIFE (PICTURE). /1996/6-A/KC356 . . . . . . **PIC 578**
SEASONS. REV. ED. (SOUND FILMSTRIP). /c1975, 1993/
K-2/KC063. . . . . **FSS 525**
SEEING THINGS (VIDEOCASSETTE). /1987/
K-3/KB913. . . . . **VCR 508**
SILVERSTEIN, A/Plants. /1996/5-A/7 KC392 . . . . **580**
TAYLOR, B/Incredible plants. /1997/3-8/8 KC393 . . . . **580**
VISUAL DICTIONARY OF PLANTS. /1992/P-A/A KC394. . . . **580**
WEBER, L/Backyard almanac. /1996/3-A/7 KB915 . . . . **508**
WHAT IS A PLANT? (VIDEOCASSETTE). /1991/
3-6/KC395. . . . . **VCR 580**
WONDERS OF GROWING PLANTS. 3RD ED. (VIDEOCASSETTE).
/1992/K-3/KC396. . . . . **VCR 580**

Plants--Development.
JOHNSON, SA/Morning glories. /1985/4-6/7 KC428 . . . . . **583**
LUCHT, I/Red poppy. /1995/1-4/5 KC430 . . . . **583**
MAESTRO, B/How do apples grow? /1992/K-2/4 KC418 . **582.16**

Plants--Experiments.
DIETL, U/Plant-and-grow project book. /1993/P-4/5 KC384 . . **580**

Plants--Fiction.
DERBY, S/Jacob and the stranger. /1994/3-5/4 KH071 . . . . . **Fic**
PULVER, R/Nobody's mother is in second grade. /1992/
K-2/2 KG293 . . . . **E**

Plants--Folklore.
BRUSCA, MC/When jaguars ate the moon: and other stories about
animals and plants of the /1995/2-3/5 KB541 . . . . **398.24**

Plants--Identification.
LERNER, C/Plant families. /1989/A/7 KC388. . . . . **580**

Plants--Miscellanea.
SOUCIE, G/What's the difference between apes and monkeys and
other living things? /1995/4-6/7 KC271. . . . . **571**

Plants--Reproduction.
OVERBECK, C/How seeds travel. /1982/2-4/6 KC389. . . . . . **580**
WHAT IS A PLANT? (VIDEOCASSETTE). /1991/
3-6/KC395. . . . . **VCR 580**

Plants--Software.
MICROSOFT EXPLORAPEDIA: THE WORLD OF NATURE.
ACADEMIC ED. (CD-ROM). /1995/1-4/KB909. . . . . . **CDR 508**

Plants, Fossil.
HENDERSON, D/Dinosaur tree. /1994/3-6/5 KC235 . . . . . . **560**

Plastics.
CASH, T/Plastics. /1990/3-5/5 KD327 . . . . **668.4**

Plastics--Experiments.
CASH, T/Plastics. /1990/3-5/5 KD327 . . . . **668.4**

Plate tectonics.
OUR CHANGING EARTH (VIDEOCASSETTE). /1991/
3-5/KC153. . . . . **VCR 551**
SATTLER, HR/Our patchwork planet: the story of plate tectonics. /
1995/A/7 KC155 . . . . **551.1**
STV: RESTLESS EARTH (VIDEODISC). /1992/
4-A/KC150 . . . . **VD 550**

Play SEE ALSO Amusements; Games; Hide-and-seek; Recreation; Sports.

Play--Fiction.
BONSALL, CN/And I mean it, Stanley. /1974/1-2/1 KF242 . . . . **E**
Day I had to play with my sister. /c1972/1-2/1 KF244 . . . . . . **E**
CASELEY, J/Noisemakers. /1992/P-1/2 KF367 . . . . **E**
CAULEY, LB/Clap your hands. /1992/P-K/2 KF373 . . . . **E**
DERBY, S/My steps. /1996/P-1/2 KF482 . . . . **E**
HENKES, K/Weekend with Wendell. /1986/P-2/2 KF712 . . . . . **E**
HUGHES, S/Bouncing. /1995/P/2 KF786 . . . . **E**
Hiding. /1996/P-K/2 KF789 . . . . **E**
JAKOB, D/My new sandbox. /1996/P-1/1 KF822 . . . . **E**
MCLERRAN, A/Roxaboxen. /1991/K-3/2 KG110. . . . . **CE E**
RAU, DM/Box can be many things. /1997/K-1/2 KG313 . . . . . . **E**
RUSSO, M/Line up book. /1986/P-1/1 KG362 . . . . **E**
RYLANT, C/Everyday children (Board book). /1993/
P-K/2 KG370. . . . . **BB E**
VAN ALLSBURG, C/Jumanji. /1981/K-A/4 KH820 . . . . **Fic**
Jumanji (Kit). /1995/K-A/KH821. . . . . **KIT Fic**
WADDELL, M/You and me, Little Bear. /1996/P-K/1 KG677 . . . **E**

Play--Social aspects.
MILLER, TR/Taking time out: recreation and play. /1996/
5-A/7 KA865 . . . . **306.4**

Play on words SEE ALSO Puns and punning.

Play on words.
TERBAN, M/Superdupers! really funny real words. /1989/
3-6/6 KB850 . . . . **428.1**

Play schools--Fiction.
WELLS, R/Edward unready for school. /1995/P-K/2 KG698 . . . . **E**

Playgrounds--Fiction.
NAYLOR, PR/King of the playground. /1991/K-3/2 KG167 . . . . **E**

Plays.
BUCHWALD, C/Puppet book: how to make and operate puppets
and stage a puppet play. /1990//KA326. . . . . **PROF 791.5**
DAVIS, O/Escape to freedom: a play about young Frederick
Douglass. /c1976, 1990/A-6/KE091 . . . . **812**
MACDONALD, MR/Skit book: 101 skits from kids. /1990/
3-6/KE092. . . . . **812**
SHAKESPEARE, W/Riverside Shakespeare. /1974/
A/KA468. . . . . **REF 822.3**
STORIES ON STAGE: SCRIPTS FOR READER'S THEATER. /1993/
/KA363. . . . . **PROF 812**
VIGIL, A/Teatro!: Hispanic plays for young people. /1996/
/KA364. . . . . **PROF 812**
WINTHER, B/Plays from African tales: one-act, royalty-free
dramatizations for young people, /1992/4-A/KE093 . . . . . . **812**

Plays--Afro-American authors.
PLAYS OF BLACK AMERICANS: THE BLACK EXPERIENCE IN
AMERICA, DRAMATIZED FOR YOUN /1994/
4-6/KE095. . . . . **812.008**

Plays--Collections.
PLAYS FROM FAVORITE FOLK TALES. /1987/
3-6/KE094. . . . . **812.008**

Plays--Fiction.
BROWN, MT/Arthur's April fool. /1983/P-3/2 KF273. . . . . . . **E**
CREW, L/Nekomah Creek Christmas. /1994/4-6/4 KH042 . . . . **Fic**

Plays--Presentation.
LAUGHLIN, MK/Readers theatre for children: scripts and script
development. /1990//KA339. . . . . **PROF 808.5**

Playwriting.
BENTLEY, N/Putting on a play: the young playwright's guide to
scripting, directing, and performing. /1996/4-6/7 KD687. . . . **792**

Pledge of Allegiance.
FISHER, LE/Stars and Stripes: our national flag. /1993/
3-6/7 KE617 . . . . **929.9**
SWANSON, J/I pledge allegiance. /1990/
2-5/4 KA909 . . . . **CE 323.6**

Plots (Drama, novel, etc.)--Software.
JUNIOR DISCOVERING AUTHORS: BIOGRAPHIES AND
PLOTLINES ON 300 MOST-STUDIED AND /1994/
5-A/KA463. . . . . **CDR REF 809**

Pluralism (Social sciences)--Periodicals.
MULTICULTURAL REVIEW: DEDICATED TO A BETTER
UNDERSTANDING OF ETHNIC, RACIAL, /1992-/
/KA125. . . . . **PER PROF 050**

Pluralism (Social sciences) in literature--Bibliography.
MILLER-LACHMANN, L/Our family, our friends, our world: /1992/
/KA020. . . . . **PROF 011.62**
VENTURE INTO CULTURES: A RESOURCE BOOK OF
MULTICULTURAL MATERIALS AND PROGRAMS. /1992/
/KA024. . . . . **PROF 011.62**

Poaching--Fiction.
DAHL, R/Danny, the champion of the world. /c1975, 1988/
4-6/6 KH054 . . . . **Fic**
FARMER, N/Warm Place. /1995/4-A/3 KH110 . . . . **Fic**

Pocahontas.
FRITZ, J/Double life of Pocahontas. /1983/
5-6/6 KE500 . . . . **B POCAHONTAS**

Pocket calculators SEE Calculating machines.

Poetics.
WAKAN, N/Haiku: one breath poetry. /1993/5-A/KE138 . . **895.6**

Poetry SEE ALSO American poetry; Canadian poetry, etc.; Ballads; Epic
poetry; Haiku; Humorous poetry; Limericks; Nonsense verses; Nursery
rhymes.

Poetry.
COLEN, K/Peas and honey: recipes for kids (with a pinch of
poetry). /1995/3-6/KD269 . . . . **641.5**
RYAN, M/How to read and write poems. /1991/
4-6/7 KD869 . . . . **808.1**
YOLEN, J/Water music: poems for children. /1995/
2-6/KE051 . . . . **811**

Poetry--Authorship.
HULME, JN/How to write, recite, and delight in all kinds of poetry.
/1996/3-6/KD867. . . . . **808.06**
LIVINGSTON, MC/Poem-making: ways to begin writing poetry. /
1991/5-6/7 KD868 . . . . **808.1**
PLACE MY WORDS ARE LOOKING FOR: WHAT POETS SAY
ABOUT AND THROUGH THEIR WORK. /1990/
3-A/KE076. . . . . **811.008**

Poetry--Collections SEE ALSO Children's poetry; Christmas poetry; Indians
of North America--Poetry; American poetry--Collections; English poetry--
Collections, etc.

Poetry--Collections.
CARLE, E/Eric Carle's animals, animals. /1989/P-3/KD880 . **808.81**
Eric Carle's dragons dragons and other creatures that never were.
/1991/K-3/KD881 . . . . **808.81**
CARNEGIE LIBRARY SCHOOL ASSOCIATION /Our holidays in
poetry. /1965/5-6/KB196. . . . . **394.26**
CHILD'S GARDEN OF VERSES AND A POTPOURRI OF POETRY:
AN INTRODUCTION TO GREAT POETS (SOUND RECORDING
CASSETTE). /n.d./2-6/KE098 . . . . **SRC 821**
DYER, J/Animal crackers: a delectable collection of pictures, poems,
and lullabies for the very young. /1996/P-1/KD882 . . . . . **808.81**
EARTH IS PAINTED GREEN: A GARDEN OF POEMS ABOUT OUR
PLANET. /1994/3-6/KD883 . . . . **808.81**
FERRIS, H/Favorite poems, old and new, selected for boys and girls.
/c1957/5-6/KA467. **REF 811.008**
FROG INSIDE MY HAT: A FIRST BOOK OF POEMS. /1993/
P-1/KD884. . . . . **808.81**

GOOD MORNING TO YOU, VALENTINE: POEMS FOR
VALENTINE'S DAY. /c1976, 1993/K-6/KE061 . . . . . . **811.008**
INNER CHIMES: POEMS ON POETRY. /1992/
2-6/KD885. . . . . **808.81**
LITTLE BOOK OF LOVE. /1995/4-6/KD886 . . . . **808.81**
MISS MARY MACK AND OTHER CHILDREN'S STREET RHYMES. /
1990/2-5/KD766 . . . . **796.1**
MY SONG IS BEAUTIFUL: POEMS AND PICTURES IN MANY
VOICES. /1994/1-4/KD887 . . . . **808.81**
PEELING THE ONION: AN ANTHOLOGY OF POEMS. /1993/
A/KD888. . . . . **808.81**
REAL MOTHER GOOSE BOOK OF AMERICAN RHYMES. /1993/
P-2/KB811. . . . . **398.8**
RIDDLE-ME RHYMES. /1994/3-5/KD738 . . . . **793.735**
SLEEP, BABY, SLEEP: LULLABIES AND NIGHT POEMS. /1994/
P-K/KD889. . . . . **808.81**
SLEEP RHYMES AROUND THE WORLD. /1994/
P-3/KD890. . . . . **808.81**
TALKING LIKE THE RAIN: A FIRST BOOK OF POEMS. /1992/
P-2/KE112 . . . . **821.008**
TALKING TO THE SUN: AN ILLUSTRATED ANTHOLOGY OF
POEMS FOR YOUNG PEOPLE. /1985/6-A/KE087 . . . . **811.008**
THANKSGIVING POEMS. /1985/K-6/KE089 . . . . **811.008**
TOMIE DE PAOLA'S BOOK OF POEMS. /1988/
K-3/KD891 . . . . **808.81**
WIND IN THE LONG GRASS: A COLLECTION OF HAIKU. /1991/
2-5/KD892. . . . . **808.81**
Poetry--Indexes.
INDEX TO POETRY FOR CHILDREN AND YOUNG PEOPLE: 1988-
1992. /1994/5-6/KA374 . . . . **REF 016.811**
Poetry--Study and teaching.
CHATTON, B/Using poetry across the curriculum: a whole language
approach. /1993/KA237. . . . . **PROF 372.64**
KOCH, K/Wishes, lies, and dreams: teaching children to write
poetry. /c1970, 1980//KA346. . . . . **PROF 808.81**
WAKAN, N/Haiku: one breath poetry. /1993/5-A/KE138 . . **895.6**
Poets--Fiction.
JARRELL, R/Bat-poet. /1996/4-A/6 KH327 . . . . **Fic**
Poets, American.
COOPER, F/Coming home: from the life of Langston Hughes. /
1994/3-5/6 KE394 . . . . **B HUGHES, L.**
GREENE, C/Eugene Field: the children's poet. /1994/
2-4/4 KE343 . . . . **B FIELD, E.**
HOPKINS, LB/Been to yesterdays: poems of a life. /1995/
3-6/KD953. . . . . **811**
MEET JACK PRELUTSKY (VIDEOCASSETTE). /1992/
3-6/KE503 . . . . **VCR B PRELUTSKY, J.**
MEET THE AUTHOR: HENRY WADSWORTH LONGFELLOW
(VIDEOCASSETTE). /1992/
5-A/KE446. . . . . **VCR B LONGFELLOW, H**
MITCHELL, B/Good morning, Mr. President: a story about Carl
Sandburg. /1988/4-6/6 KE531 . . . . **B SANDBURG, C.**
OSOFSKY, A/Free to dream: the making of a poet: Langston
Hughes. /1996/6-A/7 KE395 . . . . **B HUGHES, L.**
PLACE MY WORDS ARE LOOKING FOR: WHAT POETS SAY
ABOUT AND THROUGH THEIR WORK. /1990/
3-A/KE076. . . . . **811.008**
SHERROW, V/Phillis Wheatley. /1992/
4-6/7 KE591 . . . . **B WHEATLEY, P.**
Poets, English.
STANLEY, D/Bard of Avon: the story of William Shakespeare. /
1992/4-6/7 KE538 . . . . **B SHAKESPEARE**
Poets, Japanese.
SPIVAK, D/Grass sandals: the travels of Basho. /1997/
1-4/5 KE136 . . . . **895.6**
Poison ivy--Fiction.
MEDDAUGH, S/Hog-eye. /1995/K-3/2 KG123 . . . . **E**
Poisonous plants.
LERNER, C/Moonseed and mistletoe: a book of poisonous wild
plants. /1988/4-A/6 KC403 . . . . **581.6**
Poisons.
SKIDMORE, S/Poison! beware! be an ace poison spotter. /1991/
3-6/5 KD011 . . . . **615.9**
Polacco, Patricia.
POLACCO, P/Dream keeper (Videocassette). /1996/
2-4/KE501 . . . . **VCR B POLACCO, P.**
Poland--Fiction.
SINGER, IB/Naftali the storyteller and his horse, Sus. /1987/
5-6/5 KH712 . . . . **Fic**
Poland--German occupation, 1939-1945--Fiction.
SERRAILLIER, I/Silver sword. /c1959/5-6/6 KH699 . . . . **Fic**
Poland--History--Fiction.
KELLY, EP/Trumpeter of Krakow. New ed. /c1966, 1973/
/7 KH343 . . . . **Fic**

Poland--History--Occupation, 1939-1945--Fiction.
ORLEV, U/Island on Bird Street. /1983/5-A/6 KH566 . . . . **Fic**
Man from the other side. /1991/5-A/6 KH567 . . . . **Fic**
Poland--Social life and customs--Fiction.
KELLY, EP/Trumpeter of Krakow. New ed. /c1966, 1973/
/7 KH343 . . . . **Fic**
Polar bear.
LARSEN, T/Polar bear family book. /1996/4-6/4 KC862. **599.786**
LEPTHIEN, EU/Polar bears. /1991/2-4/5 KC863 . . . . . **599.786**
POLAR BEARS (VIDEOCASSETTE). /1986/
4-A/KC864 . . . . **VCR 599.786**
TRACQUI, V/Polar bear: master of the ice. /1994/
3-5/4 KC865 . . . . **599.786**
Polar bear--Folklore.
DABCOVICH, L/Polar bear son: an Inuit tale. /1997/
K-2/4 KB554 . . . . **398.24**
Polar expeditions SEE Antarctic regions; Arctic regions; and names of
explorers e.g. Amundsen, Roald.
Polar regions.
ARCTIC AND ANTARCTIC (VIDEOCASSETTE). /1996/
4-6/KE213. . . . . **VCR 919.8**
TAYLOR, B/Arctic and Antarctic. /1995/3-6/7 KE220 . . . . . **919.8**
Poles--Siberia.
HAUTZIG, E/Endless steppe: growing up in Siberia. /c1968/
5-6/4 KE658 . . . . **940.53**
Poles--United States--Fiction.
ESTES, E/Hundred dresses. /c1944/2-4/6 KH102 . . . . **Fic**
Polestar.
KRUPP, EC/Big dipper and you. /1989/1-6/4 KC050 . . . . . **523.8**
Police SEE ALSO Crime and criminals; Criminal investigations; Detectives.
Police.
WOMEN IN POLICING (VIDEOCASSETTE). /1994/
5-6/KB030 . . . . **VCR 363.2**
Police--Fiction.
MCKAY, H/Dog Friday. /1995/4-A/7 KH477 . . . . **Fic**
RATHMANN, P/Officer Buckle and Gloria. /1995/
K-2/3 KG310 . . . . **E**
Police dogs--Fiction.
RATHMANN, P/Officer Buckle and Gloria. /1995/
K-2/3 KG310 . . . . **E**
Policewomen.
WOMEN IN POLICING (VIDEOCASSETTE). /1994/
5-6/KB030 . . . . **VCR 363.2**
Poliomyelitis--Patients--Rehabilitation.
KEHRET, P/Small steps: the year I got polio. /1996/
2-5/5 KE414 . . . . **B KEHRET, P.**
Polis, Gary A.
PRINGLE, LP/Scorpion man: exploring the world of scorpions. /
1994/5-6/8 KC530 . . . . **595.4**
Polish Americans--Fiction.
BLOS, JW/Brooklyn doesn't rhyme. /1994/4-6/6 KG904 . . . . . **Fic**
Political leadership.
BIOGRAPHY TODAY WORLD LEADERS SERIES: PROFILES OF
PEOPLE OF INTEREST TO YOUNG /1997/-/4-6/KA407 . **REF 350**
Political participation.
LEWIS, BA/Kid's guide to social action: how to solve the social
problems you choose--and /1991/3-6/6 KA991 . . . . . . **361.2**
Political science.
WORLDMARK ENCYCLOPEDIA OF THE NATIONS. 9TH ED. /
1997/A/KA389 . . . . **REF 031**
Politicians.
LINDOP, L/Political leaders. /1996/6-A/12 KA899 . . . . **320**
STEWART, W/Aung San Suu Kyi: fearless voice of Burma. /1997/
5-A/7 KE244 . . . . **B AUNG SAN SUU**
Politics, Practical.
LEWIS, BA/Kid's guide to social action: how to solve the social
problems you choose--and /1991/3-6/6 KA991. . . . . . . **361.2**
STEINS, R/Our elections. /1994/5-6/7 KA912 . . . . **324.6**
Pollen.
LERNER, C/Plants that make you sniffle and sneeze. /1993/
5-6/9 KC404 . . . . **581.6**
Pollination by insects.
HALL, Z/Apple pie tree. /1996/1-4/2 KC413 . . . . **582.16**
Pollution SEE ALSO Air--Pollution; Hazardous wastes; Toxins; Water--
Pollution.
Pollution.
BANG, M/Chattanooga sludge. /1996/4-6/7 KD081 . . . . . **628.4**
BERGER, M/Oil spill! /1994/1-4/4 KB057 . . . . **363.73**
BLUE PLANET (VIDEOCASSETTE). /1993/
5-A/KB058. **VCR 363.73**
FRESH WATER: RESOURCE AT RISK (VIDEOCASSETTE). /1993/
6-A/KB060. **VCR 363.73**
HOFF, MK/Our endangered planet: rivers and lakes. /1991/
5-6/8 KB062 . . . . **363.73**

OUR ENDANGERED EARTH (VIDEOCASSETTE). /1990/
  3-6/KC307. . . . .   **VCR 577.27**
OUR WATERY WORLD (VIDEOCASSETTE). /1991/
  3-5/KB064. . . . .   **VCR 363.73**
POWER UP?: ENERGY IN OUR ENVIRONMENT
  (VIDEOCASSETTE). /1992/4-6/KA956 . . . .   **VCR 333.79**
YOUNT, L/Our endangered planet: air. /1995/
  4-6/8 KB069 . . . .   **363.73**

Pollution--Dictionaries.
SIMON, S/Earth words: a dictionary of the environment. /1995/
  3-6/9 KB067 . . . .   **363.73**

Pollution--Fiction.
PEET, B/Wump World. /c1970/1-3/7 KG230 . . . .   **E**
RAND, G/Prince William. /1992/2-3/4 KG300 . . . .   **E**
SEUSS, D/Lorax. /c1971/P-3/3 KG466 . . . .   **CE E**
WILDSMITH, B/Professor Noah's spaceship. /1980/
  K-2/5 KG722 . . . .   **E**

Pollution--Software.
ENVIRONMENT (MICROCOMPUTER PROGRAM). /1990/
  5-A/KB059.   **MCP 363.73**

Polyglot materials.
BROWN, R/Alphabet times four: an international ABC: English,
  Spanish, French, German. /1991/2-4/KB819. . . . .   **411**

Polynesia--Fiction.
SPERRY, A/Call it courage. /c1940/5-6/6 KH743 . . . . .   **CE Fic**

Polynesians--Folklore.
RATTIGAN, JK/Woman in the moon: a story from Hawaii. /1996/
  K-2/6 KB474 . . . .   **398.22**

Polyphemus (Greek mythology).
FISHER, LE/Cyclops. /1991/1-6/4 KA739 . . . .   **292**

Pond animals--Fiction.
FLEMING, D/In the small, small pond. /1993/P-2/1 KF555 . . . .   **E**

Pond ecology.
LOEWER, HP/Pond water zoo: an introduction to microscopic life. /
  1996/6-A/8 KC372. . . . .   **579**
PARKER, S/Pond and river. /1988/1-6/7 KC340 . . . . . .   **577.63**

Ponds--Fiction.
ROCKWELL, AF/Ducklings and pollywogs. /1994/K-2/3 KG341 .   **E**
TAFURI, N/Have you seen my duckling? /1984/P-K/1 KG590 . . .   **E**

Ponies SEE ALSO Horses.

Ponies.
EVANS, J/Horseback riding. /1992/4-A/6 KD855 . . . . . .   **798.2**
GREEN, L/Young rider. /1993/3-8/8 KD856 . . . .   **798.2**

Ponies--Fiction.
COERR, E/Chang's paper pony. /1988/2-3/2 KF400 . . . . . .   **E**
HENRY, M/Misty of Chincoteague. /c1947/3-5/4 KH244 . .   **CE Fic**
HERMAN, RA/Pal the pony. /1996/K-1/2 KF714. . . . .   **E**
KING-SMITH, D/Sophie's Lucky. /1996/3-4/8 KH356 . . . . . .   **Fic**

Pony express.
HARNESS, C/They're off!: the story of the Pony Express. /1996/
  2-5/8 KB129 . . . .   **383**
KROLL, S/Pony Express! /1996/4-6/6 KB130 . . . .   **383**

Pony express--Fiction.
COERR, E/Buffalo Bill and the Pony Express. /1995/
  1-3/2 KF399 . . . .   **E**

Pool (Game)--Fiction.
BAUER, J/Sticks. /1996/6-A/4 KG880. . . . .   **Fic**
HITE, S/Even break. /1995/5-A/6 KH266. . . . .   **Fic**

Poor--New York (N.Y.).
WOLF, B/Homeless. /1995/4-6/4 KB010 . . . .   **362.5**

Popcorn.
DE PAOLA, T/Popcorn book. /c1978/2-4/6 KD290 . . . . .   **641.6**

Popcorn--Fiction.
LOW, A/Popcorn shop. /1993/P-2/2 KG035 . . . .   **E**

Poppies.
LUCHT, I/Red poppy. /1995/1-4/5 KC430 . . . .   **583**

Popular music--History and criticism.
MEDEARIS, AS/Music. /1997/4-6/11 KD521 . . . .   **780**

Popularity--Fiction.
FARRELL, M/Marrying Malcolm Murgatroyd. /1995/
  5-A/4 KH111 . . . .   **Fic**
ORGEL, D/Don't call me Slob-o. /1996/3-5/2 KH565. . . . . .   **Fic**
SHREVE, S/Joshua T. Bates takes charge. /c1993, 1995/
  4-6/4 KH710 . . . .   **Fic**

Population.
BLASHFIELD, JF/Too many people? /1992/A/7 KA815 . . . .   **304.6**
WINCKLER, S/Our endangered planet: population growth. /1990/
  5-6/9 KA816 . . . .   **304.6**

Porcupines.
MURRAY, P/Porcupines. /1994/1-4/6 KC745 . . . .   **599.35**
SHERROW, V/Porcupine. /1991/5-6/6 KC747 . . . .   **599.35**

Porpoises.
AUDUBON SOCIETY FIELD GUIDE TO NORTH AMERICAN
  FISHES, WHALES AND DOLPHINS. /1983/A/11 KC583 . . .   **597**

Posadas (Social custom)--Fiction.
MORA, P/Gift of the poinsettia./El regalo de la flor de
  nochebuena. /1995/3-5/4 KH507. . . . .   **Fic**
Possums SEE Oppossums.
Post roads SEE ALSO names of specific post roads e.g. Boston Post Road.

Postage stamps--Collectors and collecting.
GRANGER, N/Stamp collecting. /1994/4-6/8 KD508 . . . .   **769.56**

Postal service.
POST OFFICE (VIDEOCASSETTE). /1991/1-4/KB131 . .   **VCR 383**
SKURZYNSKI, G/Here comes the mail. /1992/1-4/4 KB133 . .   **383**

Postal service--Canada.
POSTAL STATION (VIDEOCASSETTE). /1991/
  K-4/KB132.   **VCR 383**

Postal service--Fiction.
KEATS, EJ/Letter to Amy. /c1968/P-2/2 KF874. . . . . . .   **CE E**
RYLANT, C/Mr. Griggs' work. /c1989, 1993/P-2/6 KG376. . . .   **E**
SCOTT, AH/Hi. /1994/P-K/2 KG422. . . . .   **E**

Postal service--Letter carriers.
LEVINSON, NS/Snowshoe Thompson. /1992/
  K-3/2 KE564 . . . .   **B THOMPSON, S.**

Postal service--Letter carriers--Fiction.
HENKES, K/Good-bye, Curtis. /1995/P-2/2 KF704. . . . . . .   **E**

Postal service--United States--History.
HARNESS, C/They're off!: the story of the Pony Express. /1996/
  2-5/8 KB129 . . . .   **383**
KROLL, S/Pony Express! /1996/4-6/6 KB130 . . . .   **383**

Postcards--Fiction.
WILLIAMS, VB/Stringbean's trip to the shining sea. /1988/
  K-A/2 KG739.   **E**

Potatoes.
WATTS, B/Potato. /1987/2-4/2 KD172 . . . .   **635**

Potatoes--Fiction.
LIED, K/Potato: a tale from the Great Depression. /1997/
  K-3/2 KF980 . . . .   **E**

Potlatch.
HOYT-GOLDSMITH, D/Potlatch: a Tsimshian celebration. /1997/
  2-5/9 KB189 . . . .   **394.2**

Potter, Beatrix.
WALLNER, A/Beatrix Potter. /1995/
  3-5/4 KA369 . . . .   **PROF B POTTER,B**

Pottery.
BAYLOR, B/When clay sings. /c1972, 1987/3-5/6 KE748 . .   **970.1**

Pottery craft.
ANCONA, G/Earth daughter: Alicia of Acoma Pueblo. /1995/
  2-4/6 KE791 . . . .   **970.489**
DIXON, A/Clay. /1990/K-5/4 KC230 . . . .   **553.6**
SWENTZELL, R/Children of clay: a family of Pueblo potters. /1992/
  4-6/6 KE795 . . . .   **970.489**

Poultry.
SELSAM, ME/Egg to chick. Rev. ed. /1970/P-2/2 KC698 . .   **598.6**

Poultry--Fiction.
GALDONE, P/Henny Penny. /c1968/P-K/2 KF594 . . . . . .   **CE E**
HOBSON, S/Chicken Little. /1994/P-2/2 KF749. . . . .   **E**
HUTCHINS, P/Rosie's walk. /c1968/P-1/1 KF802. . . . . . .   **CE E**
SUTEEV, V/Chick and the duckling. /1972/P-1/1 KG585 . . . .   **E**

Poverty--Fiction.
ARMSTRONG, WH/Sounder. /c1969/4-A/4 KG851 . . . . .   **CE Fic**
ESTES, E/Hundred dresses. /c1944/2-4/6 KH102. . . . . . .   **Fic**
LISLE, JT/Afternoon of the elves. /1989/6-A/6 KH408 . . . . .   **Fic**
TAYLOR, MD/Song of the trees. /1975/4-6/4 KH780. . . . . .   **Fic**
UCHIDA, Y/Jar of dreams. /1981/5-6/6 KH815. . . . .   **Fic**

Powell, Colin L.
APPLEGATE, K/Story of two American generals: Benjamin O. Davis,
  Jr.; Colin L. Powell. /1995/5-6/5 KA981 . . . .   **355**
BLUE, R/Colin Powell: straight to the top. Updated ed. /1997/
  3-6/7 KE502 . . . .   **B POWELL, C.**

Powell, John Wesley.
FRASER, MA/In search of the Grand Canyon. /1995/
  3-5/6 KF068 . . . .   **979.1**

Powell, Ransom J.--Fiction.
WISLER, GC/Red Cap. /1994/5-A/7 KH873 . . . .   **Fic**

Power resources SEE ALSO Electric power; Geothermal resources; Solar
  energy; Water resources development.

Power resources.
POWER UP?: ENERGY IN OUR ENVIRONMENT
  (VIDEOCASSETTE). /1992/4-6/KA956 . . . .   **VCR 333.79**
SIMPLE THINGS YOU CAN DO TO SAVE ENERGY IN YOUR
  SCHOOL (VIDEOCASSETTE). /1995/4-6/KA957.   **VCR 333.791**
WILCOX, C/Powerhouse: inside a nuclear power plant. /1996/
  5-A/11 KD049 . . . .   **621.48**

Powhatan.
FRITZ, J/Double life of Pocahontas. /1983/
  5-6/6 KE500 . . . .   **B POCAHONTAS**

Powwows.
ANCONA, G/Powwow. /1993/3-6/6 KB194 . . . . **394.26**
BRAINE, S/Drumbeat...heartbeat: a celebration of the powwow. /
1995/5-6/9 KB178 . . . . **394**
CRUM, R/Eagle drum: on the powwow trail with a young grass
dancer. /1994/5-A/5 KB197 . . . . **394.26**
KING, S/Shannon: an Ojibway dancer. /1993/
4-6/4 KE784 . . . . **970.476**
RENDON, MR/Powwow summer: a family celebrates the circle of
life. /1996/1-3/3 KB181 . . . . **394**

Powwows--Fiction.
MITCHELL, B/Red Bird. /1996/1-3/4 KG145 . . . . **E**

Prague (Czech Republic)--Fiction.
SIS, P/Three golden keys. /1994/5-A/4 KH714 . . . . **Fic**

Prairie conservation.
GOLDSTEIN, N/Rebuilding prairies and forests. /1994/
4-6/7 KA955 . . . . **333.74**

Prairie dogs.
ARNOLD, C/Prairie dogs. /1993/4-5/4 KC749 . . . . **599.36**

Prairie ecology.
GOLDSTEIN, N/Rebuilding prairies and forests. /1994/
4-6/7 KA955 . . . . **333.74**
ROWAN, JP/Prairies and grasslands. /1983/3-6/4 KC331 . . **577.4**
STAUB, FJ/America's prairies. /1994/4-6/7 KC332 . . . . . . **577.4**
TALL GRASS PRAIRIE: AN AMERICAN STORY (VIDEOCASSETTE).
/1997/3-A/KC333 . . . . **VCR 577.4**

Prairies.
STAUB, FJ/America's prairies. /1994/4-6/7 KC332 . . . . . . **577.4**
TALL GRASS PRAIRIE: AN AMERICAN STORY (VIDEOCASSETTE).
/1997/3-A/KC333 . . . . **VCR 577.4**

Prairies--Canada.
BANNATYNE-CUGNET, J/Prairie alphabet. /1992/
2-6/6 KE811 . . . . **971.2**
Prairie year. /1994/4-6/4 KE812 . . . . **971.2**
KURELEK, W/Prairie boy's summer. /1975/3-5/7 KE813 . . . **971.2**
Prairie boy's winter. /c1973/3-6/7 KE814. . . . . . **CE 971.2**
SYMONS, RD/Grandfather Symons' homestead book. /1981/
3-5/6 KE815 . . . . **971.2**

Prairies--Fiction.
MACLACHLAN, P/Skylark. /1994/3-5/3 KH445 . . . . **Fic**

Prayers.
BAYNES, P/Thanks be to God: prayers from around the world. /
1990/3-6/KA712 . . . . **242**
FIELD, R/Prayer for a child. /1973/K-3/4 KA713 . . . . **242**

Praying mantis--Fiction.
JAMES, B/Mary Ann. /1994/K-2/3 KF823 . . . . **E**

Precipitation SEE Rain and rainfall; Snow; Storms; Weather.

Precipitation (Meteorology).
KAHL, JD/Wet weather: rain showers and snowfall. /1992/
4-6/7 KC212 . . . . **551.57**

Precognition.
GREEN, CR/Seeing the unseen. /1993/4-6/5 KA610 . . . . . **133.8**

Predation (Biology).
EAGLE AND THE SNAKE (VIDEOCASSETTE). /1993/
2-6/KC472. . . . . **VCR 591.5**

Predatory animals.
COLE, J/Cat's body. /1982/4-6/6 KC818. . . . . **599.75**
EAGLE AND THE SNAKE (VIDEOCASSETTE). /1993/
2-6/KC472. . . . . **VCR 591.5**

Pregnancy SEE ALSO Childbirth.

Pregnancy.
COLE, J/How you were born. Rev. and expanded ed. /1993/
K-3/4 KC945 . . . . **612.6**
PEARSE, P/See how you grow. /1988/K-3/5 KC954 . . . . . **612.6**
SANDEMAN, A/Babies. /1996/2-5/6 KC955 . . . . **612.6**

Prehistoric animals SEE ALSO Dinosaurs; Fossils; Mammals, Fossil;
Mammoth; Paleontology.

Prehistoric animals.
ALIKI /Wild and woolly mammoths. Rev. ed. /1996/
1-3/4 KC268 . . . . **569**
GIBBONS, G/Prehistoric animals. /1988/P-3/5 KC241 . . . . . **566**
LAUBER, P/How dinosaurs came to be. /1996/
4-A/6 KC251 . . . . **567.9**
TROLL, R/Raptors, fossils, fins, and fangs: a prehistoric creature
feature. /1996/3-6/6 KC239. . . . . **560**

Prehistoric animals--Anatomy.
SENIOR, K/X-ray picture book of dinosaurs and other prehistoric
creatures. /1995/4-8/7 KC264 . . . . **567.9**

Prehistoric animals--Dictionaries.
BENTON, M/Dinosaur and other prehistoric animal factfinder. /
1992/4-6/7 KC234 . . . . **560**

Prehistoric peobles--Fiction.
DICKINSON, P/Bone from a dry sea. /1993/6-A/7 KH075 . . . **Fic**

TURNBULL, A/Maroo of the winter caves. /c1984, 1990/
5-6/6 KH811 . . . . **Fic**

Prehistoric peoples.
ARNOLD, C/Stone Age farmers beside the sea: Scotland's
prehistoric village of Skara Brae. /1997/3-6/8 KE677. . . . **941.1**
COLE, J/Human body: how we evolved. /1987/5-6/7 KC915. **612**
GETZ, D/Frozen man. /1994/4-6/7 KE638 . . . . **937**
LESSEM, D/Iceman. /1994/4-6/6 KE640 . . . . **937**
SATTLER, HR/Hominids: a look back at our ancestors. /1988/
4-A/8 KC269 . . . . **569.9**
TANAKA, S/Discovering the Iceman: what was it like to find a
5,300-year-old mummy? /1997/3-5/4 KE642 . . . . **937**

Prejudices.
AND YOU CAN'T COME: PREJUDICE HURTS (VIDEOCASSETTE).
/1996/5-6/KA803. . . . . **VCR 303.3**
BEHIND THE MASK. REV. ED. (VIDEOCASSETTE). /1987/
1-3/KA817 . . . . **VCR 305**
COHN, J/Christmas menorahs: how a town fought hate. /1995/
3-6/5 KA818 . . . . **305**
GROARK LEARNS ABOUT PREJUDICE (VIDEOCASSETTE). /1996/
1-3/KA819 . . . . **VCR 305**
MANY VOICES (VIDEOCASSETTE). /1991/
4-6/KA851 . . . . **VCR 305.8**
PLAYING FAIR (VIDEOCASSETTE). /1991/
4-6/KA854 . . . . **VCR 305.8**
RACE (VIDEOCASSETTE). /1993/A/KA855 . . . . **VCR 305.8**
UNFORGETTABLE PEN PAL: A STORY ABOUT PREJUDICE AND
DISCRIMINATION (VIDEOCASSETTE). /1991/
3-5/KA821 . . . . **VCR 305**
WHITEWASH (VIDEOCASSETTE) /1994/3-6/KA862 . **VCR 305.8**

Prejudices--Fiction.
AAMUNDSEN, NR/Two short and one long. /1990/
4-6/5 KG811 . . . . **Fic**
BLUME, J/Blubber. /1974/4-6/3 KG906. . . . . **Fic**
CURTIS, CP/Watsons go to Birmingham--1963: a novel. /1995/
6-A/7 KH048 . . . . **CE Fic**
HIROSHIMA MAIDEN (VIDEOCASSETTE). /c1988, 1997/
5-A/KH264 . . . . **VCR Fic**
KONIGSBURG, EL/T-backs, T-shirts, COAT, and suit. /1993/
6-A/7 KH375 . . . . **Fic**
LITTLE, MO/Yoshiko and the foreigner. /1996/3-5/2 KF997 . . . **E**
MARINO, J/Day that Elvis came to town. /1993/
6-A/6 KH456 . . . . **Fic**
MOCHIZUKI, K/Baseball saved us. /1993/4-A/6 KH500 . . . . **Fic**
Heroes. /1995/3-5/4 KH501 . . . . **Fic**
NAYLOR, PR/Saving Shiloh. /1997/4-A/4 KH537 . . . . . . **Fic**
SALISBURY, G/Under the blood-red sun. /1994/6-A/4 KH672 . **Fic**
TAYLOR, MD/Friendship. /1987/4-6/5 KH776 . . . . **Fic**
Mississippi bridge. /1990/5-A/4 KH778 . . . . **Fic**
Well: David's story. /1995/5-A/4 KH781 . . . . . . **Fic**
YEP, L/City of dragons. /1995/1-3/5 KG775 . . . . **E**
Star fisher. /1991/6-A/6 KH895 . . . . **Fic**

Prejudices--Software.
PREJUDICE (MICROCOMPUTER PROGRAM). /1992/
5-A/KA820 . . . . **MCP 305**

Prelutsky, Jack.
MEET JACK PRELUTSKY (VIDEOCASSETTE). /1992/
3-6/KE503 . . . . **VCR B PRELUTSKY, J.**

Preschool children--Books and reading.
THOMAS, JL/Play, learn, and grow: an annotated guide to the best
books and materials for /1992//KA088. . . . . **PROF 028.1**

Preschool education SEE ALSO Day care centers; Kindergarten; Nursery
schools.

Presidential candidates.
SANFORD, WR/John C. Fremont: soldier and pathfinder. /1996/
5-6/4 KE357 . . . . **B FREMONT, J.**

Presidential Medal of Freedom.
BREDESON, C/Presidential Medal of Freedom winners. /1996/
5-6/10 KE850 . . . . **973**

Presidents SEE ALSO Executive power; Cabinet officers; United States--
Executive departments; also names of specific presidents e.g. Washington,
George.

Presidents.
ABRAHAM LINCOLN: THE GREAT EMANCIPATOR
(VIDEOCASSETTE). /1990/A/KE438 . . . . **VCR B LINCOLN, A.**
ADLER, DA/George Washington: father of our country. /1988/
4-5/6 KE587 . . . . **B WASHINGTON, G**
Picture book of Thomas Jefferson. /1990/
2-3/5 KE403 . . . . **B JEFFERSON, T.**
ANDREW JACKSON: THE PEOPLE'S PRESIDENT
(VIDEOCASSETTE). /1990/6-A/KE397 . . . **VCR B JACKSON, A.**
BIOGRAPHY TODAY WORLD LEADERS SERIES: PROFILES OF
PEOPLE OF INTEREST TO YOUNG /1997/-/4-6/KA407 . **REF 350**

BLASSINGAME, W/Look-it-up book of presidents. Rev. ed. /1996/
4-6/7 KE848 . . . . **973**
BRENNER, M/Abe Lincoln's hat. /1994/
1-3/2 KE439 . . . . **B LINCOLN, A.**
CARRIGAN, M/Jimmy Carter: beyond the presidency. /1995/
5-6/7 KE280 . . . . **B CARTER, J.**
CWIKLIK, R/Bill Clinton: president of the 90s. Rev. ed. /1997/
5-6/8 KE296 . . . . **B CLINTON, B.**
D'AULAIRE, I/Abraham Lincoln. /c1957, 1993/
3-4/4 KE440 . . . . **CE B LINCOLN, A.**
DARBY, J/Dwight D. Eisenhower: a man called Ike. /1989/
5-6/6 KE335 . . . . **B EISENHOWER, D**
FALKOF, L/Lyndon B. Johnson, 36th president of the United states.
/1989/6-A/9 KE406 . . . . **B JOHNSON, L.**
FISHER, LE/White House. /1989/5-6/8 KE970. . . . . **975.3**
FREEDMAN, R/Franklin Delano Roosevelt. /1990/
6-A/7 KE522 . . . . **B ROOSEVELT, F.**
    Lincoln, a photobiography. /1987/A/11 KE441 . **B LINCOLN, A.**
FRITZ, J/Bully for you, Teddy Roosevelt! /1991/
5-6/6 KE523 . . . . **B ROOSEVELT, T.**
    Great little Madison. /1989/5-A/8 KE453 . . . . **B MADISON, J.**
GEORGE WASHINGTON: THE FIRST (VIDEOCASSETTE). /1990/
6-A/KE588. . . . . **VCR B WASHINGTON, G**
GIBLIN, JC/Thomas Jefferson: a picture book biography. /1994/
3-5/5 KE404 . . . . **B JEFFERSON, T.**
HARNESS, C/Abe Lincoln goes to Washington 1837-1865. /1997/
2-4/7 KE443 . . . . **B LINCOLN, A.**
    Young Abe Lincoln: the frontier days, 1809-1837. /1996/
    2-4/5 KE442 . . . . **B LINCOLN, A.**
    Young John Quincy. /1994/3-5/6 KE226 . . . . . **B ADAMS, J.Q.**
HARRISON, B/Twilight struggle: the life of John Fitzgerald Kennedy.
/1992/6-A/8 KE418 . . . . **B KENNEDY, J.**
JUDSON, K/Ronald Reagan. /1997/
6-A/10 KE504 . . . . **B REAGAN, R.**
KENT, Z/George Bush: forty-first president of the United States. /
1989/5-6/8 KE272 . . . . **B BUSH, G.**
KUNHARDT, E/Honest Abe. /1993/1-3/4 KE444 . **B LINCOLN, A.**
LINCOLN, IN HIS OWN WORDS. /1993/A/8 KE907 . . . . . **973.7**
LINCOLN, A/Gettysburg Address. /1995/4-6/6 KE906 . . . . **973.7**
OSINSKI, A/Woodrow Wilson: twenty-eighth President of the
United States. /1989/5-A/8 KE597 . . . . **B WILSON, W.**
OUR FEDERAL GOVERNMENT: THE PRESIDENCY
(VIDEOCASSETTE). /1993/5-A/KA980 . . . . **VCR 352.23**
PASCOE, E/First facts about the presidents. /1996/
3-6/8 KE860 . . . . **973**
QUACKENBUSH, R/James Madison and Dolley Madison and their
times. /1992/4-5/7 KE894 . . . . **973.5**
RICKARBY, LA/Ulysses S. Grant and the strategy of victory. /1991/
6-A/6 KE377 . . . . **B GRANT, U.**
SANDLER, MW/Presidents. /1995/5-A/8 KE864 . . . . **973**
SCHUMAN, M/Harry S. Truman. /1997/
5-A/9 KE571 . . . . **B TRUMAN, H.**
THEODORE ROOSEVELT: THE COWBOY PRESIDENT
(VIDEOCASSETTE). /1990/6-A/KE524 . . **VCR B ROOSEVELT, T.**
ULYSSES S. GRANT (VIDEOCASSETTE). /1989/
6-A/KE378. . . . . **VCR B GRANT, U.**
WHITELAW, N/Theodore Roosevelt takes charge. /1992/
5-A/7 KE525 . . . . **B ROOSEVELT, T.**

Presidents--Assassination.
JONES, RC/President has been shot!: true stories of the attacks on
ten U.S. presidents. /1996/6-A/9 KE855 . . . . **973**
STEIN, RC/Assassination of John F. Kennedy. /1992/
5-6/7 KE921 . . . . **973.922**

Presidents--Assassination attempts.
JONES, RC/President has been shot!: true stories of the attacks on
ten U.S. presidents. /1996/6-A/9 KE855 . . . . **973**

Presidents--Election.
ELECTING A PRESIDENT: THE PROCESS (VIDEOCASSETTE). /
1993/6-A/KA913 . . . . **VCR 324.973**
ELECTING A PRESIDENT (VIDEOCASSETTE). /1995/
6-A/KA914 . . . . **VCR 324.973**
MAESTRO, B/Voice of the people: American democracy in action. /
1996/4-6/8 KA915 . . . . **324.973**

Presidents--Encyclopedias.
RUBEL, D/Scholastic encyclopedia of the presidents and their times.
Updated ed. /1997/4-A/KA492. . . . . **REF 973**

Presidents--Family.
BLUE, R/White House kids. /1995/5-6/7 KE849 . . . . **973**
LEINER, K/First children: growing up in the White House. /1996/
A/9 KE856 . . . . **973**

Presidents--History.
RUBEL, D/Scholastic encyclopedia of the presidents and their times.
Updated ed. /1997/4-A/KA492. . . . . **REF 973**

Presidents--Pictorial works.
PASCOE, E/First facts about the presidents. /1996/
3-6/8 KE860 . . . . **973**
SANDLER, MW/Presidents. /1995/5-A/8 KE864 . . . . **973**

Presidents--Poetry.
LIVINGSTON, MC/Abraham Lincoln: a man for all the people: a
ballad. /1993/K-3/KD974. . . . . **811**

Presidents--Software.
PRESIDENTS: IT ALL STARTED WITH GEORGE (CD-ROM). /
1991/2-A/KA491 . . . . **CDR REF 973**

Presidents--United States.
QUIRI, PR/White House. /1996/4-6/10 KE972 . . . . **975.3**
Presidents--Wives SEE First ladies; also names of specific First ladies e.g.
Roosevelt, Eleanor.

Presidents' Day.
PRESIDENTS' DAY (VIDEOCASSETTE). /1994/
2-5/KB215 . . . . **VCR 394.261**
Prevention of accidents SEE Safety.
Prevention of fires SEE Fire prevention.

Pride and vanity--Fiction.
CONRAD, P/Rooster's gift. /1996/K-2/3 KF414 . . . . **E**
HAYES, J/Spoon for every bite. /1996/2-4/4 KF684 . . . . **E**
SHARMAT, MW/I'm terrific. /1977/P-1/3 KF481 . . . . **E**
STEPTOE, J/Mufaro's beautiful daughters: an African tale. /1987/
K-3/5 KG552 . . . . **CE E**
THREADGALL, C/Proud rooster and the fox. /1992/
P-1/4 KG607 . . . . **E**

Pride and vanity--Folklore.
SIERRA, J/Elephant's wrestling match. /1992/
P-2/4 KB652 . . . . **398.24**
Priests SEE Clergy.

Prime ministers.
DRIEMEN, JE/Winston Churchill: an unbreakable spirit. /1990/
5-6/7 KE290 . . . . **B CHURCHILL, W.**
SEVERANCE, JB/Winston Churchill: soldier, statesman, artist. /
1996/6-A/10 KE291 . . . . **B CHURCHILL, W.**

Prince Edward Island (Canada)--Fiction.
MONTGOMERY, LM/Anne of Green Gables. /c1908, 1983/
4-A/6 KH503 . . . . **Fic**

Princes--Fiction.
ALEXANDER, L/Remarkable journey of Prince Jen. /1991/
6-A/6 KG840. . . . . **Fic**
ANDERSEN, HC/Swineherd. /1995/2-5/5 KG847 . . . . **Fic**
HUTCHINS, HJ/Prince of Tarn. /1997/4-6/5 KH308 . . . . . . **Fic**
MANN, P/Frog Princess? /1995/1-3/2 KG058 . . . . **E**
PATERSON, K/King's equal. /1992/3-6/6 KH578. . . . . **Fic**
PYLE, H/Swan Maiden. /1994/2-4/6 KG294. . . . . **E**
SCIESZKA, J/Frog Prince, continued. /1991/1-3/4 KG419 . . . . . **E**

Princes--Folklore.
TARCOV, EH/Frog prince. /c1974, 1993/P-3/2 KB376 . . . . **398.2**

Princesses.
BREWSTER, H/Anastasia's album. /1996/
5-A/7 KE234 . . . . **B ANASTASIIA**
STANLEY, D/Last princess: the story of Princess Kaiulani of Hawaii.
/1991/5-6/7 KE413 . . . . **B KAIULANI**

Princesses--Fiction.
ANDERSEN, HC/Swineherd. /1995/2-5/5 KG847 . . . . **Fic**
GILMAN, P/Gypsy princess. /1997/K-2/3 KF619 . . . . **E**
LESTER, H/Princess Penelope's parrot. /1996/K-2/2 KF965. . . . **E**
PYLE, H/King Stork. /1973/3-5/6 KH614 . . . . **Fic**
SHIELDS, CD/I am really a princess. /1993/1-3/3 KG494 . . . . **CE E**
STEVENS, J/Princess and the pea. /1982/K-2/2 KG555 . . . . **CE E**
THURBER, J/Many moons. /c1943, 1990/3-5/5 KH792. . . . . **Fic**
    Many moons. /1990/3-5/5 KH793 . . . . **Fic**
WILHELM, H/Royal raven. /1996/K-2/2 KG723. . . . . **E**

Princesses--Folklore.
CLIMO, S/Treasury of princesses: princess tales from around the
world. /1996/3-5/6 KB432 . . . . **398.22**
MAYER, M/Turandot. /1995/3-5/5 KB342 . . . . **398.2**
STEWIG, JW/Princess Florecita and the iron shoes: a Spanish fairy
tale. /1995/3-4/5 KB372 . . . . **398.2**
TARCOV, EH/Frog prince. /c1974, 1993/P-3/2 KB376 . . . **398.2**
YEP, L/Khan's daughter: a Mongolian folktale. /1997/
2-4/6 KB787 . . . . **398.27**

Printer, James--Fiction.
JACOBS, PS/James Printer: a novel of rebellion. /1997/
5-A/6 KH319 . . . . **Fic**

Printers.
FISHER, LE/Gutenberg. /1993/5-A/8 KE382 . . **B GUTENBERG, J.**

Printers--Fiction.
JACOBS, PS/James Printer: a novel of rebellion. /1997/
5-A/6 KH319 . . . . **Fic**

Printing.
ALIKI /How a book is made. /1986/K-3/3 KD345 . . . . **686**

LYNN, S/Play with paint. /1993/K-2/3 KD465. . . . . **750**

Printing--History.
FISHER, LE/Gutenberg. /1993/5-A/8 KE382 . . **B GUTENBERG, J.**
KRENSKY, S/Breaking into print: before and after the invention of
the printing press. /1996/3-5/5 KD346 . . . . **686.2**

Prints--Technique.
SOLGA, K/Make prints! /1991/P-6/4 KD504 . . . . **760**

Prints, American.
AMERICAN HISTORY: GROWING PAINS (PICTURE). /c1974/
4-6/KE912. . . . . **PIC 973.8**

Prisoners--Fiction.
BUTTERWORTH, O/Visit to the big house. /1993/
3-5/5 KG956. . . . . **Fic**
WARNER, S/Dog years. /1995/4-6/3 KH840 . . . . **Fic**

Prisoners of war.
MYERS, WD/Place called heartbreak: a story of Vietnam. /1993/
5-6/6 KE721 . . . . **959.704**

Prisoners of war--Fiction.
GREENE, B/Summer of my German soldier. /c1973, 1993/
A/8 KH197 . . . . **Fic**
MAZER, H/Last mission. /c1979, 1986/6-A/4 KH465 . . . . . . **Fic**

Prisons--Fiction.
BABBITT, N/Tuck everlasting. /c1975/4-6/4 KG873 . . . . **CE Fic**
BUTTERWORTH, O/Visit to the big house. /1993/
3-5/5 KG956. . . . . **Fic**

Privacy, Right of--Fiction.
BYARS, BC/Cartoonist. /1978/4-6/3 KG959 . . . . **Fic**
DE REGNIERS, BS/Little house of your own. /c1954/
K-1/4 KF483 . . . . **E**

Privateering.
SHERBURNE, A/Memoirs of Andrew Sherburne: patriot and
privateer of the American Revolution. /1993/5-A/8 KE886 . **973.3**

Probabilities.
CUSHMAN, J/Do you wanna bet?: your chance to find out about
probability. /1991/4-6/4 KB997. . . . . **519.2**
WYLER, R/Test your luck. /1992/5-6/4 KB998. . . . . **519.2**

Probabilities--Software.
NUMBER HEROES. SCHOOL VERSION (CD-ROM). /1996/
3-6/KB929. . . . . **CDR 510**
Problem children SEE ALSO Emotional problems.

Problem children--Fiction.
STOLZ, M/Dog on Barkham Street. /c1960/4-6/4 KH765 . . . . **Fic**

Problem solving.
CHALLENGE OF THE UNKNOWN (VIDEOCASSETTE). /1986/
5-A/KB935. . . . . **VCR 511**
DECIDING HOW CLOSE TO MEASURE (VIDEOCASSETTE). /
1982/3-5/KB996. . . . . **VCR 519**
MARKLE, S/Math mini-mysteries. /1993/3-6/7 KB928 . . . . . . **510**
MR. MARFIL'S LAST WILL AND TESTAMENT (VIDEOCASSETTE).
/1991/5-A/KB973. . . . . **VCR 513.2**
PHANTOM OF THE BELL TOWER (VIDEOCASSETTE). /1991/
5-A/KB978. . . . . **VCR 513.2**
PROBLEM SOLVING: RECOGNIZING NECESSARY
INFORMATION (VIDEOCASSETTE). /1982/
3-5/KB979. . . . . **VCR 513.2**
PROBLEM SOLVING: USING DIAGRAMS AND MODELS
(VIDEOCASSETTE). /1985/5-6/KB943 . . . . **VCR 511.3**
PROBLEM SOLVING: USING GRAPHS (VIDEOCASSETTE). /
1985/4-5/KB939. . . . . **VCR 511**
RELATING FRACTIONS AND DECIMALS (VIDEOCASSETTE). /
1982/3-5/KB981. . . . . **VCR 513.2**
USING FRACTIONS (VIDEOCASSETTE). /1982/
3-4/KB983. . . . . **VCR 513.2**
VIEW FROM THE REAR TERRACE (VIDEOCASSETTE). /1991/
A/KB984. . . . . **VCR 513.2**

Problem solving--Fiction.
MURPHY, SJ/Best vacation ever. /1997/K-2/2 KG164 . . . . **E**
RAYNER, M/Mr. and Mrs. Pig's evening out. /c1976/
K-2/4 KG317 . . . . **E**

Problem solving--Folklore.
BANG, M/Wiley and the Hairy Man: adapted from an American
folk tale. /c1976, 1987/1-3/2 KB389 . . . . **398.21**
KIMMEL, EA/Count Silvernose: a story from Italy. /1996/
3-5/5 KB504 . . . . **398.23**
MAYER, M/Turandot. /1995/3-5/5 KB342 . . . . **398.2**
SIERRA, J/Wiley and the Hairy Man. /1996/K-3/4 KB417 . **398.21**

Problem solving--Software.
BIG ANTHONY'S MIXED-UP MAGIC (CD-ROM). /1996/
K-2/KF229. . . . . **CDR E**
BUILDING PERSPECTIVE: STRATEGIES IN PROBLEM SOLVING
(MICROCOMPUTER PROGRAM). /1986/
4-A/KA637. . . . . **MCP 153.7**
CALCULATING CREW. SCHOOL VERSION. (CD-ROM). /1996/
3-6/KB955. . . . . **CDR 513.2**

CARNIVAL COUNTDOWN. SCHOOL VERSION (CD-ROM). /
1996/K-2/KB926. . . . . **CDR 510**
COLONIZATION (MICROCOMPUTER PROGRAM). /1986/
5-A/KA667 . . . . **MCP 172**
EUROPE INSPIRER (CD-ROM). /1997/4-A/KE177 . . **CDR 914**
FACTORY: EXPLORATIONS IN PROBLEM SOLVING
(MICROCOMPUTER PROGRAM). /1983/
2-4/KA635. . . . . **MCP 153.4**
GIZMOS AND GADGETS! (MICROCOMPUTER PROGRAM). /
1993/3-6/KB882. . . . . **MCP 507**
GRAPH ACTION (MICROCOMPUTER PROGRAM). /1996/
4-A/KB936. . . . . **MCP 511**
GRAPH ACTION PLUS (CD-ROM). /1996/4-A/KB937 . **CDR 511**
IMMIGRATION (MICROCOMPUTER PROGRAM). /1996/
5-A/KA917 . . . . **MCP 325**
LOGICAL JOURNEY OF THE ZOOMBINIS. SCHOOL ED. (CD-
ROM). /1996/2-5/KB938. . . . . **CDR 511**
MILLIE'S MATH HOUSE (CD-ROM). /1995/
P-2/KB971. . . . . **CDR 513.2**
MILLIE'S MATH HOUSE (MICROCOMPUTER PROGRAM). /1992/
P-2/KB972. . . . . **MCP 513.2**
NATIONAL INSPIRER (MICROCOMPUTER PROGRAM). /1997/
5-A/KE190. . . . . **MCP 917.3**
NUMBER HEROES. SCHOOL VERSION (CD-ROM). /1996/
3-6/KB929. . . . . **CDR 510**
PLAYROOM (CD-ROM). /1990/P-2/KB085. . . . . . **CDR 371.3**
PUZZLE TANKS: A GAME OF NUMBERS AND LOGIC
(MICROCOMPUTER PROGRAM). /1984/3-A/KB940. . **MCP 511**
RAINFOREST RESEARCHERS (CD-ROM). /1996/
5-A/KC323 . . . . **CDR 577.34**
REVOLUTIONARY WARS: CHOOSING SIDES (MICROCOMPUTER
PROGRAM). /1986/5-A/KA668 . . . . **MCP 172**
SAMMY'S SCIENCE HOUSE (CD-ROM). /1994/
K-3/KB870. . . . . **CDR 500**
SCIENCE BLASTER JR. TEACHER ED. (CD-ROM). /1997/
K-3/KB871. . . . . **CDR 500**
SCIENCE SLEUTHS. VOL. 1: THE MYSTERIES OF THE BLOB AND
THE EXPLODING LAWNMOWERS /1995/4-A/KB885. **CDR 507**
SEILER, B/How the west was one + three x four (Microcomputer
program). /c1987, 1989/4-A/KB951. . . . . **MCP 513**
SNAPDRAGON (MICROCOMPUTER PROGRAM). /1992/
P-1/KA636. . . . . **MCP 153.4**
STEARNS, PH/Graph Club with Fizz and Martina (Microcomputer
program). /1993/K-4/KB942 . . . . **MCP 511**
STRATEGY CHALLENGES COLLECTION 1: AROUND THE WORLD.
SCHOOL VERSION (CD-ROM). /1995/3-A/KD754. . . **CDR 794**
STRATEGY CHALLENGES COLLECTION 2: IN THE WILD. SCHOOL
VERSION (CD-ROM). /1996/4-A/KD755 . . . . **CDR 794**
THINKIN' THINGS COLLECTION 1 (MICROCOMPUTER
PROGRAM). /1993/K-3/KB080. . . . . **MCP 370.15**
THINKIN' THINGS COLLECTION 2. SCHOOL VERSION (CD-
ROM). /1995/1-6/KB081. . . . . **CDR 370.15**
THINKIN' THINGS COLLECTION 3. SCHOOL VERSION (CD-
ROM). /1995/3-A/KB082 . . . . **CDR 370.15**
TREEHOUSE (CD-ROM). /1991/K-4/KB086 . . . . **CDR 371.3**
WHERE IN SPACE IS CARMEN SANDIEGO? (MICROCOMPUTER
PROGRAM). /1993/4-A/KC005. . . . . **MCP 520**
WHERE IN THE U.S.A. IS CARMEN SANDIEGO? NEW ED. (CD-
ROM). /1996/3-A/KE182 . . . . **CDR 917**
WHERE IN THE WORLD IS CARMEN SANDIEGO? JUNIOR
DETECTIVE EDITION (CD-ROM). /1994/3-6/KE174 . . **CDR 912**
WHERE IN THE WORLD IS CARMEN SANDIEGO? NEW ED.
(CD-ROM). /1996/3-A/KE175 . . . . **CDR 912**
ZOO ZILLIONS. SCHOOL VERSION (CD-ROM). /1966/
K-2/KB986. . . . . **CDR 513.2**

Problem solving--Study and teaching.
EISENBERG, MB/Information problem-solving: the Big Six Skills
approach to library and /1990/KA063. . . . . **PROF 025.5**
MENDLER, AN/Smiling at yourself: educating young children about
stress and self-esteem. /1990/KA304. . . . . **PROF 649**

Procyonidae.
SCHMIDT, A/Bears and their forest cousins. /1991/
5-6/7 KC854 . . . . **599.78**

Program music.
PROKOFIEV, S/Peter and the wolf. /1982/
P-3/4 KD676 . . . . **CE 789.8**

Programming (Computers).
FARMER, LS/I speak HyperCard. /1992/3-A/KA573. . . . **005.265**
Programming (Microcomputers) SEE ALSO names of programming
languages e.g. BASIC (Computer program language).

Prohibition.
HINTZ, M/Farewell, John Barleycorn: prohibition in the United
States. /1996/5-6/12 KB043. **363.4**

Project Mariner.
SIMON, S/Mercury. /1992/3-6/7 KC032 . . . . **523.41**

Project method in teaching.
ARTS AND ACTIVITIES: CREATIVE ACTIVITIES FOR THE
CLASSROOM. /1932-//KA096 . . . . **PER PROF 050**

Project Voyager SEE Voyager Project.

Promises--Fiction.
BAUER, MD/On my honor. /1986/5-6/7 KG882 . . . . . . **CE Fic**
MUNSCH, R/Promise is a promise. /1988/3-5/2 KH519 . . . . . **Fic**

Promptness--Fiction.
TEAGUE, M/Secret shortcut. /1996/1-3/2 KG596 . . . . **E**

Prophecies--Fiction.
DEXTER, C/Doll who knew the future. /1994/4-6/6 KH072 . . . **Fic**

Prosthesis.
FACKLAM, M/Spare parts for people. /1987/A/9 KD035 . . . **617**

Protest movements--Fiction.
KONIGSBURG, EL/T-backs, T-shirts, COAT, and suit. /1993/
6-A/7 KH375 . . . . **Fic**

Protest songs.
SILVERMAN, J/Songs of protest and civil rights. /1992/
5-A/KD593 . . . . **789.2**

Psyche (Greek deity).
CRAFT, MC/Cupid and Psyche. /1996/4-5/6 KA737 . . . . . . **292**

Psychic trauma.
LAMB, N/One April morning: children remember the Oklahoma City
bombing. /1996/2-6/6 KF006 . . . . **976.6**

Psychical research.
DEEM, JM/How to find a ghost. /1988/4-A/7 KA604 . . . . **133.1**

Psychokinesis.
GREEN, CR/Mysterious mind powers. /1993/4-6/3 KA609 . **133.8**

Psychokinesis--Fiction.
ROBERTS, WD/Girl with the silver eyes. /1980/4-6/5 KH636 . . **Fic**

Psychotherapy.
KOPLOW, L/Tanya and the Tobo Man/Tanya y el Hombre Tobo: a
story in English and Spanish for children entering therapy /1991/
K-2/2 KD040 . . . . **618.92**

Puberty.
BOY TO MAN. 3RD ED. (VIDEOCASSETTE). /1992/
5-6/KC944 . . . . **VCR 612.6**
FEELINGS: INSIDE, OUTSIDE, UPSIDE DOWN (VIDEOCASSETTE).
/1992/6/KC946 . . . . **VCR 612.6**
HARRIS, RH/It's perfectly normal: a book about changing bodies,
growing up, and sex, /1994/5-6/6 KC949 . . . . **612.6**
LOOK WHO'S GROWING UP (VIDEOCASSETTE). /1997/
5-6/KC920 . . . . **VCR 612**
LOOKING GOOD, FEELING GOOD (VIDEOCASSETTE). /1994/
5-6/KC951 . . . . **VCR 612.6**
MADARAS, L/What's happening to my body? Book for girls. Rev.
ed. /1983/5-6/9 KC952 . . . . **612.6**
NEW, IMPROVED ME: UNDERSTANDING BODY CHANGES
(VIDEOCASSETTE). /1991/5-6/KC953 . . . . **VCR 612.6**
THEN ONE YEAR. 2ND ED. (VIDEOCASSETTE). /1992/
5-6/KC957 . . . . **VCR 612.6**

Puberty--Fiction.
BLUME, J/Then again, maybe I won't. /1971/6-A/5 KG915 . . . **Fic**

Public health SEE Communicable diseases; Hospitals; Medical care; Pollution;
Refuse and refuse disposal; Water--Pollution; Water supply.

Public lands SEE National parks and reserves.

Public relations--Libraries.
BOOKTALK! 5: MORE SELECTIONS FROM THE BOOKTALKER
FOR ALL AGES AND AUDIENCES. /1993//KA090. **PROF 028.5**

Public works.
PUBLIC WORKS (VIDEOCASSETTE). /1992/
2-4/KB055 . . . . **VCR 363.72**

Publishers and publishing.
ALIKI /How a book is made. /1986/K-3/3 KD345 . . . . . . **686**

Pueblo Indians.
CLARK, AN/In my mother's house. /c1941, 1991/
1-4/KE759 . . . . **970.3**
YUE, C/Pueblo. /1986/5-6/8 KF065 . . . . **979**

Pueblo Indians--Antiquities.
WARREN, S/Cities in the sand: the ancient civilizations of the
Southwest. /1992/5-6/8 KF064 . . . . **979**

Pueblo Indians--Biography.
KEEGAN, M/Pueblo boy: growing up in two worlds. /1991/
4-6/5 KE793 . . . . **970.489**
KREISCHER, EK/Maria Montoya Martinez: master potter. /1995/
5-6/3 KE461 . . . . **B MARTINEZ, M.**

Pueblo Indians--Folklore.
MCDERMOTT, G/Arrow to the sun. /1974/
2-4/3 KB711 . . . . **CE 398.26**

Pueblo Indians--Social life and customs.
ARNOLD, C/Ancient cliff dwellers of Mesa Verde. /1992/
5-6/8 KE790 . . . . **970.488**

KEEGAN, M/Pueblo boy: growing up in two worlds. /1991/
4-6/5 KE793 . . . . **970.489**
TRIMBLE, S/Village of blue stone. /1990/4-6/6 KF063 . . . . . **979**

Puerto Ricans--New York (N.Y.)--Fiction.
COWLEY, J/Gracias, the Thanksgiving turkey. /1996/
K-2/1 KF430 . . . . **E**

Puerto Rico.
KENT, D/Puerto Rico. /1992/5-6/6 KE847 . . . . **972.95**

Puerto Rico--Biography.
ENGEL, T/We'll never forget you, Roberto Clemente. /1997/
2-4/2 KE293 . . . . **B CLEMENTE, R.**
MACHT, NL/Roberto Clemente. /1994/
5-A/7 KE294 . . . . **B CLEMENTE, R.**

Puerto Rico--Fiction.
DELACRE, L/Vejigante masquerader. /1993/1-3/4 KF458 . . . . . **E**
PICO, F/Red comb. /1994/3-5/7 KH601 . . . . **Fic**
POMERANTZ, C/Outside dog. /1993/P-2/2 KG266 . . . . . . **CE E**

Puerto Rico--Folklore.
BERNIER-GRAND, CT/Juan Bobo: four folktales from Puerto Rico. /
1994/1-2/2 KB427 . . . . **398.22**
JAFFE, N/Golden flower: a Taino myth from Puerto Rico. /1996/
2-4/5 KB503 . . . . **398.23**
MOHR, N/Song of el coqui and other tales of Puerto Rico. /1995/
3-4/3 KB621 . . . . **398.24**
PITRE, F/Juan Bobo and the pig: a Puerto Rican folktale. /1993/
2-4/2 KB763 . . . . **398.27**

Puffins.
GIBBONS, G/Puffins are back! /1991/2-4/5 KC677 . . . . . . **598.3**
MCMILLAN, B/Nights of the pufflings. /1995/1-3/6 KC678 . **598.3**

Pumas.
GOUCK, M/Mountain lions. /1993/3-5/5 KC829 . . . . . . **599.757**

Pumpkin.
KING, E/Pumpkin patch. /1990/1-4/4 KD169 . . . . **635**

Pumpkin--Fiction.
HALL, Z/It's pumpkin time! /1994/P-2/3 KF666 . . . . **E**
JOHNSTON, T/Very scary. /1995/P-2/3 KF842 . . . . **E**
MARZOLLO, J/I'm a seed. /1996/K-2/1 KG081 . . . . **E**
SILVERMAN, E/Big pumpkin. /1992/P-2/2 KG504 . . . . **E**
TITHERINGTON, J/Pumpkin pumpkin. /1986/P-2/1 KG609 . . . . **E**

Puns and punning.
JUSTER, N/Otter nonsense. /1994/3-6/KD721 . . . . . . **793.734**

Puppet making.
BUETTER, BM/Simple puppets from everyday materials. /1997/
2-5/3 KD443 . . . . **745.592**
BULLOCH, I/I want to be a puppeteer. /1996/
3-5/5 KD444 . . . . **745.592**
MAKING AND USING PUPPETS IN THE PRIMARY GRADES
(VIDEOCASSETTE). /1992/K-6/KD446 . . . . **VCR 745.592**
WRIGHT, DA/One-person puppet plays. /1990/
/KA365 . . . . **PROF 812**

Puppet plays.
ANDERSON, D/Amazingly easy puppet plays: 42 new scripts for
one-person puppetry. /1997//KA361 . . . . **PROF 812**
BUCHWALD, C/Puppet book: how to make and operate puppets
and stage a puppet play. /1990//KA326. . . . . **PROF 791.5**
HUNT, T/Puppetry in early childhood education. /1982/
/KA327 . . . . **PROF 791.5**
PETER COTTONTAIL: HOW HE GOT HIS HOP! (VIDEOCASSTTE).
/1993/P-2/KD646 . . . . **VCR 789.3**
WRIGHT, DA/One-person puppet plays. /1990/
/KA365 . . . . **PROF 812**

Puppet plays--Fiction.
PATERSON, K/Master puppeteer. /c1975/6-A/6 KH580 . . . . . **Fic**

Puppet theater.
ANDERSON, D/Amazingly easy puppet plays: 42 new scripts for
one-person puppetry. /1997//KA361 . . . . **PROF 812**
BULLOCH, I/I want to be a puppeteer. /1996/
3-5/5 KD444 . . . . **745.592**
MAKING AND USING PUPPETS IN THE PRIMARY GRADES
(VIDEOCASSETTE). /1992/K-6/KD446 . . . . **VCR 745.592**

Puppets.
BUCHWALD, C/Puppet book: how to make and operate puppets
and stage a puppet play. /1990//KA326. . . . . **PROF 791.5**
BULLOCH, I/I want to be a puppeteer. /1996/
3-5/5 KD444 . . . . **745.592**
HUNT, T/Puppetry in early childhood education. /1982/
/KA327 . . . . **PROF 791.5**
MAKING AND USING PUPPETS IN THE PRIMARY GRADES
(VIDEOCASSETTE). /1992/K-6/KD446 . . . . **VCR 745.592**
RENFRO, N/Puppetry, language, and the special child: discovering
alternate languages. /1984//KA328 . . . . **PROF 791.5**

Puritans--Fiction.
SPEARE, EG/Witch of Blackbird Pond. /c1958/
5-6/5 KH742 . . . . **CE Fic**

Puzzles SEE ALSO Mathematical recreations; Rebuses; Riddles.
Puzzles.
    HILLMAN, LE/Nature puzzlers. /1989//KA289 . . . . . **PROF 508**
Puzzles--Dictionaries.
    EISS, HE/Dictionary of language games, puzzles, and amusements.
    /1986/4-6/KA455. . . . . **REF 793.734**
Puzzles--Fiction.
    MACAULAY, D/Black and white. /1990/3-A/5 KH432 . . . . . . **Fic**
Pyramids--Central America.
    PUTNAM, J/Pyramid. /1994/4-A/7 KD359. . . . . **690**
Pyramids--Egypt.
    BENDICK, J/Egyptian tombs. /1989/4-6/7 KE632 . . . . **932**
    MACAULAY, D/Pyramid. /1975/A/10 KD357 . . . . **CE 690**
    MANN, E/Great Pyramid. /1996/4-6/6 KE635 . . . . **932**
    PUTNAM, J/Pyramid. /1994/4-A/7 KD359. . . . . **690**
Pyramids--Mexico.
    PUTNAM, J/Pyramid. /1994/4-A/7 KD359. . . . . **690**
Pyramids--Sudan.
    PUTNAM, J/Pyramid. /1994/4-A/7 KD359. . . . . **690**
Pythons--Fiction.
    CANNON, J/Verdi. /1997/K-2/3 KF336 . . . . **E**
Quakers.
    BRILL, MT/Allen Jay and the Underground Railroad. /1993/
    4-6/4 KE898 . . . . **973.7**
Quakers--Fiction.
    AVI /Night journeys. /c1979, 1994/5-A/6 KG860 . . . . **Fic**
    TURKLE, B/Thy friend, Obadiah. /c1969/K-3/5 KG623 . . . . . . **E**
Quanah Parker, Comanche Chief.
    FREEDMAN, R/Indian chiefs. /1987/5-6/8 KE749 . . . . . . **970.1**
Quarrels.
    BULLY UP: FIGHTING FEELINGS (VIDEOCASSETTE). /c1990,
    1991/K-3/KA807 . . . . **VCR 303.6**
Quarter horse.
    STEWART, GB/Quarter horse. /1995/4-6/5 KD207 . . . . . . **636.1**
Quebec (Province)--Fiction.
    CARRIER, R/Boxing champion. /1991/4-6/2 KG976 . . . . **Fic**
    Longest home run. /1993/2-4/4 KG977 . . . . **Fic**
Quebec (Province)--Valleyfield--Fiction.
    HEWITT, M/One proud summer. /1981/A/7 KH254 . . . . **Fic**
Quechua Indians.
    PITKANEN, MA/Grandchildren of the Incas. /1991/
    4-6/6 KF110 . . . . **985**
Queen Anne's lace.
    WEXLER, J/Queen Anne's lace. /1994/2-6/6 KC433. . . . . . . **583**
Queens SEE Kings, queens, rulers, etc.
Questions and answers.
    ABC'S OF NATURE: A FAMILY ANSWER BOOK. /1984/
    P-A/KB900. . . . . **508**
    BUEHNER, C/It's a spoon, not a shovel. /1995/
    2-6/2 KB248 . . . . **395.5**
    COBB, V/Why doesn't the earth fall up? /1988/
    4-6/5 KC092 . . . . **531**
    HAUSHERR, R/What food is this? /1994/K-2/2 KD266 . . . . **641.3**
    MILLER, M/Who uses this? /1990/P-K/KA943 . . . . **331.7**
    MOORE, K/...If you lived at the time of the Civil War. /1994/
    3-5/6 KE908 . . . . **973.7**
    MOST, B/Dinosaur questions. /1995/K-4/7 KC257 . . . . . . **567.9**
    MYERS, J/What makes popcorn pop?: and other questions about
    the world around us. /c1991, 1994/3-6/7 KB868 . . . . **500**
    PETERSON, PR/Know it all: resource book for kids. /1989/
    4-A/6 KA591 . . . . **031.02**
    SOUCIE, G/What's the difference between apes and monkeys and
    other living things? /1995/4-6/7 KC271. . . . . **571**
    What's the difference between lenses and prisms and other
    scientific things? /1995/4-6/7 KB872 . . . . **500**
    SQUIRE, A/101 questions and answers about pets and people. /
    1988/5-6/7 KD192 . . . . **636.088**
    TAFURI, N/Spots, feathers, and curly tails. /1988/
    P-K/1 KD185 . . . . **636**
    WHAT IS A BELLYBUTTON?: FIRST QUESTIONS AND ANSWERS
    ABOUT THE HUMAN BODY. /1993/P-K/ KC929 . . . . . . **612**
    WOLLARD, K/How come? /1993/4-8/6 KB874 . . . . **500**
Questions and answers--Software.
    WHAT IS A BELLYBUTTON?: FUN AND INTERACTIVE
    QUESTIONS AND ANSWERS ABOUT THE /1994/
    2-6/KC930. . . . . **CDR 612**
Quetzalcoatl (Aztec deity).
    PATENT, DH/Quetzal: sacred bird of the cloud forest. /1996/
    3-6/6 KC702 . . . . **598.7**
Quetzals.
    PATENT, DH/Quetzal: sacred bird of the cloud forest. /1996/
    3-6/6 KC702 . . . . **598.7**
Quicksand.
    DE PAOLA, T/Quicksand book. /c1977/K-3/2 KC226 . . . . . . **552**

Quilting--Fiction.
    COERR, E/Josefina story quilt. /1986/1-3/2 KF401 . . . . . . **CE E**
    FLOURNOY, V/Patchwork quilt. /1985/K-3/5 KF561. . . . . **E**
    TURNER, A/Sewing quilts. /1994/1-3/6 KG628. . . . . **E**
Quiltmakers.
    FAITH RINGGOLD PAINTS CROWN HEIGHTS (VIDEOCASSETTE).
    /1995/5-A/KD461 . . . . **VCR 746.46**
Quilts.
    PAUL, AW/Seasons sewn: a year in patchwork. /1996/
    3-6/7 KD462 . . . . **746.46**
Quilts--Fiction.
    GUBACK, G/Luka's quilt. /1994/1-3/2 KF652 . . . . **E**
    HOPKINSON, D/Sweet Clara and the freedom quilt. /1993/
    1-3/4 KF770 . . . . **E**
    JONAS, A/Quilt. /1984/K-1/2 KF846 . . . . **E**
    POLACCO, P/Keeping quilt. /1988/K-3/6 KG252. . . . . . . **CE E**
    TURNER, A/Sewing quilts. /1994/1-3/6 KG628. . . . . **E**
Quinceanera (social custom).
    LANKFORD, MD/Quinceanera: a Latina's journey to womanhood. /
    1994/5-6/7 KA715 . . . . **265**
Quotations SEE ALSO Proverbs.
Quotations.
    BARTLETT, J/Bartlett's familiar quotations: a collection of passages,
    phrases and proverbs traced to sources in ancient and modern
    literature. 16th ed. /1992/A/KA458 . . . . **REF 803**
    BURLEIGH, R/Who said that?: famous Americans speak. /1997/
    4-A/7 KA597 . . . . **080**
    PROVENSEN, A/My fellow Americans: a family album. /1995/
    3-6/9 KE862 . . . . **973**
    SOMETHING RICH AND STRANGE: A TREASURY OF
    SHAKESPEARE'S VERSE. /1995/6-A/KE118 . . . . **822.3**
Rabbis SEE Clergy.
Rabbit (Legendary character).
    ROSS, G/How Rabbit tricked Otter and other Cherokee trickster
    stories. /1994/2-4/6 KB641 . . . . **CE 398.24**
    SHUTE, L/Rabbit wishes. /1995/K-2/2 KB651 . . . . **398.24**
Rabbits.
    EVANS, M/Rabbit. /1992/3-6/4 KD179 . . . . **636**
Rabbits--Fiction.
    ADAMS, R/Watership Down. /c1972, 1974/6-A/5 KG813 . . . **Fic**
    ARNOSKY, J/Rabbits and raindrops. /1997/P-2/2 KF169 . . . . **E**
    BECKER, J/Seven little rabbits. /1973/P-2/3 KF214 . . . . **E**
    BROWN, MT/Bionic Bunny Show. /1984/K-3/5 KF280 . . . . . . **E**
    Goodnight moon. /c1947/P-K/1 KF285 . . . . **CE E**
    Runaway bunny. /c1972/P-K/2 KF287 . . . . **CE E**
    DEJONG, M/Shadrach. /c1953/2-3/5 KH069. . . . . **Fic**
    EASTERLING, B/Prize in the snow. /1994/2-3/4 KF503. . . . . . **E**
    FRIEDRICH, P/Easter Bunny that overslept. /1983/P-K/KF587 . . . **E**
    GAG, W/ABC bunny. /c1933, 1997/P-K/KF591 . . . . **E**
    HEYWARD, DB/Country bunny and the little gold shoes, as told to
    Jenifer. /c1939/P-K/7 KF723 . . . . **E**
    HOBAN, T/Where is it? /c1972/P-K/1 KF747 . . . . **E**
    HOWE, D/Bunnicula: a rabbit-tale mystery. /1979/
    3-6/5 KH285 . . . . **Fic**
    HOWE, J/Rabbit-Cadabra! /1993/K-3/3 KF779 . . . . **E**
    LASKY, K/Lunch bunnies. /1996/K-2/2 KF946 . . . . **E**
    LESTER, H/Listen Buddy. /1995/K-2/2 KF964 . . . . **E**
    LOWELL, S/Tortoise and the jackrabbit. /1994/K-2/3 KG040 . . . **E**
    POTTER, B/Tale of Benjamin Bunny. /c1932, 1987/
    P-2/8 KG272 . . . . **E**
    Tale of Peter Rabbit. /n.d., 1987/P-2/6 KG278 . . . . **E**
    Tale of the Flopsy Bunnies. /c1937, 1987/P-2/7 KG281 . . . . **E**
    RATZ DE TAGYOS, P/Coney tale. /1992/2-5/5 KH620. . . . . . **Fic**
    Showdown at Lonesome Pellet. /1994/1-4/5 KH621. . . . . . **Fic**
    VAN LEEUWEN, J/Emma Bean. /1993/K-2/2 KG646 . . . . . . **E**
    WELLS, R/Bunny cakes. /1997/P-1/2 KG696 . . . . **E**
    Max and Ruby's first Greek myth: Pandora's box. /1993/
    P-1/3 KG700 . . . . **E**
    Max and Ruby's Midas: another Greek myth. /1995/
    P-1/3 KG701. . . . . **E**
    Max's chocolate chicken. /1989/P-2/2 KG702. . . . . **CE E**
    Max's Christmas. /1986/P-1/2 KG703. . . . . **CE E**
    Max's first word (Board book). /1979/P/1 KG704. . . . . . **BB E**
    WILLARD, N/Starlit somersault downhill. /1993/K-2/3 KG725 . . **E**
    WILLIAMS, M/Velveteen Rabbit; or, How toys become real. /1988/
    3-5/6 KH864 . . . . **CE Fic**
    ZOLOTOW, C/Mr. Rabbit and the lovely present. /c1962/
    P-2/2 KG804 . . . . **CE E**
Rabbits--Folklore.
    SHUTE, L/Rabbit wishes. /1995/K-2/2 KB651 . . . . **398.24**
    TORRENCE, J/Brer Rabbit stories (Sound recording cassette). /
    1984/4-5/KB666. . . . . **SRC 398.24**
Rabbits as pets--Fiction.
    NAPOLI, DJ/Bravest thing. /1995/3-5/6 KH529 . . . . **Fic**

Raccoons.
ARNOSKY, J/Raccoons and ripe corn. /c1987, 1991/
P-2/3 KC831 . . . . **599.76**

Raccoons--Fiction.
HOBAN, L/Case of the two masked robbers. /1988/
K-2/1 KF737 . . . . E
OTTO, C/Raccoon at Clear Creek Road. /1995/
K-2/3 KG202 . . . . **CE E**
WHELAN, G/Week of raccoons. /1988/K-2/5 KG710 . . . . . . E

Race awareness.
RACE (VIDEOCASSETTE). /1993/A/KA855 . . . . . . **VCR 305.8**

Race awareness--Poetry.
ADOFF, A/All the colors of the race. /1982/4-6/KD907 . . . . **811**
MAKE A JOYFUL SOUND: POEMS FOR CHILDREN BY AFRICAN-
AMERICAN POETS. /1991/1-6/KE070 . . . . **811.008**

Race horses.
STEWART, GB/Thoroughbred horse: born to run. /1995/
4-6/5 KD208 . . . . **636.1**

Race problems SEE ALSO Emigration and immigration; Intercultural
education.

Race relations.
GOLENBOCK, P/Teammates. /1990/3-6/6 KD798 . . . . . **796.357**
ROCHELLE, B/Witnesses to freedom: young people who fought for
civil rights. /1993/5-6/7 KA905 . . . . **323.1**

Race relations--Fiction.
COLEMAN, E/White socks only. /1996/3-4/4 KH014 . . . . . . **Fic**
RASCHKA, C/Yo! Yes?. /1993/P-3/1 KG307 . . . . E
ROBINET, HG/Mississippi chariot. /1994/5-A/5 KH639 . . . . **Fic**
SEBESTYEN, O/Words by heart. /1997/5-A/7 KH689 . . . **CE Fic**
TAYLOR, MD/Friendship. /1987/4-6/5 KH776. . . . . **Fic**
Mississippi bridge. /1990/5-A/4 KH778 . . . . **Fic**
Well: David's story. /1995/5-A/4 KH781 . . . . **Fic**
YOUNG, RT/Learning by heart. /1993/6-A/6 KH899 . . . . . **Fic**

Race relations--Sources.
MELTZER, M/Black Americans: a history in their own words 1619-
1983. /1984/5-6/9 KE857 . . . . **973**

Racially mixed people--Fiction.
HAMILTON, V/Plain City. /1993/6-A/5 KH217 . . . . **Fic**

Racing SEE ALSO Autombile racing; Bicycle racing; Horse racing;
Motorcycle racing; Sailboat racing.

Racing--Fiction.
CREWS, D/Bicycle race. /1985/K-2/2 KF431. . . . . E
WOLFF, A/Stella and Roy. /1993/P-1/3 KG756 . . . . E

Racism.
PLAYING FAIR (VIDEOCASSETTE). /1991/
4-6/KA854 . . . . **VCR 305.8**
WHITEWASH (VIDEOCASSETTE) /1994/3-6/KA862 . **VCR 305.8**

Racism--Software.
PREJUDICE (MICROCOMPUTER PROGRAM). /1992/
5-A/KA820 . . . . **MCP 305**

Radio--Fiction.
DORROS, A/Radio Man: a story in English and Spanish./Don
Radio: un cuento en Ingles y /1993/2-5/2 KF491 . . . . E

Radio broadcasting--Fiction.
HAMILTON, V/Willie Bea and the time the Martians landed. /
1983/5-6/3 KH219 . . . . **Fic**

Radioactive dating.
JESPERSEN, J/Mummies, dinosaurs, moon rocks: how we know how
old things are. /1996/4-6/9 KE625 . . . . **930.1**

Radioactivity--History.
PFLAUM, R/Marie Curie and her daughter Irene. /1993/
6-A/8 KC139 . . . . **539.7**

Railroad accidents--Fiction.
BODKIN, O/Banshee train. /1995/1-3/4 KF240 . . . . E

Railroads--Accidents.
SAN SOUCI, RD/Kate Shelley: bound for legend. /1995/
3-5/5 KE539 . . . . **B SHELLEY, K.**

Railroads--Fiction.
CREWS, D/Shortcut. /1992/K-2/2 KF436 . . . . E
KRENSKY, S/Iron dragon never sleeps. /1995/3-5-2 KH381. . . **Fic**
PINKNEY, GJ/Sunday outing. /1994/1-3/2 KG241 . . . . E
STEVENSON, J/All aboard! /1995/1-3/2 KG557 . . . . E

Railroads--History.
BLUMBERG, R/Full steam ahead: the race to build a transcontinental
railroad. /1996/4-6/10 KB137. . . . . **385**
BUILDING THE FIRST TRANSCONTINENTAL RAILROAD
(PICTURE). /n.d./5-6/KB138 . . . . **PIC 385**
FRASER, MA/Ten mile day and the building of the transcontinental
railroad. /c1993, 1996/5-6/7 KB139 . . . . **385**
MURPHY, J/Across America on an emigrant train. /1993/
6-A/8 KB140 . . . . **385**

Railroads--History--Fiction.
GOBLE, P/Death of the iron horse. /1987/K-3/2 KF626 . . . . . . E
YEE, P/Ghost Train. /1996/4-6/5 KH889 . . . . **Fic**

Railroads--Models--Periodicals.
MODEL RAILROADER. /1934-/4-A/KA526 . . . . **PER 050**

Railroads--Rolling stock SEE Locomotives.

Railroads--Trains.
COILEY, J/Train. /1992/5-6/8 KD072 . . . . **625.1**
GIBBONS, G/Trains. /1987/1-3/3 KD073 . . . . **625.1**
GUNNING, TG/Dream trains. /1992/4-6/6 KD074 . . . . **625.1**
LET ME TELL YOU ALL ABOUT TRAINS (VIDEOCASSETTE). /
1993/3-4/KD076 . . . . **VCR 625.2**
MAGEE, D/All aboard ABC. /1990/K-2/2 KD075 . . . . . . **625.1**
TRAINS (VIDEOCASSETTE). /1995/2-4/KD077 . . . . **VCR 625.2**

Railroads--Trains--Fiction.
HOWARD, EF/Mac and Marie and the train toss surprise. /1993/
K-2/2 KF774 . . . . E
LONDON, J/Owl who became the moon. /1993/P-2/3 KG026. . E
MCPHAIL, D/Moony B. Finch, the fastest draw in the West. /1994/
1-3/4 KG120 . . . . E
NESBIT, E/Railway children. /1994/4-5/7 KH543 . . . . **Fic**
RYLANT, C/Silver packages: an Appalachian Christmas story. /
1997/1-3/2 KG386. . . . . E
SIEBERT, D/Train song. /1990/P-3/KG501 . . . . E
TEMPLE, C/Train. /1996/K-3/2 KG599 . . . . E

Railroads--Trains--Pictorial works.
CREWS, D/Freight train. /1978/P-K/KF433 . . . . E

Rain--Poetry.
DEMING, AG/Who is tapping at my window? /c1988, 1994/
P-K/KD930 . . . . **811**

Rain and rainfall SEE ALSO Floods; Meteorology; Snow; Storms; names of
particular types of rains e.g. Monsoons.

Rain and rainfall.
BRANDT, K/What makes it rain? The story of a raindrop. /1982/
P-K/2 KC209 . . . . **551.57**
BRANLEY, FM/Flash, crash, rumble and roll. Rev. ed. /1985/
1-3/2 KC195 . . . . **CE 551.55**
Rain and hail. Rev. ed. /1983/K-3/2 KC188 . . . . . . **551.5**
KAHL, JD/Wet weather: rain showers and snowfall. /1992/
4-6/7 KC212 . . . . **551.57**
MARKLE, S/Rainy day. /1993/P-2/6 KC214 . . . . **551.57**
STEELE, P/Rain: causes and effects. /1991/3-6/7 KC215 . . **551.57**

Rain and rainfall--Fiction.
GINSBURG, M/Mushroom in the rain. /c1974, 1987/
P-2/2 KF623 . . . . E
HEST, A/In the rain with Baby Duck. /1995/P-1/2 KF718 . . . . . E
JOHNSON, A/Rain feet (Board book). /1994/P/2 KF833 . . **BB E**
KUSKIN, K/James and the rain. /1995/K-2/5 KF938 . . . . E
LONDON, J/Puddles. /1997/P-1/3 KG027 . . . . E
MARTIN, JR., B./Listen to the rain. /1988/P-2/KG077 . . . . E
SERFOZO, M/Rain talk. /1990/P-1/4 KG441 . . . . E
SHANNON, G/April showers. /1995/P-1/2 KG477 . . . . E
SHULEVITZ, U/Rain, rain rivers. /c1969, 1998/P-2/2 KG499 . . . E
SIMON, N/Wet world. /1995/P-1/3 KG508 . . . . E
STEVENSON, J/We hate rain! /1988/P-3/2 KG569 . . . . E

Rain and rainfall--Poetry.
PRELUTSKY, J/Rainy rainy Saturday. /1980/1-3/KE013 . . . . . **811**
RAINY DAY RHYMES. /1992/1-3/KE078 . . . . **811.008**

Rain forest animals.
DARLING, K/Amazon ABC. /1996/K-5/3 KC499 . . . . . . **591.981**
NAGDA, AW/Canopy crossing: a story of an Atlantic rainforest
(Kit). /1997/2-4/KC873 . . . . **KIT 599.8**
PATENT, DH/Flashy fantastic rain forest frogs. /1997/
4-6/4 KC607 . . . . **597.8**

Rain forest ecology.
GEORGE, JC/One day in the tropical rain forest. /1990/
4-6/6 KC315 . . . . **577.34**
GIBBONS, G/Nature's green umbrella: tropical rain forests. /1994/
2-6/5 KC316 . . . . **577.34**
LEWINGTON, A/Atlas of rain forests. /1997/
3-6/7 KC321 . . . . **577.34**
PRATT, KJ/Walk in the rainforest. /1992/K-6/7 KC322 . . . **577.34**
RAINFOREST (VIDEOCASSETTE). /1993/
5-A/KC324 . . . . **VCR 577.34**
SIY, A/Brazilian rain forest. /1992/4-6/6 KC326 . . . . . . **577.34**
WILLOW, D/At home in the rain forest. /1991/
K-4/6 KC328 . . . . **577.34**
YOLEN, J/Welcome to the green house. /1993/
K-3/4 KC329 . . . . **577.34**

Rain forest ecology--Amazon River Region.
GOODMAN, SE/Bats, bugs, and biodiversity: adventures in the
Amazonian rain forest. /1995/3-6/7 KC318 . . . . . . **577.34**
LESSEM, D/Inside the amazing Amazon. /1995/
2-6/7 KC319 . . . . **577.34**

Rain forest ecology--Amazon River Region--Brazil.
COBB, V/This place is wet. /1989/3-6/6 KC287 . . . . **574.5**

Rain forest ecology--Amazon River Region--Brazil--Fiction.
  CHERRY, L/Great kapok tree: a tale of the Amazon rain forest. /
  1990/2-3/4 KF380 . . . . E
    Great kapok tree (Videocassette). /1996/2-3/KF381. . . . VCR E
Rain forest ecology--Costa Rica--Software.
  SCHOLASTIC'S THE MAGIC SCHOOL BUS EXPLORES THE
  RAINFOREST. SCHOOL ED. (CD-ROM). /1997/
  6-A/KC325 . . . . CDR 577.34
Rain forest ecology--Software.
  FIELD TRIP TO THE RAINFOREST (MICROCOMPUTER
  PROGRAM). /1991/3-A/KC314 . . . . MCP 577.34
  RAINFOREST RESEARCHERS (CD-ROM). /1996/
  5-A/KC323 . . . . CDR 577.34
  STV: RAIN FOREST (VIDEODISC). /1991/
  4-A/KC327 . . . . VD 577.34
Rain forests.
  GIBBONS, G/Nature's green umbrella: tropical rain forests. /1994/
  2-6/5 KC316 . . . . 577.34
  GILLILAND, JH/River. /1993/K-3/3 KC317 . . . . 577.34
  PRATT, KJ/Walk in the rainforest. /1992/K-6/7 KC322 . . . 577.34
  SIY, A/Brazilian rain forest. /1992/4-6/6 KC326 . . . . . . 577.34
  WILLOW, D/At home in the rain forest. /1991/
  K-4/6 KC328 . . . . 577.34
  YOLEN, J/Welcome to the green house. /1993/
  K-3/4 KC329 . . . . 577.34
Rain forests--Amazon River Region.
  LESSEM, D/Inside the amazing Amazon. /1995/
  2-6/7 KC319 . . . . 577.34
Rain forests--Costa Rica--Software.
  SCHOLASTIC'S THE MAGIC SCHOOL BUS EXPLORES THE
  RAINFOREST. SCHOOL ED. (CD-ROM). /1997/
  6-A/KC325 . . . . CDR 577.34
Rain forests--Fiction.
  CHERRY, L/Great kapok tree: a tale of the Amazon rain forest. /
  1990/2-3/4 KF380 . . . . E
    Great kapok tree (Videocassette). /1996/2-3/KF381. . . . VCR E
  COWCHER, H/Rain forest. /c1988, 1990/2-4/4 KF428 . . . . . . E
  MCDERMOTT, G/Papagayo the mischief maker. /1992/
  P-2/5 KG096 . . . . E
Rain forests--Software.
  FIELD TRIP TO THE RAINFOREST (MICROCOMPUTER
  PROGRAM). /1991/3-A/KC314 . . . . MCP 577.34
  LET'S EXPLORE THE JUNGLE WITH BUZZY THE KNOWLEDGE
  BUG (CD-ROM). /1995/K-3/KC320 . . . . CDR 577.34
  RAINFOREST RESEARCHERS (CD-ROM). /1996/
  5-A/KC323 . . . . CDR 577.34
  STV: RAIN FOREST (VIDEODISC). /1991/
  4-A/KC327 . . . . VD 577.34
Rainbow--Fiction.
  KRAMER, SP/Theodoric's rainbow. /1995/3-6/4 KH380 . . . . . Fic
Ramadan.
  GHAZI, SH/Ramadan. /1996/3-5/7 KA785 297
  KERVEN, R/Id-ul-Fitr. /1997/3-5/7 KA787 297
Ramadan--Fiction.
  MATTHEWS, M/Magid fasts for Ramadan. /1996/
  4-6/4 KH462 . . . . Fic
Ramsay, Kathleen.
  DEWEY, JO/Wildlife rescue: the work of Dr. Kathleen Ramsay. /
  1994/4-6/7 KD252 . . . . 639.9
Ramsey, Alice--Fiction.
  HYATT, PR/Coast to coast with Alice. /1995/4-6/5 KH312 . . . Fic
Ranch life SEE AlSO Cowboys.
Ranch life.
  DEWEY, JO/Cowgirl dreams: a western childhood. /1995/
  3-4/4 KE320 . . . . B DEWEY, J.
Ranch life--Argentina.
  BRUSCA, MC/On the pampas. /1991/3-6/6 KF106 982
Ranch life--Fiction.
  HERMAN, RA/Pal the pony. /1996/K-1/2 KF714 . . . . E
  HERMES, P/Someone to count on: a novel. /1993/
  6-A/7 KH250 . . . . Fic
  ROUNDS, G/Once we had a horse. /1996/K-2/3 KG358 . . . . . E
  SCOTT, AH/Brand is forever. /1993/3-5/6 KH687 . . . . Fic
    One good horse: a cowpuncher's counting book. /1990/
  K-2/2 KG424 . . . . E
  WALTER, MP/Justin and the best biscuits in the world. /1986/
  4-6/6 KH839 . . . . Fic
Ranch life--New Mexico.
  ANDERSON, J/Cowboys: roundup on an American ranch. /1996/
  3-5/6 KF025 978
Rap (Music).
  SCHOOL RAP (SOUND RECORDING CASSETTE). /1990/
  2-6/KD656 . . . . SRC 789.3

Rape--Fiction.
  PECK, R/Are you in the house alone? /1989/A/6 KH592 . . . . . Fic
Raphael Sanzio.
  MUHLBERGER, R/What makes a Raphael a Raphael? /1993/
  5-A/7 KD497 . . . . 759.5
Rare and endangered species.
  ENDANGERED SPECIES (VIDEOCASSETTE). /1991/
  4-6/KC487 . . . . VCR 591.68
Rare animals SEE ALSO Extinct animals.
Rare animals.
  ARNOLD, C/Cheetah. /1989/5-6/9 KC817 . . . . 599.75
  DARLING, K/Manatee: on location. /1991/5-6/7 KC779 . . 599.55
  ENDANGERED ANIMALS: SURVIVORS ON THE BRINK
  (VIDEOCASSETTE). /1997/4-6/KC486 . . . . VCR 591.68
  ENDANGERED SPECIES (VIDEOCASSETTE). /1991/
  4-6/KC487 . . . . VCR 591.68
  ENDANGERED WILDLIFE OF THE WORLD. /1993/
  5-A/KA446 . . . . REF 578.68
  FACKLAM, M/And then there was one: the mysteries of extinction.
  /1990/5-6/7 KC488 . . . . 591.68
  HOFF, MK/Our endangered planet: life on land. /1992/
  5-6/8 KA962 . . . . 333.95
  JONAS, A/Aardvarks, disembark! /1990/2-A/4 KA963. . . 333.95
  KOCH, M/World water watch. /1993/K-2/4 KD255 . . . . . 639.9
  LONG, M/Any bear can wear glasses: the spectacled bear and
  other curious creatures. /1995/4-6/6 KC451 591
  MANATEES: RED ALERT (VIDEOCASSETTE). /1996/
  5-6/KC782 . . . . VCR 599.55
  MAYNARD, T/Rhino comes to America. /1993/
  5-6/7 KC802 . . . . 599.66
    Saving endangered mammals: a field guide to some of the earth's
    rarest animals. /1992/5-6/8 KC489 . . . . 591.68
  PATENT, DH/Gray wolf, red wolf. /1990/5-6/8 KC839 . 599.773
  POLLOCK, S/Atlas of endangered animals. /1993/
  5-6/7 KC491 . . . . 591.68
  SAVING THE MANATEE (VIDEOCASSETTE). /1993/
  2-6/KC783 . . . . VCR 599.55
Rare animals--Software.
  MICROSOFT DANGEROUS CREATURES: EXPLORE THE
  ENDANGERED WORLD OF WILDLIFE. ACADEMIC ED. (CD-
  ROM). /1994/4-A/KC490 . . . . CDR 591.68
Rare birds.
  ARNOLD, C/On the brink of extinction: the California condor. /
  1993/5-6/8 KD251 . . . . 639.9
  ENDANGERED WILDLIFE OF THE WORLD. /1993/
  5-A/KA446 . . . . REF 578.68
  PATENT, DH/Whooping crane: a comeback story. /1988/
  A/9 KD258 . . . . 639.9
Rare plants.
  HOFF, MK/Our endangered planet: life on land. /1992/
  5-6/8 KA962 . . . . 333.95
Ratites.
  ARNOLD, C/Ostriches and other flightless birds. /1990/
  5-6/7 KC690 . . . . 598.5
Rats--Fiction.
  CONLY, JL/Racso and the rats of NIMH. /1986/5-6/6 KH020 . Fic
  O'BRIEN, RC/Mrs. Frisby and the rats of NIMH. /c1971/
  4-A/6 KH556 . . . . Fic
Rats as pets--Fiction.
  GLASER, L/Rosie's birthday rat. /1996/1-3/2 KH171 . . . . . . Fic
Rattlesnakes.
  DEWEY, JO/Rattlesnake dance: true tales, mysteries, and rattlesnake
  ceremonies. /1997/4-6/4 KC634 . . . . 597.96
Ravens--Folklore.
  CAMERON, A/Raven and Snipe. /1991/3-4/6 KB546. . . . 398.24
    Raven goes berrypicking. /1991/3-4/6 KB547 . . . . 398.24
  MCDERMOTT, G/Raven: a trickster tale from the Pacific Northwest.
  /1993/1-3/3 KB618 . . . . 398.24
Readability (Literary style)--Software.
  READABILITY ANALYSIS (MICROCOMPUTER PROGRAM). /1994/
  /KA213. . . . . MCP PROF 372.4
Reader-response criticism.
  BOOK TALK AND BEYOND: CHILDREN AND TEACHERS
  RESPOND TO LITERATURE. /1995//KA235. . . . . PROF 372.64
Readers.
  MILES, B/Hey! I'm reading!: a how-to-read book for beginners. /
  1995/P-1/2 KB103 . . . . 372.4
Readers' Theater.
  FREDERICKS, AD/Frantic frogs and other frankly fractured folktales
  for readers theatre. /1993//KA362 . . . . PROF 812
  LAUGHLIN, MK/Readers theatre for children: scripts and script
  development. /1990//KA339. . . . . PROF 808.5
  ROBBINS, S/Growing rock: a Southwest Native American tale (Kit).
  /1993/P-1/KB638 . . . . KIT 398.24

STORIES ON STAGE: SCRIPTS FOR READER'S THEATER. /1993/
/KA363. . . . . **PROF 812**

Readers' Theater--Study and teaching (Elementary).
BAUER, CF/Presenting reader's theater: plays and poems to read
aloud. /1987//KA329 . . . . **PROF 792**
LAUGHLIN, MK/Social studies readers theatre for children: scripts
and script development. /1991//KA224. . . . . **PROF 372.6**

Readiness for school.
DIMIDJIAN, VJ/Early childhood at risk: actions and advocacy for
young children. /1989//KA190 . . . . **PROF 372**
Reading SEE ALSO Books and reading.

Reading.
ANDERSON, RC/Becoming a nation of readers: the report of the
Commission on Reading. /1985//KA205 . . . . **PROF 372.4**
CHALL, JS/Reading crisis: why poor children fall behind. /1990/
/KA219 . . . . **PROF 372.6**
COUNT ON READING HANDBOOK: TIPS FOR PLANNING
READING MOTIVATION PROGRAMS. /1997/
/KA206. . . . . **PROF 372.4**
ITZKOFF, SW/Children learning to read: a guide for parents and
teachers. /1996//KA209 . . . . **PROF 372.4**
MILES, B/Hey! I'm reading!: a how-to-read book for beginners. /
1995/P-1/2 KB103 . . . . **372.4**
OLSEN, ML/More creative connections: literature and the reading
program, grades 4-6. /1993//KA212 . . . . **PROF 372.4**

Reading--Fiction.
GIFF, PR/Today was a terrible day. /1980/1-2/2 KF616 . . . **CE E**
　Today was a terrible day (Kit). /1993/1-2/KF617 . . . . . . **KIT E**
GRAVES, BB/Mystery of the Tooth Gremlin. /1997/
1-3/2 KH191 . . . . **Fic**
HUTCHINS, P/Tale of Thomas Mead. /1980/1-2/2 KF804 . . **CE E**
KING-SMITH, D/School mouse. /1995/3-5/7 KH353 . . . . **Fic**
MEDDAUGH, S/Hog-eye. /1995/K-3/2 KG123 . . . . **E**
SEUSS, D/I can read with my eyes shut. /1978/P-2/2 KG463 . . **E**

Reading--Language experience approach.
LAUGHLIN, MK/Literature-based reading: children's books and
activities to enrich the K-5 curriculum. /1990/
/KA210 . . . . **PROF 372.4**
ROUTMAN, R/Invitations: changing as teachers and learners K-12.
Updated, expanded, and rev. resources and Blue pages. /c1991,
1994//KA214 . . . . **PROF 372.4**

Reading--Parent participation.
CULLINAN, BE/Read to me: raising kids who love to read. /1992/
/KA301. . . . . **PROF 649**
KROPP, P/Raising a reader: make your child a reader for life. /
c1993, 1996//KA182 . . . . **PROF 371.3028**

Reading--Research.
HARSTE, JC/New policy guidelines for reading: connecting research
and practice. /1989//KA208. . . . . **PROF 372.4**

Reading (Elementary).
BARCHERS, SI/Creating and managing the literate classroom. /
1990//KA218 . . . . **PROF 372.6**
BOSMA, B/Fairy tales, fables, legends and myths: using folk
literature in your classroom. /1992//KA177 . . . . . . **PROF 371.3**
COUNTERPOINT AND BEYOND: A RESPONSE TO BECOMING A
NATION OF READERS. /1988//KA207 . . . . **PROF 372.4**
POLETTE, N/Brain power through picture books: help children
develop with books that stimulate specific parts of their minds. /
1992//KA227 . . . . **PROF 372.6**
WATSON, DJ/Ideas and insights: language arts in the elementary
school. /1987//KA232. . . . . **PROF 372.6**

Reading (Elementary)--Language experience approach.
HELTSHE, MA/Multicultural explorations: joyous journeys with
books. /1991//KA262. . . . . **PROF 372.89**
WHOLE LANGUAGE: BELIEFS AND PRACTICES, K-8. /1989/
/KA233. . . . . **PROF 372.6**

Reading (Elementary)--Periodicals.
READING TEACHER. /1957-//KA133 . . . . **PER PROF 050**

Reading (Preschool).
NURSERY SONGS AND RHYMES (VIDEOCASSETTE). /1993/
P-2/KB104. . . . . **VCR 372.4**

Reading (Preschool)--Phonetic method.
ABC'S AND SUCH (VIDEOCASSETTE). /1993/
/KA'S . . . .
P-2/KB099. . . . . **VCR 372.4**

Reading (Preschool)--Software.
BAILEY'S BOOK HOUSE (CD-ROM). /1995/
P-2/KB100. . . . . **CDR 372.4**
BAILEY'S BOOK HOUSE (MICROCOMPUTER PROGRAM). /1993/
P-2/KB101. . . . . **MCP 372.4**
CHICKA CHICKA BOOM BOOM (CD-ROM). /1996/
P-2/KF382. . . . . **CDR E**
READER RABBIT'S READY FOR LETTERS (MICROCOMPUTER
PROGRAM). /1994/P-1/KB107. . . . . **MCP 372.4**

Reading (Primary)--Language experience approach.
SLAUGHTER, JP/Beyond storybooks: young children and the shared
book experience. /1993//KA215 . . . . **PROF 372.4**

Reading (Primary)--Software.
READ, WRITE AND TYPE! (CD-ROM). /1996/
K-2/KB105. . . . . **CDR 372.4**
READER RABBIT 3 (MICROCOMPUTER PROGRAM). /1993/
1-3/KB106. . . . . **MCP 372.4**

Reading games.
GALLINA, M/Alphabet in action: consonants and vowels taught
through song and motor activities (Sound recording cassette). /
1978/K-2/KB102. . . . . **SRC 372.4**

Reading games--Software.
CHICKA CHICKA BOOM BOOM (CD-ROM). /1996/
P-2/KF382. . . . . **CDR E**
READER RABBIT'S READY FOR LETTERS (MICROCOMPUTER
PROGRAM). /1994/P-1/KB107. . . . . **MCP 372.4**

Reading readiness.
ITZKOFF, SW/Children learning to read: a guide for parents and
teachers. /1996//KA209 . . . . **PROF 372.4**

Reagan, Ronald.
JUDSON, K/Ronald Reagan. /1997/
6-A/10 KE504 . . . . **B REAGAN, R.**

Reasoning--Software.
SNAPDRAGON (MICROCOMPUTER PROGRAM). /1992/
P-1/KA636. . . . . **MCP 153.4**

Rebuses.
NEITZEL, S/Jacket I wear in the snow. /1989/P-2/2 KG168. . . . **E**
　We're making breakfast for Mother. /1997/P-1/2 KG169 . . . . **E**
Reconstruction SEE Afro-Americans; United States--History--1865-1898.
Recording, Sound SEE Sound recording.
Recreation SEE ALSO Amusements; Games; Hobbies; Indoor games;
Outdoor recreation; Play; Sports.

Recreation.
ROWEN, L/Beyond winning: sports and games all kids want to play.
/1990//KA332. . . . . **PROF 796.1**

Recreation--History.
KALMAN, B/Early pleasures and pastimes. /1983/
4-A/8 KD680 . . . . **790.1**

Recycled products.
CHANDLER, G/Recycling. /1996/3-6/10 KB053. . . . . . . **363.72**
Recycling (Waste) SEE ALSO Refuse and refuse disposal.

Recycling (Waste).
APPELHOF, M/Worms eat my garbage. /1982/A/12 KC502 . **592**
BANG, M/Chattanooga sludge. /1996/4-6/7 KD081 . . . . . **628.4**
CAPTAIN CONSERVATION: ALL ABOUT RECYCLING (KIT). /
1992/1-3/KB052. . . . . **KIT 363.72**
CARLSON, L/EcoArt!: earth-friendly art and craft experiences for
3-to 9-year olds. /1993/K-4/KD425 . . . . **745.5**
CHANDLER, G/Recycling. /1996/3-6/10 KB053. . . . . . . **363.72**
GARBAGE STORY (VIDEOCASSETTE). /1996/
5-A/KB054. . . . . **VCR 363.72**
RECYCLING: IT'S EVERYBODY'S JOB (VIDEOCASSETTE). /1992/
5-6/KB056. . . . . **VCR 363.72**
RECYCLING: THE ENDLESS CIRCLE (VIDEOCASSETTE). /1992/
5-6/KD082. . . . . **VCR 628.4**
RECYCLING WITH WORMS (VIDEOCASSETTE). /1995/
3-6/KC507. . . . . **VCR 592**
ROSS, K/Every day is Earth Day: a craft book. /1995/
K-3/5 KD442 . . . . **745.58**
SHOWERS, P/Where does the garbage go? Rev. ed. /1994/
2-3/3 KD083 . . . . **628.4**

Recycling (Waste)--Fiction.
VAN LAAN, N/Round and round again. /1994/P-2/3 KG643 . . **E**

Recycling (Waste)--Software.
HALPERN, NA/Kids and the environment: taking responsibility for
our surroundings /1994/1-5/KB046. . . . . **CDR 363.7**

Recycling (Waste)--Songs and music.
VAN MANENS /We recycle and other songs for Earth keepers
(Sound recording cassette). /1990/K-4/KD664 . . . . . **SRC 789.3**

Recycling (Waste)--Study and teaching.
STANGL, J/Recycling activities for the primary grades. /1993/
/KA313. . . . . **PROF 745.5**

Red Cloud, Sioux Chief.
FREEDMAN, R/Indian chiefs. /1987/5-6/8 KE749 . . . . **970.1**
GOBLE, P/Brave Eagle's account of the Fetterman Fight, 21
December 1866. /c1972, 1992/5-6/6 KE913 . . . . . . **973.8**

Red Cross--History.
BURGER, L/Red Cross/Red Crescent: when help can't wait. /1996/
4-6/8 KA992 . . . . **361.7**

Red fox.
HAVARD, C/Fox: playful prowler. /1995/3-5/4 KC842 . . **599.775**
MASON, C/Wild fox: a true story. /1993/4-5/5 KC843 . **599.775**

SCHNIEPER, C/On the trail of the fox. /1986/
4-6/8 KC844 . . . . **599.775**
Red fox--Fiction.
GEORGE, JC/Vulpes, the red fox. /c1948, 1996/
5-A/5 KH160 . . . . **Fic**
Red mangrove swamps.
LAVIES, B/Mangrove wilderness: nature's nursery. /1994/
K-3/7 KC341 . . . . **577.68**
Red wolf--Fiction.
LONDON, J/Red wolf country. /1996/K-3/4 KG028 . . . . **E**
Reducing SEE Weight control.
Reese, Pee Wee.
GOLENBOCK, P/Teammates. /1990/3-6/6 KD798 . . . . . **796.357**
Reference books SEE ALSO Books and reading--Best books; Encyclopedias
and dictionaries, etc.
Reference books.
ANIMATED DICTIONARY (VIDEOCASSETTE). /1992/
3-5/KA588 . . . . **VCR 028.7**
BOOKLIST. /1905-//KA098 . . . . **PER PROF 050**
Reference books--Bibliography.
RECOMMENDED REFERENCE BOOKS FOR SMALL AND
MEDIUM-SIZED LIBRARIES AND MEDIA CENTERS. /1981-/
/KA005. . . . . **PROF 011**
Reference books--Indians--Dictionaries.
PATTERSON, L/Indian terms of the Americas. /1994/
5-A/KA478 . . . . **REF 970.004**
Reference books--Reviews.
REFERENCE BOOKS BULLETIN, 1994-1995: A COMPILATION OF
EVALUATIONS APPEARING IN "REFERENCE BOOKS
BULLETIN," SEPTEMBER 1, 1992 - AUGUST, 1993. /1995/
/KA006. . . . . **PROF 011**
Reference books--Software.
MICROSOFT BOOKSHELF: MULTIMEDIA REFERENCE LIBRARY,
1998 ED. SCHOOL ED. (CD-ROM). /1997/
3-A/KA376 . . . . **CDR REF 028.7**
Reference services (Libraries).
RECOMMENDED REFERENCE BOOKS FOR SMALL AND
MEDIUM-SIZED LIBRARIES AND MEDIA /1981-/
/KA005. . . . . **PROF 011**
Reflections--Pictorial works.
HOBAN, T/Shadows and reflections. /1990/P-6/KC112. . . . . **535**
Reflexes.
BERGER, M/Why I cough, sneeze, shiver, hiccup, and yawn. /
1983/1-3/2 KC963 . . . . **612.8**
Reformers.
ADLER, DA/Picture book of Sojourner Truth. /1994/
2-5/6 KE572 . . . . **B TRUTH, S.**
AVI /Finding Providence: the story of Roger Williams. /1997/
2-3/4 KE596 . . . . **B WILLIAMS, R.**
COLMAN, P/Mother Jones and the march of the mill children. /
1994/4-6/7 KA935 . . . . **331.3**
JACOBS, WJ/Great lives: human rights. /1990/
6-A/7 KA900 . . . . **323**
MCKISSACK, P/Sojourner Truth: ain't I a woman? /1992/
6-A/7 KE573 . . . . **B TRUTH, S.**
Refugees.
GRAFF, NP/Where the river runs: a portrait of a refugee family. /
1993/4-6/7 KA845 . . . . **305.8**
Refugees--Africa, East.
WILKES, S/One day we had to run!: refugee children tell their
stories in words and /1994/4-A/5 KB019 . . . . **362.87**
Refugees--Fiction.
GIFF, PR/Lily's crossing. /1997/5-A/5 KH165 . . . . **Fic**
TEMPLE, F/Grab hands and run. /1993/6-A/6 KH788 . . . . . . **Fic**
WATKINS, YK/My brother, my sister, and I. /1994/
A/4 KH841 . . . . **Fic**
Refugees--Kenya.
WILKES, S/One day we had to run!: refugee children tell their
stories in words and paintings. /1994/4-A/5 KB019 . . . . . **362.87**
Refuse and refuse disposal SEE ALSO Recycling (Waste); Water--Pollution.
Refuse and refuse disposal.
CAPTAIN CONSERVATION: ALL ABOUT RECYCLING (KIT). /
1992/1-3/KB052. . . . . **KIT 363.72**
GARBAGE STORY (VIDEOCASSETTE). /1996/
5-A/KB054. . . . . **VCR 363.72**
PUBLIC WORKS (VIDEOCASSETTE). /1992/
2-4/KB055. . . . . **VCR 363.72**
RECYCLING: IT'S EVERYBODY'S JOB (VIDEOCASSETTE). /1992/
5-6/KB056. . . . . **VCR 363.72**
RECYCLING: THE ENDLESS CIRCLE (VIDEOCASSETTE). /1992/
5-6/KD082. . . . . **VCR 628.4**
REDUCING, REUSING AND RECYCLING: ENVIRONMENTAL
CONCERNS (VIDEOCASSETTE). /1992/4-6/KB051. . **VCR 363.7**

SHOWERS, P/Where does the garbage go? Rev. ed. /1994/
2-3/3 KD083 . . . . **628.4**
Refuse and refuse disposal--Fiction.
KIRK, D/Trash trucks. /1997/K-2/3 KF908 . . . . **E**
Refuse and refuse disposal--Software.
ENVIRONMENT (MICROCOMPUTER PROGRAM). /1990/
5-A/KB059. . . . . **MCP 363.73**
HALPERN, NA/Kids and the environment: taking responsibility for
our surroundings /1994/1-5/KB046. . . . . **CDR 363.7**
Reggae music.
BOOKER, CM/Smilin' island of song (Sound recording cassette). /
1994/K-4/KD667 . . . . **SRC 789.4**
REGGAE FOR KIDS: A COLLECTION OF MUSIC FOR KIDS OF
ALL AGES! /1992/K-3/KD669. . . . . **SRC 789.4**
Reid Banks, Lynne.
TALK WITH LYNNE REID BANKS (VIDEOCASSETTE). /1995/
4-6/KE505. . . . . **VCR B REID BANKS, L**
Reincarnation.
GREEN, CR/Recalling past lives. /1993/4-6/3 KA611 . . . . . **133.9**
Reincarnation--Fiction.
COLE, B/Drop dead. /1996/2-4/2 KF406. . . . . **E**
Reindeer.
ARNOLD, C/Reindeer. /1993/4-5/4 KD211 . . . . **636.2**
BERNHARD, E/Reindeer. /1994/4-5/7 KC796 . . . . **599.65**
Reindeer--Fiction.
BRETT, J/Wild Christmas reindeer. /1990/K-2/2 KF263 . . . . **E**
Reiss, Johanna.
REISS, J/Upstairs room. /c1972/5-6/5 KE506 . . . . . . **B REISS, J.**
Relativity (Physics)--Fiction.
BRADBURY, R/Halloween tree. /c1982/5-A/7 KG920 . . . . . . **Fic**
Religion and mythology.
BIERHORST, J/Mythology of North America. /1985/
5-A/KA392 . . . . **REF 291.1**
Religion in the public schools.
HUBBARD, BJ/America's religions: an educator's guide to beliefs
and practices. /1997//KA160 . . . . **PROF 200**
Religions SEE ALSO Buddhism, Hinduism; Islam; Jesus Christ; Judaism;
Mythology, etc.
Religions.
FAITH AND BELIEF: FIVE MAJOR WORLD RELIGIONS
(VIDEOCASSETTE). /1992/5-A/KA722. . . . . **VCR 291**
GANERI, A/Out of the ark: stories from the world's religions. /
1996/3-6/5 KA729 . . . . **291.1**
Religions explained: a beginner's guide to world faiths. /1997/
3-5/9 KA723 . . . . **291**
GELLMAN, M/How do you spell God?: answers to the big
questions from around the world. /1995/5-A/4 KA724. . . . . **291**
MAESTRO, B/Story of religion. /1996/3-4/9 KA725 . . . . . . **291**
OSBORNE, MP/One world, many religions: the ways we worship. /
1996/4-A/7 KA726. . . . . **291**
RELIGION (VIDEOCASSETTE). /1992/3-6/KA727 . . . . **VCR 291**
SITA, L/Worlds of belief: religion and spirituality. /1995/
4-A/10 KA728 . . . . **291**
Religions--Fiction.
BLUME, J/Are you there God? It's me, Margaret. /c1970, 1982/
4-6/5 KG905 . . . . **CE Fic**
Religions--Study and teaching.
HUBBARD, BJ/America's religions: an educator's guide to beliefs
and practices. /1997//KA160 . . . . **PROF 200**
Religious life--Fiction.
RYLANT, C/Fine white dust. /1986/6-A/4 KH661. . . . . **Fic**
Remarriage--Fiction.
DANZIGER, P/Forever Amber Brown. /1996/2-4/4 KH062 . . . **Fic**
Rembrandt Harmenszoon van Rijn.
MUHLBERGER, R/What makes a Rembrandt a Rembrandt? /1993/
5-A/7 KD500 . . . . **759.9492**
PESCIO, C/Rembrandt and seventeenth-century Holland. /1995/
4-A/12 KD501 . . . . **759.9492**
SCHWARTZ, G/Rembrandt. /1992/
6-A/7 KE507 . . . . **B REMBRANDT**
Report writing.
JAMES, E/How to write a great school report. /1983/
4-6/7 KB088 . . . . **371.302**
MCINERNEY, C/Tracking the facts: how to develop research skills. /
1990/5-A/6 KB089 . . . . **371.302**
Report writing--Software.
OWENS, P/Research paper writer (Microcomputer program). /
c1990/5-A/KB090. **MCP 371.302**
STUDENT WRITING AND RESEARCH CENTER WITH COMPTON'S
CONCISE ENCYCLOPEDIA (CD-ROM). /1995/
4-A/KB091. . . . . **CDR 371.302**

Reporters and reporting SEE ALSO Newspapers; Television broadcasting of news.

Reporters and reporting--Fiction.
SCHMIDT, AM/Minnie. /1994/5-A/3 KH680. . . . . **Fic**

Reporters and reporting--Vocational guidance.
KAPLAN, A/Careers for wordsmiths. /1991/6-A/7 KA593 . . **070.4**
Representative government and representation SEE Elections.
Reproduction SEE ALSO Childbirth.

Reproduction.
BACK, C/Chicken and egg. /1986/K-3/2 KC692 . . . . **598.6**
BOY TO MAN. 3RD ED. (VIDEOCASSETTE). /1992/
5-6/KC944. . . . . **VCR 612.6**
CELL DIVISION (VIDEOCASSETTE). /1995/
5-6/KC274. . . . . **VCR 571.6**
COLE, J/Chick hatches. /1977/P-2/3 KC694 . . . . **598.6**
GIRARD, LW/You were born on your very first birthday. /1982/
P/2 KC948 . . . . **612.6**
HARRIS, RH/It's perfectly normal: a book about changing bodies,
growing up, sex, and /1994/5-6/6 KC949. . . . . **612.6**
HELLER, R/Chickens aren't the only ones. /1981/
P-K/KC282. . . . . **573.6**
Reptiles SEE ALSO Alligators; Crocodiles; Lizards; Snakes; Turtles, etc.

Reptiles.
AMPHIBIANS AND REPTILES (VIDEOCASSETTE). /1996/
5-6/KC612. . . . . **VCR 597.9**
CREAGH, C/Reptiles. /1996/3-6/8 KC613 . . . . **597.9**
EXPLORING THE WORLD OF REPTILES (VIDEOCASSETTE). /
1992/2-4/KC614. . . . . **VCR 597.9**
JOHNSTON, G/Scaly babies: reptiles growing up. /1988/
5-6/6 KC615 . . . . **597.9**

Rescue dogs.
PATENT, DH/Hugger to the rescue. /1994/3-6/5 KD226 . . **636.73**

Rescue work.
EMERGENCY 911 (VIDEOCASSETTE). /1994/
2-5/KB135. . . . . **VCR 384.6**
PATENT, DH/Hugger to the rescue. /1994/3-6/5 KD226 . . **636.73**
USING 911: PROTECT YOURSELF (VIDEOCASSETTE). /1995/
2-6/KB136. . . . . **VCR 384.6**

Research.
JAMES, E/How to write a great school report. /1983/
4-6/7 KB088 . . . . **371.302**
MCINERNEY, C/Tracking the facts: how to develop research skills. /
1990/5-A/6 KB089 . . . . **371.302**

Research--Scientific applications.
MINDS-ON SCIENCE: THE IMPACT OF DISCOVERY (VIDEODISC).
/1995/5-A/KB875. . . . . **VD 502**

Research--Software.
OWENS, P/Research paper writer (Microcomputer program). /
c1990/5-A/KB090. . . . . **MCP 371.302**
STUDENT WRITING AND RESEARCH CENTER WITH COMPTON'S
CONCISE ENCYCLOPEDIA /1995/4-A/KB091 . . . **CDR 371.302**

Respiration.
BREATH OF LIFE: OUR RESPIRATORY SYSTEM
(VIDEOCASSETTE). /1992/5-6/KC938 . . . . **VCR 612.2**

Respiratory system.
BREATH OF LIFE: OUR RESPIRATORY SYSTEM
(VIDEOCASSETTE). /1992/5-6/KC938 . . . . **VCR 612.2**
PARKER, S/Lungs and breathing. Rev. ed. /1989/
5-6/8 KC934 . . . . **612.1**
YOUR BODY: CIRCULATORY AND RESPIRATORY SYSTEMS
(VIDEOCASSETTE). /1988/5-6/KC931 . . . . **VCR 612**

Responsibility--Fiction.
GARAY, L/Pedrito's Day. /1997/1-3/2 KF598 . . . . **E**

Responsibility--Software.
TAKING RESPONSIBILITY (MICROCOMPUTER PROGRAM). /
1988/1-6/KA665 . . . . **MCP 158**

Restaurants--Fiction.
BRANDENBERG, A/Chop, simmer, season. /1997/P-1/2 KF257 . **E**
KOVALSKI, M/Pizza for breakfast. /1991/K-2/2 KF917 . . . . . . **E**
LOOMIS, C/In the diner. /1994/P-2/2 KG031. . . . . **E**
RYLANT, C/Van Gogh Cafe. /1995/5-A/7 KH664 . . . . **Fic**
Retail trade SEE ALSO Department stores; Supermarkets.

Retirement--Fiction.
HENKES, K/Good-bye, Curtis. /1995/P-2/2 KF704. . . . . **E**

Revenge--Fiction.
MYERS, WD/Righteous revenge of Artemis Bonner. /1994/
5-A/7 KH523 . . . . **Fic**

Revere, Paul.
ADLER, DA/Picture book of Paul Revere. /1995/
2-4/5 KE508 . . . . **B REVERE, P.**
FORBES, E/America's Paul Revere. /c1946/
A/7 KE509 . . . . **B REVERE, P.**
FRITZ, J/And then what happened, Paul Revere? /c1973/
5-6/6 KE510 . . . . **CE B REVERE, P.**

Revere, Paul--Fiction.
LAWSON, R/Mr. Revere and I: /c1953/5-6/7 KH389 . . . . . . **Fic**

Revere, Paul--Poetry.
LONGFELLOW, HW/Paul Revere's ride. /1990/
3-A/KD980 . . . . **CE 811**

Revolutionaries.
LAWRENCE, J/Toussaint L'Ouverture: the fight for Haiti's freedom.
/1996/4-A/8 KE569 . . . . **B TOUSSAINT**
WALLNER, A/Betsy Ross. /1994/3-4/6 KE526. . . . . . **B ROSS, B.**
WORLD LEADERS: PEOPLE WHO SHAPED THE WORLD. /1994/
5-A/KA408 . . . . **REF 350**

Revolutionists.
ADLER, DA/Picture book of Simon Bolivar. /1992/
3-4/5 KE257 . . . . **B BOLIVAR, S.**

Revolutions--Fiction.
ALEXANDER, L/Westmark. /1982/5-6/6 KG841 . . . . **Fic**

Revolutions--Software.
REVOLUTIONARY WARS: CHOOSING SIDES (MICROCOMPUTER
PROGRAM). /1986/5-A/KA668 . . . . **MCP 172**

Reynard the Fox (Legendary character).
HASTINGS, S/Reynard the Fox. /1991/2-3/6 KB586 . . . . **398.24**
WALLIS, D/Something nasty in the cabbages. /1991/
2-4/3 KB671 . . . . **398.24**

Reynoso, Anthony.
COOPER, M/Anthony Reynoso: born to rope. /1996/
3-4/4 KA841 . . . . **305.8**

Rhinoceroses.
ARNOLD, C/Rhino. /1995/4-6/7 KC801 . . . . **599.66**
MAYNARD, T/Rhino comes to America. /1993/
5-6/7 KC802 . . . . **599.66**
WALKER, SM/Rhinos. /1996/4-6/7 KC803 . . . . **599.66**

Rhinoceroses--Fiction.
KIPLING, R/How the rhinoceros got his skin; and, How the camel
got his hump (Videocassette). /1987/2-5/KH361 . . . . **VCR Fic**
How the rhinoceros got his skin (Kit). /1988/3-5/KH362 . **KIT Fic**

Rhode Island.
HEINRICHS, A/Rhode Island. /1990/4-6/9 KE932 . . . . . . **974.2**

Rhode Island--History--Colonial period, ca. 1600-1775.
FRADIN, DB/Rhode Island Colony. /1989/5-6/7 KE951. . . . **974.5**

Rhode Island--History--Revolution, 1775-1783.
FRADIN, DB/Rhode Island Colony. /1989/5-6/7 KE951. . . . **974.5**
Rhyme SEE ALSO Stories in rhyme; Poetry.
Rhymes SEE Limericks; Nonsense verses; Nursery rhymes; Poetry.

Rhythm.
JENKINS, E/Growing up with Ella Jenkins: rhythms songs and
rhymes /1990/P-2/KD628. . . . . **SRC 789.3**
This is rhythm (Compact disc). /1994/K-2/KD632. . . . **CD 789.3**
STEWART, G/Multicultural rhythm stick fun (Sound recording
cassette). /1992/P-2/KD768 . . . . **SRC 796.1**
Pre-K hooray! (Sound recording cassette). /1993/
P-K/KD659. . . . . **SRC 789.3**
Preschool favorites (Sound recording cassette). /1990/
P-K/KD660. . . . . **SRC 789.3**

Rhythm bands and orchestras.
PRESCHOOL PLAYTIME BAND (SOUND RECORDING CASSETTE).
/1987/P-K/KD651. . . . . **SRC 789.3**

Rice.
THOMSON, R/Rice. /1990/3-5/4 KD152. . . . . **633.1**

Riddles.
ADLER, DA/Calculator riddles. /1995/3-6/KD722. . . . . . **793.735**
Easy math puzzles. /1997/K-3/KD723. . . . . **793.735**
ARTELL, M/Wackiest nature riddles on earth. /1992/
3-6/KD724. . . . . **793.735**
BIXENMAN, J/Dinosaur jokes. /1991/2-4/KD725. . . . . . **793.735**
GORDON, JR/Hide and shriek: riddles about ghosts and goblins. /
1991/2-5/KD727 . . . . **793.735**
HALL, K/Batty riddles. /1993/K-3/KD728 . . . . **793.735**
HARTMAN, V/Silliest joke book ever. /1993/
2-4/5 KD729 . . . . **793.735**
KESSLER, L/Old Turtle's 90 knock-knocks, jokes, and riddles. /
1991/2-4/KD730 . . . . **793.735**
LEVINE, CA/Riddles to tell your cat. /1992/2-5/KD732. . **793.735**
LIGHTNING INSIDE YOU AND OTHER NATIVE AMERICAN
RIDDLES. /1992/3-6/KD733 . . . . **793.735**
MAESTRO, M/Riddle City, USA!: a book of geography riddles. /
1994/2-6/KD734 . . . . **793.735**
MATHEWS, J/Oh, how waffle!: riddles you can eat. /1993/
2-6/KD735. . . . . **793.735**
PHILLIPS, L/Keep 'em laughing: jokes to amuse and annoy your
friends. /1996/3-6/KD736 . . . . **793.735**
PLANET OF THE GRAPES: SHOW BIZ JOKES AND RIDDLES. /
1992/3-6/KD737 . . . . **793.735**
RIDDLE-ME RHYMES. /1994/3-5/KD738 . . . . **793.735**
SHANNON, G/Stories to solve. /1985/5-6/6 KB714 . . . . **398.26**

SWANSON, J/Summit up: riddles about mountains. /1994/
3-6/KD739. . . . . **793.735**
TAKE ME TO YOUR LITER: SCIENCE AND MATH JOKES. /1991/
3-6/KD740. . . . . **793.735**
THALER, M/Earth mirth: the ecology riddle book. /1994/
2-4/KD741. . . . . **793.735**
WOODWORTH, V/Animal jokes. /1993/2-4/KD742. . . . **793.735**
    Fairy tale jokes. /1993/2-4/KD743 . . . . **793.735**

Riddles--Fiction.
BRITTAIN, B/Mystery of the several sevens. /1994/
2-4/4 KG924 . . . . **Fic**
JACKSON, E/Impossible riddle. /1995/K-3/4 KF819. . . . . **E**
WOLFF, PR/Toll-bridge troll. /1995/1-3/2 KG759 . . . . **E**

Riddles, Spanish American.
GRANDMOTHER'S NURSERY RHYMES: LULLABIES, TONGUE
TWISTERS, AND RIDDLES FROM /1994/P-2/KB799 . . . . . **398.8**

Righteous Gentiles in the Holocaust.
MOCHIZUKI, K/Passage to freedom: the Sugihara story. /1997/
3-6/4 KE662 . . . . **940.53**
PETTIT, J/Place to hide. /1993/5-A/7 KE663 . . . . **940.53**
ROSENBERG, MB/Hiding to survive: stories of Jewish children
rescued from the Holocaust. /1994/A/6 KE665 . . . . **940.53**

Ringgold, Faith.
FAITH RINGGOLD PAINTS CROWN HEIGHTS (VIDEOCASSETTE).
/1995/5-A/KD461 . . . . **VCR 746.46**
RINGGOLD, F/Talking to Faith Ringgold. /1996/
4-6/6 KD379 . . . . **709.2**
TURNER, R/Faith Ringgold. /1993/
4-A/7 KE511 . . . . **B RINGGOLD, F.**

Rings--Fiction.
SOTO, G/Too many tamales. /1993/K-3/3 KG530 . . . . **E**

Riots--California--Los Angeles--Fiction.
BUNTING, E/Smoky night. /1994/2-5/2 KF309 . . . . **E**

Riots--Pennsylvania--Christiana--Fiction.
ROSENBURG, JM/William Parker: rebel without rights: a novel
based on fact. /1996/6-A/7 KH654 . . . . **Fic**

Ripken, Cal, Jr.
CAMPBELL, J/Cal Ripken, Jr. /1997/5-6/7 KE512 . **B RIPKEN, C.**

Rivera, Diego.
SHIRLEY, D/Diego Rivera. /1995/5-6/7 KE513 . . . **B RIVERA, D.**

Riverkeepers--Hudson River (N.Y. and N.J.).
ANCONA, G/Riverkeeper. /1990/4-6/7 KA958 . . . . **333.91**
Rivers SEE ALSO Floods; Water--Pollution; also names of rivers e.g.
Mississippi River.

Rivers--Fiction.
CONLY, JL/Trout summer. /1995/6-A/5 KH021 . . . . **Fic**
LOCKER, T/Where the river begins. /1984/K-3/5 KG016. . . . . . **E**
MICHL, R/Day on the river. /1986/1-3/4 KG133 . . . . **E**

Road construction.
GIBBONS, G/New road! /1983/1-3/4 KD078. . . . . **625.7**

Roads--History.
WHITMAN, S/Get up and go!: the history of American road travel.
/1996/4-A/10 KB160 . . . . **388.1**

Roads--Maintenance and repair--Fiction.
NIKOLA-LISA, W/One hole in the road. /1996/P-K/2 KG173. . . **E**

Roanoke Island (N.C.)--History--Fiction.
FORRESTER, S/Sound the jubilee. /1995/5-A/6 KH133 . . . . . . **Fic**

Robbers and outlaws.
WUKOVITS, JF/Jesse James. /1997/4-6/10 KE402 . **B JAMES, J.**

Robbers and outlaws--Fiction.
ADLER, DA/Cam Jansen and the ghostly mystery. /1996/
2-4/2 KG815 . . . . **Fic**
AHLBERG, J/It was a dark and stormy night. /1993/
3-5/6 KG822 . . . . **Fic**
ANTLE, N/Sam's Wild West Show. /1995/1-3/2 KF161 . . . . . . **E**
AUCH, MJ/Eggs mark the spot. /1996/K-2/3 KF176 . . . . . **CE E**
AVI /History of Helpless Harry: to which is added a variety of
amusing and entertaining adventures. /c1980, 1995/
5-A/7 KG859. . . . . **Fic**
BABBITT, N/Goody Hall. /c1971, 1992/5-6/6 KG870. . . . . . **Fic**
CHRISTELOW, E/Robbery at the Diamond Dog Diner. /1986/
K-3/4 KF389 . . . . **CE E**
CORBALIS, J/Porcellus, the flying pig. /1988/2-4/5 KH029 . . . **Fic**
FLEISCHMAN, S/Ghost on Saturday night. /1997/
3-5/4 KH122 . . . . **Fic**
MCPHAIL, D/Moony B. Finch, the fastest draw in the West. /1994/
1-3/4 KG120. . . . . **E**
PHILLIPS, M/Sign in Mendel's window. /c1985, 1996/
3-5/6 KH600 . . . . **Fic**
SATHRE, V/Leroy Potts meets the McCrooks. /1997/
1-3/2 KH677 . . . . **Fic**
STEIG, W/Real thief. /c1973/4-6/6 KH751 . . . . **Fic**
UNGERER, T/Tomi Ungerer Library (Videocassette). /1993/
K-2/KG635 . . . . **VCR E**

Robbers and outlaws--Folklore.
HOGROGIAN, N/Contest. /c1976/3-5/5 KB744 . . . . . . **398.27**

Robeson, Paul.
MCKISSACK, P/Paul Robeson: a voice to remember. /1992/
2-5/2 KE514 . . . . **B ROBESON, P.**

Robin Hood (Legendary character).
COHEN, B/Robin Hood and Little John. /1995/
2-4/4 KB433 . . . . **398.22**
CRESWICK, P/Robin Hood. /1984/6/6 KB434. . . . . . . **398.22**
CURRY, JL/Robin Hood and his Merry Men. /1994/
3-5/3 KB436 . . . . **398.22**
    Robin Hood in the greenwood. /1995/3-5/3 KB437 . . . . **398.22**

Robin Hood (Legendary character)--Fiction.
MCKINLEY, R/Outlaws of Sherwood. /1988/A/8 KH490 . . . . . **Fic**
MORPURGO, M/Robin of Sherwood. /1996/5-A/6 KH514 . . . **Fic**
TOMLINSON, T/Forestwife. /1995/6-A/5 KH797 . . . . **Fic**

Robins.
JENKINS, PB/Nest full of eggs. /1995/K-2/2 KC705 . . . . . **598.8**
WILLIS, NC/Robins in your backyard. /1996/K-3/5 KC707. . **598.8**

Robins--Fiction.
RAU, DM/Robin at Hickory Street. /1995/K-2/3 KG314 . . . **CE E**

Robinson, Jackie.
ADLER, DA/Picture book of Jackie Robinson. /1994/
2-4/6 KE515 . . . . **B ROBINSON, J.**
GOLENBOCK, P/Teammates. /1990/3-6/6 KD798 . . . . . **796.357**
RUDEEN, K/Jackie Robinson. /1996/
5-6/6 KE516 . . . . **B ROBINSON, J.**
SANTELLA, A/Jackie Robinson breaks the color line. /1996/
4-6/6 KE517 . . . . **B ROBINSON, J.**
WEIDHORN, M/Jackie Robinson. /1993/
6-A/7 KE518 . . . . **B ROBINSON, J.**

Robinson, Jackie--Fiction.
COHEN, B/Thank you, Jackie Robinson /1997/4-A/4 KH013 . . **Fic**

Robotics.
SKURZYNSKI, G/Robots: your high-tech world. /1990/
5-6/8 KD141 . . . . **629.8**

Robots.
SKURZYNSKI, G/Robots: your high-tech world. /1990/
5-6/8 KD141 . . . . **629.8**

Rock music.
RODRIGUEZ, J/Gloria Estefan. /1996/
5-6/6 KE340 . . . . **B ESTEFAN, G.**

Rocketry--History.
MAURER, R/Rocket!: how a toy launched the space age. /1995/
5-6/10 KD047 . . . . **621.43**
Rocks SEE ALSO Geology; Mineralogy; Petrology.

Rocks.
CHESTERMAN, CW/Audubon Society field guide to North
American rocks and minerals. /1978/3-6/KC225 . . . . **552**
PELLANT, C/Eyewitness handbook of rocks and minerals. /1992/
A/10 KC144 . . . . **549**
ROCKS AND MINERALS: THE HARD FACTS (VIDEOCASSETTE). /
1987/5-A/KC227 . . . . **VCR 552**

Rocks--Experiments.
VANCLEAVE, JP/Janice VanCleave's rocks and minerals: mind-
boggling experiments you can turn into science fair projects. /
1996/4-6/8 KC228 . . . . **552**

Rocks--Fiction.
POLACCO, P/My ol' man. /1995/1-3/3 KG254 . . . . **E**

Rocky Mountain goat.
NATURE'S NEWBORN: BEAR, BIGHORN SHEEP, MOUNTAIN
GOATS (VIDEOCASSETTE). /1994/1-5/KC724 . . . . . **VCR 599**
STAUB, FJ/Mountain goats. /1994/3-5/2 KC793 . . . . . **599.64**

Rocky Mountains Region.
ROCKY MOUNTAIN REGION OF THE UNITED STATES
(VIDEOCASSETTE). /1993/4-6/KF046 . . . . **VCR 978**
ROCKY MOUNTAINS (VIDEOCASSETTE). /1989/
5-6/KE181 . . . . **VCR 917**

Rocky Mountains Region--Bibliography.
EXPLORING THE MOUNTAIN STATES THROUGH LITERATURE. /
1994//KA040 . . . . **PROF 016.978**

Rodents.
JARROW, G/Naked mole-rats. /1996/4-6/7 KC744 . . . . . **599.35**

Rodeos.
COOPER, M/Anthony Reynoso: born to rope. /1996/
3-4/4 KA841 . . . . **305.8**

Rodeos--Arizona.
HOYT-GOLDSMITH, D/Apache rodeo. /1995/
4-6/7 KE798 . . . . **970.491**

Rodeos--Fiction.
HERMAN, RA/Pal the pony. /1996/K-1/2 KF714 . . . . **E**
MARTIN, JR., B/White Dynamite and Curly Kidd. /c1986, 1989/
K-3/2 KG078 . . . . **E**

Roebling, John Augustus.
  MANN, E/Brooklyn Bridge. /1996/5-6/5 KD068 624
Roebling, Washington Augustus.
  MANN, E/Brooklyn Bridge. /1996/5-6/5 KD068 624
Rogers, Will.
  SCHOTT, JA/Will Rogers. /1996/1-3/2 KE519 . . **B ROGERS, W.**
Role models--Biography.
  LETTERS FOR OUR CHILDREN: FIFTY AMERICANS SHARE
  LESSONS IN LIVING. /1996//KA158. . . . . **PROF 170**
Role models--Correspondence.
  LETTERS FOR OUR CHILDREN: FIFTY AMERICANS SHARE
  LESSONS IN LIVING. /1996//KA158. . . . . **PROF 170**
Roller hockey.
  MAYO, T/Illustrated rules of in-line hockey. /1996/
  3-6/6 KD772 . . . . 796.21
Roman numerals.
  GEISERT, A/Roman numerals I to MM./Numerabilia romana uno ad
  duo mila: liber de difficillimo computando numerum. /1996/
  K-4/6 KB988 . . . . 513.5
Rome--Antiquities.
  JAMES, S/Ancient Rome. /1990/5-6/8 KE639. 937
Rome--Civilization.
  CASELLI, G/Roman Empire and the Dark Ages. /1985/
  5-A/9 KE644 . . . . 940.1
Rome--Social life and customs.
  JAMES, S/Ancient Rome. /1990/5-6/8 KE639. 937
  MORLEY, J/Roman villa. /1992/4-6/7 KE641 937
Roosevelt, Eleanor.
  FREEDMAN, R/Eleanor Roosevelt: a life of discovery. /1993/
  6-A/7 KE521 . . . . **B ROOSEVELT, E.**
Roosevelt, Eleanor--Childhood and youth.
  COONEY, B/Eleanor. /1996/4-5/7 KE520 . . . **B ROOSEVELT, E.**
Roosevelt, Franklin Delano.
  FREEDMAN, R/Franklin Delano Roosevelt. /1990/
  6-A/7 KE522 . . . . **B ROOSEVELT, F.**
Roosevelt, Theodore.
  FRITZ, J/Bully for you, Teddy Roosevelt! /1991/
  5-6/6 KE523 . . . . **B ROOSEVELT, T.**
  THEODORE ROOSEVELT: THE COWBOY PRESIDENT
  (VIDEOCASSETTE). /1996/6-A/KE524 . . . . **VCR B ROOSEVELT, T.**
  WHITELAW, N/Theodore Roosevelt takes charge. /1992/
  5-A/7 KE525 . . . . **B ROOSEVELT, T.**
Roosters--Fiction.
  CONRAD, P/Rooster's gift. /1996/K-2/3 KF414 . . . . E
  FROEHLICH, MW/That Kookoory! /1995/K-2/3 KF588 . . . . . . E
  THREADGALL, C/Proud rooster and the fox. /1992/
  P-1/4 KG607 . . . . E
Rope skipping SEE ALSO Jump rope rhymes.
Rope skipping--Fiction.
  HRU, D/Magic moonberry jump ropes. /1996/K-2/2 KF783 . . . . E
Rosenzweig, Hilde.
  ADLER, DA/Hilde and Eli: children of the Holocaust. /1994/
  4-6/5 KE655 . . . . 940.53
Rosetta stone.
  GIBLIN, JC/Riddle of the Rosetta Stone: key to ancient Egypt. /
  1990/5-A/7 KB865 493
Rosh Hashanah.
  CHAIKIN, M/Light another candle: the story and meaning of
  Hanukkah. /c1981, 1987/5-6/8 KA770. . . . . 296.4
  KIMMEL, EA/Days of awe: stories for Rosh Hashanah and Yom
  Kippur. /1991/4-6/5 KA777 . . . . 296.4
Rosh Hashanah--Fiction.
  GOLDIN, BD/World's birthday: a Rosh Hashanah story. /1990/
  2-3/2 KH181 . . . . Fic
Ross, Betsy.
  WALLNER, A/Betsy Ross. /1994/3-4/6 KE526. . . . . . **B ROSS, B.**
Royalty SEE Kings, queens, rulers, etc.
Roybal, Timmy.
  KEEGAN, M/Pueblo boy: growing up in two worlds. /1991/
  4-6/5 KE793 . . . . 970.489
Rubber.
  COSNER, S/Rubber. /1986/5-6/9 KD337 678
Rudolph, Wilma.
  JENNINGS, J/Long shots: they beat the odds. /1990/
  5-6/6 KD762 796
  KRULL, K/Wilma unlimited: how Wilma Rudolph became the world's
  fastest woman. /1996/3-5/7 KE527 . . . . **B RUDOLPH, W.**
Rugs SEE ALSO Carpets.
Rugs--Fiction.
  BLOOD, CL/Goat in the rug. /1990/K-3/6 KF234 . . . . E
  SAY, A/Emma's rug. /1996/1-3/3 KG396 . . . . E

Rulers SEE Kings, queens, rulers, etc.
Runaways--Fiction.
  AVI /Beyond the western sea: book one: the escape from home. /
  1996/6-A/5 KG857 . . . . Fic
  Beyond the western sea: book two: Lord Kirkle's money. /1996/
  6-A/5 KG858. . . . . Fic
  Night journeys. /c1979, 1994/5-A/6 KG860 . . . . Fic
  COSSI, O/Great getaway. /1991/K-2/2 KF426. . . . . E
  CRESSWELL, H/Watchers: a mystery at Alton Towers. /1994/
  5-A/3 KH040 . . . . Fic
  FLACK, M/Story about Ping. /c1933/P-1/6 KF550 . . . . . . CE E
  KONIGSBURG, EL/From the mixed-up files of Mrs. Basil E.
  Frankweiler. /c1967/4-6/7 KH373 . . . . CE Fic
  LOWRY, L/See you around, Sam! /1996/3-6/6 KH428 . . . . . Fic
  MACKEN, W/Flight of the doves. /1992/5-A/3 KH442 . . . . . Fic
  MAZER, H/Island keeper. /1981/6-A/6 KH464 . . . . Fic
  NEUFELD, J/Gaps in stone walls. /1996/6-A/7 KH546 . . . . . Fic
  STEIG, W/Zeke Pippin. /1994/1-3/6 KG549. . . . . E
Runners (Sports).
  ADLER, DA/Picture book of Jesse Owens. /1992/
  3-4/6 KE486 . . . . **B OWENS, J.**
  GUTMAN, B/Gail Devers. /1996/5-6/6 KE319 . . . **B DEVERS, G.**
  KRULL, K/Wilma unlimited: how Wilma Rudolph became the world's
  fastest woman. /1996/3-5/7 KE527 . . . . **B RUDOLPH, W.**
Running.
  SANDELSON, R/Track athletics. /1991/4-6/7 KD811 . . . . 796.42
Running races.
  WARD, T/Track. /1996/3-6/8 KD813 . . . . 796.42
Rural families.
  WOMEN OF RURAL AMERICA (VIDEOCASSETTE). /1995/
  5-A/KA831 . . . . VCR 305.42
Rural-urban migration.
  COOPER, ML/Bound for the promised land.: the great black
  migration. /1995/6-A/9 KE851 973
Russell, Charles M. (Charles Marion).
  WINTER, J/Cowboy Charlie: the story of Charles M. Russell. /
  1995/2-5/5 KE528 . . . . **B RUSSELL, C.**
Russell, Marion Sloan.
  RUSSELL, M/Along the Santa Fe Trail: Marion Russell's own story.
  /1993/4-6/7 KE199 . . . . 917.8
Russia SEE ALSO Soviet Union.
Russia--Fiction.
  FRANKLIN, KL/Wolfhound. /1996/1-3/3 KF576. . . . . E
  JACKSON, E/Impossible riddle. /1995/K-3/4 KF819 . . . . . . E
  POLACCO, P/Babushka Baba Yaga. /1993/1-3/5 KG249 . . . . . E
Russia--Folklore.
  ARNOLD, K/Baba Yaga: a Russian folktale. /1993/
  2-3/3 KB387 . . . . 398.21
  CECIL, L/Frog princess. /1995/1-3/2 KB548 . . . . 398.24
  KIMMEL, EA/I-know-not-what, I-know-not-where: a Russian tale. /
  1994/3-4/6 KB329 . . . . 398.2
  MAYER, M/Baba Yaga and Vasilisa the Brave. /1994/
  3-5/5 KB466 . . . . 398.22
  ZIEFERT, H/Turnip. /1996/K-1/1 KB683 . . . . 398.24
Russia--History--Biography.
  BREWSTER, H/Anastasia's album. /1996/
  5-A/7 KE234 . . . . **B ANASTASIIA**
Russia, Southern--Description and travel.
  BUETTNER, D/Sovietrek: a journey by bicycle across Russia. /1994/
  4-6/8 KE692 . . . . 947.086
Russia (Federation)--Siberia--Folklore.
  BERNHARD, E/Girl who wanted to hunt: a Siberian tale. /1994/
  3-5/3 KB720 . . . . 398.27
Russia (Federation)--Social life and customs.
  KENDALL, R/Russian girl: life in an old Russian town. /1994/
  3-6/5 KE690 947
Russian Americans--Fiction.
  POLACCO, P/Trees of the dancing goats. /1996/1-3/3 KG260. . E
  Uncle Vova's tree. /1989/1-3/6 KG261 . . . . E
  PRYOR, B/Dream jar. /1996/2-3/5 KG291 . . . . E
  SACHS, M/Call me Ruth. /c1982, 1995/5-A/6 KH667 . . . . . Fic
Russian language--Vocabulary.
  AMERY, H/First thousand words in Russian. /1983/
  4-6/KB863 . . . . 491.7
Russians--United States--Fiction.
  COHEN, B/Molly's pilgrim. /1983/1-3/4 KH012 . . . . . CE Fic
  HARVEY, B/Immigrant girl: Becky of Eldridge Street. /1987/
  3-5/5 KH221 . . . . Fic
Rutan, Dick.
  ROZAKIS, L/Dick Rutan and Jeana Yeager: flying non-stop around
  the world. /1994/5-6/6 KD099 . . . . 629.13
Ruth, Babe--Fiction.
  HALL, D/When Willard met Babe Ruth. /1996/4-6/6 KH212. . . Fic

Sabbath--Fiction.
MANUSHKIN, F/Starlight and candles: the joys of the Sabbath. /
1995/1-3/2 KG061 . . . . **E**
SCHUR, MR/Day of delight: a Jewish Sabbath in Ethiopia. /1994/
1-3/4 KG412 . . . . **E**

Sabbath--Folklore.
SCHWARTZ, H/Sabbath lion: a Jewish folktale from Algeria. /
1992/4-6/6 KB511 . . . . **398.23**

Sacagawea.
ROWLAND, D/Story of Sacajawea: guide to Lewis and Clark. /
1995/5-6/6 KE529 . . . . **B SACAGAWEA**
SACAJAWEA (VIDEOCASSETTE). /1991/
2-5/KE530 . . . . **VCR B SACAGAWEA**

Sacred space--North America.
MONROE, JG/First houses: Native American homes and sacred
structures. /1993/6-A/7 KB171 . . . . **392.3**

Sacred space--Poetry.
YOLEN, J/Sacred places. /1996/3-6/KE048 . . . . **811**

Safety.
BROWN, MT/Dinosaurs, beware: a safety guide. /1982/
P-3/3 KB020 . . . . **363.1**
GIRARD, LW/Who is a stranger and what should I do? /1985/
1-3/6 KB021 . . . . **363.1**
GUTMAN, B/Hazards at home. /1996/5-6/7 KB022 . . . . . **363.1**
HOME ON YOUR OWN (VIDEOCASSETTE). /1994/
4-6/KD260 . . . . **VCR 640**
MY BODY, MY BUDDY: HEALTHY HABITS (VIDEOCASSETTE). /
1993/2-4/KD301 . . . . **VCR 646.7**
SAFETY ON WHEELS (VIDEOCASSETTE). /1994/
P-1/KB024 . . . . **VCR 363.1**

Safety--Fiction.
BERENSTAIN, S/Berenstain Bears learn about strangers. /1985/
K-2/4 KF225 . . . . **CE E**
RAND, G/Willie takes a hike. /1996/K-2/3 KG302 . . . . **E**
RATHMANN, P/Officer Buckle and Gloria. /1995/
K-2/3 KG310 . . . . **E**

Safety education SEE ALSO Bicycles and bicycling--Safety measures.

Safety education.
K.C.'S FIRST BUS RIDE (VIDEOCASSETTE). /1994/
P-1/KB023 . . . . **VCR 363.1**
SEAT BELTS ARE FOR KIDS TOO (VIDEOCASSETTE). /1987/
K-6/KD127 . . . . **VCR 629.27**

Saguaro.
BASH, B/Desert giant: the world of the saguaro cactus. /1989/
2-6/6 KC427 . . . . **583**

Sahara.
MURRAY, P/Sahara. /1994/3-6/6 KE731 . . . . **966**

Sahara--Fiction.
LONDON, J/Ali, child of the desert. /1997/K-3/3 KG019 . . . . . **E**
SAINT EXUPERY, AD/Little prince. /c1943/4-A/6 KH671 . . . . . **Fic**

Sahara--Social life and customs.
REYNOLDS, J/Sahara: vanishing cultures. /1991/
4-6/6 KE732 . . . . **966**

Sailboats--Fiction.
RAND, G/Salty dog. /1991/2-3/5 KG301 . . . . **E**

Sailing--Fiction.
CREWS, D/Sail away. /1995/P-2/2 KF434 . . . . **E**
RAND, G/Aloha, Salty! /1996/1-3/3 KG299 . . . . **E**
SMITH, EB/Seashore book. /1985/3-6/9 KH724 . . . . **Fic**
VAN ALLSBURG, C/Wreck of the Zephyr. /1983/
1-5/3 KH825 . . . . **CE Fic**

Sailing ships.
VISUAL DICTIONARY OF SHIPS AND SAILING. /1991/
4-A/6 KB154 . . . . **387.2**

Saint Helens, Mount (Wash.)--Eruption, 1980.
LAUBER, P/Volcano: the eruption and healing of Mount St. Helens.
/1986/P-A/6 KC158 . . . . **CE 551.21**

Saint Lawrence Seaway.
ARMBRUSTER, A/St. Lawrence Seaway. /1996/2-4/6 KB141. **386**
GIBBONS, G/Great St. Lawrence Seaway. /1992/
2-5/6 KB142 . . . . **386**

Saint Valentine's Day SEE Valentine's Day.

Saints.
ARMSTRONG, C/Lives and legends of the saints: with paintings
from the great museums of the world. /1995/5-A/10 KA716 . **270**
DE PAOLA, T/Christopher: the holy giant. /1994/
2-3/4 KB438 . . . . **398.22**
Mary: the mother of Jesus. /1995/3-6/5 KA699 . . . . . **232.91**
Patrick: patron saint of Ireland. /1992/
2-4/4 KE492 . . . . **B PATRICK, ST.**
HODGES, M/Brother Francis and the friendly beasts. /1991/
3-5/5 KE349 . . . . **B FRANCIS, ST.**
SABUDA, R/Saint Valentine. /1992/
4-6/4 KE581 . . . . **B VALENTINE,ST.**

WILDSMITH, B/Saint Francis. /1996/
2-4/2 KE350 . . . . **B FRANCIS, ST.**

Salamanders.
BERNHARD, E/Salamanders. /1995/2-5/6 KC598 . . . . . . **597.8**
PARKER, NW/Frogs, toads, lizards and salamanders. /1990/
5-6/7 KC606 . . . . **597.8**
SALAMANDERS (VIDEOCASSETTE). /1985/
5-6/KC609 . . . . **VCR 597.8**
WINNER, C/Salamanders. /1993/A/7 KC611 . . . . **597.8**

Salamanders--Fiction.
NOVAK, M/Newt. /1996/1-3/2 KG181 . . . . **E**

Salem (Mass.)--Fiction.
FRITZ, J/Early thunder. /c1967, 1987/5-A/6 KH144 . . . . . . **Fic**
PETRY, A/Tituba of Salem Village. /1991/5-6/4 KH599. . . . . **Fic**

Salem (Mass.)--History--Colonial period, ca. 1600-1775.
KRENSKY, S/Witch hunt: it happened in Salem Village. /1989/
3-5/4 KA606 . . . . **133.4**
ROACH, MK/In the days of the Salem witchcraft trials. /1996/
3-6/10 KE945 . . . . **974.4**

Salinan Indians--Missions--California.
BROWER, P/Missions of the inland valleys. /1997/
4-6/9 KF077 . . . . **979.4**

Salmon.
CONE, M/Come back, salmon: how a group of dedicated kids
adopted Pigeon Creek and /1992/4-6/6 KD248 . . . . **639.3**

Salutations.
ALIKI /Hello! Good-bye! /1996/P-1/2 KB244. . . . . **395.4**
BADT, KL/Greetings! /1994/3-5/6 KB245 . . . . **395.4**

Salvadoran Americans--Fiction.
ROSEN, MJ/Bonesy and Isabel. /1995/2-3/6 KG352 . . . . **E**

Salvadorans--Fiction.
TEMPLE, F/Grab hands and run. /1993/6-A/6 KH788 . . . . . . **Fic**

Salvage (Waste, etc.) SEE Recycling (Waste); Refuse and refuse disposal.

Sami (European people).
LEWIN, T/Reindeer people. /1994/4-6/6 KE695 . . . . . . **948.97**
REYNOLDS, J/Far north: vanishing cultures. /1992/
3-6/6 KE696 . . . . **948.97**

Samoan Americans--Biography.
MORGAN, T/Junior Seau: high-voltage linebacker. /1997/
5-A/10 KE532 . . . . **B SEAU, J.**

Samurai--Fiction.
HAUGAARD, EC/Samurai's tale. /1984/6-A/5 KH228 . . . . . . **Fic**
PATERSON, K/Sign of the chrysanthemum. /c1973, 1991/
5-A/6 KH581 . . . . **Fic**

San (African people)--Folklore.
LEWIS, IM/Why ostriches don't fly and other tales from the African
bush. /1997/4-6/6 KB336 . . . . **398.2**

San (African people)--Social life and customs.
LEWIS, IM/Why ostriches don't fly and other tales from the African
bush. /1997/4-6/6 KB336 . . . . **398.2**

San Blas Islands (Panama)--Social life and customs.
PRESILLA, ME/Mola: Cuna life stories and art. /1996/
3-5/7 KA832 . . . . **305.48**

San Francisco (Calif.)--Description and travel--Guides.
BROWN, T/City by the bay: a magical journey around San
Francisco. /1993/1-5/7 KE207. . . . . **917.94**

San Francisco (Calif.)--Fiction.
BURTON, VL/Maybelle the cable car. /1997/K-2/3 KF321 . . . . **E**
GREGORY, K/Earthquake at dawn. /1992/5-A/6 KH202. . . . . **Fic**
SNYDER, ZK/Black and blue magic. /c1966, 1994/
4-6/7 KH729 . . . . **Fic**
YEP, L/Child of the owl. /c1977/A/6 KH891 . . . . **Fic**

San Francisco (Calif.)--Social life and customs.
BROWN, T/Konnichiwa!: I am a Japanese-American girl. /1995/
3-5/4 KA839 . . . . **305.8**

San Nicolas Island (Calif.)--Fiction.
O'DELL, S/Island of the Blue Dolphins. /c1960/5-6/6 KH559 . . **Fic**
Island of the Blue Dolphins. /c1960, 1990/5-6/6 KH560 . . . . **Fic**

Sand tiger shark.
CARRICK, C/Sand tiger shark. /c1977/4-6/7 KC591 . . . . . **597.3**

Sandboxes--Fiction.
JAKOB, D/My new sandbox. /1996/P-1/1 KF822 . . . . **E**

Sandburg, Carl.
MITCHELL, B/Good morning, Mr. President: a story about Carl
Sandburg. /1988/4-6/6 KE531 . . . . **B SANDBURG, C.**

Sandplay--Fiction.
JONES, RC/Down at the bottom of the deep dark sea. /1991/
P-K/2 KF852 . . . . **E**

Sanitation SEE ALSO Pollution; Refuse and refuse disposal; Water--
Pollution.

Sanitation--History.
COLMAN, P/Toilets, bathtubs, sinks, and sewers: a history of the
bathroom. /1994/5-6/5 KD294 . . . . **643**

Santa Clara Pueblo (N.M.).
SWENTZELL, R/Children of clay: a family of Pueblo potters. /1992/
4-6/6 KE795 . . . . **970.489**
Santa Claus--Fiction.
BURNINGHAM, J/Harvey Slumfenburger's Christmas present. /
1993/K-2/2 KF316 . . . . **E**
JOYCE, W/Santa calls. /1993/2-4/4 KF862 . . . . **E**
LEWIS, JP/Christmas of the reddle moon. /1994/1-3/4 KF975 . . **E**
PACKARD, M/Christmas kitten. /1994/K-1/1 KG204. . . . . **E**
STEVENSON, J/Oldest elf. /1996/P-2/2 KG565 . . . . **E**
VAN ALLSBURG, C/Polar express. /1985/2-A/5 KH822 . . **CE Fic**
WELLS, R/Max's Christmas. /1986/P-1/2 KG703 . . . . **CE E**
Santa Claus--Poetry.
BORNSTEIN, H/Night before Christmas: told in sign language: an
adaptation of the original poem "A visit from St. Nicholas" by
Clement C. Moore. /1994/K-6/KD917. . . . . **811**
MOORE, CC/Grandma Moses Night before Christmas. /1991/
P-A/KD987 . . . . **811**
Twas the night before Christmas: a visit from St. Nicholas. /c1912,
1992/P-A/KD988 . . . . **811**
Santa Fe Trail.
LAVENDER, DS/Santa Fe Trail. /1995/A/6 KF037 . . . . . **978**
RUSSELL, M/Along the Santa Fe Trail: Marion Russell's own story.
/1993/4-6/7 KE199 . . . . **917.8**
Santa Fe Trail--Fiction.
HOLLING, HC/Tree in the trail. /c1942/5-6/5 KH273 . . . . . . **Fic**
Sasaki, Sadako.
COERR, E/Sadako. /1993/3-6/4 KA994 . . . . **CE 362.1**
Sasquatch.
BACH, JS/Bigfoot. /1995/3-6/7 KA562 . . . . **001.944**
Satanta, Kiowa Chief.
FREEDMAN, R/Indian chiefs. /1987/5-6/8 KE749 . . . . **970.1**
Satellites, Artificial SEE Artificial satellites.
Saturn (Planet).
SIMON, S/Saturn. /1985/3-6/6 KC039 . . . . **523.46**
Saunders, George W. (George Washington)--Fiction.
LIGHTFOOT, DJ/Trail fever: the life of a Texas cowboy. /1992/
4-6/5 KH406 . . . . **Fic**
Saving and investment--Fiction.
VIORST, J/Alexander, who used to be rich last Sunday. /c1978/
P-3/5 KG659 . . . . **CE E**
WILLIAMS, VB/Chair for my mother. /1982/P-3/3 KG734. . . . . **E**
Savitri (Hindu mythology).
SHEPARD, A/Savitri: a tale of ancient India. /1992/
3-4/4 KA766 . . . . **294.5**
Sawmills--History.
ADAMS, P/Early loggers and the sawmill. /1981/
4-6/6 KD164 . . . . **634.9**
Sayings SEE Proverbs; Quotations.
Scales (Reptiles).
LAMPRELL, K/Scaly things. /1996/4-6/5 KC616. . . . . **597.9**
Scandinavia--Folklore.
SCANDINAVIAN FOLK & FAIRY TALES. /1984/
/KA273. . . . . **PROF 398.2**
Scarecrows--Fiction.
FLEISCHMAN, S/Scarebird. /1987/1-3/5 KF552 . . . . **E**
Scenery.
MORIN, A/Newspaper theatre: creative play production for low
budgets and no budgets. /1989//KA330 . . . . **PROF 792**
SHOW TIME (VIDEOCASSETTE). /1994/K-2/KD690 . . **VCR 792**
School--Songs and music.
SCHOOL RAP (SOUND RECORDING CASSETTE). /1990/
2-6/KD656. . . . . **SRC 789.3**
School buses--Fiction.
ANDERSON, R/Bus people. /1995/6-A/6 KG850 . . . . **Fic**
CREWS, D/School bus. /1984/P-2/1 KF435 . . . . **E**
School children--Library orientation.
EISENBERG, MB/Information problem-solving: the Big Six Skills
approach to library and /1990//KA063. . . . . **PROF 025.5**
School discipline SEE ALSO Classroom management; Students--Behavior.
School drama SEE Drama in education.
School excursions.
LANKFORD, MD/Successful field trips. /1992/
/KA178. . . . . **PROF 371.3**
School excursions--Fiction.
FLEISCHMAN, P/Time train. /1994/1-3/2 KF551 . . . . **E**
School field trips--Fiction.
SLATER, T/Stay in line. /1996/K-2/2 KG516. . . . . **E**
School integration.
ELISH, D/James Meredith and school desegregation. /1994/
4-5/7 KE463 . . . . **B MEREDITH, J.**
School integration--Louisiana--New Orleans.
COLES, R/Story of Ruby Bridges. /1995/2-5/4 KA902 . . . . **323.1**

School libraries SEE ALSO Children's literature; Instructional materials
centers; Libraries, Children's.
School libraries.
FARMER, LS/Creative partnerships: librarians and teachers working
together. /1993//KA074 . . . . **PROF 027.8**
LOERTSCHER, DV/Taxonomies of the school library media program.
/1988//KA076. . . . . **PROF 027.8**
URBANIK, MK/Curriculum planning and teaching using the library
media center. /1989//KA064 . . . . **PROF 025.5**
School libraries--Activity programs.
DOLL, CA/Nonfiction books for children: activities for thinking,
learning and doing. /1990//KA072 . . . . **PROF 027.8**
FARMER, LS/Cooperative learning activities in the library media
center. /1991//KA073. . . . . **PROF 027.8**
FREEMAN, J/Books kids will sit still for: the complete read-aloud
guide. 2nd ed. /1990//KA015. . . . . **PROF 011.62**
HART, TL/Creative ideas for library media center facilities. /1990/
/KA075. . . . . **PROF 027.8**
MCELMEEL, SL/Author a month (for pennies). /1988/
/KA069. . . . . **PROF 027.62**
ZINGHER, G/At the Pirate Academy: adventures with language in
the library media center. /1990//KA081 . . . . . **PROF 027.8**
School libraries--Administration.
MORRIS, BJ/Administering the school library media center. 3rd ed.
/1992//KA077. **PROF 027.8**
School libraries--Administration--Decision making.
KARPISEK, ME/Policymaking for school library media programs. /
1989//KA050 . . . . **PROF 025.1**
School libraries--Book lists.
CHILDREN'S CATALOG. 17TH ED. /1996//KA012. **PROF 011.62**
FREEMAN, J/Books kids will sit still for: the complete read-aloud
guide. 2nd ed. /1990//KA015. . . . . **PROF 011.62**
GILLESPIE, JT/Best books for children: preschool through grade 6.
5th ed. /1994//KA084 . . . . **PROF 028.1**
PETERSON, CS/Reference books for children, 4th ed. /1992/
/KA021. . . . . **PROF 011.62**
SCIENCE BOOKS AND FILMS' BEST BOOKS FOR CHILDREN,
1992-1995. /1996//KA028 . . . . **PROF 016.5**
WYNAR, CG/Guide to reference books for school media centers.
4th ed. /1992//KA007 . . . . **PROF 011**
School libraries--Book selection.
REICHMAN, H/Censorship and selection: issues and answers for
schools. Rev. ed. /1993//KA053 . . . . **PROF 025.2**
School libraries--Censorship.
BURRESS, L/Battle of the books: literary censorship in the public
schools, 1950-1985. /1989//KA051 . . . . **PROF 025.2**
REICHMAN, H/Censorship and selection: issues and answers for
schools. Rev. ed. /1993//KA053 . . . . **PROF 025.2**
School libraries--Collection development.
VAN ORDEN, P/Collection program in schools: concepts, practices,
and information sources. 2nd ed. /1995//KA054. . . **PROF 025.2**
WRIGHT, K/Challenge of technology: action strategies for the
school library media /1993//KA080 . . . . **PROF 027.8**
School libraries--Data processing.
WRIGHT, K/Challenge of technology: action strategies for the
school library media specialist. /1993//KA080 . . . . **PROF 027.8**
School libraries--History--20th century.
GAVER, MV/Braided cord: memoirs of a school librarian. /1988/
/KA368. . . . . **PROF B GAVER, M**
School libraries--Periodicals.
BOOK LINKS: CONNECTING BOOKS, LIBRARIES AND
CLASSROOMS. /1991-//KA097 . . . . **PER PROF 050**
EMERGENCY LIBRARIAN. /1973-//KA108 . . . . . **PER PROF 050**
KNOWLEDGE QUEST. /1997-//KA119 . . . . **PER PROF 050**
LIBRARY TALK: THE MAGAZINE FOR ELEMENTARY SCHOOL
LIBRARIANS. /1988-//KA123 . . . . **PER PROF 050**
SCHOOL LIBRARIAN'S WORKSHOP. /1980-/
/KA137. . . . . **PER PROF 050**
SCHOOL LIBRARIES IN CANADA. /1974-/
/KA138. . . . . **PER PROF 050**
SCHOOL LIBRARY JOURNAL: FOR CHILDREN'S, YOUNG ADULT,
AND SCHOOL LIBRARIES. /1954-/KA139 . . . . **PER PROF 050**
SCHOOL LIBRARY MEDIA ACTIVITIES MONTHLY. /1984-/
/KA140. . . . . **PER PROF 050**
SCHOOL LIBRARY MEDIA ANNUAL. /1983-/
/KA141. . . . . **PER PROF 050**
SCHOOL LIBRARY MEDIA QUARTERLY. /1972-/
/KA142. . . . . **PER PROF 050**
School life SEE Students.
Schools SEE ALSO Education; Kindergarten; Nursery schools; also particular
types of schools e.g. Boarding schools.
Schools.
HAUSHERR, R/One-room school at Squabble Hollow. /1988/
3-6/7 KB084 . . . . **371.19**

HOW TO SUCCEED IN MIDDLE SCHOOL (VIDEOCASSETTE). /
1994/5-6/KB125. . . . . **VCR 373.2**
HOWE, J/When you go to kindergarten. Rev. and updated ed. /
1994/P-K/2 KB097 . . . . **372.21**
KUKLIN, S/Going to my nursery school. /1990/
P-3/2 KB098 . . . . **372.21**

Schools--Fiction.
ADLER, DA/Young Cam Jansen and the lost tooth. /1997/
1-2/2 KF133 . . . . **E**
ALCOTT, LM/Little men: life at Plumfield with Jo's boys. /c1947,
1982/5-A/7 KG829 . . . . **Fic**
ALLARD, H/Miss Nelson is missing. /1977/1-3/3 KF151 . . . **CE E**
AVI /Nothing but the truth: a documentary novel. /1991/
6-A/5 KG861. . . . . **Fic**
S.O.R. losers. /1984/5-A/6 KG865. . . . . **Fic**
BAWDEN, N/Granny the Pag. /1996/5-A/4 KG888. . . . . . . **Fic**
BEMELMANS, L/Madeline. /1962/P-2/4 KF218. . . . . **CE E**
Madeline's rescue. /c1953/P-2/2 KF220. . . . . **CE E**
BLUME, J/Blubber. /1974/4-6/3 KG906. . . . . **Fic**
Freckle juice. /1971/2-4/3 KG908. . . . . **CE Fic**
BROWN, MT/Arthur's April fool. /1983/P-3/2 KF273 . . . . . . **E**
Arthur's teacher trouble. /1986/K-3/4 KF277 . . . . . . **CE E**
True Francine. /1987/1-2/1 KF282 . . . . **E**
BUNTING, E/Cheyenne again. /1995/3-5/2 KG941. . . . . . . **Fic**
Our teacher's having a baby. /1992/P-1/2 KF307 . . . . . . **E**
Spying on Miss Muller. /1995/6-A/6 KG944 . . . . **Fic**
BYARS, BC/Burning questions of Bingo Brown. /1990/
5-A/5 KG958. . . . . **Fic**
CARRIER, R/Basketball player. /1996/4-6/3 KG975 . . . . . . **Fic**
CAZET, D/Fish in his pocket. /1987/P-2/2 KF374. . . . . **E**
CLEARY, B/Beezus and Ramona. /1955/2-5/3 KG992 . . . . . **Fic**
Dear Mr. Henshaw. /1983/4-A/4 KG993. . . . . **Fic**
Ellen Tebbits. /1951/2-4/3 KG994 . . . . **Fic**
Muggie Maggie. /1990/3-5/5 KG998 . . . . **Fic**
Otis Spofford. /1953/3-5/6 KG999 . . . . **Fic**
Ramona the brave. /1975/3-5/6 KH005 . . . . **Fic**
Ramona the pest. /c1968/3-5/5 KH006 . . . . **Fic**
Strider. /1991/5-A/4 KH008 . . . . **Fic**
COHEN, B/Molly's pilgrim. /1983/1-3/4 KH012 . . . . . . **CE Fic**
COHEN, M/See you in second grade! /1989/K-1/2 KF404 . **CE E**
Will I have a friend? /c1967/K-1/2 KF405 . . . . **CE E**
CREW, L/Nekomah Creek. /1991/4-A/5 KH041. . . . . **Fic**
Nekomah Creek Christmas. /1994/4-6/4 KH042. . . . . . . **Fic**
CUTLER, J/Spaceman. /1997/4-A/2 KH053. . . . . **Fic**
DAHL, R/Matilda. /1988/5-A/7 KH056 . . . . **Fic**
DANZIGER, P/Amber Brown goes fourth. /1995/
2-4/4 KH059 . . . . **Fic**
Amber Brown is not a crayon. /1994/2-4/6 KH060 . . . . . **Fic**
Amber Brown wants extra credit. /1996/2-4/4 KH061. . . . . **Fic**
Forever Amber Brown. /1996/2-4/4 KH062 . . . . **Fic**
DUBOWSKI, CE/Pirate School. /1996/1-3/2 KF499 . . . . **E**
DUFFEY, B/Utterly yours, Booker Jones. /1995/4-6/5 KH087 . . **Fic**
Virtual Cody. /1997/1-4/2 KH088 . . . . **Fic**
DYGARD, TJ/Backfield package. /1992/6-A/7 KH090 . . . . . **Fic**
Forward pass. /1989/5-A/6 KH091. . . . . **Fic**
Game plan. /1993/5-A/8 KH092 . . . . **Fic**
EVANS, D/Classroom at the end of the hall. /1996/
3-5/4 KH104 . . . . **Fic**
FITZHUGH, L/Harriet the spy. /c1964/3-5/4 KH114 . . . . **Fic**
FORD, B/Most wonderful movie in the world. /1996/
6-A/4 KH132. . . . . **Fic**
GANTOS, J/Heads or tails: stories from the sixth grade. /1994/
5-A/4 KH150. . . . . **Fic**
GIFF, PR/All about Stacy. /1988/1-2/2 KF614 . . . . **CE E**
Fourth-grade celebrity. /1981/4-6/6 KH164 . . . . **Fic**
Today was a terrible day. /1980/1-2/2 KF616 . . . . . . **CE E**
Today was a terrible day (Kit). /1993/1-2/KF617. . . . . **KIT E**
GLEITZMAN, M/Sticky Beak. /1995/3-5/4 KH176. . . . . **Fic**
GORMAN, C/Miraculous makeover of Lizard Flanagan. /c1994,
1996/5-A/4 KH182. . . . . **Fic**
GRAVES, BB/Mystery of the Tooth Gremlin. /1997/
1-3/2 KH191 . . . . **Fic**
GREENWALD, S/Rosy Cole: she grows and graduates. /1997/
3-5/4 KH200 . . . . **Fic**
HAMILTON, V/Planet of Junior Brown. /c1971/
A/6 KH218. . . . . **CE Fic**
HAVILL, J/Jamaica's blue marker. /1995/K-1/2 KF681 . . . . **E**
HAYWOOD, C/"B" is for Betsy. /c1939/2-3/3 KH230 . . . . . **Fic**
HENKES, K/Chrysanthemum. /1991/K-2/2 KF703 . . . . **E**
Lilly's purple plastic purse. /1996/K-2/2 KF708 . . . . **E**
HENNESSY, BG/School days. /1990/P-1/3 KF713. . . . . **E**
HERMAN, C/Millie Cooper and friends. /1995/3-A/7 KH247 . . **Fic**
HEYMSFELD, C/Coaching Ms. Parker. /1992/2-4/4 KH255 . . . **Fic**
HONEYCUTT, N/All new Jonah Twist. /1987/3-5/4 KH277 . . . **Fic**

HURWITZ, J/Class clown. /1987/2-4/4 KH298 . . . . **Fic**
Russell Sprouts. /1987/2-4/4 KH303 . . . . **Fic**
Teacher's pet. /1988/3-5/4 KH305 . . . . **Fic**
JACKSON, A/Blowing bubbles with the enemy. /1993/
4-6/5 KH317 . . . . **Fic**
JAMES, M/Frankenlouse. /1994/6-A/6 KH322 . . . . **Fic**
Shoebag returns. /1996/6-A/6 KH324 . . . . **Fic**
JOHNSON, D/What will Mommy do when I'm at school? /1990/
K-1/2 KF836 . . . . **E**
JONES, DW/Witch week. New ed. /c1982, 1993/
6-A/6 KH335. . . . . **Fic**
KELLER, H/Harry and Tuck. /1993/K-1/2 KF884. . . . . **E**
KING-SMITH, D/Jenius: the amazing guinea pig. /1996/
2-4/5 KH349. . . . . **Fic**
School mouse. /1995/3-5/7 KH353. . . . . **Fic**
KLINE, S/Herbie Jones and the birthday showdown. /1995/
3-4/3 KH366. . . . . **Fic**
Herbie Jones and the class gift. /1989/3-4/2 KH367. . . . . . **Fic**
Horrible Harry and the green slime. /1989/2-4/2 KH368 . . . . **Fic**
Mary Marony hides out. /1993/1-3/4 KH369. . . . . **Fic**
KONIGSBURG, EL/View from Saturday. /1996/5-A/7 KH377 . **Fic**
KORMAN, G/Zucchini warriors. /1991/5-A/7 KH378 . . . . . . **Fic**
LASKY, K/Lunch bunnies. /1996/K-2/2 KF946 . . . . **E**
LAUTURE, D/Running the road to ABC. /1996/1-3/4 KF951. . . . **E**
LEVY, E/Keep Ms. Sugarman in the fourth grade. /1992/
3-5/5 KH402 . . . . **Fic**
LOBEL, A/Rose in my garden. /1984/K-3/KG011 . . . . **E**
LONDON, J/Froggy goes to school. /1996/P-1/2 KG022 . . . . . . **E**
LOWRY, L/Anastasia, absolutely. /1995/4-A/6 KH422 . . . . . . **Fic**
MACCARONE, G/Classroom pet. /1995/K-1/2 KG046. . . . . . . **E**
MACLACHLAN, P/Three Names. /1991/2-3/5 KG055 . . . . . . **E**
MARTIN, AM/Rachel Parker, kindergarten show-off. /1992/
K-2/1 KG069. . . . . **E**
MASTERS, SR/Libby Bloom. /1995/3-5/6 KH460. . . . . **Fic**
MCCULLY, EA/School. /1987/P-K/KG095 . . . . **E**
MCDONALD, M/Insects are my life. /1995/1-3/2 KG097 . . . . . **E**
MCKENNA, CO/Good grief, third grade. /1993/
3-4/4 KH481. . . . . **Fic**
Valentine's Day can be murder. /1996/3-5/4 KH482. . . . . . **Fic**
MCKENZIE, EK/Stargone John. /1990/3-5/5 KH484. . . . . . . **Fic**
MCMILLAN, B/Mouse views: what the class pet saw. /1993/
K-3/1 KG111. . . . . **E**
MCNAUGHTON, C/Captain Abdul's pirate school. /1994/
1-3/3 KG113. . . . . **E**
MOORE, M/Under the mermaid angel. /1995/6-A/5 KH506 . . **Fic**
NOBLE, TH/Day Jimmy's boa ate the wash. /1980/
K-2/2 KG176. . . . . **CE E**
PECK, R/Lost in cyberspace. /1995/5-A/3 KH593. . . . . **Fic**
PETERSEN, PJ/Some days, other days. /1994/K-2/2 KG234 . . . **E**
PINKWATER, J/Mister Fred. /1994/5-A/4 KG606 . . . . **Fic**
PULVER, R/Nobody's mother is in second grade. /1992/
K-2/2 KG293. . . . . **E**
RATHMANN, P/Officer Buckle and Gloria. /1995/
K-2/3 KG310. . . . . **E**
Ruby the copycat. /1991/K-2/2 KG311 . . . . **E**
ROBINSON, B/Best school year ever. /1994/3-A/5 KH641 . . . **Fic**
ROCKWELL, AF/Show and tell. /1997/P-K/2 KG345 . . . . **E**
ROSEN, MJ/School for Pompey Walker. /1995/4-8/6 KH653 . **Fic**
RUSSO, M/I don't want to go back to school. /1994/
1-3/2 KG361. . . . . **E**
SACHAR, L/Dogs don't tell jokes. /1992/5-A/5 KH665 . . . . . . **Fic**
Wayside School is falling down. /1989/3-5/4 KH666 . . **CE Fic**
SALTZBERG, B/Show-and-tell. /1994/K-2/2 KG388 . . . . **E**
SAY, A/Bicycle man. /1982/K-3/4 KG395 . . . . **E**
SCHERTLE, A/Jeremy Bean's St. Patrick's Day. /1987/
K-2/4 KG404 . . . . **E**
SCHWARTZ, A/Annabelle Swift, Kindergartner. /1988/
P-2/1 KG413 . . . . **CE E**
SCIESZKA, J/Math curse. /1995/2-5/3 KG420 . . . . **Fic**
SCOTT, AH/Brave as a mountain lion. /1996/3-5/4 KH688 . . . **Fic**
SERFOZO, M/Benjamin Bigfoot. /1993/P-K/2 KG439. . . . . . . **E**
SHARMAT, MW/Getting something on Maggie Marmelstein. /
c1971/4-6/4 KH705 . . . . **Fic**
SHREVE, S/Flunking of Joshua T. Bates. /c1984, 1993/
4-6/6 KH707 . . . . **Fic**
Gift of the girl who couldn't hear. /1991/4-6/6 KH709. . . . . **Fic**
Joshua T. Bates takes charge. /c1993, 1995/4-6/6 KH710. . . . **Fic**
SIMON, C/One happy classroom. /1997/K-1/2 KG507 . . . . . . **E**
SKINNER, D/Wrecker. /1995/6-A/4 KH715 . . . . **Fic**
SLATE, J/Miss Bindergarten gets ready for kindergarten. /1996/
P-K/2 KG515. . . . . **E**
SNYDER, ZK/Egypt game. /c1967/5-6/6 KH731 . . . . **Fic**
STOEKE, JM/Minerva Louise at school. /1996/P-1/2 KG577 . . . **E**

SULLIVAN, A/Molly Maguire: wide receiver. /1992/
4-6/3 KH773 . . . . **Fic**
SURAT, MM/Angel child, dragon child. /c1983, 1989/
1-3/2 KG584 . . . . **E**
TAYLOR, W/Numbskulls. /1995/4-A/7 KH787 . . . . **Fic**
TEAGUE, M/Secret shortcut. /1996/1-3/2 KG596 . . . . **E**
TOLAN, SS/Save Halloween! /1993/5-A/7 KH794 . . . . **Fic**
VAN LEEUWEN, J/Oliver Pig at school. /1994/
K-2/1 KG648 . . . . **CE E**
VOIGT, C/Bad girls. /1996/6-A/5 KH831 . . . . **Fic**
WARNER, S/Dog years. /1995/4-6/3 KH840 . . . . **Fic**
WELLS, R/Edward unready for school. /1995/P-K/2 KG698 . . . . **E**
WILLNER-PARDO, G/Natalie Spitzer's turtles. /1992/
1-3/2 KG741 . . . . **E**
WISEMAN, B/Morris goes to school. /1970/K-2/2 KG749 . . . . **E**
WOJCIECHOWSKI, S/Don't call me Beanhead! /1994/
2-3/5 KH877 . . . . **Fic**
WOLFF, PR/Toll-bridge troll. /1995/1-3/2 KG759 . . . . **E**
YARBROUGH, C/Shimmershine Queens. /1989/5-6/6 KH887 . . **Fic**
YASHIMA, T/Crow Boy. /1955/1-3/3 KG772 . . . . **CE E**

Schools--Fiction--Software.
ARTHUR'S TEACHER TROUBLE (CD-ROM). /1992/
1-4/KF171 . . . . **CDR E**
MERCER MAYER'S LITTLE MONSTER AT SCHOOL. SCHOOL ED.
(CD-ROM). /1994/K-3/KG130 . . . . **CDR E**

Schools--Handbooks.
GUIDE TO SUMMER CAMPS AND SUMMER SCHOOLS. 26TH
ED. /1995/5-A/KA411 . . . . **REF 371.2**

Schools--History.
FISHER, LE/Schoolmasters. /1997/3-6/7 KB083 . . . . **371.1**
LOEPER, JJ/Going to school in 1776. /1973/
4-6/8 KB123 . . . . **372.973**
Going to school in 1876. /1984/3-6/7 KB124 . . . . **372.973**
STANLEY, J/Children of the Dust Bowl: the true story of the school
at Weedpatch Camp. /1992/5-A/7 KA835 . . . . **305.5**

Schools--Poetry.
DAKOS, K/Don't read this book, whatever you do!: more poems
about school. /1993/4-6/KD928 . . . . **811**
If you're not here, please raise your hand: poems about school. /
1990/2-5/KD929 . . . . **811**
HARRISON, DL/Somebody catch my homework. /1993/
2-6/KD951 . . . . **811**
I THOUGHT I'D TAKE MY RAT TO SCHOOL: POEMS FOR
SEPTEMBER TO JUNE. /1993/2-5/KE066 . . . . **811.008**
KORMAN, G/D- poems of Jeremy Bloom: a collection of poems
about school, homework, and life (sort of). /1992/
4-A/KD966 . . . . **811**
SINGER, M/All we needed to say: poems about school from Tanya
and Sophie. /1996/3-6/KE027 . . . . **811**

Schools--Songs and music.
HARLEY, B/Lunchroom tales: a natural history of the cafetorium
(Sound recording cassette). /1996/2-4/KD615 . . . . . **SRC 789.3**

Schubert, Franz--Software.
WINTER, R/Microsoft composer collection (CD-ROM). /1994/
4-A/KD525 . . . . **CDR 780**
Science SEE ALSO Astronomy; Bacteriology; Biology; Botany; Chemistry;
Ethnology; Fossils; Geology; Mathematics; Meteorology; Mineralogy;
Natural history; Paleontology; Petrology; Physics; Physiology; Zoology.

Science.
MARKLE, S/Science to the rescue. /1994/6-A/8 KB896 . . . . **507.8**
NEW BOOK OF POPULAR SCIENCE. REV. ED. /1998/
5-6/KA433 . . . . **REF 503**
PIP AND ZENA'S SCIENCE VOYAGE (VIDEODISC). /1996/
K-3/KB869 . . . . **VD 500**
STEIN, S/Science book. /1979/2-A/5 KB873 . . . . **500**

Science--Bibliography.
HEFNER, CR/Literature-based science: children's books and activities
to enrich the K-5 /1995//KA200 . . . . **PROF 372.3**
SCIENCE BOOKS AND FILMS' BEST BOOKS FOR CHILDREN,
1992-1995. /1996//KA028 . . . . **PROF 016.5**

Science--Bibliography--Periodicals.
APPRAISAL: SCIENCE BOOKS FOR YOUNG PEOPLE. /1967-/
/KA095. . . . . **PER PROF 050**
SCIENCE BOOKS AND FILMS. /1975-//KA145. . **PER PROF 050**

Science--China--History.
WILLIAMS, S/Made in China: ideas and inventions from Ancient
China. /1996/4-6/6 KE631 . . . . **931**

Science--Dictionaries.
MOUNT, E/Milestones in science and technology: the ready
reference guide to discoveries, inventions, and facts. 2nd ed. /
1994/5-A/KA441 . . . . **REF 509**
STONE, J/Julian Messner illustrated dictionary of science. /1986/
4-6/9 KB878 . . . . **503**

Science--Encyclopedias.
RAINTREE STECK-VAUGHN ILLUSTRATED SCIENCE
ENCYCLOPEDIA. NEWLY REVISED. /1997/3-5/KA434 . **REF 503**
RUBEL, D/Science. /1995/4-6/7 KB877 . . . . **503**

Science--Experiments.
ARDLEY, N/Science book of air. /1991/4-6/4 KC102 . . . . . . **533**
Science book of color. /1991/4-6/4 KC118 . . . . . . **535.6**
Science book of water. /1991/2-4/4 KC091 . . . . **531**
BEN FRANKLIN BOOK OF EASY AND INCREDIBLE EXPERIMENTS.
/1995/A/8 KB889 . . . . **507.8**
BLAKEY, N/Mudpies activity book: recipes for invention. /c1989,
1993/A/KD424 . . . . **745.5**
BOSAK, SV/Science is...2nd ed. /1991//KA285. . . . **PROF 507.8**
COBB, V/Bet you can!: science possibilities to fool you. /1990/
4-A/7 KD745 . . . . **793.8**
Bet you can't: science impossibilities to fool you. /1980/
5-6/6 KB880 . . . . **507**
Light action!: amazing experiments with optics. /1993/
2-6/7 KC108 . . . . **535**
More science experiments you can eat. /1979/A/7 KB890 . **507.8**
Science experiments you can eat. Rev. and updated. /1994/
3-5/7 KB891 . . . . **507.8**
GARDNER, R/Science in your backyard. /1987/A/6 KB881 . . **507**
HIRSCHFELD, R/Kids' science book: creative experiences for hands-
on fun. /1995/P-4/7 KB892 . . . . **507.8**
KANER, E/Balloon science. /1989/2-6/6 KC079. . . . . **530**
KENDA, M/Cooking wizardry for kids. /1990/5-6/KD273 . . **641.5**
KRAMER, SP/How to think like a scientist: answering questions by
the scientific method. /1987/4-6/6 KB883 . . . . **507**
LEVINE, S/Silly science: strange and startling projects to amaze your
family and friends. /1995/3-8/7 KB893 . . . . **507.8**
LOOK WHAT I GREW: WINDOWSILL GARDENS
(VIDEOCASSETTE). /1993/1-6/KD171 . . . . **VCR 635**
MARKLE, S/Creepy spooky science. /1996/3-6/8 KB894 . . . **507.8**
Icky squishy science. /1996/4-8/6 KB895 . . . . **507.8**
MUNSON, HR/Science experiences with everyday things. /1988/
/KA283. . . . . **PROF 507**
RAINIS, KG/Exploring with a magnifying glass. /1991/
6-A/7 KB897 . . . . **507.8**
SCIENCE ACTIVITIES FOR YOUNG PEOPLE. /1983/
5-A/9 KB884 . . . . **507**
SCIENCE FAIR PROJECTS (VIDEOCASSETTE). /1995/
5-A/KB898. . . . . **VCR 507.8**
SCIENTIFIC METHOD (VIDEOCASSETTE). /1993/
5-6/KB886. . . . . **VCR 507**
SIMON, S/Mirror magic. /1991/3-5/6 KC114. . . . . **535**
VECCHIONE, G/100 amazing make-it-yourself science fair projects.
/1995//KA287. . . . . **PROF 507.8**
WYATT, V/Weather watch. /1990/3-6/6 KC222 . . . . **551.6**
WYLER, R/Science fun with mud and dirt. /1986/
K-4/2 KB887 . . . . **507**
ZUBROWSKI, B/Balloons: building and experimenting with inflatable
toys. /1990/4-A/7 KB888. . . . . **507**
Wheels at work: building and experimenting with models of
machines. /1986/5-6/8 KD054 . . . . **621.8**

Science--Experiments--Fiction.
WIESNER, D/June 29, 1999. /1992/1-5/4 KG713 . . . . **E**

Science--Methodology.
KRAMER, SP/How to think like a scientist: answering questions by
the scientific method. /1987/4-6/6 KB883 . . . . **507**

Science--Miscellanea.
MARKLE, S/Creepy spooky science. /1996/3-6/8 KB894 . . . **507.8**
MYERS, J/What makes popcorn pop?: and other questions about
the world around us. /c1991, 1994/3-6/7 KB868 . . . . **500**
QUINLAN, SE/Case of the mummified pigs and other mysteries in
nature. /1995/4-A/7 KB911 . . . . **508**
SOUCIE, G/What's the difference between lenses and prisms and
other scientific things? /1995/4-6/7 KB872. . . . . **500**
WOLLARD, K/How come? /1993/4-8/6 KB874 . . . . **500**

Science--Models.
MINDS-ON SCIENCE: THE IMPACT OF DISCOVERY (VIDEODISC).
/1995/5-A/KB875. . . . . **VD 502**

Science--Moral and ethical aspects.
MINDS-ON SCIENCE: FOR PROFIT, FOR PLANET (VIDEODISC). /
1995/5-A/KD348 . . . . **VD 687**
MINDS-ON SCIENCE: FOR THE SAKE OF THE NATION
(VIDEODISC). /1995/5-A/KA804 . . . . **VD 303.48**
MINDS-ON SCIENCE: THE IMPACT OF DISCOVERY (VIDEODISC).
/1995/5-A/KB875. . . . . **VD 502**

Science--Periodicals.
CONNECT: HANDS-ON SCIENCE AND MATH GUIDE FOR K-8
EDUCATORS. /1988-//KA103. . . . . **PER PROF 050**
CURRENT SCIENCE. /1927-/5-6/KA513. . . . . **PER 050**
MUSE. /1997-/4-6/KA527. . . . . **PER 050**

POPULAR SCIENCE: THE WHAT'S NEW MAGAZINE. /1872-/
5-A/KA537 . . . . **PER 050**
SCIENCE NEWS. /1921-/4-6/KA539. . . . . **PER 050**
WONDERSCIENCE: FUN PHYSICAL SCIENCE ACTIVITIES FOR
CHILDREN AND ADULTS TO DO TOGETHER. /1987-/
/KA154. . . . . **PER PROF 050**
YES MAG: CANADA'S SCIENCE MAGAZINE FOR KIDS. /1996-/
4-6/KA552 . . . . **050**

Science--Software.
SAMMY'S SCIENCE HOUSE (CD-ROM). /1994/
K-3/KB870. . . . . **CDR 500**
SCIENCE BLASTER JR. TEACHER ED. (CD-ROM). /1997/
K-3/KB871. . . . . **CDR 500**

Science--Songs and music.
AXELROD, G/Songs of nature and environment (Sound recording
cassette). /1978/1-3/KC293 . . . . **SRC 577**

Science--Study and teaching.
CONNECT: HANDS-ON SCIENCE AND MATH GUIDE FOR K-8
EDUCATORS. /1988-//KA103. . . . . **PER PROF 050**
HEFNER, CR/Literature-based science: children's books and activities
to enrich the K-5 curriculum. /1995//KA200 . . . . . . **PROF 372.3**
WONDERSCIENCE: FUN PHYSICAL SCIENCE ACTIVITIES FOR
CHILDREN AND ADULTS TO DO /1987-/
/KA154. . . . . **PER PROF 050**

Science--Study and teaching--Audio-visual aids--Bibliography.
SCIENCE BOOKS AND FILMS' BEST BOOKS FOR CHILDREN,
1992-1995. /1996//KA028 . . . . **PROF 016.5**

Science--Study and teaching--Periodicals.
SCHOOL SCIENCE AND MATHEMATICS. /1901-/
/KA143. . . . . **PER PROF 050**
SCIENCE AND CHILDREN. /1963-//KA144 . . . . **PER PROF 050**

Science--Study and teaching--Software.
GIZMOS AND GADGETS! (MICROCOMPUTER PROGRAM). /
1993/3-6/KB882. . . . . **MCP 507**
SCIENCE SLEUTHS. VOL. 1: THE MYSTERIES OF THE BLOB AND
THE EXPLODING LAWNMOWERS (CD-ROM). /1995/
4-A/KB885. . . . . **CDR 507**

Science--Study and teaching--Standards--United States.
NATIONAL SCIENCE EDUCATION STANDARDS: OBSERVE,
INTERACT, CHANGE, LEARN. /1996//KA284 . . . . . . **PROF 507**

Science--Study and teaching (Elementary)--Bibliography.
RESOURCES FOR TEACHING ELEMENTARY SCHOOL SCIENCE. /
1996//KA203 . . . . **PROF 372.3**

Science--Wit and humor.
TAKE ME TO YOUR LITER: SCIENCE AND MATH JOKES. /1991/
3-6/KD740. . . . . **793.735**

Science--Yearbooks.
SCIENCE YEAR: THE WORLD ANNUAL SCIENCE SUPPLEMENT. /
1965-/A/KA435 . . . . **REF 505**

Science, Ancient.
WILLIAMS, S/Made in China: ideas and inventions from Ancient
China. /1996/4-6/6 KE631. . . . . **931**

Science fairs.
FREDERICKS, AD/Complete science fair handbook. /1990/
/KA286. . . . . **PROF 507.8**
SCIENCE FAIR PROJECTS (VIDEOCASSETTE). /1995/
5-A/KB898. . . . . **VCR 507.8**
VANCLEAVE, JP/Janice VanCleave's guide to the best science fair
projects. /1997/3-6/KB899. . . . . **507.8**

Science fiction.
CHRISTOPHER, J/Dusk of Demons. /1994/5-A/4 KG990. . . . . **Fic**
White Mountains. /1967/4-6/6 KG991 . . . . **Fic**
COVILLE, B/Aliens ate my homework. /1993/4-6/5 KH035. . . . **Fic**
FARMER, N/Ear, the Eye and the Arm: a novel. /1994/
6-A/4 KH108. . . . . **Fic**
HOOVER, HM/Only child. /1992/5-A/5 KH280. . . . . **Fic**
Winds of Mars. /1995/6-A/4 KH281 . . . . **Fic**
HUGHES, M/Golden Aquarians. /1995/5-A/6 KH287 . . . . . . **Fic**
Invitation to the game. /1993/6-A/6 KH288 . . . . **Fic**
L'ENGLE, M/Wind in the door. /c1973/5-6/7 KH393 . . . . . **Fic**
Wrinkle in time. /c1962/4-6/6 KH394 . . . . **CE Fic**
LOWRY, L/Giver. /1993/5-A/6 KH426 . . . . **Fic**
MAHY, M/Greatest show off earth. /1994/4-A/7 KH450 . **CE Fic**
MARSHALL, E/Space case. /1980/P-2/4 KG065 . . . . **E**
PATON WALSH, J/Green book. /1982/4-6/6 KH583. . . . . . **Fic**
RYAN, MC/Me two. /1993/5-A/6 KH658 . . . . **Fic**
SERVICE, PF/Stinker from space. /1988/3-5/5 KH700. . . . . . **Fic**
SKURZYNSKI, G/Virtual war. /1997/5-A/4 KH716. . . . . . . **Fic**
SLEATOR, W/Duplicate. /1990/A/6 KH717. . . . . **Fic**

Science projects.
DIETL, U/Plant-and-grow project book. /1993/P-4/5 KC384 . . **580**
LEVINE, S/Silly science: strange and startling projects to amaze your
family and friends. /1995/3-8/7 KB893 . . . . **507.8**
MARKLE, S/Science to the rescue. /1994/6-A/8 KB896. . . . **507.8**

SCIENCE FAIR PROJECTS (VIDEOCASSETTE). /1995/
5-A/KB898. . . . . **VCR 507.8**
SCIENTIFIC METHOD (VIDEOCASSETTE). /1993/
5-6/KB886. . . . . **VCR 507**
VANCLEAVE, JP/Janice VanCleave's guide to the best science fair
projects. /1997/3-6/KB899. . . . . **507.8**
Janice VanCleave's rocks and minerals: mind-boggling experiments
you can turn /1996/4-6/8 KC228 . . . . **552**
VECCHIONE, G/100 amazing make-it-yourself science fair projects.
/1995//KA287. . . . . **PROF 507.8**

Science projects--Fiction.
HUTCHINS, HJ/Anastasia Morningstar and the crystal butterfly. Rev.
ed. /1984/4-6/6 KH306. **Fic**

Scientific expeditions--History.
STEFOFF, R/Scientific explorers: travels in search of knowledge. /
1992/6-A/9 KB925 . . . . **509**

Scientific recreations.
BOSAK, SV/Science is...2nd ed. /1991//KA285. . . . **PROF 507.8**
BUSCH, PS/Backyard safaris: 52 year-round science adventures. /
1995/P-A/5 KB901 . . . . **508**
CASH, T/101 physics tricks: fun experiments with everyday
materials. /1993/4-8/7 KC077. . . . . **530**
COBB, V/Bet you can!: science possibilities to fool you. /1990/
4-A/7 KD745 . . . . **793.8**
Bet you can't: science impossibilities to fool you. /1980/
5-6/6 KB880 . . . . **507**
Wanna bet?: science challenges to fool you. /1993/
4-6/6 KD746 . . . . **793.8**
GARDNER, R/Science in your backyard. /1987/A/6 KB881 . . **507**
GRIER, K/Discover: investigate the mysteries of history with 40
practical projects probing our past. /1990/3-6/6 KA592. . . . **069**
LEVINE, S/Silly science: strange and startling projects to amaze your
family and friends. /1995/3-8/7 KB893 . . . . **507.8**
MARKLE, S/Icky squishy science. /1996/4-8/6 KB895 . . . . . **507.8**
Measuring up!: experiments, puzzles, and games exploring
measurement. /1995/5-6/6 KC086 . . . . **530.8**
OXLADE, C/Science magic with air. /1994/4-A/6 KD748. . . **793.8**
Science magic with light. /1994/3-6/5 KD749 . . . . **793.8**
Science magic with magnets. /1995/3-6/6 KD750 . . . . . **793.8**
Science magic with shapes and materials. /1995/
3-6/5 KD751 . . . . **793.8**
WATER ROCKETS I (VIDEOCASSETTE). /1994/
5-A/KA291 . . . . **VCR PROF 530**

Scientists.
ANDERSON, MJ/Isaac Newton: the greatest scientist of all time. /
1996/6-A/7 KE476 . . . . **B NEWTON, I.**
BIOGRAPHY TODAY SCIENTISTS AND INVENTORS SERIES:
PROFILES OF PEOPLE OF INTEREST TO YOUNG PEOPLE. /
1996-/4-6/KA438 . . . . **REF 509**
GEORGE WASHINGTON CARVER: A MAN OF VISION
(VIDEOCASSETTE). /1990/5-A/KE281 . . . . **VCR B CARVER, G.**
HAYDEN, RC/7 African-American scientists. Rev. and expanded ed.
/1992/6-A/6 KB923 . . . . **509**
JOHNSON, RL/Braving the frozen frontier: women working in
Antarctica. /1997/4-6/6 KE214 . . . . **919.8**
MCKISSACK, P/African-American scientists. /1994/
4-6/7 KB924 . . . . **509**
SCIENTISTS: THE LIVES AND WORKS OF 150 SCIENTISTS. /
1996/5-A/KA442 . . . . **REF 509**
SIS, P/Starry messenger: a book depicting the life of a famous
scientist. /1996/3-6/6 KE360. . . . . **CE B GALILEO**

Scientists--Dictionaries.
LAROUSSE DICTIONARY OF SCIENTISTS. /1996/
5-A/KA440 . . . . **REF 509**

Scilly, Isles of (England)--Fiction.
MORPURGO, M/Wreck of the Zanzibar. /1995/4-6/3 KH516 . **Fic**

Scoliosis--Fiction.
BLUME, J/Deenie. /1973/6/4 KG907 . . . . **Fic**
NAPOLI, DJ/Bravest thing. /1995/3-5/6 KH529. . . . . **Fic**

Scooters--Fiction.
WILLIAMS, VB/Scooter. /1993/4-A/4 KH865 . . . . **Fic**

Scorpions.
PRINGLE, LP/Scorpion man: exploring the world of scorpions. /
1994/5-6/8 KC530 . . . . **595.4**

Scotland--Antiquities.
ARNOLD, C/Stone Age farmers beside the sea: Scotland's
prehistoric village of Skara Brae. /1997/3-6/8 KE677. . . . . **941.1**

Scotland--Fiction.
BAWDEN, N/Witch's daughter. /c1966, 1991/5-A/6 KG893 . . **Fic**
COOPER, S/Boggart. /1993/6-A/7 KH026. . . . . **CE Fic**
Boggart and the monster. /1997/5-A/6 KH027 . . . . **Fic**
HUNTER, M/Third eye. /1991/A/7 KH294 . . . . **Fic**
Walking stones. /1996/6-A/8 KH295 . . . . **Fic**
KING-SMITH, D/Sophie's Lucky. /1996/3-4/8 KH356 . . . . **Fic**

STEVENSON, RL/Kidnapped: /1982/5-6/6 KH758 . . . . **Fic**

Scotland--Folklore.
COOPER, S/Tam Lin. /1991/3-4/4 KB276 . . . . **398.2**
FOREST, H/Woman who flummoxed the fairies: an old tale from
Scotland. /1990/3-4/5 KB396 . . . . **398.21**
HUNTER, M/Gilly Martin the Fox. /1994/3-4/7 KB593 . . . **398.24**
NIC LEODHAS, S/Always room for one more. /1965/
K-2/7 KB760 . . . . **398.27**
VILLAGE STEW (VIDEOCASSETTE). /1987/
K-3/KB782 . . . . **VCR 398.27**
YOLEN, J/Tam Lin. /1990/3-4/4 KB384 . . . . **398.2**

Scotland--History--18th century--Fiction.
STEVENSON, RL/David Balfour: being memoirs of the further
adventures of David Balfour at home /c1952, 1994/
6-A/6 KH757 . . . . **Fic**

Scott, Ann (Hamilton)--Fiction.
FRITZ, J/Cabin faced west. /c1958/4-6/6 KH143 . . . . **Fic**
Scouts and scouting SEE ALSO Boy Scouts; Girl Scouts.

Scouts and scouting.
BIRKBY, RC/Boy Scout handbook. 10th ed. /1990/
4-6/6 KB073 . . . . **369.43**
BOY SCOUTS OF AMERICA /Big Bear Cub Scout book. Rev. ed. /
1984/4-5/5 KB074 . . . . **369.43**
Webelos Scout book. Rev. ed. /1987/4-6/3 KB075 . . . **369.43**
Wolf Cub Scout book. Rev. ed. /1986/3-4/4 KB076 . . . . **369.43**
GIRL SCOUTS OF THE UNITED STATES OF AMERICA /Brownie
Scout handbook. /1993/1-3/KB078 . . . . **369.463**
Junior Girl Scout handbook. /1994/4-6/KB079 . . . . . **369.463**

Scribes, Jewish--Handbooks, manuals, etc.
COWAN, P/Torah is written. /1986/5-6/7 KA782 . . . . . . **296.6**

Scuba diving.
MCGOVERN, A/Down under, down under: diving adventures on
the Great Barrier Reef. /1989/3-6/5 KF120 . . . . **994.3**

Sculptors.
GARDNER, JM/Henry Moore: from bones and stones to sketches
and sculptures. /1993/3-6/6 KD397 . . . . **730**
LING, B/Maya Lin. /1997/4-6/10 KE437 . . . . . . **B LIN, M.**
Sculpture SEE ALSO Modeling; Wood carving.

Sculpture.
ROMEI, F/Story of sculpture. /1995/4-A/9 KD399 . . . . . **730**
SANCHEZ SANCHEZ, I/Dragons and prehistoric monsters. /1996/
3-6/3 KD447 . . . . **745.592**

Sculpture--History.
HESLEWOOD, J/History of Western sculpture: a young person's
guide. /1996/4-6/9 KD398 . . . . **730**
Sea SEE Ocean.

Sea in art.
ROALF, P/Seascapes. /1992/5-A/7 KD482 . . . . **758**

Sea Islands--Fiction.
SIEGELSON, KL/Terrible, wonderful tellin' at Hog Hammock. /
1996/4-6/6 KH711 . . . . **Fic**

Sea life.
BIESTY, S/Man-of-war. /1993/4-6/7 KA988 . . . . **359.1**

Sea lions.
ARNOLD, C/Sea lion. /1994/4-6/6 KC867 . . . . **599.79**
SEA ANIMALS ASHORE (VIDEOCASSETTE). /1996/
3-6/KC872 . . . . **VCR 599.79**

Sea lions--Fiction.
TAFURI, N/Follow me! /1990/P-2/KG589 . . . . **E**

Sea stories.
AVI /True confessions of Charlotte Doyle. /1990/
5-A/6 KG867 . . . . **Fic**
COHEN, D/Ghosts of the deep. /1993/4-6/7 KA600 . . . . . **133.1**
HOLLING, HC/Seabird. /c1948/5-6/5 KH272 . . . . **Fic**
SINGER, M/In the palace of the Ocean King. /1995/
2-3/5 KG509 . . . . **E**
VAN ALLSBURG, C/Wretched stone. /1991/4-A/4 KH826 . . . . **Fic**
VERNE, J/20,000 leagues under the sea. /1980/5-6/6 KH829 . **Fic**

Sea turtles.
GIBBONS, G/Sea turtles. /1995/2-4/6 KC617 . . . . **597.92**
GUIBERSON, BZ/Into the sea. /1996/1-3/3 KC618 . . . . . **597.92**
TALKING ABOUT SEA TURTLES (VIDEOCASSETTE). /1992/
4-6/KC623 . . . . **VCR 597.92**
VOYAGE OF THE LOGGERHEAD (VIDEOCASSETTE). /1995/
3-6/KC624 . . . . **VCR 597.92**

Seals (Animals).
JOHNSON, SA/Elephant seals. /1989/5-6/7 KC869 . . . . . **599.79**
MATTHEWS, D/Harp seal pups. /1997/4-6/3 KC870 . . . . **599.79**
SEA ANIMALS ASHORE (VIDEOCASSETTE). /1996/
3-6/KC872 . . . . **VCR 599.79**

Seals (Animals)--Fiction.
RAND, G/Prince William. /1992/2-3/4 KG300 . . . . **E**

Seals (Animals)--Folklore.
COOPER, S/Selkie girl. /1986/3-4/6 KB551 . . . . **CE 398.24**

Seamen.
LATHAM, JL/Carry on, Mr. Bowditch. /c1955/
5-A/3 KE260 . . . . **CE B BOWDITCH, N.**
SHERBURNE, A/Memoirs of Andrew Sherburne: patriot and
privateer of the American Revolution. /1993/5-A/8 KE886 . **973.3**

Search dogs.
PATENT, DH/Hugger to the rescue. /1994/3-6/5 KD226 . . **636.73**

Seashore.
WHAT ARE ECOSYSTEMS? (VIDEOCASSETTE). /1975/
4-6/KC299 . . . . **VCR 577**

Seashore--Fiction.
ALBERT, B/Where does the trail lead? /1991/K-2/3 KF143 . . . . **E**
ALIKI /Those summers. /1996/K-2/4 KF149 . . . . **E**
FRANKLIN, KL/Iguana Beach. /1997/P-1/2 KF575 . . . . **E**
JOHNSON, A/Joshua by the sea (Board book). /1994/
P/2 KF829 . . . . **BB E**
LAKIN, P/Dad and me in the morning. /1994/1-3/2 KF942 . . . **E**
MARTIN, AT/Famous seaweed soup. /1993/P-2/4 KG070 . . . . . **E**
MCKAY, H/Amber cat. /1997/5-8/6 KH476 . . . . **Fic**
ROCKWELL, AF/At the beach. /1987/P-3/3 KG340 . . . . **E**
ROTNER, S/Ocean day. /1993/P-2/3 KG357 . . . . **E**
SMITH, EB/Seashore book. /1985/3-6/9 KH724 . . . . **Fic**
TURKLE, B/Do not open. /1981/K-2/2 KG622 . . . . **E**

Seashore animals.
COHAT, E/Seashore. /1995/1-4/4 KC366 . . . . **578.769**

Seashore biology.
COHAT, E/Seashore. /1995/1-4/4 KC366 . . . . **578.769**
INTERTIDAL ZONE (VIDEOCASSETTE). /c1985, 1986/
5-A/KC346 . . . . **VCR 577.69**
PLUCKROSE, H/Seashore. /1994/P-2/4 KC347 . . . . **577.69**

Seashore ecology.
INTERTIDAL ZONE (VIDEOCASSETTE). /c1985, 1986/
5-A/KC346 . . . . **VCR 577.69**

Seashore ecology--Guides.
AMOS, WH/Atlantic and Gulf coasts. /1985/A/KC345 . . . **577.69**
MCCONNAUGHEY, BH/Pacific coast. /1985/A/KC296 . . . . . **577**
Seasons SEE ALSO names of specific season e.g. Autumn.

Seasons.
BOWEN, B/Gathering: a northwoods counting book. /1995/
1-3/3 KB953 . . . . **513.2**
BRANLEY, FM/Sunshine makes the season. Rev. ed. /1985/
K-2/3 KC057 . . . . **525**
BUSCH, PS/Backyard safaris: 52 year-round science adventures. /
1995/P-A/5 KB901 . . . . **508**
CHRISTIANSEN, C/Sky tree portfolio: science and art (Picture). /
1995/2-6/KC410 . . . . **PIC 582.16**
EARTH'S SEASONS/CLIMATES (VIDEOCASSETTE). /1995/
3-6/KB902 . . . . **VCR 508**
GIBBONS, G/Reasons for seasons. /1995/P-4/5 KC059 . . . . **525**
JACKSON, E/Winter solstice. /1994/3-5/6 KB211 . . . . . **394.261**
JOHNSON, SA/How leaves change. /1986/4-6/9 KC399 . . **581.4**
MAGICAL MOTHER NATURE: THE FOUR SEASONS
(VIDEOCASSETTE). /1989/2-4/KC061 . . . . **VCR 525**
OPPENHEIM, J/Have you seen trees? /1995/
P-2/3 KC420 . . . . **582.16**
RUSSO, M/Tree almanac: a year-round activity guide. /1993/
3-6/6 KC423 . . . . **582.16**
SEASONS. REV. ED. (SOUND FILMSTRIP). /c1975, 1993/
K-2/KC063 . . . . **FSS 525**
SIMON, S/Autumn across America. /1993/4-6/7 KB918 . . **508.2**
Spring across America. /1996/5-8/7 KB919 . . . . . . **508.2**
Winter across America. /1994/4-6/6 KB920 . . . . . . **508.2**
WOODS, ML/Sky tree portfolio guide: an interdisciplinary
environmental curriculum. /1995/2-6/KC424 . . . . **582.16**

Seasons--Fiction.
CARLSTROM, NW/How does the wind walk? /1993/
P-2/3 KF354 . . . . **E**
DERBY, S/My steps. /1996/P-1/2 KF482 . . . . **E**
FUCHS, DM/Bear for all seasons. /1995/K-2/2 KF589 . . . . . . **E**
GEORGE, JC/Dear Rebecca, winter is here. /1993/
1-3/3 KF605 . . . . **E**
HENDERSON, K/Year in the city. /1996/K-2/2 KF700 . . . . **E**
KROLL, VL/Seasons and Someone. /1994/K-3/5 KF935 . . . . . . **E**
LESSER, C/What a wonderful day to be a cow. /1995/
K-2/3 KF963 . . . . **E**
PALAZZO-CRAIG, J/Max and Maggie in spring. /1995/
K-1/1 KG208 . . . . **E**
PROVENSEN, A/Year at Maple Hill Farm. /1978/K-2/4 KG290 . **E**
ROCKWELL, AF/Ducklings and pollywogs. /1994/K-2/3 KG341 . **E**
SENDAK, M/Chicken soup with rice: a book of months. /c1962/
P-1/KG430 . . . . **CE E**
SIDDALS, MM/Tell me a season. /1997/P-1/1 KG500 . . . . **E**
WOLFF, A/Year of beasts. /1986/P-K/1 KG757 . . . . **E**

Seasons--Folklore.
    LARRY, C/Peboan and Seegwun. /1993/2-3/4 KB709 . . . . **398.26**
Seasons--Poetry.
    ADOFF, A/In for winter, out for spring. /1991/1-4/KD910 . . . **811**
    BRUCHAC, J/Thirteen moons on turtle's back: a Native American
        year of moons. /1992/2-6/KD919 . . . . **811**
    FROST, R/Poetry for young people. /1994/4-A/KD940 . . . . . **811**
    LEWIS, JP/July is a mad mosquito. /1994/P-3/KD972 . . . . . **811**
    LIVINGSTON, MC/Cricket never does: a collection of haiku and
        tanka. /1997/3-6/KD975 . . . . **811**
    TURNER, A/Moon for seasons. /1994/3-6/KE034 . . . . **811**
Seasons--Songs.
    JAMES, DL/Singing calendar (Sound recording cassette). /1984/
        P-1/KC071. . . . . **SRC 529**
Seau, Junior.
    MORGAN, T/Junior Seau: high-voltage linebacker. /1997/
        5-A/10 KE532 . . . . **B SEAU, J.**
Secrets.
    SENISI, EB/Secrets. /1995/K-2/2 KA643 . . . . **155.4**
Secrets--Fiction.
    RUEPP, K/Midnight Rider. /1995/3-5/2 KH657 . . . . **Fic**
    WILLNER-PARDO, G/When Jane-Marie told my secret. /1995/
        2-3/2 KH867 . . . . **Fic**
Sects--Fiction.
    AIKEN, J/Cold Shoulder Road. /1995/5-A/5 KG823 . . . . **Fic**
Seder.
    SIMON, N/Story of Passover. /1997/2-4/3 KA781 . . . . . **296.4**
Seder--Fiction.
    MANUSHKIN, F/Matzah that Papa brought home. /1995/
        1-3/2 KG059 . . . . **E**
Seeds.
    GIBBONS, G/From seed to plant. /1991/K-3/4 KC398 . . . . **581.4**
    JORDAN, HJ/How a seed grows. Rev. ed. /1992/
        P-2/1 KC387 . . . . **580**
Seeds--Dispersal.
    OVERBECK, C/How seeds travel. /1982/2-4/6 KC389. . . . . . **580**
Seeds--Experiments.
    DIETL, U/Plant-and-grow project book. /1993/P-4/5 KC384 . . **580**
Seeds--Fiction.
    KRAUSS, R/Carrot seed. /c1945/P-2/2 KF920. . . . . **CE E**
    MARZOLLO, J/I'm a seed. /1996/K-2/1 KG081 . . . . **E**
Seeing eye dogs SEE Guide dogs.
Segregation.
    BLACK IS MY COLOR: THE AFRICAN AMERICAN EXPERIENCE
        (VIDEOCASSETTE). /1992/4-6/KA838 . . . . **VCR 305.8**
    PARKS, R/Rosa Parks: my story. /1992/
        6-A/5 KE490 . . . . **B PARKS, R.**
Segregation in transportation--Alabama--Montgomery.
    STEIN, RC/Montgomery bus boycott. Rev. ed. /1993/
        5-6/6 KE998 . . . . **976.1**
Seles, Monica.
    FEHR, KS/Monica Seles: returning champion. /1997/
        4-6/10 KE533 . . . . **B SELES, M.**
Self--Fiction.
    KONIGSBURG, EL/Throwing shadows. /1979/5-6/6 KH376 . . . **Fic**
Self-acceptance.
    EVERYBODY'S DIFFERENT (VIDEOCASSETTE). /1994/
        3-6/KA639 . . . . **VCR 155.2**
    IT'S GREAT TO BE ME! INCREASING YOUR CHILD'S SELF-
        ESTEEM (VIDEOCASSETTE). /1989//KA302 . . . **VCR PROF 649**
    MENDLER, AN/Smiling at yourself: educating young children about
        stress and self-esteem. /1990//KA304. . . . . **PROF 649**
    NO ONE QUITE LIKE ME...OR YOU (VIDEOCASSETTE). /1992/
        3-6/KA640 . . . . **VCR 155.2**
Self-acceptance--Fiction.
    BALL, D/Emily Eyefinger. /1992/1-3/2 KG876. . . . . **Fic**
    COOPER, I/Buddy Love: now on video. /1995/5-A/4 KH025 . . **Fic**
    DRAANEN, WV/How I survived being a girl. /1997/
        4-A/KH084 . . . . **Fic**
    GREENWALD, S/Rosy Cole: she grows and graduates. /1997/
        3-5/4 KH200 . . . . **Fic**
    GWYNNE, F/Pondlarker. /1990/K-2/5 KF656 . . . . **E**
    HOWE, J/I wish I were a butterfly. /1987/K-3/2 KF778 . . . . . **E**
    KRAUS, R/Leo the late bloomer. /1971/P-2/2 KF918 . . . . . **CE E**
    SMITH, DB/Best girl. /1993/5-A/6 KH720 . . . . **Fic**
    WILHELM, H/Royal raven. /1996/K-2/2 KG723. . . . . **E**
Self-confidence--Fiction.
    AVI /Punch with Judy. /1993/5-A/6 KG863 . . . . **Fic**
    HOBAN, L/Big little otter (Board book). /1997/P/1 KF736. . **BB E**
    LEVY, E/Keep Ms. Sugarman in the fourth grade. /1992/
        3-5/5 KH402 . . . . **Fic**
    MASTERS, SR/Libby Bloom. /1995/3-5/6 KH460. . . . . **Fic**
    WILLIS, MS/Secret super powers of Marco. /1994/
        4-A/4 KH866 . . . . **Fic**

Self-control.
    IT'S NOT MY FAULT: A PROGRAM ABOUT CONFLICT
        RESOLUTION (VIDEOCASSETTE). /1981/
        4-6/KA628 . . . . **VCR 152.4**
    WORKING IT OUT: CONFLICT RESOLUTION (VIDEOCASSETTE).
        /1993/5-6/KA813. . . . . **VCR 303.6**
Self-esteem.
    BERGIN, DP/Zero Street (Videocassette). /1995/
        4-6/KA894 . . . . **VCR 307.76**
    JOHNSTON, A/Girls speak out: finding your true self. /1997/
        A/6 KA646 . . . . **155.5**
    SIMMONS, CW/Becoming myself: true stories about learning from
        life. /1994/5-A/6 KA664 . . . . **158**
Self-esteem--Fiction.
    CLIMO, S/Little red ant and the great big crumb: a Mexican fable.
        /1995/1-3/2 KF398 . . . . **E**
    HOWARD, E/Big seed. /1993/1-3/2 KF775 . . . . **E**
    RYAN, ME/Trouble with perfect. /1995/6-A/3 KH659. . . . . . **Fic**
Self-esteem--Songs and music.
    HARTMANN, J/One voice for children (Videocassette). /1993/
        K-4/KD618 . . . . **VCR 789.3**
Self-identity--Fiction.
    GIFF, PR/All about Stacy. /1988/1-2/2 KF614 . . . . **CE E**
Self-perception.
    EPSTEIN-KRAVIS, A/Happy to be me (Sound recording cassette). /
        1993/P-1/KA638 . . . . **SRC 155.2**
    JOHNSTON, A/Girls speak out: finding your true self. /1997/
        A/6 KA646 . . . . **155.5**
    SIMMONS, CW/Becoming myself: true stories about learning from
        life. /1994/5-A/6 KA664 . . . . **158**
Self-perception--Fiction.
    COTTONWOOD, J/Danny ain't. /1992/6-A/6 KH033 . . . . . . **Fic**
    ERNST, LC/Luckiest kid on the planet. /1994/1-3/2 KF532. . . . . **E**
    NAYLOR, PR/Agony of Alice. /1985/5-6/6 KH532. . . . . **Fic**
    SACHAR, L/Dogs don't tell jokes. /1992/5-A/5 KH665. . . . . . **Fic**
    SACHS, M/Truth about Mary Rose /1995/5-A/6 KH669. . . . . . **Fic**
    SMITH, RK/Bobby baseball. /1991/3-6/4 KH726 . . . . **Fic**
Self-protection.
    MY BODY BELONGS TO ME (VIDEOCASSETTE). /1992/
        K-3/KA170 . . . . **VCR PROF 362.7**
Self-realization--Fiction.
    MOSS, T/I want to be. /1993/1-4/3 KG159 . . . . **E**
Self-realization--Folklore.
    TALKING EGGS (VIDEOCASSETTE). /1993/
        2-5/KB420. . . . . **VCR 398.21**
Self-reliance.
    HOME ALONE: YOU'RE IN CHARGE (VIDEOCASSETTE). /1991/
        2-4/KD259. . . . . **VCR 640**
    HOME ON YOUR OWN (VIDEOCASSETTE). /1994/
        4-6/KD260. . . . . **VCR 640**
    LATCHKEY CHILDREN: WHEN YOU'RE IN CHARGE
        (VIDEOCASSETTE). /1986/5-6/KD261 . . . . **VCR 640**
    PRESCHOOL POWER!: JACKET FLIPS AND OTHER TIPS
        (VIDEOCASSETTE). /1991/P-K/KD263 . . . . **VCR 640.83**
    WORKING IT OUT: CONFLICT RESOLUTION (VIDEOCASSETTE).
        /1993/5-6/KA813. . . . . **VCR 303.6**
Self-reliance--Fiction.
    ALCOTT, LM/Rose in bloom: a sequel to Eight cousins. Uniform ed.
        /c1876, 1995/5-6/7 KG831 . . . . **Fic**
    BAWDEN, N/Humbug. /1992/5-A/5 KG891 . . . . **Fic**
    COTE, N/Palm trees. /1993/K-2/4 KF427. . . . . **E**
    FOX, P/Likely place. /c1967, 1986/4-6/4 KH135 . . . . **Fic**
    GAUCH, PL/Christina Katerina and the time she quit the family. /
        1987/K-2/6 KF600 . . . . **E**
    PATERSON, K/Lyddie. /1991/6-A/7 KH579 . . . . **Fic**
    STANEK, M/All alone after school. /1985/2-3/2 KG536 . . . . . . **E**
Self-respect.
    KAUFMAN, G/Stick up for yourself!: every kid's guide to personal
        power and positive /1990/6-A/6 KA659 . . . . **158**
Selma (Ala.)--Race relations.
    WEBB, S/Selma, Lord, Selma: girlhood memories of the civil-rights
        days. /c1980, 1997/A/7 KA906 . . . . **323.1**
Seminole Indians.
    SNEVE, V/Seminoles. /1994/4-6/7 KE775 . . . . **970.3**
Sendak, Maurice.
    SENDAK (VIDEOCASSETTE). /1993/
        4-A/KE534. **VCR B SENDAK, M.**
Seneca Indians--Folklore.
    ESBENSEN, BJ/Great buffalo race: how the buffalo got its hump: a
        Seneca tale. /1994/3-4/6 KB564 . . . . **398.24**
Senility SEE Alzheimer's disease.
Senses and sensation.
    ALIKI /My five senses. Rev. ed. /1989/K-2/2 KC962. . . . . . **612.8**

999

EYES: BRIGHT AND SAFE. REV. ED. (VIDEOCASSETTE). /1997/
3-5/KC964. . . . . **VCR 612.8**
FABULOUS FIVE: OUR SENSES (VIDEOCASSETTE). /1989/
P-2/KC917. **VCR 612**
LAUBER, P/What do you see and how do you see it?: exploring
light, color, and vision. /1994/1-6/4 KC113 . . . . **535**
MCMILLAN, B/Sense suspense: a guessing game for the five senses.
/1994/P-2/KC968. . . . . **612.8**
MILLER, M/My five senses. /1994/P-1/2 KC969 . . . . **612.8**
PARRAMON, JM/Hearing. /1985/P-1/1 KC973 . . . . **612.8**
   Sight. /1985/P-1/1 KC974. . . . . **612.8**
   Taste. /1985/P-1/2 KC975. . . . . **612.8**
   Touch. /1985/P-1/2 KC976. . . . . **612.8**
ROYSTON, A/Senses: a lift-the-flap body book. /1993/
1-3/4 KC977. . . . . **612.8**
SHOWERS, P/Look at your eyes. Rev. ed. /1992/
P-1/2 KC978. . . . . **612.8**

Separation (Psychology)--Bibliography.
RUDMAN, MK/Books to help children cope with separation and
loss: an annotated bibliography. 4th ed. /1993/
/KA025. . . . . **PROF 016.1559**

Separation anxiety--Fiction.
FOWLER, SG/I'll see you when the moon is full. /1994/
K-2/2 KF568 . . . . **E**
FREEMAN, S/Cuckoo's child. /1996/5-A/5 KH142 . . . . **Fic**
JOHNSON, D/What will Mommy do when I'm at school? /1990/
K-1/2 KF836 . . . . **E**
VIORST, J/Good-bye book. /1988/P-2/2 KG662. . . . . **E**

Sephardim--History.
FINKELSTEIN, NH/Other 1492: Jewish settlement in the new world.
/1992/5-6/8 KE687 . . . . **946**
Sequoia SEE Giant Sequoya.

Sequoyah.
KLAUSNER, J/Sequoyah's gift: a portrait of the Cherokee leader. /
1993/5-6/7 KE535 . . . . **B SEQUOYAH**

Serengeti National Park (Tanzania).
LINDBLAD, L/Serengeti migration: Africa's animals on the move. /
1994/5-6/10 KC497 . . . . **591.96**
PETERS, LW/Serengeti. /1989/4-6/6 KE738 . . . . **967.8**
Serpents SEE Snakes.

Serra, Junipero.
WHITE, FM/Story of Junipero Serra: brave adventurer. /1996/
4-6/7 KE536 . . . . **B SERRA, J.**

Service dogs--Fiction.
OSOFSKY, A/My Buddy. /1992/K-2/2 KG201 . . . . **E**

Service stations--Fiction.
KIRK, D/Lucky's 24-hour garage. /1996/K-2/4 KF907 . . . . **E**

Seven Wonders of the World.
CASELLI, G/Wonders of the world. /1992/4-A/8 KD382. . . . **720**

Sewage disposal.
COOMBS, KM/Flush!: treating wastewater. /1995/
5-6/10 KD080 . . . . **628.3**

Sewing.
HOFFMAN, C/Sewing by hand. /1994/3-5/3 KD297 . . . . . **646.2**

Sewing--Fiction.
KLINTING, L/Bruno the tailor. /1996/K-2/2 KF913 . . . . **E**
Sex SEE Reproduction.
Sex education SEE ALSO Sex instruction.

Sex in mass media.
SEXUALITY (VIDEOCASSETTE). /1995/6/KC956 . . . . **VCR 612.6**

Sex instruction.
BOY TO MAN. 3RD ED. (VIDEOCASSETTE). /1992/
5-6/KC944. **VCR 612.6**
FEELINGS: INSIDE, OUTSIDE, UPSIDE DOWN (VIDEOCASSETTE).
/1992/6/KC946. . . . . **VCR 612.6**
HARRIS, RH/It's perfectly normal: a book about changing bodies,
growing up, sex, and sexual health. /1994/5-6/6 KC949 . . **612.6**
MADARAS, L/What's happening to my body? Book for girls. Rev.
ed. /1983/5-6/9 KC952. . . . . **612.6**
NEW, IMPROVED ME: UNDERSTANDING BODY CHANGES
(VIDEOCASSETTE). /1991/5-6/KC953. . . . . . . **VCR 612.6**
SEXUALITY (VIDEOCASSETTE). /1995/6/KC956 . . . **VCR 612.6**

Sex role--Fiction.
DE PAOLA, T/Oliver Button is a sissy. /1979/K-2/2 KF477 . . . . **E**
DYGARD, TJ/Forward pass. /1989/5-A/6 KH091 . . . . **Fic**
GORMAN, C/Miraculous makeover of Lizard Flanagan. /c1994,
1996/5-A/3 KH182. . . . . **Fic**
HYATT, PR/Coast to coast with Alice. /1995/4-6/5 KH312 . . . **Fic**
JACKSON, A/Blowing bubbles with the enemy. /1993/
4-6/5 KH317 . . . . **Fic**
KING-SMITH, D/Lady Daisy (Talking book). /1995/
4-6/KH350. . . . . **TB Fic**
LATTIMORE, DN/Frida Maria: a story of the old Southwest. /
1994/1-3/2 KF949 . . . . **E**

STAPLES, SF/Shabanu, daughter of the wind. /1989/
6-A/6 KH748 . . . . **Fic**
WALTER, MP/Justin and the best biscuits in the world. /1986/
4-6/6 KH839 . . . . **Fic**

Sexually abused children.
WHEN SHOULD YOU TELL?: DEALING WITH ABUSE
(VIDEOCASSETTE). /1995/5-6/KB018 . . . . **VCR 362.76**

Shadow pictures.
WEBB, PH/Shadowgraphs anyone can make. /1991/
K-6/KD753. **793.9**

Shadows.
BULLA, CR/What makes a shadow? Rev. ed. /1994/
K-2/2 KC106 . . . . **CE 535**
GOOR, R/Shadows: here, there, and everywhere. /1981/
1-3/5 KC111 . . . . **535**

Shadows--Experiments.
ZUBROWSKI, B/Shadow play: making pictures with light and lenses.
/1995/4-8/7 KC117 . . . . **535**

Shadows--Fiction.
ASCH, F/Bear shadow. /1985/P-2/2 KF173 . . . . **E**
NARAHASHI, K/I have a friend. /1987/P-2/2 KG166 . . . . . **CE E**

Shadows--Pictorial works.
HOBAN, T/Shadows and reflections. /1990/P-6/KC112. . . . **535**
Shaka, Zula Chief SEE Chaka, Zula Chief.

Shakers.
BIAL, R/Shaker home. /1994/4-6/8 KA717 . . . . **289**
BOLICK, NO/Shaker villages. /1993/5-6/8 KA718 . . . . **289**

Shakers--Fiction.
GAEDDERT, L/Hope. /1995/5-A/6 KH148 . . . . **Fic**

Shakespeare, William.
STANLEY, D/Bard of Avon: the story of William Shakespeare. /
1992/4-6/7 KE538 . . . . **B SHAKESPEARE**

Shakespeare, William--Adaptations.
COVILLE, B/William Shakespeare's A midsummer night's dream. /
1996/4-6/4 KE114 . . . . **822.3**
LAMB, C/Tales from Shakespeare. /1979/A/9 KE115 . . . . . **822.3**
SHAKESPEARE FOR CHILDREN (SOUND RECORDING
CASSETTE). /1995/4-6/KE117 . . . . **SRC 822.3**

Shakespeare, William--Quotations.
SOMETHING RICH AND STRANGE: A TREASURY OF
SHAKESPEARE'S VERSE. /1995/6-A/KE118 . . . . . **822.3**

Shakespeare, William--Stage history.
MORLEY, J/Shakespeare's theater. /1994/4-A/7 KD689 . . . . **792**

Shakespeare, William. Macbeth.
ROSS, S/Shakespeare and Macbeth: the story behind the play. /
1994/5-A/7 KE116 . . . . **822.3**
Shape SEE ALSO Size.

Shape.
HOBAN, T/Circles, triangles, and squares. /1974/P-1/KB990 . **516**
   Dots, spots, speckles, and stripes. /1987/P-A/KA613 . . . **152.14**
   Is it red? Is it yellow? Is it blue? An adventure in color. /1978/
   P/KA614. . . . . **152.14**
   Shapes, shapes, shapes. /1986/2-6/KB991 . . . . **516**
   Shapes and things. /c1970/P-1/KA617 . . . . **152.14**
   Spirals, curves, fanshapes and lines. /1992/P-2/KB992 . . . **516**
MACDONALD, S/Sea shapes. /1994/P-2/KB993 . . . . **516**
REISS, JJ/Shapes. /c1974/P-1/KB994 . . . . **516**

Shape--Fiction.
CHARLES, NN/What am I?: looking through shapes at apples and
grapes. /1994/P-2/2 KF378 . . . . **E**
EHLERT, L/Color farm. /1990/P-K/KF515 . . . . **E**
   Color zoo. /1989/P-1/2 KF516 . . . . **E**
SERFOZO, M/There's a square: a book about shapes. /1996/
P-1/1 KG442 . . . . **E**

Sharing--Fiction.
GREENSTEIN, E/Mrs. Rose's garden. /1996/K-2/3 KF643 . . . . . **E**
HUTCHINS, P/Doorbell rang. /1986/P-2/2 KF797 . . . . **CE E**
JAKOB, D/My new sandbox. /1996/P-1/1 KF822 . . . . **E**
WALLNER, A/Alcott family Christmas. /1996/1-3/2 KG678 . . . . **E**
Sharks SEE ALSO names of specific species of shark e.g. Sevengill (Shark).

Sharks.
ABOUT SHARKS (VIDEOCASSETTE). /1981/
2-4/KC589. **VCR 597.3**
ARNOLD, C/Watch out for sharks! /1991/4-6/7 KC590 . . . **597.3**
CARRICK, C/Sand tiger shark. /c1977/4-6/7 KC591 . . . . . **597.3**
COLE, J/Hungry, hungry sharks. /1986/1-3/2 KC592 . . . . . **597.3**
GIBBONS, G/Sharks. /1992/P-3/3 KC593. . . . . **597.3**
MARKLE, S/Outside and inside sharks. /1996/
4-6/5 KC594 . . . . **597.3**
SIMON, S/Sharks. /1995/5-6/7 KC595. . . . . **597.3**

Sharks--Fiction.
MAHY, M/Great white man-eating shark: a cautionary tale. /1989/
K-4/5 KG056 . . . . **CE E**

Sharks--Folklore.
WARDLAW, L/Punia and the King of Sharks: a Hawaiian folktale. / 1997/2-3/3 KB672 . . . . **398.24**

Sharp, Timothy James--Journeys--Vietnam.
SCHMIDT, J/Two lands, one heart: an American boy's journey to his mother's Vietnam. /1995/1-3/7 KE719 . . . . **959.7**

Sharpshooters.
ANNIE OAKLEY (VIDEOCASSETTE). /1997/ 3-6/KE479. . . . . **VCR B OAKLEY, A.**
WUKOVITS, JF/Annie Oakley. /1997/ 5-6/8 KE480 . . . . **B OAKLEY, A.**

Shawnee Indians--Biography.
CONNELL, K/These lands are ours: Tecumseh's fight for the Old Northwest. /1993/5-6/7 KE559 . . . . **B TECUMSEH**

Sheep--Fiction.
KRUMGOLD, J/And now Miguel. /1953/6-A/5 KH382 . . . **CE Fic**
MACAULAY, D/Baaa. /1985/5-A/7 KH431 . . . . **Fic**
SANDERS, SR/Warm as wool. /1992/3-5/5 KH675 . . . . . . **Fic**
SHAW, N/Sheep in a jeep. /1986/K-3/2 KG489 . . . . **E**
TAYLOR, W/Agnes the sheep. /1990/5-A/6 KH786 . . . . . . **Fic**

Sheep dogs.
ANCONA, G/Sheep dog. /1985/A/8 KD227 . . . . **636.737**

Sheep ranches.
ANCONA, G/Sheep dog. /1985/A/8 KD227 . . . . **636.737**

Shelley, Kate.
SAN SOUCI, RD/Kate Shelley: bound for legend. /1995/ 3-5/5 KE539 . . . . **B SHELLEY, K.**

Shells.
FLORIAN, D/Discovering seashells. /1986/4-5/7 KC511. . . . . **594**
REHDER, HA/Audubon Society field guide to North American seashells. /1981/3-6/KC516 . . . . **594**
ZOEHFELD, KW/What lives in a shell? /1994/P-1/2 KC517 . . **594**

Shells--Fiction.
KALAN, R/Moving day. /1996/P-1/1 KF865. . . . . **E**

Shelters for the homeless.
HUBBARD, J/Lives turned upside down: homeless children in their own words and photographs. /1996/3-6/4 KB009. . . . . . **362.5**

Sherburne, Andrew.
SHERBURNE, A/Memoirs of Andrew Sherburne: patriot and privateer of the American Revolution. /1993/5-A/8 KE886 . **973.3**

Shipbuilding--Fiction.
SMITH, EB/Seashore book. /1985/3-6/9 KH724 . . . . **Fic**

Ships.
BARTON, B/Boats. /1986/P-1/2 KB151 . . . . **387.2**
GIBBONS, G/Boat book. /1983/P-2/3 KB152 . . . . **387.2**
STEELE, P/Boats. /1991/4-6/6 KD065 . . . . **623.8**
VISUAL DICTIONARY OF SHIPS AND SAILING. /1991/ 4-A/6 KB154 . . . . **387.2**

Ships--Fiction.
MACAULAY, D/Ship. /1993/5-6/8 KH433 . . . . **Fic**

Ships--Folklore.
LANG, A/Flying ship. /1995/K-3/6 KB749 . . . . **398.27**
RANSOME, A/Fool of the world and the flying ship: a Russian tale. /c1968/2-5/5 KB765. **398.27**

Ships--History.
KENTLEY, E/Boat. /1992/5-6/7 KD063 . . . . **623.8**

Shipwrecks.
BALLARD, RD/Exploring the Bismarck. /1991/ 5-6/7 KE668 . . . . **940.54**
Exploring the Titanic. /1988/4-6/8 KB025. . . . . **363.12**
COHEN, D/Ghosts of the deep. /1993/4-6/7 KA600 . . . . . **133.1**
KENT, D/Titanic. /1993/4-6/7 KB026 . . . . **363.12**
SPEDDEN, DC/Polar, the Titanic bear. /1994/4-6/7 KE158 . **910.4**
TANAKA, S/On board the Titanic. /1996/4-A/6 KB027 . . **363.12**

Shipwrecks--Fiction.
DEFOE, D/Robinson Crusoe. /1983/5-A/7 KH068 . . . . **Fic**
MACAULAY, D/Ship. /1993/5-6/8 KH433 . . . . **Fic**
MORPURGO, M/Wreck of the Zanzibar. /1995/4-6/3 KH516 . **Fic**
TAYLOR, T/Teetoncey. /c1975/5-A/5 KH784 . . . . **Fic**
Timothy of the cay. /1993/5-A/5 KH785 . . . . **Fic**

Shoes.
YOUNG, R/Sneakers: the shoes we choose! /1991/ 5-6/6 KD344 . . . . **685**
YUE, C/Shoes: their history in words and pictures. /1997/ 4-6/6 KB168 . . . . **391.4**

Shoes--Fiction.
CLEARY, B/Growing-up feet. /1987/P-3/1 KF394. . . . . **E**
HURWITZ, J/New shoes for Silvia. /1993/K-2/2 KF794. . . . . . **E**
O'BRIEN, C/Sam's sneaker search. /1997/P-2/3 KG186 . . . . . **E**
PATRICK, DL/Red dancing shoes. /1993/P-1/2 KG220 . . . . . . **E**
SAN SOUCI, RD/Red heels. /1996/3-5/6 KG393 . . . . **E**
SERFOZO, M/Benjamin Bigfoot. /1993/P-K/2 KG439. . . . . . . **E**
WINTHROP, E/Shoes. /1986/P-K/4 KG745 . . . . **CE E**

Shopping SEE ALSO Consumer education; Department stores; Supermarkets.

Shopping--Fiction.
ENDERLE, JR/What would Mama do? /1995/K-2/2 KF526 . . . . **E**
HUTCHINS, P/Don't forget the bacon! /c1976, 1987/ P-2/3 KF796 . . . . **CE E**
LOBEL, A/On Market Street. /1981/P-1/6 KG009 . . . . **E**

Short stories.
AIKEN, J/Up the chimney down and other stories. /1987/ 4-6/6 KG825 . . . . **Fic**
ALEXANDER, L/Foundling and other tales of Prydain. /c1973, 1982/4-A/5 KG835 . . . . **Fic**
ALFRED HITCHCOCK'S SUPERNATURAL TALES OF TERROR AND SUSPENSE. /c1973, 1983/A/6 KG842. . . . . **Fic**
ALL TIME FAVORITE CHILDREN'S STORIES (TALKING BOOK). / 1993/K-2/KF150. . . . . **TB E**
AMERICAN FAIRY TALES: FROM RIP VAN WINKLE TO THE ROOTABAGA STORIES. /1996/4-6/7 KG843 . . . . **Fic**
ANDERSEN, HC/Hans Christian Andersen in Central Park (Sound recording cassette). /1981/4-6/KG846 . . . . **SRC Fic**
Twelve tales. /1994/3-6/5 KG848 . . . . **Fic**
AVI /Tom, Babette, and Simon: three tales of transformation. / 1995/3-6/4 KG866. . . . . **Fic**
BABBITT, N/Devil's other storybook. /1987/5-6/8 KG868 . . . . **Fic**
Devil's storybook. /1974/3-5/4 KG869 . . . . **CE Fic**
BIRCH, C/Careful what you wish for (Sound recording cassette). / 1993/2-6/KB264. . . . . **SRC 398.2**
Happily-ever-after love stories...more or less (Sound recording cassette). /1987/2-6/KB265. . . . . **SRC 398.2**
Nightmares rising (Sound recording cassette). /1984/ 3-6/KB266. . . . . **SRC 398.2**
BIRTHDAY SURPRISES: TEN GREAT STORIES TO UNWRAP. / 1995/5-A/6 KG900 . . . . **Fic**
BOX AND TWO OTHER TITLES FOR FAMILY ENJOYMENT (VIDEOCASSETTE). /1992/1-4/KF253 . . . . **VCR E**
BROOKE, WJ/Teller of tales. /1994/5-A/5 KG927. . . . . **Fic**
Telling of the tales: five stories. /1994/5-A/7 KG928 . . . . . . **Fic**
Untold tales. /1992/6-A/7 KG929 . . . . **Fic**
BRUCHAC, J/Dog people: native dog stories. /1995/ 4-6/5 KG934 . . . . **Fic**
BRUSCA, MC/Pedro fools the gringo and other tales of a Latin American trickster. /1995/2-4/3 KB429. . . . . **398.22**
BUNTING, E/Jane Martin, dog detective. /1984/1-3/1 KF303 . . **E**
CAMERON, A/Stories Julian tells. /1981/3-4/4 KG970. . . . . . **Fic**
CARUSONE, A/Don't open the door after the sun goes down: tales of the real and unreal. /1994/4-6/4 KG982. . . . . **Fic**
CONRAD, P/Our house: the stories of Levittown. /1995/ 4-6/7 KH022 . . . . **Fic**
COOPER, AJ/Dream quest. /1987/5-A/4 KH024 . . . . **Fic**
DOYLE, AC/Adventures of Sherlock Holmes. /1992/ 6-A/7 KH082 . . . . **Fic**
EDGECOMB, D/Pattysaurus and other tales (Sound recording cassette). /1995/P-3/KF508 . . . . **SRC E**
FOX, P/Little swineherd and other tales. /1996/3-6/4 KH136 . . **Fic**
GORDH, B/Morning, noon and nighttime tales (Sound recording cassette). /1993/K-2/KD565 . . . . **SRC 789.2**
GOROG, J/In a creepy, creepy place and other scary stories. / 1996/4-6/4 KH183 . . . . **Fic**
In a messy, messy room. /1990/4-6/6 KH184 . . . . **Fic**
Please do not touch: a collection of stories. /c1993, 1995/ 6-A/7 KH185 . . . . **Fic**
GRAVEYARD TALES (SOUND RECORDING CASSETTE). /1984/ 3-6/KH193. . . . . **SRC Fic**
HAVEN, K/Fathers and sons (Sound recording cassette). /1991/ 1-4/KF679. . . . . **SRC E**
HEIDE, FP/Tales for the perfect child. /1985/2-5/2 KH233. . . . **Fic**
HEINS, E/Cat and the cook and other fables of Krylov. /1995/ 3-5/6 KH234 . . . . **Fic**
IRVING, W/Rip Van Winkle; and, The Legend of Sleepy Hollow (Talking book). /1986/5-6/KH316 . . . . **TB Fic**
JONES, DW/Stopping for a spell: three fantasies. /1993/ 5-A/6 KH334 . . . . **Fic**
KIPLING, R/Complete Just so stories. /1993/3-5/7 KH360 . . . . **Fic**
Jungle book: the Mowgli stories. /1995/6-A/7 KH363 . . . . . **Fic**
KONIGSBURG, EL/Altogether, one at a time. /c1971/ A/6 KH372 . . . . **Fic**
Throwing shadows. /1979/5-6/6 KH376 . . . . **Fic**
LESTER, J/Long journey home: stories from Black history. /c1972, 1993/6-A/6 KH395. . . . . **Fic**
LEVITT, MJ/Tales of an October moon: haunting stories from New England /1992/4-6/KH399 . . . . **SRC Fic**
LEVOY, M/Witch of Fourth Street, and other stories. /c1972/ 4-6/7 KH400 . . . . **Fic**

Witch of Fourth Street and other stories (Kit). /1978/
4-6/KH401. . . . . **KIT Fic**
LOBEL, A/Mouse tales. /c1972/K-2/2 KG008 . . . . **CE E**
MAHY, M/Horrible story and others (Talking book). /1992/
3-A/KH452 . . . . **TB Fic**
Tall story and other tales. /1992/4-6/4 KH453 . . . . **Fic**
MARSHALL, J/Rats on the range and other stories. /1993/
1-4/2 KH458 . . . . **Fic**
Rats on the roof and other stories. /1991/1-4/2 KH459 . . . . **Fic**
MARTIN, R/Rafe Martin tells his children's books (Talking book). /
1994/K-4/KB341. . . . . **TB 398.2**
MCCLOSKEY, R/Homer Price. /c1943/3-6/5 KH470 . . . . . **CE Fic**
MCKINLEY, R/Knot in the grain and other stories. /1994/
6-A/7 KH489 . . . . **Fic**
MCKISSACK, P/Dark-thirty: Southern tales of the supernatural. /
1992/5-A/6 KH491 . . . . **Fic**
MEDEARIS, AS/Haunts: five hair-raising tales. /1996/
4-6/4 KH495 . . . . **Fic**
NEWBERY HALLOWEEN: A DOZEN SCARY STORIES BY
NEWBERY AWARD-WINNING AUTHORS. /1993/
5-6/5 KH548 . . . . **Fic**
OXFORD BOOK OF SCARYTALES. /1992/6-A/7 KH569 . . . . . **Fic**
PEARCE, AP/Who's afraid? and other strange stories. /1987/
5-6/6 KH590 . . . . **Fic**
POE, EA/Poetry for young people. /1995/5-A/KD998 . . . . . **811**
POMERANTZ, C/Chalk doll. /c1989, 1993/1-3/2 KG263 . . . . . **E**
ROCKWELL, AF/Once upon a time this morning. /1997/
P-K/2 KG344 . . . . **E**
RYLANT, C/Children of Christmas: stories for the season. /c1987,
1993/4-6/6 KH660 . . . . **Fic**
SANDBURG, C/Rootabaga stories. /c1922, 1990/
1-6/7 KH674 . . . . **Fic**
SCIESZKA, J/Stinky Cheese Man and other fairly stupid tales. /
1992/4-6/4 KH686 . . . . **Fic**
SEGAL, L/Tell me a Mitzi. /c1970/K-3/6 KG426 . . . . **E**
Tell me a Trudy. /c1977, 1981/K-3/4 KG427 . . . . **E**
SEUSS, D/Yertle the turtle, and other stories. /c1958/
P-3/3 KG472 . . . . **CE E**
SINGER, IB/Naftali the storyteller and his horse, Sus. /1987/
5-6/5 KH712 . . . . **Fic**
Stories for children. /1984/5-A/6 KH713 . . . . **Fic**
SMITH, JL/Monster in the third dresser drawer and other stories
about Adam Joshua. /1981/2-4/4 KH725 . . . . **Fic**
SOTO, G/Baseball in April and other stories. /1990/
6-A/6 KH738 . . . . **Fic**
Local news. /1993/6-A/6 KH740 . . . . **Fic**
SPOOKY STORIES OF THE SUPERNATURAL. /1985/
6-A/KH745 . . . . **Fic**
STORIES FROM ASIA TODAY: COLLECTION FOR YOUNG
READERS, BOOKS ONE AND TWO. /1979/4-6/6 KH769 . . . **Fic**
SUSSMAN, S/Hanukkah: eight lights around the world. /1988/
3-5/5 KH774 . . . . **Fic**
TENDER TALE OF CINDERELLA PENGUIN (VIDEOCASSETTE). /
1990/1-3/KG600 . . . . **VCR E**
TORRENCE, J/My grandmother's treasure (Sound recording
cassette). /1993/3-5/KH799 . . . . **SRC Fic**
TREASURY OF ANIMAL STORIES. /1992/3-6/6 KH802 . . . . . **Fic**
TREASURY OF GIANT AND MONSTER STORIES. /1992/
3-5/6 KH803 . . . . **Fic**
TREASURY OF SPOOKY STORIES. /1992/4-A/6 KH804 . . . . . **Fic**
TREASURY OF STORIES FOR FIVE YEAR OLDS. /1992/
2-4/5 KH805 . . . . **Fic**
TREASURY OF STORIES FOR SEVEN YEAR OLDS. /1992/
3-5/6 KH806 . . . . **Fic**
TREASURY OF STORIES FOR SIX YEAR OLDS. /1992/
2-4/5 KH807 . . . . **Fic**
TURNER, MW/Instead of three wishes. /1995/5-A/4 KH813 . . **Fic**
VIVELO, J/Chills run down my spine. /1994/5-A/4 KH830 . . . . **Fic**
WESTALL, R/Christmas spirit: two stories. /1994/
6-A/6 KH847 . . . . **Fic**
WHITCHER, S/Real mummies don't bleed: friendly tales for October
nights. /1993/4-6/5 KH849 . . . . **Fic**
WILLARD, N/Sailing to Cythera, and other Anatole stories. /1974/
3-5/6 KH863 . . . . **Fic**
WITHIN REACH: TEN STORIES. /1993/5-A/6 KH874 . . . . **Fic**
WYNNE-JONES, T/Book of changes: stories. /1995/
6-A/3 KH885 . . . . **Fic**
Some of the kinder planets. /1995/5-A/5 KH886 . . . . **Fic**
YEE, P/Tales from Gold Mountain: stories of the Chinese in the New
World. /1989/5-A/7 KH890 . . . . **Fic**

Shoshoni Indians--Biography.
ROWLAND, D/Story of Sacajawea: guide to Lewis and Clark. /
1995/5-6/6 KE529 . . . . **B SACAGAWEA**

SACAJAWEA (VIDEOCASSETTE). /1991/
2-5/KE530. . . . . **VCR B SACAGAWEA**
Shoshoni Indians--Fiction.
SCOTT, AH/Brave as a mountain lion. /1996/3-5/2 KH688 . . . **Fic**
Shoshoni Indians--Folklore.
STEVENS, J/Old bag of bones: a coyote tale. /1996/
1-3/2 KB659 . . . . **398.24**
Show riding.
COLE, J/Riding Silver Star. /1996/3-5/2 KD854 . . . . **798.2**
LITTLE HORSE THAT COULD: THE CONNEMARA STALLION: ERIN
GO BRAGH (VIDEOCASSETTE). /1996/2-6/KD857 . **VCR 798.2**
Show-and-tell presentations--Fiction.
ROCKWELL, AF/Show and tell day. /1997/P-K/2 KG345 . . . . . **E**
Sibling rivalry.
LANDAU, E/Sibling rivalry: brothers and sisters at odds. /1994/
5-A/6 KA885 . . . . **306.875**
Sibling rivalry--Fiction.
HENKES, K/Julius, the baby of the world. /1990/K-3/2 KF707 . . **E**
POLACCO, P/My rotten redheaded older brother. /1994/
1-3/3 KG255 . . . . **E**
STEIG, W/Toy brother. /1996/2-5/6 KG547 . . . . **E**
Siblings SEE Brothers; Brothers and sisters; Sisters.
Sick SEE ALSO names of specific diseases e.g. Cold (Disease).
Sick--Family relationships--Fiction.
VIGNA, J/When Eric's mom fought cancer. /1993/
1-3/3 KG654 . . . . **E**
Sick--Fiction.
AVI /Barn. /1994/5-A/3 KG856 . . . . **Fic**
KELLEY, T/I've got chicken pox. /1994/K-3/2 KF887. . . . . . . **E**
SAY, A/River dream. /1988/K-3/4 KG399 . . . . **E**
Siegal, Aranka.
SIEGAL, A/Upon the head of the goat: a childhood in Hungary
1939-1944. /1981/4-6/8 KE691 . . . . **CE 947.084**
Sierra Madre Occidental Region (Mexico)--Social life and customs.
STAUB, FJ/Children of the Sierra Madre. /1996/
4-6/8 KE839 . . . . **972**
Sierra Nevada Mountains (California and Nevada)--Poetry.
SIEBERT, D/Sierra. /1991/2-6/KE023 . . . . **811**
Sign language SEE ALSO Indians of North America--Sign language.
Sign language.
ANCONA, G/Handtalk zoo. /1989/K-A/KB820. . . . . **419**
BORNSTEIN, H/Night before Christmas: told in sign language: an
adaptation of the original /1994/K-6/KD917 . . . . **811**
CHARLIP, R/Handtalk: an ABC of finger spelling and sign language.
/c1974, 1984/K-A/KB823. **419**
Handtalk birthday: a number and story book in sign language. /
1987/K-3/KB824. . . . . **419**
GREEDY CAT (VIDEOCASSETTE). /1987/
K-3/KB578. . . . . **VCR 398.24**
GREENE, L/Sign language talk. /1989/5-A/9 KB825 . . . . . **419**
GRYSKI, C/Hands on, thumbs up: secret handshakes, fingerprints,
sign languages, and more /1993/5-6/5 KC904 . . . . **611**
MILLER, MB/Handtalk school. /1991/K-A/KB827 . . . . **419**
PARKER, D/Sign for friends (Videocassette). /1991/
3-5/KB828. . . . . **VCR 419**
RANKIN, L/Handmade alphabet. /1991/K-3/KB829 . . . . . **419**
VILLAGE STEW (VIDEOCASSETTE). /1987/
K-3/KB782. . . . . **VCR 398.27**
Sign language--Dictionaries.
BAKER, PJ/My first book of sign. /c1986, 1995/K-3/KB821. . **419**
Sign language--Fiction.
HILL, E/Where's Spot? Sign language edition. /1987/
P-2/2 KF728 . . . . **E**
Sign language--Study and teaching.
BEGINNING AMERICAN SIGN LANGUAGE VIDEOCOURSE
(VIDEOCASSETTE). /1991/3-A/KB822 . . . . **VCR 419**
Sign language--Study and teaching (Elementary)--Activity programs.
HAFER, JC/Come sign with us: sign language activities for children.
2nd. ed. /1996//KA279 . . . . **PROF 419**
Signs and signboards SEE ALSO Traffic signs and signals.
Signs and signboards.
HOBAN, T/I read signs. /1983/P-1/KA800. . . . . **302.23**
I read symbols. /1983/P-1/KA797 . . . . **302.2**
Signs and symbols.
BARTH, E/Holly, reindeer and colored lights: the story of Christmas
symbols. /c1971/5-6/7 KB231 . . . . **394.266**
GIBBONS, G/Puff...flash...bang!: a book about signals. /1993/
1-4/4 KA796 . . . . **302.2**
HOBAN, T/I read signs. /1983/P-1/KA800. . . . . **302.23**
I read symbols. /1983/P-1/KA797 . . . . **302.2**
Signs and symbols--History.
PARKER, NW/Money, money, money: the meaning of the art and
symbols on United States paper /1995/3-6/11 KD506 . . . . **769.5**

Sihasapa Indians--Folklore.
RODANAS, K/Dance of the sacred circle: a Native American tale. /
1994/3-4/5 KB639 . . . . **398.24**

Siksika Indians--Fiction.
HUDSON, J/Sweetgrass. /1989/6-A/5 KH286 . . . . **Fic**
YOLEN, J/Sky dogs. /1990/2-3/6 KG780 . . . . **E**

Siksika Indians--Folklore.
GOBLE, P/Lost children: the boys who were neglected. /1993/
3-5/5 KB707 . . . . **398.26**

Silhouettes.
HOBAN, T/Shapes and things. /c1970/P-1/KA617 . . . . . . **152.14**

Silk--Fiction.
HONG, LT/Empress and the silkworm. /1995/1-3/6 KF766 . . . . **E**

Silk Road--History.
MAJOR, JS/Silk Route: 7,000 miles of history. /c1995, 1996/
4-6/6 KE701 . . . . **950**

Silkworms.
JOHNSON, SA/Silkworms. /1982/4-6/8 KD241 . . . . **638**

Silversmithing.
FRITZ, J/And then what happened, Paul Revere? /c1973/
5-6/6 KE510 . . . . **CE B REVERE, P.**

Similarity (Psychology).
ROTNER, S/Faces. /1994/P-1/2 KC924 . . . . **612**

Simon Rodia's Towers (Watts, Los Angeles, Calif.).
ZELVER, P/Wonderful Towers of Watts. /1994/2-4/6 KD387 . **725**

Simple machines.
SIMPLE MACHINE (VIDEOCASSETTE). /1993/
5-6/KC098. . . . . **VCR 531**
SIMPLE MACHINES: USING MECHANICAL ADVANTAGE
(VIDEOCASSETTE). /1992/5-6/KC099 . . . . **VCR 531**

Simple machines--Experiments.
ARDLEY, N/Science book of machines. /1992/
4-6/4 KD050 . . . . **621.8**

Singers.
FERRIS, J/What I had was singing: the story of Marian Anderson. /
1994/5-A/6 KE236 . . . . **B ANDERSON, M.**
MCKISSACK, P/Paul Robeson: a voice to remember. /1992/
2-5/2 KE514 . . . . **B ROBESON, P.**
RODRIGUEZ, J/Gloria Estefan. /1996/
5-6/6 KE340 . . . . **B ESTEFAN, G.**
TURK, R/Ray Charles: soul man. /1996/
5-A/8 KE286 . . . . **B CHARLES, R.**

Singing--Fiction.
BUCK, N/Sid and Sam. /1996/P-1/1 KF291 . . . . **E**

Singing--History.
SHIPTON, A/Singing. /1994/4-6/7 KD527 . . . . **782**

Singing games.
ALL-TIME FAVORITE DANCES (SOUND RECORDING CASSETTE).
/1991/K-6/KD603. . . . . **SRC 789.3**
CAMPBELL, PS/Roots and branches: a legacy of multicultural music
for children. /1994//KA320 . . . . **BA PROF 789.3**
COLE, J/Eentsy, weentsy spider: fingerplays and action rhymes. /
1991/P-K/KD706 . . . . **793.4**
GALLINA, J/A to Z, the animals and me (Sound recording
cassette). /1993/P-1/KD612 . . . . **SRC 789.3**
GLASS, H/Children's all-time Mother Goose favorites (Sound
recording cassette). /1989//KA275. . . . . **SRC PROF 398.8**
GREEN CHILI JAM BAND /Magic bike (Sound recording cassette).
/1991/P-3/KD613 . . . . **SRC 789.3**
HALLUM, R/Fingerplays and footplays (Videocassette). /1997/
P-K/KD708. . . . . **VCR 793.4**
JACK, D/Gotta hop (Sound recording cassette). /1990/
K-3/KD622 . . . . **SRC 789.3**
JENKINS, E/Ella Jenkins live!: at the Smithsonian (Videocassette). /
1991/P-K/KD627 . . . . **VCR 789.3**
Rhythm and game songs for the little ones (Sound recording
cassette). /1990/P-K/KD630 . . . . **SRC 789.3**
NGUYEN, PT/From rice paddies and temple yards: traditional music
of Vietnam. /c1990, 1992//KA317. . . . . **BA PROF 789.2**
PALMER, H/Can a cherry pie wave goodbye?: songs for learning
through music and movement /1991/P-K/KD641 . . . . **SRC 789.3**
Getting to know myself (Sound recording cassette). /1972/
P-1/KA641. . . . . **SRC 155.2**
Sammy and other songs from "Getting to know myself"
(Videocassette). /1993/P-1/KD643 . . . . **VCR 789.3**
So big: activity songs for little ones (Compact disc). /1994/
P-2/KD644. . . . . **CD 789.3**
Stepping out with Hap Palmer (Videocassette). /1994/
P-2/KD645. . . . . **VCR 789.3**
PRESCHOOL ACTION TIME (SOUND RECORDING CASSETTE). /
1988/P/KD650. . . . . **SRC 789.3**
SAM, S/Silent temples, songful hearts: traditional music of
Cambodia. /1991//KA318 . . . . **BA PROF 789.2**

**SHAKE IT TO THE ONE THAT YOU LOVE THE BEST: PLAY
SONGS AND LULLABIES FROM BLACK MUSICAL TRADITIONS.**
/1989/K-4/KD767. . . . . **BA 796.1**
STEWART, G/Multicultural rhythm stick fun (Sound recording
cassette). /1992/P-2/KD768 . . . . **SRC 796.1**
Pre-K hooray! (Sound recording cassette). /1993/
P-K/KD659. . . . . **SRC 789.3**
Preschool favorites (Sound recording cassette). /1990/
P-K/KD660. . . . . **SRC 789.3**
WEIMER, TE/Fingerplays and action chants: volume 1: animals. /
1995/P-1/KD710 . . . . **BA 793.4**
WEISSMAN, J/Joining hands with other lands: multicultural songs
and games /1993/K-3/KD666 . . . . **SRC 789.3**

Single-parent family SEE ALSO Unmarried mothers.

Single-parent family.
ROSENBERG, MB/Living with a single parent. /1992/
4-6/6 KA872 . . . . **306.85**

Single-parent family--Fiction.
ACKERMAN, K/By the dawn's early light. /1994/K-2/5 KF129 . . **E**
AUCH, MJ/Latchkey dog. /1994/3-5/4 KG855 . . . . **Fic**
BUNTING, E/In-between days. /1994/4-6/4 KG943 . . . . **Fic**
BYARS, BC/McMummy. /1993/5-A/5 KG961 . . . . **Fic**
MEAD, A/Junebug. /1995/5-A/5 KH493 . . . . **Fic**
NAYLOR, PR/Alice in rapture, sort of. /1989/6-A/6 KH533 . . . **Fic**
NESBIT, E/Railway children. /1994/4-5/7 KH543 . . . . **Fic**
PERKINS, LR/Home lovely. /1995/K-2/5 KG233 . . . . **E**
SNYDER, ZK/Fool's gold. /1993/6-A/7 KH732 . . . . **Fic**
WOLITZER, H/Toby lived here. /c1978, 1986/4-6/6 KH878 . . . **Fic**
YOUNG, RT/Moving Mama to town. /1997/6-A/4 KH900 . . . **Fic**

Single-parent family--Poetry.
CLIFTON, L/Everett Anderson's Christmas coming. /1991/
P-1/KD925. . . . . **811**
GRIMES, N/Meet Danitra Brown. /1994/2-4/KD949 . . . . . . **811**

Sioux Indians.
GOBLE, P/Red Hawk's account of Custer's last battle; the Battle of
the Little Bighorn, /c1969, 1992/5-6/6 KE914. . . . . **973.8**

Sisters--Fiction.
CLEARY, B/Beezus and Ramona. /1955/2-5/3 KG992 . . . . **Fic**
COSSI, O/Great getaway. /1991/K-2/2 KF426. . . . . **E**
HENKES, K/Sheila Rae, the brave. /1987/P-2/4 KF711 . . . . . **E**
HOLLAND, I/Journey home. /1993/6-A/6 KH270. . . . . **Fic**
JOHNSON, A/One of three. /1991/P-1/2 KF832 . . . . **E**
LATTIMORE, DN/Punga, the goddess of ugly. /1993/
3-5/4 KF950 . . . . **E**
LILLIE, P/Floppy teddy bear. /1995/P-1/2 KF982 . . . . **E**
LOH, M/Tucking mommy in. /1987/P-2/2 KG017. . . . . **E**
LOPEZ, L/Birthday swap. /1997/K-2/2 KG032. . . . . **E**
MASTERS, SR/Libby Bloom. /1995/3-5/6 KH460. . . . . **Fic**
MCKAY, H/Exiles. /1992/6-A/7 KH478 . . . . **Fic**
Exiles at home. /1994/5-A/7 KH479 . . . . **Fic**
O'CONNOR, J/Lulu and the witch baby. /1986/K-3/2 KG188 . . **E**
PARTRIDGE, E/Clara and the hoodoo man. /1996/
5-A/3 KH572 . . . . **Fic**
SCHWARTZ, A/Annabelle Swift, Kindergartner. /1988/
P-2/1 KG413 . . . . **CE E**

Sisters--Folklore.
SAN SOUCI, RD/Talking eggs. /1989/3-5/5 KB415 . . . **CE 398.21**

Sitting Bull, Sioux Chief.
ADLER, DA/Picture book of Sitting Bull. /1993/
3-4/5 KE540 . . . . **B SITTING BULL**
BRUCHAC, J/Boy called Slow: the true story of Sitting Bull. /1994/
3-4/6 KE541 . . . . **B SITTING BULL**
FREEDMAN, R/Indian chiefs. /1987/5-6/8 KE749 . . . . . . **970.1**
ST. GEORGE, J/To see with the heart: the life of Sitting Bull. /
1996/5-A/6 KE542 . . . . **B SITTING BULL**

Six Flags Great Adventure Safari Park (N.J.).
ARNOLD, C/Zebra. /1987/5-6/8 KC804 . . . . **599.665**

Size.
CLEMENT, R/Counting on Frank. /1991/1-6/5 KB927 . . . . . **510**
HOBAN, T/Is it red? Is it yellow? Is it blue? An adventure in color.
/1978/P/KA614. . . . . **152.14**
Shapes and things. /c1970/P-1/KA617 . . . . **152.14**
JOHNSON, J/How big is a whale? /1995/2-5/5 KC462 . . . **591.4**
WELLS, RE/Is a blue whale the biggest thing there is? /1993/
K-2/2 KC087 . . . . **530.8**
What's smaller than a pygmy shrew? /1995/3-6/5 KC140 . **539.7**

Size--Fiction.
COVILLE, B/Jeremy Thatcher, dragon hatcher: a magic shop book. /
1991/4-A/4 KH036. . . . . **CE Fic**
HEIDE, FP/Shrinking of Treehorn. /c1971/3-A/6 KH232. . . **CE Fic**
HENKES, K/Biggest boy. /1995/P-2/2 KF701. . . . . **E**
HERMAN, RA/Pal the pony. /1996/K-1/2 KF714. . . . . **E**
HOWARD, E/Big seed. /1993/1-3/2 KF775 . . . . **E**
HUTCHINS, P/Shrinking mouse. /1997/P-K/1 KF803 . . . . **E**

Size and shape
JONAS, A/Holes and peeks. /1984/P-K/1 KF845 . . . . E
JOYCE, W/George shrinks. /1985/P-2/2 KF860 . . . . E
KELLOGG, S/Much bigger than Martin. /c1976/K-2/2 KF891. . . E
MILLER, M/Now I'm big. /1996/P/2 KG135 . . . . E
MOLLEL, TM/Big boy. /1995/K-2/3 KG150 . . . . E
MURPHY, SJ/Best bug parade. /1996/P-1/1 KG163 . . . . E
WISLER, GC/Jericho's journey. /1993/5-A/6 KH870 . . . . **Fic**
Size and shape.
GOMI, T/Who hid it? /1991/P-K/2 KF630 . . . . E
Skara Brae Site (Scotland).
ARNOLD, C/Stone Age farmers beside the sea: Scotland's
prehistoric village of Skara Brae. /1997/3-6/8 KE677 . . . . . **941.1**
Skateboards--Fiction.
RICHEMONT, E/Magic skateboard. /1992/3-5/3 KH631 . . . . . **Fic**
Skating SEE Ice skating; Roller skating.
Skeleton.
PARKER, S/Skeleton. /1988/5-6/8 KC285 . . . . **573.7**
Skeleton and movement. Rev. ed. /1989/5-6/7 KC958 . . . **612.7**
SAUNDERSON, J/Muscles and bones. /1992/
5-6/5 KC959 . . . . **612.7**
VISUAL DICTIONARY OF THE SKELETON. /1995/
4-A/8 KC286 . . . . **573.7**
YOUR BODY: MUSCULAR AND SKELETAL SYSTEMS
(VIDEOCASSETTE). /1994/5-6/KC961 . . . . **VCR 612.7**
Skeleton--Fiction.
AHLBERG, J/Funnybones. /c1980, 1981/P-3/2 KF142 . . . . E
JOHNSTON, T/Soup bone. /1990/K-2/2 KF841 . . . . E
LOREDO, E/Boogie Bones. /1997/K-2/3 KG034 . . . . E
Skeleton--Folkore.
DEFELICE, CC/Dancing skeleton. /1996/3-6/6 KB684 . . **CE 398.25**
Skin.
SHOWERS, P/Your skin and mine. Rev. ed. /1991/
K-2/2 KC960 . . . . **612.7**
Skin diving SEE ALSO Underwater exploration.
Skinks--Fiction.
MONFRIED, L/No more animals! /1995/1-3/2 KH502 . . . . . . **Fic**
Skis and skiing.
EVANS, J/Skiing. /1992/5-A/7 KD837 . . . . **796.93**
Skunks--Fiction.
GRAY, LM/Is there room on the feather bed? /1997/
K-2/4 KF636 . . . . E
SERVICE, PF/Stinker from space. /1988/3-5/5 KH700 . . . . . . **Fic**
STEVENS, JR/Carlos and the skunk./Carlos y el zorrillo. /1997/
1-3/3 KG554 . . . . E
Sky.
WYLER, R/Starry sky. /1989/P-2/2 KC056 . . . . **523.8**
Sky--Folklore.
GERSON, M/Why the sky is far away: a Nigerian folktale. /1992/
2-4/5 KB705 . . . . **398.26**
MORONEY, L/Elinda who danced in the sky: an Estonian folktale. /
1990/3-5/5 KB407 . . . . **398.21**
Skyscrapers.
DUNN, A/Skyscrapers. /1993/3-6/7 KD383 . . . . **720**
GIBBONS, G/Up goes the skyscraper! /1986/K-3/6 KD356 . . **690**
MICHAEL, D/How skyscrapers are made. /1987/
A/10 KD358 . . . . **690**
Slang SEE English language--Slang.
Slave trade--Fiction.
FOX, P/Slave dancer: a novel. /c1973/5-6/6 KH139 . . . . . **CE Fic**
Slavery.
AMISTAD REVOLT: "ALL WE WANT IS MAKE US FREE"
(VIDEOCASSETTE). /1996/6-A/KA926 . . . . **VCR 326**
GORRELL, GK/North Star to freedom: the story of the
Underground Railroad. /1997/5-6/8 KE905 . . . . **973.7**
KATZ, WL/Breaking the chains: African-American slave resistance. /
1990/A/8 KE966 . . . . **975**
Slavery--Biography.
BARRETT, T/Nat Turner and the slave revolt. /c1993, 1995/
5-6/6 KE577 . . . . **B TURNER, N.**
ELISH, D/Harriet Tubman and the Underground Railroad. /1993/
4-6/4 KE574 . . . . **B TUBMAN, H.**
PETRY, A/Harriet Tubman: conductor on the Underground Railroad.
/c1955, 1996/A/7 KE575 . . . . **B TUBMAN, H.**
STEAL AWAY: THE HARRIET TUBMAN STORY (VIDEOCASSETTE).
/1997/4-A/KE576. . . . . **VCR B TUBMAN, H.**
YATES, E/Amos Fortune, free man. /c1950/
A/7 KE348 . . . . **B FORTUNE, A.**
Slavery--Collections.
LESTER, J/To be a slave. /c1968/A/7 KA928 . . . . **326**
Slavery--Drama.
DAVIS, O/Escape to freedom: a play about young Frederick
Douglass. /c1976, 1990/A-6/7 KE091 . . . . **812**

Slavery--Fiction.
BROTHER FUTURE (VIDEOCASSETTE). /c1991, 1997/
6-A/KG930 . . . . **VCR Fic**
COLLIER, JL/Jump ship to freedom. /1981/5-6/5 KH015 . . . . . **Fic**
War comes to Willy Freeman. /1983/5-6/6 KH017 . . . . **Fic**
CONNELLY, B/Follow the drinking gourd: a story of the
Underground Railroad (Videocassette). /1992/2-4/KF412 . **VCR E**
FOLLOW THE DRINKING GOURD. /1993/2-4/KF563 . . . . **BA E**
FORRESTER, S/Sound the jubilee. /1995/5-A/6 KH133 . . . . . **Fic**
GAEDDERT, L/Breaking free. /1994/5-A/5 KH147 . . . . **Fic**
GUCCIONE, LD/Come morning. /1995/4-6/3 KH205 . . . . . . **Fic**
HOOKS, WH/Freedom's fruit. /1996/4-6/3 KH279 . . . . **Fic**
HOPKINSON, D/Sweet Clara and the freedom quilt. /1993/
1-3/4 KF770 . . . . E
JOHNSTON, T/Wagon. /1996/2-5/2 KF843 . . . . E
LYONS, ME/Letters from a slave girl: the story of Harriet Jacobs. /
1992/4-6/4 KH430 . . . . **Fic**
MONJO, FN/Drinking gourd. Newly illustrated ed. /1993/
1-3/2 KG151 . . . . E
PATERSON, K/Jip: his story. /1996/5-A/7 KH577 . . . . **Fic**
ROSENBURG, JM/William Parker: rebel without rights: a novel
based on fact. /1996/6-A/7 KH654 . . . . **Fic**
ROSEN, MJ/School for Pompey Walker. /1995/4-8/6 KH653 . **Fic**
TURNER, A/Nettie's trip south. /1987/5-A/6 KH812 . . . . **Fic**
WRIGHT, CC/Jumping the broom. /1994/K-3/5 KG771 . . . . . E
Slavery--History.
BLACK IS MY COLOR: THE AFRICAN AMERICAN EXPERIENCE
(VIDEOCASSETTE). /1992/4-6/KA838 . . . . **VCR 305.8**
Slavery--Insurrections, etc.
MCKISSACK, P/Rebels against slavery: American slave revolts. /
1996/4-6/7 KA929 . . . . **326**
Slavery--Jamaica--Fiction.
BERRY, J/Ajeemah and his son. /1992/6-A/7 KG899 . . . . **Fic**
Slavery--United States SEE Abolitionists; Afro-Americans; Slave trade;
Underground railroad.
Slaves.
SHERROW, V/Phillis Wheatley. /1992/
4-6/7 KE591 . . . . **B WHEATLEY, P.**
Slaves--Poetry.
LAWRENCE, J/Harriet and the Promised Land. /1993/
K-3/KD969 . . . . **811**
Slaves--Social life and customs.
MCKISSACK, P/Christmas in the big house, Christmas in the
quarters. /1994/4-A/6 KE967 . . . . **975**
Slaves--Songs and music.
SILVERMAN, J/Slave songs. /1994/5-A/KD592 . . . . **789.2**
Slavic Countries--Folklore.
DE REGNIERS, BS/Little Sister and the Month Brothers. /c1976,
1994/2-3/2 KB501 . . . . **398.23**
VOJTECH, A/Marushka and the Month Brothers: a folktale. /1996/
1-3/4 KB513 . . . . **398.23**
Sled dog racing.
CRISMAN, R/Racing the Iditarod Trail. /1993/
5-6/7 KD858 . . . . **798.8**
PAULSEN, G/Puppies, dogs, and blue northers: reflections on being
raised by a pack of sled /1996/3-6/7 KD859 . . . . **798.8**
Woodsong. /1990/5-A/6 KD824 . . . . **796.5**
SHAHAN, S/Dashing through the snow: the story of the Jr.
Iditarod. /1997/4-6/7 KD860 . . . . **798.8**
Sled dog racing--Fiction.
PAULSEN, G/Dogteam. /1993/1-3/4 KG221 . . . . E
Sled dogs.
PAULSEN, G/Puppies, dogs, and blue northers: reflections on being
raised by a pack of sled /1996/3-6/7 KD859 . . . . **798.8**
Woodsong. /1990/5-A/6 KD824 . . . . **796.5**
STANDIFORD, N/Bravest dog ever: the true story of Balto. /1989/
1-3/2 KD223 . . . . **636.7**
Sled dogs--Fiction.
LONDON, J/White Fang. /c1905, 1985/6-A/6 KH417 . . . . . **Fic**
MOREY, W/Kavik, the wolf dog. /c1968/4-6/6 KH510 . . . . . **Fic**
Scrub dog of Alaska. /c1971, 1989/5-A/6 KH511 . . . . . . **Fic**
PAULSEN, G/Dogteam. /1993/1-3/4 KG221 . . . . E
PINKWATER, DM/Aunt Lulu. /1991/P-2/2 KG244 . . . . E
Sleds SEE ALSO Bobsledding.
Sleds--Fiction.
CHAPMAN, C/Snow on snow on snow. /1994/K-3/3 KF377 . . . E
WINTHROP, E/Sledding. /1989/P-K/2 KG746. . . . . E
Sleep SEE ALSO Bedtime.
Sleep.
SHOWERS, P/Sleep is for everyone. Newly illustrated ed. /1997/
K-2/3 KC979 . . . . **612.8**
ZOLOTOW, C/Sleepy book. /c1958, 1988/P-1/KC481 . . . . **591.5**
Sleep--Fiction.
APPELT, K/Bayou lullaby. /1995/P-2/5 KF163 . . . . E

BROWN, MW/Little Donkey close your eyes. /1995/
P-K/2 KF286 . . . . E
COOPER, H/Boy who wouldn't go to bed. /1997/P-1/2 KF422 . E
DALE, P/Ten out of bed. /1994/P-1/2 KF446 . . . . E
GINSBURG, M/Asleep, asleep. /1992/P/1 KF622 . . . . E
HAZELAAR, C/Zoo dreams. /1997/P-1/3 KF687 . . . . E
HOWARD, JR/When I'm sleepy. /1996/P-K/8 KF776 . . . . E
HUTCHINS, P/Good-night owl. /c1972/P-2/3 KF798 . . . . . **CE** E
SEUSS, D/I am not going to get up today! /1987/
1-3/2 KG461 . . . . E
    I am not going to get up today! plus three more Dr. Seuss classics
    (Videocassette). /1991/1-3/KG462 . . . . **VCR** E
WOOD, A/Napping house. /1984/P-2/7 KG764 . . . . . . **CE** E
Sleep--Poetry.
PRELUTSKY, J/My parents think I'm sleeping. /1985/
2-5/KE009 811
SLEEP, BABY, SLEEP: LULLABIES AND NIGHT POEMS. /1994/
P-K/KD889 . . . . 808.81
Sleeping Beauty (Ballet).
HOROSKO, M/Sleeping Beauty: the ballet story. /1994/
1-5/7 KD695 . . . . 792.8
SPATT, LE/Behind the scenes at the ballet: rehearsing and
performing "The Sleeping /1995/4-6/9 KD697 . . . . 792.8
Sleepovers--Fiction.
BROWN, MT/Arthur's first sleepover. /1994/K-2/2 KF275 . . . . . E
CASELEY, J/Slumber party! /1996/2-3/2 KF369 . . . . E
JACKSON, I/Somebody's new pajamas. /1996/3-5/4 KH318 . . **Fic**
WELLS, R/Edward's overwhelming overnight. /1995/
P-1/2 KG699 . . . . E
Sleighs and sledges SEE Sleds.
Slides (Photography)--Catalogs.
DETROIT INSTITUTE OF ARTS /Catalogue of color reproductions. /
n.d./ /KA307 . . . . **PROF 703**
Slow learning children--United States--Case studies.
STEVENS, SH/Classroom success for the LD and ADHD child. /
1997/ /KA186 . . . . **PROF 371.92**
Slugs (Mollusks)--Fiction.
EDWARDS, PD/Some smug slug. /1996/P-2/3 KF513 . . . . E
Slums SEE ALSO Housing.
Smallpox--Fiction.
HUDSON, J/Sweetgrass. /1989/6-A/5 KH286 . . . . **Fic**
ROCKWOOD, J/To spoil the sun. /c1976, 1994/
6-A/6 KH644 . . . . **Fic**
Smallpox--History.
GIBLIN, JC/When plague strikes: the Black Death, smallpox, AIDS.
/1995/A/11 KD010 . . . . 614.4
Smell.
FABULOUS FIVE: OUR SENSES (VIDEOCASSETTE). /1989/
P-2/KC917 . . . . **VCR 612**
Smith, Emmitt.
THORNLEY, S/Emmitt Smith: relentless rusher. /1997/
4-6/7 KE543 . . . . **B SMITH, E.**
Smith, John.
FRITZ, J/Double life of Pocahontas. /1983/
5-6/6 KE500 . . . . **B POCAHONTAS**
Smith, Lillian H.
LANDS OF PLEASURE: ESSAYS ON LILLIAN H. SMITH AND THE
DEVELOPMENT OF CHILDREN'S LIBRARIES. /1990/
/KA044 . . . . **PROF 020**
Smoking SEE ALSO Tobacco.
Smoking.
BILAL'S DREAM (VIDEOCASSETTE). /1990/
5-6/KD004 . . . . **VCR 613.85**
DRUG DANGER: EASY TO START, HARD TO STOP
(VIDEOCASSETTE). /1992/5-6/KC994 . . . . **VCR 613.8**
DRUG DANGER: IN THE BODY (VIDEOCASSETTE). /1992/
5-6/KD019 . . . . **VCR 616.86**
DUSTY THE DRAGON TALKS TO DR. MARGIE HOGAN ABOUT
TOBACCO (VIDEOCASSETTE). /1990/3-5/KD005 . **VCR 613.85**
KID'S GUIDE TO DRUG, ALCOHOL AND SMOKING
AWARENESS (VIDEOCASSETTE). /1985/
K-4/KA997 . . . . **VCR 362.29**
LET'S TALK ABOUT DRUGS (VIDEOCASSETTE). /1994/
1-3/KC998 . . . . **VCR 613.8**
PRINGLE, LP/Smoking: a risky business. /1996/
4-6/9 KA998 . . . . 362.29
SMOKE SIGNALS (VIDEOCASSETTE). /1995/
5-6/KD006 . . . . **VCR 613.85**
TOBACCO ACTION CURRICULUM: THE YOUNG AND THE
BREATHLESS (VIDEOCASSETTE). /1991/
5-6/KD007 . . . . **VCR 613.85**
TOBACCO FREE YOU AND ME (VIDEOCASSETTE). /1994/
4-6/KD008 . . . . **VCR 613.85**

TROUBLE WITH TOBACCO (VIDEOCASSETTE). /1996/
5-6/KD009 . . . . **VCR 613.85**
Smuggling--Fiction.
AVI /Smugglers' Island. /1994/4-6/5 KG864 . . . . **Fic**
Snails.
BUHOLZER, T/Life of the snail. /1987/4-6/7 KC510 594
JOHNSON, SA/Snails. /1982/4-6/7 KC512 594
OLESEN, J/Snail. /1986/2-4/2 KC515 594
Snails--Fiction.
CUTLER, J/Mr. Carey's garden. /1996/K-2/3 KF442 . . . . E
Snails--Folklore.
JACKSON, E/Precious gift: a Navaho creation myth. /1996/
2-3/2 KB594 . . . . 398.24
Snake River (Wyo.-Wash.).
CRAIGHEAD, C/Eagle and the river. /1994/5-6/7 KC339 . . **577.6**
Snakes SEE ALSO Poisonous snakes; names of snakes e.g. Boa constrictor.
Snakes.
ARNOLD, C/Snake. /1991/5-6/7 KC632 . . . . **597.96**
BROEKEL, R/Snakes. /1982/2-4/2 KC633 . . . . **597.96**
DEWEY, JO/Rattlesnake dance: true tales, mysteries, and rattlesnake
ceremonies. /1997/4-6/4 KC634 . . . . **597.96**
FASCINATING WORLD OF SNAKES (VIDEOCASSETTE). /1996/
5-6/KC635 . . . . **VCR 597.96**
GROSS, RB/Snakes. Rev. ed. /1990/4-6/4 KC636 . . . . . . **597.96**
LAUBER, P/Snakes are hunters. /1988/2-4/3 KC637 . . . . **597.96**
LAVIES, B/Gathering of garter snakes. /1993/
4-6/7 KC638 . . . . **597.96**
LING, M/Snake book. /1997/2-6/6 KC639 . . . . **597.96**
MAESTRO, B/Take a look at snakes. /1992/3-5/6 KC640. **597.96**
MARKLE, S/Outside and inside snakes. /1995/
4-6/4 KC641 . . . . **597.96**
PARSONS, A/Amazing snakes. /1990/2-6/5 KC642 . . . . . **597.96**
SIMON, S/Snakes. /1992/4-6/6 KC643 . . . . **597.96**
Snakes--Fiction.
BAKER, K/Hide and snake. /1991/P-1/2 KF186 . . . . E
CANNON, J/Verdi. /1997/K-2/3 KF336 . . . . E
DAVOL, MW/How Snake got his hiss: an original tale. /1996/
K-2/2 KF450 . . . . E
GRAY, LM/Small Green Snake. /1994/P-2/6 KF637 . . . . E
MCNULTY, F/Snake in the house. /1994/1-3/2 KG115 . . . . . E
NOBLE, TH/Day Jimmy's boa ate the wash. /1980/
K-2/2 KG176 . . . . **CE** E
SHANNON, G/April showers. /1995/P-1/2 KG477 . . . . E
UNGERER, T/Crictor. /c1958/K-2/KG634 . . . . E
Snakes as pets.
GRIEHL, K/Snakes: giant snakes and non-venomous snakes in the
terrarium. /1984/A/9 KD249 . . . . 639.3
Sneakers.
YOUNG, R/Sneakers: the shoes we choose! /1991/
5-6/6 KD344 685
Sneakers--Fiction.
O'BRIEN, C/Sam's sneaker search. /1997/P-2/3 KG186 . . . . . E
Snow SEE ALSO Blizzards.
Snow.
BIANCHI, J/Snow: learning for the fun of it. /1992/
5-A/9 KC208 . . . . 551.57
BRANLEY, FM/Snow is falling. Rev. ed. /1986/
K-1/2 KC210 . . . . 551.57
KAHL, JD/Wet weather: rain showers and snowfall. /1992/
4-6/7 KC212 . . . . 551.57
STEELE, P/Snow: causes and effects. /1991/3-6/7 KC216 . 551.57
Snow--Fiction.
AGELL, C/I slide into the white of winter. /1994/K-2/3 KF137 . . E
BRIGGS, R/Snowman. /1978/P-1/KF265 . . . . **CE** E
BURTON, VL/Katy and the big snow. /c1943, 1973/
P-1/4 KF319 . . . . E
CHAPMAN, C/Snow on snow on snow. /1994/K-3/3 KF377 . . . E
EHLERT, L/Snowballs. /1995/P-2/2 KF520 . . . . E
HADER, B/Big snow. /1948/K-2/5 KF658 . . . . E
HIDAKA, M/Girl from the snow country. /1986/K-2/4 KF725 . . . E
HIMMELMAN, J/Day-off machine. /1990/1-3/1 KF729 . . . . . . E
KEATS, EJ/Snowy day. /c1962, 1963/P-2/2 KF878 . . . . . **CE** E
KELLER, H/Geraldine's big snow. /1988/P-2/4 KF882 . . . . . . E
KESSLER, E/Stan the hot dog man. /1990/1-2/1 KF897 . . . . . E
LEE, HV/In the snow. /1995/1-3/2 KF955 . . . . E
LING, B/Fattest, tallest, biggest snowman ever. /1997/
K-2/2 KF987 . . . . E
LONDON, J/Froggy gets dressed. /1992/P-K/2 KG021 . . . . . . E
MEDEARIS, AS/Here comes the snow. /1996/K-1/2 KG126. . . . E
NEITZEL, S/Jacket I wear in the snow. /1989/P-2/2 KG168 . . . . E
ROCKWELL, AF/First snowfall. /1987/P-1/2 KG342 . . . . E
WELLS, R/Edward's overwhelming overnight. /1995/
P-1/2 KG699 . . . . E

Snow--Folklore.
CECH, J/First snow, magic snow. /1992/2-4/6 KB390. . . .   **398.21**
Snow--Poetry.
PRELUTSKY, J/It's snowing! It's snowing! /1984/K-3/KE005 . .   **811**
Snowman--Fiction.
CHRISTIANSEN, CB/Snowman on Sycamore Street. /1996/
2-3/2 KG989 . . . .   **Fic**
Soap.
SOAP (VIDEOCASSETTE). /1984/5-6/KD326 . . . .   **VCR 668**
Soap box derbies.
HOW TO BUILD CHAMPION PINEWOOD CARS
(VIDEOCASSETTE). /1995/2-6/KD349 . . . .   **VCR 688.6**
Soccer.
WILNER, B/Soccer. /1994/3-6/4 KD789 . . . .   **796.334**
Soccer--Fiction.
AVI /S.O.R. losers. /1984/5-A/6 KG865 . . . .   **Fic**
GILSON, J/Soccer circus. /1993/3-5/5 KH169 . . . .   **Fic**
KESSLER, L/Old Turtle's soccer team. /1988/K-3/2 KF901 . . . . .   **E**
Soccer players.
HOWARD, DE/Soccer stars. /1994/3-6/6 KD788. . . . . .   **796.334**
Social action.
LEWIS, BA/Kid's guide to social action: how to solve the social
problems you choose--and turn creative thinking into positive action.
/1991/3-6/6 KA991 . . . .   **361.2**
Social reformers.
FREEDMAN, R/Kids at work: Lewis Hine and the crusade against
child labor. /1994/5-A/8 KA937 . . . .   **331.3**
MCPHERSON, SS/Peace and bread: the story of Jane Addams. /
1993/4-6/5 KE228 . . . .   **B ADDAMS, J.**
Social sciences SEE ALSO Anthropology; Economics; subject headings
beginning with Political.
Social sciences--Periodicals.
SOCIAL EDUCATION. /1937-//KA146. . . . . . .   **PER PROF 050**
SOCIAL STUDIES AND THE YOUNG LEARNER: A QUARTERLY
FOR CREATIVE TEACHING IN /1988-//KA147 .   **PER PROF 050**
WORLD NEWSMAP OF THE WEEK: HEADLINE FOCUS. /1938-/
/KA155. . . . .   **PER PROF 050**
Social sciences--Study and teaching.
SOCIAL STUDIES AND THE YOUNG LEARNER: A QUARTERLY
FOR CREATIVE TEACHING IN GRADES K-6. /1988-/
/KA147 . . . .   **PER PROF 050**
Social sciences--Study and teaching (Elementary).
HELTSHE, MA/Multicultural explorations: joyous journeys with
books. /1991//KA262. . . . .   **PROF 372.89**
LAUGHLIN, MK/Literature-based social studies: children's books and
activities to enrich the K-5 curriculum. /1991/
/KA261. . . . .   **PROF 372.83**
Social studies readers theatre for children: scripts and script
development. /1991//KA224. . . . .   **PROF 372.6**
Social sciences--Study and teaching (Elementary)--Bibliography.
LAUGHLIN, MK/Literature-based social studies: /1991/
/KA261. . . . .   **PROF 372.83**
Social studies--Study and teaching (Elementary).
FREDERICKS, AD/Social studies through children's literature: an
integrated approach. /1991//KA260. . . . .   **PROF 372.83**
Society of Friends SEE Friends, Society of.
Sod houses.
ROUNDS, G/Sod houses on the Great Plains. /1995/
2-6/7 KD361 . . . .   **693**
Softball.
SUBLETT, A/Illustrated rules of softball. /1996/
3-6/6 KD803 . . . .   **796.357**
Software--Africa.
AFRICA TRAIL (CD-ROM). /1995/4-A/KE723 . . . .   **CDR 960**
Software--Africa--Folklore.
P.J.'S READING ADVENTURES (CD-ROM). /1996/
K-3/KB252. . . . .   **CDR 398**
Software--Alliteration.
DR. SEUSS'S ABC (CD-ROM). /1995/P-2/KF493. . . . . .   **CDR E**
Software--Alphabet.
CHICKA CHICKA BOOM BOOM (CD-ROM). /1996/
P-2/KF382. . . . .   **CDR E**
DR. SEUSS'S ABC (CD-ROM). /1995/P-2/KF493. . . . . .   **CDR E**
Software--American poetry.
NEW KID ON THE BLOCK (CD-ROM). /1993/
K-A/KD995 . . . .   **CDR 811**
Software--Animal locomotion.
ALEXANDER, RM/How animals move (CD-ROM). /1995/
4-A/KC464 . . . .   **CDR 591.47**
Software--Animals.
AMAZING ANIMALS (CD-ROM). /1997/K-3/KC444 . .   **CDR 591**
ANIMAL PLANET (CD-ROM). /1996/4-A/KC439. . . . .   **CDR 590**
MAMMALS: A MULTIMEDIA ENCYCLOPEDIA (CD-ROM). /1990/
2-A/KA450 . . . .   **CDR REF 599**

MICROSOFT EXPLORAPEDIA: THE WORLD OF NATURE.
ACADEMIC ED. (CD-ROM). /1995/1-4/KB909. . . . . .   **CDR 508**
Software--Animals--Fiction.
ARTHUR'S TEACHER TROUBLE (CD-ROM). /1992/
1-4/KF171 . . . .   **CDR E**
MARK SCHLICHTING'S HARRY AND THE HAUNTED HOUSE.
SCHOOL ED. (CD-ROM). /1994/K-3/KG063. . . . .   **CDR E**
Software--Animals--Habitats and behavior.
MICROSOFT DANGEROUS CREATURES: EXPLORE THE
ENDANGERED WORLD OF WILDLIFE. /1994/
4-A/KC490 . . . .   **CDR 591.68**
Software--Animals--Physiology.
ALEXANDER, RM/How animals move (CD-ROM). /1995/
4-A/KC464 . . . .   **CDR 591.47**
Software--Arithmetic.
CALCULATING CREW. SCHOOL VERSION. (CD-ROM). /1996/
3-6/KB955. . . . .   **CDR 513.2**
CARNIVAL COUNTDOWN. SCHOOL VERSION (CD-ROM). /
1996/K-2/KB926.   **CDR 510**
JAMES DISCOVERS MATH. SCHOOL ED. (CD-ROM). /1995/
1-3/KB962. . . . .   **CDR 513.2**
MILLIE'S MATH HOUSE (CD-ROM). /1995/
P-2/KB971 . . . .   **CDR 513.2**
MILLIE'S MATH HOUSE (MICROCOMPUTER PROGRAM). /1992/
P-2/KB972. . . . .   **MCP 513.2**
PUZZLE TANKS: A GAME OF NUMBERS AND LOGIC
(MICROCOMPUTER PROGRAM). /1984/3-A/KB940. .   **MCP 511**
SEILER, B/How the west was one + three x four (Microcomputer
program). /c1987, 1989/4-A/KB951. . . . .   **MCP 513**
ZOO ZILLIONS. SCHOOL VERSION (CD-ROM). /1966/
K-2/KB986. . . . .   **CDR 513.2**
Software--Art.
KID PIX STUDIO (CD-ROM). /1994/P-A/KD468 . . .   **CDR 750.28**
NEW KID PIX. SCHOOL VERSION (MICROCOMPUTER
PROGRAM). /1996/P-A/KD469 . . . .   **MCP 750.28**
Software--Art--Study and teaching.
WITH OPEN EYES: IMAGES FROM THE ART INSTITUTE OF
CHICAGO (CD-ROM). /1995/2-A/KD368. . . . .   **CDR 701**
Software--Art appreciation.
WITH OPEN EYES: IMAGES FROM THE ART INSTITUTE OF
CHICAGO (CD-ROM). /1995/2-A/KD368. . . . .   **CDR 701**
Software--Astronomy.
EYEWITNESS ENCYCLOPEDIA OF SPACE AND THE UNIVERSE
(CD-ROM). /1996/5-A/KC003 . . . .   **CDR 520**
MOHL, R/Planetary taxi (CD-ROM). /1993/
4-A/KC013 . . . .   **CDR 523.2**
WHERE IN SPACE IS CARMEN SANDIEGO? (MICROCOMPUTER
PROGRAM). /1993/4-A/KC005 . . . .   **MCP 520**
Software--Atlases.
MICROSOFT BOOKSHELF: MULTIMEDIA REFERENCE LIBRARY,
1998 ED. SCHOOL ED. (CD-ROM). /1997/
3-A/KA376 . . . .   **CDR REF 028.7**
MICROSOFT ENCARTA 97 WORLD ATLAS (CD-ROM). /1996/
3-A/KA472 . . . .   **CDR REF 912**
Software--Audio-visual materials--Catalogs.
ELEMENTARY SCHOOL LIBRARY COLLECTION: A GUIDE TO
BOOKS AND OTHER MEDIA, /1998/
/KA014.   **CDR PROF 011.62**
Software--Authors.
JUNIOR DISCOVERING AUTHORS: BIOGRAPHIES AND
PLOTLINES ON 300 MOST-STUDIED AND /1994/
5-A/KA463 . . . .   **CDR REF 809**
Software--Bats--Fiction.
STELLALUNA (CD-ROM). /1996/K-3/KG550. . . . .   **CDR E**
Software--Beaches--Fiction.
JUST GRANDMA AND ME (CD-ROM). /1992/
P-2/KF863. . . . .   **CDR E**
Software--Bears--Fiction.
BERENSTAIN BEARS GET IN A FIGHT. SCHOOL ED. (CD-ROM).
/1995/K-3/KF223. . . . .   **CDR E**
BERENSTAIN BEARS IN THE DARK. SCHOOL ED. (CD-ROM). /
1996/K-3/KF224. . . . .   **CDR E**
Software--Beethoven, Ludwig van.
WINTER, R/Microsoft composer collection (CD-ROM). /1994/
4-A/KD525 . . . .   **CDR 780**
Software--Behavior--Fiction.
BERENSTAIN BEARS GET IN A FIGHT. SCHOOL ED. (CD-ROM).
/1995/K-3/KF223. . . . .   **CDR E**
Software--Bilingual materials--Japanese.
JUST GRANDMA AND ME (CD-ROM). /1992/
P-2/KF863. . . . .   **CDR E**
Software--Bilingual materials--Spanish.
AESOP'S FABLE: THE TORTOISE AND THE HARE (CD-ROM). /
1993/P-A/KB522 . . . .   **CDR 398.24**

ARTHUR'S TEACHER TROUBLE (CD-ROM). /1992/
1-4/KF171. . . . . **CDR E**
BERENSTAIN BEARS GET IN A FIGHT. SCHOOL ED. (CD-ROM).
/1995/K-3/KF223. . . . . **CDR E**
BROWN, MT/Arthur's teacher trouble (Microcomputer program). /
1994/2-6/KB109. . . . . **MCP 372.6**
JUST GRANDMA AND ME (CD-ROM). /1992/
P-2/KF863. . . . . **CDR E**
KID PIX STUDIO (CD-ROM). /1994/P-A/KD468 . . . **CDR 750.28**
MARC BROWN'S ARTHUR'S BIRTHDAY. SCHOOL ED. (CD-ROM).
/1994/K-4/KG062 . . . . **CDR E**
MARK SCHLICHTING'S HARRY AND THE HAUNTED HOUSE.
SCHOOL ED. (CD-ROM). /1994/K-3/KG063. . . . . **CDR E**
MERCER MAYER'S LITTLE MONSTER AT SCHOOL. SCHOOL ED.
(CD-ROM). /1994/K-3/KG130 . . . . **CDR E**
MULTIMEDIA WORKSHOP. TEACHER ED. (CD-ROM). /1996/
3-A/KB115. **CDR 372.6**
NEW KID PIX. SCHOOL VERSION (MICROCOMPUTER
PROGRAM). /1996/P-A/KD469 . . . . **MCP 750.28**
STORYBOOK WEAVER DELUXE (CD-ROM). /1995/
1-5/KB118. **CDR 372.6**

Software--Biology.
VARIATIONS IN LIFE SCIENCE INVESTIGATIONS (CD-ROM). /
1996/6-A/KC298 . . . . **CDR 577**

Software--Biomechanics.
ALEXANDER, RM/How animals move (CD-ROM). /1995/
4-A/KC464 . . . . **CDR 591.47**

Software--Birds--Fiction.
STELLALUNA (CD-ROM). /1996/K-3/KG550. . . . . **CDR E**

Software--Birthdays--Fiction.
MARC BROWN'S ARTHUR'S BIRTHDAY. SCHOOL ED. (CD-ROM).
/1994/K-4/KG062 . . . . **CDR E**

Software--Body, Human.
SCHOLASTIC'S THE MAGIC SCHOOL BUS EXPLORES THE
HUMAN BODY. SCHOOL ED. (CD-ROM). /1995/
2-A/KC925 . . . . **CDR 612**
STV: HUMAN BODY (VIDEODISC). /1992/4-A/KC926. . **VD 612**
ULTIMATE HUMAN BODY (CD-ROM). /1996/
4-A/KC927 . . . . **CDR 612**
WHAT IS A BELLYBUTTON?: FUN AND INTERACTIVE
QUESTIONS AND ANSWERS ABOUT THE /1994/
2-6/KC930. . . . . **CDR 612**

Software--Books and reading.
READABILITY ANALYSIS (MICROCOMPUTER PROGRAM). /1994/
/KA213. . . . . **MCP PROF 372.4**

Software--Bunyan, Paul (Legendary character).
P.J.'S READING ADVENTURES (CD-ROM). /1996/
K-3/KB252. . . . . **CDR 398**

Software--Business enterprises.
CLASSROOM STOREWORKS (MICROCOMPUTER PROGRAM). /
1997/2-5/KD313 . . . . **MCP 658**

Software--Cats.
EYEWITNESS VIRTUAL REALITY: CAT (CD-ROM). /1995/
3-A/KC820 . . . . **CDR 599.75**

Software--Children's literature.
JUNIOR DISCOVERING AUTHORS: BIOGRAPHIES AND
PLOTLINES ON 300 MOST-STUDIED AND /1994/
5-A/KA463 . . . . **CDR REF 809**

Software--Children's literature--Bibliography.
ELEMENTARY SCHOOL LIBRARY COLLECTION: A GUIDE TO
BOOKS AND OTHER MEDIA, /1998/
/KA014. . . . . **CDR PROF 011.62**

Software--Chronology.
TIMELINER: HISTORY IN PERSPECTIVE (MICROCOMPUTER
PROGRAM). /1986/K-A/KE142 . . . . **MCP 902**

Software--Colonization.
COLONIZATION (MICROCOMPUTER PROGRAM). /1986/
5-A/KA667 . . . . **MCP 172**

Software--Composers.
WINTER, R/Microsoft composer collection (CD-ROM). /1994/
4-A/KD525 . . . . **CDR 780**

Software--Computer programs.
KIDDESK. SCHOOL VERSION (CD-ROM). /1995/
P-A/KA569 . . . . **CDR 004**
KIDDESK (MICROCOMPUTER PROGRAM). /1993/
K-A/KA568 . . . . **MCP 004**

Software--Construction equipment.
BIG JOB (CD-ROM). /1995/K-3/KD120. . . . . . . **CDR 629.225**

Software--Creative ability.
THINKIN' THINGS COLLECTION 2. SCHOOL VERSION (CD-
ROM). /1995/1-6/KB081. . . . . **CDR 370.15**

Software--Creative writing.
STANLEY'S STICKER STORIES. SCHOOL VERSION (CD-ROM). /
1996/P-2/KB117. . . . . **CDR 372.6**

WRITING ALONG THE OREGON TRAIL (MICROCOMPUTER
PROGRAM). /1994/4-A/KB121 . . . . **MCP 372.6**

Software--Culture.
MICROSOFT EXPLORAPEDIA: THE WORLD OF PEOPLE.
ACADEMIC ED. (CD-ROM). /1994/1-4/KA892 . . . . . **CDR 307**

Software--Decision making.
HALPERN, NA/Kids and the environment: taking responsibility for
our surroundings /1994/1-5/KB046. . . . . **CDR 363.7**
TAKING RESPONSIBILITY (MICROCOMPUTER PROGRAM). /
1988/1-6/KA665 . . . . **MCP 158**

Software--Design.
KID CAD (MICROCOMPUTER PROGRAM). /1993/
2-A/KD423 . . . . **MCP 745.4**
MULTIMEDIA WORKSHOP. TEACHER ED. (CD-ROM). /1996/
3-A/KB115. **CDR 372.6**

Software--Desktop publishing.
MICROSOFT CREATIVE WRITER 2. SCHOOL ED. (CD-ROM). /
1996/2-A/KB114 . . . . **CDR 372.6**
MULTIMEDIA WORKSHOP. TEACHER ED. (CD-ROM). /1996/
3-A/KB115. **CDR 372.6**
STANLEY'S STICKER STORIES. SCHOOL VERSION (CD-ROM). /
1996/P-2/KB117. . . . . **CDR 372.6**
STUDENT WRITING AND RESEARCH CENTER WITH COMPTON'S
CONCISE ENCYCLOPEDIA /1995/4-A/KB091 . . . **CDR 371.302**
ULTIMATE WRITING AND CREATIVITY CENTER. SCHOOL ED.
(CD-ROM). /1996/K-5/KB120. . . . . **CDR 372.6**
WRITING CENTER (MICROCOMPUTER PROGRAM). /1991/
2-A/KD347 . . . . **MCP 686.2**

Software--Dinosaurs.
MICROSOFT DINOSAURS: EXPLORE THE INCREDIBLE WORLD OF
PREHISTORIC CREATURES. /1994/2-A/KC256. . . . . **CDR 567.9**
SCHOLASTIC'S MAGIC SCHOOL BUS EXPLORES IN THE AGE OF
DINOSAURS. SCHOOL ED. /1996/1-4/KC263. . . . . **CDR 567.9**

Software--Drawing--Technique.
KID CAD (MICROCOMPUTER PROGRAM). /1993/
2-A/KD423 . . . . **MCP 745.4**

Software--Drug abuse.
SUBSTANCE ABUSE (MICROCOMPUTER PROGRAM). /1992/
4-A/KD000 . . . . **MCP 613.8**

Software--Drugs.
SUBSTANCE ABUSE (MICROCOMPUTER PROGRAM). /1992/
4-A/KD000 . . . . **MCP 613.8**

Software--Earth sciences.
SCHOLASTIC'S THE MAGIC SCHOOL BUS EXPLORES INSIDE THE
EARTH. SCHOOL ED. /1996/4-A/KC149 . . . . **CDR 550**

Software--Ecology.
ECOLOGY WITH SEUSS (MICROCOMPUTER PROGRAM). /1990/
2-5/KB112. . . . . **MCP 372.6**

Software--Educational games.
GIZMOS AND GADGETS! (MICROCOMPUTER PROGRAM). /
1993/3-6/KB882. . . . . **MCP 507**
NATIONAL INSPIRER (MICROCOMPUTER PROGRAM). /1997/
5-A/KE190. . . . . **MCP 917.3**
PLAYROOM (CD-ROM). /1990/P-2/KB085. . . . . . . **CDR 371.3**
PUZZLE TANKS: A GAME OF NUMBERS AND LOGIC
(MICROCOMPUTER PROGRAM). /1984/3-A/KB940. . **MCP 511**
SNAPDRAGON (MICROCOMPUTER PROGRAM). /1992/
P-1/KA636. . . . . **MCP 153.4**
STRATEGY CHALLENGES COLLECTION 1: AROUND THE WORLD.
SCHOOL VERSION (CD-ROM). /1995/3-A/KD754. . . **CDR 794**
STRATEGY CHALLENGES COLLECTION 2: IN THE WILD. SCHOOL
VERSION (CD-ROM). /1996/4-A/KD755 . . . . **CDR 794**
TREEHOUSE (CD-ROM). /1991/K-4/KB086. . . . . . **CDR 371.3**

Software--Elementary school libraries--Book lists.
ELEMENTARY SCHOOL LIBRARY COLLECTION: A GUIDE TO
BOOKS AND OTHER MEDIA, /1998/
/KA014. . . . . **CDR PROF 011.62**

Software--Emigration and immigration.
IMMIGRATION (MICROCOMPUTER PROGRAM). /1996/
5-A/KA917 . . . . **MCP 325**

Software--Emotions and social attitudes.
PREJUDICE (MICROCOMPUTER PROGRAM). /1992/
5-A/KA820 . . . . **MCP 305**

Software--Encyclopedias and dictionaries.
COMPTON'S MULTIMEDIA ENCYCLOPEDIA (CD-ROM). /1994/
3-6/KA381 . . . . **CDR REF 031**
MICROSOFT BOOKSHELF: MULTIMEDIA REFERENCE LIBRARY,
1998 ED. SCHOOL ED. (CD-ROM). /1997/
3-A/KA376 . . . . **CDR REF 028.7**
MICROSOFT ENCARTA 97 ENCYCLOPEDIA. DELUXE SCHOOL
ED. (CD-ROM). /1996/4-A/KA384 . . . . **CDR REF 031**
PRESIDENTS: IT ALL STARTED WITH GEORGE (CD-ROM). /
1991/2-A/KA491 . . . . **CDR REF 973**

Software--Energy (continued)
STUDENT WRITING AND RESEARCH CENTER WITH COMPTON'S CONCISE ENCYCLOPEDIA /1995/4-A/KB091 . . . **CDR 371.302**
WORLD BOOK 1997 MULTIMEDIA ENCYCLOPEDIA. DELUXE ED. (CD-ROM). /1997/3-A/KA388 . . . . **CDR REF 031**

Software--Energy.
COLONIZATION (MICROCOMPUTER PROGRAM). /1986/5-A/KA667 . . . . **MCP 172**

Software--English language--Composition and exercises.
BRIDGE TO TERABITHIA: A MULTI-MEDIA STUDY (MICROCOMPUTER PROGRAM). /1993/5-A/KB108. . . . . **MCP 372.6**
CHARLOTTE'S WEB: A WRITE ON! MULTI-MEDIA STUDY (MICROCOMPUTER PROGRAM). /1992/3-6/KB110. **MCP 372.6**
DESTINATION: OCEAN. SCHOOL VERSION (CD-ROM). /1995/1-A/KB111. . . . . **CDR 372.6**
MICROSOFT CREATIVE WRITER 2. SCHOOL ED. (CD-ROM). /1996/2-A/KB114 . . . . **CDR 372.6**
STORYBOOK WEAVER DELUXE (CD-ROM). /1995/1-5/KB118. . . . . **CDR 372.6**
WRITING ALONG THE OREGON TRAIL (MICROCOMPUTER PROGRAM). /1994/4-A/KB121 . . . . **MCP 372.6**

Software--English language--Dictionaries.
MY FIRST AMAZING WORDS AND PICTURES (CD-ROM). /1994/K-3/KA426 . . . . **CDR REF 423**

Software--English language--Grammar.
DR. SEUSS'S ABC (CD-ROM). /1995/P-2/KF493 . . . . . . **CDR E**
MY FIRST SENTENCES (MICROCOMPUTER PROGRAM). /1987/1-3/KB116 . . . . **MCP 372.6**

Software--Entrepreneurship.
CLASSROOM STOREWORKS (MICROCOMPUTER PROGRAM). /1997/2-5/KD313 . . . . **MCP 658**

Software--Environmental protection.
ENVIRONMENT (MICROCOMPUTER PROGRAM). /1990/5-A/KB059. . . . . **MCP 363.73**
GREAT OCEAN RESCUE (CD-ROM). /1996/3-A/KC349 . . . . **CDR 577.7**
HALPERN, NA/Kids and the environment: taking responsibility for our surroundings /1994/1-5/KB046. . . . . . . **CDR 363.7**

Software--Ethics.
COLONIZATION (MICROCOMPUTER PROGRAM). /1986/5-A/KA667 . . . . **MCP 172**
REVOLUTIONARY WARS: CHOOSING SIDES (MICROCOMPUTER PROGRAM). /1986/5-A/KA668 . . . . **MCP 172**

Software--Europe--Geography.
EUROPE INSPIRER (CD-ROM). /1997/4-A/KE177 . . . . **CDR 914**

Software--Fables.
AESOP'S FABLE: THE TORTOISE AND THE HARE (CD-ROM). /1993/P-A/KB522 . . . . **CDR 398.24**

Software--Fear--Fiction.
BERENSTAIN BEARS IN THE DARK. SCHOOL ED. (CD-ROM). /1996/K-3/KF224. . . . . **CDR E**

Software--Felidae.
EYEWITNESS VIRTUAL REALITY: CAT (CD-ROM). /1995/3-A/KC820 . . . . **CDR 599.75**

Software--Folklore--Africa.
P.J.'S READING ADVENTURES (CD-ROM). /1996/K-3/KB252. . . . . **CDR 398**

Software--Folklore--United States.
P.J.'S READING ADVENTURES (CD-ROM). /1996/K-3/KB252. . . . . **CDR 398**

Software--Food--Fiction.
GREEN EGGS AND HAM. SCHOOL ED. (CD-ROM). /1996/K-2/KF639. . . . . **CDR E**

Software--Food chains (Ecology).
FIELD TRIP TO THE RAINFOREST (MICROCOMPUTER PROGRAM). /1991/3-A/KC314 . . . . **MCP 577.34**

Software--Friendship--Fiction.
BERENSTAIN BEARS GET IN A FIGHT. SCHOOL ED. (CD-ROM). /1995/K-3/KF223. . . . . **CDR E**
MARC BROWN'S ARTHUR'S BIRTHDAY. SCHOOL ED. (CD-ROM). /1994/K-4/KG062. . . . . **CDR E**

Software--Frontier and pioneer life.
OREGON TRAIL II (CD-ROM). /1994/4-A/KE745 . . **CDR 970.04**

Software--Geography.
GTV: A GEOGRAPHIC PERSPECTIVE ON AMERICAN HISTORY (VIDEODISC). /c1990/5-A/KE853 . . . . **VD 973**
INTERNATIONAL INSPIRER (MICROCOMPUTER PROGRAM). /1990/5-A/KE149 . . . . **MCP 910**
MICROSOFT ENCARTA 97 WORLD ATLAS (CD-ROM). /1996/3-A/KA472 . . . . **CDR REF 912**
MY FIRST AMAZING WORLD EXPLORER (CD-ROM). /1996/1-3/KE170. . . . . **CDR 912**
NATIONAL INSPIRER (MICROCOMPUTER PROGRAM). /1997/5-A/KE190. . . . . **MCP 917.3**

TRUDY'S TIME AND PLACE HOUSE. SCHOOL VERSION (CD-ROM). /1995/P-3/KC075. . . . . **CDR 529**
WHERE IN THE U.S.A. IS CARMEN SANDIEGO? NEW ED. (CD-ROM). /1996/3-A/KE182. . . . . **CDR 917**
WHERE IN THE WORLD IS CARMEN SANDIEGO? JUNIOR DETECTIVE EDITION (CD-ROM). /1994/3-6/KE174 . . **CDR 912**
WHERE IN THE WORLD IS CARMEN SANDIEGO? NEW ED. (CD-ROM). /1996/3-A/KE175 . . . . **CDR 912**

Software--Geology.
SCHOLASTIC'S THE MAGIC SCHOOL BUS EXPLORES INSIDE THE EARTH. SCHOOL ED. /1996/4-A/KC149 . . . . **CDR 550**

Software--Geometry.
CARNIVAL COUNTDOWN. SCHOOL VERSION (CD-ROM). /1996/K-2/KB926. . . . . **CDR 510**
NUMBER HEROES. SCHOOL VERSION (CD-ROM). /1996/3-6/KB929. . . . . **CDR 510**

Software--Graphics.
PRINT SHOP DELUXE I (MICROCOMPUTER PROGRAM). /1992//KA002. . . . . **MCP PROF 006.6**

Software--Haunted houses--Fiction.
MARK SCHLICHTING'S HARRY AND THE HAUNTED HOUSE. SCHOOL ED. (CD-ROM). /1994/K-3/KG063 . . . . **CDR E**

Software--Hearing.
SCIENCE IN YOUR EAR (CD-ROM). /1996/4-A/KC104 **CDR 534**

Software--Human anatomy.
STV: HUMAN BODY (VIDEODISC). /1992/4-A/KC926. . **VD 612**
ULTIMATE HUMAN BODY (CD-ROM). /1996/4-A/KC927 . . . . **CDR 612**

Software--Human physiology.
STV: HUMAN BODY (VIDEODISC). /1992/4-A/KC926. . **VD 612**
ULTIMATE HUMAN BODY (CD-ROM). /1996/4-A/KC927 . . . . **CDR 612**
WHAT IS A BELLYBUTTON?: FUN AND INTERACTIVE QUESTIONS AND ANSWERS ABOUT THE /1994/2-6/KC930. . . . . **CDR 612**

Software--Humorous poetry.
NEW KID ON THE BLOCK (CD-ROM). /1993/K-A/KD995 . . . . **CDR 811**

Software--Hypermedia.
HYPERSTUDIO (MICROCOMPUTER PROGRAM). /1990/2-A/KA574 . . . . **MCP 006.7**

Software--Indians of Central America.
MAYAQUEST TRAIL (CD-ROM). /1996/5-A/KE845 . **CDR 972.81**

Software--Indians of North America.
500 NATIONS: STORIES OF THE NORTH AMERICAN INDIAN EXPERIENCE ACADEMIC ED. /1995/4-A/KE756. . . . **CDR 970.1**

Software--Individuality.
ON THE PLAYGROUND (MICROCOMPUTER PROGRAM). /1988/1-6/KA662 . . . . **MCP 158**

Software--Internet (Computer network)--Directories.
MICROSOFT BOOKSHELF: MULTIMEDIA REFERENCE LIBRARY, 1998 ED. SCHOOL ED. (CD-ROM). /1997/3-A/KA376 . . . . **CDR REF 028.7**

Software--Interpersonal relations.
ON THE PLAYGROUND (MICROCOMPUTER PROGRAM). /1988/1-6/KA662 . . . . **MCP 158**

Software--Inventions.
INVENTION STUDIO (CD-ROM). /1996/5-A/KC887 . . **CDR 608**

Software--Japanese language materials.
JUST GRANDMA AND ME (CD-ROM). /1992/P-2/KF863. . . . . **CDR E**

Software--Journalism.
OWENS, P/Classroom newspaper workshop (CD-ROM). /1995/4-A/KA594 . . . . **CDR 070.4**

Software--Jungles.
LET'S EXPLORE THE JUNGLE WITH BUZZY THE KNOWLEDGE BUG (CD-ROM). /1995/K-3/KC320 . . . . **CDR 577.34**

Software--Keyboarding.
MAVIS BEACON TEACHES TYPING! (MICROCOMPUTER PROGRAM). /1987/4-A/KD310 . . . . **MCP 652.3**

Software--Leopard--Fiction.
P.J.'S READING ADVENTURES (CD-ROM). /1996/K-3/KB252. . . . . **CDR 398**

Software--Life (Biology).
VARIATIONS IN LIFE SCIENCE INVESTIGATIONS (CD-ROM). /1996/6-A/KC298 . . . . **CDR 577**

Software--Literature--Criticism and interpretation.
BOOK EXCHANGE (MICROCOMPUTER PROGRAM). /1996/3-6/KD862. . . . . **MCP 808**

Software--Logic.
FACTORY: EXPLORATIONS IN PROBLEM SOLVING (MICROCOMPUTER PROGRAM). /1983/2-4/KA635 . . . . **MCP 153.4**

LOGICAL JOURNEY OF THE ZOOMBINIS. SCHOOL ED. (CD-ROM). /1996/2-5/KB938 . . . . **CDR 511**
Software--Magic tricks.
BIG ANTHONY'S MIXED-UP MAGIC (CD-ROM). /1996/K-2/KF229 . . . . **CDR E**
Software--Mammals.
MAMMALS: A MULTIMEDIA ENCYCLOPEDIA (CD-ROM). /1990/2-A/KA450 . . . . **CDR REF 599**
Software--Map drawing.
NEIGHBORHOOD MAPMACHINE (MICROCOMPUTER PROGRAM). /1997/1-5/KC066 . . . . **MCP 526**
Software--Maps.
EUROPE INSPIRER (CD-ROM). /1997/4-A/KE177 . . . . **CDR 914**
INTERNATIONAL INSPIRER (MICROCOMPUTER PROGRAM). /1990/5-A/KE149 . . . . **MCP 910**
MICROSOFT ENCARTA 97 WORLD ATLAS (CD-ROM). /1996/3-A/KA472 . . . . **CDR REF 912**
MY FIRST AMAZING WORLD EXPLORER (CD-ROM). /1996/1-3/KE170 . . . . **CDR 912**
NEIGHBORHOOD MAPMACHINE (MICROCOMPUTER PROGRAM). /1997/1-5/KC066 . . . . **MCP 526**
TRUDY'S TIME AND PLACE HOUSE. SCHOOL VERSION (CD-ROM). /1995/P-3/KC075 . . . . **CDR 529**
Software--Marine animals.
SCHOLASTIC'S THE MAGIC SCHOOL BUS EXPLORES THE OCEAN. TEACHER ED. (CD-ROM). /1995/2-A/KC369 . . . . **CDR 578.77**
Software--Marine biology.
FIELD TRIP INTO THE SEA (MICROCOMPUTER PROGRAM). /1992/3-A/KC368 . . . . **MCP 578.77**
Software--Marine ecology.
FIELD TRIP INTO THE SEA (MICROCOMPUTER PROGRAM). /1992/3-A/KC368 . . . . **MCP 578.77**
GREAT OCEAN RESCUE (CD-ROM). /1996/3-A/KC349 . . . . **CDR 577.7**
Software--Mass media--Influence.
VIOLENCE IN THE MEDIA (MICROCOMPUTER PROGRAM). /1994/5-A/KA802 . . . . **MCP 302.23**
Software--Mass media--Moral and ethical aspects.
VIOLENCE IN THE MEDIA (MICROCOMPUTER PROGRAM). /1994/5-A/KA802 . . . . **MCP 302.23**
Software--Mathematical recreations.
JAMES DISCOVERS MATH. SCHOOL ED. (CD-ROM). /1995/1-3/KB962 . . . . **CDR 513.2**
MILLIE'S MATH HOUSE (CD-ROM). /1995/P-2/KB971 . . . . **CDR 513.2**
MILLIE'S MATH HOUSE (MICROCOMPUTER PROGRAM). /1992/P-2/KB972 . . . . **MCP 513.2**
PUZZLE TANKS: A GAME OF NUMBERS AND LOGIC (MICROCOMPUTER PROGRAM). /1984/3-A/KB940. . **MCP 511**
Software--Mathematics.
CARNIVAL COUNTDOWN. SCHOOL VERSION (CD-ROM). /1996/K-2/KB926. . . . . **CDR 510**
JAMES DISCOVERS MATH. SCHOOL ED. (CD-ROM). /1995/1-3/KB962 . . . . **CDR 513.2**
LOGICAL JOURNEY OF THE ZOOMBINIS. SCHOOL ED. (CD-ROM). /1996/2-5/KB938 . . . . **CDR 511**
NUMBER HEROES. SCHOOL VERSION (CD-ROM). /1996/3-6/KB929 . . . . **CDR 510**
Software--Mathematics--Graphic methods.
GRAPH ACTION (MICROCOMPUTER PROGRAM). /1996/4-A/KB936. . . . . **MCP 511**
GRAPH ACTION PLUS (CD-ROM). /1996/4-A/KB937 . . **CDR 511**
STEARNS, PH/Graph Club with Fizz and Martina (Microcomputer program). /1993/K-4/KB942 . . . . . . **MCP 511**
Software--Mayas.
MAYAQUEST TRAIL (CD-ROM). /1996/5-A/KE845 . **CDR 972.81**
Software--Monsters--Fiction.
MERCER MAYER'S LITTLE MONSTER AT SCHOOL. SCHOOL ED. (CD-ROM). /1994/K-3/KG130 . . . . **CDR E**
Software--Mozart, Wolfgang Amadeus.
WINTER, R/Microsoft composer collection (CD-ROM). /1994/4-A/KD525 . . . . **CDR 780**
Software--Multimedia.
HYPERSTUDIO (MICROCOMPUTER PROGRAM). /1990/2-A/KA574 . . . . **MCP 006.7**
Software--Music.
PLAYROOM (CD-ROM). /1990/P-2/KB085. . . . . **CDR 371.3**
TREEHOUSE (CD-ROM). /1991/K-4/KB086 . . . . **CDR 371.3**
Software--Music--Acoustics and physics.
SCIENCE IN YOUR EAR (CD-ROM). /1996/4-A/KC104 **CDR 534**
Software--Music--Theory.
WINTER, R/Microsoft composer collection (CD-ROM). /1994/4-A/KD525 . . . . **CDR 780**

Software--Music appreciation.
WINTER, R/Microsoft composer collection (CD-ROM). /1994/4-A/KD525 . . . . **CDR 780**
Software--Nature study.
MICROSOFT EXPLORAPEDIA: THE WORLD OF NATURE. ACADEMIC ED. (CD-ROM). /1995/1-4/KB909. . . . . . **CDR 508**
Software--Newspapers.
OWENS, P/Classroom newspaper workshop (CD-ROM). /1995/4-A/KA594 . . . . **CDR 070.4**
READER RABBIT 3 (MICROCOMPUTER PROGRAM). /1993/1-3/KB106 . . . . **MCP 372.4**
Software--Night--Fiction.
BERENSTAIN BEARS IN THE DARK. SCHOOL ED. (CD-ROM). /1996/K-3/KF224 . . . . **CDR E**
Software--Occupations.
MICROSOFT EXPLORAPEDIA: THE WORLD OF PEOPLE. ACADEMIC ED. (CD-ROM). /1994/1-4/KA892 . . . . . **CDR 307**
Software--Ocean.
GREAT OCEAN RESCUE (CD-ROM). /1996/3-A/KC349 . . . . **CDR 577.7**
SCHOLASTIC'S THE MAGIC SCHOOL BUS EXPLORES THE OCEAN. TEACHER ED. (CD-ROM). /1995/2-A/KC369 . . . . **CDR 578.77**
Software--Oregon Trail.
OREGON TRAIL II (CD-ROM). /1994/4-A/KE745 . . **CDR 970.04**
WRITING ALONG THE OREGON TRAIL (MICROCOMPUTER PROGRAM). /1994/4-A/KB121 . . . . **MCP 372.6**
Software--Overland journeys to the Pacific.
OREGON TRAIL II (CD-ROM). /1994/4-A/KE745 . . **CDR 970.04**
WRITING ALONG THE OREGON TRAIL (MICROCOMPUTER PROGRAM). /1994/4-A/KB121 . . . . **MCP 372.6**
Software--Painting--Technique.
KID PIX STUDIO (CD-ROM). /1994/P-A/KD468 . . . **CDR 750.28**
NEW KID PIX. SCHOOL VERSION (MICROCOMPUTER PROGRAM). /1996/P-A/KD469 . . . . **MCP 750.28**
Software--Parties--Fiction.
MARC BROWN'S ARTHUR'S BIRTHDAY. SCHOOL ED. (CD-ROM). /1994/K-4/KG062 . . . . **CDR E**
Software--Planets.
GREAT SOLAR SYSTEM RESCUE (CD-ROM). /1996/5-A/KC009 . . . . **CDR 523.2**
SCHOLASTIC'S THE MAGIC SCHOOL BUS EXPLORES THE SOLAR SYSTEM. ACADEMIC ED. /1994/2-5/KC014 . . . . . **CDR 523.2**
Software--Plants.
MICROSOFT EXPLORAPEDIA: THE WORLD OF NATURE. ACADEMIC ED. (CD-ROM). /1995/1-4/KB909. . . . . . **CDR 508**
Software--Plots (Drama, novel, etc.).
JUNIOR DISCOVERING AUTHORS: BIOGRAPHIES AND PLOTLINES ON 300 MOST-STUDIED AND /1994/5-A/KA463 . . . . **CDR REF 809**
Software--Pollution.
ENVIRONMENT (MICROCOMPUTER PROGRAM). /1990/5-A/KB059. . . . . **MCP 363.73**
Software--Prejudices.
PREJUDICE (MICROCOMPUTER PROGRAM). /1992/5-A/KA820 . . . . **MCP 305**
Software--Presidents.
PRESIDENTS: IT ALL STARTED WITH GEORGE (CD-ROM). /1991/2-A/KA491 . . . . **CDR REF 973**
Software--Probabilities.
NUMBER HEROES. SCHOOL VERSION (CD-ROM). /1996/3-6/KB929 . . . . **CDR 510**
Software--Problem solving.
BIG ANTHONY'S MIXED-UP MAGIC (CD-ROM). /1996/K-2/KF229. . . . . **CDR E**
BUILDING PERSPECTIVE: STRATEGIES IN PROBLEM SOLVING (MICROCOMPUTER PROGRAM). /1986/4-A/KA637 . . . . **MCP 153.7**
CALCULATING CREW. SCHOOL VERSION. (CD-ROM). /1996/3-6/KB955. . . . . **CDR 513.2**
CARNIVAL COUNTDOWN. SCHOOL VERSION (CD-ROM). /1996/K-2/KB926. . . . . **CDR 510**
COLONIZATION (MICROCOMPUTER PROGRAM). /1986/5-A/KA667 . . . . **MCP 172**
EUROPE INSPIRER (CD-ROM). /1997/4-A/KE177 . . . . **CDR 914**
FACTORY: EXPLORATIONS IN PROBLEM SOLVING (MICROCOMPUTER PROGRAM). /1983/2-4/KA635 . . . . **MCP 153.4**
GIZMOS AND GADGETS! (MICROCOMPUTER PROGRAM). /1993/3-6/KB882. . . . . **MCP 507**
GRAPH ACTION (MICROCOMPUTER PROGRAM). /1996/4-A/KB936. . . . . **MCP 511**
GRAPH ACTION PLUS (CD-ROM). /1996/4-A/KB937 . **CDR 511**

IMMIGRATION (MICROCOMPUTER PROGRAM). /1996/
5-A/KA917 . . . . **MCP 325**
LOGICAL JOURNEY OF THE ZOOMBINIS. SCHOOL ED. (CD-
ROM). /1996/2-5/KB938. . . . . **CDR 511**
MILLIE'S MATH HOUSE (CD-ROM). /1995/
P-2/KB971 . . . . **CDR 513.2**
MILLIE'S MATH HOUSE (MICROCOMPUTER PROGRAM). /1992/
P-2/KB972 . . . . **MCP 513.2**
NATIONAL INSPIRER (MICROCOMPUTER PROGRAM). /1997/
5-A/KE190. . . . . **MCP 917.3**
NUMBER HEROES. SCHOOL VERSION (CD-ROM). /1996/
3-6/KB929. . . . . **CDR 510**
PLAYROOM (CD-ROM). /1990/P-2/KB085. . . . **CDR 371.3**
PUZZLE TANKS: A GAME OF NUMBERS AND LOGIC
(MICROCOMPUTER PROGRAM). /1984/3-A/KB940. . **MCP 511**
RAINFOREST RESEARCHERS (CD-ROM). /1996/
5-A/KC323 . . . . **CDR 577.34**
REVOLUTIONARY WARS: CHOOSING SIDES (MICROCOMPUTER
PROGRAM). /1986/5-A/KA668 . . . . **MCP 172**
SAMMY'S SCIENCE HOUSE (CD-ROM). /1994/
K-3/KB870. . . . . **CDR 500**
SCIENCE BLASTER JR. TEACHER ED. (CD-ROM). /1997/
K-3/KB871. . . . . **CDR 500**
SCIENCE SLEUTHS. VOL. 1: THE MYSTERIES OF THE BLOB AND
THE EXPLODING LAWNMOWERS /1995/4-A/KB885. . **CDR 507**
SEILER, B/How the west was one + three x four (Microcomputer
program). /c1987, 1989/4-A/KB951. . . . . **MCP 513**
SNAPDRAGON (MICROCOMPUTER PROGRAM). /1992/
P-1/KA636. . . . . **MCP 153.4**
STEARNS, PH/Graph Club with Fizz and Martina (Microcomputer
program). /1993/K-4/KB942. . . . . **MCP 511**
STRATEGY CHALLENGES COLLECTION 1: AROUND THE WORLD.
SCHOOL VERSION (CD-ROM). /1995/3-A/KD754. . **CDR 794**
STRATEGY CHALLENGES COLLECTION 2: IN THE WILD. SCHOOL
VERSION (CD-ROM). /1996/4-A/KD755 . . . . **CDR 794**
THINKIN' THINGS COLLECTION 1 (MICROCOMPUTER
PROGRAM). /1993/K-3/KB080. . . . . **MCP 370.15**
THINKIN' THINGS COLLECTION 2. SCHOOL VERSION (CD-
ROM). /1995/1-6/KB081. . . . . **CDR 370.15**
THINKIN' THINGS COLLECTION 3. SCHOOL VERSION (CD-
ROM). /1995/3-A/KB082 . . . . **CDR 370.15**
TREEHOUSE (CD-ROM). /1991/K-4/KB086. . . . . **CDR 371.3**
WHERE IN SPACE IS CARMEN SANDIEGO? (MICROCOMPUTER
PROGRAM). /1993/4-A/KC005 . . . . **MCP 520**
WHERE IN THE U.S.A. IS CARMEN SANDIEGO? NEW ED. (CD-
ROM). /1996/3-A/KE182 . . . . **CDR 917**
WHERE IN THE WORLD IS CARMEN SANDIEGO? JUNIOR
DETECTIVE EDITION (CD-ROM). /1994/3-6/KE174 . . **CDR 912**
WHERE IN THE WORLD IS CARMEN SANDIEGO? NEW ED.
(CD-ROM). /1996/3-A/KE175 . . . . **CDR 912**
ZOO ZILLIONS. SCHOOL VERSION (CD-ROM). /1966/
K-2/KB986. . . . . **CDR 513.2**
Software--Questions and answers.
WHAT IS A BELLYBUTTON?: FUN AND INTERACTIVE
QUESTIONS AND ANSWERS ABOUT THE /1994/
2-6/KC930. . . . . **CDR 612**
Software--Racism.
PREJUDICE (MICROCOMPUTER PROGRAM). /1992/
5-A/KA820 . . . . **MCP 305**
Software--Rain forest ecology.
FIELD TRIP TO THE RAINFOREST (MICROCOMPUTER
PROGRAM). /1991/3-A/KC314 . . . . **MCP 577.34**
RAINFOREST RESEARCHERS (CD-ROM). /1996/
5-A/KC323 . . . . **CDR 577.34**
STV: RAIN FOREST (VIDEODISC). /1991/
4-A/KC327 . . . . **VD 577.34**
Software--Rain forest ecology--Costa Rica.
SCHOLASTIC'S THE MAGIC SCHOOL BUS EXPLORES THE
RAINFOREST. SCHOOL ED. (CD-ROM). /1997/
6-A/KC325 . . . . **CDR 577.34**
Software--Rain forests.
FIELD TRIP TO THE RAINFOREST (MICROCOMPUTER
PROGRAM). /1991/3-A/KC314 . . . . **MCP 577.34**
LET'S EXPLORE THE JUNGLE WITH BUZZY THE KNOWLEDGE
BUG (CD-ROM). /1995/K-3/KC320 . . . . **CDR 577.34**
RAINFOREST RESEARCHERS (CD-ROM). /1996/
5-A/KC323 . . . . **CDR 577.34**
STV: RAIN FOREST (VIDEODISC). /1991/
4-A/KC327 . . . . **VD 577.34**
Software--Rain forests--Costa Rica.
SCHOLASTIC'S THE MAGIC SCHOOL BUS EXPLORES THE
RAINFOREST. SCHOOL ED. (CD-ROM). /1997/
6-A/KC325 . . . . **CDR 577.34**

Software--Rare animals.
MICROSOFT DANGEROUS CREATURES: EXPLORE THE
ENDANGERED WORLD OF WILDLIFE. /1994/
4-A/KC490 . . . . **CDR 591.68**
Software--Readability (Literary style).
READABILITY ANALYSIS (MICROCOMPUTER PROGRAM). /1994/
/KA213. . . . . **MCP PROF 372.4**
Software--Reading (Preschool).
BAILEY'S BOOK HOUSE (CD-ROM). /1995/
P-2/KB100. . . . . **CDR 372.4**
BAILEY'S BOOK HOUSE (MICROCOMPUTER PROGRAM). /1993/
P-2/KB101. . . . . **MCP 372.4**
CHICKA CHICKA BOOM BOOM (CD-ROM). /1996/
P-2/KF382. . . . . **CDR E**
READER RABBIT'S READY FOR LETTERS (MICROCOMPUTER
PROGRAM). /1994/P-1/KB107. . . . . **MCP 372.4**
Software--Reading (Primary).
READ, WRITE AND TYPE! (CD-ROM). /1996/
K-2/KB105. . . . . **CDR 372.4**
READER RABBIT 3 (MICROCOMPUTER PROGRAM). /1993/
1-3/KB106. . . . . **MCP 372.4**
Software--Reading games.
CHICKA CHICKA BOOM BOOM (CD-ROM). /1996/
P-2/KF382. . . . . **CDR E**
READER RABBIT'S READY FOR LETTERS (MICROCOMPUTER
PROGRAM). /1994/P-1/KB107. . . . . **MCP 372.4**
Software--Reasoning.
SNAPDRAGON (MICROCOMPUTER PROGRAM). /1992/
P-1/KA636. . . . . **MCP 153.4**
Software--Recycling (Waste).
HALPERN, NA/Kids and the environment: taking responsibility for
our surroundings /1994/1-5/KB046. . . . . **CDR 363.7**
Software--Reference books.
MICROSOFT BOOKSHELF: MULTIMEDIA REFERENCE LIBRARY,
1998 ED. SCHOOL ED. (CD-ROM). /1997/
3-A/KA376 . . . . **CDR REF 028.7**
Software--Refuse and refuse disposal.
ENVIRONMENT (MICROCOMPUTER PROGRAM). /1990/
5-A/KB059. . . . . **MCP 363.73**
HALPERN, NA/Kids and the environment: taking responsibility for
our surroundings /1994/1-5/KB046. . . . . **CDR 363.7**
Software--Report writing.
OWENS, P/Research paper writer (Microcomputer program). /
c1990/5-A/KB090. . . . . **MCP 371.302**
STUDENT WRITING AND RESEARCH CENTER WITH COMPTON'S
CONCISE ENCYCLOPEDIA /1995/4-A/KB091 . . . **CDR 371.302**
Software--Research.
OWENS, P/Research paper writer (Microcomputer program). /
c1990/5-A/KB090. . . . . **MCP 371.302**
STUDENT WRITING AND RESEARCH CENTER WITH COMPTON'S
CONCISE ENCYCLOPEDIA /1995/4-A/KB091 . . . **CDR 371.302**
Software--Responsibility.
TAKING RESPONSIBILITY (MICROCOMPUTER PROGRAM). /
1988/1-6/KA665 . . . . **MCP 158**
Software--Revolutions.
REVOLUTIONARY WARS: CHOOSING SIDES (MICROCOMPUTER
PROGRAM). /1986/5-A/KA668 . . . . **MCP 172**
Software--Schools--Fiction.
ARTHUR'S TEACHER TROUBLE (CD-ROM). /1992/
1-4/KF171. . . . . **CDR E**
MERCER MAYER'S LITTLE MONSTER AT SCHOOL. SCHOOL ED.
(CD-ROM). /1994/K-3/KG130 . . . . **CDR E**
Software--Schubert, Franz.
WINTER, R/Microsoft composer collection (CD-ROM). /1994/
4-A/KD525 . . . . **CDR 780**
Software--Science.
SAMMY'S SCIENCE HOUSE (CD-ROM). /1994/
K-3/KB870. . . . . **CDR 500**
SCIENCE BLASTER JR. TEACHER ED. (CD-ROM). /1997/
K-3/KB871. . . . . **CDR 500**
Software--Science--Study and teaching.
GIZMOS AND GADGETS! (MICROCOMPUTER PROGRAM). /
1993/3-6/KB882. . . . . **MCP 507**
SCIENCE SLEUTHS. VOL. 1: THE MYSTERIES OF THE BLOB AND
THE EXPLODING LAWNMOWERS /1995/4-A/KB885 . **CDR 507**
Software--Solar System.
EYEWITNESS ENCYCLOPEDIA OF SPACE AND THE UNIVERSE
(CD-ROM). /1996/5-A/KC003 . . . . **CDR 520**
GREAT SOLAR SYSTEM RESCUE (CD-ROM). /1996/
5-A/KC009 . . . . **CDR 523.2**
MOHL, R/Planetary taxi (CD-ROM). /1993/
4-A/KC013 . . . . **CDR 523.2**
SCHOLASTIC'S THE MAGIC SCHOOL BUS EXPLORES THE SOLAR
SYSTEM. ACADEMIC ED. /1994/2-5/KC014. . . . . . **CDR 523.2**

Software--Sound.
SCIENCE IN YOUR EAR (CD-ROM). /1996/4-A/KC104 **CDR 534**

Software--Spanish language materials.
AESOP'S FABLE: THE TORTOISE AND THE HARE (CD-ROM). /
1993/P-A/KB522 . . . . **CDR 398.24**
ARTHUR'S TEACHER TROUBLE (CD-ROM). /1992/
1-4/KF171 . . . . **CDR E**
BERENSTAIN BEARS GET IN A FIGHT. SCHOOL ED. (CD-ROM).
/1995/K-3/KF223 . . . . **CDR E**
BROWN, MT/Arthur's teacher trouble (Microcomputer program). /
1994/2-6/KB109 . . . . **MCP 372.6**
JUST GRANDMA AND ME (CD-ROM). /1992/
P-2/KF863 . . . . **CDR E**
KID PIX STUDIO (CD-ROM). /1994/P-A/KD468 . . . **CDR 750.28**
MARC BROWN'S ARTHUR'S BIRTHDAY. SCHOOL ED. (CD-ROM).
/1994/K-4/KG062 . . . . **CDR E**
MARK SCHLICHTING'S HARRY AND THE HAUNTED HOUSE.
SCHOOL ED. (CD-ROM). /1994/K-3/KG063 . . . . **CDR E**
MAYAQUEST TRAIL (CD-ROM). /1996/5-A/KE845 **CDR 972.81**
MERCER MAYER'S LITTLE MONSTER AT SCHOOL. SCHOOL ED.
(CD-ROM). /1994/K-3/KG130 . . . . **CDR E**
MULTIMEDIA WORKSHOP. TEACHER ED. (CD-ROM). /1996/
3-A/KB115 . . . . **CDR 372.6**
NEW KID PIX. SCHOOL VERSION (MICROCOMPUTER
PROGRAM). /1996/P-A/KD469 . . . . **MCP 750.28**
STORYBOOK WEAVER DELUXE (CD-ROM). /1995/
1-5/KB118 . . . . **CDR 372.6**

Software--Teachers--Fiction.
ARTHUR'S TEACHER TROUBLE (CD-ROM). /1992/
1-4/KF171 . . . . **CDR E**

Software--Technology.
MACAULAY, D/Way things work (CD-ROM). /1996/
3-A/KC882 . . . . **CDR 600**

Software--Thought and thinking.
AFRICA TRAIL (CD-ROM). /1995/4-A/KE723 . . . . **CDR 960**
BIG ANTHONY'S MIXED-UP MAGIC (CD-ROM). /1996/
K-2/KF229 . . . . **CDR E**
INVENTION STUDIO (CD-ROM). /1996/5-A/KC887 . . **CDR 608**
STRATEGY CHALLENGES COLLECTION 1: AROUND THE WORLD.
SCHOOL VERSION (CD-ROM). /1995/3-A/KD754 . . . **CDR 794**
STRATEGY CHALLENGES COLLECTION 2: IN THE WILD. SCHOOL
VERSION (CD-ROM). /1996/4-A/KD755 . . . . **CDR 794**
THINKIN' THINGS COLLECTION 1 (MICROCOMPUTER
PROGRAM). /1993/K-3/KB080 . . . . **MCP 370.15**
THINKIN' THINGS COLLECTION 2. SCHOOL VERSION (CD-
ROM). /1995/1-6/KB081 . . . . **CDR 370.15**
THINKIN' THINGS COLLECTION 3. SCHOOL VERSION (CD-
ROM). /1995/3-A/KB082 . . . . **CDR 370.15**

Software--Time.
TRUDY'S TIME AND PLACE HOUSE. SCHOOL VERSION (CD-
ROM). /1995/P-3/KC075 . . . . **CDR 529**

Software--Trucks.
BIG JOB (CD-ROM). /1995/K-3/KD120 . . . . **CDR 629.225**

Software--Typewriting.
MAVIS BEACON TEACHES TYPING! (MICROCOMPUTER
PROGRAM). /1987/4-A/KD310 . . . . **MCP 652.3**
READ, WRITE AND TYPE! (CD-ROM). /1996/
K-2/KB105 . . . . **CDR 372.4**
TYPE TO LEARN: A NEW APPROACH TO KEYBOARDING
(MICROCOMPUTER PROGRAM). /1986/
2-A/KD312 . . . . **MCP 652.3**

Software--United States--Folklore.
P.J.'S READING ADVENTURES (CD-ROM). /1996/
K-3/KB252 . . . . **CDR 398**

Software--United States--Geography.
NATIONAL INSPIRER (MICROCOMPUTER PROGRAM). /1997/
5-A/KE190 . . . . **MCP 917.3**
WHERE IN THE U.S.A. IS CARMEN SANDIEGO? NEW ED. (CD-
ROM). /1996/3-A/KE182 . . . . **CDR 917**

Software--United States--History.
GTV: A GEOGRAPHIC PERSPECTIVE ON AMERICAN HISTORY
(VIDEODISC). /c1990/5-A/KE853 . . . . **VD 973**
SKYTRIP AMERICA: AN INCREDIBLE RIDE THROUGH U.S.
HISTORY. TEACHER ED. (CD-ROM). /1996/
3-A/KE865 . . . . **CDR 973**

Software--Utilities (Computer programs).
KIDDESK. SCHOOL VERSION (CD-ROM). /1995/
P-A/KA569 . . . . **CDR 004**
KIDDESK (MICROCOMPUTER PROGRAM). /1993/
K-A/KA568 . . . . **MCP 004**

Software--Values.
TAKING RESPONSIBILITY (MICROCOMPUTER PROGRAM). /
1988/1-6/KA665 . . . . **MCP 158**

Software--Violence in mass media.
VIOLENCE IN THE MEDIA (MICROCOMPUTER PROGRAM). /
1994/5-A/KA802 . . . . **MCP 302.23**

Software--Visual perception.
BUILDING PERSPECTIVE: STRATEGIES IN PROBLEM SOLVING
(MICROCOMPUTER PROGRAM). /1986/
4-A/KA637 . . . . **MCP 153.7**

Software--Whales.
IN THE COMPANY OF WHALES (CD-ROM). /1993/
3-A/KC770 . . . . **CDR 599.5**

Software--Writing.
BAILEY'S BOOK HOUSE (CD-ROM). /1995/
P-2/KB100 . . . . **CDR 372.4**
BAILEY'S BOOK HOUSE (MICROCOMPUTER PROGRAM). /1993/
P-2/KB101 . . . . **MCP 372.4**
BRIDGE TO TERABITHIA: A MULTI-MEDIA STUDY
(MICROCOMPUTER PROGRAM). /1993/
5-A/KB108 . . . . **MCP 372.6**
BROWN, MT/Arthur's teacher trouble (Microcomputer program). /
1994/2-6/KB109 . . . . **MCP 372.6**
CHARLOTTE'S WEB: A WRITE ON! MULTI-MEDIA STUDY
(MICROCOMPUTER PROGRAM). /1992/3-6/KB110 . **MCP 372.6**
DESTINATION: OCEAN. SCHOOL VERSION (CD-ROM). /1995/
1-A/KB111 . . . . **CDR 372.6**
ECOLOGY WITH SEUSS (MICROCOMPUTER PROGRAM). /1990/
2-5/KB112 . . . . **MCP 372.6**
INDIAN IN THE CUPBOARD (MICROCOMPUTER PROGRAM). /
1991/4-6/KB113 . . . . **MCP 372.6**
MICROSOFT CREATIVE WRITER 2. SCHOOL ED. (CD-ROM). /
1996/2-A/KB114 . . . . **CDR 372.6**
MULTIMEDIA WORKSHOP. TEACHER ED. (CD-ROM). /1996/
3-A/KB115 . . . . **CDR 372.6**
MY FIRST SENTENCES (MICROCOMPUTER PROGRAM). /1987/
1-3/KB116 . . . . **MCP 372.6**
READ, WRITE AND TYPE! (CD-ROM). /1996/
K-2/KB105 . . . . **CDR 372.4**
READER RABBIT 3 (MICROCOMPUTER PROGRAM). /1993/
1-3/KB106 . . . . **MCP 372.4**
STANLEY'S STICKER STORIES. SCHOOL VERSION (CD-ROM). /
1996/P-2/KB117 . . . . **CDR 372.6**
STORYBOOK WEAVER DELUXE (CD-ROM). /1995/
1-5/KB118 . . . . **CDR 372.6**
TUCK EVERLASTING (MICROCOMPUTER PROGRAM). /1989/
4-6/KB119 . . . . **MCP 372.6**
ULTIMATE WRITING AND CREATIVITY CENTER. SCHOOL ED.
(CD-ROM). /1996/K-5/KB120 . . . . **CDR 372.6**

Soil animals.
PLUCKROSE, H/Under the ground. /1994/P-2/4 KC360 . . **578.75**

Soil biology.
LAVIES, B/Compost critters. /1993/5-6/7 KC336 . . . . **577.5**

Soil ecology.
LAVIES, B/Compost critters. /1993/5-6/7 KC336 . . . . **577.5**
PLUCKROSE, H/Under the ground. /1994/P-2/4 KC360 . . **578.75**

Soils.
BOURGEOIS, P/Amazing dirt book. /1990/4-6/6 KD148 . . **631.4**
Solar eclipse SEE Eclipse, Solar.

Solar energy--Experiments.
HILLERMAN, A/Done in the sun, solar projects for children. /1983/
2-4/7 KD048 . . . . **621.47**
Solar system SEE ALSO Comets; Earth; Moon; Planets; Sun; also names of
planets e.g. Mars (Planet), etc.

Solar system.
BENDICK, J/Sun: our very own star. /1991/1-3/5 KC044 . . **523.7**
BERGER, M/Where are the stars during the day?: a book about
stars. /1993/1-4/2 KC048 . . . . **523.8**
BRANLEY, FM/Planets in our solar system. Rev. ed. /1987/
2-4/4 KC023 . . . . **523.4**
COLE, J/Magic School Bus lost in the solar system. /1990/
2-6/4 KC008 . . . . **523.2**
COLE, N/Blast off!: a space counting book. /1994/
P-3/6 KD131 . . . . **629.43**
COUPER, H/Space atlas. /1992/3-6/6 KC002 . . . . **520**
GREAT SOLAR SYSTEM RESCUE (VIDEODISC). /1992/
5-A/KC010 . . . . **VD 523.2**
JOURNEY THROUGH THE SOLAR SYSTEM (VIDEOCASSETTE). /
1991/3-6/KC011 . . . . **VCR 523.2**
LEEDY, L/Postcards from Pluto: a tour of the solar system. /1993/
1-6/3 KC012 . . . . **523.2**
SIMON, S/Our solar system. /1992/4-8/7 KC015 . . . . . . **523.2**
SOLAR SYSTEM (PICTURE). /1990/4-A/KC016 . . . . . **PIC 523.2**
SUN, EARTH, MOON (VIDEOCASSETTE). /1995/
4-6/KC017 . . . . **VCR 523.2**
VISUAL DICTIONARY OF THE UNIVERSE. /1993/
3-A/11 KC004 . . . . **520**

WHAT'S OUT THERE?: OUR SOLAR SYSTEM AND BEYOND (VIDEOCASSETTE). /1997/5-A/KC018 . . . . **VCR 523.2**

Solar system--Software.
EYEWITNESS ENCYCLOPEDIA OF SPACE AND THE UNIVERSE (CD-ROM). /1996/5-A/KC003 . . . . **CDR 520**
GREAT SOLAR SYSTEM RESCUE (CD-ROM). /1996/ 5-A/KC009 . . . . **CDR 523.2**
MOHL, R/Planetary taxi (CD-ROM). /1993/ 4-A/KC013 . . . . **CDR 523.2**
SCHOLASTIC'S THE MAGIC SCHOOL BUS EXPLORES THE SOLAR SYSTEM. ACADEMIC ED. (CD-ROM). /1994/ 2-5/KC014. **CDR 523.2**

Soldiers.
MURPHY, J/Young patriot: the American Revolution as experienced by one boy. /1996/5-A/9 KE884. . . . . **973.3**
PFEIFER, KB/Henry O. Flipper. /1993/ 4-6/9 KE345 . . . . **B FLIPPER, H.**
REEF, C/Black fighting men: a proud history. /1994/ 5-6/6 KA982 . . . . **355**
WHITMAN, S/Uncle Sam wants you!: military men and women of World War II. /1993/A/8 KE675. . . . . **940.54**

Solomon, King of Israel.
ORGEL, D/Flower of Sheba. /1994/1-2/2 KA687 . . . . **222**
RENBERG, DH/King Solomon and the bee. /1994/ 2-3/4 KB475 . . . . **398.22**

Songhay Empire--History.
MCKISSACK, P/Royal kingdoms of Ghana, Mali, and Songhay: life in medieval Africa. /c1994, 1995/A/8 KE734 . . . . **966.2**
Songs SEE ALSO Activity songs; Ballads; Carols; Children's songs; Folk songs; Lullabies; Music; National songs.

Songs.
ALL-TIME FAVORITE DANCES (SOUND RECORDING CASSETTE). /1991/K-6/KD603. . . . . **SRC 789.3**
ALSOP, P/Plugging away (Sound recording cassette). /1990/ 1-5/KD604. **SRC 789.3**
AMERICAN MELODY SAMPLER (COMPACT DISC). /1994/ K-6/KD555 . . . . **CD 789.2**
BARCHAS, S/Pinata!: bilingual songs for children (Sound recording cassette). /1991/K-6/KD605 . . . . **SRC 789.3**
This old man/Este viejito (Sound recording cassette). /1997/ K-2/KD606 . . . . **SRC 789.3**
BETHIE /Bethie's really silly songs about animals (Sound recording cassette). /1993/K-2/KD607 . . . . **SRC 789.3**
BROADWAY KIDS SING BROADWAY (COMPACT DISC). /1994/ 2-6/KD528. **CD 782.1**
CALLINAN, T/Let's clean up our act: songs for the earth (Sound recording cassette). /1989/K-6/KD559 . . . . **SRC 789.2**
CHILD'S CELEBRATION OF SHOWTUNES (SOUND RECORDING CASSETTE). /1992/P-3/KD529. . . . . **SRC 782.1**
CHILD'S CELEBRATION OF SONG (SOUND RECORDING CASSETTE). /1992/P-3/KD608 . . . . **SRC 789.3**
COLGATE, B/Silly Willy workout (Sound recording cassette). / 1994/P-1/KD609 . . . . **SRC 789.3**
DIANE GOODE'S BOOK OF SCARY STORIES AND SONGS. / 1994/2-5/5 KB685 . . . . **398.25**
DIANE GOODE'S BOOK OF SILLY STORIES AND SONGS. / 1992/K-3/KD872 . . . . **808.8**
ELLIOTT, D/Crawdads, doodlebugs and creasy greens: songs, stories and lore celebrating the /1996/3-5/KB291 . . . . **CD 398.2**
EPSTEIN-KRAVIS, A/Happy to be me (Sound recording cassette). / 1993/P-1/KA638 . . . . **SRC 155.2**
Tot's tunes (Sound recording cassette). /c1987, 1990/ P-1/KD610. **SRC 789.3**
FARJEON, E/Morning has broken. /1996/P-2/KD611 . . . . . **789.3**
FISH THAT'S A SONG: SONGS AND STORIES FOR CHILDREN (SOUND RECORDING CASSETTE). /1990/ K-6/KD563 . . . . **SRC 789.2**
GO IN AND OUT THE WINDOW: AN ILLUSTRATED SONGBOOK FOR YOUNG PEOPLE. /1987/2-A/KD564. . . . . **789.2**
GORDH, B/Morning, noon and nighttime tales (Sound recording cassette). /1993/K-2/KD565 . . . . **SRC 789.2**
GRAHAM, S/Dear old Donegal. /1996/1-3/2 KD566 . . . . **789.2**
GREEN CHILI JAM BAND /Magic bike (Sound recording cassette). /1991/P-3/KD613. . . . . **SRC 789.3**
Starfishing (Sound recording cassette). /1993/ P-2/KD614. **SRC 789.3**
HARTMANN, J/Let's read together and other songs for sharing and caring (Sound recording cassette). /1991/P-2/KD616. **SRC 789.3**
Make a friend, be a friend: songs for growing up and growing together with /1990/K-5/KD617. . . . . **SRC 789.3**
One voice for children (Videocassette). /1993/ K-4/KD618 . . . . **VCR 789.3**
HINOJOSA, T/Cada nino./Every child (Compact disc). /1996/ 2-6/KD568. . . . . **CD 789.2**

HORTON, B/Lyrical life science (Multimedia kit). /1995/ K-A/KA295 . . . . **MMK PROF 570**
HOW SWEET THE SOUND: AFRICAN-AMERICAN SONGS FOR CHILDREN. /1995/K-6/KD571 . . . . **CE 789.2**
I'M GONNA LET IT SHINE: A GATHERING OF VOICES FOR FREEDOM (SOUND RECORDING CASSETTE). /1990/ 3-6/KD619. **SRC 789.3**
JACK, D/Dance in your pants: great songs for little kids to dance to (Sound recording cassette). /1988/K-3/KD620 . . . . . **SRC 789.3**
David Jack... live!: Makin' music, makin' friends (Videocassette). / 1991/P-2/KD621 . . . . **VCR 789.3**
Gotta hop (Sound recording cassette). /1990/ K-3/KD622 . . . . **SRC 789.3**
JANIAK, W/Basic skills for young children (Sound recording cassette). /c1980, 1990/P-K/KD623 . . . . **SRC 789.3**
JENKINS, E/African-American folk songs and rhythms (Sound recording cassette). /c1960, 1992/K-6/KD572 . . . . . **SRC 789.2**
And one and two and other songs for pre-school and primary children (Compact disc). /1995/P-K/KD624. . . . . **CD 789.3**
Call and response: rhythmic group singing (Sound recording cassette). /1990/K-3/KD625 . . . . **SRC 789.3**
Come dance by the ocean (Sound recording cassette). /1991/ P-2/KD626. **SRC 789.3**
Ella Jenkins live!: at the Smithsonian (Videocassette). /1991/ P-K/KD627 . . . . **VCR 789.3**
Growing up with Ella Jenkins: rhythms songs and rhymes (Sound recording cassette). /1990/P-2/KD628 . . . . **SRC 789.3**
Jambo and other call and response songs and chants (Sound recording cassette). /1990/K-3/KD573 . . . . **SRC 789.2**
Multicultural children's songs (Compact disc). /1995/ K-2/KD629 . . . . **CD 789.3**
Rhythm and game songs for the little ones (Sound recording cassette). /1990/P-K/KD630 . . . . **SRC 789.3**
Songs and rhythms from near and far (Sound recording cassette). /c1964, 1992/K-2/KD575 . . . . **SRC 789.2**
Songs children love to sing (Compact disc). /1996/ K-3/KD631 . . . . **CD 789.3**
This is rhythm (Compact disc). /1994/K-2/KD632 . . . . **CD 789.3**
You'll sing a song and I'll sing a song (Sound recording cassette). /c1966, 1989/P-2/KD633 . . . . **SRC 789.3**
JOHNSON, JW/Lift every voice and sing. /1993/ 2-6/5 KD672 . . . . **789.44**
JUBA THIS AND JUBA THAT. /1995//KA366 . . . . . **PROF 820.8**
JUNIPER TREE AND OTHER SONGS (SOUND RECORDING CASSETTE). /1994/K-6/KD578 . . . . **SRC 789.2**
KEEP THE SPIRIT (SOUND RECORDING CASSETTE). /1989/ K-6/KD634 . . . . **SRC 789.3**
LANGSTAFF, J/Let's sing!: John Langstaff sings with children, ages 3-7 (Videocassette). /1997//KA314 . . . . **VCR PROF 780**
Making music with children, ages 3-7 (Videocassette). /1995/ /KA315. **VCR PROF 780**
LATE LAST NIGHT (SOUND RECORDING CASSETTE). /1984/ P-2/KD635. **SRC 789.3**
LEWIS, S/Get your teddy ready (Videocassette). /1994/ P-2/KD681. **VCR 790.1**
Let's play games (Videocassette). /1994/P-2/KD709. **VCR 793.4**
LYRIC LANGUAGE: A BILINGUAL MUSIC PROGRAM: SPANISH/ ENGLISH (VIDEOCASSETTE). /1992/K-6/KD636 . . . **VCR 789.3**
MCCUTCHEON, J/Family garden (Sound recording cassette). / 1993/P-3/KD581 . . . . **SRC 789.2**
Happy adoption day! /1996/2-4/3 KD637 . . . . **789.3**
John McCutcheon's four seasons: wintersongs (Compact disc). / 1995/K-3/KD638 . . . . **CD 789.3**
MISH, M/Kid's eye view of the environment (Sound recording cassette) /1989/P-2/KB050. . . . . **SRC 363.7**
MOTHER GOOSE /Olde Mother Goose (Kit). /1993/ P-K/KB805. **KIT 398.8**
NELSON, EL/Everybody sing and dance. /1989/ /KA321. . . . . **CE PROF 789.3**
NORWORTH, J/Take me out to the ballgame. /1992/ K-2/KD639 . . . . **789.3**
NURSERY SONGS AND RHYMES (VIDEOCASSETTE). /1993/ P-2/KB104. **VCR 372.4**
ON THE ROAD AGAIN (SOUND RECORDING CASSETTE). / 1992/K-4/KD640 . . . . **SRC 789.3**
PALMER, H/Can a cherry pie wave goodbye?: songs for learning through music and movement (Sound recording cassette). /1991/ P-K/KD641. **SRC 789.3**
Getting to know myself (Sound recording cassette). /1972/ P-1/KA641. **SRC 155.2**
Sammy and other songs from "Getting to know myself" (Videocassette). /1993/P-1/KD643 . . . . **VCR 789.3**
So big: activity songs for little ones (Compact disc). /1994/ P-2/KD644. . . . . **CD 789.3**

Stepping out with Hap Palmer (Videocassette). /1994/
P-2/KD645. . . . . **VCR 789.3**
PETER COTTONTAIL: HOW HE GOT HIS HOP! (VIDEOCASSTTE).
/1993/P-2/KD646. . . . . **VCR 789.3**
POLANSKY, DS/I like dessert (Sound recording cassette). /1987/
K-6/KD647 . . . . **SRC 789.3**
POLISAR, BL/Family concert (Compact disc). /1993/
1-6/KD648. . . . . **CD 789.3**
Old dogs, new tricks (Sound recording cassette). /1993/
P-3/KD649. . . . . **SRC 789.3**
PRESCHOOL PLAYTIME BAND (SOUND RECORDING CASSETTE).
/1987/P-K/KD651. . . . . **SRC 789.3**
RAFFI /Rise and shine (Sound recording cassette). /c1982/
P-5/KD652. . . . . **SRC 789.3**
REGGAE FOR KIDS: A COLLECTION OF MUSIC FOR KIDS OF
ALL AGES! (SOUND RECORDING CASSETTE). /1992/
K-3/KD669. . . . . **SRC 789.4**
ROGERS, S/What can one little person do? (Sound recording
cassette). /1992/P-2/KD654 . . . . **SRC 789.3**
SAPP, J/We've all got stories: songs from the Dream Project
(Compact disc). /1996/K-6/KD655 . . . . **CD 789.3**
SCHOOL RAP (SOUND RECORDING CASSETTE). /1990/
2-6/KD656. . . . . **SRC 789.3**
SCRUGGS, J/Ants (Compact disc). /1994/K-3/KD657 . **CD 789.3**
SEEGER, P/Song and play time (Sound recording cassette). /1990/
K-3/KD589. . . . . **SRC 789.2**
SEUSS, D/Cat in the Hat gets grinched (Videocassette). /1982/
K-2/KG449 . . . . **VCR E**
SILVERMAN, J/Blues. /1994/5-A/KD671 . . . . **789.43**
Children's songs. /1993/5-A/KD591 . . . . **789.2**
Songs of protest and civil rights. /1992/5-A/KD593 . . . . **789.2**
SKIERA-ZUCEK, L/Save the animals, save the earth: songs about
endangered animals and the earth (Sound recording cassette). /
1991/K-4/KD658 . . . . **SRC 789.3**
STEWART, G/Multicultural rhythm stick fun (Sound recording
cassette). /1992/P-2/KD768 . . . . **SRC 796.1**
Pre-K hooray! (Sound recording cassette). /1993/
P-K/KD659. . . . . **SRC 789.3**
Preschool favorites (Sound recording cassette). /1990/
P-K/KD660. . . . . **SRC 789.3**
SUNSERI, M/Rhythm of the rocks: a multicultural musical journey
(Sound recording cassette). /1993/K-2/KD599 . . . . . **SRC 789.2**
Rhythm of the rocks songbook: a multicultural musical journey... /
1994/K-2/KD600 . . . . **789.2**
THIS OLD MAN. /1990/P-1/KD602 . . . . **789.2**
TODAY IS MONDAY. /1993/P-1/KD661 . . . . **789.3**
TRAPANI, I/Itsy bitsy spider. /1996/P-1/2 KD662 . . . . . **789.3**
VALERI, M/Mi casa es su casa/my house is your house: a bi-lingual
musical journey through Latin America (Sound recording cassette). /
1991/K-3/KD663 . . . . **SRC 789.3**
VAN MANENS /We recycle and other songs for Earth keepers
(Sound recording cassette). /1990/K-4/KD664 . . . . . **SRC 789.3**
WEEKS, S/Crocodile smile: 10 songs of the Earth as the animals see
it. /1994/P-2/KD665 . . . . **BA 789.3**
WEISS, GD/What a wonderful world. /1995/P-2/2 KG692 . . . . **E**
WEISSMAN, J/Joining hands with other lands: multicultural songs
and games (Sound recording cassette). /1993/
K-3/KD666 . . . . **SRC 789.3**
Songs--Fiction.
GERSHATOR, D/Bread is for eating. /1995/P-2/2 KF610 . . . . . **E**
Songs--Latin America.
POLLITOS DICEN: JUEGOS, RIMAS Y CANCIONES INFANTILES
DE PAISES DE HABLA /1994/P-1/2 KD584. . . . . **789.2**
Songs--Spain.
POLLITOS DICEN: JUEGOS, RIMAS Y CANCIONES INFANTILES
DE PAISES DE HABLA HISPANA./THE BABY CHICKS SING:
TRADITIONAL GAMES, NURSERY RHYMES, AND SONGS
FROM SPANISH-SPEAKING COUNTRIES. /1994/
P-1/2 KD584 . . . . **789.2**
Songs--United States.
BANGS, E/Yankee Doodle. 2nd ed. /c1976, 1996/
P-2/KD557. . . . . **789.2**
Songs, Spanish--Latin America.
DE COLORES AND OTHER LATIN-AMERICAN FOLK SONGS FOR
CHILDREN. /1994/K-3/KD561. . . . . **789.2**
Sonoran Desert.
DUNPHY, M/Here is the southwestern desert. /1995/
P-3/3 KF066 . . . . **979.1**
WRIGHT-FRIERSON, V/Desert scrapbook: dawn to dusk in the
Sonoran Desert. /1996/3-5/7 KF072 . . . . **979.1**
Sorcerers--Fiction.
COLE, J/Doctor Change. /1986/K-3/2 KF410 . . . . **E**

Sorcery SEE Occult sciences; Witchcraft.
Sound SEE ALSO Animal sounds.
Sound.
SOUND/LIGHT AND COLOR (VIDEOCASSETTE). /1994/
3-6/KC080. . . . . **VCR 530**
Sound--Experiments.
ARDLEY, N/Science book of sound. /1991/2-5/3 KC076. . . . **530**
DARLING, DJ/Sounds interesting: the science of acoustics. /1991/
6-A/8 KC103 . . . . **534**
Sound--Fiction.
CHARLES, VM/Hey! What's that sound? /1994/P-1/1 KF379 . . . **E**
JOHNSON, A/Joshua's night whispers (Board book). /1994/
P/2 KF830. . . . . **BB E**
MANUSHKIN, F/Peeping and sleeping. /1994/P-2/2 KG060 . . . **E**
MARTIN, JR., B/Listen to the rain. /1988/P-2/KG077 . . . . **E**
OGBURN, JK/Noise lullaby. /1995/P-2/2 KG190 . . . . **E**
SERFOZO, M/Joe Joe. /1993/P-K/1 KG440. . . . . **E**
SHOWERS, P/Listening walk. /c1961, 1991/P-1/1 KG495. . . . . **E**
Sound--Recording and reproducing.
SHIPTON, A/Singing. /1994/4-6/7 KD527 . . . . **782**
Sound--Software.
SCIENCE IN YOUR EAR (CD-ROM). /1996/4-A/KC104 **CDR 534**
Soup kitchens--Fiction.
DISALVO-RYAN, D/Uncle Willie and the soup kitchen. /1991/
1-3/2 KF485 . . . . **E**
Soups--Fiction.
MARTIN, AT/Famous seaweed soup. /1993/P-2/4 KG070. . . . . **E**
MEDDAUGH, S/Martha blah blah. /1996/K-2/2 KG124 . . . . . **E**
Sousa, John Philip.
GREENE, C/John Philip Sousa: the march king. /1992/
2-4/2 KE544 . . . . **B SOUSA, J.**
South Africa--Biography.
WATSON, L/Warriors, warthogs, and wisdom: growing up in
Africa. /1997/4-6/7 KE589. . . . . **B WATSON, L.**
South Africa--Fiction.
DALY, N/Not so fast, Songololo. /1986/K-3/2 KF448. . . . . **CE E**
HAARHOFF, D/Desert December. /1992/3-5/4 KH206 . . . **Fic**
ISADORA, R/At the crossroads. /1991/K-2/1 KF811 . . . . . . **E**
At the crossroads (Videocassette). /1996/K-2/KF812 . . . **VCR E**
Over the green hills. /1992/1-3/2 KF817 . . . . **E**
NAIDOO, B/No turning back: a novel of South Africa. /1997/
6-A/6 KH526 . . . . **Fic**
SISULU, E/Day Gogo went to vote: South Africa, April 1994. /
1996/1-3/2 KG513 . . . . **E**
South Africa--Folklore.
MOODIE, F/Nabulela: a South Africa folk tale. /1997/
2-4/4 KB758 . . . . **398.27**
WOLFSON, M/Marriage of the rain goddess: a South African
myth. /1996/4-5/5 KB424 . . . . **398.21**
South Africa--Race relations.
COOPER, F/Mandela: from the life of the South African statesman.
/1996/3-6/7 KE457 . . . . **B MANDELA, N.**
South Africa--Social life and customs.
ANGELOU, M/My painted house, my friendly chicken, and me. /
1994/1-3/2 KE739 . . . . **968**
South America--Fiction.
DORROS, A/Tonight is Carnaval. /1991/1-3/4 KF492 . . . . **E**
TORRES, L/Saturday sancocho. /1995/K-2/5 KG614 . . . . **E**
South America--History--Wars of Independence, 1806-1830.
ADLER, DA/Picture book of Simon Bolivar. /1992/
3-4/5 KE257 . . . . **B BOLIVAR, S.**
South Asia--Social life and customs.
VIESTI, JF/Celebrate! in South Asia. /1996/2-5/11 KB191 . . **394.2**
South Carolina.
FRADIN, DB/South Carolina. /1992/4-6/5 KE984 . . . . **975.7**
FREDEEN, C/South Carolina. /1991/4-6/6 KE986 . . . . **975.7**
South Carolina--History--Colonial period, ca. 1600-1775.
FRADIN, DB/South Carolina Colony. /1992/A/7 KE985 . . . **975.7**
South Carolina--History--Revolution, 1775-1783.
FRADIN, DB/South Carolina Colony. /1992/A/7 KE985 . . . **975.7**
South Dakota.
FRADIN, DB/South Dakota. /1995/4-6/7 KF056 . . . . **978.3**
South Dakota--Fiction.
KARR, K/Cave. /1994/5-A/4 KH341 . . . . **Fic**
South Georgia Island--Description and travel.
PONCET, S/Antarctic encounter: destination South Georgia. /1995/
4-6/6 KE217 . . . . **919.8**
Southampton Insurrection, 1831.
BARRETT, T/Nat Turner and the slave revolt. /c1993, 1995/
5-6/6 KE577 . . . . **B TURNER, N.**
Southern States--Bibliography.
EXPLORING THE SOUTHEAST STATES THROUGH LITERATURE. /
1994//KA037 . . . . **PROF 016.975**

Southern States--Fiction.
    MARINO, J/Day that Elvis came to town. /1993/
    6-A/6 KH456 . . . . **Fic**
    YOUNG, RT/Learning by heart. /1993/6-A/6 KH899 . . . . **Fic**

Southern States--Folklore.
    HAMILTON, V/When birds could talk and bats could sing: the
    adventures of Bruh Sparrow, Sis /1996/2-5/2 KB582. . . . **398.24**

Southern States--Race relations--Fiction.
    TAYLOR, MD/Friendship. /1987/4-6/5 KH776. . . . . **Fic**
    Mississippi bridge. /1990/5-A/4 KH778 . . . . **Fic**
    Roll of thunder, hear my cry. /c1976/5-6/6 KH779. . . . . **CE Fic**
    Well: David's story. /1995/5-A/4 KH781 . . . . **Fic**

Southern States--Social life and customs--1775-1865.
    MCKISSACK, P/Christmas in the big house, Christmas in the
    quarters. /1994/4-A/6 KE967 . . . . **975**

Southwest, New--Antiquities.
    WARREN, S/Cities in the sand: the ancient civilizations of the
    Southwest. /1992/5-6/8 KF064. . . . . **979**

Southwest, New--Discovery and exploration.
    SANFORD, WR/Zebulon Pike: explorer of the Southwest. /1996/
    5-6/8 KE497 . . . . **B PIKE, Z.**

Southwest, New--Fiction.
    BRIMNER, LD/Merry Christmas, Old Armadillo. /1995/
    K-2/3 KF267 . . . . **E**
    LATTIMORE, DN/Frida Maria: a story of the old Southwest. /
    1994/1-3/2 KF949. . . . . **E**
    LOWELL, S/Little Red Cowboy Hat. /1997/1-3/3 KG038. . . . . **E**
    Three little javelinas. /1992/K-2/4 KG039. . . . . **E**
    Tortoise and the jackrabbit. /1994/K-2/3 KG040 . . . . **E**

Southwest, New--Folklore.
    DUNCAN, L/Magic of Spider Woman. /1996/
    4-5/6 KB733 . . . . **398.27**
    HAYES, J/Watch out for clever women!/Cuidado con las mujeres
    astutas!: Hispanic /1994/2-5/4 KB315. . . . . **398.2**
    JACKSON, E/Precious gift: a Navaho creation myth. /1996/
    2-3/2 KB594 . . . . **398.24**
    SAN SOUCI, RD/Little seven-colored horse: a Spanish American
    folktale. /1995/3-5/5 KB648. . . . . **398.24**
    VIGIL, A/Corn woman: stories and legends of the Hispanic
    Southwest/La mujer del maiz: /1994/5-6/4 KB380. . . . **CE 398.2**
    YOUNG, R/Head on the high road: ghost stories from the
    Southwest /1993/4-6/KB698. . . . . **SRC 398.25**

Southwest, Old.
    SOUTH CENTRAL REGION: TEXAS, NEW MEXICO, OKLAHOMA
    (VIDEOCASSETTE). /1995/3-5/KE995 . . . . **VCR 976**

Southwestern States--Bibliography.
    EXPLORING THE SOUTHWEST STATES THROUGH LITERATURE. /
    1994/ . . . . **PROF 016.976**

Soviet Union--Emigration and immigration.
    BRESNICK-PERRY, R/Leaving for America. /1992/
    1-4/6 KE688 . . . . **947**

Soviet Union--Fiction.
    POLACCO, P/Rechenka's eggs. /1988/1-3/5 KG256 . . . . . **CE E**
    SEGAL, J/Place where nobody stopped. /1994/5-A/7 KH690 . **Fic**
    USHINSKY, K/How a shirt grew in the field. /1992/
    K-2/2 KG636. . . . . **E**

Soviet Union--Folklore.
    BUDBERG, M/Russian fairy tales (Talking book). /n.d./
    4-6/KB722. . . . . **TB 398.27**
    CECH, J/First snow, magic snow. /1992/2-4/6 KB390. . . . **398.21**
    GINSBURG, M/King who tried to fry an egg on his head: based on
    a Russian tale. /1994/2-4/6 KB444 . . . . **398.22**
    KIMMEL, EA/Bearhead: a Russian folktale. /1991/
    2-4/4 KB327 . . . . **398.2**
    LANG, A/Flying ship. /1995/K-3/6 KB749 . . . . **398.27**
    PROKOFIEV, S/Peter and the wolf. /1982/
    P-3/4 KD676 . . . . **CE 789.8**
    RANSOME, A/Fool of the world and the flying ship: a Russian tale.
    /c1968/2-5/5 KB765. **398.27**
    Old Peter's Russian tales. /1975/5-6/6 KB766. . . . . . . **398.27**
    ROBBINS, R/Baboushka and the three kings. /c1960/
    2-4/6 KB509 . . . . **398.23**

Soviet Union--History.
    HARVEY, M/Fall of the Soviet Union. /1995/5-A/7 KE689. . . **947**

Space and Rocket Center (Huntsville, Ala.).
    ALSTON, E/Space camp. /1990/4-5/7 KD135 . . . . **629.45**

Space and time--Fiction.
    ALCOCK, V/Red-eared ghosts. /1997/5-A/4 KG828. . . . . . . **Fic**
    CRESSWELL, H/Watchers: a mystery at Alton Towers. /1994/
    5-A/3 KH040 . . . . **Fic**
    REISS, K/Time windows. /1991/6-A/7 KH630 . . . . **Fic**

Space flight SEE ALSO Outer space--Exploration; also names of specific
    projects e.g. Apollo project.

Space flight.
    RIDE, S/To space and back. /1986/4-6/7 KD138. . . . . . **629.45**

Space flight--Fiction.
    BARTON, B/I want to be an astronaut. /1988/P-2/2 KF206. . . . **E**
    WILDSMITH, B/Professor Noah's spaceship. /1980/
    K-2/5 KG722 . . . . **E**

Space flight to Mars.
    VOGT, G/Viking and the Mars landing. /1991/
    A/10 KD132 . . . . **629.43**

Space flight to the moon--Fiction.
    ALEXANDER, M/You're a genius, Blackboard Bear. /1995/
    K-2/2 KF147 . . . . **E**

Space perception.
    HOBAN, T/Is it red? Is it yellow? Is it blue? An adventure in color.
    /1978/P/KA614 . . . . **152.14**
    Over, under and through, and other spatial concepts. /1973/
    P-K/KF745 . . . . **E**

Space perception--Fiction.
    ZIEFERT, H/Nicky upstairs and down. /c1987, 1994/
    P-1/1 KF795 . . . . **E**

Space probes.
    KERROD, R/Story of space exploration (Picture). /1994/
    4-6/KC027. . . . . **PIC 523.4**
    ROBINSON, F/Space probes to the planets. /1993/
    2-5/5 KC031 . . . . **523.4**

Space projects SEE names of specific projects e.g. Apollo project.
Space sciences SEE ALSO Astronautics; Astronomy; Outer space.

Space sciences.
    MOON/OUTER SPACE (VIDEOCASSETTE). /1994/
    3-6/KC007. . . . . **VCR 523**

Space ships--Models.
    BLOCKSMA, M/Easy-to-make spaceships that really fly. /1983/
    3-5/3 KD140 . . . . **629.47**

Space shuttles.
    DREAM IS ALIVE: A WINDOW SEAT ON THE SPACE SHUTTLE
    (VIDEOCASSETTE). /1985/5-6/KD134 . . . . **VCR 629.44**
    KETTELKAMP, L/Living in space. /1993/A/8 KD130 . . . . . **629.4**
    RIDE, S/To space and back. /1986/4-6/7 KD138. . . . . . **629.45**

Space shuttles--Experiments.
    SUMNERS, C/Toys in space: exploring science with the astronauts.
    /1997//KA282. . . . . **PROF 500.5**

Space stations.
    BERLINER, D/Living in space. /1993/5-6/9 KD139 . . . . . **629.47**
    KETTELKAMP, L/Living in space. /1993/A/8 KD130 . . . . . **629.4**

Space vehicles SEE ALSO Space shuttles; Space stations.

Spain.
    CHICOINE, S/Spain: bridge between continents. /1997/
    4-6/7 KE686 . . . . **946**

Spain--Bibliography.
    SCHON, I/Hispanic heritage, series II. /1985/
    /KA043 . . . . **PROF 016.98**

Spain--Ethnic relations.
    FINKELSTEIN, NH/Other 1492: Jewish settlement in the new world.
    /1992/5-6/8 KE687 . . . . **946**

Spain--Fiction.
    KIMMEL, EA/Bernal and Florinda: a Spanish tale. /1994/
    2-4/3 KF903 . . . . **E**
    WOJCIECHOWSKA, M/Shadow of a bull. /1964/
    5-6/6 KH875 . . . . **CE Fic**

Spain--Folklore.
    ARAUJO, FP/Nekane, the lamina and the bear: a tale of the
    Basque Pyrenees. /1993/2-3/3 KB256. . . . . **398.2**
    HAYES, J/Tales from the Southwest (Sound recording cassette). /
    1984/4-5/KB502. **SRC 398.23**
    STEWIG, JW/Princess Florecita and the iron shoes: a Spanish fairy
    tale. /1995/3-4/5 KB372 . . . . **398.2**

Spaniards--Fiction.
    ZAMORANO, A/Let's eat! /1997/P-2/1 KG786 . . . . **E**

Spanish America SEE Latin America.
Spanish Armada SEE Armada, 1588.

Spanish language--Dictionaries--English.
    LIPTON, GC/Beginning Spanish bilingual dictionary: a beginner's
    guide in words and pictures. 2nd rev. ed. /1989/3-A/KB859 . **463**

Spanish language--Vocabulary.
    ELYA, SM/Say hola to Spanish. /1996/K-2/3 KB862 . . . . . **468.1**
    KAHN, M/My everyday Spanish word book. /1982/
    1-3/KB855 . . . . **468**
    PARNWELL, EC/Oxford picture dictionary of American English.
    English/Spanish ed. /c1978, 1988/4-6/KB860. . . . . **463**

Spanish language materials SEE ALSO Bilingual materials--Spanish.
Spanish language materials.

ADA, AF/Gathering the sun: an alphabet in Spanish and English. /
1997/1-3/KE122 . . . . **861**
    Gold coin. /1991/1-3/4 KF131 . . . . **E**
    Mediopollito/Half-Chicken. /1995/K-2/2 KB521 . . . . **398.24**
ALBOROUGH, J/Where's my teddy? /1992/P-1/2 KF145 . . . . . **E**
ALIKI /My five senses. Rev. ed. /1989/K-2/2 KC962 . . . . **612.8**
ANCONA, G/Pablo remembers: the Fiesta of the Day of the Dead.
/1993/3-6/5 KB193 . . . . **394.26**
    Pinata maker./El Pinatero. /1994/3-6/6 KD450 . . . . . . **745.594**
ARMSTRONG, WH/Sounder. /c1969/4-A/4 KG851 . . . . **CE Fic**
ARROZ CON LECHE: POPULAR SONGS AND RHYMES FROM
LATIN AMERICA. /1989/P-3/KD556 . . . . **789.2**
BABBITT, N/Tuck everlasting. /c1975/4-6/4 KG873 . . . . . **CE Fic**
BADEN, R/And Sunday makes seven. /1990/
2-3/2 KB388 . . . . **398.21**
BARCHAS, S/Giant and the rabbit: six bilingual folktales from
Hispanic culture (Sound /1996/2-4/KB258 . . . . **SRC 398.2**
    Pinata!: bilingual songs for children (Sound recording cassette). /
1991/K-6/KD605 . . . . **SRC 789.3**
    This old man/Este viejito (Sound recording cassette). /1997/
K-2/KD606 . . . . **SRC 789.3**
BARRACCA, D/Adventures of taxi dog. /1990/P-2/2 KF200 **CE E**
BAUM, LF/Wonderful Wizard of Oz. /1987/4-6/4 KG886 . **CE Fic**
BEMELMANS, L/Madeline. /1962/P-2/4 KF218 . . . . **CE E**
BERNIER-GRAND, CT/Juan Bobo: four folktales from Puerto Rico. /
1994/1-2/2 KB427 . . . . **398.22**
BIESTY, S/Man-of-war. /1993/4-6/7 KA988 . . . . **359.1**
    Stephen Biesty's incredible cross-sections. /1992/
4-A/6 KC880 . . . . **600**
BLANCO, A/Angel's kite/La estrella de Angel. /1994/
2-4/6 KG902 . . . . **Fic**
BLUME, J/Are you there God? It's me, Margaret. /c1970, 1982/
4-6/5 KG905 . . . . **CE Fic**
    Blubber. /1974/4-6/3 KG906 . . . . **Fic**
    Freckle juice. /1971/2-4/3 KG910 . . . . **CE Fic**
    Otherwise known as Sheila the Great. /1972/4-6/4 KG912 . . **Fic**
    Then again, maybe I won't. /1971/6-A/5 KG915 . . . . . . **Fic**
BONSALL, CN/Case of the hungry stranger. /c1963/
1-2/2 KF243 . . . . **CE E**
BRIDWELL, N/Clifford the big red dog. /c1963, 1985/
P-2/1 KF264 . . . . **CE E**
BROWN, MT/Arthur's teacher trouble. /1986/K-3/4 KF277 . **CE E**
    Big red barn. /1956, 1989/P-1/3 KF283 . . . . **E**
    Goodnight moon. /c1947/P-K/1 KF285 . . . . **CE E**
    Runaway bunny. /c1972/P-K/2 KF287 . . . . **CE E**
    Stone soup: an old tale. /c1947/K-3/2 KB721 . . . . **CE 398.27**
BROWN, R/Alphabet times four: an international ABC: English,
Spanish, French, German. /1991/2-4/KB819 . . . . **411**
BRUSCA, MC/Three friends: a counting book./Tres amigos: un
cuento para contar. /1995/P-2/1 KB954 . . . . **513.2**
BUEHNER, C/Escape of Marvin the ape. /1992/P-2/3 KF294 . . . **E**
BURNIE, D/Tree. /1988/K-6/7 KC409 . . . . **582.16**
BURTON, VL/Mike Mulligan and his steam shovel. /c1939/
P-2/6 KF322 . . . . **CE E**
BYAM, M/Arms and armor. /1988/A/10 KA986 . . . . **355.8**
CANNON, J/Stellaluna. /1993/K-2/3 KF334 . . . . **E**
CARLE, E/Grouchy ladybug. New ed. /1996/P-2/2 KF342 . . . . **E**
CLEARY, B/Henry Huggins. /1950/3-5/4 KG996 . . . . **Fic**
    Ramona and her father. /1977/3-5/7 KH001 . . . . **Fic**
    Ramona and her mother. /1979/3-5/6 KH002 . . . . **CE Fic**
    Ramona Quimby, age 8. /1981/3-5/5 KH004 . . . . **CE Fic**
    Ramona the pest. /c1968/3-5/5 KH006 . . . . **Fic**
CLUTTON-BROCK, J/Horses. /1992/4-6/8 KD199 . . . . . . **636.1**
COERR, E/Josefina story quilt. /1986/1-3/2 KF401 . . . . . **CE E**
COHEN, B/Molly's pilgrim. /1983/1-3/4 KH012 . . . . . **CE Fic**
COLE, J/Magic School Bus at the waterworks. /1986/
2-3/4 KD079 . . . . **628.1**
    Magic School Bus in the time of the dinosaurs. /1994/
2-4/3 KC245 . . . . **567.9**
    Magic School Bus inside a hurricane. /1995/
2-4/4 KC197 . . . . **551.55**
    Magic School Bus inside the human body. /1989/
2-5/5 KC916 . . . . **612**
    Magic School Bus lost in the solar system. /1990/
2-6/4 KC008 . . . . **523.2**
    Magic School Bus on the ocean floor. /1992/
2-4/5 KC495 . . . . **591.77**
COONEY, B/Miss Rumphius. /1982/K-3/5 KF419 . . . . **E**
COWCHER, H/Rain forest. /c1988, 1990/2-4/4 KF428 . . . . . . **E**
DAHL, R/Enormous Crocodile. /c1978, 1993/1-3/4 KF444 . . . . **E**
    Matilda. /1988/5-A/7 KH056 . . . . **Fic**

DALGLIESH, A/Courage of Sarah Noble. /c1954, 1987/
3-5/3 KH058 . . . . **CE Fic**
DANZIGER, P/Amber Brown goes fourth. /1995/
2-4/4 KH059 . . . . **Fic**
    Amber Brown is not a crayon. /1994/2-4/6 KH060 . . . . **Fic**
DE COLORES AND OTHER LATIN-AMERICAN FOLK SONGS FOR
CHILDREN. /1994/K-3/KD561 . . . . **789.2**
DE PAOLA, T/Lady of Guadalupe. /1980/1-4/6 KA698 . **232.91**
    Now one foot, now the other. /1981/K-3/5 KF476 . . . . . **E**
DELACRE, L/Golden tales: myths, legends, and folktales from Latin
America. /1996/4-5/6 KB283 . . . . **398.2**
    Vejigante masquerader. /1993/1-3/4 KF458 . . . . **E**
DORRIS, M/Morning Girl. /1992/6-A/7 KH080 . . . . **Fic**
DORROS, A/Abuela. /1991/P-2/2 KF488 . . . . **E**
    Ant cities. /1987/1-4/4 KC571 . . . . **595.79**
    Isla. /1995/K-2/2 KF490 . . . . **E**
    This is my house. /1992/1-3/2 KD393 . . . . **728**
    Tonight is Carnaval. /1991/1-3/4 KF492 . . . . **E**
EHLERT, L/Cuckoo: a Mexican folktale./Cucu: un cuento folklorico
mexicano. /1997/P-2/3 KB561 . . . . **398.24**
    Feathers for lunch. /1990/P-1/2 KF517 . . . . **E**
    Moon rope: a Peruvian folktale/Un lazo a la luna: una leyenda
Peruana. /1992/1-3/2 KB563 . . . . **398.24**
EMBERLEY, R/Let's go: a book in two languages./Vamos: un libro
en dos lenguas. /1993/K-2 KB857 . . . . **463**
    My house: a book in two languages/Mi Casa: un libro en dos
lenguas. /1990/K-2/KB858 . . . . **463**
ETS, MH/Gilberto and the wind. /c1963/P-1/2 KF536 . . . **CE E**
    Nine days to Christmas. /c1959/1-3/2 KF538 . . . . **E**
EVERSOLE, R/Flute player./La Flautista. /1995/K-2/2 KF541 . . . **E**
FIENBERG, A/Wiggy and Boa. /c1988, 1990/5-6/7 KH113 . . . **Fic**
FLACK, M/Story about Ping. /c1933/P-1/6 KF550 . . . . . . **CE E**
FOX, M/Wilfrid Gordon McDonald Partridge. /1985/
K-3/6 KF574 . . . . **E**
FREEMAN, D/Corduroy. /c1968/P-2/2 KF578 . . . . **CE E**
    Pocket for Corduroy. /1978/P-2/2 KF581 . . . . **CE E**
GAG, W/Millions of cats. /c1928/P-1/6 KF592 . . . . **CE E**
GALDONE, P/Little red hen. /c1973/P-K/2 KF595 . . . . . . **CE E**
GARDNER-LOULAN, J/Period: revised and updated with a parents'
guide. /1991/5-6/7 KC947 . . . . **612.6**
GARZA, CL/Family pictures: Cuadros de familia. /1990/
2-5/6 KA866 . . . . **306.85**
GONZALEZ, LM/Bossy gallito/el gallo de bodas: a traditional
Cuban folktale. /1994/K-2 KB577 . . . . **398.24**
GRANDMOTHER'S NURSERY RHYMES: LULLABIES, TONGUE
TWISTERS, AND RIDDLES FROM /1994/P-2/KB799 . . . . . **398.8**
GUY, GF/Fiesta! /1996/P-1/1 KF655 . . . . **E**
HAFER, JC/Come sign with us: sign language activities for children.
2nd. ed. /1996/KA279 . . . . **PROF 419**
HAMILTON, V/Cousins. /1990/6-A/5 KH213 . . . . **Fic**
HART, G/Ancient Egypt. /1990/5-6/8 KE633 . . . . **932**
HAYES, J/Watch out for clever women!/Cuidado con las mujeres
astutas!: Hispanic /1994/2-5/4 KB315 . . . . **398.2**
HELLER, R/Chickens aren't the only ones. /1981/
P-K/KC282 . . . . **573.6**
HINOJOSA, T/Cada nino./Every child (Compact disc). /1996/
2-6/KD568 . . . . **CD 789.2**
HOBAN, R/Bedtime for Frances. Newly ill. ed. /1995/
P-1/2 KF739 . . . . **CE E**
HOFFMAN, M/Amazing Grace. /1991/P-2/4 KF761 . . . . . **CE E**
HOFF, S/Danny and the dinosaur. /c1958/K-2/2 KF753 . . . **CE E**
HOGROGIAN, N/One fine day. /c1971/P-2/5 KF763 . . . . **CE E**
HOWARD, JR/When I'm sleepy. /1996/P-K/8 KF776 . . . . . . **E**
HOWE, D/Bunnicula: a rabbit-tale mystery. /1979/
3-6/5 KH285 . . . . **Fic**
HOYT-GOLDSMITH, D/Day of the Dead: a Mexican-American
celebration. /1994/4-6/7 KB198 . . . . **394.26**
HUTCHINS, P/Rosie's walk. /c1968/P-1/1 KF802 . . . . **CE E**
JAMES, S/Ancient Rome. /1990/5-6/8 KE639 . . . . **937**
JOHNSON, C/Harold and the purple crayon. /c1955, 1994/
P-2/2 KF835 . . . . **CE E**
JOHNSTON, T/My Mexico--Mexico mio. /1996/K-3/KD958 . . **811**
    Tale of Rabbit and Coyote. /1994/2-3/2 KB596 . . . . . . **398.24**
JORDAN, HJ/How a seed grows. Rev. ed. /1992/
P-2/1 KC387 . . . . **580**
JUST FOR ME (VIDEOCASSETTE). /1992/
K-6/KC997 . . . . **VCR 613.8**
KALAN, R/Jump, frog, jump! New ed. /c1981, 1995/
P-1/1 KF864 . . . . **CE E**
KEATS, EJ/Letter to Amy. /c1968/P-2/2 KF874 . . . . **CE E**
    Peter's chair. /c1967/P-2/2 KF877 . . . . **CE E**
    Snowy day. /c1962, 1963/P-2/2 KF878 . . . . **CE E**
    Whistle for Willie. /c1964, 1977/P-2/3 KF880 . . . . . . **CE E**
KELLOGG, S/Island of the skog. /c1973/K-3/5 KF890 . . . . **CE E**

Paul Bunyan, a tall tale. /1984/4-6/7 KB457 . . . . **398.22**
KESSLER, L/Here comes the strikeout. /c1965/1-2/2 KF898 . **CE E**
Last one in is a rotten egg. /c1969/1-2/1 KF900 . . . . **E**
KLEVEN, E/Hooray! A pinata! /1996/K-2/2 KF910 . . . . **E**
KNOWLTON, J/Maps and globes. /1985/2-5/7 KE169 . . . . **912**
KOPLOW, L/Tanya and the Tobo Man/Tanya y el Hombre Tobo: /
1991/K-2/2 KD040 . . . . **618.92**
KRAUSS, R/Happy day. /1945, 1949/P-2/2 KF921 . . . . **E**
LAS NAVIDADES: POPULAR CHRISTMAS SONGS FROM LATIN
AMERICA. /1990/K-3/KD580 . . . . **789.2**
LEAF, M/Story of Ferdinand. /c1936/P-1/3 KF953 . . . . . . **CE E**
LEVINSON, R/Watch the stars come out. /c1985, 1995/
K-2/2 KF969 . . . . **E**
LEVY, J/Spirit of Tio Fernando: a Day of the Dead story./El espiritu
de tio Fernando: /1995/1-3/5 KH404 . . . . **Fic**
LEWIS, CS/Lion, the witch and the wardrobe. /1994/
5-A/6 KH405 . . . . **CE Fic**
LOBEL, A/Days with Frog and Toad. /1979/K-2/1 KG001 . . . . . **E**
Fables. /1980/3-A/5 KH416 . . . . **Fic**
Frog and Toad all year. /c1976/K-2/1 KG002 . . . . **CE E**
Frog and Toad are friends. /c1972/K-2/2 KG003 . . . . . . **CE E**
Frog and Toad together. /c1972/K-2/2 KG004 . . . . **CE E**
LOMAS GARZA, C/In my family./En mi familia. /1996/
2-5/6 KA870 . . . . **306.85**
LONDON, J/Froggy gets dressed. /1992/P-K/2 KG021 . . . . **E**
LONGFELLOW, HW/Hiawatha. /1983/P-A/KD979 . . . . . . **CE 811**
Paul Revere's ride. /1990/3-A/KD980 . . . . **CE 811**
LONG, L/Domino addition. /1996/P-2/2 KB966 . . . . **513.2**
LOWELL, S/Three little javelinas. /1992/K-2/4 KG039 . . . . **E**
LYRIC LANGUAGE: A BILINGUAL MUSIC PROGRAM: SPANISH/
ENGLISH (VIDEOCASSETTE). /1992/K-6/KD636 . . . **VCR 789.3**
MACHT, NL/Roberto Clemente. /1994/
5-A/7 KE294 . . . . **B CLEMENTE, R.**
MACLACHLAN, P/Sarah, plain and tall. /1985/
3-5/4 KH444 . . . . **CE Fic**
MARSHALL, E/Fox and his friends. /1994/K-2/1 KG064 . . . **CE E**
Three by the sea. /1981/K-3/1 KG066 . . . . **CE E**
MARTINEZ, AC/Woman who outshone the sun: the legend of Lucia
Zenteno./La mujer que brillaba /1991/3-5/5 KB403 . . . . . **398.21**
MCCLOSKEY, R/Lentil. /c1940/1-3/6 KG088 . . . . **CE E**
Make way for ducklings. /c1941, 1963/P-1/4 KG089 . . . . **CE E**
MCDERMOTT, G/Arrow to the sun. /1974/
2-4/3 KB711 . . . . **CE 398.26**
MCMILLAN, B/Sense suspense: a guessing game for the five senses.
/1994/P-2/KC968 . . . . **612.8**
MCPHAIL, D/Pigs aplenty, pigs galore! /1993/P-2/2 KG122 . . . **E**
MILES, M/Annie and the old one. /c1971/4-6/4 KH496 . . . . . **Fic**
MILLER, M/My five senses. /1994/P-1/2 KC969 . . . . **612.8**
MINARIK, EH/Little Bear. /c1961/P-1/2 KG141 . . . . **CE E**
MOCHIZUKI, K/Baseball saved us. /1993/4-A/6 KH500 . . . . . **Fic**
MOHR, N/Song of el coqui and other tales of Puerto Rico. /1995/
3-4/3 KB621 . . . . **398.24**
MONJO, FN/Drinking gourd. Newly illustrated ed. /1993/
1-3/2 KG151 . . . . **E**
MORA, P/Desert is my mother./El desierto es mi madre. /1994/
K-3/KD989 . . . . **811**
Gift of the poinsettia./El regalo de la flor de nochebuena. /1995/
3-5/4 KH507 . . . . **Fic**
Listen to the desert/Oye al desierto. /1994/P-1/KD990 . . . . **811**
Uno, dos, tres: one, two, three. /1996/P-1/3 KG155 . . . . . . **E**
MORRIS, A/Karate boy. /1996/2-4/5 KD832 . . . . **796.815**
NICHOL, B/Beethoven lives upstairs. /1994/4-6/4 KH549 . . . . **Fic**
NIKOLA-LISA, W/Bein' with you this way. /1994/P-2/KD996 . . **811**
NOBLE, TH/Day Jimmy's boa ate the wash. /1980/
K-2/2 KG176 . . . . **CE E**
O'BRIEN, RC/Mrs. Frisby and the rats of NIMH. /c1971/
4-A/6 KH556 . . . . **Fic**
O'DELL, S/Black pearl. /c1967/5-6/5 KH557 . . . . **CE Fic**
PALACIOS, A/Christmas surprise for Chabelita. /1993/
1-3/2 KG206 . . . . **E**
PARKER, S/Fish. /1990/5-6/7 KC584 . . . . **597**
PARRAMON, JM/Hearing. /1985/P-1/1 KC973 . . . . **612.8**
Sight. /1985/P-1/1 KC974 . . . . **612.8**
Taste. /1985/P-1/2 KC975 . . . . **612.8**
Touch. /1985/P-1/2 KC976 . . . . **612.8**
PERRAULT, C/Puss in boots. /1990/3-4/4 KB633 . . . . . . **398.24**
PETERSHAM, M/Circus baby. /c1950/P-2/3 KG235 . . . . . . **CE E**
PIPER, W/Little engine that could. /c1961/P-K/4 KG246 . . . **CE E**
POLLITOS DICEN: JUEGOS, RIMAS Y CANCIONES INFANTILES
DE PAISES DE HABLA /1994/P-1/2 KD584 . . . . **789.2**
POTTER, B/Tale of Peter Rabbit. /n.d., 1987/P-2/6 KG278 . . . . **E**
PRATT, KJ/Walk in the rainforest. /1992/K-6/7 KC322 . . . **577.34**
PROVENSEN, A/Year at Maple Hill Farm. /1978/K-2/4 KG290 . **E**

RANSOME, A/Fool of the world and the flying ship: a Russian tale.
/c1968/2-5/5 KB765 . . . . **398.27**
REY, HA/Curious George. /c1941/P-2/2 KG322 . . . . **E**
RODGERS, M/Freaky Friday. /c1972/5-6/5 KH647 . . . . . **CE Fic**
ROE, E/With my brother/Con mi hermano. /1991/
P-2/2 KG346 . . . . **E**
ROHMER, H/Atariba and Niguayona: a story from the Taino people
of Puerto Rico. /c1976, 1988/4-5/5 KB769 . . . . **398.27**
Uncle Nacho's hat: a folktale from Nicaragua/El sombrero de Tio
Nacho: /1989/2-4/2 KB770 . . . . **398.27**
ROSEN, M/We're going on a bear hunt. /1989/
P-2/2 KB814 . . . . **398.8**
RYLANT, C/Henry and Mudge: the first book. /1987/
K-3/2 KG375 . . . . **CE E**
SACRE, A/Looking for Papito: family stories from Latin America
(Sound recording /1996/1-6/KA857 . . . . **SRC 305.8**
SAN SOUCI, RD/Talking eggs. /1989/3-5/5 KB415 . . . **CE 398.21**
SCIESZKA, J/True story of the 3 little pigs. /1989/
K-3/2 KG421 . . . . **CE E**
SELDEN, G/Cricket in Times Square. /c1960/4-6/6 KH694 **CE Fic**
SENDAK, M/In the night kitchen. /c1970/K-3/3 KG432. . . . **CE E**
Where the wild things are. 25th anniv. ed. /c1963, 1988/
P-3/2 KG438 . . . . **CE E**
SEUSS, D/Lorax. /c1971/P-3/3 KG466 . . . . **CE E**
SHOWERS, P/Listening walk. /c1961, 1991/P-1/1 KG495 . . . . . **E**
SHULEVITZ, U/Treasure. /1978/2-4/4 KB778 . . . . **398.27**
SINGER, M/In the palace of the Ocean King. /1995/
2-3/5 KG509 . . . . **E**
SLOBODKINA, E/Caps for sale: a tale of a peddler, some monkeys
and their monkey business. /c1947/P-2/1 KG519 . . . . . . **CE E**
SNYDER, D/Boy of the three-year nap. /1988/K-3/6 KG525 . . . **E**
SOTO, G/Baseball in April and other stories. /1990/
6-A/6 KH738 . . . . **Fic**
Chato's kitchen. /c1995, 1997/1-3/5 KG527. . . . . **E**
SOWLER, S/Amazing armored animals. /1992/
4-6/6 KC467 . . . . **591.47**
SPERRY, A/Call it courage. /c1940/5-6/6 KH743. . . . . . . **CE Fic**
STEIG, W/Amos and Boris. /c1971/1-3/7 KG540 . . . . **CE E**
Brave Irene. /1986/K-3/3 KG541 . . . . **CE E**
Dominic. /c1972/4-6/7 KH750 . . . . **Fic**
Sylvester and the magic pebble. /c1969, 1988/
K-2/6 KG544 . . . . **CE E**
STEPTOE, J/Stevie. /c1969/K-3/3 KG553 . . . . **E**
STEVENS, JR/Carlos and the skunk./Carlos y el zorrillo. /1997/
1-3/3 KG554 . . . . **E**
STEVENSON, J/Night after Christmas. /1981/K-2/2 KG564 **CE E**
TELLO, J/Abuelo y los tres osos./Abuelo and the three bears. /
1997/K-2/2 KG598 . . . . **E**
TORRES, L/Saturday sancocho. /1995/K-2/5 KG614 . . . . **E**
TORTILLITAS PARA MAMA AND OTHER SPANISH NURSERY
RHYMES. /1981/1-3/KB816 . . . . **398.8**
TREE IS OLDER THAN YOU ARE: A BILINGUAL GATHERING OF
POEMS AND STORIES FROM /1995/5-A/KE121 . . . . . . **860.9**
TRIVIZAS, E/Three little wolves and the big bad pig. /1993/
P-3/4 KG619 . . . . **E**
TUN-TA-CA-TUN: MORE STORIES AND POEMS IN ENGLISH
AND SPANISH FOR CHILDREN. /1986/K-6/KD905 . . . . . . **810.8**
UDRY, JM/Tree is nice. /c1956/K-2/2 KG633 . . . . **E**
VALERI, M/Mi casa es su casa/my house is su casa: a bi-lingual
musical journey through /1991/K-3/KD663 . . . . **SRC 789.3**
VAN ALLSBURG, C/Polar express. /1985/2-A/5 KH822 . . **CE Fic**
Sweetest fig. /1993/3-A/3 KH823 . . . . **Fic**
Widow's broom. /1992/4-A/5 KH824 . . . . **Fic**
VAN LEEUWEN, J/Tales of Oliver Pig. /1979/K-2/1 KG649 **CE E**
VIGIL, A/Corn woman: stories and legends of the Hispanic
Southwest/La mujer del maiz: /1994/5-6/4 KB380. . . . **CE 398.2**
VIORST, J/Alexander, who used to be rich last Sunday. /c1978/
P-3/5 KG659 . . . . **CE E**
Alexander, who's not (Do you hear me? I mean it!) going to
move. /1995/1-3/2 KG660 . . . . **E**
Alexander and the terrible, horrible, no good, very bad day. /
c1972/P-3/7 KG657 . . . . **CE E**
WELLS, R/Edward in deep water. /1995/P-K/2 KG697 . . . . . . **E**
Noisy Nora. /1997/K-1/4 KG707 . . . . **CE E**
WHITE, EB/Stuart Little. /c1945/3-6/5 KH851 . . . . **Fic**
WILLIAMS, L/Little old lady who was not afraid of anything. /
1986/P-2/4 KG730 . . . . **CE E**
WILLIAMS, S/I went walking. /1990/P-1/1 KG732 . . . . . . **CE E**
WILLIAMS, VB/Music, music for everyone. /1984/P-3/4 KG737 . **E**
WORLD NEWSMAP OF THE WEEK: HEADLINE FOCUS. /1938-/
/KA155. . . . . **PER PROF 050**
ZELINSKY, PO/Rumpelstiltskin. /1986/1-4/7 KB385 . . . **CE 398.2**
ZEMACH, M/It could always be worse: a Yiddish folk tale. /1976/
2-4/4 KB792 . . . . **CE 398.27**

Little red hen, an old story. /1983/P-K/2 KG790 . . . . E
Three wishes: an old story. /1986/2-3/4 KB386 . . . . **398.2**
ZION, G/Harry the dirty dog. /c1956/P-2/2 KG800. . . . . **CE E**
ZOLOTOW, C/Mr. Rabbit and the lovely present. /c1962/
P-2/2 KG804 . . . . **CE E**
100 WORDS ABOUT ANIMALS. /1987/P-3/KC457 . . . . . **CE 591**
100 WORDS ABOUT MY HOUSE. /1988/P-3/KD296. . . . . . **645**

Spanish language materials--Software.
AESOP'S FABLE: THE TORTOISE AND THE HARE (CD-ROM). /
1993/P-A/KB522 . . . . **CDR 398.24**
ARTHUR'S TEACHER TROUBLE (CD-ROM). /1992/
1-4/KF171 . . . . **CDR E**
BERENSTAIN BEARS GET IN A FIGHT. SCHOOL ED. (CD-ROM).
/1995/K-3/KF223 . . . . **CDR E**
BROWN, MT/Arthur's teacher trouble (Microcomputer program). /
1994/2-6/KB109. . . . . **MCP 372.6**
JUST GRANDMA AND ME (CD-ROM). /1992/
P-2/KF863 . . . . **CDR E**
KID PIX STUDIO (CD-ROM). /1994/P-A/KD468 . . . **CDR 750.28**
MARC BROWN'S ARTHUR'S BIRTHDAY. SCHOOL ED. (CD-ROM).
/1994/K-4/KG062 . . . . **CDR E**
MARK SCHLICHTING'S HARRY AND THE HAUNTED HOUSE.
SCHOOL ED. (CD-ROM). /1994/K-3/KG063 . . . . **CDR E**
MAYAQUEST TRAIL (CD-ROM). /1996/5-A/KE845. . **CDR 972.81**
MERCER MAYER'S LITTLE MONSTER AT SCHOOL. SCHOOL ED.
(CD-ROM). /1994/K-3/KG130 . . . . **CDR E**
MULTIMEDIA WORKSHOP. TEACHER ED. (CD-ROM). /1996/
3-A/KB115. . . . . **CDR 372.6**
NEW KID PIX. SCHOOL VERSION (MICROCOMPUTER
PROGRAM). /1996/P-A/KD469 . . . . **MCP 750.28**
STORYBOOK WEAVER DELUXE (CD-ROM). /1995/
1-5/KB118. . . . . **CDR 372.6**

Spanish literature--Collections.
TUN-TA-CA-TUN: MORE STORIES AND POEMS IN ENGLISH
AND SPANISH FOR CHILDREN. /1986/K-6/KD905. . . . . **810.8**

Sparrows.
ARNOLD, C/House sparrows everywhere. /1992/
4-6/7 KC704 . . . . **598.8**

Special education--Fiction.
CUTLER, J/Spaceman. /1997/4-A/2 KH053 . . . . **Fic**

Special forces (Military science).
VISUAL DICTIONARY OF SPECIAL MILITARY FORCES. /1993/
4-A/8 KA987 . . . . **356**

Special Olympics.
BROWN, FG/Special Olympics. /1992/4-A/7 KD759 . . . . . **796**
DINN, S/Hearts of gold: a celebration of Special Olympics and its
heroes. /1996/4-6/9 KD760 . . . . **796**

Spedden, Daisy Corning Stone--Diaries.
SPEDDEN, DC/Polar, the Titanic bear. /1994/4-6/7 KE158 . **910.4**

Speech disorders--Fiction.
PATTERSON, NR/Shiniest rock of all. /1991/4-6/4 KH584 . . . **Fic**
SMALL, D/Ruby Mae has something to say. /1992/
1-3/4 KG523 . . . . **E**

Speeches, addresses, etc.--Afro-American authors.
AFRICAN AMERICAN VOICES. /1996/5-A/KA487 . . . . **REF 973**

Speeches, addresses, etc.--Indian authors.
NATIVE NORTH AMERICAN VOICES. /1997/
5-A/KA482 . . . . **REF 970.1**

Speed skating.
DALY, W/Bonnie Blair: power on ice. /1996/
4-6/6 KE255 . . . . **B BLAIR, B.**

Spelling SEE English language--Spelling.

Spider webs--Fiction.
CARLE, E/Very busy spider. /1985/P-2/2 KF346 . . . . **E**

Spiders.
BITE OF THE BLACK WIDOW (VIDEOCASSETTE). /1994/
5-6/KC523. . . . . **VCR 595.4**
GIBBONS, G/Spiders. /1993/1-3/4 KC525 . . . . **595.4**
HICKMAN, PM/Bugwise: thirty incredible insect investigations and
arachnid activities. /c1990, 1991/4-6/7 KC540 . . . . . . **595.7**
JOHNSON, J/Simon and Schuster children's guide to insects and
spiders. /1996/5-6/7 KC542. . . . . **595.7**
KALMAN, B/Web weavers and other spiders. /1997/
3-5/5 KC526 . . . . **595.4**
LABONTE, G/Tarantula. /1991/5-6/7 KC527 . . . . **595.4**
MARKLE, S/Outside and inside spiders. /1994/
5-6/4 KC528 . . . . **595.4**
PARSONS, A/Amazing spiders. /1990/2-6/6 KC529 . . . . . **595.4**
SCHNIEPER, C/Amazing spiders. /1989/4-6/6 KC531. . . . . **595.4**
SPIDER SURVIVAL (VIDEOCASSETTE). /1991/
4-6/KC532. . . . . **VCR 595.4**
WEAVE AND SPIN (VIDEOCASSETTE). /1986/
6-A/KC533 . . . . **VCR 595.4**

Spiders--Fiction.
BANKS, K/Spider spider. /1996/P-1/2 KF194 . . . . **E**
CARLE, E/Very busy spider. /1985/P-2/2 KF346 . . . . **E**
GRAHAM, MB/Be nice to spiders. /c1967/P-2/3 KF633 . . . . . . **E**
JUKES, M/Like Jake and me. /1984/5-6/7 KH338 . . . . **Fic**
MCNULTY, F/Lady and the spider. /1986/1-3/2 KG114 . . . . . . **E**
WHITE, EB/Charlotte's web. /c1952/3-6/6 KH850 . . . . **Fic**

Spiders--Folklore.
ARKHURST, JC/Adventures of Spider: West African folktales. /
c1964, 1992/2-3/5 KB524 . . . . **398.24**
KIMMEL, EA/Anansi and the moss-covered rock. /1988/
1-2/4 KB600 . . . . **CE 398.24**
Anansi goes fishing. /1991, c1992/K-2/2 KB602 . . . **CE 398.24**
MCDERMOTT, G/Anansi the spider: a tale from the Ashanti. /
c1972/1-3/2 KB616. . . . . **398.24**
SPIDER SPINS A STORY: FOURTEEN LEGENDS FROM NATIVE
AMERICA. /1997/2-5/6 KB371. . . . . **398.2**

Spiders--Songs and music.
TRAPANI, I/Itsy bitsy spider. /1996/P-1/2 KD662 . . . . . . **789.3**

Spielberg, Steven.
MEACHUM, V/Steven Spielberg: Hollywood filmmaker. /1996/
4-6/8 KE545 . . . . **B SPIELBERG, S.**
POWERS, T/Steven Spielberg: master storyteller. /1997/
5-A/7 KE546 . . . . **B SPIELBERG, S.**

Spies.
ROOP, P/Buttons for General Washington. /1986/
4-6/4 KE885 . . . . **973.3**
STEVENS, B/Frank Thompson: her Civil War story. /1992/
6-A/7 KE332 . . . . **B EDMONDS, S.**

Spirituals (Songs).
ALL NIGHT, ALL DAY: A CHILD'S FIRST BOOK OF AFRICAN-
AMERICAN SPIRITUALS. /1991/K-6/KD554 . . . . **789.2**
JENKINS, E/African-American folk songs and rhythms (Sound
recording cassette). /c1960, 1992/K-6/KD572 . . . . . **SRC 789.2**
SILVERMAN, J/Songs of protest and civil rights. /1992/
5-A/KD593 . . . . **789.2**
WHAT A MORNING! THE CHRISTMAS STORY IN BLACK
SPIRITUALS. /1987/K-6/KD532. . . . . **782.25**

Sponges.
ESBENSEN, BJ/Sponges are skeletons. /1993/
1-3/2 KC508 . . . . **593.4**

Sports SEE ALSO Athletics; Games; Gymnastics; Olympic games; Outdoor
life; Physical education and training; Rodeos; and names of specific sports
e.g. Hockey.

Sports.
HAMMOND, T/Sports. /1988/4-A/8 KD761 . . . . **796**

Sports--Biography.
BIOGRAPHY TODAY SPORTS SERIES: PROFILES OF PEOPLE OF
INTEREST TO YOUNG READERS. /1996/4-6/KA456. . **REF 796**
PARE, MA/Sports stars. /1994/5-A/KA457 . . . . **REF 796**

Sports--History.
MACY, S/Winning ways: a photohistory of American women in
sports. /1996/4-6/12 KD764 . . . . **796**

Sports--Periodicals.
SPORT. /1946-/4-6/KA543 . . . . **PER 050**
SPORTS ILLUSTRATED. /1954-/5-A/KA544 . . . . **PER 050**
SPORTS ILLUSTRATED FOR KIDS. /1989-/2-4/KA545 . . . . **PER 050**

Sports--Poetry.
OPENING DAYS: SPORTS POEMS. /1996/3-6/KE074. . **811.008**

Sports medicine.
PAIGE, D/Day in the life of a sports therapist. /1985/
3-5/6 KC989 . . . . **613.7**

Sportscasters.
CHADWICK, B/John Madden. /1997/
5-A/7 KE451 . . . . **B MADDEN, J.**

Sportsmanship--Fiction.
KESSLER, L/Old Turtle's soccer team. /1988/K-3/2 KF901 . . . . . **E**

Spring.
MAGICAL MOTHER NATURE: THE FOUR SEASONS
(VIDEOCASSETTE). /1989/2-4/KC061 . . . . **VCR 525**
SEASONS. REV. ED. (SOUND FILMSTRIP). /c1975, 1993/
K-2/KC063. . . . . **FSS 525**
SIMON, S/Spring across America. /1996/5-8/7 KB919. . . . **508.2**
SPRING (VIDEOCASSETTE). /1994/2-5/KC666. . . . . . **VCR 598**

Spring--Fiction.
AGELL, C/Mud makes me dance in the spring. /1994/
K-2/2 KF139 . . . . **E**
BROWN, C/In the spring. /1994/P-1/2 KF269. . . . . **E**
COLE, B/Winter wren. /1984/K-3/2 KF408 . . . . **E**
DE COTEAU ORIE, S/Did you hear Wind sing your name?: an
Oneida song of spring. /1995/K-2/3 KF454 . . . . **E**
EMBERLEY, M/Welcome back, Sun. /1993/1-3/3 KF524 . . . . . . **E**
KINSEY-WARNOCK, N/When spring comes. /1993/
P-2/3 KF906 . . . . **E**

KRAUSS, R/Happy day. /c1945, 1949/P-2/2 KF921. . . . . **E**
RAU, DM/Robin at Hickory Street. /1995/K-2/3 KG314 . . . **CE E**
RAY, ML/Mud. /1996/P-2/2 KG316 . . . . **E**
STEIG, W/Amazing bone. /1976/1-3/5 KG539 . . . . **CE E**

Spring--Poetry.
SPRING: A HAIKU STORY. /1996/1-6/KE137 . . . . **895.6**
Spy stories SEE Spies--Fiction.

Squabble Hollow School (Caledonia County, Vt.).
HAUSHERR, R/One-room school at Squabble Hollow. /1988/
3-6/7 KB084 . . . . **371.19**

Squanto.
BULLA, CR/Squanto: friend of the Pilgrims. /c1954, 1982/
3/3 KE547 . . . . **B SQUANTO**
METAXAS, E/Squanto and the first Thanksgiving (Kit). /1996/
2-6/KE548 . . . . **KIT B SQUANTO**

Square.
HOBAN, T/Circles, triangles, and squares. /1974/P-1/KB990 . **516**
Shapes, shapes, shapes. /1986/2-6/KB991 . . . . **516**

Square dancing--Fiction.
WALTON, R/Noah's square dance. /1995/K-2/3 KG687 . . . . . **E**
Squirrels SEE ALSO names of specific species e.g. Gray squirrel.

Squirrels.
LEPTHIEN, EU/Squirrels. /1992/4-6/4 KC751 . . . . **599.36**
MCDONALD, MA/Flying squirrels. /1993/1-5/5 KC753. . . **599.36**

Squirrels--Fiction.
EHLERT, L/Nuts to you! /1993/P-2/2 KF519 . . . . **E**
ERNST, LC/Squirrel Park. /1993/K-2/5 KF533 . . . . **E**
JAMES, S/Wild woods. /1996/P-2/2 KF825 . . . . **E**
LISLE, JT/Forest. /1993/5-A/7 KH409 . . . . **Fic**
POTTER, B/Tale of Squirrel Nutkin. /c1931, 1987/
P-2/7 KG280 . . . . **E**
RYDER, J/Night gliders. /1996/P-2/2 KG367 . . . . **E**
RYLANT, C/Gooseberry Park. /1995/3-5/5 KH662. . . . . . . **Fic**
STEVENSON, J/Flying Acorns. /1993/1-3/3 KG559. . . . . . . **E**

Squirrels--Folklore.
SLOAT, T/Sody sallyratus. /1997/1-3/5 KB653 . . . . **398.24**

St. Helena Island (S.C.)--Social life and customs.
KRULL, K/Bridges to change: how kids live on a South Carolina Sea
Island. /1995/4-6/7 KE987 . . . . **975.7**

St. Patrick's Day.
BARTH, E/Shamrocks, harps, and shillelaghs: the story of the St.
Patrick's Day symbols. /c1977/5-6/7 KB218 . . . . **394.262**
GIBBONS, G/St. Patrick's Day. /1994/2-5/2 KB219. . . . **394.262**

St. Patrick's Day--Fiction.
BUNTING, E/St. Patrick's Day in the morning. /1980/
K-2/2 KF310 . . . . **E**
MARKHAM, MM/St. Patrick's Day shamrock mystery. /1995/
2-4/3 KH457 . . . . **Fic**
SCHERTLE, A/Jeremy Bean's St. Patrick's Day. /1987/
K-2/4 KG404 . . . . **E**

Stage adaptations.
LAUGHLIN, MK/Readers theatre for children: scripts and script
development. /1990//KA339. . . . . **PROF 808.5**

Stage fright--Fiction.
SCOTT, AH/Brave as a mountain lion. /1996/3-5/2 KH688 . . . **Fic**

Stage props.
SHOW TIME (VIDEOCASSETTE). /1994/K-2/KD690 . . **VCR 792**

Stamp collecting.
ANSARY, MT/Stamps. /1997/1-3/2 KD507 . . . . **769.56**
Stamps SEE Postage stamps.

Stanton, Elizabeth Cady.
FRITZ, J/You want women to vote, Lizzie Stanton? /1995/
3-6/5 KE549 . . . . **B STANTON, E.**

Stanton, Elizabeth Cady--Fiction.
MCCULLY, EA/Ballot box battle. /1996/1-3/2 KH473 . . . . . . **Fic**

Star-spangled banner (Song).
ST. PIERRE, S/Our national anthem. /1992/4-A/6 KD598 . . **789.2**

Stark, John--Fiction.
DUBOIS, ML/Abenaki Captive. /1994/6-A/6 KH085. . . . . . . **Fic**
Stars SEE ALSO Constellations; Milky Way.

Stars.
BENDICK, J/Sun: our very own star. /1991/1-3/5 KC044 . . **523.7**
GIBBONS, G/Stargazers. /1992/K-2/4 KC049 . . . . **523.8**
KRUPP, EC/Big dipper and you. /1989/1-6/4 KC050 . . . . **523.8**
MAP OF THE UNIVERSE: THE NORTHERN HEMISPHERE
(PICTURE). /1980/3-A/KC051. . . . . **PIC 523.8**
REY, HA/Find the constellations. Rev. ed. /1976/
4-6/6 KC052 . . . . **523.8**
Stars: a new way to see them. /c1967/4-6/8 KC053 . . . . **523.8**
SIMON, S/Stars. /1986/4-6/6 KC054 . . . . **523.8**
STARS AND CONSTELLATIONS (VIDEOCASSETTE). /1993/
3-6/KC055. . . . . **VCR 523.8**

Stars--Fiction.
NEWMAN, L/Too far away to touch. /1995/1-3/6 KG172 . . . . **E**

Stars--Folklore.
CZERNECKI, S/Pancho's pinata. /1992/2-4/7 KB703 . . . . **398.26**
GOBLE, P/Lost children: the boys who were neglected. /1993/
3-5/5 KB707 . . . . **398.26**
LURIE, A/Heavenly zoo: legends and tales of the stars. /c1979,
1996/5-6/8 KB710 . . . . **398.26**

Stars--Formation.
APFEL, NH/Orion, the Hunter. /1995/A/10 KC047. . . . . . **523.8**

Stars--Poetry.
STAR WALK. /1995/4-8/KE085 . . . . **811.008**
TAYLOR, J/Twinkle, twinkle, little star. /1992/P-K/KE111 . . . **821**

State birds.
LANDAU, E/State birds: including the Commonwealth of Puerto
Rico. /1992/4-6/8 KC653 . . . . **598**
SHEARER, BF/State names, seals, flags, and symbols: a historical
guide. Rev. and expanded /1994/4-A/KA493. . . . . . . **REF 973**

State flowers.
LANDAU, E/State flowers: including the Commonwealth of Puerto
Rico. /1992/3-6/8 KC406. . . . . **582.13**

State songs.
SHEARER, BF/State names, seals, flags, and symbols: a historical
guide. Rev. and expanded /1994/4-A/KA493. . . . . . . **REF 973**
Statesmen SEE ALSO names of individual statesmen e.g. Franklin, Benjamin,
etc.

Statesmen.
ADLER, DA/Picture book of Paul Revere. /1995/
2-4/5 KE508 . . . . **B REVERE, P.**
D'AULAIRE, I/Benjamin Franklin. /c1950/
2-4/6 KE354 . . . . **B FRANKLIN, B.**
FORBES, E/America's Paul Revere. /c1946/
A/7 KE509 . . . . **B REVERE, P.**
FRITZ, J/And then what happened, Paul Revere? /c1973/
5-6/6 KE510 . . . . **CE B REVERE, P.**
What's the big idea, Ben Franklin? /c1976/
5-6/7 KE355 . . . . **CE B FRANKLIN, B.**
Where was Patrick Henry on the 29th of May? /c1975, 1982/
5-6/7 KE386 . . . . **CE B HENRY, P.**
Will you sign here, John Hancock? /c1976, 1997/
5-6/7 KE383 . . . . **CE B HANCOCK, J.**
WORLD LEADERS: PEOPLE WHO SHAPED THE WORLD. /1994/
5-A/KA408 . . . . **REF 350**

Statesmen--India.
FISHER, LE/Gandhi. /1995/3-6/8 KE362 . . . . . . **B GANDHI, M.**
LAZO, C/Mahatma Gandhi. /1993/4-6/7 KE363 . **B GANDHI, M.**
Statistics SEE ALSO United States--Statistics.

Statistics.
GUINNESS BOOK OF WORLD RECORDS. /1955-/
4-6/KA403 . . . . **REF 310**
STATISTICS: UNDERSTANDING MEAN, MEDIAN, AND MODE
(VIDEOCASSETTE). /1987/4-A/KB999 . . . . **VCR 519.5**
UNITED STATES. BUREAU OF PUBLIC AFFAIRS, DEPT. OF STATE.
/Background notes of the countries of the world. /n.d./
4-6/KA404 . . . . **REF 310**

Statistics--Yearbooks.
INFORMATION PLEASE ALMANAC, ATLAS & YEARBOOK. /
1947-/4-6/KA405 . . . . **REF 317.3**
WORLD ALMANAC AND BOOK OF FACTS. /1868-/
4-6/KA406 . . . . **REF 317.3**

Statue of Liberty (New York, N.Y.).
FISHER, LE/Statue of Liberty. /1985/5-6/7 KD400 . . . . . . **735**
MAESTRO, B/Story of the Statue of Liberty. /1986/
P-3/6 KD401 . . . . **735**

Statues.
FISHER, LE/Statue of Liberty. /1985/5-6/7 KD400 . . . . . . **735**
MAESTRO, B/Story of the Statue of Liberty. /1986/
P-3/6 KD401 . . . . **735**

Stealing--Fiction.
ADA, AF/Gold coin. /1991/1-3/4 KF131 . . . . **E**
ADLER, DA/Onion sundaes. /1994/2-3/2 KG819. . . . . **Fic**
CURRY, JL/Big Smith snatch. /1989/5-A/6 KH047 . . . . **Fic**

Steam.
JACOBS, L/Letting off steam. /1989/4-A/7 KC156. . . . . . **551.2**

Steam shovels--Fiction.
BURTON, VL/Mike Mulligan and his steam shovel. /c1939/
P-2/6 KF322 . . . . **CE E**

Steamboats--History.
BOWEN, AR/Head full of notions: a story about Robert Fulton. /
1997/4-5/8 KE359 . . . . **B FULTON, R.**

Steger, Will.
STEGER, W/Over the top of the world: explorer Will Steger's trek
across the Arctic. /1997/5-6/6 KE219. . . . . **919.8**

Stegosaurus.
SATTLER, HR/Stegosaurs: the solar-powered dinosaurs. /1992/
3-6/8 KC260 . . . . **567.9**

Steiff, Margarete.
  GREENE, C/Margarete Steiff: toy maker. /1993/
    2-3/2 KE550 . . . . **B STEIFF, M.**
Steig, William.
  STEIG, W/William Steig library (Videocassette). /1995/
    1-3/KG548 . . . . **VCR E**
Stencil work.
  LYNN, S/Play with paint. /1993/K-2/3 KD465. . . . . **750**
Stepfamilies--Fiction.
  HOFFMAN, M/Boundless Grace. /1995/1-3/5 KF762. . . . . . . **E**
Stepfathers--Fiction.
  JUKES, M/Like Jake and me. /1984/5-6/7 KH338 . . . . **Fic**
Stepmothers--Fiction.
  GLEITZMAN, M/Sticky Beak. /1995/3-5/4 KH176 . . . . **Fic**
  KURTZ, J/Pulling the lion's tail. /1995/1-3/6 KF937 . . . . **E**
  MACLACHLAN, P/Skylark. /1994/3-5/3 KH445 . . . . **Fic**
Stepsisters--Fiction.
  SNYDER, ZK/Headless cupid. /c1971/4-6/7 KH733 . . . . . **CE Fic**
Stevenson, James.
  STEVENSON, J/Don't you know there's a war on? /1992/
    K-3/2 KE552 . . . . **B STEVENSON, J.**
    Higher on the door. /1987/3-4/4 KE553 . . . **B STEVENSON, J.**
    When I was nine. /1986/3-4/4 KE551 . . . . . **B STEVENSON, J.**
Stevenson, Robert Louis.
  GREENE, C/Robert Louis Stevenson: author of A CHILD'S GARDEN
    OF VERSES. /1994/2-4/4 KE554. . . . . **B STEVENSON, R.**
  MEET THE AUTHOR: ROBERT LOUIS STEVENSON
    (VIDEOCASSETTE). /1989/5-6/KE555 . . **VCR B STEVENSON, R.**
  MURPHY, J/Across America on an emigrant train. /1993/
    6-A/8 KB140 . . . . **385**
Stinson, Katherine--Fiction.
  POWELL, MC/Queen of the air: the story of Katherine Stinson,
    1891-1977. /1993/4-7/7 KH613 . . . . **CE Fic**
Stone carvers.
  ANCONA, G/Cutters, carvers and the cathedral. /1995/
    5-6/7 KD392 . . . . **726.6**
Stone cutters.
  ANCONA, G/Cutters, carvers and the cathedral. /1995/
    5-6/7 KD392 . . . . **726.6**
Stores, Retail--Fiction.
  FIELD, R/General store. /c1926, 1988/P-3/KF548 . . . . **E**
Stories in rhyme.
  ADLERMAN, D/Africa calling, nighttime falling. /1996/
    P-2/KF135 . . . . **E**
  ADOFF, A/Black is brown is tan. /1973/P-3/3 KF136 . . . . **E**
  AHLBERG, J/Each peach pear plum: an "I spy" story. /1978/
    P-1/3 KF141 . . . . **CE E**
  ALBOROUGH, J/Where's my teddy? /1992/P-1/2 KF145 . . . . . **E**
  ALPERT, L/You and your dad. /1992/P-1/2 KA876 . . . . **306.874**
  ANDREWS, S/Rattlebone Rock. /1995/1-3/3 KF158 . . . . **E**
  APPELT, K/Bayou lullaby. /1995/P-2/5 KF163 . . . . **E**
  AYLESWORTH, J/Old black fly. /1992/K-2/2 KF180 . . . . **E**
  BAKER, K/Hide and snake. /1991/P-1/2 KF186 . . . . **E**
    Who is the beast? /1990/P-K/1 KF187 . . . . **E**
  BARRACCA, D/Adventures of taxi dog. /1990/P-2/2 KF200 **CE E**
    Maxi, the star. /1993/P-2/2 KF201. . . . . **E**
    Taxi Dog Christmas. /1994/P-2/3 KF202 . . . . **E**
  BECKER, J/Seven little rabbits. /1973/P-2/3 KF214 . . . . **E**
  BEMELMANS, L/Madeline. /1962/P-2/4 KF218. . . . . **CE E**
    Madeline and other Bemelmans (Talking book). /n.d./
    P-2/KF219 . . . . **TB E**
    Madeline's rescue. /c1953/P-2/2 KF220 . . . . **CE E**
  BLACKSTONE, S/Grandma went to market: a round-the-world
    counting rhyme. /1996/1-3/5 KF232. . . . . **E**
  BLOS, JW/Old Henry. /1987/K-3/2 KF237. . . . . **CE E**
  BRIMNER, LD/Brave Mary. /1996/K-1/2 KF266 . . . . **E**
  BRINK, CR/Goody O'Grumpity. /1994/K-3/3 KF268 . . . . **E**
  BROWN, MW/Big red barn. /c1956, 1989/P-1/3 KF283. . . . . **E**
    Goodnight moon. /c1947/P-K/1 KF285 . . . . **CE E**
    Little Donkey close your eyes. /1995/P-K/2 KF286 . . . . . . **E**
  BUCK, N/Oh, cats! /1997/P-1/1 KF290 . . . . **E**
  BUNTING, E/Blue and the gray. /1996/3-5/3 KF297 . . . . . . **E**
    Flower garden. /1994/P-2/3 KF299. . . . . **E**
    Scary, scary Halloween. /1986/P-K/4 KF308. . . . . **E**
    Sunflower house. /1996/P-2/2 KF311 . . . . **E**
  CARLSTROM, NW/Jesse Bear, what will you wear? /1986/
    P-K/4 KF356 . . . . **E**
    Let's count it out, Jesse Bear. /1996/P-1/2 KF357. . . . . . **E**
  CAULEY, LB/Clap your hands. /1992/P-K/2 KF373 . . . . **E**
  CHIN, C/China's bravest girl: the legend of Hua Mu Lan = [Chin
    kuo ying hsiung Hua /1993/3-5/4 KB430 . . . . **398.22**
  CHRISTELOW, E/Five little monkeys sitting in a tree. /1991/
    P-K/2 KF384 . . . . **E**

  CLIFTON, L/Everett Anderson's Christmas coming. /1991/
    P-1/KD925. . . . . **811**
  CREWS, D/Ten black dots. Rev. and redesigned ed. /c1968, 1986/
    P-2/2 KF437 . . . . **E**
  DEGEN, B/Jamberry. /1983/P-2/KF456 . . . . **CE E**
  DEMUTH, P/Busy at day care head to toe. /1996/P-K/2 KF460 . . **E**
  DRAGONWAGON, C/Itch book. /1990/K-3/KF496. . . . . **E**
  DUNBAR, J/This is the star. /1996/2-3/2 KA703 . . . . . . **232.92**
  EHLERT, L/Feathers for lunch. /1990/P-1/2 KF517 . . . . **E**
    Fish eyes: a book you can count on. /1990/P-K/1 KF518. . . . **E**
    Nuts to you! /1993/P-2/2 KF519 . . . . **E**
  ELYA, SM/Say hola to Spanish. /1996/K-2/3 KB862 . . . . **468.1**
  FIELD, R/General store. /c1926, 1988/P-3/KF548 . . . . **E**
  FISHER, LE/Kinderdike. /1994/2-4/3 KB395 . . . . **398.21**
  FLEMING, D/Barnyard banter. /1994/P-1/3 KF553 . . . . **E**
    In the small, small pond. /1993/P-2/1 KF555 . . . . **E**
    In the tall, tall grass. /1991/P-K/1 KF556 . . . . **E**
  FOX, M/Time for bed. /1993/P-1/2 KF572 . . . . **E**
  GARTEN, J/Alphabet tale. New ed., rev. and re-illustrated. /1994/
    P-K/3 KF599 . . . . **E**
  GINSBURG, M/Across the stream. /1982/P-K/2 KF621. . . . . . **E**
    Sun's asleep behind the hill. /1982/P-K/1 KF624 . . . . **E**
  GUARINO, D/Is your mama a llama? /1989/P-1/2 KF651 . . . . **E**
  GUNDERSHEIMER, K/Happy winter. /1982/P-1/3 KF653 . . . . . **E**
  HALL, K/I'm not scared. /1994/K-1/1 KF664 . . . . **E**
    Tooth fairy. /1994/K-1/1 KF665 . . . . **E**
  HAMANAKA, S/All the colors of the earth. /1994/
    P-2/4 KF667 . . . . **E**
  HARLEY, B/Sitting down to eat. /1996/P-2/2 KF672 . . . . **E**
  HENNESSY, BG/School days. /1990/P-1/3 KF713 . . . . **E**
  HOBAN, T/One little kitten. /1979/P-K/1 KF744 . . . . **E**
    Where is it? /c1972/P-K/1 KF747 . . . . **E**
  HOOPES, LL/Unbeatable bread. /1996/K-2/3 KF769 . . . . . . **E**
  HUGHES, S/Nursery collection. /c1986, 1994/P-2 KF790 . . . . . **E**
  HULME, JN/Sea sums. /1996/P-2/3 KB961 . . . . **513.2**
  HUTCHINS, P/Don't forget the bacon! /c1976, 1987/
    P-2/3 KF796 . . . . **CE E**
    Which witch is which? /1989/P-1/2 KF807 . . . . **E**
  KALAN, R/Moving day. /1996/P-1/1 KF865 . . . . **E**
  KIRK, D/Trash trucks. /1997/K-2/3 KF908 . . . . **E**
  KRAUS, R/Whose mouse are you? /c1970/P-1/1 KF919 . . . **CE E**
  KUSKIN, K/James and the rain. /1995/K-2/5 KF938 . . . . **E**
    Roar and more. /c1956, 1990/P-1/KF940 . . . . **E**
  LESIEG, T/Eye book. /c1968/1-2/1 KF958 . . . . **E**
    Ten apples up on top! /c1961/1-2/1 KF959 . . . . **E**
    Tooth book. /1981/K-2/2 KF960 . . . . **E**
    Wacky Wednesday. /c1974/1-2/1 KF961. . . . . **E**
  LINDBERGH, R/Johnny Appleseed. /1990/K-3/KD973. . . . . . **811**
    Nobody owns the sky: the story of "Brave Bessie" Coleman. /
    1996/1-3/2 KF983 . . . . **E**
  LINDEN, AM/One smiling grandma: a Caribbean counting book. /
    1995/P-1/2 KF984 . . . . **E**
  LOBEL, A/On Market Street. /1981/P-1/6 KG009 . . . . **E**
    Rose in my garden. /1984/K-3/KG011. . . . . **E**
  LONDON, J/Fireflies, fireflies, light my way. /1996/
    P-2/2 KG020 . . . . **E**
  LOOMIS, C/In the diner. /1994/P-2/2 KG031. . . . . **E**
  LOPSHIRE, R/Put me in the zoo. /c1960/K-1/1 KG033 . . . . . . **E**
  LOW, A/Popcorn shop. /1993/P-2/2 KG035 . . . . **E**
  LYON, GE/Mama is a miner. /1994/2-3/3 KG044 . . . . **E**
  MACCARONE, G/Cars! cars! cars! /1995/P-1/1 KG045 . . . . . **E**
    Classroom pet. /1995/K-1/2 KG046 . . . . **E**
    Pizza party! /1994/P-1/1 KG047 . . . . **E**
  MACDONALD, A/Cousin Ruth's tooth. /1996/K-2/2 KG048 . . . **E**
    Rachel Fister's blister. /1990/K-2/2 KG050 . . . . **E**
  MANUSHKIN, F/Matzah that Papa brought home. /1995/
    1-3/2 KG059 . . . . **E**
  MARTIN, JR., B/Barn dance! /1986/P-3/3 KG071 . . . . **E**
    Brown bear, brown bear, what do you see? /1992/
    P-K/1 KG072 . . . . **E**
    Chicka chicka boom boom. /1989/P-1/2 KG073 . . . . **E**
    Chicka chicka boom boom (Kit). /1991/P-1/KG074 . . . . . **KIT E**
    Here are my hands. /1987/P-1/2 KG076 . . . . **E**
    Listen to the rain. /1988/P-2/KG077 . . . . **E**
  MARZOLLO, J/Pretend you're a cat. /1990/P-1/KG082 . . . . . **E**
  MCCARTHY, RF/Grandfather Cherry-Blossom. /1993/
    2-3/3 KB753 . . . . **398.27**
    Inch-high samurai. /1993/3-4/4 KB754. . . . . **398.27**
    Moon princess. /1993/3-4/4 KB404 . . . . **398.21**
  MCPHAIL, D/Pigs ahoy! /1995/P-2/3 KG121 . . . . **E**
    Pigs aplenty, pigs galore! /1993/P-2/2 KG122 . . . . **E**
  MEDEARIS, AS/Here comes the snow. /1996/K-1/2 KG126. . . . **E**
  MERRIAM, E/Hole story. /1995/P-1/2 KG131 . . . . **E**
  MINTERS, F/Sleepless Beauty. /1996/2-3/3 KG142 . . . . **E**

MOFFATT, J/Who stole the cookies? /1996/P-1/1 KG149. . . . . E
MORA, P/Uno, dos, tres: one, two, three. /1996/P-1/3 KG155. . E
MOSS, L/Zin! zin! zin! a violin. /1995/K-3/3 KG157 . . . . E
MURPHY, SJ/Best bug parade. /1996/P-1/1 KG163 . . . . E
    Best vacation ever. /1997/K-2/2 KG164 . . . . E
NEITZEL, S/Jacket I wear in the snow. /1989/P-2/2 KG168. . . . E
    We're making breakfast for Mother. /1997/P-1/2 KG169 . . . . E
NOLL, S/Surprise! /1997/P-K/2 KG179 . . . . E
OCHS, CP/When I'm alone. /1993/P-2/4 KG187. . . . . E
OPPENHEIM, J/You can't catch me! /1986/P-1/KG193. . . . . . E
PACKARD, M/Christmas kitten. /1994/K-1/1 KG204. . . . . . . E
    I am king! /1994/K-1/1 KG205. . . . . E
PAULSEN, G/Worksong. /1997/K-2/2 KG222 . . . . E
PAXTON, T/Aesop's fables. /1988/3-4/KB632 . . . . **398.24**
PEET, B/Zella, Zack and Zodiac. /1986/K-3/4 KG231. . . . . . . E
PLOURDE, L/Pigs in the mud in the middle of the rud. /1997/
    K-2/2 KG247. . . . . E
ROBERTS, B/Camel caravan. /1996/P-1/3 KG335 . . . . E
ROSEN, M/We're going on a bear hunt. /1989/
    P-2/2 KB814 . . . . **398.8**
RYAN, PM/Crayon counting book. /1996/P-1/3 KB982. . . . **513.2**
RYLANT, C/Everyday children (Board book). /1993/
    P-K/2 KG370. . . . . **BB E**
    Everyday garden (Board book). /1993/P-K/2 KG371 . . . . **BB E**
    Everyday house (Board book). /1993/P-K/2 KG372 . . . . **BB E**
    Everyday pets (Board book). /1993/P-K/2 KG373 . . . . . **BB E**
    Everyday town (Board book). /1993/P-K/2 KG374 . . . . . **BB E**
SAMTON, SW/World from my window. /c1985, 1991/
    P-K/2 KG389. . . . . E
SENDAK, M/Chicken soup with rice: a book of months. /c1962/
    P-1/KG430. . . . . **CE E**
    Maurice Sendak Library (Videocassette). /1992/
    P-2/KG433. . . . . **VCR E**
    Nutshell library (Videocassette). /1987/P-2/KG434. . . . . **VCR E**
SERFOZO, M/There's a square: a book about shapes. /1996/
    P-1/1 KG442 . . . . E
SEUSS, D/And to think that I saw it on Mulberry Street. /c1937,
    1964/K-2/2 KG445. . . . . E
    Butter battle book. /1984/K-3/5 KG447. . . . . E
    Cat in the hat. /c1957/P-2/1 KG448. . . . . **CE E**
    Foot book. /c1968/P-1/1 KG452 . . . . E
    Green eggs and ham. /1960/P-2/1 KG454. . . . . **CE E**
    Horton hatches the egg. /c1940/P-3/3 KG456 . . . . **CE E**
    Horton hatches the egg./If I ran the circus (Videocassette). /
    1992/P-3/KG457 . . . . **VCR E**
    Horton hears a Who!/Thidwick the big-hearted moose
    (Videocassette). /1992/P-3/KG458 . . . . **VCR E**
    How the Grinch stole Christmas. /c1957/P-3/KG459. . . . . . E
    Hunches in bunches. /1982/K-3/2 KG460 . . . . E
    I am not going to get up today! /1987/1-3/2 KG461. . . . . . E
    I am not going to get up today! plus three more Dr. Seuss classics
    /1991/1-3/KG462 . . . . **VCR E**
    I can read with my eyes shut. /1978/P-2/2 KG463. . . . . . . E
    If I ran the circus. /c1956/P-3/4 KG464. . . . . E
    If I ran the zoo. /1950/P-3/5 KG465 . . . . E
    Lorax. /c1971/P-3/3 KG466 . . . . **CE E**
    McElligot's pool. /c1947/P-3/KG467. . . . . E
    My many colored days. /1996/K-2/2 KG468. . . . . E
    Oh, the places you'll go! /1990/1-3/2 KG469. . . . . E
    On beyond zebra. /1955/P-3/6 KG470. . . . . E
    Yertle the turtle, and other stories. /c1958/P-3/3 KG472. . **CE E**
SHAW, N/Sheep in a jeep. /1986/K-3/2 KG489. . . . . E
SIEBERT, D/Plane song. /1993/3-6/KD112 . . . . **629.133**
    Sierra. /1991/2-6/KE023 . . . . **811**
    Train song. /1990/P-3/KG501 . . . . E
    Truck song. /1984/P-1/KG502 . . . . **CE E**
SIERRA, J/House that Drac built. /1995/1-3/3 KG503 . . . . E
SLATE, J/Miss Bindergarten gets ready for kindergarten. /1996/
    P-K/2 KG515. . . . . E
SLATER, T/Stay in line. /1996/K-2/2 KG516. . . . . E
SMALL, D/Hoover's bride. /1995/1-3/5 KG521. . . . . E
STANDIFORD, N/Astronauts are sleeping. /1996/K-2/3 KG535. E
STEWART, S/Library. /1995/K-3/3 KG572. . . . . **CE E**
STURGES, P/Ten flashing fireflies. /1995/K-2/2 KG581. . . . . . . E
STUTSON, C/Prairie primer A to Z. /1996/1-3/3 KG583 . . . . . E
TEMPLE, C/Train. /1996/K-3/2 KG599 . . . . E
THIS OLD MAN. /1990/P-1/KD602 . . . . **789.2**
THOMAS, P/Stand back, said the elephant, I'm going to sneeze! /
    c1971, 1990/K-3/2 KG605. E
TRINCA, R/One woolly wombat. /1985/P-2/4 KG617 . . . . E
VAN LAAN, N/Possum come a-knockin'. /1990/K-2/2 KG642 . . E
    Round and round again. /1994/P-2/3 KG643. . . . . E
VIORST, J/Alexander and the terrible, horrible, no good, very bad
    day and other stories /1984/P-3/KG658 . . . . **TB E**

VOZAR, D/M.C. Turtle and the Hip Hop Hare: a nursery rap. /
    1997/2-3/2 KG665. . . . . E
WABER, B/Gina. /1995/1-3/2 KG666. . . . . E
WALTON, R/Noah's square dance. /1995/K-2/3 KG687. . . . . . . E
WEEKS, S/Hurricane City. /1993/K-2/2 KG691. . . . . E
WELCH, W/Playing right field. /1995/K-2/3 KG694 . . . . E
WELLS, R/Noisy Nora. /1997/K-1/4 KG707. . . . . E
    Noisy Nora (Videocassette). /1993/K-1/KG708. . . . . . . **VCR E**
WILLARD, N/Starlit somersault downhill. /1993/K-2/3 KG725 . . E
WILLIAMS, S/I went walking. /1990/P-1/1 KG732. . . . . . . **CE E**
WINTHROP, E/Shoes. /1986/P-K/4 KG745 . . . . **CE E**
    Sledding. /1989/P-K/2 KG746. . . . . E
WOOD, A/Silly Sally. /1992/P-K/2 KG766 . . . . E
YEOMAN, J/Old Mother Hubbard's dog dresses up. /c1989,
    1990/K-3/4 KG774. . . . . E
YOLEN, J/Sip of Aesop. /1995/K-3/KE050 . . . . **811**
YOSHI /Who's hiding here? /1987/K-3/2 KG784. . . . . E
YOUNG, E/Seven blind mice. /1992/K-3/2 KB681 . . . . . . **398.24**
ZEMACH, H/Judge, an untrue tale. /c1969/P-3/2 KG787 . . **CE E**

Stories without words.

ALIKI /Tabby: a story in pictures. /1995/P-1/KF148 . . . . E
ANNO, M/Anno's journey. /1978/P-A/KF159 . . . . E
BANYAI, I/Re-zoom. /1995/2-A/KF196 . . . . E
    Zoom. /1995/P-A/KF197 . . . . E
BRIGGS, R/Snowman. /1978/P-1/KF265 . . . . **CE E**
CHWAST, S/Alphabet parade. /1994/K-2/KF392. . . . . E
CREWS, D/Truck. /1980/P-K/KF438 . . . . **CE E**
DE PAOLA, T/Hunter and the animals: a wordless picture book. /
    1981/K-1/KF470. . . . . E
    Pancakes for breakfast. /1978/1-2/KF478 . . . . E
GOODALL, JS/Story of a main street. /1987/K-3/KF631 . . . . . E
HUTCHINS, P/Changes, changes. /c1971/P-1/KF795 . . . . . **CE E**
JENKINS, S/Looking down. /1995/K-3/KF827. . . . . E
MAYER, M/Boy, a dog and a frog. /c1967/P-1/KG084 . . . **CE E**
MCCULLY, EA/Picnic. /1984/P-2/KG094 . . . . **CE E**
    School. /1987/P-K/KG095. . . . . E
NOAH'S ARK. /c1977/P-2/KA681 . . . . **221.9**
ORMEROD, J/Moonlight. /1982/P-1/KG195 . . . . E
    Sunshine. /1981/P-1/KG196. E
ROHMANN, E/Time flies. /1994/1-3/KG349. . . . . E
TAFURI, N/Do not disturb. /1987/P-2/KG587. . . . . E
    Early morning in the barn. /1983/P/KG588. . . . . E
    Follow me! /1990/P-2/KG589 . . . . E

Storks--Fiction.

DEJONG, M/Wheel on the school. /c1954/4-6/3 KH070 . . . . **Fic**
O'ROURKE, F/Burton and Stanley. /1996/3-5/6 KH568 . . . . . **Fic**

Stormalong, Alfred Bulltop (Legendary character).

METAXAS, E/Stormalong (Kit). /1995/2-5/KB470 . . . **KIT 398.22**

Storms SEE ALSO Hurricanes; Meteorology; Rain and rainfall; Snow;
    Thunderstorms; Tornadoes; Winds.

Storms.

HISCOCK, B/Big storm. /1993/4-6/6 KC198. . . . . **551.55**
LAMPTON, C/Hurricane. /1991/4-6/7 KC202 . . . . **551.55**
LAUBER, P/Hurricanes: Earth's mightiest storms. /1996/
    3-6/6 KC203 . . . . **551.55**
SIMON, S/Storms. /1989/2-6/7 KC205. . . . . **551.55**
SOUZA, DM/Hurricanes. /1996/4-6/7 KC206. . . . . **551.55**

Storms--Fiction.

RAND, G/Aloha, Salty! /1996/1-3/3 KG299 . . . . E

Storytelling.

BAKER, G/Storytelling, art and technique. 3rd ed. /1995/
    /KA244. . . . . **PROF 372.67**
BALTUCK, N/Apples from heaven: multicultural folk tales and
    stories and storytellers. /1995//KA265 . . . . **PROF 398.2**
DAILEY, S/Putting the world in a nutshell: the art of the formula
    tale. /1994//KA337 . . . . **PROF 808.5**
DESPAIN, P/Tales to tell from around the world. Vol. 1 (Sound
    recording cassette). /1995/K-2/KB288. . . . . **SRC 398.2**
FOLKTELLERS /Storytelling: tales and techniques (Videocassette). /
    1994/KA245. **VCR PROF 372.67**
GRAVEYARD TALES (SOUND RECORDING CASSETTE). /1984/
    3-6/KH193. . . . . **SRC Fic**
GREEDY CAT (VIDEOCASSETTE). /1987/
    K-3/KB578. . . . . **VCR 398.24**
HOLT, D/Hogaphone and other stories (Videocassette). /1991/
    2-6/KH275. . . . . **VCR Fic**
    Why the dog chases the cat: great animal stories (Sound recording
    cassette). /1994/1-3/KB591. . . . . **SRC 398.24**
IRVING, J/Full speed ahead: stories and activities for children on
    transportation. /1988//KA223. . . . . **PROF 372.6**
JENKINS, S/Storytelling: learning and sharing (Videocassette). /
    1995//KA246. . . . . **VCR PROF 372.67**
KALLEVIG, CP/Holiday folding stories: storytelling and origami
    together for holiday fun. /1992//KA309 . . . . **PROF 736**

LEWIS, S/Get your teddy ready (Videocassette). /1994/
P-2/KD681. . . . . **VCR 790.1**
LIVO, NJ/Storytelling activities. /1987//KA247 . . . **PROF 372.67**
Storytelling folklore sourcebook. /1991//KA340. . . **PROF 808.5**
MACDONALD, MR/Celebrate the world: twenty tellable folktales
for multicultural festivals. /1994//KA270 . . . . **PROF 398.2**
PARENT, M/Tails and childhood (Sound recording cassette). /
1985/K-3/KB629. . . . . **SRC 398.24**
PELLOWSKI, A/Family storytelling handbook. /1987/
/KA070. . . . . **PROF 027.62**
Story vine: a source book of unusual and easy-to-tell stories from
around the world. /1984//KA248 . . . . **PROF 372.67**
Storytelling handbook: a young people's collection of unusual tales
and helpful hints on how to tell them. /1995/
/KA249. . . . . **PROF 372.67**
SCANDINAVIAN FOLK & FAIRY TALES. /1984/
/KA273. . . . . **PROF 398.2**
STORYTELLING TIME IS HERE (SOUND RECORDING CASSETTE).
/1992/2-4/KB374. . . . . **SRC 398.2**
STOTTER, R/Origami stories (Videocassette). /1993/
1-3/KB122 . . . . **VCR 372.67**
VILLAGE STEW (VIDEOCASSETTE). /1987/
K-3/KB782. . . . . **VCR 398.27**

Storytelling--Collections.
DESPAIN, P/Eleven nature tales: a multicultural journey. /1996/
3-5/7 KB286 . . . . **398.2**
HARLEY, B/Dinosaurs never say please and other stories (Sound
recording cassette). /c1987, 1989/1-3/KF671. . . . . **SRC E**
JUBA THIS AND JUBA THAT. /1995//KA366 . . . . . . **PROF 820.8**
MANY VOICES: TRUE TALES FROM AMERICA'S PAST. /1995/
/KA371. . . . . **PROF 973**
PELLOWSKI, A/Storytelling handbook: a young people's collection
of unusual tales and helpful /1995//KA249 . . . **PROF 372.67**
READY-TO-TELL TALES: SURE-FIRE STORIES FROM AMERICA'S
FAVORITE STORYTELLERS. /1994//KA272 . . . . . . **PROF 398.2**
TORRENCE, J/My grandmother's treasure (Sound recording
cassette). /1993/3-5/KH799 . . . . **SRC Fic**

Storytelling--Fiction.
AHLBERG, J/It was a dark and stormy night. /1993/
3-5/6 KG822 . . . . **Fic**
MARSHALL, E/Three by the sea. /1981/K-3/1 KG066 . . . . **CE E**
MYERS, WD/Story of the three kingdoms. /1995/1-3/3 KG165 . **E**
POLACCO, P/My ol' man. /1995/1-3/3 KG254 . . . . **E**
PORTE, BA/Turkey drive and other tales. /1993/1-3/2 KH611 . **Fic**
SIEGELSON, KL/Terrible, wonderful tellin' at Hog Hammock. /
1996/4-6/6 KH711 . . . . **Fic**
TOMPERT, A/Grandfather Tang's story. /1990/2-3/4 KG613. . . **E**

Storytelling--Study and teaching.
MALLAN, K/Children as storytellers. /1992//KA341 . **PROF 808.5**
Stowe, Harriet Beecher.
FRITZ, J/Harriet Beecher Stowe and the Beecher preachers. /1994/
6-A/7 KE556 . . . . **B STOWE, H.**
Strangers.
GIRARD, LW/Who is a stranger and what should I do? /1985/
1-3/6 KB021 . . . . **363.1**
Strangers--Fiction.
BERENSTAIN, S/Berenstain Bears learn about strangers. /1985/
K-2/4 KF225 . . . . **CE E**
Stravinsky, Igor.
VENEZIA, M/Igor Stravinsky. /1996/
5-6/7 KE557 . . . . **B STRAVINSKY, I**
Strawberries--Folklore.
BRUCHAC, J/First strawberries: a Cherokee story. /1993/
1-3/4 KB538 . . . . **398.24**
Stream animals--Snake River (Wyo.-Wash.).
CRAIGHEAD, C/Eagle and the river. /1994/5-6/7 KC339 . . **577.6**
Stream ecology.
PARKER, S/Pond and river. /1988/1-6/7 KC340 . . . . . . **577.63**
Street children--Fiction.
NAIDOO, B/No turning back: a novel of South Africa. /1997/
6-A/6 KH526 . . . . **Fic**
Street lines SEE Street-railroads.
Street signs.
HOBAN, T/I read signs. /1983/P-1/KA800 . . . . **302.23**
Street-railroads.
YEPSEN, R/City trains: moving through America's cities by rail. /
1993/5-6/7 KB162 . . . . **388.4**
Streetcars SEE Cable cars (Streetcars).
Streets--Pictorial works.
FLORIAN, D/City street. /1990/P-1/KA893. . . . . **307.3**
Stress (Psychology).
MENDLER, AN/Smiling at yourself: educating young children about
stress and self-esteem. /1990//KA304. . . . . **PROF 649**

STRESSBUSTERS (VIDEOCASSETTE). /1994/
3-6/KA653 . . . . **VCR 155.9**
Stress in children.
ORLICK, T/Free to feel great: teaching children to excel at living. /
1993//KA305 . . . . **PROF 649**
Strikes and lockouts.
DASH, J/We shall not be moved: the women's factory strike of
1909. /1996/6-A/8 KA939. . . . . **331.4**
Strikes and lockouts--Fiction.
KRENSKY, S/Iron dragon never sleeps. /1995/3-5/2 KH381. . . **Fic**
PEREZ, NA/Breaker. /1988/6-A/7 KH597. . . . . **Fic**
Strikes and lockouts--Textile industry--Fiction.
HEWITT, M/One proud summer. /1981/A/7 KH254 . . . . **Fic**
String--Fiction.
SCHAEFER, CL/Squiggle. /1996/P-2/3 KG402 . . . . **E**
Stringed instruments.
SHIPTON, A/Strings. /1994/4-6/7 KD548 . . . . **787**
TURNER, BC/Living violin. /1996/4-6/12 KD549 . . . . . **BA 787.2**
Structual engineering.
WILKINSON, P/Building. /1995/5-6/7 KD360 . . . . **690**
Stubblefield, Nathan Beverly--Childhood and youth--Fiction.
DENSLOW, SP/Radio boy. /1995/1-3/7 KF462 . . . . **E**
Study skills.
HOW TO STUDY (VIDEOCASSETTE). /1988/
5-6/KB087 . . . . **VCR 371.302**
MCINERNEY, C/Tracking the facts: how to develop research skills. /
1990/5-A/6 KB089 . . . . **371.302**
RADENCICH, MC/How to help your child with homework: every
caring parent's guide to encouraging /1997/
/KA181. . . . . **PROF 371.3**
STUDY SKILLS PLUS ATTITUDE: THE WINNING COMBINATION
(VIDEOCASSETTE). /1989/5-A/KB092 . . . . **VCR 371.302**
Stuffed animals SEE ALSO specific types of stuffed animals e.g. Teddy
bears.
Stuffed animals--Fiction.
MILNE, AA/House at Pooh Corner. /c1956/K-6/3 KH497 . . . . **Fic**
Winnie-the-Pooh. /1974/K-6/3 KH498 . . . . **Fic**
World of Pooh: the complete "Winnie-the-Pooh" and "The House
at Pooh Corner." /c1957/K-6/3 KH499 . . . . **Fic**
Stuttering--Fiction.
KLINE, S/Mary Marony hides out. /1993/1-3/4 KH369 . . . . . **Fic**
Subject headings--Children's literature.
FOUNTAIN, JF/Subject headings for school and public libraries: an
LCSH/Sears companion. 2nd ed. /1996//KA059. . . **PROF 025.4**
SEARS LIST OF SUBJECT HEADINGS. 16TH ED. /1997/
/KA061. . . . . **PROF 025.4**
SUBJECT HEADINGS FOR CHILDREN: A LIST OF SUBJECT
HEADINGS USED BY THE LIBRARY OF CONGRESS WITH
DEWEY NUMBERS ADDED. 2ND ED. /1998/
/KA062. . . . . **PROF 025.4**
Subject headings, Library of Congress.
SUBJECT HEADINGS FOR CHILDREN: A LIST OF SUBJECT
HEADINGS USED BY THE LIBRARY /1998//KA062. **PROF 025.4**
Submarine boats--Fiction.
VERNE, J/20,000 leagues under the sea. /1980/5-6/6 KH829 . **Fic**
Subtraction.
HULME, JN/Sea sums. /1996/P-2/3 KB961 . . . . **513.2**
Suburban life--Fiction.
BLUME, J/Are you there God? It's me, Margaret. /c1970, 1982/
4-6/5 KG905 . . . . **CE Fic**
Otherwise known as Sheila the Great. /1972/4-6/4 KG912 . . **Fic**
Subversive activities SEE Spies.
Subways.
YEPSEN, R/City trains: moving through America's cities by rail. /
1993/5-6/7 KB162 . . . . **388.4**
Subways--Fiction.
HEST, A/Jamaica Louise James. /1996/K-2/2 KF719. . . . . . . **E**
HOLMAN, F/Slake's limbo. /1974/6-A/7 KH274 . . . . **CE Fic**
Success.
GO, GO, GOALS!: HOW TO GET THERE (VIDEOCASSETTE). /
1993/4-6/KA657 . . . . **VCR 158**
LETTERS FOR OUR CHILDREN: FIFTY AMERICANS SHARE
LESSONS IN LIVING. /1996//KA158. . . . . **PROF 170**
ORLICK, T/Free to feel great: teaching children to excel at living. /
1993//KA305 . . . . **PROF 649**
Success--Fiction.
SEUSS, D/Oh, the places you'll go! /1990/1-3/2 KG469 . . . . . **E**
SHEFELMAN, J/Peddler's dream. /1992/1-3/2 KG492 . . . . **E**
Suffrage SEE Elections; also classes of people with the subdivision Suffrage
e.g. Women--Suffrage.
Suffrage.
PASCOE, E/Right to vote. /1997/4-6/12 KA910 . . . . **324.6**
Suffragists--Fiction.
MCCULLY, EA/Ballot box battle. /1996/1-3/2 KH473 . . . . **Fic**

Sugihara, Chiune.
MOCHIZUKI, K/Passage to freedom: the Sugihara story. /1997/
3-6/4 KE662 . . . . **940.53**

Sukkot.
CHAIKIN, M/Light another candle: the story and meaning of
Hanukkah. /c1981, 1987/5-6/8 KA770 . . . . **296.4**

Sukkot--Fiction.
POLACCO, P/Tikvah means hope. /1994/1-3/2 KG259 . . . . . . **E**

Sumatran rhinoceros.
MAYNARD, T/Rhino comes to America. /1993/
5-6/7 KC802 . . . . **599.66**

Summer.
KURELEK, W/Prairie boy's summer. /1975/3-5/7 KE813 . . . **971.2**
MAGICAL MOTHER NATURE: THE FOUR SEASONS
(VIDEOCASSETTE). /1989/2-4/KC061 . . . . **VCR 525**
SEASONS. REV. ED. (SOUND FILMSTRIP). /c1975, 1993/
K-2/KC063. . . . . **FSS 525**

Summer--Fiction.
AGELL, C/I wear long green hair in the summer. /1994/
K-2/2 KF138 . . . . **E**
ALIKI /Those summers. /1996/K-2/4 KF149 . . . . **E**
APPELT, K/Watermelon Day. /1996/K-2/2 KF164 . . . . **E**
CONLY, JL/Trout summer. /1995/6-A/5 KH021 . . . . **Fic**
FLORIAN, D/Winter day. /1987/P-1/1 KF560 . . . . **E**
GEORGE, LB/Around the pond: who's been here? /1996/
K-2/2 KF606 . . . . **E**
RYLANT, C/Mr. Putter and Tabby row the boat. /1997/
K-2/2 KG381 . . . . **E**

Summer--Poetry.
GIOVANNI, N/Knoxville, Tennessee. /1994/P-1/2 KD945 . . . **811**

Summer resorts--Fiction.
STEVENSON, J/Sea View Hotel. /c1978, 1994/K-3/3 KG567 . . **E**
Sun SEE ALSO Eclipse, Solar; Solar energy; Solar system.

Sun.
BENDICK, J/Sun: our very own star. /1991/1-3/5 KC044 . . **523.7**
GIBBONS, G/Sun up, sun down. /1983/P-2/2 KC045 . . . . **523.7**
HILLERMAN, A/Done in the sun, solar projects for children. /1983/
2-4/7 KD048. . . . . **621.47**
SIMON, S/Sun. /1986/P-A/7 KC046 . . . . **523.7**
SUN, EARTH, MOON (VIDEOCASSETTE). /1995/
4-6/KC017. . . . . **VCR 523.2**

Sun--Fiction.
CONRAD, P/Rooster's gift. /1996/K-2/3 KF414 . . . . **E**
EMBERLEY, M/Welcome back, Sun. /1993/1-3/3 KF524 . . . . . . **E**

Sun--Folklore.
BISHOP, G/Maui and the Sun: a Maori tale. /1996/
3-4/3 KB700 . . . . **398.26**
DAYRELL, E/Why the sun and the moon live in the sky: an African
folktale. /c1968/K-3/6 KB704 . . . . **CE 398.26**

Sunflowers.
KING, E/Backyard sunflower. /1993/1-4/4 KD174 . . . . **635.9**
WINNER, C/Sunflower family. /1996/3-6/7 KC434 . . . . **583**

Sunflowers--Fiction.
BUNTING, E/Sunflower house. /1996/P-2/2 KF311 . . . . **E**
FORD, M/Sunflower. /1995/P-1/1 KF566. . . . . **E**
Sunken treasure SEE Buried treasure.

Super Bowl (Football game).
SAMPSON, M/Football that won... /1996/K-2/2 KD786. **796.332**

Superconductivity.
ASIMOV, I/How did we find out about superconductivity? /1988/
5-A/7 KC135 . . . . **537.6**

Supermarkets.
HAUTZIG, D/At the supermarket. /1994/1-4/6 KB127 . . . . . **381**

Supermarkets--Fiction.
ADLER, DA/Onion sundaes. /1994/2-3/2 KG819 . . . . **Fic**

Supernatural.
COHEN, D/Ghosts of the deep. /1993/4-6/7 KA600 . . . . . **133.1**
DEEM, JM/How to find a ghost. /1988/4-A/7 KA604 . . . . **133.1**

Supernatural--Fiction.
ALFRED HITCHCOCK'S SUPERNATURAL TALES OF TERROR AND
SUSPENSE. /c1973, 1983/A/6 KG842. . . . . **Fic**
BELLAIRS, J/Doom of the haunted opera. /1995/
4-6/6 KG896 . . . . **Fic**
BYARS, BC/McMummy. /1993/5-A/5 KG961 . . . . **Fic**
COOPER, S/Boggart. /1993/6-A/7 KH026. . . . . **CE Fic**
Boggart and the monster. /1997/5-A/6 KH027 . . . . **Fic**
EVANS, D/Classroom at the end of the hall. /1996/
3-5/4 KH104 . . . . **Fic**
FARMER, N/Girl named Disaster. /1996/6-A/5 KH109 . . . . . **Fic**
HITE, S/Dither Farm: a novel. /1992/5-A/7 KH265 . . . . **Fic**
HUNTER, M/Walking stones. /1996/6-A/8 KH295 . . . . **Fic**
LISLE, JT/Gold dust letters. /1994/4-6/7 KH410 . . . . **Fic**
Looking for Juliette. /1994/4-6/6 KH412 . . . . **Fic**
MAHY, M/Haunting. /1982/5-A/6 KH451 . . . . **CE Fic**

MCKINLEY, R/Knot in the grain and other stories. /1994/
6-A/7 KH489 . . . . **Fic**
NIMMO, J/Griffin's castle. /1997/6-A/5 KH551 . . . . **Fic**
PEARCE, AP/Who's afraid? and other strange stories. /1987/
5-6/6 KH590 . . . . **Fic**
STEIG, W/Amazing bone. /1976/1-3/5 KG539. . . . . **CE E**
VALGARDSON, WD/Sarah and the people of Sand River. /1996/
4-6/2 KH818 . . . . **Fic**
VIVELO, J/Chills run down my spine. /1994/5-A/4 KH830 . . . . **Fic**

Supernatural--Folklore.
PIPE, J/In the footsteps of the werewolf. /1996/
4-6/7 KB635 . . . . **398.24**
RAW HEAD, BLOODY BONES: AFRICAN-AMERICAN TALES OF
THE SUPERNATURAL. /1991/4-6/4 KB361 . . . . **398.2**
SCARY BOOK. /1991/2-4/2 KB691 . . . . **398.25**

Supernatural--Literary collections.
SCARED SILLY! A BOOK FOR THE BRAVE. /1994/
K-3/KD904 . . . . **810.8**
SCARY BOOK. /1991/2-4/2 KB691 . . . . **398.25**

Supernatural--Poetry.
PRELUTSKY, J/Monday's troll: poems. /1996/K-4/KE008. . **CE 811**
Superstition SEE ALSO Astrology; Dreams; Fairies; Folklore; Fortune telling;
Ghosts; Occult sciences; Witchcraft.

Superstition.
PERL, L/Don't sing before breakfast, don't sleep in the moonlight:
everyday superstitions and how they began. /1988/
4-A/8 KA559 . . . . **001.9**

Superstition--Fiction.
DEFELICE, CC/Willy's silly grandma. /1997/1-3/2 KF455 . . . . . **E**

Surtsey (Iceland).
LASKY, K/Surtsey: the newest place on earth. /1992/
A/7 KE697 . . . . **949.12**
Survival SEE ALSO Wilderness survival.

Survival.
EVANS, J/Camping and survival. /1992/4-A/6 KD825 . . . **796.54**

Survival--Fiction.
AVI /Poppy. /1995/3-5/6 KG862. . . . . **Fic**
DEFOE, D/Robinson Crusoe. /1983/5-A/7 KH068. . . . . **Fic**
ECKERT, AW/Incident at Hawk's Hill. /1971/6-A/7 KH097. . . . **Fic**
FARMER, N/Girl named Disaster. /1996/6-A/5 KH109 . . . . . **Fic**
HENEGHAN, J/Wish me luck. /1997/6-A/5 KH237 . . . . **Fic**
HILL, D/Take it easy. /1997/6-A/4 KH260 . . . . **Fic**
HILL, K/Toughboy and sister. /1990/4-6/6 KH261 . . . . **Fic**
Winter camp. /1993/5-A/6 KH262 . . . . **Fic**
KINSEY-WARNOCK, N/Bear that heard crying. /1993/
2-3/2 KF905 . . . . **E**
MAZER, H/Island keeper. /1981/A/6 KH464 . . . . **Fic**
MCCLUNG, RM/Hugh Glass, mountain man. /1993/
6-A/7 KH472 . . . . **Fic**
O'DELL, S/Island of the Blue Dolphins. /c1960/5-6/6 KH559 . . **Fic**
Island of the Blue Dolphins. /c1960, 1990/5-6/6 KH560 . . . **Fic**
PATON WALSH, J/Green book. /1982/4-6/6 KH583. . . . . . . **Fic**
PAULSEN, G/Hatchet. /1987/5-A/6 KH587 . . . . **CE Fic**
SPERRY, A/Call it courage. /c1940/5-6/6 KH743. . . . . . . **CE Fic**
TAYLOR, T/Timothy of the cay. /1993/5-A/5 KH785 . . . . . . **Fic**
VOIGT, C/Homecoming. /1981/6-A/4 KH833 . . . . **Fic**
Survival of the fittest SEE Natural selection.

Swallows--Fiction.
POLITI, L/Song of the swallows. /c1949, 1987/
K-3/6 KG262 . . . . **CE E**

Swamp ecology.
LAVIES, B/Mangrove wilderness: nature's nursery. /1994/
K-3/7 KC341 . . . . **577.68**

Swamps--Fiction.
HURD, T/Mama don't allow. /1984/K-3/2 KF793. . . . . **CE E**
KARAS, GB/Home on the bayou: a cowboy's story. /1996/
K-2/2 KF868 . . . . **E**

Swan Lake (Ballet).
FONTEYN, M/Swan Lake. /1989/4-6/7 KD693 . . . . . . **CE 792.8**
GREGORY, C/Cynthia Gregory dances Swan Lake. /1990/
4-A/7 KD694 . . . . **792.8**

Swans.
SELSAM, ME/First look at ducks, geese, and swans. /1990/
1-3/2 KC683 . . . . **598.4**

Swans--Fiction.
ANDERSEN, HC/Ugly duckling (Videocassette). /1977/
2-5/KG849 . . . . **VCR Fic**
MITCHELL, A/Ugly Duckling. /1994/P-A/4 KG143 . . . . **E**
WHITE, EB/Trumpet of the swan. /c1970/3-6/6 KH852 . . . . . **Fic**

Sweden--Emigration and immigration--Fiction.
SANDIN, J/Long way to a new land. /1981/1-3/2 KG391 . . . . **E**

Sweden--Fiction.
HICKOX, R/Per and the Dala horse. /1995/1-3/6 KF724 . . . . . **E**

LINDGREN, A/Pippi Longstocking. /c1950, 1978/
3-5/4 KH407 . . . . **CE Fic**
Tomten. /c1965, 1997/K-2/3 KF986 . . . . **CE E**
SCHWARTZ, DM/Supergrandpa. /1991/K-3/5 KG416 . . . . **E**
Swift River (Mass.)--Fiction.
YOLEN, J/Letting Swift River go. /1992/1-3/5 KG777 . . . . . . **E**
Swimming.
BAILEY, D/Swimming. /1990/2-4/2 KD846 . . . . **797.2**
ROUSE, J/Young swimmer. /1997/3-6/6 KD848 . . . . **797.2**
VERRIER, J/Swimming and diving. /1996/3-6/8 KD849 . . . . **797.2**
WILNER, B/Swimming. /1996/3-6/6 KD850 . . . . **797.2**
Swimming--Fiction.
FRANKLIN, KL/Iguana Beach. /1997/P-1/2 KF575 . . . . **E**
KESSLER, L/Last one in is a rotten egg. /c1969/1-2/1 KF900 . . . **E**
WELLS, R/Edward in deep water. /1995/P-K/2 KG697 . . . . **E**
Swindlers and swindling--Fiction.
ABOLAFIA, Y/Fox tale. /1991/K-2/2 KF126 . . . . **E**
KIMMEL, EA/Magic dreidels: a Hanukkah story. /1996/
K-3/2 KF904 . . . . **E**
Swine SEE Pigs.
Switzerland--Fiction.
HICYILMAZ, G/Frozen waterfall. /1994/6-A/6 KH257 . . . . . **Fic**
OBLIGADO, L/Chocolate cow. /1993/K-2/2 KG185 . . . . **E**
SPYRI, J/Heidi. /1996/5-A/6 KH746 . . . . **Fic**
ULLMAN, JR/Banner in the sky (Talking book). /n.d./
4-6/KH817 . . . . **TB Fic**
Switzerland--Folklore.
EARLY, M/William Tell. /1991/4-6/6 KB440 . . . . **398.22**
FISHER, LE/William Tell. /1996/3-5/4 KB442 . . . . **398.22**
Symbiosis.
TREE: A LIVING COMMUNITY (VIDEOCASSETTE). /1988/
4-6/KC355 . . . . **VCR 577.8**
Synagogues.
ROSENBLUM, R/Old synagogue. /1989/3-6/7 KA783 . . . . **296.6**
Synonyms and antonyms--English language SEE English language--Synonyms
and antonyms.
Szenes, Hannah SEE Senesh, Hannah.
Table etiquette--History.
GIBLIN, JC/From hand to mouth, or how we invented knives, forks,
/1987/5-6/8 KB185 . . . . **394.1**
Tables--Fiction.
RUSSO, M/Under the table. /1997/P-K/2 KG363 . . . . **E**
Tableware--Fiction.
FRIEDMAN, IR/How my parents learned to eat. /1984/
1-3/2 KF586 . . . . **E**
Tableware--History.
GIBLIN, JC/From hand to mouth, or how we invented knives, forks,
/1987/5-6/8 KB185 . . . . **394.1**
Tadpoles.
PFEFFER, W/From tadpole to frog. /1994/
K-2/2 KC608 . . . . **CE 597.8**
Tadpoles--Fiction.
ASCH, F/Moonbear's pet. /1997/P-K/2 KF175 . . . . **E**
KENT, J/Caterpillar and the polliwog. /1982/K-2/4 KF896 . . **CE E**
Tail.
MACHOTKA, H/Terrific tails. /1994/3-5/7 KC272 . . . . . . **571.1**
Tail--Fiction.
ERNST, LC/Walter's tail. /1992/P-2/3 KF534 . . . . **E**
Tailors--Fiction.
FRIEDMAN, A/Cloak for the dreamer. /1995/1-3/6 KF585 . . . . **E**
KLINTING, L/Bruno the tailor. /1996/K-2/2 KF913 . . . . **E**
POTTER, B/Tailor of Gloucester. /c1931, 1987/P-3/7 KG270 . . . . **E**
Tailor of Gloucester (Videocassette). /1988/1-3/KG271 . **VCR E**
Taino Indians--Folklore.
JAFFE, N/Golden flower: a Taino myth from Puerto Rico. /1996/
2-4/5 KB503 . . . . **398.23**
ROHMER, H/Atariba and Niguayona: a story from the Taino people
of Puerto Rico. /c1976, 1988/4-5/5 KB769 . . . . **398.27**
Taiwan--Fiction.
WU, P/Abacus contest: stories from Taiwan and China. /1996/
3-5/4 KH884 . . . . **Fic**
Talented students.
EDUCATING ABLE LEARNERS (VIDEOCASSETTE). /1991/
/KA187 . . . . **VCR PROF 371.95**
Talented students--Education.
FLACK, JD/Inventing, inventions, and inventors: a teaching resource
book. /1989//KA297 . . . . **PROF 607**
Tales SEE Fairy tales; Folklore; Tall tales.
Tales.
LIVO, NJ/Storytelling folklore sourcebook. /1991/
/KA340 . . . . **PROF 808.5**
Tales--Classification.
DAILEY, S/Putting the world in a nutshell: the art of the formula
tale. /1994//KA337 . . . . **PROF 808.5**

Tall tales.
FLEISCHMAN, S/McBroom's wonderful one-acre farm: three tall
tales. /1992/3-6/4 KH124 . . . . **Fic**
ISAACS, A/Swamp Angel. /1994/2-5/6 KF810 . . . . **E**
KELLOGG, S/Mike Fink. /1992/3-4/5 KB456 . . . . **398.22**
Paul Bunyan, a tall tale. /1984/4-6/7 KB457 . . . . **398.22**
Sally Ann Thunder Ann Whirlwind Crockett: a tall tale. /1995/
2-5/5 KB458 . . . . **398.22**
LAWSON, J/If pigs could fly. /1989/5-A/6 KH387 . . . . **Fic**
MCKISSACK, P/Million fish...more or less. /c1992, 1996/
1-3/4 KG106 . . . . **E**
METAXAS, E/Stormalong (Kit). /1995/2-5/KB470 . . . . . **KIT 398.22**
ROTH, SL/Biggest frog in Australia. /1996/2-3/2 KB643 . . . **398.24**
SAN SOUCI, RD/Cut from the same cloth: American women of
myth, legend, and tall tale. /1993/5-6/6 KB481 . . . . **398.22**
SHEPARD, A/Legend of Slappy Hooper: an American tall tale. /
1993/3-5/3 KB489 . . . . **398.22**
WALKER, PR/Big men, big country: a collection of American tall
tales. /1993/4-A/7 KB493 . . . . **398.22**
WOOD, A/Bunyans. /1996/1-5/6 KG760 . . . . **E**
Tamarins.
NAGDA, AW/Canopy crossing: a story of an Atlantic rainforest
(Kit). /1997/2-4/KC873 . . . . **KIT 599.8**
Tangrams--Fiction.
TOMPERT, A/Grandfather Tang's story. /1990/2-3/4 KG613 . . . **E**
Tanks (Military science).
CHASEMORE, R/Tanks. /1996/4-6/8 KD060 . . . . **623.7**
Tanzania--Description and travel.
MARGOLIES, BA/Rehema's journey: a visit in Tanzania /c1990/
3-6/4 KE180 . . . . **916.78**
Taos Indians--Poetry.
WOOD, N/Spirit walker: poems. /1993/6-A/KE046 . . . . . . **811**
Tarahumara Indians.
STAUB, FJ/Children of the Sierra Madre. /1996/
4-6/8 KE839 . . . . **972**
Tarantulas.
LABONTE, G/Tarantula. /1991/5-6/7 KC527 . . . . **595.4**
Tarantulas--Fiction.
STOWE, C/Not-so-normal Norman. /1995/2-5/3 KH770 . . . . **Fic**
Tarasco Indians--Social life and customs.
PRESILLA, ME/Life around the lake. /1996/2-6/8 KE837 . . . **972**
Tasmanian devil.
DARLING, K/Tasmanian devil: on location. /1992/
5-6/6 KC735 . . . . **599.2**
Taste.
FABULOUS FIVE: OUR SENSES (VIDEOCASSETTE). /1989/
P-2/KC917 . . . . **VCR 612**
PARRAMON, JM/Taste. /1985/P-1/2 KC975 . . . . **612.8**
Taxicabs--Fiction.
BARRACCA, D/Adventures of taxi dog. /1990/P-2/2 KF200 **CE E**
Taxi Dog Christmas. /1994/P-2/3 KF202 . . . . **E**
Taxidermy.
CUTCHINS, J/Are those animals real?: how museums prepare
wildlife exhibits. Rev. & updated ed. /1995/3-A/7 KC443. **590.75**
Tchaikovsky, Peter Ilych.
THOMPSON, W/Pyotr Ilyich Tchaikovsky. /1993/
6-A/8 KE558 . . . . **B TCHAIKOVSKY,P**
Teacher-student relationships--Fiction.
HEYMSFELD, C/Coaching Ms. Parker. /1992/2-4/4 KH255 . . . **Fic**
KONIGSBURG, EL/View from Saturday. /1996/5-A/7 KH377 . **Fic**
LEVY, E/Keep Ms. Sugarman in the fourth grade. /1992/
3-5/5 KH402 . . . . **Fic**
NAYLOR, PR/Agony of Alice. /1985/5-6/6 KH532 . . . . **Fic**
RATHMANN, P/Ruby the copycat. /1991/K-2/2 KG311 . . . . . . **E**
Teachers.
ADLER, DA/Picture book of Louis Braille. /1997/
2-3/3 KE261 . . . . **B BRAILLE, L.**
BOOKER (VIDEOCASSETTE). /1983/
3-6/KE585 . . . . **VCR B WASHINGTON, B**
FREEDMAN, R/Out of darkness: the story of Louis Braille. /1997/
3-5/6 KE262 . . . . **B BRAILLE, L.**
HOUSTON, G/My great-aunt Arizona. /1992/
3-5/4 KE393 . . . . **B HUGHES, A.**
MCKISSACK, P/Mary McLeod Bethune. /1992/
4-6/5 KE254 . . . . **B BETHUNE, M.**
ROBERTS, JL/Booker T. Washington: educator and leader. /1995/
4-6/5 KE586 . . . . **B WASHINGTON, B**
Teachers--Bibliography.
ROUTMAN, R/Blue pages: resources for teachers from Invitations.
Updated, expanded, and rev. /1994//KA026 . . . . **PROF 016.372**
Teachers--Fiction.
ALLARD, H/Miss Nelson is missing. /1977/1-3/3 KF151 . . . **CE E**
BROWN, MT/Arthur's teacher trouble. /1986/K-3/4 KF277 . **CE E**
CLEARY, B/Ramona the brave. /1975/3-5/6 KH005 . . . . **Fic**

DENSLOW, SP/On the trail with Miss Pace. /1995/
1-3/2 KF461 . . . . **E**
HENKES, K/Lilly's purple plastic purse. /1996/K-2/2 KF708 . . . . **E**
HURWITZ, J/Teacher's pet. /1988/3-5/4 KH305 . . . . **Fic**
MCKENZIE, EK/Stargone John. /1990/3-5/5 KH484 . . . . **Fic**
PINKWATER, J/Mister Fred. /1994/5-A/4 KH606 . . . . **Fic**
YORKE, M/Miss Butterpat goes wild! /1993/3-5/5 KH898 . . . . **Fic**

Teachers--Fiction--Software.
ARTHUR'S TEACHER TROUBLE (CD-ROM). /1992/
1-4/KF171 . . . . **CDR E**

Teachers--History.
FISHER, LE/Schoolmasters. /1997/3-6/7 KB083 . . . . **371.1**

Teachers--Library orientation.
URBANIK, MK/Curriculum planning and teaching using the library
media center. /1989//KA064 . . . . **PROF 025.5**

Teachers of the deaf.
BOWEN, AR/World of knowing: a story about Thomas Hopkins
Gallaudet. /1995/3-5/6 KE361 . . . . **B GALLAUDET, T.**
Teaching SEE ALSO Child study; Classroom management; Education;
Educational innovations; Educational psychology; Kindergarten; Learning--
Psychology; Montessori method of education; Piaget, Jean; Project method
of teaching; Study, Method of; Teachers.

Teaching.
BARCHERS, SI/Creating and managing the literate classroom. /
1990//KA218 . . . . **PROF 372.6**
LAZEAR, DG/Seven pathways of learning: teaching students and
parents about multiple /1994//KA174 . . . . **PROF 370.15**

Teaching--Aids and devices.
BARRON, AE/New technologies for education: a beginner's guide.
3rd ed. /1997//KA176 . . . . **PROF 371.3**
BRODIE, CS/Bookmark book. /1996//KA310 . . . . . **PROF 741.6**
JURENKA, NE/Beyond the bean seed: gardening activities for
grades K-6. /1996//KA202 . . . . **PROF 372.3**
LAUGHLIN, MK/Literature-based social studies: /1991/
/KA261 . . . . **PROF 372.83**
STANGL, J/Recycling activities for the primary grades. /1993/
/KA313 . . . . **PROF 745.5**
STORY STARTERS. VOL. 1 (VIDEOCASSETTE). /1995/
/KA231 . . . . **VCR PROF 372.6**
URBANIK, MK/Curriculum planning and teaching using the library
media center. /1989//KA064 . . . . **PROF 025.5**
VANDERHEYDEN-TRESCONY, C/Faxing friends; a resource guide
for forming international friendships among /1992/
/KA173 . . . . **PROF 370.117**

Teaching--Aids and devices--Handbooks, manuals, etc.
RAINES, SC/Story stretchers for the primary grades: activities to
expand children's /1992//KA240 . . . . **PROF 372.64**

Teaching--Bibliography.
ROUTMAN, R/Blue pages: resources for teachers from Invitations.
Updated, expanded, and rev. /1994//KA026 . . . . **PROF 016.372**

Teaching--Computer network resources.
BARRON, AE/Internet and instruction: activities and ideas. /1996/
/KA047 . . . . **PROF 025.06**

Teaching--Handbooks, manuals, etc.
CROFT, DJ/Activities handbook for teachers of young children. 5th
ed. /1990//KA191 . . . . **PROF 372.1**

Teaching--Periodicals.
LEARNING: SUCCESSFUL TEACHING TODAY. /1972-/
/KA122 . . . . **PER PROF 050**
ONLINE--OFFLINE: THEMES AND RESOURCES K-8. /1996-/
/KA129. . . . . **PER PROF 050**
PRIMARY VOICES K-6. /1993-//KA132 . . . . . . **PER PROF 050**

Teaching, Freedom of.
REICHMAN, H/Censorship and selection: issues and answers for
schools. Rev. ed. /1993//KA053 . . . . **PROF 025.2**

Teasing--Fiction.
CAPLE, K/Biggest nose. /1985/P-2/2 KF337 . . . . **E**

Technological innovations.
JONES, CF/Accidents may happen. /1996/4-A/9 KC895. . . . **609**
STORIES OF INVENTION AND INGENUITY. VOL. 1
(VIDEOCASSETTE). /1995/3-5/KC898 . . . . **VCR 609**
Technology SEE ALSO Building; Engineering; High technology; Inventions;
Machinery; Manufactures.

Technology.
BIESTY, S/Stephen Biesty's incredible cross-sections. /1992/
4-A/6 KC880 . . . . **600**
MACAULAY, D/Way things work. /1988/A/11 KC881 . . . . . **600**
NEW BOOK OF POPULAR SCIENCE. REV. ED. /1998/
5-6/KA433 . . . . **REF 503**

Technology--China--History.
WILLIAMS, S/Made in China: ideas and inventions from Ancient
China. /1996/4-6/6 KE631 . . . . **931**

Technology--Encyclopedias.
HOW THINGS WORK. /1995/3-6/5 KC883 . . . . **603**

Technology--Government policy.
MINDS-ON SCIENCE: FOR THE SAKE OF THE NATION
(VIDEODISC). /1995/5-A/KA804 . . . . **VD 303.48**

Technology--History.
ROLAND-ENTWISTLE, T/More errata: another book of historical
errors. /1995/3-6/10 KE143. . . . . **909**

Technology--Miscellanea.
GATES, P/Nature got there first. /1995/4-8/10 KB905 . . . . . **508**
SOUCIE, G/What's the difference between lenses and prisms and
other scientific things? /1995/4-6/7 KB872. . . . . **500**

Technology--Periodicals.
YES MAG: CANADA'S SCIENCE MAGAZINE FOR KIDS. /1996-/
4-6/KA552 . . . . **050**

Technology--Software.
MACAULAY, D/Way things work (CD-ROM). /1996/
3-A/KC882 . . . . **CDR 600**

Technology--Study and teaching.
FLACK, JD/Inventing, inventions, and inventors: a teaching resource
book. /1989//KA297 . . . . **PROF 607**

Technology--Yearbooks.
SCIENCE YEAR: THE WORLD ANNUAL SCIENCE SUPPLEMENT. /
1965-/A/KA435 . . . . **REF 505**

Technology and civilization.
MINDS-ON SCIENCE: FOR THE SAKE OF THE NATION
(VIDEODISC). /1995/5-A/KA804 . . . . **VD 303.48**

Tecumseh, Shawnee Chief.
CONNELL, K/These lands are ours: Tecumseh's fight for the Old
Northwest. /1993/5-6/7 KE559 . . . . **B TECUMSEH**

Teddy bears.
MORRIS, A/How teddy bears are made: a visit to the Vermont
Teddy Bear factory. /1994/K-2/3 KD351 . . . . **688.7**
YOUNG, R/Teddy bears. /1992/5-6/6 KD354 . . . . **688.7**

Teddy bears--Fiction.
AHLBERG, J/Bear nobody wanted. /c1992, 1995/
3-6/6 KG821 . . . . **Fic**
ALBOROUGH, J/Where's my teddy? /1992/P-1/2 KF145 . . . . . **E**
KOTZWINKLE, W/Million-Dollar Bear. /1995/2-3/2 KF916. . . . . **E**
LILLIE, P/Floppy teddy bear. /1995/P-1/2 KF982. . . . . **E**
STEVENSON, J/Night after Christmas. /1981/K-2/2 KG564 **CE E**

Teenagers--Books and reading.
GILLESPIE, JT/Juniorplots 4: a book talk guide for use with readers
ages 12-16. /1993//KA091 . . . . **PROF 028.5**
KROPP, P/Raising a reader: make your child a reader for life. /
c1993, 1996//KA182 . . . . **PROF 371.3028**

Teenagers' writings.
TEN-SECOND RAINSHOWERS: POEMS BY YOUNG PEOPLE. /
1996/3-6/KE088 . . . . **811.008**
Teeth SEE ALSO Dentistry; Orthodontics.

Teeth.
YOUR TEETH (KIT). /1987/1-3/KC909 . . . . **KIT 611**

Teeth--Care and hygiene.
GOOFY OVER DENTAL HEALTH (VIDEOCASSETTE). /1991/
1-3/KD036. . . . . **VCR 617.6**

Teeth--Fiction.
ADLER, DA/Young Cam Jansen and the lost tooth. /1997/
1-2/2 KF133 . . . . **E**
BIRDSEYE, T/Air mail to the moon. /1988/K-3/5 KF231 . . . . . . **E**
BROWN, MT/Arthur's tooth. /1985/1-3/2 KF278 . . . . . . **CE E**
GIFF, PR/Rat teeth. /c1984/3-5/3 KH166 . . . . **Fic**
GRAVES, BB/Mystery of the Tooth Gremlin. /1997/
1-3/2 KH191 . . . . **Fic**
HALL, K/Tooth fairy. /1994/K-1/1 KF665 . . . . **E**
LESIEG, T/Tooth book. /1981/K-2/2 KF960 . . . . **E**
MACDONALD, A/Cousin Ruth's tooth. /1996/K-2/2 KG048 . . . **E**
MCPHAIL, D/Bear's toothache. /c1972/K-2/2 KG116 . . . . . **CE E**
Telecommunication SEE ALSO Artifical satellites; Submarines; Telegraph;
Telephone; Television.

Telecommunication.
SKURZYNSKI, G/Get the message: telecommunications in your
high-tech world. /1993/A/8 KD044 . . . . **621.38**

Telepathy.
GREEN, CR/Mysterious mind powers. /1993/4-6/3 KA609 . **133.8**

Telephone.
EMERGENCY 911 (VIDEOCASSETTE). /1994/
2-5/KB135. . . . . **VCR 384.6**
SKURZYNSKI, G/Get the message: telecommunications in your
high-tech world. /1993/A/8 KD044 . . . . **621.38**
USING 911: PROTECT YOURSELF (VIDEOCASSETTE). /1995/
2-6/KB136. . . . . **VCR 384.6**

Telephone etiquette.
PHONE MANNERS (VIDEOCASSETTE). /1991/
3-6/KB251. . . . . **VCR 395.5**

Television.
COMMUNICATIONS (VIDEOCASSETTE). /1992/
2-4/KA799 . . . . **VCR 302.23**
Television--Fiction.
BROWN, MT/Bionic Bunny Show. /1984/K-3/5 KF280 . . . . . . **E**
NOVAK, M/Mouse TV. /1994/K-2/3 KG180 . . . . **E**
POLACCO, P/Aunt Chip and the great Triple Creek Dam affair. /
1996/2-4/2 KG248 . . . . **E**
Television--History.
MCPHERSON, SS/TV's forgotten hero: the story of Philo
Farnsworth. /1996/5-A/9 KE342 . . . . **B FARNSWORTH, P**
Television actors and actresses SEE Actors and actresses.
Television advertising--Fiction.
BARRACCA, D/Maxi, the star. /1993/P-2/2 KF201 . . . . **E**
Television programs--Catalogs.
AIT CATALOG OF EDUCATIONAL MATERIALS. /1962-/
/KA003 . . . . **PROF 011**
Tell, William--Legends.
EARLY, M/William Tell. /1991/4-6/6 KB440 . . . . **398.22**
FISHER, LE/William Tell. /1996/3-5/4 KB442 . . . . **398.22**
Temperature SEE ALSO Heat.
Temperature.
HEAT, TEMPERATURE AND ENERGY (VIDEOCASSETTE). /1995/
5-6/KC128 . . . . **VCR 536**
Ten (The number).
PODWAL, M/Book of tens. /1994/5-6/7 KA769 . . . . . . **296.1**
Tennessee.
FRADIN, DB/Tennessee. /1992/4-6/2 KF009 . . . . **976.8**
Tennessee--Fiction.
ISAACS, A/Swamp Angel. /1994/2-5/6 KF810 . . . . **E**
PARTRIDGE, E/Clara and the hoodoo man. /1996/
5-A/3 KH572 . . . . **Fic**
Tennis players.
DEXTER, R/Young Arthur Ashe: brave champion. /1996/
2-3/6 KE242 . . . . **CE B ASHE, A.**
FEHR, KS/Monica Seles: returning champion. /1997/
4-6/10 KE533 . . . . **B SELES, M.**
QUACKENBUSH, R/Arthur Ashe and his match with history. /1994/
3-5/7 KE243 . . . . **B ASHE, A.**
SAVAGE, J/Andre Agassi: reaching the top--again. /1997/
4-5/7 KE229 . . . . **B AGASSI, A.**
SCHWABACHER, M/Superstars of women's tennis. /1997/
4-6/7 KD791 . . . . **796.342**
Tenzin Gyatso, Dalai Lama XIV.
STEWART, W/14th Dalai Lama: spiritual leader of Tibet. /1996/
5-A/10 KA761 . . . . **294.3**
Teotihuacan Site (San Juan Teotihuacan, Mexico).
ARNOLD, C/City of the gods: Mexico's ancient city of Teotihuacan.
/1994/5-6/7 KE828 . . . . **972**
Terban, Marvin.
VISIT WITH MARVIN TERBAN (VIDEOCASSETTE). /c1991, 1992/
5-A/KE560 . . . . **VCR B TERBAN, M.**
Teresa, Mother.
JACOBS, WJ/Mother Teresa: helping the poor. /1991/
4-6/6 KE561 . . . . **B TERESA,MOTHER**
Terrell, Mary Church.
MCKISSACK, P/Mary Church Terrell: leader for equality. /1991/
3-6/2 KE562 . . . . **B TERRELL, M.**
Terrorism--Fiction.
CROSS, G/Wolf. /1991/A/6 KH045 . . . . **Fic**
Test (Academic) SEE Examinations.
Test tube babies SEE Genetic engineering.
Teton Indians--Folklore.
GOBLE, P/Return of the buffaloes: a Plains Indian story about
famine and renewal of the Earth. /1996/3-5/3 KB575 . . . **398.24**
Tewa Indians--Dances.
MOTT, EC/Dancing rainbows: a Pueblo boy's story. /1996/
2-4/2 KE794 . . . . **970.489**
Tewa Indians--Folklore.
TAYLOR, HP/Coyote and the laughing butterflies. /1995/
2-3/5 KB662 . . . . **398.24**
Tewa Indians--Social life and customs.
MOTT, EC/Dancing rainbows: a Pueblo boy's story. /1996/
2-4/2 KE794 . . . . **970.489**
SWENTZELL, R/Children of clay: a family of Pueblo potters. /1992/
4-6/6 KE795 . . . . **970.489**
Texas.
SOUTH CENTRAL REGION: TEXAS, NEW MEXICO, OKLAHOMA
(VIDEOCASSETTE). /1995/3-5/KE995 . . . . **VCR 976**
TURNER, R/Texas traditions: the culture of the Lone Star State. /
1996/4-6/10 KF003 . . . . **976.4**
Texas--Fiction.
BURANDT, H/Tales from the homeplace: adventures of a Texas
farm girl. /1997/5-A/4 KG946 . . . . **Fic**

GIPSON, F/Old Yeller. /c1956/A/7 KH170 . . . . **CE Fic**
JOHNSTON, T/Cowboy and the black-eyed pea. /1992/
K-2/5 KF839 . . . . **E**
KARR, K/Oh, those Harper girls!; or Young and dangerous. /1992/
5-A/Y KH342 . . . . **Fic**
LIGHTFOOT, DJ/Trail fever: the life of a Texas cowboy. /1992/
4-6/5 KH406 . . . . **Fic**
MEDEARIS, AS/Haunts: five hair-raising tales. /1996/
4-6/4 KH495 . . . . **Fic**
MOORE, M/Under the mermaid angel. /1995/6-A/5 KH506 . . **Fic**
WEATHERFORD, CB/Juneteenth jamboree. /1995/
1-3/5 KG690 . . . . **E**
Texas--History.
WILLS, CA/Historical album of Texas. /1995/4-6/7 KF004 . . **976.4**
Texas--History--To 1846.
CARTER, AR/Last stand at the Alamo. /1990/4-6/7 KF001 . **976.4**
FRITZ, J/Make way for Sam Houston. /1986/
6/7 KE392 . . . . **B HOUSTON, S.**
SULLIVAN, G/Alamo! /1997/4-6/10 KF002 . . . . **976.4**
Textile factories--History.
MACAULAY, D/Mill. /1983/A/9 KD336 . . . . **677**
Textiles.
KEELER, PA/Unraveling fibers. /1995/4-6/4 KD335 . . . . . . **677**
Textures--Pictorial works.
HOBAN, T/Is it rough? Is it smooth? Is it shiny? /1984/
P-1/KF742 . . . . **E**
Thailand--Poetry.
HO, M/Hush!: a Thai lullaby. /1996/P-1/KD952 . . . . **811**
Thanksgiving cookery.
BARKIN, C/Happy Thanksgiving! /1987/3-6/6 KB221 . . . **394.264**
Thanksgiving Day.
ANDERSON, J/First Thanksgiving feast. /1984/
2-4/7 KE935 . . . . **974.4**
BARKIN, C/Happy Thanksgiving! /1987/3-6/6 KB221 . . . **394.264**
BULLA, CR/Squanto: friend of the Pilgrims. /c1954, 1982/
3/3 KE547 . . . . **B SQUANTO**
DALGLIESH, A/Thanksgiving story. /c1954/3-6/4 KB222 . **394.264**
GEORGE, JC/First Thanksgiving. /1993/4-6/6 KB223 . . . **394.264**
GIBBONS, G/Thanksgiving Day. /1983/P-2/4 KB225 . **CE 394.264**
HAYWARD, L/First Thanksgiving. /1990/
1-4/2 KB227 . . . . **CE 394.264**
METAXAS, E/Squanto and the first Thanksgiving (Kit). /1996/
2-6/KE548 . . . . **KIT B SQUANTO**
THANKSGIVING DAY (VIDEOCASSETTE). /1994/
3-6/KB229 . . . . **VCR 394.264**
Thanksgiving Day--Fiction.
ACCORSI, W/Friendship's first Thanksgiving. /1992/
P-1/2 KF127 . . . . **E**
BROWN, MT/Arthur's April fool. /1983/P-3/2 KF273 . . . . . . **E**
BUNTING, E/Turkey for Thanksgiving. /1991/P-2/2 KF312 . . . . **E**
CAPOTE, T/Thanksgiving visitor. /1996/5-A/8 KG972 . . . . . **Fic**
CARLSON, N/Visit to Grandma's. /1991/P-2/2 KF353 . . . . . . **E**
COHEN, B/Molly's pilgrim. /1983/1-3/4 KH012 . . . . . **CE Fic**
COWLEY, J/Gracias, the Thanksgiving turkey. /1996/
K-2/1 KF430 . . . . **E**
DRAGONWAGON, C/Alligator arrived with apples, a potluck
alphabet feast. /1987/K-2/5 KF494 . . . . **E**
HOBAN, L/Silly Tilly's Thanksgiving dinner. /1990/K-2/2 KF738 . **E**
KROLL, S/One tough turkey: a Thanksgiving story. /1982/
K-2/2 KF930 . . . . **E**
STEVENSON, J/Fried feathers for Thanksgiving. /1986/
P-2/2 KG560 . . . . **E**
TRYON, L/Albert's Thanksgiving. /1994/K-2/2 KG621 . . . . . . **E**
Thanksgiving Day--Poetry.
PRELUTSKY, J/It's Thanksgiving. /1982/1-3/KE006 . . . . . . **CE 811**
THANKSGIVING POEMS. /1985/K-6/KE089 . . . . **811.008**
Thanksgiving decorations.
ROSS, K/Crafts for Thanksgiving. /1995/3-5/KD457 . . . . **745.594**
Thayer, Jack.
TANAKA, S/On board the Titanic. /1996/4-A/6 KB027 . . **363.12**
Theater SEE ALSO Actors and actresses; Drama; Plays; Puppets plays;
Readers' Theater; Shadow pantomimes and plays.
Theater--Fiction.
HOFFMAN, M/Amazing Grace. /1991/P-2/4 KF761 . . . . . **CE E**
TOLAN, SS/Save Halloween! /1993/5-A/7 KH794 . . . . **Fic**
WABER, B/Lyle finds his mother. /1974/P-2/3 KG671 . . . . **E**
Theater--Production and direction.
BENTLEY, N/Putting on a play: the young playwright's guide to
scripting, directing, and /1996/4-6/7 KD687 . . . . **792**
Theaters--History.
MORLEY, J/Shakespeare's theater. /1994/4-A/7 KD689 . . . . **792**
Theodoric of Freiberg--Fiction.
KRAMER, SP/Theodoric's rainbow. /1995/3-6/4 KH380 . . . . . **Fic**

Thermodynamics.
    GOLDSMITH, S/Man who loved machines (Videocassette). /1983/
    3-A/KC127 . . . . **VCR 536**
Theseus (Greek mythology).
    FISHER, LE/Theseus and the Minotaur. /1988/5-6/6 KA741 . . **292**
    HUTTON, W/Theseus and the Minotaur. /1989/
    5-6/6 KA746 . . . . **292**
Thieves SEE Robbers and outlaws.
Thomas, Frank.
    GUTMAN, B/Frank Thomas: power hitter. /1996/
    3-5/6 KE563 . . . . **B THOMAS, F.**
Thompson, Snowshoe.
    LEVINSON, NS/Snowshoe Thompson. /1992/
    K-3/2 KE564 . . . . **B THOMPSON, S.**
Thor (Norse deity).
    CLIMO, S/Stolen thunder: a Norse myth. /1994/
    4-5/5 KA755 . . . . **293**
Thoreau, Henry David.
    RING, E/Henry David Thoreau: in step with nature. /1993/
    2-5/3 KE565 . . . . **B THOREAU, H.**
Thoreau, Henry David--Diaries.
    MURPHY, J/Into the deep forest with Henry David Thoreau. /1995/
    5-A/7 KE929 . . . . **974.1**
Thoroughbred horse.
    STEWART, GB/Thoroughbred horse: born to run. /1995/
    4-6/5 KD208 . . . . **636.1**
Thorpe, Jim.
    LIPSYTE, R/Jim Thorpe: 20th-century jock. /
    6-A/7 KE566 . . . . **B THORPE, J.**
Thought and thinking.
    KRAMER, SP/How to think like a scientist: answering questions by
    the scientific method. /1987/4-6/6 KB883 . . . . **507**
    POLETTE, N/ABC's of books and thinking skills. /1987/
    /KA156 . . . . **PROF 153.4**
Thought and thinking--Software.
    AFRICA TRAIL (CD-ROM). /1995/4-A/KE723 . . . . **CDR 960**
    BIG ANTHONY'S MIXED-UP MAGIC (CD-ROM). /1996/
    K-2/KF229 . . . . **CDR E**
    INVENTION STUDIO (CD-ROM). /1996/5-A/KC887 . . **CDR 608**
    STRATEGY CHALLENGES COLLECTION 1: AROUND THE WORLD.
    SCHOOL VERSION (CD-ROM). /1995/3-A/KD754 . . . . **CDR 794**
    STRATEGY CHALLENGES COLLECTION 2: IN THE WILD. SCHOOL
    VERSION (CD-ROM). /1996/4-A/KD755 . . . . **CDR 794**
    THINKIN' THINGS COLLECTION 1 (MICROCOMPUTER
    PROGRAM). /1993/K-3/KB080 . . . . **MCP 370.15**
    THINKIN' THINGS COLLECTION 2. SCHOOL VERSION (CD-
    ROM). /1995/1-6/KB081 . . . . **CDR 370.15**
    THINKIN' THINGS COLLECTION 3. SCHOOL VERSION (CD-
    ROM). /1995/3-A/KB082 . . . . **CDR 370.15**
Thought and thinking--Study and teaching.
    JONES, BF/Teaching thinking skills: English/language arts. /1987/
    /KA280 . . . . **PROF 428**
    LANKFORD, MD/Successful field trips. /1992/
    /KA178 . . . . **PROF 371.3**
    POLETTE, N/Brain power through picture books: /1992/
    /KA227 . . . . **PROF 372.6**
Thumb sucking SEE Finger-sucking.
Thunderstorms.
    BRANLEY, FM/Flash, crash, rumble and roll. Rev. ed. /1985/
    1-3/2 KC195 . . . . **CE 551.55**
    KAHL, JD/Thunderbolt: learning about lightning. /1993/
    4-6/9 KC207 . . . . **551.56**
Thunderstorms--Fiction.
    NIKOLA-LISA, W/Storm. /1993/P-1/2 KG174. . . . . **E**
    POLACCO, P/Thunder cake. /1990/1-3/4 KG258 . . . . **CE E**
    STOLZ, M/Storm in the night. /1988/K-3/4 KG578 . . . . **E**
Thunderstorms--Folklore.
    BRYAN, A/Story of lightning and thunder. /1993/
    K-2/2 KB702 . . . . **398.26**
Tibet (China)--History.
    STEWART, W/14th Dalai Lama: spiritual leader of Tibet. /1996/
    5-A/10 KA761 . . . . **294.3**
Tide pool ecology.
    SHAHAN, S/Barnacles eat with their feet: delicious facts about the
    tide pool food chain. /1996/3-6/5 KC348 . . . . **577.69**
Tides--Fiction.
    COLE, S/When the tide is low. /1985/P-2/3 KF411 . . . . **E**
Tigers.
    COWCHER, H/Tigress. /1991/1-3/6 KC827 . . . . **599.756**
Tigers--Fiction.
    BAKER, K/Who is the beast? /1990/P-K/1 KF187. . . . . **E**
    BANNERMAN, H/Story of Little Babaji. /1996/K-2/2 KF195 . . . **E**
    KRAUS, R/Leo the late bloomer. /1971/P-2/2 KF918 . . . . . **CE E**

    LESTER, J/Sam and the tigers: a new telling of LITTLE BLACK
    SAMBO. /1996/K-3/2 KF966 . . . . **E**
Tigers--Folklore.
    XIONG, B/Nine-in-one, grr! grr! a folktale from the Hmong people
    of Laos. /1989/P-3/4 KB677 . . . . **398.24**
Tigers--Poetry.
    BLAKE, W/Tyger. /1993/1-4/KE096 . . . . **821**
Tightrope walking--Fiction.
    MCCULLY, EA/Mirette on the high wire. /1992/1-3/2 KG093. . . **E**
Time SEE ALSO Calendars; Clocks and watches.
Time.
    BRANLEY, FM/Keeping time: from the beginning and into the 21st
    century. /1993/4-6/6 KC067 . . . . **529**
    BURNS, M/This book is about time. /1978/4-6/6 KC068 . . . . **529**
    CHAPMAN, G/Exploring time. /1995/3-6/6 KC069 . . . . **529**
    DARLING, DJ/Could you ever build a time machine? /1991/
    4-A/7 KC082 . . . . **530.1**
    GANERI, A/Story of time and clocks. /1996/4-6/8 KC070. . . **529**
    LLEWELLYN, C/My first book of time. /1992/K-3/2 KC072 . . **529**
    TICK TOCK: ALL ABOUT THE CLOCK (VIDEOCASSETTE). /1992/
    2-3/KC074. . . . . **VCR 529**
Time--Fiction.
    AXELROD, A/Pigs on a blanket. /1996/2-3/2 KF179 . . . . **E**
    BOSTON, LM/Children of Green Knowe. /c1955, 1983/
    4-A/6 KG919 . . . . **Fic**
    LEWIS, PO/P. Bear's New Year's party!: a counting book. /1989/
    K-1/3 KF978 . . . . **E**
    MCGUIRE, R/Night becomes day. /1994/1-3/1 KG104. . . . . . **E**
    PRYOR, B/House on Maple Street. /1987/K-3/4 KG292 . . . . . **E**
Time--Software.
    TRUDY'S TIME AND PLACE HOUSE. SCHOOL VERSION (CD-
    ROM). /1995/P-3/KC075. . . . . **CDR 529**
Time measurements.
    SMITH, AG/What time is it? /1992/4-A/8 KC073 . . . . **529**
Time travel.
    DARLING, DJ/Could you ever build a time machine? /1991/
    4-A/7 KC082 . . . . **530.1**
Time travel--Fiction.
    BRITTAIN, B/Wizards and the monster. /1994/2-4/4 KG926 . . **Fic**
    BROTHER FUTURE (VIDEOCASSETTE). /c1991, 1997/
    6-A/KG930 . . . . **VCR Fic**
    FLEISCHMAN, P/Time train. /1994/1-3/2 KF551 . . . . **E**
    FLEISCHMAN, S/13th floor: a ghost story. /1995/
    5-A/6 KH127 . . . . **CE Fic**
    GIFALDI, D/Gregory, Maw, and the Mean One. /1992/
    5-A/7 KH163 . . . . **Fic**
    HILDICK, EW/Case of the weeping witch. /1992/3-6/5 KH258 . **Fic**
    MACDONALD, RE/Ghosts of Austwick Manor. /c1983, 1991/
    4-A/5 KH441 . . . . **Fic**
    NOLAN, D/Dinosaur dream. /1990/2-3/5 KG178 . . . . **Fic**
    PARK, R/Playing Beatie Bow. /1982/5-A/6 KH571 . . . . **Fic**
    PATON WALSH, J/Chance child. /c1978, 1991/6-A/7 KH582 . **Fic**
    PEARCE, AP/Tom's midnight garden. /c1958, 1991/
    5-6/5 KH589 . . . . **Fic**
    PECK, R/Lost in cyberspace. /1995/5-A/3 KH593 . . . . **Fic**
    RODDA, E/Finders keepers. /1991/5-A/6 KH645 . . . . **Fic**
    SCIESZKA, J/Knights of the kitchen table. /1991/
    3-6/3 KH685 . . . . **Fic**
    WOODRUFF, E/Orphan of Ellis Island: a time-travel adventure. /
    1997/5-A/5 KH881 . . . . **Fic**
Tinamou.
    ARNOLD, C/Ostriches and other flightless birds. /1990/
    5-6/7 KC690 . . . . **598.5**
Titanic (Steamship).
    BALLARD, RD/Exploring the Titanic. /1988/4-6/8 KB025 . . **363.12**
    BLOS, JW/Heroine of the Titanic: a tale both true and otherwise of
    the life of Molly /1991/5-6/6 KE265 . . . . **B BROWN, M.**
    KENT, D/Titanic. /1993/4-6/7 KB026 . . . . **363.12**
    SPEDDEN, DC/Polar, the Titanic bear. /1994/4-6/7 KE158 . **910.4**
    TANAKA, S/On board the Titanic. /1996/4-A/6 KB027 . . **363.12**
Tituba--Fiction.
    PETRY, A/Tituba of Salem Village. /1991/5-6/4 KH599. . . . . **Fic**
Tiwi (Australian people).
    REYNOLDS, J/Down under: vanishing cultures. /1992/
    3-6/6 KF117 . . . . **994**
Tlingit Indians--Fiction.
    WISNIEWSKI, D/Wave of the Sea-Wolf. /1994/1-3/6 KG753 . . **E**
Toads.
    JULIVERT, A/Fascinating world of frogs and toads. /1993/
    4-6/6 KC605 . . . . **597.8**
    PARKER, NW/Frogs, toads, lizards and salamanders. /1990/
    5-6/7 KC606 . . . . **597.8**
Toads--Fiction.
    BROWN, R/Toad. /1997/K-2/3 KF289 . . . . **E**

LOBEL, A/Days with Frog and Toad. /1979/K-2/1 KG001 . . . . . **E**
  Frog and Toad all year. /c1976/K-2/1 KG002 . . . . **CE E**
  Frog and Toad are friends. /c1972/K-2/2 KG003 . . . . . . **CE E**
  Frog and Toad together. /c1972/K-2/2 KG004 . . . . **CE E**
Tobacco SEE ALSO Smoking.
Tobacco.
  TOBACCO ACTION CURRICULUM: THE YOUNG AND THE
  BREATHLESS (VIDEOCASSETTE). /1991/
  5-6/KD007. . . . . **VCR 613.85**
  TOBACCO FREE YOU AND ME (VIDEOCASSETTE). /1994/
  4-6/KD008. . . . . **VCR 613.85**
  TROUBLE WITH TOBACCO (VIDEOCASSETTE). /1996/
  5-6/KD009. . . . . **VCR 613.85**
Tobacco--Physiological effect.
  DUSTY THE DRAGON TALKS TO DR. MARGIE HOGAN ABOUT
  TOBACCO (VIDEOCASSETTE). /1990/3-5/KD005 . **VCR 613.85**
Tobacco habit.
  PRINGLE, LP/Smoking: a risky business. /1996/
  4-6/9 KA998 . . . . **362.29**
Tobias (Biblical figure).
  MARK, J/Tale of Tobias. /1996/1-3/2 KA693 . . . . **229**
Todd, Mary Ellen--Fiction.
  VAN LEEUWEN, J/Bound for Oregon. /1994/5-A/5 KH828. . . **Fic**
Toilets--History.
  COLMAN, P/Toilets, bathtubs, sinks, and sewers: a history of the
  bathroom. /1994/5-6/5 KD294 . . . . **643**
Tokyo (Japan).
  KENT, D/Tokyo. /1996/3-5/8 KE709. . . . . **952**
Tolkien, J.R.R. (John Ronald Reuel).
  COLLINS, DR/J.R.R. Tolkien: master of fantasy. /1992/
  6-A/6 KE567 . . . . **B TOLKIEN, J.**
Tombs--America.
  BENDICK, J/Tombs of the ancient Americas. /1993/
  3-5/8 KB174 . . . . **393**
Tombs--Egypt.
  BENDICK, J/Egyptian tombs. /1989/4-6/7 KE632 . . . . **932**
  PERL, L/Mummies, tombs, and treasure: secrets of ancient Egypt. /
  1987/5-A/8 KE636 . . . . **932**
Tonga (Zambesi people)--Folklore.
  AARDEMA, V/This for that: a Tonga tale. /1997/
  K-2/2 KB517 . . . . **398.24**
Tongue twisters.
  COLE, J/Six sick sheep: 101 tongue twisters. /3-5/KB795. . . **398.8**
  REES, E/Fast Freddie Frog and other tongue-twister rhymes. /1993/
  2-6/KB812 . . . . **398.8**
Tools SEE ALSO Agricultural machinery; Carpentry--Tools; Machinery.
Tools.
  BARTON, B/Tools (Board book). /1995/P/KF208. . . . . . . **BB E**
  GIBBONS, G/Tool book. /1982/P-K/2 KD055 . . . . **621.9**
  MILLER, M/Who uses this? /1990/P-K/KA943 . . . . **331.7**
  MORRIS, A/Tools. /1992/P-2/2 KD056 . . . . **621.9**
  ROCKWELL, AF/Toolbox. /1990/P-K/3 KD057 . . . . **621.9**
Tools--Fiction.
  KLINTING, L/Bruno the carpenter. /1996/K-2/2 KF912 . . . . **E**
Tooth fairy--Fiction.
  BIRDSEYE, T/Air mail to the moon. /1988/K-3/5 KF231 . . . . . . **E**
  HALL, K/Tooth fairy. /1994/K-1/1 KF665 . . . . **E**
Torah scrolls.
  COWAN, P/Torah is written. /1986/5-6/7 KA782 . . . . . . **296.6**
Tories SEE American loyalists.
Tornadoes SEE ALSO Storms.
Tornadoes.
  BRANLEY, FM/Tornado alert. /1988/P-4/3 KC196 . . . . . **551.55**
  HOPPING, LJ/Wild weather. Tornadoes! /1994/
  2-6/3 KC199 . . . . **551.55**
  KAHL, JD/Storm warning: tornadoes and hurricanes. /1993/
  4-7/8 KC200 . . . . **551.55**
  KRAMER, SP/Tornado. /1992/3-6/6 KC201 . . . . **551.55**
  PENNER, LR/Twisters! /1996/2-4/3 KC204 . . . . **551.55**
Tornadoes--Fiction.
  BYARS, BC/Tornado. /1996/2-5/3 KG965 . . . . **Fic**
Toronto (Ont.)--Fiction.
  CAREY, P/Big Bazoohley. /1995/3-6/5 KG973 . . . . **Fic**
Touch.
  FABULOUS FIVE: OUR SENSES (VIDEOCASSETTE). /1989/
  P-2/KC917. . . . . **VCR 612**
  PARRAMON, JM/Touch. /1985/P-1/2 KC976. . . . . **612.8**
Toulouse-Lautrec, Henry de.
  VENEZIA, M/Henri de Toulouse-Lautrec. /1995/
  4-6/8 KE568 . . . . **B TOULOUSE-LAUT**
Tourette syndrome.
  GUTMAN, B/Jim Eisenreich. /1996/
  3-5/6 KE336 . . . . **B EISENREICH, J**

Toussaint L'Ouverture.
  LAWRENCE, J/Toussaint L'Ouverture: the fight for Haiti's freedom.
  /1996/4-A/8 KE569 . . . . **B TOUSSAINT**
Tower of London (London, England).
  FISHER, LE/Tower of London. /1987/3-6/7 KE679 . . . . **942**
Toy and movable books.
  BROWNE, G/Aircraft: lift-the-flap book. /1992/
  3-6/5 KD106 . . . . **629.133**
  CARLE, E/Very busy spider. /1985/P-2/2 KF346 . . . . **E**
  Very lonely firefly. /1995/P-2/2 KF348 . . . . **E**
  CARTER, DA/In a dark, dark wood. /1991/P-2/2 KF362. . . . . **E**
  CHARLES, NN/What am I?: looking through shapes at apples and
  grapes. /1994/P-2/2 KF378 . . . . **E**
  DE PAOLA, T/First Christmas. /1984/P-4/7 KA702 . . . **232.92**
  DODDS, DA/Color box. /1992/P-K/1 KF486 . . . . **E**
  EMBERLEY, E/Go away, big green monster! /1992/
  P-1/2 KF522 . . . . **E**
  FORD, B/Hunter who was king and other African tales. /1994/
  K-3/4 KB299 . . . . **398.2**
  FORNARI, G/Inside the body: a lift-the-flap book. /1996/
  5-6/7 KC902 . . . . **611**
  HOBAN, T/Just look. /1996/P-2/KA615. . . . . **152.14**
  Look book. /1997/P-K/KD516 . . . . **779**
  JENKINS, S/Flip-flap. /1995/P-K/2 KA619 . . . . **152.14**
  JONES, C/Hare and the Tortoise. /1996/P-1/4 KB597 . . . **398.24**
  LLEWELLYN, C/My first book of time. /1992/K-3/2 KC072 . . **529**
  YOSHI /Who's hiding here? /1987/K-3/2 KG784. . . . . **E**
  ZIEFERT, H/What rhymes with eel?: a word-and-picture flap book. /
  1996/P-1/2 KG798 . . . . **E**
  Who said moo? /1996/P-1/2 KG799 . . . . **E**
Toy making.
  CORWIN, JH/Asian crafts. /1992/4-A/7 KD426 . . . . **745.5**
  CRAFTS FOR PLAY. /1993/3-6/7 KD445 . . . . **745.592**
Toy making--Fiction.
  WILLIAMS, KL/Galimoto. /1990/1-2/2 KG727 . . . . **CE E**
Toymakers.
  GREENE, C/Margarete Steiff: toy maker. /1993/
  2-3/2 KE550 . . . . **B STEIFF, M.**
Toys SEE ALSO names of specific types of toys e.g. Stuffed animals.
Toys--Design and construction.
  MORRIS, A/How teddy bears are made: a visit to the Vermont
  Teddy Bear factory. /1994/K-2/3 KD351. . . . . **688.7**
  TOYS. /1991/K-2/2 KD352 . . . . **688.7**
Toys--Fiction.
  CONRAD, P/Tub Grandfather. /1993/1-3/4 KF415 . . . . . **E**
  Tub people. /1989/1-3/4 KF416. . . . . **CE E**
  DALE, P/Ten out of bed. /1994/P-1/2 KF446 . . . . **E**
  FREEMAN, D/Corduroy. /c1968/P-2/2 KF578 . . . . **CE E**
  Pocket for Corduroy. /1978/P-2/2 KF581 . . . . **CE E**
  HOBAN, L/Arthur's honey bear. /c1964/1-3/2 KF734. . . . **CE E**
  HUGHES, S/Dogger. /c1978/P-2/3 KF788 . . . . **E**
  LEWIS, K/My friend Harry. /1995/P-1/2 KF976. . . . . **E**
  MILLER, M/Where does it go? /1992/P-K/1 KG136 . . . . **E**
  MILNE, AA/House at Pooh Corner. /c1956/K-6/3 KH497 . . . . **Fic**
  Winnie-the-Pooh. /1974/K-6/3 KH498 . . . . **Fic**
  World of Pooh: the complete "Winnie-the-Pooh" and "The House
  at Pooh Corner." /c1957/K-6/3 KH499 . . . . **Fic**
  REGAN, DC/Monsters in the attic. /1995/4-6/6 KH625. . . . . . **Fic**
  REID BANKS, L/Indian in the cupboard. /1980/
  4-6/4 KH627 . . . . **CE Fic**
  Mystery of the cupboard. /1993/5-A/6 KH628 . . . . **CE Fic**
  Return of the Indian. /1986/5-A/6 KH629 . . . . **Fic**
  RYLANT, C/Mr. Putter and Tabby fly the plane. /1997/
  K-2/2 KG378 . . . . **E**
  STEVENSON, J/Night after Christmas. /1981/K-2/2 KG564   **CE E**
  VAN LEEUWEN, J/Emma Bean. /1993/K-2/2 KG646 . . . . **E**
  WABER, B/Ira sleeps over. /c1972/K-2/2 KG668. . . . . **CE E**
  WILLIAMS, M/Velveteen Rabbit; or, How toys become real. /1988/
  3-5/6 KH864 . . . . **CE Fic**
Toys--Study and teaching.
  TAYLOR, BA/Teaching physics with toys: activities for grades K-9. /
  1995//KA204 . . . . **PROF 372.3**
Toys--Study and teaching (Elementary).
  SUMNERS, C/Toys in space: exploring science with the astronauts.
  /1997//KA282. **PROF 500.5**
Track and field.
  BAILEY, D/Track and field. /1991/1-3/4 KD809 . . . . **796.42**
  ROSENTHAL, B/Track and field. /1994/3-6/4 KD810 . . . . **796.42**
  SANDELSON, R/Track athletics. /1991/4-6/7 KD811 . . . . **796.42**
  WARD, T/Field. /1996/3-6/8 KD812 . . . . **796.42**
  Track. /1996/3-6/8 KD813 . . . . **796.42**
Track and field athletes.
  ADLER, DA/Picture book of Jesse Owens. /1992/
  3-4/6 KE486 . . . . **B OWENS, J.**

COHEN, N/Jackie Joyner-Kersee. /1992/
4-6/6 KE412 . . . . **B JOYNER-KERSEE**
GUTMAN, B/Gail Devers. /1996/5-6/6 KE319 . . . **B DEVERS, G.**
JOSEPHSON, JP/Jesse Owens: track and field legend. /1997/
5-A/8 KE487 . . . . **B OWENS, J.**
KRULL, K/Wilma unlimited: how Wilma Rudolph became the world's
fastest woman. /1996/3-5/7 KE527 . . . . **B RUDOLPH, W.**
WICKHAM, M/Superstars of women's track and field. /1997/
4-6/7 KD814 . . . . **796.42**
Tracking and trailing SEE ALSO Animal tracks.
Tracking and trailing.
MURIE, OJ/Field guide to animal tracks. 2nd ed. /1974/
A/8 KC476 . . . . **591.5**
Tractor trailers.
MARSTON, HI/Big rigs. Rev. and updated ed. /1993/
K-5/4 KD119 . . . . **629.224**
Tractors.
BROWN, C/Tractor. /1995/K-2/2 KD146 . . . . **631.3**
Tractors--Fiction.
BURTON, VL/Katy and the big snow. /c1943, 1973/
P-1/4 KF319 . . . . **E**
Trade routes--Asia--History.
MAJOR, JS/Silk Route: 7,000 miles of history. /c1995, 1996/
4-6/6 KE701 . . . . **950**
Trade unions SEE Labor unions.
Traffic signs and signals.
HOBAN, T/I read signs. /1983/P-1/KA800 . . . . **302.23**
I read symbols. /1983/P-1/KA797 . . . . **302.2**
Trail of Tears, 1838.
BEALER, AW/Only the names remain: the Cherokees and the Trail
of Tears. 2nd ed. /1996/5-6/8 KE758 . . . . **970.3**
Trail of Tears, 1838--Fiction.
STEWART, EJ/On the long trail home. /1994/4-6/4 KH762 . . . **Fic**
Trains SEE Railroads--Trains.
Transatlantic flights.
BURLEIGH, R/Flight: the journey of Charles Lindbergh. /1991/
1-4/2 KD091 . . . . **629.13**
Flight: the journey of Charles Lindbergh. /1991/
4-6/3 KD092 . . . . **629.13**
Transplantation of organs, tissues, etc.
FACKLAM, M/Spare parts for people. /1987/A/9 KD035 . . . **617**
Transportation SEE ALSO Airplanes; Automobiles; Bicycles and bicycling;
Bridges; Buses; Canals; Carriages and carts; Postal service; Railroads;
Roads; Sleds; Steamboats; Street-railroads; Trucks.
Transportation.
HERE WE GO. VOL. 1 (VIDEOCASSETTE). /1986/
1-4/KB158 . . . . **VCR 388**
HERE WE GO AGAIN! (VIDEOCASSETTE). /1986/
1-4/KB157 . . . . **VCR 388**
TRANSPORTATION (VIDEOCASSETTE). /1992/
2-4/KB159 . . . . **VCR 388**
YEPSEN, R/City trains: moving through America's cities by rail. /
1993/5-6/7 KB162 . . . . **388.4**
Transportation--Fiction.
BURNINGHAM, J/Harvey Slumfenburger's Christmas present. /
1993/K-2/2 KF316 . . . . **E**
HOWLAND, N/ABCDrive!: a car trip alphabet. /1994/
P-1/1 KF782 . . . . **E**
Transportation--History.
WHITMAN, S/Get up and go!: the history of American road travel.
/1996/4-A/10 KB160 . . . . **388.1**
Transportation--Poetry.
CASSEDY, S/Zoomrimes: poems about things that go. /1993/
3-6/KD921 . . . . **811**
ROLL ALONG: POEMS ON WHEELS. /1993/
4-A/KE080 . . . . **811.008**
Transportation--Study and teaching (Elementary).
IRVING, J/Full speed ahead: stories and activities for children on
transportation. /1988//KA223 . . . . **PROF 372.6**
Transportation in art.
MICKLETHWAIT, L/I spy a freight train: transportation in art. /
1996/P-2/2 KD473 . . . . **758**
Transportation in literature.
IRVING, J/Full speed ahead: stories and activities for children on
transportation. /1988//KA223 . . . . **PROF 372.6**
Trapp family.
RODGERS, R/Sound of music. Selections. 2nd ed. (Sound recording
cassette). /1965/K-A/KD531 . . . . **SRC 782.1**
Trash SEE Refuse and refuse disposal.
Travel.
KRUPP, RR/Let's go traveling. /1992/3-5/4 KE155 . . . . . . **910.4**
Travel--Fiction.
ROCKWELL, AF/I fly. /1997/P-1/2 KG343 . . . . **E**

WILLIAMS, VB/Stringbean's trip to the shining sea. /1988/
K-A/2 KG739 . . . . **E**
Travel--History.
WHITMAN, S/Get up and go!: the history of American road travel.
/1996/4-A/10 KB160 . . . . **388.1**
Treasure hunts--Fiction.
DUBOWSKI, CE/Pirate School. /1996/1-3/2 KF499 . . . . **E**
Treasure hunts--Folklore.
LONG, JF/Bee and the dream: a Japanese tale. /1996/
2-3/2 KB612 . . . . **398.24**
Treasure trove SEE ALSO Buried treasure.
Tree frogs.
GERHOLDT, JE/Tree frogs. /1994/3-5-5 KC602 . . . . **597.8**
JOHNSON, SA/Tree frogs. /1986/5-6/7 KC604 . . . . **597.8**
Tree houses--Fiction.
GEISERT, A/Pigs from A to Z. /1986/1-3/3 KF603 . . . . **E**
Trees SEE ALSO Forests and forestry; Leaves; Lumber and lumbering;
Plants.
Trees.
BURNIE, D/Tree. /1988/K-6/7 KC409 . . . . **582.16**
CHRISTIANSEN, C/Sky tree portfolio: science and art (Picture). /
1995/2-6/KC410 . . . . **PIC 582.16**
DOWDEN, AO/Blossom on the bough: a book of trees. /c1975,
1994/5-8/9 KC411 . . . . **582.16**
EHLERT, L/Red leaf, yellow leaf. /1991/P-1/4 KC412 . . . . **582.16**
FISCHER-NAGEL, H/Fir trees. /1989/3-6/7 KC436 . . . . **585**
JORGENSON, L/Grand trees of America: our state and champion
trees. /1992/3-6/6 KC415 . . . . **582.16**
LAUBER, P/Be a friend to trees. /1994/P-2/3 KC416 . . **CE 582.16**
MARKLE, S/Outside and inside trees. /1993/
3-6/6 KC419 . . . . **582.16**
OPPENHEIM, J/Have you seen trees? /1995/
P-2/3 KC420 . . . . **582.16**
PINE, J/Trees. /1995/3-6/3 KC421 . . . . **582.16**
PLUCKROSE, H/Trees. /1994/P-2/4 KC422 . . . . **582.16**
RUSSO, M/Tree almanac: a year-round activity guide. /1993/
3-6/6 KC423 . . . . **582.16**
THORNHILL, J/Tree in a forest. /1992/3-5/6 KC311 . . . . . . **577.3**
TREE: A LIVING COMMUNITY (VIDEOCASSETTE). /1988/
4-6/KC355 . . . . **VCR 577.8**
TRESSELT, A/Gift of the tree. /c1972, 1992/K-4/6 KC312 . **577.3**
WOODS, ML/Sky tree portfolio guide: an interdisciplinary
environmental curriculum. /1995/2-6/KC424 . . . . **582.16**
Trees--Fiction.
ATKINS, J/Aani and the tree huggers. /1995/3-5/3 KG853 . . . **Fic**
HOLLING, HC/Tree in the trail. /c1942/5-6/5 KH273 . . . . . . **Fic**
LISLE, JT/Great dimpole oak. /1987/5-6/6 KH411 . . . . **Fic**
NOBLE, TH/Apple tree Christmas. /1984/K-3/6 KG175 . . . . . **E**
TAYLOR, MD/Song of the trees. /1975/4-6/4 KH780 . . . . . . **Fic**
UDRY, JM/Tree is nice. /c1956/K-2/2 KG633 . . . . **E**
Trees--Identification.
LITTLE, JR., EL/Audubon Society field guide to North American
trees, Eastern Region. /1980/3-6/KC417 . . . . **582.16**
Trees--Life cycle.
HISCOCK, B/Big tree. /1991/1-5/6 KC414 . . . . **582.16**
Trees--North America.
LITTLE, JR., EL/Audubon Society field guide to North American
trees, Eastern Region. /1980/3-6/KC417 . . . . **582.16**
Trevino, Lee.
KRAMER, J/Lee Trevino. /1996/5-6/6 KE570 . . . **B TREVINO, L.**
Trials (Witchcraft)--Massachusetts--Salem.
ROACH, MK/In the days of the Salem witchcraft trials. /1996/
3-6/10 KE945 . . . . **974.4**
WILSON, LL/Salem witch trials. /1997/A/7 KA607 . . . . . . **133.4**
Triangle.
HOBAN, T/Circles, triangles, and squares. /1974/P-1/KB990 . **516**
Shapes, shapes, shapes. /1986/2-6/KB991 . . . . **516**
Triangle Shirtwaist Company--Fire, 1911--Fiction.
LITTLEFIELD, H/Fire at the Triangle Factory. /1996/
2-5/1 KF998 . . . . **E**
Trick roping.
COOPER, M/Anthony Reynoso: born to rope. /1996/
3-4/4 KA841 . . . . **305.8**
Tricks SEE ALSO Magic.
Tricks--Fiction.
MCKISSACK, P/Flossie and the fox. /1986/K-3/2 KG105 . . **CE E**
ROOT, P/Aunt Nancy and Old Man Trouble. /1996/
K-3/6 KG350 . . . . **E**
Tricksters--Folklore.
BRUSCA, MC/Pedro fools the gringo and other tales of a Latin
American trickster. /1995/2-4/3 KB429 . . . . **398.22**
Trillion (The number).
HOW MUCH IS A MILLION? (VIDEOCASSETTE). /1997/
K-1/KB947 . . . . **VCR 513**

SCHWARTZ, DM/How much is a million? /1985/
K-1/2 KB950 513
Trinidad and Tobago--Fiction.
JOSEPH, L/Island Christmas. /1992/1-3/2 KF855 . . . . E
Jasmine's parlour day. /1994/1-3/3 KF856 . . . . E
Trinidad and Tobago--Folklore.
JOSEPH, L/Mermaid's twin sister: more stories from Trinidad. /
1994/3-4/5 KB323 . . . . 398.2
Trojan War.
COLUM, P/Children's Homer: The Adventures of Odysseus and Tale
of Troy. /1982/A/6 KE123 883
HUTTON, W/Trojan horse. /1992/2-5/5 KE124 883
PICARD, BL/Odyssey of Homer. /c1952, 1992/5-A/7 KE126 . . 883
SUTCLIFF, R/Black ships before Troy: the story of the Iliad. /1993/
5-A/8 KE127 883
WILLIAMS, M/Iliad and the Odyssey. /1996/3-6/8 KE129. . . 883
Trolley cars SEE Street-railroads.
Trolls--Fiction.
BRETT, J/Trouble with trolls. /1992/P-1/3 KF262 . . . . E
CARRICK, C/Melanie. /1996/1-3/2 KF360 . . . . E
D'AULAIRE, I/D'Aulaires' trolls. /c1972, 1993/
4-6/6 KB280 . . . . 398.2
HICKOX, R/Per and the Dala horse. /1995/1-3/6 KF724 . . . . . E
PEET, B/Jethro and Joel were a troll. /1987/1-3/4 KG229 . . . . E
WOLFF, PR/Toll-bridge troll. /1995/1-3/2 KG759 . . . . E
Tropical fish.
BRAEMER, H/Tropical fish: a complete pet owner's manual. /1983/
5-6/9 KD247 . . . . 639.3
Trout.
COLE, J/Fish hatches. /c1978/P-A/3 KC596 . . . . 597.5
Truck drivers--Fiction.
DAY, A/Frank and Ernest on the road. /1994/2-3/2 KF451 . . . . E
Truck driving.
HORENSTEIN, H/Sam goes trucking. /1989/
2-3/3 KD118 . . . . 629.224
Trucks.
BARTON, B/Trucks. /1986/P-1/2 KB161 . . . . 388.3
BOUCHER, J/Fire truck nuts and bolts. /1993/
4-5/6 KD085 . . . . 628.9
GIBBONS, G/Trucks. /1981/P-1/1 KD117 . . . . 629.224
MARSTON, HI/Big rigs. Rev. and updated ed. /1993/
K-5/4 KD119 . . . . 629.224
SEIDEN, A/Trucks (Board book). /1983/P/KG428 . . . . BB E
Trucks--Fiction.
KIRK, D/Trash trucks. /1997/K-2/3 KF908 . . . . E
SIEBERT, D/Truck song. /1984/P-1/KG502 . . . . CE E
WILLIAMS, KL/Tap-tap. /1994/K-2/2 KG728 . . . . CE E
Trucks--Pictorial works.
CREWS, D/Truck. /1980/P-K/KF438 . . . . CE E
Trucks--Software.
BIG JOB (CD-ROM). /1995/K-3/KD120 . . . . CDR 629.225
Truman, Harry S.
SCHUMAN, M/Harry S. Truman. /1997/
5-A/9 KE571 . . . . B TRUMAN, H.
Trumpet players.
ELLIS, VF/Wynton Marsalis. /1997/
5-A/10 KE459 . . . . B MARSALIS, W.
Truth, Sojourner.
ADLER, DA/Picture book of Sojourner Truth. /1994/
2-5/6 KE572 . . . . B TRUTH, S.
MCKISSACK, P/Sojourner Truth: ain't I a woman? /1992/
6-A/7 KE573 . . . . B TRUTH, S.
Truthfulness and falsehood SEE Honesty.
Tsimshian Indians--Folklore.
MURPHY, CR/Prince and the Salmon People. /1993/
4-6/7 KB352 . . . . 398.2
Tsimshian Indians--Social life and customs.
HOYT-GOLDSMITH, D/Potlatch: a Tsimshian celebration. /1997/
2-5/9 KB189 . . . . 394.2
Tsunamis.
SOUZA, DM/Powerful waves. /1992/3-6/5 KC180 . . . . . 551.47
Tuaregs.
REYNOLDS, J/Sahara: vanishing cultures. /1991/
4-6/6 KE732 966
Tuba--Fiction.
MASTERS, SR/Libby Bloom. /1995/3-5/6 KH460. . . . . Fic
Tuberculosis--Fiction.
DEFELICE, CC/Apprenticeship of Lucas Whitaker. /1998/
5-A/6 KH066 . . . . CE Fic
Tubman, Harriet (Ross).
ELISH, D/Harriet Tubman and the Underground Railroad. /1993/
4-6/4 KE574 . . . . B TUBMAN, H.
PETRY, A/Harriet Tubman: conductor on the Underground Railroad.
/c1955, 1996/A/7 KE575 . . . . B TUBMAN, H.

STEAL AWAY: THE HARRIET TUBMAN STORY (VIDEOCASSETTE).
/1997/4-A/KE576. . . . . VCR B TUBMAN, H.
Tubman, Harriet (Ross)--Poetry.
LAWRENCE, J/Harriet and the Promised Land. /1993/
K-3/KD969 811
Tugboats.
TUGBOATS: MASTERS OF OUR HARBORS (VIDEOCASSETTE). /
1996/2-4/KB153. . . . . VCR 387.2
Tugboats--Fiction.
GRAMATKY, H/Little Toot. /1981/P-1/4 KF634 . . . . CE E
Tule elk.
ARNOLD, C/Tule elk. /1989/5-6/8 KC794 . . . . 599.65
Tundra.
HISCOCK, B/Tundra, the Arctic land. /1986/4-A/7 KC335. . 577.5
Tundra ecology.
HISCOCK, B/Tundra, the Arctic land. /1986/4-A/7 KC335. . 577.5
SIY, A/Arctic National Wildlife Refuge. /1991/
6-A/6 KC337 . . . . 577.5
Tunnels.
GIBBONS, G/Tunnels. /c1984, 1987/K-2/2 KD069 . . . . . . 624.1
PLUCKROSE, H/Under the ground. /1994/P-2/4 KC360 . . 578.75
TUNNELS (VIDEOCASSETTE). /1987/5-6/KD071. . . . VCR 624.1
Turkey--Folklore.
TREASURY OF TURKISH FOLKTALES FOR CHILDREN. /1988/
4-5/7 KB512 . . . . 398.23
Turkeys.
PATENT, DH/Wild turkey, tame turkey. /1989/
5-6/7 KC697 . . . . 598.6
TURKEYS IN THE WILD (VIDEOCASSETTE). /1991/
4-6/KC699. . . . . VCR 598.6
Turkeys--Fiction.
BUNTING, E/Turkey for Thanksgiving. /1991/P-2/2 KF312. . . . . E
COWLEY, J/Gracias, the Thanksgiving turkey. /1996/
K-2/1 KF430 . . . . E
KROLL, S/One tough turkey: a Thanksgiving story. /1982/
K-2/2 KF930 . . . . E
Turks--Switzerland--Fiction.
HICYILMAZ, G/Frozen waterfall. /1994/6-A/6 KH257 . . . . . . Fic
Turner, Nat.
BARRETT, T/Nat Turner and the slave revolt. /c1993, 1995/
5-6/6 KE577 . . . . B TURNER, N.
Turtles.
GIBBONS, G/Sea turtles. /1995/2-4/6 KC617 . . . . 597.92
GUIBERSON, BZ/Into the sea. /1996/1-3/3 KC618 . . . . . 597.92
HOLLING, HC/Minn of the Mississippi. /c1951/
5-6/6 KC619 . . . . 597.92
KUHN, D/Turtle's day. /1994/P-2/4 KC620 . . . . 597.92
PALAZZO-CRAIG, J/Turtles. /1982/P-K/1 KC621 . . . . 597.92
SCHAFER, S/Galapagos tortoise. /1992/5-6/7 KC622 . . . 597.92
TALKING ABOUT SEA TURTLES (VIDEOCASSETTE). /1992/
4-6/KC623. . . . . VCR 597.92
VOYAGE OF THE LOGGERHEAD (VIDEOCASSETTE). /1995/
3-6/KC624. . . . . VCR 597.92
Turtles--Fiction.
BLUME, J/Tales of a fourth grade nothing. /1972/
2-4/3 KG914 . . . . CE Fic
GEORGE, WT/Box turtle at Long Pond. /1989/1-3/3 KF608 . . . E
JAY, LA/Sea turtle journey: the story of a loggerhead turtle. /
1995/K-2/5 KF826 . . . . CE E
LOWELL, S/Tortoise and the jackrabbit. /1994/K-2/3 KG040 . . . E
SANFIELD, S/Great turtle drive. /1996/2-6/4 KH676 . . . . Fic
SHARMAT, MW/Nate the Great and the tardy tortoise. /1995/
1-3/2 KG487 . . . . E
VOZAR, D/M.C. Turtle and the Hip Hop Hare: a nursery rap. /
1997/2-3/2 KG665 . . . . E
WILLNER-PARDO, G/Natalie Spitzer's turtles. /1992/
1-3/2 KG741 . . . . E
Turtles--Folklore.
DESPAIN, P/Eleven turtle tales: adventure tales from around the
world. /1994/2-3/4 KB559. . . . . 398.24
MOLLEL, TM/Flying tortoise: an Igbo tale. /1994/
2-3/3 KB623 . . . . 398.24
ROSS, G/How Turtle's back was cracked: a traditional Cherokee
tale. /1995/4-5/5 KB642 . . . . 398.24
Turtles as pets.
WILKE, H/Turtles: everything about purchase, care, nutrition and
diseases. /1983/5-6/9 KD250 . . . . 639.3
Tutankhamen, King of Egypt.
FORD, B/Howard Carter: searching for King Tut. /1995/
A/9 KE279 . . . . B CARTER, H.
SABUDA, R/Tutankhamen's gift. /1994/
2-4/3 KE578 . . . . B TUTANKHAMEN

Tuttle, Merlin D.
> PRINGLE, LP/Batman: exploring the world of bats. /1991/
> 5-A/9 KC762 . . . . **599.4**

Twain, Mark.
> COX, C/Mark Twain: America's humorist, dreamer, prophet. /1995/
> 6-A/8 KE579 . . . . **B TWAIN, M.**
> QUACKENBUSH, R/Mark Twain? What kind of name is that?: a
> story of Samuel Langhorne Clemens. /1984/
> 6/8 KE580 . . . . **B TWAIN, M.**

Twelve days of Christmas (English folk song).
> TYRRELL, F/Woodland Christmas: twelve days of Christmas in the
> North Woods. /1996/K-2/KD541 . . . . **782.28**

Twelve days of Christmas (English folk song)--Adaptations.
> TRIVAS, I/Emma's Christmas: an old song. /1988/P-3/6 KG618 . **E**

Twins--Fiction.
> CLEARY, B/Growing-up feet. /1987/P-3/1 KF394 . . . . **E**
> DENSLOW, SP/On the trail with Miss Pace. /1995/
> 1-3/2 KF461 . . . . **E**
> HOBAN, L/Case of the two masked robbers. /1988/
> K-2/1 KF737 . . . . **E**
> HUTCHINS, P/Which witch is which? /1989/P-1/2 KF807 . . . . . **E**
> KELLER, H/Harry and Tuck. /1993/K-1/2 KF884 . . . . **E**
> LATTIMORE, DN/Punga, the goddess of ugly. /1993/
> 3-5/4 KF950 . . . . **E**
> MARKHAM, MM/St. Patrick's Day shamrock mystery. /1995/
> 2-4/3 KH457 . . . . **Fic**
> WISNIEWSKI, D/Warrior and the wise man. /1989/
> 1-3/5 KG752 . . . . **E**
> YORINKS, A/Oh, brother. /1989/1-4/5 KG783 . . . . **E**

Typewriting SEE ALSO Keyboarding.

Typewriting.
> MOUNTFORD, C/Kids can type too! /c1985, 1987/
> 4-6/KD311 . . . . **652.3**

Typewriting--Software.
> MAVIS BEACON TEACHES TYPING! (MICROCOMPUTER
> PROGRAM). /1987/4-A/KD310 . . . . . . **MCP 652.3**
> READ, WRITE AND TYPE! (CD-ROM). /1996/
> K-2/KB105 . . . . **CDR 372.4**
> TYPE TO LEARN: A NEW APPROACH TO KEYBOARDING
> (MICROCOMPUTER PROGRAM). /1986/
> 2-A/KD312 . . . . **MCP 652.3**

Typhoons.
> LAMPTON, C/Hurricane. /1991/4-6/7 KC202 . . . . **551.55**

Tyrannosaurus rex.
> LINDSAY, W/Tyrannosaurus. /1992/5-6/9 KC255 . . . . . . **567.9**
> SATTLER, HR/Tyrannosaurus rex and its kin: the Mesozoic monsters.
> /1989/3-6/8 KC261 . . . . **567.9**

U.S SEE United States.

U.S.S.R SEE Soviet Union.

UFOs SEE Unidentified flying objects.

Uganda--Folklore.
> SERWADDA, WM/Songs and stories from Uganda. /c1974, 1987/
> /KA319 . . . . **BA PROF 789.2**

Ukraine--Folklore.
> BRETT, J/Mitten. /1989/K-2/3 KB534 . . . . **398.24**
> KIMMEL, EA/One Eye, Two Eyes, Three Eyes: a Hutzul tale. /
> 1996/2-4/7 KB401 . . . . **398.21**

Umbrellas and parasols--Fiction.
> YASHIMA, T/Umbrella. /c1958/P-K/2 KG773 . . . . **CE E**

Uncles--Fiction.
> COTTONWOOD, J/Babcock. /1996/6-A/3 KH032 . . . . **Fic**
> DOYLE, B/Uncle Ronald. /1997/5-A/5 KH083 . . . . **Fic**
> FARMER, N/Do you know me. /1993/4-A/5 KH107 . . . . **Fic**
> FEIFFER, J/Man in the ceiling. /1993/5-A/7 KH112 . . . . . **Fic**
> HRU, D/Magic moonberry jump ropes. /1996/K-2/2 KF783 . . . . **E**
> HURWITZ, J/Roz and Ozzie. /1992/3-5/5 KH302 . . . . **Fic**
> JORDAN, M/Losing Uncle Tim. /1989/3-5/4 KH336 . . . . **Fic**
> LEVY, J/Spirit of Tio Fernando: a Day of the Dead story./El espiritu
> de tio Fernando: /1995/1-3/5 KH404 . . . . **Fic**
> LOBEL, A/Uncle Elephant. /1981/K-1/1 KG014 . . . . **E**
> MITCHELL, MK/Uncle Jed's barbershop. /1993/1-3/4 KG147 . . . **E**
> NEWMAN, L/Too far away to touch. /1995/1-3/6 KG172 . . . . **E**
> NICHOL, B/Beethoven lives upstairs. /1994/4-6/4 KH549 . . . . . **Fic**
> Beethoven lives upstairs (Videocassette). /1992/
> 4-6/KH550 . . . . **VCR Fic**
> SAY, A/River dream. /1988/K-3/4 KG399 . . . . **E**

Underachievers.
> CHALL, JS/Reading crisis: why poor children fall behind. /1990/
> /KA219 . . . . **PROF 372.6**

Underground animals.
> PLUCKROSE, H/Under the ground. /1994/P-2/4 KC360 . . **578.75**

Underground railroad SEE ALSO Slavery.

Underground railroad.
> BRILL, MT/Allen Jay and the Underground Railroad. /1993/
> 4-6/4 KE898 . . . . **973.7**
> ELISH, D/Harriet Tubman and the Underground Railroad. /1993/
> 4-6/4 KE574 . . . . **B TUBMAN, H.**
> GORRELL, GK/North Star to freedom: the story of the
> Underground Railroad. /1997/5-6/8 KE905 . . . . . . **973.7**
> HAMILTON, V/Many thousand gone: African Americans from
> slavery to freedom. /1993/4-6/7 KA927 . . . . **326**
> PETRY, A/Harriet Tubman: conductor on the Underground Railroad.
> /c1955, 1996/A/7 KE575 . . . . **B TUBMAN, H.**
> RAPPAPORT, D/Escape from slavery: five journeys to freedom. /
> 1991/4-6/4 KE863 . . . . **973**
> STEAL AWAY: THE HARRIET TUBMAN STORY (VIDEOCASSETTE).
> /1997/4-A/KE576. . . . . **VCR B TUBMAN, H.**

Underground railroad--Fiction.
> CONNELLY, B/Follow the drinking gourd: a story of the
> Underground Railroad (Videocassette). /1992/2-4/KF412 . **VCR E**
> EDWARDS, PD/Barefoot: escape on the Underground Railroad. /
> 1997/1-3/3 KF510 . . . . **E**
> FOLLOW THE DRINKING GOURD. /1993/2-4/KF563 . . . . **BA E**
> GUCCIONE, LD/Come morning. /1995/4-6/3 KH205 . . . . . . **Fic**
> MONJO, FN/Drinking gourd. Newly illustrated ed. /1993/
> 1-3/2 KG151 . . . . **E**
> RIGGIO, A/Secret signs: along the Underground Railroad. /1997/
> 2-3/2 KG331 . . . . **E**
> ROSEN, MJ/School for Pompey Walker. /1995/4-8/6 KH653 . **Fic**

Underground utility lines.
> MACAULAY, D/Underground. /1976/A/10 KD070 . . . . . . **624.1**

Underwater archaeology.
> BALLARD, RD/Exploring the Bismarck. /1991/
> 5-6/7 KE668 . . . . **940.54**
> GIBBONS, G/Sunken treasure. /1988/4-6/6 KE194 . . . . . **917.59**

Underwater archaeology--Fiction.
> MACAULAY, D/Ship. /1993/5-6/8 KH433 . . . . **Fic**

Underwater exploration SEE ALSO Marine biology; Oceanography; Skin
diving.

Underwater exploration.
> BALLARD, RD/Exploring the Titanic. /1988/4-6/8 KB025 . . **363.12**
> MARKLE, S/Pioneering ocean depths. /1995/
> 4-A/8 KC175 . . . . **551.46**
> MCGOVERN, A/Down under, down under: diving adventures on
> the Great Barrier Reef. /1989/3-6/5 KF120 . . . . . . **994.3**

Unemployed--Fiction.
> QUINLAN, P/My dad takes care of me. /1987/1-3/2 KG295. . . **E**

Unicorns--Folklore.
> GIBLIN, JC/Dwarf, the giant, and the unicorn: a tale of King Arthur.
> /1996/3-5/4 KB443 . . . . **398.22**
> Truth about unicorns. /c1991, 1996/5-A/7 KB571 . . . . . **398.24**

Unidentified flying objects.
> KETTELKAMP, L/ETs and UFOs: are they real? /1996/
> 4-6/8 KA558 . . . . **001.9**

Unidentified flying objects--Fiction.
> KITAMURA, S/UFO diary. /1989/K-2/2 KF909 . . . . **E**
> PINKWATER, DM/Fat men from space. /1977/5-A/7 KH602 . . **Fic**

Union Pacific Railroad Company--History.
> BLUMBERG, R/Full steam ahead: the race to build a transcontinental
> railroad. /1996/4-6/10 KB137. . . . . **385**

United Farm Workers--History.
> CEDENO, ME/Cesar Chavez: labor leader. /1993/
> 4-5/6 KE287 . . . . **B CHAVEZ, C.**
> DE RUIZ, DC/Causa: the migrant farmworkers' story. /1993/
> 4-6/6 KA944 . . . . **331.88**

United Nations.
> COMMON GOAL: AN INTRODUCTION TO THE UN
> (VIDEOCASSETTE). /1996/5-A/KA968. . . . . **VCR 341.23**
> STEIN, RC/United Nations. Rev. ed. /1994/4-6/7 KA969. . **341.23**
> WORLD IN OUR HANDS: IN HONOR OF THE FIFTIETH
> ANNIVERSARY OF THE UNITED NATIONS. /1995/
> 5-A/8 KA970. **341.23**

United Nations--Fiction.
> SMALL, D/Ruby Mae has something to say. /1992/
> 1-3/4 KG523 . . . . **E**

United States SEE ALSO names of individual states e.g. Alabama; also
regions of the United States e.g. New England.

United States.
> ALABAMA TO WYOMING: STATE FACT CARDS. /1997/
> 4-6/KA488 . . . . **REF 973**
> STEIN, RC/United States of America. /1994/4-A/9 KE867. . . **973**

United States--Armed Forces--Afro-Americans.
> APPLEGATE, K/Story of two American generals: Benjamin O. Davis,
> Jr.; Colin L. Powell. /1995/5-6/5 KA981 . . . . **355**

REEF, C/Black fighting men: a proud history. /1994/
5-6/6 KA982 355
United States--Armed Forces--History--World War, 1939-1945.
WHITMAN, S/Uncle Sam wants you!: military men and women of
World War II. /1993/A/8 KE675. . . . . **940.54**
United States--Armed Forces--Women.
KENT, D/Vietnam Women's Memorial. /1995/
4-6/9 KE720 . . . . **959.704**
United States--Biography.
BREDESON, C/Presidential Medal of Freedom winners. /1996/
5-6/10 KE850 . . . . **973**
United States--Civilization--Spanish influences.
HISPANIC HERITAGE (PICTURE). /1997/4-6/KA848. . . **PIC 305.8**
SINNOTT, S/Extraordinary Hispanic Americans. /1991/
5-A/7 KA860 . . . . **305.8**
United States--Civilization--19th century--Chronology.
RUBEL, D/United States in the 19th century. /1996/
4-A/8 KE895 . . . . **973.5**
United States--Civilization--20th century--Chronology.
RUBEL, D/United States in the 20th century. /1995/
4-A/8 KE916 . . . . **973.9**
United States--Constitution.
FRITZ, J/Shh! We're writing the Constitution. /1987/
3-6/6 KA971 . . . . **CE 342.73**
INDEPENDENCE: BIRTH OF A FREE NATION (VIDEOCASSETTE).
/1976/A/KE890 . . . . **VCR 973.4**
OUR CONSTITUTION: THE DOCUMENT THAT GAVE BIRTH TO A
NATION (VIDEOCASSETTE). /1988/5-A/KA975 . . **VCR 342.73**
U.S. CONSTITUTION: A DOCUMENT FOR DEMOCRACY
(VIDEOCASSETTE). /1986/5-A/KA976. . . . . **VCR 342.73**
United States--Constitutional Convention (1787).
MAESTRO, B/More perfect union: the story of our constitution. /
1987/4-6/8 KA974 . . . . 342.73
OUR CONSTITUTION: THE DOCUMENT THAT GAVE BIRTH TO A
NATION (VIDEOCASSETTE). /1988/5-A/KA975 . . **VCR 342.73**
U.S. CONSTITUTION: A DOCUMENT FOR DEMOCRACY
(VIDEOCASSETTE). /1986/5-A/KA976 . . . . **VCR 342.73**
United States--Constitutional history.
MAESTRO, B/More perfect union: the story of our constitution. /
1987/4-6/8 KA974 . . . . 342.73
United States--Constitutional law.
OUR FEDERAL GOVERNMENT: THE SUPREME COURT
(VIDEOCASSETTE). /1993/A/KA979 . . . . **VCR 347.73**
United States--Description and travel.
GEOGRAPHY OF THE U.S.A. (VIDEOCASSETTE). /1991/
4-6/KE189 . . . . **VCR 917.3**
MURPHY, J/Across America on an emigrant train. /1993/
6-A/8 KB140 385
SIMON, S/Autumn across America. /1993/4-6/7 KB918 . . . **508.2**
Spring across America. /1996/5-8/7 KB919 . . . . . **508.2**
Winter across America. /1994/4-6/6 KB920 . . . . **508.2**
United States--Description and travel--Fiction.
BARRACCA, D/Maxi, the star. /1993/P-2/2 KF201 . . . . E
SAY, A/Grandfather's journey. /1993/2-4/5 KG397 . . . . E
United States--Dictionaries and encyclopedias.
WORLDMARK ENCYCLOPEDIA OF THE STATES. 3RD ED. /1995/
A/KA494. . . . . **REF 973**
United States--Emigration and immigration.
ASHABRANNER, B/Our beckoning borders: illegal immigration to
America. /1996/5-6/12 KA924 . . . . **325.73**
To seek a better world: the Haitian minority in America. /1997/
5-6/8 KA836 . . . . **305.8**
BERGER, M/Where did your family come from?: a book about
immigrants. /1993/2-4/2 KA925 . . . . **325.73**
BRESNICK-PERRY, R/Leaving for America. /1992/
1-4/6 KE688 947
DAWSON, ML/Over here it's different: Carolina's story. /1993/
5-6/7 KA842 . . . . **305.8**
GORDON, G/My two worlds. /1993/3-6/4 KA844 . . . . . . **305.8**
IMMIGRATION (PICTURE). /n.d./5-6/KA918 . . . . **PIC 325**
KROLL, S/Ellis Island: doorway to freedom. /1995/
2-4/10 KA920 325
STANEK, M/We came from Vietnam. /1985/4-6/7 KA861 . . **305.8**
United States--Emigration and immigration--Fiction.
LEVINSON, R/Watch the stars come out. /c1985, 1995/
K-2/2 KF969 . . . . E
SANDIN, J/Long way to a new land. /1981/1-3/2 KG391 . . . . E
SORENSEN, H/New Hope. /1995/1-4/4 KG526 . . . . E
United States--Emigration and immigration--History.
AMERICA: A NATION OF IMMIGRANTS (PICTURE). /1996/
4-6/KA923 . . . . **PIC 325.73**
I WAS DREAMING TO COME TO AMERICA: MEMORIES FROM
THE ELLIS ISLAND ORAL HISTORY /1995/4-6/7 KA916 . . . 325

JACOBS, WJ/Ellis Island: new hope in a new land. /1990/
3-6/6 KA919 325
MAESTRO, B/Coming to America: the story of immigration. /1996/
1-3/8 KA921 325
SANDLER, MW/Immigrants. /1995/5-A/7 KA922 325
United States--Emigration and immigration--Pictorial works.
SANDLER, MW/Immigrants. /1995/5-A/7 KA922 325
United States--Ethnic relations--Bibliography.
VENTURE INTO CULTURES: A RESOURCE BOOK OF
MULTICULTURAL MATERIALS AND PROGRAMS. /1992/
/KA024. . . . . **PROF 011.62**
United States--Executive departments.
UNITED STATES GOVERNMENT MANUAL. /1935-/
A/KA409. . . . . **REF 353**
United States--Folklore.
BANG, M/Wiley and the Hairy Man: adapted from an American
folk tale. /c1976, 1987/1-3/2 KB389 . . . . **398.21**
BRER RABBIT AND BOSS LION (TALKING BOOK). /1992/
3-A/KB533. . . . . **TB 398.24**
CHASE, R/Grandfather tales: American-English folk tales. /c1948/
K-A/4 KB723 . . . . **398.27**
Jack tales. /c1943/K-A/3 KB724. . . . . **398.27**
Richard Chase tells three "Jack" tales from the Southern
Appalachians /n.d./K-A/KB725. . . . . **SRC 398.27**
COMPTON, J/Ashpet: an Appalachian tale. /1994/
2-3/4 KB727 . . . . **398.27**
Sody sallyratus. /K-3/3 KB550 . . . . **398.24**
DEFELICE, CC/Dancing skeleton. /1996/3-6/6 KB684 . . **CE 398.25**
DIANE GOODE BOOK OF AMERICAN FOLK TALES AND
SONGS. /1989/2-4/5 KB439 . . . . **398.22**
FOLKTELLERS /Stories for the road (Sound recording cassette). /
1992/5-A/KB297 . . . . **SRC 398.2**
Tales to grow on (Sound recording cassette). /c1981/
K-3/KB298. . . . . **SRC 398.2**
GLEESON, B/Paul Bunyan (Videocassette). /1990/
3-5/KB447 . . . . **VCR 398.22**
GONZALEZ, LM/Senor Cat's romance and other favorite stories
from Latin America. /1997/K-2/3 KB303 . . . . **398.2**
HALEY, GE/Mountain Jack tales. /1992/4-6/6 KB449 . . . . **398.22**
Two bad boys: a very old Cherokee tale. /1996/
2-5/5 KB742 . . . . **398.27**
HAMILTON, M/Haunting tales: live from the Culbertson Mansion
State Historic Site (Sound /1996/2-4/KB686 . . . . **SRC 398.25**
HASKINS, J/Headless haunt and other African-American ghost
stories. /1994/4-5/4 KB687 . . . . **398.25**
HAYES, J/Tales from the Southwest (Sound recording cassette). /
1984/4-5/KB502. . . . . **SRC 398.23**
HOOKS, WH/Snowbear Whittington: an Appalachian Beauty and
the Beast. /1994/2-3/4 KB318 . . . . **398.2**
Three little pigs and the fox. /1989/2-4/5 KB592 . . . . . . **398.24**
IRVING, W/Legend of Sleepy Hollow. /c1928, 1990/
6-A/9 KH314 . . . . **Fic**
Rip Van Winkle. /1987/4-A/9 KH315 . . . . **Fic**
Rip Van Winkle; and, The Legend of Sleepy Hollow (Talking
book). /1986/5-6/KH316 . . . . **TB Fic**
JONES, LC/Things that go bump in the night. /c1959, 1983/
A/9 KA605 . . . . 133.1
KELLOGG, S/Mike Fink. /1992/3-4/5 KB456 . . . . **398.22**
Paul Bunyan, a tall tale. /1984/4-6/7 KB457 . . . . **398.22**
Sally Ann Thunder Ann Whirlwind Crockett: a tall tale. /1995/
2-5/5 KB458 . . . . **398.22**
KESSLER, B/Brer Rabbit and Boss Lion (Kit). /1996/
3-A/KB599. . . . . **KIT 398.24**
KNAPP, M/One potato, two potato: the folklore of American
children. /1978//KA278. . . . . **PROF 398.8**
LESTER, J/John Henry. /1994/2-5/4 KB464 . . . . **398.22**
MCCORMICK, DJ/Paul Bunyan swings his axe. /c1936, 1962/
4-6/6 KB467 . . . . **398.22**
Tall timber tales: more Paul Bunyan stories. /c1939/
4-6/6 KB468 . . . . **398.22**
METAXAS, E/Stormalong (Kit). /1995/2-5/KB470 . . . **KIT 398.22**
PETERSHAM, M/Rooster crows: a book of American rhymes and
jingles. /c1945/K-2/KB810 . . . . **398.8**
ROUNDS, G/Ol' Paul, the mighty logger: /1976/
4-6/7 KB477 . . . . **398.22**
SAN SOUCI, RD/Cut from the same cloth: American women of
myth, legend, and tall tale. /1993/5-6/6 KB481 . . . . . **398.22**
Hired hand: an African-American folktale. /1997/
3-4/3 KB412 . . . . **398.21**
Talking eggs. /1989/3-5/5 KB415. . . . . **CE 398.21**
SANFIELD, S/Adventures of High John the Conqueror. /1989/
3-6/6 KB480 . . . . **398.22**
SAWYER, R/Journey cake, ho. /c1953, 1989/
P-3/5 KB776 . . . . **398.27**

SCHWARTZ, A/Scary stories to tell in the dark. /1981/
4-A/3 KB694 . . . . **CE 398.25**
SHEPARD, A/Baker's dozen: a Saint Nicholas tale. /1995/
K-2/4 KB487 . . . . **398.22**
    Legend of Slappy Hooper: an American tall tale. /1993/
    3-5/3 KB489 . . . . **398.22**
SIERRA, J/Wiley and the Hairy Man. /1996/K-3/4 KB417 . **398.21**
SLOAT, T/Sody sallyratus. /1997/1-3/5 KB653 . . . . **398.24**
TALKING EGGS (VIDEOCASSETTE). /1993/
2-5/KB420 . . . . **VCR 398.21**
TORRENCE, J/Brer Rabbit stories (Sound recording cassette). /
1984/4-5/KB666 . . . . **SRC 398.24**
    Story lady (Sound recording cassette). /1982/
    4-6/KB781 . . . . **SRC 398.27**
    Traditions: a potpourri of tales (Sound recording cassette). /1994/
    2-3/KB668 . . . . **SRC 398.24**
WAHL, J/Tailypo! /1991/4-5/4 KB421 . . . . **398.21**
WALKER, PR/Big men, big country: a collection of American tall
tales. /1993/4-A/7 KB493 . . . . **398.22**
YOUNG, R/Head on the high road: ghost stories from the
Southwest /1993/4-6/KB698 . . . . **SRC 398.25**

United States--Folklore--Collections.
FROM SEA TO SHINING SEA: A TREASURY OF AMERICAN
FOLKLORE AND FOLK SONGS. /1993/K-6/KD899 . . . . . **810.8**

United States--Folklore--Software.
P.J.'S READING ADVENTURES (CD-ROM). /1996/
K-3/KB252 . . . . **CDR 398**

United States--Foreign population--Fiction.
LEVOY, M/Witch of Fourth Street, and other stories. /c1972/
4-6/7 KH400 . . . . **Fic**
    Witch of Fourth Street and other stories (Kit). /1978/
    4-6/KH401 . . . . **KIT Fic**

United States--Foreign relations--Japan.
BLUMBERG, R/Commodore Perry in the land of the Shogun. /
1985/5-A/7 KE706 . . . . **CE 952**

United States--Geography.
GEOGRAPHY OF THE U.S.A. (VIDEOCASSETTE). /1991/
4-6/KE189 . . . . **VCR 917.3**
GEOGRAPHY OF THE UNITED STATES (VIDEOCASSETTE). /
1991/4-6/KE188 . . . . **VCR 917.3**

United States--Geography--Miscellanea.
MAESTRO, M/Riddle City, USA!: a book of geography riddles. /
1994/2-6/KD734 . . . . **793.735**

United States--Geography--Software.
NATIONAL INSPIRER (MICROCOMPUTER PROGRAM). /1997/
5-A/KE190. . . . . **MCP 917.3**
WHERE IN THE U.S.A. IS CARMEN SANDIEGO? NEW ED. (CD-
ROM). /1996/3-A/KE182 . . . . **CDR 917**

United States--History.
BLASSINGAME, W/Look-it-up book of presidents. Rev. ed. /1996/
4-6/7 KE848 . . . . **973**
HINTZ, M/Farewell, John Barleycorn: prohibition in the United
States. /1996/5-6/12 KB043. **363.4**
MCKISSACK, P/Rebels against slavery: American slave revolts. /
1996/4-6/7 KA929 . . . . **326**
PERL, L/It happened in America: true stories from the fifty states. /
1992/4-A/7 KE861 . . . . **973**
SWANSON, J/I pledge allegiance. /1990/
2-5/4 KA909 . . . . **CE 323.6**

United States--History--Anecdotes.
MANY VOICES: TRUE TALES FROM AMERICA'S PAST. /1995/
/KA371. . . . . **PROF 973**

United States--History--Biography.
HAVEN, K/Amazing American women: 40 fascinating 5-minute
reads. /1995//KA166 . . . . **PROF 305.4**

United States--History--Civil War, 1861-1865.
CIVIL WAR: THE FIERY TRIAL (VIDEOCASSETTE). /1988/
5-A/KE901 . . . . **VCR 973.7**
DAMON, D/When this cruel war is over: the Civil War home front.
/1996/5-6/10 KE902 . . . . **973.7**
GETTYSBURG (VIDEOCASSETTE). /1987/5-A/KE904. **VCR 973.7**
LINCOLN, IN HIS OWN WORDS. /1993/A/8 KE907 . . . . . **973.7**
MOORE, K/...If you lived at the time of the Civil War. /1994/
3-5/6 KE908 . . . . **973.7**
RAY, D/Behind the blue and gray: the soldier's life in the Civil War.
/1991/5-A/7 KE911 . . . . **973.7**
RICKARBY, LA/Ulysses S. Grant and the strategy of victory. /1991/
6-A/6 KE377 . . . . **B GRANT, U.**
ULYSSES S. GRANT (VIDEOCASSETTE). /1989/
6-A/KE378. . . . . **VCR B GRANT, U.**

United States--History--Civil War, 1861-1865--Afro-Americans.
KATZ, WL/Breaking the chains: African-American slave resistance. /
1990/A/8 KE966 . . . . **975**

United States--History--Civil War, 1861-1865--Biography.
ADLER, DA/Picture book of Robert E. Lee. /1994/
2-5/5 KE429 . . . . **B LEE, R.**
D'AULAIRE, I/Abraham Lincoln. /c1957, 1993/
3-4/4 KE440 . . . . **CE B LINCOLN, A.**
FREEDMAN, R/Lincoln, a photobiography. /1987/
A/11 KE441. . . . . **B LINCOLN, A.**
FRITZ, J/Stonewall. /1979/5-A/8 KE399 . . . . . . **B JACKSON, T.**
KAVANAGH, J/Robert E. Lee. /1995/4-5/6 KE430 . . . **B LEE, R.**
ROBERT E. LEE (VIDEOCASSETTE). /1989/
5-6/KE431 . . . . **VCR B LEE, R.**
STONEWALL JACKSON (VIDEOCASSETTE). /1989/
6-A/KE400. . . . . **VCR B JACKSON, T.**

United States--History--Civil War, 1861-1865--Campaigns.
BELLER, SP/To hold this ground: a desperate battle at Gettysburg.
/1995/A/9 KE897 . . . . **973.7**
CARTER, AR/Battle of Gettysburg. /1990/4-6/7 KE899. . . . **973.7**
FRITZ, J/Stonewall. /1979/5-A/8 KE399 . . . . . . **B JACKSON, T.**
GAUCH, PL/Thunder at Gettysburg. /c1975, 1990/
4-6/4 KE903 . . . . **973.7**
MURPHY, J/Long road to Gettysburg. /1992/5-A/7 KE910. **973.7**

United States--History--Civil War, 1861-1865--Campaigns--Fiction.
FLEISCHMAN, P/Bull Run. /1993/5-A/5 KH116. . . . . **Fic**

United States--History--Civil War, 1861-1865--Children.
MURPHY, J/Boys' war: Confederate and Union soldiers talk about
the Civil War. /1990/5-6/7 KE909. . . . . **973.7**

United States--History--Civil War, 1861-1865--Fiction.
ALCOTT, LM/Little women (Talking book). /1975/
5-A/KG830 . . . . **TB Fic**
BUNTING, E/Blue and the gray. /1996/3-5/3 KF297 . . . . **E**
FORRESTER, S/Sound the jubilee. /1995/5-A/6 KH133. . . . . . **Fic**
HUNT, I/Across five Aprils. /1984/5-A/5 KH291 . . . . **CE Fic**
LYON, GE/Cecil's story. /1991/K-3/2 KG042 . . . . **E**
POLACCO, P/Pink and Say. /1994/4-6/2 KH607. . . . . **Fic**
WISLER, GC/Mr. Lincoln's drummer. /1995/5-A/4 KH871 . . . **Fic**
    Mustang Flats. /1997/5-A/6 KH872. . . . . **Fic**

United States--History--Civil War, 1861-1865--Naval operations.
CARTER, AR/Battle of the ironclads: the Monitor and the
Merrimack. /1993/4-6/8 KE900. . . . . **973.7**

United States--History--Civil War, 1861-1865--Personal narratives.
MURPHY, J/Boys' war: Confederate and Union soldiers talk about
the Civil War. /1990/5-6/7 KE909. . . . . **973.7**

United States--History--Civil War, 1861-1865--Poetry.
WHITTIER, JG/Barbara Frietchie. /1992/1-3/KE040 . . . . **811**

**United States--History--Civil War, 1861-1865--Prisoners and prisons-
-Fiction.**
WISLER, GC/Red Cap. /1994/5-A/7 KH873. . . . . **Fic**

United States--History--Civil War, 1861-1865--Secret service.
STEVENS, B/Frank Thompson: her Civil War story. /1992/
6-A/7 KE332 . . . . **B EDMONDS, S.**

United States--History--Colonial period, ca. 1600-1775.
CHRISTMAS IN COLONIAL AND EARLY AMERICA. /c1996/
4-6/8 KB233 . . . . **394.266**
FISHER, LE/Cabinetmakers. /1997/3-6/7 KD343 . . . . **684.1**
    Glassmakers. /1997/3-6/7 KD323. . . . . **666**
KENT, Z/Williamsburg. /1992/4-6/5 KE871 . . . . **973.2**
STORY OF A PATRIOT (VIDEOCASSETTE). /1957/
4-6/KE888 . . . . **VCR 973.3**

United States--History--Colonial period, ca. 1600-1775--Biography.
AVI /Finding Providence: the story of Roger Williams. /1997/
2-3/4 KE596 . . . . **B WILLIAMS, R.**
D'AULAIRE, I/Benjamin Franklin. /c1950/
2-4/6 KE354 . . . . **B FRANKLIN, B.**
FRITZ, J/What's the big idea, Ben Franklin? /c1976/
5-6/7 KE355 . . . . **CE B FRANKLIN, B.**
    Where was Patrick Henry on the 29th of May? /c1975, 1982/
    5-6/7 KE386 . . . . **CE B HENRY, P.**

United States--History--Colonial period, ca. 1600-1775--Education.
FISHER, LE/Schoolmasters. /1997/3-6/7 KB083 . . . . **371.1**

United States--History--Colonial period, ca. 1600-1775--Fiction.
FRITZ, J/Early thunder. /c1967, 1987/5-A/6 KH144 . . . . **Fic**
SAN SOUCI, RD/Red heels. /1996/3-5/6 KG393 . . . . **E**
TURKLE, B/Thy friend, Obadiah. /c1969/K-3/5 KG623 . . . . . . **E**
WIBBERLEY, L/John Treegate's musket. /c1959, 1986/
5-6/7 KH855 . . . . **Fic**

United States--History--Constitutional period, 1789-1809--Biography.
FRITZ, J/Great little Madison. /1989/
5-A/8 KE453 . . . . **B MADISON, J.**

United States--History--Dictionaries.
ENCYCLOPEDIA OF AMERICAN HISTORY. 7TH ED. /1992/
5-6/KA495 . . . . **REF 973.03**

United States--History--Encyclopedias.
RUBEL, D/Scholastic encyclopedia of the presidents and their times.
Updated ed. /1997/4-A/KA492. . . . . **REF 973**

United States--History--French and Indian War, 1755-1763.
MARRIN, A/Struggle for a continent: the French and Indian wars
1690-1760. /1987/5-6/8 KE872 . . . . **973.2**
OCHOA, G/Fall of Quebec and the French and Indian War. /
1990/5-6/7 KE873 . . . . **973.2**
United States--History--Juvenile literature--Bibliography.
PEREZ-STABLE, MA/Understanding American history through
children's literature: instructional /1994//KA263. . . **PROF 372.89**
United States--History--Miscellanea.
OLD TIME AMERICA (PICTURE). /n.d./5-6/KE859 . . . . . **PIC 973**
United States--History--Periodicals.
COBBLESTONE: THE HISTORY MAGAZINE FOR YOUNG PEOPLE.
/1978-/5-6/KA510 . . . . **PER 050**
United States--History--Pictorial works.
ALBUM OF AMERICAN HISTORY. REV. ED. /1981/
5-6/KA489 . . . . **REF 973**
OLD TIME AMERICA (PICTURE). /n.d./5-6/KE859 . . . . . **PIC 973**
PROVENSEN, A/My fellow Americans: a family album. /1995/
3-6/9 KE862 . . . . **973**
SANDLER, MW/Presidents. /1995/5-A/8 KE864 . . . . **973**
United States--History--Revolution, 1775-1783.
DECLARATION OF INDEPENDENCE (VIDEOCASSETTE). /1976/
5-A/KE878. . . . . **VCR 973.3**
DOLAN, EF/American revolution: how we fought the War of
Independence. /1995/4-6/8 KE879. . . . . **973.3**
MARRIN, A/War for independence: the story of the American
Revolution. /1988/5-6/9 KE882 . . . . **973.3**
MELTZER, M/American revolutionaries: a history in their own
words--1750-1800. /1993/5-6/8 KE883 . . . . **973.3**
United States--History--Revolution, 1775-1783--Afro-Americans.
DAVIS, B/Black heroes of the American revolution. /1976/
5-6/10 KE877 . . . . **973.3**
United States--History--Revolution, 1775-1783--Biography.
ADLER, DA/Picture book of Paul Revere. /1995/
2-4/5 KE508 . . . . **B REVERE, P.**
BROWN, DP/Sybil rides for independence. /1985/
3-6/4 KE876 . . . . **973.3**
FORBES, E/America's Paul Revere. /c1946/
A/7 KE509 . . . . **B REVERE, P.**
FRITZ, J/And then what happened, Paul Revere? /c1973/
5-6/6 KE510 . . . . **CE B REVERE, P.**
Why don't you get a horse, Sam Adams? /c1974/
3-5/7 KE227 . . . . **CE B ADAMS, S.**
Will you sign here, John Hancock? /c1976, 1997/
5-6/7 KE383 . . . . **CE B HANCOCK, J.**
HARNESS, C/Young John Quincy. /1994/
3-5/6 KE226 . . . . **B ADAMS, J.Q.**
United States--History--Revolution, 1775-1783--Campaigns.
JOHNSON, N/Battle of Lexington and Concord. /1992/
4-6/7 KE881 . . . . **973.3**
MURPHY, J/Young patriot: the American Revolution as experienced
by one boy. /1996/5-A/9 KE884. . . . . **973.3**
United States--History--Revolution, 1775-1783--Campaigns--Fiction.
BENCHLEY, N/George, the drummer boy. /c1977/1-3/2 KF221 . **E**
United States--History--Revolution, 1775-1783--Causes.
STORY OF A PATRIOT (VIDEOCASSETTE). /1957/
4-6/KE888. . . . . **VCR 973.3**
United States--History--Revolution, 1775-1783--Fiction.
BENCHLEY, N/Sam the minuteman. /c1969/1-3/2 KF222. . . . . **E**
COLLIER, JL/My brother Sam is dead. /1974/5-6/5 KH016 . . . **Fic**
War comes to Willy Freeman. /1983/5-6/6 KH017. . . . . . . **Fic**
FORBES, E/Johnny Tremain: a novel for old and young. /c1943,
1971/4-6/6 KH131 . . . . **CE Fic**
GAUCH, PL/This time, Tempe Wick? /c1974, 1992/
3-5/7 KH153 . . . . **Fic**
LAWSON, R/Mr. Revere and I. /c1953/5-6/7 KH389. . . . . . **Fic**
O'DELL, S/Sarah Bishop. /1980/5-6/5 KH561 . . . . **Fic**
RAPPAPORT, D/Boston coffee party. /1988/K-3/2 KG306. . . . . **E**
TURNER, A/Katie's trunk. /1992/3-5/3 KG627 . . . . **E**
WIBBERLEY, L/John Treegate's musket. /c1959, 1986/
5-6/7 KH855 . . . . **Fic**
United States--History--Revolution, 1775-1783--Flags.
FISHER, LE/Stars and Stripes: our national flag. /1993/
3-6/7 KE617 . . . . **929.9**
United States--History--Revolution, 1775-1783--Personal narratives.
SHERBURNE, A/Memoirs of Andrew Sherburne: patriot and
privateer of the American Revolution. /1993/5-A/8 KE886 . **973.3**
United States--History--Revolution, 1775-1783--Secret Service.
ROOP, P/Buttons for General Washington. /1986/
4-6/4 KE885 . . . . **973.3**
United States--History--Revolution, 1775-1783--Songs and music.
BANGS, E/Yankee Doodle. 2nd ed. /c1976, 1996/
P-2/KD557. . . . . **789.2**

United States--History--Revolution, 1775-1783--Women.
ZEINERT, K/Those remarkable women of the American Revolution. /
1996/5-6/10 KE889 . . . . **973.3**
United States--History--Software.
GTV: A GEOGRAPHIC PERSPECTIVE ON AMERICAN HISTORY
(VIDEODISC). /c1990/5-A/KE853 . . . . **VD 973**
SKYTRIP AMERICA: AN INCREDIBLE RIDE THROUGH U.S.
HISTORY. TEACHER ED. (CD-ROM). /1996/
3-A/KE865. . . . . **CDR 973**
United States--History--Songs and music.
BATES, KL/America the beautiful. /1993/K-3/KD558. . . . . . **789.2**
JENKINS, E/We are America's children (Compact disc). /1989/
1-6/KD577. . . . . **CD 789.2**
United States--History--Study and teaching (Elementary).
PEREZ-STABLE, MA/Understanding American history through
children's literature: instructional units and activities for grades K-8.
/1994//KA263. . . . . **PROF 372.89**
United States--History--War of 1812--Fiction.
LAWSON, J/If pigs could fly. /1989/5-A/6 KH387 . . . . **Fic**
United States--History--War of 1898.
MARRIN, A/Spanish-American War. /1991/A/7 KE915. . . . **973.8**
United States--History--1865-1898--Pictorial works.
AMERICAN HISTORY: GROWING PAINS (PICTURE). /c1974/
4-6/KE912. . . . . **PIC 973.8**
United States--History--19th century.
GAN, G/Communication. /1997/5-6/9 KA795. . . . . **302.2**
United States--History--19th century--Children.
TOYNTON, E/Growing up in America, 1830-1860. /1995/
A/7 KE896 . . . . **973.5**
United States--History--19th century--Chronology.
RUBEL, D/United States in the 19th century. /1996/
4-A/8 KE895 . . . . **973.5**
United States--History--19th century--Fiction.
AVI /Beyond the western sea: book two: Lord Kirkle's money. /
1996/6-A/5 KG858 . . . . **Fic**
United States--History--1919-1933--Fiction.
LEVOY, M/Witch of Fourth Street, and other stories. /c1972/
4-6/7 KH400 . . . . **Fic**
Witch of Fourth Street and other stories (Kit). /1978/
4-6/KH401. . . . . **KIT Fic**
MITCHELL, MK/Uncle Jed's barbershop. /1993/1-3/4 KG147. . . **E**
United States--History--1933-1945.
DUST BOWL (PICTURE). /n.d./5-6/KE917 . . . . . . **PIC 973.917**
STEIN, RC/Great Depression. Rev. ed. /1993/
4-6/7 KE918 . . . . **973.917**
United States--History--1933-1945--Fiction.
ARMSTRONG, WH/Sounder. /c1969/4-A/4 KG851 . . . . **CE Fic**
KIRK, D/Lucky's 24-hour garage. /1996/K-2/4 KF907 . . . . **E**
ROBINET, HG/Mississippi chariot. /1994/5-A/5 KH639 . . . . . . **Fic**
United States--History--1969- --Chronology.
MARTINET, J/Year you were born, 1983. /1992/
4-6/7 KE922 . . . . **973.927**
United States--History--20th century.
WOMEN OF RURAL AMERICA (VIDEOCASSETTE). /1995/
5-A/KA831 . . . . **VCR 305.42**
United States--History--20th century--Chronology.
RUBEL, D/United States in the 20th century. /1995/
4-A/8 KE919 . . . . **973.9**
United States--History, Military.
APPLEGATE, K/Story of two American generals: Benjamin O. Davis,
Jr.; Colin L. Powell. /1995/5-6/5 KA981 . . . . **355**
REEF, C/Black fighting men: a proud history. /1994/
5-6/6 KA982 . . . . **355**
United States--Literary collections.
FROM SEA TO SHINING SEA: A TREASURY OF AMERICAN
FOLKLORE AND FOLK SONGS. /1993/K-6/KD899 . . . . . **810.8**
United States--Maps.
NATIONAL GEOGRAPHIC PICTURE ATLAS OF OUR FIFTY
STATES. /1994/4-A/KA475 . . . . **REF 912.73**
United States--Poetry.
CELEBRATE AMERICA IN POETRY AND ART. /1994/
3-6/KE054. . . . . **811.008**
HAND IN HAND: AN AMERICAN HISTORY THROUGH POETRY. /
1994/2-6/KE063. . . . . **811.008**
United States--Politics and government.
KRONENWETTER, M/Congress of the United States. /1996/
5-A/10 KA932 . . . . **328.73**
STEINS, R/Our elections. /1994/5-6/7 KA912. . . . . **324.6**
UNITED STATES GOVERNMENT MANUAL. /1935-/
A/KA409. . . . . **REF 353**
United States--Politics and government--1775-1783.
STEIN, RC/Declaration of Independence. /1995/
5-A/7 KE887 . . . . **973.3**

United States--Politics and government--1789-1797.
INDEPENDENCE: BIRTH OF A FREE NATION (VIDEOCASSETTE).
/1976/A/KE890 . . . . **VCR 973.4**

United States--Race relations.
CWIKLIK, R/Malcolm X and black pride. /1991/
5-6/6 KE455 . . . . **B MALCOLM X**
DUNCAN, AF/National Civil Rights Museum celebrates everyday
people. /1995/3-6/8 KA903 . . . . **323.1**

United States--Relations--Mexico.
PASCOE, E/Mexico and the United States: cooperation and conflict.
/1996/6-A/11 KA805 . . . . **303.48**

United States--Religion.
HUBBARD, BJ/America's religions: an educator's guide to beliefs
and practices. /1997//KA160 . . . . **PROF 200**

United States--Social life and customs.
ALBUM OF AMERICAN HISTORY. REV. ED. /1981/
5-6/KA489 . . . . **REF 973**
CANEY, S/Steven Caney's Kids' America. /1978/
4-6/7 KE920 . . . . **973.92**

United States--Social life and customs--Pictorial works.
AMERICAN HISTORY: GROWING PAINS (PICTURE). /c1974/
4-6/KE912 . . . . **PIC 973.8**

United States--Social life and customs--To 1775.
BARRETT, T/Growing up in colonial America. /1995/
4-6/9 KE869 . . . . **973.2**
CHRISTMAS IN COLONIAL AND EARLY AMERICA. /c1996/
4-6/8 KB233 . . . . **394.266**
LOEPER, JJ/Going to school in 1776. /1973/
4-6/8 KB123 . . . . **372.973**
PERL, L/Slumps, grunts, and snickerdoodles: what Colonial America
ate and why. /1975/4-6/9 KD276 . . . . **641.5**
STEVENS, BS/Colonial American craftspeople. /1993/
5-6/8 KD339 . . . . **680**

United States--Social life and customs--1775-1783.
BRENNER, B/If you were there in 1776. /1994/
5-6/6 KE875 . . . . **973.3**
MELTZER, M/American revolutionaries: a history in their own
words--1750-1800. /1993/5-6/8 KE883 . . . . **973.3**

United States--Social life and customs--1783-1865.
TOYNTON, E/Growing up in America, 1830-1860. /1995/
A/7 KE896 . . . . **973.5**
TUNIS, E/Frontier living. /c1961/5-6/9 KE893 . . . . **973.4**

United States--Social life and customs--1865-1918.
LOEPER, JJ/Going to school in 1876. /1984/
3-6/7 KB124 . . . . **372.973**

United States--Social life and customs--1865-1918--Fiction.
HALL, D/Lucy's Christmas. /1994/1-3/6 KF662 . . . . **E**

**United States--Social life and customs--20th century, 1900-1999--
Fiction.**
RYLANT, C/When I was young in the mountains. /1982/
K-3/6 KG387 . . . . **CE E**

United States--Statistics.
TESAR, J/New view almanac: the first all-visual resource of vital
facts and statistics! /1996/4-A/KA391 . . . . **REF 031.02**
WORLD ALMANAC AND BOOK OF FACTS. /1868-/
4-6/KA406 . . . . **REF 317.3**

United States--Territorial expansion.
HERB, AM/Beyond the Mississippi: early westward expansion of the
United States. /1996/4-6/10 KF032 . . . . **978**

United States. Army--Fiction.
HOFF, S/Captain Cat: story and pictures. /1993/K-2/2 KF752 . . **E**

United States. Army--History--Civil War, 1861-1865.
RAY, D/Behind the blue and gray: the soldier's life in the Civil War.
/1991/5-A/7 KE911 . . . . **973.7**

**United States. Bureau of Land Management. Adopt-A-Horse or
Burro.**
ANCONA, G/Man and mustang. /1992/5-6/6 KD197 . . . . **636.1**

United States. Congress.
KRONENWETTER, M/Congress of the United States. /1996/
5-A/10 KA932 . . . . **328.73**
OUR FEDERAL GOVERNMENT: THE LEGISLATIVE BRANCH
(VIDEOCASSETTE). /1993/5-A/KA933 . . . . **VCR 328.73**

United States. Congress. House--Biography.
ADLER, DA/Picture book of Davy Crockett. /1996/
2-3/7 KE310 . . . . **B CROCKETT, D.**
PATRICK-WEXLER, D/Barbara Jordan. /1996/
4-6/8 KE408 . . . . **B JORDAN, B.**

United States. Constitutional Convention (1787).
FRITZ, J/Shh! We're writing the Constitution. /1987/
3-6/6 KA971 . . . . **CE 342.73**

United States. Constitutional Convention (1787)--Fiction.
COLLIER, JL/Jump ship to freedom. /1981/5-6/5 KH015 . . . . . **Fic**

United States. Declaration of Independence.
BRENNER, B/If you were there in 1776. /1994/
5-6/6 KE875 . . . . **973.3**
DECLARATION OF INDEPENDENCE (VIDEOCASSETTE). /1976/
5-A/KE878. . . . . **VCR 973.3**
INDEPENDENCE: BIRTH OF A FREE NATION (VIDEOCASSETTE).
/1976/A/KE890 . . . . **VCR 973.4**
STEIN, RC/Declaration of Independence. /1995/
5-A/7 KE887 . . . . **973.3**

United States. Marine Corps.
WARNER, JF/U.S. Marine Corps. /1991/5-6/7 KA990 . . . . **359.9**

United States. Office of the Federal Register.
UNITED STATES GOVERNMENT MANUAL. /1935-/
A/KA409 . . . . **REF 353**

United States. Supreme Court.
KRONENWETTER, M/Supreme Court of the United States. /1996/
5-A/10 KA978 . . . . **347.73**
OUR FEDERAL GOVERNMENT: THE SUPREME COURT
(VIDEOCASSETTE). /1993/A/KA979 . . . . **VCR 347.73**

United States. Supreme Court--Biography.
MACHT, NL/Sandra Day O'Connor. /1992/
4-5/8 KE481 . . . . **B O'CONNOR, S.**

United States in art.
CELEBRATE AMERICA IN POETRY AND ART. /1994/
3-6/KE054 . . . . **811.008**

United States Naval Expedition to Japan (1852-1854).
BLUMBERG, R/Commodore Perry in the land of the Shogun. /
1985/5-A/7 KE706 . . . . **CE 952**

Universe SEE ALSO Astronomy; Creation; Earth; Life on other planets.

Unmarried mothers--Fiction.
SMITH, DB/Return to Bitter Creek. /1988/5-A/5 KH721 . . . . . **Fic**

Uranus (Planet).
SIMON, S/Uranus. /1987/4-6/6 KC040 . . . . **523.47**

Urban animals.
BASH, B/Urban roosts: where birds nest in the city. /1990/
3-6/7 KC672 . . . . **598.156**
SWANSON, D/Coyotes in the crosswalk: true tales of animal life in
the wilds...of the city! /1995/4-6/6 KC494 . . . . . **591.75**
Urban areas SEE Cities and towns.

Urban ecology (Biology).
HENDERSON AVENUE BUG PATROL (VIDEOCASSETTE). /1984/
1-6/KB867 . . . . **VCR 500**

Ursa Major.
KRUPP, EC/Big dipper and you. /1989/1-6/4 KC050 . . . . . **523.8**
USSR SEE Soviet Union.

Utah.
SIRVAITIS, K/Utah. /1991/4-6/6 KF073 . . . . **979.2**

Ute Indians--Folklore.
STEVENS, J/Coyote steals the blanket: a Ute tale. /1993/
2-4/2 KB657 . . . . **398.24**

Utilities (Computer programs)--Software.
KIDDESK. SCHOOL VERSION (CD-ROM). /1995/
P-A/KA569 . . . . **CDR 004**
KIDDESK (MICROCOMPUTER PROGRAM). /1993/
K-A/KA568 . . . . **MCP 004**

Vacations.
EMBERLEY, R/Let's go: a book in two languages./Vamos: un libro
en dos lenguas. /1993/K-2/2 KB857 . . . . **463**

Vacations--Fiction.
BLUME, J/Fudge-a-mania. /1990/4-6/3 KG909 . . . . **CE Fic**
BROWN, R/Our puppy's vacation. /1987/P-1/1 KF288 . . . . . **E**
CUSHMAN, D/Aunt Eater's mystery vacation. /1992/
1-3/2 KF441 . . . . **E**
GILSON, J/Hobie Hanson, you're weird. /1987/3-5/6 KH168. . **Fic**
HORVATH, P/Occasional cow. /1989/5-6/8 KH284 . . . . **Fic**
MACLACHLAN, P/Arthur, for the very first time. /1980/
4-6/7 KH443 . . . . **Fic**
MURPHY, SJ/Best vacation ever. /1997/K-2/2 KG164 . . . . **E**
NETHERY, M/Hannah and Jack. /1996/K-2/2 KG170 . . . . **E**
STEVENSON, J/Sea View Hotel. /c1978, 1994/K-3/3 KG567 . . **E**

Vacuum cleaners--Fiction.
SMALL, D/Hoover's bride. /1995/1-3/5 KG521 . . . . **E**

Valentine, Saint.
SABUDA, R/Saint Valentine. /1992/
4-6/4 KE581 . . . . **B VALENTINE,ST.**

Valentine's Day.
GIBBONS, G/Valentine's Day. /1986/1-6/5 KB207 . . **CE 394.261**
GRAHAM-BARBER, L/Mushy! the complete book of Valentine
words. /1991/5-6/8 KB209 . . . . **394.261**

Valentine's Day--Fiction.
BROWN, MT/Arthur's April fool. /1983/P-3/2 KF273 . . . . **E**
DE GROAT, D/Roses are pink, your feet really stink. /1996/
K-2/2 KF457 . . . . **E**

MCKENNA, CO/Valentine's Day can be murder. /1996/
3-5/4 KH482 . . . . **Fic**
STEVENSON, J/Village full of valentines. /1995/1-3/2 KG568 . . **E**

Valentine's Day--Poetry.
GOOD MORNING TO YOU, VALENTINE: POEMS FOR
VALENTINE'S DAY. /c1976, 1993/K-6/KE061 . . . . **811.008**
PRELUTSKY, J/It's Valentine's Day. /1983/K-2/KE007 . . . . . . **811**

Valentines.
GIBBONS, G/Valentine's Day. /1986/1-6/5 KB207 . . **CE 394.261**

Valentines--Fiction.
DE GROAT, D/Roses are pink, your feet really stink. /1996/
K-2/2 KF457 . . . . **E**
MCKENNA, CO/Valentine's Day can be murder. /1996/
3-5/4 KH482 . . . . **Fic**
STEVENSON, J/Village full of valentines. /1995/1-3/2 KG568 . . **E**

Values.
COOPERATION (VIDEOCASSETTE). /1990/4-6/KA655 **VCR 158**

Values--Fiction.
LOWRY, L/Anastasia, absolutely. /1995/4-A/6 KH422 . . . . . **Fic**

Values--Software.
TAKING RESPONSIBILITY (MICROCOMPUTER PROGRAM). /
1988/1-6/KA665 . . . . **MCP 158**

Vampires--Fiction.
HOWE, D/Bunnicula: a rabbit-tale mystery. /1979/
3-6/5 KH285 . . . . **Fic**
HOWE, J/Rabbit-Cadabra! /1993/K-3/3 KF779 . . . . **E**
KWITZ, MD/Little Vampire and the Midnight Bear. /1995/
1-3/2 KF941 . . . . **E**

Van Gogh, Vincent SEE Gogh, Vincent van.

Van Meter, Vicki.
VAN METER, V/Taking flight: my story. /1995/
3-6/6 KD101 . . . . **629.13**

Vanishing animals SEE Rare animals.

Variation (Biology) SEE ALSO Adaptation (Biology); Animals--Color;
Evolution; Natural selection.

Vegetable gardening.
KUHN, D/More than just a vegetable garden. /1990/
4-5/5 KD170 . . . . **635**

Vegetables.
BROWN, LK/Vegetable show. /1995/P-2/2 KD289 . . . . . . **641.6**
MCMILLAN, B/Growing colors. /1988/P-1/KC124 . . . . . **535.6**

Vegetables--Fiction.
CASELEY, J/Grandpa's garden lunch. /1990/P-1/2 KF364 . . . . . **E**
GREENSTEIN, E/Mrs. Rose's garden. /1996/K-2/3 KF643 . . . . . **E**
WIESNER, D/June 29, 1999. /1992/1-5/4 KG713 . . . . **E**

Vegetarianism--Fiction.
HURWITZ, J/Aldo Applesauce. /1979/4-6/6 KH296 . . . . . . **Fic**

Vehicles.
GIBBONS, G/Emergency! /1994/P-1/6 KB032 . . . . **363.3**
SMITH, JH/Most rugged all-terrain vehicles. /1995/
5-6/6 KD830 . . . . **796.7**

Vehicles--Fiction.
ROBERTS, B/Camel caravan. /1996/P-1/3 KG335 . . . . **E**

Vehicles--Poetry.
ROLL ALONG: POEMS ON WHEELS. /1993/
4-A/KE080. . . . . **811.008**

Vehicles, Military.
CHASEMORE, R/Tanks. /1996/4-6/8 KD060 . . . . **623.7**

Venezuela--Fiction.
KURUSA /Streets are free. Rev. ed. /1995/3-4/5 KH383 . . . . . **Fic**

Venus (Planet).
SCHLOSS, M/Venus. /1991/4-6/8 KC033 . . . . **523.42**
SIMON, S/Venus. /1992/3-6/8 KC034 . . . . **523.42**

Verdi, Giuseppe.
PRICE, L/Aida. /1990/4-A/6 KD530 . . . . **782.1**

Vermont.
FRADIN, DB/Vermont. /1993/4-6/4 KE934 . . . . **974.3**

Vermont--Description and travel.
ARNOSKY, J/Nearer nature. /1996/A/6 KE933 . . . . **974.3**

Vermont--Fiction.
PECK, RN/Soup. /1974/4-6/6 KH594 . . . . **Fic**

Verne, Jules.
TEETERS, P/Jules Verne: the man who invented tomorrow. /1992/
5-A/6 KE582 . . . . **B VERNE, J.**

Vertebrates SEE ALSO Amphibians; Birds; Fishes; Mammals; Reptiles.

Vertebrates.
SILVERSTEIN, A/Vertebrates. /1996/A/9 KC581 . . . . **596**

Vertebrates, Fossil.
GIBBONS, G/Prehistoric animals. /1988/P-3/5 KC241 . . . . . **566**

Veterinarians.
GIBBONS, G/Say woof!: the day of a country veterinarian. /1992/
P-2/2 KD194 . . . . **636.089**
MAZE, S/I want to be... a veterinarian. /1997/
5-6/9 KD195 . . . . **636.089**

PAIGE, D/Day in the life of a zoo veterinarian. /1985/
2-5/6 KD196 . . . . **CE 636.089**

Veterinary hospitals.
KUKLIN, S/Taking my cat to the vet. /1988/P-K/4 KD234 . . **636.8**

Veterinary medicine.
GIBBONS, G/Say woof!: the day of a country veterinarian. /1992/
P-2/2 KD194 . . . . **636.089**
KUKLIN, S/Taking my cat to the vet. /1988/P-K/4 KD234 . . **636.8**

Vice-Presidents.
STEFOFF, R/Al Gore, vice president. /1994/
4-5/6 KE374 . . . . **B GORE, A.**

Victims of famine--Fiction.
LUTZEIER, E/Coldest winter. /1991/6-A/7 KH429 . . . . **Fic**

Video discs--Catalogs.
VIDEO SOURCE BOOK. /1979-//KA030 . . . . . . **PROF 016.791**

Video games.
SKURZYNSKI, G/Know the score: video games in your high-tech
world. /1994/3-6/8 KD757 . . . . **794.8**

Video recordings--Production and direction.
BENTLEY, N/Young producer's video book: how to write, direct,
and shoot your own video. /1995/3-6/4 KD686 . . . . . . **791.45**

Video recordings for the hearing impaired.
BEGINNING AMERICAN SIGN LANGUAGE VIDEOCOURSE
(VIDEOCASSETTE). /1991/3-A/KB822 . . . . **VCR 419**

Videocassettes--Catalogs.
AIT CATALOG OF EDUCATIONAL MATERIALS. /1962-/
/KA003. . . . . **PROF 011**

Videotapes--Catalogs.
VIDEO SOURCE BOOK. /1979-//KA030 . . . . . . **PROF 016.791**

Vienna. Spanish Riding School--Fiction.
HENRY, M/White stallion of Lipizza. /c1964, 1994/
4-6/6 KH246 . . . . **Fic**

Vietnam.
GARLAND, S/Vietnam: rebuilding a nation. /1990/
5-6/7 KE717 . . . . **959.7**

Vietnam--Description and travel.
SCHMIDT, J/Two lands, one heart: an American boy's journey to
his mother's Vietnam. /1995/1-3/7 KE719 . . . . **959.7**

Vietnam--Fiction.
KELLER, H/Grandfather's dream. /1994/K-2/2 KF883 . . . . **E**

Vietnam--Folklore.
VUONG, LD/Sky legends of Vietnam. /1993/
3-5/7 KB717 . . . . **398.26**

Vietnam--Social life and customs.
HUYNH, QN/Land I lost: adventures of a boy in Vietnam. /1982/
5-6/7 KE718 . . . . **959.7**

Vietnam Women's Memorial (Washington, D.C.).
KENT, D/Vietnam Women's Memorial. /1995/
4-6/7 KE720 . . . . **959.704**

Vietnamese--United States.
STANEK, M/We came from Vietnam. /1985/4-6/7 KA861. . **305.8**

Vietnamese--United States--Fiction.
SURAT, MM/Angel child, dragon child. /c1983, 1989/
1-3/2 KG584 . . . . **E**

Vietnamese Americans.
HOYT-GOLDSMITH, D/Hoang Anh: a Vietnamese-American boy. /
1992/3-6/6 KA849 . . . . **305.8**

**Vietnamese Conflict, 1961-1975--Prisoners and prisons, North
Vietnamese.**
MYERS, WD/Place called heartbreak: a story of Vietnam. /1993/
5-6/6 KE721 . . . . **959.704**

Vietnamese Conflict, 1961-1975--Women--United States.
KENT, D/Vietnam Women's Memorial. /1995/
4-6/7 KE720 . . . . **959.704**

Vietnamese language materials.
HILL, E/Where's Spot? Sign language edition. /1987/
P-2/2 KF728 . . . . **E**

Viking Mars Program.
VOGT, G/Viking and the Mars landing. /1991/
A/10 KD132 . . . . **629.43**

Vikings.
MARGESON, SM/Viking. /1994/4-6/7 KE693 . . . . **948**
PITKANEN, MA/Grandchildren of the Vikings. /1996/
4-6/8 KE694 . . . . **948**

Vikings--Folklore.
WISNIEWSKI, D/Elfwyn's saga. /1990/4-6/6 KB422 . . . . **398.21**

Villages SEE ALSO Local government.

Violence in mass media--Software.
VIOLENCE IN THE MEDIA (MICROCOMPUTER PROGRAM). /
1994/5-A/KA802 . . . . **MCP 302.23**

Violin.
TURNER, BC/Living violin. /1996/4-6/12 KD549 . . . . . **BA 787.2**

Violin--Fiction.
NAMIOKA, L/Yang the youngest and his terrible ear. /1994/
5-A/5 KH528 . . . . **Fic**

Virgin Islands of the United States--Folklore.
GERSHATOR, P/Tukama Tootles the flute: a tale from the Antilles.
/1994/K-2/5 KB398 . . . . **398.21**

Virginia.
SIRVAITIS, K/Virginia. /1991/4-6/6 KE981 . . . . . . **975.5**

Virginia--Buildings, structures, etc.
MOUNT VERNON: HOME OF GEORGE WASHINGTON
(VIDEOCASSETTE). /1989/4-6/KE980 . . . . **VCR 975.5**

Virginia--Fiction.
FLOURNOY, V/Tanya's reunion. /1995/K-3/3 KF562 . . . . **E**
HITE, S/Dither Farm: a novel. /1992/5-A/7 KH265. . . . . . . **Fic**
RANSOM, CF/When the whippoorwill calls. /1995/
1-3/2 KG305 . . . . **E**

Virginia--History.
COCKE, W/Historical album of Virginia. /1995/
4-6/7 KE976 . . . . **975.5**

Virginia--History--Colonial period, ca. 1600-1775.
FRADIN, DB/Virginia Colony. /1986/A/10 KE977 . . . . **975.5**
FRITZ, J/Double life of Pocahontas. /1983/
5-6/6 KE500 . . . . **B POCAHONTAS**

Virginia--History--Revolution, 1775-1783.
FRADIN, DB/Virginia Colony. /1986/A/10 KE977 . . . . **975.5**

Virginia--Politics and government--1775-1783.
GOOR, R/Williamsburg: cradle of the revolution. /1994/
5-A/7 KE978 . . . . **975.5**

Virtual reality--Fiction.
CROSS, G/New world. /1995/6-A/5 KH044 . . . . **Fic**
SKURZYNSKI, G/Virtual war. /1997/5-A/4 KH716. . . . . . . **Fic**

Virus diseases.
FACKLAM, H/Viruses. /1994/5-A/8 KC377. . . . . **579.2**
NOURSE, AE/Virus invaders. /1992/A/10 KD012 . . . . . . **616**
VIRUS! (VIDEOCASSETTE). /1994/A/KD013. . . . . . . **VCR 616**

Viruses.
BERGER, M/Germs make me sick! Rev. ed. /1995/
1-3/5 KD021 . . . . **616.9**
FACKLAM, H/Viruses. /1994/5-A/8 KC377. . . . . **579.2**
IMMUNE SYSTEM: OUR INTERNAL DEFENDER
(VIDEOCASSETTE). /1991/4-5/KD014. . . . . **VCR 616.07**
NOURSE, AE/Virus invaders. /1992/A/10 KD012 . . . . . . **616**
REALMS OF LIFE (PICTURE). /1996/6-A/KC356 . . . . . . **PIC 578**
VIRUS! (VIDEOCASSETTE). /1994/A/KD013. . . . . . . **VCR 616**

Vision.
EYES: BRIGHT AND SAFE. REV. ED. (VIDEOCASSETTE). /1997/
3-5/KC964. . . . . **VCR 612.8**
FABULOUS FIVE: OUR SENSES (VIDEOCASSETTE). /1989/
P-2/KC917. . . . . **VCR 612**
JEDROSZ, A/Eyes. /1992/5-6/6 KC965. . . . . **612.8**
LAUBER, P/What do you see and how do you see it?: exploring
light, color, and vision. /1994/1-6/4 KC113 . . . . **535**
PARKER, S/Eye and seeing. Rev. ed. /1989/A/8 KC972 . . . **612.8**
PARRAMON, JM/Sight. /1985/P-1/1 KC974 . . . . **612.8**
SHOWERS, P/Look at your eyes. Rev. ed. /1992/
P-1/2 KC978 . . . . **612.8**

Visits of state.
ALIKI /Medieval feast. /1983/2-5/5 KB183. . . . . **CE 394.1**

Visual perception.
GOMI, T/Who hid it? /1991/P-K/2 KF630 . . . . **E**
HOBAN, T/Just look. /1996/P-2/KA615. . . . . **152.14**
Look book. /1997/P-K/KD516 . . . . **779**
Look up, look down. /1992/P-1/KF743 . . . . **E**
Look! look! look! /1988/P-3/KA616. . . . . **152.14**
Take another look. /1981/P-A/KA618 . . . . **152.14**
JENKINS, S/Flip-flap. /1995/P-K/2 KA619 . . . . **152.14**
MAGIC EYE: A NEW WAY OF LOOKING AT THE WORLD. /
1993/3-A/KA620 . . . . **152.14**
MCMILLAN, B/Mouse views: what the class pet saw. /1993/
K-3/1 KG111 . . . . **E**
WESTRAY, K/Picture puzzler. /1994/1-6/7 KA621. . . . . . **152.14**

Visual perception--Experiments.
DOHERTY, P/Cheshire cat and other eye-popping experiments on
how we see the world. /1995/4-A/5 KA612 . . . . **152.14**

Visual perception--Fiction.
BANYAI, I/Re-zoom. /1995/2-A/KF196 . . . . **E**
Zoom. /1995/P-A/KF197 . . . . **E**
HUTCHINS, P/Shrinking mouse. /1997/P-K/1 KF803 . . . . **E**
JENKINS, S/Looking down. /1995/K-3/KF827 . . . . **E**

Visual perception--Software.
BUILDING PERSPECTIVE: STRATEGIES IN PROBLEM SOLVING
(MICROCOMPUTER PROGRAM). /1986/
4-A/KA637 . . . . **MCP 153.7**

Vivariums SEE ALSO Terrariums.
Vocabulary SEE ALSO Word games.
Vocabulary.
BADT, KL/Greetings! /1994/3-5/6 KB245 . . . . **395.4**
BARTON, B/Big machines (Board book). /1995/P/KF204. . . **BB E**
Tools (Board book). /1995/P/KF208 . . . . **BB E**
Zoo animals (Board book). /1995/P/KF209 . . . . **BB E**
CORBEIL, J/Facts on File visual dictionary. /1986/
6-A/KA390 . . . . **REF 031.02**
EMBERLEY, R/Let's go: a book in two languages./Vamos: un libro
en dos lenguas. /1993/K-2/2 KB857 . . . . **463**
My house: a book in two languages/Mi Casa: un libro en dos
lenguas. /1990/K-2/KB858 . . . . **463**
HOBAN, T/Over, under and through, and other spatial concepts. /
1973/P-K/KF745. . . . . **E**
KINGFISHER FIRST DICTIONARY. /1995/1-2/KA424 . . . **REF 423**
MICKLETHWAIT, L/Child's book of art: great pictures, first words. /
1993/P-1/KD366 . . . . **701**
ROCKWELL, AF/What we like. /1992/P/KB849 . . . . . . **428.1**
ROOT, B/My first dictionary. /1993/P-2/KB835. . . . . . . **423**
TERBAN, M/Superdupers! really funny real words. /1989/
3-6/6 KB850 . . . . **428.1**
WILKES, A/My first word book. /1991/P-2/KB839. . . . . . **423**
100 WORDS ABOUT MY HOUSE. /1988/P-3/KD296. . . . . . **645**

Vocabulary--Fiction.
ZIEFERT, H/What rhymes with eel?: a word-and-picture flap book. /
1996/P-1/2 KG798 . . . . **E**

Vocabulary--Study and teaching.
NAGY, WE/Teaching vocabulary to improve reading comprehension.
/1988//KA211 . . . . **PROF 372.4**

Vocal music--History.
SHIPTON, A/Singing. /1994/4-6/7 KD527 . . . . **782**

Vocational guidance SEE ALSO Occupations; and name of specific
occupation e.g. Physician; Journalism.
Vocational guidance.
KALMAN, M/Chicken soup, boots. /1993/P-K/3 KA941 . . . **331.7**
KAPLAN, A/Careers for outdoor types. /1991/
4-A/8 KA952 . . . . **333.7**
MAYNARD, C/Jobs people do. /1997/P-1/4 KA942 . . . . **331.7**
MAZE, S/I want to be... an astronaut. /1997/
5-6/9 KD137 . . . . **629.45**

Vocational guidance--Agriculture.
KAPLAN, A/Careers for outdoor types. /1991/
4-A/8 KA952 . . . . **333.7**

Vocational guidance--Computers.
KAPLAN, A/Careers for computer buffs. /1991/5-6/9 KA567. **004**

Vocational guidance--Data processing.
KAPLAN, A/Careers for computer buffs. /1991/5-6/9 KA567. **004**

Vocational guidance--Farming.
ANDERSON, J/American family farm. /1989/
5-6/8 KD145 . . . . **630.973**

Vocational guidance--Graphic arts.
SO YOU WANT TO BE?: NEWSPAPER ARTIST
(VIDEOCASSETTE). /1994/5-6/KA595 . . . . **VCR 070.4**

Vocational guidance--Journalism.
KAPLAN, A/Careers for wordsmiths. /1991/6-A/7 KA593 . . **070.4**
SO YOU WANT TO BE?: NEWSPAPER ARTIST
(VIDEOCASSETTE). /1994/5-6/KA595 . . . . **VCR 070.4**

Vocational guidance--Law.
SO YOU WANT TO BE?: JUDGE (VIDEOCASSETTE). /1994/
5-6/KA977 . . . . **VCR 347**

Vocational guidance--Outdoor recreation.
KAPLAN, A/Careers for outdoor types. /1991/
4-A/8 KA952 . . . . **333.7**

Vocational guidance--Reporters and reporting.
KAPLAN, A/Careers for wordsmiths. /1991/6-A/7 KA593 . . **070.4**

Voice SEE ALSO Respiration; Singing; Speech.
Volcanoes.
LAMPTON, C/Volcano. /1991/4-6/7 KC157 . . . . **551.21**
LAUBER, P/Volcano: the eruption and healing of Mount St. Helens.
/1986/P-A/6 KC158 . . . . **CE 551.21**
SIMON, S/Volcanoes. /1988/3-6/6 KC159 . . . . **551.21**
STV: RESTLESS EARTH (VIDEODISC). /1992/
4-A/KC150 . . . . **VD 550**
VAN ROSE, S/Volcano and earthquake. /1992/
3-6/7 KC160 . . . . **551.21**

Voting SEE ALSO Elections; Women--Suffrage.
Voting.
MAESTRO, B/Voice of the people: American democracy in action. /
1996/4-6/8 KA915 . . . . **324.973**
PASCOE, E/Right to vote. /1997/4-6/12 KA910 . . . . **324.6**

Voting--Fiction.
MITCHELL, MK/Granddaddy's gift. /1997/1-3/2 KG146 . . . . . . **E**

SISULU, E/Day Gogo went to vote: South Africa, April 1994. /
  1996/1-3/2 KG513 . . . . **E**
Voyager (Airplane).
  ROZAKIS, L/Dick Rutan and Jeana Yeager: flying non-stop around
  the world. /1994/5-6/6 KD099 . . . . **629.13**
Voyager Project.
  APFEL, NH/Voyager to the planets. /1991/3-6/7 KC022 . . . **523.4**
  BURROWS, WE/Mission to deep space: Voyagers' journey of
  discovery. /1993/4-8/11 KC024 . . . . **523.4**
  HARRIS, AW/Great Voyager adventure: a guided tour through the
  solar system. /1990/A/9 KC026 . . . . **523.4**
  RIDE, S/Voyager: an adventure to the edge of the solar system. /
  1992/3-6/7 KC030 . . . . **523.4**
Voyages and travels SEE ALSO Adventure and adventurers; Discoveries (in
  geography); Explorers; Overland journeys to the Pacific; Seamen;
  Shipwrecks; Space flight; Travel; Whaling.
Voyages and travels.
  BLOS, JW/Heroine of the Titanic: a tale both true and otherwise of
  the life of Molly /1991/5-6/6 KE265 . . . . **B BROWN, M.**
  KRUPP, RR/Let's go traveling. /1992/3-5/4 KE155 . . . . **910.4**
  LASKY, K/Searching for Laura Ingalls: a reader's journey. /1993/
  3-6/6 KE198 . . . . **917.8**
  O'DELL, S/Cruise of the Arctic Star. /c1973/5-6/6 KE208 . **917.94**
Voyages and travels--Fiction.
  BLACKSTONE, S/Grandma went to market: a round-the-world
  counting rhyme. /1996/1-3/5 KF232 . . . . **E**
  BLOS, JW/Nellie Bly's monkey: his remarkable story in his own
  words. /1996/2-5/9 KF236 . . . . **E**
  HENEGHAN, J/Wish me luck. /1997/6-A/5 KH237 . . . . **Fic**
  MCPHAIL, D/Pigs ahoy! /1995/P-2/3 KG121 . . . . **E**
  PENE DU BOIS, W/Twenty-one balloons. /c1947/
  4-6/7 KH595 . . . . **CE Fic**
  PRICEMAN, M/How to make an apple pie and see the world. /
  1994/K-2/3 KG288 . . . . **E**
  SAY, A/Grandfather's journey. /1993/2-4/5 KG397 . . . . **E**
  STEIG, W/Dominic. /c1972/4-6/7 KH750 . . . . **Fic**
  WILD, M/Going home. /1993/1-3/3 KG716 . . . . **E**
Vultures SEE ALSO Birds of prey.
Waka.
  LIVINGSTON, MC/Cricket never does: a collection of haiku and
  tanka. /1997/3-6/KD975 . . . . **811**
Waldorf method of education.
  CHILD'S SEASONAL TREASURY. /1996//KA193 . . **PROF 372.13**
Wales--Fiction.
  BAWDEN, N/Carrie's war. /c1973/4-6/4 KG887 . . . . **Fic**
  NIMMO, J/Griffin's castle. /1997/6-A/5 KH551 . . . . **Fic**
Walker, C.J., Madam.
  COLMAN, P/Madam C.J. Walker: building a business empire. /
  1994/4-6/7 KE583 . . . . **B WALKER, C.J.**
  MADAM C.J. WALKER (VIDEOCASSETTE). /1992/
  5-A/KE584. . . . . **VCR B WALKER, C.J.**
Walking--Fiction.
  SIS, P/Waving: a counting book. /1988/P-2/KG512 . . . . **E**
  WILLIAMS, S/I went walking. /1990/P-1/1 KG732 . . . . . . **CE E**
Walruses.
  DARLING, K/Walrus: on location. /1991/5-6/6 KC868 . . . **599.79**
  ROTTER, C/Walruses. /1993/3-5/3 KC871 . . . . **599.79**
  SEA ANIMALS ASHORE (VIDEOCASSETTE). /1996/
  3-6/KC872. . . . . **VCR 599.79**
Walt Disney Company.
  HAHN, D/Animation magic: a behind-the-scenes look at how an
  animated film is made. /1996/4-6/9 KD685 . . . . **791.43**
  PEET, B/Bill Peet: an autobiography. /1989/
  6-A/8 KE494 . . . . **B PEET, B.**
Wampanoag Indians.
  SEWALL, M/People of the breaking day. /1990/
  3-6/5 KA858 . . . . **305.8**
  WATERS, K/Tapenum's day: a Wampanoag Indian boy in pilgrim
  times. /1996/3-5/2 KE950 . . . . **974.4**
Wampanoag Indians--Folklore.
  MEDICINE STORY /Children of the Morning Light: Wampanoag
  tales. /1994/4-5/7 KB348 . . . . **398.2**
Wampanoag Indians--History.
  SEWALL, M/Thunder from the clear sky. /1995/
  4-6/7 KE874 . . . . **973.2**
Wampanoag Indians--Religion and mythology.
  MEDICINE STORY /Children of the Morning Light: Wampanoag
  tales. /1994/4-5/7 KB348 . . . . **398.2**
Wampanoag Indians--Rites and ceremonies.
  PETERS, RM/Clambake: a Wampanoag tradition. /1992/
  4-6/5 KE780 . . . . **970.444**
War--Fiction.
  LYON, GE/Cecil's story. /1991/K-3/2 KG042 . . . . **E**
  SEUSS, D/Butter battle book. /1984/K-3/5 KG447 . . . . **E**

SKURZYNSKI, G/Virtual war. /1997/5-A/4 KH716 . . . . **Fic**
TURNER, P/War between the Vowels and the Consonants. /1996/
  1-3/3 KG630 . . . . **E**
War--Folklore.
  MACDONALD, MR/Peace tales: world folktales to talk about. /
  1992//KA271 . . . . **PROF 398.2**
War--Poetry.
  GRANFIELD, L/In Flanders Fields: the story of the poem by John
  McCrae. /1995/4-6/7 KD947 . . . . **811**
Warsaw (Poland)--Fiction.
  ORLEV, U/Island on Bird Street. /1983/5-A/6 KH566 . . . . . . **Fic**
  SERRAILLIER, I/Silver sword. /c1959/5-6/6 KH699 . . . . **Fic**
Warthog.
  ROTHAUS, D/Warthogs. /1995/4-6/8 KC787 . . . . **599.63**
Washakie, Shoshoni Chief.
  FREEDMAN, R/Indian chiefs. /1987/5-6/8 KE749 . . . . **970.1**
Washington, Booker T.
  BOOKER (VIDEOCASSETTE). /1983/
  3-6/KE585. . . . . **VCR B WASHINGTON, B**
  ROBERTS, J/Booker T. Washington: educator and leader. /1995/
  4-6/5 KE586 . . . . **B WASHINGTON, B**
Washington, Booker T.--Fiction.
  BRADBY, M/More than anything else. /1995/1-3/3 KF256 . . . . . **E**
Washington, George.
  ADLER, DA/George Washington: father of our country. /1988/
  4-5/6 KE587 . . . . **B WASHINGTON, G**
  GEORGE WASHINGTON: THE FIRST (VIDEOCASSETTE). /1990/
  6-A/KE588. . . . . **VCR B WASHINGTON, G**
  MOUNT VERNON: HOME OF GEORGE WASHINGTON
  (VIDEOCASSETTE). /1989/4-6/KE980 . . . . **VCR 975.5**
Washington (D.C.).
  CLIMO, S/City! Washington, D.C. /1991/4-6/7 KE193 . . . **917.53**
  JOHNSTON, J/Washington, D.C. /1993/4-6/7 KE971 . . . . **975.3**
  MIDDLE ATLANTIC REGION: NEW YORK, NEW JERSEY,
  DELAWARE, MARYLAND, PENNSYLVANIA, /1996/
  4-6/KE924 . . . . **VCR 974**
Washington (D.C.)--Buildings, structures, etc.
  QUIRI, PR/White House. /1996/4-6/10 KE972 . . . . **975.3**
Washington (D.C.)--Guides.
  STEINS, R/Our national capital. /1994/4-6/9 KE973 . . . . . **975.3**
Washington (D.C.)--History.
  STEINS, R/Our national capital. /1994/4-6/9 KE973 . . . . . **975.3**
Washington (State).
  FRADIN, DB/Washington. /1994/4-6/4 KF093 . . . . **979.7**
  POWELL, ES/Washington. /1993/4-6/6 KF094 . . . . **979.7**
Washington (State)--History.
  COCKE, W/Historical album of Washington. /1995/
  4-6/7 KF092 . . . . **979.7**
Wasps.
  JOHNSON, SA/Wasps. /1984/5-6/8 KC574 . . . . **595.79**
Waste products SEE ALSO Refuse and refuse disposal; Hazardous waste;
Toxins.
Water SEE ALSO Drinking water; Floods; Glaciers; Lakes; Ocean; Rain and
rainfall; Rivers; Snow.
Water.
  BRANDT, K/What makes it rain? The story of a raindrop. /1982/
  P-K/2 KC209 . . . . **551.57**
  FOWLER, A/It could still be water. /1992/P-2/2 KC231 . . . **553.7**
  HATHORN, L/Wonder thing. /1996/P-2/KC181 . . . . **551.48**
  HOFF, MK/Our endangered planet: rivers and lakes. /1991/
  5-6/8 KB062 . . . . **363.73**
  HOFFMAN, M/Earth, fire, water, air. /1995/2-6/7 KA814 . **304.2**
  OUR WATERY WORLD (VIDEOCASSETTE). /1991/
  3-5/KB064 . . . . **VCR 363.73**
  WALKER, SM/Water up, water down: the hydrologic cycle. /1992/
  4-6/7 KC184 . . . . **551.48**
  WALPOLE, B/Water. /1990/K-2/5 KC141 . . . . **546**
  WICK, W/Drop of water: a book of science and wonder. /1997/
  K-6/6 KC142 . . . . **546**
Water--Experiments.
  ARDLEY, N/Science book of water. /1991/2-4/4 KC091 . . . **531**
  MURPHY, B/Experiment with water. /1991/K-3/4 KC101 . . . . **532**
  RYBOLT, TR/Environmental experiments about water. /1993/
  5-6/7 KB066 . . . . **363.73**
  WALPOLE, B/Water. /1990/K-2/5 KC141 . . . . **546**
  WATER ROCKETS I (VIDEOCASSETTE). /1994/
  5-A/KA291 . . . . **VCR PROF 530**
  WICK, W/Drop of water: a book of science and wonder. /1997/
  K-6/6 KC142 . . . . **546**
Water--Fiction.
  SCHMID, E/Water's journey. /1989/2-4/7 KG408 . . . . **E**
Water--Poetry.
  YOLEN, J/Water music: poems for children. /1995/
  2-6/KE051. . . . . **811**

Water--Pollution.
  CHERRY, L/River ran wild: an environmental history. /1992/
  4-6/6 KE937 . . . . **974.4**
  FRESH WATER: RESOURCE AT RISK (VIDEOCASSETTE). /1993/
  6-A/KB060. . . . . **VCR 363.73**
  HOFF, MK/Our endangered planet: rivers and lakes. /1991/
  5-6/8 KB062 . . . . **363.73**
  OUR WATERY WORLD (VIDEOCASSETTE). /1991/
  3-5/KB064. . . . . **VCR 363.73**
  SOURCE OF LIFE?: WATER IN OUR ENVIRONMENT
  (VIDEOCASSETTE). /1992/4-6/KB068 . . . . **VCR 363.73**
Water--Pollution--Experiments.
  RYBOLT, TR/Environmental experiments about water. /1993/
  5-6/7 KB066 . . . . **363.73**
Water--Pollution--Hudson River (N.Y. and N.J.).
  ANCONA, G/Riverkeeper. /1990/4-6/7 KA958 . . . . **333.91**
Water--Purification--Experiments.
  RYBOLT, TR/Environmental experiments about water. /1993/
  5-6/7 KB066 . . . . **363.73**
Water, Underground.
  HOFF, MK/Our endangered planet: groundwater. /1991/
  5-6/8 KA959 . . . . **333.91**
Water birds.
  ARNOSKY, J/Watching water birds. /1997/
  4-6/6 KC674 . . . . **598.176**
  BROWN, MB/Wings along the waterway. /1992/
  5-6/6 KC675 . . . . **598.176**
Water in art.
  MCHUGH, C/Water. /1993/4-A/7 KD375 . . . . **704.9**
Water quality management.
  FRESH WATER: RESOURCE AT RISK (VIDEOCASSETTE). /1993/
  6-A/KB060. . . . . **VCR 363.73**
Water skiing.
  WALKER, C/Waterskiing and kneeboarding. /1992/
  4-A/7 KD851 . . . . **797.3**
Water supply.
  FRESH WATER: RESOURCE AT RISK (VIDEOCASSETTE). /1993/
  6-A/KB060. . . . . **VCR 363.73**
  SOURCE OF LIFE?: WATER IN OUR ENVIRONMENT
  (VIDEOCASSETTE). /1992/4-6/KB068 . . . . **VCR 363.73**
Water treatment plants.
  COLE, J/Magic School Bus at the waterworks. /1986/
  2-3/4 KD079 . . . . **628.1**
  PUBLIC WORKS (VIDEOCASSETTE). /1992/
  2-4/KB055. . . . . **VCR 363.72**
Watermelons--Fiction.
  APPELT, K/Watermelon Day. /1996/K-2/2 KF164 . . . . **E**
Watkins, Yoko Kawashima--Fiction.
  WATKINS, YK/My brother, my sister, and I. /1994/
  A/4 KH841 . . . . **Fic**
    So far from the bamboo grove. /c1986, 1994/5-A/5 KH842 . **Fic**
Watson, Lyall--Childhood and youth.
  WATSON, L/Warriors, warthogs, and wisdom: growing up in
  Africa. /1997/4-6/7 KE589. . . . . **B WATSON, L.**
Waves SEE Light; Sound waves.
Waves--Experiments.
  ZUBROWSKI, B/Making waves: finding out about rhythmic motion.
  /1994/5-A/7 KC081 . . . . **530**
Wealth--Fiction.
  HAYES, J/Spoon for every bite. /1996/2-4/4 KF684 . . . . **E**
Weapons SEE Arms and armour; Firearms.
Weapons.
  MELTZER, M/Weapons and warfare: from the stone age to the
  space age. /1996/4-6/8 KA983. . . . . **355.02**
Weasels--Fiction.
  ERNST, LC/Zinnia and Dot. /1992/P-1/2 KF535 . . . . **E**
  LOBEL, A/Mouse soup. /c1977/K-2/1 KG007 . . . . **CE E**
  MOUSE SOUP (VIDEOCASSETTE). /1992/K-2/KG161 . . . **VCR E**
  SEIDLER, T/Wainscott weasel. /1993/4-6/5 KH691 . . . . **Fic**
Weather SEE ALSO Climate; Meteorology; Rain and rainfall; Snow; Storms;
  Winds.
Weather.
  ATMOSPHERE: ON THE AIR (VIDEOCASSETTE). /1993/
  5-6/KC186. . . . . **VCR 551.5**
  BERGER, M/How's the weather?: a look at weather and how it
  changes. /1993/K-5/2 KC187 . . . . **551.5**
  CASEY, D/Weather everywhere. /1995/P-2/6 KC189 . . . . . **551.5**
  COLE, J/Magic School Bus inside a hurricane. /1995/
  2-4/4 KC197 . . . . **551.55**
  COOPER, K/Too many rabbits and other fingerplays about animals,
  nature, weather, and the /1995/P-1/KD707 . . . . **793.4**
  DAY, JA/Peterson first guide to clouds and weather. /1991/
  3-6/A KC211 . . . . **551.57**

DICKINSON, T/Exploring the sky by day: the equinox guide to
  weather and the atmosphere. /1988/3-A/7 KC217 . . . . . **551.6**
  HISCOCK, B/Big storm. /1993/4-6/6 KC198 . . . . **551.55**
  KAHL, JD/Weatherwise: learning about the weather. /1992/
  4-6/6 KC219 . . . . **551.6**
    Wet weather: rain showers and snowfall. /1992/
  4-6/7 KC212 . . . . **551.57**
  MCMILLAN, B/Weather sky. /1991/5-A/7 KC220 . . . . **551.6**
  PLUCKROSE, H/Weather. /1994/P-2/4 KC192 . . . . **551.5**
  ROGERS, P/What will the weather be like today? /1990/
  P-1/2 KC221 . . . . **551.6**
  SIMON, S/Weather. /1993/3-6/7 KC193 . . . . **551.5**
  TELLING THE WEATHER (VIDEOCASSETTE). /1996/
  4-6/KC194. . . . . **VCR 551.5**
  WYATT, V/Weather watch. /1990/3-6/6 KC222 . . . . **551.6**
  3-2-1 CONTACT: EXPLORING WEATHER, CLIMATE AND
  SEASONS (VIDEOCASSETTE). /1988/2-A/KC223 . . **VCR 551.6**
Weather--Bibliography.
  PERRY, PJ/World's regions and weather: linking fiction to nonfiction.
  /1996//KA294. . . . . **PROF 551.6**
Weather--Experiments.
  ARDLEY, N/Science book of weather. /1992/K-3/3 KC185 . **551.5**
Weather--Fiction.
  BARRETT, J/Cloudy with a chance of meatballs. /1978/
  P-2/7 KF203 . . . . **E**
  BELLAIRS, J/Dark secret of Weatherend. /c1984/
  6-A/6 KG895 . . . . **Fic**
Weather--Miscellanea.
  LOCKHART, G/Weather companion. /1988//KA293 . **PROF 551.5**
Weather--Poetry.
  HOPKINS, LB/Weather: poems. /1994/K-3/KE064 . . . . . **811.008**
Weather--Study and teaching.
  PERRY, PJ/World's regions and weather: linking fiction to nonfiction.
  /1996//KA294. . . . . **PROF 551.6**
Weather--Terminology.
  GIBBONS, G/Weather words and what they mean. /1990/
  K-4/4 KC218 . . . . **551.6**
Weather forecasting.
  GIBBONS, G/Weather forecasting. /1987/2-4/7 KC224 . . **551.63**
  TELLING THE WEATHER (VIDEOCASSETTE). /1996/
  4-6/KC194. . . . . **VCR 551.5**
Weather vanes--Folklore.
  ADA, AF/Mediopollito/Half-Chicken. /1995/K-2/2 KB521 . **398.24**
Weaving--Fiction.
  BLOOD, CL/Goat in the rug. /1990/K-3/6 KF234 . . . . **E**
Weaving--Folklore.
  OUGHTON, J/Magic weaver of rugs: a tale of the Navajo. /1994/
  2-4/3 KB627 . . . . **398.24**
Webb, Sheyann.
  WEBB, S/Selma, Lord, Selma: girlhood memories of the civil-rights
  days. /c1980, 1997/A/7 KA906 . . . . **323.1**
Webb, Spud.
  JENNINGS, J/Long shots: they beat the odds. /1990/
  5-6/6 KD762 . . . . **796**
Webber, Chris.
  KNAPP, R/Chris Webber: star forward. /1997/
  5-6/7 KE590 . . . . **B WEBBER, C.**
Weddings--Fiction.
  HEINE, H/Pigs' wedding. /c1978, 1986/P-2/6 KF697 . . . . . **CE E**
  SOTO, G/Snapshots from the wedding. /1997/K-2/2 KG529 . . . **E**
  VAN LAAN, N/Boda: a Mexican wedding celebration. /1996/
  1-3/2 KG641 . . . . **E**
  WRIGHT, CC/Jumping the broom. /1994/K-3/5 KG771 . . . . . . **E**
Weight control SEE ALSO Diet.
Weight control--Fiction.
  BLUME, J/Blubber. /1974/4-6/3 KG906. . . . . **Fic**
Weightlessness.
  SKURZYNSKI, G/Zero gravity. /1994/3-6/5 KC100 . . . . **531**
Weightlessness--Experiments.
  SUMNERS, C/Toys in space: exploring science with the astronauts.
  /1997//KA282. . . . . **PROF 500.5**
Weights and measures SEE ALSO Measurements; Metric system.
Weights and measures--Fiction.
  ENDERLE, JR/What would Mama do? /1995/K-2/2 KF526 . . . . **E**
Wells, Randall S.
  PRINGLE, LP/Dolphin man: exploring the world of dolphins. /1995/
  5-6/11 KC776 . . . . **599.5**
Werewolves.
  PIPE, J/In the footsteps of the werewolf. /1996/
  4-6/7 KB635 . . . . **398.24**
West (U.S.)--Biography.
  BLACK WEST (VIDEOCASSETTE). /1992/5-6/KF028 . . **VCR 978**
  FABER, D/Calamity Jane: her life and her legend. /1992/
  4-6/8 KE274 . . . . **B CALAMITY JANE**

MILLER, RH/Cowboys. /1991/4-6/6 KF039. . . . . **978**
ROBISON, N/Buffalo Bill. /1991/5-6/6 KE267 . **B BUFFALO BILL**
SANFORD, WR/Kit Carson: frontier scout. /1996/
5-6/7 KE277 . . . . **B CARSON, K.**
SCHLISSEL, L/Black frontiers: a history of African American heroes
in the Old West. /1995/4-6/8 KF048 . . . . **978**

West (U.S.)--Description and travel--Guides.
AMERICA'S WESTERN NATIONAL PARKS (VIDEOCASSETTE). /
1990/4-6/KE200. . . . . **VCR 917.804**

West (U.S.)--Description and travel--To 1848.
STEWART, GR/Pioneers go west. /c1982, 1997/
4-6/7 KF051 . . . . **978**

West (U.S.)--Discovery and exploration.
ACROSS THE SEA OF GRASS (VIDEOCASSETTE). /1991/
A/KF024. . . . . **VCR 978**
HERB, AM/Beyond the Mississippi: early westward expansion of the
United States. /1996/4-6/10 KF032 . . . . **978**
KROLL, S/Lewis and Clark: explorers of the American West. /1994/
4-6/6 KE203 . . . . **917.804**
LEWIS AND CLARK EXPEDITION (VIDEOCASSETTE). /1992/
5-6/KE204. . . . . **VCR 917.804**
SANFORD, WR/Zebulon Pike: explorer of the Southwest. /1996/
5-6/8 KE497. . . . . **B PIKE, Z.**
STEFOFF, R/Lewis and Clark. /1992/5-6/5 KE206 . . . . . **917.804**

West (U.S.)--Fiction.
ANTLE, N/Sam's Wild West Show. /1995/1-3/2 KF161 . . . . . . **E**
BLANC, ES/Berchick. /1989/3-5/5 KG901 . . . . **Fic**
BYARS, BC/Golly sisters go West. /1986/1-3/1 KF325 . . . . **CE E**
DENSLOW, SP/On the trail with Miss Pace. /1995/
1-3/2 KF461 . . . . **E**
FLEISCHMAN, S/Ghost on Saturday night. /1997/
3-5/4 KH122 . . . . **Fic**
Jim Ugly. /1992/4-A/6 KH123. . . . . **Fic**
GIFALDI, D/Gregory, Maw, and the Mean One. /1992/
5-A/7 KH163 . . . . **Fic**
HARVEY, B/Cassie's journey: going West in the 1860s. /1988/
1-3/5 KF677. . . . . **E**
My prairie Christmas. /1990/2-4/4 KH222 . . . . **Fic**
HOLLAND, I/Journey home. /1993/6-A/6 KH270. . . . . **Fic**
HOOKER, R/Matthew the cowboy. /1990/K-2/2 KF767 . . . . . . **E**
JOHNSTON, T/Cowboy and the black-eyed pea. /1992/
K-2/5 KF839. . . . . **E**
LIGHTFOOT, DJ/Trail fever: the life of a Texas cowboy. /1992/
4-6/5 KH406 . . . . **Fic**
MACLACHLAN, P/Three Names. /1991/2-3/5 KG055 . . . . **E**
MCCLUNG, RM/Hugh Glass, mountain man. /1993/
6-A/7 KH472. . . . . **Fic**
MYERS, WD/Righteous revenge of Artemis Bonner. /1994/
5-A/7 KH523. . . . . **Fic**
PAULSEN, G/Call me Francis Tucket. /1995/5-A/5 KH585. . . . **Fic**
Mr. Tucket. /1994/5-A/5 KH588 . . . . **Fic**
RATZ DE TAGYOS, P/Showdown at Lonesome Pellet. /1994/
1-4/5 KH621 . . . . **Fic**
SCOTT, AH/One good horse: a cowpuncher's counting book. /
1990/K-2/2 KG424. . . . . **E**
SHARMAT, MW/Gila monsters meet you at the airport. /1980/
K-2/2 KG480. . . . . **E**
SHUB, E/White stallion. /1982/1-3/2 KG497 . . . . **E**
STANLEY, D/Saving Sweetness. /1996/1-3/4 KG538 . . . . **E**
WILLIAMS, VB/Stringbean's trip to the shining sea. /1988/
K-A/2 KG739. . . . . **E**

West (U.S.)--History.
FREEDMAN, R/Children of the wild west. /1983/
4-6/8 KA824 . . . . **305.23**
HARNESS, C/They're off!: the story of the Pony Express. /1996/
2-5/8 KB129 . . . . **383**
HILTON, S/Miners, merchants, and maids. /1995/
4-6/8 KF033 . . . . **978**
HOMESTEADING: 70 YEARS ON THE GREAT PLAINS, 1862-1932
(VIDEOCASSETTE). /1992/4-6/KF034 . . . . **VCR 978**
INTO THE SHINING MOUNTAINS (VIDEOCASSETTE). /1991/
A/KF035. . . . . **VCR 978**
KROLL, S/Pony Express! /1996/4-6/6 KB130 . . . . **383**
MURPHY, VR/Across the plains in the Donner Party. /1996/
5-6/7 KF041 . . . . **978**
RITCHIE, D/Frontier life. /1996/5-6/9 KF045. . . . . **978**
STEFOFF, R/Children of the westward trail. /1996/
4-6/KF050 . . . . **978**
WUKOVITS, JF/Jesse James. /1997/4-6/10 KE402 . **B JAMES, J.**

West (U.S.)--History--Pictorial works.
AMERICAN HISTORY: GROWING PAINS (PICTURE). /c1974/
4-6/KE912. . . . . **PIC 973.8**

West (U.S.)--History--Songs and music.
COWBOY SONGS (SOUND RECORDING CASSETTE). /1992/
4-A/KD560 . . . . **SRC 789.2**

West (U.S.)--History--To 1848.
HERB, AM/Beyond the Mississippi: early westward expansion of the
United States. /1996/4-6/10 KF032 . . . . **978**

West (U.S.)--History--1848-1860.
PATENT, DH/West by covered wagon: retracing the pioneer trails.
/1995/2-4/8 KF043 . . . . **978**

West (U.S.)--History--1860-1890.
WRIGHT, CC/Wagon train: a family goes West in 1865. /1995/
4-6/3 KF052 . . . . **978**

West (U.S.)--Social life and customs.
BIAL, R/Frontier home. /1993/4-6/8 KF027. . . . . **978**
BLACK WEST (VIDEOCASSETTE). /1992/5-6/KF028 . . **VCR 978**
FREEDMAN, R/Children of the wild west. /1983/
4-6/8 KA824 . . . . **305.23**
Cowboys of the wild west. /1985/5-A/7 KF029. . . . . **978**
GREENWOOD, B/Pioneer sampler: the daily life of a pioneer family
in 1840. /1995/4-6/6 KF031 . . . . **978**
MILLER, RH/Cowboys. /1991/4-6/6 KF039. . . . . **978**
SCOTT, AH/Cowboy country. /1993/3-6/3 KF049 . . . . **978**

West (U.S.)--Songs and music.
HORSE SENSE FOR KIDS AND OTHER PEOPLE (SOUND
RECORDING CASSETTE). /1992/2-4/KD668. . . . . . **SRC 789.4**

West (U.S.) in art.
WINTER, J/Cowboy Charlie: the story of Charles M. Russell. /
1995/2-5/5 KE528 . . . . **B RUSSELL, C.**

West Africa SEE Africa, West.
West Indies SEE ALSO Caribbean area.

West Indies--Fiction.
RAHAMAN, V/O Christmas tree. /1996/1-3/4 KG298 . . . . . . **E**

West Indies--Folklore.
BRYAN, A/Turtle knows your name. /1989/K-3/6 KB545. . **398.24**

West Virginia.
FRADIN, DB/West Virginia. /1994/4-6/7 KE975 . . . . **975.4**

West Virginia--Fiction.
NAYLOR, PR/Saving Shiloh. /1997/4-A/4 KH537 . . . . **Fic**
Shiloh. /1991/4-6/6 KH538. . . . . **CE Fic**
Shiloh season. /1996/4-A/4 KH539. . . . . **Fic**
RYLANT, C/Missing May. /1992/5-A/7 KH663 . . . . **Fic**

West Virginia--Social life and customs.
ANDERSON, J/Pioneer children of Appalachia. /1986/
4-6/6 KE974 . . . . **975.4**

Westinghouse, George.
NOONAN, J/Nineteenth-century inventors. /1992/
5-6/7 KC897 . . . . **609**

Wetland ecology.
LIPTAK, K/Saving our wetlands and their wildlife. /1991/
4-6/8 KA960 . . . . **333.91**
LUENN, N/Squish!: a wetland walk. /1994/P-2/3 KC342. . **577.68**
OUR WONDERFUL WETLANDS (VIDEOCASSETTE). /1993/
4-6/KC344. . . . . **VCR 577.68**

Wetlands.
LIPTAK, K/Saving our wetlands and their wildlife. /1991/
4-6/8 KA960 . . . . **333.91**
LUENN, N/Squish!: a wetland walk. /1994/P-2/3 KC342. . **577.68**
OUR WONDERFUL WETLANDS (VIDEOCASSETTE). /1993/
4-6/KC344. . . . . **VCR 577.68**

Whales SEE ALSO names of specific species e.g. Humpback whales.
Whales.
ARNOLD, C/Killer whale. /1994/4-6/7 KC764. . . . . **599.5**
AUDUBON SOCIETY FIELD GUIDE TO NORTH AMERICAN
FISHES, WHALES AND DOLPHINS. /1983/A/11 KC583 . . . **597**
BEHRENS, J/Whales of the world. /1987/3-5/4 KC765. . . . **599.5**
Whalewatch. /1978/2-4/4 KC766. . . . . **599.5**
CARRICK, C/Whaling days. /1993/4-5/6 KD243 . . . . **639.2**
DAVIES, N/Big blue whale. /1997/K-4/3 KC767 . . . . **599.5**
ESBENSEN, BJ/Baby whales drink milk. /1994/
1-3/2 KC768 . . . . **599.5**
GIBBONS, G/Whales. /1991/K-4/3 KC769 . . . . **599.5**
KIM, M/Blue whale. /1993/3-5/7 KC772 . . . . **599.5**
LAUBER, P/Great whales: the gentle giants. /1993/
4-5/4 KC773 . . . . **599.5**
MILTON, J/Whales: the gentle giants. /1989/1-3/2 KC774 . **599.5**
PATENT, DH/Killer whales. /1993/4-6/6 KC775. . . . . . . **599.5**
SIMON, S/Whales. /1989/5-6/6 KC777. . . . . **599.51**

Whales--Arctic regions.
KALMAN, B/Arctic whales and whaling. /1988/
5-6/6 KC771 . . . . **599.5**

Whales--Fiction.
ESTERL, A/Okino and the whales. /1995/3-5/3 KH101 . . . . . **Fic**
LEWIS, PO/Davy's dream. /1988/1-3/3 KF977 . . . . **E**

Whales--Folklore.
MCCLOSKEY, R/Burt Dow, deep-water man: a tale of the sea in the classic tradition. /c1963/P-A/6 KH468. . . . . **CE Fic**
STEIG, W/Amos and Boris. /c1971/1-3/7 KG540 . . . . **CE E**

Whales--Folklore.
LEWIS, PO/Storm boy. /1995/2-4/3 KB610 . . . . **398.24**

Whales--Software.
IN THE COMPANY OF WHALES (CD-ROM). /1993/
3-A/KC770 . . . . **CDR 599.5**

Whaling.
CARRICK, C/Whaling days. /1993/4-5/6 KD243 . . . . . . **639.2**
STANLEY, D/True adventure of Daniel Hall. /1995/
2-5/7 KE159 . . . . **910.4**

Whaling--Arctic regions.
KALMAN, B/Arctic whales and whaling. /1988/
5-6/6 KC771 . . . . **599.5**

Whaling--Arctic regions--History.
KALMAN, B/Arctic whales and whaling. /1988/
5-6/6 KC771 . . . . **599.5**

Whaling--Fiction.
HOLLING, HC/Seabird. /c1948/5-6/5 KH272 . . . . **Fic**

Wheat.
JOHNSON, SA/Wheat. /1990/5-6/7 KD151 . . . . **633.1**

Wheatley, Phillis.
SHERROW, V/Phillis Wheatley. /1992/
4-6/7 KE591 . . . . **B WHEATLEY, P.**

Wheels.
ROTNER, S/Wheels around. /1995/P-2/3 KD053 . . . . **621.8**

Wheels--Poetry.
ROLL ALONG: POEMS ON WHEELS. /1993/
4-A/KE080. . . . . **811.008**

Whistler, James.
BERMAN, A/James McNeil Whistler. /1993/
5-A/7 KE592 . . . . **B WHISTLER, J.**

Whistling--Fiction.
KEATS, EJ/Whistle for Willie. /c1964, 1977/P-2/3 KF880 . . **CE E**

White, E.B. (Elwyn Brooks).
GHERMAN, B/E.B. White: some writer! /1992/
6-A/8 KE593 . . . . **B WHITE, E.B.**

White, Ryan.
WHITE, R/Ryan White: my own story. /1991/
5-A/5 KE594 . . . . **B WHITE, R.**

White House (Washington, D.C.).
BLUE, R/White House kids. /1995/5-6/7 KE849 . . . . . . **973**
FISHER, LE/White House. /1989/5-6/8 KE970 . . . . **975.3**
LEINER, K/First children: growing up in the White House. /1996/
A/9 KE856 . . . . **973**
QUIRI, PR/White House. /1996/4-6/10 KE972 . . . . **975.3**

White-tailed deer.
BARE, CS/Never grab a deer by the ear. /1993/
4-5/5 KC795 . . . . **599.65**

White-water canoeing.
EVANS, J/Whitewater kayaking. /1992/4-A/7 KD845 . . . . **797.1**

Whooping cranes.
OWENS, MB/Counting cranes. /1993/P-4/3 KB976 . . . . . **513.2**
PATENT, DH/Whooping crane: a comeback story. /1988/
A/9 KD258 . . . . **639.9**

Wied, Maximilian, Prinz von--Journeys--Missouri River Valley.
FREEDMAN, R/Indian winter. /1992/A/9 KE202 . . . . . **917.804**

Wild animals as pets SEE Pets; also names of specific animals e.g. Snakes.

Wild animals as pets.
GEORGE, JC/Tarantula in my purse and 172 other wild pets. /
1996/4-6/4 KE366 . . . . **B GEORGE, J.**

Wild boar.
NICHOLSON, D/Wild boars. /1987/5-6/9 KC786 . . . . . . **599.63**

Wild flowers.
KELLY, MA/Child's book of wildflowers. /1992/
3-5/5 KC405 . . . . **582.13**
NIERING, WA/Audubon Society field guide to North American
wildflowers, Eastern Region. /1979/3-6/KC407 . . . . . . **582.13**
SPELLENBERG, R/Audubon Society field guide to North American
wildflowers, Western Region. /1979/3-6/KC408 . . . . . . **582.13**

Wild horse adoption.
ANCONA, G/Man and mustang. /1992/5-6/6 KD197 . . . . **636.1**

Wild horses.
HONDA, T/Wild horse winter. /1992/K-3/4 KC806 . . . . **599.665**
PATENT, DH/Where the wild horses roam. /1989/
5-6/7 KD257 . . . . **639.9**

Wild plants, Edible.
FORSYTH, A/How monkeys make chocolate: foods and medicines
from the rainforest. /1995/4-8/7 KC402 . . . . **581.6**

Wild rice--Harvesting.
REGGUINTI, G/Sacred harvest: Ojibway wild rice gathering. /
1992/4-6/6 KE785 . . . . **970.476**

Wild turkeys.
PATENT, DH/Wild turkey, tame turkey. /1989/
5-6/7 KC697 . . . . **598.6**
TURKEYS IN THE WILD (VIDEOCASSETTE). /1991/
4-6/KC699. **VCR 598.6**

Wilder, Laura Ingalls.
LASKY, K/Searching for Laura Ingalls: a reader's journey. /1993/
3-6/6 KE198 . . . . **917.8**
WADSWORTH, G/Laura Ingalls Wilder: storyteller of the prairie. /
1997/4-A/5 KE595 . . . . **B WILDER, L.**
WALKER, BM/Little House cookbook: frontier foods from Laura
Ingalls Wilder's classic. /1995/4-6/9 KD282 . . . . **641.5**

Wilder, Laura Ingalls--Correspondence.
DEAR LAURA: LETTERS FROM CHILDREN TO LAURA INGALLS
WILDER. /1996/3-6/KD893 . . . . **808.86**

Wilder, Laura Ingalls--Family--Fiction.
WILKES, MD/Little house in Brookfield. /1996/4-6/5 KH861. . . **Fic**

Wilder, Laura Ingalls--Fiction.
MACBRIDE, RL/Little house on Rocky Ridge. /1993/
4-6/6 KH436 . . . . **Fic**

Wilder, Laura Ingalls--Homes and haunts.
ANDERSON, W/Little House guidebook. /1996/
3-5/10 KE196 . . . . **917.8**

Wilderness areas--Fiction.
ECKERT, AW/Incident at Hawk's Hill. /1971/6-A/7 KH097. . . . **Fic**

Wilderness survival.
EVANS, J/Camping and survival. /1992/4-A/6 KD825 . . . **796.54**

Wilderness survival--Fiction.
GEORGE, JC/Julie of the wolves. /c1972/6-A/6 KH157 . . **CE Fic**
Julie of the wolves (Talking book). /1993/6-A/KH158. . . **TB Fic**
STEIG, W/Abel's island. /1976/4-6/6 KH749 . . . . **CE Fic**

Wilderness survival--Handbooks, manuals, etc.
MCMANNERS, H/Outdoor adventure handbook. /1996/
4-6/6 KD823 . . . . **796.5**

Wildfires.
CONE, P/Wildfire. /1997/4-A/6 KB040 . . . . **363.37**

Wildlife--Periodicals.
CHICKADEE: THE CANADIAN MAGAZINE FOR YOUNG
CHILDREN. /1979/-P-3/KA506 . . . . **PER 050**
OWL: THE DISCOVERY MAGAZINE FOR CHILDREN. /1976/
2-4/KA535 . . . . **PER 050**

Wildlife attracting.
FLEMING, D/Where once there was a wood. /1996/
1-4/3 KD253 . . . . **639.9**
JOHNSON, K/Worm's eye view: make your own wildlife refuge. /
1991/2-4/5 KC294 . . . . **577**

Wildlife conservation SEE ALSO Forest and forestry; Game and game
birds; National parks and reserves; Natural resources; Rare animals; Rare
and endangered species; Rare birds.

Wildlife conservation.
ANCONA, G/Man and mustang. /1992/5-6/6 KD197 . . . . **636.1**
ARNOLD, C/On the brink of extinction: the California condor. /
1993/5-6/8 KD251 . . . . **639.9**
BLASHFIELD, JF/Rescuing endangered species. /1994/
4-6/7 KA961 . . . . **333.95**
COWCHER, H/Tigress. /1991/1-3/6 KC827 . . . . **599.756**
ELEPHANT DIARY (VIDEOCASSETTE). /1990/
3-5/KC809. **VCR 599.67**
ENDANGERED SPECIES (VIDEOCASSETTE). /1991/
4-6/KC487 . . . . **VCR 591.68**
ENDANGERED WILDLIFE OF THE WORLD. /1993/
5-A/KA446 . . . . **REF 578.68**
FACKLAM, M/And then there was one: the mysteries of extinction.
/1990/5-6/7 KC488 . . . . **591.68**
FLEMING, D/Where once there was a wood. /1996/
1-4/3 KD253 . . . . **639.9**
HOFF, MK/Our endangered planet: life on land. /1992/
5-6/8 KA962 . . . . **333.95**
JONAS, A/Aardvarks, disembark! /1990/2-A/4 KA963. . . **333.95**
KIM, M/Mountain gorilla. /1993/4-5/8 KC875 . . . . . . **599.884**
KOCH, M/World water watch. /1993/K-2/4 KD255 . . . . **639.9**
MAYNARD, T/Rhino comes to America. /1993/
5-6/7 KC802 . . . . **599.66**
Saving endangered mammals: a field guide to some of the earth's
rarest animals. /1992/5-6/8 KC489 . . . . **591.68**
MOUNTAIN GORILLAS: GENTLE GIANTS (VIDEOCASSETTE). /
1993/4-6/KC876 . . . . **VCR 599.884**
NIRGIOTIS, N/No more dodos: how zoos help endangered wildlife.
/1996/A/6 KD256 . . . . **639.9**
PATENT, DH/Gray wolf, red wolf. /1990/5-6/8 KC839 . **599.773**
Places of refuge: our national wildlife refuge system. /1992/
4-6/7 KA966 . . . . **333.95**
Way of the grizzly. /1987/5-6/8 KC860 . . . . **599.784**
Whooping crane: a comeback story. /1988/A/9 KD258 . . **639.9**

POLLOCK, S/Atlas of endangered animals. /1993/
5-6/7 KC491 . . . . **591.68**
TALKING ABOUT SEA TURTLES (VIDEOCASSETTE). /1992/
4-6/KC623. . . . . **VCR 597.92**
TRACQUI, V/Polar bear: master of the ice. /1994/
3-5/4 KC865 . . . . **599.786**

Wildlife conservation--Fiction.
HENRY, M/Mustang, wild spirit of the West. /c1966, 1992/
5-6/5 KH245 . . . . **Fic**
ORR, K/My grandpa and the sea. /1990/K-2/2 KG198 . . . **E**
PEET, B/Farewell to Shady Glade. /c1966/K-2/KG227 . . . . . . **E**

Wildlife conservation--Periodicals.
INTERNATIONAL WILDLIFE. /1971-/4-6/KA520 . . . **PER 050**
NATIONAL WILDLIFE. /1962-/A/KA532 . . . . . . **PER 050**
WILDLIFE CONSERVATION. /1897-/K-A/KA551 . . . . . **PER 050**

Wildlife conservation--Songs and music.
SKIERA-ZUCEK, L/Save the animals, save the earth: /1991/
K-4/KD658 . . . . **SRC 789.3**

Wildlife management.
PATENT, DH/Buffalo: the American Bison today. /1986/
5-6/8 KA965 . . . . **333.95**
Where the wild horses roam. /1989/5-6/7 KD257 . . . . . **639.9**

Wildlife refuges.
PATENT, DH/Places of refuge: our national wildlife refuge system. /
1992/4-6/7 KA966 . . . . **333.95**

Wildlife reintroduction.
BLASHFIELD, JF/Rescuing endangered species. /1994/
4-6/7 KA961 . . . . **333.95**
NIRGIOTIS, N/No more dodos: how zoos help endangered wildlife.
/1996/A/6 KD256 . . . . **639.9**

Wildlife rescue.
ARNOLD, C/Sea lion. /1994/4-6/6 KC867 . . . . **599.79**
CRICKET, TIGLET AND FRIENDS (VIDEOCASSETTE). /1984/
4-6/KC712. . . . . **VCR 598.9**
DEWEY, JO/Wildlife rescue: the work of Dr. Kathleen Ramsay. /
1994/4-6/7 KD252 . . . . **639.9**
ELEPHANT DIARY (VIDEOCASSETTE). /1990/
3-5/KC809. . . . . **VCR 599.67**

Wildlife rescue--Fiction.
CANNON, A/Bat in the boot. /1996/1-3/2 KF333. . . . . . . **E**
KELLER, H/Island baby. /1992/P-2/3 KF885 . . . . **E**
RAND, G/Prince William. /1992/2-3/4 KG300 . . . . **E**

Wildlife watching.
SELSAM, ME/Keep looking. /1989/P-3/2 KC728 . . . . **599**

Williams, Roger.
AVI /Finding Providence: the story of Roger Williams. /1997/
2-3/4 KE596 . . . . **B WILLIAMS, R.**

Williamsburg (Va.)--History.
KENT, Z/Williamsburg. /1992/4-6/5 KE871 . . . . **973.2**
STORY OF A PATRIOT (VIDEOCASSETTE). /1957/
4-6/KE888. . . . . **VCR 973.3**

Williamsburg (Va.)--Social life and customs.
GOOR, R/Williamsburg: cradle of the revolution. /1994/
5-A/7 KE978 . . . . **975.5**

Wilson, Woodrow.
OSINSKI, A/Woodrow Wilson: twenty-eighth President of the
United States. /1989/5-A/8 KE597. . . . . **B WILSON, W.**

Wind instruments.
TURNER, BC/Living clarinet. /1996/4-6/12 KD552 . . . . **BA 788.6**
Living flute. /1996/4-6/11 KD551 . . . . **BA 788.3**

Windigos.
ROSS, G/Legend of the Windigo: a tale from native North
America. /1996/2-3/6 KB410 . . . . **398.21**
Winds SEE ALSO Hurricanes; Storms; Tornadoes.

Winds.
DORROS, A/Feel the wind. /1989/P-2/2 KC190 . . . . **551.5**

Winds--Fiction.
CARLSTROM, NW/How does the wind walk? /1993/
P-2/3 KF354 . . . . **E**
ETS, MH/Gilberto and the wind. /c1963/P-1/2 KF536 . . . . **CE E**
MCKISSACK, P/Mirandy and Brother Wind. /1988/
1-3/6 KG107 . . . . **CE E**
SATHRE, V/Mouse chase. /1995/P-1/2 KG394 . . . . **E**

Wings.
CREAGH, C/Things with wings. /1996/4-6/5 KC445 . . . . . . **591**

Winning and losing--Fiction.
BLEDSOE, LJ/Big bike race. /1995/3-6/2 KG903 . . . . **Fic**

Winter.
BANCROFT, H/Animals in winter. Rev. ed. /1997/
K-2/2 KC482 . . . . **591.56**
DUNPHY, M/Here is the Arctic winter. /1993/
K-4/2 KC731 . . . . **599.17**
HONDA, T/Wild horse winter. /1992/K-3/4 KC806 . . . . **599.665**
KURELEK, W/Prairie boy's winter. /c1973/3-6/7 KE814. . **CE 971.2**

MAGICAL MOTHER NATURE: THE FOUR SEASONS
(VIDEOCASSETTE). /1989/2-4/KC061 . . . . **VCR 525**
SEASONS. REV. ED. (SOUND FILMSTRIP). /c1975, 1993/
K-2/KC063. . . . . **FSS 525**
SELSAM, ME/Keep looking. /1989/P-3/2 KC728. . . . . **599**
SIMON, S/Winter across America. /1994/4-6/6 KB920. . . . **508.2**
STOKES, DW/Guide to nature in winter, northeast and north central
North America. /c1976, 1979/6-A/8 KB921. . . . . **508.2**
WHERE DO ANIMALS GO IN WINTER? (VIDEOCASSETTE). /
1995/3-6/KC463 . . . . **VCR 591.4**
WINTER (VIDEOCASSETTE). /1994/2-5/KC669. . . . . . **VCR 598**

Winter--Fiction.
AGELL, C/I slide into the white of winter. /1994/K-2/3 KF137 . . **E**
CHRISTELOW, E/Five-dog night. /1993/1-3/3 KF386 . . . . **E**
CHRISTIANSEN, CB/Snowman on Sycamore Street. /1996/
2-3/2 KG989 . . . . **Fic**
EHLERT, L/Snowballs. /1995/P-2/2 KF520 . . . . **E**
FLEMING, D/Time to sleep. /1997/P-1/2 KF558 . . . . **E**
FLORIAN, D/Winter day. /1987/P-1/1 KF560 . . . . **E**
GEORGE, JC/Dear Rebecca, winter is here. /1993/
1-3/3 KF605 . . . . **E**
GEORGE, LB/In the snow: who's been here? /1995/
1-3/2 KF607 . . . . **E**
GUNDERSHEIMER, K/Happy winter. /1982/P-1/3 KF653 . . . . **E**
HASLER, E/Winter magic. /1989/K-3/4 KF678 . . . . **E**
LINDGREN, A/Tomten. /c1965, 1997/K-2/3 KF986 . . . . . . **CE E**
MEDEARIS, AS/Here comes the snow. /1996/K-1/2 KG126. . . . **E**
SHEA, PD/New moon. /1996/P-2/2 KG490 . . . . **E**
STOEKE, JM/Hat for Minerva Louise. /1994/P-K/2 KG576 . . . . **E**
WILLARD, N/Starlit somersault downhill. /1993/K-2/3 KG725 . . **E**

Winter--Poetry.
FROST, R/Stopping by the woods on a snowy evening. /1978/
P-A/KD941 . . . . **811**
PRELUTSKY, J/It's snowing! It's snowing! /1984/K-3/KE005 . . **811**

Winter--Songs.
MCCUTCHEON, J/John McCutcheon's four seasons: wintersongs
(Compact disc). /1995/K-3/KD638 . . . . **CD 789.3**

Winter Olympics.
SANDELSON, R/Ice sports. /1991/4-6/7 KD835 . . . . **796.9**

Winter solstice.
JACKSON, E/Winter solstice. /1994/3-5/6 KB211 . . . . . **394.261**

Winter sports.
SANDELSON, R/Ice sports. /1991/4-6/7 KD835 . . . . **796.9**

Wisconsin.
BRATVOLD, G/Wisconsin. /1991/4-6/7 KF019 . . . . **977.5**

Wisconsin--Fiction.
BRINK, CR/Caddie Woodlawn. New ed. /1973/
4-6/6 KG922 . . . . **CE Fic**
ENRIGHT, E/Thimble summer. /1966/4-6/6 KH100 . . . . . **CE Fic**
WILDER, LI/Dance at Grandpa's. /1994/K-3/4 KG719 . . . . . . **E**
Winter days in the Big Woods. /1994/K-3/4 KG720. . . . . . **E**
WILKES, MD/Little house in Brookfield. /1996/4-6/5 KH861. . . **Fic**

Wishes--Fiction.
BRITTAIN, B/Wish giver. /1983/3-6/7 KG925 . . . . **Fic**
BROWN, J/Stanley and the magic lamp. /1996/2-4/3 KG932 . **Fic**
DEXTER, C/Gertie's green thumb. /1995/3-5/4 KH073 . . . . . **Fic**
EGAN, T/Burnt toast on Davenport Street. /1997/1-3/2 KF514 . **E**
GERSHATOR, P/Rata-pata-scata-fata: a Caribbean story. /1994/
K-2/2 KF611 . . . . **E**
GRIFFITH, HV/Emily and the enchanted frog. /1989/
2-4/2 KF646 . . . . **E**
HUTCHINS, HJ/Three and many wishes of Jason Reid. /1988/
4-6/6 KH310 . . . . **Fic**
KOVALSKI, M/Pizza for breakfast. /1991/K-2/2 KF917 . . . . . . **E**
WALTER, MP/Brother to the wind. /1985/1-3/2 KG684 . . . . . **E**
ZIEFERT, H/Three wishes. /c1993, 1996/P-1/1 KG797 . . . . . . **E**

Wit and humor SEE ALSO Humorous stories; Jokes; Limericks; Nonsense
verses; Riddles; Satire.

Wit and humor.
LAUGHING TOGETHER: GIGGLES AND GRINS FROM AROUND
THE GLOBE. /c1977, 1992/3-A/KD731 . . . . **793.735**
PHILLIPS, L/Keep 'em laughing: jokes to amuse and annoy your
friends. /1996/3-6/KD736 . . . . **793.735**
Witchcraft SEE ALSO Occult sciences.

Witchcraft--Fiction.
BELLAIRS, J/House with a clock in its walls. /c1973/
4-6/5 KG897 . . . . **Fic**
HILDICK, EW/Case of the weeping witch. /1992/3-6/5 KH258 . **Fic**
JONES, DW/Witch week. New ed. /c1982, 1993/
6-A/6 KH335 . . . . **Fic**
KONIGSBURG, EL/Jennifer, Hecate, Macbeth, William McKinley,
and me, Elizabeth. /c1967/3-6/4 KH374 . . . . **CE Fic**
NORTON, M/Bed-knob and broomstick. /c1957/4-6/5 KH553 . **Fic**
PETRY, A/Tituba of Salem Village. /1991/5-6/4 KH599. . . . . **Fic**

SPEARE, EG/Witch of Blackbird Pond. /c1958/
5-6/5 KH742 . . . . **CE Fic**

Witchcraft--Massachusetts--Salem.
KRENSKY, S/Witch hunt: it happened in Salem Village. /1989/
3-5/4 KA606 . . . . **133.4**
ROACH, MK/In the days of the Salem witchcraft trials. /1996/
3-6/10 KE945 . . . . **974.4**
WILSON, LL/Salem witch trials. /1997/A/7 KA607 . . . . . . **133.4**

Witches--Fiction.
BRITTAIN, B/Dr. Dredd's wagon of wonders. /1987/
3-6/5 KG923 . . . . **Fic**
DE PAOLA, T/Merry Christmas, Strega Nona. /1986/
K-3/5 KF473 . . . . **E**
  Merry Christmas, Strega Nona (Talking book). /1991/
  K-3/KF474 . . . . **TB E**
  Strega Nona meets her match. /1993/1-3/2 KF479 . . . . **E**
HEARN, DD/Bad Luck Boswell. /1995/1-3/5 KF690 . . . . **E**
HOWE, J/Scared silly: a Halloween treat. /1989/K-3/3 KF780 . . **E**
KRAAN, H/Tales of the wicked witch. /1995/3-5/3 KH379 . . . **Fic**
KROLL, S/Candy witch. /1979/K-1/6 KF927 . . . . **E**
MAZER, A/Accidental witch. /1995/3-5/4 KH463 . . . . **Fic**
MEDDAUGH, S/Witches' supermarket. /1991/1-3/2 KG125 . . . **E**
O'CONNOR, J/Lulu and the witch baby. /1986/K-3/2 KG188 . . **E**
PALATINI, M/Piggie Pie! /1995/1-5/2 KG207 . . . . **E**
PEET, B/Big bad Bruce. /1977/K-3/3 KG224. . . . . **E**
SAN SOUCI, RD/Red heels. /1996/3-5/6 KG393 . . . . **E**
SILVERMAN, E/Big pumpkin. /1992/P-2/2 KG504 . . . . **E**
SNYDER, ZK/Witches of Worm. /c1965/4-6/7 KH735 . . . . . . **Fic**
STEVENSON, J/Fried feathers for Thanksgiving. /1986/
P-2/2 KG560 . . . . **E**
WOOD, A/Heckedy peg. /1987/K-3/3 KG762 . . . . **E**

Witches--Folklore.
BADEN, R/And Sunday makes seven. /1990/
2-3/2 KB388 . . . . **398.21**
DE PAOLA, T/Strega Nona: an old tale. /1975/
1-4/6 KB394 . . . . **CE 398.21**
GRIMM, J/Hansel and Gretel: a tale from the Brothers Grimm. /
1984/5/6 KB740 . . . . **CE 398.27**
KIMMEL, EA/Witch's face: a Mexican tale. /1993/
3-5/2 KB402 . . . . **398.21**

Wizards--Fiction.
BELLAIRS, J/Doom of the haunted opera. /1995/
4-6/6 KG896 . . . . **Fic**
STRICKLAND, B/Hand of the necromancer. /1996/
5-A/6 KH772 . . . . **Fic**
YOLEN, J/Wizard's Hall. /1991/4-6/6 KH897 . . . . **Fic**

Wolves.
BRANDENBURG, J/To the top of the world: adventures with arctic
wolves. /1993/5-6/7 KC834 . . . . **599.773**
JOHNSON, SA/Wolf pack: tracking wolves in the wild. /1985/
6/10 KC836. **599.773**
LAWRENCE, RD/Wolves. /1990/5-6/7 KC837. . . . . **599.773**
LEPTHIEN, EU/Wolves. /1991/2-4/5 KC838 . . . . **599.773**
PATENT, DH/Gray wolf, red wolf. /1990/5-6/8 KC839 . **599.773**
SIMON, S/Wolves. /1993/4-6/7 KC840 . . . . **599.773**
WOLPERT, T/Wolf magic for kids. /c1990, 1991/
5-6/5 KC841 . . . . **599.773**

Wolves--Alaska.
GEORGE, JC/Moon of the gray wolves. New ed. /1991/
5-6/6 KC835 . . . . **599.773**

Wolves--Fiction.
BLADES, A/Mary of Mile 18. /1971/1-3/3 KF233 . . . . **CE E**
BUNTING, E/On Call Back Mountain. /1997/1-3/2 KF306 . . . . . **E**
BURGESS, M/Cry of the wolf. /1994/5-A/7 KG948. . . . . . . **Fic**
BUSHNELL, J/Circus of the wolves. /1994/4-6/5 KG952 . . . . . **Fic**
CROSS, G/Wolf. /1991/A/6 KH045 . . . . **Fic**
ERNST, LC/Little Red Riding Hood: a newfangled prairie tale. /
1995/K-2/4 KF531 . . . . **E**
GEORGE, JC/Julie. /1994/5-A/3 KH156 . . . . **Fic**
  Julie of the wolves. /c1972/6-A/6 KH157. . . . . **CE Fic**
  Julie of the wolves (Talking book). /1993/6-A/KH158. . . **TB Fic**
GOBLE, P/Dream wolf. /1990/K-3/4 KF627 . . . . **E**
KASZA, K/Wolf's chicken stew. /1987/P-2/2 KF870 . . . . **E**
LONDON, J/Red wolf country. /1996/K-3/4 KG028 . . . . **E**
  White Fang. /c1905, 1985/6-A/6 KH417 . . . . **Fic**
LOWELL, S/Little Red Cowboy Hat. /1997/1-3/3 KG038. . . . . . **E**
MEDDAUGH, S/Hog-eye. /1995/K-3/2 KG123 . . . . **E**
PATERSON, K/King's equal. /1992/3-6/6 KH578 . . . . **Fic**
SCIESZKA, J/True story of the 3 little pigs. /1989/
K-3/2 KG421. . . . . **CE E**
TRIVIZAS, E/Three little wolves and the big bad pig. /1993/
P-3/4 KG619 . . . . **E**

Wolves--Folklore.
ROUNDS, G/Three little pigs and the big bad wolf. /1992/
K-3/4 KB645 . . . . **398.24**
YOUNG, E/Lon Po Po: A Red-Riding Hood story from China. /
1989/3-4/4 KB679 . . . . **398.24**
Women SEE ALSO Girls; Grandmothers; Mothers; Stepmothers.

Women--Biography.
HAVEN, K/Amazing American women: 40 fascinating 5-minute
reads. /1995//KA166 . . . . **PROF 305.4**
JOHNSON, RL/Braving the frozen frontier: women working in
Antarctica. /1997/4-6/6 KE214 . . . . **919.8**

Women--Employment--History.
COLMAN, P/Rosie the Riveter: women working on the home front
in World War II. /1995/5-A/7 KA938 . . . . **331.4**
DASH, J/We shall not be moved: the women's factory strike of
1909. /1996/6-A/8 KA939. . . . . **331.4**

Women--Folklore.
FOREST, H/Songspinner: folktales and fables sung and told (Sound
recording cassette). /1982/2-4/KB735. . . . . **SRC 398.27**
HAMILTON, V/Her stories: African-American folktales, fairy tales,
and true tales. /1995/4-6/3 KB312 . . . . **398.2**
HAYES, J/Watch out for clever women!/Cuidado con las mujeres
astutas!: Hispanic /1994/2-5/4 KB315 . . . . **398.2**
SAN SOUCI, RD/Cut from the same cloth: American women of
myth, legend, and tall tale. /1993/5-6/6 KB481 . . . . **398.22**

Women--History.
BROWN, FG/Daisy and the Girl Scouts: the story of Juliette
Gordon Low. /1996/3-6/7 KE448 . . . . **B LOW, J.**
WOMEN OF RURAL AMERICA (VIDEOCASSETTE). /1995/
5-A/KA831 . . . . **VCR 305.42**

Women--History--Miscellanea.
WOMEN'S ALMANAC. /1997/5-A/KA397 . . . . **REF 305.4**

Women--Miscellanea.
WOMEN'S ALMANAC. /1997/5-A/KA397 . . . . **REF 305.4**

Women--Suffrage.
SMITH, BC/Women win the vote. /1989/5-6/9 KA911 . . . . **324.6**

Women--Suffrage--Fiction.
MCCULLY, EA/Ballot box battle. /1996/1-3/2 KH473 . . . . **Fic**

Women--Suffrage--History.
FRITZ, J/You want women to vote, Lizzie Stanton? /1995/
3-6/5 KE549 . . . . **B STANTON, E.**

Women--United States--History--18th century.
ZEINERT, K/Those remarkable women of the American Revolution. /
1996/5-6/10 KE889 . . . . **973.3**

Women--West (U.S.).
WUKOVITS, JF/Annie Oakley. /1997/
5-6/8 KE480 . . . . **B OAKLEY, A.**

Women--West (U.S.)--History--19th century.
HILTON, S/Miners, merchants, and maids. /1995/
4-6/8 KF033 . . . . **978**

Women air pilots.
BRIGGS, CS/At the controls: women in aviation. /1991/
6-A/10 KD090 . . . . **629.13**
BROWN, D/Ruth Law thrills a nation. /1993/
2-3/4 KE428 . . . . **B LAW, R.**
HART, PS/Up in the air: the story of Bessie Coleman. /1996/
4-6/8 KE299 . . . . **B COLEMAN, B.**
KERBY, M/Amelia Earhart: courage in the sky. /1990/
3-4/5 KE327 . . . . **B EARHART, A.**
KULLING, M/Vanished!: the mysterious disappearance of Amelia
Earhart. /1996/2-4/7 KE328 . . . . **B EARHART, A.**
SZABO, C/Sky pioneer: a photobiography of Amelia Earhart. /
1997/4-6/12 KE329 . . . . **B EARHART, A.**
VAN METER, V/Taking flight: my story. /1995/
3-6/6 KD101 . . . . **629.13**

Women air pilots--Fiction.
LINDBERGH, R/Nobody owns the sky: the story of "Brave Bessie"
Coleman. /1996/1-3/2 KF983 . . . . **E**
POWELL, MC/Queen of the air: the story of Katherine Stinson,
1891-1977. /1993/4-7/7 KH613 . . . . **CE Fic**

Women artists.
BIOGRAPHY TODAY ARTISTS SERIES: PROFILES OF INTEREST
TO YOUNG READERS. /1996/-4-6/KA453 . . . . **REF 709.2**
CUSH, C/Artists who created great works. /1995/
4-A/8 KD377 . . . . **709.2**
FAITH RINGGOLD PAINTS CROWN HEIGHTS (VIDEOCASSETTE).
/1995/5-A/KD461 . . . . **VCR 746.46**
LING, B/Maya Lin. /1997/4-6/10 KE437 . . . . **B LIN, M.**
LOWERY, L/Georgia O'Keeffe. /1996/
2-3/2 KE482 . . . . **B O'KEEFFE, G.**
MEYER, SE/Mary Cassatt. /1990/6-A/8 KE283 . . **B CASSATT, M.**
MUHLBERGER, R/What makes a Cassatt a Cassatt? /1994/
5-A/7 KD489 . . . . **759.13**

RINGGOLD, F/Talking to Faith Ringgold. /1996/
4-6/6 KD379 . . . . **709.2**
SILLS, L/Inspirations: stories about women artists. /1989/
5-A/7 KD486 . . . . **759.1**
    Visions: stories about women artists. /1993/4-A/6 KD380 . **709.2**
TURNER, R/Faith Ringgold. /1993/
4-A/7 KE511 . . . . **B RINGGOLD, F.**
WALLNER, A/Beatrix Potter. /1995/
3-5/4 KA369 . . . . **PROF B POTTER,B**

Women astronomers.
CAMP, CA/American astronomers: searchers and wonderers. /
1996/A/10 KC000 . . . . **520**
MCPHERSON, SS/Rooftop astronomer: a story about Maria
Mitchell. /1990/4-5/6 KE465 . . . . **B MITCHELL, M.**

Women athletes.
BAIUL, O/Oksana: my own story. /1997/
3-6/4 KE247 . . . . **B BAIUL, O.**
BIOGRAPHY TODAY SPORTS SERIES: PROFILES OF PEOPLE OF
INTEREST TO YOUNG READERS. /1996-/4-6/KA456 . . **REF 796**
COHEN, JH/Superstars of women's gymnastics. /1997/
4-6/7 KD815 . . . . **796.44**
COHEN, N/Jackie Joyner-Kersee. /1992/
4-6/6 KE412 . . . . **B JOYNER-KERSEE**
DALY, W/Bonnie Blair: power on ice. /1996/
4-6/6 KE255 . . . . **B BLAIR, B.**
FEHR, KS/Monica Seles: returning champion. /1997/
4-6/10 KE533 . . . . **B SELES, M.**
GALT, MF/Up to the plate: the All American Girls Professional
Baseball League. /1995/4-6/6 KD797 . . . . **796.357**
GUTMAN, B/Gail Devers. /1996/5-6/6 KE319 . . . **B DEVERS, G.**
    Julie Krone. /1996/5-6/5 KE425. . . . . . . **B KRONE, J.**
KRULL, K/Wilma unlimited: how Wilma Rudolph became the world's
fastest woman. /1996/3-5/7 KE527 . . . . **B RUDOLPH, W.**
LINDOP, L/Athletes. /1996/4-6/7 KD763 . . . . **796**
PARE, MA/Sports stars. /1994/5-A/KA457 . . . . **REF 796**
SANFORD, WR/Babe Didrikson Zaharias. /1993/
4-5/4 KE608 . . . . **B ZAHARIAS, B.**
SAVAGE, J/Kristi Yamaguchi: pure gold. /1993/
3-5/7 KE603 . . . . **B YAMAGUCHI, K.**
SMITH, P/Superstars of women's figure skating. /1997/
4-6/7 KD836 . . . . **796.91**
WICKHAM, M/Superstars of women's track and field. /1997/
4-6/7 KD814 . . . . **796.42**
WILNER, B/Superstars of women's golf. /1997/
4-6/7 KD792 . . . . **796.352**

Women athletes--History.
MACY, S/Winning ways: a photohistory of American women in
sports. /1996/4-6/12 KD764 . . . . **796**

Women authors.
BIOGRAPHY TODAY AUTHOR SERIES: PROFILES OF PEOPLE OF
INTEREST TO YOUNG READERS. /1996-/4-6/KA461 . . **REF 809**

Women authors, American.
BUNTING, E/Once upon a time. /1995/
2-5/3 KE268 . . . . **B BUNTING, E.**
CLEARY, B/Girl from Yamhill. /1988/5-6/7 KE292 . **B CLEARY, B.**
DEWEY, JO/Cowgirl dreams: a western childhood. /1995/
3-4/4 KE320 . . . . **B DEWEY, J.**
    Rattlesnake dance: true tales, mysteries, and rattlesnake
    ceremonies. /1997/4-6/4 KC634. . . . . **597.96**
EHLERT, L/Under my nose. /1996/3-6/2 KE333 . . . **B EHLERT, L.**
FRITZ, J/Harriet Beecher Stowe and the Beecher preachers. /1994/
6-A/7 KE556 . . . . **B STOWE, H.**
KEHRET, P/Small steps: the year I got polio. /1996/
2-5/5 KE414 . . . . **B KEHRET, P.**
KUSKIN, K/Thoughts, pictures, and words. /1995/
2-5/6 KE426 . . . . **B KUSKIN, K.**
LESTER, H/Author: a true story. /1997/
2-5/2 KE436 . . . . **B LESTER, H.**
LYON, GE/Wordful child. /1996/4-5/4 KE450 . . . **B LYON, G. E.**
LYONS, ME/Sorrow's kitchen: the life and folklore of Zora Neale
Hurston. /1990/6-A/6 KE396 . . . . **B HURSTON, Z.**
MEIGS, C/Invincible Louisa. /1933/5-6/8 KE232 . . **B ALCOTT, L.**
PETTIT, J/Maya Angelou: journey of the heart. /1996/
4-6/8 KE237 . . . . **B ANGELOU, M.**
POLACCO, P/Dream keeper (Videocassette). /1996/
2-4/KE501 . . . . **VCR B POLACCO, P.**
TALK WITH BETSY BYARS (VIDEOCASSETTE). /1995/
4-6/KE273. . . . . **VCR B BYARS, B.**
TALK WITH JEAN FRITZ (VIDEOCASSETTE). /1993/
5-6/KE358 . . . . **VCR B FRITZ, J.**
VISIT WITH EVE BUNTING (VIDEOCASSETTE). /1991/
4-6/KE269. . . . . **VCR B BUNTING, E.**
WADSWORTH, G/Laura Ingalls Wilder: storyteller of the prairie. /
1997/4-A/5 KE595 . . . . **B WILDER, L.**

Women authors, American--Correspondence.
DEAR LAURA: LETTERS FROM CHILDREN TO LAURA INGALLS
WILDER. /1996/3-6/KD893 . . . . **808.86**

Women authors, Canadian.
ANDRONIK, CM/Kindred spirit: a biography of L. M. Montgomery,
creator of Anne of Green /1993/
5-A/6 KE469 . . . . **B MONTGOMERY, L**
LUCY MAUD MONTGOMERY: THREADS FROM THE QUILT
(VIDEOCASSETTE). /1993/
6-A/KE470. . . . . **VCR B MONTGOMERY, L**
MIND'S EYE: JEAN LITTLE (VIDEOCASSETTE). /1996/
5-6/KE445. . . . . **VCR B LITTLE, J.**

Women authors, English.
TALK WITH LYNNE REID BANKS (VIDEOCASSETTE). /1995/
4-6/KE505. . . . . **VCR B REID BANKS, L**
WALLNER, A/Beatrix Potter. /1995/
3-5/4 KA369 . . . . **PROF B POTTER,B**

Women authors, New Zealand.
MAHY, M/My mysterious world. /1995/
2-4/6 KE454 . . . . **B MAHY, M.**

Women basketball players.
KELLY, J/Superstars of women's basketball. /1997/
4-6/7 KD775 . . . . **796.323**

Women biologists.
RANSOM, CF/Listening to crickets: a story about Rachel Carson. /
1993/5-6/6 KE278 . . . . **B CARSON, R.**

Women chemists.
POYNTER, M/Marie Curie: discoverer of radium. /1994/
4-6/4 KE311 . . . . **B CURIE, M.**

Women civil rights workers.
MCKISSACK, P/Mary Church Terrell: leader for equality. /1991/
3-6/2 KE562 . . . . **B TERRELL, M.**
MEDEARIS, AS/Dare to dream: Coretta Scott King and the civil
rights movement. /1994/3-5/3 KE419 . . . . **B KING, C.S.**
PARKS, R/Rosa Parks: my story. /1992/
6-A/5 KE490 . . . . **B PARKS, R.**

Women conservationists.
BRYANT, J/Marjory Stoneman Douglas: voice of the Everglades. /
1992/4-5/6 KE324 . . . . **B DOUGLAS, M.**

Women educators.
MCKISSACK, P/Mary McLeod Bethune. /1992/
4-6/5 KE254 . . . . **B BETHUNE, M.**
O'CONNOR, B/Mammolina: a story about Maria Montessori. /
1993/4-6/6 KE467 . . . . **B MONTESSORI, M**
SHEPHARD, MT/Maria Montessori: teacher of teachers. /1996/
A/9 KE468 . . . . **B MONTESSORI, M**

Women entertainers.
ADAMS, MA/Whoopi Goldberg: from street to stardom. /1993/
4-6/7 KE371 . . . . **B GOLDBERG, W.**
ANNIE OAKLEY (VIDEOCASSETTE). /1997/
3-6/KE479. . . . . **VCR B OAKLEY, A.**

Women environmentalists.
SIRCH, WA/Eco-women: protectors of the earth. /1996/
4-6/7 KA953 . . . . **333.7**

Women executives.
JEFFREY, LS/Great American businesswomen. /1996/
5-6/9 KD315 . . . . **658.4**

Women illustrators.
DEWEY, JO/Cowgirl dreams: a western childhood. /1995/
3-4/4 KE320 . . . . **B DEWEY, J.**
HELLER, R/Fine lines. /1996/4-6/2 KE385. . . . . . . **B HELLER, R.**
POLACCO, P/Dream keeper (Videocassette). /1996/
2-4/KE501 . . . . **VCR B POLACCO, P.**

Women in agriculture.
WOMEN OF RURAL AMERICA (VIDEOCASSETTE). /1995/
5-A/KA831 . . . . **VCR 305.42**

Women in Judaism.
GOLDIN, BD/Bat mitzvah: a Jewish girl's coming of age. /1995/
5-A/10 KA773 . . . . **296.4**

Women in politics.
LINDOP, L/Political leaders. /1996/6-A/12 KA899 . . . . . **320**
PATRICK-WEXLER, D/Barbara Jordan. /1996/
4-6/8 KE408 . . . . **B JORDAN, B.**
POLLACK, JS/Shirley Chisholm. /1994/
5-6/10 KE289 . . . . **B CHISHOLM, S.**
STEWART, W/Aung San Suu Kyi: fearless voice of Burma. /1997/
5-A/7 KE244 . . . . **B AUNG SAN SUU**

Women in the Bible.
MCDONOUGH, YZ/Eve and her sisters: women of the Old
Testament. /1994/3-4/7 KA680. . . . . **221.9**

Women inventors.
JEFFREY, LS/American inventors of the 20th century. /1996/
4-6/12 KC894 . . . . **609**

Women journalists.
KENDALL, ME/Nellie Bly: reporter for the world. /1992/
4-6/5 KE256 . . . . **B BLY, N.**

Women judges.
MACHT, NL/Sandra Day O'Connor. /1992/
4-5/8 KE481 . . . . **B O'CONNOR, S.**

Women lighthouse keepers.
FLEMING, C/Women of the lights. /1996/4-6/6 KB148. . . . **387.1**

Women mathematicians.
CELEBRATING WOMEN IN MATHEMATICS AND SCIENCE. /
1996/A/11 KA439 . . . . **REF 509**

Women musicians.
REDIGER, P/Great African Americans in music. /1996/
3-6/8 KD524 . . . . **780**

Women musicians--Poetry.
LIVINGSTON, MC/Keep on singing: a ballad of Marian Anderson.
/1994/1-3/KD977 . . . . **811**

Women naturalists.
GEORGE, JC/Tarantula in my purse and 172 other wild pets. /
1996/4-6/4 KE366 . . . . **B GEORGE, J.**

Women photographers.
TURNER, R/Dorothea Lange. /1994/5-A/7 KE427 . . **B LANGE, D.**

Women physicians.
BUTTS, ER/May Chinn: the best medicine. /1995/
5-A/8 KE288 . . . . **B CHINN, M.**

Women pioneers.
KATZ, WL/Black women of the Old West. /1995/
5-6/9 KF036 . . . . **978**
KNIGHT, AS/Way west: journal of a pioneer woman. /1993/
5-6/5 KE197 . . . . **917.8**
RILEY, J/Prairie cabin: a Norwegian pioneer woman's story
(Videocassette). /1991/A/KF012 . . . . **VCR 977**
SEAVER, JE/Captured by Indians: the life of Mary Jemison. /1995/
5-A/8 KE405 . . . . **B JEMISON, M.**

Women pirates.
MCCULLY, EA/Pirate queen. /1995/3-5/5 KE156 . . . . **910.4**

Women poets, American.
SHERROW, V/Phillis Wheatley. /1992/
4-6/7 KE591 . . . . **B WHEATLEY, P.**

Women reformers.
ADLER, DA/Picture book of Sojourner Truth. /1994/
2-5/6 KE572 . . . . **B TRUTH, S.**
MCKISSACK, P/Sojourner Truth: ain't I a woman? /1992/
6-A/7 KE573 . . . . **B TRUTH, S.**
YATES, E/Prudence Crandall: woman of courage. 2nd ed. /1996/
6-A/6 KE306 . . . . **B CRANDALL, P.**

Women revolutionaries.
WALLNER, A/Betsy Ross. /1994/3-4/6 KE526 . . . . . **B ROSS, B.**

Women scientists.
BIOGRAPHY TODAY SCIENTISTS AND INVENTORS SERIES:
PROFILES OF PEOPLE OF INTEREST /1996-/
4-6/KA438 . . . . **REF 509**
CELEBRATING WOMEN IN MATHEMATICS AND SCIENCE. /
1996/A/11 KA439 . . . . **REF 509**
DUNLAP, J/Birds in the bushes: a story about Margaret Morse
Nice. /1996/3-5/9 KE477 . . . . **B NICE, M.**
PFLAUM, R/Marie Curie and her daughter Irene. /1993/
6-A/8 KC139 . . . . **539.7**
PRINGLE, LP/Jackal woman: exploring the world of jackals. /1993/
5-6/6 KC833 . . . . **599.77**

Women singers.
FERRIS, J/What I had was singing: the story of Marian Anderson. /
1994/5-A/6 KE236 . . . . **B ANDERSON, M.**
RODRIGUEZ, J/Gloria Estefan. /1996/
5-6/6 KE340 . . . . **B ESTEFAN, G.**

Women social reformers.
COLMAN, P/Mother Jones and the march of the mill children. /
1994/4-6/7 KA935 . . . . **331.3**
MCPHERSON, SS/Peace and bread: the story of Jane Addams. /
1993/4-6/5 KE228 . . . . **B ADDAMS, J.**

Women spies.
STEVENS, B/Frank Thompson: her Civil War story. /1992/
6-A/7 KE332 . . . . **B EDMONDS, S.**

Women tennis players.
HARRINGTON, DJ/Top 10 women tennis players. /1995/
3-6/7 KD790 . . . . **796.342**
SCHWABACHER, M/Superstars of women's tennis. /1997/
4-6/7 KD791 . . . . **796.342**

Women veterinarians.
DEWEY, JO/Wildlife rescue: the work of Dr. Kathleen Ramsay. /
1994/4-6/7 KD252 . . . . **639.9**
PAIGE, D/Day in the life of a zoo veterinarian. /1985/
2-5/6 KD196 . . . . **CE 636.089**

Women zoologists.
MEACHUM, V/Jane Goodall: protector of chimpanzees. /1997/
5-A/7 KE372 . . . . **B GOODALL, J.**

Women's computer network resources.
TECH GIRL'S INTERNET ADVENTURE. /1997/
4-A/KA580 . . . . **BC 025.04**

Women's rights.
SMITH, BC/Women win the vote. /1989/5-6/9 KA911 . . . . **324.6**

Women's rights--History.
BLUMBERG, R/Bloomers!. /1993/3-5/6 KA830 . . . . **305.42**
FRITZ, J/You want women to vote, Lizzie Stanton? /1995/
3-6/5 KE549 . . . . **B STANTON, E.**

Wood.
WOOD (VIDEOCASSETTE). /1985/5-6/KD330 . . . . . . **VCR 674**

Wood, Grant.
DUGGLEBY, J/Artist in overalls: the life of Grant Wood. /1995/
5-A/6 KE599 . . . . **B WOOD, G.**

Wood-carvers--Fiction.
ROSEN, MJ/Elijah's angel: a story for Chanukah and Christmas. /
1992/3-6/7 KH652 . . . . **Fic**

Wood-carving--Fiction.
BULLA, CR/Daniel's duck. /1979/1-2/1 KF296 . . . . **E**
ROSE, DL/Rose horse. /1995/3-5/6 KH651 . . . . **Fic**
WOJCIECHOWSKI, S/Christmas miracle of Jonathan Toomey. /
1995/4-6/5 KH876 . . . . **Fic**

Woodchucks.
LEPTHIEN, EU/Woodchucks. /1992/3-4/4 KC752 . . . . . . **599.36**

Woodchucks--Fiction.
BANG, M/Goose. /1996/P-2/2 KF190 . . . . **E**
KOSCIELNIAK, B/Geoffrey Groundhog predicts the weather. /
1995/K-2/2 KF915 . . . . **E**
KROLL, S/It's groundhog day! /1987/K-2/4 KF929 . . . . **E**

Woodland Indians--Folklore.
EHLERT, L/Mole's hill: a woodland tale. /1994/
K-2/3 KB562 . . . . **398.24**

Woods, Tiger.
KRAMER, S/Tiger Woods: golfing to greatness. /1997/
2-6/6 KE600 . . . . **B WOODS, T.**

Woodson, Carter Godwin.
MCKISSACK, P/Carter G. Woodson: the father of black history. /
1991/3-6/2 KE601 . . . . **B WOODSON, C.**

Woodwind instruments.
SHIPTON, A/Woodwinds. /1994/4-6/7 KD550 . . . . **788.2**

Woodwork SEE ALSO Carpentry; Furniture.

Woodwork.
LEAVITT, J/Easy carpentry projects for children. /c1959, 1986/
5-6/4 KD340 . . . . **684**
MCGUIRE, K/Woodworking for kids: 40 fabulous, fun and useful
things for kids to make. /1993/5-A/KD341 . . . . **684**

Wool.
DE PAOLA, T/Charlie needs a cloak. /1982/
P-2/3 KD299 . . . . **CE 646.4**

Woolly mammoth.
ALIKI /Wild and woolly mammoths. Rev. ed. /1996/
1-3/4 KC268 . . . . **569**

Word games SEE ALSO Puns and punning.

Word games.
BOURKE, L/Eye spy: a mysterious alphabet. /1991/
1-4/KD720. . . . . **793.734**
HEPWORTH, C/ANTics!: an alphabetical anthology. /1992/
2-6/KB831 . . . . **421**

Word games--Dictionaries.
EISS, HE/Dictionary of language games, puzzles, and amusements.
/1986/4-6/KA455. . . . . **REF 793.734**

Word games--Fiction.
BONSALL, CN/Piggle. /1973/P-2/2 KF246. . . . . **E**
MOST, B/Hippopotamus hunt. /1994/1-3/2 KG160 . . . . **E**

Word problems.
RELATING FRACTIONS AND DECIMALS (VIDEOCASSETTE). /
1982/3-5/KB981. . . . . **VCR 513.2**

Wordless books SEE Stories without words.

Work SEE ALSO Occupations; Vocational guidance; and name of specific
type of occupation e.g. Journalism--Vocational guidance; Zoology--
Vocational guidance.

Work.
BARKIN, C/Jobs for kids: the guide to having fun and making
money. /1990/5-6/7 KD305 . . . . **650.1**

Work--Fiction.
BARKER, M/Magical hands. /1989/1-3/5 KF199 . . . . **E**
BEST, C/Red light, green light, Mama and me. /1995/
K-2/2 KF228 . . . . **E**
BULLA, CR/Shoeshine girl. /1975/3-5/2 KG938 . . . . **Fic**
BUNTING, E/Day's work. /1994/1-3/2 KF298. . . . . **E**
HAZEN, BS/Mommy's office. /1992/P-2/2 KF688 . . . . **E**

HOBAN, J/Buzby. /1992/K-2/2 KF731 . . . . **CE E**
LYON, GE/Mama is a miner. /1994/2-3/3 KG044 . . . . **E**
PARISH, P/Come back, Amelia Bedelia. Newly illustrated ed. /
   1995/K-2/2 KG213 . . . . **E**
PATERSON, K/Lyddie. /1991/6-A/7 KH579 . . . . **Fic**
PAULSEN, G/Worksong. /1997/K-2/2 KG222 . . . . **E**
WABER, B/Lyle at the office. /1994/K-2/3 KG670 . . . . **E**

Working dogs.
ANCONA, G/Sheep dog. /1985/A/8 KD227 . . . . **636.737**
CLUTTON-BROCK, J/Dog. /1991/A/8 KD217 . . . . **636.7**

Working parents SEE ALSO Children of working parents.
World history SEE ALSO Geography; History, Ancient; History, Modern.

World history.
ANCIENT CIVILIZATIONS (PICTURE). /1991/4-6/KE620 . **PIC 930**
MARTELL, H/Kingfisher book of the ancient world: from the Ice Age
   to the fall of Rome. /1995/4-6/10 KE621 . . . . **930**

World politics.
UNITED STATES. BUREAU OF PUBLIC AFFAIRS, DEPT. OF STATE.
   /Background notes of the countries of the world. /n.d./
   4-6/KA404 . . . . **REF 310**

World records.
MATTHEWS, R/Record breakers of the sea. /1990/
   2-4/6 KA590 . . . . **031.02**

World War, 1914-1918.
MCGOWEN, T/World War I. /1993/4-6/8 KE653 . . . . . . **940.3**

World War, 1914-1918--Aerial operations.
LIEBERMAN, S/Intrepid birdmen: the fighter pilots of World War I
   (Sound recording cassette). /1993/A/KE654 . . . . . . **SRC 940.4**

World War, 1914-1918--Campaigns.
MARRIN, A/Yanks are coming: the United States in the First World
   War. /1986/A/7 KE652 . . . . **940.3**

World War, 1914-1918--Fiction.
RABIN, S/Casey over there. /1994/2-4/4 KG297 . . . . **E**

World War, 1914-1918--Literature and the war.
GRANFIELD, L/In Flanders Fields: the story of the poem by John
   McCrae. /1995/4-6/7 KD947 . . . . **811**

World War, 1914-1918--United States.
DOLAN, EF/America in World War I. /1996/5-A/7 KE651 . **940.3**
MARRIN, A/Yanks are coming: the United States in the First World
   War. /1986/A/7 KE652 . . . . **940.3**

World War, 1914-1918--United States--Fiction.
HOUSTON, G/Year of the perfect Christmas tree. /1988/
   K-3/6 KF771 . . . . **E**
ROSTKOWSKI, MI/After the dancing days. /1986/
   6-A/4 KH656 . . . . **Fic**

World War, 1939-1945.
MCGOWEN, T/World War II. /1993/4-6/8 KE673 . . . . . **940.54**
WHITMAN, S/Uncle Sam wants you!: military men and women of
   World War II. /1993/A/8 KE675 . . . . **940.54**

World War, 1939-1945--Aerial operations--Fiction.
MAZER, H/Last mission. /c1979, 1986/6-A/4 KH465 . . . . **Fic**

World War, 1939-1945--Antiquities.
BALLARD, RD/Exploring the Bismarck. /1991/
   5-6/7 KE668 . . . . **940.54**

World War, 1939-1945--Children.
MARX, T/Echoes of World War II. /1994/A/7 KE660. . . . **940.53**
TUNNELL, MO/Children of Topaz: the story of a Japanese-
   American internment camp: based on a /1996/
   5-6/8 KE667 . . . . **940.53**

World War, 1939-1945--Children--Fiction.
HAUGAARD, EC/Little fishes. /c1967, 1987/A/6 KH227 . . . . . **Fic**

World War, 1939-1945--Denmark--Fiction.
LOWRY, L/Number the stars. /1989/5-6/5 KH427 . . . . **Fic**

World War, 1939-1945--Evacuation of civilians--Fiction.
UCHIDA, Y/Journey to Topaz. /c1971, 1984/5-A/7 KH816 . . . **Fic**

World War, 1939-1945--Evacuation of civilians--Great Britain--Fiction.
PEARSON, K/Sky is falling. /1995/5-A/6 KH591 . . . . **Fic**

World War, 1939-1945--Fiction.
MOCHIZUKI, K/Baseball saved us. /1993/4-A/6 KH500 . . . . . **Fic**
SALISBURY, G/Under the blood-red sun. /1994/6-A/4 KH672 . **Fic**
WATKINS, YK/So far from the bamboo grove. /c1986, 1994/
   5-A/5 KH842 . . . . **Fic**

World War, 1939-1945--France--Fiction.
MORPURGO, M/Waiting for Anya. /1991/5-A/7 KH515 . . . . **Fic**

World War, 1939-1945--Germany--Fiction.
RICHTER, HP/Friedrich. /c1970, 1987/5-A/5 KH633 . . . . **Fic**

World War, 1939-1945--Great Britain.
FOREMAN, M/War boy: a country childhood. /1990/
   4-A/6 KE347 . . . . **B FOREMAN, M.**

World War, 1939-1945--Great Britain--Fiction.
BORDEN, L/Little ships: the heroic rescue at Dunkirk in World War
   II. /1997/3-5/3 KF251 . . . . **E**
HENEGHAN, J/Wish me luck. /1997/6-A/5 KH237 . . . . **Fic**

World War, 1939-1945--Greece--Fiction.
BAWDEN, N/Real Plato Jones. /1993/6-A/6 KG892 . . . . . . **Fic**

World War, 1939-1945--Hungary.
SIEGAL, A/Upon the head of the goat: a childhood in Hungary
   1939-1944. /1981/4-6/8 KE691 . . . . **CE 947.084**

World War, 1939-1945--Japan.
MARUKI, T/Hiroshima no pika. /1982/4-6/5 KE672 . . . . **940.54**

World War, 1939-1945--Jews.
ADLER, DA/We remember the holocaust. /c1989, 1995/
   5-6/8 KE656 . . . . **940.53**
MELTZER, M/Never to forget: the Jews of the Holocaust. /c1976/
   A/7 KE674 . . . . **940.54**

World War, 1939-1945--Jews--Fiction.
RICHTER, HP/Friedrich. /c1970, 1987/5-A/5 KH633 . . . . **Fic**
SERRAILLIER, I/Silver sword. /c1959/5-6/6 KH699 . . . . **Fic**

World War, 1939-1945--Jews--Rescue.
MELTZER, M/Rescue: the story of how Gentiles saved Jews in the
   Holocaust. /1988/5-A/7 KE661 . . . . **940.53**
MOCHIZUKI, K/Passage to freedom: the Sugihara story. /1997/
   3-6/4 KE662 . . . . **940.53**
PETTIT, J/Place to hide. /1993/5-A/7 KE663 . . . . **940.53**

World War, 1939-1945--Jews--Rescue--Fiction.
LOWRY, L/Number the stars. /1989/5-6/5 KH427 . . . . **Fic**
VOS, I/Hide and seek. /c1981, 1991/5-A/4 KH835 . . . . **Fic**

World War, 1939-1945--Naval operations.
MARRIN, A/Victory in the Pacific. /1983/4-6/7 KE671 . . . **940.54**

World War, 1939-1945--Netherlands.
FRANK, A/Diary of a young girl. /c1967/
   4-6/6 KE352 . . . . **B FRANK, A.**

World War, 1939-1945--Netherlands--Fiction.
VOS, I/Hide and seek. /c1981, 1991/5-A/4 KH835 . . . . **Fic**

World War, 1939-1945--Northern Ireland--Belfast--Fiction.
BUNTING, E/Spying on Miss Muller. /1995/6-A/6 KG944 . . . **Fic**

World War, 1939-1945--Pacific Ocean.
MARRIN, A/Victory in the Pacific. /1983/4-6/7 KE671 . . . **940.54**

World War, 1939-1945--Participation, Indian.
DAILY, R/Code talkers: American Indians in World War II. /1995/
   4-6/9 KE669 . . . . **940.54**

World War, 1939-1945--Personal narratives.
DAHL, R/Boy: tales of childhood. /1984/
   5-6/6 KE312 . . . . **B DAHL, R.**
FOREMAN, M/War boy: a country childhood. /1990/
   4-A/6 KE347 . . . . **B FOREMAN, M.**
HAUTZIG, E/Endless steppe: growing up in Siberia. /c1968/
   5-6/4 KE658 . . . . **940.53**
MARX, T/Echoes of World War II. /1994/A/7 KE660. . . . **940.53**
REISS, J/Upstairs room. /c1972/5-6/5 KE506 . . . . . . **B REISS, J.**

World War, 1939-1945--Poland--Fiction.
ORLEV, U/Island on Bird Street. /1983/5-A/6 KH566 . . . . . . **Fic**
   Man from the other side. /1991/5-A/6 KH567 . . . . **Fic**

World War, 1939-1945--Refugees--Fiction.
LEVITIN, S/Journey to America. /c1970, 1993/5-A/5 KH398 . . **Fic**
WATKINS, YK/My brother, my sister, and I. /1994/
   A/4 KH841 . . . . **Fic**

World War, 1939-1945--Underground movements.
MELTZER, M/Never to forget: the Jews of the Holocaust. /c1976/
   A/7 KE674 . . . . **940.54**

World War, 1939-1945--United States.
COLMAN, P/Rosie the Riveter: women working on the home front
   in World War II. /1995/5-A/7 KA938 . . . . **331.4**
KRULL, K/V is for victory: America remembers World War II. /
   1995/A/7 KE659 . . . . **940.53**
STANLEY, J/I am an American: a true story of Japanese internment.
   /1994/5-A/8 KE666 . . . . **940.53**
STEVENSON, J/Don't you know there's a war on? /1992/
   K-3/2 KE552 . . . . **B STEVENSON, J.**
WHITMAN, S/V is for victory: the American home front during
   World War II. /1993/5-6/8 KE919. . . . . **973.917**

World War, 1939-1945--United States--Fiction.
CUTLER, J/My wartime summers. /1994/5-A/4 KH052 . . . . . . **Fic**
GIFF, PR/Lily's crossing. /1997/5-A/5 KH165 . . . . **Fic**
GREENE, B/Summer of my German soldier. /c1973, 1993/
   A/8 KH197 . . . . **Fic**
LEE, M/Nim and the war effort. /1997/2-4/5 KH391 . . . . . . **Fic**
UCHIDA, Y/Bracelet. /1993/2-5/3 KG631 . . . . **E**

World Wide Web (Information retrieval system).
AHMAD, N/Cybersurfer: the Owl Internet guide for kids. /1996/
   3-A/8 KA575 . . . . **BC 025.04**
BRIMNER, LD/World Wide Web. /1997/2-6/6 KA577 . . **025.04**
KIDS RULE THE NET: THE ONLY GUIDE TO THE INTERNET
   WRITTEN BY KIDS. /1996/3-A/7 KA579 . . . . **025.04**
SALZMAN, M/Kids on-line: 150 ways for kids to surf the net for
   fun and information. /1995/3-6/6 KA572 . . . . **004.67**

World Wide Web (Information retrieval system)--Directories.
GIAGNOCAVO, G/Educator's Internet companion: CLASSROOM CONNECT's complete guide to educational /1996/ /KA049. . . . . **BC PROF 025.06**
HARRIS, J/Way of the ferret: finding and using educational resources on the Internet. /1995//KA046. . . . . . **PROF 025.04**

World Wide Web (Information retrieval system)--Handbooks, manuals, etc.
EDUCATORS' ESSENTIAL INTERNET TRAINING SYSTEM (MULTIMEDIA KIT). /1996//KA001 . . . . . . **MMK PROF 004.67**

World Wide Web (Information retrieval system)--Periodicals.
CLASSROOM CONNECT. /1994-//KA102 . . . . . **PER PROF 050**

Worms SEE ALSO Earthworms.

Worms.
RECYCLING WITH WORMS (VIDEOCASSETTE). /1995/ 3-6/KC507. . . . . **VCR 592**

Worms--Fiction.
ROCKWELL, T/How to eat fried worms. /1973/4-6/5 KH643 . . **Fic**

Worry.
FLEMING, A/What, me worry?: how to hang in when your problems stress you out. /1992/4-6/8 KA624. . . . . **152.4**

Worry--Fiction.
GLEITZMAN, M/Puppy fat. /1995/5-A/5 KH175. . . . . **Fic**

Wound healing.
COLE, J/Cuts, breaks, bruises and burns: how your body heals. / 1985/4-6/6 KC932 . . . . **612.1**

Wounds and injuries--Fiction.
MACDONALD, A/Rachel Fister's blister. /1990/K-2/2 KG050. . . **E**

Wozniak, Stephen Gary.
GREENBERG, KE/Steven Jobs and Stephen Wozniak: creating the Apple computer. /1994/4-6/7 KD046 . . . . **621.39**

Wright, Orville.
FREEDMAN, R/Wright brothers: how they invented the airplane. / 1991/A/7 KD094 . . . . **629.13**
MARQUARDT, M/Wilbur and Orville and the flying machine. / 1989/1-3/1 KD096 . . . . **629.13**

Wright, Wilbur.
FREEDMAN, R/Wright brothers: how they invented the airplane. / 1991/A/7 KD094 . . . . **629.13**
MARQUARDT, M/Wilbur and Orville and the flying machine. / 1989/1-3/1 KD096 . . . . **629.13**

Writing SEE ALSO Alphabet; Ciphers; Cryptography; Typewriting; Journalism; Letter writing.

Writing--Software.
BAILEY'S BOOK HOUSE (CD-ROM). /1995/ P-2/KB100. . . . . **CDR 372.4**
BAILEY'S BOOK HOUSE (MICROCOMPUTER PROGRAM). /1993/ P-2/KB101. . . . . **MCP 372.4**
BRIDGE TO TERABITHIA: A MULTI-MEDIA STUDY (MICROCOMPUTER PROGRAM). /1993/ 5-A/KB108. . . . . **MCP 372.6**
BROWN, MT/Arthur's teacher trouble (Microcomputer program). / 1994/2-6/KB109. . . . . **MCP 372.6**
CHARLOTTE'S WEB: A WRITE ON! MULTI-MEDIA STUDY (MICROCOMPUTER PROGRAM). /1992/3-6/KB110. **MCP 372.6**
DESTINATION: OCEAN. SCHOOL VERSION (CD-ROM). /1995/ 1-A/KB111. . . . . **CDR 372.6**
ECOLOGY WITH SEUSS (MICROCOMPUTER PROGRAM). /1990/ 2-5/KB112. . . . . **MCP 372.6**
INDIAN IN THE CUPBOARD (MICROCOMPUTER PROGRAM). / 1991/4-6/KB113. . . . . **MCP 372.6**
MICROSOFT CREATIVE WRITER 2. SCHOOL ED. (CD-ROM). / 1996/2-A/KB114 . . . . **CDR 372.6**
MULTIMEDIA WORKSHOP. TEACHER ED. (CD-ROM). /1996/ 3-A/KB115. . . . . **CDR 372.6**
MY FIRST SENTENCES (MICROCOMPUTER PROGRAM). /1987/ 1-3/KB116. . . . . **MCP 372.6**
READ, WRITE AND TYPE! (CD-ROM). /1996/ K-2/KB105. . . . . **CDR 372.4**
READER RABBIT 3 (MICROCOMPUTER PROGRAM). /1993/ 1-3/KB106. . . . . **CDR 372.4**
STANLEY'S STICKER STORIES. SCHOOL VERSION (CD-ROM). / 1996/P-2/KB117. . . . . **CDR 372.6**
STORYBOOK WEAVER DELUXE (CD-ROM). /1995/ 1-5/KB118. . . . . **CDR 372.6**
TUCK EVERLASTING (MICROCOMPUTER PROGRAM). /1989/ 4-6/KB119. . . . . **MCP 372.6**
ULTIMATE WRITING AND CREATIVITY CENTER. SCHOOL ED. (CD-ROM). /1996/K-5/KB120. . . . . **CDR 372.6**

Writing (Authorship) SEE Authorship; Creative writing; Journalism; Letter writing.

Wyeth, Andrew.
MERYMAN, R/Andrew Wyeth. /1991/ 6-A/7 KE602 . . . . **B WYETH, A.**

Wyoming.
FRISCH, C/Wyoming. /1994/4-6/7 KF059 . . . . **978.7**

Wyoming--Fiction.
BLANC, ES/Berchick. /1989/3-5/5 KG901 . . . . **Fic**

Yamaguchi, Kristi.
SAVAGE, J/Kristi Yamaguchi: pure gold. /1993/ 3-5/7 KE603 . . . . **B YAMAGUCHI, K.**

Yanomamo Indians.
REYNOLDS, J/Amazon Basin: vanishing cultures. /1993/ 3-6/7 KF104 . . . . **981**
SCHWARTZ, DM/Yanomami: people of the Amazon. /1995/ 4-6/7 KF105 . . . . **981**

Yard sales SEE Garage sales.

Yeager, Jeana.
ROZAKIS, L/Dick Rutan and Jeana Yeager: flying non-stop around the world. /1994/5-6/6 KD099 . . . . **629.13**

Yellowstone National Park.
CALABRO, M/Operation grizzly bear. /1989/ 5-6/7 KC858 . . . . **599.784**
PRINGLE, LP/Fire in the forest: a cycle of growth and renewal. / 1995/A/8 KC305 . . . . **577.2**
STAUB, FJ/Yellowstone's cycle of fire. /1993/4-6/8 KC306 . **577.2**

Yep, Laurence.
YEP, L/Lost garden. /1996/5-A/7 KE604 . . . . **B YEP, L.**

Yom Kippur.
CHAIKIN, M/Light another candle: the story and meaning of Hanukkah. /c1981, 1987/5-6/8 KA770 . . . . **296.4**
KIMMEL, EA/Days of awe: stories for Rosh Hashanah and Yom Kippur. /1991/4-6/5 KA777 . . . . **296.4**

Yorkshire (England)--Fiction.
BURNETT, FH/Secret garden. /c1911, 1987/3-6/5 KG951. **CE Fic**

Yoruba (African people).
KOSLOW, P/Yorubaland: the flowering of genius. /1996/ 6-A/12 KE726 . . . . **960**

Yoruba (African people)--Folklore.
ANDERSON, DA/Origin of life on Earth: an African creation myth. /1991/4-5/4 KA730 . . . . **291.2**
GERSHATOR, P/Iroko-man: a Yoruba folktale. /1994/ 2-3/6 KB397 . . . . **398.21**

Young, Brigham.
SANFORD, WR/Brigham Young: pioneer and Mormon leader. / 1996/5-6/8 KE605 . . . . **B YOUNG, B.**

Young, Butch.
GREENBERG, KE/Out of the gang. /1992/4-6/6 KB071 . . . **364.1**

Young, Steve.
CHRISTOPHER, M/In the huddle with...Steve Young. /1996/ 3-5/8 KE606 . . . . **B YOUNG, S.**
GUTMAN, B/Steve Young: NFL passing wizard. /1996/ 4-6/7 KE607 . . . . **B YOUNG, S.**

Young adult literature--Bibliography.
GILLESPIE, JT/Juniorplots 4: a book talk guide for use with readers ages 12-16. /1993//KA091 . . . . **PROF 028.5**
LYNN, RN/Fantasy literature for children and young adults: an annotated bibliography. /1994//KA032. . . . . . **PROF 016.80883**
MIDDLE AND JUNIOR HIGH SCHOOL LIBRARY CATALOG. 7TH ED. /1995//KA019. . . . . **PROF 011.62**
MILLER-LACHMANN, L/Our family, our friends, our world: /1992/ /KA020. . . . . **PROF 011.62**
YOUR READING: AN ANNOTATED BOOKLIST FOR MIDDLE SCHOOL AND JUNIOR HIGH. 1995-96 ED. /1996/ 5-A/KA373 . . . . **REF 011.62**

Young adult literature--Stories, plots, etc.
GILLESPIE, JT/Juniorplots 4: a book talk guide for use with readers ages 12-16. /1993//KA091 . . . . **PROF 028.5**

Youth SEE ALSO Adolescence; Boys; Children; Girls; Runaways.

Youth--Poetry.
HOPKINS, LB/Been to yesterdays: poems of a life. /1995/ 3-6/KD953. . . . . **811**

Youths' periodicals--Bibliography.
MAGAZINES FOR KIDS AND TEENS: REV. ED. /1997/ /KA018. . . . . **PROF 011.62**

Youths' writings.
RISING VOICES: WRITINGS OF YOUNG NATIVE AMERICANS. / 1992/5-A/7 KD903 . . . . **810.8**

Yucatan (Mexico: State)--Social life and customs.
STAUB, FJ/Children of Yucatan. /1996/4-6/7 KE840 . . . . . . **972**

Yucatan Peninsula.
SUEMI'S STORY: MY MODERN MAYAN HOME (VIDEOCASSETTE). /c1991/5-A/KE841 . . . . **VCR 972**

Yukon River (Yukon and Alaska)--Description and travel.
LOURIE, P/Yukon River: an adventure to the gold fields of the Klondike. /1992/4-6/6 KE210 . . . . **917.98**

Yukon River Valley (Yukon and Alaska)--Description and travel.
LOURIE, P/Yukon River: an adventure to the gold fields of the
Klondike. /1992/4-6/6 KE210 . . . . **917.98**
Yukon Territory--Fiction.
HILL, K/Toughboy and sister. /1990/4-6/6 KH261 . . . . **Fic**
Yvain (Legendary character).
HOWE, J/Knight with the lion: the story of Yvain. /1996/
5-6/6 KB455 . . . . **398.22**
Zaharias, Babe Didrikson.
SANFORD, WR/Babe Didrikson Zaharias. /1993/
4-5/4 KE608 . . . . **B ZAHARIAS, B.**
Zambia--Folklore.
LESTER, J/Man who knew too much: a moral tale from the Baila of
Zambia. /1994/4-5/3 KB607 . . . . **398.24**
Zapotec Indians--Folklore.
MARTINEZ, AC/Woman who outshone the sun: the legend of Lucia
Zenteno./La mujer que brillaba /1991/3-5/5 KB403 . . . . . **398.21**
Zapotec Indians--Social life and customs--Fiction.
VAN LAAN, N/Boda: a Mexican wedding celebration. /1996/
1-3/2 KG641 . . . . **E**
Zebras.
ARNOLD, C/Zebra. /1987/5-6/8 KC804 . . . . **599.665**
LEPTHIEN, EU/Zebras. /1994/3-5/4 KC807 . . . . **599.665**
Zebras--Fiction.
PEET, B/Zella, Zack and Zodiac. /1986/K-3/4 KG231 . . . . **E**
Zebras--Migration.
LINDBLAD, L/Serengeti migration: Africa's animals on the move. /
1994/5-6/10 KC497 . . . . **591.96**
Zenteno, Lucia (Legendary character).
MARTINEZ, AC/Woman who outshone the sun: the legend of Lucia
Zenteno./La mujer que brillaba aun mas que el sol: la leyenda de
Lucia Zenteno. /1991/3-5/5 KB403. . . . . **398.21**
Zhang, Song Nan.
ZHANG, SN/Little tiger in the Chinese night: an autobiography in
art. /4-6/6 KE609 . . . . **B ZHANG, S.**
Zimbabwe--Fiction.
FARMER, N/Do you know me. /1993/4-A/5 KH107 . . . . **Fic**
Ear, the Eye and the Arm: a novel. /1994/6-A/4 KH108 . . . . **Fic**
Girl named Disaster. /1996/6-A/5 KH109 . . . . **Fic**
STOCK, C/Where are you going Manyoni? /1993/
K-3/3 KG575 . . . . **E**
Zodiac SEE ALSO Astrology.
Zodiac.
MAP OF THE UNIVERSE: THE NORTHERN HEMISPHERE
(PICTURE). /1980/3-A/KC051 . . . . **PIC 523.8**
YOUNG, E/Cat and Rat: the legend of the Chinese zodiac. /1995/
K-6/4 KA608 . . . . **133.5**
Zoo animals.
AMAZING ANIMALS (VIDEOCASSETTE). /1994/
3-6/KD188. . . . . **VCR 636.008**
ANCONA, G/Handtalk zoo. /1989/K-A/KB820. . . . . **419**
BARTON, B/Zoo animals (Board book). /1995/P/KF209 . . . **BB E**
BIG ZOO (VIDEOCASSETTE). /1995/2-5/KC440. . . **VCR 590.73**
ORMEROD, J/When we went to the zoo. /1991/
P-2/3 KC442 . . . . **590.73**
Zoo animals--Fiction.
HAZELAAR, C/Zoo dreams. /1997/P-1/3 KF687 . . . . **E**
RATHMANN, P/Good night, Gorilla. /1994/K-2/1 KG309. . . . . **E**
WILD, M/Going home. /1993/1-3/3 KG716. . . . . **E**
Zoological models.
CUTCHINS, J/Are those animals real?: how museums prepare
wildlife exhibits. Rev. & updated /1995/3-A/7 KC443 . . . **590.75**
Zoologists.
MEACHUM, V/Jane Goodall: protector of chimpanzees. /1997/
5-A/7 KE372 . . . . **B GOODALL, J.**
PRINGLE, LP/Dolphin man: exploring the world of dolphins. /1995/
5-6/11 KC776 . . . . **599.5**
Jackal woman: exploring the world of jackals. /1993/
5-6/6 KC833 . . . . **599.77**
Zoology.
DORIS, E/Invertebrate zoology. /1993/5-6/8 KC503 . . . . . . **592**
LACEY, EA/What's the difference?: a guide to some familiar animal
look-alikes. /1993/5-6/8 KC450. . . . . **591**
Zoology--Africa.
HARTMANN, W/One sun rises: an African wildlife counting book. /
1994/P-2/3 KB959 . . . . **513.2**
Zoology--Amazon River Region.
DARLING, K/Amazon ABC. /1996/K-5/3 KC499 . . . . . **591.981**
Zoology--Antarctic regions.
MCMILLAN, B/Summer ice: life along the Antarctic Peninsula. /
1995/A/8 KE216 . . . . **919.8**
PONCET, S/Antarctic encounter: destination South Georgia. /1995/
4-6/6 KE217 . . . . **919.8**

Zoology--Arctic regions.
DUNPHY, M/Here is the Arctic winter. /1993/
K-4/2 KC731 . . . . **599.17**
KALMAN, B/Arctic animals. /1988/4-6/8 KC501 . . . . . . **591.998**
MATTHEWS, D/Arctic summer. /1993/5-6/3 KC732. . . . . **599.17**
Zoology--Australia--Fiction.
TRINCA, R/One woolly wombat. /1985/P-2/4 KG617 . . . . **E**
VAUGHAN, MK/Snap! /1996/K-2/2 KG651. . . . . **E**
Zoology--Central America.
MURIE, OJ/Field guide to animal tracks. 2nd ed. /1974/
A/8 KC476 . . . . **591.5**
Zoology--Iceland.
MCMILLAN, B/Nights of the pufflings. /1995/1-3/6 KC678 . **598.3**
Zoology--Nepal.
HIMALAYAN ADVENTURE (VIDEOCASSETTE). /1994/
K-6/KE712 . . . . **VCR 954.96**
Zoology--North America.
MURIE, OJ/Field guide to animal tracks. 2nd ed. /1974/
A/8 KC476 . . . . **591.5**
THORNHILL, J/Wildlife A-B-C: a nature alphabet book. /1990/
P-2/3 KC498 . . . . **591.97**
Zoology--Polar regions.
TAYLOR, B/Arctic and Antarctic. /1995/3-6/7 KE220 . . . . . **919.8**
Zoology--South Georgia Island.
PONCET, S/Antarctic encounter: destination South Georgia. /1995/
4-6/6 KE217 . . . . **919.8**
Zoos.
AMAZING ANIMALS (VIDEOCASSETTE). /1994/
3-6/KD188. . . . . **VCR 636.008**
BIG ZOO (VIDEOCASSETTE). /1995/2-5/KC440. . . **VCR 590.73**
GIBBONS, G/Zoo. /1991/K-2/4 KC441. . . . . **CE 590.73**
ORMEROD, J/When we went to the zoo. /1991/
P-2/3 KC442 . . . . **590.73**
PAIGE, D/Day in the life of a zoo veterinarian. /1985/
2-5/6 KD196 . . . . **CE 636.089**
Zoos--Fiction.
FARMER, N/Warm Place. /1995/4-A/3 KH110 . . . . **Fic**
GRAHAM, MB/Be nice to spiders. /c1967/P-2/3 KF633 . . . . . **E**
HAZELAAR, C/Zoo dreams. /1997/P-1/3 KF687 . . . . **E**
LOBEL, A/Zoo for Mister Muster. /c1962/P-1/5 KG015 . . . . . **E**
RATHMANN, P/Good night, Gorilla. /1994/K-2/1 KG309. . . . . **E**
SEUSS, D/If I ran the zoo. /1950/P-3/5 KG465 . . . . **E**
SLATER, T/Stay in line. /1996/K-2/2 KG516. . . . . **E**
Zoos--Periodicals.
ZOONOOZ. /1926-/4-6/KA554 . . . . **PER 050**
Zulu (African people)--Folklore.
WOLFSON, M/Marriage of the rain goddess: a South African
myth. /1996/4-5/5 KB424 . . . . **398.21**
Zulus--Biography.
STANLEY, D/Shaka, king of the Zulus. /1988/
4-6/6 KE537 . . . . **B SHAKA, KING**
Zuni Indians--Folklore.
HULPACH, V/Ahaiyute and Cloud Eater. /1996/
3-4/5 KB708 . . . . **398.26**
POLLOCK, P/Turkey girl: a Zuni Cinderella story. /1996/
2-4/6 KB764 . . . . **398.27**
RODANAS, K/Dragonfly's tale. /1992/2-3/4 KB767 . . . . . **398.27**

APPENDIXES

MATERIALS FOR PRESCHOOL CHILDREN

The following is a list of books and audiovisual materials which have been marked with a P interest level in the Classified Catalog. For easy access, they are listed here alphabetically under author (or main entry) with a short title. Full information may be found by looking under the call number given for each entry.

398.24	AARDEMA, V.	*Borreguita and the coyote: a tale from Ayutla, Mexico.*
CE 398.24	AARDEMA, V.	*How the ostrich got its long neck: a tale from the Akamba of Kenya.*
VCR 372.4		*ABC'S AND SUCH (Videocassette).*
508		*ABC'S OF NATURE: A FAMILY ANSWER BOOK.*
E	ACCORSI, W.	*Friendship's first Thanksgiving.*
E	ADLERMAN, D.	*Africa calling, nighttime falling.*
E	ADOFF, A.	*Black is brown is tan.*
811	ADOFF, A.	*Eats.*
CDR 398.24		*AESOP'S FABLE: THE TORTOISE AND THE HARE (CD-ROM).*
CE E	AHLBERG, J.	*Each peach pear plum: an " I spy" story.*
E	AHLBERG, J.	*Funnybones.*
E	ALBOROUGH, J.	*Where's my teddy?*
395.4	ALIKI.	*Hello! Good-bye!*
612.6	ALIKI.	*I'm growing!*
612	ALIKI.	*My feet.*
612	ALIKI.	*My hands. Rev. ed.*
E	ALIKI.	*Tabby: a story in pictures.*
VCR 811		*ALLIGATOR PIE (Videocassette).*
306.874	ALPERT, L.	*You and your dad.*
E	ANDERSON, P. P.	*Time for bed, the babysitter said.*
394.266	ANGLUND, J. W.	*Christmas is a time of giving.*
305.232	ANHOLT, C.	*Here come the babies.*
SRC 398.24		*ANIMAL TALES (Sound recording cassette).*
513	ANNO, M.	*Anno's counting book.*
E	ANNO, M.	*Anno's journey.*
513.4	ANNO, M.	*Anno's magic seeds.*
512	ANNO, M.	*Anno's mysterious multiplying jar.*
E	ANTLE, N.	*Good bad cat.*
E	APPELT, K.	*Bayou lullaby.*
PER 050		*ARIZONA HIGHWAYS.*
E	ARNOLD, T.	*No jumping on the bed!*
599.35	ARNOSKY, J.	*Come out, muskrats.*
598	ARNOSKY, J.	*Crinkleroot's 25 birds every child should know.*
E	ARNOSKY, J.	*Every autumn comes the bear.*
E	ARNOSKY, J.	*Rabbits and raindrops.*
599.76	ARNOSKY, J.	*Raccoons and ripe corn.*
E	ARNOSKY, J.	*Watching foxes.*
789.2		*ARROZ CON LECHE: POPULAR SONGS AND RHYMES FROM LATIN AMERICA.*
398.24	ARUEGO, J.	*Rockabye crocodile.*
E	ARUEGO, J.	*We hide, you seek.*
E	ASCH, F.	*Bear shadow.*
CE E	ASCH, F.	*Bear's bargain.*
CE E	ASCH, F.	*Happy birthday, moon.*
E	ASCH, F.	*Moonbear's pet.*
CE E	ASCH, F.	*Moongame.*

811	AYLESWORTH, J.	*Cat and the fiddle and more.*
E	AYLESWORTH, J.	*Two terrible frights.*
E	BABBITT, N.	*Bub, or, The very best thing.*
CDR 372.4		*BAILEY'S BOOK HOUSE (CD-ROM).*
MCP 372.4		*BAILEY'S BOOK HOUSE (Microcomputer program).*
E	BAKER, K.	*Hide and snake.*
E	BAKER, K.	*Who is the beast?*
E	BANG, M.	*Goose.*
E	BANG, M.	*Ten, nine, eight.*
789.2	BANGS, E.	*Yankee Doodle. 2nd ed.*
E	BANKS, K.	*Spider spider.*
E	BANYAI, I.	*Zoom.*
636	BARE, C. S.	*Guinea pigs don't read books.*
CE E	BARRACCA, D.	*Adventures of taxi dog.*
CE E	BARRACCA, D.	*Aventuras de Maxi, el perro taxista.*
CE E	BARRACCA, D.	*Maxi, the hero.*
E	BARRACCA, D.	*Maxi, the star.*
E	BARRACCA, D.	*Taxi Dog Christmas.*
387.7	BARTON, B.	*Airplanes.*
BB E	BARTON, B.	*Big machines (Board book).*
387.2	BARTON, B.	*Boats.*
690	BARTON, B.	*Building a house.*
BB E	BARTON, B.	*Dinosaurs (Board book).*
E	BARTON, B.	*I want to be an astronaut.*
E	BARTON, B.	*Machines at work.*
398.24	BARTON, B.	*Three bears.*
BB E	BARTON, B.	*Tools (Board book).*
388.3	BARTON, B.	*Trucks.*
BB E	BARTON, B.	*Zoo animals (Board book).*
E	BASE, G.	*Animalia.*
E	BECKER, J.	*Seven little rabbits.*
CE E	BEMELMANS, L.	*Madeline.*
CE E	BEMELMANS, L.	*Madeline (Big book).*
TB E	BEMELMANS, L.	*Madeline and other Bemelmans (Talking book).*
CE E	BEMELMANS, L.	*Madeline's rescue.*
811	BENJAMIN, A.	*Nickel buys a rhyme.*
398.8		*BIG FAT HEN.*
796.357	BLACKSTONE, M.	*This is baseball.*
E	BLOOM, S.	*Family for Jamie: an adoption story.*
E	BONSALL, C. N.	*Piggle.*
E	BONSALL, C. N.	*Who's a pest?*
E	BONSALL, C. N.	*Who's afraid of the dark?*
E	BRANDENBERG, A.	*Chop, simmer, season.*
E	BRANDENBERG, A.	*I am me!*
551.57	BRANDT, K.	*What makes it rain? The story of a raindrop.*
551.55	BRANLEY, F. M.	*Tornado alert.*
E	BRETT, J.	*Trouble with trolls.*
CE E	BRIDWELL, N.	*Clifford, we love you.*
CE E	BRIDWELL, N.	*Clifford at the circus.*
CE E	BRIDWELL, N.	*Clifford gets a job.*
CE E	BRIDWELL, N.	*Clifford takes a trip.*

CE E	BRIDWELL, N.	*Clifford the big red dog.*
CE E	BRIDWELL, N.	*Clifford the small red puppy.*
CE E	BRIDWELL, N.	*Clifford's good deeds.*
CE E	BRIDWELL, N.	*Clifford's Halloween.*
CE E	BRIDWELL, N.	*Clifford's sports day.*
CE E	BRIGGS, R.	*Snowman.*
398.2	BROOKE, L. L.	*Golden goose book: a fairy tale picture book.*
E	BROWN, C.	*In the spring.*
641.6	BROWN, L. K.	*Vegetable show.*
E	BROWN, M. T.	*Arthur's April fool.*
E	BROWN, M. T.	*Arthur's Christmas.*
E	BROWN, M. T.	*Arthur's Halloween.*
E	BROWN, M. T.	*Arthur's Thanksgiving.*
E	BROWN, M. T.	*Arthur's Valentine.*
E	BROWN, M. T.	*D.W. all wet.*
E	BROWN, M. T.	*D.W. flips.*
E	BROWN, M. T.	*D.W. rides again!*
E	BROWN, M. T.	*D.W. the picky eater.*
E	BROWN, M. T.	*D.W. thinks big.*
363.1	BROWN, M. T.	*Dinosaurs, beware: a safety guide.*
E	BROWN, M. W.	*Big red barn.*
E	BROWN, M. W.	*Child's good night book.*
232.92	BROWN, M. W.	*Christmas in the barn.*
CE E	BROWN, M. W.	*Conejito andarin.*
CE E	BROWN, M. W.	*Goodnight moon.*
CE E	BROWN, M. W.	*Gran granero rojo.*
E	BROWN, M. W.	*Little Donkey close your eyes.*
CE E	BROWN, M. W.	*Runaway bunny.*
811	BROWN, M. W.	*Under the sun and the moon and other poems.*
E	BROWN, R.	*Our puppy's vacation.*
152.4	BROWN, T.	*Someone special, just like you.*
513.2	BRUSCA, M. C.	*Three friends: a counting book./ Tres amigos: un cuento para contar.*
E	BUCK, N.	*Oh, cats!*
E	BUCK, N.	*Sid and Sam.*
E	BUCKLEY, H. E.	*Grandfather and I.*
E	BUCKLEY, H. E.	*Grandmother and I.*
E	BUEHNER, C.	*Escapada de Marvin el mono.*
E	BUEHNER, C.	*Escape of Marvin the ape.*
E	BUNTING, E.	*Flower garden.*
E	BUNTING, E.	*Ghost's hour, spook's hour.*
CE E	BUNTING, E.	*Mother's Day mice.*
E	BUNTING, E.	*Our teacher's having a baby.*
E	BUNTING, E.	*Scary, scary Halloween.*
E	BUNTING, E.	*Sunflower house.*
E	BUNTING, E.	*Turkey for Thanksgiving.*
CE E	BURNINGHAM, J.	*Come away from the water, Shirley.*
CE E	BURNINGHAM, J.	*Mr. Gumpy's motor car.*
CE E	BURNINGHAM, J.	*Mr. Gumpy's outing.*
E	BURTON, V. L.	*Katy and the big snow.*
CE E	BURTON, V. L.	*Mike Mulligan and his steam shovel.*
VCR E		*CALDECOTT VIDEO LIBRARY. VOL. I (Videocassette).*
VCR E		*CALDECOTT VIDEO LIBRARY. VOL. II (Videocassette).*
VCR E		*CALDECOTT VIDEO LIBRARY. VOL. III (Videocassette).*
VCR 398.2		*CALDECOTT VIDEO LIBRARY. VOL. IV (Videocassette).*
E	CAPLE, K.	*Biggest nose.*
E	CAPUCILLI, A.	*Biscuit.*
E	CAPUCILLI, A.	*Biscuit finds a friend.*
E	CARLE, E.	*Do you want to be my friend?*
808.81	CARLE, E.	*Eric Carle's animals, animals.*
E	CARLE, E.	*From head to toe.*
E	CARLE, E.	*Grouchy ladybug. New ed.*
E	CARLE, E.	*Have you seen my cat?*
E	CARLE, E.	*House for Hermit Crab.*
E	CARLE, E.	*Mariquita malhumorada.*
E	CARLE, E.	*Rooster's off to see the world.*
E	CARLE, E.	*Very busy spider.*
E	CARLE, E.	*Very hungry caterpillar.*
E	CARLE, E.	*Very lonely firefly.*
E	CARLE, E.	*1, 2, 3 to the zoo.*
CE E	CARLSON, N.	*Making the team.*
CE E	CARLSON, N.	*Mysterious valentine.*
CE E	CARLSON, N.	*Perfect family.*
CE E	CARLSON, N.	*Talent show.*
E	CARLSON, N.	*Visit to Grandma's.*
CE E	CARLSON, N.	*Witch lady.*
E	CARLSTROM, N. W.	*Better not get wet, Jesse Bear.*
E	CARLSTROM, N. W.	*Happy birthday, Jesse Bear!*
E	CARLSTROM, N. W.	*How do you say it today, Jesse Bear?*
E	CARLSTROM, N. W.	*How does the wind walk?*
E	CARLSTROM, N. W.	*I'm not moving, Mama!*
E	CARLSTROM, N. W.	*Jesse Bear, what will you wear?*
E	CARLSTROM, N. W.	*Let's count it out, Jesse Bear.*
811	CARLSTROM, N. W.	*Who said boo?: Halloween poems for the very young.*
E	CARTER, D. A.	*In a dark, dark wood.*
E	CASELEY, J.	*Grandpa's garden lunch.*
E	CASELEY, J.	*Noisemakers.*
E	CASELEY, J.	*Sophie and Sammy's library sleepover.*
551.5	CASEY, D.	*Weather everywhere.*
E	CASEY, P.	*My cat Jack.*
E	CAULEY, L. B.	*Clap your hands.*
E	CAZET, D.	*Fish in his pocket.*
E	CHARLES, N. N.	*What am I?: looking through shapes at apples and grapes.*
E	CHARLES, V. M.	*Hey! What's that sound?*
646.4	CHERNOFF, G. T.	*Easy costumes you don't have to sew.*
CDR E		*CHICKA CHICKA BOOM BOOM (CD-ROM).*
PER 050		*CHICKADEE: THE CANADIAN MAGAZINE FOR YOUNG CHILDREN.*
SRC 782.1		*CHILD'S CELEBRATION OF SHOWTUNES (Sound recording cassette).*
SRC 789.3		*CHILD'S CELEBRATION OF SONG (Sound recording cassette).*
REF 031		*CHILDCRAFT: THE HOW AND WHY LIBRARY.*
398.8		*CHINESE MOTHER GOOSE RHYMES.*
E	CHRISTELOW, E.	*Don't wake up Mama!*
E	CHRISTELOW, E.	*Five little monkeys sitting in a tree.*
E	CHRISTELOW, E.	*Five little monkeys with nothing to do.*
E	CLEARY, B.	*Growing-up feet.*
E	CLEARY, B.	*Janet's thingamajigs.*
E	CLEARY, B.	*Real hole.*
E	CLEARY, B.	*Two dog biscuits.*
811	CLIFTON, L.	*Everett Anderson's Christmas coming.*
E	COFFELT, N.	*Good night, Sigmund.*
E	COLE, B.	*Giant's toe.*
598.6	COLE, J.	*Chick hatches.*
793.4	COLE, J.	*Eentsy, weentsy spider: fingerplays and action rhymes.*
597.5	COLE, J.	*Fish hatches.*
597.8	COLE, J.	*Frog's body.*
636.8	COLE, J.	*My new kitten.*
636.7	COLE, J.	*My puppy is born. Rev. and expanded ed.*
629.43	COLE, N.	*Blast off!: a space counting book.*
E	COLE, S.	*When the tide is low.*
SRC 789.3	COLGATE, B.	*Silly Willy workout (Sound recording cassette).*
E	COOPER, H.	*Boy who wouldn't go to bed.*
793.4	COOPER, K.	*Too many rabbits and other fingerplays about animals, nature, weather, and the universe.*
E	COREY, D.	*Will there be a lap for me?*
398.24	COWLEY, J.	*Mouse bride.*
E	CREWS, D.	*Carousel.*
629.13	CREWS, D.	*Flying.*
E	CREWS, D.	*Freight train.*
623.8	CREWS, D.	*Harbor.*
394.2	CREWS, D.	*Parade.*
E	CREWS, D.	*Sail away.*
E	CREWS, D.	*School bus.*

E	CREWS, D.	Ten black dots. Rev. and redesigned ed.
CE E	CREWS, D.	Truck.
VCR 362.76		*CRITTER JITTERS (Videocassette).*
VCR 306.89		*DADDY DOESN'T LIVE WITH US (Videocassette).*
E	DALE, P.	Ten out of bed.
E	DE BRUNHOFF, J.	Babar and his children.
E	DE BRUNHOFF, J.	Story of Babar, the little elephant.
CE 646.4	DE PAOLA, T.	Charlie needs a cloak.
398.8	DE PAOLA, T.	Favorite nursery tales.
232.92	DE PAOLA, T.	First Christmas.
398.21	DE PAOLA, T.	Jamie O'Rourke and the big potato: an Irish folktale.
398.8	DE PAOLA, T.	Tomie De Paola's Mother Goose.
CE 398.27	DE REGNIERS, B. S.	Red Riding Hood.
CE E	DEGEN, B.	Jamberry.
811	DEMING, A. G.	Who is tapping at my window?
E	DEMUTH, P.	Busy at day care head to toe.
E	DENTON, K. M.	Would they love a lion?
E	DERBY, S.	My steps.
580	DIETL, U.	Plant-and-grow project book.
REF 031		*DINOSAURS: A SUPPLEMENT TO CHILDCRAFT--THE HOW AND WHY LIBRARY.*
E	DODDS, D. A.	Color box.
E	DONNELLY, L.	Dinosaur day.
E	DORROS, A.	Abuela.
VCR E	DORROS, A.	Abuela (Videocassette).
551.5	DORROS, A.	Feel the wind.
CDR E		*DR. SEUSS'S ABC (CD-ROM).*
E	DUBANEVICH, A.	Pig William.
979.1	DUNPHY, M.	Here is the southwestern desert.
808.81	DYER, J.	Animal crackers: a delectable collection of pictures, poems, and lullabies for the very young.
E	EASTMAN, P. D.	Are you my mother?
VCR E	EASTMAN, P. D.	Are you my mother? plus two more P.D. Eastman classics (Videocassette).
E	EASTMAN, P. D.	Go, dog, go!
E	EASTMAN, P. D.	Sam and the firefly.
SRC E	EDGECOMB, D.	Pattysaurus and other tales (Sound recording cassette).
E	EDWARDS, P. D.	Some smug slug.
E	EHLERT, L.	Color farm.
E	EHLERT, L.	Color zoo.
398.24	EHLERT, L.	Cuckoo: a Mexican folktale./Cucu: un cuento folklorico mexicano.
E	EHLERT, L.	Feathers for lunch.
E	EHLERT, L.	Fish eyes: a book you can count on.
E	EHLERT, L.	Nuts to you!
582.16	EHLERT, L.	Red leaf, yellow leaf.
E	EHLERT, L.	Snowballs.
636.8	EISLER, C.	Cats know best.
E	EMBERLEY, E.	Go away, big green monster!
E	EMBERLEY, R.	Three cool kids.
SRC 155.2	EPSTEIN-KRAVIS, A.	Happy to be me (Sound recording cassette).
SRC 789.3	EPSTEIN-KRAVIS, A.	Tot's tunes (Sound recording cassette).
E	ERNST, L. C.	Letters are lost!
E	ERNST, L. C.	Walter's tail.
E	ERNST, L. C.	Zinnia and Dot.
CE E	ETS, M. H.	Gilberto and the wind.
CE E	ETS, M. H.	Gilberto y el viento.
E	ETS, M. H.	In the forest.
CE E	ETS, M. H.	Play with me.
REF 031		*EXPLORING THE OCEAN: A SUPPLEMENT TO CHILDCRAFT--THE HOW AND WHY LIBRARY.*
VCR 612		*FABULOUS FIVE: OUR SENSES (Videocassette).*
E	FALWELL, C.	We have a baby.
789.3	FARJEON, E.	Morning has broken.
636		*FARM ANIMALS.*
996	FEENEY, S.	Hawaii is a rainbow.

591.5	FELDMAN, E. B.	Animals don't wear pajamas: a book about sleeping.
E	FIELD, R.	General store.
398.8		*FIVE LITTLE DUCKS: AN OLD RHYME.*
CE E	FLACK, M.	Ask Mr. Bear.
CE E	FLACK, M.	Historia de Ping.
CE E	FLACK, M.	Story about Ping.
E	FLEMING, D.	Barnyard banter.
E	FLEMING, D.	Count!
E	FLEMING, D.	In the small, small pond.
E	FLEMING, D.	In the tall, tall grass.
E	FLEMING, D.	Lunch.
E	FLEMING, D.	Time to sleep.
629.28	FLORIAN, D.	Auto mechanic.
307.3	FLORIAN, D.	City street.
508.3	FLORIAN, D.	Nature walk.
E	FLORIAN, D.	Summer day.
E	FLORIAN, D.	Winter day.
745		*FOLK ART COUNTING BOOK.*
E	FORD, M.	Little elephant.
E	FORD, M.	Sunflower.
508.2	FOWLER, A.	How do you know it's fall?
508.2	FOWLER, A.	How do you know it's spring?
508.2	FOWLER, A.	How do you know it's summer?
508.2	FOWLER, A.	How do you know it's winter?
553.7	FOWLER, A.	It could still be water.
E	FOX, M.	Hattie and the fox.
TB E	FOX, M.	Mem Fox reads (Talking book).
E	FOX, M.	Possum magic.
E	FOX, M.	Time for bed.
305.8	FOX, M.	Whoever you are.
E	FRANKLIN, K. L.	Iguana Beach.
E	FRASIER, D.	On the day you were born.
CE E	FREEMAN, D.	Corduroy.
CE E	FREEMAN, D.	Pocket for Corduroy.
E	FRENCH, V.	Red Hen and Sly Fox.
E	FRIEDRICH, P.	Easter Bunny that overslept.
598	FRISKEY, M.	Birds we know.
808.81		*FROG INSIDE MY HAT: A FIRST BOOK OF POEMS.*
811	FROST, R.	Stopping by the woods on a snowy evening.
E	GAG, W.	ABC bunny.
CE E	GAG, W.	Millions of cats.
CE 398.27	GALDONE, P.	Gingerbread boy.
CE E	GALDONE, P.	Henny Penny.
CE E	GALDONE, P.	Little red hen.
E	GALDONE, P.	Magic porridge pot.
398.8	GALDONE, P.	Three little kittens.
SRC 789.3	GALLINA, J.	A to Z, the animals and me (Sound recording cassette).
E	GARTEN, J.	Alphabet tale. New ed., rev. and re-illustrated.
E	GERINGER, L.	Three hat day.
E	GERSHATOR, D.	Bread is for eating.
811	GHIGNA, C.	Tickle Day: poems from Father Goose.
387.2	GIBBONS, G.	Boat book.
CE 567.9	GIBBONS, G.	Dinosaurs.
363.3	GIBBONS, G.	Emergency!
628.9	GIBBONS, G.	Fire! Fire!
CE 394.264	GIBBONS, G.	Halloween.
566	GIBBONS, G.	Prehistoric animals.
525	GIBBONS, G.	Reasons for seasons.
636.089	GIBBONS, G.	Say woof!: the day of a country veterinarian.
597.3	GIBBONS, G.	Sharks.
523.7	GIBBONS, G.	Sun up, sun down.
CE 394.264	GIBBONS, G.	Thanksgiving Day.
621.9	GIBBONS, G.	Tool book.
629.224	GIBBONS, G.	Trucks.
513.5	GIGANTI, JR., P.	Each orange had 8 slices: a counting book.
E	GILLILAND, J. H.	Not in the house, Newton!
E	GINSBURG, M.	Across the stream.
E	GINSBURG, M.	Asleep, asleep.
E	GINSBURG, M.	Sun's asleep behind the hill.
811	GIOVANNI, N.	Knoxville, Tennessee.

612.6	GIRARD, L. W.	*You were born on your very first birthday.*
635	GLASER, L.	*Compost!: growing gardens from your garbage.*
513.2	GOENNEL, H.	*Odds and evens: a numbers book.*
573.6	GOLDSEN, L.	*Egg.*
634	GOLDSEN, L.	*Fruit.*
E	GOMI, T.	*Who hid it?*
E	GOODE, D.	*Where's our mama?*
E	GRAHAM, M. B.	*Be nice to spiders.*
CE E	GRAMATKY, H.	*Little Toot.*
398.8		*GRANDMOTHER'S NURSERY RHYMES: LULLABIES, TONGUE TWISTERS, AND RIDDLES FROM SOUTH AMERICA/NANAS DE ABUELITA: CANCIONES DE CUNA,*
E	GRAVOIS, J. M.	*Quickly, Quigley.*
E	GRAY, L. M.	*Small Green Snake.*
SRC 789.3	GREEN CHILI JAM BAND.	*Magic bike (Sound recording cassette).*
SRC 789.3	GREEN CHILI JAM BAND.	*Starfishing (Sound recording cassette).*
E	GRIFFITH, H. V.	*Mine will, said John. New ed.*
E	GROSSMAN, P.	*Night ones.*
E	GUARINO, D.	*Is your mama a llama?*
E	GUNDERSHEIMER, K.	*Happy winter.*
811	GUNNING, M.	*Not a copper penny in me house: poems from the Caribbean.*
CD 789.2	GUTHRIE, W.	*Nursery days (Compact disc).*
E	GUY, G. F.	*Fiesta!*
E	HADITHI, M.	*Crafty chameleon.*
E	HALL, Z.	*It's pumpkin time!*
VCR 793.4	HALLUM, R.	*Fingerplays and footplays (Videocassette).*
513.2	HALSEY, M.	*3 pandas planting.*
E	HAMANAKA, S.	*All the colors of the earth.*
E	HAMM, D. J.	*Grandma drives a motor bed.*
E	HAMM, D. J.	*Laney's lost momma.*
398.24	HAN, S. C.	*Rabbit's escape/Kusa ilsaenghan tookki.*
398.24	HANSARD, P.	*Jig, Fig, and Mrs. Pig.*
E	HARLEY, B.	*Sitting down to eat.*
E	HARPER, I.	*My cats Nick and Nora.*
E	HARPER, I.	*My dog Rosie.*
E	HARPER, I.	*Our new puppy.*
E	HARRIS, R. H.	*Happy birth day!*
SRC 789.3	HARTMANN, J.	*Let's read together and other songs for sharing and caring (Sound recording cassette).*
513.2	HARTMANN, W.	*One sun rises: an African wildlife counting book.*
551.48	HATHORN, L.	*Wonder thing.*
E	HAVILL, J.	*Treasure nap.*
595.76	HAWES, J.	*Fireflies in the night. Rev. ed.*
E	HAYES, S.	*Eat up, Gemma.*
E	HAYES, S.	*Happy Christmas Gemma.*
E	HAZELAAR, C.	*Zoo dreams.*
E	HAZEN, B. S.	*Mommy's office.*
E	HEATH, A.	*Sofie's role.*
CE E	HEINE, H.	*Pigs' wedding.*
E	HELLER, N.	*This little piggy.*
428.1	HELLER, R.	*Cache of jewels and other collective nouns.*
573.6	HELLER, R.	*Chickens aren't the only ones.*
573.6	HELLER, R.	*Las gallinas no son las unicas.*
E	HENKES, K.	*Biggest boy.*
E	HENKES, K.	*Good-bye, Curtis.*
E	HENKES, K.	*Grandpa and Bo.*
E	HENKES, K.	*Owen.*
VCR E	HENKES, K.	*Owen (Videocassette).*
E	HENKES, K.	*Sheila Rae, the brave.*
E	HENKES, K.	*Weekend with Wendell.*
232.92	HENNESSY, B. G.	*First night.*
796.48	HENNESSY, B. G.	*Olympics!*
E	HENNESSY, B. G.	*School days.*
398.24	HEO, Y.	*Green frogs: a Korean folktale.*
E	HEST, A.	*Baby Duck and the bad eyeglasses.*

E	HEST, A.	*In the rain with Baby Duck.*
E	HEST, A.	*You're the boss, Baby Duck!*
VCR 306.875		*HEY, WHAT ABOUT ME? (Videocassette).*
E	HEYWARD, D. B.	*Country bunny and the little gold shoes, as told to Jenifer.*
PER 050		*HIGHLIGHTS FOR CHILDREN.*
E	HILL, E.	*Ki con dau roi nhi.*
E	HILL, E.	*Where's Spot? Sign language edition.*
REF 423	HILLERICH, R. L.	*American Heritage picture dictionary.*
507.8	HIRSCHFELD, R.	*Kids' science book: creative experiences for hands-on fun.*
811	HO, M.	*Hush!: a Thai lullaby.*
BB E	HOBAN, L.	*Big little otter (Board book).*
CE E	HOBAN, R.	*Baby sister for Frances. Newly ill. ed.*
CE E	HOBAN, R.	*Bargain for Frances. Newly ill. ed.*
CE E	HOBAN, R.	*Bedtime for Frances. Newly ill. ed.*
CE E	HOBAN, R.	*Best friends for Frances. Newly ill. ed.*
E	HOBAN, R.	*Birthday for Frances.*
CE E	HOBAN, R.	*Bread and jam for Frances. Newly ill. ed.*
CE E	HOBAN, R.	*Gran negocio de Francisca.*
CE E	HOBAN, R.	*Hora de acostarse de Francisca.*
CE E	HOBAN, R.	*Nueva hermanita de Francisca.*
CE E	HOBAN, R.	*Pan y mermelada para Francisca.*
428.2	HOBAN, T.	*All about where.*
591	HOBAN, T.	*Children's zoo.*
516	HOBAN, T.	*Circles, triangles, and squares.*
535.6	HOBAN, T.	*Colors everywhere.*
E	HOBAN, T.	*Count and see.*
629.225	HOBAN, T.	*Dig, drill, dump, fill.*
152.14	HOBAN, T.	*Dots, spots, speckles, and stripes.*
428.1	HOBAN, T.	*Exactly the opposite.*
302.23	HOBAN, T.	*I read signs.*
302.2	HOBAN, T.	*I read symbols.*
152.14	HOBAN, T.	*Is it red? Is it yellow? Is it blue? An adventure in color.*
E	HOBAN, T.	*Is it rough? Is it smooth? Is it shiny?*
152.14	HOBAN, T.	*Just look.*
779	HOBAN, T.	*Look book.*
E	HOBAN, T.	*Look up, look down.*
152.14	HOBAN, T.	*Look! look! look!*
535.6	HOBAN, T.	*Of colors and things.*
E	HOBAN, T.	*One little kitten.*
E	HOBAN, T.	*Over, under and through, and other spatial concepts.*
E	HOBAN, T.	*Push, pull, empty, full: a book of opposites.*
535	HOBAN, T.	*Shadows and reflections.*
152.14	HOBAN, T.	*Shapes and things.*
516	HOBAN, T.	*Spirals, curves, fanshapes and lines.*
152.14	HOBAN, T.	*Take another look.*
E	HOBAN, T.	*Where is it?*
E	HOBAN, T.	*26 letters and 99 cents.*
E	HOBSON, S.	*Chicken Little.*
CE E	HOFFMAN, M.	*Amazing Grace.*
CE E	HOGROGIAN, N.	*Buen dia.*
CE E	HOGROGIAN, N.	*One fine day.*
E	HOLABIRD, K.	*Angelina and Alice.*
E	HOLABIRD, K.	*Angelina and the princess.*
E	HOLABIRD, K.	*Angelina Ballerina.*
TB E	HOLABIRD, K.	*Angelina Ballerina and other stories (Talking book).*
E	HOLABIRD, K.	*Angelina ice skates.*
E	HOLABIRD, K.	*Angelina on stage.*
E	HOLABIRD, K.	*Angelina's baby sister.*
E	HOLABIRD, K.	*Angelina's birthday surprise.*
E	HOLABIRD, K.	*Angelina's Christmas.*
E	HOWARD, J. R.	*When I'm sleepy.*
E	HOWE, J.	*There's a monster under my bed.*
372.21	HOWE, J.	*When you go to kindergarten. Rev. and updated ed.*
E	HOWLAND, N.	*ABCDrive!: a car trip alphabet.*
E	HUGHES, S.	*Alfie gets in first.*
E	HUGHES, S.	*Big Alfie and Annie Rose storybook.*

E	HUGHES, S.	*Big Alfie out of doors storybook.*
E	HUGHES, S.	*Bouncing.*
E	HUGHES, S.	*Chatting.*
E	HUGHES, S.	*Dogger.*
E	HUGHES, S.	*Hiding.*
E	HUGHES, S.	*Nursery collection.*
821	HUGHES, S.	*Rhymes for Annie Rose.*
513.2	HULME, J. N.	*Sea sums.*
PER 050		*HUMPTY DUMPTY'S MAGAZINE.*
CE E	HUTCHINS, P.	*Changes, changes.*
CE E	HUTCHINS, P.	*Don't forget the bacon!*
CE E	HUTCHINS, P.	*Doorbell rang.*
CE E	HUTCHINS, P.	*Good-night owl.*
E	HUTCHINS, P.	*Little Pink Pig.*
CE E	HUTCHINS, P.	*Llaman a la puerta.*
E	HUTCHINS, P.	*One hunter.*
CE E	HUTCHINS, P.	*Paseo de Rosie.*
CE E	HUTCHINS, P.	*Rosie's walk.*
E	HUTCHINS, P.	*Shrinking mouse.*
CE E	HUTCHINS, P.	*Silly Billy!*
E	HUTCHINS, P.	*Tidy Titch.*
E	HUTCHINS, P.	*Titch and Daisy.*
CE E	HUTCHINS, P.	*Very worst monster.*
CE E	HUTCHINS, P.	*Where's the baby?*
E	HUTCHINS, P.	*Which witch is which?*
E	HUTCHINS, P.	*You'll soon grow into them, Titch.*
221.9	HUTTON, W.	*Moses in the bulrushes.*
REF 031		*I WAS WONDERING: A SUPPLEMENT TO CHILDCRAFT--THE HOW AND WHY LIBRARY.*
VCR E		*INTRODUCTION TO LETTERS AND NUMERALS (Videocassette).*
E	ISADORA, R.	*City seen from A to Z.*
E	ISADORA, R.	*Lili at ballet.*
VCR 789.3	JACK, D.	*David Jack... live!: Makin' music, makin' friends (Videocassette).*
E	JACKSON, E.	*Brown cow, green grass, yellow mellow sun.*
E	JAKOB, D.	*My new sandbox.*
SRC 529	JAMES, D. L.	*Singing calendar (Sound recording cassette).*
E	JAMES, S.	*Wild woods.*
SRC 789.3	JANIAK, W.	*Basic skills for young children (Sound recording cassette).*
CD 789.3	JENKINS, E.	*And one and two and other songs for pre-school and primary children (Compact disc).*
SRC 789.3	JENKINS, E.	*Come dance by the ocean (Sound recording cassette).*
SRC 513	JENKINS, E.	*Counting games and rhythms for the little ones, vol. 1 (Sound recording cassette).*
VCR 789.3	JENKINS, E.	*Ella Jenkins live!: at the Smithsonian (Videocassette).*
SRC 789.3	JENKINS, E.	*Growing up with Ella Jenkins: rhythms songs and rhymes (Sound recording cassette).*
CD 394.26	JENKINS, E.	*Holiday times (Compact disc).*
SRC 789.3	JENKINS, E.	*Rhythm and game songs for the little ones (Sound recording cassette).*
SRC 789.3	JENKINS, E.	*You'll sing a song and I'll sing a song (Sound recording cassette).*
152.14	JENKINS, S.	*Flip-flap.*
BB E	JOHNSON, A.	*Joshua by the sea (Board book).*
BB E	JOHNSON, A.	*Joshua's night whispers (Board book).*
E	JOHNSON, A.	*Julius.*
E	JOHNSON, A.	*One of three.*
BB E	JOHNSON, A.	*Rain feet (Board book).*
E	JOHNSON, A.	*When I am old with you.*
CE E	JOHNSON, C.	*Harold and the purple crayon.*
CE E	JOHNSON, C.	*Harold y el lapiz color morado.*
CE E	JOHNSON, C.	*Harold's ABC.*
CE E	JOHNSON, C.	*Harold's fairy tale: further adventures with the purple crayon.*
CE E	JOHNSON, C.	*Harold's trip to the sky.*
CE E	JOHNSON, C.	*Picture for Harold's room.*
E	JOHNSON, P. B.	*Farmers' market.*
E	JOHNSTON, T.	*Quilt story.*
E	JOHNSTON, T.	*Very scary.*
E	JONAS, A.	*Color dance.*
E	JONAS, A.	*Holes and peeks.*
E	JONAS, A.	*Splash!*
E	JONAS, A.	*Trek.*
E	JONAS, A.	*When you were a baby.*
398.24	JONES, C.	*Hare and the Tortoise.*
E	JONES, R. C.	*Down at the bottom of the deep dark sea.*
E	JOOSSE, B. M.	*Mama, do you love me?*
580	JORDAN, H. J.	*Como crece una semilla.*
580	JORDAN, H. J.	*How a seed grows. Rev. ed.*
E	JOYCE, W.	*George shrinks.*
CDR E		*JUST GRANDMA AND ME (CD-ROM).*
VCR 363.1		*K.C.'s first bus ride (Videocassette).*
CE E	KALAN, R.	*Jump, frog, jump! New ed.*
E	KALAN, R.	*Moving day.*
CE E	KALAN, R.	*Salta, ranita, salta!*
158	KALMAN, B.	*Fun with my friends.*
331.7	KALMAN, M.	*Chicken soup, boots.*
E	KARLIN, N.	*I see, you saw.*
E	KASZA, K.	*Wolf's chicken stew.*
641.5	KATZEN, M.	*Pretend soup and other real recipes: a cookbook for preschoolers and up.*
VCR E	KEATS, E. J.	*Ezra Jack Keats Library (Videocassette).*
CE E	KEATS, E. J.	*Hi, cat!*
CE E	KEATS, E. J.	*Letter to Amy.*
E	KEATS, E. J.	*Maggie and the pirate.*
CE E	KEATS, E. J.	*Pet show.*
CE E	KEATS, E. J.	*Peter's chair.*
CE E	KEATS, E. J.	*Silla de Pedro.*
CE E	KEATS, E. J.	*Snowy day.*
CE E	KEATS, E. J.	*Whistle for Willie.*
E	KELLER, H.	*Geraldine's big snow.*
E	KELLER, H.	*Island baby.*
E	KELLOGG, S.	*Mystery of the missing red mitten.*
E	KELLOGG, S.	*Mystery of the stolen blue paint.*
CE E	KELLOGG, S.	*Pinkerton, behave.*
E	KELLOGG, S.	*Prehistoric Pinkerton.*
CE E	KELLOGG, S.	*Rose for Pinkerton.*
CE E	KELLOGG, S.	*Tallyho, Pinkerton.*
E	KHALSA, D. K.	*I want a dog.*
CDR 004		*KIDDESK. School version (CD-ROM).*
E	KINSEY-WARNOCK, N.	*When spring comes.*
E	KLINTING, L.	*Bruno the baker.*
306.87	KNIGHT, M. B.	*Welcoming babies.*
E	KNUTSON, K.	*Ska-tat!*
CE E	KRAUS, R.	*Come out and play, little mouse.*
CE E	KRAUS, R.	*Leo the late bloomer.*
CE E	KRAUS, R.	*Where are you going little mouse?*
CE E	KRAUS, R.	*Whose mouse are you?*
CE E	KRAUSS, R.	*Carrot seed.*
E	KRAUSS, R.	*Dia feliz.*
E	KRAUSS, R.	*Happy day.*
CE E	KRAUSS, R.	*Hole is to dig: a first book of first definitions.*
E	KRAUSS, R.	*Very special house.*
597.92	KUHN, D.	*Turtle's day.*
372.21	KUKLIN, S.	*Going to my nursery school.*
636.8	KUKLIN, S.	*Taking my cat to the vet.*
610.69	KUKLIN, S.	*When I see my doctor.*
E	KUSKIN, K.	*Roar and more.*
PER 050		*LADYBUG: THE MAGAZINE FOR YOUNG CHILDREN.*
CE 789.2	LANGSTAFF, J.	*Frog went a-courtin'.*
811	LANSKY, B.	*New adventures of Mother Goose: gentle rhymes for happy times.*
E	LANTON, S.	*Daddy's chair.*
SRC 789.3		*LATE LAST NIGHT (Sound recording cassette).*
CE 582.16	LAUBER, P.	*Be a friend to trees.*

567.9	LAUBER, P.	*News about dinosaurs.*
CE 551.21	LAUBER, P.	*Volcano: the eruption and healing of Mount St. Helens.*
395	LEAF, M.	*Four-and-twenty watchbirds.*
CE E	LEAF, M.	*Story of Ferdinand.*
821	LEAR, E.	*Owl and the Pussy-cat.*
E	LEE, J. M.	*Silent Lotus.*
E	LEVINSON, R.	*Emperor's new clothes.*
811	LEWIS, J. P.	*July is a mad mosquito.*
E	LEWIS, K.	*My friend Harry.*
VCR 790.1	LEWIS, S.	*Get your teddy ready (Videocassette).*
VCR 793.4	LEWIS, S.	*Let's play games (Videocassette).*
E	LILLIE, P.	*Everything has a place.*
E	LILLIE, P.	*Floppy teddy bear.*
E	LINDEN, A. M.	*One smiling grandma: a Caribbean counting book.*
E	LIONNI, L.	*Alexander and the wind-up mouse.*
E	LIONNI, L.	*Frederick.*
E	LIONNI, L.	*Frederick's fables: a Leo Lionni treasury of favorite stories. Rev. ed.*
VCR E	LIONNI, L.	*Leo Lionni's Caldecotts (Videocassette).*
E	LOBEL, A.	*Alison's zinnia.*
398.8	LOBEL, A.	*Arnold Lobel book of Mother Goose.*
E	LOBEL, A.	*On Market Street.*
E	LOBEL, A.	*Treeful of pigs.*
E	LOBEL, A.	*Zoo for Mister Muster.*
E	LOH, M.	*Tucking mommy in.*
E	LONDON, J.	*Fireflies, fireflies, light my way.*
E	LONDON, J.	*Froggy gets dressed.*
E	LONDON, J.	*Froggy goes to school.*
E	LONDON, J.	*Froggy se viste.*
E	LONDON, J.	*Let's go, Froggy!*
E	LONDON, J.	*Lion who had asthma.*
E	LONDON, J.	*Owl who became the moon.*
E	LONDON, J.	*Puddles.*
E	LONG, E.	*Gone fishing.*
513.2	LONG, L.	*Domino addition.*
513.2	LONG, L.	*Sumemos con el domino.*
CE 811	LONGFELLOW, H. W.	*Hiawatha.*
REF 031		*LOOK INTO SPACE: A SUPPLEMENT TO CHILDCRAFT--THE HOW AND WHY LIBRARY.*
E	LOOMIS, C.	*In the diner.*
398.2	LOTTRIDGE, C. B.	*Ten small tales.*
SRC 789.8	LOUCHARD, R.	*Hey, Ludwig!: classical piano solos for playful times (Sound recording cassette).*
E	LOW, A.	*Popcorn shop.*
E	LOW, J.	*Mice twice.*
577.68	LUENN, N.	*Squish!: a wetland walk.*
E	MACCARONE, G.	*Cars! cars! cars!*
E	MACCARONE, G.	*Pizza party!*
E	MACDONALD, A.	*Little Beaver and The Echo.*
E	MACDONALD, S.	*Alphabatics.*
591	MACDONALD, S.	*Peck slither and slide.*
516	MACDONALD, S.	*Sea shapes.*
E	MACK, S.	*10 bears in my bed: a goodnight countdown.*
428.1	MAESTRO, B.	*All aboard overnight: a book of compound words.*
386	MAESTRO, B.	*Ferryboat.*
735	MAESTRO, B.	*Story of the Statue of Liberty.*
CE 581.4	MAESTRO, B.	*Why do leaves change color?*
548	MAKI, C.	*Snowflakes, sugar, and salt: crystals up close.*
398.8	MANSON, C.	*Tree in the wood: an old nursery song.*
E	MANUSHKIN, F.	*Peeping and sleeping.*
551.57	MARKLE, S.	*Rainy day.*
E	MARSHALL, E.	*Space case.*
CE E	MARSHALL, J.	*George and Martha.*
CE E	MARSHALL, J.	*George and Martha 'round and 'round.*
CE E	MARSHALL, J.	*George and Martha back in town.*
CE E	MARSHALL, J.	*George and Martha encore.*
CE E	MARSHALL, J.	*George and Martha one fine day.*
CE E	MARSHALL, J.	*George and Martha rise and shine.*
E	MARTIN, A. T.	*Famous seaweed soup.*
E	MARTIN, JR., B.	*Barn dance!*
E	MARTIN, JR., B.	*Brown bear, brown bear, what do you see?*
E	MARTIN, JR., B.	*Chicka chicka boom boom.*
KIT E	MARTIN, JR., B.	*Chicka chicka boom boom (Kit).*
E	MARTIN, JR., B.	*Here are my hands.*
E	MARTIN, JR., B.	*Listen to the rain.*
E	MARTIN, JR., B.	*Polar bear, polar bear, what do you hear?*
398.8	MARTIN, S. C.	*Comic adventures of Old Mother Hubbard and her dog.*
E	MARZOLLO, J.	*Pretend you're a cat.*
E	MASUREL, C.	*No, no, Titus!*
CE E	MAYER, M.	*Boy, a dog and a frog.*
CE E	MAYER, M.	*Frog goes to dinner.*
CE E	MAYER, M.	*Frog on his own.*
CE E	MAYER, M.	*Frog where are you?*
CE E	MAYER, M.	*One frog too many.*
E	MAYER, M.	*There's an alligator under my bed.*
331.7	MAYNARD, C.	*Jobs people do.*
398.24	MAYO, M.	*Tortoise's flying lesson.*
CE E	MCCLOSKEY, R.	*Blueberries for Sal.*
CE FIC	MCCLOSKEY, R.	*Burt Dow, deep-water man: a tale of the sea in the classic tradition.*
CE E	MCCLOSKEY, R.	*Make way for ducklings.*
CE E	MCCLOSKEY, R.	*Time of wonder.*
CE E	MCCULLY, E. A.	*Picnic.*
E	MCCULLY, E. A.	*School.*
SRC 789.2	MCCUTCHEON, J.	*Family garden (Sound recording cassette).*
398.24	MCDERMOTT, G.	*Coyote: a trickster tale from the American Southwest.*
E	MCDERMOTT, G.	*Papagayo the mischief maker.*
595.3	MCDONALD, M.	*Is this a house for hermit crab?*
E	MCDONNELL, F.	*Flora McDonnell's ABC.*
E	MCDONNELL, F.	*I love animals.*
E	MCDONNELL, F.	*I love boats.*
CE E	MCLEOD, E. W.	*Bear's bicycle.*
428	MCMILLAN, B.	*Dry or wet?*
513.2	MCMILLAN, B.	*Eating fractions.*
535.6	MCMILLAN, B.	*Growing colors.*
612.8	MCMILLAN, B.	*Sense suspense: a guessing game for the five senses.*
E	MCMULLAN, K.	*If you were my bunny.*
E	MCPHAIL, D.	*Cerdos a montones, cerdos a granel!*
E	MCPHAIL, D.	*Farm morning.*
E	MCPHAIL, D.	*Lost!*
E	MCPHAIL, D.	*Pigs ahoy!*
E	MCPHAIL, D.	*Pigs aplenty, pigs galore!*
811	MERRIAM, E.	*Halloween A B C.*
811	MERRIAM, E.	*Higgle wiggle: happy rhymes.*
E	MERRIAM, E.	*Hole story.*
701	MICKLETHWAIT, L.	*Child's book of art: great pictures, first words.*
758	MICKLETHWAIT, L.	*I spy a freight train: transportation in art.*
758	MICKLETHWAIT, L.	*I spy a lion: animals in art.*
513.2	MICKLETHWAIT, L.	*I spy two eyes: numbers in art.*
759	MICKLETHWAIT, L.	*I spy: an alphabet in art.*
372.4	MILES, B.	*Hey! I'm reading!: a how-to-read book for beginners.*
612.8	MILLER, M.	*My five senses.*
E	MILLER, M.	*Now I'm big.*
E	MILLER, M.	*Where does it go?*
331.7	MILLER, M.	*Who uses this?*
391.4	MILLER, M.	*Whose hat?*
391.4	MILLER, M.	*Whose shoe?*
CDR 513.2		*MILLIE'S MATH HOUSE (CD-ROM).*
MCP 513.2		*MILLIE'S MATH HOUSE (Microcomputer program).*
821	MILNE, A. A.	*World of Christopher Robin: the complete When we were very young and Now we are six.*
E	MINARIK, E. H.	*Am I beautiful?*
CE E	MINARIK, E. H.	*Amigos de Osito.*
CE E	MINARIK, E. H.	*Father Bear comes home.*
CE E	MINARIK, E. H.	*Kiss for Little Bear.*

Call No.	Author	Title
CE E	MINARIK, E. H.	Little Bear.
CE E	MINARIK, E. H.	Little Bear's friend.
CE E	MINARIK, E. H.	Little Bear's visit.
CE E	MINARIK, E. H.	Osito.
CE E	MINARIK, E. H.	Papa Oso vuelve a casa.
CE E	MINARIK, E. H.	Visita de Osito.
SRC 363.7	MISH, M.	Kid's eye view of the environment (Sound recording cassette)
E	MITCHELL, A.	Ugly Duckling.
674	MITGUTSCH, A.	From tree to table.
E	MOFFATT, J.	Who stole the cookies?
398.24	MOLLEL, T. M.	Rhinos for lunch and elephants for supper!: a Masai tale.
E	MOON, N.	Lucy's picture.
811	MOORE, C. C.	Grandma Moses Night before Christmas.
811	MOORE, C. C.	Twas the night before Christmas: a visit from St. Nicholas.
811	MORA, P.	Listen to the desert/Oye al desierto.
E	MORA, P.	Uno, dos, tres: one, two, three.
VCR 640.83		MORE PRESCHOOL POWER! (Videocassette).
621.9	MORRIS, A.	Tools.
599.78	MORRIS, J.	Bears, bears, and more bears.
398.27	MOSEL, A.	Tikki Tikki Tembo.
398.8	MOTHER GOOSE.	Glorious Mother Goose.
398.8	MOTHER GOOSE.	Michael Foreman's Mother Goose.
KIT 398.8	MOTHER GOOSE.	Olde Mother Goose (Kit).
398.8	MOTHER GOOSE.	Real Mother Goose.
398.8	MOTHER GOOSE.	Ring o'roses: a nursery rhyme picture book.
E	MUELLER, V.	Halloween mask for Monster.
SRC 595.7	MURPHY, J.	Songs about insects, bugs and squiggly things (Sound recording cassette).
E	MURPHY, S. J.	Best bug parade.
153.14	MURPHY, S. J.	Pair of socks.
513.2	MURPHY, S. J.	Too many kangaroo things to do!
398.8		MY VERY FIRST MOTHER GOOSE.
CE E	NARAHASHI, K.	I have a friend.
E	NEITZEL, S.	Dress I'll wear to the party.
E	NEITZEL, S.	Jacket I wear in the snow.
E	NEITZEL, S.	We're making breakfast for Mother.
VCR 306.875		NEW BABY IN MY HOUSE (Videocassette).
MCP 750.28		NEW KID PIX. School version (Microcomputer program).
811	NIKOLA-LISA, W.	Alegria de ser tu y yo.
811	NIKOLA-LISA, W.	Bein' with you this way.
E	NIKOLA-LISA, W.	One hole in the road.
E	NIKOLA-LISA, W.	Storm.
221.9		NOAH'S ARK.
VCR 221.9		NOAH'S ARK (Videocassette).
E	NODSET, J. L.	Go away, dog.
E	NOLL, S.	Surprise!
VCR 372.4		NURSERY SONGS AND RHYMES (Videocassette).
398.2		NURSERY TALES AROUND THE WORLD.
E	O'BRIEN, C.	Sam's sneaker search.
E	O'CONNOR, J.	Nina, Nina ballerina.
E	OCHS, C. P.	When I'm alone.
E	OGBURN, J. K.	Noise lullaby.
398.8		OLD MOTHER HUBBARD AND HER WONDERFUL DOG.
636.2	OLDER, J.	Cow.
VCR E		ON THE DAY YOU WERE BORN (Videocassette).
582.16	OPPENHEIM, J.	Have you seen trees?
E	OPPENHEIM, J.	You can't catch me!
E	ORMEROD, J.	Moonlight.
E	ORMEROD, J.	Sunshine.
590.73	ORMEROD, J.	When we went to the zoo.
E	ORMEROD, J.	101 things to do with a baby.
REF 031		OUR AMAZING BODIES: A SUPPLEMENT TO CHILDCRAFT--THE HOW AND WHY LIBRARY.
513.2	OWENS, M. B.	Counting cranes.
E	OXENBURY, H.	Grandma and grandpa.
597.92	PALAZZO-CRAIG, J.	Turtles.
SRC 789.3	PALMER, H.	Can a cherry pie wave goodbye?: songs for learning through music and movement (Sound recording cassette).
SRC 789.3	PALMER, H.	Child's world of lullabies: multicultural songs for quiet times (Sound recording cassette).
SRC 155.2	PALMER, H.	Getting to know myself (Sound recording cassette).
VCR 793	PALMER, H.	Learning basic skills (Videocassette).
VCR 789.3	PALMER, H.	Sammy and other songs from "Getting to know myself" (Videocassette).
CD 789.3	PALMER, H.	So big: activity songs for little ones (Compact disc).
VCR 789.3	PALMER, H.	Stepping out with Hap Palmer (Videocassette).
E	PARNALL, P.	Feet!
612.8	PARRAMON, J. M.	Hearing.
612.8	PARRAMON, J. M.	Sight.
612.8	PARRAMON, J. M.	Taste.
612.8	PARRAMON, J. M.	Touch.
E	PATRICK, D. L.	Red dancing shoes.
224	PATTERSON, G.	Jonah and the whale.
E	PELLEGRINI, N.	Families are different.
REF 031		PEOPLE TO KNOW: A SUPPLEMENT TO CHILDCRAFT--THE HOW AND WHY LIBRARY.
CD 789.2	PETER, PAUL & MARY.	Peter, Paul and Mommy, too (Compact disc).
VCR 789.3		PETER COTTONTAIL: HOW HE GOT HIS HOP! (Videocasstte).
CE E	PETERSHAM, M.	Circus baby.
REF 031		PETS AND OTHER ANIMALS: A SUPPLEMENT TO CHILDCRAFT--THE HOW AND WHY LIBRARY.
VCR E	PINDAL, K.	Peep and the big wide world (Videocassette).
TB 808.8	PINDER, M.	People with one heart (Talking book).
E	PINKWATER, D. M.	Aunt Lulu.
CE E	PIPER, W.	Little engine that could.
CDR 371.3		PLAYROOM (CD-ROM).
577.69	PLUCKROSE, H.	Seashore.
582.16	PLUCKROSE, H.	Trees.
578.75	PLUCKROSE, H.	Under the ground.
551.5	PLUCKROSE, H.	Weather.
808.8	POLACCO, P.	Babushka's Mother Goose.
SRC 789.3	POLISAR, B. L.	Old dogs, new tricks (Sound recording cassette).
789.2		POLLITOS DICEN: JUEGOS, RIMAS Y CANCIONES INFANTILES DE PAISES DE HABLA HISPANA./THE BABY CHICKS SING: TRADITIONAL GAMES, NURSERY
E	POMERANTZ, C.	One duck, another duck.
CE E	POMERANTZ, C.	Outside dog.
E	POTTER, B.	Hill top tales.
E	POTTER, B.	Tailor of Gloucester.
E	POTTER, B.	Tale of Benjamin Bunny.
E	POTTER, B.	Tale of Jemima Puddle-Duck.
E	POTTER, B.	Tale of Johnny Town-Mouse.
E	POTTER, B.	Tale of Mrs. Tiggy-Winkle.
E	POTTER, B.	Tale of Mrs. Tittlemouse.
E	POTTER, B.	Tale of Peter Rabbit.
TB E	POTTER, B.	Tale of Peter Rabbit, and four other stories (Talking book).
E	POTTER, B.	Tale of Squirrel Nutkin.
E	POTTER, B.	Tale of the Flopsy Bunnies.
E	POTTER, B.	Tale of Tom Kitten.
E	POTTER, B.	Tale of two bad mice.
591	POWELL, C.	Bold carnivore: an alphabet of predators.
E	POYDAR, N.	Busy Bea.
811	PRELUTSKY, J.	Ride a purple pelican.

SRC 789.3		*PRESCHOOL ACTION TIME* (Sound recording cassette).
SRC 789.3		*PRESCHOOL PLAYTIME BAND* (Sound recording cassette).
VCR 640.83		*PRESCHOOL POWER 3!* (Videocassette).
VCR 640.83		*PRESCHOOL POWER!: JACKET FLIPS AND OTHER TIPS* (Videocassette).
CE 789.8	PROKOFIEV, S.	Peter and the wolf.
223		*PSALM TWENTY-THREE.*
E	RABE, B.	Where's Chimpy?
629.04	RADFORD, D.	Cargo machines and what they do.
SRC 782.28	RAFFI.	Raffi's Christmas album (Sound recording cassette).
SRC 789.3	RAFFI.	Rise and shine (Sound recording cassette).
789.3	RAFFI.	Wheels on the bus.
CD 789.2		*RAINBOW SIGN (Compact disc).*
E	RANSOM, C. F.	Big green pocketbook.
E	RASCHKA, C.	Yo! Yes?.
E	RAY, M. L.	Mud.
811.008		*READ-ALOUD RHYMES FOR THE VERY YOUNG.*
MCP 372.4		*READER RABBIT'S READY FOR LETTERS (Microcomputer program).*
810.8		*READY...SET...READ!: THE BEGINNING READER'S TREASURY.*
398.8		*REAL MOTHER GOOSE BOOK OF AMERICAN RHYMES.*
598	REIDEL, M.	From egg to bird.
595.78	REIDEL, M.	From egg to butterfly.
E	REISER, L.	Beach feet.
E	REISER, L.	Surprise family.
E	REISER, L.	Two mice in three fables.
E	REISS, J. J.	Numbers.
516	REISS, J. J.	Shapes.
E	REY, H. A.	Curious George.
TB E	REY, H. A.	Curious George and other stories about Curious George (Talking book).
E	REY, H. A.	Curious George gets a medal.
E	REY, H. A.	Curious George learns the alphabet.
CE E	REY, H. A.	Curious George rides a bike.
E	REY, H. A.	Curious George takes a job.
E	REY, M.	Curious George flies a kite.
E	REY, M.	Curious George goes to the hospital.
E	RICE, E.	Benny bakes a cake.
591.47	RILEY, L. C.	Elephants swim.
398.8		*RING-A-RING O' ROSES AND A DING, DONG, BELL: A BOOK OF NURSERY RHYMES.*
E	ROBART, R.	Cake that Mack ate.
KIT 398.24	ROBBINS, S.	Growing rock: a Southwest Native American tale (Kit).
E	ROBERTS, B.	Camel caravan.
E	ROBERTS, B.	Halloween mice!
398.2	ROCKWELL, A. F.	Acorn tree and other folktales.
E	ROCKWELL, A. F.	At the beach.
629.222	ROCKWELL, A. F.	Cars.
628.9	ROCKWELL, A. F.	Fire engines.
E	ROCKWELL, A. F.	First snowfall.
E	ROCKWELL, A. F.	I fly.
E	ROCKWELL, A. F.	Once upon a time this morning.
641.5	ROCKWELL, A. F.	Pots and pans.
E	ROCKWELL, A. F.	Show and tell day.
621.9	ROCKWELL, A. F.	Toolbox.
428.1	ROCKWELL, A. F.	What we like.
617.6	ROCKWELL, H.	My dentist.
E	ROE, E.	With my brother/Con mi hermano.
E	ROGERS, J.	Runaway mittens.
551.6	ROGERS, P.	What will the weather be like today?
SRC 789.3	ROGERS, S.	What can one little person do? (Sound recording cassette).
423	ROOT, B.	My first dictionary.
E	ROOT, P.	Coyote and the magic words.
398.8	ROSEN, M.	We're going on a bear hunt.

E	ROTH, S. L.	My love for you.
612	ROTNER, S.	Faces.
306.874	ROTNER, S.	Lots of dads.
306.874	ROTNER, S.	Lots of moms.
508	ROTNER, S.	Nature spy.
E	ROTNER, S.	Ocean day.
621.8	ROTNER, S.	Wheels around.
978	ROUNDS, G.	Cowboys.
398.24	ROUNDS, G.	Three billy goats Gruff.
398.2	ROWE, J. A.	Gingerbread Man: an old English folktale.
629.222	ROYSTON, A.	Cars.
629.225	ROYSTON, A.	Diggers and dump trucks.
591.734	ROYSTON, A.	Jungle animals.
E	RUBINSTEIN, G.	Dog in, cat out.
E	RUSSO, M.	Line up book.
E	RUSSO, M.	Under the table.
E	RUURS, M.	Emma's eggs.
513.2	RYAN, P. M.	Crayon counting book.
E	RYDER, J.	Night gliders.
E	RYLANT, C.	Birthday presents.
BB E	RYLANT, C.	Everyday children (Board book).
BB E	RYLANT, C.	Everyday garden (Board book).
BB E	RYLANT, C.	Everyday house (Board book).
BB E	RYLANT, C.	Everyday pets (Board book).
BB E	RYLANT, C.	Everyday town (Board book).
E	RYLANT, C.	Mr. Griggs' work.
VCR 363.1		*SAFETY ON WHEELS* (Videocassette).
E	SAMTON, S. W.	World from my window.
E	SATHRE, V.	Mouse chase.
398.27	SAWYER, R.	Journey cake, ho.
398.27	SAY, A.	Under the cherry blossom tree: an old Japanese tale.
E	SCHAEFER, C. L.	Squiggle.
E	SCHEER, J.	Rain makes applesauce.
E	SCHINDEL, J.	What's for lunch?
303.6	SCHOLES, K.	Peace begins with you.
CE E	SCHWARTZ, A.	Annabelle Swift, Kindergartner.
E	SCHWARTZ, A.	Teeny tiny baby.
E	SCHWARTZ, H.	How I captured a dinosaur.
REF 031		*SCIENCE, SCIENCE EVERYWHERE: A SUPPLEMENT TO CHILDCRAFT--THE HOW AND WHY LIBRARY.*
811	SCIESZKA, J.	Book that Jack wrote.
E	SCOTT, A. H.	Hi.
E	SCOTT, A. H.	On mother's lap.
BB E	SEIDEN, A.	Trucks (Board book).
598.6	SELSAM, M. E.	Egg to chick. Rev. ed.
599	SELSAM, M. E.	Keep looking.
CE E	SENDAK, M.	Alligators all around: an alphabet.
CE E	SENDAK, M.	Chicken soup with rice: a book of months.
398.8	SENDAK, M.	Hector Protector and As I went over the water: two nursery rhymes with pictures.
VCR E	SENDAK, M.	Maurice Sendak Library (Videocassette).
VCR E	SENDAK, M.	Nutshell library (Videocassette).
CE E	SENDAK, M.	One was Johnny: a counting book.
CE E	SENDAK, M.	Pierre: a cautionary tale in five chapters and a prologue.
CE E	SENDAK, M.	Where the wild things are. 25th anniv. ed.
TB E	SENDAK, M.	Where the wild things are and other stories (Talking book).
E	SERFOZO, M.	Benjamin Bigfoot.
E	SERFOZO, M.	Joe Joe.
E	SERFOZO, M.	Rain talk.
E	SERFOZO, M.	There's a square: a book about shapes.
E	SERFOZO, M.	What's what?: a guessing game.
E	SERFOZO, M.	Who said red?
PER 050		*SESAME STREET MAGAZINE.*
E	SEUSS, D.	Bartholomew and the oobleck.
CE E	SEUSS, D.	Cat in the hat.
CE E	SEUSS, D.	Cat in the hat comes back.
CE E	SEUSS, D.	Dr. Seuss's ABC.

E	SEUSS, D.	*Foot book.*
E	SEUSS, D.	*Fox in socks.*
CE E	SEUSS, D.	*Green eggs and ham.*
E	SEUSS, D.	*Hop on pop.*
CE E	SEUSS, D.	*Horton hatches the egg.*
VCR E	SEUSS, D.	*Horton hatches the egg./If I ran the circus (Videocassette).*
CE E	SEUSS, D.	*Horton hears a Who.*
VCR E	SEUSS, D.	*Horton hears a Who!/Thidwick the big-hearted moose (Videocassette).*
E	SEUSS, D.	*How the Grinch stole Christmas.*
E	SEUSS, D.	*I can read with my eyes shut.*
E	SEUSS, D.	*If I ran the circus.*
E	SEUSS, D.	*If I ran the zoo.*
CE E	SEUSS, D.	*Lorax.*
E	SEUSS, D.	*McElligot's pool.*
E	SEUSS, D.	*On beyond zebra.*
E	SEUSS, D.	*One fish, two fish, red fish, blue fish.*
CE E	SEUSS, D.	*Yertle the turtle, and other stories.*
E	SEUSS, D.	*500 hats of Bartholomew Cubbins.*
E	SHANNON, G.	*April showers.*
811	SHAPIRO, A.	*Mice squeak, we speak: a poem.*
E	SHARMAT, M. W.	*I'm terrific.*
E	SHEA, P. D.	*New moon.*
E	SHOWERS, P.	*Listening walk.*
612.8	SHOWERS, P.	*Look at your eyes. Rev. ed.*
E	SHOWERS, P.	*Sonidos a mi alrededor.*
E	SHULEVITZ, U.	*Rain, rain rivers.*
E	SIDDALS, M. M.	*Tell me a season.*
E	SIEBERT, D.	*Train song.*
CE E	SIEBERT, D.	*Truck song.*
398.24	SIERRA, J.	*Elephant's wrestling match.*
E	SILVERMAN, E.	*Big pumpkin.*
E	SILVERMAN, E.	*Don't fidget a feather!*
811	SILVERSTEIN, S.	*Falling up: poems and drawings.*
811	SILVERSTEIN, S.	*Light in the attic.*
811	SILVERSTEIN, S.	*Where the sidewalk ends: the poems and drawings of Shel Silverstein.*
155.4	SIMON, N.	*I am not a crybaby.*
152.4	SIMON, N.	*I was so mad.*
E	SIMON, N.	*Wet world.*
523.7	SIMON, S.	*Sun.*
E	SIS, P.	*Going up! A color counting book.*
E	SIS, P.	*Waving: a counting book.*
E	SLATE, J.	*Miss Bindergarten gets ready for kindergarten.*
789.2	SLAVIN, B.	*Cat came back: a traditional song.*
808.81		*SLEEP, BABY, SLEEP: LULLABIES AND NIGHT POEMS.*
808.81		*SLEEP RHYMES AROUND THE WORLD.*
VCR E		*SLIGHTLY SCARY STORIES (Videocassette).*
CE E	SLOBODKINA, E.	*Caps for sale: a tale of a peddler, some monkeys and their monkey business.*
CE E	SLOBODKINA, E.	*Venden gorras: la historia de un vendedor ambulante, unos monos y sus travesuras.*
CE E	SMALL, D.	*Imogene's antlers.*
MCP 153.4		*SNAPDRAGON (Microcomputer program).*
811.008		*SNUFFLES AND SNOUTS: POEMS.*
760	SOLGA, K.	*Make prints!*
398.24	SOUHAMI, J.	*Leopard's drum: an Asante tale from West Africa.*
E	SPIER, P.	*Dreams.*
E	SPIER, P.	*Peter Spier's circus!*
CDR 372.6		*STANLEY'S STICKER STORIES. School version (CD-ROM).*
CE E	STEIG, W.	*Doctor De Soto.*
CE E	STEIG, W.	*Doctor De Soto goes to Africa.*
E	STEIG, W.	*Toby, where are you?*
305.232	STEIN, S.	*Oh, baby!*
E	STEVENSON, H.	*Grandpa's house.*
E	STEVENSON, J.	*Fried feathers for Thanksgiving.*
E	STEVENSON, J.	*Oldest elf.*
E	STEVENSON, J.	*Rolling Rose.*
E	STEVENSON, J.	*We hate rain!*
821	STEVENSON, R. L.	*Child's garden of verses.*
SRC 613.7	STEWART, G.	*Good morning exercises for kids (Sound recording cassette).*
SRC 796.1	STEWART, G.	*Multicultural rhythm stick fun (Sound recording cassette).*
SRC 789.3	STEWART, G.	*Pre-K hooray! (Sound recording cassette).*
SRC 789.3	STEWART, G.	*Preschool favorites (Sound recording cassette).*
E	STOCK, C.	*Birthday present.*
E	STOCK, C.	*Christmas time.*
E	STOCK, C.	*Easter surprise.*
E	STOCK, C.	*Halloween monster.*
E	STOCK, C.	*Thanksgiving treat.*
E	STOEKE, J. M.	*Hat for Minerva Louise.*
E	STOEKE, J. M.	*Minerva Louise at school.*
VCR 577.3	STOLTZ, W. J.	*Come walk with me (Videocassette).*
811.008		*SUNFLAKES: POEMS FOR CHILDREN.*
E	SUTEEV, V.	*Chick and the duckling.*
SRC 577	SUZUKI, D.	*Connections: finding out about the environment (Sound recording cassette).*
E	SYKES, J.	*This and that.*
E	TAFURI, N.	*Do not disturb.*
E	TAFURI, N.	*Early morning in the barn.*
E	TAFURI, N.	*Follow me!*
E	TAFURI, N.	*Have you seen my duckling?*
636	TAFURI, N.	*Spots, feathers, and curly tails.*
E	TAFURI, N.	*This is the farmer.*
E	TAFURI, N.	*Who's counting?*
821.008		*TALKING LIKE THE RAIN: A FIRST BOOK OF POEMS.*
398.2	TARCOV, E. H.	*Frog prince.*
821	TAYLOR, J.	*Twinkle, twinkle, little star.*
E	TEJIMA, K.	*Fox's dream.*
789.2		*THIS OLD MAN.*
828	THOMAS, D.	*Child's Christmas in Wales.*
E	THOMAS, S. M.	*Putting the world to sleep.*
591.5	THORNHILL, J.	*Wild in the city.*
591.97	THORNHILL, J.	*Wildlife A-B-C: a nature alphabet book.*
591	THORNHILL, J.	*Wildlife 1 2 3: a nature counting book.*
E	THREADGALL, C.	*Proud rooster and the fox.*
VCR 398.24		*THREE BILLY GOATS GRUFF; AND, THE THREE LITTLE PIGS (Videocassette).*
E	TITHERINGTON, J.	*Place for Ben.*
E	TITHERINGTON, J.	*Pumpkin pumpkin.*
E	TITHERINGTON, J.	*Where are you going, Emma?*
E	TITUS, E.	*Kitten who couldn't purr.*
789.3		*TODAY IS MONDAY.*
398.2		*TOM TIT TOT: AN ENGLISH FOLK TALE.*
SRC 398.24	TORRENCE, J.	*Classic children's tales (Sound recording cassette).*
789.3	TRAPANI, I.	*Itsy bitsy spider.*
808.8		*TREASURY OF CHILDREN'S LITERATURE.*
E	TRINCA, R.	*One woolly wombat.*
E	TRIVAS, I.	*Emma's Christmas: an old song.*
E	TRIVIZAS, E.	*Three little wolves and the big bad pig.*
E	TRIVIZAS, E.	*Tres lobitos y el cochino feroz.*
CDR 529		*TRUDY'S TIME AND PLACE HOUSE. School version (CD-ROM).*
E	TRYON, L.	*Albert's alphabet.*
E	TRYON, L.	*Albert's ballgame.*
E	TRYON, L.	*Albert's field trip.*
E	TRYON, L.	*Albert's play.*
394.26	TUDOR, T.	*Time to keep: the Tasha Tudor book of holidays.*
CE E	TURNER, A.	*Through moon and stars and night skies.*
KIT 394	TURNER, M.	*Come on everybody! Let's go to the fair (Kit).*

782.28		*TWELVE DAYS OF CHRISTMAS.*
782.28		*TWELVE DAYS OF CHRISTMAS.*
VCR 782.28		*TWELVE DAYS OF CHRISTMAS (Videocassette).*
E	UDRY, J. M.	*Let's be enemies.*
811	UPDIKE, J.	*Helpful alphabet of friendly objects: poems.*
E	VAN LAAN, N.	*Round and round again.*
E	VAN LAAN, N.	*Sleep, sleep, sleep: a lullaby for little ones around the world.*
398.8	VAN RYNBACH, I.	*Five little pumpkins.*
570	VANCLEAVE, J. P.	*Biology for every kid: 101 easy experiments that really work.*
E	VAUGHAN, M. K.	*Wombat stew.*
E	VIGNA, J.	*I wish Daddy didn't drink so much.*
E	VINCENT, G.	*Ernest and Celestine.*
E	VINCENT, G.	*Ernest and Celestine at the circus.*
E	VINCENT, G.	*Ernest and Celestine's picnic.*
E	VINCENT, G.	*Where are you, Ernest and Celestine?*
CE E	VIORST, J.	*Alexander, who used to be rich last Sunday.*
CE E	VIORST, J.	*Alexander and the terrible, horrible, no good, very bad day.*
TB E	VIORST, J.	*Alexander and the terrible, horrible, no good, very bad day and other stories and poems (Talking book).*
E	VIORST, J.	*Good-bye book.*
E	VIORST, J.	*My mama says there aren't any zombies, ghosts, vampires, creatures, demons, monsters, fiends, goblins, or things.*
E	WABER, B.	*Funny, funny Lyle.*
E	WABER, B.	*House on East 88th Street.*
CE E	WABER, B.	*Lovable Lyle.*
CE E	WABER, B.	*Lyle, Lyle, crocodile.*
E	WABER, B.	*Lyle and the birthday party.*
E	WABER, B.	*Lyle finds his mother.*
E	WADDELL, M.	*Can't you sleep, Little Bear? 2nd ed.*
E	WADDELL, M.	*Farmer duck.*
E	WADDELL, M.	*Let's go home, Little Bear.*
E	WADDELL, M.	*You and me, Little Bear.*
591	WADSWORTH, G.	*One on a web: counting animals at home.*
VCR 636.7		*WAGGING TAILS: THE DOG AND PUPPY MUSIC VIDEO (Videocassette).*
E	WALSH, E. S.	*Hop jump.*
E	WALSH, E. S.	*Mouse paint.*
E	WALSH, E. S.	*You silly goose.*
E	WALTER, M. P.	*My mama needs me.*
E	WATSON, C.	*AppleBet; an ABC.*
BA 789.3	WEEKS, S.	*Crocodile smile: 10 songs of the Earth as the animals see it.*
BA 793.4	WEIMER, T. E.	*Fingerplays and action chants: volume 1: animals.*
E	WEISS, G. D.	*What a wonderful world.*
E	WELLS, R.	*Bunny cakes.*
E	WELLS, R.	*Edward in deep water.*
E	WELLS, R.	*Edward unready for school.*
E	WELLS, R.	*Edward's overwhelming overnight.*
E	WELLS, R.	*Max and Ruby's first Greek myth: Pandora's box.*
E	WELLS, R.	*Max and Ruby's Midas: another Greek myth.*
CE E	WELLS, R.	*Max's chocolate chicken.*
CE E	WELLS, R.	*Max's Christmas.*
BB E	WELLS, R.	*Max's first word (Board book).*
BB E	WELLS, R.	*Max's new suit.*
BB E	WELLS, R.	*Max's ride.*
CE 811	WESTCOTT, N. B.	*I know an old lady who swallowed a fly.*
398.8	WESTCOTT, N. B.	*Lady with the alligator purse.*
612		*WHAT IS A BELLYBUTTON?: FIRST QUESTIONS AND ANSWERS ABOUT THE HUMAN BODY.*
793.73	WICK, W.	*I spy Christmas: a book of picture riddles.*
793.73	WICK, W.	*I spy spooky night: a book of picture riddles.*
E	WIDMAN, C.	*Lemon drop jar.*
E	WIESNER, D.	*Tuesday.*
E	WIKLER, L.	*Alfonse, where are you?*
E	WILD, M.	*Our granny.*
E	WILDSMITH, B.	*Brian Wildsmith's ABC.*
597	WILDSMITH, B.	*Fishes.*
423	WILKES, A.	*Mi primer libro de palabras en Espanol.*
423	WILKES, A.	*Mon premier livre de mots en Francais.*
423	WILKES, A.	*My first word book.*
CE E	WILLIAMS, L.	*Little old lady who was not afraid of anything.*
CE E	WILLIAMS, L.	*Viejecita que no le tenia miedo a nada.*
CE E	WILLIAMS, S.	*I went walking.*
CE E	WILLIAMS, S.	*Sali de paseo.*
E	WILLIAMS, V. B.	*Algo especial para mi.*
E	WILLIAMS, V. B.	*Chair for my mother.*
E	WILLIAMS, V. B.	*More more more, said the baby.*
E	WILLIAMS, V. B.	*Music, music for everyone.*
E	WILLIAMS, V. B.	*Something special for me.*
E	WINTHROP, E.	*Bear and Mrs. Duck.*
E	WINTHROP, E.	*Bear's Christmas surprise.*
CE E	WINTHROP, E.	*Shoes.*
E	WINTHROP, E.	*Sledding.*
E	WITTMAN, S.	*Special trade.*
E	WOLFF, A.	*Stella and Roy.*
E	WOLFF, A.	*Year of beasts.*
CE E	WOOD, A.	*King Bidgood's in the bathtub.*
CE E	WOOD, A.	*Napping house.*
TB E	WOOD, A.	*Napping house and other stories (Talking book).*
E	WOOD, A.	*Silly Sally.*
398.24	WOOD, A. J.	*Lion and the mouse: an Aesop's fable.*
E	WOOD, D.	*Piggies.*
E	WOOD, J.	*Dads are such fun.*
591.59	WOOD, J.	*Jakki Wood's animal hullabaloo: a wildlife noisy book.*
E	WORMELL, C.	*Number of animals.*
523.8	WYLER, R.	*Starry sky.*
398.24	XIONG, B.	*Nine-in-one, grr! grr! a folktale from the Hmong people of Laos.*
CE E	YASHIMA, T.	*Umbrella.*
513.2	YEKTAI, N.	*Bears at the beach: counting 10 to 20.*
CE E	YOLEN, J.	*Owl moon.*
E	ZALBEN, J. B.	*Beni's first Chanukah.*
E	ZALBEN, J. B.	*Leo and Blossom's sukkah.*
E	ZAMORANO, A.	*Let's eat!*
SRC 508	ZEITLIN, P.	*Spin, spider, spin: songs for a greater appreciation of nature (Sound recording cassette).*
CE E	ZEMACH, H.	*Judge, an untrue tale.*
E	ZEMACH, H.	*Mommy, buy me a china doll.*
E	ZEMACH, H.	*Little red hen, an old story.*
398.24	ZEMACH, M.	*Three little pigs.*
E	ZIEFERT, H.	*Clown games.*
E	ZIEFERT, H.	*Nicky upstairs and down.*
E	ZIEFERT, H.	*Three wishes.*
E	ZIEFERT, H.	*What rhymes with eel?: a word-and-picture flap book.*
E	ZIEFERT, H.	*Who said moo?*
CE E	ZION, G.	*Harry, no quiere rosas!*
CE E	ZION, G.	*Harry and the lady next door.*
CE E	ZION, G.	*Harry by the sea.*
CE E	ZION, G.	*Harry el perrito sucio.*
CE E	ZION, G.	*Harry the dirty dog.*
CE E	ZION, G.	*No roses for Harry.*
594	ZOEHFELD, K. W.	*What lives in a shell?*
CE E	ZOLOTOW, C.	*Mr. Rabbit and the lovely present.*
E	ZOLOTOW, C.	*Over and over.*
CE E	ZOLOTOW, C.	*Senor Conejo y el hermoso regalo.*
591.5	ZOLOTOW, C.	*Sleepy book.*
E	ZOLOTOW, C.	*William's doll.*

BOOKS FOR INDEPENDENT READING

This special list is limited to books only and consists of those titles in the Classified Catalog which can be recommended for use by beginning readers. The reading levels: 1-1, 1-2, 2-1, and 2-2 have been determined by application of the Spache Reading Formula which is recommended as especially effective for use in testing primary grade reading materials. For complete information and descriptive annotations of each title, the reader is referred to the citation under the call number in the Classified Catalog.

Books for Independent Reading Level 1-1

E	ANTLE, N.	*Good bad cat.*
E	BERENSTAIN, S.	*Inside, outside, upside down.*
398.8		*BIG FAT HEN.*
E	BONSALL, C. N.	*And I mean it, Stanley.*
E	BONSALL, C. N.	*Day I had to play with my sister.*
E	BONSALL, C. N.	*Who's afraid of the dark?*
CE E	BROWN, M. W.	*Goodnight moon.*
E	BUCK, N.	*Oh, cats!*
E	BUCK, N.	*Sid and Sam.*
E	CARLE, E.	*Have you seen my cat?*
E	CREWS, D.	*School bus.*
E	FALWELL, C.	*We have a baby.*
E	FLEMING, D.	*In the tall, tall grass.*
E	FLORIAN, D.	*Summer day.*
E	FLORIAN, D.	*Winter day.*
745		*FOLK ART COUNTING BOOK.*
E	FORD, M.	*Little elephant.*
E	GINSBURG, M.	*Asleep, asleep.*
E	GUY, G. F.	*Fiesta!*
E	HEILBRONER, J.	*Robert the rose horse.*
E	HOBAN, T.	*Where is it?*
E	HOFF, S.	*Who will be my friends?*
CE E	HUTCHINS, P.	*Rosie's walk.*
E	KALAN, R.	*Stop, thief!*
E	KARLIN, N.	*I see, you saw.*
E	LESIEG, T.	*Eye book.*
E	LILLIE, P.	*Everything has a place.*
E	MACCARONE, G.	*Cars! cars! cars!*
E	MACCARONE, G.	*Pizza party!*
E	MCGUIRE, R.	*Night becomes day.*
513.2	MCMILLAN, B.	*Eating fractions.*
E	MILLER, M.	*Where does it go?*
599.78	MORRIS, J.	*Bears, bears, and more bears.*
E	MUELLER, V.	*Halloween mask for Monster.*
E	MURPHY, S. J.	*Best bug parade.*
E	NODSET, J. L.	*Go away, dog.*
E	POMERANTZ, C.	*One duck, another duck.*
E	RASCHKA, C.	*Yo! Yes?.*
E	RATHMANN, P.	*Good night, Gorilla.*
E	ROBART, R.	*Cake that Mack ate.*
E	RUBINSTEIN, G.	*Dog in, cat out.*
E	SERFOZO, M.	*Joe Joe.*
E	SEUSS, D.	*Foot book.*
E	SEUSS, D.	*Hop on pop.*
E	SEUSS, D.	*One fish, two fish, red fish, blue fish.*
E	SIDDALS, M. M.	*Tell me a season.*
E	SPIRN, M.	*Know-Nothing birthday.*
E	TAFURI, N.	*Have you seen my duckling?*
636	TAFURI, N.	*Spots, feathers, and curly tails.*
CE E	WILLIAMS, S.	*I went walking.*
E	ZIEFERT, H.	*Clown games.*
E	ZIEFERT, H.	*Nicky upstairs and down.*

Books for Independent Reading Level 1-2

E	ANDERSON, P. P.	*Time for bed, the babysitter said.*
E	ARNOSKY, J.	*Watching foxes.*
E	ARUEGO, J.	*We hide, you seek.*
E	BAKER, B.	*One Saturday morning.*
E	BAKER, B.	*Staying with Grandmother.*
E	BAKER, K.	*Who is the beast?*
398.24	BARTON, B.	*Three bears.*
398.24	BENITEZ, M.	*How spider tricked snake.*
E	BERENSTAIN, S.	*Berenstain Bears and the spooky old tree.*
E	BONSALL, C. N.	*Mine's the best. Newly illustrated ed.*
E	BRANDENBERG, A.	*I am me!*
CE E	BRENNER, B.	*Wagon wheels.*
CE E	BRIDWELL, N.	*Clifford, we love you.*
CE E	BRIDWELL, N.	*Clifford gets a job.*
CE E	BRIDWELL, N.	*Clifford the big red dog.*
CE E	BRIDWELL, N.	*Clifford the small red puppy.*
E	BROWN, L. K.	*Rex and Lilly family time.*
E	BROWN, M. T.	*D.W. flips.*
E	BROWN, M. T.	*True Francine.*
E	BROWN, R.	*Our puppy's vacation.*
513.2	BRUSCA, M. C.	*Three friends: a counting book. / Tres amigos: un cuento para contar.*
E	BUCKLEY, H. E.	*Grandfather and I.*
E	BULLA, C. R.	*Daniel's duck.*
E	BUNTING, E.	*Jane Martin, dog detective.*
E	BYARS, B. C.	*Ant plays Bear.*
CE E	BYARS, B. C.	*Golly sisters go West.*
CE E	BYARS, B. C.	*Golly sisters ride again.*
CE E	BYARS, B. C.	*Hooray for the Golly sisters!*
E	BYARS, B. C.	*Joy boys.*
E	BYARS, B. C.	*My brother, Ant.*
E	CAPUCILLI, A.	*Biscuit.*
E	CAPUCILLI, A.	*Biscuit finds a friend.*
E	CARLE, E.	*From head to toe.*
E	CARLSTROM, N. W.	*I'm not moving, Mama!*
E	CHARLES, V. M.	*Hey! What's that sound?*
E	CLEARY, B.	*Growing-up feet.*
E	COWLEY, J.	*Gracias, the Thanksgiving turkey.*
E	DELANEY, A.	*Pearl's first prize plant.*
E	DENTON, K. M.	*Would they love a lion?*
E	DODDS, D. A.	*Color box.*
E	DONNELLY, L.	*Dinosaur day.*
E	DUBANEVICH, A.	*Pig William.*
E	EASTMAN, P. D.	*Are you my mother?*
E	EASTMAN, P. D.	*Go, dog, go!*
E	EASTMAN, P. D.	*Sam and the firefly.*
E	EHLERT, L.	*Fish eyes: a book you can count on.*
636.8	EISLER, C.	*Cats know best.*
398.8		*FIVE LITTLE DUCKS: AN OLD RHYME.*
E	FLEMING, D.	*In the small, small pond.*
E	FORD, M.	*Sunflower.*
305.8	FOX, M.	*Whoever you are.*
629.224	GIBBONS, G.	*Trucks.*
E	GINSBURG, M.	*Sun's asleep behind the hill.*
E	GRAY, N.	*Country far away.*
E	GRIFFITH, H. V.	*Grandaddy's place.*
E	HALL, K.	*I'm not scared.*
E	HALL, K.	*Tooth fairy.*

E	HARPER, I.	*My dog Rosie.*
E	HARPER, I.	*Our new puppy.*
E	HAZEN, B. S.	*Tight times.*
E	HEST, A.	*Baby Duck and the bad eyeglasses.*
E	HILL, E.	*Where's Spot? Sign language edition.*
E	HIMMELMAN, J.	*Day-off machine.*
BB E	HOBAN, L.	*Big little otter (Board book).*
E	HOBAN, L.	*Case of the two masked robbers.*
E	HOBAN, T.	*One little kitten.*
E	HOFF, S.	*Barkley.*
E	HOFF, S.	*Julius.*
E	HOWLAND, N.	*ABCDrive!: a car trip alphabet.*
E	HUTCHINS, P.	*Shrinking mouse.*
E	ISADORA, R.	*At the crossroads.*
E	JAKOB, D.	*My new sandbox.*
E	JONAS, A.	*Color dance.*
E	JONAS, A.	*Holes and peeks.*
E	JONAS, A.	*Splash!*
E	JONAS, A.	*13th clue.*
580	JORDAN, H. J.	*How a seed grows. Rev. ed.*
CE E	KALAN, R.	*Jump, frog, jump! New ed.*
E	KALAN, R.	*Moving day.*
E	KESSLER, E.	*Stan the hot dog man.*
E	KESSLER, L.	*Big mile race.*
E	KESSLER, L.	*Last one in is a rotten egg.*
CE E	KRAUS, R.	*Come out and play, little mouse.*
CE E	KRAUS, R.	*Whose mouse are you?*
E	KRAUSS, R.	*Very special house.*
E	LAPOINTE, C.	*Out of sight! Out of mind!*
E	LESIEG, T.	*Ten apples up on top!*
E	LESIEG, T.	*Wacky Wednesday.*
E	LEVINSON, N. S.	*Clara and the bookwagon.*
E	LEXAU, J. M.	*Rooftop mystery.*
E	LITTLEFIELD, H.	*Fire at the Triangle Factory.*
E	LOBEL, A.	*Days with Frog and Toad.*
CE E	LOBEL, A.	*Frog and Toad all year.*
CE E	LOBEL, A.	*Ming Lo moves the mountain.*
CE E	LOBEL, A.	*Mouse soup.*
E	LOBEL, A.	*Owl at home.*
E	LOBEL, A.	*Uncle Elephant.*
E	LONG, E.	*Gone fishing.*
E	LOPSHIRE, R.	*Put me in the zoo.*
B KELLER, H.	LUNDELL, M.	*Girl named Helen Keller.*
E	MACDONALD, A.	*Little Beaver and The Echo.*
591	MACDONALD, S.	*Peck slither and slide.*
E	MACK, S.	*10 bears in my bed: a goodnight countdown.*
629.13	MARQUARDT, M.	*Wilbur and Orville and the flying machine.*
CE E	MARSHALL, E.	*Fox and his friends.*
CE E	MARSHALL, E.	*Three by the sea.*
CE E	MARSHALL, E.	*Three up a tree.*
E	MARSHALL, J.	*Fox be nimble.*
E	MARTIN, A. M.	*Rachel Parker, kindergarten show-off.*
E	MARTIN, JR., B.	*Brown bear, brown bear, what do you see?*
E	MARZOLLO, J.	*I'm a seed.*
E	MCCLINTOCK, M.	*Stop that ball.*
398.24	MCDERMOTT, G.	*Zomo the rabbit: a trickster tale from West Africa.*
E	MCMILLAN, B.	*Mouse views: what the class pet saw.*
759	MICKLETHWAIT, L.	*I spy: an alphabet in art.*
750	MICKLETHWAIT, L.	*Spot a dog.*
CE E	MINARIK, E. H.	*Kiss for Little Bear.*
E	MOFFATT, J.	*Who stole the cookies?*
391.4	MORRIS, A.	*Hats, hats, hats.*
E	O'CONNOR, J.	*Nina, Nina ballerina.*
E	PACKARD, M.	*Christmas kitten.*
E	PACKARD, M.	*I am king!*
E	PALAZZO-CRAIG, J.	*Max and Maggie in autumn.*
E	PALAZZO-CRAIG, J.	*Max and Maggie in spring.*
E	PALAZZO-CRAIG, J.	*Max and Maggie in summer.*
E	PALAZZO-CRAIG, J.	*Max and Maggie in winter.*
597.92	PALAZZO-CRAIG, J.	*Turtles.*
CE E	PARISH, P.	*Amelia Bedelia goes camping.*
E	PARISH, P.	*Be ready at eight.*
CE E	PARISH, P.	*Merry Christmas, Amelia Bedelia.*
E	PARISH, P.	*No more monsters for me!*
E	PARISH, P.	*Scruffy.*
CE E	PARISH, P.	*Teach us, Amelia Bedelia.*
E	PARNALL, P.	*Feet!*
612.8	PARRAMON, J. M.	*Hearing.*
612.8	PARRAMON, J. M.	*Sight.*
E	REY, M.	*Curious George flies a kite.*
E	ROBINS, J.	*Addie meets Max.*
629.222	ROCKWELL, A. F.	*Cars.*
CE B BURGESS, A	ROOP, P.	*Keep the lights burning, Abbie.*
306.874	ROTNER, S.	*Lots of moms.*
E	RUSSO, M.	*Line up book.*
CE E	SCHWARTZ, A.	*Annabelle Swift, Kindergartner.*
398.25	SCHWARTZ, A.	*In a dark, dark room and other scary stories.*
E	SERFOZO, M.	*There's a square: a book about shapes.*
CE E	SEUSS, D.	*Cat in the hat.*
CE E	SEUSS, D.	*Cat in the hat comes back.*
CE E	SEUSS, D.	*Green eggs and ham.*
E	SHARMAT, M. W.	*I'm the best!*
E	SHARMAT, M. W.	*Mitchell is moving.*
CE E	SHARMAT, M. W.	*Nate the Great and the phony clue.*
E	SHARMAT, M. W.	*Nate the Great and the pillowcase.*
E	SHAW, N.	*Sheep in a shop.*
E	SHAW, N.	*Sheep on a ship.*
E	SHOWERS, P.	*Listening walk.*
598	SILL, C.	*About birds: a guide for children.*
E	SIRACUSA, C.	*Bingo, the best dog in the world.*
CE E	SLOBODKINA, E.	*Caps for sale: a tale of a peddler, some monkeys and their monkey business.*
E	SPOHN, K.	*Dog and Cat shake a leg.*
E	STEVENSON, J.	*National worm day.*
E	SUTEEV, V.	*Chick and the duckling.*
912	SWEENEY, J.	*Me on the map.*
E	TAFURI, N.	*This is the farmer.*
E	TITHERINGTON, J.	*Pumpkin pumpkin.*
E	TITUS, E.	*Kitten who couldn't purr.*
CE E	TURNER, A.	*Through moon and stars and night skies.*
CE E	VAN LEEUWEN, J.	*Amanda Pig, schoolgirl.*
CE E	VAN LEEUWEN, J.	*Amanda Pig and her big brother, Oliver.*
CE E	VAN LEEUWEN, J.	*More tales of Amanda Pig.*
CE E	VAN LEEUWEN, J.	*Oliver, Amanda, and Grandmother Pig.*
CE E	VAN LEEUWEN, J.	*Oliver and Amanda and the big snow.*
CE E	VAN LEEUWEN, J.	*Oliver Pig at school.*
CE E	VAN LEEUWEN, J.	*Tales of Amanda Pig.*
CE E	VAN LEEUWEN, J.	*Tales of Oliver Pig.*
E	VINCENT, G.	*Ernest and Celestine.*
E	VINCENT, G.	*Ernest and Celestine's picnic.*
E	WADDELL, M.	*You and me, Little Bear.*
E	WALTER, M. P.	*My mama needs me.*
BB E	WELLS, R.	*Max's first word (Board book).*
BB E	WELLS, R.	*Max's new suit.*
BB E	WELLS, R.	*Max's ride.*
E	WIKLER, L.	*Alfonse, where are you?*
E	WINTHROP, E.	*Bear and Mrs. Duck.*
E	WISEMAN, B.	*Morris and Boris.*
E	WISEMAN, B.	*Morris and Boris at the circus.*
E	WOLFF, A.	*Year of beasts.*
CE E	WOOD, A.	*King Bidgood's in the bathtub.*
E	WOOD, D.	*Piggies.*
E	WOOD, J.	*Dads are such fun.*
E	ZAMORANO, A.	*Let's eat!*
E	ZEMACH, H.	*Mommy, buy me a china doll.*
E	ZIEFERT, H.	*Jason's bus ride.*
E	ZIEFERT, H.	*Mike and Tony: best friends.*
E	ZIEFERT, H.	*Princess and the pea.*
E	ZIEFERT, H.	*Three wishes.*
398.24	ZIEFERT, H.	*Turnip.*

Books for Independent Reading Level 2-1

398.24	AARDEMA, V.	*This for that: a Tonga tale.*	
E	ABOLAFIA, Y.	*Fox tale.*	
E	ADLER, D. A.	*Young Cam Jansen and the dinosaur game.*	
E	ADLER, D. A.	*Young Cam Jansen and the lost tooth.*	
E	AHLBERG, J.	*Funnybones.*	
E	ALBOROUGH, J.	*Where's my teddy?*	
E	ALEXANDER, M.	*How my library grew by Dinah.*	
E	ALEXANDER, M.	*You're a genius, Blackboard Bear.*	
560	ALIKI.	*Fossils tell of long ago. Rev. ed.*	
612.6	ALIKI.	*I'm growing!*	
395	ALIKI.	*Manners.*	
637	ALIKI.	*Milk from cow to carton. Rev. ed.*	
612.8	ALIKI.	*My five senses. Rev. ed.*	
CE E	ALLEN, L. J.	*Rollo and Tweedy and the ghost at Dougal Castle.*	
512	ANNO, M.	*Anno's mysterious multiplying jar.*	
398.24	ARUEGO, J.	*Rockabye crocodile.*	
CE E	ASCH, F.	*Happy birthday, moon.*	
E	ASCH, F.	*Moonbear's pet.*	
583	BACK, C.	*Bean and plant.*	
598.6	BACK, C.	*Chicken and egg.*	
E	BAKER, K.	*Hide and snake.*	
E	BANG, M.	*Goose.*	
398.21	BANG, M.	*Wiley and the Hairy Man: adapted from an American folk tale.*	
E	BANNERMAN, H.	*Story of Little Babaji.*	
E	BARTON, B.	*Machines at work.*	
E	BENCHLEY, N.	*George, the drummer boy.*	
551.5	BERGER, M.	*How's the weather?: a look at weather and how it changes.*	
523.8	BERGER, M.	*Where are the stars during the day?: a book about stars.*	
325.73	BERGER, M.	*Where did your family come from?: a book about immigrants.*	
912	BERGER, M.	*Whole world in your hands: looking at maps.*	
398.22	BERNIER-GRAND, C. T.	*Juan Bobo: four folktales from Puerto Rico.*	
E	BEST, C.	*Red light, green light, Mama and me.*	
796.357	BLACKSTONE, M.	*This is baseball.*	
CE E	BLUME, J.	*One in the middle is the green kangaroo.*	
E	BOLAND, J.	*Dog named Sam.*	
CE E	BONSALL, C. N.	*Case of the cat's meow.*	
CE E	BONSALL, C. N.	*Case of the double cross.*	
CE E	BONSALL, C. N.	*Case of the hungry stranger.*	
CE E	BONSALL, C. N.	*Case of the scaredy cats.*	
E	BONSALL, C. N.	*Piggle.*	
E	BONSALL, C. N.	*Tell me some more.*	
E	BOYD, C. D.	*Daddy, Daddy, be there.*	
B LINCOLN, A.	BRENNER, M.	*Abe Lincoln's hat.*	
E	BRETT, J.	*Annie and the wild animals.*	
CE E	BRIDWELL, N.	*Clifford at the circus.*	
CE E	BRIDWELL, N.	*Clifford takes a trip.*	
CE E	BRIDWELL, N.	*Clifford's good deeds.*	
E	BRIMNER, L. D.	*Brave Mary.*	
597.96	BROEKEL, R.	*Snakes.*	
E	BROWN, C.	*In the spring.*	
631.3	BROWN, C.	*Tractor.*	
CE E	BROWN, M. T.	*Arthur babysits.*	
CE E	BROWN, M. T.	*Arthur goes to camp.*	
CE E	BROWN, M. T.	*Arthur meets the president.*	
E	BROWN, M. T.	*Arthur writes a story.*	
E	BROWN, M. T.	*Arthur's April fool.*	
E	BROWN, M. T.	*Arthur's baby.*	
CE E	BROWN, M. T.	*Arthur's birthday.*	
CE E	BROWN, M. T.	*Arthur's eyes.*	
E	BROWN, M. T.	*Arthur's first sleepover.*	
E	BROWN, M. T.	*Arthur's Halloween.*	
CE E	BROWN, M. T.	*Arthur's new puppy.*	
CE E	BROWN, M. T.	*Arthur's nose.*	
CE E	BROWN, M. T.	*Arthur's pet business.*	
E	BROWN, M. T.	*Arthur's Thanksgiving.*	
CE E	BROWN, M. T.	*Arthur's tooth.*	
E	BROWN, M. T.	*Arthur's TV trouble.*	
E	BROWN, M. T.	*Arthur's Valentine.*	
E	BROWN, M. T.	*D.W. rides again!*	
E	BROWN, M. T.	*D.W. thinks big.*	
E	BROWN, M. W.	*Little Donkey close your eyes.*	
CE E	BROWN, M. W.	*Runaway bunny.*	
398.24	BRYAN, A.	*Cat's purr.*	
FIC	BULLA, C. R.	*Chalk box kid.*	
FIC	BULLA, C. R.	*Pirate's promise.*	
CE 535	BULLA, C. R.	*What makes a shadow? Rev. ed.*	
FIC	BULLA, C. R.	*White bird.*	
FIC	BUNTING, E.	*Cheyenne again.*	
E	BUNTING, E.	*Fly away home.*	
E	BUNTING, E.	*Going home.*	
E	BUNTING, E.	*Our teacher's having a baby.*	
E	BUNTING, E.	*Turkey for Thanksgiving.*	
CE E	BURNINGHAM, J.	*Come away from the water, Shirley.*	
CE E	BURNINGHAM, J.	*Mr. Gumpy's motor car.*	
CE E	BURNINGHAM, J.	*Mr. Gumpy's outing.*	
FIC	BUSSER, M.	*King Bobble.*	
FIC	CAMERON, A.	*Julian's glorious summer.*	
E	CAPLE, K.	*Biggest nose.*	
E	CARLE, E.	*Very busy spider.*	
E	CARLE, E.	*Very lonely firefly.*	
E	CARLSON, N.	*Sit still!*	
E	CARLSON, N.	*Visit to Grandma's.*	
E	CARLSTROM, N. W.	*How do you say it today, Jesse Bear?*	
E	CARLSTROM, N. W.	*Let's count it out, Jesse Bear.*	
CE E	CARRICK, C.	*What happened to Patrick's dinosaurs?*	
E	CASELEY, J.	*Harry and Willy and Carrothead.*	
E	CASELEY, J.	*Noisemakers.*	
E	CAULEY, L. B.	*Clap your hands.*	
E	CHARLES, N. N.	*What am I?: looking through shapes at apples and grapes.*	
E	CHRISTIAN, M. B.	*Toady and Dr. Miracle.*	
FIC	CHRISTIANSEN, C. B.	*Snowman on Sycamore Street.*	
E	CLEARY, B.	*Two dog biscuits.*	
CE E	COERR, E.	*Josefina story quilt.*	
E	COFFELT, N.	*Good night, Sigmund.*	
CE E	COHEN, M.	*No good in art.*	
CE E	COHEN, M.	*See you in second grade!*	
CE E	COHEN, M.	*Will I have a friend?*	
E	COLE, B.	*Giant's toe.*	
E	COLE, J.	*Doctor Change.*	
362.73	COLE, J.	*How I was adopted: Samantha's story.*	
597.3	COLE, J.	*Hungry, hungry sharks.*	
636.7	COLE, J.	*My puppy is born. Rev. and expanded ed.*	
E	COOPER, H.	*Boy who wouldn't go to bed.*	
E	COREY, D.	*Will there be a lap for me?*	
398.27	CRAIG, M. J.	*Three wishes.*	
E	CREWS, D.	*Bicycle race.*	
E	CREWS, D.	*Ten black dots. Rev. and redesigned ed.*	
E	CUSHMAN, D.	*Aunt Eater's mystery Christmas.*	
E	CUSHMAN, D.	*Aunt Eater's mystery vacation.*	
E	DALE, P.	*Ten out of bed.*	
CE E	DALY, N.	*Not so fast, Songololo.*	
E	DE GROAT, D.	*Roses are pink, your feet really stink.*	
E	DE PAOLA, T.	*Baby sister.*	
E	DE PAOLA, T.	*Tom.*	
E	DE PAOLA, T.	*Watch out for the chicken feet in your soup.*	
E	DEMUTH, P.	*Busy at day care head to toe.*	
E	DISALVO-RYAN, D.	*Uncle Willie and the soup kitchen.*	
E	DRAGONWAGON, C.	*Annie flies the birthday bike.*	
E	DUBOWSKI, C. E.	*Pirate School.*	
E	DUFFEY, B.	*Camp Knock Knock.*	
FIC	DUFFEY, B.	*Virtual Cody.*	
CE E	DUVOISIN, R.	*Petunia's Christmas.*	
E	EGAN, T.	*Burnt toast on Davenport Street.*	
E	EHLERT, L.	*Color zoo.*	

398.24	EHLERT, L.	*Moon rope: a Peruvian folktale/Un lazo a la luna: una leyenda Peruana.*
E	EHLERT, L.	*Nuts to you!*
FIC	ELSTE, J.	*True Blue.*
E	EMBERLEY, E.	*Go away, big green monster!*
E	ERNST, L. C.	*Letters are lost!*
CE E	ETS, M. H.	*Gilberto and the wind.*
E	ETS, M. H.	*Nine days to Christmas.*
CE E	FLACK, M.	*Ask Mr. Bear.*
E	FLEISCHMAN, P.	*Time train.*
E	FLEMING, D.	*Lunch.*
E	FLEMING, D.	*Time to sleep.*
508.2	FOWLER, A.	*How do you know it's spring?*
508.2	FOWLER, A.	*How do you know it's summer?*
508.2	FOWLER, A.	*How do you know it's winter?*
E	FOX, M.	*Hattie and the fox.*
E	FOX, M.	*Time for bed.*
E	FOX, M.	*Tough Boris.*
CE E	FREEMAN, D.	*Pocket for Corduroy.*
398.2	FRENCH, V.	*Lazy Jack.*
E	FRENCH, V.	*Red Hen and Sly Fox.*
E	FRIEDMAN, I. R.	*How my parents learned to eat.*
E	GACKENBACH, D.	*Mag the magnificent.*
E	GAGE, W.	*My stars, it's Mrs. Gaddy!: the three Mrs. Gaddy stories.*
E	GERSHATOR, P.	*Rata-pata-scata-fata: a Caribbean story.*
E	GERSHATOR, P.	*Sambalena show-off.*
E	GERSHATOR, P.	*Sweet, sweet fig banana.*
CE E	GIFF, P. R.	*All about Stacy.*
E	GIFF, P. R.	*Garbage juice for breakfast.*
CE E	GIFF, P. R.	*Stacy says good-bye.*
CE E	GIFF, P. R.	*Today was a terrible day.*
513.5	GIGANTI, JR., P.	*Each orange had 8 slices: a counting book.*
E	GINSBURG, M.	*Across the stream.*
811	GIOVANNI, N.	*Knoxville, Tennessee.*
612.6	GIRARD, L. W.	*You were born on your very first birthday.*
513.2	GOENNEL, H.	*Odds and evens: a numbers book.*
FIC	GOLDIN, B. D.	*World's birthday: a Rosh Hashanah story.*
634	GOLDSEN, L.	*Fruit.*
E	GOMI, T.	*Who hid it?*
E	GOODE, D.	*Where's our mama?*
E	GRAVOIS, J. M.	*Quickly, Quigley.*
B BACH, J.	GREENE, C.	*Johann Sebastian Bach: great man of music.*
B SOUSA, J.	GREENE, C.	*John Philip Sousa: the march king.*
B STEIFF, M.	GREENE, C.	*Margarete Steiff: toy maker.*
B CAMPANELLA,	GREENE, C.	*Roy Campanella: major-league champion.*
E	GRIFFITH, H. V.	*Emily and the enchanted frog.*
E	GRIFFITH, H. V.	*Mine will, said John. New ed.*
E	GROSSMAN, P.	*Night ones.*
E	GUARINO, D.	*Is your mama a llama?*
E	GUBACK, G.	*Luka's quilt.*
E	HAAS, J.	*Sugaring.*
582.16	HALL, Z.	*Apple pie tree.*
E	HAMM, D. J.	*Grandma drives a motor bed.*
E	HARLEY, B.	*Sitting down to eat.*
E	HARPER, I.	*My cats Nick and Nora.*
E	HAVILL, J.	*Jamaica and Brianna.*
E	HAVILL, J.	*Jamaica's find.*
E	HAYES, S.	*Eat up, Gemma.*
CE 394.264	HAYWARD, L.	*First Thanksgiving.*
FIC	HEIDE, F. P.	*Tales for the perfect child.*
E	HENKES, K.	*Biggest boy.*
E	HERMAN, R. A.	*Pal the pony.*
E	HEST, A.	*In the rain with Baby Duck.*
E	HEST, A.	*Jamaica Louise James.*
E	HEST, A.	*You're the boss, Baby Duck!*
E	HIMMELMAN, J.	*Clover County carrot contest.*
E	HIMMELMAN, J.	*Great leaf blast-off.*
E	HIMMELMAN, J.	*Super camper caper.*
636.8	HIRSCHI, R.	*What is a cat?*
CE E	HOBAN, J.	*Buzby.*
E	HOBAN, L.	*Arthur's funny money.*
CE E	HOBAN, L.	*Arthur's great big valentine.*

CE E	HOBAN, L.	*Arthur's Halloween costume.*
CE E	HOBAN, L.	*Arthur's honey bear.*
CE E	HOBAN, L.	*Arthur's loose tooth.*
E	HOBAN, L.	*Arthur's pen pal.*
CE E	HOBAN, L.	*Arthur's prize reader.*
E	HOBAN, L.	*Silly Tilly and the Easter Bunny.*
E	HOBAN, L.	*Silly Tilly's Thanksgiving dinner.*
CE E	HOBAN, R.	*Bargain for Frances. Newly ill. ed.*
CE E	HOBAN, R.	*Bedtime for Frances. Newly ill. ed.*
E	HOBSON, S.	*Chicken Little.*
CE E	HOFF, S.	*Danny and the dinosaur.*
E	HOFF, S.	*Danny and the dinosaur go to camp.*
E	HOFF, S.	*Happy birthday, Danny and the dinosaur!*
E	HOFF, S.	*Horse in Harry's room.*
E	HOFF, S.	*Mrs. Brice's mice.*
E	HOOKER, R.	*Matthew the cowboy.*
E	HOWARD, E. F.	*Aunt Flossie's hats (and crab cakes later).*
E	HOWE, J.	*Hot fudge.*
E	HOWE, J.	*There's a monster under my bed.*
E	HUGHES, S.	*Bouncing.*
E	HUGHES, S.	*Hiding.*
CE E	HUTCHINS, P.	*Doorbell rang.*
E	HUTCHINS, P.	*Little Pink Pig.*
CE E	HUTCHINS, P.	*Silly Billy!*
CE E	HUTCHINS, P.	*Tale of Thomas Mead.*
E	HUTCHINS, P.	*Tidy Titch.*
E	HUTCHINS, P.	*Titch and Daisy.*
CE E	HUTCHINS, P.	*Very worst monster.*
E	HUTCHINS, P.	*You'll soon grow into them, Titch.*
E	ISADORA, R.	*Over the green hills.*
E	JACKSON, E.	*Brown cow, green grass, yellow mellow sun.*
FIC	JAM, T.	*Charlotte stories.*
E	JAMES, S.	*Leon and Bob.*
E	JAMES, S.	*Wild woods.*
152.14	JENKINS, S.	*Flip-flap.*
E	JENNINGS, S.	*Jeremiah and Mrs. Ming.*
BB E	JOHNSON, A.	*Joshua by the sea (Board book).*
BB E	JOHNSON, A.	*Joshua's night whispers (Board book).*
E	JOHNSON, A.	*One of three.*
BB E	JOHNSON, A.	*Rain feet (Board book).*
E	JOHNSON, D.	*What will Mommy do when I'm at school?*
E	JOHNSTON, T.	*Soup bone.*
E	JONAS, A.	*Quilt.*
E	JONAS, A.	*When you were a baby.*
E	JOSEPH, L.	*Island Christmas.*
158	KALMAN, B.	*Fun with my friends.*
E	KASZA, K.	*Wolf's chicken stew.*
CE E	KEATS, E. J.	*Letter to Amy.*
E	KEATS, E. J.	*Maggie and the pirate.*
CE E	KEATS, E. J.	*Snowy day.*
CE E	KEATS, E. J.	*Trip.*
E	KELLER, H.	*Geraldine first.*
E	KELLER, H.	*Harry and Tuck.*
E	KELLOGG, S.	*Mystery of the missing red mitten.*
E	KELLOGG, S.	*Mystery of the stolen blue paint.*
CE E	KELLOGG, S.	*Pinkerton, behave.*
E	KESSLER, L.	*Kick, pass, and run.*
E	KESSLER, L.	*Old Turtle's soccer team.*
CE 398.24	KIMMEL, E. A.	*Anansi goes fishing.*
E	KIMMEL, E. A.	*Magic dreidels: a Hanukkah story.*
398.24	KIMMEL, E. A.	*Old woman and her pig.*
E	KLEVEN, E.	*Hooray! A pinata!*
FIC	KLINE, S.	*Horrible Harry's secret.*
618.92	KOPLOW, L.	*Tanya and the Tobo Man/Tanya y el Hombre Tobo: a story in English and Spanish for children entering therapy.*
CE E	KRAUSS, R.	*Hole is to dig: a first book of first definitions.*
E	KRENSKY, S.	*Lionel and Louise.*
E	KRENSKY, S.	*Lionel at large.*
E	KRENSKY, S.	*Three blind mice mystery.*
E	KROLL, S.	*One tough turkey: a Thanksgiving story.*

372.21	KUKLIN, S.	*Going to my nursery school.*
E	KWITZ, M. D.	*Little Vampire and the Midnight Bear.*
E	LASKY, K.	*Lunch bunnies.*
525	LAUBER, P.	*How we learned the earth is round.*
577	LAUBER, P.	*Who eats what?: food chains and food webs.*
513.2	LEEDY, L.	*Mission: addition.*
E	LEEDY, L.	*Monster money book.*
306.85	LEEDY, L.	*Who's who in my family.*
E	LESIEG, T.	*Tooth book.*
E	LESTER, H.	*Listen Buddy.*
B THOMPSON, S.	LEVINSON, N. S.	*Snowshoe Thompson.*
E	LEVINSON, R.	*Watch the stars come out.*
E	LEVITT, S.	*Mighty Movers.*
E	LIED, K.	*Potato: a tale from the Great Depression.*
E	LILLIE, P.	*Floppy teddy bear.*
E	LINDGREN, A.	*Lotta's Christmas surprise.*
CE E	LINDGREN, A.	*Tomten and the fox.*
E	LING, B.	*Fattest, tallest, biggest snowman ever.*
E	LITTLE, J.	*Revenge of the small Small.*
E	LITTLE, M. O.	*Yoshiko and the foreigner.*
CE E	LOBEL, A.	*Frog and Toad are friends.*
CE E	LOBEL, A.	*Grasshopper on the road.*
CE E	LOBEL, A.	*Mouse tales.*
E	LOH, M.	*Tucking mommy in.*
E	LONDON, J.	*Fireflies, fireflies, light my way.*
E	LONDON, J.	*Froggy goes to school.*
E	LOOMIS, C.	*In the diner.*
E	LOPEZ, L.	*Birthday swap.*
CE E	LUENN, N.	*Nessa's fish.*
E	MACCARONE, G.	*Classroom pet.*
FIC	MACDONALD, M.	*No room for Francie.*
386	MAESTRO, B.	*Ferryboat.*
398.8	MANSON, C.	*Tree in the wood: an old nursery song.*
E	MANUSHKIN, F.	*Matzah that Papa brought home.*
229	MARK, J.	*Tale of Tobias.*
CE E	MARSHALL, E.	*Four on the shore.*
CE E	MARSHALL, E.	*Fox all week.*
CE E	MARSHALL, E.	*Fox on stage.*
E	MARSHALL, J.	*Fox on the job.*
E	MARSHALL, J.	*Fox outfoxed.*
CE E	MARSHALL, J.	*George and Martha 'round and 'round.*
CE E	MARSHALL, J.	*George and Martha back in town.*
E	MARTIN, JR., B.	*Chicka chicka boom boom.*
E	MARTIN, JR., B.	*Ghost-eye tree.*
CE E	MARTIN, R.	*Will's mammoth.*
E	MASUREL, C.	*No, no, Titus!*
E	MAYER, M.	*There's an alligator under my bed.*
398.24	MCDERMOTT, G.	*Coyote: a trickster tale from the American Southwest.*
B WOODSON, C.	MCKISSACK, P.	*Carter G. Woodson: the father of black history.*
B TERRELL, M.	MCKISSACK, P.	*Mary Church Terrell: leader for equality.*
B ROBESON, P.	MCKISSACK, P.	*Paul Robeson: a voice to remember.*
B PAIGE, S.	MCKISSACK, P.	*Satchel Paige: the best arm in baseball.*
CE E	MCLEOD, E. W.	*Bear's bicycle.*
E	MCPHAIL, D.	*Lost!*
FIC	MEDEARIS, A. S.	*Adventures of Sugar and Junior.*
E	MEDEARIS, A. S.	*Here comes the snow.*
E	MERRIAM, E.	*Hole story.*
758	MICKLETHWAIT, L.	*I spy a freight train: transportation in art.*
758	MICKLETHWAIT, L.	*I spy a lion: animals in art.*
750	MICKLETHWAIT, L.	*Spot a cat.*
E	MILLER, M.	*Now I'm big.*
599.5	MILTON, J.	*Whales: the gentle giants.*
CE E	MINARIK, E. H.	*Father Bear comes home.*
CE E	MINARIK, E. H.	*Little Bear.*
CE E	MINARIK, E. H.	*Little Bear's friend.*
CE E	MINARIK, E. H.	*Little Bear's visit.*
E	MITCHELL, M. K.	*Granddaddy's gift.*
E	MODELL, F.	*Look out, it's April Fools' Day.*
E	MONSON, A. M.	*Wanted: best friend.*
641.8	MORRIS, A.	*Bread, bread, bread.*
306.874	MORRIS, A.	*Loving.*
621.9	MORRIS, A.	*Tools.*
599.53	MORRIS, R. A.	*Dolphin.*
E	MOST, B.	*Hippopotamus hunt.*
E	MURPHY, S. J.	*Best vacation ever.*
398.8		*MY VERY FIRST MOTHER GOOSE.*
CE E	NARAHASHI, K.	*I have a friend.*
E	NAYLOR, P. R.	*King of the playground.*
E	NEITZEL, S.	*Jacket I wear in the snow.*
E	NEITZEL, S.	*We're making breakfast for Mother.*
E	NETHERY, M.	*Hannah and Jack.*
CE E	NOBLE, T. H.	*Day Jimmy's boa ate the wash.*
E	NOLL, S.	*Surprise!*
E	NOVAK, M.	*Newt.*
E	O'CONNOR, J.	*Lulu and the witch baby.*
E	O'MALLEY, K.	*Who killed Cock Robin?*
E	OBLIGADO, L.	*Chocolate cow.*
594	OLESEN, J.	*Snail.*
FIC	ORGEL, D.	*Don't call me Slob-o.*
E	OXENBURY, H.	*Grandma and grandpa.*
E	PALMER, H.	*Fish out of water.*
E	PARISH, H.	*Bravo, Amelia Bedelia!*
E	PARISH, P.	*Come back, Amelia Bedelia. Newly illustrated ed.*
E	PARISH, P.	*Play ball, Amelia Bedelia.*
612.8	PARRAMON, J. M.	*Taste.*
612.8	PARRAMON, J. M.	*Touch.*
E	PELLEGRINI, N.	*Families are different.*
E	PINKWATER, D. M.	*Aunt Lulu.*
E	PINKWATER, D. M.	*Doodle flute.*
E	PLOURDE, L.	*Pigs in the mud in the middle of the rud.*
E	PORTE, B. A.	*Harry gets an uncle.*
E	PORTE, B. A.	*Harry's birthday.*
E	PORTE, B. A.	*Harry's dog.*
E	PRAGER, A.	*Baseball birthday party.*
E	PRAGER, A.	*Spooky Halloween party.*
E	PULVER, R.	*Nobody's mother is in second grade.*
E	QUINLAN, P.	*My dad takes care of me.*
E	RAPPAPORT, D.	*Boston coffee party.*
E	RAU, D. M.	*Box can be many things.*
E	REISER, L.	*Beach feet.*
E	RICE, E.	*Benny bakes a cake.*
E	ROBINS, J.	*Addie's bad day.*
E	ROCKWELL, A. F.	*Once upon a time this morning.*
E	ROCKWELL, A. F.	*Show and tell day.*
E	ROE, E.	*With my brother/Con mi hermano.*
551.6	ROGERS, P.	*What will the weather be like today?*
398.27	ROHMER, H.	*Uncle Nacho's hat: a folktale from Nicaragua/El sombrero de Tio Nacho: un cuento de Nicaragua.*
398.8	ROSEN, M.	*We're going on a bear hunt.*
E	ROSENBERG, L.	*Big and little alphabet.*
E	ROTH, S. L.	*My love for you.*
428.2	ROTNER, S.	*Action alphabet.*
612	ROTNER, S.	*Faces.*
306.874	ROTNER, S.	*Lots of dads.*
E	RYLANT, C.	*Birthday presents.*
BB E	RYLANT, C.	*Everyday children (Board book).*
CE E	RYLANT, C.	*Henry and Mudge and the bedtime thumps.*
CE E	RYLANT, C.	*Henry and Mudge and the forever sea.*
CE E	RYLANT, C.	*Henry and Mudge and the happy cat.*
CE E	RYLANT, C.	*Henry and Mudge and the long weekend.*
CE E	RYLANT, C.	*Henry and Mudge and the wild wind.*
CE E	RYLANT, C.	*Henry and Mudge get the cold shivers.*
CE E	RYLANT, C.	*Henry and Mudge in puddle trouble.*
CE E	RYLANT, C.	*Henry and Mudge take the big test.*
CE E	RYLANT, C.	*Henry and Mudge: the first book.*

E	RYLANT, C.	*Mr. Putter and Tabby bake the cake.*
E	RYLANT, C.	*Mr. Putter and Tabby fly the plane.*
E	RYLANT, C.	*Poppleton.*
796.332	SAMPSON, M.	*Football that won...*
929.4	SANDERS, M.	*What's your name?: from Ariel to Zoe.*
E	SANDIN, J.	*Long way westward.*
FIC	SATHRE, V.	*Leroy Potts meets the McCrooks.*
FIC	SAY, A.	*Allison.*
E	SAY, A.	*Lost lake.*
398.25		*SCARY BOOK.*
FIC	SCHECTER, E.	*Big idea.*
E	SCHEER, J.	*Rain makes applesauce.*
E	SCHINDEL, J.	*Dear Daddy.*
E	SCHINDEL, J.	*What's for lunch?*
428.2	SCHNEIDER, R. M.	*Add it, dip it, fix it: a book of verbs.*
CE 398.25	SCHWARTZ, A.	*Ghosts!: ghostly tales from folklore.*
E	SCHWARTZ, A.	*Oma and Bobo.*
FIC	SCOTT, A. H.	*Brave as a mountain lion.*
E	SCOTT, A. H.	*On mother's lap.*
E	SCOTT, A. H.	*One good horse: a cowpuncher's counting book.*
394.264	SCOTT, G.	*Labor Day.*
599.64	SELSAM, M. E.	*First look at animals with horns.*
598.4	SELSAM, M. E.	*First look at ducks, geese, and swans.*
CE E	SENDAK, M.	*Where the wild things are. 25th anniv. ed.*
155.4	SENISI, E. B.	*Secrets.*
E	SEUSS, D.	*And to think that I saw it on Mulberry Street.*
CE E	SEUSS, D.	*Dr. Seuss's ABC.*
E	SEUSS, D.	*Fox in socks.*
E	SEUSS, D.	*I am not going to get up today!*
E	SEUSS, D.	*I can read with my eyes shut.*
E	SEUSS, D.	*My many colored days.*
E	SEUSS, D.	*Oh, the places you'll go!*
CE E	SHARMAT, M. W.	*Nate the Great.*
E	SHARMAT, M. W.	*Nate the Great and the crunchy Christmas.*
CE E	SHARMAT, M. W.	*Nate the Great and the stolen base.*
E	SHARMAT, M. W.	*Nate the Great and the tardy tortoise.*
CE E	SHARMAT, M. W.	*Nate the Great goes undercover.*
CE E	SHARMAT, M. W.	*Nate the Great stalks stupidweed.*
612.8	SHOWERS, P.	*Look at your eyes. Rev. ed.*
612.7	SHOWERS, P.	*Your skin and mine. Rev. ed.*
E	SHUB, E.	*Seeing is believing.*
E	SHUB, E.	*White stallion.*
E	SHULEVITZ, U.	*Dawn.*
398.24	SHULEVITZ, U.	*Golden goose.*
E	SILVERMAN, E.	*Big pumpkin.*
E	SIMON, C.	*One happy classroom.*
152.4	SIMON, N.	*I was so mad.*
E	SKOFIELD, J.	*Detective Dinosaur.*
398.24	SOUHAMI, J.	*Leopard's drum: an Asante tale from West Africa.*
636.7	STANDIFORD, N.	*Bravest dog ever: the true story of Balto.*
599.64	STAUB, F. J.	*Mountain goats.*
E	STEIG, W.	*Toby, where are you?*
E	STEVENSON, J.	*All aboard!*
E	STEVENSON, J.	*Fried feathers for Thanksgiving.*
B STEVENSON, J	STEVENSON, J.	*I had a lot of wishes.*
E	STEVENSON, J.	*Mud Flat mystery.*
CE E	STEVENSON, J.	*Night after Christmas.*
E	STEVENSON, J.	*Rolling Rose.*
CE E	STEVENSON, J.	*That terrible Halloween night.*
E	STEVENSON, J.	*Village full of valentines.*
E	STEVENSON, J.	*Worst goes South.*
FIC	STEVENSON, J.	*Yard sale.*
E	STOCK, C.	*Christmas time.*
E	STOCK, C.	*Easter surprise.*
E	STOCK, C.	*Thanksgiving treat.*
E	STOEKE, J. M.	*Hat for Minerva Louise.*
E	STOEKE, J. M.	*Minerva Louise at school.*
E	STURGES, P.	*Ten flashing fireflies.*
398.2	TARCOV, E. H.	*Frog prince.*
E	TELLO, J.	*Abuelo y los tres osos./Abuelo and the three bears.*
E	THOMAS, P.	*Stand back, said the elephant, I'm going to sneeze!*
E	TITHERINGTON, J.	*Place for Ben.*
789.3	TRAPANI, I.	*Itsy bitsy spider.*
E	TURKLE, B.	*Do not open.*
E	TURNER, A.	*Dust for dinner.*
E	UDRY, J. M.	*Let's be enemies.*
FIC	VALGARDSON, W. D.	*Sarah and the people of Sand River.*
CE E	VAN LEEUWEN, J.	*Amanda Pig on her own.*
CE E	VAN LEEUWEN, J.	*Oliver and Amanda's Christmas.*
CE E	VAN LEEUWEN, J.	*Oliver and Amanda's Halloween.*
398.8	VAN RYNBACH, I.	*Five little pumpkins.*
E	VIGNA, J.	*I wish Daddy didn't drink so much.*
E	VINCENT, G.	*Ernest and Celestine at the circus.*
E	VINCENT, G.	*Where are you, Ernest and Celestine?*
E	VIORST, J.	*Tenth good thing about Barney.*
CE E	WABER, B.	*Ira sleeps over.*
E	WADDELL, M.	*Farmer duck.*
398.27	WAHL, J.	*Little Eight John.*
E	WALSH, E. S.	*Hop jump.*
E	WALSH, E. S.	*Mouse paint.*
E	WALTER, M. P.	*Brother to the wind.*
598.8	WATTS, B.	*Birds' nest.*
599.35	WATTS, B.	*Hamster.*
635	WATTS, B.	*Potato.*
E	WELLS, R.	*Bunny cakes.*
E	WELLS, R.	*Edward in deep water.*
E	WELLS, R.	*Edward unready for school.*
E	WELLS, R.	*Edward's overwhelming overnight.*
CE E	WELLS, R.	*Max's chocolate chicken.*
CE E	WELLS, R.	*Max's Christmas.*
E	WHEELER, C.	*Bookstore cat.*
E	WILLIAMS, S.	*Edwin and Emily.*
E	WILLIAMS, V. B.	*Stringbean's trip to the shining sea.*
E	WILLNER-PARDO, G.	*Natalie Spitzer's turtles.*
E	WING, N.	*Jalapeno bagels.*
E	WINTHROP, E.	*Bear's Christmas surprise.*
E	WISEMAN, B.	*Morris goes to school.*
CE E	WISEMAN, B.	*Morris the Moose.*
E	WOLF, J.	*Daddy, could I have an elephant?*
E	WOOD, A.	*Silly Sally.*
523.8	WYLER, R.	*Starry sky.*
E	YOSHI.	*Who's hiding here?*
398.24	YOUNG, E.	*Seven blind mice.*
E	ZEMACH, H.	*Penny a look.*
E	ZEMACH, M.	*Little red hen, an old story.*
E	ZIEFERT, H.	*Little red hen.*
E	ZIEFERT, H.	*What rhymes with eel?: a word-and-picture flap book.*
E	ZIEFERT, H.	*Who said moo?*
CE E	ZION, G.	*Harry and the lady next door.*
CE E	ZION, G.	*No roses for Harry.*
594	ZOEHFELD, K. W.	*What lives in a shell?*
CE E	ZOLOTOW, C.	*Mr. Rabbit and the lovely present.*
E	ZOLOTOW, C.	*My grandson Lew.*
E	ZOLOTOW, C.	*Old dog. Rev. and newly illustrated ed.*

Books for Independent Reading Level 2-2

E	ACCORSI, W.	*Friendship's first Thanksgiving.*
398.24	ADA, A. F.	*Mediopollito/Half-Chicken.*
FIC	ADLER, D. A.	*Cam Jansen and the ghostly mystery.*
513.2	ADLER, D. A.	*Fraction fun.*
FIC	ADLER, D. A.	*Onion sundaes.*
E	ADLER, D. A.	*Young Cam Jansen and the missing cookie.*
E	AGELL, C.	*I wear long green hair in the summer.*
E	AGELL, C.	*Mud makes me dance in the spring.*
395.4	ALIKI.	*Hello! Good-bye!*
612	ALIKI.	*My feet.*
612	ALIKI.	*My hands. Rev. ed.*
CE E	ALLARD, H.	*Miss Nelson has a field day.*
E	ALLARD, H.	*Stupids die.*
E	ALLARD, H.	*Stupids take off.*
306.874	ALPERT, L.	*You and your dad.*
FIC	ANAYA, R.	*Farolitos of Christmas.*
968	ANGELOU, M.	*My painted house, my friendly chicken, and me.*
305.232	ANHOLT, C.	*Here come the babies.*
769.56	ANSARY, M. T.	*Stamps.*
E	ANTLE, N.	*Sam's Wild West Show.*
E	ANTLE, N.	*Staying cool.*
E	APPELT, K.	*Watermelon Day.*
531	ARDLEY, N.	*Science book of gravity.*
536	ARDLEY, N.	*Science book of hot and cold.*
538	ARDLEY, N.	*Science book of magnets.*
531	ARDLEY, N.	*Science book of motion.*
599.35	ARNOSKY, J.	*Come out, muskrats.*
E	ARNOSKY, J.	*Every autumn comes the bear.*
599.769	ARNOSKY, J.	*Otters under water.*
E	ARNOSKY, J.	*Rabbits and raindrops.*
E	ASCH, F.	*Bear shadow.*
CE E	ASCH, F.	*Bear's bargain.*
CE E	ASCH, F.	*Moongame.*
E	AVERILL, E.	*Fire cat.*
E	AXELROD, A.	*Pigs on a blanket.*
E	AYLESWORTH, J.	*Old black fly.*
E	BABBITT, N.	*Bub, or, The very best thing.*
398.21	BADEN, R.	*And Sunday makes seven.*
796.6	BAILEY, D.	*Cycling.*
799.1	BAILEY, D.	*Fishing.*
797.2	BAILEY, D.	*Swimming.*
E	BAKER, K. L.	*Seneca.*
FIC	BALL, D.	*Emily Eyefinger.*
591.56	BANCROFT, H.	*Animals in winter. Rev. ed.*
E	BANG, M.	*Dawn.*
E	BANG, M.	*Tye May and the magic brush.*
E	BANKS, K.	*Spider spider.*
636.8	BARE, C. S.	*Toby the tabby kitten.*
CE E	BARRACCA, D.	*Adventures of taxi dog.*
CE E	BARRACCA, D.	*Maxi, the hero.*
E	BARRACCA, D.	*Maxi, the star.*
387.7	BARTON, B.	*Airplanes.*
387.2	BARTON, B.	*Boats.*
690	BARTON, B.	*Building a house.*
E	BARTON, B.	*I want to be an astronaut.*
388.3	BARTON, B.	*Trucks.*
E	BARTONE, E.	*Peppe the lamplighter.*
362.1		*BE A FRIEND: CHILDREN WHO LIVE WITH HIV SPEAK.*
E	BEDARD, M.	*Emily.*
CE E	BEMELMANS, L.	*Madeline's rescue.*
E	BENCHLEY, N.	*Sam the minuteman.*
E	BERENSTAIN, S.	*Berenstain Bears and the sitter.*
E	BERENSTAIN, S.	*Berenstain Bears get in a fight.*
E	BERENSTAIN, S.	*Berenstain Bears go to camp.*
E	BERENSTAIN, S.	*Berenstain Bears visit the dentist.*
E	BERENSTAIN, S.	*Berenstain Bears' moving day.*
332.4	BERGER, M.	*Round and round the money goes: what money is and how we use it.*
612.8	BERGER, M.	*Why I cough, sneeze, shiver, hiccup, and yawn.*
FIC	BLEDSOE, L. J.	*Big bike race.*
E	BLOOM, S.	*Family for Jamie: an adoption story.*

CE E	BLOS, J. W.	*Old Henry.*
CE FIC	BLUME, J.	*Superfudge.*
CE E	BONSALL, C. N.	*Case of the dumb bells.*
E	BONSALL, C. N.	*Who's a pest?*
E	BRANDENBERG, A.	*Chop, simmer, season.*
551.57	BRANDT, K.	*What makes it rain? The story of a raindrop.*
CE 551.55	BRANLEY, F. M.	*Flash, crash, rumble and roll. Rev. ed.*
551.5	BRANLEY, F. M.	*Rain and hail. Rev. ed.*
551.57	BRANLEY, F. M.	*Snow is falling. Rev. ed.*
599.78	BRENNER, B.	*Two orphan cubs.*
E	BRETT, J.	*Berlioz the bear.*
E	BRETT, J.	*Wild Christmas reindeer.*
CE E	BRIDWELL, N.	*Clifford's sports day.*
641.6	BROWN, L. K.	*Vegetable show.*
CE 398.27	BROWN, M.	*Stone soup: an old tale.*
CE E	BROWN, M. T.	*Arthur's chicken pox.*
CE E	BROWN, M. T.	*Arthur's family vacation.*
E	BROWN, M. W.	*Child's good night book.*
398.24	BRUCHAC, J.	*Great ball game: a Muskogee story.*
398.26	BRYAN, A.	*Story of lightning and thunder.*
E	BUCKLEY, H. E.	*Grandmother and I.*
395.5	BUEHNER, C.	*It's a spoon, not a shovel.*
FIC	BUNTING, E.	*Dandelions.*
E	BUNTING, E.	*Day's work.*
E	BUNTING, E.	*Ghost's hour, spook's hour.*
E	BUNTING, E.	*Man who could call down owls.*
CE E	BUNTING, E.	*Mother's Day mice.*
E	BUNTING, E.	*On Call Back Mountain.*
E	BUNTING, E.	*Smoky night.*
E	BUNTING, E.	*St. Patrick's Day in the morning.*
E	BUNTING, E.	*Sunflower house.*
629.13	BURLEIGH, R.	*Flight: the journey of Charles Lindbergh.*
E	BURNINGHAM, J.	*Harvey Slumfenburger's Christmas present.*
CE E	BURTON, V. L.	*Little house.*
E	BUSH, T.	*Grunt!: the primitive cave boy.*
FIC	BUSSER, M.	*On the road with Poppa Whopper.*
E	CALHOUN, M.	*Flood.*
E	CALHOUN, M.	*High-wire Henry.*
636.7	CALMENSON, S.	*Rosie, a visiting dog's story.*
FIC	CAMERON, A.	*More stories Huey tells.*
FIC	CAMERON, A.	*Stories Huey tells.*
E	CANNON, A.	*Bat in the boot.*
E	CARLE, E.	*Grouchy ladybug. New ed.*
E	CARLE, E.	*House for Hermit Crab.*
E	CARLE, E.	*Rooster's off to see the world.*
E	CARLSON, N.	*How to lose all your friends.*
CE E	CARLSON, N.	*Making the team.*
CE E	CARLSON, N.	*Mysterious valentine.*
CE E	CARLSON, N.	*Perfect family.*
CE E	CARLSON, N.	*Witch lady.*
E	CARLSTROM, N. W.	*Happy birthday, Jesse Bear!*
E	CARRICK, C.	*Left behind.*
E	CARRICK, C.	*Melanie.*
E	CARTER, D. A.	*In a dark, dark wood.*
E	CASELEY, J.	*Dear Annie.*
E	CASELEY, J.	*Grandpa's garden lunch.*
E	CASELEY, J.	*Priscilla twice.*
E	CASELEY, J.	*Slumber party!*
E	CASEY, P.	*My cat Jack.*
E	CAZET, D.	*Fish in his pocket.*
398.24	CECIL, L.	*Frog princess.*
513.2	CHALLONER, J.	*Science book of numbers.*
E	CHAMPION, J.	*Emily and Alice.*
E	CHAMPION, J.	*Emily and Alice again.*
394.261	CHOCOLATE, D. M. N.	*My first Kwanzaa book.*
E	CHRISTELOW, E.	*Don't wake up Mama!*
E	CHRISTELOW, E.	*Five little monkeys sitting in a tree.*
E	CHRISTELOW, E.	*Five little monkeys with nothing to do.*
E	CHRISTELOW, E.	*Great pig escape.*
808.06	CHRISTELOW, E.	*What do authors do?*
E	CLEARY, B.	*Real hole.*

E	CLIMO, S.	*Little red ant and the great big crumb: a Mexican fable.*
E	COERR, E.	*Buffalo Bill and the Pony Express.*
E	COERR, E.	*Chang's paper pony.*
CE E	COHEN, M.	*Real-skin rubber monster mask.*
E	COLE, B.	*Drop dead.*
E	COLE, B.	*Winter wren.*
595.79	COLE, J.	*Magic School Bus inside a beehive.*
636.8	COLE, J.	*My new kitten.*
798.2	COLE, J.	*Riding Silver Star.*
618.92	COLLINS, P. L.	*Waiting for baby Joe.*
E	CONRAD, P.	*Call me Ahnighito.*
E	COOPER, S.	*Danny and the kings.*
E	COSSI, O.	*Great getaway.*
E	COWEN-FLETCHER, J.	*It takes a village.*
398.24	COWLEY, J.	*Mouse bride.*
CE B CREWS, D.	CREWS, D.	*Bigmama's.*
E	CREWS, D.	*Sail away.*
E	CREWS, D.	*Shortcut.*
E	CROLL, C.	*Too many Babas.*
FIC	CUTLER, J.	*Spaceman.*
E	DAVOL, M. W.	*Batwings and the curtain of night.*
E	DAVOL, M. W.	*How Snake got his hiss: an original tale.*
E	DAY, A.	*Frank and Ernest on the road.*
398.24	DAY, N. Y.	*Kancil and the crocodiles: a tale from Malaysia.*
636.8	DE PAOLA, T.	*Kids' cat book.*
E	DE PAOLA, T.	*Little Grunt and the big egg: a prehistoric fairy tale.*
E	DE PAOLA, T.	*Oliver Button is a sissy.*
552	DE PAOLA, T.	*Quicksand book.*
E	DE PAOLA, T.	*Strega Nona meets her match.*
398.23	DE REGNIERS, B. S.	*Little Sister and the Month Brothers.*
E	DEFELICE, C. C.	*Willy's silly grandma.*
398.2	DEMI.	*Magic gold fish: a Russian folktale.*
E	DENSLOW, S. P.	*On the trail with Miss Pace.*
E	DERBY, S.	*My steps.*
E	DORROS, A.	*Abuela.*
551.5	DORROS, A.	*Feel the wind.*
E	DORROS, A.	*Isla.*
E	DORROS, A.	*Radio Man: a story in English and Spanish./Don Radio: un cuento en Ingles y Espanol.*
728	DORROS, A.	*This is my house.*
FIC	DRAANEN, W. V.	*How I survived being a girl.*
784.192	DREW, H.	*My first music book.*
930.1	DUKE, K.	*Archaeologists dig for clues.*
232.92	DUNBAR, J.	*This is the star.*
599.17	DUNPHY, M.	*Here is the Arctic winter.*
E	EDWARDS, M.	*Chicken man.*
E	EDWARDS, P. D.	*Livingstone Mouse.*
E	EHLERT, L.	*Feathers for lunch.*
E	EHLERT, L.	*Snowballs.*
B EHLERT, L.	EHLERT, L.	*Under my nose.*
463	EMBERLEY, R.	*Let's go: a book in two languages./ Vamos: un libro en dos lenguas.*
E	ENDERLE, J. R.	*What would Mama do?*
B CLEMENTE, R.	ENGEL, T.	*We'll never forget you, Roberto Clemente.*
E	ENGLISH, K.	*Neeny coming, Neeny going.*
E	ERNST, L. C.	*Luckiest kid on the planet.*
E	ERNST, L. C.	*Zinnia and Dot.*
599.5	ESBENSEN, B. J.	*Baby whales drink milk.*
593.4	ESBENSEN, B. J.	*Sponges are skeletons.*
E	ETS, M. H.	*In the forest.*
CE E	ETS, M. H.	*Play with me.*
E	EVERETT, P.	*One that got away.*
E	EVERSOLE, R.	*Flute player./La Flautista.*
398.27	FARLEY, C. J.	*Mr. Pak buys a story.*
636		*FARM ANIMALS.*
263	FISHER, A. L.	*Story of Easter.*
381	FLANAGAN, A.	*Busy day at Mr. Kang's grocery store.*
598.47	FLETCHER, N.	*Penguin.*
508.2	FOWLER, A.	*How do you know it's fall?*
553.7	FOWLER, A.	*It could still be water.*
637	FOWLER, A.	*Thanks to cows.*
E	FOWLER, S. G.	*I'll see you when the moon is full.*
976.8	FRADIN, D. B.	*Tennessee.*
E	FRANKLIN, K. L.	*Iguana Beach.*
CE E	FREEMAN, D.	*Corduroy.*
CE E	FREEMAN, D.	*Dandelion.*
E	FRENCH, F.	*Anancy and Mr. Dry-Bone.*
598	FRISKEY, M.	*Birds we know.*
E	FUCHS, D. M.	*Bear for all seasons.*
CE E	GALDONE, P.	*Henny Penny.*
CE E	GALDONE, P.	*Little red hen.*
598.156	GANS, R.	*How do birds find their way?*
E	GANTOS, J.	*Rotten Ralph's show and tell.*
E	GARAY, L.	*Pedrito's Day.*
371.92	GEHRET, J.	*Don't-give-up Kid and learning differences. 2nd ed.*
E	GEISERT, A.	*Etcher's studio.*
E	GEORGE, L. B.	*Around the pond: who's been here?*
E	GEORGE, L. B.	*In the snow: who's been here?*
E	GERINGER, L.	*Three hat day.*
E	GERSHATOR, D.	*Bread is for eating.*
630	GIBBONS, G.	*Farming.*
629.13	GIBBONS, G.	*Flying.*
636.089	GIBBONS, G.	*Say woof!: the day of a country veterinarian.*
394.262	GIBBONS, G.	*St. Patrick's Day.*
523.7	GIBBONS, G.	*Sun up, sun down.*
621.9	GIBBONS, G.	*Tool book.*
624.1	GIBBONS, G.	*Tunnels.*
E	GIFF, P. R.	*Powder puff puzzle.*
E	GILLILAND, J. H.	*Not in the house, Newton!*
E	GINSBURG, M.	*Mushroom in the rain.*
FIC	GLASER, L.	*Rosie's birthday rat.*
E	GLASSMAN, P.	*Wizard next door.*
E	GOBLE, P.	*Death of the iron horse.*
398.24	GOLDIN, B. D.	*Coyote and the fire stick: a Pacific Northwest Indian tale.*
535.6	GOLDSEN, L.	*Colors.*
573.6	GOLDSEN, L.	*Egg.*
789.2	GRAHAM, S.	*Dear old Donegal.*
FIC	GRAVES, B. B.	*Mystery of the Tooth Gremlin.*
CE E	GREEN, N. B.	*Hole in the dike.*
B KIPLING, R.	GREENE, C.	*Rudyard Kipling: author of the "Jungle books."*
E	GREENFIELD, E.	*Grandpa's face.*
E	GREENWOOD, P. D.	*What about my goldfish?*
E	GRIFFITH, H. V.	*Grandaddy and Janetta.*
E	GRIFFITH, H. V.	*Grandaddy's stars.*
398.2	GRIMM, J.	*Rumpelstiltskin.*
FIC	HAAS, J.	*Be well, Beware.*
513.2	HALSEY, M.	*3 pandas planting.*
398.24	HAMILTON, V.	*When birds could talk and bats could sing: the adventures of Bruh Sparrow, Sis Wren, and their friends.*
E	HAMM, D. J.	*Laney's lost momma.*
790.1	HANKIN, R.	*What was it like before television?*
641.3	HAUSHERR, R.	*What food is this?*
398.2	HAUTZIG, D.	*Aladdin and the magic lamp.*
E	HAVILL, J.	*Jamaica's blue marker.*
E	HAVILL, J.	*Treasure nap.*
E	HAYES, S.	*Happy Christmas Gemma.*
E	HAZEN, B. S.	*Mommy's office.*
E	HEARNE, B.	*Seven brave women.*
E	HEATH, A.	*Sofie's role.*
595.78	HEILIGMAN, D.	*From caterpillar to butterfly.*
E	HELLER, N.	*This little piggy.*
B HELLER, R.	HELLER, R.	*Fine lines.*
E	HENDERSON, K.	*Year in the city.*
E	HENKES, K.	*Chrysanthemum.*
E	HENKES, K.	*Good-bye, Curtis.*
E	HENKES, K.	*Grandpa and Bo.*
E	HENKES, K.	*Julius, the baby of the world.*
E	HENKES, K.	*Lilly's purple plastic purse.*
E	HENKES, K.	*Owen.*
E	HENKES, K.	*Weekend with Wendell.*
398.24	HEO, Y.	*Green frogs: a Korean folktale.*
E	HEROLD, M. R.	*Very important day.*
646.4	HERSHBERGER, P.	*Make costumes!: for creative play.*
FIC	HESSE, K.	*Lavender.*

E	HIGHTOWER, S.	*Twelve snails to one lizard: a tale of mischief and measurement.*
E	HILL, E. S.	*Evan's corner.*
E	HOBAN, J.	*Buzby to the rescue.*
CE E	HOBAN, L.	*Arthur's camp-out.*
CE E	HOBAN, L.	*Arthur's Christmas cookies.*
CE E	HOBAN, R.	*Best friends for Frances. Newly ill. ed.*
E	HOBAN, R.	*Birthday for Frances.*
E	HOFF, S.	*Arturo's baton.*
E	HOFF, S.	*Captain Cat: story and pictures.*
E	HOFF, S.	*Grizzwold.*
E	HOOPER, M.	*Cow, a bee, a cookie, and me.*
E	HOWARD, E.	*Big seed.*
E	HOWARD, E. F.	*Mac and Marie and the train toss surprise.*
E	HOWE, J.	*I wish I were a butterfly.*
372.21	HOWE, J.	*When you go to kindergarten. Rev. and updated ed.*
E	HRU, D.	*Magic moonberry jump ropes.*
E	HUGHES, S.	*Alfie gets in first.*
E	HUGHES, S.	*Chatting.*
E	HUGHES, S.	*Nursery collection.*
E	HURD, E. T.	*I dance in my red pajamas.*
E	HURD, T.	*Art dog.*
CE E	HURD, T.	*Mama don't allow.*
E	HURWITZ, J.	*New shoes for Silvia.*
E	HUTCHINS, P.	*Which witch is which?*
E	ISADORA, R.	*Lili at ballet.*
398.24	JACKSON, E.	*Precious gift: a Navaho creation myth.*
599.55	JACOBS, F.	*Sam the sea cow.*
CE E	JAFFE, N.	*In the month of Kislev: a story for Hanukkah.*
598.8	JENKINS, P. B.	*Nest full of eggs.*
E	JOHNSON, A.	*Julius.*
CE E	JOHNSON, C.	*Harold and the purple crayon.*
CE E	JOHNSON, C.	*Harold's ABC.*
CE E	JOHNSON, C.	*Harold's fairy tale: further adventures with the purple crayon.*
CE E	JOHNSON, C.	*Harold's trip to the sky.*
CE E	JOHNSON, C.	*Picture for Harold's room.*
E	JOHNSON, P. B.	*Farmers' market.*
E	JOHNSTON, T.	*Quilt story.*
398.24	JOHNSTON, T.	*Tale of Rabbit and Coyote.*
E	JOHNSTON, T.	*Wagon.*
CE E	JONAS, A.	*Round trip.*
E	JONES, R. C.	*Down at the bottom of the deep dark sea.*
E	JONES, R. C.	*Great Aunt Martha.*
E	JOOSSE, B. M.	*Mama, do you love me?*
E	KARAS, G. B.	*Home on the bayou: a cowboy's story.*
CE E	KEATS, E. J.	*Goggles!*
CE E	KEATS, E. J.	*Hi, cat!*
CE E	KEATS, E. J.	*Pet show.*
CE E	KEATS, E. J.	*Peter's chair.*
E	KELLER, H.	*Grandfather's dream.*
E	KELLER, H.	*Rosata.*
E	KELLEY, T.	*I've got chicken pox.*
E	KELLOGG, S.	*Best friends.*
E	KELLOGG, S.	*Much bigger than Martin.*
CE E	KELLOGG, S.	*Rose for Pinkerton.*
CE E	KELLOGG, S.	*Tallyho, Pinkerton.*
CE E	KESSLER, L.	*Here comes the strikeout.*
CE 398.24	KIMMEL, E. A.	*Anansi and the talking melon.*
398.21	KIMMEL, E. A.	*Boots and his brothers: a Norwegian tale.*
398.21	KIMMEL, E. A.	*Witch's face: a Mexican tale.*
FIC	KING-SMITH, D.	*Mr. Potter's pet.*
E	KINSEY-WARNOCK, N.	*Bear that heard crying.*
E	KITAMURA, S.	*UFO diary.*
FIC	KLINE, S.	*Horrible Harry and the green slime.*
E	KLINTING, L.	*Bruno the baker.*
E	KLINTING, L.	*Bruno the carpenter.*
E	KLINTING, L.	*Bruno the tailor.*
306.87	KNIGHT, M. B.	*Welcoming babies.*
E	KOSCIELNIAK, B.	*Geoffrey Groundhog predicts the weather.*
E	KOTZWINKLE, W.	*Million-Dollar Bear.*
E	KOVALSKI, M.	*Pizza for breakfast.*
CE E	KRAUS, R.	*Leo the late bloomer.*
CE E	KRAUSS, R.	*Carrot seed.*
E	KRAUSS, R.	*Happy day.*
FIC	KRENSKY, S.	*Iron dragon never sleeps.*
E	KRENSKY, S.	*Lionel in the winter.*
E	KROEGER, M. K.	*Paperboy.*
E	KROLL, S.	*Happy Father's Day.*
231	KROLL, V. L.	*I wanted to know all about God.*
E	LAKIN, P.	*Dad and me in the morning.*
E	LANTON, S.	*Daddy's chair.*
E	LATIMER, J.	*Moose and friends.*
E	LATTIMORE, D. N.	*Flame of peace, a tale of the Aztecs.*
E	LATTIMORE, D. N.	*Frida Maria: a story of the old Southwest.*
E	LEE, H. V.	*In the snow.*
513.2	LEEDY, L.	*Fraction action.*
395.4	LEEDY, L.	*Messages in the mailbox: how to write a letter.*
513.2	LEEDY, L.	*2 x 2 = boo!: a set of spooky multiplication stories.*
B LESTER, H.	LESTER, H.	*Author: a true story.*
E	LESTER, H.	*Princess Penelope's parrot.*
E	LESTER, J.	*Sam and the tigers: a new telling of LITTLE BLACK SAMBO.*
E	LEWIN, B.	*Booby hatch.*
E	LEWIS, K.	*My friend Harry.*
E	LINDBERGH, R.	*Nobody owns the sky: the story of "Brave Bessie" Coleman.*
E	LINDEN, A. M.	*One smiling grandma: a Caribbean counting book.*
E	LIONNI, L.	*Extraordinary egg.*
E	LIONNI, L.	*Frederick.*
529	LLEWELLYN, C.	*My first book of time.*
E	LOBEL, A.	*Alison's zinnia.*
CE E	LOBEL, A.	*Frog and Toad together.*
E	LOBEL, A.	*Small pig.*
E	LONDON, J.	*Froggy gets dressed.*
E	LONDON, J.	*Let's go, Froggy!*
E	LONDON, J.	*Lion who had asthma.*
398.24	LONG, J. F.	*Bee and the dream: a Japanese tale.*
513.2	LONG, L.	*Domino addition.*
398.2	LOTTRIDGE, C. B.	*Ten small tales.*
E	LOW, A.	*Popcorn shop.*
B O'KEEFFE, G.	LOWERY, L.	*Georgia O'Keeffe.*
649	LURIE, J.	*Allison's story: a book about homeschooling.*
E	LYON, G. E.	*Cecil's story.*
E	LYON, G. E.	*Come a tide.*
E	MACDONALD, A.	*Cousin Ruth's tooth.*
E	MACDONALD, A.	*Rachel Fister's blister.*
CE 581.4	MAESTRO, B.	*Why do leaves change color?*
625.1	MAGEE, D.	*All aboard ABC.*
E	MANN, P.	*Frog Princess?*
E	MANUSHKIN, F.	*Peeping and sleeping.*
E	MANUSHKIN, F.	*Starlight and candles: the joys of the Sabbath.*
FIC	MARSHALL, J.	*Rats on the range and other stories.*
FIC	MARSHALL, J.	*Rats on the roof and other stories.*
CE 398.24	MARSHALL, J.	*Three little pigs.*
E	MARTIN, JR., B.	*Polar bear, polar bear, what do you hear?*
E	MARTIN, JR., B.	*White Dynamite and Curly Kidd.*
FIC	MCCULLY, E. A.	*Ballot box battle.*
E	MCCULLY, E. A.	*Mirette on the high wire.*
398.24	MCDERMOTT, G.	*Anansi the spider: a tale from the Ashanti.*
398.27	MCDERMOTT, G.	*Daniel O'Rourke: an Irish tale.*
E	MCDONALD, M.	*Insects are my life.*
E	MCDONNELL, F.	*I love animals.*
E	MCGEORGE, C. W.	*Boomer's big day.*
E	MCGOVERN, A.	*Lady in the box.*
CE E	MCKISSACK, P.	*Flossie and the fox.*
CE E	MCLERRAN, A.	*Roxaboxen.*
332.4	MCMILLAN, B.	*Jelly beans for sale.*
E	MCNULTY, F.	*Snake in the house.*
CE E	MCPHAIL, D.	*Bear's toothache.*

E	MCPHAIL, D.	*Farm morning.*
E	MCPHAIL, D.	*Pigs aplenty, pigs galore!*
E	MEDDAUGH, S.	*Hog-eye.*
E	MEDDAUGH, S.	*Martha blah blah.*
E	MEDDAUGH, S.	*Witches' supermarket.*
372.4	MILES, B.	*Hey! I'm reading!: a how-to-read book for beginners.*
612.8	MILLER, M.	*My five senses.*
E	MILLER, S. S.	*Three stories you can read to your cat.*
E	MILLS, C.	*Phoebe's parade.*
E	MINARIK, E. H.	*Am I beautiful?*
E	MITCHELL, B.	*Down Buttermilk Lane.*
674	MITGUTSCH, A.	*From tree to table.*
FIC	MONFRIED, L.	*No more animals!*
E	MONJO, F. N.	*Drinking gourd. Newly illustrated ed.*
E	MOON, N.	*Lucy's picture.*
E	MOORE, E.	*Grandma's promise.*
E	MOSS, M.	*Mel's Diner.*
970.489	MOTT, E. C.	*Dancing rainbows: a Pueblo boy's story.*
FIC	MUNSCH, R.	*Promise is a promise.*
153.14	MURPHY, S. J.	*Pair of socks.*
513.2	MURPHY, S. J.	*Too many kangaroo things to do!*
612		*MY BODY.*
E	NEITZEL, S.	*Dress I'll wear to the party.*
E	NIKOLA-LISA, W.	*One hole in the road.*
E	NIKOLA-LISA, W.	*Storm.*
CE E	NOBLE, T. H.	*Jimmy's boa and the big splash birthday bash.*
CE E	NOBLE, T. H.	*Jimmy's boa bounces back.*
E	NUMEROFF, L. J.	*Why a disguise?*
E	OBERMAN, S.	*Always Prayer Shawl.*
FIC	OBERMAN, S.	*White stone in the castle wall.*
E	OGBURN, J. K.	*Noise lullaby.*
636.2	OLDER, J.	*Cow.*
398.23	OPPENHEIM, J.	*Christmas Witch: an Italian legend.*
E	OPPENHEIM, S. L.	*Hundredth name.*
222	ORGEL, D.	*Flower of Sheba.*
E	ORR, K.	*My grandpa and the sea.*
E	OSOFSKY, A.	*My Buddy.*
E	PALACIOS, A.	*Christmas surprise for Chabelita.*
E	PALATINI, M.	*Piggie Pie!*
CE E	PARISH, P.	*Good work, Amelia Bedelia.*
CE E	PARISH, P.	*Thank you, Amelia Bedelia. Rev. ed.*
E	PATRICK, D. L.	*Red dancing shoes.*
E	PAULSEN, G.	*Worksong.*
421	PELLETIER, D.	*Graphic alphabet.*
974.4	PENNER, L. R.	*Pilgrims at Plymouth.*
E	PETERSEN, P. J.	*Some days, other days.*
CE 597.8	PFEFFER, W.	*From tadpole to frog.*
E	PILKEY, D.	*Hallo-wiener.*
E	PILKEY, D.	*Paperboy.*
E	PINKNEY, G. J.	*Sunday outing.*
E	PINKNEY, J. B.	*JoJo's flying side kick.*
616.4	PIRNER, C. W.	*Even little kids get diabetes.*
398.27	PITRE, F.	*Juan Bobo and the pig: a Puerto Rican folktale.*
E	POLACCO, P.	*Aunt Chip and the great Triple Creek Dam affair.*
E	POLACCO, P.	*Chicken Sunday.*
E	POLACCO, P.	*Mrs. Katz and Tush.*
FIC	POLACCO, P.	*Pink and Say.*
E	POLACCO, P.	*Tikvah means hope.*
789.2		*POLLITOS DICEN: JUEGOS, RIMAS Y CANCIONES INFANTILES DE PAISES DE HABLA HISPANA./THE BABY CHICKS SING: TRADITIONAL GAMES, NURSERY*
E	POMERANTZ, C.	*Chalk doll.*
CE E	POMERANTZ, C.	*Outside dog.*
E	PORTE, B. A.	*Harry's pony.*
FIC	PORTE, B. A.	*Turkey drive and other tales.*
E	POTTER, B.	*Hill top tales.*
E	POYDAR, N.	*Busy Bea.*
E	RABE, B.	*Where's Chimpy?*
E	RANSOM, C. F.	*Big green pocketbook.*

E	RANSOM, C. F.	*Shooting star summer.*
E	RANSOM, C. F.	*When the whippoorwill calls.*
E	RASKIN, E.	*Nothing ever happens on my block.*
E	RATHMANN, P.	*Ruby the copycat.*
E	RATTIGAN, J. K.	*Dumpling soup.*
E	RAVEN, M.	*Angels in the dust.*
E	RAY, M. L.	*Mud.*
598	REIDEL, M.	*From egg to bird.*
E	REISER, L.	*Surprise family.*
E	REY, H. A.	*Curious George.*
E	REY, H. A.	*Curious George learns the alphabet.*
E	REY, M.	*Curious George goes to the hospital.*
E	RIGGIO, A.	*Secret signs: along the Underground Railroad.*
398.8		*RING-A-RING O' ROSES AND A DING, DONG, BELL: A BOOK OF NURSERY RHYMES.*
398.2	ROCKWELL, A. F.	*Acorn tree and other folktales.*
E	ROCKWELL, A. F.	*First snowfall.*
E	ROCKWELL, A. F.	*I fly.*
617.6	ROCKWELL, H.	*My dentist.*
E	ROOT, P.	*Coyote and the magic words.*
599.78	ROSENTHAL, M.	*Bears.*
398.24	ROTH, S. L.	*Biggest frog in Australia.*
398.24	ROUNDS, G.	*Three billy goats Gruff.*
398.2	ROWE, J. A.	*Gingerbread Man: an old English folktale.*
629.222	ROYSTON, A.	*Cars.*
FIC	RUEPP, K.	*Midnight Rider.*
E	RUSSO, M.	*Grandpa Abe.*
E	RUSSO, M.	*I don't want to go back to school.*
E	RUSSO, M.	*Under the table.*
E	RUURS, M.	*Emma's eggs.*
E	RYDER, J.	*Night gliders.*
E	RYLANT, C.	*Bookshop dog.*
BB E	RYLANT, C.	*Everyday garden (Board book).*
BB E	RYLANT, C.	*Everyday house (Board book).*
BB E	RYLANT, C.	*Everyday pets (Board book).*
BB E	RYLANT, C.	*Everyday town (Board book).*
CE E	RYLANT, C.	*Henry and Mudge and the best day of all.*
CE E	RYLANT, C.	*Henry and Mudge and the careful cousin.*
CE E	RYLANT, C.	*Henry and Mudge in the green time.*
CE E	RYLANT, C.	*Henry and Mudge in the sparkle days.*
CE E	RYLANT, C.	*Henry and Mudge under the yellow moon.*
E	RYLANT, C.	*Mr. Putter and Tabby pick the pears.*
E	RYLANT, C.	*Mr. Putter and Tabby pour the tea.*
E	RYLANT, C.	*Mr. Putter and Tabby row the boat.*
E	RYLANT, C.	*Mr. Putter and Tabby walk the dog.*
E	RYLANT, C.	*Old woman who named things.*
E	RYLANT, C.	*Silver packages: an Appalachian Christmas story.*
CE 595.79	SABIN, F.	*Amazing world of ants.*
394.261	SAINT JAMES, S.	*Gifts of Kwanzaa.*
E	SALTZBERG, B.	*Show-and-tell.*
E	SAMTON, S. W.	*World from my window.*
398.24	SAN SOUCI, R. D.	*Pedro and the monkey.*
E	SANDIN, J.	*Long way to a new land.*
398.27	SANFIELD, S.	*Bit by bit.*
E	SATHRE, V.	*Mouse chase.*
398.22	SCHECTER, E.	*Warrior maiden: a Hopi legend.*
B ROGERS, W.	SCHOTT, J. A.	*Will Rogers.*
296.4	SCHOTTER, R.	*Hanukkah!*
E	SCHOTTER, R.	*Passover magic.*
E	SCHWARTZ, A.	*Teeny tiny baby.*
FIC	SCHWARTZ, A.	*Yossel Zissel and the wisdom of Chelm.*
513	SCHWARTZ, D. M.	*How much is a million?*
E	SCHWARTZ, H.	*How I captured a dinosaur.*
E	SCHWARTZ, H. B.	*When Artie was little.*
CE E	SCIESZKA, J.	*True story of the 3 little pigs.*
E	SCOTT, A. H.	*Hi.*
E	SEABROOK, E.	*Cabbage and kings.*
598.6	SELSAM, M. E.	*Egg to chick. Rev. ed.*
599	SELSAM, M. E.	*Keep looking.*

E	SERFOZO, M.	*Benjamin Bigfoot.*
E	SERFOZO, M.	*What's what?: a guessing game.*
E	SEUSS, D.	*Hunches in bunches.*
E	SEYMOUR, T.	*Hunting the white cow.*
E	SHANNON, G.	*April showers.*
E	SHANNON, G.	*Seeds.*
E	SHANNON, G.	*Tomorrow's alphabet.*
FIC	SHARMAT, M. W.	*Genghis Khan: a dog star is born.*
FIC	SHARMAT, M. W.	*Genghis Khan: dog-gone Hollywood.*
E	SHARMAT, M. W.	*Gila monsters meet you at the airport.*
E	SHAW, N.	*Sheep in a jeep.*
E	SHAW, N.	*Sheep out to eat.*
E	SHEA, P. D.	*New moon.*
E	SHEFELMAN, J.	*Peddler's dream.*
398.22	SHEPARD, A.	*Gifts of Wali Dad: a tale of India and Pakistan.*
612.1	SHOWERS, P.	*Drop of blood. Rev. ed.*
E	SHULEVITZ, U.	*Rain, rain rivers.*
398.24	SHUTE, L.	*Rabbit wishes.*
E	SILVERMAN, E.	*Don't fidget a feather!*
E	SILVERMAN, E.	*Gittel's hands.*
398.26	SIMMS, L.	*Moon and Otter and Frog.*
155.4	SIMON, N.	*I am not a crybaby.*
E	SISULU, E.	*Day Gogo went to vote: South Africa, April 1994.*
E	SLATE, J.	*Miss Bindergarten gets ready for kindergarten.*
E	SLATER, T.	*Stay in line.*
789.2	SLAVIN, B.	*Cat came back: a traditional song.*
E	SLEPIAN, J.	*Lost moose.*
E	SMALL, D.	*Fenwick's suit.*
E	SOTO, G.	*Old man and his door.*
E	SOTO, G.	*Snapshots from the wedding.*
E	STANEK, M.	*All alone after school.*
398.24	STEVENS, J.	*Coyote steals the blanket: a Ute tale.*
398.24	STEVENS, J.	*Old bag of bones: a coyote tale.*
CE E	STEVENS, J.	*Princess and the pea.*
398.24	STEVENS, J.	*Tops and bottoms.*
E	STEVENSON, H.	*Grandpa's house.*
B STEVENSON, J	STEVENSON, J.	*Don't you know there's a war on?*
E	STEVENSON, J.	*Mud Flat Olympics.*
E	STEVENSON, J.	*Oldest elf.*
E	STEVENSON, J.	*We hate rain!*
CE E	STEVENSON, J.	*What's under my bed.*
E	STEVENSON, J.	*Worse than the worst.*
E	STEWART, S.	*Gardener.*
E	STOCK, C.	*Birthday present.*
E	STOCK, C.	*Halloween monster.*
E	STRETE, C. K.	*They thought they saw him.*
398.24	SUMMERS, K.	*Milly and Tilly: the story of a town mouse and a country mouse.*
E	SURAT, M. M.	*Angel child, dragon child.*
E	SYKES, J.	*This and that.*
E	TAMAR, E.	*Garden of happiness.*
E	TEAGUE, M.	*Field beyond the outfield.*
E	TEAGUE, M.	*Pigsty.*
E	TEAGUE, M.	*Secret shortcut.*
E	TEMPLE, C.	*Train.*
398.24	TEMPLE, F.	*Tiger soup: an Anansi story from Jamaica.*
E	TESTA, M.	*Thumbs up, Rico!*
E	THAYER, J.	*Puppy who wanted a boy.*
E	THOMAS, S. M.	*Putting the world to sleep.*
FIC	TORNQVIST, R.	*Christmas carp.*
688.7		*TOYS.*
E	TRYON, L.	*Albert's ballgame.*
E	TRYON, L.	*Albert's Thanksgiving.*
E	UDRY, J. M.	*Tree is nice.*
E	USHINSKY, K.	*How a shirt grew in the field.*
E	VAN LAAN, N.	*Boda: a Mexican wedding celebration.*
E	VAN LAAN, N.	*Possum come a-knockin'.*
E	VAN LEEUWEN, J.	*Emma Bean.*
E	VAN LEEUWEN, J.	*Fourth of July on the plains.*
E	VAUGHAN, M. K.	*Snap!*
E	VIORST, J.	*Alexander, who's not (Do you hear me? I mean it!) going to move.*
E	VIORST, J.	*Earrings!*
E	VIORST, J.	*Good-bye book.*
E	VOZAR, D.	*M.C. Turtle and the Hip Hop Hare: a nursery rap.*
E	WABER, B.	*Gina.*
E	WABER, B.	*You look ridiculous said the rhinoceros to the hippopotamus.*
636.5	WALLACE, K.	*My hen is dancing.*
E	WALLNER, A.	*Alcott family Christmas.*
E	WALSH, E. S.	*Samantha.*
E	WALSH, E. S.	*You silly goose.*
E	WALTER, M. P.	*Ty's one-man band.*
394.261	WATERS, K.	*Lion dancer: Ernie Wan's Chinese New Year.*
974.4	WATERS, K.	*Tapenum's day: a Wampanoag Indian boy in pilgrim times.*
579.6	WATTS, B.	*Mushroom.*
E	WEEKS, S.	*Hurricane City.*
E	WEISS, G. D.	*What a wonderful world.*
E	WEISS, N.	*Stone men.*
E	WELLS, R.	*McDuff comes home.*
E	WELLS, R.	*McDuff moves in.*
530.8	WELLS, R. E.	*Is a blue whale the biggest thing there is?*
612		*WHAT IS A BELLYBUTTON?: FIRST QUESTIONS AND ANSWERS ABOUT THE HUMAN BODY.*
E	WIDMAN, C.	*Lemon drop jar.*
E	WIESNER, D.	*Hurricane.*
B FRANCIS, ST.	WILDSMITH, B.	*Saint Francis.*
E	WILHELM, H.	*Royal raven.*
CE E	WILLIAMS, K. L.	*Galimoto.*
CE E	WILLIAMS, K. L.	*Tap-tap.*
E	WILLIAMS, K. L.	*When Africa was home.*
E	WILLIAMS, S. A.	*Working cotton.*
E	WILLIAMS, V. B.	*Cherries and cherry pits.*
E	WILLIAMS, V. B.	*More more more, said the baby.*
E	WILLIAMS, V. B.	*Something special for me.*
FIC	WILLNER-PARDO, G.	*When Jane-Marie told my secret.*
E	WINTHROP, E.	*Sledding.*
E	WINTHROP, E.	*Very noisy girl.*
398.26	WOLF-SAMPATH, G.	*Mala: a women's folktale.*
E	WOLFF, F.	*Seven loaves of bread.*
E	WOLFF, P. R.	*Toll-bridge troll.*
398.27	WOLKSTEIN, D.	*White Wave: a Chinese tale. Rev. ed.*
507	WYLER, R.	*Science fun with mud and dirt.*
591.47	YAMASHITA, K.	*Paws, wings, and hooves: mammals on the move.*
FIC	YARBROUGH, C.	*Tamika and the wisdom rings.*
CE E	YASHIMA, T.	*Umbrella.*
CE E	YOLEN, J.	*Owl moon.*
636.088	ZIEFERT, H.	*Let's get a pet.*
CE E	ZION, G.	*Harry by the sea.*
CE E	ZION, G.	*Harry the dirty dog.*
577	ZOEHFELD, K. W.	*What's alive?*
E	ZOLOTOW, C.	*Hating book.*
E	ZOLOTOW, C.	*Over and over.*

AUTHOR'S SERIES

Many authors carry familiar characters through many different experiences. The titles do not always fall together in the Classified Catalog nor can they always be included in one entry. For the purpose of this appendix, a series is defined as three or more books written by an author about a particular character or characters. The listing is in alphabetical order by author with the titles under the series name. If there is no specific name for the series, one has been created using the name of the predominate character(s). Refer to the main entry for complete information.

Adler, D.A. . . . . **Cam Jansen adventure series**
Cam Jansen and the ghostly mystery.
Cam Jansen and the mystery at the haunted house.
Cam Jansen and the mystery at the monkey house.
Cam Jansen and the mystery of flight 54.
Cam Jansen and the mystery of the Babe Ruth baseball.
Cam Jansen and the mystery of the carnival prize.
Cam Jansen and the mystery of the circus clown.
Cam Jansen and the mystery of the dinosaur bones.
Cam Jansen and the mystery of the gold coins.
Cam Jansen and the mystery of the monster movie.
Cam Jansen and the mystery of the stolen diamonds.
Cam Jansen and the mystery of the television dog.
Cam Jansen and the mystery of the UFO.

Adler, D.A. . . . . **Young Cam Jansen**
Young Cam Jansen and the dinosaur game.
Young Cam Jansen and the lost tooth.
Young Cam Jansen and the missing cookie.

Aiken, J. . . . . **Wolves chronicles**
Cold Shoulder Road.
Is underground.
Wolves of Willoughby Chase.

Alexander, L. . . . . **Prydain chronicles**
Black cauldron.
Book of three.
Castle of Llyr.
Foundling and other tales of Prydain.
Taran wanderer.

Alexander, L. . . . . **Vesper Holly**
Drackenberg adventure.
El Dorado adventure.
Illyrian adventure.
Jedera adventure.
Philadelphia adventure.

Allard, H. . . . . **Miss Nelson**
Miss Nelson has a field day.
Miss Nelson is back.
Miss Nelson is missing.

Allard, H. . . . . **Stupids**
Stupids die.
Stupids have a ball.
Stupids step out.
Stupids take off.

Arnosky, J. . . . . **Crinkleroot's nature guides**
Crinkleroot's guide to knowing animal habitats.
Crinkleroot's guide to knowing butterflies and moths.
Crinkleroot's guide to knowing the birds.
Crinkleroot's 25 birds every child should know.

Asch, F. . . . . **Frank Asch bear story**
Bear's bargain.
Happy birthday, moon.
Moongame.

Barracca, D. . . . . **Taxi Dog**
Adventures of taxi dog.
Aventuras de Maxi, el perro taxista.
Maxi, the hero.
Maxi, the star.
Taxi Dog Christmas.

Baum, L.F. . . . . **Oz**
Emerald City of Oz.
Mago de Oz.
Ozma of Oz.
Patchwork girl of Oz.
Road to Oz.
Tik-Tok of Oz.
Wonderful Wizard of Oz.

Bellairs, J. . . . . **Anthony Monday and Miss Eells**
Dark secret of Weatherend.
Mansion in the mist.
Treasure of Alpheus Winterborn.

Bellairs, J. . . . . **Lewis**
Doom of the haunted opera.
Figure in the shadows.
Ghost in the mirror.
House with a clock in its walls.
Letter, the witch, and the ring.

Berenstain, S. . . . . **Berenstain Bears**
Berenstain Bears and the sitter.
Berenstain Bears and the spooky old tree.
Berenstain Bears and too much birthday.
Berenstain Bears get in a fight.
BERENSTAIN BEARS GET IN A FIGHT. School ed. (CD-ROM).
Berenstain Bears go to camp.
BERENSTAIN BEARS IN THE DARK. School ed. (CD-ROM).
Berenstain Bears learn about strangers.
Berenstain Bears visit the dentist.
Berenstain Bears: no girls allowed.
Berenstain Bears' moving day.
Inside, outside, upside down.
Los osos Berenstain y demasiada fiesta.
Osos Berenstain dia de mudanza.

Blume, J. . . . . **Peter and Fudge**
Fudge-a-mania.
Superfudge (Spanish version).
Superfudge.
Tales of a fourth grade nothing.

Bond, M. . . . . **Paddington**
    Bear called Paddington.
    Paddington on screen.
    Paddington takes the test.

Bonsall, C. . . . . **Wizard, Tubby, Skinny & Snitch**
    Case of the cat's meow.
    Case of the double cross.
    Case of the dumb bells.
    Case of the hungry stranger.
    Case of the scaredy cats.
    Caso del forastero hambriento.

Boston, L.M. . . . . **Children of Green Knowe**
    Children of Green Knowe.
    Enemy at Green Knowe.
    River at Green Knowe.
    Stranger at Green Knowe.

Bridwell, N. . . . . **Clifford**
    Buenas acciones de Clifford.
    Clifford at the circus.
    Clifford el grand perro colorado.
    Clifford gets a job.
    Clifford takes a trip.
    Clifford the big red dog.
    Clifford the small red puppy.
    Clifford va de viaje.
    Clifford, we love you.
    Clifford's good deeds.
    Clifford's Halloween.
    Clifford's sports day.

Brown, L.K. . . . . **Dinosaurs' guide**
    Dinosaurs alive and well! a guide to good health.
    Dinosaurs divorce: a guide for changing families.
    Dinosaurs to the rescue!: a guide to protecting our planet.
    Dinosaurs, beware: a safety guide.
    When dinosaurs die: a guide to understanding death.

Brown, M.T. . . . . **Arthur adventure**
    Arthur babysits.
    Arthur goes to camp.
    Arthur meets the president.
    Arthur writes a story.
    Arthur's April fool.
    Arthur's baby.
    Arthur's birthday.
    Arthur's chicken pox.
    Arthur's Christmas.
    Arthur's eyes.
    Arthur's family vacation.
    Arthur's first sleepover.
    Arthur's Halloween.
    Arthur's new puppy.
    Arthur's nose.
    Arthur's pet business.
    Arthur's teacher trouble.
    Arthur's Thanksgiving.
    Arthur's tooth.
    Arthur's TV trouble.
    Arthur's Valentine.
    Arturo y sus problemas con el profesor.

Brown, M.T. . . . . **D.W.**
    D.W. all wet.
    D.W. flips.
    D.W. rides again!
    D.W. the picky eater.
    D.W. thinks big.

Byars, B. . . . . **Golly sisters**
    Golly sisters go West.
    Golly sisters ride again.
    Hooray for the Golly sisters!

Byars, B.C. . . . . **Bingo Brown**
    Burning questions of Bingo Brown.

Byars, B.C. . . . . **Blossom Family**
    Blossom promise.
    Blossoms and the Green Phantom.
    Blossoms meet the Vulture Lady.
    Not-just-anybody family.
    Wanted...Mud Blossom.

Calhoun, M. . . . . **Henry**
    Cross-country cat.
    Henry the sailor cat.
    High-wire Henry.
    Hot-air Henry.

Cameron, A. . . . . **Julian**
    Julian, dream doctor.
    Julian's glorious summer.
    More stories Julian tells.
    Stories Julian tells.

Carlson, N. . . . . **Louanne Pig**
    Making the team.
    Mysterious valentine.
    Perfect family.
    Talent show.
    Witch lady.

Carlstrom, N.W. . . . . **Jesse Bear**
    Better not get wet, Jesse Bear.
    Happy birthday, Jesse Bear!
    How do you say it today, Jesse Bear?
    Jesse Bear, what will you wear?
    Let's count it out, Jesse Bear.

Caseley, J. . . . . **Kane family**
    Chloe in the know.
    Dorothy's darkest days.
    Harry and Arney.
    Hurricane Harry.

Christelow, E. . . . . **Five little monkeys**
    Don't wake up Mama!
    Five little monkeys sitting in a tree.
    Five little monkeys with nothing to do.

Christopher, J. . . . . **Tripod series**
    City of gold and lead.
    Pool of fire.
    White Mountains.

Cleary, B. . . . . **Beezus and Ramona**
    Beezus and Ramona.
    Ramona and her father.
    Ramona and her mother.
    Ramona Empieza el curso.
    Ramona forever.
    Ramona la chinche.
    Ramona Quimby, age 8.
    Ramona the brave.
    Ramona the pest.
    Ramona y su madre.
    Ramona y su padre.

Cleary, B. . . . . **Henry Huggins**
    Henry and Beezus.
    Henry and Ribsy.
    Henry and the paper route.
    Henry Huggins (Spanish version).
    Henry Huggins.
    Ribsy.

Cleary, B. . . . . **Jimmy and Janet**
    Janet's thingamajigs.
    Real hole.
    Two dog biscuits.

Cleary, B. . . . . **Ralph S. Mouse**
    Mouse and the motorcycle.
    Ralph S. Mouse.
    Runaway Ralph.

Cohen, M. . . . .   **First grade**
   Don't eat too much turkey!
   Liar, liar, pants on fire!
   No good in art.
   Real-skin rubber monster mask.
   See you in second grade!
   When will I read?
   Will I have a friend?

Cole, J. . . . .   **Magic School Bus**
   Autobus magico dentro de un huracan.
   Autobus magico en el cuerpo humano.
   Autobus magico en el fondo del mar.
   Autobus magico en el interior de la tierra.
   Autobus magico en el sistema solar.
   Autobus magico en tiempos de los dinosaurios.
   Autobus magico viaja por el agua.
   Magic School Bus at the waterworks.
   Magic School Bus in the time of the dinosaurs.
   Magic School Bus inside a beehive.
   Magic School Bus inside a hurricane.
   Magic School Bus inside the earth.
   Magic School Bus inside the human body.
   Magic School Bus lost in the solar system.
   Magic School Bus on the ocean floor.

Cooper, S. . . . .   **Will Stanton**
   Greenwitch.
   Over sea, under stone.
   Silver on the tree.

Cottonwood, J. . . . .   **San Puerco, California**
   Adventures of Boone Barnaby.
   Babcock.
   Danny ain't.

Danziger, P. . . . .   **Amber Brown**
   Ambar en cuarto y sin su amigo.
   Amber Brown goes fourth.
   Amber Brown is not a crayon.
   Amber Brown wants extra credit.
   Forever Amber Brown.
   Sequiremos siendo amigos.

Farley, W. . . . .   **Black Stallion**
   Black Stallion and Flame.
   Black Stallion mystery.
   Black Stallion.
   Black Stallion's ghost.
   Young Black Stallion.

Gannett, R.S. . . . .   **Dragons**
   Dragons of Blueland.
   Elmer and the dragon.
   My father's dragon.

Gantos, J. . . . .   **Rotten Ralph**
   Happy birthday Rotten Ralph.
   Rotten Ralph.
   Rotten Ralph's show and tell.

Giff, P.R. . . . .   **Casey**
   Fourth-grade celebrity.
   Girl who knew it all.
   Left-handed shortstop.
   Winter worm business.

Giff, P.R. . . . .   **New kids at the Polk Street School**
   All about Stacy.
   B-E-S-T friends.
   Stacy says good-bye.

Gilson, J. . . . .   **Hobie Hanson**
   Hobie Hanson, greatest hero of the mall.
   Hobie Hanson, you're weird.
   Soccer circus.
   Sticks and stones and skeleton bones.

Gleitzman, M. . . . .   **Keith Shipley**
   Misery guts.
   Puppy fat.
   Worry warts.

Griffith, H.V. . . . .   **Janetta**
   Grandaddy and Janetta.
   Grandaddy's place.
   Grandaddy's stars.

Havill, J. . . . .   **Jamaica**
   Jamaica and Brianna.
   Jamaica's blue marker.
   Jamaica's find.

Haywood, C. . . . .   **Betsy**
   "B" is for Betsy.
   Betsy and Billy.
   Betsy and the boys.

Heide, F.P. . . . .   **Treehorn**
   Shrinking of Treehorn.

Henry, M. . . . .   **Misty of Chincoteague**
   Misty of Chincoteague.
   Sea-Star: orphan of Chincoteague.
   Stormy, Misty's foal.

Hest, A. . . . .   **Baby Duck**
   Baby Duck and the bad eyeglasses.
   In the rain with Baby Duck.
   You're the boss, Baby Duck!

Himmelman, J. . . . .   **Fix-it family**
   Clover County carrot contest.
   Day-off machine.
   Great leaf blast-off.
   Super camper caper.

Hoban, L. . . . .   **Arthur**
   Arthur's camp-out.
   Arthur's Christmas cookies.
   Arthur's funny money.
   Arthur's great big valentine.
   Arthur's Halloween costume.
   Arthur's honey bear.
   Arthur's loose tooth.
   Arthur's pen pal.
   Arthur's prize reader.

Hoban, R. . . . .   **Frances**
   Baby sister for Frances. Newly ill. ed.
   Bargain for Frances. Newly ill. ed.
   Bedtime for Frances. Newly ill. ed.
   Best friends for Frances. Newly ill. ed.
   Birthday for Frances.
   Bread and jam for Frances. Newly ill. ed.
   Gran negocio de Francisca.
   Hora de acostarse de Francisca.
   Nueva hermanita de Francisca.
   Pan y mermelada para Francisca.

Hoban, Tana . . . .   **"Look" books**
   Just look.
   Look book.
   Look up, look down.
   Look! look! look!
   Take another look.

Hoff, S. . . . .   **Danny and the dinosaur**
   Danny and the dinosaur go to camp.
   Danny and the dinosaur.
   Happy birthday, Danny and the dinosaur!

Holabird, K. . . . .   **Angelina**
   Angelina and Alice.
   Angelina and the princess.
   Angelina Ballerina and other stories (Talking book).

Holabird, K. (Continued)
Angelina Ballerina.
Angelina ice skates.
Angelina on stage.
Angelina's baby sister.
Angelina's birthday surprise.
Angelina's Christmas.

Honeycutt, N. . . . . **Jonah Twist**
All new Jonah Twist.
Best-laid plans of Jonah Twist.
Juliet Fisher and the foolproof plan.

Howe, D. & J. . . . . **Harold and Chester**
Bonicula.
Bunnicula: a rabbit-tale mystery.
Celery stalks at midnight.
Creepy-crawly birthday.
Hot fudge.
Howliday Inn.
Return to Howliday Inn.
Scared silly: a Halloween treat.

Hughes, S. . . . . **Alfie**
Alfie gets in first.
Big Alfie and Annie Rose storybook.
Big Alfie out of doors storybook.

Hurwitz, J. . . . . **Aldo**
Aldo Applesauce.
Aldo Ice Cream.
Aldo Peanut Butter.
Much ado about Aldo.

Hurwitz, J. . . . . **Lucas Cott**
Class clown.
Class president.
School spirit.
School's out.
Teacher's pet.

Hurwitz, J. . . . . **Russell**
E is for Elisa.
Elisa in the middle.
Make room for Elisa.
Russell and Elisa.
Russell Sprouts.

Hutchins, P. . . . . **Billy the monster**
Silly Billy!
Very worst monster.
Where's the baby?

Hutchins, P. . . . . **Titch**
Tidy Titch.
Titch and Daisy.
You'll soon grow into them, Titch.

Jansson, T. . . . . **Moomintroll**
Comet in Moominland.
Finn Family Moomintroll.
Moominland midwinter.
Moominpappa at sea.
Moominpappa's memoirs.
Moominsummer madness.
Tales from Moominvalley.

Johnson, A. . . . . **Joshua**
Joshua by the sea (Board book).
Joshua's night whispers (Board book).
Rain feet (Board book).

Johnson, C. . . . . **Harold**
Harold and the purple crayon.
Harold y el lapiz color morado.
Harold's ABC.
Harold's fairy tale: further adventures with the purple crayon.
Harold's trip to the sky.

Johnson, C. (Continued)
Picture for Harold's room.

Keats, E.J. . . . . **Peter**
Dia de nieve.
Goggles!
Letter to Amy.
Peter's chair.
Silba por Willie.
Silla de Pedro.
Snowy day.
Whistle for Willie.

Kellogg, S. . . . . **Pinkerton**
Pinkerton, behave.
Prehistoric Pinkerton.
Rose for Pinkerton.
Tallyho, Pinkerton.

Kennedy, X.J. . . . . **Brats**
Brats.
Drat these brats!
Fresh brats.

King-Smith, D. . . . . **Sophie**
Sophie hits six.
Sophie in the saddle.
Sophie's Lucky.
Sophie's Tom.

Kline, S. . . . . **Herbie Jones**
Herbie Jones and Hamburger Head.
Herbie Jones and the birthday showdown.
Herbie Jones and the class gift.

Klinting, L. . . . . **Bruno**
Bruno the baker.
Bruno the carpenter.
Bruno the tailor.

Korman, G. . . . . **Bruno and Boots**
Go jump in the pool!
Something fishy at Macdonald Hall.
This can't be happening at Macdonald Hall!
Zucchini warriors.

Kraus, R. . . . . **Little Mouse**
Come out and play, little mouse.
Where are you going little mouse?
Whose mouse are you?

Krensky, S. . . . . **Lionel**
Lionel and Louise.
Lionel at large.
Lionel in the winter.

Le Guin, U.K. . . . . **Earthsea**
Farthest shore.
Tehanu: the last book of Earthsea.
Wizard of Earthsea.

Levitin, S. . . . . **Annie**
Annie's promise.
Journey to America.
Silver days.

Levy, E. . . . . **Something queer**
Something queer at the haunted school.
Something queer at the lemonade stand.
Something queer at the scary movie.
Something queer in outer space.
Something queer is going on (a mystery).

Lewis, C.S. . . . . **Chronicles of Narnia**
Caballo y su jinete.
Horse and his boy.
Last battle.
Leon, la bruja, y el armario.

Lewis, C.S. (Continued)
Lion, the witch and the wardrobe.
Magician's nephew.
Prince Caspian: the return to Narnia.
Principe Caspio.
Sillon de plata.
Silver chair.
Ultima batalla.
Viaje del Amanecer.
Voyage of the Dawn Treader.

Lobel, A. . . . . **Frog and Toad**
Days with Frog and Toad.
Dias con Sapo y Sepo.
Frog and Toad all year.
Frog and Toad are friends.
Frog and Toad together.
Sapo y Sepo inseparables.
Sapo y Sepo son amigos.
Sapo y Sepo un ano entero.

London, J. . . . . **Froggy**
Froggy gets dressed.
Froggy goes to school.
Froggy se viste.
Let's go, Froggy!

Lowry, L. . . . . **Anastasia Krupnik**
All about Sam.
Anastasia again.
Anastasia ask your analyst.
Anastasia at this address.
Anastasia at your service.
Anastasia has the answers.
Anastasia Krupnik (Spanish version).
Anastasia Krupnik.
Anastasia on her own.
Anastasia, absolutely.
Anastasia's chosen career.
Attaboy, Sam!

Markle, S. . . . . **Outside and inside**
Outside and inside birds.
Outside and inside sharks.
Outside and inside snakes.
Outside and inside spiders.
Outside and inside trees.
Outside and inside you.

Marshall, E. . . . . **Fox**
Fox all week.
Fox and his friends.
Fox in love.
Fox on stage.
Zorro y sus amigos.

Marshall, E. . . . . **Lolly, Sam and Spider**
Four on the shore.
Pandilla en la orilla.
Three by the sea.
Three up a tree.
Tres en un arbol.

Marshall, J. . . . . **Fox**
Fox be nimble.
Fox on the job.
Fox outfoxed.

Marshall, J. . . . . **George and Martha**
George and Martha 'round and 'round.
George and Martha back in town.
George and Martha encore.
George and Martha one fine day.
George and Martha rise and shine.
George and Martha.

Mayer, M. . . . . **Boy and frog**
Boy, a dog and a frog.
Frog goes to dinner.

Mayer, M. (Continued)
Frog on his own.
Frog where are you?
One frog too many.

McCaffrey, A. . . . . **Menolly**
Dragondrums.
Dragonsinger.
Dragonsong.

Micklethwait, L. . . . . **I spy...**
I spy a freight train: transportation in art.
I spy a lion: animals in art.
I spy two eyes: numbers in art.
I spy: an alphabet in art.

Minarik, E.H. . . . . **Little Bear**
Amigos de Osito.
Father Bear comes home.
Kiss for Little Bear.
Little Bear.
Little Bear's friend.
Little Bear's visit.
Osito.
Papa Oso vuelve a casa.
Visita de Osito.

Montgomery, L.M. . . . . **Anne**
Anne of Avonlea.
Anne of Green Gables.
Anne of Ingleside.
Anne of the island.
Anne of the island: an Anne of Green Gables story.
Anne of Windy Poplars.
Anne's house of dreams.
Rainbow Valley.
Rilla of Ingleside.

Naylor, P. . . . . **Shiloh trilogy**
Saving Shiloh.
Shiloh season.
Shiloh.

Naylor, P.R. . . . . **Alice**
Agony of Alice.
Alice in April.
Alice in rapture, sort of.
Alice the brave.
All but Alice.
Reluctantly Alice.

Noble, T.H. . . . . **Jimmy's boa**
Day Jimmy's boa ate the wash.
Dia que la boa de Jimmy se comio la ropa.
Jimmy's boa and the big splash birthday bash.
Jimmy's boa bounces back.

Norton, M. . . . . **Borrowers**
Borrowers afield.
Borrowers afloat.
Borrowers aloft.
Borrowers avenged.
Borrowers.

Parish, P. . . . . **Amelia Bedelia**
Amelia Bedelia goes camping.
Amelia Bedelia's family album.
Come back, Amelia Bedelia. Newly illustrated ed.
Good work, Amelia Bedelia.
Merry Christmas, Amelia Bedelia.
Play ball, Amelia Bedelia.
Teach us, Amelia Bedelia.
Thank you, Amelia Bedelia. Rev. ed.

Porte, B.A. . . . . **Harry**
Harry gets an uncle.
Harry in trouble.
Harry's birthday.

Porte, B.A. (Continued)
Harry's dog.
Harry's pony.

Rand, G. . . . . **Salty**
Aloha, Salty!

Rayner, M. . . . . **Pig Family**
Garth Pig and the ice cream lady.
Mr. and Mrs. Pig's evening out.
Mrs. Pig's bulk buy.

Reid Banks, L.. . . . . **Indian in the cupboard**
Indian in the cupboard.
Mystery of the cupboard.
Return of the Indian.
Secret of the Indian.

Rey, H.A. & M.. . . . . **Curious George**
Curious George flies a kite.
Curious George gets a medal.
Curious George goes to the hospital.
Curious George learns the alphabet.
Curious George rides a bike.
Curious George takes a job.
Curious George.
Jorge el Curioso.

Rylant, C. . . . . **Henry and Mudge**
Henry and Mudge and the bedtime thumps.
Henry and Mudge and the best day of all.
Henry and Mudge and the careful cousin.
Henry and Mudge and the forever sea.
Henry and Mudge and the happy cat.
Henry and Mudge and the long weekend.
Henry and Mudge and the wild wind.
Henry and Mudge get the cold shivers.
Henry and Mudge in puddle trouble.
Henry and Mudge in the green time.
Henry and Mudge in the sparkle days.
Henry and Mudge take the big test.
Henry and Mudge under the yellow moon.
Henry and Mudge: the first book.
Henry y Mudge con barro hasta el rabo.
Henry y mudge y el mejor dia del ano.

Rylant, C. . . . . **Mr. Putter and Tabby**
Mr. Putter and Tabby bake the cake.
Mr. Putter and Tabby fly the plane.
Mr. Putter and Tabby pick the pears.
Mr. Putter and Tabby pour the tea.
Mr. Putter and Tabby row the boat.
Mr. Putter and Tabby walk the dog.

San Souci, R.D. . . . . **Arthurian cycle**
Young Guinevere.
Young Lancelot.
Young Merlin.

Scieszka, J. . . . . **Time warp trio**
Good, the bad, and the goofy.
Knights of the kitchen table.
Not-so-jolly Roger.
Tut, tut.
Your mother was a Neanderthal.

Selden, G. . . . . **Chester Cricket**
Chester Cricket's new home.
Chester Cricket's pigeon ride.
Cricket in Times Square.
Old meadow.

Selden, G. . . . . **Harry Cat & Tucker Mouse**
Harry Kitten and Tucker Mouse.
Tucker's countryside.

Sendak, M. . . . . **Nutshell library**
Alligators all around: an alphabet.

Sendak, M. (Continued)
Chicken soup with rice: a book of months.
Nutshell library (Videocassette).
One was Johnny: a counting book.
Pierre: a cautionary tale in five chapters and a prologue.

Sharmat, M.W. . . . . **Nate the Great**
Nate the Great and the crunchy Christmas.
Nate the Great and the Halloween hunt.
Nate the Great and the lost list.
Nate the Great and the phony clue.
Nate the Great and the pillowcase.
Nate the Great and the stolen base.
Nate the Great and the tardy tortoise.
Nate the Great goes undercover.
Nate the Great stalks stupidweed.
Nate the Great.

Shaw, N. . . . . **Sheep**
Sheep in a jeep.
Sheep in a shop.
Sheep on a ship.
Sheep out to eat.

Smith, J.L. . . . . **Adam Joshua**
Kid next door and other headaches.
Monster in the third dresser drawer and other stories about Adam Joshua.
Serious science: an Adam Joshua story.
Show and tell war.
Turkey's side of it: Adam Joshua's Thanksgiving.

Sobol, D.J. . . . . **Encyclopedia Brown**
Encyclopedia Brown and the case of Pablo's nose.
Encyclopedia Brown and the case of the dead eagles.
Encyclopedia Brown and the case of the midnight visitor.
Encyclopedia Brown and the case of the mysterious handprints.
Encyclopedia Brown and the case of the secret pitch.
Encyclopedia Brown and the case of the treasure hunt.
Encyclopedia Brown finds the clues.
Encyclopedia Brown gets his man.
Encyclopedia Brown keeps the peace.
Encyclopedia Brown lends a hand.
Encyclopedia Brown saves the day.
Encyclopedia Brown sets the pace.
Encyclopedia Brown solves them all.
Encyclopedia Brown takes the case.
Encyclopedia Brown tracks them down.
Encyclopedia Brown, boy detective.

Stevenson, J. . . . . **Autobiographical sketches**
Fun no fun.
Higher on the door.
I had a lot of wishes.
July.
When I was nine.

Stevenson, J. . . . . **Grandpa, Mary Ann and Louie**
Could be worse.
That terrible Halloween night.
We hate rain!
What's under my bed.

Stevenson, J. . . . . **Mud Flat adventures**
Mud Flat mystery.
Mud Flat Olympics.
Yard sale.

Stevenson, J. . . . . **Worst person**
Worse than the worst.
Worst goes South.
Worst person in the world.

Stock, C.. . . . . **Festive year**
Birthday present.
Christmas time.
Easter surprise.
Halloween monster.
Thanksgiving treat.

Taylor, M.D. . . . . **Logan Family**
  Friendship.
  Let the circle be unbroken.
  Mississippi bridge.
  Roll of thunder, hear my cry.
  Song of the trees.
  Well: David's story.

Taylor, S. . . . . **All-of-a-Kind Family**
  All-of-a-kind family uptown.
  All-of-a-kind family.
  Ella of all-of-a-kind family.
  More all-of-a-kind family.

Taylor, T. . . . . **Teetoncey and Ben**
  Odyssey of Ben O'Neal.
  Teetoncey and Ben O'Neal.
  Teetoncey.

Travers, P.L. . . . . **Mary Poppins**
  Mary Poppins comes back.
  Mary Poppins in Cherry Tree Lane.
  Mary Poppins. Rev. ed.

Tryon, L. . . . . **Albert**
  Albert's alphabet.
  Albert's ballgame.
  Albert's field trip.
  Albert's play.
  Albert's Thanksgiving.

Uchida, Y. . . . . **Rinko**
  Best bad thing.
  Happiest ending.
  Jar of dreams.

Van Leeuwen, J. . . . . **Amanda Pig & Oliver**
  Amanda Pig and her big brother, Oliver.
  Amanda Pig on her own.
  Amanda Pig, schoolgirl.
  Cuentos del cerdito Oliver.
  More tales of Amanda Pig.
  Oliver and Amanda and the big snow.
  Oliver and Amanda's Christmas.
  Oliver and Amanda's Halloween.
  Oliver Pig at school.
  Oliver, Amanda, and Grandmother Pig.
  Tales of Amanda Pig.
  Tales of Oliver Pig.

Vincent, G. . . . . **Ernest and Celestine**
  Ernest and Celestine at the circus.
  Ernest and Celestine.
  Ernest and Celestine's picnic.
  Where are you, Ernest and Celestine?

Waber, B. . . . . **Lyle**
  Funny, funny Lyle.
  House on East 88th Street.
  Lovable Lyle.
  Lyle and the birthday party.
  Lyle at the office.
  Lyle finds his mother.
  Lyle, Lyle, crocodile.

Waddell, M. . . . . **Little Bear/Big Bear**
  Can't you sleep, Little Bear? 2nd ed.
  Let's go home, Little Bear.
  You and me, Little Bear.

Waugh, S. . . . . **Mennyms**
  Mennyms alone.
  Mennyms in the wilderness.
  Mennyms under siege.
  Mennyms.

Wells, R. . . . . **Max & Ruby**
  Bunny cakes.
  Max and Ruby's first Greek myth: Pandora's box.

Wells, R. (Continued)
  Max and Ruby's Midas: another Greek myth.
  Max's chocolate chicken.
  Max's Christmas.
  Max's first word (Board book).
  Max's new suit.
  Max's ride.

Wilder, L.I. . . . . **Little House**
  By the shores of Silver Lake.
  *DEAR LAURA: LETTERS FROM CHILDREN TO LAURA
    INGALLS WILDER.*
  Farmer boy.
  First four years.
  Little house in the Big Woods.
  Little house on the prairie.
  Little town on the prairie.
  Long winter.
  On the banks of Plum Creek.
  These happy golden years.

Williams, V.B. . . . . **Rosa**
  Algo especial para mi.
  Chair for my mother.
  Music, music for everyone.
  Musica para todo el mundo!
  Sillon para mi mama.
  Something special for me.

Wiseman, B. . . . . **Morris and Boris**
  Morris and Boris at the circus.
  Morris and Boris.
  Morris goes to school.
  Morris has a cold.
  Morris the Moose.

Yeoman, J., & Blake, Q. . . . . **Old Mother Hubbard's dog**
  Old Mother Hubbard's dog dresses up.
  Old Mother Hubbard's dog learns to play.
  Old Mother Hubbard's dog needs a doctor.
  Old Mother Hubbard's dog takes up sport.

Yolen, J. . . . . **Piggins**
  Picnic with Piggins.
  Piggins and the royal wedding.
  Piggins.

Zion, G. . . . . **Harry**
  Harry and the lady next door.
  Harry by the sea.
  Harry el perrito sucio.
  Harry the dirty dog.
  Harry, no quiere rosas!
  No roses for Harry.

PUBLISHER'S SERIES

This appendix lists publisher's series in alphabetical order by series name. A short author/title listing for each recommended title is given. Refer to the main entry for complete information.

Abbeville anthology . . . . **Abbeville Kids**
    EVETTS-SECKER, J. *Mother and daughter tales.*
    RIORDAN, J. *Stories from the sea.*

Achievers . . . . **Lerner**
    ANDERSON, C. C. *Jackie Kennedy Onassis: woman of courage.*
    DIPPOLD, J. *Troy Aikman: quick-draw quarterback.*
    HUGHES, M. E. *Mario Lemieux: beating the odds.*
    KRAMER, B. *Ken Griffey Junior: all-around all-star.*
    SAVAGE, J. *Barry Bonds: Mr. Excitement.*
    SAVAGE, J. *Mike Piazza: hard-hitting catcher.*

Achievers: African Americans in science & tech. **Twenty-First Century**
    HAYDEN, R. C. *11 African-American doctors. Rev. and expanded ed.*
    HAYDEN, R. C. *7 African-American scientists. Rev. and expanded ed.*
    HAYDEN, R. C. *9 African-American inventors. Rev. and expanded ed.*

Action sports . . . . **Capstone Press**
    WALKER, C. *Waterskiing and kneeboarding.*

Active minds series . . . . **Broderbund**
    JAMES DISCOVERS MATH. School ed. (CD-ROM).
    LOGICAL JOURNEY OF THE ZOOMBINIS. School ed. (CD-ROM).

Adventurers . . . . **Crestwood House**
    EVANS, J. *Camping and survival.*
    EVANS, J. *Horseback riding.*
    EVANS, J. *Skiing.*
    EVANS, J. *Whitewater kayaking.*

Adventures of safety frog . . . . **AIMS Media**
    SEAT BELTS ARE FOR KIDS TOO (Videocassette).

African American artists . . . . **L & S Video**
    FAITH RINGGOLD PAINTS CROWN HEIGHTS (Videocassette).
    JACOB LAWRENCE: THE GLORY OF EXPRESSION (Videocassette).

African American life . . . . **Rourke**
    MACK-WILLIAMS, K. *Food and our history.*
    WOODYARD, S. *Music and song.*

African American reference library . . . . **U X L**
    AFRICAN AMERICAN BIOGRAPHY.

African-American achievers . . . . **Chelsea House**
    WILKER, J. *Harlem Globetrotters.*

African-American arts . . . . **Twenty-First Century**
    MEDEARIS, A. S. *Dance.*

African-American arts (Continued)
    MEDEARIS, A. S. *Music.*

African-American biographies . . . . **Enslow**
    JOSEPHSON, J. P. *Jesse Owens: track and field legend.*
    OLD, W. C. *Duke Ellington: giant of jazz.*

African-American soldiers . . . . **Twenty-First Century**
    PFEIFER, K. B. *Henry O. Flipper.*
    REEF, C. *Black fighting men: a proud history.*
    SUPER, N. *Daniel "Chappie" James.*

Against the odds . . . . **Films for the Humanities**
    HELEN KELLER (Videocassette).

All aboard reading . . . . **Grosset & Dunlap**
    DUBOWSKI, C. E. *Pirate School.*
    ELSTE, J. *True Blue.*
    HERMAN, R. A. *Pal the pony.*
    MOFFATT, J. *Who stole the cookies?*
    O'CONNOR, J. *Nina, Nina ballerina.*

ALSC program support publications . . **American Library Association**
    WATKINS, J. *Programming author visits.*

Amazing amphibians . . . . **Abdo & Daughters**
    GERHOLDT, J. E. *Frogs.*
    GERHOLDT, J. E. *Tree frogs.*

Amazing animals . . . . **DK Vision**
    ANIMAL APPETITES (Videocassette).
    ANIMAL JOURNEYS (Videocassette).
    ANIMAL WEAPONS (Videocassette).
    NIGHTTIME ANIMALS (Videocassette).

America the beautiful . . . . **Childrens Press**
    HEINRICHS, A. *Alaska.*
    HEINRICHS, A. *Arizona.*
    HEINRICHS, A. *Montana.*
    HEINRICHS, A. *Rhode Island.*
    KENT, D. *Iowa.*
    KENT, D. *Puerto Rico.*
    KENT, Z. *Idaho.*
    KENT, Z. *Kansas.*
    LILLEGARD, D. *Nevada.*

America's special days . . . . **GPN**
    NEW YEAR'S DAY (Videocassette).
    PRESIDENTS' DAY (Videocassette).
    THANKSGIVING DAY (Videocassette).

American children . . . . **Millbrook Press**
    BARRETT, T. *Growing up in colonial America.*

American discovery . . . . **FM Productions**
    BEING AN EXPLORER (Videocassette).

American discovery (Continued)
    SCIENCE OF EXPLORATION (Videocassette).
    STORIES OF INVENTION AND INGENUITY. VOL. 1
    (Videocassette).
    STORIES OF INVENTION AND INGENUITY. VOL. 2
    (Videocassette).

American government in action . . . . **Enslow**
    KRONENWETTER, M. *Congress of the United States.*
    KRONENWETTER, M. *Supreme Court of the United States.*

American heroes and legends . . . . **Rabbit Ears**
    BRER RABBIT AND BOSS LION (Talking book).
    CONNELLY, B. *Follow the drinking gourd: a story of the*
    Underground Railroad (Videocassette).
    FOLLOW THE DRINKING GOURD.
    KESSLER, B. *Brer Rabbit and Boss Lion (Kit).*
    KUNSTLER, J. H. *Johnny Appleseed (Videocassette).*
    METAXAS, E. *Stormalong (Kit).*

American history through folksong . . . . **WEM Records**
    COWBOY SONGS (Sound recording cassette).

American portraits . . . . **Clearvue/EAV**
    ABRAHAM LINCOLN: THE GREAT EMANCIPATOR
    (Videocassette).
    ANDREW JACKSON: THE PEOPLE'S PRESIDENT
    (Videocassette).
    GEORGE WASHINGTON: THE FIRST (Videocassette).
    THEODORE ROOSEVELT: THE COWBOY PRESIDENT
    (Videocassette).

American profiles . . . . **Facts on File**
    AASENG, N. *Twentieth-century inventors.*
    NOONAN, J. *Nineteenth-century inventors.*

American religious experience . . . . **Watts**
    WILLIAMS, J. K. *Amish.*

American story series . . . . **Woodside Avenue Music Productions**
    SACRE, A. *Looking for Papito: family stories from Latin*
    America (Sound recording cassette).

American storytelling . . . . **August House**
    READY-TO-TELL TALES: SURE-FIRE STORIES FROM
    AMERICA'S FAVORITE STORYTELLERS.

American war . . . . **Enslow**
    KENT, Z. *Persian Gulf War: "the mother of all battles."*

Animal classes . . . . **National Geographic**
    AMPHIBIANS AND REPTILES (Videocassette).

Animal close-ups . . . . **Charlesbridge**
    DUPONT, P. *Cheetah: fast as lightning.*
    FONTANEL, B. *Penguin: a funny bird.*
    HAVARD, C. *Fox: playful prowler.*
    TRACQUI, V. *Polar bear: master of the ice.*

Animal families . . . . **Gareth Stevens**
    KAPPELER, M. *Big cats.*
    KAPPELER, M. *Dogs: wild and domestic.*
    KAPPELER, M. *Owls.*
    SCHMIDT, A. *Bears and their forest cousins.*

Animal family series . . . . **North-South Books**
    HOFER, A. *Lion family book.*
    HOSHINO, M. *Grizzly bear family book.*
    LARSEN, T. *Polar bear family book.*
    LAUKEL, H. G. *Desert fox family book.*

Animal habitats . . . . **Gareth Stevens**
    LINDLEY, M. *Lizard in the jungle.*

Animal magic for kids . . . . **Gareth Stevens**
    FAIR, J. *Black bear magic for kids.*
    GIECK, C. *Bald eagle magic for kids.*
    KLEIN, T. *Loon magic for kids.*

Animal magic for kids (Continued)
    WOLPERT, T. *Wolf magic for kids.*

Animals Q & A . . . . **Ideals**
    GREENWAY, S. *Can you see me?*
    GREENWAY, S. *Whose baby am I?*

Annick young novels . . . . **Annick Press**
    HUTCHINS, H. J. *Anastasia Morningstar and the crystal*
    butterfly. Rev. ed.
    HUTCHINS, H. J. *Cat of Artimus Pride.*
    HUTCHINS, H. J. *Prince of Tarn.*
    HUTCHINS, H. J. *Within a painted past.*

Appointment with nature . . . . **Pfeifer-Hamilton**
    WEBER, L. *Backyard almanac.*

Arctic world . . . . **Crabtree**
    KALMAN, B. *Arctic animals.*
    KALMAN, B. *Arctic whales and whaling.*

Art and activities for kids . . . . **North Light**
    HERSHBERGER, P. *Make costumes!: for creative play.*
    SOLGA, K. *Draw!*
    SOLGA, K. *Make cards!*
    SOLGA, K. *Make prints!*
    SOLGA, K. *Paint!*

Art explorations . . . . **SRA/McGraw-Hill**
    MEXICAN FOLK ART (Videocassette).

Art for young people . . . . **Sterling**
    HARRISON, P. *Claude Monet.*
    HARRISON, P. *Vincent van Gogh.*

Art's place . . . . **Films for the Humanities & Sciences**
    SHOW TIME (Videocassette).

Asian American experience . . . . **Chelsea House**
    RAGAZA, A. *Lives of notable Asian Americans: business,*
    politics, science.

Asian copublication programme . . . . **Weatherhill/dist. by Tuttle**
    STORIES FROM ASIA TODAY: COLLECTION FOR
    YOUNG READERS, BOOKS ONE AND TWO.

ASPCA pet care guides for kids . . . . **DK Publishing**
    EVANS, M. *Guinea pigs.*
    EVANS, M. *Rabbit.*

Aspects of learning . . . . **National Education Association**
    WHOLE LANGUAGE: BELIEFS AND PRACTICES, K-8.

Assistant professor . . . . **Allied Video**
    HOW TO READ MUSIC. 2ND ED. (Videocassette).

Audubon Society field guides . . . . **Knopf**
    AUDUBON SOCIETY FIELD GUIDE TO NORTH
    AMERICAN FISHES, WHALES AND DOLPHINS.
    BULL, J. *Audubon Society field guide to North American*
    birds--Eastern Region.
    CHESTERMAN, C. W. *Audubon Society field guide to North*
    American rocks and minerals.
    NIERING, W. A. *Audubon Society field guide to North*
    American wildflowers, Eastern Region.
    REHDER, H. A. *Audubon Society field guide to North*
    American seashells.
    SPELLENBERG, R. *Audubon Society field guide to North*
    American wildflowers, Western Region.
    THOMPSON, I. *Audubon Society field guide to North*
    American fossils.
    UDVARDY, M. D. *Audubon Society field guide to North*
    American birds--Western Region.
    WHITAKER, J. O. *Audubon Society field guide to North*
    American mammals. Rev. & expanded.

Audubon Society nature guides . . . . **Knopf**
    AMOS, W. H. *Atlantic and Gulf coasts.*

Audubon Society nature guides (Continued)
BROWN, L. *Grasslands.*
MACMAHON, J. *Deserts.*
MCCONNAUGHEY, B. H. *Pacific coast.*
WHITNEY, S. *Western forests.*

Author and artist series . . . . **Houghton Mifflin-Clarion**
VISIT WITH EVE BUNTING (Videocassette).
VISIT WITH MARVIN TERBAN (Videocassette).

Baby animal series . . . . **Morrow**
ARNOLD, C. *Bat.*

Baby zoo animals . . . . **Morrow**
ARNOLD, C. *Camel.*
ARNOLD, C. *Cheetah.*
ARNOLD, C. *Elephant.*
ARNOLD, C. *Fox.*
ARNOLD, C. *Hippo.*
ARNOLD, C. *Killer whale.*
ARNOLD, C. *Koala.*
ARNOLD, C. *Llama.*
ARNOLD, C. *Panda.*
ARNOLD, C. *Sea lion.*
ARNOLD, C. *Snake.*
ARNOLD, C. *Zebra.*

Bank Street ready-to-read . . . . **Bantam Doubleday Dell**
OPPENHEIM, J. *Christmas Witch: an Italian legend.*
ORGEL, D. *Flower of Sheba.*
SCHECTER, E. *Warrior maiden: a Hopi legend.*

Baseball legends . . . . **Chelsea House**
CAMPBELL, J. *Cal Ripken, Jr.*
GRABOWSKI, J. *Stan Musial.*
MACHT, N. L. *Lou Gehrig.*

Beginner book video . . . . **Random House Home Video**
EASTMAN, P. D. *Are you my mother? plus two more P.D. Eastman classics (Videocassette).*
SEUSS, D. *I am not going to get up today! plus three more Dr. Seuss classics (Videocassette).*

Beginner books . . . . **Random House**
CAT IN THE HAT BEGINNER BOOK DICTIONARY.
EASTMAN, P. D. *Are you my mother?*
EASTMAN, P. D. *Corre, perro, corre!*
EASTMAN, P. D. *Go, dog, go!*
EASTMAN, P. D. *Sam and the firefly.*
LESIEG, T. *Ten apples up on top!*
LOPSHIRE, R. *Put me in the zoo.*
PALMER, H. *Fish out of water.*
SEUSS, D. *Cat in the hat comes back.*
SEUSS, D. *Cat in the hat.*
SEUSS, D. *Fox in socks.*
SEUSS, D. *Green eggs and ham.*
SEUSS, D. *Hop on pop.*
SEUSS, D. *Huevos verdes con jamon.*
SEUSS, D. *I am not going to get up today!*
SEUSS, D. *I can read with my eyes shut.*
SEUSS, D. *One fish, two fish, red fish, blue fish.*

Beyond the horizons . . . . **Raintree Steck-Vaughn**
TWIST, C. *Charles Darwin: on the trail of evolution.*

Bill Nye the science guy: classroom edition . . . . **Disney Educational**
EARTH'S SEASONS/CLIMATES (Videocassette).
MOON/OUTER SPACE (Videocassette).
SOUND/LIGHT AND COLOR (Videocassette).

Bio-science series . . . . **National Geographic Society**
CHICK EMBRYOLOGY (Videocassette).
LIFE CYCLE OF THE HONEYBEE (Videocassette).

Biographical history . . . . **Peter Bedrick**
CHILD, J. *Rise of Islam.*

Biology live! . . . . **Yellow Brick Road/Human Relations Media**
PLANTS: ANGIOSPERMS (Videocassette).

Biovideo series . . . . **Carolina Biological Supply**
LOCOMOTION (Videocassette).

Black Americans of achievement . . . . **Chelsea House**
RENNERT, R. S. *Henry Aaron.*

Black Americans of achievement video collection . . . . . **Schlessinger**
FREDERICK DOUGLASS (Videocassette).
MADAM C.J. WALKER (Videocassette).
MATTHEW HENSON (Videocassette).

Body books . . . . **Copper Beech**
SANDEMAN, A. *Babies.*

Books of wonder . . . . **Morrow**
BAUM, L. F. *Mago de Oz.*
BAUM, L. F. *Wonderful Wizard of Oz.*
CARROLL, L. *Alice's adventures in Wonderland.*
CARROLL, L. *Through the looking-glass and what Alice found there.*
DOYLE, A. C. *Adventures of Sherlock Holmes.*
IRVING, W. *Rip Van Winkle.*
JUSTER, N. *Otter nonsense.*
NESBIT, E. *Enchanted castle.*
TWAIN, M. *Adventures of Tom Sawyer.*
WIGGIN, K. D. *Rebecca of Sunnybrook Farm.*

Booktalk! . . . . **Wilson**
BOOKTALK! 2: BOOKTALKING FOR ALL AGES AND AUDIENCES. 2ND ED.
BOOKTALK! 3: MORE BOOKTALKS FOR ALL AGES AND AUDIENCES.
BOOKTALK! 4: SELECTIONS FROM THE BOOKTALKER FOR ALL AGES AND AUDIENCES.
BOOKTALK! 5: MORE SELECTIONS FROM THE BOOKTALKER FOR ALL AGES AND AUDIENCES.

Boston Children's Museum activity book . . . . **Little, Brown**
ZUBROWSKI, B. *Bubbles.*

Boston Children's Museum activity book . . . . **Morrow**
ZUBROWSKI, B. *Balloons: building and experimenting with inflatable toys.*
ZUBROWSKI, B. *Making waves: finding out about rhythmic motion.*
ZUBROWSKI, B. *Mirrors: finding out about the properties of light.*
ZUBROWSKI, B. *Shadow play: making pictures with light and lenses.*
ZUBROWSKI, B. *Wheels at work: building and experimenting with models of machines.*

Breakthrough . . . . **Raintree Steck-Vaughn**
HOOPER, T. *Electricity.*
HOOPER, T. *Genetics.*

Bright and early book . . . . **Random House**
BERENSTAIN, S. *Berenstain Bears and the spooky old tree.*
BERENSTAIN, S. *Inside, outside, upside down.*
LESIEG, T. *Eye book.*
LESIEG, T. *Tooth book.*
SEUSS, D. *Foot book.*

Brown paper school book . . . . **Little, Brown**
ALLISON, L. *Blood and guts: a working guide to your own insides.*
BURNS, M. *Math for smarty pants.*
BURNS, M. *This book is about time.*

Building America . . . . **Blackbirch Press**
DOHERTY, C. A. *Golden Gate Bridge.*

Building history series . . . . **Lucent**
MCNEESE, T. *Panama Canal.*

Building students' thinking skills . . . National Education Association
JONES, B. F. *Teaching thinking skills: English/language arts.*

Bullseye biography . . . . Random House
DALY, W. *Bonnie Blair: power on ice.*

Caedmon children's classic. . . . . Caedmon
BUDBERG, M. *Russian fairy tales (Talking book).*

California missions . . . . Lerner
ABBINK, E. *Missions of the Monterey Bay Area.*
BEHRENS, J. *Missions of the central coast.*
BROWER, P. *Missions of the inland valleys.*
LEMKE, N. *Missions of the Southern Coast.*
MACMILLAN, D. *Missions of the Los Angeles Area.*
WHITE, T. N. *Missions of the San Francisco Bay Area.*

Calling all safety scouts . . . . . Films for the Humanities & Sciences
SAFETY ON WHEELS (Videocassette).

Can be fun books . . . . HarperCollins
LEAF, M. *Manners can be fun. Rev. ed.*

Carolrhoda creative minds book . . . . Carolrhoda
BOWEN, A. R. *Head full of notions: a story about Robert Fulton.*
BOWEN, A. R. *World of knowing: a story about Thomas Hopkins Gallaudet.*
COLLINS, D. R. *Pioneer plowmaker: a story about John Deere.*
CROFFORD, E. *Frontier surgeons: a story about the Mayo Brothers.*
DUNLAP, J. *Birds in the bushes: a story about Margaret Morse Nice.*
DUNLAP, J. *Eye on the wild: a story about Ansel Adams.*
MCPHERSON, S. S. *Rooftop astronomer: a story about Maria Mitchell.*
MITCHELL, B. *Good morning, Mr. President: a story about Carl Sandburg.*
MITCHELL, B. *Raggin', a story about Scott Joplin.*
MITCHELL, B. *We'll race you, Henry: a story about Henry Ford.*
MITCHELL, B. *Wizard of sound: a story about Thomas Edison.*
O'CONNOR, B. *Mammolina: a story about Maria Montessori.*
RANSOM, C. F. *Listening to crickets: a story about Rachel Carson.*
STREISSGUTH, T. *Say it with music: a story about Irving Berlin.*

Carolrhoda earth watch book . . . . Carolrhoda
JACOBS, L. *Letting off steam.*
STAUB, F. J. *America's prairies.*
STAUB, F. J. *Yellowstone's cycle of fire.*
WALKER, S. M. *Water up, water down: the hydrologic cycle.*

Carolrhoda nature watch book . . . . Carolrhoda
ARNOLD, C. *House sparrows everywhere.*
ARNOLD, C. *Ostriches and other flightless birds.*
ARNOLD, C. *Saving the peregrine falcon.*
ARNOLD, C. *Tule elk.*
ARNOLD, C. *Watching desert wildlife.*
BERMAN, R. *American bison.*
BUHOLZER, T. *Life of the snail.*
BURGEL, P. H. *Gorillas.*
EPPLE, W. *Barn owls.*
FISCHER-NAGEL, H. *Fir trees.*
FISCHER-NAGEL, H. *Housefly.*
FISCHER-NAGEL, H. *Life of the honeybee.*
FISCHER-NAGEL, H. *Life of the ladybug.*
FISCHER-NAGEL, H. *Look through the mouse hole.*
HANSEN, E. *Guinea pigs.*
ISENBART, H. *Birth of a foal.*
JARROW, G. *Naked mole-rats.*
JOHNSON, S. A. *Albatrosses of Midway Island.*
JOHNSON, S. A. *Ferrets.*
MACMILLAN, D. *Elephants: our last land giants.*
NICHOLSON, D. *Wild boars.*
SCHNIEPER, C. *Amazing spiders.*

Carolrhoda nature watch book (Continued)
SCHNIEPER, C. *Apple tree through the year.*
SCHNIEPER, C. *Chameleons.*
SCHNIEPER, C. *On the trail of the fox.*
STONE, L. M. *Grizzlies.*
STUART, D. *Astonishing armadillo.*
WALKER, S. M. *Rhinos.*
WINNER, C. *Salamanders.*
WINNER, C. *Sunflower family.*

Carolrhoda on my own book . . . . Carolrhoda
LITTLEFIELD, H. *Fire at the Triangle Factory.*
LOWERY, L. *Georgia O'Keeffe.*
LOWERY, L. *Wilma Mankiller.*
SCHOTT, J. A. *Will Rogers.*
SWANSON, J. *I pledge allegiance.*

Carolrhoda start to finish book . . . . Carolrhoda
MITGUTSCH, A. *From tree to table.*
REIDEL, M. *From egg to bird.*
REIDEL, M. *From egg to butterfly.*

Cartwheel learning bookshelf . . . . Scholastic
JONES, G. *My first book of how things are made: crayons, jeans, peanut butter, guitars, and more.*
KUHN, D. *My first book of nature: how living things grow.*

Celebrating our differences . . . . National Geographic Society
RACE (Videocassette).
RELIGION (Videocassette).

Cell series . . . . Rainbow Educational
CELL DIVISION (Videocassette).

Children of other lands . . . . Rainbow Educational
SHEENA AZAK OF CANADA (Videocassette).

Children's adventure videos . . . . Forney Miller Film & Video
WAGGING TAILS: THE DOG AND PUPPY MUSIC VIDEO (Videocassette).

Children's literature series . . . . SRA McGraw-Hill
BROWN, L. K. *Dinosaurs divorce: a guide for changing families.*
CHERRY, L. *Great kapok tree (Videocassette).*
DORROS, A. *Abuela (Videocassette).*
ISADORA, R. *At the crossroads (Videocassette).*
ROSENBERG, L. *Monster mama (Videocassette).*

Children's world series . . . . Friendship Press
WORLD OF CHILDREN'S SONGS.

Choices . . . . Millbrook Press
KAPLAN, A. *Careers for computer buffs.*
KAPLAN, A. *Careers for outdoor types.*
KAPLAN, A. *Careers for wordsmiths.*

Choices, choices . . . . Tom Snyder Productions
HALPERN, N. A. *Kids and the environment: taking responsibility for our surroundings (Microcomputer program).*
ON THE PLAYGROUND (Microcomputer program).
TAKING RESPONSIBILITY (Microcomputer program).

Christmas around the world . . . . World Book
CHRISTMAS IN CANADA.
CHRISTMAS IN COLONIAL AND EARLY AMERICA.

Cincinnati Zoo book . . . . Watts
MAYNARD, T. *Rhino comes to America.*
MAYNARD, T. *Saving endangered mammals: a field guide to some of the earth's rarest animals.*

Circle of life . . . . Dillon
SIY, A. *Brazilian rain forest.*
SIY, A. *Great Astrolabe Reef.*

Cities of the world . . . . Children's Press
KENT, D. *Dublin.*

Cities of the world (Continued)
KENT, D. *New York City.*
KENT, D. *Tokyo.*
STEIN, R. C. *London.*
STEIN, R. C. *Paris.*

Civil War . . . . **Atlas Video**
CIVIL WAR: THE FIERY TRIAL (Videocassette).

Civil War Generals. . . . . **Atlas Video**
ROBERT E. LEE (Videocassette).
STONEWALL JACKSON (Videocassette).
ULYSSES S. GRANT (Videocassette).

Collectibles . . . . **Dillon**
YOUNG, R. *Dolls.*
YOUNG, R. *Teddy bears.*

Collective biographies . . . . **Enslow**
AASENG, N. *American dinosaur hunters.*
BREDESON, C. *Presidential Medal of Freedom winners.*
CAMP, C. A. *American astronomers: searchers and wonderers.*
JEFFREY, L. S. *American inventors of the 20th century.*
JEFFREY, L. S. *Great American businesswomen.*

Colonial America . . . . **Watts**
STEVENS, B. S. *Colonial American craftspeople.*

Colonial American craftsmen . . . . **Godine**
FISHER, L. E. *Tanners.*

Colonial craftsmen . . . . **Benchmark Books**
FISHER, L. E. *Cabinetmakers.*
FISHER, L. E. *Glassmakers.*
FISHER, L. E. *Schoolmasters.*

Come look with me. . . . . **Thomasson-Grant**
BLIZZARD, G. S. *Come look with me: world of play.*
TUCKER, J. S. *Come look with me: discovering photographs with children.*

Coming to America. . . . . **Millbrook Press**
CAVAN, S. *Irish-American experience.*
WU, D. Y. *Chinese-American experience.*

Composer's world. . . . . **Viking Penguin**
THOMPSON, W. *Claude Debussy.*
THOMPSON, W. *Pyotr Ilyich Tchaikovsky.*

Concept book. . . . . **Whitman**
GIRARD, L. W. *Who is a stranger and what should I do?*
LITCHFIELD, A. B. *Words in our hands.*
STANEK, M. *All alone after school.*

Concepts in nature series. . . . . **Altschul Group Corporation**
INSTINCTS IN ANIMALS (Videocassette).

Concise collection. . . . . **Grange Books**
LLOYD, M. *Military badges and insignia.*

Conquering the media maze . . . . . **International Marketing Exchange**
SEXUALITY (Videocassette).
SUBSTANCE ABUSE (Videocassette).

Contemporary African Americans. . . . . **Raintree Steck-Vaughn**
ELLIS, V. F. *Wynton Marsalis.*
PATRICK-WEXLER, D. *Barbara Jordan.*
PATRICK-WEXLER, D. *Walter Dean Myers.*
SIMMONS, A. *Ben Carson.*
SIMMONS, A. *John Lucas.*

Contemporary Asian Americans . . . . **Raintree Steck-Vaughn**
LING, B. *Maya Lin.*

Contemporary Hispanic Americans. . . . . **Raintree Steck-Vaughn**
RODRIGUEZ, J. *Gloria Estefan.*

Contemporary Native Americans . . . . **Raintree Steck-Vaughn**
WEIL, A. *Michael Dorris.*

Cool collections . . . . **Rigby**
ANSARY, M. T. *Stamps.*

Cool tools . . . . **Davidson**
MULTIMEDIA WORKSHOP BILINGUAL. Teacher ed. (CD-ROM).
MULTIMEDIA WORKSHOP. Teacher ed. (CD-ROM).

Cornerstones of freedom . . . . **Childrens Press**
HARVEY, M. *Fall of the Soviet Union.*
KENT, D. *Titanic.*
KENT, D. *Vietnam Women's Memorial.*
KENT, Z. *Williamsburg.*
MCKISSACK, P. *Mary McLeod Bethune.*
SANTELLA, A. *Jackie Robinson breaks the color line.*
STEIN, R. C. *Assassination of John F. Kennedy.*
STEIN, R. C. *Declaration of Independence.*
STEIN, R. C. *Great Depression. Rev. ed.*
STEIN, R. C. *Montgomery bus boycott. Rev. ed.*
STEIN, R. C. *United Nations. Rev. ed.*

Country insights. . . . . **Raintree Steck-Vaughn**
BORNOFF, N. *Japan.*

Crabapples. . . . . **Crabtree**
KALMAN, B. *Giraffes.*
KALMAN, B. *Web weavers and other spiders.*
SOTZEK, H. *Koala is not a bear!*

Craft topics . . . . **Watts**
WRIGHT, R. *Knights: facts, things to make, activities.*

Creature club. . . . . **Ideals Children's Books**
KIM, M. *Blue whale.*
KIM, M. *Mountain gorilla.*

Creatures all around us. . . . . **Carolrhoda**
SOUZA, D. M. *Catch me if you can.*

Cruisin'. . . . . **Capstone Press**
CARSER, S. X. *Motocross cycles.*
CONNOLLY, M. *Dragsters.*

Culture crafts . . . . **Lerner**
TEMKO, F. *Traditional crafts from Africa.*
TEMKO, F. *Traditional crafts from Mexico and Central America.*

Cut 'n clip series . . . . **Libraries Unlimited**
BRODIE, C. S. *Bookmark book.*

Dalemark quartet. . . . . **Greenwillow**
JONES, D. W. *Cart and cwidder.*
JONES, D. W. *Crown of Dalemark.*
JONES, D. W. *Drowned Ammet.*
JONES, D. W. *Spellcoats.*

David Suzuki's looking at . . . . **Wiley**
SUZUKI, D. *Looking at insects.*

Day in the life of . . . . **Troll**
MARTIN, J. H. *Day in the life of a carpenter.*
MICHELS, P. *Day in the life of a beekeeper.*
PAIGE, D. *Day in the life of a sports therapist.*
PAIGE, D. *Day in the life of a zoo veterinarian.*

Decision is yours book . . . . **Parenting Press**
CRARY, E. *Finders, keepers?*

Decisions, decisions . . . . **Tom Snyder Productions**
COLONIZATION (Microcomputer program).
ENVIRONMENT (Microcomputer program).
IMMIGRATION (Microcomputer program).
PREJUDICE (Microcomputer program).

Decisions, decisions (Continued)
REVOLUTIONARY WARS: CHOOSING SIDES (Microcomputer program).
SUBSTANCE ABUSE (Microcomputer program).
VIOLENCE IN THE MEDIA (Microcomputer program).

Detective stories for math problem solving. . Human Relations Media
MR. MARFIL'S LAST WILL AND TESTAMENT (Videocassette).
PHANTOM OF THE BELL TOWER (Videocassette).

Dial easy-to-read . . . . **Dial**
ANTLE, N.   *Sam's Wild West Show.*
BOLAND, J.   *Dog named Sam.*
HALL, K.   *Batty riddles.*
KRENSKY, S.   *Lionel and Louise.*
KRENSKY, S.   *Lionel at large.*
KRENSKY, S.   *Lionel in the winter.*
KWITZ, M. D.   *Little Vampire and the Midnight Bear.*
MARSHALL, E.   *Fox all week.*
MARSHALL, E.   *Fox and his friends.*
MARSHALL, E.   *Fox in love.*
MARSHALL, E.   *Fox on stage.*
MARSHALL, E.   *Zorro y sus amigos.*
MARSHALL, J.   *Fox be nimble.*
MARSHALL, J.   *Fox on the job.*
MARSHALL, J.   *Fox outfoxed.*
PARKS, R.   *I am Rosa Parks.*
VAN LEEUWEN, J.   *Cuentos del cerdito Oliver.*
VAN LEEUWEN, J.   *Tales of Oliver Pig.*

Dillon remarkable animals book . . . . **Dillon**
DAY, N.   *Horseshoe crab.*
HARRIS, L.   *Caribou.*
LABONTE, G.   *Tarantula.*
O'CONNOR, K.   *Herring gull.*
PEMBLETON, S.   *Armadillo.*
SCHAFER, S.   *Galapagos tortoise.*
SCHAFER, S.   *Komodo dragon.*
SHERROW, V.   *Porcupine.*
STONE, L. M.   *Pelican.*

Dino easy reader . . . . **Little, Brown**
BROWN, L. K.   *Rex and Lilly family time.*

Disaster! . . . . **Millbrook Press**
LAMPTON, C.   *Earthquake.*
LAMPTON, C.   *Hurricane.*
LAMPTON, C.   *Volcano.*

Discover Canada . . . . **Childrens Press**
EMMOND, K.   *Manitoba.*
GANN, M.   *New Brunswick.*
HANCOCK, L.   *Northwest Territories.*
LOTZ, J.   *Nova Scotia.*
MACKAY, K.   *Ontario.*
NANTON, I.   *British Columbia.*

Discovering art . . . . **Thomson Learning**
MCHUGH, C.   *Animals.*
MCHUGH, C.   *Faces.*
MCHUGH, C.   *Water.*

Discovering books . . . . **Scribner's**
FLORIAN, D.   *Discovering seashells.*

Discovering our heritage . . . . **Dillon**
GARLAND, S.   *Vietnam: rebuilding a nation:*
PETERSON, M.   *Argentina: a wild west heritage. New ed.*

Discovery . . . . **Lerner**
JOHNSON, S. A.   *Manada de lobos: siguiendo las huellas de los lobos en su entorno natural.*
JOHNSON, S. A.   *Wolf pack: tracking wolves in the wild.*

Discovery readers . . . . **Ideals Children's Books**
BERGER, M.   *How's the weather?: a look at weather and how it changes.*

Discovery readers (Continued)
BERGER, M.   *Round and round the money goes: what money is and how we use it.*
BERGER, M.   *Where are the stars during the day?: a book about stars.*
BERGER, M.   *Where did your family come from?: a book about immigrants.*
BERGER, M.   *Whole world in your hands: looking at maps.*

Disney Archives . . . . **Disney Press**
CARROLL, L.   *Jabberwocky.*

Dover children's thrift classics . . . . **Dover**
JAPANESE FAIRY TALES.

Dr. Seuss video classics. . . . . **Random House**
SEUSS, D.   *Horton hatches the egg./If I ran the circus* (Videocassette).
SEUSS, D.   *Horton hears a Who!/Thidwick the big-hearted moose* (Videocassette).

Draw 50 . . . . **Doubleday**
AMES, L. J.   *Draw 50 airplanes, aircraft and spacecraft.*
AMES, L. J.   *Draw 50 animals.*
AMES, L. J.   *Draw 50 beasties and yugglies and turnover uglies and things that go bump in the night.*
AMES, L. J.   *Draw 50 boats, ships, trucks and trains.*
AMES, L. J.   *Draw 50 cars, trucks, and motorcycles.*
AMES, L. J.   *Draw 50 dinosaurs.*
AMES, L. J.   *Draw 50 dogs.*
AMES, L. J.   *Draw 50 horses.*

Draw, model, and paint . . . . **Gareth Stevens**
SANCHEZ SANCHEZ, I.   *Dragons and prehistoric monsters.*
SANCHEZ SANCHEZ, I.   *Drawing dinosaurs.*
SANCHEZ SANCHEZ, I.   *Dreadful creatures.*
SANCHEZ SANCHEZ, I.   *Modeling dinosaurs.*
SANCHEZ SANCHEZ, I.   *Monsters and extraterrestrials.*
SANCHEZ SANCHEZ, I.   *Painting and coloring dinosaurs.*

Dutton easy reader . . . . **Dutton**
BAKER, B.   *One Saturday morning.*
BAKER, B.   *Staying with Grandmother.*

Dynamic modern women . . . . **Twenty-First Century**
LINDOP, L.   *Athletes.*
LINDOP, L.   *Political leaders.*

Early bird . . . . **Millbrook Press**
BENDICK, J.   *Sun: our very own star.*

Early bird nature books . . . . **Lerner**
STAUB, F. J.   *Mountain goats.*

Early I can read book . . . . **HarperCollins**
BONSALL, C. N.   *And I mean it, Stanley.*
BONSALL, C. N.   *Day I had to play with my sister.*
BONSALL, C. N.   *Who's afraid of the dark?*
HOFF, S.   *Barkley.*
HOFF, S.   *Horse in Harry's room.*
HOFF, S.   *Who will be my friends?*
ROBINS, J.   *Addie meets Max.*
WISEMAN, B.   *Morris the Moose.*

Early learning house . . . . **Edmark**
BAILEY'S BOOK HOUSE (CD-ROM).
BAILEY'S BOOK HOUSE (Microcomputer program).
MILLIE'S MATH HOUSE (CD-ROM).
MILLIE'S MATH HOUSE (Microcomputer program).
SAMMY'S SCIENCE HOUSE (CD-ROM).
STANLEY'S STICKER STORIES. School version (CD-ROM).
TRUDY'S TIME AND PLACE HOUSE. School version (CD-ROM).

Early settler life . . . . **Crabtree**
ADAMS, P.   *Early loggers and the sawmill.*
KALMAN, B.   *Early artisans.*
KALMAN, B.   *Early pleasures and pastimes.*

Earth at risk environmental video series . . . . **Schlessinger Video**
RAINFOREST (Videocassette).

Earth keepers . . . . **Twenty-First Century**
BRYANT, J.   *Marjory Stoneman Douglas: voice of the*
   Everglades.
REEF, C.   *Jacques Cousteau: champion of the sea.*

Easy menu ethnic cookbooks . . . . **Lerner**
CORONADA, R.   *Cooking the African way.*
CORONADA, R.   *Cooking the Caribbean way.*
CORONADA, R.   *Cooking the French way.*
CORONADA, R.   *Cooking the German way.*
CORONADA, R.   *Cooking the Greek way.*
CORONADA, R.   *Cooking the Hungarian way.*
CORONADA, R.   *Cooking the Indian way.*
CORONADA, R.   *Cooking the Irish way.*
CORONADA, R.   *Cooking the Israeli way.*
CORONADA, R.   *Cooking the Italian way.*
CORONADA, R.   *Cooking the Japanese way.*
CORONADA, R.   *Cooking the Korean way.*
CORONADA, R.   *Cooking the Lebanese way.*
CORONADA, R.   *Cooking the Mexican way.*
CORONADA, R.   *Cooking the Polish way.*
CORONADA, R.   *Cooking the Russian way.*
CORONADA, R.   *Cooking the Thai way.*
CORONADA, R.   *Cooking the Vietnamese way.*

Ecozones . . . . **Rourke**
STONE, L. M.   *Temperate forests.*

Educating able learners . . . . . . **Agency for Instructional Technology**
ACADEMICALLY GIFTEDNESS (Videocassette).
ARTISTICALLY GIFTED (Videocassette).
COUNSELING (Videocassette).
CREATIVITY (Videocassette).
DEVELOPMENTAL EDUCATIONAL PROGRAMS
   (Videocassette).
EDUCATING ABLE LEARNERS (Videocassette).
GIFTEDNESS (Videocassette).
INTELLECTUAL GIFTEDNESS (Videocassette).
LEADERSHIP--MENTORING (Videocassette).
LEADERSHIP--MENTORING (Videocassette).
PULL-OUT PROGRAMS (Videocassette).
REGULAR CLASSROOM (Videocassette).
UNDER-REPRESENTED GIFTED (Videocassette).

Education and psychology of the gifted . . . . . **Teachers College Press**
PATTERNS OF INFLUENCE ON GIFTED LEARNERS: THE
   HOME, SELF, AND THE SCHOOL.

Educational Dimensions . . . . **SRA/McGraw-Hill**
LOOKING AT ART (Videocassette).

Edward the unready . . . . **Dial**
WELLS, R.   *Eduardo cumpleanos en la piscina.*
WELLS, R.   *Eduardo: el primer dia de colegio.*
WELLS, R.   *Edward in deep water.*
WELLS, R.   *Edward unready for school.*
WELLS, R.   *Edward's overwhelming overnight.*

Enchantment of the world . . . . **Childrens Press**
STEIN, R. C.   *United States of America.*

Encyclopedia of presidents . . . . **Childrens Press**
KENT, Z.   *George Bush: forty-first president of the United*
   States.
OSINSKI, A.   *Woodrow Wilson: twenty-eighth President of the*
   United States.

Everyday book . . . . **Bradbury**
RYLANT, C.   *Everyday children (Board book).*
RYLANT, C.   *Everyday garden (Board book).*
RYLANT, C.   *Everyday house (Board book).*
RYLANT, C.   *Everyday pets (Board book).*
RYLANT, C.   *Everyday town (Board book).*

Experiment! . . . . **Dillon**
DARLING, D. J.   *Making light work: the science of optics.*

Experiment! (Continued)
DARLING, D. J.   *Sounds interesting: the science of acoustics.*

Exploration series . . . . **Microsoft**
MICROSOFT DANGEROUS CREATURES: EXPLORE THE
   ENDANGERED WORLD OF WILDLIFE. Academic ed.
   (CD-ROM).
MICROSOFT DINOSAURS: EXPLORE THE INCREDIBLE
   WORLD OF PREHISTORIC CREATURES. Academic ed.
   (CD-ROM).

Exploratorium science snackbook series . . . . **Wiley**
DOHERTY, P.   *Cheshire cat and other eye-popping experiments*
   on how we see the world.
DOHERTY, P.   *Cool hot rod and other electrifying experiments*
   on energy and matter.
DOHERTY, P.   *Magic wand and other bright experiments on*
   light and color.
DOHERTY, P.   *Spinning blackboard and other dynamic*
   experiments on force and motion.

Exploring cultures of the world . . . . . . **Benchmark Books/Marshall**
CHICOINE, S.   *Spain: bridge between continents.*
KENT, D.   *Mexico: rich in spirit and tradition.*
KING, D. C.   *Egypt: ancient traditions, modern hopes.*
MARKHAM, L.   *Colombia: the gateway to South America.*

Exploring music . . . . **Raintree Steck-Vaughn**
SHIPTON, A.   *Brass.*
SHIPTON, A.   *Percussion.*
SHIPTON, A.   *Singing.*
SHIPTON, A.   *Strings.*
SHIPTON, A.   *Woodwinds.*

Exploring the animal kingdom . . . . **National Geographic Society**
HOW ANIMALS MOVE (Videocassette).

Exploring the United States through literature . . . . **Oryx**
EXPLORING THE GREAT LAKES STATES THROUGH
   LITERATURE.
EXPLORING THE MOUNTAIN STATES THROUGH
   LITERATURE.
EXPLORING THE NORTHEAST STATES THROUGH
   LITERATURE.
EXPLORING THE PACIFIC STATES THROUGH
   LITERATURE.
EXPLORING THE PLAINS STATES THROUGH
   LITERATURE.
EXPLORING THE SOUTHEAST STATES THROUGH
   LITERATURE.
EXPLORING THE SOUTHWEST STATES THROUGH
   LITERATURE.

Exploring the unknown . . . . **Enslow**
GREEN, C. R.   *Mysterious mind powers.*
GREEN, C. R.   *Recalling past lives.*
GREEN, C. R.   *Seeing the unseen.*

Exploring the unknown . . . . **Lucent**
BACH, J. S.   *Bigfoot.*
STEFFENS, B.   *Loch Ness Monster.*

Extraordinary explorers . . . . **Oxford University Press**
STEFOFF, R.   *Scientific explorers: travels in search of*
   knowledge.

Extraordinary people . . . . **Children's Press**
AVERY, S.   *Extraordinary American Indians.*
BRILL, M. T.   *Extraordinary young people.*
SINNOTT, S.   *Extraordinary Asian Pacific Americans.*
SINNOTT, S.   *Extraordinary Hispanic Americans.*

Eye openers . . . . **Aladdin/Macmillan**
FARM ANIMALS.
ROYSTON, A.   *Cars.*
ROYSTON, A.   *Diggers and dump trucks.*
ROYSTON, A.   *Dinosaurs.*
ROYSTON, A.   *Jungle animals.*

Eyewitness books . . . . **Knopf**
BAQUEDANO, E.   *Aztec, Inca and Maya.*
BROOKFIELD, K.   *Book.*
BURNIE, D.   *Arbol.*
BURNIE, D.   *Bird.*
BURNIE, D.   *Plant.*
BURNIE, D.   *Tree.*
BYAM, M.   *Armas y armaduras.*
BYAM, M.   *Arms and armor.*
CLARKE, B.   *Amphibian.*
CLUTTON-BROCK, J.   *Caballos.*
CLUTTON-BROCK, J.   *Dog.*
CLUTTON-BROCK, J.   *Horses.*
COILEY, J.   *Train.*
COTTERELL, A.   *Ancient China.*
CRAMPTON, W. G.   *Flag.*
CRIBB, J.   *Money.*
GRAVETT, C.   *Knight.*
HAMMOND, T.   *Sports.*
HART, G.   *Ancient Egypt.*
HART, G.   *Antiguo Egipto.*
JAMES, S.   *Ancient Rome.*
JAMES, S.   *Antigua Roma.*
KENTLEY, E.   *Boat.*
MACQUITTY, M.   *Desert.*
MACQUITTY, M.   *Ocean.*
MARGESON, S. M.   *Viking.*
MATTHEWS, R.   *Explorer.*
MCINTOSH, J.   *Archeology.*
MOUND, L.   *Insect.*
MURDOCH, D. H.   *Cowboy.*
MURDOCH, D. H.   *North American Indian.*
NORMAN, D.   *Dinosaur.*
PARKER, S.   *Fish.*
PARKER, S.   *Mammal.*
PARKER, S.   *Peces.*
PARKER, S.   *Pond and river.*
PARKER, S.   *Skeleton.*
PLATT, R.   *Pirate.*
PUTNAM, J.   *Mummy.*
PUTNAM, J.   *Pyramid.*
REDMOND, I.   *Elephant.*
ROWLAND-WARNE, L.   *Costume.*
TAYLOR, B.   *Arctic and Antarctic.*
TAYLOR, P. D.   *Fossil.*
VAN ROSE, S.   *Volcano and earthquake.*
WHALLEY, P.   *Butterfly and moth.*
WILKINSON, P.   *Building.*

Eyewitness handbooks . . . . **DK Publishing**
PELLANT, C.   *Eyewitness handbook of rocks and minerals.*

Eyewitness juniors . . . . **Knopf**
KERROD, R.   *Amazing flying machines.*
LINCOLN, M.   *Amazing boats.*
LORD, T.   *Amazing bikes.*
PARSONS, A.   *Amazing birds.*
PARSONS, A.   *Amazing mammals.*
PARSONS, A.   *Amazing snakes.*
PARSONS, A.   *Amazing spiders.*
SOWLER, S.   *Amazing armored animals.*
SOWLER, S.   *Asombrosos animales acorazados.*

Eyewitness living earth . . . . DK Vision
ARCTIC AND ANTARCTIC (Videocassette).

Eyewitness natural world . . . . DK Vision
DOG (Videocassette).

Eyewitness science . . . . **DK Publishing**
BURNIE, D.   *Light.*
COOPER, C.   *Matter.*
LAFFERTY, P.   *Force and motion.*
PARKER, S.   *Electricity.*

Eyewitness videos . . . . DK Vision
MAMMAL (Videocassette).

Eyewitness virtual reality . . . . **DK Multimedia**
EYEWITNESS VIRTUAL REALITY: CAT (CD-ROM).

Eyewitness visual dictionaries . . . . **DK Publishing**
VISUAL DICTIONARY OF ANCIENT CIVILIZATIONS.
VISUAL DICTIONARY OF DINOSAURS.
VISUAL DICTIONARY OF MILITARY UNIFORMS.
VISUAL DICTIONARY OF PLANTS.
VISUAL DICTIONARY OF SHIPS AND SAILING.
VISUAL DICTIONARY OF SPECIAL MILITARY FORCES.
VISUAL DICTIONARY OF THE EARTH.
VISUAL DICTIONARY OF THE HORSE.
VISUAL DICTIONARY OF THE HUMAN BODY.
VISUAL DICTIONARY OF THE SKELETON.
VISUAL DICTIONARY OF THE UNIVERSE.

Face to face with science . . . . **Crown**
RIDE, S.   *Voyager: an adventure to the edge of the solar system.*

Famous artists . . . . **Barron's**
HUGHES, A.   *Van Gogh.*

Famous lives . . . . **Chelsea House**
ROWLAND, D.   *Story of Sacajawea: guide to Lewis and Clark.*

Famous lives . . . . **Gareth Stevens**
APPLEGATE, K.   *Story of two American generals: Benjamin O. Davis, Jr.; Colin L. Powell.*
WEINER, E.   *Story of Frederick Douglass: voice of freedom.*
WHITE, F. M.   *Story of Junipero Serra: brave adventurer.*

Fascinating world of . . . . **Stoney-Wolf Productions**
FASCINATING WORLD OF SNAKES (Videocassette).

Female sports stars . . . . **Chelsea House**
COHEN, J. H.   *Superstars of women's gymnastics.*
KELLY, J.   *Superstars of women's basketball.*
SCHWABACHER, M.   *Superstars of women's tennis.*
SMITH, P.   *Superstars of women's figure skating.*
WICKHAM, M.   *Superstars of women's track and field.*
WILNER, B.   *Superstars of women's golf.*

First Americans book . . . . **Holiday House**
SNEVE, V.   *Apaches.*
SNEVE, V.   *Cherokees.*
SNEVE, V.   *Cheyennes.*
SNEVE, V.   *Hopis.*
SNEVE, V.   *Iroquois.*
SNEVE, V.   *Navajos.*
SNEVE, V.   *Nez Perce.*
SNEVE, V.   *Seminoles.*
SNEVE, V.   *Sioux.*

First biography . . . . **Holiday House**
ADLER, D. A.   *Christopher Columbus: great explorer.*
ADLER, D. A.   *George Washington: father of our country.*

First book . . . . **Watts**
ANDERSON, M. K.   *Nez Perce.*
ARMBRUSTER, A.   *American flag.*
BASKIN-SALZBERG, A.   *Flightless birds.*
BENDICK, J.   *Egyptian tombs.*
BENDICK, J.   *Tombs of the ancient Americas.*
BROWN, F. G.   *Owls.*
BROWN, F. G.   *Special Olympics.*
CARTER, A. R.   *Battle of Gettysburg.*
CARTER, A. R.   *Battle of the ironclads: the Monitor and the Merrimack.*
CARTER, A. R.   *Last stand at the Alamo.*
COCHRANE, K.   *Internet.*
CORBIN, C. L.   *Knights.*
DAILY, R.   *Code talkers: American Indians in World War II.*
GREENBERG, L.   *AIDS: how it works in the body.*
GREENE, J. D.   *Maya.*
GREENE, L.   *Sign language talk.*
LABONTE, G.   *Leeches, lampreys, and other cold-blooded bloodsuckers.*
LANDAU, E.   *Cherokees.*
LIPTAK, K.   *North American Indian ceremonies.*

First book (Continued)
    LIPTAK, K.   *North American Indian sign language.*
    LIPTAK, K.   *Saving our wetlands and their wildlife.*
    MCGOWEN, T.   *World War I.*
    MCGOWEN, T.   *World War II.*
    MYERS, A.   *Cheyenne.*
    NEWMAN, S. P.   *Incas.*
    NEWMAN, S. P.   *Inuits.*
    NIELSEN, N. J.   *Carnivorous plants.*
    POLLACK, J. S.   *Shirley Chisholm.*
    QUIRI, P. R.   *Algonquians.*
    QUIRI, P. R.   *White House.*
    ROBISON, N.   *Buffalo Bill.*
    RYAN, M.   *How to read and write poems.*
    SCHLOSS, M.   *Venus.*
    SHEPHERD, D. W.   *Auroras: light shows in the night sky.*
    SHEPHERD, D. W.   *Aztecs.*

First discovery book . . . . **Scholastic**
    COHAT, E.   *Seashore.*
    GOLDSEN, L.   *Colors.*
    GOLDSEN, L.   *Egg.*
    GOLDSEN, L.   *Fruit.*
    GOLDSEN, L.   *Ladybug and other insects.*
    KRULIK, N. E.   *Birds.*

First facts about... . . . . **Blackbirch**
    PASCOE, E.   *First facts about the presidents.*

First guide. . . . . **Millbrook Press**
    GRANGER, N.   *Stamp collecting.*
    PHOTOGRAPHY.

First impressions . . . . **Abrams**
    BERMAN, A.   *James McNeil Whistler.*
    GREENFELD, H.   *Marc Chagall.*
    MCLANATHAN, R.   *Leonardo da Vinci.*
    MERYMAN, R.   *Andrew Wyeth.*
    MEYER, S. E.   *Edgar Degas.*
    MEYER, S. E.   *Mary Cassatt.*
    SCHWARTZ, G.   *Rembrandt.*

First look at . . . . **Walker**
    SELSAM, M. E.   *First look at animals with horns.*
    SELSAM, M. E.   *First look at ducks, geese, and swans.*

First picture word book. . . . . **Usborne/EDC**
    AMERY, H.   *First thousand words in Russian.*

First stepping stone book. . . . . **Random House**
    SHARMAT, M. W.   *Genghis Khan: a dog star is born.*
    SHARMAT, M. W.   *Genghis Khan: dog-gone Hollywood.*
    YARBROUGH, C.   *Tamika and the wisdom rings.*

First time book . . . . **Random House**
    BERENSTAIN, S.   *Berenstain Bears and the sitter.*
    BERENSTAIN, S.   *Berenstain Bears and too much birthday.*
    BERENSTAIN, S.   *Berenstain Bears get in a fight.*
    BERENSTAIN, S.   *Berenstain Bears go to camp.*
    BERENSTAIN, S.   *Berenstain Bears visit the dentist.*
    BERENSTAIN, S.   *Berenstain Bears: no girls allowed.*
    BERENSTAIN, S.   *Berenstain Bears' moving day.*
    BERENSTAIN, S.   *Los osos Berenstain y demasiada fiesta.*
    BERENSTAIN, S.   *Osos Berenstain dia de mudanza.*

Five senses . . . . **Barron's**
    PARRAMON, J. M.   *El gusto.*
    PARRAMON, J. M.   *El oido.*
    PARRAMON, J. M.   *El tacto.*
    PARRAMON, J. M.   *Hearing.*
    PARRAMON, J. M.   *Sight.*
    PARRAMON, J. M.   *Taste.*
    PARRAMON, J. M.   *Touch.*
    PARRAMON, J. M.   *Vista.*

Focus on safety . . . . **Twenty-First Century**
    GUTMAN, B.   *Hazards at home.*

Folk dances for children . . . . **Can-Ed Media**
    FOLK DANCES FOR CHILDREN (Sound recording cassette).

Football legends . . . . **Chelsea House**
    CHADWICK, B.   *John Madden.*

Four-to-go . . . . **Smarty Pants**
    *ALL TIME FAVORITE CHILDREN'S STORIES (Talking
    book).*

From sea to shining sea. . . . . **Childrens Press**
    FRADIN, D. B.   *Arkansas.*
    FRADIN, D. B.   *Colorado.*
    FRADIN, D. B.   *Connecticut.*
    FRADIN, D. B.   *Delaware.*
    FRADIN, D. B.   *Indiana.*
    FRADIN, D. B.   *Louisiana.*
    FRADIN, D. B.   *Maine.*
    FRADIN, D. B.   *Maryland.*
    FRADIN, D. B.   *Minnesota.*
    FRADIN, D. B.   *Missouri.*
    FRADIN, D. B.   *New York.*
    FRADIN, D. B.   *North Dakota.*
    FRADIN, D. B.   *Oklahoma.*
    FRADIN, D. B.   *Oregon.*
    FRADIN, D. B.   *South Carolina.*
    FRADIN, D. B.   *South Dakota.*
    FRADIN, D. B.   *Tennessee.*
    FRADIN, D. B.   *Vermont.*
    FRADIN, D. B.   *Washington.*
    FRADIN, D. B.   *West Virginia.*

Gale biographical index series . . . . **Gale**
    *CHILDREN'S AUTHORS AND ILLUSTRATORS: AN
    INDEX TO BIOGRAPHICAL DICTIONARIES.*

Gateway biography . . . . **Millbrook Press**
    BLUE, R.   *Colin Powell: straight to the top. Updated ed.*
    COLMAN, P.   *Madam C.J. Walker: building a business empire.*
    CWIKLIK, R.   *Bill Clinton: president of the 90s. Rev. ed.*
    JACOBS, W. J.   *Mother Teresa: helping the poor.*
    KENDALL, M. E.   *Nellie Bly: reporter for the world.*
    LEVERT, S.   *Hillary Rodham Clinton, first lady.*
    STEFOFF, R.   *Al Gore, vice president.*

Gateway civil rights . . . . **Millbrook Press**
    BARRETT, T.   *Nat Turner and the slave revolt.*
    COLLINS, J. L.   *John Brown and the fight against slavery.*
    CWIKLIK, R.   *Malcolm X and black pride.*
    ELISH, D.   *Harriet Tubman and the Underground Railroad.*
    ELISH, D.   *James Meredith and school desegregation.*
    ROBERTS, J. L.   *Booker T. Washington: educator and leader.*

Gateway green biography . . . . **Millbrook Press**
    NADEN, C. J.   *John Muir: saving the wilderness.*
    RING, E.   *Henry David Thoreau: in step with nature.*

Get to know... . . . . **Harcourt Brace**
    GET TO KNOW BERNARD MOST (Videocassette).
    GET TO KNOW KEITH BAKER (Videocassette).

Getting to know the world's greatest artists . . . . **Children's Press**
    VENEZIA, M.   *Francisco Goya.*
    VENEZIA, M.   *Henri de Toulouse-Lautrec.*
    VENEZIA, M.   *Salvador Dali.*

Getting to know the world's greatest composers . . . . **Children's Press**
    VENEZIA, M.   *Aaron Copland.*
    VENEZIA, M.   *George Gershwin.*
    VENEZIA, M.   *Igor Stravinsky.*

Gifted treasury. . . . . **Teacher Ideas Press/Libraries Unlimited**
    FLACK, J. D.   *Inventing, inventions, and inventors: a teaching
    resource book.*

Golden gate junior book . . . . **Childrens Press**
    BEHRENS, J.   *Whalewatch.*

Gone forever . . . . Crestwood House/Macmillan
    MORRISON, S. D. *Passenger pigeon.*

Good conversation! . . . . Tim Podell Productions
    TALK WITH AVI (Videocassette).
    TALK WITH BETSY BYARS (Videocassette).
    TALK WITH JEAN FRITZ (Videocassette).
    TALK WITH LYNNE REID BANKS (Videocassette).

Great African Americans . . . . Enslow
    MCKISSACK, P. *Carter G. Woodson: the father of black history.*
    MCKISSACK, P. *Mary Church Terrell: leader for equality.*
    MCKISSACK, P. *Paul Robeson: a voice to remember.*
    MCKISSACK, P. *Satchel Paige: the best arm in baseball.*

Great animal stories . . . . Berlet Films & Video
    SEA ANIMALS ASHORE (Videocassette).
    TURKEYS IN THE WILD (Videocassette).

Great Black heroes . . . . Scholastic
    HUDSON, W. *Five notable inventors.*

Great creatures of the world . . . . Facts on File
    LUMPKIN, S. *Big cats.*
    LUMPKIN, S. *Small cats.*

Great episodes . . . . Gulliver/Harcourt Brace Jovanovich
    GREGORY, K. *Earthquake at dawn.*

Great lives . . . . Scribner's
    FABER, D. *Great lives: nature and the environment.*
    JACOBS, W. J. *Great lives: human rights.*
    LOMASK, M. *Great lives: invention and technology.*

Great minds of science . . . . Enslow
    ANDERSON, M. J. *Charles Darwin: naturalist.*
    ANDERSON, M. J. *Isaac Newton: the greatest scientist of all time.*
    POYNTER, M. *Marie Curie: discoverer of radium.*
    YOUNT, L. *Antoni van Leeuwenhoek: first to see microscopic life.*

Greatest stories ever told . . . . Rabbit Ears
    GLEESON, B. *Joseph and his brothers (Videocassette).*
    GLEESON, B. *Savior is born (Kit).*
    METAXAS, E. *David and Goliath (Videocassette).*

Greenwillow read-alone . . . . Greenwillow
    BANG, M. *Tye May and the magic brush.*
    BRUUN, R. D. *Brain--what it is, what it does.*
    HUTCHINS, P. *Tale of Thomas Mead.*
    KESSLER, L. *Big mile race.*
    KESSLER, L. *Old Turtle's soccer team.*
    PARISH, P. *Amelia Bedelia goes camping.*
    PARISH, P. *Good work, Amelia Bedelia.*
    PARISH, P. *Merry Christmas, Amelia Bedelia.*
    PARISH, P. *Teach us, Amelia Bedelia.*
    PORTE, B. A. *Harry gets an uncle.*
    PORTE, B. A. *Harry in trouble.*
    PORTE, B. A. *Harry's birthday.*
    PORTE, B. A. *Harry's dog.*
    PORTE, B. A. *Harry's pony.*
    PRELUTSKY, J. *It's Halloween.*
    PRELUTSKY, J. *It's Thanksgiving.*
    PRELUTSKY, J. *It's Valentine's Day.*
    PRELUTSKY, J. *Rainy rainy Saturday.*
    SEIXAS, J. S. *Alcohol--what it is, what it does.*
    SEIXAS, J. S. *Allergies - what they are, what they do.*
    SHUB, E. *Seeing is believing.*

Harcourt Brace contemporary classic . . . . Harcourt Brace
    THURBER, J. *Great Quillow.*

HarperCollins nature study book . . . . HarperCollins
    PINE, J. *Trees.*

Hello Canada . . . . Lerner
    BARNES, M. *Ontario.*
    BOWERS, V. *British Columbia.*
    HANCOCK, L. *Nunavut.*
    JACKSON, L. *Newfoundland and Labrador.*

Hello math reader . . . . Scholastic
    LING, B. *Fattest, tallest, biggest snowman ever.*
    SLATER, T. *Stay in line.*

Hello reader! . . . . Scholastic
    HOPPING, L. J. *Wild weather. Tornadoes!*
    LOW, A. *Popcorn shop.*
    LUNDELL, M. *Girl named Helen Keller.*
    MACCARONE, G. *Classroom pet.*
    MACCARONE, G. *Pizza party!*
    MEDEARIS, A. S. *Here comes the snow.*
    MOORE, E. *Buddy: the first seeing eye dog.*
    TARCOV, E. H. *Frog prince.*

Hello reading! . . . . Viking Penguin
    ZIEFERT, H. *Clown games.*
    ZIEFERT, H. *Jason's bus ride.*
    ZIEFERT, H. *Mike and Tony: best friends.*
    ZIEFERT, H. *Three wishes.*

Hello science reader! . . . . Scholastic
    MARZOLLO, J. *I'm a seed.*

Hello U.S.A. . . . . Lerner
    BLEDSOE, S. *Colorado.*
    BRATVOLD, G. *Wisconsin.*
    BROWN, D. *Alabama.*
    BROWN, D. *Kentucky.*
    BROWN, D. *New Hampshire.*
    DI PIAZZA, D. *Arkansas.*
    ENGFER, L. *Maine.*
    FILBIN, D. *Arizona.*
    FREDEEN, C. *Kansas.*
    FREDEEN, C. *New Jersey.*
    FREDEEN, C. *South Carolina.*
    FRISCH, C. *Wyoming.*
    JOHNSTON, J. *Alaska.*
    JOHNSTON, J. *Washington, D.C.*
    LADOUX, R. C. *Georgia.*
    PELTA, K. *California.*
    POWELL, E. S. *Washington.*
    SCHULZ, A. *North Carolina.*
    SIRVAITIS, K. *Florida.*
    SIRVAITIS, K. *Michigan.*
    SIRVAITIS, K. *Utah.*
    SIRVAITIS, K. *Virginia.*
    SWAIN, G. *Pennsylvania.*

Hello! From around the world! . . . . Ernst Interactive Media
    JAPAN: ASIA, VOLUME 2 (Videocassette).

Herculeah Jones mystery . . . . Viking
    BYARS, B. C. *Dark stairs.*
    BYARS, B. C. *Dead letter.*
    BYARS, B. C. *Death's door.*
    BYARS, B. C. *Tarot says beware.*

Here's how! . . . . TVOntario
    CHEWING GUM (Videocassette).
    LIGHT BULBS (Videocassette).
    POSTAL STATION (Videocassette).
    SOUP (Videocassette).

High energy fitness series . . . . Educational Activities
    COLGATE, B. *Silly Willy workout (Sound recording cassette).*

Hispanic heritage . . . . Millbrook Press
    CEDENO, M. E. *Cesar Chavez: labor leader.*

Historic communities . . . . Crabtree
    KALMAN, B. *Colonial crafts.*
    KALMAN, B. *Home crafts.*
    KALMAN, B. *Kitchen.*

Historic communities (Continued)
  KALMAN, B.   *Pioneer projects.*
  KALMAN, B.   *18th century clothing.*
  KALMAN, B.   *19th century clothing.*

Historical albums . . . . **Millbrook Press**
  AVAKIAN, M.   *Historical album of Massachusetts.*
  AVAKIAN, M.   *Historical album of New York.*
  CARLSON, J. D.   *Historical album of Minnesota.*
  COCKE, W.   *Historical album of Virginia.*
  COCKE, W.   *Historical album of Washington.*
  SMITH, A.   *Historical album of Kentucky.*
  TOPPER, F.   *Historical album of New Jersey.*
  WILLS, C. A.   *Historical album of Alabama.*
  WILLS, C. A.   *Historical album of California.*
  WILLS, C. A.   *Historical album of Colorado.*
  WILLS, C. A.   *Historical album of Connecticut.*
  WILLS, C. A.   *Historical album of Florida.*
  WILLS, C. A.   *Historical album of Illinois.*
  WILLS, C. A.   *Historical album of Michigan.*
  WILLS, C. A.   *Historical album of Nebraska.*
  WILLS, C. A.   *Historical album of Ohio.*
  WILLS, C. A.   *Historical album of Oregon.*
  WILLS, C. A.   *Historical album of Pennsylvania.*
  WILLS, C. A.   *Historical album of Texas.*

History of everyday things . . . . **Bedrick/Blackie**
  CASELLI, G.   *Middle Ages.*
  CASELLI, G.   *Roman Empire and the Dark Ages.*

History of the Civil War . . . . **Silver Burdett**
  RICKARBY, L. A.   *Ulysses S. Grant and the strategy of victory.*

History through art and architecture . . . . **Alarion**
  AMERICAN ART AND ARCHITECTURE (Videocassette).

Hockey superstars . . . . **Morrow**
  DUPLACEY, J.   *Amazing forwards.*
  DUPLACEY, J.   *Great goalies.*
  DUPLACEY, J.   *Top rookies.*

Holiday classics . . . . **Bogner Entertainment**
  PETER COTTONTAIL: HOW HE GOT HIS HOP!
  (Videocasstte).

Holiday classics . . . . **Rabbit Ears**
  POTTER, B.   *Tailor of Gloucester (Videocassette).*

Holiday crafts for kids . . . . **Millbrook Press**
  ROSS, K.   *Crafts for Christmas.*
  ROSS, K.   *Crafts for Easter.*
  ROSS, K.   *Crafts for Halloween.*
  ROSS, K.   *Crafts for Hanukkah.*
  ROSS, K.   *Crafts for Kwanzaa.*
  ROSS, K.   *Crafts for Thanksgiving.*
  ROSS, K.   *Every day is Earth Day: a craft book.*

Holiday on my own book . . . . **Carolrhoda**
  SCOTT, G.   *Labor Day.*

Holidays and festivals series . . . . **Crabtree**
  SMITH, D.   *Holidays and festivals activities.*

Horn Book papers . . . . **Horn Book**
  HORN BOOK MAGAZINE.   *Newbery Medal books: 1922-1955: with their authors' acceptance papers, biographies, and related materials chiefly from the Horn*

Houdini Club magic mystery . . . . **Random House**
  ADLER, D. A.   *Onion sundaes.*

How did we find out . . . . **Walker**
  ASIMOV, I.   *How did we find out about microwaves?*
  ASIMOV, I.   *How did we find out about photosynthesis?*
  ASIMOV, I.   *How did we find out about superconductivity?*

How do we know . . . . **Raintree Steck-Vaughn**
  GANERI, A.   *What's inside us?*

How history is invented . . . . **Lerner**
  PELTA, K.   *Discovering Christopher Columbus.*
  WILSON, L. L.   *Salem witch trials.*

How it is made . . . . **Facts on File**
  MICHAEL, D.   *How skyscrapers are made.*

How it works . . . . **Simon & Schuster**
  GANERI, A.   *Creature features.*
  GANERI, A.   *Funny bones.*

How it's made . . . . **Lerner**
  ERLBACH, A.   *Peanut butter.*

How to play the all-star way . . . . **Raintree Steck-Vaughn**
  FRANCIS, J.   *Bicycling.*
  HARRIS, L.   *Hockey.*
  NARDI, T. J.   *Karate and judo.*
  NORMILE, D.   *Gymnastics.*
  RAFFO, D.   *Football.*
  ROSENTHAL, B.   *Track and field.*
  TEIRSTEIN, M. A.   *Baseball.*
  WILNER, B.   *Soccer.*
  WILNER, B.   *Swimming.*
  WITHERS, T.   *Basketball.*

How we work . . . . **Greenwillow**
  FLORIAN, D.   *Auto mechanic.*
  FLORIAN, D.   *Chef.*
  FLORIAN, D.   *Fisher.*
  FLORIAN, D.   *Painter.*

How-to-do-it manuals for libraries . . . . **Neal-Schuman**
  FECKO, M. B.   *Cataloging nonbook resources: a how-to-do-it manual for librarians.*

How's the weather? . . . . **Lerner**
  KAHL, J. D.   *Storm warning: tornadoes and hurricanes.*
  KAHL, J. D.   *Thunderbolt: learning about lightning.*
  KAHL, J. D.   *Weatherwise: learning about the weather.*
  KAHL, J. D.   *Wet weather: rain showers and snowfall.*

Human body . . . . **National Geographic**
  DIGESTIVE SYSTEM (Videocassette).
  NERVOUS SYSTEM (Videocassette).
  YOUR BODY: CIRCULATORY AND RESPIRATORY SYSTEMS (Videocassette).
  YOUR BODY: MUSCULAR AND SKELETAL SYSTEMS (Videocassette).

Human body . . . . **Watts**
  PARKER, S.   *Ear and hearing. Rev. ed.*
  PARKER, S.   *Eye and seeing. Rev. ed.*
  PARKER, S.   *Food and digestion. Rev. ed.*
  PARKER, S.   *Heart and blood. Rev. ed.*
  PARKER, S.   *Lungs and breathing. Rev. ed.*
  PARKER, S.   *Skeleton and movement. Rev. ed.*

Human Race Club . . . . **Kids' Media Group/Guidance Associates**
  CASEY'S REVENGE: A STORY ABOUT FIGHTING AND DISAGREEMENTS (Videocassette).
  UNFORGETTABLE PEN PAL: A STORY ABOUT PREJUDICE AND DISCRIMINATION (Videocassette).

Hyperion chapters . . . . **Hyperion**
  GERSTEIN, M.   *Behind the couch.*
  GRAVES, B. B.   *Mystery of the Tooth Gremlin.*
  MACDONALD, M.   *No room for Francie.*
  WILLIAMS, S.   *Edwin and Emily.*

I am reading book . . . . **Pantheon**
  PRAGER, A.   *Spooky Halloween party.*

I can read book . . . . HarperCollins
  ALLEN, L. J. *Rollo and Tweedy and the ghost at Dougal Castle.*
  AVERILL, E. *Fire cat.*
  BERNIER-GRAND, C. T. *Juan Bobo: four folktales from Puerto Rico.*
  BONSALL, C. N. *Tell me some more.*
  BONSALL, C. N. *Who's a pest?*
  BULLA, C. R. *Daniel's duck.*
  BYARS, B. C. *Golly sisters go West.*
  BYARS, B. C. *Golly sisters ride again.*
  BYARS, B. C. *Hooray for the Golly sisters!*
  COERR, E. *Buffalo Bill and the Pony Express.*
  COERR, E. *Chang's paper pony.*
  COERR, E. *Josefina story quilt.*
  COERR, E. *Josefina y la colcha de retazos.*
  CROLL, C. *Too many Babas.*
  CUSHMAN, D. *Aunt Eater's mystery Christmas.*
  CUSHMAN, D. *Aunt Eater's mystery vacation.*
  HOBAN, J. *Buzby to the rescue.*
  HOBAN, J. *Buzby.*
  HOBAN, L. *Arthur's camp-out.*
  HOBAN, L. *Arthur's Christmas cookies.*
  HOBAN, L. *Arthur's funny money.*
  HOBAN, L. *Arthur's great big valentine.*
  HOBAN, L. *Arthur's Halloween costume.*
  HOBAN, L. *Arthur's honey bear.*
  HOBAN, L. *Arthur's loose tooth.*
  HOBAN, L. *Arthur's prize reader.*
  HOBAN, L. *Case of the two masked robbers.*
  HOBAN, L. *Silly Tilly and the Easter Bunny.*
  HOBAN, L. *Silly Tilly's Thanksgiving dinner.*
  HOFF, S. *Captain Cat: story and pictures.*
  HOFF, S. *Danny and the dinosaur go to camp.*
  HOFF, S. *Danny and the dinosaur.*
  HOFF, S. *Grizzwold.*
  HOFF, S. *Happy birthday, Danny and the dinosaur!*
  HOFF, S. *Julius.*
  HOPKINS, L. B. *Weather: poems.*
  KESSLER, E. *Stan the hot dog man.*
  LEVINSON, N. S. *Clara and the bookwagon.*
  LEVINSON, N. S. *Snowshoe Thompson.*
  LOBEL, A. *Days with Frog and Toad.*
  LOBEL, A. *Dias con Sapo y Sepo.*
  LOBEL, A. *Frog and Toad all year.*
  LOBEL, A. *Frog and Toad are friends.*
  LOBEL, A. *Frog and Toad together.*
  LOBEL, A. *Grasshopper on the road.*
  LOBEL, A. *Mouse soup.*
  LOBEL, A. *Mouse tales.*
  LOBEL, A. *Owl at home.*
  LOBEL, A. *Sapo y Sepo inseparables.*
  LOBEL, A. *Sapo y Sepo son amigos.*
  LOBEL, A. *Sapo y Sepo un ano entero.*
  LOBEL, A. *Small pig.*
  LOBEL, A. *Uncle Elephant.*
  MINARIK, E. H. *Amigos de Osito.*
  MINARIK, E. H. *Father Bear comes home.*
  MINARIK, E. H. *Kiss for Little Bear.*
  MINARIK, E. H. *Little Bear.*
  MINARIK, E. H. *Little Bear's friend.*
  MINARIK, E. H. *Little Bear's visit.*
  MINARIK, E. H. *Osito.*
  MINARIK, E. H. *Papa Oso vuelve a casa.*
  MINARIK, E. H. *Visita de Osito.*
  MONJO, F. N. *Drinking gourd. Newly illustrated ed.*
  MONJO, F. N. *Osa menor: una historia del ferrocarril subterraneo.*
  MORRIS, R. A. *Dolphin.*
  NOVAK, M. *Newt.*
  O'CONNOR, J. *Lulu and the witch baby.*
  PARISH, P. *Come back, Amelia Bedelia. Newly illustrated ed.*
  PARISH, P. *No more monsters for me!*
  PARISH, P. *Play ball, Amelia Bedelia.*
  PARISH, P. *Scruffy.*
  PARISH, P. *Thank you, Amelia Bedelia. Rev. ed.*
  POMERANTZ, C. *Outside dog.*
  RAPPAPORT, D. *Boston coffee party.*
  ROBINS, J. *Addie's bad day.*
  SCHWARTZ, A. *Ghosts!: ghostly tales from folklore.*

I can read book (Continued)
  SCHWARTZ, A. *In a dark, dark room and other scary stories.*
  SIRACUSA, C. *Bingo, the best dog in the world.*
  SKOFIELD, J. *Detective Dinosaur.*
  SPIRN, M. *Know-Nothing birthday.*
  TURNER, A. *Dust for dinner.*
  WISEMAN, B. *Morris goes to school.*

I can read chapter book . . . . HarperCollins
  AVI. *Finding Providence: the story of Roger Williams.*

I can read history book . . . . HarperCollins
  BENCHLEY, N. *George, the drummer boy.*
  BENCHLEY, N. *Sam the minuteman.*
  BRENNER, B. *Wagon wheels.*
  SANDIN, J. *Long way to a new land.*
  SANDIN, J. *Long way westward.*

I can read it all by myself . . . . Random House
  HEILBRONER, J. *Robert the rose horse.*
  MCCLINTOCK, M. *Stop that ball.*
  SEUSS, D. *Dr. Seuss's ABC.*

I can read mystery . . . . HarperCollins
  BONSALL, C. N. *Case of the cat's meow.*
  BONSALL, C. N. *Case of the double cross.*
  BONSALL, C. N. *Case of the dumb bells.*
  BONSALL, C. N. *Case of the hungry stranger.*
  BONSALL, C. N. *Case of the scaredy cats.*
  BONSALL, C. N. *Caso del forastero hambriento.*
  LEXAU, J. M. *Rooftop mystery.*

I know America . . . . Millbrook Press
  ST. PIERRE, S. *Our national anthem.*
  STEINS, R. *Our elections.*
  STEINS, R. *Our national capital.*

I love the seasons . . . . Tilbury House
  AGELL, C. *I slide into the white of winter.*
  AGELL, C. *I wear long green hair in the summer.*
  AGELL, C. *Mud makes me dance in the spring.*
  AGELL, C. *Wind spins me around in the fall.*

I spy books . . . . Scholastic
  WICK, W. *I spy Christmas: a book of picture riddles.*
  WICK, W. *I spy fantasy: a book of picture riddles.*
  WICK, W. *I spy school days: a book of picture riddles.*
  WICK, W. *I spy spooky night: a book of picture riddles.*

I want to be. . . . . World Book
  BULLOCH, I. *I want to be a puppeteer.*
  BULLOCH, I. *I want to be an actor.*

I want to be... book series . . . . Harcourt Brace
  MAZE, S. *I want to be... a veterinarian.*
  MAZE, S. *I want to be... an astronaut.*

I was there . . . . Hyperion
  TANAKA, S. *Discovering the Iceman: what was it like to find a 5,300-year-old mummy?*
  TANAKA, S. *On board the Titanic.*

Illustrated junior library . . . . Grosset & Dunlap
  ALCOTT, L. M. *Jo's boys.*
  ALCOTT, L. M. *Little men: life at Plumfield with Jo's boys.*

Imagination express . . . . Edmark
  DESTINATION: CASTLE. School version (CD-ROM).
  DESTINATION: NEIGHBORHOOD. School version (CD-ROM).
  DESTINATION: OCEAN. School version (CD-ROM).
  DESTINATION: PYRAMIDS. School version (CD-ROM).
  DESTINATION: RAIN FOREST. School version (CD-ROM).
  DESTINATION: TIME TRIP, USA. School version (CD-ROM).

Imagine living here . . . . Walker
  COBB, V. *This place is lonely.*
  COBB, V. *This place is wet.*

In my world. . . . . **Crabtree**
KALMAN, B. *Fun with my friends.*

Information management, policy, services . . . . **Ablex**
EISENBERG, M. B. *Information problem-solving: the Big Six Skills approach to library and information skills instruction.*

Inside guides . . . . **DK Publishing**
TAYLOR, B. *Incredible plants.*

Inside story . . . . **Peter Bedrick**
MACDONALD, F. *Greek temple.*
MACDONALD, F. *Medieval castle.*
MACDONALD, F. *Medieval cathedral.*
MACDONALD, F. *16th century mosque.*
MORLEY, J. *Roman villa.*
MORLEY, J. *Shakespeare's theater.*

Inside-outside. . . . . **Dutton**
MUNRO, R. *Inside-outside book of London.*
MUNRO, R. *Inside-outside book of Paris.*

Instructor Books . . . . **Scholastic Professional Books**
ORLANDO, L. *Multicultural game book: more than 70 traditional games from 30 countries.*

Interactive writing tools . . . . **Learning Company**
READ, WRITE AND TYPE! (CD-ROM).
STUDENT WRITING AND RESEARCH CENTER WITH COMPTON'S CONCISE ENCYCLOPEDIA (CD-ROM).
ULTIMATE WRITING AND CREATIVITY CENTER. School ed. (CD-ROM).

International cooperation. . . . . **Lerner**
BURGER, L. *Red Cross/Red Crescent: when help can't wait.*

Introduction to the microscope. . . . . **Clearvue/EAV**
HOW TO USE THE COMPOUND MICROSCOPE (Videocassette).

Invaders . . . . **Twenty-First Century**
FACKLAM, H. *Bacteria.*
FACKLAM, H. *Viruses.*

Inventions that changed our lives . . . . **Walker**
COSNER, S. *Rubber.*
FORD, B. *Automobile.*

Investigators of the unknown . . . . **Orchard Books**
LISLE, J. T. *Gold dust letters.*
LISLE, J. T. *Looking for Juliette.*

Isaac Asimov's pioneers of science and exploration . . **Gareth Stevens**
ASIMOV, I. *Christopher Columbus: navigator to the New World.*

It figures. . . . . **Agency for Instructional Technology**
DECIDING HOW CLOSE TO MEASURE (Videocassette).
PROBLEM SOLVING: RECOGNIZING NECESSARY INFORMATION (Videocassette).
RELATING FRACTIONS AND DECIMALS (Videocassette).
USING FRACTIONS (Videocassette).

Jackdaws . . . . **Golden Owl**
CALIFORNIA GOLD RUSH: 1849 (Multimedia kit).
OKLAHOMA LAND RUSH (Multimedia kit).

Janice VanCleave's science for every kid. . . . . **Wiley**
VANCLEAVE, J. P. *Biology for every kid: 101 easy experiments that really work.*
VANCLEAVE, J. P. *Janice VanCleave's math for every kid: easy activities that make learning math fun.*
VANCLEAVE, J. P. *Janice VanCleave's oceans for every kid: easy activities that make learning science fun.*
VANCLEAVE, J. P. *Janice VanCleave's the human body for every kid: easy activities that make learning science fun.*

Janice VanCleave's spectacular science projects . . . . **Wiley**
VANCLEAVE, J. P. *Janice VanCleave's rocks and minerals: mind-boggling experiments you can turn into science fair projects.*

JPS young biography . . . . **Jewish Publication Society**
HURWITZ, J. *Leonard Bernstein: a passion for music.*

Junior field trips . . . . **Humongous Entertainment**
LET'S EXPLORE THE JUNGLE WITH BUZZY THE KNOWLEDGE BUG (CD-ROM).

Junior world biographies . . . . **Chelsea House**
KAVANAGH, J. *Robert E. Lee.*
MACHT, N. L. *Muhammad Ali.*
MACHT, N. L. *Roberto Clemente (Spanish version).*
MACHT, N. L. *Roberto Clemente.*
MACHT, N. L. *Sandra Day O'Connor.*
SHERROW, V. *Phillis Wheatley.*
SHIRLEY, D. *Diego Rivera.*
SONNEBORN, L. *Clara Barton.*
STEFOFF, R. *Lewis and Clark.*

Just for a day . . . . **Morrow**
RYDER, J. *Lizard in the sun.*

Kingdom of plants . . . . **National Geographic Society**
HOW PLANTS ARE USED (Videocassette).
WHAT IS A LEAF? (Videocassette).
WHAT IS A PLANT? (Videocassette).

Kingdoms of Africa . . . . **Chelsea House**
KOSLOW, P. *Dahomey: the warrior kings.*
KOSLOW, P. *Yorubaland: the flowering of genius.*

Kingdoms of life. . . . . **Twenty-First Century**
SILVERSTEIN, A. *Fungi.*
SILVERSTEIN, A. *Monerans and protists.*
SILVERSTEIN, A. *Plants.*
SILVERSTEIN, A. *Vertebrates.*

Know about. . . . . **Walker**
HYDE, M. O. *Know about AIDS. 3rd ed.*

Knowing nature . . . . **Farrar Straus & Giroux**
BROOKS, B. *Nature by design.*

Kodansha children's classics. . . . . **Kodansha International**
MCCARTHY, R. F. *Grandfather Cherry-Blossom.*
MCCARTHY, R. F. *Inch-high samurai.*
MCCARTHY, R. F. *Moon princess.*

Kolowalu book. . . . . **University of Hawaii Press**
BROWN, M. *Backbone of the king: the story of Paka'a and his son Ku.*
FEENEY, S. *Hawaii is a rainbow.*
THOMPSON, V. L. *Hawaiian legends of tricksters and riddlers.*
THOMPSON, V. L. *Hawaiian tales of heroes and champions.*

Lamb Chop's play-along! . . . . **A&M Video**
LEWIS, S. *Get your teddy ready (Videocassette).*
LEWIS, S. *Let's play games (Videocassette).*

Land of the eagle . . . . **PBS Video**
ACROSS THE SEA OF GRASS (Videocassette).
CONFRONTING THE WILDERNESS (Videocassette).
CONQUERING THE SWAMPS (Videocassette).
FIRST AND LAST FRONTIER (Videocassette).
GREAT ENCOUNTER (Videocassette).
INTO THE SHINING MOUNTAINS (Videocassette).
LIVING ON THE EDGE (Videocassette).
SEARCHING FOR PARADISE (Videocassette).

Land of the free. . . . . **Millbrook Press**
KING, D. C. *Freedom of assembly.*
KING, D. C. *Right to speak out.*
PASCOE, E. *Right to vote.*
SHERROW, V. *Freedom of worship.*

Landmark books. . . . . **Random House**
STEWART, G. R.   *Pioneers go west.*

Landmark editions . . . . **Landmark**
MOORE, A.   *Broken Arrow boy.*

Languages and lifestyles . . . . **Gessler Publishing**
BONJOUR DE PARIS (French Version) (Videocassette).
BONJOUR DE PARIS (Videocassette).

Learn to draw . . . . **Peel Productions**
DUBOSQUE, D.   *Learn to draw 3-D.*

Learning about horses. **Capstone Press**
STEWART, G. B.   *Appaloosa horse.*
STEWART, G. B.   *Arabian horse.*
STEWART, G. B.   *Quarter horse.*
STEWART, G. B.   *Thoroughbred horse: born to run.*

Learning through folklore . . . . **Teacher Ideas Press**
LIVO, L. J.   *Of bugs and beasts: fact, folklore, and activities.*

Legendary heroes of the Wild West . . . . **Enslow**
SANFORD, W. R.   *Brigham Young: pioneer and Mormon
leader.*
SANFORD, W. R.   *John C. Fremont: soldier and pathfinder.*
SANFORD, W. R.   *Kit Carson: frontier scout.*
SANFORD, W. R.   *Zebulon Pike: explorer of the Southwest.*

Legends from Mexico and Central America . . . **Fearon Teacher Aids**
PARKE, M.   *Quetzalcoatl tale of corn.*

Legends of the West. . . . . **Chelsea House**
WUKOVITS, J. F.   *Annie Oakley.*
WUKOVITS, J. F.   *Jesse James.*

Legends of the world . . . . **Troll**
REASONER, C.   *Night owl and the rooster: a Haitian legend.*

Lerner biography . . . . **Lerner**
DARBY, J.   *Dwight D. Eisenhower: a man called Ike.*
SHEPHARD, M. T.   *Maria Montessori: teacher of teachers.*

Lerner natural science book. **Lerner**
JOHNSON, S. A.   *Apple trees.*
JOHNSON, S. A.   *Bats.*
JOHNSON, S. A.   *Crabs.*
JOHNSON, S. A.   *Elephant seals.*
JOHNSON, S. A.   *Fireflies.*
JOHNSON, S. A.   *Hermit crabs.*
JOHNSON, S. A.   *How leaves change.*
JOHNSON, S. A.   *Inside an egg.*
JOHNSON, S. A.   *Ladybugs.*
JOHNSON, S. A.   *Morning glories.*
JOHNSON, S. A.   *Mosses.*
JOHNSON, S. A.   *Silkworms.*
JOHNSON, S. A.   *Snails.*
JOHNSON, S. A.   *Tree frogs.*
JOHNSON, S. A.   *Wasps.*
JOHNSON, S. A.   *Water insects.*
JOHNSON, S. A.   *Wheat.*
OVERBECK, C.   *Ants.*
OVERBECK, C.   *Carnivorous plants.*
OVERBECK, C.   *How seeds travel.*

Lerner's armed services. . . . . **Lerner**
WARNER, J. F.   *U.S. Marine Corps.*

Lerner's sports legacy series . . . . **Lerner**
GALT, M. F.   *Up to the plate: the All American Girls
Professional Baseball League.*

Let me tell you... . . . . **Traditional Images**
LET ME TELL YOU ALL ABOUT PLANES (Videocassette).
LET ME TELL YOU ALL ABOUT TRAINS (Videocassette).

Let's explore series. . . . . **Barbara Lawrence Productions**
STORY STARTERS. Vol. 1 (Videocassette).

Let's investigate . . . . **Marshall Cavendish**
SMOOTHEY, M.   *Calculators.*
SMOOTHEY, M.   *Graphs.*

Let's visit . . . . **Troll**
ALSTON, E.   *Space camp.*
COREY, M.   *Spaghetti factory.*

Let's-read-and-find-out science book . . . . **HarperCollins**
ALIKI.   *Corn is maize: the gift of the Indians.*
ALIKI.   *Fossils tell of long ago. Rev. ed.*
ALIKI.   *I'm growing!*
ALIKI.   *Milk from cow to carton. Rev. ed.*
ALIKI.   *Mis cinco sentidos. Ed. rev.*
ALIKI.   *My feet.*
ALIKI.   *My five senses. Rev. ed.*
ALIKI.   *My hands. Rev. ed.*
ALIKI.   *My visit to the dinosaurs. Rev. ed.*
BANCROFT, H.   *Animals in winter. Rev. ed.*
BERGER, M.   *Germs make me sick! Rev. ed.*
BERGER, M.   *Oil spill!*
BERGER, M.   *Switch on, switch off.*
BERGER, M.   *Why I cough, sneeze, shiver, hiccup, and yawn.*
BRANLEY, F. M.   *Earthquakes.*
BRANLEY, F. M.   *Flash, crash, rumble and roll. Rev. ed.*
BRANLEY, F. M.   *Rain and hail. Rev. ed.*
BRANLEY, F. M.   *Snow is falling. Rev. ed.*
BRANLEY, F. M.   *Sunshine makes the season. Rev. ed.*
BRANLEY, F. M.   *Tornado alert.*
BRANLEY, F. M.   *What happened to the dinosaurs?*
BULLA, C. R.   *What makes a shadow? Rev. ed.*
COLE, J.   *Evolution.*
DORROS, A.   *Ant cities.*
DORROS, A.   *Ciudades de hormigas.*
DORROS, A.   *Feel the wind.*
DUKE, K.   *Archaeologists dig for clues.*
EARLE, A.   *Zipping, zapping, zooming bats.*
ESBENSEN, B. J.   *Baby whales drink milk.*
ESBENSEN, B. J.   *Sponges are skeletons.*
GANS, R.   *How do birds find their way?*
HAWES, J.   *Fireflies in the night. Rev. ed.*
HEILIGMAN, D.   *From caterpillar to butterfly.*
JENKINS, P. B.   *Nest full of eggs.*
JORDAN, H. J.   *Como crece una semilla.*
JORDAN, H. J.   *How a seed grows. Rev. ed.*
LAUBER, P.   *Be a friend to trees.*
LAUBER, P.   *How we learned the earth is round.*
LAUBER, P.   *Octopus is amazing.*
LAUBER, P.   *Snakes are hunters.*
LAUBER, P.   *Who eats what?: food chains and food webs.*
LAUBER, P.   *You're aboard spaceship Earth.*
MAESTRO, B.   *How do apples grow?*
MAESTRO, B.   *Why do leaves change color?*
PFEFFER, W.   *From tadpole to frog.*
PFEFFER, W.   *What's it like to be a fish?*
SHOWERS, P.   *Drop of blood. Rev. ed.*
SHOWERS, P.   *Look at your eyes. Rev. ed.*
SHOWERS, P.   *Sleep is for everyone. Newly illustrated ed.*
SHOWERS, P.   *What happens to a hamburger? Rev. ed.*
SHOWERS, P.   *Where does the garbage go? Rev. ed.*
SHOWERS, P.   *Your skin and mine. Rev. ed.*
ZOEHFELD, K. W.   *How mountains are made.*
ZOEHFELD, K. W.   *What lives in a shell?*
ZOEHFELD, K. W.   *What's alive?*

Library of first questions and answers. . . . . . **Time-Life for Children**
*WHAT IS A BELLYBUTTON?: FIRST QUESTIONS AND
ANSWERS ABOUT THE HUMAN BODY.*

Library service to children. . . . . **Canadian Library Association**
GAGNON, A.   *Guidelines for children's services.*

Life in America 100 years ago . . . . **Chelsea House**
GAN, G.   *Communication.*
RITCHIE, D.   *Frontier life.*

Life lessons . . . . **Film Ideas**
CHEATING, LYING AND STEALING (Videocassette).
HURTFUL WORDS (Videocassette).

Life lessons (Continued)
THAT'S WHAT FRIENDS ARE FOR (Videocassette).
WHEN I GET MAD (Videocassette).

Lighter look . . . . **Millbrook Press**
JOHNSON, K. *Worm's eye view: make your own wildlife refuge.*
SKIDMORE, S. *Poison! beware! be an ace poison spotter.*

Literature bridges to science series . . . . **Teacher Ideas Press**
PERRY, P. J. *World's regions and weather: linking fiction to nonfiction.*

Little House: the Brookfield years . . . . **HarperCollins**
WILKES, M. D. *Little house in Brookfield.*
WILKES, M. D. *Little town at the crossroads.*

Little House: the Rocky Ridge years . . . . **HarperCollins**
MACBRIDE, R. L. *In the land of the big red apple.*
MACBRIDE, R. L. *Little farm in the Ozarks.*
MACBRIDE, R. L. *Little house on Rocky Ridge.*
MACBRIDE, R. L. *Little town in the Ozarks.*
MACBRIDE, R. L. *On the other side of the hill.*

Living books . . . . **Broderbund**
AESOP'S FABLE: THE TORTOISE AND THE HARE (CD-ROM).
ARTHUR'S TEACHER TROUBLE (CD-ROM).
BERENSTAIN BEARS GET IN A FIGHT. School ed. (CD-ROM).
BERENSTAIN BEARS IN THE DARK. School ed. (CD-ROM).
DR. SEUSS'S ABC (CD-ROM).
GREEN EGGS AND HAM. School ed. (CD-ROM).
JUST GRANDMA AND ME (CD-ROM).
MARC BROWN'S ARTHUR'S BIRTHDAY. School ed. (CD-ROM).
MARK SCHLICHTING'S HARRY AND THE HAUNTED HOUSE. School ed. (CD-ROM).
MERCER MAYER'S LITTLE MONSTER AT SCHOOL. School ed. (CD-ROM).
NEW KID ON THE BLOCK (CD-ROM).
STELLALUNA (CD-ROM).

Living dangerously . . . . **Garrett Educational**
MCDONALD, K. *Divers.*

Living music series . . . . **Knopf/EMI**
TURNER, B. C. *Living clarinet.*
TURNER, B. C. *Living flute.*
TURNER, B. C. *Living piano.*
TURNER, B. C. *Living violin.*

Look inside cross-sections . . . . **DK Publishing**
CHASEMORE, R. *Tanks.*
JENSSEN, H. *Jets.*

Look up . . . . **Films for the Humanities**
OTHER THINGS THAT FLY (Videocassette).

Looking at paintings . . . . **Hyperion**
ROALF, P. *Cats.*
ROALF, P. *Circus.*
ROALF, P. *Dancers.*
ROALF, P. *Families.*
ROALF, P. *Flowers.*
ROALF, P. *Horses.*
ROALF, P. *Landscapes.*
ROALF, P. *Seascapes.*

Louise Lindsey Merrick Texas environment series . . . . **Texas A&M**
HILLER, I. *Introducing mammals to young naturalists: from Texas Parks & Wildlife Magazine.*

Magic eye . . . . **Andrews and McMeel**
MAGIC EYE II: NOW YOU SEE IT....
MAGIC EYE: A NEW WAY OF LOOKING AT THE WORLD.

Making a better world . . . . **Twenty-First Century**
CHANDLER, G. *Recycling.*

Making music with John Langstaff . . . . **Langstaff Video Project**
LANGSTAFF, J. *Let's sing!: John Langstaff sings with children, ages 3-7* (Videocassette).
LANGSTAFF, J. *Let's sing!: John Langstaff sings with children, ages 3-7. Teacher's guide.*
LANGSTAFF, J. *Making music with children, ages 3-7* (Videocassette).

Many voices . . . . **TVOntario**
FOOD FOR THOUGHT (Videocassette).
HAIR SCARE (Videocassette).
MANY VOICES (Videocassette).
MOTHER TONGUE (Videocassette).
POSITIVELY NATIVE (Videocassette).
QUICK TO JUDGE (Videocassette).
SARI TALE (Videocassette).
TO JEW IS NOT A VERB (Videocassette).
WHAT'S IN A NAME (Videocassette).
WORLD AT MY DOOR (Videocassette).

Many voices, one song . . . . **Childrens Press**
ALTMAN, S. *Followers of the North Star: rhymes about African American heroes, heroines, and historical times.*
CUMPIAN, C. *Latino rainbow: poems about Latino Americans.*
IZUKI, S. *Believers in America: poems about Americans of Asian and Pacific islander descent.*

Master storyteller series . . . . **Chip Taylor Communications**
STOTTER, R. *Origami stories* (Videocassette).

Masters of art . . . . **Peter Bedrick**
CORRAIN, L. *Giotto and medieval art: the lives and works of the medieval artists.*
CRISPINO, E. *Van Gogh.*
DI CAGNO, G. *Michelangelo.*
LORIA, S. *Pablo Picasso.*
PESCIO, C. *Rembrandt and seventeenth-century Holland.*
ROMEI, F. *Story of sculpture.*
SALVI, F. *Impressionists: the origins of modern painting.*

Math fun . . . . **Messner**
WYLER, R. *Math fun with a pocket calculator.*
WYLER, R. *Math fun with tricky lines and shapes.*
WYLER, R. *Test your luck.*

Math works . . . . **Agency for Instructional Technology**
PROBLEM SOLVING: USING DIAGRAMS AND MODELS (Videocassette).
PROBLEM SOLVING: USING GRAPHS (Videocassette).

Mathnet mysteries . . . . **Children's Television Workshop**
VIEW FROM THE REAR TERRACE (Videocassette).

MathStart . . . . **HarperCollins**
MURPHY, S. J. *Best bug parade.*
MURPHY, S. J. *Best vacation ever.*
MURPHY, S. J. *Pair of socks.*
MURPHY, S. J. *Too many kangaroo things to do!*

Matt Christopher sports biographies . . . . **Little, Brown**
CHRISTOPHER, M. *At the plate with...Ken Griffey Jr.*
CHRISTOPHER, M. *In the huddle with...Steve Young.*
CHRISTOPHER, M. *On the court with...Michael Jordan.*
CHRISTOPHER, M. *On the ice with...Wayne Gretzky.*
CHRISTOPHER, M. *On the mound with...Greg Maddux.*

Meet the author . . . . **Richard C. Owen**
BUNTING, E. *Once upon a time.*
EHLERT, L. *Under my nose.*
HELLER, R. *Fine lines.*
KUSKIN, K. *Thoughts, pictures, and words.*
LYON, G. E. *Wordful child.*
MAHY, M. *My mysterious world.*

Meet the author . . . .   SRA/McGraw-Hill
    MEET ASHLEY BRYAN: STORYTELLER, ARTIST,
      WRITER (Videocassette).
    MEET JACK PRELUTSKY (Videocassette).
    MEET THE AUTHOR: HENRY WADSWORTH
      LONGFELLOW (Videocassette).
    MEET THE AUTHOR: ROBERT LOUIS STEVENSON
      (Videocassette).

Meet the author/illustrator . . . .   School Services of Canada
    MIND'S EYE: JEAN LITTLE (Videocassette).

Meet the Newbery author . . . .   SRA/McGraw-Hill
    MEET THE NEWBERY AUTHOR: RUSSELL FREEDMAN
      (Videocassette).

Meeting the challenge . . . .   Lerner
    LURIE, J.   *Allison's story: a book about homeschooling.*

Microsoft Explorapedia series . . . .   Microsoft
    MICROSOFT EXPLORAPEDIA: THE WORLD OF NATURE.
      Academic ed. (CD-ROM).
    MICROSOFT EXPLORAPEDIA: THE WORLD OF PEOPLE.
      Academic ed. (CD-ROM).

Mighty easy motivators . . . .   American Library Association
    BAUER, C. F.   *Leading kids to books through magic.*

Mighty math . . . .   Edmark
    CALCULATING CREW. School version. (CD-ROM).
    CARNIVAL COUNTDOWN. School version (CD-ROM).
    NUMBER HEROES. School version (CD-ROM).
    ZOO ZILLIONS. School version (CD-ROM).

Millbrook arts library . . . .   Millbrook Press
    CRAFTS FOR DECORATION.
    CRAFTS FOR PLAY.

Millbrook sports world . . . .   Millbrook Press
    GUTMAN, B.   *Frank Thomas: power hitter.*
    GUTMAN, B.   *Grant Hill: basketball's high flier.*
    GUTMAN, B.   *Hakeem Olajuwon: superstar center.*
    GUTMAN, B.   *Michael Jordan: basketball to baseball and back.*
      Rev. ed.
    GUTMAN, B.   *Steve Young: NFL passing wizard.*

Minding your manners series . . . .   Rainbow Educational
    MINDING YOUR MANNERS AT SCHOOL (Videocassette).

Minds-on science . . . .   Smithsonian Institution
    MINDS-ON SCIENCE: FOR PROFIT, FOR PLANET
      (Videodisc).
    MINDS-ON SCIENCE: FOR THE SAKE OF THE NATION
      (Videodisc).
    MINDS-ON SCIENCE: THE IMPACT OF DISCOVERY
      (Videodisc).

Missions in space . . . .   Millbrook Press
    VOGT, G.   *Viking and the Mars landing.*

Mulberry read-alones . . . .   Mulberry
    PARISH, P.   *Mind your manners!*

Multicultural junior biographies . . . .   Enslow
    HERMANN, S.   *R.C. Gorman: Navajo artist.*
    RILEY, G. B.   *Wah Ming Chang: artist and master of special*
      effects.

Music box . . . .   Films for the Humanities & Sciences
    METER (Videocassette).
    PITCH (Videocassette).

My first I can read book . . . .   HarperCollins
    BONSALL, C. N.   *Mine's the best. Newly illustrated ed.*
    BUCK, N.   *Oh, cats!*
    BUCK, N.   *Sid and Sam.*
    CAPUCILLI, A.   *Biscuit finds a friend.*
    CAPUCILLI, A.   *Biscuit.*

My first I can read book (Continued)
    KARLIN, N.   *I see, you saw.*

My first Little House books . . . .   HarperCollins
    WILDER, L. I.   *Dance at Grandpa's.*
    WILDER, L. I.   *Winter days in the Big Woods.*

My first reader . . . .   Childrens Press
    HALL, K.   *I'm not scared.*
    HALL, K.   *Tooth fairy.*
    PACKARD, M.   *I am king!*

My very own holiday books . . . .   Carolrhoda
    WEST, R.   *My very own Halloween: a book of cooking and*
      crafts.

Mysteries of science . . . .   Scientific American
    ARONSON, B.   *They came from DNA.*

Mystery of... . . . .   Crestwood House
    ABELS, H.   *Bermuda triangle.*

Mythology of the Americas . . . .   Morrow
    BIERHORST, J.   *Mythology of Mexico and Central America.*
    BIERHORST, J.   *Mythology of North America.*
    BIERHORST, J.   *Mythology of South America.*

National park & monument series. . . . .   Finley-Holiday Films
    AMERICA'S WESTERN NATIONAL PARKS (Videocassette).

National parks . . . .   Crestwood House
    PETERS, L. W.   *Serengeti.*

Native American biographies . . . .   Enslow
    HERMANN, S.   *Geronimo: Apache freedom fighter.*

Native Americans . . . .   Courage Books
    PRESS, P.   *Indians of the Northwest: traditions, history,*
      legends, and life.
    SITA, L.   *Indians of the Great Plains: traditions, history,*
      legends, and life.
    SITA, L.   *Indians of the Northeast: traditions, history, legends,*
      and life.
    SITA, L.   *Indians of the Southwest: traditions, history, legends,*
      and life.

Native dwellings . . . .   Tundra
    SHEMIE, B.   *Mounds of earth and shell: the Southeast.*

Nature close-up . . . .   Blackbirch
    PASCOE, E.   *Butterflies and moths.*
    PASCOE, E.   *Earthworms.*

Nature Company discoveries library . . . .   Time-Life Books
    CREAGH, C.   *Reptiles.*
    DOW, L.   *Incredible plants.*
    LYNCH, A.   *Great buildings.*

Nature Company guide . . . .   Time Life
    FORSHAW, J.   *Birding.*

Nature Company young discoveries library . . . .   Time Life
    CREAGH, C.   *Things with wings.*
    LAMPRELL, K.   *Scaly things.*

Nature in action . . . .   Carolrhoda
    CONE, P.   *Wildfire.*
    KRAMER, S. P.   *Avalanche.*
    KRAMER, S. P.   *Tornado.*
    SOUZA, D. M.   *Hurricanes.*
    SOUZA, D. M.   *Northern lights.*
    SOUZA, D. M.   *Powerful waves.*

Nature watch . . . .   TVOntario
    CHIPMUNK (Videocassette).

Nature's newborn . . . . Stoney-Wolf Productions
   NATURE'S NEWBORN: BEAR, BIGHORN SHEEP,
     MOUNTAIN GOATS (Videocassette).
   NATURE'S NEWBORN: ELK, MOOSE, DEER (Videocassette).

Naturebooks . . . . Child's World
   GOUCK, M. *Mountain lions.*
   MCDONALD, M. A. *Flying squirrels.*
   MURRAY, P. *Hummingbirds.*
   MURRAY, P. *Parrots.*
   MURRAY, P. *Porcupines.*
   PATTON, D. *Armadillos.*
   PATTON, D. *Flamingos.*
   PATTON, D. *Iguanas.*
   ROTHAUS, D. *Moray eels.*
   ROTHAUS, D. *Warthogs.*
   ROTTER, C. *Walruses.*

NCTE bibliography series . . National Council of Teachers of English
   ADVENTURING WITH BOOKS: A BOOKLIST FOR PRE-K-
     GRADE 6. 1997 ed.
   YOUR READING: AN ANNOTATED BOOKLIST FOR
     MIDDLE SCHOOL AND JUNIOR HIGH. 1995-96 ed.

NEA Professional library . . . . National Education Association
   DIMIDJIAN, V. J. *Early childhood at risk: actions and*
     advocacy for young children.
   TOWER, C. C. *Homeless students.*

Neal-Schuman NetGuide series. . . . . Neal-Schuman
   BENSON, A. C. *Connecting kids and the Internet: a handbook*
     for librarians, teachers, and parents.

Need to know library . . . . Rosen
   BRATMAN, F. *Everything you need to know when a parent*
     dies.

NetBooks . . . . Wolff New Media
   KIDS RULE THE NET: THE ONLY GUIDE TO THE
   INTERNET WRITTEN BY KIDS.

New true book . . . . Childrens Press
   BROEKEL, R. *Snakes.*
   FRADIN, D. B. *Earth.*
   FRISKEY, M. *Birds we know.*
   HENDERSON, K. *Great Lakes.*
   LEPTHIEN, E. U. *Beavers.*
   LEPTHIEN, E. U. *Buffalo.*
   LEPTHIEN, E. U. *Elk.*
   LEPTHIEN, E. U. *Manatees.*
   LEPTHIEN, E. U. *Polar bears.*
   LEPTHIEN, E. U. *Squirrels.*
   LEPTHIEN, E. U. *Wolves.*
   LEPTHIEN, E. U. *Woodchucks.*
   LEPTHIEN, E. U. *Zebras.*
   NOFSINGER, R. *Pigeons and doves.*
   PETERSEN, D. *Moose.*
   POSELL, E. *Horses.*
   ROSENTHAL, M. *Bears.*
   ROWAN, J. P. *Prairies and grasslands.*
   SCHEMENAUER, E. *Canada.*

New York Public Library answer books for kids series . . . . . . Wiley
   CAMPBELL, A. *New York Public Library amazing space: a*
     book of answers for kids.

Newsmakers . . . . Lerner
   POWERS, T. *Steven Spielberg: master storyteller.*
   STEWART, W. *14th Dalai Lama: spiritual leader of Tibet.*
   TURK, R. *Ray Charles: soul man.*

Nguzo Saba folklore series . . . . Beacon Films
   NOEL'S LEMONADE STAND (UJAMAA) (Videocassette).

Nice mice . . . . WhistleStop/Troll
   PALAZZO-CRAIG, J. *Max and Maggie in autumn.*
   PALAZZO-CRAIG, J. *Max and Maggie in spring.*
   PALAZZO-CRAIG, J. *Max and Maggie in summer.*
   PALAZZO-CRAIG, J. *Max and Maggie in winter.*

Notes Alive! StoryConcert series . . . . Minnesota Orchestra
   ON THE DAY YOU WERE BORN (Videocassette).

Now I know . . . . Troll
   PALAZZO-CRAIG, J. *Turtles.*

Olympic library . . . . Rigby
   READHEAD, L. *Gymnastics.*
   TAMES, R. *Ancient Olympics.*
   TAMES, R. *Modern Olympics.*
   VERRIER, J. *Swimming and diving.*
   WARD, T. *Field.*
   WARD, T. *Track.*

Olympic sports. . . . . Crestwood House/Macmillan
   SANDELSON, R. *Track athletics.*

On location . . . . Lothrop, Lee & Shepard
   DARLING, K. *Komodo dragon: on location.*
   DARLING, K. *Tasmanian devil: on location.*
   DARLING, K. *Walrus: on location.*

On my own adventure. . . . . Intervideo
   LOOK WHAT I GREW: WINDOWSILL GARDENS
     (Videocassette).
   LOOK WHAT I MADE: PAPER, PLAYTHINGS AND GIFTS
     (Videocassette).

Opening of the American West . . . . Delphi Productions
   LEWIS AND CLARK EXPEDITION (Videocassette).

Oryx multicultural folktale series. . . . . Oryx
   KNOCK AT THE DOOR.

Our endangered planet . . . . Lerner
   HOFF, M. K. *Our endangered planet: atmosphere.*
   HOFF, M. K. *Our endangered planet: groundwater.*
   HOFF, M. K. *Our endangered planet: life on land.*
   HOFF, M. K. *Our endangered planet: oceans.*
   HOFF, M. K. *Our endangered planet: rivers and lakes.*
   WINCKLER, S. *Nuestro planeta en peligro: la Antartida.*
   WINCKLER, S. *Our endangered planet: Antarctica.*
   WINCKLER, S. *Our endangered planet: population growth.*
   YOUNT, L. *Our endangered planet: air.*

Our human family . . . . Blackbirch Press
   MILLER, T. R. *Taking time out: recreation and play.*
   SITA, L. *Worlds of belief: religion and spirituality.*

Our national heritage . . . . Finley-Holiday Films
   INDEPENDENCE: BIRTH OF A FREE NATION
     (Videocassette).
   MOUNT VERNON: HOME OF GEORGE WASHINGTON
     (Videocassette).

Our neighborhood. . . . . Children's Press
   FLANAGAN, A. *Busy day at Mr. Kang's grocery store.*

Outdoor science book . . . . Messner
   WYLER, R. *Starry sky.*

Outside story with Slim Goodbody . . . . . AIT/Slim Goodbody Corp.
   OUR WATERY WORLD (Videocassette).

Outstanding African Americans . . . . Crabtree
   REDIGER, P. *Great African Americans in music.*

Overcoming the odds . . . . Raintree Steck-Vaughn
   GUTMAN, B. *Gail Devers.*
   GUTMAN, B. *Jim Eisenreich.*
   GUTMAN, B. *Julie Krone.*
   KRAMER, J. *Bo Jackson.*
   KRAMER, J. *Jim Abbott.*
   KRAMER, J. *Lee Trevino.*

Overview. . . . . Lucent
   BLOYD, S. *Animal rights.*
   YOUNT, L. *Cancer.*

OWL discovery film . . . .   Bullfrog films
  POLAR BEARS (Videocassette).
  SLEEPING BEARS (Videocassette).

Oxford myths and legends . . . .   Oxford University Press
  PICARD, B. L.   *Odyssey of Homer.*

Pacts & treaties . . . .   Twenty-First Century
  GOLD, S. D.   *Indian treaties.*

Pantheon fairy tale & folklore library . . . .   Pantheon
  FAVORITE FOLKTALES FROM AROUND THE WORLD.

Parabola storytime series . . . .   Parabola
  EVANS, R.   *Inktomi and the ducks and other Assiniboin trickster stories* (Talking book).

Partners . . . .   Blackbirch
  GREENBERG, K. E.   *Steven Jobs and Stephen Wozniak: creating the Apple computer.*
  ROZAKIS, L.   *Dick Rutan and Jeana Yeager: flying non-stop around the world.*

Partners with the earth curriculum . .   Heritage Education Foundation
  WOODS, M. L.   *Sky tree portfolio guide: an interdisciplinary environmental curriculum.*

Peacemakers . . . .   Dillon
  LAZO, C.   *Mahatma Gandhi.*

People in focus . . . .   Dillon
  DRIEMEN, J. E.   *Winston Churchill: an unbreakable spirit.*

People to know . . . .   Enslow
  COLE, M. D.   *Walt Disney: creator of Mickey Mouse.*
  MEACHUM, V.   *Jane Goodall: protector of chimpanzees.*
  MEACHUM, V.   *Steven Spielberg: Hollywood filmmaker.*

People's history . . . .   Lerner
  CURRIE, S.   *We have marched together: the working children's crusade.*
  CZECH, K. P.   *Snapshot: America discovers the camera.*
  DAMON, D.   *When this cruel war is over: the Civil War home front.*
  HINTZ, M.   *Farewell, John Barleycorn: prohibition in the United States.*
  WHITMAN, S.   *Get up and go!: the history of American road travel.*
  WHITMAN, S.   *Uncle Sam wants you!: military men and women of World War II.*
  WHITMAN, S.   *V is for victory: the American home front during World War II.*

Perennial library . . . .   HarperCollins
  KOCH, K.   *Wishes, lies, and dreams: teaching children to write poetry.*

Pet care . . . .   Barron's
  BRAEMER, H.   *Tropical fish: a complete pet owner's manual.*
  GRIEHL, K.   *Snakes: giant snakes and non-venomous snakes in the terrarium.*
  WILKE, H.   *Turtles: everything about purchase, care, nutrition and diseases.*

Peterson field guide series . . . .   Houghton Mifflin
  BORROR, D. J.   *Field guide to the insects of America north of Mexico.*
  MURIE, O. J.   *Field guide to animal tracks. 2nd ed.*
  PETERSON, R. T.   *Field guide to the birds: a completely new guide to all birds of eastern and central*
  PETERSON, R. T.   *Field guide to western birds. 3rd ed.*

Peterson first guide . . . .   Houghton Mifflin
  ALDEN, P.   *Peterson first guide to mammals of North America.*
  DAY, J. A.   *Peterson first guide to clouds and weather.*
  LEAHY, C. W.   *Peterson first guide to insects of North America.*

Physical geography of North America . .   National Geographic Society
  CENTRAL LOWLANDS (Videocassette).
  EAST (Videocassette).
  NORTHLANDS (Videocassette).
  PACIFIC EDGE (Videocassette).
  ROCKY MOUNTAINS (Videocassette).
  WESTERN DRY LANDS (Videocassette).

Physical geography of the continents . . .   National Geographic Society
  AFRICA (Videocassette).
  ANTARCTICA (Videocassette).
  ASIA (Videocassette).
  AUSTRALIA (Videocassette).

Picture book biography . . . .   Holiday House
  ADLER, D. A.   *Libro ilustrado sobre Cristobal Colon.*
  ADLER, D. A.   *Libro ilustrado sobre Martin Luther King, Hijo.*
  ADLER, D. A.   *Picture book of Anne Frank.*
  ADLER, D. A.   *Picture book of Christopher Columbus.*
  ADLER, D. A.   *Picture book of Davy Crockett.*
  ADLER, D. A.   *Picture book of Florence Nightingale.*
  ADLER, D. A.   *Picture book of Jackie Robinson.*
  ADLER, D. A.   *Picture book of Jesse Owens.*
  ADLER, D. A.   *Picture book of Louis Braille.*
  ADLER, D. A.   *Picture book of Martin Luther King, Jr.*
  ADLER, D. A.   *Picture book of Paul Revere.*
  ADLER, D. A.   *Picture book of Robert E. Lee.*
  ADLER, D. A.   *Picture book of Simon Bolivar.*
  ADLER, D. A.   *Picture book of Sitting Bull.*
  ADLER, D. A.   *Picture book of Sojourner Truth.*
  ADLER, D. A.   *Picture book of Thomas Alva Edison.*
  ADLER, D. A.   *Picture book of Thomas Jefferson.*

Picture book parade . . . .   Weston Woods
  SENDAK, M.   *Nutshell library* (Videocassette).
  SLIGHTLY SCARY STORIES (Videocassette).

Picture landmark books . . . .   Random House
  PENNER, L. R.   *Pilgrims at Plymouth.*

Picture-story biographies . . . .   Childrens Press
  CARRIGAN, M.   *Jimmy Carter: beyond the presidency.*
  SIMON, C.   *Seiji Ozawa: symphony conductor.*

Places in American history . . . .   Dillon
  REEF, C.   *Monticello.*

Playing fair . . . .   National Film Board of Canada
  CAROL'S MIRROR (Videocassette).
  HEY, KELLY (Videocassette).
  MELA'S LUNCH (Videocassette).
  PLAYING FAIR (Videocassette).
  WALKER (Videocassette).

Plots series . . . .   Bowker
  GILLESPIE, J. T.   *Introducing bookplots 3: a book talk guide for use with readers ages 8-12.*
  GILLESPIE, J. T.   *Introducing more books: a guide for the middle grades.*
  GILLESPIE, J. T.   *Juniorplots 3: a book talk guide for use with readers ages 12-16.*
  GILLESPIE, J. T.   *Juniorplots 4: a book talk guide for use with readers ages 12-16.*
  GILLESPIE, J. T.   *Juniorplots: a book talk manual for teachers and librarians.*
  GILLESPIE, J. T.   *Middleplots 4: a book talk guide for use with readers ages 8-12.*
  GILLESPIE, J. T.   *More juniorplots: a guide for teachers and librarians.*
  THOMAS, R. L.   *Primaryplots 2: a book talk guide for use with readers ages 4-8.*
  THOMAS, R. L.   *Primaryplots: a book talk guide for use with readers age 4-8.*

Pocket facts . . . .   Crestwood House
  STEELE, P.   *Boats.*
  STEELE, P.   *Insects.*
  STEELE, P.   *Planes.*

Portraits of the nations . . . . HarperCollins
    MALCOLM, A. H.   *Land and people of Canada.*

Portraits of women artists for children . . . . Little, Brown
    TURNER, R.   *Dorothea Lange.*
    TURNER, R.   *Faith Ringgold.*

Prejudice series . . . . Rainbow Educational
    AND YOU CAN'T COME: PREJUDICE HURTS
    (Videocassette).

Preschool power! . . . . Concept Associates
    EVEN MORE PRESCHOOL POWER (Videocassette).
    MORE PRESCHOOL POWER! (Videocassette).
    PRESCHOOL POWER 3! (Videocassette).
    PRESCHOOL POWER!: JACKET FLIPS AND OTHER TIPS
    (Videocassette).

Presidents of the United States . . . . Garrett
    FALKOF, L.   *Lyndon B. Johnson, 36th president of the United states.*

Prevent violence with Groark . . . . . Elkind & Sweet Communications
    GROARK LEARNS ABOUT BULLYING (Videocassette).
    GROARK LEARNS ABOUT PREJUDICE (Videocassette).
    GROARK LEARNS TO WORK OUT CONFLICTS
    (Videocassette).

Pro/Con . . . . Lerner
    OWEN, M.   *Animal rights: yes or no?*

Professional growth series . . . . Linworth Publishing
    FARMER, L. S. J.   *Creative partnerships: librarians and teachers working together.*

Proud heritage . . . . Millbrook Press
    MCKISSACK, P.   *African-American scientists.*

Puffin easy-to-read . . . . Puffin Books
    ZIEFERT, H.   *Nicky upstairs and down.*

Puppetry in education . . . . Nancy Renfro Studios
    HUNT, T.   *Puppetry in early childhood education.*
    RENFRO, N.   *Puppetry, language, and the special child: discovering alternate languages.*

Race car legends . . . . Chelsea House
    BRINSTER, R.   *Jeff Gordon.*

Raffi songs to read . . . . Crown
    RAFFI.   *Wheels on the bus.*

Rainbow biography . . . . Lodestar/Dutton
    MEDEARIS, A. S.   *Dare to dream: Coretta Scott King and the civil rights movement.*
    MEDEARIS, A. S.   *Little Louis and the jazz band: the story of Louis "Satchmo" Armstrong.*
    PETTIT, J.   *Maya Angelou: journey of the heart.*

Rand McNally for kids . . . . Rand McNally
    JOHNSON, J.   *How big is a whale?*

Read all about it . . . . Steck-Vaughn
    HANKIN, R.   *What was it like before television?*

Read and discover photo-illustrated biographies . . . . Bridgestone
    MCLOONE, M.   *George Washington Carver: a photo-illustrated biography.*

Read and wonder . . . . Candlewick
    CASEY, P.   *My cat Jack.*
    KING-SMITH, D.   *I love guinea pigs.*
    WALLACE, K.   *My hen is dancing.*
    WALLACE, K.   *Think of a beaver.*

Read with me . . . . Scholastic
    MARZOLLO, J.   *I'm tyrannosaurus!: a book of dinosaur rhymes.*

Read-aloud book . . . . Kingfisher
    TREASURY OF ANIMAL STORIES.
    TREASURY OF GIANT AND MONSTER STORIES.
    TREASURY OF SPOOKY STORIES.
    TREASURY OF STORIES FOR FIVE YEAR OLDS.
    TREASURY OF STORIES FOR SEVEN YEAR OLDS.
    TREASURY OF STORIES FOR SIX YEAR OLDS.

Reading Rainbow . . . . GPN/WNED-TV
    HOW MUCH IS A MILLION? (Videocassette).

Ready-to-read . . . . Simon & Schuster
    BANG, M.   *Wiley and the Hairy Man.*
    BANG, M.   *Wiley and the Hairy Man: adapted from an American folk tale.*
    CHRISTIAN, M. B.   *Toady and Dr. Miracle.*
    KRENSKY, S.   *Striking it rich: the story of the California gold rush.*
    PARISH, P.   *Be ready at eight.*
    SHARMAT, M. W.   *Mitchell is moving.*

Real kids real science books . . . . Thames & Hudson
    DORIS, E.   *Invertebrate zoology.*

Real readers . . . . Raintree/Steck-Vaughn
    BENITEZ, M.   *How spider tricked snake.*
    MARQUARDT, M.   *Wilbur and Orville and the flying machine.*
    MARTINO, T.   *Pizza!*

Really silly series . . . . Discovery Music
    BETHIE.   *Bethie's really silly songs about animals (Sound recording cassette).*

Record breakers . . . . Troll
    MATTHEWS, R.   *Record breakers of the air.*
    MATTHEWS, R.   *Record breakers of the land.*
    MATTHEWS, R.   *Record breakers of the sea.*

Redfeather book . . . . Henry Holt
    BENDICK, J.   *Caves!: underground worlds.*
    BRUSCA, M. C.   *Pedro fools the gringo and other tales of a Latin American trickster.*
    FRASER, M. A.   *In search of the Grand Canyon.*
    GETZ, D.   *Frozen man.*
    GUIBERSON, B. Z.   *Lighthouses: watchers at sea.*
    HESSE, K.   *Lavender.*
    HESSE, K.   *Sable.*
    LAUBER, P.   *Great whales: the gentle giants.*
    MASTERS, S. R.   *Libby Bloom.*
    MCKENZIE, E. K.   *King, the princess, and the tinker.*
    MCKENZIE, E. K.   *Stargone John.*

Reflections of a Black cowboy . . . . Silver Burdett
    MILLER, R. H.   *Buffalo Soldiers.*
    MILLER, R. H.   *Cowboys.*

Restoring nature: success stories . . . . Childrens Press
    BLASHFIELD, J. F.   *Rescuing endangered species.*
    GOLDSTEIN, N.   *Rebuilding prairies and forests.*
    WILLIS, T.   *Healing the land.*

Rookie biography . . . . Childrens Press
    GREENE, C.   *Eugene Field: the children's poet.*
    GREENE, C.   *Johann Sebastian Bach: great man of music.*
    GREENE, C.   *John Philip Sousa: the march king.*
    GREENE, C.   *Margarete Steiff: toy maker.*
    GREENE, C.   *Robert Louis Stevenson: author of A CHILD'S GARDEN OF VERSES.*
    GREENE, C.   *Roy Campanella: major-league champion.*
    GREENE, C.   *Rudyard Kipling: author of the "Jungle books."*

Rookie read-about science . . . . Childrens Press
    FOWLER, A.   *Como sabes que es otono?*
    FOWLER, A.   *Como sabes que es primavera?*
    FOWLER, A.   *Como sabes que es verano?*
    FOWLER, A.   *How do you know it's fall?*
    FOWLER, A.   *How do you know it's spring?*
    FOWLER, A.   *How do you know it's summer?*
    FOWLER, A.   *How do you know it's winter?*

Rookie read-about science (Continued)
FOWLER, A.   *It could still be water.'*
FOWLER, A.   *Thanks to cows.*
FOWLER, A.   *Y aun podria ser agua.*

Rookie reader . . . . **Children's Press**
BRIMNER, L. D.   *Brave Mary.*
RAU, D. M.   *Box can be many things.*
SIMON, C.   *One happy classroom.*

Royal Ontario Museum book . . . . **Addison-Wesley**
GRIER, K.   *Discover: investigate the mysteries of history with 40 practical*

Rusty and Rosy . . . . **Waterford Institute**
ABC'S AND SUCH (Videocassette).

Save-the-Earth book . . . . **Morrow**
PRINGLE, L. P.   *Oil spills: damage, recovery, and prevention.*

Saving planet Earth . . . . **Childrens Press**
BLASHFIELD, J. F.   *Too many people?*

Scholastic biography . . . . **Scholastic**
BULLA, C. R.   *Squanto: friend of the Pilgrims.*
ENGEL, T.   *We'll never forget you, Roberto Clemente.*
PETTIT, J.   *Place to hide.*

Scholastic first encyclopedia . . . . **Scholastic Reference**
HOW THINGS WORK.

Scholastic guides . . . . **Scholastic**
TERBAN, M.   *Checking your grammar.*

Scholastic homework reference series . . . . **Scholastic**
ZEMAN, A.   *Everything you need to know about math homework.*

Scholastic kid's encyclopedia . . . . **Scholastic**
RUBEL, D.   *Science.*

Scholastic timelines . . . . **Scholastic Reference**
RUBEL, D.   *United States in the 19th century.*
RUBEL, D.   *United States in the 20th century.*

Scholastic's the Magic School Bus explores . . . . **Microsoft**
SCHOLASTIC'S MAGIC SCHOOL BUS EXPLORES IN THE AGE OF DINOSAURS. School ed. (CD-ROM).
SCHOLASTIC'S THE MAGIC SCHOOL BUS EXPLORES INSIDE THE EARTH. School ed. (CD-ROM).
SCHOLASTIC'S THE MAGIC SCHOOL BUS EXPLORES THE HUMAN BODY. School ed. (CD-ROM).
SCHOLASTIC'S THE MAGIC SCHOOL BUS EXPLORES THE OCEAN. Teacher ed. (CD-ROM).
SCHOLASTIC'S THE MAGIC SCHOOL BUS EXPLORES THE RAINFOREST. School ed. (CD-ROM).
SCHOLASTIC'S THE MAGIC SCHOOL BUS EXPLORES THE SOLAR SYSTEM. Academic ed. (CD-ROM).

School library media programs. Focus on trends and issues . . . . **ALA**
WRIGHT, K.   *Challenge of technology: action strategies for the school library media specialist.*
ZINGHER, G.   *At the Pirate Academy: adventures with language in the library media center.*

School library media series . . . . **Scarecrow**
BURGUNDER, A.   *Zoolutions: a mathematical expedition with topics for grades 4 through 8.*

Science all around you . . . . **Lerner**
MAKI, C.   *Snowflakes, sugar, and salt: crystals up close.*
YAMASHITA, K.   *Paws, wings, and hooves: mammals on the move.*

Science and its secrets . . . . **Raintree**
DOLPHINS.

Science book of . . . . **Gulliver/Harcourt Brace Jovanovich**
ARDLEY, N.   *Science book of gravity.*
ARDLEY, N.   *Science book of hot and cold.*
ARDLEY, N.   *Science book of motion.*
ARDLEY, N.   *Science book of things that grow.*
ARDLEY, N.   *Science book of weather.*
CHALLONER, J.   *Science book of numbers.*

Science experiments . . . . **Lerner**
MURPHY, B.   *Experiment with water.*

Science experiments for young people . . . . **Enslow**
RYBOLT, T. R.   *Environmental experiments about air.*
RYBOLT, T. R.   *Environmental experiments about water.*

Science I can read book . . . . **HarperCollins**
SELSAM, M. E.   *Egg to chick. Rev. ed.*

Science magic . . . . **Barron's**
OXLADE, C.   *Science magic with air.*
OXLADE, C.   *Science magic with light.*
OXLADE, C.   *Science magic with shapes and materials.*

Science spotlight . . . . **Raintree Steck-Vaughn**
GRAHAM, I.   *Crime-fighting.*
GRAHAM, I.   *Fakes and forgeries.*

Science superstars . . . . **W. H. Freeman**
BUTTS, E. R.   *May Chinn: the best medicine.*
FORD, B.   *Howard Carter: searching for King Tut.*
LESSEM, D.   *Jack Horner: living with dinosaurs.*

Science walk with David Suzuki . . . . . **Beacon Films/Altschul Group**
SEEING THINGS (Videocassette).

Seasons across America . . . . **Hyperion**
SIMON, S.   *Autumn across America.*
SIMON, S.   *Spring across America.*
SIMON, S.   *Winter across America.*

See & explore library . . . . **DK Publishing**
CASELLI, G.   *Wonders of the world.*
PARKER, S.   *Body and how it works.*

See how they grow . . . . **DK Publishing**
FLETCHER, N.   *Penguin.*

See through history . . . . **Viking**
WOOD, T.   *Aztecs.*

Self-help for kids . . . . **Free Spirit**
CUMMINGS, R. W.   *School survival guide for kids with LD (Learning differences).*

Serving special needs . . . . **Bowker**
RUDMAN, M. K.   *Books to help children cope with separation and loss: an annotated bibliography. 4th ed.*

Settling the West . . . . **Twenty-First Century**
HILTON, S.   *Miners, merchants, and maids.*

Shamu and you . . . . **Video Treasures**
EXPLORING THE WORLD OF REPTILES (Videocassette).

Shorewood art programs for education . . . **Shorewood Reproductions**
AMERICAN HISTORY: GROWING PAINS (Picture).

Sierra Club wildlife library . . . . **Sierra Club**
GRACE, E. S.   *Elephants.*
LAWRENCE, R. D.   *Wolves.*
STIRLING, I.   *Bears.*

Signs of the times . . . . **Oxford University Press**
GANERI, A.   *Story of time and clocks.*

Silver seedling easy reader . . . . **Silver Press/Silver Burdett**
HIMMELMAN, J.   *Clover County carrot contest.*
HIMMELMAN, J.   *Day-off machine.*

Silver seedling easy reader (Continued)
    HIMMELMAN, J.   *Great leaf blast-off.*
    HIMMELMAN, J.   *Super camper caper.*

Smart talk . . . .   **Troll**
    KARLSBERG, E.   *Eating pretty.*

Smithsonian oceanic collection . . . .   **Soundprints**
    BOYLE, D.   *Coral reef hideaway: the story of a clown*
    anemonefish.
    JAY, L. A.   *Sea turtle journey: the story of a loggerhead turtle.*

Smithsonian's backyard . . . .   **Soundprints**
    OTTO, C.   *Raccoon at Clear Creek Road.*
    RAU, D. M.   *Robin at Hickory Street.*

So you want to be? . . . .   **Pyramid**
    SO YOU WANT TO BE?: JUDGE (Videocassette).
    SO YOU WANT TO BE?: NEWSPAPER ARTIST
    (Videocassette).

Solve it . . . .   **Agency for Instructional Technology**
    GEOMETRY AND MEASUREMENT: MEASURING
    ANGLES (Videocassette).
    MENTAL COMPUTATION: USING MENTAL
    COMPUTATION FOR MULTIPLICATION (Videocassette).
    RATIO/PROPORTION/PERCENT: THE MEANING OF
    PERCENT (Videocassette).
    STATISTICS: UNDERSTANDING MEAN, MEDIAN, AND
    MODE (Videocassette).

Soundways to reading . . . .   **Listening Library**
    LEVOY, M.   *Witch of Fourth Street and other stories (Kit).*

Speedsters . . . .   **Dutton**
    MONFRIED, L.   *No more animals!*

Spirit Bay . . . .   **Annick/Firefly**
    COOPER, A. J.   *Dream quest.*

Spirit of America . . . .   **CBS News Production**
    DECLARATION OF INDEPENDENCE (Videocassette).

Sports I can read book . . . .   **HarperCollins**
    KESSLER, L.   *Aqui viene el que se poncha!*
    KESSLER, L.   *Here comes the strikeout.*
    KESSLER, L.   *Kick, pass, and run.*
    KESSLER, L.   *Last one in is a rotten egg.*
    KESSLER, L.   *Ultimo en tirarse es un miedoso.*

Sports immortals . . . .   **Crestwood House**
    SANFORD, W. R.   *Babe Didrikson Zaharias.*

Sports reports . . . .   **Enslow**
    KNAPP, R.   *Chris Webber: star forward.*
    MACNOW, G.   *Shaquille O'Neal: star center.*
    SULLIVAN, M. J.   *Mark Messier: star center.*

Sports top 10 . . . .   **Enslow**
    HARRINGTON, D. J.   *Top 10 women tennis players.*
    KNAPP, R.   *Top 10 basketball centers.*
    KNAPP, R.   *Top 10 basketball scorers.*
    KNAPP, R.   *Top 10 hockey scorers.*
    LACE, W. W.   *Top 10 football quarterbacks.*
    LACE, W. W.   *Top 10 football rushers.*
    SULLIVAN, M. J.   *Top 10 baseball pitchers.*

Sports triumphs . . . .   **Silver Burdett**
    JENNINGS, J.   *Long shots: they beat the odds.*

Sports world . . . .   **Steck-Vaughn**
    BAILEY, D.   *Cycling.*
    BAILEY, D.   *Fishing.*
    BAILEY, D.   *Swimming.*
    BAILEY, D.   *Track and field.*

Standard catalog series . . . .   **Wilson**
    CHILDREN'S CATALOG. 17th ed.

Standard catalog series (Continued)
    MIDDLE AND JUNIOR HIGH SCHOOL LIBRARY
    CATALOG. 7th ed.

Start to read . . . .   **School Zone**
    ANTLE, N.   *Good bad cat.*

Step into reading . . . .   **Random House**
    BRENNER, M.   *Abe Lincoln's hat.*
    COLE, J.   *Hungry, hungry sharks.*
    HAUTZIG, D.   *Aladdin and the magic lamp.*
    HAYWARD, L.   *First Thanksgiving.*
    KRAMER, S. A.   *Ty Cobb: bad boy of baseball.*
    KRENSKY, S.   *Witch hunt: it happened in Salem Village.*
    KULLING, M.   *Vanished!: the mysterious disappearance of*
    Amelia Earhart.
    MILTON, J.   *Whales: the gentle giants.*
    O'CONNOR, J.   *Comeback!: four true stories.*
    PENNER, L. R.   *Twisters!*
    PRAGER, A.   *Baseball birthday party.*
    STANDIFORD, N.   *Bravest dog ever: the true story of Balto.*
    WHEELER, C.   *Bookstore cat.*

Stephen Biesty's cross-sections . . . .   **DK Publishing**
    BIESTY, S.   *Barco de guerra del siglo XVIII.*
    BIESTY, S.   *Man-of-war.*

Stepping stone book . . . .   **Random House**
    BULLA, C. R.   *Chalk box kid.*
    BULLA, C. R.   *White bird.*
    CAMERON, A.   *Julian's glorious summer.*
    WHELAN, G.   *Next spring an oriole.*

Stopwatch books . . . .   **Silver Burdett**
    BACK, C.   *Bean and plant.*
    BACK, C.   *Chicken and egg.*
    OLESEN, J.   *Snail.*
    WATTS, B.   *Birds' nest.*
    WATTS, B.   *Butterfly and caterpillar.*
    WATTS, B.   *Hamster.*
    WATTS, B.   *Ladybug.*
    WATTS, B.   *Mushroom.*
    WATTS, B.   *Potato.*

Stories from the attic . . . .   **Sign-A-Vision**
    GREEDY CAT (Videocassette).
    VILLAGE STEW (Videocassette).

Stories of America . . . .   **Raintree Steck-Vaughn**
    CONNELL, K.   *These lands are ours: Tecumseh's fight for the*
    Old Northwest.
    DE RUIZ, D. C.   *Causa: the migrant farmworkers' story.*
    MYERS, W. D.   *Place called heartbreak: a story of Vietnam.*

Stories to remember . . . .   **Lightyear Entertainment**
    BEAUTY AND THE BEAST (Videocassette).
    NOAH'S ARK (Videocassette).
    PEGASUS (Videocassette).

Story corner . . . .   **Scholastic**
    MACCARONE, G.   *Cars! cars! cars!*
    MCMULLAN, K.   *If you were my bunny.*
    SERFOZO, M.   *There's a square: a book about shapes.*

Story in a picture . . . .   **Ideals**
    RICHMOND, R.   *Story in a picture: animals in art.*
    RICHMOND, R.   *Story in a picture: children in art.*

Story stretchers . . . .   **Gryphon House**
    RAINES, S. C.   *More story stretchers: more activities to expand*
    children's favorite books.
    RAINES, S. C.   *Story stretchers for the primary grades:*
    activities to expand children's favorite books.
    RAINES, S. C.   *450 more story stretchers for the primary*
    grades: activities to expand children's favorite books.

Storybook classics . . . . **Rabbit Ears**
    KIPLING, R. *How the rhinoceros got his skin; and, How the camel got his hump* (Videocassette).
    THREE BILLY GOATS GRUFF; AND, THE THREE LITTLE PIGS (Videocassette).

Storytelling circle . . . . **Weston Woods**
    FOREST, H. *Songspinner: folktales and fables sung and told* (Sound recording cassette).
    FOREST, H. *Tales of womenfolk* (Sound recording cassette).
    TORRENCE, J. *Story lady* (Sound recording cassette).

Strategy series . . . . **Edmark**
    STRATEGY CHALLENGES COLLECTION 1: AROUND THE WORLD. School version (CD-ROM).
    STRATEGY CHALLENGES COLLECTION 2: IN THE WILD. School version (CD-ROM).

Structures . . . . **Thomson Learning**
    DUNN, A. *Skyscrapers.*

Study skills . . . . **Lerner**
    MCINERNEY, C. *Tracking the facts: how to develop research skills.*

Successful sports . . . . **Rigby**
    LITKE, R. *Ice hockey.*

Super solvers . . . . **Learning Company**
    GIZMOS AND GADGETS! (Microcomputer program).

Superstar lineup . . . . **HarperCollins**
    LIPSYTE, R. *Jim Thorpe: 20th-century jock.*
    LIPSYTE, R. *Joe Louis: a champ for all America.*
    LIPSYTE, R. *Michael Jordan: a life above the rim.*

SVE basic skill booster . . . . **Society for Visual Education**
    ANIMATED ALMANAC (Videocassette).
    ANIMATED ATLAS (Videocassette).
    ANIMATED ENCYCLOPEDIA (Videocassette).
    CANADA: PORTRAIT OF A NATION (Videocassette).
    ENDANGERED SPECIES (Videocassette).

Take a look 2 . . . . **TVOntario**
    DAIRY FARM (Videocassette).

Taking part . . . . **Dillon**
    ADAMS, M. A. *Whoopi Goldberg: from street to stardom.*
    SAVAGE, J. *Kristi Yamaguchi: pure gold.*

Tales of King Arthur . . . . **Morrow**
    TALBOTT, H. *King Arthur and the Round Table.*

Tales of the Americas . . . . **Children's Book Press**
    ROHMER, H. *Atariba and Niguayona: a story from the Taino people of Puerto Rico.*

Taxicab tales . . . . **Greenwillow**
    PORTE, B. A. *Turkey drive and other tales.*

Teachers' secrets . . . . **DK Publishing**
    YORKE, M. *Miss Butterpat goes wild!*

Teddy board books . . . . **Grosset & Dunlap**
    SEIDEN, A. *Trucks* (Board book).

Thinkin' things series . . . . **Edmark**
    THINKIN' THINGS COLLECTION 1 (Microcomputer program).
    THINKIN' THINGS COLLECTION 2. School version (CD-ROM).
    THINKIN' THINGS COLLECTION 3. School version (CD-ROM).

Thirteen colonies . . . . **Childrens Press**
    FRADIN, D. B. *Georgia Colony.*
    FRADIN, D. B. *New Hampshire Colony.*
    FRADIN, D. B. *New Jersey Colony.*

Thirteen colonies (Continued)
    FRADIN, D. B. *New York Colony.*
    FRADIN, D. B. *North Carolina Colony.*
    FRADIN, D. B. *Pennsylvania Colony.*
    FRADIN, D. B. *Rhode Island Colony.*
    FRADIN, D. B. *South Carolina Colony.*
    FRADIN, D. B. *Virginia Colony.*

Thirteen moons . . . . **HarperCollins**
    GEORGE, J. C. *Moon of the gray wolves. New ed.*

Thorndike-Barnhart dictionary . . . . **World Book**
    WORLD BOOK DICTIONARY.

Threads . . . . **Garrett**
    CASH, T. *Plastics.*
    DIXON, A. *Clay.*
    DIXON, A. *Paper.*
    THOMSON, R. *Rice.*
    WALPOLE, B. *Water.*

Through the seasons with birds . . . . **Journal Films**
    SPRING (Videocassette).
    WINTER (Videocassette).

Time for a tale storytelling series . . . . **High Windy Audio**
    HOLT, D. *Why the dog chases the cat: great animal stories* (Sound recording cassette).

Time quest book . . . . **Scholastic**
    BALLARD, R. D. *Exploring the Bismarck.*

Toucan tales . . . . **Rayve Productions**
    ARAUJO, F. P. *Nekane, the lamina and the bear: a tale of the Basque Pyrenees.*

Traditional Black music . . . . **Chelsea House**
    SILVERMAN, J. *African roots.*
    SILVERMAN, J. *Blues.*
    SILVERMAN, J. *Children's songs.*
    SILVERMAN, J. *Christmas songs.*
    SILVERMAN, J. *Slave songs.*
    SILVERMAN, J. *Songs of protest and civil rights.*

Trailblazers . . . . **Carolrhoda**
    FERRIS, J. *What I had was singing: the story of Marian Anderson.*
    MCPHERSON, S. S. *Ordinary genius: the story of Albert Einstein.*

Transportation series . . . . **Film Ideas**
    TRAINS (Videocassette).
    TUGBOATS: MASTERS OF OUR HARBORS (Videocassette).

Treasury of children's classics . . . . **Scribner's**
    STEVENSON, R. L. *Treasure Island.*

Tree tales . . . . **Sierra Club**
    BASH, B. *Ancient ones: the world of the old-growth Douglas fir.*
    BASH, B. *Desert giant: the world of the saguaro cactus.*

Troll first-start biography . . . . **Troll**
    DEXTER, R. *Young Arthur Ashe: brave champion.*

Trophy chapter book . . . . **HarperTrophy**
    BROWN, J. *Stanley and the magic lamp.*
    BULLA, C. R. *Pirate's promise.*
    RUDEEN, K. *Jackie Robinson.*

True book . . . . **Children's Press**
    ARMBRUSTER, A. *St. Lawrence Seaway.*
    BRIMNER, L. D. *World Wide Web.*
    FOWLER, A. *Library of Congress.*
    KAZUNAS, C. *Internet for kids.*

Turning points in American history . . . . **Silver Burdett**
    OCHOA, G. *Fall of Quebec and the French and Indian War.*

Turning points in American history (Continued)
   SMITH, B. C.   *Women win the vote.*

U.S. geography from sea to shining sea . . . .   **Preview Media**
   MIDDLE ATLANTIC REGION: NEW YORK, NEW JERSEY,
      DELAWARE, MARYLAND, PENNSYLVANIA, DISTRICT
      OF COLUMBIA (Videocassette).
   SOUTH CENTRAL REGION: TEXAS, NEW MEXICO,
      OKLAHOMA (Videocassette).

United States presidents . . . .   **Enslow**
   JUDSON, K.   *Ronald Reagan.*
   SCHUMAN, M.   *Harry S. Truman.*

Unlovables. . . . .   **National Geographic**
   WILD, WONDERFUL ANIMALS IN THE WOODS
      (Videocassette).

Vanishing cultures . . . .   **Harcourt Brace**
   REYNOLDS, J.   *Amazon Basin: vanishing cultures.*
   REYNOLDS, J.   *Down under: vanishing cultures.*
   REYNOLDS, J.   *Far north: vanishing cultures.*
   REYNOLDS, J.   *Frozen land: vanishing cultures.*
   REYNOLDS, J.   *Himalaya: vanishing cultures.*
   REYNOLDS, J.   *Mongolia: vanishing cultures.*
   REYNOLDS, J.   *Sahara: vanishing cultures.*

Vanishing peoples. . . . .   **Lothrop, Lee & Shepard**
   SCHWARTZ, D. M.   *Yanomami: people of the Amazon.*

Venture book. . . . .   **Watts**
   NOURSE, A. E.   *Virus invaders.*
   RAINIS, K. G.   *Exploring with a magnifying glass.*

Very-first-step-to-reading book . . . .   **Crowell/HarperCollins**
   CARLE, E.   *Do you want to be my friend?*

Video history of the civil war. . . . .   **Osterlund/Regency Home Video**
   GETTYSBURG (Videocassette).

Videos for parents . . . .   **Boys Town**
   CHANGE FOR THE BETTER: TEACHING CORRECT
      BEHAVIOR (Videocassette).
   IT'S GREAT TO BE ME! INCREASING YOUR CHILD'S
      SELF-ESTEEM (Videocassette).

VideoTours history collection. . . . .   **VideoTours**
   FREEDOM TRAIL (Videocassette).
   OLD STURBRIDGE VILLAGE (Videocassette).

Viking easy-to-read. . . . .   **Viking**
   ADLER, D. A.   *Young Cam Jansen and the dinosaur game.*
   ADLER, D. A.   *Young Cam Jansen and the lost tooth.*
   ADLER, D. A.   *Young Cam Jansen and the missing cookie.*
   BYARS, B. C.   *Ant plays Bear.*
   BYARS, B. C.   *My brother, Ant.*
   SPOHN, K.   *Dog and Cat shake a leg.*
   ZIEFERT, H.   *Turnip.*

Viking easy-to-read classic. . . . .   **Viking**
   ZIEFERT, H.   *Little red hen.*
   ZIEFERT, H.   *Princess and the pea.*

Vision book. . . . .   **Child's World**
   GOUCK, M.   *Great Barrier Reef.*
   MURRAY, P.   *Amazon.*
   MURRAY, P.   *Everglades.*
   MURRAY, P.   *Sahara.*

Visual almanac series . . . .   **Voyager**
   MOHL, R.   *Planetary taxi (CD-ROM).*

Visual guides . . . .   **Watts**
   BARRETT, N. S.   *Flying machines.*

Walkabout. . . . .   **Childrens Press**
   PLUCKROSE, H.   *Seashore.*
   PLUCKROSE, H.   *Trees.*

Walkabout (Continued)
   PLUCKROSE, H.   *Under the ground.*
   PLUCKROSE, H.   *Weather.*

Walt Morey adventure library . . . .   **Blue Heron Publishing**
   MOREY, W.   *Home is the North.*
   MOREY, W.   *Scrub dog of Alaska.*

We all have tales . . . .   **Rabbit Ears**
   GLEESON, B.   *Anansi (Kit).*
   GLEESON, B.   *Finn McCoul (Videocassette).*
   GLEESON, B.   *Koi and the kola nuts (Kit).*
   KUNSTLER, J. H.   *Aladdin and the magic lamp (Kit).*
   METAXAS, E.   *Peachboy (Videocassette).*
   METAXAS, E.   *Puss in Boots (Kit).*

We are still here: Native Americans today . . . .   **Lerner**
   BRAINE, S.   *Drumbeat...heartbeat: a celebration of the*
      powwow.
   KING, S.   *Shannon: an Ojibway dancer.*
   PETERS, R. M.   *Clambake: a Wampanoag tradition.*
   REGGUINTI, G.   *Sacred harvest: Ojibway wild rice gathering.*
   ROESSEL, M.   *Kinaalda: a Navajo girl grows up.*
   ROESSEL, M.   *Songs from the loom: a Navajo girl learns to*
      weave.
   SWENTZELL, R.   *Children of clay: a family of Pueblo potters.*
   WITTSTOCK, L. W.   *Ininatig's gift of sugar: traditional native*
      sugarmaking.

Weather watch. . . . .   **Watts**
   STEELE, P.   *Rain: causes and effects.*
   STEELE, P.   *Snow: causes and effects.*

Weekly reader presents . . . .   **Harcourt Brace Jovanovich**
   TAYLOR, B.   *Be an inventor.*

Weird and wacky science. . . . .   **Enslow**
   AASENG, N.   *Meat-eating plants.*
   GOLDENSTERN, J.   *Lost cities.*
   POYNTER, M.   *Killer asteroids.*

West Side kids. . . . .   **Hyperion**
   ORGEL, D.   *Don't call me Slob-o.*
   SCHECTER, E.   *Big idea.*

What do we know about . . . .   **Peter Bedrick**
   GANERI, A.   *What do we know about Hinduism?*
   HUSAIN, S.   *What do we know about Islam?*

What makes a...a...? . . . .   **Metropolitan Museum of Art**
   MUHLBERGER, R.   *What makes a Bruegel a Bruegel?*
   MUHLBERGER, R.   *What makes a Cassatt a Cassatt?*
   MUHLBERGER, R.   *What makes a Degas a Degas?*
   MUHLBERGER, R.   *What makes a Goya a Goya?*
   MUHLBERGER, R.   *What makes a Leonardo a Leonardo?*
   MUHLBERGER, R.   *What makes a Monet a Monet?*
   MUHLBERGER, R.   *What makes a Picasso a Picasso?*
   MUHLBERGER, R.   *What makes a Raphael a Raphael?*
   MUHLBERGER, R.   *What makes a Rembrandt a Rembrandt?*

What's inside? . . . .   **DK Publishing**
   MY BODY.
   TOYS.

What's the difference . . . .   **Wiley**
   SOUCIE, G.   *What's the difference between apes and monkeys*
      and other living things?
   SOUCIE, G.   *What's the difference between lenses and prisms*
      and other scientific things?

Wheels . . . .   **Capstone Press**
   SMITH, J. H.   *Most rugged all-terrain vehicles.*

When disaster strikes . . . .   **Twenty-First Century**
   OTFINOSKI, S.   *Blizzards.*
   ROZENS, A.   *Floods.*
   SPIES, K. B.   *Earthquakes.*
   WOOD, L.   *Fires.*

Where in the world. . . . . **Learning Matters**
    KIDS EXPLORE ALASKA (Videocassette).
    KIDS EXPLORE AMERICA'S NATIONAL PARKS
      (Videocassette).
    KIDS EXPLORE KENYA (Videocassette).
    KIDS EXPLORE MEXICO (Videocassette).

Wiley science editions. . . . . **Wiley**
    LOCKHART, G.   *Weather companion.*

Windmill book. **Crowell/HarperCollins**
    KRAUS, R.   *Leo the late bloomer.*

Women of our time. . . . . **Viking Penguin**
    KERBY, M.   *Amelia Earhart: courage in the sky.*

Women's history and literature media. . . . . **Her Own Words**
    RILEY, J.   *Prairie cabin: a Norwegian pioneer woman's story*
      (Videocassette).
    WOMEN IN POLICING (Videocassette).

Wonders of discovery series. . . . . **Churchill Media**
    WONDERS OF GROWING PLANTS. 3rd ed. (Videocassette).
    WONDERS OF GROWING PLANTS. 3rd ed. (Videodisc).

Wonders of learning. . . . . **National Geographic Society**
    CAPTAIN CONSERVATION: ALL ABOUT RECYCLING
      (Kit).
    YOUR TEETH (Kit).

Wonders of the world book. . . . . **Mikay Press**
    MANN, E.   *Brooklyn Bridge.*
    MANN, E.   *Great Pyramid.*

WonderWorks. . . . . **Public Media**
    BROTHER FUTURE (Videocassette).
    HECTOR'S BUNYIP (Videocassette).
    HIROSHIMA MAIDEN (Videocassette).
    HOME AT LAST (Videocassette).

Wonderworks family movie. . . . . **WQED, Pittsburgh**
    BOOKER (Videocassette).

Wonderworks of nature. . . . . **Gareth Stevens**
    WOOD, J.   *Caves: an underground wonderland.*

World around us. . . . . **Kingfisher**
    GABB, M.   *Human body.*

World Cup soccer. . . . . **Childrens Press**
    HOWARD, D. E.   *Soccer stars.*

World folklore series. . . . . **Libraries Unlimited**
    KIRCHNER, A. B.   *In days gone by: folklore and traditions of*
      the Pennsylvania Dutch.
    LEWIS, I. M.   *Why ostriches don't fly and other tales from the*
      African bush.
    MCNEIL, H.   *Hyena and the moon: stories to listen to from*
      Kenya (Talking book).
    MCNEIL, H.   *Hyena and the moon: stories to tell from Kenya.*
    VIGIL, A.   *Corn woman: stories and legends of the Hispanic*
      Southwest/La mujer del maiz: cuentos y leyendas del sudoeste
      Hispano.

World history series. . . . . **Lucent**
    FROST, M. P.   *Mexican Revolution.*
    ITO, T.   *California gold rush.*
    MEXICAN WAR OF INDEPENDENCE.

World of difference. . . . . **Childrens Press**
    BADT, K. L.   *Good morning, let's eat!*
    BADT, K. L.   *Greetings!*
    BADT, K. L.   *Hair there and everywhere.*
    BADT, K. L.   *Pass the bread!*
    CORBETT, S.   *Shake, rattle, and strum.*
    WHITE, S.   *Welcome home!*

World of holidays. . . . . **Raintree Steck-Vaughn**
    KADODWALA, D.   *Holi.*
    KERVEN, R.   *Id-ul-Fitr.*

World of my own. . . . . **Lodestar/Dutton**
    KRULL, K.   *Bridges to change: how kids live on a South*
      Carolina Sea Island.
    KRULL, K.   *One nation, many tribes: how kids live in*
      Milwaukee's Indian community.

World of nature. . . . . **Beacon Films**
    CICADAS: THE 17-YEAR INVASION (Videocassette).
    MOUNTAIN GORILLAS: GENTLE GIANTS (Videocassette).
    PLIGHT OF THE ASIAN ELEPHANT (Videocassette).
    SAVING THE MANATEE (Videocassette).

World stories. . . . . **Fulcrum Kids**
    BRUCHAC, J.   *Dog people: native dog stories.*
    FLOOD, N. B.   *From the mouth of the monster eel: stories from*
      Micronesia.
    MADRIGAL, A. H.   *Eagle and the rainbow: timeless tales from*
      Mexico.
    WU, P.   *Abacus contest: stories from Taiwan and China.*

World's children. . . . . **Carolrhoda**
    BEIRNE, B.   *Children of the Ecuadorean Highlands.*
    GOODSMITH, L.   *Children of Mauritania: days in the desert*
      and by the river shore.
    HERMES, J.   *Children of Bolivia.*
    HERMES, J.   *Children of India.*
    HERMES, J.   *Children of Micronesia.*
    HERMES, J.   *Children of Morocco.*
    KINKADE, S.   *Children of the Philippines.*
    PITKANEN, M. A.   *Grandchildren of the Incas.*
    PITKANEN, M. A.   *Grandchildren of the Vikings.*
    STAUB, F. J.   *Children of Cuba.*
    STAUB, F. J.   *Children of the Sierra Madre.*
    STAUB, F. J.   *Children of Yucatan.*

Write on! . . . . **Humanities Software**
    BRIDGE TO TERABITHIA: A MULTI-MEDIA STUDY
      (Microcomputer program).
    BROWN, M. T.   *Arthur's teacher trouble (Microcomputer*
      program).
    CHARLOTTE'S WEB: A WRITE ON! MULTI-MEDIA
      STUDY (Microcomputer program).
    ECOLOGY WITH SEUSS (Microcomputer program).
    INDIAN IN THE CUPBOARD (Microcomputer program).
    MY FIRST SENTENCES (Microcomputer program).
    TUCK EVERLASTING (Microcomputer program).

X-ray picture book. . . . . **Watts**
    SENIOR, K.   *X-ray picture book of dinosaurs and other*
      prehistoric creatures.

Yearling first choice chapter book. . . . . **Delacorte**
    BYARS, B. C.   *Joy boys.*
    DUFFEY, B.   *Camp Knock Knock.*
    GLASER, L.   *Rosie's birthday rat.*
    KRENSKY, S.   *Three blind mice mystery.*
    SATHRE, V.   *Leroy Potts meets the McCrooks.*

York state book. . . . . **Syracuse University Press**
    JONES, L. C.   *Things that go bump in the night.*

You and your body. . . . . **Troll**
    JEDROSZ, A.   *Eyes.*
    MATHERS, D.   *Brain.*
    MATHERS, D.   *Ears.*
    SAUNDERSON, J.   *Heart and lungs.*
    SAUNDERSON, J.   *Muscles and bones.*

You can choose. . . . . **Live Wire Video**
    APPRECIATING YOURSELF (Videocassette).
    ASKING FOR HELP (Videocassette).
    BEING FRIENDS (Videocassette).
    BEING RESPONSIBLE (Videocassette).
    COOPERATION (Videocassette).
    DEALING WITH DISAPPOINTMENT (Videocassette).

You can choose (Continued)
DEALING WITH FEELINGS (Videocassette).
DOING THE RIGHT THING (Videocassette).
RESOLVING CONFLICTS (Videocassette).
SAYING NO (Videocassette).

You must be joking . . . . **Lerner**
SWANSON, J.   Summit up: riddles about mountains.

Young artist . . . . **DK Publishing**
WATERS, E.   Painting: a young artist's guide.
WELTON, J.   Drawing: a young artist's guide.

Young pet owner's guide . . . . **Barron's**
PIERS, H.   Taking care of your gerbils.

Young readers' history of the Civil War . . . . **Lodestar/Dutton**
RAY, D.   Behind the blue and gray: the soldier's life in the Civil War.

Young readers' history of the West . . . . **Lodestar/Dutton**
HERB, A. M.   Beyond the Mississippi: early westward expansion of the United States.

Your high-tech world . . . . **Bradbury**
SKURZYNSKI, G.   Get the message: telecommunications in your high-tech world.
SKURZYNSKI, G.   Know the score: video games in your high-tech world.
SKURZYNSKI, G.   Robots: your high-tech world.

Your town . . . . **National Geographic Society**
COMMUNICATIONS (Videocassette).
FIRE STATION (Videocassette).
HOSPITAL (Videocassette).
LIBRARY (Videocassette).
POST OFFICE (Videocassette).
PUBLIC WORKS (Videocassette).
TRANSPORTATION (Videocassette).

Your world explained . . . . **Henry Holt**
GANERI, A.   Religions explained: a beginner's guide to world faiths.

Zoo life with Jack Hanna . . . . **Ingle Productions**
AMAZING ANIMALS (Videocassette).
HIMALAYAN ADVENTURE (Videocassette).

20 events . . . . **Raintree Steck-Vaughn**
CUSH, C.   Artists who created great works.
SINGER, D.   Structures that changed the way the world looked.

DIRECTORY OF PUBLISHERS, PRODUCERS, AND DISTRIBUTORS

Following are the addresses of publishers, producers, and distributors of the audiovisual materials, O.D. (order direct) titles, and periodicals which are included in this edition.

ABC Clio
130 Cremona Dr
Santa Barbara CA 93117
800-422-2546
805-968-1911
805-685-9685 (FAX)
http://www.abc-clio.com

Agency for Instructional Technology
(AIT)
Box A
Bloomington IN 47402-0120
800-457-4509
812-339-2203
812-333-4278 (FAX)

Air Age
PO Box 428
Mt Morris IL 61054
800-837-0323
815-734-1223 (FAX)
http://www.man@airage.com

ALA Video/Library Network Video
320 York Rd
Towson MD 21204-5179
800-441-8273
410-887-2082
410-887-2091 (FAX)
lvn@mail.bcpl.lib.md.us

Alarion Press Inc
PO Box 1882
Boulder CO 80306
800-523-9177
303-443-9098 (FAX)

Alaska Publishing Properties
PO Box 2036
Marion OH 43306-2136
800-288-5892

Alfred Higgins Productions
6350 Laurel Canyon Blvd
North Hollywood CA 91606
800-766-5353
818-762-3300
818-762-8223 (FAX)

All Media Productions
15307 Concord Dr
Spring Lake MI 49456
800-800-4354
616-844-4006
616-844-4009 (FAX)
http://www.allmediaproductions.com

Altschul Group
1560 Sherman Ave Ste 100
Evanston IL 60201-9971
800-323-9084
847-328-6700
847-328-6706 (FAX)
agc@mcs.net
http://www.agcmedia.com

Ambrose Video
28 W 44th St Ste 2100
New York NY 10036
800-526-4663
212-768-7373
212-768-9282 (FAX)

American Assn for the Advancement
of Science
Dept SBF Box 3000
Denville NJ 07834
202-326-6454

American Association of School
Librarians (AASL)
50 E Huron St
Chicago IL 60611
800-545-2433
312-944-2641 (FAX)

American Chemical Society
ACS Sales
PO Box 2537
Kearneysville WV 25430
800-209-0423
800-525-5562 (FAX)

American Girl
PO Box 37311
Boone IA 50037-2311
800-234-1278
608-831-7089 (FAX)

American Indian Art
7314 E Osborn Dr
Scottsdale AZ 85251
602-994-5445

American Library Association
50 E Huron St
Chicago IL 60611
800-545-2433
312-944-2641 (FAX)

American Library Association
Book Order Fulfillment
155 N Wacker Dr
Chicago IL 60606-1719
800-545-2433, ext 7
312-836-9958 (FAX)
http://www.ala.org/alaeditions

American Melody Records
PO Box 270
Guilford CT 06437
800-220-5557
203-457-0881
203-457-2085 (FAX)

American Museum of Natural History
Central Park W at 79th St
New York NY 10024-5192
800-220-5557
212-769-5500
212-769-5511 (FAX)

Anna Epstein-Kravis
PO Box 1449
Melville NY 11747
516-673-8805
516-421-5716 (FAX)

Anti-Defamation League of B'nai
B'rith
22-D Hollywood Ave
Ho Ho Kus NJ 07423
800-343-5540
201-652-1973 (FAX)

Arizona Highways
2039 W Lewis Ave
Phoenix AZ 85009
602-258-6641
602-254-4505 (FAX)
http://www.arizhwys.com

Assn for Educational
Communications & Technology
1025 Vermont Ave NW Ste 820
Washington DC 20005
202-347-7834
202-347-7839 (FAX)
aect@aect.org
http://www.aect.org

Audio Book Contractors
PO Box 40115
Washington DC 20016-0115
202-363-3429
FAX--USE LOCAL NUMBER

Bantam Doubleday Dell
1540 Broadway
New York NY 10036
800-223-5780
800-233-3294 (FAX)
800-223-5780

Bantam Doubleday Dell
105 Bond St
Toronto Ontario M5B 1Y3 Canada
800-223-5780
800-233-3294 (FAX)

Barbara Lawrence Productions
3203 Overland Ave #6157
Los Angeles CA 90034
310-836-9224
310-836-6992 (FAX)
explore1@aol.com

BeJo Sales
7050B Bramalea Rd Unit 52
Mississauga Ontario L5S 1S9 Canada
800-668-7932 (Ontario)
800-268-9973 (All others)
416-677-0905 (Toronto only)
905-677-0905 (FAX)

Benchmark Books
Marshall Cavendish Corporation
99 White Plains Rd
Tarrytown NY 10591-9001
800-821-9881
914-332-8888
914-332-1082 (FAX)

Berkley Publishing
Mail Order Dept
PO Box 12289
Newark NJ 07101-5289
800-788-6262
201-933-2316 (FAX)

Berlet Films & Video
1646 Kimmel Rd
Jackson MI 49201-9772
517-784-6969
517-796-2646 (FAX)

Bess Press
3565 Harding Ave
Honolulu HI 96816
800-910-2377
808-734-7159
808-732-3627 (FAX)
email@besspress.com
http://www.besspress.com

Bethany Sciences
PO Box 3726
New Haven CT 06525-0726
800-525-1052
203-393-3395
203-393-2457 (FAX)
bethanysci@aol.com

BFA Educational Media
2349 Chaffee Dr
St Louis MO 63146
800-221-1274
314-569-0211
314-569-2834 (FAX)
BFAeduc@worldnet.att.net

Bloch and Company
PO Box 18058
Cleveland OH 44118
216-371-0979

Bogner Entertainment
PO Box 641428
Los Angeles CA 90064
310-473-0139
310-473-6417 (FAX)

Book Links
434 W Downers
Aurora IL 60506
630-892-7465

Book Lures
Box 0455
O'Fallon MO 63366
800-844-0455
314-272-4242
FAX--USE LOCAL NUMBER

Boy Scouts of America
PO Box 152350
Irving TX 75015-2079
972-580-2000
972-588-2079 (FAX)

Braille Institute
Communications Dept
Attn: Braille Press
741 N Vermont Ave
Los Angeles CA 90029-3594
213-663-1111
213-666-0867 (FAX)

Brodart Co
500 Arch St
Williamsport PA 17705
800-233-8467 ext 784
717-326-2461 ext 784
717-326-1479 (FAX)

Broderbund Software
PO Box 6125
Novato CA 94948-6121
800-521-6263 (Orders only)
415-382-4700
415-382-4419 (FAX)
http://www.broderbund.com

Bullfrog Films
Box 149
Oley PA 19547
800-543-3764
610-779-8226
610-370-1978 (FAX)
bullfrog@igc.com
http://www.bullfrogfilms.com

Cambridge Educational
PO Box 2153
Charleston WV 25328-2153
800-468-4227
800-329-6687 (FAX)
304-744-9323
304-744-9351 (FAX)
http://www.cambridgeol.com/
cambridge

Can Ed Media
43 Moccasin Trail
Don Mills Ontario M3C 1Y5 Canada
416-445-3900
416-445-9976 (FAX)

Canadian Childrens Literature Assn
University of Guelph Dept of English
Guelph Ontario N1G 2W1 Canada
519-824-4120 ext 3189
519-837-1315 (FAX)
ccl@uoguelph.ca
http://www.uoguelph.ca/englit/ccl/

Canadian Library Assn
200 Elgin St Ste 602
Ottawa Ontario K2P 1L5 Canada
613-232-9625
613-563-9895 (FAX--Canada)
604-321-2453 (FAX--U.S.)
http://www.cla.amlibs.ca

Carolina Biological Supply Co
2700 York Rd
Burlington NC 27215-3398
800-334-5551
800-222-7112 (FAX)
910-584-0381
910-584-7686 (FAX)

Carus Corporation
Box 7433
Red Oak IA 51591-4434
800-827-0227
515-246-1020 (FAX)

Cascade Pass Inc
10734 Jefferson Blvd Ste 235
Culver City CA 90230-3235
310-202-1468
http://www.cascadepass.com

Celestial Arts
PO Box 7123
Berkeley CA 94707
800-841-2665
510-559-1600
510-524-1629 (FAX)

Century Publishing Co
PO Box 569
Mt Morris IL 61054-0569
800-877-5893
708-491-6440

Charlesbridge
85 Main St
Watertown MA 02172-4411
800-225-3214
800-926-5775 (FAX)
617-926-0329
617-926-5720 (FAX)
http://www.charlesbridge.com

Childrens Art Foundation
PO Box 83
Santa Cruz CA 95063
408-426-5557
408-426-1161 (FAX)
http://www.stonesoup.com

Childrens Better Health Institute
PO Box 420235
Palm Coast FL 32142
800-829-5579
904-445-2728 (FAX)

Childrens Book Council
568 Broadway Ste 404
New York NY 10012-3225
800-999-2160
212-966-1990
212-966-2073 (FAX)

Children's Press/Grolier
School and Library
PO Box 1331
Danbury CT 06813-1331
800-621-1115
203-797-3657 (FAX)
800-361-5873
514-747-5000
514-747-0440 (FAX)

Childrens Television Workshop
PO Box 53349
Boulder CO 80322
800-678-0613
212-595-3456
212-875-6105 (FAX)

Child's World
PO Box 326
Chanhassen MN 55317
800-599-7323
612-906-3939
612-906-3940 (FAX)

Chip Taylor Communications
15 Spollett Dr
Derry NH 03038
800-876-2447
603-434-9262
603-432-2723 (FAX)
sales@chiptaylor.com
http://www.chiptaylor.com

Christopher Gordon Publishers
1502 Providence Highway Ste 12
Norwood MA 02062
800-934-8322
617-762-5577
617-762-2110 (FAX)

Classroom Connect
1866 Colonial Village Ln
PO Box 10488
Lancaster PA 17605-0488
800-638-1639
717-393-1000
717-393-5752 or 717-391-7186 (FAX)
connect@classroom.net
http://www.classroom.net

Clearvue EAV
6465 N Avondale Ave
Chicago IL 60631-1996
800-253-2788
800-444-9855 (FAX)
773-775-9433
http://www.clearvue.com

Cobblestone Publishing
7 School St
Peterborough NH 03458
800-821-0115
603-924-7209
603-924-7380 (FAX)

Coldwater Press
9806 Coldwater Circle
Dallas TX 75228
214-328-7612
214-320-2480 (FAX)
neilaann@aol.com

Consumer Information Center
Pueblo CO 81009

Consumers Union of the
United States
PO Box 54861
Boulder CO 80322-4861
800-234-1645

Council for Canadian Learning
Resources
Resource Links
101-1001 W Broadway Ste 353
Vancouver British Columbia V6H 4E4
Canada
604-925-0266
604-925-0566 (FAX)
cclr@rockland.com

Council for Exceptional Children
1920 Association Dr
Reston VA 22091
703-620-3660
703-264-9494 (FAX)
http://www.cec.sped.org

Coyote Creek Productions
2419 E Mission Rd
Fallbrook CA 92028
800-492-4041
760-731-3184
760-731-3008 (FAX)
pstevens@coycreek.com
http://www.coycreek.com

Creative Editions
Harcourt Brace Trade Order
Fulfillment
6277 Sea Harbor Dr
Orlando FL 32887-4300
800-543-1918
800-235-0256 (FAX)
407-345-4001
407-345-2727 (FAX)

Davidson & Associates
c/o Educational Resources
1550 Executive Dr
Elgin IL 60121
800-624-2926
847-888-8300
http://www.education.com

Davis Publications Inc
50 Portland St Printers Bldg
Worcester MA 01608
800-533-2847
508-754-7201
508-753-3834 (FAX)
davispub@aol.com

DeBeck Educational Video
3873 Airport Way PO Box 9754
Bellingham WA 98227-9754
604-739-7696
604-739-7609 (FAX)
604-739-7696

DeBeck Educational Video
Box 33738 Station D
Vancouver British Columbia
V6J 4L6
Canada
604-739-7696
604-739-7609 (FAX)

Delos International Inc.
Hollywood & Vine Plaza
1645 N Vine St Ste 340
Hollywood CA 90028
800-364-0645
213-962-2626
213-962-2636 (FAX)
http://www.delosmus.com

Delta Education
12 Simon St PO Box 3000
Nashua NH 03061-3000
800-442-5444
800-282-9560 (FAX)
603-598-7170
http://www.delta-ed.com

Detroit Institute of Arts
Attn: Photography Dept
5200 Woodward Ave
Detroit MI 48202
313-833-7913
313-833-9161 (FAX)

Dimension 5
Kingsbridge Sta Box 403
Bronx NY 10463
718-548-6112

Direct Cinema Limited
PO Box 10003
Santa Monica CA 90410-9003
800-525-0000
310-636-8200
310-636-8228 (FAX)
directcinema@attmail.com

Discovery Channel Multimedia
PO Box 1089
Florence KY 41022
800-678-3343 (U.S. only)
606-342-5630 (FAX)
http://www.discovery.com

Disney Educational Productions
105 Terry Dr Ste 120
Newtown PA 18940
800-295-5010
215-579-8589 (FAX)

Distican
35 Fulton Way
Richmond Hill Ontario L4B 2N4
Canada
800-268-3212
905-764-0073
905-764-0086 (FAX)

DK Multimedia
c/o PRI
1224 Heil Quaker Blvd
La Vergne TN 37086
888-342-5357
800-774-6733 (FAX)
http://www.dk.com

Documentary Photo Aids
PO Box 956
Mt Dora FL 32757
800-255-0763
352-383-8435
352-383-5679 (FAX)

Douglas & McIntyre
1615 Venables St
Vancouver British Columbia V5L 2H1
Canada
800-667-6902 (WEST ONLY)
800-565-9523 (EAST ONLY)
604-254-7191 (ALL ORDERS)

Droll Yankees Inc
27 Mill Rd
Foster RI 02825
800-352-9164
401-647-3324
401-647-7620 (FAX)
drollbird@aol.com

Durrin Productions Inc
4926 Sedgwick St NW
Washington DC 20016-2326
800-536-6843
202-237-6700
202-237-6738 (FAX)
durrinprod@aol.com

E C Publications
PO Box 52344
Boulder CO 80323
800-462-3624
303-661-1994 (FAX)
dcosubs@aol.com

Early Years
PO Box 54805
Boulder CO 80323-4805
800-678-8793

Editorial Projects in Education
PO Box 2083
Marion OH 43306
800-728-2790
202-364-4114
info@epe.org
http://www.edweek.org

Edmark Corporation
PO Box 97021
Redmond WA 98073-9721
800-362-2890
425-556-8400
425-556-8430 (FAX)
http://www.edmark.com

Education Center Inc
PO Box 54293
Boulder CO 80322
800-753-1843
910-273-9409
303-661-1994 (FAX)
edcenter@spyder.net
http://www.theeducationcenter.com

Educational Activities
PO Box 87
Baldwin NY 11510
800-645-3739
516-223-4666
516-623-9282 (FAX)
learn@edact.com

Educational Graphics Press
PO Box 180476
Austin TX 78718
800-274-8804
512-345-4664
512-345-9734 (FAX)

Encyclopedia Britannica Educational
Corp
310 S Michigan Ave
Chicago IL 60604
800-554-9862
312-347-7900
312-347-7966 (FAX)
http://www.ebec.eb.com

Ernst Interactive Media
6847 Rt 21
Naples NY 14512
800-554-3556

Facts on File Inc
11 Penn Plaza, 15th fl
New York NY 10001-2006
800-322-8755
800-678-3633 (FAX)
212-967-8800
212-967-9311 (FAX)

Family PC
PO Box 55411
Boulder CO 80323-5411
800-825-6450
familypc@aol.com

Farrar Straus & Giroux
19 Union Sq W
New York NY 10003
800-631-8571
212-741-6900
212-633-9385 (FAX)

Film Ideas
3710 Commercial Ave Ste 13
Northbrook IL 60062
800-475-3456
847-480-5760
847-480-7496 (FAX)
fi inc@aol.com

Films for the Humanities & Sciences
Inc
PO Box 2053
Princeton NJ 08543-2053
800-257-5126
609-275-1400
609-275-3767 (FAX)
custserv@films.com
http://www.films.com

Finley Holiday Films
PO Box 619
Whittier CA 90601
800-345-6707
562-945-3325
562-693-4756 (FAX)
finley-holiday@finley-holiday
http://www.finley-holiday.com

Firefly Books
3680 Victoria Pk Ave
Willowdale Ontario M2H 3K1
Canada
800-387-5085
800-565-6034 (FAX)
416-499-8412
FAX--USE LOCAL NUMBER

Fitzhenry & Whiteside
195 Allstate Pkwy
Markham Ontario L3R 4T8 Canada
800-387-9776
905-477-9700
905-477-9179 (FAX)
godwit@fitzhenry.ca
http://www.fitzhenry.ca

Five Owls
2004 Sheridan Ave S
Minneapolis MN 55405
612-644-7377
612-377-4816 (FAX)

Folk Legacy Records
85 Sharon Mtn Rd
Sharon CT 06069
800-836-0901
860-364-5661
860-364-1050 (FAX)
folklegacy@snet.net
http://www.folklegacy.com

Fondo de Cultura Economica
2293 Verus St
San Diego CA 92154
800-532-3872
619-429-0455
619-429-0827 (FAX)
sales@fceusa.com
http://www.fceusa.com

Friends Street Music
6505 SE 28th St
Mercer Island WA 98040
206-232-1078
FAX--USE LOCAL NUMBER

Friendship Press
Distribution Office
PO Box 37844
Cincinnati OH 45222-0844
800-889-5733
513-948-8733

Frostfire
Carol L. Birch, Storyteller
PO Box 32
Southbury CT 06488
203-264-3800
914-238-3597 (FAX)

G/C/T Publishing
c/o Prufrock Press
PO Box 8813
Waco TX 76714-8813
800-998-2208
800-240-0333 (FAX)
http://www.prufrock.com

Gale Research
PO Box 33477
Detroit MI 48232-5477
800-877-4253
800-414-5043 (FAX)
galeord@gale.com
800-701-9130 (Canada)
416-752-9646 (FAX--Canada)

Gamco Educational Materials
PO Box 1911
Big Spring TX 79721-9945
800-351-1404
800-896-1760 (FAX)
915-267-6327
915-267-7480 (FAX)
http://www.gamco.com

Girl Scouts of America
420 Fifth Ave
New York NY 10018
800-811-9342
800-643-0639 (FAX)
http://www.home.girl scouts.org

GPN
PO Box 80669
Lincoln NE 68501-0669
800-228-4630
800-306-2330 (FAX)
402-472-2007
402-472-4076 (FAX)
gpn@unl.edu
http://www.gpn.unl.edu/index.html

Great American Music
David S Polansky
PO Box 5061
Cochituate MA 01778
508-655-5046
508-650-4758 (FAX)
http://www.galaxymall.com/stores/
music.html

Greathall Productions Inc
PO Box 813
Benicia CA 94510
800-477-6234
707-745-5820 (FAX)

Greenwood Press
88 Post Road W Box 5007
Westport CT 06881
800-225-5800 (Orders only)
203-226-3571
203-222-1502 (FAX)
http://www.greenwood.com

Grolier Educational Corp
PO Box 1716
Danbury CT 06813-1331
800-243-7256
203-797-3500
203-797-3657 (FAX)
http://www.publishing.grolier.com

Grolier Limited
45 Montpelier Blvd
Montreal Quebec H4N 3H6 Canada
800-361-5873
514-747-5000
514-747-0440 (FAX)

Guidance Associates
Box 1000
Mt Kisco NY 10549-0010
800-431-1242 (Alaska call collect)
800-901-2847 (FAX)
914-666-4100
914-666-5319 (FAX)
http://www.guidanceassociates.com

H W Wilson Co
950 University Ave
Bronx NY 10452-4224
800-367-6770(U.S. & Canada)
800-590-1617 (FAX--U.S. & Canada)
718-588-8400(Outside U.S. & Canada)
718-590-1617 (FAX--Outside U.S. & Canada)
custserv@info.hwwilson.com

Hansen Planetarium
1845 South 300 West #A
Salt Lake City UT 84115
800-321-2369
801-483-5400
801-483-5484 (FAX)
rrauch@utah.uswest.net

Harcourt Brace
6277 Sea Harbor Dr
Orlando FL 32887-4300
800-543-1918
800-235-0256 (FAX)

HarperCollins Publishers
Order Dept
100 Keystone Industrial Pk
Scranton PA 18512-4621
800-242-7737
800-822-4090 (FAX)

HarperCollins Publishers Ltd
1995 Markham Rd
Scarborough Ontario M1B 5M8
Canada
800-387-0117 (Canada only)
416-321-2241
800-668-5788 (FAX--Canada only)
416-321-3033 (FAX)
http://www.harperchildrens.com

Harris Communications
15159 Technology Dr
Eden Prairie MN 55344
800-825-6758
612-906-9144
612-906-9099 (FAX)

Hartley Courseware
9920 Pacific Heights Blvd Ste 500
San Diego CA 92121
800-247-1380
619-587-0087
619-622-7873 (FAX)

Hawkhill Associates
125 E Gillman St Dept W
PO Box 1029
Madison WI 53701-1029
800-422-4295
608-251-3924 (FAX)
http://www.hawkhill.com

Hearst Book Group of Canada
2061 McCowan Rd Ste 210
Scarborough Ontario M1S 3Y6
Canada
800-268-3531
800-274-2113 (FAX)
416-293-9404 (Toronto)

Heinemann
PO Box 5007
88 Post Rd W
Westport CT 06881
800-793-2154
800-847-0938 (FAX)
http://www.heinemann.com
416-660-0611 (Canada)
905-445-5967 (FAX--Canada)

Her Own Words
PO Box 5264
Madison WI 53705
608-271-7083
herownword@aol.com

Heritage Educational Foundation
7821 W Morris St
Indianapolis IN 46231
800-827-4374 ext 2972
317-486-2972
317-243-4382 (FAX)

Hidden Spring
65 Springhill Rd
Frankfort KY 40601
800-438-4390
502-223-4523
FAX--USE LOCAL NUMBER

High Haven Music
Educational Record Center
3233 Burnt Mill Dr Ste 100
Wilmington NC 28403-2698
800-438-1637
888-438-1637 (FAX)
910-251-1235
erc-inc.@worldnet.att.net
http://www.erc-inc.com

High Windy Audio
PO Box 553
Fairview NC 28730
800-637-8679
704-628-1728
704-628-4435 (FAX)
highwindy@aol.com
http://www.highwindy.com

Highlights for Children
PO Box 269
Columbus OH 43216
800-848-8922
614-486-0631
614-487-0762 (FAX)

Hispanic Books Distributors Inc
1328 W Prince Rd
Tucson AZ 85705
800-634-2124
520-690-0643
520-690-6574 (FAX)

Hoctor Dance Recordings
PO Box 38
Waldwick NJ 07463
800-462-8679
201-652-7767
201-652-2599 (FAX)
caravan.pdta@worldnet.att.net
http://www.dancecaravan.com

Holiday House
425 Madison Ave
New York NY 10017
212-688-0085
212-421-6134 (FAX)

Hopscotch
PO Box 164
Blufton OH 45817-0164
800-358-4732 (Orders only)
419-358-4610
419-358-5027 (FAX)

Horn Book Inc
11 Beacon St Ste 1000
Boston MA 02108
800-325-1170
617-227-1555
617-523-0299 (FAX)
info@hbook.com

Houghton Mifflin
PO Box 7050
181 Ballardvale St
Wilmington MA 01887
800-225-3362 (Schools)
800-634-7568 (FAX)
212-351-5954
http://www.hmco.com

Hudson's Bay
478 167 Lombard Ave
Winnipeg Manitoba R3B 0T6 Canada
800-816-6777 (U.S. & Canada)
204-988-9300
204-988-9309 (FAX)
beaver@cyberspace.mb.ca
http://www.beaver@cyberspace.mb.ca- otmw-cnhs-cnhs.html

Human Kinetics Publishers Inc
Box 5076
Champaign IL 61825-5076
800-747-4457
217-351-5076
217-351-1549 (FAX)
humankinetic.com
http://www.humankinetic.com

Human Relations Media
175 Tompkins Ave
Pleasantville NY 10570-9973
800-431-2050
914-769-7496
914-747-1744 (FAX)
http://www.hrmvideo.com

Humongous Entertainment
PO Box 180
Woodinville WA 98072
800-499-8386
425-806-0480 (FAX)
http://www.humongous.com

IDOC Productions
301 E 64th St Suite 4D
New York NY 10021
800-791-5133
212-737-5737
212-535-0741 (FAX)

Informed Democracy
PO Box 67
Santa Cruz CA 95063
800-827-0949
408-426-3921
408-426-2312 (FAX)
http://www.sadako.com

Ingram Library Services
One Ingram Blvd
LaVergne TN 37086
800-937-5300
800-677-5116 (FAX)
615-793-5000

Insights Visual Productions Inc
PO Box 230644
Encinitas CA 92023
800-942-0528
760-942-0528
760-942-0803 (FAX)
info@sciencevideos.com
http://www.sciencevideos.com

Instructional Resources Company
PO Box 111704
Anchorage AK 99511-1704
907-345-6689
FAX--USE LOCAL NUMBER
santhony@alaska.net

Instructor Publications
Professional Magazines
PO Box 53896
Boulder CO 80322
800-544-2917
303-604-7455 (FAX)

InterAct Story Theatre
11401 Encore Dr
Silver Springs MD 20901
800-276-8087
301-681-0875
301-681-9257 (FAX)

International Reading Assn
PO Box 8139
Newark DE 19714-8139
302-731-1600
302-731-1057 (FAX)
http://www.reading.org

International Society for Technology
in Education
Customer Service Office
480 Charnelton St
Eugene OR 97401-2626
800-336-5191 (U.S. & Canada)
541-302-3777(International)
541-302-3778

IRI/Skylight
2626 S Clearbrook Dr
Arlington Heights IL 60005-5310
800-348-4474
847-290-6600
847-290-6609 (FAX)
info@iriskylight.com
http://www.iriskylight.com

Jackdaws
PO Box 503
Amawalk NY 10501-0503
800-789-0022
800-962-9101 (FAX)
914-962-6911
914-962-0034 (FAX)

Jim Gill Music
PO Box 2263
Oak Park IL 60303
708-763-9864
708-763-9888 (FAX)

Junior Scholastic
PO Box 3710
Jefferson City MO 65102
800-631-1586
314-635-7630 (FAX)

Kalmbach Publishing
Box 1612
Waukesha WI 53187-1612
800-446-5489
414-796-8776
414-796-1615 (FAX)
http://www.modelrailroad.com

Kar-Ben Copies Inc
6800 Tildenwood Ln
Rockville MD 20852
800-452-7236
301-984-8733
301-881-9195 (FAX)
karben@aol.com
http://www.karben.com

Karol Media
PO Box 7600
Wilkes-Barre PA 18773-7600
800-884-0555
717-822-8899
717-822-8226 (FAX)
http://www.karolmedia.com

Kaw Valley Films & Video
Box 3541
Shawnee KS 66203
800-332-5060
913-631-3040
913-631-4320 (FAX)

Kids Shop
PO Box 1909
New York NY 10025
212-691-0633
212-691-4670 (FAX)

KidSafety of America
4750 Chino Ave Suite D
Chino CA 91710
800-524-1156
909-902-1340
909-902-1343 (FAX)
kidsafety-america@compuserv.com

KIDVIDZ
618 Centre St
Newton MA 02158
617-965-3345
617-965-3640 (FAX)
http://www.kidvidz.com

Kimbo Educational
PO Box 477
Long Branch NJ 07740-0477
800-631-2187
732-229-4949
732-870-3340 (FAX)
http://www.kimboed.com

Knowledge Unlimited
PO Box 52
Madison WI 53701-0052
800-356-2303
800-618-1570 (FAX)
608-836-6660
608-831-1570 (FAX)

Landmark Media
3450 Slade Run Dr
Falls Church VA 22042
800-342-4336
703-241-2030
703-536-9540 (FAX)

Langstaff Video Project
683 Santa Barbara Rd
Berkeley CA 94707
510-452-9334
510-452-9335 (FAX)
sfbayrevels@earthlink.net

Lawrence Productions
1800 S 35th St
Galesburg MI 49053-0458
800-421-4157
616-665-7075
616-665-7060 (FAX)
http://www.lpi.com

Leapfrog Productions
515 N Flagler Dr Ste 700
West Palm Beach FL 33401
561-642-5257
FAX--USE LOCAL NUMBER
derbydoc@aol.com

Learning Beat
10 Pineview Dr
Media PA 19063
800-232-8244
610-892-7055 (FAX)

Learning Company
School Division
6160 Summit Dr N
Minneapolis MN 55430-4003
800-685-6322 (U.S.)
612-569-1500
612-569-1755 (FAX)
800-663-7731 (Canada)

Learning in Motion
500 Seabright Ave Ste 105
Santa Cruz CA 95062
800-560-5670
408-457-5600
408-459-6876 (FAX)
helpdesk@learn.motion.com

Learning Matters
PO Box 6589
Portland OR 97228
800-540-9487
503-224-9401
503-274-9476 (FAX)
gadamsinc@aol.com

Lectorum Publications Inc
111 8th Ave Ste 804
New York NY 10011
800-345-5946
212-929-2833
212-727-3035 (FAX)
http://www.lectorum.com

Lee & Low (Spanish)
c/o Publishers Group West
4065 Hollis St
Emeryville CA 94662
800-788-3123
510-658-1934 (FAX)
info@leeandlow.com

Lerner Publishing Group
1251 Washington Ave N
Minneapolis MN 55401
800-328-4929
800-332-1132 (FAX)
800-387-9776
905-477-9700
905-477-9179 (FAX)

Libraries Unlimited
Dept 9798 PO Box 6633
Englewood CA 80155-6633
800-237-6124
303-770-1220
303-220-8843 (FAX)
lu-books@lu.com
http://www.lu.com

Library Learning Resources
Box 87
Berkeley Heights NJ 07922
201-635-1833
201-635-2614 (FAX)
rootbr@juno.com

Linnet/Shoe String Press
PO Box 657
2 Linsley Street
North Haven CT 06473-2517
203-239-2702
203-239-2568 (FAX)
sspbooks@aol.com

Linworth Publishing
480 E Wilson Bridge Rd Ste L
Worthing OH 43085
800-786-5017
614-436-7107
614-436-9490 (FAX)
newslin@aol.com
http://www.linworth.com

Listening Library
One Park Ave
Old Greenwich CT 06870-1727
800-243-4504
800-454-0606 (FAX)
203-637-3616
203-698-1998 (FAX)
moreinfo@listeninglib.com

Live Oak Media
PO Box 652
Pine Plains NY 12567
518-398-1010
518-398-1070 (FAX)

Live Wire Media
3450 Sacramento St
San Francisco CA 94118
800-359-5437
415-764-9500
415-665-8006 (FAX)
http://www.livewiremedia.com

LMS Associates
17 E Henrietta St
Baltimore MD 21230
410-685-8621

Lucent Technologies/AT&T
5151 Blazer Pkwy
Dublin OH 43017
800-452-0042
614-764-5206
614-764-5328 (FAX)
jejohnson4@lucent.com

Mama T Artists
PO Box 2898
Asheville NC 28802
800-864-0299
704-258-1113
704-253-0100 (FAX)

Marshall Cavendish
99 White Plains Rd PO Box 2001
Tarrytown NY 10591
800-332-1082
914-332-8888
914-332-1082 (FAX)
800-821-9881
905-851-4660

Marshall Cavendish
PO Box 56510 93B Woodbridge Ave
Woodbridge Ontario L4L 8V3 Canada
800-821-9881
905-851-4660
905-851-5507 (FAX)

Marshmedia
PO Box 8082
Shawnee Mission KS 66208
800-821-3303
816-523-1059
816-333-7421 (FAX)
info@marshmedia.com

McClelland & Stewart
Canbook Distributing Services
1220 Nicholson Rd
New Market Ontario L3Y 7V1
Canada
800-399-6858
800-363-2665 (FAX)

Media Bus
Box 718
Woodstock NY 12498
914-679-7739
FAX--USE LOCAL NUMBER

Media Projects
5215 Homer St
Dallas TX 75206
214-826-3863
214-826-3919 (FAX)
cynfilm@aol.com

Mercury Press
143 Cream Hill Rd
Cornwall CT 06796
860-672-6376
860-672-2643 (FAX)

MicroSoft Canada Inc
320 Matheson Blvd W
Mississauga Ontario L54 3R1 Canada
800-549-6653

MicroSoft Corp
For the authorized educational
reseller nearest you, contact
MicroSoft Pre-sales Information
Directory
800-426-9400
800-549-6653

Miller Freeman
600 Harrison St
San Francisco CA 94107
800-607-4410
415-908-6613
937-890-0221 (FAX)
http://www.techlearning.com

Minnesota Orchestra Visual
Entertainment
1111 Nicollet Mall
Minneapolis MN 55403-9895
888-666-6837
612-371-7123
612-371-7170 (FAX)
http://www.mnorch.org

Mish Mash Music
PO Box 3477
Ashland OR 97520
541-482-6578
541-482-5636 (FAX)
http://www.websails.com/mish

Monarch Avalon
4517 Harford Rd
Baltimore MD 21214
800-999-3222
410-254-9200
410-254-0991(FAX)
girllife@aol.com
http://www.girlslife.com

Moose School Productions
Box 960
Topanga CA 90290
800-676-5480
310-455-2318
310-455-4192 (FAX)
peteralsop@earthlink.net
http://www.caboodle.com

Morrow
Wilmor/Order Dept
PO Box 1219 39 Plymouth St
Fairfield NJ 07007
800-843-9389 (Orders only)
888-775-3260 (FAX)
201-227-7200
201-227-6849 (FAX)
800-268-3531
800-274-2113 (FAX)
416-293-9404 (Toronto)

MPI Home Video
16101 S 108th Ave
Orland Park IL 60467
800-323-0442
708-460-0555
708-460-0175 (FAX)
http://www.mpimedia.com

Muse
PO Box 7468
Red Oak IA 51591-2468
800-827-0227

Music Educators National Conference
Subscription Sales
1806 Robert Fulton Dr
Reston VA 20191
800-336-3768
703-860-4000
703-860-2652 (FAX)
http://www.menc.org

Music for Little People
Box 1460
Redway CA 95560-1460
800-346-4445
707-923-3991
707-923-3241 (FAX)
mlp@igc.apc.org

Nancy Renfro Studios
3312 Pecan Springs Rd
Austin, TX 78723
800-933-5512
512-927-7090
FAX--USE LOCAL NUMBER
puppets@fc.net
http://www.fc.net/~puppets/

National Audubon Society
Box 52529
Boulder CO 80322
800-274-4201
303-604-7455 (FAX)

National Council for the Social
Studies
3501 Newark St NW
Washington DC 20016
800-296-7840
202-966-7840
202-966-2061 (FAX)

National Council of Teachers of
English
1111 W Kenyon Rd
Urbana IL 61801-3870
800-369-6283
217-328-3870
217-328-9645 (FAX)
http://www.ncte.org

National Council of Teachers of
Mathematics
1906 Association Dr
Reston VA 20191-1593
800-235-7566
703-620-9840
703-476-2970 (FAX)
infocentral@nctm.org
http://www.nctm.org

National Education Goals Panel
1255 22nd St NW Ste 502
Washington DC 20037
202-724-0015
202-632-0957 (FAX)
http://www.ngep.gov

National Film Board of Canada
22D Hollywood Ave
Ho Ho Kus NJ 07423
800-542-2164
201-652-1973 (FAX)
http://www.nfb.ca
800-267-7710

National Film Board of Canada
Box 6100 Centreville
Montreal Quebec H3C 3H5 Canada
800-267-7710
http://www.nfb.ca

National Gallery of Art
Extension Service
Washington DC 20565
202-842-6273
http://www.nga.gov

National Geographic Society
Education Services
PO Box 98018
Washington DC 20090-8018
800-368-2728
202-828-5664
301-921-1575 (FAX)
http://www.nationalgeographic.com

National Library Service
for the Blind and Physically
Handicapped
Library of Congress
Washington DC 20542
800-424-9100
202-707-0722

National Parks and Conservation
Assn
1776 Massachusetts Ave NW Ste 200
Washington DC 20036
800-628-7275
202-223-6722
202-659-8178 (FAX)
http://www.npca.org

National Science Teachers Assn
Publication Sales Dept
1840 Wilson Blvd
Arlington VA 22201
800-722-6782
703-243-7100
703-243-7177 (FAX)
http://www.nsta.org

National Storytellers Association
116 W Main St
Jonesborough TN 37659
423-753-2171
423-753-9331 (FAX)
nsa@tricon.net
http://www.storynet.org

National Wildlife Federation
Box 777
Mt Morris IL 61054-0777
800-588-1650

Native Ground Music
109 Bell Rd
Asheville NC 28805
800-752-2656
704-299-7031
704-298-5607 (FAX)

New Castle Communications
229 King St
Chappaqua NY 10514
800-723-1263
914-238-0600
914-238-8445 (FAX)

Northeastern University
403 Richards Hall
Boston MA 02216
617-373-7539
appraisal@lynx.new.edu

NorthWord Press Inc
PO Box 1360
Minocqua WI 54548
800-336-6398
715-356-9800
715-356-9762 (FAX)

Nystrom
3333 Elston Ave
Chicago IL 60618
800-621-8086
773-463-1144
773-463-0515 (FAX)
http://www.nystromnet.com

NYZS Wildlife Conservation
PO Box 534
Mt Morris IL 61054-0534
718-220-6876
718-584-2625 (FAX)
http://www.wsc.org/news/magazine

Old City Press
1715 La Loma Ave
Berkeley CA 94709
510-464-4466
510-883-0888 (FAX)
http://www.storypage.com

Ondeck Home Entertainment
14546 Hesby St
Sherman Oaks CA 19403
818-906-3306
818-906-7806 (FAX)
ondeck123@aol.com

One Step Records
PO Box 6078
Auburn CA 95604
800-746-3371
916-269-0760
916-269-1208 (FAX)
postbox@onesteprecords.com

Parents Choice Foundation
PO Box 185
Waban MA 02168
617-965-5913
617-965-4516 (FAX)
http://www.ctw.org./parents

PBS Video
1320 Broddock Pl
Alexandria VA 22314-1698
800-344-3337
703-739-5380
703-739-5269 (FAX)

Peaceable Kingdom Press
707B Heinz Ave
Berkeley CA 94710
800-444-7778
510-644-9801
510-644-9805 (FAX)
http://www.pkpress.com

Penguin Books Canada, Limited
10 Alcorn Ave Ste 300
Toronto Ontario M4V 3B2 Canada
416-925-2249
416-925-0068 (FAX)

Penguin USA
Order Dept Box 120
Bergenfield NJ 07621-0120
800-526-0275
800-227-9604 (FAX)
212-366-2000
201-385-6521 (FAX)
http://www.penguin.com/usa
416-925-2249
416-925-0068 (FAX)

People Records
8929 Apache Dr
Beulah CO 81023
800-381-3191
719-485-3191
719-485-3500 (FAX)
dvanman@fone.net

Peter Piper Publishing
4175 Francisco Place
Victoria British Columbia V8N 6H1
Canada
250-477-5543
FAX--USE LOCAL NUMBER
yesmag@islandnet.com

Petersen Publishing Co
6420 Wilshire Blvd
Los Angeles CA 90048
800-800-8326
213-782-2000

Phi Delta Kappa Educational
Foundation
Box 789
Bloomington IN 47402-0789
800-766-1156
812-339-1156
812-339-0018 (FAX)
orders@pdkintl.org
http://www.pdkintl.org

Pied Piper/AIMS Multimedia
9710 DeSoto Ave
Chatsworth CA 91311-9734
800-367-2467
818-773-4300
818-341-6700 (FAX)

Pierian Press
PO Box 1808
Ann Arbor MI 48106
800-678-2435
313-434-5530
313-434-6409 (FAX)
http://www.pierianpress.com

Plays Inc
120 Boylston St
Boston MA 02116-4615
617-423-3157
617-423-2168 (FAX)
writer@user.channel1.com
http://www.channel1.com/thewriter

Prakken Publications
Box 8623
Ann Arbor MI 48107
800-530-9673
313-975-2800
313-975-2787 (FAX)
http://www.ededit@cybrzone/inc.com

Pro Ed Publishing
8700 Shoal Creek
Austin TX 78757
800-897-3202
800-897-7633 (FAX)
512-451-3246
http://www.proedinc.com

Public Media Education
4411 N Ravenswood Ave 3rd Flr
Chicago IL 60640-5802
800-343-4312
773-878-2600
773-878-8406 (FAX)
classics@homevision.public
media.com

Publishers Development Corp
591 Camino de la Reina Ste 200
San Diego CA 92108
619-297-8032
619-297-5353 (FAX)

Puppet Concepts Publishing
PO Box 15203
Portland OR 97215
503-236-4034

Putnam
One Grosset Dr
Kirkwood NY 13795
800-847-5515
607-775-1740
607-775-5586 (FAX)
800-668-7932 (Ontario)
800-268-9973 (All others)
416-677-0905 (Toronto only)

Pyramid Media
PO Box 1048
Santa Monica CA 90406-1048
800-421-2304
310-828-7577
310-453-9083 (FAX)

R R Bowker
Subscription Dept
121 Chanlon Rd
New Providence NJ 07974
800-521-8110
908-665-6688 (FAX)

Rainbow Educational Media
4540 Preslyn Dr
Raleigh NC 27616-3177
800-331-4047
919-954-7550
919-954-7554 (FAX)

Rainbow Morning Music
2121 Fairland Rd
Silver Spring MD 20904
800-888-4741
301-384-9207
barrylou@ziplink.net
http://www.ziplink.net\~barrylou

RAS Records Inc
PO Box 42517
Washington DC 20015
301-588-9641 or 5135
301-588-7108 (FAX)
smith@rounder.com

RCA Records
Contact your local RCA retailer

Reading Adventures
Varsity Reading Services
PO Box 261431
Columbus OH 43226-1431

Reading & O'Reilly
PO Box 302
Wilton CT 06897-0302
800-458-4274
203-762-2854
203-762-8295 (FAX)
http://www.WILTONART.com

Recorded Books
270 Skipjack Rd
Prince Frederick MD 20678
800-638-1304
410-535-5499 (FAX)
recordedbk@aol.com
http://www.recordedbooks.com

Regency Home Video
9911 W Pico Blvd Ste E
Los Angeles CA 90035
310-552-2660
310-552-9039 (FAX)

Research Press
2612 N Mattis Ave
Champaign IL 61821
800-519-2707
217-352-3273
217-352-1221 (FAX)
rp@researchpress.com
http://www.researchpress.com

Rigby Interactive Library
PO Box 1650
Crystal Lake IL 60039-1650
800-822-8661
800-427-4429 (FAX)
815-477-3880
815-477-3990 (FAX)

Rock Hill Press
14 Rock Hill Rd
Bala Cynwyd PA 19004
888-762-5445
610-667-2040
610-667-2291 (FAX)
info@rockhillpress.com
http://www.rockhillpress.com

Rockland Press
Box 34069 Dept 284
Seattle WA 98124-1069
604-876-3377
eml@rockland.com
604-925-0266
604-925-0566 (FAX)

Rockland Press
101-1001 W Broadway Ste 343
Vancouver British Columbia V6H 4E4
Canada
604-925-0266
604-925-0566 (FAX)
eml@rockland.com

Roger Wagner Publishing
1050 Pioneer Way Step Ste P
El Cajon CA 92020
800-421-6526 ext 73
619-442-0522
619-442-0525 (FAX)
care@hyperstudio.com
http://www.hyperstudio.com

Round River Records
301 Jacob St
Seekonk MA 02771
800-682-9522
508-336-9703
508-336-2254 (FAX)
jane@billharley.com
http://www.billharley.com

Rounder Records
1 Camp St
Cambridge MA 02140
800-443-4727
617-354-0700
617-491-1970 (FAX)

Rourke Publishing Group
PO Box 3328
Vero Beach FL 32964
800-394-7055
561-234-6001
561-234-6622 (FAX)

Sally Rogers
PO Box 98
Abington CT 06230
860-974-3089
salrog@neca.com

Santillana
2105 NW 86th Ave
Miami FL 33122
800-245-8584
305-591-9145 (FAX)

Scholastic Canada Ltd
123 Newkirk Rd
Richmond Hill Ontario L4C 3G5
Canada
416-883-5300 (CALL COLLECT)

Scholastic Inc (Books)
PO Box 7502
Jefferson City MO 65102
800-325-6149
800-223-4011 (FAX)
573-636-5271
416-883-5300 (CALL COLLECT)

Scholastic Inc (Magazines)
PO Box 3710
Jefferson City MO 65102
800-631-1586

School Library Journal
PO Box 57559
Boulder CO 80322
800-456-9409
303-604-7455 (FAX)

School Science and Mathematics
Assn
Donald Pratt Curriculum and
Foundations
400 E 2nd St
Bloomsburg PA 17815
717-389-4915
pratt@bf486.bloom.edu

School Services of Canada
176 Albany Ave
Toronto Ontario M5V 2M8 Canada
800-387-2084
416-410-7465 (Toronto only)
FAX--USE LOCAL NUMBER
ssc@echo-on.net

Science Service
PO Box 1925
Marion OH 43305
800-552-4412
614-382-5866 (FAX)

Sea Studios
810 Cannery Row
Monterey CA 93940
408-649-5152
408-649-1380 (FAX)
http://www.seastudios@
seastudios.com

Select Media
22-D Hollywood Ave
Ho Ho Kus NJ 07423
800-343-5540
201-652-1973 (FAX)

Shadow Play Records & Video
PO Box 180476
Austin TX 78718
800-274-8804
512-345-4664
512-345-9734 (FAX)

Shengold
18 W 45th St
New York NY 10036
212-944-2555
212-944-2589 (FAX)

Shorewood Art Reproductions
33 River Rd
Cos Cob CT 06807
800-494-3824
203-426-8100
203-661-2480 (FAX)

Sign Enhancers Inc
PO Box 12687
Salem OR 97309-0687
800-767-4461
503-304-4530
503-304-1063 (FAX)
http://www.teleport.com\.~sign

Silo Music
PO Box 429
Waterbury VT 05676
800-342-0295
802-244-7856
802-244-6128 (FAX)
sales@silo-alcazar.com

Simon & Schuster
1230 Ave of Americas
New York NY 10020
800-223-2336
800-445-6991 (FAX)
212-698-4351
212-698-4350 (FAX)
800-268-3212
905-764-0073
905-764-0086 (FAX)

Sky Tree Press
Dept B 8700 Riverview St
Stuyvesant NY 12173
518-758-6671
518-822-1223 (FAX)

Smarty Pants Audio & Video
15104 Detroit Ave Ste 2
Lakewood OH 44107
216-221-5300
216-221-5348 (FAX)

Smithsonian Associates
900 Jefferson Dr
Washington DC 20560
800-766-2149
202-357-2888
202-786-2564 (FAX)
http://www.smithsonian.si.edu

Smithsonian Folkways
414 Hungerford Dr Ste 444
Rockville MD 20850
800-410-9815
301-443-2314
301-443-1819 (FAX)
http://www.si.edu/folkways

Software Toolworks/MindScape
88 Roland Way
Novato CA 94945
800-234-3088
415-897-9900
415-897-9956 (FAX)
msales@mindscape.com

Spoken Arts Inc
8 Lawn Ave
New Rochelle NY 10801
800-326-4090
914-633-4516
914-633-4602 (FAX)

Sports Illustrated
PO Box 60001
Tampa FL 33660-0001
800-528-5000
212-522-1212

Sports Illustrated for Kids
820 Tom Martin Dr
Birmingham AL 35211
800-992-0196
205-877-6504 (FAX)

Squeaky Wheel Productions
PO Box 30723
Albuquerque NM 87190
505-296-0863
FAX--USE LOCAL NUMBER
http://www.greenchilijam.com
/kidzmusic

SRA McGraw Hill
220 E Danieldale Rd
DeSoto TX 75115-2490
800-843-8855 or 888-772-4543
972-224-1111
972-228-1982 (FAX)
http://www.mcgraw-hill.com
(Information only)

Story Street USA
1155 Hart Ln
Fulton CA 95439
707-577-0259
FAX--USE LOCAL NUMBER
kenhaven@aol.com

Sunburst Communications
101 Castleton St
Pleasantville NY 10570-9807
800-431-1934
914-769-5030
914-769-2109 (FAX)
service@nysunburst.com
http://www.SUNBURSTonline.com

SVE/Churchill Media
6677 N Northwest Hwy
Chicago IL 60631
800-829-1900
800-624-1678 (FAX)
773-775-9550
http://www.svemedia.com

Syd Lieberman
SL Productions
2522 Ashland
Evanston IL 60201
847-328-6281

Ta Dum Productions
PO Box 4077
Leucadia CA 92024
800-328-4352
760-438-7523
760-438-4360 (FAX)
http://www.davidjack.com

Teachers Laboratory Inc
PO Box 6480
Brattleboro VT 05302-6480
800-769-6199
802-254-3457
802-254-5233 (FAX)
connect@sover.net

Tickle Tune Typhoon
4649 Sunnyside Ave N Ste 122
Seattle WA 98103
206-632-9466
206-632-9548 (FAX)

Tim Podell Productions
PO Box 244
Scarborough NY 10510
800-642-4181
914-762-4286
914-944-8110 (FAX)
timpod@msn.com

Time Inc
PO Box 60001
Tampa FL 33660-0001
800-777-8600
800-777-3400 (FAX)
timeforkids@time.com
http://www.timeforkids.com

Time Inc
Customer Service
PO Box 60001
Tampa FL 33660-0001
800-843-8463
http://pathfinder.com/time

Time-Life Education
PO Box 85026
Richmond VA 23285-5026
800-449-2010
800-449-2011 (FAX)
http://www.timelifeedu.com

Times Mirror Magazines
PO Box 51268
Boulder CO 80322
800-289-9399
303-661-1181 (FAX)

Tom Snyder Productions
80 Coolidge Hill Rd
Watertown MA 02172-2817
800-342-0236
617-926-6000
617-926-6222 (FAX)

Toni Simmons
1248 Regents Park Court
DeSoto TX 75115
972-230-0616
972-230-5535 (FAX)
astoryteller@webtv.net

Toucan Valley Publications
142 N Milpitas Blvd Ste 260
Milpitas CA 95035
800-236-7946
510-498-1009
510-498-1010 (FAX)
orders@toucanvalley.com

Tricycle Press
PO Box 7123
Berkeley CA 94707
800-841-2665
510-559-1629 (FAX)

Troll Associates
100 Corporate Dr
Mahwah NJ 07430
800-929-8765
800-979-8765 (FAX)
201-529-4000
http://www.troll.com

Tundra Books Inc
c/o Canbook Distribution Services
1220 Nicholson Rd
New Market Ontario L3Y 7V1
Canada
800-399-6858 (U.S. & Canada)
800-363-2665 (FAX)

TVOntario
Ontario Educational Communications
Authority (OCEA)
1140 Kildaire Farm Rd
Cary NC 27511
800-331-9566
919-380-0747
919-380-0961 (FAX)
416-484-2600

TVOntario
Ontario Educational Communications
Authority (OCEA)
Box 200 Sta Q
Toronto Ontario M4T 2T1 Canada
416-484-2600
416-484-2896 (FAX)

United Learning
6633 W Howard St Box 48718
Niles IL 60714-0718
800-424-0362
847-647-0918 (FAX)
http://www.unitedlearning.com

University of Illinois Press
1325 S Oak St
Champaign IL 61820
217-244-0626
217-244-8082 (FAX)

US Government Printing Office
Superintendent of Documents
Washington DC 20402
202-512-1800
202-512-1355 (FAX)

Vermont Story Works
PO Box 3278
338 Northgate Rd
Burlington VT 05401
800-206-8383
802-865-2735
802-660-8112 (FAX)

Video Enterprise
336 Leffingwell Ste 100
St Louis MO 63122
314-821-4551
314-821-2052 (FAX)

Video Project
200 Estates Drive
Ben Lomond CA 95005
800-475-2638
408-336-0160
408-336-2168 (FAX)
videoproject@igc.org
http://www.videoproject.org

Video Specialties
3805 Pontchartrain Dr Ste 19
Slidell LA 70458
800-643-2750
504-643-2758

Video Treasures
For the retailer nearest you,
contact Video Treasures Hotline
800-745-1145

Videodiscovery
1700 Westlake Ave N Ste 600
Seattle WA 98109
800-548-3472
206-285-5400
206-285-9245 (FAX)
http://www.videodiscovery.com
800-548-3472 ext 401
604-525-8246
604-525-8298 (FAX)

Videodiscovery
1220 Quayside Dr #404
New Westminister British Columbia
V3M
6H1 Canada
800-548-3472 ext 401
604-525-8246
604-525-8298 (FAX)
http://www.videodiscovery.com

VideoTours Inc/Animal Adventures
1070 Commerce Dr
Perrysburg OH 43551
800-477-7385
419-872-3305 (FAX)

Voyager Co
PO Box 2284
S Burlington VT 05407
800-446-2001
802-864-9846 (FAX)
http://www.voyagerco.com

Warner Brothers
Contact your local music dealer

Waterford Institute
1590 E 9400 South
Sandy UT 84093
800-767-9976
801-576-4900
801-572-1667 (FAX)
office@waterford.org

Weekly Reader Corp
3001 Cindel Dr
Delran NJ 08370
800-446-3355
609-786-3360 (FAX)
webmaster@weeklyreader.com
http://www.weeklyreader.com

Weston Woods
PO Box 2193
Norwalk CT 06852-2193
800-243-5020
203-226-3355
203-845-0498 (FAX)

Wilderwalks Productions
PO Box 365422
Hyde Park MA 02136
781-455-1926
617-522-4335 (FAX)
wilderwalk@aol.com
http://www.lightlink.com/acstudio/
wwalk.htm

WOMBAT
1560 Sherman Ave Ste 100
Evanston IL 60201
800-323-9084
708-328-6700
708-328-6706 (FAX)
gc@mcs.net
http://www.agcmedia.com

World Book Educational Products of
Canada
School & Library Division
34 Armstrong Ave
Georgetown Ontario L7G 4R9
Canada
800-837-5365
903-873-6170 (FAX)

World Book Inc
School & Library Division
525 W Monroe 20th Flr
Chicago IL 60661
800-975-3250
312-258-3950 (FAX)
800-837-5365

World Future Society
7910 Woodmont Ave Ste 450
Bethesda MD 20814
800-989-8274
301-656-8274
301-951-0394 (FAX)
http://www.wfs.org/wfs

World Music Press
PO Box 2565
Danbury CT 06813-2565
800-810-2040
203-748-1131
203-748-3432 (FAX)

Yellin Tabor Visual Productions
5916 Howe St Ste C-1
Pittsburgh PA 15232
412-231-5933
cindyt@aol.com

Yellow Moon Press
PO Box 381316
Cambridge MA 02238
800-497-4385
617-776-2230
617-776-8246 (FAX)
ymp@tiac.net
http://www.yellowmoon.com

Young Naturalist Foundation
35 Riviera Dr Unit 17
Markham Ontario L3R 8N4 Canada
800-387-4379
905-946-1174
905-946-0410 (FAX)

Zoological Society of San Diego
PO Box 551
San Diego CA 92112
619-231-1515 ext 4900
619-685-3290 (FAX)
http://www.sandiegozoo.org

~NOTES~

~NOTES~

~NOTES~

~NOTES~

~NOTES~